Contents

SECTION

PRICE £18.50

PERSONAL INDEX

DISTRESS	15:1
WEATHER — BBC SERVICES	18:29
FIRST AID	17:1

A SUPPLEMENT TO THIS ALMANAC WILL BE PUBLISHED IN APRIL. TO KEEP UP TO DATE PLEASE COMPLETE AND SEND US THE FORM INCLUDED IN THIS SECTION.

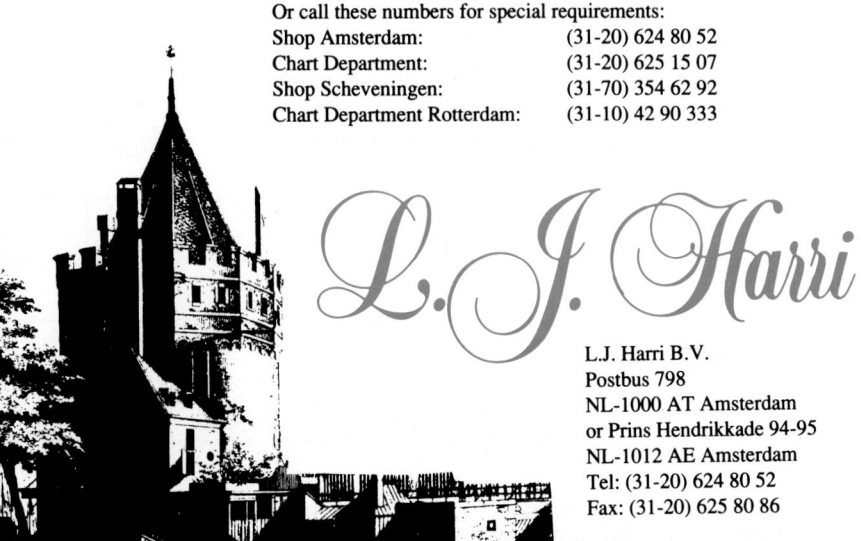

Reed's Nautical Books

REED'S
NAUTICAL
ALMANAC
1992

61st YEAR OF PUBLICATION

Editorial Director: **Jean Fowler** M.R.I.N.

Assistant Editors:
Lt. Cdr. Harry J. Baker, R.D., R.N.R., M.R.I.N.
Arthur Somers, C.ENG., M.I.E.E.
Thomas B. Stableford, Master Mariner, M.R.I.N.

Hydrographic Adviser: Robin Ekblom, F.R.I.C.S.

Price £18.50

ISBN 0 947637 96 6   ISSN 0144-5936

THOMAS REED
PUBLICATIONS LTD

Weir House, Hurst Road, East Molesey, Surrey KT8 9AQ
Tel: 081-941 8090   Fax: 081-941 8046   Telex: 883526 REED G

Printed in Great Britain

PREFACE

Many changes have been made to the 1992 edition of Reed's Nautical Almanac, including the much improved quality of the cover and, the paper on which the Almanac is printed.

A particular feature this year is that the Visual Navigational Aids & Port Information sections have been reset to double column format throughout, leading to improved clarity.

A major reshuffle means that sections on weather, radiobeacons, radio communications, tides, lights & buoys and, port information including marinas and yacht harbours are now located together for ease of reference.

NEW for 1992:

120 page section of Visual Navigational Aids and Port information including 19 Chartlets, covering the area from SE Norway to the Southern Baltic, plus radiobeacons, racons and weather broadcasts for the same area.

Additional tidal predictions/differences for the ports of St. Malo, Esbjerg and Bergen.

A 6 page informative article on the use of radar in small craft.

A full description of the courses available under the RYA National Training Schemes, both motor and sail.

Detailed list of Customs Post Boxes throughout the UK. for deposit of Form C1328.

This 61st edition of 'The Yachtsman's Bible' is greater value than ever before.

REMINDER: The half-yearly Supplement to Reed's will be published in April 1992. Please fill in and send us the application form, located in Section 1, in good time to ensure that you receive this updating service.

Wishing you good sailing in 1992.

JF.

INTERNATIONAL PORT TRAFFIC SIGNALS
(to be introduced worldwide as circumstances permit)

MAIN MESSAGE

1	FLASHING	SERIOUS EMERGENCY— ALL VESSELS TO STOP OR DIVERT ACCORDING TO INSTRUCTIONS
2		VESSELS SHALL NOT PROCEED
3		VESSELS MAY PROCEED. ONE WAY TRAFFIC
4	FIXED OR SLOW OCCULTING	VESSELS MAY PROCEED. TWO WAY TRAFFIC
5		A VESSEL MAY PROCEED ONLY WHEN IT HAS RECEIVED SPECIFIC ORDERS TO DO SO

EXEMPTION SIGNALS AND MESSAGES

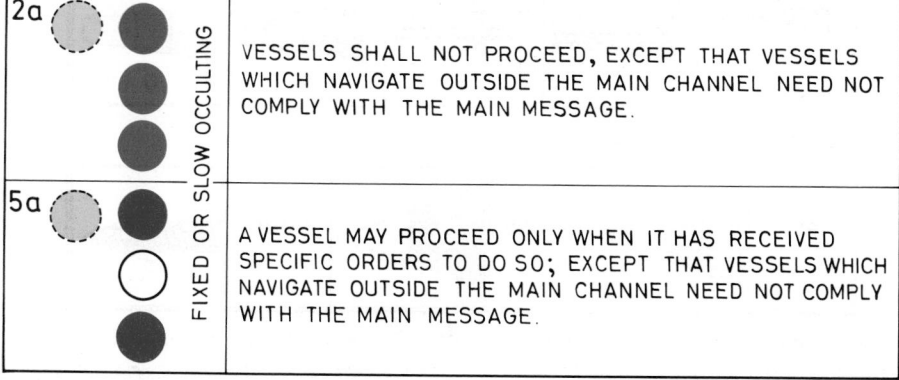

2a	FIXED OR SLOW OCCULTING	VESSELS SHALL NOT PROCEED, EXCEPT THAT VESSELS WHICH NAVIGATE OUTSIDE THE MAIN CHANNEL NEED NOT COMPLY WITH THE MAIN MESSAGE.
5a		A VESSEL MAY PROCEED ONLY WHEN IT HAS RECEIVED SPECIFIC ORDERS TO DO SO; EXCEPT THAT VESSELS WHICH NAVIGATE OUTSIDE THE MAIN CHANNEL NEED NOT COMPLY WITH THE MAIN MESSAGE.

INTERNATIONAL
CODE OF SIGNALS

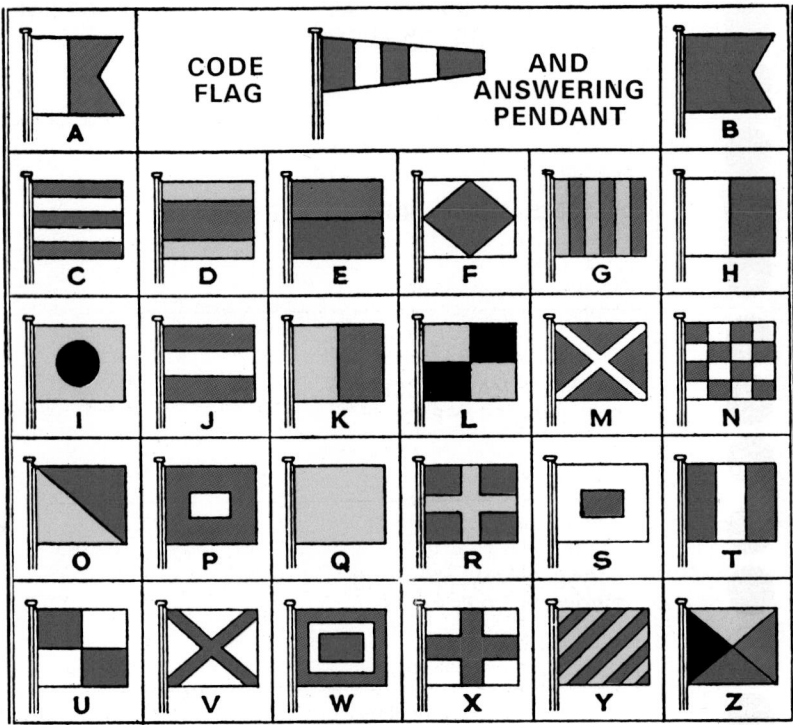

NUMERAL PENDANTS

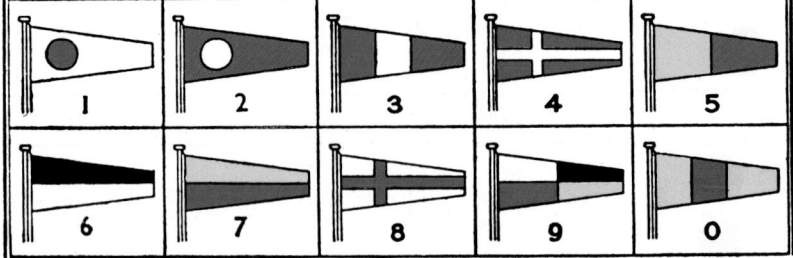

SUBSTITUTES

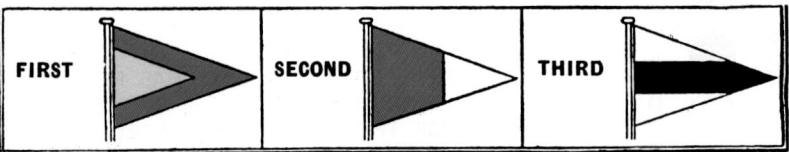

The meanings of all Single Letter Flags, A to Z, are shown on the opposite page.

INTERNATIONAL CODE OF SIGNALS

SINGLE LETTER SIGNALS BY FLAG, LIGHT, OR SOUND

The most important Code signals of all—the single letter signals—consist of Very Urgent signals or those in common use. Seamen should know these by heart, so that there may be no hesitation in acting on them.

The following may be made by any method of signalling, but those marked (*) when made by sound may only be made in compliance with the International Regulations for Preventing Collisions at Sea, Rules 34 and 35.

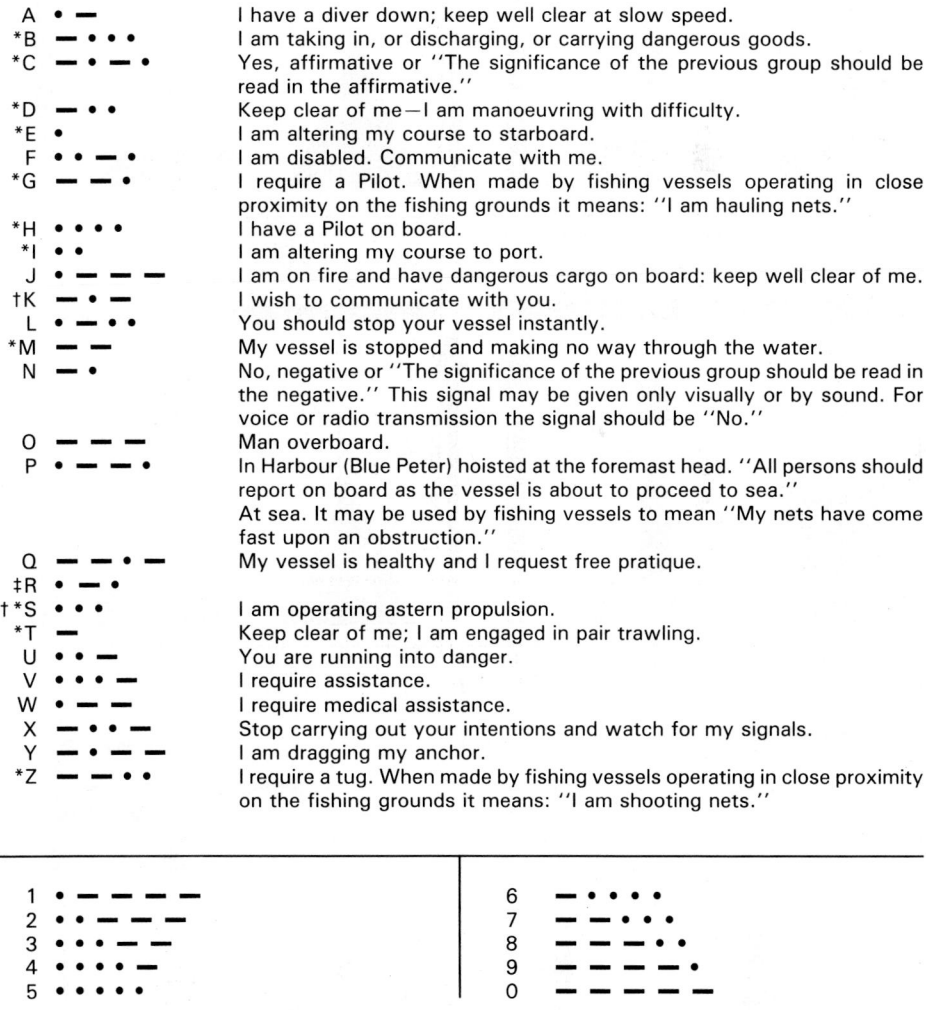

A	• —	I have a diver down; keep well clear at slow speed.
*B	— • • •	I am taking in, or discharging, or carrying dangerous goods.
*C	— • — •	Yes, affirmative or "The significance of the previous group should be read in the affirmative."
*D	— • •	Keep clear of me—I am manoeuvring with difficulty.
*E	•	I am altering my course to starboard.
F	• • — •	I am disabled. Communicate with me.
*G	— — •	I require a Pilot. When made by fishing vessels operating in close proximity on the fishing grounds it means: "I am hauling nets."
*H	• • • •	I have a Pilot on board.
*I	• •	I am altering my course to port.
J	• — — —	I am on fire and have dangerous cargo on board: keep well clear of me.
†K	— • —	I wish to communicate with you.
L	• — • •	You should stop your vessel instantly.
*M	— —	My vessel is stopped and making no way through the water.
N	— •	No, negative or "The significance of the previous group should be read in the negative." This signal may be given only visually or by sound. For voice or radio transmission the signal should be "No."
O	— — —	Man overboard.
P	• — — •	In Harbour (Blue Peter) hoisted at the foremast head. "All persons should report on board as the vessel is about to proceed to sea." At sea. It may be used by fishing vessels to mean "My nets have come fast upon an obstruction."
Q	— — • —	My vessel is healthy and I request free pratique.
‡R	• — •	
†*S	• • •	I am operating astern propulsion.
*T	—	Keep clear of me; I am engaged in pair trawling.
U	• • —	You are running into danger.
V	• • • —	I require assistance.
W	• — —	I require medical assistance.
X	— • • —	Stop carrying out your intentions and watch for my signals.
Y	— • — —	I am dragging my anchor.
*Z	— — • •	I require a tug. When made by fishing vessels operating in close proximity on the fishing grounds it means: "I am shooting nets."

1	• — — — —		6	— • • • •
2	• • — — —		7	— — • • •
3	• • • — —		8	— — — • •
4	• • • • —		9	— — — — •
5	• • • • •		0	— — — — —

†Signals "K" and "S" have special meanings as landing signals for small boats with crews or persons in distress. See Section 19. ‡Single letter Signal R has so far not been allocated a Signal meaning as this already has a meaning in Rule 35 of the Collision Regulations.

IALA MARITIME BUOYAGE SYSTEM

LATERAL MARKS OF REGION A

(EUROPE, AFRICA, INDIA, AUSTRALIA, MOST OF ASIA)

PORT HAND	STARBOARD HAND
LIGHT: RED ANY RHYTHM	LIGHT: GREEN ANY RHYTHM

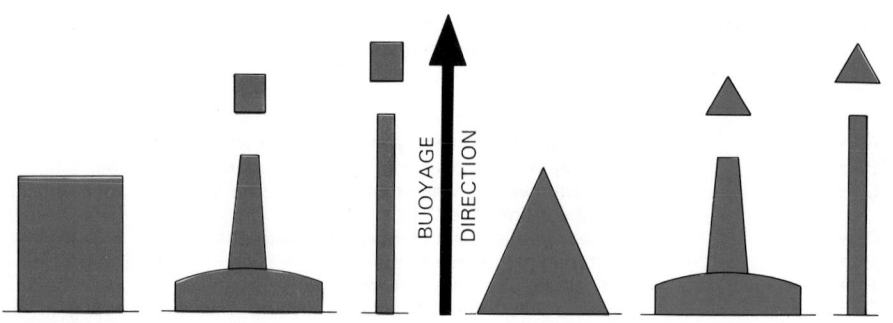

PREFERRED CHANNEL TO STARBOARD	PREFERRED CHANNEL TO PORT
LIGHT: COMPOSITE GROUP FLASHING (2 + 1) RED	LIGHT: COMPOSITE GROUP FLASHING (2 + 1) GREEN

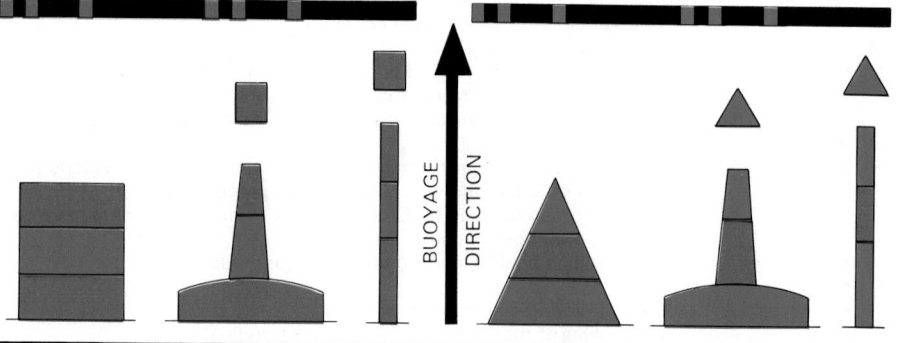

ISOLATED DANGER MARKS	SAFE WATER MARKS
LIGHT: WHITE GP. FL. (2)	LIGHT: WHITE ISOPHASE, OCCULTING, LONG FLASH EV. 10 S. OR MORSE A.

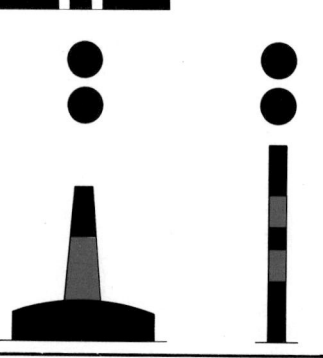
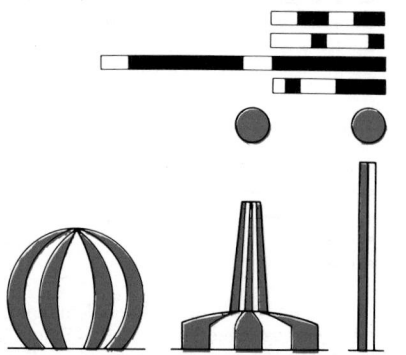

IALA MARITIME BUOYAGE SYSTEM 'A'

SPECIAL MARKS

LIGHT: YELLOW

SHAPE OPTIONAL

CARDINAL MARKS

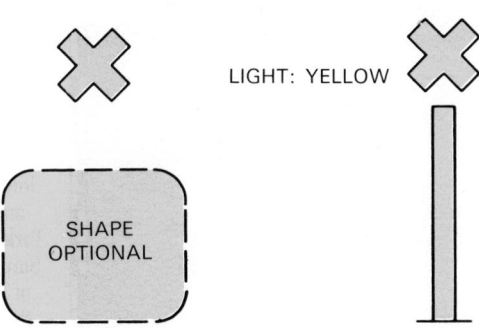

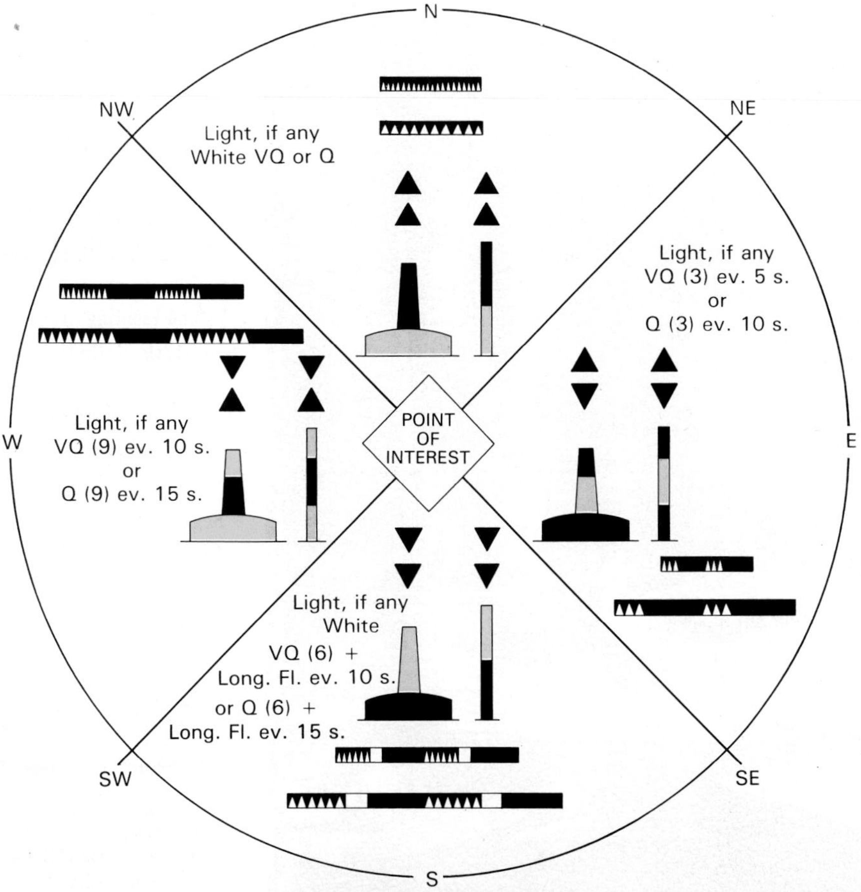

N

NW

NE

Light, if any
White VQ or Q

Light, if any
VQ (3) ev. 5 s.
or
Q (3) ev. 10 s.

W

POINT OF INTEREST

E

Light, if any
VQ (9) ev. 10 s.
or
Q (9) ev. 15 s.

Light, if any
White
VQ (6) +
Long. Fl. ev. 10 s.
or Q (6) +
Long. Fl. ev. 15 s.

SW

SE

S

THE IALA MARITIME BUOYAGE SYSTEM 'A' IS FULLY EXPLAINED IN SECTION 22.

RECOGNITION OF LIGHTS AND SHAPES
(Complete details in Collision Regulations)

LIGHTS

ASTERN   AHEAD

SAILING VESSEL UNDERWAY — NOT USING POWER

Red and green all round mast head lights may be shown in addition to side lights. Under 20 m. in length, side lights and sternlight may be combined in tricolour lantern at mast head, e.g.  → Ahead

Under 7 m. in length, if not practicable to exhibit these lights, shall have a white light ready to display to avoid collision.

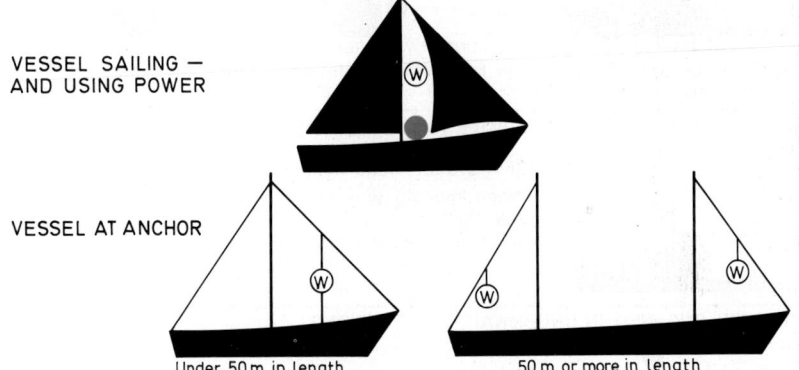

VESSEL SAILING — AND USING POWER

VESSEL AT ANCHOR

Under 50 m. in length   50 m. or more in length

A vessel of 100 m. or more shall also illuminate her decks.
A vessel of less than 7 m. in length when at anchor, not in or near a narrow channel, fairway, or anchorage, shall not be required to exhibit these lights.

POWER DRIVEN VESSEL UNDERWAY

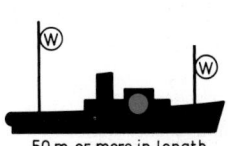 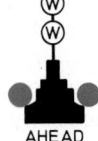  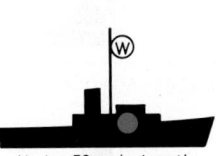

50 m. or more in length   AHEAD   ASTERN   Under 50 m. in length

Under 12 m. may exhibit all round white light and side lights.

Less than 7 m. and maximum speed not exceeding 7 knots an all round white light may be shown, and if practicable side lights.

HOVERCRAFT

Normal lights as for power driven vessels and when in non–displacement mode an all round flashing yellow light.

VESSELS TOWING

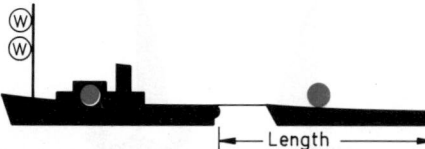
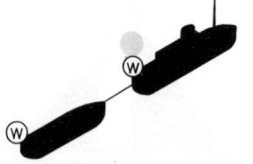

|← Length →|

Tow length 200 m. or less, two mast head lights shown; over 200 m. three lights. Yellow towing light shown over stern light. Towed vessels show side and stern lights.

PILOT VESSEL ON DUTY

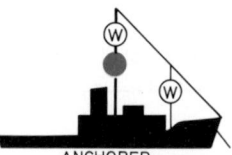
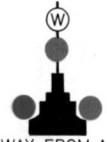

ANCHORED   UNDERWAY, FROM AHEAD   UNDERWAY, FROM ASTERN

2 all round lights, white over red. When underway shows stern and side lights instead of anchor light.

VESSELS RESTRICTED IN ABILITY TO MANOEUVRE

Shows 3 all round lights, red over white over red.
When making way shows mast head, stern and side lights.
When at anchor shows an anchor light.

VESSEL ENGAGED IN UNDERWATER OPERATIONS

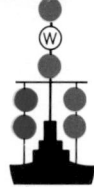

PASS THIS SIDE   OBSTRUCTION THIS SIDE

When making way also shows mast head, stern and side lights.
When at anchor does NOT show anchor light.

VESSEL AGROUND

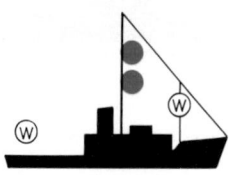

Two all round red lights and anchor light(s).
A vessel of less than 12 m. in length shall not be required to exhibit these lights.

VESSEL CONSTRAINED BY HER DRAUGHT

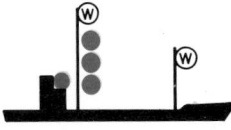

Three all round red lights,
with normal navigation lights

VESSEL ENGAGED IN MINESWEEPING

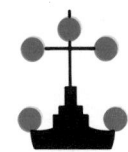

Three all round green lights,
with normal navigation lights

VESSEL TRAWLING

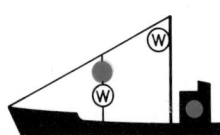

Two all round lights green over white,
with normal navigation lights.
Mast head light optional under 50 m.

VESSEL FISHING, OTHER THAN TRAWLING

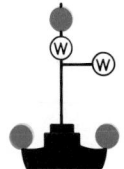

Two all round lights red over white with one
all round white light in direction of gear if it
extends more than 150 m. horizontally.
Each vessel engaged in 'pair trawling' may direct
a searchlight forward and in direction of other
vessel.

VESSEL NOT UNDER COMMAND

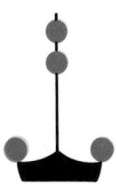

Two all round red lights and when making way
stern and side lights.

REMEMBER:

A sailing vessel when using its engine —with or without sails—
is a power driven vessel within the meaning of the Rules
and must act accordingly, showing the appropriate shapes
and lights.
Therefore a tricolour lantern may not be used when under power.

DAYMARKS

VESSEL SAILING AND USING POWER

Black cone, point down.

VESSEL AT ANCHOR

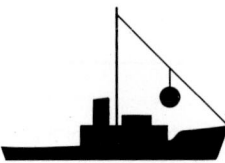

Black ball.

A vessel of less than 7m. in length when at anchor, not in or near a narrow channel, fairway or anchorage, shall not be required to exhibit the ball.

VESSEL TOWING

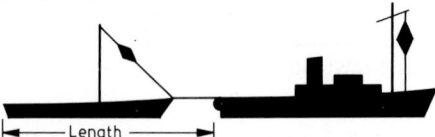

|←———— Length ————→|

If length of tow exceeds 200 m. a black diamond shape to be exhibited on each vessel.

VESSEL RESTRICTED IN ABILITY TO MANOEUVRE

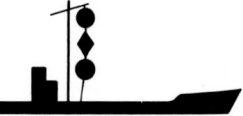

Black ball over black diamond over black ball.

VESSEL ENGAGED IN UNDERWATER OPERATIONS

PASS
THIS
SIDE

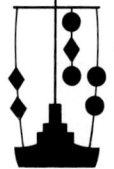

OBSTRUCTION
THIS SIDE

Two black balls on the side of obstruction.

Two black diamonds on side on which vessels may pass.

If vessel is too small to exhibit above shapes a rigid replica of code flag A shall be flown. White and blue.

VESSEL AGROUND

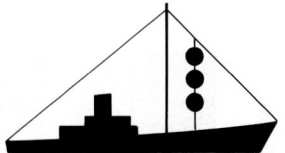

Three black balls to be exhibited.
Not required for vessel under 12 m.

VESSEL CONSTRAINED BY HER DRAUGHT

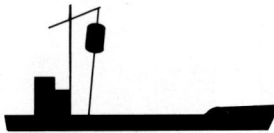

A black cylinder

VESSEL ENGAGED IN MINESWEEPING

Three black balls

VESSEL ENGAGED IN FISHING

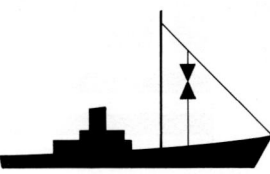

Two black cones, points together.
May be replaced by basket if under 20 m.

If outlying gear extends more than 150 m.
horizontally, a black cone point up is shown
in direction of gear, e.g.

VESSEL NOT UNDER COMMAND

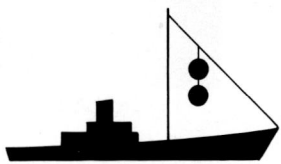

Two black balls

SOME ENSIGNS OF THE WORLD

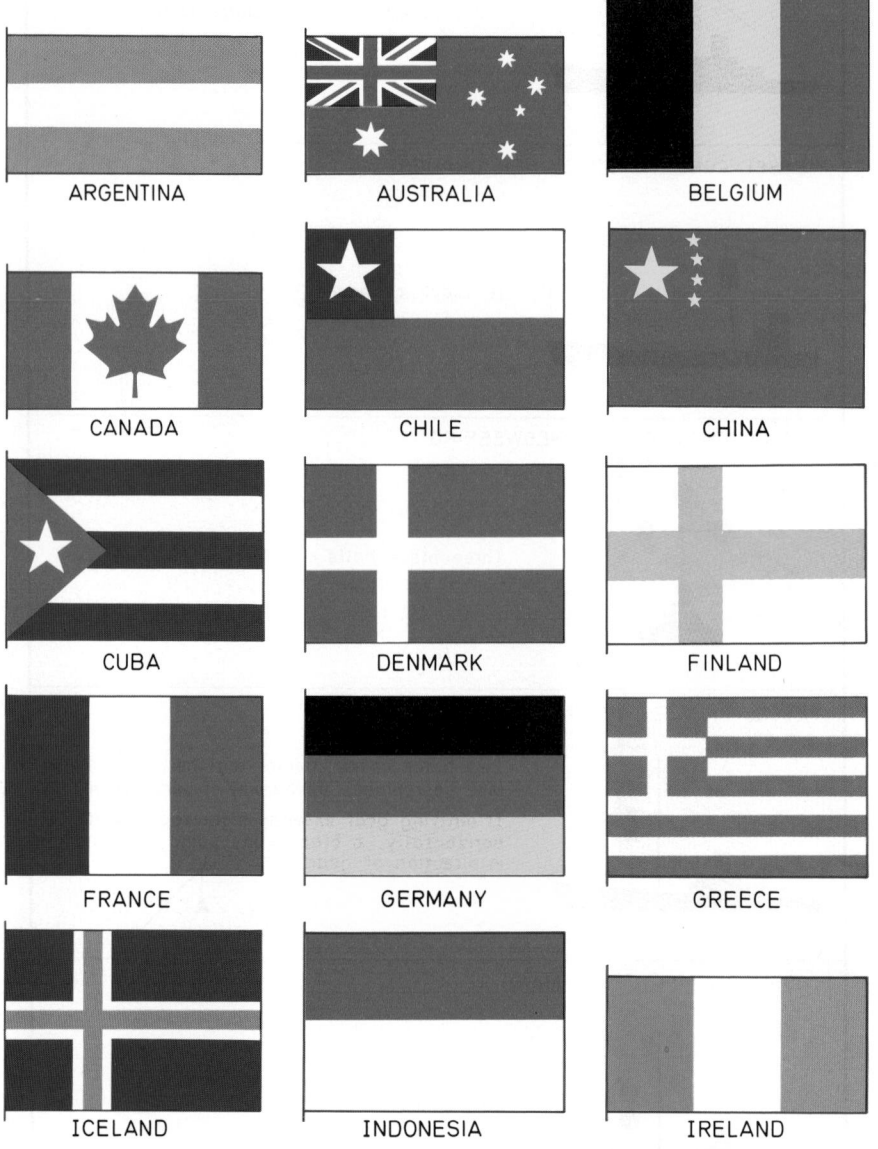

ARGENTINA   AUSTRALIA   BELGIUM

CANADA   CHILE   CHINA

CUBA   DENMARK   FINLAND

FRANCE   GERMANY   GREECE

ICELAND   INDONESIA   IRELAND

SOME ENSIGNS OF THE WORLD

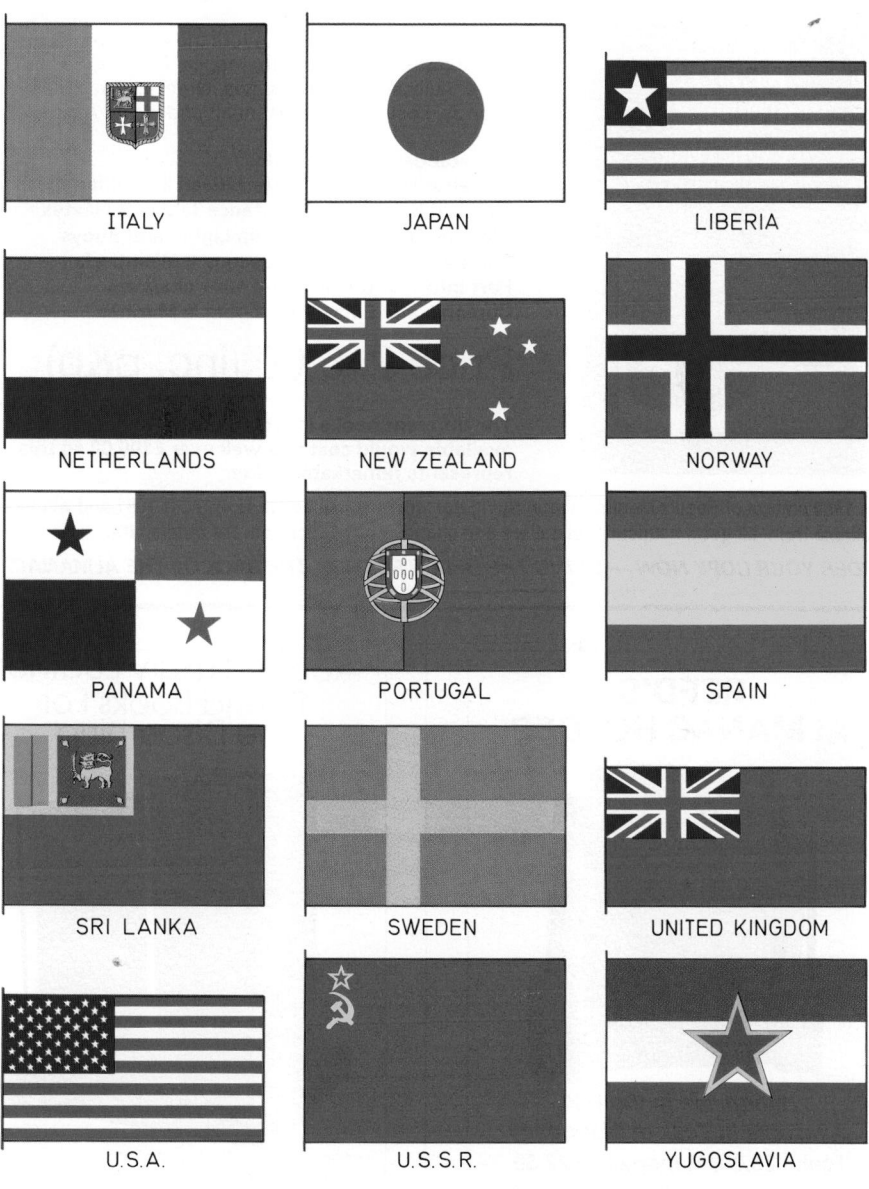

ITALY	JAPAN	LIBERIA
NETHERLANDS	NEW ZEALAND	NORWAY
PANAMA	PORTUGAL	SPAIN
SRI LANKA	SWEDEN	UNITED KINGDOM
U.S.A.	U.S.S.R.	YUGOSLAVIA

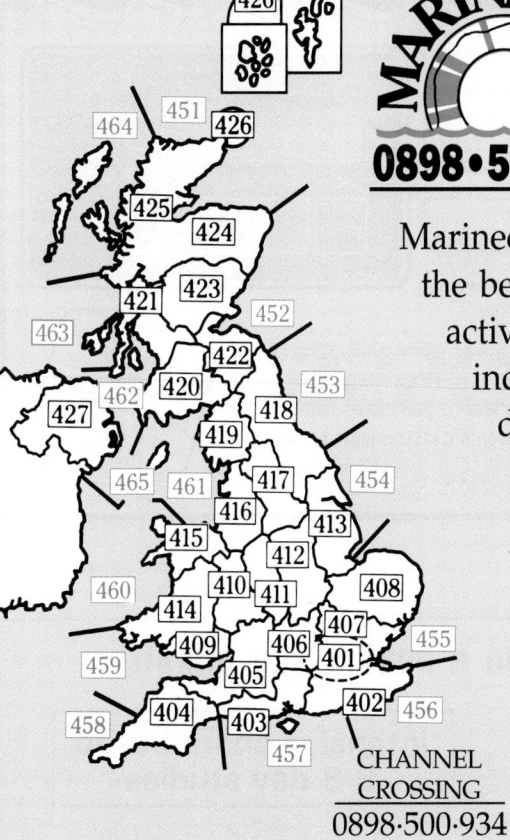

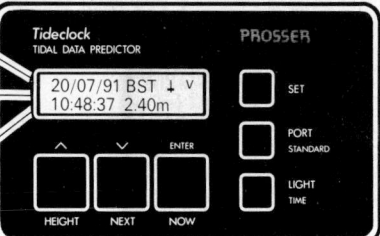

Super'92
Yacht

FOR THE CONNOISSEUR

The 2nd International Super Yacht Conference & Exhibition

The Acropolis • Nice • The French Riviera

Wednesday 4th March 1992
Thursday 5th March 1992
Friday 6th March 1992

Organisers:
Gillan Beach Limited
Stanley House, Stanley Road
Wembley, Middlesex HA0 4JB
England

SPONSORED BY
Yachting

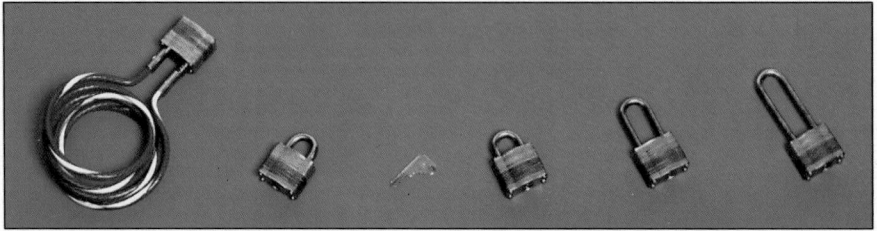
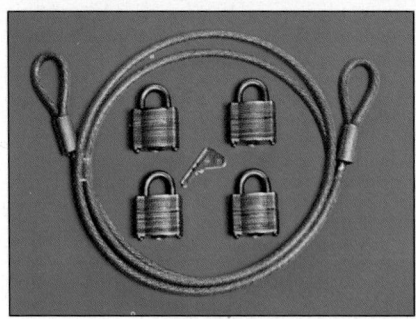
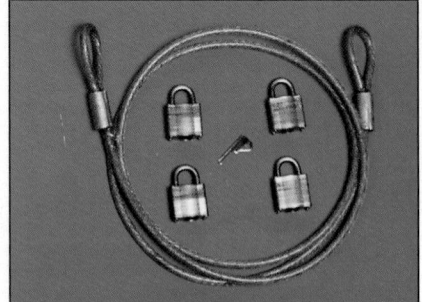

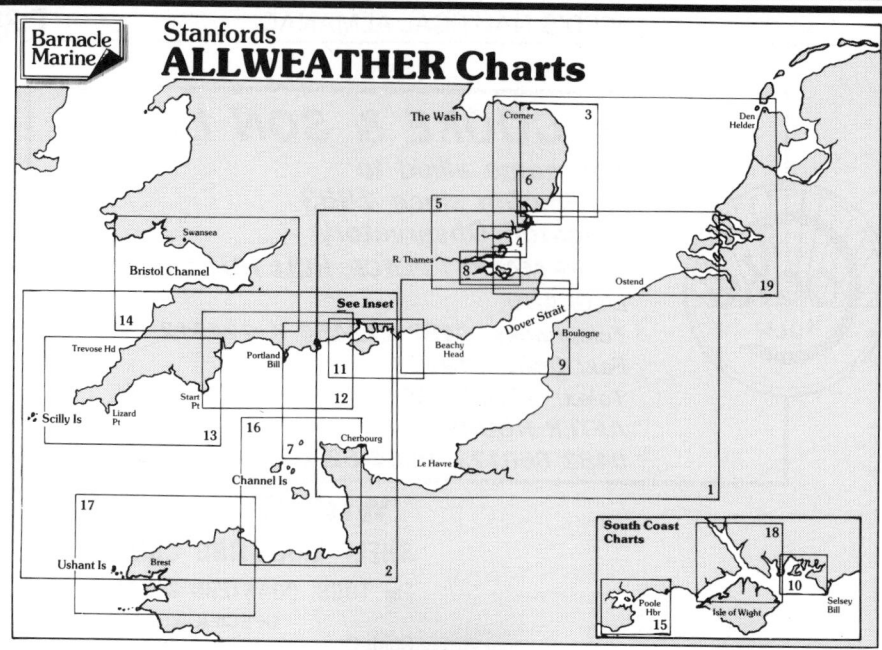

OPEN LEARNING FOR YACHTSMEN

The Open Learning method of teaching has in the past 25 years become the main medium for programmed distance learning. Open Learning has been used with considerable success by the Open University for instruction at degree level courses, and now the Open College is developing Open Learning courses for technical training. With Open Learning for Yachtsmen we are applying the Open Learning principles to the training of the amateur seaman.

Course Structure

Open Learning for Yachtsmen is based on the RYA training syllabus for the Day Skipper Certificate and has been divided into three modules covering the following subjects:

- Module 1: Prevention of Collision Regulations and IALA Buoyage System
- Module 2: Coastal Navigation
- Module 3: Basic Seamanship and Safety Equipment.

Teaching Materials

The teaching materials suppled for each module will be a text book with a supporting video programme.

The Text Book

The main instructional medium for each module will be the text book. The text book is divided into a number of lessons. Each lesson consisting of:

- a set of tutorial notes with explanatory exercises where necessary
- self test questions and answers. The number of self test exercises in a lesson will depend on the depth of study required for the subject.
- tutor assessment paper

Video Programme

The video programme is designed to support the text book. The video programme is used to:

- expand the main points in the tutorial notes
- to give practical demonstrations
- to develop points that are difficult to show in the written format

Text Book £20.00.
(Packing and postage £3.02 (Home)
£4.65 (Overseas).

Video £21.00.
(Packing and postage £1.50 (Home)
£1.86 (Overseas).
Plus VAT £3.91 (U.K. only).

Text Book and Video £39.50.
Post Paid U.K.   £4.12 (Overseas).
Plus VAT — Video Element £2.98 (U.K. only).

*Available from:—***BROWN, SON & FERGUSON, LTD.**, 4-10 Darnley Street, Glasgow, G41 2SD

NOW AVAILABLE

- A5 size (210 x 148mm)
- Gold Blocked on blue bonded leather
- Week to view
- 176 pages
- 27 pages of photographs - Keith Beken's personal selection from Beken's unique photographic collection
- Weather Forecast Areas, Coastal Radio Stations, Dover High Water etc.
- At all good bookshops and chandlers or direct from the publishers

- -

ORDER YOUR COPY NOW!

Name (please Print)..

Address..

....

.... Postcode..................

Signature...

❑ I enclose a Cheque/BankDraft/International Money Order to the value of £10.50 (to include postage) made payable to:
THOMAS REED PUBLICATIONS Ltd.**or**

❑ Please debit my credit card to the value of £10.50

❑ ACCESS   ❑ VISA   ❑ AMERICAN EXPRESS

A/c No. ☐☐☐☐☐ ☐☐☐☐☐ ☐☐☐☐☐ ☐☐☐☐☐   Expiry Date............

Send this completed coupon to: Thomas Reed Publications Ltd.,
Weir House, Hurst Road, East Molesey, Surrey KT8 9AQ, U.K. RNACWP

The magazine with more Boats and Planes for sale than any other

Notices to Navigators

1

(Gives changes to navaids and other data up to the time of publication since the body of the book was printed. Compiled from information available at July 1991.)

The discovery of new or suspected dangers to navigation or of defects in Aids to Navigation should immediately be notified to The Hydrographer of the Navy, Hydrographic Office, Ministry of Defence, Taunton, Somerset.

WARNING ON USE OF FLOATING AIDS
THE PRUDENT NAVIGATOR WILL NOT RELY SOLELY ON ANY SINGLE AID TO NAVIGATION, PARTICULARLY ON FLOATING AIDS.

ADMIRALTY PUBLICATIONS

SAILING DIRECTIONS

NP		NP	
1	Africa Pilot Vol. I	55	North Sea (East) Pilot
18	Baltic Pilot Vol. I	56	Norway Pilot Volume I
19	Baltic Pilot Vol. II	57A	Norway Pilot Vol. IIA
20	Baltic Pilot Vol. III	57B	Norway Pilot Vol. IIB
22	Bay of Biscay Pilot	58A	Norway Pilot Vol. IIIA
27	Channel Pilot	58B	Norway Pilot Vol. IIIB
28	Dover Strait Pilot	66	West Coast of Scotland Pilot
37	West Coast of England Pilot	67	West Coast of Spain and
40	Irish Coast Pilot		Portugal Pilot
52	North Coast of Scotland Pilot	100	The Mariner's Handbook
54	North Sea (West) Pilot	136	Ocean Passages for the World

ADMIRALTY LIST OF LIGHTS AND FOG SIGNALS

NP 74 Volume A,   *NP* 75 Volume B,   *NP* 76 Volume C,   *NP* 77 Volume D

ADMIRALTY LIST OF RADIO SIGNALS
NP

281(1)	Vol. 1 Coast Radio Stations: Part 1: Europe, Africa and Asia
282	Vol. 2 Radio Navigational Aids, Electronic Position Fixing Systems & Radio Time Signals.
283	Vol. 3 Radio Weather Services and Navigational Warnings.
284	Vol. 4 Meteorological Observation Stations
	Vol. 6 Vessel Traffic Services, Port Operations and Pilot Services.
286(1)	Part 1: NW Europe and the Mediterranean
286(2)	Part 2: Africa and Asia, Australasia, the Americas, Greenland & Iceland

TIDAL PUBLICATIONS
NP

201	*Admiralty Tide Tables.* Vol. I European Waters, *Admiralty Tidal Stream Atlases*
209	Orkney and Shetland Islands
218	North Coast of Ireland, West Coast of Scotland
219	Portsmouth Harbour and Approaches
220	Rosyth Harbour and Approaches
221	Plymouth Harbour and Approaches
233	Dover Strait
249	Thames Estuary (with Co-Tidal Charts)
250	The English & Bristol Channels
251	North Sea, Southern Part
252	North Sea, Northern Part
253	North Sea, Eastern Part
256	Irish Sea
257	Approaches to Portland
264	The Channel Islands and the Adjacent Coasts of France
265	France, West Coast
337	The Solent and Adjacent Waters

HALF YEARLY SUPPLEMENT
TO REED'S NAUTICAL ALMANAC, 1992

The Almanac, which commences to be used on January 1st, 1992, has to be printed and distributed throughout the world by this date. It is therefore corrected only up to the time of going to press.

In order that the greatest benefit may be derived from having up-to-date information on board, a half yearly supplement is issued giving alterations or corrections to Lights, Buoys, Radio Stations, etc., which have taken place since the Almanac went to press and up to March 1st, 1992. This supplement will be published early April 1992 and will be sent to you free of charge on receipt of this form.

(PLEASE USE BLOCK CAPITALS)

IMPORTANT PLEASE STAMP FORM THIS SIDE OR WE CANNOT GUARANTEE TO SUPPLY SUPPLEMENT. OVERSEAS READERS MAY SEND INTERNATIONAL REPLY COUPON AVAILABLE FROM LOCAL POST OFFICE.

> AFFIX STAMP FOR RETURN POSTAGE Under 60g

CUT HERE

NAME ....

ADDRESS ....

....

....

....POSTAL CODE........................

Please tick appropriate box and complete.

Yachtsman ☐ Make of craft .... LOA ...... Age of craft ......

Motor Yachtsman ☐ Make of craft .... LOA ...... Age of craft ......

Fisherman ☐ Make of craft .... LOA ...... Age of craft ......

Other ☐ Please state ....

How often do you buy REED'S? ....

Thank you

SUGGESTIONS

We welcome any suggestions to increase the usefulness of this Almanac. Please write on reverse side of this form.

HALF YEARLY SUPPLEMENT
TO REED'S NAUTICAL ALMANAC, 1992
TO OBTAIN YOUR FREE COPY
COMPLETE AND RETURN
THIS FORM TO US
NOW!

Cut carefully along the line at the side of the page. Then fold down the long vertical line marked First Fold.

Fold the two short lines inwards, Folds 2 and 3, tucking one flap into the other.

Make sure our address is kept on the outside.

SECOND FOLD

IMPORTANT PLEASE STAMP FORM THIS SIDE
OR WE CANNOT GUARANTEE TO SUPPLY SUPPLEMENT

PLEASE
AFFIX
STAMP

FIRST FOLD

THOMAS REED PUBLICATIONS LIMITED,

WEIR HOUSE, HURST ROAD,

EAST MOLESEY,

SURREY KT8 9AQ.

U.K.

THIRD FOLD AND TUCK

SOME USEFUL ADDRESSES

British Marine Industries Federation, Meadlake Place, Thorpe Lea Road, Egham, Surrey TW20 8HE. Tel: 0784 473377. Fax: 0784 439678.

British Sub-Aqua Club, Telford's Quay, Ellesmere Port, South Wirral, Cheshire L65 4FY. Tel: 051-357 1951.

British Telecom Maritime Radio Services, 43 Bartholomew Close, London EC1A 7HP. Tel: 071-583 9416.

British Waterways Board, Greycaine Road, Watford, Herts WD2 4JR. Tel: 0923 226422.

Clyde Cruising Club, c/o R.A. Clements & Co. 29 St. Vincent Place, Glasgow G1 2DT. Tel: 041-221 0068.

HM Coastguard, Department of Transport, Sunley House, 90-93 High Holborn, London WC1V 6LP. Tel: 071-405 6911.

Cruising Association, Ivory House, St. Katharine's Dock, World Trade Centre, London E1 9AT. Tel: 071-481 0881.

HM Customs and Excise, Dorset House, Stamford Street, London SE1 9PS. Tel: 071-865 4743.

Hydrographic Office, Ministry of Defence, Taunton, Somerset TA1 2DN. Tel: 0823 337900.

International Maritime Organisation, 4 Albert Embankment, London SE1. Tel: 071-735 7611.

Lloyds of London Press, Sheepen Place, Colchester, Essex CO3 3LP. Tel: 0206 772277.

Lloyd's Register of Shipping, Yacht and Small Craft Department, 71 Fenchurch Street, London EC3M 4BS. Tel: 071-709 9166.

Meteorological Office, London Road, Bracknell, Berkshire RG12 2SZ. Tel: 0344 420242.

National Yacht Harbour Association, Hardy House, Somerset Road, Ashford, Kent TN24 8EW. Tel: 0233 643837.

Port of London Authority, Tilbury Dock, Tilbury, Essex RM18 7EH. Tel: 0474 560444.

Proudman Oceanographic Laboratory, Bidston Observatory, Birkenhead, Cheshire L43 7RA. Tel: 051-653 8633.

Royal Institute of Navigation, 1 Kensington Gore, London SW7 2AT. Tel: 071-589 5021.

Royal National Lifeboat Institution, West Quay Road, Poole, Dorset BH15 1HZ. Tel: 0202 671133.

Royal Naval Sailing Association, c/o Royal Naval Club, Pembroke Road, Portsmouth, Hants PO1 2NT. Tel: 0705 823524.

Royal Yachting Association, RYA House, Romsey Road, Eastleigh, Hants. SO5 4YA. Tel: 0703 629962.

Royal Yachting Association (Scotland), Caledonia House, South Gyle, Edinburgh EH12 9DQ. Tel: 031-317 7388.

Solent Cruising and Racing Association, 18 Bath Road, Cowes, I.O.W. Tel: 0983 295744.

Trinity House, Corporation of, Trinity House, Tower Hill, London EC3N 4DH. Tel: 071-480 6601.

UK Offshore Boating Association, 16A Station Approach, West Byfleet, Surrey KT14 6NF. Tel: 0932 336597.

Yacht Charter Association, 60 Silverdale, New Milton, Hants BH25 7DE. Tel: 0425 619004. Fax: 0425 610967.

PERSONAL NOTES

TELEPHONE DIALLING CODES

Country	Code	Int. Prefix	Country	Code	Int. Prefix
Belgium	32	(00..44)	Netherlands	31	(09..44)
Denmark	45	(00944)	Norway	47	(09544)
Eire	353*	(03)†	Poland	48	(0..044)
France	33	(19..44)	Portugal	351	(0044)
Germany	49	(0044)	Spain	34	(07..44)
Gibraltar	350	(0044)	Sweden	46	(00944)
Iceland	354	(9044)	United Kingdom	44	(010)

From the UK: dial the international prefix (010), followed by the country code, e.g. France 010 33, then the area code and telephone number.
* For Dublin dial 0001 followed by the number required.

Dialling the UK: dial the international prefix and country code (shown in brackets), e.g. from France 19..44, followed by the area code and number required (but omit the initial '0' in the area code).

NOTE: where dots are shown (..) wait for second dialling tone.
†Dial 03, followed by area code and number required, e.g. 03-071 0012.

NATIONAL HOLIDAYS 1992

Belgium	Jan. 1; Apr. 4*, 5†; May 1; June 11, 12, 19; July 1, 5†, 10; Sept. 9; Nov. 1†,
Denmark	Jan. 1; Apr. 16, 17, 20; May 15, 28; June 5, 8; Dec. 25, 26*.
France	Jan. 1; Apr. 20; May 1, 8, 28; June 8; July 14; Aug. 15*; Nov. 1†, 11; Dec. 25.
Germany	Jan. 1; Apr. 17, 20; May 1, 28; June 8; Oct. 3*; Nov. 18; Dec. 25, 26*.
Gibraltar	Jan. 1; Mar. 9; Apr. 17, 20; May 4; June 8; Aug. 31; Dec. 25, 26*, 28.
Iceland	Jan. 1; Apr. 16, 17, 19†, 20, 23; May 1, 28; June 7†, 8, 17; Aug. 3; Dec. 25, 26*.
Netherlands	Jan. 1; Apr. 17, 20; May 28; June 8; Dec. 25, 26*.
Norway	Jan. 1; Apr. 12†, 16, 17, 19†, 20.
Poland	Jan. 1; Apr. 20; May 1; June 18; Aug 15*; Nov. 1†, 11; Dec. 25, 26*.
Portugal	Jan. 1; Mar. 3; Apr. 17, 19†, 25*; May 1 June 10, 18; Aug. 15*; Oct. 5; Nov. 1†; Dec. 1, 8, 25.
Spain	Jan. 1, 6; Mar. 19; Apr. 16, 17; May 1; June 18; July 25*, Aug. 15*; Oct. 12; Nov. 1†, 2; Dec. 6†, 7, 8, 25.
Sweden	Jan. 1, 6; Apr. 17, 20; May 1, 28; June 8, 20*; Oct. 31*; Dec. 25, 26*.
United Kingdom	Jan. 1; Apr. 17, 20; May 4, 25; Aug. 31; Dec. 25, 26*, 28.

† = Sun.   * = Sat.   All dates subject to revision

SIMPLE FORM OF SALVAGE AGREEMENT
"NO CURE — NO PAY"

(Incorporating Lloyd's Open Form)

Date

On board the yacht

IT IS HEREBY AGREED BETWEEN

for and on behalf of the Owners of the
(hereinafter called "the Owners")

AND   for and on behalf of
(hereinafter called "the Contractor")

1. That the Contractor will use his best endeavours to salve the
and take her into

or such other place as may hereinafter be agreed or if no place is named or agreed to
a place of safety.

2. That the services shall be rendered by the Contractor and accepted by the owner
as salvage services upon the principle of "No cure — No pay" subject to the terms
conditions and provisions (including those relating to Arbitration and the providing of
security) of the current Standard Form of Salvage Agreement approved and published
by the Council of Lloyd's of London and known as Lloyd's Open Form.

3. In the event of success the Contractor's remuneration shall be £   or
if no sum be mutually agreed between the parties or entered herein same shall be
fixed by arbitration in London in the manner prescribed in Lloyd's Open Form.

4. The Owners their servants and agents shall cooperate fully with the Contractor in
and about the salvage including obtaining entry to the place named in Clause 1 hereof
or the place of safety. The Contractor may make reasonable use of the vessel's
machinery gear equipment anchors chains stores and other appurtenances during
and for the purpose of the services free of expense but shall not unnecessarily
damage abandon or sacrifice the same or any property the subject of this Agreement.

For and on behalf of the Owners of property to be salved

....

For and on behalf of the Contractor

....

Note   Full copies of the Lloyd's Open Form Salvage Agreement can be obtained
from the Salvage Arbitration Branch, Lloyd's of London, One Lime Street,
London EC3M 7HA. Tel: (071) 623 7100, Ext. 5849, who should be notified of
the services only when no agreement can be reached as to remuneration.

LATEST CORRECTIONS TO NAVIGATIONAL AIDS

Page	
19:16	111 Cap d'Alprech Lt: amend mode to A1A.
	165 Outer Gabbard Lt.V: delete station.
19:17	216 Bressay Lt.Ho. Shetlands: delete station.
19:28	589 Eckmuhl Lt.Ho. Pte. Penmarc'h: amend mode to A1A.
19:34	R95 East Channel Lt. Float: delete station and replace by
	R95 East Channel Lt.By. 49°58'.7 2°28'.9 T - 10 'b'.
19:35	R203 Outer Gabbard Lt.V: delete station and replace by
	R203 Outer Gabbard Lt.By.51°57'.8 2°04'.3 0 - - -10 'f'.
	R210 Winterton Old Lt.Ho: delete 90s, insert footnote ref 'f'.
19:37	R745 Mavholmsbaden Lt: amend ident to M - - (0.45) and range to 3 miles.
20:9	Insert above Celtic: Burnham 51°15'N 3°00'W VHF 25 (working channel). Direct Calling Station.
22:13	Penninis Head Lt. now 12M
22:22	Delete Shagstone Lt.
22:50	Cowes. Amend Tel. Nos: H.M. & Pilots (0983) 293952.Mon-Fri. and 0800-1700 Sat-Sun. or (0983) 293812 H24. Fax: (0983) 290018.
	Radio-Pilot: VHF Ch. 16, 9, 12, 69 Mon-Fri 0830-1700 and when vessel expected.
	Newport. Add Tel. No: 520000. Radio-Port now Chan. 16, 69 0800-1600 when office manned.
22:54	E. Winner By. now Winner By.
22:65	Train Ferry Dock Jetty Head Lt: delete fog signal.
22:68	Delete Bow Creek Tidal Barrier. Add: River Lea Bridge: vertical clearance 9.1m.
22:78	Add below Otterham, Bartlett etc:
	Chatham Locks (N) 145.2m x 28.65m x 9.6m MHWN.
	(S) 145.2m x 25.6m x 9.1m MHWN.
22:79	Insert above Conyer creek: Emley By.Conical G.
22:89	Brightlingsea. Ldg.Lts. now 041° (Front) F.R. 4M. Or. □ W.stripe 7m. 020°-080° (Rear) F.R. 4M. Or. □ W. stripe 10m.
	Insert below Ldg.Lts:
	Lt.Q. ⚓ on B.Y.Bn.
	Hardway Head Lt. 2 F.R. on post 2m.
	New Jetty Lt. 2 F.R.
	Olivers Wharf Lt. 2 F.R.
22:98	Newarp Lanby range now 21M.
22:102	Boston. Delete Entry Signals
22:103	Delete Dowsing Lt.V.
22:111	Insert below Amethyst Field A2D:
	C1D 53°38'.7N 0°36'.2E
	B1D 53°33'.6N 0°52'.8E
22:118	Blyth: add Pilots (0670) 353137.
22:123	Braefoot Bay Terminal Ldg.Lts. 019°24'. Add: Shown for vessels using terminal. Q.Y. (strobe) for tankers.
22:131	Kinnairds Head Lt. now 18M. 25m.
22:140	Kirkabister Ness Lt: delete RC.
22:166	Rhu South Lt.By. now Rhu SE Lt.By.

LATEST CORRECTIONS TO NAVIGATIONAL AIDS

Page
22:175   Victoria Pier head: delete RC.
             Barrow. Tel. Nos. Amend to: Dock (0229) 822911. H.M. (0229) 820155.
22:199   Breaksea Lt.F. now 12M.
22:209   Instow Ldg.Lts. sector now 104.5°-131.5°. H24.
22:211   Hayle. Amend as follows:
             Perch Lt. F.G.
             Perch Lt. F.G. on Col.
             Chapel Anjou Point Lt. F.G. on Col.
22:215   Insert above Haulbowline Island: No: 22 Lt.By. Fl.R.5 sec. Can R.
22:240   Insert above Beginish Bar Channel Lt. Harbour Rock Lt.
             Q. (3) 10 sec. 5M. ϑ on B.Y.B.Bn. 4m. 080°-040°.
23:25   E. Channel Lt.By. Amend Long. to: 02°28'.9W.
23:53   Delete Landing Stage Lt. and insert: RoRo Berth Head Lt. Oc. (2) R.6 sec. 6M
             R.mast 7m.
23:69   Delete ATT-ARC Lt.By.
23:79   Darsena No: 1 Wharf Head Lt. now Oc.G.2.5 sec.G.Col.7m.
23:101   Ponta do Topo Lt. now Fl.(2) 10 sec.
24:6   Schelde. Steenbank Pilot now VHF Chan.6, 64.
24:9   Vlissingen Radio. Amend VHF Chan.14 to 64.
24:49   Amrun Hafen Ldg.Lts. now 272°.
25:44   Foto Lts. in line 265° now Lt.Fl.(2)W.R.G.6 sec. W.9M. R.7M. G.6M. Or.mast
             6m. G.236°-259°; W.-262°; R.-293°.
             Delete 2nd Lts. in line 265°.
25:56   Insert below Marstal Havn Ldg.Lts.254°:
             S. Channel Ldg.Lts.319°24' (Front) Iso.2 sec. 7M. Tr.6m. 303.4°-335.4°. (Rear)
             Iso.4 sec. 7M.Tr.10m. 303.4°-355.4°.
             Lt. Oc.W.R.G.5 sec. W.7M. R.5M. G.5M. mast 6m. G.281.4°-286.4°; W.-290.4°;
             R-294.4°; G.-301.4°.
25:82   Hoganas Pier Head Lt. range now W.9M. R.7M. G.6M.
25:96   N. Point Lt. now Oc.G.4 sec.
25:98   Delete Basen Mlynski Lt.
             Delete Wyspa Gryfia S.End Lt.
25:99   Ostrow Grabowski N.End Lt. Add: F.Lt.110m.SW and 80m.E. Dolphins 300m
             SE, W.Side 2 F.G.vert. E.Side 2 F.R. vert.
             Lt.Oc.5 sec. Add: Dolphins 450m NNW, W.side 2 F.G. vert. E.Side 2 F.R.vert.

NEW CHARTS for the area covered by this Almanac

35	112	133	192	278	304	825	1237	1349	1491	1594	1753
1856	1858	1872	1892	1951	1953	1957	1970	1975	1977	1978	2010
2050	2114	2390	2450	2451	2656	2748	2904	3159	3283	3290	3490

JANUARY 1992 PLANNER	FEBRUARY 1992 PLANNER
1 W	1 Sa
2 Th	2 **Su**
3 F	3 M
4 Sa	4 Tu
5 **Su**	5 W
6 M	6 Th
7 Tu	7 F
8 W	8 Sa
9 Th	9 **Su**
10 F	10 M
11 Sa	11 Tu
12 **Su**	12 W
13 M	13 Th
14 Tu	14 F
15 W	15 Sa
16 Th	16 **Su**
17 F	17 M
18 Sa	18 Tu
19 **Su**	19 W
20 M	20 Th
21 Tu	21 F
22 W	22 Sa
23 Th	23 **Su**
24 F	24 M
25 Sa	25 Tu
26 **Su**	26 W
27 M	27 Th
28 Tu	28 F
29 W	29 Sa
30 Th	
31 F	

MARCH 1992 PLANNER	APRIL 1992 PLANNER
1 **Su**	1 W
2 M	2 Th
3 Tu	3 F
4 W	4 Sa
5 Th	5 **Su**
6 F	6 M
7 Sa	7 Tu
8 **Su**	8 W
9 M	9 Th
10 Tu	10 F
11 W	11 Sa
12 Th	12 **Su**
13 F	13 M
14 Sa	14 Tu
15 **Su**	15 W
16 M	16 Th
17 Tu	17 F
18 W	18 Sa
19 Th	19 **Su**
20 F	20 M
21 Sa	21 Tu
22 **Su**	22 W
23 M	23 Th
24 Tu	24 F
25 W	25 Sa
26 Th	26 **Su**
27 F	27 M
28 Sa	28 Tu
29 **Su**	29 W
30 M	30 Th
31 Tu	

MAY 1992 PLANNER	JUNE 1992 PLANNER
1 F	1 M
2 Sa	2 Tu
3 **Su**	3 W
4 M	4 Th
5 Tu	5 F
6 W	6 Sa
7 Th	7 **Su**
8 F	8 M
9 Sa	9 Tu
10 **Su**	10 W
11 M	11 Th
12 Tu	12 F
13 W	13 Sa
14 Th	14 **Su**
15 F	15 M
16 Sa	16 Tu
17 **Su**	17 W
18 M	18 Th
19 Tu	19 F
20 W	20 Sa
21 Th	21 **Su**
22 F	22 M
23 Sa	23 Tu
24 **Su**	24 W
25 M	25 Th
26 Tu	26 F
27 W	27 Sa
28 Th	28 **Su**
29 F	29 M
30 Sa	30 Tu
31 **Su**	

JULY 1992 PLANNER	AUGUST 1992 PLANNER
1 W	1 Sa
2 Th	2 **Su**
3 F	3 M
4 Sa	4 Tu
5 **Su**	5 W
6 M	6 Th
7 Tu	7 F
8 W	8 Sa
9 Th	9 **Su**
10 F	10 M
11 Sa	11 Tu
12 **Su**	12 W
13 M	13 Th
14 Tu	14 F
15 W	15 Sa
16 Th	16 **Su**
17 F	17 M
18 Sa	18 Tu
19 **Su**	19 W
20 M	20 Th
21 Tu	21 F
22 W	22 Sa
23 Th	23 **Su**
24 F	24 M
25 Sa	25 Tu
26 **Su**	26 W
27 M	27 Th
28 Tu	28 F
29 W	29 Sa
30 Th	30 **Su**
31 F	31 M

SEPTEMBER 1992 PLANNER	OCTOBER 1992 PLANNER
1 Tu	1 Th
2 W	2 F
3 Th	3 Sa
4 F	4 **Su**
5 Sa	5 M
6 **Su**	6 Tu
7 M	7 W
8 Tu	8 Th
9 W	9 F
10 Th	10 Sa
11 F	11 **Su**
12 Sa	12 M
13 **Su**	13 Tu
14 M	14 W
15 Tu	15 Th
16 W	16 F
17 Th	17 Sa
18 F	18 **Su**
19 Sa	19 M
20 **Su**	20 Tu
21 M	21 W
22 Tu	22 Th
23 W	23 F
24 Th	24 Sa
25 F	25 **Su**
26 Sa	26 M
27 **Su**	27 Tu
28 M	28 W
29 Tu	29 Th
30 W	30 F
	31 Sa

NOVEMBER 1992 PLANNER

1 **Su**	
2 M	
3 Tu	
4 W	
5 Th	
6 F	
7 Sa	
8 **Su**	
9 M	
10 Tu	
11 W	
12 Th	
13 F	
14 Sa	
15 **Su**	
16 M	
17 Tu	
18 W	
19 Th	
20 F	
21 Sa	
22 **Su**	
23 M	
24 Tu	
25 W	
26 Th	
27 F	
28 Sa	
29 **Su**	
30 M	

DECEMBER 1992 PLANNER

1 Tu	
2 W	
3 Th	
4 F	
5 Sa	
6 **Su**	
7 M	
8 Tu	
9 W	
10 Th	
11 F	
12 Sa	
13 **Su**	
14 M	
15 Tu	
16 W	
17 Th	
18 F	
19 Sa	
20 **Su**	
21 M	
22 Tu	
23 W	
24 Th	
25 F	
26 Sa	
27 **Su**	
28 M	
29 Tu	
30 W	
31 Th	

Nautical Astronomy

2

NAUTICAL ASTRONOMY
(Astro Navigation)
and the
NAUTICAL ALMANAC

Nautical Astronomy or Astro Navigation as it is now more commonly known, is that part of Astronomy which uses the Heavenly Bodies to calculate—when out of sight of land—the position of a vessel in the waters of the Earth. In the same way also, the Error of the magnetic Compass may at any time be found so that the mariner may, with accuracy, steer from one point to another.

The heavenly bodies used are the Sun, the Moon; the Planets—Venus, Jupiter, Mars and Saturn—and more than 60 bright Stars.

The function of an Astronomical Calendar—that is the Nautical Ephemeris portion of a Nautical Almanac—is to present in the most legible and easily understood manner the position of these heavenly bodies at all times throughout the year.

Reed's Nautical Almanac has for half a century given these positions in terms of Declination and G.H.A. (Greenwich Hour Angle). It will be seen by the diagram on p. 2:4 that the Earth and Celestial Sphere have the same axis and centre; therefore angles on one correspond to angles on the other; so that the Dec. and G.H.A. of a body in the Celestial Sphere corresponds to the Latitude and Longitude of a position, vertically below it on the Earth.

Owing to the rotation of the Earth daily and to its annual movement round the Sun, also of course to the body's own movement, the whole layout of the Nautical Ephemeris, and the Correction Tables, has been designed so that with the greatest accuracy in the shortest possible time the exact position of a heavenly body may be found at the required time of Observation.

It is, of course, necessary to have a knowledge of Navigation to be able to use the data provided; but for the assistance of Navigators generally—professional and amateur alike—a full explanation of how to use the information for all Navigational purposes is given with many examples in the following sections.

The Sun—pre-eminent body—needs no finding, neither does the Moon, of course; but the times of Sunrise and Sunset, Moonrise and Moonset are given on the monthly pages, as unless these bodies are visible they cannot naturally be of any Navigational assistance.

The four Planets—Venus, Jupiter, Mars and Saturn—are extremely important in Navigation, so all data for these is provided on one monthly page, and further notes to help to identify them are given on p. 2:32.

The Stars are the modern Navigator's greatest friends, because in the daytime only one Sun can ever be visible even under the best conditions; but many—approximately 60—quite bright Stars give the Observer, if not always a choice, a far better chance to secure definite and more accurate observations for ascertaining his position.

CELESTIAL SIGNS AND ABBREVIATIONS

SIGNS OF THE PLANETS

⊙	The Sun.	⊕	The Earth.	♄	Saturn.
☾	The Moon.	♂	Mars.	♅	Uranus.
☿	Mercury.	♃	Jupiter.	♆	Neptune
♀	Venus.				

SIGNS OF THE ZODIAC

The Zodiac is the belt or zone extending 8° on either side of the Ecliptic, which contains the apparent paths of the Sun, Moon and the principal planets. It is divided into twelve angular portions of 30° (equalling the circle of 360°), each portion containing one constellation or sign, termed collectively The Signs of the Zodiac.

The seasons associated with these signs are given below, however, owing to the precession of the equinoxes the vernal equinox now actually occurs during Pisces instead of marking the First Point of Aries.

Northern Signs

Spring Signs.
- 1. ♈ Aries .... 0°
- 2. ♉ Taurus .... 30°
- 3. ♊ Gemini .... 60°

Summer Signs.
- 4. ♋ Cancer .... 90°
- 5. ♌ Leo .... 120°
- 6. ♍ Virgo .... 150°

Southern Signs

Autumn Signs.
- 7. ♎ Libra .... 180°
- 8. ♏ Scorpio .... 210°
- 9. ♐ Sagittarius .... 240°

Winter Signs.
- 10. ♑ Capricornus .... 270°
- 11. ♒ Aquarius ....: 300°
- 12. ♓ Pisces .... 330°

ASPECTS

☌ Conjunction, or having the same Longitude or Right Ascension.
☐ Quadrature, or differing ±90° in Longitude or Right Ascension.
☍ Opposition, or differing 180° in Longitude or Right Ascension.

ABBREVIATIONS

☊	Ascending Node	°	Degrees
☋	Descending Node	′	Minutes of Arc
N	North	″	Seconds of Arc
S	South	h	Hours
E	East	m	Minutes of Time
W	West	s	Seconds of Time

GREEK ALPHABET

Letter	Name	Letter	Name	Letter	Name
α	Alpha	ι	Iota	ρ	Rho
β	Beta	κ	Kappa	σ	Sigma
γ	Gamma	λ	Lambda	τ	Tau
δ	Delta	μ	Mu	υ	Upsilon
ε	Epsilon	ν	Nu	φ	Phi
ζ	Zeta	ξ	Xi	χ	Chi
η	Eta	ο	Omicron	ψ	Psi
θ	Theta	π	Pi	ω	Omega

A SHORT GLOSSARY OF TERMS USED

IN NAUTICAL ASTRONOMY AND

ASTRO NAVIGATION

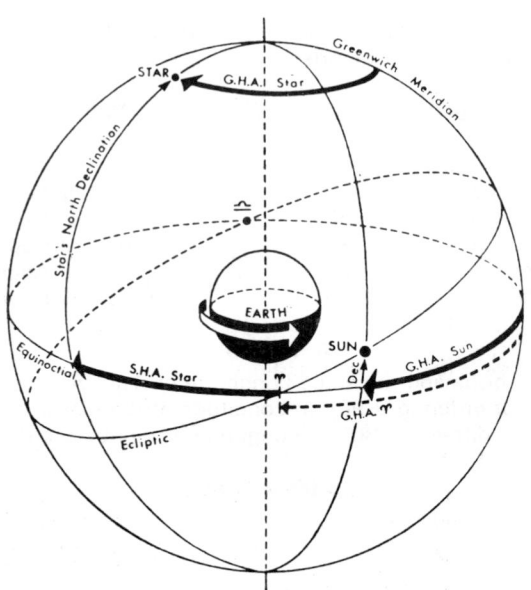

The Celestial Sphere

The Celestial Sphere (also termed the Celestial Concave—or the Heavens) illustrated above, is really the "Space" around the Earth into which we gaze at the Stars. Although it has no defined outline, being so far away it is assumed for practical purposes to be a hollow sphere, of very large radius, having the Earth at its centre, and all heavenly bodies located on its surface.

Owing to the Earth's radius being so small in comparison, the observer's eye may be assumed to be at the centre of the Earth. Positions on the Earth's surface may be projected from the centre outwards on to the celestial sphere, also Parallels of Latitude and Meridians of Longitude.

Altitude. The Observed Altitude is the angular height of an object above the visible horizon, measured on a Vertical Circle (which is a great Circle perpendicular to the horizon) by a Sextant. After correcting this Observed Altitude for Dip, Refraction, Semi-Diameter and Parallax (all embodied in a Total Correction Table in this Almanac) the True Altitude is obtained.

Amplitude. The bearing of a heavenly body when rising or setting measured from the east or west points of the observer's horizon.

Apogee. The position in the orbit of the Moon which is farthest from the Earth. (Tabulated as the date on each monthly page of this Almanac) — opposite to Perigee.

Aphelion. When the Earth or other Planet is at the farthest point (in its orbit) from the Sun, opposite to Perihelion.

Apparent Time. Time measured by the Apparent Sun.

Apparent Sun, The, is the "True" and actually visible Sun of which observations can be taken.

An Apparent Solar Day is the interval between two consecutive transits of the Apparent Sun over an observer's meridian.

Apparent Noon at a place is the time when the Apparent Sun is on the Meridian of that place.

Ship Apparent Time (S.A.T.) **or Local Apparent Time** at any instant is the L.H.A. of the True (or actual) Sun $\pm$ 12h., S.A.T. is reckoned Westwards (0h. to 24h.) from the antimeridian of the place.
The measurement of Apparent Solar Time at any place is simply the measurement of the Apparent Sun's angular distance from the antimeridian of that place. As the Apparent Sun does not move uniformly, it is of no use as a standard time-keeper so another unit is adopted, called Mean Time (q.v.)

Arc. A part of the circumference of any circle.

Aries. One of the constellations of the Zodiac (see First Point of Aries).

Ascension (Right). See Right Ascension.

Astronomical Day, The, is composed of 24 mean solar hours, and begins at midnight on the civil day. It is reckoned from 0h. to 24h.

Autumnal Equinox. The time of the year — September 23rd — when the Sun crosses the Equator from North to South declinations.

Azimuth of a body is the arc of the horizon contained between the observer's meridian and a vertical circle through the centre of the body. It is simply the bearing of a Heavenly Body measured from the North or South points of the horizon.

Azimuth Tables. A set of Tables to determine the true bearing of a Heavenly Body for any Latitude and time.

Calendar Month. The ordinary month having 30, 31 or 28 (and in leap year 29) days in general use.

Celestial Poles, The, are the N. and S. poles of the Earth projected from the Earth's centre on to the Celestial Sphere.

Circumpolar Stars. Stars which never set below the horizon at the place of observation and to get this phenomenon the Latitude of the place must be more than the Polar distance of such Stars. Hence, there are no circumpolar stars at the Terrestrial Equator; but at the Terrestrial Poles all the Stars visible are circumpolar.

Civil Time is composed of 24 mean solar hours divided into two equal portions, the first marked A.M., from midnight to noon, the second marked P.M., from noon to midnight.

The civil year is 365 days (366 to every 4 years — Leap Year).

Conjunction. When two Celestial bodies are in the same direction from the Earth they are said to be in conjunction.

Constellations. The groups into which the stars are divided for identification purposes; the ancients gave these groups names of a fish, bird or figure which they were thought to resemble.

Culmination. The time of a Heavenly body reaching its highest altitude in the Heavens, when it crosses the observer's meridian or ''culminates''.

Cycle. The period of time between some celestial phenomena and its repetition.

Day. See Apparent Time, Mean Day and Sidereal Day.

Declination. The Declination (Dec.) of a body is its angular distance North (N) or South (S) of the Celestial Equator. Declination on the Celestial Sphere corresponds to Latitude on the Earth. North is sometimes written as + (plus) and South as − (minus), but this form of notation is not in general use.

Eclipse. The period when one Celestial body passes through the shadow of another. (See also data at beginning of Ephemeris.)

The Ecliptic is the Great circle on the Celestial Sphere in which the Sun appears to move during its annual movement round the Earth. Its plane is inclined 23° 27′ (which is the Sun's maximum Declination) to the plane of the Celestial Equator, which angle is called the Obliquity of the Ecliptic.

Elevated Pole. The Celestial Pole which is above the observer's horizon.

Ephemeris (Ephemerides). The special calendar showing the predicted timetable of the moving Celestial Bodies.

Ephemeris Time (E.T.). A conception of time for presentation of Ephemerides of the Sun, Moon and Planets.

Equation of Time (Eq.T.). The excess of Mean Solar Time over Apparent Solar Time. When Apparent Time is greater than Mean Time the equation of time is a negative quantity and is prefixed with a minus sign. (See page 2:15.)

Equinoctial (or Celestial Equator). The Equinoctial is a Great Circle dividing the Celestial Sphere into two equal parts. It is in the same plane as the Earth's Equator.

Equinox. See Autumnal Equinox, also Vernal Equinox.

First Point of Libra. The Autumnal Equinoctial Point; the point where the Sun's centre crosses the Equinoctial as it moves along the Ecliptic and changes its Declination from North to South on the 23rd of September each year. It is diametrically opposite to the First point of Aries.

First Point of Aries. The starting point for measuring right ascensions. The point where the Sun's centre crosses the Celestial Equator (Equinoctial) when moving along the Ecliptic and changing from South to North Declination on March 21st. It is called the Vernal (or Spring) Equinox.

At this time the lengths of the day and night are equal throughout the world. See also Transit of Aries, page 2:10.

Full Moon. When the Moon is in "opposition" to the Sun, or on the Sun's antimeridian; i.e., when it is on the Meridian about midnight—12 hours different from the Sun.

Geographical Position (The) of a Heavenly body is the point on the Earth's surface directly underneath that object (i.e., the object is in this position's Zenith). Its actual position is found by its Declination (i.e., Latitude) and its G.H.A. (i.e., Longitude), both of which elements are tabulated in this Almanac.

G.H.A. in the Heavens corresponds to the Longitude (measured 0° to 360° westwards from the Prime Meridian) of the Geographical Position of the body.

Gibbous Moon. The phases of the Moon when the Moon's disc is more than half illuminated; i.e., between First Quarter and Full Moon and also between Full Moon and Last Quarter.

Greenwich Mean Time (G.M.T.) is the Time at Greenwich by the Mean Sun and is the standard to which all observations can be referred.

Greenwich Hour Angle, The, is the angle at the pole between the Meridian at Greenwich and the Meridian or hour circle through the body. As can be seen clearly from the figure (p. 2:4), it may also be measured Westward from 0° to 360° along the Celestial Equator from the Celestial Meridian of Greenwich.

Greenwich Sidereal Time (G.S.T.) is the same as G.H.A. Aries.

Hemisphere. Half of the Sphere. A plane (Equator) passing through the centre of a Sphere (the Earth) divides it into two equal parts (the Northern and Southern Hemispheres).

Harvest Moon. The Full Moon nearest the Autumnal Equinox (Sept. 23rd).

Horizontal Parallax (H.P.). Any Heavenly body on an observer's horizon would have no altitude, but if observed from the Earth's centre there would be an altitude as it would be above the horizon from the different viewpoint. The angle between these two positions is termed the Horizontal Parallax. (Given on the monthly pages for the Moon in this Almanac.)

Hour Angle (of the Heavenly Bodies). The Hour Angle of a heavenly body is the angle at the Pole between the observer's meridian and the meridian through the Body. It is purely a system of measurement, but because it often expresses "time" it is termed the Hour Angle, and when it is measured Westward from the Meridian (0° to 360° in arc or 0 to 24 hours in time) it is called "Local Hour Angle" (L.H.A.); but if measured Eastwards from the Meridian it is called "Easterly Hour Angle" and labelled E.H.A.
As the earth is rotating slowly unceasingly, the hour angle of any body that is fixed in the celestial concave will increase constantly during the 24 hours. When the body is on the observer's meridian the Hour Angle is 0 hours; and it is 24 hours later when it again returns to the observer's meridian.

The Local Hour Angle (L.H.A.) of the True (or actual) Sun is denoted by L.H.A.T.S. and that of the Mean Sun by L.H.A.M.S. (See also under Greenwich Hour Angle above.)
The L.H.A. of a Heavenly Body is also the sum of the L.H.A. of the First Point of Aries (i.e., the local Sidereal time) and the Sidereal Hour Angle (S.H.A.) of the body.

Hunter's Moon. The Full Moon nearest October 21st; but it is not so pronounced as the phenomenon of the Harvest Moon.

Inferior Planet. A Planet whose orbit round the Sun is between the Earth and the Sun. Only Mercury and Venus are Inferior Planets.

Latitude. (Terrestrial). The angular distance of a place on the Earth's surface North or South of the Equator.

Latitude. (Celestial). The angular distance of a Celestial Body North or South of the Ecliptic.

Leap Year. The year really consists of $365\frac{1}{4}$ days; but as the Civil year consists of 365 days, the extra 6 hours ($\frac{1}{4}$ day) is added at the end of the fourth year as an extra day in February to give Leap Year.

Line (The). The Seamen's name for the Equator. When a vessel moves from South to North Latitude or vice versa she is said to ''Cross the Line''.

Limb. The edge (Upper or Lower) of the Sun, Moon or Planet's disc.

Local Hour Angle (L.H.A.) (or the Hour Angle at the ship), is the difference between the Longitude of the Geographical Position of the body and the Longitude of the Observer. It is measured WESTWARDS (0° to 360°) from the Observer's Meridian.

The modern Navigator who determines his position by celestial observation and ''position lines'' is first and foremost concerned with obtaining his Local Hour Angle (L.H.A.).

Longitude. The angular distance between the Greenwich Meridian and the meridian passing through any place, measured along the Equator, and named E or W of Greenwich from 0° to 180°.

Longitude of Time is the difference between S.M.T. and G.M.T. and the difference of longitude between two places is the difference between the local mean times of the places. From which statements we get the rhyme (shown on p. 2:16) which gives the rule for turning Ship Time into Greenwich Time (and vice-versa). As the Mean Sun moves westwards through 360° of longitude in 24 hours, the difference in time between the two places 15° of longitude apart is 1h. and so on in proportion. In other words time can be converted into arc at the rate of 15° to 1h., 1° to 4min., or 1' to 4sec. (See table on pp. 4:2-4:3.) As the earth rotates from West to East, Easterly meridians will pass under the Mean Sun before that of Greenwich; hence the time for a place East of Greenwich is in advance of Greenwich time, i.e., S.M.T. is for any instant greater than G.M.T. for the same instant.

Local Mean Time. The mean time at any place on the Earth's surface (see Ship Mean Time).

Local Sidereal Time (or Sidereal time of a place at any instant) is the L.H.A. of the First Point of Aries at that instant reckoned (0-24 hours) Westward from the meridian of the place. It is also the angular distance of the meridian Eastward from the First Point of Aries of the Right Ascension of the meridian (R.A.M.).

Lunar Distance. The angular distance of the Moon from other Heavenly Bodies.

Lunar—of the Moon. (A Lunar Day is the time between two successive transits of the Moon over the same meridian.)

Magnitude. Relative brightness of a Star or Planet.

Mean Time. The Mean Solar Day, which is the average of all the Apparent solar days throughout a large number of years, may also be defined as the interval of time between two consecutive transits of the Mean Sun over an observer's meridian. This Mean Sun is an imaginary celestial body supposed to move along the celestial equator with a uniform speed equal to the average speed of the true Sun in the ecliptic.

Ship Mean Time (S.M.T.) or **Local Mean Time** at any instant is the H.A. of the Mean Sun ± 12h. S.M.T. is reckoned Westward (0h. to 24h.) from the antimeridian of the ship.

Meridian. An imaginary great circle extending from North to South Pole. Any heavenly body reaching the highest point of its arc is said to be "on the Meridian" of any observer.

Meridian Altitude. The highest altitude above the horizon of a heavenly body when "on the Meridian".

Meridian, Prime. The Meridian of Greenwich (England) — Longitude 0°.

Moon's Age. The Moon's Age is the number of days that have passed since the previous New Moon.

Nadir. The point opposite to the Zenith, i.e., the point of the heavens directly below the observer.

New Moon. When the Sun and Moon are on the same celestial longitude, i.e., are in conjunction, it is called "New Moon". Is often incorrectly applied to the time when the Moon is first visible as a crescent in the West after Sunset.

Noon (Apparent). When the centre of the actual Sun is on the observer's meridian.

Obliquity of the Ecliptic. See Ecliptic.

Occultation. When one heavenly body eclipses another.

Opposition. When a heavenly body is 180° of Longitude from another. At Full Moon the Moon is in opposition to the Sun.

Orbit. The elliptical path of one heavenly body round another body.

Parallax. The apparent movement of an object when viewed from two different positions.

Perigee. The position in the Moon's orbit nearest to the Earth, opposite to Apogee.

Perihelion. The point in the orbit of the Earth or other Planet when it is nearest to the Sun, opposite to Aphelion.

Phase. The particular aspects of a heavenly body as Phases of the Moon, etc.

Polar Distance. The angular distance of a heavenly body from the nearer celestial Pole.

Prime Meridian . See Meridian, Prime.

Prime Vertical. Vertical Circle of the celestial sphere passing through East and West points of the horizon. A heavenly body is on the "Prime Vertical" when it bears East or West (true).

Quadrature. When the positions of the heavenly bodies differ by 90° of longitude. At First Quarter and Last Quarter the Moon is in Quadrature.

Quarter, First and Last. At "Half Moon", when the Sun and Moon are 90° apart — the Phases of the Moon when the body is half illuminated.

Right Ascension. The Right Ascension (R.A.) of a heavenly body is the angular distance Eastward from the First Point of Aries, to the point where the Great Circle through the Pole and the body cuts the Equator, always expressed in hours 0-24.

Rising. The appearance of a heavenly body above the horizon of the observer. Owing to refraction, the object appears above the horizon when it is really still below it.

Seasons. The variation in the length of day and night is due to the inclining of the Earth's axis to the plane of its orbit.

Semi-Diameter (S.D.). Half the angular diameter of a heavenly body. The S.D. of the Sun and Moon is roughly 16'. Accurate values for each are tabulated in this Almanac.

Sun's Semi-Diameter. The Sun has a perceptible disc and so its centre cannot be observed. The part of the circumference actually observed is called the Limb. If the lower limb be observed in an altitude, the semi-diameter must be added to get the altitude of the centre; but from an altitude of the upper limb, the semi-diameter must be subtracted.

Sidereal. In relation to the Stars. Time is an element of the highest importance in all observations of heavenly bodies. One unit of time is provided by the rotation of the earth on its axis from West to East. Thus:

A Sidereal Day is the time occupied in one complete rotation of the Earth upon its axis, or more particularly it is the interval between two successive transits of the First Point of Aries over an observer's meridian. (See First Point of Aries.) Sidereal Time is used by astronomers.

Sidereal Hour Angle (The) S.H.A. of a star, is the angle at the pole measured (from 0° to 360°) from the meridian of Aries to the meridian of the Star in a WESTERLY direction.

Signs of the Zodiac. The twelve constellations through which the Ecliptic runs.

Solstices. When the Sun is farthest from the Celestial Equator (i.e., Declination $23\frac{1}{2}°$ North or South) June 21st, December 22nd, the "longest" and "shortest" days, respectively, in northern latitudes.

Superior Planets. Those Planets whose orbits are outside that of the Earth, and farthest from the Sun. That is all Planets except Mercury and Venus.

Time. See Apparent, Mean, Sidereal.

Transit. The passage of a heavenly body across the observer's Meridian.

Transit of Aries. The Transit of the First Point of Aries and of the fixed Stars occurs approximately 4 minutes earlier on each successive day; so that every month the Transit occurs 2 hours (approx.) earlier and thus 24 hours per year in completing the cycle.

Twilight. The periods of the day when, although the Sun is below the visible horizon, the observer does not experience complete darkness because indirect light is received from the Sun through reflection and scattering by the upper atmosphere. Complete darkness occurs when the Sun's centre is 18° below the horizon. Civil Twilight begins or ends when the Sun is 6° below the horizon, at which time the sea horizon is clear and the brightest stars are visible—the most favourable time for stellar observations. The times of Civil Twilight are tabulated in this Almanac.

Universal Time (U.T.). Another name for G.M.T. (Greenwich Mean Time).

Vernal Equinox. Also called the Spring Equinox, when the Sun crosses the Equinoctial from South to North (about March 21st). See First Point of Aries.

Waxing and waning. The Moon is said to be waxing between New Moon and Full Moon when its light increases and waning when its light decreases between Full Moon and New Moon.

Zenith, Zenith Distance is the angular distance of an object from the observer's Zenith (the point vertically overhead in the celestial sphere). It is the complement of the Altitude, i.e., 90° minus the Altitude. Zenith is opposite to Nadir.

Zodiac. An imaginary belt of sky along the Ecliptic, in which the Sun, Moon and larger Planets perform their revolutions.

HOW TO USE THE NAUTICAL EPHEMERIS

Examples of how to find and use the elements of the Nautical Ephemeris given in this Almanac are shown on the pages listed below.

THE NAUTICAL ALMANAC, 1992

The Nautical Ephemerides (pages 3:10-3:81) contain full navigational elements for finding a vessel's position at sea by the Sun, Moon, Planets and Stars. Whilst in this limited number of pages it is not possible to tabulate the positions of these celestial bodies at hourly intervals, nevertheless, with care and a little more interpolation, results are obtained practically identical to those found from the fuller daily tabulations of the movements of the bodies.

In the layout of the Nautical Almanac, six pages have been devoted each month to the movements of the heavenly bodies.

The accuracy to which all the data are given is 0'.1, which is much better than the normal accuracy obtainable when using a sextant at sea. Thus errors arising through interpolating the figures approximately are negligible.

Ephemeris of the Sun

On the first monthly page the top half is devoted to elements of the Sun – including the Equation of Time – twice daily; the time of the Sun's Transit, and the daily Semi-diameter. The times of Sunrise, Sunset and morning and evening Twilight for the Latitude of Greenwich are given, with a constant correction table adjacent, to correct these times for any Latitude other than Greenwich.

The two centre pages – 3:12 and 3:13 for January – contain all the Sun elements required for the whole of January tabulated at 2 hourly intervals. The G.H.A of the Sun is given to 0.1 of a minute of arc; and the Declination of the Sun is also given to this accuracy. A special correction table for Sun G.H.A given on page 4:7 is easy to use and of quite sufficient accuracy.

Ephemerides of the Stars

The second monthly page is devoted to the fullest details of 60 of the brighter and more used Navigational Stars. Each Star is numbered and given its name used by seamen (and not its astronomical constellation name) together with its magnitude. The approximate time of the Transit of each Star is given for the first day of the month and an adjacent table shows the correction to apply for each subsequent day of the month with examples. The Declination (Dec.), Right Ascension (R.A.) and Sidereal Hour Angle (S.H.A.) for each star are given also. The Monthly Diary is also included.

On the third and fourth pages of each month under the heading ARIES is tabulated the G.H.A. Aries to an accuracy of 0'.1 for every 2 hours of G.M.T.

Aries is shown on the second page at the head of the Stars with its approximate time of Transit and its G.H.A. for the first of the month at Oh. The special Star correction table (p. 4:8) enables the G.H.A. Aries to be found at any other particular moment.

Because we believe many Navigators prefer to use the same data for all bodies – and this is one of the virtues of G.H.A. (Greenwich Hour Angle) – Reed's Almanac tabulates also the G.H.A of each Star for midnight on the first of the month. Using the unique Correction Table on page 4:8, by a simple addition sum the G.H.A. required for any day, hour, minute and second in the month, can be found at once for any of the 60 Stars.

The clearness of setting and the wealth of information shown in column form on this monthly page is believed to represent the most complete Star data extant given in the smallest space.

The Pole Star
Although the full data are provided on the Star page for Polaris, a special table is given on page 5:18, so that by simply applying one correction, the approximate Latitude of the vessel may be found at any time from the Pole Star. The True Bearing of Polaris at any time can be found from a table on page 5:19.

Ephemerides of the Planets
The fifth monthly pages contain all necessary data for the only four Navigational Planets: Venus, Jupiter, Mars and Saturn. The G.H.A. (and its variation), Declination (and its variation) together with the time of its Meridian Passage is given for each of the Planets at 0 hours G.M.T. on each day of the month. Correction Tables are given on pages 4:9-4:13, so that by a simple addition sum the G.H.A. and Dec. required at any moment for any Planet may be found.

Notes on the Planet Mercury are included also for interest only.

This page also includes notes on each Planet, giving its magnitude and showing whether it is a Morning or Evening Planet and where to find it.

Ephemeris of the Moon
On the lower half of the first monthly page are given all data required for the Moon except its position; this includes the Age of the Moon; its Transit time; Semi-diameter and Horizontal Parallax. The important—to seamen—Phases of the Moon are shown with times of Apogee and Perigee. The times of Moonrise and Moonset are given also for the Latitude of Greenwich. A table to correct this for home waters and Mediterranean Latitudes is given on p. 4:20.

The sixth monthly page shows the Moon G.H.A. and Declination with the hourly Variations. Special correction tables are given to enable the position at any moment to be found. (See pages 4:15-4:18).

Although the Moon may be used for Navigation, compared with the Sun and Stars which are always visible (given good meteorological conditions) the Moon is less available to the Navigator. For this reason the Moon — which has greater movement than any other celestial body — is only tabulated at every six hours — special Moon correction tables in the body of the book giving by simple addition the required G.H.A. and Dec. of the Moon at any particular moment.

Instructions on how to find the astronomical data for the Sun and Stars are provided on page 3:82 for the months of 1993 for those without access to the new year's Almanac.

The explanations in this Section are confined to showing how to use the figures given in the Nautical Ephemeris section of Reed's Nautical Almanac for 1992.

THE NAUTICAL ALMANAC

The Almanac is based on Greenwich Mean Time in 24 hours notation. In all cases 0000 hours and 2400 hours is midnight

EPHEMERIS OF THE SUN

The various elements tabulated in Reed's Nautical Almanac may be found for any particular instant of time as follows:

SUN'S DECLINATION (DEC.)

The Sun's Declination is tabulated at two hourly intervals throughout the year in degrees, minutes and decimals of a minute of arc on monthly pages 3:12-3:13 (January), 3:18-3:19 (February), etc.

The quantity is worked out from the nearest 2nd hour to the required time, and the intervening time between any two hours is found by simple mental interpolation to 0.1 of a minute of arc.

Example I.—Find the Declination of the Sun for April 26th, 1992, at 7h. 00min. G.M.T. As this is an exact hour, it may be taken out at sight as half way between the quantities tabulated for 8 hours and 6 hours. It will be found to be 13° 37'.2N. The suffix N denotes that the Declination is North.

Example II.—Required the Declination of the Sun for Oct. 29th. 1992, at 15h. 20min. G.M.T. The declination by mental interpolation is 13° 40'.4S.

SUN'S GREENWICH HOUR ANGLE (G.H.A.)

The G.H.A. of the Sun is tabulated at 2 hourly intervals throughout the year in degrees, minutes and decimals of a minute of arc. For all general purposes the quantity is looked out for the 2 hours less than the required G.M.T. and the balance between the tabulated 2 hours and the exact minute of observation is found from the Sun's G.H.A. Correction Table on page 4:7. Greenwich Hour Angle of the Sun (always Westerly) is thus obtained at that particular instant.

As, however, the Correction Table is based on a fixed average change of G.H.A. per hour throughout the year, if absolute accuracy is desired in the working, then the G.H.A. should first be looked out for the nearest 2 hours and the correction applied back from the higher 2 hour tabulations if the time is nearer the higher 2 hours than the lower (as shown in Example II to follow). If this is not done then at certain times during the year G.H.A. as looked out from the 2 hourly tabulations under the largest excess of time over the 2 hours (say 1h. 45min.) might be as much as 0.3 of a minute of arc in error. This is obviated if the nearest 2 hours is worked to.

Example I. —Find the Sun's G.H.A. for July 9th, 1992, at 16h, 22min. 15s. G.M.T.

Sun G.H.A. (page 3:48) for 16h.	58°	41'.2W
Corr. for 22 min. (page 4:7)	+ 5°	30'.0
" " 15s.		03'.8
Sun's G.H.A. July 9th, 16h. 22min. 15s.	64°	15'.0W

Example II. —Find the Sun's G.H.A. for Jan 2nd, 1992, at 9h. 40m. 20s. G.M.T.

Sun G.H.A. (page 3:12) for 10h.	329°	04'.0W
Corr. for 19m. 40s. (page 4:7)	− 4°	55'.0
Sun's G.H.A. Jan. 2nd, 9h. 40min. 20s. G.M.T.	324°	09'.0W

In this case, as the required time is much nearer to 10 hours than 8 hours, the correction is looked out for the minutes and seconds less than 10 hours and these are subtracted from the G.H.A. for 10 hours.

EQUATION OF TIME

Whilst with a G.H.A. Almanac the Equation of Time is not really required, to suit the convenience of all who have grown used to working with it, the Equation of Time is tabulated twice daily on the monthly pages for 0h. and 12h. G.M.T. The quantity can be taken out at sight, to the nearest second of time.

The Equation of Time is the amount by which Mean Time exceeds Apparent Time (i.e. L.H.A.M.S.—L.H.A.T.S. or the correction that should be applied to the time given on a sundial). If the Equation of Time is +6min. 30s. and the Apparent Time is 12h. 00min. 00s. then the Mean Time is 12h. 06min. 30s. If the Equation of Time is –4min. 30s. then the Mean Time is 11h. 55min. 30s.

But in astro-navigation the Mean Time is usually known and one may want to establish the Apparent Time, therefore the calculation is in fact reversed, e.g. if the Equation of Time is +6min. 30s. and the Mean Time is 12h. 00min. 00s. the Apparent Time is 11h. 53min. 30s. Alternatively if the Equation of Time is –4min. 30s. then the Apparent Time is 12h. 04min. 30s.

TO FIND THE SHIP APPARENT TIME (OR HOUR

ANGLE OF THE SUN)

If the Longitude of a place is known approximately, it is easy to calculate the S.A.T. (Ship Apparent Time); also the L.H.A.T.S. (see page 2:16).

In modern navigation Greenwich Mean Time (G.M.T.) is always available and from this the S.A.T. and L.H.A.T.S. may be obtained.

S.A.T. (Ship Apparent Time)

The Ship Apparent Time may be needed to set the ship's clocks to S.A.T. (where this is kept), and to use the various volumes of Azimuth Tables. It may be found as shown below using the Equation of Time.

L.H.A.T.S. (Local Hour Angle of True Sun)

The L.H.A.T.S. (being reckoned from the previous noon instead of midnight) always differs from the S.A.T. by 12 hours. Thus 12 hours may be added or subtracted from the S.A.T. to get L.H.A.T.S.

The method of finding the S.A.T. and Hour Angle are detailed below.

Example I.—An Azimuth of the Sun was taken on July 10th, 1992, in Longitude 15° 33'E at 19h. 35min. G.M.T. Required the S.A.T. to use the Azimuth Tables.

Using Equation of Time

G.M.T. 10th July.......................		19h.	35min. 00s.
Long in Time	+	1	2 12
S.M.T.		20	37 12
Equation of Time	–		5 25
S.A.T...............................		20h.	31min. 47s.

The Ship Apparent Time is 20h. 32min. (nearly) on 10th July, as "Time" is reckoned from midnight. The Hour Angle is of course reckoned Westwards from noon so as the L.H.A.T.S is 8h. 32min. the time is 20h. 32min.

Longitude is turned from Arc into Time by the Table on pages 4:2-4:3. The E.T. is + therefore it must be subtracted from the mean time to give apparent time.

Remember all Local Hour Angles of the Sun are reckoned Westerly from noon i.e., when the Sun is on the Observer's Meridian.

TO FIND LOCAL HOUR ANGLE OF THE SUN (USING G.H.A.)

The expression Local Hour Angle holds good for all heavenly bodies and is simply the Hour Angle of the body reckoned from the ship, always Westerly.

The Local Hour Angle of the Sun may be found very simply from its G.H.A.

From the following examples it can be seen that the G.H.A. method may be used to find the Hour Angle without any knowledge of Equation of Time. In the particular problem, of course, where we want the Hour Angle in time, or S.A.T. to enter the Azimuth Tables, the Local Hour Angle has to be converted into "Time" by the table on pages 4:2-4:3 and thus the full benefit of the Local Hour Angle being in arc is not felt. In the actual problem where an observation is taken for position such as by Longitude by Chronometer or Marcq St. Hilaire, then the Hour Angle is required in Arc which reduces the working as no conversion from time into Arc is required.

Those who use G.H.A. however will, even so, probably prefer to use the method given below; because everything is worked in exactly the same way and uniformity of working lessens the chance of error.

Example I.—Having taken an Azimuth of the Sun at 19h. 35min. G.M.T. on July 10th, 1992, in Long. 15° 33′E, required the Local Hour Angle.

Sun G.H.A., July 10th, 18h.	=	88°	39′.0W
Corr. for 1h. 35min.	+	23°	45′.0
G.H.A., 19h. 35min.	=	112°	24′.0W
Longitude East.	+	15°	33′.0
Local Hour Angle.	=	127°	57′.0W

Which in time is (8h. 28 min. + 3min. 48s.) = 8h. 31min. 48s
Which agrees with the answer arrived at on page 2:15.

In using this method it is extremely simple to find the Hour Angle. The G.H.A. is looked out for the lower 2nd hour in the monthly pages and is corrected by the table on page 4:7 for the exact hours and minutes (and seconds if necessary). To this exact G.H.A. the D.R. Longitude is applied directly in arc and this gives the Hour Angle (always Westerly).

The longitude is applied according to the usual rhyme—

Longitude East, Greenwich Time least,

Longitude West, Greenwich Time best.

Therefore, Westerly Longitude is always subtracted from G.H.A. (adding 360° to this if necessary); and Easterly Longitude is always added to G.H.A. (subtracting 360° from the result if necessary).

Further examples will make this quite clear.

It will be noted that the L.H.A., if more than 180°, may be subtracted from 360° and named East (E.H.A.). L.H.A. 300° is the same as E.H.A. 60°.

Example II.—An Ex-Meridian altitude was taken on July 10th, 1992, at 15h. 40min. 36s. G.M.T. in Longitude 58° 45'W. What was the Local Hour Angle?

Sun G.H.A., July 10th, 14h.	= 28°	39'.3W
Corr. for 1h. 40min.	+ 25°	00'.0
„ „ 36s.	+	9'.0
G.H.A. for 10d. 15h. 40min. 36s	= 53°	48'.3W
	+ 360°	
	413°	48'.3W
Longitude W.	− 58°	45'.0
Local Hour Angle	= 355°	03'.3W
or in time	= 23h. 40min. 13s.	

As the Longitude is subtracted from the G.H.A. and in this case is greater than G.H.A., 360° is added in first.

Even though in the above examples the full benefit of the G.H.A. being in arc is not derived because we still think in "time", it will be advantageous to use this method because the same working is used for all observations of heavenly bodies and uniformity of working reduces errors.

TRANSIT OF SUN

The times of Transit of the Sun are given daily on each monthly page.

Example.—On January 11th, the Sun's Meridian passage occurs at 12h. 08min. (Ship Mean Time).

TO FIND THE SUN'S MERIDIAN PASSAGE OR TRANSIT

The Transit (or Meridian Passage) of any heavenly body is the G.M.T. when the Hour Angle is 0.

Example I.—Required the G.M.T. of Sun's transit on Oct. 29th, 1992, at Greenwich. Page 3:67, Oct. 29th, shows at 12 hours G.M.T. the G.H.A. of the Sun is 4° 04'.1, so when the G.H.A. is 0° the G.M.T. will be less than 1200 hours. By the table on page 4:2 we find that 4° 04'.1 in time is 16min 16.4s. so 12 hours minus 16min 16s. gives 11h. 43min 44s. as the G.M.T. of Apparent Noon.

This can also be found, of course, by applying the Equation of Time to the Apparent Time at Ship, i.e., 12.00 minus 16min. 16s. = 11h. 43min. 44s. or more simply by the Sun's Transit time on page 3:64 = 11h. 44min.

Example II.—Required to know the G.M.T. at which to observe the Sun's Meridian Altitude in Lat. D.R. 49° 20'N, Long. D.R. 7° 35'W on July 11th, 1992.

July 11th, 12 hours G.H.A.		358°	37'.5	
		360°	00'.0	
	Diff. =	1°	22'.5W	
So Noon occurs at		1°	22'.5	after 1200 hours Ship Mean Time
Long.W	+	7°	35'.0W	
G.M.T.	12 h. +	8°	57'.5W	= 12h. 35min. 50s

Or more simply by taking the Sun's Transit time on page 3:46–12h. 05min. and applying the Longitude as usual (+30min.) to get 12h. 35min. G.M.T.

TO FIND SUN'S SEMI-DIAMETER

This is tabulated daily on each monthly page under the Sun.

Example.—Required the Sun's Semi-Diameter for March 12th, 1992. Page 3:22 shows this as 16.1'.

TO FIND THE TIMES OF SUNRISE, SUNSET AND TWILIGHT

The Times of Visible Sunrise and Sunset of the Sun's Upper Limb are given on the monthly pages for the Latitude of Greenwich (Latitude 52°N). These are for practical purposes S.M.T. (Ship Mean Time), to which the Longitude must be applied if G.M.T. is required.

The daily times of the Morning and Evening Civil Twilight are also given (and these are the times when the Sun is 6° below the Horizon).

The reason for giving the times of Civil Twilight is because under ordinary atmospheric conditions the amount of light at this time is nearly the ideal for Stellar observations; that is, when the first magnitude Stars and the Planets will be visible and the horizon still clearly defined. Thus the approximate time to arrange a programme for taking Star sights is the time given for Civil Twilight.

These times may be corrected for the Latitude of the Ship between Latitude 70°N and 50°S by the small table on each monthly page. They are strictly accurate only for the middle of the month, but are sufficiently accurate for all practical purposes for the whole of the month.

Example I.—Required the time of Sunrise on January 11th, 1992, in Lat. 30°N. Sunrise 8h. 05min. (for Lat. 52°N) –1h. 05min. = 7h. 00min. (see page 3:10).

Example II.—What time should the Star sight programme be arranged for on January 11th, 1991, at dawn in Latitude 45°N? Twilight 7h. 25min. (for Lat. 52°N) –0h. 20min. = 7h. 05min. (See page 3:10).

EPHEMERIDES OF THE STARS

PROPER NAMES AND MAGNITUDES

For uniform purposes the 60 brightest navigational stars have been chosen and these stars used exclusively in the various monthly tabulations. Each star has been given a number which is used throughout Reed's Almanac to obviate errors. Polaris has been included because of its importance and not because of its brilliance.

LIST OF THE NAMES AND NUMBERS OF THE STARS

Page 2:24 contains the Alphabetical List of the 60 Principal Stars used in the Almanac with their Mean Positions. This list is alphabetical, and shows both the Proper and Constellation name of each Star. Their magnitudes are given also together with their Reed's Almanac Number. As Stars are practically "fixed" and their movement in Right Ascension and declination is so small, a mean (average) quantity is tabulated on this page. This table will be found extremely useful when wishing to ascertain approximate Declination, Right Ascension or S.H.A. at a glance.

THE FIXED STARS

These are called "fixed" as their position in relation to one another changes but a fraction. All stars appear to move across the sky from East to West, and across the meridian about four minutes earlier each day. They do not move about the heavens at random as the Moon and the Planets appear to do. The Stars are at an immense distance from the Earth and, unlike the Moon and Planets, which shine with the reflected light of the Sun, shine with their own light.

At first sight there appears to be an immense number of Stars in the heavens; but on due examination it will be seen that there are relatively few bright Stars and only some hundreds of smaller ones, which latter, of course, are of no use for Navigational purposes.

Stellar Magnitudes: The stars are classified according to the amount of light which is received from them on Earth. The magnitude of a star is a measure of its relative brilliance; the actual grading being based on the definition that "a star of magnitude 1 is one from which the Earth receives 100 times as much light as it receives from a star of magnitude 6". Thus a star of magnitude 2 is 100 times brighter than a star of magnitude 7; a star of magnitude 3 is 100 times brighter than a star of magnitude 8. It follows therefore that a star of magnitude 0 is 100 times brighter than a star of magnitude 5, and a star which is 100 times brighter than a star of magnitude 4 must have a magnitude of −1. Sirius, the brightest star in the heavens, has a magnitude of −1.6.

In practice, the terms "stars of the first magnitude" (of which there are 12 only) refers to all those whose magnitude is less than 1.0.

Note: A sixth-magnitude star is only just visible to the naked eye.

The Planets Venus and Jupiter have variable minus magnitudes in the nature of −3.5 and −2.0, respectively. An interesting comparison also is that of the Sun and the Full Moon which have magnitudes of −26.7 and −12.5 respectively.

Constellations: From ancient times Stars have been divided into groups called Constellations; and as it would be impossible to name each Star with a proper name the Stars were named according to their Constellation. The brightest Star in a constellation is prefixed with the Greek Letter α (alpha), and the second brightest Star is prefixed β (Beta); and so on in order of their brightness as, for example, α Andromedae and β Andromedae.

Proper Names have also been given to the brightest of the Fixed Stars—especially in the Northern Hemisphere—as, for example, Alpheratz (α Andromedae); Mirach (β Andromedae); Vega (Alpha Lyrae); Altair (Alpha Aquiliae); Canopus (Alpha * Carinae); and Denebola (Beta Leonis), etc.

It is frequently of advantage to be able to judge the angular distance between heavenly bodies, and this can be done by comparing the distance with the known angular distance between specified stars or arcs.

The following examples of varying sized angles may be useful to serve as a guide to the estimation of apparent distances in the sky when using Star Charts.

360°	All round the horizon.
180°	East to West along the horizon or through Zenith.
90°	Horizon to Zenith.
60°	Dubhe (Great Bear) to Caph (β Cassiopeiae).
30°	Polaris to Caph (β Cassiopeiae).
23°	Vega to Deneb.
20°	Betelguese to Rigel (Orion).
5°	Merak to Dubhe (Pointers to the Plough).
4°	Castor to Pollux.

*Formerly Argus

HOW TO FIND THE PRINCIPAL FIXED STARS

LISTED IN REED'S NAUTICAL ALMANAC

The Navigator will usually find a Star Map or Atlas of great benefit, especially if he is not able to take Star Sights often; but as many Star Maps are still graduated in Right Ascension, for the purposes of identification, we give the R.A. of each Star as well as its S.H.A.

Generally, of course, the brighter Planets and Stars are used to take observations and Azimuths, so Reed's Almanac has tabulated each month the position, i.e., Declination and G.H.A., etc. of 60 Principal Stars. Each of these Stars is numbered, and to assist the beginner especially, we give the following notes on how to find every one of these navigational Stars in the same numerical order as in the Almanac.

Pronunciations are also given for some of the Stars. Always accent the syllable marked.

Star No.

(1) Alpheratz. A line from the Pole Star through β Cassiopeiae (Caph) and produced the same distance beyond leads to Alpheratz (α Andromedae), which together with the Stars Markab, Algenib and Scheat form the Square of Pegasus with Markab at the south-west corner. These are all bright Stars, and make almost an exact square which is easily found.

(2) Ankaa. (α Phoenicis). A second magnitude Star situated just east of a line from Achernar to Fomalhaut.

(3) Schedar. The brightest Star in Cassiopeiae. This constellation is on the opposite side of the Pole to the Plough and about the same distance away. It is in the shape of a 'W' and is known as Cassiopeiae's Chair.

When the Great Bear (or Plough) is on the meridian above the Pole, Cassiopeiae is on the meridian below the Pole, and the two constellations appear to revolve round the Pole Star at equi-distances. A line drawn from Aldebaran through Algol will intersect Schedar.

(4) Diphda. A Star of second magnitude which lies by itself about half way between the Square of Pegasus and Achernar.

(5) Achernar. (Ak'-er-nar). The brightest Star in the constellation Eridanus in the Southern Hemisphere. Lies about 70° west of Canopus just off a line between Canopus and Fomalhaut.

(6) POLARIS (or POLE STAR). See diagram of the Great Bear and description on page 2:25.

(7) Hamal. The brightest Star in the constellation Aries. A line from Betelgeuse through Aldebaran leads to Hamal which lies midway between Aldebaran and the Great Square of Pegasus.

(8) Acamar. A third magnitude Star situated about 20° N.E. of Achernar.

(9) Menkar. A second magnitude Star which lies S.W. of Aldebaran and forms the apex of a triangle (upside down) with Aldebaran and Hamal. A line from Sirius through Rigel about the same distance beyond points to Menkar (α Ceti).

Star No.

(10) Mirfak. Lies North of Algol and on a line from Capella to Cassiopeiae.

(11) Aldebaran (Al-deb'-ar-an). See the diagram of the constellation of Orion on p. 2:25. This very bright red Star lies to the North of Orion just a little off the line of the Belt. It lies at the top of one of the arms of a V-shaped cluster of small Stars — the Hyades. The Pleiades, a well defined cluster of Stars (The Seven Sisters) lie close to the Hyades, and form a valuable skymark.

(12) Rigel (Ri'-jel). See diagram of the constellation of Orion on p. 2:25.

(13) Capella (Ca-pel'-la). A line drawn from the Pole Star away from the Great Bear but perpendicular to the Pointers leads to Capella. It will readily be recognised as a bright yellow Star.
A line from Polaris to Rigel nearly intersects Capella, which is 45° from the Pole Star and 55° from Rigel. It may be recognised also from being in a line from Menkar through the Pleiades about 30° N.E. of that cluster of Stars.

(14) Bellatrix (Bel'-la-trix). See the diagram of the constellation of Orion on p. 2:25.

(15) Elnath (Nath). The second brightest Star to Aldebaran in the constellation Taurus, and lies about halfway along a line between Orion's Belt and Capella.

(16) Alnilam. The middle Star of the three bright Stars in the centre of Orion forming the Belt.

(17) Betelgeuse (Bet'-el-joox). See the diagram of the constellation of Orion. Betelgeuse has a reddish appearance rather like Aldebaran.

(18) Canopus (Can-o'-pus). α Carinae (formerly Argus). The second brightest Star in the sky, but situated in 52° South declination. A line drawn from Bellatrix through the northern star in Orion's Belt passes to Canopus. It is almost due South from Sirius and a pale blue colour.

(19) Sirius (Sir'-e-us). The Dog Star — is magnificent — in that he is the brightest Star in the sky (surpassing in brilliance the Planets Mars and Saturn), and has a gorgeous pale blue colour. The three Stars in the Belt of Orion lead directly away from Aldebaran to Sirius which lies S.E. of Orion.
A fine heavenly curve is formed by Capella, Castor, Pollux, Procyon and Sirius. See diagram of the constellation of Orion.

(20) Adhara. This is a first magnitude star which lies about 10° South of Sirius.

(21) Castor and Pollux (Kas'-ter and Pol'-lux). Known as the Twins — these two Stars lie nearly halfway between the Plough and Orion. A line from Rigel through the centre Star in Orion's Belt points to Castor. Pollux (the brighter Star of the two) will be found $4\frac{1}{2}$° to the southward.

(22) Procyon (Pro'-se-on). A line drawn from Castor and Pollux to Sirius passes almost through Procyon, the little Dog Star.

(23) Pollux. See No. 21 above.

(24) Avior. This first magnitude Star lies far South (60° declination) about 30° S.E. of Canopus and a little to the east of a line joining Canopus to Miaplacidus.

(25) Suhail (ν Velorum). A second magnitude Star South of Alphard and E.N.E. of Canopus.

(26) Miaplacidus (β Carinae formerly Argus). A far southerly first magnitude Star, situated about halfway between Canopus and Acrux, but about 10° S.W. of a line joining them.

Star No.

(27)   Alphard. This second magnitude Star lies on a line drawn from the Great Bear Star Alioth through Regulus and about 20° beyond to the S.S.W. Its name means "the solitary one" because there is no other bright star near it.

(28)   Regulus (Reg'-u-lus). A line from the Pole Star through the Pointers of the Plough, and continued about 45° leads close to Regulus. This Star may be found easily, as it is situated at the end of the "handle" of the "Sickle" (which shape the constellation Leo takes), and is the brightest Star in the group.

(29)   Dubhe. The northern and brightest of the two Pointers of the Great Bear.

(30)   Denebola (De-neb'-o-la). The second brightest Star in the constellation of Leo. Lies about halfway along a line from Arcturus to Regulus.

(31)   Gienah (γ Corvi). A second magnitude Star situated S.W. of Spica.

(32)   Acrux. The brightest and most Southerly Star in the Southern Cross or Crux. Together with the bright Stars, α and β Centauri, the Southern Cross, or Crux, forms the most remarkable constellation in the Southern Hemisphere. It is unfortunately not visible far North, and only shows up over the horizon when sailing South and the Latitude 20's are reached.

(33)   Gacrux (γ Crucis) is nearly as bright as Mimosa (β Crux) and is situated at the top (North) of the Cross.

(34)   Mimosa. (γ Crucis). Is the second brightest Star in the Crux and lies at the eastern arm of the Cross.

(35)   Alioth. One of the Stars in the Tail of the Great Bear.

(36)   Spica (Spi'-ka). When the curve of the three Stars in the Tail of the Great Bear is continued through Arcturus, and about 30° beyond it passes through Spica, a first magnitude Star. Just South-West of Spica are four Stars which look exactly like a Spanker sail, and are known as Spica's Spanker, the gaff of which always points to Spica.

(37) Alkaid (Benetnasch). A first magnitude Star situated at the extreme Tail of the Great Bear.

(38)   Hadar (β Centauri). The two Stars β and α Centauri lie close Eastward of the Southern Cross, and are called the Southern Cross Pointers. β Centauri is the nearer of the two to Crux.

(39)   Menkent (θ Centauri). A second magnitude Star situated about halfway between Spica and β Centauri and slightly east of a direct line.

(40)   Arcturus (Ark-tu-rus). If the Great Bear is followed southwards away from the Pole Star for the same distance as the length of the Plough itself, it will lead to Arcturus (a yellow Star). There are three small Stars just to the Westward of Arcturus which form a small triangle. Arcturus is the second brightest Star in the Northern heavens.

(41)   Rigil Kent (α Centauri). See No. 38 above. α Centauri is the nearest fixed Star to the Earth.

(42)   Zuben'ubi (α Librae). A second magnitude Star situated on a line about halfway between Spica and Antares.

(43)   Kochab. A second magnitude Star in Ursa Minor.

(44)   Alphecca. A second magnitude Star in the constellation Corona Borealis but the brightest in the heavenly jewel, the Northern Crown. A line drawn from Megrez through Alkaid (the last Star in the tail of the Great Bear) leads to Alphecca in the Northern Crown—an almost perfect semi-circular group of small Stars. It lies a third of the distance from Arcturus to Vega about 20° E.N.E. of Arcturus.

Star No.

(45) Antares (An'-ta-rez). A line from Regulus through Spica the same distance beyond leads to Antares—a bright red Star. It lies about 45° S.W. of Altair.

(46) Atria (α Trianguli Australis). A first magnitude Star and the brightest of the three Stars lying at the S.E. apex of the Southern Triangle, which lies S.E. of Centaurus and about 45° due South of Antares.

(47) Sabik (η Ophuchi). A second magnitude Star situated N.E. of Antares about a quarter of the way towards Altair.

(48) Shaula. A first magnitude Star lying 15° S.E. of Antares about a quarter of the way on a line drawn from Antares to Peacock (α Pavonis).

(49) Rasalhague. A second magnitude Star lying about 25° W.N.W. of Altair. It lies also on a line between Vega and Antares. It forms a triangle with Altair and Vega.

(50) Eltanin. A second magnitude Star lying about 10° N.N.W. of Vega on a line from Altair through Vega.

(51) Kaus Australis. A second magnitude Star lying with the many Stars of the constellation of Sagittarius. It is difficult to identify and lies about 25° E.S.E. of Antares, but East of a line from Antares to Peacock (No. 55).

(52) Vega (Ve'-ga). A line drawn through the Stars Dubhe, Megrez, Alioth and Mizar (see diagram of the Great Bear, p. 2:25) in the direction of the tail of the Bear leads directly to Vega—the brightest and most beautiful Star in the Northern heavens, and of a fine pale blue colour. Vega may also be found by a line from Arcturus through the Northern Crown Star (Alphecca) and extending about 40° beyond.

(53) Nunki. A second magnitude Star lying amongst many others of the constellation Sagittarius about 35° due East of Antares.

(54) Altair (Al-tair'). Is easily recognised as a bright Star lying between two smaller Stars which are close in line and point in the direction of Vega. A line from the Pole Star between Vega and Deneb and extended the same distance beyond leads to Altair.

(55) Peacock. This second magnitude Star lies alone in 57° South declination about halfway between Achernar and Centauri on the same parallel of latitude (West from Achernar). It lies S.E. of Antares and S.W. of Fomalhaut and about 65° due South of Altair.

(56) Deneb (Den'-eb). This first magnitude Star lies E.N.E. of Vega and is the brightest Star in the constellation of Cygnus (the Swan). A line drawn from Castor and Pollux through the Pole Star and extended the same distance beyond passes through Deneb, which is readily found as it is at the top of a "Cross" of Stars (very similar to the Southern Cross). The constellation is usually known as the "Kite"—it is exactly this shape. It lies about 25° Eastward of Vega.

(57) Enif (ε Pegasi). A second magnitude Star situated about halfway between Altair and Markab (Square of Pegasus).

(58) Al Na'ir (α Gruis). This second magnitude Star lies West of β Gruis and is situated on a line about halfway between Fomalhaut and Peacock.

(59) Fomalhaut (Fom'-al-haut). A line drawn from Scheat through Markab (which Stars form one side of the Great Square of Pegasus) passes through Fomalhaut, which may be found readily as it has a small square of Stars near it. Situated about 45° South of Markab.

(60) Markab. Is in the S.W. corner of the Square of Pegasus. A line from Altair N.E. through the Dolphin 50° from Altair will lead to Scheat. It lies about 45° to the east of Altair and about 45° North of Fomalhaut.

★ ALPHABETICAL INDEX OF PRINCIPAL STARS ★

With their approximate places, 1992

PROPER NAME	Constellation Name	Mag.	R.A.	Dec.	S.H.A.	No.
			h. m.	°	°	
Acamar	θ Eridani	3.1	2 58	S 40	316	8
Achernar	α Eridani	0.6	1 37	S 57	336	5
Acrux	α Crucis	1.1	12 26	S 63	173	32
Adhara	ε Canis Majoris	1.6	6 58	S 29	255	20
Aldebaran	α Tauri	1.1	4 35	N 16	291	11
Alioth	ε Ursae Majoris	1.7	12 54	N 56	167	35
Alkaid	η Ursae Majoris	1.9	13 47	N 49	153	37
Al Na'ir	α Gruis	2.2	22 08	S 47	28	58
Alnilam	ε Orionis	1.8	5 36	S 1	276	16
Alphard	α Hydrae	2.2	9 27	S 9	218	27
Alphecca	α Coronae Bor.	2.3	15 34	N 27	126	44
Alpheratz	α Andromedae	2.2	0 08	N 29	358	1
Altair	α Aquilae	0.9	19 50	N 9	62	54
Ankaa	α Phoenicis	2.4	0 26	S 42	354	2
Antares	α Scorpii	1.2	16 29	S 26	113	45
Arcturus	α Bootis	0.2	14 15	N 19	146	40
Atria	α Triang Aust.	1.9	16 48	S 69	108	46
Avior	ε Carinae	1.7	8 22	S 59	234	24
Bellatrix	γ Orionis	1.7	5 25	N 6	279	14
Betelgeuse	α Orionis	0.1-1.2	5 55	N 7	271	17
Canopus	α Carinae	-0.9	6 24	S 53	264	18
Capella	α Aurgae	0.2	5 16	N 46	281	13
Castor	α Geminorum	1.6	7 34	N 32	246	21
Deneb	α Cygni	1.3	20 41	N 45	50	56
Denebola	β Leonis	2.2	11 49	N 15	183	30
Diphda	β Ceti	2.2	0 43	S 18	349	4
Dubhe	α Ursae Majoris	2.0	11 03	N 62	194	29
Elnath	β Tauri	1.8	5 26	N 29	279	15
Eltanin	γ Draconis	2.4	17 56	N 51	91	50
Enif	ε Pegasi	2.5	21 44	N 10	34	57
Fomalhaut	α Piscis Aust.	1.3	22 57	S 30	16	59
Gacrux	γ Crucis	1.6	12 31	S 57	172	33
Gienah	λ Corvi	2.8	12 15	S 18	176	31
Hadar	β Centauri	0.9	14 03	S 60	149	38
Hamal	α Arietis	2.2	2 07	N 23	328	7
Kaus Aust.	ε Sagittarii	2.0	18 24	S 34	84	51
Kochab	β Ursae Minoris	2.2	14 51	N 74	137	43
Markab	α Pegasi	2.6	23 04	N 15	14	60
Menkar	α Ceti	2.8	3 02	N 4	315	9
Menkent	θ Centauri	2.3	14 06	S 36	148	39
Miaplacidus	β Carinae	1.8	9 13	S 70	222	26
Mimosa	β Crucis	1.5	12 47	S 60	168	34
Mirfak	α Persei	1.9	3 24	N 50	309	10
Nunki	σ Sagittarii	2.1	18 55	S 26	76	53
Peacock	α Pavonis	2.1	20 25	S 57	54	55
POLARIS	α Ursae Minoris	2.1	2 24	N 89	324	6
Pollux	β Geminorum	1.2	7 45	N 28	244	23
Procyon	α Canis Minoris	0.5	7 39	N 5	245	22
Rasalhague	α Ophiuchi	2.1	17 35	N 13	96	49
Regulus	α Leonis	1.3	10 08	N 12	208	28
Rigel	β Orionis	0.3	5 14	S 8	281	12
Rigil Kent	α Centauri	0.1	14 39	S 61	140	41
Sabik	η Ophiuchi	2.6	17 10	S 16	103	47
Schedar	α Cassiopeiae	2.5	0 40	N 56	350	3
Shaula	λ Scorpii	1.7	17 33	S 37	97	48
Sirius	α Canis Majoris	-1.6	6 45	S 17	259	19
Spica	α Virginis	1.2	13 25	S 11	159	36
Suhail	λ Velorum	2.2	9 08	S 43	223	25
Vega	α Lyrae	0.1	18 37	N 39	81	52
Zuben'ubi	α Librae	2.9	14 50	S 16	137	42

The last column refers to the number given to the Star in this Almanac. The Star's exact position may be found according to this number on the monthly pages 3:11, 3:17, 3:23, etc. Full instructions how to find the above Stars are given in Section 2.

AUXILIARY STAR CHARTS
POLE–PLOUGH–DUBHE–BENETNASCH–KOCHAB

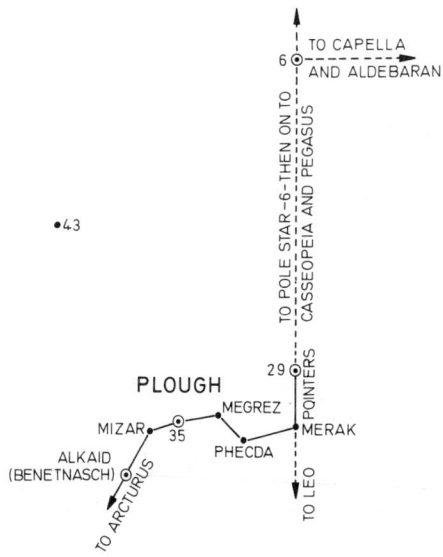

No. 6. POLARIS.
No. 29. DUBHE.
No. 35. ALIOTH.
No. 43. KOCHAB.
No. 11. ALDEBARAN.
No. 13. CAPELLA.

Polaris—the Pole Star—familiar in the Northern Hemisphere is always seen in the same part of the heavens, over the Pole of the Earth. It is the brightest star in the Little Bear (Ursa Minor). The position of Polaris in the Little Bear corresponds to the position of Alkaid (Benetnasch) 37, in the Great Bear. The Plough or Great Bear (Ursa Major) is the easiest recognisable constellation in the northern heavens, a straight line through Merak and Dubhe—the Pointers—leads to the Pole Star.

CAPELLA–POLLUX–SIRIUS–ORION–ALDEBARAN

No. 11. ALDEBARAN.
No. 12. RIGEL.
No. 13. CAPELLA.
No. 14. BELLATRIX.
No. 17. BETELGEUSE.
No. 19. SIRIUS.
No. 21. CASTOR.
No. 22. PROCYON.
No. 23. POLLUX.

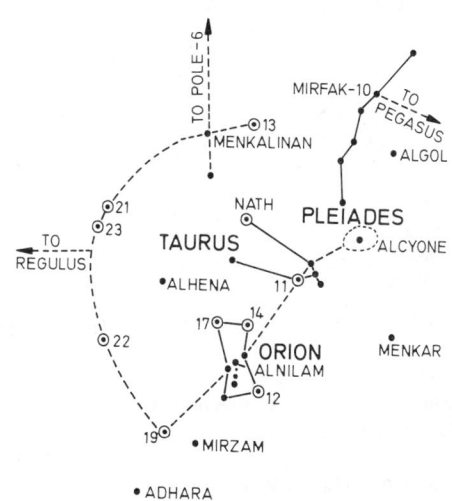

Orion is the finest constellation visible in the northern hemisphere, is easily recognised, and the many fine stars around it make it invaluable. The three bright stars in line form Orion's belt with Alnilam at the centre and the sword hanging down below the belt. Four bright stars surround Orion—Betelgeuse, Bellatrix, Rigel and Saiph. Orion is near the meridian at midnight late in the year, and therefore is only visible in northern latitudes in winter and early spring.

Further instructions will be found on pages 2:20-2:23 under star numbers.

STAR CHART No. 1

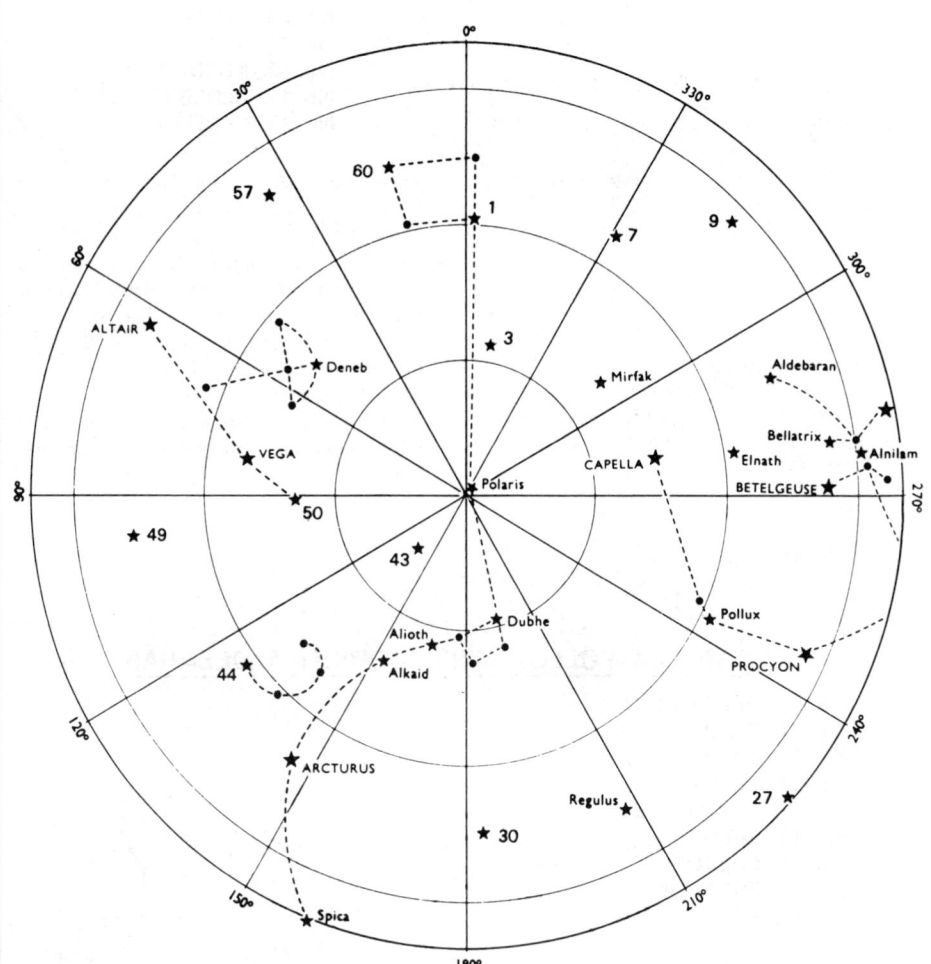

NORTHERN HEMISPHERE

* **Stars of the first magnitude (capital letters).**

* **Stars of magnitude 2.0 to 1.0 (small letters).**

Key to numbered stars

1 Alpheratz	27 Alphard	49 Rasalhague
3 Schedar	30 Denebola	50 Eltanin
7 Hamal	43 Kochab	57 Enif
9 Menkar	44 Alphecca	60 Markab

STAR CHART No. 2

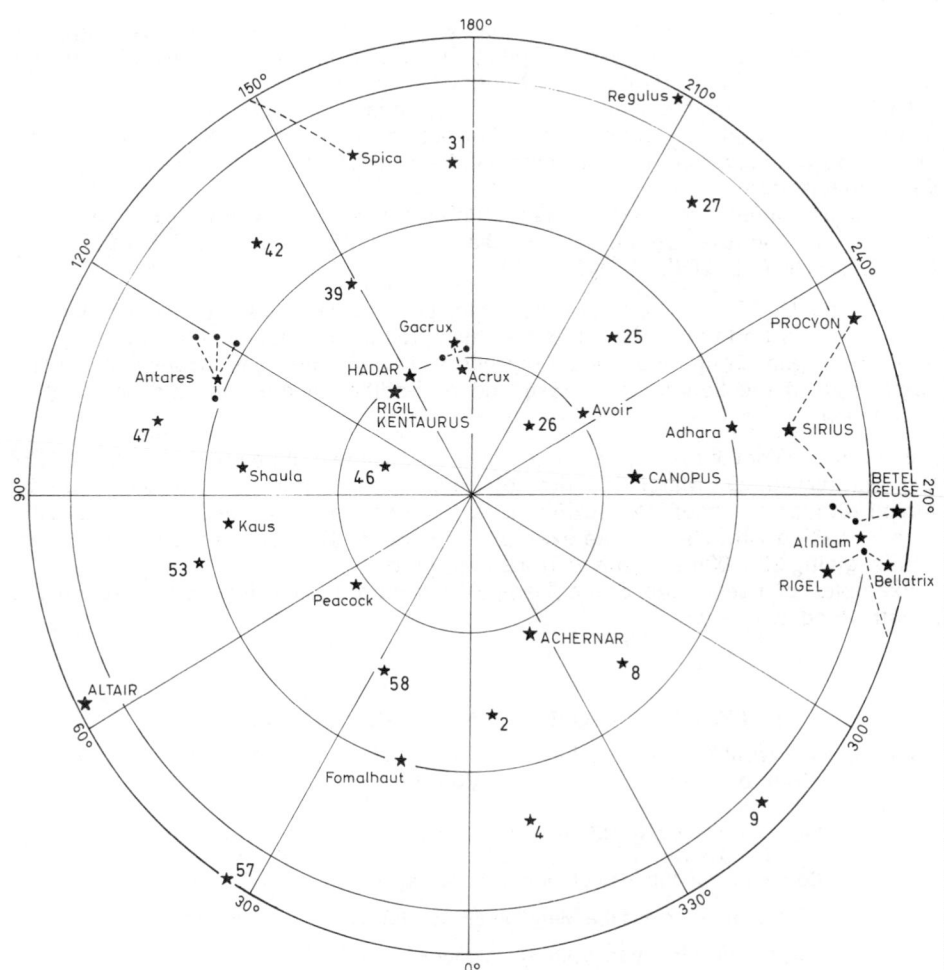

SOUTHERN HEMISPHERE

* Stars which are less bright than mag. 2.0 but are listed and numbered as Selected Stars.	Key to numbered stars
● Stars of lesser magnitude, included to help identification of some constellations.	

Key to numbered stars

2 Ankaa	26 Miaplacidus	46 Atria
4 Diphda	27 Alphard	47 Sabik
8 Acamar	31 Gienah	53 Nunki
9 Menkar	39 Menkent	57 Enif
25 Suhail	42 Zuben'ubi	58 Al Na'ir

TO FIND THE APPROXIMATE MEAN TIME OF MERIDIAN
TRANSIT OF THE 60 PRINCIPAL STARS AT GREENWICH

Often at twilight, the opportunity occurs to take a "sight" of a Star to obtain immediately the ship's latitude, and frequently, when approaching the coast, this knowledge is invaluable.

The information becomes useful at once when it is decided to take a Star sight for Latitude, because it tells IN ADVANCE what time each Star will cross the Meridian, and which therefore will be suitable for "shooting".

The Times of Transit are given on the monthly pages (3:11, 3:17, etc.) for the first day of the month, and the Stars Transit Correction Table on the same page gives immediately the correction to subtract to find the G.M.T. of Transit for any subsequent day of that month.

It must be noticed particularly that the Almanac gives the G.M.T. of Meridian Transit of each Star on the Greenwich Meridian, but THIS TIME IS APPROXIMATELY CORRECT FOR ALL OTHER LONGITUDES.

To find the G.M.T. of a Star's Meridian Transit on any day of the month for any other longitude, first find the G.M.T. of its Meridian Transit at Greenwich for that day, and apply the usual Longitude Time Correction (1° = 04min., see pages 4:2-4:3); by subtraction, if the Longitude is East, and by addition if the Longitude is West of Greenwich.

Example.—What is the approximate time of Transit of Dubhe on March 20th, 1992? Dubhe (Star No. 29), March 1st, Time of Transit is 0h. 27min., but the correction for March 20th (same page), viz. 1h. 15min., is greater so increase the 0h. 27min. by 23h. 56min. making 24h. 23min. (see example on page 3:11). Subtract the correction 1h. 15min. giving 23h. 08min. Time of Transit required.

Examples of use of the Star's Transit Correction Tables are given also on the monthly pages.

TO FIND STARS TO OBSERVE FOR MERIDIAN ALTITUDE

Example I.—What Star is available at 6.07 a.m. on October 15th, 1992, in Latitude 48° 00'N to observe for Latitude by Meridian Altitude? What is its Magnitude?

	h.	min.
Page 3:65 shows No. 22 October 1st		
M.T. of Transit	6	58
Correction for 15th day of month (same page)	−0	55
∴ Procyon will cross the Meridian on Oct. 15th at	6	03 a.m.

Magnitude of Procyon is 0.5 (same page)

Page 3:65 shows also Pollux, No. 23, October 1st		
M.T. of Transit	7	04
Correction for 15th day of month	−0	55
∴ Pollux crosses Meridian at	6	09 a.m.

Magnitude of Pollux is 1.2

Both of these Stars (having Declinations of 5°N and 28°N respectively) are above the horizon in Lat. 48°N and therefore above the horizon at time of transit.

Example II.—What Stars are available for Meridian Altitude Observations about 18.15h. on March 28th, 1992, in Latitude 47° 30'N?

Having deducted from the Time of Transit, March 1st, 1h. 46min. (for the 28th day), Canopus transits at 17h. 58min., Sirius transits at 18h. 19min.

It will be seen by a glance at the table on page 3:23 that Canopus, Sirius and Adhara will all be on the Meridian about the required time. By a further glance at their Declinations on page 3:23, however, it can be at once seen that Canopus having a Dec. of $52\frac{1}{2}°$S will be below the horizon ($52\frac{1}{2}°$S + $47\frac{1}{2}°$N = 100°), and that Adhara has a Dec. of 29°S. Now (29°S + $47\frac{1}{2}°$N = $76\frac{1}{2}°$) will put this Star only $13\frac{1}{2}°$ above the horizon. Whilst a Latitude MIGHT be obtained from a sight of this Star, in view of the fact that Sirius (the brightest Star in the sky) has a Dec. of only $16\frac{1}{2}°$S and would therefore ($16\frac{1}{2}°$S + $47\frac{1}{2}°$N = 64°) be well up at a convenient altitude, it is obvious that Sirius would be used.

	h. min.
Page 3:65 shows Sirius No. 19, March 1st	
M.T. of Transit	20 05
Correction for 28th day of month...............................	−1 46
∴ Sirius will cross the Meridian on 28th March at	18 19

TO FIND A STAR'S DECLINATION (DEC.)

The Declination of the Principal Stars are given for the first days of each month on the monthly pages, and, of course, this quantity does not alter throughout the month.

Example.—Required the Declination of Vega on March 10th, 1992. Page 3:23 gives the Dec. for March as (Star No. 52) N38° 46'.3.

GREENWICH HOUR ANGLE (G.H.A.) OF THE STARS

For all general purposes of Sights or Azimuths the brighter Stars are used always, so the G.H.A. is tabulated direct for the 60 principal Stars numbered in Reed's Almanac, at 0h. for the first of each month.

The correct G.H.A. at the instant of time of the observation is found by applying a correction for the day of the month, the hour, the minute and the second; always additive. These corrections are given in a special Star G.H.A. Correction Table on page 4:8. When using the direct tabulation of a Star's G.H.A. then the columns for the Date, Hour, Minute and Second are used. If however the G.H.A. Aries method is being used then as the working is from the nearest two hours, the columns for "1 Hour + minutes," minutes and seconds must be used (Page 4:8).

Example I.—Required the G.H.A. of Sirius on February 22nd, 1992, at 19h. 20min. Page 3:17 (February) shows Sirius (Star No. 19) G.H.A. = 029° 30'.4W on February 1st.

Feb. 1st, 0h. Sirius G.H.A.	= 029°	15'.4
Page 4:8 Corr. for 22nd	+ 20°	41'.9
19h..	+ 285°	46'.8
20min.	+ 5°	00'.8
G.H.A. of Sirius	= 340°	44'.9

The G.H.A. of any other of the 60 Stars may be found at any time in the same way.

TO FIND LOCAL HOUR ANGLE OF A STAR
FROM STAR'S G.H.A.

Example.—On July 15th, 1992, in Lat. 48° 20'N, Long. 38° 15'W at G.M.T. 3h. 40min. 10s., having taken sights; what is Local Hour Angle of (a) Sirius and (b) Aldebaran?

(a) Sirius				(b) Aldebaran			
Page 3:47 July 1st, 0h.				Page 3:47 July 1st, 0h.			
Sirius G.H.A.		= 178°	05'.7W	Aldebaran G.H.A.		= 210°	25'.5W
Page 4:8				Page 4:8			
Corr. for	15d	+ 13°	48'.0	Corr. for	15d	+ 13°	48'.0
" "	3h.	+ 45°	07'.4	" "	3h.	+ 45°	07'.4
" "	40min.	+ 10°	01'.6	" "	40min.	+ 10°	01'.6
" "	10s.	+	02'.5	" "	10s.	+	02'.5
G.H.A. of Sirius		247°	05'.2W	G.H.A. of Aldebaran		279°	25'.0W
Long. W		− 38°	15'.0W	Long. W		− 38°	15'.0W
Local Hour Angle		208°	50'.2W	Local Hour Angle		241°	10'.0W

The simplicity of the G.H.A. method is here clearly demonstrated.

Be careful when using the G.H.A. Correction Table on p. 4:8 to ignore the "Corr. for 1 hour + Minute" column and use the Date, Hour, Minute and Second columns only.

TO FIND HOUR ANGLE FROM ARIES

On each of the monthly pages (Nos. 3:12-3:13; 3:18-3:19, etc.) on which the Sun's Dec. and G.H.A. are tabulated at 2 hourly intervals, the G.H.A. of Aries (the First Point of Aries) is tabulated in degrees and minutes at 2 hourly intervals throughout the year. The special column "Hours and minutes" in the G.H.A. Correction Table on p. 4:8 is used to find the G.H.A. of Aries at the exact instant of observation.

Having found the correct G.H.A. of Aries then by adding the S.H.A. (Sidereal Hour Angle) of any Star the G.H.A. of that Star may be found. The application of the Longitude in the usual way will give the Local Hour Angle.

This Sidereal Hour Angle of a Star is simply 360° minus the R.A. (Right Ascension) of the Star in Arc.

TO FIND G.H.A. OF STAR FROM ARIES

Example I.—Required the G.H.A. of Sirius on February 22nd, 1992, at 19h. 20min. Page 3:17 (February) shows the S.H.A. of Sirius (No. 19) to be 258° 47'.5W.

Page 3:19 G.H.A. Aries...........................	18h.	=	61° 54'.2W
Corr. for 1h. 20min. (Page 4:8)		+	20° 03'.3
G.H.A. Aries at obs.			81° 57'.5
Sirius S.H.A.)		+	258° 47'.5
G.H.A. Sirius.			340° 45'.0W

Which agrees with the answer found from the direct tabulation of G.H.A. on p. 2:29.

TO FIND LOCAL HOUR ANGLE OF STAR FROM ARIES

Example I.—On July 15th, 1992, in Lat. 48° 20'N, Long. 38° 15'W, at G.M.T. 3h. 40min. 10s., having taken sights; what is the L.H.A. of (a) Sirius (b) Aldebaran?

(a) Sirius			(b) Aldebaran		
G.H.A. Aries 2h.	323°	10'.8W	G.H.A. Aries 2h.	323°	10'.8
Corr. for 1h. 40min. 10s.	+ 25°	06'.6	Corr. for 1h. 40min. 10s.	+ 25°	06'.6
G.H.A. Aries at 3h. 40min. 10s	348°	17'.4W	G.H.A. Aries at 3h. 40min. 10s	348°	17'.4W
Sirius S.H.A.	+ 258°	47'.8	Aldebaran S.H.A.	+ 291°	07'.6
G.H.A. Sirius	607°	05'.2W	G.H.A. Aldebaran	639°	25'.0W
(Reject 360°)	− 360°		(Reject 360°)	− 360°	
G.H.A. Sirius	247°	05'.2W	G.H.A. Aldebaran	279°	25'.0W
Long. W	− 38°	15'.0	Long. W	− 38°	15'.0
L.H.A. Sirius	208°	50'.2W	L.H.A. Aldebaran	241°	10'.0W

Which agrees with the answers from the direct tabulation of G.H.A. on p. 2:30.
Be careful to use the correct columns from the table on p. 4:8.

TO FIND STAR'S RIGHT ASCENSION

This may be found roughly for identification purposes with a Star Chart or by p. 2:24 from the Alphabetical List, but more accurately from the 60 principal Stars listed in Reed's Almanac on each monthly page.

Example.—Required the R.A. of Canopus on July 10th, 1992. Page 3:47 shows this to be (Star No. 18) 6h. 24min.
Should the Right Ascension be required accurately (though it is unnecessary with a G.H.A. Almanac) it may be found by subtracting the S.H.A. from 360° and converting this from arc to time.
S.H.A. Canopus (No. 18 is 264° 03'.6) ... 360° 00' − 264° 03'.6 = 95° 56'.4, which in time (by the table on p. 4:2-4:3) is 6h. 23min. 46s., which is R.A. of Canopus.

TO FIND R.A.M. (Right Ascension of the Meridian) or SIDEREAL TIME

For Star Atlas purposes the R.A.M. is found from G.H.A. Aries.

Example.—Required R.A.M. at 08h. 21min. G.M.T. on Jan. 20th, 1992, in Long. 15°W.

G.H.A. Aries 8h.	=	238°	58'.0W
Corr. for 21min. (Page 4:8)	+	5°	15'.9
G.H.A. Aries at 8h. 21min.		244°	13'.9W
Long. W	−	15°	00'.0
L.H.A. Aries	=	229°	13'.9
Which in time (see p. 4:3) = R.A.M.		15h.	16min. 56s.

TO FIND THE R.A. OF SUN, MOON, OR PLANET

The Right Ascension of Greenwich equals the G.H.A. Aries (converted from Arc into Time by the table on page 4:2-4:3).
To find the Right Ascension of the Sun, Moon or a Planet, subtract the G.H.A. of the Body from the G.H.A. of Aries, and convert from arc to time.

HOW TO RECOGNISE THE PLANETS

The principal planets are Mercury (☿), Venus (♀), the Earth (⊕ or ♁), Mars (♂), Jupiter (♃), Saturn (♄), Uranus (♅) and Neptune (♆).

Planets are heavenly bodies of which our Earth is an example—which revolve round the Sun in their own particular orbits (or paths). These planets are situated at varying distances from the Sun and thus have entirely different periods of revolution. They are all, however, situated in a belt of the celestial sphere about 8° on either side of the Ecliptic called the Zodiac.

The planets, like the Earth's satellite—the Moon—(and the Comets when visible), all receive their light from the reflected rays of the Sun. Those between the Earth and the Sun are Mercury and Venus and are called Inferior planets, the others are outside the Earth's Orbit and are called Superior planets.

On account of their position varying so much in comparison with the fixed stars, the planets are often termed "wandering stars."

None of the visible planets ever twinkle like the Stars so they may readily be recognised in consequence.

Mercury is very close to the Sun and being seldom seen is of little use to the Navigator. Uranus on the other hand, is not visible, except perhaps with a telescope, so is of no service either. The remainder of the planets are never visible to the naked eye, except Venus, Jupiter, Mars and Saturn, which are all four of great importance and assistance to the practical Navigator.

Venus is only visible for a short time after sunset and before sunrise, because its orbit is between the Earth and the Sun, and it appears to cross and recross the Sun continually. In practice, the time of the meridian passage of Venus is constantly changing from about 9 a.m. to 3 p.m. As Venus is so bright, she can, at all times, during clear weather and when not too near the Sun, be observed during the daytime, even though not visible to the naked eye. Many Navigators get a splendid position during the day by taking Venus on the meridian crossed with a Sun position line.

Venus has a bluish light and with the exception of the Sun and Moon, is by far the brightest object in the heavens. She is outstanding for easy navigation and may readily be observed during twilight.

Jupiter, whilst not so bright as Venus, is nevertheless brighter than any fixed star and may be used for a daytime fix with a powerful sextant telescope.

Mars' distance from the Earth varies and in consequence is sometimes very bright and at others very faint. Mars has a reddish colour.

Saturn is the least bright of the four planets and shines at the equivalent of a first magnitude star. Saturn has a yellowish colour.

The diameter of Jupiter is quite appreciable and is about three times that of Saturn. As their semi-diameters vary, it is customary to observe the centre of the planet to avoid any correction for semi-diameter.

The notes on monthly Planet page 3:14 (and each succeeding sixth page to page 3:80 for December) show whether the Planet is a Morning or Evening Planet and whether it is too close to the Sun for observation and give an indication of its position in the heavens.

When the meridian passage (given daily) occurs at midnight the body is in Opposition to the Sun and is visible all night so may be observed in both morning and evening twilights; it bears to the east of the meridian before meridian passage.

THE POLE STAR (POLARIS)

Polaris is listed as one of the principal Stars—No. 6 to be exact—and the data are given for this on each monthly Star page.

Example.—Required the Declination, and G.H.A. of Polaris on February 20th, 1992, at G.M.T. 4h. 27min. 40s. Page 3:17, Star No. 6, gives Polaris Dec. N89° 14'.2 (which, of course, is the same for the whole month).

	G.H.A. 0h. Feb. 1st is	94° 39'.8W	(G.H.A. is always
	20d.	+ 18° 43'.6	West)
Page 4:8	,, 4h.	+ 60° 09'.9	
	,, 27min.	+ 6° 46'1.	
	,, 40s.	+ 10'.0	
	G.H.A. of Polaris Feb. 20th, 4h. 27min. 40s. ...	180° 29'4W	

Examples of how to find the Latitude by Polaris are given on page 5:17, and Azimuth of Polaris on page 5:19.

EPHEMERIDES OF THE PLANETS

On each monthly page, 3:14, 3:20, 3:26, etc., is given the G.M.T. of the Meridian Passage of the four navigational Planets, Venus, Mars, Jupiter and Saturn, over the Meridian of Greenwich, which is for all practical purposes the Ship Mean Time of Transit over any other Meridian. This page not only gives the time each day of the Planet's Transit over the Meridian of Greenwich as mentioned but, at the foot of the Planet's data, gives the magnitude of the Planet and its position in the heavens during that month.

This information coupled with the description of the Planets given on page 2:32, will identify the Planets for Sights or Azimuths.

This monthly page gives also the Planet's position, i.e., the Declination (and its mean Variation per hour) and the G.H.A. (and its Variation per hour), for each of the four Planets every day throughout the month at 0h. G.M.T.

Appropriate Correction Tables are given on pages 4:9-4:13.

The S.H.A. of each navigational Planet is given 6 times a month.

Example.—Required the Dec. and G.H.A. of Mars on July 10th, 1992, at 19h. 36min. G.M.T. What is the time of the Meridian Passage.

The Meridian Passage of Mars, July 10th, is 07h. 52min. G.M.T. (page 3:50).

To find the Declination

Page 3:50, Mars, July 10th, Dec. at		
G.M.T. 0h. is	16° 17'.4N	Var. per hour
Page 4:13, Corr. for 19h. 36min. .... +	09'.8	+0.5
Dec. July 10th at 19h. 36 min.	16° 27'.2N	

To find the G.H.A.

Page 3:50 G.H.A. at G.M.T. 0h. is	241° 59'.9W	Var. per hour
Page 4:9, Var 15° 0'.7, 19h. .... + 285° 13'.3		15° 0'.7
Page 4:11, Var. 15° 0'.7, 36min .... + 9° 00'.4		
	536° 13'.6	
	- 360° 00'.0	
G.H.A. July 10th at 19h. 36 min.	176° 13'.6	

The Table on page 4:9-4:10 (always additive) is used to correct the G.H.A. for 19h. (interpolating for exactness) and the extra 36min. is found on page 4:11 according to the Mean Var. per hour.

The Horizontal Parallax of the Planets is for navigational purposes considered negligible.

The Local Hour Angle is found as already described by applying Longitude (by the usual rhyme) to G.H.A.; in the same way that by the Time method the R.A. of the Planet compared with the R.A.M. gives the Hour Angle. The G.H.A. method—being always additive—will, with practice, certainly be found more simple.

Note—Owing to the movement of the Planets the data should be taken out as accurately as possible.

S.H.A. OF PLANETS

Should the approx. Sidereal Hour Angle (S.H.A.) of a Planet be required, i.e., to use with a Star Chart, it may be found from Aries.

Subtract the G.H.A. of Aries from the G.H.A. of the Planet. If necessary add 360° to G.H.A. of the Planet before subtraction.

Example.—Required the S.H.A. of Mars at G.M.T. 0h. on March 8th, 1992.

G.H.A. of Mars at 0h. on March 8th	208° 41'.7
G.H.A. of Aries at 0h. on March 8th	165° 56'.9
S.H.A. of Mars at 0h. on March 8th	42° 44'.8

EPHEMERIS OF THE MOON

On the first page of each month (3:10, 3:16, 3:22, etc.), elements will be found giving the Moon's Age, times of Moonrise and Moonset at London, the Moon's Semi-Diameter and Horizontal Parallax and the Moon's Meridian Passage times, together with its difference. A complete Moon page is given monthly in addition (3:15, 3:21, 3:27, etc.), where the Moon's G.H.A. and Declination is given for each six hours throughout the month, together with the mean variations per hour.

TO FIND THE MOON'S DECLINATION

Example.—Required the Dec. of the Moon on March 12th, 1992, at 15h. 12min. G.M.T.

Page 3:27, Dec. 12h.	=	24° 14'.0N	Var. in 1 hour
Corr. 3h. i.e., 3 x –2'.8.	–	8'.4	–2'.8
Page 4:18, Corr. 12min. i.e., 0.2 x –2'.8	–	0'.6	
Dec. at 15h. 12min.		24° 05'.0N	

TO FIND THE MOON'S G.H.A.

Example.—Required the G.H.A. of the Moon on March 2nd, 1992, at 9h. 12min. G.M.T.

Page 3:27, G.H.A. at 6h.		292° 19'.8W	Var. in 1 hour
Page 4:15, Corr. for 3h.	+	43° 42'.3	14° 34'.1
Page 4:17, Corr. for 12min.	+	2° 54'.8	
G.H.A. at 9h. 12 min..		338° 56'.9W	

The nearest 6 hours should normally be worked to, being careful to apply the correction in the correct way. The Local Hour Angle of the Moon can be found in exactly the same way as for the Sun.

TO FIND THE MOON'S AGE

This is the number of days elapsed since New Moon. It is given on the monthly pages. On March 18th, 1992, the Age is 14 days (page 3:22).

TO FIND THE MOON'S MERIDIAN PASSAGE OF TIME

The monthly pages contain the G.M.T. of the Moon's Upper Meridian Passage (Transit) over the Meridian of Greenwich with the daily difference.

Example.—What is the Ship Mean Time of the Moon's Meridian Passage on March 21st, 1992, in Longitude 65°W?

Page 3:22, March 21st G.M.T. of Moon's Mer.

Pass. is	01h. 55min.	Diff. 53min.*
Page 4:19, Diff. 53min. Long. 65°W .... +	9min.	
Mer. Pass. in Long. 65°W S.M.T.	02h. 04min.	

Example II.—What is the Ship Mean Time of the Moon's Meridian Passage in Longitude 70°E on March 21st, 1992?

Page 3:22, March 21st G.M.T. of Moon's Mer.

Pass. is	01h. 55min.	Diff. 51min.*
Page 4:19, Diff. 51min. Long. 70°E S.M.T....... −	10min.	
Mer. Pass. in Long. 70°E S.M.T.	01h. 45min.	

*When longitude is East, use the difference between the Meridian Passage on the day in question and that of the day previous. In West longitude, take the difference between the day in question and the following day.

TO FIND THE MOON'S SEMI-DIAMETER

This is given on each monthly page.
Page 3:10 shows this to be 15'.1 on January 11th, 1992.

TO FIND THE MOON'S HORIZONTAL PARALLAX

This is given on each monthly page.
Page 3:10 shows this to be 55'.4 on January 11th, 1992, at 12h. 00min.

TO FIND THE TIMES OF MOONRISE AND MOONSET

The daily G.M.T.'s of Moonrise and Moonset are given for the position of Latitude 52°N on the Meridian of Greenwich on the Moon's monthly pages.

To find the L.M.T. on any other meridian apply the correction from the Table on page 4:19 using the same rules as those given for times of Moon's Meridian passage.

Page 3:22 shows that on March 18th, the Moon rises in that position at 14h. 41min. and sets at 07h. 31min. on the following day.

THE MOON'S PHASES

These are shown on the monthly and Moon pages, and in March Full Moon is shown to be on the 19th day at 21h. 28min. See also page 2:36-2:37.

The Moon is said to be in Apogee (when her Semi-Diameter is smallest—about 14.7') and in March this occurs on the 6th day at 12h. and in Perigee (when the Semi-diameter is largest, about 16'.3) and in March this occurs on the 19th day at 22h.

The time required for the Moon to make one orbit using the Sun as a reference point, i.e., the interval between two successive New Moons, is approximately $29\frac{1}{2}$ days and is called a Synodical Month or a Lunation.

A Sidereal Month is the time taken for one complete orbit with reference to a fixed star. It is the time interval from Perigee to Perigee or Apogee to Apogee, and is approximately 27 days.

A Lunar Day is the time interval between two successive transits of the Moon over the same meridian. It averages about 24 hours and 50 minutes. The minutes in excess of 24 hours vary from 38 to 66 minutes due to the irregular speed of the Moon along its orbit.

Because the Moon crosses the meridian later each day, there is always a day in each synodical month in which there is no meridian passage, another in which there is no moonrise and another with no moonset. For example, if Moonrise occurs at, say, 2330 on a Monday, the following Moonrise may not occur until 0020 on Wednesday.

AN EXPLANATION OF THE MOON'S PHASES

The Moon's Phases are changes in the appearance of the Moon's disc due to variations in its position with reference to the Earth and Sun. Some knowledge of this is of good practical use to the seaman because, at a single glance at the Moon he will know without reference to books or tables, its phase, rough time of meridian passage and the state of the tides in regard to Springs and Neaps.

Spring Tides do not occur in European waters until about 2 days after the New and Full Moon. Similarly Neaps occur about 2 days after the Moon's Quarters.

The Sun is so far away from us that, for all practical purposes, its light is considered to reach the whole of the Earth-Moon system in parallel rays.

Figure 1—looking down onto the North pole of the Earth—shows 8 successive positions of the Moon as it orbits the Earth in an anticlockwise direction. It also shows how at all times one hemisphere of the Moon is illuminated by the Sun's rays whilst the opposite hemisphere is in total darkness. The 8 positions are numbered consecutively commencing at the New Moon, Position 1.

Figure 2 illustrates the appearance of the Moon's disc corresponding to each of the positions, numbered 1 to 8, in Figure 1. This shows how the Moon looks to an observer in, say, the British Isles or in any latitude from which the Moon bears South at its meridian passage.

When comparing Figures 1 and 2, remember that an observer looks from the Earth towards the Moon. Thus if Figure 1 is turned upside down to look at the Moon in Position 7, its corresponding appearance in Figure 2 (not upside down) is obvious.

Figure 2, when turned upside down, shows the appearance of the Moon at each phase (keeping the same numbers as before) when seen from latitudes in which it passes North of the observer at meridian passage.

PHASES OF THE MOON

Referring again to Figures 1 and 2:

Position No.	Moon's Phase	Age	Time of Mer. Pass (Approx)	Remarks
		Days	Hrs.	
1	New Moon	0	1200	Sun and Moon "in conjunction". Moon not visible because only the dark hemisphere faces the Earth.
2	Between New Moon and First Quarter	3-4	1500	Visible as a crescent with its bow towards the West. Waxing.
3	First Quarter	7	1800	Moon 90° East of Sun (in East Quadrature). Visible as a half-disc with its bow towards the West. Waxing.
4	Between First Quarter and Full Moon	11-12	2100	Three quarters of the disc visible (called a Gibbous Moon), the more rounded side towards the West. Waxing.
5	Full Moon	15	2400	Moon on Sun's antimeridian, i.e., "in opposition". The whole of the illuminated hemisphere is visible.
6	Between Full Moon and Last Quarter	18-19	0300	Three quarters of the disc visible (called a Gibbous Moon), the more rounded side towards the East. Waning.
7	Last Quarter	22	0600	Moon 90° West of the Sun (in West Quadrature). Visible as a half-disc with its bow towards the East. Waning.
8	Between Last Quarter and New Moon	25-26	0900	Visible as a crescent with its bow towards the East. Waning.

In low latitudes, Moonrise and Moonset occur a few minutes more than 6 hours before and after mer. pass., respectively. In high latitudes the times vary with changes in the Moon's Declination.

THE MOON'S PHASES

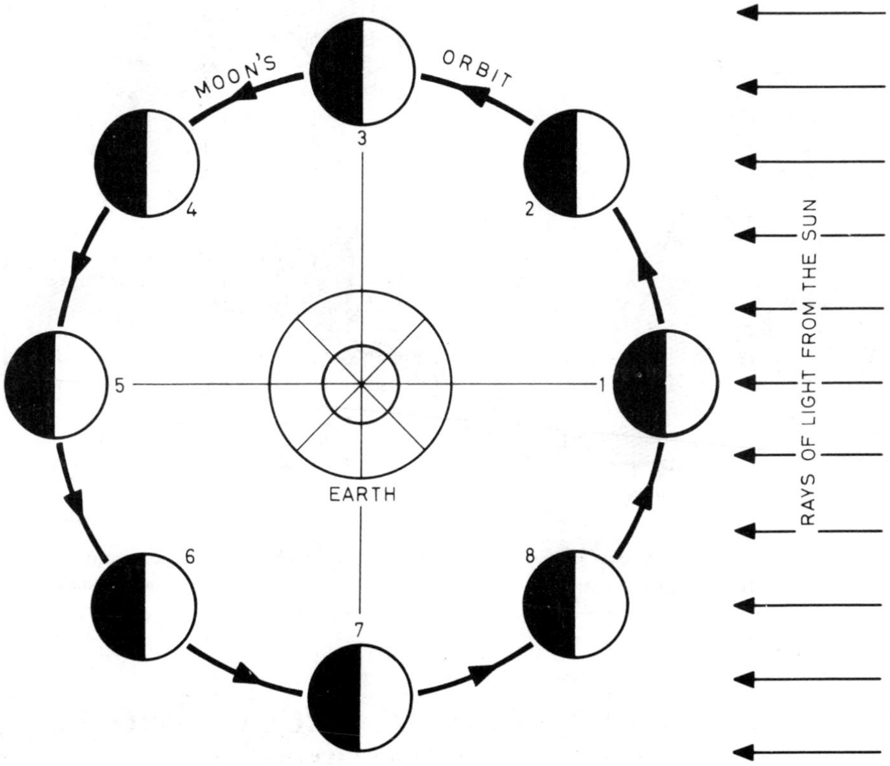

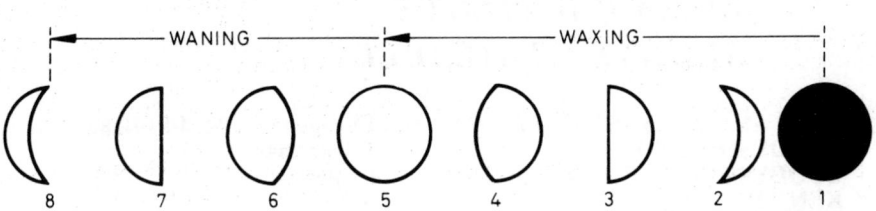

Figure 1
Successive positions (1 to 8) of the Moon along its orbit round the Earth.

Figure 2
Phases of the Moon as viewed from the Earth's surface.

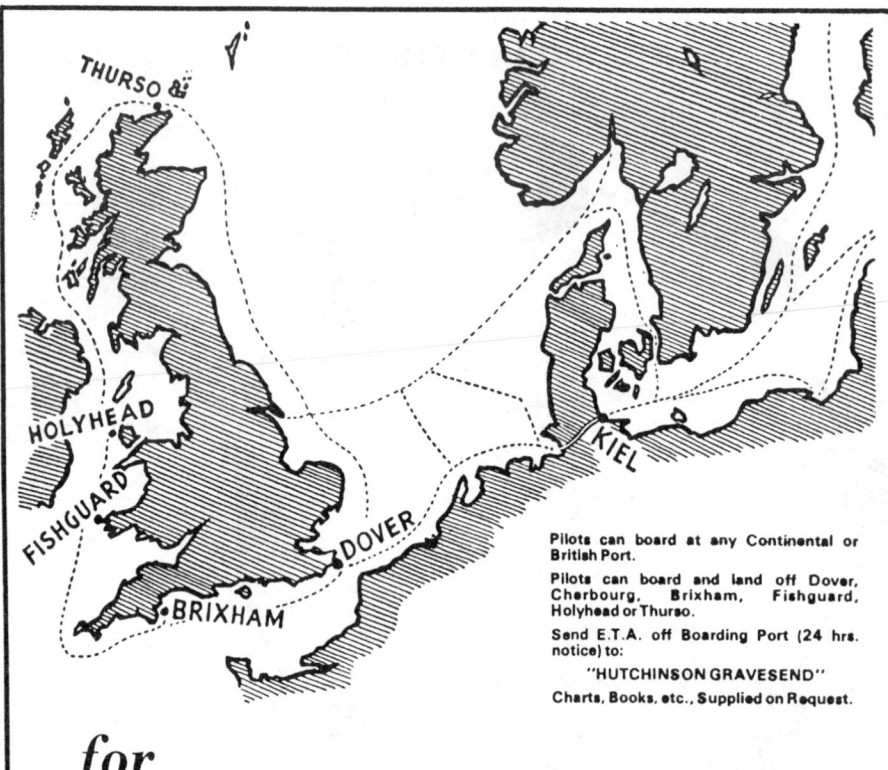

Nautical Almanac for 1992

3

CALENDAR — 1992

JANUARY				
Sun		5	12	19	26
Mon		6	13	20	27
Tue		7	14	21	28
Wed	1	8	15	22	29
Thu	2	9	16	23	30
Fri	3	10	17	24	31
Sat	4	11	18	25	

FEBRUARY				
Sun		2	9	16	23
Mon		3	10	17	24
Tue		4	11	18	25
Wed		5	12	19	26
Thu		6	13	20	27
Fri		7	14	21	28
Sat	1	8	15	22	29

MARCH					
Sun	1	8	15	22	29
Mon	2	9	16	23	30
Tue	3	10	17	24	31
Wed	4	11	18	25	
Thu	5	12	19	26	
Fri	6	13	20	27	
Sat	7	14	21	28	

APRIL				
Sun		5	12	19	26
Mon		6	13	20	27
Tue		7	14	21	28
Wed	1	8	15	22	29
Thu	2	9	16	23	30
Fri	3	10	17	24	
Sat	4	11	18	25	

MAY					
Sun		3	10	17	24	31
Mon		4	11	18	25	
Tue		5	12	19	26	
Wed		6	13	20	27	
Thu		7	14	21	28	
Fri	1	8	15	22	29	
Sat	2	9	16	23	30	

JUNE				
Sun		7	14	21	28
Mon	1	8	15	22	29
Tue	2	9	16	23	30
Wed	3	10	17	24	
Thu	4	11	18	25	
Fri	5	12	19	26	
Sat	6	13	20	27	

JULY				
Sun		5	12	19	26
Mon		6	13	20	27
Tue		7	14	21	28
Wed	1	8	15	22	29
Thu	2	9	16	23	30
Fri	3	10	17	24	31
Sat	4	11	18	25	

AUGUST					
Sun		2	9	16	23	30
Mon		3	10	17	24	31
Tue		4	11	18	25	
Wed		5	12	19	26	
Thu		6	13	20	27	
Fri		7	14	21	28	
Sat	1	8	15	22	29	

SEPTEMBER				
Sun		6	13	20	27
Mon		7	14	21	28
Tue	1	8	15	22	29
Wed	2	9	16	23	30
Thu	3	10	17	24	
Fri	4	11	18	25	
Sat	5	12	19	26	

OCTOBER				
Sun		4	11	18	25
Mon		5	12	19	26
Tue		6	13	20	27
Wed		7	14	21	28
Thu	1	8	15	22	29
Fri	2	9	16	23	30
Sat	3	10	17	24	31

NOVEMBER				
Sun	1	8	15	22	29
Mon	2	9	16	23	30
Tue	3	10	17	24	
Wed	4	11	18	25	
Thu	5	12	19	26	
Fri	6	13	20	27	
Sat	7	14	21	28	

DECEMBER				
Sun		6	13	20	27
Mon		7	14	21	28
Tue	1	8	15	22	29
Wed	2	9	16	23	30
Thu	3	10	17	24	31
Fri	4	11	18	25	
Sat	5	12	19	26	

FESTIVALS AND ANNIVERSARIES, 1992

RELIGIOUS CALENDARS

Epiphany	January 6
Septuagesima Sunday	February 16
Quinquagesima Sunday	March 1
Shrove Tuesday (Pancake Day)	March 3
Ash Wednesday	March 4
Quadragesima Sunday	March 8
Palm Sunday	April 12
Good Friday	April 17
Easter Day	April 19
Low Sunday	April 26
Rogation Sunday	May 24
Ascension Day — Holy Thursday	May 28
Whit Sunday — Pentecost	June 7
Trinity Sunday	June 14
Corpus Christi	June 18
Feast of the Assumption	August 15
First Sunday in Advent	Novrmber 29
Christmas Day	December 25
Passover, First day of (Pesach)	April 18
Feast of Weeks (Shavuot)	June 7
Jewish New Year 5753 (Rosh Hashanah)	September 28
Day of Atonement (Yom Kippur)	October 7
Tabernacles, First day of (Succoth)	October 12
Ramadan, First day of (tabular)	March 5
Islamic New Year (1413)	July 2

CIVIL CALENDAR — UNITED KINGDOM

Bank Holiday in England, Wales & N. Ireland	January 1
Bank Holiday in Scotland	January 1 & 2
Accession of Queen Elizabeth II	February 6
St. David (Wales)	March 1
Commonwealth Day	March 9
St. Patrick (Ireland)	March 17
Bank Holiday in Northern Ireland	March 17
Bank Holiday in Scotland	March 17
Bank Holiday in England, Wales and Northern Ireland	April 20
Birthday of Queen Elizabeth II	April 21
St. George (England)	April 23
Bank Holiday in England, Wales and Northern Ireland	May 4 & 25
Bank Holiday in Scotland	May 4 & 25
Coronation Day	June 2
The Queen's Official Birthday	June 13
Birthday of Prince Philip, Duke of Edinburgh	June 10
Bank Holiday in Northern Ireland	July 12
Bank Holiday in Scotland	August 3
Bank Holiday in England, Wales and Northern Ireland	August 31
Trafalgar Day	October 21
Remembrance Sunday	November 8
Birthday of the Prince of Wales	November 14
St. Andrew (Scotland)	November 30
Bank Holiday in Scotland	December 25 & 28
Bank Holiday in England, Wales and Northern Ireland	December 25, 26 & 28

CIVIL CALENDAR — UNITED STATES OF AMERICA

New Year's Day	January 1
Martin Luther King's Birthday	January 20
Lincoln's Birthday	February 12
Washington's Birthday	February 17
Memorial Day	May 25
Independence Day	July 4
Labor Day	September 7
Columbus Day	October 12
Election Day (in certain States)	November 3
Veterans Day	November 11
Thanksgiving Day	November 26

PHENOMENA 1992
SEASONS 1992

Vernal Equinox—
Spring commences when Sun enters Aries, March 20d. 08h. 48min,
Summer Solstice—
Summer commences when Sun enters Cancer, June 21d. 03h. 14min.
Autumnal Equinox—
Autumn commences when Sun enters Libra, September 22d. 18h. 43min,
Winter Solstice—
Winter commences when Sun enters Capricornus, December 21d. 14h. 43min.
The longest day is June 21. The shortest day is December 21.

POSITION OF THE EARTH

Earth at Perihelion (at its least distance from the Sun) January 3.
Earth at Aphelion (at its greatest distance from the Sun) July 3.

FESTIVALS

Epiphany—The twelfth Night, that is twelve days after Christmas, is commemorated on 6th of January.
Lent — Lent (a fast of forty days before Easter) begins on the Wednesday of the seventh week before Easter. Ash Wednesday is the first day of Lent.
Palm Sunday — The Sunday before Easter.
Good Friday — The Friday before Easter Sunday.
Easter — The Vernal Equinox is March 21st and Easter is the Sunday following the full moon on, or next after, the Vernal Equinox. Should the full moon be on a Sunday, Easter is on the Sunday following.

Whitsun Day, or Pentecost, is seven weeks after Easter.
Advent covers four Sundays, the first of which is the Sunday nearest November 30th

DATE OR CALENDAR LINE

The Date or Calendar Line is a modification of the line of the 180th meridian, which is drawn so as to include islands of any one group, etc., on the same side of the line. It may be traced by joining up the following positions:

Lat. 60° 00'S.	Long. 180° 00'	Lat. 65° 30'N. Long. 169° 00'W.
" 51° 00'S.	" 180° 00'	Thence through the centre of the
" 45° 00'S.	" 172° 30'W.	Diomede Islands to:
" 15° 00'S.	" 172° 30'W.	Lat. 68° 00'N. Long. 169° 00'W.
" 5° 00'S.	" 180° 00'	Thence passing east of Herold Island
" 48° 00'N.	" 180° 00'	to:
" 52° 00'N.	" 170° 00'E.	Lat. 75° 00'N. Long. 180° 00'

When crossing this line on a Westerly Course a day is lost and the date must be advanced one day. When crossing it on an Easterly Course, a day is gained and the date must be retarded one day.

DAY OF THE YEAR

The figures given in this column on the monthly pages (3:10, 3:16, etc.) are useful in determining the length of a voyage. For instance, if a ship leaves port on May 6th and returns on December 6th of the same year, the voyage will have occupied 340 (day of year for Dec. 6th) minus 126 (day of year for May 6th) = 214 days.

ECLIPSES 1992

There are five eclipses, three of the Sun and two of the Moon.

1. **January 4-5**. Annular Eclipse of the Sun. Eclipse begins on January 4 at 20h.03min and ends on January 5 at 02.05min. The annular phase begins on Jan 4 at 21h.16min. and ends on January 5 at 00h.53min. Visible in Oceania, Philippines, Japan, extreme coast of NE Asia, N. Australia, W. coast of N. America.

2. **June 15**. Partial Eclipse of the Moon. Eclipse begins at 02h.09min. and ends at 07.44min. The time of maximum eclipse is 04h.57min. when 0.687 of the Moon's diameter is obscured. Visible in Antarctica, E. Africa, S. tip of Greenland, S. America, N. America (except N.W.), Central America, E. New Zealand.

3. **June 30**. Total Eclipse of the Sun. Eclipse begins at 09h.50min. and ends at 14h.29min. The total phase begins at 11h.01min. and ends at 13h.18min. Visible in Central S. America and S.W. Africa.

4. **Dec. 9-10**. Total Eclipse of the Moon. Eclipse begins at 20h.55min. and ends at 02h.32min. The total phase begins on Dec. 9 at 23h.06min. and ends on Dec. 10 at 00h.21min. Visible in Asia (except extreme E.) Europe including British Isles, Africa, Iceland, Greenland, S. America (except S.) Central America, N. America (except W. Coast).

5. **Dec. 23-24**. Partial eclipse of the Sun. Eclipse begins on Dec. 23 at 22h.20min. and ends on Dec. 24 at 02h.40min. (Max. eclipse 00h.30min. magnitude 0.843) Visible E. China, Korea, Japan, extreme E. of U.S.S.R., S.W. Alaska.

An eclipse is the name given to the phenomenom which occurs when one celestial object by its movement obstructs our view of another celestial object. There are two types of eclipses: (1) in which the eclipsed body is self-luminous, and (2) when it shines by reflected light.

1. The Sun is a self-luminous body and a Solar eclipse is caused by the Earth's satellite The Moon — coming between the Sun and the Earth during its revolution round the earth each month. When this occurs the three bodies, Sun, Earth and Moon are in the same straight line. If the plane of the Moon's orbit coincided with that of the Sun there would be a Solar eclipse at each New Moon. The moon's orbit, however, is inclined about 5° to the Ecliptic (i.e. Sun's apparent orbit or path) and so generally the Moon will be outside the Sun's path. Occasionally, however, when the Moon is near one of the points where it crosses the Ecliptic then it may cause a Solar Eclipse.

There are 3 degrees of Eclipses (i.e., Total, Partial, and Annular). A Total Eclipse occurs when the Sun is totally obscured by the Moon. A Partial Eclipse is when the Sun's face is only partially obscured. An Annular Eclipse occurs when the Sun is obscured except for an 'Annulus' or bright ring circling the darker Sun's disc. The degree of an eclipse depends somewhat on the observer's position on the sphere, for a partial eclipse at one place may be seen as a total eclipse at another.

2. The Moon is not self-luminous and an eclipse of such a body occurs when the reflected light by which it shines is cut off from it. A Lunar eclipse occurs when, at Full Moon, the Earth intercepts the light from the Sun and sends the Moon into total or partial shade. Due to the inclination of the Moon's path to the Ecliptic, lunar eclipses are infrequent as generally the Moon passes to the north or south of the shadow without entering it.

Solar Eclipses occur more frequently than Lunar Eclipses. In a period of 20 years there are about 80 eclipses; 47 of the Sun and 33 of the Moon.

STANDARD TIMES AND SUMMER TIMES

Standard Time is the same as Zone Time e.g., in Britain it is Greenwich Mean Time.

Some countries, closely linked with another country, adopt the time of that country, which is different from their Zone Time. This is known as Clock Time.

In the following Tables where the Clock Time of a country differs from its Zone Time, Clock Time is given.

COUNTRIES NORMALLY KEEPING GREENWICH MEAN TIME

Ascension Island	Iceland	Principe
Bourkina-Faso	†Ireland, Northern	St. Helena
*Canary Islands	†Irish Republic	São Tomé
†Channel Islands	Ivory Coast	Senegal
*Faeroes	Liberia	Sierra Leone
Gambia	*Maderia	Togo Republic
Ghana	Maili	Tristan da Cunha
†Great Britian	Mauritania	
Guinea Bissau	Morocco	
Guinea Republic	*Portugal	

COUNTRIES KEEPING TIMES FAST (OR EAST) ON GMT

	fast		fast		fast
*Albania 1h.	"	Fiji 12h	"	Mozambique 2h.	"
Algeria 1h.	"	*Finland 2h.	"	*New Zealand 12h.	"
Andaman Is.		*France 1h.	"	Nigeria 1h.	"
5h. 30min.	"	*Germany 1h.	"	*Norway 1h.	"
Angola 1h.	"	*Gibraltar 1h.	"	Pakistan 5h.	
Australia:		*Greece 2h.	"	*Philippine Is. 8h.	"
*Victoria, N.S.W. 10h	"	*Holland 1h.	"	*Poland 1h.	"
*Tasmania 10h.	"	Hong Kong 8h.		*Romania 2h.	"
*Queensland	"	*Hungary 1h.	"	Seychelles 4h.	"
*South 9h. 30min.	"	India 5h. 30min.	"	*Sicily 1h.	"
N. Territory		Iran 3h. 30min.	"	Singapore 8h.	"
9h. 30min.	"	*Iraq 3h.	"	Solomon Is. 11h.	"
West 8h.	"	*Israel 2h.	"	Somalia 3h.	"
*Austria 1h.	"	*Italy 1h.	"	South Africa 2h.	"
Bahrain 3h.	"	Japan 9h.	"	*Spain 1h.	"
*Balearic Is. 1h.	"	*Jordan 2h.	"	Sri Lanka 5h. 30min.	"
Bangladesh 6h.	"	Kenya 3h.	"	*Sweden 1h.	"
*Belgium 1h.	"	Korea 9h.	"	*Switzerland 1h.	"
*Bulgaria 2h	"	Laos 7h.	"	*Syria 2h.	"
Burma 6h. 30min.	"	*Lebanon 2h.	"	*Taiwan 8h.	"
Cameroon 1h.	"	Libya 2h.	"	Tanzania 3h.	"
*China 8h.	"	*Liechtenstein 1h.	"	Thailand 7h.	"
Congo 1h.	"	*Luxembourg 1h.	"	*Tunisia 1h.	"
*Corsica 1h.	"	Madagascar 3h.	"	*Turkey 2h.	"
*Crete 2h.	"	Malawi 2h.	"	Uganda 3h.	"
*Cyprus 2h.	"	Malaysia 8h.	"	U.S.S.R. 3 to 12h.	"
*Czechoslovakia 1h.	"	*Malta 1h.	"	Vietnam 7h.	"
*Denmark 1h.	"	Marshall Is. 12h.	"	*Yugoslavia 1h.	"
*Egypt 2h	"	Mauritius 4h.	"	Zambia 2h.	"
Ethiopia 3h.	"	*Monaco 1h.	"	Zimbabwe 2h.	"

Add to GMT for Standard Time and subtract from Standard Time for GMT.

*May keep Summer Time or Daylight Saving Time.
†Summer Time, one hour in advance of GMT, is kept from March 29 01h. to October 25 01h. GMT.

COUNTRIES KEEPING TIMES SLOW (OR WEST) ON GMT

	slow		slow		slow
Argentina 3h.	"	*Cook Is. 10h.	"	Niue Is. 11h.	"
*Azores 1h.	"	*Costa Rica 6h.	"	Panama 5h.	"
*Bahamas 4h.	"	*Cuba 5h.	"	*Paraguay 4h.	"
Barbados 4h.	"	Curaco 4h.	"	Peru 5h.	"
Belize 6h.	"	Dominican		Puerto Rico 4h.	"
*Bermuda 4h.	"	Republic 4h.	"	*St Pierre and	
Brazil E. 3h.	"	Ecuador 5h.	"	Miquelon 3h.	"
Brazil W. 4h.	"	El Salvador 6h.	"	Samoa 11h.	"
Canada:		*Falkland Is. 4h.	"	South Georgia 2h.	"
*Alberta 7h.	"	French Guiana 3h.	"	Trinadad &	
*British Columbia 8h.	"	Greenland 1-4h.	"	Tobago 4h.	"
*Labrador 4h.	"	Grenada 4h.	"	*Turks and Caicos Is.5h.	"
*Manitoba 6h.	"	Guadeloupe 4h.	"	United States:	
*New Brunswick 4h.	"	Guatemala 6h.	"	*Eastern Zone 5h.	"
*Newfoundland 3½h.	"	Guayana 3h.	"	*Central Zone 6h.	"
*Nova Scotia 4h.	"	*Haiti 5h.	"	*Pacific Zone 8h.	"
*Ontario 5h.	"	Honduras 6h.	"	Mountain Zone 7h.	"
*Quebec 5h.	"	Jamaica 5h.	"	Hawaiian Is. 10h.	"
*Yukon 8h.	"	Leeward Is. 4h.	"	*Uruguay 3h.	"
Cape Verde Is. 1h.	"	Mexico 6-8h.	"	Venezuela 4h.	"
*Chile 4h.	"	Midway Is. 11h.	"	Virgin Is. 4h.	"
Columbia 5h.	"	Nicaragua 6h.	"	Windward Is. 4h.	"

Subtract from GMT for Standard Time and add to Standard Time for GMT.

*May keep Summer Time or Daylight Saving Time.

MEASUREMENT OF TIME

Days

1 Mean Solar Day = 24 Mean Solar Hours.
1 Sidereal Day = 23h. 56min. 04.1 sec. of Mean Solar Time.
1 Lunar Day averages approx. 24h. 50min. of Mean Solar Time.

Months

A Calendar Month = 28, 29, 30 or 31 days, depending on which month.
A Lunar Month (or Lunation, or Synodical Month) is the time interval between successive New Moons, i.e. one revolution of the Moon with reference to the Sun — about 29½ Mean Solar Days.
A Sidereal Month is the average time taken for the Moon to complete one orbit with reference to a star, a period of approx. 27⅓ Mean Solar Days.

Years

The common year has 365 calendar days. Leap Years which have 366 calendar days, are those years which are divisible by 4 (as 1988, 1992, etc.) except those century years not divisible by 400 (e.g. 1900). The year 2000 A.D. will be a leap year but 2100 A.D. a common year. If there were no leap years the calendar date would gradually fall out of step with the seasons and, in course of time, midsummer would occur in January. One complete cycle of the Gregorian Calendar takes 400 years, viz. in 400 years there are:

$$
\begin{array}{lcr}
\text{97 (leap) years of 366 days each} & = & 35,502 \\
\text{and 303 years of 365 days each} & = & 110,595 \\
\hline
\text{Therefore the total number of days} & = & 146,097 \\
\hline
\end{array}
$$

Hence the Civil Year $= \dfrac{146,097}{400} = 365.2425$ days

TIME ZONES

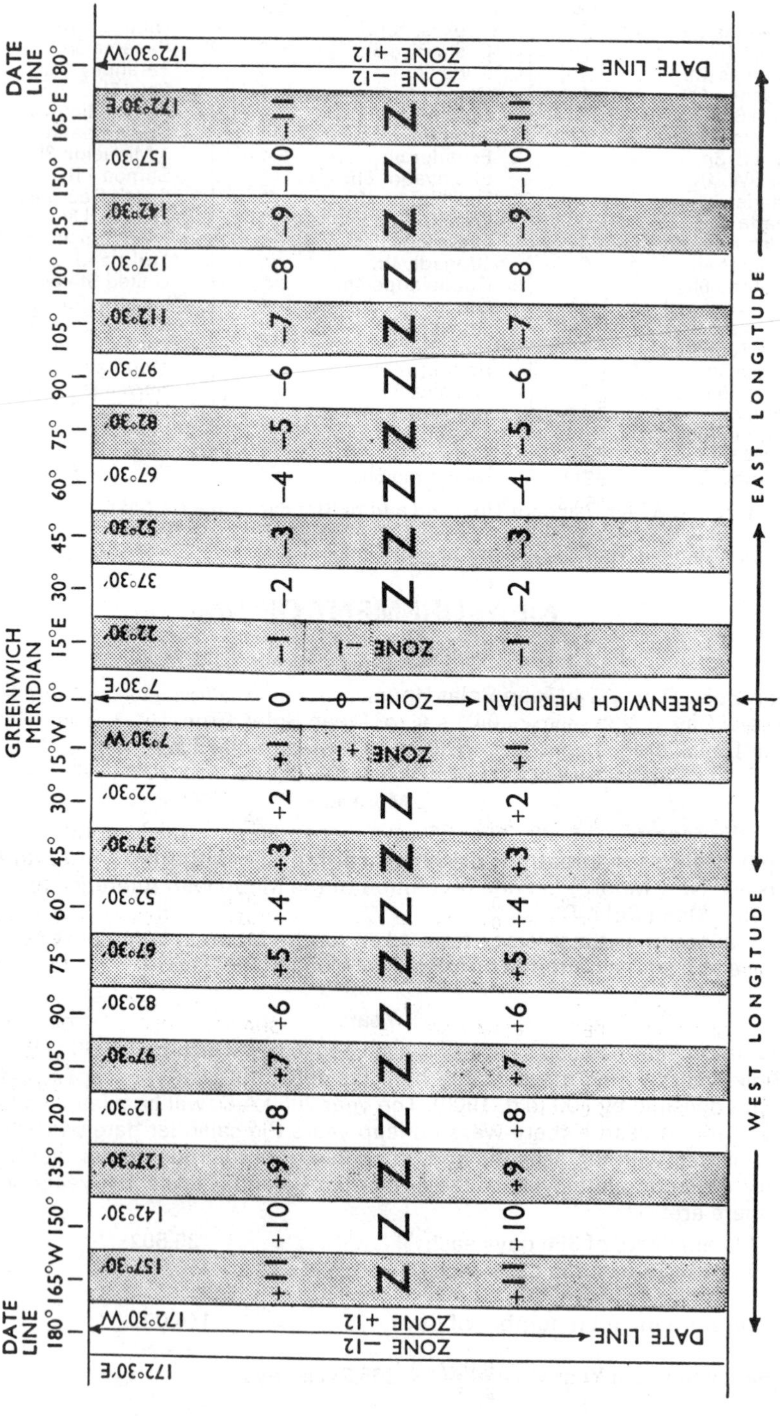

GREENWICH MERIDIAN

DATE LINE

ZONE +12
ZONE −12
DATE LINE

ZONE −1
ZONE +1

GREENWICH MERIDIAN — ZONE 0

EAST LONGITUDE

WEST LONGITUDE

Longitude	Zone
172°30′W / 180°	+12 / −12
172°30′E / 165°E	−11
157°30′ / 150°	−10
142°30′ / 135°	−9
127°30′ / 120°	−8
112°30′ / 105°	−7
97°30′ / 90°	−6
82°30′ / 75°	−5
67°30′ / 60°	−4
52°30′ / 45°	−3
37°30′ / 30°	−2
22°30′ / 15°E	−1
7°30′E / 0°	0
7°30′W / 15°W	+1
22°30′ / 30°	+2
37°30′ / 45°	+3
52°30′ / 60°	+4
67°30′ / 75°	+5
82°30′ / 90°	+6
97°30′ / 105°	+7
112°30′ / 120°	+8
127°30′ / 135°	+9
142°30′ / 150°	+10
157°30′ / 165°W	+11
172°30′W / 180°	+12 / −12
172°30′E	

Sets of monthly polynomial coefficients are provided for calculating the Greenwich Hour Angle (GHA) and Declination (Dec.) of the Sun for 1992. They are intended for use with small electronic calculators.

The date and time in GMT are used to form the interpolation factor p=d/32 where d is the sum of the month and decimal of a day. Then GHA-GMT in hours and Dec. in degrees are calculated from polynomial expressions of the form

$$a_0+a_1p+a_2p^2+a_3p^3+a_4p^4$$

where p is the interpolating factor. This is most efficiently evaluated in the nested form

$$(((a_4p+a_3)p+a_2)p+a_1)p+a_0$$

EXAMPLE: Calculate GHA and Dec. of Sun on July 23, 1992, at 17h 02m 15s GMT.

GMT =	17h.0375 and the interpolation factor is
p =	(23 + 17.0375/24)/32 = 0.740934
GHA-GMT =	11h.94055 – 0h.10689p + 0h.03845p² + 0h.03061p³ – 0h.00773p⁴
=	11h.89258
Hence GHA =	11h.89258 + GMT = 11h.89258 + 17h.0375

Remove multiples of 24h from GHA and multiply by 15 to convert from hours to degrees.

Then GHA =	73°.9512
=	73°57'.1
Dec =	23°.1704 – 1°.9444p – 3°.4587p² + 0°.1661p³ + 0°.0750p⁴
=	19°.9211
=	N19°55.3

Semi-diameter of the Sun

Jan. 1-Feb. 4	16'.3	Apr. 19-May 13	15'.9	Oct. 12-Nov. 2	16'.1
Feb. 5-Mar. 4	16'.2	May 14-Aug. 25	15'.8	Nov. 3-Dec. 2	16'.2
Mar. 5-Mar. 27	16'.1	Aug. 26-Sept. 19	15'.9	Dec. 3-Dec. 31	16'.3
Mar. 28-Apr. 18	16'.0	Sept. 20-Oct. 11	16'.0

In critical cases ascend

To correct for the effect of parallax of the Sun it is normally sufficient to add 0'.1 to all observed altitudes less than 70°. If greater accuracy is required, the correction is 0'.15 cosine (altitude).

MONTHLY POLYNOMIAL COEFFICIENTS FOR THE SUN, 1992

	JANUARY GHA-GMT (h)	DEC. (°)	FEBRUARY GHA-GMT (h)	DEC. (°)	MARCH GHA-GMT (h)	DEC. (°)	APRIL GHA-GMT (h)	DEC. (°)
Sun a_0	11.95712	−23.1492	11.77840	−17.6464	11.79015	−7.9497	11.92937	4.1691
a_1	−0.25733	2.1544	−0.08719	8.7883	0.09813	12.1083	0.15869	12.3979
a_2	0.03329	3.9903	0.11815	2.6865	0.07482	0.9792	−0.01038	−0.6738
a_3	0.06024	−0.2778	0.00106	−0.6581	−0.02494	−0.6184	−0.03010	−0.5148
a_4	−0.01755	−0.0868	−0.01043	0.0233	−0.00386	0.0366	0.00271	0.0105
check sum	11.77577	−17.3691	11.79999	−6.8064	11.93430	4.5560	12.05029	15.3889

	MAY GHA-GMT (h)	DEC. (°)	JUNE GHA-GMT (h)	DEC. (°)	JULY GHA-GMT (h)	DEC. (°)	AUGUST GHA-GMT (h)	DEC. (°)
Sun a_0	12.04630	14.7838	12.04003	21.9202	11.94055	23.1704	11.89412	18.2579
a_1	0.06826	9.8123	−0.07875	4.5432	−0.10689	−1.9444	0.02526	−7.9079
a_2	−0.07227	−2.0931	−0.05566	−3.2572	0.03845	−3.4587	0.09373	−2.5132
a_3	−0.01285	−0.4881	0.02555	−0.2777	0.03061	0.1661	−0.00996	0.3992
a_4	0.00805	0.0441	0.00286	0.1068	−0.00773	0.0750	−0.00385	0.0314
check sum	12.03749	22.0590	11.93403	23.0353	11.89499	18.0084	11.99930	8.2674

	SEPTEMBER GHA-GMT (h)	DEC. (°)	OCTOBER GHA-GMT (h)	DEC. (°)	NOVEMBER GHA-GMT (h)	DEC. (°)	DECEMBER GHA-GMT (h)	DEC. (°)
Sun a_0	11.99411	8.6293	12.16584	−2.8119	12.27248	−14.1185	12.18957	−21.6488
a_1	0.16449	−11.5422	0.17301	−12.4355	0.02024	−10.3672	−0.19368	−5.1866
a_2	0.05213	−1.1279	−0.02980	0.2833	−0.10324	1.9208	−0.09005	3.4986
a_3	−0.03660	0.4083	−0.04447	0.4708	−0.03107	0.6374	0.02605	0.4976
a_4	0.00241	0.0446	0.00843	0.0527	0.01871	−0.0316	0.01101	−0.1781
check sum	12.17654	−3.5879	12.27301	−14.4406	12.17712	−21.9591	11.94290	−23.0173

Prepared by H.M. Nautical Almanac Office, Royal Greenwich Observatory, reproduced with permission from data supplied by the Science and Engineering Research Council

JANUARY, 1992

☉ SUN ☉

DATE			Equation of Time		Transit	Semi-diam.	Lat. 52°N.				Lat. Corr. to Sunrise, Sunset, etc.				
Day of			0 h.	12 h.			Twilight	Sunrise	Sunset	Twilight	Lat.	Twilight	Sunrise	Sunset	Twilight
Yr.	Mth.	Week	m. s.	m. s.	h. m.	′	h. m.	h. m.	h. m.	h. m.	°	h. m.	h. m.	h. m.	h. m.
1	1	Wed.	+03 03	+03 17	12 03	16.3	07 28	08 08	15 59	16 39	N70	+1 57	S.B.H.	S.B.H.	−0 56
2	2	Th.	+03 32	+03 46	12 04	16.3	07 28	08 08	16 00	16 40	68	+1 32	+2 34	−2 33	−1 32
3	3	Fri.	+04 00	+04 14	12 04	16.3	07 28	08 08	16 01	16 41	66	+1 13	+1 53	−1 53	−1 13
4	4	Sat.	+04 28	+04 42	12 05	16.3	07 28	08 08	16 02	16 42	64	+0 57	+1 25	−1 25	−0 57
5	5	Sun.	+04 55	+05 09	12 05	16.3	07 27	08 08	16 03	16 43	62	+0 44	+1 04	−1 04	−0 44
6	6	Mon.	+05 23	+05 36	12 06	16.3	07 27	08 07	16 05	16 44	N60	+0 32	+0 47	−0 47	−0 33
7	7	Tu.	+05 49	+06 02	12 06	16.3	07 27	08 07	16 06	16 46	58	+0 22	+0 33	−0 32	−0 23
8	8	Wed.	+06 15	+06 28	12 06	16.3	07 26	08 06	16 07	16 47	56	+0 14	+0 21	−0 20	−0 14
9	9	Th.	+06 41	+06 54	12 07	16.3	07 26	08 06	16 08	16 48	54	+0 07	+0 10	−0 09	−0 07
10	10	Fri.	+07 06	+07 19	12 07	16.3	07 26	08 06	16 10	16 50	50	−0 06	−0 08	+0 09	+0 06
11	11	Sat.	+07 31	+07 43	12 08	16.3	07 25	08 05	16 11	16 51	N45	−0 20	−0 26	+0 27	+0 20
12	12	Sun.	+07 55	+08 07	12 08	16.3	07 25	08 05	16 13	16 52	40	−0 33	−0 41	+0 42	+0 32
13	13	Mon.	+08 18	+08 30	12 08	16.3	07 24	08 04	16 14	16 54	35	−0 43	−0 54	+0 54	+0 42
14	14	Tu.	+08 41	+08 52	12 09	16.3	07 23	08 03	16 15	16 55	30	−0 52	−1 05	+1 05	+0 52
15	15	Wed.	+09 03	+09 14	12 09	16.3	07 23	08 02	16 17	16 56	20	−1 08	−1 24	+1 24	+1 08
16	16	Th.	+09 24	+09 35	12 10	16.3	07 22	08 01	16 19	16 58	N10	−1 24	−1 41	+1 41	+1 24
17	17	Fri.	+09 45	+09 55	12 10	16.3	07 21	08 00	16 20	16 59	0	−1 39	−1 56	+1 56	+1 39
18	18	Sat.	+10 05	+10 15	12 10	16.3	07 21	07 59	16 22	17 01	S10	−1 55	−2 13	+2 11	+1 55
19	19	Sun.	+10 25	+10 34	12 11	16.3	07 20	07 58	16 23	17 02	20	−2 14	−2 30	+2 28	+2 14
20	20	Mon.	+10 43	+10 52	12 11	16.3	07 19	07 57	16 25	17 04	30	−2 36	−2 49	+2 48	+2 36
21	21	Tu.	+11 01	+11 10	12 11	16.3	07 18	07 56	16 27	17 05	S35	−2 49	−3 01	+3 00	+2 49
22	22	Wed.	+11 18	+11 27	12 11	16.3	07 17	07 55	16 28	17 07	40	−3 06	−3 13	+3 13	+3 06
23	23	Th.	+11 35	+11 43	12 12	16.3	07 16	07 54	16 30	17 08	45	−3 26	−3 31	+3 29	+3 26
24	24	Fri.	+11 50	+11 58	12 12	16.3	07 14	07 52	16 32	17 10	S50	−3 51	−3 51	+3 49	+3 52
25	25	Sat.	+12 05	+12 12	12 12	16.3	07 13	07 51	16 34	17 11					
26	26	Sun.	+12 19	+12 26	12 12	16.3	07 12	07 50	16 36	17 13					
27	27	Mon.	+12 33	+12 39	12 13	16.3	07 11	07 48	16 38	17 15					
28	28	Tu.	+12 45	+12 51	12 13	16.3	07 10	07 47	16 39	17 16					
29	29	Wed.	+12 57	+13 02	12 13	16.3	07 09	07 46	16 41	17 18					
30	30	Th.	+13 08	+13 13	12 13	16.3	07 07	07 44	16 43	17 20					
31	31	Fri.	+13 18	+13 23	12 13	16.3	07 06	07 43	16 44	17 21					

NOTES

The corrections to sunrise, sunset, etc., are for Jan. 15.

S.B.H. = The Sun is below the Horizon. Examples on the use of the above data are given on page 2:11 onwards.

Equation of Time is the excess of Mean Time over Apparent Time (See explanation and examples on p. 2:15)

☾ MOON ☽

DATE			Age	Transit Diff. (Upper)		Semi-diam.	Hor. Par. 12 h.	Lat. 52°N.		MOON'S PHASES
Day of			days					Moonrise	Moonset	
Yr.	Mth.	Week		h. m.	m.	′	′	h. m.	h. m.	
1	1	Wed.	26	09 11	51	15.0	55.0	05 17	13 00	
2	2	Th.	27	10 02	51	14.9	54.6	06 19	13 43	
3	3	Fri.	28	10 53	49	14.8	54.3	07 11	14 36	
4	4	Sat.	29	11 42	48	14.7	54.1	07 52	15 37	
5	5	Sun.	01	12 30	46	14.7	54.0	08 24	16 44	
6	6	Mon.	02	13 16	44	14.7	53.9	08 48	17 52	
7	7	Tu.	03	14 00	42	14.7	54.0	09 08	19 01	
8	8	Wed.	04	14 42	41	14.8	54.1	09 25	20 10	
9	9	Th.	05	15 23	41	14.8	54.4	09 40	21 18	
10	10	Fri.	06	16 04	42	14.9	54.8	09 54	22 27	
11	11	Sat.	07	16 46	44	15.1	55.4	10 08	23 38	
12	12	Sun.	08	17 30	46	15.3	56.1	10 24	– –	
13	13	Mon.	09	18 17	47	15.5	56.9	10 43	00 52	
14	14	Tu.	10	19 09	52	15.7	57.8	11 07	02 09	
15	15	Wed.	11	20 05	56	16.0	58.8	11 39	03 27	
16	16	Th.	12	21 06	61	16.3	59.7	12 24	04 44	
17	17	Fri.	13	22 10	64	16.5	60.5	13 25	05 53	
18	18	Sat.	14	23 14	64	16.7	61.1	14 41	06 49	
19	19	Sun.	15	24 16	62	16.7	61.5	16 09	07 31	
20	20	Mon.	16	00 16	–	16.7	61.4	17 41	08 03	
21	21	Tu.	17	01 14	58	16.6	61.1	19 11	08 27	
22	22	Wed.	18	02 09	55	16.5	60.4	20 38	08 47	
23	23	Th.	19	03 00	51	16.2	59.6	22 01	09 05	
24	24	Fri.	20	03 50	48	16.0	58.6	23 23	09 23	
25	25	Sat.	21	04 38	49	15.7	57.7	– –	09 42	
26	26	Sun.	22	05 27	50	15.5	56.8	00 41	10 03	
27	27	Mon.	23	06 17	50	15.3	56.0	01 57	10 29	
28	28	Tu.	24	07 07	50	15.1	55.3	03 08	11 01	
29	29	Wed.	25	07 58	51	14.9	54.8	04 13	11 41	
30	30	Th.	26	08 49	51	14.8	54.4	05 08	12 31	
31	31	Fri.	27	09 39	50	14.7	54.1	05 52	13 30	

MOON'S PHASES

	d.	h.	m.
● New Moon	4	23	10
☽ First Quarter	13	02	32
○ Full Moon	19	21	28
☾ Last Quarter	26	15	27

	d.	h.
Apogee	6	12
Perigee	19	22

NOTES

Moon's G.H.A. and Dec. are given on page 3:15.
A table for correcting Moonrise and Moonset for latitude is on page 4:20.
A table for correcting Moon's meridian passage for longitude is on page 4:19.
Examples on the use of the above data are given on page 2:11 onwards.

0h. = midnight. For explanation of use of above data see page 2:11 onwards.

No.	Name	Mag.	Transit (approx.)	DEC.	G.H.A.	R.A.	S.H.A.
			h. m.	° ′	° ′	h. m.	° ′
♈	ARIES	–	17 18	–	99 54.6	–	–
1	Alpheratz	2.2	17 25	N29 03.0	97 54.8	0 08	358 00.2
2	Ankaa	2.4	17 43	S42 21.1	93 26.1	0 26	353 31.5
3	Schedar........	2.5	17 57	N56 30.0	89 53.7	0 40	349 59.1
4	Diphda	2.2	18 01	S18 01.9	89 06.6	0 43	349 12.0
5	Achernar	0.6	18 55	S57 16.8	75 33.1	1 37	335 38.5
6	POLARIS	2.1	19 41	N89 14.1	63 55.4	2 24	324 00.8
7	Hamal	2.2	19 24	N23 25.7	68 13.4	2 07	328 18.8
8	Acamar........	3.1	20 15	S40 20.3	55 24.8	2 58	315 30.2
9	Menkar	2.8	20 19	N 4 03.6	54 26.3	3 02	314 31.7
10	Mirfak	1.9	20 41	N49 50.3	48 57.7	3 24	309 03.1
11	Aldebaran	1.1	21 52	N16 29.7	31 02.1	4 36	291 07.5
12	Rigel	0.3	22 31	S 8 12.7	21 21.7	5 14	281 27.1
13	Capella	0.2	22 33	N45 59.6	20 52.3	5 16	280 57.7
14	Bellatrix	1.7	22 41	N 6 20.6	18 43.5	5 25	278 48.9
15	Elnath	1.8	22 42	N28 36.1	18 27.1	5 26	278 32.5
16	Alnilam	1.8	22 52	S 1 12.4	15 56.9	5 36	276 02.3
17	Betelgeuse ...	{ 0.1 1.2	23 11	N 7 24.3	11 12.9	5 55	271 18.3
18	Canopus	–0.9	23 40	S52 41.6	3 57.3	6 24	264 02.7
19	Sirius	–1.6	00 05	S16 42.4	358 42.0	6 45	258 47.4
20	Adhara	1.6	00 19	S28 57.7	355 19.3	6 58	255 24.7
21	Castor	1.6	00 54	N31 54.3	346 22.5	7 34	246 27.9
22	Procyon........	0.5	00 59	N 5 14.7	345 10.7	7 39	245 16.1
23	Pollux	1.2	01 05	N28 02.7	343 41.4	7 45	243 46.8
24	Avior	1.7	01 42	S59 29.0	334 18.6	8 22	234 24.0
25	Suhail	2.2	02 28	S43 24.0	322 58.4	9 08	223 03.8
26	Miaplacidus ...	1.8	02 33	S69 41.0	321 36.9	9 13	221 42.3
27	Alphard........	2.2	02 47	S 8 37.5	318 06.1	9 27	218 11.5
28	Regulus	1.3	03 28	N12 00.2	307 54.8	10 08	208 00.2
29	Dubhe	2.0	04 23	N61 47.3	294 05.2	11 03	194 10.6
30	Denebola	2.2	05 08	N14 36.7	282 44.4	11 49	182 49.8
31	Gienah	2.8	05 35	S17 29.9	276 03.3	12 15	176 08.7
32	Acrux...........	1.1	05 46	S63 03.2	273 21.8	12 26	173 27.2
33	Gacrux	1.6	05 50	S57 04.0	272 13.4	12 31	172 18.8
34	Mimosa........	1.5	06 07	S59 38.6	268 05.4	12 47	168 10.8
35	Alioth........	1.7	06 13	N55 59.7	266 29.0	12 54	166 34.4
36	Spica	1.2	06 44	S11 07.3	258 42.7	13 25	158 48.1
37	Alkaid	1.9	07 06	N49 20.8	253 06.0	13 47	153 11.4
38	Hadar...........	0.9	07 22	S60 19.9	249 05.5	14 03	149 10.9
39	Menkent	2.3	07 25	S36 19.8	248 21.2	14 06	148 26.6
40	Arcturus	0.2	07 34	N19 13.1	246 04.9	14 15	146 10.3
41	Rigil Kent.	0.1	07 58	S60 48.0	240 08.5	14 39	140 13.9
42	Zuben'ubi......	2.9	08 09	S16 00.6	237 17.9	14 50	137 23.3
43	Kochab........	2.2	08 10	N74 10.9	237 14.2	14 51	137 19.6
44	Alphecca	2.3	08 53	N26 44.2	226 19.3	15 34	126 24.7
45	Antares........	1.2	09 48	S26 24.9	212 40.8	16 29	112 46.2
46	Atria	1.9	10 07	S69 00.7	207 57.5	16 48	108 02.9
47	Sabik...........	2.6	10 29	S15 43.0	202 25.8	17 10	102 31.2
48	Shaula	1.7	10 52	S37 05.9	196 38.6	17 33	96 44.0
49	Rasalhague ...	2.1	10 53	N12 33.8	196 16.2	17 35	96 21.6
50	Eltanin	2.4	11 15	N51 29.2	190 48.7	17 56	90 54.1
51	Kaus Aust. ...	2.0	11 42	S34 23.3	184 00.0	18 24	84 05.4
52	Vega	0.1	11 55	N38 46.5	180 44.8	18 37	80 50.2
53	Nunki...........	2.1	12 13	S26 18.4	176 13.1	18 55	76 18.5
54	Altair	0.9	13 09	N 8 50.8	162 18.8	19 50	62 24.2
55	Peacock........	2.1	13 43	S56 45.7	153 39.4	20 25	53 44.8
56	Deneb	1.3	13 59	N45 15.2	149 37.5	20 41	49 42.9
57	Enif...........	2.5	15 02	N 9 50.4	133 57.7	21 44	34 03.1
58	Al Na'ir	2.2	15 26	S47 00.1	127 58.6	22 08	28 04.0
59	Fomalhaut	1.3	16 15	S29 39.9	115 36.4	22 57	15 41.8
60	Markab	2.6	16 22	N15 09.9	113 49.1	23 04	13 54.5

Stars Transit Correction Table

D. of Mth.	Corr (Sub.)	D. of Mth.	Corr. (Sub.)
	h. m.		h. m.
1	–0 00	17	–1 03
2	–0 04	18	–1 07
3	–0 08	19	–1 11
4	–0 12	20	–1 15
5	–0 16	21	–1 19
6	–0 20	22	–1 23
7	–0 24	23	–1 27
8	–0 28	24	–1 30
9	–0 31	25	–1 34
10	–0 35	26	–1 38
11	–0 39	27	–1 42
12	–0 43	28	–1 46
13	–0 47	29	–1 50
14	–0 51	30	–1 54
15	–0 55	31	–1 58
16	–0 59		

STAR'S TRANSIT

To find the approx. time of Transit of a Star for any day of the month use above table.

If the quantity taken from the table is greater than the time of Transit for the first of the month, add 23h. 56min. to the time of transit before subtracting the correction below.

Example: What time will Adhara (No 20) be on the Meridian on January 30th?

	h.min.
Transit on January 1st ...	00 19
	+23 56
	24 15
Corr. for January 30th ...	–01 54
Transit on January 30th ...	22 21

d. h. JANUARY DIARY

1 12 Venus 5°N of Moon
3 01 Mercury 3°N of Moon
3 10 Mars 0°.8N of Moon Occn.
3 15 Earth at perihelion
4 23 New Moon Eclipse
6 12 Moon at apogee
6 23 Saturn 3°S of Moon
7 19 Venus 7°N of Antares
10 20 Mercury 0°.6N of Mars
13 03 First Quarter
19 21 Full Moon
19 22 Moon at perigee
23 01 Jupiter 7°N of Moon
26 15 Last Quarter
29 22 Saturn in conjunction with Sun
31 17 Venus 1°.0N of Moon Occn.

STAR TIME

The best time to take Star observations is shown in the a.m. and p.m. TWILIGHT columns on the opposite page – corrected for Latitude.

For Lighting-up Time (ashore) add 30 mins to Sunset Times.

For Star's G.H.A. Correction Table, see page 4:8.

For Alphabetical List of Stars with Constellation names, see page 2:24.

For Examples on the use of the above data, see page 2:11.

For full directions for finding the above 60 Stars, see p. 2:20 onwards. For Special Pole Star tables see pages 5:17-5:19.

G.M.T.	SUN G.H.A.	Dec.	ARIES G.H.A.	G.M.T.	SUN G.H.A.	Dec.	ARIES G.H.A.	G.M.T.	SUN G.H.A.	Dec.	ARIES G.H.A.	G.M.T.

Wednesday, 1st January | | | **Monday, 6th January** | | | **Saturday, 11th January** | | |

h	° '	° '	° '	h	° '	° '	° '	h	° '	° '	° '	h
00	179 14.1	S23 04.7	99 54.6	00	178 39.2	S22 36.4	104 50.3	00	178 07.2	S21 57.0	109 46.0	00
02	209 13.5	23 04.3	129 59.6	02	208 38.7	22 35.8	134 55.3	02	208 06.7	21 56.2	139 51.0	02
04	239 12.9	23 03.9	160 04.5	04	238 38.1	22 35.3	165 00.2	04	238 06.2	21 55.5	169 55.9	04
06	269 12.3	23 03.5	190 09.4	06	268 37.6	22 34.7	195 05.1	06	268 05.7	21 54.7	200 00.8	06
08	299 11.7	23 03.2	220 14.3	08	298 37.0	22 34.1	225 10.0	08	298 05.2	21 54.0	230 05.7	08
10	329 11.1	23 02.8	250 19.3	10	328 36.4	22 33.5	255 15.0	10	328 04.7	21 53.2	260 10.7	10
12	359 10.5	23 02.4	280 24.2	12	358 35.9	22 33.0	285 19.9	12	358 04.2	21 52.4	290 15.6	12
14	29 09.9	23 02.0	310 29.1	14	28 35.3	22 32.4	315 24.8	14	28 03.7	21 51.7	320 20.5	14
16	59 09.3	23 01.6	340 34.1	16	58 34.8	22 31.8	345 29.8	16	58 03.2	21 50.9	350 25.5	16
18	89 08.7	23 01.2	10 39.0	18	88 34.2	22 31.2	15 34.7	18	88 02.7	21 50.1	20 30.4	18
20	119 08.1	23 00.8	40 43.9	20	118 33.7	22 30.6	45 39.6	20	118 02.2	21 49.4	50 35.3	20
22	149 07.5	S23 00.3	70 48.8	22	148 33.1	S22 30.0	75 44.5	22	148 01.7	S21 48.6	80 40.2	22

Thursday, 2nd January | | | **Tuesday, 7th January** | | | **Sunday, 12th January** | | |

h	° '	° '	° '	h	° '	° '	° '	h	° '	° '	° '	h
00	179 06.9	S22 59.9	100 53.8	00	178 32.6	S22 29.4	105 49.5	00	178 01.2	S21 47.8	110 45.2	00
02	209 06.3	22 59.5	130 58.7	02	208 32.0	22 28.8	135 54.4	02	208 00.7	21 47.0	140 50.1	02
04	239 05.7	22 59.1	161 03.6	04	238 31.5	22 28.2	165 59.3	04	238 00.2	21 46.2	170 55.0	04
06	269 05.1	22 58.7	191 08.6	06	268 30.9	22 27.6	196 04.3	06	267 59.7	21 45.4	201 00.0	06
08	299 04.6	22 58.3	221 13.5	08	298 30.4	22 27.0	226 09.2	08	297 59.2	21 44.6	231 04.9	08
10	329 04.0	22 57.8	251 18.4	10	328 29.8	22 26.3	256 14.1	10	327 58.7	21 43.8	261 09.8	10
12	359 03.4	22 57.4	281 23.3	12	358 29.3	22 25.7	286 19.0	12	357 58.3	21 43.0	291 14.7	12
14	29 02.8	22 57.0	311 28.3	14	28 28.7	22 25.1	316 24.0	14	27 57.8	21 42.2	321 19.7	14
16	59 02.2	22 56.5	341 33.2	16	58 28.2	22 24.5	346 28.9	16	57 57.3	21 41.4	351 24.6	16
18	89 01.6	22 56.1	11 38.1	18	88 27.6	22 23.8	16 33.8	18	87 56.8	21 40.6	21 29.5	18
20	119 01.0	22 55.6	41 43.1	20	118 27.1	22 23.2	46 38.8	20	117 56.3	21 39.8	51 34.4	20
22	149 00.4	S22 55.2	71 48.0	22	148 26.6	S22 22.6	76 43.7	22	147 55.8	S21 39.0	81 39.4	22

Friday, 3rd January | | | **Wednesday, 8th January** | | | **Monday, 13th January** | | |

h	° '	° '	° '	h	° '	° '	° '	h	° '	° '	° '	h
00	178 59.9	S22 54.7	101 52.9	00	178 26.0	S22 21.9	106 48.6	00	177 55.4	S21 38.2	111 44.3	00
02	208 59.3	22 54.3	131 57.8	02	208 25.5	22 21.3	136 53.5	02	207 54.9	21 37.4	141 49.2	02
04	238 58.7	22 53.8	162 02.8	04	238 24.9	22 20.7	166 58.5	04	237 54.4	21 36.5	171 54.2	04
06	268 58.1	22 53.4	192 07.7	06	268 24.4	22 20.0	197 03.4	06	267 53.9	21 35.7	201 59.1	06
08	298 57.5	22 52.9	222 12.6	08	298 23.9	22 19.4	227 08.3	08	297 53.4	21 34.9	232 04.0	08
10	328 56.9	22 52.4	252 17.6	10	328 23.3	22 18.7	257 13.3	10	327 53.0	21 34.1	262 08.9	10
12	358 56.4	22 52.0	282 22.5	12	358 22.8	22 18.1	287 18.2	12	357 52.5	21 33.2	292 13.9	12
14	28 55.8	22 51.5	312 27.4	14	28 22.3	22 17.4	317 23.1	14	27 52.0	21 32.4	322 18.8	14
16	58 55.2	22 51.0	342 32.3	16	58 21.7	22 16.7	347 28.0	16	57 51.5	21 31.6	352 23.7	16
18	88 54.6	22 50.5	12 37.3	18	88 21.2	22 16.1	17 33.0	18	87 51.1	21 30.7	22 28.7	18
20	118 54.0	22 50.0	42 42.2	20	118 20.7	22 15.4	47 37.9	20	117 50.6	21 29.9	52 33.6	20
22	148 53.5	S22 49.6	72 47.1	22	148 20.1	S22 14.7	77 42.8	22	147 50.1	S21 29.0	82 38.5	22

Saturday, 4th January | | | **Thursday, 9th January** | | | **Tuesday, 14th January** | | |

h	° '	° '	° '	h	° '	° '	° '	h	° '	° '	° '	h
00	178 52.9	S22 49.1	102 52.1	00	178 19.6	S22 14.1	107 47.7	00	177 49.7	S21 28.2	112 43.4	00
02	208 52.3	22 48.6	132 57.0	02	208 19.1	22 13.4	137 52.7	02	207 49.2	21 27.3	142 48.4	02
04	238 51.7	22 48.1	163 01.9	04	238 18.6	22 12.7	167 57.6	04	237 48.7	21 26.5	172 53.3	04
06	268 51.2	22 47.6	193 06.8	06	268 18.0	22 12.0	198 02.5	06	267 48.3	21 25.6	202 58.2	06
08	298 50.6	22 47.1	223 11.8	08	298 17.5	22 11.3	228 07.5	08	297 47.8	21 24.7	233 03.2	08
10	328 50.0	22 46.6	253 16.7	10	328 17.0	22 10.6	258 12.4	10	327 47.3	21 23.9	263 08.1	10
12	358 49.4	22 46.1	283 21.6	12	358 16.4	22 09.9	288 17.3	12	357 46.9	21 23.0	293 13.0	12
14	28 48.9	22 45.6	313 26.6	14	28 15.9	22 09.3	318 22.2	14	27 46.4	21 22.1	323 17.9	14
16	58 48.3	22 45.0	343 31.5	16	58 15.4	22 08.6	348 27.2	16	57 46.0	21 21.3	353 22.9	16
18	88 47.7	22 44.5	13 36.4	18	88 14.9	22 07.9	18 32.1	18	87 45.5	21 20.4	23 27.8	18
20	118 47.1	22 44.0	43 41.3	20	118 14.4	22 07.1	48 37.0	20	117 45.1	21 19.5	53 32.7	20
22	148 46.6	S22 43.5	73 46.3	22	148 13.8	S22 06.4	78 42.0	22	147 44.6	S21 18.6	83 37.7	22

Sunday, 5th January | | | **Friday, 10th January** | | | **Wednesday, 15th January** | | |

h	° '	° '	° '	h	° '	° '	° '	h	° '	° '	° '	h
00	178 46.0	S22 43.0	103 51.2	00	178 13.3	S22 05.7	108 46.9	00	177 44.1	S21 17.7	113 42.6	00
02	208 45.4	22 42.4	133 56.1	02	208 12.8	22 05.0	138 51.8	02	207 43.7	21 16.8	143 47.5	02
04	238 44.9	22 41.9	164 01.0	04	238 12.3	22 04.3	168 56.7	04	237 43.2	21 16.0	173 52.4	04
06	268 44.3	22 41.4	194 06.0	06	268 11.8	22 03.6	199 01.7	06	267 42.8	21 15.1	203 57.4	06
08	298 43.7	22 40.8	224 10.9	08	298 11.3	22 02.9	229 06.6	08	297 42.3	21 14.2	234 02.3	08
10	328 43.2	22 40.3	254 15.8	10	328 10.7	22 02.1	259 11.5	10	327 41.9	21 13.3	264 07.2	10
12	358 42.6	22 39.7	284 20.8	12	358 10.2	22 01.4	289 16.5	12	357 41.4	21 12.4	294 12.2	12
14	28 42.0	22 39.2	314 25.7	14	28 09.7	22 00.7	319 21.4	14	27 41.0	21 11.5	324 17.1	14
16	58 41.5	22 38.6	344 30.6	16	58 09.2	21 59.9	349 26.3	16	57 40.6	21 10.5	354 22.0	16
18	88 40.9	22 38.1	14 35.5	18	88 08.7	21 59.2	19 31.2	18	87 40.1	21 09.6	24 26.9	18
20	118 40.3	22 37.5	44 40.5	20	118 08.2	21 58.5	49 36.2	20	117 39.7	21 08.7	54 31.9	20
22	148 39.8	S22 37.0	74 45.4	22	148 07.7	S21 57.7	79 41.1	22	147 39.2	S21 07.8	84 36.8	22

To interpolate SUN G.H.A. see page 4:7   To interpolate ARIES G.H.A. see page 4:8

Thursday, 16th January

G.M.T. h	SUN G.H.A.	SUN Dec.	ARIES G.H.A.	G.M.T. h
00	177 38.8	S21 06.9	114 41.7	00
02	207 38.4	21 06.0	144 46.6	02
04	237 37.9	21 05.0	174 51.6	04
06	267 37.5	21 04.1	204 56.5	06
08	297 37.0	21 03.2	235 01.4	08
10	327 36.6	21 02.3	265 06.4	10
12	357 36.2	21 01.3	295 11.3	12
14	27 35.7	21 00.4	325 16.2	14
16	57 35.3	20 59.4	355 21.1	16
18	87 34.9	20 58.5	25 26.1	18
20	117 34.5	20 57.5	55 31.0	20
22	147 34.0	S20 56.6	85 35.9	22

Friday, 17th January

G.M.T. h	SUN G.H.A.	SUN Dec.	ARIES G.H.A.	G.M.T. h
00	177 33.6	S20 55.6	115 40.9	00
02	207 33.2	20 54.7	145 45.8	02
04	237 32.8	20 53.7	175 50.7	04
06	267 32.3	20 52.8	205 55.6	06
08	297 31.9	20 51.8	236 00.6	08
10	327 31.5	20 50.8	266 05.5	10
12	357 31.1	20 49.9	296 10.4	12
14	27 30.7	20 48.9	326 15.4	14
16	57 30.2	20 47.9	356 20.3	16
18	87 29.8	20 46.9	26 25.2	18
20	117 29.4	20 46.0	56 30.1	20
22	147 29.0	S20 45.0	86 35.1	22

Saturday, 18th January

G.M.T. h	SUN G.H.A.	SUN Dec.	ARIES G.H.A.	G.M.T. h
00	177 28.6	S20 44.0	116 40.0	00
02	207 28.2	20 43.0	146 44.9	02
04	237 27.8	20 42.0	176 49.9	04
06	267 27.4	20 41.0	206 54.8	06
08	297 27.0	20 40.0	236 59.7	08
10	327 26.6	20 39.0	267 04.6	10
12	357 26.2	20 38.0	297 09.6	12
14	27 25.8	20 37.0	327 14.5	14
16	57 25.4	20 36.0	357 19.4	16
18	87 25.0	20 35.0	27 24.4	18
20	117 24.6	20 34.0	57 29.3	20
22	147 24.2	S20 33.0	87 34.2	22

Sunday, 19th January

G.M.T. h	SUN G.H.A.	SUN Dec.	ARIES G.H.A.	G.M.T. h
00	177 23.8	S20 31.9	117 39.1	00
02	207 23.4	20 30.9	147 44.1	02
04	237 23.0	20 29.9	177 49.0	04
06	267 22.6	20 28.9	207 53.9	06
08	297 22.2	20 27.8	237 58.9	08
10	327 21.8	20 26.8	268 03.8	10
12	357 21.4	20 25.8	298 08.7	12
14	27 21.0	20 24.7	328 13.6	14
16	57 20.6	20 23.7	358 18.6	16
18	87 20.3	20 22.7	28 23.5	18
20	117 19.9	20 21.6	58 28.4	20
22	147 19.5	S20 20.6	88 33.3	22

Monday, 20th January

G.M.T. h	SUN G.H.A.	SUN Dec.	ARIES G.H.A.	G.M.T. h
00	177 19.1	S20 19.5	118 38.3	00
02	207 18.7	20 18.5	148 43.2	02
04	237 18.3	20 17.4	178 48.1	04
06	267 18.0	20 16.3	208 53.1	06
08	297 17.6	20 15.3	238 58.0	08
10	327 17.2	20 14.2	269 02.9	10
12	357 16.8	20 13.2	299 07.8	12
14	27 16.5	20 12.1	329 12.8	14
16	57 16.1	20 11.0	359 17.7	16
18	87 15.7	20 09.9	29 22.6	18
20	117 15.4	20 08.9	59 27.6	20
22	147 15.0	S20 07.8	89 32.5	22

Tuesday, 21st January

G.M.T. h	SUN G.H.A.	SUN Dec.	ARIES G.H.A.	G.M.T. h
00	177 14.6	S20 06.7	119 37.4	00
02	207 14.3	20 05.6	149 42.3	02
04	237 13.9	20 04.5	179 47.3	04
06	267 13.5	20 03.4	209 52.2	06
08	297 13.2	20 02.3	239 57.1	08
10	327 12.8	20 01.3	270 02.1	10
12	357 12.5	20 00.2	300 07.0	12
14	27 12.1	19 59.1	330 11.9	14
16	57 11.8	19 57.9	0 16.8	16
18	87 11.4	19 56.8	30 21.8	18
20	117 11.1	19 55.7	60 26.7	20
22	147 10.7	S19 54.6	90 31.6	22

Wednesday, 22nd January

G.M.T. h	SUN G.H.A.	SUN Dec.	ARIES G.H.A.	G.M.T. h
00	177 10.4	S19 53.5	120 36.6	00
02	207 10.0	19 52.4	150 41.5	02
04	237 09.7	19 51.3	180 46.4	04
06	267 09.3	19 50.2	210 51.3	06
08	297 09.0	19 49.0	240 56.3	08
10	327 08.6	19 47.9	271 01.2	10
12	357 08.3	19 46.8	301 06.1	12
14	27 07.9	19 45.6	331 11.1	14
16	57 07.6	19 44.5	1 16.0	16
18	87 07.3	19 43.4	31 20.9	18
20	117 06.9	19 42.2	61 25.8	20
22	147 06.6	S19 41.1	91 30.8	22

Thursday, 23rd January

G.M.T. h	SUN G.H.A.	SUN Dec.	ARIES G.H.A.	G.M.T. h
00	177 06.3	S19 39.9	121 35.7	00
02	207 05.9	19 38.8	151 40.6	02
04	237 05.6	19 37.6	181 45.6	04
06	267 05.3	19 36.5	211 50.5	06
08	297 04.9	19 35.3	241 55.4	08
10	327 04.6	19 34.2	272 00.3	10
12	357 04.3	19 33.0	302 05.3	12
14	27 04.0	19 31.9	332 10.2	14
16	57 03.6	19 30.7	2 15.1	16
18	87 03.3	19 29.5	32 20.0	18
20	117 03.0	19 28.4	62 25.0	20
22	147 02.7	S19 27.2	92 29.9	22

Friday, 24th January

G.M.T. h	SUN G.H.A.	SUN Dec.	ARIES G.H.A.	G.M.T. h
00	177 02.3	S19 26.0	122 34.8	00
02	207 02.0	19 24.8	152 39.8	02
04	237 01.7	19 23.7	182 44.7	04
06	267 01.4	19 22.5	212 49.6	06
08	297 01.1	19 21.3	242 54.5	08
10	327 00.8	19 20.1	272 59.5	10
12	357 00.5	19 18.9	303 04.4	12
14	27 00.2	19 17.7	333 09.3	14
16	56 59.9	19 16.5	3 14.3	16
18	86 59.5	19 15.3	33 19.2	18
20	116 59.2	19 14.1	63 24.1	20
22	146 58.9	S19 12.9	93 29.0	22

Saturday, 25th January

G.M.T. h	SUN G.H.A.	SUN Dec.	ARIES G.H.A.	G.M.T. h
00	176 58.6	S19 11.7	123 34.0	00
02	206 58.3	19 10.5	153 38.9	02
04	236 58.0	19 09.3	183 43.8	04
06	266 57.7	19 08.1	213 48.8	06
08	296 57.4	19 06.9	243 53.7	08
10	326 57.1	19 05.7	273 58.6	10
12	356 56.8	19 04.4	304 03.5	12
14	26 56.6	19 03.2	334 08.5	14
16	56 56.3	19 02.0	4 13.4	16
18	86 56.0	19 00.8	34 18.3	18
20	116 55.7	18 59.5	64 23.3	20
22	146 55.4	S18 58.3	94 28.2	22

Sunday, 26th January

G.M.T. h	SUN G.H.A.	SUN Dec.	ARIES G.H.A.	G.M.T. h
00	176 55.1	S18 57.1	124 33.1	00
02	206 54.8	18 55.8	154 38.0	02
04	236 54.5	18 54.6	184 43.0	04
06	266 54.3	18 53.4	214 47.9	06
08	296 54.0	18 52.1	244 52.8	08
10	326 53.7	18 50.9	274 57.8	10
12	356 53.4	18 49.6	305 02.7	12
14	26 53.1	18 48.4	335 07.6	14
16	56 52.9	18 47.1	5 12.5	16
18	86 52.6	18 45.9	35 17.5	18
20	116 52.3	18 44.6	65 22.4	20
22	146 52.1	S18 43.3	95 27.3	22

Monday, 27th January

G.M.T. h	SUN G.H.A.	SUN Dec.	ARIES G.H.A.	G.M.T. h
00	176 51.8	S18 42.1	125 32.2	00
02	206 51.5	18 40.8	155 37.2	02
04	236 51.3	18 39.6	185 42.1	04
06	266 51.0	18 38.3	215 47.0	06
08	296 50.7	18 37.0	245 52.0	08
10	326 50.5	18 35.7	275 56.9	10
12	356 50.2	18 34.5	306 01.8	12
14	26 49.9	18 33.2	336 06.7	14
16	56 49.7	18 31.9	6 11.7	16
18	86 49.4	18 30.6	36 16.6	18
20	116 49.2	18 29.3	66 21.5	20
22	146 48.9	S18 28.0	96 26.5	22

Tuesday, 28th January

G.M.T. h	SUN G.H.A.	SUN Dec.	ARIES G.H.A.	G.M.T. h
00	176 48.7	S18 26.8	126 31.4	00
02	206 48.4	18 25.5	156 36.3	02
04	236 48.2	18 24.2	186 41.2	04
06	266 47.9	18 22.9	216 46.2	06
08	296 47.7	18 21.6	246 51.1	08
10	326 47.4	18 20.3	276 56.0	10
12	356 47.2	18 19.0	307 01.0	12
14	26 46.9	18 17.7	337 05.9	14
16	56 46.7	18 16.3	7 10.8	16
18	86 46.4	18 15.0	37 15.7	18
20	116 46.2	18 13.7	67 20.7	20
22	146 46.0	S18 12.4	97 25.6	22

Wednesday, 29th January

G.M.T. h	SUN G.H.A.	SUN Dec.	ARIES G.H.A.	G.M.T. h
00	176 45.7	S18 11.1	127 30.5	00
02	206 45.5	18 09.8	157 35.5	02
04	236 45.3	18 08.4	187 40.4	04
06	266 45.0	18 07.1	217 45.3	06
08	296 44.8	18 05.8	247 50.2	08
10	326 44.6	18 04.5	277 55.2	10
12	356 44.3	18 03.1	308 00.1	12
14	26 44.1	18 01.8	338 05.0	14
16	56 43.9	18 00.5	8 10.0	16
18	86 43.7	17 59.1	38 14.9	18
20	116 43.4	17 57.8	68 19.8	20
22	146 43.2	S17 56.4	98 24.7	22

Thursday, 30th January

G.M.T. h	SUN G.H.A.	SUN Dec.	ARIES G.H.A.	G.M.T. h
00	176 43.0	S17 55.1	128 29.7	00
02	206 42.8	17 53.7	158 34.6	02
04	236 42.6	17 52.4	188 39.5	04
06	266 42.4	17 51.0	218 44.5	06
08	296 42.1	17 49.7	248 49.4	08
10	326 41.9	17 48.3	278 54.3	10
12	356 41.7	17 47.0	308 59.2	12
14	26 41.5	17 45.6	339 04.2	14
16	56 41.3	17 44.2	9 09.1	16
18	86 41.1	17 42.9	39 14.0	18
20	116 40.9	17 41.5	69 18.9	20
22	146 40.7	S17 40.1	99 23.9	22

Friday, 31st January

G.M.T. h	SUN G.H.A.	SUN Dec.	ARIES G.H.A.	G.M.T. h
00	176 40.5	S17 38.8	129 28.8	00
02	206 40.3	17 37.4	159 33.7	02
04	236 40.1	17 36.0	189 38.7	04
06	266 39.9	S17 34.6	219 43.6	06
08	296 39.7	S17 33.3	249 48.5	08
10	326 39.5	17 31.9	279 53.4	10
12	356 39.3	17 30.5	309 58.4	12
14	26 39.1	S17 29.1	340 03.3	14
16	56 38.9	S17 27.7	10 08.2	16
18	86 38.7	17 26.3	40 13.2	18
20	116 38.5	17 24.9	70 18.1	20
22	146 38.3	S17 23.5	100 23.0	22

To interpolate SUN G.H.A. see page 4:7   To interpolate ARIES G.H.A. see page 4:8

♀ VENUS ♀ / ♃ JUPITER ♃

Mer. Pass.	G.H.A.	Mean Var. 14°	Dec.	Mean Var.	M	Day of Week	G.H.A	Mean Var. 15°	Dec.	Mean Var.	Mer. Pass
h. m.	° ′	′	° ′	′			° ′	′	° ′	′	h. m.
09 16	221 10.2	59.4	S18 10.0	0.7	1	Wed.	293 36.7	2.5	N 7 08.1	0.0	04 25
09 17	220 55.1	59.4	S18 26.2	0.7	2	Th.	294 36.1	2.5	N 7 08.5	0.0	04 21
09 18	220 39.7	59.3	S18 42.1	0.6	3	Fri.	295 35.6	2.5	N 7 08.9	0.0	04 17
09 19	220 24.0	59.3	S18 57.4	0.6	4	Sat.	296 35.2	2.5	N 7 09.4	0.0	04 13
09 20	220 08.0	59.3	S19 12.3	0.6	5	SUN.	297 35.1	2.5	N 7 10.0	0.0	04 09
09 21	219 51.7	59.3	S19 26.7	0.6	6	Mon.	298 35.2	2.5	N 7 10.7	0.0	04 05
09 22	219 35.2	59.3	S19 40.7	0.6	7	Tu.	299 35.4	2.5	N 7 11.5	0.0	04 01
09 23	219 18.3	59.3	S19 54.1	0.5	8	Wed.	300 35.8	2.5	N 7 12.3	0.0	03 57
09 24	219 01.2	59.3	S20 07.0	0.5	9	Th.	301 36.4	2.5	N 7 13.2	0.0	03 53
09 26	218 43.9	59.3	S20 19.3	0.5	10	Fri.	302 37.2	2.5	N 7 14.2	0.0	03 49
09 27	218 26.3	59.3	S20 31.2	0.5	11	Sat.	303 38.1	2.5	N 7 15.2	0.0	03 45
09 28	218 08.4	59.2	S20 42.5	0.4	12	SUN.	304 39.2	2.6	N 7 16.3	0.1	03 41
09 29	217 50.3	59.2	S20 53.2	0.4	13	Mon.	305 40.5	2.6	N 7 17.5	0.1	03 37
09 30	217 32.0	59.2	S21 03.3	0.4	14	Tu.	306 42.0	2.6	N 7 18.8	0.1	03 33
09 32	217 13.4	59.2	S21 12.9	0.4	15	Wed.	307 43.7	2.6	N 7 20.1	0.1	03 28
09 33	216 54.7	59.2	S21 21.9	0.4	16	Th.	308 45.5	2.6	N 7 21.5	0.1	03 24
09 34	216 35.7	59.2	S21 30.3	0.3	17	Fri.	309 47.5	2.6	N 7 23.0	0.1	03 20
09 35	216 16.5	59.2	S21 38.1	0.3	18	Sat.	310 49.7	2.6	N 7 24.5	0.1	03 16
09 37	215 57.2	59.2	S21 45.3	0.3	19	SUN.	311 52.0	2.6	N 7 26.1	0.1	03 12
09 38	215 37.7	59.2	S21 51.9	0.2	20	Mon.	312 54.5	2.6	N 7 27.8	0.1	03 08
09 39	215 18.0	59.2	S21 57.8	0.2	21	Tu.	313 57.2	2.6	N 7 29.5	0.1	03 04
09 41	214 58.1	59.2	S22 03.2	0.2	22	Wed.	315 00.0	2.6	N 7 31.3	0.1	02 59
09 42	214 38.2	59.2	S22 07.9	0.2	23	Th.	316 03.0	2.6	N 7 33.2	0.1	02 55
09 43	214 18.1	59.2	S22 11.9	0.1	24	Fri.	317 06.1	2.6	N 7 35.1	0.1	02 51
09 45	213 57.9	59.2	S22 15.3	0.1	25	Sat.	318 09.4	2.6	N 7 37.1	0.1	02 47
09 46	213 37.6	59.2	S22 18.1	0.1	26	SUN.	319 12.9	2.6	N 7 39.1	0.1	02 43
09 47	213 17.2	59.1	S22 20.2	0.1	27	Mon.	320 16.5	2.7	N 7 41.3	0.1	02 38
09 49	212 56.7	59.1	S22 21.7	0.0	28	Tu.	321 20.3	2.7	N 7 43.4	0.1	02 34
09 50	212 36.2	59.1	S22 22.5	0.0	29	Wed.	322 24.2	2.7	N 7 45.6	0.1	02 30
09 52	212 15.7	59.1	S22 22.6	0.0	30	Th.	323 28.3	2.7	N 7 47.9	0.1	02 26
09 53	211 55.1	59.1	S22 22.1	0.0	31	Fri.	324 32.5	2.7	N 7 50.2	0.1	02 21

♀ VENUS. Av. Mag. −4.0. A Morning Star. S.H.A. Jan. 5 116°; 10 110°; 15 104°; 20 97°; 25 90°; 30 84°.

♃ JUPITER. Av. Mag. −2.3. A Morning Star. S.H.A. Jan. 5 194°; 10 195°; 15 193°; 20 194°; 25 196°; 30 194°.

♂ MARS ♂ / ♄ SATURN ♄

Mer. Pass.	G.H.A.	Mean Var. 15°	Dec.	Mean Var.	M	Day of Week	G.H.A	Mean Var. 15°	Dec.	Mean Var.	Mer. Pass
h. m.	° ′	′	° ′	′			° ′	′	° ′	′	h. m.
10 53	196 41.9	0.5	S23 45.4	0.1	1	Wed.	151 31.9	2.2	S19 22.4	0.1	13 52
10 52	196 52.9	0.4	S23 48.0	0.1	2	Th.	152 24.1	2.2	S19 20.8	0.1	13 48
10 51	197 03.7	0.4	S23 50.3	0.1	3	Fri.	153 16.3	2.2	S19 19.2	0.1	13 45
10 51	197 14.5	0.4	S23 52.4	0.1	4	Sat.	154 08.5	2.2	S19 17.6	0.1	13 41
10 50	197 25.3	0.4	S23 54.2	0.1	5	SUN.	155 00.6	2.2	S19 15.9	0.1	13 38
10 49	197 35.9	0.4	S23 55.8	0.1	6	Mon.	155 52.7	2.2	S19 14.3	0.1	13 35
10 49	197 46.5	0.4	S23 57.1	0.0	7	Tu.	156 44.8	2.2	S19 12.6	0.1	13 31
10 48	197 57.1	0.4	S23 58.2	0.0	8	Wed.	157 36.9	2.2	S19 10.9	0.1	13 28
10 47	198 07.6	0.4	S23 59.0	0.0	9	Th.	158 28.9	2.2	S19 09.2	0.1	13 24
10 46	198 18.0	0.4	S23 59.6	0.0	10	Fri.	159 21.0	2.2	S19 07.5	0.1	13 21
10 46	198 28.4	0.4	S24 00.0	0.0	11	Sat.	160 12.9	2.2	S19 05.8	0.1	13 17
10 45	198 38.8	0.4	S24 00.0	0.0	12	SUN.	161 04.9	2.2	S19 04.1	0.1	13 14
10 44	198 49.1	0.4	S23 59.9	0.0	13	Mon.	161 56.9	2.2	S19 02.4	0.1	13 10
10 44	198 59.3	0.4	S23 59.4	0.1	14	Tu.	162 48.8	2.2	S19 00.6	0.1	13 07
10 43	199 09.5	0.4	S23 58.8	0.1	15	Wed.	163 40.7	2.2	S18 58.9	0.1	13 03
10 42	199 19.7	0.4	S23 57.8	0.1	16	Th.	164 32.7	2.2	S18 57.1	0.1	13 00
10 42	199 29.9	0.4	S23 56.6	0.1	17	Fri.	165 24.5	2.2	S18 55.4	0.1	12 56
10 41	199 40.0	0.4	S23 55.2	0.1	18	Sat.	166 16.4	2.2	S18 53.6	0.1	12 53
10 40	199 50.1	0.4	S23 53.5	0.1	19	SUN.	167 08.3	2.2	S18 51.8	0.1	12 50
10 40	200 00.2	0.4	S23 51.5	0.1	20	Mon.	168 00.2	2.2	S18 50.0	0.1	12 46
10 39	200 10.3	0.4	S23 49.3	0.1	21	Tu.	168 52.0	2.2	S18 48.3	0.1	12 43
10 38	200 20.3	0.4	S23 46.8	0.1	22	Wed.	169 43.8	2.2	S18 46.5	0.1	12 39
10 38	200 30.4	0.4	S23 44.1	0.1	23	Th.	170 35.7	2.2	S18 44.7	0.1	12 36
10 37	200 40.4	0.4	S23 41.1	0.1	24	Fri.	171 27.5	2.2	S18 42.8	0.1	12 32
10 36	200 50.5	0.4	S23 37.9	0.1	25	Sat.	172 19.3	2.2	S18 41.0	0.1	12 29
10 36	201 00.5	0.4	S23 34.4	0.2	26	SUN.	173 11.1	2.2	S18 39.2	0.1	12 25
10 35	201 10.5	0.4	S23 30.6	0.2	27	Mon.	174 03.0	2.2	S18 37.4	0.1	12 22
10 34	201 20.6	0.4	S23 26.6	0.2	28	Tu.	174 54.8	2.2	S18 35.6	0.1	12 19
10 34	201 30.6	0.4	S23 22.4	0.2	29	Wed.	175 46.6	2.2	S18 33.7	0.1	12 15
10 33	201 40.7	0.4	S23 17.9	0.2	30	Th.	176 38.4	2.2	S18 31.9	0.1	12 12
10 32	201 50.8	0.4	S23 13.1	0.2	31	Fri.	177 30.2	2.2	S18 30.1	0.1	12 08

♂ MARS. Av. Mag. +1.4. A Morning Star. In conjunction with Mercury on January 10. S.H.A. Jan. 5 94°; 10 90°; 15 85°; 20 81°; 25 77°; 30 73°.

♄ SATURN. Av. Mag. +0.6. Visible in the evening sky until mid-Jan. when it is too close to the sun for observation. S.H.A. Jan. 5 51°; 10 51°; 15 49°; 20 49°; 25 50° 30 47°.

MERCURY. Visible low in the east before sunrise until January 30. Do not confuse with Mars during first half of January. Mars has a reddish tint.

For Planets Correction Tables see pages 4:9-4:13. See also 'How to Recognise the Planets' on page 2:32.
Mean Var. means Variation per Hour.

Day of M. W.	G.M.T. h	G.H.A. ° ′	Mean Var. per Hour 14°,+	Dec. ° ′	Mean Var. per Hour ′
1 Wed.	0	227 00.2	29.5	S22 51.3	5.0
	6	313 57.1	29.3	S23 21.6	4.3
	12	40 53.2	29.3	S23 47.6	3.5
	18	127 48.7	29.2	S24 09.3	2.8
2 Th.	0	214 43.9	29.2	S24 26.6	2.1
	6	301 38.8	29.2	S24 39.5	1.4
	12	28 33.7	29.2	S24 47.9	0.6
	18	115 28.8	29.3	S24 51.9	0.1
3 Fri.	0	202 24.2	29.3	S24 51.5	0.8
	6	289 20.3	29.5	S24 46.7	1.5
	12	16 17.1	29.6	S24 37.5	2.3
	18	103 14.9	29.9	S24 24.1	3.0
4 Sat.	0	190 13.9	30.0	S24 06.5	3.7
	6	277 14.2	30.3	S23 44.8	4.4
	12	4 16.0	30.6	S23 19.1	5.0
	18	Eclipse of the Sun occurs today			
5 Sun.	0	178 24.5	31.2	S22 16.3	6.2
	6	265 31.4	31.5	S21 39.4	6.7
	12	352 40.2	31.8	S20 59.1	7.4
	18	79 50.8	32.1	S20 15.4	7.9
6 Mon.	0	167 03.4	32.5	S19 28.7	8.3
	6	254 17.9	32.7	S18 39.0	8.8
	12	341 34.3	33.0	S17 46.4	9.3
	18	68 52.5	33.3	S16 51.3	9.6
7 Tu.	0	156 12.5	33.6	S15 53.6	10.0
	6	243 34.2	33.9	S14 53.6	10.4
	12	330 57.4	34.1	S13 51.5	10.7
	18	58 22.1	34.4	S12 47.3	11.1
8 Wed.	0	145 48.2	34.5	S11 41.4	11.3
	6	233 15.4	34.7	S10 33.7	11.6
	12	320 43.7	34.9	S 9 24.5	11.8
	18	48 12.9	35.0	S 8 13.9	12.0
9 Th.	0	135 42.8	35.1	S 7 02.0	12.2
	6	223 13.3	35.2	S 5 49.1	12.4
	12	310 44.1	35.2	S 4 35.2	12.4
	18	38 15.0	35.1	S 3 20.5	12.6
10 Fri.	0	125 45.9	35.1	S 2 05.1	12.6
	6	213 16.5	35.0	S 0 49.2	12.7
	12	300 46.7	34.9	N 0 27.0	12.7
	18	28 16.1	34.8	N 1 43.5	12.8
11 Sat.	0	115 44.7	34.6	N 3 00.1	12.7
	6	203 12.1	34.3	N 4 16.6	12.7
	12	290 38.1	34.1	N 5 32.9	12.7
	18	18 02.5	33.7	N 6 48.7	12.6
12 Sun.	0	105 25.0	33.4	N 8 04.0	12.4
	6	192 45.5	33.0	N 9 18.5	12.2
	12	280 03.6	32.5	N10 32.0	12.0
	18	7 19.1	32.1	N11 44.4	11.9
13 Mon.	0	94 31.8	31.6	N12 55.3	11.6
	6	181 41.4	31.0	N14 04.7	11.3
	12	268 47.8	30.5	N15 12.1	10.8
	18	355 50.8	29.8	N16 17.4	10.4
14 Tu.	0	82 50.0	29.2	N17 20.3	9.9
	6	169 45.4	28.5	N18 20.5	9.5
	12	256 36.9	27.9	N19 17.6	9.0
	18	343 24.3	27.1	N20 11.4	8.3
15 Wed.	0	70 07.6	26.4	N21 01.5	7.6
	6	156 46.7	25.8	N21 47.6	6.9
	12	243 21.7	25.1	N22 29.3	6.1
	18	329 52.7	24.5	N23 06.3	5.2
16 Th.	0	56 19.8	23.8	N23 38.2	4.3
	6	142 43.3	23.3	N24 04.8	3.4
	12	229 03.4	22.8	N24 25.6	2.4
	18	315 20.5	22.4	N24 40.6	1.4
17 Fri.	0	41 35.0	22.0	N24 49.3	0.3
	6	127 47.3	21.8	N24 51.6	0.8
	12	213 58.0	21.6	N24 47.3	2.0
	18	300 07.7	21.5	N24 36.3	3.1
18 Sat.	0	26 16.8	21.5	N24 18.7	4.2
	6	112 25.9	21.7	N23 54.3	5.3
	12	198 35.6	21.8	N23 23.4	6.4
	18	284 46.3	22.1	N22 45.9	7.3
19 Sun.	0	10 58.7	22.5	N22 02.0	8.4
	6	97 13.0	22.8	N21 12.5	9.3
	12	183 29.6	23.3	N20 17.0	10.2
	18	269 48.9	23.8	N19 16.2	11.0
20 Mon.	0	356 11.1	24.3	N18 10.3	11.8
	6	82 36.3	24.8	N16 59.9	12.5
	12	169 04.7	25.3	N15 45.4	13.1
	18	255 36.3	25.9	N14 27.1	13.6
21 Tu.	0	342 11.2	26.4	N13 05.6	14.1
	6	68 49.1	26.8	N11 41.3	14.5
	12	155 30.1	27.3	N10 14.7	14.7
	18	242 14.1	27.8	N 8 46.2	15.1
22 Wed.	0	329 00.8	28.3	N 7 16.2	15.2
	6	55 50.1	28.7	N 5 45.2	15.3
	12	142 41.7	29.0	N 4 13.6	15.3
	18	229 35.6	29.3	N 2 41.7	15.3
23 Th.	0	316 31.3	29.6	N 1 09.9	15.2
	6	43 28.8	29.8	S 0 21.4	15.1
	12	130 27.7	30.1	S 1 51.9	14.9
	18	217 27.9	30.3	S 3 21.3	14.7
24 Fri.	0	304 29.2	30.4	S 4 49.3	14.3
	6	31 31.2	30.4	S 6 15.7	14.1
	12	118 33.9	30.6	S 7 40.2	13.7
	18	205 36.9	30.6	S 9 02.6	13.2
25 Sat.	0	292 40.1	30.6	S10 22.5	12.8
	6	19 43.4	30.5	S11 40.0	12.4
	12	106 46.6	30.5	S12 54.6	12.0
	18	193 49.5	30.4	S14 06.3	11.4
26 Sun.	0	280 52.0	30.3	S15 14.9	10.8
	6	7 54.0	30.3	S16 20.2	10.3
	12	94 55.5	30.2	S17 22.2	9.7
	18	181 56.2	30.0	S18 20.5	9.0
27 Mon.	0	268 56.3	29.9	S19 15.1	8.5
	6	355 55.7	29.7	S20 06.0	7.8
	12	82 54.3	29.7	S20 52.9	7.1
	18	169 52.2	29.5	S21 35.8	6.4
28 Tu.	0	256 49.4	29.5	S22 14.6	5.7
	6	343 46.1	29.4	S22 49.1	5.0
	12	70 42.2	29.2	S23 19.4	4.3
	18	157 38.0	29.3	S23 45.4	3.5
29 Wed.	0	244 33.4	29.2	S24 07.1	2.8
	6	331 28.8	29.2	S24 24.3	2.0
	12	58 24.1	29.2	S24 37.1	1.3
	18	145 19.6	29.3	S24 45.5	0.6
30 Th.	0	232 15.4	29.4	S24 49.5	0.1
	6	319 11.7	29.5	S24 49.2	0.9
	12	46 08.7	29.7	S24 44.5	1.5
	18	133 06.5	29.8	S24 35.5	2.3
31 Fri.	0	220 05.4	30.0	S24 22.3	2.9
	6	307 05.3	30.2	S24 04.9	3.6
	12	34 06.6	30.4	S23 43.5	4.3
	18	121 09.3	30.7	S23 18.2	4.9

PHASES OF THE MOON

	d. h/min		d. h/min
● New Moon	4 23 10	○ Full Moon	19 21 28
☽ First Quarter	13 02 32	☾ Last Quarter	26 15 27
Apogee	6 12	Perigee	19 22

FEBRUARY, 1992
(29 days)

☉ SUN ☉

DATE Yr.	Mth.	Week	Equation of Time 0 h.	12 h.	Transit	Semi-diam.	Lat. 52°N. Twilight	Sunrise	Sunset	Twilight	Lat. Corr. Lat.	Twilight	Sunrise	Sunset	Twilight
			m. s.	m. s.	h. m.	′	h. m.	h. m.	h. m.	h. m.	°	h. m.	h. m.	h. m.	h. m.
32	1	Sat.	+13 27	+13 32	12 14	16.3	07 04	07 41	16 46	17 23	N70	+0 48	+1 23	-1 22	-0 49
33	2	Sun.	+13 36	+13 40	12 14	16.3	07 03	07 39	16 48	17 25	68	+0 39	+1 06	-1 06	-0 40
34	3	Mon.	+13 43	+13 47	12 14	16.3	07 01	07 38	16 50	17 26	66	+0 32	+0 53	-0 53	-0 32
35	4	Tu.	+13 50	+13 53	12 14	16.3	07 00	07 36	16 52	17 28	64	+0 26	+0 42	-0 41	-0 26
36	5	Wed.	+13 56	+13 59	12 14	16.3	06 58	07 34	16 54	17 30	62	+0 20	+0 32	-0 32	-0 20
37	6	Th.	+14 02	+14 04	12 14	16.2	06 57	07 33	16 56	17 32	N60	+0 15	+0 25	-0 25	-0 16
38	7	Fri.	+14 06	+14 08	12 14	16.2	06 55	07 31	16 58	17 34	58	+0 10	+0 17	-0 17	-0 11
39	8	Sat.	+14 10	+14 11	12 14	16.2	06 53	07 29	17 00	17 36	56	+0 06	+0 11	-0 11	-0 07
40	9	Sun.	+14 13	+14 14	12 14	16.2	06 52	07 28	17 01	17 37	54	+0 03	+0 05	-0 05	-0 04
41	10	Mon.	+14 15	+14 15	12 14	16.2	06 50	07 26	17 03	17 39	50	-0 03	-0 05	+0 04	+0 03
42	11	Tu.	+14 16	+14 16	12 14	16.2	06 48	07 24	17 05	17 41	N45	-0 10	-0 15	+0 15	+0 10
43	12	Wed.	+14 16	+14 16	12 14	16.2	06 47	07 22	17 07	17 42	40	-0 16	-0 23	+0 23	+0 16
44	13	Th.	+14 16	+14 15	12 14	16.2	06 45	07 20	17 09	17 44	35	-0 22	-0 30	+0 31	+0 21
45	14	Fri.	+14 15	+14 14	12 14	16.2	06 43	07 18	17 11	17 46	30	-0 27	-0 37	+0 37	+0 26
46	15	Sat.	+14 13	+14 12	12 14	16.2	06 42	07 17	17 12	17 47	20	-0 36	-0 48	+0 48	+0 35
47	16	Sun.	+14 10	+14 09	12 14	16.2	06 40	07 15	17 14	17 49	N10	-0 45	-0 59	+0 58	+0 44
48	17	Mon.	+14 07	+14 05	12 14	16.2	06 38	07 13	17 16	17 51	0	-0 55	-1 08	+1 07	+0 54
49	18	Tu.	+14 03	+14 01	12 14	16.2	06 36	07 11	17 18	17 53	S10	-1 05	-1 18	+1 16	+1 04
50	19	Wed.	+13 58	+13 55	12 14	16.2	06 34	07 09	17 20	17 55	20	-1 16	-1 28	+1 26	+1 15
51	20	Th.	+13 53	+13 50	12 14	16.2	06 32	07 07	17 22	17 57	30	-1 31	-1 40	+1 38	+1 30
52	21	Fri.	+13 47	+13 43	12 14	16.2	06 30	07 05	17 24	17 58	S35	-1 40	-1 48	+1 45	+1 49
53	22	Sat.	+13 40	+13 36	12 14	16.2	06 28	07 03	17 26	18 00	40	-1 50	-1 55	+1 53	+1 49
54	23	Sun.	+13 32	+13 27	12 13	16.2	06 26	07 01	17 28	18 02	45	-2 05	-2 05	+2 02	+2 00
55	24	Mon.	+13 24	+13 20	12 13	16.2	06 24	06 58	17 29	18 03	S50	-2 17	-2 16	+2 13	+2 16
56	25	Tu.	+13 16	+13 11	12 13	16.2	06 22	06 56	17 31	18 05					
57	26	Wed.	+13 06	+13 02	12 13	16.2	06 20	06 54	17 33	18 07					
58	27	Th.	+12 57	+12 52	12 13	16.2	06 18	06 52	17 34	18 08					
59	28	Fri.	+12 46	+12 41	12 13	16.2	06 16	06 50	17 36	18 10					
60	29	Sat.	+12 35	+12 30	12 12	16.2	06 14	06 48	17 38	18 12					

NOTES

The corrections to sunrise, sunset, etc., are for Feb. 15. Examples on the use of the above data are given on page 2:11 onwards.

Equation of Time is the excess of Mean Time over Apparent Time (See explanation and examples on p. 2:15)

☽ MOON ☾

DATE Yr.	Mth.	Week	Age days	Transit Diff. (Upper) h. m.	m.	Semi-diam.	Hor. Par. 12 h.	Lat. 52°N. Moonrise	Moonset
				h. m.	m.	′	′	h. m.	h. m.
32	1	Sat.	28	10 27	47	14.7	54.0	06 26	14 34
33	2	Sun.	29	11 14	44	14.7	53.9	06 53	15 42
34	3	Mon.	30	11 58	43	14.7	54.0	07 15	16 51
35	4	Tu.	01	12 41	41	14.7	54.1	07 33	18 00
36	5	Wed.	02	13 22	41	14.8	54.3	07 48	19 09
37	6	Th.	03	14 03	42	14.9	54.6	08 03	20 18
38	7	Fri.	04	14 45	43	15.0	55.0	08 17	21 28
39	8	Sat.	05	15 28	45	15.1	55.5	08 32	22 39
40	9	Sun.	06	16 13	49	15.3	56.1	08 50	23 53
41	10	Mon.	07	17 02	53	15.5	56.7	09 11	– –
42	11	Tu.	08	17 55	57	15.7	57.5	09 39	01 09
43	12	Wed	09	18 52	60	15.9	58.4	10 16	02 24
44	13	Th.	10	19 52	61	16.1	59.2	11 07	03 34
45	14	Fri.	11	20 53	62	16.3	60.0	12 14	04 34
46	15	Sat.	12	21 55	59	16.5	60.7	13 34	05 22
47	16	Sun.	13	22 54	56	16.6	61.1	15 02	05 58
48	17	Mon.	14	23 50	54	16.7	61.2	16 33	06 26
49	18	Tu.	15	24 44	–	16.6	61.1	18 02	06 49
50	19	Wed.	16	00 44	52	16.5	60.6	19 29	07 08
51	20	Th.	17	01 36	51	16.3	59.8	20 54	07 27
52	21	Fri.	18	02 27	51	16.1	58.9	22 17	07 46
53	22	Sat.	19	03 18	51	15.8	58.0	23 37	08 07
54	23	Sun.	20	04 09	51	15.5	57.0	– –	08 31
55	24	Mon.	21	05 00	52	15.3	56.2	00 53	09 02
56	25	Tu.	22	05 52	52	15.1	55.4	02 01	09 40
57	26	Wed.	23	06 44	50	14.9	54.8	03 01	10 27
58	27	Th.	24	07 34	49	14.8	54.4	03 49	11 22
59	28	Fri.	25	08 23	47	14.8	54.1	04 27	12 25
60	29	Sat.	26	09 10	45	14.7	54.0	04 57	13 32

MOON'S PHASES

		d.	h.	m.
●	New Moon	3	19	00
☽	First Quarter	11	16	15
○	Full Moon	18	08	04
☾	Last Quarter	25	07	56

	d.	h.
Apogee	2	12
Perigee	17	11
Apogee	29	21

NOTES

Moon's G.H.A. and Dec. are given on page 3:21.

A table for correcting Moonrise and Moonset for latitude is on page 4:20.

A table for correcting Moon's meridian passage for longitude is on page 4:19.

Examples on the use of the above data are given on page 2:11 onwards.

0h. = midnight. For explanation of use of above data see page 2:11 onwards.

0h. G.M.T. FEBRUARY 1 ★ ★ STARS ★ ★ 0h. G.M.T. FEBRUARY 1

No.	Name	Mag.	Transit (approx.) h. m.	DEC. ° '	G.H.A. ° '	R.A. h. m.	S.H.A. ° '
♈	ARIES	–	15 16	–	130 27.9	–	–
1	Alpheratz	2.2	15 24	N29 02.9	128 28.2	0 08	358 00.3
2	Ankaa	2.4	15 41	S42 21.0	123 59.5	0 26	353 31.6
3	Schedar	2.5	15 56	N56 29.9	120 27.2	0 40	349 59.3
4	Diphda	2.2	15 59	S18 01.8	119 39.9	0 43	349 12.0
5	Achernar	0.6	16 53	S57 16.8	106 06.6	1 37	335 38.7
6	POLARIS	2.1	17 38	N89 14.2	94 39.8	2 23	324 11.9
7	Hamal	2.2	17 22	N23 25.7	98 46.8	2 07	328 18.9
8	Acamar	3.1	18 13	S40 20.4	85 58.3	2 58	315 30.4
9	Menkar	2.8	18 17	N 4 03.6	84 59.6	3 02	314 31.7
10	Mirfak	1.9	18 39	N49 50.3	79 31.2	3 24	309 03.3
11	Aldebaran	1.1	19 50	N16 29.7	61 35.5	4 35	291 07.6
12	Rigel	0.3	20 29	S 8 12.7	51 55.1	5 14	281 27.2
13	Capella	0.2	20 31	N45 59.6	51 25.7	5 16	280 57.8
14	Bellatrix	1.7	20 39	N 6 20.5	49 16.8	5 25	278 48.9
15	Elnath	1.8	20 41	N28 36.2	49 00.5	5 26	278 32.6
16	Alnilam	1.8	20 51	S 1 12.5	46 30.3	5 36	276 02.4
17	Betelgeuse	{ 0.1 1.2 }	21 09	N 7 24.3	41 46.2	5 55	271 18.3
18	Canopus	-0.9	21 38	S52 41.7	34 30.7	6 24	264 02.8
19	Sirius	-1.6	21 59	S16 42.5	29 15.4	6 45	258 47.5
20	Adhara	1.6	22 13	S28 57.9	25 52.6	6 58	255 24.7
21	Castor	1.6	22 49	N31 54.3	16 55.7	7 34	246 27.8
22	Procyon	0.5	22 53	N 5 14.6	15 44.0	7 39	245 16.1
23	Pollux	1.2	22 59	N28 02.7	14 14.7	7 45	243 46.8
24	Avior	1.7	23 37	S59 29.2	4 51.9	8 22	234 24.0
25	Suhail	2.2	00 26	S43 24.2	353 31.7	9 08	223 03.8
26	Miaplacidus	1.8	00 31	S69 41.2	352 10.2	9 13	221 42.3
27	Alphard	2.2	00 45	S 8 37.6	348 39.3	9 27	218 11.4
28	Regulus	1.3	01 26	N12 00.1	338 28.0	10 08	208 00.1
29	Dubhe	2.0	02 21	N61 47.3	324 38.2	11 03	194 10.3
30	Denebola	2.2	03 06	N14 36.7	313 17.5	11 49	182 49.6
31	Gienah	2.8	03 33	S17 30.1	306 36.4	12 15	176 08.5
32	Acrux	1.1	03 44	S63 03.3	303 54.7	12 26	173 26.8
33	Gacrux	1.6	03 48	S57 04.1	302 46.3	12 31	172 18.4
34	Mimosa	1.5	04 05	S59 38.7	298 38.3	12 47	168 10.4
35	Alioth	1.7	04 11	N55 59.8	297 02.0	12 54	166 34.1
36	Spica	1.2	04 42	S11 07.4	289 15.8	13 25	158 47.9
37	Alkaid	1.9	05 05	N49 20.7	283 39.0	13 47	153 11.1
38	Hadar	0.9	05 21	S60 20.0	279 38.4	14 03	149 10.5
39	Menkent	2.3	05 23	S36 19.9	278 54.2	14 06	148 26.3
40	Arcturus	0.2	05 33	N19 13.1	276 38.0	14 15	146 10.1
41	Rigil Kent	0.1	05 56	S60 48.0	270 41.3	14 39	140 13.4
42	Zuben'ubi	2.9	06 08	S16 00.7	267 50.9	14 50	137 23.0
43	Kochab	2.2	06 08	N74 10.8	267 46.8	14 51	137 18.9
44	Alphecca	2.3	06 51	N26 44.1	256 52.4	15 34	126 24.5
45	Antares	1.2	07 46	S26 24.9	243 13.8	16 29	112 45.9
46	Atria	1.9	08 05	S69 00.7	238 30.2	16 48	108 02.3
47	Sabik	2.6	08 27	S15 43.0	232 58.9	17 10	102 31.0
48	Shaula	1.7	08 50	S37 05.9	227 11.6	17 33	96 43.7
49	Rasalhague	2.1	08 51	N12 33.7	226 49.3	17 35	96 21.4
50	Eltanin	2.4	09 13	N51 29.1	221 21.7	17 56	90 53.8
51	Kaus Aust.	2.0	09 40	S34 23.3	214 33.1	18 24	84 05.2
52	Vega	0.1	09 53	N38 46.3	211 17.9	18 37	80 50.0
53	Nunki	2.1	10 11	S26 18.4	206 46.2	18 55	76 18.3
54	Altair	0.9	11 07	N 8 50.7	192 52.0	19 50	62 24.1
55	Peacock	2.1	11 41	S56 45.6	184 12.6	20 25	53 44.7
56	Deneb	1.3	11 57	N45 15.1	180 10.7	20 41	49 42.8
57	Enif	2.5	13 00	N 9 50.3	164 31.0	21 44	34 03.1
58	Al Na'ir	2.2	13 24	S47 00.0	158 31.9	22 08	28 04.0
59	Fomalhaut	1.3	14 13	S29 39.9	146 09.7	22 57	15 41.8
60	Markab	2.6	14 20	N15 09.8	144 22.4	23 04	13 54.5

Stars Transit Correction Table

D. of Mth.	Corr (Sub.) h. m.	D. of Mth.	Corr. (Sub.) h. m.
1	–0 00	17	–1 03
2	–0 04	18	–1 07
3	–0 08	19	–1 11
4	–0 08	20	–1 15
5	–0 16	21	–1 19
6	–0 20	22	–1 23
7	–0 24	23	–1 27
8	–0 28	24	–1 30
9	–0 31	25	–1 34
10	–0 35	26	–1 38
11	–0 39	27	–1 42
12	–0 43	28	–1 46
13	–0 47		
14	–0 51		
15	–0 55		
16	–0 59		

STAR'S TRANSIT

To find the approx. time of Transit of a Star for any day of the month use above table.

If the quantity taken from the table is greater than the time of Transit for the first of the month, add 23h. 56min. to the time of transit before subtracting the correction below.

Example: Will Rigel (No 12) be on the Meridian between 1700h. and 1900h. on February 28th?

	h.min.
Transit on February 1st ...	20 29
Corr. for 28th	–01 46
Transit on February 28th	18 43

FEBRUARY DIARY

d.	h.	
1	13	Mars 1°.5S of Moon
2	12	Moon at apogee
3	19	New Moon
11	16	First Quarter
12	09	Mercury in superior conjunction
17	11	Moon at perigee
18	08	Full Moon
19	07	Jupiter 6°N. of Moon
19	22	Venus 0°.9N. of Mars
25	08	Last Quarter
29	01	Jupiter at opposition
29	02	Venus 0°.1N. of Saturn
29	21	Moon at apogee

STAR TIME

The best time to take Star observations is shown in the a.m. and p.m. TWILIGHT columns on the opposite page - corrected for Latitude.

For **Lighting-up Time** (ashore) add 30 mins to Sunset Times.

For Star's G.H.A. Correction Table, see page 4:8.

For Alphabetical List of Stars with Constellation names, see page 2:24.

For Examples on the use of the above data, see page 2:11.

For full directions for finding the above 60 Stars, see p. 2:20 onwards. For Special Pole Star tables see pages 5:17-5:19.

Saturday, 1st February

GMT h	SUN G.H.A.	Dec.	ARIES G.H.A.
00	176 38.1	S17 22.1	130 27.9
02	206 38.0	17 20.7	160 32.9
04	236 37.8	17 19.3	190 37.8
06	266 37.6	17 17.9	220 42.7
08	296 37.4	17 16.5	250 47.7
10	326 37.2	17 15.1	280 52.6
12	356 37.1	17 13.7	310 57.5
14	26 36.9	17 12.3	341 02.4
16	56 36.7	17 10.9	11 07.4
18	86 36.5	17 09.5	41 12.3
20	116 36.4	17 08.0	71 17.2
22	146 36.2	S17 06.6	101 22.2

Sunday, 2nd February

GMT h	SUN G.H.A.	Dec.	ARIES G.H.A.
00	176 36.0	S17 05.2	131 27.1
02	206 35.9	17 03.8	161 32.0
04	236 35.7	17 02.3	191 36.9
06	266 35.5	17 00.9	221 41.9
08	296 35.4	16 59.5	251 46.8
10	326 35.2	16 58.1	281 51.7
12	356 35.0	16 56.6	311 56.7
14	26 34.9	16 55.2	342 01.6
16	56 34.7	16 53.7	12 06.5
18	86 34.6	16 52.3	42 11.4
20	116 34.4	16 50.9	72 16.4
22	146 34.3	S16 49.4	102 21.3

Monday, 3rd February

GMT h	SUN G.H.A.	Dec.	ARIES G.H.A.
00	176 34.1	S16 48.0	132 26.2
02	206 34.0	16 46.5	162 31.2
04	236 33.8	16 45.1	192 36.1
06	266 33.7	16 43.6	222 41.0
08	296 33.5	16 42.1	252 45.9
10	326 33.4	16 40.7	282 50.9
12	356 33.2	16 39.2	312 55.8
14	26 33.1	16 37.8	343 00.7
16	56 32.9	16 36.3	13 05.6
18	86 32.8	16 34.8	43 10.6
20	116 32.7	16 33.4	73 15.5
22	146 32.5	S16 31.9	103 20.4

Tuesday, 4th February

GMT h	SUN G.H.A.	Dec.	ARIES G.H.A.
00	176 32.4	S16 30.4	133 25.4
02	206 32.3	16 29.0	163 30.3
04	236 32.1	16 27.5	193 35.2
06	266 32.0	16 26.0	223 40.1
08	296 31.9	16 24.5	253 45.1
10	326 31.7	16 23.0	283 50.0
12	356 31.6	16 21.6	313 54.9
14	26 31.5	16 20.1	343 59.9
16	56 31.4	16 18.6	14 04.8
18	86 31.2	16 17.1	44 09.7
20	116 31.1	16 15.6	74 14.6
22	146 31.0	S16 14.1	104 19.6

Wednesday, 5th February

GMT h	SUN G.H.A.	Dec.	ARIES G.H.A.
00	176 30.9	S16 12.6	134 24.5
02	206 30.8	16 11.1	164 29.4
04	236 30.6	16 09.6	194 34.4
06	266 30.5	16 08.1	224 39.3
08	296 30.4	16 06.6	254 44.2
10	326 30.3	16 05.1	284 49.1
12	356 30.2	16 03.6	314 54.1
14	26 30.1	16 02.1	344 59.0
16	56 30.0	16 00.6	15 03.9
18	86 29.9	15 59.1	45 08.9
20	116 29.8	15 57.5	75 13.8
22	146 29.7	S15 56.0	105 18.7

Thursday, 6th February

GMT h	SUN G.H.A.	Dec.	ARIES G.H.A.
00	176 29.6	S15 54.5	135 23.6
02	206 29.5	15 53.0	165 28.6
04	236 29.4	15 51.5	195 33.5
06	266 29.3	15 49.9	225 38.4
08	296 29.2	15 48.4	255 43.4
10	326 29.1	15 46.9	285 48.3
12	356 29.0	15 45.4	315 53.2
14	26 28.9	15 43.8	345 58.1
16	56 28.8	15 42.3	16 03.1
18	86 28.7	15 40.8	46 08.0
20	116 28.6	15 39.2	76 12.9
22	146 28.5	S15 37.7	106 17.8

Friday, 7th February

GMT h	SUN G.H.A.	Dec.	ARIES G.H.A.
00	176 28.5	S15 36.1	136 22.8
02	206 28.4	15 34.6	166 27.7
04	236 28.3	15 33.1	196 32.6
06	266 28.2	15 31.5	226 37.6
08	296 28.1	15 30.0	256 42.5
10	326 28.1	15 28.4	286 47.4
12	356 28.0	15 26.9	316 52.3
14	26 27.9	15 25.3	346 57.3
16	56 27.8	15 23.7	17 02.2
18	86 27.8	15 22.2	47 07.1
20	116 27.7	15 20.6	77 12.1
22	146 27.6	S15 19.1	107 17.0

Saturday, 8th February

GMT h	SUN G.H.A.	Dec.	ARIES G.H.A.
00	176 27.5	S15 17.5	137 21.9
02	206 27.5	15 15.9	167 26.8
04	236 27.4	15 14.4	197 31.8
06	266 27.4	15 12.8	227 36.7
08	296 27.3	15 11.2	257 41.6
10	326 27.2	15 09.7	287 46.6
12	356 27.2	15 08.1	317 51.5
14	26 27.1	15 06.5	347 56.4
16	56 27.1	15 04.9	18 01.3
18	86 27.0	15 03.4	48 06.3
20	116 27.0	15 01.8	78 11.2
22	146 26.9	S15 00.2	108 16.1

Sunday, 9th February

GMT h	SUN G.H.A.	Dec.	ARIES G.H.A.
00	176 26.8	S14 58.6	138 21.1
02	206 26.8	14 57.0	168 26.0
04	236 26.7	14 55.4	198 30.9
06	266 26.7	14 53.8	228 35.8
08	296 26.7	14 52.3	258 40.8
10	326 26.6	14 50.7	288 45.7
12	356 26.6	14 49.1	318 50.6
14	26 26.5	14 47.5	348 55.6
16	56 26.5	14 45.9	19 00.5
18	86 26.5	14 44.3	49 05.4
20	116 26.4	14 42.7	79 10.3
22	146 26.4	S14 41.1	109 15.3

Monday, 10th February

GMT h	SUN G.H.A.	Dec.	ARIES G.H.A.
00	176 26.3	S14 39.5	139 20.2
02	206 26.3	14 37.9	169 25.1
04	236 26.3	14 36.3	199 30.1
06	266 26.3	14 34.6	229 35.0
08	296 26.2	14 33.0	259 39.9
10	326 26.2	14 31.4	289 44.8
12	356 26.2	14 29.8	319 49.8
14	26 26.1	14 28.2	349 54.7
16	56 26.1	14 26.6	19 59.6
18	86 26.1	14 24.9	50 04.5
20	116 26.1	14 23.3	80 09.5
22	146 26.1	S14 21.7	110 14.4

Tuesday, 11th February

GMT h	SUN G.H.A.	Dec.	ARIES G.H.A.
00	176 26.0	S14 20.1	140 19.3
02	206 26.0	14 18.4	170 24.3
04	236 26.0	14 16.8	200 29.2
06	266 26.0	14 15.2	230 34.1
08	296 26.0	14 13.6	260 39.0
10	326 26.0	14 11.9	290 44.0
12	356 26.0	14 10.3	320 48.9
14	26 26.0	14 08.7	350 53.8
16	56 25.9	14 07.0	20 58.8
18	86 25.9	14 05.4	51 03.7
20	116 25.9	14 03.7	81 08.6
22	146 25.9	S14 02.1	111 13.5

Wednesday, 12th February

GMT h	SUN G.H.A.	Dec.	ARIES G.H.A.
00	176 25.9	S14 00.4	141 18.5
02	206 25.9	13 58.8	171 23.4
04	236 25.9	13 57.2	201 28.3
06	266 25.9	13 55.5	231 33.3
08	296 25.9	13 53.9	261 38.2
10	326 25.9	13 52.2	291 43.1
12	356 26.0	13 50.5	321 48.0
14	26 26.0	13 48.9	351 53.0
16	56 26.0	13 47.2	21 57.9
18	86 26.0	13 45.6	52 02.8
20	116 26.0	13 43.9	82 07.8
22	146 26.0	S13 42.3	112 12.7

Thursday, 13th February

GMT h	SUN G.H.A.	Dec.	ARIES G.H.A.
00	176 26.0	S13 40.6	142 17.6
02	206 26.0	13 38.9	172 22.5
04	236 26.1	13 37.3	202 27.5
06	266 26.1	13 35.6	232 32.4
08	296 26.1	13 33.9	262 37.3
10	326 26.1	13 32.2	292 42.3
12	356 26.1	13 30.6	322 47.2
14	26 26.2	13 28.9	352 52.1
16	56 26.2	13 27.2	22 57.0
18	86 26.2	13 25.5	53 02.0
20	116 26.2	13 23.9	83 06.9
22	146 26.3	S13 22.2	113 11.8

Friday, 14th February

GMT h	SUN G.H.A.	Dec.	ARIES G.H.A.
00	176 26.3	S13 20.5	143 16.7
02	206 26.3	13 18.8	173 21.7
04	236 26.4	13 17.1	203 26.6
06	266 26.4	13 15.5	233 31.5
08	296 26.4	13 13.8	263 36.5
10	326 26.5	13 12.1	293 41.4
12	356 26.5	13 10.4	323 46.3
14	26 26.6	13 08.7	353 51.2
16	56 26.6	13 07.0	23 56.2
18	86 26.6	13 05.3	54 01.1
20	116 26.7	13 03.6	84 06.0
22	146 26.7	S13 01.9	114 11.0

Saturday, 15th February

GMT h	SUN G.H.A.	Dec.	ARIES G.H.A.
00	176 26.8	S13 00.2	144 15.9
02	206 26.8	12 58.5	174 20.8
04	236 26.9	12 56.8	204 25.7
06	266 26.9	12 55.1	234 30.7
08	296 27.0	12 53.4	264 35.6
10	326 27.0	12 51.7	294 40.5
12	356 27.1	12 50.0	324 45.5
14	26 27.1	12 48.3	354 50.4
16	56 27.2	12 46.6	24 55.3
18	86 27.3	12 44.8	55 00.2
20	116 27.3	12 43.1	85 05.2
22	146 27.4	S12 41.4	115 10.1

To interpolate **SUN** G.H.A. see page 4:7   To interpolate **ARIES** G.H.A. see page 4:8

Sunday, 16th February

G.M.T. h	SUN G.H.A. ° '	SUN Dec. ° '	ARIES G.H.A. ° '
00	176 27.4	S12 39.7	145 15.0
02	206 27.5	12 38.0	175 20.0
04	236 27.6	12 36.3	205 24.9
06	266 27.6	12 34.5	235 29.8
08	296 27.7	12 32.8	265 34.7
10	326 27.8	12 31.1	295 39.7
12	356 27.8	12 29.4	325 44.6
14	26 27.9	12 27.6	355 49.5
16	56 28.0	12 25.9	25 54.5
18	86 28.1	12 24.2	55 59.4
20	116 28.1	12 22.4	86 04.3
22	146 28.2	S12 20.7	116 09.2

Monday, 17th February

G.M.T. h	SUN G.H.A.	SUN Dec.	ARIES G.H.A.
00	176 28.3	S12 19.0	146 14.2
02	206 28.4	12 17.2	176 19.1
04	236 28.4	12 15.5	206 24.0
06	266 28.5	12 13.8	236 29.0
08	296 28.6	12 12.0	266 33.9
10	326 28.7	12 10.3	296 38.8
12	356 28.8	12 08.6	326 43.7
14	26 28.9	12 06.8	356 48.7
16	56 28.9	12 05.1	26 53.6
18	86 29.0	12 03.3	56 58.5
20	116 29.1	12 01.6	87 03.4
22	146 29.2	S11 59.8	117 08.4

Tuesday, 18th February

G.M.T. h	SUN G.H.A.	SUN Dec.	ARIES G.H.A.
00	176 29.3	S11 58.1	147 13.3
02	206 29.4	11 56.3	177 18.2
04	236 29.5	11 54.6	207 23.2
06	266 29.6	11 52.8	237 28.1
08	296 29.7	11 51.1	267 33.0
10	326 29.8	11 49.3	297 37.9
12	356 29.9	11 47.5	327 42.9
14	26 30.0	11 45.8	357 47.8
16	56 30.1	11 44.0	27 52.7
18	86 30.2	11 42.3	57 57.7
20	116 30.3	11 40.5	88 02.6
22	146 30.4	S11 38.7	118 07.5

Wednesday, 19th February

G.M.T. h	SUN G.H.A.	SUN Dec.	ARIES G.H.A.
00	176 30.5	S11 37.0	148 12.4
02	206 30.6	11 35.2	178 17.4
04	236 30.7	11 33.4	208 22.3
06	266 30.8	11 31.7	238 27.2
08	296 30.9	11 29.9	268 32.2
10	326 31.0	11 28.1	298 37.1
12	356 31.2	11 26.4	328 42.0
14	26 31.3	11 24.6	358 46.9
16	56 31.4	11 22.8	28 51.9
18	86 31.5	11 21.0	58 56.8
20	116 31.6	11 19.2	89 01.7
22	146 31.7	S11 17.5	119 06.7

Thursday, 20th February

G.M.T. h	SUN G.H.A.	SUN Dec.	ARIES G.H.A.
00	176 31.9	S11 15.7	149 11.6
02	206 32.0	11 13.9	179 16.5
04	236 32.1	11 12.1	209 21.4
06	266 32.2	11 10.3	239 26.4
08	296 32.4	11 08.6	269 31.3
10	326 32.5	11 06.8	299 36.2
12	356 32.6	11 05.0	329 41.2
14	26 32.7	11 03.2	359 46.1
16	56 32.9	11 01.4	29 51.0
18	86 33.0	10 59.6	59 55.9
20	116 33.1	10 57.8	90 00.9
22	146 33.3	S10 56.0	120 05.8

Friday, 21st February

G.M.T. h	SUN G.H.A.	SUN Dec.	ARIES G.H.A.
00	176 33.4	S10 54.2	150 10.7
02	206 33.5	10 52.4	180 15.7
04	236 33.7	10 50.6	210 20.6
06	266 33.8	10 48.8	240 25.5
08	296 34.0	10 47.0	270 30.4
10	326 34.1	10 45.2	300 35.4
12	356 34.2	10 43.4	330 40.3
14	26 34.4	10 41.6	0 45.2
16	56 34.5	10 39.8	30 50.1
18	86 34.7	10 38.0	60 55.1
20	116 34.8	10 36.2	91 00.0
22	146 35.0	S10 34.4	121 04.9

Saturday, 22nd February

G.M.T. h	SUN G.H.A.	SUN Dec.	ARIES G.H.A.
00	176 35.1	S10 32.6	151 09.9
02	206 35.3	10 30.8	181 14.8
04	236 35.4	10 29.0	211 19.7
06	266 35.6	10 27.2	241 24.6
08	296 35.7	10 25.3	271 29.6
10	326 35.9	10 23.5	301 34.5
12	356 36.0	10 21.7	331 39.4
14	26 36.2	10 19.9	1 44.4
16	56 36.3	10 18.1	31 49.3
18	86 36.5	10 16.3	61 54.2
20	116 36.6	10 14.4	91 59.1
22	146 36.8	S10 12.6	122 04.1

Sunday, 23rd February

G.M.T. h	SUN G.H.A.	SUN Dec.	ARIES G.H.A.
00	176 37.0	S10 10.8	152 09.0
02	206 37.1	10 09.0	182 13.9
04	236 37.3	10 07.2	212 18.9
06	266 37.4	10 05.3	242 23.8
08	296 37.6	10 03.5	272 28.7
10	326 37.8	10 01.7	302 33.6
12	356 37.9	9 59.8	332 38.6
14	26 38.1	9 58.0	2 43.5
16	56 38.3	9 56.2	32 48.4
18	86 38.5	9 54.4	62 53.4
20	116 38.6	9 52.5	92 58.3
22	146 38.8	S 9 50.7	123 03.2

Monday, 24th February

G.M.T. h	SUN G.H.A.	SUN Dec.	ARIES G.H.A.
00	176 39.0	S 9 48.8	153 08.1
02	206 39.1	9 47.0	183 13.1
04	236 39.3	9 45.2	213 18.0
06	266 39.5	9 43.3	243 22.9
08	296 39.7	9 41.5	273 27.9
10	326 39.9	9 39.7	303 32.8
12	356 40.0	9 37.8	333 37.7
14	26 40.2	9 36.0	3 42.6
16	56 40.4	9 34.1	33 47.6
18	86 40.6	9 32.3	63 52.5
20	116 40.8	9 30.4	93 57.4
22	146 40.9	S 9 28.6	124 02.3

Tuesday, 25th February

G.M.T. h	SUN G.H.A.	SUN Dec.	ARIES G.H.A.
00	176 41.1	S 9 26.7	154 07.3
02	206 41.3	9 24.9	184 12.2
04	236 41.5	9 23.1	214 17.1
06	266 41.7	9 21.2	244 22.1
08	296 41.9	9 19.3	274 27.0
10	326 42.1	9 17.5	304 31.9
12	356 42.3	9 15.6	334 36.8
14	26 42.5	9 13.8	4 41.8
16	56 42.7	9 11.9	34 46.7
18	86 42.9	9 10.1	64 51.6
20	116 43.0	9 08.2	94 56.6
22	146 43.2	S 9 06.4	125 01.5

Wednesday, 26th February

G.M.T. h	SUN G.H.A.	SUN Dec.	ARIES G.H.A.
00	176 43.4	S 9 04.5	155 06.4
02	206 43.6	9 02.6	185 11.3
04	236 43.8	9 00.8	215 16.3
06	266 44.0	8 58.9	245 21.2
08	296 44.2	8 57.1	275 26.1
10	326 44.4	8 55.2	305 31.1
12	356 44.6	8 53.3	335 36.0
14	26 44.9	8 51.5	5 40.9
16	56 45.1	8 49.6	35 45.8
18	86 45.3	8 47.7	65 50.8
20	116 45.5	8 45.9	95 55.7
22	146 45.7	S 8 44.0	126 00.6

Thursday, 27th February

G.M.T. h	SUN G.H.A.	SUN Dec.	ARIES G.H.A.
00	176 45.9	S 8 42.1	156 05.6
02	206 46.1	8 40.3	186 10.5
04	236 46.3	8 38.4	216 15.4
06	266 46.5	8 36.5	246 20.3
08	296 46.7	8 34.6	276 25.3
10	326 47.0	8 32.8	306 30.2
12	356 47.2	8 30.9	336 35.1
14	26 47.4	8 29.0	6 40.1
16	56 47.6	8 27.1	36 45.0
18	86 47.8	8 25.2	66 49.9
20	116 48.0	8 23.4	96 54.8
22	146 48.3	S 8 21.5	126 59.8

Friday, 28th February

G.M.T. h	SUN G.H.A.	SUN Dec.	ARIES G.H.A.
00	176 48.5	S 8 19.6	157 04.7
02	206 48.7	8 17.7	187 09.6
04	236 48.9	8 15.8	217 14.6
06	266 49.1	8 14.0	247 19.5
08	296 49.4	8 12.1	277 24.4
10	326 49.6	8 10.2	307 29.3
12	356 49.8	8 08.3	337 34.3
14	26 50.0	8 06.4	7 39.2
16	56 50.3	8 04.5	37 44.1
18	86 50.5	8 02.6	67 49.0
20	116 50.7	8 00.8	97 54.0
22	146 51.0	S 7 58.9	127 58.9

Saturday, 29th February

G.M.T. h	SUN G.H.A.	SUN Dec.	ARIES G.H.A.
00	176 51.2	S 7 57.0	158 03.8
02	206 51.4	7 55.1	188 08.8
04	236 51.7	7 53.2	218 13.7
06	266 51.9	7 51.3	248 18.6
08	296 52.1	7 49.4	278 23.5
10	326 52.4	7 47.5	308 28.5
12	356 52.6	7 45.6	338 33.4
14	26 52.8	7 43.7	8 38.3
16	56 53.1	7 41.8	38 43.3
18	86 53.3	7 39.9	68 48.2
20	116 53.5	7 38.0	98 53.1
22	146 53.8	S 7 36.1	128 58.0

To interpolate SUN G.H.A. see page 4:7 To interpolate ARIES G.H.A. see page 4:8

♀ VENUS ♀ / ♃ JUPITER ♃

Mer. Pass. h. m.	G.H.A. ° ′	Mean Var. 14° ′	Dec. ° ′	Mean Var. ′	M	Day of Week	G.H.A ° ′	Mean Var. 15° ′	Dec. ° ′	Mean Var. ′	Mer. Pass h. m.
09 54	211 34.5	59.1	S22 20.9	0.1	1	Sat.	325 36.8	2.7	N 7 52.6	0.1	02 17
09 56	211 13.9	59.1	S22 19.0	0.1	2	SUN.	326 41.3	2.7	N 7 55.1	0.1	02 13
09 57	210 53.3	59.1	S22 16.5	0.1	3	Mon.	327 45.9	2.7	N 7 57.5	0.1	02 09
09 58	210 32.8	59.1	S22 13.4	0.2	4	Tu.	328 50.6	2.7	N 8 00.1	0.1	02 04
10 00	210 12.3	59.1	S22 09.5	0.2	5	Wed.	329 55.5	2.7	N 8 02.6	0.1	02 00
10 01	209 51.8	59.2	S22 05.0	0.2	6	Th.	331 00.5	2.7	N 8 05.2	0.1	01 56
10 02	209 31.5	59.2	S21 59.9	0.2	7	Fri.	332 05.6	2.7	N 8 07.9	0.1	01 51
10 04	209 11.2	59.2	S21 54.1	0.3	8	Sat.	333 10.8	2.7	N 8 10.6	0.1	01 47
10 05	208 51.0	59.2	S21 47.6	0.3	9	SUN.	334 16.1	2.7	N 8 13.3	0.1	01 43
10 06	208 30.9	59.2	S21 40.5	0.3	10	Mon.	335 21.5	2.7	N 8 16.1	0.1	01 38
10 08	208 11.0	59.2	S21 32.8	0.4	11	Tu.	336 27.0	2.7	N 8 18.9	0.1	01 34
10 09	207 51.2	59.2	S21 24.4	0.4	12	Wed.	337 32.7	2.7	N 8 21.7	0.1	01 30
10 10	207 31.5	59.2	S21 15.3	0.4	13	Th.	338 38.4	2.7	N 8 24.6	0.1	01 25
10 12	207 12.0	59.2	S21 05.7	0.4	14	Fri.	339 44.2	2.7	N 8 27.5	0.1	01 21
10 13	206 52.7	59.2	S20 55.4	0.5	15	Sat.	340 50.0	2.8	N 8 30.4	0.1	01 16
10 14	206 33.5	59.2	S20 44.5	0.5	16	SUN.	341 56.0	2.8	N 8 33.3	0.1	01 12
10 16	206 14.5	59.2	S20 33.0	0.5	17	Mon.	343 02.0	2.8	N 8 36.3	0.1	01 08
10 17	205 55.7	59.2	S20 20.9	0.5	18	Tu.	344 08.1	2.8	N 8 39.2	0.1	01 03
10 18	205 37.1	59.2	S20 08.1	0.6	19	Wed.	345 14.2	2.8	N 8 42.2	0.1	00 59
10 19	205 18.7	59.2	S19 54.8	0.6	20	Th.	346 20.5	2.8	N 8 45.3	0.1	00 54
10 20	205 00.6	59.3	S19 40.9	0.6	21	Fri.	347 26.7	2.8	N 8 48.3	0.1	00 50
10 22	204 42.6	59.3	S19 26.5	0.6	22	Sat.	348 33.0	2.8	N 8 51.3	0.1	00 46
10 23	204 24.9	59.3	S19 11.4	0.6	23	SUN.	349 39.4	2.8	N 8 54.4	0.1	00 41
10 24	204 07.4	59.3	S18 55.8	0.7	24	Mon.	350 45.8	2.8	N 8 57.4	0.1	00 37
10 25	203 50.2	59.3	S18 39.7	0.7	25	Tu.	351 52.2	2.8	N 9 00.5	0.1	00 32
10 26	203 33.2	59.3	S18 23.0	0.7	26	Wed.	352 58.6	2.8	N 9 03.5	0.1	00 28
10 27	203 16.5	59.3	S18 05.8	0.7	27	Th.	354 05.1	2.8	N 9 06.6	0.1	00 24
10 28	203 00.0	59.3	S17 48.1	0.8	28	Fri.	355 11.6	2.8	N 9 09.6	0.1	00 19
10 30	202 43.7	59.3	S17 29.8	0.8	29	Sat.	356 18.1	2.8	N 9 12.7	0.1	00 15

♀ VENUS. Av. Mag. –4.0. A **Morning Star.** In conjunction with Mars on February 19 and Saturn on February 29. **S.H.A.** February 5 76°; 10 69°; 15 62°; 20 56°; 25 50°; 29 45°.

♃ JUPITER. Av. Mag. –2.5. A **Morning Star.** At opposition on February 29. **S.H.A.** February 5 194°; 10 196°; 15 198°; 20 196°; 25 198°; 29 197°.

♂ MARS ♂ / ♄ SATURN ♄

Mer. Pass. h. m.	G.H.A. ° ′	Mean Var. 15° ′	Dec. ° ′	Mean Var. ′	M	Day of Week	G.H.A ° ′	Mean Var. 15° ′	Dec. ° ′	Mean Var. ′	Mer. Pass h. m.
10 32	202 00.9	0.4	S23 08.1	0.2	1	Sat.	178 22.0	2.2	S18 28.2	0.1	12 05
10 31	202 11.0	0.4	S23 02.8	0.2	2	SUN.	179 13.9	2.2	S18 26.4	0.1	12 01
10 30	202 21.2	0.4	S22 57.3	0.2	3	Mon.	180 05.7	2.2	S18 24.5	0.1	11 58
10 30	202 31.4	0.4	S22 51.6	0.3	4	Tu.	180 57.5	2.2	S18 22.7	0.1	11 54
10 29	202 41.6	0.4	S22 45.6	0.3	5	Wed.	181 49.4	2.2	S18 20.8	0.1	11 51
10 28	202 51.9	0.4	S22 39.3	0.3	6	Th.	182 41.3	2.2	S18 19.0	0.1	11 48
10 28	203 02.2	0.4	S22 32.8	0.3	7	Fri.	183 33.1	2.2	S18 17.1	0.1	11 44
10 27	203 12.5	0.4	S22 26.0	0.3	8	Sat.	184 25.0	2.2	S18 15.2	0.1	11 41
10 26	203 22.9	0.4	S22 19.1	0.3	9	SUN.	185 16.9	2.2	S18 13.4	0.1	11 37
10 25	203 33.4	0.4	S22 11.8	0.3	10	Mon.	186 08.8	2.2	S18 11.5	0.1	11 34
10 25	203 43.9	0.4	S22 04.3	0.3	11	Tu.	187 00.7	2.2	S18 09.7	0.1	11 30
10 24	203 54.4	0.4	S21 56.6	0.3	12	Wed.	187 52.7	2.2	S18 07.8	0.1	11 27
10 23	204 05.0	0.4	S21 48.7	0.3	13	Th.	188 44.6	2.2	S18 05.9	0.1	11 23
10 23	204 15.7	0.4	S21 40.5	0.3	14	Fri.	189 36.6	2.2	S18 04.1	0.1	11 20
10 22	204 26.4	0.4	S21 32.1	0.4	15	Sat.	190 28.6	2.2	S18 02.2	0.1	11 16
10 21	204 37.2	0.4	S21 23.4	0.4	16	SUN.	191 20.6	2.2	S18 00.4	0.1	11 13
10 20	204 48.1	0.5	S21 14.6	0.4	17	Mon.	192 12.6	2.2	S17 58.5	0.1	11 10
10 20	204 59.0	0.5	S21 05.5	0.4	18	Tu.	193 04.7	2.2	S17 56.7	0.1	11 06
10 19	205 10.0	0.5	S20 56.1	0.4	19	Wed.	193 56.8	2.2	S17 54.8	0.1	11 03
10 18	205 21.1	0.5	S20 46.6	0.4	20	Th.	194 48.9	2.2	S17 53.0	0.1	10 59
10 18	205 32.2	0.5	S20 36.8	0.4	21	Fri.	195 41.0	2.2	S17 51.1	0.1	10 56
10 17	205 43.5	0.5	S20 26.8	0.4	22	Sat.	196 33.2	2.2	S17 49.3	0.1	10 52
10 16	205 54.8	0.5	S20 16.6	0.4	23	SUN.	197 25.4	2.2	S17 47.5	0.1	10 49
10 15	206 06.1	0.5	S20 06.1	0.4	24	Mon.	198 17.6	2.2	S17 45.7	0.1	10 45
10 15	206 17.6	0.5	S19 55.5	0.5	25	Tu.	199 09.8	2.2	S17 43.8	0.1	10 42
10 14	206 29.1	0.5	S19 44.6	0.5	26	Wed.	200 02.1	2.2	S17 42.0	0.1	10 38
10 13	206 40.7	0.5	S19 33.6	0.5	27	Th.	200 54.4	2.2	S17 40.2	0.1	10 35
10 12	206 52.4	0.5	S19 22.3	0.5	28	Fri.	201 46.8	2.2	S17 38.4	0.1	10 31
10 11	207 04.2	0.5	S19 10.8	0.5	29	Sat.	202 39.2	2.2	S17 36.6	0.1	10 28

♂ MARS. Av. Mag. +1.3. A **Morning Star.** Do not confuse with Venus from mid-month. Venus is the brighter object. **S.H.A.** February 5 68°; 10 64°; 15 60°; 20 56°; 25 52°; 29 49°.

♄ SATURN. Av. Mag. +0.7. Too close to the sun for observation until February 16 when it appears in the morning sky. Do not confuse with Venus in late February. **S.H.A.** February 5 47°; 10 47°; 15 47°; 20 45°; 25 45°; 29 44°.

MERCURY. Too close to the sun for observation until February 23 when it is visible low in the west after sunset.

For Planets Correction Tables see pages 4:9-4:13. See also 'How to Recognise the Planets' on page 2:32.
Mean Var. means Variation per Hour.

Day of M. W. T.	G. M. T.	G.H.A.	Mean Var. per Hour	Dec.	Mean Var. per Hour	Day of M. W. T.	G. M. T.	G.H.A.	Mean Var. per Hour	Dec.	Mean Var. per Hour
	h	° ′	14°,+	° ′	′		h	° ′	14°,+	° ′	′
1 Sat.	0	208 13.5	30.9	S22 49.0	5.6	17 Mon.	0	15 51.1	25.5	N15 37.9	13.0
	6	295 19.3	31.2	S22 16.2	6.2		6	102 24.2	25.9	N14 20.4	13.5
	12	22 26.7	31.6	S21 39.7	6.7		12	188 59.7	26.3	N12 59.5	14.0
	18	109 35.9	31.8	S20 59.8	7.2		18	275 37.6	26.7	N11 35.5	14.4
2 Sun.	0	196 46.9	32.2	S20 16.6	7.8	18 Tu.	0	2 17.9	27.1	N10 09.0	14.8
	6	283 59.6	32.5	S19 30.2	8.2		6	89 00.3	27.4	N 8 40.3	15.1
	12	11 14.1	32.7	S18 40.9	8.7		12	175 44.9	27.8	N 7 09.8	15.3
	18	98 30.3	33.0	S17 48.7	9.2		18	262 31.5	28.1	N 5 38.1	15.5
3 Mon.	0	185 48.2	33.3	S16 53.8	9.6	19 Wed.	0	349 19.9	28.4	N 4 05.5	15.5
	6	273 07.8	33.5	S15 56.4	10.0		6	76 09.9	28.6	N 2 32.4	15.5
	12	0 28.9	33.8	S14 56.6	10.4		12	163 01.4	28.8	N 0 59.2	15.5
	18	87 51.6	34.0	S13 54.6	10.7		18	249 54.2	28.9	S 0 33.7	15.4
4 Tu.	0	175 15.6	34.3	S12 50.5	11.0	20 Th.	0	336 48.0	29.1	S 2 05.9	15.1
	6	262 40.8	34.4	S11 44.6	11.3		6	63 42.7	29.2	S 3 37.1	14.9
	12	350 07.2	34.6	S10 36.9	11.5		12	150 38.2	29.4	S 5 06.9	14.7
	18	77 34.7	34.8	S 9 27.7	11.8		18	237 34.2	29.4	S 6 35.0	14.3
5 Wed.	0	165 03.0	34.8	S 8 17.1	12.0	21 Fri.	0	324 30.5	29.4	S 8 01.2	14.0
	6	252 32.0	35.0	S 7 05.2	12.2		6	51 27.0	29.4	S 9 25.0	13.6
	12	340 01.6	35.0	S 5 52.2	12.3		12	138 23.7	29.5	S10 46.4	13.1
	18	67 31.5	35.1	S 4 38.2	12.4		18	225 20.2	29.4	S12 04.9	12.5
6 Th.	0	155 01.7	35.0	S 3 23.5	12.6	22 Sat.	0	312 16.5	29.3	S13 20.4	12.0
	6	242 32.0	35.0	S 2 08.1	12.7		6	39 12.6	29.3	S14 32.7	11.5
	12	330 02.1	34.9	S 0 52.3	12.7		12	126 08.2	29.2	S15 41.6	10.8
	18	57 31.9	34.9	N 0 23.8	12.7		18	213 03.5	29.1	S16 46.9	10.2
7 Fri.	0	145 01.2	34.8	N 1 40.1	12.7	23 Sun.	0	299 58.2	29.0	S17 48.4	9.5
	6	232 29.7	34.6	N 2 56.3	12.7		6	26 52.5	28.9	S18 46.0	8.9
	12	319 57.4	34.4	N 4 12.4	12.6		12	113 46.3	28.9	S19 39.5	8.2
	18	47 23.9	34.2	N 5 28.2	12.6		18	200 39.6	28.8	S20 28.9	7.5
8 Sat.	0	134 49.1	34.0	N 6 43.4	12.4	24 Mon.	0	287 32.5	28.7	S21 13.9	6.7
	6	222 12.8	33.6	N 7 57.9	12.3		6	14 25.1	28.8	S21 54.7	6.0
	12	309 34.7	33.3	N 9 11.5	12.1		12	101 17.4	28.7	S22 31.0	5.2
	18	36 54.7	33.0	N10 24.1	11.8		18	188 09.4	28.6	S23 02.8	4.5
9 Sun.	0	124 12.6	32.6	N11 35.3	11.6	25 Tu.	0	275 01.5	28.7	S23 30.2	3.8
	6	211 28.1	32.1	N12 45.1	11.3		6	1 53.6	28.8	S23 53.0	3.0
	12	298 41.0	31.7	N13 53.2	11.0		12	88 45.9	28.8	S24 11.2	2.2
	18	25 51.3	31.2	N14 59.3	10.6		18	175 38.6	28.8	S24 24.9	1.5
10 Mon.	0	112 58.6	30.7	N16 03.3	10.3	26 Wed.	0	262 31.8	29.0	S24 34.1	0.7
	6	200 02.8	30.2	N17 04.9	9.8		6	349 25.7	29.1	S24 38.8	0.0
	12	287 03.8	29.6	N18 03.8	9.3		12	76 20.4	29.3	S24 39.0	0.8
	18	14 01.5	29.0	N18 59.8	8.7		18	163 16.1	29.5	S24 34.9	1.5
11 Tu.	0	100 55.7	28.4	N19 52.7	8.2	27 Th.	0	250 13.0	29.7	S24 26.4	2.2
	6	187 46.5	27.8	N20 42.0	7.5		6	337 11.0	29.9	S24 13.7	2.9
	12	274 33.6	27.2	N21 27.6	6.9		12	64 10.5	30.2	S23 56.9	3.5
	18	1 17.2	26.6	N22 09.2	6.2		18	151 11.4	30.4	S23 36.1	4.2
12 Wed.	0	87 57.3	26.0	N22 46.4	5.4	28 Fri.	0	238 13.9	30.7	S23 11.4	4.9
	6	174 34.0	25.5	N23 19.0	4.6		6	325 18.0	31.0	S22 42.8	5.5
	12	261 07.4	25.0	N23 46.8	3.7		12	52 23.8	31.3	S22 10.6	6.0
	18	347 37.6	24.5	N24 09.4	2.7		18	139 31.4	31.6	S21 34.8	6.5
13 Th.	0	74 05.0	24.1	N24 26.6	1.8	29 Sat.	0	226 40.8	31.9	S20 55.6	7.1
	6	160 29.9	23.7	N24 38.2	0.9		6	313 51.9	32.2	S20 13.2	7.7
	12	246 52.4	23.4	N24 43.9	0.1		12	41 04.8	32.4	S19 27.6	8.2
	18	333 13.1	23.1	N24 43.7	1.1		18	128 19.4	32.8	S18 39.0	8.7
14 Fri.	0	59 32.3	23.0	N24 37.4	2.2						
	6	145 50.4	22.9	N24 24.9	3.3						
	12	232 07.9	22.8	N24 06.1	4.2						
	18	318 25.1	22.9	N23 41.1	5.3						
15 Sat.	0	44 42.5	23.0	N23 09.8	6.3						
	6	131 00.6	23.2	N22 32.5	7.3						
	12	217 19.7	23.4	N21 49.2	8.3						
	18	303 40.1	23.7	N21 00.1	9.2						
16 Sun.	0	30 02.2	24.0	N20 05.5	10.1						
	6	116 26.1	24.3	N19 05.7	10.9						
	12	202 52.2	24.8	N18 00.9	11.7						
	18	289 20.5	25.2	N16 51.5	12.3						

PHASES OF THE MOON

	d. h/min		d. h/min
● New Moon	3 19 00	○ Full Moon	18 08 04
) First Quarter	11 16 15	(Last Quarter	25 07 56
Apogee	2 12	Perigee	17 11
		Apogee	29 21

MARCH, 1992

G.M.T. (31 days) G.M.T.

☉ SUN ☉

DATE Yr.	Mth.	Week	Equation of Time 0 h.	12 h.	Transit	Semi-diam.	Lat. 52°N. Twilight	Sunrise	Sunset	Twilight	Lat. Corr. Lat.	Twilight	Sunrise	Sunset	Twilight
			m. s.	m. s.	h. m.	′	h. m.	h. m.	h. m.	h. m.	°	h. m.	h. m.	h. m.	h. m.
61	1	Sun.	+12 24	+12 18	12 12	16.2	06 11	06 45	17 40	18 14	N70	−0 18	+0 08	−0 06	+0 19
62	2	Mon.	+12 12	+12 06	12 12	16.2	06 09	06 43	17 42	18 16	68	−0 15	+0 06	−0 05	+0 15
63	3	Tu.	+12 00	+11 54	12 12	16.2	06 07	06 41	17 44	18 18	66	−0 12	+0 05	−0 04	+0 13
64	4	Wed.	+11 47	+11 41	12 12	16.1	06 05	06 39	17 45	18 19	64	−0 09	+0 04	−0 03	+0 10
65	5	Th.	+11 34	+11 27	12 11	16.1	06 03	06 37	17 47	18 21	62	−0 06	+0 03	−0 02	+0 07
66	6	Fri.	+11 20	+11 13	12 11	16.1	06 01	06 35	17 49	18 23	N60	−0 04	+0 03	−0 02	+0 05
67	7	Sat.	+11 06	+10 59	12 11	16.1	05 58	06 32	17 51	18 24	58	−0 03	+0 02	−0 02	+0 04
68	8	Sun.	+10 52	+10 44	12 11	16.1	05 56	06 30	17 53	18 26	56	−0 01	+0 01	−0 01	+0 02
69	9	Mon.	+10 37	+10 29	12 10	16.1	05 54	06 28	17 55	18 28	54	−0 01	+0 01	−0 01	+0 01
70	10	Tu.	+10 22	+10 14	12 10	16.1	05 51	06 25	17 56	18 30	50	+0 01	0 00	0 00	−0 01
71	11	Wed.	+10 06	+09 58	12 10	16.1	05 49	06 23	17 58	18 32	N45	+0 03	−0 01	+0 02	−0 02
72	12	Th.	+09 50	+09 42	12 10	16.1	05 47	06 21	18 00	18 34	40	+0 05	−0 02	+0 02	−0 04
73	13	Fri.	+09 34	+09 26	12 09	16.1	05 45	06 18	18 01	18 35	35	+0 06	−0 03	+0 03	−0 05
74	14	Sat.	+09 17	+09 09	12 09	16.1	05 43	06 16	18 03	18 37	30	+0 07	−0 04	+0 04	−0 06
75	15	Sun.	+09 01	+08 52	12 09	16.1	05 41	06 14	18 05	18 39	20	+0 07	−0 05	+0 05	−0 06
76	16	Mon.	+08 44	+08 35	12 09	16.1	05 38	06 11	18 06	18 40	N10	+0 07	−0 07	+0 06	−0 06
77	17	Tu.	+08 26	+08 18	12 08	16.1	05 36	06 09	18 08	18 42	0	+0 06	−0 08	+0 07	−0 05
78	18	Wed.	+08 09	+08 00	12 08	16.1	05 34	06 07	18 10	18 44	S10	+0 04	−0 09	+0 09	−0 03
79	19	Th.	+07 51	+07 42	12 08	16.1	05 31	06 04	18 12	18 45	20	+0 01	−0 11	+0 10	0 00
80	20	Fri.	+07 33	+07 24	12 07	16.1	05 29	06 02	18 14	18 47	30	−0 03	−0 14	+0 12	+0 04
81	21	Sat.	+07 15	+07 06	12 07	16.1	05 27	06 00	18 16	18 49	S35	−0 06	−0 15	+0 14	+0 07
82	22	Sun.	+06 57	+06 48	12 07	16.1	05 24	05 57	18 17	18 51	40	−0 10	−0 17	+0 15	+0 11
83	23	Mon.	+06 39	+06 30	12 07	16.1	05 22	05 55	18 19	18 53	45	−0 13	−0 18	+0 17	+0 14
84	24	Tu.	+06 21	+06 12	12 06	16.1	05 20	05 53	18 21	18 55	S50	−0 18	−0 20	+0 19	+0 20
85	25	Wed.	+06 03	+05 54	12 06	16.1	05 17	05 50	18 22	18 56					
86	26	Th.	+05 45	+05 36	12 06	16.1	05 15	05 48	18 24	18 58					
87	27	Fri.	+05 27	+05 18	12 05	16.1	05 12	05 46	18 26	19 00					
88	28	Sat.	+05 08	+04 59	12 05	16.0	05 10	05 43	18 27	19 01					
89	29	Sun.	+04 50	+04 41	12 05	16.0	05 07	05 41	18 29	19 03					
90	30	Mon.	+04 32	+04 23	12 04	16.0	05 05	05 39	18 31	19 05					
91	31	Tu.	+04 14	+04 05	12 04	16.0	05 02	05 37	18 32	19 07					

NOTES

The Lat. corr. to sunrise, etc., is for the middle of March. Examples of how to use the above data are given on page 2:11 onwards.

Equation of Time is the excess of Mean Time over Apparent Time
(See explanation and examples on p. 2:15)

☾ MOON ☽

DATE Yr.	Mth.	Week	Age days	Transit Diff. (Upper)		Semi-diam.	Hor. Par. 12 h.	Lat. 52°N. Moonrise	Moonset	MOON'S PHASES
				h. m.	m.	′	′	h. m.	h. m.	
61	1	Sun.	27	09 55	44	14.7	54.0	05 20	14 40	
62	2	Mon.	28	10 39	44	14.8	54.2	05 39	15 49	d. h. m.
63	3	Tu.	29	11 21	42	14.8	54.4	05 56	16 58	● New Moon 4 13 22
64	4	Wed.	30	12 02	41	14.9	54.7	06 11	18 07	☽ First Quarter........... 12 02 36
65	5	Th.	01	12 44	42	15.0	55.1	06 25	19 17	○ Full Moon 18 18 18
66	6	Fri.	02	13 27	43	15.1	55.5	06 41	20 29	☾ Last Quarter........... 26 02 30
67	7	Sat.	03	14 12	45	15.2	55.9	06 58	21 43	
68	8	Sun.	04	15 00	48	15.4	56.4	07 18	22 58	
69	9	Mon.	05	15 51	51	15.5	57.0	07 44	— —	d. h.
70	10	Tu.	06	16 45	54	15.7	57.6	08 18	00 12	Perigee 16 18
71	11	Wed.	07	17 43	58	15.9	58.2	09 03	01 23	Apogee 28 14
72	12	Th.	08	18 42	59	16.0	58.8	10 02	02 25	
73	13	Fri	09	19 41	59	16.2	59.4	11 14	03 15	
74	14	Sat.	10	20 39	58	16.3	60.0	12 35	03 55	
75	15	Sun.	11	21 35	56	16.4	60.3	14 02	04 25	
76	16	Mon.	12	22 29	54	16.5	60.5	15 29	04 49	
77	17	Tu.	13	23 21	52	16.5	60.4	16 56	05 10	
78	18	Wed.	14	24 12	51	16.4	60.1	18 21	05 29	NOTES
79	19	Th.	15	00 12	52	16.2	59.6	19 46	05 48	Moon's G.H.A. and Dec. are given
80	20	Fri.	16	01 04	52	16.0	58.8	21 09	06 08	on page 3:27.
81	21	Sat.	17	01 55	51	15.8	58.0	22 28	06 32	A table for correcting Moonrise and
82	22	Sun	18	02 48	53	15.6	57.1	23 42	07 00	Moonset for latitude is on page 4:20.
83	23	Mon	19	03 42	54	15.3	56.3	— —	07 36	A table for correcting Moon's meri-
84	24	Tu.	20	04 35	53	15.1	55.6	00 47	08 20	dian passage for longitude is on page
85	25	Wed.	21	05 27	52	15.0	55.0	01 41	09 14	4:19.
86	26	Th.	22	06 17	48	14.9	54.5	02 24	10 15	Examples on the use of the above
87	27	Fri.	23	07 05	46	14.8	54.3	02 57	11 20	data are given on page 2:11 onwards.
88	28	Sat.	24	07 51	44	14.8	54.2	03 23	12 28	
89	29	Sun.	25	08 35	42	14.8	54.2	03 44	13 36	
90	30	Mon.	26	09 17	42	14.8	54.4	04 01	14 45	
91	31	Tu.	27	09 59	42	14.9	54.7	04 17	15 54	

0h. = midnight. For explanation of use of above data see page 2:11 onwards.

0h. G.M.T. MARCH 1　　★ ★ STARS ★ ★　　0h. G.M.T. MARCH 1

No.	Name	Mag.	Transit (approx.) h. m.	DEC. ° '	G.H.A. ° '	R.A. h. m.	S.H.A. ° '
♈	ARIES	–	13 22		159 03.0	–	–
1	Alpheratz	2.2	13 30	N29 02.9	157 03.3	0 08	358 00.3
2	Ankaa	2.4	13 47	S42 20.9	152 34.6	0 26	353 31.6
3	Schedar	2.5	14 02	N56 29.8	149 02.4	0 40	349 59.4
4	Diphda	2.2	14 05	S18 01.8	148 15.1	0 43	349 12.1
5	Achernar	0.6	14 59	S57 16.7	134 41.9	1 37	335 38.9
6	POLARIS	2.1	15 44	N89 14.1	123 24.2	2 23	324 21.2
7	Hamal	2.2	15 28	N23 25.6	127 22.0	2 07	328 19.0
8	Acamar	3.1	16 19	S40 20.3	114 33.6	2 58	315 30.6
9	Menkar	2.8	16 23	N 4 03.6	113 34.9	3 02	314 31.9
10	Mirfak	1.9	16 45	N49 50.2	108 06.5	3 24	309 03.5
11	Aldebaran	1.1	17 56	N16 29.7	90 10.7	4 35	291 07.7
12	Rigel	0.3	18 35	S 8 12.7	80 30.3	5 14	281 27.3
13	Capella	0.2	18 37	N45 59.6	80 01.0	5 16	280 58.0
14	Bellatrix	1.7	18 45	N 6 20.5	77 52.0	5 25	278 49.0
15	Elnath	1.8	18 47	N28 36.2	77 35.7	5 26	278 32.7
16	Alnilam	1.8	18 57	S 1 12.5	75 05.5	5 36	276 02.5
17	Betelgeuse	{ 0.1 1.2	19 15	N 7 24.3	70 21.4	5 55	271 18.4
18	Canopus	-0.9	19 44	S52 41.8	63 06.1	6 24	264 03.1
19	Sirius	-1.6	20 05	S16 42.5	57 50.6	6 45	258 47.6
20	Adhara	1.6	20 19	S28 57.9	54 27.9	6 58	255 24.9
21	Castor	1.6	20 55	N31 54.4	45 30.9	7 34	246 27.9
22	Procyon	0.5	20 59	N 5 14.6	44 19.1	7 39	245 16.1
23	Pollux	1.2	21 05	N28 02.7	42 49.9	7 45	243 46.9
24	Avior	1.7	21 43	S59 29.4	33 27.2	8 22	234 24.2
25	Suhail	2.2	22 28	S43 24.3	22 06.8	9 08	223 03.8
26	Miaplacidus	1.8	22 33	S69 41.4	20 45.5	9 13	221 42.5
27	Alphard	2.2	22 47	S 8 37.7	17 14.4	9 27	218 11.4
28	Regulus	1.3	23 28	N12 00.1	7 03.1	10 08	208 00.1
29	Dubhe	2.0	00 27	N61 47.5	353 13.2	11 03	194 10.2
30	Denebola	2.2	01 12	N14 36.7	341 52.5	11 49	182 49.5
31	Gienah	2.8	01 39	S17 30.2	335 11.3	12 15	176 08.3
32	Acrux	1.1	01 50	S63 03.5	332 29.6	12 26	173 26.6
33	Gacrux	1.6	01 54	S57 04.3	331 21.2	12 31	172 18.2
34	Mimosa	1.5	02 11	S59 38.9	327 13.2	12 47	168 10.2
35	Alioth	1.7	02 17	N55 59.8	325 36.9	12 54	166 33.9
36	Spica	1.2	02 48	S11 07.5	317 50.7	13 25	158 47.7
37	Alkaid	1.9	03 11	N49 20.8	312 13.9	13 47	153 10.9
38	Hadar	0.9	03 27	S60 20.2	308 13.1	14 03	149 10.1
39	Menkent	2.3	03 29	S36 20.0	307 29.1	14 06	148 26.1
40	Arcturus	0.2	03 39	N19 13.1	305 12.9	14 15	146 09.9
41	Rigil Kent	0.1	04 02	S60 48.1	299 16.1	14 39	140 13.1
42	Zuben'ubi	2.9	04 14	S16 00.8	296 25.8	14 50	137 22.8
43	Kochab	2.2	04 14	N74 10.9	296 21.4	14 51	137 18.4
44	Alphecca	2.3	04 57	N26 44.1	285 27.2	15 34	126 24.2
45	Antares	1.2	05 52	S26 25.0	271 48.7	16 29	112 45.7
46	Atria	1.9	06 11	S69 00.7	267 04.7	16 48	108 01.7
47	Sabik	2.6	06 33	S15 43.0	261 33.7	17 10	102 30.7
48	Shaula	1.7	06 56	S37 05.9	255 46.5	17 33	96 43.5
49	Rasalhague	2.1	06 57	N12 33.7	255 24.2	17 35	96 21.2
50	Eltanin	2.4	07 19	N51 29.0	249 56.9	17 56	90 53.6
51	Kaus Aust.	2.0	07 46	S34 23.3	243 07.9	18 24	84 04.9
52	Vega	0.1	07 59	N38 46.3	239 52.8	18 37	80 49.8
53	Nunki	2.1	08 17	S26 18.4	235 21.1	18 55	76 18.1
54	Altair	0.9	09 13	N 8 50.7	221 26.9	19 50	62 23.9
55	Peacock	2.1	09 47	S56 45.5	212 47.4	20 25	53 44.4
56	Deneb	1.3	10 03	N45 14.9	208 45.7	20 41	49 42.7
57	Enif	2.5	11 06	N 9 50.3	193 06.0	21 44	34 03.0
58	Al Na'ir	2.2	11 30	S46 59.9	187 06.9	22 08	28 03.9
59	Fomalhaut	1.3	12 19	S29 39.8	174 44.7	22 57	15 41.7
60	Markab	2.6	12 26	N15 09.8	172 57.5	23 04	13 54.5

Stars Transit Correction Table

D. of Mth.	Corr (Sub.) h. m.	D. of Mth.	Corr. (Sub.) h. m.
1	-0 00	17	-1 03
2	-0 04	18	-1 07
3	-0 08	19	-1 11
4	-0 12	20	-1 15
5	-0 16	21	-1 19
6	-0 20	22	-1 23
7	-0 24	23	-1 27
8	-0 28	24	-1 30
9	-0 31	25	-1 34
10	-0 35	26	-1 38
11	-0 39	27	-1 42
12	-0 43	28	-1 46
13	-0 47	29	-1 50
14	-0 51	30	-1 54
15	-0 55	31	-1 58
16	-0 59		

STAR'S TRANSIT

To find the approx. time of Transit of a Star for any day of the month use above table.

If the quantity taken from the table is greater than the time of Transit for the first of the month, add 23h. 56min. to the time of transit before subtracting the correction below.

Example: A bright star in the Southern hemisphere is observed on the Meridian at 19h. 24min. on March 6th. What is it?

	h.min.
Transit on March 6th	19 24
Corr. for the 6th	+00 20
Transit on March 1st	19 44

Answer: Canopus (No: 18) Mag. –0.9

MARCH DIARY

d.	h.	
1	18	Mars 4°S. of Moon
2	01	Saturn 4°S. of Moon
2	06	Venus 4°S. of Moon
4	13	New Moon
6	06	Mercury 4°S. of Moon
6	13	Mars 0°.4S. of Saturn
9	21	Mercury greatest elong. E.(18°)
12	03	First Quarter
16	15	Mercury stationary
16	18	Moon at perigee
17	12	Jupiter 6°N. of Moon
18	18	Full Moon
20	09	Equinox
26	02	Last Quarter
26	15	Mercury in inferior conjunction
28	14	Moon at apogee
29	14	Saturn 4°S. of Moon
31	01	Mars 6°S. of Moon

STAR TIME

The best time to take Star observations is shown in the a.m. and p.m. TWILIGHT columns on the opposite page – corrected for Latitude.

For **Lighting-up Time** (ashore) add 30 mins to Sunset Times.

For Star's G.H.A. Correction Table, see page 4:8.

For Alphabetical List of Stars with Constellation names, see page 2:24.

For Examples on the use of the above data, see page 2:11.

For full directions for finding the above 60 Stars, see p. 2:20 onwards. For Special Pole Star tables see pages 5:17-5:19.

Sunday, 1st March

h	SUN G.H.A.	Dec.	ARIES G.H.A.
00	176 54.0	S 7 34.2	159 03.0
02	206 54.3	7 32.3	189 07.9
04	236 54.5	7 30.4	219 12.8
06	266 54.8	7 28.5	249 17.8
08	296 55.0	7 26.6	279 22.7
10	326 55.3	7 24.7	309 27.6
12	356 55.5	7 22.8	339 32.5
14	26 55.7	7 20.9	9 37.5
16	56 56.0	7 19.0	39 42.4
18	86 56.2	7 17.1	69 47.3
20	116 56.5	7 15.2	99 52.3
22	146 56.7	S 7 13.3	129 57.2

Monday, 2nd March

h	SUN G.H.A.	Dec.	ARIES G.H.A.
00	176 57.0	S 7 11.4	160 02.1
02	206 57.2	7 09.5	190 07.0
04	236 57.5	7 07.5	220 12.0
06	266 57.8	7 05.6	250 16.9
08	296 58.0	7 03.7	280 21.8
10	326 58.3	7 01.8	310 26.8
12	356 58.5	6 59.9	340 31.7
14	26 58.8	6 58.0	10 36.6
16	56 59.0	6 56.1	40 41.5
18	86 59.3	6 54.1	70 46.5
20	116 59.6	6 52.2	100 51.4
22	146 59.8	S 6 50.3	130 56.3

Tuesday, 3rd March

h	SUN G.H.A.	Dec.	ARIES G.H.A.
00	177 00.1	S 6 48.4	161 01.2
02	207 00.3	6 46.5	191 06.2
04	237 00.6	6 44.6	221 11.1
06	267 00.9	6 42.6	251 16.0
08	297 01.1	6 40.7	281 21.0
10	327 01.4	6 38.8	311 25.9
12	357 01.7	6 36.9	341 30.8
14	27 01.9	6 35.0	11 35.7
16	57 02.2	6 33.0	41 40.7
18	87 02.5	6 31.1	71 45.6
20	117 02.7	6 29.2	101 50.5
22	147 03.0	S 6 27.3	131 55.5

Wednesday, 4th March

h	SUN G.H.A.	Dec.	ARIES G.H.A.
00	177 03.3	S 6 25.3	162 00.4
02	207 03.5	6 23.4	192 05.3
04	237 03.8	6 21.5	222 10.2
06	267 04.1	6 19.6	252 15.2
08	297 04.4	6 17.6	282 20.1
10	327 04.6	6 15.7	312 25.0
12	357 04.9	6 13.8	342 30.0
14	27 05.2	6 11.8	12 34.9
16	57 05.5	6 09.9	42 39.8
18	87 05.7	6 08.0	72 44.7
20	117 06.0	6 06.0	102 49.7
22	147 06.3	S 6 04.1	132 54.6

Thursday, 5th March

h	SUN G.H.A.	Dec.	ARIES G.H.A.
00	177 06.6	S 6 02.2	162 59.5
02	207 06.9	6 00.3	193 04.5
04	237 07.1	5 58.3	223 09.4
06	267 07.4	5 56.4	253 14.3
08	297 07.7	5 54.4	283 19.2
10	327 08.0	5 52.5	313 24.2
12	357 08.3	5 50.6	343 29.1
14	27 08.6	5 48.6	13 34.0
16	57 08.9	5 46.7	43 39.0
18	87 09.1	5 44.8	73 43.9
20	117 09.4	5 42.8	103 48.8
22	147 09.7	S 5 40.9	133 53.7

Friday, 6th March

h	SUN G.H.A.	Dec.	ARIES G.H.A.
00	177 10.0	S 5 39.0	163 58.7
02	207 10.3	5 37.0	194 03.6
04	237 10.6	5 35.1	224 08.5
06	267 10.9	5 33.1	254 13.5
08	297 11.2	5 31.2	284 18.4
10	327 11.5	5 29.2	314 23.3
12	357 11.7	5 27.3	344 28.2
14	27 12.0	5 25.4	14 33.2
16	57 12.3	5 23.4	44 38.1
18	87 12.6	5 21.5	74 43.0
20	117 12.9	5 19.5	104 47.9
22	147 13.2	S 5 17.6	134 52.9

Saturday, 7th March

h	SUN G.H.A.	Dec.	ARIES G.H.A.
00	177 13.5	S 5 15.6	164 57.8
02	207 13.8	5 13.7	195 02.7
04	237 14.1	5 11.8	225 07.7
06	267 14.4	5 09.8	255 12.6
08	297 14.7	5 07.9	285 17.5
10	327 15.0	5 05.9	315 22.4
12	357 15.3	5 04.0	345 27.4
14	27 15.6	5 02.0	15 32.3
16	57 15.9	5 00.1	45 37.2
18	87 16.2	4 58.1	75 42.2
20	117 16.5	4 56.2	105 47.1
22	147 16.8	S 4 54.2	135 52.0

Sunday, 8th March

h	SUN G.H.A.	Dec.	ARIES G.H.A.
00	177 17.1	S 4 52.3	165 56.9
02	207 17.4	4 50.3	196 01.9
04	237 17.8	4 48.4	226 06.8
06	267 18.1	4 46.4	256 11.7
08	297 18.4	4 44.5	286 16.7
10	327 18.7	4 42.5	316 21.6
12	357 19.0	4 40.6	346 26.5
14	27 19.3	4 38.6	16 31.4
16	57 19.6	4 36.6	46 36.4
18	87 19.9	4 34.7	76 41.3
20	117 20.2	4 32.7	106 46.2
22	147 20.5	S 4 30.8	136 51.2

Monday, 9th March

h	SUN G.H.A.	Dec.	ARIES G.H.A.
00	177 20.9	S 4 28.8	166 56.1
02	207 21.2	4 26.9	197 01.0
04	237 21.5	4 24.9	227 05.9
06	267 21.8	4 23.0	257 10.9
08	297 22.1	4 21.0	287 15.8
10	327 22.4	4 19.0	317 20.7
12	357 22.7	4 17.1	347 25.7
14	27 23.1	4 15.1	17 30.6
16	57 23.4	4 13.2	47 35.5
18	87 23.7	4 11.2	77 40.4
20	117 24.0	4 09.2	107 45.4
22	147 24.3	S 4 07.3	137 50.3

Tuesday, 10th March

h	SUN G.H.A.	Dec.	ARIES G.H.A.
00	177 24.7	S 4 05.3	167 55.2
02	207 25.0	4 03.4	198 00.1
04	237 25.3	4 01.4	228 05.1
06	267 25.6	3 59.4	258 10.0
08	297 25.9	3 57.5	288 14.9
10	327 26.3	3 55.5	318 19.9
12	357 26.6	3 53.6	348 24.8
14	27 26.9	3 51.6	18 29.7
16	57 27.2	3 49.6	48 34.6
18	87 27.6	3 47.7	78 39.6
20	117 27.9	3 45.7	108 44.5
22	147 28.2	S 3 43.7	138 49.4

Wednesday, 11th March

h	SUN G.H.A.	Dec.	ARIES G.H.A.
00	177 28.6	S 3 41.8	168 54.4
02	207 28.9	3 39.8	198 59.3
04	237 29.2	3 37.9	229 04.2
06	267 29.5	3 35.9	259 09.1
08	297 29.9	3 33.9	289 14.1
10	327 30.2	3 32.0	319 19.0
12	357 30.5	3 30.0	349 23.9
14	27 30.9	3 28.0	19 28.9
16	57 31.2	3 26.1	49 33.8
18	87 31.5	3 24.1	79 38.7
20	117 31.9	3 22.1	109 43.6
22	147 32.2	S 3 20.2	139 48.6

Thursday, 12th March

h	SUN G.H.A.	Dec.	ARIES G.H.A.
00	177 32.5	S 3 18.2	169 53.5
02	207 32.9	3 16.2	199 58.4
04	237 33.2	3 14.3	230 03.4
06	267 33.5	3 12.3	260 08.3
08	297 33.9	3 10.3	290 13.2
10	327 34.2	3 08.4	320 18.1
12	357 34.5	3 06.4	350 23.1
14	27 34.9	3 04.4	20 28.0
16	57 35.2	3 02.4	50 32.9
18	87 35.6	3 00.5	80 37.9
20	117 35.9	2 58.5	110 42.8
22	147 36.2	S 2 56.5	140 47.7

Friday, 13th March

h	SUN G.H.A.	Dec.	ARIES G.H.A.
00	177 36.6	S 2 54.6	170 52.6
02	207 36.9	2 52.6	200 57.6
04	237 37.3	2 50.6	231 02.5
06	267 37.6	2 48.7	261 07.4
08	297 38.0	2 46.7	291 12.4
10	327 38.3	2 44.7	321 17.3
12	357 38.6	2 42.7	351 22.2
14	27 39.0	2 40.8	21 27.1
16	57 39.3	2 38.8	51 32.1
18	87 39.7	2 36.8	81 37.0
20	117 40.0	2 34.9	111 41.9
22	147 40.4	S 2 32.9	141 46.8

Saturday, 14th March

h	SUN G.H.A.	Dec.	ARIES G.H.A.
00	177 40.7	S 2 30.9	171 51.8
02	207 41.1	2 28.9	201 56.7
04	237 41.4	2 27.0	232 01.6
06	267 41.8	2 25.0	262 06.6
08	297 42.1	2 23.0	292 11.5
10	327 42.5	2 21.1	322 16.4
12	357 42.8	2 19.1	352 21.3
14	27 43.2	2 17.1	22 26.3
16	57 43.5	2 15.1	52 31.2
18	87 43.9	2 13.2	82 36.1
20	117 44.2	2 11.2	112 41.1
22	147 44.6	S 2 09.2	142 46.0

Sunday, 15th March

h	SUN G.H.A.	Dec.	ARIES G.H.A.
00	177 44.9	S 2 07.2	172 50.9
02	207 45.3	2 05.3	202 55.8
04	237 45.6	2 03.3	233 00.8
06	267 46.0	2 01.3	263 05.7
08	297 46.3	1 59.3	293 10.6
10	327 46.7	1 57.4	323 15.6
12	357 47.0	1 55.4	353 20.5
14	27 47.4	1 53.4	23 25.4
16	57 47.7	1 51.4	53 30.3
18	87 48.1	1 49.5	83 35.3
20	117 48.5	1 47.5	113 40.2
22	147 48.8	S 1 45.5	143 45.1

To interpolate **SUN** G.H.A. see page 4:7   To interpolate **ARIES** G.H.A. see page 4:8

Monday, 16th March

h	SUN G.H.A.	Dec.	ARIES G.H.A.
00	177 49.2	S 1 43.5	173 50.1
02	207 49.5	1 41.6	203 55.0
04	237 49.9	1 39.6	233 59.9
06	267 50.3	1 37.6	264 04.8
08	297 50.6	1 35.6	294 09.8
10	327 51.0	1 33.7	324 14.7
12	357 51.3	1 31.7	354 19.6
14	27 51.7	1 29.7	24 24.6
16	57 52.1	1 27.7	54 29.5
18	87 52.4	1 25.8	84 34.4
20	117 52.8	1 23.8	114 39.3
22	147 53.1	S 1 21.8	144 44.3

Tuesday, 17th March

h	SUN G.H.A.	Dec.	ARIES G.H.A.
00	177 53.5	S 1 19.8	174 49.2
02	207 53.9	1 17.9	204 54.1
04	237 54.2	1 15.9	234 59.0
06	267 54.6	1 13.9	265 04.0
08	297 55.0	1 11.9	295 08.9
10	327 55.3	1 10.0	325 13.8
12	357 55.7	1 08.0	355 18.8
14	27 56.0	1 06.0	25 23.7
16	57 56.4	1 04.0	55 28.6
18	87 56.8	1 02.0	85 33.5
20	117 57.1	1 00.1	115 38.5
22	147 57.5	S 0 58.1	145 43.4

Wednesday, 18th March

h	SUN G.H.A.	Dec.	ARIES G.H.A.
00	177 57.9	S 0 56.1	175 48.3
02	207 58.2	0 54.1	205 53.3
04	237 58.6	0 52.2	235 58.2
06	267 59.0	0 50.2	266 03.1
08	297 59.3	0 48.2	296 08.0
10	327 59.7	0 46.2	326 13.0
12	358 00.1	0 44.3	356 17.9
14	28 00.4	0 42.3	26 22.8
16	58 00.8	0 40.3	56 27.8
18	88 01.2	0 38.3	86 32.7
20	118 01.6	0 36.4	116 37.6
22	148 01.9	S 0 34.4	146 42.5

Thursday, 19th March

h	SUN G.H.A.	Dec.	ARIES G.H.A.
00	178 02.3	S 0 32.4	176 47.5
02	208 02.7	0 30.4	206 52.4
04	238 03.0	0 28.5	236 57.3
06	268 03.4	0 26.5	267 02.3
08	298 03.8	0 24.5	297 07.2
10	328 04.1	0 22.5	327 12.1
12	358 04.5	0 20.6	357 17.0
14	28 04.9	0 18.6	27 22.0
16	58 05.3	0 16.6	57 26.9
18	88 05.6	0 14.6	87 31.8
20	118 06.0	0 12.7	117 36.8
22	148 06.4	S 0 10.7	147 41.7

Friday, 20th March

h	SUN G.H.A.	Dec.	ARIES G.H.A.
00	178 06.8	S 0 08.7	177 46.6
02	208 07.1	0 06.7	207 51.5
04	238 07.5	0 04.7	237 56.5
06	268 07.9	0 02.8	268 01.4
08	298 08.2	0 00.8	298 06.3
10	328 08.6	N 0 01.2	328 11.3
12	358 09.0	0 03.2	358 16.2
14	28 09.4	0 05.1	28 21.1
16	58 09.7	0 07.1	58 26.0
18	88 10.1	0 09.1	88 31.0
20	118 10.5	0 11.0	118 35.9
22	148 10.9	N 0 13.0	148 40.8

Saturday, 21st March

h	SUN G.H.A.	Dec.	ARIES G.H.A.
00	178 11.2	N 0 15.0	178 45.7
02	208 11.6	0 17.0	208 50.7
04	238 12.0	0 18.9	238 55.6
06	268 12.4	0 20.9	269 00.5
08	298 12.7	0 22.9	299 05.5
10	328 13.1	0 24.9	329 10.4
12	358 13.5	0 26.8	359 15.3
14	28 13.9	0 28.8	29 20.2
16	58 14.2	0 30.8	59 25.2
18	88 14.6	0 32.8	89 30.1
20	118 15.0	0 34.7	119 35.0
22	148 15.4	N 0 36.7	149 40.0

Sunday, 22nd March

h	SUN G.H.A.	Dec.	ARIES G.H.A.
00	178 15.7	N 0 38.7	179 44.9
02	208 16.1	0 40.7	209 49.8
04	238 16.5	0 42.6	239 54.7
06	268 16.9	0 44.6	269 59.7
08	298 17.3	0 46.6	300 04.6
10	328 17.6	0 48.5	330 09.5
12	358 18.0	0 50.5	0 14.5
14	28 18.4	0 52.5	30 19.4
16	58 18.8	0 54.5	60 24.3
18	88 19.1	0 56.4	90 29.2
20	118 19.5	0 58.4	120 34.2
22	148 19.9	N 1 00.4	150 39.1

Monday, 23rd March

h	SUN G.H.A.	Dec.	ARIES G.H.A.
00	178 20.3	N 1 02.3	180 44.0
02	208 20.6	1 04.3	210 49.0
04	238 21.0	1 06.3	240 53.9
06	268 21.4	1 08.2	270 58.8
08	298 21.8	1 10.2	301 03.7
10	328 22.2	1 12.2	331 08.7
12	358 22.5	1 14.2	1 13.6
14	28 22.9	1 16.1	31 18.5
16	58 23.3	1 18.1	61 23.5
18	88 23.7	1 20.1	91 28.4
20	118 24.0	1 22.0	121 33.3
22	148 24.4	N 1 24.0	151 38.2

Tuesday, 24th March

h	SUN G.H.A.	Dec.	ARIES G.H.A.
00	178 24.8	N 1 26.0	181 43.2
02	208 25.2	1 27.9	211 48.1
04	238 25.6	1 29.9	241 53.0
06	268 25.9	1 31.9	271 57.9
08	298 26.3	1 33.8	302 02.9
10	328 26.7	1 35.8	332 07.8
12	358 27.1	1 37.8	2 12.7
14	28 27.5	1 39.7	32 17.7
16	58 27.8	1 41.7	62 22.6
18	88 28.2	1 43.7	92 27.5
20	118 28.6	1 45.6	122 32.4
22	148 29.0	N 1 47.6	152 37.4

Wednesday, 25th March

h	SUN G.H.A.	Dec.	ARIES G.H.A.
00	178 29.3	N 1 49.6	182 42.3
02	208 29.7	1 51.5	212 47.2
04	238 30.1	1 53.5	242 52.2
06	268 30.5	1 55.5	272 57.1
08	298 30.9	1 57.4	303 02.0
10	328 31.2	1 59.4	333 06.9
12	358 31.6	2 01.4	3 11.9
14	28 32.0	2 03.3	33 16.8
16	58 32.4	2 05.3	63 21.7
18	88 32.8	2 07.2	93 26.7
20	118 33.1	2 09.2	123 31.6
22	148 33.5	N 2 11.2	153 36.5

Thursday, 26th March

h	SUN G.H.A.	Dec.	ARIES G.H.A.
00	178 33.9	N 2 13.1	183 41.4
02	208 34.3	2 15.1	213 46.4
04	238 34.6	2 17.1	243 51.3
06	268 35.0	2 19.0	273 56.2
08	298 35.4	2 21.0	304 01.2
10	328 35.8	2 22.9	334 06.1
12	358 36.2	2 24.9	4 11.0
14	28 36.5	2 26.9	34 15.9
16	58 36.9	2 28.8	64 20.9
18	88 37.3	2 30.8	94 25.8
20	118 37.7	2 32.7	124 30.7
22	148 38.0	N 2 34.7	154 35.7

Friday, 27th March

h	SUN G.H.A.	Dec.	ARIES G.H.A.
00	178 38.4	N 2 36.7	184 40.6
02	208 38.8	2 38.6	214 45.5
04	238 39.2	2 40.6	244 50.4
06	268 39.6	2 42.5	274 55.4
08	298 39.9	2 44.5	305 00.3
10	328 40.3	2 46.4	335 05.2
12	358 40.7	2 48.4	5 10.2
14	28 41.1	2 50.3	35 15.1
16	58 41.5	2 52.3	65 20.0
18	88 41.8	2 54.3	95 24.9
20	118 42.2	2 56.2	125 29.9
22	148 42.6	N 2 58.2	155 34.8

Saturday, 28th March

h	SUN G.H.A.	Dec.	ARIES G.H.A.
00	178 43.0	N 3 00.1	185 39.7
02	208 43.4	3 02.1	215 44.6
04	238 43.7	3 04.0	245 49.6
06	268 44.1	3 06.0	275 54.5
08	298 44.5	3 07.9	305 59.4
10	328 44.9	3 09.9	336 04.4
12	358 45.2	3 11.8	6 09.3
14	28 45.6	3 13.8	36 14.2
16	58 46.0	3 15.7	66 19.1
18	88 46.4	3 17.7	96 24.1
20	118 46.8	3 19.6	126 29.0
22	148 47.1	N 3 21.6	156 33.9

Sunday, 29th March

h	SUN G.H.A.	Dec.	ARIES G.H.A.
00	178 47.5	N 3 23.5	186 38.9
02	208 47.9	3 25.5	216 43.8
04	238 48.3	3 27.4	246 48.7
06	268 48.6	3 29.4	276 53.6
08	298 49.0	3 31.3	306 58.6
10	328 49.4	3 33.3	337 03.5
12	358 49.8	3 35.2	7 08.4
14	28 50.1	3 37.2	37 13.4
16	58 50.5	3 39.1	67 18.3
18	88 50.9	3 41.0	97 23.2
20	118 51.3	3 43.0	127 28.1
22	148 51.6	N 3 44.9	157 33.1

Monday, 30th March

h	SUN G.H.A.	Dec.	ARIES G.H.A.
00	178 52.0	N 3 46.9	187 38.0
02	208 52.4	3 48.8	217 42.9
04	238 52.8	3 50.8	247 47.9
06	268 53.1	3 52.7	277 52.8
08	298 53.5	3 54.6	307 57.7
10	328 53.9	3 56.6	338 02.6
12	358 54.3	3 58.5	8 07.6
14	28 54.6	4 00.5	38 12.5
16	58 55.0	4 02.4	68 17.4
18	88 55.4	4 04.3	98 22.4
20	118 55.8	4 06.3	128 27.3
22	148 56.1	N 4 08.2	158 32.2

Tuesday, 31st March

h	SUN G.H.A.	Dec.	ARIES G.H.A.
00	178 56.5	N 4 10.2	188 37.1
02	208 56.9	4 12.1	218 42.1
04	238 57.3	4 14.0	248 47.0
06	268 57.6	N 4 16.0	278 51.9
08	298 58.0	N 4 17.9	308 56.8
10	328 58.4	4 19.8	339 01.8
12	358 58.8	4 21.8	9 06.7
14	28 59.1	N 4 23.7	39 11.6
16	58 59.5	N 4 25.6	69 16.6
18	88 59.9	4 27.6	99 21.5
20	119 00.3	4 29.5	129 26.4
22	149 00.6	N 4 31.4	159 31.3

To interpolate SUN G.H.A. see page 4:7   To interpolate ARIES G.H.A. see page 4:8

♀ VENUS ♀ / ♃ JUPITER ♃

Mer. Pass. h. m.	G.H.A. Mean Var. 14°	Dec.	Mean Var.	M	Day of Week	G.H.A Mean Var. 15°	Dec.	Mean Var.	Mer. Pass h. m.
10 31	202 27.7 59.3	S17 11.1	0.8	1	SUN.	357 24.6 2.8	N 9 15.7	0.1	00 10
10 32	202 12.0 59.4	S16 51.9	0.8	2	Mon.	358 31.1 2.8	N 9 18.7	0.1	00 06
10 33	201 56.5 59.4	S16 32.2	0.8	3	Tu.	359 37.5 2.8	N 9 21.7	0.1	00 01
10 34	201 41.3 59.4	S16 12.0	0.9	4	Wed.	0 44.0 2.8	N 9 24.7	0.1	23 53
10 35	201 26.4 59.4	S15 51.4	0.9	5	Th.	1 50.5 2.8	N 9 27.7	0.1	23 48
10 36	201 11.7 59.4	S15 30.3	0.9	6	Fri.	2 56.9 2.8	N 9 30.7	0.1	23 44
10 37	200 57.3 59.4	S15 08.8	0.9	7	Sat.	4 03.3 2.8	N 9 33.6	0.1	23 39
10 38	200 43.1 59.4	S14 46.9	0.9	8	SUN.	5 09.7 2.8	N 9 36.6	0.1	23 35
10 38	200 29.2 59.4	S14 24.6	0.9	9	Mon.	6 16.1 2.8	N 9 39.4	0.1	23 31
10 39	200 15.6 59.4	S14 01.9	1.0	10	Tu.	7 22.4 2.8	N 9 42.3	0.1	23 26
10 40	200 02.2 59.5	S13 38.7	1.0	11	Wed.	8 28.6 2.8	N 9 45.2	0.1	23 22
10 41	199 49.1 59.5	S13 15.3	1.0	12	Th.	9 34.8 2.8	N 9 48.0	0.1	23 17
10 42	199 36.2 59.5	S12 51.4	1.0	13	Fri.	10 40.9 2.8	N 9 50.8	0.1	23 13
10 43	199 23.6 59.5	S12 27.2	1.0	14	Sat.	11 47.0 2.8	N 9 53.5	0.1	23 09
10 44	199 11.2 59.5	S12 02.7	1.0	15	SUN.	12 53.0 2.8	N 9 56.2	0.1	23 04
10 44	198 59.0 59.5	S11 37.8	1.1	16	Mon.	13 59.0 2.7	N 9 58.9	0.1	23 00
10 45	198 47.1 59.5	S11 12.6	1.1	17	Tu.	15 04.8 2.7	N10 01.5	0.1	22 55
10 46	198 35.4 59.5	S10 47.1	1.1	18	Wed.	16 10.6 2.7	N10 04.1	0.1	22 51
10 47	198 23.9 59.5	S10 21.3	1.1	19	Th.	17 16.3 2.7	N10 06.6	0.1	22 47
10 47	198 12.6 59.5	S 9 55.3	1.1	20	Fri.	18 21.9 2.7	N10 09.1	0.1	22 42
10 48	198 01.5 59.5	S 9 28.9	1.1	21	Sat.	19 27.3 2.7	N10 11.6	0.1	22 38
10 49	197 50.6 59.6	S 9 02.3	1.1	22	SUN.	20 32.7 2.7	N10 14.0	0.1	22 34
10 50	197 39.9 59.6	S 8 35.5	1.1	23	Mon.	21 38.0 2.7	N10 16.4	0.1	22 29
10 50	197 29.3 59.6	S 8 08.4	1.1	24	Tu.	22 43.2 2.7	N10 18.7	0.1	22 25
10 51	197 18.9 59.6	S 7 41.1	1.1	25	Wed.	23 48.3 2.7	N10 20.9	0.1	22 21
10 52	197 08.7 59.6	S 7 13.6	1.2	26	Th.	24 53.2 2.7	N10 23.2	0.1	22 16
10 52	196 58.7 59.6	S 6 45.9	1.2	27	Fri.	25 58.1 2.7	N10 25.3	0.1	22 12
10 53	196 48.8 59.6	S 6 18.0	1.2	28	Sat.	27 02.8 2.7	N10 27.4	0.1	22 08
10 54	196 39.0 59.6	S 5 50.0	1.2	29	SUN.	28 07.4 2.7	N10 29.4	0.1	22 04
10 54	196 29.4 59.6	S 5 21.7	1.2	30	Mon.	29 11.9 2.7	N10 31.4	0.1	21 59
10 55	196 19.8 59.6	S 4 53.3	1.2	31	Tu.	30 16.2 2.7	N10 33.4	0.1	21 55

♀ **VENUS.** Av. Mag. –3.9. A **Morning Star.** Do not confuse with Mars and Saturn early in March. In both cases Venus is the brighter object. **S.H.A.** March 5 38°; 10 32°; 15 27°; 20 20°; 25 14°; 30 9°.

♃ **JUPITER.** Av. Mag. –2.5. Can be seen throughout the night sky. **S.H.A.** March 5 199°; 10 201°; 15 199°; 20 201°; 25 202°; 30 200°.

♂ MARS ♂ / ♄ SATURN ♄

Mer. Pass. h. m.	G.H.A. Mean Var. 15°	Dec.	Mean Var.	M	Day of Week	G.H.A Mean Var. 15°	Dec.	Mean Var.	Mer. Pass h. m.
10 11	207 16.1 0.5	S18 59.1	0.5	1	SUN.	203 31.6 2.2	S17 34.8	0.1	10 24
10 10	207 28.0 0.5	S18 47.3	0.5	2	Mon.	204 24.0 2.2	S17 33.0	0.1	10 21
10 09	207 40.1 0.5	S18 35.2	0.5	3	Tu.	205 16.5 2.2	S17 31.2	0.1	10 17
10 08	207 52.2 0.5	S18 22.9	0.5	4	Wed.	206 09.1 2.2	S17 29.5	0.1	10 14
10 07	208 04.5 0.5	S18 10.5	0.5	5	Th.	207 01.6 2.2	S17 27.7	0.1	10 10
10 07	208 16.8 0.5	S17 57.9	0.5	6	Fri.	207 54.3 2.2	S17 26.0	0.1	10 07
10 06	208 29.2 0.5	S17 45.0	0.5	7	Sat.	208 46.9 2.2	S17 24.2	0.1	10 03
10 05	208 41.7 0.5	S17 32.0	0.5	8	SUN.	209 39.6 2.2	S17 22.5	0.1	10 00
10 04	208 54.3 0.5	S17 18.8	0.6	9	Mon.	210 32.4 2.2	S17 20.8	0.1	09 56
10 03	209 07.0 0.5	S17 05.5	0.6	10	Tu.	211 25.2 2.2	S17 19.0	0.1	09 53
10 02	209 19.8 0.5	S16 51.9	0.6	11	Wed.	212 18.0 2.2	S17 17.3	0.1	09 49
10 01	209 32.7 0.5	S16 38.2	0.6	12	Th.	213 10.9 2.2	S17 15.6	0.1	09 46
10 01	209 45.7 0.5	S16 24.4	0.6	13	Fri.	214 03.8 2.2	S17 14.0	0.1	09 42
10 00	209 58.8 0.6	S16 10.3	0.6	14	Sat.	214 56.8 2.2	S17 12.3	0.1	09 39
09 59	210 12.0 0.6	S15 56.1	0.6	15	SUN.	215 49.8 2.2	S17 10.6	0.1	09 35
09 58	210 25.3 0.6	S15 41.8	0.6	16	Mon.	216 42.9 2.2	S17 09.0	0.1	09 32
09 57	210 38.6 0.6	S15 27.2	0.6	17	Tu.	217 36.1 2.2	S17 07.4	0.1	09 28
09 56	210 52.1 0.6	S15 12.6	0.6	18	Wed.	218 29.2 2.2	S17 05.7	0.1	09 25
09 55	211 05.7 0.6	S14 57.8	0.6	19	Th.	219 22.5 2.2	S17 04.1	0.1	09 21
09 54	211 19.3 0.6	S14 42.8	0.6	20	Fri.	220 15.8 2.2	S17 02.6	0.1	09 18
09 53	211 33.1 0.6	S14 27.7	0.6	21	Sat.	221 09.2 2.2	S17 01.0	0.1	09 14
09 52	211 46.9 0.6	S14 12.4	0.6	22	SUN.	222 02.6 2.2	S16 59.4	0.1	09 10
09 52	212 00.9 0.6	S13 57.0	0.6	23	Mon.	222 56.1 2.2	S16 57.9	0.1	09 07
09 51	212 14.9 0.6	S13 41.5	0.6	24	Tu.	223 49.6 2.2	S16 56.3	0.1	09 03
09 50	212 29.0 0.6	S13 25.9	0.7	25	Wed.	224 43.2 2.2	S16 54.8	0.1	09 00
09 49	212 43.2 0.6	S13 10.1	0.7	26	Th.	225 36.8 2.2	S16 53.3	0.1	08 56
09 48	212 57.5 0.6	S12 54.2	0.7	27	Fri.	226 30.6 2.2	S16 51.9	0.1	08 53
09 47	213 11.9 0.6	S12 38.1	0.7	28	Sat.	227 24.3 2.2	S16 50.4	0.1	08 49
09 46	213 26.3 0.6	S12 22.0	0.7	29	SUN.	228 18.2 2.2	S16 48.9	0.1	08 45
09 45	213 40.9 0.6	S12 05.7	0.7	30	Mon.	229 12.1 2.3	S16 47.4	0.1	08 42
09 44	213 55.6 0.6	S11 49.3	0.7	31	Tu.	230 06.1 2.3	S16 46.1	0.1	08 38

♂ **MARS.** Av. Mag. +1.2. A **Morning Star.** Do not confuse with Saturn during first half of month when Mars is the brighter object. **S.H.A.** March 5 45°; 10 41°; 15 37°; 20 34°; 25 30°; 30 26°.

♄ **SATURN.** Av. Mag. +0.8. A **Morning Star.** In conjunction with Mars on March 6. **S.H.A.** March 5 44°; 10 44°; 15 42°; 20 42°; 25 43°; 30 41°.

MERCURY. Visible low in the west after sunset until March 19 when it becomes too close to the sun for observation.

Day of M. W.	G.M.T.	G.H.A.		Mean Var. per Hour	Dec.	Mean Var. per Hour	Day of M. W.	G.M.T.	G.H.A.		Mean Var. per Hour	Dec.	Mean Var. per Hour
	h	°	′	14°,+	° ′	′		h	°	′	14°,+	° ′	′
1 Sun.	0	215	35.7	33.0	S17 47.6	9.1	17 Tu.	0	22	00.3	28.4	N 6 44.9	15.0
	6	302	53.6	33.3	S16 53.5	9.5		6	108	50.4	28.6	N 5 15.3	15.2
	12	30	13.1	33.5	S15 56.8	9.9		12	195	41.7	28.7	N 3 44.6	15.2
	18	117	34.0	33.7	S14 57.7	10.3		18	282	33.9	28.8	N 2 13.3	15.2
2 Mon.	0	204	56.3	34.0	S13 56.4	10.6	18 Wed.	0	9	26.9	29.0	N 0 41.7	15.3
	6	292	19.8	34.1	S12 53.0	10.9		6	96	20.5	29.0	S 0 49.7	15.2
	12	19	44.5	34.3	S11 47.7	11.2		12	183	14.6	29.0	S 2 20.7	15.0
	18	107	10.2	34.5	S10 40.5	11.5		18	270	09.0	29.1	S 3 50.9	14.8
3 Tu.	0	194	36.8	34.6	S 9 31.7	11.7	19 Th.	0	357	03.5	29.1	S 5 19.9	14.6
	6	282	04.2	34.6	S 8 21.4	12.0		6	83	58.0	29.1	S 6 47.5	14.3
	12	9	32.1	34.8	S 7 09.8	12.2		12	170	52.3	29.0	S 8 13.1	13.9
	18	97	00.5	34.8	S 5 57.0	12.3		18	257	46.3	28.9	S 9 36.7	13.5
4 Wed.	0	184	29.1	34.8	S 4 43.2	12.5	20 Fri.	0	344	39.8	28.9	S10 57.8	13.0
	6	271	57.8	34.8	S 3 28.6	12.6		6	71	32.9	28.8	S12 16.1	12.5
	12	359	26.5	34.7	S 2 13.2	12.6		12	158	25.4	28.6	S13 31.5	12.0
	18	86	55.0	34.6	S 0 57.3	12.7		18	245	17.2	28.6	S14 43.6	11.4
5 Th.	0	174	23.0	34.5	N 0 18.9	12.7	21 Sat.	0	332	08.3	28.4	S15 52.2	10.8
	6	261	50.5	34.4	N 1 35.3	12.8		6	58	58.7	28.3	S16 57.1	10.1
	12	349	17.2	34.3	N 2 51.8	12.7		12	145	48.5	28.1	S17 58.1	9.4
	18	76	43.0	34.1	N 4 08.0	12.7		18	232	37.5	28.1	S18 55.0	8.7
6 Fri.	0	164	07.6	33.9	N 5 23.9	12.5	22 Sun.	0	319	26.0	28.0	S19 47.7	8.0
	6	251	31.0	33.6	N 6 39.3	12.4		6	46	13.9	27.9	S20 36.0	7.2
	12	338	52.8	33.4	N 7 53.9	12.3		12	133	01.4	27.8	S21 19.8	6.5
	18	66	13.0	33.1	N 9 07.5	12.0		18	219	48.6	27.8	S21 59.1	5.7
7 Sat.	0	153	31.4	32.7	N10 20.1	11.9	23 Mon.	0	306	35.7	27.9	S22 33.7	4.9
	6	240	47.7	32.4	N11 31.2	11.6		6	33	22.8	27.8	S23 03.5	4.1
	12	328	01.8	32.0	N12 40.8	11.3		12	120	10.0	28.0	S23 28.7	3.3
	18	55	13.6	31.5	N13 48.5	10.9		18	206	57.6	28.0	S23 49.1	2.5
8 Sun.	0	142	22.9	31.1	N14 54.3	10.5	24 Tu.	0	293	45.7	28.2	S24 04.7	1.7
	6	229	29.6	30.6	N15 57.7	10.1		6	20	34.6	28.3	S24 15.7	1.0
	12	316	33.5	30.1	N16 58.7	9.7		12	107	24.3	28.5	S24 21.9	0.3
	18	43	34.6	29.7	N17 56.8	9.2		18	194	15.1	28.7	S24 23.6	0.5
9 Mon.	0	130	32.8	29.1	N18 52.0	8.6	25 Wed.	0	281	07.2	28.9	S24 20.8	1.3
	6	217	28.0	28.6	N19 43.9	8.1		6	8	00.7	29.2	S24 13.5	2.0
	12	304	20.2	28.2	N20 32.3	7.3		12	94	55.8	29.5	S24 01.9	2.7
	18	31	09.4	27.7	N21 16.9	6.7		18	181	52.5	29.8	S23 46.0	3.4
10 Tu.	0	117	55.6	27.1	N21 57.4	6.0	26 Th.	0	268	51.0	30.1	S23 26.1	4.1
	6	204	38.8	26.7	N22 33.7	5.2		6	355	51.3	30.4	S23 02.2	4.7
	12	291	19.3	26.3	N23 05.5	4.5		12	82	53.6	30.7	S22 34.5	5.3
	18	17	57.2	25.8	N23 32.6	3.7		18	169	57.9	31.0	S22 03.1	5.9
11 Wed.	0	104	32.6	25.5	N23 54.7	2.8	27 Fri.	0	257	04.1	31.4	S21 28.2	6.4
	6	191	05.7	25.1	N24 11.6	1.9		6	344	12.4	31.7	S20 49.8	6.9
	12	277	36.8	24.9	N24 23.3	1.0		12	71	22.6	32.0	S20 08.3	7.5
	18	4	06.2	24.6	N24 29.4	0.0		18	158	34.8	32.4	S19 23.6	8.0
12 Th.	0	90	34.2	24.5	N24 30.0	1.0	28 Sat.	0	245	48.9	32.7	S18 35.9	8.4
	6	177	01.1	24.3	N24 24.9	1.9		6	333	04.8	32.9	S17 45.4	8.9
	12	263	27.3	24.3	N24 14.0	2.8		12	60	22.4	33.2	S16 52.3	9.3
	18	349	53.0	24.3	N23 57.4	3.8		18	147	41.6	33.4	S15 56.7	9.7
13 Fri.	0	76	18.7	24.3	N23 35.0	4.8	29 Sun.	0	235	02.4	33.7	S14 58.6	10.1
	6	162	44.7	24.4	N23 06.9	5.7		6	322	24.6	34.0	S13 58.4	10.5
	12	249	11.2	24.6	N22 33.1	6.7		12	49	48.1	34.1	S12 56.0	10.7
	18	335	38.6	24.8	N21 53.8	7.5		18	137	12.7	34.3	S11 51.7	11.1
14 Sat.	0	62	07.1	25.0	N21 09.2	8.4	30 Mon.	0	224	38.3	34.4	S10 45.6	11.3
	6	148	37.0	25.2	N20 19.3	9.2		6	312	04.8	34.5	S 9 37.8	11.5
	12	235	08.4	25.5	N19 24.5	10.0		12	39	31.9	34.6	S 8 28.5	11.8
	18	321	41.4	25.9	N18 24.9	10.7		18	126	59.5	34.7	S 7 17.8	12.0
15 Sun.	0	48	16.3	26.1	N17 20.8	11.4	31 Tu.	0	214	27.5	34.7	S 6 05.9	12.2
	6	134	53.0	26.5	N16 12.6	12.1		6	301	55.7	34.7	S 4 52.8	12.4
	12	221	31.6	26.7	N15 00.4	12.7		12	29	23.8	34.7	S 3 38.9	12.5
	18	308	12.0	27.0	N13 44.7	13.2		18	116	51.8	34.6	S 2 24.1	12.6
16 Mon.	0	34	54.3	27.3	N12 25.8	13.7							
	6	121	38.4	27.7	N11 04.0	14.1							
	12	208	24.2	27.9	N 9 39.6	14.5							
	18	295	11.5	28.1	N 8 13.2	14.7							

PHASES OF THE MOON

		d. h/min			d. h/min
●	New Moon	4 13 22	○	Full Moon	18 18 18
◗	First Quarter	12 02 36	◖	Last Quarter	26 02 30
	Perigee	16 18		Apogee	28 14

G.M.T.   (30 days)   G.M.T.

☉ SUN ☉

Yr.	Mth.	Week	Eq. of Time 0 h.	Eq. of Time 12 h.	Transit	Semi-diam.	Twilight	Sunrise	Sunset	Twilight	Lat.	Twilight	Sunrise	Sunset	Twilight
			m. s.	m. s.	h. m.	′	h. m.	h. m.	h. m.	h. m.	°	h. m.	h. m.	h. m.	h. m.
92	1	Wed.	+03 56	+03 47	12 04	16.0	05 00	05 35	18 34	19 09	N70	−1 50	−1 05	+1 09	+1 50
93	2	Th.	+03 39	+03 30	12 03	16.0	04 58	05 33	18 36	19 11	68	−1 26	−0 53	+0 55	+1 27
94	3	Fri.	+03 21	+03 12	12 03	16.0	04 55	05 30	18 37	19 12	66	−1 07	−0 42	+0 44	+1 08
95	4	Sat.	+03 03	+02 55	12 03	16.0	04 53	05 28	18 39	19 14	64	−0 52	−0 33	+0 35	+0 53
96	5	Sun.	+02 46	+02 38	12 03	16.0	04 51	05 26	18 41	19 16	62	−0 40	−0 26	+0 27	+0 41
97	6	Mon.	+02 29	+02 21	12 02	16.0	04 48	05 23	18 42	19 17	N60	−0 30	−0 19	+0 20	+0 30
98	7	Tu.	+02 12	+02 04	12 02	16.0	04 46	05 21	18 44	19 19	58	−0 21	−0 13	+0 14	+0 21
99	8	Wed.	+01 55	+01 47	12 02	16.0	04 44	05 19	18 46	19 21	56	−0 13	−0 08	+0 09	+0 13
100	9	Th.	+01 39	+01 31	12 02	16.0	04 41	05 16	18 48	19 23	54	−0 06	−0 04	+0 04	+0 06
101	10	Fri.	+01 23	+01 15	12 01	16.0	04 39	05 14	18 50	19 25	50	+0 05	+0 04	−0 04	−0 05
102	11	Sat.	+01 07	+00 59	12 01	16.0	04 37	05 12	18 52	19 27	N45	+0 17	+0 12	−0 11	−0 17
103	12	Sun.	+00 51	+00 43	12 01	16.0	04 34	05 09	18 53	19 28	40	+0 26	+0 19	−0 18	−0 25
104	13	Mon.	+00 35	+00 28	12 00	16.0	04 32	05 07	18 55	19 30	35	+0 33	+0 25	−0 24	−0 33
105	14	Tu.	+00 20	+00 13	12 00	16.0	04 30	05 05	18 57	19 32	30	+0 40	+0 30	−0 29	−0 40
106	15	Wed.	+00 05	−00 02	12 00	16.0	04 27	05 03	18 58	19 34	20	+0 51	+0 38	−0 38	−0 50
107	16	Th.	−00 09	−00 16	12 00	16.0	04 25	05 01	19 00	19 36	N10	+0 59	+0 45	−0 42	−0 59
108	17	Fri.	−00 23	−00 30	11 59	16.0	04 23	04 59	19 02	19 38	0	+1 07	+0 52	−0 53	−1 07
109	18	Sat.	−00 37	−00 44	11 59	15.9	04 20	04 56	19 03	19 40	S10	+1 12	+0 59	−0 59	−1 13
110	19	Sun.	−00 50	−00 57	11 59	15.9	04 18	04 54	19 05	19 42	20	+1 18	+1 05	−1 06	−1 18
111	20	Mon.	−01 03	−01 10	11 59	15.9	04 16	04 52	19 07	19 44	30	+1 24	+1 13	−1 15	−1 27
112	21	Tu.	−01 16	−01 22	11 59	15.9	04 13	04 50	19 08	19 45	S35	+1 27	+1 17	−1 19	−1 27
113	22	Wed.	−01 28	−01 34	11 58	15.9	04 11	04 48	19 10	19 47	40	+1 30	+1 22	−1 24	−1 30
114	23	Th.	−01 40	−01 45	11 58	15.9	04 09	04 46	19 12	19 49	45	+1 34	+1 28	−1 30	−1 34
115	24	Fri.	−01 51	−01 56	11 58	15.9	04 06	04 44	19 13	19 51	S50	+1 38	+1 35	−1 36	−1 38
116	25	Sat.	−02 01	−02 06	11 58	15.9	04 04	04 42	19 15	19 53					
117	26	Sun.	−02 11	−02 16	11 58	15.9	04 02	04 40	19 17	19 55					
118	27	Mon.	−02 21	−02 26	11 58	15.9	04 00	04 38	19 18	19 57					
119	28	Tu.	−02 30	−02 34	11 57	15.9	03 58	04 36	19 20	19 59					
120	29	Wed.	−02 39	−02 43	11 57	15.9	03 56	04 34	19 22	20 01					
121	30	Th.	−02 47	−02 50	11 57	15.9	03 53	04 32	19 23	20 02					

NOTES

*Equation of time changes its sign from plus to minus on the 15th. The Lat. Corr. to sunrise, sunset, etc., is for the middle of April. Examples of how to use the above data are given on page 2:11 onwards.

Equation of Time is the excess of Mean Time over Apparent Time
(See explanation and examples on p. 2:15)

☾ MOON ☽

Yr.	Mth.	Week	Age days	Transit (Upper) h. m.	Diff. m.	Semi-diam.	Hor. Par. 12 h.	Moonrise	Moonset
				h. m.	m.	′	′	h. m.	h. m.
92	1	Wed.	28	10 41	43	15.0	55.2	04 32	17 04
93	2	Th.	29	11 24	45	15.2	55.6	04 47	18 15
94	3	Fri.	00	12 09	47	15.3	56.1	05 04	19 29
95	4	Sat.	01	12 56	51	15.4	56.6	05 24	20 45
96	5	Sun.	02	13 47	54	15.6	57.1	05 49	22 01
97	6	Mon.	03	14 41	57	15.7	57.6	06 20	23 13
98	7	Tu.	04	15 38	59	15.8	58.1	07 02	– –
99	8	Wed.	05	16 37	58	15.9	58.5	07 57	00 18
100	9	Th.	06	17 35	57	16.0	58.9	09 05	01 12
101	10	Fri.	07	18 32	55	16.1	59.2	10 22	01 54
102	11	Sat.	08	19 27	53	16.2	59.4	11 45	02 26
103	12	Sun	09	20 20	51	16.2	59.6	13 09	02 52
104	13	Mon.	10	21 11	50	16.2	59.6	14 32	03 13
105	14	Tu.	11	22 01	50	16.2	59.5	15 56	03 32
106	15	Wed.	12	22 51	51	16.1	59.2	17 18	03 51
107	16	Th.	13	23 42	53	16.0	58.8	18 41	04 10
108	17	Fri.	14	24 35	–	15.9	58.2	20 02	04 32
109	18	Sat.	15	00 35	53	15.7	57.6	21 19	04 59
110	19	Sun.	16	01 28	54	15.5	56.9	22 29	05 31
111	20	Mon.	17	02 22	54	15.3	56.2	23 29	06 13
112	21	Tu.	18	03 16	52	15.1	55.5	– –	07 03
113	22	Wed.	19	04 08	50	15.0	55.0	00 17	08 02
114	23	Th.	20	04 58	47	14.9	54.6	01 23	09 07
115	24	Fri.	21	05 45	44	14.8	54.3	01 46	10 14
116	25	Sat	22	06 29	43	14.8	54.2	02 05	11 22
117	26	Sun.	23	07 12	42	14.8	54.4	02 22	12 30
118	27	Mon.	24	07 54	42	14.9	54.6	02 37	13 38
119	28	Tu.	25	08 36	42	15.0	55.0	02 52	14 47
120	29	Wed.	26	09 18	44	15.1	55.5	03 09	15 58
121	30	Th.	27	10 02	47	15.3	56.2	03 25	17 11

MOON'S PHASES

		d.	h.	m.
●	New Moon	3	05	01
☽	First Quarter...........	10	10	06
○	Full Moon	17	04	42
☾	Last Quarter	24	21	40

		d.	h.
	Perigee	13	07
	Apogee	25	10

NOTES

Moon's G.H.A. and Dec. are given on page 3:33.
A table for correcting Moonrise and Moonset for latitude is on page 4:20.
A table for correcting Moon's meridian passage for longitude is on page 4:19.
Examples on the use of the above data are given on page 2:11 onwards.

0h. = midnight. For explanation of use of above data see page 2:11 onwards.

0h. G.M.T. APRIL 1   ★ ★ STARS ★ ★   **0h. G.M.T. APRIL 1**

No.	Name	Mag.	Transit (approx.)	DEC.	G.H.A.	R.A.	S.H.A.
			h. m.	° ′	° ′	h. m.	° ′
♈	ARIES	–	11 20	–	189 36.3	–	–
1	Alpheratz	2.2	11 28	N29 02.8	187 36.6	0 08	358 00.3
2	Ankaa	2.4	11 46	S42 20.8	183 07.9	0 26	353 31.6
3	Schedar........	2.5	12 00	N56 29.7	179 35.6	0 40	349 59.3
4	Diphda	2.2	12 03	S18 01.7	178 48.3	0 43	349 12.0
5	Achernar	0.6	12 57	S57 16.5	165 15.2	1 37	335 38.9
6	POLARIS	2.1	13 42	N89 13.9	154 02.0	2 22	324 25.7
7	Hamal	2.2	13 26	N23 25.6	157 55.3	2 07	328 19.0
8	Acamar	3.1	14 17	S40 20.2	145 07.0	2 58	315 30.7
9	Menkar	2.8	14 21	N 4 03.6	144 08.2	3 02	314 31.9
10	Mirfak	1.9	14 43	N49 50.2	13 39.9	3 24	309 03.6
11	Aldebaran.....	1.1	15 54	N16 29.7	120 44.1	4 35	291 07.8
12	Rigel	0.3	16 33	S 8 12.7	111 03.8	5 14	281 27.5
13	Capella	0.2	16 35	N45 59.6	110 34.4	5 16	280 58.1
14	Bellatrix	1.7	16 44	N 6 20.5	108 25.5	5 25	278 49.2
15	Elnath	1.8	16 45	N28 36.1	108 09.1	5 26	278 32.8
16	Alnilam	1.8	16 55	S 1 12.5	105 38.9	5 36	276 02.6
17	Betelgeuse ...	{ 0.1 / 1.2 }	17 14	N 7 24.3	100 54.9	5 55	271 18.6
18	Canopus	-0.9	17 42	S52 41.8	93 39.7	6 24	264 03.4
19	Sirius	-1.6	18 03	S16 42.5	88 24.0	6 45	258 47.7
20	Adhara	1.6	18 17	S28 57.9	85 01.3	6 58	255 25.0
21	Castor	1.6	18 53	N31 54.4	76 04.4	7 34	246 28.1
22	Procyon........	0.5	18 57	N 5 14.6	74 52.6	7 39	245 16.3
23	Pollux	1.2	19 03	N28 02.7	73 23.3	7 45	243 47.0
24	Avior	1.7	19 41	S59 29.5	64 00.8	8 22	234 24.5
25	Suhail	2.2	20 26	S43 24.4	52 40.3	9 08	223 04.0
26	Miaplacidus ...	1.8	20 31	S69 41.5	51 19.1	9 13	221 42.8
27	Alphard........	2.2	20 45	S 8 37.7	47 47.8	9 27	218 11.5
28	Regulus........	1.3	21 26	N12 00.2	37 36.4	10 08	208 00.1
29	Dubhe	2.0	22 21	N61 47.6	23 46.6	11 03	194 10.3
30	Denebola	2.2	23 06	N14 36.7	12 25.8	11 49	182 49.5
31	Gienah	2.8	23 33	S17 30.2	5 44.6	12 15	176 08.3
32	Acrux..........	1.1	23 44	S63 03.7	3 02.9	12 26	173 26.6
33	Gacrux	1.6	23 48	S57 04.5	1 54.5	12 31	172 18.2
34	Mimosa........	1.5	00 09	S59 39.0	357 46.4	12 47	168 10.1
35	Alioth..........	1.7	00 15	N56 00.0	356 10.1	12 54	166 33.8
36	Spica	1.2	00 46	S11 07.5	348 23.9	13 25	158 47.6
37	Alkaid	1.9	01 09	N49 20.9	342 47.0	13 47	153 10.7
38	Hadar..........	0.9	01 25	S60 20.3	338 46.2	14 03	149 09.9
39	Menkent	2.3	01 28	S36 20.1	338 02.2	14 06	148 25.9
40	Arcturus	0.2	01 37	N19 13.1	335 46.1	14 15	146 09.8
41	Rigil Kent.....	0.1	02 00	S60 48.3	329 49.1	14 39	140 12.8
42	Zuben'ubi	2.9	02 12	S16 00.8	326 59.0	14 50	137 22.7
43	Kochab	2.2	02 12	N74 11.0	326 54.3	14 51	137 18.0
44	Alphecca	2.3	02 55	N26 44.2	316 00.4	15 34	126 24.1
45	Antares	1.2	03 50	S26 25.0	302 21.7	16 29	112 45.4
46	Atria	1.9	04 09	S69 00.7	297 37.5	16 48	108 01.2
47	Sabik	2.6	04 31	S15 43.0	292 06.8	17 10	102 30.5
48	Shaula	1.7	04 54	S37 05.9	286 19.5	17 33	96 43.2
49	Rasalhague ...	2.1	04 55	N12 33.7	285 57.3	17 35	96 21.0
50	Eltanin	2.4	05 17	N51 29.1	280 29.6	17 56	90 53.3
51	Kaus Aust. ...	2.0	05 44	S34 23.3	273 40.9	18 24	84 04.6
52	Vega	0.1	05 57	N38 46.3	270 25.9	18 37	80 49.6
53	Nunki..........	2.1	06 15	S26 18.4	265 54.1	18 55	76 17.8
54	Altair	0.9	07 11	N 8 50.7	252 00.0	19 50	62 23.7
55	Peacock........	2.1	07 45	S56 45.4	243 20.4	20 25	53 44.1
56	Deneb	1.3	08 01	N45 14.9	239 18.7	20 41	49 42.4
57	Enif	2.5	09 04	N 9 50.3	223 39.1	21 44	34 02.8
58	Al Na'ir	2.2	09 28	S46 59.7	217 40.0	22 08	28 03.7
59	Fomalhaut	1.3	10 17	S29 39.7	205 17.9	22 57	15 41.6
60	Markab	2.6	10 24	N15 09.7	203 30.7	23 04	13 54.4

Stars Transit Correction Table

D. of Mth.	Corr (Sub.)	D. of Mth.	Corr. (Sub.)
	h. m.		h. m.
1	–0 00	17	–1 03
2	–0 04	18	–1 07
3	–0 08	19	–1 11
4	–0 12	20	–1 15
5	–0 16	21	–1 19
6	–0 20	22	–1 23
7	–0 24	23	–1 27
8	–0 28	24	–1 30
9	–0 31	25	–1 34
10	–0 35	26	–1 38
11	–0 39	27	–1 42
12	–0 43	28	–1 46
13	–0 47	29	–1 50
14	–0 51	30	–1 54
15	–0 55		
16	–0 59		

STAR'S TRANSIT

To find the approx. time of Transit of a Star for any day of the month use above table.

If the quantity taken from the table is greater than the time of Transit for the first of the month, add 23h. 56min. to the time of transit before subtracting the correction below.

Example: Required the time of transit of Hamal (No 7) on April 8th?

	h.min.
Transit on April 1st	13 26
Corr. for April 8th	–00 28
Transit on April 8th	12 58

APRIL DIARY

d. h.
1 19 Venus 7°S. of Moon
2 08 Mercury 4°S. of Moon
3 05 New Moon
5 23 Mercury 2°N. of Venus
8 01 Mercury stationary
10 10 First Quarter
13 07 Moon at perigee
13 16 Jupiter 6°N. of Moon
17 05 Full Moon
23 15 Mercury greatest elong. W.(27°)
24 22 Last Quarter
25 10 Moon at apogee
26 02 Saturn 5°S. of Moon
29 07 Mars 7°S. of Moon
30 21 Mercury 8°S. of Moon

STAR TIME

The best time to take Star observations is shown in the a.m. and p.m. TWILIGHT columns on the opposite page – corrected for Latitude.

For **Lighting-up Time** (ashore) add 30 mins to Sunset Times.

For Star's G.H.A. Correction Table, see page 4:8.

For Alphabetical List of Stars with Constellation names, see page 2:24.

For Examples on the use of the above data, see page 2:11.

For full directions for finding the above 60 Stars, see p. 2:20 onwards. For Special Pole Star tables see pages 5:17-5:19.

Wednesday, 1st April

G.M.T. (h)	SUN G.H.A.	Dec.	ARIES G.H.A.
00	179 01.0	N 4 33.4	189 36.3
02	209 01.4	4 35.3	219 41.2
04	239 01.7	4 37.2	249 46.1
06	269 02.1	4 39.1	279 51.1
08	299 02.5	4 41.1	309 56.0
10	329 02.9	4 43.0	340 00.9
12	359 03.2	4 44.9	10 05.8
14	29 03.6	4 46.9	40 10.8
16	59 04.0	4 48.8	70 15.7
18	89 04.3	4 50.7	100 20.6
20	119 04.7	4 52.6	130 25.6
22	149 05.1	N 4 54.6	160 30.5

Thursday, 2nd April

G.M.T. (h)	SUN G.H.A.	Dec.	ARIES G.H.A.
00	179 05.4	N 4 56.5	190 35.4
02	209 05.8	4 58.4	220 40.3
04	239 06.2	5 00.3	250 45.3
06	269 06.5	5 02.2	280 50.2
08	299 06.9	5 04.2	310 55.1
10	329 07.3	5 06.1	341 00.1
12	359 07.6	5 08.0	11 05.0
14	29 08.0	5 09.9	41 09.9
16	59 08.4	5 11.8	71 14.8
18	89 08.7	5 13.8	101 19.8
20	119 09.1	5 15.7	131 24.7
22	149 09.5	N 5 17.6	161 29.6

Friday, 3rd April

G.M.T. (h)	SUN G.H.A.	Dec.	ARIES G.H.A.
00	179 09.8	N 5 19.5	191 34.6
02	209 10.2	5 21.4	221 39.5
04	239 10.6	5 23.3	251 44.4
06	269 10.9	5 25.2	281 49.3
08	299 11.3	5 27.2	311 54.3
10	329 11.7	5 29.1	341 59.2
12	359 12.0	5 31.0	12 04.1
14	29 12.4	5 32.9	42 09.1
16	59 12.8	5 34.8	72 14.0
18	89 13.1	5 36.7	102 18.9
20	119 13.5	5 38.6	132 23.8
22	149 13.9	N 5 40.5	162 28.8

Saturday, 4th April

G.M.T. (h)	SUN G.H.A.	Dec.	ARIES G.H.A.
00	179 14.2	N 5 42.4	192 33.7
02	209 14.6	5 44.3	222 38.6
04	239 14.9	5 46.2	252 43.5
06	269 15.3	5 48.2	282 48.5
08	299 15.7	5 50.1	312 53.4
10	329 16.0	5 52.0	342 58.3
12	359 16.4	5 53.9	13 03.3
14	29 16.7	5 55.8	43 08.2
16	59 17.1	5 57.7	73 13.1
18	89 17.5	5 59.6	103 18.0
20	119 17.8	6 01.5	133 23.0
22	149 18.2	N 6 03.4	163 27.9

Sunday, 5th April

G.M.T. (h)	SUN G.H.A.	Dec.	ARIES G.H.A.
00	179 18.5	N 6 05.3	193 32.8
02	209 18.9	6 07.2	223 37.8
04	239 19.3	6 09.1	253 42.7
06	269 19.6	6 11.0	283 47.6
08	299 20.0	6 12.9	313 52.5
10	329 20.3	6 14.7	343 57.5
12	359 20.7	6 16.6	14 02.4
14	29 21.0	6 18.5	44 07.3
16	59 21.4	6 20.4	74 12.3
18	89 21.8	6 22.3	104 17.2
20	119 22.1	6 24.2	134 22.1
22	149 22.5	N 6 26.1	164 27.0

Monday, 6th April

G.M.T. (h)	SUN G.H.A.	Dec.	ARIES G.H.A.
00	179 22.8	N 6 28.0	194 32.0
02	209 23.2	6 29.9	224 36.9
04	239 23.5	6 31.8	254 41.8
06	269 23.9	6 33.7	284 46.8
08	299 24.2	6 35.5	314 51.7
10	329 24.6	6 37.4	344 56.6
12	359 24.9	6 39.3	15 01.5
14	29 25.3	6 41.2	45 06.5
16	59 25.7	6 43.1	75 11.4
18	89 26.0	6 45.0	105 16.3
20	119 26.4	6 46.8	135 21.3
22	149 26.7	N 6 48.7	165 26.2

Tuesday, 7th April

G.M.T. (h)	SUN G.H.A.	Dec.	ARIES G.H.A.
00	179 27.1	N 6 50.6	195 31.1
02	209 27.4	6 52.5	225 36.0
04	239 27.8	6 54.4	255 41.0
06	269 28.1	6 56.2	285 45.9
08	299 28.5	6 58.1	315 50.8
10	329 28.8	7 00.0	345 55.7
12	359 29.2	7 01.9	16 00.7
14	29 29.5	7 03.7	46 05.6
16	59 29.8	7 05.6	76 10.5
18	89 30.2	7 07.5	106 15.5
20	119 30.5	7 09.4	136 20.4
22	149 30.9	N 7 11.2	166 25.3

Wednesday, 8th April

G.M.T. (h)	SUN G.H.A.	Dec.	ARIES G.H.A.
00	179 31.2	N 7 13.1	196 30.2
02	209 31.6	7 15.0	226 35.2
04	239 31.9	7 16.8	256 40.1
06	269 32.3	7 18.7	286 45.0
08	299 32.6	7 20.6	316 50.0
10	329 33.0	7 22.4	346 54.9
12	359 33.3	7 24.3	16 59.8
14	29 33.6	7 26.2	47 04.7
16	59 34.0	7 28.0	77 09.7
18	89 34.3	7 29.9	107 14.6
20	119 34.7	7 31.7	137 19.5
22	149 35.0	N 7 33.6	167 24.5

Thursday, 9th April

G.M.T. (h)	SUN G.H.A.	Dec.	ARIES G.H.A.
00	179 35.4	N 7 35.5	197 29.4
02	209 35.7	7 37.3	227 34.3
04	239 36.0	7 39.2	257 39.2
06	269 36.4	7 41.0	287 44.2
08	299 36.7	7 42.9	317 49.1
10	329 37.1	7 44.8	347 54.0
12	359 37.4	7 46.6	17 59.0
14	29 37.7	7 48.5	48 03.9
16	59 38.1	7 50.3	78 08.8
18	89 38.4	7 52.2	108 13.7
20	119 38.8	7 54.0	138 18.7
22	149 39.1	N 7 55.9	168 23.6

Friday, 10th April

G.M.T. (h)	SUN G.H.A.	Dec.	ARIES G.H.A.
00	179 39.4	N 7 57.7	198 28.5
02	209 39.8	7 59.6	228 33.5
04	239 40.1	8 01.4	258 38.4
06	269 40.4	8 03.2	288 43.3
08	299 40.8	8 05.1	318 48.2
10	329 41.1	8 06.9	348 53.2
12	359 41.4	8 08.8	18 58.1
14	29 41.8	8 10.6	49 03.0
16	59 42.1	8 12.5	79 07.9
18	89 42.4	8 14.3	109 12.9
20	119 42.8	8 16.1	139 17.8
22	149 43.1	N 8 18.0	169 22.7

Saturday, 11th April

G.M.T. (h)	SUN G.H.A.	Dec.	ARIES G.H.A.
00	179 43.4	N 8 19.8	199 27.7
02	209 43.8	8 21.7	229 32.6
04	239 44.1	8 23.5	259 37.5
06	269 44.4	8 25.3	289 42.4
08	299 44.8	8 27.2	319 47.4
10	329 45.1	8 29.0	349 52.3
12	359 45.4	8 30.8	19 57.2
14	29 45.7	8 32.6	50 02.2
16	59 46.1	8 34.5	80 07.1
18	89 46.4	8 36.3	110 12.0
20	119 46.7	8 38.1	140 16.9
22	149 47.0	N 8 40.0	170 21.9

Sunday, 12th April

G.M.T. (h)	SUN G.H.A.	Dec.	ARIES G.H.A.
00	179 47.4	N 8 41.8	200 26.8
02	209 47.7	8 43.6	230 31.7
04	239 48.0	8 45.4	260 36.7
06	269 48.3	8 47.3	290 41.6
08	299 48.7	8 49.1	320 46.5
10	329 49.0	8 50.9	350 51.4
12	359 49.3	8 52.7	20 56.4
14	29 49.6	8 54.5	51 01.3
16	59 50.0	8 56.3	81 06.2
18	89 50.3	8 58.2	111 11.2
20	119 50.6	9 00.0	141 16.1
22	149 50.9	N 9 01.8	171 21.0

Monday, 13th April

G.M.T. (h)	SUN G.H.A.	Dec.	ARIES G.H.A.
00	179 51.2	N 9 03.6	201 25.9
02	209 51.6	9 05.4	231 30.9
04	239 51.9	9 07.2	261 35.8
06	269 52.2	9 09.0	291 40.7
08	299 52.5	9 10.8	321 45.7
10	329 52.8	9 12.7	351 50.6
12	359 53.1	9 14.5	21 55.5
14	29 53.5	9 16.3	52 00.4
16	59 53.8	9 18.1	82 05.4
18	89 54.1	9 19.9	112 10.3
20	119 54.4	9 21.7	142 15.2
22	149 54.7	N 9 23.5	172 20.2

Tuesday, 14th April

G.M.T. (h)	SUN G.H.A.	Dec.	ARIES G.H.A.
00	179 55.0	N 9 25.3	202 25.1
02	209 55.3	9 27.1	232 30.0
04	239 55.7	9 28.9	262 34.9
06	269 56.0	9 30.7	292 39.9
08	299 56.3	9 32.5	322 44.8
10	329 56.6	9 34.3	352 49.7
12	359 56.9	9 36.1	22 54.6
14	29 57.2	9 37.8	52 59.6
16	59 57.5	9 39.6	83 04.5
18	89 57.8	9 41.4	113 09.4
20	119 58.1	9 43.2	143 14.4
22	149 58.4	N 9 45.0	173 19.3

Wednesday, 15th April

G.M.T. (h)	SUN G.H.A.	Dec.	ARIES G.H.A.
00	179 58.7	N 9 46.8	203 24.2
02	209 59.0	9 48.6	233 29.1
04	239 59.4	9 50.4	263 34.1
06	269 59.7	9 52.1	293 39.0
08	300 00.0	9 53.9	323 43.9
10	330 00.3	9 55.7	353 48.9
12	0 00.6	9 57.5	23 53.8
14	30 00.9	9 59.3	53 58.7
16	60 01.2	10 01.0	84 03.6
18	90 01.5	10 02.8	114 08.6
20	120 01.8	10 04.6	144 13.5
22	150 02.1	N10 06.4	174 18.4

To interpolate SUN G.H.A. see page 4:7   To interpolate ARIES G.H.A. see page 4:8

Thursday, 16th April

G.M.T.	SUN G.H.A.	Dec.	ARIES G.H.A.	G.M.T.
00	180 02.4	N10 08.1	204 23.4	00
02	210 02.7	10 09.9	234 28.3	02
04	240 03.0	10 11.7	264 33.2	04
06	270 03.3	10 13.5	294 38.1	06
08	300 03.6	10 15.2	324 43.1	08
10	330 03.9	10 17.0	354 48.0	10
12	0 04.1	10 18.8	24 52.9	12
14	30 04.4	10 20.5	54 57.9	14
16	60 04.7	10 22.3	85 02.8	16
18	90 05.0	10 24.1	115 07.7	18
20	120 05.3	10 25.8	145 12.6	20
22	150 05.6	N10 27.6	175 17.6	22

Friday, 17th April

G.M.T.	SUN G.H.A.	Dec.	ARIES G.H.A.	G.M.T.
00	180 05.9	N10 29.3	205 22.5	00
02	210 06.2	10 31.1	235 27.4	02
04	240 06.5	10 32.8	265 32.4	04
06	270 06.8	10 34.6	295 37.3	06
08	300 07.1	10 36.4	325 42.2	08
10	330 07.3	10 38.1	355 47.1	10
12	0 07.6	10 39.9	25 52.1	12
14	30 07.9	10 41.6	55 57.0	14
16	60 08.2	10 43.4	86 01.9	16
18	90 08.5	10 45.1	116 06.8	18
20	120 08.8	10 46.9	146 11.8	20
22	150 09.1	N10 48.6	176 16.7	22

Saturday, 18th April

G.M.T.	SUN G.H.A.	Dec.	ARIES G.H.A.	G.M.T.
00	180 09.3	N10 50.3	206 21.6	00
02	210 09.6	10 52.1	236 26.6	02
04	240 09.9	10 53.8	266 31.5	04
06	270 10.2	10 55.6	296 36.4	06
08	300 10.5	10 57.3	326 41.3	08
10	330 10.7	10 59.1	356 46.3	10
12	0 11.0	11 00.8	26 51.2	12
14	30 11.3	11 02.5	56 56.1	14
16	60 11.6	11 04.3	87 01.1	16
18	90 11.9	11 06.0	117 06.0	18
20	120 12.1	11 07.7	147 10.9	20
22	150 12.4	N11 09.5	177 15.8	22

Sunday, 19th April

G.M.T.	SUN G.H.A.	Dec.	ARIES G.H.A.	G.M.T.
00	180 12.7	N11 11.2	207 20.8	00
02	210 13.0	11 12.9	237 25.7	02
04	240 13.2	11 14.6	267 30.6	04
06	270 13.5	11 16.4	297 35.6	06
08	300 13.8	11 18.1	327 40.5	08
10	330 14.0	11 19.8	357 45.4	10
12	0 14.3	11 21.5	27 50.3	12
14	30 14.6	11 23.3	57 55.3	14
16	60 14.9	11 25.0	88 00.2	16
18	90 15.1	11 26.7	118 05.1	18
20	120 15.4	11 28.4	148 10.1	20
22	150 15.7	N11 30.1	178 15.0	22

Monday, 20th April

G.M.T.	SUN G.H.A.	Dec.	ARIES G.H.A.	G.M.T.
00	180 15.9	N11 31.8	208 19.9	00
02	210 16.2	11 33.5	238 24.8	02
04	240 16.4	11 35.3	268 29.8	04
06	270 16.7	11 37.0	298 34.7	06
08	300 17.0	11 38.7	328 39.6	08
10	330 17.2	11 40.4	358 44.6	10
12	0 17.5	11 42.1	28 49.5	12
14	30 17.8	11 43.8	58 54.4	14
16	60 18.0	11 45.5	88 59.3	16
18	90 18.3	11 47.2	119 04.3	18
20	120 18.5	11 48.9	149 09.2	20
22	150 18.8	N11 50.6	179 14.1	22

Tuesday, 21st April

G.M.T.	SUN G.H.A.	Dec.	ARIES G.H.A.	G.M.T.
00	180 19.0	N11 52.3	209 19.1	00
02	210 19.3	11 54.0	239 24.0	02
04	240 19.6	11 55.7	269 28.9	04
06	270 19.8	11 57.4	299 33.8	06
08	300 20.1	11 59.1	329 38.8	08
10	330 20.3	12 00.8	359 43.7	10
12	0 20.6	12 02.5	29 48.6	12
14	30 20.8	12 04.1	59 53.5	14
16	60 21.1	12 05.8	89 58.5	16
18	90 21.3	12 07.5	120 03.4	18
20	120 21.6	12 09.2	150 08.3	20
22	150 21.8	N12 10.9	180 13.3	22

Wednesday, 22nd April

G.M.T.	SUN G.H.A.	Dec.	ARIES G.H.A.	G.M.T.
00	180 22.1	N12 12.6	210 18.2	00
02	210 22.3	12 14.2	240 23.1	02
04	240 22.5	12 15.9	270 28.0	04
06	270 22.8	12 17.6	300 33.0	06
08	300 23.0	12 19.3	330 37.9	08
10	330 23.3	12 21.0	0 42.8	10
12	0 23.5	12 22.6	30 47.8	12
14	30 23.8	12 24.3	60 52.7	14
16	60 24.0	12 26.0	90 57.6	16
18	90 24.2	12 27.6	121 02.5	18
20	120 24.5	12 29.3	151 07.5	20
22	150 24.7	N12 31.0	181 12.4	22

Thursday, 23rd April

G.M.T.	SUN G.H.A.	Dec.	ARIES G.H.A.	G.M.T.
00	180 24.9	N12 32.6	211 17.3	00
02	210 25.2	12 34.3	241 22.3	02
04	240 25.4	12 36.0	271 27.2	04
06	270 25.7	12 37.6	301 32.1	06
08	300 25.9	12 39.3	331 37.0	08
10	330 26.1	12 40.9	1 42.0	10
12	0 26.4	12 42.6	31 46.9	12
14	30 26.6	12 44.2	61 51.8	14
16	60 26.8	12 45.9	91 56.8	16
18	90 27.0	12 47.5	122 01.7	18
20	120 27.3	12 49.2	152 06.6	20
22	150 27.5	N12 50.8	182 11.5	22

Friday, 24th April

G.M.T.	SUN G.H.A.	Dec.	ARIES G.H.A.	G.M.T.
00	180 27.7	N12 52.5	212 16.5	00
02	210 27.9	12 54.1	242 21.4	02
04	240 28.2	12 55.8	272 26.3	04
06	270 28.4	12 57.4	302 31.3	06
08	300 28.6	12 59.1	332 36.2	08
10	330 28.8	13 00.7	2 41.1	10
12	0 29.1	13 02.3	32 46.0	12
14	30 29.3	13 04.0	62 51.0	14
16	60 29.5	13 05.6	92 55.9	16
18	90 29.7	13 07.2	123 00.8	18
20	120 29.9	13 08.9	153 05.7	20
22	150 30.2	N13 10.5	183 10.7	22

Saturday, 25th April

G.M.T.	SUN G.H.A.	Dec.	ARIES G.H.A.	G.M.T.
00	180 30.4	N13 12.1	213 15.6	00
02	210 30.6	13 13.8	243 20.5	02
04	240 30.8	13 15.4	273 25.5	04
06	270 31.0	13 17.0	303 30.4	06
08	300 31.2	13 18.6	333 35.3	08
10	330 31.4	13 20.3	3 40.2	10
12	0 31.7	13 21.9	33 45.2	12
14	30 31.9	13 23.5	63 50.1	14
16	60 32.1	13 25.1	93 55.0	16
18	90 32.3	13 26.7	124 00.0	18
20	120 32.5	13 28.4	154 04.9	20
22	150 32.7	N13 30.0	184 09.8	22

Sunday, 26th April

G.M.T.	SUN G.H.A.	Dec.	ARIES G.H.A.	G.M.T.
00	180 32.9	N13 31.6	214 14.7	00
02	210 33.1	13 33.2	244 19.7	02
04	240 33.3	13 34.8	274 24.6	04
06	270 33.5	13 36.4	304 29.5	06
08	300 33.7	13 38.0	334 34.5	08
10	330 33.9	13 39.6	4 39.4	10
12	0 34.1	13 41.2	34 44.3	12
14	30 34.3	13 42.8	64 49.2	14
16	60 34.5	13 44.4	94 54.2	16
18	90 34.7	13 46.0	124 59.1	18
20	120 34.9	13 47.6	155 04.0	20
22	150 35.1	N13 49.2	185 09.0	22

Monday, 27th April

G.M.T.	SUN G.H.A.	Dec.	ARIES G.H.A.	G.M.T.
00	180 35.3	N13 50.8	215 13.9	00
02	210 35.5	13 52.4	245 18.8	02
04	240 35.7	13 54.0	275 23.7	04
06	270 35.9	13 55.6	305 28.7	06
08	300 36.1	13 57.1	335 33.6	08
10	330 36.3	13 58.7	5 38.5	10
12	0 36.5	14 00.3	35 43.5	12
14	30 36.6	14 01.9	65 48.4	14
16	60 36.8	14 03.5	95 53.3	16
18	90 37.0	14 05.0	125 58.2	18
20	120 37.2	14 06.6	156 03.2	20
22	150 37.4	N14 08.2	186 08.1	22

Tuesday, 28th April

G.M.T.	SUN G.H.A.	Dec.	ARIES G.H.A.	G.M.T.
00	180 37.6	N14 09.8	216 13.0	00
02	210 37.8	14 11.3	246 18.0	02
04	240 37.9	14 12.9	276 22.9	04
06	270 38.1	14 14.5	306 27.8	06
08	300 38.3	14 16.0	336 32.7	08
10	330 38.5	14 17.6	6 37.7	10
12	0 38.7	14 19.2	36 42.6	12
14	30 38.8	14 20.7	66 47.5	14
16	60 39.0	14 22.3	96 52.4	16
18	90 39.2	14 23.9	126 57.4	18
20	120 39.4	14 25.4	157 02.3	20
22	150 39.5	N14 27.0	187 07.2	22

Wednesday, 29th April

G.M.T.	SUN G.H.A.	Dec.	ARIES G.H.A.	G.M.T.
00	180 39.7	N14 28.5	217 12.2	00
02	210 39.9	14 30.1	247 17.1	02
04	240 40.0	14 31.6	277 22.0	04
06	270 40.2	14 33.2	307 26.9	06
08	300 40.4	14 34.7	337 31.9	08
10	330 40.6	14 36.3	7 36.8	10
12	0 40.7	14 37.8	37 41.7	12
14	30 40.9	14 39.3	67 46.7	14
16	60 41.1	14 40.9	97 51.6	16
18	90 41.2	14 42.4	127 56.5	18
20	120 41.4	14 44.0	158 01.4	20
22	150 41.5	N14 45.5	188 06.4	22

Thursday, 30th April

G.M.T.	SUN G.H.A.	Dec.	ARIES G.H.A.	G.M.T.
00	180 41.7	N14 47.0	218 11.3	00
02	210 41.9	14 48.6	248 16.2	02
04	240 42.0	14 50.1	278 21.2	04
06	270 42.2	14 51.6	308 26.1	06
08	300 42.3	14 53.1	338 31.0	08
10	330 42.5	14 54.7	8 35.9	10
12	0 42.7	14 56.2	38 40.9	12
14	30 42.8	14 57.7	68 45.8	14
16	60 43.0	14 59.2	98 50.7	16
18	90 43.1	15 00.8	128 55.7	18
20	120 43.3	15 02.3	159 00.6	20
22	150 43.4	N15 03.8	189 05.5	22

To interpolate SUN G.H.A. see page 4:7   To interpolate ARIES G.H.A. see page 4:8

♀ VENUS ♀   —   ♃ JUPITER ♃

Mer. Pass. h.m.	♀ G.H.A. ° ′	Mean Var. 14°	Dec. ° ′	Mean Var. ′	M	Day of Week	♃ G.H.A ° ′	Mean Var. 15°	Dec. ° ′	Mean Var. ′	Mer. Pass h.m.
10 56	196 10.4	59.6	S 4 24.8	1.2	1	Wed.	31 20.4	2.7	N10 35.3	0.1	21 51
10 56	196 01.1	59.6	S 3 56.1	1.2	2	Th.	32 24.4	2.7	N10 37.1	0.1	21 47
10 57	195 51.9	59.6	S 3 27.4	1.2	3	Fri.	33 28.4	2.7	N10 38.8	0.1	21 42
10 57	195 42.8	59.6	S 2 58.5	1.2	4	Sat.	34 32.1	2.6	N10 40.5	0.1	21 38
10 58	195 33.8	59.6	S 2 29.5	1.2	5	SUN.	35 35.7	2.6	N10 42.1	0.1	21 34
10 59	195 24.8	59.6	S 2 00.5	1.2	6	Mon.	36 39.2	2.6	N10 43.7	0.1	21 30
10 59	195 15.9	59.6	S 1 31.4	1.2	7	Tu.	37 42.5	2.6	N10 45.2	0.1	21 25
11 00	195 07.0	59.6	S 1 02.2	1.2	8	Wed.	38 45.7	2.6	N10 46.6	0.1	21 21
11 00	194 58.2	59.6	S 0 33.0	1.2	9	Th.	39 48.7	2.6	N10 48.0	0.1	21 17
11 01	194 49.4	59.6	S 0 03.8	1.2	10	Fri.	40 51.5	2.6	N10 49.3	0.1	21 13
11 02	194 40.6	59.6	N 0 25.5	1.2	11	Sat.	41 54.2	2.6	N10 50.5	0.0	21 09
11 02	194 31.8	59.6	N 0 54.8	1.2	12	SUN.	42 56.7	2.6	N10 51.6	0.0	21 05
11 03	194 23.1	59.6	N 1 24.0	1.2	13	Mon.	43 59.1	2.6	N10 52.7	0.0	21 00
11 03	194 14.3	59.6	N 1 53.3	1.2	14	Tu.	45 01.3	2.6	N10 53.8	0.0	20 56
11 04	194 05.5	59.6	N 2 22.6	1.2	15	Wed.	46 03.3	2.6	N10 54.7	0.0	20 52
11 04	193 56.7	59.6	N 2 51.8	1.2	16	Th.	47 05.1	2.6	N10 55.6	0.0	20 48
11 05	193 47.8	59.6	N 3 20.9	1.2	17	Fri.	48 06.8	2.6	N10 56.4	0.0	20 44
11 06	193 38.9	59.6	N 3 50.0	1.2	18	Sat.	49 08.3	2.6	N10 57.2	0.0	20 40
11 06	193 29.9	59.6	N 4 19.1	1.2	19	SUN.	50 09.7	2.5	N10 57.9	0.0	20 36
11 07	193 20.8	59.6	N 4 48.0	1.2	20	Mon.	51 10.9	2.5	N10 58.5	0.0	20 32
11 08	193 11.7	59.6	N 5 16.9	1.2	21	Tu.	52 11.9	2.5	N10 59.0	0.0	20 28
11 08	193 02.5	59.6	N 5 45.6	1.2	22	Wed.	53 12.7	2.5	N10 59.5	0.0	20 24
11 09	192 53.1	59.6	N 6 14.2	1.2	23	Th.	54 13.3	2.5	N10 59.9	0.0	20 20
11 09	192 43.7	59.6	N 6 42.7	1.2	24	Fri.	55 13.8	2.5	N11 00.3	0.0	20 16
11 10	192 34.1	59.6	N 7 11.1	1.2	25	Sat.	56 14.1	2.5	N11 00.5	0.0	20 12
11 11	192 24.4	59.6	N 7 39.3	1.2	26	SUN.	57 14.3	2.5	N11 00.7	0.0	20 08
11 11	192 14.5	59.6	N 8 07.3	1.2	27	Mon.	58 14.2	2.5	N11 00.9	0.0	20 04
11 12	192 04.5	59.6	N 8 35.2	1.2	28	Tu.	59 14.0	2.5	N11 00.9	0.0	20 00
11 13	191 54.4	59.6	N 9 02.9	1.1	29	Wed.	60 13.6	2.5	N11 00.9	0.0	19 56
11 13	191 44.1	59.6	N 9 30.4	1.1	30	Th.	61 13.0	2.5	N11 00.9	0.0	19 52

♀ **VENUS.** Av. Mag. –3.9. A **Morning Star.** In conjunction with Mercury on April 5. **S.H.A.** April 5 2°; 10 356°; 15 351°; 20 345°; 25 339°; 30 333°.

♃ **JUPITER.** Av. Mag. –2.3. An **Evening Star.** S.H.A. April 5 201°; 10 202°; 15 204°; 20 202°; 25 203°; 30 204°.

♂ MARS ♂   —   ♄ SATURN ♄

Mer. Pass. h.m.	♂ G.H.A. ° ′	Mean Var. 15°	Dec. ° ′	Mean Var. ′	M	Day of Week	♄ G.H.A ° ′	Mean Var. 15°	Dec. ° ′	Mean Var. ′	Mer. Pass h.m.
09 43	214 10.3	0.6	S11 32.8	0.7	1	Wed.	231 00.1	2.3	S16 44.7	0.1	08 35
09 42	214 25.1	0.6	S11 16.2	0.7	2	Th.	231 54.2	2.3	S16 43.4	0.1	08 31
09 41	214 40.0	0.6	S10 59.5	0.7	3	Fri.	232 48.4	2.3	S16 42.0	0.1	08 27
09 40	214 54.9	0.6	S10 42.7	0.7	4	Sat.	233 42.7	2.3	S16 40.7	0.1	08 24
09 39	215 10.0	0.6	S10 25.9	0.7	5	SUN.	234 37.0	2.3	S16 39.4	0.1	08 20
09 38	215 25.1	0.6	S10 08.9	0.7	6	Mon.	235 31.4	2.3	S16 38.1	0.1	08 17
09 37	215 40.4	0.6	S 9 51.8	0.7	7	Tu.	236 25.8	2.3	S16 36.8	0.1	08 13
09 36	215 55.7	0.6	S 9 34.6	0.7	8	Wed.	237 20.4	2.3	S16 35.6	0.1	08 09
09 35	216 11.1	0.6	S 9 17.4	0.7	9	Th.	238 15.0	2.3	S16 34.3	0.1	08 06
09 34	216 26.5	0.6	S 9 00.1	0.7	10	Fri.	239 09.7	2.3	S16 33.1	0.0	08 02
09 33	216 42.1	0.7	S 8 42.7	0.7	11	Sat.	240 04.4	2.3	S16 31.9	0.1	07 58
09 32	216 57.7	0.7	S 8 25.2	0.7	12	SUN.	240 59.3	2.3	S16 30.8	0.1	07 55
09 31	217 13.4	0.7	S 8 07.6	0.7	13	Mon.	241 54.2	2.3	S16 29.6	0.0	07 51
09 30	217 29.1	0.7	S 7 50.0	0.7	14	Tu.	242 49.2	2.3	S16 28.5	0.0	07 48
09 29	217 45.0	0.7	S 7 32.4	0.7	15	Wed.	243 44.2	2.3	S16 27.4	0.0	07 44
09 28	218 00.9	0.7	S 7 14.6	0.7	16	Th.	244 39.4	2.3	S16 26.3	0.0	07 40
09 26	218 16.8	0.7	S 6 56.8	0.7	17	Fri.	245 34.6	2.3	S16 25.3	0.0	07 37
09 25	218 32.8	0.7	S 6 39.0	0.7	18	Sat.	246 29.9	2.3	S16 24.3	0.0	07 33
09 24	218 48.9	0.7	S 6 21.1	0.8	19	SUN.	247 25.3	2.3	S16 23.3	0.0	07 29
09 23	219 05.0	0.7	S 6 03.1	0.8	20	Mon.	248 20.8	2.3	S16 22.3	0.0	07 25
09 22	219 21.2	0.7	S 5 45.1	0.8	21	Tu.	249 16.3	2.3	S16 21.3	0.0	07 22
09 21	219 37.5	0.7	S 5 27.1	0.8	22	Wed.	250 12.0	2.3	S16 20.4	0.0	07 18
09 20	219 53.8	0.7	S 5 09.0	0.8	23	Th.	251 07.7	2.3	S16 19.5	0.0	07 14
09 19	220 10.1	0.7	S 4 50.9	0.8	24	Fri.	252 03.5	2.3	S16 18.6	0.0	07 11
09 18	220 26.5	0.7	S 4 32.8	0.8	25	Sat.	252 59.4	2.3	S16 17.8	0.0	07 07
09 17	220 43.0	0.7	S 4 14.6	0.8	26	SUN.	253 55.4	2.3	S16 17.0	0.0	07 03
09 16	220 59.5	0.7	S 3 56.4	0.8	27	Mon.	254 51.4	2.3	S16 16.2	0.0	06 59
09 15	221 16.0	0.7	S 3 38.2	0.8	28	Tu.	255 47.6	2.3	S16 15.4	0.0	06 56
09 13	221 32.6	0.7	S 3 19.9	0.8	29	Wed.	256 43.8	2.4	S16 14.7	0.0	06 52
09 12	221 49.2	0.7	S 3 01.7	0.8	30	Th.	257 40.2	2.3	S16 14.0	0.0	06 48

♂ **MARS.** Av. Mag. +1.1. A **Morning Star.** S.H.A. April 5 21°; 10 18°; 15 15°; 20 10°; 25 7°; 30 4°.

♄ **SATURN.** Av. Mag. +0.8. A **Morning Star.** S.H.A. April 5 40°; 10 41°; 15 41°; 20 39°; 25 40°; 30 40°.

MERCURY. Too close to the sun for observation until April 3 when it is visible low in the east before sunrise. Do not confuse with Venus in early April. Venus is the brighter object.

For Planets Correction Tables see pages 4:9-4:13. See also 'How to Recognise the Planets' on page 2:32.
Mean Var. means Variation per Hour.

Day of M. W. T.	G.M.T. h	G.H.A. ° '	Mean Var. per Hour 14°,+	Dec. ° '	Mean Var. per Hour '	Day of M. W. T.	G.M.T. h	G.H.A. ° '	Mean Var. per Hour 14°,+	Dec. ° '	Mean Var. per Hour '
1 Wed.	0	204 19.4	34.5	S 1 08.7	12.6	17 Fri.	0	4 16.2	28.7	S13 55.3	11.6
	6	291 46.4	34.4	N 0 07.1	12.7		6	91 08.2	28.5	S15 05.1	11.0
	12	19 12.7	34.2	N 1 23.3	12.7		12	177 59.1	28.3	S16 11.5	10.4
	18	106 38.0	34.0	N 2 39.5	12.7		18	264 48.9	28.1	S17 14.2	9.7
2 Th.	0	194 02.3	33.9	N 3 55.7	12.7	18 Sat.	0	351 37.7	28.0	S18 13.1	9.1
	6	281 25.2	33.5	N 5 11.7	12.5		6	78 25.3	27.8	S19 08.0	8.4
	12	8 46.7	33.3	N 6 27.1	12.4		12	165 12.1	27.6	S19 58.7	7.6
	18	96 06.5	32.9	N 7 42.0	12.3		18	251 58.0	27.6	S20 45.0	6.9
3 Fri.	0	183 24.5	32.7	N 8 55.9	12.2	19 Sun.	0	338 43.3	27.5	S21 26.8	6.1
	6	270 40.5	32.3	N10 08.8	11.9		6	65 28.0	27.4	S22 03.9	5.3
	12	357 54.2	31.8	N11 20.4	11.6		12	152 12.5	27.4	S22 36.3	4.6
	18	85 05.7	31.5	N12 30.3	11.3		18	238 56.8	27.4	S23 04.0	3.7
4 Sat.	0	172 14.7	31.0	N13 38.5	11.0	20 Mon.	0	325 41.2	27.5	S23 26.8	2.9
	6	259 21.1	30.6	N14 44.7	10.6		6	52 25.9	27.6	S23 44.8	2.2
	12	346 24.7	30.1	N15 48.5	10.1		12	139 11.3	27.7	S23 57.9	1.3
	18	73 25.6	29.7	N16 49.7	9.7		18	225 57.4	27.9	S24 06.2	0.6
5 Sun.	0	160 23.6	29.1	N17 48.1	9.2	21 Tu.	0	312 44.5	28.1	S24 09.8	0.3
	6	247 18.7	28.6	N18 43.4	8.6		6	39 32.9	28.3	S24 08.7	1.1
	12	334 10.8	28.1	N19 35.4	8.0		12	126 22.7	28.6	S24 03.1	1.8
	18	61 00.0	27.7	N20 23.6	7.3		18	213 14.1	28.9	S23 52.9	2.4
6 Mon.	0	147 46.4	27.2	N21 08.0	6.7	22 Wed.	0	300 07.3	29.2	S23 38.5	3.2
	6	234 29.9	26.8	N21 48.2	6.0		6	27 02.4	29.5	S23 19.7	3.8
	12	321 10.6	26.3	N22 24.0	5.1		12	113 59.6	29.9	S22 57.0	4.5
	18	47 49.3	26.0	N22 55.1	4.3		18	200 58.9	30.3	S22 30.2	5.2
7 Tu.	0	134 25.4	25.6	N23 21.5	3.5	23 Th.	0	288 00.4	30.7	S21 59.8	5.8
	6	220 59.5	25.4	N23 42.7	2.6		6	15 04.2	31.0	S21 25.7	6.3
	12	307 31.8	25.1	N23 58.8	1.7		12	102 10.2	31.4	S20 48.2	6.9
	18	34 02.5	25.0	N24 09.5	0.8		18	189 18.4	31.8	S20 07.4	7.4
8 Wed.	0	120 32.1	24.7	N24 14.7	0.1	24 Fri.	0	276 28.8	32.1	S19 23.4	7.9
	6	207 00.8	24.7	N24 14.5	1.1		6	3 41.4	32.5	S18 36.6	8.3
	12	293 29.1	24.7	N24 08.6	2.0		12	90 56.0	32.8	S17 46.9	8.8
	18	19 57.1	24.7	N23 57.1	2.9		18	178 12.6	33.2	S16 54.6	9.1
9 Th.	0	106 25.3	24.8	N23 40.0	3.8	25 Sat.	0	265 31.1	33.4	S15 59.8	9.6
	6	192 54.0	25.0	N23 17.3	4.8		6	352 51.4	33.7	S15 02.7	9.9
	12	279 23.5	25.1	N22 49.2	5.7		12	80 13.2	33.9	S14 03.4	10.3
	18	5 54.1	25.3	N22 15.8	6.5		18	167 36.5	34.1	S13 02.1	10.6
10 Fri.	0	92 25.9	25.6	N21 37.2	7.4	26 Sun.	0	255 01.2	34.3	S11 58.8	10.9
	6	178 59.3	25.9	N20 53.5	8.2		6	342 26.9	34.5	S10 53.5	11.1
	12	265 34.4	26.2	N20 05.0	8.9		12	69 53.7	34.6	S 9 47.1	11.4
	18	352 11.3	26.5	N19 11.9	9.6		18	157 21.2	34.7	S 8 38.9	11.6
11 Sat.	0	78 50.1	26.8	N18 14.4	10.3	27 Mon.	0	244 49.4	34.8	S 7 29.4	11.8
	6	165 30.8	27.1	N17 12.8	10.9		6	332 18.0	34.8	S 6 18.6	12.0
	12	252 13.6	27.5	N16 07.3	11.5		12	59 46.8	34.8	S 5 06.8	12.2
	18	338 58.3	27.8	N14 58.3	12.1		18	147 15.6	34.8	S 3 54.0	12.3
12 Sun.	0	65 45.0	28.1	N13 45.9	12.6	28 Tu.	0	234 44.3	34.7	S 2 40.3	12.4
	6	152 33.4	28.4	N12 30.5	13.0		6	322 12.6	34.6	S 1 26.0	12.5
	12	239 23.6	28.7	N11 12.5	13.4		12	49 40.4	34.5	S 0 11.1	12.6
	18	326 15.4	28.9	N 9 52.0	13.8		18	137 07.3	34.3	N 1 04.1	12.6
13 Mon.	0	53 08.7	29.1	N 8 29.5	14.1	29 Wed.	0	224 33.3	34.1	N 2 19.6	12.6
	6	140 03.3	29.3	N 7 05.2	14.3		6	311 58.0	33.9	N 3 35.1	12.5
	12	226 59.0	29.5	N 5 39.4	14.5		12	39 21.4	33.6	N 4 50.4	12.5
	18	313 55.7	29.6	N 4 12.5	14.6		18	126 43.2	33.3	N 6 05.5	12.5
14 Tu.	0	40 53.1	29.7	N 2 44.8	14.7	30 Th.	0	214 03.1	33.0	N 7 20.0	12.3
	6	127 51.1	29.8	N 1 16.6	14.7		6	301 21.0	32.6	N 8 33.9	12.1
	12	214 49.5	29.8	S 0 11.7	14.7		12	28 36.8	32.2	N 9 46.8	12.0
	18	301 48.0	29.8	S 1 39.9	14.6		18	115 50.1	31.8	N10 58.5	11.7
15 Wed.	0	28 46.6	29.7	S 3 07.7	14.4						
	6	115 45.0	29.6	S 4 34.6	14.3						
	12	202 43.0	29.6	S 6 00.4	14.0						
	18	289 40.6	29.5	S 7 24.9	13.7						
16 Th.	0	16 37.5	29.4	S 8 47.6	13.4						
	6	103 33.6	29.2	S10 08.3	13.0						
	12	190 28.8	29.0	S11 26.6	12.6						
	18	277 23.0	28.9	S12 42.4	12.1						

PHASES OF THE MOON

	d. h/min		d. h/min
● New Moon	3 05 01	○ Full Moon	17 04 42
) First Quarter	10 10 06	(Last Quarter	24 21 40
Perigee	13 07	Apogee	25 10

MAY, 1992

(31 days)

☉ SUN ☉

DATE			Equation of Time		Transit	Semi-diam.	Lat. 52°N.				Lat. Corr. to Sunrise, Sunset, etc.				
Day of							Twi-light	Sun-rise	Sun-set	Twi-light		Twi-light	Sun-rise	Sun-set	Twi-light
Yr.	Mth.	Week	0 h.	12 h.							Lat.				
			m. s.	m. s.	h. m.	′	h. m.	h. m.	h. m.	h. m.	°	h. m.	h. m.	h. m.	h. m.
122	1	Fri.	−02 54	−02 58	11 57	15.9	03 51	04 30	19 25	20 04	N70	T.A.N.	−3 17	+3 32	T.A.N.
123	2	Sat.	−03 01	−03 04	11 57	15.9	03 49	04 28	19 27	20 06	68	T.A.N.	−2 16	+2 20	T.A.N.
124	3	Sun.	−03 08	−03 11	11 57	15.9	03 47	04 26	19 28	20 08	66	T.A.N.	−1 42	+1 45	T.A.N.
125	4	Mon.	−03 13	−03 16	11 57	15.9	03 45	04 24	19 30	20 10	64	−2 12	−1 17	+1 20	+2 13
126	5	Tu.	−03 19	−03 21	11 57	15.9	03 43	04 22	19 32	20 12	62	−1 31	−0 58	+1 01	+1 31
127	6	Wed.	−03 23	−03 26	11 57	15.9	03 41	04 21	19 33	20 14	N60	−1 04	−0 43	+0 44	+1 03
128	7	Th.	−03 28	−03 30	11 57	15.9	03 39	04 19	19 35	20 16	58	−0 42	−0 30	+0 30	+0 45
129	8	Fri.	−03 31	−03 33	11 56	15.9	03 37	04 17	19 37	20 18	56	−0 27	−0 18	+0 19	+0 27
130	9	Sat.	−03 34	−03 36	11 56	15.9	03 35	04 16	19 38	20 19	54	−0 12	−0 08	+0 09	+0 12
131	10	Sun.	−03 37	−03 38	11 56	15.9	03 33	04 14	19 40	20 21	50	+0 11	+0 08	−0 08	−0 11
132	11	Mon.	−03 39	−03 40	11 56	15.9	03 31	04 12	19 42	20 23	N45	+0 33	+0 25	−0 24	−0 32
133	12	Tu.	−03 40	−03 41	11 56	15.9	03 29	04 11	19 43	20 25	40	+0 50	+0 39	−0 38	−0 49
134	13	Wed.	−03 41	−03 42	11 56	15.9	03 27	04 09	19 45	20 27	35	+1 04	+0 50	−0 50	−1 03
135	14	Th.	−03 42	−03 42	11 56	15.9	03 25	04 07	19 46	20 29	30	+1 17	+1 00	−1 00	−1 16
136	15	Fri.	−03 41	−03 41	11 56	15.8	03 24	04 06	19 48	20 30	20	+1 35	+1 17	−1 17	−1 35
137	16	Sat.	−03 41	−03 40	11 56	15.8	03 22	04 04	19 49	20 32	N10	+1 51	+1 32	−1 32	−1 51
138	17	Sun.	−03 39	−03 38	11 56	15.8	03 20	04 03	19 51	20 34	0	+2 06	+1 46	−1 46	−2 06
139	18	Mon.	−03 37	−03 36	11 56	15.8	03 19	04 01	19 52	20 35	S10	+2 19	+1 59	−2 00	−2 19
140	19	Tu.	−03 35	−03 33	11 56	15.8	03 17	04 00	19 54	20 37	20	+2 32	+2 13	−2 15	−2 32
141	20	Wed.	−03 32	−03 30	11 56	15.8	03 15	03 59	19 55	20 39	30	+2 46	+2 30	−2 31	−2 47
142	21	Th.	−03 28	−03 26	11 57	15.8	03 14	03 57	19 57	20 40	S35	+2 54	+2 39	−2 41	−2 54
143	22	Fri.	−03 24	−03 22	11 57	15.8	03 12	03 56	19 58	20 42	40	+3 03	+2 50	−2 52	−3 03
144	23	Sat.	−03 20	−03 17	11 57	15.8	03 11	03 55	19 59	20 44	45	+3 13	+3 03	−3 04	−3 13
145	24	Sun.	−03 14	−03 12	11 57	15.8	03 09	03 54	20 01	20 45	S50	+3 24	+3 18	−3 20	−3 24
146	25	Mon.	−03 09	−03 06	11 57	15.8	03 08	03 53	20 02	20 47					
147	26	Tu.	−03 02	−02 59	11 57	15.8	03 07	03 52	20 03	20 49			NOTES		
148	27	Wed.	−02 56	−02 52	11 57	15.8	03 05	03 50	20 05	20 50					
149	28	Th.	−02 49	−02 45	11 57	15.8	03 04	03 49	20 06	20 52					
150	29	Fri.	−02 41	−02 37	11 57	15.8	03 03	03 49	20 07	20 53					
151	30	Sat.	−02 33	−02 29	11 58	15.8	03 01	03 48	20 08	20 55					
152	31	Sun.	−02 24	−02 20	11 58	15.8	03 00	03 47	20 09	20 56					

The Lat. Corr. to sunrise, sunset, etc., is for the middle of May. T.A.N. means Twilight all night. Examples are given on page 2:11 onwards.

Equation of Time is the excess of Mean Time over Apparent Time
(See explanation and examples on p. 2:15)

☾ MOON ☽

DATE			Age	Transit Diff. (Upper)		Semi-diam.	Hor. Par. 12 h.	Lat. 52°N.		MOON'S PHASES
Day of			days					Moon-rise	Moon-set	
Yr.	Mth.	Week								
				h. m.	m.	′	′	h. m.	h. m.	
122	1	Fri.	28	10 49	50	15.5	56.8	03 28	18 26	
123	2	Sat.	29	11 39	54	15.6	57.4	03 51	19 43	● New Moon 2 17 44
124	3	Sun.	01	12 33	58	15.8	58.0	04 20	20 59	
125	4	Mon.	02	13 31	59	15.9	58.5	04 59	22 08	☽ First Quarter........... 9 15 43
126	5	Tu.	03	14 30	60	16.0	58.9	05 51	23 07	
127	6	Wed.	04	15 30	58	16.1	59.1	06 56	23 53	○ Full Moon 16 16 03
128	7	Th.	05	16 28	56	16.2	59.3	08 12	– –	
129	8	Fri.	06	17 24	52	16.2	59.3	09 34	00 28	☾ Last Quarter........... 24 15 53
130	9	Sat.	07	18 16	51	16.2	59.3	10 57	00 56	
131	10	Sun.	08	19 07	49	16.1	59.2	12 19	01 18	
132	11	Mon.	09	19 56	49	16.1	59.0	13 40	01 38	d. h.
133	12	Tu.	10	20 45	49	16.0	58.7	15 01	01 56	Perigee 8 12
134	13	Wed.	11	21 34	51	15.9	58.3	16 21	02 14	Apogee 23 05
135	14	Th.	12	22 25	52	15.8	57.9	17 41	02 35	
136	15	Fri.	13	23 17	54	15.6	57.4	18 59	02 59	
137	16	Sat.	14	24 11	–	15.5	56.9	20 11	03 29	
138	17	Sun.	15	00 11	54	15.3	56.3	21 16	04 06	
139	18	Mon.	16	01 05	53	15.2	55.7	22 09	04 53	
140	19	Tu.	17	01 58	51	15.0	55.2	22 51	05 49	
141	20	Wed.	18	02 49	49	14.9	54.8	23 23	06 52	NOTES
142	21	Th.	19	03 38	45	14.8	54.5	23 48	07 59	Moon's G.H.A. and Dec. are given
143	22	Fri.	20	04 23	44	14.8	54.3	– –	09 07	on page 3:39.
144	23	Sat.	21	05 07	42	14.8	54.2	00 09	10 15	A table for correcting Moonrise and
145	24	Sun.	22	05 49	41	14.8	54.4	00 26	11 23	Moonset for latitude is on page 4:20.
146	25	Mon.	23	06 30	41	14.9	54.7	00 42	12 31	A table for correcting Moon's meri-
147	26	Tu.	24	07 11	43	15.0	55.2	00 57	13 40	dian passage (transit) for longitude is
148	27	Wed.	25	07 54	45	15.2	55.8	01 13	14 51	on page 4:19.
149	28	Th.	26	08 39	47	15.4	56.5	01 30	16 04	Examples on the use of the above
150	29	Fri.	27	09 28	52	15.6	57.3	01 51	17 21	data are given on page 2:11 onwards.
151	30	Sat.	28	10 20	57	15.8	58.0	02 18	18 38	
152	31	Sun.	29	11 17	60	16.0	58.8	02 53	19 51	

0h. = midnight. For explanation of use of above data see page 2:11 onwards.

No.	Name	Mag.	Transit (approx.)	DEC.	G.H.A.	R.A.	S.H.A.
			h. m.	° ′	° ′	h. m.	° ′
♈	ARIES	–	09 22	–	219 10.4	–	–
1	Alpheratz	2.2	09 30	N29 02.8	217 10.5	0 08	358 00.1
2	Ankaa	2.4	09 48	S42 20.6	212 41.8	0 26	353 31.4
3	Schedar........	2.5	10 02	N56 29.6	209 09.5	0 40	349 59.1
4	Diphda	2.2	10 05	S18 01.6	208 22.3	0 43	349 11.9
5	Achernar	0.6	10 59	S57 16.3	194 49.2	1 37	335 38.8
6	POLARIS	2.1	11 44	N89 13.8	183 33.2	2 22	324 22.8
7	Hamal	2.2	11 28	N23 25.6	187 29.3	2 07	328 18.9
8	Acamar	3.1	12 19	S40 20.0	174 41.1	2 58	315 30.7
9	Menkar	2.8	12 23	N 4 03.6	173 42.3	3 02	314 31.9
10	Mirfak	1.9	12 45	N49 50.1	168 13.9	3 24	309 03.5
11	Aldebaran......	1.1	13 56	N16 29.7	150 18.2	4 35	291 07.8
12	Rigel	0.3	14 35	S 8 12.7	140 37.9	5 14	281 27.5
13	Capella	0.2	14 37	N45 59.5	140 08.6	5 16	280 58.2
14	Bellatrix	1.7	14 46	N 6 20.6	137 59.6	5 25	278 49.2
15	Elnath	1.8	14 47	N28 36.1	137 43.3	5 26	278 32.9
16	Alnilam	1.8	14 57	S 1 12.4	135 13.1	5 36	276 02.7
17	Betelgeuse ...	{ 0.1 1.2 }	15 16	N 7 24.3	130 29.0	5 55	271 18.6
18	Canopus	–0.9	15 44	S52 41.7	123 14.0	6 24	264 03.6
19	Sirius	–1.6	16 05	S16 42.5	117 58.2	6 45	258 47.8
20	Adhara	1.6	16 19	S28 57.9	114 35.6	6 58	255 25.2
21	Castor	1.6	16 55	N31 54.4	105 38.6	7 34	246 28.2
22	Procyon........	0.5	16 59	N 5 14.6	104 26.8	7 39	245 16.4
23	Pollux	1.2	17 05	N28 02.7	102 57.5	7 45	243 47.1
24	Avior	1.7	17 43	S59 29.4	93 35.2	8 22	234 24.8
25	Suhail	2.2	18 28	S43 24.4	82 14.6	9 08	223 04.2
26	Miaplacidus ...	1.8	18 33	S69 41.6	80 53.7	9 13	221 43.3
27	Alphard........	2.2	18 47	S 8 37.7	77 22.0	9 27	218 11.6
28	Regulus........	1.3	19 28	N12 00.2	67 10.6	10 08	208 00.2
29	Dubhe	2.0	20 23	N61 47.7	53 20.9	11 03	194 10.5
30	Denebola	2.2	21 09	N14 36.8	41 59.9	11 49	182 49.5
31	Gienah	2.8	21 35	S17 30.2	35 18.8	12 15	176 08.4
32	Acrux...........	1.1	21 46	S63 03.8	32 37.1	12 26	173 26.7
33	Gacrux........	1.6	21 50	S57 04.6	31 28.7	12 31	172 18.3
34	Mimosa........	1.5	22 07	S59 39.2	27 20.6	12 47	168 10.2
35	Alioth...........	1.7	22 13	N56 00.1	25 44.3	12 54	166 33.9
36	Spica	1.2	22 44	S11 07.4	17 58.0	13 25	158 47.6
37	Alkaid	1.9	23 07	N49 21.0	12 21.2	13 47	153 10.8
38	Hadar...........	0.9	23 23	S60 20.4	8 20.3	14 03	149 09.9
39	Menkent	2.3	23 26	S36 20.2	7 36.3	14 06	148 25.9
40	Arcturus	0.2	23 35	N19 13.2	5 20.2	14 15	146 09.8
41	Rigil Kent	0.1	00 02	S60 48.4	359 23.1	14 39	140 12.7
42	Zuben'ubi.....	2.9	00 14	S16 00.8	356 33.0	14 50	137 22.6
43	Kochab	2.2	00 14	N74 11.2	356 28.4	14 51	137 18.0
44	Alphecca	2.3	00 58	N26 44.3	345 34.4	15 34	126 24.0
45	Antares.........	1.2	01 52	S26 25.0	331 55.7	16 29	112 45.3
46	Atria	1.9	02 11	S69 00.9	327 11.2	16 48	108 00.8
47	Sabik	2.6	02 33	S15 43.0	321 40.7	17 10	102 30.3
48	Shaula	1.7	02 56	S37 05.9	315 53.4	17 33	96 43.0
49	Rasalhague ...	2.1	02 57	N12 33.8	315 31.2	17 35	96 20.8
50	Eltanin	2.4	03 19	N51 29.2	310 03.4	17 56	90 53.0
51	Kaus Aust. ...	2.0	03 46	S34 23.3	303 14.8	18 24	84 04.4
52	Vega	0.1	03 59	N38 46.4	299 59.7	18 37	80 49.3
53	Nunki...........	2.1	04 17	S26 18.3	295 28.0	18 55	76 17.6
54	Altair...........	0.9	05 13	N 8 50.8	281 33.8	19 50	62 23.4
55	Peacock........	2.1	05 47	S56 45.3	272 54.1	20 25	53 43.7
56	Deneb	1.3	06 04	N45 15.0	268 52.5	20 41	49 42.1
57	Enif..............	2.5	07 06	N 9 50.3	253 13.0	21 44	34 02.6
58	Al Na'ir........	2.2	07 30	S46 59.6	247 13.8	22 08	28 03.4
59	Fomalhaut ...	1.3	08 19	S29 39.6	234 51.8	22 57	15 41.4
60	Markab	2.6	08 26	N15 09.8	233 04.6	23 04	13 54.2

Stars Transit Correction Table

D. of Mth.	Corr (Sub.)	D. of Mth.	Corr. (Sub.)
	h. m.		h. m.
1	–0 00	17	–1 03
2	–0 04	18	–1 07
3	–0 08	19	–1 11
4	–0 12	20	–1 15
5	–0 16	21	–1 19
6	–0 20	22	–1 23
7	–0 24	23	–1 27
8	–0 28	24	–1 30
9	–0 31	25	–1 34
10	–0 35	26	–1 38
11	–0 39	27	–1 42
12	–0 43	28	–1 46
13	–0 47	29	–1 50
14	–0 51	30	–1 54
15	–0 55	31	–1 58
16	–0 59		

STAR'S TRANSIT

To find the approx. time of Transit of a Star for any day of the month use above table.

If the quantity taken from the table is greater than the time of Transit for the first of the month, add 23h. 56min. to the time of transit before subtracting the correction below.

Example: The time is 1900h. on May 13th. What stars would be suitable for a Meridian altitude sight within the next hour, latitude 40°N?

	h.min.
Present time	19 00
Corr. for 13th	+00 47
Transit on May 1st	19 47
	+01 00
	20 47

Required a star Dec. N. Transit between 1947h. and 2047h. **Answer:** Dubhe (No 29) only.

d. h. MAY DIARY

1 05 Jupiter stationary
2 18 New Moon
8 12 Moon at perigee
9 16 First Quarter
10 22 Jupiter 6°N. of Moon
16 16 Full Moon
23 05 Moon at apogee
23 12 Saturn 5°S. of Moon
24 16 Last Quarter
28 09 Mars 7°S of Moon
29 03 Saturn stationary
31 16 Mercury in superior conjunction

STAR TIME

The best time to take Star observations is shown in the a.m. and p.m. TWILIGHT columns on the opposite page – corrected for Latitude.

For **Lighting-up Time** (ashore) add 30 mins to Sunset Times.

For Star's G.H.A. Correction Table, see page 4:8.

For Alphabetical List of Stars with Constellation names, see page 2:24.

For Examples on the use of the above data, see page 2:11.

For full directions for finding the above 60 Stars, see p. 2:20 onwards. For Special Pole Star tables see pages 5:17-5:19.

Friday, 1st May

h	SUN G.H.A.	SUN Dec.	ARIES G.H.A.
00	180 43.6	N15 05.3	219 10.4
02	210 43.7	15 06.8	249 15.4
04	240 43.9	15 08.3	279 20.3
06	270 44.0	15 09.8	309 25.2
08	300 44.2	15 11.3	339 30.2
10	330 44.3	15 12.8	9 35.1
12	0 44.5	15 14.3	39 40.0
14	30 44.6	15 15.8	69 44.9
16	60 44.8	15 17.3	99 49.9
18	90 44.9	15 18.8	129 54.8
20	120 45.0	15 20.3	159 59.7
22	150 45.2	N15 21.8	190 04.6

Saturday, 2nd May

h	SUN G.H.A.	SUN Dec.	ARIES G.H.A.
00	180 45.3	N15 23.3	220 09.6
02	210 45.5	15 24.8	250 14.5
04	240 45.6	15 26.3	280 19.4
06	270 45.7	15 27.8	310 24.4
08	300 45.9	15 29.3	340 29.3
10	330 46.0	15 30.7	10 34.2
12	0 46.1	15 32.2	40 39.1
14	30 46.3	15 33.7	70 44.1
16	60 46.4	15 35.2	100 49.0
18	90 46.5	15 36.7	130 53.9
20	120 46.7	15 38.1	160 58.9
22	150 46.8	N15 39.6	191 03.8

Sunday, 3rd May

h	SUN G.H.A.	SUN Dec.	ARIES G.H.A.
00	180 46.9	N15 41.1	221 08.7
02	210 47.0	15 42.5	251 13.6
04	240 47.2	15 44.0	281 18.6
06	270 47.3	15 45.5	311 23.5
08	300 47.4	15 46.9	341 28.4
10	330 47.5	15 48.4	11 33.4
12	0 47.7	15 49.9	41 38.3
14	30 47.8	15 51.3	71 43.2
16	60 47.9	15 52.8	101 48.1
18	90 48.0	15 54.2	131 53.1
20	120 48.1	15 55.7	161 58.0
22	150 48.3	N15 57.1	192 02.9

Monday, 4th May

h	SUN G.H.A.	SUN Dec.	ARIES G.H.A.
00	180 48.4	N15 58.6	222 07.9
02	210 48.5	16 00.0	252 12.8
04	240 48.6	16 01.5	282 17.7
06	270 48.7	16 02.9	312 22.6
08	300 48.8	16 04.4	342 27.6
10	330 48.9	16 05.8	12 32.5
12	0 49.1	16 07.2	42 37.4
14	30 49.2	16 08.7	72 42.4
16	60 49.3	16 10.1	102 47.3
18	90 49.4	16 11.5	132 52.2
20	120 49.5	16 13.0	162 57.1
22	150 49.6	N16 14.4	193 02.1

Tuesday, 5th May

h	SUN G.H.A.	SUN Dec.	ARIES G.H.A.
00	180 49.7	N16 15.8	223 07.0
02	210 49.8	16 17.2	253 11.9
04	240 49.9	16 18.7	283 16.8
06	270 50.0	16 20.1	313 21.8
08	300 50.1	16 21.5	343 26.7
10	330 50.2	16 22.9	13 31.6
12	0 50.3	16 24.3	43 36.6
14	30 50.4	16 25.8	73 41.5
16	60 50.5	16 27.2	103 46.4
18	90 50.6	16 28.6	133 51.3
20	120 50.7	16 30.0	163 56.3
22	150 50.8	N16 31.4	194 01.2

Wednesday, 6th May

h	SUN G.H.A.	SUN Dec.	ARIES G.H.A.
00	180 50.9	N16 32.8	224 06.1
02	210 51.0	16 34.2	254 11.1
04	240 51.1	16 35.6	284 16.0
06	270 51.2	16 37.0	314 20.9
08	300 51.3	16 38.4	344 25.8
10	330 51.3	16 39.8	14 30.8
12	0 51.4	16 41.2	44 35.7
14	30 51.5	16 42.6	74 40.6
16	60 51.6	16 43.9	104 45.6
18	90 51.7	16 45.3	134 50.5
20	120 51.8	16 46.7	164 55.4
22	150 51.9	N16 48.1	195 00.3

Thursday, 7th May

h	SUN G.H.A.	SUN Dec.	ARIES G.H.A.
00	180 51.9	N16 49.5	225 05.3
02	210 52.0	16 50.9	255 10.2
04	240 52.1	16 52.2	285 15.1
06	270 52.2	16 53.6	315 20.1
08	300 52.3	16 55.0	345 25.0
10	330 52.3	16 56.4	15 29.9
12	0 52.4	16 57.7	45 34.8
14	30 52.5	16 59.1	75 39.8
16	60 52.6	17 00.5	105 44.7
18	90 52.6	17 01.8	135 49.6
20	120 52.7	17 03.2	165 54.6
22	150 52.8	N17 04.5	195 59.5

Friday, 8th May

h	SUN G.H.A.	SUN Dec.	ARIES G.H.A.
00	180 52.9	N17 05.9	226 04.4
02	210 52.9	17 07.3	256 09.3
04	240 53.0	17 08.6	286 14.3
06	270 53.1	17 10.0	316 19.2
08	300 53.1	17 11.3	346 24.1
10	330 53.2	17 12.6	16 29.1
12	0 53.3	17 14.0	46 34.0
14	30 53.3	17 15.3	76 38.9
16	60 53.4	17 16.7	106 43.8
18	90 53.5	17 18.0	136 48.8
20	120 53.5	17 19.4	166 53.7
22	150 53.6	N17 20.7	196 58.6

Saturday, 9th May

h	SUN G.H.A.	SUN Dec.	ARIES G.H.A.
00	180 53.6	N17 22.0	227 03.5
02	210 53.7	17 23.4	257 08.5
04	240 53.8	17 24.7	287 13.4
06	270 53.8	17 26.0	317 18.3
08	300 53.9	17 27.3	347 23.3
10	330 53.9	17 28.7	17 28.2
12	0 54.0	17 30.0	47 33.1
14	30 54.0	17 31.3	77 38.0
16	60 54.1	17 32.6	107 43.0
18	90 54.1	17 33.9	137 47.9
20	120 54.2	17 35.2	167 52.8
22	150 54.2	N17 36.6	197 57.8

Sunday, 10th May

h	SUN G.H.A.	SUN Dec.	ARIES G.H.A.
00	180 54.3	N17 37.9	228 02.7
02	210 54.3	17 39.2	258 07.6
04	240 54.4	17 40.5	288 12.5
06	270 54.4	17 41.8	318 17.5
08	300 54.5	17 43.1	348 22.4
10	330 54.5	17 44.4	18 27.3
12	0 54.5	17 45.7	48 32.3
14	30 54.6	17 47.0	78 37.2
16	60 54.6	17 48.3	108 42.1
18	90 54.7	17 49.5	138 47.0
20	120 54.7	17 50.8	168 52.0
22	150 54.7	N17 52.1	198 56.9

Monday, 11th May

h	SUN G.H.A.	SUN Dec.	ARIES G.H.A.
00	180 54.8	N17 53.4	229 01.8
02	210 54.8	17 54.7	259 06.8
04	240 54.8	17 56.0	289 11.7
06	270 54.9	17 57.2	319 16.6
08	300 54.9	17 58.5	349 21.5
10	330 54.9	17 59.8	19 26.5
12	0 55.0	18 01.1	49 31.4
14	30 55.0	18 02.3	79 36.3
16	60 55.0	18 03.6	109 41.3
18	90 55.0	18 04.9	139 46.2
20	120 55.1	18 06.1	169 51.1
22	150 55.1	N18 07.4	199 56.0

Tuesday, 12th May

h	SUN G.H.A.	SUN Dec.	ARIES G.H.A.
00	180 55.1	N18 08.6	230 01.0
02	210 55.1	18 09.9	260 05.9
04	240 55.2	18 11.2	290 10.8
06	270 55.2	18 12.4	320 15.7
08	300 55.2	18 13.7	350 20.7
10	330 55.2	18 14.9	20 25.6
12	0 55.3	18 16.1	50 30.5
14	30 55.3	18 17.4	80 35.5
16	60 55.3	18 18.6	110 40.4
18	90 55.3	18 19.9	140 45.3
20	120 55.3	18 21.1	170 50.2
22	150 55.3	N18 22.3	200 55.2

Wednesday, 13th May

h	SUN G.H.A.	SUN Dec.	ARIES G.H.A.
00	180 55.3	N18 23.6	231 00.1
02	210 55.4	18 24.8	261 05.0
04	240 55.4	18 26.0	291 10.0
06	270 55.4	18 27.3	321 14.9
08	300 55.4	18 28.5	351 19.8
10	330 55.4	18 29.7	21 24.7
12	0 55.4	18 30.9	51 29.7
14	30 55.4	18 32.1	81 34.6
16	60 55.4	18 33.4	111 39.5
18	90 55.4	18 34.6	141 44.5
20	120 55.4	18 35.8	171 49.4
22	150 55.4	N18 37.0	201 54.3

Thursday, 14th May

h	SUN G.H.A.	SUN Dec.	ARIES G.H.A.
00	180 55.4	N18 38.2	231 59.2
02	210 55.4	18 39.4	262 04.2
04	240 55.4	18 40.6	292 09.1
06	270 55.4	18 41.8	322 14.0
08	300 55.4	18 43.0	352 19.0
10	330 55.4	18 44.2	22 23.9
12	0 55.4	18 45.4	52 28.8
14	30 55.4	18 46.6	82 33.7
16	60 55.4	18 47.8	112 38.7
18	90 55.4	18 49.0	142 43.6
20	120 55.4	18 50.2	172 48.5
22	150 55.4	N18 51.3	202 53.5

Friday, 15th May

h	SUN G.H.A.	SUN Dec.	ARIES G.H.A.
00	180 55.4	N18 52.5	232 58.4
02	210 55.3	18 53.7	263 03.3
04	240 55.3	18 54.9	293 08.2
06	270 55.3	18 56.0	323 13.2
08	300 55.3	18 57.2	353 18.1
10	330 55.3	18 58.4	23 23.0
12	0 55.3	18 59.6	53 28.0
14	30 55.3	19 00.7	83 32.9
16	60 55.2	19 01.9	113 37.8
18	90 55.2	19 03.0	143 42.7
20	120 55.2	19 04.2	173 47.7
22	150 55.2	N19 05.4	203 52.6

To interpolate SUN G.H.A. see page 4:7   To interpolate ARIES G.H.A. see page 4:8

Saturday, 16th May

G.M.T. h	SUN G.H.A. ° '	Dec. ° '	ARIES G.H.A. ° '	G.M.T. h
00	180 55.2	N19 06.5	233 57.5	00
02	210 55.1	19 07.7	264 02.4	02
04	240 55.1	19 08.8	294 07.4	04
06	270 55.1	19 10.0	324 12.3	06
08	300 55.1	19 11.1	354 17.2	08
10	330 55.0	19 12.2	24 22.2	10
12	0 55.0	19 13.4	54 27.1	12
14	30 55.0	19 14.5	84 32.0	14
16	60 54.9	19 15.7	114 36.9	16
18	90 54.9	19 16.8	144 41.9	18
20	120 54.9	19 17.9	174 46.8	20
22	150 54.8	N19 19.1	204 51.7	22

Sunday, 17th May

G.M.T. h	SUN G.H.A. ° '	Dec. ° '	ARIES G.H.A. ° '	G.M.T. h
00	180 54.8	N19 20.2	234 56.7	00
02	210 54.8	19 21.3	265 01.6	02
04	240 54.7	19 22.4	295 06.5	04
06	270 54.7	19 23.5	325 11.4	06
08	300 54.7	19 24.7	355 16.4	08
10	330 54.6	19 25.8	25 21.3	10
12	0 54.6	19 26.9	55 26.2	12
14	30 54.6	19 28.0	85 31.2	14
16	60 54.5	19 29.1	115 36.1	16
18	90 54.5	19 30.2	145 41.0	18
20	120 54.4	19 31.3	175 45.9	20
22	150 54.4	N19 32.4	205 50.9	22

Monday, 18th May

G.M.T. h	SUN G.H.A. ° '	Dec. ° '	ARIES G.H.A. ° '	G.M.T. h
00	180 54.3	N19 33.5	235 55.8	00
02	210 54.3	19 34.6	266 00.7	02
04	240 54.2	19 35.7	296 05.7	04
06	270 54.2	19 36.8	326 10.6	06
08	300 54.1	19 37.9	356 15.5	08
10	330 54.1	19 39.0	26 20.4	10
12	0 54.0	19 40.1	56 25.4	12
14	30 54.0	19 41.1	86 30.3	14
16	60 53.9	19 42.2	116 35.2	16
18	90 53.9	19 43.3	146 40.2	18
20	120 53.8	19 44.4	176 45.1	20
22	150 53.8	N19 45.5	206 50.0	22

Tuesday, 19th May

G.M.T. h	SUN G.H.A. ° '	Dec. ° '	ARIES G.H.A. ° '	G.M.T. h
00	180 53.7	N19 46.5	236 54.9	00
02	210 53.7	19 47.6	266 59.9	02
04	240 53.6	19 48.7	297 04.8	04
06	270 53.5	19 49.7	327 09.7	06
08	300 53.5	19 50.8	357 14.6	08
10	330 53.4	19 51.8	27 19.6	10
12	0 53.4	19 52.9	57 24.5	12
14	30 53.3	19 54.0	87 29.4	14
16	60 53.2	19 55.0	117 34.4	16
18	90 53.2	19 56.1	147 39.3	18
20	120 53.1	19 57.1	177 44.2	20
22	150 53.0	N19 58.2	207 49.1	22

Wednesday, 20th May

G.M.T. h	SUN G.H.A. ° '	Dec. ° '	ARIES G.H.A. ° '	G.M.T. h
00	180 53.0	N19 59.2	237 54.1	00
02	210 52.9	20 00.2	267 59.0	02
04	240 52.8	20 01.3	298 03.9	04
06	270 52.7	20 02.3	328 08.9	06
08	300 52.7	20 03.3	358 13.8	08
10	330 52.6	20 04.4	28 18.7	10
12	0 52.5	20 05.4	58 23.6	12
14	30 52.5	20 06.4	88 28.6	14
16	60 52.4	20 07.5	118 33.5	16
18	90 52.3	20 08.5	148 38.4	18
20	120 52.2	20 09.5	178 43.4	20
22	150 52.1	N20 10.5	208 48.3	22

Thursday, 21st May

G.M.T. h	SUN G.H.A. ° '	Dec. ° '	ARIES G.H.A. ° '	G.M.T. h
00	180 52.1	N20 11.5	238 53.2	00
02	210 52.0	20 12.5	268 58.1	02
04	240 51.9	20 13.6	299 03.1	04
06	270 51.8	20 14.6	329 08.0	06
08	300 51.7	20 15.6	359 12.9	08
10	330 51.6	20 16.6	29 17.9	10
12	0 51.6	20 17.6	59 22.8	12
14	30 51.5	20 18.6	89 27.7	14
16	60 51.4	20 19.6	119 32.6	16
18	90 51.3	20 20.6	149 37.6	18
20	120 51.2	20 21.5	179 42.5	20
22	150 51.1	N20 22.5	209 47.4	22

Friday, 22nd May

G.M.T. h	SUN G.H.A. ° '	Dec. ° '	ARIES G.H.A. ° '	G.M.T. h
00	180 51.0	N20 23.5	239 52.4	00
02	210 50.9	20 24.5	269 57.3	02
04	240 50.8	20 25.5	300 02.2	04
06	270 50.8	20 26.5	330 07.1	06
08	300 50.7	20 27.4	0 12.1	08
10	330 50.6	20 28.4	30 17.0	10
12	0 50.5	20 29.4	60 21.9	12
14	30 50.4	20 30.3	90 26.8	14
16	60 50.3	20 31.3	120 31.8	16
18	90 50.2	20 32.3	150 36.7	18
20	120 50.1	20 33.2	180 41.6	20
22	150 50.0	N20 34.2	210 46.6	22

Saturday, 23rd May

G.M.T. h	SUN G.H.A. ° '	Dec. ° '	ARIES G.H.A. ° '	G.M.T. h
00	180 49.9	N20 35.2	240 51.5	00
02	210 49.8	20 36.1	270 56.4	02
04	240 49.7	20 37.1	301 01.3	04
06	270 49.6	20 38.0	331 06.3	06
08	300 49.4	20 39.0	1 11.2	08
10	330 49.3	20 39.9	31 16.1	10
12	0 49.2	20 40.8	61 21.1	12
14	30 49.1	20 41.8	91 26.0	14
16	60 49.0	20 42.7	121 30.9	16
18	90 48.9	20 43.6	151 35.8	18
20	120 48.8	20 44.6	181 40.8	20
22	150 48.7	N20 45.5	211 45.7	22

Sunday, 24th May

G.M.T. h	SUN G.H.A. ° '	Dec. ° '	ARIES G.H.A. ° '	G.M.T. h
00	180 48.6	N20 46.4	241 50.6	00
02	210 48.5	20 47.4	271 55.6	02
04	240 48.3	20 48.3	302 00.5	04
06	270 48.2	20 49.2	332 05.4	06
08	300 48.1	20 50.1	2 10.3	08
10	330 48.0	20 51.0	32 15.3	10
12	0 47.9	20 51.9	62 20.2	12
14	30 47.7	20 52.8	92 25.1	14
16	60 47.6	20 53.8	122 30.1	16
18	90 47.5	20 54.7	152 35.0	18
20	120 47.4	20 55.6	182 39.9	20
22	150 47.3	N20 56.5	212 44.8	22

Monday, 25th May

G.M.T. h	SUN G.H.A. ° '	Dec. ° '	ARIES G.H.A. ° '	G.M.T. h
00	180 47.1	N20 57.4	242 49.8	00
02	210 47.0	20 58.3	272 54.7	02
04	240 46.9	20 59.1	302 59.6	04
06	270 46.8	21 00.0	333 04.6	06
08	300 46.6	21 00.9	3 09.5	08
10	330 46.5	21 01.8	33 14.4	10
12	0 46.4	21 02.7	63 19.3	12
14	30 46.2	21 03.6	93 24.3	14
16	60 46.1	21 04.4	123 29.2	16
18	90 46.0	21 05.3	153 34.1	18
20	120 45.8	21 06.2	183 39.1	20
22	150 45.7	N21 07.1	213 44.0	22

Tuesday, 26th May

G.M.T. h	SUN G.H.A. ° '	Dec. ° '	ARIES G.H.A. ° '	G.M.T. h
00	180 45.6	N21 07.9	243 48.9	00
02	210 45.4	21 08.8	273 53.8	02
04	240 45.3	21 09.6	303 58.8	04
06	270 45.2	21 10.5	334 03.7	06
08	300 45.0	21 11.4	4 08.6	08
10	330 44.9	21 12.2	34 13.5	10
12	0 44.8	21 13.1	64 18.5	12
14	30 44.6	21 13.9	94 23.4	14
16	60 44.5	21 14.8	124 28.3	16
18	90 44.3	21 15.6	154 33.3	18
20	120 44.2	21 16.4	184 38.2	20
22	150 44.0	N21 17.3	214 43.1	22

Wednesday, 27th May

G.M.T. h	SUN G.H.A. ° '	Dec. ° '	ARIES G.H.A. ° '	G.M.T. h
00	180 43.9	N21 18.1	244 48.0	00
02	210 43.8	21 19.0	274 53.0	02
04	240 43.6	21 19.8	304 57.9	04
06	270 43.5	21 20.6	335 02.8	06
08	300 43.3	21 21.4	5 07.8	08
10	330 43.2	21 22.3	35 12.7	10
12	0 43.0	21 23.1	65 17.6	12
14	30 42.9	21 23.9	95 22.5	14
16	60 42.7	21 24.7	125 27.5	16
18	90 42.6	21 25.5	155 32.4	18
20	120 42.4	21 26.3	185 37.3	20
22	150 42.3	N21 27.1	215 42.3	22

Thursday, 28th May

G.M.T. h	SUN G.H.A. ° '	Dec. ° '	ARIES G.H.A. ° '	G.M.T. h
00	180 42.1	N21 28.0	245 47.2	00
02	210 41.9	21 28.8	275 52.1	02
04	240 41.8	21 29.6	305 57.0	04
06	270 41.6	21 30.4	336 02.0	06
08	300 41.5	21 31.1	6 06.9	08
10	330 41.3	21 31.9	36 11.8	10
12	0 41.1	21 32.7	66 16.8	12
14	30 41.0	21 33.5	96 21.7	14
16	60 40.8	21 34.3	126 26.6	16
18	90 40.7	21 35.1	156 31.5	18
20	120 40.5	21 35.9	186 36.5	20
22	150 40.3	N21 36.6	216 41.4	22

Friday, 29th May

G.M.T. h	SUN G.H.A. ° '	Dec. ° '	ARIES G.H.A. ° '	G.M.T. h
00	180 40.2	N21 37.4	246 46.3	00
02	210 40.0	21 38.2	276 51.3	02
04	240 39.8	21 39.0	306 56.2	04
06	270 39.7	21 39.7	337 01.1	06
08	300 39.5	21 40.5	7 06.0	08
10	330 39.3	21 41.2	37 11.0	10
12	0 39.2	21 42.0	67 15.9	12
14	30 39.0	21 42.8	97 20.8	14
16	60 38.8	21 43.5	127 25.7	16
18	90 38.7	21 44.3	157 30.7	18
20	120 38.5	21 45.0	187 35.6	20
22	150 38.3	N21 45.8	217 40.5	22

Saturday, 30th May

G.M.T. h	SUN G.H.A. ° '	Dec. ° '	ARIES G.H.A. ° '	G.M.T. h
00	180 38.1	N21 46.5	247 45.5	00
02	210 38.0	21 47.2	277 50.4	02
04	240 37.8	21 48.0	307 55.3	04
06	270 37.6	21 48.7	338 00.2	06
08	300 37.4	21 49.4	8 05.2	08
10	330 37.3	21 50.2	38 10.1	10
12	0 37.1	21 50.9	68 15.0	12
14	30 36.9	21 51.6	98 20.0	14
16	60 36.7	21 52.3	128 24.9	16
18	90 36.5	21 53.1	158 29.8	18
20	120 36.4	21 53.8	188 34.7	20
22	150 36.2	N21 54.5	218 39.7	22

Sunday, 31st May

G.M.T. h	SUN G.H.A. ° '	Dec. ° '	ARIES G.H.A. ° '	G.M.T. h
00	180 36.0	N21 55.2	248 44.6	00
02	210 35.8	21 55.9	278 49.5	02
04	240 35.6	21 56.6	308 54.5	04
06	270 35.4	N21 57.3	338 59.4	06
08	300 35.3	N21 58.0	8 04.3	08
10	330 35.1	21 58.7	39 09.2	10
12	0 34.9	21 59.4	69 14.2	12
14	30 34.7	N22 00.1	99 19.1	14
16	60 34.5	N22 00.8	129 24.0	16
18	90 34.3	22 01.5	159 29.0	18
20	120 34.1	22 02.2	189 33.9	20
22	150 33.9	N22 02.9	219 38.8	22

♀ VENUS ♀   ♃ JUPITER ♃

Mer. Pass.	G.H.A.	Mean Var. 14°	Dec.	Mean Var.	M	Day of Week	G.H.A	Mean Var. 15°	Dec.	Mean Var.	Mer. Pass
h. m.	° ′	′	° ′	′			° ′	′	° ′	′	h. m.
11 14	191 33.6	59.6	N 9 57.6	1.1	1	Fri.	62 12.3	2.5	N11 00.7	0.0	19 48
11 15	191 22.9	59.5	N10 24.7	1.1	2	Sat.	63 11.4	2.5	N11 00.5	0.0	19 44
11 16	191 12.0	59.5	N10 51.5	1.1	3	SUN.	64 10.3	2.4	N11 00.2	0.0	19 40
11 16	191 01.0	59.5	N11 18.0	1.1	4	Mon.	65 09.0	2.4	N10 59.9	0.0	19 36
11 17	190 49.7	59.5	N11 44.3	1.1	5	Tu.	66 07.6	2.4	N10 59.5	0.0	19 32
11 18	190 38.2	59.5	N12 10.3	1.1	6	Wed.	67 06.0	2.4	N10 59.0	0.0	19 28
11 19	190 26.5	59.5	N12 36.1	1.1	7	Th.	68 04.2	2.4	N10 58.5	0.0	19 25
11 19	190 14.6	59.5	N13 01.5	1.0	8	Fri.	69 02.2	2.4	N10 57.8	0.0	19 21
11 20	190 02.5	59.5	N13 26.6	1.0	9	Sat.	70 00.1	2.4	N10 57.2	0.0	19 17
11 21	189 50.1	59.5	N13 51.4	1.0	10	SUN.	70 57.8	2.4	N10 56.4	0.0	19 13
11 22	189 37.5	59.5	N14 15.9	1.0	11	Mon.	71 55.3	2.4	N10 55.6	0.0	19 09
11 23	189 24.6	59.5	N14 40.0	1.0	12	Tu.	72 52.7	2.4	N10 54.7	0.0	19 05
11 24	189 11.5	59.4	N15 03.8	1.0	13	Wed.	73 49.9	2.4	N10 53.8	0.0	19 02
11 25	188 58.1	59.4	N15 27.2	1.0	14	Th.	74 46.9	2.4	N10 52.8	0.0	18 58
11 25	188 44.4	59.4	N15 50.2	0.9	15	Fri.	75 43.8	2.4	N10 51.7	0.0	18 54
11 26	188 30.5	59.4	N16 12.8	0.9	16	Sat.	76 40.5	2.4	N10 50.6	0.0	18 50
11 27	188 16.4	59.4	N16 35.0	0.9	17	SUN.	77 37.0	2.3	N10 49.4	0.1	18 47
11 28	188 01.9	59.4	N16 56.8	0.9	18	Mon.	78 33.4	2.3	N10 48.1	0.1	18 43
11 29	187 47.2	59.4	N17 18.2	0.9	19	Tu.	79 29.6	2.3	N10 46.8	0.1	18 39
11 30	187 32.2	59.4	N17 39.1	0.9	20	Wed.	80 25.6	2.3	N10 45.4	0.1	18 35
11 31	187 16.9	59.3	N17 59.5	0.8	21	Th.	81 21.5	2.3	N10 44.0	0.1	18 32
11 32	187 01.3	59.3	N18 19.5	0.8	22	Fri.	82 17.3	2.3	N10 42.4	0.1	18 28
11 33	186 45.4	59.3	N18 39.0	0.8	23	Sat.	83 12.9	2.3	N10 40.9	0.1	18 24
11 35	186 29.3	59.3	N18 58.1	0.8	24	SUN.	84 08.3	2.3	N10 39.2	0.1	18 21
11 36	186 12.9	59.3	N19 16.6	0.8	25	Mon.	85 03.6	2.3	N10 37.6	0.1	18 17
11 37	185 56.2	59.3	N19 34.6	0.7	26	Tu.	85 58.7	2.3	N10 35.8	0.1	18 13
11 38	185 39.2	59.3	N19 52.1	0.7	27	Wed.	86 53.7	2.3	N10 34.0	0.1	18 10
11 39	185 22.0	59.3	N20 09.1	0.7	28	Th.	87 48.5	2.3	N10 32.1	0.1	18 06
11 40	185 04.4	59.3	N20 25.5	0.7	29	Fri.	88 43.2	2.3	N10 30.2	0.1	18 02
11 41	184 46.6	59.3	N20 41.3	0.6	30	Sat.	89 37.7	2.3	N10 28.2	0.1	17 59
11 43	184 28.6	59.2	N20 56.6	0.6	31	SUN.	90 32.1	2.3	N10 26.2	0.1	17 55

♀ **VENUS.** Av. Mag. –3.9. A **Morning Star** until May 7 when it is too close to the sun for observation. **S.H.A.** May 5 328°; 10 322°; 15 316°; 20 310°; 25 303°; 30 297°.

♃ **JUPITER.** Av. Mag. –2.1. An **Evening Star.** S.H.A. May 5 202°; 10 203°; 15 204°; 20 202°; 25 202°; 30 203°.

♂ MARS ♂   ♄ SATURN ♄

Mer. Pass.	G.H.A.	Mean Var. 15°	Dec.	Mean Var.	M	Day of Week	G.H.A	Mean Var. 15°	Dec.	Mean Var.	Mer. Pass
h. m.	° ′	′	° ′	′			° ′	′	° ′	′	h. m.
09 11	222 05.9	0.7	S 2 43.4	0.8	1	Fri.	258 36.6	2.4	S16 13.3	0.0	06 45
09 10	222 22.6	0.7	S 2 25.1	0.8	2	Sat.	259 33.1	2.4	S16 12.6	0.0	06 41
09 09	222 39.4	0.7	S 2 06.8	0.8	3	SUN.	260 29.7	2.4	S16 12.0	0.0	06 37
09 08	222 56.2	0.7	S 1 48.5	0.8	4	Mon.	261 26.4	2.4	S16 11.4	0.0	06 33
09 07	223 13.1	0.7	S 1 30.2	0.8	5	Tu.	262 23.2	2.4	S16 10.8	0.0	06 29
09 06	223 29.9	0.7	S 1 11.9	0.8	6	Wed.	263 20.1	2.4	S16 10.3	0.0	06 26
09 04	223 46.9	0.7	S 0 53.7	0.8	7	Th.	264 17.0	2.4	S16 09.8	0.0	06 22
09 03	224 03.8	0.7	S 0 35.4	0.8	8	Fri.	265 14.1	2.4	S16 09.3	0.0	06 18
09 02	224 20.8	0.7	S 0 17.1	0.8	9	Sat.	266 11.3	2.4	S16 08.9	0.0	06 14
09 01	224 37.8	0.7	N 0 01.1	0.8	10	SUN.	267 08.5	2.4	S16 08.4	0.0	06 10
09 00	224 54.8	0.7	N 0 19.4	0.8	11	Mon.	268 05.9	2.4	S16 08.0	0.0	06 07
08 59	225 11.9	0.7	N 0 37.6	0.8	12	Tu.	269 03.3	2.4	S16 07.7	0.0	06 03
08 58	225 29.0	0.7	N 0 55.8	0.8	13	Wed.	270 00.8	2.4	S16 07.3	0.0	05 59
08 57	225 46.1	0.7	N 1 13.9	0.8	14	Th.	270 58.5	2.4	S16 07.0	0.0	05 55
08 55	226 03.2	0.7	N 1 32.1	0.8	15	Fri.	271 56.2	2.4	S16 06.8	0.0	05 51
08 54	226 20.3	0.7	N 1 50.2	0.8	16	Sat.	272 54.0	2.4	S16 06.5	0.0	05 47
08 53	226 37.5	0.7	N 2 08.3	0.8	17	SUN.	273 51.9	2.4	S16 06.3	0.0	05 44
08 52	226 54.6	0.7	N 2 26.3	0.8	18	Mon.	274 49.9	2.4	S16 06.1	0.0	05 40
08 51	227 11.8	0.7	N 2 44.3	0.7	19	Tu.	275 48.0	2.4	S16 06.0	0.0	05 36
08 50	227 29.0	0.7	N 3 02.2	0.7	20	Wed.	276 46.2	2.4	S16 05.9	0.0	05 32
08 48	227 46.2	0.7	N 3 20.1	0.7	21	Th.	277 44.5	2.4	S16 05.8	0.0	05 28
08 47	228 03.4	0.7	N 3 38.0	0.7	22	Fri.	278 42.9	2.4	S16 05.7	0.0	05 24
08 46	228 20.6	0.7	N 3 55.8	0.7	23	Sat.	279 41.4	2.4	S16 05.7	0.0	05 20
08 45	228 37.9	0.7	N 4 13.5	0.7	24	SUN.	280 40.0	2.4	S16 05.7	0.0	05 16
08 44	228 55.1	0.7	N 4 31.2	0.7	25	Mon.	281 38.7	2.5	S16 05.7	0.0	05 13
08 43	229 12.3	0.7	N 4 48.8	0.7	26	Tu.	282 37.5	2.5	S16 05.8	0.0	05 09
08 42	229 29.6	0.7	N 5 06.4	0.7	27	Wed.	283 36.4	2.5	S16 05.9	0.0	05 05
08 40	229 46.8	0.7	N 5 23.9	0.7	28	Th.	284 35.4	2.5	S16 06.0	0.0	05 01
08 39	230 04.0	0.7	N 5 41.3	0.7	29	Fri.	285 34.5	2.5	S16 06.2	0.0	04 57
08 38	230 21.3	0.7	N 5 58.6	0.7	30	Sat.	286 33.6	2.5	S16 06.4	0.0	04 53
08 37	230 38.5	0.7	N 6 15.9	0.7	31	SUN.	287 32.9	2.5	S16 06.6	0.0	04 49

♂ **MARS.** Av. Mag. +1.0. A **Morning Star. S.H.A.** May 5 0°; 10 357°; 15 353°; 20 349°; 25 346°; 30 343°.

♄ **SATURN.** Av. Mag. +0.7. A **Morning Star. S.H.A.** May 5 38°; 10 39°; 15 40°; 20 38°; 25 39°; 30 40°.

MERCURY. Visible low in the east before sunrise until May 24 when it is too close to the sun for observation.

For Planets Correction Tables see pages 4:9-4:13. See also 'How to Recognise the Planets' on page 2:32.
Mean Var. means Variation per Hour.

Day of M. W.	G.M.T. h	G.H.A.	Mean Var. per Hour 14°,+	Dec.	Mean Var. per Hour	Day of M. W.	G.M.T. h	G.H.A.	Mean Var. per Hour 14°,+	Dec.	Mean Var. per Hour
1 Fri.	0	203 00.8	31.3	N12 08.9	11.5	17 Sun.	0	357 22.1	27.5	S22 48.8	3.9
	6	290 08.9	30.8	N13 17.6	11.1		6	84 06.9	27.5	S23 13.1	3.2
	12	17 14.0	30.3	N14 24.4	10.8		12	170 51.7	27.5	S23 32.7	2.4
	18	104 16.2	29.8	N15 29.0	10.4		18	257 36.7	27.6	S23 47.5	1.6
2 Sat.	0	191 15.2	29.3	N16 31.1	9.9	18 Mon.	0	344 22.1	27.7	S23 57.5	0.8
	6	278 11.1	28.7	N17 30.5	9.4		6	71 08.2	27.9	S24 02.7	0.1
	12	5 03.7	28.2	N18 26.8	8.8		12	157 55.2	28.1	S24 03.2	0.7
	18	91 53.0	27.6	N19 19.8	8.2		18	244 43.4	28.3	S23 59.1	1.5
3 Sun.	0	178 39.1	27.1	N20 09.1	7.5	19 Tu.	0	331 33.0	28.6	S23 50.4	2.3
	6	265 22.0	26.6	N20 54.5	6.8		6	58 24.2	28.8	S23 37.3	3.0
	12	352 01.9	26.2	N21 35.7	6.1		12	145 17.2	29.1	S23 19.8	3.7
	18	78 38.9	25.7	N22 12.4	5.2		18	232 12.2	29.5	S22 58.2	4.3
4 Mon.	0	165 13.1	25.2	N22 44.3	4.4	20 Wed.	0	319 09.3	29.9	S22 32.5	4.9
	6	251 44.9	24.9	N23 11.3	3.5		6	46 08.5	30.3	S22 03.0	5.5
	12	338 14.4	24.6	N23 33.0	2.7		12	133 10.0	30.6	S21 29.8	6.1
	18	64 42.1	24.3	N23 49.3	1.7		18	220 13.9	31.0	S20 53.0	6.7
5 Tu.	0	151 08.3	24.2	N24 00.1	0.7	21 Th.	0	307 20.1	31.5	S20 12.9	7.3
	6	237 33.4	24.0	N24 05.2	0.2		6	34 28.6	31.8	S19 29.7	7.7
	12	323 57.7	24.0	N24 04.6	1.1		12	121 39.4	32.2	S18 43.4	8.2
	18	50 21.7	24.0	N23 58.2	2.1		18	208 52.4	32.6	S17 54.3	8.7
6 Wed.	0	136 45.7	24.1	N23 46.0	3.1	22 Fri.	0	296 07.7	32.9	S17 02.6	9.1
	6	223 10.3	24.3	N23 28.1	4.0		6	23 25.0	33.2	S16 08.4	9.5
	12	309 35.7	24.4	N23 04.5	4.9		12	110 44.3	33.6	S15 11.8	9.8
	18	36 02.2	24.7	N22 35.4	5.8		18	198 05.4	33.8	S14 13.1	10.1
7 Th.	0	122 30.3	25.0	N22 00.9	6.7	23 Sat.	0	285 28.2	34.1	S13 12.4	10.5
	6	209 00.2	25.3	N21 21.2	7.5		6	12 52.6	34.3	S12 09.8	10.7
	12	295 32.1	25.7	N20 36.6	8.3		12	100 18.3	34.5	S11 05.6	11.0
	18	22 06.1	26.1	N19 47.2	9.0		18	187 45.3	34.7	S 9 59.7	11.2
8 Fri.	0	108 42.5	26.5	N18 53.3	9.8	24 Sun.	0	275 13.3	34.8	S 8 52.4	11.4
	6	195 21.3	26.9	N17 55.2	10.4		6	2 42.1	34.9	S 7 43.8	11.6
	12	282 02.5	27.3	N16 53.2	11.0		12	90 11.6	35.0	S 6 34.0	11.8
	18	8 46.2	27.7	N15 47.6	11.6		18	177 41.5	35.0	S 5 23.2	11.9
9 Sat.	0	95 32.2	28.1	N14 38.6	12.0	25 Mon.	0	265 11.7	35.0	S 4 11.4	12.1
	6	182 20.6	28.4	N13 26.6	12.5		6	352 41.9	35.0	S 2 58.9	12.2
	12	269 11.2	28.9	N12 11.8	12.9		12	80 11.9	34.9	S 1 45.8	12.3
	18	356 03.9	29.2	N10 54.7	13.3		18	167 41.5	34.8	S 0 32.1	12.3
10 Sun.	0	82 58.6	29.4	N 9 35.4	13.5	26 Tu.	0	255 10.5	34.7	N 0 42.0	12.4
	6	169 55.0	29.7	N 8 14.3	13.7		6	342 38.7	34.5	N 1 56.3	12.4
	12	256 53.0	29.9	N 6 51.7	14.0		12	70 05.8	34.3	N 3 10.6	12.4
	18	343 52.4	30.1	N 5 27.8	14.1		18	157 31.6	34.1	N 4 24.9	12.4
11 Mon.	0	70 52.9	30.2	N 4 03.1	14.2	27 Wed.	0	244 55.9	33.7	N 5 39.0	12.3
	6	157 54.4	30.3	N 2 37.6	14.3		6	332 18.4	33.4	N 6 52.7	12.2
	12	244 56.7	30.5	N 1 11.9	14.3		12	59 39.0	33.0	N 8 05.8	12.0
	18	331 59.4	30.6	S 0 14.0	14.3		18	146 57.4	32.7	N 9 18.1	11.9
12 Tu.	0	59 02.5	30.5	S 1 39.6	14.2	28 Th.	0	234 13.4	32.2	N10 29.4	11.7
	6	146 05.7	30.5	S 3 04.8	14.1		6	321 26.8	31.8	N11 39.5	11.4
	12	233 08.7	30.5	S 4 29.2	13.9		12	48 37.4	31.3	N12 48.2	11.2
	18	320 11.5	30.3	S 5 52.6	13.7		18	135 44.9	30.7	N13 55.2	10.8
13 Wed.	0	47 13.7	30.1	S 7 14.7	13.4	29 Fri.	0	222 49.3	30.1	N15 00.2	10.5
	6	134 15.3	30.1	S 8 35.2	13.1		6	309 50.4	29.5	N16 03.1	10.1
	12	221 16.1	29.9	S 9 53.9	12.8		12	36 48.1	29.0	N17 03.4	9.5
	18	308 15.8	29.8	S11 10.4	12.3		18	123 42.1	28.4	N18 00.9	9.0
14 Th.	0	35 14.5	29.6	S12 24.7	11.9	30 Sat.	0	210 32.6	27.7	N18 55.3	8.5
	6	122 12.0	29.3	S13 36.3	11.4		6	297 19.4	27.1	N19 46.3	7.8
	12	209 08.2	29.2	S14 45.1	10.9		12	24 02.6	26.5	N20 33.6	7.1
	18	296 03.1	28.9	S15 50.8	10.3		18	110 42.2	26.0	N21 16.8	6.5
15 Fri.	0	22 56.6	28.7	S16 53.1	9.7	31 Sun.	0	197 18.4	25.5	N21 55.6	5.6
	6	109 48.7	28.5	S17 51.9	9.2		6	283 51.3	25.0	N22 29.8	4.8
	12	196 39.6	28.2	S18 47.0	8.5		12	10 21.1	24.5	N22 59.0	3.9
	18	283 29.1	28.1	S19 38.1	7.8		18	96 48.1	24.1	N23 23.1	3.1
16 Sat.	0	10 17.5	27.8	S20 25.1	7.0						
	6	97 04.8	27.7	S21 07.8	6.4						
	12	183 51.2	27.6	S21 46.0	5.6						
	18	270 36.9	27.5	S22 19.7	4.8						

PHASES OF THE MOON

	d. h/min		d. h/min
● New Moon	2 17 44	○ Full Moon	16 16 03
☽ First Quarter	9 15 43	☾ Last Quarter	24 15 53
Perigee	8 12	Apogee	23 05

G.M.T.   (30 days)   G.M.T.

☉ SUN ☉

DATE			Equation of Time		Transit	Semidiam.	Lat. 52°N.				Lat. Corr. to Sunrise, Sunset, etc.				
Day of			0 h.	12 h.			Twilight	Sunrise	Sunset	Twilight	Lat.	Twilight	Sunrise	Sunset	Twilight
Yr.	Mth.	Week													
			m. s.	m. s.	h. m.	′	h. m.	h. m.	h. m.	h. m.	°	h. m.	h. m.	h. m.	h. m.
153	1	Mon.	−02 15	−02 11	11 58	15.8	02 59	03 46	20 10	20 57	N70	S.A.H.	S.A.H.	S.A.H.	S.A.H.
154	2	Tu.	−02 06	−02 01	11 58	15.8	02 58	03 45	20 12	20 59	68	S.A.H.	S.A.H.	S.A.H.	S.A.H.
155	3	Wed.	−01 56	−01 51	11 58	15.8	02 57	03 44	20 13	21 00	66	S.A.H.	S.A.H.	S.A.H.	S.A.H.
156	4	Th.	−01 46	−01 41	11 58	15.8	02 57	03 44	20 14	21 01	64	T.A.N.	S.A.H.	S.A.H.	S.A.H.
157	5	Fri.	−01 35	−01 31	11 58	15.8	02 56	03 43	20 15	21 02	62	T.A.N.	−2 06	+2 07	T.A.N.
158	6	Sat.	−01 25	−01 19	11 59	15.8	02 55	03 42	20 16	21 03	N60	−1 57	−1 29	+1 30	+1 58
159	7	Sun.	−01 14	−01 08	11 59	15.8	02 55	03 42	20 16	21 04	58	−1 09	−0 43	+0 43	+1 11
160	8	Mon.	−01 02	−00 56	11 59	15.8	02 54	03 42	20 17	21 05	56	−0 39	−0 26	+0 26	+0 40
161	9	Tu.	−00 51	−00 45	11 59	15.8	02 53	03 41	20 18	21 06	54	−0 17	−0 12	+0 12	+0 18
162	10	Wed.	−00 39	−00 33	11 59	15.8	02 53	03 41	20 18	21 07	50	+0 16	+0 11	−0 11	−0 15
163	11	Th.	−00 27	−00 21	12 00	15.8	02 52	03 41	20 19	21 08	N45	+0 45	+0 33	−0 34	−0 46
164	12	Fri.	−00 15	−00 08	12 00	15.8	02 51	03 40	20 20	21 09	40	+1 07	+0 51	−0 51	−0 07
165	13	Sat.	−00 02	+00 04	12 00	15.8	02 51	03 40	20 20	21 09	35	+1 25	+1 06	−1 06	−1 25
166	14	Sun.	+00 10	+00 17	12 00	15.8	02 51	03 40	20 20	21 10	30	+1 40	+1 19	−1 20	−1 40
167	15	Mon.	+00 23	+00 29	12 00	15.8	02 51	03 39	20 22	21 10	20	+2 05	+1 41	−1 41	−2 05
168	16	Tu.	+00 36	+00 42	12 01	15.8	02 51	03 39	20 22	21 11	N10	+2 26	+2 00	−2 00	−2 26
169	17	Wed.	+00 48	+00 55	12 01	15.8	02 51	03 39	20 22	21 11	0	+2 44	+2 18	−2 18	−2 44
170	18	Th.	+01 01	+01 08	12 01	15.8	02 50	03 39	20 23	21 12	S10	+3 01	+2 35	−2 36	−3 01
171	19	Fri.	+01 14	+01 21	12 01	15.8	02 50	03 39	20 23	21 12	20	+3 18	+2 54	−2 54	−3 18
172	20	Sat.	+01 27	+01 34	12 02	15.8	02 50	03 39	20 23	21 12	30	+3 37	+3 15	−3 15	−3 37
173	21	Sun.	+01 40	+01 47	12 02	15.8	02 51	03 40	20 24	21 13	S35	+3 48	+3 27	−3 28	−3 48
174	22	Mon.	+01 53	+02 00	12 02	15.8	02 51	03 40	20 24	21 13	40	+4 00	+3 41	−3 42	−3 59
175	23	Tu.	+02 06	+02 13	12 02	15.8	02 51	03 40	20 24	21 13	45	+4 13	+3 58	−3 58	−4 13
176	24	Wed.	+02 19	+02 26	12 02	15.8	02 52	03 41	20 24	21 13	S50	+4 29	+4 19	−4 19	−4 29
177	25	Th.	+02 32	+02 38	12 03	15.8	02 52	03 41	20 24	21 13					
178	26	Fri.	+02 45	+02 51	12 03	15.8	02 52	03 41	20 24	21 13					
179	27	Sat	+02 57	+03 04	12 03	15.8	02 53	03 42	20 24	21 13					
180	28	Sun.	+03 10	+03 16	12 03	15.8	02 53	03 42	20 24	21 13					
181	29	Mon.	+03 22	+03 28	12 03	15.8	02 54	03 43	20 24	21 13					
182	30	Tu.	+03 34	+03 40	12 04	15.8	02 55	03 44	20 23	21 12					

NOTES

Equation of Time changes its sign from minus to plus on the 13th. The Lat. Corr. to sunrise, sunset, etc. is for the middle of June. S.A.H. means Sun above horizon. T.A.N. means Twilight all night. Examples are given on page 2:11 onwards.

Equation of Time is the excess of Mean Time over Apparent Time
(See explanation and examples on p. 2:15)

☾ MOON ☽

DATE			Age	Transit Diff. (Upper)		Semidiam.	Hor. Par. 12 h.	Lat. 52°N.		MOON'S PHASES
Day of			days					Moonrise	Moonset	
Yr.	Mth.	Week		h. m.	m.	′	′	h. m.	h. m.	
153	1	Mon.	00	12 17		16.2	59.3	03 40	20 56	
154	2	Tu.	01	13 18	61	16.3	59.8	04 41	21 48	
155	3	Wed.	02	14 19	61	16.3	60.0	05 55	22 28	
156	4	Th.	03	15 17	58	16.3	60.0	07 18	22 59	
157	5	Fri.	04	16 12	55	16.3	59.8	08 43	23 23	
158	6	Sat.	05	17 04	52	16.2	59.5	10 07	23 44	
159	7	Sun.	06	17 54	50	16.1	59.1	11 29	— —	
160	8	Mon.	07	18 42	48	16.0	58.7	12 50	00 02	
161	9	Tu.	08	19 31	49	15.8	58.2	14 09	00 21	
162	10	Wed.	09	20 20	49	15.7	57.6	15 28	00 40	
163	11	Th.	10	21 11	51	15.6	57.1	16 45	01 03	
164	12	Fri.	11	22 04	53	15.4	56.6	17 58	01 30	
165	13	Sat.	12	22 57	53	15.3	56.1	19 05	02 03	
166	14	Sun.	13	23 50	53	15.2	55.7	20 02	02 46	
167	15	Mon.	14	24 42	52	15.0	55.2	20 48	03 38	
168	16	Tu.	15	00 42	—	14.9	54.8	21 23	04 39	
169	17	Wed.	16	01 31	49	14.8	54.5	21 51	05 45	
170	18	Th.	17	02 18	47	14.8	54.3	22 13	06 53	
171	19	Fri.	18	03 03	45	14.8	54.1	22 32	08 01	
172	20	Sat.	19	03 45	42	14.8	54.1	22 48	09 09	
173	21	Sun.	20	04 26	41	14.8	54.3	23 03	10 17	
174	22	Mon.	21	05 07	41	14.9	54.6	23 18	11 24	
175	23	Tu.	22	05 48	41	15.0	55.1	23 34	12 33	
176	24	Wed.	23	06 31	43	15.2	55.8	23 53	13 44	
177	25	Th.	24	07 17	46	15.4	56.6	—	14 58	
178	26	Fri	25	08 07	50	15.6	57.4	00 16	16 13	
179	27	Sat.	26	09 01	54	15.8	58.3	00 45	17 28	
180	28	Sun.	27	09 59	58	16.1	59.2	01 27	18 38	
181	29	Mon.	28	11 00	61	16.3	59.9	02 21	19 37	
182	30	Tu.	29	12 03	63	16.5	60.5	03 30	20 23	
					61					

MOON'S PHASES

	d.	h.	m.
● New Moon	1	03	57
☽ First Quarter..........	7	20	47
○ Full Moon	15	04	50
☾ Last Quarter..........	23	08	11
● New Moon	30	12	18

	d.	h.
Perigee	4	02
Apogee	19	22

NOTES

Moon's G.H.A. and Dec. are given on page 3:45.
A table for correcting Moonrise and Moonset for latitude is on page 4:20.
A table for correcting Moon's meridian passage (transit) for longitude is on page 4:19.
Examples on the use of the above data are given on page 2:11 onwards.

0h. = midnight. For explanation of use of above data see page 2:11 onwards.

0h. G.M.T. JUNE 1   ★ ★ STARS ★ ★   0h. G.M.T. JUNE 1

No.	Name	Mag.	Transit (approx.) h. m.	DEC. ° ′	G.H.A. ° ′	R.A. h. m.	S.H.A. ° ′
♈	ARIES	–	07 20	–	249 43.7	–	–
1	Alpheratz	2.2	07 28	N29 02.9	247 43.5	0 08	357 59.8
2	Ankaa	2.4	07 46	S42 20.5	243 14.9	0 26	353 31.2
3	Schedar	2.5	08 00	N56 29.6	239 42.4	0 40	349 58.7
4	Diphda	2.2	08 03	S18 01.5	238 55.4	0 43	349 11.7
5	Achernar	0.6	08 57	S57 16.2	225 22.3	1 37	335 38.6
6	POLARIS	2.1	09 43	N89 13.7	213 58.6	2 23	324 14.3
7	Hamal	2.2	09 26	N23 25.6	218 02.4	2 07	328 18.7
8	Acamar	3.1	10 17	S40 19.9	205 14.2	2 58	315 30.5
9	Menkar	2.8	10 21	N 4 03.7	204 15.4	3 02	314 31.7
10	Mirfak	1.9	10 43	N49 50.0	198 47.1	3 24	309 03.4
11	Aldebaran	1.1	11 55	N16 29.7	180 51.4	4 35	291 07.7
12	Rigel	0.3	12 33	S 8 12.6	171 11.2	5 14	281 27.5
13	Capella	0.2	12 35	N45 59.4	170 41.8	5 16	280 58.1
14	Bellatrix	1.7	12 44	N 6 20.6	168 32.9	5 25	278 49.2
15	Elnath	1.8	12 45	N28 36.1	168 16.5	5 26	278 32.8
16	Alnilam	1.8	12 55	S 1 12.4	165 46.3	5 36	276 02.6
17	Betelgeuse	{ 0.1 / 1.2 }	13 14	N 7 24.4	161 02.3	5 55	271 18.6
18	Canopus	–0.9	13 43	S52 41.6	153 47.3	6 24	264 03.6
19	Sirius	–1.6	14 04	S16 42.4	148 31.6	6 45	258 47.9
20	Adhara	1.6	14 17	S28 57.8	145 08.9	6 58	255 25.2
21	Castor	1.6	14 53	N31 54.4	136 11.9	7 34	246 28.2
22	Procyon	0.5	14 58	N 5 14.6	135 00.1	7 39	245 16.4
23	Pollux	1.2	15 03	N28 02.7	133 30.9	7 45	243 47.2
24	Avior	1.7	15 41	S59 29.4	124 08.7	8 22	234 25.0
25	Suhail	2.2	16 26	S43 24.4	112 48.0	9 08	223 04.3
26	Miaplacidus	1.8	16 31	S69 41.5	111 27.4	9 13	221 43.7
27	Alphard	2.2	16 46	S 8 37.7	107 55.4	9 27	218 11.7
28	Regulus	1.3	17 26	N12 00.2	97 44.0	10 08	208 00.3
29	Dubhe	2.0	18 21	N61 47.7	83 54.5	11 03	194 10.8
30	Denebola	2.2	19 07	N14 36.8	72 33.3	11 49	182 49.6
31	Gienah	2.8	19 33	S17 30.2	65 52.1	12 15	176 08.4
32	Acrux	1.1	19 44	S63 03.9	63 10.6	12 26	173 26.9
33	Gacrux	1.6	19 49	S57 04.7	62 02.1	12 31	172 18.4
34	Mimosa	1.5	20 05	S59 39.2	57 54.0	12 47	168 10.3
35	Alioth	1.7	20 11	N56 00.2	56 17.8	12 54	166 34.1
36	Spica	1.2	20 42	S11 07.5	48 31.4	13 25	158 47.7
37	Alkaid	1.9	21 05	N49 21.2	42 54.6	13 47	153 10.9
38	Hadar	0.9	21 21	S60 20.5	38 53.6	14 03	149 09.9
39	Menkent	2.3	21 24	S36 20.3	38 09.6	14 06	148 25.9
40	Arcturus	0.2	21 33	N19 13.3	35 53.5	14 15	146 09.8
41	Rigil Kent	0.1	21 57	S60 48.5	29 56.5	14 39	140 12.8
42	Zuben'ubi	2.9	22 08	S16 00.8	27 06.3	14 50	137 22.6
43	Kochab	2.2	22 08	N74 11.3	27 02.0	14 51	137 18.3
44	Alphecca	2.3	22 52	N26 44.4	16 07.6	15 34	126 23.9
45	Antares	1.2	23 46	S26 25.0	2 28.9	16 29	112 45.2
46	Atria	1.9	00 09	S69 01.0	357 44.3	16 48	108 00.6
47	Sabik	2.6	00 31	S15 43.0	352 13.9	17 10	102 30.2
48	Shaula	1.7	00 54	S37 06.0	346 26.5	17 33	96 42.8
49	Rasalhague	2.1	00 56	N12 33.9	346 04.4	17 35	96 20.7
50	Eltanin	2.4	01 17	N51 29.4	340 36.6	17 56	90 52.9
51	Kaus Aust.	2.0	01 45	S34 23.3	333 47.9	18 24	84 04.2
52	Vega	0.1	01 57	N38 46.5	330 32.9	18 37	80 49.2
53	Nunki	2.1	02 16	S26 18.3	326 01.1	18 55	76 17.4
54	Altair	0.9	03 11	N 8 50.9	312 06.9	19 50	62 23.2
55	Peacock	2.1	03 46	S56 45.3	303 27.0	20 25	53 43.3
56	Deneb	1.3	04 02	N45 15.1	299 25.6	20 41	49 41.9
57	Enif	2.5	05 04	N 9 50.4	283 46.1	21 44	34 02.4
58	Al Na'ir	2.2	05 28	S46 59.5	277 46.8	22 08	28 03.1
59	Fomalhaut	1.3	06 17	S29 39.5	265 24.8	22 57	15 41.1
60	Markab	2.6	06 24	N15 09.9	263 37.6	23 04	13 53.9

Stars Transit Correction Table

D. of Mth.	Corr (Sub.) h. m.	D. of Mth.	Corr. (Sub.) h. m.
1	–0 00	17	–1 03
2	–0 04	18	–1 07
3	–0 08	19	–1 11
4	–0 12	20	–1 15
5	–0 16	21	–1 19
6	–0 20	22	–1 23
7	–0 24	23	–1 27
8	–0 28	24	–1 30
9	–0 31	25	–1 34
10	–0 35	26	–1 38
11	–0 39	27	–1 42
12	–0 43	28	–1 46
13	–0 47	29	–1 50
14	–0 51	30	–1 54
15	–0 55		
16	–0 59		

STAR'S TRANSIT

To find the approx. time of Transit of a Star for any day of the month use above table.

If the quantity taken from the table is greater than the time of Transit for the first of the month, add 23h. 56min. to the time of transit before subtracting the correction below.

Example: Required the time of the Meridian passage of Alioth (No 35) on June 26th.

	h.min.
Transit on the 1st	20 11
Corr. for the 26th	–01 38
Transit on the 26th	18 33

JUNE DIARY

d.	h.	
1	04	New Moon
4	02	Moon at perigee
7	07	Jupiter 7°N. of Moon
7	21	First Quarter
13	16	Venus in superior conjunction
15	05	Full Moon Eclipse
19	19	Saturn 5°S. of Moon
19	22	Moon at apogee
21	03	Solstice
23	02	Mercury 5°S. of Pollux
23	08	Last Quarter
26	08	Mars 6°S. of Moon
30	12	New Moon Eclipse

STAR TIME

The best time to take Star observations is shown in the a.m. and p.m. TWILIGHT columns on the opposite page – corrected for Latitude.

For **Lighting-up Time** (ashore) add 30 mins to Sunset Times.

For Star's G.H.A. Correction Table, see page 4:8.

For Alphabetical List of Stars with Constellation names, see page 2:24.

For Examples on the use of the above data, see page 2:11.

For full directions for finding the above 60 Stars, see p. 2:20 onwards. For Special Pole Star tables see pages 5:17-5:19.

Monday, 1st June

G.M.T. (h)	SUN G.H.A.	Dec.	ARIES G.H.A.	G.M.T. (h)
00	180 33.7	N22 03.5	249 43.7	00
02	210 33.6	22 04.2	279 48.7	02
04	240 33.4	22 04.9	309 53.6	04
06	270 33.2	22 05.6	339 58.5	06
08	300 33.0	22 06.2	10 03.5	08
10	330 32.8	22 06.9	40 08.4	10
12	0 32.6	22 07.5	70 13.3	12
14	30 32.4	22 08.2	100 18.2	14
16	60 32.2	22 08.8	130 23.2	16
18	90 32.0	22 09.5	160 28.1	18
20	120 31.8	22 10.2	190 33.0	20
22	150 31.6	N22 10.8	220 37.9	22

Tuesday, 2nd June

G.M.T. (h)	SUN G.H.A.	Dec.	ARIES G.H.A.	G.M.T. (h)
00	180 31.4	N22 11.5	250 42.9	00
02	210 31.2	22 12.1	280 47.8	02
04	240 31.0	22 12.8	310 52.7	04
06	270 30.8	22 13.4	340 57.7	06
08	300 30.6	22 14.0	11 02.6	08
10	330 30.4	22 14.7	41 07.5	10
12	0 30.2	22 15.3	71 12.4	12
14	30 30.0	22 15.9	101 17.4	14
16	60 29.8	22 16.6	131 22.3	16
18	90 29.6	22 17.2	161 27.2	18
20	120 29.4	22 17.8	191 32.2	20
22	150 29.2	N22 18.4	221 37.1	22

Wednesday, 3rd June

G.M.T. (h)	SUN G.H.A.	Dec.	ARIES G.H.A.	G.M.T. (h)
00	180 29.0	N22 19.0	251 42.0	00
02	210 28.7	22 19.6	281 46.9	02
04	240 28.5	22 20.2	311 51.9	04
06	270 28.3	22 20.9	341 56.8	06
08	300 28.1	22 21.5	12 01.7	08
10	330 27.9	22 22.1	42 06.7	10
12	0 27.7	22 22.7	72 11.6	12
14	30 27.5	22 23.3	102 16.5	14
16	60 27.3	22 23.8	132 21.4	16
18	90 27.1	22 24.4	162 26.4	18
20	120 26.8	22 25.0	192 31.3	20
22	150 26.6	N22 25.6	222 36.2	22

Thursday, 4th June

G.M.T. (h)	SUN G.H.A.	Dec.	ARIES G.H.A.	G.M.T. (h)
00	180 26.4	N22 26.2	252 41.2	00
02	210 26.2	22 26.8	282 46.1	02
04	240 26.0	22 27.3	312 51.0	04
06	270 25.8	22 27.9	342 55.9	06
08	300 25.6	22 28.5	13 00.9	08
10	330 25.3	22 29.1	43 05.8	10
12	0 25.1	22 29.6	73 10.7	12
14	30 24.9	22 30.2	103 15.7	14
16	60 24.7	22 30.7	133 20.6	16
18	90 24.5	22 31.3	163 25.5	18
20	120 24.2	22 31.9	193 30.4	20
22	150 24.0	N22 32.4	223 35.4	22

Friday, 5th June

G.M.T. (h)	SUN G.H.A.	Dec.	ARIES G.H.A.	G.M.T. (h)
00	180 23.8	N22 33.0	253 40.3	00
02	210 23.6	22 33.5	283 45.2	02
04	240 23.4	22 34.1	313 50.2	04
06	270 23.1	22 34.6	343 55.1	06
08	300 22.9	22 35.1	14 00.0	08
10	330 22.7	22 35.7	44 04.9	10
12	0 22.5	22 36.2	74 09.9	12
14	30 22.2	22 36.7	104 14.8	14
16	60 22.0	22 37.3	134 19.7	16
18	90 21.8	22 37.8	164 24.6	18
20	120 21.6	22 38.3	194 29.6	20
22	150 21.3	N22 38.8	224 34.5	22

Saturday, 6th June

G.M.T. (h)	SUN G.H.A.	Dec.	ARIES G.H.A.	G.M.T. (h)
00	180 21.1	N22 39.3	254 39.4	00
02	210 20.9	22 39.9	284 44.4	02
04	240 20.6	22 40.4	314 49.3	04
06	270 20.4	22 40.9	344 54.2	06
08	300 20.2	22 41.4	14 59.1	08
10	330 20.0	22 41.9	45 04.1	10
12	0 19.7	22 42.4	75 09.0	12
14	30 19.5	22 42.9	105 13.9	14
16	60 19.3	22 43.4	135 18.9	16
18	90 19.0	22 43.9	165 23.8	18
20	120 18.8	22 44.4	195 28.7	20
22	150 18.6	N22 44.8	225 33.6	22

Sunday, 7th June

G.M.T. (h)	SUN G.H.A.	Dec.	ARIES G.H.A.	G.M.T. (h)
00	180 18.3	N22 45.3	255 38.6	00
02	210 18.1	22 45.8	285 43.5	02
04	240 17.9	22 46.3	315 48.4	04
06	270 17.6	22 46.8	345 53.4	06
08	300 17.4	22 47.2	15 58.3	08
10	330 17.2	22 47.7	46 03.2	10
12	0 16.9	22 48.2	76 08.1	12
14	30 16.7	22 48.6	106 13.1	14
16	60 16.5	22 49.1	136 18.0	16
18	90 16.2	22 49.5	166 22.9	18
20	120 16.0	22 50.0	196 27.9	20
22	150 15.7	N22 50.5	226 32.8	22

Monday, 8th June

G.M.T. (h)	SUN G.H.A.	Dec.	ARIES G.H.A.	G.M.T. (h)
00	180 15.5	N22 50.9	256 37.7	00
02	210 15.3	22 51.4	286 42.6	02
04	240 15.0	22 51.8	316 47.6	04
06	270 14.8	22 52.2	346 52.5	06
08	300 14.5	22 52.7	16 57.4	08
10	330 14.3	22 53.1	47 02.4	10
12	0 14.1	22 53.5	77 07.3	12
14	30 13.8	22 54.0	107 12.2	14
16	60 13.6	22 54.4	137 17.1	16
18	90 13.3	22 54.8	167 22.1	18
20	120 13.1	22 55.2	197 27.0	20
22	150 12.8	N22 55.7	227 31.9	22

Tuesday, 9th June

G.M.T. (h)	SUN G.H.A.	Dec.	ARIES G.H.A.	G.M.T. (h)
00	180 12.6	N22 56.1	257 36.8	00
02	210 12.4	22 56.5	287 41.8	02
04	240 12.1	22 56.9	317 46.7	04
06	270 11.9	22 57.3	347 51.6	06
08	300 11.6	22 57.7	17 56.6	08
10	330 11.4	22 58.1	48 01.5	10
12	0 11.1	22 58.5	78 06.4	12
14	30 10.9	22 58.9	108 11.3	14
16	60 10.6	22 59.3	138 16.3	16
18	90 10.4	22 59.7	168 21.2	18
20	120 10.1	23 00.1	198 26.1	20
22	150 09.9	N23 00.5	228 31.1	22

Wednesday, 10th June

G.M.T. (h)	SUN G.H.A.	Dec.	ARIES G.H.A.	G.M.T. (h)
00	180 09.6	N23 00.9	258 36.0	00
02	210 09.4	23 01.2	288 40.9	02
04	240 09.1	23 01.6	318 45.8	04
06	270 08.9	23 02.0	348 50.8	06
08	300 08.6	23 02.4	18 55.7	08
10	330 08.4	23 02.7	49 00.6	10
12	0 08.1	23 03.1	79 05.6	12
14	30 07.9	23 03.5	109 10.5	14
16	60 07.6	23 03.8	139 15.4	16
18	90 07.4	23 04.2	169 20.3	18
20	120 07.1	23 04.5	199 25.3	20
22	150 06.9	N23 04.9	229 30.2	22

Thursday, 11th June

G.M.T. (h)	SUN G.H.A.	Dec.	ARIES G.H.A.	G.M.T. (h)
00	180 06.6	N23 05.2	259 35.1	00
02	210 06.4	23 05.6	289 40.1	02
04	240 06.1	23 05.9	319 45.0	04
06	270 05.9	23 06.3	349 49.9	06
08	300 05.6	23 06.6	19 54.8	08
10	330 05.4	23 06.9	49 59.8	10
12	0 05.1	23 07.3	80 04.7	12
14	30 04.9	23 07.6	110 09.6	14
16	60 04.6	23 07.9	140 14.6	16
18	90 04.4	23 08.2	170 19.5	18
20	120 04.1	23 08.6	200 24.4	20
22	150 03.8	N23 08.9	230 29.3	22

Friday, 12th June

G.M.T. (h)	SUN G.H.A.	Dec.	ARIES G.H.A.	G.M.T. (h)
00	180 03.6	N23 09.2	260 34.3	00
02	210 03.3	23 09.5	290 39.2	02
04	240 03.1	23 09.8	320 44.1	04
06	270 02.8	23 10.1	350 49.1	06
08	300 02.6	23 10.4	20 54.0	08
10	330 02.3	23 10.7	50 58.9	10
12	0 02.0	23 11.0	81 03.8	12
14	30 01.8	23 11.3	111 08.8	14
16	60 01.5	23 11.6	141 13.7	16
18	90 01.3	23 11.9	171 18.6	18
20	120 01.0	23 12.2	201 23.5	20
22	150 00.8	N23 12.5	231 28.5	22

Saturday, 13th June

G.M.T. (h)	SUN G.H.A.	Dec.	ARIES G.H.A.	G.M.T. (h)
00	180 00.5	N23 12.8	261 33.4	00
02	210 00.2	23 13.0	291 38.3	02
04	240 00.0	23 13.3	321 43.3	04
06	269 59.7	23 13.6	351 48.2	06
08	299 59.5	23 13.9	21 53.1	08
10	329 59.2	23 14.1	51 58.0	10
12	359 58.9	23 14.4	82 03.0	12
14	29 58.7	23 14.6	112 07.9	14
16	59 58.4	23 14.9	142 12.8	16
18	89 58.2	23 15.2	172 17.8	18
20	119 57.9	23 15.4	202 22.7	20
22	149 57.6	N23 15.7	232 27.6	22

Sunday, 14th June

G.M.T. (h)	SUN G.H.A.	Dec.	ARIES G.H.A.	G.M.T. (h)
00	179 57.4	N23 15.9	262 32.5	00
02	209 57.1	23 16.2	292 37.5	02
04	239 56.8	23 16.4	322 42.4	04
06	269 56.6	23 16.6	352 47.3	06
08	299 56.3	23 16.9	22 52.3	08
10	329 56.1	23 17.1	52 57.2	10
12	359 55.8	23 17.3	83 02.1	12
14	29 55.5	23 17.6	113 07.0	14
16	59 55.3	23 17.8	143 12.0	16
18	89 55.0	23 18.0	173 16.9	18
20	119 54.7	23 18.2	203 21.8	20
22	149 54.5	N23 18.4	233 26.8	22

Monday, 15th June

G.M.T. (h)	SUN G.H.A.	Dec.	ARIES G.H.A.	G.M.T. (h)
00	179 54.2	N23 18.6	263 31.7	00
02	209 53.9	23 18.9	293 36.6	02
04	239 53.7	23 19.1	323 41.5	04
06	269 53.4	23 19.3	353 46.5	06
08	299 53.2	23 19.5	23 51.4	08
10	329 52.9	23 19.7	53 56.3	10
12	359 52.6	23 19.9	84 01.3	12
14	29 52.4	23 20.1	114 06.2	14
16	59 52.1	23 20.2	144 11.1	16
18	89 51.8	23 20.4	174 16.0	18
20	119 51.6	23 20.6	204 21.0	20
22	149 51.3	N23 20.8	234 25.9	22

To interpolate SUN G.H.A. see page 4:7   To interpolate ARIES G.H.A. see page 4:8

G.M.T.	SUN G.H.A.	SUN Dec.	ARIES G.H.A.	G.M.T.

Tuesday, 16th June

h	G.H.A.	Dec.	G.H.A.	h
00	179 51.0	N23 21.0	264 30.8	00
02	209 50.8	23 21.1	294 35.7	02
04	239 50.5	23 21.3	324 40.7	04
06	269 50.2	23 21.5	354 45.6	06
08	299 50.0	23 21.7	24 50.5	08
10	329 49.7	23 21.8	54 55.5	10
12	359 49.4	23 22.0	85 00.4	12
14	29 49.2	23 22.1	115 05.3	14
16	59 48.9	23 22.3	145 10.2	16
18	89 48.6	23 22.4	175 15.2	18
20	119 48.4	23 22.6	205 20.1	20
22	149 48.1	N23 22.7	235 25.0	22

Sunday, 21st June

h	G.H.A.	Dec.	G.H.A.	h
00	179 34.9	N23 26.4	269 26.5	00
02	209 34.6	23 26.4	299 31.4	02
04	239 34.3	23 26.4	329 36.4	04
06	269 34.1	23 26.4	359 41.3	06
08	299 33.8	23 26.4	29 46.2	08
10	329 33.5	23 26.4	59 51.2	10
12	359 33.3	23 26.4	89 56.1	12
14	29 33.0	23 26.4	120 01.0	14
16	59 32.7	23 26.4	150 05.9	16
18	89 32.4	23 26.3	180 10.9	18
20	119 32.2	23 26.3	210 15.8	20
22	149 31.9	N23 26.3	240 20.7	22

Friday, 26th June

h	G.H.A.	Dec.	G.H.A.	h
00	179 18.8	N23 21.5	274 22.2	00
02	209 18.5	23 21.4	304 27.1	02
04	239 18.2	23 21.2	334 32.1	04
06	269 18.0	23 21.0	4 37.0	06
08	299 17.7	23 20.8	34 41.9	08
10	329 17.4	23 20.7	64 46.8	10
12	359 17.2	23 20.5	94 51.8	12
14	29 16.9	23 20.3	124 56.7	14
16	59 16.7	23 20.1	155 01.6	16
18	89 16.4	23 19.9	185 06.6	18
20	119 16.1	23 19.7	215 11.5	20
22	149 15.9	N23 19.5	245 16.4	22

Wednesday, 17th June

h	G.H.A.	Dec.	G.H.A.	h
00	179 47.8	N23 22.9	265 30.0	00
02	209 47.6	23 23.0	295 34.9	02
04	239 47.3	23 23.2	325 39.8	04
06	269 47.0	23 23.3	355 44.7	06
08	299 46.7	23 23.4	25 49.7	08
10	329 46.5	23 23.6	55 54.6	10
12	359 46.2	23 23.7	85 59.5	12
14	29 45.9	23 23.8	116 04.5	14
16	59 45.7	23 23.9	146 09.4	16
18	89 45.4	23 24.1	176 14.3	18
20	119 45.1	23 24.2	206 19.2	20
22	149 44.9	N23 24.3	236 24.2	22

Monday, 22nd June

h	G.H.A.	Dec.	G.H.A.	h
00	179 31.6	N23 26.3	270 25.7	00
02	209 31.4	23 26.2	300 30.6	02
04	239 31.1	23 26.2	330 35.5	04
06	269 30.8	23 26.2	0 40.4	06
08	299 30.5	23 26.1	30 45.4	08
10	329 30.3	23 26.1	60 50.3	10
12	359 30.0	23 26.0	90 55.2	12
14	29 29.7	23 26.0	121 00.2	14
16	59 29.5	23 25.9	151 05.1	16
18	89 29.2	23 25.9	181 10.0	18
20	119 28.9	23 25.8	211 14.9	20
22	149 28.7	N23 25.8	241 19.9	22

Saturday, 27th June

h	G.H.A.	Dec.	G.H.A.	h
00	179 15.6	N23 19.3	275 21.3	00
02	209 15.3	23 19.1	305 26.3	02
04	239 15.1	23 18.9	335 31.2	04
06	269 14.8	23 18.7	5 36.1	06
08	299 14.6	23 18.5	35 41.1	08
10	329 14.3	23 18.3	65 46.0	10
12	359 14.0	23 18.1	95 50.9	12
14	29 13.8	23 17.8	125 55.8	14
16	59 13.5	23 17.6	156 00.8	16
18	89 13.3	23 17.4	186 05.7	18
20	119 13.0	23 17.2	216 10.6	20
22	149 12.8	N23 16.9	246 15.6	22

Thursday, 18th June

h	G.H.A.	Dec.	G.H.A.	h
00	179 44.6	N23 24.4	266 29.1	00
02	209 44.3	23 24.5	296 34.0	02
04	239 44.1	23 24.6	326 39.0	04
06	269 43.8	23 24.7	356 43.9	06
08	299 43.5	23 24.8	26 48.8	08
10	329 43.3	23 24.9	56 53.7	10
12	359 43.0	23 25.0	86 58.7	12
14	29 42.7	23 25.1	117 03.6	14
16	59 42.4	23 25.2	147 08.5	16
18	89 42.2	23 25.2	177 13.5	18
20	119 41.9	23 25.3	207 18.4	20
22	149 41.6	N23 25.4	237 23.3	22

Tuesday, 23rd June

h	G.H.A.	Dec.	G.H.A.	h
00	179 28.4	N23 25.7	271 24.8	00
02	209 28.1	23 25.6	301 29.7	02
04	239 27.8	23 25.6	331 34.6	04
06	269 27.6	23 25.5	1 39.6	06
08	299 27.3	23 25.4	31 44.5	08
10	329 27.0	23 25.4	61 49.4	10
12	359 26.8	23 25.3	91 54.4	12
14	29 26.5	23 25.2	121 59.3	14
16	59 26.2	23 25.1	152 04.2	16
18	89 26.0	23 25.0	182 09.1	18
20	119 25.7	23 24.9	212 14.1	20
22	149 25.4	N23 24.8	242 19.0	22

Sunday, 28th June

h	G.H.A.	Dec.	G.H.A.	h
00	179 12.5	N23 16.7	276 20.5	00
02	209 12.2	23 16.5	306 25.4	02
04	239 12.0	23 16.3	336 30.3	04
06	269 11.7	23 16.0	6 35.3	06
08	299 11.5	23 15.7	36 40.2	08
10	329 11.2	23 15.5	66 45.1	10
12	359 11.0	23 15.2	96 50.1	12
14	29 10.7	23 15.0	126 55.0	14
16	59 10.4	23 14.7	156 59.9	16
18	89 10.2	23 14.5	187 04.8	18
20	119 09.9	23 14.2	217 09.8	20
22	149 09.7	N23 13.9	247 14.7	22

Friday, 19th June

h	G.H.A.	Dec.	G.H.A.	h
00	179 41.4	N23 25.5	267 28.2	00
02	209 41.1	23 25.6	297 33.2	02
04	239 40.8	23 25.6	327 38.1	04
06	269 40.6	23 25.7	357 43.0	06
08	299 40.3	23 25.8	27 47.9	08
10	329 40.0	23 25.8	57 52.9	10
12	359 39.7	23 25.9	87 57.8	12
14	29 39.5	23 25.9	118 02.7	14
16	59 39.2	23 26.0	148 07.7	16
18	89 38.9	23 26.0	178 12.6	18
20	119 38.7	23 26.1	208 17.5	20
22	149 38.4	N23 26.1	238 22.4	22

Wednesday, 24th June

h	G.H.A.	Dec.	G.H.A.	h
00	179 25.2	N23 24.7	272 23.9	00
02	209 24.9	23 24.6	302 28.9	02
04	239 24.6	23 24.5	332 33.8	04
06	269 24.4	23 24.4	2 38.7	06
08	299 24.1	23 24.3	32 43.6	08
10	329 23.8	23 24.2	62 48.6	10
12	359 23.6	23 24.1	92 53.5	12
14	29 23.3	23 24.0	122 58.4	14
16	59 23.0	23 23.8	153 03.4	16
18	89 22.8	23 23.7	183 08.3	18
20	119 22.5	23 23.6	213 13.2	20
22	149 22.2	N23 23.5	243 18.1	22

Monday, 29th June

h	G.H.A.	Dec.	G.H.A.	h
00	179 09.4	N23 13.7	277 19.6	00
02	209 09.2	23 13.4	307 24.6	02
04	239 08.9	23 13.1	337 29.5	04
06	269 08.7	23 12.8	7 34.4	06
08	299 08.4	23 12.6	37 39.3	08
10	329 08.2	23 12.3	67 44.3	10
12	359 07.9	23 12.0	97 49.2	12
14	29 07.7	23 11.7	127 54.1	14
16	59 07.4	23 11.4	157 59.0	16
18	89 07.2	23 11.1	188 04.0	18
20	119 06.9	23 10.8	218 08.9	20
22	149 06.7	N23 10.5	248 13.8	22

Saturday, 20th June

h	G.H.A.	Dec.	G.H.A.	h
00	179 38.1	N23 26.2	268 27.4	00
02	209 37.8	23 26.2	298 32.3	02
04	239 37.6	23 26.2	328 37.2	04
06	269 37.3	23 26.3	358 42.2	06
08	299 37.0	23 26.3	28 47.1	08
10	329 36.8	23 26.3	58 52.0	10
12	359 36.5	23 26.3	88 56.9	12
14	29 36.2	23 26.4	119 01.9	14
16	59 36.0	23 26.4	149 06.8	16
18	89 35.7	23 26.4	179 11.7	18
20	119 35.4	23 26.4	209 16.7	20
22	149 35.1	N23 26.4	239 21.6	22

Thursday, 25th June

h	G.H.A.	Dec.	G.H.A.	h
00	179 22.0	N23 23.3	273 23.1	00
02	209 21.7	23 23.2	303 28.0	02
04	239 21.4	23 23.1	333 32.9	04
06	269 21.2	23 22.9	3 37.9	06
08	299 20.9	23 22.8	33 42.8	08
10	329 20.6	23 22.6	63 47.7	10
12	359 20.4	23 22.5	93 52.6	12
14	29 20.1	23 22.3	123 57.6	14
16	59 19.8	23 22.2	154 02.5	16
18	89 19.6	23 22.0	184 07.4	18
20	119 19.3	23 21.9	214 12.4	20
22	149 19.0	N23 21.7	244 17.3	22

Tuesday, 30th June

h	G.H.A.	Dec.	G.H.A.	h
00	179 06.4	N23 10.2	278 18.8	00
02	209 06.2	23 09.9	308 23.7	02
04	239 05.9	23 09.6	338 28.6	04
06	269 05.7	23 09.3	8 33.5	06
08	299 05.4	23 09.0	38 38.5	08
10	329 05.2	23 08.7	68 43.4	10
12	359 04.9	23 08.3	98 48.3	12
14	29 04.7	23 08.0	128 53.3	14
16	59 04.4	23 07.7	158 58.2	16
18	89 04.2	23 07.4	189 03.1	18
20	119 03.9	23 07.0	219 08.0	20
22	149 03.7	N23 06.7	249 13.0	22

To interpolate SUN G.H.A. see page 4:7   To interpolate ARIES G.H.A. see page 4:8

♀ VENUS ♀ — ♃ JUPITER ♃

Mer. Pass. (h. m.)	VENUS G.H.A. ° '	Mean Var 14° '	Dec. ° '	Mean Var '	M	Day of Week	JUPITER G.H.A ° '	Mean Var 15° '	Dec. ° '	Mean Var '	Mer. Pass (h. m.)
11 44	184 10.3	59.2	N21 11.3	0.6	1	Mon.	91 26.3	2.3	N10 24.1	0.1	17 52
11 45	183 51.7	59.2	N21 25.5	0.6	2	Tu.	92 20.4	2.3	N10 21.9	0.1	17 48
11 46	183 32.9	59.2	N21 39.0	0.5	3	Wed.	93 14.4	2.2	N10 19.7	0.1	17 44
11 48	183 13.9	59.2	N21 51.9	0.5	4	Th.	94 08.2	2.2	N10 17.5	0.1	17 41
11 49	182 54.6	59.2	N22 04.2	0.5	5	Fri.	95 01.9	2.2	N10 15.2	0.1	17 37
11 50	182 35.1	59.2	N22 15.9	0.5	6	Sat.	95 55.5	2.2	N10 12.8	0.1	17 34
11 52	182 15.4	59.2	N22 27.0	0.4	7	SUN.	96 48.9	2.2	N10 10.4	0.1	17 30
11 53	181 55.5	59.2	N22 37.4	0.4	8	Mon.	97 42.2	2.2	N10 07.9	0.1	17 27
11 54	181 35.4	59.2	N22 47.2	0.4	9	Tu.	98 35.3	2.2	N10 05.4	0.1	17 23
11 56	181 15.1	59.2	N22 56.3	0.4	10	Wed.	99 28.4	2.2	N10 02.8	0.1	17 20
11 57	180 54.7	59.1	N23 04.8	0.3	11	Th.	100 21.3	2.2	N10 00.2	0.1	17 16
11 58	180 34.1	59.1	N23 12.6	0.3	12	Fri.	101 14.0	2.2	N 9 57.5	0.1	17 13
12 00	180 13.3	59.1	N23 19.7	0.3	13	Sat.	102 06.7	2.2	N 9 54.8	0.1	17 09
12 01	179 52.4	59.1	N23 26.2	0.2	14	SUN.	102 59.2	2.2	N 9 52.0	0.1	17 06
12 03	179 31.4	59.1	N23 31.9	0.2	15	Mon.	103 51.6	2.2	N 9 49.2	0.1	17 02
12 04	179 10.3	59.1	N23 37.0	0.2	16	Tu.	104 43.9	2.2	N 9 46.3	0.1	16 59
12 05	178 49.1	59.1	N23 41.4	0.2	17	Wed.	105 36.1	2.2	N 9 43.4	0.1	16 55
12 07	178 27.8	59.1	N23 45.1	0.1	18	Th.	106 28.2	2.2	N 9 40.4	0.1	16 52
12 08	178 06.4	59.1	N23 48.0	0.1	19	Fri.	107 20.1	2.2	N 9 37.4	0.1	16 48
12 10	177 45.0	59.1	N23 50.3	0.1	20	Sat.	108 11.9	2.2	N 9 34.4	0.1	16 45
12 11	177 23.5	59.1	N23 51.9	0.0	21	SUN.	109 03.7	2.1	N 9 31.3	0.1	16 41
12 13	177 02.0	59.1	N23 52.8	0.0	22	Mon.	109 55.3	2.1	N 9 28.1	0.1	16 38
12 14	176 40.5	59.1	N23 52.9	0.0	23	Tu.	110 46.8	2.1	N 9 24.9	0.1	16 35
12 15	176 19.0	59.1	N23 52.4	0.1	24	Wed.	111 38.2	2.1	N 9 21.7	0.1	16 31
12 17	175 57.5	59.1	N23 51.1	0.1	25	Th.	112 29.5	2.1	N 9 18.4	0.1	16 28
12 18	175 36.0	59.1	N23 49.1	0.1	26	Fri.	113 20.7	2.1	N 9 15.1	0.1	16 24
12 20	175 14.5	59.1	N23 46.5	0.1	27	Sat.	114 11.7	2.1	N 9 11.7	0.1	16 21
12 21	174 53.2	59.1	N23 43.1	0.2	28	SUN.	115 02.7	2.1	N 9 08.3	0.1	16 18
12 23	174 31.9	59.1	N23 39.0	0.2	29	Mon.	115 53.6	2.1	N 9 04.9	0.1	16 14
12 24	174 10.7	59.1	N23 34.2	0.2	30	Tu.	116 44.4	2.1	N 9 01.4	0.2	16 11

♀ **VENUS.** Av. Mag. –3.9. Too close to the sun for observation throughout the month. **S.H.A.** June 5 289°; 10 283°; 15 276°; 20 269°; 25 263°; 30 256°.

♃ **JUPITER.** Av. Mag. –1.9. An **Evening Star. S.H.A.** June 5 202°; 10 200°; 15 200°; 20 201°; 25 198°; 30 198°.

♂ MARS ♂ — ♄ SATURN ♄

Mer. Pass. (h. m.)	MARS G.H.A. ° '	Mean Var 15° '	Dec. ° '	Mean Var '	M	Day of Week	SATURN G.H.A ° '	Mean Var 15° '	Dec. ° '	Mean Var '	Mer. Pass (h. m.)
08 36	230 55.8	0.7	N 6 33.1	0.7	1	Mon.	288 32.3	2.5	S16 06.8	0.0	04 45
08 35	231 13.0	0.7	N 6 50.2	0.7	2	Tu.	289 31.7	2.5	S16 07.1	0.0	04 41
08 34	231 30.2	0.7	N 7 07.3	0.7	3	Wed.	290 31.3	2.5	S16 07.4	0.0	04 37
08 32	231 47.4	0.7	N 7 24.2	0.7	4	Th.	291 31.0	2.5	S16 07.7	0.0	04 33
08 31	232 04.7	0.7	N 7 41.1	0.7	5	Fri.	292 30.7	2.5	S16 08.1	0.0	04 29
08 30	232 21.9	0.7	N 7 57.8	0.7	6	Sat.	293 30.6	2.5	S16 08.5	0.0	04 25
08 29	232 39.1	0.7	N 8 14.5	0.7	7	SUN.	294 30.5	2.5	S16 08.9	0.0	04 21
08 28	232 56.3	0.7	N 8 31.1	0.7	8	Mon.	295 30.6	2.5	S19 09.3	0.0	04 17
08 27	233 13.5	0.7	N 8 47.6	0.7	9	Tu.	296 30.7	2.5	S16 09.8	0.0	04 13
08 26	233 30.7	0.7	N 9 04.0	0.7	10	Wed.	297 30.9	2.5	S16 10.3	0.0	04 09
08 24	233 47.9	0.7	N 9 20.3	0.7	11	Th.	298 31.2	2.5	S16 10.9	0.0	04 05
08 23	234 05.0	0.7	N 9 36.4	0.7	12	Fri.	299 31.7	2.5	S16 11.4	0.0	04 01
08 22	234 22.2	0.7	N 9 52.5	0.7	13	Sat.	300 32.2	2.5	S16 12.0	0.0	03 57
08 21	234 39.3	0.7	N10 08.5	0.7	14	SUN.	301 32.8	2.5	S16 12.6	0.0	03 53
08 20	234 56.4	0.7	N10 24.3	0.7	15	Mon.	302 33.5	2.5	S16 13.3	0.0	03 49
08 19	235 13.6	0.7	N10 40.0	0.7	16	Tu.	303 34.2	2.5	S16 14.0	0.0	03 45
08 18	235 30.7	0.7	N10 55.7	0.6	17	Wed.	304 35.1	2.5	S16 14.7	0.0	03 41
08 16	235 47.7	0.7	N11 11.1	0.6	18	Th.	305 36.1	2.5	S16 15.4	0.0	03 37
08 15	236 04.8	0.7	N11 26.5	0.6	19	Fri.	306 37.1	2.6	S16 16.2	0.0	03 33
08 14	236 21.9	0.7	N11 41.8	0.6	20	Sat.	307 38.3	2.5	S16 16.9	0.0	03 29
08 13	236 38.9	0.7	N11 56.9	0.6	21	SUN.	308 39.5	2.6	S16 17.8	0.0	03 25
08 12	236 55.9	0.7	N12 11.9	0.6	22	Mon.	309 40.8	2.6	S16 18.6	0.0	03 21
08 11	237 12.9	0.7	N12 26.7	0.6	23	Tu.	310 42.2	2.6	S16 19.4	0.0	03 17
08 10	237 29.9	0.7	N12 41.5	0.6	24	Wed.	311 43.6	2.6	S16 20.3	0.0	03 13
08 08	237 46.8	0.7	N12 56.1	0.6	25	Th.	312 45.2	2.6	S16 21.2	0.0	03 08
08 07	238 03.8	0.7	N13 10.5	0.6	26	Fri.	313 46.8	2.6	S16 22.2	0.0	03 04
08 06	238 20.7	0.7	N13 24.8	0.6	27	Sat.	314 48.6	2.6	S16 23.1	0.0	03 00
08 05	238 37.6	0.7	N13 39.0	0.6	28	SUN.	315 50.4	2.6	S16 24.1	0.0	02 56
08 04	238 54.5	0.7	N13 53.1	0.6	29	Mon.	316 52.2	2.6	S16 25.1	0.0	02 52
08 03	239 11.4	0.7	N14 06.9	0.6	30	Tu.	317 54.2	2.6	S16 26.1	0.0	02 48

♂ **MARS.** Av. Mag. +0.9. A **Morning Star. S.H.A.** June 5 339°; 10 335°; 15 331°; 20 328°; 25 324°; 30 321°.

♄ **SATURN.** Av. Mag. +0.5. A **Morning Star. S.H.A.** June 5 40°; 10 38°; 15 39°; 20 40°; 25 38°; 30 40°.

MERCURY. Too close to the sun for observation until June 8 when it is visible in the west after sunset.

For Planets Correction Tables see pages 4:9-4:13. See also 'How to Recognise the Planets' on page 2:32.
Mean Var. means Variation per Hour.

Day of M. W. T.	G.M.T. h	G.H.A. ° '	Mean Var. per Hour 14°,+	Dec. ° '	Mean Var. per Hour '
1 Mon.	0	183 12.6	23.7	N23 41.6	2.1
	6	269 35.0	23.4	N23 54.6	1.1
	12	355 55.7	23.2	N24 01.7	0.1
	18	82 15.2	23.1	N24 02.8	0.9
2 Tu.	0	168 33.9	23.1	N23 58.0	1.9
	6	254 52.3	23.1	N23 47.0	2.9
	12	341 10.8	23.2	N23 30.1	3.9
	18	67 30.0	23.4	N23 07.1	4.9
3 Wed.	0	153 50.2	23.6	N22 38.3	5.8
	6	240 11.8	23.9	N22 03.8	6.8
	12	326 35.2	24.3	N21 23.8	7.6
	18	53 00.7	24.7	N20 38.5	8.5
4 Th.	0	139 28.6	25.1	N19 48.2	9.2
	6	225 59.1	25.5	N18 53.2	10.0
	12	312 32.2	26.0	N17 53.9	10.6
	18	39 08.1	26.5	N16 50.4	11.3
5 Fri.	0	125 46.8	27.0	N15 43.2	11.8
	6	212 28.3	27.4	N14 32.7	12.3
	12	299 12.6	27.9	N13 19.1	12.8
	18	25 59.5	28.3	N12 02.8	13.1
6 Sat.	0	112 48.9	28.6	N10 44.2	13.5
	6	199 40.8	29.1	N 9 23.7	13.7
	12	286 34.8	29.4	N 8 01.4	13.9
	18	13 30.9	29.7	N 6 37.9	14.1
7 Sun.	0	100 28.8	29.9	N 5 13.3	14.2
	6	187 28.2	30.2	N 3 48.0	14.3
	12	274 29.1	30.4	N 2 22.3	14.3
	18	1 31.0	30.5	N 0 56.5	14.3
8 Mon.	0	88 33.9	30.6	S 0 29.2	14.2
	6	175 37.5	30.7	S 1 54.4	14.1
	12	262 41.5	30.7	S 3 19.0	13.9
	18	349 45.7	30.7	S 4 42.6	13.7
9 Tu.	0	76 50.0	30.6	S 6 05.0	13.5
	6	163 54.1	30.6	S 7 25.9	13.1
	12	250 57.8	30.5	S 8 45.2	12.8
	18	338 00.9	30.4	S10 02.5	12.5
10 Wed.	0	65 03.3	30.2	S11 17.7	12.1
	6	152 04.8	30.1	S12 30.5	11.7
	12	239 05.3	29.9	S13 40.7	11.2
	18	326 04.8	29.7	S14 48.1	10.7
11 Th.	0	53 03.0	29.5	S15 52.4	10.2
	6	140 00.0	29.2	S16 53.6	9.5
	12	226 55.7	29.1	S17 51.3	9.0
	18	313 50.1	28.8	S18 45.4	8.3
12 Fri.	0	40 43.2	28.6	S19 35.7	7.6
	6	127 35.1	28.4	S20 22.0	7.0
	12	214 25.9	28.3	S21 04.3	6.3
	18	301 15.7	28.1	S21 42.3	5.6
13 Sat.	0	28 04.6	28.0	S22 15.9	4.8
	6	114 52.8	27.9	S22 45.1	4.0
	12	201 40.5	27.9	S23 09.7	3.2
	18	288 27.8	27.9	S23 29.7	2.5
14 Sun.	0	15 15.1	28.0	S23 45.1	1.7
	6	102 02.5	28.0	S23 55.7	1.0
	12	188 50.3	28.1	S24 01.8	0.2
	18	275 38.7	28.2	S24 03.1	0.6
15 Mon.	0	2 28.0	28.5	S23 59.9	1.3
	6	89 18.4	28.6	S23 52.2	2.1
	12	176 10.1	28.9	S23 40.1	2.9
	18	263 03.3	29.2	S23 23.6	3.5
16 Tu.	0	349 58.3	29.5	S23 02.9	4.1
	6	76 55.1	29.9	S22 38.2	4.8
	12	163 53.9	30.2	S22 09.5	5.5
	18	250 54.8	30.5	S21 37.1	6.0

Day of M. W. T.	G.M.T. h	G.H.A. ° '	Mean Var. per Hour 14°,+	Dec. ° '	Mean Var. per Hour '
17 Wed.	0	337 57.9	30.9	S21 01.1	6.6
	6	65 03.2	31.3	S20 21.7	7.2
	12	152 10.8	31.7	S19 39.0	7.7
	18	239 20.7	32.1	S18 53.3	8.1
18 Th.	0	326 32.8	32.4	S18 04.8	8.6
	6	53 47.0	32.8	S17 13.5	9.0
	12	141 03.5	33.1	S16 19.7	9.4
	18	228 21.9	33.4	S15 23.5	9.7
19 Fri.	0	315 42.4	33.8	S14 25.2	10.1
	6	43 04.6	34.1	S13 24.8	10.4
	12	130 28.5	34.2	S12 22.6	10.7
	18	217 54.0	34.5	S11 18.7	10.9
20 Sat.	0	305 20.8	34.7	S10 13.3	11.2
	6	32 48.9	34.8	S 9 06.5	11.4
	12	120 18.0	35.1	S 7 58.4	11.6
	18	207 48.0	35.1	S 6 49.2	11.7
21 Sun.	0	295 18.7	35.2	S 5 39.0	11.9
	6	22 49.9	35.2	S 4 27.9	12.0
	12	110 21.3	35.2	S 3 16.2	12.1
	18	197 52.8	35.2	S 2 03.9	12.1
22 Mon.	0	285 24.2	35.2	S 0 51.1	12.2
	6	12 55.3	35.1	N 0 22.0	12.2
	12	100 25.8	35.0	N 1 35.2	12.2
	18	187 55.4	34.8	N 2 48.5	12.2
23 Tu.	0	275 24.1	34.6	N 4 01.8	12.1
	6	2 51.6	34.3	N 5 14.7	12.1
	12	90 17.6	34.0	N 6 27.3	12.0
	18	177 41.9	33.7	N 7 39.3	11.9
24 Wed.	0	265 04.3	33.3	N 8 50.6	11.7
	6	352 24.5	33.0	N10 01.0	11.6
	12	79 42.4	32.6	N11 10.2	11.3
	18	166 57.6	32.0	N12 18.2	11.1
25 Th.	0	254 10.1	31.5	N13 24.7	10.7
	6	341 19.6	31.0	N14 29.4	10.4
	12	68 25.9	30.4	N15 32.1	10.0
	18	155 28.8	29.8	N16 32.6	9.7
26 Fri.	0	242 28.2	29.2	N17 30.6	9.1
	6	329 24.0	28.6	N18 25.8	8.6
	12	56 16.0	28.0	N19 17.9	8.1
	18	143 04.3	27.3	N20 06.7	7.4
27 Sat.	0	229 48.7	26.7	N20 51.7	6.7
	6	316 29.4	26.1	N21 32.8	6.0
	12	43 06.3	25.5	N22 09.5	5.3
	18	129 39.7	25.0	N22 41.6	4.5
28 Sun.	0	216 09.7	24.4	N23 08.8	3.6
	6	302 36.5	23.9	N23 30.8	2.7
	12	29 00.5	23.5	N23 47.3	1.7
	18	115 22.0	23.2	N23 58.2	0.7
29 Mon.	0	201 41.4	22.9	N24 03.2	0.3
	6	287 59.1	22.8	N24 02.2	1.3
	12	14 15.7	22.7	N23 55.0	2.3
	18	100 31.5	22.6	N23 41.7	3.4
30 Tu.	0	186 47.1	22.7	N23 22.1	4.4
	6	273 02.9	22.8	N22 56.4	5.3
	12	Eclipse of the Sun occurs today			
	18	85 37.1	23.3	N21 46.9	7.3

PHASES OF THE MOON

	d. h/min		d. h/min
● New Moon	1 03 57	○ Full Moon	15 04 50
☽ First Quarter	7 20 47	☾ Last Quarter	23 08 11
		● New Moon	30 12 18
Perigee	4 02	Apogee	19 22

JULY, 1992

(31 days)

☉ SUN ☉

DATE			Equation of Time		Transit	Semi-diam.	Lat. 52°N.				Lat. Corr. to Sunrise, Sunset, etc.				
Day of							Twilight	Sunrise	Sunset	Twilight		Twilight	Sunrise	Sunset	Twilight
Yr.	Mth.	Week	0 h.	12 h.							Lat.				
			m. s.	m. s.	h. m.	′	h. m.	h. m.	h. m.	h. m.	°	h. m.	h. m.	h. m.	h. m.
183	1	Wed.	+03 46	+03 52	12 04	15.8	02 56	03 44	20 23	21 12	N70	S.A.H.	S.A.H.	S.A.H.	S.A.H.
184	2	Th.	+03 58	+04 03	12 04	15.8	02 57	03 45	20 23	21 11	68	S.A.H.	S.A.H.	S.A.H.	S.A.H.
185	3	Fri.	+04 09	+04 14	12 04	15.8	02 58	03 46	20 22	21 10	66	T.A.N.	-2 21	+2 19	T.A.N.
186	4	Sat.	+04 20	+04 25	12 04	15.8	02 59	03 46	20 22	21 10	64	T.A.N.	-1 42	+1 40	T.A.N.
187	5	Sun.	+04 30	+04 36	12 05	15.8	03 00	03 47	20 22	21 09	62	-2 21	-1 14	+1 14	+2 21
188	6	Mon.	+04 41	+04 46	12 05	15.8	03 01	03 48	20 21	21 08	N60	-1 27	-0 54	+0 54	+1 27
189	7	Tu.	+04 51	+04 55	12 05	15.8	03 02	03 49	20 21	21 07	58	-0 55	-0 37	+0 37	+0 56
190	8	Wed.	+05 00	+05 05	12 05	15.8	03 03	03 50	20 20	21 06	56	-0 33	-0 22	+0 23	+0 34
191	9	Th.	+05 09	+05 13	12 05	15.8	03 04	03 51	20 19	21 05	54	-0 15	-0 10	+0 11	+0 15
192	10	Fri.	+05 18	+05 22	12 05	15.8	03 05	03 52	20 18	21 04	50	+0 13	+0 10	-0 10	-0 13
193	11	Sat.	+05 26	+05 30	12 05	15.8	03 07	03 54	20 17	21 03	N45	+0 39	+0 30	-0 30	-0 39
194	12	Sun.	+05 34	+05 37	12 06	15.8	03 08	03 55	20 16	21 02	40	+0 59	+0 46	-0 46	-0 59
195	13	Mon.	+05 41	+05 44	12 06	15.8	03 09	03 56	20 15	21 01	35	+1 16	+1 00	-0 59	-1 16
196	14	Tu.	+05 48	+05 51	12 06	15.8	03 11	03 57	20 14	20 59	30	+1 30	+1 12	-1 11	-1 30
197	15	Wed.	+05 54	+05 57	12 06	15.8	03 12	03 58	20 13	20 58	20	+1 53	+1 32	-1 31	-1 52
198	16	Th.	+06 00	+06 03	12 06	15.8	03 14	03 59	20 12	20 57	N10	+2 12	+1 46	-1 48	-2 11
199	17	Fri.	+06 05	+06 08	12 06	15.8	03 15	04 01	20 11	20 55	0	+2 28	+2 05	-2 04	-2 27
200	18	Sat.	+06 10	+06 12	12 06	15.8	03 17	04 02	20 10	20 54	S10	+2 43	+2 21	-2 19	-2 43
201	19	Sun.	+06 14	+06 16	12 06	15.8	03 19	04 03	20 09	20 53	20	+2 59	+2 38	-2 36	-2 59
202	20	Mon.	+06 18	+06 19	12 06	15.8	03 20	04 05	20 07	20 51	30	+3 15	+2 57	-2 54	-3 15
203	21	Tu.	+06 21	+06 22	12 06	15.8	03 22	04 06	20 06	20 50	S35	+3 25	+3 08	-3 06	-3 25
204	22	Wed.	+06 24	+06 25	12 06	15.8	03 24	04 07	20 05	20 48	40	+3 35	+3 21	-3 18	-3 35
205	23	Th.	+06 26	+06 26	12 06	15.8	03 25	04 09	20 03	20 47	45	+3 38	+3 36	-3 33	-3 47
206	24	Fri.	+06 27	+06 28	12 06	15.8	03 27	04 10	20 02	20 45	S50	+4 02	+3 55	-3 51	-4 02
207	25	Sat.	+06 28	+06 28	12 06	15.8	03 29	04 11	20 01	20 43					
208	26	Sun.	+06 28	+06 28	12 06	15.8	03 30	04 13	19 59	20 42					
209	27	Mon.	+06 28	+06 28	12 06	15.8	03 32	04 14	19 58	20 40					
210	28	Tu.	+06 27	+06 27	12 06	15.8	03 34	04 16	19 56	20 38					
211	29	Wed.	+06 26	+06 25	12 06	15.8	03 35	04 17	19 55	20 36					
212	30	Th.	+06 24	+06 23	12 06	15.8	03 37	04 19	19 53	20 34					
213	31	Fri.	+06 21	+06 20	12 06	15.8	03 39	04 20	19 51	20 32					

Equation of Time is the excess of Mean Time over Apparent Time
(See explanation and examples on p. 2:15)

NOTES

The Lat. Corr. to sunrise, sunset, etc., is for the middle of July. S.A.H. means Sun above horizon. T.A.N. means Twilight all night. Examples on the use of the above data are given on page 2:11 onwards.

☾ MOON ☽

DATE			Age	Transit Diff. (Upper)		Semi-diam.	Hor. Par. 12 h.	Lat. 52°N.		MOON'S PHASES
Day of								Moonrise	Moonset	
Yr.	Mth.	Week	days							
				h. m.	m.	′	′	h. m.	h. m.	
183	1	Wed.	01	13 04	58	16.6	60.8	04 52	20 59	
184	2	Th.	02	14 02	55	16.6	60.8	06 19	21 26	☽ First Quarter........... 7 02 43
185	3	Fri.	03	14 57	52	16.5	60.5	07 47	21 49	○ Full Moon 14 19 06
186	4	Sat.	04	15 49	50	16.4	60.0	09 12	22 08	☾ Last Quarter........... 22 22 12
187	5	Sun.	05	16 39	49	16.2	59.4	10 36	22 27	● New Moon 29 19 35
188	6	Mon.	06	17 28	50	16.0	58.7	11 57	22 47	
189	7	Tu.	07	18 18	50	15.8	58.0	13 17	23 08	
190	8	Wed.	08	19 08	52	15.6	57.3	14 35	23 33	
191	9	Th.	09	20 00	52	15.4	56.6	15 49	— —	d. h.
192	10	Fri.	10	20 52	53	15.3	56.1	16 57	00 05	Perigee 2 01
193	11	Sat.	11	21 45	51	15.1	55.5	17 57	00 44	Apogee 17 11
194	12	Sun.	12	22 36	50	15.0	55.1	18 46	01 33	Perigee 30 08
195	13	Mon.	13	23 26	48	14.9	54.7	19 25	02 30	
196	14	Tu.	14	24 14	—	14.8	54.4	19 55	03 34	
197	15	Wed.	15	01 04	45	14.8	54.2	20 19	04 41	
198	16	Th.	16	00 59	44	14.7	54.1	20 38	05 49	
199	17	Fri.	17	01 43	41	14.7	54.0	20 55	06 58	
200	18	Sat.	18	02 24	41	14.7	54.1	21 10	08 05	
201	19	Sun.	19	03 05	40	14.8	54.3	21 25	09 12	
202	20	Mon.	20	03 45	42	14.9	54.6	21 41	10 20	NOTES
203	21	Tu.	21	04 27	44	15.0	55.1	21 58	11 29	Moon's G.H.A. and Dec. are given
204	22	Wed.	22	05 11	47	15.2	55.7	22 19	12 39	on page 3:51.
205	23	Th.	23	05 58	50	15.4	56.5	22 44	13 52	A table for correcting Moonrise and
206	24	Fri.	24	06 48	55	15.6	57.3	23 19	15 06	Moonset for latitude is on page 4:20.
207	25	Sat.	25	07 43	59	15.9	58.3	— —	16 17	A table for correcting Moon's meri-dian passage (transit) for longitude is
208	26	Sun.	26	08 42	61	16.1	59.2	00 05	17 20	on page 4:19.
209	27	Mon.	27	09 43	62	16.4	60.1	01 06	18 12	Examples on the use of the above
210	28	Tu.	28	10 45	60	16.6	60.8	02 21	18 53	data are given on page 2:11 onwards.
211	29	Wed.	29	11 45	57	16.7	61.2	03 46	19 25	
212	30	Th.	01	12 42	55	16.7	61.3	05 15	19 51	
213	31	Fri.	02	13 37	53	16.6	61.1	06 44	20 12	

0h. = midnight. For explanation of use of above data see page 2:11 onwards.

No.	Name	Mag.	Transit (approx.) h. m.	DEC. ° ′	G.H.A. ° ′	R.A. h. m.	S.H.A. ° ′
♈	ARIES	–	05 22	–	279 17.9	–	–
1	Alpheratz	2.2	05 30	N29 03.0	277 17.5	0 08	357 59.6
2	Ankaa	2.4	05 48	S42 20.4	272 48.8	0 26	353 30.9
3	Schedar........	2.5	06 02	N56 29.7	269 16.3	0 40	349 58.4
4	Diphda	2.2	06 05	S18 01.4	268 29.3	0 43	349 11.4
5	Achernar	0.6	06 59	S57 16.1	254 56.2	1 37	335 38.3
6	POLARIS	2.1	07 45	N89 13.6	243 20.3	2 24	324 02.4
7	Hamal	2.2	07 28	N23 25.7	247 36.4	2 07	328 18.5
8	Acamar	3.1	08 19	S40 19.7	234 48.2	2 58	315 30.3
9	Menkar	2.8	08 23	N 4 03.8	233 49.4	3 02	314 31.5
10	Mirfak	1.9	08 45	N49 50.0	228 21.0	3 24	309 03.1
11	Aldebaran......	1.1	09 57	N16 29.7	210 25.5	4 35	291 07.6
12	Rigel	0.3	10 35	S 8 12.5	200 45.2	5 14	281 27.3
13	Capella	0.2	10 37	N45 59.4	200 15.8	5 16	280 57.9
14	Bellatrix	1.7	10 46	N 6 20.6	198 06.9	5 25	278 49.0
15	Elnath	1.8	10 47	N28 36.1	197 50.6	5 26	278 32.7
16	Alnilam	1.8	10 57	S 1 12.3	195 20.4	5 36	276 02.5
17	Betelgeuse ...	{ 0.1 / 1.2 }	11 16	N 7 24.4	190 36.4	5 55	271 18.5
18	Canopus	–0.9	11 45	S52 41.4	183 21.5	6 24	264 03.6
19	Sirius............	–1.6	12 06	S16 42.3	178 05.7	6 45	258 47.8
20	Adhara	1.6	12 19	S28 57.7	174 43.1	6 58	255 25.2
21	Castor	1.6	12 55	N31 54.3	165 46.1	7 34	246 28.2
22	Procyon........	0.5	13 00	N 5 14.7	164 34.3	7 39	245 16.4
23	Pollux	1.2	13 06	N28 02.7	163 05.0	7 45	243 47.1
24	Avior	1.7	13 43	S59 29.2	153 43.0	8 22	234 25.1
25	Suhail	2.2	14 28	S43 24.3	142 22.3	9 08	223 04.4
26	Miaplacidus ...	1.8	14 33	S69 41.4	141 01.8	9 13	221 43.9
27	Alphard........	2.2	14 48	S 8 37.6	137 29.6	9 27	218 11.7
28	Regulus	1.3	15 28	N12 00.2	127 18.2	10 08	208 00.3
29	Dubhe	2.0	16 23	N61 47.6	113 28.9	11 03	194 11.0
30	Denebola	2.2	17 09	N14 36.8	102 07.6	11 49	182 49.7
31	Gienah	2.8	17 35	S17 30.2	95 26.4	12 15	176 08.5
32	Acrux...........	1.1	17 46	S63 03.9	92 45.0	12 26	173 27.1
33	Gacrux.........	1.6	17 51	S57 04.7	91 36.5	12 31	172 18.6
34	Mimosa........	1.5	18 07	S59 39.3	87 28.4	12 47	168 10.5
35	Alioth...........	1.7	18 14	N56 00.2	85 52.2	12 54	166 34.3
36	Spica	1.2	18 45	S11 07.5	78 05.6	13 25	158 47.7
37	Alkaid	1.9	19 07	N49 21.2	72 28.9	13 47	153 11.0
38	Hadar...........	0.9	19 23	S60 20.6	68 28.0	14 03	149 10.1
39	Menkent	2.3	19 26	S36 20.3	67 43.9	14 06	148 26.0
40	Arcturus	0.2	19 35	N19 13.3	65 27.8	14 15	146 09.9
41	Rigil Kent....	0.1	19 59	S60 48.6	59 30.8	14 39	140 12.9
42	Zuben'ubi......	2.9	20 10	S16 00.8	56 40.5	14 50	137 22.6
43	Kochab	2.2	20 10	N74 11.4	56 36.7	14 51	137 18.8
44	Alphecca	2.3	20 54	N26 44.5	45 41.9	15 34	126 24.0
45	Antares.........	1.2	21 48	S26 25.1	32 03.1	16 29	112 45.2
46	Atria	1.9	22 07	S69 01.1	27 18.5	16 48	108 00.6
47	Sabik	2.6	22 29	S15 43.0	21 48.1	17 10	102 30.2
48	Shaula	1.7	22 52	S37 06.0	16 00.6	17 33	96 42.7
49	Rasalhague ...	2.1	22 54	N12 34.0	15 38.5	17 35	96 20.6
50	Eltanin	2.4	23 15	N51 29.5	10 10.8	17 56	90 52.9
51	Kaus Aust. ...	2.0	23 43	S34 23.3	3 22.0	18 24	84 04.1
52	Vega	0.1	23 56	N38 46.7	0 07.0	18 37	80 49.1
53	Nunki...........	2.1	00 18	S26 18.3	355 35.2	18 55	76 17.3
54	Altair...........	0.9	01 13	N 8 51.0	341 41.0	19 50	62 23.1
55	Peacock........	2.1	01 48	S56 45.4	333 01.0	20 25	53 43.1
56	Deneb	1.3	02 04	N45 15.3	328 59.6	20 41	49 41.7
57	Enif..............	2.5	03 06	N 9 50.6	313 20.1	21 44	34 02.2
58	Al Na'ir........	2.2	03 30	S46 59.5	307 20.7	22 08	28 02.8
59	Fomalhaut ...	1.3	04 19	S29 39.4	294 58.8	22 57	15 40.9
60	Markab	2.6	04 26	N15 10.0	293 11.6	23 04	13 53.7

Stars Transit Correction Table

D. of Mth.	Corr. (Sub.) h. m.	D. of Mth.	Corr. (Sub.) h. m.
1	–0 00	17	–1 03
2	–0 04	18	–1 07
3	–0 08	19	–1 11
4	–0 12	20	–1 15
5	–0 16	21	–1 19
6	–0 20	22	–1 23
7	–0 24	23	–1 27
8	–0 28	24	–1 30
9	–0 31	25	–1 34
10	–0 35	26	–1 38
11	–0 39	27	–1 42
12	–0 43	28	–1 46
13	–0 47	29	–1 50
14	–0 51	30	–1 54
15	–0 55	31	–1 58
16	–0 59		

STAR'S TRANSIT

To find the approx. time of Transit of a Star for any day of the month use above table.

If the quantity taken from the table is greater than the time of Transit for the first of the month, add 23h. 56min. to the time of transit before subtracting the correction below.

Example: Find the time of Transit of Kochab (No 43) on July 17th.

	h.min.
Transit on the 1st	20 10
Corr. for the 17th	–01 03
Transit on the 17th	19 07

d. h. JULY DIARY

2 01 Moon at perigee
2 10 Mercury 4°N. of Moon
3 12 Earth at aphelion
4 20 Jupiter 7°N. of Moon
6 01 Mercury greatest elong. E.(26°)
7 03 First Quarter
14 19 Full Moon
16 23 Saturn 5°S. of Moon
17 11 Moon at apogee
19 03 Mercury stationary
22 22 Last Quarter
25 04 Mars 4°S. of Moon
25 15 Mercury 6°S. of Venus
29 20 New Moon
30 08 Moon at perigee

STAR TIME

The best time to take Star observations is shown in the a.m. and p.m. TWILIGHT columns on the opposite page - corrected for Latitude.

For **Lighting-up Time** (ashore) add 30 mins to Sunset Times.

For Star's G.H.A. Correction Table, see page 4:8.

For Alphabetical List of Stars with Constellation names, see page 2:24.

For Examples on the use of the above data, see page 2:11.

For full directions for finding the above 60 Stars, see p. 2:20 onwards. For Special Pole Star tables see pages 5:17-5:19.

Wednesday, 1st July

G.M.T. (h)	SUN G.H.A.	SUN Dec.	ARIES G.H.A.
00	179 03.4	N23 06.4	279 17.9
02	209 03.2	23 06.0	309 22.8
04	239 03.0	23 05.7	339 27.8
06	269 02.7	23 05.3	9 32.7
08	299 02.5	23 05.0	39 37.6
10	329 02.2	23 04.7	69 42.5
12	359 02.0	23 04.3	99 47.5
14	29 01.8	23 03.9	129 52.4
16	59 01.5	23 03.6	159 57.3
18	89 01.3	23 03.2	190 02.3
20	119 01.0	23 02.9	220 07.2
22	149 00.8	N23 02.5	250 12.1

Thursday, 2nd July

G.M.T. (h)	SUN G.H.A.	SUN Dec.	ARIES G.H.A.
00	179 00.6	N23 02.1	280 17.0
02	209 00.3	23 01.8	310 22.0
04	239 00.1	23 01.4	340 26.9
06	268 59.8	23 01.0	10 31.8
08	298 59.6	23 00.6	40 36.8
10	328 59.4	23 00.2	70 41.7
12	358 59.1	22 59.8	100 46.6
14	28 58.9	22 59.5	130 51.5
16	58 58.7	22 59.1	160 56.5
18	88 58.4	22 58.7	191 01.4
20	118 58.2	22 58.3	221 06.3
22	148 58.0	N22 57.9	251 11.3

Friday, 3rd July

G.M.T. (h)	SUN G.H.A.	SUN Dec.	ARIES G.H.A.
00	178 57.7	N22 57.5	281 16.2
02	208 57.5	22 57.1	311 21.1
04	238 57.3	22 56.7	341 26.0
06	268 57.1	22 56.2	11 31.0
08	298 56.8	22 55.8	41 35.9
10	328 56.6	22 55.4	71 40.8
12	358 56.4	22 55.0	101 45.7
14	28 56.1	22 54.6	131 50.7
16	58 55.9	22 54.1	161 55.6
18	88 55.7	22 53.7	192 00.5
20	118 55.5	22 53.3	222 05.5
22	148 55.2	N22 52.9	252 10.4

Saturday, 4th July

G.M.T. (h)	SUN G.H.A.	SUN Dec.	ARIES G.H.A.
00	178 55.0	N22 52.4	282 15.3
02	208 54.8	22 52.0	312 20.2
04	238 54.6	22 51.5	342 25.2
06	268 54.3	22 51.1	12 30.1
08	298 54.1	22 50.6	42 35.0
10	328 53.9	22 50.2	72 40.0
12	358 53.7	22 49.7	102 44.9
14	28 53.5	22 49.3	132 49.8
16	58 53.2	22 48.8	162 54.7
18	88 53.0	22 48.4	192 59.7
20	118 52.8	22 47.9	223 04.6
22	148 52.6	N22 47.4	253 09.5

Sunday, 5th July

G.M.T. (h)	SUN G.H.A.	SUN Dec.	ARIES G.H.A.
00	178 52.4	N22 47.0	283 14.5
02	208 52.1	22 46.5	313 19.4
04	238 51.9	22 46.0	343 24.3
06	268 51.7	22 45.5	13 29.2
08	298 51.5	22 45.1	43 34.2
10	328 51.3	22 44.6	73 39.1
12	358 51.1	22 44.1	103 44.0
14	28 50.9	22 43.6	133 49.0
16	58 50.6	22 43.1	163 53.9
18	88 50.4	22 42.6	193 58.8
20	118 50.2	22 42.1	224 03.7
22	148 50.0	N22 41.6	254 08.7

Monday, 6th July

G.M.T. (h)	SUN G.H.A.	SUN Dec.	ARIES G.H.A.
00	178 49.8	N22 41.1	284 13.6
02	208 49.6	22 40.6	314 18.5
04	238 49.4	22 40.1	344 23.5
06	268 49.2	22 39.6	14 28.4
08	298 49.0	22 39.1	44 33.3
10	328 48.7	22 38.6	74 38.2
12	358 48.5	22 38.1	104 43.2
14	28 48.3	22 37.5	134 48.1
16	58 48.1	22 37.0	164 53.0
18	88 47.9	22 36.5	194 57.9
20	118 47.7	22 36.0	225 02.9
22	148 47.5	N22 35.4	255 07.8

Tuesday, 7th July

G.M.T. (h)	SUN G.H.A.	SUN Dec.	ARIES G.H.A.
00	178 47.3	N22 34.9	285 12.7
02	208 47.1	22 34.4	315 17.7
04	238 46.9	22 33.8	345 22.6
06	268 46.7	22 33.3	15 27.5
08	298 46.5	22 32.7	45 32.4
10	328 46.3	22 32.2	75 37.4
12	358 46.1	22 31.6	105 42.3
14	28 45.9	22 31.1	135 47.2
16	58 45.7	22 30.5	165 52.2
18	88 45.5	22 29.9	195 57.1
20	118 45.3	22 29.4	226 02.0
22	148 45.2	N22 28.8	256 06.9

Wednesday, 8th July

G.M.T. (h)	SUN G.H.A.	SUN Dec.	ARIES G.H.A.
00	178 45.0	N22 28.3	286 11.9
02	208 44.8	22 27.7	316 16.8
04	238 44.6	22 27.1	346 21.7
06	268 44.4	22 26.5	16 26.7
08	298 44.2	22 26.0	46 31.6
10	328 44.0	22 25.4	76 36.5
12	358 43.8	22 24.8	106 41.4
14	28 43.6	22 24.2	136 46.4
16	58 43.4	22 23.6	166 51.3
18	88 43.3	22 23.0	196 56.2
20	118 43.1	22 22.4	227 01.2
22	148 42.9	N22 21.8	257 06.1

Thursday, 9th July

G.M.T. (h)	SUN G.H.A.	SUN Dec.	ARIES G.H.A.
00	178 42.7	N22 21.2	287 11.0
02	208 42.5	22 20.6	317 15.9
04	238 42.3	22 20.0	347 20.9
06	268 42.1	22 19.4	17 25.8
08	298 42.0	22 18.8	47 30.7
10	328 41.8	22 18.2	77 35.7
12	358 41.6	22 17.6	107 40.6
14	28 41.4	22 17.0	137 45.5
16	58 41.2	22 16.3	167 50.4
18	88 41.1	22 15.7	197 55.4
20	118 40.9	22 15.1	228 00.3
22	148 40.7	N22 14.5	258 05.2

Friday, 10th July

G.M.T. (h)	SUN G.H.A.	SUN Dec.	ARIES G.H.A.
00	178 40.5	N22 13.8	288 10.2
02	208 40.4	22 13.2	318 15.1
04	238 40.2	22 12.6	348 20.0
06	268 40.0	22 11.9	18 24.9
08	298 39.8	22 11.3	48 29.9
10	328 39.7	22 10.6	78 34.8
12	358 39.5	22 10.0	108 39.7
14	28 39.3	22 09.3	138 44.6
16	58 39.1	22 08.7	168 49.6
18	88 39.0	22 08.0	198 54.5
20	118 38.8	22 07.4	228 59.4
22	148 38.6	N22 06.7	259 04.4

Saturday, 11th July

G.M.T. (h)	SUN G.H.A.	SUN Dec.	ARIES G.H.A.
00	178 38.5	N22 06.1	289 09.3
02	208 38.3	22 05.4	319 14.2
04	238 38.1	22 04.7	349 19.1
06	268 38.0	22 04.0	19 24.1
08	298 37.8	22 03.4	49 29.0
10	328 37.6	22 02.7	79 33.9
12	358 37.5	22 02.0	109 38.9
14	28 37.3	22 01.3	139 43.8
16	58 37.2	22 00.7	169 48.7
18	88 37.0	22 00.0	199 53.6
20	118 36.8	21 59.3	229 58.6
22	148 36.7	N21 58.6	260 03.5

Sunday, 12th July

G.M.T. (h)	SUN G.H.A.	SUN Dec.	ARIES G.H.A.
00	178 36.5	N21 57.9	290 08.4
02	208 36.4	21 57.2	320 13.4
04	238 36.2	21 56.5	350 18.3
06	268 36.1	21 55.8	20 23.2
08	298 35.9	21 55.1	50 28.1
10	328 35.8	21 54.4	80 33.1
12	358 35.6	21 53.7	110 38.0
14	28 35.4	21 53.0	140 42.9
16	58 35.3	21 52.3	170 47.9
18	88 35.1	21 51.5	200 52.8
20	118 35.0	21 50.8	230 57.7
22	148 34.9	N21 50.1	261 02.6

Monday, 13th July

G.M.T. (h)	SUN G.H.A.	SUN Dec.	ARIES G.H.A.
00	178 34.7	N21 49.4	291 07.6
02	208 34.6	21 48.6	321 12.5
04	238 34.4	21 47.9	351 17.4
06	268 34.3	21 47.2	21 22.4
08	298 34.1	21 46.4	51 27.3
10	328 34.0	21 45.7	81 32.2
12	358 33.8	21 45.0	111 37.1
14	28 33.7	21 44.2	141 42.1
16	58 33.6	21 43.5	171 47.0
18	88 33.4	21 42.7	201 51.9
20	118 33.3	21 42.0	231 56.8
22	148 33.1	N21 41.2	262 01.8

Tuesday, 14th July

G.M.T. (h)	SUN G.H.A.	SUN Dec.	ARIES G.H.A.
00	178 33.0	N21 40.5	292 06.7
02	208 32.9	21 39.7	322 11.6
04	238 32.7	21 38.9	352 16.6
06	268 32.6	21 38.2	22 21.5
08	298 32.4	21 37.4	52 26.4
10	328 32.3	21 36.6	82 31.3
12	358 32.2	21 35.9	112 36.3
14	28 32.1	21 35.1	142 41.2
16	58 32.0	21 34.3	172 46.1
18	88 31.8	21 33.5	202 51.1
20	118 31.7	21 32.8	232 56.0
22	148 31.6	N21 32.0	263 00.9

Wednesday, 15th July

G.M.T. (h)	SUN G.H.A.	SUN Dec.	ARIES G.H.A.
00	178 31.4	N21 31.2	293 05.8
02	208 31.3	21 30.4	323 10.8
04	238 31.2	21 29.6	353 15.7
06	268 31.1	21 28.8	23 20.6
08	298 30.9	21 28.0	53 25.6
10	328 30.8	21 27.2	83 30.5
12	358 30.7	21 26.4	113 35.4
14	28 30.6	21 25.6	143 40.3
16	58 30.5	21 24.8	173 45.3
18	88 30.4	21 24.0	203 50.2
20	118 30.2	21 23.2	233 55.1
22	148 30.1	N21 22.4	264 00.1

To interpolate SUN G.H.A. see page 4:7   To interpolate ARIES G.H.A. see page 4:8

Thursday, 16th July

h	SUN G.H.A.	Dec.	ARIES G.H.A.	h
00	178 30.0	N21 21.6	294 05.0	00
02	208 29.9	21 20.7	324 09.9	02
04	238 29.8	21 19.9	354 14.8	04
06	268 29.7	21 19.1	24 19.8	06
08	298 29.6	21 18.3	54 24.7	08
10	328 29.4	21 17.4	84 29.6	10
12	358 29.3	21 16.6	114 34.6	12
14	28 29.2	21 15.8	144 39.5	14
16	58 29.1	21 14.9	174 44.4	16
18	88 29.0	21 14.1	204 49.3	18
20	118 28.9	21 13.2	234 54.3	20
22	148 28.8	N21 12.4	264 59.2	22

Tuesday, 21st July

h	SUN G.H.A.	Dec.	ARIES G.H.A.	h
00	178 24.8	N20 27.9	299 00.7	00
02	208 24.7	20 27.0	329 05.6	02
04	238 24.6	20 26.0	359 10.5	04
06	268 24.6	20 25.0	29 15.5	06
08	298 24.5	20 24.1	59 20.4	08
10	328 24.5	20 23.1	89 25.3	10
12	358 24.4	20 22.1	119 30.2	12
14	28 24.4	20 21.1	149 35.2	14
16	58 24.3	20 20.1	179 40.1	16
18	88 24.3	20 19.1	209 45.0	18
20	118 24.2	20 18.2	239 50.0	20
22	148 24.2	N20 17.2	269 54.9	22

Sunday, 26th July

h	SUN G.H.A.	Dec.	ARIES G.H.A.	h
00	178 22.9	N19 25.7	303 56.4	00
02	208 22.9	19 24.6	334 01.3	02
04	238 22.9	19 23.5	4 06.2	04
06	268 22.9	19 22.4	34 11.2	06
08	298 22.9	19 21.3	64 16.1	08
10	328 22.9	19 20.2	94 21.0	10
12	358 22.9	19 19.0	124 25.9	12
14	28 22.9	19 17.9	154 30.9	14
16	58 22.9	19 16.8	184 35.8	16
18	88 22.9	19 15.7	214 40.7	18
20	118 22.9	19 14.6	244 45.7	20
22	148 22.9	N19 13.4	274 50.6	22

Friday, 17th July

h	SUN G.H.A.	Dec.	ARIES G.H.A.	h
00	178 28.7	N21 11.5	295 04.1	00
02	208 28.6	21 10.7	325 09.0	02
04	238 28.5	21 09.8	355 14.0	04
06	268 28.4	21 09.0	25 18.9	06
08	298 28.3	21 08.1	55 23.8	08
10	328 28.2	21 07.3	85 28.8	10
12	358 28.1	21 06.4	115 33.7	12
14	28 28.0	21 05.5	145 38.6	14
16	58 27.9	21 04.7	175 43.5	16
18	88 27.8	21 03.8	205 48.5	18
20	118 27.7	21 02.9	235 53.4	20
22	148 27.6	N21 02.1	265 58.3	22

Wednesday, 22nd July

h	SUN G.H.A.	Dec.	ARIES G.H.A.	h
00	178 24.1	N20 16.2	299 59.8	00
02	208 24.1	20 15.2	330 04.7	02
04	238 24.0	20 14.2	0 09.7	04
06	268 24.0	20 13.2	30 14.6	06
08	298 23.9	20 12.2	60 19.5	08
10	328 23.9	20 11.2	90 24.5	10
12	358 23.8	20 10.2	120 29.4	12
14	28 23.8	20 09.1	150 34.3	14
16	58 23.7	20 08.1	180 39.2	16
18	88 23.7	20 07.1	210 44.2	18
20	118 23.7	20 06.1	240 49.1	20
22	148 23.6	N20 05.1	270 54.0	22

Monday, 27th July

h	SUN G.H.A.	Dec.	ARIES G.H.A.	h
00	178 23.0	N19 12.3	304 55.5	00
02	208 23.0	19 11.2	335 00.4	02
04	238 23.0	19 10.0	5 05.4	04
06	268 23.0	19 08.9	35 10.3	06
08	298 23.0	19 07.7	65 15.2	08
10	328 23.0	19 06.6	95 20.2	10
12	358 23.0	19 05.5	125 25.1	12
14	28 23.1	19 04.3	155 30.0	14
16	58 23.1	19 03.2	185 34.9	16
18	88 23.1	19 02.0	215 39.9	18
20	118 23.1	19 00.9	245 44.8	20
22	148 23.1	N18 59.7	275 49.7	22

Saturday, 18th July

h	SUN G.H.A.	Dec.	ARIES G.H.A.	h
00	178 27.5	N21 01.2	296 03.3	00
02	208 27.4	21 00.3	326 08.2	02
04	238 27.3	20 59.4	356 13.1	04
06	268 27.2	20 58.5	26 18.0	06
08	298 27.1	20 57.6	56 23.0	08
10	328 27.1	20 56.8	86 27.9	10
12	358 27.0	20 55.9	116 32.8	12
14	28 26.9	20 55.0	146 37.8	14
16	58 26.8	20 54.1	176 42.7	16
18	88 26.7	20 53.2	206 47.6	18
20	118 26.6	20 52.3	236 52.5	20
22	148 26.5	N20 51.4	266 57.5	22

Thursday, 23rd July

h	SUN G.H.A.	Dec.	ARIES G.H.A.	h
00	178 23.6	N20 04.1	300 59.0	00
02	208 23.6	20 03.0	331 03.9	02
04	238 23.5	20 02.0	1 08.8	04
06	268 23.5	20 01.0	31 13.7	06
08	298 23.5	19 59.9	61 18.7	08
10	328 23.4	19 58.9	91 23.6	10
12	358 23.4	19 57.9	121 28.5	12
14	28 23.4	19 56.8	151 33.5	14
16	58 23.3	19 55.8	181 38.4	16
18	88 23.3	19 54.8	211 43.3	18
20	118 23.3	19 53.7	241 48.2	20
22	148 23.2	N19 52.7	271 53.2	22

Tuesday, 28th July

h	SUN G.H.A.	Dec.	ARIES G.H.A.	h
00	178 23.2	N18 58.5	305 54.6	00
02	208 23.2	18 57.4	335 59.6	02
04	238 23.2	18 56.2	6 04.5	04
06	268 23.2	18 55.1	36 09.4	06
08	298 23.3	18 53.9	66 14.4	08
10	328 23.3	18 52.7	96 19.3	10
12	358 23.3	18 51.6	126 24.2	12
14	28 23.3	18 50.4	156 29.1	14
16	58 23.4	18 49.2	186 34.1	16
18	88 23.4	18 48.0	216 39.0	18
20	118 23.4	18 46.9	246 43.9	20
22	148 23.5	N18 45.7	276 48.9	22

Sunday, 19th July

h	SUN G.H.A.	Dec.	ARIES G.H.A.	h
00	178 26.5	N20 50.5	297 02.4	00
02	208 26.4	20 49.5	327 07.3	02
04	238 26.3	20 48.6	357 12.3	04
06	268 26.2	20 47.7	27 17.2	06
08	298 26.1	20 46.8	57 22.1	08
10	328 26.1	20 45.9	87 27.0	10
12	358 26.0	20 45.0	117 32.0	12
14	28 25.9	20 44.0	147 36.9	14
16	58 25.8	20 43.1	177 41.8	16
18	88 25.8	20 42.2	207 46.8	18
20	118 25.7	20 41.2	237 51.7	20
22	148 25.6	N20 40.3	267 56.6	22

Friday, 24th July

h	SUN G.H.A.	Dec.	ARIES G.H.A.	h
00	178 23.2	N19 51.6	301 58.1	00
02	208 23.2	19 50.6	332 03.0	02
04	238 23.2	19 49.5	2 07.9	04
06	268 23.1	19 48.4	32 12.9	06
08	298 23.1	19 47.4	62 17.8	08
10	328 23.1	19 46.3	92 22.7	10
12	358 23.1	19 45.3	122 27.7	12
14	28 23.1	19 44.2	152 32.6	14
16	58 23.0	19 43.1	182 37.5	16
18	88 23.0	19 42.1	212 42.4	18
20	118 23.0	19 41.0	242 47.4	20
22	148 23.0	N19 39.9	272 52.3	22

Wednesday, 29th July

h	SUN G.H.A.	Dec.	ARIES G.H.A.	h
00	178 23.5	N18 44.5	306 53.8	00
02	208 23.5	18 43.3	336 58.7	02
04	238 23.6	18 42.1	7 03.6	04
06	268 23.6	18 40.9	37 08.6	06
08	298 23.7	18 39.7	67 13.5	08
10	328 23.7	18 38.5	97 18.4	10
12	358 23.7	18 37.3	127 23.4	12
14	28 23.8	18 36.2	157 28.3	14
16	58 23.8	18 35.0	187 33.2	16
18	88 23.9	18 33.7	217 38.1	18
20	118 23.9	18 32.5	247 43.1	20
22	148 24.0	N18 31.3	277 48.0	22

Monday, 20th July

h	SUN G.H.A.	Dec.	ARIES G.H.A.	h
00	178 25.5	N20 39.4	298 01.5	00
02	208 25.5	20 38.4	328 06.5	02
04	238 25.4	20 37.5	358 11.4	04
06	268 25.3	20 36.5	28 16.3	06
08	298 25.3	20 35.6	58 21.3	08
10	328 25.2	20 34.7	88 26.2	10
12	358 25.1	20 33.7	118 31.1	12
14	28 25.1	20 32.7	148 36.0	14
16	58 25.0	20 31.8	178 41.0	16
18	88 24.9	20 30.8	208 45.9	18
20	118 24.9	20 29.9	238 50.8	20
22	148 24.8	N20 28.9	268 55.7	22

Saturday, 25th July

h	SUN G.H.A.	Dec.	ARIES G.H.A.	h
00	178 23.0	N19 38.8	302 57.2	00
02	208 23.0	19 37.7	333 02.2	02
04	238 23.0	19 36.7	3 07.1	04
06	268 22.9	19 35.6	33 12.0	06
08	298 22.9	19 34.5	63 16.9	08
10	328 22.9	19 33.4	93 21.9	10
12	358 22.9	19 32.3	123 26.8	12
14	28 22.9	19 31.2	153 31.7	14
16	58 22.9	19 30.1	183 36.7	16
18	88 22.9	19 29.0	213 41.6	18
20	118 22.9	19 27.9	243 46.5	20
22	148 22.9	N19 26.8	273 51.4	22

Thursday, 30th July

h	SUN G.H.A.	Dec.	ARIES G.H.A.	h
00	178 24.0	N18 30.1	307 52.9	00
02	208 24.1	18 28.9	337 57.9	02
04	238 24.1	18 27.7	8 02.8	04
06	268 24.2	18 26.5	38 07.7	06
08	298 24.2	18 25.3	68 12.6	08
10	328 24.3	18 24.1	98 17.6	10
12	358 24.3	18 22.8	128 22.5	12
14	28 24.4	18 21.6	158 27.4	14
16	58 24.4	18 20.4	188 32.4	16
18	88 24.5	18 19.2	218 37.3	18
20	118 24.6	18 17.9	248 42.2	20
22	148 24.6	N18 16.7	278 47.1	22

Friday, 31st July

h	SUN G.H.A.	Dec.	ARIES G.H.A.	h
00	178 24.7	N18 15.5	308 52.1	00
02	208 24.7	18 14.2	338 57.0	02
04	238 24.8	18 13.0	9 01.9	04
06	268 24.9	N18 11.8	39 06.8	06
08	298 24.9	N18 10.5	69 11.8	08
10	328 25.0	18 09.3	99 16.7	10
12	358 25.1	18 08.0	129 21.6	12
14	28 25.1	N18 06.8	159 26.6	14
16	58 25.2	N18 05.5	189 31.5	16
18	88 25.3	18 04.3	219 36.4	18
20	118 25.3	18 03.0	249 41.3	20
22	148 25.4	N18 01.8	279 46.3	22

To interpolate SUN G.H.A. see page 4:7   To interpolate ARIES G.H.A. see page 4:8

♀ VENUS ♀ / ♃ JUPITER ♃

Mer. Pass. h.m.	G.H.A. ° '	Mean Var. 14°	Dec. ° '	Mean Var.	M	Day of Week	G.H.A ° '	Mean Var. 15°	Dec. ° '	Mean Var.	Mer. Pass h.m.
12 25	173 49.5	59.1	N23 28.7	0.3	1	Wed.	117 35.1	2.1	N 8 57.8	0.1	16 07
12 27	173 28.6	59.1	N23 22.6	0.3	2	Th.	118 25.7	2.1	N 8 54.3	0.2	16 04
12 28	173 07.7	59.1	N23 15.7	0.3	3	Fri.	119 16.2	2.1	N 8 50.6	0.1	16 01
12 30	172 47.0	59.1	N23 08.1	0.3	4	Sat.	120 06.6	2.1	N 8 47.0	0.2	15 57
12 31	172 26.4	59.2	N22 59.9	0.4	5	SUN.	120 56.9	2.1	N 8 43.3	0.2	15 54
12 32	172 06.1	59.2	N22 51.0	0.4	6	Mon.	121 47.2	2.1	N 8 39.6	0.2	15 51
12 34	171 45.9	59.2	N22 41.4	0.4	7	Tu.	122 37.3	2.1	N 8 35.8	0.2	15 47
12 35	171 25.9	59.2	N22 31.1	0.5	8	Wed.	123 27.4	2.1	N 8 32.0	0.2	15 44
12 36	171 06.1	59.2	N22 20.2	0.5	9	Th.	124 17.4	2.1	N 8 28.2	0.2	15 41
12 38	170 46.5	59.2	N22 08.7	0.5	10	Fri.	125 07.3	2.1	N 8 24.3	0.2	15 37
12 39	170 27.1	59.2	N21 56.5	0.5	11	Sat.	125 57.1	2.1	N 8 20.4	0.2	15 34
12 40	170 08.0	59.2	N21 43.6	0.6	12	SUN.	126 46.8	2.1	N 8 16.4	0.2	15 31
12 41	169 49.1	59.2	N21 30.2	0.6	13	Mon.	127 36.5	2.1	N 8 12.4	0.2	15 27
12 43	169 30.5	59.2	N21 16.1	0.6	14	Tu.	128 26.1	2.1	N 8 08.4	0.2	15 24
12 44	169 12.1	59.2	N21 01.4	0.6	15	Wed.	129 15.6	2.1	N 8 04.4	0.2	15 21
12 45	168 54.0	59.3	N20 46.1	0.7	16	Th.	130 05.0	2.1	N 8 00.3	0.2	15 18
12 46	168 36.2	59.3	N20 30.2	0.7	17	Fri.	130 54.4	2.1	N 7 56.2	0.2	15 14
12 47	168 18.6	59.3	N20 13.7	0.7	18	Sat.	131 43.7	2.0	N 7 52.1	0.2	15 11
12 49	168 01.3	59.3	N19 56.6	0.7	19	SUN.	132 32.9	2.1	N 7 47.9	0.2	15 08
12 50	167 44.3	59.3	N19 39.0	0.8	20	Mon.	133 22.1	2.0	N 7 43.7	0.2	15 04
12 51	167 27.6	59.3	N19 20.9	0.8	21	Tu.	134 11.2	2.0	N 7 39.4	0.2	15 01
12 52	167 11.1	59.3	N19 02.1	0.8	22	Wed.	135 00.2	2.0	N 7 35.2	0.2	14 58
12 53	166 55.0	59.3	N18 42.9	0.8	23	Th.	135 49.1	2.0	N 7 30.9	0.2	14 55
12 54	166 39.1	59.4	N18 23.1	0.8	24	Fri.	136 38.0	2.0	N 7 26.6	0.2	14 51
12 55	166 23.6	59.4	N18 02.9	0.9	25	Sat.	137 26.9	2.0	N 7 22.2	0.2	14 48
12 56	166 08.3	59.4	N17 42.1	0.9	26	SUN.	138 15.6	2.0	N 7 17.8	0.2	14 45
12 57	165 53.3	59.4	N17 20.8	0.9	27	Mon.	139 04.3	2.0	N 7 13.4	0.2	14 42
12 58	165 38.6	59.4	N16 59.1	0.9	28	Tu.	139 53.0	2.0	N 7 09.0	0.2	14 38
12 59	165 24.3	59.4	N16 36.9	0.9	29	Wed.	140 41.6	2.0	N 7 04.5	0.2	14 35
13 00	165 10.2	59.4	N16 14.2	1.0	30	Th.	141 30.1	2.0	N 7 00.1	0.2	14 32
13 01	164 56.4	59.4	N15 51.1	1.0	31	Fri.	142 18.6	2.0	N 6 55.6	0.2	14 29

♀ VENUS. Av. Mag. −3.9. Too close to the sun for observation until July 20 when it appears in the evening sky. In conjunction with Mercury on July 25. S.H.A. July 10 243°; 15 236°; 20 229°; 25 224°; 30 217°.

♃ JUPITER. Av. Mag. −1.8. An **Evening Star**.. S.H.A. July 5 199°; 10 196°; 15 196°; 20 196°; 25 194°; 30 194°.

♂ MARS ♂ / ♄ SATURN ♄

Mer. Pass. h.m.	G.H.A. ° '	Mean Var. 15°	Dec. ° '	Mean Var.	M	Day of Week	G.H.A ° '	Mean Var. 15°	Dec. ° '	Mean Var.	Mer. Pass h.m.
08 02	239 28.3	0.7	N14 20.7	0.6	1	Wed.	318 56.2	2.6	S16 27.2	0.0	02 44
08 01	239 45.2	0.7	N14 34.3	0.6	2	Th.	319 58.3	2.6	S16 28.3	0.0	02 40
07 59	240 02.0	0.7	N14 47.7	0.6	3	Fri.	321 00.5	2.6	S16 29.4	0.0	02 36
07 58	240 18.9	0.7	N15 01.0	0.5	4	Sat.	322 02.7	2.6	S16 30.5	0.0	02 31
07 57	240 35.7	0.7	N15 14.1	0.5	5	SUN.	323 05.1	2.6	S16 31.6	0.1	02 27
07 56	240 52.6	0.7	N15 27.1	0.5	6	Mon.	324 07.5	2.6	S16 32.8	0.0	02 23
07 55	241 09.4	0.7	N15 39.9	0.5	7	Tu.	325 09.9	2.6	S16 33.9	0.0	02 19
07 54	241 26.3	0.7	N15 52.6	0.5	8	Wed.	326 12.4	2.6	S16 35.1	0.1	02 15
07 53	241 43.1	0.7	N16 05.1	0.5	9	Th.	327 15.0	2.6	S16 36.3	0.1	02 11
07 52	241 59.9	0.7	N16 17.4	0.5	10	Fri.	328 17.6	2.6	S16 37.5	0.1	02 06
07 51	242 16.7	0.7	N16 29.6	0.5	11	Sat.	329 20.3	2.6	S16 38.7	0.1	02 02
07 49	242 33.5	0.7	N16 41.6	0.5	12	SUN.	330 23.1	2.6	S16 40.0	0.1	01 58
07 48	242 50.4	0.7	N16 53.4	0.5	13	Mon.	331 25.9	2.6	S16 41.2	0.1	01 54
07 47	243 07.2	0.7	N17 05.1	0.5	14	Tu.	332 28.8	2.6	S16 42.5	0.1	01 50
07 46	243 24.0	0.7	N17 16.6	0.5	15	Wed.	333 31.7	2.6	S16 43.8	0.1	01 46
07 45	243 40.8	0.7	N17 28.0	0.5	16	Th.	334 34.7	2.6	S16 45.1	0.1	01 41
07 44	243 57.6	0.7	N17 39.1	0.5	17	Fri.	335 37.7	2.6	S16 46.4	0.1	01 37
07 43	244 14.4	0.7	N17 50.1	0.5	18	Sat.	336 40.8	2.6	S16 47.7	0.1	01 33
07 42	244 31.2	0.7	N18 01.0	0.4	19	SUN.	337 44.0	2.6	S16 49.1	0.1	01 29
07 40	244 48.0	0.7	N18 11.6	0.4	20	Mon.	338 47.1	2.6	S16 50.4	0.1	01 25
07 39	245 04.9	0.7	N18 22.1	0.4	21	Tu.	339 50.3	2.6	S16 51.8	0.1	01 20
07 38	245 21.7	0.7	N18 32.4	0.4	22	Wed.	340 53.6	2.6	S16 53.1	0.1	01 16
07 37	245 38.5	0.7	N18 42.5	0.4	23	Th.	341 56.9	2.6	S16 54.5	0.1	01 12
07 36	245 55.4	0.7	N18 52.4	0.4	24	Fri.	343 00.2	2.6	S16 55.9	0.1	01 08
07 35	246 12.3	0.7	N19 02.2	0.4	25	Sat.	344 03.6	2.6	S16 57.3	0.1	01 04
07 34	246 29.2	0.7	N19 11.8	0.4	26	SUN.	345 07.0	2.6	S16 58.7	0.1	00 59
07 33	246 46.1	0.7	N19 21.2	0.4	27	Mon.	346 10.4	2.6	S17 00.1	0.1	00 55
07 31	247 03.1	0.7	N19 30.4	0.4	28	Tu.	347 13.8	2.6	S17 01.5	0.1	00 51
07 30	247 20.1	0.7	N19 39.5	0.4	29	Wed.	348 17.3	2.6	S17 02.9	0.1	00 47
07 29	247 37.1	0.7	N19 48.3	0.4	30	Th.	349 20.8	2.6	S17 04.3	0.1	00 42
07 28	247 54.2	0.7	N19 57.0	0.4	31	Fri.	350 24.3	2.6	S17 05.7	0.1	00 38

♂ MARS. Av. Mag. +0.8. A **Morning Star**. S.H.A. July 5 318°; 10 314°; 15 310°; 20 307°; 25 303°; 30 300°.

♄ SATURN. Av. Mag. +0.4. A **Morning Star**. S.H.A. July 5 41°; 10 39°;15 40°; 20 42°; 25 40°; 30 41°.

MERCURY. Visible low in the west after sunset until July 26 when it is too close to the sun for observation.

For Planets Correction Tables see pages 4:9-4:13. See also 'How to Recognise the Planets' on page 2:32.
Mean Var. means Variation per Hour.

Day of M. W.	G.M.T. h	G.H.A. ° '	Mean Var. per Hour 14°,+	Dec. ° '	Mean Var. per Hour '
1 Wed.	0	171 56.4	23.5	N21 03.5	8.3
	6	258 17.5	23.9	N20 14.7	9.1
	12	344 40.8	24.3	N19 20.6	9.9
	18	71 06.6	24.7	N18 21.7	10.6
2 Th.	0	157 34.9	25.2	N17 18.2	11.3
	6	244 05.9	25.7	N16 10.6	11.9
	12	330 39.8	26.1	N14 59.2	12.5
	18	57 16.4	26.6	N13 44.4	13.0
3 Fri.	0	143 55.8	27.0	N12 26.6	13.4
	6	230 38.0	27.5	N11 06.1	13.8
	12	317 22.7	27.9	N 9 43.5	14.1
	18	44 09.9	28.3	N 8 19.1	14.3
4 Sat.	0	130 59.4	28.6	N 6 53.2	14.5
	6	217 51.1	29.0	N 5 26.3	14.6
	12	304 44.6	29.2	N 3 58.6	14.6
	18	31 39.9	29.5	N 2 30.6	14.7
5 Sun.	0	118 36.7	29.7	N 1 02.6	14.6
	6	205 34.8	29.9	S 0 25.2	14.5
	12	292 33.9	30.0	S 1 52.4	14.3
	18	19 33.9	30.1	S 3 18.7	14.2
6 Mon.	0	106 34.5	30.2	S 4 43.8	13.9
	6	193 35.4	30.2	S 6 07.5	13.6
	12	280 36.6	30.2	S 7 29.6	13.3
	18	7 37.8	30.2	S 8 49.7	13.0
7 Tu.	0	94 38.9	30.1	S10 07.7	12.6
	6	181 39.6	30.0	S11 23.3	12.1
	12	268 39.8	29.9	S12 36.3	11.7
	18	355 39.4	29.8	S13 46.6	11.2
8 Wed.	0	82 38.2	29.6	S14 53.8	10.6
	6	169 36.3	29.5	S15 57.9	10.1
	12	256 33.4	29.3	S16 58.6	9.5
	18	343 29.5	29.1	S17 55.8	8.8
9 Th.	0	70 24.7	29.0	S18 49.4	8.2
	6	157 19.0	28.9	S19 39.0	7.6
	12	244 12.2	28.7	S20 24.8	6.9
	18	331 04.6	28.6	S21 06.4	6.2
10 Fri.	0	57 56.2	28.5	S21 43.8	5.5
	6	144 47.2	28.4	S22 16.9	4.7
	12	231 37.5	28.3	S22 45.6	4.0
	18	318 27.4	28.3	S23 09.9	3.2
11 Sat.	0	45 17.1	28.3	S23 29.6	2.5
	6	132 06.8	28.3	S23 44.8	1.7
	12	218 56.5	28.4	S23 55.5	0.9
	18	305 46.7	28.5	S24 01.6	0.2
12 Sun.	0	32 37.3	28.5	S24 03.1	0.5
	6	119 28.8	28.7	S24 00.2	1.3
	12	206 21.2	29.0	S23 52.8	2.0
	18	293 14.8	29.2	S23 41.1	2.7
13 Mon.	0	20 09.7	29.4	S23 25.2	3.4
	6	107 06.2	29.8	S23 05.1	4.0
	12	194 04.3	30.0	S22 41.0	4.8
	18	281 04.2	30.4	S22 13.0	5.4
14 Tu.	0	8 06.1	30.7	S21 41.2	5.9
	6	95 09.9	31.0	S21 05.9	6.6
	12	182 15.8	31.4	S20 27.2	7.1
	18	269 23.8	31.7	S19 45.1	7.6
15 Wed.	0	356 33.8	32.0	S19 00.1	8.0
	6	83 46.0	32.4	S18 12.0	8.5
	12	171 00.3	32.7	S17 21.3	8.9
	18	258 16.6	33.1	S16 28.0	9.3
16 Th.	0	345 34.8	33.3	S15 32.2	9.6
	6	72 55.0	33.7	S14 34.3	10.1
	12	160 16.9	33.9	S13 34.3	10.3
	18	247 40.5	34.2	S12 32.5	10.6
17 Fri.	0	335 05.6	34.5	S11 28.9	10.9
	6	62 32.2	34.6	S10 23.7	11.1
	12	150 00.1	34.9	S 9 17.2	11.3
	18	237 29.0	35.0	S 8 09.4	11.5
18 Sat.	0	324 59.0	35.2	S 7 00.5	11.6
	6	52 29.7	35.2	S 5 50.6	11.8
	12	140 01.1	35.3	S 4 39.9	11.9
	18	227 32.9	35.3	S 3 28.6	12.0
19 Sun.	0	315 04.9	35.3	S 2 16.7	12.0
	6	42 37.0	35.3	S 1 04.5	12.1
	12	130 09.0	35.3	N 0 08.0	12.1
	18	217 40.7	35.2	N 1 20.7	12.1
20 Mon.	0	305 11.8	35.1	N 2 33.3	12.1
	6	32 42.2	34.9	N 3 45.7	12.0
	12	120 11.7	34.7	N 4 57.8	12.0
	18	207 40.0	34.5	N 6 09.5	11.9
21 Tu.	0	295 07.0	34.2	N 7 20.6	11.7
	6	22 32.4	34.0	N 8 30.9	11.5
	12	109 56.0	33.6	N 9 40.2	11.3
	18	197 17.6	33.2	N10 48.5	11.2
22 Wed.	0	284 37.1	32.8	N11 55.4	10.9
	6	11 54.1	32.4	N13 00.9	10.6
	12	99 08.5	31.9	N14 04.8	10.3
	18	186 20.1	31.4	N15 06.7	10.0
23 Th.	0	273 28.7	30.9	N16 06.6	9.5
	6	0 34.2	30.3	N17 04.1	9.1
	12	87 36.5	29.7	N17 59.1	8.6
	18	174 35.3	29.1	N18 51.2	8.1
24 Fri.	0	261 30.6	28.5	N19 40.2	7.6
	6	348 22.3	28.0	N20 25.9	7.0
	12	75 10.4	27.4	N21 08.0	6.4
	18	161 54.9	26.8	N21 46.1	5.6
25 Sat.	0	248 35.8	26.2	N22 20.0	4.8
	6	335 13.3	25.7	N22 49.5	4.0
	12	61 47.4	25.1	N23 14.2	3.2
	18	148 18.4	24.6	N23 33.9	2.3
26 Sun.	0	234 46.4	24.2	N23 48.4	1.4
	6	321 11.9	23.9	N23 57.3	0.4
	12	47 35.1	23.5	N24 00.6	0.6
	18	133 56.3	23.3	N23 58.0	1.5
27 Mon.	0	220 16.0	23.1	N23 49.5	2.5
	6	306 34.6	23.0	N23 34.9	3.6
	12	32 52.6	22.9	N23 14.3	4.6
	18	119 10.2	23.0	N22 47.5	5.5
28 Tu.	0	205 28.1	23.1	N22 14.8	6.5
	6	291 46.6	23.2	N21 36.1	7.5
	12	18 06.1	23.5	N20 57.3	8.4
	18	104 26.8	23.7	N20 01.7	9.2
29 Wed.	0	190 49.2	24.1	N19 06.5	10.1
	6	277 13.4	24.4	N18 06.2	10.9
	12	3 39.6	24.7	N17 01.2	11.6
	18	90 08.1	25.1	N15 51.8	12.3
30 Th.	0	176 38.9	25.6	N14 38.5	12.8
	6	263 12.0	26.0	N13 21.6	13.4
	12	349 47.5	26.3	N12 01.5	13.9
	18	76 25.3	26.7	N10 38.6	14.2
31 Fri.	0	163 05.3	27.1	N 9 13.4	14.6
	6	249 47.6	27.4	N 7 46.3	14.8
	12	336 31.9	27.8	N 6 17.7	15.0
	18	63 18.1	28.0	N 4 48.0	15.1

PHASES OF THE MOON

	d. h/min		d. h/min
☽ First Quarter	7 02 43	☾ Last Quarter	22 22 12
○ Full Moon	14 19 06	● New Moon	29 19 35
Perigee	2 01	Apogee	17 11
		Perigee	30 08

AUGUST, 1992

G.M.T.   (31 days)   G.M.T.

☉ SUN ☉

DATE			Equation of Time		Transit	Semi-diam.	Lat. 52°N.				Lat. Corr. to Sunrise, Sunset, etc.				
Day of							Twilight	Sunrise	Sunset	Twilight		Twilight	Sunrise	Sunset	Twilight
Yr.	Mth.	Week	0 h.	12 h.							Lat.				
			m. s.	m. s.	h. m.	′	h. m.	h. m.	h. m.	h. m.	°	h. m.	h. m.	h. m.	h. m.
214	1	Sat.	+06 18	+06 16	12 06	15.8	03 40	04 22	19 50	20 31	N70	T.A.N.	−1 50	+1 46	T.A.N.
215	2	Sun.	+06 14	+06 12	12 06	15.8	03 42	04 23	19 48	20 29	68	−2 28	−1 26	+1 23	+2 26
216	3	Mon.	+06 10	+06 07	12 06	15.8	03 44	04 25	19 46	20 27	66	−1 48	−1 08	+1 06	+1 47
217	4	Tu.	+06 05	+06 02	12 06	15.8	03 46	04 26	19 45	20 25	64	−1 21	−0 53	+0 51	+1 20
218	5	Wed.	+05 59	+05 56	12 06	15.8	03 48	04 28	19 43	20 23	62	−1 01	−0 41	+0 39	+1 00
219	6	Th.	+05 53	+05 49	12 06	15.8	03 50	04 30	19 41	20 21	N60	−0 45	−0 30	+0 29	+0 44
220	7	Fri.	+05 46	+05 42	12 06	15.8	03 51	04 31	19 39	20 18	58	−0 32	−0 21	+0 21	+0 30
221	8	Sat.	+05 38	+05 34	12 06	15.8	03 53	04 33	19 37	20 16	56	−0 20	−0 13	+0 13	+0 18
222	9	Sun.	+05 30	+05 26	12 05	15.8	03 55	04 35	19 35	20 14	54	−0 10	−0 06	+0 06	+0 09
223	10	Mon.	+05 21	+05 17	12 05	15.8	03 57	04 36	19 33	20 12	50	+0 07	+0 06	−0 06	−0 04
224	11	Tu.	+05 12	+05 07	12 05	15.8	03 59	04 38	19 31	20 10	N45	+0 23	+0 18	−0 18	−0 27
225	12	Wed.	+05 02	+04 57	12 05	15.8	04 01	04 40	19 29	20 08	40	+0 36	+0 28	−0 28	−0 38
226	13	Th.	+04 51	+04 46	12 05	15.8	04 02	04 41	19 27	20 06	35	+0 47	+0 37	−0 37	−0 48
227	14	Fri.	+04 40	+04 35	12 05	15.8	04 04	04 43	19 25	20 04	30	+0 57	+0 44	−0 45	−0 58
228	15	Sat.	+04 29	+04 23	12 04	15.8	04 06	04 44	19 23	20 02	20	+1 12	+0 57	−0 57	−1 13
229	16	Sun.	+04 17	+04 11	12 04	15.8	04 08	04 46	19 21	19 59	N10	+1 24	+1 09	−1 08	−1 25
230	17	Mon.	+04 04	+03 58	12 04	15.8	04 10	04 47	19 19	19 57	0	+1 35	+1 19	−1 18	−1 35
231	18	Tu.	+03 51	+03 44	12 04	15.8	04 12	04 49	19 17	19 55	S10	+1 44	+1 29	−1 28	−1 46
232	19	Wed.	+03 38	+03 31	12 04	15.8	04 13	04 50	19 15	19 52	20	+1 54	+1 40	−1 39	−1 56
233	20	Th.	+03 23	+03 16	12 03	15.8	04 15	04 52	19 13	19 50	30	+2 05	+1 52	−1 51	−2 06
234	21	Fri.	+03 09	+03 02	12 03	15.8	04 17	04 54	19 11	19 48	S35	+2 10	+2 00	−1 57	−2 11
235	22	Sat.	+02 54	+02 46	12 03	15.8	04 19	04 55	19 09	19 45	40	+2 16	+2 07	−2 05	−2 17
236	23	Sun.	+02 39	+02 31	12 03	15.8	04 21	04 57	19 07	19 43	45	+2 23	+2 17	−2 15	−2 24
237	24	Mon.	+02 23	+02 15	12 02	15.8	04 23	04 59	19 05	19 41	S50	+2 30	+2 27	−2 26	−2 32
238	25	Tu.	+02 07	+01 59	12 02	15.9	04 24	05 00	19 02	19 38					
239	26	Wed.	+01 50	+01 42	12 02	15.9	04 26	05 02	19 00	19 36					
240	27	Th.	+01 33	+01 24	12 01	15.9	04 28	05 04	18 58	19 34					
241	28	Fri.	+01 16	+01 07	12 01	15.9	04 29	05 05	18 55	19 31					
242	29	Sat	+00 58	+00 49	12 01	15.9	04 31	05 07	18 53	19 29					
243	30	Sun.	+00 40	+00 31	12 01	15.9	04 33	05 09	18 51	19 27					
244	31	Mon.	+00 21	+00 12	12 00	15.9	04 35	05 10	18 49	19 24					

NOTES

The Lat. Corr. to sunrise, sunset, etc., is for the middle of August.

T.A.N. means Twilight all night.

Examples on the use of the above data are given on page 2:11 onwards.

Equation of Time is the excess of Mean Time over Apparent Time
(See explanation and examples on p. 2:15)

☽ MOON ☾

DATE			Age	Transit Diff. (Upper)		Semi-diam.	Hor. Par. 12 h.	Lat. 52°N.		MOON'S PHASES
Day of			days					Moonrise	Moonset	
Yr.	Mth.	Week								
				h. m.	m.	′	′	h. m.	h. m.	
214	1	Sat.	03	14 30	52	16.5	60.6	08 12	20 32	d. h. m.
215	2	Sun.	04	15 22	51	16.3	59.9	09 37	20 52	☽ First Quarter............ 5 10 58
216	3	Mon.	05	16 13	51	16.1	59.0	11 00	21 13	○ Full Moon 13 10 27
217	4	Tu.	06	17 04	52	15.8	58.1	12 20	21 38	☾ Last Quarter............ 21 10 01
218	5	Wed.	07	17 56	53	15.6	57.3	13 37	22 08	● New Moon 28 02 42
219	6	Th.	08	18 49	52	15.4	56.5	14 49	22 44	
220	7	Fri.	09	19 41	52	15.2	55.8	15 55	23 30	
221	8	Sat.	10	20 33	50	15.0	55.2	16 44	– –	d. h.
222	9	Sun.	11	21 23	49	14.9	54.8	17 25	00 24	Apogee 13 16
223	10	Mon.	12	22 12	45	14.8	54.4	17 58	01 26	Perigee 27 18
224	11	Tu.	13	22 57	44	14.8	54.2	18 24	02 32	
225	12	Wed.	14	23 41	42	14.7	54.0	18 45	03 40	
226	13	Th.	15	24 23	–	14.7	54.0	19 02	04 48	
227	14	Fri.	16	00 23	41	14.7	54.0	19 18	05 55	
228	15	Sat.	17	01 04	41	14.7	54.1	19 33	07 02	
229	16	Sun.	18	01 45	41	14.8	54.3	19 49	08 10	
230	17	Mon.	19	02 26	43	14.9	54.7	20 05	09 18	
231	18	Tu.	20	03 09	45	15.0	55.1	20 25	10 27	
232	19	Wed.	21	03 54	48	15.2	55.7	20 48	11 38	
233	20	Th.	22	04 42	51	15.4	56.4	21 18	12 50	NOTES
234	21	Fri.	23	05 33	56	15.6	57.2	21 58	14 00	Moon's G.H.A. and Dec. are given on page 3:57.
235	22	Sat.	24	06 29	58	15.8	58.1	22 50	15 05	A table for correcting Moonrise and Moonset for latitude is on page 4:20.
236	23	Sun.	25	07 27	59	16.1	59.0	23 56	16 00	A table for correcting Moon's meridian passage (transit) for longitude is on page 4:19.
237	24	Mon.	26	08 26	60	16.3	59.8	– –	16 46	Examples on the use of the above data are given on page 2:11 onwards.
238	25	Tu.	27	09 26	58	16.5	60.6	01 14	17 21	
239	26	Wed.	28	10 24	57	16.7	61.1	02 40	17 49	
240	27	Th.	29	11 21	54	16.7	61.3	04 09	18 13	
241	28	Fri.	00	12 15	53	16.7	61.3	05 38	18 34	
242	29	Sat.	01	13 08	53	16.6	60.9	07 06	18 55	
243	30	Sun.	02	14 01	53	16.4	60.2	08 33	19 16	
244	31	Mon.	03	14 54	54	16.2	59.3	09 57	19 40	

0h. = midnight. For explanation of use of above data see page 2:11 onwards.

No.	Name	Mag.	Transit (approx.)	DEC.	G.H.A.	R.A.	S.H.A.
			h. m.	° '	° '	h. m.	° '
♈	ARIES	–	03 20	–	309 51.2	–	–
1	Alpheratz	2.2	03 28	N29 03.1	307 50.6	0 08	357 59.4
2	Ankaa	2.4	03 46	S42 20.4	303 21.8	0 26	353 30.6
3	Schedar	2.5	04 00	N56 29.8	299 49.2	0 40	349 58.0
4	Diphda	2.2	04 03	S18 01.3	299 02.4	0 43	349 11.2
5	Achernar	0.6	04 57	S57 16.0	285 29.1	1 37	335 37.9
6	POLARIS	2.1	05 44	N89 13.7	273 40.6	2 25	323 49.4
7	Hamal	2.2	05 26	N23 25.7	278 09.4	2 07	328 18.2
8	Acamar	3.1	06 18	S40 19.7	265 21.2	2 58	315 30.0
9	Menkar	2.8	06 21	N 4 03.8	264 22.5	3 02	314 31.3
10	Mirfak	1.9	06 43	N49 50.0	258 53.9	3 24	309 02.7
11	Aldebaran	1.1	07 55	N16 29.8	240 58.5	4 36	291 07.3
12	Rigel	0.3	08 33	S 8 12.4	231 18.3	5 14	281 27.1
13	Capella	0.2	08 35	N45 59.4	230 48.9	5 16	280 57.7
14	Bellatrix	1.7	08 44	N 6 20.7	228 40.0	5 25	278 48.8
15	Elnath	1.8	08 45	N28 36.1	228 23.7	5 26	278 32.5
16	Alnilam	1.8	08 55	S 1 12.2	225 53.5	5 36	276 02.3
17	Betelgeuse	{ 0.1 / 1.2 }	09 14	N 7 24.4	221 09.5	5 55	271 18.3
18	Canopus	–0.9	09 43	S52 41.3	213 54.6	6 24	264 03.4
19	Sirius	–1.6	10 04	S16 42.2	208 38.8	6 45	258 47.6
20	Adhara	1.6	10 17	S28 57.6	205 16.2	6 58	255 25.0
21	Castor	1.6	10 53	N31 54.3	196 19.2	7 34	246 28.0
22	Procyon	0.5	10 58	N 5 14.7	195 07.5	7 39	245 16.3
23	Pollux	1.2	11 04	N28 02.6	193 38.2	7 45	243 47.0
24	Avior	1.7	11 41	S59 29.1	184 16.2	8 22	234 25.0
25	Suhail	2.2	12 26	S43 24.2	172 55.6	9 08	223 04.4
26	Miaplacidus	1.8	12 32	S69 41.2	171 35.2	9 13	221 44.0
27	Alphard	2.2	12 46	S 8 37.6	168 02.9	9 27	218 11.7
28	Regulus	1.3	13 26	N12 00.2	157 51.5	10 08	208 00.3
29	Dubhe	2.0	14 21	N61 47.5	144 02.3	11 03	194 11.1
30	Denebola	2.2	15 07	N14 36.8	132 40.9	11 49	182 49.7
31	Gienah	2.8	15 33	S17 30.1	125 59.8	12 15	176 08.6
32	Acrux	1.1	15 44	S63 03.8	123 18.6	12 26	173 27.4
33	Gacrux	1.6	15 49	S57 04.6	122 10.0	12 31	172 18.8
34	Mimosa	1.5	16 05	S59 39.2	118 02.0	12 47	168 10.8
35	Alioth	1.7	16 12	N56 00.1	116 25.7	12 54	166 34.5
36	Spica	1.2	16 43	S11 07.4	108 39.0	13 25	158 47.8
37	Alkaid	1.9	17 05	N49 21.2	103 02.4	13 47	153 11.2
38	Hadar	0.9	17 21	S60 20.6	99 01.5	14 03	149 10.3
39	Menkent	2.3	17 24	S36 20.2	98 17.3	14 06	148 26.1
40	Arcturus	0.2	17 33	N19 13.3	96 01.2	14 15	146 10.0
41	Rigil Kent.	0.1	17 57	S60 48.6	90 04.4	14 39	140 13.2
42	Zuben'ubi	2.9	18 08	S16 00.8	87 13.9	14 50	137 22.7
43	Kochab	2.2	18 08	N74 11.4	87 10.6	14 51	137 19.4
44	Alphecca	2.3	18 52	N26 44.5	76 15.3	15 34	126 24.1
45	Antares	1.2	19 46	S26 25.1	62 36.4	16 29	112 45.2
46	Atria	1.9	20 05	S69 01.2	57 52.1	16 48	108 00.9
47	Sabik	2.6	20 27	S15 43.0	52 21.4	17 10	102 30.2
48	Shaula	1.7	20 50	S37 06.0	46 34.0	17 33	96 42.8
49	Rasalhague	2.1	20 52	N12 34.1	46 11.9	17 35	96 20.7
50	Eltanin	2.4	21 14	N51 29.6	40 44.2	17 56	90 53.0
51	Kaus Aust.	2.0	21 41	S34 23.3	33 55.3	18 24	84 04.1
52	Vega	0.1	21 54	N38 46.8	30 40.4	18 37	80 49.2
53	Nunki	2.1	22 12	S26 18.3	26 08.5	18 55	76 17.3
54	Altair	0.9	23 07	N 8 51.1	12 14.3	19 50	62 23.1
55	Peacock	2.1	23 42	S56 45.5	3 34.2	20 25	53 43.0
56	Deneb	1.3	00 02	N45 15.4	359 32.9	20 41	49 41.7
57	Enif	2.5	01 04	N 9 50.7	343 53.3	21 44	34 02.1
58	Al Na'ir	2.2	01 28	S46 59.6	337 53.8	22 08	28 02.6
59	Fomalhaut	1.3	02 17	S29 39.4	325 31.9	22 57	15 40.7
60	Markab	2.6	02 25	N15 10.1	323 44.7	23 04	13 53.5

Stars Transit Correction Table

D. of Mth.	Corr (Sub.)	D. of Mth.	Corr. (Sub.)
	h. m.		h. m.
1	–0 00	17	–1 03
2	–0 04	18	–1 07
3	–0 08	19	–1 11
4	–0 12	20	–1 15
5	–0 16	21	–1 19
6	–0 20	22	–1 23
7	–0 24	23	–1 27
8	–0 28	24	–1 30
9	–0 31	25	–1 34
10	–0 35	26	–1 38
11	–0 39	27	–1 42
12	–0 43	28	–1 46
13	–0 47	29	–1 50
14	–0 51	30	–1 54
15	–0 55	31	–1 58
16	–0 59		

STAR'S TRANSIT

To find the approx. time of Transit of a Star for any day of the month use above table.

If the quantity taken from the table is greater than the time of Transit for the first of the month, add 23h. 56min. to the time of transit before subtracting the correction below.

Example: Required the time of Transit of Al Na'ir (No 58) on August 26th.

	h.min.
Transit on the 1st	01 28
	+23 56
	25 24
Corr. for the 26th	–01 38
Transit on the 26th	23 46

d. h. AUGUST DIARY

1 12	Jupiter 7°N. of Moon
2 21	Mercury in inferior conjunction
5 11	First Quarter
6 18	Venus 1°.1N. of Regulus
7 10	Saturn at opposition
11 09	Mars 5°N. of Aldebaran
12 13	Mercury stationary
13 01	Saturn 5°S. of Moon
13 10	Full Moon
13 16	Moon at apogee
21 02	Mercury greatest elong. W.(18°)
21 10	Last Quarter
22 21	Mars 1°.4S. of Moon
23 03	Venus 0°.3N. of Jupiter
27 01	Mercury 5°N. of Moon
27 18	Moon at perigee
28 03	New Moon
29 19	Venus 7°N. of Moon

STAR TIME

The best time to take Star observations is shown in the a.m. and p.m. TWILIGHT columns on the opposite page – corrected for Latitude.

For **Lighting-up Time** (ashore) add 30 mins to Sunset Times.

For Star's G.H.A. Correction Table, see page 4:8.

For Alphabetical List of Stars with Constellation names, see page 2:24.

For Examples on the use of the above data, see page 2:11.

3:54 ☉ SUN — August, 1992 — ARIES ♈

Saturday, 1st August

G.M.T.	SUN G.H.A.	Dec.	ARIES G.H.A.	G.M.T.
00	178 25.5	N18 00.5	309 51.2	00
02	208 25.6	17 59.2	339 56.1	02
04	238 25.6	17 58.0	10 01.1	04
06	268 25.7	17 56.7	40 06.0	06
08	298 25.8	17 55.4	70 10.9	08
10	328 25.9	17 54.2	100 15.8	10
12	358 26.0	17 52.9	130 20.8	12
14	28 26.0	17 51.6	160 25.7	14
16	58 26.1	17 50.4	190 30.6	16
18	88 26.2	17 49.1	220 35.6	18
20	118 26.3	17 47.8	250 40.5	20
22	148 26.4	N17 46.5	280 45.4	22

Sunday, 2nd August

G.M.T.	SUN G.H.A.	Dec.	ARIES G.H.A.	G.M.T.
00	178 26.5	N17 45.2	310 50.3	00
02	208 26.5	17 44.0	340 55.3	02
04	238 26.6	17 42.7	11 00.2	04
06	268 26.7	17 41.4	41 05.1	06
08	298 26.8	17 40.1	71 10.1	08
10	328 26.9	17 38.8	101 15.0	10
12	358 27.0	17 37.5	131 19.9	12
14	28 27.1	17 36.2	161 24.8	14
16	58 27.2	17 34.9	191 29.8	16
18	88 27.3	17 33.6	221 34.7	18
20	118 27.4	17 32.3	251 39.6	20
22	148 27.5	N17 31.0	281 44.6	22

Monday, 3rd August

G.M.T.	SUN G.H.A.	Dec.	ARIES G.H.A.	G.M.T.
00	178 27.6	N17 29.7	311 49.5	00
02	208 27.7	17 28.4	341 54.4	02
04	238 27.8	17 27.1	11 59.3	04
06	268 27.9	17 25.8	42 04.3	06
08	298 28.0	17 24.5	72 09.2	08
10	328 28.1	17 23.1	102 14.1	10
12	358 28.2	17 21.8	132 19.0	12
14	28 28.3	17 20.5	162 24.0	14
16	58 28.4	17 19.2	192 28.9	16
18	88 28.5	17 17.9	222 33.8	18
20	118 28.6	17 16.5	252 38.8	20
22	148 28.7	N17 15.2	282 43.7	22

Tuesday, 4th August

G.M.T.	SUN G.H.A.	Dec.	ARIES G.H.A.	G.M.T.
00	178 28.9	N17 13.9	312 48.6	00
02	208 29.0	17 12.5	342 53.5	02
04	238 29.1	17 11.2	12 58.5	04
06	268 29.2	17 09.9	43 03.4	06
08	298 29.3	17 08.5	73 08.3	08
10	328 29.4	17 07.2	103 13.3	10
12	358 29.6	17 05.9	133 18.2	12
14	28 29.7	17 04.5	163 23.1	14
16	58 29.8	17 03.2	193 28.0	16
18	88 29.9	17 01.8	223 33.0	18
20	118 30.0	17 00.5	253 37.9	20
22	148 30.2	N16 59.1	283 42.8	22

Wednesday, 5th August

G.M.T.	SUN G.H.A.	Dec.	ARIES G.H.A.	G.M.T.
00	178 30.3	N16 57.8	313 47.8	00
02	208 30.4	16 56.4	343 52.7	02
04	238 30.6	16 55.1	13 57.6	04
06	268 30.7	16 53.7	44 02.5	06
08	298 30.8	16 52.3	74 07.5	08
10	328 30.9	16 51.0	104 12.4	10
12	358 31.1	16 49.6	134 17.3	12
14	28 31.2	16 48.3	164 22.3	14
16	58 31.3	16 46.9	194 27.2	16
18	88 31.5	16 45.5	224 32.1	18
20	118 31.6	16 44.1	254 37.0	20
22	148 31.7	N16 42.8	284 42.0	22

Thursday, 6th August

G.M.T.	SUN G.H.A.	Dec.	ARIES G.H.A.	G.M.T.
00	178 31.9	N16 41.4	314 46.9	00
02	208 32.0	16 40.0	344 51.8	02
04	238 32.2	16 38.6	14 56.8	04
06	268 32.3	16 37.3	45 01.7	06
08	298 32.5	16 35.9	75 06.6	08
10	328 32.6	16 34.5	105 11.5	10
12	358 32.7	16 33.1	135 16.5	12
14	28 32.9	16 31.7	165 21.4	14
16	58 33.0	16 30.3	195 26.3	16
18	88 33.2	16 28.9	225 31.3	18
20	118 33.3	16 27.5	255 36.2	20
22	148 33.5	N16 26.1	285 41.1	22

Friday, 7th August

G.M.T.	SUN G.H.A.	Dec.	ARIES G.H.A.	G.M.T.
00	178 33.6	N16 24.7	315 46.0	00
02	208 33.8	16 23.3	345 51.0	02
04	238 33.9	16 21.9	15 55.9	04
06	268 34.1	16 20.5	46 00.8	06
08	298 34.2	16 19.1	76 05.7	08
10	328 34.4	16 17.7	106 10.7	10
12	358 34.6	16 16.3	136 15.6	12
14	28 34.7	16 14.9	166 20.5	14
16	58 34.9	16 13.5	196 25.5	16
18	88 35.0	16 12.1	226 30.4	18
20	118 35.2	16 10.7	256 35.3	20
22	148 35.4	N16 09.3	286 40.2	22

Saturday, 8th August

G.M.T.	SUN G.H.A.	Dec.	ARIES G.H.A.	G.M.T.
00	178 35.5	N16 07.8	316 45.2	00
02	208 35.7	16 06.4	346 50.1	02
04	238 35.9	16 05.0	16 55.0	04
06	268 36.0	16 03.6	47 00.0	06
08	298 36.2	16 02.1	77 04.9	08
10	328 36.4	16 00.7	107 09.8	10
12	358 36.5	15 59.3	137 14.7	12
14	28 36.7	15 57.9	167 19.7	14
16	58 36.9	15 56.4	197 24.6	16
18	88 37.0	15 55.0	227 29.5	18
20	118 37.2	15 53.5	257 34.5	20
22	148 37.4	N15 52.1	287 39.4	22

Sunday, 9th August

G.M.T.	SUN G.H.A.	Dec.	ARIES G.H.A.	G.M.T.
00	178 37.6	N15 50.7	317 44.3	00
02	208 37.7	15 49.2	347 49.2	02
04	238 37.9	15 47.8	17 54.2	04
06	268 38.1	15 46.3	47 59.1	06
08	298 38.3	15 44.9	78 04.0	08
10	328 38.5	15 43.4	108 09.0	10
12	358 38.6	15 42.0	138 13.9	12
14	28 38.8	15 40.5	168 18.8	14
16	58 39.0	15 39.1	198 23.7	16
18	88 39.2	15 37.6	228 28.7	18
20	118 39.4	15 36.2	258 33.6	20
22	148 39.6	N15 34.7	288 38.5	22

Monday, 10th August

G.M.T.	SUN G.H.A.	Dec.	ARIES G.H.A.	G.M.T.
00	178 39.8	N15 33.2	318 43.5	00
02	208 40.0	15 31.8	348 48.4	02
04	238 40.1	15 30.3	18 53.3	04
06	268 40.3	15 28.8	48 58.2	06
08	298 40.5	15 27.4	79 03.2	08
10	328 40.7	15 25.9	109 08.1	10
12	358 40.9	15 24.4	139 13.0	12
14	28 41.1	15 23.0	169 17.9	14
16	58 41.3	15 21.5	199 22.9	16
18	88 41.5	15 20.0	229 27.8	18
20	118 41.7	15 18.5	259 32.7	20
22	148 41.9	N15 17.1	289 37.7	22

Tuesday, 11th August

G.M.T.	SUN G.H.A.	Dec.	ARIES G.H.A.	G.M.T.
00	178 42.1	N15 15.6	319 42.6	00
02	208 42.3	15 14.1	349 47.5	02
04	238 42.5	15 12.6	19 52.4	04
06	268 42.7	15 11.1	49 57.4	06
08	298 42.9	15 09.6	80 02.3	08
10	328 43.1	15 08.1	110 07.2	10
12	358 43.3	15 06.6	140 12.2	12
14	28 43.5	15 05.1	170 17.1	14
16	58 43.7	15 03.7	200 22.0	16
18	88 43.9	15 02.2	230 26.9	18
20	118 44.2	15 00.7	260 31.9	20
22	148 44.4	N14 59.2	290 36.8	22

Wednesday, 12th August

G.M.T.	SUN G.H.A.	Dec.	ARIES G.H.A.	G.M.T.
00	178 44.6	N14 57.7	320 41.7	00
02	208 44.8	14 56.2	350 46.7	02
04	238 45.0	14 54.6	20 51.6	04
06	268 45.2	14 53.1	50 56.5	06
08	298 45.4	14 51.6	81 01.4	08
10	328 45.7	14 50.1	111 06.4	10
12	358 45.9	14 48.6	141 11.3	12
14	28 46.1	14 47.1	171 16.2	14
16	58 46.3	14 45.6	201 21.2	16
18	88 46.5	14 44.1	231 26.1	18
20	118 46.8	14 42.5	261 31.0	20
22	148 47.0	N14 41.0	291 35.9	22

Thursday, 13th August

G.M.T.	SUN G.H.A.	Dec.	ARIES G.H.A.	G.M.T.
00	178 47.2	N14 39.5	320 40.9	00
02	208 47.4	14 38.0	351 45.8	02
04	238 47.7	14 36.5	21 50.7	04
06	268 47.9	14 34.9	51 55.7	06
08	298 48.1	14 33.4	82 00.6	08
10	328 48.3	14 31.9	112 05.5	10
12	358 48.6	14 30.3	142 10.4	12
14	28 48.8	14 28.8	172 15.4	14
16	58 49.0	14 27.3	202 20.3	16
18	88 49.3	14 25.7	232 25.2	18
20	118 49.5	14 24.2	262 30.2	20
22	148 49.7	N14 22.7	292 35.1	22

Friday, 14th August

G.M.T.	SUN G.H.A.	Dec.	ARIES G.H.A.	G.M.T.
00	178 50.0	N14 21.1	322 40.0	00
02	208 50.2	14 19.6	352 44.9	02
04	238 50.4	14 18.0	22 49.9	04
06	268 50.7	14 16.5	52 54.8	06
08	298 50.9	14 14.9	82 59.7	08
10	328 51.1	14 13.4	113 04.6	10
12	358 51.4	14 11.8	143 09.6	12
14	28 51.6	14 10.3	173 14.5	14
16	58 51.9	14 08.7	203 19.4	16
18	88 52.1	14 07.2	233 24.4	18
20	118 52.4	14 05.6	263 29.3	20
22	148 52.6	N14 04.1	293 34.2	22

Saturday, 15th August

G.M.T.	SUN G.H.A.	Dec.	ARIES G.H.A.	G.M.T.
00	178 52.9	N14 02.5	323 39.1	00
02	208 53.1	14 00.9	353 44.1	02
04	238 53.3	13 59.4	23 49.0	04
06	268 53.6	13 57.8	53 53.9	06
08	298 53.8	13 56.2	83 58.9	08
10	328 54.1	13 54.7	114 03.8	10
12	358 54.3	13 53.1	144 08.7	12
14	28 54.6	13 51.5	174 13.6	14
16	58 54.9	13 50.0	204 18.6	16
18	88 55.1	13 48.4	234 23.5	18
20	118 55.4	13 46.8	264 28.4	20
22	148 55.6	N13 45.2	294 33.4	22

To interpolate SUN G.H.A. see page 4:7   To interpolate ARIES G.H.A. see page 4:8

Sunday, 16th August

G.M.T. (h)	SUN G.H.A.	Dec.	ARIES G.H.A.	G.M.T. (h)
00	178 55.9	N13 43.6	324 38.3	00
02	208 56.1	13 42.1	354 43.2	02
04	238 56.4	13 40.5	24 48.1	04
06	268 56.6	13 38.9	54 53.1	06
08	298 56.9	13 37.3	84 58.0	08
10	328 57.2	13 35.7	115 02.9	10
12	358 57.4	13 34.1	145 07.9	12
14	28 57.7	13 32.6	175 12.8	14
16	58 58.0	13 31.0	205 17.7	16
18	88 58.2	13 29.4	235 22.6	18
20	118 58.5	13 27.8	265 27.6	20
22	148 58.8	N13 26.2	295 32.5	22

Friday, 21st August

G.M.T. (h)	SUN G.H.A.	Dec.	ARIES G.H.A.	G.M.T. (h)
00	179 12.8	N12 06.3	328 34.0	00
02	209 13.1	12 04.6	358 38.9	02
04	239 13.4	12 02.9	29 43.8	04
06	269 13.8	12 01.3	59 48.8	06
08	299 14.1	11 59.6	89 53.7	08
10	329 14.4	11 57.9	119 58.6	10
12	359 14.7	11 56.3	150 03.5	12
14	29 15.0	11 54.6	180 08.5	14
16	59 15.3	11 52.9	210 13.4	16
18	89 15.6	11 51.2	240 18.3	18
20	119 15.9	11 49.5	270 23.3	20
22	149 16.3	N11 47.9	300 28.2	22

Wednesday, 26th August

G.M.T. (h)	SUN G.H.A.	Dec.	ARIES G.H.A.	G.M.T. (h)
00	179 32.6	N10 24.1	334 29.7	00
02	209 32.9	10 22.3	4 34.6	02
04	239 33.3	10 20.6	34 39.5	04
06	269 33.6	10 18.9	64 44.5	06
08	299 34.0	10 17.1	94 49.4	08
10	329 34.4	10 15.4	124 54.3	10
12	359 34.7	10 13.6	154 59.2	12
14	29 35.1	10 11.9	185 04.2	14
16	59 35.4	10 10.1	215 09.1	16
18	89 35.8	10 08.4	245 14.0	18
20	119 36.1	10 06.6	275 19.0	20
22	149 36.5	N10 04.9	305 23.9	22

Monday, 17th August

G.M.T. (h)	SUN G.H.A.	Dec.	ARIES G.H.A.	G.M.T. (h)
00	178 59.0	N13 24.6	325 37.4	00
02	208 59.3	13 23.0	355 42.4	02
04	238 59.6	13 21.4	25 47.3	04
06	268 59.8	13 19.8	55 52.2	06
08	299 00.1	13 18.2	85 57.1	08
10	329 00.4	13 16.6	116 02.1	10
12	359 00.6	13 15.0	146 07.0	12
14	29 00.9	13 13.4	176 11.9	14
16	59 01.2	13 11.8	206 16.8	16
18	89 01.5	13 10.2	236 21.8	18
20	119 01.7	13 08.5	266 26.7	20
22	149 02.0	N13 06.9	296 31.6	22

Saturday, 22nd August

G.M.T. (h)	SUN G.H.A.	Dec.	ARIES G.H.A.	G.M.T. (h)
00	179 16.6	N11 46.2	330 33.1	00
02	209 16.9	11 44.5	0 38.0	02
04	239 17.2	11 42.8	30 43.0	04
06	269 17.5	11 41.1	60 47.9	06
08	299 17.8	11 39.5	90 52.8	08
10	329 18.2	11 37.8	120 57.8	10
12	359 18.5	11 36.1	151 02.7	12
14	29 18.8	11 34.4	181 07.6	14
16	59 19.1	11 32.7	211 12.5	16
18	89 19.5	11 31.0	241 17.5	18
20	119 19.8	11 29.3	271 22.4	20
22	149 20.1	N11 27.6	301 27.3	22

Thursday, 27th August

G.M.T. (h)	SUN G.H.A.	Dec.	ARIES G.H.A.	G.M.T. (h)
00	179 36.8	N10 03.1	335 28.8	00
02	209 37.2	10 01.4	5 33.7	02
04	239 37.6	9 59.6	35 38.7	04
06	269 37.9	9 57.9	65 43.6	06
08	299 38.3	9 56.1	95 48.5	08
10	329 38.7	9 54.3	125 53.5	10
12	359 39.0	9 52.6	155 58.4	12
14	29 39.4	9 50.8	186 03.3	14
16	59 39.7	9 49.1	216 08.2	16
18	89 40.1	9 47.3	246 13.2	18
20	119 40.5	9 45.5	276 18.1	20
22	149 40.8	N 9 43.8	306 23.0	22

Tuesday, 18th August

G.M.T. (h)	SUN G.H.A.	Dec.	ARIES G.H.A.	G.M.T. (h)
00	179 02.3	N13 05.3	326 36.6	00
02	209 02.6	13 03.7	356 41.5	02
04	239 02.9	13 02.1	26 46.4	04
06	269 03.1	13 00.5	56 51.3	06
08	299 03.4	12 58.8	86 56.3	08
10	329 03.7	12 57.2	117 01.2	10
12	359 04.0	12 55.6	147 06.1	12
14	29 04.3	12 54.0	177 11.1	14
16	59 04.5	12 52.3	207 16.0	16
18	89 04.8	12 50.7	237 20.9	18
20	119 05.1	12 49.1	267 25.8	20
22	149 05.4	N12 47.5	297 30.8	22

Sunday, 23rd August

G.M.T. (h)	SUN G.H.A.	Dec.	ARIES G.H.A.	G.M.T. (h)
00	179 20.4	N11 25.9	331 32.3	00
02	209 20.7	11 24.2	1 37.2	02
04	239 21.1	11 22.5	31 42.1	04
06	269 21.4	11 20.8	61 47.0	06
08	299 21.7	11 19.1	91 52.0	08
10	329 22.1	11 17.4	121 56.9	10
12	359 22.4	11 15.7	152 01.8	12
14	29 22.7	11 14.0	182 06.8	14
16	59 23.0	11 12.3	212 11.7	16
18	89 23.4	11 10.6	242 16.6	18
20	119 23.7	11 08.9	272 21.5	20
22	149 24.0	N11 07.2	302 26.5	22

Friday, 28th August

G.M.T. (h)	SUN G.H.A.	Dec.	ARIES G.H.A.	G.M.T. (h)
00	179 41.2	N 9 42.0	336 27.9	00
02	209 41.6	9 40.2	6 32.9	02
04	239 41.9	9 38.5	36 37.8	04
06	269 42.3	9 36.7	66 42.7	06
08	299 42.7	9 34.9	96 47.7	08
10	329 43.0	9 33.2	126 52.6	10
12	359 43.4	9 31.4	156 57.5	12
14	29 43.8	9 29.6	187 02.4	14
16	59 44.1	9 27.8	217 07.4	16
18	89 44.5	9 26.1	247 12.3	18
20	119 44.9	9 24.3	277 17.2	20
22	149 45.3	N 9 22.5	307 22.2	22

Wednesday, 19th August

G.M.T. (h)	SUN G.H.A.	Dec.	ARIES G.H.A.	G.M.T. (h)
00	179 05.7	N12 45.8	327 35.7	00
02	209 06.0	12 44.2	357 40.6	02
04	239 06.3	12 42.6	27 45.6	04
06	269 06.6	12 40.9	57 50.5	06
08	299 06.8	12 39.3	87 55.4	08
10	329 07.1	12 37.7	118 00.3	10
12	359 07.4	12 36.0	148 05.3	12
14	29 07.7	12 34.4	178 10.2	14
16	59 08.0	12 32.7	208 15.1	16
18	89 08.3	12 31.1	238 20.1	18
20	119 08.6	12 29.4	268 25.0	20
22	149 08.9	N12 27.8	298 29.9	22

Monday, 24th August

G.M.T. (h)	SUN G.H.A.	Dec.	ARIES G.H.A.	G.M.T. (h)
00	179 24.4	N11 05.5	332 31.4	00
02	209 24.7	11 03.8	2 36.3	02
04	239 25.0	11 02.1	32 41.3	04
06	269 25.4	11 00.3	62 46.2	06
08	299 25.7	10 58.6	92 51.1	08
10	329 26.1	10 56.9	122 56.0	10
12	359 26.4	10 55.2	153 01.0	12
14	29 26.7	10 53.5	183 05.9	14
16	59 27.1	10 51.8	213 10.8	16
18	89 27.4	10 50.0	243 15.7	18
20	119 27.8	10 48.3	273 20.7	20
22	149 28.1	N10 46.6	303 25.6	22

Saturday, 29th August

G.M.T. (h)	SUN G.H.A.	Dec.	ARIES G.H.A.	G.M.T. (h)
00	179 45.6	N 9 20.7	337 27.1	00
02	209 46.0	9 19.0	7 32.0	02
04	239 46.4	9 17.2	37 36.9	04
06	269 46.8	9 15.4	67 41.9	06
08	299 47.1	9 13.6	97 46.8	08
10	329 47.5	9 11.8	127 51.7	10
12	359 47.9	9 10.1	157 56.7	12
14	29 48.3	9 08.3	188 01.6	14
16	59 48.6	9 06.5	218 06.5	16
18	89 49.0	9 04.7	248 11.4	18
20	119 49.4	9 02.9	278 16.4	20
22	149 49.8	N 9 01.1	308 21.3	22

Thursday, 20th August

G.M.T. (h)	SUN G.H.A.	Dec.	ARIES G.H.A.	G.M.T. (h)
00	179 09.2	N12 26.1	328 34.8	00
02	209 09.5	12 24.5	358 39.8	02
04	239 09.8	12 22.8	28 44.7	04
06	269 10.1	12 21.2	58 49.6	06
08	299 10.4	12 19.5	88 54.6	08
10	329 10.7	12 17.9	118 59.5	10
12	359 11.0	12 16.2	149 04.4	12
14	29 11.3	12 14.6	179 09.3	14
16	59 11.6	12 12.9	209 14.3	16
18	89 11.9	12 11.3	239 19.2	18
20	119 12.2	12 09.6	269 24.1	20
22	149 12.5	N12 07.9	299 29.1	22

Tuesday, 25th August

G.M.T. (h)	SUN G.H.A.	Dec.	ARIES G.H.A.	G.M.T. (h)
00	179 28.4	N10 44.9	333 30.5	00
02	209 28.8	10 43.1	3 35.5	02
04	239 29.1	10 41.4	33 40.4	04
06	269 29.5	10 39.7	63 45.3	06
08	299 29.8	10 38.0	93 50.2	08
10	329 30.2	10 36.2	123 55.2	10
12	359 30.5	10 34.5	154 00.1	12
14	29 30.9	10 32.8	184 05.0	14
16	59 31.2	10 31.0	214 10.0	16
18	89 31.5	10 29.3	244 14.9	18
20	119 31.9	10 27.6	274 19.8	20
22	149 32.2	N10 25.8	304 24.7	22

Sunday, 30th August

G.M.T. (h)	SUN G.H.A.	Dec.	ARIES G.H.A.	G.M.T. (h)
00	179 50.2	N 8 59.3	338 26.2	00
02	209 50.5	8 57.5	8 31.2	02
04	239 50.9	8 55.7	38 36.1	04
06	269 51.3	8 53.9	68 41.0	06
08	299 51.7	8 52.2	98 45.9	08
10	329 52.1	8 50.4	128 50.9	10
12	359 52.5	8 48.6	158 55.8	12
14	29 52.8	8 46.8	189 00.7	14
16	59 53.2	8 45.0	219 05.7	16
18	89 53.6	8 43.2	249 10.6	18
20	119 54.0	8 41.4	279 15.5	20
22	149 54.4	N 8 39.6	309 20.4	22

Monday, 31st August

G.M.T. (h)	SUN G.H.A.	Dec.	ARIES G.H.A.	G.M.T. (h)
00	179 54.8	N 8 37.8	339 25.4	00
02	209 55.2	8 36.0	9 30.3	02
04	239 55.6	8 34.2	39 35.2	04
06	269 55.9	N 8 32.4	69 40.2	06
08	299 56.3	N 8 30.5	99 45.1	08
10	329 56.7	8 28.7	129 50.0	10
12	359 57.1	8 26.9	159 54.9	12
14	29 57.5	N 8 25.1	189 59.9	14
16	59 57.9	N 8 23.3	220 04.8	16
18	89 58.3	8 21.5	250 09.7	18
20	119 58.7	8 19.7	280 14.6	20
22	149 59.1	N 8 17.9	310 19.6	22

To interpolate SUN G.H.A. see page 4:7   To interpolate ARIES G.H.A. see page 4:8

♀ VENUS ♀   ♃ JUPITER ♃

Mer. Pass.	G.H.A.	Mean Var. 14°	Dec.	Mean Var.	M	Day of Week	G.H.A	Mean Var. 15°	Dec.	Mean Var.	Mer. Pass
h. m.	° ′	′	° ′	′			° ′	′	° ′	′	h. m.
13 02	164 42.9	59.4	N15 27.6	1.0	1	Sat...........	143 07.0	2.0	N 6 51.0	0.2	14 26
13 02	164 29.6	59.5	N15 03.7	1.0	2	SUN.........	143 55.4	2.0	N 6 46.5	0.2	14 22
13 03	164 16.7	59.5	N14 39.4	1.0	3	Mon.........	144 43.7	2.0	N 6 41.9	0.2	14 19
13 04	164 04.0	59.5	N14 14.6	1.0	4	Tu...........	145 32.0	2.0	N 6 37.3	0.2	14 16
13 05	163 51.7	59.5	N13 49.5	1.1	5	Wed.........	146 20.2	2.0	N 6 32.6	0.2	14 13
13 06	163 39.6	59.5	N13 24.0	1.1	6	Th.	147 08.4	2.0	N 6 28.0	0.2	14 10
13 07	163 27.7	59.5	N12 58.2	1.1	7	Fri.	147 56.6	2.0	N 6 23.3	0.2	14 06
13 07	163 16.1	59.5	N12 32.0	1.1	8	Sat...........	148 44.7	2.0	N 6 18.6	0.2	14 03
13 08	163 04.8	59.5	N12 05.5	1.1	9	SUN.........	149 32.7	2.0	N 6 13.9	0.2	14 00
13 09	162 53.7	59.6	N11 38.7	1.1	10	Mon.........	150 20.7	2.0	N 6 09.2	0.2	13 57
13 10	162 42.9	59.6	N11 11.5	1.1	11	Tu...........	151 08.7	2.0	N 6 04.4	0.2	13 54
13 10	162 32.3	59.6	N10 44.1	1.2	12	Wed.........	151 56.6	2.0	N 5 59.7	0.2	13 50
13 11	162 21.9	59.6	N10 16.4	1.2	13	Th.	152 44.5	2.0	N 5 54.9	0.2	13 47
13 12	162 11.7	59.6	N 9 48.4	1.2	14	Fri.	153 32.3	2.0	N 5 50.0	0.2	13 44
13 12	162 01.8	59.6	N 9 20.2	1.2	15	Sat...........	154 20.1	2.0	N 5 45.2	0.2	13 41
13 13	161 52.0	59.6	N 8 51.7	1.2	16	SUN.........	155 07.9	2.0	N 5 40.4	0.2	13 38
13 14	161 42.4	59.6	N 8 22.9	1.2	17	Mon.........	155 55.6	2.0	N 5 35.5	0.2	13 34
13 14	161 33.1	59.6	N 7 54.0	1.2	18	Tu...........	156 43.3	2.0	N 5 30.6	0.2	13 31
13 15	161 23.9	59.6	N 7 24.8	1.2	19	Wed.........	157 31.0	2.0	N 5 25.7	0.2	13 28
13 15	161 14.8	59.6	N 6 55.5	1.2	20	Th.	158 18.7	2.0	N 5 20.8	0.2	13 25
13 16	161 05.9	59.6	N 6 25.9	1.2	21	Fri.	159 06.3	2.0	N 5 15.9	0.2	13 22
13 17	160 57.2	59.6	N 5 56.2	1.2	22	Sat...........	159 53.9	2.0	N 5 11.0	0.2	13 19
13 17	160 48.6	59.6	N 5 26.3	1.3	23	SUN.........	160 41.4	2.0	N 5 06.0	0.2	13 15
13 18	160 40.1	59.7	N 4 56.3	1.3	24	Mon.........	161 28.9	2.0	N 5 01.0	0.2	13 12
13 18	160 31.8	59.7	N 4 26.1	1.3	25	Tu...........	162 16.4	2.0	N 4 56.0	0.2	13 09
13 19	160 23.5	59.7	N 3 55.8	1.3	26	Wed.........	163 03.9	2.0	N 4 51.1	0.2	13 06
13 19	160 15.4	59.7	N 3 25.4	1.3	27	Th.	163 51.4	2.0	N 4 46.1	0.2	13 03
13 20	160 07.3	59.7	N 2 54.9	1.3	28	Fri.	164 38.8	2.0	N 4 41.0	0.2	13 00
13 20	159 59.3	59.7	N 2 24.3	1.3	29	Sat...........	165 26.2	2.0	N 4 36.0	0.2	12 57
13 21	159 51.4	59.7	N 1 53.6	1.3	30	SUN.........	166 13.6	2.0	N 4 31.0	0.2	12 53
13 21	159 43.5	59.7	N 1 22.8	1.3	31	Mon.........	167 01.0	2.0	N 4 25.9	0.2	12 50

♀ VENUS. Av. Mag. –3.9. An **Evening Star**. In conjunction with Jupiter on August 23. **S.H.A.** August 5 210°; 10 204°; 15 199°; 20 193°; 25 187°; 30 182°.

♃ JUPITER. Av. Mag. –1.7. An **Evening Star**. Do not confuse with Venus in late August. Venus is the brighter object. **S.H.A.** August 5 193°; 10 192°; 15 190°; 20 190°; 25 190°; 30 187°.

♂ MARS ♂   ♄ SATURN ♄

Mer. Pass.	G.H.A.	Mean Var. 15°	Dec.	Mean Var.	M	Day of Week	G.H.A	Mean Var. 15°	Dec.	Mean Var.	Mer. Pass
h. m.	° ′	′	° ′	′			° ′	′	° ′	′	h. m.
07 27	248 11.3	0.7	N20 05.5	0.3	1	Sat...........	351 27.9	2.6	S17 07.1	0.1	00 34
07 26	248 28.4	0.7	N20 13.8	0.3	2	SUN.........	352 31.4	2.6	S17 08.5	0.1	00 30
07 25	248 45.6	0.7	N20 21.9	0.3	3	Mon.........	353 35.0	2.6	S17 09.9	0.1	00 26
07 23	249 02.8	0.7	N20 29.8	0.3	4	Tu...........	354 38.6	2.6	S17 11.4	0.1	00 21
07 22	249 20.1	0.7	N20 37.6	0.3	5	Wed.........	355 42.2	2.7	S17 12.8	0.1	00 17
07 21	249 37.4	0.7	N20 45.2	0.3	6	Th.	356 45.8	2.6	S17 14.2	0.1	00 13
07 20	249 54.8	0.7	N20 52.6	0.3	7	Fri.	357 49.4	2.6	S17 15.6	0.1	00 09
07 19	250 12.2	0.7	N20 59.8	0.3	8	Sat...........	358 53.0	2.6	S17 17.0	0.1	00 04
07 18	250 29.7	0.7	N21 06.8	0.3	9	SUN.........	359 56.6	2.6	S17 18.4	0.1	00 00
07 16	250 47.3	0.7	N21 13.6	0.3	10	Mon.........	1 00.2	2.7	S17 19.8	0.1	23 52
07 15	251 04.9	0.7	N21 20.3	0.3	11	Tu...........	2 03.8	2.6	S17 21.2	0.1	23 48
07 14	251 22.6	0.7	N21 26.7	0.3	12	Wed.........	3 07.4	2.7	S17 22.6	0.1	23 43
07 13	251 40.4	0.7	N21 33.0	0.3	13	Th.	4 11.0	2.6	S17 23.9	0.1	23 39
07 12	251 58.2	0.7	N21 39.1	0.3	14	Fri.	5 14.5	2.7	S17 25.3	0.1	23 35
07 11	252 16.1	0.8	N21 45.1	0.2	15	Sat...........	6 18.1	2.7	S17 26.7	0.1	23 31
07 09	252 34.1	0.8	N21 50.8	0.2	16	SUN.........	7 21.7	2.6	S17 28.0	0.1	23 26
07 08	252 52.1	0.8	N21 56.4	0.2	17	Mon.........	8 25.2	2.6	S17 29.4	0.1	23 22
07 07	253 10.3	0.8	N22 01.8	0.2	18	Tu...........	9 28.7	2.6	S17 30.7	0.1	23 18
07 06	253 28.5	0.8	N22 07.0	0.2	19	Wed	10 32.2	2.6	S17 32.0	0.1	23 14
07 05	253 46.9	0.8	N22 12.0	0.2	20	Th.	11 35.6	2.6	S17 33.3	0.1	23 10
07 03	254 05.3	0.8	N22 16.9	0.2	21	Fri.	12 39.1	2.6	S17 34.6	0.1	23 05
07 02	254 23.8	0.8	N22 21.5	0.2	22	Sat...........	13 42.5	2.6	S17 35.9	0.1	23 01
07 01	254 42.5	0.8	N22 26.0	0.2	23	SUN.........	14 45.8	2.6	S17 37.2	0.1	22 57
07 00	255 01.2	0.8	N22 30.4	0.2	24	Mon.........	15 49.2	2.6	S17 38.5	0.0	22 53
06 58	255 20.1	0.8	N22 34.5	0.2	25	Tu...........	16 52.5	2.6	S17 39.7	0.1	22 48
06 57	255 39.1	0.8	N22 38.5	0.2	26	Wed.........	17 55.7	2.6	S17 41.0	0.0	22 44
06 56	255 58.2	0.8	N22 42.3	0.2	27	Th.	18 59.0	2.6	S17 42.2	0.1	22 40
06 54	256 17.5	0.8	N22 46.0	0.1	28	Fri.	20 02.1	2.6	S17 43.4	0.0	22 36
06 53	256 36.8	0.8	N22 49.5	0.1	29	Sat...........	21 05.3	2.6	S17 44.6	0.0	22 32
06 52	256 56.4	0.8	N22 52.8	0.1	30	SUN.........	22 08.4	2.6	S17 45.7	0.1	22 28
06 51	257 16.0	0.8	N22 55.9	0.1	31	Mon.........	23 11.4	2.6	S17 46.9	0.0	22 23

♂ MARS. Av. Mag. +0.7. A **Morning Star**. S.H.A. August 5 296°; 10 292°; 15 288°; 20 285°; 25 282°; 30 278°.

♄ SATURN. Av. Mag. +0.2. A **Morning Star**. At opposition on August 7 when it is visible throughout the night. **S.H.A.** August 5 42°; 10 43°; 15 42°; 20 43°; 25 44°; 30 43°.

MERCURY. Too close to the sun for observation until August 11 when it is visible low in the east before sunrise.

For Planets Correction Tables see pages 4:9-4:13. See also 'How to Recognise the Planets' on page 2:32.
Mean Var. means Variation per Hour.

Day of M. W.	G.M.T.	G.H.A.	Mean Var. per Hour	Dec.	Mean Var. per Hour	Day of M. W.	G.M.T.	G.H.A.	Mean Var. per Hour	Dec.	Mean Var. per Hour
	h	° ′	14°,+	° ′	′		h	° ′	14°,+	° ′	′
1 Sat.	0	150 06.0	28.3	N 3 17.6	15.1	17 Mon.	0	324 30.5	34.6	N 6 00.6	11.7
	6	236 55.4	28.5	N 1 47.0	15.1		6	51 58.0	34.3	N 7 11.1	11.6
	12	323 46.2	28.7	N 0 16.4	15.0		12	139 24.2	34.1	N 8 20.8	11.5
	18	50 38.2	28.9	S 1 13.8	14.9		18	226 48.8	33.8	N 9 29.4	11.3
2 Sun.	0	137 31.2	29.0	S 2 43.1	14.7	18 Tu.	0	314 11.8	33.5	N10 36.9	11.0
	6	224 25.0	29.1	S 4 11.3	14.4		6	41 32.8	33.1	N11 43.1	10.8
	12	311 19.4	29.1	S 5 38.0	14.1		12	128 51.8	32.8	N12 47.7	10.5
	18	38 14.2	29.2	S 7 03.0	13.8		18	216 08.6	32.4	N13 50.6	10.2
3 Mon.	0	125 09.3	29.1	S 8 26.0	13.4	19 Wed.	0	303 23.0	32.0	N14 51.7	9.8
	6	212 04.4	29.2	S 9 46.7	12.9		6	30 34.8	31.5	N15 50.6	9.4
	12	298 59.5	29.2	S11 04.8	12.5		12	117 44.0	31.0	N16 47.2	9.0
	18	25 54.4	29.1	S12 20.1	12.1		18	204 50.3	30.5	N17 41.3	8.5
4 Tu.	0	112 49.0	29.0	S13 32.4	11.4	20 Th.	0	291 53.7	30.0	N18 32.6	8.0
	6	199 43.2	28.9	S14 41.5	10.9		6	18 54.1	29.5	N19 21.0	7.5
	12	286 36.9	28.9	S15 47.2	10.3		12	105 51.4	29.0	N20 06.2	6.9
	18	13 30.0	28.7	S16 49.3	9.7		18	192 45.6	28.5	N20 47.9	6.3
5 Wed.	0	100 22.6	28.7	S17 47.6	9.0	21 Fri.	0	279 36.7	28.0	N21 25.9	5.6
	6	187 14.5	28.6	S18 42.1	8.4		6	6 24.6	27.4	N22 00.1	4.9
	12	274 05.9	28.5	S19 32.5	7.6		12	93 09.4	26.9	N22 30.0	4.2
	18	0 56.7	28.3	S20 18.8	6.9		18	179 51.3	26.4	N22 55.6	3.4
6 Th.	0	87 47.1	28.3	S21 00.8	6.3	22 Sat.	0	266 30.3	26.1	N23 16.6	2.7
	6	174 37.0	28.3	S21 38.4	5.5		6	353 06.7	25.6	N23 32.7	1.7
	12	261 26.6	28.2	S22 11.7	4.7		12	79 40.5	25.2	N23 43.8	0.9
	18	348 15.9	28.2	S22 40.4	4.0		18	166 12.1	24.9	N23 49.7	0.0
7 Fri.	0	75 05.3	28.3	S23 04.6	3.2	23 Sun.	0	252 41.7	24.6	N23 50.2	0.9
	6	161 54.7	28.3	S23 24.3	2.5		6	339 09.6	24.4	N23 45.2	1.9
	12	248 44.3	28.3	S23 39.4	1.7		12	65 36.1	24.2	N23 34.6	2.8
	18	335 34.4	28.5	S23 50.0	1.0		18	152 01.6	24.1	N23 18.3	3.8
8 Sat.	0	62 25.0	28.6	S23 56.0	0.2	24 Mon.	0	238 26.4	24.0	N22 56.3	4.7
	6	149 16.5	28.8	S23 57.5	0.5		6	324 50.8	24.1	N22 28.5	5.6
	12	236 08.8	28.9	S23 54.6	1.2		12	51 15.1	24.1	N21 55.1	6.6
	18	323 02.3	29.2	S23 47.4	1.9		18	137 39.7	24.2	N21 16.1	7.5
9 Sun.	0	49 57.1	29.3	S23 35.8	2.7	25 Tu.	0	224 04.9	24.3	N20 31.6	8.4
	6	136 53.2	29.6	S23 20.1	3.3		6	310 30.9	24.5	N19 41.8	9.2
	12	223 51.0	30.0	S23 00.3	4.0		12	36 58.0	24.7	N18 46.9	10.0
	18	310 50.4	30.2	S22 36.6	4.7		18	123 26.3	25.0	N17 47.1	10.9
10 Mon.	0	37 51.5	30.6	S22 09.0	5.3	26 Wed.	0	209 56.0	25.2	N16 42.7	11.5
	6	124 54.6	30.9	S21 37.8	5.8		6	296 27.3	25.5	N15 33.9	12.2
	12	211 59.5	31.1	S21 03.0	6.4		12	23 00.3	25.7	N14 21.1	12.7
	18	299 06.5	31.5	S20 24.8	6.9		18	109 34.9	26.1	N13 04.7	13.3
11 Tu.	0	26 15.4	31.8	S19 43.4	7.5	27 Th.	0	196 11.1	26.3	N11 45.0	13.8
	6	113 26.3	32.1	S18 59.0	7.9		6	282 49.1	26.6	N10 22.3	14.2
	12	200 39.2	32.5	S18 11.6	8.4		12	9 28.6	26.9	N 8 57.2	14.6
	18	287 54.0	32.8	S17 21.5	8.9		18	96 09.7	27.1	N 7 29.9	14.9
12 Wed.	0	15 10.7	33.1	S16 28.8	9.2	28 Fri.	0	182 52.1	27.3	N 6 00.9	15.0
	6	102 29.3	33.4	S15 33.7	9.6		6	269 35.9	27.5	N 4 30.7	15.2
	12	189 49.6	33.7	S14 36.3	10.0		12	356 20.9	27.7	N 2 59.6	15.2
	18	277 11.6	33.9	S13 36.9	10.3		18	83 06.9	27.8	N 1 28.0	15.3
13 Th.	0	4 35.1	34.1	S12 35.6	10.5	29 Sat.	0	169 53.8	27.9	S 0 03.6	15.2
	6	92 00.1	34.4	S11 32.5	10.8		6	256 41.3	28.1	S 1 34.9	15.1
	12	179 26.5	34.6	S10 27.7	11.0		12	343 29.5	28.1	S 3 05.4	14.9
	18	266 54.0	34.7	S 9 21.6	11.2		18	70 18.0	28.1	S 4 34.8	14.6
14 Fri.	0	354 22.6	35.0	S 8 14.2	11.4	30 Sun.	0	157 06.8	28.1	S 6 02.7	14.4
	6	81 52.1	35.1	S 7 05.6	11.6		6	243 55.7	28.2	S 7 28.8	14.0
	12	169 22.4	35.2	S 5 56.0	11.7		12	330 44.7	28.1	S 8 52.8	13.5
	18	256 53.2	35.3	S 4 45.7	11.9		18	57 33.4	28.1	S10 14.3	13.1
15 Sat.	0	344 24.6	35.3	S 3 34.6	11.9	31 Mon.	0	144 21.9	28.0	S11 33.1	12.6
	6	71 56.2	35.3	S 2 23.0	12.0		6	231 10.2	28.0	S12 48.8	12.0
	12	159 27.9	35.3	S 1 11.0	12.0		12	317 58.0	27.9	S14 01.2	11.5
	18	246 59.5	35.2	N 0 01.2	12.0		18	44 45.3	28.0	S15 10.1	10.8
16 Sun.	0	334 30.9	35.1	N 1 13.5	12.0						
	6	62 01.9	35.0	N 2 25.8	12.0						
	12	149 32.3	34.9	N 3 37.8	11.9						
	18	237 01.9	34.7	N 4 49.5	11.9						

PHASES OF THE MOON

		d. h/min			d. h/min
))	First Quarter	5 10 58	(	Last Quarter	21 10 01
O	Full Moon	13 10 27	●	New Moon	28 02 42
	Apogee	13 16		Perigee	27 18

☉ SUN ☉

DATE			Equation of Time		Transit	Semi-diam.	Lat. 52°N.				Lat. Corr. to Sunrise, Sunset, etc.				
Day of							Twi-light	Sun-rise	Sun-set	Twi-light		Twi-light	Sun-rise	Sun-set	Twi-light
Yr.	Mth.	Week	0 h.	12 h.							Lat.				
			m. s.	m. s.	h. m.	′	h. m.	h. m.	h. m.	h. m.	°	h. m.	h. m.	h. m.	h. m.
245	1	Tu.	+00 03	−00 07	12 00	15.9	04 37	05 12	18 47	19 22	N70	−0 53	−0 21	+0 20	+0 51
246	2	Wed.	−00 17	−00 26	12 00	15.9	04 39	05 14	18 45	19 20	68	−0 42	−0 17	+0 16	+0 41
247	3	Th.	−00 36	−00 46	11 59	15.9	04 40	05 15	18 42	19 17	66	−0 34	−0 14	+0 13	+0 32
248	4	Fri.	−00 56	−01 05	11 59	15.9	04 42	05 17	18 40	19 15	64	−0 27	−0 11	+0 10	+0 25
249	5	Sat.	−01 15	−01 25	11 59	15.9	04 44	05 19	18 38	19 13	62	−0 20	−0 08	+0 08	+0 19
250	6	Sun.	−01 36	−01 46	11 58	15.9	04 45	05 20	18 35	19 10	N60	−0 15	−0 06	+0 06	+0 15
251	7	Mon.	−01 56	−02 06	11 58	15.9	04 47	05 22	18 33	19 08	58	−0 11	−0 04	+0 05	+0 10
252	8	Tu.	−02 16	−02 27	11 58	15.9	04 49	05 24	18 31	19 05	56	−0 07	−0 02	+0 03	+0 07
253	9	Wed.	−02 37	−02 48	11 57	15.9	04 50	05 25	18 28	19 03	54	−0 03	−0 01	+0 02	+0 03
254	10	Th.	−02 58	−03 09	11 57	15.9	04 52	05 27	18 26	19 00	50	+0 03	+0 02	−0 01	−0 03
255	11	Fri.	−03 19	−03 30	11 57	15.9	04 54	05 28	18 24	18 58	N45	+0 09	+0 04	−0 03	−0 09
256	12	Sat.	−03 40	−03 51	11 56	15.9	04 55	05 30	18 21	18 55	40	+0 12	+0 06	−0 06	−0 13
257	13	Sun.	−04 02	−04 12	11 56	15.9	04 57	05 31	18 19	18 53	35	+0 16	+0 08	−0 08	−0 17
258	14	Mon.	−04 23	−04 34	11 55	15.9	04 59	05 33	18 17	18 51	30	+0 20	+0 10	−0 09	−0 20
259	15	Tu.	−04 44	−04 55	11 55	15.9	05 00	05 34	18 14	18 48	20	+0 24	+0 13	−0 12	−0 25
260	16	Wed.	−05 06	−05 17	11 55	15.9	05 02	05 36	18 12	18 46	N10	+0 28	+0 16	−0 14	−0 28
261	17	Th.	−05 27	−05 38	11 54	15.9	05 04	05 38	18 10	18 44	0	+0 31	+0 18	−0 16	−0 31
262	18	Fri.	−05 49	−05 59	11 54	16.0	05 05	05 39	18 07	18 41	S10	+0 33	+0 19	−0 17	−0 32
263	19	Sat.	−06 10	−06 21	11 54	16.0	05 07	05 41	18 05	18 39	20	+0 33	+0 21	−0 19	−0 33
264	20	Sun.	−06 31	−06 42	11 53	16.0	05 09	05 43	18 03	18 37	30	+0 34	+0 24	−0 20	−0 33
265	21	Mon.	−06 53	−07 03	11 53	16.0	05 10	05 44	18 00	18 34	S35	+0 34	+0 26	−0 21	−0 32
266	22	Tu.	−07 14	−07 24	11 53	16.0	05 12	05 46	17 58	18 32	40	+0 33	+0 27	−0 23	−0 32
267	23	Wed.	−07 35	−07 45	11 52	16.0	05 14	05 48	17 56	18 30	45	+0 32	+0 28	−0 24	−0 31
268	24	Th.	−07 56	−08 06	11 52	16.0	05 15	05 49	17 53	18 27	S50	+0 31	+0 30	−0 26	−0 30
269	25	Fri.	−08 16	−08 27	11 52	16.0	05 17	05 51	17 51	18 25					
270	26	Sat.	−08 37	−08 47	11 51	16.0	05 19	05 53	17 49	18 23					
271	27	Sun.	−08 57	−09 07	11 51	16.0	05 20	05 54	17 46	18 20		NOTES			
272	28	Mon.	−09 17	−09 27	11 51	16.0	05 22	05 56	17 44	18 18					
273	29	Tu.	−09 37	−09 47	11 50	16.0	05 24	05 58	17 42	18 16					
274	30	Wed.	−09 57	−10 07	11 50	16.0	05 25	05 59	17 39	18 13					

NOTES

*Equation of Time changes its sign on the 1st. The Lat. Corr. to sunrise, sunset, etc., is for the middle of September. Examples on the use of the above data are given on page 2:11 onwards.

Equation of Time is the excess of Mean Time over Apparent Time
(See explanation and examples on p. 2:15)

☾ MOON ☽

DATE			Age	Transit Diff. (Upper)		Semi-diam.	Hor. Par. 12 h.	Lat. 52°N.		MOON'S PHASES
Day of								Moon-rise	Moon-set	
Yr.	Mth.	Week	days							
				h. m.	m.	′	′	h. m.	h. m.	
245	1	Tu.	04	15 48	54	15.9	58.4	11 18	20 09	d. h. m.
246	2	Wed.	05	16 42	54	15.6	57.4	12 34	20 44	☽ First Quarter........... 3 22 39
247	3	Th.	06	17 36	53	15.4	56.5	13 42	21 27	○ Full Moon 12 02 17
248	4	Fri.	07	18 29	51	15.2	55.8	14 38	22 19	☾ Last Quarter........... 19 19 53
249	5	Sat.	08	19 20	49	15.0	55.1	15 24	23 19	● New Moon 26 10 40
250	6	Sun.	09	20 09	46	14.9	54.6	16 00	− −	
251	7	Mon.	10	20 55	44	14.8	54.3	16 28	00 24	
252	8	Tu.	11	21 39	43	14.7	54.1	16 50	01 31	
253	9	Wed.	12	22 22	41	14.7	54.0	17 09	02 38	
254	10	Th.	13	23 03	41	14.7	54.0	17 26	03 46	d. h.
255	11	Fri.	14	23 44	42	14.8	54.1	17 41	04 53	Apogee 9 19
256	12	Sat.	15	24 26		14.8	54.3	17 57	06 00	Perigee 25 03
257	13	Sun.	16	00 26	42	14.9	54.6	18 14	07 08	
258	14	Mon.	17	01 08	44	15.0	55.0	18 32	08 17	
259	15	Tu.	18	01 52	47	15.1	55.4	18 54	09 28	
260	16	Wed.	19	02 39	50	15.2	55.9	19 22	10 39	
261	17	Th.	20	03 29	54	15.4	56.5	19 58	11 49	
262	18	Fri.	21	04 23	55	15.6	57.2	20 45	12 54	
263	19	Sat.	22	05 18	57	15.8	57.9	21 44	13 52	
264	20	Sun.	23	06 15	58	16.0	58.6	22 55	14 39	NOTES
265	21	Mon.	24	07 13	57	16.2	59.4	− −	15 17	Moon's G.H.A. and Dec. are given on page 3:63.
266	22	Tu.	25	08 10	55	16.4	60.0	00 14	15 48	A table for correcting Moonrise and Moonset for latitude is on page 4:20.
267	23	Wed.	26	09 05	54	16.5	60.6	01 39	16 13	A table for correcting Moon's meri-
268	24	Th.	27	09 59	54	16.6	60.9	03 06	16 35	dian passage (transit) for longitude is
269	25	Fri.	28	10 53	53	16.6	60.9	04 33	16 56	on page 4:19.
270	26	Sat.	00	11 46	53	16.5	60.6	05 59	17 17	Examples on the use of the above
271	27	Sun.	01	12 39	55	16.4	60.1	07 25	17 41	data are given on page 2:11 onwards.
272	28	Mon.	02	13 34	55	16.2	59.4	08 50	18 08	
273	29	Tu.	03	14 29	56	15.9	58.5	10 11	18 41	
274	30	Wed.	04	15 25	55	15.7	57.6	11 24	19 22	

0h. = midnight. For explanation of use of above data see page 2:11 onwards.

0h. G.M.T. SEPTEMBER 1 ★ ★ STARS ★ ★ 0h. G.M.T. SEPTEMBER 1

No.	Name	Mag.	Transit (approx.)	DEC.	G.H.A.	R.A.	S.H.A.
			h. m.	° ′	° ′	h. m.	° ′
♈	ARIES	–	01 18	–	340 24.5	–	–
1	Alpheratz	2.2	01 26	N29 03.2	338 23.7	0 08	357 59.2
2	Ankaa	2.4	01 44	S42 20.5	333 55.0	0 26	353 30.5
3	Schedar	2.5	01 58	N56 30.0	330 22.3	0 40	349 57.8
4	Diphda	2.2	02 01	S18 01.3	329 35.6	0 43	349 11.1
5	Achernar	0.6	02 55	S57 16.1	316 02.1	1 37	335 37.6
6	POLARIS	2.1	03 43	N89 13.8	304 02.6	2 25	323 38.1
7	Hamal	2.2	03 25	N23 25.8	308 42.5	2 07	328 18.0
8	Acamar	3.1	04 16	S40 19.7	295 54.3	2 58	315 29.8
9	Menkar	2.8	04 20	N 4 03.9	294 55.6	3 02	314 31.1
10	Mirfak	1.9	04 41	N49 50.1	289 26.9	3 24	309 02.4
11	Aldebaran	1.1	05 53	N16 29.8	271 31.6	4 36	291 07.1
12	Rigel	0.3	06 32	S 8 12.4	261 51.4	5 14	281 26.9
13	Capella	0.2	06 33	N45 59.4	261 21.9	5 16	280 57.4
14	Bellatrix	1.7	06 42	N 6 20.7	259 13.1	5 25	278 48.6
15	Elnath	1.8	06 43	N28 36.1	258 56.7	5 26	278 32.2
16	Alnilam	1.8	06 53	S 1 12.2	256 26.6	5 36	276 02.1
17	Betelgeuse	{ 0.1 / 1.2 }	07 12	N 7 24.5	251 42.6	5 55	271 18.1
18	Canopus	–0.9	07 41	S52 41.2	244 27.6	6 24	264 03.1
19	Sirius	–1.6	08 02	S16 42.2	239 12.0	6 45	258 47.5
20	Adhara	1.6	08 15	S28 57.5	235 49.3	6 58	255 24.8
21	Castor	1.6	08 51	N31 54.2	226 52.3	7 34	246 27.8
22	Procyon	0.5	08 56	N 5 14.7	225 40.6	7 39	245 16.1
23	Pollux	1.2	09 02	N28 02.6	224 11.3	7 45	243 46.8
24	Avior	1.7	09 39	S59 29.0	214 49.3	8 22	234 24.8
25	Suhail	2.2	10 24	S43 24.0	203 28.7	9 08	223 04.2
26	Miaplacidus	1.8	10 30	S69 41.1	202 08.3	9 13	221 43.8
27	Alphard	2.2	10 44	S 8 37.5	198 36.1	9 27	218 11.6
28	Regulus	1.3	11 24	N12 00.2	188 24.8	10 08	208 00.3
29	Dubhe	2.0	12 20	N61 47.3	174 35.6	11 03	194 11.1
30	Denebola	2.2	13 05	N14 36.8	163 14.2	11 49	182 49.7
31	Gienah	2.8	13 32	S17 30.1	156 33.1	12 15	176 08.6
32	Acrux	1.1	13 42	S63 03.6	153 52.0	12 26	173 27.5
33	Gacrux	1.6	13 47	S57 04.5	152 43.4	12 31	172 18.9
34	Mimosa	1.5	14 03	S59 39.1	148 35.4	12 47	168 10.9
35	Alioth	1.7	14 10	N56 00.0	146 59.1	12 54	166 34.6
36	Spica	1.2	14 41	S11 07.4	139 12.4	13 25	158 47.9
37	Alkaid	1.9	15 03	N49 21.1	133 35.9	13 47	153 11.4
38	Hadar	0.9	15 19	S60 20.5	129 35.1	14 03	149 10.6
39	Menkent	2.3	15 22	S36 20.2	128 50.7	14 06	148 26.2
40	Arcturus	0.2	15 31	N19 13.3	126 34.6	14 15	146 10.1
41	Rigil Kent	0.1	15 55	S60 48.5	120 37.9	14 39	140 13.4
42	Zuben'ubi	2.9	16 06	S16 00.7	117 47.3	14 50	137 22.8
43	Kochab	2.2	16 06	N74 11.3	117 44.4	14 51	137 19.9
44	Alphecca	2.3	16 50	N26 44.5	106 48.8	15 34	126 24.3
45	Antares	1.2	17 44	S26 25.0	93 09.9	16 29	112 45.4
46	Atria	1.9	18 03	S69 01.2	88 25.8	16 48	108 01.3
47	Sabik	2.6	18 25	S15 43.0	82 54.8	17 10	102 30.3
48	Shaula	1.7	18 48	S37 06.0	77 07.5	17 33	96 43.0
49	Rasalhague	2.1	18 50	N12 34.1	76 45.3	17 35	96 20.8
50	Eltanin	2.4	19 12	N51 29.7	71 17.8	17 56	90 53.3
51	Kaus Aust.	2.0	19 39	S34 23.4	64 28.7	18 24	84 04.2
52	Vega	0.1	19 52	N38 46.9	61 13.8	18 37	80 49.3
53	Nunki	2.1	20 10	S26 18.4	56 41.9	18 55	76 17.4
54	Altair	0.9	21 05	N 8 51.1	42 47.7	19 50	62 23.2
55	Peacock	2.1	21 40	S56 45.6	34 07.6	20 25	53 43.1
56	Deneb	1.3	21 56	N45 15.6	30 06.2	20 41	49 41.7
57	Enif	2.5	22 58	N 9 50.7	14 26.5	21 44	34 02.0
58	Al Na'ir	2.2	23 22	S46 59.7	8 27.1	22 08	28 02.6
59	Fomalhaut	1.3	00 16	S29 39.5	356 05.1	22 57	15 40.6
60	Markab	2.6	00 23	N15 10.2	354 18.0	23 04	13 53.5

Stars Transit Correction Table

D. of Mth.	Corr (Sub.)	D. of Mth.	Corr. (Sub.)
	h. m.		h. m.
1	–0 00	17	–1 03
2	–0 04	18	–1 07
3	–0 08	19	–1 11
4	–0 12	20	–1 15
5	–0 16	21	–1 19
6	–0 20	22	–1 23
7	–0 24	23	–1 27
8	–0 28	24	–1 30
9	–0 31	25	–1 34
10	–0 35	26	–1 38
11	–0 39	27	–1 42
12	–0 43	28	–1 46
13	–0 47	29	–1 50
14	–0 51	30	–1 54
15	–0 55		
16	–0 59		

STAR'S TRANSIT

To find the approx. time of Transit of a Star for any day of the month use above table.

If the quantity taken from the table is greater than the time of Transit for the first of the month, add 23h. 56min. to the time of transit before subtracting the correction below.

Example: Required the brightest star to cross the Meridian between 1900h. and 2000h. on September 13th

h.min.
Corr. for 13th .... –00 47
... Corresponding time on the 1st is between 1947h. and 2047h.
Answer: Vega (No 52) Mag. 0.1.

d. h. SEPTEMBER DIARY

2 23 Mercury 1°.2N. of Regulus
3 23 First Quarter
9 03 Saturn 5°S. of Moon
9 19 Moon at apogee
12 02 Full Moon
15 04 Mercury in superior conjunction
17 19 Jupiter in conjunction with Sun
19 05 Venus 3°N. of Spica
19 20 Last Quarter
20 09 Mars 0°.9N. of Moon Occn.
22 19 Equinox
25 03 Moon at perigee
26 11 New Moon
28 15 Venus 4°N. of Moon

STAR TIME

The best time to take Star observations is shown in the a.m. and p.m. TWILIGHT columns on the opposite page – corrected for Latitude.

For **Lighting-up Time** (ashore) add 30 mins to Sunset Times.

For Star's G.H.A. Correction Table, see page 4:8.

For Alphabetical List of Stars with Constellation names, see page 2:24.

For Examples on the use of the above data, see page 2:11.

G.M.T.	SUN G.H.A.	Dec.	ARIES G.H.A.

Tuesday, 1st September

h	SUN G.H.A.	Dec.	ARIES G.H.A.	h
00	179 59.5	N 8 16.1	340 24.5	00
02	209 59.9	8 14.3	10 29.4	02
04	240 00.3	8 12.4	40 34.4	04
06	270 00.6	8 10.6	70 39.3	06
08	300 01.0	8 08.8	100 44.2	08
10	330 01.4	8 07.0	130 49.1	10
12	0 01.8	8 05.2	160 54.1	12
14	30 02.2	8 03.4	190 59.0	14
16	60 02.6	8 01.5	221 03.9	16
18	90 03.0	7 59.7	251 08.9	18
20	120 03.4	7 57.9	281 13.8	20
22	150 03.8	N 7 56.1	311 18.7	22

Sunday, 6th September

h	SUN G.H.A.	Dec.	ARIES G.H.A.	h
00	180 24.0	N 6 25.7	345 20.2	00
02	210 24.4	6 23.8	15 25.1	02
04	240 24.8	6 22.0	45 30.1	04
06	270 25.3	6 20.1	75 35.0	06
08	300 25.7	6 18.3	105 39.9	08
10	330 26.1	6 16.4	135 44.8	10
12	0 26.5	6 14.5	165 49.8	12
14	30 27.0	6 12.7	195 54.7	14
16	60 27.4	6 10.8	225 59.6	16
18	90 27.8	6 08.9	256 04.6	18
20	120 28.2	6 07.0	286 09.5	20
22	150 28.7	N 6 05.2	316 14.4	22

Friday, 11th September

h	SUN G.H.A.	Dec.	ARIES G.H.A.	h
00	180 49.9	N 4 32.7	350 15.9	00
02	210 50.3	4 30.8	20 20.8	02
04	240 50.8	4 28.9	50 25.7	04
06	270 51.2	4 27.0	80 30.7	06
08	300 51.7	4 25.1	110 35.6	08
10	330 52.1	4 23.2	140 40.5	10
12	0 52.5	4 21.3	170 45.5	12
14	30 53.0	4 19.4	200 50.4	14
16	60 53.4	4 17.5	230 55.3	16
18	90 53.9	4 15.6	261 00.2	18
20	120 54.3	4 13.7	291 05.2	20
22	150 54.8	N 4 11.8	321 10.1	22

Wednesday, 2nd September

h	SUN G.H.A.	Dec.	ARIES G.H.A.	h
00	180 04.2	N 7 54.2	341 23.6	00
02	210 04.6	7 52.4	11 28.6	02
04	240 05.0	7 50.6	41 33.5	04
06	270 05.4	7 48.8	71 38.4	06
08	300 05.8	7 46.9	101 43.4	08
10	330 06.2	7 45.1	131 48.3	10
12	0 06.6	7 43.3	161 53.2	12
14	30 07.0	7 41.4	191 58.1	14
16	60 07.5	7 39.6	222 03.1	16
18	90 07.9	7 37.8	252 08.0	18
20	120 08.3	7 36.0	282 12.9	20
22	150 08.7	N 7 34.1	312 17.9	22

Monday, 7th September

h	SUN G.H.A.	Dec.	ARIES G.H.A.	h
00	180 29.1	N 6 03.3	346 19.3	00
02	210 29.5	6 01.4	16 24.3	02
04	240 29.9	5 59.6	46 29.2	04
06	270 30.4	5 57.7	76 34.1	06
08	300 30.8	5 55.8	106 39.1	08
10	330 31.2	5 53.9	136 44.0	10
12	0 31.6	5 52.1	166 48.9	12
14	30 32.1	5 50.2	196 53.8	14
16	60 32.5	5 48.3	226 58.8	16
18	90 32.9	5 46.4	257 03.7	18
20	120 33.4	5 44.6	287 08.6	20
22	150 33.8	N 5 42.7	317 13.5	22

Saturday, 12th September

h	SUN G.H.A.	Dec.	ARIES G.H.A.	h
00	180 55.2	N 4 09.9	351 15.0	00
02	210 55.6	4 08.0	21 20.0	02
04	240 56.1	4 06.1	51 24.9	04
06	270 56.5	4 04.2	81 29.8	06
08	300 57.0	4 02.2	111 34.7	08
10	330 57.4	4 00.3	141 39.7	10
12	0 57.9	3 58.4	171 44.6	12
14	30 58.3	3 56.5	201 49.5	14
16	60 58.7	3 54.6	231 54.5	16
18	90 59.2	3 52.7	261 59.4	18
20	120 59.6	3 50.8	292 04.3	20
22	151 00.1	N 3 48.9	322 09.2	22

Thursday, 3rd September

h	SUN G.H.A.	Dec.	ARIES G.H.A.	h
00	180 09.1	N 7 32.3	342 22.8	00
02	210 09.5	7 30.4	12 27.7	02
04	240 09.9	7 28.6	42 32.6	04
06	270 10.3	7 26.8	72 37.6	06
08	300 10.7	7 24.9	102 42.5	08
10	330 11.1	7 23.1	132 47.4	10
12	0 11.5	7 21.3	162 52.4	12
14	30 11.9	7 19.4	192 57.3	14
16	60 12.3	7 17.6	223 02.2	16
18	90 12.7	7 15.7	253 07.1	18
20	120 13.2	7 13.9	283 12.1	20
22	150 13.6	N 7 12.1	313 17.0	22

Tuesday, 8th September

h	SUN G.H.A.	Dec.	ARIES G.H.A.	h
00	180 34.2	N 5 40.8	347 18.5	00
02	210 34.7	5 38.9	17 23.4	02
04	240 35.1	5 37.0	47 28.3	04
06	270 35.5	5 35.2	77 33.3	06
08	300 35.9	5 33.3	107 38.2	08
10	330 36.4	5 31.4	137 43.1	10
12	0 36.8	5 29.5	167 48.0	12
14	30 37.2	5 27.6	197 53.0	14
16	60 37.7	5 25.7	227 57.9	16
18	90 38.1	5 23.9	258 02.8	18
20	120 38.5	5 22.0	288 07.8	20
22	150 39.0	N 5 20.1	318 12.7	22

Sunday, 13th September

h	SUN G.H.A.	Dec.	ARIES G.H.A.	h
00	181 00.5	N 3 47.0	352 14.2	00
02	211 01.0	3 45.0	22 19.1	02
04	241 01.4	3 43.1	52 24.0	04
06	271 01.8	3 41.2	82 29.0	06
08	301 02.3	3 39.3	112 33.9	08
10	331 02.7	3 37.4	142 38.8	10
12	1 03.2	3 35.5	172 43.7	12
14	31 03.6	3 33.5	202 48.7	14
16	61 04.1	3 31.6	232 53.6	16
18	91 04.5	3 29.7	262 58.5	18
20	121 05.0	3 27.8	293 03.5	20
22	151 05.4	N 3 25.9	323 08.4	22

Friday, 4th September

h	SUN G.H.A.	Dec.	ARIES G.H.A.	h
00	180 14.0	N 7 10.2	343 21.9	00
02	210 14.4	7 08.4	13 26.8	02
04	240 14.8	7 06.5	43 31.8	04
06	270 15.2	7 04.7	73 36.7	06
08	300 15.6	7 02.8	103 41.6	08
10	330 16.0	7 01.0	133 46.6	10
12	0 16.5	6 59.1	163 51.5	12
14	30 16.9	6 57.3	193 56.4	14
16	60 17.3	6 55.4	224 01.3	16
18	90 17.7	6 53.6	254 06.3	18
20	120 18.1	6 51.7	284 11.2	20
22	150 18.5	N 6 49.9	314 16.1	22

Wednesday, 9th September

h	SUN G.H.A.	Dec.	ARIES G.H.A.	h
00	180 39.4	N 5 18.2	348 17.6	00
02	210 39.8	5 16.3	18 22.5	02
04	240 40.3	5 14.4	48 27.5	04
06	270 40.7	5 12.5	78 32.4	06
08	300 41.1	5 10.6	108 37.3	08
10	330 41.6	5 08.8	138 42.3	10
12	0 42.0	5 06.9	168 47.2	12
14	30 42.5	5 05.0	198 52.1	14
16	60 42.9	5 03.1	228 57.0	16
18	90 43.3	5 01.2	259 02.0	18
20	120 43.8	4 59.3	289 06.9	20
22	150 44.2	N 4 57.4	319 11.8	22

Monday, 14th September

h	SUN G.H.A.	Dec.	ARIES G.H.A.	h
00	181 05.9	N 3 24.0	353 13.3	00
02	211 06.3	3 22.0	23 18.2	02
04	241 06.7	3 20.1	53 23.2	04
06	271 07.2	3 18.2	83 28.1	06
08	301 07.6	3 16.3	113 33.0	08
10	331 08.1	3 14.4	143 38.0	10
12	1 08.5	3 12.4	173 42.9	12
14	31 09.0	3 10.5	203 47.8	14
16	61 09.4	3 08.6	233 52.7	16
18	91 09.9	3 06.7	263 57.7	18
20	121 10.3	3 04.7	294 02.6	20
22	151 10.8	N 3 02.8	324 07.5	22

Saturday, 5th September

h	SUN G.H.A.	Dec.	ARIES G.H.A.	h
00	180 19.0	N 6 48.0	344 21.1	00
02	210 19.4	6 46.2	14 26.0	02
04	240 19.8	6 44.3	44 30.9	04
06	270 20.2	6 42.5	74 35.8	06
08	300 20.6	6 40.6	104 40.8	08
10	330 21.0	6 38.7	134 45.7	10
12	0 21.5	6 36.9	164 50.6	12
14	30 21.9	6 35.0	194 55.6	14
16	60 22.3	6 33.2	225 00.5	16
18	90 22.7	6 31.3	255 05.4	18
20	120 23.1	6 29.4	285 10.3	20
22	150 23.6	N 6 27.6	315 15.3	22

Thursday, 10th September

h	SUN G.H.A.	Dec.	ARIES G.H.A.	h
00	180 44.6	N 4 55.5	349 16.8	00
02	210 45.0	4 53.6	19 21.7	02
04	240 45.5	4 51.7	49 26.6	04
06	270 45.9	4 49.8	79 31.5	06
08	300 46.4	4 47.9	109 36.5	08
10	330 46.8	4 46.0	139 41.4	10
12	0 47.3	4 44.1	169 46.3	12
14	30 47.7	4 42.2	199 51.3	14
16	60 48.1	4 40.3	229 56.2	16
18	90 48.6	4 38.4	260 01.1	18
20	120 49.0	4 36.5	290 06.0	20
22	150 49.5	N 4 34.6	320 11.0	22

Tuesday, 15th September

h	SUN G.H.A.	Dec.	ARIES G.H.A.	h
00	181 11.2	N 3 00.9	354 12.4	00
02	211 11.7	2 59.0	24 17.4	02
04	241 12.1	2 57.1	54 22.3	04
06	271 12.5	2 55.1	84 27.2	06
08	301 13.0	2 53.2	114 32.2	08
10	331 13.4	2 51.3	144 37.1	10
12	1 13.9	2 49.4	173 42.0	12
14	31 14.3	2 47.4	204 46.9	14
16	61 14.8	2 45.5	234 51.9	16
18	91 15.2	2 43.6	264 56.8	18
20	121 15.7	2 41.6	295 01.7	20
22	151 16.1	N 2 39.7	325 06.7	22

G.M.T.	SUN G.H.A.	SUN Dec.	ARIES G.H.A.	G.M.T.

Wednesday, 16th September

h	SUN G.H.A.	SUN Dec.	ARIES G.H.A.	h
00	181 16.6	N 2 37.8	355 11.6	00
02	211 17.0	2 35.9	25 16.5	02
04	241 17.5	2 33.9	55 21.4	04
06	271 17.9	2 32.0	85 26.4	06
08	301 18.3	2 30.1	115 31.3	08
10	331 18.8	2 28.1	145 36.2	10
12	1 19.2	2 26.2	175 41.2	12
14	31 19.7	2 24.3	205 46.1	14
16	61 20.1	2 22.4	235 51.0	16
18	91 20.6	2 20.4	265 55.9	18
20	121 21.0	2 18.5	296 00.9	20
22	151 21.5	N 2 16.6	326 05.8	22

Thursday, 17th September

h	SUN G.H.A.	SUN Dec.	ARIES G.H.A.	h
00	181 21.9	N 2 14.6	356 10.7	00
02	211 22.4	2 12.7	26 15.7	02
04	241 22.8	2 10.8	56 20.6	04
06	271 23.3	2 08.8	86 25.5	06
08	301 23.7	2 06.9	116 30.4	08
10	331 24.2	2 05.0	146 35.4	10
12	1 24.6	2 03.0	176 40.3	12
14	31 25.0	2 01.1	206 45.2	14
16	61 25.5	1 59.2	236 50.2	16
18	91 25.9	1 57.2	266 55.1	18
20	121 26.4	1 55.3	297 00.0	20
22	151 26.8	N 1 53.3	327 04.9	22

Friday, 18th September

h	SUN G.H.A.	SUN Dec.	ARIES G.H.A.	h
00	181 27.3	N 1 51.4	357 09.9	00
02	211 27.7	1 49.5	27 14.8	02
04	241 28.2	1 47.5	57 19.7	04
06	271 28.6	1 45.6	87 24.6	06
08	301 29.1	1 43.7	117 29.6	08
10	331 29.5	1 41.7	147 34.5	10
12	1 30.0	1 39.8	177 39.4	12
14	31 30.4	1 37.9	207 44.4	14
16	61 30.8	1 35.9	237 49.3	16
18	91 31.3	1 34.0	267 54.2	18
20	121 31.7	1 32.0	297 59.1	20
22	151 32.2	N 1 30.1	328 04.1	22

Saturday, 19th September

h	SUN G.H.A.	SUN Dec.	ARIES G.H.A.	h
00	181 32.6	N 1 28.2	358 09.0	00
02	211 33.1	1 26.2	28 13.9	02
04	241 33.5	1 24.3	58 18.9	04
06	271 34.0	1 22.3	88 23.8	06
08	301 34.4	1 20.4	118 28.7	08
10	331 34.8	1 18.5	148 33.6	10
12	1 35.3	1 16.5	178 38.6	12
14	31 35.7	1 14.6	208 43.5	14
16	61 36.2	1 12.6	238 48.4	16
18	91 36.6	1 10.7	268 53.4	18
20	121 37.1	1 08.8	298 58.3	20
22	151 37.5	N 1 06.8	329 03.2	22

Sunday, 20th September

h	SUN G.H.A.	SUN Dec.	ARIES G.H.A.	h
00	181 38.0	N 1 04.9	359 08.1	00
02	211 38.4	1 02.9	29 13.1	02
04	241 38.8	1 01.0	59 18.0	04
06	271 39.3	0 59.0	89 22.9	06
08	301 39.7	0 57.1	119 27.9	08
10	331 40.2	0 55.2	149 32.8	10
12	1 40.6	0 53.2	179 37.7	12
14	31 41.1	.0 51.3	209 42.6	14
16	61 41.5	0 49.3	239 47.6	16
18	91 41.9	0 47.4	269 52.5	18
20	121 42.4	0 45.4	299 57.4	20
22	151 42.8	N 0 43.5	330 02.4	22

Monday, 21st September

h	SUN G.H.A.	SUN Dec.	ARIES G.H.A.	h
00	181 43.3	N 0 41.6	0 07.3	00
02	211 43.7	0 39.6	30 12.2	02
04	241 44.1	0 37.7	60 17.1	04
06	271 44.6	0 35.7	90 22.1	06
08	301 45.0	0 33.8	120 27.0	08
10	331 45.5	0 31.8	150 31.9	10
12	1 45.9	0 29.9	180 36.9	12
14	31 46.3	0 27.9	210 41.8	14
16	61 46.8	0 26.0	240 46.7	16
18	91 47.2	0 24.1	270 51.6	18
20	121 47.7	0 22.1	300 56.6	20
22	151 48.1	N 0 20.2	331 01.5	22

Tuesday, 22nd September

h	SUN G.H.A.	SUN Dec.	ARIES G.H.A.	h
00	181 48.5	N 0 18.2	1 06.4	00
02	211 49.0	0 16.3	31 11.3	02
04	241 49.4	0 14.3	61 16.3	04
06	271 49.9	0 12.4	91 21.2	06
08	301 50.3	0 10.4	121 26.1	08
10	331 50.7	0 08.5	151 31.1	10
12	1 51.2	0 06.5	181 36.0	12
14	31 51.6	0 04.6	211 40.9	14
16	61 52.1	0 02.6	241 45.8	16
18	91 52.5	0 00.7	271 50.8	18
20	121 52.9	S 0 01.3	301 55.7	20
22	151 53.4	S 0 03.2	332 00.6	22

Wednesday, 23rd September

h	SUN G.H.A.	SUN Dec.	ARIES G.H.A.	h
00	181 53.8	S 0 05.1	2 05.6	00
02	211 54.2	0 07.1	32 10.5	02
04	241 54.7	0 09.0	62 15.4	04
06	271 55.1	0 11.0	92 20.3	06
08	301 55.5	0 12.9	122 25.3	08
10	331 56.0	0 14.9	152 30.2	10
12	1 56.4	0 16.8	182 35.1	12
14	31 56.8	0 18.8	212 40.1	14
16	61 57.3	0 20.7	242 45.0	16
18	91 57.7	0 22.7	272 49.9	18
20	121 58.2	0 24.6	302 54.8	20
22	151 58.6	S 0 26.6	332 59.8	22

Thursday, 24th September

h	SUN G.H.A.	SUN Dec.	ARIES G.H.A.	h
00	181 59.0	S 0 28.5	3 04.7	00
02	211 59.5	0 30.5	33 09.6	02
04	241 59.9	0 32.4	63 14.6	04
06	272 00.3	0 34.4	93 19.5	06
08	302 00.8	0 36.3	123 24.4	08
10	332 01.2	0 38.3	153 29.3	10
12	2 01.6	0 40.2	183 34.3	12
14	32 02.0	0 42.2	213 39.2	14
16	62 02.5	0 44.1	243 44.1	16
18	92 02.9	0 46.1	273 49.1	18
20	122 03.3	0 48.0	303 54.0	20
22	152 03.8	S 0 50.0	333 58.9	22

Friday, 25th September

h	SUN G.H.A.	SUN Dec.	ARIES G.H.A.	h
00	182 04.2	S 0 51.9	4 03.8	00
02	212 04.6	0 53.9	34 08.8	02
04	242 05.1	0 55.8	64 13.7	04
06	272 05.5	0 57.7	94 18.6	06
08	302 05.9	0 59.7	124 23.5	08
10	332 06.3	1 01.6	154 28.5	10
12	2 06.8	1 03.6	184 33.4	12
14	32 07.2	1 05.5	214 38.3	14
16	62 07.6	1 07.5	244 43.3	16
18	92 08.1	1 09.4	274 48.2	18
20	122 08.5	1 11.4	304 53.1	20
22	152 08.9	S 1 13.3	334 58.0	22

Saturday, 26th September

h	SUN G.H.A.	SUN Dec.	ARIES G.H.A.	h
00	182 09.3	S 1 15.3	5 03.0	00
02	212 09.8	1 17.2	35 07.9	02
04	242 10.2	1 19.2	65 12.8	04
06	272 10.6	1 21.1	95 17.8	06
08	302 11.0	1 23.1	125 22.7	08
10	332 11.5	1 25.0	155 27.6	10
12	2 11.9	1 27.0	185 32.5	12
14	32 12.3	1 28.9	215 37.5	14
16	62 12.7	1 30.9	245 42.4	16
18	92 13.2	1 32.8	275 47.3	18
20	122 13.6	1 34.8	305 52.3	20
22	152 14.0	S 1 36.7	335 57.2	22

Sunday, 27th September

h	SUN G.H.A.	SUN Dec.	ARIES G.H.A.	h
00	182 14.4	S 1 38.7	6 02.1	00
02	212 14.8	1 40.6	36 07.0	02
04	242 15.3	1 42.6	66 12.0	04
06	272 15.7	1 44.5	96 16.9	06
08	302 16.1	1 46.5	126 21.8	08
10	332 16.5	1 48.4	156 26.8	10
12	2 16.9	1 50.3	186 31.7	12
14	32 17.4	1 52.3	216 36.6	14
16	62 17.8	1 54.2	246 41.5	16
18	92 18.2	1 56.2	276 46.5	18
20	122 18.6	1 58.1	306 51.4	20
22	152 19.0	S 2 00.1	336 56.3	22

Monday, 28th September

h	SUN G.H.A.	SUN Dec.	ARIES G.H.A.	h
00	182 19.5	S 2 02.0	7 01.3	00
02	212 19.9	2 04.0	37 06.2	02
04	242 20.3	2 05.9	67 11.1	04
06	272 20.7	2 07.9	97 16.0	06
08	302 21.1	2 09.8	127 21.0	08
10	332 21.5	2 11.8	157 25.9	10
12	2 21.9	2 13.7	187 30.8	12
14	32 22.4	2 15.7	217 35.8	14
16	62 22.8	2 17.6	247 40.7	16
18	92 23.2	2 19.5	277 45.6	18
20	122 23.6	2 21.5	307 50.5	20
22	152 24.0	S 2 23.4	337 55.5	22

Tuesday, 29th September

h	SUN G.H.A.	SUN Dec.	ARIES G.H.A.	h
00	182 24.4	S 2 25.4	8 00.4	00
02	212 24.8	2 27.3	38 05.3	02
04	242 25.3	2 29.3	68 10.2	04
06	272 25.7	2 31.2	98 15.2	06
08	302 26.1	2 33.2	128 20.1	08
10	332 26.5	2 35.1	158 25.0	10
12	2 26.9	2 37.0	188 30.0	12
14	32 27.3	2 39.0	218 34.9	14
16	62 27.7	2 40.9	248 39.8	16
18	92 28.1	2 42.9	278 44.7	18
20	122 28.5	2 44.8	308 49.7	20
22	152 28.9	S 2 46.8	338 54.6	22

Wednesday, 30th September

h	SUN G.H.A.	SUN Dec.	ARIES G.H.A.	h
00	182 29.3	S 2 48.7	8 59.5	00
02	212 29.8	2 50.6	39 04.5	02
04	242 30.2	2 52.6	69 09.4	04
06	272 30.6	2 54.5	99 14.3	06
08	302 31.0	2 56.5	129 19.2	08
10	332 31.4	2 58.4	159 24.2	10
12	2 31.8	3 00.4	189 29.1	12
14	32 32.2	3 02.3	219 34.0	14
16	62 32.6	3 04.2	249 39.0	16
18	92 33.0	3 06.2	279 43.9	18
20	122 33.4	3 08.1	309 48.8	20
22	152 33.8	S 3 10.1	339 53.7	22

To interpolate SUN G.H.A. see page 4:7   To interpolate ARIES G.H.A. see page 4:8

♀ VENUS ♀   ♃ JUPITER ♃

Mer. Pass.	G.H.A.	Mean Var. 14°	Dec.	Mean Var.	M	Day of Week	G.H.A	Mean Var. 15°	Dec.	Mean Var.	Mer. Pass
h. m.	° ′	′	° ′	′			° ′	′	° ′	′	h. m.
13 22	159 35.7	59.7	N 0 52.0	1.3	1	Tu.	167 48.3	2.0	N 4 20.9	0.2	12 47
13 22	159 27.9	59.7	N 0 21.1	1.3	2	Wed.	168 35.6	2.0	N 4 15.8	0.2	12 44
13 23	159 20.2	59.7	S 0 09.7	1.3	3	Th.	169 22.9	2.0	N 4 10.7	0.2	12 41
13 23	159 12.4	59.7	S 0 40.7	1.3	4	Fri.	170 10.2	2.0	N 4 05.7	0.2	12 38
13 24	159 04.7	59.7	S 1 11.6	1.3	5	Sat.	170 57.5	2.0	N 4 00.6	0.2	12 35
13 24	158 57.0	59.7	S 1 42.5	1.3	6	SUN.	171 44.8	2.0	N 3 55.5	0.2	12 31
13 25	158 49.2	59.7	S 2 13.4	1.3	7	Mon.	172 32.1	2.0	N 3 50.4	0.2	12 28
13 26	158 41.4	59.7	S 2 44.2	1.3	8	Tu.	173 19.3	2.0	N 3 45.3	0.2	12 25
13 26	158 33.6	59.7	S 3 15.1	1.3	9	Wed.	174 06.6	2.0	N 3 40.2	0.2	12 22
13 27	158 25.8	59.7	S 3 45.8	1.3	10	Th.	174 53.8	2.0	N 3 35.1	0.2	12 19
13 27	158 17.8	59.7	S 4 16.6	1.3	11	Fri.	175 41.0	2.0	N 3 29.9	0.2	12 16
13 28	158 09.9	59.7	S 4 47.2	1.3	12	Sat.	176 28.2	2.0	N 3 24.8	0.2	12 13
13 28	158 01.8	59.7	S 5 17.7	1.3	13	SUN.	177 15.4	2.0	N 3 19.7	0.2	12 09
13 29	157 53.6	59.7	S 5 48.2	1.3	14	Mon.	178 02.6	2.0	N 3 14.6	0.2	12 06
13 29	157 45.4	59.6	S 6 18.5	1.3	15	Tu.	178 49.8	2.0	N 3 09.4	0.2	12 03
13 30	157 37.0	59.6	S 6 48.7	1.3	16	Wed.	179 37.0	2.0	N 3 04.3	0.2	12 00
13 30	157 28.5	59.6	S 7 18.8	1.2	17	Th.	180 24.2	2.0	N 2 59.2	0.2	11 57
13 31	157 19.9	59.6	S 7 48.7	1.2	18	Fri.	181 11.4	2.0	N 2 54.1	0.2	11 54
13 32	157 11.2	59.6	S 8 18.5	1.2	19	Sat.	181 58.6	2.0	N 2 48.9	0.2	11 51
13 32	157 02.3	59.6	S 8 48.1	1.2	20	SUN.	182 45.8	2.0	N 2 43.8	0.2	11 47
13 33	156 53.2	59.6	S 9 17.5	1.2	21	Mon.	183 33.0	2.0	N 2 38.7	0.2	11 44
13 33	156 44.0	59.6	S 9 46.7	1.2	22	Tu.	184 20.2	2.0	N 2 33.5	0.2	11 41
13 34	156 34.5	59.6	S10 15.7	1.2	23	Wed.	185 07.4	2.0	N 2 28.4	0.2	11 38
13 35	156 24.9	59.6	S10 44.5	1.2	24	Th.	185 54.6	2.0	N 2 23.3	0.2	11 35
13 35	156 15.1	59.6	S11 13.0	1.2	25	Fri.	186 41.8	2.0	N 2 18.2	0.2	11 32
13 36	156 05.1	59.6	S11 41.3	1.2	26	Sat.	187 29.1	2.0	N 2 13.1	0.2	11 29
13 37	155 54.9	59.6	S12 09.4	1.2	27	SUN.	188 16.3	2.0	N 2 08.0	0.2	11 25
13 37	155 44.4	59.6	S12 37.1	1.1	28	Mon.	189 03.5	2.0	N 2 02.9	0.2	11 22
13 38	155 33.7	59.5	S13 04.6	1.1	29	Tu.	189 50.8	2.0	N 1 57.8	0.2	11 19
13 39	155 22.8	59.5	S13 31.8	1.1	30	Wed.	190 38.1	2.0	N 1 52.7	0.2	11 16

♀ VENUS. Av. Mag. –3.9. An **Evening Star. S.H.A.** September 5 175°; 10 169°; 15 163°; 20 158°; 25 152°; 30 146°.

♃ JUPITER. Av. Mag. –1.7. An **Evening Star** until September 4 and is then too close to the sun for observation for the rest of the month. **S.H.A.** September 5 186°; 10 186°; 15 185°; 20 183°; 25 183°; 30 182°.

♂ MARS ♂   ♄ SATURN ♄

Mer. Pass.	G.H.A.	Mean Var. 15°	Dec.	Mean Var.	M	Day of Week	G.H.A	Mean Var. 15°	Dec.	Mean Var.	Mer. Pass
h. m.	° ′	′	° ′	′			° ′	′	° ′	′	h. m.
06 49	257 35.8	0.8	N22 58.9	0.1	1	Tu.	24 14.4	2.6	S17 48.0	0.0	22 19
06 48	257 55.8	0.8	N23 01.1	0.1	2	Wed.	25 17.4	2.6	S17 49.1	0.0	22 15
06 47	258 15.9	0.8	N23 04.4	0.1	3	Th.	26 20.2	2.6	S17 50.2	0.0	22 11
06 45	258 36.2	0.8	N23 06.9	0.1	4	Fri.	27 23.1	2.6	S17 51.3	0.0	22 07
06 44	258 56.6	0.9	N23 09.3	0.1	5	Sat.	28 25.8	2.6	S17 52.4	0.0	22 02
06 42	259 17.2	0.9	N23 11.5	0.1	6	SUN.	29 28.6	2.6	S17 53.4	0.0	21 58
06 41	259 38.0	0.9	N23 13.6	0.1	7	Mon.	30 31.2	2.6	S17 54.4	0.0	21 54
06 40	259 58.9	0.9	N23 15.5	0.1	8	Tu.	31 33.8	2.6	S17 55.4	0.0	21 50
06 38	260 20.0	0.9	N23 17.3	0.1	9	Wed.	32 36.3	2.6	S17 56.4	0.0	21 46
06 37	260 41.3	0.9	N23 18.9	0.1	10	Th.	33 38.8	2.6	S17 57.4	0.0	21 42
06 35	261 02.8	0.9	N23 20.4	0.1	11	Fri.	34 41.1	2.6	S17 58.3	0.0	21 38
06 34	261 24.5	0.9	N23 21.7	0.1	12	Sat.	35 43.5	2.6	S17 59.2	0.0	21 33
06 33	261 46.4	0.9	N23 22.9	0.0	13	SUN.	36 45.7	2.6	S18 00.1	0.0	21 29
06 31	262 08.4	0.9	N23 24.0	0.0	14	Mon.	37 47.9	2.6	S18 00.9	0.0	21 25
06 30	262 30.7	0.9	N23 24.9	0.0	15	Tu.	38 50.0	2.6	S18 01.8	0.0	21 21
06 28	262 53.2	0.9	N23 25.8	0.0	16	Wed.	39 52.0	2.6	S18 02.6	0.0	21 17
06 27	263 15.9	1.0	N23 26.4	0.0	17	Th.	40 53.9	2.6	S18 03.4	0.0	21 13
06 25	263 38.8	1.0	N23 27.0	0.0	18	Fri.	41 55.8	2.6	S18 04.1	0.0	21 09
06 23	264 01.9	1.0	N23 27.5	0.0	19	Sat.	42 57.5	2.6	S18 04.9	0.0	21 05
06 22	264 25.2	1.0	N23 27.8	0.0	20	SUN.	43 59.2	2.6	S18 05.6	0.0	21 00
06 20	264 48.8	1.0	N23 28.0	0.0	21	Mon.	45 00.8	2.6	S18 06.3	0.0	20 56
06 19	265 12.7	1.0	N23 28.1	0.0	22	Tu.	46 02.3	2.6	S18 06.9	0.0	20 52
06 17	265 36.7	1.0	N23 28.1	0.0	23	Wed.	47 03.8	2.6	S18 07.6	0.0	20 48
06 16	266 01.1	1.0	N23 28.0	0.0	24	Th.	48 05.1	2.6	S18 08.2	0.0	20 44
06 14	266 25.7	1.0	N23 27.8	0.0	25	Fri.	49 06.4	2.5	S18 08.8	0.0	20 40
06 12	266 50.5	1.0	N23 27.5	0.0	26	Sat.	50 07.5	2.5	S18 09.3	0.0	20 36
06 11	267 15.6	1.1	N23 27.1	0.0	27	SUN.	51 08.6	2.5	S18 09.8	0.0	20 32
06 09	267 41.0	1.1	N23 26.6	0.0	28	Mon.	52 09.6	2.5	S18 10.3	0.0	20 28
06 07	268 06.7	1.1	N23 26.1	0.0	29	Tu.	53 10.5	2.5	S18 10.8	0.0	20 24
06 05	268 32.7	1.1	N23 25.4	0.0	30	Wed.	54 11.3	2.5	S18 11.3	0.0	20 20

♂ MARS. Av. Mag. +0.5. A **Morning Star. S.H.A.** September 5 274°; 10 271°; 15 269°; 20 265°; 25 262°; 30 260°.

♄ SATURN. Av. Mag. +0.4. An **Evening Star** throughout the month. **S.H.A.** September 5 43°; 10 44°; 15 46°; 20 44°; 25 45°; 30 46°.

MERCURY. Visible low in the east before sunrise until September 6 when it is too close to the sun for observation. Reappears in the evening sky on September 27.

For Planets Correction Tables see pages 4:9-4:13. See also 'How to Recognise the Planets' on page 2:32.
Mean Var. means Variation per Hour.

Day of M. W.	G.M.T. h	G.H.A. ° '	Mean Var. per Hour 14°,+	Dec. ° '	Mean Var. per Hour '	Day of M. W.	G.M.T. h	G.H.A. ° '	Mean Var. per Hour 14°,+	Dec. ° '	Mean Var. per Hour '
1 Tu.	0	131 32.3	27.8	S16 15.3	10.2	17 Th.	0	309 26.6	28.8	N20 35.6	6.2
	6	218 18.7	27.6	S17 16.5	9.5		6	36 20.1	28.4	N21 12.8	5.5
	12	305 04.7	27.6	S18 13.7	8.7		12	123 10.9	28.0	N21 46.1	4.8
	18	31 50.3	27.5	S19 06.6	8.0		18	209 59.2	27.6	N22 15.3	4.1
2 Wed.	0	118 35.5	27.5	S19 55.1	7.2	18 Fri.	0	296 45.0	27.3	N22 40.3	3.3
	6	205 20.5	27.5	S20 39.1	6.5		6	23 28.5	26.9	N23 00.9	2.6
	12	292 05.4	27.5	S21 18.5	5.7		12	110 09.9	26.5	N23 16.8	1.8
	18	18 50.2	27.5	S21 53.3	5.0		18	196 49.3	26.2	N23 27.9	1.0
3 Th.	0	105 35.2	27.5	S22 23.4	4.2	19 Sat.	0	283 26.9	26.0	N23 34.1	0.2
	6	192 20.4	27.6	S22 48.7	3.4		6	10 03.0	25.8	N23 35.3	0.7
	12	279 06.1	27.8	S23 09.3	2.6		12	96 37.8	25.7	N23 31.3	1.6
	18	5 52.4	27.8	S23 25.2	1.8		18	183 11.5	25.5	N23 22.1	2.4
4 Fri.	0	92 39.4	28.0	S23 36.4	1.1	20 Sun.	0	269 44.5	25.4	N23 07.7	3.3
	6	179 27.5	28.2	S23 42.9	0.3		6	356 17.0	25.4	N22 47.9	4.2
	12	266 16.6	28.4	S23 44.9	0.5		12	82 49.2	25.4	N22 22.9	5.2
	18	353 07.1	28.7	S23 42.4	1.2		18	169 21.4	25.4	N21 52.6	6.0
5 Sat.	0	79 58.9	28.9	S23 35.4	1.9	21 Mon.	0	255 53.9	25.5	N21 17.1	6.8
	6	166 52.4	29.2	S23 24.2	2.6		6	342 26.9	25.6	N20 36.5	7.7
	12	253 47.6	29.5	S23 08.7	3.3		12	69 00.4	25.8	N19 51.0	8.5
	18	340 44.6	29.9	S22 49.3	3.9		18	155 34.9	25.9	N19 00.6	9.2
6 Sun.	0	67 43.5	30.2	S22 25.8	4.6	22 Tu.	0	242 10.3	26.1	N18 05.6	10.0
	6	154 44.4	30.5	S21 58.6	5.2		6	328 46.7	26.2	N17 06.1	10.7
	12	241 47.3	30.8	S21 27.8	5.7		12	55 24.3	26.5	N16 02.4	11.3
	18	328 52.3	31.2	S20 53.4	6.3		18	142 03.1	26.7	N14 54.7	12.0
7 Mon.	0	55 59.4	31.6	S20 15.8	6.8	23 Wed.	0	228 43.1	26.9	N13 43.4	12.5
	6	143 08.6	31.9	S19 34.9	7.3		6	315 24.3	27.1	N12 28.6	13.0
	12	230 19.7	32.2	S18 51.0	7.8		12	42 06.7	27.2	N11 10.7	13.5
	18	317 32.9	32.5	S18 04.3	8.3		18	128 50.1	27.5	N 9 50.0	13.9
8 Tu.	0	44 48.1	32.8	S17 14.8	8.7	24 Th.	0	215 34.6	27.5	N 8 26.9	14.2
	6	132 05.1	33.2	S16 22.8	9.1		6	302 20.0	27.7	N 7 01.7	14.5
	12	219 24.0	33.5	S15 28.5	9.4		12	29 06.2	27.8	N 5 34.8	14.7
	18	306 44.5	33.7	S14 31.8	9.8		18	115 53.0	27.9	N 4 06.5	14.9
9 Wed.	0	34 06.6	33.9	S13 33.1	10.2	25 Fri.	0	202 40.4	28.0	N 2 37.2	15.0
	6	121 30.3	34.2	S12 32.5	10.4		6	289 28.1	28.0	N 1 07.4	15.0
	12	208 55.3	34.4	S11 30.1	10.7		12	16 16.1	28.0	S 0 22.7	15.0
	18	296 21.5	34.6	S10 26.1	10.9		18	103 04.1	28.0	S 1 52.7	14.9
10 Th.	0	23 48.8	34.8	S 9 20.6	11.1	26 Sat.	0	189 52.1	27.9	S 3 22.0	14.7
	6	111 17.1	34.9	S 8 13.8	11.3		6	276 39.9	27.9	S 4 50.5	14.5
	12	198 46.2	34.9	S 7 05.8	11.5		12	3 27.3	27.8	S 6 17.7	14.3
	18	286 15.9	35.0	S 5 56.7	11.7		18	90 14.3	27.7	S 7 43.1	13.9
11 Fri.	0	13 46.1	35.1	S 4 46.8	11.8	27 Sun.	0	177 00.7	27.6	S 9 06.6	13.4
	6	101 16.7	35.1	S 3 36.2	11.9		6	263 46.5	27.5	S10 27.7	13.1
	12	188 47.5	35.1	S 2 25.0	11.9		12	350 31.5	27.4	S11 46.1	12.5
	18	276 18.3	35.1	S 1 13.4	12.0		18	77 15.7	27.3	S13 01.5	12.0
12 Sat.	0	3 48.9	35.1	S 0 01.4	12.0	28 Mon.	0	163 59.1	27.0	S14 13.5	11.3
	6	91 19.2	35.0	N 1 10.6	12.0		6	250 41.8	26.9	S15 22.0	10.7
	12	178 49.1	34.8	N 2 22.6	11.9		12	337 23.6	26.9	S16 26.7	10.1
	18	266 18.3	34.7	N 3 34.4	11.9		18	64 04.7	26.7	S17 27.3	9.3
13 Sun.	0	353 46.6	34.5	N 4 45.9	11.9	29 Tu.	0	150 45.1	26.7	S18 23.6	8.6
	6	81 14.1	34.4	N 5 56.8	11.7		6	237 25.0	26.5	S19 15.5	7.8
	12	168 40.3	34.1	N 7 07.1	11.6		12	324 04.5	26.5	S20 02.8	7.1
	18	256 05.3	33.9	N 8 16.5	11.3		18	50 43.6	26.5	S20 45.3	6.2
14 Mon.	0	343 28.7	33.6	N 9 24.9	11.1	30 Wed.	0	137 22.7	26.5	S21 23.0	5.4
	6	70 50.6	33.3	N10 32.1	10.9		6	224 01.9	26.6	S21 55.8	4.5
	12	158 10.7	33.0	N11 37.9	10.7		12	310 41.4	26.7	S22 23.7	3.8
	18	245 28.8	32.7	N12 42.1	10.4		18	37 21.3	26.8	S22 46.6	2.9
15 Tu.	0	332 44.9	32.3	N13 44.5	10.0						
	6	59 58.8	31.9	N14 45.0	9.7						
	12	147 10.4	31.5	N15 43.2	9.3						
	18	234 19.6	31.1	N16 39.1	8.9						
16 Wed.	0	321 26.2	30.6	N17 32.5	8.4						
	6	48 30.3	30.3	N18 23.0	7.9						
	12	135 31.7	29.7	N19 10.5	7.4						
	18	222 30.5	29.3	N19 54.8	6.8						

PHASES OF THE MOON

	d.	h/min		d.	h/min
) First Quarter	3	22 39	(Last Quarter	19	19 53
O Full Moon	12	02 17	● New Moon	26	10 40
Apogee	9	19	Perigee	25	03

3:64   OCTOBER, 1992

G.M.T.   (31 days)   **G.M.T.**

☉ SUN ☉

DATE			Equation of Time		Transit	Semi-diam.	Lat. 52°N.				Lat. Corr. to Sunrise, Sunset, etc.				
Day of							Twi-light	Sun-rise	Sun-set	Twi-light	Lat.	Twi-light	Sun-rise	Sun-set	Twi-light
Yr.	Mth.	Week	0 h.	12 h.											
			m. s.	m. s.	h. m.	′	h. m.	h. m.	h. m.	h. m.	°	h. m.	h. m.	h. m.	h. m.
275	1	Th.	−10 16	−10 26	11 50	16.0	05 27	06 01	17 37	18 11	N70	+0 19	+0 49	−0 51	−0 20
276	2	Fri.	−10 36	−10 45	11 49	16.0	05 29	06 03	17 35	18 09	68	+0 16	+0 40	−0 41	−0 16
277	3	Sat.	−10 54	−11 04	11 49	16.0	05 31	06 04	17 32	18 06	66	+0 13	+0 32	−0 33	−0 14
278	4	Sun.	−11 13	−11 22	11 49	16.0	05 33	06 06	17 30	18 04	64	+0 10	+0 25	−0 27	−0 11
279	5	Mon.	−11 31	−11 40	11 48	16.0	05 35	06 08	17 28	18 02	62	+0 08	+0 20	−0 21	−0 09
280	6	Tu.	−11 49	−11 58	11 48	16.0	05 36	06 09	17 25	17 59	N60	+0 06	+0 14	−0 16	−0 07
281	7	Wed.	−12 07	−12 15	11 48	16.0	05 38	06 11	17 23	17 57	58	+0 05	+0 10	−0 11	−0 05
282	8	Th.	−12 24	−12 32	11 47	16.0	05 40	06 13	17 21	17 55	56	+0 03	+0 06	−0 07	−0 04
283	9	Fri.	−12 40	−12 49	11 47	16.0	05 41	06 14	17 19	17 52	54	+0 01	+0 03	−0 04	−0 02
284	10	Sat.	−12 57	−13 05	11 47	16.0	05 43	06 16	17 17	17 50	50	−0 02	−0 03	+0 03	+0 01
285	11	Sun.	−13 12	−13 20	11 47	16.0	05 45	06 18	17 15	17 48	N45	−0 05	−0 10	+0 09	+0 05
286	12	Mon.	−13 28	−13 35	11 46	16.1	05 46	06 20	17 12	17 46	40	−0 08	−0 15	+0 14	+0 07
287	13	Tu.	−13 42	−13 50	11 46	16.1	05 48	06 22	17 10	17 44	35	−0 11	−0 19	+0 19	+0 10
288	14	Wed.	−13 57	−14 04	11 46	16.1	05 50	06 24	17 08	17 42	30	−0 14	−0 23	+0 23	+0 13
289	15	Th.	−14 11	−14 17	11 46	16.1	05 51	06 25	17 05	17 40	20	−0 18	−0 30	+0 30	+0 18
290	16	Fri.	−14 24	−14 30	11 46	16.1	05 53	06 27	17 03	17 38	N10	−0 24	−0 36	+0 37	+0 23
291	17	Sat.	−14 36	−14 42	11 45	16.1	05 55	06 29	17 01	17 36	0	−0 29	−0 42	+0 43	+0 29
292	18	Sun.	−14 48	−14 54	11 45	16.1	05 56	06 30	16 59	17 33	S10	−0 36	−0 49	+0 49	+0 36
293	19	Mon.	−14 59	−15 05	11 45	16.1	05 58	06 32	16 57	17 31	20	−0 43	−0 55	+0 57	+0 44
294	20	Tu.	−15 10	−15 15	11 45	16.1	06 00	06 34	16 55	17 29	30	−0 53	−1 03	+1 05	+0 54
295	21	Wed.	−15 20	−15 25	11 45	16.1	06 01	06 35	16 53	17 27	S35	−1 00	−1 08	+1 10	+1 00
296	22	Th.	−15 29	−15 34	11 44	16.1	06 03	06 37	16 51	17 25	40	−1 07	−1 13	+1 15	+1 08
297	23	Fri.	−15 38	−15 42	11 44	16.1	06 05	06 39	16 49	17 23	45	−1 16	−1 19	+1 21	+1 16
298	24	Sat.	−15 46	−15 50	11 44	16.1	06 06	06 43	16 45	17 20	S50	−1 27	−1 27	+1 28	+1 26
299	25	Sun.	−15 53	−15 57	11 44	16.1	06 08	06 43	16 45	17 20					
300	26	Mon.	−16 00	−16 03	11 44	16.1	06 10	06 45	16 43	17 18					
301	27	Tu.	−16 05	−16 08	11 44	16.1	06 11	06 46	16 41	17 16					
302	28	Wed.	−16 10	−16 13	11 44	16.1	06 13	06 48	16 39	17 14					
303	29	Th.	−16 15	−16 18	11 44	16.1	06 15	06 50	16 37	17 12					
304	30	Fri.	−16 18	−16 20	11 44	16.1	06 16	06 51	16 35	17 11					
305	31	Sat.	−16 21	−16 22	11 44	16.1	06 18	06 53	16 33	17 09					

NOTES

The Lat. Corr. to sunrise, sunset, etc., is for the middle of October. Examples on the use of the above data are given on page 2:11 onwards.

Equation of Time is the excess of Mean Time over Apparent Time
(See explanation and examples on p. 2:15)

☾ MOON ☽

DATE			Age	Transit Diff. (Upper)		Semi-diam.	Hor. Par. 12 h.	Lat. 52°N.		MOON'S PHASES
Day of			days					Moon-rise	Moon-set	
Yr.	Mth.	Week								
				h. m.	m.	′	′	h. m.	h. m.	
275	1	Th.	05	16 20	53	15.4	56.7	12 27	20 12	
276	2	Fri.	06	17 13	50	15.2	55.9	13 18	21 10	☽ First Quarter.......... 3 14 12
277	3	Sat.	07	18 03	48	15.0	55.2	13 58	22 14	
278	4	Sun.	08	18 51	45	14.9	54.7	14 29	23 20	○ Full Moon 11 18 03
279	5	Mon.	09	19 36	43	14.8	54.3	14 54	– –	
280	6	Tu.	10	20 19	42	14.8	54.1	15 14	00 28	☾ Last Quarter.......... 19 04 12
281	7	Wed.	11	21 01	41	14.7	54.1	15 32	01 35	
282	8	Th.	12	21 42	41	14.8	54.2	15 48	02 42	● New Moon 25 20 34
283	9	Fri.	13	22 23	43	14.8	54.4	16 04	03 49	
284	10	Sat.	14	23 06	44	14.9	54.7	16 20	04 57	
285	11	Sun.	15	23 50	47	15.0	55.1	16 38	06 06	d. h.
286	12	Mon.	16	24 37		15.1	55.5	17 00	07 17	
287	13	Tu.	17	00 37	49	15.3	56.0	17 26	08 28	Apogee 7 06
288	14	Wed.	18	01 26	53	15.4	56.5	18 00	09 39	Perigee 23 05
289	15	Th.	19	02 19	55	15.5	57.0	18 44	10 46	
290	16	Fri.	20	03 14	56	15.7	57.5	19 39	11 46	
291	17	Sat.	21	04 10	57	15.8	58.0	20 45	12 36	
292	18	Sun.	22	05 07	55	15.9	58.5	22 01	13 17	
293	19	Mon.	23	06 02	54	16.1	59.0	23 21	13 49	
294	20	Tu.	24	06 56	53	16.2	59.5	– –	14 15	
295	21	Wed.	25	07 49	52	16.3	59.8	00 43	14 37	NOTES
296	22	Th.	26	08 41	51	16.4	60.1	02 07	14 58	Moon's G.H.A. and Dec. are given
297	23	Fri.	27	09 32	52	16.4	60.1	03 31	15 19	on page 3:69.
298	24	Sat.	28	10 24	54	16.3	59.9	04 55	15 40	A table for correcting Moonrise and
299	25	Sun.	29	11 18	55	16.2	59.5	06 19	16 06	Moonset for latitude is on page 4:20.
300	26	Mon.	01	12 13	57	16.1	59.0	07 42	16 36	A table for correcting Moon's meri-
301	27	Tu.	02	13 10	56	15.9	58.2	09 00	17 14	dian passage (transit) for longitude is
302	28	Wed.	03	14 06	55	15.7	57.4	10 09	18 01	on page 4:19.
303	29	Th.	04	15 01	53	15.4	56.6	11 07	18 57	Examples on the use of the above
304	30	Fri.	05	15 54	50	15.2	55.9	11 52	20 00	data are given on page 2:11 onwards.
305	31	Sat.	06	16 44	47	15.1	55.2	12 28	21 06	

0h. = midnight. For explanation of use of above data see page 2:11 onwards.

No.	Name	Mag.	Transit (approx.)	DEC.	G.H.A.	R.A.	S.H.A.
			h. m.	° ′	° ′	h. m.	° ′
♈	ARIES	–	23 16	–	9 58.7	–	–
1	Alpheratz	2.2	23 24	N29 03.3	7 57.9	0 08	357 59.2
2	Ankaa	2.4	23 42	S42 20.6	3 29.1	0 26	353 30.4
3	Schedar	2.5	00 00	N56 30.1	359 56.4	0 40	349 57.7
4	Diphda	2.2	00 03	S18 01.4	359 09.7	0 43	349 11.0
5	Achernar	0.6	00 57	S57 16.2	345 36.2	1 38	335 37.5
6	POLARIS	2.1	01 46	N89 14.0	333 29.4	2 26	323 30.7
7	Hamal	2.2	01 27	N23 25.9	338 16.6	2 07	328 17.9
8	Acamar	3.1	02 18	S40 19.8	325 28.3	2 58	315 29.6
9	Menkar	2.8	02 22	N 4 03.9	324 29.6	3 02	314 30.9
10	Mirfak	1.9	02 44	N49 50.2	319 00.8	3 24	309 02.1
11	Aldebaran	1.1	03 55	N16 29.8	301 05.6	4 36	291 06.9
12	Rigel	0.3	04 34	S 8 12.4	291 25.4	5 14	281 26.7
13	Capella	0.2	04 36	N45 59.4	290 55.7	5 16	280 57.0
14	Bellatrix	1.7	04 44	N 6 20.7	288 47.1	5 25	278 48.4
15	Elnath	1.8	04 45	N28 36.1	288 30.7	5 26	278 32.0
16	Alnilam	1.8	04 55	S 1 12.2	286 00.6	5 36	276 01.9
17	Betelgeuse	{ 0.1 / 1.2	05 14	N 7 24.5	281 16.6	5 55	271 17.9
18	Canopus	–0.9	05 43	S52 41.2	274 01.5	6 24	264 02.8
19	Sirius	–1.6	06 04	S16 42.2	268 45.9	6 45	258 47.2
20	Adhara	1.6	06 17	S28 57.5	265 23.3	6 58	255 24.6
21	Castor	1.6	06 53	N31 54.2	256 26.3	7 34	246 27.6
22	Procyon	0.5	06 58	N 5 14.7	255 14.6	7 39	245 15.9
23	Pollux	1.2	07 04	N28 02.6	253 45.3	7 45	243 46.6
24	Avior	1.7	07 41	S59 28.9	244 23.2	8 22	234 24.5
25	Suhail	2.2	08 26	S43 24.0	233 02.7	9 08	223 04.0
26	Miaplacidus	1.8	08 32	S69 41.0	231 42.1	9 13	221 43.4
27	Alphard	2.2	08 46	S 8 37.6	228 10.1	9 27	218 11.4
28	Regulus	1.3	09 27	N12 00.1	217 58.8	10 08	208 00.1
29	Dubhe	2.0	10 22	N61 47.2	204 09.6	11 03	194 10.9
30	Denebola	2.2	11 07	N14 36.7	192 48.4	11 49	182 49.7
31	Gienah	2.8	11 34	S17 30.1	186 07.3	12 15	176 08.6
32	Acrux	1.1	11 44	S63 03.5	183 26.1	12 26	173 27.4
33	Gacrux	1.6	11 49	S57 04.3	182 17.5	12 31	172 18.8
34	Mimosa	1.5	12 05	S59 38.9	178 09.6	12 47	168 10.9
35	Alioth	1.7	12 12	N55 59.9	176 33.4	12 54	166 34.7
36	Spica	1.2	12 43	S11 07.4	168 46.6	13 25	158 47.9
37	Alkaid	1.9	13 05	N49 21.0	163 10.2	13 47	153 11.5
38	Hadar	0.9	13 21	S60 20.4	159 09.3	14 03	149 10.6
39	Menkent	2.3	13 24	S36 20.1	158 25.0	14 06	148 26.3
40	Arcturus	0.2	13 33	N19 13.2	156 08.8	14 15	146 10.1
41	Rigil Kent	0.1	13 57	S60 48.4	150 12.3	14 39	140 13.6
42	Zuben'ubi	2.9	14 08	S16 00.7	147 21.6	14 50	137 22.9
43	Kochab	2.2	14 08	N74 11.2	147 19.0	14 51	137 20.3
44	Alphecca	2.3	14 52	N26 44.4	136 23.1	15 34	126 24.4
45	Antares	1.2	15 46	S26 25.0	122 44.2	16 29	112 45.5
46	Atria	1.9	16 05	S69 01.1	118 00.3	16 48	108 01.6
47	Sabik	2.6	16 27	S15 42.9	112 29.2	17 10	102 30.5
48	Shaula	1.7	16 50	S37 06.0	106 41.8	17 33	96 43.1
49	Rasalhague	2.1	16 52	N12 34.1	106 19.7	17 35	96 21.0
50	Eltanin	2.4	17 14	N51 29.7	100 52.2	17 56	90 53.5
51	Kaus Aust.	2.0	17 41	S34 23.4	94 03.1	18 24	84 04.4
52	Vega	0.1	17 54	N38 46.9	90 48.2	18 37	80 49.5
53	Nunki	2.1	18 12	S26 18.4	86 16.2	18 55	76 17.5
54	Altair	0.9	19 07	N 8 51.2	72 22.0	19 50	62 23.3
55	Peacock	2.1	19 42	S56 45.6	63 42.0	20 25	53 43.3
56	Deneb	1.3	19 58	N45 15.6	59 40.6	20 41	49 41.9
57	Enif	2.5	21 00	N 9 50.8	44 00.8	21 44	34 02.1
58	Al Na'ir	2.2	21 24	S46 59.8	38 01.4	22 08	28 02.7
59	Fomalhaut	1.3	22 14	S29 39.5	25 39.4	22 57	15 40.7
60	Markab	2.6	22 21	N15 10.3	23 52.2	23 04	13 53.5

Stars Transit Correction Table

D. of Mth.	Corr (Sub.)	D. of Mth.	Corr. (Sub.)
	h. m.		h. m.
1	–0 00	17	–1 03
2	–0 04	18	–1 07
3	–0 08	19	–1 11
4	–0 12	20	–1 15
5	–0 16	21	–1 19
6	–0 20	22	–1 23
7	–0 24	23	–1 27
8	–0 28	24	–1 30
9	–0 31	25	–1 34
10	–0 35	26	–1 38
11	–0 39	27	–1 42
12	–0 43	28	–1 46
13	–0 47	29	–1 50
14	–0 51	30	–1 54
15	–0 55	31	–1 58
16	–0 59		

STAR'S TRANSIT

To find the approx. time of Transit of a Star for any day of the month use above table.

If the quantity taken from the table is greater than the time of Transit for the first of the month, add 23h. 56min. to the time of transit before subtracting the correction below.

Example: It is 0130h. on October 15th. How soon will you be able to get a Meridian altitude sight, and of which star?

	h.min.
Present time	01 30
Corr. for the 15th	+00 55
Corresponding time on the 1st	02 25

Answer: 19 min. Mirfak (No 10).

OCTOBER DIARY

d.	h.	
2	22	Mercury 2°N of Spica
3	14	First Quarter
6	08	Saturn 5°S of Moon
7	06	Moon at apogee.
11	18	Full Moon
16	04	Saturn stationary
18	15	Mars 3°N of Moon
19	04	Last Quarter
23	05	Moon at perigee
24	00	Jupiter 7°N of Moon
25	21	New Moon
27	07	Venus 3°N of Antares
27	15	Mercury 0°.5S of Moon Occn.
28	15	Venus 0°.4S of Moon Occn.
31	16	Mercury greatest elong. E (24°)

STAR TIME

The best time to take Star observations is shown in the a.m. and p.m. TWILIGHT columns on the opposite page – corrected for Latitude.

For **Lighting-up Time** (ashore) add 30 mins to Sunset Times.

For Star's G.H.A. Correction Table, see page 4:8.

For Alphabetical List of Stars with Constellation names, see page 2:24.

For Examples on the use of the above data, see page 2:11.

Thursday, 1st October

G.M.T. (h)	SUN G.H.A.	SUN Dec.	ARIES G.H.A.	G.M.T. (h)
00	182 34.2	S 3 12.0	9 58.7	00
02	212 34.6	3 13.9	40 03.6	02
04	242 35.0	3 15.9	70 08.5	04
06	272 35.4	3 17.8	100 13.5	06
08	302 35.8	3 19.8	130 18.4	08
10	332 36.2	3 21.7	160 23.3	10
12	2 36.6	3 23.6	190 28.2	12
14	32 37.0	3 25.6	220 33.2	14
16	62 37.4	3 27.5	250 38.1	16
18	92 37.8	3 29.5	280 43.0	18
20	122 38.2	3 31.4	310 48.0	20
22	152 38.6	S 3 33.3	340 52.9	22

Friday, 2nd October

G.M.T. (h)	SUN G.H.A.	SUN Dec.	ARIES G.H.A.	G.M.T. (h)
00	182 39.0	S 3 35.3	10 57.8	00
02	212 39.4	3 37.2	41 02.7	02
04	242 39.8	3 39.1	71 07.7	04
06	272 40.2	3 41.1	101 12.6	06
08	302 40.6	3 43.0	131 17.5	08
10	332 41.0	3 44.9	161 22.4	10
12	2 41.3	3 46.9	191 27.4	12
14	32 41.7	3 48.8	221 32.3	14
16	62 42.1	3 50.8	251 37.2	16
18	92 42.5	3 52.7	281 42.2	18
20	122 42.9	3 54.6	311 47.1	20
22	152 43.3	S 3 56.6	341 52.0	22

Saturday, 3rd October

G.M.T. (h)	SUN G.H.A.	SUN Dec.	ARIES G.H.A.	G.M.T. (h)
00	182 43.7	S 3 58.5	11 56.9	00
02	212 44.1	4 00.4	42 01.9	02
04	242 44.5	4 02.4	72 06.8	04
06	272 44.9	4 04.3	102 11.7	06
08	302 45.2	4 06.2	132 16.7	08
10	332 45.6	4 08.1	162 21.6	10
12	2 46.0	4 10.1	192 26.5	12
14	32 46.4	4 12.0	222 31.4	14
16	62 46.8	4 13.9	252 36.4	16
18	92 47.2	4 15.9	282 41.3	18
20	122 47.6	4 17.8	312 46.2	20
22	152 47.9	S 4 19.7	342 51.2	22

Sunday, 4th October

G.M.T. (h)	SUN G.H.A.	SUN Dec.	ARIES G.H.A.	G.M.T. (h)
00	182 48.3	S 4 21.7	12 56.1	00
02	212 48.7	4 23.6	43 01.0	02
04	242 49.1	4 25.5	73 05.9	04
06	272 49.5	4 27.4	103 10.9	06
08	302 49.9	4 29.4	133 15.8	08
10	332 50.2	4 31.3	163 20.7	10
12	2 50.6	4 33.2	193 25.7	12
14	32 51.0	4 35.2	223 30.6	14
16	62 51.4	4 37.1	253 35.5	16
18	92 51.8	4 39.0	283 40.4	18
20	122 52.1	4 40.9	313 45.4	20
22	152 52.5	S 4 42.9	343 50.3	22

Monday, 5th October

G.M.T. (h)	SUN G.H.A.	SUN Dec.	ARIES G.H.A.	G.M.T. (h)
00	182 52.9	S 4 44.8	13 55.2	00
02	212 53.3	4 46.7	44 00.2	02
04	242 53.6	4 48.6	74 05.1	04
06	272 54.0	4 50.5	104 10.0	06
08	302 54.4	4 52.5	134 14.9	08
10	332 54.8	4 54.4	164 19.9	10
12	2 55.1	4 56.3	194 24.8	12
14	32 55.5	4 58.2	224 29.7	14
16	62 55.9	5 00.2	254 34.7	16
18	92 56.2	5 02.1	284 39.6	18
20	122 56.6	5 04.0	314 44.5	20
22	152 57.0	S 5 05.9	344 49.4	22

Tuesday, 6th October

G.M.T. (h)	SUN G.H.A.	SUN Dec.	ARIES G.H.A.	G.M.T. (h)
00	182 57.3	S 5 07.8	14 54.4	00
02	212 57.7	5 09.8	44 59.3	02
04	242 58.1	5 11.7	75 04.2	04
06	272 58.4	5 13.6	105 09.1	06
08	302 58.8	5 15.5	135 14.1	08
10	332 59.2	5 17.4	165 19.0	10
12	2 59.5	5 19.3	195 23.9	12
14	32 59.9	5 21.3	225 28.9	14
16	63 00.3	5 23.2	255 33.8	16
18	93 00.6	5 25.1	285 38.7	18
20	123 01.0	5 27.0	315 43.6	20
22	153 01.4	S 5 28.9	345 48.6	22

Wednesday, 7th October

G.M.T. (h)	SUN G.H.A.	SUN Dec.	ARIES G.H.A.	G.M.T. (h)
00	183 01.7	S 5 30.8	15 53.5	00
02	213 02.1	5 32.7	45 58.4	02
04	243 02.4	5 34.6	76 03.4	04
06	273 02.8	5 36.6	106 08.3	06
08	303 03.2	5 38.5	136 13.2	08
10	333 03.5	5 40.4	166 18.1	10
12	3 03.9	5 42.3	196 23.1	12
14	33 04.2	5 44.2	226 28.0	14
16	63 04.6	5 46.1	256 32.9	16
18	93 04.9	5 48.0	286 37.9	18
20	123 05.3	5 49.9	316 42.8	20
22	153 05.6	S 5 51.8	346 47.7	22

Thursday, 8th October

G.M.T. (h)	SUN G.H.A.	SUN Dec.	ARIES G.H.A.	G.M.T. (h)
00	183 06.0	S 5 53.7	16 52.6	00
02	213 06.3	5 55.6	46 57.6	02
04	243 06.7	5 57.6	77 02.5	04
06	273 07.0	5 59.5	107 07.4	06
08	303 07.4	6 01.4	137 12.4	08
10	333 07.7	6 03.3	167 17.3	10
12	3 08.1	6 05.2	197 22.2	12
14	33 08.4	6 07.1	227 27.1	14
16	63 08.8	6 09.0	257 32.1	16
18	93 09.1	6 10.9	287 37.0	18
20	123 09.5	6 12.8	317 41.9	20
22	153 09.8	S 6 14.7	347 46.9	22

Friday, 9th October

G.M.T. (h)	SUN G.H.A.	SUN Dec.	ARIES G.H.A.	G.M.T. (h)
00	183 10.2	S 6 16.6	17 51.8	00
02	213 10.5	6 18.5	47 56.7	02
04	243 10.9	6 20.4	78 01.6	04
06	273 11.2	6 22.3	108 06.6	06
08	303 11.5	6 24.2	138 11.5	08
10	333 11.9	6 26.1	168 16.4	10
12	3 12.2	6 28.0	198 21.3	12
14	33 12.5	6 29.9	228 26.3	14
16	63 12.9	6 31.8	258 31.2	16
18	93 13.2	6 33.7	288 36.1	18
20	123 13.6	6 35.5	318 41.1	20
22	153 13.9	S 6 37.4	348 46.0	22

Saturday, 10th October

G.M.T. (h)	SUN G.H.A.	SUN Dec.	ARIES G.H.A.	G.M.T. (h)
00	183 14.2	S 6 39.3	18 50.9	00
02	213 14.6	6 41.2	48 55.8	02
04	243 14.9	6 43.1	79 00.8	04
06	273 15.2	6 45.0	109 05.7	06
08	303 15.6	6 46.9	139 10.6	08
10	333 15.9	6 48.8	169 15.6	10
12	3 16.2	6 50.7	199 20.5	12
14	33 16.5	6 52.6	229 25.4	14
16	63 16.9	6 54.5	259 30.3	16
18	93 17.2	6 56.3	289 35.3	18
20	123 17.5	6 58.2	319 40.2	20
22	153 17.8	S 7 00.1	349 45.1	22

Sunday, 11th October

G.M.T. (h)	SUN G.H.A.	SUN Dec.	ARIES G.H.A.	G.M.T. (h)
00	183 18.2	S 7 02.0	19 50.1	00
02	213 18.5	7 03.9	49 55.0	02
04	243 18.8	7 05.8	79 59.9	04
06	273 19.1	7 07.6	110 04.8	06
08	303 19.5	7 09.5	140 09.8	08
10	333 19.8	7 11.4	170 14.7	10
12	3 20.1	7 13.3	200 19.6	12
14	33 20.4	7 15.2	230 24.6	14
16	63 20.7	7 17.1	260 29.5	16
18	93 21.0	7 18.9	290 34.4	18
20	123 21.4	7 20.8	320 39.3	20
22	153 21.7	S 7 22.7	350 44.3	22

Monday, 12th October

G.M.T. (h)	SUN G.H.A.	SUN Dec.	ARIES G.H.A.	G.M.T. (h)
00	183 22.0	S 7 24.6	20 49.2	00
02	213 22.3	7 26.4	50 54.1	02
04	243 22.6	7 28.3	80 59.1	04
06	273 22.9	7 30.2	111 04.0	06
08	303 23.2	7 32.1	141 08.9	08
10	333 23.5	7 33.9	171 13.8	10
12	3 23.9	7 35.8	201 18.8	12
14	33 24.2	7 37.7	231 23.7	14
16	63 24.5	7 39.6	261 28.6	16
18	93 24.8	7 41.4	291 33.6	18
20	123 25.1	7 43.3	321 38.5	20
22	153 25.4	S 7 45.2	351 43.4	22

Tuesday, 13th October

G.M.T. (h)	SUN G.H.A.	SUN Dec.	ARIES G.H.A.	G.M.T. (h)
00	183 25.7	S 7 47.0	21 48.3	00
02	213 26.0	7 48.9	51 53.3	02
04	243 26.3	7 50.8	81 58.2	04
06	273 26.6	7 52.6	112 03.1	06
08	303 26.9	7 54.5	142 08.0	08
10	333 27.2	7 56.4	172 13.0	10
12	3 27.5	7 58.2	202 17.9	12
14	33 27.8	8 00.1	232 22.8	14
16	63 28.1	8 02.0	262 27.8	16
18	93 28.4	8 03.8	292 32.7	18
20	123 28.7	8 05.7	322 37.6	20
22	153 29.0	S 8 07.5	352 42.5	22

Wednesday, 14th October

G.M.T. (h)	SUN G.H.A.	SUN Dec.	ARIES G.H.A.	G.M.T. (h)
00	183 29.2	S 8 09.4	22 47.5	00
02	213 29.5	8 11.3	52 52.4	02
04	243 29.8	8 13.1	82 57.3	04
06	273 30.1	8 15.0	113 02.3	06
08	303 30.4	8 16.8	143 07.2	08
10	333 30.7	8 18.7	173 12.1	10
12	3 31.0	8 20.6	203 17.0	12
14	33 31.3	8 22.4	233 22.0	14
16	63 31.5	8 24.3	263 26.9	16
18	93 31.8	8 26.1	293 31.8	18
20	123 32.1	8 28.0	323 36.8	20
22	153 32.4	S 8 29.8	353 41.7	22

Thursday, 15th October

G.M.T. (h)	SUN G.H.A.	SUN Dec.	ARIES G.H.A.	G.M.T. (h)
00	183 32.7	S 8 31.7	23 46.6	00
02	213 33.0	8 33.5	53 51.5	02
04	243 33.2	8 35.4	83 56.5	04
06	273 33.5	8 37.2	114 01.4	06
08	303 33.8	8 39.1	144 06.3	08
10	333 34.1	8 40.9	174 11.3	10
12	3 34.3	8 42.7	204 16.2	12
14	33 34.6	8 44.6	234 21.1	14
16	63 34.9	8 46.4	264 26.0	16
18	93 35.1	8 48.3	294 31.0	18
20	123 35.4	8 50.1	324 35.9	20
22	153 35.7	S 8 52.0	354 40.8	22

To interpolate SUN G.H.A. see page 4:7   To interpolate ARIES G.H.A. see page 4:8

G.M.T.	SUN G.H.A.	ARIES Dec.	G.H.A.	G.M.T.

Friday, 16th October

h	° '	° '	° '	h
00	183 35.9	S 8 53.8	24 45.8	00
02	213 36.2	8 55.6	54 50.7	02
04	243 36.5	8 57.5	84 55.6	04
06	273 36.7	8 59.3	115 00.5	06
08	303 37.0	9 01.1	145 05.5	08
10	333 37.3	9 03.0	175 10.4	10
12	3 37.5	9 04.8	205 15.3	12
14	33 37.8	9 06.7	235 20.3	14
16	63 38.0	9 08.5	265 25.2	16
18	93 38.3	9 10.3	295 30.1	18
20	123 38.6	9 12.2	325 35.0	20
22	153 38.8	S 9 14.0	355 40.0	22

Saturday, 17th October

h	° '	° '	° '	h
00	183 39.1	S 9 15.8	25 44.9	00
02	213 39.3	9 17.6	55 49.8	02
04	243 39.6	9 19.5	85 54.7	04
06	273 39.8	9 21.3	115 59.7	06
08	303 40.1	9 23.1	146 04.6	08
10	333 40.3	9 24.9	176 09.5	10
12	3 40.6	9 26.8	206 14.5	12
14	33 40.8	9 28.6	236 19.4	14
16	63 41.1	9 30.4	266 24.3	16
18	93 41.3	9 32.2	296 29.2	18
20	123 41.6	9 34.1	326 34.2	20
22	153 41.8	S 9 35.9	356 39.1	22

Sunday, 18th October

h	° '	° '	° '	h
00	183 42.1	S 9 37.7	26 44.0	00
02	213 42.3	9 39.5	56 49.0	02
04	243 42.5	9 41.3	86 53.9	04
06	273 42.8	9 43.1	116 58.8	06
08	303 43.0	9 45.0	147 03.7	08
10	333 43.3	9 46.8	177 08.7	10
12	3 43.5	9 48.6	207 13.6	12
14	33 43.7	9 50.4	237 18.5	14
16	63 44.0	9 52.2	267 23.5	16
18	93 44.2	9 54.0	297 28.4	18
20	123 44.4	9 55.8	327 33.3	20
22	153 44.7	S 9 57.6	357 38.2	22

Monday, 19th October

h	° '	° '	° '	h
00	183 44.9	S 9 59.4	27 43.2	00
02	213 45.1	10 01.2	57 48.1	02
04	243 45.4	10 03.0	87 53.0	04
06	273 45.6	10 04.8	117 58.0	06
08	303 45.8	10 06.7	148 02.9	08
10	333 46.0	10 08.5	178 07.8	10
12	3 46.3	10 10.3	208 12.7	12
14	33 46.5	10 12.1	238 17.7	14
16	63 46.7	10 13.9	268 22.6	16
18	93 46.9	10 15.6	298 27.5	18
20	123 47.1	10 17.4	328 32.5	20
22	153 47.4	S10 19.2	358 37.4	22

Tuesday, 20th October

h	° '	° '	° '	h
00	183 47.6	S10 21.0	28 42.3	00
02	213 47.8	10 22.8	58 47.2	02
04	243 48.0	10 24.6	88 52.2	04
06	273 48.2	10 26.4	118 57.1	06
08	303 48.4	10 28.2	149 02.0	08
10	333 48.6	10 30.0	179 06.9	10
12	3 48.9	10 31.8	209 11.9	12
14	33 49.1	10 33.6	239 16.8	14
16	63 49.3	10 35.3	269 21.7	16
18	93 49.5	10 37.1	299 26.7	18
20	123 49.7	10 38.9	329 31.6	20
22	153 49.9	S10 40.7	359 36.5	22

Wednesday, 21st October

h	° '	° '	° '	h
00	183 50.1	S10 42.5	29 41.4	00
02	213 50.3	10 44.3	59 46.4	02
04	243 50.5	10 46.0	89 51.3	04
06	273 50.7	10 47.8	119 56.2	06
08	303 50.9	10 49.6	150 01.2	08
10	333 51.1	10 51.4	180 06.1	10
12	3 51.3	10 53.1	210 11.0	12
14	33 51.5	10 54.9	240 15.9	14
16	63 51.7	10 56.7	270 20.9	16
18	93 51.8	10 58.5	300 25.8	18
20	123 52.0	11 00.2	330 30.7	20
22	153 52.2	S11 02.0	0 35.7	22

Thursday, 22nd October

h	° '	° '	° '	h
00	183 52.4	S11 03.8	30 40.6	00
02	213 52.6	11 05.5	60 45.5	02
04	243 52.8	11 07.3	90 50.4	04
06	273 53.0	11 09.1	120 55.4	06
08	303 53.1	11 10.8	151 00.3	08
10	333 53.3	11 12.6	181 05.2	10
12	3 53.5	11 14.3	211 10.2	12
14	33 53.7	11 16.1	241 15.1	14
16	63 53.9	11 17.9	271 20.0	16
18	93 54.0	11 19.6	301 24.9	18
20	123 54.2	11 21.4	331 29.9	20
22	153 54.4	S11 23.1	1 34.8	22

Friday, 23rd October

h	° '	° '	° '	h
00	183 54.6	S11 24.9	31 39.7	00
02	213 54.7	11 26.6	61 44.7	02
04	243 54.9	11 28.4	91 49.6	04
06	273 55.1	11 30.1	121 54.5	06
08	303 55.2	11 31.9	151 59.4	08
10	333 55.4	11 33.6	182 04.4	10
12	3 55.6	11 35.4	212 09.3	12
14	33 55.7	11 37.1	242 14.2	14
16	63 55.9	11 38.9	272 19.2	16
18	93 56.1	11 40.6	302 24.1	18
20	123 56.2	11 42.4	332 29.0	20
22	153 56.4	S11 44.1	2 33.9	22

Saturday, 24th October

h	° '	° '	° '	h
00	183 56.5	S11 45.8	32 38.9	00
02	213 56.7	11 47.6	62 43.8	02
04	243 56.8	11 49.3	92 48.7	04
06	273 57.0	11 51.0	122 53.6	06
08	303 57.2	11 52.8	152 58.6	08
10	333 57.3	11 54.5	183 03.5	10
12	3 57.5	11 56.2	213 08.4	12
14	33 57.6	11 58.0	243 13.4	14
16	63 57.8	11 59.7	273 18.3	16
18	93 57.9	12 01.4	303 23.2	18
20	123 58.0	12 03.2	333 28.1	20
22	153 58.2	S12 04.9	3 33.1	22

Sunday, 25th October

h	° '	° '	° '	h
00	183 58.3	S12 06.6	33 38.0	00
02	213 58.5	12 08.3	63 42.9	02
04	243 58.6	12 10.1	93 47.9	04
06	273 58.8	12 11.8	123 52.8	06
08	303 58.9	12 13.5	153 57.7	08
10	333 59.0	12 15.2	184 02.6	10
12	3 59.2	12 16.9	214 07.6	12
14	33 59.3	12 18.6	244 12.5	14
16	63 59.4	12 20.4	274 17.4	16
18	93 59.6	12 22.1	304 22.4	18
20	123 59.7	12 23.8	334 27.3	20
22	153 59.8	S12 25.5	4 32.2	22

Monday, 26th October

h	° '	° '	° '	h
00	183 59.9	S12 27.2	34 37.1	00
02	214 00.1	12 28.9	64 42.1	02
04	244 00.2	12 30.6	94 47.0	04
06	274 00.3	12 32.3	124 51.9	06
08	304 00.4	12 34.0	154 56.9	08
10	334 00.6	12 35.7	185 01.8	10
12	4 00.7	12 37.4	215 06.7	12
14	34 00.8	12 39.1	245 11.6	14
16	64 00.9	12 40.8	275 16.6	16
18	94 01.0	12 42.5	305 21.5	18
20	124 01.1	12 44.2	335 26.4	20
22	154 01.3	S12 45.9	5 31.4	22

Tuesday, 27th October

h	° '	° '	° '	h
00	184 01.4	S12 47.6	35 36.3	00
02	214 01.5	12 49.3	65 41.2	02
04	244 01.6	12 51.0	95 46.1	04
06	274 01.7	12 52.7	125 51.1	06
08	304 01.8	12 54.3	155 56.0	08
10	334 01.9	12 56.0	186 00.9	10
12	4 02.0	12 57.7	216 05.8	12
14	34 02.1	12 59.4	246 10.8	14
16	64 02.2	13 01.1	276 15.7	16
18	94 02.3	13 02.7	306 20.6	18
20	124 02.4	13 04.4	336 25.6	20
22	154 02.5	S13 06.1	6 30.5	22

Wednesday, 28th October

h	° '	° '	° '	h
00	184 02.6	S13 07.8	36 35.4	00
02	214 02.7	13 09.5	66 40.3	02
04	244 02.8	13 11.1	96 45.3	04
06	274 02.9	13 12.8	126 50.2	06
08	304 03.0	13 14.5	156 55.1	08
10	334 03.1	13 16.1	187 00.1	10
12	4 03.2	13 17.8	217 05.0	12
14	34 03.3	13 19.5	247 09.9	14
16	64 03.3	13 21.1	277 14.8	16
18	94 03.4	13 22.8	307 19.8	18
20	124 03.5	13 24.4	337 24.7	20
22	154 03.6	S13 26.1	7 29.6	22

Thursday, 29th October

h	° '	° '	° '	h
00	184 03.7	S13 27.8	37 34.6	00
02	214 03.8	13 29.4	67 39.5	02
04	244 03.8	13 31.1	97 44.4	04
06	274 03.9	13 32.7	127 49.3	06
08	304 04.0	13 34.4	157 54.3	08
10	334 04.1	13 36.0	187 59.2	10
12	4 04.1	13 37.7	218 04.1	12
14	34 04.2	13 39.3	248 09.1	14
16	64 04.3	13 41.0	278 14.0	16
18	94 04.3	13 42.6	308 18.9	18
20	124 04.4	13 44.3	338 23.8	20
22	154 04.5	S13 45.9	8 28.8	22

Friday, 30th October

h	° '	° '	° '	h
00	184 04.5	S13 47.5	38 33.7	00
02	214 04.6	13 49.2	68 38.6	02
04	244 04.7	13 50.8	98 43.6	04
06	274 04.7	13 52.4	128 48.5	06
08	304 04.8	13 54.1	158 53.4	08
10	334 04.9	13 55.7	188 58.3	10
12	4 04.9	13 57.3	219 03.3	12
14	34 05.0	13 59.0	249 08.2	14
16	64 05.0	14 00.6	279 13.1	16
18	94 05.1	14 02.2	309 18.1	18
20	124 05.1	14 03.9	339 23.0	20
22	154 05.2	S14 05.5	9 27.9	22

Saturday, 31st October

h	° '	° '	° '	h
00	184 05.2	S14 07.1	39 32.8	00
02	214 05.3	14 08.7	69 37.8	02
04	244 05.3	14 10.3	99 42.7	04
06	274 05.4	S14 11.9	129 47.6	06
08	304 05.4	S14 13.6	159 52.5	08
10	334 05.4	14 15.2	189 57.5	10
12	4 05.5	14 16.8	220 02.4	12
14	34 05.5	S14 18.4	250 07.3	14
16	64 05.5	S14 20.0	280 12.3	16
18	94 05.6	14 21.6	310 17.2	18
20	124 05.7	14 23.2	340 22.1	20
22	154 05.7	S14 24.8	10 27.0	22

To interpolate SUN G.H.A. see page 4:7

To interpolate ARIES G.H.A. see page 4:8

♀ VENUS ♀ / ♃ JUPITER ♃

Mer. Pass.	G.H.A.	Mean Var. 14°	Dec.	Mean Var.	M	Day of Week	G.H.A	Mean Var. 15°	Dec.	Mean Var.	Mer. Pass
h. m.	° '	'	° '	'			° '	'	° '	'	h. m.
13 40	155 11.6	59.5	S 13 58.6	1.1	1	Th.	191 25.3	2.0	N 1 47.6	0.2	11 13
13 40	155 00.2	59.5	S 14 25.2	1.1	2	Fri.	192 12.6	2.0	N 1 42.5	0.2	11 10
13 41	154 48.5	59.5	S 14 51.4	1.1	3	Sat.	192 59.9	2.0	N 1 37.5	0.2	11 07
13 42	154 36.6	59.5	S 15 17.3	1.1	4	SUN.	193 47.3	2.0	N 1 32.4	0.2	11 03
13 43	154 24.4	59.5	S 15 42.7	1.1	5	Mon.	194 34.6	2.0	N 1 27.4	0.2	11 00
13 44	154 11.9	59.5	S 16 07.9	1.0	6	Tu.	195 22.0	2.0	N 1 22.3	0.2	10 57
13 45	153 59.1	59.5	S 16 32.6	1.0	7	Wed.	196 09.4	2.0	N 1 17.3	0.2	10 54
13 45	153 46.1	59.4	S 16 56.9	1.0	8	Th.	196 56.8	2.0	N 1 12.3	0.2	10 51
13 46	153 32.8	59.4	S 17 20.8	1.0	9	Fri.	197 44.2	2.0	N 1 07.3	0.2	10 48
13 47	153 19.3	59.4	S 17 44.3	1.0	10	Sat.	198 31.6	2.0	N 1 02.3	0.2	10 44
13 48	153 05.4	59.4	S 18 07.4	0.9	11	SUN.	199 19.1	2.0	N 0 57.3	0.2	10 41
13 49	152 51.2	59.4	S 18 30.0	0.9	12	Mon.	200 06.6	2.0	N 0 52.4	0.2	10 38
13 50	152 36.8	59.4	S 18 52.1	0.9	13	Tu.	200 54.2	2.0	N 0 47.4	0.2	10 35
13 51	152 22.0	59.4	S 19 13.7	0.9	14	Wed.	201 41.7	2.0	N 0 42.5	0.2	10 32
13 52	152 07.0	59.4	S 19 34.9	0.9	15	Th.	202 29.3	2.0	N 0 37.6	0.2	10 29
13 53	151 51.6	59.4	S 19 55.6	0.8	16	Fri.	203 16.9	2.0	N 0 32.6	0.2	10 25
13 54	151 36.0	59.3	S 20 15.7	0.8	17	Sat.	204 04.6	2.0	N 0 27.7	0.2	10 22
13 55	151 20.0	59.3	S 20 35.3	0.8	18	SUN.	204 52.2	2.0	N 0 22.9	0.2	10 19
13 56	151 03.8	59.3	S 20 54.4	0.8	19	Mon.	205 40.0	2.0	N 0 18.0	0.2	10 16
13 57	150 47.3	59.3	S 21 12.9	0.8	20	Tu.	206 27.7	2.0	N 0 13.2	0.2	10 13
13 59	150 30.5	59.3	S 21 30.9	0.7	21	Wed.	207 15.5	2.0	N 0 08.4	0.2	10 10
14 00	150 13.4	59.3	S 21 48.3	0.7	22	Th.	208 03.3	2.0	N 0 03.6	0.2	10 06
14 01	149 56.1	59.3	S 22 05.1	0.7	23	Fri.	208 51.2	2.0	S 0 01.2	0.2	10 03
14 02	149 38.4	59.3	S 22 21.3	0.7	24	Sat.	209 39.1	2.0	S 0 06.0	0.2	10 00
14 03	149 20.5	59.2	S 22 37.0	0.6	25	SUN.	210 27.0	2.0	S 0 10.7	0.2	09 57
14 05	149 02.3	59.2	S 22 52.0	0.6	26	Mon.	211 15.0	2.0	S 0 15.4	0.2	09 54
14 06	148 43.9	59.2	S 23 06.3	0.6	27	Tu.	212 03.0	2.0	S 0 20.1	0.2	09 50
14 07	148 25.2	59.2	S 23 20.1	0.5	28	Wed.	212 51.1	2.0	S 0 24.8	0.2	09 47
14 08	148 06.3	59.2	S 23 33.1	0.5	29	Th.	213 39.2	2.0	S 0 29.4	0.2	09 44
14 10	147 47.2	59.2	S 23 45.6	0.5	30	Fri.	214 27.4	2.0	S 0 34.0	0.2	09 41
14 11	147 27.9	59.2	S 23 57.4	0.5	31	Sat.	215 15.6	2.0	S 0 38.6	0.2	09 38

♀ VENUS. Av. Mag. –4.0. An **Evening Star**. S.H.A. October 5 141°; 10 134°; 15 128°; 20 122°; 25 116°; 30 109°.

♃ JUPITER. Av. Mag. –1.7. A **Morning Star** throughout the month. S.H.A. October 5 180°; 10 180°; 15 180°; 20 177°; 25 177°; 30 177°.

♂ MARS ♂ / ♄ SATURN ♄

Mer. Pass.	G.H.A.	Mean Var. 15°	Dec.	Mean Var.	M	Day of Week	G.H.A	Mean Var. 15°	Dec.	Mean Var.	Mer. Pass
h. m.	° '	'	° '	'			° '	'	° '	'	h. m.
06 04	268 59.0	1.1	N23 24.7	0.0	1	Th.	55 12.0	2.5	S18 11.7	0.0	20 16
06 02	269 25.5	1.1	N23 23.8	0.0	2	Fri.	56 12.6	2.5	S18 12.1	0.0	20 12
06 00	269 52.4	1.1	N23 23.0	0.0	3	Sat.	57 13.1	2.5	S18 12.4	0.0	20 08
05 58	270 19.6	1.1	N23 22.0	0.0	4	SUN.	58 13.5	2.5	S18 12.8	0.0	20 04
05 56	270 47.1	1.2	N23 21.0	0.0	5	Mon.	59 13.8	2.5	S18 13.1	0.0	20 00
05 55	271 14.9	1.2	N23 19.9	0.0	6	Tu.	60 14.0	2.5	S18 13.3	0.0	19 56
05 53	271 43.1	1.2	N23 18.8	0.1	7	Wed.	61 14.1	2.5	S18 13.6	0.0	19 52
05 51	272 11.6	1.2	N23 17.6	0.1	8	Th.	62 14.1	2.5	S18 13.8	0.0	19 48
05 49	272 40.4	1.2	N23 16.4	0.1	9	Fri.	63 14.1	2.5	S18 14.0	0.0	19 44
05 47	273 09.5	1.2	N23 15.1	0.1	10	Sat.	64 13.9	2.5	S18 14.2	0.0	19 40
05 45	273 39.0	1.2	N23 13.8	0.1	11	SUN.	65 13.6	2.5	S18 14.3	0.0	19 36
05 43	274 08.8	1.3	N23 12.5	0.1	12	Mon.	66 13.2	2.5	S18 14.4	0.0	19 32
05 41	274 39.0	1.3	N23 11.1	0.1	13	Tu.	67 12.7	2.5	S18 14.5	0.0	19 28
05 39	275 09.6	1.3	N23 09.7	0.1	14	Wed.	68 12.2	2.5	S18 14.5	0.0	19 24
05 37	275 40.5	1.3	N23 08.3	0.1	15	Th.	69 11.5	2.5	S18 14.6	0.0	19 20
05 35	276 11.9	1.3	N23 06.8	0.1	16	Fri.	70 10.7	2.5	S18 14.5	0.0	19 16
05 33	276 43.6	1.3	N23 05.4	0.1	17	Sat.	71 09.8	2.5	S18 14.5	0.0	19 12
05 30	277 15.7	1.4	N23 03.9	0.1	18	SUN.	72 08.8	2.5	S18 14.4	0.0	19 08
05 28	277 48.2	1.4	N23 02.5	0.1	19	Mon.	73 07.7	2.4	S18 14.4	0.0	19 04
05 26	278 21.2	1.4	N23 01.0	0.1	20	Tu.	74 06.5	2.4	S18 14.2	0.0	19 00
05 24	278 54.5	1.4	N22 59.5	0.1	21	Wed.	75 05.2	2.4	S18 14.1	0.0	18 57
05 22	279 28.3	1.4	N22 58.1	0.1	22	Th.	76 03.8	2.4	S18 13.9	0.0	18 53
05 19	280 02.6	1.4	N22 56.7	0.1	23	Fri.	77 02.3	2.4	S18 13.7	0.0	18 49
05 17	280 37.3	1.5	N22 55.3	0.1	24	Sat.	78 00.6	2.4	S18 13.4	0.0	18 45
05 15	281 12.5	1.5	N22 53.9	0.1	25	SUN.	78 58.9	2.4	S18 13.2	0.0	18 41
05 12	281 48.1	1.5	N22 52.6	0.1	26	Mon.	79 57.1	2.4	S18 12.9	0.0	18 37
05 10	282 24.2	1.5	N22 51.3	0.1	27	Tu.	80 55.2	2.4	S18 12.5	0.0	18 33
05 07	283 00.9	1.5	N22 50.0	0.0	28	Wed.	81 53.1	2.4	S18 12.2	0.0	18 29
05 05	283 38.0	1.6	N22 48.8	0.0	29	Th.	82 51.0	2.4	S18 11.8	0.0	18 26
05 02	284 15.6	1.6	N22 47.7	0.0	30	Fri.	83 48.2	2.4	S18 11.4	0.0	18 22
05 00	284 53.8	1.6	N22 46.6	0.0	31	Sat.	84 46.5	2.4	S18 11.0	0.0	18 18

♂ MARS. Av. Mag. +0.1. A **Morning Star**. S.H.A. October 5 256°; 10 254°; 15 252°; 20 249°; 25 248°; 30 246°.

♄ SATURN. Av. Mag. +0.5. An **Evening Star**. S.H.A. October 5 44°; 10 45°; 15 46°; 20 44°; 25 45°; 30 46°.

MERCURY. Visible low in the west after sunset throughout the month.

For Planets Correction Tables see pages 4:9-4:13. See also 'How to Recognise the Planets' on page 2:32.
Mean Var. means Variation per Hour.

Day of M. W.	G.M.T. (h)	G.H.A. (° ')	Mean Var. per Hour (14°,+)	Dec. (° ')	Mean Var. per Hour (')
1 Th.	0	124 02.1	27.0	S23 04.5	2.1
	6	210 43.7	27.2	S23 17.5	1.3
	12	297 26.5	27.4	S23 25.7	0.5
	18	24 10.7	27.6	S23 29.1	0.3
2 Fri.	0	110 56.4	28.0	S23 27.7	1.0
	6	197 43.9	28.3	S23 21.8	1.8
	12	284 33.3	28.6	S23 11.5	2.6
	18	11 24.7	29.0	S22 56.8	3.2
3 Sat.	0	98 18.3	29.3	S22 37.9	3.9
	6	185 14.1	29.7	S22 15.1	4.5
	12	272 12.2	30.1	S21 48.4	5.1
	18	359 12.7	30.5	S21 18.0	5.7
4 Sun.	0	86 15.5	30.9	S20 44.1	6.3
	6	173 20.8	31.3	S20 06.9	6.7
	12	260 28.3	31.7	S19 26.5	7.3
	18	347 38.2	32.0	S18 43.0	7.8
5 Mon.	0	74 50.3	32.4	S17 56.8	8.2
	6	162 04.6	32.8	S17 07.9	8.6
	12	249 20.9	33.1	S16 16.5	9.0
	18	336 39.2	33.4	S15 22.7	9.3
6 Tu.	0	63 59.3	33.7	S14 26.8	9.7
	6	151 21.1	33.9	S13 28.8	10.0
	12	238 44.5	34.1	S12 28.9	10.3
	18	326 09.3	34.4	S11 27.3	10.5
7 Wed.	0	53 35.4	34.5	S10 24.0	10.8
	6	141 02.6	34.7	S 9 19.3	11.0
	12	228 30.8	34.9	S 8 13.3	11.2
	18	315 59.7	34.9	S 7 06.1	11.4
8 Th.	0	43 29.2	35.0	S 5 57.8	11.5
	6	130 59.2	35.1	S 4 48.6	11.6
	12	218 29.5	35.1	S 3 38.7	11.8
	18	305 59.8	35.0	S 2 28.1	11.8
9 Fri.	0	33 30.1	35.0	S 1 17.1	11.9
	6	121 00.1	34.9	S 0 05.7	11.9
	12	208 29.7	34.8	N 1 05.9	11.9
	18	295 58.7	34.7	N 2 17.5	11.9
10 Sat.	0	23 26.9	34.5	N 3 29.0	11.8
	6	110 54.2	34.3	N 4 40.2	11.7
	12	198 20.3	34.1	N 5 51.0	11.7
	18	285 45.2	33.9	N 7 01.1	11.5
11 Sun.	0	13 08.6	33.6	N 8 10.4	11.3
	6	100 30.4	33.3	N 9 18.8	11.1
	12	187 50.4	33.0	N10 26.0	10.9
	18	275 08.6	32.6	N11 31.8	10.7
12 Mon.	0	2 24.6	32.3	N12 36.0	10.4
	6	89 38.6	31.9	N13 38.5	10.1
	12	176 50.2	31.5	N14 39.0	9.7
	18	263 59.5	31.1	N15 37.3	9.3
13 Tu.	0	351 06.3	30.7	N16 33.1	8.8
	6	78 10.6	30.3	N17 26.3	8.3
	12	165 12.4	29.8	N18 16.7	7.8
	18	252 11.5	29.4	N19 03.9	7.3
14 Wed.	0	339 08.1	29.0	N19 47.8	6.6
	6	66 02.1	28.6	N20 28.2	6.1
	12	152 53.7	28.1	N21 04.8	5.4
	18	239 42.9	27.8	N21 37.5	4.7
15 Th.	0	326 29.8	27.4	N22 06.0	4.0
	6	53 14.5	27.1	N22 30.2	3.3
	12	139 57.3	26.8	N22 49.9	2.5
	18	226 38.4	26.6	N23 05.0	1.6
16 Fri.	0	313 17.9	26.3	N23 15.2	0.8
	6	39 56.2	26.2	N23 20.6	0.0
	12	126 33.4	26.0	N23 20.9	0.8
	18	213 09.8	26.0	N23 16.2	1.7
17 Sat.	0	299 45.7	25.9	N23 06.5	2.6
	6	26 21.4	26.0	N22 51.6	3.4
	12	112 57.1	26.0	N22 31.7	4.2
	18	199 33.0	26.0	N22 06.7	5.1
18 Sun.	0	286 09.4	26.2	N21 36.8	5.9
	6	12 46.6	26.3	N21 02.0	6.7
	12	99 24.6	26.5	N20 22.4	7.4
	18	186 03.6	26.7	N19 38.2	8.1
19 Mon.	0	272 43.8	26.9	N18 49.6	8.9
	6	359 25.2	27.2	N17 56.6	9.5
	12	86 08.0	27.4	N16 59.6	10.2
	18	172 52.0	27.5	N15 58.7	10.8
20 Tu.	0	259 37.4	27.8	N14 54.1	11.4
	6	346 24.1	28.1	N13 46.2	11.9
	12	73 12.1	28.2	N12 35.0	12.4
	18	160 01.2	28.3	N11 21.0	12.8
21 Wed.	0	246 51.4	28.6	N10 04.4	13.2
	6	333 42.5	28.7	N 8 45.4	13.5
	12	60 34.5	28.8	N 7 24.3	13.8
	18	147 27.1	28.9	N 6 01.5	14.1
22 Th.	0	234 20.2	29.0	N 4 37.3	14.2
	6	321 13.7	29.0	N 3 11.9	14.4
	12	48 07.3	28.9	N 1 45.7	14.4
	18	135 01.0	28.9	N 0 19.0	14.5
23 Fri.	0	221 54.4	28.9	S 1 07.8	14.4
	6	308 47.5	28.7	S 2 34.5	14.4
	12	35 40.1	28.6	S 4 00.6	14.2
	18	122 31.9	28.5	S 5 25.9	14.0
24 Sat.	0	209 23.0	28.4	S 6 50.0	13.7
	6	296 13.0	28.1	S 8 12.6	13.4
	12	23 02.0	27.9	S 9 33.3	13.1
	18	109 49.8	27.7	S10 51.7	12.6
25 Sun.	0	196 36.4	27.5	S12 07.7	12.2
	6	283 21.6	27.3	S13 20.8	11.6
	12	10 05.5	27.0	S14 30.8	11.0
	18	96 48.1	26.9	S15 37.3	10.4
26 Mon.	0	183 29.4	26.6	S16 40.1	9.7
	6	270 09.5	26.5	S17 38.9	9.1
	12	356 48.4	26.3	S18 33.5	8.3
	18	83 26.4	26.2	S19 23.7	7.5
27 Tu.	0	170 03.6	26.1	S20 09.3	6.7
	6	256 40.1	26.1	S20 50.1	5.9
	12	343 16.3	26.0	S21 26.1	5.1
	18	69 52.3	26.0	S21 57.0	4.3
28 Wed.	0	156 28.4	26.1	S22 23.0	3.4
	6	243 04.8	26.2	S22 43.8	2.5
	12	329 41.9	26.4	S22 59.6	1.7
	18	56 20.0	26.6	S23 10.4	0.9
29 Th.	0	142 59.2	26.8	S23 16.1	0.0
	6	229 39.2	27.1	S23 17.0	0.7
	12	316 22.2	27.4	S23 13.0	1.5
	18	43 06.5	27.8	S23 04.4	2.3
30 Fri.	0	129 52.9	28.2	S22 51.2	3.0
	6	216 41.5	28.5	S22 33.7	3.7
	12	303 32.6	28.9	S22 12.0	4.3
	18	30 26.2	29.4	S21 46.2	5.0
31 Sat.	0	117 22.3	29.9	S21 16.7	5.6
	6	204 21.2	30.2	S20 43.5	6.2
	12	291 22.6	30.8	S20 06.8	6.7
	18	18 26.7	31.1	S19 26.9	7.2

PHASES OF THE MOON

	d. h/min		d. h/min
☽ First Quarter	3 14 12	☾ Last Quarter	19 04 12
○ Full Moon	11 18 03	● New Moon	25 20 34
Apogee	7 06	Perigee	23 05

NOVEMBER, 1992

G.M.T.   (30 days)   G.M.T.

☉ SUN ☉

DATE Day of			Equation of Time		Transit	Semi-diam.	Lat. 52°N.				Lat. Corr. to Sunrise, Sunset, etc.				
Yr.	Mth.	Week	0 h.	12 h.			Twilight	Sunrise	Sunset	Twilight	Lat.	Twilight	Sunrise	Sunset	Twilight
			m. s.	m. s.	h. m.	'	h. m.	h. m.	h. m.	h. m.	°	h. m.	h. m.	h. m.	h. m.
306	1	Sun.	−16 23	−16 24	11 44	16.1	06 20	06 55	16 31	17 07	N70	+1 27	+2 27	−2 27	−1 27
307	2	Mon.	−16 24	−16 24	11 44	16.2	06 21	06 57	16 30	17 06	68	+1 09	+1 52	−1 52	−1 10
308	3	Tu.	−16 25	−16 24	11 44	16.2	06 23	06 59	16 28	17 04	66	+0 56	+1 27	−1 26	−0 57
309	4	Wed.	−16 24	−16 24	11 44	16.2	06 25	07 01	16 26	17 02	64	+0 44	+1 07	−0 07	−0 45
310	5	Th.	−16 23	−16 22	11 44	16.2	06 26	07 02	16 24	17 01	62	+0 34	+0 51	−0 51	−0 35
311	6	Fri.	−16 21	−16 20	11 44	16.2	06 28	07 04	16 22	16 59	N60	+0 26	+0 38	−0 38	−0 26
312	7	Sat.	−16 18	−16 17	11 44	16.2	06 30	07 06	16 20	16 57	58	+0 19	+0 26	−0 26	−0 18
313	8	Sun.	−16 15	−16 12	11 44	16.2	06 31	07 08	16 19	16 56	56	+0 12	+0 17	−0 16	−0 12
314	9	Mon.	−16 10	−16 08	11 44	16.2	06 33	07 10	16 17	16 54	54	+0 06	+0 08	−0 08	−0 06
315	10	Tu.	−16 05	−16 02	11 44	16.2	06 35	07 12	16 16	16 53	50	−0 06	−0 07	+0 07	+0 06
316	11	Wed.	−15 59	−15 55	11 44	16.2	06 36	07 13	16 14	16 51	N45	−0 17	−0 22	+0 22	+0 16
317	12	Th.	−15 52	−15 48	11 48	16.2	06 38	07 15	16 13	16 50	40	−0 26	−0 34	+0 34	+0 26
318	13	Fri.	−15 44	−15 39	11 44	16.2	06 40	07 17	16 12	16 49	35	−0 34	−0 45	+0 45	+0 34
319	14	Sat.	−15 35	−15 30	11 44	16.2	06 41	07 18	16 10	16 47	30	−0 42	−0 54	+0 54	+0 42
320	15	Sun.	−15 25	−15 20	11 45	16.2	06 43	07 20	16 09	16 46	20	−0 56	−1 10	+1 10	+0 57
321	16	Mon.	−15 15	−15 09	11 45	16.2	06 44	07 22	16 08	16 45	N10	−1 09	−1 24	+1 25	+1 10
322	17	Tu.	−15 03	−14 57	11 45	16.2	06 46	07 23	16 06	16 43	0	−1 21	−1 37	+1 38	+1 22
323	18	Wed.	−14 51	−14 45	11 45	16.2	06 47	07 25	16 05	16 42	S10	−1 36	−1 50	+1 51	+1 35
324	19	Th.	−14 38	−14 31	11 45	16.2	06 49	07 27	16 04	16 41	20	−1 52	−2 05	+2 06	+1 51
325	20	Fri.	−14 24	−14 17	11 46	16.2	06 50	07 28	16 02	16 40	30	−2 10	−2 21	+2 23	+2 10
326	21	Sat.	−14 10	−14 02	11 46	16.2	06 52	07 30	16 01	16 39	S35	−2 22	−2 31	+2 33	+2 22
327	22	Sun.	−13 54	−13 46	11 46	16.2	06 54	07 32	16 00	16 39	40	−2 36	−2 42	+2 44	+2 36
328	23	Mon.	−13 38	−13 29	11 47	16.2	06 55	07 33	15 59	16 38	45	−2 52	−2 55	+2 57	+2 53
329	24	Tu.	−13 21	−13 12	11 47	16.2	06 57	07 35	15 58	16 37	S50	−3 14	−3 12	+3 13	+3 13
330	25	Wed.	−13 03	−12 54	11 47	16.2	06 58	07 37	15 57	16 36					
331	26	Th.	−12 44	−12 35	11 47	16.2	07 00	07 38	15 56	16 35					
332	27	Fri.	−12 25	−12 15	11 48	16.2	07 01	07 40	15 55	16 34					
333	28	Sat.	−12 05	−11 54	11 48	16.2	07 02	07 42	15 55	16 34					
334	29	Sun.	−11 44	−11 33	11 48	16.2	07 04	07 43	15 54	16 33					
335	30	Mon.	−11 23	−11 12	11 49	16.2	07 05	07 45	15 53	16 32					

NOTES

The Lat. Corr. to sunrise, sunset, etc., is for the middle of November. Examples on the use of the above data are given on page 2:11 onwards.

Equation of Time is the excess of Mean Time over Apparent Time (See explanation and examples on p. 2:15)

☾ MOON ☽

DATE Day of			Age days	Transit Diff. (Upper)		Semi-diam.	Hor. Par. 12 h.	Lat. 52°N.		MOON'S PHASES
Yr.	Mth.	Week						Moonrise	Moonset	
				h. m.	m.	'	'	h. m.	h. m.	
306	1	Sun.	07	17 31	44	14.9	54.7	12 55	22 14	
307	2	Mon.	08	18 15	42	14.8	54.4	13 17	23 22	
308	3	Tu.	09	18 57	41	14.8	54.2	13 36	– –	
309	4	Wed.	10	19 38	41	14.8	54.2	13 53	00 29	
310	5	Th.	11	20 19	42	14.8	54.4	14 09	01 35	
311	6	Fri.	12	21 01	44	14.9	54.7	14 25	02 43	
312	7	Sat.	13	21 45	46	15.0	55.1	14 43	03 51	
313	8	Sun.	14	22 31	49	15.2	55.6	15 03	05 01	
314	9	Mon.	15	23 20	52	15.3	56.2	15 28	06 13	
315	10	Tu.	16	24 12	–	15.5	56.7	16 00	07 25	
316	11	Wed.	17	00 12	56	15.6	57.3	16 41	08 35	
317	12	Th.	18	01 08	57	15.7	57.8	17 33	09 39	
318	13	Fri.	19	02 05	57	15.9	58.2	18 40	10 33	
319	14	Sat.	20	03 02	57	16.0	58.5	19 51	11 17	
320	15	Sun.	21	03 59	54	16.0	58.8	21 10	11 51	
321	16	Mon.	22	04 53	52	16.1	59.1	22 31	12 19	
322	17	Tu.	23	05 45	51	16.1	59.2	23 52	12 42	
323	18	Wed.	24	06 36	50	16.2	59.3	– –	13 03	
324	19	Th.	25	07 26	50	16.2	59.3	01 14	13 22	
325	20	Fri.	26	08 16	51	16.1	59.2	02 35	13 43	
326	21	Sat.	27	09 07	53	16.1	59.0	03 57	14 06	
327	22	Sun.	28	10 00	55	16.0	58.6	05 18	14 33	
328	23	Mon.	29	10 55	56	15.9	58.2	06 37	15 07	
329	24	Tu.	00	11 51	56	15.7	57.6	07 50	15 50	
330	25	Wed.	01	12 47	55	15.5	57.0	08 53	16 42	
331	26	Th.	02	13 42	52	15.3	56.3	09 44	17 43	
332	27	Fri.	03	14 34	49	15.2	55.7	10 24	18 49	
333	28	Sat.	04	15 23	45	15.0	55.1	10 55	19 58	
334	29	Sun.	05	16 08	44	14.9	54.7	11 20	21 06	
335	30	Mon.	06	16 52	41	14.8	54.4	11 40	22 14	

MOON'S PHASES

	d.	h.	m.
☽ First Quarter...........	2	09	11
○ Full Moon..............	10	09	20
☾ Last Quarter..........	17	11	39
● New Moon	24	09	11

	d.	h.
Apogee	3	23
Perigee	19	00

NOTES

Moon's G.H.A. and Dec. are given on page 3:75.
A table for correcting Moonrise and Moonset for latitude is on page 4:20.
A table for correcting Moon's meridian passage (transit) for longitude is given on page 4:19.
Examples on the use of the above data are given on page 2:11 onwards.

0h. = midnight. For explanation of use of above data see page 2:11 onwards.

No.	Name	Mag.	Transit (approx.)	DEC.	G.H.A.	R.A.	S.H.A.
			h. m.	° ′	° ′	h. m.	° ′
♈	ARIES	–	21 14	–	40 32.0	–	–
1	Alpheratz	2.2	21 22	N29 03.4	38 31.2	0 08	357 59.2
2	Ankaa	2.4	21 40	S42 20.7	34 02.5	0 26	353 30.5
3	Schedar.........	2.5	21 54	N56 30.2	30 29.8	0 40	349 57.8
4	Diphda	2.2	21 58	S18 01.4	29 43.0	0 43	349 11.0
5	Achernar	0.6	22 52	S57 16.4	16 09.6	1 37	335 37.6
6	POLARIS	2.1	23 40	N89 14.1	4 00.5	2 26	323 28.5
7	Hamal	2.2	23 21	N23 25.9	8 49.8	2 07	328 17.8
8	Acamar	3.1	00 16	S40 19.9	356 01.5	2 58	315 29.5
9	Menkar	2.8	00 20	N 4 03.9	355 02.8	3 02	314 30.8
10	Mirfak	1.9	00 42	N49 50.3	349 34.0	3 24	309 02.0
11	Aldebaran......	1.1	01 53	N16 29.8	331 38.7	4 36	291 06.7
12	Rigel	0.3	02 32	S 8 12.5	321 58.5	5 14	281 26.5
13	Capella	0.2	02 34	N45 59.4	321 28.8	5 16	280 56.8
14	Bellatrix	1.7	02 42	N 6 20.7	319 20.2	5 25	278 48.2
15	Elnath	1.8	02 43	N28 36.1	319 03.7	5 26	278 31.7
16	Alnilam	1.8	02 53	S 1 12.3	316 33.7	5 36	276 01.7
17	Betelgeuse ...	{ 0.1 / 1.2 }	03 12	N 7 24.4	311 49.7	5 55	271 17.7
18	Canopus	–0.9	03 41	S52 41.3	304 34.5	6 24	264 02.5
19	Sirius	–1.6	04 02	S16 42.3	299 19.0	6 45	258 47.0
20	Adhara	1.6	04 16	S28 57.6	295 56.4	6 58	255 24.4
21	Castor	1.6	04 51	N31 54.1	286 59.3	7 34	246 27.3
22	Procyon.........	0.5	04 56	N 5 14.6	285 47.6	7 39	245 15.6
23	Pollux	1.2	05 02	N28 02.5	284 18.3	7 45	243 46.3
24	Avior	1.7	05 39	S59 29.0	274 56.1	8 22	234 24.1
25	Suhail	2.2	06 25	S43 24.0	263 35.7	9 08	223 03.7
26	Miaplacidus ...	1.8	06 30	S69 41.0	262 14.9	9 13	221 42.9
27	Alphard.........	2.2	06 44	S 8 37.6	258 43.2	9 27	218 11.2
28	Regulus	1.3	07 25	N12 00.0	248 31.9	10 08	207 59.9
29	Dubhe	2.0	08 20	N61 47.0	234 42.6	11 03	194 10.6
30	Denebola	2.2	09 05	N14 36.6	223 21.5	11 49	182 49.5
31	Gienah	2.8	09 32	S17 30.1	216 40.4	12 15	176 08.4
32	Acrux	1.1	09 42	S63 03.4	213 59.1	12 26	173 27.1
33	Gacrux	1.6	09 47	S57 04.2	212 50.6	12 31	172 18.6
34	Mimosa.........	1.5	10 04	S59 38.8	208 42.6	12 47	168 10.6
35	Alioth............	1.7	10 10	N55 59.7	207 06.5	12 54	166 34.5
36	Spica	1.2	10 41	S11 07.4	199 19.8	13 25	158 47.8
37	Alkaid	1.9	11 03	N49 20.8	193 43.4	13 47	153 11.4
38	Hadar............	0.9	11 19	S60 20.3	189 42.5	14 03	149 10.5
39	Menkent	2.3	11 22	S36 20.0	188 58.2	14 06	148 26.2
40	Arcturus	0.2	11 31	N19 13.1	186 42.1	14 15	146 10.1
41	Rigil Kent .	0.1	11 55	S60 48.3	180 45.5	14 39	140 13.5
42	Zuben'ubi......	2.9	12 06	S16 00.7	177 54.8	14 50	137 22.8
43	Kochab	2.2	12 07	N74 11.0	177 52.5	14 51	137 20.5
44	Alphecca	2.3	12 50	N26 44.3	166 56.4	15 34	126 24.4
45	Antares.........	1.2	13 45	S26 25.0	153 17.5	16 29	112 45.5
46	Atria	1.9	14 03	S69 01.0	148 33.8	16 48	108 01.8
47	Sabik	2.6	14 25	S15 42.9	143 02.5	17 10	102 30.5
48	Shaula	1.7	14 49	S37 06.0	137 15.2	17 33	96 43.2
49	Rasalhague ...	2.1	14 50	N12 34.0	136 53.0	17 35	96 21.0
50	Eltanin	2.4	15 12	N51 29.6	131 25.7	17 56	90 53.7
51	Kaus Aust. ...	2.0	15 39	S34 23.3	124 36.5	18 24	84 04.5
52	Vega	0.1	15 52	N38 46.8	121 21.7	18 37	80 49.7
53	Nunki	2.1	16 10	S26 18.4	116 49.6	18 55	76 17.6
54	Altair............	0.9	17 05	N 8 51.1	102 55.4	19 50	62 23.4
55	Peacock.........	2.1	17 40	S56 45.6	94 15.5	20 25	53 43.5
56	Deneb	1.3	17 56	N45 15.7	90 14.1	20 41	49 42.1
57	Enif	2.5	18 59	N 9 50.8	74 34.2	21 44	34 02.2
58	Al Na'ir	2.2	19 22	S46 59.8	68 34.9	22 08	28 02.9
59	Fomalhaut ...	1.3	20 12	S29 39.6	56 12.8	22 57	15 40.8
60	Markab	2.6	20 19	N15 10.3	54 25.6	23 04	13 53.6

Stars Transit Correction Table

D. of Mth.	Corr (Sub.)	D. of Mth.	Corr. (Sub.)
	h. m.		h. m.
1	–0 00	17	–1 03
2	–0 04	18	–1 07
3	–0 08	19	–1 11
4	–0 12	20	–1 15
5	–0 16	21	–1 19
6	–0 20	22	–1 23
7	–0 24	23	–1 27
8	–0 28	24	–1 30
9	–0 31	25	–1 34
10	–0 35	26	–1 38
11	–0 39	27	–1 42
12	–0 43	28	–1 46
13	–0 47	29	–1 50
14	–0 51	30	–1 54
15	–0 55		
16	–0 59		

STAR'S TRANSIT

To find the approx. time of Transit of a Star for any day of the month use above table.

If the quantity taken from the table is greater than the time of Transit for the first of the month, add 23h. 56min. to the time of transit before subtracting the correction below.

Example: Required the time of Transit of Aldebaran (No 11) on November 17th.

	h.min.
Transit on the 1st	01 53
Corr. for the 17th	–01 03
Transit on the 17th	00 50

d. h. NOVEMBER DIARY

2 09 First Quarter
2 16 Saturn 5°S of Moon
3 23 Moon at apogee
4 21 Mars 5°S of Pollux
10 09 Full Moon
11 14 Mercury stationary
15 12 Mars 5°N of Moon
17 12 Last Quarter
19 00 Moon at perigee
20 16 Jupiter 7°N of Moon
21 22 Mercury in inferior
   conjunction
24 09 New Moon
27 21 Venus 5°S of Moon
29 16 Mars stationary
30 03 Saturn 5°S of Moon

STAR TIME

The best time to take Star observations is shown in the a.m. and p.m. TWILIGHT columns on the opposite page – corrected for Latitude.

For **Lighting-up Time** (ashore) add 30 mins to Sunset Times.

For Star's G.H.A. Correction Table, see page 4:8.

For Alphabetical List of Stars with Constellation names, see page 2:24.

For Examples on the use of the above data, see page 2:11.

For full directions for finding the above 60 Stars, see p. 2:20 onwards. For Special Pole Star tables see pages 5:17-5:19.

Sunday, 1st November

G.M.T. (h)	SUN G.H.A.	Dec.	ARIES G.H.A.
00	184 05.7	S14 26.4	40 32.0
02	214 05.8	14 28.0	70 36.9
04	244 05.8	14 29.6	100 41.8
06	274 05.8	14 31.2	130 46.8
08	304 05.8	14 32.8	160 51.7
10	334 05.9	14 34.4	190 56.6
12	4 05.9	14 36.0	221 01.5
14	34 05.9	14 37.6	251 06.5
16	64 05.9	14 39.2	281 11.4
18	94 06.0	14 40.8	311 16.3
20	124 06.0	14 42.4	341 21.3
22	154 06.0	S14 43.9	11 26.2

Monday, 2nd November

G.M.T. (h)	SUN G.H.A.	Dec.	ARIES G.H.A.
00	184 06.0	S14 45.5	41 31.1
02	214 06.0	14 47.1	71 36.0
04	244 06.1	14 48.7	101 41.0
06	274 06.1	14 50.3	131 45.9
08	304 06.1	14 51.8	161 50.8
10	334 06.1	14 53.4	191 55.8
12	4 06.1	14 55.0	222 00.7
14	34 06.1	14 56.5	252 05.6
16	64 06.1	14 58.1	282 10.5
18	94 06.1	14 59.7	312 15.5
20	124 06.1	15 01.2	342 20.4
22	154 06.1	S15 02.8	12 25.3

Tuesday, 3rd November

G.M.T. (h)	SUN G.H.A.	Dec.	ARIES G.H.A.
00	184 06.1	S15 04.4	42 30.3
02	214 06.1	15 05.9	72 35.2
04	244 06.1	15 07.5	102 40.1
06	274 06.1	15 09.1	132 45.0
08	304 06.1	15 10.6	162 50.0
10	334 06.1	15 12.2	192 54.9
12	4 06.1	15 13.7	222 59.8
14	34 06.1	15 15.3	253 04.8
16	64 06.1	15 16.8	283 09.7
18	94 06.1	15 18.4	313 14.6
20	124 06.1	15 19.9	343 19.5
22	154 06.0	S15 21.4	13 24.5

Wednesday, 4th November

G.M.T. (h)	SUN G.H.A.	Dec.	ARIES G.H.A.
00	184 06.0	S15 23.0	43 29.4
02	214 06.0	15 24.5	73 34.3
04	244 06.0	15 26.1	103 39.2
06	274 06.0	15 27.6	133 44.2
08	304 06.0	15 29.1	163 49.1
10	334 05.9	15 30.7	193 54.0
12	4 05.9	15 32.2	223 59.0
14	34 05.9	15 33.7	254 03.9
16	64 05.9	15 35.3	284 08.8
18	94 05.8	15 36.8	314 13.7
20	124 05.8	15 38.3	344 18.7
22	154 05.8	S15 39.8	14 23.6

Thursday, 5th November

G.M.T. (h)	SUN G.H.A.	Dec.	ARIES G.H.A.
00	184 05.7	S15 41.3	44 28.5
02	214 05.7	15 42.9	74 33.5
04	244 05.7	15 44.4	104 38.4
06	274 05.6	15 45.9	134 43.3
08	304 05.6	15 47.4	164 48.2
10	334 05.6	15 48.9	194 53.2
12	4 05.5	15 50.4	224 58.1
14	34 05.5	15 51.9	255 03.0
16	64 05.4	15 53.4	285 08.0
18	94 05.4	15 54.9	315 12.9
20	124 05.3	15 56.4	345 17.8
22	154 05.3	S15 57.9	15 22.7

Friday, 6th November

G.M.T. (h)	SUN G.H.A.	Dec.	ARIES G.H.A.
00	184 05.2	S15 59.4	45 27.7
02	214 05.2	16 00.9	75 32.6
04	244 05.1	16 02.4	105 37.5
06	274 05.1	16 03.9	135 42.5
08	304 05.0	16 05.4	165 47.4
10	334 05.0	16 06.9	195 52.3
12	4 04.9	16 08.4	225 57.2
14	34 04.9	16 09.9	256 02.2
16	64 04.8	16 11.4	286 07.1
18	94 04.7	16 12.8	316 12.0
20	124 04.7	16 14.3	346 17.0
22	154 04.6	S16 15.8	16 21.9

Saturday, 7th November

G.M.T. (h)	SUN G.H.A.	Dec.	ARIES G.H.A.
00	184 04.5	S16 17.3	46 26.8
02	214 04.5	16 18.7	76 31.7
04	244 04.4	16 20.2	106 36.7
06	274 04.3	16 21.7	136 41.6
08	304 04.3	16 23.2	166 46.5
10	334 04.2	16 24.6	196 51.4
12	4 04.1	16 26.1	226 56.4
14	34 04.0	16 27.5	257 01.3
16	64 04.0	16 29.0	287 06.2
18	94 03.9	16 30.5	317 11.2
20	124 03.8	16 31.9	347 16.1
22	154 03.7	S16 33.4	17 21.0

Sunday, 8th November

G.M.T. (h)	SUN G.H.A.	Dec.	ARIES G.H.A.
00	184 03.6	S16 34.8	47 25.9
02	214 03.5	16 36.3	77 30.9
04	244 03.5	16 37.7	107 35.8
06	274 03.4	16 39.2	137 40.7
08	304 03.3	16 40.6	167 45.7
10	334 03.2	16 42.1	197 50.6
12	4 03.1	16 43.5	227 55.5
14	34 03.0	16 44.9	258 00.4
16	64 02.9	16 46.4	288 05.4
18	94 02.8	16 47.8	318 10.3
20	124 02.7	16 49.2	348 15.2
22	154 02.6	S16 50.7	18 20.2

Monday, 9th November

G.M.T. (h)	SUN G.H.A.	Dec.	ARIES G.H.A.
00	184 02.5	S16 52.1	48 25.1
02	214 02.4	16 53.5	78 30.0
04	244 02.3	16 55.0	108 34.9
06	274 02.2	16 56.4	138 39.9
08	304 02.1	16 57.8	168 44.8
10	334 02.0	16 59.2	198 49.7
12	4 01.9	17 00.6	228 54.7
14	34 01.7	17 02.1	258 59.6
16	64 01.6	17 03.5	289 04.5
18	94 01.5	17 04.9	319 09.4
20	124 01.4	17 06.3	349 14.4
22	154 01.3	S17 07.7	19 19.3

Tuesday, 10th November

G.M.T. (h)	SUN G.H.A.	Dec.	ARIES G.H.A.
00	184 01.2	S17 09.1	49 24.2
02	214 01.0	17 10.5	79 29.2
04	244 00.9	17 11.9	109 34.1
06	274 00.8	17 13.3	139 39.0
08	304 00.7	17 14.7	169 43.9
10	334 00.5	17 16.1	199 48.9
12	4 00.4	17 17.5	229 53.8
14	34 00.3	17 18.9	259 58.7
16	64 00.2	17 20.3	290 03.7
18	94 00.0	17 21.7	320 08.6
20	123 59.9	17 23.0	350 13.5
22	153 59.8	S17 24.4	20 18.4

Wednesday, 11th November

G.M.T. (h)	SUN G.H.A.	Dec.	ARIES G.H.A.
00	183 59.6	S17 25.8	50 23.4
02	213 59.5	17 27.2	80 28.3
04	243 59.3	17 28.6	110 33.2
06	273 59.2	17 29.9	140 38.1
08	303 59.1	17 31.3	170 43.1
10	333 58.9	17 32.7	200 48.0
12	3 58.8	17 34.0	230 52.9
14	33 58.6	17 35.4	260 57.9
16	63 58.5	17 36.8	291 02.8
18	93 58.3	17 38.1	321 07.7
20	123 58.2	17 39.5	351 12.6
22	153 58.0	S17 40.8	21 17.6

Thursday, 12th November

G.M.T. (h)	SUN G.H.A.	Dec.	ARIES G.H.A.
00	183 57.9	S17 42.2	51 22.5
02	213 57.7	17 43.6	81 27.4
04	243 57.5	17 44.9	111 32.4
06	273 57.4	17 46.3	141 37.3
08	303 57.2	17 47.6	171 42.2
10	333 57.1	17 48.9	201 47.1
12	3 56.9	17 50.3	231 52.1
14	33 56.7	17 51.6	261 57.0
16	63 56.6	17 53.0	292 01.9
18	93 56.4	17 54.3	322 06.9
20	123 56.2	17 55.6	352 11.8
22	153 56.0	S17 57.0	22 16.7

Friday, 13th November

G.M.T. (h)	SUN G.H.A.	Dec.	ARIES G.H.A.
00	183 55.9	S17 58.3	52 21.6
02	213 55.7	17 59.6	82 26.6
04	243 55.5	18 00.9	112 31.5
06	273 55.3	18 02.3	142 36.4
08	303 55.2	18 03.6	172 41.4
10	333 55.0	18 04.9	202 46.3
12	3 54.8	18 06.2	232 51.2
14	33 54.6	18 07.5	262 56.1
16	63 54.4	18 08.8	293 01.1
18	93 54.2	18 10.2	323 06.0
20	123 54.1	18 11.5	353 10.9
22	153 53.9	S18 12.8	23 15.9

Saturday, 14th November

G.M.T. (h)	SUN G.H.A.	Dec.	ARIES G.H.A.
00	183 53.7	S18 14.1	53 20.8
02	213 53.5	18 15.4	83 25.7
04	243 53.3	18 16.7	113 30.6
06	273 53.1	18 18.0	143 35.6
08	303 52.9	18 19.3	173 40.5
10	333 52.8	18 20.6	203 45.4
12	3 52.5	18 21.8	233 50.4
14	33 52.3	18 23.1	263 55.3
16	63 52.1	18 24.4	294 00.2
18	93 51.9	18 25.7	324 05.1
20	123 51.7	18 27.0	354 10.1
22	153 51.5	S18 28.3	24 15.0

Sunday, 15th November

G.M.T. (h)	SUN G.H.A.	Dec.	ARIES G.H.A.
00	183 51.3	S18 29.5	54 19.9
02	213 51.0	18 30.8	84 24.8
04	243 50.8	18 32.1	114 29.8
06	273 50.6	18 33.3	144 34.7
08	303 50.4	18 34.6	174 39.6
10	333 50.2	18 35.9	204 44.6
12	3 50.0	18 37.1	234 49.5
14	33 49.8	18 38.4	264 54.4
16	63 49.5	18 39.7	294 59.3
18	93 49.3	18 40.9	325 04.3
20	123 49.1	18 42.2	355 09.2
22	153 48.9	S18 43.4	25 14.1

To interpolate **SUN** G.H.A. see page 4:7   To interpolate **ARIES** G.H.A. see page 4:8

Monday, 16th November

G.M.T. (h)	SUN G.H.A.	SUN Dec.	ARIES G.H.A.	h
00	183 48.6	S18 44.7	55 19.1	00
02	213 48.4	18 45.9	85 24.0	02
04	243 48.2	18 47.2	115 28.9	04
06	273 47.9	18 48.4	145 33.8	06
08	303 47.7	18 49.6	175 38.8	08
10	333 47.5	18 50.9	205 43.7	10
12	3 47.2	18 52.1	235 48.6	12
14	33 47.0	18 53.3	265 53.6	14
16	63 46.8	18 54.6	295 58.5	16
18	93 46.5	18 55.8	326 03.4	18
20	123 46.3	18 57.0	356 08.3	20
22	153 46.0	S18 58.3	26 13.3	22

Tuesday, 17th November

G.M.T. (h)	SUN G.H.A.	SUN Dec.	ARIES G.H.A.	h
00	183 45.8	S18 59.5	56 18.2	00
02	213 45.5	19 00.7	86 23.1	02
04	243 45.3	19 01.9	116 28.1	04
06	273 45.0	19 03.1	146 33.0	06
08	303 44.8	19 04.3	176 37.9	08
10	333 44.6	19 05.5	206 42.8	10
12	3 44.3	19 06.7	236 47.8	12
14	33 44.0	19 08.0	266 52.7	14
16	63 43.8	19 09.2	296 57.6	16
18	93 43.5	19 10.4	327 02.6	18
20	123 43.3	19 11.5	357 07.5	20
22	153 43.0	S19 12.7	27 12.4	22

Wednesday, 18th November

G.M.T. (h)	SUN G.H.A.	SUN Dec.	ARIES G.H.A.	h
00	183 42.7	S19 13.9	57 17.3	00
02	213 42.5	19 15.1	87 22.3	02
04	243 42.2	19 16.3	117 27.2	04
06	273 41.9	19 17.5	147 32.1	06
08	303 41.7	19 18.7	177 37.1	08
10	333 41.4	19 19.9	207 42.0	10
12	3 41.1	19 21.0	237 46.9	12
14	33 40.9	19 22.2	267 51.8	14
16	63 40.6	19 23.4	297 56.8	16
18	93 40.3	19 24.6	328 01.7	18
20	123 40.0	19 25.7	358 06.6	20
22	153 39.7	S19 26.9	28 11.5	22

Thursday, 19th November

G.M.T. (h)	SUN G.H.A.	SUN Dec.	ARIES G.H.A.	h
00	183 39.5	S19 28.1	58 16.5	00
02	213 39.2	19 29.2	88 21.4	02
04	243 38.9	19 30.4	118 26.3	04
06	273 38.6	19 31.5	148 31.3	06
08	303 38.3	19 32.7	178 36.2	08
10	333 38.0	19 33.8	208 41.1	10
12	3 37.8	19 35.0	238 46.0	12
14	33 37.5	19 36.1	268 51.0	14
16	63 37.2	19 37.3	298 55.9	16
18	93 36.9	19 38.4	329 00.8	18
20	123 36.6	19 39.6	359 05.8	20
22	153 36.3	S19 40.7	29 10.7	22

Friday, 20th November

G.M.T. (h)	SUN G.H.A.	SUN Dec.	ARIES G.H.A.	h
00	183 36.0	S19 41.8	59 15.6	00
02	213 35.7	19 43.0	89 20.5	02
04	243 35.4	19 44.1	119 25.5	04
06	273 35.1	19 45.2	149 30.4	06
08	303 34.8	19 46.3	179 35.3	08
10	333 34.5	19 47.5	209 40.3	10
12	3 34.2	19 48.6	239 45.2	12
14	33 33.9	19 49.7	269 50.1	14
16	63 33.6	19 50.8	299 55.0	16
18	93 33.3	19 51.9	330 00.0	18
20	123 32.9	19 53.0	0 04.9	20
22	153 32.6	S19 54.1	30 09.8	22

Saturday, 21st November

G.M.T. (h)	SUN G.H.A.	SUN Dec.	ARIES G.H.A.	h
00	183 32.3	S19 55.2	60 14.8	00
02	213 32.0	19 56.3	90 19.7	02
04	243 31.7	19 57.4	120 24.6	04
06	273 31.4	19 58.5	150 29.5	06
08	303 31.0	19 59.6	180 34.5	08
10	333 30.7	20 00.7	210 39.4	10
12	3 30.4	20 01.8	240 44.3	12
14	33 30.1	20 02.9	270 49.3	14
16	63 29.7	20 04.0	300 54.2	16
18	93 29.4	20 05.1	330 59.1	18
20	123 29.1	20 06.1	1 04.0	20
22	153 28.8	S20 07.2	31 09.0	22

Sunday, 22nd November

G.M.T. (h)	SUN G.H.A.	SUN Dec.	ARIES G.H.A.	h
00	183 28.4	S20 08.3	61 13.9	00
02	213 28.1	20 09.4	91 18.8	02
04	243 27.8	20 10.4	121 23.7	04
06	273 27.4	20 11.5	151 28.7	06
08	303 27.1	20 12.6	181 33.6	08
10	333 26.8	20 13.6	211 38.5	10
12	3 26.4	20 14.7	241 43.5	12
14	33 26.1	20 15.7	271 48.4	14
16	63 25.7	20 16.8	301 53.3	16
18	93 25.4	20 17.8	331 58.2	18
20	123 25.0	20 18.9	2 03.2	20
22	153 24.7	S20 19.9	32 08.1	22

Monday, 23rd November

G.M.T. (h)	SUN G.H.A.	SUN Dec.	ARIES G.H.A.	h
00	183 24.3	S20 21.0	62 13.0	00
02	213 24.0	20 22.0	92 18.0	02
04	243 23.6	20 23.0	122 22.9	04
06	273 23.3	20 24.1	152 27.8	06
08	303 22.9	20 25.1	182 32.7	08
10	333 22.6	20 26.1	212 37.7	10
12	3 22.2	20 27.2	242 42.6	12
14	33 21.9	20 28.2	272 47.5	14
16	63 21.5	20 29.2	302 52.5	16
18	93 21.2	20 30.2	332 57.4	18
20	123 20.8	20 31.2	3 02.3	20
22	153 20.4	S20 32.3	33 07.2	22

Tuesday, 24th November

G.M.T. (h)	SUN G.H.A.	SUN Dec.	ARIES G.H.A.	h
00	183 20.1	S20 33.3	63 12.2	00
02	213 19.7	20 34.3	93 17.1	02
04	243 19.3	20 35.3	123 22.0	04
06	273 19.0	20 36.3	153 27.0	06
08	303 18.6	20 37.3	183 31.9	08
10	333 18.2	20 38.3	213 36.8	10
12	3 17.9	20 39.3	243 41.7	12
14	33 17.5	20 40.3	273 46.7	14
16	63 17.1	20 41.3	303 51.6	16
18	93 16.7	20 42.2	333 56.5	18
20	123 16.4	20 43.2	4 01.5	20
22	153 16.0	S20 44.2	34 06.4	22

Wednesday, 25th November

G.M.T. (h)	SUN G.H.A.	SUN Dec.	ARIES G.H.A.	h
00	183 15.6	S20 45.2	64 11.3	00
02	213 15.2	20 46.2	94 16.2	02
04	243 14.8	20 47.1	124 21.2	04
06	273 14.5	20 48.1	154 26.1	06
08	303 14.1	20 49.1	184 31.0	08
10	333 13.7	20 50.0	214 36.0	10
12	3 13.3	20 51.0	244 40.9	12
14	33 12.9	20 52.0	274 45.8	14
16	63 12.5	20 52.9	304 50.7	16
18	93 12.1	20 53.9	334 55.7	18
20	123 11.7	20 54.8	5 00.6	20
22	153 11.3	S20 55.8	35 05.5	22

Thursday, 26th November

G.M.T. (h)	SUN G.H.A.	SUN Dec.	ARIES G.H.A.	h
00	183 10.9	S20 56.7	65 10.4	00
02	213 10.5	20 57.7	95 15.4	02
04	243 10.1	20 58.6	125 20.3	04
06	273 09.7	20 59.6	155 25.2	06
08	303 09.3	21 00.5	185 30.2	08
10	333 08.9	21 01.4	215 35.1	10
12	3 08.5	21 02.4	245 40.0	12
14	33 08.1	21 03.3	275 44.9	14
16	63 07.7	21 04.2	305 49.9	16
18	93 07.3	21 05.1	335 54.8	18
20	123 06.9	21 06.0	5 59.7	20
22	153 06.5	S21 07.0	36 04.7	22

Friday, 27th November

G.M.T. (h)	SUN G.H.A.	SUN Dec.	ARIES G.H.A.	h
00	183 06.1	S21 07.9	66 09.6	00
02	213 05.7	21 08.8	96 14.5	02
04	243 05.3	21 09.7	126 19.4	04
06	273 04.9	21 10.6	156 24.4	06
08	303 04.4	21 11.5	186 29.3	08
10	333 04.0	21 12.4	216 34.2	10
12	3 03.6	21 13.3	246 39.2	12
14	33 03.2	21 14.2	276 44.1	14
16	63 02.8	21 15.1	306 49.0	16
18	93 02.4	21 16.0	336 53.9	18
20	123 01.9	21 16.9	6 58.9	20
22	153 01.5	S21 17.7	37 03.8	22

Saturday, 28th November

G.M.T. (h)	SUN G.H.A.	SUN Dec.	ARIES G.H.A.	h
00	183 01.1	S21 18.6	67 08.7	00
02	213 00.7	21 19.5	97 13.7	02
04	243 00.2	21 20.4	127 18.6	04
06	272 59.8	21 21.3	157 23.5	06
08	302 59.4	21 22.1	187 28.4	08
10	332 58.9	21 23.0	217 33.4	10
12	2 58.5	21 23.9	247 38.3	12
14	32 58.1	21 24.7	277 43.2	14
16	62 57.6	21 25.6	307 48.2	16
18	92 57.2	21 26.4	337 53.1	18
20	122 56.8	21 27.3	7 58.0	20
22	152 56.3	S21 28.1	38 02.9	22

Sunday, 29th November

G.M.T. (h)	SUN G.H.A.	SUN Dec.	ARIES G.H.A.	h
00	182 55.9	S21 29.0	68 07.9	00
02	212 55.5	21 29.8	98 12.8	02
04	242 55.0	21 30.7	128 17.7	04
06	272 54.6	21 31.5	158 22.7	06
08	302 54.1	21 32.3	188 27.6	08
10	332 53.7	21 33.2	218 32.5	10
12	2 53.2	21 34.0	248 37.4	12
14	32 52.8	21 34.8	278 42.4	14
16	62 52.3	21 35.6	308 47.3	16
18	92 51.9	21 36.5	338 52.2	18
20	122 51.4	21 37.3	8 57.1	20
22	152 51.0	S21 38.1	39 02.1	22

Monday, 30th November

G.M.T. (h)	SUN G.H.A.	SUN Dec.	ARIES G.H.A.	h
00	182 50.5	S21 38.9	69 07.0	00
02	212 50.1	21 39.7	99 11.9	02
04	242 49.6	21 40.5	129 16.9	04
06	272 49.2	21 41.3	159 21.8	06
08	302 48.7	21 42.1	189 26.7	08
10	332 48.3	21 42.9	219 31.6	10
12	2 47.8	21 43.7	249 36.6	12
14	32 47.3	21 44.5	279 41.5	14
16	62 46.9	21 45.3	309 46.4	16
18	92 46.4	21 46.1	339 51.4	18
20	122 45.9	21 46.9	9 56.3	20
22	152 45.4	S21 47.7	40 01.2	22

To interpolate SUN G.H.A. see page 4:7   To interpolate ARIES G.H.A. see page 4:8

♀ VENUS ♀ — ♃ JUPITER ♃

Mer. Pass. (h. m.)	G.H.A. (°)	Mean Var. 14° (')	Dec. (°)	Mean Var. (')	M	Day of Week	G.H.A (°)	Mean Var. 15° (')	Dec. (°)	Mean Var. (')	Mer. Pass (h. m.)
14 12	147 08.4	59.2	S24 08.5	0.4	1	SUN.	216 03.9	2.0	S 0 43.2	0.2	09 34
14 14	146 48.7	59.2	S24 18.9	0.4	2	Mon.	216 52.2	2.0	S 0 47.7	0.2	09 31
14 15	146 28.9	59.2	S24 28.6	0.4	3	Tu.	217 40.6	2.0	S 0 52.3	0.2	09 28
14 16	146 08.8	59.2	S24 37.6	0.4	4	Wed.	218 29.0	2.0	S 0 56.7	0.2	09 25
14 18	145 48.7	59.2	S24 46.0	0.3	5	Th.	219 17.5	2.0	S 1 01.2	0.2	09 22
14 19	145 28.4	59.1	S24 53.6	0.3	6	Fri.	220 06.1	2.0	S 1 05.6	0.2	09 18
14 20	145 08.0	59.1	S25 00.5	0.3	7	Sat.	220 54.7	2.0	S 1 10.0	0.2	09 15
14 22	144 47.6	59.1	S25 06.7	0.2	8	SUN.	221 43.3	2.0	S 1 14.4	0.2	09 12
14 23	144 27.0	59.1	S25 12.2	0.2	9	Mon.	222 32.1	2.0	S 1 18.7	0.2	09 09
14 24	144 06.4	59.1	S25 16.9	0.2	10	Tu.	223 20.9	2.0	S 1 23.0	0.2	09 05
14 26	143 45.7	59.1	S25 20.9	0.1	11	Wed.	224 09.7	2.0	S 1 27.3	0.2	09 02
14 27	143 25.0	59.1	S25 24.2	0.1	12	Th.	224 58.6	2.0	S 1 31.6	0.2	08 59
14 29	143 04.3	59.1	S25 26.8	0.1	13	Fri.	225 47.6	2.0	S 1 35.8	0.2	08 56
14 30	142 43.6	59.1	S25 28.6	0.0	14	Sat.	226 36.7	2.0	S 1 39.9	0.2	08 52
14 31	142 22.9	59.1	S25 29.7	0.0	15	SUN.	227 25.8	2.1	S 1 44.1	0.2	08 49
14 33	142 02.2	59.1	S25 30.0	0.0	16	Mon.	228 15.0	2.1	S 1 48.2	0.2	08 46
14 34	141 41.6	59.1	S25 29.6	0.0	17	Tu.	229 04.3	2.1	S 1 52.3	0.2	08 43
14 35	141 21.1	59.1	S25 28.4	0.1	18	Wed.	229 53.7	2.1	S 1 56.3	0.2	08 39
14 37	141 00.6	59.2	S25 26.5	0.1	19	Th.	230 43.1	2.1	S 2 00.3	0.2	08 36
14 38	140 40.3	59.2	S25 23.9	0.1	20	Fri.	231 32.6	2.1	S 2 04.2	0.2	08 33
14 39	140 20.1	59.2	S25 20.6	0.2	21	Sat.	232 22.2	2.1	S 2 08.2	0.2	08 29
14 41	140 00.1	59.2	S25 16.5	0.2	22	SUN.	233 11.9	2.1	S 2 12.0	0.2	08 26
14 42	139 40.2	59.2	S25 11.7	0.2	23	Mon.	234 01.6	2.1	S 2 15.9	0.2	08 23
14 43	139 20.5	59.2	S25 06.1	0.3	24	Tu.	234 51.4	2.1	S 2 19.7	0.2	08 19
14 45	139 00.9	59.2	S24 59.9	0.3	25	Wed.	235 41.4	2.1	S 2 23.4	0.2	08 16
14 46	138 41.6	59.2	S24 52.9	0.3	26	Th.	236 31.4	2.1	S 2 27.1	0.2	08 13
14 47	138 22.6	59.2	S24 45.3	0.4	27	Fri.	237 21.5	2.1	S 2 30.8	0.1	08 09
14 49	138 03.8	59.2	S24 36.9	0.4	28	Sat.	238 11.7	2.1	S 2 34.4	0.2	08 06
14 50	137 45.2	59.2	S24 27.8	0.4	29	SUN.	239 02.0	2.1	S 2 38.0	0.2	08 03
14 51	137 26.9	59.3	S24 18.1	0.4	30	Mon.	239 52.3	2.1	S 2 41.6	0.1	07 59

♀ VENUS. Av. Mag. –4.0. An **Evening Star**. S.H.A. November 5 101°; 10 95°; 15 88°; 20 81°; 25 75°; 30 68°.

♃ JUPITER. Av. Mag. –1.8. A **Morning Star**. S.H.A. November 5 176°; 10 173°; 15 173°; 20 173°; 25 171°; 30 171°.

♂ MARS ♂ — ♄ SATURN ♄

Mer. Pass. (h. m.)	G.H.A. (°)	Mean Var. 15° (')	Dec. (°)	Mean Var. (')	M	Day of Week	G.H.A (°)	Mean Var. 15° (')	Dec. (°)	Mean Var. (')	Mer. Pass (h. m.)
04 57	285 32.5	1.6	N22 45.6	0.0	1	SUN.	85 44.0	2.4	S18 10.5	0.0	18 14
04 55	286 11.7	1.7	N22 44.6	0.0	2	Mon.	86 41.5	2.4	S18 10.0	0.0	18 10
04 52	286 51.5	1.7	N22 43.7	0.0	3	Tu.	87 38.8	2.4	S18 09.5	0.0	18 07
04 49	287 31.8	1.7	N22 42.9	0.0	4	Wed.	88 36.1	2.4	S18 08.9	0.0	18 03
04 47	288 12.7	1.7	N22 42.2	0.0	5	Th.	89 33.3	2.4	S18 08.3	0.0	17 59
04 44	288 54.1	1.8	N22 41.5	0.0	6	Fri.	90 30.3	2.4	S18 07.7	0.0	17 55
04 41	289 36.2	1.8	N22 41.0	0.0	7	Sat.	91 27.3	2.4	S18 07.1	0.0	17 51
04 38	290 18.8	1.8	N22 40.6	0.0	8	SUN.	92 24.2	2.4	S18 06.4	0.0	17 48
04 35	291 02.1	1.8	N22 40.2	0.0	9	Mon.	93 21.0	2.4	S18 05.7	0.0	17 44
04 32	291 45.9	1.9	N22 40.0	0.0	10	Tu.	94 17.6	2.4	S18 05.0	0.0	17 40
04 29	292 30.4	1.9	N22 39.9	0.0	11	Wed.	95 14.2	2.4	S18 04.2	0.0	17 36
04 26	293 15.5	1.9	N22 39.9	0.0	12	Th.	96 10.7	2.3	S18 03.5	0.0	17 33
04 23	294 01.3	1.9	N22 40.0	0.0	13	Fri.	97 07.1	2.3	S18 02.7	0.0	17 29
04 20	294 47.8	2.0	N22 40.3	0.0	14	Sat.	98 03.4	2.3	S18 01.8	0.0	17 25
04 17	295 34.9	2.0	N22 40.7	0.0	15	SUN.	98 59.6	2.3	S18 01.0	0.0	17 21
04 14	296 22.8	2.0	N22 41.2	0.0	16	Mon.	99 55.7	2.3	S18 00.1	0.0	17 18
04 11	297 11.3	2.1	N22 41.9	0.0	17	Tu.	100 51.7	2.3	S17 59.2	0.0	17 14
04 07	298 00.6	2.1	N22 42.7	0.0	18	Wed.	101 47.6	2.3	S17 58.3	0.0	17 10
04 04	298 50.7	2.1	N22 43.7	0.0	19	Th.	102 43.5	2.3	S17 57.3	0.0	17 06
04 01	299 41.4	2.1	N22 44.8	0.1	20	Fri.	103 39.2	2.3	S17 56.3	0.0	17 03
03 57	300 33.0	2.2	N22 46.1	0.1	21	Sat.	104 34.9	2.3	S17 55.3	0.0	16 59
03 54	301 25.3	2.2	N22 47.6	0.1	22	SUN.	105 30.4	2.3	S17 54.3	0.0	16 55
03 50	302 18.4	2.2	N22 49.2	0.1	23	Mon.	106 25.9	2.3	S17 53.2	0.0	16 52
03 47	303 12.3	2.3	N22 51.0	0.1	24	Tu.	107 21.3	2.3	S17 52.1	0.0	16 48
03 43	304 07.1	2.3	N22 53.0	0.1	25	Wed.	108 16.6	2.3	S17 51.0	0.0	16 44
03 39	305 02.7	2.4	N22 55.2	0.1	26	Th.	109 11.8	2.3	S17 49.9	0.1	16 41
03 35	305 59.1	2.4	N22 57.5	0.1	27	Fri.	110 07.0	2.3	S17 48.7	0.0	16 37
03 32	306 56.3	2.4	N23 00.0	0.1	28	Sat.	111 02.0	2.3	S17 47.5	0.0	16 33
03 28	307 54.4	2.5	N23 02.6	0.1	29	SUN.	111 57.0	2.3	S17 46.3	0.1	16 30
03 24	308 53.4	2.5	N23 05.5	0.1	30	Mon.	112 51.9	2.3	S17 45.1	0.1	16 26

♂ MARS. Av. Mag. -0.4. A **Morning Star**. S.H.A. November 5 244°; 10 242°; 15 241°; 20 241°; 25 239°; 30 240°.

♄ SATURN. Av. Mag. +0.7. An **Evening Star**. S.H.A. November 5 46°; 10 44°; 15 45°; 20 45°; 25 43°; 30 44°.

MERCURY. Visible low in the west after sunset until November 16. Reappears low in the east before sunrise on November 28.

For Planets Correction Tables see pages 4:9-4:13. See also 'How to Recognise the Planets' on page 2:32.
Mean Var. means Variation per Hour.

Day of M. W.	G.M.T. h	G.H.A. ° '	Mean Var. per Hour 14°,+	Dec. ° '	Mean Var. per Hour '	Day of M. W.	G.M.T. h	G.H.A. ° '	Mean Var. per Hour 14°,+	Dec. ° '	Mean Var. per Hour '
1 Sun.	0	105 33.4	31.5	S18 44.0	7.7	17 Tu.	0	276 44.0	29.0	N11 06.4	12.6
	6	192 42.7	32.0	S17 58.1	8.1		6	3 37.7	29.2	N 9 51.1	12.9
	12	279 54.4	32.4	S17 09.6	8.6		12	90 32.6	29.4	N 8 33.7	13.2
	18	7 08.5	32.8	S16 18.6	8.9		18	177 28.8	29.5	N 7 14.5	13.4
2 Mon.	0	94 24.9	33.1	S15 25.2	9.3	18 Wed.	0	264 25.9	29.7	N 5 53.8	13.7
	6	181 43.4	33.4	S14 29.6	9.6		6	351 23.9	29.8	N 4 31.9	13.8
	12	269 03.8	33.8	S13 32.1	9.9		12	78 22.4	29.8	N 3 09.1	13.9
	18	356 26.1	34.0	S12 32.7	10.2		18	165 21.4	29.8	N 1 45.6	14.0
3 Tu.	0	83 50.0	34.2	S11 31.6	10.5	19 Th.	0	252 20.6	29.8	N 0 21.7	14.0
	6	171 15.5	34.5	S10 28.9	10.7		6	339 19.7	29.8	S 1 02.3	14.0
	12	258 42.2	34.7	S 9 24.8	11.0		12	66 18.7	29.8	S 2 26.1	13.9
	18	346 10.1	34.8	S 8 19.4	11.1		18	153 17.3	29.7	S 3 49.4	13.8
4 Wed.	0	73 38.9	34.9	S 7 12.9	11.3	20 Fri.	0	240 15.2	29.6	S 5 11.9	13.6
	6	161 08.5	35.0	S 6 05.4	11.4		6	327 12.4	29.4	S 6 33.4	13.4
	12	248 38.6	35.1	S 4 57.0	11.6		12	54 08.7	29.2	S 7 53.5	13.0
	18	336 09.1	35.1	S 3 47.8	11.7		18	141 03.8	28.9	S 9 12.0	12.8
5 Th.	0	63 39.8	35.1	S 2 38.0	11.7	21 Sat.	0	227 57.8	28.7	S10 28.5	12.4
	6	151 10.5	35.0	S 1 27.7	11.7		6	314 50.3	28.5	S11 42.9	12.0
	12	238 41.0	35.0	S 0 17.1	11.8		12	41 41.4	28.2	S12 54.7	11.5
	18	326 11.0	34.9	N 0 53.8	11.8		18	128 30.9	28.0	S14 03.7	11.0
6 Fri.	0	53 40.4	34.8	N 2 04.7	11.8	22 Sun.	0	215 18.9	27.7	S15 09.7	10.4
	6	141 09.0	34.6	N 3 15.6	11.8		6	302 05.3	27.4	S16 12.4	9.8
	12	228 36.7	34.4	N 4 26.3	11.7		12	28 50.1	27.2	S17 11.4	9.1
	18	316 03.1	34.2	N 5 36.6	11.6		18	115 33.4	26.9	S18 06.7	8.5
7 Sat.	0	43 28.2	33.9	N 6 46.4	11.5	23 Mon.	0	202 15.2	26.7	S18 57.9	7.7
	6	130 51.6	33.6	N 7 55.5	11.3		6	288 55.8	26.6	S19 44.8	7.0
	12	218 13.4	33.3	N 9 03.8	11.2		12	15 35.2	26.4	S20 27.3	6.2
	18	305 33.2	33.0	N10 10.9	10.9		18	102 13.6	26.3	S21 05.1	5.4
8 Sun.	0	32 50.9	32.5	N11 16.9	10.7	24 Tu.	0	188 51.3	26.2	S21 38.2	4.7
	6	120 06.4	32.1	N12 21.3	10.4		6	275 28.5	26.2	S22 06.5	3.8
	12	207 19.5	31.7	N13 24.1	10.2		12	2 05.4	26.2	S22 29.8	3.0
	18	294 30.1	31.2	N14 25.0	9.8		18	88 42.4	26.2	S22 48.1	2.2
9 Mon.	0	21 38.1	30.8	N15 23.8	9.4	25 Wed.	0	175 19.8	26.4	S23 01.3	1.3
	6	108 43.4	30.4	N16 20.3	8.9		6	261 57.7	26.5	S23 09.6	0.5
	12	195 45.8	29.9	N17 14.2	8.4		12	348 36.2	26.7	S23 13.0	0.3
	18	282 45.4	29.4	N18 05.2	8.0		18	75 16.8	27.0	S23 11.4	1.1
10 Tu.	0	9 42.2	29.0	N18 53.2	7.4	26 Th.	0	161 58.5	27.2	S23 05.0	1.9
	6	96 36.1	28.5	N19 37.8	6.8		6	248 41.9	27.6	S22 54.0	2.7
	12	183 27.2	28.0	N20 18.9	6.1		12	335 27.3	28.0	S22 38.4	3.4
	18	270 15.6	27.6	N20 56.2	5.5		18	62 14.9	28.4	S22 18.5	4.1
11 Wed.	0	357 01.4	27.2	N21 29.5	4.8	27 Fri.	0	149 04.8	28.8	S21 54.3	4.8
	6	83 44.7	26.8	N21 58.5	4.1		6	235 57.2	29.2	S21 26.1	5.4
	12	170 25.7	26.5	N22 23.0	3.2		12	322 52.3	29.6	S20 54.1	5.9
	18	257 04.7	26.1	N22 43.0	2.5		18	49 49.9	30.1	S20 18.5	6.6
12 Th.	0	343 41.8	25.9	N22 58.1	1.6	28 Sat.	0	136 50.3	30.5	S19 39.4	7.1
	6	70 17.4	25.7	N23 08.2	0.8		6	223 53.4	31.0	S18 57.2	7.5
	12	156 51.7	25.6	N23 13.3	0.1		12	310 59.3	31.5	S18 11.9	8.1
	18	243 25.1	25.4	N23 13.3	1.0		18	38 07.7	31.9	S17 23.9	8.5
13 Fri.	0	329 57.9	25.4	N23 08.1	1.8	29 Sun.	0	125 18.7	32.3	S16 33.2	8.9
	6	56 30.4	25.4	N22 57.6	2.7		6	212 32.2	32.7	S15 40.2	9.2
	12	143 02.9	25.5	N22 42.0	3.5		12	299 48.1	33.1	S14 44.9	9.6
	18	229 35.8	25.6	N22 21.1	4.4		18	27 06.2	33.4	S13 47.6	9.9
14 Sat.	0	316 09.3	25.8	N21 55.2	5.2	30 Mon.	0	114 26.5	33.7	S12 48.4	10.1
	6	42 43.7	25.9	N21 24.3	6.0		6	201 48.6	34.0	S11 47.5	10.5
	12	129 19.2	26.2	N20 48.5	6.9		12	289 12.6	34.3	S10 45.1	10.6
	18	215 56.0	26.4	N20 08.0	7.6		18	16 38.2	34.5	S 9 41.2	10.9
15 Sun.	0	302 34.4	26.7	N19 23.0	8.3						
	6	29 14.4	27.0	N18 33.7	8.9						
	12	115 56.2	27.3	N17 40.2	9.6						
	18	202 39.7	27.5	N16 42.8	10.3						
16 Mon.	0	289 25.1	27.9	N15 41.8	10.8						
	6	16 12.2	28.2	N14 37.4	11.3						
	12	103 01.2	28.4	N13 29.9	11.8						
	18	189 51.8	28.7	N12 19.5	12.3						

PHASES OF THE MOON

	d. h/min		d. h/min
) First Quarter	2 09 11	(Last Quarter	17 11 39
O Full Moon	10 09 20	● New Moon	24 09 11
Apogee	3 23	Perigee	19 00

DECEMBER, 1992

G.M.T.   **(31 days)**   **G.M.T.**

☉ SUN ☉

DATE			Equation of Time		Transit	Semi-diam.	Lat. 52°N.				Lat. Corr. to Sunrise, Sunset, etc.				
Day of							Twi-light	Sun-rise	Sun-set	Twi-light		Twi-light	Sun-rise	Sun-set	Twi-light
Yr.	Mth.	Week	0 h.	12 h.							Lat.				
			m. s.	m. s.	h. m.	′	h. m.	h. m.	h. m.	h. m.	°	h. m.	h. m.	h. m.	h. m.
336	1	Tu.	−11 01	−10 49	11 49	16.2	07 06	07 46	15 53	16 32	N70	+2 26	S.B.H.	S.B.H.	−2 26
337	2	Wed.	−10 38	−10 26	11 50	16.3	07 08	07 48	15 52	16 32	68	+1 52	S.B.H.	S.B.H.	−1 52
338	3	Th.	−10 14	−10 03	11 50	16.3	07 09	07 49	15 51	16 31	66	+1 27	+2 25	−2 26	−1 27
339	4	Fri.	−09 51	−09 38	11 50	16.3	07 10	07 50	15 51	16 31	64	+1 08	+1 44	−1 45	−1 08
340	5	Sat.	−09 26	−09 14	11 51	16.3	07 11	07 52	15 51	16 31	62	+0 52	+1 16	−1 17	−0 52
341	6	Sun.	−09 01	−08 48	11 51	16.3	07 12	07 53	15 50	16 30	N60	+0 38	+0 55	−0 56	−0 38
342	7	Mon.	−08 36	−08 23	11 52	16.3	07 13	07 54	15 50	16 30	58	+0 27	+0 38	−0 39	−0 27
343	8	Tu.	−08 10	−07 56	11 52	16.3	07 15	07 55	15 50	16 30	56	+0 17	+0 23	−0 24	−0 17
344	9	Wed.	−07 43	−07 30	11 53	16.3	07 16	07 56	15 49	16 29	54	+0 08	+0 11	−0 11	−0 08
345	10	Th.	−07 16	−07 03	11 53	16.3	07 17	07 57	15 49	16 29	50	−0 08	−0 10	+0 10	+0 08
346	11	Fri.	−06 49	−06 35	11 53	16.3	07 18	07 58	15 49	16 29	N45	−0 23	−0 30	+0 30	+0 23
347	12	Sat.	−06 21	−06 07	11 54	16.3	07 19	07 59	15 48	16 29	40	−0 37	−0 47	+0 47	+0 37
348	13	Sun.	−05 53	−05 39	11 54	16.3	07 19	08 00	15 48	16 29	35	−0 48	−1 01	+1 01	+0 48
349	14	Mon.	−05 25	−05 10	11 55	16.3	07 20	08 01	15 48	16 29	30	−0 59	−1 13	+1 13	+0 59
350	15	Tu.	−04 56	−04 41	11 55	16.3	07 21	08 02	15 49	16 29	20	−1 17	−1 34	+1 34	+1 18
351	16	Wed.	−04 27	−04 12	11 56	16.3	07 21	08 02	15 49	16 29	N10	−1 34	−1 53	+1 53	+1 35
352	17	Th.	−03 58	−03 43	11 56	16.3	07 22	08 03	15 49	16 29	0	−1 51	−2 10	+2 10	+1 52
353	18	Fri.	−03 28	−03 14	11 57	16.3	07 23	08 04	15 49	16 30	S10	−2 09	−2 27	+2 27	+2 10
354	19	Sat.	−02 59	−02 44	11 57	16.3	07 23	08 04	15 49	16 30	20	−2 30	−2 46	+2 46	+2 31
355	20	Sun.	−02 29	−02 14	11 58	16.3	07 24	08 05	15 50	16 31	30	−2 54	−3 08	+3 08	+2 15
356	21	Mon.	−01 59	−01 44	11 58	16.3	07 25	08 06	15 51	16 32	S35	−3 09	−3 21	+3 21	+3 16
357	22	Tu.	−01 29	−01 14	11 59	16.3	07 25	08 06	15 51	16 32	40	−3 29	−3 36	+3 36	+3 29
358	23	Wed.	−00 59	−00 44	11 59	16.3	07 25	08 06	15 51	16 32	45	−3 49	−3 53	+3 54	+3 51
359	24	Th.	−00 29	−00 14	12 00	16.3	07 26	08 07	15 52	16 33	S50	−4 18	−4 16	+4 16	+4 20
360	25	Fri.	+00 01	+00 01	12 00	16.3	07 26	08 07	15 53	16 33					
361	26	Sat.	+00 30	+00 45	12 01	16.3	07 26	08 07	15 54	16 34					
362	27	Sun.	+01 00	+01 15	12 01	16.3	07 27	08 08	15 55	16 35					
363	28	Mon.	+01 30	+01 44	12 02	16.3	07 27	08 08	15 55	16 36					
364	29	Tu.	+01 59	+02 14	12 02	16.3	07 27	08 08	15 56	16 37					
365	30	Wed.	+02 28	+02 43	12 03	16.3	07 28	08 08	15 57	16 38					
366	31	Th.	+02 57	+03 11	12 03	16.3	07 28	08 08	15 57	16 38					

NOTES

Equation of time changes its sign on the 25th. The Lat. Corr. to sunrise, sunset, etc., is for the middle of December. S.B.H. means Sun below Horizon. Examples on the use of the above data are given on page 2:11 onwards.

Equation of Time is the excess of Mean Time over Apparent Time (See explanation and examples on p. 2:15)

☾ MOON ☽

DATE			Age	Transit Diff. (Upper)		Semi-diam.	Hor. Par. 12 h.	Lat. 52°N.		MOON'S PHASES
Day of								Moon-rise	Moon-set	
Yr.	Mth.	Week	days							
				h. m.	m.	′	′	h. m.	h. m.	
336	1	Tu.	07	17 33	41	14.8	54.2	11 57	23 20	
337	2	Wed.	08	18 14	41	14.8	54.3	12 14	– –	
338	3	Th.	09	18 55	42	14.8	54.5	12 29	00 27	
339	4	Fri.	10	19 37	45	14.9	54.8	12 46	01 34	
340	5	Sat.	11	20 22	47	15.1	55.4	13 05	02 43	
341	6	Sun.	12	21 09	51	15.3	56.0	13 28	03 53	
342	7	Mon.	13	22 00	55	15.4	56.7	13 56	05 05	
343	8	Tu.	14	22 55	58	15.6	57.4	14 33	06 17	
344	9	Wed.	15	23 53	59	15.8	58.1	15 22	07 25	
345	10	Th.	16	24 52	–	16.0	58.7	16 23	08 24	
346	11	Fri.	17	00 52	59	16.1	59.1	17 35	09 13	
347	12	Sat.	18	01 51	58	16.2	59.4	18 55	09 52	
348	13	Sun.	19	02 47	54	16.2	59.6	20 18	10 22	
349	14	Mon.	20	03 41	52	16.2	59.6	21 41	10 47	
350	15	Tu.	21	04 33	50	16.2	59.4	23 02	11 09	
351	16	Wed.	22	05 23	50	16.1	59.2	– –	11 29	
352	17	Th.	23	06 13	50	16.0	58.9	00 23	11 49	
353	18	Fri.	24	07 03	51	16.0	58.5	01 43	12 11	
354	19	Sat.	25	07 54	53	15.8	58.1	03 03	12 36	
355	20	Sun.	26	08 47	54	15.7	57.7	04 21	13 06	
356	21	Mon.	27	09 41	56	15.6	57.3	05 34	13 44	
357	22	Tu.	28	10 37	54	15.5	56.8	06 40	14 31	
358	23	Wed.	29	11 31	53	15.3	56.3	07 36	15 28	
359	24	Th.	00	12 24	50	15.2	55.8	08 20	16 32	
360	25	Fri.	01	13 14	47	15.1	55.3	08 55	17 40	
361	26	Sat.	02	14 01	45	14.9	54.8	09 22	18 49	
362	27	Sun.	03	14 46	42	14.8	54.5	09 44	19 58	
363	28	Mon.	04	15 28	41	14.8	54.2	10 03	21 05	
364	29	Tu.	05	16 09	41	14.8	54.1	10 19	22 12	
365	30	Wed.	06	16 50	41	14.8	54.2	10 35	23 18	
366	31	Th.	07	17 31	42	14.8	54.4	10 51	– –	

MOON'S PHASES

	d.	h.	m.
☽ First Quarter	2	06	17
○ Full Moon	9	23	41
☾ Last Quarter	16	19	13
● New Moon	24	00	43

	d.	h.
Apogee	1	20
Perigee	13	21
Apogee	29	17

NOTES

Moon's G.H.A. and Dec. are given on page 3:81.

A table for correcting Moonrise and Moonset for latitude is given on page 4:20.

A table for correcting Moon's meridian passage (transit) for longitude is given on page 4:19.

Examples on the use of the above data are given on page 2:11 onwards.

0h. = midnight. For explanation of use of above data see page 2:11 onwards.

No.	Name	Mag.	Transit (approx.)	DEC.	G.H.A.	R.A.	S.H.A.
			h. m.	° ′	° ′	h. m.	° ′
♈	ARIES	–	19 16	–	70 06.1	–	–
1	Alpheratz	2.2	19 24	N29 03.4	68 05.4	0 08	357 59.3
2	Ankaa	2.4	19 42	S42 20.8	63 36.7	0 26	353 30.6
3	Schedar........	2.5	19 56	N56 30.3	60 04.0	0 40	349 57.9
4	Diphda	2.2	20 00	S18 01.5	59 17.2	0 43	349 11.1
5	Achernar	0.6	20 54	S57 16.5	45 43.8	1 37	335 37.7
6	POLARIS	2.1	21 42	N89 14.3	33 39.1	2 26	323 33.0
7	Hamal	2.2	21 23	N23 26.0	38 24.0	2 07	328 17.9
8	Acamar	3.1	22 14	S40 20.0	25 35.7	2 58	315 29.6
9	Menkar	2.8	22 18	N 4 03.8	24 36.9	3 02	314 30.8
10	Mirfak	1.9	22 40	N49 50.4	19 08.0	3 24	309 01.9
11	Aldebaran......	1.1	23 51	N16 29.8	1 12.7	4 36	291 06.6
12	Rigel	0.3	00 34	S 8 12.6	351 32.5	5 14	281 26.4
13	Capella	0.2	00 36	N45 59.5	351 02.7	5 16	280 56.6
14	Bellatrix	1.7	00 44	N 6 20.6	348 54.2	5 25	278 48.1
15	Elnath	1.8	00 45	N28 36.1	348 37.7	5 26	278 31.6
16	Alnilam	1.8	00 55	S 1 12.4	346 07.7	5 36	276 01.6
17	Betelgeuse ...	{ 0.1 / 1.2 }	01 14	N 7 24.4	341 23.6	5 55	271 17.5
18	Canopus	–0.9	01 43	S52 41.5	334 08.5	6 24	264 02.4
19	Sirius	–1.6	02 04	S16 42.4	328 52.9	6 45	258 46.8
20	Adhara	1.6	02 18	S28 57.7	325 30.3	6 58	255 24.2
21	Castor	1.6	02 53	N31 54.1	316 33.2	7 34	246 27.1
22	Procyon........	0.5	02 58	N 5 14.5	315 21.5	7 39	245 15.4
23	Pollux	1.2	03 04	N28 02.5	313 52.2	7 45	243 46.1
24	Avior	1.7	03 41	S59 29.1	304 29.9	8 22	234 23.8
25	Suhail	2.2	04 27	S43 24.1	293 09.6	9 08	223 03.5
26	Miaplacidus ...	1.8	04 32	S69 41.1	291 48.5	9 13	221 42.4
27	Alphard........	2.2	04 46	S 8 37.7	288 17.0	9 27	218 10.9
28	Regulus	1.3	05 27	N11 59.9	278 05.7	10 08	207 59.6
29	Dubhe	2.0	06 22	N61 46.9	264 16.3	11 03	194 10.2
30	Denebola	2.2	07 07	N14 36.5	252 55.4	11 49	182 49.3
31	Gienah	2.8	07 34	S17 30.2	246 14.2	12 15	176 08.1
32	Acrux...........	1.1	07 45	S63 03.4	243 32.8	12 26	173 26.7
33	Gacrux.........	1.6	07 49	S57 04.2	242 24.3	12 31	172 18.2
34	Mimosa........	1.5	08 06	S59 38.8	238 16.4	12 47	168 10.3
35	Alioth..........	1.7	08 12	N55 59.5	236 43.3	12 54	166 34.2
36	Spica	1.2	08 43	S11 07.5	228 53.7	13 25	158 47.6
37	Alkaid	1.9	09 05	N49 20.6	223 17.3	13 47	153 11.2
38	Hadar..........	0.9	09 21	S60 20.2	219 16.3	14 03	149 10.2
39	Menkent	2.3	09 24	S36 20.0	218 32.1	14 06	148 26.0
40	Arcturus	0.2	09 33	N19 13.0	216 16.0	14 15	146 09.9
41	Rigil Kent.....	0.1	09 57	S60 48.2	210 19.3	14 39	140 13.2
42	Zuben'ubi	2.9	10 08	S16 00.8	207 28.8	14 50	137 22.7
43	Kochab	2.2	10 09	N74 10.8	207 26.3	14 51	137 20.2
44	Alphecca	2.3	10 52	N26 44.2	196 30.4	15 34	126 24.3
45	Antares........	1.2	11 47	S26 25.0	182 51.5	16 29	112 45.4
46	Atria	1.9	12 05	S69 00.9	178 07.7	16 48	108 01.6
47	Sabik	2.6	12 28	S15 43.0	172 36.6	17 10	102 30.5
48	Shaula	1.7	12 51	S37 05.9	166 49.2	17 33	96 43.1
49	Rasalhague ...	2.1	12 52	N12 33.9	166 27.1	17 35	96 21.0
50	Eltanin	2.4	13 14	N51 29.4	160 59.9	17 56	90 53.8
51	Kaus Aust. ...	2.0	13 41	S34 23.3	154 10.6	18 24	84 04.5
52	Vega	0.1	13 54	N38 46.7	150 55.9	18 37	80 49.8
53	Nunki	2.1	14 12	S26 18.3	146 23.7	18 55	76 17.6
54	Altair	0.9	15 08	N 8 51.1	132 29.6	19 50	62 23.5
55	Peacock........	2.1	15 42	S56 45.6	123 49.8	20 25	53 43.7
56	Deneb	1.3	15 58	N45 15.6	119 48.4	20 41	49 42.3
57	Enif	2.5	17 01	N 9 50.7	104 08.4	21 44	34 02.3
58	Al Na'ir	2.2	17 25	S46 59.8	98 09.1	22 08	28 03.0
59	Fomalhaut ...	1.3	18 14	S29 39.6	85 47.0	22 57	15 40.9
60	Markab	2.6	18 21	N15 10.3	83 59.7	23 04	13 53.6

Stars Transit Correction Table

D. of Mth.	Corr (Sub.)	D. of Mth.	Corr. (Sub.)
	h. m.		h. m.
1	–0 00	17	–1 03
2	–0 04	18	–1 07
3	–0 08	19	–1 11
4	–0 12	20	–1 15
5	–0 16	21	–1 19
6	–0 20	22	–1 23
7	–0 24	23	–1 27
8	–0 28	24	–1 30
9	–0 31	25	–1 34
10	–0 35	26	–1 38
11	–0 39	27	–1 42
12	–0 43	28	–1 46
13	–0 47	29	–1 50
14	–0 51	30	–1 54
15	–0 55	31	–1 58
16	–0 59		

STAR'S TRANSIT

To find the approx. time of Transit of a Star for any day of the month use above table.

If the quantity taken from the table is greater than the time of Transit for the first of the month, add 23h. 56min. to the time of transit before subtracting the correction below.

Example: What time will Bellatrix (No 14) be on the Meridian on December 9th?

	h.min.
Transit on the 1st	00 44
Corr. for 9th	–00 31
Transit on the 9th	00 13

d. h. DECEMBER DIARY

1 06 Mercury stationary
1 20 Moon at apogee
2 06 First Quarter
9 14 Mercury greatest elong. W (21°)
10 00 Full Moon   Eclipse
12 19 Mars 6°S of Moon
13 21 Moon at perigee
16 19 Last Quarter
18 05 Jupiter 7°N of Moon
19 03 Mercury 6°N of Antares
21 15 Solstice
21 16 Venus 1°.1S of Saturn
22 14 Mercury 1°.5N of Moon
22 21 Mars 3°S of Pollux
24 01 New Moon   Eclipse
27 17 Saturn 6°S of Moon
28 07 Venus 7°S of Moon
29 17 Moon at apogee

STAR TIME

The best time to take Star observations is shown in the a.m. and p.m. TWILIGHT columns on the opposite page – corrected for Latitude.

For **Lighting-up Time** (ashore) add 30 mins to Sunset Times.

For Star's G.H.A. Correction Table, see page 4:8.

For Alphabetical List of Stars with Constellation names, see page 2:24.

For Examples on the use of the above data, see page 2:11.

For full directions for finding the above 60 Stars, see p. 2:20 onwards. For Special Pole Star tables see pages 5:17-5:19.

Tuesday, 1st December

G.M.T. h	SUN G.H.A. ° ′	SUN Dec. ° ′	ARIES G.H.A. ° ′	G.M.T. h
00	182 45.0	S21 48.4	70 06.1	00
02	212 44.5	21 49.2	100 11.1	02
04	242 44.1	21 50.0	130 16.0	04
06	272 43.6	21 50.8	160 20.9	06
08	302 43.1	21 51.5	190 25.9	08
10	332 42.7	21 52.3	220 30.8	10
12	2 42.2	21 53.0	250 35.7	12
14	32 41.7	21 53.8	280 40.6	14
16	62 41.2	21 54.6	310 45.6	16
18	92 40.8	21 55.3	340 50.5	18
20	122 40.3	21 56.1	10 55.4	20
22	152 39.8	S21 56.8	41 00.4	22

Sunday, 6th December

G.M.T. h	SUN G.H.A. ° ′	SUN Dec. ° ′	ARIES G.H.A. ° ′	G.M.T. h
00	182 15.2	S22 29.7	75 01.8	00
02	212 14.6	22 30.3	105 06.8	02
04	242 14.1	22 30.9	135 11.7	04
06	272 13.6	22 31.5	165 16.6	06
08	302 13.0	22 32.1	195 21.6	08
10	332 12.5	22 32.7	225 26.5	10
12	2 12.0	22 33.3	255 31.4	12
14	32 11.4	22 33.8	285 36.3	14
16	62 10.9	22 34.4	315 41.3	16
18	92 10.4	22 35.0	345 46.2	18
20	122 09.8	22 35.5	15 51.1	20
22	152 09.3	S22 36.1	45 56.0	22

Friday, 11th December

G.M.T. h	SUN G.H.A. ° ′	SUN Dec. ° ′	ARIES G.H.A. ° ′	G.M.T. h
00	181 42.1	S23 00.0	79 57.5	00
02	211 41.5	23 00.4	110 02.5	02
04	241 40.9	23 00.9	140 07.4	04
06	271 40.3	23 01.3	170 12.3	06
08	301 39.8	23 01.7	200 17.2	08
10	331 39.2	23 02.1	230 22.2	10
12	1 38.6	23 02.5	260 27.1	12
14	31 38.0	23 02.8	290 32.0	14
16	61 37.5	23 03.2	320 37.0	16
18	91 36.9	23 03.6	350 41.9	18
20	121 36.3	23 04.0	20 46.8	20
22	151 35.7	S23 04.4	50 51.7	22

Wednesday, 2nd December

G.M.T. h	SUN G.H.A. ° ′	SUN Dec. ° ′	ARIES G.H.A. ° ′	G.M.T. h
00	182 39.3	S21 57.5	71 05.3	00
02	212 38.9	21 58.3	101 10.2	02
04	242 38.4	21 59.0	131 15.1	04
06	272 37.9	21 59.8	161 20.1	06
08	302 37.4	22 00.5	191 25.0	08
10	332 36.9	22 01.2	221 29.9	10
12	2 36.4	22 01.9	251 34.9	12
14	32 35.9	22 02.7	281 39.8	14
16	62 35.5	22 03.4	311 44.7	16
18	92 35.0	22 04.1	341 49.6	18
20	122 34.5	22 04.8	11 54.6	20
22	152 34.0	S22 05.5	41 59.5	22

Monday, 7th December

G.M.T. h	SUN G.H.A. ° ′	SUN Dec. ° ′	ARIES G.H.A. ° ′	G.M.T. h
00	182 08.8	S22 36.7	76 01.0	00
02	212 08.2	22 37.2	106 05.9	02
04	242 07.7	22 37.8	136 10.8	04
06	272 07.2	22 38.3	166 15.8	06
08	302 06.6	22 38.9	196 20.7	08
10	332 06.1	22 39.4	226 25.6	10
12	2 05.5	22 40.0	256 30.5	12
14	32 05.0	22 40.5	286 35.5	14
16	62 04.4	22 41.1	316 40.4	16
18	92 03.9	22 41.6	346 45.3	18
20	122 03.4	22 42.1	16 50.3	20
22	152 02.8	S22 42.7	46 55.2	22

Saturday, 12th December

G.M.T. h	SUN G.H.A. ° ′	SUN Dec. ° ′	ARIES G.H.A. ° ′	G.M.T. h
00	181 35.1	S23 04.7	80 56.7	00
02	211 34.6	23 05.1	111 01.6	02
04	241 34.0	23 05.5	141 06.5	04
06	271 33.4	23 05.9	171 11.5	06
08	301 32.8	23 06.2	201 16.4	08
10	331 32.2	23 06.6	231 21.3	10
12	1 31.6	23 06.9	261 26.2	12
14	31 31.1	23 07.3	291 31.2	14
16	61 30.5	23 07.6	321 36.1	16
18	91 29.9	23 08.0	351 41.0	18
20	121 29.3	23 08.3	21 46.0	20
22	151 28.7	S23 08.7	51 50.9	22

Thursday, 3rd December

G.M.T. h	SUN G.H.A. ° ′	SUN Dec. ° ′	ARIES G.H.A. ° ′	G.M.T. h
00	182 33.5	S22 06.2	72 04.4	00
02	212 33.0	22 06.9	102 09.4	02
04	242 32.5	22 07.6	132 14.3	04
06	272 32.0	22 08.3	162 19.2	06
08	302 31.5	22 09.0	192 24.1	08
10	332 30.9	22 09.7	222 29.1	10
12	2 30.5	22 10.4	252 34.0	12
14	32 30.0	22 11.1	282 38.9	14
16	62 29.5	22 11.8	312 43.8	16
18	92 29.0	22 12.5	342 48.8	18
20	122 28.5	22 13.1	12 53.7	20
22	152 28.0	S22 13.8	42 58.6	22

Tuesday, 8th December

G.M.T. h	SUN G.H.A. ° ′	SUN Dec. ° ′	ARIES G.H.A. ° ′	G.M.T. h
00	182 02.3	S22 43.2	77 00.1	00
02	212 01.7	22 43.7	107 05.0	02
04	242 01.2	22 44.2	137 10.0	04
06	272 00.6	22 44.7	167 14.9	06
08	302 00.1	22 45.3	197 19.8	08
10	331 59.5	22 45.8	227 24.8	10
12	1 59.0	22 46.3	257 29.7	12
14	31 58.4	22 46.8	287 34.6	14
16	61 57.9	22 47.3	317 39.5	16
18	91 57.3	22 47.8	347 44.5	18
20	121 56.8	22 48.3	17 49.4	20
22	151 56.2	S22 48.8	47 54.3	22

Sunday, 13th December

G.M.T. h	SUN G.H.A. ° ′	SUN Dec. ° ′	ARIES G.H.A. ° ′	G.M.T. h
00	181 28.1	S23 09.0	81 55.8	00
02	211 27.5	23 09.3	112 00.7	02
04	241 26.9	23 09.7	142 05.7	04
06	271 26.3	23 10.0	172 10.6	06
08	301 25.8	23 10.3	202 15.5	08
10	331 25.2	23 10.6	232 20.5	10
12	1 24.6	23 11.0	262 25.4	12
14	31 24.0	23 11.3	292 30.3	14
16	61 23.4	23 11.6	322 35.2	16
18	91 22.8	23 11.9	352 40.2	18
20	121 22.2	23 12.2	22 45.1	20
22	151 21.6	S23 12.5	52 50.0	22

Friday, 4th December

G.M.T. h	SUN G.H.A. ° ′	SUN Dec. ° ′	ARIES G.H.A. ° ′	G.M.T. h
00	182 27.5	S22 14.5	73 03.6	00
02	212 27.0	22 15.2	103 08.5	02
04	242 26.5	22 15.8	133 13.4	04
06	272 26.0	22 16.5	163 18.3	06
08	302 25.5	22 17.2	193 23.3	08
10	332 25.0	22 17.8	223 28.2	10
12	2 24.5	22 18.5	253 33.1	12
14	32 24.0	22 19.1	283 38.1	14
16	62 23.5	22 19.8	313 43.0	16
18	92 22.9	22 20.4	343 47.9	18
20	122 22.4	22 21.0	13 52.8	20
22	152 21.9	S22 21.7	43 57.8	22

Wednesday, 9th December

G.M.T. h	SUN G.H.A. ° ′	SUN Dec. ° ′	ARIES G.H.A. ° ′	G.M.T. h
00	181 55.6	S22 49.3	77 59.3	00
02	211 55.1	22 49.7	108 04.2	02
04	241 54.5	22 50.2	138 09.1	04
06	271 54.0	22 50.7	168 14.0	06
08	301 53.4	22 51.2	198 19.0	08
10	331 52.8	22 51.6	228 23.9	10
12	1 52.3	22 52.1	258 28.8	12
14	31 51.7	22 52.6	288 33.8	14
16	61 51.2	22 53.0	318 38.7	16
18	91 50.6	22 53.5	348 43.6	18
20	121 50.0	22 54.0	18 48.5	20
22	151 49.5	S22 54.4	48 53.5	22

Monday, 14th December

G.M.T. h	SUN G.H.A. ° ′	SUN Dec. ° ′	ARIES G.H.A. ° ′	G.M.T. h
00	181 21.0	S23 12.8	82 55.0	00
02	211 20.4	23 13.1	112 59.9	02
04	241 19.8	23 13.4	143 04.8	04
06	271 19.2	23 13.7	173 09.7	06
08	301 18.6	23 14.0	203 14.7	08
10	331 18.0	23 14.2	233 19.6	10
12	1 17.4	23 14.5	263 24.5	12
14	31 16.8	23 14.8	293 29.4	14
16	61 16.2	23 15.1	323 34.4	16
18	91 15.6	23 15.3	353 39.3	18
20	121 15.0	23 15.6	23 44.2	20
22	151 14.4	S23 15.9	53 49.2	22

Saturday, 5th December

G.M.T. h	SUN G.H.A. ° ′	SUN Dec. ° ′	ARIES G.H.A. ° ′	G.M.T. h
00	182 21.4	S22 22.3	74 02.7	00
02	212 20.9	22 23.0	104 07.6	02
04	242 20.4	22 23.6	134 12.6	04
06	272 19.9	22 24.2	164 17.5	06
08	302 19.3	22 24.8	194 22.4	08
10	332 18.8	22 25.5	224 27.3	10
12	2 18.3	22 26.1	254 32.3	12
14	32 17.8	22 26.7	284 37.2	14
16	62 17.2	22 27.3	314 42.1	16
18	92 16.7	22 27.9	344 47.1	18
20	122 16.2	22 28.5	14 52.0	20
22	152 15.7	S22 29.1	44 56.9	22

Thursday, 10th December

G.M.T. h	SUN G.H.A. ° ′	SUN Dec. ° ′	ARIES G.H.A. ° ′	G.M.T. h
00	181 48.9	S22 54.9	78 58.4	00
02	211 48.3	22 55.3	109 03.3	02
04	241 47.8	22 55.8	139 08.3	04
06	271 47.2	22 56.2	169 13.2	06
08	301 46.6	22 56.6	199 18.1	08
10	331 46.1	22 57.1	229 23.0	10
12	1 45.5	22 57.5	259 28.0	12
14	31 44.9	22 57.9	289 32.9	14
16	61 44.4	22 58.4	319 37.8	16
18	91 43.8	22 58.8	349 42.7	18
20	121 43.2	22 59.2	19 47.7	20
22	151 42.6	S22 59.6	49 52.6	22

Tuesday, 15th December

G.M.T. h	SUN G.H.A. ° ′	SUN Dec. ° ′	ARIES G.H.A. ° ′	G.M.T. h
00	181 13.8	S23 16.1	83 54.1	00
02	211 13.2	23 16.4	113 59.0	02
04	241 12.6	23 16.6	144 03.9	04
06	271 12.0	23 16.9	174 08.9	06
08	301 11.4	23 17.1	204 13.8	08
10	331 10.8	23 17.4	234 18.7	10
12	1 10.2	23 17.6	264 23.7	12
14	31 09.6	23 17.9	294 28.6	14
16	61 09.0	23 18.1	324 33.5	16
18	91 08.4	23 18.3	354 38.4	18
20	121 07.8	23 18.5	24 43.4	20
22	151 07.2	S23 18.8	54 48.3	22

To interpolate SUN G.H.A. see page 4:7   To interpolate ARIES G.H.A. see page 4:8

Wednesday, 16th December

G.M.T. h	SUN G.H.A.	Dec.	ARIES G.H.A.	G.M.T. h
00	181 06.6	S23 19.0	84 53.2	00
02	211 06.0	23 19.2	114 58.2	02
04	241 05.4	23 19.4	145 03.1	04
06	271 04.8	23 19.6	175 08.0	06
08	301 04.2	23 19.8	205 12.9	08
10	331 03.5	23 20.0	235 17.9	10
12	1 02.9	23 20.2	265 22.8	12
14	31 02.3	23 20.4	295 27.7	14
16	61 01.7	23 20.6	325 32.7	16
18	91 01.1	23 20.8	355 37.6	18
20	121 00.5	23 21.0	25 42.5	20
22	150 59.9	S23 21.2	55 47.4	22

Thursday, 17th December

G.M.T. h	SUN G.H.A.	Dec.	ARIES G.H.A.	G.M.T. h
00	180 59.3	S23 21.4	85 52.4	00
02	210 58.7	23 21.6	115 57.3	02
04	240 58.1	23 21.7	146 02.2	04
06	270 57.4	23 21.9	176 07.2	06
08	300 56.8	23 22.1	206 12.1	08
10	330 56.2	23 22.2	236 17.0	10
12	0 55.6	23 22.4	266 21.9	12
14	30 55.0	23 22.6	296 26.9	14
16	60 54.4	23 22.7	326 31.8	16
18	90 53.8	23 22.9	356 36.7	18
20	120 53.2	23 23.0	26 41.7	20
22	150 52.5	S23 23.2	56 46.6	22

Friday, 18th December

G.M.T. h	SUN G.H.A.	Dec.	ARIES G.H.A.	G.M.T. h
00	180 51.9	S23 23.3	86 51.5	00
02	210 51.3	23 23.5	116 56.4	02
04	240 50.7	23 23.6	147 01.4	04
06	270 50.1	23 23.7	177 06.3	06
08	300 49.5	23 23.9	207 11.2	08
10	330 48.8	23 24.0	237 16.1	10
12	0 48.2	23 24.1	267 21.1	12
14	30 47.6	23 24.2	297 26.0	14
16	60 47.0	23 24.3	327 30.9	16
18	90 46.4	23 24.5	357 35.9	18
20	120 45.8	23 24.6	27 40.8	20
22	150 45.1	S23 24.7	57 45.7	22

Saturday, 19th December

G.M.T. h	SUN G.H.A.	Dec.	ARIES G.H.A.	G.M.T. h
00	180 44.5	S23 24.8	87 50.6	00
02	210 43.9	23 24.9	117 55.6	02
04	240 43.3	23 25.0	148 00.5	04
06	270 42.7	23 25.1	178 05.4	06
08	300 42.0	23 25.2	208 10.4	08
10	330 41.4	23 25.3	238 15.3	10
12	0 40.8	23 25.4	268 20.2	12
14	30 40.2	23 25.4	298 25.1	14
16	60 39.6	23 25.5	328 30.1	16
18	90 38.9	23 25.6	358 35.0	18
20	120 38.3	23 25.6	28 39.9	20
22	150 37.7	S23 25.7	58 44.9	22

Sunday, 20th December

G.M.T. h	SUN G.H.A.	Dec.	ARIES G.H.A.	G.M.T. h
00	180 37.1	S23 25.8	88 49.8	00
02	210 36.5	23 25.8	118 54.7	02
04	240 35.8	23 25.9	148 59.6	04
06	270 35.2	23 25.9	179 04.6	06
08	300 34.6	23 26.0	209 09.5	08
10	330 34.0	23 26.0	239 14.4	10
12	0 33.4	23 26.1	269 19.4	12
14	30 32.7	23 26.1	299 24.3	14
16	60 32.1	23 26.2	329 29.2	16
18	90 31.5	23 26.2	359 34.1	18
20	120 30.9	23 26.2	29 39.1	20
22	150 30.2	S23 26.3	59 44.0	22

Monday, 21st December

G.M.T. h	SUN G.H.A.	Dec.	ARIES G.H.A.	G.M.T. h
00	180 29.6	S23 26.3	89 48.9	00
02	210 29.0	23 26.3	119 53.9	02
04	240 28.4	23 26.3	149 58.8	04
06	270 27.8	23 26.4	180 03.7	06
08	300 27.1	23 26.4	210 08.6	08
10	330 26.5	23 26.4	240 13.6	10
12	0 25.9	23 26.4	270 18.5	12
14	30 25.3	23 26.4	300 23.4	14
16	60 24.6	23 26.4	330 28.4	16
18	90 24.0	23 26.4	0 33.3	18
20	120 23.4	23 26.4	30 38.2	20
22	150 22.8	S23 26.4	60 43.1	22

Tuesday, 22nd December

G.M.T. h	SUN G.H.A.	Dec.	ARIES G.H.A.	G.M.T. h
00	180 22.1	S23 26.3	90 48.1	00
02	210 21.5	23 26.3	120 53.0	02
04	240 20.9	23 26.3	150 57.9	04
06	270 20.3	23 26.3	181 02.8	06
08	300 19.7	23 26.3	211 07.8	08
10	330 19.0	23 26.2	241 12.7	10
12	0 18.4	23 26.2	271 17.6	12
14	30 17.8	23 26.2	301 22.6	14
16	60 17.2	23 26.1	331 27.5	16
18	90 16.5	23 26.1	1 32.4	18
20	120 15.9	23 26.0	31 37.3	20
22	150 15.3	S23 26.0	61 42.3	22

Wednesday, 23rd December

G.M.T. h	SUN G.H.A.	Dec.	ARIES G.H.A.	G.M.T. h
00	180 14.7	S23 25.9	91 47.2	00
02	210 14.0	23 25.9	121 52.1	02
04	240 13.4	23 25.8	151 57.1	04
06	270 12.8	23 25.8	182 02.0	06
08	300 12.2	23 25.7	212 06.9	08
10	330 11.5	23 25.6	242 11.8	10
12	0 10.9	23 25.5	272 16.8	12
14	30 10.3	23 25.5	302 21.7	14
16	60 09.7	23 25.4	332 26.6	16
18	90 09.0	23 25.3	2 31.6	18
20	120 08.4	23 25.2	32 36.5	20
22	150 07.8	S23 25.1	62 41.4	22

Thursday, 24th December

G.M.T. h	SUN G.H.A.	Dec.	ARIES G.H.A.	G.M.T. h
00	180 07.2	S23 25.0	92 46.3	00
02	210 06.6	23 24.9	122 51.3	02
04	240 05.9	23 24.8	152 56.2	04
06	270 05.3	23 24.7	183 01.1	06
08	300 04.7	23 24.6	213 06.1	08
10	330 04.1	23 24.5	243 11.0	10
12	0 03.4	23 24.4	273 15.9	12
14	30 02.8	23 24.3	303 20.8	14
16	60 02.2	23 24.2	333 25.8	16
18	90 01.6	23 24.1	3 30.7	18
20	120 01.0	23 23.9	33 35.6	20
22	150 00.3	S23 23.8	63 40.6	22

Friday, 25th December

G.M.T. h	SUN G.H.A.	Dec.	ARIES G.H.A.	G.M.T. h
00	179 59.7	S23 23.7	93 45.5	00
02	209 59.1	23 23.5	123 50.4	02
04	239 58.5	23 23.4	153 55.3	04
06	269 57.8	23 23.3	184 00.3	06
08	299 57.2	23 23.1	214 05.2	08
10	329 56.6	23 23.0	244 10.1	10
12	359 56.0	23 22.8	274 15.1	12
14	29 55.4	23 22.7	304 20.0	14
16	59 54.7	23 22.5	334 24.9	16
18	89 54.1	23 22.3	4 29.8	18
20	119 53.5	23 22.2	34 34.8	20
22	149 52.9	S23 22.0	64 39.7	22

Saturday, 26th December

G.M.T. h	SUN G.H.A.	Dec.	ARIES G.H.A.	G.M.T. h
00	179 52.3	S23 21.8	94 44.6	00
02	209 51.6	23 21.7	124 49.5	02
04	239 51.0	23 21.5	154 54.5	04
06	269 50.4	23 21.3	184 59.4	06
08	299 49.8	23 21.1	215 04.3	08
10	329 49.2	23 20.9	245 09.3	10
12	359 48.5	23 20.8	275 14.2	12
14	29 47.9	23 20.6	305 19.1	14
16	59 47.3	23 20.4	335 24.0	16
18	89 46.7	23 20.2	5 29.0	18
20	119 46.1	23 20.0	35 33.9	20
22	149 45.4	S23 19.8	65 38.8	22

Sunday, 27th December

G.M.T. h	SUN G.H.A.	Dec.	ARIES G.H.A.	G.M.T. h
00	179 44.8	S23 19.5	95 43.8	00
02	209 44.2	23 19.3	125 48.7	02
04	239 43.6	23 19.1	155 53.6	04
06	269 43.0	23 18.9	185 58.5	06
08	299 42.4	23 18.7	216 03.5	08
10	329 41.7	23 18.4	246 08.4	10
12	359 41.1	23 18.2	276 13.3	12
14	29 40.5	23 18.0	306 18.3	14
16	59 39.9	23 17.8	336 23.2	16
18	89 39.3	23 17.5	6 28.1	18
20	119 38.7	23 17.3	36 33.0	20
22	149 38.1	S23 17.0	66 38.0	22

Monday, 28th December

G.M.T. h	SUN G.H.A.	Dec.	ARIES G.H.A.	G.M.T. h
00	179 37.4	S23 16.8	96 42.9	00
02	209 36.8	23 16.5	126 47.8	02
04	239 36.2	23 16.3	156 52.8	04
06	269 35.6	23 16.0	186 57.7	06
08	299 35.0	23 15.8	217 02.6	08
10	329 34.4	23 15.5	247 07.5	10
12	359 33.8	23 15.2	277 12.5	12
14	29 33.2	23 15.0	307 17.4	14
16	59 32.5	23 14.7	337 22.3	16
18	89 31.9	23 14.4	7 27.3	18
20	119 31.3	23 14.1	37 32.2	20
22	149 30.7	S23 13.8	67 37.1	22

Tuesday, 29th December

G.M.T. h	SUN G.H.A.	Dec.	ARIES G.H.A.	G.M.T. h
00	179 30.1	S23 13.5	97 42.0	00
02	209 29.5	23 13.3	127 47.0	02
04	239 28.9	23 13.0	157 51.9	04
06	269 28.3	23 12.7	187 56.8	06
08	299 27.7	23 12.4	218 01.8	08
10	329 27.1	23 12.1	248 06.7	10
12	359 26.5	23 11.7	278 11.6	12
14	29 25.8	23 11.4	308 16.5	14
16	59 25.2	23 11.1	338 21.5	16
18	89 24.6	23 10.8	8 26.4	18
20	119 24.0	23 10.5	38 31.3	20
22	149 23.4	S23 10.2	68 36.2	22

Wednesday, 30th December

G.M.T. h	SUN G.H.A.	Dec.	ARIES G.H.A.	G.M.T. h
00	179 22.8	S23 09.8	98 41.2	00
02	209 22.2	23 09.5	128 46.1	02
04	239 21.6	23 09.2	158 51.0	04
06	269 21.0	23 08.8	188 56.0	06
08	299 20.4	23 08.5	219 00.9	08
10	329 19.8	23 08.2	249 05.8	10
12	359 19.2	23 07.8	279 10.7	12
14	29 18.6	23 07.5	309 15.7	14
16	59 18.0	23 07.1	339 20.6	16
18	89 17.4	23 06.8	9 25.5	18
20	119 16.8	23 06.4	39 30.5	20
22	149 16.2	S23 06.0	69 35.4	22

Thursday, 31st December

G.M.T. h	SUN G.H.A.	Dec.	ARIES G.H.A.	G.M.T. h
00	179 15.6	S23 05.7	99 40.3	00
02	209 15.0	23 05.3	129 45.2	02
04	239 14.4	23 04.9	159 50.2	04
06	269 13.8	S23 04.6	189 55.1	06
08	299 13.2	S23 04.2	220 00.0	08
10	329 12.6	23 03.8	250 05.0	10
12	359 12.0	23 03.4	280 09.9	12
14	29 11.4	S23 03.0	310 14.8	14
16	59 10.8	S23 02.6	340 19.7	16
18	89 10.2	23 02.3	10 24.7	18
20	119 09.7	23 01.9	40 29.6	20
22	149 09.1	S23 01.5	70 34.5	22

To interpolate SUN G.H.A. see page 4:7   To interpolate ARIES G.H.A. see page 4:8

Mer. Pass.	♀ VENUS G.H.A.	Mean Var. 14°	Dec.	Mean Var.	M	Day of Week	♃ JUPITER G.H.A	Mean Var. 15°	Dec.	Mean Var.	Mer. Pass
h. m.	° ′	′	° ′	′			° ′	′	° ′	′	h. m.
14 52	137 09.0	59.3	S24 07.6	0.5	1	Tu.	240 42.8	2.1	S 2 45.1	0.1	07 56
14 53	136 51.3	59.3	S23 56.5	0.5	2	Wed.	241 33.4	2.1	S 2 48.5	0.1	07 53
14 54	136 34.0	59.3	S23 44.8	0.5	3	Th.	242 24.1	2.1	S 2 51.9	0.1	07 49
14 56	136 17.0	59.3	S23 32.3	0.5	4	Fri.	243 14.8	2.1	S 2 55.3	0.1	07 46
14 57	136 00.3	59.3	S23 19.3	0.6	5	Sat.	244 05.7	2.1	S 2 58.6	0.1	07 43
14 58	135 44.1	59.3	S23 05.6	0.6	6	SUN.	244 56.7	2.1	S 3 01.8	0.1	07 39
14 59	135 28.1	59.4	S22 51.2	0.6	7	Mon.	245 47.8	2.1	S 3 05.0	0.1	07 36
15 00	135 12.6	59.4	S22 36.3	0.6	8	Tu.	246 39.0	2.1	S 3 08.2	0.1	07 32
15 01	134 57.5	59.4	S22 20.8	0.7	9	Wed.	247 30.3	2.1	S 3 11.3	0.1	07 29
15 02	134 42.8	59.4	S22 04.6	0.7	10	Th.	248 21.7	2.1	S 3 14.4	0.1	07 25
15 03	134 28.5	59.4	S21 47.9	0.7	11	Fri.	249 13.2	2.2	S 3 17.4	0.1	07 22
15 04	134 14.6	59.4	S21 30.6	0.7	12	Sat.	250 04.9	2.2	S 3 20.3	0.1	07 19
15 04	134 01.1	59.5	S21 12.8	0.8	13	SUN.	250 56.6	2.2	S 3 23.2	0.1	07 15
15 05	133 48.1	59.5	S20 54.4	0.8	14	Mon.	251 48.5	2.2	S 3 26.0	0.1	07 12
15 06	133 35.5	59.5	S20 35.5	0.8	15	Tu.	252 40.5	2.2	S 3 28.8	0.1	07 08
15 07	133 23.4	59.5	S20 16.0	0.8	16	Wed.	253 32.6	2.2	S 3 31.6	0.1	07 05
15 08	133 11.7	59.5	S19 56.0	0.9	17	Th.	254 24.9	2.2	S 3 34.2	0.1	07 01
15 08	133 00.5	59.6	S19 35.6	0.9	18	Fri.	255 17.2	2.2	S 3 36.9	0.1	06 58
15 09	132 49.7	59.6	S19 14.7	0.9	19	Sat.	256 09.7	2.2	S 3 39.4	0.1	06 54
15 10	132 39.4	59.6	S18 53.3	0.9	20	SUN.	257 02.4	2.2	S 3 41.9	0.1	06 51
15 10	132 29.6	59.6	S18 31.4	0.9	21	Mon.	257 55.1	2.2	S 3 44.4	0.1	06 47
15 11	132 20.2	59.6	S18 09.1	0.9	22	Tu.	258 48.0	2.2	S 3 46.8	0.1	06 44
15 12	132 11.3	59.6	S17 46.3	1.0	23	Wed.	259 41.0	2.2	S 3 49.1	0.1	06 40
15 12	132 02.8	59.7	S17 23.2	1.0	24	Th.	260 34.2	2.2	S 3 51.3	0.1	06 37
15 13	131 54.9	59.7	S16 59.6	1.0	25	Fri.	261 27.5	2.2	S 3 53.6	0.1	06 33
15 13	131 47.4	59.7	S16 35.7	1.0	26	Sat.	262 20.9	2.2	S 3 55.7	0.1	06 30
15 14	131 40.4	59.7	S16 11.4	1.0	27	SUN.	263 14.5	2.2	S 3 57.8	0.1	06 26
15 14	131 33.9	59.7	S15 46.7	1.0	28	Mon.	264 08.2	2.2	S 3 59.8	0.1	06 23
15 14	131 27.8	59.8	S15 21.6	1.1	29	Tu.	265 02.1	2.3	S 4 01.8	0.1	06 19
15 15	131 22.3	59.8	S14 56.3	1.1	30	Wed.	265 56.1	2.3	S 4 03.7	0.1	06 15
15 15	131 17.2	59.8	S14 30.6	1.1	31	Th.	266 50.2	2.3	S 4 05.5	0.1	06 12

♀ VENUS. Av. Mag. –4.2. An Evening Star. In conjunction with Saturn on December 21. S.H.A. December 5 62°; 10 56; 15 50°; 20 44°; 25 38°; 30 33°.

♃ JUPITER. Av. Mag. –1.9. A Morning Star. S.H.A. December 5 171°; 10 169°; 15 169°; 20 169°; 25 167°; 30 167°.

Mer. Pass.	♂ MARS G.H.A.	Mean Var. 15°	Dec.	Mean Var.	M	Day of Week	♄ SATURN G.H.A	Mean Var. 15°	Dec.	Mean Var.	Mer. Pass
h. m.	° ′	′	° ′	′			° ′	′	° ′	′	h. m.
03 20	309 53.2	2.5	N23 08.5	0.1	1	Tu.	113 46.7	2.3	S17 43.8	0.1	16 22
03 16	310 54.0	2.6	N23 11.7	0.1	2	Wed.	114 41.4	2.3	S17 42.5	0.1	16 19
03 12	311 55.6	2.6	N23 15.1	0.1	3	Th.	115 36.1	2.3	S17 41.2	0.1	16 15
03 08	312 58.1	2.6	N23 18.7	0.2	4	Fri.	116 30.7	2.3	S17 39.9	0.1	16 12
03 03	314 01.5	2.7	N23 22.4	0.2	5	Sat.	117 25.2	2.3	S17 38.6	0.1	16 08
02 59	315 05.8	2.7	N23 26.3	0.2	6	SUN.	118 19.6	2.3	S17 37.2	0.1	16 04
02 55	316 11.0	2.8	N23 30.4	0.2	7	Mon.	119 14.0	2.3	S17 35.8	0.1	16 01
02 50	317 17.2	2.8	N23 34.6	0.2	8	Tu.	120 08.2	2.3	S17 34.4	0.1	15 57
02 46	318 24.2	2.8	N23 39.0	0.2	9	Wed.	121 02.4	2.3	S17 32.9	0.1	15 53
02 41	319 32.1	2.9	N23 43.5	0.2	10	Th.	121 56.6	2.3	S17 31.5	0.1	15 50
02 37	320 41.0	2.9	N23 48.2	0.2	11	Fri.	122 50.6	2.3	S17 30.0	0.1	15 46
02 32	321 50.8	2.9	N23 53.0	0.2	12	Sat.	123 44.6	2.3	S17 28.5	0.1	15 43
02 27	323 01.5	3.0	N23 58.0	0.2	13	SUN.	124 38.6	2.2	S17 26.9	0.1	15 39
02 23	324 13.0	3.0	N24 03.0	0.2	14	Mon.	125 32.4	2.2	S17 25.4	0.1	15 36
02 18	325 25.5	3.1	N24 08.2	0.2	15	Tu.	126 26.2	2.2	S17 23.8	0.1	15 32
02 13	326 38.9	3.1	N24 13.5	0.2	16	Wed.	127 20.0	2.2	S17 22.2	0.1	15 28
02 08	327 53.1	3.1	N24 18.9	0.2	17	Th.	128 13.7	2.2	S17 20.6	0.1	15 25
02 03	329 08.2	3.2	N24 24.4	0.2	18	Fri.	129 07.3	2.2	S17 19.0	0.1	15 21
01 58	330 24.2	3.2	N24 30.0	0.2	19	Sat.	130 00.8	2.2	S17 17.3	0.1	15 18
01 53	331 41.0	3.2	N24 35.6	0.2	20	SUN.	130 54.3	2.2	S17 15.7	0.1	15 14
01 48	332 58.5	3.3	N24 41.3	0.2	21	Mon.	131 47.7	2.2	S17 14.0	0.1	15 11
01 42	334 16.9	3.3	N24 47.0	0.2	22	Tu.	132 41.1	2.2	S17 12.3	0.1	15 07
01 37	335 36.0	3.3	N24 52.7	0.2	23	Wed.	133 34.4	2.2	S17 10.6	0.1	15 03
01 32	336 55.8	3.4	N24 58.4	0.2	24	Th.	134 27.7	2.2	S17 08.8	0.1	15 00
01 27	338 16.4	3.4	N25 04.2	0.2	25	Fri.	135 20.9	2.2	S17 07.1	0.1	14 56
01 21	339 37.5	3.4	N25 09.9	0.2	26	Sat.	136 14.1	2.2	S17 05.3	0.1	14 53
01 16	340 59.3	3.4	N25 15.6	0.2	27	SUN.	137 07.2	2.2	S17 03.5	0.1	14 49
01 10	342 21.7	3.5	N25 21.2	0.2	28	Mon.	138 00.2	2.2	S17 01.7	0.1	14 46
01 05	343 44.5	3.5	N25 26.8	0.2	29	Tu.	138 53.2	2.2	S16 59.8	0.1	14 42
00 59	345 07.9	3.5	N25 32.3	0.2	30	Wed	139 46.2	2.2	S16 57.9	0.1	14 39
00 54	346 31.7	3.5	N25 37.8	0.2	31	Th.	140 39.1	2.2	S16 56.1	0.1	14 35

♂ MARS. Av. Mag. -1.1. A Morning Star. S.H.A. December 5 241°; 10 239°; 15 242°; 20 24°; 25 243°; 30 246°

♄ SATURN. Av. Mag. +0.7. An Evening Star. Do not confuse with Venus on December 21. Venus is the brighter object. S.H.A. December 5 44°; 10 42°; 15 43°; 20 43°; 25 41°; 30 41°.

MERCURY. Visible low in the east before sunrise throughout the month.

For Planets Correction Tables see pages 4:9-4:13. See also 'How to Recognise the Planets' on page 2:32.
Mean Var. means Variation per Hour.

Day of M. W. T.	G.M.T. h	G.H.A. ° '	Mean Var. per Hour 14°,+	Dec. ° '	Mean Var. per Hour '
1 Tu.	0	104 05.1	34.7	S 8 36.2	11.0
	6	191 33.3	34.9	S 7 30.0	11.2
	12	279 02.6	35.0	S 6 22.9	11.4
	18	6 32.7	35.1	S 5 15.0	11.4
2 Wed.	0	94 03.5	35.2	S 4 06.3	11.5
	6	181 34.6	35.3	S 2 57.1	11.7
	12	269 06.0	35.2	S 1 47.5	11.7
	18	356 37.5	35.2	S 0 37.5	11.7
3 Th.	0	84 08.7	35.1	N 0 32.7	11.7
	6	171 39.6	35.0	N 1 42.9	11.7
	12	259 09.8	34.9	N 2 53.1	11.7
	18	346 39.2	34.8	N 4 03.1	11.6
4 Fri.	0	74 07.6	34.5	N 5 12.8	11.5
	6	161 34.7	34.2	N 6 21.9	11.4
	12	249 00.4	33.9	N 7 30.5	11.3
	18	336 24.4	33.6	N 8 38.3	11.2
5 Sat.	0	63 46.6	33.4	N 9 45.1	11.0
	6	151 06.7	32.9	N10 50.8	10.7
	12	238 24.6	32.5	N11 55.2	10.5
	18	325 40.1	32.1	N12 58.1	10.2
6 Sun.	0	52 53.0	31.6	N13 59.3	9.9
	6	140 03.1	31.1	N14 58.6	9.5
	12	227 10.3	30.7	N15 55.8	9.1
	18	314 14.6	30.1	N16 50.5	8.6
7 Mon.	0	41 15.8	29.6	N17 42.7	8.2
	6	128 13.8	29.1	N18 32.0	7.7
	12	215 08.6	28.5	N19 18.1	7.1
	18	302 00.2	28.0	N20 00.9	6.5
8 Tu.	0	28 48.6	27.5	N20 40.0	5.8
	6	115 34.0	27.0	N21 15.2	5.1
	12	202 16.3	26.5	N21 46.3	4.3
	18	288 55.9	26.1	N22 12.9	3.6
9 Wed.	0	15 32.8	25.7	N22 35.0	2.8
	6	102 07.3	25.4	N22 52.2	2.0
	12	188 39.8	25.1	N23 04.4	1.1
	18	275 10.4	24.9	N23 11.4	0.2
10 Th.	0	1 39.6	24.7	N23 13.1	0.7
	6	88 07.6	24.5	N23 09.5	1.6
	12	174 35.0	24.5	N23 00.3	2.5
	18	261 02.0	24.5	N22 45.7	3.4
11 Fri.	0	347 29.1	24.5	N22 25.7	4.3
	6	73 56.6	24.7	N22 00.2	5.2
	12	160 24.8	24.9	N21 29.5	6.1
	18	246 54.1	25.1	N20 53.6	6.9
12 Sat.	0	333 24.7	25.4	N20 12.7	7.7
	6	59 56.9	25.7	N19 27.0	8.5
	12	146 30.9	26.0	N18 36.7	9.2
	18	233 06.9	26.3	N17 42.1	9.8
13 Sun.	0	319 44.9	26.7	N16 43.4	10.5
	6	46 25.1	27.1	N15 41.0	11.0
	12	133 07.5	27.5	N14 35.1	11.6
	18	219 52.0	27.8	N13 26.1	12.0
14 Mon.	0	306 38.6	28.2	N12 14.2	12.4
	6	33 27.2	28.4	N10 59.7	12.8
	12	120 17.8	28.8	N 9 43.0	13.1
	18	207 10.1	29.0	N 8 24.4	13.4
15 Tu.	0	294 04.2	29.3	N 7 04.2	13.6
	6	20 59.6	29.4	N 5 42.7	13.8
	12	107 56.4	29.7	N 4 20.2	13.9
	18	194 54.3	29.8	N 2 57.0	14.0
16 Wed.	0	281 53.0	30.0	N 1 33.4	14.0
	6	8 52.4	30.0	N 0 09.7	14.0
	12	95 52.3	30.0	S 1 13.9	13.9
	18	182 52.5	30.0	S 2 37.0	13.8

Day of M. W. T.	G.M.T. h	G.H.A. ° '	Mean Var. per Hour 14°,+	Dec. ° '	Mean Var. per Hour '
17 Th.	0	269 52.7	30.0	S 3 59.5	13.6
	6	356 52.7	29.9	S 5 20.9	13.4
	12	83 52.4	29.9	S 6 41.1	13.1
	18	170 51.5	29.7	S 7 59.9	12.8
18 Fri.	0	257 49.9	29.6	S 9 16.9	12.5
	6	344 47.5	29.4	S10 31.9	12.1
	12	71 44.0	29.2	S11 44.6	11.7
	18	158 39.3	29.0	S12 54.8	11.3
19 Sat.	0	245 33.4	28.8	S14 02.3	10.7
	6	332 26.2	28.6	S15 06.9	10.2
	12	59 17.5	28.3	S16 08.2	9.6
	18	146 07.5	28.1	S17 06.2	9.0
20 Sun.	0	232 56.0	27.8	S18 00.5	8.4
	6	319 43.1	27.7	S18 50.9	7.7
	12	46 28.9	27.4	S19 37.4	7.0
	18	133 13.4	27.2	S20 19.7	6.2
21 Mon.	0	219 56.9	27.0	S20 57.6	5.5
	6	306 39.4	26.9	S21 31.0	4.7
	12	33 21.2	26.9	S21 59.9	3.9
	18	120 02.4	26.8	S22 24.1	3.2
22 Tu.	0	206 43.3	26.9	S22 43.4	2.4
	6	293 24.2	26.8	S22 58.0	1.6
	12	20 05.3	26.9	S23 07.8	0.7
	18	106 46.8	27.0	S23 12.8	0.0
23 Wed.	0	193 29.1	27.2	S23 12.9	0.8
	6	280 12.5	27.4	S23 08.4	1.6
	12	6 57.1	27.7	S22 59.2	2.4
	18	93 43.2	28.0	S22 45.5	3.0
24 Th.	0	Eclipse of the Sun occurs today			
	6	267 20.9	28.7	S22 05.0	4.5
	12	354 12.8	29.1	S21 38.5	5.1
	18	81 06.9	29.4	S21 08.1	5.7
25 Fri.	0	168 03.4	29.9	S20 33.9	6.3
	6	255 02.4	30.3	S19 56.2	6.9
	12	342 03.9	30.7	S19 15.2	7.5
	18	69 07.9	31.1	S18 31.0	7.9
26 Sat.	0	156 14.4	31.5	S17 43.9	8.4
	6	243 23.4	31.9	S16 54.0	8.8
	12	330 34.9	32.4	S16 01.6	9.1
	18	57 48.7	32.8	S15 06.9	9.5
27 Sun.	0	145 04.9	33.1	S14 10.0	9.8
	6	232 23.2	33.5	S13 11.2	10.1
	12	319 43.6	33.7	S12 10.6	10.4
	18	47 05.9	34.0	S11 08.4	10.6
28 Mon.	0	134 29.9	34.3	S10 04.8	10.9
	6	221 55.6	34.5	S 8 59.9	11.0
	12	309 22.7	34.8	S 7 53.9	11.1
	18	36 51.0	34.9	S 6 46.9	11.3
29 Tu.	0	124 20.5	35.0	S 5 39.2	11.4
	6	211 50.9	35.2	S 4 30.8	11.5
	12	299 21.9	35.2	S 3 21.8	11.6
	18	26 53.5	35.3	S 2 12.5	11.6
30 Wed.	0	114 25.4	35.3	S 1 02.9	11.6
	6	201 57.4	35.3	N 0 06.9	11.6
	12	289 29.3	35.2	N 1 16.7	11.6
	18	17 00.9	35.2	N 2 26.3	11.5
31 Th.	0	104 32.1	35.0	N 3 35.7	11.5
	6	192 02.5	34.9	N 4 44.8	11.4
	12	279 32.0	34.7	N 5 53.3	11.3
	18	7 00.4	34.5	N 7 01.3	11.2

PHASES OF THE MOON

	d. h/min		d. h/min
) First Quarter	2 06 17	(Last Quarter	16 19 13
O Full Moon	9 23 41	● New Moon	24 00 43
Apogee	1 20	Perigee	13 21
		Apogee	29 17

ASTRONOMICAL DATA FOR 1993

It may occur, especially on a long voyage, that the new year's Nautical Almanac may not be available by January 1st. In such cases the necessary data for the Sun and Stars may be obtained from this 1992 Almanac approximately, but of quite sufficient accuracy for navigational purposes, as shown below, any error would be unlikely to exceed 0'.4.

The Almanac cannot be used in this way for the Moon or the Planets.

SUN

Take out the G.H.A. and Dec. for the same date but, for January and February , for a time 18h. 12min. 00sec. *later* and, for March to December, for a time 5h. 48 min. 00sec. *earlier* than the G.M.T. of observation; in both cases *add* 87°00' to the G.H.A. so obtained.

STARS

Calculate the G.H.A. and Dec. for the same date and the same time, but for January and February *add* 44'.0 and for March to December *subtract* 15'.1 from the G.H.A. so found.

MOON RISE AND MOON SET TIMES

In the practice of normal navigation precise times of Moonrise and Moonset are rarely required, so it is not considered necessary to give the considerable amount of space required to include this for all Latitudes. If these are required for a special purpose the Admiralty Nautical Almanac should be consulted.

ABBREVIATIONS

Alt:	Altitude	**L.H.A.T.S.**	Local Hour Angle of True Sun
Az:	Azimuth	**Lat:**	Latitude
Cor:	Correction	**Long:**	Longitude
C.P.	Chosen Position	**L.L.**	Lower Limb (of sun or moon)
C.Z.D.	Calculated Zenith Distance	**L.M.T.**	Local Mean Time
Dec:	Declination	**M**	Mile(s)
Dep:	Departure	**m**	Metre(s)
D.Lat:	Difference in Latitude	**M.P.**	Meridional Parts
D.Long:	Difference in Longitude	**Mer: Alt:**	Meridian Altitude
D.M.P.	Difference in Meridional Parts	**Mer: Pass:**	Meridian Passage
D.R.	Dead Reckoning (position by)	**O.P.**	Observed Position
D.W.E.	Deck Watch Error	**P.L.**	Position Line
E.H.A.	Easterly Hour Angle	**P.V.**	Prime Vertical
E.P.	Estimated Position	**R.A.**	Right Ascension
G.D.	Greenwich Date	**R.A.M.**	Right Ascension of the
G.H.A.	Greenwich Hour Angle		Meridian
G.M.T.	Greenwich Mean Time	**S.A.T.**	Ship's Apparent Time
G.P.	Geographical Position	**S.H.A.**	Sidereal Hour Angle
H.A.	Hour Angle	**S.M.T.**	Ship's Mean Time
H.P.	Horizontal Parallax	**T.Z.D.**	True Zenith Distance
I.E.	Index Error (of sextant)	**U.L.**	Upper Limb (sun or moon)
L.H.A.	Local Hour Angle	**U.T.**	Universal Time
L.H.A.M.S.	Local Hour Angle	**Z.D.**	Zenith Distance
	of Mean Sun	**Z.T.**	Zone Time

CALENDAR — 1993

JANUARY					
Sun	31	3	10	17	24
Mon		4	11	18	25
Tue		5	12	19	26
Wed		6	13	20	27
Thu		7	14	21	28
Fri	1	8	15	22	29
Sat	2	9	16	23	30

FEBRUARY					
Sun		7	14	21	28
Mon	1	8	15	22	
Tue	2	9	16	23	
Wed	3	10	17	24	
Thu	4	11	18	25	
Fri	5	12	19	26	
Sat	6	13	20	27	

MARCH					
Sun		7	14	21	28
Mon	1	8	15	22	29
Tue	2	9	16	23	30
Wed	3	10	17	24	31
Thu	4	11	18	25	
Fri	5	12	19	26	
Sat	6	13	20	27	

APRIL					
Sun		4	11	18	25
Mon		5	12	19	26
Tue		6	13	20	27
Wed		7	14	21	28
Thu	1	8	15	22	29
Fri	2	9	16	23	30
Sat	3	10	17	24	

MAY					
Sun	30	2	9	16	23
Mon	31	3	10	17	24
Tue		4	11	18	25
Wed		5	12	19	26
Thu		6	13	20	27
Fri		7	14	21	28
Sat	1	8	15	22	29

JUNE					
Sun		6	13	20	27
Mon		7	14	21	28
Tue	1	8	15	22	29
Wed	2	9	16	23	30
Thu	3	10	17	24	
Fri	4	11	18	25	
Sat	5	12	19	26	

JULY					
Sun		4	11	18	25
Mon		5	12	19	26
Tue		6	13	20	27
Wed		7	14	21	28
Thu	1	8	15	22	29
Fri	2	9	16	23	30
Sat	3	10	17	24	31

AUGUST					
Sun	1	8	15	22	29
Mon	2	9	16	23	30
Tue	3	10	17	24	31
Wed	4	11	18	25	
Thu	5	12	19	26	
Fri	6	13	20	27	
Sat	7	14	21	28	

SEPTEMBER					
Sun		5	12	19	26
Mon		6	13	20	27
Tue		7	14	21	28
Wed	1	8	15	22	29
Thu	2	9	16	23	30
Fri	3	10	17	24	
Sat	4	11	18	25	

OCTOBER					
Sun	31	3	10	17	24
Mon		4	11	18	25
Tue		5	12	19	26
Wed		6	13	20	27
Thu		7	14	21	28
Fri	1	8	15	22	29
Sat	2	9	16	23	30

NOVEMBER					
Sun		7	14	21	28
Mon	1	8	15	22	29
Tue	2	9	16	23	30
Wed	3	10	17	24	
Thu	4	11	18	25	
Fri	5	12	19	26	
Sat	6	13	20	27	

DECEMBER					
Sun		5	12	19	26
Mon		6	13	20	27
Tue		7	14	21	28
Wed	1	8	15	22	29
Thu	2	9	16	23	30
Fri	3	10	17	24	31
Sat	4	11	18	25	

NOTES

Nautical Ephemeris Tables

4

TABLES FOR CONVERTING ARC INTO TIME OR TIME INTO ARC

The Table on pages 4:2 and 4:3 is of considerable practical value as it enables Longitude in Arc to be turned into Longitude in Time and the reverse. Set in three separate columns for degrees, minutes and seconds it is simplicity itself to use.

As the decimal system is used throughout this Almanac, the last panel, "Secs. of Arc into Secs. of Time," shows the equivalent in seconds of arc to each tenth minute of arc.

Example I. Turn Longitude in Arc (7° 25′ 40″ **East) into Time.**

7° =	0h. 28min. 00s.
25′ =	1min. 40
40″ =	2.7
Time =	0h. 29min. 42.7 East

Example II. If the Longitude in Time is 3h. 53min. 20s. West, what is the Longitude in Arc?

3h. 52min. =	58° 00′
1min. =	15′
20s. =	5′
Arc =	58° 20′ West

4:1

CONVERTING ARC INTO TIME & VICE-VERSA

Secs. (& decimals) of Arc into Secs. of Time

"	s
0 = 0·0	0·00
1	0·07
2	0·13
3	0·20
4	0·27
5	0·33
6 = 0·1	0·40
7	0·47
8	0·53
9	0·60
10	0·67
11	0·73
12 = 0·2	0·80
13	0·87
14	0·93
15	1·00
16	1·07
17	1·13
18 = 0·3	1·20
19	1·27
20	1·33
21	1·40
22	1·47
23	1·53
24 = 0·4	1·60
25	1·67
26	1·73
27	1·80
28	1·87
29	1·93
30 = 0·5	2·00

Mins. of Arc into Mins. and Secs. of Time

'	min.	s
0	0	0
1	0	4
2	0	8
3	0	12
4	0	16
5	0	20
6	0	24
7	0	28
8	0	32
9	0	36
10	0	40
11	0	44
12	0	48
13	0	52
14	0	56
15	1	0
16	1	4
17	1	8
18	1	12
19	1	16
20	1	20
21	1	24
22	1	28
23	1	32
24	1	36
25	1	40
26	1	44
27	1	48
28	1	52
29	1	56
30	2	0

DEGREES OF ARC INTO HOURS AND MINUTES.

°	h.min	°	h.min	°	h.min	°	h.min	°	h.min	°	h.min
300	20 00	240	16 00	180	12 00	120	8 00	60	4 00	0	0 00
301	20 04	241	16 04	181	12 04	121	8 04	61	4 04	1	0 04
302	20 08	242	16 08	182	12 08	122	8 08	62	4 08	2	0 08
303	20 12	243	16 12	183	12 12	123	8 12	63	4 12	3	0 12
304	20 16	244	16 16	184	12 16	124	8 16	64	4 16	4	0 16
305	20 20	245	16 20	185	12 20	125	8 20	65	4 20	5	0 20
306	20 24	246	16 24	186	12 24	126	8 24	66	4 24	6	0 24
307	20 28	247	16 28	187	12 28	127	8 28	67	4 28	7	0 28
308	20 32	248	16 32	188	12 32	128	8 32	68	4 32	8	0 32
309	20 36	249	16 36	189	12 36	129	8 36	69	4 36	9	0 36
310	20 40	250	16 40	190	12 40	130	8 40	70	4 40	10	0 40
311	20 44	251	16 44	191	12 44	131	8 44	71	4 44	11	0 44
312	20 48	252	16 48	192	12 48	132	8 48	72	4 48	12	0 48
313	20 52	253	16 52	193	12 52	133	8 52	73	4 52	13	0 52
314	20 56	254	16 56	194	12 56	134	8 56	74	4 56	14	0 56
315	21 00	255	17 00	195	13 00	135	9 00	75	5 00	15	1 00
316	21 04	256	17 04	196	13 04	136	9 04	76	5 04	16	1 04
317	21 08	257	17 08	197	13 08	137	9 08	77	5 08	17	1 08
318	21 12	258	17 12	198	13 12	138	9 12	78	5 12	18	1 12
319	21 16	259	17 16	199	13 16	139	9 16	79	5 16	19	1 16
320	21 20	260	17 20	200	13 20	140	9 20	80	5 20	20	1 20
321	21 24	261	17 24	201	13 24	141	9 24	81	5 24	21	1 24
322	21 28	262	17 28	202	13 28	142	9 28	82	5 28	22	1 28
323	21 32	263	17 32	203	13 32	143	9 32	83	5 32	23	1 32
324	21 36	264	17 36	204	13 36	144	9 36	84	5 36	24	1 36
325	21 40	265	17 40	205	13 40	145	9 40	85	5 40	25	1 40
326	21 44	266	17 44	206	13 44	146	9 44	86	5 44	26	1 44
327	21 48	267	17 48	207	13 48	147	9 48	87	5 48	27	1 48
328	21 52	268	17 52	208	13 52	148	9 52	88	5 52	28	1 52
329	21 56	269	17 56	209	13 56	149	9 56	89	5 56	29	1 56
330	22 00	270	18 00	210	14 00	150	10 00	90	6 00	30	2 00

For explanation of use of above table see page 4:1

CONVERTING ARC INTO TIME & VICE-VERSA

Secs. (& decimals) of Arc into Secs. of Time

"	s
31	2·07
32	2·13
33	2·20
34	2·27
35	2·33
36 = 0·6	2·40
37	2·47
38	2·53
39	2·60
40	2·67
41	2·73
42 = 0·7	2·80
43	2·87
44	2·93
45	3·00
46	3·07
47	3·13
48 = 0·8	3·20
49	3·27
50	3·33
51	3·40
52	3·47
53	3·53
54 = 0·9	3·60
55	3·67
56	3·73
57	3·80
58	3·87
59	3·93
60 = 1·0	4·00

Mins. of Arc into Mins. and Secs. of Time

'	min.	s
31	2	04
32	2	08
33	2	12
34	2	16
35	2	20
36	2	24
37	2	28
38	2	32
39	2	36
40	2	40
41	2	44
42	2	48
43	2	52
44	2	56
45	3	00
46	3	04
47	3	08
48	3	12
49	3	16
50	3	20
51	3	24
52	3	28
53	3	32
54	3	36
55	3	40
56	3	44
57	3	48
58	3	52
59	3	56
60	4	00

DEGREES OF ARC INTO HOURS AND MINUTES.

°	h.min.	°	h.min.	°	h.min.	°	h.min.	°	h.min.	°	h.min.
331	22 04	271	18 04	211	14 04	151	10 04	91	6 04	31	2 04
332	22 08	272	18 08	212	14 08	152	10 08	92	6 08	32	2 08
333	22 12	273	18 12	213	14 12	153	10 12	93	6 12	33	2 12
334	22 16	274	18 16	214	14 16	154	10 16	94	6 16	34	2 16
335	22 20	275	18 20	215	14 20	155	10 20	95	6 20	35	2 20
336	22 24	276	18 24	216	14 24	156	10 24	96	6 24	36	2 24
337	22 28	277	18 28	217	14 28	157	10 28	97	6 28	37	2 28
338	22 32	278	18 32	218	14 32	158	10 32	98	6 32	38	2 32
339	22 36	279	18 36	219	14 36	159	10 36	99	6 36	39	2 36
340	22 40	280	18 40	220	14 40	160	10 40	100	6 40	40	2 40
341	22 44	281	18 44	221	14 44	161	10 44	101	6 44	41	2 44
342	22 48	282	18 48	222	14 48	162	10 48	102	6 48	42	2 48
343	22 52	283	18 52	223	14 52	163	10 52	103	6 52	43	2 52
344	22 56	284	18 56	224	14 56	164	10 56	104	6 56	44	2 56
345	23 00	285	19 00	225	15 00	165	11 00	105	7 00	45	3 00
346	23 04	286	19 04	226	15 04	166	11 04	106	7 04	46	3 04
347	23 08	287	19 08	227	15 08	167	11 08	107	7 08	47	3 08
348	23 12	288	19 12	228	15 12	168	11 12	108	7 12	48	3 12
349	23 16	289	19 16	229	15 16	169	11 16	109	7 16	49	3 16
350	23 20	290	19 20	230	15 20	170	11 20	110	7 20	50	3 20
351	23 24	291	19 24	231	15 24	171	11 24	111	7 24	51	3 24
352	23 28	292	19 28	232	15 28	172	11 28	112	7 28	52	3 28
353	23 32	293	19 32	233	15 32	173	11 32	113	7 32	53	3 32
354	23 36	294	19 36	234	15 36	174	11 36	114	7 36	54	3 36
355	23 40	295	19 40	235	15 40	175	11 40	115	7 40	55	3 40
356	23 44	296	19 44	236	15 44	176	11 44	116	7 44	56	3 44
357	23 48	297	19 48	237	15 48	177	11 48	117	7 48	57	3 48
358	23 52	298	19 52	238	15 52	178	11 52	118	7 52	58	3 52
359	23 56	299	19 56	239	15 56	179	11 56	119	7 56	59	3 56
360	24 0	300	20 0	240	16 0	180	12 0	120	8 0	60	4 0

For example of use of above table see page 4:1

REFRACTION AND DIP TABLES

MEAN REFRACTION
Subtractive

App. Alt.	Refr.	App. Alt	Refr.	App. Alt.	Refr.	App. Alt.	Refr.
o '	'	o '	'	o '	'	o '	'
0 00	34.9	5 00	9.8	10 00	5.3	16 30	3.2
10	32.8	10	9.5	10	5.2	17 00	3.1
20	30.9	20	9.3	20	5.1	17 30	3.0
30	29.1	30	9.0	30	5.0	18 00	2.9
40	27.4	40	8.8	40	5.0	18 30	2.9
50	25.8	50	8.6	50	4.9	19 00	2.8
1 00	24.4	6 00	8.4	11 00	4.8	20	2.6
10	23.1	10	8.2	10	4.7	21	2.5
20	21.9	20	8.0	20	4.7	22	2.4
30	20.9	30	7.8	30	4.6	23	2.3
40	19.9	40	7.7	40	4.5	24	2.2
50	19.0	50	7.5	50	4.5	26	2.0
2 00	18.1	7 00	7.3	12 00	4.4	28	1.8
10	17.4	10	7.2	10	4.4	30	1.7
20	16.7	20	7.0	20	4.3	32	1.5
30	16.0	30	6.9	30	4.2	34	1.4
40	15.4	40	6.8	40	4.2	36	1.3
50	14.8	50	6.6	50	4.1	38	1.2
3 00	14.2	8 00	6.5	13 00	4.1	40	1.1
10	13.7	10	6.4	10	4.0	43	1.0
20	13.3	20	6.3	20	4.0	46	0.9
30	12.8	30	6.1	30	3.9	50	0.8
40	12.4	40	6.0	40	3.9	55	0.7
50	12.0	50	5.9	50	3.8	60	0.6
4 00	11.7	9 00	5.8	14 00	3.8	65	0.5
10	11.3	10	5.7	20	3.7	70	0.4
20	11.0	20	5.6	40	3.6	75	0.3
30	10.7	30	5.5	15 00	3.5	80	0.2
40	10.4	40	5.4	30	3.4	85	0.1
50	10.1	50	5.4	16 00	3.3	90	0.0

DIP OF SEA HORIZON
Subtractive

H.E.	Dip	H.E.	H.E.	Dip	H.E.
Ft.	'	m.	Ft.	'	m.
2	1.5	0.6	44	6.5	13.4
3	1.8	0.9	46	6.7	14.0
4	2.0	1.2	48	6.8	14.6
5	2.2	1.5	50	6.9	15.2
6	2.4	1.8	52	7.1	15.9
7	2.6	2.1	54	7.2	16.5
8	2.8	2.4	56	7.3	17.0
9	2.9	2.7	58	7.5	17.7
10	3.1	3.0	60	7.6	18.3
11	3.3	3.4	65	7.9	19.8
12	3.4	3.7	70	8.2	21.3
13	3.5	4.0	80	8.8	24.4
14	3.7	4.3	90	9.3	27.4
15	3.8	4.6	100	9.6	30.5
16	3.9	4.9	120	10.7	36.6
17	4.0	5.2	140	11.6	42.7
18	4.2	5.5	160	12.4	49.8
19	4.3	5.8	180	13.2	54.9
20	4.4	6.1	200	13.7	61.0
22	4.6	6.7	220	14.5	67.1
24	4.8	7.3	240	15.2	73.2
26	5.0	7.9	260	15.8	79.3
28	5.2	8.5	280	16.4	85.3
30	5.4	9.1	300	17.0	91.4
32	5.5	9.8	350	18.3	107
34	5.7	10.4	400	19.6	122
36	5.9	11.0	450	20.8	137
38	6.0	11.6	500	21.9	152
40	6.2	12.2			
42	6.4	12.8			

SUN'S PARALLAX in ALTITUDE

App. Alt.	Additive Plx.	App. Alt.	Additive Plx.	App. Alt.	Additive Plx.	App. Alt.	Additive Plx.
o	'	o	'	o	'	o	'
0	0.15	20	0.14	40	0.11	70	0.06
5	0.15	25	0.13	50	0.10	80	0.03
10	0.14	30	0.12	60	0.08	90	0.00
15	0.14						

The Sun's **Semi-Diameter** will be found on each monthly page—3:10, 3:16, 3:22.

SUN ALTITUDE TOTAL CORRECTION TABLE
For correcting the Observed Altitude of the Sun's Lower Limb

ALWAYS ADDITIVE (+)
Height of the eye above the sea. Top line metres, lower line feet

Obs. Alt.	0.9 / 3	1.8 / 6	2.4 / 8	3 / 10	3.7 / 12	4.3 / 14	4.9 / 16	5.5 / 18	6 / 20	7.6 / 25	9 / 30	12 / 40	15 / 50	18 / 60	21 / 70	24 / 80
9°	8.6	8.0	7.6	7.2	6.9	6.6	6.4	6.2	5.9	5.4	4.9	4.1	3.4	2.7	2.1	1.5
10	9.1	8.5	8.1	7.9	7.5	7.2	7.0	6.7	6.6	6.0	5.5	4.7	3.9	3.3	2.7	2.1
11	9.6	9.0	8.6	8.3	8.0	7.7	7.4	7.2	7.0	6.4	6.0	5.2	4.4	3.7	3.1	2.5
12	10.0	9.4	9.0	8.7	8.4	8.1	7.8	7.6	7.4	6.8	6.4	5.6	4.8	4.1	3.5	2.9
13	10.3	9.7	9.3	9.0	8.7	8.4	8.2	7.9	7.7	7.2	6.7	5.9	5.2	4.5	3.9	3.3
14	10.6	10.0	9.6	9.3	9.0	8.7	8.5	8.2	8.0	7.5	7.0	6.2	5.5	4.8	4.2	3.6
15	10.9	10.2	9.9	9.5	9.2	9.0	8.7	8.5	8.2	7.7	7.2	6.4	5.7	5.0	4.4	3.8
16	11.1	10.5	10.1	9.7	9.5	9.2	8.9	8.7	8.5	7.9	7.5	6.7	5.9	5.2	4.6	4.1
17	11.3	10.7	10.3	10.0	9.7	9.4	9.1	8.9	8.7	8.2	7.7	6.9	6.1	5.5	4.9	4.3
18	11.5	10.8	10.5	10.1	9.9	9.6	9.3	9.1	8.9	8.3	7.9	7.0	6.3	5.6	5.0	4.5
19	11.6	11.0	10.6	10.3	10.0	9.7	9.5	9.2	9.0	8.5	8.0	7.2	6.5	5.8	5.2	4.6
20	11.8	11.2	10.8	10.4	10.2	9.9	9.6	9.4	9.2	8.6	8.2	7.4	6.6	5.9	5.3	4.8
21	11.9	11.3	10.9	10.6	10.3	10.0	9.8	9.5	9.3	8.8	8.3	7.5	6.8	6.1	5.5	4.9
22	12.0	11.4	11.0	10.7	10.4	10.1	9.9	9.7	9.4	8.9	8.4	7.6	6.9	6.2	5.6	5.0
23	12.1	11.5	11.1	10.8	10.5	10.2	10.0	9.8	9.5	9.0	8.5	7.7	7.0	6.3	5.7	5.1
24	12.2	11.6	11.2	10.9	10.6	10.3	10.1	9.9	9.6	9.1	8.6	7.8	7.1	6.4	5.8	5.2
25	12.3	11.7	11.3	11.0	10.7	10.4	10.2	10.0	9.7	9.2	8.7	7.9	7.2	6.5	5.9	5.3
26	12.4	11.8	11.4	11.1	10.8	10.5	10.3	10.1	9.8	9.3	8.8	8.0	7.3	6.6	6.0	5.4
27	12.5	11.9	11.5	11.2	10.9	10.6	10.4	10.1	9.9	9.4	8.9	8.1	7.4	6.7	6.1	5.5
28	12.6	12.0	11.6	11.3	11.0	10.7	10.4	10.2	10.0	9.5	9.0	8.2	7.4	6.8	6.2	5.6
30	12.7	12.1	11.7	11.4	11.1	10.8	10.6	10.4	10.1	9.6	9.1	8.3	7.6	6.9	6.3	5.7
32	12.9	12.2	11.9	11.5	11.2	11.0	10.7	10.5	10.2	9.7	9.3	8.4	7.7	7.0	6.4	5.8
34	13.0	12.3	12.0	11.6	11.3	11.1	10.8	10.6	10.3	9.8	9.4	8.5	7.8	7.1	6.5	5.9
36	13.1	12.4	12.1	11.7	11.4	11.2	10.9	10.7	10.4	9.9	9.5	8.6	7.9	7.2	6.6	6.0
38	13.2	12.5	12.1	11.8	11.5	11.2	11.0	10.8	10.5	10.0	9.5	8.7	8.0	7.3	6.7	6.1
40	13.3	12.6	12.2	11.9	11.6	11.3	11.1	10.8	10.6	10.1	9.6	8.8	8.1	7.4	6.8	6.2
42	13.4	12.7	12.3	12.0	11.7	11.4	11.2	10.9	10.7	10.2	9.7	8.9	8.2	7.5	6.9	6.3
44	13.4	12.7	12.4	12.0	11.7	11.5	11.2	11.0	10.7	10.2	9.8	8.9	8.2	7.5	6.9	6.3
46	13.5	12.8	12.4	12.1	11.8	11.5	11.3	11.0	10.8	10.3	9.8	9.0	8.3	7.6	7.0	6.4
48	13.6	12.9	12.5	12.2	11.9	11.6	11.3	11.1	10.9	10.4	9.9	9.1	8.3	7.7	7.1	6.4
50	13.6	12.9	12.5	12.2	11.9	11.6	11.4	11.1	10.9	10.4	9.9	9.1	8.4	7.7	7.1	6.5
52	13.6	13.0	12.6	12.3	12.0	11.7	11.4	11.2	11.0	10.5	10.0	9.2	8.4	7.8	7.2	6.5
54	13.7	13.0	12.6	12.3	12.0	11.7	11.5	11.3	11.0	10.5	10.0	9.2	8.5	7.8	7.2	6.6
56	13.7	13.1	12.7	12.4	12.1	11.8	11.5	11.3	11.1	10.6	10.1	9.3	8.5	7.9	7.3	6.7
58	13.8	13.1	12.7	12.4	12.1	11.8	11.6	11.3	11.1	10.6	10.1	9.3	8.6	7.9	7.3	6.8
60	13.8	13.1	12.8	12.4	12.1	11.9	11.6	11.4	11.1	10.6	10.2	9.3	8.6	7.9	7.3	6.8
62	13.9	13.2	12.8	12.5	12.2	11.9	11.7	11.4	11.2	10.7	10.2	9.4	8.7	8.0	7.4	6.8
64	13.9	13.2	12.8	12.5	12.2	11.9	11.7	11.5	11.2	10.7	10.2	9.4	8.7	8.0	7.4	6.9
66	14.0	13.2	12.9	12.5	12.3	12.0	11.7	11.5	11.3	10.7	10.3	9.5	8.7	8.1	7.5	7.0
70	14.1	13.3	12.9	12.6	12.3	12.0	11.8	11.6	11.3	10.8	10.3	9.5	8.8	8.1	7.5	7.0
80	14.2	13.5	13.1	12.8	12.5	12.2	11.9	11.7	11.5	11.0	10.5	9.7	8.9	8.3	7.7	7.1
90	14.3	13.6	13.2	12.9	12.6	12.3	12.1	11.9	11.6	11.1	10.6	9.8	9.1	8.4	7.8	7.2

MONTHLY CORRECTION

Jan.	Feb.	Mar.	Apr.	May	June	July	Aug.	Sept.	Oct.	Nov.	Dec.
+0'.3	+0'.2	+0'.1	0'.0	−0'.1	−0'.2	−0'.2	−0'.2	−0'.1	+0'.1	+0'.2	+0'.3

SUN ALTITUDE TOTAL CORRECTION TABLE

The Table on page 4:5 shows the combined effect of the usual Sun's corrections for Dip of the Horizon, Refraction, Parallax and Semi-Diameter. The corrections have been reduced to minutes and tenths, these tenths may be reduced to seconds by multiplying them by six.

Owing to the fact that the Table has been calculated for a fixed Semi-Diameter, it is necessary to apply a small monthly correction (given at the foot of the Table) if accuracy is desired.

If the Sun's Upper Limb has been observed, subtract twice the Sun's Semi-Diameter (given on the monthly pages) from the Altitude and then use this Table in the usual way.

Example: Having taken a Meridian Altitude of the Sun for Latitude at noon on July 20th, required the True Altitude. Height of eye 4.6 metres above the sea. Observed Altitude 42° 25.5'.

Observed Altitude of Sun's Lower Limb	42° +25.5'
Correction from Table. Alt. 43° and H.E. 4.6m (July)	+ 11.1'
True Altitude	42° 36.6'

STAR OR PLANET ALTITUDE TOTAL CORRECTION TABLE

ALWAYS SUBTRACTIVE (−)

Height of Eye above the Sea. Top line metres — lower line feet

Obs. Alt.	1.5	3	4.6	6	7.6	9	10.7	12	13.7	15	16.8	18	21.3
	5	10	15	20	25	30	35	40	45	50	55	60	70
9°	8.0	8.9	9.6	10.3	10.7	11.2	11.6	12.0	12.4	12.8	13.1	13.5	14.1
10°	7.4	8.4	9.1	9.7	10.2	10.6	11.1	11.5	11.8	12.2	12.5	12.9	13.5
11°	7.0	7.9	8.6	9.2	9.7	10.2	10.6	11.0	11.4	11.8	12.0	12.4	13.0
12°	6.6	7.5	8.2	8.8	9.3	9.8	10.2	10.6	11.0	11.4	11.6	12.0	12.6
13°	6.2	7.2	7.9	8.4	9.0	9.4	9.9	10.3	10.6	11.0	11.3	11.6	12.3
14°	5.9	6.9	7.6	8.1	8.6	9.2	9.6	10.0	10.3	10.7	11.0	11.3	12.0
15°	5.7	6.6	7.3	7.9	8.4	8.9	9.3	9.7	10.1	10.4	10.8	11.1	11.7
16°	5.5	6.4	7.1	7.7	8.2	8.7	9.1	9.5	9.9	10.2	10.5	10.9	11.5
17°	5.3	6.2	6.9	7.5	8.0	8.5	8.9	9.3	9.7	10.0	10.3	10.7	11.3
18°	5.1	6.0	6.7	7.3	7.8	8.3	8.7	9.1	9.5	9.8	10.2	10.5	11.1
19°	4.9	5.8	6.5	7.1	7.6	8.1	8.5	8.9	9.3	9.7	10.0	10.3	11.0
20°	4.8	5.7	6.4	7.0	7.5	8.0	8.4	8.8	9.2	9.6	9.9	10.2	10.8
25°	4.2	5.1	5.8	6.4	6.9	7.4	7.8	8.2	8.6	9.0	9.3	9.6	10.2
30°	3.8	4.7	5.4	6.0	6.5	7.0	7.4	7.8	8.2	8.6	8.9	9.2	9.8
35°	3.5	4.4	5.1	5.7	6.3	6.7	7.2	7.6	7.9	8.3	8.6	8.9	9.5
40°	3.3	4.2	4.9	5.5	6.0	6.5	6.9	7.3	7.7	8.1	8.4	8.7	9.3
50°	3.0	3.9	4.6	5.2	5.7	6.2	6.6	7.0	7.4	7.7	8.1	8.4	9.0
60°	2.7	3.6	4.4	4.9	5.5	5.9	6.4	6.8	7.1	7.5	7.8	8.1	8.8
70°	2.5	3.4	4.1	4.7	5.3	5.7	6.2	6.6	6.9	7.3	7.6	7.9	8.6
80°	2.3	3.3	4.0	4.6	5.1	5.5	6.0	6.4	6.7	7.1	7.4	7.8	8.4
90°	2.2	3.1	3.8	4.4	4.9	5.4	5.8	6.2	6.6	6.9	7.3	7.6	8.2

The above table contains the combined effects of Dip of the Horizon and Refraction and is therefore a total correction table for a Star or Planet. It is always subtractive.

Example: The observed altitude of a star was 32° 50'; and the height of observer's eye was 20 feet. What was the star's True Altitude?

Star's Observed Altitude	32° 50.0'
Correction from Table	− 5.8'
Star's True Altitude	32° 44.2'

☉ SUN G.H.A. CORRECTION TABLE ☉

Min. or Sec.	Add for Minutes	Add for 1 Hour +Minutes	Add for Secs.		Min. or Sec.	Add for Minutes	Add for 1 Hour +Minutes	Add for Secs.
	° ′	° ′	′			° ′	° ′	′
0	0 0.0	15 0.0	0.0		30	7 30.0	22 30.0	7.5
1	0 15.0	15 15.0	0.3		31	7 45.0	22 45.0	7.8
2	0 30.0	15 30.0	0.5		32	8 0.0	23 0.0	8.0
3	0 45.0	15 45.0	0.8		33	8 15.0	23 15.0	8.3
4	1 0.0	16 0.0	1.0		34	8 30.0	23 30.0	8.5
5	1 15.0	16 15.0	1.3		35	8 45.0	23 45.0	8.8
6	1 30.0	16 30.0	1.5		36	9 0.0	24 0.0	9.0
7	1 45.0	16 45.0	1.8		37	9 15.0	24 15.0	9.3
8	2 0.0	17 0.0	2.0		38	9 30.0	24 30.0	9.5
9	2 15.0	17 15.0	2.3		39	9 45.0	24 45.0	9.8
10	2 30.0	17 30.0	2.5		40	10 0.0	25 0.0	10.0
11	2 45.0	17 45.0	2.8		41	10 15.0	25 15.0	10.3
12	3 0.0	18 0.0	3.0		42	10 30.0	25 30.0	10.5
13	3 15.0	18 15.0	3.3		43	10 45.0	25 45.0	10.8
14	3 30.0	18 30.0	3.5		44	11 0.0	26 0.0	11.0
15	3 45.0	18 45.0	3.8		45	11 15.0	26 15.0	11.3
16	4 0.0	19 0.0	4.0		46	11 30.0	26 30.0	11.5
17	4 15.0	19 15.0	4.3		47	11 45.0	26 45.0	11.8
18	4 30.0	19 30.0	4.5		48	12 0.0	27 0.0	12.0
19	4 45.0	19 45.0	4.8		49	12 15.0	27 15.0	12.3
20	5 0.0	20 0.0	5.0		50	12 30.0	27 30.0	12.5
21	5 15.0	20 15.0	5.3		51	12 45.0	27 45.0	12.8
22	5 30.0	20 30.0	5.5		52	13 0.0	28 0.0	13.0
23	5 45.0	20 45.0	5.8		53	13 15.0	28 15.0	13.3
24	6 0.0	21 0.0	6.0		54	13 30.0	28 30.0	13.5
25	6 15.0	21 15.0	6.3		55	13 45.0	28 45.0	13.8
26	6 30.0	21 30.0	6.5		56	14 0.0	29 0.0	14.0
27	6 45.0	21 45.0	6.8		57	14 15.0	29 15.0	14.3
28	7 0.0	22 0.0	7.0		58	14 30.0	29 30.0	14.5
29	7 15.0	22 15.0	7.3		59	14 45.0	29 45.0	14.8
					60	15 0.0	30 0.0	15.0

The above table is calculated on the assumption that the Sun changes her G.H.A. 15° in one hour, which it does on an average throughout the year. At certain times however, it may differ nearly 0.2 of a minute of arc from this. Little error will be occasioned for ordinary navigation if the lesser 2 hours is always worked from, when the above table will be additive.

Example of Use of above Table

(1) Required the Sun G.H.A. October 29th, 1992, at 9h. 27min. 38s. G.M.T.

October 29th 1992, G.M.T. 8h. (see p. 3:67) .... G.H.A. = 304° 04'.0

Correction from the above table for 1h. 27min. .... + = 21° 45'.0

″   ″   ″   ″   ″   ″   38s. .... + = 9'.5

October 29th, 1992, at 9h. 27 min. 38s.   .... G.H.A. = 325° 58'.5

Correction for DATE

Greenwich Date	Correction ° '
1st	+ 0 0.0
2nd	+ 0 59.1
3rd	+ 1 58.2
4th	+ 2 57.3
5th	+ 3 56.5
6th	+ 4 55.6
7th	+ 5 54.8
8th	+ 6 54.0
9th	+ 7 53.1
10th	+ 8 52.2
11th	+ 9 51.4
12th	+ 10 50.5
13th	+ 11 49.6
14th	+ 12 48.8
15th	+ 13 48.0
16th	+ 14 47.1
17th	+ 15 46.2
18th	+ 16 45.3
19th	+ 17 44.5
20th	+ 18 43.6
21st	+ 19 42.7
22nd	+ 20 41.9
23rd	+ 21 41.0
24th	+ 22 40.1
25th	+ 23 39.3
26th	+ 24 38.4
27th	+ 25 37.6
28th	+ 26 36.7
29th	+ 27 35.8
30th	+ 28 35.0
31st	+ 29 34.1

Correction for HOURS

Hours	Correction ° '
0	+ 0 0.0
1	+ 15 2.5
2	+ 30 4.9
3	+ 45 7.4
4	+ 60 9.9
5	+ 75 12.3
6	+ 90 14.8
7	+ 105 17.2
8	+ 120 19.7
9	+ 135 22.2
10	+ 150 24.6
11	+ 165 27.1
12	+ 180 29.6
13	+ 195 32.0
14	+ 210 34.5
15	+ 225 37.0
16	+ 240 39.4
17	+ 255 41.9
18	+ 270 44.4
19	+ 285 46.8
20	+ 300 49.3
21	+ 315 51.7
22	+ 330 54.2
23	+ 345 56.7
24	+ 360 59.1

Corr. for 1 HOUR+MIN. / Correction for MINS. / Corr. for SECONDS

1 hr. + mins.	Correction ° '	Mins.	Correction ° '	Secs.	Correction '
0	+ 15 2.5	0	+ 0 0.0	0	+ 0.0
1	+ 15 17.5	1	+ 0 15.0	1	+ 0.3
2	+ 15 32.6	2	+ 0 30.1	2	+ 0.5
3	+ 15 47.6	3	+ 0 45.1	3	+ 0.8
4	+ 16 2.7	4	+ 1 0.2	4	+ 1.0
5	+ 16 17.7	5	+ 1 15.2	5	+ 1.3
6	+ 16 32.7	6	+ 1 30.2	6	+ 1.5
7	+ 16 47.8	7	+ 1 45.3	7	+ 1.8
8	+ 17 2.8	8	+ 2 0.3	8	+ 2.0
9	+ 17 17.9	9	+ 2 15.4	9	+ 2.3
10	+ 17 32.9	10	+ 2 30.4	10	+ 2.5
11	+ 17 48.0	11	+ 2 45.5	11	+ 2.8
12	+ 18 3.0	12	+ 3 0.5	12	+ 3.0
13	+ 18 18.0	13	+ 3 15.5	13	+ 3.3
14	+ 18 33.1	14	+ 3 30.6	14	+ 3.5
15	+ 18 48.1	15	+ 3 45.6	15	+ 3.8
16	+ 19 3.2	16	+ 4 0.7	16	+ 4.0
17	+ 19 18.2	17	+ 4 15.7	17	+ 4.3
18	+ 19 33.2	18	+ 4 30.7	18	+ 4.5
19	+ 19 48.3	19	+ 4 45.8	19	+ 4.8
20	+ 20 3.3	20	+ 5 0.8	20	+ 5.0
21	+ 20 18.4	21	+ 5 15.9	21	+ 5.3
22	+ 20 33.4	22	+ 5 30.9	22	+ 5.5
23	+ 20 48.4	23	+ 5 45.9	23	+ 5.8
24	+ 21 3.5	24	+ 6 1.0	24	+ 6.0
25	+ 21 18.5	25	+ 6 16.0	25	+ 6.3
26	+ 21 33.6	26	+ 6 31.1	26	+ 6.5
27	+ 21 48.6	27	+ 6 46.1	27	+ 6.8
28	+ 22 3.6	28	+ 7 1.1	28	+ 7.0
29	+ 22 18.7	29	+ 7 16.2	29	+ 7.3
30	+ 22 33.7	30	+ 7 31.2	30	+ 7.5
31	+ 22 48.8	31	+ 7 46.3	31	+ 7.8
32	+ 23 3.8	32	+ 8 1.3	32	+ 8.0
33	+ 23 18.9	33	+ 8 16.4	33	+ 8.3
34	+ 23 33.9	34	+ 8 31.4	34	+ 8.5
35	+ 23 48.9	35	+ 8 46.4	35	+ 8.8
36	+ 24 4.0	36	+ 9 1.5	36	+ 9.0
37	+ 24 19.0	37	+ 9 16.5	37	+ 9.3
38	+ 24 34.1	38	+ 9 31.6	38	+ 9.5
39	+ 24 49.1	39	+ 9 46.6	39	+ 9.8
40	+ 25 4.1	40	+ 10 1.6	40	+ 10.0
41	+ 25 19.2	41	+ 10 16.7	41	+ 10.3
42	+ 25 34.2	42	+ 10 31.7	42	+ 10.5
43	+ 25 49.3	43	+ 10 46.8	43	+ 10.8
44	+ 26 4.3	44	+ 11 1.8	44	+ 11.0
45	+ 26 19.3	45	+ 11 16.8	45	+ 11.3
46	+ 26 34.4	46	+ 11 31.9	46	+ 11.5
47	+ 26 49.4	47	+ 11 46.9	47	+ 11.8
48	+ 27 4.5	48	+ 12 2.0	48	+ 12.0
49	+ 27 19.5	49	+ 12 17.0	49	+ 12.3
50	+ 27 34.6	50	+ 12 32.1	50	+ 12.5
51	+ 27 49.6	51	+ 12 47.1	51	+ 12.8
52	+ 28 4.6	52	+ 13 2.1	52	+ 13.0
53	+ 28 19.7	53	+ 13 17.2	53	+ 13.3
54	+ 28 34.7	54	+ 13 32.2	54	+ 13.5
55	+ 28 49.8	55	+ 13 47.3	55	+ 13.8
56	+ 29 4.8	56	+ 14 2.3	56	+ 14.0
57	+ 29 19.8	57	+ 14 17.3	57	+ 14.3
58	+ 29 34.9	58	+ 14 32.4	58	+ 14.5
59	+ 29 49.9	59	+ 14 47.4	59	+ 14.8
60	+ 30 4.9	60	+ 15 2.5	60	+ 15.0

This Table is to be used for both Stars and Aries.
The first full page column (Corr. for 1 hour + min.) is required
only when finding G.H.A. of a Star from G.H.A. ARIES
For Examples on the use of this Table see page 2:29 onwards.

PLANETS G.H.A. CORRECTION TABLE
ALWAYS ADDITIVE

Time	Variation per Hour								
	14°58'.8	14°59'.0	14°59'.1	14°59'.3	14°59'.4	14°59'.6	14°59'.7	14°59'.9	15°0'.0
Hrs.	° ′	° ′	° ′	° ′	° ′	° ′	° ′	° ′	° ′
0	0 00.0	0 00.0	0 00.0	0 00.0	0 00.0	0 00.0	0 00.0	0 00.0	0 00.0
1	14 58.8	14 59.0	14 59.1	15 59.3	14 59.4	14 59.6	14 59.7	14 59.9	15 00.0
2	29 57.6	29 58.0	29 58.2	29 58.6	29 58.8	29 59.2	29 59.4	29 59.8	30 00.0
3	44 56.4	44 57.0	44 57.3	44 57.9	44 58.2	44 58.8	44 59.1	44 59.7	45 00.0
4	59 55.2	59 56.0	59 56.4	59 57.2	59 57.6	59 58.4	59 58.8	59 59.6	60 00.0
5	74 54.0	74 55.0	74 55.5	74 56.5	74 57.0	74 58.0	74 58.5	74 59.5	75 00.0
6	89 52.8	89 54.0	89 54.6	89 55.8	89 56.4	89 57.6	89 58.2	89 59.4	90 00.0
7	104 51.6	104 53.0	104 53.7	104 55.1	104 55.8	104 57.2	104 57.9	104 59.3	105 00.0
8	119 50.4	119 52.0	119 52.8	119 54.4	119 55.2	119 56.8	119 57.6	119 59.2	120 00.0
9	134 49.2	134 51.0	134 51.9	134 53.7	134 54.6	134 56.4	134 57.3	134 59.1	135 00.0
10	149 48.0	149 50.0	149 51.0	149 53.0	149 54.0	149 56.0	149 57.0	149 59.0	150 00.0
11	164 46.8	164 49.0	164 50.1	164 52.3	164 53.4	164 55.6	164 56.7	164 58.9	165 00.0
12	179 45.6	179 48.0	179 49.2	179 51.6	179 52.8	179 55.2	179 56.4	179 58.8	180 00.0
13	194 44.4	194 47.0	194 48.3	194 50.9	194 52.2	194 54.8	194 56.1	194 58.7	195 00.0
14	209 43.2	209 46.0	209 47.4	209 50.2	209 51.6	209 54.4	209 55.8	209 58.6	210 00.0
15	224 42.0	224 45.0	224 46.5	224 49.5	224 51.0	224 54.0	224 55.5	224 58.5	225 00.0
16	239 40.8	239 44.0	239 45.6	239 48.8	239 50.4	239 53.6	239 55.2	239 58.4	240 00.0
17	254 39.6	254 43.0	254 44.7	254 48.1	254 49.8	254 53.2	254 54.9	254 58.3	255 00.0
18	269 38.4	269 42.0	269 43.8	269 47.4	269 49.2	269 52.8	269 54.6	269 58.2	270 00.0
19	284 37.2	284 41.0	284 42.9	284 46.7	284 48.6	284 52.4	284 54.3	284 58.1	285 00.0
20	299 36.0	299 40.0	299 42.0	299 46.0	299 48.0	299 52.0	299 54.0	299 58.0	300 00.0
21	314 34.8	314 39.0	314 41.1	314 45.3	314 47.4	314 51.6	314 53.7	314 57.9	315 00.0
22	329 33.6	329 38.0	329 40.2	329 44.6	329 46.8	329 51.2	329 53.4	329 57.8	330 00.0
23	344 32.4	344 37.0	344 39.3	344 43.7	344 46.2	344 50.8	344 53.1	344 57.7	345 00.0
24	359 31.2	359 36.0	359 38.4	359 43.2	359 45.6	359 50.4	359 52.8	359 57.6	0 00.0

ALWAYS ADDITIVE

Time	Variation per Hour								
	15°0'.2	15°0'.3	15°0'.5	15°0'.6	15°0'.8	15°0'.9	15°1'.1	15°1'.2	15°1'.4
Hrs.	° ′	° ′	° ′	° ′	° ′	° ′	° ′	° ′	° ′
0	0 00.0	0 00.0	0 00.0	0 00.0	0 00.0	0 00.0	0 00.0	0 00.0	0 00.0
1	15 00.2	15 00.3	15 00.5	15 00.6	15 00.8	15 00.9	15 01.1	15 01.2	15 01.4
2	30 00.4	30 00.6	30 01.0	30 01.2	30 01.6	30 01.8	30 02.2	30 02.4	30 02.8
3	45 00.6	45 00.9	45 01.5	45 01.8	45 02.4	45 02.7	45 03.3	45 03.6	45 04.2
4	60 00.8	06 01.2	60 02.0	60 02.4	60 03.2	60 03.6	60 04.4	60 04.8	60 05.6
5	75 01.0	75 01.5	75 02.5	75 03.0	75 04.0	75 04.5	75 05.5	75 06.0	75 07.0
6	90 01.2	90 01.8	90 03.0	90 03.6	90 04.8	90 05.4	90 06.6	90 07.2	90 08.4
7	105 01.4	105 02.1	105 03.5	105 04.2	105 05.6	105 06.3	105 07.7	105 08.4	105 09.8
8	120 01.6	120 02.4	120 04.0	120 04.8	120 06.4	120 07.2	120 08.8	120 09.6	120 11.2
9	135 01.8	135 02.7	135 04.5	135 05.4	135 07.2	135 08.1	135 09.9	135 10.8	135 12.6
10	150 02.0	150 03.0	150 05.0	150 06.0	150 08.0	150 09.0	150 11.0	150 12.0	150 14.0
11	165 02.2	165 03.3	165 05.5	165 06.6	165 08.8	165 09.9	165 12.1	165 13.2	165 15.4
12	180 02.4	180 03.6	180 06.0	180 07.2	180 09.6	180 10.8	180 13.2	180 14.4	180 16.8
13	195 02.6	195 03.9	195 06.5	195 07.8	195 10.4	195 11.7	195 14.3	195 15.6	195 18.2
14	210 02.8	210 04.2	210 07.0	210 08.4	210 11.1	210 12.6	210 15.4	210 16.8	210 19.6
15	225 03.0	225 04.5	225 07.5	225 09.0	225 12.0	225 13.5	225 16.5	225 18.5	225 21.0
16	240 03.2	240 04.8	240 08.0	240 09.6	240 12.8	240 14.4	240 17.6	240 19.2	240 22.4
17	255 03.4	255 05.1	255 08.5	255 10.2	255 13.6	255 15.3	255 18.7	255 20.4	255 23.8
18	270 03.6	270 05.4	270 09.0	270 10.8	270 14.4	270 16.2	270 19.8	270 21.6	270 25.2
19	285 03.8	285 05.7	285 09.5	285 11.4	285 15.2	285 17.1	285 20.9	285 22.8	285 26.6
20	300 04.0	300 06.0	300 10.0	300 12.0	300 16.0	300 18.0	300 22.0	300 24.0	300 28.0
21	315 04.2	315 06.3	315 10.5	315 12.6	315 16.8	315 18.9	315 23.1	315 25.2	315 29.4
22	330 04.4	330 06.6	330 11.0	330 13.2	330 17.6	330 19.8	330 24.2	330 26.4	330 30.8
23	345 04.6	345 06.9	345 11.5	345 13.8	345 18.4	345 20.7	345 25.3	345 27.6	345 32.2
24	0 04.8	0 07.2	0 12.0	0 14.4	0 19.2	0 21.6	0 26.4	0 28.8	0 33.6

PLANETS G.H.A. CORRECTION TABLE
ALWAYS ADDITIVE

Time	Variation per Hour								
	15°1'.5	15°1'.7	15°1'.8	15°2'.0	15°2'.1	15°2'.3	15°2'.4	15°2'.6	15°2'.7
Hrs.	° '	° '	° '	° '	° '	° '	° '	° '	° '
0	0 00.0	0 00.0	0 00.0	0 00.0	0 00.0	0 00.0	0 00.0	0 00.0	0 00.0
1	15 01.5	15 01.7	15 01.8	15 02.0	15 02.1	15 02.3	15 02.4	15 02.6	15 02.7
2	30 03.0	30 03.4	30 03.6	30 04.0	30 04.2	30 04.6	30 04.8	30 05.2	30 05.4
3	45 04.5	45 05.1	45 05.4	45 06.0	45 06.3	45 06.9	45 07.2	45 07.8	45 08.1
4	60 06.0	60 06.8	60 07.2	60 08.0	60 08.4	60 09.2	60 09.6	60 10.4	60 10.8
5	75 07.5	75 08.5	75 09.0	75 10.0	75 10.5	75 11.5	75 12.0	75 13.0	75 13.5
6	90 09.0	90 10.2	90 10.8	90 12.0	90 12.6	90 13.8	90 14.4	90 15.6	90 16.2
7	105 10.5	105 11.9	105 12.6	105 14.0	105 14.7	105 16.1	105 16.8	105 18.2	105 18.9
8	120 12.0	120 13.6	120 14.4	120 16.0	120 16.8	120 18.4	120 19.2	120 20.8	120 21.6
9	135 13.5	135 15.3	135 16.2	135 18.0	135 18.9	135 20.7	135 21.6	135 23.4	135 24.3
10	150 15.0	150 17.0	150 18.0	150 20.0	150 21.0	150 23.0	150 24.0	150 26.0	150 27.0
11	165 16.5	165 18.7	165 19.8	165 22.0	165 23.1	165 25.8	165 26.4	165 28.6	165 29.7
12	180 18.0	180 20.4	180 21.6	180 24.0	180 25.2	180 27.6	180 28.8	180 31.2	180 32.4
13	195 19.5	195 22.1	195 23.4	195 26.0	195 27.3	195 29.9	195 31.2	195 33.8	195 35.1
14	210 21.0	210 23.8	210 25.2	210 28.0	210 29.4	210 32.2	210 33.6	210 36.4	210 37.8
15	225 22.5	225 25.5	225 27.0	225 30.0	225 31.5	225 34.5	225 36.0	225 39.0	225 40.5
16	240 24.0	240 27.2	240 28.8	240 32.0	240 33.6	240 36.8	240 38.4	240 41.6	240 43.2
17	255 25.5	255 28.9	255 30.6	255 34.0	255 35.7	255 39.1	255 40.8	255 44.8	255 45.9
18	270 27.0	270 30.6	270 32.4	270 36.0	270 37.8	270 41.4	270 43.2	270 46.8	270 48.6
19	285 28.5	285 32.3	285 34.2	285 38.0	285 39.9	285 43.7	285 45.6	285 49.4	285 51.3
20	300 30.0	300 34.0	300 36.0	300 40.0	300 42.0	300 46.0	300 48.0	300 52.0	300 54.0
21	315 31.5	315 35.7	315 37.8	315 42.0	315 44.1	315 48.3	315 50.4	315 54.6	315 56.7
22	330 33.0	330 37.4	330 39.6	330 44.0	330 46.2	330 50.6	330 52.8	330 57.2	330 59.4
23	345 34.5	345 39.1	345 41.4	345 46.0	345 48.3	345 52.9	345 55.2	345 59.8	346 02.1
24	0 36.0	0 40.8	0 43.2	0 48.0	0 50.4	0 55.2	0 57.6	1 02.4	1 04.8

ALWAYS ADDITIVE

Time	Variation per Hour								
	15°2'.9	15°3'.0	15°3'.2	15°3'.3	15°3'.5	15°3'.6	15°3'.8	15°3'.9	15°4'.1
Hrs.	° '	° '	° '	° '	° '	° '	° '	° '	° '
0	0 00.0	0 00.0	0 00.0	0 00.0	0 00.0	0 00.0	0 00.0	0 00.0	0 00.0
1	15 02.9	15 03.0	15 03.2	15 03.3	15 03.5	15 03.6	15 03.8	15 03.9	15 04.1
2	30 05.8	30 06.0	30 06.4	30 06.6	30 07.0	30 07.2	30 07.6	30 07.8	30 08.2
3	45 08.7	45 09.0	45 09.6	45 09.9	45 10.5	45 10.8	45 11.4	45 11.7	45 12.3
4	60 11.6	60 12.0	60 12.8	60 13.2	60 14.0	60 14.4	60 15.2	60 15.6	60 16.4
5	75 14.5	75 15.0	75 16.0	75 16.5	75 17.5	75 18.0	75 19.0	75 19.5	75 20.5
6	90 17.4	90 18.0	90 19.2	90 19.8	90 19.8	90 21.6	90 22.8	90 23.4	90 24.6
7	105 20.3	105 21.0	105 22.4	105 23.1	105 24.5	105 25.2	105 26.6	105 27.3	105 28.7
8	120 23.2	120 24.0	120 25.6	120 26.4	120 28.0	120 28.8	120 30.4	120 31.2	120 32.8
9	135 26.1	135 27.0	135 28.8	135 29.7	135 31.5	135 32.4	135 34.2	135 35.1	135 36.9
10	150 29.0	150 30.0	150 32.0	150 33.0	150 35.0	150 36.0	150 38.0	150 39.0	150 41.0
11	165 31.9	165 33.0	165 35.2	165 36.3	165 38.5	165 39.6	165 41.8	165 42.9	165 45.1
12	180 34.8	180 36.0	180 38.4	180 39.6	180 42.0	180 43.2	180 45.6	180 46.8	180 49.2
13	195 37.7	195 39.0	195 41.6	195 42.9	195 45.5	195 46.8	195 49.4	195 50.7	195 53.3
14	210 40.6	210 42.0	210 44.8	210 46.2	210 49.0	210 50.4	210 53.2	210 54.6	210 57.4
15	225 43.5	225 45.0	225 48.0	225 49.5	225 52.5	225 54.0	225 57.0	225 58.5	226 01.5
16	240 46.4	240 48.0	240 51.2	240 52.8	240 56.0	240 57.6	241 00.8	241 02.4	241 05.6
17	255 49.3	255 51.0	255 54.4	255 56.1	255 59.5	256 01.2	256 04.6	256 06.3	256 09.7
18	270 52.2	270 54.0	270 57.6	270 59.4	271 03.0	271 04.8	271 08.4	271 10.2	271 13.8
19	285 55.1	285 57.0	286 00.8	286 02.7	286 06.5	286 08.4	286 12.2	286 14.1	286 17.9
20	300 58.0	301 00.0	301 04.0	301 06.0	301 10.0	301 12.0	301 16.0	301 18.0	301 22.0
21	316 00.9	316 03.0	316 07.2	316 09.3	316 13.5	316 15.6	316 19.8	316 21.9	316 26.1
22	331 03.8	331 06.0	331 10.4	331 12.6	331 17.0	331 19.2	331 23.6	331 25.8	331 30.2
23	346 06.7	346 09.0	346 13.6	346 15.9	346 20.5	346 22.8	346 27.4	346 29.7	346 34.3
24	001 09.6	001 12.0	001 16.8	001 19.2	001 24.0	001 26.4	001 31.2	001 33.6	001 38.4

PLANETS G.H.A. CORRECTION TABLE
ALWAYS ADDITIVE

Time	14°58'.8	14°59'.4	15°00'.0	15°00'.6	15°01'.2	15°01'.8	15°02'.4	15°03'.0	15°03'.6	Sec.	Corr.
min.	° '	° '	° '	° '	° '	° '	° '	° '	° '		
0	0 0.0	0 0.0	0 0.0	0 0.0	0 0.0	0 0.0	0 0.0	0 0.0	0 0.0	0	0.0
1	0 15.0	0 15.0	0 15.0	0 15.0	0 15.0	0 15.0	0 15.0	0 15.0	0 15.1	1	0.3
2	0 30.0	0 30.0	0 30.0	0 30.0	0 30.0	0 30.1	0 30.1	0 30.1	0 30.1	2	0.5
3	0 44.9	0 45.0	0 45.0	0 45.0	0 45.1	0 45.1	0 45.1	0 45.1	0 45.2	3	0.8
4	0 59.9	1 0.0	1 0.0	1 0.0	1 0.1	1 0.1	1 0.2	1 0.2	1 0.2	4	1.0
5	1 14.9	1 14.9	1 15.0	1 15.0	1 15.1	1 15.2	1 15.2	1 15.2	1 15.3	5	1.3
6	1 29.9	1 29.9	1 30.0	1 30.1	1 30.1	1 30.2	1 30.2	1 30.3	1 30.4	6	1.5
7	1 44.9	1 44.9	1 45.0	1 45.1	1 45.1	1 45.2	1 45.3	1 45.3	1 45.4	7	1.8
8	1 59.8	1 59.9	2 0.0	2 0.1	2 0.2	2 0.2	2 0.3	2 0.4	2 0.5	8	2.0
9	2 14.8	2 14.9	2 15.0	2 15.1	2 15.2	2 15.3	2 15.4	2 15.4	2 15.5	9	2.3
10	2 29.8	2 29.9	2 30.0	2 30.1	2 30.2	2 30.3	2 30.4	2 30.5	2 30.6	10	2.5
11	2 44.8	2 44.9	2 45.0	2 45.1	2 45.2	2 45.3	2 45.4	2 45.5	2 45.7	11	2.8
12	2 59.8	2 59.9	3 0.0	3 0.1	3 0.2	3 0.4	3 0.5	3 0.6	3 0.7	12	3.0
13	3 14.7	3 14.9	3 15.0	3 15.1	3 15.3	3 15.4	3 15.5	3 15.6	3 15.8	13	3.3
14	3 29.7	3 29.9	3 30.0	3 30.1	3 30.3	3 30.4	3 30.6	3 30.7	3 30.8	14	3.5
15	3 44.7	3 44.8	3 45.0	3 45.2	3 45.3	3 45.4	3 45.6	3 45.7	3 45.9	15	3.8
16	3 59.7	3 59.8	4 0.0	4 0.2	4 0.3	4 0.5	4 0.6	4 0.8	4 1.0	16	4.0
17	4 14.7	4 14.8	4 15.0	4 15.2	4 15.3	4 15.5	4 15.7	4 15.8	4 16.0	17	4.3
18	4 29.6	4 29.8	4 30.0	4 30.2	4 30.4	4 30.5	4 30.7	4 30.9	4 31.1	18	4.5
19	4 44.6	4 44.8	4 45.0	4 45.2	4 45.4	4 45.6	4 45.8	4 45.9	4 46.1	19	4.8
20	4 59.6	4 59.8	5 0.0	5 0.2	5 0.4	5 0.6	5 0.8	5 1.0	5 1.2	20	5.0
21	5 14.6	5 14.8	5 15.0	5 15.2	5 15.4	5 15.6	5 15.8	5 16.0	5 16.3	21	5.3
22	5 29.6	5 29.8	5 30.0	5 30.2	5 30.4	5 30.7	5 30.9	5 31.1	5 31.3	22	5.5
23	5 44.5	5 44.8	5 45.0	5 45.2	5 45.5	5 45.7	5 45.9	5 46.1	5 46.4	23	5.8
24	5 59.5	5 59.8	6 0.0	6 0.2	6 0.5	6 0.7	6 1.0	6 1.2	6 1.4	24	6.0
25	6 14.5	6 14.8	6 15.0	6 15.2	6 15.5	6 15.7	6 16.0	6 16.2	6 16.5	25	6.3
26	6 29.5	6 29.7	6 30.0	6 30.3	6 30.5	6 30.8	6 31.0	6 31.3	6 31.6	26	6.5
27	6 44.5	6 44.7	6 45.0	6 45.3	6 45.5	6 45.8	6 46.1	6 46.3	6 46.6	27	6.8
28	6 59.4	6 59.7	7 0.0	7 0.3	7 0.6	7 0.8	7 1.1	7 1.4	7 1.7	28	7.0
29	4 14.4	7 14.7	7 15.0	7 15.3	7 15.6	7 15.9	7 16.2	7 16.4	7 16.7	29	7.3
30	7 29.4	7 29.7	7 30.0	7 30.3	7 30.6	7 30.9	7 31.2	7 31.5	7 31.8	30	7.5
31	7 44.4	7 44.7	7 45.0	7 45.3	7 45.6	7 45.9	7 46.2	7 46.5	7 46.9	31	7.8
32	7 59.4	7 59.7	8 0.0	8 0.3	8 0.6	8 1.0	8 1.3	8 1.6	8 1.9	32	8.0
33	8 14.3	8 14.7	8 15.0	8 15.3	8 15.7	8 16.0	8 16.3	8 16.6	8 17.0	33	8.3
34	8 29.3	8 29.7	8 30.0	8 30.3	8 30.7	8 31.0	8 31.4	8 31.7	8 32.0	34	8.5
35	8 44.3	8 44.6	8 45.0	8 45.5	8 45.7	8 46.0	8 46.4	8 46.7	8 47.1	35	8.8
36	8 59.3	8 59.6	9 0.0	9 0.4	9 0.7	9 1.1	9 1.4	9 1.8	9 2.2	36	9.0
37	9 14.3	9 14.6	9 15.0	9 15.4	9 15.7	9 16.1	9 16.5	9 16.8	9 17.2	37	9.3
38	9 29.2	9 29.6	9 30.0	9 30.4	9 30.8	9 31.1	9 31.5	9 31.9	9 32.3	38	9.5
39	9 44.2	9 44.6	9 45.0	9 45.4	9 45.8	9 46.2	9 46.6	9 46.9	9 47.3	39	9.8
40	9 59.2	9 59.6	10 0.0	10 0.4	10 0.8	10 1.2	10 1.6	10 2.0	10 2.4	40	10.0
41	10 14.2	10 14.6	10 15.0	10 15.4	10 15.8	10 16.2	10 16.6	10 17.0	10 17.5	41	10.3
42	10 29.2	10 29.6	10 30.0	10 30.4	10 30.8	10 31.3	10 31.7	10 32.1	10 32.5	42	10.5
43	10 44.1	10 44.6	10 45.0	10 45.4	10 45.9	10 46.3	10 46.7	10 47.1	10 47.6	43	10.8
44	10 59.1	10 59.6	11 0.0	11 0.4	11 0.9	11 1.3	11 1.8	11 2.2	11 2.6	44	11.0
45	11 14.1	11 14.6	11 15.0	11 15.4	11 15.9	11 16.3	11 16.8	11 17.2	11 17.7	45	11.3
46	11 29.1	11 29.5	11 30.0	11 30.5	11 30.9	11 31.4	11 31.8	11 32.3	11 32.8	46	11.5
47	11 44.1	11 44.5	11 45.0	11 45.5	11 45.9	11 46.4	11 46.9	11 47.3	11 47.8	47	11.8
48	11 59.0	11 59.5	12 0.0	12 0.5	12 1.0	12 1.4	12 1.9	12 2.4	12 2.9	48	12.0
49	12 14.0	12 14.5	12 15.0	12 15.5	12 16.0	12 16.5	12 17.0	12 17.4	12 17.9	49	12.3
50	12 29.0	12 29.5	12 30.0	12 30.5	12 31.0	12 31.5	12 32.0	12 32.5	12 33.0	50	12.5
51	12 44.0	12 44.5	12 45.0	12 45.5	12 46.0	12 46.5	12 47.0	12 47.5	12 48.1	51	12.8
52	12 59.0	12 59.5	13 0.0	13 0.5	13 1.0	13 1.6	13 2.1	13 2.6	13 3.1	52	13.1
53	13 13.9	13 14.5	13 15.0	13 15.5	13 16.1	13 16.6	13 17.1	13 17.6	13 18.2	53	13.3
54	13 28.9	13 29.5	13 30.0	13 30.5	13 31.1	13 31.6	13 32.2	13 32.7	13 33.2	54	13.5
55	13 43.9	13 44.4	13 45.0	13 45.6	13 46.1	13 46.6	13 47.2	13 47.7	13 48.3	55	13.8
56	13 58.9	13 59.4	14 0.0	14 0.6	14 1.1	14 1.7	14 2.2	14 2.8	14 3.4	56	14.0
57	14 13.9	14 14.4	14 15.0	14 15.6	14 16.1	14 16.7	14 17.3	14 17.8	14 18.4	57	14.3
58	14 28.8	14 29.4	14 30.0	14 30.6	14 31.2	14 31.7	14 32.3	14 32.9	14 33.5	58	14.5
59	14 43.8	14 44.4	14 45.0	14 45.6	14 46.2	14 46.8	14 47.4	14 47.9	14 48.5	59	14.8
60	14 58.8	14 59.4	15 0.0	15 0.6	15 1.2	15 1.8	15 2.4	15 3.0	15 3.6	60	15.0

PLANETS DECLINATION CORRECTION TABLE

Time	\Variation per Hour															
	0'.0	0'.1	0'.2	0'.3	0'.4	0'.5	0'.6	0'.7	0'.8	0'.9	1'.0	1'.1	1'.2	1'.3	1'.4	1'.5
h min.																
0 00	0.0	0.0	0.0	0.0	0.0	0.0	0.0	0.0	0.0	0.0	0.0	0.0	0.0	0.0	0.0	0.0
12	0.0	0.0	0.0	0.1	0.1	0.1	0.1	0.1	0.2	0.2	0.2	0.2	0.2	0.3	0.3	0.3
24	0.0	0.0	0.1	0.1	0.2	0.2	0.2	0.3	0.3	0.4	0.4	0.4	0.5	0.5	0.6	0.6
36	0.0	0.1	0.1	0.2	0.2	0.3	0.4	0.4	0.5	0.5	0.6	0.7	0.7	0.8	0.8	0.9
48	0.0	0.1	0.2	0.2	0.3	0.4	0.5	0.6	0.6	0.7	0.8	0.9	1.0	1.0	1.1	1.2
1 00	0.0	0.1	0.2	0.3	0.4	0.5	0.6	0.7	0.8	0.9	1.0	1.1	1.2	1.3	1.4	1.5
12	0.0	0.1	0.2	0.4	0.5	0.6	0.7	0.8	1.0	1.1	1.2	1.3	1.4	1.6	1.7	1.8
24	0.0	0.1	0.3	0.4	0.6	0.7	0.8	1.0	1.1	1.3	1.4	1.5	1.7	1.8	2.0	2.1
36	0.0	0.2	0.3	0.5	0.6	0.8	1.0	1.1	1.3	1.4	1.6	1.8	1.9	2.1	2.2	2.4
48	0.0	0.2	0.4	0.5	0.7	0.9	1.1	1.3	1.4	1.6	1.8	2.0	2.2	2.3	2.5	2.7
2 00	0.0	0.2	0.4	0.6	0.8	1.0	1.2	1.4	1.6	1.8	2.0	2.2	2.4	2.6	2.8	3.0
12	0.0	0.2	0.4	0.7	0.9	1.1	1.3	1.5	1.8	2.0	2.2	2.4	2.6	2.9	3.1	3.3
24	0.0	0.2	0.5	0.7	1.0	1.2	1.4	1.7	1.9	2.2	2.4	2.6	2.9	3.1	3.4	3.6
36	0.0	0.3	0.5	0.8	1.0	1.3	1.6	1.8	2.1	2.3	2.6	2.9	3.1	3.4	3.6	3.9
48	0.0	0.3	0.6	0.8	1.1	1.4	1.7	2.0	2.2	2.5	2.8	3.1	3.4	3.6	3.9	4.2
3 00	0.0	0.3	0.6	0.9	1.2	1.5	1.8	2.1	2.4	2.7	3.0	3.3	3.6	3.9	4.2	4.5
12	0.0	0.3	0.6	1.0	1.3	1.6	1.9	2.2	2.6	2.9	3.2	3.5	3.8	4.2	4.5	4.8
24	0.0	0.3	0.7	1.0	1.4	1.7	2.0	2.4	2.7	3.1	3.4	3.7	4.1	4.4	4.8	5.1
36	0.0	0.4	0.7	1.1	1.4	1.8	2.2	2.5	2.9	3.2	3.6	4.0	4.3	4.7	5.0	5.4
48	0.0	0.4	0.8	1.1	1.5	1.9	2.3	2.7	3.0	3.4	3.8	4.2	4.6	4.9	5.3	5.7
4 00	0.0	0.4	0.8	1.2	1.6	2.0	2.4	2.8	3.2	3.6	4.0	4.4	4.8	5.2	5.6	6.0
12	0.0	0.4	0.8	1.3	1.7	2.1	2.5	2.9	3.4	3.8	4.2	4.6	5.0	5.5	5.9	6.3
24	0.0	0.4	0.9	1.3	1.8	2.2	2.6	3.1	3.5	4.0	4.4	4.8	5.3	5.7	6.2	6.6
36	0.0	0.5	0.9	1.4	1.8	2.3	2.8	3.2	3.7	4.1	4.6	5.1	5.5	6.0	6.4	6.9
48	0.0	0.5	1.0	1.4	1.9	2.4	2.9	3.4	3.8	4.3	4.8	5.3	5.8	6.2	6.7	7.2
5 00	0.0	0.5	1.0	1.5	2.0	2.5	3.0	3.5	4.0	4.5	5.0	5.5	6.0	6.5	7.0	7.5
12	0.0	0.5	1.0	1.6	2.1	2.6	3.1	3.6	4.2	4.7	5.2	5.7	6.2	6.8	7.3	7.8
24	0.0	0.5	1.1	1.6	2.2	2.7	3.2	3.8	4.3	4.9	5.4	5.9	6.5	7.0	7.6	8.1
36	0.0	0.6	1.1	1.7	2.2	2.8	3.4	3.9	4.5	5.0	5.6	6.2	6.7	7.3	7.8	8.4
48	0.0	0.6	1.2	1.7	2.3	2.9	3.5	4.1	4.6	5.2	5.8	6.4	7.0	7.5	8.1	8.7
6 00	0.0	0.6	1.2	1.8	2.4	3.0	3.6	4.2	4.8	5.4	6.0	6.6	7.2	7.8	8.4	9.0
12	0.0	0.6	1.2	1.9	2.5	3.1	3.7	4.3	5.0	5.6	6.2	6.8	7.4	8.1	8.7	9.3
24	0.0	0.6	1.3	1.9	2.6	3.2	3.8	4.5	5.1	5.8	6.4	7.0	7.7	8.3	9.0	9.6
36	0.0	0.7	1.3	2.0	2.6	3.3	4.0	4.6	5.3	5.9	6.6	7.3	7.9	8.6	9.2	9.9
48	0.0	0.7	1.4	2.0	2.7	3.4	4.1	4.8	5.4	6.1	6.8	7.5	8.2	8.8	9.5	10.2
7 00	0.0	0.7	1.4	2.1	2.8	3.5	4.2	4.9	5.6	6.3	7.0	7.7	8.4	9.1	9.8	10.5
12	0.0	0.7	1.4	2.2	2.9	3.6	4.3	5.0	5.8	6.5	7.2	7.9	8.6	9.4	10.1	10.8
24	0.0	0.7	1.5	2.2	3.0	3.7	4.4	5.2	5.9	6.7	7.4	8.1	8.9	9.6	10.4	11.1
36	0.0	0.8	1.5	2.3	3.0	3.8	4.6	5.3	6.1	6.8	7.6	8.4	9.1	9.9	10.6	11.4
48	0.0	0.8	1.6	2.3	3.1	3.9	4.7	5.5	6.2	7.0	7.8	8.6	9.4	10.1	10.9	11.7
8 00	0.0	0.8	1.6	2.4	3.2	4.0	4.8	5.6	6.4	7.2	8.0	8.8	9.6	10.4	11.2	12.0
12	0.0	0.8	1.6	2.5	3.3	4.1	4.9	5.7	6.6	7.4	8.2	9.0	9.8	10.7	11.5	12.3
24	0.0	0.8	1.7	2.5	3.4	4.2	5.0	5.9	6.7	7.6	8.4	9.2	10.1	10.9	11.8	12.6
36	0.0	0.9	1.7	2.6	3.4	4.3	5.2	6.0	6.9	7.7	8.6	9.5	10.3	11.2	12.0	12.9
48	0.0	0.9	1.8	2.6	3.5	4.4	5.3	6.2	7.0	7.9	8.8	9.7	10.6	11.4	12.3	13.2
9 00	0.0	0.9	1.8	2.7	3.6	4.5	5.4	6.3	7.2	8.1	9.0	9.9	10.8	11.7	12.6	13.5
12	0.0	0.9	1.8	2.8	3.7	4.6	5.5	6.4	7.4	8.3	9.2	10.1	11.0	12.0	12.9	13.8
24	0.0	0.9	1.9	2.8	3.8	4.7	5.6	6.6	7.5	8.5	9.4	10.3	11.3	12.2	13.2	14.1
36	0.0	1.0	1.9	2.9	3.8	4.8	5.8	6.7	7.7	8.6	9.6	10.6	11.5	12.5	13.4	14.4
48	0.0	1.0	2.0	2.9	3.9	4.9	5.9	6.9	7.8	8.8	9.8	10.8	11.8	12.7	13.7	14.7
10 00	0.0	1.0	2.0	3.0	4.0	5.0	6.0	7.0	8.0	9.0	10.0	11.0	12.0	13.0	14.0	15.0
12	0.0	1.0	2.0	3.1	4.1	5.1	6.1	7.1	8.2	9.2	10.2	11.2	12.2	13.2	14.3	15.3
24	0.0	1.0	2.1	3.1	4.2	5.2	6.2	7.3	8.3	9.4	10.4	11.4	12.5	13.5	14.6	15.6
36	0.0	1.1	2.1	3.2	4.2	5.3	6.4	7.4	8.5	9.5	10.6	11.7	12.7	13.8	14.8	15.9
48	0.0	1.1	2.2	3.2	4.3	5.4	6.5	7.6	8.6	9.7	10.8	11.9	13.0	14.0	15.1	16.2
11 00	0.0	1.1	2.2	3.3	4.4	5.5	6.6	7.7	8.8	9.9	11.0	12.1	13.2	14.3	15.4	16.5
12	0.0	1.1	2.2	3.4	4.5	5.6	6.7	7.8	9.0	10.1	11.2	12.3	13.4	14.6	15.7	16.8
24	0.0	1.1	2.3	3.4	4.6	5.7	6.8	8.0	9.1	10.3	11.4	12.5	13.7	14.8	16.0	17.1
36	0.0	1.2	2.3	3.5	4.6	5.8	7.0	8.1	9.3	10.4	11.6	12.8	13.9	15.1	16.2	17.4
48	0.0	1.2	2.4	3.5	4.7	5.9	7.1	8.3	9.4	10.6	11.8	13.0	14.2	15.3	16.5	17.7
12 00	0.0	1.2	2.4	3.6	4.8	6.0	7.2	8.4	9.6	10.8	12.0	13.2	14.4	15.6	16.8	18.0

PLANETS DECLINATION CORRECTION TABLE

Time	Variation per Hour															
	0'.0	0'.1	0'.2	0'.3	0'.4	0'.5	0'.6	0'.7	0'.8	0'.9	1'.0	1'.1	1'.2	1'.3	1'.4	1'.5
h min.	'	'	'	'	'	'	'	'	'	'	'	'	'	'	'	'
12 00	0.0	1.2	2.4	3.6	4.8	6.0	7.2	8.4	9.6	10.8	12.0	13.2	14.4	15.6	16.8	18.0
12	0.0	1.2	2.4	3.7	4.9	6.1	7.3	8.5	9.8	11.0	12.2	13.4	14.6	15.9	17.1	18.3
24	0.0	1.2	2.5	3.7	5.0	6.2	7.4	8.7	9.9	11.2	12.4	13.6	14.9	16.1	17.4	18.6
36	0.0	1.3	2.5	3.8	5.0	6.3	7.6	8.8	10.1	11.3	12.6	13.9	15.1	16.4	17.6	18.9
48	0.0	1.3	2.6	3.8	5.1	6.4	7.7	9.0	10.2	11.5	12.8	14.1	15.4	16.6	17.9	19.2
13 00	0.0	1.3	2.6	3.9	5.2	6.5	7.8	9.1	10.4	11.7	13.0	14.3	15.6	16.9	18.2	19.5
12	0.0	1.3	2.6	4.0	5.3	6.6	7.9	9.2	10.6	11.9	13.2	14.5	15.8	17.2	18.5	19.8
24	0.0	1.3	2.7	4.0	5.4	6.7	8.0	9.4	10.7	12.1	13.4	14.7	16.1	17.4	18.8	20.1
36	0.0	1.4	2.7	4.1	5.4	6.8	8.2	9.5	10.9	12.2	13.6	15.0	16.3	17.7	19.0	20.4
48	0.0	1.4	2.8	4.1	5.5	6.9	8.3	9.7	11.0	12.4	13.8	15.2	16.6	17.9	19.3	20.7
14 00	0.0	1.4	2.8	4.2	5.6	7.0	8.4	9.8	11.2	12.6	14.0	15.4	16.8	18.2	19.6	21.0
12	0.0	1.4	2.8	4.3	5.7	7.1	8.5	9.9	11.4	12.8	14.2	15.6	17.0	18.5	19.9	21.3
24	0.0	1.4	2.9	4.3	5.8	7.2	8.6	10.1	11.5	13.0	14.4	15.8	17.3	18.7	20.2	21.6
36	0.0	1.5	2.9	4.4	5.8	7.3	8.8	10.2	11.7	13.1	14.6	16.1	17.5	19.0	20.4	21.9
48	0.0	1.5	3.0	4.4	5.9	7.4	8.9	10.4	11.8	13.3	14.8	16.3	17.8	19.2	20.7	22.2
15 00	0.0	1.5	3.0	4.5	6.0	7.5	9.0	10.5	12.0	13.5	15.0	16.5	18.0	19.5	21.0	22.5
12	0.0	1.5	3.0	4.6	6.1	7.6	9.1	10.6	12.2	13.7	15.2	16.7	18.2	19.8	21.3	22.8
24	0.0	1.5	3.1	4.6	6.2	7.7	9.2	10.8	12.3	13.9	15.4	16.9	18.5	20.0	21.6	23.1
36	0.0	1.6	3.1	4.7	6.2	7.8	9.4	10.9	12.5	14.0	15.6	17.2	18.7	20.3	21.8	23.4
48	0.0	1.6	3.2	4.7	6.3	7.9	9.5	11.1	12.6	14.2	15.8	17.4	19.0	20.5	22.1	23.7
16 00	0.0	1.6	3.2	4.8	6.4	8.0	9.6	11.2	12.8	14.4	16.0	17.6	19.2	20.8	22.4	24.0
12	0.0	1.6	3.2	4.9	6.5	8.1	9.7	11.3	13.0	14.6	16.2	17.8	19.4	21.1	22.7	24.3
24	0.0	1.6	3.3	4.9	6.6	8.2	9.8	11.5	13.1	14.8	16.4	18.0	19.7	21.3	23.0	24.6
36	0.0	1.7	3.3	5.0	6.6	8.3	10.0	11.6	13.3	14.9	16.6	18.3	19.9	21.6	23.2	24.9
48	0.0	1.7	3.4	5.0	6.7	8.4	10.1	11.8	13.4	15.1	16.8	18.5	20.2	21.8	23.5	25.2
17 00	0.0	1.7	3.4	5.1	6.8	8.5	10.2	11.9	13.6	15.3	17.0	18.7	20.4	22.1	23.8	25.5
12	0.0	1.7	3.4	5.2	6.9	8.6	10.3	12.0	13.8	15.5	17.2	18.9	20.6	22.4	24.1	25.8
24	0.0	1.7	3.5	5.2	7.0	8.7	10.4	12.2	13.9	15.7	17.4	19.1	20.9	22.6	24.4	26.1
36	0.0	1.8	3.5	5.3	7.0	8.8	10.6	12.3	14.1	15.8	17.6	19.4	21.1	22.9	24.6	26.4
48	0.0	1.8	3.6	5.3	7.1	8.9	10.7	12.5	14.2	16.0	17.8	19.6	21.4	23.1	24.9	26.7
18 00	0.0	1.8	3.6	5.4	7.2	9.0	10.8	12.6	14.4	16.2	18.0	19.8	21.6	23.4	25.2	27.0
12	0.0	1.8	3.6	5.5	7.3	9.1	10.9	12.7	14.6	16.4	18.2	20.0	21.8	23.7	25.5	27.3
24	0.0	1.8	3.7	5.5	7.4	9.2	11.0	12.9	14.7	16.6	18.4	20.2	22.1	23.9	25.8	27.6
36	0.0	1.9	3.7	5.6	7.4	9.3	11.2	13.0	14.9	16.7	18.6	20.5	22.3	24.2	26.0	27.9
48	0.0	1.9	3.8	5.6	7.5	9.4	11.3	13.2	15.0	16.9	18.8	20.7	22.6	24.4	26.3	28.2
19 00	0.0	1.9	3.8	5.7	7.6	9.5	11.4	13.3	15.2	17.1	19.0	20.9	22.8	24.7	26.6	28.5
12	0.0	1.9	3.8	5.8	7.7	9.6	11.5	13.4	15.4	17.3	19.2	21.1	23.0	25.0	26.9	28.8
24	0.0	1.9	3.9	5.8	7.8	9.7	11.6	13.6	15.5	17.5	19.4	21.3	23.3	25.2	27.2	29.1
36	0.0	2.0	3.9	5.9	7.8	9.8	11.8	13.7	15.7	17.6	19.6	21.6	23.5	25.5	27.4	29.4
48	0.0	2.0	4.0	5.9	7.9	9.9	11.9	13.9	15.8	17.8	19.8	21.8	23.8	25.7	27.7	29.7
20 00	0.0	2.0	4.0	6.0	8.0	10.0	12.0	14.0	16.0	18.0	20.0	22.0	24.0	26.0	28.0	30.0
12	0.0	2.0	4.0	6.1	8.1	10.1	12.1	14.1	16.2	18.2	20.2	22.2	24.2	26.3	28.3	30.3
24	0.0	2.0	4.1	6.1	8.2	10.2	12.2	14.3	16.3	18.4	20.4	22.4	24.5	26.5	28.6	30.6
36	0.0	2.1	4.1	6.2	8.2	10.3	12.4	14.4	16.5	18.5	20.6	22.7	24.7	26.8	28.8	30.9
48	0.0	2.1	4.2	6.2	8.3	10.4	12.5	14.6	16.6	18.7	20.8	22.9	25.0	27.0	29.1	31.2
21 00	0.0	2.1	4.2	6.3	8.4	10.5	12.6	14.7	16.8	18.9	21.0	23.1	25.2	27.3	29.4	31.5
12	0.0	2.1	4.2	6.4	8.5	10.6	12.7	14.8	17.0	19.1	21.2	23.3	25.4	27.6	29.7	31.8
24	0.0	2.1	4.3	6.4	8.6	10.7	12.8	15.0	17.1	19.3	21.4	23.5	25.7	27.8	30.0	32.1
36	0.0	2.2	4.3	6.5	8.6	10.8	13.0	15.1	17.3	19.4	21.6	23.8	25.9	28.1	30.2	32.4
48	0.0	2.2	4.4	6.5	8.7	10.9	13.1	15.3	17.4	19.6	21.8	24.0	26.2	28.3	30.5	32.7
22 00	0.0	2.2	4.4	6.6	8.8	11.0	13.2	15.4	17.6	19.8	22.0	24.2	26.4	28.6	30.8	33.0
12	0.0	2.2	4.4	6.7	8.9	11.1	13.3	15.5	17.8	20.0	22.2	24.4	26.6	28.9	31.1	33.3
24	0.0	2.2	4.5	6.7	9.0	11.2	13.4	15.7	17.9	20.2	22.4	24.6	26.9	29.1	31.4	33.6
36	0.0	2.3	4.5	6.8	9.0	11.3	13.6	15.8	18.1	20.3	22.6	24.9	27.1	29.4	31.6	33.9
48	0.0	2.3	4.6	6.8	9.1	11.4	13.7	16.0	18.2	20.5	22.8	25.1	27.4	29.6	31.9	34.2
23 00	0.0	2.3	4.6	6.9	9.2	11.5	13.8	16.1	18.4	20.7	23.0	25.3	27.6	29.9	32.2	34.5
12	0.0	2.3	4.6	7.0	9.3	11.6	13.9	16.2	18.6	20.9	23.2	25.5	27.8	30.2	32.5	34.8
24	0.0	2.3	4.7	7.0	9.4	11.7	14.0	16.4	18.7	21.1	23.4	25.7	28.1	30.4	32.8	35.1
36	0.0	2.4	4.7	7.1	9.4	11.8	14.2	16.5	18.9	21.2	23.6	26.0	28.3	30.7	33.0	35.4
48	0.0	2.4	4.8	7.1	9.5	11.9	14.3	16.7	19.0	21.4	23.8	26.2	28.6	30.9	33.3	35.7
24 00	0.0	2.4	4.8	7.2	9.6	12.0	14.4	16.8	19.2	21.6	24.0	26.4	28.8	31.2	33.6	36.0

Moon Altitude Total Correction Table

(Upper Limb Add/Subtract D										(Lower Limb Add D							
	Horizontal Parallax									Horizontal Parallax							
Obs. Alt.	54'	55'	56'	57'	58'	59'	60'	61'	Obs. Alt.	54'	55'	56'	57'	58'	59'	60'	61'
10	23.4	24.0	24.6	25.5	26.0	26.7	27.5	28.3	10	52.7	54.0	55.3	56.5	57.7	59.0	60.2	61.5
12	23.8	24.6	25.2	26.0	26.5	27.2	28.0	28.7	12	53.2	54.5	55.7	57.0	58.4	59.5	60.7	62.0
14	24.0	24.8	25.4	26.1	26.7	27.5	28.3	29.0	14	53.5	54.7	56.0	57.3	58.5	59.8	61.0	62.3
16	24.0	24.8	25.5	26.1	26.7	27.5	28.3	28.8	16	53.5	54.6	56.0	57.3	58.5	59.8	61.0	62.2
18	23.8	24.6	25.2	26.0	26.5	27.3	28.0	28.6	18	53.4	54.6	55.7	57.0	58.4	59.5	60.6	62.0
20	23.6	24.2	25.0	25.5	26.2	27.0	27.5	28.2	20	53.0	54.4	55.5	56.8	58.0	59.0	60.4	61.5
22	23.2	23.8	24.6	25.0	25.7	26.5	27.0	27.8	22	52.5	53.7	55.0	56.3	57.5	58.8	60.0	61.0
24	22.7	23.2	24.0	24.5	25.3	25.8	26.5	27.0	24	52.0	53.3	54.5	55.5	56.7	58.0	59.4	60.5
26	22.0	22.6	23.4	24.0	24.5	25.0	25.7	26.5	26	51.5	52.5	53.7	55.0	56.3	57.5	58.0	59.8
28	21.4	22.0	22.6	23.3	23.8	24.5	25.0	25.5	28	50.7	52.0	53.0	54.4	55.5	56.5	57.8	59.0
30	20.6	21.2	21.8	22.3	23.0	23.5	24.3	24.7	30	50.0	51.0	52.3	53.5	54.5	55.7	57.0	58.0
32	19.8	20.2	21.0	21.3	22.0	22.5	23.2	23.7	32	49.3	50.4	51.3	52.5	53.7	54.8	56.0	57.0
34	19.0	19.4	20.0	20.5	21.0	21.5	22.2	22.7	34	48.3	49.5	50.5	51.5	52.7	53.7	55.0	56.0
36	18.0	18.4	19.0	19.5	20.0	20.5	21.0	21.7	36	47.3	48.5	49.5	50.5	51.7	52.7	54.0	55.0
38	16.8	17.4	17.8	18.5	19.0	19.5	20.0	20.4	38	46.4	47.4	48.5	49.5	50.5	51.5	52.7	53.8
40	15.8	16.2	16.8	17.3	17.7	18.2	18.8	19.2	40	45.3	46.3	47.3	48.3	49.5	50.5	51.5	52.5
42	14.7	15.2	15.6	16.0	16.5	17.0	17.5	18.0	42	44.0	45.0	46.0	47.0	48.0	49.0	50.0	51.0
44	13.5	13.8	14.2	14.6	15.0	15.5	16.0	16.5	44	42.7	43.7	44.7	45.7	46.7	47.7	48.7	49.7
46	12.0	12.6	13.0	13.4	13.8	14.2	14.5	15.0	46	41.5	42.5	43.5	44.5	45.5	46.5	47.5	48.5
48	10.5	11.2	11.6	12.0	12.4	12.8	13.2	13.5	48	40.2	41.2	42.2	43.0	44.0	45.0	46.0	47.0
50	9.3	10.0	10.2	10.6	11.0	11.3	11.7	12.0	50	39.0	40.0	41.0	41.8	42.6	43.6	44.5	45.5
52	8.0	8.4	8.6	9.2	9.5	9.7	10.0	10.5	52	37.5	38.5	39.3	40.2	41.0	42.0	42.8	43.7
54	6.7	6.8	7.2	7.5	7.8	8.2	8.5	8.7	54	36.0	37.0	38.0	38.8	39.5	40.5	41.3	42.0
56	5.2	5.5	5.6	6.0	6.3	6.5	7.0	7.0	56	34.5	35.5	36.2	37.0	38.0	38.7	39.5	40.5
58	3.7	3.7	4.2	4.5	4.5	5.0	5.0	5.5	58	33.0	34.0	34.7	35.5	36.3	37.0	38.0	38.8
60	2.0	2.2	2.5	2.7	3.0	3.2	3.5	3.5	60	31.5	32.4	33.0	34.0	34.5	35.5	36.0	37.0
62	+0.5	+0.7	+0.8	+1.0	+1.2	+1.5	+1.5	+1.7	62	30.0	30.5	31.5	32.0	33.0	33.5	34.5	35.0
64	-1.2	-1.0	-1.0	-0.8	-0.6	-0.5	-0.3	-0.1	64	28.3	29.0	29.6	30.5	31.0	31.8	32.5	33.3
66	3.0	2.8	2.6	2.5	2.4	2.3	2.0	2.0	66	26.5	27.3	28.0	28.5	29.3	30.0	30.7	31.5
68	4.5	4.5	4.4	4.3	4.2	4.0	4.0	4.0	68	25.0	25.5	26.3	26.8	27.5	28.0	28.8	29.5
70	6.3	6.2	6.2	6.1	6.0	6.0	5.8	5.8	70	23.3	23.8	24.5	25.0	25.5	26.2	27.0	27.5
72	8.0	8.0	8.0	8.0	8.0	8.0	7.8	7.8	72	21.5	22.0	22.5	23.3	23.8	24.5	25.0	25.5
74	9.7	9.7	9.7	9.7	9.7	9.7	9.7	9.7	74	19.7	20.3	20.7	21.2	22.0	22.5	23.0	23.5
76	11.5	11.5	11.5	11.5	11.6	11.7	11.7	11.7	76	18.0	18.5	19.0	19.5	20.0	20.5	21.0	21.5
78	13.5	13.5	13.5	13.6	13.6	13.7	13.7	13.7	78	16.0	16.5	17.0	17.5	18.0	18.5	19.0	19.5
80	15.4	15.4	15.4	15.5	15.6	15.7	15.7	16.0	80	14.2	14.7	15.3	15.5	16.0	16.5	17.0	17.5
82	17.0	17.0	17.2	17.3	17.5	17.7	17.8	18.0	82	12.5	13.0	13.3	13.5	14.0	14.5	15.0	15.5
84	18.8	19.0	19.2	19.3	19.5	19.7	19.9	20.0	84	10.5	11.0	11.5	11.7	12.0	12.5	13.0	13.4
86	20.8	21.0	21.0	21.2	21.5	21.7	22.0	22.0	86	8.8	9.0	9.5	9.8	10.0	10.5	11.0	11.3
88	22.6	22.8	23.0	23.2	23.4	23.7	24.0	24.2	88	7.0	7.2	7.5	8.0	8.3	8.5	8.7	9.0
90									90								

HEIGHT OF EYE CORRECTION—ADD

Height of Eye in Metres	0	1.5	3	4.6	6	7.6	9	10.7	12	14	15	17	18	20	21	23	24	26	27	29	30
in feet	0	5	10	15	20	25	30	35	40	45	50	55	60	65	70	75	80	85	90	95	100
Correction +	9.8	7.6	6.7	6.0	5.5	5.0	4.5	4.0	3.5	3.2	3.0	2.5	2.3	2.0	1.7	1.3	1.0	0.8	0.5	0.2	0.0

MOON G.H.A. CORRECTION TABLE (1-6 HOURS)

Hrs.	Variation per Hour								
	14° 20′	14° 20.5′	14° 21′	14° 21.5′	14° 22′	14° 22.5′	14° 23′	14° 23.5′	14° 24′
1	14 20	14 20.5	14 21	14 21.5	14 22	14 22.5	14 23	14 23.5	14 24
2	28 40	28 41	28 42	28 43	28 44	28 45	28 46	28 47	28 48
3	43 00	43 01.5	43 03	43 04.5	43 06	43 07.5	43 09	43 10.5	43 12
4	57 20	57 22	57 24	57 26	57 28	57 30	57 32	57 34	57 36
5	71 40	71 42.5	71 45	71 47.5	71 50	71 52.5	71 55	71 57.5	72 00

Hrs.	Variation per Hour								
	14° 24.5′	14° 25′	14° 25.5′	14° 26′	14° 26.5′	14° 27′	14° 27.5′	14° 28′	14° 28.5′
1	14 24.5	14 25	14 25.5	14 26	14 26.5	14 27	14 27.5	14 28	14 28.5
2	28 49	28 50	28 51	28 52	28 53	28 54	28 55	28 56	28 57
3	43 13.5	43 15	43 16.5	43 18	43 19.5	43 21	43 22.5	43 24	43 25.5
4	57 38	57 40	57 42	57 44	57 46	57 48	57 50	57 52	57 54
5	72 02.5	72 05	72 07.5	72 10	72 12.5	72 15	72 17.5	72 20	72 22.5

Hrs.	Variation per Hour								
	14° 29′	14° 29.5′	14° 30′	14° 30.5′	14° 31′	14° 31.5′	14° 32′	14° 32.5′	14° 33′
1	14 29	14 29.5	14 30	14 30.5	14 31	14 31.5	14 32	14 32.5	14 33
2	28 58	28 59	29 00	29 01	29 02	29 03	29 04	29 05	29 06
3	43 27	43 28.5	43 30	43 31.5	43 33	43 34.5	43 36	43 37.5	43 39
4	57 56	57 58	58 00	58 02	58 04	58 06	58 08	58 10	58 12
5	72 25	72 27.5	72 30	72 32.5	72 35	72 37.5	72 40	72 42.5	72 45

Hrs.	Variation per Hour								
	14° 33.5′	14° 34′	14° 34.5′	14° 35′	14° 35.5′	14° 36′	14° 36.5′	14° 37′	14° 37.5′
1	14 33.5	14 34	14 34.5	14 35	14 35.5	14 36	14 36.5	14 37	14 37.5
2	29 07	29 08	29 09	29 10	29 11	29 12	29 13	29 14	29 15
3	43 40.5	43 42	43 43.5	43 45	43 46.5	43 48	43 49.5	43 51	43 52.5
4	58 14	58 16	58 18	58 20	58 22	58 24	58 26	58 28	58 30
5	72 47.5	72 50	72 52.5	72 55	72 57.5	73 00	73 02.5	73 05	73 07.5

The Moon G.H.A. Correction Table in minutes is on p.4:16.

MOON G.H.A. CORRECTION TABLE

Min.	14°20'	14°21'	14°22'	14°23'	14°24'	14°25'	14°26'	14°27'	14°28'	Diff. 1'	Sec.	Corr.
0	0 0.0	0 0.0	0 0.0	0 0.0	0 0.0	0 0.0	0 0.0	0 0.0	0 0.0	.0	0	0.0
1	0 14.3	0 14.4	0 14.4	0 14.4	0 14.4	0 14.4	0 14.4	0 14.4	0 14.5	.0	1	0.2
2	0 28.7	0 28.7	0 28.7	0 28.8	0 28.8	0 28.8	0 28.9	0 28.9	0 28.9	.0	2	0.5
3	0 43.0	0 43.0	0 43.1	0 43.2	0 43.2	0 43.2	0 43.3	0 43.4	0 43.4	.0	3	0.7
4	0 57.3	0 57.4	0 57.5	0 57.5	0 57.6	0 57.7	0 57.7	0 57.8	0 57.9	.1	4	1.0
5	1 11.7	1 11.8	1 11.8	1 11.9	1 12.0	1 12.1	1 12.2	1 12.2	1 12.3	.1	5	1.2
6	1 26.0	1 26.1	1 26.2	1 26.3	1 26.4	1 26.5	1 26.6	1 26.7	1 26.8	.1	6	1.4
7	1 40.3	1 40.4	1 40.6	1 40.7	1 40.8	1 40.9	1 41.2	1 41.2	1 41.3	.1	7	1.7
8	1 54.7	1 54.8	1 54.9	1 55.1	1 55.2	1 55.3	1 55.5	1 55.6	1 55.7	.1	8	1.9
9	2 9.0	2 9.2	2 9.3	2 9.4	2 9.6	2 9.8	2 9.9	2 10.0	2 10.2	.2	9	2.2
10	2 23.3	2 23.5	2 23.7	2 23.8	2 24.0	2 24.2	2 24.3	2 24.5	2 24.7	.2	10	2.4
11	2 37.7	2 37.8	2 38.0	2 38.2	2 38.4	2 38.6	2 38.8	2 39.0	2 39.1	.2	11	2.6
12	2 52.0	2 52.2	2 52.4	2 52.6	2 52.8	2 53.0	2 53.2	2 53.4	2 53.6	.2	12	2.9
13	3 6.3	3 6.6	3 6.8	3 7.0	3 7.2	3 7.4	3 7.6	3 7.8	3 8.1	.2	13	3.1
14	3 20.7	3 20.9	3 21.1	3 21.4	3 21.6	3 21.8	3 22.1	3 22.3	3 22.5	.2	14	3.4
15	3 35.0	3 35.2	3 35.5	3 35.8	3 36.0	3 36.2	3 36.5	3 36.8	3 37.0	.2	15	3.6
16	3 49.3	3 49.6	3 49.9	3 50.1	3 50.4	3 50.7	3 50.9	3 51.2	3 51.5	.3	16	3.8
17	4 3.7	4 4.0	4 4.2	4 4.5	4 4.5	4 5.1	4 5.4	4 5.6	4 5.9	.3	17	4.1
18	4 18.0	4 18.3	4 18.6	4 18.9	4 19.2	4 19.5	4 19.8	4 20.1	4 20.4	.3	18	4.3
19	4 32.3	4 32.6	4 33.0	4 33.3	4 33.6	4 33.9	4 34.2	4 34.6	4 34.9	.3	19	4.6
20	4 46.7	4 47.0	4 47.3	4 47.7	4 48.0	4 48.3	4 48.7	4 49.0	4 49.3	.3	20	4.8
21	5 1.0	5 1.4	5 1.7	5 2.0	5 2.4	5 2.8	5 3.1	5 3.4	5 3.8	.4	21	5.0
22	5 15.3	5 15.7	5 16.1	5 16.4	5 16.8	5 17.2	5 17.5	5 17.9	5 18.3	.4	22	5.3
23	5 29.7	5 30.0	5 30.4	5 30.8	5 31.2	5 31.6	5 32.0	5 32.4	5 32.7	.4	23	5.5
24	5 44.0	5 44.4	5 44.8	5 45.2	5 45.6	5 46.0	5 46.4	5 46.8	5 47.2	.4	24	5.8
25	5 58.3	5 58.8	5 59.2	5 59.6	6 0.0	6 0.4	6 0.8	6 1.2	6 1.7	.4	25	6.0
26	6 12.7	6 13.1	6 13.5	6 14.0	6 14.4	6 14.8	6 15.3	6 15.7	6 16.1	.4	26	6.2
27	6 27.0	6 27.4	6 27.9	6 28.4	6 28.8	6 29.2	6 29.7	6 30.2	6 30.6	.4	27	6.5
28	6 41.3	6 41.8	6 42.3	6 42.7	6 43.2	6 43.7	6 44.1	6 44.6	6 45.1	.5	28	6.7
29	6 55.7	6 56.2	6 56.6	6 57.1	6 57.6	6 58.1	6 58.6	6 59.0	6 59.5	.5	29	7.0
30	7 10.0	7 10.5	7 11.0	7 11.5	7 12.0	7 12.5	7 13.0	7 13.5	7 14.0	.5	30	7.2
31	7 24.3	7 24.8	7 25.4	7 25.9	7 26.4	7 26.9	7 27.4	7 28.0	7 28.5	.5	31	7.4
32	7 38.7	7 39.2	7 39.7	7 40.3	7 40.8	7 41.3	7 41.9	7 42.4	7 42.9	.5	32	7.7
33	7 53.0	7 53.6	7 54.1	7 54.6	7 55.2	7 55.8	7 56.3	7 56.8	7 57.4	.6	33	7.9
34	8 7.3	8 7.9	8 8.5	8 9.0	8 9.6	8 10.2	8 10.7	8 11.3	8 11.9	.6	34	8.2
35	8 21.7	8 22.2	8 22.8	8 23.4	8 24.0	8 24.6	8 25.2	8 25.8	8 26.3	.6	35	8.4
36	8 36.0	8 36.6	8 37.2	8 37.8	8 38.4	8 39.0	8 39.6	8 40.2	8 40.8	.6	36	8.6
37	8 50.3	8 51.0	8 51.6	8 52.2	8 52.8	8 53.4	8 54.0	8 54.6	8 55.3	.6	37	8.9
38	9 4.7	9 5.3	9 5.9	9 6.6	9 7.2	9 7.8	9 8.5	9 9.1	9 9.7	.6	38	9.1
39	9 19.0	9 19.6	9 20.3	9 21.0	9 21.6	9 22.2	9 22.9	9 23.6	9 24.2	.6	39	9.4
40	9 33.3	9 34.0	9 34.7	9 35.3	9 36.0	9 36.7	9 37.3	9 38.0	9 38.7	.7	40	9.6
41	9 47.7	9 48.4	9 49.0	9 49.7	9 50.4	9 51.1	9 51.8	9 52.4	9 53.1	.7	41	9.8
42	10 2.0	10 2.7	10 3.4	10 4.1	10 4.8	10 5.5	10 6.2	10 6.9	10 7.6	.7	42	10.1
43	10 16.3	10 17.0	10 17.8	10 18.5	10 19.2	10 19.9	10 20.6	10 21.4	10 22.1	.7	43	10.3
44	10 30.7	10 31.4	10 32.1	10 32.9	10 33.6	10 34.3	10 35.1	10 35.8	10 36.5	.7	44	10.6
45	10 45.0	10 45.8	10 46.5	10 47.2	10 48.0	10 48.8	10 49.5	10 50.2	10 51.0	.8	45	10.8
46	10 59.3	11 0.1	11 0.9	11 1.6	11 2.4	11 3.2	11 3.9	11 4.7	11 5.5	.8	46	11.0
47	11 13.7	11 14.4	11 15.2	11 16.0	11 16.8	11 17.6	11 18.4	11 19.2	11 19.9	.8	47	11.3
48	11 28.0	11 28.8	11 29.6	11 30.4	11 31.2	11 32.0	11 32.8	11 33.6	11 34.4	.8	48	11.5
49	11 42.3	11 43.2	11 44.0	11 44.8	11 45.6	11 46.4	11 47.2	11 48.0	11 48.9	.8	49	11.8
50	11 56.7	11 57.5	11 58.3	11 59.2	12 0.0	12 0.8	12 1.7	12 2.5	12 3.3	.8	50	12.0
51	12 11.0	12 11.8	12 12.7	12 13.6	12 14.4	12 15.2	12 16.1	12 17.0	12 17.8	.8	51	12.2
52	12 25.3	12 26.2	12 27.1	12 27.9	12 28.8	12 29.7	12 30.5	12 31.4	12 32.3	.9	52	12.5
53	12 39.7	12 40.6	12 41.4	12 42.3	12 43.2	12 44.1	12 45.0	12 45.8	12 46.7	.9	53	12.7
54	12 54.0	12 54.9	12 55.8	12 56.7	12 57.6	12 58.5	12 59.4	13 0.3	13 1.2	.9	54	13.0
55	13 8.3	13 9.2	13 10.2	13 11.1	13 12.0	13 12.9	13 13.8	13 14.8	13 15.7	.9	55	13.2
56	13 22.7	13 23.6	13 24.5	13 25.5	13 26.4	13 27.3	13 28.3	13 29.2	13 30.1	.9	56	13.4
57	13 37.0	13 38.0	13 38.9	13 39.8	13 40.8	13 41.8	13 42.7	13 43.6	13 44.6	1.0	57	13.7
58	13 51.3	13 52.3	13 53.3	13 54.2	13 55.2	13 56.2	13 57.1	13 58.1	13 59.1	1.0	58	13.9
59	14 5.7	14 6.6	14 7.6	14 8.6	14 9.6	14 10.6	14 11.6	14 12.6	14 13.5	1.0	59	14.1
60	14 20.0	14 21.0	14 22.0	14 23.0	14 24.0	14 25.0	14 26.0	14 27.0	14 28.0	1.0	60	14.4

MOON G.H.A. CORRECTION TABLE

Min.	Variation per Hour									Diff. 1'	Sec.	Corr.
	14°29'	14°30'	14°31'	14°32'	14°33'	14°34'	14°35'	14°36'	14°37'			
	° '	° '	° '	° '	° '	° '	° '	° '	'			
0	0 0.0	0 0.0	0 0.0	0 0.0	0 0.0	0 0.0	0 0.0	0 0.0	0 0.0	.0	0	0.0
1	0 14.5	0 14.5	0 14.5	0 14.6	0 14.6	0 14.6	0 14.6	0 14.6	0 14.6	.0	1	0.2
2	0 29.0	0 29.0	0 29.0	0 29.1	0 29.1	0 29.1	0 29.2	0 29.2	0 29.2	.0	2	0.5
3	0 43.4	0 43.5	0 43.6	0 43.6	0 43.6	0 43.7	0 43.8	0 43.8	0 43.8	.0	3	0.7
4	0 57.9	0 58.0	0 58.1	0 58.1	0 58.2	0 58.3	0 58.3	0 58.4	0 58.5	.1	4	1.0
5	1 12.4	1 12.5	1 12.6	1 12.7	1 12.8	1 12.8	1 12.9	1 13.0	1 13.1	.1	5	1.2
6	1 26.9	1 27.0	1 27.1	1 27.2	1 27.3	1 27.4	1 27.5	1 27.6	1 27.7	.1	6	1.5
7	1 41.4	1 41.5	1 41.6	1 41.7	1 41.8	1 42.0	1 42.1	1 42.2	1 42.3	.1	7	1.7
8	1 55.9	1 56.0	1 56.1	1 56.3	1 56.4	1 56.5	1 56.7	1 56.8	1 56.9	.1	8	1.9
9	2 10.4	2 10.5	2 10.6	2 10.8	2 11.0	2 11.1	2 11.2	2 11.4	2 11.6	.2	9	2.2
10	2 24.8	2 25.0	2 25.2	2 25.3	2 25.5	2 25.7	2 25.8	2 26.0	2 26.2	.2	10	2.4
11	2 39.3	2 39.5	2 39.7	2 39.9	2 40.0	2 40.2	2 40.4	2 40.6	2 40.8	.2	11	2.7
12	2 53.8	2 54.0	2 54.2	2 54.4	2 54.6	2 54.8	2 55.0	2 55.2	2 55.4	.2	12	2.9
13	3 8.3	3 8.5	3 8.7	3 8.9	3 9.2	3 9.4	3 9.6	3 9.8	3 10.0	.2	13	3.2
14	3 22.8	3 23.0	3 23.2	3 23.5	3 23.7	3 23.9	3 24.2	3 24.4	3 24.6	.2	14	3.4
15	3 37.2	3 37.5	3 37.8	3 38.0	3 38.2	3 38.5	3 38.8	3 39.0	3 39.2	.2	15	3.6
16	3 51.7	3 52.0	3 52.3	3 52.5	3 52.8	3 53.1	3 53.3	3 53.6	3 53.9	.3	16	3.9
17	4 6.2	4 6.5	4 6.8	4 7.1	4 7.4	4 7.6	4 7.9	4 8.2	4 8.5	.3	17	4.1
18	4 20.7	4 21.0	4 21.3	4 21.6	4 21.9	4 22.2	4 22.5	4 22.8	4 23.1	.3	18	4.4
19	4 35.2	4 35.5	4 35.8	4 36.1	4 36.4	4 36.8	4 37.1	4 37.4	4 37.7	.3	19	4.6
20	4 49.7	4 50.0	4 50.3	4 50.7	4 51.0	4 51.3	4 51.7	4 52.0	4 52.3	.3	20	4.9
21	5 4.2	5 4.5	5 4.8	5 5.2	5 5.6	5 5.9	5 6.2	5 6.6	5 7.0	.4	21	5.1
22	5 18.6	5 19.0	5 19.4	5 19.7	5 20.1	5 20.5	5 20.8	5 21.2	5 21.6	.4	22	5.3
23	5 33.1	5 33.5	5 33.9	5 34.3	5 34.6	5 35.0	5 35.4	5 35.8	5 36.2	.4	23	5.6
24	5 47.6	5 48.0	5 48.4	5 48.8	5 49.2	5 49.6	5 50.0	5 50.4	5 50.8	.4	24	5.8
25	6 2.1	6 2.5	6 2.9	6 3.3	6 3.8	6 4.2	6 4.6	6 5.0	6 5.4	.4	25	6.1
26	6 16.6	6 17.0	6 17.4	6 17.9	6 18.3	6 18.7	6 19.2	6 19.6	6 20.0	.4	26	6.3
27	6 31.0	6 31.5	6 32.0	6 32.4	6 32.8	6 33.3	6 33.8	6 34.2	6 34.6	.4	27	6.5
28	6 45.5	6 46.0	6 46.5	6 46.9	6 47.4	6 47.9	6 48.3	6 48.8	6 49.3	.5	28	6.8
29	7 0.0	7 0.5	7 1.0	7 1.5	7 2.0	7 2.4	7 2.9	7 3.4	7 3.9	.5	29	7.0
30	7 14.5	7 15.0	7 15.5	7 16.0	7 16.5	7 17.0	7 17.5	7 18.0	7 18.5	.5	30	7.3
31	7 29.0	7 29.5	7 30.0	7 30.5	7 31.0	7 31.6	7 32.1	7 32.6	7 33.1	.5	31	7.5
32	7 43.5	7 44.0	7 44.5	7 45.1	7 45.6	7 46.1	7 46.7	7 47.2	7 47.7	.5	32	7.8
33	7 58.0	7 58.5	7 59.0	7 59.6	8 0.2	8 0.7	8 1.2	8 1.8	8 2.4	.6	33	8.0
34	8 12.4	8 13.0	8 13.6	8 14.1	8 14.7	8 15.3	8 15.8	8 16.4	8 17.0	.6	34	8.2
35	8 26.9	8 27.5	8 28.1	8 28.7	8 29.2	8 29.8	8 30.4	8 31.0	8 31.6	.6	35	8.5
36	8 41.4	8 42.0	8 42.6	8 43.2	8 43.8	8 44.4	8 45.0	8 45.6	8 46.2	.6	36	8.7
37	8 55.9	8 56.5	8 57.1	8 57.7	8 58.4	8 59.0	8 59.6	9 0.2	9 0.8	.6	37	9.0
38	9 10.4	9 11.0	9 11.6	9 12.3	9 12.9	9 13.5	9 14.2	9 14.8	9 15.4	.6	38	9.2
39	9 24.8	9 25.5	9 26.2	9 26.8	9 27.4	9 28.1	9 28.8	9 29.4	9 30.0	.6	39	9.5
40	9 39.3	9 40.0	9 40.7	9 41.3	9 42.0	9 42.7	9 43.3	9 44.0	9 44.7	.7	40	9.7
41	9 53.8	9 54.5	9 55.2	9 55.9	9 56.6	9 57.2	9 57.9	9 58.6	9 59.3	.7	41	9.9
42	10 8.3	10 9.0	10 9.7	10 10.4	10 11.1	10 11.8	10 12.5	10 13.2	10 13.9	.7	42	10.2
43	10 22.8	10 23.5	10 24.2	10 24.9	10 25.6	10 26.4	10 27.1	10 27.8	10 28.5	.7	43	10.4
44	10 37.3	10 38.0	10 38.7	10 39.5	10 40.2	10 40.9	10 41.7	10 42.2	10 43.1	.7	44	10.7
45	10 51.8	10 52.5	10 53.2	10 54.0	10 54.8	10 55.5	10 56.2	10 57.0	10 57.8	.8	45	10.9
46	11 6.2	11 7.0	11 7.8	11 8.5	11 9.3	11 10.1	11 10.8	11 11.6	11 12.4	.8	46	11.2
47	11 20.7	11 21.5	11 22.3	11 23.1	11 23.8	11 24.6	11 25.4	11 26.2	11 27.0	.8	47	11.4
48	11 35.2	11 36.0	11 36.8	11 37.6	11 38.4	11 39.2	11 40.0	11 40.8	11 41.6	.8	48	11.6
49	11 49.7	11 50.5	11 51.3	11 52.1	11 53.0	11 53.8	11 54.6	11 55.4	11 56.2	.8	49	11.9
50	12 4.2	12 5.0	12 5.8	12 6.7	12 7.5	12 8.3	12 9.2	12 10.0	12 10.8	.8	50	12.1
51	12 18.6	12 19.5	12 20.4	12 21.2	12 22.0	12 22.9	12 23.8	12 24.6	12 25.4	.8	51	12.4
52	12 33.1	12 34.0	12 34.9	12 35.7	12 36.6	12 37.5	12 38.3	12 39.2	12 40.1	.9	52	12.6
53	12 47.6	12 48.5	12 49.4	12 50.3	12 51.2	12 52.0	12 52.9	12 53.8	12 54.7	.9	53	12.9
54	13 2.1	13 3.0	13 3.9	13 4.8	13 5.7	13 6.6	13 7.5	13 8.4	13 9.3	.9	54	13.1
55	13 16.6	13 17.5	13 18.4	13 19.3	13 20.2	13 21.2	13 22.1	13 23.0	13 23.9	.9	55	13.3
56	13 31.1	13 32.0	13 32.9	13 33.9	13 34.8	13 35.7	13 36.7	13 37.6	13 38.5	.9	56	13.6
57	13 45.6	13 46.5	13 47.4	13 48.4	13 49.4	13 50.3	13 51.2	13 52.2	13 53.2	1.0	57	13.9
58	14 0.0	14 1.0	14 2.0	14 2.9	14 3.9	14 4.9	14 5.8	14 6.8	14 7.8	1.0	58	14.1
59	14 14.5	14 15.5	14 16.5	14 17.5	14 18.4	14 19.4	14 20.4	14 21.4	14 22.4	1.0	59	14.3
60	14 29.0	14 30.0	14 31.0	14 32.0	14 33.0	14 34.0	14 35.0	14 36.0	14 37.0	1.0	60	14.6

MOON DECLINATION CORRECTION TABLE

Min.	0	10	20	30	40	50	60	70	80	90	100	110	120	130	140	150	160	170	180
										Variation per Hour									
0	0	0	0	0	0	0	0	0	0	0	0	0	0	0	0	0	0	0	0
1	0	0	0	0	1	1	1	1	1	2	2	2	2	2	2	2	3	3	3
2	0	0	1	1	1	2	2	2	3	3	3	4	4	4	5	5	5	6	6
3	0	0	1	2	2	2	3	4	4	4	5	6	6	7	8	8	8	9	9
4	0	1	1	2	3	3	4	5	5	6	7	7	8	9	9	10	11	11	12
5	0	1	2	2	3	4	5	6	7	8	8	9	10	11	12	12	13	14	15
6	0	1	2	3	4	5	6	7	8	9	10	11	12	13	14	15	16	17	18
7	0	1	2	4	5	6	7	8	9	10	12	13	14	15	16	18	19	20	21
8	0	1	3	4	5	7	8	9	11	12	13	15	16	17	19	20	21	23	24
9	0	2	3	4	6	8	9	10	12	14	15	16	18	20	21	22	24	26	27
10	0	2	3	5	7	8	10	12	13	15	17	18	20	22	23	25	27	28	30
11	0	2	4	6	7	9	11	13	15	16	18	20	22	24	26	28	29	31	33
12	0	2	4	6	8	10	12	14	16	18	20	22	24	26	28	30	32	34	36
13	0	2	4	6	9	11	13	15	17	20	22	24	26	28	30	32	35	37	39
14	0	2	5	7	9	12	14	16	19	21	23	26	28	30	33	35	37	40	42
15	0	2	5	8	10	12	15	18	20	22	25	28	30	32	35	38	40	42	45
16	0	3	5	8	11	13	16	19	21	24	27	29	32	35	37	40	43	45	48
17	0	3	6	8	11	14	17	20	23	26	28	31	34	37	40	42	45	48	51
18	0	3	6	9	12	15	18	21	24	27	30	33	36	39	42	45	48	51	54
19	0	3	6	10	13	16	19	22	25	28	32	35	38	41	44	48	51	54	57
20	0	3	7	10	13	17	20	23	27	30	33	37	40	43	47	50	53	57	60
21	0	4	7	10	14	18	21	24	28	32	35	38	42	46	49	52	56	60	63
22	0	4	7	11	15	18	22	26	29	33	37	40	44	48	51	55	59	62	66
23	0	4	8	12	15	19	23	27	31	34	38	42	46	50	54	58	61	65	69
24	0	4	8	12	16	20	24	28	32	36	40	44	48	52	56	60	64	68	72
25	0	4	8	12	17	21	25	29	33	38	42	46	50	54	58	62	67	71	75
26	0	4	9	13	17	22	26	30	35	39	43	48	52	56	61	65	69	74	78
27	0	4	9	13	18	22	27	32	36	40	45	50	54	58	63	68	72	76	81
28	0	5	9	14	19	23	28	33	37	42	47	51	56	61	65	70	75	79	84
29	0	5	10	14	19	24	29	34	39	44	48	53	58	63	68	72	77	82	87
30	0	5	10	15	20	25	30	35	40	45	50	55	60	65	70	75	80	85	90
31	0	5	10	16	21	26	31	36	41	46	52	57	62	67	72	78	83	88	93
32	0	5	11	16	21	27	32	37	43	48	53	59	64	69	75	80	85	91	96
33	0	6	11	16	22	28	33	38	44	50	55	60	66	72	77	82	88	94	99
34	0	6	11	17	23	28	34	40	45	51	57	62	68	74	79	85	91	96	102
35	0	6	12	18	23	29	35	41	47	52	58	64	70	76	82	88	93	99	105
36	0	6	12	18	24	30	36	42	48	54	60	66	72	78	84	90	96	102	108
37	0	6	12	18	25	31	37	43	49	56	62	68	74	80	86	92	99	105	111
38	0	6	13	19	25	32	38	44	51	57	63	70	76	82	89	95	101	108	114
39	0	6	13	20	26	32	39	46	52	58	65	72	78	84	91	98	104	110	117
40	0	7	13	20	27	33	40	47	53	60	67	73	80	87	93	100	107	113	120
41	0	7	14	20	27	34	41	48	55	62	68	75	82	89	96	102	109	116	123
42	0	7	14	21	28	35	42	49	56	63	70	77	84	91	98	105	112	119	126
43	0	7	14	22	29	36	43	50	57	64	72	79	86	93	100	108	115	122	129
44	0	7	15	22	29	37	44	51	59	66	73	81	88	95	103	110	117	125	132
45	0	8	15	22	30	38	45	52	60	68	75	82	90	98	105	112	120	128	135
46	0	8	15	23	31	38	46	54	61	69	77	84	92	100	107	115	123	130	138
47	0	8	16	24	31	39	47	55	63	70	78	86	94	102	110	118	125	133	141
48	0	8	16	24	32	40	48	56	64	72	80	88	96	104	112	120	128	136	144
49	0	8	16	24	33	41	49	57	65	74	82	90	98	106	114	122	131	139	147
50	0	8	17	25	33	42	50	58	67	75	83	92	100	108	117	125	133	142	150
51	0	8	17	26	34	42	51	60	68	76	85	94	102	110	119	128	136	144	153
52	0	9	17	26	35	43	52	61	69	78	87	95	104	113	121	130	139	147	156
53	0	9	18	26	35	44	53	62	71	80	88	97	106	115	124	132	141	150	159
54	0	9	18	27	36	45	54	63	72	81	90	99	108	117	126	135	144	153	162
55	0	9	18	28	37	46	55	64	73	82	92	101	110	119	128	138	147	156	165
56	0	9	19	28	37	47	56	65	75	84	93	103	112	121	131	140	149	159	168
57	0	10	19	28	38	48	57	66	76	86	95	104	114	124	133	142	152	162	171
58	0	10	19	29	39	48	58	68	77	87	97	106	116	126	135	145	155	164	174
59	0	10	20	30	39	49	59	69	79	88	98	108	118	128	138	148	157	167	177
60	0	10	20	30	40	50	60	70	80	90	100	110	120	130	140	150	160	170	180

Moon Meridian Passage (Transit) Correction Table

This table is necessary when taking a Meridian Altitude of the Moon, because the SHIP time of Transit is necessary for the observation and the G.M.T. of Transit for correcting the Moon Declination. Take the Time of the Moon Upper Transit from the monthly page of the Almanac and the Difference (Diff.) from the adjoining column.

Long.	39 min.	42 min.	45 min.	48 min.	51 min.	54 min.	57 min.	60 min.	63 min.	66 min.	69 min.	Long.
				Daily Difference of Meridian Passage (in minutes)								
0°	0	0	0	0	0	0	0	0	0	0	0	0°
10°	1	1	1	1	1	1	2	2	2	2	2	10°
20°	2	2	2	3	3	3	3	3	3	4	4	20°
30°	3	3	4	4	4	4	5	5	5	5	6	30°
40°	4	5	5	5	6	6	6	7	7	7	8	40°
50°	5	6	6	7	7	7	8	8	9	9	10	50°
60°	6	7	7	8	8	9	9	10	10	11	11	60°
70°	8	8	9	9	10	10	11	12	12	13	13	70°
80°	9	9	10	11	11	12	13	13	14	15	15	80°
90°	10	10	11	12	13	13	14	15	16	16	17	90°
100°	11	12	12	13	14	15	16	17	17	18	19	100°
110°	12	13	14	15	16	16	17	18	19	20	21	110°
120°	13	14	15	16	17	18	19	20	21	22	23	120°
130°	14	15	16	17	18	19	21	22	23	24	25	130°
140°	15	16	17	19	20	21	22	23	24	26	27	140°
150°	16	17	19	20	21	22	24	25	26	27	29	150°
160°	17	19	20	21	23	24	25	27	28	29	31	160°
170°	18	20	21	23	24	25	27	28	30	31	33	170°
180°	19	21	22	24	25	27	28	30	31	33	34	180°

Correction **Plus** to Time of Meridian Passage (Transit) in West Long. **Minus** in East Long.

Moon Altitude Total Correction Table

The corrections given on page 4:14 are total corrections to be applied to the Observed Altitude of the Moon's Upper (or Lower) Limb, and include for Semi-Diameter, Parallax and Refraction. The table has been prepared (as in other Nautical Tables) for a height of eye of 100 feet (30.4m) which enables the height of eye correction at the foot of the page (which correction must not be neglected) always to be added.

Example: The observed altitude of the Moon's Upper Limb on a certain date was 30° 20'; what was the True Altitude? Height of eye 15 feet (4.6m) H.P. (Horizontal Parallax) from monthly page was 61'0.

```
Obs. Alt. ......  30° 20'
Corr. + .........      24.5
H.E. Corr. + ..        6.0

True Alt. ......  30° 50'.5
```

MOON RISING AND SETTING TABLE

Lat °N	DECLINATION—N or S													Lat °N
	2°	4°	6°	8°	10°	12°	14°	16°	18°	20°	22°	24°	26°	28°	
							Minutes								
24	6	14	20	27	34	41	48	57	65	74	84	93	105	117	24
26	6	13	19	25	32	39	46	54	62	70	80	89	100	112	26
28	6	12	18	24	30	37	44	51	58	66	75	84	95	106	28
30	5	12	17	22	29	35	41	48	55	62	71	79	90	101	30
32	5	11	16	21	27	32	38	45	51	58	67	74	84	94	32
34	5	10	15	20	26	31	36	43	48	55	63	71	79	89	34
36	5	9	14	19	24	29	34	40	46	52	58	66	73	83	36
38	4	8	13	17	22	26	31	36	41	47	53	60	67	75	38
40	4	7	11	15	19	23	27	32	37	42	47	54	60	68	40
41	4	7	10	14	18	21	26	30	34	39	44	50	57	64	41
42	3	6	9	13	16	20	24	28	32	36	41	46	53	60	42
43	3	6	9	12	15	18	22	25	29	33	38	43	49	55	43
44	3	5	8	11	14	17	20	23	26	30	34	39	44	50	44
45	2	5	7	10	12	15	18	20	23	27	31	35	40	45	45
46	2	4	6	8	11	13	15	18	20	24	27	31	35	40	46
47	2	3	5	7	9	11	13	15	17	20	23	26	30	34	47
48	1	3	4	6	7	9	11	12	14	16	19	21	24	28	48
49	1	2	3	4	6	7	8	9	11	13	14	16	19	22	49
50	1	2	2	3	4	5	6	6	7	9	10	11	13	15	50
50½	1	1	1	2	3	3	4	5	5	7	7	9	10	11	50½
51	0	1	1	1	2	2	3	3	4	4	5	6	7	8	51
51½	0	0	1	1	1	1	1	2	2	2	2	3	3	4	51½
52	0	0	0	0	0	0	0	0	0	0	0	0	0	0	52
52½	0	0	1	1	1	1	1	2	2	2	2	3	3	4	52½
53	0	1	1	1	2	3	3	3	4	4	5	6	7	8	53
53½	1	1	2	2	3	4	4	5	7	7	8	9	11	13	53½
54	1	2	2	3	4	5	6	7	8	10	11	13	15	17	54
54½	1	2	3	4	5	6	8	9	11	12	14	16	19	22	54½
55	1	3	4	5	6	8	9	11	13	15	17	20	23	27	55
55½	1	3	4	6	8	9	11	13	15	18	20	23	27	33	55½
56	2	3	5	7	9	11	13	15	18	20	24	27	32	38	56
56½	2	4	6	8	10	12	15	17	20	23	27	31	37	44	56½
57	2	4	7	9	11	14	17	20	23	26	31	35	42	51	57
57½	2	5	7	10	13	15	19	22	25	30	34	40	47	57	57½
58	3	5	8	11	14	17	21	24	28	33	38	45	53	65	58

Rule.—Enter the table with latitude on the left and declination along the top. This gives the number of minutes to add or subtract (according to the rules at the foot of the table) to the times given for Latitude 52°N. on the monthly pages.

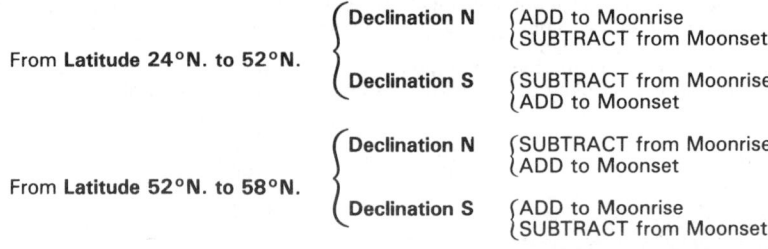

From **Latitude 24°N. to 52°N.**
- Declination N {ADD to Moonrise / SUBTRACT from Moonset
- Declination S {SUBTRACT from Moonrise / ADD to Moonset

From **Latitude 52°N. to 58°N.**
- Declination N {SUBTRACT from Moonrise / ADD to Moonset
- Declination S {ADD to Moonrise / SUBTRACT from Moonset

Astro Navigation

5

NAVIGATION

THE ART OF NAVIGATION

The Art of Navigation is the means by which vessels of any size are sailed from one safe place to another. The art is the same essentially, whether the vessel is large or small or under sail or power. Larger vessels carry more responsibilities; but smaller vessels, where conditions are much more difficult — owing to space and motion — call for the same art of navigation; but it is carried out in a different manner.

The knowledge required may conveniently be split up into two parts — the practice of navigation in sight of (or close to) the land, generally termed Coastal navigation; whilst the practice of navigation out of sight of land over the boundless ocean is termed Celestial, Ocean, Deep Sea or Astro (Astronomical) navigation, or frequently and perhaps more correctly, just navigation.

Pilotage is generally defined as the art of navigating a vessel in enclosed waters or in harbours and estuaries.

As it is obvious that Coastal navigation cannot be carried out without a knowledge of pilotage — one must enter harbour sometimes — it is equally clear that Ocean navigation cannot be carried out without a knowledge of Coastal navigation — as one must leave and arrive from some coastline.

Where countries or islands are adjacent, or separated by short distances, then the two types of navigation mentioned overlap somewhat and short voyages can be carried out without the instruments required for longer voyages. Conversely the instruments or knowledge required essentially for long voyages can be employed usefully on the coast.

It is essential also that anyone who wishes to navigate anywhere must acquire the art of seamanship. Each art is really dependent on the other. One may be able to navigate successfully in all weathers; but if for example the navigator cannot handle his ship — then there probably will not be any ship left to navigate.

ASTRO NAVIGATION

Astro navigation has two main functions:

1) To determine the azimuth (bearing) of the sun (star, planet, moon) and thereby establish the compass error and

2) To determine a position line when coastal methods of fixing are not available.

(Note, two or more position lines are necessary to fix the observer's position.)

Astro navigation has the advantage that it is cheap — all you need is Reed's Almanac, a sextant and a watch accurate to the nearest second or so, and you have a system that can be used anywhere at any time, provided the cloud is not too dense.

Beginners to Astro navigation must not let the theory or the threat of massive calculations deter them. The theory can be largely ignored if simple routines are adopted and the calculations considerably reduced by a variety of ways, many of which are indicated on the following pages.

The beginner should start by finding the latitude from the sun and pole star.

THE NAVIGATIONAL TRIANGLE

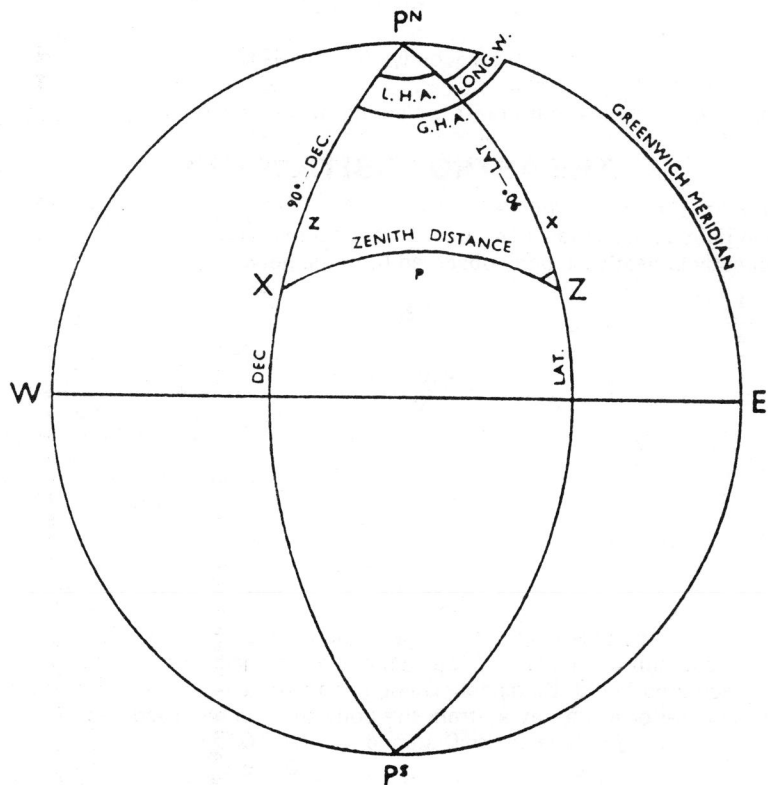

A Glossary of Terms used in astro navigation is given on p. 2:4-2:10.

PRINCIPLES OF ASTRO POSITION LINE NAVIGATION

To obtain a position line from a celestial body the following principles are involved.

The actual distance of the heavenly bodies from the earth are disregarded (as only angular measurements from the earth's centre are involved), and all bodies are assumed to be on the surface of an imaginary sphere, "the Celestial Sphere", with the centre of the earth at the centre. Angular measurements on the celestial sphere correspond to those on the earth, *i.e.*, the celestial equator is on the same plane as the terrestrial equator and north or south latitude (called Declination on the Celestial Sphere) correspond. Longitude on the celestial sphere, or hour angle, is the angle at the pole measured from the meridian of Greenwich westward from 0° to 360°.

The Navigational Triangle

Thus, as shown in the diagram above, it can be seen that obtaining a "Position Line" from a celestial observation requires resolving a spherical triangle PZX, the "Navigational Triangle". All calculations for celestial observations are related to this PZX triangle as will be readily appreciated throughout the following examples.

In the triangle, the angle ZPX is the angle at the nearest Pole (N or S) between the observer's meridian (longitude) and the meridian of the body at the time of observation. It is therefore the Local Hour Angle (LHA) of the body and is found as shown on p. 2:16 for the sun.

Z is the position of the observer, the Observer's Zenith; X is the position of the observed body.

PZ is the arc of the observer's meridian between the Pole and the Observer's Zenith and is therefore the Observer's Latitude subtracted from 90°. (Co-latitude.)

PX is the arc of the body's meridian between the Pole and the observed body and is therefore the body's Declination subtracted from 90° (Polar Distance).

ZX is the Zenith Distance, or the arc of a great circle contained between the Observer's Zenith and the observed body, it is therefore the altitude of the body subtracted from 90°.

The angle PZX is the Azimuth or True Bearing of the observed body.

THE ASTRO POSITION LINE

The corrected sextant altitude subtracted from 90 does therefore give you the distance in nautical miles (as 1' of arc = 1 nautical mile) from the point on the earth's surface directly beneath the body observed (*i.e.*, the geographical position (see p. 2:6))

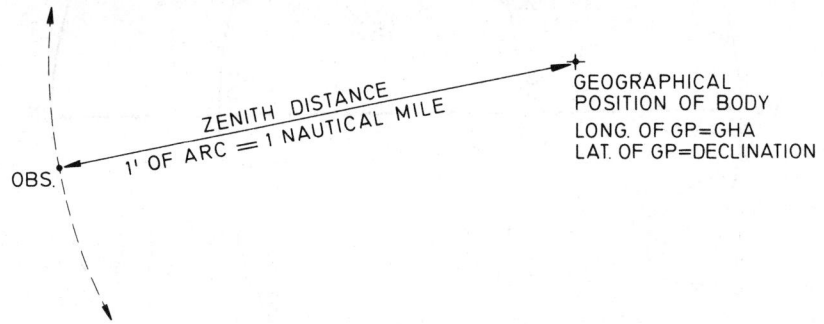

In practice this zenith distance is too large to plot so the observer compares his actual distance (True Zenith Distance) with the distance he has calculated from some assumed position (Calculated Zenith Distance). This comparison tells the observer that he is so many miles nearer or further away from the body than he had assumed.

$$\textit{i.e. True Zenith Distance} = 40 \quad 10$$
$$\text{Calc} \quad ,, \quad ,, \quad = 40 \quad 5$$
$$\text{Intercept 5 miles}$$
$$\text{away} \ldots$$

that is the observer is five miles further away from the G.P. than he had assumed.

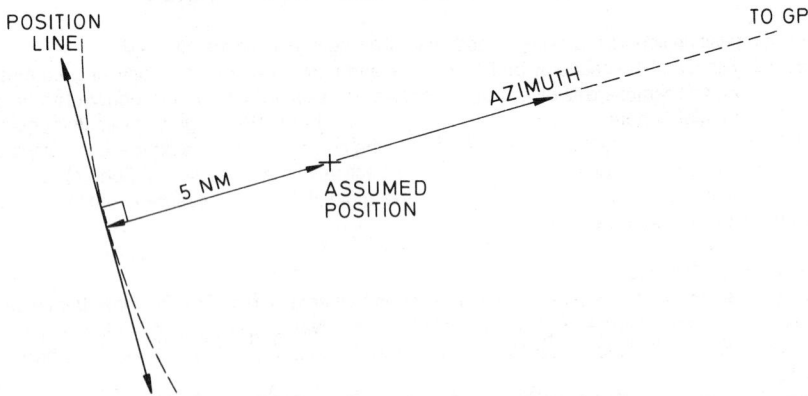

As the radius of the position circle is so large the small section the observer is concerned with, can be drawn as a straight line at right angles to the Azimuth.

Note, the easiest position line to obtain is when the body lies due north or south. In this case the calculation is minimal and the position line obtained can be assumed to be the latitude.

See pages 5:15-5:28.

AMPLITUDES

The bearing of the sun when rising or setting is known as its Amplitude.
It is the quickest and easiest method of obtaining the compass error as "Time" does not enter into the problem at all. Also the Amplitude is the only astronomical sight that can be made accurately without the aid of any instrument (other than the compass), Nature's own instrument—the horizon being used.

All that is required is to know the approximate latitude from the chart, and the approximate declination from this Almanac, see p. 2:14.

With these quantities a simple inspection of the table given on pages 5:6-5:7 will give the True Bearing of the Sun at Sunrise or Sunset in any part of the world up to Latitude 66°; which, when compared with the compass bearing at sunrise or sunset will give the error of the compass. The Deviation can then be found immediately.

To take the observation

The "Theoretical Sunrise" is considered to take place at the moment when its centre is on the edge of the horizon to the eastward, and the setting when its centre is on the edge of the horizon to the westward.

In consequence of refraction (i.e., the bending of rays of light when passing through the atmosphere) the sun appears higher than it actually is and it must therefore be remembered that it apparently rises before it is actually above the horizon, and it is actually set when you can still see a small portion of the limb.

Amplitudes should therefore be taken, both at rising and setting, when the sun's lower limb is about half the sun's diameter above the horizon, as it is then that the centre of the sun may be taken as being on the horizon.

This table can also be used for true bearing at rising and setting of any celestial body other than the moon, within these declinations.

Example—On November 18th, in latitude 18°N. declination 19°S. the sun rose bearing by compass N88°E (or 088°). The Variation from the chart was 24°E. Find the deviation.

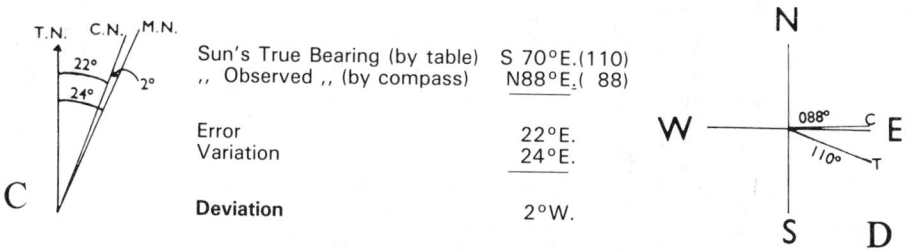

Sun's True Bearing (by table)	S 70°E.(110)
,, Observed ,, (by compass)	N88°E.(88)
Error	22°E.
Variation	24°E.
Deviation	2°W.

To name the deviation.   To name the error

Draw diagrams as shown to help in naming the error (D) and deviation (C).

Further Examples of the Use of the Table on pages 5:6-5:7

1. In latitude 20°N. and declination 10°N. what is the sun's true bearing at sunrise? On page 5:6 it will be seen to be 79.4, which by the footnote is N 79.4°E.

2. In latitude 29°S. and declination 19°S., what is the sun's true bearing at sunset? On page 5:7 it will be seen to be 68.2, which by the footnote is S 68.2°W.

REED'S NAUTICAL ALMANAC

SUN'S TRUE BEARING AT SUNRISE AND SUNSET
LATITUDES 0° to 66°   DECLINATIONS 0° to 11°

LAT.	0°	1°	2°	3°	4°	5°	6°	7°	8°	9°	10°	11°
0° to 5°	90	89	88	87	86	85	84	83	82	81	80	79
6°	90	89	88	87	86	85	84	83	82	81	79.9	78.9
7°	90	89	88	87	86	85	84	83	81.9	80.9	79.9	78.9
8°	90	89	88	87	86	85	84	82.9	81.9	80.9	79.9	78.9
9°	90	89	88	87	86	85	83.9	82.9	81.9	80.9	79.8	78.9
10°	90	89	88	87	86	84.9	83.9	82.9	81.9	80.9	79.8	78.8
11°	90	89	88	87	86	84.9	83.9	82.9	81.9	80.8	79.8	78.8
12°	90	89	88	87	85.9	84.9	83.9	82.9	81.8	80.8	79.8	78.8
13°	90	89	88	86.9	86.9	84.9	83.8	82.8	81.8	80.8	79.7	78.7
14°	90	89	88	86.9	85.9	84.8	83.8	82.8	81.8	80.7	79.7	78.7
15°	90	89	88	86.9	85.9	84.8	83.8	82.8	81.7	80.7	79.6	78.6
16°	90	89	87.9	86.9	85.8	84.8	83.8	82.7	81.7	80.6	79.6	78.6
17°	90	89	87.9	86.9	85.8	84.8	83.7	82.7	81.6	80.6	79.5	78.5
18°	90	89	87.9	86.9	85.8	84.8	83.7	82.6	81.6	80.5	79.5	78.4
19°	90	89	87.9	86.8	85.8	84.7	83.7	82.6	81.5	80.5	79.4	78.4
20°	90	88.9	87.9	86.8	85.8	84.7	83.6	82.6	81.5	80.4	79.4	78.3
21°	90	88.9	87.9	86.8	85.7	84.7	83.6	82.5	81.4	80.4	79.3	78.2
22°	90	88.9	87.9	86.8	85.7	84.6	83.5	82.5	81.4	80.3	79.2	78.1
23°	90	88.9	87.9	86.7	85.7	84.6	83.5	82.4	81.3	80.2	79.1	78.0
24°	90	88.9	87.8	86.7	85.6	84.5	83.4	82.3	81.2	80.1	79.0	78.0
25°	90	88.9	87.8	86.7	85.6	84.5	83.4	82.3	81.2	80.1	79.0	77.9
26°	90	88.9	87.8	86.7	85.5	84.4	83.3	82.2	81.1	80.0	78.9	77.8
27°	90	88.9	87.8	86.6	85.5	84.4	83.3	82.1	81.0	79.9	78.8	77.6
28°	90	88.9	87.8	86.6	85.5	84.4	83.2	82.1	80.9	79.8	78.7	77.5
29°	90	88.9	87.8	86.6	85.5	84.3	83.1	82.0	80.9	79.7	78.6	77.4
30°	90	88.9	87.7	86.5	85.4	84.2	83.1	81.9	80.8	79.6	78.5	77.3
31°	90	88.9	87.7	86.5	85.4	84.2	83.0	81.8	80.7	79.5	78.3	77.1
32°	90	88.9	87.7	86.5	85.3	84.1	82.9	81.7	80.6	79.4	78.2	77.0
33°	90	88.8	87.7	86.4	85.3	84.0	82.8	81.7	80.5	79.3	78.0	76.9
34°	90	88.8	87.6	86.4	85.2	84.0	82.7	81.5	80.3	79.1	77.9	76.7
35°	90	88.8	87.5	86.3	85.1	83.9	82.7	81.4	80.2	79.0	77.8	76.5
36°	90	88.8	87.5	86.3	85.0	83.8	82.6	81.3	80.1	78.8	77.6	76.3
37°	90	88.7	87.5	86.2	85.0	83.7	82.5	81.2	80.0	78.7	77.4	76.2
38°	90	88.7	87.5	86.2	84.9	83.6	82.4	81.1	79.8	78.5	77.3	76.0
39°	90	88.7	87.4	86.1	84.8	83.6	82.3	81.0	79.7	78.4	77.1	75.8
40°	90	88.7	87.4	86.1	84.8	83.5	82.1	80.8	79.5	78.2	76.9	75.6
41°	90	88.7	87.3	86.0	84.7	83.4	82.0	80.7	79.4	78.0	76.7	75.3
42°	90	88.6	87.3	86.0	84.6	83.3	81.9	80.6	79.2	77.8	76.5	75.1
43°	90	88.6	87.3	85.9	84.5	83.1	81.8	80.4	79.0	77.6	76.3	74.9
44°	90	88.6	87.2	85.8	84.4	83.0	81.6	80.2	78.8	77.4	76.0	74.6
45°	90	88.6	87.2	85.7	84.3	82.9	81.5	80.1	78.6	77.2	75.8	74.3
46°	90	88.6	87.1	85.7	84.2	82.8	81.3	79.9	78.4	77.0	75.5	74.0
47°	90	88.5	87.1	85.6	84.1	82.6	81.2	79.7	78.2	76.7	75.2	73.7
48°	90	88.5	87.0	85.5	84.0	82.5	81.0	79.5	78.0	76.5	75.0	73.4
49°	90	88.5	86.9	85.4	83.9	82.4	80.8	79.3	77.7	76.2	74.6	73.1
50°	90	88.4	86.9	85.3	83.8	82.2	80.6	79.1	77.5	75.9	74.3	72.7
51°	90	88.4	86.8	85.2	83.6	82.0	80.4	78.8	77.2	75.6	74.0	72.3
52°	90	88.4	86.7	85.1	83.5	81.9	80.2	78.6	76.9	75.3	73.6	71.9
53°	90	88.3	86.7	85.0	83.3	81.7	80.0	78.3	76.6	74.9	73.2	71.5
54°	90	88.3	86.6	84.9	83.2	81.5	79.7	78.0	76.3	74.6	72.8	71.0
55°	90	88.2	86.5	84.8	83.0	81.3	79.5	77.7	75.9	74.2	72.4	70.6
56°	90	88.2	86.4	84.6	82.8	81.0	79.2	77.4	75.6	73.7	71.9	70.0
57°	90	88.2	86.3	84.5	82.6	80.8	78.9	77.1	75.2	73.3	71.4	69.5
58°	90	88.1	86.2	84.3	82.4	80.5	78.6	76.7	74.8	72.8	70.9	68.9
59°	90	88.0	86.1	84.2	82.2	80.2	78.3	76.3	74.3	72.3	70.3	68.2
60°	90	88.0	86.0	84.0	82.0	80.0	77.9	75.9	73.8	71.8	69.7	67.6
61°	90	87.9	85.9	83.8	81.7	79.6	77.5	75.4	73.3	71.2	69.0	66.8
62°	90	87.9	85.7	83.6	81.4	79.3	77.1	74.9	72.7	70.5	68.3	66.0
63°	90	87.8	85.6	83.3	81.2	78.9	76.7	74.4	72.1	69.8	67.5	65.1
64°	90	87.7	85.4	83.1	80.8	78.5	76.2	73.9	71.5	69.1	66.7	64.2
65°	90	87.6	85.3	82.9	80.5	78.1	75.7	73.2	70.8	68.3	65.7	63.2
66°	90	87.5	85.1	82.6	80.1	77.6	75.1	72.6	70.0	67.4	64.7	62.0

Name the Bearing the same as the Declination NORTH or SOUTH and EAST if rising, WEST if setting. For example of use of this Table see p.5:5

SUN'S TRUE BEARING AT SUNRISE AND SUNSET
LATITUDES 0° to 66°   DECLINATIONS 12° to 23°

LAT.	12°	13°	14°	15°	16°	17°	18°	19°	20°	21°	22°	23°
	°	°	°	°	°	°	°	°	°	°	°	°
0° to 5°	77.9	76.9	75.9	74.9	73.9	72.9	71.9	70.9	69.9	68.9	67.9	66.9
6°	77.9	76.9	75.9	74.9	73.9	72.9	71.9	70.9	69.9	68.9	67.9	66.9
7°	77.9	76.9	75.9	74.9	73.9	72.9	71.9	70.9	69.8	68.8	67.8	66.8
8°	77.9	76.9	75.9	74.8	73.8	72.8	71.8	70.8	69.8	68.8	67.8	66.8
9°	77.8	76.8	75.8	74.8	73.8	72.8	71.8	70.7	69.7	68.7	67.7	66.7
10°	77.8	76.8	75.8	74.8	73.7	72.7	71.7	70.7	69.7	68.7	67.6	66.6
11°	77.8	76.8	75.7	74.7	73.7	72.7	71.6	70.6	69.6	68.6	67.6	66.5
12°	77.7	76.7	75.7	74.6	73.6	72.6	71.6	70.6	69.5	68.5	67.5	66.4
13°	77.7	76.6	75.6	74.6	73.6	72.5	71.5	70.5	69.4	68.4	67.4	66.4
14°	77.6	76.6	75.6	74.5	73.5	72.5	71.4	70.4	69.4	68.3	67.3	66.2
15°	77.6	76.5	75.5	74.4	73.4	72.4	71.3	70.3	69.3	68.2	67.2	66.1
16°	77.5	76.5	75.4	74.4	73.3	72.3	71.2	70.2	69.1	68.1	67.1	66.0
17°	77.4	76.4	75.3	74.3	73.3	72.2	71.1	70.1	69.0	68.0	66.9	65.9
18°	77.4	76.3	75.3	74.2	73.2	72.1	71.0	70.0	68.9	67.9	66.8	65.7
19°	77.4	76.2	75.2	74.1	73.0	72.0	70.9	69.9	68.8	67.7	66.7	65.6
20°	77.2	76.1	75.1	74.0	72.9	71.9	70.8	69.7	68.6	67.6	66.5	65.4
21°	77.1	76.0	75.0	73.9	72.8	71.7	70.7	69.6	68.5	67.4	66.3	65.2
22°	77.0	76.0	74.9	73.8	72.7	71.6	70.5	69.4	68.3	67.3	66.2	65.1
23°	76.9	75.9	74.8	73.7	72.6	71.5	70.4	69.3	68.2	67.1	66.0	64.9
24°	76.8	75.7	74.6	73.5	72.5	71.3	70.2	69.1	68.0	66.9	65.8	64.7
25°	76.7	75.6	74.5	73.4	72.3	71.2	70.1	68.9	67.8	66.7	65.6	64.5
26°	76.6	75.5	74.4	73.3	72.1	71.0	69.9	68.8	67.6	66.5	65.4	64.2
27°	76.5	75.4	74.3	73.1	72.0	70.8	69.7	68.6	67.4	66.3	65.1	64.0
28°	76.4	75.2	74.1	73.0	71.8	70.7	69.5	68.4	67.2	66.1	64.9	63.8
29°	76.2	75.1	73.9	72.8	71.6	70.5	69.3	68.2	67.0	65.8	64.6	63.5
30°	76.1	75.0	73.8	72.6	71.4	70.3	69.1	67.9	66.7	65.5	64.4	63.2
31°	76.0	74.8	73.6	72.4	71.2	70.0	68.9	67.6	66.5	65.3	64.1	62.9
32°	75.8	74.6	73.4	72.2	71.0	69.8	68.6	67.4	66.2	65.0	63.8	62.6
33°	75.7	74.4	73.2	72.0	70.8	69.6	68.4	67.1	65.9	64.7	63.5	62.2
34°	75.5	74.2	73.0	71.8	70.6	69.3	68.1	66.9	65.6	64.4	63.1	61.9
35°	75.3	74.1	72.8	71.6	70.3	69.1	67.8	66.6	65.3	64.0	62.8	61.5
36°	75.1	73.8	72.6	71.3	70.1	68.8	67.5	66.3	65.0	63.7	62.4	61.1
37°	74.9	73.6	72.4	71.1	69.8	68.5	67.2	65.9	64.6	63.3	62.0	60.7
38°	74.7	73.4	72.1	70.8	69.5	68.2	66.9	65.6	64.3	62.9	61.6	60.3
39°	74.5	73.2	71.9	70.5	69.2	67.9	66.6	65.2	63.9	62.5	61.2	59.8
40°	74.2	72.9	71.6	70.2	68.9	67.6	66.2	64.8	63.5	62.1	60.7	59.3
41°	74.0	72.7	71.3	70.0	68.6	67.2	65.8	64.4	63.0	61.6	60.2	58.8
42°	73.7	72.4	71.0	69.6	68.2	66.8	65.4	64.0	62.6	61.2	59.7	58.3
43°	73.5	72.1	70.7	69.3	67.9	66.4	65.0	63.6	62.1	60.7	59.2	57.7
44°	73.2	71.8	70.3	68.9	67.5	66.0	64.6	63.1	61.6	60.1	58.6	57.1
45°	72.9	71.4	70.0	68.5	67.0	65.6	64.1	62.6	61.1	59.5	58.0	56.4
46°	72.6	71.1	69.6	68.1	66.6	65.1	63.6	62.1	60.5	58.9	57.4	55.8
47°	72.2	70.7	69.2	67.7	66.2	64.6	63.0	61.5	59.9	58.3	56.7	55.0
48°	71.9	70.3	68.8	67.2	65.7	64.1	62.5	60.9	59.3	57.6	55.9	54.3
49°	71.5	69.9	68.4	66.8	65.1	63.5	61.9	60.2	58.6	56.9	55.2	53.4
50°	71.1	69.5	67.9	66.2	64.6	63.0	61.3	59.6	57.8	56.1	54.3	52.6
51°	70.7	69.0	67.4	65.7	64.0	62.3	60.6	58.8	57.1	55.3	53.5	51.6
52°	70.3	68.6	66.9	65.1	63.4	61.6	59.9	58.1	56.2	54.4	52.5	50.6
53°	69.8	68.0	66.3	64.5	62.7	60.9	59.1	57.2	55.4	53.4	51.5	49.5
54°	69.3	67.5	65.7	63.9	62.0	60.2	58.3	56.4	54.4	52.4	50.4	48.3
55°	68.7	66.9	65.0	63.2	61.3	59.3	57.4	55.4	53.4	51.3	49.2	47.1
56°	68.2	66.3	64.4	62.4	60.5	58.5	56.4	54.4	52.3	50.1	47.9	45.7
57°	67.6	65.6	63.6	61.6	59.6	57.5	55.4	53.3	51.1	48.8	46.5	44.2
58°	66.9	64.9	62.8	60.8	58.6	56.5	54.3	52.1	49.8	47.4	45.0	42.5
59°	66.2	64.1	62.0	59.8	57.6	55.4	53.1	50.8	48.4	45.9	43.3	40.6
60°	65.4	63.3	61.1	58.8	56.5	54.2	51.8	49.4	46.8	44.2	41.5	38.6
61°	64.6	62.3	60.1	57.7	55.3	52.9	50.4	47.8	45.1	42.3	39.4	36.3
62°	63.7	61.4	59.0	56.5	54.0	51.5	48.8	46.1	43.2	40.2	37.1	33.7
63°	62.7	60.3	57.8	55.2	52.6	49.9	47.1	44.2	41.1	37.9	34.4	30.6
64°	61.7	59.1	56.5	53.8	51.0	48.2	45.2	42.0	38.7	35.2	31.3	27.0
65°	60.5	57.8	55.1	52.2	49.3	46.2	43.0	39.6	36.0	32.0	27.6	22.4
66°	59.2	56.4	53.5	50.5	47.3	44.0	40.5	36.8	32.8	28.2	22.9	16.1

**Name the Bearing the same as the Declination NORTH or SOUTH
and EAST if rising, WEST if setting.**

THE AZIMUTH

The azimuth is another name for the bearing of a celestial body. It is of importance in navigation firstly because the position line found from a sight is always at right angles to the azimuth, which is therefore needed when the position line is plotted on the chart. Secondly, the azimuth can be used to ascertain the compass error, by comparing the compass bearing of a celestial body with the true azimuth. This bearing could always be calculated from the PZX or navigational triangle, but the degree of accuracy which this method affords is rarely necessary. In practice, the true azimuth is usually obtained from either ABC tables, special azimuth tables or from the Weir Azimuth Diagram.

It matters little which method is used; the Weir Azimuth Diagram is simple, but one requires the special chart; azimuth tables necessitate the purchase of a separate volume of tables; the ABC tables are easy to use and with a little interpolation give sufficient accuracy for most navigational purposes.

The requirements to work out the azimuth (or bearing) from the ABC tables are:
1. the vessel's approximate latitude
2. the local hour angle of the celestial body
3. the declination of the celestial body

It is difficult to take accurate compass bearings of celestial bodies when they are high in the heavens, and so it is best not to take a bearing to ascertain the compass error when the altitude of the body is more than about 45°.

EXPLANATION OF THE ABC TABLES

The tables are very simple to use and as the true azimuth required for establishing a compass error or for plotting the position line is usually only needed to the nearest degree, interpolation can be by eye.

Table A is entered with latitude and hour angle as arguments. The resultant value is named + or - depending on whether the hour angle was found at the top or the bottom of the table.

Table B is entered with declination and hour angle as arguments. The resultant value is named respectively – or + depending on whether or not the latitude and declination have the same (*i.e.* both North or both South) or different names (*i.e.* one North and one South).

The sum of A and B gives C. (when both + or both – add, when one + and one – take smaller from greater and give sign of greater).

Table C is entered with the value obtained from this addition of A and B, and the latitude. The azimuth angle is given in the body of the table. The appropriate quadrant is then identified from the information given at the bottom of the page.

Example 1.   Lat. 50°N. Sun's Dec. 21°N. LHA=300°.

Lat. 50°N.	A = + 0.688 + as HA at top of page
Dec. 21°N.	B = – 0.443 – as Lat. and Dec. same names
Add to get	C = + 0.245

(Note: we are adding a + and a - number)

If table C is entered with 0.245 and Lat. 50° the azimuth angle is found to be 81°.1 (say 81°). By following the instructions at the bottom of the page it can be identified as S81°E as "+= South in North Latitudes" and "the hour angle is greater than 180°", S81°E=099°(T)

Answer 099°(T)

Example 2.

In Latitude 43°47'N. Sun's Dec. 11°50'S. LHA=49°. What is the true azimuth?

Lat. 44°N.	A = + 0.840 + as HA at top of page
Dec. 12°S.	B = + 0.281 + as Lat. and Dec. are different names
Add to get	C = + 1.121

If table C is entered with 1.121 and Lat. 44° the azimuth angle is found to be 51°. By following the instructions at the bottom of the page it can be identified as S51°N as "+= South in North Latitudes" and "the hour angle is LESS than 180°", S51°W=231°(T)

Answer 231°(T)

Example 3.

In Latitude 48°S. Star's Dec. 62°S. LHA=138°. What is the azimuth?

Lat. 48°S.	A = – 1.23 (Note hour angle is at bottom of page so A is –).
Dec. 62°S.	B = – 2.81
Add to get	C = – 4.04

If table C is entered with 4.04 and Lat. 48° the azimuth angle is found to be 20°.3 (say 20°½). By following the instructions at the bottom of the page it can be identified as S20 ½ W"– = South in South Latitudes" and "the hour angle is less than 180°", S20° ½ W = 200° ½ (T).

Answer 200° ½ (T)

A — HOUR ANGLE at top + / Hour angle at bottom −

LAT.	1° 359°	2° 358°	3° 357°	4° 356°	5° 355°	6° 354°	7° 353°	8° 352°	9° 351°	10° 350°	11° 349°	12° 348°	13° 347°	14° 346°	15° 345°
0°	0.00	.000	.000	.000	.000	.000	.000	.000	.000	.000	.000	.000	.000	.000	.000
3	3.00	1.50	1.00	.749	.599	.499	.427	.373	.331	.297	.270	.247	.227	.210	.196
6	6.02	3.01	2.01	1.50	1.20	1.00	.856	.748	.664	.596	.541	.494	.455	.422	.392
9	9.07	4.54	3.02	2.27	1.81	1.51	1.29	1.13	1.00	.898	.815	.745	.686	.635	.591
12	12.2	6.09	4.06	3.04	2.43	2.02	1.73	1.51	1.34	1.21	1.09	1.00	.921	.853	.793
15	15.4	7.67	5.11	3.83	3.06	2.55	2.18	1.91	1.69	1.52	1.38	1.26	1.16	1.07	1.00
18	18.6	9.30	6.20	4.65	3.71	3.09	2.65	2.31	2.05	1.84	1.67	1.53	1.41	1.30	1.21
21	22.0	11.0	7.32	5.49	4.39	3.65	3.13	2.73	2.42	2.18	1.97	1.81	1.66	1.54	1.43
24	25.5	12.7	8.50	6.37	5.09	4.24	3.63	3.17	2.81	2.53	2.29	2.09	1.93	1.79	1.66
27	29.2	14.6	9.72	7.29	5.82	4.85	4.15	3.63	3.22	2.89	2.62	2.40	2.21	2.04	1.90
30	33.1	16.5	11.0	8.26	6.60	5.49	4.70	4.11	3.65	3.27	2.97	2.72	2.50	2.32	2.15
33	37.2	18.6	12.4	9.29	7.42	6.18	5.29	4.62	4.10	3.68	3.34	3.06	2.81	2.61	2.42
36	41.6	20.8	13.9	10.4	8.30	6.91	5.92	5.17	4.59	4.12	3.74	3.42	3.15	2.91	2.71
38	44.8	22.4	14.9	11.2	8.93	7.43	6.36	5.56	4.93	4.43	4.02	3.68	3.38	3.13	2.92
40	48.1	24.0	16.0	12.0	9.59	7.98	6.83	5.97	5.30	4.76	4.32	3.95	3.63	3.37	3.13
42	51.6	25.8	17.2	12.9	10.3	8.57	7.33	6.41	5.69	5.11	4.63	4.24	3.90	3.61	3.36
44	55.3	27.7	18.4	13.8	11.0	9.19	7.86	6.87	6.10	5.48	4.97	4.54	4.18	3.87	3.60
46	59.3	29.7	19.8	14.8	11.8	9.85	8.43	7.37	6.54	5.87	5.33	4.87	4.49	4.15	3.86
48	63.6	31.8	21.2	15.9	12.7	10.6	9.05	7.90	7.01	6.30	5.71	5.23	4.81	4.45	4.14
50	68.3	34.1	22.7	17.0	13.6	11.3	9.71	8.48	7.52	6.76	6.13	5.61	5.16	4.78	4.45
52	73.3	36.7	24.4	18.3	14.6	12.2	10.4	9.11	8.08	7.26	6.58	6.02	5.55	5.13	4.78
54	78.9	39.4	26.3	19.7	15.7	13.1	11.2	9.79	8.69	7.81	7.08	6.48	5.96	5.52	5.14
56	84.9	42.5	28.3	21.2	16.9	14.1	12.1	10.5	9.36	8.41	7.63	6.97	6.42	5.95	5.53
58	91.7	45.8	30.5	22.9	18.3	15.2	13.0	11.4	10.1	9.08	8.23	7.53	6.93	6.42	5.97
60	99.2	49.6	33.0	24.8	19.8	16.5	14.1	12.3	10.9	9.82	8.91	8.15	7.50	6.95	6.46
62	108	53.9	35.9	26.9	21.5	17.9	15.3	13.4	11.9	10.7	9.68	8.85	8.15	7.54	7.02
64	117	58.7	39.1	29.3	23.4	19.5	16.7	14.6	12.9	11.6	10.5	9.65	8.88	8.22	7.65
66	129	64.3	42.9	32.1	25.7	21.4	18.3	16.0	14.2	12.7	11.6	10.6	9.72	9.01	8.38
LAT.	179° 181°	178° 182°	177° 183°	176° 184°	175° 185°	174° 186°	173° 187°	172° 188°	171° 189°	170° 190°	169° 191°	168° 192°	167° 193°	166° 194°	165° 195°

B — Lat. and Dec. SAME NAME − / Lat. and Dec. DIFFERENT NAMES +

DEC.	1° 359°	2° 358°	3° 357°	4° 356°	5° 355°	6° 354°	7° 353°	8° 352°	9° 351°	10° 350°	11° 349°	12° 348°	13° 347°	14° 346°	15° 345°
0°	0.00	.000	.000	.000	.000	.000	.000	.000	.000	.000	.000	.000	.000	.000	.000
3	3.00	1.50	1.00	.751	.601	.501	.430	.377	.335	.302	.275	.252	.233	.217	.202
6	6.02	3.01	2.01	1.51	1.21	1.01	.862	.755	.672	.605	.551	.506	.467	.434	.406
9	9.08	4.54	3.03	2.27	1.82	1.52	1.30	1.14	1.01	.912	.830	.762	.704	.655	.612
12	12.2	6.09	4.06	3.05	2.44	2.03	1.74	1.53	1.36	1.22	1.11	1.02	.945	.879	.821
15	15.4	7.68	5.12	3.84	3.07	2.56	2.20	1.93	1.71	1.54	1.40	1.29	1.19	1.11	1.04
18	18.6	9.31	6.21	4.66	3.73	3.11	2.67	2.33	2.08	1.87	1.70	1.56	1.44	1.34	1.26
21	22.0	11.0	7.33	5.50	4.40	3.67	3.15	2.76	2.45	2.21	2.01	1.85	1.71	1.59	1.48
24	25.5	12.8	8.51	6.38	5.11	4.26	3.65	3.20	2.85	2.56	2.33	2.14	1.98	1.84	1.72
27	29.2	14.6	9.74	7.30	5.85	4.87	4.18	3.66	3.26	2.93	2.67	2.45	2.27	2.11	1.97
30	33.1	16.5	11.0	8.28	6.62	5.52	4.74	4.15	3.69	3.32	3.03	2.78	2.57	2.39	2.23
33	37.2	18.6	12.4	9.31	7.45	6.21	5.33	4.67	4.15	3.74	3.40	3.12	2.89	2.68	2.51
36	41.6	20.8	13.9	10.4	8.34	6.95	5.96	5.22	4.64	4.18	3.81	3.49	3.23	3.00	2.81
38	44.8	22.4	14.9	11.2	8.96	7.47	6.41	5.61	4.99	4.50	4.09	3.76	3.47	3.23	3.02
40	48.1	24.0	16.0	12.0	9.63	8.03	6.89	6.03	5.36	4.83	4.40	4.04	3.73	3.47	3.24
42	51.6	25.8	17.2	12.9	10.3	8.61	7.39	6.47	5.76	5.19	4.72	4.33	4.00	3.72	3.48
44	55.3	27.7	18.5	13.8	11.1	9.24	7.92	6.94	6.17	5.56	5.06	4.64	4.29	3.99	3.73
46	59.3	29.7	19.8	14.8	11.9	9.91	8.50	7.44	6.62	5.96	5.43	4.98	4.60	4.28	4.00
48	63.6	31.8	21.3	15.9	12.7	10.6	9.11	7.98	7.10	6.40	5.82	5.34	4.94	4.59	4.29
50	68.3	34.1	22.8	17.1	13.7	11.4	9.78	8.56	7.62	6.86	6.25	5.73	5.30	4.93	4.60
52	73.3	36.7	24.5	18.3	14.7	12.2	10.5	9.20	8.18	7.37	6.71	6.16	5.69	5.29	4.95
54	78.9	39.4	26.3	19.7	15.8	13.2	11.3	9.89	8.80	7.93	7.21	6.62	6.12	5.69	5.32
56	84.9	42.5	28.3	21.3	17.0	14.2	12.2	10.7	9.48	8.54	7.77	7.13	6.59	6.13	5.73
58	91.7	45.9	30.6	22.9	18.4	15.3	13.1	11.5	10.2	9.22	8.39	7.70	7.11	6.62	6.18
60	99.2	49.6	33.1	24.8	19.9	16.6	14.2	12.5	11.1	9.97	9.08	8.33	7.70	7.16	6.69
62	108	53.9	35.9	27.0	21.6	18.0	15.4	13.5	12.0	10.8	9.86	9.05	8.36	7.77	7.27
DEC.	179° 181°	178° 182°	177° 183°	176° 184°	175° 185°	174° 186°	173° 187°	172° 188°	171° 189°	170° 190°	169° 191°	168° 192°	167° 193°	166° 194°	165° 195°

A — HOUR ANGLE at top $+$ Hour angle at bottom $-$

LAT.	16° 344°	17° 343°	18° 342°	19° 341°	20° 340°	21° 339°	22° 338°	23° 337°	24° 336°	25° 335°	26° 334°	27° 333°	28° 332°	29° 331°	30° 330°
0°	.000	.000	.000	.000	.000	.000	.000	.000	.000	.000	.000	.000	.000	.000	.000
3	.183	.171	.161	.152	.144	.137	.130	.123	.118	.112	.107	.103	.099	.095	.091
6	.367	.344	.323	.305	.289	.274	.260	.248	.236	.225	.215	.206	.198	.190	.182
9	.552	.518	.487	.460	.435	.413	.392	.373	.356	.340	.325	.311	.298	.286	.274
12	.741	.695	.654	.617	.584	.554	.526	.501	.477	.456	.436	.417	.400	.383	.368
15	.934	.876	.825	.778	.736	.698	.663	.631	.602	.575	.549	.526	.504	.483	.464
18	1.13	1.06	1.00	.944	.893	.846	.804	.765	.730	.697	.666	.638	.611	.586	.563
21	1.34	1.26	1.18	1.11	1.05	1.00	.950	.904	.862	.823	.787	.753	.722	.693	.665
24	1.55	1.46	1.37	1.29	1.22	1.16	1.10	1.05	1.00	.955	.913	.874	.837	.803	.771
27	1.78	1.67	1.57	1.48	1.40	1.33	1.26	1.20	1.14	1.09	1.04	1.00	.958	.919	.883
30	2.01	1.89	1.78	1.68	1.59	1.50	1.43	1.36	1.30	1.24	1.18	1.13	1.09	1.04	1.00
33	2.26	2.12	2.00	1.89	1.78	1.69	1.61	1.53	1.46	1.39	1.33	1.27	1.22	1.17	1.12
36	2.53	2.38	2.24	2.11	2.00	1.89	1.80	1.71	1.63	1.56	1.49	1.43	1.37	1.31	1.26
38	2.72	2.56	2.40	2.27	2.15	2.04	1.93	1.84	1.75	1.68	1.60	1.53	1.47	1.41	1.35
40	2.93	2.74	2.58	2.44	2.31	2.19	2.08	1.98	1.88	1.80	1.72	1.65	1.58	1.51	1.45
42	3.14	2.95	2.77	2.61	2.47	2.35	2.23	2.12	2.02	1.93	1.85	1.77	1.69	1.62	1.56
44	3.37	3.16	2.97	2.80	2.65	2.52	2.39	2.28	2.17	2.07	1.98	1.90	1.82	1.74	1.67
46	3.61	3.39	3.19	3.01	2.85	2.70	2.56	2.44	2.33	2.22	2.12	2.03	1.95	1.87	1.79
48	3.87	3.63	3.42	3.23	3.05	2.89	2.75	2.62	2.49	2.38	2.28	2.18	2.09	2.00	1.92
50	4.16	3.90	3.67	3.46	3.27	3.10	2.95	2.81	2.68	2.56	2.44	2.34	2.24	2.15	2.06
52	4.46	4.19	3.94	3.72	3.52	3.33	3.17	3.02	2.87	2.74	2.62	2.51	2.41	2.31	2.22
54	4.80	4.50	4.24	4.00	3.78	3.59	3.41	3.24	3.09	2.95	2.82	2.70	2.59	2.48	2.38
56	5.17	4.85	4.56	4.31	4.07	3.86	3.67	3.49	3.33	3.18	3.04	2.91	2.79	2.67	2.57
58	5.58	5.23	4.93	4.65	4.40	4.17	3.96	3.77	3.59	3.43	3.28	3.14	3.01	2.89	2.77
60	6.04	5.67	5.33	5.03	4.76	4.51	4.29	4.08	3.89	3.71	3.55	3.40	3.26	3.12	3.00
62	6.56	6.15	5.79	5.46	5.17	4.90	4.65	4.43	4.22	4.03	3.86	3.69	3.54	3.39	3.26
64	7.15	6.71	6.31	5.95	5.63	5.34	5.07	4.83	4.61	4.40	4.20	4.02	3.86	3.70	3.55
66	7.83	7.35	6.91	6.52	6.17	5.85	5.56	5.29	5.04	4.82	4.61	4.41	4.22	4.05	3.89
LAT.	164° 196°	163° 197°	162° 198°	161° 199°	160° 200°	159° 201°	158° 202°	157° 203°	156° 204°	155° 205°	154° 206°	153° 207°	152° 208°	151° 209°	150° 210°

B — Lat. and Dec. SAME NAME $-$ Lat. and Dec. DIFFERENT NAMES $+$

DEC.	16° 344°	17° 343°	18° 342°	19° 341°	20° 340°	21° 339°	22° 338°	23° 337°	24° 336°	25° 335°	26° 334°	27° 333°	28° 332°	29° 331°	30° 330°
0°	.000	.000	.000	.000	.000	.000	.000	.000	.000	.000	.000	.000	.000	.000	.000
3	.190	.179	.170	.161	.153	.146	.140	.134	.129	.124	.120	.115	.112	.108	.105
6	.381	.359	.340	.323	.307	.293	.281	.269	.258	.249	.240	.232	.224	.217	.210
9	.575	.542	.513	.486	.463	.442	.423	.405	.389	.375	.361	.349	.337	.327	.317
12	.771	.727	.688	.653	.621	.593	.567	.544	.523	.503	.485	.468	.453	.438	.425
15	.972	.916	.867	.823	.783	.748	.715	.686	.659	.634	.611	.590	.571	.553	.536
18	1.18	1.11	1.05	.998	.950	.907	.867	.832	.799	.769	.741	.716	.692	.670	.650
21	1.39	1.31	1.24	1.18	1.12	1.07	1.02	.982	.944	.908	.876	.846	.818	.792	.768
24	1.62	1.52	1.44	1.37	1.30	1.24	1.19	1.14	1.09	1.05	1.02	.981	.948	.918	.890
27	1.85	1.74	1.65	1.57	1.49	1.42	1.36	1.30	1.25	1.21	1.16	1.12	1.09	1.05	1.02
30	2.09	1.97	1.87	1.77	1.69	1.61	1.54	1.48	1.42	1.37	1.32	1.27	1.23	1.19	1.15
33	2.36	2.22	2.10	1.99	1.90	1.81	1.73	1.66	1.60	1.54	1.48	1.43	1.38	1.34	1.30
36	2.64	2.48	2.35	2.23	2.12	2.03	1.94	1.86	1.79	1.72	1.66	1.60	1.55	1.50	1.45
38	2.83	2.67	2.53	2.40	2.28	2.18	2.09	2.00	1.92	1.85	1.78	1.72	1.66	1.61	1.56
40	3.04	2.87	2.72	2.58	2.45	2.34	2.24	2.15	2.06	1.99	1.91	1.85	1.79	1.73	1.68
42	3.27	3.08	2.91	2.77	2.63	2.51	2.40	2.30	2.21	2.13	2.05	1.98	1.92	1.86	1.80
44	3.50	3.30	3.13	2.97	2.82	2.69	2.58	2.47	2.37	2.29	2.20	2.13	2.06	1.99	1.93
46	3.76	3.54	3.35	3.18	3.03	2.89	2.76	2.65	2.55	2.45	2.36	2.28	2.21	2.14	2.07
48	4.03	3.80	3.59	3.41	3.25	3.10	2.96	2.84	2.73	2.63	2.53	2.45	2.37	2.29	2.22
50	4.32	4.08	3.86	3.66	3.48	3.33	3.18	3.05	2.93	2.82	2.72	2.63	2.54	2.46	2.38
52	4.64	4.38	4.14	3.93	3.74	3.57	3.42	3.28	3.15	3.03	2.92	2.82	2.73	2.64	2.56
54	4.99	4.71	4.45	4.23	4.02	3.84	3.67	3.52	3.38	3.26	3.14	3.03	2.93	2.84	2.75
56	5.38	5.07	4.80	4.55	4.33	4.14	3.96	3.79	3.65	3.51	3.38	3.27	3.16	3.06	2.97
58	5.81	5.47	5.18	4.92	4.68	4.47	4.27	4.10	3.93	3.79	3.65	3.53	3.41	3.30	3.20
60	6.28	5.92	5.61	5.32	5.06	4.83	4.62	4.43	4.26	4.10	3.95	3.82	3.69	3.57	3.46
62	6.82	6.43	6.09	5.78	5.50	5.25	5.02	4.81	4.62	4.45	4.29	4.14	4.01	3.88	3.76
DEC.	164° 196°	163° 197°	162° 198°	161° 199°	160° 200°	159° 201°	158° 202°	157° 203°	156° 204°	155° 205°	154° 206°	153° 207°	152° 208°	151° 209°	150° 210°

A HOUR ANGLE at top +
Hour angle at bottom −

LAT.	32° 328°	34° 326°	36° 324°	38° 322°	40° 320°	42° 318°	44° 316°	46° 314°	48° 312°	50° 310°	52° 308°	54° 306°	56° 304°	58° 302°	60° 300°
0°	.000	.000	.000	.000	.000	.000	.000	.000	.000	.000	.000	.000	.000	.000	.000
3	.084	.078	.072	.067	.062	.058	.054	.051	.047	.044	.041	.038	.035	.033	.030
6	.168	.156	.145	.135	.125	.117	.109	.101	.095	.088	.082	.076	.071	.066	.061
9	.253	.235	.218	.203	.189	.176	.164	.153	.143	.133	.124	.115	.107	.099	.091
12	.340	.315	.293	.272	.253	.236	.220	.205	.191	.178	.166	.154	.143	.133	.123
15	.429	.397	.369	.343	.319	.298	.277	.259	.241	.225	.209	.195	.181	.167	.155
18	.520	.482	.447	.416	.387	.361	.336	.314	.293	.273	.254	.236	.219	.203	.188
21	.614	.569	.528	.491	.457	.426	.398	.371	.346	.322	.300	.279	.259	.240	.222
24	.713	.660	.613	.570	.531	.494	.461	.430	.401	.374	.348	.323	.300	.278	.257
27	.815	.755	.701	.652	.607	.566	.528	.492	.459	.428	.398	.370	.344	.318	.294
30	.924	.856	.795	.739	.688	.641	.598	.558	.520	.484	.451	.419	.389	.361	.333
33	1.04	.963	.894	.831	.774	.721	.672	.627	.585	.545	.507	.472	.438	.406	.375
36	1.16	1.08	1.00	.930	.866	.807	.752	.702	.654	.610	.568	.528	.490	.454	.419
38	1.25	1.16	1.08	1.00	.931	.868	.809	.754	.703	.656	.610	.568	.527	.488	.451
40	1.34	1.24	1.15	1.07	1.00	.932	.869	.810	.756	.704	.656	.610	.566	.524	.484
42	1.44	1.33	1.24	1.15	1.07	1.00	.932	.870	.811	.756	.703	.654	.607	.563	.520
44	1.55	1.43	1.33	1.24	1.15	1.07	1.00	.933	.870	.810	.754	.702	.651	.603	.558
46	1.66	1.54	1.43	1.33	1.23	1.15	1.07	1.00	.932	.869	.809	.752	.698	.647	.598
48	1.78	1.65	1.53	1.42	1.32	1.23	1.15	1.07	1.00	.932	.868	.807	.749	.694	.641
50	1.91	1.77	1.64	1.53	1.42	1.32	1.23	1.15	1.07	1.00	.931	.866	.804	.745	.688
52	2.05	1.90	1.76	1.64	1.53	1.42	1.33	1.24	1.15	1.07	1.00	.930	.863	.800	.739
54	2.20	2.04	1.89	1.76	1.64	1.53	1.43	1.33	1.24	1.15	1.08	1.00	.928	.860	.795
56	2.37	2.20	2.04	1.90	1.77	1.65	1.54	1.43	1.33	1.24	1.16	1.08	1.00	.926	.856
58	2.56	2.37	2.20	2.05	1.91	1.78	1.66	1.55	1.44	1.34	1.25	1.16	1.08	1.00	.924
60	2.77	2.57	2.38	2.22	2.06	1.92	1.79	1.67	1.56	1.45	1.35	1.26	1.17	1.08	1.00
62	3.01	2.79	2.59	2.41	2.24	2.09	1.95	1.82	1.69	1.58	1.47	1.37	1.27	1.18	1.09
64	3.28	3.04	2.82	2.62	2.44	2.28	2.12	1.98	1.85	1.72	1.60	1.49	1.38	1.28	1.18
66	3.59	3.33	3.09	2.87	2.68	2.49	2.33	2.17	2.02	1.88	1.75	1.63	1.52	1.40	1.30
LAT.	148° 212°	146° 214°	144° 216°	142° 218°	140° 220°	138° 222°	136° 224°	134° 226°	132° 228°	130° 230°	128° 232°	126° 234°	124° 236°	122° 238°	120° 240°

B Lat. and Dec. SAME NAME −
Lat. and Dec. DIFFERENT NAMES +

DEC.	32° 328°	34° 326°	36° 324°	38° 322°	40° 320°	42° 318°	44° 316°	46° 314°	48° 312°	50° 310°	52° 308°	54° 306°	56° 304°	58° 302°	60° 300°
0°	.000	.000	.000	.000	.000	.000	.000	.000	.000	.000	.000	.000	.000	.000	.000
3	.099	.094	.089	.085	.082	.078	.075	.073	.071	.068	.067	.065	.063	.062	.061
6	.198	.188	.179	.171	.164	.157	.151	.146	.141	.137	.133	.130	.127	.124	.121
9	.299	.283	.269	.257	.246	.237	.228	.220	.213	.207	.201	.196	.191	.187	.183
12	.401	.380	.362	.345	.331	.318	.306	.295	.286	.277	.270	.263	.256	.251	.245
15	.506	.479	.456	.435	.417	.400	.386	.372	.361	.350	.340	.331	.323	.316	.309
18	.613	.581	.553	.528	.505	.486	.468	.452	.437	.424	.412	.402	.392	.383	.375
21	.724	.686	.653	.623	.597	.574	.553	.534	.517	.501	.487	.474	.463	.453	.443
24	.840	.796	.757	.723	.693	.665	.641	.619	.599	.581	.565	.550	.537	.525	.514
27	.962	.911	.867	.828	.793	.761	.733	.708	.686	.665	.647	.630	.615	.601	.588
30	1.09	1.03	.982	.938	.898	.863	.831	.803	.777	.754	.733	.714	.696	.681	.667
33	1.23	1.16	1.11	1.05	1.01	.971	.935	.903	.874	.848	.824	.803	.783	.766	.750
36	1.37	1.30	1.24	1.18	1.13	1.09	1.05	1.01	.978	.948	.922	.898	.876	.857	.839
38	1.47	1.40	1.33	1.27	1.22	1.17	1.12	1.09	1.05	1.02	.991	.966	.942	.921	.902
40	1.58	1.50	1.43	1.36	1.31	1.25	1.21	1.17	1.13	1.10	1.06	1.04	1.01	.989	.969
42	1.70	1.61	1.53	1.46	1.40	1.35	1.30	1.25	1.21	1.18	1.14	1.11	1.09	1.06	1.04
44	1.82	1.73	1.64	1.57	1.50	1.44	1.39	1.34	1.30	1.26	1.23	1.19	1.16	1.14	1.12
46	1.95	1.85	1.76	1.68	1.61	1.55	1.49	1.44	1.39	1.35	1.31	1.28	1.25	1.22	1.20
48	2.10	1.99	1.89	1.80	1.73	1.66	1.60	1.54	1.49	1.45	1.41	1.37	1.34	1.31	1.28
50	2.25	2.13	2.03	1.94	1.85	1.78	1.72	1.66	1.60	1.56	1.51	1.47	1.44	1.41	1.38
52	2.42	2.29	2.18	2.08	1.99	1.91	1.84	1.78	1.72	1.67	1.62	1.58	1.54	1.51	1.48
54	2.60	2.46	2.34	2.24	2.14	2.06	1.98	1.91	1.85	1.80	1.75	1.70	1.66	1.62	1.59
56	2.80	2.65	2.52	2.41	2.31	2.22	2.13	2.06	2.00	1.94	1.88	1.83	1.79	1.75	1.71
58	3.02	2.86	2.72	2.60	2.49	2.39	2.30	2.22	2.15	2.09	2.03	1.98	1.93	1.89	1.85
60	3.27	3.10	2.95	2.81	2.69	2.59	2.49	2.41	2.33	2.26	2.20	2.14	2.09	2.04	2.00
62	3.55	3.36	3.20	3.05	2.93	2.81	2.71	2.61	2.53	2.46	2.39	2.32	2.27	2.22	2.17
DEC.	148° 212°	146° 214°	144° 216°	142° 218°	140° 220°	138° 222°	136° 224°	134° 226°	132° 228°	130° 230°	128° 232°	126° 234°	124° 236°	122° 238°	120° 240°

A   HOUR ANGLE at top +
        Hour angle at bottom —

LAT.	62°/298°	64°/296°	66°/294°	68°/292°	70°/290°	72°/288°	74°/286°	76°/284°	78°/282°	80°/280°	82°/278°	84°/276°	86°/274°	88°/272°	90°/270°
0°	.000	.000	.000	.000	.000	.000	.000	.000	.000	.000	.000	.000	.000	.000	.000
3	.028	.026	.023	.021	.019	.017	.015	.013	.011	.009	.007	.006	.004	.002	.000
6	.056	.051	.047	.043	.038	.034	.030	.026	.022	.019	.015	.011	.007	.004	.000
9	.084	.077	.071	.064	.058	.051	.045	.039	.034	.028	.022	.017	.011	.006	.000
12	.113	.104	.095	.086	.077	.069	.061	.053	.045	.037	.030	.022	.015	.007	.000
15	.142	.131	.119	.108	.098	.087	.077	.067	.057	.047	.038	.028	.019	.009	.000
18	.173	.158	.145	.131	.118	.106	.093	.081	.069	.057	.046	.034	.023	.012	.000
21	.204	.187	.171	.155	.140	.125	.110	.096	.082	.068	.054	.040	.027	.013	.000
24	.237	.217	.198	.180	.162	.145	.128	.111	.095	.079	.063	.047	.031	.016	.000
27	.271	.249	.227	.206	.185	.166	.146	.127	.108	.090	.072	.054	.036	.018	.000
30	.307	.282	.257	.233	.210	.188	.166	.144	.123	.102	.081	.061	.040	.020	.000
33	.345	.317	.289	.262	.236	.211	.186	.162	.138	.115	.091	.068	.045	.023	.000
36	.386	.354	.323	.294	.264	.236	.208	.181	.154	.128	.102	.076	.051	.025	.000
38	.415	.381	.348	.316	.284	.254	.224	.195	.166	.138	.110	.082	.055	.027	.000
40	.446	.409	.374	.339	.305	.273	.241	.209	.178	.148	.118	.088	.059	.029	.000
42	.479	.439	.401	.364	.328	.293	.258	.224	.191	.159	.127	.095	.063	.031	.000
44	.513	.471	.430	.390	.351	.314	.277	.241	.205	.170	.136	.101	.068	.034	.000
46	.551	.505	.461	.418	.377	.336	.297	.258	.220	.183	.146	.109	.072	.036	.000
48	.591	.542	.494	.449	.404	.361	.318	.277	.236	.196	.156	.117	.078	.039	.000
50	.634	.581	.531	.481	.434	.387	.342	.297	.253	.210	.167	.125	.083	.042	.000
52	.681	.624	.570	.517	.466	.416	.367	.319	.272	.226	.180	.135	.090	.045	.000
54	.732	.671	.613	.556	.501	.447	.395	.343	.293	.243	.193	.145	.096	.048	.000
56	.788	.723	.660	.603	.540	.482	.425	.370	.315	.261	.208	.156	.104	.052	.000
58	.851	.781	.713	.647	.582	.520	.459	.399	.340	.282	.225	.168	.112	.056	.000
60	.921	.845	.771	.700	.630	.563	.497	.432	.368	.305	.243	.182	.121	.060	.000
62	1.00	.917	.837	.760	.685	.611	.539	.469	.400	.332	.264	.198	.132	.066	.000
64	1.09	1.00	.913	.828	.746	.666	.588	.511	.436	.362	.288	.215	.143	.072	.000
66	1.19	1.10	1.00	.907	.817	.730	.644	.560	.477	.396	.316	.236	.157	.078	.000
LAT.	118°/242°	116°/244°	114°/246°	112°/248°	110°/250°	108°/252°	106°/254°	104°/256°	102°/258°	100°/260°	98°/262°	96°/264°	94°/266°	92°/268°	90°/270°

B   Lat. and Dec. SAME NAME —
        Lat. and Dec. DIFFERENT NAMES +

	62°/298°	64°/296°	66°/294°	68°/292°	70°/290°	72°/288°	74°/286°	76°/284°	78°/282°	80°/280°	82°/278°	84°/276°	86°/274°	88°/272°	90°/270°
0°	.000	.000	.000	.000	.000	.000	.000	.000	.000	.000	.000	.000	.000	.000	.000
3	.059	.058	.057	.057	.056	.055	.055	.054	.054	.053	.053	.053	.053	.052	.052
6	.119	.117	.115	.113	.112	.111	.109	.108	.107	.107	.106	.106	.105	.105	.105
9	.179	.176	.173	.171	.169	.167	.165	.163	.162	.161	.160	.159	.159	.158	.158
12	.241	.236	.233	.229	.226	.223	.221	.219	.217	.216	.215	.214	.213	.213	.213
15	.303	.298	.293	.289	.285	.282	.279	.276	.274	.272	.271	.269	.269	.268	.268
18	.368	.362	.356	.350	.346	.342	.338	.335	.332	.330	.328	.327	.326	.325	.325
21	.435	.427	.420	.414	.408	.404	.399	.396	.392	.390	.388	.386	.385	.384	.384
24	.504	.495	.487	.480	.474	.468	.463	.459	.455	.452	.450	.448	.446	.446	.445
27	.577	.567	.558	.550	.542	.536	.530	.525	.521	.517	.515	.512	.511	.510	.510
30	.654	.642	.632	.623	.614	.607	.601	.595	.590	.586	.583	.581	.579	.578	.577
33	.735	.723	.711	.700	.691	.683	.676	.669	.664	.659	.656	.653	.651	.650	.649
36	.823	.808	.795	.784	.773	.764	.756	.749	.743	.738	.734	.731	.728	.727	.727
38	.885	.869	.855	.843	.831	.821	.813	.805	.799	.793	.789	.786	.783	.782	.781
40	.950	.934	.919	.905	.893	.882	.873	.865	.858	.852	.847	.844	.841	.840	.839
42	1.02	1.00	.986	.971	.958	.947	.937	.928	.921	.914	.909	.905	.903	.901	.900
44	1.09	1.07	1.06	1.04	1.03	1.02	1.00	.995	.987	.981	.975	.971	.968	.966	.966
46	1.17	1.15	1.13	1.12	1.10	1.09	1.08	1.07	1.06	1.05	1.05	1.04	1.04	1.04	1.04
48	1.26	1.24	1.22	1.20	1.18	1.17	1.16	1.14	1.14	1.13	1.12	1.12	1.11	1.11	1.11
50	1.35	1.33	1.30	1.29	1.27	1.25	1.24	1.23	1.22	1.21	1.20	1.20	1.19	1.19	1.19
52	1.45	1.42	1.40	1.38	1.36	1.35	1.33	1.32	1.31	1.30	1.29	1.29	1.28	1.28	1.28
54	1.56	1.53	1.51	1.48	1.46	1.45	1.43	1.42	1.41	1.40	1.39	1.38	1.38	1.38	1.38
56	1.68	1.65	1.62	1.60	1.58	1.56	1.54	1.53	1.52	1.51	1.50	1.49	1.49	1.48	1.48
58	1.81	1.78	1.75	1.73	1.70	1.68	1.66	1.65	1.64	1.63	1.62	1.61	1.60	1.60	1.60
60	1.96	1.93	1.90	1.87	1.84	1.82	1.80	1.79	1.77	1.76	1.75	1.74	1.74	1.73	1.73
62	2.13	2.09	2.06	2.03	2.00	1.98	1.96	1.94	1.92	1.91	1.90	1.89	1.89	1.88	1.88
DEC.	118°/242°	116°/244°	114°/246°	112°/248°	110°/250°	108°/252°	106°/254°	104°/256°	102°/258°	100°/260°	98°/262°	96°/264°	94°/266°	92°/268°	90°/270°

C

C = A ± B

AZIMUTH

Lat. °	.00	.05	.10	.15	.20	.25	.30	.35	.40	.45	.50	.55	.60	.70	.80	.90	1.00	1.10	1.20	1.40	1.60	Lat. °
0	90.0	87.1	84.3	81.5	78.7	76.0	73.3	70.7	68.2	65.8	63.4	61.2	59.0	55.0	51.3	48.0	45.0	42.3	39.8	35.5	32.0	0
10	90.0	87.2	84.4	81.6	78.9	76.2	73.5	71.0	68.5	66.1	63.8	61.6	59.4	55.4	51.8	48.4	45.4	42.7	40.2	36.0	32.4	10
20	90.0	87.3	84.6	82.0	79.4	76.8	74.3	71.8	69.4	67.1	64.8	62.7	60.6	56.7	53.1	49.8	46.8	44.1	41.6	37.2	33.6	20
24	90.0	87.4	84.8	82.2	79.6	77.1	74.7	72.3	69.9	67.7	65.5	63.3	61.3	57.4	53.8	50.6	47.6	44.9	42.4	38.0	34.4	24
28	90.0	87.5	85.0	82.5	80.0	77.6	75.2	72.8	70.5	68.3	66.2	64.1	62.1	58.3	54.8	51.5	48.6	45.8	43.3	39.0	35.3	28
30	90.0	87.5	85.1	82.6	80.2	77.8	75.4	73.1	70.9	68.7	66.6	64.5	62.5	58.8	55.3	52.1	49.1	46.4	43.9	39.5	35.8	30
32	90.0	87.6	85.2	82.8	80.4	78.0	75.7	73.5	71.3	69.1	67.0	65.0	63.0	59.3	55.8	52.7	49.7	47.0	44.5	40.1	36.4	32
34	90.0	87.6	85.3	82.9	80.6	78.3	76.0	73.8	71.7	69.5	67.5	65.5	63.6	59.9	56.4	53.3	50.3	47.6	45.1	40.7	37.0	34
36	90.0	87.7	85.4	83.1	80.8	78.6	76.4	74.2	72.1	70.0	68.0	66.0	64.1	60.5	57.1	53.9	51.0	48.3	45.8	41.4	37.7	36
38	90.0	87.7	85.5	83.3	81.0	78.9	76.7	74.6	72.5	70.5	68.5	66.6	64.7	61.1	57.8	54.7	51.8	49.1	46.6	42.2	38.4	38
40	90.0	87.8	85.6	83.4	81.3	79.2	77.1	75.0	73.0	71.0	69.0	67.2	65.3	61.8	58.5	55.4	52.5	49.9	47.4	43.0	39.2	40
42	90.0	87.9	85.7	83.6	81.5	79.5	77.4	75.4	73.4	71.5	69.6	67.8	66.0	62.5	59.3	56.2	53.4	50.8	48.3	43.9	40.1	42
44	90.0	87.9	85.9	83.8	81.8	79.8	77.8	75.9	73.9	72.1	70.2	68.4	66.7	63.3	60.1	57.1	54.3	51.6	49.2	44.8	41.0	44
46	90.0	88.0	86.0	84.1	82.1	80.1	78.2	76.3	74.5	72.6	70.8	69.1	67.4	64.1	60.9	58.0	55.2	52.6	50.2	45.8	42.0	46
48	90.0	88.1	86.2	84.3	82.4	80.5	78.6	76.8	75.0	73.2	71.5	69.8	68.1	64.9	61.8	58.9	56.2	53.6	51.2	46.9	43.0	48
50	90.0	88.2	86.3	84.5	82.7	80.9	79.1	77.3	75.6	73.9	72.2	70.5	68.9	65.8	62.8	60.0	57.3	54.7	52.4	48.0	44.2	50
52	90.0	88.3	86.5	84.7	83.0	81.2	79.5	77.8	76.2	74.5	72.9	71.3	69.7	66.7	63.8	61.0	58.4	55.9	53.5	49.2	45.4	52
54	90.0	88.3	86.6	85.0	83.3	81.6	80.0	78.4	76.8	75.2	73.6	72.1	70.6	67.6	64.8	62.1	59.6	57.1	54.8	50.6	46.8	54
56	90.0	88.4	86.8	85.2	83.6	82.0	80.5	78.9	77.4	75.9	74.4	72.9	71.5	68.6	65.9	63.3	60.8	58.4	56.1	51.9	48.2	56
58	90.0	88.5	87.0	85.5	84.0	82.5	81.0	79.5	78.0	76.6	75.2	73.8	72.4	69.6	67.0	64.5	62.1	59.8	57.5	53.4	49.7	58
60	90.0	88.6	87.1	85.7	84.3	82.9	81.5	80.1	78.7	77.3	76.0	74.6	73.3	70.7	68.2	65.8	63.4	61.2	59.0	55.0	51.3	60
62	90.0	88.7	87.3	86.0	84.6	83.3	82.0	80.7	79.4	78.1	76.8	75.5	74.3	71.8	69.4	67.1	64.9	62.7	60.6	56.7	53.1	62
64	90.0	88.7	87.5	86.2	85.0	83.7	82.5	81.3	80.1	78.8	77.6	76.4	75.3	72.9	70.7	68.5	66.3	64.3	62.3	58.5	55.0	64
66	90.0	88.8	87.7	86.5	85.3	84.2	83.0	81.9	80.8	79.6	78.5	77.4	76.3	74.1	72.0	69.9	67.9	65.9	64.0	60.3	56.9	66
68	90.0	88.9	87.9	86.8	85.7	84.6	83.6	82.5	81.5	80.4	79.4	78.4	77.3	75.3	73.3	71.4	69.5	67.6	65.8	62.3	59.1	68
Lat. °	.00	.05	.10	.15	.20	.25	.30	.35	.40	.45	.50	.55	.60	.70	.80	.90	1.00	1.10	1.20	1.40	1.60	Lat. °

C CORRECTION

TO NAME AZIMUTH

+   SOUTH in N. Latitudes
    NORTH in S. Latitudes   Hour Angle LESS than 180° = WEST

−   NORTH in N. Latitudes
    SOUTH in S. Latitudes   Hour Angle GREATER than 180° = EAST

C

C = A ± B

AZIMUTH

Lat.	1.60	1.80	2.00	2.20	2.40	2.60	2.80	3.20	3.60	4.00	4.50	5.00	6.00	7.00	8.00	9.00	10.0	15.0	20.0	40.0	Lat.
0	0°	0°	0°	0°	0°	0°	0°	0°	0°	0°	0°	0°	0°	0°	0°	0°	0°	0°	0°	0°	0
10	32.4	29.4	26.9	24.8	22.9	21.3	19.9	17.6	15.8	14.2	12.7	11.5	9.6	8.3	7.2	6.4	5.8	3.9	2.9	1.5	10
20	33.6	30.6	28.0	25.8	23.9	22.3	20.8	18.4	16.5	14.9	13.3	12.0	10.1	8.6	7.6	6.7	6.1	4.1	3.0	1.5	20
24	34.4	31.3	28.7	26.5	24.5	22.8	21.4	18.9	16.9	15.3	13.7	12.3	10.3	8.9	7.8	6.9	6.2	4.2	3.1	1.6	24
28	35.3	32.2	29.5	27.2	25.3	23.5	22.0	19.5	17.5	15.8	14.1	12.8	10.7	9.2	8.1	7.2	6.5	4.3	3.2	1.6	28
30	35.8	32.7	30.0	27.7	25.7	23.9	22.4	19.8	17.8	16.1	14.4	13.0	10.9	9.4	8.2	7.3	6.6	4.4	3.3	1.7	30
32	36.4	33.2	30.5	28.2	26.2	24.4	22.8	20.2	18.1	16.4	14.7	13.3	11.1	9.6	8.4	7.5	6.7	4.5	3.4	1.7	32
34	37.0	33.8	31.1	28.7	26.7	24.9	23.3	20.7	18.5	16.8	15.0	13.6	11.4	9.8	8.6	7.6	6.9	4.6	3.5	1.7	34
36	37.7	34.5	31.7	29.3	27.3	25.4	23.8	21.1	19.0	17.2	15.4	13.9	11.6	10.0	8.8	7.8	7.0	4.7	3.5	1.8	36
38	38.4	35.2	32.4	30.0	27.9	26.0	24.4	21.6	19.4	17.6	15.8	14.2	11.9	10.3	9.0	8.0	7.2	4.8	3.6	1.8	38
40	39.2	36.0	33.1	30.7	28.5	26.7	25.0	22.2	19.9	18.1	16.2	14.6	12.3	10.6	9.3	8.3	7.4	5.0	3.7	1.9	40
42	40.1	36.8	33.9	31.5	29.3	27.4	25.7	22.8	20.5	18.6	16.7	15.1	12.7	10.9	9.5	8.5	7.7	5.1	3.8	1.9	42
44	41.0	37.7	34.8	32.3	30.1	28.1	26.4	23.5	21.1	19.2	17.2	15.5	13.0	11.2	9.9	8.8	7.9	5.3	4.0	2.0	44
46	42.0	38.7	35.7	33.2	31.0	29.0	27.2	24.2	21.8	19.8	17.8	16.0	13.5	11.6	10.2	9.1	8.2	5.5	4.1	2.0	46
48	43.0	39.7	36.8	34.2	31.9	29.9	28.1	25.0	22.5	20.5	18.4	16.6	14.0	12.1	10.6	9.4	8.5	5.7	4.3	2.1	48
50	44.2	40.8	37.9	35.3	33.0	30.9	29.1	25.9	23.4	21.3	19.1	17.3	14.5	12.5	11.0	9.8	8.8	5.9	4.4	2.2	50
52	45.4	42.1	39.1	36.4	34.1	32.0	30.1	26.9	24.3	22.1	19.9	18.0	15.1	13.1	11.5	10.2	9.2	6.2	4.6	2.3	52
54	46.4	43.4	40.4	37.7	35.4	33.2	31.3	28.0	25.3	23.1	20.7	18.8	15.8	13.7	12.0	10.7	9.7	6.5	4.9	2.4	54
56	48.2	44.8	41.8	39.1	36.7	34.5	32.6	29.2	26.4	24.1	21.7	19.7	16.6	14.3	12.6	11.2	10.1	6.8	5.1	2.6	56
58	49.7	46.4	43.4	40.6	38.2	36.0	34.0	30.5	27.7	25.3	22.8	20.7	17.5	15.1	13.3	11.8	10.7	7.2	5.4	2.7	58
60	51.3	48.0	45.0	42.3	39.8	37.6	35.5	32.0	29.1	26.6	24.0	21.8	18.4	15.9	14.0	12.5	11.3	7.6	5.7	2.9	60
62	53.1	49.8	46.8	44.1	41.6	39.3	37.3	33.6	30.6	28.0	25.3	23.1	19.6	16.9	14.9	13.3	12.0	8.1	6.1	3.0	62
64	55.0	51.7	48.8	46.0	43.5	41.3	39.2	35.5	32.3	29.7	26.9	24.5	20.8	18.1	15.9	14.2	12.8	8.6	6.5	3.3	64
66	56.9	53.8	50.9	48.2	45.7	43.4	41.3	37.6	34.3	31.6	28.7	26.2	22.3	19.4	17.1	15.3	13.8	9.3	7.0	3.5	66
68	59.1	56.0	53.2	50.5	48.0	45.8	43.6	39.8	36.6	33.7	30.7	28.1	24.0	20.9	18.5	16.5	14.9	10.1	7.6	3.8	68

C CORRECTION

TO NAME AZIMUTH

+ SOUTH in N. Latitudes / NORTH in S. Latitudes

NORTH in N. Latitudes / SOUTH in S. Latitudes

Hour Angle LESS than 180° = WEST

Hour Angle GREATER than 180° = EAST

Finding the vessel's latitude by the meridian altitude of the sun is by far the simplest and on the whole the most accurate method of obtaining a single position line from a celestial body.

The position line found from a meridian altitude is exactly the same as found from any other altitude; but the great advantage of this special meridian altitude lies with the absence of all normal calculations.

The sun rises in the east and sets in the west the world over and as it crosses each imaginary meridian the sun has then reached its highest altitude and is said to be "on the meridian". In the regions of the equator the altitude will be very high depending how nearly the ship is below the sun, but the altitude will be much lower in higher latitudes.

When the sun is "on the meridian," the time is NOON anywhere in the world, the sun appears to "stop" for a moment at its highest altitude and the sextant observation is then taken, checked, and written down at once. Its bearing which will be on your meridian must be recorded also. North of the Tropic of Cancer it always bears south (S) of course, but off Cape Horn — if visible at all — it would always bear north (N), and if on March 21st when the sun's declination (i.e., latitude in the heavens), is 0° — i.e., it is over the equator — a ship on the equator would have a meridian altitude of 90° which would be almost impossible to observe accurately and star observations would be taken normally.

Generally speaking however the sun crosses the meridian at a reasonable altitude for observers in European latitudes. The altitude will be large however around much of the coast of the USA during early summer.

It is unnecessary to know the exact time if the sun is constantly visible because in slow moving vessels when the sun reaches its highest altitude and appears to stop for a moment or so — this must be the correct meridian altitude and as soon as the sun is observed to fall — "It's away" is the expression — it is then after noon.

It is much more convenient of course to know the correct time to save a long period of watching with the sextant; but if time was not available (if, for example the clock or chronometer had stopped), then by frequent reading of the sun's rising altitude on the sextant a continual watch could be kept so that when the sun's rise has stopped then noon could be ascertained quite accurately enough for the latitude to be found by this meridian altitude.

To find the Time of the Sun's Meridian Transit

The sun transits at noon sun time, and this will not of course be 12 o'clock if your clock is set to zone time (see p. 3:8) or G.M.T. A complete description is given on p. 2:17 of finding the time by your clock to take the meridian altitude.

To find the data to complete the problem

Find your height of eye above the sea and record this in the log book to save night measurements — provided you can take all observations from the same height!

The sun's total correction is found from the table on p. 4:5 and added to the sextant altitude to obtain the true meridian altitude; which subtracted from 90° gives the angle of sun from overhead (Z.D.), changing the direction from S to N (or vice-versa in southern latitudes). The sun's declination for the correct time is found as described on p. 2:14. These two elements are additive or subtractive according to the following simple rule.

(a) **SAME NAMES ADD,** and give same name.

(b) **DIFFERENT NAMES (one N and one S), SUBTRACT** and name same as greater.

To find the meridian altitude

The beginner with the sextant will of course commence by taking sights of the sun with the sextant. In higher latitudes round the coasts of the United Kingdom, for example, it is by no means certain that the sun will be visible, as rain storms, or thick cloud may intervene just when the sun is "on the meridian" — whereas in lower latitudes he stays out all day blazing away — but even so there is only one time to secure a meridian altitude observation of the sun.

Facility with the use of the sextant is most important with all astro navigation — for with the sun, rapid changing of the coloured mirror shades is frequently necessary when clouds pass quickly over the sun.

EXAMPLE I.

Sun's Obs. Mer. Alt.	55°	20'S
Sun's Total Correction (plus)	+	12'
Sun's True Mer. Alt.	55°	32'S
	90°	
Zenith Distance (Z.D.)	34°	28'N
Sun's Declination (Dec.)	17°	24'S
Latitude of Ship	17°	04'N

The Position Line would be laid due E. and W. along 17° 04'N.

EXAMPLE II.

On a certain date, in D.R. Position 17°21'S. 35°30'E. Meridian Altitude of the Sun's Lower Limb was observed by Sextant to be 55°22' Sun Bearing North. Observers Height of eye 12 feet (3.7m). G.M.T., by Chronometer 9h 46min. Compute the Latitude.

Sun Obs. Mer. Alt.	55°	22'N
Sun's Total Correction (plus)	+	12'
Sun True Mer. Alt.	55°	34'N
	90°	
Zenith Distance (Z.D.)	34°	26.0'S
Sun's Declination (Dec.)	17°	17.6'N
Latitude of Ship	17°	08.4'S

The P.L. would run 90°-270° along the Line of Latitude 17°08.4'S.

How to use the Latitude found

As the sun bears exactly south at noon the AZIMUTH is 180° (south), so P.L. (position line) runs 090° − 270° (due east and west).

This would be plotted on the chart as an exact Line of latitude and if crossed with a shore bearing or a radio bearing, or a corrected sounding, a fix would be obtained; otherwise you have only just the one line of position running due east and west, but this knowledge may be of the greatest benefit to a vessel bound northerly or southerly or approaching a coastline as used in conjunction with the DR longitude should normally give a good approximate position.

Never neglect this easy observation as it still rules the lives of most ocean going seafarers as it no doubt did in the days of Columbus.

SHORT METHOD FOR RAPID NOON OBSERVATION

The latitude at noon can be found in a few seconds, at the instant of noon observation, if the working is prepared in advance as follows (working more or less backwards). It is necessary only to write down the Obs. Mer. Alt. and the latitude is found immediately. Using Example 1 above:

	90°	00'	
Total Corr.	−	12'	(always subtractive)
	89°	48'	
Sun Declination	17°	24'	
Total	72°	24'	(prepared ready for noon)
Obs. Mer. Alt.	55°	20'	(written down at noon)
Latitude of Ship	17°	04'	

What could be simpler?

Polaris is of the greatest value to the navigator in northern waters, as at any time during clear weather, from evening to morning twilight, a single sight will give the approximate latitude.

Being situated less than 1° from the north celestial pole, a small correction applied to the sextant altitude will give the latitude at any time. The Pole Star is not a "special" problem, but is really just another form of ex-meridian. It is desirable to take the observation when the horizon is clearly defined; but as Polaris is only a moderately bright star (magnitude 2.1) it is frequently invisible to the naked eye until the horizon is too dark to get an accurate sight. It is customary therefore at twilight to clamp the index of the sextant to the degree of dead reckoning latitude, and sweep the horizon to the north, when the star will usually be seen quite clearly.

A sextant altitude of the Pole Star is taken in the usual way and the G.M.T. noted. Whilst it is naturally best to have this as accurately as possible, correct time within a few minutes is sufficient, as an error of, say, fifteen minutes will only produce an error of two or three miles.

Example 1. Wishing to ascertain a vessel's latitude, an altitude of the Pole Star was taken at 2240 hours G.M.T. on June 15th, 1992. Lat. (D.R.) 51° 48'N. Long (D.R.) 5° 45'W. The height of the observer's eye above the water was 4.5m. The observed altitude was 51° 02'N.

G.H.A. Aries June 15th ..			Obs. Alt. Polaris	51°	02'.ON
22h. G.M.T.	234°	25'.9	Star Total Corr	−	4'.6
Corr for 40 min.	+ 10°	01'.6			
G.H.A. of Aries	244°	27'.5	True Alt	50°	57'.4
Long West	− 5°	45'.0	Pole Star Correction	+	42'.4
L.H.A. of Aries	238°	42'.5	Latitude	51°	39'.8

Which shows the vessel to be 8.2 miles South of her D.R. latitude.

Explanation of above working

The G.H.A. of Aries is found from the monthly page for June, for 22h. G.M.T. As the G.M.T. is 22h. 40min. the correction for the increase on the G.H.A. for 40min. is found from page 4:8. Apply the longitude by the usual rule (add for east longitude and subtract for west). The result is the local hour angle of Aries. The Pole Star correction is found according to the local hour angle of Aries from the special single table on page 5:18, which when applied according to its sign to the true altitude gives the latitude of the vessel.

Example 2. On June 1st 1992, a vessel in latitude (D.R.) 52° 16'N. longitude (D.R.) 3° 15'E. required her latitude at 4h. 16min. a.m. G.M.T. The observed altitude of the Pole Star was 52° 40'N. No index error. Height of eye, 3m.

G.H.A. Aries June 1st			Obs. Alt. Polaris	52°	40'.ON
04h. G.M.T.	309°	53'.6	Star Total Corr	−	3'.8
Corr for 16 min.	+ 4°	00'.7			
G.H.A. of Aries at obs. ...	313°	54'.3	True Alt	52°	36'.2
Long East	+ 3°	15'.0	Pole Star Correction	−	8'.4
L.H.A. of Aries	317°	09'.3	Latitude	52°	27'.8

Which shows the vessel to be 11.8 miles North of her D.R. latitude.

The above examples show that this method of obtaining the approximate latitude from an altitude of the Pole Star is extremely simple, and as stars are visible so frequently when the sun has been clouded at noon, offers the navigator a glorious opportunity to check his latitude, that should never be overlooked.

HOW TO FIND THE POLE STAR

At night when at sea, especially in a small vessel it is very comforting to know that for all practical purposes the Pole Star may be regarded as being situated over the N. Pole and thus is giving in the whole Northern Hemisphere - when stars are visible - a very simple way of finding direction on the earth's surface from the True North Pole.

An Auxiliary Star Chart on page 2:25 gives an illustration of how to find the Pole Star.

Compass Error by Pole Star

The Error of the Compass may be found in lower northern latitudes by taking a bearing of Polaris: For rough calculations this may be assumed to be True North 000° (or 360°). Should accuracy be desired the table on page 5:19 - True bearing of the Pole Star, 1992 - will indicate at the required time how much away from True North, Polaris is at any given moment.

The Pole Star is indeed a friend to the northern hemisphere sailors, airmen and travellers.

REED'S NAUTICAL ALMANAC

LATITUDE BY POLE STAR 1992

TABLE FOR DETERMINING APPROXIMATE LATITUDE
FROM TRUE ALTITUDE OF POLARIS

L.H.A. Aries	Corr.	L.H.A. Aries	Corr.	L.H.A. Aries	Corr.	L.H.A. Aries	Corr.	L.H.A. Aries	Corr.	L.H.A. Aries	Corr.	L.H.A. Aries	Corr.	L.H.A. Aries	Corr.
0	-37.1	45	-45.4	90	-26.8	135	+7.5	180	+37.3	225	+45.4	270	+27.3	315	-6.8
1	-37.5	46	-45.3	91	-26.2	136	+8.2	181	+37.8	226	+45.3	271	+26.7	316	-7.6
2	-38.0	47	-45.1	92	-25.5	137	+9.1	182	+38.2	227	+45.2	272	+26.0	317	-8.4
3	-38.4	48	-45.0	93	-24.8	138	+9.9	183	+38.7	228	+45.0	273	+25.3	318	-9.2
4	-38.9	49	-44.8	94	-24.1	139	+10.9	184	+39.1	229	+44.8	274	+24.7	319	-10.0
5	-39.3	50	-44.6	95	-23.5	140	+11.4	185	+39.5	230	+44.7	275	+24.0	320	-10.7
6	-39.7	51	-44.4	96	-22.8	141	+12.2	186	+39.9	231	+44.5	276	+23.3	321	-11.5
7	-40.1	52	-44.2	97	-22.1	142	+13.0	187	+40.3	232	+44.3	277	+22.6	322	-12.3
8	-40.5	53	-44.0	98	-21.3	143	+13.7	188	+40.7	233	+44.0	278	+21.9	323	-13.1
9	-40.9	54	-43.9	99	-20.6	144	+14.5	189	+41.0	234	+43.8	279	+21.2	324	-13.8
10	-41.3	55	-43.5	100	-19.9	145	+15.3	190	+41.4	235	+43.5	280	+20.5	325	-14.6
11	-41.6	56	-43.2	101	-19.2	146	+16.0	191	+41.7	236	+43.3	281	+19.8	326	-15.4
12	-41.9	57	-42.9	102	-18.4	147	+16.8	192	+42.1	237	+43.0	282	+19.1	327	-16.1
13	-42.3	58	-42.6	103	-17.7	148	+17.5	193	+42.4	238	+42.7	283	+18.3	328	-16.9
14	-42.6	59	-42.3	104	-17.0	149	+18.2	194	+42.7	239	+42.4	284	+17.6	329	-17.6
15	-42.9	60	-42.0	105	-16.2	150	+19.0	195	+43.0	240	+42.1	285	+16.8	330	-18.4
16	-43.2	61	-41.6	106	-15.4	151	+19.7	196	+43.3	241	+41.8	286	+16.1	331	-19.1
17	-43.1	62	-41.3	107	-14.7	152	+20.4	197	+43.5	242	+41.4	287	+15.3	332	-19.8
18	-43.7	63	-40.9	108	-13.9	153	+21.1	198	+43.8	243	+41.1	288	+14.6	333	-20.6
19	-43.9	64	-40.6	109	-13.2	154	+21.8	199	+44.0	244	+40.7	289	+13.8	334	-21.3
20	-44.2	65	-40.2	110	-12.4	155	+22.5	200	+44.2	245	+40.3	290	+13.1	335	-22.0
21	-44.4	66	-39.8	111	-11.6	156	+23.2	201	+44.4	246	+39.9	291	+12.3	336	-22.7
22	-44.6	67	-39.4	112	-10.8	157	+23.9	202	+44.6	247	+39.5	292	+11.5	337	-23.4
23	-44.8	68	-38.9	113	-10.0	158	+24.6	203	+44.8	248	+39.1	293	+10.7	338	-24.1
24	-45.0	69	-38.5	114	-9.3	159	+25.3	204	+45.0	249	+38.7	294	+9.9	339	-24.8
25	-45.1	70	-38.0	115	-8.5	160	+25.9	205	+45.2	250	+38.3	295	+9.2	340	-25.4
26	-45.3	71	-37.6	116	-7.7	161	+26.6	206	+45.3	251	+37.8	296	+8.4	341	-26.1
27	-45.4	72	-37.1	117	-6.9	162	+27.2	207	+45.4	252	+37.4	297	+7.6	342	-26.8
28	-45.5	73	-36.6	118	-6.1	163	+27.9	208	+45.6	253	+36.9	298	+6.8	343	-27.4
29	-45.6	74	-36.1	119	-5.3	164	+28.5	209	+45.7	254	+36.4	299	+6.0	344	-28.1
30	-45.7	75	-35.6	120	-4.5	165	+29.1	210	+45.7	255	+35.9	300	+5.2	345	-28.7
31	-45.8	76	-35.1	121	-3.7	166	+29.8	211	+45.8	256	+35.4	301	+4.4	346	-29.3
32	-45.9	77	-34.6	122	-2.9	167	+30.4	212	+45.9	257	+34.9	302	+3.6	347	-29.9
33	-45.9	78	-34.0	123	-2.1	168	+31.0	213	+45.9	258	+34.4	303	+2.8	348	-30.5
34	-46.0	79	-33.5	124	-1.3	169	+31.5	214	+46.0	259	+33.8	304	+2.0	349	-31.1
35	-46.0	80	-32.9	125	-0.5	170	+32.1	215	+46.0	260	+33.3	305	+1.2	350	-31.7
36	-46.0	81	-32.4	126	+0.3	171	+32.7	216	+46.0	261	+32.7	306	+0.4	351	-32.3
37	-46.0	82	-31.8	127	+1.1	172	+33.2	217	+46.0	262	+32.2	307	-0.4	352	-32.9
38	-46.0	83	-31.2	128	+1.9	173	+33.8	218	+46.0	263	+31.6	308	-1.2	353	-33.4
39	-45.9	84	-30.6	129	+2.7	174	+34.3	219	+45.9	264	+31.0	309	-2.0	354	-34.0
40	-45.9	85	-30.0	130	+3.5	175	+34.8	220	+45.9	265	+30.4	310	-2.8	355	-34.5
41	-45.8	86	-29.4	131	+4.3	176	+35.4	221	+45.8	266	+29.8	311	-3.6	356	-35.1
42	-45.7	87	-28.8	132	+5.1	177	+35.9	222	+45.8	267	+29.2	312	-4.4	357	-35.6
43	-45.7	88	-28.1	133	+5.9	178	+36.4	223	+45.7	268	+28.6	313	-5.2	358	-36.1
44	-45.6	89	-27.5	134	-6.7	179	+36.8	224	+45.6	269	+27.9	314	-6.0	359	-36.6

1. The above single table gives the correction with its sign, in minutes of arc, to be applied to the True Altitude of Polaris to obtain the approximate Latitude.

2. It is entered with the L.H.A. of Aries - the Correction interpolated where necessary.

3. It is designed for Latitudes 0° – 60°. For the higher Latitudes more exact tables are necessary.

4. To find L.H.A. of Aries - see page 5:17

TRUE BEARING OF POLE STAR 1992

L.H.A. Aries ◆	LATITUDE							L.H.A. Aries ◆
	0°	20°	40°	50°	55°	60°	65°	
5	000.4	000.4	000.5	000.6	000.7	000.8	001.0	5
15	000.3	000.3	000.4	000.4	000.5	000.6	000.7	15
25	000.1	000.2	000.2	000.2	000.3	000.3	000.3	25
35	000.0	000.0	000.0	000.0	000.0	000.0	000.0	35
45	359.9	359.9	359.8	359.8	359.8	359.7	359.7	45
55	359.7	359.7	359.7	359.6	359.5	359.5	359.4	55
65	359.6	359.6	359.5	359.4	359.3	359.2	359.1	65
75	359.5	359.5	359.4	359.2	359.1	359.0	358.8	75
85	359.4	359.4	359.2	359.1	359.0	358.8	358.6	85
95	359.3	359.3	359.1	359.0	358.8	358.7	358.4	95
105	359.3	359.2	359.1	358.9	358.7	358.5	358.3	105
115	359.2	359.2	359.0	358.8	358.7	358.5	358.2	115
125	359.2	359.2	359.0	358.8	358.7	358.5	358.2	125
135	359.2	359.2	359.0	358.8	358.7	358.5	358.2	135
145	359.3	359.2	359.1	358.9	358.7	358.6	358.3	145
155	359.3	359.3	359.1	359.0	358.8	358.7	358.4	155
165	359.4	359.4	359.2	359.1	359.0	358.8	358.6	165
175	359.5	359.5	359.3	359.2	359.1	359.0	358.8	175
185	359.6	359.6	359.5	359.4	359.3	359.2	359.1	185
195	359.7	359.7	359.6	359.6	359.5	359.5	359.4	195
205	359.9	359.8	359.8	359.8	359.8	359.7	359.7	205
215	000.0	000.0	000.0	000.0	000.0	000.0	000.0	215
225	000.1	000.1	000.2	000.2	000.2	000.2	000.3	225
235	000.3	000.3	000.3	000.4	000.4	000.5	000.6	235
245	000.4	000.4	000.5	000.6	000.7	000.9	000.9	245
255	000.5	000.5	000.6	000.8	000.8	001.0	001.1	255
265	000.6	000.6	000.8	000.9	001.0	001.2	001.4	265
275	000.7	000.7	000.9	001.0	001.1	001.3	001.5	275
285	000.7	000.8	000.9	001.1	001.2	001.4	001.7	285
195	000.8	000.8	001.0	001.2	001.3	001.5	001.8	195
305	000.8	000.8	001.0	001.2	001.3	001.5	001.8	305
315	000.8	000.8	001.0	001.2	001.3	001.5	001.8	315
325	000.7	000.8	001.0	001.1	001.3	001.5	001.7	325
335	000.7	000.7	000.9	001.1	001.2	001.4	001.6	335
345	000.6	000.6	000.8	000.9	001.1	001.2	001.4	345
355	000.5	000.5	000.7	000.8	000.9	001.0	001.2	355

TO FIND THE TRUE BEARING OF POLARIS

(1) Find L.H.A. Aries ϒ as shown on page 5:17.
(2) Enter the table with the arguments Latitude (approx) at the top and L.H.A. Aries at the side. The True Bearing is given in degrees and decimals of 360° notation.

Example 1. Lat. 51°N., L.H.A. ϒ 73° gives True Bearing 359.3°.
Example 2. Lat. 19°N., L.H.A. ϒ 262° gives True Bearing 000.5°.

LATITUDE BY STAR, MOON OR PLANET
MERIDIAN ALTITUDE

The sun as we know (see p. 5:15), being on the meridian at the same time at noon is always observed for meridian-altitude, and because of its simplicity the Pole Star also represents a very special case to northern hemisphere navigators, but a little explanation is necessary to understand when the other heavenly bodies are or can be utilised.

The moon is inconsistent in that sometimes it is available for observation and sometimes is not, so being unreliable in this respect is only used by navigators when they feel a moon observation is of special benefit as for example when it is visible in the day-time to cross with the sun — and when no stars are visible.

The observation would be worked out as a position line as with any other body, but of course using the moon yearly elements as described on p. 2:35 and 2:36. The Moon Altitude Correction Table is on p. 4:14 and Meridian Passage Correction Table on p. 4:19.

The planets (see also page 2:32), are very valuable to the navigator because Venus and Jupiter are always so much brighter than the normal star and can thus be more easily seen. Also Venus may at certain times of the year be observed as a simple meridian altitude during the day-time. Where the meridian altitude of a planet occurs at a useful time, this should always be observed, as the position line found may be able to be "run forward" to another P.L. from another source or crossed with a radio bearing, or other means found to secure a position. At "star time" consideration would always be given to including one or more planets in the observations.

The yearly elements for each planet would of course be used as described on page 2:33.

The stars are used to obtain a meridian altitude when it is considered necessary or when perhaps due to bad weather a proper star observation programme cannot be carried out. Normally modern navigators think it is much easier to get a position line from a star at the time other stars are being taken rather than to wait for the star to be on the meridian. On the other hand if when star time arrives a bright star is on or near the meridian, it can be "shot" for latitude or an ex-meridian position line. Used in conjunction with a Pole Star observation it should give a very accurate latitude to use in calculating longitude from other star observations.

A meridian altitude of a star could be taken at night in bright moonlight, but unless the horizon is clearly defined as at morning and evening twilight the latitude found should be regarded only as approximate and used with caution.

So much depends on circumstances, but if in real need and the horizon is clear (or reasonably so if in dire distress), then remember that this Almanac tabulates the exact positions of 60 bright stars each month and their times of transit.

The yearly elements for each star would of course be used as described on p. 2:28 to 2:31.

Finding the Latitude

The latitude from one of the above mentioned bodies is found from its own data for the correct time of observation and worked out exactly as described for the sun on p. 5:15.

Example. D.R. lat. 49° 20'N. the observed meridian altitude of the star Bellatrix (Dec. 6° 20.6'N.) was found to be 46° 53.5'S. Height of eye 25 feet (7.6 m). Find the latitude.

		NOTES	
*Obs. Alt.	46° 53.5'S.	
*Total Corr. (p. 4:6)	− 5.8	(a) Use Star Corr. Table—always subtractive.
*True Alt.	46° 47.7'S.	(b) Change name when subtracting from 90°.
	90°	
*Zen. Dist.	43° 12.3'N.	(c) Same rule as Sun p. 5:15 same names add.
*Dec.	6° 20.6'N.	
Latitude by Obs.	49° 32.9'N.	∴ **Vessel is 12.0m. N of the D.R. Latitude.**

All Meridian Altitude Observations are worked out in the same way.

POSITION LINE FROM A CELESTIAL OBSERVATION USING AN ELECTRONIC CALCULATOR

Almost any scientific calculator can be used for celestial navigation providing it produces accurate results, you press enough keys and know what you are doing. For celestial applications a memory is useful - but the back of an envelope or a note in your sightbook will do. The more memories there are the better as they reduce the number of key operations required and fewer keystrokes mean greater accuracy and less possibility of making an error. If you can afford a programmable calculator so much the better, but the important thing is that you can use the calculator with confidence.

The minimum functions required are: +, −, x, ÷, Sin, Cos and Arc (shown on some calculators as INV). In addition, a key which converts degrees, minutes and seconds (DDMMSS) to degrees and decimal parts of a degree (D.d) is highly desirable, but by no means essential. If this is not available divide the minutes by 60 on the calculator to decimalise.

If you are using a programmable calculator perhaps the easiest procedure is to use the longitude method and run it through twice with the same data, except in the second run enter a different latitude. This will give two positions on the position line which enables it to be plotted without the need of an Azimuth.

INTERCEPT METHOD

Note this is exactly the same problem as indicated on pages 5:25 and 5:26 except the arithmetic is done on the calculator using a formula more suited to this device.

$$\text{Sin Alt} = \text{Cos LHA} \times \text{Cos LAT} \times \text{Cos DEC} \pm \text{Sin LAT} \times \text{Sin Dec}$$

Note: The (+) sign is used if both LATITUDE and DECLINATION have the same name, *i.e.* are both NORTH or both SOUTH.

The (−) sign is used if the LATITUDE and DECLINATION have different names, i.e. one is NORTH and the other is SOUTH.

If the LHA is between 090 and 270 which is unlikely, the first expression containing Cos LHA will be negative (−).

EXAMPLE At 09h 10m 28s GMT on 25 April 1992 the SUN's lower limb was observed as 27° 56'.0. Height of eye 6ft. Log 83. Course 045°(T).

DR position 50° 10'N 20° 03'W. Find the intercept and Azimuth?

LHA 298° 05'.2	LAT 50° 10'N	DEC.N. 13°19'.6
= 298.0867°	= 50.1667°	= N. 13.3267°
True Altitude 28° 08'.0		
= 28.1333°		

Notes: Key STO transfers a quantity to store or memory. (If no key or store make a note of it.)

Key RCL recalls a quantity from store.

Some calculators use keys M or MS for transferring a quantity to store and MR or M = for recall from store and M+ or M- to sum and store. You should consult your manufacturer's handbook before using and fully understand what happens especially with those calculators that sum and store positively and negatively, *i.e.* M+ or M–.

Dependent on the type of calculator used, the procedures may have to be modified slightly. Parenthesis keys can be used in many of the calculations as an alternative procedure to using a memory or store. RPN logic machines will require a different entry procedure for data.

Quantity		Entry	Reading
LHA 298°05'.2	→	298.0867	298.0867
		Cos	0.4708
		x	0.4708
LAT 50°10'	→	50.1667	50.1667
		Cos	0.6406
		x	0.3016
DEC. 13°19'.6	→	13.3267	13.3267
		Cos	0.9731
		=	0.2935
		STO 1	0.2935
LAT 50°10'	→	50.1667	50.1667
		Sin	0.7679
		x	0.7679
DEC. 13° 19'.6	→	13.3267	13.3267
		Sin	0.2305
		+	0.1770
		RCL 1	0.2935
		=	0.4705
		ARC Sin	28.0644

Note: To convert decimals of a degree to minutes multiply by 60

i.e. 0.0644 x 60 = 3.8640   Calc. Alt. = 28° 03'.9

Calculated Altitude	28°	03'.9
True Altitude	28°	08'.0
Intercept		4.1 Towards

Plot as on page 5:26

Note: There may be a slight difference between the results obtained from the tables and a calculator. The calculator will be more accurate, provided of course that you haven't pressed any wrong keys and your batteries are not run down.

AZIMUTH

The easiest and quickest way to find the Azimuth is still probably using the ABC tables or Weir's diagram (Admiralty Chart No. 5000) as before, unless you have a programmable calculator. However, for those who want to use their calculator one formula is:

$$\text{Sin Azimuth} = \frac{\text{Sin LHA} \times \text{Cos DEC}}{\text{Cos Alt}}$$

Quantity	Entry	Reading
LHA (using EHA*)	61.9133	61.9133
	Sin	0.8822
	x	0.8822
Dec N 13° 19'.6	13.3267	13.3267
	Cos	0.9731
	÷	0.8585
Alt 28°.08'.0	28.1333	28.1333
	Cos	0.8819
	=	0.9735
	Arc Sin	76.7790
Az	=	76.8

Note: The Azimuth will be easterly as the LHA is easterly. The body lies south of the observer. The question as to whether it is N76'.8 E or S76'.8E is perhaps best resolved by noting the approximate bearing of the body at the time of taking the sight.

* Easterly Hour Angle i.e., 360° minus LHA.

LONGITUDE METHOD OF OBTAINING A POSITION LINE

$$\text{Use the formulae: } \quad \text{Cos LHA} = \frac{\text{Sin True Alt} \pm \text{Sin LAT} \times \text{Sin DEC}}{\text{Cos LAT} \times \text{Cos DEC}}$$

The (–) sign is used if both the latitude and declination have the same name, *i.e.,* are both north or south.

The (+) sign is used if the latitude and declination have different names, *i.e.,* one is north and the other is south.

Note: A negative result indicates the LHA is between 90 and 270.

Working the same example as on page 5:28.

LAT 50° 10'N   DEC 13° 19'.6N   ALT 28° 08'.0
= 50°.1667°   =13.3267   = 28.1333°

Quantity		Entry	Reading
DEC. 13°19'.6	→	13.3267	13.3267
		Sin	0.2305
		x	0.2305
LAT 50°10'	→	50.1667	50.1667
		Sin	0.7679
		=	0.1770
		STO 1	0.1770
Alt 28°08'		28.1333	28.1333
		Sin	0.4715
		−	0.4715
		RCL 1	0.1770
		=	0.2945
		÷	0.2945
DEC. 13° 19'.6	→	13.3267	13.3267
		Cos	0.9731
		÷	0.3027
LAT 50°10'	→	50.1667	50.1667
		Cos	0.6406
		=	0.4725
		ARC Cos	61.8027
		−	61.8027
		61	61
		=	0.8027
		x	0.8027
		60	60
		=	48.1610

LHA = 61° 48'.2 (EHA)
or (360° - 61° 48'.2)
= 298° 11'.8

Then proceed as on page 5:28

For the real enthusiast the following formula is included to determine the azimuth if the altitude is not available.

$$\text{Cot Azimuth} = \frac{\text{Cos LAT x Tan DEC}}{\text{Sin LHA}} \pm \frac{\text{Sin LAT}}{\text{Tan LHA}}$$

If LHA is between 180° and 360° use (360-LHA)
(−) if Latitude and Declination are same names.
(+) if Latitude and Declination are different names.

If the result is negative (−) subtract the angle found from 180.
Measure the angle from N or S depending on the name of Declination.
Measure East or West depending on the hour angle.
Note: If your calculator has no COT key then use 1/x key followed by Inv. Tan key.

POSITION LINE FROM A CELESTIAL
OBSERVATION USING THE VERSINE* TABLE

In the diagram on page 5:3 it can be seen that obtaining a Position Line from a celestial observation requires resolving a spherical triangle. In the method described below, the known factors are the angle ZPX (Local Hour Angle); the side x, the co-lat (90° - the latitude); and the side z, the Polar Distance (90° - the Declination). These factors are used to obtain the side "p" which is the Zenith Distance or the body's altitude subtracted from 90°. This angle, the Calculated Zenith Distance, is compared with the Observed Zenith Distance (from the body's True Altitude taken by Sextant measurement) and the difference is known as the Intercept.

Formula: Versine 0 = Versine P sin x sin z + Versine (x - z) or in practice

Versine Zenith Distance = Versine LHA cos lat. cos dec + Versine (lat ± dec).

This Intercept is measured from the Dead Reckoning Position used in the calculation to a point along the True bearing of the body at the time of observation and the resultant Position Line is a line drawn at right angles to the bearing through that point.

This bearing could always be calculated from the PZX or navigational triangle but it can now be readily obtained from the ABC tables which are explained on page 5:8

The Versine formula is shown on page 5:42. It is of course unnecessary to understand exactly what these trigonometrical functions mean. The seaman has simply to use the figures provided and set out the above formula as is shown on page 5:26.

The Table on pages 5:29 to 5.42 give Versines, and pages 5:43 to 5:48 give Log Cosines - these latter pages also give Log Sines but they are not required with the particular formula used.

Examining page 5:29 it will be seen that all Log. Versines are set in heavy black type, whilst the corresponding Nat. Versines are set in ordinary type. Log. means a Logarithm and Nat. a Natural number.

The columns are read with degrees at the top and mins. of arc (') 0-60 at the left hand side up to page 5:42. The larger degrees move backwards from page 5:42 at the bottom with minutes of arc (') on the right hand side.

Page 5:29 shows that the Log Vers. of 6° 45' is 7.8408, whilst the adjacent Nat. Versine of 6° 45' is 0.0069. Page 5:38 gives the Log. Vers. of 75° 22' as 9.8735 and the Nat. Vers. as 0.7473. Note in this as 22' is not given - to save space - you must interpolate as nearly as possible for the nearest minute required. It is necessary to write down the Log. prefix of 9 (or whatever it is shown on the page), but is only shown on each second column and it is necessary always to write down the Nat. prefix 0 or 1. The Nat. Vers. of 255° 37' on page 5:39 is 1.2484 whilst the adjacent Log. Vers is 0.0964. Extreme accuracy to decimal points is unnecessary. Simply take the amount the last figures alter for the four minutes of arc on either side of the minute you want and work out carefully the required figures. Be as accurate as possible is all that is necessary.

The Log. Cosine Table is entered only from the top of the page from 1° to 90° with minutes of arc (') down the left hand column. For example page 5:45 shows the Log. Cos. of 40° 21' to be 9.8820 and on page 5:48 the Log. Cos. of 84° 40' to be 8.9682. Be careful not to take out the Log. Sines from the bottom of the page - they are not required at all.

The Table of Versines should produce solutions of the Astronomical triangle to a resultant position accuracy of 1' arc; providing the interpolation between two consecutive values is carefully carried out. They hold good for observations at any time, day or night, on any bearing, in any part of the world, using any heavenly Body.

*Note: the haversine method is EXACTLY the same - simply use haversines where the following examples use versines.

AN INTERCEPT METHOD

Example. At 09 hours 10 minutes 28 seconds G.M.T. on the 25th April 1992, the sun's lower limb was observed at 27° 56'.0. Height of eye 6 feet. Log 83. Course 045° True. D.R. position 50° 10'N. 20° 03'W. Required intercept and azimuth.

G.H.A. Sun 08h.	300°	31'.2W	Obs. Alt.	27°	56'.0
Increment for 1h 10m	+17°	30'	Total Corr	+	12'.0
Increment for 28sec.	+	7'			
			True Alt	28°	08'.0
G.H.A. 09h 10m 28s.	318°	08'.2W		90°	
Long D.R.	−20°	0.3'.0W			
			True Zen. Dist. (T.Z.D.)	61°	52'.0
Local Hour Angle (LHA)	298°	05'.2W			

(360° - LHA) = EHA =   61°   54'.8

Easterly Hour Angle	(E.H.A.)	61° 54'.8E	Log. Versine	9.7236	These are added
Latitude	(Lat.)	50° 10'.0N	Log. Cosine	9.8066	and the tens unit dropped
Declination	(Dec.)	13° 19.6N	Log. Cosine	9.9881	

Log. Versine   9.5183 —— Nat. Versine 0.3299

(a) Lat.-Dec. = 36° 50'.4 ———— Nat. Versine 0.1997

Calculated Zenith Distance (Z.D.) 61° 56'.3 ———— Nat. Versine 0.5296

(b)	True Z.T. (T.Z.D.)	61° 52'.0	*(c)*	**Sun True Bearing (Azimuth) 103°**
	Calculated Z.D. (C.Z.D.)	61° 56'.3		∴**Position Line Runs 013° - 193°**
	INTERCEPT =	4'.3		**Towards *(b)*** Sun.

(a) Lat. and Dec. are the same name (both N.) so are subtracted.
(b) True Z.D. is less than Cal. Z.D. so INTERCEPT is TOWARDS. C.G.T. = **Calculated Greater Towards.**
(c) Sun True Bearing find as on page 5:8 or as calculateᵈ on page 5:23.

Plot of Morning Sun Sight
    The Plot illustrated below represents the final part of Sight whether worked (a) by Pre-computed Tables, (b) the Haversine formula, (c) Reed's Versine Table, or (d) Electronic Calculator.
    The Intercept is drawn from the latitude and longitude used as a D.R. position, or an adjusted D.R. pos. on a bearing of 103.0° True.
    The position lines from all methods - Pre-computed Tables Haversines or Versines - are the same.

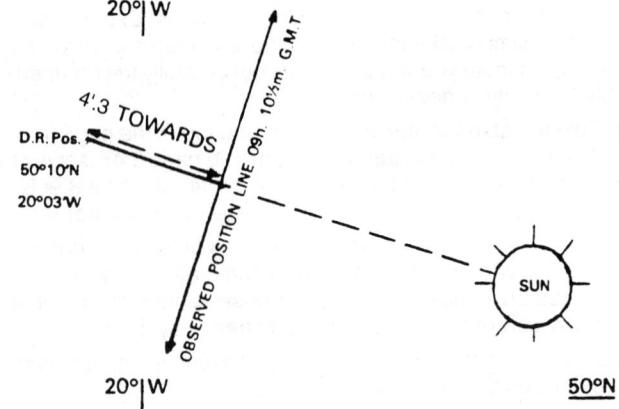

50°N   20°|W   50°N

THE SIGHT FORM

for use with Sights worked by Reed's Versine Table

Date	Time	Ht. of Eye	Body Obs.	
Lat. left	Long. left	Course	°(T) Distance	run since to sights

(a) To find the D.R. Position

D.R. Position from	Lat. left	° ′	Long. left	° ′
Chart or Run	d. Lat.	′	d. Long.	′
	Sights D.R. Lat.	° ′	Sights D.R. Long.	° ′

(b) To find G.M.T. and G.H.A.

	G.H.A.	° ′W		
Chron. Time	Corr. for		Obs. Alt.	° ′
Error		——	Total Corr.	
G.M.T.	G.H.A. at Obs.	° ′W	True Alt.	
	Longitude	° ′		90°
	(L.H.A.)	° ′W	True Zen. Dist.	
	or E.H.A.	° ′E	(T.Z.D.)	

(c) To find the INTERCEPT

L.H.A.	(L.H.A.)	° ′	Log. Versine
Latitude	(Lat.)	° ′	Log. Cosine
Declination	(Dec.)	° ′	Log. Cosine

Log. Versine → Nat. Versine ————

*Lat. + or − Dec. ° ′ ——————— → Nat. Versine ————

Calculated Zenith Distance (C.Z.D.) ° ′← − Nat. Versine ————

(d) To name the INTERCEPT

True Z.D. (T.Z.D.)	° ′
Cal. Z.D. (C.Z.D.)	° ′
Intercept	Away†
	Towards†

∴ Intercept

(e) To find the TRUE BEARING:

A =
B =
C =

Az =

∴ P.L. runs

(f) To find the observed position

To obtain the vessels position two position lines (at least) are of course necessary. A popular and simple method is to work a sun observation, as above, before noon (say 2 to 3 hours before). This position line is run up to noon and crossed with the Sun's meridian altitude (when the latitude obtained becomes the position line). However a position line by any other method will do, provided of course that it does not run parallel or nearly parallel with the first.

REMARKS FOR RECORDS

It is not suggested that this method is simpler than the usual Nautical Tables or the pre-computed Tables, but it does give the same results, so for those who have no other books (or have sailed without them), Reed's now enables 'Sights' to be worked as required.

*Delete one sign. Same names Subtract. Different names Add.
†Delete one or the other. True Z.D. greater Intercept AWAY. True Z.D. smaller Intercept TOWARDS.

LONGITUDE BY CHRONOMETER
An alternative method

It must be realised that the navigational triangle can be used in a number of ways and under modern Position Line Navigation the Versine formula is used to find the Calculated Zenith Distance. By transposing the Versine formula however and using the True (observed) Zenith Distance, the Local Hour Angle (ZPX) can be calculated, which when compared with the Greenwich Hour Angle (G.H.A.) for the time of the sight will give the observed longitude of the ship at the D.R. Latitude through which the Position Line passes — the Position Line being a line 90° to the Azimuth of the body.

Transposing the versine formula on page 5:25 we get

$$\text{Versine LHA} = \frac{[\text{Versine Zenith Distance} - \text{Versine (Lat} + \text{ or } - \text{ dec)}]}{\text{Cos Lat. Cos Dec}}$$

Working with the same example as on page 5:26

Example. At 09 hours 10 minutes 28 seconds G.M.T. on the 25th April 1992 the Sun's lower limb was observed as 27° 56'.0 Height of Eye 6 feet. Log 83. Course 045° True. D.R. Position 50° 10'N. 20° 03'W Required Position Line.

		Nat Vers ZD 61° 52.0	= 0.5285
		Nat Vers (L–D) 36° 50'.4	= 0.1997
Log Cos Lat 50° 10'	= 9.8066	Diff	= 0.3288
Log Cos Decl 13° 19'.6	= 9.9881	Log Diff (above)	= 9.5170
Log sum	= 9.7947	Log sum -	= 9.7947
		Diff = Log Versine LHA	= 9.7223

LHA = 298° 11'.5
GHA 09h 10m 28s = 318° 8'.2
Longitude through which P/L passes   19° 56'.7 W

Az 103° Position Line runs 013° — 193°

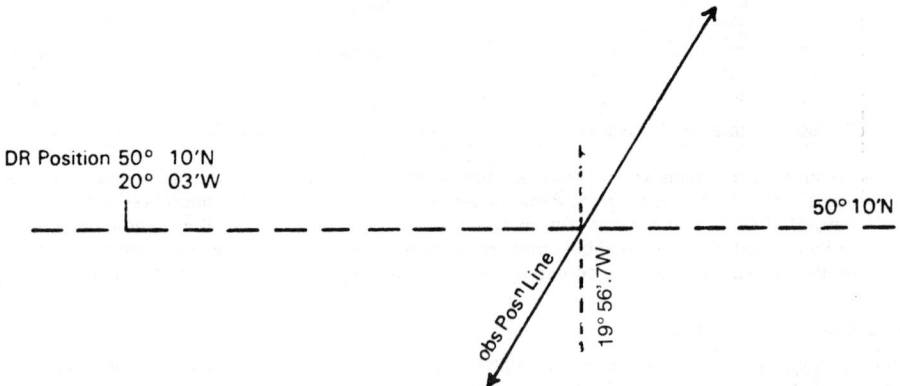

DR Position 50° 10'N
20° 03'W

50° 10'N

This position line is the same as that obtained on page 5:26. If the Latitude used is the ship's actual Latitude then the Longitude found will be the ship's Longitude

VERSINES

′	1° LOG.	NAT.	2° LOG.	NAT.	3° LOG.	NAT.	4° LOG.	NAT.	5° LOG.	NAT.	6° LOG.	NAT.	7° LOG.	NAT.	′
− ∞	− ∞	0.0000	1827	0002	6.7847	0006	1369	0014	7.3867	0024	5804	0038	7.7386	0.0055	60
1	2.6264	0.0000	1971	0002	6.7919	0006	1417	0014	7.3903	0025	5833	0038	7.7410	0.0055	59
2	3.2285	0.0000	2112	0002	6.7991	0006	1465	0014	7.3939	0025	5862	0039	7.7434	0.0055	58
3	3.5807	0.0000	2251	0002	6.8062	0006	1512	0014	7.3975	0025	5890	0039	7.7458	0.0056	57
4	3.8305	0.0000	2388	0002	6.8132	0007	1560	0014	7.4010	0025	5919	0039	7.7482	0.0056	56
5	4.0244	0.0000	2522	0002	6.8202	0007	1607	0014	7.4046	0025	5947	0039	7.7506	0.0056	55
6	4.1827	0.0000	2655	0002	6.8271	0007	1653	0015	7.4081	0026	5976	0040	7.7530	0.0057	54
7	4.3166	0.0000	2786	0002	6.8340	0007	1700	0015	7.4116	0026	6004	0040	7.7553	0.0057	53
8	4.4326	0.0000	2914	0002	6.8408	0007	1746	0015	7.4151	0026	6032	0040	7.7577	0.0057	52
9	4.5349	0.0000	3041	0002	6.8476	0007	1792	0015	7.4186	0026	6060	0040	7.7601	0.0058	51
10	4.6264	0.0000	3166	0002	6.8543	0007	1838	0015	7.4221	0026	6089	0041	7.7624	0.0058	50
11	4.7092	0.0000	3289	0002	6.8609	0007	1884	0015	7.4256	0027	6116	0041	7.7647	0.0058	49
12	4.7848	0.0000	3411	0002	6.8675	0007	1929	0016	7.4290	0027	6144	0041	7.7671	0.0058	48
13	4.8543	0.0000	3531	0002	6.8741	0007	1974	0016	7.4325	0027	6172	0041	7.7694	0.0059	47
14	4.9187	0.0000	3649	0002	6.8806	0008	2019	0016	7.4359	0027	6200	0042	7.7717	0.0059	46
15	4.9786	0.0000	3765	0002	6.8870	0008	2064	0016	7.4393	0028	6227	0042	7.7741	0.0059	45
16	5.0347	0.0000	3880	0002	6.8934	0008	2108	0016	7.4427	0028	6255	0042	7.7764	0.0060	44
17	5.0873	0.0000	3994	0003	6.8998	0008	2152	0016	7.4461	0028	6282	0042	7.7787	0.0060	43
18	5.1370	0.0000	4106	0003	6.9061	0008	2196	0017	7.4495	0028	6310	0043	7.7810	0.0060	42
19	5.1839	0.0000	4217	0003	6.9124	0008	2240	0017	7.4528	0028	6337	0043	7.7833	0.0061	41
20	5.2285	0.0000	4326	0003	6.9186	0008	2284	0017	7.4562	0029	6364	0043	7.7855	0.0061	40
21	5.2709	0.0000	4434	0003	6.9248	0009	2327	0017	7.4595	0029	6391	0044	7.7878	0.0061	39
22	5.3113	0.0000	4540	0003	6.9309	0009	2370	0017	7.4628	0029	6418	0044	7.7901	0.0062	38
23	5.3499	0.0000	4646	0003	6.9370	0009	2413	0017	7.4661	0029	6445	0044	7.7924	0.0062	37
24	5.3868	0.0000	4750	0003	6.9431	0009	2456	0018	7.4694	0029	6472	0044	7.7946	0.0062	36
25	5.4223	0.0000	4852	0003	6.9491	0009	2498	0018	7.4727	0030	6499	0045	7.7969	0.0063	35
26	5.4564	0.0000	4954	0003	6.9551	0009	2540	0018	7.4760	0030	6525	0045	7.7991	0.0063	34
27	5.4891	0.0000	5054	0003	6.9610	0009	2582	0018	7.4792	0030	6552	0045	7.8014	0.0063	33
28	5.5207	0.0000	5154	0003	6.9669	0009	2624	0018	7.4825	0030	6578	0045	7.8036	0.0064	32
29	5.5512	0.0000	5252	0003	6.9727	0010	2666	0019	7.4857	0031	6605	0046	7.8059	0.0064	31
30	5.5807	0.0000	5349	0003	6.9785	0010	2707	0019	7.4889	0031	6631	0046	7.8081	0.0064	30
31	5.6091	0.0000	5445	0003	6.9843	0010	2749	0019	7.4921	0031	6657	0046	7.8103	0.0065	29
32	5.6367	0.0000	5540	0004	6.9900	0010	2790	0019	7.4953	0031	6684	0047	7.8125	0.0065	28
33	5.6634	0.0000	5634	0004	6.9957	0010	2830	0019	7.4985	0032	6710	0047	7.8147	0.0065	27
34	5.6894	0.0000	5727	0004	7.0014	0010	2871	0019	7.5017	0032	6736	0047	7.8169	0.0066	26
35	5.7146	0.0001	5818	0004	7.0070	0010	2912	0020	7.5049	0032	6762	0047	7.8191	0.0066	25
36	5.7390	0.0001	5909	0004	7.0126	0010	2952	0020	7.5080	0032	6788	0048	7.8213	0.0066	24
37	5.7628	0.0001	5999	0004	7.0181	0010	2992	0020	7.5111	0032	6813	0048	7.8235	0.0067	23
38	5.7860	0.0001	6088	0004	7.0237	0011	3032	0020	7.5143	0033	6839	0048	7.8257	0.0067	22
39	5.8085	0.0001	6177	0004	7.0291	0011	3072	0020	7.5174	0033	6865	0049	7.8279	0.0067	21
40	5.8305	0.0001	6264	0004	7.0346	0011	3111	0020	7.5205	0033	6890	0049	7.8301	0.0068	20
41	5.8520	0.0001	6350	0004	7.0400	0011	3151	0021	7.5236	0033	6916	0049	7.8322	0.0068	19
42	5.8729	0.0001	6436	0004	7.0454	0011	3190	0021	7.5267	0034	6941	0049	7.8344	0.0068	18
43	5.8934	0.0001	6521	0005	7.0507	0011	3229	0021	7.5298	0034	6967	0050	7.8365	0.0069	17
44	5.9133	0.0001	6605	0005	7.0560	0011	3268	0021	7.5328	0034	6992	0050	7.8387	0.0069	16
45	5.9328	0.0001	6688	0005	7.0613	0012	3306	0021	7.5359	0034	7017	0050	7.8408	0.0069	15
46	5.9519	0.0001	6770	0005	7.0666	0012	3345	0022	7.5389	0035	7042	0051	7.8430	0.0070	14
47	5.9706	0.0001	6852	0005	7.0718	0012	3383	0022	7.5419	0035	7067	0051	7.8451	0.0070	13
48	5.9889	0.0001	6932	0005	7.0770	0012	3421	0022	7.5450	0035	7092	0051	7.8472	0.0070	12
49	6.0068	0.0001	7012	0005	7.0821	0012	3459	0022	7.5480	0035	7117	0051	7.8494	0.0071	11
50	6.0244	0.0001	7092	0005	7.0872	0012	3497	0022	7.5510	0036	7142	0052	7.8515	0.0071	10
51	6.0416	0.0001	7170	0005	7.0923	0012	3535	0023	7.5539	0036	7167	0052	7.8536	0.0071	9
52	6.0584	0.0001	7248	0005	7.0974	0013	3572	0023	7.5569	0036	7191	0052	7.8557	0.0072	8
53	6.0750	0.0001	7325	0005	7.1024	0013	3610	0023	7.5599	0036	7216	0053	7.8578	0.0072	7
54	6.0912	0.0001	7402	0005	7.1074	0013	3647	0023	7.5629	0037	7240	0053	7.8599	0.0072	6
55	6.1071	0.0001	7478	0006	7.1124	0013	3684	0023	7.5658	0037	7265	0053	7.8620	0.0073	5
56	6.1228	0.0001	7553	0006	7.1174	0013	3721	0024	7.5687	0037	7289	0054	7.8641	0.0073	4
57	6.1382	0.0001	7628	0006	7.1223	0013	3757	0024	7.5717	0037	7314	0054	7.8662	0.0073	3
58	6.1533	0.0001	7701	0006	7.1272	0013	3794	0024	7.5746	0038	7338	0054	7.8682	0.0074	2
59	6.1681	0.0001	7775	0006	7.1320	0014	3830	0024	7.5775	0038	7362	0054	7.8703	0.0074	1
60	6.1827	0.0002	7847	0006	7.1369	0014	3867	0024	7.5804	0038	7386	0055	7.8724	0.0075	0

LOG.	NAT.	LOG.	NAT.	LOG.	NAT.	LOG.	NAT.	LOG.	NAT.	LOG.	NAT.	LOG.	NAT.	′
359°		358°		357°		356°		355°		354°		353°		

For an explanation of the use of above Tables see p. 5:25.

VERSINES

/	7° LOG.	NAT.	8° LOG.	NAT.	9° LOG.	NAT.	10° LOG.	NAT.	11° LOG.	NAT.	12° LOG.	NAT.	13° LOG.	NAT.	
0	7.8724	0.0075	7.9882	0097	0903	0123	1816	0152	2642	0184	8.3395	0219	8.4087	0.0256	60
1	7.8744	0.0075	7.9900	0098	0919	0124	1831	0152	2655	0184	8.3407	0219	8.4099	0.0257	59
2	7.8765	0.0075	7.9918	0098	0935	0124	1845	0153	2668	0185	8.3419	0220	8.4110	0.0258	58
3	7.8786	0.0076	7.9936	0099	0951	0124	1859	0153	2681	0185	8.3431	0220	8.4121	0.0258	57
4	7.8806	0.0076	7.9954	0099	0967	0125	1874	0154	2694	0186	8.3443	0221	8.4132	0.0259	56
5	7.8826	0.0076	7.9972	0099	0983	0125	1888	0154	2707	0187	8.3455	0222	8.4143	0.0260	55
6	7.8847	0.0077	7.9990	0100	0999	0126	1902	0155	2720	0187	8.3467	0222	8.4154	0.0260	54
7	7.8867	0.0077	8.0008	0100	1015	0126	1917	0155	2733	0188	8.3479	0223	8.4165	0.0261	53
8	7.8887	0.0077	8.0025	0101	1031	0127	1931	0156	2746	0188	8.3491	0223	8.4176	0.0262	52
9	7.8908	0.0078	8.0043	0101	1046	0127	1945	0157	2759	0189	8.3502	0224	8.4187	0.0262	51
10	7.8928	0.0078	8.0061	0101	1062	0128	1959	0157	2772	0189	8.3514	0225	8.4198	0.0263	50
11	7.8948	0.0078	8.0078	0102	1078	0128	1974	0158	2785	0190	8.3526	0225	8.4209	0.0264	49
12	7.8968	0.0079	8.0096	0102	1094	0129	1988	0158	2798	0190	8.3538	0226	8.4220	0.0264	48
13	7.8988	0.0079	8.0114	0103	1109	0129	2002	0159	2811	0191	8.3550	0226	8.4230	0.0265	47
14	7.9008	0.0080	8.0131	0103	1125	0130	2016	0159	2824	0192	8.3562	0227	8.4241	0.0266	46
15	7.9028	0.0080	8.0149	0103	1141	0130	2030	0160	2836	0192	8.3573	0228	8.4252	0.0266	45
16	7.9048	0.0080	8.0166	0104	1156	0131	2044	0160	2849	0193	8.3585	0228	8.4263	0.0267	44
17	7.9068	0.0081	8.0184	0104	1172	0131	2058	0161	2862	0193	9.3597	0229	8.4274	0.0268	43
18	7.9088	0.0081	8.0201	0105	1187	0131	2072	0161	2875	0194	8.3609	0230	8.4285	0.0268	42
19	7.9108	0.0081	8.0219	0105	1203	0132	2086	0162	2887	0194	8.3620	0230	8.4296	0.0269	41
20	7.9127	0.0082	8.0236	0106	1218	0132	2100	0162	2900	0195	8.3632	0231	8.4306	0.0270	40
21	7.9147	0.0082	8.0253	0106	1234	0133	2114	0163	2913	0196	8.3644	0231	8.4317	0.0270	39
22	7.9167	0.0083	8.0271	0106	1249	0133	2128	0163	2926	0196	8.3655	0232	8.4328	0.0271	38
23	7.9186	0.0083	8.0288	0107	1265	0134	2142	0164	2938	0197	8.3667	0233	8.4339	0.0272	37
24	7.9206	0.0083	8.0305	0107	1280	0134	2156	0164	2951	0197	8.3679	0233	8.4350	0.0272	36
25	7.9225	0.0084	8.0322	0108	1295	0135	2170	0165	2964	0198	8.3690	0234	8.4360	0.0273	35
26	7.9245	0.0084	8.0339	0108	1311	0135	2184	0165	2976	0198	8.3702	0235	8.4371	0.0274	34
27	7.9264	0.0084	8.0357	0109	1326	0136	2198	0166	2989	0199	8.3714	0235	8.4382	0.0274	33
28	7.9284	0.0085	8.0374	0109	1341	0136	2211	0166	3001	0200	8.3725	0236	8.4392	0.0275	32
29	7.9303	0.0085	8.0391	0109	1357	0137	2225	0167	3014	0200	8.3737	0236	8.4403	0.0276	31
30	7.9322	0.0086	8.0408	0110	1372	0137	2239	0167	3027	0201	8.3748	0237	8.4414	0.0276	30
31	7.9342	0.0086	8.0425	0110	1387	0138	2253	0168	3039	0201	8.3760	0238	8.4424	0.0277	29
32	7.9361	0.0086	8.0442	0111	1402	0138	2266	0169	3052	0202	8.3771	0238	8.4435	0.0278	28
33	7.9380	0.0087	8.0459	0111	1417	0139	2280	0169	3064	0203	8.3783	0239	8.4446	0.0278	27
34	7.9399	0.0087	8.0475	0112	1432	0139	2294	0170	3077	0203	8.3794	0240	8.4456	0.0279	26
35	7.9418	0.0087	8.0492	0112	1447	0140	2307	0170	3089	0204	8.3806	0240	8.4467	0.0280	25
36	7.9437	0.0088	8.0509	0112	1463	0140	2321	0171	3102	0204	8.3817	0241	8.4478	0.0280	24
37	7.9456	0.0088	8.0526	0113	1478	0141	2335	0171	3114	0205	8.3829	0241	8.4488	0.0281	23
38	7.9475	0.0089	8.0543	0113	1493	0141	2348	0172	3126	0205	8.3840	0242	8.4499	0.0282	22
39	7.9494	0.0089	8.0559	0114	1508	0142	2362	0172	3139	0206	8.3851	0243	8.4509	0.0282	21
40	7.9513	0.0089	8.0576	0114	1522	0142	2375	0173	3151	0206	8.3863	0243	8.4520	0.0283	20
41	7.9532	0.0090	8.0593	0115	1537	0142	2389	0173	3164	0207	8.3874	0244	8.4530	0.0284	19
42	7.9551	0.0090	8.0609	0115	1552	0143	2402	0174	3176	0208	8.3886	0245	8.4541	0.0285	18
43	7.9569	0.0091	8.0626	0116	1567	0143	2416	0174	3188	0208	8.3897	0245	8.4551	0.0285	17
44	7.9588	0.0091	8.0642	0116	1582	0144	2429	0175	3200	0209	8.3908	0246	8.4562	0.0286	16
45	7.9607	0.0091	8.0659	0116	1597	0144	2443	0176	3213	0210	8.3920	0247	8.4572	0.0287	15
46	7.9625	0.0092	8.0675	0117	1612	0145	2456	0176	3225	0210	8.3931	0247	8.4583	0.0287	14
47	7.9644	0.0092	8.0692	0117	1626	0145	2469	0177	3237	0211	8.3942	0248	8.4593	0.0288	13
48	7.9662	0.0093	8.0708	0118	1641	0146	2483	0177	3250	0211	8.3953	0249	8.4604	0.0289	12
49	7.9681	0.0093	8.0725	0118	1656	0146	2496	0178	3262	0212	8.3965	0249	8.4614	0.0289	11
50	7.9699	0.0093	8.0741	0119	1671	0147	2510	0178	3274	0213	8.3976	0250	8.4625	0.0290	10
51	7.9718	0.0094	8.0757	0119	1685	0147	2523	0179	3286	0213	8.3987	0250	8.4635	0.0291	9
52	7.9736	0.0094	8.0774	0120	1700	0148	2536	0179	3298	0214	8.3998	0251	8.4645	0.0291	8
53	7.9755	0.0095	8.0790	0120	1715	0148	2549	0180	3310	0214	8.4010	0252	8.4656	0.0292	7
54	7.9773	0.0095	8.0806	0121	1729	0149	2563	0180	3323	0215	8.4021	0252	8.4666	0.0293	6
55	7.9791	0.0095	8.0823	0121	1744	0149	2576	0181	3335	0216	8.4032	0253	8.4677	0.0294	5
56	7.9809	0.0096	8.0839	0121	1758	0150	2589	0182	3347	0216	8.4043	0254	8.4687	0.0294	4
57	7.9828	0.0096	8.0855	0122	1773	0150	2602	0182	3359	0217	8.4054	0254	8.4697	0.0295	3
58	7.9846	0.0097	8.0871	0122	1787	0151	2615	0183	3371	0217	8.4065	0255	8.4708	0.0296	2
59	7.9864	0.0097	8.0887	0123	1802	0151	2629	0183	3383	0218	8.4076	0256	8.4718	0.0296	1
60	7.9882	0.0097	8.0903	0123	1816	0152	2642	0184	3395	0219	8.4087	0256	8.4728	0.0297	0

LOG.	NAT.	LOG.	NAT.	LOG.	NAT.	LOG.	NAT.	LOG.	NAT.	LOG.	NAT.	LOG.	NAT.	/
352°		**351°**		**350°**		**349°**		**348°**		**347°**		**346°**		

For an explanation of the use of above Tables see p. 5:25.

VERSINES

/	14° LOG.	NAT.	15° LOG.	NAT.	16° LOG.	NAT.	17° LOG.	NAT.	18° LOG.	NAT.	19° LOG.	NAT.	20° LOG.	NAT.	
0	8.4728	0.0297	5324	0341	8.5881	0387	6404	0437	8.6897	0489	7362	0545	8.7804	0.0603	60
1	8.4738	0.0298	5334	0341	8.5890	0388	6413	0438	8.6905	0490	7370	0546	8.7811	0.0604	59
2	8.4749	0.0298	5343	0342	8.5899	0389	6421	0439	8.6913	0491	7378	0547	8.7818	0.0605	58
3	8.4759	0.0299	5353	0343	8.5908	0390	6430	0440	8.6921	0492	7385	0548	8.7825	0.0606	57
4	8.4769	0.0300	5363	0344	8.5917	0391	6438	0440	8.6929	0493	7393	0549	8.7832	0.0607	56
5	8.4779	0.0301	5372	0345	8.5926	0391	6447	0441	8.6937	0494	7400	0550	8.7839	0.0608	55
6	8.4790	0.0301	5382	0345	8.5935	0392	6455	0442	8.6945	0495	7408	0551	8.7847	0.0609	54
7	8.4800	0.0302	5391	0346	8.5944	0393	6463	0443	8.6953	0496	7415	0551	8.7854	0.0610	53
8	8.4810	0.0303	5401	0347	8.5953	0394	6472	0444	8.6961	0497	7423	0552	8.7861	0.0611	52
9	8.4820	0.0303	5410	0348	8.5962	0395	6480	0445	8.6968	0498	7430	0553	8.7868	0.0612	51
10	8.4830	0.0304	5420	0348	8.5971	0395	6488	0445	8.6976	0498	7438	0554	8.7875	0.0613	50
11	8.4841	0.0305	5429	0349	8.5980	0396	6497	0446	8.6984	0499	7445	0555	8.7882	0.0614	49
12	8.4851	0.0306	5439	0350	8.5989	0397	6505	0447	8.6992	0500	7453	0556	8.7889	0.0615	48
13	8.4861	0.0306	5448	0351	8.5997	0398	6514	0448	8.7000	0501	7460	0557	8.7896	0.0616	47
14	8.4871	0.0307	5458	0351	8.6006	0399	6522	0449	8.7008	0502	7468	0558	8.7903	0.0617	46
15	8.4881	0.0308	5467	0352	8.6015	0399	6530	0450	8.7016	0503	7475	0559	8.7910	0.0618	45
16	8.4891	0.0308	5476	0353	8.6024	0400	6539	0451	8.7024	0504	7482	0560	8.7918	0.0619	44
17	8.4901	0.0309	5486	0354	8.6033	0401	6547	0452	8.7031	0505	7490	0561	8.7925	0.0620	43
18	8.4911	0.0310	5495	0354	8.6042	0402	6555	0452	8.7039	0506	7497	0562	8.7932	0.0621	42
19	8.4921	0.0311	5505	0355	8.6051	0403	6563	0453	8.7047	0507	7505	0563	8.7939	0.0622	41
20	8.4932	0.0311	5514	0356	8.6059	0404	6572	0454	8.7055	0508	7512	0564	8.7946	0.0623	40
21	8.4942	0.0312	5523	0357	8.6068	0404	6580	0455	8.7063	0508	7520	0565	8.7953	0.0624	39
22	8.4952	0.0313	5533	0358	8.6077	0405	6588	0456	8.7071	0509	7527	0566	8.7960	0.0625	38
23	8.4962	0.0313	5542	0358	8.6086	0406	6597	0457	8.7078	0510	7534	0567	8.7967	0.0626	37
24	8.4972	0.0314	5551	0359	8.6094	0407	6605	0458	8.7086	0511	7542	0568	8.7974	0.0627	36
25	8.4982	0.0315	5561	0360	8.6103	0408	6613	0458	8.7094	0512	7549	0569	8.7981	0.0628	35
26	8.4992	0.0316	5570	0361	8.6112	0409	6621	0459	8.7102	0513	7557	0570	8.7988	0.0629	34
27	8.5002	0.0316	5579	0361	8.6121	0409	6630	0460	8.7110	0514	7564	0571	8.7995	0.0630	33
28	8.5012	0.0317	5589	0362	8.6129	0410	6638	0461	8.7117	0515	7571	0572	8.8002	0.0631	32
29	8.5021	0.0318	5598	0363	8.6138	0411	6646	0462	8.7125	0516	7579	0573	8.8009	0.0632	31
30	8.5031	0.0319	5607	0364	8.6147	0412	6654	0463	8.7133	0517	7586	0574	8.8016	0.0633	30
31	8.5041	0.0319	5617	0364	8.6156	0413	6662	0464	8.7141	0518	7593	0575	8.8023	0.0634	29
32	8.5051	0.0320	5626	0365	8.6164	0413	6671	0465	8.7148	0519	7601	0576	8.8030	0.0635	28
33	8.5061	0.0321	5635	0366	8.6173	0414	6679	0465	8.7156	0520	7608	0577	8.8037	0.0636	27
34	8.5071	0.0321	5644	0367	8.6182	0415	6687	0466	8.7164	0520	7615	0577	8.8044	0.0637	26
35	8.5081	0.0322	5654	0368	8.6190	0416	6695	0467	8.7172	0521	7623	0578	8.8051	0.0638	25
36	8.5091	0.0323	5663	0368	8.6199	0417	6703	0468	8.7179	0522	7630	0579	8.8058	0.0639	24
37	8.5101	0.0324	5672	0369	8.6208	0418	6711	0469	8.7187	0523	7637	0580	8.8065	0.0640	23
38	8.5110	0.0324	5681	0370	8.6216	0418	6720	0470	8.7195	0524	7645	0581	8.8072	0.0641	22
39	8.5120	0.0325	5691	0371	8.6225	0419	6728	0471	8.7202	0525	7652	0582	8.8079	0.0642	21
40	8.5130	0.0326	5700	0372	8.6234	0420	6736	0472	8.7210	0526	7659	0583	8.8086	0.0644	20
41	8.5140	0.0327	5709	0372	8.6242	0421	6744	0473	8.7218	0527	7666	0584	8.8092	0.0645	19
42	8.5150	0.0327	5718	0373	8.6251	0422	6752	0473	8.7225	0528	7674	0585	8.8099	0.0646	18
43	8.5160	0.0328	5727	0374	8.6259	0423	6760	0474	8.7233	0529	7681	0586	8.8106	0.0647	17
44	8.5169	0.0329	5736	0375	8.6268	0423	6768	0475	8.7241	0530	7688	0587	8.8113	0.0648	16
45	8.5179	0.0330	5745	0375	8.6277	0424	6776	0476	8.7248	0531	7696	0588	8.8120	0.0649	15
46	8.5189	0.0330	5755	0376	8.6285	0425	6785	0477	8.7256	0532	7703	0589	8.8127	0.0650	14
47	8.5199	0.0331	5764	0377	8.6294	0426	6793	0478	8.7264	0533	7710	0590	8.8134	0.0651	13
48	8.5208	0.0332	5773	0378	8.6302	0427	6801	0479	8.7271	0534	7717	0591	8.8141	0.0652	12
49	8.5218	0.0333	5782	0379	8.6311	0428	6809	0480	8.7279	0534	7725	0592	8.8148	0.0653	11
50	8.5228	0.0333	5791	0379	8.6319	0428	6817	0480	8.7287	0535	7732	0593	8.8155	0.0654	10
51	8.5237	0.0334	5800	0380	8.6328	0429	6825	0481	8.7294	0536	7739	0594	8.8161	0.0655	9
52	8.5247	0.0335	5809	0381	8.6336	0430	6833	0482	8.7302	0537	7746	0595	8.8168	0.0656	8
53	8.5257	0.0335	5818	0382	8.6345	0431	6841	0483	8.7309	0538	7753	0596	8.8175	0.0657	7
54	8.5266	0.0336	5827	0383	8.6353	0432	6849	0484	8.7317	0539	7761	0597	8.8182	0.0658	6
55	9.5276	0.0337	5836	0383	8.6362	0433	6857	0485	8.7325	0540	7768	0598	8.8189	0.0659	5
56	8.5286	0.0338	5845	0384	8.6370	0434	6865	0486	8.7332	0541	7775	0599	8.8196	0.0660	4
57	8.5295	0.0338	5854	0385	8.6379	0434	6873	0487	8.7340	0542	7782	0600	8.8202	0.0661	3
58	8.5305	0.0339	5863	0386	8.6387	0435	6881	0488	8.7347	0543	7789	0601	8.8209	0.0662	2
59	8.5315	0.0340	5872	0387	8.6396	0436	6889	0489	8.7355	0544	7797	0602	8.8216	0.0663	1
60	8.5324	0.0341	5881	0387	8.6404	0437	6897	0489	8.7362	0545	7804	0603	8.8223	0.0664	0
	LOG.	NAT.	LOG.	NAT.	LOG.	NAT.	LOG.	NAT.	LOG.	NAT.	LOG.	NAT.	LOG.	NAT.	/
	345°		344°		343°		342°		341°		340°		339°		

For an explanation of the use of above Tables see p. 5:25.

VERSINES

/	21° LOG.	NAT.	22° LOG.	NAT.	23° LOG.	NAT.	24° LOG.	NAT.	25° LOG.	NAT.	26° LOG.	NAT.	27° LOG.	NAT.	
0	8.8223	0.0664	8622	0728	8.9003	0795	9368	0865	8.9717	0937	0052	1012	9.0374	0.1090	60
1	8.8230	0.0665	8629	0729	8.9010	0796	9374	0866	8.9723	0938	0058	1013	9.0379	0.1091	59
2	8.8237	0.0666	8635	0730	8.9016	0797	9380	0867	8.9728	0939	0063	1015	9.0385	0.1093	58
3	8.8243	0.0667	8642	0731	8.9022	0798	9386	0868	8.9734	0941	0068	1016	9.0390	0.1094	57
4	8.8250	0.0668	8648	0733	8.9028	0800	9392	0869	8.9740	0942	0074	1017	9.0395	0.1095	56
5	8.8257	0.0669	8655	0734	8.9034	0801	9398	0870	8.9745	0943	0079	1018	9.0400	0.1097	55
6	8.8264	0.0670	8661	0735	8.9041	0802	9403	0872	8.9751	0944	0085	1020	9.0406	0.1098	54
7	8.8271	0.0672	8668	0736	8.9047	0803	9409	0873	8.9757	0946	0090	1021	9.0411	0.1099	53
8	8.8277	0.0673	8674	0737	8.9053	0804	9415	0874	8.9762	0947	0096	1022	9.0416	0.1101	52
9	8.8284	0.0674	8681	0738	8.9059	0805	9421	0875	8.9768	0948	0101	1024	9.0421	0.1102	51
10	8.8291	0.0675	8687	0739	8.9065	0806	9427	0876	8.9774	0949	0107	1025	9.0426	0.1103	50
11	8.8298	0.0676	8693	0740	8.9071	0808	9433	0878	8.9779	0950	0112	1026	9.0432	0.1105	49
12	8.8304	0.0677	8700	0741	8.9078	0809	9439	0879	8.9785	0952	0117	1027	9.0437	0.1106	48
13	8.8311	0.0678	8706	0742	8.9084	0810	9445	0880	8.9791	0953	0123	1029	9.0442	0.1107	47
14	8.8318	0.0679	8713	0743	8.9090	0811	9451	0881	8.9796	0954	0128	1030	9.0447	0.1108	46
15	8.8325	0.0680	8719	0745	8.9096	0812	9457	0882	8.9802	0955	0134	1031	9.0453	0.1110	45
16	8.8331	0.0681	8726	0746	8.9102	0813	9462	0884	8.9808	0957	0139	1033	9.0458	0.1111	44
17	8.8338	0.0682	8732	0747	8.9108	0815	9468	0885	8.9813	0958	0145	1034	9.0463	0.1112	43
18	8.8345	0.0683	8738	0748	8.9114	0816	9474	0886	8.9819	0959	0150	1035	9.0468	0.1114	42
19	8.8351	0.0684	8745	0749	8.9121	0817	9480	0887	8.9825	0960	0155	1036	9.0473	0.1115	41
20	8.8358	0.0685	8751	0750	8.9127	0818	9486	0888	8.9830	0962	0161	1038	9.0479	0.1116	40
21	8.8365	0.0686	8758	0751	8.9133	0819	9492	0890	8.9836	0963	0166	1039	9.0484	0.1118	39
22	8.8372	0.0687	8764	0752	8.9139	0820	9498	0891	8.9841	0964	0172	1040	9.0489	0.1119	38
23	8.8378	0.0688	8770	0753	8.9145	0821	9503	0892	8.9847	0965	0177	1042	9.0494	0.1121	37
24	8.8385	0.0689	8777	0755	8.9151	0822	9509	0893	8.9853	0967	0182	1043	9.0499	0.1122	36
25	8.8392	0.0691	8783	0756	8.9157	0824	9515	0894	8.9858	0968	0188	1044	9.0505	0.1123	35
26	8.8398	0.0692	8790	0757	8.9163	0825	9521	0896	8.9864	0969	0193	1045	9.0510	0.1125	34
27	8.8405	0.0693	8796	0758	8.9169	0826	9527	0897	8.9869	0970	0198	1047	9.0515	0.1126	33
28	8.8412	0.0694	8802	0759	8.9175	0827	9533	0898	8.9875	0972	0204	1048	9.0520	0.1127	32
29	8.8418	0.0695	8809	0760	8.9182	0828	9538	0899	8.9881	0973	0209	1049	9.0525	0.1129	31
30	8.8425	0.0696	8815	0761	8.9188	0829	9544	0900	8.9886	0974	0215	1051	9.0530	0.1130	30
31	8.8432	0.0697	8821	0762	8.9194	0831	9550	0902	8.9892	0975	0220	1052	9.0536	0.1131	29
32	8.8438	0.0698	8828	0763	8.9200	0832	9556	0903	8.9897	0977	0225	1053	9.0541	0.1133	28
33	8.8445	0.0699	8834	0765	8.9206	0833	9562	0904	8.9903	0978	0231	1055	9.0546	0.1134	27
34	8.8452	0.0700	8840	0766	8.9212	0834	9568	0905	8.9909	0979	0236	1056	9.0551	0.1135	26
35	8.8458	0.0701	8847	0767	8.9218	0835	9573	0906	8.9914	0980	0241	1057	9.0556	0.1137	25
36	8.8465	0.0702	8853	0768	8.9224	0836	9579	0908	8.9920	0982	0247	1058	9.0561	0.1138	24
37	8.8471	0.0703	8859	0769	8.9230	0838	9585	0909	8.9925	0983	0252	1060	9.0566	0.1139	23
38	8.8478	0.0704	8866	0770	8.9236	0839	9591	0910	8.9931	0984	0257	1061	9.0572	0.1141	22
39	8.8485	0.0705	8872	0771	8.9242	0840	9596	0911	8.9936	0985	0263	1062	9.0577	0.1142	21
40	8.8491	0.0707	8878	0772	8.9248	0841	9602	0912	8.9942	0987	0268	1064	9.0582	0.1143	20
41	8.8498	0.0708	8885	0773	8.9254	0842	9608	0914	8.9947	0988	0273	1065	9.0587	0.1145	19
42	8.8504	0.0709	8891	0775	8.9260	0843	9614	0915	8.9953	0989	0279	1066	9.0592	0.1146	18
43	8.8511	0.0710	8897	0776	8.9266	0845	9620	0916	8.9959	0990	0284	1068	9.0597	0.1147	17
44	8.8518	0.0711	8903	0777	8.9272	0846	9625	0917	8.9964	0992	0289	1069	9.0602	0.1149	16
45	8.8524	0.0712	8910	0778	8.9278	0847	9631	0919	8.9970	0993	0295	1070	9.0607	0.1150	15
46	8.8531	0.0713	8916	0779	8.9284	0848	9637	0920	8.9975	0994	0300	1072	9.0613	0.1151	14
47	8.8537	0.0714	8922	0780	8.9290	0849	9643	0921	8.9981	0996	0305	1073	9.0618	0.1153	13
48	8.8544	0.0715	8929	0781	8.9296	0850	9648	0922	8.9986	0997	0311	1074	9.0623	0.1154	12
49	8.8550	0.0716	8935	0782	8.9302	0852	9654	0923	8.9992	0998	0316	1075	9.0628	0.1156	11
50	8.8557	0.0717	8941	0784	8.9308	0853	9660	0925	8.9997	0999	0321	1077	9.0633	0.1157	10
51	8.8564	0.0718	8947	0785	8.9314	0854	9666	0926	9.0003	1001	0327	1078	9.0638	0.1158	9
52	8.8570	0.0719	8954	0786	8.9320	0855	9671	0927	9.0008	1002	0332	1079	9.0643	0.1160	8
53	8.8577	0.0721	8960	0787	8.9326	0856	9677	0928	9.0014	1003	0337	1081	9.0648	0.1161	7
54	8.8583	0.0722	8966	0788	8.9332	0857	9683	0930	9.0019	1004	0342	1082	9.0653	0.1162	6
55	8.8590	0.0723	8972	0789	8.9338	0859	9688	0931	9.0025	1006	0348	1083	9.0658	0.1164	5
56	8.8596	0.0724	8979	0790	8.9344	0860	9694	0932	9.0030	1007	0353	1085	9.0664	0.1165	4
57	8.8603	0.0725	8985	0792	8.9350	0861	9700	0933	9.0036	1008	0358	1086	9.0669	0.1166	3
58	8.8609	0.0726	8991	0793	8.9356	0862	9706	0934	9.0041	1010	0363	1087	9.0674	0.1168	2
59	8.8616	0.0727	8997	0794	8.9362	0863	9711	0936	9.0047	1011	0369	1089	9.0679	0.1169	1
60	8.8622	0.0728	9003	0795	8.9368	0865	9717	0937	9.0052	1012	0374	1090	9.0684	0.1171	0
	LOG.	NAT.	LOG.	NAT.	LOG.	NAT.	LOG.	NAT.	LOG.	NAT.	LOG.	NAT.	LOG.	NAT.	/
	338°		337°		336°		335°		334°		333°		332°		

For an explanation of the use of above Tables see p. 5:25.

VERSINES

/	28° LOG.	NAT.	29° LOG.	NAT.	30° LOG.	NAT.	31° LOG.	NAT.	32° LOG.	NAT.	33° LOG.	NAT.	34° LOG.	NAT.	
0	9.0684	0.1171	0982	1254	9.1270	1340	1548	1428	9.1817	1520	2077	1613	9.2329	0.1710	60
1	9.0689	0.1172	0987	1255	9.1275	1341	1553	1430	9.1821	1521	2081	1615	9.2333	0.1711	59
2	9.0694	0.1173	0992	1257	9.1280	1343	1557	1431	9.1826	1523	2086	1616	9.2337	0.1713	58
3	9.0699	0.1175	0997	1258	9.1284	1344	1562	1433	9.1830	1524	2090	1618	9.2341	0.1715	57
4	9.0704	0.1176	1002	1259	9.1289	1346	1566	1434	9.1835	1526	2094	1620	9.2346	0.1716	56
5	9.0709	0.1177	1007	1261	9.1294	1347	1571	1436	9.1839	1527	2098	1621	9.2350	0.1718	55
6	9.0714	0.1179	1012	1262	9.1298	1348	1576	1437	9.1843	1529	2103	1623	9.2354	0.1719	54
7	9.0719	0.1180	1016	1264	9.1303	1350	1580	1439	9.1848	1530	2107	1624	9.2358	0.1721	53
8	9.0724	0.1181	1021	1265	9.1308	1351	1585	1440	9.1852	1532	2111	1626	9.2362	0.1723	52
9	9.0729	0.1183	1026	1267	9.1313	1353	1589	1442	9.1857	1533	2115	1628	9.2366	0.1724	51
10	9.0734	0.1184	1031	1268	9.1317	1354	1594	1443	9.1861	1535	2120	1629	9.2370	0.1726	50
11	9.0739	0.1186	1036	1269	9.1322	1356	1598	1445	9.1865	1537	2124	1631	9.2374	0.1728	49
12	9.0744	0.1187	1041	1271	9.1327	1357	1603	1446	9.1870	1538	2128	1632	9.2378	0.1729	48
13	9.0749	0.1188	1046	1272	9.1331	1359	1607	1448	9.1874	1540	2132	1634	9.2383	0.1731	47
14	9.0754	0.1190	1050	1274	9.1336	1360	1612	1449	9.1879	1541	2137	1636	9.2387	0.1732	46
15	9.0759	0.1191	1055	1275	9.1341	1362	1616	1451	9.1883	1543	2141	1637	9.2391	0.1734	45
16	9.0764	0.1192	1060	1276	9.1345	1363	1621	1452	9.1887	1544	2145	1639	9.2395	0.1736	44
17	9.0769	0.1194	1065	1278	9.1350	1365	1625	1454	9.1892	1546	2149	1640	9.2399	0.1737	43
18	9.0775	0.1195	1070	1279	9.1355	1366	1630	1455	9.1896	1547	2154	1642	9.2403	0.1739	42
19	9.0780	0.1197	1075	1281	9.1359	1368	1634	1457	9.1900	1549	2158	1644	9.2407	0.1741	41
20	9.0785	0.1198	1079	1282	9.1364	1369	1639	1458	9.1905	1550	2162	1645	9.2411	0.1742	40
21	9.0790	0.1199	1084	1284	9.1369	1370	1643	1460	9.1909	1552	2166	1647	9.2415	0.1744	39
22	9.0795	0.1201	1089	1285	9.1373	1372	1648	1461	9.1913	1554	2170	1648	9.2419	0.1746	38
23	9.0800	0.1202	1094	1286	9.1378	1373	1652	1463	9.1918	1555	2175	1650	9.2423	0.1747	37
24	9.0805	0.1204	1099	1288	9.1383	1375	1657	1464	9.1922	1557	2179	1652	9.2428	0.1749	36
25	9.0810	0.1205	1104	1289	9.1387	1376	1661	1466	9.1926	1558	2183	1653	9.2432	0.1751	35
26	9.0814	0.1206	1108	1291	9.1392	1378	1666	1468	9.1931	1560	2187	1655	9.2436	0.1752	34
27	9.0819	0.1208	1113	1292	9.1397	1379	1670	1469	9.1935	1561	2191	1656	9.2440	0.1754	33
28	9.0824	0.1209	1118	1294	9.1401	1381	1675	1471	9.1939	1563	2196	1658	9.2444	0.1755	32
29	9.0829	0.1210	1123	1295	9.1406	1382	1679	1472	9.1944	1565	2200	1660	9.2448	0.1757	31
30	9.0834	0.1212	1128	1296	9.1410	1384	1684	1474	9.1948	1566	2204	1661	9.2452	0.1759	30
31	9.0839	0.1213	1132	1298	9.1415	1385	1688	1475	9.1952	1567	2208	1663	9.2456	0.1760	29
32	9.0844	0.1215	1137	1299	9.1420	1387	1693	1477	9.1957	1569	2212	1664	9.2460	0.1762	28
33	9.0849	0.1216	1142	1301	9.1424	1388	1698	1478	9.1961	1571	2217	1666	9.2464	0.1764	27
34	9.0854	0.1217	1147	1302	9.1429	1390	1702	1480	9.1965	1572	2221	1668	9.2468	0.1765	26
35	9.0859	0.1219	1151	1304	9.1434	1391	1706	1481	9.1970	1574	2225	1669	9.2472	0.1767	25
36	9.0864	0.1220	1156	1305	9.1438	1393	1711	1483	9.1974	1575	2229	1671	9.2476	0.1769	24
37	9.0869	0.1222	1161	1306	9.1443	1394	1715	1484	9.1978	1577	2233	1672	9.2480	0.1770	23
38	9.0874	0.1223	1166	1308	9.1447	1396	1720	1486	9.1983	1578	2238	1674	9.2484	0.1772	22
39	9.0879	0.1224	1171	1309	9.1452	1397	1724	1487	9.1987	1580	2242	1676	9.2489	0.1774	21
40	9.0884	0.1226	1175	1311	9.1457	1399	1728	1489	9.1991	1582	2246	1677	9.2493	0.1775	20
41	9.0889	0.1227	1180	1312	9.1461	1400	1733	1490	9.1996	1583	2250	1679	9.2497	0.1777	19
42	9.0894	0.1229	1185	1314	9.1466	1401	1737	1492	9.2000	1585	2254	1680	9.2501	0.1779	18
43	9.0899	0.1230	1190	1315	9.1470	1403	1742	1493	9.2004	1586	2258	1682	9.2505	0.1780	17
44	9.0904	0.1231	1194	1317	9.1475	1404	1746	1495	9.2009	1588	2263	1684	9.2509	0.1782	16
45	9.0909	0.1233	1199	1318	9.1480	1406	1751	1496	9.2013	1590	2267	1685	9.2513	0.1784	15
46	9.0914	0.1234	1204	1319	9.1484	1407	1755	1498	9.2017	1591	2271	1687	9.2517	0.1785	14
47	9.0919	0.1236	1209	1321	9.1489	1409	1760	1500	9.2022	1593	2275	1689	9.2521	0.1787	13
48	9.0923	0.1237	1213	1322	9.1493	1410	1764	1501	9.2026	1594	2279	1690	9.2525	0.1789	12
49	9.0928	0.1238	1218	1324	9.1498	1412	1768	1503	9.2030	1596	2283	1692	9.2529	0.1790	11
50	9.0933	0.1240	1223	1325	9.1503	1413	1773	1504	9.2034	1597	2288	1693	9.2533	0.1792	10
51	9.0938	0.1241	1228	1327	9.1507	1415	1777	1506	9.2039	1599	2292	1695	9.2537	0.1793	9
52	9.0943	0.1242	1232	1328	9.1512	1416	1782	1507	9.2043	1601	2296	1697	9.2541	0.1795	8
53	9.0948	0.1244	1237	1330	9.1516	1418	1786	1509	9.2047	1602	2300	1698	9.2545	0.1797	7
54	9.0953	0.1245	1242	1331	9.1521	1419	1791	1510	9.2052	1604	2304	1700	9.2549	0.1798	6
55	9.0958	0.1247	1247	1332	9.1525	1421	1795	1512	9.2056	1605	2308	1702	9.2553	0.1800	5
56	9.0963	0.1248	1251	1334	9.1530	1422	1799	1513	9.2060	1607	2312	1703	9.2557	0.1802	4
57	9.0968	0.1250	1256	1335	9.1535	1424	1804	1515	9.2064	1609	2317	1705	9.2561	0.1803	3
58	9.0973	0.1251	1261	1337	9.1539	1425	1808	1516	9.2069	1610	2321	1706	9.2565	0.1805	2
59	9.0977	0.1252	1266	1338	9.1544	1427	1813	1518	9.2073	1612	2325	1708	9.2569	0.1807	1
60	9.0982	0.1254	1270	1340	9.1548	1428	1817	1520	9.2077	1613	2329	1710	9.2573	0.1808	0

LOG. NAT.	LOG. NAT.	LOG. NAT.	LOG. NAT.	LOG. NAT.	LOG. NAT.	LOG. NAT.	/
331°	330°	329°	328°	327°	326°	325°	

For an explanation of the use of above Tables see p. 5:25.

VERSINES

/	35° LOG.	35° NAT.	36° LOG.	36° NAT.	37° LOG.	37° NAT.	38° LOG.	38° NAT.	39° LOG.	39° NAT.	40° LOG.	40° NAT.	41° LOG.	41° NAT.	
0	9.2573	0.1808	2810	1910	9.3040	2014	3263	2120	9.3480	2229	3691	2340	9.3897	0.2453	60
1	9.2577	0.1810	2814	1912	9.3044	2015	3267	2122	9.3484	2230	3695	2341	9.3900	0.2455	59
2	9.2581	0.1812	2818	1913	9.3047	2017	3270	2123	9.3487	2232	3698	2343	9.3904	0.2457	58
3	9.2585	0.1813	2822	1915	9.3051	2019	3274	2125	9.3491	2234	3702	2345	9.3907	0.2459	57
4	9.2589	0.1815	2825	1917	9.3055	2021	3278	2127	9.3494	2236	3705	2347	9.3910	0.2461	56
5	9.2593	0.1817	2829	1918	9.3059	2022	3281	2129	9.3498	2238	3709	2349	9.3914	0.2462	55
6	9.2597	0.1819	2833	1920	9.3062	2024	3285	2131	9.3502	2240	3712	2351	9.3917	0.2464	54
7	9.2601	0.1820	2837	1922	9.3066	2026	3289	2132	9.3505	2241	3716	2353	9.3920	0.2466	53
8	9.2605	0.1822	2841	1924	9.3070	2028	3292	2134	9.3509	2243	3719	2355	9.3924	0.2468	52
9	9.2609	0.1824	2845	1925	9.3074	2029	3296	2136	9.3512	2245	3723	2356	9.3927	0.2470	51
10	9.2613	0.1825	2849	1927	9.3077	2031	3300	2138	9.3516	2247	3726	2358	9.3931	0.2472	50
11	9.2617	0.1827	2853	1929	9.3081	2033	3303	2140	9.3519	2249	3729	2360	9.3934	0.2474	49
12	9.2621	0.1829	2856	1930	9.3085	2035	3307	2141	9.3523	2251	3733	2362	9.3937	0.2476	48
13	9.2625	0.1830	2860	1932	9.3089	2036	3311	2143	9.3526	2252	3736	2364	9.3941	0.2478	47
14	9.2629	0.1832	2864	1934	9.3092	2038	3314	2145	9.3530	2254	3740	2366	9.3944	0.2480	46
15	9.2633	0.1834	2868	1936	9.3096	2040	3318	2147	9.3534	2256	3743	2368	9.3947	0.2482	45
16	9.2637	0.1835	2872	1937	9.3100	2042	3322	2149	9.3537	2258	3747	2370	9.3951	0.2484	44
17	9.2641	0.1837	2876	1939	9.3104	2044	3325	2150	9.3541	2260	3750	2371	9.3954	0.2485	43
18	9.2645	0.1839	2880	1941	9.3107	2045	3329	2152	9.3544	2262	3754	2373	9.3957	0.2487	42
19	9.2649	0.1840	2883	1942	9.3111	2047	3333	2154	9.3548	2263	3757	2375	9.3961	0.2489	41
20	9.2653	0.1842	2887	1944	9.3115	2049	3336	2156	9.3551	2265	3760	2377	9.3964	0.2491	40
21	9.2657	0.1844	2891	1946	9.3119	2051	3340	2158	9.3555	2267	3764	2379	9.3967	0.2493	39
22	9.2661	0.1845	2895	1948	9.3122	2052	3343	2159	9.3558	2269	3767	2381	9.3971	0.2495	38
23	9.2665	0.1847	2899	1949	9.3126	2054	3347	2161	9.3562	2271	3771	2383	9.3974	0.2497	37
24	9.2669	0.1849	2903	1951	9.3130	2056	3351	2163	9.3565	2273	3774	2385	9.3977	0.2499	36
25	9.2673	0.1850	2907	1953	9.3134	2058	3354	2165	9.3569	2275	3778	2387	9.3981	0.2501	35
26	9.2677	0.1852	2910	1955	9.3137	2059	3358	2167	9.3572	2276	3781	2388	9.3984	0.2503	34
27	9.2681	0.1854	2914	1956	9.3141	2061	3362	2168	9.3576	2278	3784	2390	9.3987	0.2505	33
28	9.2685	0.1855	2918	1958	9.3145	2063	3365	2170	9.3579	2280	3788	2392	9.3991	0.2507	32
29	9.2688	0.1857	2922	1960	9.3149	2065	3369	2172	9.3583	2282	3791	2394	9.3994	0.2509	31
30	9.2692	0.1859	2926	1961	9.3152	2067	3372	2174	9.3586	2284	3795	2396	9.3998	0.2510	30
31	9.2696	0.1861	2930	1963	9.3156	2068	3376	2176	9.3590	2286	3798	2398	9.4001	0.2512	29
32	9.2700	0.1862	2933	1965	9.3160	2070	3380	2178	9.3594	2287	3802	2400	9.4004	0.2514	28
33	9.2704	0.1864	2937	1967	9.3163	2072	3383	2179	9.3597	2289	3805	2402	9.4008	0.2516	27
34	9.2708	0.1866	2941	1968	9.3167	2074	3387	2181	9.3601	2291	3808	2404	9.4011	0.2518	26
35	9.2712	0.1867	2945	1970	9.3171	2075	3390	2183	9.3604	2293	3812	2405	9.4014	0.2520	25
36	9.2716	0.1869	2949	1972	9.3175	2077	3394	2185	9.3608	2295	3815	2407	9.4017	0.2522	24
37	9.2720	0.1871	2953	1974	9.3178	2079	3398	2185	9.3611	2297	3819	2409	9.4021	0.2524	23
38	9.2724	0.1872	2956	1975	9.3182	2081	3401	2188	9.3615	2299	3822	2411	9.4024	0.2526	22
39	9.2728	0.1874	2960	1977	9.3186	2082	3405	2190	9.3618	2300	3826	2413	9.4027	0.2528	21
40	9.2732	0.1876	2964	1979	9.3189	2084	3409	2192	9.3622	2302	3829	2415	9.4031	0.2530	20
41	9.2736	0.1877	2968	1981	9.3193	2086	3412	2194	9.3625	2304	3832	2417	9.4034	0.2532	19
42	9.2740	0.1879	2972	1982	9.3197	2088	3416	2196	9.3629	2306	3836	2419	9.4037	0.2534	18
43	9.2744	0.1881	2975	1984	9.3201	2090	3419	2198	9.3632	2308	3839	2421	9.4041	0.2536	17
44	9.2747	0.1883	2979	1986	9.3204	2091	3423	2199	9.3636	2310	3843	2422	9.4044	0.2537	16
45	9.2751	0.1884	2983	1987	9.3208	2093	3427	2201	9.3639	2312	3846	2424	9.4047	0.2539	15
46	9.2755	0.1886	2987	1989	9.3212	2095	3430	2203	9.3643	2313	3849	2426	9.4051	0.2541	14
47	9.2759	0.1888	2991	1991	9.3215	2097	3434	2205	9.3646	2315	3853	2428	9.4054	0.2543	13
48	9.2763	0.1889	2994	1993	9.3219	2099	3437	2207	9.3650	2317	3856	2430	9.4057	0.2545	12
49	9.2767	0.1891	2998	1994	9.3223	2100	3441	2208	9.3653	2319	3860	2432	9.4061	0.2547	11
50	9.2771	0.1893	3002	1996	9.3226	2102	3444	2210	9.3657	2321	3863	2434	9.4064	0.2549	10
51	9.2775	0.1894	3006	1998	9.3230	2104	3448	2212	9.3660	2323	3866	2436	9.4067	0.2551	9
52	9.2779	0.1896	3010	2000	9.3234	2106	3452	2214	9.3664	2325	3870	2438	9.4071	0.2553	8
53	9.2783	0.1898	3013	2001	9.3237	2107	3455	2216	9.3667	2326	3873	2440	9.4074	0.2555	7
54	9.2787	0.1900	3017	2003	9.3241	2109	3459	2218	9.3670	2328	3877	2441	9.4077	0.2557	6
55	9.2790	0.1901	3021	2005	9.3245	2111	3462	2219	9.3674	2330	3880	2443	9.4080	0.2559	5
56	9.2794	0.1903	3025	2007	9.3248	2113	3466	2221	9.3677	2332	3883	2445	9.4084	0.2561	4
57	9.2798	0.1905	3028	2008	9.3252	2115	3469	2223	9.3681	2334	3887	2447	9.4087	0.2563	3
58	9.2802	0.1906	3032	2010	9.3256	2116	3473	2225	9.3684	2336	3890	2449	9.4090	0.2565	2
59	9.2806	0.1908	3036	2012	9.3259	2118	3477	2227	9.3688	2338	3893	2451	9.4094	0.2567	1
60	9.2810	0.1910	3040	2014	9.3263	2120	3480	2229	9.3691	2340	3897	2453	9.4097	0.2569	0

LOG.	NAT.	LOG.	NAT.	LOG.	NAT.	LOG.	NAT.	LOG.	NAT.	LOG.	NAT.	LOG.	NAT.	/
324°		**323°**		**322°**		**321°**		**320°**		**319°**		**318°**		

For an explanation of the use of above Tables see p. 5:25.

VERSINES

I	42° LOG.	42° NAT.	43° LOG.	43° NAT.	44° LOG.	44° NAT.	45° LOG.	45° NAT.	46° LOG.	46° NAT.	47° LOG.	47° NAT.	48° LOG.	48° NAT.	
0	9.4097	0.2569	4292	2686	9.4482	2807	4667	2929	9.4848	3053	5024	3180	9.5197	0.3309	60
1	9.4100	0.2570	4295	2688	9.4485	2809	4670	2931	9.4851	3056	5027	3182	9.5199	0.3311	59
2	9.4103	0.2572	4298	2690	9.4488	2811	4673	2933	9.4854	3058	5030	3184	9.5202	0.3313	58
3	9.4107	0.2574	4301	2692	9.4491	2813	4676	2935	9.4857	3060	5033	3186	9.5205	0.3315	57
4	9.4110	0.2576	4305	2694	9.4494	2815	4679	2937	9.4860	3062	5036	3189	9.5208	0.3317	56
5	9.4113	0.2578	4308	2696	9.4497	2817	4682	2939	9.4863	3064	5039	3191	9.5211	0.3320	55
6	9.4117	0.2580	4311	2698	9.4501	2819	4685	2941	9.4866	3066	5042	3193	9.5214	0.3322	54
7	9.4120	0.2582	4314	2700	9.4504	2821	4688	2943	9.4869	3068	5045	3195	9.5216	0.3324	53
8	9.4123	0.2584	4317	2702	9.4507	2823	4691	2945	9.4872	3070	5048	3197	9.5219	0.3326	52
9	9.4126	0.2586	4321	2704	9.4510	2825	4694	2947	9.4875	3072	5050	3199	9.5222	0.3328	51
10	9.4130	0.2588	4324	2706	9.4513	2827	4698	2950	9.4878	3074	5053	3201	9.5225	0.3330	50
11	9.4133	0.2590	4327	2708	9.4516	2829	4701	2952	9.4881	3076	5056	3203	9.5228	0.3333	49
12	9.4136	0.2592	4330	2710	9.4519	2831	4704	2954	9.4883	3079	5059	3206	9.5231	0.3335	48
13	9.4140	0.2594	4333	2712	9.4522	2833	4707	2956	9.4886	3081	5062	3208	9.5233	0.3337	47
14	9.4143	0.2596	4337	2714	9.4525	2835	4710	2958	9.4889	3083	5065	3210	9.5236	0.3339	46
15	9.4146	0.2598	4340	2716	9.4529	2837	4713	2960	9.4892	3085	5068	3212	9.5239	0.3341	45
16	9.4149	0.2600	4343	2718	9.4532	2839	4716	2962	9.4895	3087	5071	3214	9.5242	0.3343	44
17	9.4153	0.2602	4346	2720	9.4535	2841	4719	2964	9.4898	3089	5074	3216	9.5245	0.3346	43
18	9.4156	0.2604	4349	2722	9.4538	2843	4722	2966	9.4901	3091	5076	3218	9.5247	0.3348	42
19	9.4159	0.2606	4352	2724	9.4541	2845	4725	2968	9.4904	3093	5079	3221	9.5250	0.3350	41
20	9.4162	0.2608	4356	2726	9.4544	2847	4728	2970	9.4907	3095	5082	3223	9.5253	0.3352	40
21	9.4166	0.2610	4359	2728	9.4547	2849	4731	2972	9.4910	3097	5085	3225	9.5256	0.3354	39
22	9.4169	0.2612	4362	2730	9.4550	2851	4734	2974	9.4913	3100	5088	3227	9.5259	0.3356	38
23	9.4172	0.2613	4365	2732	9.4553	2853	4737	2976	9.4916	3102	5091	3229	9.5262	0.3359	37
24	9.4175	0.2615	4368	2734	9.4556	2855	4740	2978	9.4919	3104	5094	3231	9.5264	0.3361	36
25	9.4179	0.2617	4372	2736	9.4560	2857	4743	2981	9.4922	3106	5097	3233	9.5267	0.3363	35
26	9.4182	0.2619	4375	2738	9.4563	2959	4746	2983	9.4925	3108	5099	3236	9.5270	0.3365	34
27	9.4185	0.2621	4378	2740	9.4566	2861	4749	2985	9.4928	3110	5102	3238	9.5273	0.3367	33
28	9.4188	0.2623	4381	2742	9.4569	2863	4752	2987	9.4931	3112	5105	3240	9.5276	0.3369	32
29	9.4192	0.2625	4384	2744	9.4572	2865	4755	2989	9.4934	3114	5108	3242	9.5278	0.3372	31
30	9.4195	0.2627	4387	2746	9.4575	2867	4758	2991	9.4937	3116	5111	3244	9.5281	0.3374	30
31	9.4198	0.2629	4391	2748	9.4578	2870	4761	2993	9.4940	3119	5114	3246	9.5284	0.3376	29
32	9.4201	0.2631	4394	2750	9.4581	2872	4764	2995	9.4942	3121	5117	3248	9.5287	0.3378	28
33	9.4205	0.2633	4397	2752	9.4584	2874	4767	2997	9.4945	3123	5120	3251	9.5290	0.3380	27
34	9.4208	0.2635	4400	2754	9.4587	2876	4770	2999	9.4948	3125	5122	3253	9.5292	0.3383	26
35	9.4211	0.2637	4403	2756	9.4590	2878	4773	3001	9.4951	3127	5125	3255	9.5295	0.3385	25
36	9.4214	0.2639	4406	2758	9.4594	2880	4776	3003	9.4954	3129	5128	3257	9.5298	0.3387	24
37	9.4218	0.2641	4410	2760	9.4597	2882	4779	3005	9.4957	3131	5131	3259	9.5301	0.3389	23
38	9.4221	0.2643	4413	2762	9.4600	2884	4782	3008	9.4960	3133	5134	3261	9.5304	0.3391	22
39	9.4224	0.2645	4416	2764	9.4603	2886	4785	3010	9.4963	3135	5137	3263	9.5306	0.3393	21
40	9.4227	0.2647	4419	2766	9.4606	2888	4788	3012	9.4966	3138	5140	3266	9.5309	0.3396	20
41	9.4231	0.2649	4422	2768	9.4609	2890	4791	3014	9.4969	3140	5142	3268	9.5312	0.3398	19
42	9.4234	0.2651	4425	2770	9.4612	2892	4794	3016	9.4972	3142	5145	3270	9.5315	0.3400	18
43	9.4237	0.2653	4428	2772	9.4615	2894	4797	3018	9.4975	3144	5148	3272	9.5318	0.3402	17
44	9.4240	0.2655	4432	2774	9.4618	2896	4800	3020	9.4978	3146	5151	3274	9.5320	0.3404	16
45	9.4244	0.2657	4435	2776	9.4621	2898	4803	3022	9.4981	3148	5154	3276	9.5323	0.3407	15
46	9.4247	0.2659	4438	2778	9.4624	2900	4806	3024	9.4984	3150	5157	3278	9.5326	0.3409	14
47	9.4250	0.2661	4441	2780	9.4627	2902	4809	3026	9.4986	3152	5160	3281	9.5329	0.3411	13
48	9.4253	0.2663	4444	2782	9.4630	2904	4812	3028	9.4989	3155	5162	3283	9.5331	0.3413	12
49	9.4256	0.2665	4447	2784	9.4633	2906	4815	3030	9.4992	3157	5165	3285	9.5334	0.3415	11
50	9.4260	0.2667	4450	2786	9.4637	2908	4818	3033	9.4995	3159	5168	3287	9.5337	0.3417	10
51	9.4263	0.2669	4454	2788	9.4640	2910	4821	3035	9.4998	3161	5171	3289	9.5340	0.3420	9
52	9.4266	0.2671	4457	2790	9.4643	2912	4824	3037	9.5001	3163	5174	3291	9.5343	0.3422	8
53	9.4269	0.2673	4460	2792	9.4646	2915	4827	3039	9.5004	3165	5177	3294	9.5345	0.3424	7
54	9.4273	0.2675	4463	2794	9.4649	2917	4830	3041	9.5007	3167	5180	3296	9.5348	0.3426	6
55	9.4276	0.2677	4466	2797	9.4652	2919	4833	3043	9.5010	3169	5182	3298	9.5351	0.3428	5
56	9.4279	0.2679	4469	2799	9.4655	2921	4836	3045	9.5013	3172	5185	3300	9.5354	0.3431	4
57	9.4282	0.2681	4472	2801	9.4658	2923	4839	3047	9.5016	3174	5188	3302	9.5357	0.3433	3
58	9.4285	0.2682	4476	2803	9.4661	2925	4842	3049	9.5018	3176	5191	3304	9.5359	0.3435	2
59	9.4289	0.2684	4479	2805	9.4664	2927	4845	3051	9.5021	3178	5194	3307	9.5362	0.3437	1
60	9.4292	0.2686	4482	2807	9.4667	2929	4848	3053	9.5024	3180	5197	3309	9.5365	0.3439	0

LOG.	NAT.	LOG.	NAT.	LOG.	NAT.	LOG.	NAT.	LOG.	NAT.	LOG.	NAT.	LOG.	NAT.	I
317°		**316°**		**315°**		**314°**		**313°**		**312°**		**311°**		

For an explanation of the use of above Tables see p. 5:25.

VERSINES

/	49° LOG.	49° NAT.	50° LOG.	50° NAT.	51° LOG.	51° NAT.	52° LOG.	52° NAT.	53° LOG.	53° NAT.	54° LOG.	54° NAT.	55° LOG.	55° NAT.	
0	9.5365	0.3439	5529	3572	9.5690	3707	5847	3843	9.6001	3982	6151	4122	9.6298	0.4264	60
1	9.5368	0.3442	5532	3574	9.5693	3709	5850	3846	9.6003	3984	6154	4125	9.6301	0.4267	59
2	9.5370	0.3444	5535	3577	9.5695	3711	5852	3848	9.6006	3986	6156	4127	9.6303	0.4269	58
3	9.5373	0.3446	5537	3579	9.5698	3714	5855	3850	9.6008	3989	6159	4129	9.6306	0.4271	57
4	9.5376	0.3448	5540	3581	9.5701	3716	5857	3853	9.6011	3991	6161	4132	9.6308	0.4274	56
5	9.5379	0.3450	5543	3583	9.5703	3718	5860	3855	9.6014	3993	6164	4134	9.6311	0.4276	55
6	9.5381	0.3453	5546	3586	9.5706	3720	5863	3857	9.6016	3996	6166	4136	9.6313	0.4279	54
7	9.5384	0.3455	5548	3588	9.5709	3723	5865	3859	9.6019	3998	6169	4139	9.6315	0.4281	53
8	9.5387	0.3457	5551	3590	9.5711	3725	5868	3862	9.6021	4000	6171	4141	9.6318	0.4283	52
9	9.5390	0.3459	5554	3592	9.5714	3727	5870	3864	9.6024	4003	6174	4143	9.6320	0.4286	51
10	9.5393	0.3461	5556	3594	9.5716	3729	5873	3866	9.6026	4005	6176	4146	9.6323	0.4288	50
11	9.5395	0.3464	5559	3597	9.5719	3732	5876	3869	9.6029	4007	6178	4148	9.6325	0.4290	49
12	9.5398	0.3466	5562	3599	9.5722	3734	5878	3871	9.6031	4010	6181	4150	9.6327	0.4293	48
13	9.5401	0.3468	5564	3601	9.5724	3736	5881	3873	9.6034	4012	6183	4153	9.6330	0.4295	47
14	9.5404	0.3470	5567	3603	9.5727	3738	5883	3876	9.6036	4014	6186	4155	9.6332	0.4298	46
15	9.5406	0.3472	5570	3606	9.5730	3741	5886	3878	9.6039	4017	6188	4158	9.6335	0.4300	45
16	9.5409	0.3475	5572	3608	9.5732	3743	5888	3880	9.6041	4019	6191	4160	9.6337	0.4302	44
17	9.5412	0.3477	5575	3610	9.5735	3745	5891	3882	9.6044	4021	6193	4162	9.6340	0.4305	43
18	9.5415	0.3479	5578	3615	9.5738	3748	5894	3885	9.6046	4024	6196	4165	9.6342	0.4307	42
19	9.5417	0.3481	5581	3612	9.5740	3750	5896	3887	9.6049	4026	6198	4167	9.6344	0.4310	41
20	9.5420	0.3483	5583	3617	9.5743	3752	5899	3889	9.6051	4028	6201	4169	9.6347	0.4312	40
21	9.5423	0.3486	5586	3619	9.5745	3754	5901	3892	9.6054	4031	6203	4172	9.6349	0.4314	39
22	9.5426	0.3488	5589	3621	9.5748	3757	5904	3894	9.6056	4033	6206	4174	9.6352	0.4317	38
23	9.5428	0.3490	5591	3624	9.5751	3759	5906	3896	9.6059	4035	6208	4176	9.6354	0.4319	37
24	9.5431	0.3492	5594	3626	9.5753	3761	5909	3899	9.6061	4038	6210	4179	9.6356	0.4322	36
25	9.5434	0.3494	5597	3628	9.5756	3763	5912	3901	9.6064	4040	6213	4181	9.6359	0.4324	35
26	9.5437	0.3497	5599	3630	9.5759	3766	5914	3903	9.6066	4042	6215	4184	9.6361	0.4326	34
27	9.5439	0.3499	5602	3632	9.5761	3768	5917	3905	9.6069	4045	6218	4186	9.6364	0.4329	33
28	9.5442	0.3501	5605	3635	9.5764	3770	5919	3908	9.6071	4047	6220	4188	9.6366	0.4331	32
29	9.5445	0.3503	5607	3637	9.5766	3773	5922	3910	9.6074	4049	6223	4191	9.6368	0.4334	31
30	9.5448	0.3506	5610	3639	9.5769	3775	5924	3912	9.6076	4052	6225	4193	9.6371	0.4336	30
31	9.5450	0.3508	5613	3641	9.5772	3777	5927	3915	9.6079	4054	6228	4195	9.6373	0.4338	29
32	9.5453	0.3510	5615	3644	9.5774	3779	5930	3917	9.6081	4056	6230	4198	9.6376	0.4341	28
33	9.5456	0.3512	5618	3646	9.5777	3782	5932	3919	9.6084	4059	6233	4200	9.6378	0.4343	27
34	9.5458	0.3514	5621	3648	9.5779	3784	5935	3922	9.6086	4061	6235	4202	9.6380	0.4346	26
35	9.5461	0.3517	5623	3650	9.5782	3786	5937	3924	9.6089	4063	6237	4205	9.6383	0.4348	25
36	9.5464	0.3519	5626	3653	9.5785	3789	5940	3926	9.6091	4066	6240	4207	9.6385	0.4350	24
37	9.5467	0.3521	5629	3655	9.5787	3791	5942	3929	9.6094	4068	6242	4210	9.6388	0.4353	23
38	9.5469	0.3523	5631	3657	9.5790	3793	5945	3931	9.6096	4070	6245	4212	9.6390	0.4355	22
39	9.5472	0.3525	5634	3659	9.5793	3795	5947	3933	9.6099	4073	6247	4214	9.6392	0.4358	21
40	9.5475	0.3528	5637	3662	9.5795	3798	5950	3935	9.6101	4075	6250	4217	9.6395	0.4360	20
41	9.5477	0.3530	5639	3664	9.5798	3800	5953	3938	9.6104	4078	6252	4219	9.6397	0.4362	19
42	9.5480	0.3532	5642	3666	9.5800	3802	5955	3940	9.6106	4080	6255	4221	9.6400	0.4365	18
43	9.5483	0.3534	5645	3668	9.5803	3804	5958	3942	9.6109	4082	6257	4224	9.6402	0.4367	17
44	9.5486	0.3537	5647	3671	9.5806	3807	5960	3945	9.6111	4085	6259	4226	9.6404	0.4370	16
45	9.5489	0.3539	5650	3673	9.5808	3809	5963	3947	9.6114	4087	6262	4229	9.6407	0.4372	15
46	9.5491	0.3541	5653	3675	9.5811	3811	5965	3949	9.6116	4089	6264	4231	9.6409	0.4374	14
47	9.5494	0.3543	5655	3677	9.5813	3814	5968	3952	9.6119	4092	6267	4233	9.6412	0.4377	13
48	9.5497	0.3545	5658	3680	9.5816	3816	5970	3954	9.6121	4094	6269	4236	9.6414	0.4379	12
49	9.5499	0.3548	5661	3682	9.5819	3818	5973	3956	9.6124	4096	6272	4238	9.6416	0.4382	11
50	9.5502	0.3550	5663	3684	9.5821	3820	5975	3959	9.6126	4099	6274	4240	9.6419	0.4384	10
51	9.5505	0.3552	5666	3686	9.5824	3823	5978	3961	9.6129	4101	6277	4243	9.6421	0.4386	9
52	9.5508	0.3554	5669	3689	9.5826	3825	5981	3963	9.6131	4103	6279	4245	9.6423	0.4389	8
53	9.5510	0.3557	5671	3691	9.5829	3827	5983	3966	9.6134	4106	6281	4248	9.6426	0.4391	7
54	9.5513	0.3559	5674	3693	9.5832	3830	5986	3968	9.6136	4108	6284	4250	9.6428	0.4394	6
55	9.5516	0.3561	5677	3696	9.5834	3832	5988	3970	9.6139	4110	6286	4252	9.6431	0.4396	5
56	9.5518	0.3563	5679	3698	9.5837	3834	5991	3973	9.6141	4113	6289	4255	9.6433	0.4398	4
57	9.5521	0.3565	5682	3700	9.5839	3837	5993	3975	9.6144	4115	6291	4257	9.6435	0.4401	3
58	9.5524	0.3568	5685	3702	9.5842	3839	5996	3977	9.6146	4117	6294	4259	9.6438	0.4403	2
59	9.5527	0.3570	5687	3705	9.5845	3841	5998	3980	9.6149	4120	6296	4262	9.6440	0.4406	1
60	9.5529	0.3572	5690	3707	9.5847	3843	6001	3982	9.6151	4122	6298	4264	9.6442	0.4408	0

LOG. NAT.	LOG. NAT.	LOG. NAT.	LOG. NAT.	LOG. NAT.	LOG. NAT.	LOG. NAT. /
310°	309°	308°	307°	306°	305°	304°

For an explanation of the use of above Tables see p. 5:25.

VERSINES

′	56° LOG.	NAT.	57° LOG.	NAT.	58° LOG.	NAT.	59° LOG.	NAT.	60° LOG.	NAT.	61° LOG.	NAT.	62° LOG.	NAT.	′
0	9.6442	0.4408	6584	4554	9.6722	4701	6857	4850	9.6990	5000	7120	5152	9.7247	0.5305	60
1	9.6445	0.4410	6586	4556	9.6724	4703	6859	4852	9.6992	5003	7122	5154	9.7249	0.5308	59
2	9.6447	0.4413	6588	4558	9.6726	4706	6862	4855	9.6994	5005	7124	5157	9.7251	0.5310	58
3	9.6450	0.4415	6591	4561	9.6729	4708	6864	4857	9.6996	5008	7126	5160	9.7253	0.5313	57
4	9.6452	0.4418	6593	4563	9.6731	4711	6866	4860	9.6998	5010	7128	5162	9.7255	0.5316	56
5	9.6454	0.4420	6595	4566	9.6733	4713	6868	4862	9.7001	5013	7130	5165	9.7258	0.5318	55
6	9.6457	0.4423	6598	4568	9.6735	4716	6870	4865	9.7003	5015	7133	5167	9.7260	0.5321	54
7	9.6459	0.4425	6600	4571	9.6738	4718	6873	4867	9.7005	5018	7135	5170	9.7262	0.5323	53
8	9.6461	0.4427	6602	4573	9.6740	4721	6875	4870	9.7007	5020	7137	5172	9.7264	0.5326	52
9	9.6464	0.4430	6604	4576	9.6742	4723	6877	4872	9.7009	5023	7139	5175	9.7266	0.5328	51
10	9.6466	0.4432	6607	4578	9.6744	4725	6879	4875	9.7012	5025	7141	5177	9.7268	0.5331	50
11	9.6469	0.4435	6609	4580	9.6747	4728	6882	4877	9.7014	5028	7143	5180	9.7270	0.5334	49
12	9.6471	0.4437	6611	4583	9.6749	4730	6884	4880	9.7016	5030	7145	5182	9.7272	0.5336	48
13	9.6473	0.4439	6614	4585	9.6751	4733	6886	4882	9.7018	5033	7147	5185	9.7274	0.5339	47
14	9.6476	0.4442	6616	4588	9.6754	4735	6888	4885	9.7020	5035	7150	5188	9.7276	0.5341	46
15	9.6478	0.4444	6618	4590	9.6756	4738	6890	4887	9.7022	5038	7152	5190	9.7279	0.5344	45
16	9.6480	0.4447	6621	4593	9.6758	4740	6893	4890	9.7025	5040	7154	5193	9.7281	0.5346	44
17	9.6483	0.4449	6623	4595	9.6760	4743	6895	4892	9.7027	5043	7156	5195	9.7283	0.5349	43
18	9.6485	0.4452	6625	4598	9.6763	4745	6897	4895	9.7029	5045	7158	5198	9.7285	0.5352	42
19	9.6487	0.4454	6628	4600	9.6765	4748	6899	4897	9.7031	5048	7160	5200	9.7287	0.5354	41
20	9.6490	0.4456	6630	4602	9.6767	4750	6902	4900	9.7033	5050	7162	5203	9.7289	0.5357	40
21	9.6492	0.4459	6632	4605	9.6769	4753	6904	4902	9.7035	5053	7165	5205	9.7291	0.5359	39
22	9.6495	0.4461	6635	4607	9.6772	4755	6906	4905	9.7038	5056	7167	5208	9.7293	0.5362	38
23	9.6497	0.4464	6637	4610	9.6774	4758	6908	4907	9.7040	5058	7169	5211	9.7295	0.5364	37
24	9.6499	0.4466	6639	4612	9.6776	4760	6910	4910	9.7042	5061	7171	5213	9.7297	0.5367	36
25	9.6502	0.4469	6641	4615	9.6778	4763	6913	4912	9.7044	5063	7173	5216	9.7299	0.5370	35
26	9.6504	0.4471	6644	4617	9.6781	4765	6915	4915	9.7046	5066	7175	5218	9.7302	0.5372	34
27	9.6506	0.4473	6646	4620	9.6783	4768	6917	4917	9.7049	5068	7177	5221	9.7304	0.5375	33
28	9.6509	0.4476	6648	4622	9.6785	4770	6919	4920	9.7051	5071	7179	5223	9.7306	0.5377	32
29	9.6511	0.4478	6651	4625	9.6787	4773	6922	4922	9.7053	5073	7182	5226	9.7308	0.5380	31
30	9.6513	0.4481	6653	4627	9.6790	4775	6924	4925	9.7055	5076	7184	5228	9.7310	0.5383	30
31	9.6516	0.4483	6655	4629	9.6792	4777	6926	4927	9.7057	5078	7186	5231	9.7312	0.5385	29
32	9.6518	0.4485	6658	4632	9.6794	4780	6928	4930	9.7059	5081	7188	5234	9.7314	0.5388	28
33	9.6520	0.4488	6660	4634	9.6797	4782	6930	4932	9.7062	5083	7190	5236	9.7316	0.5390	27
34	9.6523	0.4490	6662	4637	9.6799	4785	6933	4935	9.7064	5086	7192	5239	9.7318	0.5393	26
35	9.6525	0.4493	6665	4639	9.6801	4787	6935	4937	9.7066	5088	7194	5241	9.7320	0.5395	25
36	9.6527	0.4495	6667	4642	9.6803	4790	6937	4940	9.7068	5091	7196	5244	9.7322	0.5398	24
37	9.6530	0.4498	6669	4644	9.6806	4792	6939	4942	9.7070	5093	7199	5246	9.7324	0.5401	23
38	9.6532	0.4500	6671	4647	9.6808	4795	6941	4945	9.7072	5096	7201	5249	9.7326	0.5403	22
39	9.6535	0.4502	6674	4649	9.6810	4797	6944	4947	9.7074	5099	7203	5251	9.7329	0.5406	21
40	9.6537	0.4505	6676	4652	9.6812	4800	6946	4950	9.7077	5101	7205	5254	9.7331	0.5408	20
41	9.6539	0.4507	6678	4654	9.6815	4802	6948	4952	9.7079	5104	7207	5257	9.7333	0.5411	19
42	9.6542	0.4510	6681	4656	9.6817	4805	6950	4955	9.7081	5106	7209	5259	9.7335	0.5414	18
43	9.6544	0.4512	6683	4659	9.6819	4807	6952	4957	9.7083	5109	7211	5262	9.7337	0.5416	17
44	9.6546	0.4515	6685	4661	9.6821	4810	6955	4960	9.7085	5111	7213	5264	9.7339	0.5419	16
45	9.6549	0.4517	6687	4664	9.6823	4812	6957	4962	9.7087	5114	7215	5267	9.7341	0.5421	15
46	9.6551	0.4520	6690	4666	9.6826	4815	6959	4965	9.7090	5116	7218	5269	9.7343	0.5424	14
47	9.6553	0.4522	6692	4669	9.6828	4817	6961	4967	9.7092	5119	7220	5272	9.7345	0.5426	13
48	9.6556	0.4524	6694	4671	9.6830	4820	6963	4970	9.7094	5121	7222	5274	9.7347	0.5429	12
49	9.6558	0.4527	6697	4674	9.6832	4822	6966	4972	9.7096	5124	7224	5277	9.7349	0.5432	11
50	9.6560	0.4529	6699	4676	9.6835	4825	6968	4975	9.7098	5126	7226	5280	9.7351	0.5434	10
51	9.6563	0.4532	6701	4679	9.6837	4827	6970	4977	9.7100	5129	7228	5282	9.7353	0.5437	9
52	9.6565	0.4534	6703	4681	9.6839	4830	6972	4980	9.7102	5132	7230	5285	9.7355	0.5439	8
53	9.6567	0.4537	6706	4684	9.6841	4832	6974	4982	9.7105	5134	7232	5287	9.7358	0.5442	7
54	9.6570	0.4539	6708	4686	9.6844	4835	6977	4985	9.7107	5137	7234	5290	9.7360	0.5445	6
55	9.6572	0.4541	6710	4688	9.6846	4837	6979	4987	9.7109	5139	7237	5292	9.7362	0.5447	5
56	9.6574	0.4544	6713	4691	9.6848	4840	6981	4990	9.7111	5142	7239	5295	9.7364	0.5450	4
57	9.6577	0.4546	6715	4693	9.6850	4842	6983	4992	9.7113	5144	7241	5298	9.7366	0.5452	3
58	9.6579	0.4549	6717	4696	9.6853	4845	6985	4995	9.7115	5147	7243	5300	9.7368	0.5455	2
59	9.6581	0.4551	6719	4698	9.6855	4847	6988	4997	9.7118	5149	7245	5303	9.7370	0.5458	1
60	9.6584	0.4554	6722	4701	9.6857	4850	6990	5000	9.7120	5152	7247	5305	9.7372	0.5460	0
	LOG.	NAT.	LOG.	NAT.	LOG.	NAT.	LOG.	NAT.	LOG.	NAT.	LOG.	NAT.	LOG.	NAT.	′
	303°		**302°**		**301°**		**300°**		**299°**		**298°**		**297°**		

For an explanation of the use of above Tables see p. 5:25.

VERSINES

/	63° LOG.	NAT.	64° LOG.	NAT.	65° LOG.	NAT.	66° LOG.	NAT.	67° LOG.	NAT.	68° LOG.	NAT.	69° LOG.	NAT.	
0	9.7372	0.5460	7494	5616	9.7615	5774	7732	5933	9.7848	6093	7962	6254	9.8073	0.6416	60
4	9.7380	0.5470	7503	5627	9.7623	5784	7740	5943	9.7856	6103	7969	6265	9.8080	0.6427	56
8	9.7388	0.5481	7511	5637	9.7630	5795	7748	5954	9.7863	6114	7976	6276	9.8088	0.6438	52
12	9.7397	0.5491	7519	5648	9.7638	5805	7756	5965	9.7871	6125	7984	6286	9.8095	0.6449	48
16	9.7405	0.5502	7527	5658	9.7646	5816	7764	5975	9.7879	6136	7991	6297	9.8102	0.6460	44
20	9.7413	0.5512	7535	5669	9.7654	5827	7771	5986	9.7886	6146	7999	6308	9.8110	0.6471	40
24	9.7421	0.5522	7543	5679	9.7662	5837	7779	5997	9.7894	6157	8006	6319	9.8117	0.6482	36
28	9.7428	0.5533	7551	5690	9.7670	5848	7787	6007	9.7901	6168	8014	6330	9.8124	0.6492	32
32	9.7438	0.5543	7559	5700	9.7678	5858	7794	6018	9.7909	6179	8021	6340	9.8131	0.6503	28
36	9.7446	0.5554	7567	5711	9.7686	5869	7802	6029	9.7916	6189	8029	6351	9.8139	0.6514	24
40	9.7454	0.5564	7575	5721	9.7693	5880	7810	6039	9.7924	6200	8036	6362	9.8146	0.6525	20
44	9.7462	0.5575	7583	5732	9.7701	5890	7817	6050	9.7931	6211	8043	6373	9.8153	0.6536	16
48	9.7470	0.5585	7591	5742	9.7709	5901	7825	6061	9.7939	6222	8051	6384	9.8160	0.6547	12
52	9.7478	0.5595	7599	5753	9.7717	5911	7833	6071	9.7947	6232	8058	6395	9.8168	0.6558	8
56	9.7486	0.5606	7607	5763	9.7725	5922	7840	6082	9.7954	6243	8066	6405	9.8175	0.6569	4
60	9.7494	0.5616	7615	5774	9.7732	5933	7848	6093	9.7962	6254	8073	6416	9.8182	0.6580	0

296°　295°　294°　293°　292°　291°　290°　/

/	70° LOG.	NAT.	71° LOG.	NAT.	72° LOG.	NAT.	73° LOG.	NAT.	74° LOG.	NAT.	75° LOG.	NAT.	76° LOG.	NAT.	
0	9.8182	0.6580	8289	6744	9.8395	6910	8498	7076	9.8600	7244	8699	7412	9.8797	0.7581	60
4	9.8189	0.6591	8296	6755	9.8402	6921	8505	7087	9.8606	7255	8706	7423	9.8804	0.7592	56
8	9.8197	0.6602	8304	6766	9.8409	6932	8512	7099	9.8613	7266	8712	7434	9.8810	0.7603	52
12	9.8204	0.6613	8311	6777	9.8416	6943	8519	7110	9.8620	7277	8719	7446	9.8817	0.7615	48
16	9.8211	0.6624	8318	6788	9.8422	6954	8525	7121	9.8626	7288	8726	7457	9.8823	0.7625	44
20	9.8218	0.6635	8325	6799	9.8429	6965	8532	7132	9.8633	7300	8732	7468	9.8829	0.7637	40
24	9.8225	0.6645	8332	6810	9.8436	6976	8539	7143	9.8640	7311	8739	7479	9.8836	0.7649	36
28	9.8232	0.6656	8339	6821	9.8443	6987	8546	7154	9.8646	7322	8745	7491	9.8842	0.7660	32
32	9.8240	0.6667	8346	6832	9.8450	6998	8552	7165	9.8653	7333	8752	7502	9.8849	0.7671	28
36	9.8247	0.6678	8353	6844	9.8457	7010	8559	7177	9.8660	7344	8758	7513	9.8855	0.7683	24
40	9.8254	0.6689	8360	6855	9.8464	7021	8566	7188	9.8666	7356	8765	7524	9.8861	0.7694	20
44	9.8261	0.6700	8367	6866	9.8471	7032	8573	7199	9.8673	7367	8771	7536	9.8868	0.7705	16
48	9.8268	0.6711	8374	6877	9.8478	7043	8579	7210	9.8679	7378	8778	7547	9.8874	0.7716	12
52	9.8275	0.6722	8381	6888	9.8484	7054	8586	7221	9.8686	7389	8784	7558	9.8881	0.7728	8
56	9.8282	0.6733	8388	6899	9.8491	7065	8593	7232	9.8693	7401	8791	7569	9.8887	0.7739	4
60	9.8289	0.6744	8395	6910	9.8498	7076	8600	7244	9.8699	7412	8797	7581	9.8893	0.7750	0

289°　288°　287°　286°　285°　284°　283°　/

/	77° LOG.	NAT.	78° LOG.	NAT.	79° LOG.	NAT.	80° LOG.	NAT.	81° LOG.	NAT.	82° LOG.	NAT.	83° LOG.	NAT.	
0	9.8893	0.7750	8988	7921	9.9081	8092	9172	8264	9.9261	8436	9349	8608	9.9436	0.8781	60
4	9.8900	0.7762	8994	7932	9.9087	8103	9178	8275	9.9267	8447	9355	8620	9.9441	0.8793	56
8	9.8906	0.7773	9000	7944	9.9093	8115	9184	8286	9.9273	8459	9361	8631	9.9447	0.8804	52
12	9.8912	0.7785	9006	7955	9.9099	8126	9190	8298	9.9279	8470	9367	8643	9.9453	0.8816	48
16	9.8919	0.7796	9013	7966	9.9105	8138	9196	8309	9.9285	8482	9372	8654	9.9458	0.8828	44
20	9.8925	0.7807	9019	7978	9.9111	8149	9202	8321	9.9291	8493	9378	8666	9.9464	0.8839	40
24	9.8931	0.7819	9025	7989	9.9117	8160	9208	8332	9.9297	8505	9384	8677	9.9470	0.8851	36
28	9.8938	0.7830	9031	8001	9.9123	8172	9214	8344	9.9302	8516	9390	8689	9.9475	0.8862	32
32	9.8944	0.7841	9037	8012	9.9129	8183	9220	8355	9.9308	8528	9395	8701	9.9481	0.8874	28
36	9.8950	0.7853	9044	8023	9.9135	8195	9226	8367	9.9314	8539	9401	8712	9.9487	0.8885	24
40	9.8956	0.7864	9050	8035	9.9141	8206	9232	8378	9.9320	8551	9407	8724	9.9492	0.8897	20
44	9.8963	0.7875	9056	8046	9.9148	8218	9237	8390	9.9326	8562	9413	8735	9.9498	0.8908	16
48	9.8969	0.7887	9062	8058	9.9154	8229	9243	8401	9.9332	8574	9418	8747	9.9504	0.8920	12
52	9.8975	0.7898	9068	8069	9.9160	8241	9249	8413	9.9338	8585	9424	8758	9.9509	0.8932	8
56	9.8981	0.7910	9074	8080	9.9166	8252	9255	8424	9.9343	8597	9430	8770	9.9515	0.8943	4
60	9.8988	0.7921	9081	8092	9.9172	8264	9261	8436	9.9349	8608	9436	8781	9.9521	0.8955	0

| | LOG. | NAT. | LOG. | NAT. | LOG. | NAT. | LOG. | NAT. | LOG. | NAT. | LOG. | NAT. | LOG. | NAT. | |

282°　281°　280°　279°　278°　277°　276°

For an explanation of the use of above Tables see p. 5:25.

VERSINES

/	84° LOG.	NAT.	85° LOG.	NAT.	86° LOG.	NAT.	87° LOG.	NAT.	88° LOG.	NAT.	89° LOG.	NAT.	90° LOG.	NAT.	
0	9.9521	0.8955	9604	9128	9.9686	9302	9767	9477	9.9846	9651	9924	9825	0.0000	1.0000	60
4	9.9526	0.8966	9609	9140	9.9691	9314	9772	9488	9.9851	9663	9929	9837	0.0005	1.0012	56
8	9.9532	0.8978	9615	9152	9.9697	9326	9777	9500	9.9856	9674	9934	9849	0.0010	1.0023	52
12	9.9537	0.8989	9620	9163	9.9702	9337	9782	9512	9.9861	9686	9939	9860	0.0015	1.0035	48
16	9.9543	0.9001	9626	9175	9.9708	9349	9788	9523	9.9867	9698	9944	9872	0.0020	1.0047	44
20	9.9548	0.9013	9631	9186	9.9713	9360	9793	9535	9.9872	9709	9949	9884	0.0025	1.0058	40
24	9.9554	0.9024	9637	9198	9.9718	9372	9798	9546	9.9877	9721	9954	9895	0.0030	1.0070	36
28	9.9560	0.9036	9642	9210	9.9724	9384	9804	9558	9.9882	9732	9959	9907	0.0035	1.0081	32
32	9.9565	0.9047	9648	9221	9.9729	9395	9809	9570	9.9887	9744	9964	9919	0.0040	1.0093	28
36	9.9571	0.9059	9653	9233	9.9734	9407	9814	9581	9.9893	9756	9970	9930	0.0045	1.0105	24
40	9.9576	0.9070	9659	9244	9.9740	9419	9819	9593	9.9898	9767	9975	9942	0.0050	1.0116	20
44	9.9582	0.9082	9664	9256	9.9745	9430	9825	9604	9.9903	9779	9980	9953	0.0055	1.0128	16
48	9.9587	0.9094	9670	9268	9.9751	9442	9830	9616	9.9908	9791	9985	9965	0.0060	1.0140	12
52	9.9593	0.9105	9675	9279	9.9756	9453	9835	9628	9.9913	9802	9990	9977	0.0065	1.0151	8
56	9.9598	0.9117	9681	9291	9.9761	9465	9840	9639	9.9918	9814	9995	9988	0.0070	1.0163	4
60	9.9604	0.9128	9686	9302	9.9767	9477	9846	9651	9.9924	9825	0000	0000	0.0075	1.0175	0

	275°	274°	273°	272°	271°	270°	269°	/

/	91°	92°	93°	94°	95°	96°	97°	

/	91° LOG.	NAT.	92° LOG.	NAT.	93° LOG.	NAT.	94° LOG.	NAT.	95° LOG.	NAT.	96° LOG.	NAT.	97° LOG.	NAT.	
0	0.0075	1.0175	0149	0349	0.0222	0523	0293	0698	0.0363	0872	0432	1045	0.0499	1.1219	60
4	0.0080	1.0186	0154	0361	0.0226	0535	0298	0709	0.0368	0883	0436	1057	0.0504	1.1230	56
8	0.0085	1.0198	0159	0372	0.0231	0547	0302	0721	0.0372	0895	0441	1068	0.0508	1.1242	52
12	0.0090	1.0209	0164	0384	0.0236	0558	0307	0732	0.0377	0906	0445	1080	0.0513	1.1253	48
16	0.0095	1.0221	0168	0396	0.0241	0570	0312	0744	0.0381	0918	0450	1092	0.0517	1.1265	44
20	0.0100	1.0233	0173	0407	0.0245	0581	0316	0756	0.0386	0929	0454	1103	0.0522	1.1276	40
24	0.0105	1.0244	0178	0419	0.0250	0593	0321	0767	0.0391	0941	0459	1115	0.0526	1.1288	36
28	0.0110	1.0256	0183	0430	0.0255	0605	0326	0779	0.0395	0953	0463	1126	0.0531	1.1299	32
32	0.0115	1.0268	0188	0442	0.0260	0616	0330	0790	0.0400	0964	0468	1138	0.0535	1.1311	28
36	0.0120	1.0279	0193	0454	0.0264	0628	0335	0802	0.0404	0976	0473	1149	0.0539	1.1323	24
40	0.0125	1.0291	0197	0465	0.0269	0640	0340	0814	0.0409	0987	0477	1161	0.0544	1.1334	20
44	0.0129	1.0302	0202	0477	0.0274	0651	0344	0825	0.0414	0999	0481	1172	0.0548	1.1346	16
48	0.0134	1.0314	0207	0488	0.0279	0663	0349	0837	0.0418	1011	0486	1184	0.0553	1.1357	12
52	0.0139	1.0326	0212	0500	0.0283	0674	0354	0848	0.0423	1022	0490	1196	0.0557	1.1369	8
56	0.0144	1.0337	0217	0512	0.0288	0686	0358	0860	0.0427	1034	0495	1207	0.0562	1.1380	4
60	0.0149	1.0349	0222	0523	0.0293	0698	0363	0872	0.0432	1045	0499	1219	0.0566	1.1392	0

	268°	267°	266°	265°	264°	263°	262°	/

/	98°	99°	100°	101°	102°	103°	104°	

/	98° LOG.	NAT.	99° LOG.	NAT.	100° LOG.	NAT.	101° LOG.	NAT.	102° LOG.	NAT.	103° LOG.	NAT.	104° LOG.	NAT.	
0	0.0566	1.1392	0631	1564	0.0695	1736	0758	1908	0.0820	2079	0881	2250	0.0941	1.2419	60
4	0.0570	1.1403	0636	1576	0.0700	1748	0763	1920	0.0824	2090	0885	2261	0.0945	1.2431	56
8	0.0575	1.1415	0640	1587	0.0704	1759	0767	1931	0.0829	2102	0889	2272	0.0949	1.2442	52
12	0.0579	1.1426	0644	1599	0.0708	1771	0771	1942	0.0833	2113	0893	2284	0.0953	1.2453	48
16	0.0583	1.1438	0648	1610	0.0712	1782	0775	1954	0.0837	2125	0897	2295	0.0957	1.2464	44
20	0.0588	1.1449	0653	1622	0.0717	1794	0779	1965	0.0841	2136	0901	2306	0.0961	1.2476	40
24	0.0592	1.1461	0657	1633	0.0721	1805	0783	1977	0.0845	2147	0905	2317	0.0965	1.2487	36
28	0.0597	1.1472	0661	1645	0.0725	1817	0787	1988	0.0849	2159	0909	2329	0.0968	1.2498	32
32	0.0601	1.1484	0666	1656	0.0729	1828	0792	1999	0.0853	2170	0913	2340	0.0972	1.2509	28
36	0.0605	1.1495	0670	1668	0.0733	1840	0796	2011	0.0857	2181	0917	2351	0.0976	1.2521	24
40	0.0610	1.1507	0674	1679	0.0738	1851	0800	2022	0.0861	2193	0921	2363	0.0980	1.2532	20
44	0.0614	1.1518	0678	1691	0.0742	1862	0804	2034	0.0865	2204	0925	2374	0.0984	1.2543	16
48	0.0618	1.1530	0683	1702	0.0746	1874	0808	2045	0.0869	2215	0929	2385	0.0988	1.2554	12
52	0.0623	1.1541	0687	1714	0.0750	1885	0812	2056	0.0873	2227	0933	2397	0.0992	1.2566	8
56	0.0627	1.1553	0691	1725	0.0754	1897	0816	2068	0.0877	2238	0937	2408	0.0996	1.2577	4
60	0.0631	1.1564	0695	1736	0.0758	1908	0820	2079	0.0881	2250	0941	2419	0.1000	1.2588	0

LOG.	NAT.	LOG.	NAT.	LOG.	NAT.	LOG.	NAT.	LOG.	NAT.	LOG.	NAT.	LOG.	NAT.	/
261°		260°		259°		258°		257°		256°		255°		

For an explanation of the use of above Tables see p. 5:25.

VERSINES

′	105° LOG.	NAT.	106° LOG.	NAT.	107° LOG.	NAT.	108° LOG.	NAT.	109° LOG.	NAT.	110° LOG.	NAT.	111° LOG.	NAT.	
0	0.1000	1.2588	1057	2756	0.1114	2924	1169	3090	0.1224	3256	1278	3420	0.1330	1.3584	60
4	0.1004	1.2599	1061	2768	0.1118	2935	1173	3101	0.1228	3267	1281	3431	0.1334	1.3595	56
8	0.1007	1.2611	1065	2779	0.1121	2946	1177	3112	0.1231	3278	1285	3442	0.1337	1.3605	52
12	0.1011	1.2622	1069	2790	0.1125	2957	1180	3123	0.1235	3289	1288	3453	0.1341	1.3616	48
16	0.1015	1.2633	1072	2801	0.1129	2968	1184	3134	0.1238	3300	1292	3464	0.1344	1.3627	44
20	0.1019	1.2644	1076	2812	0.1133	2979	1188	3145	0.1242	3311	1295	3475	0.1347	1.3638	40
24	0.1023	1.2656	1080	2823	0.1136	2990	1191	3156	0.1246	3322	1299	3486	0.1351	1.3649	36
28	0.1027	1.2667	1084	2835	0.1140	3002	1195	3168	0.1249	3333	1302	3497	0.1354	1.3660	32
32	0.1031	1.2678	1088	2846	0.1144	3013	1199	3179	0.1253	3344	1306	3508	0.1358	1.3670	28
36	0.1034	1.2689	1091	2857	0.1147	3024	1202	3190	0.1256	3355	1309	3518	0.1361	1.3681	24
40	0.1038	1.2700	1095	2868	0.1151	3035	1206	3201	0.1260	3365	1313	3529	0.1365	1.3692	20
44	0.1042	1.2712	1099	2879	0.1155	3046	1210	3212	0.1263	3376	1316	3540	0.1368	1.3703	16
48	0.1046	1.2723	1103	2890	0.1158	3057	1213	3223	0.1267	3387	1320	3551	0.1372	1.3714	12
52	0.1050	1.2734	1106	2901	0.1162	3068	1217	3234	0.1271	3398	1323	3562	0.1375	1.3724	8
56	0.1053	1.2745	1110	2913	0.1166	3079	1220	3245	0.1274	3409	1327	3573	0.1378	1.3735	4
60	0.1057	1.2756	1114	2924	0.1169	3090	1224	3256	0.1278	3420	1330	3584	0.1382	1.3746	0

254°   253°   252°   251°   250°   249°   248°   ′

′	112° LOG.	NAT.	113° LOG.	NAT.	114° LOG.	NAT.	115° LOG.	NAT.	116° LOG.	NAT.	117° LOG.	NAT.	118° LOG.	NAT.	
0	0.1382	1.3746	1432	3907	0.1482	4067	1531	4226	0.1579	4384	1626	4540	0.1672	1.4695	60
4	0.1385	1.3757	1436	3918	0.1485	4078	1534	4237	0.1582	4394	1629	4550	0.1675	1.4705	56
8	0.1389	1.3768	1439	3929	0.1489	4089	1537	4247	0.1585	4405	1632	4561	0.1678	1.4715	52
12	0.1392	1.3778	1442	3939	0.1492	4099	1541	4258	0.1588	4415	1635	4571	0.1681	1.4726	48
16	0.1395	1.3789	1446	3950	0.1495	4110	1544	4268	0.1591	4425	1638	4581	0.1684	1.4736	44
20	0.1399	1.3800	1449	3961	0.1498	4120	1547	4279	0.1594	4436	1641	4592	0.1687	1.4746	40
24	0.1402	1.3811	1452	3971	0.1502	4131	1550	4289	0.1598	4446	1644	4602	0.1690	1.4756	36
28	0.1406	1.3821	1456	3982	0.1505	4142	1553	4300	0.1601	4457	1647	4612	0.1693	1.4766	32
32	0.1409	1.3832	1459	3993	0.1508	4152	1557	4310	0.1604	4467	1650	4623	0.1696	1.4777	28
36	0.1412	1.3843	1462	4003	0.1511	4163	1560	4321	0.1607	4478	1653	4633	0.1699	1.4787	24
40	0.1416	1.3854	1466	4014	0.1515	4173	1563	4331	0.1610	4488	1656	4643	0.1702	1.4797	20
44	0.1419	1.3864	1469	4025	0.1518	4184	1566	4342	0.1613	4498	1659	4654	0.1705	1.4807	16
48	0.1422	1.3875	1472	4035	0.1521	4195	1569	4352	0.1616	4509	1662	4664	0.1708	1.4818	12
52	0.1426	1.3886	1476	4046	0.1524	4205	1572	4363	0.1619	4519	1666	4674	0.1711	1.4828	8
56	0.1429	1.3897	1479	4057	0.1528	4216	1576	4373	0.1623	4530	1669	4684	0.1714	1.4838	4
60	0.1432	1.3907	1482	4067	0.1531	4226	1579	4384	0.1626	4540	1672	4694	0.1717	1.4848	0

247°   246°   245°   244°   243°   242°   241°   ′

′	119° LOG.	NAT.	120° LOG.	NAT.	121° LOG.	NAT.	122° LOG.	NAT.	123° LOG.	NAT.	124° LOG.	NAT.	125° LOG.	NAT.	
0	0.1717	1.4848	1761	5000	0.1804	5150	1847	5299	0.1888	5446	1929	5592	0.1969	1.5736	60
4	0.1720	1.4858	1764	5010	0.1807	5160	1849	5309	0.1891	5456	1932	5602	0.1972	1.5745	56
8	0.1723	1.4868	1767	5020	0.1810	5170	1852	5319	0.1894	5466	1934	5611	0.1974	1.5755	52
12	0.1726	1.4879	1770	5030	0.1813	5180	1855	5329	0.1896	5476	1937	5621	0.1977	1.5764	48
16	0.1729	1.4889	1773	5040	0.1816	5190	1858	5339	0.1899	5485	1940	5630	0.1979	1.5774	44
20	0.1732	1.4899	1775	5050	0.1818	5200	1861	5348	0.1902	5495	1942	5640	0.1982	1.5783	40
24	0.1734	1.4909	1778	5060	0.1821	5210	1863	5358	0.1905	5505	1945	5650	0.1985	1.5793	36
28	0.1737	1.4919	1781	5070	0.1824	5220	1866	5368	0.1907	5515	1948	5659	0.1987	1.5802	32
32	0.1740	1.4929	1784	5080	0.1827	5230	1869	5378	0.1910	5524	1950	5669	0.1990	1.5812	28
36	0.1743	1.4939	1787	5090	0.1830	5240	1872	5388	0.1913	5534	1953	5678	0.1992	1.5821	24
40	0.1746	1.4950	1790	5100	0.1833	5250	1875	5398	0.1916	5544	1956	5688	0.1995	1.5831	20
44	0.1749	1.4960	1793	5110	0.1835	5260	1877	5407	0.1918	5553	1958	5698	0.1998	1.5840	16
48	0.1752	1.4970	1796	5120	0.1838	5270	1880	5417	0.1921	5563	1961	5707	0.2000	1.5850	12
52	0.1755	1.4980	1799	5130	0.1841	5279	1883	5427	0.1924	5573	1964	5717	0.2003	1.5859	8
56	0.1758	1.4990	1801	5140	0.1844	5289	1886	5437	0.1926	5582	1966	5726	0.2005	1.5868	4
60	0.1761	1.5000	1804	5150	0.1847	5299	1888	5446	0.1929	5592	1969	5736	0.2008	1.5878	0

LOG. NAT.   LOG. NAT.   LOG. NAT.   LOG. NAT.   LOG. NAT.   LOG. NAT.   LOG. NAT.   ′

240°   239°   238°   237°   236°   235°   234°

For an explanation of the use of above Tables see p. 5:25.

VERSINES

/	126° LOG.	NAT.	127° LOG.	NAT.	128° LOG.	NAT.	129° LOG.	NAT.	130° LOG.	NAT.	131° LOG.	NAT.	132° LOG.	NAT.	
0	0.2008	1.5878	2046	6018	0.2084	6157	2120	6293	0.2156	6428	2191	6561	0.2225	1.6691	60
6	0.2012	1.5892	2050	6032	0.2087	6170	2124	6307	0.2159	6441	2194	6574	0.2228	1.6704	54
12	0.2016	1.5906	2054	6046	0.2091	6184	2127	6320	0.2163	6455	2198	6587	0.2232	1.6717	48
18	0.2019	1.5920	2057	6060	0.2095	6198	2131	6334	0.2166	6468	2201	6600	0.2235	1.6730	42
24	0.2023	1.5934	2061	6074	0.2098	6211	1234	6347	0.2170	6481	2205	6613	0.2238	1.6743	36
30	0.2027	1.5948	2065	6088	0.2102	6225	2138	6361	0.2173	6494	2208	6626	0.2242	1.6756	30
36	0.2031	1.5962	2069	6101	0.2106	6239	2142	6374	0.2177	6508	2211	6639	0.2245	1.6769	24
42	0.2035	1.5976	2072	6115	0.2109	6252	2145	6388	0.2180	6521	2215	6652	0.2248	1.6782	18
48	0.2039	1.5990	2076	6129	0.2113	6266	2149	6401	0.2184	6534	2218	6665	0.2252	1.6794	12
54	0.2042	1.6004	2080	6143	0.2116	6280	2152	6415	0.2187	6547	2222	6678	0.2255	1.6807	6
60	0.2046	1.6018	2084	6157	0.2120	6293	2156	6428	0.2191	6561	2225	6691	0.2258	1.6820	0

233°   232°   231°   230°   229°   228°   227° /

/	133° LOG.	NAT.	134° LOG.	NAT.	135° LOG.	NAT.	136° LOG.	NAT.	137° LOG.	NAT.	138° LOG.	NAT.	139° LOG.	NAT.	
0	0.2258	1.6820	2291	6947	0.2323	7071	2354	7193	0.2384	7314	2413	7431	0.2242	1.7547	60
6	0.2262	1.6833	2294	6959	0.2326	7083	2357	7206	0.2387	7325	2416	7443	0.2445	1.7559	54
12	0.2265	1.6845	2297	6972	0.2329	7096	2360	7218	0.2390	7337	2419	7455	0.2448	1.7570	48
18	0.2268	1.6858	2300	6984	0.2332	7108	2363	7230	0.2393	7349	2422	7466	0.2451	1.7581	42
24	0.2271	1.6871	2304	6997	0.2335	7120	2366	7242	0.2396	7361	2425	7478	0.2453	1.7593	36
30	0.2275	1.6884	2307	7009	0.2338	7133	2369	7254	0.2399	7373	2428	7490	0.2456	1.7604	30
36	0.2278	1.6896	2310	7022	0.2341	7145	2372	7266	0.2402	7385	2431	7501	0.2459	1.7615	24
42	0.2281	1.6909	2313	7034	0.2344	7157	2375	7278	0.2405	7396	2434	7513	0.2462	1.7627	18
48	0.2284	1.6921	2316	7046	0.2347	7169	2378	7290	0.2408	7408	2436	7524	0.2464	1.7638	12
54	0.2288	1.6934	2319	7059	0.2351	7181	2381	7302	0.2410	7420	2439	7536	0.2467	1.7649	6
60	0.2291	1.6947	2323	7071	0.2354	7193	2384	7314	0.2413	7431	2442	7547	0.2470	1.7660	0

226°   225°   224°   223°   222°   221°   220° /

/	140° LOG.	NAT.	141° LOG.	NAT.	142° LOG.	NAT.	143° LOG.	NAT.	144° LOG.	NAT.	145° LOG.	NAT.	146° LOG.	NAT.	
0	0.2470	1.7660	2497	7771	0.2524	7880	2549	7986	0.2574	8090	2599	8192	0.2622	1.8290	60
6	0.2473	1.7672	2500	7782	0.2526	7891	2552	7997	0.2577	8100	2601	8202	0.2625	1.8300	54
12	0.2476	1.7683	2503	7793	0.2529	7902	2554	8007	0.2579	8111	2603	8211	0.2627	1.8310	48
18	0.2478	1.7694	2505	7804	0.2531	7912	2557	8018	0.2582	8121	2606	8221	0.2629	1.8320	42
24	0.2481	1.7705	2508	7815	0.2534	7923	2560	8028	0.2584	8131	2608	8231	0.2631	1.8329	36
30	0.2484	1.7716	2511	7826	0.2537	7934	2562	8039	0.2587	8141	2611	8241	0.2634	1.8339	30
36	0.2486	1.7727	2513	7837	0.2539	7944	2565	8049	0.2589	8151	2613	8251	0.2636	1.8348	24
42	0.2489	1.7738	2516	7848	0.2542	7955	2567	8059	0.2591	8161	2615	8261	0.2638	1.8358	18
48	0.2492	1.7749	2518	7859	0.2544	7965	2569	8070	0.2594	8171	2618	8271	0.2641	1.8368	12
54	0.2495	1.7760	2521	7869	0.2547	7976	2572	8080	0.2596	8182	2620	8281	0.2643	1.8377	6
60	0.2497	1.7771	2524	7880	0.2549	7986	2574	8090	0.2599	8192	2622	8290	0.2645	1.8387	0

219°   218°   217°   216°   215°   214°   213° /

/	147° LOG.	NAT.	148° LOG.	NAT.	149° LOG.	NAT.	150° LOG.	NAT.	151° LOG.	NAT.	152° LOG.	NAT.	153° LOG.	NAT.	
0	0.2645	1.8387	2667	8480	0.2689	8572	2709	8660	0.2729	8746	2748	8829	0.2767	1.8910	60
6	0.2647	1.8396	2669	8490	0.2691	8581	2711	8669	0.2731	8755	2750	8838	0.2769	1.8918	54
12	0.2650	1.8406	2671	8499	0.2693	8590	2713	8678	0.2733	8763	2752	8846	0.2771	1.8926	48
18	0.2652	1.8415	2674	8508	0.2695	8599	2715	8686	0.2735	8771	2754	8854	0.2772	1.8934	42
24	0.2654	1.8425	2676	8517	0.2697	8607	2717	8695	0.2737	8780	2756	8862	0.2774	1.8942	36
30	0.2656	1.8434	2678	8526	0.2699	8616	2719	8704	0.2739	8788	2758	8870	0.2776	1.8949	30
36	0.2658	1.8443	2680	8536	0.2701	8625	2721	8712	0.2741	8796	2760	8878	0.2778	1.8957	24
42	0.2661	1.8453	2682	8545	0.2703	8634	2723	8721	0.2743	8805	2761	8886	0.2779	1.8965	18
48	0.2663	1.8462	2684	8554	0.2705	8643	2725	8729	0.2745	8813	2763	8894	0.2781	1.8973	12
54	0.2665	1.8471	2686	8563	0.2707	8652	2727	8738	0.2746	8821	2765	8902	0.2783	1.8980	6
60	0.2667	1.8480	2689	8572	0.2709	8660	2729	8746	0.2748	8829	2767	8910	0.2785	1.8988	0

LOG. NAT.	LOG. NAT.	LOG. NAT.	LOG. NAT.	LOG. NAT.	LOG. NAT.	LOG. NAT. /
212°	211°	210°	209°	208°	207°	206°

For an explanation of the use of above Tables see p. 5:25.

VERSINES

/	154° LOG.	NAT.	155° LOG.	NAT.	156° LOG.	NAT.	157° LOG.	NAT.	158° LOG.	NAT.	159° LOG.	NAT.	160° LOG.	NAT.	
0	0.2785	1.8988	2802	9063	0.2818	9135	2834	9205	0.2849	9272	2864	9336	0.2877	1.9397	60
6	0.2787	1.8996	2804	9070	0.2820	9143	2836	9212	0.2851	9278	2865	9342	0.2879	1.9403	54
12	0.2788	1.9003	2805	9078	0.2822	9150	2837	9219	0.2852	9285	2866	9348	0.2880	1.9409	48
18	0.2790	1.9011	2807	9085	0.2823	9157	2839	9225	0.2854	9291	2868	9354	0.2881	1.9415	42
24	0.2792	1.9018	2809	9092	0.2825	9164	2840	9232	0.2855	9298	2869	9361	0.2883	1.9421	36
30	0.2793	1.9026	2810	9100	0.2826	9171	2842	9239	0.2857	9307	2871	9367	0.2884	1.9426	30
36	0.2795	1.9033	2812	9107	0.2828	9178	2843	9245	0.2858	9311	2872	9373	0.2885	1.9432	24
42	0.2797	1.9041	2814	9114	0.2829	9184	2845	9252	0.2859	9317	2873	9379	0.2887	1.9438	18
48	0.2799	1.9048	2815	9121	0.2831	9191	2846	9259	0.2861	9323	2875	9385	0.2888	1.9444	12
54	0.2800	1.9056	2817	9128	0.2833	9198	2848	9265	0.2862	9330	2876	9391	0.2889	1.9449	6
60	0.2802	1.9063	2818	9135	0.2834	9205	2849	9272	0.2864	9336	2877	9397	0.2890	1.9455	0

205°   204°   203°   202°   201°   200°   199°   /

/	161°	NAT.	162°	NAT.	163°	NAT.	164°	NAT.	165°	NAT.	166°	NAT.	167°	NAT.	
0	0.2890	1.9455	2903	9511	0.2914	9563	2925	9613	0.2936	9659	2945	9703	0.2954	1.9744	60
6	0.2892	1.9461	2904	9516	0.2915	9568	2926	9617	0.2937	9664	2946	9707	0.2955	1.9748	54
12	0.2893	1.9466	2905	9521	0.2917	9573	2927	9622	0.2938	9668	2947	9711	0.2956	1.9751	48
18	0.2894	1.9472	2906	9527	0.2918	9578	2929	9627	0.2939	9673	2948	9715	0.2957	1.9755	42
24	0.2895	1.9478	2907	9532	0.2919	9583	2930	9632	0.2940	9677	2949	9720	0.2958	1.9759	36
30	0.2897	1.9483	2909	9537	0.2920	9588	2931	9636	0.2941	9681	2950	9724	0.2959	1.9763	30
36	0.2898	1.9489	2910	9542	0.2921	9593	2932	9641	0.2942	9686	2951	9728	0.2959	1.9767	24
42	0.2899	1.9494	2911	9548	0.2922	9598	2933	9646	0.2942	9690	2952	9732	0.2960	1.9770	18
48	0.2900	1.9500	2912	9553	0.2923	9603	2934	9650	0.2943	9694	2953	9736	0.2961	1.9774	12
54	0.2901	1.9505	2913	9558	0.2924	9608	2935	9655	0.2944	9699	2953	9740	0.2962	1.9778	6
60	0.2903	1.9511	2914	9563	0.2925	9613	2936	9659	0.2945	9703	2954	9744	0.2963	1.9781	0

198°   197°   196°   195°   194°   193°   192°

/	168°	NAT.	169°	NAT.	170°	NAT.	171°	NAT.	172°	NAT.	173°	NAT.	174°	NAT.	
0	0.2963	1.9781	2970	9816	0.2977	9848	2983	9877	0.2989	9903	2994	9925	0.2998	1.9945	60
6	0.2963	1.9785	2971	9820	0.2978	9851	2984	9880	0.2990	9905	2995	9928	0.2999	1.9947	54
12	0.2964	1.9789	2972	9823	0.2979	9854	2985	9882	0.2990	9907	2995	9930	0.2999	1.9949	48
18	0.2965	1.9792	2972	9826	0.2979	9857	2985	9885	0.2991	9910	2995	9932	0.3000	1.9951	42
24	0.2966	1.9796	2973	9829	0.2980	9860	2986	9888	0.2991	9912	2996	9934	0.3000	1.9952	36
30	0.2966	1.9799	2974	9833	0.2980	9863	2986	9890	0.2992	9914	2996	9936	0.3000	1.9954	30
36	0.2967	1.9803	2974	9836	0.2981	9866	2987	9893	0.2992	9917	2997	9938	0.3001	1.9956	24
42	0.2968	1.9806	2975	9839	0.2982	9869	2987	9895	0.2993	9919	2997	9940	0.3001	1.9957	18
48	0.2969	1.9810	2976	9842	0.2982	9871	2988	9898	0.2993	9921	2998	9942	0.3001	1.9959	12
54	0.2969	1.9813	2977	9845	0.2983	9874	2989	9900	0.2994	9923	2998	9943	0.3002	1.9960	6
60	0.2970	1.9816	2977	9848	0.2983	9877	2989	9903	0.2994	9925	2998	9945	0.3002	1.9962	0

191°   190°   189°   188°   187°   186°   185°

/	175°	NAT.	176°	NAT.	177°	NAT.	178°	NAT.	179°	NAT.	
0	0.3002	1.9962	3005	9976	0.3007	9986	3009	9994	0.3010	1.9998	60
6	0.3002	1.9963	3005	9977	0.3008	9987	3009	9995	0.3010	1.9999	54
12	0.3003	1.9965	3006	9978	0.3008	9988	3009	9995	0.3010	1.9999	48
18	0.3003	1.9966	3006	9979	0.3008	9989	3009	9996	0.3010	1.9999	42
24	0.3003	1.9968	3006	9980	0.3008	9990	3009	9996	0.3010	1.9999	36
30	0.3004	1.9969	3006	9981	0.3008	9990	3010	9997	0.3010	2.0000	30
36	0.3004	1.9971	3006	9982	0.3008	9991	3010	9997	0.3010	2.0000	24
42	0.3004	1.9972	3007	9983	0.3009	9992	3010	9997	0.3010	2.0000	18
48	0.3004	1.9973	3007	9984	0.3009	9993	3010	9998	0.3010	2.0000	12
54	0.3005	1.9974	3007	9985	0.3009	9993	3010	9998	0.3010	2.0000	6
60	0.3005	1.9976	3007	9986	0.3009	9994	3010	9998	0.3010	2.0000	0

The versine = 1−Cosine = twice the Haversine
The Altitude = 90°−ZD
and since
HAV.ZD = HAV.P.COS.L.COS.D + HAV.(L − D)
then
VERS.ZD = VERS.P.COS.L.COS.D + VERS (L − D)
Where Lat. & Dec. are of the same name, subtract the lesser from the greater. Where they are of contrary names add the two together.

LOG.	NAT.	LOG.	NAT.	LOG.	NAT.	LOG.	NAT.	LOG.	NAT.	/
184°		183°		182°		181°		180°		

For an explanation of the use of above Tables see p. 5:25.

LOG COSINES

/	0°	1°	2°	3°	4°	5°	6°	7°	8°	9°	10°	11°	12°	13°	14°	
0	0.0000	9999	9997	9994	9989	9.9983	9976	9968	9958	9.9946	9934	9919	9904	9887	9.9869	60
1	0.0000	9999	9997	9994	9989	9.9983	9976	9967	9957	9.9946	9933	9919	9904	9887	9.9869	59
2	0.0000	9999	9997	9994	9989	9.9983	9976	9967	9957	9.9946	9933	9919	9904	9887	9.9868	58
3	0.0000	9999	9997	9994	9989	9.9983	9976	9967	9957	9.9946	9933	9919	9903	9886	9.9868	57
4	0.0000	9999	9997	9994	9989	9.9983	9976	9967	9957	9.9945	9933	9918	9903	9886	9.9868	56
5	0.0000	9999	9997	9994	9989	9.9983	9975	9967	9957	9.9945	9932	9918	9903	9886	9.9867	55
6	0.0000	9999	9997	9994	9989	9.9983	9975	9967	9956	9.9945	9932	9918	9902	9885	9.9867	54
7	0.0000	9999	9997	9994	9989	9.9983	9975	9966	9956	9.9945	9932	9918	9902	9885	9.9867	53
8	0.0000	9999	9997	9994	9989	9.9983	9975	9966	9956	9.9945	9932	9917	9902	9885	9.9867	52
9	0.0000	9999	9997	9993	9989	9.9982	9975	9966	9956	9.9944	9931	9917	9902	9885	9.9866	51
10	0.0000	9999	9997	9993	9989	9.9982	9975	9966	9956	9.9944	9931	9917	9901	9884	9.9866	50
11	0.0000	9999	9997	9993	9988	9.9982	9975	9966	9956	9.9944	9931	9917	9901	9884	9.9866	49
12	0.0000	9999	9997	9993	9988	9.9982	9975	9966	9955	9.9944	9931	9916	9901	9884	9.9865	48
13	0.0000	9999	9997	9993	9988	9.9982	9974	9965	9955	9.9944	9931	9916	9901	9883	9.9865	47
14	0.0000	9999	9997	9993	9988	9.9982	9974	9965	9955	9.9943	9930	9916	9900	9883	9.9865	46
15	0.0000	9999	9997	9993	9988	9.9982	9974	9965	9955	9.9943	9930	9916	9900	9883	9.9864	45
16	0.0000	9999	9997	9993	9988	9.9982	9974	9965	9955	9.9943	9930	9915	9900	9883	9.9864	44
17	0.0000	9999	9997	9993	9988	9.9982	9974	9965	9954	9.9943	9930	9915	9899	9882	9.9864	43
18	0.0000	9999	9996	9993	9988	9.9981	9974	9965	9954	9.9943	9929	9915	9899	9882	9.9863	42
19	0.0000	9999	9996	9993	9988	9.9981	9974	9964	9954	9.9942	9929	9915	9899	9882	9.9863	41
20	0.0000	9999	9996	9993	9988	9.9981	9973	9964	9954	9.9942	9929	9914	9899	9881	9.9863	40
21	0.0000	9999	9996	9993	9987	9.9981	9973	9964	9954	9.9942	9929	9914	9898	9881	9.9862	39
22	0.0000	9999	9996	9992	9987	9.9981	9973	9964	9954	9.9942	9929	9914	9898	9881	9.9862	38
23	0.0000	9999	9996	9992	9987	9.9981	9973	9964	9953	9.9941	9928	9914	9898	9880	9.9862	37
24	0.0000	9999	9996	9992	9987	9.9981	9973	9964	9953	9.9941	9928	9913	9897	9880	9.9861	36
25	0.0000	9999	9996	9992	9987	9.9981	9973	9964	9953	9.9941	9928	9913	9897	9880	9.9861	35
26	0.0000	9999	9996	9992	9987	9.9980	9973	9963	9953	9.9941	9928	9913	9897	9879	9.9861	34
27	0.0000	9999	9996	9992	9987	9.9980	9972	9963	9953	9.9941	9927	9913	9897	9879	9.9860	33
28	0.0000	9999	9996	9992	9987	9.9980	9972	9963	9952	9.9440	9927	9912	9896	9879	9.9860	32
29	0.0000	9999	9996	9992	9987	9.9980	9972	9963	9952	9.9940	9927	9912	9896	9879	9.9860	31
30	0.0000	9999	9996	9992	9987	9.9980	9972	9963	9952	9.9940	9927	9912	9896	9878	9.9859	30
31	0.0000	9998	9996	9992	9986	9.9980	9972	9963	9952	9.9940	9926	9912	9896	9878	9.9859	29
32	0.0000	9998	9996	9992	9986	9.9980	9972	9962	9952	9.9940	9926	9911	9895	9878	9.9859	28
33	0.0000	9998	9996	9992	9986	9.9980	9972	9962	9951	9.9939	9926	9911	9895	9877	9.9858	27
34	0.0000	9998	9996	9992	9986	9.9979	9971	9962	9951	9.9939	9926	9911	9895	9877	9.9858	26
35	0.0000	9998	9996	9992	9986	9.9979	9971	9962	9951	9.9939	9925	9911	9894	9877	9.9858	25
36	0.0000	9998	9996	9991	9986	9.9979	9971	9962	9951	9.9939	9925	9910	9894	9876	9.9857	24
37	0.0000	9998	9995	9991	9986	9.9979	9971	9962	9951	9.9939	9925	9910	9894	9876	9.9857	23
38	0.0000	9998	9995	9991	9986	9.9979	9971	9961	9951	9.9938	9925	9910	9894	9876	9.9857	22
39	0.0000	9998	9995	9991	9986	9.9979	9971	9961	9950	9.9938	9925	9910	9893	9876	9.9856	21
40	0.0000	9998	9995	9991	9986	9.9979	9971	9961	9950	9.9938	9924	9909	9893	9875	9.9856	20
41	0.0000	9998	9995	9991	9985	9.9979	9970	9961	9950	9.9938	9924	9909	9893	9875	9.9856	19
42	0.0000	9998	9995	9991	9985	9.9978	9970	9961	9950	9.9937	9924	9909	9892	9875	9.9855	18
43	0.0000	9998	9995	9991	9985	9.9978	9970	9960	9950	9.9937	9924	9909	9892	9874	9.9855	17
44	0.0000	9998	9995	9991	9985	9.9978	9970	9960	9949	9.9937	9923	9908	9892	9874	9.9855	16
45	0.0000	9998	9995	9991	9985	9.9978	9970	9960	9949	9.9937	9923	9908	9892	9874	9.9854	15
46	0.0000	9998	9995	9991	9985	9.9978	9970	9960	9949	9.9937	9923	9908	9891	9873	9.9854	14
47	0.0000	9998	9995	9991	9985	9.9978	9969	9960	9949	9.9936	9923	9908	9891	9873	9.9854	13
48	0.0000	9998	9995	9990	9985	9.9978	9969	9960	9949	9.9936	9922	9907	9891	9873	9.9853	12
49	0.0000	9998	9995	9990	9985	9.9978	9969	9959	9948	9.9936	9922	9907	9890	9872	9.9853	11
50	0.0000	9998	9995	9990	9985	9.9977	9969	9959	9948	9.9936	9922	9907	9890	9872	9.9853	10
51	0.0000	9998	9995	9990	9984	9.9977	9969	9959	9948	9.9936	9922	9906	9890	9872	9.9852	9
52	0.0000	9998	9995	9990	9984	9.9977	9969	9959	9948	9.9935	9921	9906	9890	9872	9.9852	8
53	9.9999	9998	9994	9990	9984	9.9977	9969	9959	9948	9.9935	9921	9906	9889	9871	9.9852	7
54	9.9999	9998	9994	9990	9984	9.9977	9968	9959	9947	9.9935	9921	9906	9889	9871	9.9851	6
55	9.9999	9998	9994	9990	9984	9.9977	9968	9958	9947	9.9935	9921	9905	9889	9871	9.9851	5
56	9.9999	9998	9994	9990	9984	9.9977	9968	9958	9947	9.9934	9920	9905	9888	9870	9.9851	4
57	9.9999	9997	9994	9990	9984	9.9977	9968	9958	9947	9.9934	9920	9905	9888	9870	9.9850	3
58	9.9999	9997	9994	9990	9984	9.9976	9968	9958	9947	9.9934	9920	9905	9888	9870	9.9850	2
59	9.9999	9997	9994	9989	9984	9.9976	9968	9958	9946	9.9934	9920	9904	9888	9869	9.9850	1
60	9.9999	9997	9994	9989	9983	9.9976	9968	9958	9946	9.9934	9919	9904	9887	9869	9.9849	0

89° 88° 87° 86° 85° 84° 83° 82° 81° 80° 79° 78° 77° 76° 75° /

LOG SINES

For an explanation of the use of above Tables see p. 5:25.

LOG COSINES

′	15°	16°	17°	18°	19°	20°	21°	22°	23°	24°	25°	26°	27°	28°	29°	
0	9.9849	9828	9806	9782	9757	9.9730	9702	9672	9640	9.9607	9573	9537	9499	9459	9.9418	60
1	9.9849	9828	9806	9782	9756	9.9729	9701	9671	9640	9.9607	9572	9536	9498	9459	9.9417	59
2	9.9849	9828	9805	9781	9756	9.9729	9701	9671	9639	9.9606	9572	9535	9498	9458	9.9417	58
3	9.9848	9827	9805	9781	9755	9.9728	9700	9670	9639	9.9606	9571	9535	9497	9457	9.9416	57
4	9.9848	9827	9804	9780	9755	9.9728	9700	9670	9638	9.9605	9570	9534	9496	9457	9.9415	56
5	9.9848	9827	9804	9780	9755	9.9728	9699	9669	9638	9.9604	9570	9534	9496	9456	9.9415	55
6	9.9847	9826	9804	9780	9754	9.9727	9699	9669	9637	9.9604	9569	9533	9495	9455	9.9414	54
7	9.9847	9826	9803	9779	9754	9.9727	9698	9668	9636	9.9603	9569	9532	9494	9455	9.9413	53
8	9.9847	9826	9803	9779	9753	9.9726	9698	9668	9636	9.9693	9568	9532	9494	9454	9.9413	52
9	9.9846	9825	9802	9778	9753	9.9726	9697	9667	9635	9.9602	9567	9531	9493	9453	9.9412	51
10	9.9846	9825	9802	9778	9752	9.9725	9697	9667	9635	9.9692	9567	9530	9492	9453	9.9411	50
11	9.9846	9824	9802	9778	9752	9.9725	9696	9666	9634	9.9601	9566	9530	9492	9452	9.9410	49
12	9.8845	9824	9801	9777	9751	9.9724	9696	9666	9634	9.9601	9566	9529	9491	9451	9.9410	48
13	9.9845	9824	9801	9777	9751	9.9724	9695	9665	9633	9.9600	9565	9529	9490	9451	9.9409	47
14	9.9845	9823	9801	9776	9751	9.9723	9695	9664	9633	9.9599	9564	9528	9490	9450	9.9408	46
15	9.9844	9823	9800	9776	9750	9.9723	9694	9664	9632	9.9599	9564	9527	9489	9449	9.9408	45
16	9.9844	9823	9800	9775	9750	9.9722	9694	9663	9632	9.9598	9563	9527	9488	9449	9.9407	44
17	9.9844	9822	9799	9775	9749	9.9722	9693	9663	9631	9.9598	9563	9526	9488	9448	9.9406	43
18	9.9843	9822	9799	9775	9749	9.9722	9693	9662	9631	9.9597	9562	9525	9487	9447	9.9406	42
19	9.9843	9821	9799	9774	9748	9.9721	9692	9662	9630	9.9597	9561	9525	9486	9447	9.9405	41
20	9.9843	9821	9798	9774	9748	9.9721	9692	9661	9629	9.9596	9561	9524	9486	9446	9.9404	40
21	9.9842	9821	9798	9773	9747	9.9720	9691	9661	9629	9.9595	9560	9524	9485	9445	9.9403	39
22	9.9842	9820	9797	9773	9747	9.9720	9691	9660	9628	9.9595	9560	9523	9484	9444	9.9403	38
23	9.9842	9820	9797	9773	9747	9.9719	9690	9660	9628	9.9594	9559	9522	9484	9444	9.9402	37
24	9.9841	9820	9797	9772	9746	9.9719	9690	9659	9627	9.9594	9558	9522	9483	9443	9.9401	36
25	9.9841	9819	9796	9772	9746	9.9718	9689	9659	9627	9.9593	9558	9521	9483	9442	9.9401	35
26	9.9841	9819	9796	9771	9745	9.9718	9689	9658	9626	9.9593	9557	9520	9482	9442	9.9400	34
27	9.9840	9818	9795	9771	9745	9.9717	9688	9658	9626	9.9592	9557	9520	9481	9441	9.9399	33
28	9.9840	9818	9795	9770	9744	9.9717	9688	9657	9625	9.9591	9556	9519	9481	9440	9.9398	32
29	9.9839	9818	9795	9770	9744	9.9716	9687	9657	9625	9.9591	9555	9519	9480	9440	9.9398	31
30	9.9839	9817	9794	9770	9743	9.9716	9687	9656	9624	9.9590	9555	9518	9479	9439	9.9397	30
31	9.9839	9817	9794	9769	9743	9.9715	9686	9656	9623	9.9590	9554	9517	9479	9438	9.9396	29
32	9.9838	9817	9793	9769	9742	9.9715	9686	9655	9623	9.9589	9554	9517	9478	9438	9.9396	28
33	9.9838	9816	9793	9768	9742	9.9714	9685	9655	9622	9.9589	9553	9516	9477	9437	9.9395	27
34	9.9838	9816	9793	9768	9742	9.9714	9685	9654	9622	9.9588	9552	9515	9477	9436	9.9394	26
35	9.9837	9815	9792	9767	9741	9.9714	9684	9654	9621	9.9587	9552	9515	9476	9436	9.9393	25
36	9.9837	9815	9792	9767	9741	9.9713	9684	9653	9621	9.9587	9551	9514	9475	9435	9.9393	24
37	9.9837	9815	9791	9767	9740	9.9713	9683	9652	9620	9.9586	9551	9513	9475	9434	9.9392	23
38	9.9836	9814	9791	9766	9740	9.9712	9683	9652	9620	9.9586	9550	9513	9474	9433	9.9391	22
39	9.9836	9814	9791	9766	9739	9.9712	9682	9651	9619	9.9585	9549	9512	9473	9433	9.9391	21
40	9.9836	9814	9790	9765	9739	9.9711	9682	9651	9618	9.9584	9549	9512	9473	9432	9.9390	20
41	9.9835	9813	9790	9765	9739	9.9711	9681	9650	9618	9.9584	9548	9511	9472	9431	9.9389	19
42	9.9835	9813	9789	9764	9738	9.9710	9681	9650	9617	9.9583	9548	9510	9471	9431	9.9388	18
43	9.9835	9812	9789	9764	9738	9.9710	9680	9649	9617	9.9583	9547	9510	9471	9430	9.9388	17
44	9.9834	9812	9789	9764	9737	9.9709	9680	9649	9616	9.9582	9546	9509	9470	9429	9.9387	16
45	9.9834	9812	9788	9763	9737	9.9709	9679	9648	9616	9.9582	9546	9508	9469	9429	9.9386	15
46	9.9833	9811	9788	9763	9736	9.9708	9679	9648	9615	9.9581	9545	9508	9469	9428	9.9385	14
47	9.9833	9811	9787	9762	9736	9.9708	9678	9647	9615	9.9580	9545	9507	9468	9427	9.9385	13
48	9.9833	9811	9787	9762	9735	9.9707	9678	9647	9614	9.9580	9544	9507	9467	9427	9.9384	12
49	9.9832	9810	9787	9761	9735	9.9707	9677	9646	9613	9.9579	9543	9506	9467	9426	9.9383	11
50	9.9832	9810	9786	9761	9734	9.9706	9677	9646	9613	9.9579	9543	9505	9466	9425	9.9383	10
51	9.9832	9809	9786	9761	9734	9.9706	9676	9645	9612	9.9578	9542	9505	9465	9424	9.9382	9
52	9.9831	9809	9785	9760	9734	9.9705	9676	9645	9612	9.9577	9542	9504	9465	9424	9.9381	8
53	9.9831	9809	9785	9760	9733	9.9705	9675	9644	9611	9.9577	9541	9503	9464	9423	9.9380	7
54	9.9831	9808	9785	9759	9733	9.9704	9675	9643	9610	9.9576	9540	9503	9463	9422	9.9380	6
55	9.9830	9808	9784	9759	9732	9.9704	9674	9643	9610	9.9576	9540	9502	9463	9422	9.9379	5
56	9.9830	9808	9784	9758	9732	9.9703	9674	9642	9610	9.9575	9539	9501	9462	9421	9.9378	4
57	9.9830	9807	9783	9758	9731	9.9703	9673	9642	9609	9.9575	9538	9501	9461	9420	9.9377	3
58	9.9829	9807	9783	9758	9731	9.9702	9673	9641	9608	9.9574	9538	9500	9461	9420	9.9377	2
59	9.9829	9806	9782	9757	9730	9.9702	9672	9641	9608	9.9573	9537	9499	9460	9419	9.9376	1
60	9.9828	9806	9782	9757	9730	9.9702	9672	9640	9607	9.9573	9537	9499	9459	9418	9.9375	0

74° 73° 72° 71° 70° 69° 68° 67° 66° 65° 64° 63° 62° 61° 60° ′

LOG SINES

For an explanation of the use of above Tables see p. 5:25.

LOG COSINES

′	30°	31°	32°	33°	34°	35°	36°	37°	38°	39°	40°	41°	42°	43°	44°	
0	9.9375	9330	9283	9235	9185	9.9134	9080	9023	8965	9.8905	8843	8778	8711	8641	9.8569	60
1	9.9375	9330	9283	9235	9185	9.9133	9079	9023	8964	9.8904	8841	8777	8710	8640	9.8568	59
2	9.9374	9329	9283	9234	9184	9.9132	9078	9022	8963	9.8903	8840	8776	8708	8639	9.8567	58
3	9.9373	9328	9282	9233	9183	9.9131	9077	9021	8962	9.8902	8839	8775	8707	8638	9.8566	57
4	9.9372	9328	9281	9233	9182	9.9130	9076	9020	8961	9.8901	8838	8773	8706	8637	9.8564	56
5	9.9372	9327	9280	9232	9181	9.9129	9075	9019	8960	9.8900	8837	8772	8705	8635	9.8563	55
6	9.9371	9326	9279	9231	9181	9.9128	9074	9018	8959	9.8899	8836	8771	8704	8634	9.8562	54
7	9.9370	9325	9279	9230	9180	9.9127	9073	9017	8958	9.8898	8835	8770	8703	8633	9.8561	53
8	9.9369	9325	9278	9229	9179	9.9127	9072	9016	8957	9.8897	8834	8769	8702	8632	9.8560	52
9	9.9369	9324	9277	9229	9178	9.9126	9071	9015	8956	9.8896	8833	8768	8700	8631	9.8558	51
10	9.9368	9323	9276	9228	9177	9.9125	9070	9014	8955	9.8895	8832	8767	8699	8629	9.8557	50
11	9.9367	9322	9275	9227	9176	9.9124	9069	9013	8954	9.8894	8831	8766	8698	8628	9.8556	49
12	9.9367	9322	9275	9226	9175	9.9123	9069	9012	8953	9.8893	8830	8765	8697	8627	9.8555	48
13	9.9366	9321	9274	9225	9175	9.9122	9068	9011	8952	9.8892	8829	8763	8696	8626	9.8553	47
14	9.9365	9320	9273	9224	9174	9.9121	9067	9010	8951	9.8891	8828	8762	8695	8625	9.8552	46
15	9.9364	9319	9272	9224	9173	9.9120	9066	9009	8950	9.8890	8827	8761	8694	8624	9.8551	45
16	9.9364	9318	9272	9223	9172	9.9119	9065	9008	8949	9.8889	8825	8760	8692	8622	9.8550	44
17	9.9363	9318	9271	9222	9171	9.9119	9064	9007	8948	9.8888	8824	8759	8691	8621	9.8548	43
18	9.9362	9317	9270	9221	9170	9.9118	9063	9006	8947	9.8887	8823	8758	8690	8620	9.8547	42
19	9.9361	9316	9269	9220	9169	9.9117	9062	9005	8946	9.8885	8822	8757	8689	8619	9.8546	41
20	9.9361	9315	9268	9219	9169	9.9116	9061	9004	8945	9.8884	8821	8756	8688	8618	9.8545	40
21	9.9360	9315	9268	9219	9168	9.9115	9060	9003	8944	9.8883	8820	8755	8687	8616	9.8544	39
22	9.9359	9314	9267	9218	9167	9.9114	9059	9002	8943	9.8882	8819	8753	8686	8615	9.8542	38
23	9.9358	9313	9266	9217	9166	9.9113	9058	9001	8942	9.8881	8818	8752	8684	8614	9.8541	37
24	9.9358	9312	9265	9216	9165	9.9112	9057	9000	8941	9.8880	8817	8751	8683	8613	9.8540	36
25	9.9357	9312	9264	9215	9164	9.9111	9056	9000	8940	9.8879	8816	8750	8682	8612	9.8539	35
26	9.9356	9311	9264	9214	9163	9.9110	9056	8999	8939	9.8878	8815	8749	8681	8610	9.8537	34
27	9.9355	9310	9263	9214	9163	9.9110	9055	8998	8938	9.8877	8814	8748	8680	8609	9.8536	33
28	9.9355	9309	9262	9213	9162	9.9109	9054	8997	8937	9.8876	8813	8747	8679	8608	9.8535	32
29	9.9354	9308	9261	9212	9161	9.9108	9053	8996	8936	9.8875	8812	8746	8677	8607	9.8534	31
30	9.9353	9308	9260	9211	9160	9.9107	9052	8995	8935	9.8874	8810	8745	8676	8606	9.8532	30
31	9.9352	9307	9259	9210	9159	9.9106	9051	8994	8934	9.8873	8809	8743	8675	8604	9.8531	29
32	9.9352	9306	9259	9209	9158	9.9105	9050	8993	8933	9.8872	8808	8742	8674	8603	9.8530	28
33	9.9351	9305	9258	9209	9157	9.9104	9049	8992	8932	9.8871	8807	8741	8673	8602	9.8529	27
34	9.9350	9305	9257	9208	9156	9.9103	9048	8991	8931	9.8870	8806	8740	8672	8601	9.8527	26
35	9.9349	9304	9256	9207	9156	9.9102	9047	8990	8930	9.8869	8805	8739	8671	8600	9.8526	25
36	9.9349	9303	9255	9206	9155	9.9101	9046	8989	8929	9.8868	8804	8738	8669	8598	9.8525	24
37	9.9348	9302	9255	9205	9154	9.9101	9045	8988	8928	9.8867	8803	8737	8668	8597	9.8524	23
38	9.9347	9301	9254	9204	9153	9.9100	9044	8987	8927	9.8866	8802	8736	8667	8596	9.8522	22
39	9.9346	9301	9253	9204	9152	9.9099	9043	8986	8926	9.8865	8801	8734	8666	8595	9.8521	21
40	9.9346	9300	9252	9203	9151	9.9098	9042	8985	8925	9.8864	8800	8733	8665	8594	9.8520	20
41	9.9345	9299	9251	9202	9150	9.9097	9041	8984	8924	9.8863	8799	8732	8664	8592	9.8519	19
42	9.9344	9298	9251	9201	9149	9.9096	9041	8983	8923	9.8862	8797	8731	8662	8591	9.8517	18
43	9.9343	9298	9250	9200	9149	9.9095	9040	8982	8922	9.8860	8796	8730	8661	8590	9.8516	17
44	9.9343	9297	9249	9199	9148	9.9094	9039	8981	8921	9.8859	8795	8729	8660	8589	9.8515	16
45	9.9342	9296	9248	9198	9147	9.9093	9038	8980	8920	9.8858	8794	8728	8659	8588	9.8514	15
46	9.9341	9295	9247	9198	9146	9.9092	9037	8979	8919	9.8857	8793	8727	8658	8586	9.8512	14
47	9.9340	9294	9247	9197	9145	9.9091	9036	8978	8918	9.8856	8792	8725	8657	8585	9.8511	13
48	9.9340	9294	9246	9196	9144	9.9091	9035	8977	8917	9.8855	8791	8724	8655	8584	9.8510	12
49	9.9339	9293	9245	9195	9143	9.9090	9034	8976	8916	9.8854	8790	8723	8654	8583	9.8509	11
50	9.9338	9292	9244	9194	9142	9.9089	9033	8975	8915	9.8853	8789	8722	8653	8582	9.8507	10
51	9.9337	9291	9243	9193	9142	9.9088	9032	8974	8914	9.8852	8788	8721	8652	8580	9.8506	9
52	9.9337	9291	9242	9193	9141	9.9087	9031	8973	8913	9.8851	8787	8720	8651	8579	9.8505	8
53	9.9336	9290	9242	9192	9140	9.9086	9030	8972	8912	9.8850	8785	8719	8650	8578	9.8504	7
54	9.9335	9289	9241	9191	9139	9.9085	9029	8971	8911	9.8849	8784	8718	8648	8577	9.8502	6
55	9.9334	9288	9240	9190	9138	9.9084	9028	8970	8910	9.8848	8783	8716	8647	8575	9.8501	5
56	9.9334	9287	9239	9189	9137	9.9083	9027	8969	8909	9.8847	8782	8715	8646	8574	9.8500	4
57	9.9333	9287	9238	9188	9136	9.9082	9026	8968	8908	9.8846	8781	8714	8645	8573	9.8499	3
58	9.9332	9286	9238	9187	9135	9.9081	9025	8967	8907	9.8845	8780	8713	8644	8572	9.8497	2
59	9.9331	9285	9237	9187	9135	9.9080	9024	8966	8906	9.8844	8779	8712	8642	8571	9.8496	1
60	9.9331	9284	9236	9186	9134	9.9080	9023	8965	8905	9.8843	8778	8711	8641	8569	9.8495	0

59° 58° 57° 56° 55° 54° 53° 52° 51° 50° 49° 48° 47° 46° 45° ′

LOG SINES

For an explanation of the use of above Tables see p. 5:25.

LOG COSINES

′	45°	46°	47°	48°	49°	50°	51°	52°	53°	54°	55°	56°	57°	58°	59°	
0	9.8495	8418	8338	8255	8169	9.8081	7989	7893	7795	9.7692	7586	7476	7361	7242	9.7118	60
1	9.8494	8416	8336	8254	8168	9.8079	7987	7892	7793	9.7690	7584	7474	7359	7240	9.7116	59
2	9.8492	8415	8335	8252	8167	9.8078	7886	7890	7791	9.7689	7582	7472	7357	7238	9.7114	58
3	9.8491	8414	8334	8251	8165	9.8076	7984	7889	7790	9.7687	7580	7470	7355	7236	9.7112	57
4	9.8490	8412	8332	8249	8164	9.8075	7982	7887	7788	9.7685	7579	7468	7353	7234	9.7110	56
5	9.8489	8411	8331	8248	8162	9.8073	7981	7885	7786	9.7683	7577	7466	7351	7232	9.7108	55
6	9.8487	8410	8330	8247	8161	9.8072	7979	7884	7785	9.7682	7575	7464	7349	7230	9.7106	54
7	9.8486	8409	8328	8245	8159	9.8070	7978	7882	7783	9.7680	7573	7462	7347	7228	9.7104	53
8	9.8485	8407	8327	8244	8158	9.8069	7976	7880	7781	9.7678	7571	7461	7345	7226	9.7102	52
9	9.8483	8406	8326	8242	8156	9.8067	7975	7879	7780	9.7676	7570	7459	7344	7224	9.7099	51
10	9.8482	8405	8324	8241	8155	9.8066	7973	7877	7778	9.7675	7568	7457	7342	7222	9.7097	50
11	9.8481	8403	8323	8240	8153	9.8064	7972	7876	7776	9.7673	7566	7455	7340	7220	9.7095	49
12	9.8480	8402	8322	8238	8152	9.8063	7970	7874	7774	9.7671	7564	7453	7338	7218	9.7093	48
13	9.8478	8401	8320	8237	8150	9.8061	7968	7872	7773	9.7669	7562	7451	7336	7216	9.7091	47
14	9.8477	8399	8319	8235	8149	9.8060	7967	7871	7771	9.7668	7561	7449	7334	7214	9.7089	46
15	9.8476	8398	8317	8234	8148	9.8058	7965	7869	7769	9.7666	7559	7447	7332	7212	9.7087	45
16	9.8475	8397	8316	8233	8146	9.8056	7964	7867	7768	9.7664	7557	7445	7330	7210	9.7085	44
17	9.8473	8395	8315	8231	8145	9.8055	7962	7866	7766	9.7662	7555	7444	7328	7208	9.7082	43
18	9.8472	8394	8313	8230	8143	9.8053	7960	7864	7764	9.7661	7553	7442	7326	7205	9.7080	42
19	9.8471	8393	8312	8228	8142	9.8052	7959	7863	7763	9.7659	7551	7440	7324	7203	9.7078	41
20	9.8469	8391	8311	8227	8140	9.8050	7957	7861	7761	9.7657	7550	7438	7322	7201	9.7076	40
21	9.8468	8390	8309	8225	8139	9.8049	7956	7859	7759	9.7655	7548	7436	7320	7199	9.7074	39
22	9.8467	8389	8308	8224	8137	9.8047	7954	7858	7758	9.7654	7546	7434	7318	7197	9.7072	38
23	9.8466	8387	8306	8223	8136	9.8046	7953	7856	7756	9.7652	7544	7432	7316	7195	9.7070	37
24	9.8464	8386	8305	8221	8134	9.8044	7951	7854	7754	9.7650	7542	7430	7314	7193	9.7068	36
25	9.8463	8385	8304	8220	8133	9.8043	7949	7853	7752	9.7648	7540	7428	7312	7191	9.7065	35
26	9.8462	8383	8302	8218	8131	9.8041	7948	7851	7751	9.7647	7539	7427	7310	7189	9.7063	34
27	9.8460	8382	8301	8217	8130	9.8040	7946	7849	7749	9.7645	7537	7425	7308	7187	9.7061	33
28	9.8459	8381	8300	8216	8128	9.8038	7945	7848	7747	9.7643	7535	7423	7306	7185	9.7059	32
29	9.8458	8379	8298	8214	8127	9.8037	7943	7846	7746	9.7641	7533	7421	7304	7183	9.7057	31
30	9.8457	8378	8297	8213	8125	9.8035	7941	7844	7744	9.7640	7531	7419	7302	7181	9.7055	30
31	9.8455	8377	8295	8211	8124	9.8034	7940	7843	7742	9.7638	7529	7417	7300	7179	9.7053	29
32	9.8454	8375	8294	8210	8122	9.8032	7938	7841	7740	9.7636	7528	7415	7298	7177	9.7050	28
33	9.8453	8374	8293	8208	8121	9.8031	7937	7840	7739	9.7634	7526	7413	7296	7175	9.7048	27
34	9.8451	8373	8291	8207	8120	9.8029	7935	7838	7737	9.7632	7524	7411	7294	7173	9.7046	26
35	9.8450	8371	8290	8205	8118	9.8027	7934	7836	7735	9.7631	7522	7409	7292	7171	9.7044	25
36	9.8449	8370	8289	8204	8117	9.8026	7932	7835	7734	9.7629	7520	7407	7290	7168	9.7042	24
37	9.8448	8369	8287	8203	8115	9.8024	7930	7833	7732	9.7627	7518	7406	7288	7166	9.7040	23
38	9.8446	8367	8286	8201	8114	9.8023	7929	7831	7730	9.7625	7517	7404	7286	7164	9.7037	22
39	9.8445	8366	8284	8200	8112	9.8021	7927	7830	7728	9.7624	7515	7402	7284	7162	9.7035	21
40	9.8444	8365	8283	8198	8111	9.8020	7926	7828	7727	9.7622	7513	7400	7282	7160	9.7033	20
41	9.8442	8363	8282	8197	8109	9.8018	7924	7826	7725	9.7620	7511	7398	7280	7158	9.7031	19
42	9.8441	8362	8280	8195	8108	9.8017	7922	7825	7723	9.7618	7509	7396	7278	7156	9.7029	18
43	9.8440	8361	8279	8194	8106	9.8015	7921	7823	7722	9.7616	7507	7394	7276	7154	9.7027	17
44	9.8439	8359	8277	8193	8105	9.8014	7919	7821	7720	9.7615	7505	7392	7274	7152	9.7025	16
45	9.8437	8358	8276	8191	8103	9.8012	7918	7820	7718	9.7613	7504	7390	7272	7150	9.7022	15
46	9.8436	8357	8275	8190	8102	9.8010	7916	7818	7716	9.7611	7502	7388	7270	7148	9.7020	14
47	9.8435	8355	8273	8188	8100	9.8009	7914	7816	7715	9.7609	7500	7386	7268	7146	9.7018	13
48	9.8433	8354	8272	8187	8099	9.8007	7913	7815	7713	9.7607	7498	7384	7266	7144	9.7016	12
49	9.8432	8353	8270	8185	8097	9.8006	7911	7813	7711	9.7606	7496	7382	7264	7141	9.7014	11
50	9.8431	8351	8269	8184	8096	9.8004	7910	7811	7710	9.7604	7494	7380	7262	7139	9.7012	10
51	9.8429	8350	8268	8182	8094	9.8003	7908	7810	7708	9.7602	7492	7379	7260	7137	9.7009	9
52	9.8428	8349	8266	8181	8093	9.8001	7906	7808	7706	9.7600	7491	7377	7258	7135	9.7007	8
53	9.8427	8347	8265	8180	8091	9.8000	7905	7806	7704	9.7599	7489	7375	7256	7133	9.7005	7
54	9.8426	8346	8264	8178	8090	9.7998	7903	7805	7703	9.7597	7487	7373	7254	7131	9.7003	6
55	9.8424	8345	8262	8177	8088	9.7997	7901	7803	7701	9.7595	7485	7371	7252	7129	9.7001	5
56	9.8423	8343	8261	8175	8087	9.7995	7900	7801	7699	9.7593	7483	7369	7250	7127	9.6998	4
57	9.8422	8342	8259	8174	8085	9.7993	7898	7800	7697	9.7591	7481	7367	7248	7125	9.6996	3
58	9.8420	8341	8258	8172	8084	9.7992	7897	7798	7696	9.7590	7479	7365	7246	7123	9.6994	2
59	9.8419	8339	8257	8171	8082	9.7990	7895	7796	7694	9.7588	7477	7363	7244	7120	9.6992	1
60	9.8418	8338	8255	8169	8081	9.7989	7893	7795	7692	9.7586	7476	7361	7242	7118	9.6990	0

44°	43°	42°	41°	40°	39°	38°	37°	36°	35°	34°	33°	32°	31°	30°	′

LOG SINES

For an explanation of the use of above Tables see p. 5:25.

LOG COSINES

′	60°	61°	62°	63°	64°	65°	66°	67°	68°	69°	70°	71°	72°	73°	74°	
0	9.6990	6856	6716	6570	6418	9.6259	6093	5919	5736	9.5543	5341	5126	4900	4659	9.4403	60
1	9.6988	6853	6714	6568	6416	9.6257	6090	5916	5733	9.5540	5337	5123	4896	4655	9.4399	59
2	9.6985	6851	6711	6566	6413	9.6254	6087	5913	5729	9.5537	5334	5119	4892	4651	9.4395	58
3	9.6983	6849	6709	6563	6411	9.6251	6085	5910	5726	9.5533	5330	5115	4888	4647	9.4390	57
4	9.6981	6847	6707	6561	6408	9.6249	6082	5907	5723	9.5530	5327	5112	4884	4643	9.4386	56
5	9.6979	6844	6704	6558	6405	9.6246	6079	5904	5720	9.5527	5323	5108	4880	4639	9.4381	55
6	9.6977	6842	6702	6556	6403	9.6243	6076	5901	5717	9.5523	5320	5104	4876	4634	9.4377	54
7	9.6974	6840	6699	6553	6400	9.6240	6073	5898	5714	9.5520	5316	5101	4873	4630	9.4372	53
8	9.6972	6837	6697	6551	6398	9.6238	6070	5895	5711	9.5517	5313	5097	4869	4626	9.4368	52
9	9.6970	6835	6695	6548	6395	9.6235	6068	5892	5708	9.5514	5309	5093	4865	4622	9.4364	51
10	9.6968	6833	6692	6546	6392	9.6232	6065	5889	5704	9.5510	5306	5090	4861	4618	9.4359	50
11	9.6966	6831	6690	6543	6390	9.6230	6062	5886	5701	9.5507	5302	5086	4857	4614	9.4355	49
12	9.6963	6828	6687	6541	6387	9.6227	6059	5883	5698	9.5504	5299	5082	4853	4609	9.4350	48
13	9.6961	6826	6685	6538	6385	9.6224	6056	5880	5695	9.5500	5295	5078	4849	4605	9.4346	47
14	9.6959	6824	6683	6536	6382	9.6221	6053	5877	5692	9.5497	5292	5075	4845	4601	9.4341	46
15	9.6957	6821	6680	6533	6379	9.6219	6050	5874	5689	9.5494	5288	5071	4841	4597	9.4337	45
16	9.6955	6819	6678	6531	6377	9.6216	6047	5871	5685	9.5490	5285	5067	4837	4593	9.4332	44
17	9.6952	6817	6675	6528	6374	9.6213	6045	5868	5682	9.5487	5281	5064	4833	4588	9.4328	43
18	9.6950	6814	6673	6526	6371	9.6210	6042	5865	5679	9.5484	5278	5060	4829	4584	9.4323	42
19	9.6948	6812	6671	6523	6369	9.6208	6039	5862	5676	9.5480	5274	5056	4825	4580	9.4319	41
20	9.6946	6810	6668	6521	6366	9.6205	6036	5859	5673	9.5477	5270	5052	4821	4576	9.4314	40
21	9.6943	6808	6666	6518	6364	9.6202	6033	5856	5670	9.5474	5267	5049	4817	4572	9.4310	39
22	9.6941	6805	6663	6515	6361	9.6199	6030	5853	5666	9.5470	5263	5045	4813	4567	9.4305	38
23	9.6939	6803	6661	6513	6358	9.6197	6027	5850	5663	9.5467	5260	5041	4809	4563	9.4301	37
24	9.6937	6801	6659	6510	6356	9.6194	6024	5847	5660	9.5463	5256	5037	4805	4559	9.4296	36
25	9.6935	6798	6656	6508	6353	9.6191	6021	5844	5657	9.5460	5253	5034	4801	4555	9.4292	35
26	9.6932	6796	6654	6505	6350	9.6188	6019	5841	5654	9.5457	5249	5030	4797	4550	9.4287	34
27	9.6930	6794	6651	6503	6348	9.6186	6016	5838	5650	9.5453	5246	5026	4793	4546	9.4283	33
28	9.6928	6791	6649	6500	6345	9.6183	6013	5834	5647	9.5450	5242	5022	4789	4542	9.4278	32
29	9.6926	6789	6646	6498	6342	9.6180	6010	5831	5644	9.5447	5239	5019	4785	4538	9.4274	31
30	9.6923	6787	6644	6495	6340	9.6177	6007	5828	5641	9.5443	5235	5015	4781	4533	9.4269	30
31	9.6921	6784	6642	6493	6337	9.6174	6004	5825	5638	9.5440	5231	5011	4777	4529	9.4264	29
32	9.6919	6782	6639	6490	6335	9.6172	6001	5822	5634	9.5436	5228	5007	4773	4525	9.4260	28
33	9.6917	6780	6637	6488	6332	9.6169	5998	5819	5631	9.5433	5224	5003	4769	4521	9.4255	27
34	9.6914	6777	6634	6485	6329	9.6166	5995	5816	5628	9.5430	5221	5000	4765	4516	9.4251	26
35	9.6912	6775	6632	6483	6327	9.6163	5992	5813	5625	9.5426	5217	4996	4761	4512	9.4246	25
36	9.6910	6773	6629	6480	6324	9.6161	5990	5810	5621	9.5423	5213	4992	4757	4508	9.4242	24
37	9.6908	6770	6627	6477	6321	9.6158	5987	5807	5618	9.5420	5210	4988	4753	4503	9.4237	23
38	9.6905	6768	6625	6475	6319	9.6155	5984	5804	5615	9.5416	5206	4984	4749	4499	9.4232	22
39	9.6903	6766	6622	6472	6316	9.6152	5981	5801	5612	9.5413	5203	4981	4745	4495	9.4228	21
40	9.6901	6763	6620	6470	6313	9.6149	5978	5798	5609	9.5409	5199	4977	4741	4491	9.4223	20
41	9.6899	6761	6617	6467	6311	9.6147	5975	5795	5605	9.5406	5196	4973	4737	4486	9.4219	19
42	9.6896	6759	6615	6465	6308	9.6144	5972	5792	5602	9.5402	5192	4969	4733	4482	9.4214	18
43	9.6894	6756	6612	6462	6305	9.6141	5969	5789	5599	9.5399	5188	4965	4729	4478	9.4209	17
44	9.6892	6754	6610	6460	6303	9.6138	5966	5785	5596	9.5396	5185	4962	4725	4473	9.4205	16
45	9.6890	6752	6607	6457	6300	9.6135	5963	5782	5592	9.5392	5181	4958	4721	4469	9.4200	15
46	9.6887	6749	6605	6454	6297	9.6133	5960	5779	5589	9.5389	5177	4954	4717	4465	9.4195	14
47	9.6885	6747	6603	6452	6295	9.6130	5957	5776	5586	9.5385	5174	4950	4713	4460	9.4191	13
48	9.6883	6744	6600	6449	6292	9.6127	5954	5773	5583	9.5382	5170	4946	4709	4456	9.4186	12
49	9.6881	6742	6598	6447	6289	9.6124	5951	5770	5579	9.5379	5167	4942	4705	4452	9.4181	11
50	9.6878	6740	6595	6444	6286	9.6121	5948	5767	5576	9.5376	5163	4939	4700	4447	9.4177	10
51	9.6876	6737	6593	6442	6284	9.6119	5945	5764	5573	9.5372	5159	4935	4696	4443	9.4172	9
52	9.6874	6735	6590	6439	6281	9.6116	5943	5761	5570	9.5368	5156	4931	4692	4438	9.4168	8
53	9.6872	6733	6588	6437	6278	9.6113	5940	5758	5566	9.5365	5152	4927	4688	4434	9.4163	7
54	9.6869	6730	6585	6434	6276	9.6110	5937	5754	5563	9.5361	5148	4923	4684	4430	9.4158	6
55	9.6867	6728	6583	6431	6273	9.6107	5934	5751	5560	9.5358	5145	4919	4680	4425	9.4153	5
56	9.6865	6726	6580	6429	6270	9.6104	5931	5748	5556	9.5354	5141	4915	4676	4421	9.4149	4
57	9.6863	6723	6578	6426	6268	9.6102	5928	5745	5553	9.5351	5137	4911	4672	4417	9.4144	3
58	9.6860	6721	6575	6424	6265	9.6099	5925	5742	5550	9.5347	5134	4908	4668	4412	9.4139	2
59	9.6858	6718	6573	6421	6262	9.6096	5922	5739	5547	9.5344	5130	4904	4663	4408	9.4135	1
60	9.6856	6716	6570	6418	6259	9.6093	5919	5736	5543	9.5341	5126	4900	4659	4403	9.4130	0

| 29° | 28° | 27° | 26° | 25° | 24° | 23° | 22° | 21° | 20° | 19° | 18° | 17° | 16° | 15° | ′ |

LOG SINES

For an explanation of the use of above Tables see p. 5:25.

LOG COSINES

′	75°	76°	77°	78°	79°	80°	81°	82°	83°	84°	85°	86°	87°	88°	89°	
0	9.4130	3837	3521	3179	2806	9.2397	1943	1436	0859	9.0192	9403	8436	7188	5428	8.2419	60
1	9.4125	3832	3515	3173	2799	9.2390	1935	1427	0849	9.0180	9388	8418	7164	5392	8.2346	59
2	9.4121	3827	3510	3167	2793	9.2382	1927	1418	0838	9.0168	9374	8400	7140	5355	8.2271	58
3	9.4116	3822	3504	3161	2786	9.2375	1919	1409	0828	9.0156	9359	8381	7115	5318	8.2196	57
4	9.4111	3816	3499	3155	2780	9.2368	1911	1399	0818	9.0144	9345	8363	7090	5281	9.2119	56
5	9.4106	3811	3493	3149	2773	9.2361	1903	1390	0807	9.0132	9330	8345	7066	5243	8.2041	55
6	9.4102	3806	3488	3143	2767	9.2353	1895	1381	0797	9.0120	9315	8326	7041	5206	8.1961	54
7	9.4097	3801	3482	3137	2760	9.2346	1887	1372	0786	9.0107	9301	8307	7016	5167	8.1880	53
8	9.4092	3796	3477	3131	2754	9.2339	1879	1363	0776	9.0095	9286	8289	6991	5129	8.1797	52
9	9.4087	3791	3471	3125	2747	9.2332	1871	1354	0765	9.0083	9271	8270	6965	5090	8.1713	51
10	9.4083	3786	3466	3119	2740	9.2324	1863	1345	0755	9.0070	9256	8251	6940	5050	8.1627	50
11	9.4078	3781	3460	3113	2734	9.2317	1855	1336	0744	9.0058	9241	8232	6914	5011	8.1539	49
12	9.4073	3775	3455	3107	2727	9.2310	1847	1326	0734	9.0046	9226	8213	6889	4971	8.1450	48
13	9.4068	3770	3449	3101	2721	9.2303	1838	1317	0723	9.0033	9211	8194	6863	4930	8.1358	47
14	9.4063	3765	3444	3095	2714	9.2295	1830	1308	0712	9.0021	9196	8175	6837	4890	8.1265	46
15	9.4059	3760	3438	3089	2707	9.2288	1822	1299	0702	9.0008	9181	8156	6810	4848	8.1169	45
16	9.4054	3755	3432	3083	2701	9.2280	1814	1289	0691	8.9996	9166	8137	6784	4807	8.1072	44
17	9.4049	3750	3427	3077	2694	9.2273	1806	1280	0680	8.9983	9150	8117	6758	4765	8.0972	43
18	9.4044	3745	3421	3070	2687	9.2266	1797	1271	0670	8.9970	9135	8098	6731	4723	8.0870	42
19	9.4039	3739	3416	3064	2681	9.2258	1789	1261	0659	8.9958	9119	8078	6704	4680	8.0765	41
20	9.4035	3734	3410	3058	2674	9.2251	1781	1252	0648	8.9945	9104	8059	6677	4637	8.0658	40
21	9.4030	3729	3404	3052	2667	9.2243	1772	1242	0637	8.9932	9089	8039	6650	4593	8.0548	39
22	9.4025	3724	3399	3046	2661	9.2236	1764	1233	0626	8.9919	9073	8019	6622	4549	8.0435	38
23	9.4020	3719	3393	3040	2654	9.2229	1756	1224	0616	8.9907	9057	7999	6595	4504	8.0319	37
24	9.4015	3713	3387	3034	2647	9.2221	1747	1214	0605	8.9894	9042	7979	6567	4459	8.0200	36
25	9.4010	3708	3382	3027	2640	9.2214	1739	1205	0594	8.9881	9026	7959	6539	4414	8.0078	35
26	9.4005	3703	3376	3021	2634	9.2206	1731	1195	0583	8.9868	9010	7939	6511	4368	7.9952	34
27	9.4001	3698	3370	3015	2627	9.2199	1722	1186	0572	8.9855	8994	7918	6483	4322	7.9822	33
28	9.3996	3692	3365	3009	2620	9.2191	1714	1176	0561	8.9842	8978	7898	6454	4275	7.9689	32
29	9.3991	3687	3359	3003	2613	9.2184	1705	1167	0550	8.9829	8962	7877	6426	4227	7.9551	31
30	9.3986	3682	3353	2997	2606	9.2176	1697	1157	0539	8.9816	8946	7857	6397	4179	7.9408	30
31	9.3981	3677	3348	2990	2600	9.2169	1689	1147	0527	8.9803	8930	7836	6368	4131	7.9261	29
32	9.3976	3671	3342	2984	2593	9.2161	1680	1138	0516	8.9789	8914	7815	6339	4082	7.9109	28
33	9.3971	3666	3336	2978	2586	9.2153	1672	1128	0505	8.9776	8898	7794	6309	4032	7.8951	27
34	9.3966	3661	3331	2972	2579	9.2146	1663	1118	0494	8.9763	8882	7773	6279	3982	7.8787	26
35	9.3961	3655	3325	2965	2572	9.2138	1655	1109	0483	8.9750	8865	7752	6250	3931	7.8617	25
36	9.3957	3650	3319	2959	2565	9.2131	1646	1099	0472	8.9736	8849	7731	6220	3880	7.8439	24
37	9.3952	3645	3313	2953	2558	9.2123	1637	1089	0460	8.9723	8833	7710	6189	3828	7.8255	23
38	9.3947	3640	3308	2947	2551	9.2115	1629	1080	0449	8.9709	8816	7688	6159	3775	7.8061	22
39	9.3942	3634	3302	2940	2545	9.2108	1620	1070	0438	8.9696	8799	7667	6128	3722	7.7859	21
40	9.3937	3629	3296	2934	2538	9.2100	1612	1060	0426	8.9682	8783	7645	6097	3668	7.7648	20
41	9.3932	3624	3290	2928	2531	9.2092	1603	1050	0415	8.9669	8766	7623	6066	3613	7.7425	19
42	9.3927	3618	3284	2921	2524	9.2085	1594	1040	0403	8.9655	8749	7602	6035	3558	7.7190	18
43	9.3922	3613	3279	2915	2517	9.2077	1586	1030	0392	8.9642	8733	7580	6003	3502	7.6942	17
44	9.3917	3608	3273	2909	2510	9.2069	1577	1020	0380	8.9628	8716	7557	5972	3445	7.6678	16
45	9.3912	3602	3267	2902	2503	9.2061	1568	1011	0369	8.9614	8689	7535	5939	3388	7.6398	15
46	9.3907	3597	3261	2896	2496	9.2054	1560	1001	0357	8.9601	8682	7513	5907	3329	7.6099	14
47	9.3902	3591	3255	2890	2489	9.2046	1551	0991	0346	8.9587	8665	7491	5875	3270	7.5777	13
48	9.3897	3586	3250	2883	2482	9.2038	1542	0981	0334	8.9573	8647	7468	5842	3210	7.5429	12
49	9.3892	3581	3244	2877	2475	9.2030	1533	0971	0323	8.9559	8630	7445	5809	3150	7.5051	11
50	9.3887	3575	3238	2870	2468	9.2022	1525	0961	0311	8.9545	8613	7423	5776	3088	7.4637	10
51	9.3882	3570	3232	2864	2461	9.2015	1516	0951	0299	8.9531	8595	7400	5742	3025	7.4180	9
52	9.3877	3564	3226	2858	2454	9.2007	1507	0940	0287	8.9517	8578	7377	5708	2962	7.3668	8
53	9.3872	3559	3220	2851	2447	9.1999	1498	0930	0276	8.9503	8560	7354	5674	2898	7.3088	7
54	9.3867	3554	3214	2845	2439	9.1991	1489	0920	0264	8.9489	8543	7330	5640	2832	7.2419	6
55	9.3862	3548	3208	2838	2432	9.1983	1480	0910	0252	8.9475	8525	7307	5605	2766	7.1627	5
56	9.3857	3543	3202	2832	2425	9.1975	1471	0900	0240	8.9460	8508	7283	5571	2699	7.0658	4
57	9.3852	3537	3197	2825	2418	9.1967	1462	0890	0228	8.9446	8490	7260	5535	2630	6.9409	3
58	9.3847	3532	3191	2819	2411	9.1959	1453	0879	0216	8.9432	8472	7236	5500	2561	6.7648	2
59	9.3842	3526	3185	2812	2404	9.1951	1445	0869	0204	8.9417	8454	7212	5464	2490	6.4637	1
60	9.3837	3521	3179	2806	2397	9.1943	1436	0859	0192	8.9403	8436	7188	5428	2419	∞	0

| 14° | 13° | 12° | 11° | 10° | 9° | 8° | 7° | 6° | 5° | 4° | 3° | 2° | 1° | 0° | ′ |

LOG SINES

For an explanation of the use of above Tables see p. 5:25.

DEPARTURE INTO D. LONG AND VICE VERSA

DEP = D. LONG COS. MEAN LAT.   D. LONG = DEP. SEC. LAT.

MEAN LAT	COS. LAT	SEC. LAT	MEAN LAT	COS. LAT	SEC. LAT
0.00	1.00	1.00	38.00	0.79	1.27
5.00	1.00	1.00	39.00	0.78	1.29
10.00	0.98	1.02	40.00	0.77	1.31
12.00	0.98	1.02	41.00	0.75	1.33
14.00	0.97	1.03	42.00	0.74	1.35
15.00	0.97	1.04	43.00	0.73	1.37
16.00	0.96	1.04	44.00	0.72	1.39
17.00	0.96	1.05	45.00	0.71	1.41
18.00	0.95	1.05	46.00	0.69	1.44
19.00	0.95	1.06	47.00	0.68	1.47
20.00	0.94	1.06	48.00	0.67	1.49
21.00	0.93	1.07	49.00	0.66	1.52
22.00	0.93	1.08	50.00	0.64	1.56
23.00	0.92	1.09	51.00	0.63	1.59
24.00	0.91	1.09	52.00	0.62	1.62
25.00	0.91	1.10	53.00	0.60	1.66
26.00	0.90	1.11	54.00	0.59	1.70
27.00	0.89	1.12	55.00	0.57	1.74
28.00	0.88	1.13	56.00	0.56	1.79
29.00	0.87	1.14	57.00	0.54	1.84
30.00	0.87	1.15	58.00	0.53	1.89
31.00	0.86	1.17	59.00	0.52	1.94
32.00	0.85	1.18	60.00	0.50	2.00
33.00	0.84	1.19	61.00	0.48	2.06
34.00	0.83	1.21	62.00	0.47	2.13
35.00	0.82	1.22	63.00	0.45	2.20
36.00	0.81	1.24	64.00	0.44	2.28
37.00	0.80	1.25	65.00	0.42	2.37

Therefore to find the departure simply multiply the cos. Mean Latitude by the D. Long e.g. Mean Lat 27, D. Long 247, Dep = 247 × 0.89 = 219.8
To convert departure into D. Long multiply the departure by the secant of the Latitude, e.g. Mean Lat 51, Dep 150, D. Long = 150 × 1.59 = 238.5.

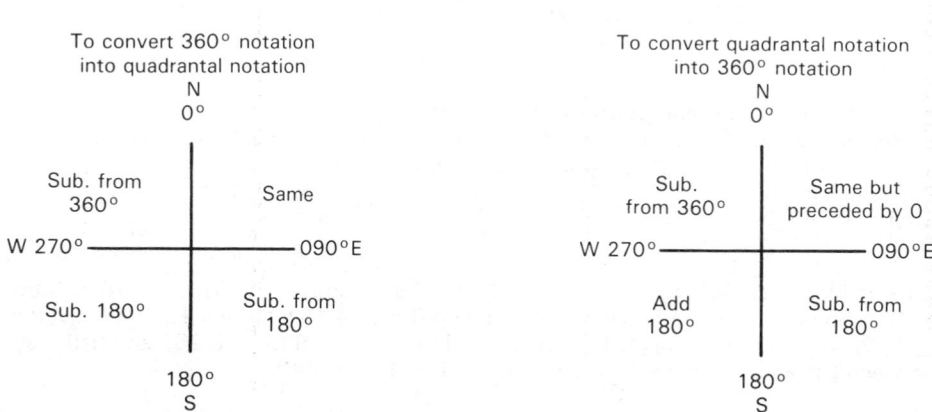

To convert 360° notation into quadrantal notation

To convert quadrantal notation into 360° notation

EXAMPLE:
320° → N 40°W   220° → S 40°W   140° → S 40°E Note with values from 0°–90° although numerically the same they are written as N 40 E or 040°.

TRAVERSE TABLES
For those with scientific calculators see page 5:55

These Tables have many uses but briefly it may be said that if the values for any two of the four things, viz. the Course, Distance, Difference of Latitude and the Departure be given, and these two be found together in the Tables, the values for the two remaining parts will be found in their respective places on the same page.

As the Tables are abbreviated, when any of the given parts (excepting the Course, which should never be multiplied or divided) exceed the table limits, any aliquot part, as a half, third, fourth or tenth, may be taken and the corresponding figures found are to be doubled, trebled, etc., that is multiplied by the same figure that the given number is divided by.

The Tables will be found useful for the run between sights where a large scale chart is not available — also to find the vessel's D.R. position at any time, or to find the Course to steer and distance to run over Short Navigation Distances of a few hundred miles or less.

The Tables are entered by using the Mean Latitude between any two positions, the Difference of Latitude (D. Lat.) in minutes of arc; and the Departure (Dep.) in nautical miles. Departure is the Distance made good in an east-west direction in nautical miles.

DEPARTURE MAY BE CHANGED INTO DIFFERENCE OF LONGITUDE BY USING THE TABLE ON PAGE 5:49.

EXAMPLE (A). To find vessel's D.R. Position
A vessel in Lat. 17°20'N., Long. 38°41'W. steers 320°. Distance 54 miles. What position has she arrived at? From example on page 5:49 we see that 320° = N 40°W.

So we require the D. Lat. and Dep. for 40° and 54 miles; It is easier to divide the distance by 2 (and multiply the figures found by 2) so on page 5:53 we find:

Under 40° and 27' D. Lat. = 20.7 × 2 = 41.4 and Dep. 17.4 × 2 = 34.8.

Now Lat. from = 17°20'N	Mean Lat. is therefore 18° by	Now. Long. from = 38°41'W
D. Lat... 41'.4N	the table on page 5:49 against	D. Long.. 36'.5W
Lat. in... 18°01'.4N	Lat. 18 the Secant = 1.05	Long. in.. 39°17'.5W
	D. Long = 34.8 × 1.05 = 36.5	

Hence the vessel's position is Lat. 18°01'.4N., Long. 39°17'.5W. (approx.)

EXAMPLE (B). To find the Course and Distance
What is the True Course and Distance to steer from Lat. 49°57'N., Long. 6°00'W. to Lat. 43°04'N., Long. 9°38'W. Mean Lat. is about 46°?

Lat. from 49°57'N.		Long. from 6°00'W.	
Lat. to 43°04'N.		Long. to 9°38'W.	
D. Lat. = 6°53'S. × 60 = 413'S.		D. Long. = 3°38'W. × 60 = 218'W.	

Using Mean Lat. 46° we find that cos 46 is 0.69. Therefore the Dep. = 218 × 0.69 = 150. So we search the Traverse Table to find D. Lat. 4.13 and Dep. 1.5 (both divided by 100). We find them adjacent on page 5:51 on the line of Course 20° and half way between Distance columns 4' and 5', i.e., 4.4 × 100 = 440.

So the Course is S20°W. and the Distance 440 miles.

Practice with interpolation will give greater accuracy, but the table — abbreviated as it is — will give quite close results with care.

TRAVERSE TABLES

COURSE	1' D.Lat	1' Dep	2' D.Lat	2' Dep	3' D.Lat	3' Dep	4' D.Lat	4' Dep	5' D.Lat	5' Dep	6' D.Lat	6' Dep	7' D.Lat	7' Dep	8' D.Lat	8' Dep	9' D.Lat	9' Dep	10' D.Lat	10' Dep	11' D.Lat	11' Dep	COURSE
0	1.0	0.0	2.0	0.0	3.0	0.0	4.0	0.0	5.0	0.0	6.0	0.0	7.0	0.0	8.0	0.0	9.0	0.0	10.0	0.0	11.0	0.0	90
1	1.0	0.0	2.0	0.0	3.0	0.1	4.0	0.1	5.0	0.1	6.0	0.1	7.0	0.1	8.0	0.1	9.0	0.2	10.0	0.2	11.0	0.2	89
2	1.0	0.0	2.0	0.1	3.0	0.1	4.0	0.1	5.0	0.2	6.0	0.2	7.0	0.2	8.0	0.3	9.0	0.3	10.0	0.3	11.0	0.4	88
3	1.0	0.1	2.0	0.1	3.0	0.2	4.0	0.2	5.0	0.3	6.0	0.3	7.0	0.4	8.0	0.4	9.0	0.5	10.0	0.5	11.0	0.6	87
4	1.0	0.1	2.0	0.1	3.0	0.2	4.0	0.3	5.0	0.3	6.0	0.4	7.0	0.5	8.0	0.6	9.0	0.6	10.0	0.7	11.0	0.8	86
5	1.0	0.1	2.0	0.2	3.0	0.3	4.0	0.3	5.0	0.4	6.0	0.5	7.0	0.6	8.0	0.7	9.0	0.8	10.0	0.9	11.0	1.0	85
6	1.0	0.1	2.0	0.2	3.0	0.3	4.0	0.4	5.0	0.5	6.0	0.6	7.0	0.7	8.0	0.8	9.0	0.9	9.9	1.0	10.9	1.1	84
7	1.0	0.1	2.0	0.2	3.0	0.4	4.0	0.5	5.0	0.6	6.0	0.7	6.9	0.9	7.9	1.0	8.9	1.1	9.9	1.2	10.9	1.3	83
8	1.0	0.1	2.0	0.3	3.0	0.4	4.0	0.6	5.0	0.7	5.9	0.8	6.9	1.0	7.9	1.1	8.9	1.3	9.9	1.4	10.9	1.5	82
9	1.0	0.2	2.0	0.3	3.0	0.5	4.0	0.6	4.9	0.8	5.9	0.9	6.9	1.1	7.9	1.3	8.9	1.4	9.9	1.6	10.9	1.7	81
10	1.0	0.2	2.0	0.3	3.0	0.5	3.9	0.7	4.9	0.9	5.9	1.0	6.9	1.2	7.9	1.4	8.9	1.6	9.8	1.7	10.8	1.9	80
11	1.0	0.2	2.0	0.4	2.9	0.6	3.9	0.8	4.9	1.0	5.9	1.1	6.9	1.3	7.9	1.5	8.8	1.7	9.8	1.9	10.8	2.1	79
12	1.0	0.2	2.0	0.4	2.9	0.6	3.9	0.8	4.9	1.0	5.9	1.2	6.8	1.5	7.8	1.7	8.8	1.9	9.8	2.1	10.8	2.3	78
13	1.0	0.2	1.9	0.4	2.9	0.7	3.9	0.9	4.9	1.1	5.8	1.3	6.8	1.6	7.8	1.8	8.8	2.0	9.7	2.2	10.7	2.5	77
14	1.0	0.2	1.9	0.5	2.9	0.7	3.9	1.0	4.9	1.2	5.8	1.5	6.8	1.7	7.8	1.9	8.7	2.2	9.7	2.4	10.7	2.7	76
15	1.0	0.3	1.9	0.5	2.9	0.8	3.9	1.0	4.8	1.3	5.8	1.6	6.8	1.8	7.7	2.1	8.7	2.3	9.7	2.6	10.6	2.8	75
16	1.0	0.3	1.9	0.6	2.9	0.8	3.8	1.1	4.8	1.4	5.8	1.7	6.7	1.9	7.7	2.2	8.7	2.5	9.6	2.8	10.6	3.0	74
17	1.0	0.3	1.9	0.6	2.9	0.9	3.8	1.2	4.8	1.5	5.7	1.8	6.7	2.0	7.7	2.3	8.6	2.6	9.6	2.9	10.5	3.2	73
18	1.0	0.3	1.9	0.6	2.9	0.9	3.8	1.2	4.8	1.5	5.7	1.9	6.7	2.2	7.6	2.5	8.6	2.8	9.5	3.1	10.5	3.4	72
19	0.9	0.3	1.9	0.7	2.8	1.0	3.8	1.3	4.7	1.6	5.7	2.0	6.6	2.3	7.6	2.6	8.5	2.9	9.5	3.3	10.4	3.6	71
20	0.9	0.3	1.9	0.7	2.8	1.0	3.8	1.4	4.7	1.7	5.6	2.1	6.6	2.4	7.5	2.7	8.5	3.1	9.4	3.4	10.3	3.8	70
21	0.9	0.4	1.9	0.7	2.8	1.1	3.7	1.4	4.7	1.8	5.6	2.2	6.5	2.5	7.5	2.9	8.4	3.2	9.3	3.6	10.3	3.9	69
22	0.9	0.4	1.9	0.7	2.8	1.1	3.7	1.5	4.6	1.9	5.6	2.2	6.5	2.6	7.4	3.0	8.3	3.4	9.3	3.7	10.2	4.1	68
23	0.9	0.4	1.8	0.8	2.8	1.2	3.7	1.6	4.6	2.0	5.5	2.3	6.4	2.7	7.4	3.1	8.3	3.5	9.2	3.9	10.1	4.3	67
24	0.9	0.4	1.8	0.8	2.7	1.2	3.7	1.6	4.6	2.0	5.5	2.4	6.4	2.8	7.3	3.3	8.2	3.7	9.1	4.1	10.0	4.5	66
25	0.9	0.4	1.8	0.8	2.7	1.3	3.6	1.7	4.5	2.1	5.4	2.5	6.3	3.0	7.3	3.4	8.2	3.8	9.1	4.2	10.0	4.6	65
26	0.9	0.4	1.8	0.9	2.7	1.3	3.6	1.8	4.5	2.2	5.4	2.6	6.3	3.1	7.2	3.5	8.1	3.9	9.0	4.4	9.9	4.8	64
27	0.9	0.5	1.8	0.9	2.7	1.4	3.6	1.8	4.5	2.3	5.3	2.7	6.2	3.2	7.1	3.6	8.0	4.1	8.9	4.5	9.8	5.0	63
28	0.9	0.5	1.8	0.9	2.6	1.4	3.5	1.9	4.4	2.3	5.3	2.8	6.2	3.3	7.1	3.8	7.9	4.2	8.8	4.7	9.7	5.2	62
29	0.9	0.5	1.7	1.0	2.6	1.5	3.5	1.9	4.4	2.4	5.2	2.9	6.1	3.4	7.0	3.9	7.9	4.4	8.7	4.8	9.6	5.3	61
30	0.9	0.5	1.7	1.0	2.6	1.5	3.5	2.0	4.3	2.5	5.2	3.0	6.1	3.5	6.9	4.0	7.8	4.5	8.7	5.0	9.5	5.5	60
31	0.9	0.5	1.7	1.0	2.6	1.5	3.4	2.1	4.3	2.6	5.1	3.1	6.0	3.6	6.9	4.1	7.7	4.6	8.6	5.2	9.4	5.7	59
32	0.8	0.5	1.7	1.1	2.5	1.6	3.4	2.1	4.2	2.6	5.1	3.2	5.9	3.7	6.8	4.2	7.6	4.8	8.5	5.3	9.3	5.8	58
33	0.8	0.5	1.7	1.1	2.5	1.6	3.4	2.2	4.2	2.7	5.0	3.3	5.9	3.8	6.7	4.4	7.5	4.9	8.4	5.4	9.2	6.0	57
34	0.8	0.6	1.7	1.1	2.5	1.7	3.3	2.2	4.1	2.8	5.0	3.4	5.8	3.9	6.6	4.5	7.5	5.0	8.3	5.6	9.1	6.2	56
35	0.8	0.6	1.6	1.1	2.5	1.7	3.3	2.3	4.1	2.9	4.9	3.4	5.7	4.0	6.6	4.6	7.4	5.2	8.2	5.7	9.0	6.3	55
36	0.8	0.6	1.6	1.2	2.4	1.8	3.2	2.4	4.0	2.9	4.9	3.5	5.7	4.1	6.5	4.7	7.3	5.3	8.1	5.9	8.9	6.5	54
37	0.8	0.6	1.6	1.2	2.4	1.8	3.2	2.4	4.0	3.0	4.8	3.6	5.6	4.2	6.4	4.8	7.2	5.4	8.0	6.0	8.8	6.6	53
38	0.8	0.6	1.6	1.2	2.4	1.8	3.2	2.5	3.9	3.1	4.7	3.7	5.5	4.3	6.3	4.9	7.1	5.5	7.9	6.2	8.7	6.8	52
39	0.8	0.6	1.6	1.3	2.3	1.9	3.1	2.5	3.9	3.1	4.7	3.8	5.4	4.4	6.2	5.0	7.0	5.7	7.8	6.3	8.5	6.9	51
40	0.8	0.6	1.5	1.3	2.3	1.9	3.1	2.6	3.8	3.2	4.6	3.9	5.4	4.5	6.1	5.1	6.9	5.8	7.7	6.4	8.4	7.1	50
41	0.8	0.7	1.5	1.3	2.3	2.0	3.0	2.6	3.8	3.3	4.5	3.9	5.3	4.6	6.0	5.2	6.8	5.9	7.5	6.6	8.3	7.2	49
42	0.7	0.7	1.5	1.3	2.2	2.0	3.0	2.7	3.7	3.3	4.5	4.0	5.2	4.7	5.9	5.4	6.7	6.0	7.4	6.7	8.2	7.4	48
43	0.7	0.7	1.5	1.4	2.2	2.0	2.9	2.7	3.7	3.4	4.4	4.1	5.1	4.8	5.9	5.5	6.6	6.1	7.3	6.8	8.0	7.5	47
44	0.7	0.7	1.4	1.4	2.2	2.1	2.9	2.8	3.6	3.5	4.3	4.2	5.0	4.9	5.8	5.6	6.5	6.3	7.2	6.9	7.9	7.6	46
45	0.7	0.7	1.4	1.4	2.1	2.1	2.8	2.8	3.5	3.5	4.2	4.2	4.9	4.9	5.7	5.7	6.4	6.4	7.1	7.1	7.8	7.8	45

| COURSE | 1' Dep | 1' D.Lat | 2' Dep | 2' D.Lat | 3' Dep | 3' D.Lat | 4' Dep | 4' D.Lat | 5' Dep | 5' D.Lat | 6' Dep | 6' D.Lat | 7' Dep | 7' D.Lat | 8' Dep | 8' D.Lat | 9' Dep | 9' D.Lat | 10' Dep | 10' D.Lat | 11' Dep | 11' D.Lat | COURSE |

DISTANCE

Read the columns downwards for Courses 0° − 45° and upwards from 45° − 90°

TRAVERSE TABLES

COURSE	12' D.Lat.	12' Dep.	13' D.Lat.	13' Dep.	14' D.Lat.	14' Dep.	15' D.Lat.	15' Dep.	16' D.Lat.	16' Dep.	17' D.Lat.	17' Dep.	18' D.Lat.	18' Dep.	19' D.Lat.	19' Dep.	20' D.Lat.	20' Dep.	COURSE
0	12.0	0.0	13.0	0.0	14.0	0.0	15.0	0.0	16.0	0.0	17.0	0.0	18.0	0.0	19.0	0.0	20.0	0.0	90
1	12.0	0.2	13.0	0.2	14.0	0.2	15.0	0.3	16.0	0.3	17.0	0.3	18.0	0.3	19.0	0.3	20.0	0.3	89
2	12.0	0.4	13.0	0.5	14.0	0.5	15.0	0.5	16.0	0.6	17.0	0.6	18.0	0.6	19.0	0.7	20.0	0.7	88
3	12.0	0.6	13.0	0.7	14.0	0.7	15.0	0.8	16.0	0.8	17.0	0.9	18.0	0.9	19.0	1.0	20.0	1.0	87
4	12.0	0.8	13.0	0.9	14.0	1.0	15.0	1.0	16.0	1.1	17.0	1.2	18.0	1.3	19.0	1.3	20.0	1.4	86
5	12.0	1.0	13.0	1.1	13.9	1.2	14.9	1.3	15.9	1.4	16.9	1.5	17.9	1.6	18.9	1.7	19.9	1.7	85
6	11.9	1.3	12.9	1.4	13.9	1.5	14.9	1.6	15.9	1.7	16.9	1.8	17.9	1.9	18.9	2.0	19.9	2.1	84
7	11.9	1.5	12.9	1.6	13.9	1.7	14.9	1.8	15.9	1.9	16.9	2.1	17.9	2.2	18.9	2.3	19.9	2.4	83
8	11.9	1.7	12.8	1.8	13.9	1.9	14.9	2.1	15.8	2.2	16.8	2.4	17.8	2.5	18.8	2.6	19.8	2.8	82
9	11.9	1.9	12.8	2.0	13.8	2.2	14.8	2.3	15.8	2.5	16.8	2.7	17.8	2.8	18.8	3.0	19.8	3.1	81
10	11.8	2.1	12.8	2.3	13.8	2.4	14.8	2.6	15.7	2.8	16.7	3.0	17.7	3.1	18.7	3.3	19.7	3.5	80
11	11.8	2.3	12.8	2.5	13.7	2.7	14.7	2.9	15.7	3.1	16.7	3.2	17.7	3.4	18.7	3.6	19.6	3.8	79
12	11.7	2.5	12.7	2.7	13.7	2.9	14.7	3.1	15.7	3.3	16.6	3.5	17.6	3.7	18.6	4.0	19.6	4.2	78
13	11.7	2.7	12.7	2.9	13.6	3.1	14.6	3.4	15.6	3.6	16.6	3.8	17.5	4.0	18.5	4.3	19.5	4.5	77
14	11.6	2.9	12.6	3.1	13.6	3.4	14.6	3.6	15.5	3.9	16.5	4.1	17.5	4.4	18.4	4.6	19.4	4.8	76
15	11.6	3.1	12.6	3.4	13.5	3.6	14.5	3.9	15.4	4.1	16.4	4.4	17.4	4.7	18.4	4.9	19.3	5.2	75
16	11.5	3.3	12.5	3.6	13.5	3.9	14.4	4.1	15.4	4.4	16.3	4.7	17.3	5.0	18.3	5.2	19.2	5.5	74
17	11.5	3.5	12.4	3.8	13.4	4.1	14.3	4.4	15.3	4.7	16.3	5.0	17.2	5.3	18.2	5.6	19.1	5.8	73
18	11.4	3.7	12.4	4.0	13.3	4.3	14.3	4.6	15.2	4.9	16.2	5.3	17.1	5.6	18.1	5.9	19.0	6.2	72
19	11.3	3.9	12.3	4.2	13.2	4.6	14.2	4.9	15.1	5.2	16.1	5.5	17.0	5.9	18.0	6.2	18.9	6.5	71
20	11.3	4.1	12.2	4.4	13.2	4.8	14.1	5.1	15.0	5.5	16.0	5.8	16.9	6.2	17.9	6.5	18.8	6.8	70
21	11.2	4.3	12.1	4.7	13.1	5.0	14.0	5.4	14.9	5.7	15.9	6.1	16.8	6.5	17.7	6.8	18.7	7.2	69
22	11.1	4.5	12.1	4.9	13.0	5.2	13.9	5.6	14.8	6.0	15.8	6.4	16.7	6.7	17.6	7.1	18.5	7.5	68
23	11.0	4.7	12.0	5.1	12.9	5.5	13.8	5.9	14.7	6.3	15.6	6.6	16.6	7.0	17.5	7.4	18.4	7.8	67
24	11.0	4.9	11.9	5.3	12.8	5.7	13.7	6.1	14.6	6.5	15.5	6.9	16.4	7.3	17.4	7.7	18.3	8.1	66
25	10.9	5.1	11.8	5.5	12.7	5.9	13.6	6.3	14.5	6.8	15.4	7.2	16.3	7.6	17.2	8.0	18.1	8.5	65
26	10.8	5.3	11.7	5.7	12.6	6.1	13.5	6.6	14.4	7.0	15.3	7.5	16.2	7.9	17.1	8.3	18.0	8.8	64
27	10.7	5.4	11.6	5.9	12.5	6.4	13.4	6.8	14.3	7.3	15.1	7.7	16.0	8.2	16.9	8.6	17.8	9.1	63
28	10.6	5.6	11.5	6.1	12.4	6.6	13.2	7.0	14.1	7.5	15.0	8.0	15.9	8.5	16.8	8.9	17.7	9.4	62
29	10.5	5.8	11.4	6.3	12.2	6.8	13.1	7.3	14.0	7.8	14.9	8.2	15.7	8.7	16.6	9.2	17.5	9.7	61
30	10.4	6.0	11.3	6.5	12.1	7.0	13.0	7.5	13.9	8.0	14.7	8.5	15.6	9.0	16.5	9.5	17.3	10.0	60
31	10.3	6.2	11.1	6.7	12.0	7.2	12.9	7.7	13.7	8.2	14.6	8.8	15.4	9.3	16.3	9.8	17.1	10.3	59
32	10.2	6.4	11.0	6.9	11.9	7.4	12.7	7.9	13.6	8.5	14.4	9.0	15.3	9.5	16.1	10.1	17.0	10.6	58
33	10.1	6.5	10.9	7.1	11.7	7.6	12.6	8.2	13.4	8.7	14.3	9.3	15.1	9.8	15.9	10.3	16.8	10.9	57
34	9.9	6.7	10.8	7.3	11.6	7.8	12.4	8.4	13.3	8.9	14.1	9.5	14.9	10.1	15.8	10.6	16.6	11.2	56
35	9.8	6.9	10.6	7.5	11.5	8.0	12.3	8.6	13.1	9.2	13.9	9.8	14.7	10.3	15.6	10.9	16.4	11.5	55
36	9.7	7.1	10.5	7.6	11.3	8.2	12.1	8.8	12.9	9.4	13.8	10.0	14.6	10.6	15.4	11.2	16.2	11.8	54
37	9.6	7.2	10.4	7.8	11.2	8.4	12.0	9.0	12.8	9.6	13.6	10.2	14.4	10.8	15.2	11.4	16.0	12.0	53
38	9.5	7.4	10.2	8.0	11.0	8.6	11.8	9.2	12.6	9.9	13.4	10.5	14.2	11.1	15.0	11.7	15.8	12.3	52
39	9.3	7.6	10.1	8.2	10.9	8.8	11.7	9.4	12.4	10.1	13.2	10.7	14.0	11.3	14.8	12.0	15.5	12.6	51
40	9.2	7.7	10.0	8.4	10.7	9.0	11.5	9.6	12.3	10.3	13.0	10.9	13.8	11.6	14.6	12.2	15.3	12.9	50
41	9.1	7.9	9.8	8.5	10.6	9.2	11.3	9.8	12.1	10.5	12.8	11.2	13.6	11.8	14.3	12.5	15.1	13.1	49
42	8.9	8.0	9.7	8.7	10.4	9.4	11.1	10.0	11.9	10.7	12.6	11.4	13.4	12.0	14.1	12.7	14.9	13.4	48
43	8.8	8.2	9.5	8.9	10.2	9.5	11.0	10.2	11.7	10.9	12.4	11.6	13.2	12.3	13.9	13.0	14.6	13.6	47
44	8.6	8.3	9.4	9.0	10.1	9.7	10.8	10.4	11.5	11.1	12.2	11.8	12.9	12.5	13.7	13.2	14.4	13.9	46
45	8.5	8.5	9.2	9.2	9.9	9.9	10.6	10.6	11.3	11.3	12.0	12.0	12.7	12.7	13.4	13.4	14.1	14.1	45

| | Dep. | D.Lat. | Dep. | D.Lat. | Dep. | D.Lat. | Dep. | D.Lat. | Dep. | D.Lat. | Dep. | D.Lat. | Dep. | D.Lat. | Dep. | D.Lat. | Dep. | D.Lat. | |
| | 12' | | 13' | | 14' | | 15' | | 16' | | 17' | | 18' | | 19' | | 20' | | COURSE |

DISTANCE

Read the columns downwards for Courses 0° −45° and upwards from 45° −90°

TRAVERSE TABLES

COURSE	DISTANCE																	COURSE
	21'		22'		23'		24'		25'		26'		27'		28'		29'	
	D. Lat.	Dep.	D. Lat.	Dep.	D. Lat.	Dep.	D. Lat.	Dep.	D. Lat.	Dep.	D. Lat.	Dep.	D. Lat.	Dep.	D. Lat.	Dep.	D. Lat.	Dep.	
0	21.0	0.0	22.0	0.0	23.0	0.0	24.0	0.0	25.0	0.0	26.0	0.0	27.0	0.0	28.0	0.0	29.0	0.0	90
1	21.0	0.4	22.0	0.4	23.0	0.4	24.0	0.4	25.0	0.4	26.0	0.5	27.0	0.5	28.0	0.5	29.0	0.5	89
2	21.0	0.7	22.0	0.8	23.0	0.8	24.0	0.8	25.0	0.9	26.0	0.9	27.0	0.9	28.0	1.0	29.0	1.0	88
3	21.0	1.1	22.0	1.2	23.0	1.2	24.0	1.3	25.0	1.3	26.0	1.4	27.0	1.4	28.0	1.5	29.0	1.5	87
4	20.9	1.5	21.9	1.5	22.9	1.6	23.9	1.7	24.9	1.7	25.9	1.8	26.9	1.9	27.9	2.0	28.9	2.0	86
5	20.9	1.8	21.9	1.9	22.9	2.0	23.9	2.1	24.9	2.2	25.9	2.3	26.9	2.4	27.9	2.4	28.9	2.5	85
6	20.9	2.2	21.9	2.3	22.9	2.4	23.9	2.5	24.9	2.6	25.9	2.7	26.9	2.8	27.8	2.9	28.8	3.0	84
7	20.8	2.6	21.8	2.7	22.8	2.8	23.8	2.9	24.8	3.0	25.8	3.2	26.8	3.3	27.8	3.4	28.8	3.5	83
8	20.8	2.9	21.8	3.1	22.8	3.2	23.8	3.3	24.8	3.5	25.7	3.6	26.7	3.8	27.7	3.9	28.7	4.0	82
9	20.7	3.3	21.7	3.4	22.7	3.6	23.7	3.8	24.7	3.9	25.7	4.1	26.7	4.2	27.7	4.4	28.6	4.5	81
10	20.7	3.6	21.7	3.8	22.7	4.0	23.6	4.2	24.6	4.3	25.6	4.5	26.6	4.7	27.6	4.9	28.6	5.0	80
11	20.6	4.0	21.6	4.2	22.6	4.4	23.6	4.6	24.5	4.8	25.5	5.0	26.5	5.2	27.5	5.3	28.5	5.5	79
12	20.5	4.4	21.5	4.6	22.5	4.8	23.5	5.0	24.5	5.2	25.4	5.4	26.4	5.6	27.4	5.8	28.4	6.0	78
13	20.5	4.7	21.4	4.9	22.4	5.2	23.4	5.4	24.4	5.6	25.3	5.8	26.3	6.1	27.3	6.3	28.3	6.5	77
14	20.4	5.1	21.3	5.3	22.3	5.6	23.3	5.8	24.3	6.0	25.2	6.3	26.2	6.5	27.2	6.8	28.1	7.0	76
15	20.3	5.4	21.3	5.7	22.2	6.0	23.2	6.2	24.1	6.5	25.1	6.7	26.1	7.0	27.0	7.2	28.0	7.5	75
16	20.2	5.8	21.1	6.1	22.1	6.3	23.1	6.6	24.0	6.9	25.0	7.2	26.0	7.4	26.9	7.7	27.9	8.0	74
17	20.1	6.1	21.0	6.4	22.0	6.7	23.0	7.0	23.9	7.3	24.9	7.6	25.8	7.9	26.8	8.2	27.7	8.5	73
18	20.0	6.5	20.9	6.8	21.9	7.1	22.8	7.4	23.8	7.7	24.7	8.0	25.7	8.3	26.6	8.7	27.6	9.0	72
19	19.9	6.8	20.8	7.2	21.7	7.5	22.7	7.8	23.6	8.1	24.6	8.5	25.5	8.8	26.5	9.1	27.4	9.4	71
20	19.7	7.2	20.7	7.5	21.6	7.9	22.6	8.2	23.5	8.6	24.4	8.9	25.4	9.2	26.3	9.6	27.3	9.9	70
21	19.6	7.5	20.5	7.9	21.5	8.2	22.4	8.6	23.3	9.0	24.3	9.3	25.2	9.7	26.1	10.0	27.1	10.4	69
22	19.5	7.9	20.4	8.2	21.3	8.6	22.3	9.0	23.2	9.4	24.1	9.7	25.0	10.1	26.0	10.5	26.9	10.9	68
23	19.3	8.2	20.3	8.6	21.2	9.0	22.1	9.4	23.0	9.8	23.9	10.2	24.9	10.5	25.8	10.9	26.7	11.3	67
24	19.2	8.5	20.1	8.9	21.0	9.4	21.9	9.8	22.8	10.2	23.8	10.6	24.7	11.0	25.6	11.4	26.5	11.8	66
25	19.0	8.9	19.9	9.3	20.8	9.7	21.8	10.1	22.7	10.6	23.6	11.0	24.5	11.4	25.4	11.8	26.3	12.3	65
26	18.9	9.2	19.8	9.6	20.7	10.1	21.6	10.5	22.5	11.0	23.4	11.4	24.3	11.8	25.2	12.3	26.1	12.7	64
27	18.7	9.5	19.6	10.0	20.5	10.4	21.4	10.9	22.3	11.3	23.2	11.8	24.1	12.3	24.9	12.7	25.8	13.2	63
28	18.5	9.9	19.4	10.3	20.3	10.8	21.2	11.3	22.1	11.7	23.0	12.2	23.8	12.7	24.7	13.1	25.6	13.6	62
29	18.4	10.2	19.2	10.7	20.1	11.2	21.0	11.6	21.9	12.1	22.7	12.6	23.6	13.1	24.5	13.6	25.4	14.1	61
30	18.2	10.5	19.1	11.0	19.9	11.5	20.8	12.0	21.7	12.5	22.5	13.0	23.4	13.5	24.2	14.0	25.1	14.5	60
31	18.0	10.8	18.9	11.3	19.7	11.8	20.6	12.4	21.4	12.9	22.3	13.4	23.1	13.9	24.0	14.4	24.9	14.9	59
32	17.8	11.1	18.7	11.7	19.5	12.2	20.4	12.7	21.2	13.2	22.0	13.8	22.9	14.3	23.7	14.8	24.6	15.4	58
33	17.6	11.4	18.5	12.0	19.3	12.5	20.1	13.1	21.0	13.6	21.8	14.2	22.6	14.7	23.5	15.2	24.3	15.8	57
34	17.4	11.7	18.2	12.3	19.1	12.9	19.9	13.4	20.7	14.0	21.6	14.5	22.4	15.1	23.2	15.7	24.0	16.2	56
35	17.2	12.0	18.0	12.6	18.8	13.2	19.7	13.8	20.5	14.3	21.3	14.9	22.1	15.5	22.9	16.1	23.8	16.6	55
36	17.0	12.3	17.8	12.9	18.6	13.5	19.4	14.1	20.2	14.7	21.0	15.3	21.8	15.9	22.7	16.5	23.5	17.0	54
37	16.8	12.6	17.6	13.2	18.4	13.8	19.2	14.4	20.0	15.0	20.8	15.6	21.6	16.2	22.4	16.9	23.2	17.5	53
38	16.5	12.9	17.3	13.5	18.1	14.2	18.9	14.8	19.7	15.4	20.5	16.0	21.3	16.6	22.1	17.2	22.8	17.9	52
39	16.3	13.2	17.1	13.8	17.9	14.5	18.7	15.1	19.4	15.7	20.2	16.4	21.0	17.0	21.8	17.6	22.5	18.3	51
40	16.1	13.5	16.9	14.1	17.6	14.8	18.4	15.4	19.2	16.1	19.9	16.7	20.7	17.4	21.4	18.0	22.2	18.6	50
41	15.8	13.8	16.6	14.4	17.4	15.1	18.1	15.7	18.9	16.4	19.6	17.1	20.4	17.7	21.1	18.4	21.9	19.0	49
42	15.6	14.1	16.3	14.7	17.1	15.4	17.8	16.1	18.6	16.7	19.3	17.4	20.1	18.1	20.8	18.7	21.6	19.4	48
43	15.4	14.3	16.1	15.0	16.8	15.7	17.6	16.4	18.3	17.0	19.0	17.7	19.7	18.4	20.5	19.1	21.2	19.8	47
44	15.1	14.6	15.8	15.3	16.5	16.0	17.3	16.7	18.0	17.4	18.7	18.1	19.4	18.8	20.1	19.5	20.9	20.1	46
45	14.8	14.8	15.6	15.6	16.3	16.3	17.0	17.0	17.7	17.7	18.4	18.4	19.1	19.1	19.8	19.8	20.5	20.5	45
	Dep.	D. Lat.	Dep.	D. Lat.	Dep.	D. Lat.	Dep.	D. Lat.	Dep.	D. Lat.	Dep.	D. Lat.	Dep.	D. Lat.	Dep.	D. Lat.	Dep.	D. Lat.	COURSE
	21'		22'		23'		24'		25'		26'		27'		28'		29'	

DISTANCE

Read the columns downwards for Courses 0° −45° and upwards from 45° −90°

TRAVERSE TABLES

C O U R S E	DISTANCE																	C O U R S E
	30′		40′		50′		60′		70′		80′		90′		100′		200′	
	D. Lat.	Dep.	D. Lat.	Dep.	D. Lat.	Dep.	D. Lat.	Dep.	D. Lat.	Dep.	D. Lat.	Dep.	D. Lat.	Dep.	D. Lat.	Dep.	D. Lat.	Dep.	
0	30.0	0.0	40.0	0.0	50.0	0.0	60.0	0.0	70.0	0.0	80.0	0.0	90.0	0.0	100.0	0.0	200.0	0.0	90
1	30.0	0.5	40.0	0.7	50.0	0.9	60.0	1.0	70.0	1.2	80.0	1.4	90.0	1.6	100.0	1.7	200.0	3.5	89
2	30.0	1.0	40.0	1.4	50.0	1.7	60.0	2.1	70.0	2.4	80.0	2.8	89.9	3.1	99.9	3.5	199.9	7.0	88
3	30.0	1.6	39.9	2.1	49.9	2.6	59.9	3.1	69.9	3.7	79.9	4.2	89.9	4.7	99.9	5.2	199.7	10.5	87
4	29.9	2.1	39.9	2.8	49.9	3.5	59.9	4.2	69.8	4.9	79.8	5.6	89.8	6.3	99.8	7.0	199.5	14.0	86
5	29.9	2.6	39.8	3.5	49.8	4.4	59.8	5.2	69.7	6.1	79.7	7.0	89.7	7.8	99.6	8.7	199.2	17.4	85
6	29.8	3.1	39.8	4.2	49.7	5.2	59.7	6.3	69.6	7.3	79.6	8.4	89.5	9.4	99.5	10.5	198.9	20.9	84
7	29.8	3.7	39.7	4.9	49.6	6.1	59.6	7.3	69.5	8.5	79.4	9.7	89.3	11.0	99.3	12.2	198.5	24.4	83
8	29.7	4.2	39.6	5.6	49.5	7.0	59.4	8.4	69.3	9.7	79.2	11.1	89.1	12.5	99.0	13.9	198.1	27.8	82
9	29.6	4.7	39.5	6.3	49.4	7.8	59.3	9.4	69.1	11.0	79.0	12.5	88.9	14.1	98.8	15.6	197.5	31.3	81
10	29.5	5.2	39.4	6.9	49.2	8.7	59.1	10.4	68.9	12.2	78.8	13.9	88.6	15.6	98.5	17.4	197.0	34.7	80
11	29.4	5.7	39.3	7.6	49.1	9.5	58.9	11.4	68.7	13.4	78.5	15.3	88.3	17.2	98.2	19.1	196.3	38.2	79
12	29.3	6.2	39.1	8.3	48.9	10.4	58.7	12.5	68.5	14.6	78.3	16.6	88.0	18.7	97.8	20.8	195.6	41.6	78
13	29.2	6.7	39.0	9.0	48.7	11.2	58.5	13.5	68.2	15.7	77.9	18.0	87.7	20.2	97.4	22.5	194.9	45.0	77
14	29.1	7.3	38.8	9.7	48.5	12.1	58.2	14.5	67.9	16.9	77.6	19.4	87.3	21.8	97.0	24.2	194.1	48.4	76
15	29.0	7.8	38.6	10.4	48.3	12.9	58.0	15.5	67.6	18.1	77.3	20.7	86.9	23.3	96.6	25.9	193.2	51.8	75
16	28.8	8.3	38.5	11.0	48.1	13.8	57.7	16.5	67.3	19.3	76.9	22.1	86.5	24.8	96.1	27.6	192.3	55.1	74
17	28.7	8.8	38.3	11.7	47.8	14.6	57.4	17.5	66.9	20.5	76.5	23.4	86.1	26.3	95.6	29.2	191.3	58.5	73
18	28.5	9.3	38.0	12.4	47.6	15.5	57.1	18.5	66.6	21.6	76.1	24.7	85.6	27.8	95.1	30.9	190.2	61.8	72
19	28.4	9.8	37.8	13.0	47.3	16.3	56.7	19.5	66.2	22.8	75.6	26.0	85.1	29.3	94.6	32.6	189.1	65.1	71
20	28.2	10.3	37.6	13.7	47.0	17.1	56.4	20.5	65.8	23.9	75.2	27.4	84.6	30.8	94.0	34.2	187.9	68.4	70
21	28.0	10.8	37.3	14.3	46.7	17.9	56.0	21.5	65.4	25.1	74.7	28.7	84.0	32.3	93.4	35.8	186.7	71.7	69
22	27.8	11.2	37.1	15.0	46.4	18.7	55.6	22.5	64.9	26.2	74.2	30.0	83.4	33.7	92.7	37.5	185.4	74.9	68
23	27.6	11.7	36.8	15.6	46.0	19.5	55.2	23.4	64.4	27.4	73.6	31.3	82.8	35.2	92.1	39.1	184.1	78.1	67
24	27.4	12.2	36.5	16.3	45.7	20.3	54.8	24.4	63.9	28.5	73.1	32.5	82.2	36.6	91.4	40.7	182.7	81.3	66
25	27.2	12.7	36.3	16.9	45.3	21.1	54.4	25.4	63.4	29.6	72.5	33.8	81.6	38.0	90.6	42.3	181.3	84.5	65
26	27.0	13.2	36.0	17.5	44.9	21.9	53.9	26.3	62.9	30.7	71.9	35.1	80.9	39.5	89.9	43.8	179.8	87.7	64
27	26.7	13.6	35.6	18.2	44.6	22.7	53.5	27.2	62.4	31.8	71.3	36.3	80.2	40.9	89.1	45.4	178.2	90.8	63
28	26.5	14.1	35.3	18.8	44.1	23.5	53.0	28.2	61.8	32.9	70.6	37.6	79.5	42.3	88.3	46.9	176.6	93.9	62
29	26.2	14.5	35.0	19.4	43.7	24.2	52.5	29.1	61.2	33.9	70.0	38.8	78.7	43.6	87.5	48.5	174.9	97.0	61
30	26.0	15.0	34.6	20.0	43.3	25.0	52.0	30.0	60.6	35.0	69.3	40.0	77.9	45.0	86.6	50.0	173.2	100.0	60
31	25.7	15.5	34.3	20.6	42.9	25.8	51.4	30.9	60.0	36.1	68.6	41.2	77.1	46.4	85.7	51.5	171.4	103.0	59
32	25.4	15.9	33.9	21.2	42.4	26.5	50.9	31.8	59.4	37.1	67.8	42.4	76.3	47.7	84.8	53.0	169.6	106.0	58
33	25.2	16.3	33.5	21.8	41.9	27.2	50.3	32.7	58.7	38.1	67.1	43.6	75.5	49.0	83.9	54.5	167.7	108.9	57
34	24.9	16.8	33.2	22.4	41.5	28.0	49.7	33.6	58.0	39.1	66.3	44.7	74.6	50.3	82.9	55.9	165.8	111.8	56
35	24.6	17.2	32.8	22.9	41.0	28.7	49.1	34.4	57.3	40.2	65.5	45.9	73.7	51.6	81.9	57.4	163.8	114.7	55
36	24.3	17.6	32.4	23.5	40.5	29.4	48.5	35.3	56.6	41.1	64.7	47.0	72.8	52.9	80.9	58.8	161.8	117.6	54
37	24.0	18.1	31.9	24.1	39.9	30.1	47.9	36.1	55.9	42.1	63.9	48.1	71.9	54.2	79.9	60.2	159.7	120.4	53
38	23.6	18.5	31.5	24.6	39.4	30.8	47.3	36.9	55.2	43.1	63.0	49.3	70.9	55.4	78.8	61.6	157.6	123.1	52
39	23.3	18.9	31.1	25.2	38.9	31.5	46.6	37.8	54.4	44.1	62.2	50.3	69.9	56.6	77.7	62.9	155.4	125.9	51
40	23.0	19.3	30.6	25.7	38.3	32.1	46.0	38.6	53.6	45.0	61.3	51.4	68.9	57.9	76.6	64.3	153.2	128.6	50
41	22.6	19.7	30.2	26.2	37.7	32.8	45.3	39.4	52.8	45.9	60.4	52.5	67.9	59.0	75.5	65.6	150.9	131.2	49
42	22.3	20.1	29.7	26.8	37.2	33.5	44.6	40.1	52.0	46.8	59.5	53.5	66.9	60.2	74.3	66.9	148.6	133.8	48
43	21.9	20.5	29.3	27.3	36.6	34.1	43.9	40.9	51.2	47.7	58.5	54.6	65.8	61.4	73.1	68.2	146.3	136.4	47
44	21.6	20.8	28.8	27.8	36.0	34.7	43.2	41.7	50.4	48.6	57.5	55.6	64.7	62.5	71.9	69.5	143.9	138.9	46
45	21.2	21.2	28.3	28.3	35.4	35.4	42.4	42.4	49.5	49.5	56.6	56.6	63.6	63.6	70.7	70.7	141.4	141.4	45
	Dep.	D. Lat.	Dep.	D. Lat.	Dep.	D. Lat.	Dep.	D. Lat.	Dep.	D. Lat.	Dep.	D. Lat.	Dep.	D. Lat.	Dep.	D. Lat.	Dep.	D. Lat.	C O U R S E
	30′		40′		50′		60′		70′		80′		90′		100′		200′		

DISTANCE

Read the columns downwards for Courses 0° − 45° and upwards from 45° − 90°

TO FIND THE D.R. POSITION AND COURSE AND DISTANCE BY CALCULATOR

The same results as obtained by the Traverse Tables can be achieved very simply by the use of a scientific calculator.

The same examples as given on page 5:50 are repeated below. The working as shown may look somewhat lengthy but with practice the calculation can be done very quickly and accurately.

EXAMPLE (A) To find vessel's D.R. Position
A vessel in Lat. 17°20′N., Long. 38°41′W. steers 320°(N.40°W.) for 54 miles. What position has she arrived at?

To find D. Lat.   D. Lat. = Distance × cos Co.

Quantity		Entry	Reading
Course	→	40	40
		cos	0.76604
		STO 1	0.76604
Dist.	→	54	54
		×	54
		RCL 1	0.76604
D. Lat.	←	=	41.4

To find Dep.   Dep. = Dist. × sin Co.

Quantity		Entry	Reading
Course	→	40	40
		sin	0.64279
		STO 1	0.64279
Dist.	→	54	54
		×	54
		RCL 1	0.64279
Dep.	←	=	34.7

To find D. Long.   D. Long. $= \dfrac{\text{Dep.}}{\cos \text{Mean Lat.}}$

Mean Lat. = Initial Lat. + ½ D. Lat. = 17°20′N. + 20′.5 = 17°40′.5N. (N.B. a mental approximation for Mean Lat. will do.)

Quantity		Entry	Reading
Mean Lat.	→	17.68	17.68
		cos	0.95277
		STO 1	0.95277
Dep.	→	34.7	34.7
		÷	34.7
		RCL 1	0.95277
D. Long.	←	=	36.4

Lat. from	17°20′N.		Long. from	38°41′W.
D. Lat.	41′.4N.		D. Long.	36′.4W.
D.R. Position	18°01′.4N.			39°17′.4W.

EXAMPLE (B) To find the Course and Distance
What is the True Course and Distance to steer from Lat. 49°57′N., Long. 6°00′W. to Lat. 43°04′N., Long. 9°38′W.

Lat. from	49°57′N.	Long. from	6°00′W.
Lat. to	43°04′N.	Long. to	9°38′W.
D. Lat.	6°53′S. = 413′S	D. Long.	3°38′W. = 218′W.

Mean Lat. = 43°04′ + 3°26′.5 = 46°30′.5N. (N.B. a mental approximation for Mean Lat. will do.)

To find Dep.   Departure = D. Long. × cos. Mean Lat.

Quantity		Entry	Reading
Mean Lat.	→	46.5	46.5
		cos	0.68835
		STO 1	0.68835
D. Long.	→	218	218
		×	218
		RCL 1	0.68835
Dep.	←	=	150

To find the Course. $\tan \text{Co.} = \dfrac{\text{Dep.}}{\text{D. Lat.}}$

Quantity		Entry	Reading
Dep.	→	150	150
		÷	150
D. Lat.	→	413	413
		=	0.3632
		arc	0.3632
Course	←	tan	20

Therefore the Course is S.20°W.

To find the Distance. $\text{Distance} = \dfrac{\text{D. Lat.}}{\cos \text{Co.}}$

Quantity		Entry	Reading
Course	→	20	20
		cos	0.93969
		STO 1	0.93969
D. Lat.	→	413	413
		÷	413
		RCL 1	0.93969
Distance	←	=	439.5

So the Course is S.20°W. and the Distance 439.5 miles.

Note: These formulae assume that the earth is flat which is why this routine is often referred to as Plane Sailing. This assumption is reasonable for distances up to 500 or 600 miles. Therefore do not use for distances greater than this.

MIDDLE LATITUDE SAILING

For distances greater than 500-600 miles the same procedures can be followed except that a correction has to be applied to the mean latitude.

This corrected MEAN latitude is called the MIDDLE latitude.

Mean Lat.	DIFFERENCE OF LATITUDE																Mean Lat.
°	2°	4°	6°	8°	10°	11°	12°	13°	14°	15°	16°	17°	18°	19°	20°	21°	°
11	−129	−125	−118	−110	−100	−93	−87	−80	−72	−64	−57	−48	−38	−29	−18	−8	11
12	−114	−111	−105	−98	−89	−83	−77	−71	−64	−57	−49	−42	−33	−23	−15	−5	12
13	−102	−100	−95	−88	−79	−75	−69	−63	−57	−51	−43	−36	−27	−20	−12	−3	13
14	−93	−90	−86	−80	−72	−67	−62	−57	−51	−45	−38	−31	−24	−16	−9	0	14
15	−85	−83	−79	−73	−65	−61	−56	−51	−46	−40	−34	−27	−21	−13	−6	+1	15
16	−79	−76	−72	−66	−60	−56	−51	−46	−41	−36	−30	−24	−17	−10	−4	+4	16
17	−72	−70	−66	−61	−55	−51	−47	−42	−37	−32	−27	−21	−15	−8	−2	+6	17
18	−67	−65	−61	−56	−50	−46	−43	−38	−34	−29	−24	−18	−12	−6	+1	+8	18
19	−62	−60	−57	−52	−46	−43	−39	−35	−30	−25	−21	−15	−9	−3	+3	+10	19
20	−58	−56	−53	−48	−42	−39	−35	−31	−27	−22	−18	−13	−7	−1	+5	+13	20
22	−50	−48	−45	−41	−36	−33	−29	−25	−22	−17	−13	−8	−3	+3	+9	+15	22
24	−44	−42	−40	−36	−31	−28	−24	−21	−17	−13	−8	−4	+1	+6	+12	+17	24
26	−39	−37	−35	−31	−26	−23	−20	−16	−13	−9	−5	0	+5	+10	+15	+21	26
28	−34	−32	−30	−26	−22	−19	−16	−12	−9	−5	−1	+3	+8	+13	+18	+23	28
30	−30	−29	−26	−22	−18	−15	−12	−9	−6	−2	+2	+6	+11	+16	+21	+26	30
35	−22	−21	−18	−15	−10	−7	−5	−1	+2	+6	+10	+14	+18	+23	+28	+33	35
40	−16	−14	−12	−8	−4	−1	+2	+5	+8	+12	+16	+20	+25	+29	+34	+40	40
45	−11	−10	−7	−3	+1	+4	+7	+11	+14	+18	+22	+27	+31	+36	+41	+47	45
50	−8	−6	−3	+1	+6	+9	+12	+16	+20	+24	+28	+33	+38	+44	+49	+55	50
55	−5	−3	0	+5	+10	+14	+17	+21	+25	+30	+35	+40	+46	+52	+58	+65	55
60	−3	−1	+3	+8	+14	+18	+22	+27	+32	+37	+43	+49	+55	+62	+69	+77	60

Correction to apply to MEAN LAT. to obtain MIDDLE LAT.

Examples:
To find course and distance from 42°03′N 70°04′W to 36°59′N 25°10′W.

Departure position	42°03′N	70°04′W
Destination position	36°59′N	25°10′W

D. Lat.   5°04′S   D. Long 44°54′E
,, = 304   ,, = 2694
Mean Lat. = 39°31′N
(from table) corr. = − 13′
Middle Lat.   39°18′

To find Departure
Dep = d.long Cos middle Lat.

Quantity		Entry	Reading
Middle Lat.	→	39.3	39.3
		cos	0.77384
		STO 1	0.77384
D. Long.	→	2694	2694
		×	2694
		RCL 1	0.77384
Departure	←	=	2084.73

To find course   Tan course = $\dfrac{\text{Departure}}{\text{D. Lat.}}$

Quantity		Entry	Reading
Dep.	→	2084.73	2084.73
		÷	2084.73
D. Lat.	→	304	304
		=	6.85765
		avc Tan	81.7035

Course = S 81°42'.17E

To find distance   Dist = $\dfrac{\text{D. Lat.}}{\cos \text{course}}$

Quantity		Entry	Reading
Course	→	81.7035	81.7035
		cos	0.14430
		STO 1	0.14430
D. Lat.	→	304	304
		÷	304
		RCL 1	0.14430
Dist.	←	=	2106.77

Distance = 2106.8

   Conversely suppose the vessel starts from a position 42°03'N 70°04'W and steers S81°42'E for a distance of 2106.8 miles. What would be her D.R.

To find D. Lat.   D. Lat. = distance × cos Co.

Quantity		Entry	Reading
Course	→	81.7	81.7
		cos	0.14436
		STO 1	0.14436
Distance	→	2106.8	2106.8
		×	
		RCL 1	0.14436
D. Lat.	←	=	304.13

Latitude departure	= 42°03'N	Mean Lat.	= 39°31'
D. Lat. (304)	= 5°04'S	Corr.	= − 13'
Arrival D.R. Lat.	= 36°59'N	Middle Lat.	= 39°18'

To find Departure   Dep. = Dist × Sin Co

Quantity		Entry	Reading
Course	→	81.7	81.7
		sin	0.98953
		STO 1	0.98953
Distance	→	2106.8	2106.8
		×	2106.8
		RCL 1	0.98953
Departure	←	=	2084.73

To find D. Long   D. Long. = $\dfrac{\text{Dep.}}{\cos \text{mid. lat.}}$

Quantity		Entry	Reading
Mid. Lat.	→	39.3	39.3
		cos	0.77384
		STO 1	0.77384
Dep.	→	2084.5	2084.73
		÷	2084.73
		RCL 1	0.77384
D. Long.	←	=	2694

Longitude departure	= 70°04'W
D. Long. 2694	= 44°54'E
Arrival D.R. Long.	= 25°10'W

Coastal Navigation

6

COASTAL NAVIGATION

This section is not intended to be an advanced or even an elementary course on coastal navigation. Those readers who wish to study the subject should read *Coastal Navigation* in the Reed's Yacht Master Series which is aimed at preparing the student for the Yacht Master Certificate examination and consequently contains all the information required by the aspiring coastal navigator.

The primary object of this section is to act as a general *aide memoire* for the inexperienced navigator, with the hope that the more experienced one may find it useful at times. The tables included in this section will of course be of equal use to the newcomer and the experienced navigator.

It may not perhaps be out of place to emphasise that the essence of good navigation in small ships is adequate preparation before the start of the voyage, careful observation and recording, thus enabling the dead reckoning to be kept up to date at regular intervals. It is essential to be able to state with confidence and accuracy one's position on the chart at any time, a consoling thought if fog should suddenly appear.

THE NAVIGATOR'S EQUIPMENT

The following list of equipment is not necessarily exhaustive, neither must it be considered that every item is essential — this depends on the type of voyaging the owner has in mind. The list does, however, contain equipment which the prudent navigator would be well advised to consider very carefully. Satellite Navigation Systems, Decca and Loran are not included at this stage as it is essential for any navigator to be thoroughly familiar with basic principles before contemplating the use of sophisticated hi-tech systems.

CHARTS
    The basic essential for navigation — dealt with more fully later.

TIDAL ATLAS
    Issued by the Admiralty, various editions for different areas give hour by hour diagrams of tidal stream direction and strength. Extremely useful for the small ship navigator.

SAILING DIRECTIONS
    Many available, issued by the Admiralty, as Admiralty Pilots, etc., and many commercially published ones. Highly desirable for reading before a trip into unfamiliar waters and should be available on passage.

NAUTICAL ALMANAC
    Is essential to provide all the information required relating to tides, lights, buoys, radio aids and navigational tables, etc.

SHIP'S LOG BOOK
    It is important to record all the information relating to the navigation of the ship as well as the D.R. position on the chart. A ship's position about which the navigator is subsequently doubtful can thus be rechecked if the facts and calculations are readily available. It is customary to keep a rough or "deck" log, entering it up in the ship's log at the end of the day or other suitable interval.

DIVIDERS AND PENCIL COMPASSES
    Essential for chart work.

PARALLEL RULER OR PATENT PROTRACTOR
    The traditional instrument for laying off courses on the chart is the parallel ruler, but for small ship navigation where motion may be violent and space restricted the patent protractor is more convenient with less chance of error. The patent protractor consists of a compass rose on a perspex base with a rotating arm which permits a course to be read or laid off without reference to the chart rose. There is also the excellent Nautrack Chart Plotting System and Bearing Plotter from GNAV Marine Products.

STATION POINTER
Useful for fixing the ship's position from bearings taken on fixed objects.

CHART MAGNIFIER
An illuminated chart magnifier can be extremely useful for reading fine detail on a chart under difficult conditions.

CLOCK
A good marine clock is a useful item of equipment as is a stopwatch for timing the frequency of lights.

BAROMETER
A good marine barometer is necessary to maintain a check on the weather situation. Remember that shipping forecasts are invaluable but that they cover a large area — it is useful and it may be vital to know the trend of pressure locally.

COMPASS
A good compass is an essential piece of equipment in any vessel and there are types and sizes to meet all requirements. A particularly useful type for use in small vessels with possibly inexperienced helmsmen is the grid compass. In this type the compass bowl is surmounted by a perspex plate with an annular ring marked with 0-360°. The course is set by rotating the annular ring on to the desired heading and the helmsman then keeps the N-S line on the compass card parallel to two lines engraved on the perspex grid. This renders the helmsman's task much easier, especially at night and when fatigue sets in, and can therefore contribute to the peace of mind of the navigator.

A small hand bearing compass is invaluable for position fixing from fixed objects and lights.

PATENT LOG
A Walker patent log or one of the many impeller type distance recorders will help immeasurably with the dead reckoning calculations.

POCKET CALCULATORS
Useful for rapid calculations. The scientific type, programmed for calculating SIN, COS and TAN are especially useful in navigation provided the navigator understands the fundamentals involved.

ECHO SOUNDER
Apart from the useful ability to predict when the ship is likely to run aground, the electronic echo sounder is a very useful aid to navigation, especially in fog.

SEXTANT
Not an essential item of equipment for the coastal navigator but useful for measuring horizontal and vertical angles for fixing positions. Dealt with more fully later.

RADIO AIDS
A radio set for weather forecasts is really essential. R.D.F. sets are of considerable assistance to navigators but should never be relied on to the exclusion of normal navigational methods.

THE CHART

The chart is obviously the key piece of equipment required by the navigator and should be treated as such and kept up to date.

Notices to Mariners are issued weekly for H.M. ships and merchant ships and can be obtained from chart agents. This weekly notice contains navigational warnings — amendments to dangerous areas, corrections to Admiralty Lists of Lights, fog signals, radio signals and any important navigational alterations or additions necessary to safe navigation. The navigator should always carry a number of charts to cover the area of the projected voyage, together with those necessary to cover any area to which the vessel may be driven by reason of bad weather. In the case of a fairly lengthy trip, for example from Burnham to Ijmuiden in Holland, one small scale passage chart to cover the whole trip is required together with larger scale charts covering the coastline and port approaches.

TYPES OF CHARTS

There are basically two different types of navigational chart issued by the Admiralty, the difference being in the method of construction or "projection". These two projections are called the Mercator and the Gnomonic projections, the latter being used for large scale charts covering small areas. From the small ship navigator's point of view, the projection has no practical significance in coastal navigation. If further information is desired, Reed's Coastal Navigation should be consulted.

The Admiralty publish a chart catalogue covering the whole of the world's surface and listing the charts covering the various areas. The charts can be roughly divided into three main groups, general charts on a small scale covering large areas, i.e. the Atlantic Ocean; coastal charts of larger scale and detailed charts of harbours and estuaries, etc. A "home" section of this chart catalogue covering the British Isles and the N.W. coast of Europe as far as the Kiel Canal is issued separately. It is important when ordering charts to quote the number as well as the title.

In addition to the navigational charts issued by the Admiralty, charts for special purposes such as Decca, Consol and Loran charts are also issued which deal with commercial radio navigational systems. Various other specialised charts such as magnetic variation, track charts and tidal stream are also obtainable.

METRIC CHARTS

British Admiralty charts are now being republished with depths and heights in metres; on these charts extensive use is made of colour, an invaluable aid for quick reference by the small ship navigator.

DISTANCES

The Nautical Mile and its relation to the Cable are unaltered. Ten cables still equals one Sea (or Nautical) Mile.

The Admiralty, have however, adopted the International Nautical Mile of 6076.12 feet for survey work and this equals 1,852 metres. This small change from 6,080 feet (which was an approximate average adopted as a convenient standard at Latitude 48°) can make no practical difference whatever to the Sea Navigator.

COMPASS ROSE
Compass Roses are True 0°-360° — very large and clear with a small line with half an arrow head reaching out from the centre of the rose pointing to the N. Magnetic Pole with the legend printed — Mag. Var. 5°W. decreasing about 8' annually. (Note: These figures will vary according to the particular area covered by the Charts.)

DEPTHS
All depths are given below Chart Datum and the units are stated under the title; the legend "DEPTHS IN METRES" is printed in colour outside the top and bottom borders of the chart also. In places where there is no appreciable tide, depths are given below sea level. Chart datum, originally M.L.W.S. is now adjusted to the level of the predicted lowest astronomical tide (L.A.T.)
Depths of more than 21 are always given in whole metres, whereas depths of less than 21 are given in metres and decimetres — e.g., 5_3 which means 5.3 metres.

HEIGHTS
Heights, other than drying heights are given IN METRES above M.H.W.S., except in places where there is no appreciable tide, in such cases heights are referred to sea level.
Drying Heights are given in metres and decimetres above Chart Datum and underlined, thus $\underline{1}_6$, $\underline{0}_9$, etc. Should there be insufficient space for printing the figures in the drying area, such height may be stated alongside the area; e.g., *"Dries 1.6 m."*

DEPTH CONTOURS (called "Fathom Lines" on older charts).
Depth contours are drawn in fine firm lines, broken in places where there are figures indicating the depth in metres, e.g. 30, 100, 1,000, 2,000, etc.

VERTICAL CLEARANCES
Vertical clearances (under bridges, etc.) are given in metres, the figures are printed with a line over the top and in brackets, thus $(\overline{\tfrac{}{10}})$.

SUBMERGED WRECKS
Sounded or swept depths over wrecks are given in metres, or metres and decimetres. The criterion for dangerous wrecks is less than 28 m. clearance.

TINTS AND COLOURS
The land tint is buff and drying areas are green. The 10 metres contour is edged on the inside with a narrow blue ribbon, and all sea areas contained within the 5 metre contour are blue. Blue tints however, may be shown to different limits according to the scale of the chart.

On both borders of the chart there is a ruled Conversion Scale with feet and fathoms on either side of the centre vertical metres scale from 1 to 30 metres (i.e. 100 feet and $16\tfrac{1}{3}$ fathoms) so conversion is simple.

CHART SYMBOLS
For a full understanding of all symbols used in British Admiralty charts, reference should be made to Admiralty Chart No. 5011 now published in book form. This gives full details of every symbol and abbreviation used and should be included in the equipment of everyone who takes their navigation seriously. A few useful chart symbols and abbreviations are shown overleaf.
Owing to the considerable number of symbols now employed on Admiralty Charts, it is not possible or sensible to try to commit them all to memory. It is infinitely preferable to try to remember the really important ones.

USEFUL CHART SYMBOLS AND ABBREVIATIONS

④ $\mathcal{O}(4)$ •(4)   ·(0·6)
Rock which does not cover
(elevation above MHWS or MHHW,
or where there is no tide, above MSL)

Rock which covers and uncovers (1_2) ✳ (1_2)
(elevation above chart datum)

Rock awash at level of chart datum

1_2 R   +   ⊕   (+ + +)
Underwater rock with 2 m. or less water
at chart datum, or rock ledge where
depths are known to be 2 m. or less,
or rock or rock ledge over which the exact
depth is unknown but could be dangerous
to surface navigation

10_7 R 16_5 R $+ (16_5)$

Shoal sounding on isolated rock

6_4 11_2

Underwater danger, depth cleared by
wire drag

Wk

Large scale charts

Wreck showing at level of chart datum

+++ Masts   ○ Mast (1·2)
     ○ Funnel
     ○ Mast (2_1)

Large scale charts

Wreck, masts only visible

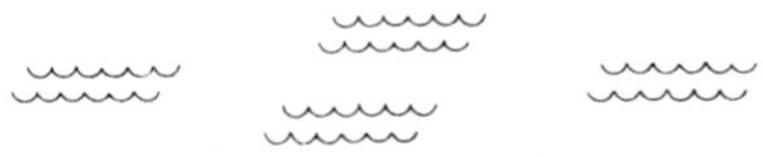

Overfalls and tide-rips

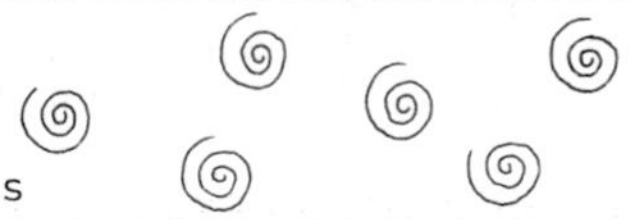

Eddies

Well   35 Well
Submerged wellhead (with least depth
where known)

Obstn.

Obstruction or danger to navigation

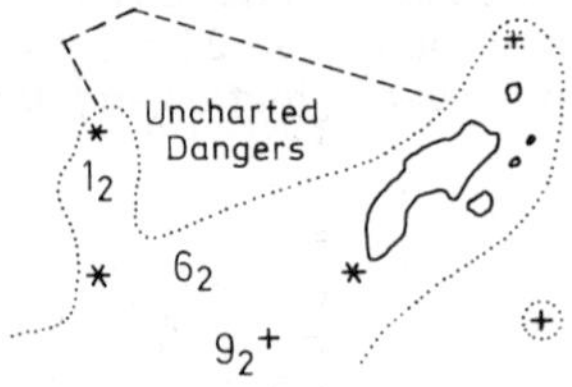

Uncharted
Dangers
1_2
6_2
9_2+

Danger line

○ RC   Non-directional radiobeacon

RD   RD 269°30'   Directional radiobeacon

○ Aero RC   Aeronautical radiobeacon

○ RG   Radio direction finding station

Radar reflector   Lifeboat station

Pilot boarding place   Oil or gas production platform

Ch   Church   Tr   Tower

Position of light   Light-vessel

Wk	Wreck	Gd	Ground
PA	Position approx.	Oz	Ooze
Bk	Bank	S	Silt
Sh	Shoal	Sh	Shells
Rf	Reef	Sn	Shingle
Le	Ledge	St	Stones
S	Sand	Wd	Weed
M	Mud	m	Medium
P	Pebbles	f	Fine
R	Rock	c	Coarse
Bo	Boulders	so	Soft
G	Gravel	h	Hard

VARIATION AND DEVIATION

Basically variation is the angle between the Magnetic North Pole and the True Pole — which could perhaps be described as the Geometric Pole. This angle varies over the earth's surface and at present is of the order of 5°W in the North Sea area and is decreasing about 8' annually.

Deviation is an error induced in a vessel's compass by local conditions, *i.e.*, magnetic material near to the compass. This error varies with the ship's heading and should therefore be known on all points of the compass for which purpose a deviation card is required. This card can be prepared by a professional compass adjuster or, with care, by the mariner himself. One method of preparing such a card is described later.

METHOD OF APPLYING VARIATION

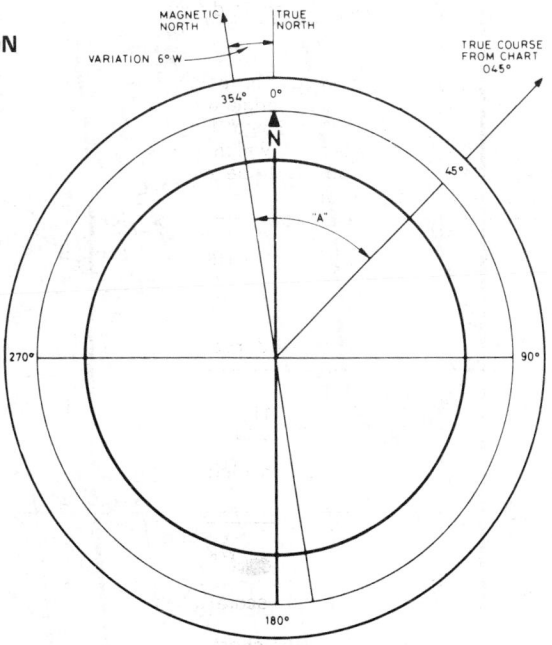

When the *True* course has been laid off on the chart, it is then necessary to convert it to a *Magnetic* course for use on the mariner's compass. Consider the diagram right and assume a course of 045° *True* is required. It will be observed that the *Variation* angle in this example is 6° West, *i.e.*, *Magnetic North* is 6° West of *True North*.

The angle between the *True* course of 45° and the *Magnetic North* is therefore 45° + 6° = 51° (angle A). The course to be steered on the compass is therefore 51° Magnetic. Similarly, if the Variation angle was to be East of *True North* it will be seen that the Variation is subtracted from the True Course, *i.e.*, if the variation was 6° East the above-mentioned course of 45° True would become 45° True − 6° = 39° Magnetic.

To assist in remembering this fact when converting from True to Magnetic courses under difficult conditions the following may help:

"West is best (*i.e.* greater); East is least (*i.e.* less)."

APPLYING VARIATION AND DEVIATION

The same rule applies to Deviation. For example a True Course of 254°T, Variation 6°W; Magnetic Course will be 254°T + 6°W = 260°M, and from the Deviation Card (p. 206) Dev. for this course will be 4°E. ∴ Compass Course will be 254°T + 6°W Var. = 260° − 4°E. Dev. = 256°C.

The two components, Var. & Dev. can be combined, *i.e.* + 6°W. − 4°E = 2° Compass error for the particular course. 254°T + 2° = 256°C.

It is essential when converting from True to Compass to apply Var. and Dev. in that order.

MAGNETIC VARIATION CHART 1985

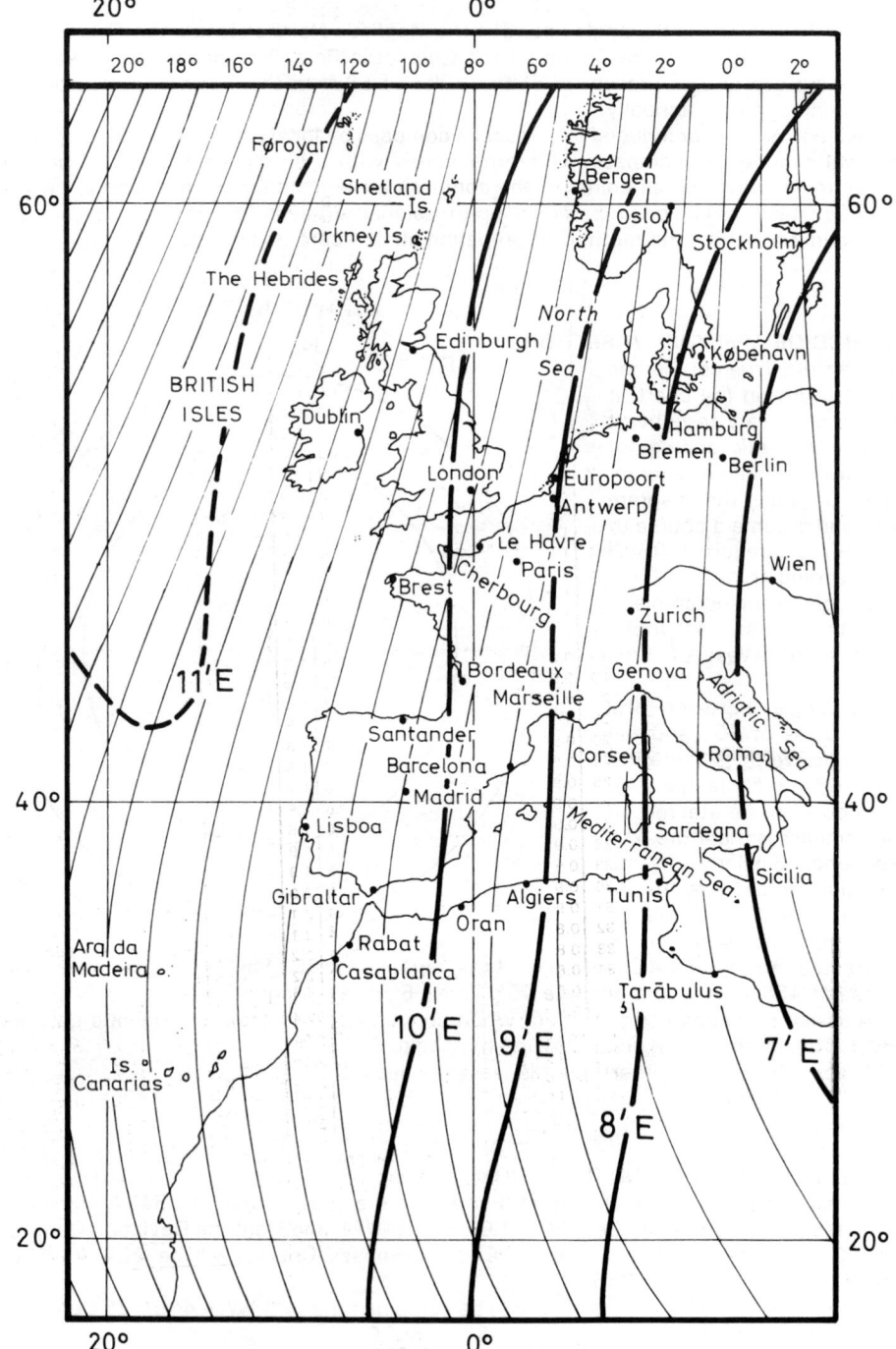

WESTERLY VARIATION 0°–20° (ISOGONIC LINES)
ANNUAL CHANGE (ISALLOGONIC LINES) AN INCREASE OF 6'–10' IN THE EASTERLY
COMPONENT, THEREBY REDUCING THE WESTERLY VARIATION FIGURE.

PREPARING A DEVIATION CARD

It is important that the master of any vessel should know the deviation of the ship's compass (unless it is a gyro compass where this error does not arise). It is also very useful if the owner of the smaller vessel has sufficient knowledge and confidence in his ability to produce his own deviation card. Full information relating to compass deviation will be found in more detailed books on navigation and of course in Reed's Coastal Navigation. One useful method for producing a reasonably accurate deviation card when no known transit is readily available is described below.

A Pelorus is required for the exercise but if not available, with reasonable care can easily be constructed with materials readily to hand. A sheet of plywood approximately 12" to 18" square is prepared with a lubber line clearly marked along the centre. On the centre of this square is glued a compass rose from an old Admiralty chart with the magnetic North and South line accurately lined up on the lubber line. A circle of say 12" diameter is then marked on the plywood square using the centre of the compass rose for the purpose. Lines are then drawn through each 5° point on the rose to the outer circle mentioned above. It is important to ensure that the ruler edge forms a line through the rose centre and the desired degree mark to ensure maximum accuracy. The degree marks then obtained on the outer ring can be further subdivided but it will probably be found that readings can be quite accurately estimated by eye. A small wooden pointer about 9" long with appropriate sighting marks is then mounted in the centre of the rose and the Pelorus is complete.

The Pelorus is then mounted in such a position that the lubber line is on the fore and aft line of the vessel and sights can be taken all round. It will be appreciated that the purpose of the Pelorus is to take bearings of an object relative to the ship's head.

A position is then selected where the vessel can be manoeuvred through 360° as far as possible in the same position, for example near a buoy, and bearings taken on a distant object, ideally at least 5 miles away. The magnetic bearing of this object is immaterial at this stage. The procedure is as follows:

The ship is swung until her head is on due North (Compass) and the bearing of the object is noted on the Pelorus. This procedure is repeated for each quadrant of the compass so that 8 bearings of the object are obtained relative to the main compass headings. The compass bearings of the object with the ship's head on the different compass headings can then be calculated and the deviation card prepared in the usual way. For example, with the ship's head on compass North, the Pelorus reading will be the actual bearing of the object as it would be read from the ship's compass. Assume that this figure is 250°. The ship's head would then be swung to 45° and the Pelorus bearing would become say 200°. The compass bearing of the object would thus be 200° + 45° = 245°. Carrying on in this way a series of roughly similar Pelorus bearings would be obtained and the average of these would give the correct magnetic bearing of the object, *i.e.*, in effect a transit.

By adjustment, *i.e.*, adding or subtracting each ship's head bearing from the Pelorus bearing (it will be obvious when the figures are obtained what to do) corrected bearings are obtained which when compared with the mean bearing give the difference necessary on each heading to enable the deviation curve to be prepared.

DEVIATION CARD

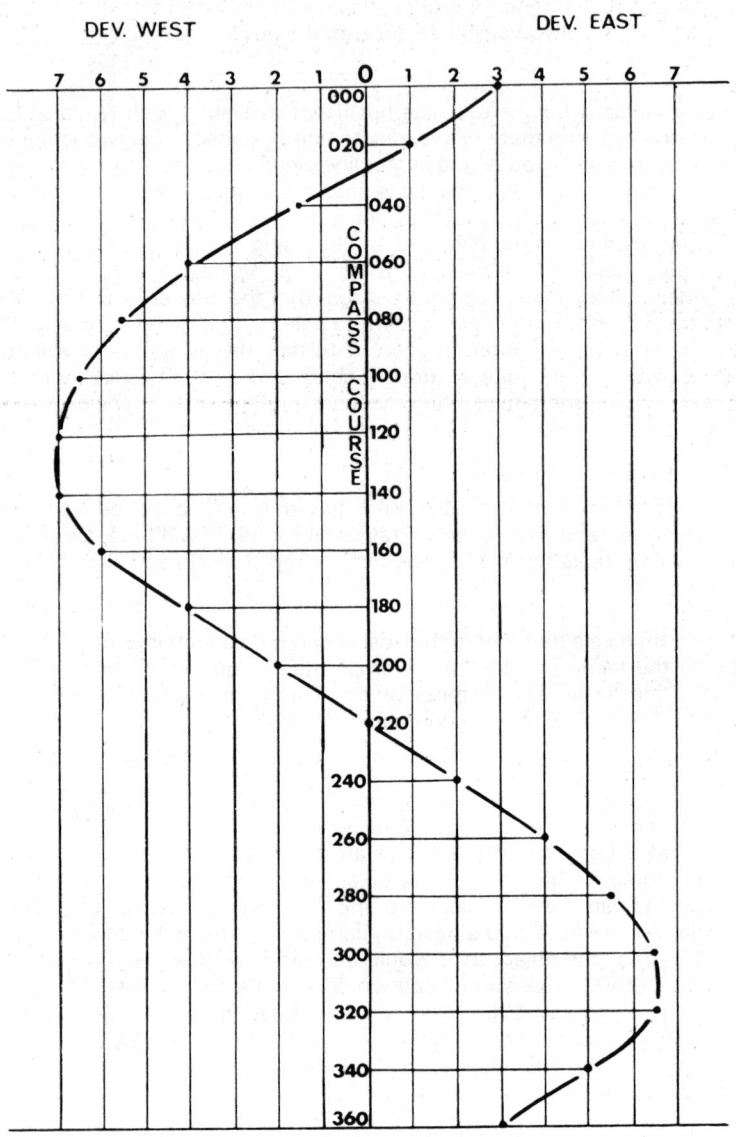

A typical deviation card which shows the method of construction.

THE SEXTANT

The sextant is an optical instrument used for measuring angles and is an essential item of equipment for the ocean navigator. It is, however, of considerable assistance to the coastal navigator, mainly in the field of position fixing by means of vertical and horizontal angles of terrestrial objects such as lighthouses, etc. Position fixing by observations of celestial bodies is dealt with in Section V. Like most instruments practice is necessary to achieve proficiency in its use — coastal navigation will afford plenty of opportunity. Those wishing to attain a high standard of proficiency should refer to *The Sextant Simplified* by Captain O. M. Watts, published by Reed's.

INDEX ERROR

Any residual error left in the sextant after it has been properly adjusted is called *Index Error* and this value should be applied as a correction to all sextant readings. There are several methods by which Index Error can be found, one simple method is:

To find Index Error by the sea horizon
1. Clamp the index at approximately zero.
2. Hold the sextant vertically and look through the telescope at the sea horizon.
3. Turn the tangent screw until the true and reflected horizons together form an unbroken line.
4. The *reading* on the sextant now indicates the Index Error which should be applied as a subtractive correction if the reading is on the arc, and additive if off the arc.

A clear horizon is essential to ensure accurate results.

TAKING HORIZONTAL AND VERTICAL SEXTANT ANGLES

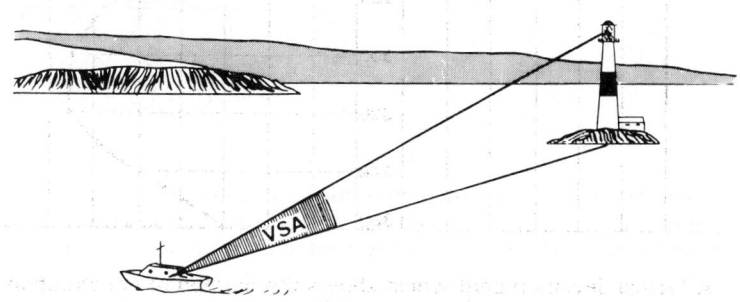

Fig. A. Vertical Sextant Angle

TO MEASURE VERTICAL SEXTANT ANGLES (e.g. those of the lighthouse in Fig. A).

The Telescope is shipped in its collar and the Index set to zero. Hold the Sextant vertically and view the centre of the light through the Telescope. The light will be seen direct through the plane (or unsilvered) part of the Horizon Glass, *i.e.* the TRUE image. It will also be seen as a REFLECTED image in the silvered part. (Figs. C and D.) Both True and Reflected images should coincide.

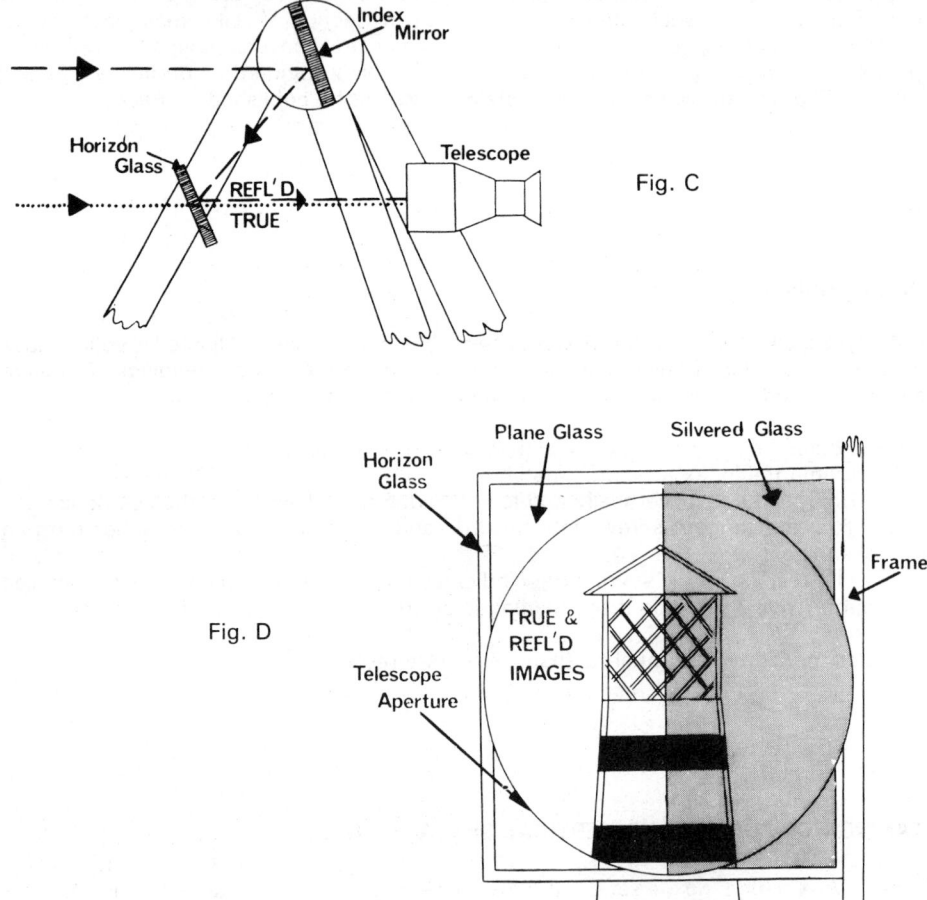

Fig. C

Fig. D

The Micrometer Head is now turned with the Left hand so that the Index moves along the Arc, away from the Telescope end. As soon as the Micrometer is turned the True and Reflected images will separate, the Reflected image moving downwards. (Fig. E.)

As the Reflected image of the light "falls" the Sextant is tilted downwards to follow its movement. When the centre of the light reaches the shore line the reading is noted. (Fig. F.)

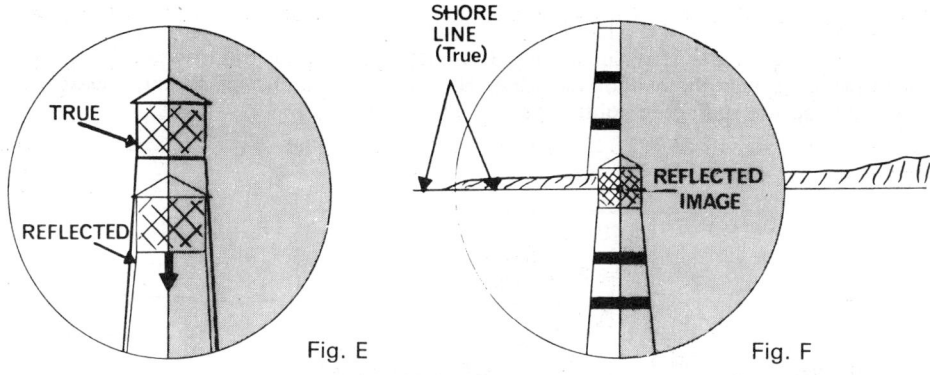

Fig. E   Fig. F

Using the sextant should first be practised on dry land and then on a yacht. Try bringing a chimney top down to the base of a wall to begin with.

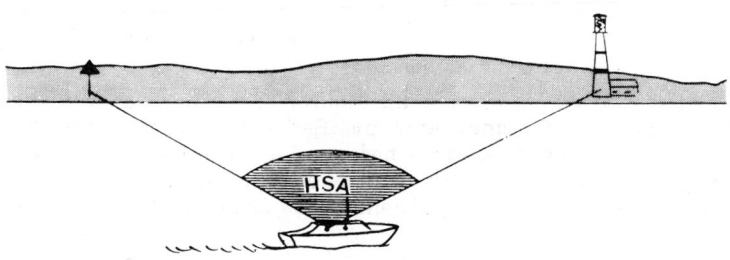

Fig. B Horizontal Sextant Angle

TO MEASURE HORIZONTAL SEXTANT ANGLES (Fig. B)

The Horizontal Sextant Angle between, say, a lighthouse and a beacon is measured by holding the Sextant horizontally with the Handle downwards. As with the Vertical Sextant Angle the Index is set to zero. The Telescope is now pointed at the Right hand object, in Fig. G, the Lighthouse.

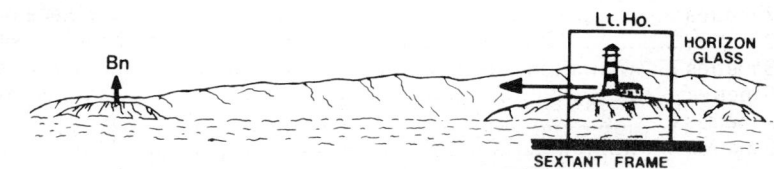

Fig. G

Since the angle to be measured will be relatively large the Index is now moved along the Arc by means of the Quick Release Clamp. Make sure a firm pressure is exerted on the clamp otherwise the gear teeth may be damaged.

The Reflected image of the Lighthouse will appear to move towards the LEFT, so that by letting it follow the True coastline in the unsilvered part of the Horizon Glass it will eventually approach the beacon (Bn.) (Fig. H). The Sextant must be swung towards the LEFT to keep the Reflected lighthouse in view.

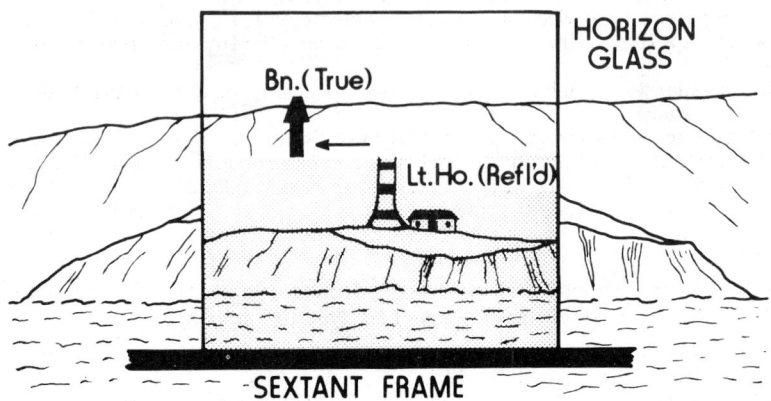

Fig. H

As soon as the beacon is seen in the Horizon Glass the clamp is released. The Micrometer Head is now turned until the Reflected image of the lighthouse is superimposed on the True image of the beacon. The angle may then be read.

Some navigators prefer to point the sextant initially at the left hand object and move the index bar forward so that the right hand object eventually comes into view.

THE MARKING OF A METRIC LEAD LINE

2 metres	two strips of leather
3 metres	three strips of leather
5 metres	a piece of white duck
7 metres	a piece of red bunting
10 metres	a piece of leather with a hole in it
13 metres	a piece of blue serge
15 metres	a piece of white duck
17 metres	a piece of red bunting
20 metres	two knots

then repeat up to 40 metres.

The above are the marks suggested by the Admiralty Manual of Seamanship. For yachting purposes any owner is, of course, free to mark his lead line to suit his own convenience.

BRITISH NAUTICAL INSTRUMENT TRADE ASSOCIATION
105 West George Street, Glasgow G2 1QP

The prime object of this Association is: "To originate, develop and promote all means within the scope of the trade for ensuring and increasing the safety and efficiency of navigation and shipping" — Rule 3D.

This short summary of efficient services promoted by members of the Association indicates the constant endeavour to fulfil their obligation to the Shipping Industry.

Magnetic Compasses — Advice on compass problems and the supply of the most suitable compasses for any requirements. Maintenance of an efficient and speedy repair service throughout UK.

Siting and Installation — Selection of the best magnetic position on the bridge and the supervision of installation.

Compass Adjusting — The services of a DoT Certified Compass Adjuster at any time of the day or night. It should be noted that proper adjustment of compasses and associated equipment including remote heading references, is a task which calls for the employment of precise and complex professional skills, and that the only professional qualification in the UK for full time professional compass adjusters is the Certificate of Competency as Compass Adjuster issued by the DoT after examination following a period of practical training in making, repairing and adjusting compasses. The adjustment of compasses is not something that should be attempted by unqualified persons, and for a fully professional service only DoT Certificated Adjusters should be employed. Member firms who offer such facilities are marked * in the succeeding lists.

Charts — The supply of single charts or world outfits to special folio requirements from comprehensive stocks corrected up to the date of issue.

Chart Tracings — The supply of chart correction tracings supplementary to the Admiralty Notices to Mariners.

Chart Service — Examination and correction of charts at appropriate intervals by full-time qualified Chart Correctors, operating with the co-operation of the Hydrographic Department.

Nautical Publications — The latest "Pilot" or Hydrographic publication. It is almost certain that this Almanac was supplied by a member of the Association.

Chartroom Instruments — A range for Coastal, Home or World Trading voyages.

Sextants — The choice of a new sextant from a full range of instruments and a competent repair service in most Ports.

Binoculars and Telescopes — The cleaning, adjusting or repair of prismatic binoculars, or a wide variety of binoculars and telescopes from which a selection can be made for all needs.

Meteorological Instruments — Supply and repair of mercurial or aneroid barometers and barographs and associated instruments.

Sounding Machines — Stocks of complete sounding machine outfits and the supply of Sounding Tubes, refills and all accessories.

Ships Logs — Comprehensive range of Logs with all accessories, and full stock of manufacturers' spares for the maintenance of all models.

Clocks and Chronometers — The rating and cleaning of chronometers and the supply of clocks for all marine purposes.

Signalling Apparatus — Supply and repair of all signalling apparatus to DoT standards.

OVERSEAS MEMBERS

NOTE. Firms marked * employ DoT Certificated Adjusters. Other overseas firms listed employ Adjusters holding locally equivalent qualifications.

AUSTRALIA	Messrs. A. H. Pickles & Co., P.O. Box 320, Fremantle, Western Australia 6160.
BELGIUM	*Bogerd Navtec NV, Oude Leeuwenrui 37, 2000 Antwerp.
	*Martin & Co., Oude Leeuwenrui 37, 2000 Antwerp.
DENMARK	Iver C. Weilbach & Co., A/S, 35 Toldbodgade, Postbox 2051, DK-1253, Copenhagen K.
HOLLAND	*Datema Delfzijl BV, Oude Schans 11, 9934 Delfzijl.
HONG KONG	George Falconer (Nautical) Ltd., The Hong Kong Jewellery Building, 178-180 Queen's Road, Central.
	Hong Kong Ships Supplies Co., Room 1614, Melbourne Plaza, 33 Queen's Road, Central.
NORWAY	A/S Navicharts Masteveien 3, N-1481 Hagan.
	J. C. Krohn & Sons, A/S, Postboks 1953, N5011 Bergen.
PORTUGAL	J. Garraio & Co. Lda., Avenida 24 de Julho, 2-1° D-1200, Lisbon.
SINGAPORE	Motion Smith, Marina House, 70 Shenton Way, 02-03 Singapore 0207.
SWEDEN	AB Ramantenn, Knipplagatan 12, S-414 74 Gothenburg.
URUGUAY	Marine Technical Services, Port of Montevideo, Florida 1562, 11100 Montevideo

PORTS WHERE SHIPS' COMPASSES ARE ADJUSTED

Names of member firms. Those marked * have DoT Certificated Compass Adjusters available for
Adjustment of Compasses day or night.

Port or District	Name and Address	Telephone
ABERDEEN	*Thomas Gunn Navigation Services, 62 Marischal Street, AB1 2AL.	0224 595045
AVONMOUTH	W. F. Price & Co., Ltd., 24 Gloucester Road, BS11 9AG. *Severnside Consultants, Imperial Chambers, 2nd Floor, Gloucester Road, BS11 9AQ.	0272 823888 0272 827184
CARDIFF	*Blairs Nautical Supplies Ltd., Unit 3, 7-11 West Bute Street, CF1 6EN *T. J. Williams & Son, (Cardiff) Ltd., 19 & 19A West Bute Street, The Docks, CF1 6EP.	0222 487746 0222 487676
FALMOUTH	*Marine Instruments, The Bosun's Locker, Upton Slip TR11 3DQ.	0326 312414
GLASGOW	Brown, Son & Ferguson Ltd, 4-10 Darnley Street, G41 2SD.	041-429 1234
HULL	N. Carmichael, Shiptech Buildings, St Andrews Dock. *B. Cooke & Son Limited, Kingston Observatory, 58/59 Market Place, HU1 1RH.	0482 29916 0482 223454
KENT	Robertson Autopilots UK, Station Road, Harrietsham, Maidstone ME17 1JA *S.I.R.S. Navigation Limited, 186a Milton Road, Swanscombe, DA10 0LX.	0622 858885 0322 843672
LIVERPOOL	Dubois-Phillips & McCallum Ltd., Oriel Chambers, Covent Garden L2 8UD.	051-236 2776
LONDON	Brown & Perring, Sestrel House, 36/44 Tabernacle Street, EC2A 4DT. *Kelvin Hughes Charts and Maritime Supplies, New North Road, Hainault, Ilford, Essex IG6 2UR. 145 Minories, EC3N 1NH. Thomas Reed Publications Ltd., Weir House, Hurst Road, E. Molesey, Surrey KT8 9AQ. Silva (UK) Limited, 15 Bolney Way, Feltham, Middlesex TW13 6DB. A. M. Smith (Marine) Ltd., 33 Epping Way, Chingford E4 7PB.	071-253 4517 081-500 6166 071-709 9076 081-941 8090 081-898 6901 081-529 6988
LOWESTOFT	*Seath Instruments Ltd., Unit 30, Colville Road Works, Colville Road, NR33 9QS.	0502 573811
NORTH SHIELDS	*John Lilley & Gillie (incorporating T. L. Ainsley Ltd.), Clive Street NE29 6LF.	091-257 2217
PORTRUSH	Todd Chart Agency, North Quay, The Harbour, Portrush, Co. Antrim BT56 8DF.	0265 824176
SOUTHAMPTON	*R. J. Muir, 22 Seymour Close, Chandlers Ford, Eastleigh SO5 2JE. Frederick Ford, Esq., 15 Heath Road North, Locks Heath SO3 6PP. Wessex Marine Equipment Ltd., 49-51 Millbrook Road East, SO1 0HN.	0703 261042 048-95 84425 0703 220735

Coastal Passage Making

7

NAVIGATOR'S CHECK LIST

The following check list may be helpful to those making a coastal passage for the first time. Remember that pre-sailing planning materially reduces the possibility of making a navigational error when the situation is difficult.

BEFORE YOU SAIL

Check on the competence of the crew and on the general seaworthiness of the vessel to embrace engine, fuel, provisions and equipment.

Have you made a quick reference list of lights and buoys with their ranges, etc, for use in the cockpit if necessary?

Check that all charts required are available on board and corrected up to date.

Are the desired course lines marked on the charts to assist navigation at sea?

Have alternative courses been considered in case stress of weather dictates a departure from the planned trip?

Have you an up to date copy of Reed's Nautical Almanac on board? (Don't forget the Spring Supplement.)

A Tidal Atlas for the area is a most useful addition to the reference books. If not available the information is shown on the tidal stream charts in this Almanac but of necessity the scale is much smaller.

Do you know your compass deviation and have you prepared a deviation card?

POINTS TO CONSIDER WHEN ON PASSAGE

(i) It is important to plot estimated position on the chart at regular intervals of say one hour. In the event of difficulties such as fog or bad weather it engenders confidence in one's decision if the ship's position is accurately known.

(ii) Never pass a light or buoy without positively identifying it if reasonably possible. Remember that dangers such as sandbanks may have several buoys with the same name but different prefixes.

(iii) Remember that tidal streams vary in force and direction from place to place and also according to the time relative to HW. It is also important to remember the effect of Springs and Neaps on the force of the tidal stream.

(iv) Don't forget leeway angle when setting courses and don't overlook the effect of surface drift which may occur due to a hard and prolonged blow.

(v) When navigating in fog if it is not possible to anchor in safety out of shipping lanes try to maintain a constant speed — it makes calculations easier.

(vi) Remember the copy book approach to an unfamiliar but well lighted shore — close the coast before dawn to obtain an accurate fix from lights and then make your entry with daylight.

(vii) Finally — when approaching an unfamiliar destination, if uncertain of your position and there is a possibility of danger as a result — heave to or stand out to sea again until you have sorted out the situation.

THE VESSEL'S COURSE

One of the first essentials before commencing a trip is to decide upon the different courses to be made good between the start and the finishing point. The standard terms used in connection with the vessel's course are given below and it is recommended that these should always be used, particularly in discussions between the navigator and helmsman — a misunderstanding could be disastrous.

The word "course" by itself can have several quite different meanings. It may refer to a course to steer, a leeway course, a required course, or a course to make good, which is not always the same thing as the required course. Misunderstanding could be dangerous and to avoid confusion the following terms, which are used by many professional navigators, are strongly recommended.

HEADING refers only to the vessel's fore-and-aft line. It is the direction in which she is pointing, regardless of her actual track, and is designated as True (T), Magnetic (M) or Compass (C), as appropriate. Whenever the true heading is plotted on the chart, the line should be marked for identification with a single arrow head pointing in the appropriate direction.

TRACK refers to the direction of the ship's track over the sea bed. It may be designated as True (T) or Magnetic (M), as convenient, and when drawn on the chart should be marked for identification with two arrow heads and clearly labelled, e.g. 286° (T). The Required Track is the direction of the intended track between two points. The line drawn on the chart to indicate the required track is often referred to as the "course line".

TIDAL STREAM — when plotted on the chart should be marked with three arrow heads.

COURSE TO STEER is the heading required to make good a specified track.

COURSE STEERED refers to the heading that was steered over a specified time.

LEEWAY is the angle between the ship's fore-and-aft line and her line of movement through the water.

LEEWAY COURSE OR WAKE COURSE is the direction of the vessel's line of movement through the water. Thus when she is making leeway the wake course always lies to leeward of the true heading; and if there is a significant current, too, the track may be different to both the heading and wake course.

PLOTTING THE REQUIRED TRACK

Any reader wishing to use a calculator should, after studying the following basic information, refer to The Electronic Calculator in Coastal Navigation, later in this section.

On a coastal passage the configuration of the coastline may necessitate many changes of course and it is a wise practice to plot all the required courses on the chart before the commencement of the passage. The prudent navigator will also plot the courses of any "escape route" that may be necessitated by bad weather.

A close examination of the course lines should then be made to ensure that adequate clearance is given to all possible dangers. The courses can be marked in on the course lines or preferably noted in a notebook with the other navigational details such as lights, etc, which should be readily available on the trip. The reason for not writing them on the chart is to ensure that it is as uncluttered as possible before the normal chartwork of recording estimated positions, etc, commences as the passage progresses.

SETTING THE COURSE

WITH ALLOWANCE FOR LEEWAY ONLY:

Some sea-going experience and a knowledge of the ship's likely behaviour under existing conditions is required when estimating the allowance to be made for leeway. For any one course this allowance must be adjusted from time to time as dictated by change in the force and/or direction of the wind.

The leeway angle is the angle between the fore and aft line of the vessel and her wake and should be measured or estimated for various speeds and sea conditions.

To determine the true course to steer: apply leeway to windward of the required true track.

To determine the true track being made good: apply leeway to leeward of the true course being steered.

Always apply leeway angle before deviation and variation have been applied to the course to steer.

When there is no current or tidal effect, the track and the wake course are the same.

ALLOWANCE FOR TIDE OR CURRENT AND LEEWAY

The term speed refers always to the ship's speed through the water; her speed over the sea bed is called effective speed.

EXAMPLE: It is required to set course to make good a track of 080°(T) when the tidal stream is setting 180° at 3 knots, wind northerly and leeway 5°. If the vessel's speed is 9 knots, what course should she steer, and what will be her effective speed?

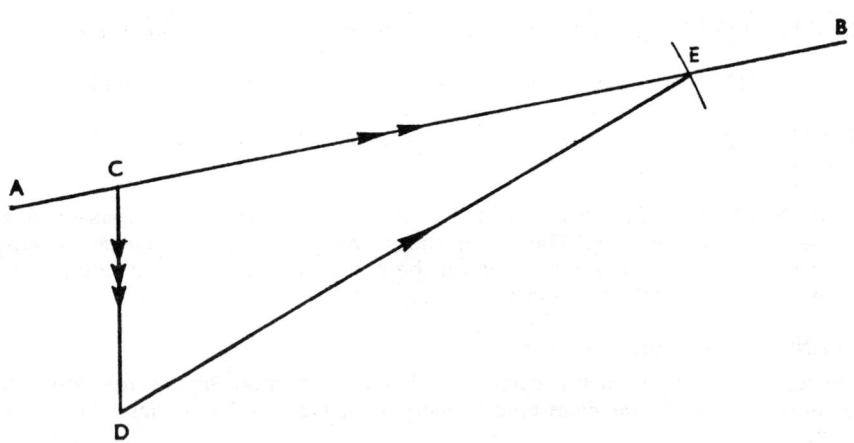

ALLOWING FOR BOTH LEEWAY AND EFFECT OF CURRENT:

In the diagram AB represents the required track drawn on the chart.

1. Take any convenient point C and lay off the current vector CD representing 3 kts. (using units from any convenient scale) at 180°(T).

2. With centre D and radius equal to ship's speed of 9 kts. strike an arc cutting AB at E.

3. DE represents True Course required, i.e. 061°(T).
4. Apply Southerly leeway angle of 5°; course will be 056°(T).
5. Compass course will be 056° + 6°Var. W. −3°Dev. E. = 059°(C).
6. CE measured in the same units as CD gives 8 kts. − the effective speed.

When out of sight of land or in low visibility with no navigational fixing aids available, allowance for leeway and tide should be adjusted continually, as required, so as to "make good" the required track over the sea bed. In continued low visibility, soundings taken at regular intervals often provide a useful check on the distance off the coast.

POSITION LINES

A "Fix" is obtained by the intersection of two or more position lines; more than two should be used whenever possible. If the position lines are obtained all at the same time it is commonly called a Simultaneous Fix. If, however, there is a significant time interval between the observations, so that the first position time has to be transferred up to the time of the last one, it is termed a Running Fix. All other things being equal, a simultaneous fix is more reliable than a running fix.

There are many types of position lines; some are obtained only by the use of very sophisticated and expensive equipment, but those which are normally available to the average yacht are obtained by:

(1) A compass bearing of a fixed object ashore;

(2) A transit bearing i.e., two fixed objects seen in line with one another, e.g., a point of land in line with a conspicuous chimney − very accurate;

(3) A vertical sextant angle of an object of known height − very accurate;

(4) A horizontal sextant angle between two fixed objects − very accurate;

(5) A dipping range;

(6) A sounding corresponding to a clearly defined fathom line (e.g., 20 fathoms) on the chart;

(7) A radio D/F bearing;

(8) An astronomical observation.

A fix can be obtained by any combination of the position lines listed above. A quick and accurate method by day is to combine the distance off an object (e.g., headland or lighthouse) obtained from a vertical sextant angle with the simultaneous bearing of the object.

Compass bearings are obtained with the use of an Azimuth Mirror or, in the case of smaller vessels, by means of a Hand Bearing Compass.

There are many occasions when a single position line may prove useful, for example:

(a) A position line which is parallel or nearly parallel to the required track shows whether or not the vessel is maintaining that track.

(b) A position line which cuts the track at or near 90° will often provide a good check on effective speed and ETA at the next point.

(c) Two marks or beacons in transit may provide a leading line into a harbour, or clear a danger.

(d) A single bearing may be used as a clearing line − danger being avoided by keeping in one side of the bearing line.

FIXING THE POSITION

When making a passage it is necessary to have an accurate assessment of the vessel's position at all times — especially important in coastal navigation. The ocean navigator may only plot his position at noon each day — the coastal navigator should plot his at least once each hour. The standard terms used in position fixing are:

DEAD RECKONING (DR) — a position obtained from the course steered by the vessel and her speed through the water and no other factors. The distance run through the water is laid off along the course line steered and the position so obtained marked with a small cross, the letters DR and the time, thus — +DR 1030.

ESTIMATED POSITION (EP) — a position obtained by adjusting the DR position for the effects of leeway and current. It is marked on the chart by means of a dot in a triangle thus △ EP 1030.

A FIX — provided by reliable observations of terrestrial or celestial bodies and is shown thus ⊙ Fix 1030.

With practice the symbols only should be used — clarity on the chart reduces the chances of error.

The figure below illustrates the different kinds of position as defined above. Assuming point A to be the last reliable fix (obtained at, say, 1300 hours), AB the course steered and the log distance for one hour; then B is the DR position for 1400 hours — *i.e.*, the position the vessel would be in if there was no leeway, no current, the course had been accurately steered and the distance run through the water accurately indicated.

If the ship had been making leeway (angle BAC) due to a northerly wind, but was not affected by current; then C would be the EP at 1400 hours. Note that the distances AB and AC are always the same.

If, however, a current setting (say) 200°(T) at 3 knots was expected, then the set and drift for one hour (200°(T) − 3 miles) would be laid off on the chart from point C — *i.e.*, CD, and point D is now the EP for 1400 hours. Note that the effect of current is marked by three arrow heads.

Should a reliable fix, E, be obtained at 1400 hours, the current actually experienced during the last hour would be determined by measuring the direction and distance from C to E (not drawn in figure). The track and distance made good, and the effective speed, would be determined by the straight line AE.

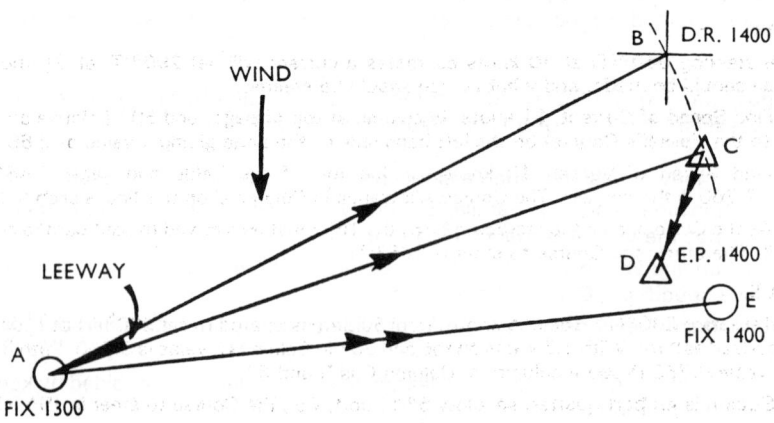

COURSE CORRECTION

Every prudent Shipmaster and Navigator when setting a Course makes allowance for Leeway, and the effects of a Tidal Stream or Current.

The following Table has been designed to save the Navigator of a small vessel having to work the problem on the Chart to find out what Course Allowance he should make to counteract the effect of a Tidal Stream or Current of an estimated speed according to the speed of his vessel.

It will be realised, of course, that the slower the vessel's speed the more it will be affected by any Current; and the more this Tidal Stream or Current is abeam, the more it will push the vessel sideways from her Course, and, therefore, the more allowance that must be made. Should the Stream be directly ahead or astern, no Course Allowance need be made, but the speed will be advanced or retarded according to the speed of the Current.

The Table — in addition to giving in the shortest time the allowance to be made to the Course — gives also the Speed made good over the Ground. Whilst this latter may sometimes be required, it is more necessary always in practical navigation to find the Course Allowance to be made at frequent intervals.

This Table saves any chart plotting and enables the Course Allowance for Tidal Stream or Current to be found mentally in the quickest possible manner.

HOW TO FIND THE COURSE TO STEER TO COUNTERACT THE EFFECT OF TIDE OR CURRENT

(1). Find the Speed of Tidal Stream (or Current) at the top of the page and with the relative angle of the Tidal Stream (or Current) from the desired track to be made good in the left hand column, C, read value from the Table.

(2). Find at the top of the Table the Speed of the Vessel (through the water) and look down this column until the value in (1) above is found (or closely approximated). Then read off in the left hand column C, the number of degrees allowance to be made to the Course.

(3). Allow this Course Correction to the same side, port or starboard, as the Tidal Stream or Current; *i.e.,* in order to counteract a Current setting towards the vessel on the starboard side, you naturally make the Course Allowance towards the starboard side.

Example I.

Vessel steering 060°(T) at 10 knots estimates a current will set 290°(T) at 3½ knots. What allowance should be made, and what course should be steered?

(1). Find Speed of Current, 3½ knots, in column at top of page, and 50° (relative angle of the Current to the Vessel's Course) on the left hand side of the page giving a value of 2.681.

(2). Find Speed of vessel, 10 knots, at the top of the Table and value 2.681 in this column—2,760 is the nearest. The Course Allowance in Column C on this line is seen to be 16°C.

(3). As the Current is on the starboard bow, the 16° must be allowed to starboard to counteract its effect. Therefore, the Course to steer is 076°(T).

Example II.

Vessel steering 200°(T), Speed 8 knots, Tidal Stream estimated to set 230°(T) at 1½ knots (*i.e.,* 30° from dead astern). With 1.5 knots on top and 30° in Column C, value is 0.750. With 8 knots on top and value 0.750 in same column, in Column C is found 5°.

Tidal Stream is on port quarter, so allow 5° to port, *i.e.,* the Course to steer is 195°(T).

Example III.

Vessel steering 337° at $14\frac{1}{2}$ knots, Tidal Stream setting 247° at $2\frac{1}{2}$ knots. What Course should the vessel steer to counteract the effect of the Tidal Stream?

With $2\frac{1}{2}$ knots on top and 90° in Column C. value is 2.500. With $14\frac{1}{2}$ knots on top and value 2.500 in the same column, in Column C is found 10°.

Tidal Stream is abeam to starboard so allow 10° to starboard. Course to steer therefore is 347°.

HOW TO FIND THE SPEED MADE GOOD OVER THE GROUND (EFFECTIVE SPEED)

(1). Enter Table from the top with speed of Tidal Stream (or Current) and from the right hand column S with relative angle of the Stream. Read from the Table the Factor and name it T.C. (Tidal Contribution to vessel's speed over ground).

(2). Enter Table from the top with ship's speed (through the water) and from the right hand column S with Course Correction. Read from the Table the Factor and name it S.C. (Ship's Contribution to vessel's speed over ground).

(3). If Tidal Stream (or Current) is on the bow, (*i.e.*, before the Beam) the vessel's effective speed is the difference between S.C. and T.C.

If Tidal Stream (or Current) is on the Quarter (*i.e.*, abaft the Beam), the vessel's effective speed is the sum of S.C. and T.C.

Example I. (as page 7:7).

Vessel's speed 10 knots, Current $3\frac{1}{2}$ knots, 50° on the starboard bow. What is the vessel's speed over the ground?

(1). With $3\frac{1}{2}$ knots at top and 50° on the right in Column S, gives (by interpolation) 2.249.

(2). With 10 knots at the top and 16° (see Example I opposite) Course Correction on the T.C. right in Column S gives (by interpolation) S.C. 9.608.

(3). As the Current is ahead of the vessel (*i.e.*, 50° on the starboard bow) and pushing her back, the difference between S.C. and T.C. −9.608 and 2.249 gives 7.359* knots, the vessel's effective speed.

Should the Current have been on the starboard quarter (*i.e.*, helping the vessel along) the sum of T.C. and S.C., *i.e.*, 11.857 knots, would have been the effective speed.

*If interpolation had not been done but the nearest tabulated figures used, *i.e.*, T.C.2.203 and S.C.9.660, the result would be 7.457, which is quite accurate enough for ordinary purposes.

Example II. (as page 7:7).

Vessel's speed, 8 knots. Tidal Stream speed, $1\frac{1}{2}$ knots, 30° on the quarter. Course allowance 5°. What speed did the vessel make good over the ground?

1. With $1\frac{1}{2}$ knots and 30° T.C. equals 1.300.
2. With 8 knots and 5° S.C. equals 7.970.
3. As Stream is behind vessel, the sum 9.27 is the effective speed.

Example III. (above).

Vessel's speed $14\frac{1}{2}$ knots. Tidal Stream $2\frac{1}{2}$ knots abeam. Course allowance 10°. What was the vessel's effective speed?

1. With $2\frac{1}{2}$ knots and 90° T.C. equals 0.
2. With $14\frac{1}{2}$ knots and 10° S.C. equals $14\frac{1}{4}$.

As Stream is abeam the sum (or difference) is $14\frac{1}{4}$, so vessel's speed over the ground is $14\frac{1}{4}$ knots.

COURSE CORRECTION TABLE
(Designed by R. C. Fisher)

SPEED OF TIDAL STREAM (OR CURRENT) OVER THE GROUND AND SHIP'S SPEED THROUGH THE WATER

C	Knots 0.5	1.0	1.5	2.0	Knots 2.5	3.0	3.5	4.0	4.5	Knots 5.0	S
0	0	0	0	0	0	0	0	0	0	0	90
1	0.009	0.019	0.026	0.035	0.044	0.052	0.061	0.070	0.079	0.087	89
2	0.017	0.035	0.052	0.070	0.087	0.105	0.122	0.139	0.157	0.174	88
3	0.026	0.052	0.079	0.105	0.131	0.157	0.183	0.209	0.236	0.262	87
4	0.035	0.070	0.105	0.140	0.174	0.209	0.244	0.279	0.314	0.349	86
5	0.044	0.087	0.131	0.174	0.218	0.261	0.305	0.349	0.392	0.436	85
6	0.052	0.105	0.157	0.209	0.261	0.314	0.366	0.418	0.470	0.523	84
8	0.070	0.139	0.209	0.278	0.348	0.418	0.487	0.557	0.626	0.696	82
10	0.087	0.174	0.260	0.347	0.434	0.521	0.608	0.695	0.781	0.868	80
12	0.104	0.208	0.312	0.416	0.520	0.624	0.728	0.832	0.936	1.040	78
14	0.121	0.242	0.363	0.484	0.605	0.726	0.847	0.968	1.089	1.210	76
16	0.138	0.276	0.413	0.551	0.689	0.827	0.965	1.103	1.240	1.378	74
18	0.155	0.309	0.464	0.618	0.773	0.927	1.082	1.236	1.391	1.545	72
21	0.179	0.358	0.538	0.717	0.896	1.075	1.254	1.433	1.613	1.792	69
24	0.203	0.407	0.610	0.813	1.017	1.220	1.424	1.627	1.830	2.034	66
27	0.227	0.454	0.681	0.908	1.135	1.362	1.589	1.816	2.043	2.270	63
30	0.250	0.500	0.750	1.000	1.250	1.500	1.750	2.000	2.250	2.500	60
33	0.272	0.545	0.817	1.089	1.362	1.634	1.906	2.179	2.451	2.723	57
36	0.294	0.588	0.882	1.176	1.469	1.763	2.057	2.351	2.645	2.939	54
39	0.315	0.629	0.944	1.259	1.573	1.888	2.203	2.517	2.832	3.147	51
42	0.335	0.669	1.004	1.338	1.673	2.007	2.342	2.667	3.011	3.346	48
46	0.360	0.719	1.079	1.439	1.798	2.158	2.518	2.877	3.237	3.597	44
50	0.383	0.766	1.149	1.532	1.915	2.298	2.681	3.064	3.447	3.830	40
54	0.405	0.809	1.214	1.618	2.023	2.427	2.832	3.236	3.641	4.045	36
58	0.424	0.848	1.272	1.696	2.120	2.540	2.986	3.392	3.816	4.240	32
62	0.442	0.883	1.324	1.766	2.207	2.649	3.090	3.532	3.973	4.415	28
66	0.457	0.914	1.370	1.827	2.284	2.741	3.197	3.754	4.111	4.568	24
70	0.470	0.940	1.410	1.879	2.349	2.819	3.289	3.759	4.229	4.698	20
75	0.483	0.966	1.449	1.932	2.415	2.898	3.381	3.864	4.347	4.830	15
80	0.492	0.985	1.477	1.970	2.462	2.954	3.447	3.939	4.432	4.924	10
85	0.498	0.996	1.494	1.992	2.490	2.989	3.487	3.985	4.483	4.981	5
90	0.500	1.000	1.500	2.000	2.500	3.000	3.500	4.000	4.500	5.000	0
C	0.5	1.0	1.5	2.0	2.5	3.0	3.5	4.0	4.5	5.0	S
					Knots						

C	Knots 6	7	8	9	Knots 10	12	14	16	18	Knots 20	S
0	0	0	0	0	0	0	0	0	0	0	90
1	0.105	0.120	0.140	0.160	0.170	0.210	0.240	0.280	0.310	0.350	89
2	0.209	0.240	0.280	0.310	0.350	0.420	0.490	0.560	0.503	0.700	88
3	0.314	0.370	0.420	0.470	0.520	0.630	0.730	0.840	0.940	1.050	87
4	0.419	0.490	0.560	0.630	0.700	0.840	0.980	1.120	1.260	1.400	86
5	0.523	0.610	0.700	0.780	0.870	1.050	1.220	1.390	1.570	1.740	85
6	0.627	0.730	0.840	0.940	1.050	1.250	1.460	1.670	1.880	2.080	84
8	0.835	0.970	1.110	1.250	1.390	1.670	1.950	2.230	2.510	2.780	82
10	1.040	1.220	1.390	1.560	1.740	2.080	2.430	2.780	3.130	3.470	80
12	1.247	1.460	1.660	1.870	2.080	2.490	2.910	3.330	3.740	4.160	78
14	1.452	1.690	1.940	2.180	2.420	2.900	3.390	3.870	4.350	4.840	76
16	1.654	1.930	2.210	2.480	2.760	3.310	3.860	4.410	4.960	5.510	74
18	1.854	2.160	2.470	2.780	3.090	3.710	4.330	4.940	5.560	6.180	72
21	2.150	2.510	2.870	3.230	3.580	4.300	5.020	5.730	6.450	7.170	69
24	2.440	2.850	3.250	3.660	4.070	4.880	5.690	6.510	7.320	8.130	66
27	2.724	3.180	3.630	4.090	4.540	5.450	6.360	7.260	8.170	9.080	63
30	3.000	3.500	4.000	4.500	5.000	6.000	7.000	8.300	9.000	10.00	60
33	3.268	3.810	4.360	4.900	5.450	6.540	7.620	8.710	9.800	10.89	57
36	3.527	4.110	4.700	5.290	5.880	7.050	8.230	9.400	10.58	11.76	54
39	3.776	4.410	5.030	5.660	6.290	7.550	8.810	10.07	11.33	12.59	51
42	4.015	4.680	5.350	6.020	6.690	8.030	9.370	10.71	12.04	13.38	48
46	4.316	5.040	5.750	6.470	7.190	8.630	10.07	11.51	12.95	14.39	44
50	4.596	5.360	6.130	6.890	7.660	9.190	10.72	12.26	13.79	15.32	40
54	4.854	5.660	6.470	7.280	8.090	9.710	11.33	12.94	14.56	16.18	36
58	5.088	5.940	6.780	7.630	8.480	10.18	11.87	13.57	15.26	16.96	32
62	5.298	6.180	7.060	7.950	8.830	10.60	12.36	14.13	15.89	17.66	28
66	5.481	6.390	7.310	8.220	9.140	10.96	12.79	14.62	16.44	18.27	24
70	5.638	6.580	7.520	8.460	9.400	11.28	13.16	15.04	16.91	18.79	20
75	5.796	6.760	7.730	8.690	9.660	11.59	13.52	15.45	17.39	19.32	15
80	5.909	6.890	7.880	8.860	9.850	11.82	13.79	15.76	17.73	19.70	10
85	5.977	6.970	7.970	8.970	9.960	11.95	13.95	15.94	17.93	19.92	5
90	6.000	7.000	8.000	9.000	10.00	12.00	14.00	16.00	18.00	20.00	0
C	6	7	8	9	10	12	14	16	18	20	S
					Knots						

THE RUNNING FIX

A Running Fix is primarily for use on those frequent occasions (particularly during night passage) when only one known object is visible, so that simultaneous cross bearings cannot be obtained. Although less reliable than a simultaneous fix, it does have many valuable applications which should never be neglected.

To obtain a Running Fix from bearings of the same object with a time interval between them:

(1). Take the first bearing and note the reading on the patent log, plot the position line on the chart and mark it with a single arrowhead at one end and also the time at which the observation was made.

(2). When the bearing has altered enough to make a good angle of "cut" with the first position line repeat the procedure.

(3). From any convenient point on the first position line lay off the "run" (the run being the track and distance made good over the ground during the time interval between the bearings).

(4). Through the end of the run draw a line parallel to the first position line. This line is the first position line " transferred", and it should be marked by two arrow heads at each end.

(5). The point where the transferred position line cuts the second bearing is the "fix" and should be marked accordingly.

Important Notes:—

(a) The accuracy of this method of fixing is dependent, not only on the accuracy of the bearings and their angle of cut, but also on the accuracy with which the "run" between the bearings has been estimated — remember leeway and effect of tide.

(b) The reliability of a running fix can be better assessed when two bearings are transferred up to the time of a third. A small "cocked hat" thus formed can generally be treated with a greater degree of confidence than a running fix from only two bearings.

(c) The principle of the running fix applies whether or not the position lines are obtained from the same point of origin. A bearing of one object may be transferred to cross with a bearing of a different object which was not sighted until after the first one was lost to view.

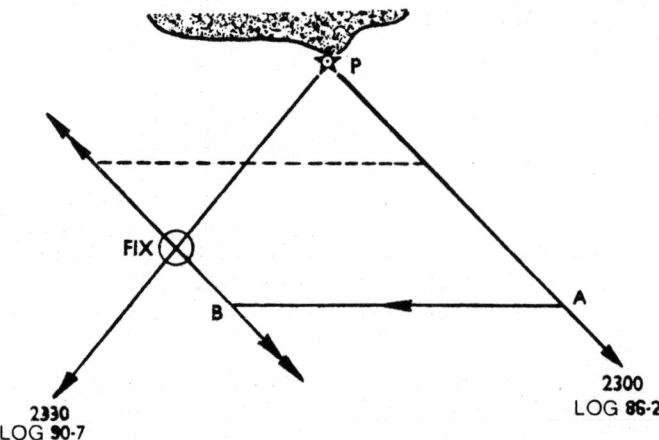

Fig. 1

Example of a Running Fix when there is no tide: Fig. 1

Vessel steering 270°(T) and making no leeway. At 2300 hrs. a lighthouse, P, bore 315°(T), Patent Log read 86.2. At 2330 hrs. the same light bore 040°(T), Patent Log read 90.7. If the tidal effect was estimated to be nil during the interval between the bearings, what was the ship's position at 2330 hours?

(1). Plot the two position lines as described above.

(2). From any convenient point A on the first position line lay off the run (AB) 270° 4.5 miles.

(3). Through B draw the transferred position line parallel to PA, and the point where it cuts the second bearing is the fix.

Example of a Running Fix in a tidal stream: Fig. 2

Vessel steering 270°(T) and making 5° leeway due to a northerly wind. At 2300 hours a Light House, P, bore 315°(T), Patent Log reading 86.2. At 2330 hours the same light bore 040°(T), Patent Log reading 90.7. The tidal stream was estimated to be setting 010° at 2 knots. Required: the vessel's position at 2330 hours.

Referring to the figure below:

(1). Plot the two position lines as described above.

(2). From any convenient point A on the first position line lay off AB (4.5 miles along the Wake Course—265°).

(3). From point B lay off BC the tidal effect for 30 minutes (set 010°, drift 1 mile). The estimated run then is AC.

(4). Through point C draw the transferred position line parallel to PA, and the point where it cuts the second bearing is the fix.

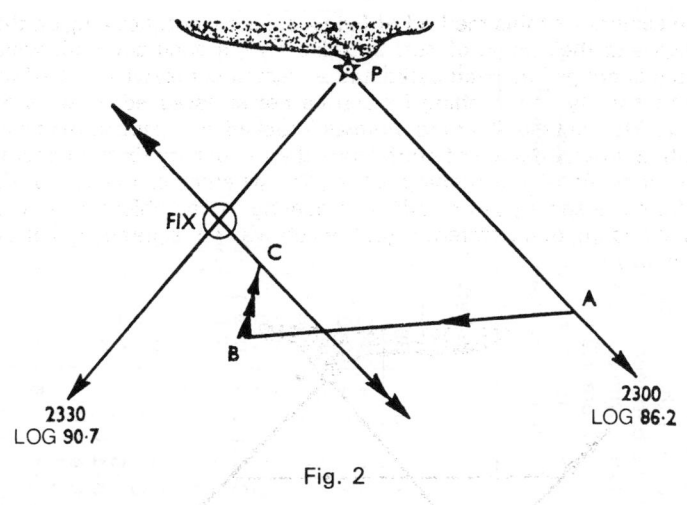

Fig. 2

SOME USEFUL VARIATIONS IN THE RUNNING FIX METHOD

One particular advantage of any of the methods which follow is that the approximate distance off a terrestrial object can be found before it comes abeam and, if necessary, the track can be altered at once to avoid passing too close to a danger.

Another important feature is that the approximate "distance off" any fixed object can be found even though the observed object cannot be located and identified on the chart.

Running Fix Table: To avoid having to plot these bearings on the chart, a special table has been included overleaf.

RUNNING FIX TABLE

DISTANCE OFF (at Second Bearing) By TWO BEARINGS AND RUN BETWEEN THEM

EXAMPLE OF USING TABLE. At 0600 steering East (Magnetic) a vessel takes a bearing of a lighthouse 160°(M). Patent Log 56. Half an hour later the Patent Log reads 60 and the bearing is found to be 210°(M). Find the distance off at the second bearing. Angle between Course Line and First bearing equals 70°. Angle between First and Second bearing equals 50°. Using Table, with above angles 70° at top and 50° at side, gives 1.2M. Distance run between bearings (P L 60 − 56) = 4 miles. Therefore 1.2 × 4 = 4.8 miles.

Vessel's bearing and distance from the Lighthouse is therefore 210°, distance 4.8 miles. Speed must be estimated as accurately as possible if Patent Log is not available.

Angle between Course Line (i.e. Ship's Head) and First Bearing

Angle between 1st and 2nd Bearings	20°	25°	30°	35°	40°	45°	50°	55°	60°	65°	70°	75°	80°	85°	90°	Angle between 1st and 2nd Bearings
10°	2·0	2·4	2·9	3·3	3·7	4·1	4·4	4·7	5·0	5·2	5·4	5·5	5·7	5·7	5·8	160°
15°	1·3	1·6	1·9	2·2	2·5	2·7	3·0	3·2	3·3	3·5	3·7	3·8	4·0	4·0	4·0	155°
20°	1·0	1·2	1·5	1·7	1·9	2·1	2·2	2·4	2·5	2·6	2·7	2·8	2·9	2·9	2·9	150°
25°	0·8	1·0	1·2	1·4	1·6	1·7	1·8	1·9	2·0	2·1	2·2	2·3	2·3	2·4	2·4	145°
30°	0·7	0·9	1·0	1·1	1·3	1·4	1·5	1·6	1·7	1·8	1·9	1·9	2·0	2·0	2·0	140°
35°	0·6	0·8	0·9	1·0	1·1	1·3	1·4	1·4	1·5	1·6	1·6	1·7	1·7	1·7	1·7	135°
40°	0·5	0·6	0·8	0·8	1·0	1·1	1·2	1·3	1·3	1·4	1·4	1·5	1·5	1·6	1·6	130°
45°	0·5	0·6	0·7	0·8	0·9	1·0	1·1	1·2	1·2	1·3	1·3	1·4	1·4	1·4	1·4	125°
50°	0·4	0·5	0·7	0·7	0·8	0·9	1·0	1·1	1·1	1·1	1·2	1·2	1·2	1·3	1·3	120°
55°	0·4	0·5	0·6	0·7	0·8	0·9	0·9	1·0	1·0	1·1	1·1	1·1	1·1	1·2	1·2	115°
60°	0·4	0·5	0·5	0·6	0·7	0·8	0·9	0·9	1·0	1·0	1·0	1·0	1·1	1·1	1·1	110°
65°	0·4	0·4	0·5	0·6	0·7	0·8	0·8	0·9	0·9	0·9	1·0	1·0	1·0	1·0		105°
70°	0·3	0·4	0·5	0·6	0·7	0·7	0·8	0·8	0·9	0·9	0·9	1·0	1·0			100°
75°	0·3	0·4	0·5	0·6	0·6	0·7	0·8	0·8	0·9	0·9	0·9	1·0				95°
80°	0·3	0·4	0·5	0·6	0·6	0·7	0·8	0·8	0·9	0·9						90°
	160°	155°	150°	145°	140°	135°	130°	125°	120°	115°	110°	105°	100°	95°	90°	

Angle between Course Line (i.e. Ship's Head) and First Bearing

Note: When the angles exceed 90° use the right vertical column for the difference between bearings and the bottom horizontal row for the angle between Course Line and First Bearing. Interpolate for accuracy.

Bearing-Angles on the Bow: If, through bad weather or other cause, it is not possible to use tables the following special bow bearings may be very valuable.

Provided the same track is maintained and the distance run over the ground during the interval between the two bearings is known, the "distance off" that the vessel will pass the object (of which the bearings were taken) when it is abeam can be determined by observing any pair of the following angles on the bow:

Pairs of Angles: (a) 22° and 34°; (b) 25° and 41°; (c) 26½° and 45°; (d) 32° and 59°; (e) 35° and 67°; (f) 37° and 72°; (g) 45° and 90°.

The distance off when abeam of the object will be equal to the distance run (over the ground) between the bearings in any one pair.

CAUTION: These methods (including the special cases described below are accurate only when: (a) there is no tidal effect; (b) no leeway; (c) the bearings are accurate; (d) the course is accurately steered from the instant of the first bearing until the vessel is abeam of the object; and (e) the distance run over the ground between the bearings is accurately known.

In tidal waters and/or when the vessel is making leeway the "angle on the bow" should be substituted by the "angle between the true bearing of the object and the true track", because in these circumstances the heading is likely to be very different to the track. The "abeam" bearing should always be at 90° to the track.

When the track and/or effective speed is uncertain, running fixes should be treated with the utmost caution.

SPECIAL CASES OF RUNNING FIXES

Although tables will give the distance off for any bearings, it requires pencil, paper, and, of course, the table itself. The following well-known methods of fixing a vessel's position can be used mentally hence their great value in small vessels.

(1) The Four Point Bearing.   (2) Doubling the Angle on the Bow.

1.—The Four Point Bearing

It is customary in Coastal Navigation (where no special dangers lie near the Course Line) to fix the position when a point of land or a light is abeam as it is then the Track is usually altered.

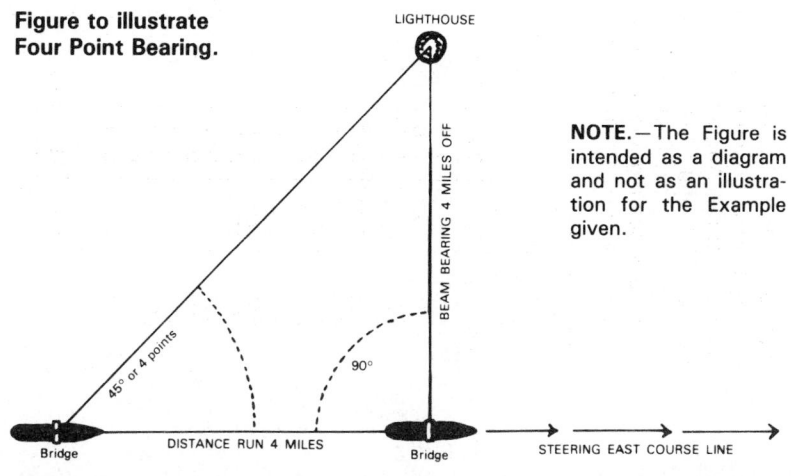

Figure to illustrate Four Point Bearing.

LIGHTHOUSE

BEAM BEARING 4 MILES OFF

NOTE.—The Figure is intended as a diagram and not as an illustration for the Example given.

45° or 4 points

90°

DISTANCE RUN 4 MILES

Bridge   Bridge   STEERING EAST COURSE LINE

METHOD.—Take a bearing of an object when it bears 4 points (*i.e.*, 45°) on the bow (assuming there is no leeway or current, otherwise take the bearing when it makes an angle of 45° with the track) and note the time and Patent Log. Again take the time and log when it is abeam (*i.e.*, at 90° to the track). Then—the distance made good over the ground in the interval between the two bearings equals the distance off when abeam.

Example.—Steering 022° at 8½ knots, a lighthouse bears 067° at 1638 Log 36. At 1704 it came abeam (Log 39½). What was the distance off when abeam? At 8½ knots in 26 mins. vessel goes 3.7 miles (see Time Speed and Distance Tables) check by the Log which shows 3½ miles has been run. Therefore the vessel is 3½ miles off.

2.—DOUBLING THE ANGLE ON THE BOW

The 4-point bearing method gives the distance off when abeam, but by "doubling the angle on the bow" the vessel's position may be found in advance, and therefore how far off a point the vessel will be when it comes abeam.

Method.—Take a bearing of an object when more than 2 points (22½°) on the bow and take the time and Log. Note down this angle and watch the compass bearing carefully until it is exactly doubled then note the log and time again. Then the distance made good over the ground between the bearings is the distance off at the time of taking the second bearing.

Example.—Steering 231° at 5 knots a lighthouse bears 259°. One hour 13 minutes later it bears 287°. What is the position at the second bearing?

As the first angle on the bow had been doubled, *i.e.*, 28° to 56° the distance run must be the distance off.

In 1hr. 13min. at 5 knots the vessel steams 6.1 miles therefore the vessel's position is with the lighthouse bearing 287° 6.1 miles off.

POSITION BY VERTICAL SEXTANT ANGLE

For the benefit of those who are not familiar with this method of fixing a vessel's position, it should be explained that if the height of any object is known, the distance off may at once be found in the daytime by taking a vertical sextant angle of it. If at the same time the bearing of the object is taken by compass the vessel's position is ascertained exactly.

This method gives an ABSOLUTE FIX and should, when practicable, be used in preference to all other methods of fixing position when in tidal waters as it gives the position at once without the possibility of error that may occur with the 4 point and other bearing fixes.

When observing the sextant angle of a lighthouse, it should be borne in mind that it is the centre of the glass lamp that must be reflected down to the sea (high water mark to be strictly accurate) and not the top of the lighthouse.

In practice no allowance is made for height of tide or height of eye, as by ignoring these the observer is led to believe he is closer to the object than he really is and therefore in most cases is given an added margin of safety.

If especial accuracy is desired, always, take the mean of the readings "on and off" the arc. This eliminates any sextant index error.

The heights of the lighthouse, beacons, etc., are given in the Section on Navigational Aids. They are also shown on the chart.

The angle observed is that which is subtended by the object and its sea level base point. Therefore where a long fore shore intervenes, the result should be accepted with caution.

TABLE FOR FINDING "DISTANCE OFF" UP TO 7 MILES

The following table gives the "distance off" by inspection of an object whose height is known and of which a sextant angle has been obtained. Where the height of the object is small, the distances cannot be found beyond 6 miles, so for this reason the first page extends only to 6 miles. The columns are for every 3m. (10ft.) up to 122m. (400ft.) and every 15m. (50ft.) thence to 213m. (700ft.) The distance column is for every cable up to 3 miles and every 2 cables from 3 to 6 miles.

Example 1. The sextant angle of a lighthouse 40m. above H.W. was taken and found to be 0° 24'. Required, the distance off. First find the column for 40m. Glance down this column until the "angle off" is sighted, i.e., 24'. Cast the eye along this line to the left when the "Distance off" in miles and cables will be seen—in this case 3 miles exactly. The distance off is therefore 3 miles.

Example 2. After a rain squall, a lighthouse 70m. above H.W. suddenly showed up, and wishing to be certain the vessel would clear the rocks, it was desired to know the exact position. A sextant angle of the lighthouse was found to be 1° 26' and the compass bearing 022°.

Under 70m. the nearest figure given for 1° 26' is 1° 27' which gives 1 mile 5 cables. The position of the vessel is therefore on a bearing of 202° from the lighthouse, 1.5 miles off—a reliable fix if the bearing is reasonably accurate.

Having now ascertained your position and wishing to keep 1 mile off the lighthouse as you round it, the Vertical Danger Angle may be ascertained from the table. Using the same height column for 70m., the angle shown on the line for 1 mile off is 2°10'. Therefore if this vertical angle of the lighthouse is maintained on the sextant, then the vessel will be kept definitely at the desired distance of 1 mile.

As the height of the object is known the Almanac may be opened in advance at the correct page, and having ascertained the sextant angle of the object, the "distance off" is found immediately. As no calculations whatsoever are required, this method of finding the "distance off" is invaluable.

The table is calculated using the plane trigonometric relationship of $d = H \cot \Theta$. (d = distance off, H = height and Θ = vertical angle). This formula is perfectly accurate for the limits of height and distance given in the table. If you wish to use heights or distances beyond the limits of the table use the formula.

$$d = H \cot (\Theta + \text{correction})$$

This correction in minutes of arc = .417 × estimated distance off. The correction allows for refraction and the curvature of the earth.

TABLE FOR FINDING DISTANCE OFF WITH SEXTANT
UP TO 6 MILES

Distance in Miles & Cables	HEIGHT OF OBJECT, TOP LINE METRES – LOWER LINE FEET												Distance in Miles & Cables
m c	12 / 40	15 / 50	18 / 60	21 / 70	24 / 80	27 / 90	30 / 100	33 / 110	37 / 120	40 / 130	43 / 140	46 / 150	m c
	° ′	° ′	° ′	° ′	° ′	° ′	° ′	° ′	° ′	° ′	° ′	° ′	
0 1	3 46	4 42	5 38	6 34	7 30	8 25	9 20	10 15	11 10	12 04	12 58	13 52	0 1
0 2	1 53	2 21	2 49	3 18	3 46	4 14	4 42	5 10	5 38	6 06	6 34	7 02	0 2
0 3	1 15	1 34	1 53	2 12	2 31	2 49	3 08	3 27	3 46	4 05	4 23	4 42	0 3
0 4	0 57	1 11	1 25	1 39	1 53	2 07	2 21	2 35	2 49	3 04	3 18	3 32	0 4
0 5	0 45	0 57	1 08	1 19	1 30	1 42	1 53	2 04	2 16	2 27	2 38	2 49	0 5
0 6	0 38	0 47	0 57	1 06	1 15	1 25	1 34	1 44	1 53	2 02	2 12	2 21	0 6
0 7	0 32	0 40	0 48	0 57	1 05	1 13	1 21	1 29	1 37	1 45	1 53	2 01	0 7
0 8	0 28	0 35	0 42	0 49	0 57	1 04	1 11	1 18	1 25	1 32	1 39	1 46	0 8
0 9	0 25	0 31	0 38	0 44	0 50	0 57	1 03	1 09	1 15	1 22	1 28	1 34	0 9
1 0	0 23	0 28	0 34	0 40	0 45	0 51	0 57	1 02	1 08	1 14	1 19	1 25	1 0
1 1	0 21	0 26	0 31	0 36	0 41	0 46	0 51	0 57	1 02	1 07	1 12	1 17	1 1
1 2	0 19	0 24	0 28	0 33	0 38	0 42	0 47	0 52	0 57	1 01	1 06	1 11	1 2
1 3	0 17	0 22	0 26	0 30	0 35	0 39	0 44	0 48	0 52	0 57	1 01	1 05	1 3
1 4	0 16	0 20	0 24	0 28	0 32	0 36	0 40	0 44	0 48	0 53	0 57	1 01	1 4
1 5	0 15	0 19	0 23	0 26	0 30	0 34	0 38	0 41	0 45	0 49	0 53	0 57	1 5
1 6	0 14	0 18	0 21	0 25	0 28	0 32	0 35	0 39	0 42	0 46	0 49	0 53	1 6
1 7	0 13	0 17	0 20	0 23	0 27	0 30	0 33	0 37	0 40	0 43	0 47	0 50	1 7
1 8	0 13	0 16	0 19	0 22	0 25	0 28	0 31	0 35	0 38	0 41	0 44	0 47	1 8
1 9	0 12	0 15	0 18	0 21	0 24	0 27	0 30	0 33	0 36	0 39	0 42	0 45	1 9
2 0	0 11	0 14	0 17	0 20	0 23	0 25	0 28	0 31	0 34	0 37	0 40	0 42	2 0
2 1	0 10	0 14	0 16	0 19	0 22	0 24	0 27	0 30	0 32	0 35	0 38	0 40	2 1
2 2	0 10	0 13	0 15	0 18	0 21	0 23	0 26	0 28	0 31	0 33	0 36	0 39	2 2
2 3	0 10	0 12	0 14	0 17	0 20	0 22	0 25	0 27	0 30	0 32	0 34	0 37	2 3
2 4	0 10	0 12	0 14	0 17	0 19	0 21	0 24	0 26	0 28	0 31	0 33	0 35	2 4
2 5	0 9	0 11	0 13	0 16	0 18	0 20	0 23	0 25	0 27	0 29	0 32	0 34	2 5
2 6	0 9	0 11	0 13	0 15	0 17	0 20	0 22	0 24	0 26	0 28	0 30	0 33	2 6
2 7	0 9	0 10	0 12	0 15	0 17	0 19	0 21	0 23	0 25	0 27	0 29	0 31	2 7
2 8	0 8	0 10	0 12	0 14	0 16	0 18	0 20	0 22	0 24	0 26	0 28	0 30	2 8
2 9	0 8	0 10	0 11	0 14	0 16	0 18	0 20	0 21	0 23	0 25	0 27	0 29	2 9
3 0	0 8	0 9	0 10	0 13	0 15	0 17	0 19	0 21	0 23	0 24	0 26	0 28	3 0
3 2				0 12	0 14	0 16	0 18	0 19	0 21	0 23	0 25	0 27	3 2
3 4				0 12	0 13	0 15	0 17	0 18	0 20	0 22	0 23	0 25	3 4
3 6				0 11	0 13	0 14	0 16	0 17	0 19	0 20	0 22	0 24	3 6
3 8				0 10	0 12	0 13	0 15	0 16	0 18	0 19	0 21	0 22	3 8
4 0				0 10	0 11	0 13	0 14	0 16	0 17	0 18	0 20	0 21	4 0
4 2					0 12	0 14	0 15	0 16	0 17	0 19	0 20		4 2
4 4					0 12	0 13	0 14	0 15	0 17	0 18	0 19		4 4
4 6					0 11	0 13	0 14	0 15	0 16	0 17	0 18		4 6
4 8					0 11	0 12	0 13	0 14	0 15	0 16	0 18		4 8
5 0					0 10	0 11	0 12	0 14	0 15	0 16	0 17		5 0
5 2							0 12	0 13	0 14	0 15	0 16		5 2
5 4							0 12	0 13	0 14	0 15	0 16		5 4
5 6							0 11	0 12	0 13	0 14	0 15		5 6
5 8							0 11	0 12	0 13	0 14	0 15		5 8
6 0							0 10	0 11	0 12	0 13	0 14		6 0

TABLE FOR FINDING DISTANCE OFF WITH SEXTANT UP TO 7 MILES

Distance in Miles & Cables	HEIGHT OF OBJECT, TOP LINE METRES—LOWER LINE FEET												Distance in Miles & Cables
	49 / 160	52 / 170	55 / 180	58 / 190	61 / 200	64 / 210	67 / 220	70 / 230	73 / 240	76 / 250	79 / 260	82 / 270	
m c	° '	° '	° '	° '	° '	° '	° '	° '	° '	° '	° '	° '	m c
0 1	14 45	15 37	16 29	17 21	18 13	19 03	19 54	20 43	21 32	22 21	23 09	23 57	0 1
0 2	7 30	7 58	8 25	8 53	9 20	9 48	10 15	10 43	11 10	11 37	12 04	12 31	0 2
0 3	5 01	5 19	5 38	5 57	6 15	6 34	6 53	7 11	7 30	7 48	8 07	8 25	0 3
0 4	3 46	4 00	4 14	4 28	4 42	4 56	5 10	5 24	5 38	5 52	6 06	6 20	0 4
0 5	3 01	3 12	3 23	3 35	3 46	3 57	4 08	4 20	4 31	4 42	4 53	5 05	0 5
0 6	2 31	2 40	2 49	2 59	3 08	3 18	3 27	3 36	3 46	3 55	4 05	4 14	0 6
0 7	2 09	2 17	2 25	2 33	2 41	2 49	2 58	3 06	3 14	3 22	3 30	3 38	0 7
0 8	1 53	2 00	2 07	2 14	2 21	2 28	2 35	2 42	2 49	2 57	3 04	3 11	0 8
0 9	1 40	1 47	1 53	1 59	2 06	2 12	2 18	2 24	2 31	2 37	2 43	2 49	0 9
1 0	1 30	1 36	1 42	1 47	1 53	1 59	2 04	2 10	2 16	2 21	2 27	2 33	1 0
1 1	1 22	1 27	1 33	1 38	1 43	1 48	1 53	1 58	2 03	2 08	2 14	2 19	1 1
1 2	1 15	1 20	1 25	1 30	1 34	1 39	1 44	1 48	1 53	1 58	2 02	2 07	1 2
1 3	1 10	1 14	1 18	1 23	1 27	1 31	1 36	1 40	1 44	1 49	1 53	1 57	1 3
1 4	1 05	1 09	1 13	1 17	1 21	1 25	1 29	1 33	1 37	1 41	1 45	1 49	1 4
1 5	1 00	1 04	1 8	1 12	1 15	1 19	1 23	1 27	1 30	1 34	1 38	1 42	1 5
1 6	0 57	1 00	1 04	1 07	1 11	1 14	1 18	1 21	1 25	1 28	1 32	1 35	1 6
1 7	0 53	0 57	1 00	1 03	1 07	1 10	1 13	1 16	1 20	1 23	1 26	1 30	1 7
1 8	0 50	0 53	0 57	1 00	1 03	1 06	1 09	1 12	1 15	1 19	1 22	1 25	1 8
1 9	0 48	0 51	0 54	0 57	1 00	1 02	1 05	1 08	1 11	1 14	1 17	1 20	1 9
2 0	0 45	0 48	0 51	0 54	0 57	0 59	1 02	1 05	1 08	1 11	1 14	1 16	2 0
2 1	0 43	0 46	0 48	0 51	0 54	0 57	0 59	1 02	1 05	1 07	1 10	1 13	2 1
2 2	0 41	0 44	0 46	0 49	0 51	0 54	0 57	0 59	1 02	1 04	1 07	1 09	2 2
2 3	0 39	0 42	0 44	0 47	0 49	0 52	0 54	0 57	0 59	1 01	1 04	1 06	2 3
2 4	0 38	0 40	0 42	0 45	0 47	0 49	0 52	0 54	0 57	0 59	1 01	1 04	2 4
2 5	0 36	0 38	0 41	0 43	0 45	0 48	0 50	0 52	0 54	0 57	0 59	1 01	2 5
2 6	0 35	0 37	0 39	0 41	0 44	0 46	0 48	0 50	0 52	0 54	0 57	0 59	2 6
2 7	0 34	0 36	0 38	0 40	0 42	0 44	0 46	0 48	0 50	0 52	0 54	0 57	2 7
2 8	0 32	0 34	0 36	0 38	0 40	0 42	0 44	0 46	0 48	0 50	0 53	0 55	2 8
2 9	0 31	0 33	0 35	0 37	0 39	0 41	0 43	0 45	0 47	0 49	0 51	0 53	2 9
3 0	0 30	0 32	0 34	0 36	0 38	0 40	0 41	0 43	0 45	0 47	0 49	0 51	3 0
3 2	0 28	0 30	0 32	0 34	0 35	0 37	0 39	0 41	0 42	0 44	0 46	0 48	3 2
3 4	0 27	0 28	0 30	0 32	0 33	0 35	0 37	0 38	0 40	0 42	0 43	0 45	3 4
3 6	0 25	0 27	0 28	0 30	0 31	0 33	0 35	0 36	0 38	0 39	0 41	0 42	3 6
3 8	0 24	0 25	0 27	0 28	0 30	0 31	0 33	0 34	0 36	0 37	0 39	0 40	3 8
4 0	0 23	0 24	0 25	0 27	0 28	0 30	0 31	0 33	0 34	0 35	0 37	0 38	4 0
4 2	0 22	0 23	0 24	0 26	0 27	0 28	0 30	0 31	0 32	0 34	0 35	0 36	4 2
4 4	0 21	0 22	0 23	0 24	0 26	0 27	0 28	0 30	0 31	0 32	0 33	0 35	4 4
4 6	0 20	0 21	0 22	0 23	0 25	0 26	0 27	0 28	0 30	0 31	0 32	0 33	4 6
4 8	0 19	0 20	0 21	0 22	0 24	0 25	0 26	0 27	0 28	0 30	0 31	0 32	4 8
5 0	0 18	0 19	0 20	0 21	0 23	0 24	0 25	0 26	0 27	0 28	0 29	0 31	5 0
5 2	0 17	0 18	0 20	0 21	0 22	0 23	0 24	0 25	0 26	0 27	0 28	0 29	5 2
5 4	0 17	0 18	0 19	0 20	0 21	0 22	0 23	0 24	0 25	0 26	0 27	0 28	5 4
5 6	0 16	0 17	0 18	0 19	0 20	0 21	0 22	0 23	0 24	0 25	0 26	0 27	5 6
5 8	0 16	0 17	0 18	0 19	0 19	0 20	0 21	0 22	0 23	0 24	0 25	0 26	5 8
6 0	0 15	0 16	0 17	0 18	0 19	0 20	0 21	0 22	0 23	0 24	0 25	0 25	6 0
6 2					0 18	0 19	0 20	0 21	0 22	0 23	0 24	0 25	6 2
6 4					0 18	0 19	0 20	0 21	0 21	0 22	0 23	0 24	6 4
6 6					0 17	0 18	0 19	0 20	0 21	0 21	0 22	0 23	6 6
6 8					0 17	0 18	0 18	0 19	0 20	0 21	0 22	0 22	6 8
7 0					0 16	0 17	0 18	0 19	0 19	0 20	0 21	0 22	7 0

TABLE FOR FINDING DISTANCE OFF WITH SEXTANT UP TO 7 MILES

Distance in Miles & Cables	HEIGHT OF OBJECT, TOP LINE METRES—LOWER LINE FEET												Distance in Miles & Cables
	85 280	88 290	91 300	94 310	97 320	101 330	104 340	107 350	110 360	113 370	116 380	119 390	
m c	° '	° '	° '	° '	° '	° '	° '	° '	° '	° '	° '	° '	m c
0 1	24 44	25 30	26 16	26 01	27 46	28 29	29 13	29 56	30 38	31 19	32 00	32 41	0 1
0 2	12 58	13 25	13 52	14 08	14 45	15 11	15 37	16 03	16 29	16 55	17 21	17 47	0 2
0 3	8 44	9 02	9 20	9 39	9 57	10 15	10 34	10 52	11 10	11 28	11 46	12 04	0 3
0 4	6 34	6 48	7 02	7 16	7 30	7 44	7 58	8 11	8 25	8 39	8 53	9 07	0 4
0 5	5 16	5 27	5 38	5 49	6 01	6 12	6 23	6 34	6 45	6 56	7 08	7 19	0 5
0 6	4 23	4 33	4 42	4 51	5 01	5 10	5 19	5 29	5 38	5 47	5 47	6 06	0 6
0 7	3 46	3 54	4 02	5 10	4 18	4 26	4 43	4 42	4 50	4 58	5 06	5 14	0 7
0 8	3 18	3 25	3 32	3 39	3 46	3 53	4 00	4 07	4 14	4 21	4 28	4 35	0 8
0 9	2 56	3 02	3 08	3 15	3 21	3 27	3 33	3 40	3 46	3 52	3 58	4 05	0 9
1 0	2 38	2 44	2 49	2 55	3 01	3 06	3 12	3 18	3 23	3 29	3 35	3 40	1 0
1 1	2 24	2 29	2 34	2 39	2 44	2 49	2 55	3 00	3 05	3 10	3 15	3 20	1 1
1 2	2 12	2 17	2 21	2 26	2 31	2 35	2 40	2 45	2 49	2 54	2 59	3 04	1 2
1 3	2 02	2 06	2 10	2 15	2 19	2 23	2 28	2 32	2 36	2 41	2 45	2 49	1 3
1 4	1 53	1 57	2 01	2 05	2 09	2 13	2 17	2 21	2 25	2 29	2 37	2 37	1 4
1 5	1 46	1 49	1 53	1 57	2 01	2 04	2 08	2 12	2 16	2 19	2 23	2 27	1 5
1 6	1 39	1 42	1 46	1 50	1 53	1 57	2 00	2 04	2 07	2 11	2 14	2 18	1 6
1 7	1 33	1 36	1 40	1 43	1 46	1 50	1 53	1 56	2 00	2 03	2 06	2 10	1 7
1 8	1 28	1 31	1 34	1 37	1 40	1 44	1 47	1 50	1 53	1 56	1 59	2 02	1 8
1 9	1 23	1 26	1 29	1 32	1 35	1 38	1 41	1 44	1 47	1 50	1 53	1 56	1 9
2 0	1 19	1 22	1 25	1 28	1 30	1 33	1 36	1 39	1 42	1 45	1 47	1 50	2 0
2 1	1 15	1 18	1 21	1 23	1 26	1 29	1 32	1 34	1 37	1 40	1 42	1 45	2 1
2 2	1 12	1 15	1 17	1 20	1 22	1 25	1 27	1 30	1 33	1 35	1 38	1 40	2 2
2 3	1 09	1 11	1 14	1 16	1 19	1 21	1 24	1 26	1 29	1 31	1 33	1 36	2 3
2 4	1 06	1 08	1 11	1 13	1 15	1 18	1 20	1 22	1 25	1 27	1 30	1 32	2 4
2 5	1 03	1 06	1 08	1 10	1 12	1 15	1 17	1 19	1 21	1 24	1 26	1 28	2 5
2 6	1 01	1 03	1 05	1 07	1 10	1 12	1 14	1 16	1 18	1 20	1 23	1 25	2 6
2 7	0 59	1 01	1 03	1 05	1 07	1 09	1 11	1 13	1 15	1 17	1 20	1 23	2 7
2 8	0 57	0 59	1 01	1 03	1 05	1 07	1 09	1 11	1 13	1 15	1 17	1 19	2 8
2 9	0 55	0 57	0 58	1 00	1 02	1 04	1 06	1 08	1 10	1 12	1 14	1 16	2 9
3 0	0 53	0 55	0 57	0 58	1 00	1 02	1 04	1 06	1 08	1 10	1 12	1 14	3 0
3 2	0 49	0 51	0 53	0 55	0 57	0 58	1 00	1 02	1 04	1 05	1 07	1 09	3 2
3 4	0 47	0 48	0 50	0 52	0 53	0 55	0 57	0 58	1 00	1 02	1 03	1 05	3 4
3 6	0 44	0 46	0 47	0 49	0 50	0 52	0 53	0 55	0 57	0 58	1 00	1 01	3 6
3 8	0 42	0 43	0 45	0 46	0 48	0 49	0 51	0 52	0 54	0 55	0 57	0 58	3 8
4 0	0 40	0 41	0 42	0 44	0 45	0 47	0 48	0 49	0 51	0 52	0 54	0 55	4 0
4 2	0 38	0 39	0 40	0 42	0 43	0 44	0 46	0 47	0 48	0 50	0 51	0 53	4 2
4 4	0 36	0 37	0 39	0 40	0 41	0 42	0 44	0 45	0 46	0 48	0 49	0 50	4 4
4 6	0 34	0 36	0 37	0 38	0 39	0 41	0 42	0 43	0 44	0 45	0 47	0 48	4 6
4 8	0 33	0 34	0 35	0 37	0 38	0 39	0 40	0 41	0 42	0 44	0 45	0 46	4 8
5 0	0 32	0 33	0 34	0 35	0 36	0 37	0 38	0 40	0 41	0 42	0 43	0 44	5 0
5 2	0 30	0 32	0 33	0 34	0 35	0 36	0 37	0 38	0 39	0 40	0 41	0 42	5 2
5 4	0 29	0 30	0 31	0 32	0 34	0 34	0 36	0 37	0 38	0 39	0 40	0 41	5 4
5 6	0 28	0 29	0 30	0 31	0 32	0 33	0 34	0 35	0 36	0 37	0 38	0 39	5 6
5 8	0 27	0 28	0 29	0 30	0 31	0 32	0 33	0 34	0 35	0 36	0 37	0 38	5 8
6 0	0 26	0 27	0 28	0 29	0 30	0 31	0 32	0 33	0 34	0 35	0 36	0 37	6 0
6 2	0 26	0 26	0 27	0 28	0 29	0 30	0 31	0 32	0 33	0 34	0 35	3 06	6 2
6 4	0 25	0 26	0 27	0 27	0 28	0 29	0 30	0 31	0 32	0 33	0 34	0 34	6 4
6 6	0 24	0 25	0 26	0 27	0 27	0 28	0 29	0 30	0 31	0 32	0 33	0 33	6 6
6 8	0 23	0 24	0 25	0 26	0 27	0 27	0 28	0 29	0 30	0 31	0 32	0 32	6 8
7 0	0 23	0 23	0 24	0 25	0 26	0 27	0 37	0 38	0 29	0 30	0 31	0 31	7 0

TABLE FOR FINDING DISTANCE OFF WITH SEXTANT UP TO 7 MILES

Distance in Miles & Cables	122 / 400	137 / 450	152 / 500	168 / 550	183 / 600	198 / 650	213 / 700	244 / 800	274 / 900	305 / 1000	457 / 1500	610 / 2000	Distance in Miles & Cables
m c	o ′	o ′	o ′	o ′	o ′	o ′	o ′	o ′	o ′	o ′	o ′	o ′	m c
0 1	33 20	36 30	39 26	42 08	44 37								0 1
0 2	18 13	20 18	22 21	24 20	26 16	28 08	29 56	33 20	36 30	39 26			0 2
0 3	12 22	13 52	15 20	16 47	18 13	19 37	21 00	23 41	26 16	28 44			0 3
0 4	9 20	10 29	11 37	12 45	13 52	14 58	16 03	18 13	20 18	22 21			0 4
0 5	7 30	8 25	9 20	10 15	11 10	12 04	12 58	14 45	16 30	18 13	26 15		0 5
0 6	6 15	7 02	7 48	8 34	9 20	10 06	10 52	12 22	13 52	15 20	22 20	28 44	0 6
0 7	5 22	6 02	6 42	7 22	8 01	8 41	9 20	10 39	11 56	13 13	19 25	25 10	0 7
0 8	4 42	5 17	5 52	6 27	7 02	7 37	8 11	9 20	10 29	11 37	17 08	22 21	0 8
0 9	4 11	4 42	5 13	5 44	6 15	6 46	7 17	8 19	9 20	10 21	15 19	20 05	0 9
1 0	3 46	4 14	4 42	5 10	5 38	6 06	6 34	7 30	8 25	9 20	13 51	18 13	1 0
1 1	3 25	3 51	4 17	4 42	5 08	5 33	5 59	6 49	7 40	8 30	12 38	16 39	1 1
1 2	3 08	3 32	3 55	4 19	4 42	5 05	5 29	6 15	7 02	7 48	11 37	15 20	1 2
1 3	2 54	3 16	3 37	3 59	4 20	4 42	5 04	5 47	6 30	7 13	10 45	14 12	1 3
1 4	2 41	3 02	3 22	3 42	4 02	4 22	4 42	5 22	6 02	6 42	10 00	13 13	1 4
1 5	2 31	2 49	3 08	3 27	3 46	4 05	4 23	5 01	5 38	6 15	9 20	12 22	1 5
1 6	2 21	2 39	2 57	3 14	3 32	3 49	4 07	4 42	5 17	5 52	8 46	11 37	1 6
1 7	2 13	2 30	2 46	3 03	3 19	3 36	3 52	4 26	4 59	5 32	8 15	10 57	1 7
1 8	2 06	2 21	2 37	2 53	3 08	3 24	3 40	4 11	4 42	5 13	7 48	10 21	1 8
1 9	1 59	2 14	2 29	2 44	2 58	3 13	3 28	3 58	4 27	4 57	7 25	9 50	1 9
2 0	1 53	2 07	2 21	2 35	2 49	3 04	3 18	3 46	4 14	4 42	7 02	9 20	2 0
2 1	1 48	2 01	2 15	2 28	2 41	2 55	3 08	3 35	4 02	4 29	6 41	8 53	2 1
2 2	1 43	1 56	2 08	2 21	2 34	2 47	3 00	3 25	3 51	4 17	6 23	8 30	2 2
2 3	1 38	1 51	2 03	2 15	2 27	2 40	2 52	3 16	3 41	4 05	6 07	8 09	2 3
2 4	1 34	1 46	1 58	2 10	2 21	2 33	2 45	3 08	3 32	3 55	5 52	7 48	2 4
2 5	1 30	1 42	1 53	2 04	2 16	2 27	2 38	3 01	3 23	3 46	5 38	7 30	2 5
2 6	1 27	1 38	1 49	2 00	2 10	2 21	2 32	2 54	3 16	3 37	5 25	7 13	2 6
2 7	1 24	1 34	1 45	1 55	2 06	2 16	2 27	2 47	3 08	3 29	5 13	6 57	2 7
2 8	1 21	1 31	1 41	1 51	2 01	2 11	2 21	2 41	3 02	3 22	5 02	6 42	2 8
2 9	1 18	1 28	1 37	1 47	1 57	2 07	2 16	2 36	2 55	3 15	4 52	6 28	2 9
3 0	1 15	1 25	1 34	1 44	1 53	2 02	2 12	2 31	2 49	3 08	4 42	6 15	3 0
3 2	1 11	1 20	1 28	1 37	1 46	1 55	2 04	2 21	2 39	2 57	4 24	5 52	3 2
3 4	1 07	1 15	1 23	1 31	1 40	1 48	1 56	2 13	2 30	2 46	4 09	5 32	3 4
3 6	1 03	1 11	1 19	1 26	1 34	1 42	1 50	2 06	2 21	2 37	3 55	5 13	3 6
3 8	1 00	1 07	1 14	1 22	1 29	1 37	1 44	1 59	2 14	2 29	3 43	4 57	3 8
4 0	0 57	1 04	1 11	1 18	1 25	1 32	1 39	1 53	2 07	2 21	3 31	4 42	4 0
4 2	0 54	1 01	1 07	1 14	1 21	1 28	1 34	1 48	2 01	2 15	3 21	4 29	4 2
4 4	0 51	0 58	1 04	1 11	1 17	1 24	1 30	1 43	1 56	2 08	3 12	4 17	4 4
4 6	0 49	0 55	1 01	1 08	1 14	1 20	1 26	1 38	1 51	2 03	3 04	4 05	4 6
4 8	0 47	0 53	0 59	1 05	1 11	1 17	1 22	1 34	1 46	1 58	2 57	3 55	4 8
5 0	0 45	0 51	0 57	1 02	1 08	1 14	1 19	1 30	1 42	1 53	2 50	3 46	5 0
5 2	0 43	0 49	0 54	1 00	1 05	1 11	1 16	1 27	1 38	1 49	2 44	3 38	5 2
5 4	0 42	0 47	0 52	0 58	1 03	1 08	1 13	1 24	1 34	1 45	2 28	3 30	5 4
5 6	0 40	0 45	0 50	0 56	1 01	1 06	1 11	1 21	1 31	1 41	2 32	3 22	5 6
5 8	0 39	0 44	0 49	0 54	0 58	1 03	1 08	1 18	1 28	1 37	2 26	3 15	5 8
6 0	0 38	0 42	0 47	0 52	0 57	1 01	1 06	1 15	1 25	1 34	2 21	3 09	6 0
6 2	0 36	0 41	0 46	1 50	1 55	0 59	1 04	1 13	1 22	1 31	2 16	3 02	6 2
6 4	0 35	0 40	0 44	0 49	0 53	0 57	1 02	1 11	1 20	1 28	2 12	2 57	6 4
6 6	0 34	0 38	0 43	0 47	0 51	0 56	1 00	1 09	1 17	1 26	2 08	2 51	6 6
6 8	0 33	0 37	0 42	0 46	0 50	0 54	0 58	1 07	1 15	1 23	2 04	2 46	6 8
7 0	0 32	0 36	0 40	0 44	0 48	0 53	0 57	1 05	1 13	1 21	2 01	2 42	7 0

HEIGHT OF OBJECT, TOP LINE METRES — LOWER LINE FEET

HORIZONTAL SEXTANT ANGLE FIX

By Radius of Position Circle instead of the Station Pointer

The time honoured Three Point Problem (or Station Pointer Fix) will, if the objects be well chosen, give the most accurate Fix of any. It is so valuable in Navigation because it is not subject to errors arising from imperfect knowledge of the compass error, improper log reading or the effects of tidal streams or currents, as are the other Fixing methods.

Three objects as presented on the chart are selected, and with the aid of the Sextant the angles are measured between the centre object and each of the other two objects. The position is then plotted by means of the Station Pointer (or a sheet of tracing paper), as described in all books on Navigation. The following table, however, permits the use of this valuable method of Fixing without the need of any other aids to Navigation than the most common ones, *i.e.*, rulers, dividers (or compasses) and Reed's.

Excellent Fixes with this method (quite independent of the means by which it is being used) will be obtained:

1.   When the centre object of the three lies between the observer and a line joining the other two, or lies nearer than either of the other two.

2.   When the sum of the right and left angles is equal to or greater than 180°.

3.   When two of the objects are equidistant from the observer, or nearly so, and the angle to the third is not less than 30°.

4.   When the three objects are on or nearly on the same straight line.

A condition that limits all of these is that the angles should be large, at least as large as 30°, exempting Case 3, but even then the other angle must be of good size, just the same.

It should be emphasised that the above limitations are not peculiar to the new method proposed, but are mathematical peculiarities of the problem as such.

In general, the practical Navigator, when coasting, will find little difficulty in selecting conspicuous objects, that will fulfil the above conditions, but it must be realised that the method requires smooth operating conditions. In a small vessel, even with moderate sea conditions a reliable three point fix becomes extremely difficult.

Remember, practice makes perfect.

Explanation and examples of how to use the Tables on following pages

The diagram following illustrates a vessel (S) whose Navigator, when coasting, has taken simultaneous (or nearly so) horizontal sextant angles. The first angle taken was between the centre object a Church (✴) and the right hand object — a high Rock (R); and the second angle was taken immediately between the same centre object, a Church (✴) and the left hand object, a Lighthouse (L), all marked conspicuously on the chart and clearly visible to the Navigator.

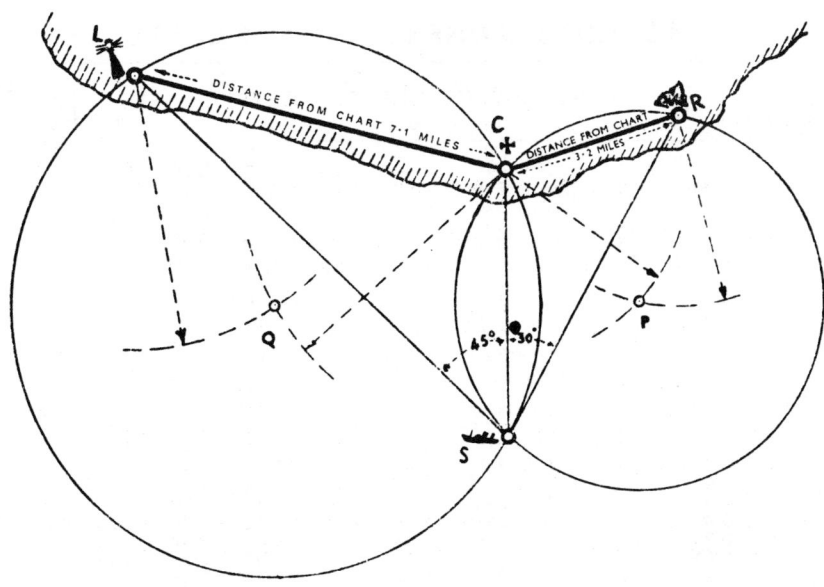

Example.
Angle between Rock (R) and Church (C) (right hand angle) = 30°. Distance between R and C = 3.2 miles. Angle between Lighthouse (L) and Church (C) (left hand angle) = 45°, and Distance between L and C = 7.1 miles.

Instructions
With the angle RSC (30°), subtended by the right hand and centre objects enter the table on page 232 from the side and find the Radius of one of the Position Circles in the column headed by the Distance between the aforesaid objects. In this case with 30° at the side and 3.2 miles at the top the Radius (by simple interpolation) is 3.2. Therefore with 3.2 miles in the compasses (or dividers as substitute) as Radius strike short arcs from both R and C and mark P—their point of intersection. With the same radius describe round P the circle RCS.

Proceeding in a similar way, describe with Radius 5 miles (found from the table following) the circle LCS.

The intersection of the two circles (S in the figure) gives the desired Fix and the Ship's position.

Note: The distances, tabulated at the top and bottom of the table are for full miles. For tenfolds and decimals of full miles use ten times or tenths respectively, of the tabulated radii and add, thus:

Subtended Angle 50°
Distances between objects 23.7 miles.

For 20 miles (ten times two) 10x1.31	13.1	miles
,, 3 miles (from table)	1.96	miles
,, 0.7 miles (column 7 divided by 10)	0.46	miles
Radius	15.5	miles

In general no interpolation between the tabulated angles will be necessary and in any case most Navigators would prefer to interpolate at sight.

HORIZONTAL SEXTANT ANGLE FIX

Angle Subtended by Objects		Distance between Objects									Angle Subtended by Objects	
°	′	1	2	3	4	5	6	7	8	9	°	′
30		1.00	2.00	3.00	4.00	5.00	6.00	7.00	8.00	9.00	150	
	10	1.00	1.99	2.99	3.98	4.98	5.97	6.97	7.96	8.96		50
	20	0.99	1.98	2.97	3.96	4.95	5.94	6.93	7.92	8.91		40
	30	0.99	1.97	2.96	3.94	4.93	5.91	6.90	7.88	8.87		30
	40	0.98	1.96	2.94	3.92	4.90	5.88	6.86	7.84	8.83		20
	50	0.98	1.95	2.93	3.90	4.88	5.85	6.83	7.80	8.78		10
31		0.97	1.94	2.91	3.88	4.86	5.83	6.80	7.77	8.74	149	
	10	0.97	1.93	2.90	3.86	4.83	5.80	6.76	7.73	8.70		
	20	0.96	1.92	2.89	3.85	4.81	5.77	6.73	7.70	8.65		50
	30	0.96	1.91	2.87	3.83	4.79	5.74	6.70	7.66	8.61		40
	40	0.95	1.91	2.86	3.81	4.76	5.72	6.67	7.62	8.57		30
	50	0.95	1.90	2.84	3.79	4.74	5.69	6.64	7.58	8.53		20
												10
32		0.94	1.89	2.83	3.77	4.72	5.66	6.61	7.55	8.49	148	
	10	0.94	1.88	2.82	3.76	4.70	5.63	6.57	7.51	8.45		50
	20	0.94	1.87	2.81	3.74	4.68	5.61	6.55	7.48	8.42		40
	30	0.93	1.86	2.79	3.72	4.65	5.58	6.51	7.44	8.38		30
	40	0.93	1.85	2.78	3.71	4.63	5.56	6.49	7.41	8.34		20
	50	0.92	1.84	2.77	3.69	4.61	5.53	6.45	7.38	8.30		10
33		0.92	1.84	2.75	3.67	4.59	5.51	6.43	7.34	8.26	147	
	10	0.92	1.83	2.75	3.66	4.58	5.49	6.41	7.32	8.24		50
	20	0.91	1.82	2.73	3.64	4.55	5.46	6.37	7.28	8.19		40
	30	0.91	1.81	2.72	3.62	4.53	5.44	6.34	7.25	8.15		30
	40	0.90	1.80	2.71	3.61	4.51	5.41	6.31	7.22	8.12		20
	50	0.90	1.80	2.69	3.59	4.49	5.39	6.29	7.18	8.08		10
34		0.89	1.79	2.68	3.58	4.47	5.36	6.26	7.15	8.05	146	
	10	0.89	1.78	2.67	3.56	4.45	5.34	6.23	7.12	8.02		50
	20	0.89	1.77	2.66	3.55	4.43	5.32	6.21	7.09	7.98		40
	30	0.88	1.77	2.65	3.53	4.42	5.30	6.18	7.06	7.95		30
	40	0.88	1.76	2.64	3.52	4.40	5.27	6.15	7.03	7.91		20
	50	0.88	1.75	2.63	3.50	4.38	5.25	6.13	7.00	7.88		10
35		0.87	1.74	2.62	3.49	4.36	5.23	6.10	6.97	7.84	145	
	12	0.87	1.74	2.60	3.47	4.34	5.21	6.07	6.94	7.81		48
	24	0.86	1.73	2.59	3.45	4.32	5.18	6.04	6.90	7.77		36
	36	0.86	1.72	2.58	3.44	4.30	5.15	6.01	6.87	7.73		24
	48	0.86	1.71	2.57	3.42	4.28	5.13	5.99	6.84	7.70		12
36		0.85	1.70	2.55	3.40	4.25	5.10	5.95	6.80	7.66	144	
	12	0.85	1.69	2.54	3.39	4.23	5.08	5.93	6.77	7.62		48
	24	0.84	1.69	2.53	3.37	4.21	5.06	5.90	6.74	7.58		36
	36	0.84	1.68	2.52	3.35	4.19	5.03	5.87	6.71	7.55		24
	48	0.83	1.67	2.50	3.34	4.17	5.01	5.84	6.68	7.51		12
37		0.83	1.66	2.49	3.32	4.16	4.99	5.82	6.65	7.48	143	
	12	0.83	1.65	2.48	3.31	4.14	4.96	5.79	6.62	7.44		48
	24	0.82	1.65	2.47	3.29	4.12	4.94	5.76	6.58	7.41		36
	36	0.82	1.64	2.46	3.28	4.10	4.92	5.74	6.56	7.38		24
	48	0.82	1.63	2.45	3.26	4.08	4.90	5.71	6.53	7.34		12
38		0.81	1.62	2.44	3.25	4.06	4.87	5.68	6.50	7.31	142	
	12	0.81	1.62	2.43	3.23	4.04	4.85	5.66	6.47	7.28		48
	24	0.81	1.61	2.42	3.22	4.03	4.83	5.64	6.44	7.25		36
	36	0.80	1.60	2.41	3.21	4.01	4.81	5.61	6.41	7.21		24
	48	0.80	1.60	2.39	3.19	3.99	4.79	5.59	6.38	7.18		12
39		0.79	1.59	2.38	3.18	3.97	4.77	5.56	6.36	7.15	141	
	12	0.79	1.58	2.37	3.16	3.96	4.75	5.54	6.33	7.12		48
	24	0.79	1.58	2.36	3.15	3.94	4.73	5.52	6.30	7.09		36
	36	0.79	1.57	2.35	3.14	3.92	4.71	5.49	6.28	7.06		24
	48	0.78	1.56	2.34	3.12	3.91	4.69	5.47	6.25	7.03		12
40		0.78	1.56	2.33	3.11	3.89	4.67	5.45	6.22	7.00	140	
	20	0.77	1.55	2.32	3.09	3.86	4.64	5.41	6.18	6.95		40
	40	0.77	1.54	2.30	3.07	3.84	4.61	5.37	6.14	6.91		20
41		0.76	1.52	2.29	3.05	3.81	4.57	5.33	6.10	6.86	139	
	20	0.76	1.51	2.27	3.03	3.79	4.54	5.30	6.06	6.81		40
	40	0.75	1.50	2.26	3.01	3.76	4.51	5.26	6.02	6.77		20
42		0.75	1.50	2.24	2.99	3.74	4.49	5.23	5.98	6.73	138	
	20	0.74	1.49	2.23	2.97	3.71	4.46	5.20	5.94	6.68		40
	40	0.74	1.48	2.21	2.95	3.69	4.43	5.17	5.90	6.64		20
43		0.73	1.47	2.20	2.93	3.67	4.40	5.13	5.86	6.60	137	
°	′										°	′

HORIZONTAL SEXTANT ANGLE FIX

Angle Subtended by Objects		Distance between Objects									Angle Subtended by Objects	
°	′	1	2	3	4	5	6	7	8	9	°	′
43		0.73	1.47	2.20	2.93	3.67	4.40	5.13	5.86	6.60	137	
	20	0.73	1.46	2.19	2.91	3.64	4.37	5.10	5.83	6.56		40
	40	0.72	1.45	2.17	2.90	3.62	4.34	5.07	5.79	6.52		20
44		0.72	1.44	2.16	2.88	3.60	4.32	5.04	5.76	6.48	136	
	20	0.72	1.43	2.15	2.86	3.58	4.29	5.01	5.72	6.44		40
	40	0.71	1.42	2.14	2.85	3.56	4.27	4.98	5.69	6.40		20
45		0.71	1.41	2.12	2.83	3.54	4.24	4.95	5.66	6.36	135	
	20	0.70	1.41	2.11	2.81	3.52	4.22	4.92	5.62	6.33		40
	40	0.70	1.40	2.10	2.80	3.50	4.19	4.89	5.59	6.29		20
46		0.70	1.39	2.09	2.78	3.48	4.17	4.87	5.56	6.26	134	
	20	0.69	1.38	2.07	2.76	3.46	4.15	4.84	5.53	6.22		40
	40	0.69	1.38	2.06	2.75	3.44	4.13	4.81	5.50	6.19		20
47		0.68	1.37	2.05	2.73	3.42	4.10	4.79	5.47	6.15	133	
	20	0.68	1.36	2.04	2.72	3.40	4.08	4.76	5.44	6.12		40
	40	0.68	1.35	2.03	2.71	3.38	4.06	4.74	5.41	6.09		20
48		0.67	1.35	2.02	2.69	3.37	4.04	4.71	5.38	6.06	132	
	20	0.67	1.34	2.01	2.68	3.35	4.02	4.69	5.36	6.03		40
	40	0.67	1.33	2.00	2.66	3.33	4.00	4.66	5.33	5.99		20
49		0.66	1.33	2.00	2.65	3.31	3.98	4.64	5.30	5.96	131	
	20	0.66	1.32	1.98	2.64	3.30	3.95	4.61	5.27	5.93		40
	40	0.66	1.31	1.97	2.62	3.28	3.94	4.59	5.25	5.90		20
50		0.65	1.31	1.96	2.61	3.26	3.92	4.57	5.22	5.87	130	
	30	0.65	1.30	1.94	2.59	3.24	3.89	4.54	5.18	5.83		30
51		0.64	1.29	1.93	2.57	3.22	3.86	4.51	5.15	5.79	129	
	30	0.64	1.28	1.92	2.56	3.20	3.83	4.47	5.11	5.75		30
52		0.63	1.27	1.90	2.54	3.17	3.81	4.44	5.08	5.71	128	
	30	0.63	1.26	1.89	2.52	3.15	3.78	4.41	5.04	5.68		30
53		0.63	1.25	1.88	2.50	3.13	3.76	4.38	5.01	5.63	127	
	30	0.62	1.24	1.87	2.49	3.11	3.73	4.35	4.98	5.60		30
54		0.62	1.24	1.85	2.47	3.09	3.71	4.33	4.94	5.56	126	
	30	0.61	1.23	1.84	2.46	3.07	3.68	4.30	4.91	5.53		30
55		0.61	1.22	1.83	2.44	3.05	3.66	4.27	4.88	5.50	125	
	30	0.61	1.21	1.82	2.43	3.03	3.64	4.25	4.85	5.46		30
56		0.60	1.21	1.81	2.41	3.02	3.62	4.22	4.82	5.43	124	
	30	0.60	1.20	1.80	2.40	3.00	3.60	4.20	4.80	5.40		30
57		0.60	1.19	1.79	2.38	2.98	3.58	4.17	4.77	5.36	123	
	30	0.59	1.19	1.78	2.37	2.97	3.56	4.15	4.74	5.34		30
58		0.59	1.18	1.77	2.36	2.95	3.54	4.13	4.72	5.31	122	
	30	0.59	1.17	1.76	2.35	2.93	3.52	4.11	4.69	5.28		30
59		0.58	1.17	1.75	2.33	2.92	3.50	4.09	4.67	5.25	121	
	30	0.58	1.16	1.74	3.32	2.90	3.48	4.06	4.64	5.23		30
60		0.58	1.16	1.73	2.31	2.89	3.47	4.04	4.62	5.20	120	
61		0.57	1.14	1.72	2.29	2.86	3.43	4.00	4.57	5.14	119	
62		0.57	1.13	1.70	2.27	2.83	3.40	3.97	4.53	5.10	118	
63		0.56	1.12	1.68	2.24	2.81	3.37	3.93	4.49	5.05	117	
64		0.56	1.11	1.67	2.23	2.78	3.34	3.90	4.45	5.01	116	
65		0.55	1.10	1.66	2.21	2.76	3.31	3.86	4.41	4.96	115	
66		0.55	1.10	1.64	2.19	2.74	3.29	3.83	4.38	4.93	114	
67		0.54	1.09	1.63	2.17	2.72	3.26	3.80	4.34	4.89	113	
68		0.54	1.08	1.62	2.16	2.70	3.24	3.78	4.32	4.86	112	
69		0.54	1.07	1.61	2.14	2.68	3.21	3.75	4.28	4.82	111	
70		0.53	1.06	1.60	2.13	2.66	3.19	3.72	4.26	4.79	110	
71		0.53	1.06	1.59	2.12	2.65	3.17	3.70	4.23	4.76	109	
72		0.53	1.05	1.58	2.10	2.63	3.16	3.68	4.21	4.73	108	
73		0.52	1.05	1.57	2.09	2.62	3.14	3.66	4.18	4.71	107	
74		0.52	1.04	1.56	2.08	2.60	3.12	3.64	4.16	4.68	106	
76		0.52	1.03	1.55	2.06	2.58	3.09	3.61	4.12	4.64	104	
78		0.51	1.02	1.53	2.04	2.56	3.07	3.58	4.09	4.60	102	
80		0.51	1.02	1.52	2.03	2.54	3.05	3.55	4.06	4.57	100	
82		0.51	1.01	1.52	2.02	2.53	3.03	3.54	4.04	4.55	98	
84		0.50	1.01	1.51	2.01	2.52	3.02	3.52	4.02	4.53	96	
86		0.50	1.00	1.50	2.00	2.51	3.01	3.51	4.01	4.51	94	
90		0.50	1.00	1.50	2.00	2.50	3.00	3.50	4.00	4.50	90	
°	′										°	′

FINDING THE DISTANCE OF OBJECTS AT SEA

Owing to the Earth's curvature, the distance to the sea horizon is governed by the height of the observer's eye. The figure below illustrates this and also that, in conditions of clear visibility, the distance at which the top of an object first shows itself on the horizon depends upon its height as well as the height of eye. In this case the distance of the ship from the taller of the two lighthouses is $(6 + 14\frac{1}{2}) = 20\frac{1}{2}$ miles.

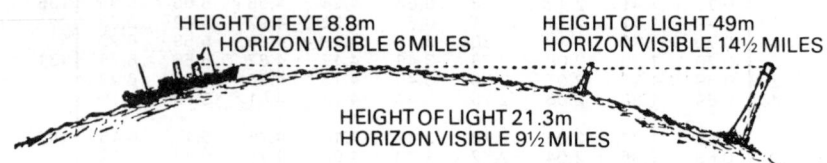

HEIGHT OF EYE 8.8m
HORIZON VISIBLE 6 MILES

HEIGHT OF LIGHT 49m
HORIZON VISIBLE 14½ MILES

HEIGHT OF LIGHT 21.3m
HORIZON VISIBLE 9½ MILES

Range of lights

Luminous range is the maximum distance at which a light can be seen at a given time, as determined by the intensity of the light and the meteorological visibility prevailing at the time; it takes no account of elevation, observer's height of eye or the curvature of the earth.

Nominal range is the luminous range when the meteorological visibility is 10 sea miles.

Geographical range is the maximum distance at which light from a light can theoretically reach an observer, as limited only by the curvature of the earth and the refraction of the atmosphere, and by the elevation of the light and the height of the observer. Geographical ranges on charts are based on a height of eye of 15ft (5 metres).

The range shown on charts published after 1972 for northern European waters is the nominal range. The range on charts published for a few years prior to 1972 was the lesser of these ranges, which for most powerful lights in European waters would be the Geographical range. On very old charts only the Geographical range will be given.

Caution: If using old charts, geographical ranges will be given for lights not sufficiently powerful to be seen from the horizon.

All heights of lights are given above High Water. Allowance for the state of the tides should be made with lights of small elevation.

Tables I and II allow for the effect of normal atmospheric refraction but would be of no use when conditions are abnormal.

Glare from background lighting will reduce considerably the range at which lights are sighted. A light of 100 000 candelas has a nominal range of about 20 miles; with minor background lighting as from a populated coastline this range will be reduced to about 14 miles, and with major background lighting as from a city or from harbour installations to about 9 miles.

Yachtsmen with a near horizon and utilising the powerful lights around the European Coastline will probably be more concerned with the Geographical Range of lights.

To find the Geographical range of a light: The height of a light is 44m and its charted visibility is 18 miles. At what distance should it be sighted if the observer's eye is 18.3m above the sea?

Distance to horizon from light 44m (143ft) .... 13.7 miles
Distance to horizon from a height of 18.3m (60ft) .... 8.9 miles
                                                                                                                      _____
Distance at which light should be sighted .... 22.6 miles
                                                                                                                      _____

The example given above refers to Tables I and II.

TABLE I = DISTANCE OF SEA HORIZON IN NAUTICAL MILES

Height in Metres	Height in Feet	Distance in Miles	Height in Metres	Height in Feet	Distance in Miles	Height in Metres	Height in Feet	Distance in Miles	Height in Metres	Height in Feet	Distance in Miles
0.3	1	1.15	4.3	14	4.30	12.2	40	7.27	55	180	15.4
0.6	2	1.62	4.9	16	4.60	12.8	42	7.44	61	200	16.2
0.9	3	1.99	5.5	18	4.87	13.4	44	7.62	73	240	17.8
1.2	4	2.30	6.1	20	5.14	14.0	46	7.79	85	280	19.2
1.5	5	2.57	6.7	22	5.39	14.6	48	7.96	98	320	20.5
1.8	6	2.81	7.3	24	5.62	15.2	50	8.1	110	360	21.8
2.1	7	3.04	7.9	26	5.86	18	60	8.9	122	400	23.0
2.4	8	3.25	8.5	28	6.08	20	70	9.6	137	450	24.3
2.7	9	3.45	9.1	30	6.30	24	80	10.3	152	500	25.7
3.0	10	3.63	9.8	32	6.50	27	90	10.9	183	600	28.1
3.4	11	3.81	10.4	34	6.70	30	100	11.5	213	700	30.4
3.7	12	3.98	11.0	36	6.90	40	130	13.1	244	800	32.5
4.0	13	4.14	11.6	38	7.09	46	150	14.1			

TABLE II – TO FIND DISTANCE OFF LIGHTS RISING OR DIPPING

Height of Light		HEIGHT OF EYE												
		Metres												
		1.5	3	4.6	6.1	7.6	9.1	10.7	12.2	13.7	15.2	16.8	18.3	19.8
		Feet												
		5	10	15	20	25	30	35	40	45	50	55	60	65
m	**ft**													
12	**40**	9¾	11	11¾	12½	13	13½	14	14½	15	15½	15¾	16¼	16½
15	**50**	10¾	11¾	12½	13¼	14	14½	15	15½	15¾	16¼	16¾	17	17½
18	**60**	11½	12½	13½	14	14¾	15¼	15¾	16¼	16½	17	17½	17¾	18¼
21	**70**	12¼	13¼	14	14¾	15½	16	16½	17	17¼	17¾	18	18½	19
24	**80**	13	14	14¾	15½	16	16½	17	17½	18	18½	18¾	19¼	19½
27	**90**	13½	14½	15½	16	16¾	17¼	17¾	18¼	18½	19	19½	19¾	20¼
30	**100**	14	15	16	16½	17¼	17¾	18¼	18¾	19¼	19½	20	20½	20¾
34	**110**	14½	15¾	16½	17¼	17¾	18¼	19	19¼	19¾	20¼	20½	21	21¼
37	**120**	15¼	16¼	17	17¾	18¼	19	19½	20	20¼	20¾	21	21½	22
40	**130**	15¾	16¾	17½	18¼	19	19½	20	20½	20¾	21¼	21½	22	22½
43	**140**	16¼	17¼	18	18¾	19½	20	20½	21	21¼	21¾	22	22½	23
46	**150**	16¾	17¾	18½	19¼	19¾	20½	21	21¼	21¾	22¼	22½	23	23¼
49	**160**	17	18¼	19	19¾	20¼	20¾	21½	21¾	22¼	22¾	23	23½	23¾
52	**170**	17½	18½	19½	20	20¾	21¼	21¾	22¼	22¾	23	23½	24	24¼
55	**180**	18	19	20	20½	21¼	21¾	22¼	22¾	23	23½	24	24¼	24¾
58	**190**	18½	19½	20¼	21	21½	22	22¾	23	23½	24	24½	24¾	25
61	**200**	18¾	20	20¾	21½	22	22½	23	23½	24	24½	24¾	25¼	25½
64	**210**	19¼	20¼	21	21¾	22½	23	23½	24	24½	24¾	25¼	25½	26
67	**220**	19½	20¾	21½	22¼	22¾	23¼	24	24¼	24¾	25¼	25½	26	26¼
70	**230**	20	21	22	22½	23¼	23¾	24¼	24¾	25	25½	26	26¼	26¾
73	**240**	20½	21½	22¼	23	23½	24	24½	25	25½	26	26¼	26¾	27
76	**250**	20¾	21¾	22½	23¼	24	24½	25	25½	26	26¼	26¾	27	27½
79	**260**	21	22¼	23	23¾	24¼	24¾	25¼	25¾	26¼	26¾	27	27½	27¾
82	**270**	21½	22½	23¼	24	24½	25¼	25¾	26¼	26½	27	27½	27¾	28¼
85	**280**	21¾	23	23¾	24½	25	25½	26	26½	27	27½	27¾	28	28½
88	**290**	22	23¼	24	24¾	25¼	26	26½	26¾	27¼	27¾	28	28½	28¾
91	**300**	22½	23½	24½	25	25¾	26¼	26¾	27¼	27½	28	28½	28¾	29¼
95	**310**	22¾	24	24¾	25½	26	26½	27	27½	28	28½	28¾	29	29½
98	**320**	23	24¼	25	25¾	26¼	27	27½	27¾	28¼	28¾	29	29½	29¾
100	**330**	23½	24½	25¼	26	26½	27¼	27¾	28	28½	29	29½	29¾	30
104	**340**	23¾	24¾	25¾	26¼	27	27½	28	28½	29	29¼	29¾	30	30½
107	**350**	24	25	26	26¾	27¼	27¾	28¼	28¾	29¼	29½	30	30½	30¾
122	**400**	25½	26½	27½	28	28¾	29¼	29¾	30¼	30¾	31	31½	32	32¼
137	**450**	27	28	28¾	29½	30	30¾	31¼	31¾	32	32½	33	33¼	33¾

FINDING THE DISTANCE OF OBJECTS AT SEA — Cont.

To check whether or not a newly sighted light (when you have not previously seen the loom) is actually on the horizon, if practicable, lower the eye immediately to find out if the light dips below the horizon again. In clear visibility and a heavy swell the light should alternately rise above and dip below the horizon with the ship's movement. The distance off from the light at this moment is often referred to as the "dipping range" or "dipping distance."

Table II will be found very useful for finding the dipping range of a light immediately by inspection.

Fix by dipping range and bearing: The light "X" has just appeared on the horizon in clear visibility and bearing 068°. If the height of eye is 25 ft what is the ship's position?

The Visual Aids to Navigation Section gives the height of Light "X" as 126 ft and the charted visibility as 17 miles. With height of eye 25 ft at the top and 126 ft at the side, Table II gives 18¾ miles.

The ship's position is, therefore, 18¾ miles 248° from Light "X".

TABLE FOR CONVERTING THE POWER OF A LIGHT INTO NOMINAL RANGE

Nominal Range Sea miles	1	2	5	10	20	30
Luminous Intensity (candelas)	1	5	77	1,400	110,000	5,000,000

LENGTH IN NAUTICAL MILES OF A DEGREE OF LONGITUDE IN LATITUDES 0° TO 90°

Lat°	Length	Lat°	Length	Lat°	Length	Lat°	Length
0	60.41	23	55.55	46	41.80	69	21.52
1	60.40	24	55.12	47	41.04	70	20.54
2	60.37	25	55.68	48	40.27	71	19.55
3	60.33	26	54.22	49	39.48	72	18.55
4	60.26	27	53.75	50	38.69	73	17.55
5	60.18	28	53.26	51	37.88	74	16.55
6	60.07	29	52.75	52	37.06	75	15.54
7	59.95	30	52.23	53	36.23	76	14.52
8	59.81	31	51.69	54	35.39	77	13.50
9	59.65	32	51.13	55	34.53	78	12.48
10	59.48	33	50.56	56	33.67	79	11.45
11	59.28	34	49.98	57	32.79	80	10.42
12	59.07	35	49.37	58	31.91	81	9.39
13	58.84	36	48.76	59	31.02	82	8.35
14	58.59	37	48.13	60	30.11	83	7.31
15	58.32	38	47.48	61	29.20	84	6.27
16	58.04	39	46.82	62	28.28	85	5.23
17	57.74	40	46.15	63	27.34	86	4.19
18	57.42	41	45.46	64	26.40	87	3.14
19	57.08	42	44.76	65	25.46	88	2.09
20	56.72	43	44.04	66	24.52	89	1.05
21	56.35	44	43.31	67	23.47	90	0.0
22	55.96	45	42.55	68	22.50		.

MEASURED DISTANCES

At a number of places on the coast marks have been erected which indicate accurately measured distances, which are of great practical utility in that they enable the speeds of vessels to be obtained.

A vessel on a voyage passing a measured distance has only to note down the exact second of time when the first two marks are in line and again when the last two are in transit. The elapsed time should be used to look out the speed in knots from the Measured Mile Table.

Remember that with a single run allowance must be made for any estimated Tidal Stream which may be running.

The practice when running speed trials in a vessel is to take several runs each way on the measured mile.

Once the up stream time and the down stream time have been measured, the ship's speed through the water and also the speed of the stream over the ground may be found as follows:

1.　The ship's down stream speed over ground (G Knots), is found by dividing the distance by the down stream time.

2.　The ship's up stream speed over ground (g Knots), is found by dividing the distance by the up stream time.

3.　The ship's speed through the water is equal to one half of the sum (G + g).

4.　Speed of stream over ground is equal to one half of the difference (G − g).

LOG SPEED TABLE
Speed Table for use with Walker's Excelsior IV Log

TIME IN SECONDS OF 50 REVOLUTIONS

SPEED (KNOTS)

**Time 50 revolutions as indicated by the white patch
on the governor wheel and read off speed from the table**

MEASURED MILE
Time and Knot Table

Ascertain the time taken on the measured mile in minutes and seconds and look up the table (minutes at the top and seconds at the side) to find the vessel's speed in knots.

Example. — Having covered the measured mile in 6 minutes 18 seconds, what is the speed? This will be found to be 9.524 knots.

For speeds lower than 5 knots simply halve the time taken and then halve the speed found, e.g., if the time taken on the mile is 17 minutes then look out under $8\frac{1}{2}$ mins. (8m. 30s.) the speed given for $8\frac{1}{2}$m. is 7.059 which divided by 2 gives the speed of 3.529 knots (i.e., $3\frac{1}{2}$ knots).

If the speed through the water determined by the Patent Log is required; record accurately the time taken to travel one mile; then read off the speed in knots from the table.

MEASURED MILE (TIME AND KNOT) TABLE

Secs.	2 min.	3 min.	4 min.	5 min.	6 min.	7 min.	8 min.	9 min.	10 min.	11 min.
0	30.000	20.000	15.000	12.000	10.000	8.571	7.500	6.667	6.000	5.455
1	29.752	19.890	14.938	11.960	9.972	8.551	7.484	6.654	5.990	5.446
2	29.508	19.780	14.876	11.921	9.945	8.531	7.469	6.642	5.980	5.438
3	29.268	19.672	14.815	11.881	9.917	8.511	7.453	6.630	5.970	5.430
4	29.032	19.565	14.754	11.842	9.890	8.491	7.438	6.618	5.960	5.422
5	28.800	19.459	14.694	11.803	9.863	8.471	7.423	6.606	5.950	5.414
6	28.571	19.355	14.634	11.765	9.836	8.451	7.407	6.593	5.941	5.405
7	28.346	19.251	14.575	11.726	9.809	8.431	7.392	6.581	5.931	5.397
8	28.125	19.149	14.516	11.688	9.783	8.411	7.377	6.569	5.921	5.389
9	27.907	19.048	14.458	11.650	9.756	8.392	7.362	6.557	5.911	5.381
10	27.692	18.947	14.400	11.613	9.730	8.372	7.347	6.545	5.902	5.373
11	27.481	18.848	14.343	11.576	9.704	8.353	7.332	6.534	5.892	5.365
12	27.273	18.750	14.286	11.538	9.677	8.333	7.317	6.522	5.882	5.357
13	27.068	18.653	14.229	11.502	9.651	8.314	7.302	6.510	5.873	5.349
14	26.866	18.557	14.173	11.465	9.626	8.295	7.287	6.498	5.863	5.341
15	26.667	18.461	14.118	11.429	9.600	8.276	7.273	6.486	5.854	5.333
16	26.471	18.367	14.062	11.392	9.574	8.257	7.258	6.475	5.844	5.325
17	26.277	18.274	14.008	11.356	9.549	8.238	7.243	6.463	5.835	5.318
18	26.087	18.182	13.953	11.321	9.524	8.219	7.229	6.452	5.825	5.310
19	25.899	18.090	13.900	11.285	9.499	8.200	7.214	6.440	5.816	5.302
20	25.714	18.000	13.846	11.250	9.474	8.182	7.200	6.429	5.806	5.294
21	25.532	17.910	13.793	11.215	9.449	8.163	7.186	6.417	5.797	5.286
22	25.352	17.822	13.740	11.180	9.424	8.145	7.171	6.406	5.788	5.279
23	25.175	17.734	13.688	11.146	9.399	8.126	7.157	6.394	5.778	5.271
24	25.000	17.647	13.636	11.111	9.375	8.108	7.143	6.383	5.769	5.263
25	24.828	17.561	13.585	11.077	9.351	8.090	7.129	6.372	5.760	5.255
26	24.658	17.476	13.534	11.043	9.326	8.072	7.115	6.360	5.751	5.248
27	24.490	17.391	13.483	11.009	9.302	8.054	7.101	6.349	5.742	5.240
28	24.324	17.308	13.433	10.976	9.278	8.036	7.087	6.338	5.732	5.233
29	24.161	17.225	13.383	10.942	9.254	8.018	7.073	6.327	5.723	5.225
30	24.000	17.143	13.333	10.909	9.231	8.000	7.059	6.316	5.714	5.217
31	23.841	17.062	13.284	10.876	9.207	7.982	7.045	6.305	5.705	5.210
32	23.684	16.981	13.235	10.843	9.184	7.965	7.031	6.294	5.696	5.202
33	23.529	16.901	13.187	10.811	9.160	7.947	7.018	6.283	5.687	5.195
34	23.377	16.822	13.139	10.778	9.137	7.930	7.004	6.272	5.678	5.187
35	23.226	16.744	13.091	10.746	9.114	7.912	6.990	6.261	5.669	5.180
36	23.077	16.667	13.043	10.714	9.091	7.895	6.977	6.250	5.660	5.172
37	22.930	16.590	12.996	10.682	9.068	7.877	6.963	6.239	5.651	5.165
38	22.785	16.514	12.950	10.651	9.045	7.860	6.950	6.228	5.643	5.158
39	22.642	16.438	12.903	10.619	9.023	7.843	6.936	6.218	5.634	5.150
40	22.500	16.364	12.857	10.588	9.000	7.826	6.923	6.207	5.625	5.143
41	22.360	16.290	12.811	10.557	8.978	7.809	6.910	6.196	5.616	5.136
42	22.222	16.216	12.766	10.526	8.955	7.792	6.897	6.186	5.607	5.128
43	22.086	16.143	12.721	10.496	8.933	7.775	6.883	6.175	5.599	5.121
44	21.951	16.071	12.676	10.465	8.911	7.759	6.870	6.164	5.590	5.114
45	21.818	16.000	12.632	10.435	8.889	7.742	6.857	6.154	5.581	5.106
46	21.687	15.929	12.587	10.405	8.867	7.725	6.844	6.143	5.573	5.099
47	21.557	15.859	12.544	10.375	8.845	7.709	6.831	6.133	5.564	5.092
48	21.429	15.789	12.500	10.345	8.824	7.692	6.818	6.122	5.556	5.085
49	21.302	15.721	12.457	10.315	8.802	7.676	6.805	6.112	5.547	5.078
50	21.176	15.652	12.414	10.286	8.780	7.660	6.792	6.102	5.538	5.070
51	21.053	15.584	12.371	10.256	8.759	7.643	6.780	6.091	5.530	5.063
52	20.930	15.517	12.329	10.227	8.738	7.627	6.767	6.081	5.521	5.056
53	20.809	15.451	12.287	10.198	8.717	7.611	6.754	6.071	5.513	5.049
54	20.690	15.385	12.245	10.169	8.696	7.595	6.742	6.061	5.505	5.042
55	20.571	15.319	12.203	10.141	8.675	7.579	6.729	6.050	5.496	5.035
56	20.455	15.254	12.162	10.112	8.654	7.563	6.716	6.040	5.488	5.028
57	20.339	15.190	12.121	10.084	8.633	7.547	6.704	6.030	5.479	5.021
58	20.225	15.126	12.081	10.056	8.612	7.531	6.691	6.020	5.471	5.014
59	20.112	15.063	12.040	10.028	8.592	7.516	6.679	6.010	5.463	5.007
Secs.	2 min.	3 min.	4 min.	5 min.	6 min.	7 min.	8 min.	9 min.	10 min.	11 min.

The above figures indicate the speed in knots according to a particular time in minutes and seconds

TIME, SPEED and DISTANCE TABLE

for finding distance run in a given time at various Speeds, $2\frac{1}{2}$ to 22 knots

Min	$2\frac{1}{2}$	3	$3\frac{1}{2}$	4	$4\frac{1}{2}$	5	$5\frac{1}{2}$	6	$6\frac{1}{2}$	7	$7\frac{1}{2}$	8	$8\frac{1}{2}$	Min
						KNOTS								
1	0.1	0.1	0.1	0.1	0.1	0.1	0.1	0.1	0.1	0.1	0.1	0.1	0.2	1
2	0.1	0.1	0.1	0.2	0.2	0.2	0.2	0.2	0.2	0.2	0.3	0.3	0.3	2
3	0.1	0.2	0.2	0.2	0.3	0.3	0.3	0.3	0.3	0.3	0.4	0.4	0.4	3
4	0.1	0.2	0.3	0.3	0.3	0.3	0.4	0.4	0.4	0.5	0.5	0.5	0.6	4
5	0.2	0.3	0.3	0.4	0.4	0.4	0.5	0.5	0.6	0.6	0.6	0.7	0.7	5
6	0.3	0.3	0.4	0.4	0.5	0.5	0.6	0.6	0.7	0.7	0.8	0.8	0.9	6
7	0.3	0.4	0.4	0.5	0.6	0.6	0.6	0.7	0.8	0.8	0.9	0.9	1.0	7
8	0.4	0.4	0.5	0.6	0.6	0.7	0.7	0.8	0.9	0.9	1.0	1.0	1.1	8
9	0.4	0.5	0.6	0.6	0.7	0.8	0.8	0.9	1.0	1.1	1.1	1.2	1.3	9
10	0.4	0.5	0.6	0.7	0.8	0.8	0.9	1.0	1.1	1.2	1.3	1.3	1.4	10
11	0.5	0.6	0.7	0.8	0.9	0.9	1.0	1.1	1.2	1.3	1.4	1.5	1.6	11
12	0.5	0.6	0.7	0.8	0.9	1.0	1.1	1.2	1.3	1.4	1.5	1.6	1.7	12
13	0.6	0.7	0.8	0.9	1.0	1.1	1.2	1.3	1.4	1.5	1.6	1.7	1.8	13
14	0.6	0.7	0.8	1.0	1.1	1.2	1.3	1.4	1.5	1.6	1.8	1.9	2.0	14
15	0.7	0.8	0.9	1.0	1.2	1.3	1.4	1.5	1.6	1.8	1.9	2.0	2.1	15
16	0.7	0.8	1.0	1.1	1.2	1.3	1.5	1.6	1.7	1.9	2.0	2.1	2.3	16
17	0.7	0.9	1.0	1.2	1.3	1.4	1.6	1.7	1.8	2.0	2.1	2.3	2.4	17
18	0.8	0.9	1.1	1.2	1.4	1.5	1.7	1.8	2.0	2.1	2.3	2.4	2.6	18
19	0.8	1.0	1.1	1.3	1.5	1.6	1.7	1.9	2.1	2.2	2.4	2.5	2.7	19
20	0.9	1.0	1.2	1.4	1.5	1.7	1.8	2.0	2.2	2.3	2.5	2.7	2.8	20
21	0.9	1.1	1.3	1.4	1.6	1.8	1.9	2.1	2.3	2.5	2.6	2.8	3.0	21
22	0.9	1.1	1.3	1.5	1.7	1.8	2.0	2.2	2.4	2.6	2.8	2.9	3.1	22
23	1.0	1.2	1.4	1.6	1.8	1.9	2.1	2.3	2.5	2.7	2.9	3.0	3.3	23
24	1.0	1.2	1.4	1.6	1.8	2.0	2.2	2.4	2.6	2.8	3.0	3.2	3.4	24
25	1.1	1.3	1.5	1.7	1.9	2.1	2.3	2.5	2.7	2.9	3.1	3.3	3.5	25
26	1.1	1.3	1.5	1.8	2.0	2.2	2.4	2.6	2.8	3.0	3.3	3.5	3.7	26
27	1.2	1.4	1.6	1.8	2.1	2.3	2.5	2.7	2.9	3.2	3.4	3.6	3.9	27
28	1.2	1.4	1.7	1.9	2.1	2.3	2.6	2.8	3.0	3.3	3.5	3.7	4.0	28
29	1.2	1.5	1.7	2.0	2.2	2.4	2.7	2.9	3.1	3.4	3.6	3.9	4.1	29
30	1.3	1.5	1.8	2.0	2.3	2.5	2.8	3.0	3.3	3.5	3.8	4.0	4.3	30
31	1.3	1.6	1.8	2.1	2.4	2.6	2.8	3.1	3.4	3.6	3.9	4.1	4.4	31
32	1.4	1.6	1.9	2.2	2.4	2.7	2.9	3.2	3.5	3.7	4.0	4.3	4.5	32
33	1.4	1.7	2.0	2.3	2.5	2.8	3.0	3.3	3.6	3.9	4.1	4.4	4.7	33
34	1.4	1.7	2.0	2.3	2.6	2.9	3.1	3.4	3.7	4.0	4.3	4.5	4.8	34
35	1.5	1.8	2.1	2.4	2.7	2.9	3.2	3.5	3.8	4.1	4.4	4.7	5.0	35
36	1.5	1.8	2.1	2.4	2.7	3.0	3.3	3.6	3.9	4.2	4.5	4.8	5.1	36
37	1.6	1.9	2.2	2.5	2.8	3.1	3.4	3.7	4.0	4.3	4.6	4.9	5.2	37
38	1.6	1.9	2.2	2.6	2.9	3.2	3.5	3.8	4.1	4.4	4.8	5.0	5.4	38
39	1.7	2.0	2.3	2.6	2.9	3.3	3.6	3.9	4.2	4.6	4.9	5.2	5.5	39
40	1.7	2.0	2.4	2.7	3.0	3.3	3.7	4.0	4.3	4.7	5.0	5.3	5.7	40
41	1.7	2.1	2.4	2.8	3.1	3.4	3.8	4.1	4.4	4.8	5.1	5.5	5.8	41
42	1.8	2.1	2.5	2.8	3.2	3.5	3.9	4.2	4.6	4.9	5.3	5.6	6.0	42
43	1.8	2.2	2.5	2.9	3.3	3.6	3.9	4.3	4.7	5.0	5.4	5.7	6.1	43
44	1.9	2.2	2.6	3.0	3.3	3.7	4.0	4.4	4.8	5.1	5.5	5.9	6.2	44
45	1.9	2.3	2.7	3.0	3.4	3.8	4.1	4.5	4.9	5.3	5.6	6.0	6.4	45
46	1.9	2.3	2.7	3.1	3.5	3.8	4.2	4.6	5.0	5.4	5.8	6.1	6.5	46
47	2.0	2.4	2.8	3.2	3.6	3.9	4.3	4.7	5.1	5.5	5.9	6.3	6.7	47
48	2.0	2.4	2.8	3.2	3.6	4.0	4.4	4.8	5.2	5.6	6.0	6.4	6.8	48
49	2.1	2.5	2.9	3.3	3.7	4.1	4.5	4.9	5.3	5.7	6.1	6.5	6.9	49
50	2.1	2.5	2.9	3.4	3.8	4.2	4.6	5.0	5.4	5.8	6.3	6.7	7.1	50
51	2.2	2.6	3.0	3.4	3.9	4.3	4.7	5.1	5.5	6.0	6.4	6.8	7.2	51
52	2.2	2.6	3.1	3.5	3.9	4.3	4.8	5.2	5.6	6.1	6.5	6.9	7.4	52
53	2.2	2.7	3.1	3.6	4.0	4.4	4.9	5.3	5.7	6.2	6.6	7.0	7.5	53
54	2.3	2.7	3.2	3.6	4.1	4.5	5.0	5.4	5.9	6.3	6.8	7.1	7.6	54
55	2.3	2.8	3.2	3.7	4.2	4.6	5.0	5.5	6.0	6.4	6.9	7.3	7.8	55
56	2.4	2.8	3.3	3.8	4.2	4.7	5.1	5.6	6.1	6.5	7.0	7.5	7.9	56
57	2.4	2.9	3.4	3.8	4.3	4.8	5.2	5.7	6.2	6.7	7.1	7.6	8.1	57
58	2.4	2.9	3.4	3.9	4.4	4.8	5.3	5.8	6.3	6.8	7.3	7.7	8.2	58
59	2.5	3.0	3.5	3.9	4.5	4.9	5.4	5.9	6.4	6.9	7.4	7.9	8.4	59
60	2.5	3.0	3.5	4.0	4.5	5.0	5.5	6.0	6.5	7.0	7.5	8.0	8.5	60
Min	$2\frac{1}{2}$	3	$3\frac{1}{2}$	4	$4\frac{1}{2}$	5	$5\frac{1}{2}$	6	$6\frac{1}{2}$	7	$7\frac{1}{2}$	8	$8\frac{1}{2}$	Min

Example 1. If steaming $7\frac{1}{2}$ knots, what distance has been covered in 41 minutes?   Answer = 5.1 miles.

TIME, SPEED and DISTANCE TABLE

Min	9	9½	10	10½	11	11½	12	12½	13	13½	14	14½	15	Min
						KNOTS								
1	0.2	0.2	0.2	0.2	0.2	0.2	0.2	0.2	0.2	0.2	0.2	0.2	0.3	1
2	0.3	0.3	0.3	0.4	0.4	0.4	0.4	0.4	0.5	0.5	0.5	0.5	0.5	2
3	0.5	0.5	0.5	0.5	0.6	0.6	0.6	0.6	0.7	0.7	0.7	0.7	0.8	3
4	0.6	0.6	0.7	0.7	0.7	0.8	0.8	0.8	0.9	0.9	0.9	1.0	1.0	4
5	0.8	0.8	0.8	0.9	0.9	1.0	1.0	1.1	1.1	1.2	1.2	1.2	1.3	5
6	0.9	1.0	1.0	1.1	1.1	1.2	1.2	1.3	1.3	1.4	1.4	1.5	1.5	6
7	1.1	1.1	1.2	1.2	1.3	1.3	1.4	1.5	1.5	1.6	1.6	1.7	1.8	7
8	1.2	1.3	1.3	1.4	1.5	1.5	1.6	1.7	1.7	1.8	1.9	1.9	2.0	8
9	1.4	1.4	1.5	1.6	1.7	1.7	1.8	1.9	2.0	2.0	2.1	2.2	2.3	9
10	1.5	1.6	1.7	1.8	1.8	1.9	2.0	2.1	2.2	2.3	2.3	2.4	2.5	10
11	1.7	1.7	1.8	1.9	2.0	2.1	2.2	2.3	2.4	2.5	2.6	2.7	2.8	11
12	1.8	1.9	2.0	2.1	2.2	2.3	2.4	2.5	2.6	2.7	2.8	2.9	3.0	12
13	2.0	2.1	2.2	2.3	2.4	2.5	2.6	2.7	2.8	2.9	3.0	3.1	3.2	13
14	2.1	2.2	2.3	2.5	2.6	2.7	2.8	2.9	3.0	3.2	3.3	3.4	3.5	14
15	2.3	2.4	2.5	2.6	2.8	2.9	3.0	3.1	3.3	3.4	3.5	3.6	3.8	15
16	2.4	2.5	2.7	2.8	2.9	3.1	3.2	3.3	3.5	3.6	3.7	3.9	4.0	16
17	2.6	2.7	2.8	3.0	3.1	3.3	3.4	3.5	3.7	3.8	4.0	4.1	4.3	17
18	2.7	2.9	3.0	3.2	3.3	3.5	3.6	3.8	3.9	4.1	4.2	4.4	4.5	18
19	2.9	3.1	3.2	3.3	3.5	3.6	3.8	4.0	4.2	4.3	4.4	4.6	4.8	19
20	3.0	3.2	3.3	3.5	3.7	3.8	4.0	4.2	4.4	4.5	4.7	4.8	5.0	20
21	3.2	3.3	3.5	3.7	3.9	4.0	4.2	4.4	4.6	4.7	4.9	5.1	5.3	21
22	3.3	3.5	3.7	3.9	4.0	4.2	4.4	4.6	4.8	5.0	5.1	5.3	5.5	22
23	3.5	3.6	3.8	4.0	4.2	4.4	4.6	4.8	5.0	5.2	5.4	5.6	5.7	23
24	3.6	3.8	4.0	4.2	4.4	4.6	4.8	5.0	5.2	5.4	5.6	5.8	6.0	24
25	3.8	4.0	4.2	4.4	4.6	4.8	5.0	5.2	5.4	5.6	5.8	6.1	6.3	25
26	3.9	4.1	4.3	4.6	4.8	5.0	5.2	5.4	5.6	5.9	6.1	6.3	6.5	26
27	4.1	4.3	4.5	4.7	5.0	5.2	5.4	5.6	5.9	6.1	6.3	6.5	6.8	27
28	4.2	4.4	4.7	4.9	5.1	5.4	5.6	5.8	6.1	6.3	6.5	6.8	7.0	28
29	4.4	4.6	4.8	5.1	5.3	5.6	5.8	6.0	6.3	6.5	6.8	7.0	7.3	29
30	4.5	4.8	5.0	5.3	5.5	5.8	6.0	6.3	6.5	6.8	7.0	7.3	7.5	30
31	4.7	4.9	5.2	5.4	5.7	5.9	6.2	6.5	6.7	7.0	7.2	7.5	7.8	31
32	4.8	5.0	5.3	5.6	5.9	6.1	6.4	6.7	6.9	7.2	7.5	7.7	8.0	32
33	5.0	5.2	5.5	5.8	6.1	6.3	6.6	6.9	7.2	7.4	7.7	8.0	8.3	33
34	5.1	5.4	5.7	6.0	6.2	6.5	6.8	7.1	7.4	7.7	8.0	8.2	8.5	34
35	5.3	5.5	5.8	6.1	6.4	6.7	7.0	7.3	7.6	7.9	8.2	8.5	8.8	35
36	5.4	5.7	6.0	6.3	6.6	6.9	7.2	7.5	7.8	8.1	8.4	8.7	9.0	36
37	5.6	5.9	6.2	6.5	6.8	7.1	7.4	7.7	8.0	8.3	8.6	8.9	9.3	37
38	5.7	6.0	6.3	6.7	7.0	7.3	7.6	7.9	8.2	8.6	8.9	9.2	9.5	38
39	5.9	6.2	6.5	6.8	7.1	7.5	7.8	8.1	8.5	8.8	9.1	9.4	9.8	39
40	6.0	6.3	6.7	7.0	7.3	7.7	8.0	8.3	8.7	9.0	9.3	9.7	10.0	40
41	6.2	6.5	6.8	7.3	7.5	7.9	8.2	8.5	8.9	9.2	9.6	9.9	10.3	41
42	6.3	6.7	7.0	7.4	7.7	8.1	8.4	8.8	9.1	9.5	9.8	10.2	10.5	42
43	6.5	6.8	7.2	7.5	7.9	8.2	8.6	9.0	9.3	9.7	10.0	10.4	10.8	43
44	6.6	7.0	7.3	7.7	8.0	8.4	8.8	9.2	9.5	9.9	10.3	10.6	11.0	44
45	6.8	7.1	7.5	7.9	8.2	8.6	9.0	9.4	9.8	10.1	10.5	10.9	11.3	45
46	6.9	7.3	7.7	8.1	8.4	8.8	9.2	9.6	10.0	10.4	10.7	11.1	11.5	46
47	7.1	7.4	7.8	8.2	8.6	9.0	9.4	9.8	10.2	10.6	11.0	11.4	11.8	47
48	7.2	7.6	8.0	8.4	8.8	9.2	9.6	10.0	10.4	10.8	11.2	11.6	12.0	48
49	7.4	7.8	8.2	8.6	9.0	9.4	9.8	10.2	10.6	11.0	11.4	11.8	12.3	49
50	7.5	7.9	8.3	8.7	9.1	9.6	10.0	10.4	10.8	11.3	11.7	12.1	12.5	50
51	7.7	8.1	8.5	8.9	9.4	9.8	10.2	10.6	11.1	11.5	11.9	12.3	12.8	51
52	7.8	8.2	8.7	9.1	9.5	10.0	10.4	10.8	11.3	11.7	12.1	12.6	13.0	52
53	8.0	8.4	8.8	9.3	9.7	10.2	10.6	11.0	11.5	11.9	12.4	12.8	13.3	53
54	8.1	8.6	9.0	9.5	9.9	10.4	10.8	11.3	11.7	12.2	12.6	13.1	13.5	54
55	8.3	8.7	9.2	9.6	10.0	10.5	11.0	11.5	11.9	12.4	12.8	13.3	13.8	55
56	8.4	8.9	9.3	9.8	10.2	10.7	11.2	11.7	12.1	12.6	13.1	13.5	14.0	56
57	8.6	9.0	9.5	10.0	10.5	10.9	11.4	11.9	12.4	12.8	13.3	13.8	14.3	57
58	8.7	9.2	9.7	10.2	10.6	11.1	11.6	12.1	12.6	13.1	13.5	14.0	14.5	58
59	8.9	9.3	9.8	10.3	10.8	11.3	11.8	12.3	12.8	13.3	13.8	14.3	14.8	59
60	9.0	9.5	10.0	10.5	11.0	11.5	12.0	12.5	13.0	13.5	14.0	14.5	15.0	60
Min	9	9½	10	10½	11	11½	12	12½	13	13½	14	14½	15	Min

Example 2. How long will it take to steam 6.8 miles (when the course is to be altered)? Vessel's speed, 10½ knots. Answer = 39 minutes.

TIME, SPEED and DISTANCE TABLE

Min	15½	16	16½	17	17½	18	18½	19	19½	20	20½	21	21½	22	Min
						KNOTS									
1	0.3	0.3	0.3	0.3	0.3	0.3	0.3	0.3	0.3	0.3	0.3	0.4	0.4	0.4	1
2	0.5	0.5	0.5	0.6	0.6	0.6	0.6	0.6	0.6	0.6	0.7	0.7	0.7	0.7	2
3	0.8	0.8	0.8	0.9	0.9	0.9	0.9	1.0	1.0	1.0	1.0	1.1	1.1	1.1	3
4	1.0	1.1	1.1	1.1	1.1	1.2	1.2	1.3	1.3	1.3	1.3	1.4	1.4	1.5	4
5	1.3	1.3	1.3	1.4	1.4	1.5	1.5	1.6	1.6	1.7	1.7	1.8	1.8	1.8	5
6	1.5	1.6	1.6	1.7	1.7	1.8	1.8	1.9	1.9	2.0	2.0	2.1	2.1	2.2	6
7	1.8	1.9	1.9	2.0	2.0	2.1	2.1	2.2	2.2	2.3	2.4	2.5	2.5	2.6	7
8	2.0	2.1	2.2	2.3	2.3	2.4	2.4	2.5	2.6	2.7	2.7	2.8	2.8	2.9	8
9	2.3	2.4	2.5	2.6	2.6	2.7	2.8	2.9	2.9	3.0	3.1	3.2	3.2	3.3	9
10	2.6	2.7	2.7	2.8	2.9	3.0	3.1	3.2	3.2	3.3	3.4	3.5	3.6	3.7	10
11	2.8	2.9	3.0	3.1	3.2	3.3	3.4	3.5	3.6	3.7	3.8	3.9	3.9	4.0	11
12	3.1	3.2	3.3	3.4	3.5	3.6	3.7	3.8	3.9	4.0	4.1	4.2	4.3	4.4	12
13	3.4	3.5	3.6	3.7	3.8	3.9	4.0	4.1	4.2	4.3	4.4	4.6	4.7	4.8	13
14	3.6	3.7	3.8	4.0	4.1	4.2	4.3	4.4	4.5	4.7	4.8	4.9	5.0	5.1	14
15	3.9	4.0	4.1	4.3	4.4	4.5	4.6	4.8	4.9	5.0	5.1	5.3	5.4	5.5	15
16	4.2	4.3	4.4	4.5	4.6	4.8	4.9	5.1	5.2	5.3	5.4	5.6	5.7	5.9	16
17	4.4	4.5	4.6	4.8	4.9	5.1	5.2	5.4	5.5	5.7	5.8	6.0	6.1	6.2	17
18	4.7	4.8	4.9	5.1	5.2	5.4	5.5	5.7	5.8	6.0	6.1	6.3	6.4	6.6	18
19	4.9	5.1	5.2	5.4	5.5	5.7	5.8	6.0	6.1	6.3	6.5	6.7	6.8	7.0	19
20	5.1	5.3	5.5	5.7	5.8	6.0	6.1	6.3	6.5	6.7	6.8	7.0	7.1	7.3	20
21	5.4	5.6	5.8	6.0	6.1	6.3	6.5	6.7	6.8	7.0	7.2	7.4	7.5	7.7	21
22	5.7	5.9	6.0	6.2	6.4	6.6	6.8	7.0	7.1	7.3	7.5	7.7	7.9	8.1	22
23	5.9	6.1	6.3	6.5	6.7	6.9	7.1	7.3	7.5	7.7	7.9	8.1	8.2	8.4	23
24	6.2	6.4	6.6	6.8	7.0	7.2	7.4	7.6	7.8	8.0	8.2	8.4	8.6	8.8	24
25	6.5	6.7	6.9	7.1	7.3	7.5	7.7	7.9	8.1	8.3	8.5	8.8	9.0	9.2	25
26	6.7	6.9	7.1	7.4	7.6	7.8	8.0	8.2	8.4	8.7	8.9	9.1	9.3	9.5	26
27	7.0	7.2	7.4	7.7	7.9	8.1	8.3	8.6	8.8	9.0	9.2	9.5	9.7	9.9	27
28	7.2	7.5	7.7	7.9	8.1	8.4	8.6	8.9	9.1	9.3	9.5	9.8	10.0	10.3	28
29	7.5	7.7	7.9	8.2	8.4	8.7	8.9	9.2	9.4	9.7	9.9	10.2	10.4	10.6	29
30	7.8	8.0	8.2	8.5	8.7	9.0	9.2	9.5	9.7	10.0	10.2	10.5	10.7	11.0	30
31	8.0	8.3	8.5	8.8	9.0	9.3	9.5	9.8	10.0	10.3	10.6	10.9	11.1	11.4	31
32	8.2	8.5	8.8	9.1	9.3	9.6	9.9	10.2	10.4	10.7	10.9	11.2	11.4	11.7	32
33	8.5	8.8	9.1	9.4	9.6	9.9	10.2	10.5	10.7	11.0	11.3	11.6	11.8	12.1	33
34	8.8	9.1	9.3	9.6	9.9	10.2	10.5	10.8	11.0	11.3	11.6	11.9	12.2	12.5	34
35	9.0	9.3	9.6	9.9	10.2	10.5	10.8	11.1	11.4	11.7	12.0	12.3	12.5	12.8	35
36	9.3	9.6	9.9	10.2	10.5	10.8	11.1	11.4	11.7	12.0	12.3	12.6	12.9	13.2	36
37	9.6	9.9	10.2	10.5	10.8	11.1	11.4	11.7	12.0	12.3	12.6	13.0	13.3	13.6	37
38	9.8	10.1	10.4	10.8	11.1	11.4	11.7	12.0	12.3	12.7	13.0	13.3	13.6	13.9	38
39	10.1	10.4	10.7	11.1	11.4	11.7	12.0	12.4	12.7	13.0	13.3	13.7	14.0	14.3	39
40	10.4	10.7	11.0	11.3	11.7	12.0	12.3	12.7	13.0	13.3	13.6	14.0	14.3	14.7	40
41	10.6	10.9	11.2	11.6	12.0	12.3	12.6	13.0	13.3	13.7	14.0	14.4	14.7	15.0	41
42	10.8	11.2	11.5	11.9	12.3	12.6	12.9	13.3	13.6	14.0	14.3	14.7	15.0	15.4	42
43	11.1	11.5	11.8	12.2	12.5	12.9	13.2	13.6	13.9	14.3	14.7	15.1	15.4	15.8	43
44	11.3	11.7	12.1	12.5	12.8	13.2	13.5	13.9	14.3	14.7	15.0	15.4	15.7	16.1	44
45	11.6	12.0	12.4	12.8	13.1	13.5	13.8	14.3	14.6	15.0	15.4	15.8	16.1	16.5	45
46	11.9	12.3	12.6	13.0	13.4	13.8	14.2	14.6	14.9	15.3	15.7	16.1	16.5	16.9	46
47	12.2	12.5	12.9	13.3	13.7	14.1	14.5	14.9	15.3	15.7	16.1	16.5	16.8	17.2	47
48	12.4	12.8	13.2	13.6	14.0	14.4	14.8	15.2	15.6	16.0	16.4	16.8	17.2	17.6	48
49	12.7	13.1	13.5	13.9	14.3	14.7	15.1	15.5	15.9	16.3	16.7	17.2	17.6	18.0	49
50	12.9	13.3	13.7	14.2	14.6	15.0	15.4	15.8	16.2	16.7	17.1	17.5	17.9	18.3	50
51	13.2	13.6	14.0	14.5	14.9	15.3	15.7	16.2	16.6	17.0	17.5	17.9	18.3	18.7	51
52	13.5	13.9	14.3	14.7	15.1	15.6	16.0	16.5	16.9	17.3	17.8	18.2	18.6	19.1	52
53	13.7	14.1	14.5	15.0	15.4	15.9	16.3	16.8	17.2	17.7	18.1	18.6	19.0	19.4	53
54	14.0	14.4	14.8	15.3	15.7	16.2	16.6	17.1	17.5	18.0	18.4	18.9	19.3	19.8	54
55	14.2	14.7	15.1	15.6	16.0	16.5	16.9	17.4	17.8	18.3	18.8	19.3	19.7	20.2	55
56	14.4	14.9	15.4	15.9	16.3	16.8	17.2	17.7	18.2	18.7	19.1	19.6	20.0	20.5	56
57	14.7	15.2	15.7	16.2	16.6	17.1	17.6	18.1	18.5	19.0	19.5	20.0	20.4	20.9	57
58	15.0	15.5	16.0	16.4	16.9	17.4	17.9	18.4	18.8	19.3	19.8	20.3	20.8	21.3	58
59	15.2	15.7	16.2	16.7	17.2	17.7	18.2	18.7	19.2	19.7	20.2	20.7	21.1	21.6	59
60	15.5	16.0	16.5	17.0	17.5	18.0	18.5	19.0	19.5	20.0	20.5	21.0	21.5	22.0	60
Min	15½	16	16½	17	17½	18	18½	19	19½	20	20½	21	21½	22	Min

Example 3. How far will a vessel steam at 17.5 knots in 25 minutes? Answer = 7.3 miles.

VOYAGE—DISTANCE—SPEED—TIME TABLE

Dist-ance	SPEED IN KNOTS												
	4	5	6	7	8	9	10	11	12	13	14	15	16
Miles													
5	1.2	1.0	0.8	0.7	0.6	0.6	0.5	0.5	0.4	0.4	0.3	0.3	0.3
10	2.5	2.0	1.7	1.4	1.2	1.1	1.0	0.9	0.8	0.8	0.7	0.6	0.6
15	3.8	3.0	2.5	2.1	1.9	1.7	1.5	1.4	1.2	1.2	1.1	1.0	0.9
20	5.0	4.0	3.3	2.9	2.5	2.2	2.0	1.8	1.7	1.5	1.4	1.3	1.2
25	6.2	5.0	4.2	3.6	3.1	2.8	2.5	2.3	2.1	1.9	1.8	1.7	1.6
50	12.5	10.0	8.3	7.1	6.2	5.6	5.0	4.5	4.2	3.8	3.6	3.3	3.1
75	18.7	15.0	12.5	10.7	9.4	8.3	7.5	6.8	6.2	5.8	5.3	5.0	4.7
100	25.0	20.0	16.7	14.3	12.5	11.1	10.0	9.1	8.3	7.7	7.1	6.6	6.2
150	37.5	30.0	25.0	21.4	18.7	16.7	15.0	13.6	12.5	11.6	10.7	10.0	9.4
200	50.0	40.0	33.3	28.6	25.0	22.2	20.0	18.2	16.7	15.4	14.3	13.3	12.5
250	62.5	50.0	41.8	35.7	31.2	27.8	25.0	22.7	20.8	19.1	17.8	16.6	15.6
300	75.0	60.0	50.0	42.8	37.5	33.3	30.0	27.3	25.0	23.1	21.4	20.0	18.7
350	87.5	70.0	58.3	50.0	43.7	38.9	35.0	31.8	29.2	26.9	25.0	23.3	21.8
400	100.0	80.0	66.6	57.1	50.0	44.4	40.0	36.4	33.3	30.8	28.6	26.6	25.0
450	112.5	90.0	75.0	64.3	56.2	50.0	45.0	40.9	37.5	34.6	32.1	30.0	28.1
500	125.0	100.0	83.3	71.4	62.5	55.5	50.0	45.5	41.7	38.4	35.7	33.3	31.2
550	137.5	110.0	91.7	78.6	68.7	61.1	55.0	50.0	45.8	42.3	39.3	36.6	34.4
600	150.0	120.0	100.0	85.7	75.0	66.6	60.0	54.5	50.0	46.2	42.8	40.0	37.5
650	162.5	130.0	108.3	92.9	81.2	72.2	65.0	59.1	54.2	50.0	46.4	43.3	40.6
700	175.0	140.0	116.7	100.0	87.5	77.7	70.0	63.6	58.3	53.8	50.0	46.6	43.8
750	187.5	150.0	125.0	107.1	93.7	83.3	75.0	68.2	62.5	57.7	53.6	50.0	46.9
800	200.0	160.0	133.3	114.3	100.0	88.8	80.0	72.7	66.6	61.5	57.1	53.3	50.0
850	212.5	170.0	141.7	121.4	106.2	94.4	85.0	77.3	70.8	65.4	60.7	56.6	53.1
900	225.0	180.0	150.0	128.6	112.5	100.0	90.0	81.8	75.0	69.2	64.3	60.0	56.3
950	237.5	190.0	158.3	135.9	118.7	105.5	95.0	86.4	79.2	73.1	67.9	63.3	59.4
1000	250.0	200.0	166.6	142.9	125.0	111.1	100.0	90.9	83.3	76.9	71.4	66.6	62.5
2000	500.0	400.0	333.3	285.7	250.0	222.2	200.0	181.8	166.6	153.8	142.8	133.3	125.0

H	Hrs.:	24	48	72	96	120	144	168	192	216	240
	Day:	1	2	3	4	5	6	7	8	9	10

This table will be found useful to save working out "the time" required for any voyage up to 2,000 miles at speeds from 4 to 16 knots. For greater distances two or more times from the table added together will give the approximate time needed in hours and decimals of an hour.

Example (a) How long will it take a vessel with average speed 7 knots to sail 291 miles?

Against 300 miles in the left hand column and 7 knots at the top the time required is 42.8 hours. For 9 miles less, deduct (at 7 knots) 1.3h. so (42.8 − 1.3) = 41.5 hours, or 1 day 17.5 hours.

Example (b) At 8 knots how long will it take to sail 673 miles?

650 miles at 8 knots = 81.2 hours $\left.\right\}$ = 84 hours.
23 miles at 8 knots = 2.8 hours

The small table H above shows that 84 hours equals 3 days 12 hours.

DAILY AVERAGE SPEED TABLE

SPEED IN KNOTS

	6	7	8	9	10	11	12	13	14	15	16	17	18	19	20	21	22	23	24	25
.000	144	168	192	216	240	264	288	312	336	360	384	408	432	456	480	504	528	552	576	600
.041	145	169	193	217	241	265	289	313	337	361	385	409	433	457	481	505	529	553	577	601
.083	146	170	194	218	242	266	290	314	338	362	386	410	434	458	482	506	530	554	578	602
.125	147	171	195	219	243	267	291	315	339	363	387	411	435	459	483	507	531	555	579	603
.166	148	172	196	220	244	268	292	316	340	364	388	412	436	460	484	508	532	556	580	604
.208	149	173	197	221	245	269	293	317	341	365	389	413	437	461	485	509	533	557	581	605
.25	150	174	198	222	246	270	294	318	342	366	390	414	438	462	486	510	534	558	582	606
.291	151	175	199	223	247	271	295	319	343	367	391	415	439	463	487	511	535	559	583	607
.333	152	176	200	224	248	272	296	320	344	368	392	416	440	464	488	512	536	560	584	608
.375	153	177	201	225	249	273	297	321	345	369	393	417	441	465	489	513	537	561	585	609
.416	154	178	202	226	250	274	298	322	346	370	394	418	442	466	490	514	538	562	586	610
.458	155	179	203	227	251	275	299	323	347	371	395	419	443	467	491	515	539	563	587	611
.5	156	180	204	228	252	276	300	324	348	372	396	420	444	468	492	516	540	564	588	612
.541	157	181	205	229	253	277	301	325	349	373	397	421	445	469	493	517	541	565	589	613
.583	158	182	206	230	254	278	302	326	350	374	398	422	446	470	494	518	542	566	590	614
.625	159	183	207	231	255	279	303	327	351	375	399	423	447	471	495	519	543	567	591	615
.666	160	184	208	232	256	280	304	328	352	376	400	424	448	472	496	520	544	568	592	616
.708	161	185	209	233	257	281	305	329	353	377	401	425	449	473	497	521	545	569	593	617
.75	162	186	210	234	258	282	306	330	354	378	402	426	450	474	498	522	546	570	594	618
.791	163	187	211	235	259	283	307	331	355	379	403	427	451	475	499	523	547	571	595	619
.833	164	188	212	236	260	284	308	332	356	380	404	428	452	476	500	524	548	572	596	620
.875	165	189	213	237	261	285	309	333	357	381	405	429	453	477	501	525	549	573	597	621
.916	166	190	214	238	262	286	310	334	358	382	406	430	454	478	502	526	550	574	598	622
.958	167	191	215	239	263	287	311	335	359	383	407	431	455	479	503	527	551	575	599	623

The table above gives the vessel's average daily speed in the 24 hours from noon to noon, being arranged with the speed shown in knots at the top of each column and decimals of a knot in the left-hand column, according to the miles run shown in the table.

EXAMPLE: From noon one day to noon the next, a vessel makes good a distance of 301 miles. What is the vessel's daily average speed?

ANSWER: 12.541 knots.

THE ELECTRONIC CALCULATOR
IN COASTAL NAVIGATION

Coastal Navigation can be an almost continuous process and aids which can be utilised for rapid calculation should be seriously considered. It must always be understood, however, that the calculator is an aid — it is a piece of electronic equipment which is fallible, but useful for supplementing the basic skills of the navigator by enabling rapid checks to be carried out to calculations already made, and as confidence grows, of carrying out initial calculations. It would be most unwise to use a calculator without fully understanding the fundamental principles involved and being able to work out the problem in longhand. Appropriate tables should therefore always be carried on board.

Calculators can be divided into three main groups — the inexpensive arithmetical type with a decimal base, the scientific or slide rule calculator with algebraic, trigonometrical and logarithmic functions and a number of memories, and the most expensive calculators which can be programmed for repetition work either manually or by the insertion of magnetic card and sometimes have printout facilities.

The middle range of scientific or slide rule calculators with trigonometrical and logarithmic functions, square root, exponents and reciprocals, with two to three memories, would fulfil the needs of the average coastal navigator. The better the calculator the fewer the key sequences required. Key sequences and functions vary with different calculators and the maker's handbook should always first be studied.

The examples in this section have all been worked using sin, cos, tan and inverse (sometimes shown as ARC) keys together with the normal arithmetical functions, all of which are included on most scientific calculators.

BASIC TRIGONOMETRICAL FUNCTIONS

Before using these functions consider the method by which they are derived as this will assist in the solution of triangular problems. Given any right angle triangle ABC (Fig. 1) trigonometrical functions are:

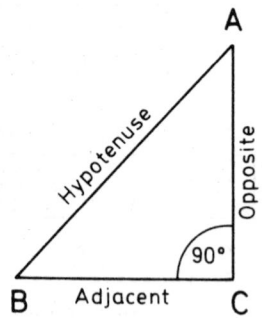

$$\sin \text{ angle ABC} = \frac{\text{opposite}}{\text{hypotenuse}} = \frac{AC}{AB}$$

$$\cos \text{ angle ABC} = \frac{\text{adjacent}}{\text{hypotenuse}} = \frac{BC}{AB}$$

$$\tan \text{ angle} = \frac{\text{opposite}}{\text{adjacent}} = \frac{AC}{BC}$$

Fig. 1

For example:

$$\sin \text{ angle BAC} = \frac{\text{opposite}}{\text{hypotenuse}} = \frac{BC}{AB}$$

These functions are the same for angle BAC except that adjacent and opposite sides are different.

Thus it will be seen that triangular problems can easily be solved if they can be reduced to right angle triangles.

SIMPLE NAVIGATIONAL PROBLEMS

Distance Off

Consider now the solution of one of the simplest navigational problems, finding the distance "off" from a fixed point. If using the "four points" rule or "doubling the angle" on the bow one has to wait for specific bearings to appear, i.e., 45° or 30° and 60°.

Using trigonometrical functions, however, the navigator can take the initial bearing at any suitable time. Consider the example in Fig. 2 where the vessel is on a course of 105°T and requires to know the distance off the headland when abeam.

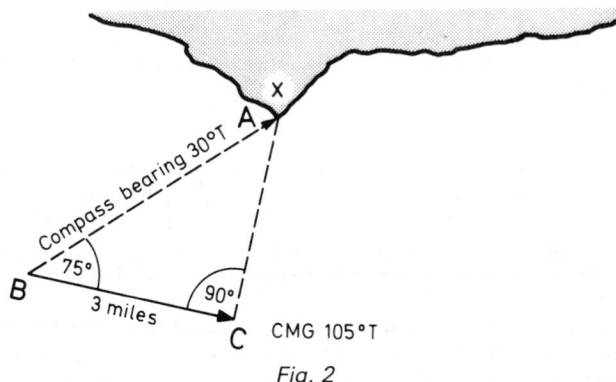

Fig. 2

In this example tidal set and leeway angle are ignored for the sake of simplicity.

$$\text{Vessel's course} = 105°\text{T}.$$

$$\text{Compass bearing of A} = 030°\text{T}.$$

$$\therefore \text{Relative Bearing (RB)} = 75° \text{ (Angle ABC)}.$$

When the vessel is abeam of the fixed point A the relative bearing will be 90° and the log reads 3 miles.

From Fig. 1 it will be seen that:

$$\frac{AC}{BC} = \text{tan angle ABC}$$

$$\therefore AC = BC \times \tan 75$$

$$AC = 3 \times 3.732$$

$$= \underline{11.19 \text{ miles.}}$$

Using the calculator to solve the problem the following steps are necessary:

Quantity	Entry	Reading
Clear calculator	C	0
Enter Relative Bearing (RB)	75	75
	tan	3.732
	×	3.732
Distance Run	3	3
Answer	=	11.19

Distance off = 11.19 miles

It will be appreciated that the distance run must be the distance over the ground and the log reading must therefore be adjusted for tidal set and leeway angle (see on for method of calculating this).

In many cases the navigator will wish to know his "distance off" before reaching the abeam position if for example there are outlying dangers as in the following example (Fig. 3).

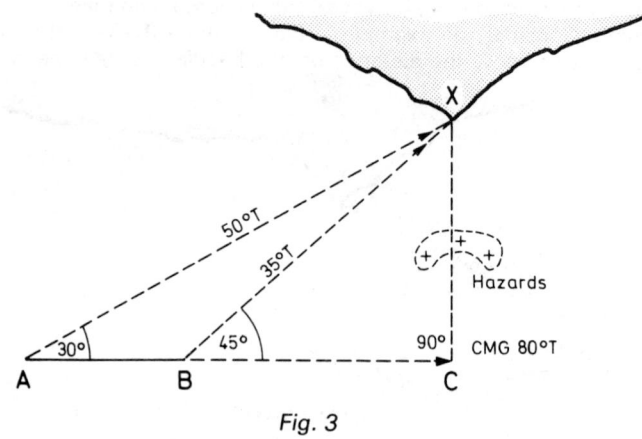

Fig. 3

The vessel is somewhere in vicinity of A on a course of 080°T and wishes to know if this will clear outlying danger.

> At A first compass bearing is 050°T.
> ∴ first RB = 30°
>
> Second compass bearing after 3 miles run is 035°T
> ∴ second RB = 45°

Now consider the solution to obtain both a "fix" and a probable distance off using trigonometrical functions. (This working will be used to derive a formula which will considerably simplify later calculations.)

In Fig. 4 the triangle ABD is completed by drawing BD at right angles to AX.

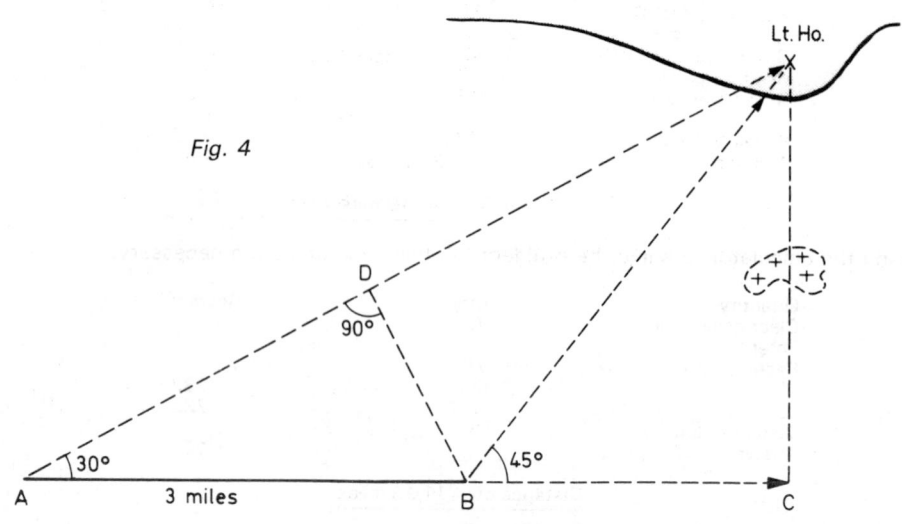

Fig. 4

To find XC it is first necessary to evaluate BD and then BX

(1) To find DB referring again to Fig. 1 it will be seen that:

$$\sin 30° = \frac{DB}{AB} = \frac{DB}{3}$$

$$\therefore 3 \times 0.5 = 1.5m$$

(2) To find XB angle DXB is first required. This is (45-30) = 15°

$$\sin 15° = \frac{DB}{XB} = 0.258$$

$$\therefore XB = \frac{DB}{0.258} = \frac{1.5}{0.258} = 5.8m.$$

(3) To find XC

$$\sin 45° = \frac{XC}{5.8}$$

$$\therefore XC = \sin 45° \times 5.8 = 4.1m.$$

Referring to Fig. 4 the position at B can be established by describing a circle of radius 5.8 miles with centre at X and then drawing XB, the True bearing (*not* the relative bearing) and the point of intersection is the fix. Similarly with XC, giving the probable position when abeam.

Consider now the key sequences necessary on the calculator, first using the somewhat lengthy calculation shown above.

Quantity	Entry	Reading
Clear calculator	C	0
Enter first RB	30°	30°
	sin	0.5
	×	0.5
Enter Distance Run	3	3
	=	1.5
Store — Memory 1	M1 +	1.5
Clear Display	C	0
Enter angle DXB	15°	15°
	sin	0.2588
Store — Memory 2	M2 +	0.2588
Clear Display	C	0
Recall Memory 1	MR1	1.5
	÷	1.5
Recall Memory 2	MR2	0.2588
Answer	=	5.8

Distance off first bearing 5.8 miles

The key sequences for distance off when abeam will be:

Quantity	Entry	Reading
Clear calculator	C	0
Enter second RB	45°	45°
	sin	0.7071
	×	0.7071
Enter distance off at second RB	5.8	5.8
	=	4.1

Distance off when abeam = 4 miles.

These somewhat lengthy calculations can be reduced and simplified to the following two formulae, thus obviating the necessity for any chartwork until the final fix is obtained.

Formula for Distance Off at 2nd Bearing

D2 = Distance off at 2nd Bearing.

R = Distance between 1st and 2nd Bearings.

RB1 = First Relative Bearing.

RB2 = Second Relative Bearing.

$$D2 = \frac{R \sin RB1}{\sin (RB2 - RB1)}$$

In the case above the calculations will therefore be: $\dfrac{3 \sin 30°}{\sin (45\text{-}30)} = \dfrac{3 \times 0.5}{0.258}$

$= 5.8$ miles.

Formula for Distance Off When Abeam

D2 = Distance off at Second Bearing.

RB2 = 2nd Relative Bearing.

DA = Distance off when abeam.

$DA = D2 \sin RB2$

$= 5.8 \times \sin 45°$

$= 4.1$ miles.

From the calculations above it will be seen that the formula derived from the original rather lengthy calculations reduces the work to a short key sequence which is rapidly performed and requires no plotting until the navigator wishes to plot his position on the chart.

Tide Correction Angle and Speed Made Good (Fig. 5)

Similarly a formula can be derived for calculating the tidal correction angle. Omitting the step by step calculation this formula is:

$$\sin \theta = \frac{TS \times \sin RA}{SS}$$

where θ = Tidal Correction Angle
TS = Tide Speed
RA = Relative angle between tide and course to be made good.
SS = Ships Speed.

Example:

Tidal Stream 3.5kts. 280°T
Ships Speed 5kts.
Course to be made good 210°T

$\therefore$ RA = 70°

$CB = CA \times \sin 70°$

$\therefore \sin \theta = \dfrac{CA \times \sin 70°}{CD}$

$= \dfrac{3.5 \sin 70°}{5} = \dfrac{3.5 \times 0.94}{5} = 0.658$

$\theta = 41°$

NOTE: To convert 0.658 use invert and sine keys. Method may vary with different types of calculator.

Fig. 5

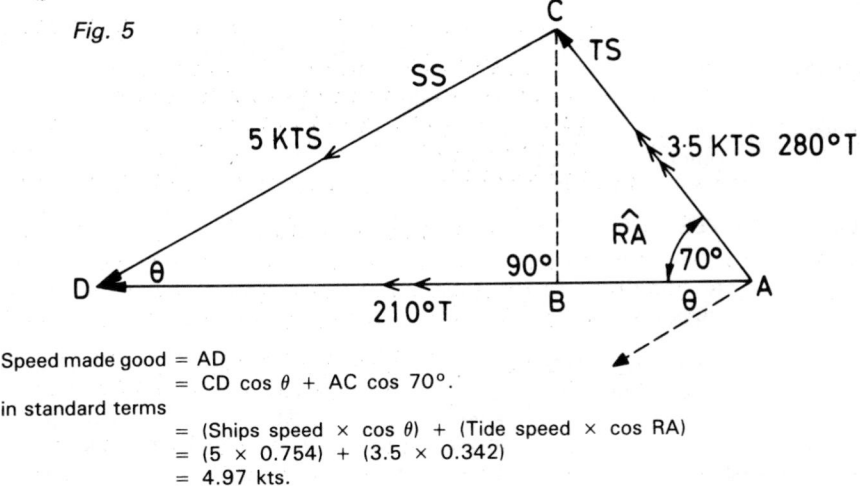

Speed made good = AD
$\quad\quad\quad\quad\quad\quad\quad$ = CD cos θ + AC cos 70°.
in standard terms
$\quad\quad\quad\quad\quad\quad\quad$ = (Ships speed $\times$ cos θ) + (Tide speed $\times$ cos RA)
$\quad\quad\quad\quad\quad\quad\quad$ = (5 $\times$ 0.754) + (3.5 $\times$ 0.342)
$\quad\quad\quad\quad\quad\quad\quad$ = 4.97 kts.

When $\hat{R}A$ is greater than 90° the complementary angle is used (eg. $\hat{R}A$ = 150°, complementary angle = 180–150 = 30°) in both correction angle and speed calculations. The latter formula becomes SS cos θ – TS cos $\hat{R}A$ where $\hat{R}A$ is the complementary angle.

HORIZONTAL ANGLE FIX

A quick method of calculating the radius of the circle required in the horizontal angle fix omitting the step by step calculation is:

$$\text{Radius} = \frac{\frac{1}{2}AB}{\text{SIN } \theta}$$

Where AB is the horizontal distance between the two points and θ is the angle subtended at the vessel.

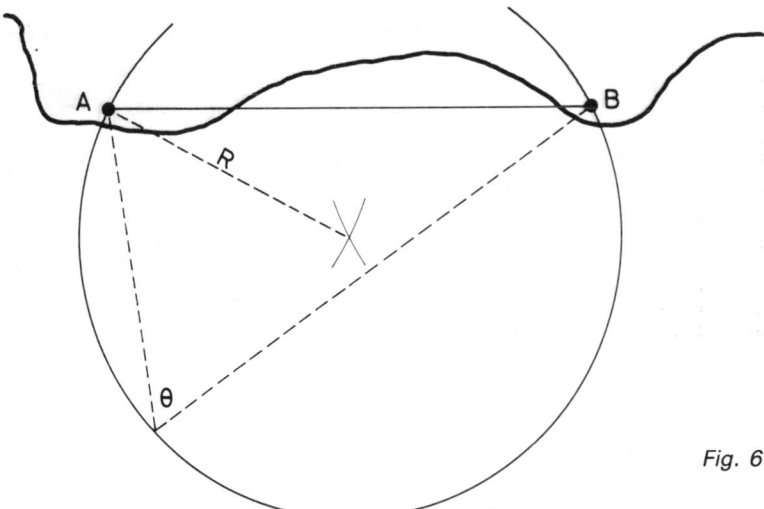

Fig. 6

In the example, if the distance AB = 7 miles and angle θ is 55°

$$\text{Radius} = \frac{AB}{2 \text{ SIN } \theta} = \frac{7}{2 \times .819} = 4.27m$$

It will be appreciated that a position line cutting the circle will give a fix.

TO FIND THE DIFFERENCE IN HEIGHT OF TIDE AT A PARTICULAR TIME, USING A CALCULATOR

(Describing the simple tide curve)

Data required   Range of tide (in metres)
Duration (in hours and minutes)
Interval from nearest Low Water, before or after.

Algorithm $\text{DIFFERENCE} = (\text{Sin} \dfrac{90 \times \text{Interval}}{\text{Duration}})^2 \times \text{Range}$

Worked example   Note: Enter hours and minutes on your calculator as you would enter degrees and minutes.

Range   4.0m
Duration   6hr. 40min.
Interval   5hr. 20min.

Quantity	Entry	Display
Interval from LW	5.20	5.20
Change to decimal	→H	5.33
	÷	5.33
Duration of tide	6.40	6.40
Change to decimal	→H	6.67
	×	0.80
	90	90
	=	72.00
	SIN	0.95
	$\times^2$	0.90
	×	0.90
Range	4	4
DIFFERENCE	=	3.62

THE DIFFERENCE MUST NOW BE ADDED TO THE PREDICTED HEIGHT OF LOW WATER.

If you have a programmable calculator, you may use one of the following programs.

Using algebraic logic Entry	Quantity	Using RPN logic Entry
Clear PGM		Clear PGM
RCL 1	Interval in hr. and min.	RCL 1
→ H	Change to decimal	→ H
÷		
RCL 2	Duration in hr. and min.	RCL 2
→ H	Change to decimal	→ H
=		÷
×		90
90		×
=		Sin
Sin		x^2
x^2		
×		
RCL 3	Range	RCL 3
=		×
R/S		RTN

This is the simplest program approach. Further sophistication is possible.
The answer must be added to the predicted height of low water.

International Regulations for Preventing Collisions at Sea

8

Explanatory notes are added to individual rules in the Steering and Sailing Rules Section, whilst general comments only are made in parts C (Lights and Shapes) and part D (Sound and Light Signals). These notes are intended for the less experienced skippers of small craft.

It is important for anyone going to sea to fully understand the rules, and the ability to recognise lights and shapes and understand sound signals is vital. It should never be necessary in an emergency to consult a book to identify a particular group of lights or a signal.

As a matter of interest the newcomer to sailing may consider it odd to refer to arcs of lights in half degrees, when steering to half a degree is impracticable e.g. "the stern light shall be visible 22½° abaft the beam". Originally magnetic compasses were marked in 32 cardinal points thus each point equated to 11¼°. Whilst the use of degrees became universal the old arcs of visibility were retained, thus "2 points abaft the beam" became "22½° abaft the beam" in the modern nomenclature.

INTERNATIONAL REGULATIONS FOR

PREVENTING COLLISIONS AT SEA, 1972

(Including 1983 & 1989 Amendments)

PART A — GENERAL

Rule 1 *Application*

(a) These Rules shall apply to all vessels upon the high seas and in all waters connected therewith navigable by seagoing vessels.

(b) Nothing in these Rules shall interfere with the operation of special rules made by an appropriate authority for roadsteads, harbours, rivers, lakes or inland waterways connected with the high seas and navigable by seagoing vessels. Such special rules shall conform as closely as possible to these rules.

(c) Nothing in these Rules shall interfere with the operation of any special rules made by the Government of any State with respect to additional station or signal lights, shapes or whistle signals for ships of war and vessels proceeding under convoy, or with respect to additional station or signal lights or shapes for fishing vessels engaged in fishing as a fleet. These additional station or signal lights, shapes or whistle signals shall, so far as possible, be such that they cannot be mistaken for any light, shape or signal authorised elsewhere under these Rules.

(d) Traffic separation schemes may be adopted by the Organisation for the purpose of these Rules.

(e) Whenever the Government concerned shall have determined that a vessel of special construction or purpose cannot comply fully with the provisions of any of these Rules with respect to the number, position, range or arc of visibility of lights or shapes, as well as to the disposition and characteristics of sound-signalling applicances, such vessel shall comply with such other provisions in regard to the number, position, range or arc of visibility of lights or shapes, as well as to the disposition and characteristics of sound-signalling applicances, as her Government shall have determined to be the closest possible compliance with these Rules in respect of that vessel.

Rule 2 *Responsibility*
(a) Nothing in these Rules shall exonerate any vessel, or the owner, master or crew thereof, from the consequences of any neglect to comply with these Rules or of the neglect of any precaution which may be required by the ordinary practice of seamen, or by the special circumstances of the case.

(b) In construing and complying with these Rules due regard shall be had to all dangers of navigation and collision and to any special circumstances, including the limitations of the vessels involved, which may make a departure from these Rules necessary to avoid immediate danger.

NOTE TO RULE 2
It must be remembered that rules do not give absolute right of way to any vessel. Right of way is conferred by one vessel to another by an alteration of course and speed, but both vessels have responsibility to avoid a collision. In certain circumstances the "give way" vessel may be unable to take avoiding action and then the "stand on" vessel is required to take the necessary action.

Rule 3 *General Definitions*

For the purpose of these Rules, except where the context otherwise requires:

(a) The word "vessel" includes every description of water craft, including non-displacement craft and seaplanes, used or capable of being used as a means of transportation on water.

(b) The term "power-driven vessel" means any vessel propelled by machinery.

(c) The term "sailing vessel" means any vessel under sail provided that propelling machinery, if fitted, is not being used.

(d) The term "vessel engaged in fishing" means any vessel fishing with nets, lines, trawls or other fishing apparatus which restrict manoeuvrability, but does not include a vessel fishing with trolling lines or other fishing apparatus which do not restrict manoeuvrability.

(e) The word "seaplane" includes any aircraft designed to manoeuvre on the water.

(f) The term "vessel not under command" means a vessel which through some exceptional circumstance is unable to manoeuvre as required by these Rules and is therefore unable to keep out of the way of another vessel.

(g) The term "vessel restricted in her ability to manoeuvre" means a vessel which from the nature of her work is restricted in her ability to manoeuvre as required by these Rules and is therefore unable to keep out of the way of another vessel.

The term "vessels restricted in their ability to manoeuvre" shall include but not be limited to:

(i) a vessel engaged in laying, servicing or picking up a navigation mark, submarine cable or pipeline;

(ii) a vessel engaged in dredging, surveying or underwater operations;

(iii) a vessel engaged in replenishment or transferring persons, provisions or cargo while underway;

(iv) a vessel engaged in the launching or recovery of aircraft;

(v) a vessel engaged in mine clearance operations;

(vi) a vessel engaged in a towing operation such as severely restricts the towing vessel and her tow in their ability to deviate from their course.

(h) The term "vessel constrained by her draught" means a power-driven vessel which because of her draught in relation to the available depth and width of navigable water is severely restricted in her ability to deviate from the course she is following.

(i) The word "underway" means that a vessel is not at anchor, or made fast to the shore, or aground.

(j) The words "length" and "breadth" of a vessel mean her length overall and greatest breadth.

(k) Vessels shall be deemed to be in sight of one another only when one can be observed visually from the other.

(l) The term "restricted visibility" means any condition in which visibility is restricted by fog, mist, falling snow, heavy rainstorms, sandstorms or any other similar causes.

NOTE TO RULE 3
A useful explanation of various terms which occur in the rules and should be known and understood by those in charge of any seagoing vessel.

PART B — STEERING AND SAILING RULES

SECTION 1 — CONDUCT OF VESSELS IN ANY CONDITION OF VISIBILITY

Rule 4   *Application*

Rules in this Section apply in any condition of visibility.

Rule 5   *Lookout*

Every vessel shall at all times maintain a proper lookout by sight and hearing as well as by all available means appropriate in the prevailing circumstances and conditions so as to make a full appraisal of the situation and of the risk of collision.

NOTE TO RULE 5
Keeping a proper look out at all times is one of the most important duties of any vessel. It is particularly difficult in a sailing yacht with a long footed headsail especially when heeled but it is vital to keep a good look out to leeward in these circumstances. Watchkeeping at night also presents problems insofar as the lights on the vessel are concerned. Chart table lights and any internal lights visible to the helmsman should be red which reduces night vision by a relatively small amount. Deck lights for sail changing at night constitute a real difficulty for the lookout both at the time and for a short while afterwards. In conditions of poor visibility a good listening watch is also important – it cannot be kept from inside a closed wheelhouse.

Rule 6 *Safe Speed*

Every vessel shall at all times proceed at a safe speed so that she can take proper and effective action to avoid collision and be stopped within a distance appropriate to the prevailing circumstances and conditions.

In determining a safe speed the following factors shall be among those taken into account:

(a) By all vessels:

    (i) the state of visibility;

    (ii) the traffic density including concentrations of fishing vessels or any other vessels;

    (iii) the manoeuvrability of the vessel with special reference to stopping distance and turning ability in the prevailing conditions;

    (iv) at night the presence of background light such as from shore lights or from back scatter of her own lights;

    (v) the state of wind, sea and current, and the proximity of navigational hazards;

    (vi) the draught in relation to the available depth of water.

(b) Additionally, by vessels with operational radar:

    (i) the characteristics, efficiency and limitations of the radar equipment;

    (ii) any constraints imposed by the radar range scale in use;

    (iii) the effect on radar detection of the sea state, weather and other sources of interference;

    (iv) the possibility that small vessels, ice and other floating objects may not be detected by radar at an adequate range;

    (v) the number, location and movement of vessels detected by radar;

    (vi) the more exact assessment of the visibility that may be possible when radar is used to determine the range of vessels or other objects in the vicinity.

NOTE TO RULE 6
This rule refers to a "safe speed" i.e. not necessarily high speed. High speed in a sailing yacht is rarely a contributory factor in a collision situation but slow speed may be. The essence of the Rule is to have complete control and manoeuvrability at all times. A sailing yacht carrying a spinnaker at night in a congested traffic situation would not be conforming to the spirit of this Rule, she should be sailing more slowly under plain sail but with complete manoeuvrability. For the fast motor yacht high speed in a tight situation may be a danger as it effectively reduces "thinking time".

Rule 7   *Risk of Collision*

(a) Every vessel shall use all available means appropriate to the prevailing circumstances and conditions to determine if risk of collision exists. If there is any doubt such risk shall be deemed to exist.

(b) Proper use shall be made of radar equipment if fitted and operational, including long-range scanning to obtain early warning of risk of collision and radar plotting or equivalent systematic observation of detected objects.

(c) Assumptions shall not be made on the basis of scanty information, especially scanty radar information.

(d) In determining if risk of collision exists the following considerations shall be among those taken into account:

(i) such risk shall be deemed to exist if the compass bearing of an approaching vessel does not appreciably change;

(ii) such risk may sometimes exist even when an appreciable bearing change is evident, particularly when approaching a very large vessel or a tow or when approaching a vessel at close range.

NOTE TO RULE 7
In the situation of an approaching or crossing vessel the first step is to take a compass bearing of the vessel and repeat it at suitable intervals. If the bearing does not change, risk of collision exists. Note that it is the compass bearing, not the relative bearing that is crucial.

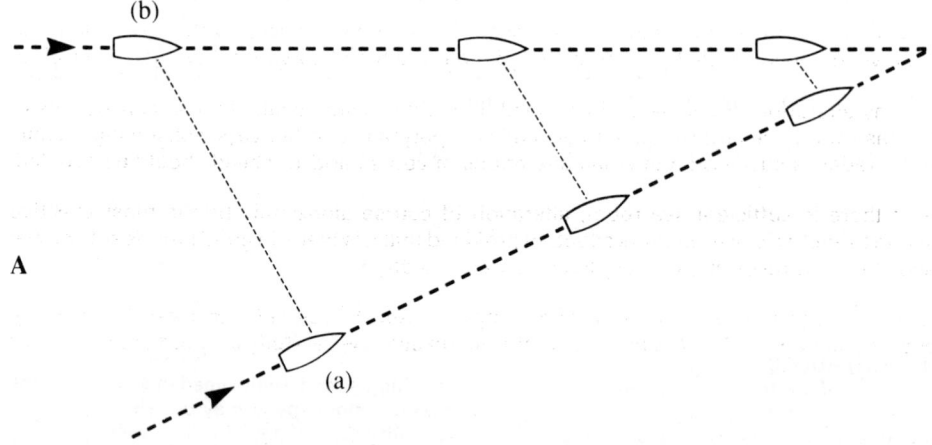

In A. the compass bearing of (a) relative to (b) is constant and therefore risk of collision exists. In this particular case the relative bearing of (a) to (b) is also constant.

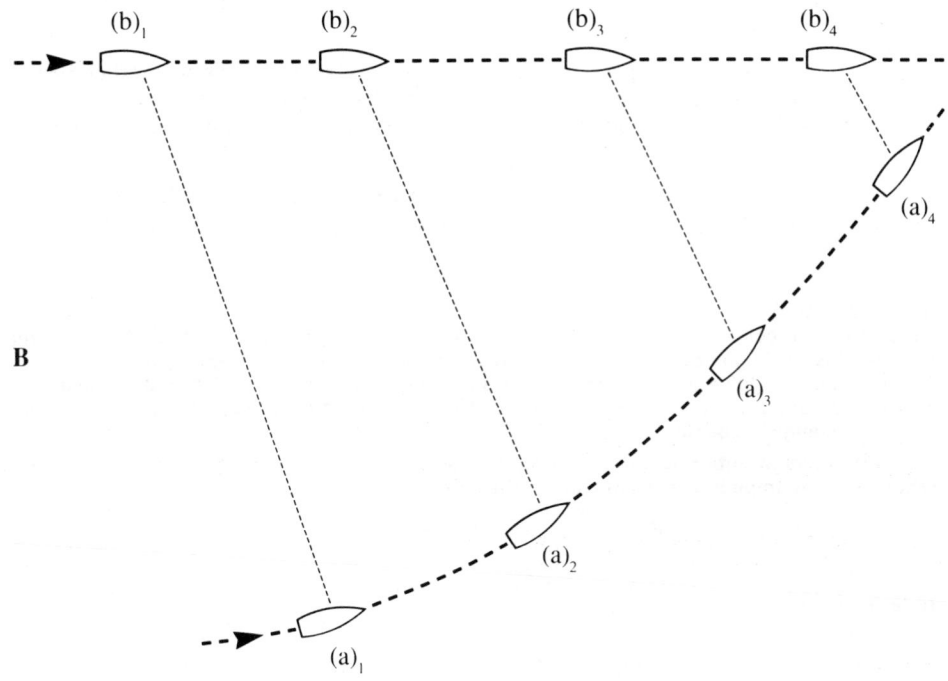

In B. the relative bearing of (b)$_1$ from (a)$_1$ is abaft the beam. At (a)$_2$ the bearing is approximately abeam and at (a)$_3$ and (a)$_4$ is moving ahead of the beam. The compass bearing however, remains constant and therefore risk of collision exists.

Rule 8   *Action to avoid Collision*

(a) Any action taken to avoid collision shall, if the circumstances of the case admit, be positive, made in ample time and with due regard to the observance of good seamanship.

(b) Any alteration of course and/or speed to avoid collision shall, if the circumstances of the case admit, be large enough to be readily apparent to another vessel observing visually or by radar; a succession of small alterations of course and/or speed should be avoided.

(c) If there is sufficient sea room, alteration of course alone may be the most effective action to avoid a close-quarters situation provided that it is made in good time, is substantial and does not result in another close-quarters situation.

(d) Action taken to avoid collision with another vessel shall be such as to result in passing at a safe distance. The effectiveness of the action shall be carefully checked until the other vessel is finally past and clear.

(e) If necessary to avoid collision or allow more time to assess the situation, a vessel shall slacken her speed or take all way off by stopping or reversing her means of propulsion.

(f)   (i) A vessel which, by any of these rules, is required not to impede the passage or safe passage of another vessel shall, when required by the circumstances of the case, take early action to allow sufficient sea room for the safe passage of the other vessel.

(ii) A vessel required not to impede the passage or safe passage of another vessel is not relieved of this obligation if approaching the other vessel so as to involve risk of collision and shall, when taking action, have full regard to the action which may be required by the rules of this part.

(iii) A vessel the passage of which is not to be impeded remains fully obliged to comply with the rules of this part when the two vessels are approaching one another so as to involve risk of collision.

NOTE TO RULE 8
Action to avoid collision must be taken in good time and in such a manner that the "stand on" vessel is left in no doubt that the "give way" vessel is taking avoiding action. In the case of the "give way" vessel being a small yacht any alteration in speed is unlikely to be obvious from any distance. The action therefore must be to alter the profile of the yacht by a marked change of course.
Rule 8(f) draws attention to the importance of small vessels navigating in traffic separation schemes not to impede vessels moving in the lane.

Rule 9   *Narrow Channels*

(a) A vessel proceeding along the course of a narrow channel or fairway shall keep as near to the outer limit of the channel or fairway which lies on her starboard side as is safe and practicable.

(b) A vessel of less than 20 metres in length or a sailing vessel shall not impede the passage of a vessel which can safely navigate only within a narrow channel or fairway.

(c) A vessel engaged in fishing shall not impede the passage of any other vessel navigating within a narrow channel or fairway.

(d) A vessel shall not cross a narrow channel or fairway if such crossing impedes the passage of a vessel which can safely navigate only within such channel or fairway. The latter vessel may use the sound signal prescribed in Rule 34(d) if in doubt as to the intention of the crossing vessel.

(e)   (i) In a narrow channel or fairway when overtaking can take place only if the vessel to be overtaken has to take action to permit safe passing, the vessel intending to overtake shall indicate her intention by sounding the appropriate signal prescribed in Rule 34(c)(i). The vessel to be overtaken shall, if in agreement, sound the appropriate signal prescribed in Rule 34(c)(ii) and take steps to permit safe passing. If in doubt she may sound the signals prescribed in Rule 34(d).

      (ii) This Rule does not relieve the overtaking vessel of her obligation under Rule 13.

(f) A vessel nearing a bend or an area of a narrow channel or fairway where other vessels may be obscured by an intervening obstruction shall navigate with particular alertness and caution and shall sound the appropriate signal prescribed in Rule 34(e).

(g) Any vessel shall, if the circumstances of the case admit, avoid anchoring in a narrow channel.

NOTE TO RULE 9
On occasion doubt may arise whether one is in a "narrow channel" – usually it is obvious, but if not, any channel which has port and starboard hand buoys will be regarded as a narrow channel by ocean-going vessels. Hence all other vessels should have regard to the requirements of this rule when in such a channel. It is important to note that 9(a) refers to "a vessel", hence a sailing yacht is also required to keep as near as possible to the starboard side of the channel and avoid impeding the passage of a vessel which can only navigate with safety in a narrow channel.

Rule 10   *Traffic Separation Schemes*

(a) This Rule applies to traffic separation schemes adopted by the Organisation and does not relieve any vessel of her obligation under any other rule.

(b) A vessel using a traffic separation scheme shall:

(i) proceed in the appropriate traffic lane in the general direction of traffic flow for that lane;

(ii) so far as practicable keep clear of a traffic separation line or separation zone;

(iii) normally join or leave a traffic lane at the termination of the lane, but when joining or leaving from either side shall do so at as small an angle to the general direction of traffic flow as practicable.

(c) A vessel shall so far as practicable avoid crossing traffic lanes, but if obliged to do so shall cross on a heading as nearly as practicable at right angles to the general direction of traffic flow.

(d)   (i) A vessel shall not use an inshore traffic zone when she can safely use the appropriate traffic lane within the adjacent traffic separation scheme. However, vessels of less than 20 metres in length, sailing vessels and vessels engaged in fishing may use the inshore traffic zone.

(ii) Notwithstanding sub-paragraph (d)(i) a vessel may use an inshore traffic zone when en route to or from a port, offshore installation or structure, pilot station or any other place situated within the inshore traffic zone, or to avoid immediate danger.

(e) A vessel other than a crossing vessel or a vessel joining or leaving a lane, shall not normally enter a separation zone or cross a separation line except:

(i) in cases of emergency to avoid immediate danger;

(ii) to engage in fishing within a separation zone.

(f) A vessel navigating in areas near the terminations of traffic separation schemes shall do so with particular caution.

(g) A vessel shall so far as practicable avoid anchoring in a traffic separation scheme or in areas near its terminations.

(h) A vessel not using a traffic separation scheme shall avoid it by as wide a margin as is practicable.

(i) A vessel engaged in fishing shall not impede the passage of any vessel following a traffic lane.

(j) A vessel of less than 20 metres in length or a sailing vessel shall not impede the safe passage of a power-driven vessel following a traffic lane.

(k) A vessel restricted in her ability to manoeuvre when engaged in an operation for the maintenance of safety of navigation in a traffic separation scheme is exempted from complying with this Rule to the extent necessary to carry out the operation.

(l) A vessel restricted in her ability to manoeuvre when engaged in an operation for the laying, servicing or picking up of a submarine cable, within a traffic separation scheme, is exempted from complying with this Rule to the extent necessary to carry out the operation.

NOTE TO RULE 10
This is an extremely important rule and there are two aspects of it which are particularly important to sailing yachts.
Firstly it is important to cross the lane as quickly as possible and it may therefore be necessary to use the auxilliary to maintain the highest speed in the circumstances.
Secondly it is essential to present a full profile to traffic in the lane, i.e. the vessel's fore and aft line should be as near to a right angle to the lane as possible – not her track across the lane.

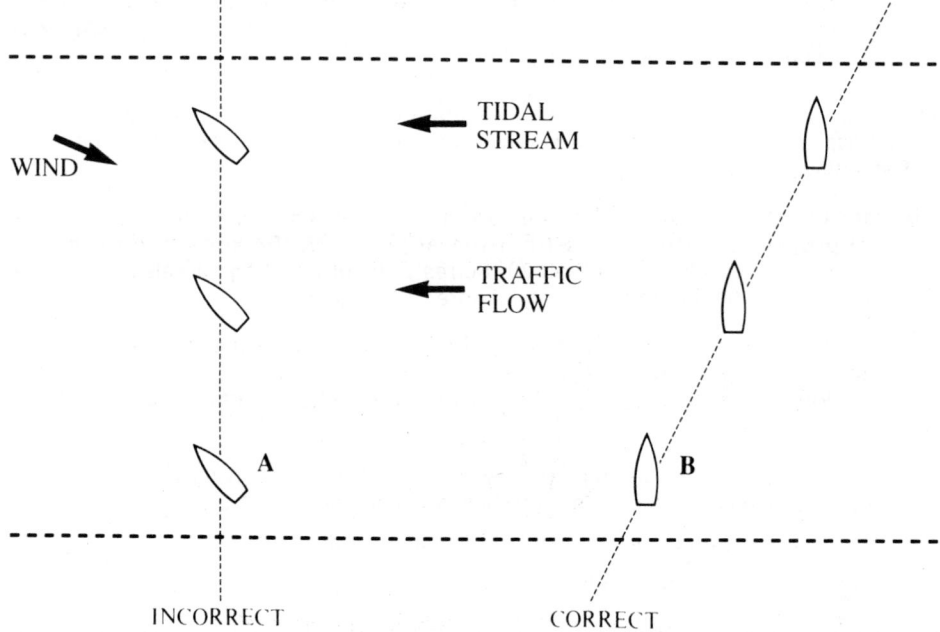

In the sketch, Yacht A is utilising wind and tide to cross the traffic lane on a course at 90° to the lane but is not presenting a full profile to the traffic – this is incorrect.

Yacht B is presenting her full profile to the traffic, i.e. her fore and aft line is at 90° to the lane and her passage time will be faster than A's. This is the correct approach.

In the event of crossing the lane against a head wind and motoring is not practical the yacht should sail close hauled on that tack which makes her heading as close as possible to 90° to the traffic flow.

Bearing in mind the above points, the objective should be to cross the lane as quickly as possible.

SECTION II — CONDUCT OF VESSELS IN SIGHT OF ONE ANOTHER

Rule 11 *Application*

Rules in this Section apply to vessels in sight of one another.

Rule 12 *Sailing Vessels*

(a) When two sailing vessels are approaching one another, so as to involve risk of collision, one of them shall keep out of the way of the other as follows:

(i) when each has the wind on a different side, the vessel which has the wind on the port side shall keep out of the way of the other;

(ii) when both have the wind on the same side, the vessel which is to windward shall keep out of the way of the vessel which is to leeward;

(iii) if a vessel with the wind on the port side sees a vessel to windward and cannot determine with certainty whether the other vessel has the wind on the port or on the starboard side, she shall keep out of the way of the other.

(b) For the purposes of this Rule the windward side shall be deemed to be the side opposite to that on which the mainsail is carried or, in the case of a square-rigged vessel, the side opposite to that on which the largest fore-and-aft sail is carried.

NOTE TO RULE 12

a(i) and a(ii) are quite clear and are well known but a(iii) must be fully understood. A yacht close hauled on the port tack approaching a yacht running free and unable to determine her tack must keep clear. The windward boat may be carrying a spinnaker which makes it difficult to determine her tack and in any case at night quite impossible. In these circumstances it is the duty of the close hauled port tack vessel to keep clear.

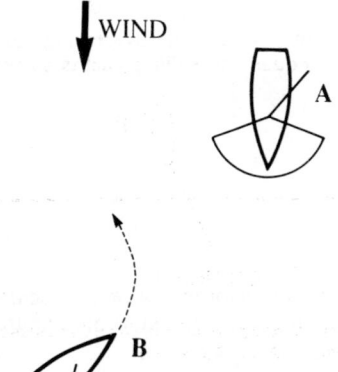

↓WIND

A

B

When B is in doubt about A's tack it is the responsibility of B to keep clear.

Rule 13 *Overtaking*

(a) Notwithstanding anything contained in the Rules of Part B, Sections I and II any vessel overtaking any other shall keep out of the way of the vessel being overtaken.

(b) A vessel shall be deemed to be overtaking when coming up with another vessel from a direction more than 22.5 degrees abaft her beam, that is, in such a position with reference to the vessel she is overtaking, that at night she would be able to see only the sternlight of that vessel but neither of her sidelights.

(c) When a vessel is in any doubt as to whether she is overtaking another, she shall assume that this is the case and act accordingly.

(d) Any subsequent alteration of the bearing between the two vessels shall not make the overtaking vessel a crossing vessel within the meaning of these Rules or relieve her of the duty of keeping clear of the overtaken vessel until she is finally past and clear.

NOTE TO RULE 13

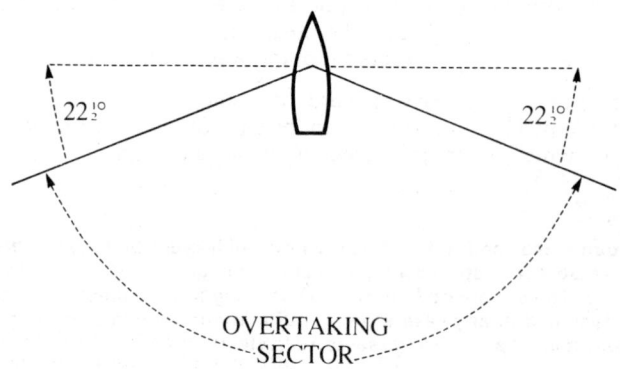

It is important to note the final sentence of this rule, i.e. that the overtaking vessel shall keep clear until she is "past and clear". This applies equally to sailing yachts as well as power-driven craft.

Rule 14 *Head-on Situation*

(a) When two power-driven vessels are meeting on reciprocal or nearly reciprocal courses so as to involve risk of collision each shall alter her course to starboard so that each shall pass on the port side of the other.

(b) Such a situation shall be deemed to exist when a vessel sees the other ahead or nearly ahead and by night she could see the masthead lights of the other in a line or nearly in a line and/or both sidelights and by day she observes the corresponding aspect of the other vessel.

(c) When a vessel is in any doubt as to whether such a situation exists she shall assume that it does exist and act accordingly.

NOTE TO RULE 14

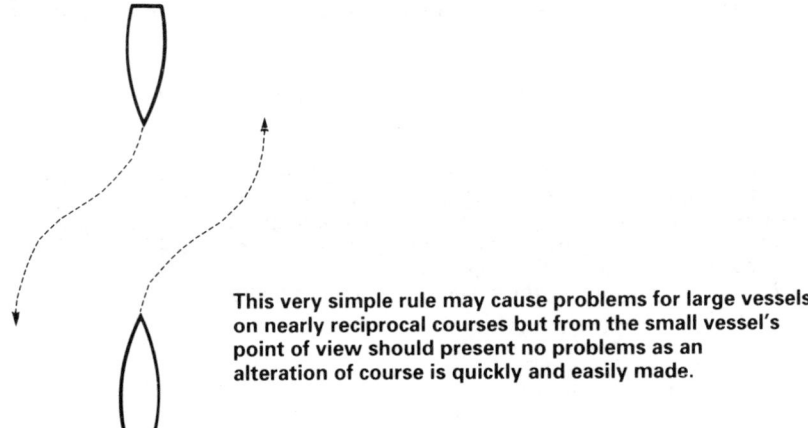

This very simple rule may cause problems for large vessels on nearly reciprocal courses but from the small vessel's point of view should present no problems as an alteration of course is quickly and easily made.

Rule 15 *Crossing Situation*

When two power-driven vessels are crossing so as to involve risk of collision, the vessel which has the other on her own starboard side shall keep out of the way and shall, if the circumstances of the case admit, avoid crossing ahead of the other vessel.

NOTE TO RULE 15

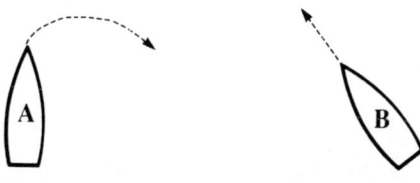

The normally correct action for A is to alter course to starboard and pan under B's stern.

Rule 16 *Action by Give-way Vessel*

Every vessel which is directed to keep out of the way of another vessel shall, so far as possible, take early and substantial action to keep well clear.

Rule 17 *Action by Stand-on Vessel*

(a)   (i) Where one of two vessels is to keep out of the way the other shall keep her course and speed.

(ii) The latter vessel may however take action to avoid collision by her manoeuvre alone, as soon as it becomes apparent to her that the vessel required to keep out of the way is not taking appropriate action in compliance with these Rules.

(b) When, from any cause, the vessel required to keep her course and speed finds herself so close that collision cannot be avoided by the action of the give-way vessel alone, she shall take such action as will best aid to avoid collision.

(c) A power-driven vessel which takes action in a crossing situation in accordance with sub-paragraph (a)(ii) of this Rule to avoid collision with another power-driven vessel shall, if the circumstances of the case admit, not alter course to port for a vessel on her own port side.

(d) This Rule does not relieve the give-way vessel of her obligation to keep out of the way.

NOTE TO RULE 17
This is an important rule as it requires the "stand on" vessel to take avoiding action if it appears that the "give way" vessel is not acting in accordance with the rules.
This may pose problems for a small vessel meeting a large ship, particularly at night; the small vessel may well have right of way according to the rules but would be foolish to "stand on" as she may not be visible to the large ship.
The sensible course of action for the small vessel in this situation is to turn completely away from the large ship.

Rule 18 *Responsibilities between Vessels*

Except where Rules 9, 10 and 13 otherwise require:

(a) A power-driven vessel underway shall keep out of the way of:

(i) a vessel not under command;

(ii) a vessel restricted in her ability to manoeuvre;

(iii) a vessel engaged in fishing;

(iv) a sailing vessel.

(b) A sailing vessel underway shall keep out of the way of:

(i) a vessel not under command;

(ii) a vessel restricted in her ability to manoeuvre;

(iii) a vessel engaged in fishing.

(c) A vessel engaged in fishing when underway shall, so far as possible, keep out of the way of:

(i) a vessel not under command;

(ii) a vessel restricted in her ability to manoeuvre.

(d) (i) Any vessel other than a vessel not under command or a vessel restricted in her ability to manoeuvre shall, if the circumstances of the case admit, avoid impeding the safe passage of a vessel constrained by her draught, exhibiting the signals in Rule 28.

(ii) A vessel constrained by her draught shall navigate with particular caution having full regard to her special condition.

(e) A seaplane on the water shall, in general keep well clear of all vessels and avoid impeding their navigation. In circumstances, however, where risk of collision exists, she shall comply with the Rules of this Part.

NOTE TO RULE 18
Basically this rule very sensibly means that the more manoeuvrable vessel shall keep out of the way of the less manoeuvrable one.

SECTION III — CONDUCT OF VESSELS IN
RESTRICTED VISIBILITY

Rule 19   *Conduct of Vessels in Restricted Visibility*

(a) This Rule applies to vessels not in sight of one another when navigating in or near an area of restricted visibility.

(b) Every vessel shall proceed at a safe speed adapted to the prevailing circumstances and conditions of restricted visibility. A power-driven vessel shall have her engines ready for immediate manoeuvre.

(c) Every vessel shall have due regard to the prevailing circumstances and conditions of restricted visibility when complying with the Rules of Section I of this Part.

(d) A vessel which detects by radar alone the presence of another vessel shall determine if a close-quarters situation is developing and/or risk of collision exists. If so, she shall take avoiding action in ample time, provided that when such action consists of an alteration of course, so far as possible the following shall be avoided:

(i) an alteration of course to port for a vessel forward of the beam, other than for a vessel being overtaken;

(ii) an alteration of course towards a vessel abeam or abaft the beam.

(e) Except where it has been determined that a risk of collision does not exist, every vessel which hears apparently forward of her beam the fog signal of another vessel, or which cannot avoid a close-quarters situation with another vessel forward of her beam, shall reduce her speed to the minimum at which she can be kept on her course. She shall if necessary take all her way off and in any event navigate with extreme caution until danger of collision is over.

NOTE TO RULE 19
It is obviously impossible to lay down a rule where there are so many imponderables. From the yachtsman's point of view the following points are vital.

(a) Have a radar reflector of proven efficiency mounted as high as possible.
(b) Keep a good lookout, both visual and aural, if underway with an auxilliary going, a lookout should be well forward away from the sound of the engine.
(c) Keep clear of shipping lanes and if possible move into water too shallow for larger vessels.
(d) Be ready for immediate action.

PART C — LIGHTS AND SHAPES

NOTE
The rules in this section are clear and explicit and need no classification. However, one important rule which is regrettably not always observed by small vessels is the use of the correct signals when anchored (Rule 30). It is not necessarily obvious to a large vessel whether a small yacht is anchored if she is not displaying the correct signals.

Rule 20 *Application*

(a) Rules in this Part shall be complied with in all weathers.

(b) The Rules concerning lights shall be complied with from sunset to sunrise, and during such times no other lights shall be exhibited, except such lights as cannot be mistaken for the lights specified in these Rules or do not impair their visibility or distinctive character, or interfere with the keeping of a proper look-out.

(c) The lights prescribed by these Rules shall, if carried, also be exhibited from sunrise to sunset in restricted visibility and may be exhibited in all other circumstances when it is deemed necessary.

(d) The Rules concerning shapes shall be complied with by day.

(e) The lights and shapes specified in these Rules shall comply with the provisions of Annex I to these Regulations.

Rule 21 *Definitions*

(a) "Masthead light" means a white light placed over the fore and aft centreline of the vessel showing an unbroken light over an arc of the horizon of 225 degrees and so fixed as to show the light from right ahead to 22.5 degrees abaft the beam on either side of the vessel.

(b) "Sidelights" means a green light on the starboard side and a red light on the port side each showing an unbroken light over an arc of the horizon of 112.5 degrees and so fixed as to show the light from right ahead to 22.5 degrees abaft the beam on its respective side. In a vessel of less than 20 metres in length the sidelights may be combined in one lantern carried on the fore and aft centreline of the vessel.

(c) "Sternlight" means a white light placed as nearly as practicable at the stern showing an unbroken light over an arc of the horizon of 135 degrees and so fixed as to show the light 67.5 degrees from right aft on each side of the vessel.

(d) "Towing light" means a yellow light having the same characteristics as the "sternlight" defined in paragraph (c) of this Rule.

(e) "All-round light" means a light showing an unbroken light over an arc of the horizon of 360 degrees.

(f) "Flashing light" means a light flashing at regular intervals at a frequency of 120 flashes or more per minute.

Rule 22　*Visibility of Lights*

The lights prescribed in these Rules shall have an intensity as specified in Section 8 of Annex I to these Regulations so as to be visible at the following minimum ranges:

(a) In vessels of 50 metres or more in length:

　　—a masthead light, 6 miles;
　　—a sidelight, 3 miles;
　　—a sternlight, 3 miles;
　　—a towing light, 3 miles;
　　—a white, red, green or yellow all-round light, 3 miles.

(b) In vessels of 12 metres or more in length but less than 50 metres in length;

　　—a masthead light, 5 miles; except that where the length of the vessel is less than 20 metres, 3 miles;
　　—a sidelight, 2 miles;
　　—a sternlight, 2 miles;
　　—a towing light, 2 miles;
　　—a white, red, green or yellow all-round light, 2 miles.

(c) In vessels of less than 12 metres in length:

　　—a masthead light, 2 miles;
　　—a sidelight, 1 mile;
　　—a sternlight, 2 miles;
　　—a towing light, 2 miles;
　　—a white, red, green or yellow all-round light, 2 miles.

(d) In inconspicuous, partly submerged vessels or objects being towed:
　　—a white all-round light, 3 miles.

Rule 23　*Power-driven Vessels underway*

(a) A power-driven vessel underway shall exhibit:

(i) a masthead light forward;

(ii) a second masthead light abaft of and higher than the forward one; except that a vessel of less than 50 metres in length shall not be obliged to exhibit such light but may do so;

(iii) sidelights;

(iv) a sternlight.

(b) An air-cushion vessel when operating in the non-displacement mode shall, in addition to the lights prescribed in paragraph (a) of this Rule, exhibit an all-round flashing yellow light.

(c) (i) A power-driven vessel of less than 12 metres in length may, in lieu of the lights prescribed in paragraph (a) of this Rule, exhibit an all-round white light and sidelights;

(ii) a power-driven vessel of less than 7 metres in length whose maximum speed does not exceed 7 knots may in lieu of the lights prescribed in paragraph (a) of this Rule exhibit an all-round white light and shall, if practicable, also exhibit sidelights;

(iii) the masthead light or all-round white light on a power-driven vessel of less than 12 metres in length may be displaced from the fore and aft centreline of the vessel if centreline fitting is not practicable, provided that the sidelights are combined in one lantern which shall be carried on the fore and aft centreline of the vessel or located as nearly as practicable in the same fore and aft line as the masthead light or the all-round white light.

Rule 24 *Towing and Pushing*

(a) A power-driven vessel when towing shall exhibit:

(i) instead of the light prescribed in Rule 23(a)(i) or (a)(ii), two masthead lights in a vertical line. When the length of the tow, measuring from the stern of the towing vessel to the after end of the tow exceeds 200 metres, three such lights in a vertical line;

(ii) sidelights;

(iii) a sternlight;

(iv) a towing light in a vertical line above the sternlight;

(v) when the length of the tow exceeds 200 metres, a diamond shape where it can best be seen.

(b) When a pushing vessel and a vessel being pushed ahead are rigidly connected in a composite unit they shall be regarded as a power-driven vessel and exhibit the lights prescribed in Rule 23.

(c) A power-driven vessel when pushing ahead or towing alongside, except in the case of a composite unit, shall exhibit:

(i) instead of the light prescribed in Rule 23(a)(i) or (a)(ii), two masthead lights in a vertical line;

(ii) sidelights;

(iii) a sternlight.

(d) A power-driven vessel to which paragraphs (a) or (c) of this Rule apply shall also comply with Rule 23(a)(ii).

(e) A vessel or object being towed, other than those mentioned in paragraph (g) of this Rule, shall exhibit:

(i) sidelights;

(ii) a sternlight;

(iii) when the length of the tow exceeds 200 metres, a diamond shape where it can best be seen.

(f) Provided that any number of vessels being towed alongside or pushed in a group shall be lighted as one vessel,

(i) a vessel being pushed ahead, not being part of a composite unit, shall exhibit at the forward end, sidelights;

(ii) a vessel being towed alongside shall exhibit a sternlight and at the forward end, sidelights.

(g) An inconspicuous, partly submerged vessel or object, or combination of such vessels or objects being towed, shall exhibit:

(i) if it is less than 25 metres in breadth, one all-round white light at or near the forward end and one at or near the after end except that dracones need not exhibit a light at or near the forward end;

(ii) if it is 25 metres or more in breadth, two additional all-round white lights at or near the extremities of its breadth;

(iii) if it exceeds 100 metres in length, additional all-round white lights between the lights prescribed in subparagraphs (i) and (ii) so that the distance between the lights shall not exceed 100 metres;

(iv) a diamond shape at or near the aftermost extremity of the last vessel or object being towed and if the length of the tow exceeds 200 metres an additional diamond shape where it can best be seen and located as far forward as is practicable.

(h) Where from any sufficient cause it is impracticable for a vessel or object being towed to exhibit the lights or shapes prescribed in paragraph (e) or (g) of this Rule, all possible measures shall be taken to light the vessel or object towed or at least to indicate the presence of such vessel or object.

(i) Where from any sufficient cause it is impracticable for a vessel not normally engaged in towing operations to display the lights prescribed in paragraph (a) or (c) of this Rule, such vessel shall not be required to exhibit those lights when engaged in towing another vessel in distress or otherwise in need of assistance. All possible measures shall be taken to indicate the nature of the relationship between the towing vessel and the vessel being towed as authorised by Rule 36, in particular by illuminating the towline.

Rule 25 *Sailing Vessels underway and Vessels under Oars*

(a) A sailing vessel underway shall exhibit:

(i) sidelights;

(ii) a sternlight.

(b) In a sailing vessel of less than 20 metres in length the lights prescribed in paragraph (a) of this Rule may be combined in one lantern carried at or near the top of the mast where it can best be seen.

(c) A sailing vessel underway may, in addition to the lights prescribed in paragraph (a) of this Rule, exhibit at or near the top of the mast, where they can best be seen, two all-round lights in a vertical line, the upper being red and the lower green, but these lights shall not be exhibited in conjunction with the combined lantern permitted by paragraph (b) of this Rule.

(d)   (i) A sailing vessel of less than 7 metres in length shall, if practicable, exhibit the lights prescribed in paragraph (a) or (b) of this Rule, but if she does not, she shall have ready at hand an electric torch or lighted lantern showing a white light which shall be exhibited in sufficient time to prevent collision.

(ii) A vessel under oars may exhibit the lights prescribed in this Rule for sailing vessels, but if she does not, she shall have ready at hand an electric torch or lighted lantern showing a white light which shall be exhibited in sufficient time to prevent collision.

(e) A vessel proceeding under sail when also being propelled by machinery shall exhibit forward where it can best be seen a conical shape, apex downwards.

Rule 26 *Fishing Vessels*

(a) A vessel engaged in fishing, whether underway or at anchor, shall exhibit only the lights and shapes prescribed in this Rule.

(b) A vessel when engaged in trawling, by which is meant the dragging through the water of a dredge net or other apparatus used as a fishing appliance, shall exhibit:

(i) two all-round lights in a vertical line, the upper being green and the lower white, or a shape consisting of two cones with their apexes together in a vertical line one above the other; a vessel of less than 20 metres in length may instead of this shape exhibit a basket;

(ii) a masthead light abaft of and higher than the all-round green light; a vessel of less than 50 metres in length shall not be obliged to exhibit such a light but may do so;

(iii) when making way through the water, in addition to the lights prescribed in this paragraph, sidelights and a sternlight.

(c) A vessel engaged in fishing, other than trawling, shall exhibit:

(i) two all-round lights in a vertical line, the upper being red and the lower white, or a shape consisting of two cones with their apexes together in a vertical line one above the other; a vessel of less than 20 metres in length may instead of this shape exhibit a basket;

(ii) when there is outlying gear extending more than 150 metres horizontally from the vessel, an all-round white light or a cone apex upwards in the direction of the gear;

(iii) when making way through the water, in addition to the lights prescribed in this paragraph, side lights and a sternlight.

(d) A vessel engaged in fishing in close proximity to other vessels engaged in fishing may exhibit the additional signals described in Annex II to these Regulations.

(e) A vessel when not engaged in fishing shall not exhibit the lights or shapes prescribed in this Rule, but only those prescribed for a vessel of her length.

Rule 27 *Vessels not under Command or Restricted in their ability to Manoeuvre*

(a) A vessel not under command shall exhibit:

(i) two all-round red lights in a vertical line where they can best be seen:

(ii) two balls or similar shapes in a vertical line where they can best be seen;

(iii) when making way through the water, in addition to the lights prescribed in this paragraph, sidelights and a sternlight.

(b) A vessel restricted in her ability to manoeuvre, except a vessel engaged in mine clearance operations, shall exhibit:

(i) three all-round lights in a vertical line where they can best be seen. The highest and lowest of these lights shall be red and the middle light shall be white;

(ii) three shapes in a vertical line where they can best be seen. The highest and lowest of these shapes shall be balls and the middle one a diamond;

(iii) when making way through the water, a masthead light or lights, sidelights and a sternlight, in addition to the lights prescribed in sub-paragraph (i);

(iv) When at anchor, in addition to the lights or shapes prescribed in sub-paragraphs (i) and (ii), the light, lights or shape prescribed in Rule 30.

(c) A power-driven vessel engaged in a towing operation such as severely restricts the towing vessel and her tow in their ability to deviate from their course shall, in addition to the lights or shapes prescribed in Rule 24(a), exhibit the lights or shapes prescribed in subparagraphs (b)(i) and (ii) of this Rule.

(d) A vessel engaged in dredging or underwater operations, when restricted in her ability to manoeuvre, shall exhibit the lights and shapes prescribed in subparagraphs (b)(i), (ii) and (iii) of this Rule and shall in addition, when an obstruction exists, exhibit:

(i) two all-round red lights or two balls in a vertical line to indicate the side on which the obstruction exists;

(ii) two all-round green lights or two diamonds in a vertical line to indicate the side on which another vessel may pass;

(iii) when at anchor, the lights or shapes prescribed in this paragraph instead of the lights or shape prescribed in Rule 30.

(e) Whenever the size of a vessel engaged in diving operations makes it impracticable to exhibit all lights and shapes prescribed in paragraph (d) of this Rule, the following shall be exhibited:

(i) three all-round lights in a vertical line where they can best be seen. The highest and lowest of these lights shall be red and the middle light shall be white;

(ii) a rigid replica of the International Code flag 'A' not less than 1 metre in height. Measures shall be taken to ensure its all-round visibility.

(f) A vessel engaged in mine clearance operations shall, in addition to the lights prescribed for a power-driven vessel in Rule 23 or to the lights or shape prescribed for a vessel at anchor in Rule 30 as appropriate, exhibit three all-round green lights or three balls. One of these lights or shapes shall be exhibited near the foremast head and one at each end of the fore yard. These lights or shapes indicate that it is dangerous for another vessel to approach within 1,000 metres of the mine clearance vessel.

(g) Vessels of less than 12 metres in length, except those engaged in diving operations, shall not be required to exhibit the lights and shapes prescribed in this Rule.

(h) The signals prescribed in this Rule are not signals of vessels in distress and requiring assistance. Such signals are contained in Annex IV to these Regulations.

Rule 28   *Vessels constrained by their Draught*

A vessel constrained by her draught may, in addition to the lights prescribed for power-driven vessels in Rule 23, exhibit where they can best be seen three all-round red lights in a vertical line, or a cylinder.

Rule 29   *Pilot Vessels*

(a) A vessel engaged on pilotage duty shall exhibit:

(i) at or near the masthead, two all-round lights in a vertical line, the upper being white and the lower red;

(ii) when underway, in addition, sidelights and a sternlight;

(iii) when at anchor, in addition to the lights prescribed in sub-paragraph (i), the light, lights or shape prescribed in Rule 30 for vessels at anchor.

(b) A pilot vessel when not engaged on pilotage duty shall exhibit the lights or shapes prescribed for a similar vessel of her length.

Rule 30   *Anchored Vessels and Vessels aground*

(a) A vessel at anchor shall exhibit where it can best be seen:

(i) in the fore part, an all-round white light or one ball;

(ii) at or near the stern and at a lower level than the light prescribed in sub-paragraph (i), an all-round white light.

(b) A vessel of less than 50 metres in length may exhibit an all-round white light where it can best be seen instead of the lights prescribed in paragraph (a) of this Rule.

(c) A vessel at anchor may, and a vessel of 100 metres and more in length shall, also use the available working or equivalent lights to illuminate her decks.

(d) A vessel aground shall exhibit the lights prescribed in paragraph (a) or (b) of this Rule and in addition, where they can best be seen:

(i) two all-round red lights in a vertical line;

(ii) three balls in a vertical line.

(e) A vessel of less than 7 metres in length, when at anchor, not in or near a narrow channel, fairway or anchorage, or where other vessels normally navigate, shall not be required to exhibit the lights or shape prescribed in paragraphs (a) and (b) of this Rule.

(f) A vessel of less than 12 metres in length, when aground, shall not be required to exhibit the lights or shapes prescribed in subparagraphs (d)(i) and (ii) of this Rule.

Rule 31   *Seaplanes*

Where it is impracticable for a seaplane to exhibit lights and shapes of the characteristics or in the positions prescribed in the Rules of this Part she shall exhibit lights and shapes as closely similar in characteristics and position as is possible.

PART D — SOUND AND LIGHT SIGNALS

NOTE
The rules are clear and explicit and, from the yachtsman's point of view the most important aspects are, firstly to have the most effective fog signal that can be used on board and secondly to carry a supply of white flares or a Very pistol with white cartridges. At night or in fog it is important and reassuring to make one's presence known in a close quarters situation.

A point to note in Sound Signals is Rule 34 — 3 short blasts — "I am operating astern propulsion". In the case of a large vessel she may carry her way for an appreciable time after putting the engines astern. This can appear confusing and should not be overlooked.

Rule 32 *Definitions*

(a) The word "whistle" means any sound signalling appliance capable of producing the prescribed blasts and which complies with the specifications in Annex III to these Regulations.

(b) The term "short blast" means a blast of about one second's duration.

(c) The term "prolonged blast" means a blast of from four to six seconds' duration.

Rule 33 *Equipment for Sound Signals*

(a) A vessel of 12 metres or more in length shall be provided with a whistle and a bell and a vessel of 100 metres or more in length shall, in addition, be provided with a gong, the tone and sound of which cannot be confused with that of the bell. The whistle, bell and gong shall comply with the specifications in Annex III to these Regulations. The bell or gong or both may be replaced by other equipment having the same respective sound characteristics, provided that manual sounding of the prescribed signals shall always be possible.

(b) A vessel of less than 12 metres in length shall not be obliged to carry the sound signalling appliances prescribed in paragraph (a) of this Rule but if she does not, she shall be provided with some other means of making an efficient sound signal.

Rule 34 *Manoeuvring and Warning Signals*

(a) When vessels are in sight of one another, a power-driven vessel underway, when manoeuvring as authorised or required by these Rules, shall indicate that manoeuvre by the following signals on her whistle:

   —one short blast to mean "I am altering my course to starboard";

   —two short blasts to mean "I am altering my course to port";

   —three short blasts to mean "I am operating astern propulsion".

(b) Any vessel may supplement the whistle signals prescribed in paragraph (a) of this Rule by light signals, repeated as appropriate, whilst the manoeuvre is being carried out:

   (i) these light signals shall have the following significance:

      —one flash to mean "I am altering my course to starboard";

      —two flashes to mean "I am altering my course to port";

      —three flashes to mean "I am operating astern propulsion";

(ii) the duration of each flash shall be about one second, the interval between flashes shall be about one second, and the interval between successive signals shall be not less than ten seconds;

(iii) the light used for this signal shall, if fitted, be an all-round white light, visible at a minimum range of 5 miles, and shall comply with the provisions of Annex I to these Regulations.

(c) When in sight of one another in a narrow channel or fairway:

(i) a vessel intending to overtake another shall in compliance with Rule 9(e)(i) indicate her intention by the following signals on her whistle:

—two prolonged blasts followed by one short blast to mean ''I intend to overtake you on your starboard side'';

—two prolonged blasts followed by two short blasts to mean ''I intend to overtake you on your port side'';

(ii) the vessel about to be overtaken when acting in accordance with Rule 9(e)(i) shall indicate her agreement by the following signal on her whistle:

—one prolonged, one short, one prolonged and one short blast, in that order.

(d) When vessels in sight of one another are approaching each other and from any cause either vessel fails to understand the intentions or actions of the other, or is in doubt whether sufficient action is being taken by the other to avoid collision, the vessel in doubt shall immediately indicate such doubt by giving at least five short and rapid blasts on the whistle. Such signal may be supplemented by a light signal of at least five short and rapid flashes.

(e) A vessel nearing a bend or an area of a channel or fairway where other vessels may be obscured by an intervening obstruction shall sound one prolonged blast. Such signal shall be answered with a prolonged blast by any approaching vessel that may be within hearing around the bend or behind the intervening obstruction.

(f) If whistles are fitted on a vessel at a distance apart of more than 100 metres, one whistle only shall be used for giving manoeuvring and warning signals.

Rule 35   *Sound Signals in restricted Visibility*

In or near an area of restricted visibility, whether by day or night, the signals prescribed in this Rule shall be used as follows:

(a) A power-driven vessel making way through the water shall sound at intervals of not more than 2 minutes one prolonged blast.

(b) A power-driven vessel underway but stopped and making no way through the water shall sound at intervals of not more than 2 minutes two prolonged blasts in succession with an interval of about 2 seconds between them.

(c) A vessel not under command, a vessel restricted in her ability to manoeuvre, a vessel constrained by her draught, a sailing vessel, a vessel engaged in fishing and a vessel engaged in towing or pushing another vessel shall, instead of the signals prescribed in paragraphs (a) or (b) of this Rule, sound at intervals of not more than 2 minutes three blasts in succession, namely one prolonged followed by two short blasts.

(d) A vessel engaged in fishing, when at anchor, and a vessel restricted in her ability to manoeuvre when carrying out her work at anchor, shall instead of the signals prescribed in paragraph (g) of this Rule sound the signal prescribed in paragraph (c) of this Rule.

(e) A vessel towed or if more than one vessel is towed the last vessel of the tow, if manned, shall at intervals of not more than 2 minutes sound four blasts in succession, namely one prolonged followed by three short blasts. When practicable, this signal shall be made immediately after the signal made by the towing vessel.

(f) When a pushing vessel and a vessel being pushed ahead are rigidly connected in a composite unit they shall be regarded as a power-driven vessel and shall give the signals prescribed in paragraphs (a) or (b) of this Rule.

(g) A vessel at anchor shall at intervals of not more than one minute ring the bell rapidly for about 5 seconds. In a vessel of 100 metres or more in length the bell shall be sounded in the forepart of the vessel and immediately after the ringing of the bell the gong shall be sounded rapidly for about 5 seconds in the after part of the vessel. A vessel at anchor may in addition sound three blasts in succession, namely one short, one prolonged and one short blast, to give warning of her position and of the possibility of collision to an approaching vessel.

(h) A vessel aground shall give the bell signal and if required the gong signal prescribed in paragraph (g) of this Rule and shall, in addition, give three separate and distinct strokes on the bell immediately before and after the rapid ringing of the bell. A vessel aground may in addition sound an appropriate whistle signal.

(i) A vessel of less than 12 metres in length shall not be obliged to give the above-mentioned signals but, if she does not, shall make some other efficient sound signal at intervals of not more than 2 minutes.

(j) A pilot vessel when engaged on pilotage duty may in addition to the signals prescribed in paragraphs (a), (b) or (g) of this Rule sound an identity signal consisting of four short blasts.

Rule 36 *Signals to attract Attention*

If necessary to attract the attention of another vessel any vessel may make light or sound signals that cannot be mistaken for any signal authorised elsewhere in these

Rules, or may direct the beam of her searchlight in the direction of the danger, in such a way as not to embarrass any vessel. Any light to attract the attention of another vessel shall be such that it cannot be mistaken for any aid to navigation. For the purpose of this Rule the use of high intensity intermittent or revolving lights, such as strobe lights, shall be avoided.

Rule 37   *Distress Signals*

When a vessel is in distress and requires assistance she shall use or exhibit the signals described in Annex IV to these Regulations.

PART E — EXEMPTIONS

Rule 38   *Exemptions*

Any vessel (or class of vessels) provided that she complies with the requirements of the International Regulations for Preventing Collisions at Sea, 1960, the keel of which is laid or which is at a corresponding stage of construction before the entry into force of these Regulations may be exempted from compliance therewith as follows:

(a) The installation of lights with ranges prescribed in Rule 22, until four years after the date of entry into force of these Regulations.

(b) The installation of lights with colour specifications as prescribed in Section 7 of Annex I to these Regulations, until four years after the date of entry into force of these Regulations.

(c) The repositioning of lights as a result of conversion from Imperial to metric units and rounding off measurement figures, permanent exemption.

(d)   (i) The repositioning of masthead lights on vessels of less than 150 metres in length, resulting from the prescriptions of Section 3(a) of Annex I to these Regulations, permanent exemption.

(ii) The repositioning of masthead lights on vessels of 150 metres or more in length, resulting from the prescriptions of Section 3(a) of Annex I to these Regulations, until nine years after the date of entry into force of these Regulations.

(e) The repositioning of masthead lights resulting from the prescriptions of Section 2(b) of Annex I to these Regulations, until nine years after the date of entry into force of these Regulations.

(f) The repositioning of sidelights resulting from the prescriptions of Sections 2(g) and 3(b) of Annex I to these Regulations, until nine years after the date of entry into force of these Regulations.

(g) The requirements for sound signal appliances prescribed in Annex III to these Regulations, until nine years after the date of entry into force of these Regulations.

(h) The repositioning of all-round lights resulting from the prescription of Section 9(b) of Annex I to these Regulations, permanent exemption.

ANNEX I

POSITIONING AND TECHNICAL DETAILS OF LIGHTS AND SHAPES

1. **Definition**

The term "height above the hull" means height above the uppermost continuous deck. This height shall be measured from the position vertically beneath the location of the light.

2. **Vertical positioning and spacing of lights**

(a) On a power-driven vessel of 20 metres or more in length the masthead lights shall be placed as follows:

(i) the forward masthead light, or if only one masthead light is carried, then that light, at a height above the hull of not less than 6 metres, and, if the breadth of the vessel exceeds 6 metres, then at a height above the hull not less than such breadth, so however that the light need not be placed at a greater height above the hull than 12 metres;

(ii) when two masthead lights are carried the after one shall be at least 4.5 metres vertically higher than the forward one.

(b) The vertical separation of masthead lights of power-driven vessels shall be such that in all normal conditions of trim the after light will be seen over and separate from the forward light at a distance of 1,000 metres from the stem when viewed from sea level.

(c) The masthead light of a power-driven vessel of 12 metres but less than 20 metres in length shall be placed at a height above the gunwale of not less then 2.5 metres.

(d) A power-driven vessel of less than 12 metres in length may carry the uppermost light at a height of less than 2.5 metres above the gunwale. When however a masthead light is carried in addition to sidelights and a sternlight or the all-round light prescribed in rule 23(c)(i) is carried in addition to sidelights, then such masthead light or all-round light shall be carried at least 1 metre higher than the sidelights.

(e) One of the two or three masthead lights prescribed for a power-driven vessel when engaged in towing or pushing another vessel shall be placed in the same position as either the forward masthead light or the after masthead light; provided that, if carried on the aftermast, the lowest after masthead light shall be at least 4.5 metres vertically higher than the forward masthead light.

(f)   (i) The masthead light or lights prescribed in Rule 23(a) shall be so placed as to be above and clear of all other lights and obstructions except as described in subparagraph(ii).

(ii) When it is impracticable to carry the all-round lights prescribed by Rule 27(b)(i) or Rule 28 below the masthead lights, they may be carried above the after masthead light(s) or vertically in between the forward masthead light(s) and after masthead light(s), provided that in the latter case the requirement of Section 3(c) of this Annex shall be complied with.

(g) The sidelights of a power-driven vessel shall be placed at a height above the hull not greater than three quarters of that of the forward masthead light. They shall not be so low as to be interfered with by deck lights.

(h) The sidelights, if in a combined lantern and carried on a power-driven vessel of less than 20 metres in length, shall be placed not less than 1 metre below the masthead light.

(i) When the Rules prescribe two or three lights to be carried in a vertical line, they shall be spaced as follows:

(i) on a vessel of 20 metres in length or more such lights shall be spaced not less than 2 metres apart, and the lowest of these lights shall, except where a towing light is required, be placed at a height of not less than 4 metres above the hull;

(ii) on a vessel of less than 20 metres in length such lights shall be spaced not less than 1 metre apart and the lowest of these lights shall, except where a towing light is required, be placed at a height of not less than 2 metres above the gunwale;

(iii) when three lights are carried they shall be equally spaced.

(j) The lower of the two all-round lights prescribed for a vessel when engaged in fishing shall be at a height above the sidelights not less than twice the distance between the two vertical lights.

(k) The forward anchor light prescribed in Rule 30(a)(i), when two are carried, shall not be less than 4.5 metres above the after one. On a vessel of 50 metres or more in length this forward anchor light shall be placed at a height of not less than 6 metres above the hull.

3. **Horizontal position and spacing of lights**

(a) When two masthead lights are prescribed for a power-driven vessel, the horizontal distance between them shall not be less than one half of the length of the vessel but need not be more than 100 metres. The forward light shall be placed not more than one quarter of the length of the vessel from the stem.

(b) On a power-driven vessel of 20 metres or more in length the sidelights shall not be placed in front of the forward masthead lights. They shall be placed at or near the side of the vessel.

(c) When the lights prescribed in Rule 27(b)(i) or Rule 28 are placed vertically between the forward masthead light(s) and the after masthead light(s) these all-round lights shall be placed at a horizontal distance of not less than 2 metres from the fore and aft centreline of the vessel in the athwartship direction.

4. Details of location of direction-indicating lights for fishing vessels, dredgers and vessels engaged in underwater operations

(a) The light indicating the direction of the outlying gear from a vessel engaged in fishing as prescribed in Rule 26(c)(ii) shall be placed at a horizontal distance of not less than 2 metres and not more than 6 metres away from the two all-round red and white lights. This light shall be placed not higher than the all-round white light prescribed in Rule 26(c)(i) and not lower than the sidelights.

(b) The lights and shapes on a vessel engaged in dredging or underwater operations to indicate the obstructed side and/or the side on which it is safe to pass, as prescribed in Rule 27(d)(i) and (ii), shall be placed at the maximum practical horizontal distance, but in no case less than 2 metres, from the lights or shapes prescribed in Rule 27(b)(i) and (ii). In no case shall the upper of these lights or shapes be at a greater height than the lower of the three lights or shapes prescribed in Rule 27(b)(i) and (ii).

5. Screens for sidelights

The sidelights of vessels of 20 metres or more in length shall be fitted with inboard screens painted matt black, and meeting the requirements of Section 9 of this Annex. On vessels of less than 20 metres in length the sidelights, if necessary to meet the requirements of Section 9 of this Annex, shall be fitted with inboard matt black screens. With a combined lantern, using a single vertical filament and a very narrow division between the green and red sections, external screens need not be fitted.

6. Shapes

(a) Shapes shall be black and of the following sizes:

    (i) a ball shall have a diameter of not less than 0.6 metre;

    (ii) a cone shall have a base diameter of not less than 0.6 metre and a height equal to its diameter;

    (iii) a cylinder shall have a diameter of at least 0.6 metre and a height of twice its diameter;

    (iv) a diamond shape shall consist of two cones as defined in (ii) above having a common base.

(b) The vertical distance between shapes shall be at least 1.5 metres.

(c) In a vessel of less than 20 metres in length shapes of lesser dimensions but commensurate with the size of the vessel may be used and the distance apart may be correspondingly reduced.

7. Colour specification of lights

The chromaticity of all navigation lights shall conform to the following standards, which lie within the boundaries of the area of the diagram specified for each colour by the International Commission on Illumination (CIE).

The boundaries of the area for each colour are given by indicating the corner co-ordinates, which are as follows:

(i) *white*

x	0.525	0.525	0.452	0.310	0.310	0.443
y	0.382	0.440	0.440	0.348	0.283	0.382

(ii) *Green*

x	0.028	0.009	0.300	0.203
y	0.385	0.723	0.511	0.356

(iii) *Red*

x	0.680	0.660	0.735	0.721
y	0.320	0.320	0.265	0.259

(iv) *Yellow*

x	0.612	0.618	0.575	0.575
y	0.382	0.382	0.425	0.406

8. Intensity of lights

(a) The minimum luminous intensity of lights shall be calculated by using the formula:

$$I = 3.43 \times 10^6 \times T \times D^2 \times K^{-D}$$

where

    I   is luminous intensity in candelas under service conditions,

    T   is threshold factor 2×10^{-7} lux,

    D   is range of visibility (luminous range) of the light in nautical miles,

    K   is atmospheric transmissivity.

    For prescribed lights the value of K shall be 0.8, corresponding to a meteorological visibility of approximately 13 nautical miles.

(b) A selection of figures derived from the formula is given in the following table:

Range of visibility (luminous range) of light in nautical miles D	Luminous intensity of light in candelas for K = 0.8 I
1	0.9
2	4.3
3	12
4	27
5	52
6	94

NOTE: The maximum luminous intensity of navigation lights should be limited to avoid undue glare. This shall not be achieved by a variable control of the luminous intensity.

9. Horizontal sectors

(a) (i) In the forward direction, sidelights as fitted on the vessel shall show the minimum required intensities. The intensities shall decrease to reach practical cut-off between 1 degree and 3 degrees outside the prescribed sectors.

(ii) For sternlights and masthead lights and at 22.5 degrees abaft the beam for sidelights, the minimum required intensities shall be maintained over the arc of the horizon up to 5 degrees within the limits of the sectors prescribed in Rule 21. From 5 degrees within the prescribed sectors the intensity may decrease by 50 per cent up to the prescribed limits; it shall decrease steadily to reach practical cut-off at not more than 5 degrees outside the prescribed sectors.

(b) All-round lights shall be so located as not to be obscured by masts, topmasts or structures within angular sectors of more than 6 degrees, except anchor lights prescribed in Rule 30, which need not be placed at an impracticable height above the hull.

10. Vertical sectors

(a) The vertical sectors of electric lights as fitted, with the exception of lights on sailing vessels underway shall ensure that:

(i) at least the required minimum intensity is maintained at all angles from 5 degrees above to 5 degrees below the horizontal;

(ii) at least 60 per cent of the required minimum intensity is maintained from 7.5 degrees above to 7.5 degrees below the horizontal.

(b) In the case of sailing vessels underway the vertical sectors of electric lights as fitted shall ensure that:

(i) at least the required minimum intensity is maintained at all angles from 5 degrees above to 5 degrees below the horizontal;

(ii) at least 50 per cent of the required minimum intensity is maintained from 25 degrees above to 25 degrees below the horizontal.

(c) In the case of lights other than electric these specifications shall be met as closely as possible.

11. Intensity of non-electric lights

Non-electric lights shall so far as practicable comply with the minimum intensities, as specified in the Table given in Section 8 of this Annex.

12. Manoeuvring light

Notwithstanding the provisions of paragraph 2(f) of this Annex the manoeuvring light described in Rule 34(b) shall be placed in the same fore and aft vertical plane as the masthead light or lights and, where practicable, at a minimum height of 2 metres vertically above the forward masthead light, provided that it shall be carried not less than 2 metres vertically above or below the after masthead light. On a vessel where only one masthead light is carried the manoeuvring light, if fitted, shall be carried where it can best be seen, not less than 2 metres vertically apart from the masthead light.

13. Approval

The construction of lights and shapes and the installation of lights on board the vessel shall be to the satisfaction of the appropriate authority of the State whose flag the vessel is entitled to fly.

ANNEX II
ADDITIONAL SIGNALS FOR FISHING VESSELS
FISHING IN CLOSE PROXIMITY

1. General

The lights mentioned herein shall, if exhibited in pursuance of Rule 26(d), be placed where they can best be seen. They shall be at least 0.9 metre apart but at a lower level than lights prescribed in Rule 26(b)(i) and (c)(i). The lights shall be visible all round the horizon at a distance of at least 1 mile but at a lesser distance than the lights prescribed by these Rules for fishing vessels.

2. Signals for trawlers

(a) Vessels when engaged in trawling, whether using demersal or pelagic gear, may exhibit:

(i)   when shooting their nets: two white lights in a vertical line;

(ii)   when hauling their nets: one white light over one red light in a vertical line;

(iii) when the net has come fast upon an obstruction: two red lights in a vertical line.

(b) Each vessel engaged in pair trawling may exhibit:

(i)   by night, a searchlight directed forward and in the direction of the other vessel of the pair;

(ii)   when shooting or hauling their nets or when their nets have come fast upon an obstruction, the lights prescribed in 2(a) above.

3. Signals for purse seiners

Vessels engaged in fishing with purse seine gear may exhibit two yellow lights in a vertical line. These lights shall flash alternately every second and with equal light and occultation duration. These lights may be exhibited only when the vessel is hampered by its fishing gear.

ANNEX III

TECHNICAL DETAILS OF SOUND SIGNAL APPLIANCES

1. Whistles

(a) *Frequencies and range of audibility*

The fundamental frequency of the signal shall lie within the range 70-700 Hz.

The range of audibility of the signal from a whistle shall be determined by those frequencies, which may include the fundamental and/or one or more higher frequencies, which lie within the range 180-700 Hz (±1 per cent) and which provide the sound pressure levels specified in paragraph 1(c) below.

(b) *Limits of fundamental frequencies*

To ensure a wide variety of whistle characteristics, the fundamental frequency of a whistle shall be between the following limits:

(i) 70-200 Hz, for a vessel 200 metres or more in length;

(ii) 130-350 Hz, for a vessel 75 metres but less than 200 metres in length;

(iii) 250-700 Hz, for a vessel less than 75 metres in length.

(c) *Sound signal intensity and range of audibility*

A whistle fitted in a vessel shall provide, in the direction of maximum intensity of the whistle and at a distance of 1 metre from it, a sound pressure level in at least one $\frac{1}{3}$rd-octave band within the range of frequencies 180-700 Hz (±1 per cent) of not less than the appropriate figure given in the table below.

Length of vessel in metres	$\frac{1}{3}$rd-octave band level at 1 metre in dB referred to 2×10^{-5} N/m^2	Audibility range in nautical miles
200 or more	143	2
75 but less than 200	138	1.5
20 but less than 75	130	1
Less than 20	120	0.5

The range of audibility in the table above is for information and is approximately the range at which a whistle may be heard on its forward axis with 90 per cent probability in conditions of still air on board a vessel having average background noise level at the listening posts (taken to be 68 dB in the octave band centred on 250 Hz and 63 dB in the octave band centred on 500 Hz).

In practice the range at which a whistle may be heard is extremely variable and depends critically on weather conditions; the values given can be regarded as typical but under conditions of strong wind or high ambient noise level at the listening post the range may be much reduced.

(d) *Directional properties*
The sound pressure level of a directional whistle shall be not more than 4 dB below the prescribed sound pressure level on the axis at any direction in the horizontal plane within ± 45 degrees of the axis. The sound pressure level at any other direction in the horizontal plane shall be not more than 10 dB below the prescribed sound pressure level on the axis, so that the range in any direction will be at least half the range on the forward axis. The sound pressure level shall be measured in that $\frac{1}{3}$rd-octave band which determines the audibility range.

(e) *Positioning of whistles*
When a directional whistle is to be used as the only whistle on a vessel, it shall be installed with its maximum intensity directed straight ahead.

A whistle shall be placed as high as practicable on a vessel, in order to reduce interception of the emitted sound by obstructions and also to minimise hearing damage risk to personnel. The sound pressure level of the vessel's own signal at listening posts shall not exceed 110 dB (A) and so far as practicable should not exceed 100 dB (A).

(f) *Fitting of more than one whistle*
If whistles are fitted at a distance apart of more than 100 metres, it shall be so arranged that they are not sounded simultaneously.

(g) *Combined whistle systems*
If due to the presence of obstructions the sound field of a single whistle or of one of the whistles referred to in paragraph 1(f) above is likely to have a zone of greatly reduced signal level, it is recommended that a combined whistle system be fitted so as to overcome this reduction. For the purposes of the Rules a combined whistle system is to be regarded as a single whistle. The whistles of a combined system shall be located at a distance apart of not more than 100 metres and arranged to be sounded simultaneously. The frequency of any one whistle shall differ from those of the others by at least 10 Hz.

2. Bell or gong

(a) *Intensity of signal*
A bell or gong, or other device having similar sound characteristics shall produce a sound pressure level of not less than 110 dB at a distance of 1 metre from it.

(b) *Construction*

Bells and gongs shall be made of corrosion-resistant material and designed to give a clear tone. The diameter of the mouth of the bell shall be not less than 300 mm for vessels of 20 metres or more in length, and shall be not less than 200 mm for vessels of 12 metres or more but of less than 20 metres in length. Where practicable, a power-driven bell striker is recommended to ensure constant force but manual operation shall be possible. The mass of the striker shall be not less than 3 per cent of the mass of the bell.

3. Approval

The construction of sound signal appliances, their performance and their installation on board the vessel shall be to the satisfaction of the appropriate authority of the State whose flag the vessel is entitled to fly.

ANNEX IV

DISTRESS SIGNALS

1. The following signals, used or exhibited either together or separately, indicate distress and need of assistance:

(a) a gun or other explosive signal fired at intervals of about a minute;
(b) continuous sounding with any fog-signalling apparatus;
(c) rockets or shells, throwing red stars fired one at a time at short intervals;
(d) a signal made by radiotelegraphy or by other signalling method consisting of the group · · · − − − · · · (SOS) in the Morse Code;
(e) a signal sent by radiotelephony consisting of the spoken word "Mayday";
(f) the International Code Signal of distress indicated by N.C.;
(g) a signal consisting of a square flag having above or below it a ball or anything resembling a ball;
(h) flames on the vessel (as from a burning tar barrel, oil barrel, etc.);
(i) a rocket parachute flare or a hand flare showing a red light;
(j) a smoke signal giving off orange-coloured smoke;
(k) slowly and repeatedly raising and lowering arms outstretched to each side;
(l) the radiotelegraph alarm signal;
(m) the radiotelephone alarm signal;
(n) signals transmitted by emergency position-indicating radio beacons.
(o) approved signals transmitted by radio communication systems.

2. The use or exhibition of any of the foregoing signals except for the purpose of indicating distress and need of assistance and the use of other signals which may be confused with any of the above signals is prohibited.

3. Attention is drawn to the relevant sections of the International Code of Signals, the Merchant Ship Search and Rescue Manual and the following signals:
(a) a piece of orange-coloured canvas with either a black square and circle or other appropriate symbol (for identification from the air);

(b) a dye marker.

Navigable Distances

9

Home Waters — Ushant to Gibraltar

DISTANCES IN HOME WATERS
IN NAUTICAL MILES

The distances given between the following principal ports are by the usual commercial routes. In some cases it may be necessary to add distances together as follows:
What is the distance from Glasgow to Rosslare?

Glasgow to Greenock (p. 9:6)	21	miles
Greenock to Dun Laoghaire (p. 9:6)	166	"
Dun Laoghaire to Rosslare (p. 9:5)	68	"
Total......	255	miles

ABERDEEN to

	Miles.
Antwerp	465
Ardrossan	485
Arendal	372
Belfast	464
Blyth	128
Boston	282
Bremerhaven	436
Burghead	91
Cardiff	740
Christeansand	355
Christiansund	479
Cromarty	110
Cuxhaven	428
Dover	415
Dundee	61
Dunkirk	438
Emden	399
Flushing	415
Fredrikshaven	439
Gravesend	408
Grimsby	249
Hamburg	480
Hartlepool	153
Harwich	360
Helgoland	387
Hook of Holland	374
Hull	260
Inverness	121
Kirkwall (Orkneys)	130
Leith	85
Lerwick (Shetlands)	186
Middlesbrough	161
Montrose	32
The Naze of Norway	303
Narvik	869
Ostende	415
Oslo	488
Rosyth	93
Scapa	125
Sheerness	398
Sunderland	138
Stonehaven	14
Stromness (Orkneys)	127
Thorshaven (Faeroes)	328
Texel (The)	342
Tyne (The) (Ent.)	131
Whitby	185
Wick	101
Wilhelmshaven	420
Yarmouth (Gt.)	308
Ymuiden	363

BELFAST to

	Miles
Berehaven	328
Brest	416
Bristol (Avonmouth)	311
Campbeltown	53
Cardiff	297
Douglas	79
Dun Laoghaire	102
Fishguard	172
Galway	314
Greenock	90
Holyhead	102
Lamlash	60
Liverpool	137
Lundy Is.	246
Milford Haven	215
Queenstown	256
Rosslare	169
Rothesay	79
Sligo	186
Stornoway	236
Waterford	200

BEREHAVEN to

Belfast	328
Brest	304
Bristol (Avonmouth)	288
Campeltown	362
Cardiff	272
Cobh	82
Douglas	294
Dun Laoghaire	233
Fishguard	204
Galway	148
Greenock	390
Holyhead	251
Inishteraght	52
Inverary	410
Lamlash	363
Liverpool	315
Longships	188
Lundy Is.	211
Milford Haven	195
Portree	446
Rosslare	164

BEREHAVEN to

	Miles
Rothesay	384
Shannon River (Tarbet Roads)	116
Sligo	243
Stornoway	458
Waterford	132

BLYTH to

Aalesund	518
Aberdeen	128
Bergen	404
Boston	162
Bremerhaven	370
Cromarty	235
Cuxhaven	366
Dover	290
Dundee	102
Dunkirk	306
Ekersind	327
Emden	330
Flushing	302
Gravesend	297
Grimsby	125
Hartlepool	30
Harwich	246
Helgoland	331
Hook of Holland	279
Hull	141
Hungesund	350
Kirkwall	247
Leith	95
Lerwick	302
Middlesbrough	38
Montrose	105
Naze, The (Norway)	329
Ostende	286
Peterhead	145
Rosyth	105
Scapa	239
Sheerness	280
Stavanger	349
Sunderland	15
Texel (The)	255
Tyne (The) (Ent.)	8
Wick	218
Wilhelmshaven	360
Yarmouth (Gt.)	190
Ymuiden	270

BOSTON (Lincs.) to
Miles.
Aberdeen	282
Bergen	484
Blyth	162
Bremerhaven	315
Cromarty	381
Cuxhaven	310
Dover	178
Dundee	261
Dunkirk	194
Emden	262
Flushing	181
Gravesend	180
Grimsby	57
Hartlepool	134
Harwich	131
Helgoland	283
Hook of Holland	165
Hull	70
Hungesund	429
Kirkwall	404
Leith	258
Lerwick	442
Middlesbrough	142
Montrose	268
Naze, The (Norway)	380
Ostende	176
Peterhead	296
Rosyth	267
Scapa	394
Sheerness	165
Stavanger	425
Sunderland	150
Texel (The)	171
Tyne (The) (Entrance)	154
Wick	368
Yarmouth (Gt.)	78
Ymuiden	168

BREMERHAVEN to
Aberdeen	436
Bergen	454
Blyth	370
Boston	315
Bremen	35
Cromarty	516
Cuxhaven	63
Dover	338
Dundee	444
Dunkirk	316
Ekersund	313
Emden	138
Flushing	307
Gravesend	356
Grimsby	324
Hartlepool	362
Harwich	312
Helgoland	51
Hook of Holland	239
Hull	338
Hungesund	384
Kirkwall	510
Leith	446
Lerwick	509
Middlesbrough	362
Montrose	432

BREMERHAVEN to
Miles.
Naze (The) (Norway)	280
Ostende	286
Peterhead	434
Rosyth	453
Scapa	513
Sheerness	346
Stavanger	374
Sunderland	368
Texel (The)	182
Tyne (The) (Entrance)	370
Wick	493
Wilhelmshaven	62
Yarmouth (Gt.)	275
Ymuiden	210

BRISTOL (Avonmouth) to
Ardrossan	363
Barrow	285
Barry	22
Belfast	311
Berehaven	288
Brest	276
Campbeltown	347
Cardiff	18
Cherbourg	322
Cobh	216
Dartmouth	258
Dublin	225
Dun Laoghaire	220
Douglas	274
Falmouth	198
Fishguard	156
Fort William	440
Galway	416
Greenock	378
Havre	395
Holyhead	228
Inishteraght	329
Inverary	398
Ilfracombe	58
Lamlash	347
Limerick	421
Liverpool	290
Loch Alsh (Balmacara)	478
Loch Broom (Ullapool)	540
Loch Nevis	465
Loch Ryan (Stranraer)	328
Longships	154
Lough Foyle (Moville)	374
Lough Swilly	406
Lundy Is.	83
Milford	99
Newport	10
Portland	288
Port Talbot	60
Rosslare	167
St. Malmo	330
Swansea	55
St. Nazaire	416

BRISTOL (Avonmouth) to
Miles.
Shannon River (Tarbert Roads)	389
Sligo	482
Troon	358
Waterford	176

CAMPBELTOWN to
Belfast	53
Berehaven	362
Brest	448
Bristol (Avonmouth)	347
Cardiff	332
Cobh	289
Douglas	106
Dun Laoghaire	136
Fastnet Rock	339
Fishguard	209
Fort William	125
Galway	302
Greenock	53
Holyhead	134
Inishteraght	330
Inishtrahull	71
Inverary	55
Lamlash	23
Liverpool	166
Loch Alsh (Balmacara)	166
Loch Broom (Ullapool)	228
Loch Nevis	151
Loch Ryan (Stranraer)	34
Longships	326
Lough Foyle (Moville)	66
Lough Swilly	98
Lundy Island	379
Milford Haven	249
Rosslare	205
Rothesay	43
St. Nazaire	568
Shannon River (Tarbert Roads)	325
Sligo	173
Tobermory	115
Waterford	237

CARDIFF to
Avonmouth	18
Barry	9
Bristol	26
Belfast	297
Berehaven	272
Brest	260
Campbeltown	332
Cobh	205
Dublin	201
Douglas	254
Dun Laoghaire	204
Fastnet Rock	248
Fishguard	130
Fort William	425
Galway	405
Greenock	362

CARDIFF to

	Miles.
Glasgow	402
Holyhead	210
Inishteraght	313
Inverary	380
Lamlash	330
Liverpool	272
Loch Alsh (Balmacara)	460
Loch Broom (Ullapool)	523
Loch Nevis	451
Loch Ryan (Stranraer)	310
Longships	136
Lough Foyle (Moville)	358
Lough Swilly	391
Lundy Is.	67
Milford Haven	84
Newport	10
Plymouth	215
Port Talbot	38
Rosslare	145
Rothesay	350
St. Nazaire	400
Shannon River (Tarbert Roads)	378
Sligo	467
Stornoway	516
Sharpness	36
Swansea	40
Tobermory	412
Waterford	160

COBH (Eire) to

Ardrossan	316
Barrow	260
Belfast	256
Berehaven	82
Boulogne	435
Brest	267
Bristol (Avonmouth)	216
Campbeltown	289
Cardiff	205
Cherbourg	305
Douglas	220
Dieppe	405
Dublin	165
Dun Laoghaire	159
Falmouth	197
Fishguard	128
Fort William	381
Galway	225
Greenock	316
Havre	379
Holyhead	181
Inishteraght	124
Inverary	339
Lamlash	289
Limerick	231
Liverpool	240
Loch Alsh (Balmacara)	419
Loch Broom (Ullapool)	482
Loch Nevis	409
Loch Ryan (Stranraer)	270

COBH (Eire) to

	Miles.
Longships	140
Lough Foyle (Moville)	316
Lough Swilly	348
Lundy Is.	144
Milford Haven	145
Rosslare	91
Rothesay	309
St. Nazaire	399
Shannon River (Tarbert Roads)	189
Sligo	314
Stornoway	474
Swansea	182
Tobermory	371
Waterford	60

DARTMOUTH to

Alderney (Braye)	64
Boulogne	200
Brest	149
Calais	215
Cherbourg	85
Dieppe	182
Dover	199
Dunkirk	230
Falmouth	65
Folkestone	194
Havre	151
Longships	98
Newhaven	139
Penzance	89
Plymouth	36
Portland	51
Portsmouth	105
St. Helier	96
St. Malo	120
St. Mary's	117
Southampton	101
Torquay	11

DOUGLAS (Isle of Man) to

Bayonne	690
Belfast	79
Berehaven	294
Brest	378
Bristol (Avonmouth)	274
Campbeltown	106
Cardiff	254
Cobh	220
Dun Laoghaire	77
Fishguard	130
Fort William	200
Galway	371
Greenock	141
Holyhead	50
Inishteraght	330
Inishtrahull	145
Inverary	156
Lamlash	109
Liverpool	68
Loch Alsh (Balmacara)	240
Loch Broom (Ullapool)	302

DOUGLAS (Isle of Man) to

	Miles.
Loch Nevis	227
Loch Ryan (Stranraer)	84
Longships	252
Lough Foyle (Moville)	136
Lough Swilly	168
Lundy Is.	204
Milford Haven	174
Rosslare	132
Rothesay	130
St. Nazaire	513
Sligo	244
Stornoway	295
Tobermory	195
Waterford	168

DOVER to

Aberdeen	406
Antwerp	137
Bergen	590
Blyth	290
Boulogne	26
Brest	316
Bremerhaven	338
Boston	178
Calais	22
Cardiff	435
Cherbourg	150
Cromarty	504
Cuxhaven	334
Dartmouth	199
Dieppe	72
Dunkirk	38
Dundee	390
Dublin	513
Emden	285
Falmouth	258
Flushing	87
Folkestone	6
Gravesend	70
Grimsby	190
Hamburg	391
Havre	120
Hartlepool	264
Harwich	64
Helgoland	309
Hook of Holland	116
Holyhead	504
Hull	203
Kirkwall	526
Leith	390
Lerwick	565
Limerick	609
Longships	297
Middlesbrough	270
Milford Haven	396
Naze (The) (Norway)	454
Newcastle	296
Newhaven	59
Ostende	60
Penzance	281
Peterhead	419
Plymouth	225
Portland	159

DOVER to

	Miles
Portsmouth	104
Rosyth	390
Rotterdam	135
St. Helier	200
St. Malo	229
Sheerness	53
Southampton	120
Swansea	410
Sunderland	280
Texel (The)	168
Tyne (Entrance)	286
Torquay	200
Waterford	430
Wick	491
Wilhelmshaven	330
Yarmouth (Gt.)	98
Ymuiden	158

DUBLIN to

Ardrossan	156
Barrow	139
Barry	200
Belfast	112
Cherbourg	370
Douglas	86
Dun Laoghaire	7
Falmouth	250
Havre	452
Holyhead	63
Londonderry	194
Milford Haven	123
Swansea	172
Wicklow	28
Whitehaven	130

DUNDEE to

Aberdeen	61
Bergen	360
Blyth	102
Boston	261
Bremerhaven	444
Cromarty	172
Cuxhaven	433
Dover	390
Dunkirk	410
Emden	406
Flushing	406
Gravesend	395
Grimsby	228
Hartlepool	130
Harwich	344
Helgoland	390
Hook of Holland	369
Hull	240
Kirkwall	188
Leith	50
Lerwick	240
Middlesbrough	138
Naze (The) (Norway)	343
Ostende	390
Peterhead	85
Rosyth	60
Scapa	183
Sheerness	378
Sunderland	116
Texel (The)	338

DUNDEE to

	Miles.
Tyne (Entrance)	112
Wick	158
Wilhelmshaven	430
Yarmouth (Gt.)	295
Ymuiden	361

DUN LAOGHAIRE (Eire) to

Bayonne	643
Belfast	102
Berehaven	233
Brest	321
Bristol (Avonmouth)	220
Campbeltown	136
Cardiff	204
Cobh	159
Douglas	77
Fishguard	89
Fort William	228
Galway (S. about)	365
Galway (N. about)	397
Greenock	166
Holyhead	56
Inishteraght	270
Inishtrahull	177
Inverary	184
Lamlash	136
Liverpool	113
Loch Alsh (Balmacara)	267
Loch Broom (Ullapool)	326
Loch Nevis	250
Loch Ryan (Stranraer)	114
Longships	199
Lough Foyle (Moville)	160
Lough Swilly	193
Lundy Is.	151
Milford Haven	122
Rosslare	68
Rothesay	155
St. Nazaire	460
Shannon River (Tarbert Roads)	334
Sligo	271
Stornoway	317
Tobermory	216
Waterford	107

FALMOUTH to

Boulogne	257
Brest	124
Calais	269
Cherbourg	137
Dartmouth	65
Dieppe	230
Dover	258
Dunkirk	291
Folkestone	254
Havre	200
Longships	40
Milford Haven	140
Newhaven	201
Penzance	33
Plymouth	38
Portland	112

FALMOUTH to

	Miles.
Portsmouth	165
St. Helier	131
St. Malmo	149
Scilly Is. (St. Mary's)	60
Southampton	160
Torquay	73

FOLKESTONE to

Boulogne	26
Brest	312
Calais	25
Cherbourg	138
Dartmouth	194
Dieppe	68
Dover	6
Dunkirk	43
Falmouth	254
Havre	110
Longships	285
Newhaven	53
Penzance	275
Plymouth	224
Portland	151
Portsmouth	101
St. Helier	195
St. Malo	224
Scilly Is. (St. Mary's)	300
Southampton	117
Torquay	194

GRAVESEND to

Aberdeen	408
Bergen	594
Blyth	297
Boston	180
Bremerhaven	356
Cromarty	513
Dover	70
Dundee	395
Dunkerque	91
Emden	300
Flushing	128
Grimsby	197
Hartlepool	271
Harwich	65
Helgoland	328
Hook of Holland	149
Hull	209
Hungesund	540
Kirkwall	536
Leith	390
Lerwick	566
Middlesbrough	274
Naze (The) (Norway)	469
Ostende	99
Peterhead	423
Rosyth	402
Sheerness	22
Sunderland	287
Texel (The)	187
Tyne (Entrance)	293
Wick	497
Wilhelmshaven	347
Yarmouth (Gt.)	102
Ymuiden	174

GREENOCK to

	Miles
Ardrossan	27
Barrow	159
Barry	372
Bayonne	794
Belfast	90
Berehaven	390
Brest	480
Bristol (Avonmouth)	378
Campbeltown	53
Cardiff	362
Cobh	316
Douglas	141
Dublin	173
Dun Laoghaire	166
Fishguard	240
Fort William	166
Galway	344
Glasgow	21
Holyhead	166
Inishteraght	374
Inishtrahull	118
Inverness	209
Inverary	62
Lamlash	31
Liverpool	200
Limerick	441
Londonderry	128
Loch Alsh (Balmacara)	206
Loch Broom (Ullapool)	268
Loch Nevis	198
Loch Ryan (Stranraer)	65
Longships	353
Lough Foyle (Moville)	110
Lough Swilly	144
Lundy Is.	305
Milford Haven	275
Port Patrick	93
Rothesay	14
Shannon River (Tarbert Roads)	370
Sligo	218
Stornoway	263
Stranraer	63
Tobermory	160
Troon	34
Waterford	268
Whitehaven	145

For Distances from Glasgow add 21 miles to Distances from Greenock.

GRIMSBY to

Aberdeen	249
Bergen	454
Blyth	125
Boston	57
Bremerhaven	324
Cromarty	353
Cuxhaven	320
Dover	190
Dundee	228
Dunkirk	209

GRIMSBY to

	Miles.
Emden	271
Flushing	206
Gravesend	197
Hartlepool	101
Harwich	149
Helgoland	287
Hook of Holland	180
Hull	13
Hungesund	401
Kirkwall	370
Leith	228
Lerwick	412
Middlesbrough	104
Naze (The) (Norway)	382
Ostende	191
Peterhead	264
Rosyth	235
Sheerness	184
Sunderland	116
Texel (The)	176
Tyne (Entrance)	121
Wick	337
Wilhelmshaven	312
Yarmouth (Gt.)	96
Ymuiden	182

HARTLEPOOL to

Aberdeen	165
Antwerp	330
Bergen	402
Belfast	622
Blyth	30
Boston	134
Bremerhaven	362
Cuxhaven	356
Dover	264
Dundee	130
Dunkirk	280
Emden	310
Flushing	280
Gravesend	271
Grimsby	101
Glasgow	663
Harwich	221
Hamburg	409
Helgoland	318
Hook of Holland	248
Hull	115
Hungesund	351
Kirkwall	280
Leith	124
Lerwick	330
Middlesbrough	11
Naze (The) (Norway)	341
Ostende	267
Peterhead	174
Rotterdam	286
Rosyth	135
Sheerness	255
Sunderland	17
Texel (The)	235
Tyne (Entrance)	22

HARTLEPOOL to

	Miles.
Whitby	24
Wick	247
Wilhelmshaven	349
Yarmouth (Gt.)	171
Ymuiden	245

HARWICH to

Aberdeen	360
Antwerp	143
Bergen	542
Blyth	246
Boston	131
Bremerhaven	312
Cuxhaven	310
Dover	64
Dundee	344
Dunkirk	81
Emden	253
Flushing	93
Gravesend	65
Grimsby	149
Hamburg	361
Hartlepool	221
Helgoland	281
Hook of Holland	105
Hull	161
Hungesund	488
Kirkwall	489
Leith	340
Lerwick	516
Middlesbrough	221
Naze (The) (Norway)	414
Ostende	79
Peterhead	376
Rosyth	350
Rotterdam	123
Sheerness	50
Sunderland	234
Texel (The)	141
Tyne (Entrance)	241
Wick	446
Wilhelmshaven	300
Yarmouth (Gt.)	51
Ymuiden	127

HOLYHEAD to

Belfast	102
Berehaven	251
Brest	331
Bristol (Avonmouth)	228
Campbeltown	134
Cardiff	210
Cobh	181
Douglas	50
Dun Laoghaire	56
Fishguard	83
Fort William	227
Greenock	166
Inishteraght	290
Inishtrahull	171
Inverary	184
Lamlash	137

HOLYHEAD to

	Miles.
Liverpool	68
Loch Alsh (Balmacara) ..	267
Loch Broom (Ullapool) ..	230
Loch Nevis	254
Loch Ryan (Stranraer) ..	114
Longships	204
Lough Foyle (Moville) ...	164
Lough Swilly	192
Lundy Is.	159
Milford Haven	127
Rosslare	91
Rothesay	154
Shannon River	
(Tarbert Roads)	356
Sligo	273
Stornoway	318
Tobermory	216
Waterford	124

HULL to

Aberdeen	260
Antwerp	267
Bergen	472
Blyth	141
Boston	70
Bremen	371
Bremerhaven	338
Bruges	209
Cuxhaven	329
Dover	203
Dundee	240
Dunkirk	222
Emden	280
Flushing	217
Fredrickstad	518
Gravesend	209
Grimsby	13
Ghent	250
Hartlepool	115
Harwich	161
Hamburg	386
Harlingen	319
Helgoland	298
Hook of Holland	193
Hungesund	417
Kirkwall	379
Leith	239
Lerwick	425
Middlesbrough	121
Naze (The) (Norway)	374
Newcastle	136
Ostende	200
Peterhead	273
Rosyth	246
Rotterdam	210
Sheerness	195
Shields	135
Sunderland	127
Texel (The)	189
Tyne (Entrance)	135
Whitby	87
Wick	349
Wilhelmshaven	325
Yarmouth (Gt.)	107
Ymuiden	193
Zeebrugge	199

KIRKWALL to

Aberdeen	130
Bergen	277
Blyth	247
Boston	404
Bremerhaven	510
Cromarty	100
Cuxhaven	496
Dover	526
Dundee	188
Dunkirk	543
Emden	499
Flushing	520
Gravesend	536
Grimsby	370
Hartlepool	280
Harwich	489
Helgoland	464
Hook of Holland	490
Hull	379
Hungesund	253
Leith	212
Lerwick	98
Middlesbrough	280
Naze (The) (Norway)	323
Ostende	521
Peterhead	102
Rosyth	220
Sheerness	520
Sunderland	260
Texel (The)	450
Tyne (Entrance)	260
Wick	44
Wilhelmshaven	502
Yarmouth (Gt.)	433
Ymuiden	470

LEITH to

Aberdeen	85
Antwerp	454
Bergen	386
Berwick	52
Blyth	95
Bremerhaven	446
Cromarty	197
Dover	390
Dundee	50
Dunkirk	406
Emden	403
Flushing	404
Grangemouth	19
Gravesend	390
Grimsby	228
Hartlepool	124
Harwich	340
Hamburg	490
Helgoland	400
Hook of Holland	362
Hull	239
Hungesund	344
Inverness	203
Kirkwall	212
Lerwick	269
Middlesbrough	131
Naze (The) (Norway)	356

LEITH to

	Miles.
Newcastle	114
Ostende	386
Peterhead	106
Rotterdam	384
Rosyth	10
Sheerness	377
Sunderland	110
Texel (The)	335
Tyne (Entrance)	103
Wick	181
Wilhelmshaven	431
Yarmouth (Gt.)	293
Ymuiden	354

LIVERPOOL (Landing Stage) to

Ardrossan	176
Barrow	48
Barry	264
Belfast	137
Berehaven	315
Brest	396
Bristol (Avonmouth) ..	290
Campbeltown	166
Cardiff	272
Cobh	240
Douglas	68
Dublin	126
Dunkirk	605
Dundee (N. about)	626
Dun Laoghaire	113
Falmouth	324
Fishguard	148
Fort William	260
Galway (N. about)	440
Galway (S. about)	445
Greenock	200
Holyhead	68
Inishteraght	356
Inishtrahull	200
Inverary	217
Lamlash	172
Limerick	468
Londonderry	215
Loch Alsh (Balmacara) ..	300
Loch Broom (Ullapool) ..	365
Loch Nevis	288
Loch Ryan (Stranraer) ..	146
Longships	269
Lough Foyle (Moville) ...	197
Lough Swilly	229
Lundy Is.	221
Manchester	40
Milford Haven	188
Newcastle (N. about) ...	736
Plymouth	353
Rosslare	154
Rothesay	190
Shields (N. about)	728
Stornoway	342
St. Nazaire	530
Swansea	242
Shannon River	
(N. about)	458

LIVERPOOL (Landing Stage) to

	Miles.
Shannon River (S. about)	414
Sligo	304
Tobermory	251
Waterford	192
Whitehaven	77

LONDON (Tower Bridge) to

Aberdeen	430
Antwerp	196
Ardrossan	721
Barrow	649
Belfast	665
Bergen	604
Blyth	303
Boulogne	97
Bremerhaven	381
Bristol	525
Bruges	143
Calais	96
Cuxhaven	382
Dover	91
Dublin	590
Dundee	416
Dunkirk	116
Flushing	146
Gravesend	23
Hamburg	422
Hartlepool	290
Harwich	87
Hull	228
Leith	431
Middlesbrough	296
Newcastle	316
Ostende	122
Rotterdam	187
Sheerness	45
Yarmouth (Gt.)	132
Zeebrugge	133

MIDDLESBROUGH to

Aberdeen	161
Bergen	416
Blyth	38
Boston	142
Bremerhaven	362
Cromarty	264
Cuxhaven	360
Dover	270
Dundee	138
Dunkirk	290
Emden	310
Flushing	286
Gravesend	274
Grimsby	104
Hartlepool	11
Harwich	221
Helgoland	325
Hook of Holland	256
Hull	120
Hungesund	361
Kirkwall	280

MIDDLESBROUGH to

	Miles.
Leith	130
Lerwick	330
Naze (The) (Norway)	340
Ostende	260
Peterhead	180
Rosyth	143
Sheerness	259
Sunderland	25
Texel (The)	235
Tyne (Entrance)	32
Wick	255
Wilhelmshaven	351
Yarmouth (Gt.)	174
Ymuiden	249

MILFORD HAVEN to

Aberdeen	657
Ardrossan	267
Barrow	207
Barry Dock	86
Bideford	56
Boulogne	396
Brest	242
Calais	410
Cape Finisterre	564
Cherbourg	272
Dieppe	371
Dunkirk	432
Folkestone	391
Galway	337
Gravesend	466
Havre	336
Hull	600
Inishtrahull	286
Leith	736
Limerick	338
Lowestoft	481
Newhaven	341
Newport	101
Ostend	455
Portishead	104
Portsmouth	298
St. Helier	262
Sheerness	449
Sligo	391
Southampton	296
Sunderland	676
Yarmouth Gt.	491

PETERHEAD to

Aberdeen	25
Bergen	286
Blyth	145
Boston	296
Bremerhaven	434
Cromarty	87
Cuxhaven	416
Dover	419
Dundee	85

PETERHEAD to

	Miles
Dunkirk	440
Emden	402
Flushing	418
Gravesend	423
Grimsby	264
Hartlepool	174
Harwich	376
Helgoland	381
Hook of Holland	391
Hull	273
Hungesund	248
Kirkwall	102
Leith	106
Lerwick	155
Middlesbrough	181
Naze (The) (Norway)	286
Ostende	421
Rosyth	117
Sheerness	406
Sunderland	161
Texel (The)	350
Tyne (Entrance)	156
Wick	73
Wilhelmshaven	420
Yarmouth (Gt.)	324
Ymuiden	370

PLYMOUTH to

Ardrossan	488
Barrow	352
Barry	208
Boulogne	227
Brest	138
Calais	242
Cherbourg	107
Dartmouth	36
Dieppe	212
Dover	225
Dunkirk	263
Falmouth	38
Folkestone	224
Galway	404
Greenock	446
Holyhead	280
Havre	175
Longships	72
Limerick	394
Milford Haven	192
Newport	230
Newhaven	165
Penzance	66
Portland	80
Portsmouth	134
St. Malo	135
St. Mary's	94
Southampton	135
Swansea	199
Torquay	41
Waterford	214
Whitehaven	360

SHEERNESS to

	Miles
Aberdeen	398
Bergen	573
Blyth	280
Boston	165
Bremerhaven	346
Chatham	8
Cromarty	490
Cuxhaven	341
Dover	53
Dundee	378
Dunkirk	74
Emden	285
Flushing	108
Gravesend	22
Grimsby	184
Hartlepool	255
Harwich	50
Helgoland	314
Hook of Holland	130
Hull	195
Hungesund	514
Kirkwall	520
Leith	377
Lerwick	550
Middlesbrough	259
Naze (The) (Norway)	455
Ostende	85
Peterhead	406
Rosyth	386
Sunderland	277
Texel (The)	169
Tyne (Entrance)	280
Wick	478
Wilhelmshaven	332
Yarmouth (Gt.)	86
Ymuiden	156

SOUTHAMPTON to

Boulogne	121
Brest	228
Calais	136
Cherbourg	90
Cowes	11
Dartmouth	101
Dieppe	118
Dover	120
Dunkirk	162
Falmouth	160
Folkestone	117
Guernsey	104
Havre	105
Longships	188
Newhaven	62
Penzance	184
Plymouth	135
Portland	55
Portsmouth	18
Ryde	13
St. Malo	166
St. Helier	128
St. Mary's	212
Torquay	97

SUNDERLAND to

	Miles
Aberdeen	138
Antwerp	342
Bergen	400
Blyth	15
Boston (Lincs.)	150
Bremerhaven	368
Cromarty	243
Cuxhaven	360
Dover	280
Dundee	116
Dunkirk	300
Emden	320
Flushing	292
Gravesend	287
Grimsby	116
Hamburg	419
Hartlepool	17
Harwich	234
Helgoland	324
Hook of Holland	260
Hull	127
Hungesund	345
Kirkwall	260
Leith	110
Lerwick	314
London	284
Middlesbrough	25
Naze (The) (Norway)	335
Newcastle	16
Ostende	279
Peterhead	161
Rosyth	120
Sheerness	277
Texel (The)	242
Tyne (Entrance)	6½
Whitby	36
Wick	231
Wilhelmshaven	359
Yarmouth (Gt.)	186
Ymuiden	256

WATERFORD to

Belfast	200
Berehaven	132
Brest	258
Bristol (Avonmouth)	176
Campbeltown	237
Cardiff	160
Cobh	60
Douglas	168
Dun Laoghaire	107
Fishguard	75

WATERFORD to

	Miles.
Fort William	329
Galway	266
Greenock	268
Holyhead	124
Inishteraght	173
Inverary	287
Lamlash	238
Liverpool	192
Loch Alsh (Balmcara)	369
Loch Broom (Ullapool)	430
Loch Nevis	356
Loch Ryan (Stranraer)	216
Longships	132
Lough Foyle (Moville)	264
Lundy Is.	104
Milford Haven	75
Rosslare	39
Rothesay	256
St. Nazaire	394
Shannon River (Tarbert Roads)	238
Stornoway	423
Tobermory	321

YARMOUTH (GREAT) (Norfolk) to

Aberdeen	308
Bergen	494
Blyth	200
Boston (Lincs.)	78
Bremerhaven	275
Cromarty	410
Cuxhaven	273
Dover	98
Dundee	295
Dunkirk	116
Emden	218
Flushing	113
Gravesend	102
Grimsby	96
Hartlepool	171
Harwich	51
Helgoland	244
Hook of Holland	95
Hull	107
Hungesund	437
Kirkwall	433
Leith	293
Lerwick	476
Middlesbrough	174
Naze (The) (Norway)	395
Ostende	100
Peterhead	326
Rosyth	303
Sheerness	86
Sunderland	186
Texel (The)	100
Tyne (Entrance)	192
Wick	402
Wilhelmshaven	206
Ymuiden	114

BRITISH ISLES — WEST COAST

LONGSHIPS LT. TO LUNDY ISLAND

Longships Lt. (Lands End)	Longships Lt. (Lands End)					
Pendeen Lt.	6	Pendeen Lt.				
Godrevy Lt.	18	12	Godrevy Lt.			
St. Agnes Hd.	25½	19½	7½	St. Agnes Hd.		
Trevose Hd.	41½	35½	23½	16	Trevose Hd.	
Hartland Pt.	75½	69½	57½	50	34	Hartland Pt.
Lundy Island	85½	79½	67½	60	44	10	Lundy Island

LUNDY ISLAND TO KISH BANK LT. HO. (Dublin Bay)

Lundy Island	Lundy Island					
St. Gowan Lt. V.	21½	St. Gowan Lt. V.				
Smalls	50½	29	Smalls			
Tuskar Rock	85½	64	35	Tuskar Rock		
Arklow LANBY	114½	93	64	29	Arklow LANBY	
Wicklow Hd.	133½	112	83	48	19	Wicklow Hd.
Kish Bank Lt. Ho. (Dublin Bay)	154½	133	104	69	40	21	Kish Bank Lt. Ho.

KISH BANK LT. HO. (Dublin Bay) TO RATHLIN ISLE

Kish Bank Lt. Ho. (Dublin Bay)	Kish Bank Lt. Ho.					
Skerries Isle	17	Skerries Isle				
Lough Carlingford	40	23	Lough Carlingford			
S. Rock Lt. F.	75	58	35	S. Rock Lt. F.		
Mew Isle (Belfast Lough End)	94	77	54	19	Mew Isle (Belfast Lough End)	
Maidens	110	93	70	35	16	Maidens
Rathlin Isle	136	119	96	61	42	26	Rathlin Isle

ST. GOWAN LT. V. TO BARDSEY ISLE

St. Gowan Lt. V.	St. Gowan Lt. V.					
St. Anns Hd.	12½	St. Anns Hd.				
St. Davids Hd.	28½	16	St. Davids Hd.			
Strumble Head	45	28	12	Strumble Head		
Aberystwyth	83½	71	55	43	Aberystwyth	
Aberdovey	91½	79	63	51	8	Aberdovey
Bardsey Isle	120½	108	92	80	37	29	Bardsey Isle

BARDSEY ISLE TO AILSA CRAIG

Bardsey Isle	Bardsey Isle					
South Stack	34	South Stack				
Chicken Rk. (I.o.M.)	77	43	Chicken Rk. (I.o.M.)			
Mull of Galloway	112	78	35	Mull of Galloway		
Port Patrick	128	94	51	16	Port Patrick	
Corsewall Point	140	106	63	28	12	Corsewall Pt.
Ailsa Craig	155	121	78	43	27	15	Ailsa Craig

LONGSHIPS LT. TO WHITEHAVEN

Longships Lt.	Longships Lt.					
Smalls	99	Smalls				
Bardsey Isle	169	70	Bardsey Isle			
South Stack	203	104	34	South Stack		
Skerries (Anglesey)	211	112	42	8	Skerries (Anglesey)	
Douglas (I.o.M.)	254	155	85	51	43	Douglas (I.o.M.)
Whitehaven	293	194	124	90	82	39	Whitehaven

BRITISH ISLES — EAST COAST

GT. NORE TO CROSS SAND LANBY.

Gt. Nore	Gt. Nore					
Whitaker By.	17	Whitaker By.				
Orfordness Lt. Ho.	45	28	Orfordness Lt. Ho.			
Southwold Lt. Ho.	60	43	15	Southwold Lt. Ho.		
Lowestoft Lt.	69	52	24	9	Lowestoft Lt. Ho.	
Cross Sand By.	80	63	35	20	11	Cross Sand By.

CROSS SAND BY. TO SPURN LT. F.

Cross Sand By.	Cross Sand By.					
Newarp Lt. F.	10	Newarp Lt. F.				
Dudgeon Lt. V.	$47\frac{1}{2}$	$37\frac{1}{2}$	Dudgeon Lt. V.			
Dowsing Lt. V.	71	61	$23\frac{1}{2}$	Dowsing Lt. V.		
Humber Lt. V.	87	77	$39\frac{1}{2}$	16	Humber Lt. V.	
Spurn Lt. F.	93	83	$45\frac{1}{2}$	22	6	Spurn Lt. F.

SPURN LT. F. TO R. TYNE ENTRANCE (N. PIER)

Spurn Lt. F.	Spurn Lt. F.					
Flamborough Hd. Lt. Ho.	35	Flamborough Hd. Lt. Ho.				
Whitby Lt. Ho.	65	30	Whitby Lt. Ho.			
R. Tees Entrance	85	50	20	R. Tees Entrance		
Hartlepool (The Heugh)	89	54	24	4	Hartlepool (The Heugh)	
Sunderland (Roker Pier)	104	69	34	19	15	Sunderland (Roker Pier)
R. Tyne Ent. (N. Pier)	110	75	40	25	21	6	R. Tyne Ent. (N. Pr.)

R. TYNE ENTRANCE (N. PIER) TO BELL ROCK LT. HO.

R. Tyne Ent. (N. Pier)	R. Tyne Entrance (N. Pier)					
Blyth	7	Blyth				
Coquet Lt. Ho.	20	13	Coquet Lt. Ho.			
Farne (Longstone) Lt. Ho.	38	31	18	Farne (Longstone) Lt. Ho.		
St. Abbs Hd. Lt. Ho.	63	56	43	25	St. Abbs Hd. Lt. Ho.	
May Island	85	78	65	47	22	May Island
Bell Rock Lt. Ho.	101	94	81	63	38	16	Bell Rock Lt. Ho.

BELL ROCK LT. HO. TO KINNAIRDS HEAD LT. HO.

Bell Rock Lt. Ho.	Bell Rock Lt. Ho.					
Montrose	16	Montrose				
Tod Hd. Lt. Ho.	29	13	Tod Hd. Lt. Ho.			
Girdle Ness Lt. Ho.	40	30	17	Girdle Ness Lt. Ho.		
Buchan Ness Lt. Ho.	68	52	39	22	Buchan Ness Lt. Ho.	
Rattray Hd. Lt. Ho.	78	62	49	32	10	Rattray Hd. Lt. Ho.
Kinnairds Hd. Lt. Ho.	88	72	59	42	20	10	Kinnairds Hd. Lt. Ho.

KINNAIRDS HD. LT. HO. TO DUNNET HD. LT. HO.

Kinnairds Hd. Lt. Ho.	Kinnairds Hd. Lt. Ho.					
Lossiemouth	42	Lossiemouth				
Tarbot Ness Lt. Ho.	58	16	Tarbot Ness Lt. Ho.			
Clythness Lt. Ho.	92	50	34	Clythness Lt. Ho.		
Wick	102	60	44	10	Wick	
Duncansby Hd. Lt. Ho.	113	71	55	21	11	Duncansby Hd. Lt. Ho.
Dunnet Hd. Lt. Ho.	135	83	67	33	23	12	Dunnet Hd. Lt. Ho.

RIVER THAMES DISTANCES — Nautical Miles

TOWER BRIDGE TO STONE NESS LIGHT HOUSE

Distances in nautical miles. Column numbers correspond to the same place names listed in the rows.

	1	2	3	4	5	6	7	8	9	10	11	12	13	14	15	16	17
1. Tower Bridge																	
2. London Dock—Wapping Ent.	0.5																
3. Tunnel Pier	0.9	0.4															
4. London Dock—Shadwell Ent.	1.3	0.8	0.4														
5. Limehouse Pier	1.9	1.4	1.0	0.6													
6. Commercial Dock Pier	2.4	1.9	1.5	1.1	0.5												
7. Greenwich Pier	3.7	3.2	2.8	2.4	1.8	1.3											
8. Blackwall Tunnel	5.1	4.6	4.2	3.8	3.2	2.7	1.4										
9. East India Dock	5.4	4.9	4.5	4.1	3.5	3.0	1.7	0.3									
10. Royal Victoria Dock	5.8	5.3	4.9	4.5	3.9	3.4	2.1	0.7	0.4								
11. Woolwich Ferry	8.0	7.5	7.1	6.7	6.1	5.6	4.3	2.9	2.6	2.2							
12. Gallion's Point	8.7	8.2	7.8	7.4	6.8	6.3	5.0	3.6	3.3	2.9	0.7						
13. Margaret Ness Lt. Ho.	9.4	8.9	8.5	8.1	7.5	7.0	5.7	4.3	4.0	3.6	1.4	0.7					
14. Crossness Pt. Lt. Ho.	10.9	10.4	10.0	9.6	9.0	8.5	7.2	5.8	5.5	5.1	2.9	2.2	1.5				
15. Ford's Jetty	11.7	11.2	10.8	10.4	9.8	9.3	8.0	6.6	6.3	5.9	3.7	3.0	2.3	0.8			
16. Jenningtree Pt. Lt. Ho.	12.5	12.0	11.6	11.2	10.6	10.1	8.8	7.4	7.1	6.7	4.5	3.8	3.1	1.6	0.8		
17. Coldharbour Pt. Lt. Ho.	13.9	13.4	13.0	12.6	12.0	11.5	10.2	8.8	8.5	8.1	5.9	5.2	4.5	3.0	2.2	1.4	
18. Stone Ness Lt. Ho.	18.0	17.5	17.1	16.7	16.1	15.6	14.3	12.9	12.6	12.2	10.0	9.3	8.6	7.1	6.3	5.5	4.1

STONE NESS LIGHT HOUSE TO GREAT NORE

Distances in nautical miles. Column numbers correspond to the same place names listed in the rows.

	1	2	3	4	5	6	7	8	9	10	11	12	13	14	15
1. Stone Ness Lt. Ho.															
2. Broadness Lt. Ho.	1.5														
3. Lower Northfleet Lt. Ho.	2.9	1.4													
4. Tilbury Ness	3.1	1.6	0.2												
5. Tilbury Pier (North Bank)	4.2	2.7	1.3	1.1											
6. Gravesend Pier (South Bank)	4.2	2.7	1.3	1.1	1.1										
7. Ovens By.	7.0	5.5	4.1	3.9	2.8	2.8									
8. Mucking No. 5 By.	8.5	7.0	5.6	5.4	4.3	4.3	1.5								
9. Mucking No. 1 By.	9.9	8.4	7.0	6.8	5.7	5.7	2.9	1.4							
10. West Blyth By.	10.4	8.9	7.5	7.3	6.2	6.2	3.4	1.9	0.5						
11. Middle Blyth By. (Holehaven)	12.3	10.8	9.4	9.2	8.1	8.1	5.3	3.8	2.4	1.9					
12. Chapman By.	14.8	13.3	11.9	11.7	10.6	10.6	7.8	6.3	4.9	4.4	2.5				
13. Sea Reach No. 6 By.	16.6	15.1	13.7	13.5	12.4	12.4	9.6	8.1	6.7	6.2	4.3	1.8			
14. Sea Reach No. 5 By.	17.6	16.1	14.7	14.5	13.4	13.4	10.6	9.1	7.7	7.2	5.3	2.8	1.0		
15. Sea Reach No. 3 By.	21.6	20.1	18.7	18.5	17.4	17.4	14.6	13.1	11.7	11.2	9.3	6.8	5.0	4.0	
16. Sea Reach No. 1 By.	25.1	23.6	22.2	22.0	20.9	20.9	18.1	16.6	15.2	14.7	12.8	10.3	8.5	7.5	3.5

RIVER HUMBER DISTANCE TABLE — Nautical Miles

	Humber Lt. V.	Spurn Lt. F.	Spurn Head	Grimsby Docks Ent.	Immingham Docks	Thorngumbald Clough	Salt End	Hull (King George Dk. Ent.)	Hull (Alexandra Dk. Ent.)	Hull (Victoria Dk. Ent.)	Hull (Victoria Pier)	Hull (St. Andrews Dk. Ent.)	Barton Hn.	Winteringham Hn.	Brough Hn.	Faxfleet Ness	Blacktoft Pier	Whitgift	Swinefleet
Humber Lt. V.																			
Spurn Lt. F.	5½																		
Spurn Head	10½	5																	
Grimsby Docks Ent.	16½	11	6																
Immingham Docks	21¼	15¾	10¾	4¾															
Thorngumbald Clough	26	20½	15½	9½	4¾														
Salt End	27¼	21¾	16¾	10¾	6	1¼													
Hull (King George Dk. Ent.)	28¼	22¾	17¾	11¾	6¾	2¼	1												
Hull (Alexandra Dk. Ent.)	29	23½	18½	12½	7½	3	1¾	¾											
Hull (Victoria Dk. Ent.)	29¾	24¼	19¼	13¼	8¼	3¾	2½	1¼	¾										
Hull (Victoria Pier)	30¼	24¾	19¾	13¾	8¾	4½	3	2	1¼	½									
Hull (St. Andrews Dk. Ent.)	31½	26	21	15	10	5¾	4¼	3¼	2½	1¾	1¼								
Barton Hn.	34½	29	24	18	13	8¾	7¼	6¼	5½	4¾	4¼	3							
Winteringham Hn.	40½	35	30	24	19	14¾	13¼	12¼	11½	10¾	10¼	9	6						
Brough Hn.	41½	36	31	25	20	15¾	14¼	13¼	12½	11¾	11¼	10	7	1					
*Faxfleet Ness (Trent Falls)	45¾	40¼	35¼	29¼	24¼	20	18½	17½	16¾	16	15½	14¼	11¼	5¼	4¼				
Blacktoft Pier	46½	41	36	30	25	20¾	19¼	18¼	17½	16¾	16¼	15	12	6	5	¾			
Whitgift	48½	43	38	32	27	22¾	21¼	20¼	19½	18¾	18¼	17	14	8	7	2¾	2		
Swinefleet	52	46½	41½	35½	30½	26¼	24¾	23¾	23	22¼	21¾	20½	17½	11¼	10½	6¼	5½	3½	
Goole	55	49½	44½	38½	33½	29¼	27¾	26¾	26	25¼	24¾	23½	20½	14½	13½	9¼	8½	6½	3

*Trent Falls is the junction with River Humber and River Trent.
Trent Falls to Keadby about 10M; to Gainsborough 26½ M; to Newark (about) 55 M.
The distance from Hull to Goole is constantly varying owing to changes in the Channel.
Distance from Goole to York about 35 M; Hull to Goole is about 26 M.

RIVER TYNE DISTANCES

NAUTICAL MILES

DUNSTON STAITHES (East) TO TYNE PIER ENDS

	Dunston Staithes (East)	Redheugh Bridge	High Level Bridge	Ouseburn Entrance	St. Anthony's Point	Wallsend Landing	Jarrow Landing	Tyne Dock Ent.	Albert Edward Dk. Ent.	Ferry L. (N. Sh.)	Lloyd's S.S.	Pier Ends
Dunston Staithes (East)												
Redheugh Bridge	½											
High Level Bridge	1	½										
Ouseburn Entrance	1¾	1	¾									
St. Anthony's Point	3	2½	2	1¼								
Wallsend Landing	5	4	3¾	3	1¾							
Jarrow Landing	6½	6	5½	5	3½	1¾						
Tyne Dock Ent.	7¾	7	6½	6	4¾	3	1					
Albert Edward Dk. Ent.	8¼	7½	7¼	6½	5¼	3½	1¾	½				
Ferry Landing (N. Shields)	8¾	8	7½	7	5½	4	2	1	½			
Lloyd's Sig. Station	9½	8¾	8¼	7½	6¼	4½	2¾	1½	1	¾		
Pier Ends	10¼	9¾	9¼	8½	7¼	5½	3¾	2½	2	1¾	1	

FIRTH OF FORTH DISTANCES

NAUTICAL MILES

NORTH SIDE

	N. Carr Lt. By.	Fifeness	Crail	Anstruther Easter	Elieness	Methil	Kinghorn Ness	Oxcars Lt. Ho.	Forth Bridge
N. Carr Lt. By.									
Fifeness	2								
Crail	4	2							
Anstruther Easter	7¼	5¼	3¼						
Elieness	11¾	9¾	7¾	4½					
Methil	18¼	16¼	14¼	11	6½				
Kinghorn Ness	27¼	25¼	23¼	20	15½	9			
Oxcars Lt. Ho.	31¼	29¼	27¼	24	19½	13	4		
Forth Bridge	35	33	31	27¾	23¼	16¾	7¾	3¾	

SOUTH SIDE (including above Forth Bridge)

	St. Abbs Head	Bass Rock	Fidra	Leith (Entrance)	Inch Keith Lt. Ho.	Oxcars Lt. Ho.	Forth Bridge	Borrowstounness	Grangemouth Dks.
St. Abbs Head									
Bass Rock	20								
Fidra	24¾	4¾							
Leith (Entrance)	38¾	18¾	14						
Inch Keith Lt. Ho.	36½	16½	12	3					
Oxcars Lt. Ho.	41½	21¼	16¾	3¾	4¾				
Forth Bridge	45¼	25	20½	7½	8½	3¾			
Borrowstounness	52¾	32½	28	15	16	11¼	7½		
Grangemouth Docks	55¾	35½	31	18	19	14¼	10½	3	

CALEDONIAN CANAL

This delightful waterway saves a small vessel the more arduous voyage through Pentland Firth, about 350 miles longer. It is just over 50 miles from sea to sea; Lochs Ness, Lochy, and Oich, total 30 miles and the Canal Reaches, 20 miles. The Canal admits vessels of the following dimensions:—Length 45.8 m., Beam 10.6 m., Draught 4.1 m., for through passage, but if restricted to 2.7 m., the length can be 48.8 m. For Corpach Sea Lock and Basin only to 62 × 10.6 × 4.1 m. Maximum Mast Height 36.6 m.

The Canal has 29 locks and runs from Corpach at Fort William (Loch Linnhe), through Banavie, Loch Lochy, Loch Oich, Fort Augustus, Loch Ness, Foyers, and ends at Clacknaharry near **Inverness.** Particulars from Canal Office, Inverness.

RIVER CLYDE, FIRTH OF CLYDE and APPROACHES
DISTANCE TABLES (Nautical Miles)

GLASGOW BRIDGE TO PORT GLASGOW LT.

Glasgow Bridge	Glasgow Bridge						
Finnieston Quay	1	Finnieston Quay					
Govan Ferry	2	1	Govan Ferry				
Whiteinch	3	2	1	Whiteinch			
Renfrew Ferry	4½	3½	2½	1½	Renfrew Ferry		
Dumbarton Castle	11½	10½	9½	8½	7	Dumbarton Castle	
Port Glasgow Lt.	15½	14½	13½	12½	11	4	Port Glasgow Lt.

PORT GLASGOW LT. TO GIRVAN

Port Glasgow Lt.	Port Glasgow Lt.						
Greenock Pier Lt.	3	Greenock Pier Lt.					
Gourock Pier	5	2	Gourock Pier				
Cloch Lt. Ho.	7½	4½	2½	Cloch Lt. Ho.			
Toward Point Lt. Ho.	13½	10½	8½	6	Toward Point Lt. Ho.		
Cumbrae Lt. Ho.	22	19	17	14½	8½	Cumbrae Lt. Ho.	
Girvan	50½	47½	45½	43	37	28½	Girvan

CUMBRAE LT. HO. TO AILSA CRAIG

Cumbrae Lt. Ho.	Cumbrae Lt. Ho.						
Ardrossan Hr.	8	Ardrossan Hr.					
Irvine	13	5	Irvine				
Troon Hr.	17	9	4	Troon Hr.			
Ayr Hr.	22	14	9	5	Ayr Hr.		
Turnberry Pt. Lt.	33	25	20	16	11	Turnberry Pt. Lt.	
Ailsa Craig	43	35	30	26	21	10	Ailsa Craig

CUMBRAE LT. HO. TO STRANRAER

Cumbrae Lt. Ho.	Cumbrae Lt. Ho.						
Lamlash	12½	Lamlash					
Holy Isle Lt.	14½	2	Holy Isle Lt.				
Pladda Is.	20	7½	5½	Pladda Is.			
Ailsa Craig	30½	18	16	10½	Ailsa Craig		
Loch Ryan Entrance	44½	32	30	24½	14	Loch Ryan Entrance	
Stranraer	52	39½	37½	32	21½	7½	Stranraer

PLADDA IS. TO LOUGH FOYLE ENTRANCE

Pladda Is.	Pladda Is.						
Sanda Is.	18	Sanda Is.					
Mull of Kintyre	26	8	Mull of Kintyre				
Rathlin Is. Rue Pt.	40	22	14	Rathlin Is. Rue Pt.			
Bengore Hd.	49	31	23	9	Bengore Hd.		
Portrush	56	38	30	16	7	Portrush	
Lough Foyle Entrance	66	48	40	26	17	10	Lough Foyle Ent.

CUMBRAE LT. HO. TO SANDA IS. — Via BUTE and KILBRENNAN SOUNDS

Cumbrae Lt. Ho.	Cumbrae Lt. Ho.						
Garroch Hd.	4	Garroch Hd.					
Skipness	15	11	Skipness				
Carradale Pt.	26½	22½	11½	Carradale Pt.			
Campbeltown	35½	31½	20½	9	Campbeltown		
Dunnighn Pt.	42	38	27	15½	6½	Dunnighn Pt.	
Sanda Is.	45	41	30	18½	9½	3	Sanda Is.

RIVER MERSEY and LIVERPOOL APPROACHES

DISTANCE TABLES Nautical Miles

CANNING HALF TIDE DOCK TO BAR LANBY.

Canning Half Tide Dock	Canning Half Tide Dock					
Seacombe Landing Stage	$\frac{3}{4}$	Seacombe Landing Stage				
New Brighton Lt.	$2\frac{3}{4}$	2	New Brighton Lt.			
Rock Ferry	$3\frac{1}{4}$	$2\frac{1}{2}$	$\frac{1}{2}$	Rock Ferry		
Crosby Lt. F.	8	$7\frac{1}{4}$	$5\frac{1}{4}$	$4\frac{3}{4}$	Crosby Lt. F.	
Formby Lt. F.	$12\frac{1}{2}$	$11\frac{3}{4}$	$9\frac{3}{4}$	$9\frac{1}{4}$	$4\frac{1}{2}$	Formby Lt. F.
Bar LANBY	$17\frac{1}{4}$	$16\frac{1}{2}$	$14\frac{1}{2}$	14	$9\frac{1}{4}$	$4\frac{3}{4}$	Bar LANBY

BAR LANBY TO LLANDDWYN IS. Through Menai Strait

Bar LANBY	Bar LANBY					
Gt. Ormes Hd.	$22\frac{1}{2}$	Gt. Ormes Hd.				
Puffin Is.	$27\frac{1}{2}$	5	Puffin Is.			
Bangor	$33\frac{1}{2}$	11	6	Bangor		
Port Dinorwic	$38\frac{1}{2}$	16	11	5	Port Dinorwic	
Caernarvon	42	$19\frac{1}{2}$	$14\frac{1}{2}$	$8\frac{1}{2}$	$3\frac{1}{2}$	Caernarvon
Llanddwyn Is.	47	$24\frac{1}{2}$	$19\frac{1}{2}$	$13\frac{1}{2}$	$8\frac{1}{2}$	5	Llanddwyn Is.

BAR LANBY TO BARDSEY IS.

Bar LANBY	Bar LANBY				
Pt. Lynas	$33\frac{1}{2}$	Pt. Lynas			
Skerries	$44\frac{1}{2}$	11	Skerries		
Holyhead	51	$17\frac{1}{2}$	$6\frac{1}{2}$	Holyhead	
S. Stack	56	$22\frac{1}{2}$	$11\frac{1}{2}$	5	S. Stack	
Bardsey	90	$56\frac{1}{2}$	$45\frac{1}{2}$	39	34	Bardsey

CHICKEN ROCK I.o.M. TO CUMBRAE LT. HO.

Chicken Rock I.o.M.	Chicken Rock I.o.M.					
Peel	$12\frac{1}{2}$	Peel				
Mull of Galloway	$38\frac{1}{2}$	26	Mull of Galloway			
Port Patrick	$55\frac{1}{2}$	43	17	Port Patrick		
Corsewall Point	$67\frac{1}{2}$	55	9	12	Corsewall Point	
Ailsa Craig	$82\frac{1}{2}$	70	44	27	15	Ailsa Craig
Cumbrae Lt. Ho.	$112\frac{1}{2}$	100	74	57	45	30	Cumbrae Lt. Ho.

BAR LANBY TO MEW ISLAND Belfast Lough Entrance
N. of Isle of Man

Bar LANBY	Bar LANBY			
Formby Lt. F.	$4\frac{1}{2}$	Formby Lt. F.		
St. Bees Hd.	66	$61\frac{1}{2}$	St. Bees Hd.	
Mull of Galloway	10	$105\frac{1}{2}$	44	Mull of Galloway
Mew Is. Belfast L. Ent.	138	$133\frac{1}{2}$	72	28	Mew Is. Belfast L. Ent.

Isle of Man – Mail Boat Distances

Douglas I.o.M. to Liverpool 70 miles and to Heysham 57 miles

BRISTOL CHANNEL DISTANCES

Nautical Miles

RIVER SEVERN FROM SHARPNESS TO WORCESTER 45 MILES

SHARPNESS TO BREAKSEA LANBY

Sharpness	Sharpness					
Aust Ferry Chepstow	9.4	Aust Ferry				
Avonmouth	16.9	7.5	Avonmouth			
Welsh Hook Buoy	23.2	13.8	6.3	Welsh Hook Buoy		
English & Welsh Grounds Lt F.	28.6	19.2	11.7	5.4	English & Welsh Grounds Lt. F.	
Flat Holm	34.8	25.4	17.9	11.6	6.2	Flat Holm
Breaksea LANBY	41.8	32.4	24.9	18.6	13.2	7.0	Breaksea LANBY

Newport to Breaksea LANBY 24.0		Penarth to Breaksea LANBY 9.4	
Cardiff Dock to Breaksea LANBY 10.5		Barry to Breaksea LANBY 3.6	

BREAKSEA LANBY TO SMALLS LT. HO.

Breaksea LANBY	Breaksea LANBY				
Nash Pt. Lt. Ho. 2 M. S. of	9.8	Nash Point Lt. Ho.			
St. Gowan Lt. V. 2.4 M. S. of	63.6	53.8	39.8	21.2	St. Gowan Lt. V.
Smalls Lt. Ho.	93.1	83.3	69.3	50.7	29.5	Smalls Lt. Ho.

BREAKSEA LANBY TO LUNDY ISLAND

Breaksea LANBY	Breaksea LANBY				
Foreland 2.5 M. N. of	18.8	Foreland			
Ilfracombe 2.7 M. N. of	31.6	12.8	Ilfracombe		
Bull Point 3.6 M. N. of	35.3	16.5	3.7	Bull Point	
Lundy Island	52.3	33.0	20.7	17.0	Lundy Island

LUNDY ISLAND TO LANDS END

Lundy Island	Lundy Island					
Hartland Pt. 12.8 M. W. of	12.8	Hartland Point				
Trevose Hd. 11 M. W. of ..	44.8	32.0	Trevose Head			
Godrevy Is. 8.5 M. W. of ..	65.4	52.6	20.6	Godrevy Island		
Pendeen Lt. 1.4 M. W. of ..	71.4	58.6	26.6	6.0	Pendeen Lt.	
Longships Lt. Ho.	75.9	63.1	31.1	10.5	5.5	Longships Lt. Ho.

CROSS BRISTOL CHANNEL DISTANCES

Avonmouth to Newport	15.8	Swansea to Lundy Island	38.0
Avonmouth to Cardiff	21.8	Swansea to Bideford	42.7
Cardiff to Weston Super Mare	10.0	Bideford to Lundy Island	22.5
Barry to Burnham	16.6	Tenby to Lundy Island	29.0
Barry to Watchet	12.8	Milford Haven to Lundy Island	34.0
Barry to Minehead	13.4	Milford Haven to Bideford	54.0
Porthcawl to Ilfracombe Lt.	22.5	Milford Haven to Padstow	69.0
Swansea to Ilfracombe	24.3	Milford Haven to Longships Lt. Ho.	100.0

ENGLISH CHANNEL DISTANCES — Nautical Miles

From	TB	Gr	GN	TST	SG	Do	Dn	RS	BH	Nh	OL	Po	So	SC	Ne	Sh	PB	Ca	Da	St	Pr	Pl	Ed	Fo	Dod	Fa	Li	Pe	Lo
Tower Bridge																													
Gravesend	23																												
Great Nore	43	19																											
Tongue Sand Towers	60	38	19																										
S. Goodwin Lt. F.	84	63	43	24																									
Dover	91	68	48	29	6																								
Dungeness	109	86	67	48	23	18																							
Royal Sovereign Lt. Tr.	131	108	90	71	47	41	23																						
Beachy Head	140	116	99	78	55	50	31	8																					
Newhaven	148	125	106	86	62	58	40	16	8																				
Owers LANBY	175	152	133	113	89	85	66	44	36	28																			
Portsmouth	194	171	152	133	108	104	86	62	55	48	20																		
Southampton	208	185	166	147	123	120	100	76	69	60	34	14																	
St. Catherine's	199	176	158	137	114	110	91	69	61	53	25	21	34																
Needles	214	191	173	154	130	106	84	74	70	40	21	22	13																
Shambles Lt. By.	238	217	198	179	155	150	131	109	94	66	51	52	40	30															
Portland Bill	242	222	203	182	160	155	114	104	99	71	55	56	46	34	5														
Casquets	256	232	214	196	172	167	149	119	114	85	86	87	67	64	48	48													
Dartmouth	287	264	245	226	202	196	178	126	124	113	101	102	86	79	64	60	44												
Start Pt.	292	269	249	230	206	202	184	159	152	145	118	104	106	93	83	49	48	9											
Prawle Pt.	295	272	252	233	209	205	187	162	155	149	121	108	109	95	86	57	57	12	3										
Plymouth	318	295	276	257	233	210	179	172	169	141	132	133	120	110	80	75	79	36	26	23									
Eddystone	314	292	272	253	230	225	207	183	176	169	141	129	130	117	106	78	79	33	24	22	11								
Fowey	330	307	288	274	246	240	223	199	191	185	157	144	145	132	123	93	88	48	39	36	20	17							
Dodman Pt.	336	313	294	277	229	204	196	191	163	150	151	138	129	99	93	55	46	42	27	21	9								
Falmouth	345	321	304	286	261	255	238	213	206	159	147	138	160	147	138	108	103	63	55	51	38	30	20	11					
Lizard	353	331	311	291	269	264	245	223	215	209	181	167	168	156	146	116	111	71	62	60	48	39	32	22	15				
Penzance	370	347	328	308	285	280	261	239	231	225	197	183	184	172	161	132	127	88	79	76	64	55	48	39	32	16			
Longships	378	355	336	316	293	287	268	247	239	233	205	191	192	180	170	135	134	96	87	84	72	62	56	47	40	25	15		
Bishop Rk.	402	379	360	341	317	311	293	271	257	229	216	215	204	194	164	159	120	111	108	96	87	80	71	64	49	42	31		

Distance	n.m.
Dungeness–St. Vincent	1029
Dungeness–Europa	1220
Dungeness–Ushant	281
Dungeness–C. Finisterre	673
Casquets–Ushant	135
Ushant–C. Finisterre	390
C. Finisterre–St. Vincent	346
St. Vincent–Europa	215

CROSS CHANNEL DISTANCES

Route	n.m.
Penzance–Scilly Isles	35
Weymouth–Guernsey	65
Weymouth–Jersey	82
Southampton–Guernsey	99
Southampton–Jersey	109
Southampton–Havre	108
Southampton–St. Malo	153
Southampton–Caen	110
Newhaven–Dieppe	64
Folkestone–Boulogne	26
Dover–Calais	21
Dover–Ostend	60

USHANT TO EUROPA PT. (GIBRALTAR)

DISTANCE TABLES (Nautical Miles)

DISTANCES TO USHANT

From Gt. Nore	356	From Portland Bill	158
Dover	308	Start Pt.	119
Dungeness	281	Eddystone Lt. Ho.	110
Beachy Head	255	Falmouth	108
Owers LANBY	222	Lizard	98
St. Catherines Lt. Ho.	193	Longships	90
Anvil Pt.	180	Casquets	135

USHANT TO EUROPA PT.

	Ushant	C. Finisterre	C. Roca	St. Vincent	Trafalgar	Tarifa	Europa Pt.
Ushant	Ushant						
C. Finisterre	390	C. Finisterre					
C. Roca	638	248	C. Roca				
St. Vincent	746	356	108	St. Vincent			
Trafalgar	898	508	284	176	Trafalgar		
Tarifa	922	532	308	200	24	Tarifa	
Europa Pt.	937	547	323	215	39	15	Europa Pt.

USHANT TO S. SEBASTIAN

	Ushant	Belle Ile	Ile D'Yeu	I'De Oléron	Arcachon	C. Breton	S. Sebastian
Ushant	Ushant						
Belle Ile	110	Belle Ile					
Ile D'Yeu	160	50	Ile D'Yeu				
I'De Oléron	216	106	56	I'De Oléron			
Arcachon	311	201	151	95	Arcachon		
C. Breton	367	257	207	151	56	C. Breton	
S. Sebastian	393	283	233	177	82	26	S. Sebastian

S. SEBASTIAN TO C. FINISTERRE

	S. Sebastian	Bilbao	Santander	C. De Peñas	Estaca Pt.	Coruña	C. Finisterre
S. Sebastian	S. Sebastian						
Bilbao	50	Bilbao					
Santander	95	45	Santander				
C. De Peñas	195	145	100	C. De Peñas			
Estaca Pt.	277	227	182	82	Estaca Pt.		
Coruña	327	277	232	132	50	Coruña	
C. Finisterre	392	342	297	197	115	65	C. Finisterre

C. FINISTERRE TO ST. VINCENT

	C. Finisterre	C. Silleiro	Rio Douro	Figueira	Berlenga Ile	C. Roca	St. Vincent
C. Finisterre	C. Finisterre						
C. Silleiro	40	C. Silleiro					
Rio Douro	100	60	Rio Douro				
Figueira	160	120	60	Figueira			
Berlenga Ile	210	170	110	50	Berlenga Ile		
C. Roca	248	208	148	88	38	C. Roca	
St. Vincent	356	316	256	196	146	108	St. Vincent

ST. VINCENT TO EUROPA PT.

	St. Vincent	C. Sta. Maria	Rio Guadiana	Cadiz	Trafalgar	Tarifa	Europa Pt.
St. Vincent	St. Vincent						
C. Sta. Maria	55	C. Sta. Maria					
Rio Guadiana	85	30	Rio Guadiana				
Cadiz	150	95	65	Cadiz			
Trafalgar	176	121	91	26	Trafalgar		
Tarifa	200	145	115	50	24	Tarifa	
Europa Pt.	215	160	130	65	39	15	Europa Pt.

DON'T SMUGGLE ANIMALS

Smuggling animals into the British Isles could bring rabies in, putting human and animal lives at risk.

If you're going abroad, don't take pets with you.
If you're coming in, don't bring any animals with you.

The penalties are severe.

If you smuggle an animal into the British Isles, you could face an unlimited fine and up to a year in prison.

The animal itself may have to be destroyed.

This law applies even if the animal is vaccinated against rabies.

All animal imports must be licensed.

BRINGING IT IN IS MADNESS

Ministry of Agriculture,
Fisheries and Food

MAFF

Ship Master's Business

10

TONNAGE

The words "tons" and "tonnage" can have so many meanings that a clear indication of which tonnage is referred to is necessary. The following notes — necessarily brief — are intended as a guide to the general use of the terms.

The word tonnage is handed down from early days when dues were collected on vessels carrying wine in "tuns" (a tun is still the recognised wine measure of 252 gallons). Since this time the words have become to be regarded as a means of indicating the size of vessels, both in terms of capacity and weight.

Registered Tonnage

Basically this is the internal capacity of a vessel; a registered ton originally being 100 cubic feet of internal measurement. Ever since this type of tonnage was introduced, over a century ago, different countries developed slightly different rules for assessing Registered Tonnages. However in 1969 an internationally agreed method for determining these tonnages was devised by the I.M.O. which came into force in July, 1982.

Under this new system every ship will continue to be assigned two tonnages (i.e. a GROSS TONNAGE and a NET TONNAGE).

The GROSS TONNAGE will be a realistic indication of the ship's size. It is based on the moulded volume of the entire ship (hull plus erections and all enclosed places) and there are no deductions, exemptions or special allowances therefrom.

The NET TONNAGE will be a general indication of the ship's earning capacity. This value is derived from a formula based upon the moulded volume of the cargo spaces, the number of passengers carried, the moulded depth of the ship and the summer draught.

These values are to be expressed simply as the GROSS TONNAGE and NET TONNAGE and the word ton should not be used in this connection.

Ships built before July 1982 may use their existing gross and net tonnages until the 17th of July, 1994.

Until there was an internationally agreed loadline, which did not come into being until 1930, these tonnages based on capacity were the only ones available. It is therefore customary for harbour and other dues to be paid on either the Gross or Net tonnage.

Displacement Tonnage

The actual weight of the ship which is equal to the weight of the water displaced by the vessel.

Light displacement refers to the weight of vessel and her equipment and machinery. Loaded displacement refers to the weight of a vessel loaded with her water, cargo, bunkers, stores and passengers.

The Displacement tonnage is found by calculating the volume of water displaced by Simpson's Rules. The weight of the water displaced can then be determined and may be expressed in either tons or tonnes.

Deadweight Tonnage

The difference between the Light and Loaded displacements is the Dead Weight carrying capacity of the vessel in tons or tonnes.

Freight Tonnage

The freight or charge for carrying the cargo may be assessed on weight or volume. If the cargo is more than 40 cu. ft. per ton or 1 cu. metre per tonne the shipper pays on volume, e.g. cargo stowing at 80 cu. ft. to the ton would be considered as 80/40 or 2 freight tons.

THAMES MEASUREMENT TONNAGE

All small vessels and yachts are measured for the purposes of "official" registration and Certificate of Registry.

"Thames Measurement" however is an entirely different tonnage designed as a means of obtaining much more accurate comparisons of size, as between one yacht and another, than is possible by comparing "Registered" tonnages.

The formula is $$\frac{(L-B) \times B \times \frac{1}{2} B}{94}$$

Thus the Length (L) of the yacht (measured at deck level from the fore side of the stem to the after side of the stern post on deck); with the breadth (B) deducted; multiplied by the breadth and again by the half breadth, when divided by 94 gives the Thames Tonnage.

(B = the extreme breadth on deck – excluding rubbing strakes or belting).

NOTE.–The sternpost in a yacht with a transom stern and an inboard rudder is the central upright timber or iron of stern incorporated in the transom.

Although tonnage details of measurement for tonnage are not international the majority of countries use similar methods to the British. Full details as to how the measurements are carried out exactly are contained in the official DoT handbook "Instructions as to the Tonnage Measurement of Ships".

TON CUPS

The word "Ton" when used in relation to Ton Cups is a derivation from a French tonnage rule of 1892.

The One Ton Cup was first presented in 1898 by members of the Cercle de la Voile de Paris for match racing between France and Great Britain of small inshore keel boats rating at One Ton under the 1892 French tonnage rules.

Between 1906 and 1962, after the formation of the International Yacht Racing Union, the One Ton Cup was presented for the International Six Metre Class. In 1965, Jean Peytel, after whom the Three-Quarter Ton Trophy has been named, put the One Ton Cup for competition between yachts of 22 feet R.O.R.C. Rating with no time allowance. In 1968 the Offshore Racing Council was founded and since 1969 the One Ton Cup has, together with other Ton Cups, been presented for world championships of yachts of a specified maximum International Offshore Rule Rating. There are now six Ton Cups, and world championships are held annually. Maximum I.O.R. rating limits are:

		where to be held in	
		1992	1993
TWO TON	35.05 ft	USA (Hawaii)	UK
ONE TON	30.55 ft	Denmark	UK
THREE-QUARTER TON	24.55 ft	UK	Spain (Med.)
HALF TON	22.05 ft	Italy	Spain (Atlantic)
QUARTER TON	18.55 ft	Italy	Spain (Atlantic)
MINI TON	16.55 ft	Italy	Spain (Atlantic)

Further details can be obtained from the Offshore Racing Council, 19 St James's Place, London SW1A 1NN.

Light Dues

These are payments made by ships for the maintenance of the lighthouses, lightvessels and buoys. Certain small vessels in addition to H.M. Ships and vessels in ballast (i.e. neither loading nor unloading and not earning freight) are exempted, but otherwise all vessels pay these on the tonnage of the vessel. The Light Dues Bill and Receipt should always be kept on board with the Certificate of Registry to be shown on demand to any officer of H.M. Customs.

All Yachts if 20 tons or over pay light dues annually (unless they sign an exemption form that the yacht will not be used at sea for the following 12 months).

REGISTRATION OF BRITISH SHIPS

Under the Merchant Shipping Acts 1894/1988 all British-owned merchant vessels or yachts are entitled to be registered, although this is no longer compulsory. It is advisable that vessels going foreign should be registered as most foreign administrations require this.

The Merchant Shipping Act 1983 allows an alternative mode of registration for vessels less than 24 metres (79 ft.) in length. This small ship register offers a much cheaper and simpler option. It provides evidence of nationality of the ship but not title, nor will it enable mortgages to be recorded. See section on Alternative Registration on page 10.5. British subjects resident overseas cannot use the small ships register.

Standard Registration for Commercial Ships:

This is a general guide to the requirements to be observed, by persons or bodies corporate entitled to own a British ship, before registry can be effected:

1. An application for registry to be made by the owner, or authorised agent, to the Registrar of British Ships at the registry port of his choice.

2. Approval of the ship's name by the Department of Transport.

3. Survey of the ship by a Department of Transport Marine Surveyor or other person appointed by organisations authorised for the purpose by that Department.

4. Satisfactory evidence of title to ownership, which for British and foreign built ships consists of the Builder's Certificate and documents of sale prior to registry if the vessel has passed through more than one owner's hands before registry. Provision is made however for waiving of the Builder's Certificate for a foreign built ship if at the time of making his Declaration of Ownership, which all owners are required to complete, the applicant declares that the time and place of building are unknown to him or that the Builder's Certificate cannot be procured, in which case title is founded in the bill of sale by which the vessel was first acquired by a British Subject from the foreigner and any subsequent documents of sale up to that vesting ownership in the applicant for registry. For a British built ship purchased from a foreigner title is founded in the foreign bill of sale and any subsequent documents of sale between the various parties.

When these particulars have been approved a Carving Note is issued to the Owner who instructs the builder to identify the vessel according to the requirement of this form. The official Number must be cut in the vessel's main beam together with the appropriate tonnage and these normally remain constant throughout the life of the vessel. Upon completion the Note is to be signed appropriately and returned to the Registrar. Then on payment of the prescribed fee the Registrar issues the Certificate of Registry which is a most important document as it is the vessel's identification Certificate containing all details already outlined.

When a Master is appointed to the vessel his name is endorsed on the Certificate of Registry by the Registrar and his appointment is not recognised until this is done. When a vessel is issued with SIGNAL LETTERS these are endorsed on her Certificate of Registry and never alter. A vessel's Radio Call signals are now identical with her visual Signal Letters.

The Name of a British Registered vessel will only be approved provided no other vessel of that name is Registered already.

STANDARD REGISTRATION OF PLEASURE CRAFT UNDER 45 FEET IN LENGTH
(From Merchant Shipping Notice No. M1162)

The steps which an owner has to take before a pleasure yacht can be registered are as follows:

1. He must apply in writing to the Registrar of British Ships at the registry port of his choice, for registration of the yacht. The Registrar is normally located in the Custom House. If the owner is a member of a yacht club, he should when applying so inform the Registrar, and give the name of the club.

2. He must produce to the Registrar documents of title which establish ownership. A certificate from the builder of the yacht will meet this requirement if it is in a specified form and provided the yacht has not changed hands since building. Many builders of yachts know the form of certificate required. Should a yacht have been built in stages by different builders, then a separate certificate for each stage will be required. For yachts which have changed hands since building, the Bill of Sale in respect of each transfer of ownership will also be required. Official forms of Bill of Sale can be obtained from any Registrar.

3. He must obtain approval of the pleasure yacht's name from the Registrar General of Shipping and Seamen, Department of Transport, Llantrisant Road, Cardiff CF5 2YS. Approval must be sought on the official form which can be obtained either from any Registrar or direct from the Registrar General of Shipping and Seamen.

4. He must arrange for tonnage measurement, which leads to the issue of a Certificate of Survey (Tonnage Measurement) for the yacht*.

5. He must make a declaration of ownership on the appropriate form obtainable from any Registrar.

6. When the Registrar is satisfied that all these requirements have been met he will issue a Carving and Marking Note to the owner. This Note indicates how the pleasure yacht is to be marked for identification purposes. The owner must arrange for the carving and marking to be performed in accordance with the directions on the Carving and Marking Note and when these have been so completed he should sign the Note and return it to the Registrar.

7. On request, he must pay the registry fee at the Office of H.M. Customs and Excise at which the Registrar is located. This fee is in addition to the fee payable for tonnage measurement and is chargeable at the rate in force when the Registrar is in a position to complete the registration, i.e. when all the above formalities have been satisfactorily completed.

When these requirements have been met the Registrar will register the pleasure yacht and issue the Certificate of Registry.

ALTERNATIVE REGISTRATION FOR SHIPS BELOW 24 METRES IN LENGTH (SSR)

The application should be made in writing to: Royal Yachting Association, RYA House, Romsey Road, Eastleigh, Hampshire SO5 4YA, who will require the owner to complete a simple form stating:

a) The overall length of the ship . . . 'self measurement' will do.

b) The name of the ship . . . there is no requirement for uniqueness of name but 'undesirable' names will not be allowed.

c) The name and address of every owner.

This registration shall be valid for a period of five years or until change of ownership and application for renewal should be made during the period of six months prior to the date of expiration.

The Registration Fee is £10.

---

*As the payment of Harbour and other dues for small craft are not normally based upon cubic capacity (i.e. tonnage), during 1975 the Department of Trade simplified the survey required for pleasure craft under 45 ft length overall, and also authorised YBDSA, Lloyds and RYA measurers to carry out the necessary survey on the Department's behalf.

Most of the information now taken by the measurer is to enable the craft or yacht to be easily identified in cases of theft, etc., however, the gross and nett tonnage (both the same) are still calculated by 0.0045 × length × breadth × internal height, all measured in feet.

OFFICIAL MARKINGS ON SMALL CRAFT

Ships registered under the alternative system for small ships must have clearly painted or affixed to the exterior of the ship the number of its registration preceded by the letters SSR.

Under the Merchant Shipping Act (circular 1968), pleasure yachts, barges (other than sea-going barges), pilot vessels and vessels employed solely in river navigation are exempted from having the name marked on the bows and a scale of feet on the stem and stern post. In addition, power-driven pilot vessels are exempted from having the name marked on the stern, and yachts belonging to specified clubs from having the name and port of registry marked on the stern. Royal National Lifeboats are exempted also.

NOTES ON MOORINGS

In many small harbours and rivers due to the lack of space available moorings are laid for vessels to lie to. The chains of these moorings normally foul the sea bed so that a vessel cannot use her anchor. Under these circumstances yachts are usually allotted space and put down their own moorings or they may be hired from the harbour authority.

It should be realised that these are private property and except of necessity must not be picked up and used "as a right". It is essential that the visiting yachtsman should carefully check that the strength of the mooring is adequate for the size of his vessel. In these circumstances it is customary for no objection to be made to the visiting yachtsman picking up an unattended mooring for a short period — indeed it is a universal custom which smooths the path of the cruising yachtsman. A point sometimes overlooked is that because of convenience an owner uses a "mooring" instead of an anchor, but if in tidal waters he cannot claim absolute right to the stretch of water the moorings occupy; and as he has really "obstructed" anyone else wishing to anchor there he cannot object to someone using his mooring — provided they do not damage it.

It is of course assumed that one man able to handle the vessel will remain on board and vacate the mooring immediately on request on the return of the owner. It is wrong however to pick up a mooring without authority, and leave the vessel there unattended. If an owner returns under such circumstances it is best for him either to pick up the adjacent mooring temporarily or to tie up alongside. He must not let the other vessel adrift as he would be liable for any damage done.

If difficulty exists consult the Harbour Master — if there is one — but otherwise courtesy and tolerance on both sides will make a somewhat complicated problem present no real difficulty.

The position in common law is that if another owner returns and finds an unattended vessel on his mooring he is entitled to remove it to a place of safety **provided** that due care is exercised and no damage results. He is moving another man's property and in the event of damage occurring the burden of proof will be upon him to show that he took all reasonable care to prevent such damage.

Obviously to move another man's vessel in his absence should only be undertaken as a last resort in view of the possible difficulties that could arise.

Merchant Shipping (Life Saving Appliances) Rules

These are most important as a vessel may be detained unless they are complied with. It is important to realise that the Rules apply to all vessels of any size, including fishing vessels, sea going sailing vessels, and Yachts exceeding 15 tons burden. The Merchant Shipping (Life Saving Appliances) Rules do not apply to pleasure craft of less than 13.7 metres (45 feet) and such craft are subject to no equipment regulations.

However, in 1990 The Department of Transport stated that it would regard as a "pleasure craft" only one used exclusively for the private pleasure purposes of the owner. Thus craft used for chartering or training, even if under 13.7 metres in length, may be required to comply with the 1990 Department of Transport Code of Practice.

NOTES ON TOWAGE AND SALVAGE

Towage is the amount payable to a tug or other vessel by agreement for towing a vessel anywhere.

Salvage is quite another matter however and is the act of saving or helping to save vessels or maritime property of any sort when in danger. This is a voluntary act so members of the crew cannot claim salvage for saving their own vessels, neither can passengers, pilots, or crews of tugs on ordinary duty. Salvage is not payable when life is saved only.

Provided no damage is done to the salvor's vessel we hope that Yachtsmen will always help one another without thought of monetary reward; but as any vessel may at any time need assistance through no fault of her own the following notes may be helpful to avoid an excessive claim or at least inform small craft owners of the important features of SALVAGE.

(a) The R.N.L.I. never itself claims salvage or makes a charge. Lifeboatmen, in common with anyone who saves property, are legally entitled to claim salvage for themselves, but they very rarely do so. If they did, they would forfeit any R.N.L.I. reward and be required to pay the costs of the rescue and any damage sustained by the lifeboat, irrespective of whether or not their claim was successful.

(b) If a breakdown occurs under favourable conditions always ask for a tow to a mutually agreed place and arrange the payment for this in advance if possible. Do not accept any tow unless agreement has been made in advance.

(c) Unless in physical difficulties do not allow any of the rescuers' men to board your vessel.

(d) Unless "parish rigged" or "schooner rigged" (means cheaply rigged), never take a salvors' rope — always pass him your rope and also always — if practicable — steer your own vessel, give orders, have your anchor ready and in fact assume command of the whole situation.

(e) Unless actually in distress do not use the recognised distress signals; but ask for assistance by flags, lamp, whistle or radio. If danger does exist, naturally the Distress Signals shown in Section 15 should be used.

(f) If salvage is claimed on the spot, always endeavour to get an agreement (and in writing if possible) or have a witness to what is said.

(g) If this cannot be arranged endeavour to get agreement to have the reward decided according to the provisions of Lloyd's Open Form.

(h) Unless danger exists, no claim can be made for Salvage, nor can claim be made in general, if the attempt is unsuccessful or if it results in the vessel being put into a worse position than she was in originally.

(i) If salvage is performed always endeavour to produce the chart with the vessel's position noted thereon and the Log Book will be excellent evidence; because a "moderate breeze" may quickly become a "whole gale" in a Salvage claim.

(j) If a vessel runs ashore in a narrow creek on a falling tide never accept a "pluck off" from a stranger without saying — with thanks — that you are not in distress and do not need a tow and will run a kedge anchor away until the tide rises. Otherwise what may appear to you to be a friendly gesture may turn out unfortunately to lead to a Salvage claim.

Also if an owner accepts the "loan" of a heavy anchor and rope he must agree a sum for its "loan"; otherwise a Salvage claim may result.

(k) If salvage is inevitable and a bargain unobtainable — never disclose the value of your vessel or the fact of whether you are insured or not.

The laws on Towage and Salvage are governed by legal action (which is always costly) so if, by prior thought, either can be avoided (except by proper arrangements) it is a wise policy to do so. Better be sure than sorry.

CUSTOMS AND EXCISE

OWNERS AND PERSONS RESPONSIBLE FOR PLEASURE CRAFT BASED IN THE UNITED KINGDOM

I   GENERAL

Pleasure craft arriving in, or departing from, the United Kingdom from or to places abroad are subject to the Pleasure Craft (Arrival and Report) Regulations, 1990. In these Regulations a pleasure craft means:

(a)   A vessel which, at the time of its arrival from abroad at a port in the United Kingdom, is being used for private recreational purposes, and of which the total complement, including passengers and crew, does not exceed 12 persons; or

(b)   Any vessel which an officer allows, after application is made to him in person or in writing, to be treated as a pleasure craft for the purposes of these Regulations.

The 'person responsible' means the person on board a pleasure craft under whose command or subject to whose personal direction it has arrived or will depart.

The procedures will apply throughout the United Kingdom and the Isle of Man. Compliance with the system will reduce or eliminate delays in Customs clearance.

II   DEPARTURES

Registration

Pleasure craft based in the United Kingdom which proceed abroad are required to be registered under the Merchant Shipping Acts, 1894 and 1983. Information on registration can be obtained from the Registrar of British Ships at any registry port in the United Kingdom, or the Royal Yachting Association for inclusion on the Small Ships Register. See also section in Almanac on Registration.

Notice of Intended Departure

As far in advance as possible, the proposed date of each intended departure from the United Kingdom must be notified to HM Customs and Excise on Part I of Form C1328, which is a three part, carbon interleaved form. When completed, Part I, which constitutes a Notice of Intended Departure should be delivered to the Customs office nearest to the place of departure **to arrive prior to the expected time of departure.** Customs and Excise post boxes are available for this purpose (See page 10:14). The Notice of Intended Departure is valid for up to 48 hours after the stated time of departure.

Failure to give notice of intended departure may result not only in delay and inconvenience on return to the United Kingdom but may in certain circumstances, lead to prosecution and a fine of up to £400 on summary conviction. The person in charge of the pleasure craft during the voyage must take with him Parts II and III of Form C1328. These will constitute the arrival documents when the return voyage is completed.

Should the voyage be abandoned after despatch or lodgement of Part I of Form C1328, Parts II and III of the form marked 'voyage abandoned' should be sent to the Customs office to which Part I was originally sent.

Shipment of Stores

In general, no restriction is placed upon the shipment of reasonable quantities of foodstuffs, fuel and other stores on which all duties and VAT have been paid. The shipment of duty free stores is normally restricted but subject to certain conditions, such stores may be shipped on yachts departing for a port beyond certain limits, viz: south of Brest or north of the north bank of the Eider. Prior application is necessary and information on the procedure for shipping stores or to reship previously landed surplus duty free stores may be obtained from any Customs office, listed in Appendix 'B' of Customs Public Notice 8.

Prohibited and Restricted goods
Certain goods such as arms, strategic goods (eg computers) and items over fifty years old are prohibited to be exported from the United Kingdom except under cover of a Department of Trade and Industry export licence. The licencing requirements will however be waived where Customs are satisfied that the goods are being shipped solely for use on board the vessel as stores, or, in the case of firearms, where the owner can produce to Customs a valid firearm or shotgun certificate and the ultimate destination is not South Africa or Namibia.

Cargo
Vessels carrying goods other than personal effects and bona fide stores do *not* qualify as pleasure craft. Customs Public Notice No. 69 explains the procedures to be followed by commercial vessels.

Immigration Regulations
The person responsible for the vessel must ensure that the embarkation of any non-EC nationals is notified to the Immigration Officer prior to departure, unless the vessel is proceeding to the Channel Islands, Republic of Ireland or Isle of Man. In most yachting centres, Customs officers perform the duties of Immigration officers.

Passports
The person in charge of a vessel departing for a place outside the Channel Islands, Republic of Ireland or Isle of Man is advised that to take advantage of the quick report procedure on return to the United Kingdom, all persons on board must be EC nationals carrying a valid passport.

Pleasure craft sailed by persons other than owners
Persons hiring, chartering or loaning a vessel which may depart from the United Kingdom on a foreign voyage should ensure that the person responsible for the vessel is aware of the details required in respect of the VAT status of the vessel and that these details have been completed on Part I of Form C1328 prior to departure. Failure to complete this section of the form will inhibit the use of the quick report procedure on the return of the vessel to the United Kingdom and may result in follow-up enquiries in respect of its VAT position.

British-owned pleasure craft visiting France (including vessels towed upon trailers or carried upon vehicles)
The French authorities require all foreign pleasure craft visiting France to carry documents identifying their nationality and ownership. In the case of British-owned vessels this document is the Certificate of British Registry.

The certificate of registration available from the Small Ships Register is an official document issued by Her Majesty's Government through the Royal Yachting Association. It constitutes the evidence of nationality required under international law and will be acceptable to authorities abroad.

Small Craft Licences
The statutory requirement to obtain a Small Craft Licence for chartered or hired pleasure craft going abroad is no longer required.

III ARRIVALS

Warning: A pleasure craft is liable to be searched by Customs officers at any time. The penalties for smuggling are severe and in some instances may include forfeiture of the pleasure craft in addition to monetary penalties or imprisonment for the person(s) concerned.

General

On arrival from abroad (including the Channel Islands and the Republic of Ireland), all pleasure craft are subject to Customs control and the person responsible must make written report on Form C1328. They may also be subject to Public and Animal Health and Immigration requirements when appropriate.

The arrival of an animal brought to the UK from the Channel Islands, Isle of Man and Republic of Ireland is not restricted provided that where an animal originated from outside these countries, it has served its full quarantine.

Persons responsible for pleasure craft who are uncertain of their responsibilities in respect of the health regulations should refer to the Health Departments of the United Kingdom Form Port 38.

PROCEDURE ON ARRIVAL

Summary: All yachts must fly the yellow "Q" flag on arrival in territorial waters and complete the declaration on Form C1328

Yachts with *nothing to declare* must post the declaration in a Customs post-box, lodge it at a Customs office or hand it to a Customs officer. When this has been done all persons on board may go home. No telephone report is required.

Yachtsmen with *goods to declare* must telephone the nearest Customs office immediately on arrival. (Note that Freephone Customs Yachts is discontinued.) They will be told whether or not a Customs officer will board the vessel, and any Customs charges will be assessed over the phone.

All yachts, whether in ports or territorial waters, remain liable to Customs anti-smuggling checks.

Signals

On entering United Kingdom territorial waters, since 1 October 1987 twelve miles from land, a yellow flag (the 'Q' flag in the International Code of Signals), must be flown conspicuously until such time as report has been made. During the hours of darkness the flag should be suitably illuminated.

Failure to fly a yellow flag on entering United Kingdom territorial waters is an offence and may, in certain circumstances, lead to prosecution and a fine of up to £400 on summary conviction. You should also complete Form C1328 at this point. Failure to complete Form C1328 when entering territorial waters is an offence and may, in certain circumstances, lead to prosecution and a fine of up to £400 on summary conviction.

If animal or public health clearance is also required the procedure in paragraph 3 of the Health Departments of the United Kingdom Form Port 38 should be followed.

Procedure for making report

If duty and/or VAT is payable on the vessel or if the vessel:

(a)   has on board any goods on which duty and/or VAT is payable; or

(b)   has had any repairs, modifications or additions whilst abroad; or

(c)   has on board any live animals or birds (including domestic pets); or

(d)   has on board any goods the importation of which is subject to any prohibition or restriction; or

(e)   has on board any person who is not a patrial or if a patrial is not carrying a valid British passport (except in the case of arrivals from the Channel Islands or Republic of Ireland); or

(f)   departed on its last voyage from the United Kingdom more than a year ago; or
(g)   was not on its voyage from the United Kingdom cleared outwards on Part I of Form C1328; or
(h)   has any death or notifiable illness or sickness on board as defined in Form Port 38; then the person responsible must make report of the vessel by ensuring that he telephones the nearest Customs Office. You may use your Radio Telephone for this. The completed form is to be handed to the officer on his arrival.

Procedure for report with nothing to declare
This method may be used when none of the conditions above apply and animal and health clearance is NOT required.
In this case the person responsible is to complete Parts II and III of Form C1328 and, if the vessel is not visited by a Customs officer, deliver Part II to a Customs office (or post it in a Customs post box, see page 10:14) and retain Part III for reference. All persons may then leave the vessel.

Vessel boarded on arrival
If your vessel is boarded on arrival the officer will require the person responsible to complete all reporting formalities immediately. Under these circumstances a separate notification of arrival to the Customs office will *not*, of course, be required

Customs duty on pleasure craft
Vessels of less than 12 metres in length arriving in the United Kingdom from outside the EEC (European Economic Community) are liable to Customs duty but a vessel built in the EEC or a vessel shown to have previously departed from the EEC may be admitted into the United Kingdom free of duty subject to the following conditions:
(a)   the vessel is being imported within three years of the date of its departure from the EEC;
(b)   the vessel is being imported by or at the instance of its previous exporter;
(c)   no refund of Customs duty was obtained on the vessel at export and any Customs duty previously relieved on incorporated parts has been repaid;
(d)   the vessel was not exported in order to be processed or repaired; and
(e)   any repair outside the EEC was unforeseen at the time of exportation and
(i)   merely restored the vessel to its condition at exportation; and
(ii)   did not enhance its export value.
A declaration certifying that these conditions are fulfilled signed by the person responsible may be called for by the Customs officer on arrival if duty free importation is claimed. Particulars of any process, repairs or alterations must be declared on Part II of Form C1328.
If a person resident in the United Kingdom buys a pleasure craft while outside the EEC or if a vessel is brought to this country for the purpose of being sold or for hire, to anyone in the United Kingdom, the vessel must be produced to the Customs officer on arrival (i.e. the full report procedure must be followed) and full details of the transaction (actual or prospective) declared.
British registration of a vessel does not in itself establish title to duty free admission into the United Kingdom.

Liability to Value Added Tax (VAT)
Vessels of less than 15 tons gross and ALL vessels designed or adapted for pleasure or recreation, whatever their tonnage or age, are liable to VAT on importation.
Vessels returning from a voyage abroad are entitled to VAT free reimportation if ALL the following conditions are satisfied. If any of these conditions are not satisfied a full report must be made as described above.
(a)   the importer is not a registered taxable person or, if he is, the vessel is imported otherwise than in the course of his business;
(b)   the vessel was last exported by him or on his behalf;

(c)   the vessel (i) was supplied in or imported into the United Kingdom before its export, and any purchase tax or VAT due on that supply or importation was paid and neither has been, nor will be, refunded; or
    (ii)   is imported by the person who made it;
(d)   the vessel was not zero-rated on export or exported free of purchase tax;
(e)   the vessel has not been subject to any process or repair abroad except as allowed by (e) of previous paragraph; and
(f)   the vessel: (i) was at the time of exportation intended to be re-imported; or
    (ii)   has been returned for repair or refit; or
    (iii)   was in the private use and possession of its present owner in the United Kingdom (excluding the Channel Islands) before it was exported.

Importation of goods

All goods which may be subject to a prohibition or restriction must be declared to a Customs officer. Excess goods are to be declared on the reverse of Parts II and III of Form C1328 by each person on board. Ship's surplus stores remaining are to be declared on the reverse of Parts II and III by the owner or person responsible.

Some goods are subject to duty and/or levies and import licensing control and most goods are liable to VAT. Failure to declare goods may render them liable to forfeiture and the person(s) involved to heavy penalties. No goods must be landed or transferred to another vessel until permission is given by a Customs officer or report formalities have been completed.

Animals and Birds (including domestic pets)

Rabies susceptible mammals including dogs, cats, rabbits, mice, guinea pigs, etc, must only be landed if an agricultural department licence has previously been issued. Live birds must only be landed if an agricultural department licence has previously been issued.

Certain non-domestic species of live animals and birds (including tortoises and most species of parrot) can only be imported or exported with a valid permit " contact the Department of Environment for more information.

There are severe penalties including imprisonment and heavy fines for not meeting this requirement.

Prohibited and Restricted Goods

In order to protect health and the environment, certain goods cannot freely be imported. The main items are as follows:

Flick knives, radio transmitters (walkie-talkies, CB radios, cordless telephones, etc.) not approved for use in the United Kingdom, plants and parts thereof, plant produce including trees and shrubs, potatoes and certain other vegetables, fruit, bulbs and seeds.

If you wish to bring back articles from an overseas voyage and feel that there may be some difficulty at importation, consult a Customs officer before departure. This may save problems later!

Immigration Regulations

All non-EC nationals need the permission of an Immigration officer to enter when they arrive from outside the United Kingdom, the Channel Islands or the Republic of Ireland. The person responsible must ensure that permission is obtained.

Currency Regulations

There is no restriction on the importation of any currency notes, including United Kingdom bank notes.

Personal Duty Free Allowances
Persons arriving in the United Kingdom by pleasure craft are allowed the same personal duty free allowances as those arriving by other means of transport. These allowances, and those for paid crew members, are shown at Appendix A of Customs Notice 8.
Note. Persons under the age of 17 years are NOT allowed duty free allowances of tobacco products or alcoholic drinks.

Notices & Forms
Copies of Customs Notice 8 and Form C1328 can be obtained at most Customs offices. Where copies cannot be obtained locally, enquiries should be addressed to HM Customs & Excise, CDE1, Dorset House, Stamford Street, London SE1 9PS.

IV   OWNERS AND PERSONS RESPONSIBLE FOR PLEASURE CRAFT NOT BASED IN THE UNITED KINGDOM
Slightly different procedures will apply to pleasure craft not based in the United Kingdom and these are explained in Customs Notice 8A. The main differences are that Form C1329 is to be completed instead of C1328. The automatic clearance facility is not available; clearance can only be granted by the Customs officer boarding the vessel.
Further information on points of detail and copies of Public Notice 8A and Form C1329 can be obtained at most Customs offices. Where additional copies or information cannot be obtained locally, enquiries should be addressed to HM Customs & Excise, CDE1, Dorset House, Stamford Street, London SE1 9PS.

HEALTH CLEARANCE — Vessels Arriving from Abroad

This is now dealt with by the Port Health Authority, and full details are set out in Form Port 38 obtainable from the local Port Health Authority or from Department of Health & Social Security, Alexander Fleming House, Elephant & Castle, London SE1 6BY. Basically if there are no indications of infectious disease on board there is no need to obtain health clearance.

INTERNATIONAL CODE OF SIGNALS

ZS or Q	My vessel is 'healthy' and I request free pratique.
* QQ	I require health clearance.
ZU	My maritime Declaration of Health has a positive answer to question(s) . . . (indicated by appropriate number[s]).
ZW	I require Port Medical Officer.
	ZW1 Port Medical Officer will be available at (time indicated).
ZY	You have health clearance.
ZZ	You should proceed to anchorage for health clearance (at place indicated).
	ZZ1 Where is the anchorage for health clearance?
	I have a doctor on board. AL
	Have you a doctor? AM.

* By night, a red light over a white light may be shown by vessels requiring health clearance. These lights should be about 2 m. apart, should be exhibited when within the precincts of a port, and should be visible all round the horizon as nearly as possible.

Health clearance may be given in three ways:
   a) Wholly in plain language.
   b) Partly in above signal code; remainder in plain language.
   c) Wholly in the above signal code.

CUSTOMS POST BOXES IN THE UNITED KINGDOM

Location	Description	Location	Description
RAMSGATE	HARBOUR MARINA	WEYMOUTH	OSTLE COVE
SANDWICH	QUAY	PORTLAND	BOSCOWAN SAILING CENTRE
DOVER	GRANVILLE DOCK		
DOVER	WELLINGTON DOCK	WEST BAY	H M OFFICE
RYE	HARBOUR	LYME REGIS	H M OFFICE
NEWHAVEN	MARINA OFFICE	EXMOUTH	DOCKS
SHOREHAM	CUSTOM HOUSE	TORQUAY	MARINA
SHOREHAM	SUSSEX YACHT CLUB	BRIXHAM	CUSTOM HOUSE
LITTLEHAMPTON	ARUN Y.C.	DARTMOUTH	TOWN QUAY
LITTLEHAMPTON	CUSTOMS OFFICE	DARTMOUTH	DART MARINA
BRIGHTON MARINA	ADMINISTRATION BUILDING	KINGSWEAR	DARTHAVEN
		STARCROSS	CRUISING CLUB
BRIGHTON MARINA	WEST JETTY	SALCOMBE	WHITESTRAND
CHICHESTER	HARBOUR CONSERVANCY OFFICE	NEWTON FERRERS	PUBLIC JETTY
		PLYMOUTH	MAYFLOWER MARINA
CHICHESTER	YACHT BASIN	PLYMOUTH	QUEEN ANNE'S BATTERY
BIRDHAM	POOL	PLYMOUTH	SUTTON MARINA
EMSWORTH	MARINA	PLYMOUTH	CLOVELLY BAY MARINA
NORTHNEY	MARINA	LOOE	H M OFFICE
SPARKES	MARINA	FOWEY	CUSTOM HOUSE
LANGSTONE	MARINA	PAR	DOCK OFFICE
GOSPORT	JSSC	CHARLESTOWN	QUAYSIDE
GOSPORT	CAMPER & NICHOLSON	MEVAGISSEY	HARBOUR
GOSPORT	C S SAILING CLUB	FALMOUTH	MARINA
GOSPORT	HARDWAY SAILING CLUB	FALMOUTH	ROYAL CORNWALL Y C
FAREHAM	SAILING CLUB	FALMOUTH	H M PONTOON
PORTCHESTER	WICOR MARINE	MYLOR	
PORTCHESTER	SAILING CLUB	HELFORD RIVER	
PORT SOLENT	MARINA	PORTHLEVEN	H M OFFICE
COWES	ANCASTER MARINE	PENZANCE	H M OFFICE
EAST COWES	MARINA	NEWLYN	NEW PIER
YARMOUTH	CUSTOMS OFFICE	ST IVES	H M OFFICE
FOLLY	H M OFFICE	ST MARYS IOS	H M OFFICE
BEMBRIDGE	H M OFFICE	TRESCO	NEW GRIMSBY
WARSASH	H M OFFICE	ILFRACOMBE	H M OFFICE
HAMBLE	HAMBLE POINT MARINA	BRISTOL	CITY DOCKS
HAMBLE	COUGAR MARINE	SHARPNESS	CUSTOM HOUSE
HAMBLE	PORT HAMBLE	NEWPORT	ALEXANDRA DOCK
HAMBLE	MERCURY MARINA	CARDIFF	ROATH BASIN
HAMBLE	UNIVERSAL SHIPYARD	SWANSEA	CUSTOM HOUSE
HAMBLE	MOODY'S MARINA	SWANSEA	YACHT HAVEN
SOUTHAMPTON	SHAMROCK QUAY	PEMBROKE DOCK	CUSTOM HOUSE
SOUTHAMPTON	OCEAN VILLAGE	MILFORD HAVEN	NEYLAND MARINA
HYTHE	MARINA	FISHGUARD	CUSTOM HOUSE
BEAULIEU	H M OFFICE	PORTMADOC	
BEAULIEU	GIN'S FARM	PWLLHELI	MARINA
LYMINGTON	H M OFFICE	PWLLHELI	H M OFFICE
LYMINGTON	YACHT HAVEN	ABERSOCH	
LYMINGTON	BERTHON	BARMOUTH	
KEYHAVEN	SAILING CLUB	CAERNARFON	
CHRISTCHURCH	SAILING CLUB	HOLYHEAD	SAILING CLUB
WAREHAM	RIDGE WHARF	LLANDULAS	
POOLE	COBBS QUAY	MOSTYN	
POOLE	YACHT CLUB	SHOTTON	STEELWORKS
POOLE	SALTERNS MARINA	FLEETWOOD	DOCKS
POOLE	R M Y C	BARROW IN FURNESS	CUSTOM HOUSE
WEYMOUTH	CUSTOM HOUSE QUAY	WHITEHAVEN	H M OFFICE
WEYMOUTH	HARBOUR COVE	WORKINGTON	DOCK OFFICE

CUSTOMS POST BOXES IN THE UNITED KINGDOM

MARYPORT	MARINA	FELIXSTOWE	CUSTOM HOUSE
SILLOTH	BOX	LEVINGTON	MARINA OFFICE
LOCH ALINE		IPSWICH	HAVEN HOUSE
CORPACH LOCK		IPSWICH	WHERRY QUAY
MALLAIG		IPSWICH	DOCKHEAD OFFICE
LOCHINVER		IPSWICH	FOX'S MARINA
KYLESTROME		WOOLVERSTONE	MARINA
KINLOCKBERVIE		SHOTLEY	MARINA
SCRABSTER		HARWICH	CUSTOM HOUSE
STROMNESS		WALTON ON THE NAZE	WALTON Y C
LERWICK	CHARLOTTE HOUSE	WALTON ON THE NAZE	TITCHMARSH MARINA
ELGIN	GORDON STREET	BRIGHTLINGSEA	JAMES & STONE
BUCKIE	QUEEN STREET	COLCHESTER	CUSTOM HOUSE
MACDUFF	HARBOUR OFFICE	WESTMERSEA	MERSEA MARINA
FRASERBURGH	SALTOUN CHAMBERS	TOLLESBURY	YACHT HARBOUR
PETERHEAD	ASCO NORTH & SOUTH	MALDON	CUSTOMS OFFICE
ABERDEEN	CUSTOM HOUSE	BRADWELL ON SEA	MARINA OFFICE
MONTROSE	NORTHSIDE & SOUTHSIDE	BURNHAM ON COUCH	CUSTOMS OFFICE
DUNDEE	CUSTOM HOUSE	SHELLHAVEN	REFINERY
KIRKCALDY	CUSTOM HOUSE	TILBURY	CUSTOM HOUSE
GRANTON	H M OFFICE	ST KATHARINE HAVEN	LOCK OFFICE
EYEMOUTH	F M A OFFICE	TEDDINGTON LOCK	LOCK OFFICE
BERWICK	CUSTOM HOUSE	SOUTH DOCK MARINA	LOCK OFFICE
AMBLE	MARINA	DARTFORD	CUSTOMS OFFICE
BLYTHE	CUSTOM HOUSE	GRAVESEND	CUSTOM HOUSE
NORTH SHIELDS	CUSTOM HOUSE		PONTOON
SEAHAM HARBOUR	CUSTOM OFFICE	HOO	MARINA
HARTLEPOOL	CUSTOM HOUSE	STROOD	YACHT CLUB
TEESPORT	CUSTOM HOUSE	ROCHESTER	CRUISING CLUB
WHITBY	CUSTOM HOUSE	ROCHESTER	ELMHAVEN MARINA
WHITBY	ENDEAVOUR WHARF	ROCHESTER	MEDWAY Y C
WHITBY	MARINA	CUXTON	MARINA
SCARBOROUGH	H M OFFICE	CUXTON	AUTOMARINE LTD
BRIDLINGTON	H M OFFICE	GILLINGHAM	MARINA
HULL	CUSTOM HOUSE	SHEERNESS	QUEENBOROUGH
HULL	MARINA	CONYER	MARINA
GOOLE	CUSTOM HOUSE	CONYER	SWALE MARINA
SCUNTHORPE	OSWALD ROAD	HARTY FERRY	NORTH & SOUTH SIDE
GRIMSBY	CUSTOM HOUSE	OARE CREEK	MARINA
BOSTON	CUSTOM HOUSE	FAVERSHAM	HOLLOWSHORE MARINA
WISBECH	PORT MANAGER'S OFFICE		
KING'S LYNN	CUSTOM HOUSE		
WELLS-ON-SEA	H M OFFICE	NORTHERN IRELAND:	
GREAT YARMOUTH	HAVENBRIDGE HOUSE		
LOWESTOFT	RISHTON HOUSE	BANGOR	MARINA OFFICE
LOWESTOFT	RN&S YC	CARRICKFERGUS	MARINA OFFICE
SOUTHWOLD	LIFEBOAT STATION	COLERAINE	SEATONS MARINA
ALDEBURGH	UPSON'S BOATYARD	COLERAINE	COLERAINE MARINA
ORFORD	QUAY	LARNE	CUSTOM HOUSE
RAMSHOLT	QUAY	PORTRUSH	HARBOUR OFFICE
WOODBRIDGE	H M OFFICE	STRANGFORD	FERRY TERMINAL

GENERAL SUMMARY OF ENTRY REQUIREMENTS FOR WESTERN EUROPE

1) Most countries require evidence of ownership and in Spain, France, Malta, Italy and Greece this must be in the form of a document of Registration. However, now the Small Ships Register makes Registration so cheap and easy to obtain this is obviously the most convenient way to cover all eventualities in this area.

2) Some countries, particularly concerning their inland waterways, require that the Skipper has some recognised qualification, if the Skipper does not have a Yachtmaster or Coastal Skipper Certificate, he/she should apply to the RYA for the Helmsmans (Overseas) Certificate of Competence.

3) Prepare crew lists and ensure all crew have a valid Passport, Take the charter contract if one is involved and be prepared to 'declare your intentions' when you arrive. The French authorities interpret the expression 'Private and Pleasure Only' very strictly and even crew members contributing to voyage expenses may make them consider you a commercial craft.

4) Flying the Q flag only seems to be necessary when first entering the UK, Ireland, Belgium and Spain, unless the yacht is carrying dutiable stores, or goods, which it is intended to land.

5) Virtually all countries except France (unless the yacht is carrying dutiable stores, or goods, in excess of the personal allowance limits), require you to report to the Customs at the first port of ca'l in that country. Because of this many countries require your first point of entry to be a port where such facilities exist.

6) The Q flag must be flown when visiting the Channel Islands from anywhere outside the UK, but when returning to the UK from the Channel Islands the usual arrival procedures must be followed.

7) The Italian authorities require all visiting craft (whether by sea or road) to carry third party insurance and to have aboard available for Inspection at all times, a certified translation of the Insurance Certificate.

See RYA booklets 'Foreign Cruising Notes' for further specific details. Available from Royal Yachting Association, RYA House, Romsey Road, Eastleigh, Hants. SO5 4YA. Tel: 0703 629962. Also from Cruising Association, Ivory House, St. Katharine Dock, London E1 9AT. Tel: 071-481 0881.

Conversions

11

Language Conversions

Conversion Tables

FIVE LANGUAGE GLOSSARY

ENGLISH–FRENCH–GERMAN–SPANISH–DUTCH

Compiled by Arthur Somers

TRANSLATIONS ARE GIVEN UNDER THE FOLLOWING HEADINGS

1 PROHIBITIONS

2 TYPES OF VESSEL		12 FUEL, ETC	
3 PARTS OF VESSEL		13 METALS	
4 MASTS AND SPARS		14 LIGHTS	
5 RIGGING		15 SHIPS' PAPERS	
6 SAILS		16 TOOLS	
7 BELOW DECK		17 CHANDLERY	
8 NAVIGATION EQUIPMENT		18 FOOD	
9 ENGINES		19 SHOPS AND PLACES ASHORE	
10 ENGINE ACCESSORIES		20 IN HARBOUR	
11 ELECTRICS		21 FIRST AID	

ENGLISH	FRENCH	GERMAN	SPANISH	DUTCH
1 PROHIBITIONS				
Prohibited area	Zone interdite	Verbotenes gebiet	Zona prohibida	Verboden gebied
Anchoring prohibited	Defense de mouiller	Ankern verboten	Fondeadero prohibido	Verboden ankerplaats
Mooring prohibited	Accostage interdite	Anlegen verboten	Amarradero prohibido	Verboden aan te leggen
2 TYPES OF VESSEL (Private)				
Sloop	Sloop	Slup	Balandra	Sloep
Cutter	Cotre	Kutter	Cúter	Kotter
Ketch	Ketch	Ketsch	Queche	Kits
Yawl	Yawl	Yawl	Yola	Yawl
Schooner	Goélette	Schoner	Goleta	Schoener
Motor sailer	Bateau mixte	Motorsegler	Moto-velero	Motorzeiljacht

ENGLISH	FRENCH	GERMAN	SPANISH	DUTCH
Dinghy	Youyou, prame	Beiboot	Balandro	Jol, bijboot
Launch	Chaloupe	Barkasse	Lancha	Barkas
Motor boat	Bateau a moteur	Motoryacht	Motora, bote a motor	Motorboot
Lifeboat	Bateau, canot de sauvetage	Rettungsboot	Bote salvadidas	Reddingboot
(Commercial)				
Trawler	Chalutier	Fischereifahrzeug	Pesquero	Stoomtreiler
Tanker	Bateau-citerne	Tanker	Petrolero	Tankschip
Merchantman	Navire marchand	Handelsschiff	Buque mercante	Koopvaardijschip
Ferry	Transbordeur, bac	Fähre	Transbordador	Pont, veerboot
Tug	Remorqueur	Schlepper	Remolcador	Sleepboot

3 PARTS OF VESSEL

Stem	Étrave	Vorsteven	Roda	Voorsteven
Stern	Poupe	Heck	Popa	Achtersteven
Forecastle (fo'c's'le)	Gaillard d'avant	Vorschiff, back	Castillo de proa	Vooronder
Fore peak	Pic avant	Vorpiek	Pique de proa	Voorpiek
Cabin	Cabine	Kajute	Camarote	Kajuit
Chain locker	Puits à chaines	Kettenkasten	Caja de cadenas	Kettingbak
Saloon	Salon	Messe	Salón (Cámara)	Salon
Lavatory	Toilette	Toilette	Retrete	W.C.
Galley	Cuisine	Kombuse	Cocina	Kombuis
Chartroom	Salle des cartes	Kartenraum	Caseta de derrota	Kaartenkamer
Bunk	Couchette	Koje	Litera	Kooi
Pipe cot	Cadre	Gasrohrkoje	Catre	Pijkooi
Engine room	Chambre des machines	Maschinenraum	Cámara de máquinas	Motorruim
Locker	Coffre	Schrank	Taquilla	Kastje
Bulkhead	Cloison	Schott	Mamparo	Schot
Hatch	Écoutille	Luk	Escotilla	Luik
Cockpit	Cockpit	Cockpit	Cabina	Kuip
Sail locker	Soute à voiles	Segellast	Panol de velas	Zeilkooi
Freshwater tank	Reservoir d'eau douce	Frischwassertank	Tanque de agua potable	Drinkwatertank
Rudder	Gouvernail	Ruder	Timón	Roer
Propeller	Hélice	Propeller	Hélice	Schroef
Bilges	Cale	Bilge	Sentina	Kim
Keel	Quille	Kiel	Quilla	Kiel
Gunwhale	Plat-bord	Schandeck	Borda, regala	Dolboord
Rubbing strake	Bourrelet de défense	Scheuerleiste	Verduguillo	Berghout
Tiller	Barre	Ruderpinne	Cana	Helmstok
Stanchions	Chandelier	Reelingstütze	Candelero	Scepters
Bilge pump	Pompe de cale	Lenzpumpe	Bombas de achique de sentina	Lenspomp
Pulpit	Balcon avant	Bugkorb	Púlpito	Preekstoel
Pushpit	Balcon arrière	Heckkorb	Púlpito de popa	Hekstoel

4 MASTS AND SPARS

Mast	Mât	Mast	Palo	Mast
Foremast	Mât de misaine	Grossmast	Trinquete	Fokkemast
Mizzen mast	Mât d'artimon	Besanmast	Palo mesana	Bezaans mast
Boom	Bôme	Baum	Botavara	Giek
Bowsprit	Beaupré	Bugspriet	Baupres	Boegspriet
Bumpkin	Bout-dehors	Ausleger, achtern	Pescante amura trinquette	Papegaaistok
Spinnaker boom	Tangon de spi	Spinnakerbaum	Tangon del espinaquer	Nagel-of spinnakerboom
Gaff	Corne	Gaffel	Pico (de vela cangreja)	Gaffel

ENGLISH	FRENCH	GERMAN	SPANISH	DUTCH
Cross trees	Barres de flèche	Salinge	Crucetas	Dwarszaling
Jumper struts	Guignol	Jumpstagstrebe	Contrete	Knikstagen
Truck	Pomme	Topp	Tope (galleta)	Top
Slide	Coulisseau	Rutscher	Corredera	Slede
Roller reefing	Bôme à rouleau	Patentreff	Rizo de catalina	Patentrif
Worm gear	Vis sans fin	Schneckenreff	Husillo	Worm en wormwiel
Solid	Massif	Voll	Macizo	Massief
Hollow	Creux	Hohl	Hueco	Hol
Derrick	Grue	Ladebaum	Pluma de carga	Dirk of Kraanlijn

5 RIGGING
(Standing)

ENGLISH	FRENCH	GERMAN	SPANISH	DUTCH
Forestay	Étai avant, étai de trinquette	Vorstag	Estay de proa	Voorstag
Aft stay	Étai arriere	Preventer	Stay de popa	Achterstag
Shrouds	Haubans	Wanten	Obenques	Want
Stay	Étai	Stag	Estay	Stag
Bob stay	Sous-barbe	Wasserstag	Barbiquejo	Waterstag
Backstay	Galhauban	Achterstag	Brandal	Bakstagen
Guy	Retenue	Achterholer	Retenida (Cabo de retenida viento)	Bulletalie

(Running)

ENGLISH	FRENCH	GERMAN	SPANISH	DUTCH
Halyard	Drisse	Fall	Driza	Val
Foresail halyard	Drisse de misaine	Vorsegelfall	Driza de trinquetilla	Voorzeil val
Throat halyard	Attache de drisse	Klaufall	Driza de boca	Klauwval
Peak halyard	Drisse de pic	Piekfall	Driza de pico	Piekeval
Burgee halyard	Drisse de guidon	Standerfall	Driza de grimpola	Clubstandaardval
Topping lift	Balancine	Dirk	Amantillo	Dirk
Main sheet	Écoute de grand voile	Gross-Schot	Escota mayor	Grootschoot
Foresail sheet	Écoute de Misaine	Vorschot	Trinquetilla (escota de)	Voorzeil of Fokke-schoot
Kicking strap	Hale-bas de bôme	Niederholer	Trapa	Neerhouder
Rope	Cordage	Tauwerk	Cabulleria	Touw
Single block	Poulie simple	Einscheibenblock	Motón de una cajera	Eenschijfsblok
Double block	Poulie double	Zweischeibenblock	Motón de dos cajeras	Tweeschijfsblok
Sheave	Réa	Scheibe	Roldana	Schijf
Shackle	Manille	Schäkel	Grillete	Sluiting
Pin	Goupille	Bolzen	Perno, cabilla	Bout
"D" Shackle	Manille Droite	"U" Schäkel	Grillete en D	Harpsluiting
Snap shackle	Manille rapide	Schnappschäkel	Grillete de escape	Patent sluiting

6 SAILS

ENGLISH	FRENCH	GERMAN	SPANISH	DUTCH
Mainsail	Grand voile	Gross-Segel	Vela mayor	Grootzeil
Foresail	Voile de misaine	Vorsegel	Vela trinquete	Voorzeil
Jib	Foc	Klüver	Foque	Fok
Storm jib	Tourmentin	Sturmklüver	Foque de capa	Stormfok
Trysail	Voile de cape	Trysegel	Vela de cangrejo	Stormzeil
Genoa	Génois	Genua	Foque génova	Genua
Spinnaker	Spinnaker	Spinnaker	Espinaquer (foque balón)	Spinnaker
Topsail	Flèche	Toppsegel	Gavia	Topzeil
Mizzen sail	Artimon	Besan	Mesana	Druil of bezaan
Lugsail	Voile de fortune	Luggersegel	Vela al tercio	Emmerzeil

(Parts of sail)

ENGLISH	FRENCH	GERMAN	SPANISH	DUTCH
Head	Point de drisse	Kopf	Puno de driza	Top
Tack	Point d'amure	Hals	Puno de amura	Hals

ENGLISH	FRENCH	GERMAN	SPANISH	DUTCH
Clew	Point d'écoute	Schothorn	Puno de escota	Schoothoorn
Luff	Guidant	Vorliek	Gratil	Voorlijk
Leech	Chute arrière	Achterliek	Apagapenol	Achterlijk
Foot	Bordure	Unterliek	Pujamen	Onderlijk
Roach	Rond echancrure	Rundung des Achterlieks	Alunamiento	Gilling
Peak	Pic	Piek	Pico	Piek
Throat	Gorge	Klau	Puno de driza	Klauw
Batten pocket	Étui, gaine de latte	Lattentasche	Bolsa del sable	Zeillatzak
Batten	Latte	Latte	Enjaretado	Zeillat
Cringle	Anneau, patte de bouline	Kausch	Garruncho de cabo	Grommer
Seam	Couture	Naht	Costura	Naad
Sailbag	Sac à voile	Segelsack	Saco de vela	Zeilzak

7 BELOW DECK

Toilet	Toilette	Toilette	Retretes	W.C.
Lavatory paper	Papier hygiénique	Toilettenpapier	Papel higiénico	Toilet-papier
Towel	Serviette	Handtuch	Toalla	Handdoek
Soap	Savon	Seife	Jabón	Zeep
Cabin	Cabine	Kajüte	Camarote	Kajuit
Mattress	Matelas	Matratze	Colchón	Matras
Sleeping bag	Sac de couchage	Schlafsack	Saco de dormir	Slaapzak
Sheet	Drap	Bettlaken	Sábana	Laken
Blanket	Couverture	Decke	Manta	Wollen deken
Galley	Cuisine	Kombüse	Cocina	Kombuis
Cooker	Cuisinière	Kocher	Fogón	Kookpan
Frying pan	Poêle à frire	Bratpfanne	Sartén	Braadpan
Saucepan	Casserole	Kochtopf	Cacerola	Steelpan of Stoofpan
Kettle	Bouilloire	Kessel	Caldero	Ketel
Tea pot	Théière	Teekanne	Tetera	Theepot
Coffee pot	Cafetière	Kaffekanne	Cafetera	Koffiepot
Knives	Couteaux	Messer	Cuchillos	Messen
Forks	Fourchettes	Gabel	Tenedores	Vorken
Spoons	Cuillères	Löffel	Cucharas	Lepels
Tin opener	Ouvre-boites	Dosenöffner	Abrelatas	Blikopener
Corkscrew	Tire-bouchon	Korkenzieher	Sacacorchos	Kurketrekker
Matches	Allumettes	Striechhölzer	Cerillas	Lucifers
Washing-up liquid	Détergent	Abwaschmittel	Detergente	Afwasmiddel

8 NAVIGATION EQUIPMENT

Chart table	Table à cartes	Kartentisch	Planero	Kaartentafel
Chart	Carte marine	Seekarte	Carta Náutica	Zeekaart
Parallel ruler	Règles parallèles	Parallel-lineal	Regla de paralelas	Parallel Liniaal
Protractor	Rapporteur	Winkelmesser	Transportador	Gradenboog
Pencil	Crayon	Bleistift	Lápiz	Potlood
Rubber	Gomme	Radiergummi	Goma	Vlakgom
Dividers	Pointes sèches	Kartenzirkel	Compas de puntas	Verdeelpasser
Binoculars	Jumelles	Fernglas	Gemelos	Kijker
Compass	Compas	Kompass	Compás	Kompas
Hand bearing compass	Compas de relèvement	Handpeilkompass	Alidada	Handpeilkompas
Echo sounder	Echosondeur	Echolot	Sondador acústico	Echolood
Radio receiver	Poste récepteur	Empfangsgerät	Receptor de radio	Radio-ontvangtoestel
Direction finding radio	Récepteur goniométrique	Funkpeiler	Radio goniómetro	Radio peil-toestel
Patent log	Loch enregistreur	Patent Log	Corredera de patente	Patent Log
Sextant	Sextant	Sextant	Sextante	Sextant

11:6

REED'S NAUTICAL ALMANAC

ENGLISH	FRENCH	GERMAN	SPANISH	DUTCH
9 ENGINES				
Petrol engine	Moteur à essence	Benzinmotor	Motor de gasolina	Benzinemotor
Diesel engine	Moteur diesel	Dieselmotor	Motor diesel	Dieselmotor
Two stroke	À deuxtemps	Zweitakt	Dos tiempos	Tweetakt
Four stroke	À quatre temps	Viertakt	Cuatro tiempos	Viertakt
Exhaust pipe	Tuyau déchappement	Auspuffrohr	Tubo de escape	Uitlaatpijp
Gear box	Boîte de vitesse	Getriebekasten	Caja de engranajes	Versnellingsbak
Gear lever	Levier des vitesses	Schalthebel	Palanca de cambio	Versnellingshandel
Throttle	Accelérateur	Gashebel	Estrangulador	Manette
Clutch	Embrayage	Kupplung	Embrague	Koppeling
Stern tube	Tube d'étambot, arbre	Stevenrohr	Bocina	Schroefaskoker
Fuel pump	Pompe à combustible	Brennstoffpumpe	Bomba de alimentación	Brandstofpomp
Carburettor	Carburateur	Vergaser	Carburado	Carburateur
Fuel tank	Réservoir de combustible	Brennstofftank	Tanque de combustible	Brandstoftank
10 ENGINE ACCESSORIES				
Cylinder head	Culasse	Zylinderkopf	Culata	Cilinderkop
Jointing compound	Pâte à joint	Dichtungsmasse	Junta de culata	Vloeibare pakking
Nut	Ecrou	Schraubenmutter	Tuerca	Moer
Bolt	Boulon	Bolzen	Perno	Bout
Washer	Rondelle	Unterlegsscheibe	Arandela	Ring
Split pin	Coupille fendue	Splint	Pasador abierto	Splitpen
Asbestos tape	Ruban d'amiante	Asbestband	Cinta de amianto	Asbestband
Copper pipe	Tuyau de cuivre	Kupferrohr	Tubo de cobre	Koperpijp
Plastic pipe	Tuyau de plastique	Plastikrohr	Tubo de plastico	Plastikpijp
11 ELECTRICS				
Voltage	Tension	Spannung	Voltaje	Spanning
Amp	Ampères	Ampere	Amperio	Ampère
Sparking plug	Bougie	Zündkerze	Bujia	Bougie
Dynamo	Dynamo	Lichtmaschine	Dinamo	Dynamo
Magneto	Magnéto	Magnetzündung	Magneto	Magneet
Dynamo belt	Courroie de dynamo	Keilriemen	Correa de dinamo	Dynamoriem
Battery	Accumulateur	Batterie	Bateria	Accu
Contact breaker	Interrupteur	Unterbrecher-kontakt	Disyuntor	Contactonder-breker
Fuse box	Boite à fusibles	Sicherungskasten	Caja de fusibles	Zekeringskast
Switch	Commutateur	Schalter	Interruptor	Schakelaar
Bulb	Ampoule	Glühbirne	Bombilla	Lampje
Copper wire	File de cuivre	Kupferdraht	Cable de cobre	Koperdraad
Distilled water	Eau distillée	Destilliertes Wasser	Agua destilada	Gedistilleerd water
Solder	Soudure	Lötmetall	Soldadura	Soldeer
Fluxite	Flux	Flussmittel	Flux	Smeltmiddel
Insulating tape	Ruban isolant	Isolierband	Cinta aislante	Isolatieband
12 FUEL, ETC.				
Petrol	Essence	Benzin	Gasolina	Benzine
Paraffin	Pétrole lampant	Petroleum	Petroleo	Petroleum
Diesel oil	Gas-oil	Diesel kraftstoff	Gasoil	Dieselolie
T.V.O.	Pétrole carburant	Rohpetroleum	T.V.O. petroleo	Tractor-petroleum
Methylated spirit	Alcool à brûler	Brennspiritus	Alcool desnaturalizado	Spiritus
Lubricating oil	Huile	Schmieröl	Aceite de lubricación	Smeerolie
Two stroke oil	Huile deux temps	Zweitakter Öl	Aceite de motor 2 tiempos	Tweetaktolie
Penetrating oil	Huile penetrante, dégrippant	Rostlösendes Öl	Aceite penetrante	Kruipolie
Grease	Graissé	Schmierfett	Grasa	Vet

ENGLISH	FRENCH	GERMAN	SPANISH	DUTCH
13 METALS				
Galvanised iron	Fer galvanisé	Verzinktes Eisen	Hierro galvanizado	Gegalvaniseerd Ijzer
Stainless steel	Acier inoxydable	Rostfreier Stahl	Acero inoxidable	Roestvrij staal
Iron	Fer	Eisen	Hierro	Ijzer
Steel	Acier	Stahl	Acero	Staal
Copper	Cuivre	Kupfer	Cobre	Koper
Brass	Laiton	Messing	Latón	Messing
Aluminium	Aluminium	Aluminium	Aluminio	Aluminium
Bronze	Bronze	Bronze	Bronce	Brons
14 LIGHTS				
Navigation lights	Feux de bord	Positionslampen	Luces de navegación	Navigatie lichten
Mast head light	Feu de téte de mât	Topplicht	Luz del tope de proa	Toplicht
Spreader light	Feu de barre de flèche	Salinglampe	Luz de verga	Zalinglicht
Port light	Feu de babord	Backbordlampe	Luz de babor	Bakboordlicht
Starboard light	Feu de tribord	Steuerbordlampe	Luz de estribor	Stuurboordlicht
Stern light	Feu arrière	Hecklicht	Luz de alcance	Heklicht
Cabin lamp	Lampe de cabine	Kajütslampe	Lámpera de camarote	Kajuitlamp
Lamp glass	Verre de lampe	Glaszylinder	Lámpara de cristal	Lampeglas
Wick	Mèche	Docht	Mecha (para engrase)	Kous
15 SHIPS' PAPERS				
Certificate of Registry	Acte de francisation	Schiffszertificate	Patente de Navegación	Zeebrief
Pratique	Libre-pratique	Verkehrserlaubnis	Plática	Verlof tot Ontscheping
Ships Log	Livre de bord	Schiffstagebuch	Cuaderno de bitácora	Journaal
Insurance certificate	Certificat d'assurance	Versicherungs-police	Poliza de seguro	Verzekeringsbewijs
Passport	Passeport	Reisepass	Passaporte	Paspoort
Customs clearance	Dédouanement	Zollpapier	Despacho de aduana	Bewijs van inklaring door douane
16 TOOLS				
Hammer	Marteau	Hammer	Martillo	Hamer
Wood chisel	Ciseau à bois	Stechbeitel	Formón	Beitel
Cold chisel	Ciseau à froid	Meissel	Cortafrio	Koubeitel
Screwdriver	Tournevis	Schraubenzieher	Destornillador	Schroevedraaier
Spanner	Clé	Schrauben-schlüssel	Llave para tuercas	Sleutel
Adjustable spanner	Cle anglaise	Verstellbarer Schrauben-schlüssel	Llave adjustable	Verstelbare sleutel
Saw	Scie	Säge	Sierra	Zaag
Hacksaw	Scie à métaux	Metallsäge	Sierra para metal	IJzerzaag
Hand drill	Chignolle à main	Handbohrmaschine	Taladro de mano	Handboor
File	Lime	Feile	Lima	Vijl
Wire cutters	Pinces coupantes	Drahtschere	Cortador de alambre	Draadschaar
Pliers	Pinces	Zange	Alicates	Buigtang
Wrench	Tourne-à-gauche	Schrauben-schlüssel	Llave de boca	Waterpomptang
17 CHANDLERY				
Burgee	Guidon	Klubstander	Grimpola	Clubstandaard
Ensign	Pavillon	Nationalflagge	Pabellón	Natie vlag
Courtesy flag	Fanion de courtoisie	Gastlandflagge	Pabellón extranjero	Vreemde natievlag
Q flag	Pavillon Q	Quarantäneflagge	Bandera Q	Quarantaine Vlag

ENGLISH	FRENCH	GERMAN	SPANISH	DUTCH
Signal flag	Pavillon (alphabetique)	Signalflagge	Bandera de senales	Seinvlag
Anchor	Ancre	Anker	Ancla	Anker
Anchor chain	Chaîne d'ancre	Ankerkette	Cadena del ancla	Ankerketting
Rope	Cordage	Tauwerk	Cabullería	Touw
Hawser	Cable d'acier	Drahttauwerk	Estacha, amarra	Staaldraad
Synthetic rope	Cordage synthétique	Synthetisches tauwerk	Cabullería sintetica	Synthetisch touw
Nylon rope	Cordage de nylon	Nylontauwerk	Cabullería de nylon	Nylon touw
Terylene rope	Cordage de Tergal	Diolentauwerk	Cabullería de terylene	Terylene touw
Hemp rope	Cordage de chanvre	Hanftauwerk	Cabullería de canamo	Henneptouw
Fender	Defense	Fender	Defensa	Stootkusse, wiln
Life buoy	Bouee de sauvetage	Rettungsboje	Guindola	Redding boei
Cleat	Taquet	Klampe	Cornamusa	Klamp
Winch	Winch	Winde	Chigre	Lier
Boat hook	Gaffe	Bootshaken	Bichero	Pikhaak
Oar	Aviron	Riemen	Remo	Riem
Fair lead	Chaumard	Lippe	Guía	Verhaalkam
Eye bolt	Piton de filière	Augbolzen	Cáncamo	Oogbout
Paint	Peinture	Farbe	Pintura	Verf
Varnish	Vernis	Lack	Barniz	Lak
Glass paper	Papier de verre	Schleifpapier	Papel de lija	Schuurpapier
Foghorn	Corne de brume	Nebelhorn	Bocina de niebla	Misthoorn

18 FOOD

Cheese	Fromage	Käse	Queso	Kaas
Butter	Beurre	Butter	Mantequilla	Boter
Bread	Pain	Brot	Pan	Brood
Milk	Lait	Milch	Leche	Melk
Jam	Confiture	Marmelade	Compota	Jam
Marmalade	Confiture d'oranges	Orangen marmelade	Mermelada	Marmelade
Mustard	Moutarde	Senf	Mostaza	Mosterd
Salt	Sel	Salz	Sal	Zout
Pepper	Poivre	Pfeffer	Pimienta	Peper
Vinegar	Vinaigre	Essig	Vinagre	Azijn
Meat	Viande	Fleisch	Carne	Vlees
Fish	Poisson	Fisch	Pescado	Vis
Fruit	Fruits	Obst	Frutas	Fruit
Vegetables	Légumes	Gemüse	Legumbres	Groenten
Sausages	Saucisses	Würstchen	Embutidos	Worstjes
Ham	Jambon	Schinken	Jamón	Ham
Beef	Boeuf	Rindfleisch	Carne de vaca	Rundvlees
Pork	Porc	Schweinefleisch	Carne de cerdo	Varkensvlees
Mutton	Mouton	Hammelfleisch	Carne de cernero	Schapenvlees
Bacon	Lard fumé	Speck	Tocino	Spek
Eggs	Oeufs	Eier	Huevos	Eieren
Fresh water	Eau douce	Süsswasser	Agua dulce	Zoetwater

19 SHOPS AND PLACES ASHORE

Grocer	Épicier	Krämer	Tendero de Comestibles	Kruidenier
Greengrocer	Marchand de légumes	Gemüsehändler	Verdulero	Groente handelaar
Butcher	Boucher	Metzger	Carnicero	Slager
Baker	Boulanger	Bäcker	Panadero	Bakker
Fishmonger	Marchand de poisson	Fischhändler	Pescadero	Vishandel
Ironmonger	Quincaillerie	Eisenwarenhändler	Ferretero	Ijzerwarenwinkel
Supermarket	Supermarché	Supermarkt	Supermercado	Supermarkt
Market	Marché	Markt	Mercado	Markt

ENGLISH	FRENCH	GERMAN	SPANISH	DUTCH
Yacht chandler	Fournisseur de marine	Yachtausrüster	Almacén de efectos navales	Scheepsleverancier
Sailmaker	Voilier	Segelmacher	Velero	Zeilmaker
Garage	Garage	Autowerkstatt	Garaje	Garage
Railway station	Gare	Bahnhof	Estación	Station
Bus	Autobus	Bus	Autobus	Bus
Post Office	Poste	Postamt	Correos	Postkantoor
Bank	Banque	Bank	Banco	Bank
Chemist	Pharmacien	Apotheke	Farmaceútico	Apotheek
Hospital	Hôpital	Kránkenhaus	Hospital	Ziekenhuis
Doctor	Médecin	Arzt	Medico	Dokter
Dentist	Dentiste	Zahnarzt	Dentista	Tandarts

20 IN HARBOUR

ENGLISH	FRENCH	GERMAN	SPANISH	DUTCH
Harbour	Bassin	Hafen	Puerto	Haven
Yacht harbour	Bassin pour yachts	Yachthafen	Puerto de yates	Jachthaven
Fishing harbour	Port de pêché	Fischereihafen	Puerto pesquero	Vissershaven
Harbour master	Capitaine de port	Hafenkapitän	Capitan de puerto	Havenmeester
Harbour master's office	Bureau du capitaine de port	Büro des Hafenkapitäns	Comandancia de puerto	Havenkantoor
Immigration officer	Agent du service de l'immigration	Beamter der Passkontrolle	Oficial de inmigración	Immigratie Beamte
Customs office	Bureau de douane	Zollamt	Aduana	Douanekantoor
Prohibited area	Zone interdite	Verbotenes gebiet	Zona prohibida	Verboden gebied
Anchoring prohibited	Défense de mouiller	Ankern verboten!	Fondeadero prohibido	Verboden ankerplaats
Mooring prohibited	Accostage interdit	Anlegen verboten	Amarradero prohibido	Verboden aan te leggen
Lock	Écluse	Schleuse	Esclusa	Sluis
Canal	Canal	Kanal	Canal	Kanaal
Mooring place	Point d'accostage	Liegeplatz im Bojenfeld	Amarradero	Aanlegplaats
Movable bridge	Pont mobile	Bewegliche Brücke	Puente móvil	Beweegbare brug
Swing bridge	Pont tournant	Drehbrücke	Puente giratorio	Draaibrug
Lifting bridge	Pont basculant	Hubbrücke	Puente levadizo	Hefbrug
Ferry	Bac	Fähre	Transbordador	Veer
Harbour steps	Éscalier du quai	Kaitreppe	Escala Real	Haventrappen

21 FIRST AID

ENGLISH	FRENCH	GERMAN	SPANISH	DUTCH
Bandage	Bandage	Binde	Venda	Verband
Lint	Pansement	Verbandsmull	Hilacha	Pluksel
Sticking plaster	Pansement adhésif	Heftplaster	Esparadrapo	Kleefpleister
Cotton wool	Ouate	Watte	Algodón	Watten
Scissors	Ciseaux	Schere	Tijeras	Schaar
Safety pin	Épingle de sûreté	Sicherheitsnadel	Imperdibles	Veiligheidsspeld
Tweezers	Pince à échardes	Pinzette	Pinzas	Pincet
Thermometer	Thermométre	Thermometer	Termómetro	Thermometer
Disinfectant	Désinfectant	Desinfektionsmittel	Desinfectante	Desinfecterend middel
Aspirin tablets	Aspirine	Aspirintabletten	Pastillas de aspirina	Aspirine
Laxative	Laxatif	Abführmittel	Laxante	Laxeermiddel
Indigestion tablets	Pillules contre l'indigestion	Tabletten gegen Darmstörungen	Pastillas laxantes	Laxeertabletten
Antiseptic cream	Onguent antiseptique	Antiseptische Salbe	Pomada antiséptica	Antiseptische zalf
Anti-seasickness pills	Remède contre le mal de mer	Antiseekrankheitsmittel	Pildoras contra el mareo	Pillen tegen zeeziekte
Calamine lotion	Lotion a la calamine	Zink-Tinktur	Locion de calamina	Anti-jeuk middel
Wound dressing	Pansement stérilisé	Verbandzeug	Botiquin para heridas	Noodverband
Stomach upset	Mal à l'estomac	Magen-und Darmbeschwerden	Corte de digestion	Last van de maag

ENGLISH & FOREIGN CHART TERMS

ENGLISH	FRENCH	GERMAN	SPANISH	DUTCH
1. LIGHT CHARACTERISTICS				
F.	Fixe	F.	F.	V.
Oc.	Occ.	Ubr.	Oc.	O.
Iso	Iso	Glt.	Iso./Isof.	Iso.
Fl.	É	Blz/Blk.	D.	S.
Q	Scint	Fkl.	Ct.	Fl.
IQ	Scint. dis.	Fkl. unt.	Gp. Ct.	Int. Fl.
Al.	Alt.	Wchs.	Alt.	Alt.
Oc(..)	... Occ.	Urb(..) Urb. Grp.	Gp.Oc. Gr.Oc.	GO.
Fl(..)	... É	Blz(..)/Blk(..)	Gp. D.	GS.
		Blz.Grp./Blk.Grp.		
Mo	—	Mo	Mo	—
FFl	Fixe É	F. & Blz. Mi.	F.D.	V&S
FFl(..)	Fixe..É	F. & Blz(..) Mi.	F.Gp.D./Gp.DyF.	V&GS

2. COMPASS POINTS				
North(N) South(S)	Nord(N) Sud(S)	Nord(N) Süd(S)	Norte(N) Sur(S)	Noord(N) Zuid(Z)
East(E) West(W)	Est(E) Ouest(O)	Ost(O) West(W)	Este, Leste(E) Oeste(W)	Oost(O) West(W)
North East(NE)	Nordé(NE)	Nord-Ost(NO)	Nordeste(NE)	Noord-oost(NO)
North-North East (NNE)	Nord-Nordé(NNE)	Nord-Nord-Ost (NNO)	Nornordeste (NNE)	Noord-noord-oost (NNO)
North by East	Nord quart Nordé	Nord zum Osten(NzO)	Norte cuarta al Este(N¼NE)	Noord ten oosten(N-t-O)

3. COLOURS				
Black	Noir (n)	Schwarz (s)	Negro (n)	Zwart (Z)
Red	Rouge (r)	Rot (r)	Rojo (r)	Rood (R)
Green	Vert (v)	Grün (gn)	Verde (v)	Groen (Gn)
Yellow	Jaune (j)	Gelb (g)	Amarillo (am)	Geel (Gl)
White	Blanc (b)	Weiß (w)	Blanco (b)	Wit (w)
Orange	Orange (org)	Orange (or)	Naranja	Oranje (or)
Blue	Bleu (bl)	Blau (bl)	Azul (az)	Blauw (B)
Brown	Brun	Braun (br)	Pardo (p)	Bruin
Violet	Violet (vio)	Violet (viol)	Violeta	Violet (Vi)

4. RADIO AND AURAL AIDS				
Radiobeacon	Radiophare	Funkfeuer	Radiofaro	Radiobaken
Diaphone	Diaphone	Kolbensirene	Diafono	Diafoon
Horn	Nautophone	Nautofon	Nautofono	Nautofoon
Siren	Siène	Sirene	Sirena	Mistsirene
Reed	Trompette	Zungenhorn	Bocina	Mistfluit
Explosive	Explosion	Nebelknallsignal	Explosivo	Knalmistsein
Bell	Cloche	Glocke	Campana	Mistklok
Gong	Gong	Gong	Gong	Mistgong
Whistle	Sifflet	Heuler	Silbato	Mistfluit

5. STRUCTURE OR FLOAT				
Dolphin	Duc d'Albe	Dalben	Dugue de Alba	Ducdalf
Light	Feu	Leuchtfeuer	Luz	Licht
Lighthouse	Phare	Leuchtturm	Faro	Lichttoren
Light vessel	Bateau feu	Feuerschiff	Faro flotanto	Lichtschip
Light float	Feu flottant	Leuchtfloß	Luzflotante	Lichtvlot
Beacon	Balise	Bake	Baliza	Baken
Column	Colonne	Laternenträger	Columna	Lantaarnpaal
Dwelling	Maison	Wohnhaus	Casa	Huis
Framework Tower	Pylone	Gittermast	Armazon	Traliemast
House	Bâtiment	Haus	Casa	Huis
Hut	Cabane	Hutte	Caseta	Huisje
Mast	Mât	Mast	Mastil	Mast
Post	Poteau	Laternenpfahl	Poste	Lantaarnpaal
Tower	Tour	Turm	Torre	Toren
Mooring Buoy	Coffre d'ammrage corps-mort	Festmachtonne	Boya de amarre muerto	Meerboei
Buoy	Bouée	Tonne	Boya	Ton

ENGLISH	FRENCH	GERMAN	SPANISH	DUTCH
6. TYPE OF MARKING				
Band	Bande	waagerecht gestreift	fajas horizontales	Horizontaal gestreept
Stripe	Raie	senkrecht gestreift	Fajas verticales	Vertikaal gestreept
Chequered	à damier	gewurfelt	Damero	Geblokt
Top mark	Voyant	Toppzeichen	Marea de Tope	Topteken
7. SHAPE				
Round	Circulaire	rund	Redondo	Rond
Conical	Conique	Kegelformig	Conico	Kegelvormig
Diamond	Losange	Raute	Rombo	Ruitvormig
Square	Carré	Viereck	Cuadrangular	Vierkant
Triangle	Triangle	Dreieck	Triangulo	Driehoek
8. DESCRIPTION				
Destroyed	Détruit	zerstort	Destruido	Vernield
Occasional	Feu occasionnel	gelégentlich	Ocasional	Facultatief
Temporary	Temporaire	votubergehend	Temporal	Tijdelijk
Extinguished	Éteint	geloscht	Apagada	Gedoofd
9. TIDE				
High Water	Pleine mer	Hochwasser	Pleamar	Hoogwater
Low Water	Basse mer	Niedrigwasser	Bajamar	Laagwater
Flood	Marée montante	Flut	Entrante	Vloed
Ebb	Marée decendante	Ebbe	Vaciante	Eb
Stand	Étale	Wasserstand	Margen	Stilwater
Range	Amplitude	Tidenhub	Repunte	Verval
Spring tide	Vive eau	Springtide	Marea viva	Springtij
Neap tide	Morte eau	Nipptide	Aguas Muertas	Doodtij
Sea level	Niveau	Wasserstand	Nivel	Waterstand
Mean	Moyen	Mittlere	Media	Gemiddeld
Current	Courant	Strom	Corriente	Stroom
10. CHART DANGERS				
Sunken rock	Roche submergée	Unterwasserklippe (klp)	Roca siempre cubierta	Blinde klip
Wreck	Épave	Wrack	Naufragio (Nauf)	Wrak
Shoal	Haut fond (Ht.Fd.)	Untiefe (Untf.)	Bajo (Bo)	Droogte, ondiepte (Dre.)
Obstruction	Obstruction (Obs.)	Schiffahrts-Hindernis (Sch-H.)	Obstrución (Obston.)	Belemmering van de vaart, hindernis (Obstr.)
Overfalls	Remous et clapotis	Stromkabbelung	Escarceos, hileros	Stroomrafeling
Dries	Assèche	Trockenfallend (tr.)	Que vela en bajamar	Droogvallend
Isolated Danger	Danger isolé	Einzelliegende Gefahr	Peligro aislado	Losliggend gevaar
11. WEATHER				
Weather Forecast	Prévisions météo	Wettervorhersage	Previsión meteorologica	Weersvoorspelling
Gale	Coup de vent	Stürmischer wind	Duro	Storm
Squall	Grain	Bö	Turbonada	Bui
Fog	Brouillard	Nebel	Niebla	Mist
Mist	Brume légere ou mouillée	Feuchter Dunst, diesig	Neblina	Nevel
12. DIMENSIONS				
Height	Tirant d'air	Durchfahrtshöhe	Altura	Doorvaarthoogte
Breadth	Largeur, de large	Breite	Ancho, anchura	Breedte
Depth	Profondeur	Tiefe	Fondo, profundidad	Diepte
Draught	Tirant d'eau	Tiefgang	Calado	Diepgang

LINEAR CONVERSION TABLE

INTERNATIONAL NAUTICAL MILES, STATUTE MILES AND KILOMETRES

INM	Km	SM	Km	INM	SM	SM	Km	INM
1	1.852	1.15078	1	0.53996	0.62137	1	1.60934	0.86898
2	3.70	2.30	2	1.08	1.24	2	3.22	1.74
3	5.56	3.45	3	1.62	1.86	3	4.83	2.61
4	7.41	4.60	4	2.16	2.49	4	6.44	3.48
5	9.26	5.75	5	2.70	3.11	5	8.05	4.34
6	11.11	6.90	6	3.24	3.73	6	9.66	5.21
7	12.96	8.06	7	3.78	4.35	7	11.27	6.08
8	14.82	9.21	8	4.32	4.97	8	12.87	6.95
9	16.67	10.36	9	4.86	5.59	9	14.48	7.82
10	18.52	11.51	10	5.40	6.21	10	16.09	8.69
11	20.37	12.66	11	5.94	6.84	11	17.70	9.56
12	22.22	13.81	12	6.48	7.46	12	19.31	10.43
13	24.08	14.96	13	7.02	8.08	13	20.92	11.30
14	25.93	16.11	14	7.56	8.70	14	22.53	12.17
15	27.78	17.26	15	8.10	9.32	15	23.14	13.03
16	29.63	18.41	16	8.64	9.94	16	25.75	13.90
17	31.48	19.56	17	9.18	10.56	17	27.36	14.77
18	33.34	20.71	18	9.72	11.18	18	28.97	15.64
19	35.19	21.86	19	10.26	11.81	19	30.58	16.51
20	37.04	23.02	20	10.80	12.43	20	32.19	17.38
21	38.89	24.17	21	11.34	13.05	21	33.80	18.25
22	40.74	25.32	22	11.88	13.67	22	35.41	19.12
23	42.60	26.47	23	12.42	14.29	23	37.01	19.99
24	44.45	27.62	24	12.96	14.91	24	38.62	20.86
25	46.30	28.77	25	13.50	15.53	25	40.23	21.72
26	48.15	29.92	26	14.04	16.16	26	41.84	22.59
27	50.00	31.07	27	14.58	16.78	27	43.45	23.46
28	51.86	32.22	28	15.12	17.40	28	45.06	24.33
29	53.71	33.37	29	15.66	18.02	29	46.67	25.20
30	55.56	34.52	30	16.20	18.64	30	48.28	26.07
31	57.41	35.67	31	16.74	19.26	31	49.89	26.94
32	59.26	36.82	32	17.28	19.88	32	51.50	27.81
33	61.12	37.98	33	17.82	20.51	33	53.11	28.68
34	62.97	39.13	34	18.36	21.13	34	54.72	29.55
35	64.82	40.28	35	18.90	21.75	35	56.33	30.41
36	66.67	41.43	36	19.44	22.37	36	57.94	31.28
37	68.52	42.58	37	19.98	22.99	37	59.55	32.15
38	70.38	43.73	38	20.52	23.61	38	61.15	33.02
39	72.23	44.88	39	21.06	24.23	39	62.76	33.89
40	74.08	46.03	40	21.60	24.85	40	64.37	34.76
45	83.34	51.79	45	24.30	27.96	45	72.42	39.10
50	92.60	57.54	50	27.00	31.07	50	80.47	43.45
55	101.86	63.29	55	29.70	34.18	55	88.51	47.79
60	111.12	69.05	60	32.40	37.28	60	96.56	52.14
65	120.38	74.80	65	35.10	40.39	65	104.61	56.48
70	129.64	80.55	70	37.80	43.50	70	112.65	60.83
75	138.90	86.31	75	40.50	46.60	75	120.70	65.17
80	148.16	92.06	80	43.20	49.71	80	128.75	69.52
85	157.42	97.82	85	45.90	52.82	85	136.79	73.86
90	166.68	103.57	90	48.60	55.92	90	144.84	78.21
95	175.94	109.32	95	51.30	59.03	95	152.89	82.55
100	185.20	115.08	100	54.00	62.14	100	160.93	86.90

FEET TO METRES

Feet	Metres	Feet	Metres
1	0.30	26	7.92
2	0.61	27	8.23
3	0.91	28	8.53
4	1.22	29	8.84
5	1.52	30	9.14
6	1.83	31	9.45
7	2.13	32	9.75
8	2.44	33	10.06
9	2.74	34	10.36
10	3.05	35	10.67
11	3.35	36	10.97
12	3.66	37	11.28
13	3.96	38	11.58
14	4.27	39	11.89
15	4.57	40	12.19
16	4.88	41	12.50
17	5.18	42	12.80
18	5.49	43	13.11
19	5.79	44	13.41
20	6.10	45	13.72
21	6.40	46	14.02
22	6.71	47	14.33
23	7.01	48	14.63
24	7.32	49	14.94
25	7.62	50	15.24

METRES TO FEET

Metres	Feet	Metres	Feet
1	3.28	26	85.30
2	6.56	27	88.58
3	9.84	28	91.86
4	13.12	29	95.14
5	16.40	30	98.43
6	19.69	31	101.71
7	22.97	32	104.99
8	26.25	33	108.27
9	29.53	34	111.55
10	32.81	35	114.83
11	36.09	36	118.11
12	39.37	37	121.39
13	42.65	38	124.67
14	45.93	39	127.95
15	49.21	40	131.23
16	52.49	41	134.51
17	55.77	42	137.80
18	59.06	43	141.08
19	62.34	44	144.36
20	65.62	45	147.64
21	68.90	46	150.92
22	72.18	47	154.20
23	75.46	48	157.48
24	78.74	49	160.76
25	82.02	50	164.04

FATHOMS TO METRES

Fathoms	Metres	Fathoms	Metres
1	1.83	26	47.55
2	3.66	27	49.38
3	5.49	28	51.21
4	7.32	29	53.04
5	9.14	30	54.86
6	10.97	31	56.69
7	12.80	32	58.52
8	14.63	33	60.35
9	16.46	34	62.18
10	18.29	35	64.00
11	20.12	36	65.84
12	21.95	37	67.67
13	23.77	38	69.49
14	25.60	39	71.32
15	27.43	40	73.15
16	29.26	41	74.98
17	31.09	42	76.81
18	32.92	43	78.64
19	34.75	44	80.47
20	36.58	45	82.30
21	38.40	46	84.12
22	40.23	47	85.95
23	42.06	48	87.78
24	43.89	49	89.61
25	45.72	50	91.44

METRES TO FATHOMS

Metres	Fathoms	Metres	Fathoms
1	0.547	26	14.217
2	1.094	27	14.764
3	1.640	28	15.311
4	2.187	29	15.857
5	2.734	30	16.404
6	3.281	31	16.951
7	3.828	32	17.498
8	4.374	33	18.045
9	4.921	34	18.591
10	5.468	35	19.138
11	6.015	36	19.685
12	6.562	37	20.232
13	7.108	38	20.779
14	7.655	39	21.325
15	8.202	40	21.872
16	8.749	41	22.419
17	9.296	42	22.966
18	9.842	43	23.513
19	10.389	44	24.059
20	10.936	45	24.606
21	11.483	46	25.153
22	12.030	47	25.700
23	12.577	48	26.247
24	13.123	49	26.793
25	13.670	50	27.340

INCHES TO MILLIMETRES   MILLIMETRES TO INCHES

Inches	mm	Inches	mm	mm	Inches	mm	Inches
1	25.40	15	381.00	1	0.0394	15	0.5906
2	50.80	20	508.00	2	0.0787	20	0.7874
3	76.20	25	635.00	3	0.1181	25	0.9843
4	101.60	30	762.00	4	0.1575	30	1.1811
5	127.00	35	889.00	5	0.1969	35	1.3780
10	254.00	40	1016.00	10	0.3937	40	1.5748

10 MILLIMETRES = 1 CENTIMETRE   100 CENTIMETRES (1000 MM) = 1 METRE = 39.37 INCHES (3.3 FEET)

INCHES TO METRES   METRES TO INCHES

Inches	Metres	Inches	Metres	Metres	Inches	Metres	Inches
1	0.0254	7	0.1778	0.1	3.937	0.7	27.559
2	0.0508	8	0.2032	0.2	7.874	0.8	31.496
3	0.0762	9	0.2286	0.3	11.811	0.9	35.433
4	0.1016	10	0.2540	0.4	15.748	1.0	39.370
5	0.1270	11	0.2794	0.5	19.685	1.1	43.307
6	0.1524	12	0.3048	0.6	23.622	1.2	47.244

To convert metres to centimetres: move decimal point two places to the right

YARDS TO METRES   METRES TO YARDS

Yds	Metres	Yds	Metres	Metres	Yds	Metres	Yds
1	0.91440	6	5.48640	1	1.09361	6	6.56168
2	1.82880	7	6.40080	2	2.18723	7	7.65529
3	2.74320	8	7.31520	3	3.28084	8	8.74891
4	3.65760	9	8.22960	4	4.37445	9	9.84252
5	4.57200	10	9.14400	5	5.46807	10	10.93614

Move decimal point for higher values — eg, 6,000 metres = 6,561.68 yards

POUNDS TO KILOGRAMMES   KILOGRAMMES TO POUNDS

lb	kg	lb	kg	kg	lb	kg	lb
1	0.454	6	2.722	1	2.205	6	13.228
2	0.907	7	3.175	2	4.409	7	15.432
3	1.361	8	3.629	3	6.614	8	17.637
4	1.814	9	4.082	4	8.818	9	19.842
5	2.268	10	4.536	5	11.023	10	22.046

GALLONS TO LITRES   LITRES TO GALLONS

Gallons	Litres	Gallons	Litres	Litres	Gallons	Litres	Gallons
1	4.5461	10	45.4609	1	0.2200	60	13.1982
2	9.0922	20	90.9218	2	0.4399	90	19.7972
3	13.6383	30	136.3826	5	1.0998	120	26.3963
4	18.1844	40	181.8435	10	2.1997	150	32.9954
5	22.7304	50	227.3044	20	4.3994	180	39.5945

PINTS TO LITRES   LITRES TO PINTS

Pints	Litres	Pints	Litres	Litres	Pints	Litres	Pints
1	0.568	6	3.409	1	1.760	6	10.559
2	1.136	7	3.978	2	3.520	7	12.319
3	1.705	8	4.546	3	5.279	8	14.078
4	2.273	9	5.114	4	7.039	9	15.838
5	2.841	10	5.682	5	8.799	10	17.598

SOME USEFUL CONVERSIONS

1 fathom	=	6 feet
1 shackle	=	15 fathoms
1 cable	=	608ft (approx 100 fathoms)
10 cables	=	1 international nautical mile
1 international nautical mile	=	6076.12ft = 1.15 statute miles = 1852m
1 statute mile	=	5280ft = 1760yd = 0.87 sea miles

Length

kilometre(km)	=	1093.61yd
metre(m)	=	39.37in.
centimetre(cm)	=	0.3937in.
millimetre(mm)	=	0.03937in.

Weight

tonne	=	2204.6lb
kilogram(kg)	=	2.2046lb
gram(g)	=	0.0353oz

Area

sq metre(m^2)	=	1.196yd^2
sq centimetre(cm^2)	=	0.1550in.^{2}
sq millimetre(mm^2)	=	0.00155in.^{2}

Volume

cubicmetre(m^3)	=	220 gallons = 1000 litres = 1.308yd^3
litre	=	1.7598 pints
centilitre(cl)	=	0.352fl oz
millilitre(ml)	=	0.035fl oz

For **wind speed, temperature and barometer** conversions, see Section 18.

OTHER MEASURES

Weight

1 long ton (British) = 2240lb = 1.12 short tons = 1.016 tonne
1 short ton (USA and Canada) = 20 centals of 100lb each = 2000lb = 0.893 long tons = 0.907 tonne
1 tonne = 2204.6lb = 1.1023 short tons = 0.9842 long tons = 1000kg

Nautical

1 ton (displacement) = 35cu ft salt water or 36cu ft fresh water
1 ton (register) = 100cu ft   1 ton (measurement) = 40cu ft

Fresh water

1cu ft = 6$\frac{1}{4}$ gallons and weighs 62.5lb
36cu ft = 224 gallons and weighs 1 ton
1 gallon = 4.546 litres and weighs 10lb
10 British gallons = approx 12 American gallons
1000 litres = 1cu m
1 litre weighs approx 1kg

Salt water

1cu ft weighs 64lb   35cu ft weighs 1 ton

BRITISH/CONTINENTAL CLOTHING SIZES

Women's Shoes	3(35$\frac{1}{2}$) 4(36$\frac{1}{2}$) 5(38) 6(39$\frac{1}{2}$) 7(40$\frac{1}{2}$) 8(42) 9(43)
Suits & Dresses	10(38) 12(40) 14(42) 16(44) 18(46) 20(48) 22(50)
Men's Shoes	7(41) 8(42) 9(43) 10(44) 11(45$\frac{1}{2}$) 12(47) 13(48)
Shirts	14(36) 14$\frac{1}{2}$(37) 15(38) 15$\frac{1}{2}$(39/40) 16(41) 16$\frac{1}{2}$(42) 17(43) 17$\frac{1}{2}$(44)
Suits/Overcoats	37-38(94-97) 39-40(99-102) 41-42(104-107) 43-44(109-112)

PERSONAL CONVERSION NOTES

Sea Signalling

IMPORTANT SIGNALS

Important Sound Signals are given on p. 12:2, but as not all the other signals (which it is of vital importance to know the meaning of **at once**) are given in this Section their page or Section numbers are grouped below for easy checking)

Distress Signals by Vessels (Collision Regulations) .... See Section 8

Signals by Vessels 'not under command' .... See Section 8

Health Clearance .... See Section 10

Signals for a Pilot .... See Section 22

Important Single Letter Code Signals .... Front of Almanac and 12:8

Distress & Emergency Signals .... See Section 15

Distress Signals from Lightvessels and Lighthouses in UK .... See Section 15

Fog Signals by Lighthouses, etc., 'Aids to Navigation' .... See Section 22

12:1

IMPORTANT SOUND SIGNALS

Although signalling between vessels may be carried out by whistle or siren using the Morse Code, it is a slow method, and unless in open waters should never be resorted to. Confusion as to any Sound Signals given or its misinterpretation can have most disastrous results, so Sound Signals should be used with the utmost discretion.

On the other hand they should be used decisively and correctly whenever they are required by the Collision Regulations or when the circumstances of the occasion require. The following Sound Signals occur in ordinary Navigation:

FOG SIGNALS BY LIGHTHOUSES, LIGHTVESSELS, BUOYS, ETC.

These cannot of course be memorised—except by Pilots in their own Pilotage area—but should be consulted as required in the "Navigational Aids" Section.

SOUND SIGNALS BY YOUR OWN AND OTHER VESSELS IN FOG OR THICK WEATHER

These must be known instinctively as described in the Collision Regulations, Rule 35.*

SOUND SIGNALS BY VESSELS MANOEUVRING

These are not given in Fog, but must be used by vessels manoeuvring in sight of other vessels, so must be known without hesitation. See the Collision Regulations, Rule 34.*

Note carefully the provision under Rule 34 of the "in doubt" or "wake up" signal of five or more short and rapid blasts.

DISTRESS SIGNALS

Shown fully in Annex IV of the Collision Regulations.*

PILOT SIGNALS IN FOG

These are given in Section 22. In a majority of U.K. ports, but by no means all, vessels make the Morse letter G (– – ·) when requiring a Pilot and the Pilot vessel waiting to put the Pilot on board sounds 4 short blasts (· · · ·) as prescribed by Rule 35 of the Collision Regulations.*

RIVER APPROACH SIGNAL

A prolonged warning blast by a vessel approaching a bend in a river as described in Rule 9 of the Collision Regulations.

URGENT AND IMPORTANT SIGNALS

For single-letter signals which may be made by any method of signalling see front of Almanac.

It is of the utmost importance that all Owners or Masters in charge of small craft should commit these signals to memory so that they can be used or recognised instantly, without reference.

FOG CLOSE QUARTERS WARNING SIGNAL

"R" (· – ·), made by sound signal only, may be used by a vessel at anchor in fog to give warning of her position to an approaching vessel. This signal would be made in addition to her normal sound signal. See Rule 35.*

"U" DANGER WARNING SIGNAL

"U" (· · –) should never be neglected—many vessels "standing" towards a sandbank or rocky coast have been saved from disaster by the vigilance of others.

*The International Regulations for Preventing Collisions are given in Section 8.

SIGNAL FOR VESSEL TURNING

Although not contained in the Collision Regulations it is the "ordinary practice of seamen" in the River Thames—and other crowded waterways—to use a special signal for "turning" (either when turning completely round or simply turning athwart the channel) of—4 short blasts followed after a very short interval by One short blast if turning to Starboard, or Two short blasts if turning to Port.

KEEP CLEAR OF ME—I AM MANOEUVRING WITH DIFFICULTY

The Sound Signal D(- · ·) "keep clear of me—I am manoeuvring with difficulty"—is a single letter Code Signal, which should be used if necessary in crowded waters.

IMPORTANT DAY AND NIGHT SIGNALS, U.K. LIFESAVING STATION SIGNALS.

These most important signals between lifesaving personnel ashore, and a ship-wrecked vessel or crew, are fully described in Section 15 and should be well understood.

DISTRESS SIGNALS by Vessels at Sea

Hardly a day goes by on the shores of the United Kingdom, without the ever watchful Coastguard or another vessel sighting a genuine distress signal, and it is true to say that without this signal being given, many vessels would not be rescued, and lives lost needlessly. So, all seagoing personnel in charge of vessels of every size must know what these signals are and how to use them. Section 15 gives most valuable information on this subject.

COASTGUARD RESCUE EQUIPMENT

It is vital that the Master of any vessel—and this includes all fishing vessels and yachts—should know precisely what to do in an emergency—which most probably could occur at night. The rules are simple, but must be clearly understood. Consult Section 15 for this information.

INTERNATIONAL DIVING FLAG

The International Code flag A means:
"I HAVE A DIVER DOWN; KEEP WELL CLEAR
AT SLOW SPEED."
In view of the increasing number of underwater swimmers and diving parties operating on the coasts and in harbour approaches, Mariners are asked to keep well clear whenever they see this DIVING FLAG — which is the International Code flag A. Give the vessel flying this flag a very wide berth at slow speed as it means that divers are down.

All persons in charge of craft are asked to keep well clear of the immediate area where this flag is flown, so that divers' lives may not be put in hazard and so that their own craft may not become fouled on lifelines, ropes or other temporary underwater obstructions ancillary to diving.

Club diving parties will do their best to avoid all recognised fairways, although some diving may be expected in fair-ways when the object is a survey or recovery operation. Local branches of the British Sub-Aqua Club are often able to assist other organisations in such work.

SIGNALLING AT SEA

Signalling at sea in all large vessels is normally carried on by radio, and only when signalling to vessels close to or to small vessels would other means be employed.

Small vessels do not always carry radio and, although many are equipped with radiotelephones, these may be out of order or other circumstances may make the use of visual signalling necessary.

Vessels in sight or hearing of one another may use Sound Signals, Code Flags, or Flashing.

CODE FLAGS

All signals are given in one, two or three letter hoists. The International Code Book is published in the nine most commonly used languages and thus communication between different nationals presents no difficulty. As all urgent or important signals are now made with one or two flags it is practicable for small vessels to carry a few flags which would enable them to make essential distress signals.

FLASHING

Signalling by flashing is carried out by using the Morse Code — which is also International — so it is only necessary to learn the symbols and their meanings and to practice sending and receiving by this method to be able to talk to any other vessel, up to several miles range by day and night.

The signalling lamp — generally the Aldis lamp — is of great use to small vessels. It is portable and may be plugged into any 12 volt battery or the vessel's 24 volt main supply.

The lamp is held in the arm and pointed in any direction by movement of the operator's body. Sights are attached to secure the correct "line" of vision on the target for the signal. It has a good range of several miles both by day and night. It may also be used for rescues or for picking up a mooring at night.

INTERNATIONAL MORSE CODE

Letter	Character	Letter	Character	Num'l	Character	
						Ä (German) = AE (Danish)
A	· —	N	— ·	1	· — — — —	· — · —
B	— · · ·	O	— — —	2	· · — — —	Á or Å (Spanish or Scandinavian)
C	— · — ·	P	· — — ·	3	· · · — —	· — — · —
D	— · ·	Q	— — · —	4	· · · · —	Ch (German or Scandinavian)
E	·	R	· — ·	5	· · · · ·	— — — —
F	· · — ·	S	· · ·	6	— · · · ·	É (French)
G	— — ·	T	—	7	— — · · ·	· · — · ·
H	· · · ·	U	· · —	8	— — — · ·	Ñ (Spanish)
I	· ·	V	· · · —	9	— — — — ·	— — · — —
J	· — — —	W	· — —	0	— — — — —	Ö (German = Ø Danish)
K	— · —	X	— · · —			— — — ·
L	· — · ·	Y	— · — —			Ü (German)
M	— —	Z	— — · ·			· · — —

THE INTERNATIONAL CODE OF SIGNALS

A VESSEL'S IDENTITY

It is often necessary, to inform other vessels of your vessel's name and nationality, for identification purposes. The Ensign ordinarily indicates the nationality of the signalling vessel, but in addition, most registered vessels, warships, and certain other vessels are allotted a combination signal of four flags, the top flag or flags indicating their nationality. For example in British vessels the top flag is either G, M, or 2 while in vessels of the United States of America the top flag is either A, K, N or W. The four flags are always kept bent together on the Bridge for instant use and are known as the vessel's "number". The same four letters or numbers are also the vessel's radio call sign.

THE CODE FLAG AND ANSWERING PENNANT (or Pendant)

Known as Code Flag, when flown singly — indicates International Code being used.

When used to answer hoists of flags from another vessel it is termed the Answering Pennant. When any flag hoist is sighted, the Answering Pennant should be hoisted immediately at the "dip" (about half-way up the halliards) and when the Code Book has been consulted and the Signal thoroughly understood, the Answering Pennant is at once hoisted "close up" (at the top of the halliards). After the other vessel has hauled down her hoist the Answering Pennant is lowered to the "dip" again to await another hoist from the other signalling vessel.

It may be used also as a decimal point.

THE THREE SUBSTITUTES

To avoid the necessity of carrying more than one set of Flags, Substitutes are used. The first substitute always repeats the uppermost flag of that class of flag which immediately precedes it. The second and third substitutes similarly repeat the second or third flag of that class of flags which immediately precede them. No substitute can be used more than once in a hoist.

Example. Longitude 11°11′ = G Numeral 1 first substitute; second substitute; third substitute. Example. MTT = MT second substitute.

SINGLE-LETTER SIGNALS WITH COMPLEMENTS

A — with three numerals	—	AZIMUTH or BEARING
C — with three numerals	—	COURSE
D — with two, four or six numerals	—	DATE
G — with four or five numerals	—	LONGITUDE (last two mins, rest deg.)
K — with one numeral	—	I wish to COMMUNICATE by · · · (Semaphore)
L — with four numerals	—	LATITUDE (first two deg., rest mins.)
R — with one or more numerals	—	DISTANCE in nautical miles
S — with one or more numerals	—	SPEED in knots
T — with four numerals	—	LOCAL TIME (first two hours, rest mins.)
V — with one or more numerals	—	SPEED in kilometres per hour
Z — with four numerals	—	GMT (first two hours, rest mins.)

PROCEDURE SIGNALS

A bar over the letters composing a signal denotes that the letters are to be made as one symbol.

SIGNALS FOR VOICE TRANSMISSIONS

Signal	Pronounced as	Meaning
Interco	IN-TER-CO	International Code group(s) follow(s)
Stop	STOP	Full Stop.
Decimal	DAY-SEE-MAL	Decimal point
Correction	KOR REK SHUN	Cancel my last word or group. The correct word or group follows.

SIGNALS FOR FLASHING-LIGHT TRANSMISSION

$\overline{AA}\ \overline{AA}\ \overline{AA}$ etc.   Call for unknown station or general call

$\overline{EEEEE}$ etc.   Erase signal

$\overline{AAA}$ Full stop or decimal point

$\overline{TTTT}$ etc   Answering signal

T   Word or group received.

SIGNALS FOR FLAGS, RADIOTELEPHONY AND RADIOTELEGRAPHY TRANSMISSIONS

CQ   Call for unknown station(s) or general call to all stations

When this signal is used in voice transmission, it should be pronounced in accordance with the letter-spelling table.

SIGNALS FOR USE WHERE APPROPRIATE
IN ALL FORMS OF TRANSMISSION

AA   "All after..." (used after the "Repeat signal" (RPT), means "Repeat all after...".

AB   "All before..." (used after the "Repeat signal" (RPT)) means "Repeat all before...".

AR   Ending signal or End of Transmission or signal.

AS   Waiting signal or period.

BN   "All between...and..." (used after the "Repeat signal" (RPT)) means "Repeat all between...and...".

C   Affirmative—YES or "The significance of the previous group should be read in the affirmative".

CS   "What is the name or identity signal of your vessel (or station)?"

DE   "From..." (used to precede the name or identity signal of the calling station).

K   "I wish to communicate with you" or "Invitation to transmit".

NO   Negative—NO or "The significance of the previous group should be read in the negative". When used in voice transmission the pronunciation should be "NO".

OK   Acknowledging a correct repetition or "It is correct".

RQ   Interrogative, or, "The significance of the previous group should be read as a question".

R   "Received" or "I have received your last signal".

RPT   Repeat signal "I repeat" or "Repeat what you have sent" or "Repeat what you have received".

WA   "Word or group after..." (used after the "Repeat signal" (RPT)) means "Repeat word or group after...".

WB   "Word or group before..." (used after the "Repeat signal" (RPT)) means "Repeat word or group before...".

The procedure signals "C", "NO" and "RQ" cannot be used in conjunction with single-letter signals.

SINGLE LETTER SIGNALS

A I have a diver down; keep well clear at slow speed.

*B I am taking in, or discharging, or carrying dangerous goods.

*C Yes, affirmative or "The significance of the previous group should be read in the affirmative."

*D Keep clear of me — I am manoeuvring with difficulty.

*E I am altering my course to starboard.

F I am disabled. Communicate with me.

*G I require a Pilot. When made by fishing vessels operating in close proximity on the fishing grounds it means: "I am hauling nets."

*H I have a Pilot on board.

*I I am altering my course to port.

J I am on fire and have dangerous cargo on board; keep well clear of me.

†K I wish to communicate with you.

L You should stop your vessel instantly.

*M My vessel is stopped and making no way through the water.

N NO, negative or "The significance of the previous group should be read in the negative." This signal may be given only visually or by sound. For voice or radio transmission the signal should be "NO."

O Man overboard.

P In Harbour (Blue Peter) hoisted at the foremast head. "All persons should report on board as the vessel is about to proceed to sea." At Sea. It may be used by fishing vessels to mean "My nets have come fast upon an obstruction."

Q My vessel is healthy and I request free pratique.

‡R

†*S I am operating astern propulsion.

*T Keep clear of me; I am engaged in pair trawling.

U You are running into danger.

V I require assistance.

W I require medical assistance.

X Stop carrying out your intentions and watch for my signals.

Y I am dragging my anchor.

*Z I require a tug. When made by fishing vessels operating in close proximity on the fishing grounds it means: "I am shooting nets."

†K and S have special meanings as landing signals for small boats with crews or persons in distress.
‡Single letter R has not been allocated a Signal meaning as this has a meaning in Rule 35 of Collision Regulations. *When made by Sound must comply with Rules 34 and 35 of Collision Regulations.

Flags

ENSIGNS OF THE WORLD

FLAG ETIQUETTE

FLAGS OF THE UNITED KINGDOM

THE ROYAL BANNER

The Royal Banner, generally but incorrectly known as the Royal Standard, is the personal flag of the Sovereign.

Other immediate members of the Sovereign's family have a similar banner which is defaced with their personal emblem. This defacement consists of a narrow white strip from fly to hoist, down to the first horizontal. For example, Prince Edward has a banner on which the white horizontal is divided into three "tabs" on the centre one of which is a red rose with a yellow centre and green barbs.

THE NATIONAL FLAG

The Union Flag, frequently but incorrectly referred to as the Union Jack, is never worn at sea except by Royalty or specified officers of the Royal Navy.

ENSIGNS

1. **White**— Red Cross of St George on a white field. Union Flag in upper canton. Worn by the Royal Yacht, Royal Navy and Royal Squadron, and sometimes with Royal Cypher used as a Standard.

2. **Blue**— Dark blue field with Union Flag in upper canton. The fly is frequently defaced by badge of the office or organisation wearing it, e.g.: Royal Fleet Auxiliary, H.M. Customs etc. An Admiralty warrant for the vessel is required before an undefaced or defaced Blue Ensign may be worn. Many Yacht Club members have this privilege, some with defaced and some with undefaced Ensigns.

3. **Red**— Red field with Union Flag in the upper canton. Worn by Merchant Navy and private craft of British subjects. Sometimes defaced in fly. Worn with defacement in fly by some Yacht Clubs (e.g. Lloyd's Y.C.) with Admiralty Warrant.

4. **Royal Air Force** vessels wear a Light Blue Ensign with the Union Flag in the upper canton and with a defacement of Red, White and Dark Blue Roundels (small red in the centre).

5. **Civil Air**. Dark Blue St. George's Cross with White border on a Light Blue field with the Union Flag in the upper canton.

ROYAL NAVY

1. **All Ships and Establishments**— White Ensign.

2. **Lord High Admiral and Lords Commissioners**. Crimson (Maroon) field charged with gold anchor and cable. Also worn on foremast of Royal Yacht when the Sovereign is aboard.

3. **Admiral of the Fleet**— Union Flag.

4. **Admiral**— White field charged with Red Cross of St. George.

5. **Vice Admiral**— As Admiral plus red ball in the upper canton.

6. **Rear Admiral**— As Vice Admiral plus red ball in the lower canton.

7. **Commodore**— As Vice Admiral but slight taper ending with swallow tail.

8. **Commanding Officer Small Craft**— White pendant with Red Cross of St. George in the hoist.

TRINITY HOUSE

1. Jack— Red Cross of St. George, old sailing ships in quarters.
2. Ensign— Red Ensign, defaced by Jack in fly.
3. Burgee— As Jack on a red field.

H.M. CUSTOMS

1. Ensign— Blue defaced by crown over portcullis.
2. Burgee— White with red border on upper and lower edges, defaced crown over portcullis.

MISCELLANEOUS

1. **Queen's Harbour Master**— Union Flag with white border, charged with white circle with Q.H.M. in black; Imperial Crown over.
2. **Thames Conservancy**— St. George's Cross charged with arms of T.C.
3. **Port of London Authority**— St. George's Cross charged with arms of P.L.A. or Blue Ensign defaced.
4. **Examination Service Vessels**— Blue or White Ensign and Special flag White over Red horizontal surrounded by a Blue border.
5. **Royal Mail**— White pendant charged with "ROYAL MAIL" cypher and horn.
6. **North Sea Fisheries**— Pendant quartered, Blue above Yellow in hoist, reverse in fly.
7. **Pilots—Pilot Flag**, upper half white, lower half Red.
8. **The Jack**— A small flag worn on a jackstaff on the stem of Naval Vessels. The Royal Navy wears the Union Flag and other Commonwealth countries wear their National Colours. Only worn at anchor or in harbour. This is the only occasion when it is correct to describe the flag as the Union Jack.
9. **The Pilot Jack**— This consists of the Union Flag having a White border one fifth of the size of the flag. Originally the International signal for a Pilot it was discontinued as such when the International Code of Signals was introduced. It is rarely used nowadays but may be flown by any registered British ship from a Jackstaff in the bows when the vessel is at anchor or in harbour and wearing her Ensign. It should be raised and lowered at the same time as colours.

SEA FLAG ETIQUETTE

Flags worn at sea by British vessels comprise:

1. **Ensigns**
    (a) The Royal Navy and Royal Yacht Squadron wear the White Ensign. Red and Blue Ensigns, either undefaced or defaced, are worn by all other British vessels.
    The Red Ensign undefaced is the correct wear for any British vessel unless she has been granted an Admiralty Warrant (or in the case of a yacht — a Yacht Certificate) for a privilege Ensign.
    The Blue Ensign undefaced may be worn by a Merchant vessel providing she fulfils certain conditions laid down by the Ministry of Defence regarding the presence of Naval Reserve officers in her complement, when an Admiralty Warrant will be issued to this ship. Blue Ensigns undefaced are also worn by a few Yacht

Clubs such as the Royal Cruising Club which have in the past been granted an Ensign Warrant for this purpose.

Under the terms of the Merchant Shipping Act a vessel of 50 tons gross or larger is compelled to wear her colours when entering or leaving a British port and all vessels (unless registered as fishermen) must wear their National colours when entering or leaving a foreign port.

(b) Individual Yacht Permits are issued which permit the holder to wear a privilege Ensign (White, Blue defaced or plain and Red defaced). The owner must first be a member of a Yacht Club which holds a special Ensign Warrant issued by the Ministry of Defence. This warrant empowers the Secretary of the Club to issue a Yacht Permit to a member whose yacht satisfies the qualifying conditions of the Small Ships Register or those yachts registered under the Merchant Shipping Act 1894. Yachts qualifying by virtue of entry on the S.S.R. must measure not less than 7m in length. Yachts which are the property of a Limited Company are eligible for a Yacht Permit provided that they are not used for business, professional or commercial purposes and that the name does not incorporate a name, product or trade mark used for business or commercial purposes. This applies only to yachts registered under the Merchant Shipping Act 1894 as the S.S.R. is not open to yachts owned by Limited Companies. A permit may be issued for a yacht under charter to a club member for a period at the discretion of the Club. Yachts registered under the Merchant Shipping Act will be issued with a permit which is valid until such time as the ownership of the vessel changes, when a new permit will be required (assuming the new owner is a member of an approved Club). The permit issued to a yacht registered on the S.S.R. *will* be valid until the expiry of the Registration Certificate. *i.e.* for a maximum of five years, or until change of ownership occurs. Warrants already issued for vessels registered under the Merchant Shipping Act will continue to be valid until such time as the ownership of the vessel changes. The new owner will then have to apply to the appropriate Yacht Club Secretary for a permit. It is important to remember that the privilege Ensign may only be worn when the particular Yacht Club Burgee is flown. A yacht tender, provided it can be hoisted on board, may wear the special Ensign as long as the parent vessel is wearing hers. Severe penalties exist for the improper use of privilege Ensigns. Under the Merchant Shipping Act 1894 the illegal wearing of a Privilege Ensign renders the vessel's owner liable to a fine not exceeding £1,000. A Naval Officer or Customs Officer is entitled to demand sight of the Admiralty Warrant granting the right to wear the Ensign. If this is not forthcoming the Ensign will be confiscated and the matter referred to the Civil Courts.

2. Yacht Club Burgees and Flag Officers' Broad Pennants

A Burgee is a triangular flag with a design adopted by the particular Yacht Club, the design of which must be such that it cannot be confused with any other Burgee, flag or Ensign. The Burgee should be worn at the masthead but nowadays the increasing amount of instrumentation at the truck renders this very difficult and it is becoming increasingly common to wear it at the starboard yard arm. It should be worn with a Red Ensign except in the case of very small yachts or those yachts which have an Admiralty Warrant for a special Ensign.

When an owner is a member of several clubs the first rule is that the senior club's Burgee has precedence over the others and also that a "Royal" club is senior to a "non Royal" club. In the owner's home waters it is however a matter of courtesy to wear the Burgee of his local club. In this case if his local club does not have an Admiralty Warrant for a special Ensign then the Red Ensign must be worn with the local Burgee. If an owner belongs to a Yacht Club and an Association and wishes to fly both Burgees the Yacht Club should take precedence and its Burgee should be worn at the masthead with the other at the starboard yard arm. An exception to this rule is the Cruising Association, a very old established Yacht Club with London headquarters, and which has an Admiralty Warrant for a defaced Blue Ensign. When a yachtsman belongs to a foreign Yacht Club and wishes to wear its Burgee in the club's home port, it must displace his British Yacht Club's Burgee at the masthead, unless his yacht has two masts when the foreign Burgee should be worn at the foremast and the British Burgee at the aftermast.

The Flag Officers of a club normally comprise the Commodore, Vice Commodore and Rear Commodore (in some clubs there may be more than one Rear Commodore). The Commodore wears a swallow tail flag incorporating the club's Burgee design, the Vice Commodore wears a similar flag with a ball of distinctive colour in the upper canton, while the Rear Commodore has a similar flag with two balls which may be side by side or more usually one in the upper canton and one in the lower. These swallow tail flags are known as Broad Pennants and in a sailing yacht must always be flown at the masthead.

Some Yacht Clubs have special appointments such as Admiral, President, or Past Commodore, and these officers fly a rectangular flag with similar design to the club Burgee. In some clubs the Secretary is regarded as a Flag Officer and usually wears a triangular club Burgee with some additional distinguishing marks on it, such as one ball in the upper canton.

3. House Flags

A House flag is a rectangular flag of special design and is in effect the personal flag of the owner. It may be of any design as long as it cannot be confused with any existing Ensign, flag or Burgee. In the Merchant Navy it is customary for each shipping line to have its own house flag.

House flags are seldom used in sailing yachts, being usually confined to the larger power yachts. An exception to this is the Royal Yachting Association flag flown by members of the R.Y.A. when in harbour. It does not denote ownership but indicates that the owner is a member of the R.Y.A.

4. Special Flags

(a) *Courtesy Ensigns:* It is traditional for a vessel visiting a foreign country to show her respect by flying the maritime flag of that country in a conspicuous position, usually the starboard yard arm. The courtesy Ensign is usually about one third the size of the vessel's National Ensign.

In the provinces of some countries it will be observed that the local yachts wear the provincial flag instead of the National flag. An example of this is in Friesland where many local yachts fly the Friesland flag instead of the Dutch flag. In such cases it is a pleasant gesture and much appreciated by local yachtsmen if visiting yachts fly the Provincial flag in addition to the National Ensign. It must be appreciated that the National Maritime flag is the only correct courtesy flag and if a Provincial flag is flown it must be in addition and inferior to the National flag.

The correct Courtesy Ensign for foreign yachts visiting the United Kingdom is the Red Ensign — not the Union flag.

(b) *The Euro flag:* It is important to understand that the Euro flag is not a National flag but a flag representing an association of nations, in other words an association flag.

Some Continental nations are using it as a defaced Ensign, i.e. a Euro flag with a small edition of their National flag in the upper canton (similar to a Red Ensign with the small Union flag in the upper canton).

While this may be permissable under their particular constitution, it would not be so in the United Kingdom. The Merchant Shipping Act of 1894 specifically states that the Red Ensign is the proper National flag for British ships. (This is amended by Admiralty Warrants for Red and Blue defaced Ensigns).

The wearing of a Euro flag as an Ensign in a British ship, whether defaced or not, is therefore prohibited and can lead to a fine of £500.

Its use as a courtesy flag is rather different. A courtesy flag is the flag of a foreign nation worn on the starboard yard arm of a yacht when visting that particular country. It cannot be replaced by the Euro flag as this is not the flag of any particular country.

However, it would be regarded as a pleasant gesture if the Euro flag was worn inferior to (below) the correct courtesy flag when visiting a foreign country which is a member of the European Community.

(c) Racing Flags: When a yacht is racing the club Burgee is replaced with the owner's racing flag, square in shape and of any design and colour. It is not now obligatory to fly a racing flag unless prescribed by the club rules due to the difficulties incurred with instrumentation at the masthead. The Ensign is never worn while racing, being handed down at the 5 minute gun and rehoisted at the conclusion of the race, or if the yacht withdraws, to indicate that she is no longer racing.

The prize flag is usually a smaller version of the owner's racing flag. The second prize flag is triangular, blue with a white 2 marked on it and the third prize is a red triangular flag with a white 3.

The protest flag may be specified by the organising club (the R.Y.A. does not specify any particular flag), the International Yacht Racing Union suggests the use of International Code Flag B.

(d) *International Code Flags:* These flags, together with the International Code Book enable vessels of any nationality to communicate with each other irrespective of language difficulties. It is unusual for the smaller cruising yacht to carry the full set unless she wishes to "dress overall" on ceremonial occasions but it is useful for certain flags with single letter meanings to be carried on board. An example is "W" — I require medical assistance. It is important to remember that the flags must be of such a size as to be clearly visible at a reasonable distance. Any registered British vessel may be allotted a four flag hoist — known as her "number" and which is the same as her radio call sign. This hoist is used when she wishes to identify herself at sea.

The code flag most frequently used by yachts is the "Q" flag meaning: My vessel is healthy and I request free pratique. This is used universally as a request for Customs clearance when a vessel is entering a foreign port from another country and also when returning to her own country from abroad.

When Flags are Worn

Flags worn at sea comprise the Ensign, club Burgee or house flag. The Ensign may be hauled down at night and when on passage out of sight of land or other ships, but should be hoisted when passing another vessel.

When entering or leaving a foreign port a British vessel must wear her "colours" and those of 50 tons gross and upwards must do likewise when entering or leaving a British port.

In harbour the Burgee and special Ensigns are worn when the owner is on board or in effective control of the vessel (similarly with any house flag which the owner may fly).

Ensigns, Burgees and house flags are hoisted at 0800 in summer and 0900 in winter and lowered at sunset or 2100 hours whichever is earlier. Flag Officers' Broad Pennants, following the Royal Navy custom, are flown throughout the 24 hours when the owner is on board. There is no strict rule regarding the raising and lowering of Burgees and it is now common practice to fly the Burgee throughout the 24 hours. The times in some foreign countries may vary and whenever possible the time should be taken from any Naval vessel in port or the local Yacht Club.

Where Flags are Worn

The Ensign, being the most important flag on board, must always be worn in the after part of the vessel on its own staff on the taffrail. If for any reason this is impossible it may be worn at a position ⅔ up the leech of the mainsail in the case of single masted vessels and in similar position in two masted vessels where the aftermast is as tall or taller than the foremast. Where the aftermast is shorter than the foremast the Ensign may be worn on a staff at the mizzen masthead.

The Burgee or Flag Officer's Pennant should be flown from the main masthead although if the masthead is cluttered with instrumentation the Burgee may be flown from the starboard yard arm but a Flag Officer's Pennant must never be flown from any position other than the main masthead.

Saluting

It has always been traditional for Ensigns to be "dipped" when passing any Naval vessel, Royal yacht, or the flag officer of a yacht club when the yacht saluting is wearing the Burgee of the Flag officer's club. The salute is made by lowering the Ensign to a position about ⅓ from the lower end of the hoist and rehoisting when the vessel being saluted rehoists hers.

Nowadays, this is hardly practicable in certain situations, e.g. a crowded summer weekend on the Solent. When at sea, however, it is pleasant and courteous to maintain this ancient tradition.

Dressing Ship

Dressing overall can take place on three types of ocasion, a British national festival, a foreign festival and local occasions such as regattas, and there are minor variations in the flag arrangements for each. Ships only dress overall when in harbour or anchored. The International code flags are worn on a line stretching from stem to stern, over the masthead or heads. The order in which the flags are attached is as follows and commences at the Stem (the reason for a particular order is to ensure variety of shape and colour):

E Q p3 G p8 Z p4 W p6 P p1 1 CODE T Y B X 1st H
3rd D F 2nd U A O M R p2 J p0 N p9 K p7 V p5 L C S

If the vessel is two masted the line between the mastheads starts with Y and finishes with 0.

In the case of a British national festival the Ensign will be worn in its usual place, i.e. taffrail or mizzen masthead with the addition of an Ensign at the masthead, with the Club Burgee side by side. In the case of a Flag Officer his personal Pennant only will be flown from the masthead.

For foreign national festivals the appropriate National flag should be flown at the masthead with the Club Burgee alongside. If however the vessel is two masted the foreign national flag is flown at the lower masthead. In the event of the owner being a Flag Officer his personal Pennant only is flown at the main masthead the foreign Ensign being flown at the starboard crosstree if the vessel is single masted.

When the owner is entitled to wear the special Ensign of a privileged yacht club he may fly either the Red Ensign or the privilege Ensign but if the latter, the same privilege Ensign must be worn at the taffrail or at the masthead.

In the case of local festivals, regattas, etc. no Ensign is flown from the masthead, only the Club Burgee or Flag Officer's Pennant.

Seamanship

14

ROPE — ITS USE AND CARE

Types of Construction

There are three main methods of rope construction, laid or twisted ropes (cable laid), the traditional form of manufacture used when natural fibre ropes were in general use, and plaited and braided ropes. Plaited ropes, usually 4, 8 or 16 plait have the great advantage of being far less liable to kink than a traditional laid rope and are thus useful for anchor and mooring ropes where long lengths may require to be rapidly stowed in fairly small places as they will flake down with no tendency to kink. Multiplait ropes have very little tendency to kink and are smooth running. This type of construction does of course require specialist splicing techniques.

Types of Material

There are three main types of man made fibre, nylon, polyester and polypropylene.

Nylon is the strongest of the three followed by polyester and then polypropylene. Nylon, as well as being very strong is also elastic and is thus most suitable for dealing with shock loads, for example with anchors, but is unsuitable for halyards where minimum stretch is essential.

Polyester has the useful combination of strength with a low stretch characteristic which thus makes it suitable for most purposes on board — it is also available as pre-stretched which is ideal for halyards, in both plaited or 3 strand construction.

The main advantage of polypropylene is that it floats and is thus the most useful rope to use for dinghy painters and mooring lines where a submerged rope could offer hazards to propellers.

A fourth material polythene is relatively cheap and has a "waxy" feel, very popular for fishing net construction but of no great interest to yachtsmen, other than for mooring lines. (Unsuitable where it is necessary to tie knots due to slippery finish.) The latest additions to the man made fibre groups are 'Spectra' (brand name of Allied Chemicals) and 'Kevlar' (brand name of Du Pont). Both are very light with immensely strong filaments.

In their present form, both ropes are mainly of interest to the racing yachtsmen where great strength and lightness are highly desirable and cost and working life of lesser importance than they are to the cruising man. Reference should be made to the manufacturers' publications when it is proposed to use any of such new generation products in view of the varying characteristics and requirements. For example Kevlar is very susceptible to damage by chafe and bending and must be protected from sunlight whereas with Spectra variants with adequate resistance to long term creep must be selected.

Generally speaking, man made fibre ropes used in yachts are larger than is necessary from a strength point of view in order to facilitate ease of handling, for example the modern equivalent strength wise of the old $1\frac{1}{2}$ inch circumference manilla ropes would be far too small to handle comfortably if used for sheets. The surface of the rope also has considerable bearing on its handling properties, ropes formed with a continuous filament (never possible with natural fibres) are immensely strong and very shiny in appearance, whilst rope formed of the staple or shorter filament has slightly lower strength than the continuous filament rope but has a matt finish which is obviously more desirable where the rope is frequently handled, as in the case of sheets. With self tailers or stoppers the shiny Marlow braid should be used to facilitate long life.

Handling and Care of Ropes

The majority of man made fibres as well as being much stronger than natural fibres are very tolerant of those factors which reduced the working life of the latter, for example the former can be stored away damp and will not rot although mildew may appear.

Physical damage must be guarded against as with natural fibres, particularly bearing in mind that rope under tension is easily damaged by chafe. Ropes under tension but static (*e.g.* mooring lines) should be protected at any angular point or rough service by plastic tubing over the rope or parcelling with canvas, etc.

The effects of chafe from normal friction surfaces such as sheaves, fairleads and cleats is considerably reduced if the bearing surfaces are large. In the case of sheaves the diameter should be not less than five times the diameter of the rope and preferably more. The groove of a sheave should have such a radius that it supports one third of the rope's circumference. Whenever possible sharp "nips" in a rope should be avoided but if a rope has to be led through a sharp angle the bearing surface of the lead should be at least that required of a sheave and smooth. Rope can be severely damaged if led through a thin shackle or eye bolt, particularly if the angle is sharp.

When coiling a rope always commence at the end which is made fast so that any twists or kinks can be chased along and run out at the far end. It is particularly important to ensure that load is never applied to rope when there is a kink in it as this will almost inevitably damage and weaken it. Rope which has been badly overloaded in any way may indicate this by being unusually hard in parts, this hardness is caused by the heat produced by the overload friction fusing some of the filaments together.

Always avoid heavy shock loads if possible, for example when passing a tow rope between a stationary vessel and a moving one never make both ends fast at once. The resulting jerk imposes a tremendous strain on the rope which if it does not damage it may rip a cleat or bollard out. When one end has been made fast the correct procedure at the other end is to make a figure of eight turn round the bitts, or a round turn on a bollard and allow the rope to render smoothly as the load comes on, then check steadily and make fast as the vessel gathers way.

Unless ropes are properly coiled kinks will occur with subsequent snags when the rope is run out. Nearly all laid ropes are right handed and should be coiled clockwise to ensure smooth running out.

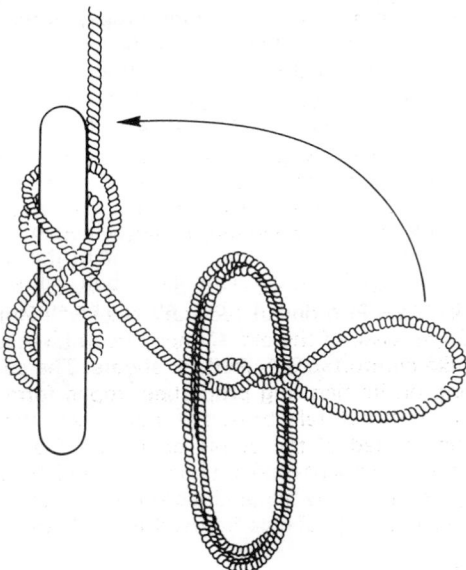

Fig. 1

In practice it is seldom that cleats on yachts are large enough to allow the fall of the halyard to be looped over the horn of the cleat without slipping off and becoming a confused tangle. When the halyard has been made up on the cleat and coiled, hold it close to the cleat, pull a short length through the coil, twist and then loop it over the horn of the cleat (Sketch 1). Alternatively a buntline hitch can be used. After coiling and looping the last loop can be pushed through the centre of the coil, capsized over the top and drawn tight (Sketch 2). A very useful hitch to use when hanging spare warps up in a cockpit locker.

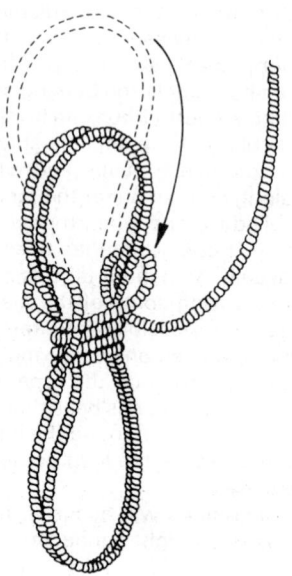

Fig. 2

A point to remember in connection with mooring ropes is that the eye of the rope should not be dropped over any lines already on the bollard. The eye should be passed up through the eyes of lines already there and then dropped over the bollard. This will facilitate the removal of any line without disturbing the others.

It is desirable to ensure uniformity of wear in ropes whenever possible by changing end for end occasionally.

Cleaning

The life of a rope can be extended considerably by washing in fresh water to get rid of salt crystal, grit and dirt. This should be done at the end of the season when laying up and will ensure that not only will the rope look clean but will remain soft and pliable. Detergents should not be used, soap powder only should be employed to clean the rope.

(From information supplied by Marlow Ropes).

KNOTS, BENDS AND HITCHES

The following simple bends and hitches are but a few of those used by the professional seaman — they should, however, serve to meet most of the requirements of those working yachts and small boats.

A **Bend** is used to join the ends of two ropes.
A **Hitch** secures a rope to another object.

THE ROUND TURN
Although this is only the first movement in securing a rope to a permanent fixture there is much virtue in a Round Turn not always appreciated by small boat owners. Always remember that a considerable weight can be held with relatively little effort by taking a round turn about the bitts or other secure object. A round turn should always be taken about an open ended protrusion, such as bitts as this does not necessitate letting go of the rope. When in the act of coming alongside a round turn or two will take the weight without the danger of jambing.

In emergency a quick turn round some strong object on board (and the rope then held away tight), will frequently prevent the bow or stern swinging out into the tide at the wrong moment. Having stopped the vessel's movement by the round turn a judicious "slacking away" or "hauling in" using the bollard, bitt or cleat as a "hold" temporarily, is excellent seamanship — when the emergency is over, the rope can be secured or removed as desired.

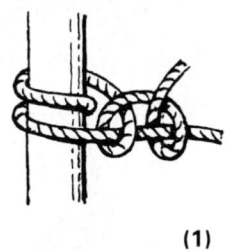  

(1)   **(2)**   **(3)**

(1) **Round Turn and Two Half Hitches.** For securing a dinghy painter to a mooring ring, etc. If leaving a vessel moored to a buoy by this — the best method — have loose hitches — not too close to the buoy and lay the loose end along the standing part of the rope and frap together — it will never come adrift, but is easy to untie.

(2) **Clove Hitch.** A good hitch for securing a rope at intermediate points. It is not safe with a short end. Difficult to untie after being subjected to heavy strain, especially when wet.

(3) **Sheet Bend.** Serves many purposes. Used for making a rope fast to the bight of another — i.e. bending the sheets to the sails — securing the end of a small rope to that of a larger. If used to join ropes which are made of different materials, the ends should be seized back or the bend is liable to come adrift. (See also Double Sheet Bend.)

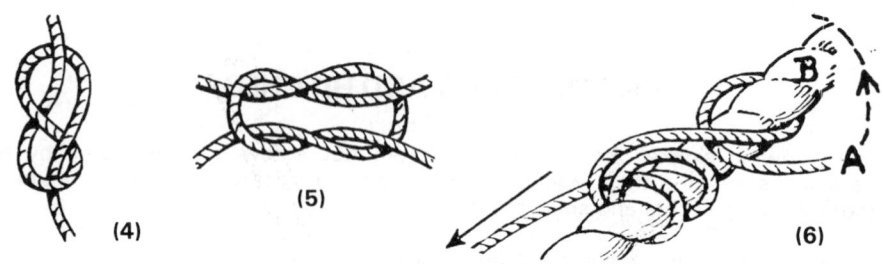

(4)

(5)

(6)

(4) **Figure of Eight Knot.** To prevent the end of a small rope from accidentally running through a block or the deck lead for jib sheets, etc.

(5) **Reef Knot.** Has many uses. Is excellent as a "binder" knot, joining the ends of small ropes — e.g. reef points when reefing and furling sail. Before leaving signal halliards or any "running ropes" not in use — always join both ends together in case wind blows them off the cleat and they become unrove. CAUTION: Do not use a reef knot as a bend for tying two ropes together. If the ropes are of different size, or different materials, or one is stiffer than the other, the knot is very liable to capsize.

(6) **Rolling Hitch.** A most practical knot much used at sea for all purposes. After commencing as a clove hitch an additional hitch is made over the first between this and the standing part of the rope which effectively jambs the hitch and prevents sideways pull — the simple form is finished off with a further hitch away from the strain as shown in Fig. 6. Used for securing the tail of a block to a larger rope, hanging off a rope on a stopper, flag swivel sticks, etc. It does not slip or "roll" under normal loading but if subjected to heavy strain — as when stoppering off a mooring rope — the end (A) which does not carry the load should be "backed and dogged", i.e. backed against the hitch and twisted round the first rope (B) in long lays. The end is then held or stopped until the load can be transferred back to the larger rope.

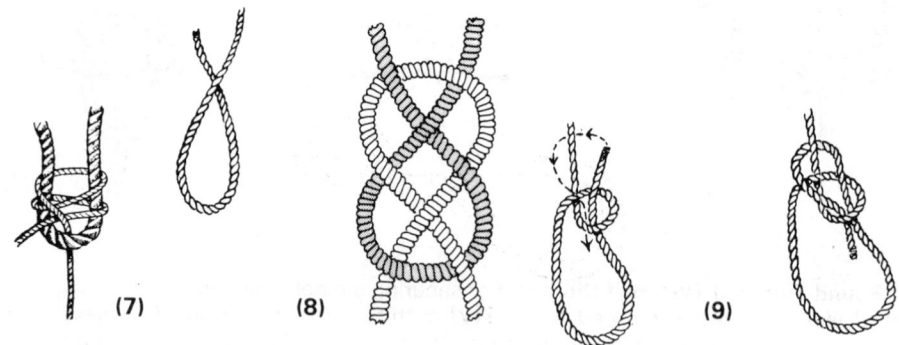

(7)

(8)

(9)

(7) **Double Sheet Bend.** For securing "Bosun's Chair" and for the same purposes as the sheet bend. The working end is rove twice to give extra security.

(8) **Carrick Bend.** For bending two hawsers or wire ropes together. Very secure and unlikely to jamb. Each end tucks under/over four times.

(9) **Bowline.** The most commonly used loop knot. Will never capsize if properly formed. Used to make a loop in the end of a rope without splicing — made quickly and without hesitation when sending small mooring lines ashore.

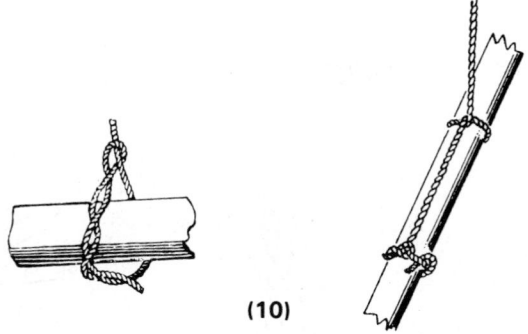

(10)

(10) **Timber Hitch.** Used for lifting a spar, timber, bale or plank, etc. The turns should always be dogged with the lay of the rope. When used for towing a spar, or to keep a piece of timber pointing in one direction when being lifted, it should be used with a half-hitch as illustrated.

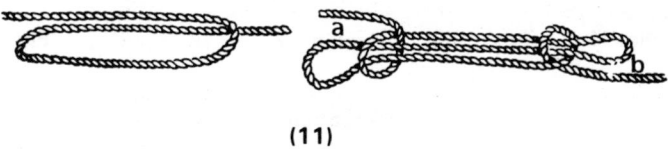

(11)

(11) **Sheepshank.** Used for shortening a rope temporarily. To make more secure, especially if not subjected to a steady pull, the loops should be stopped to the standing part at points a and b.

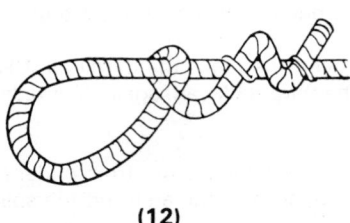

(12)

(12) **Lighterman's Hitch.** Used by lightermen to make a towing eye in the end of a barge rope. The lighterman's hitch consists of a loop secured by a half-hitch with two back tucks on the standing part, and will hold as well as any splice.

A few knots known and used correctly and instantly, shows a better seaman than one who knows all the names of the lesser used knots; but who is slow or inaccurate in their execution.

ROPE SPLICING

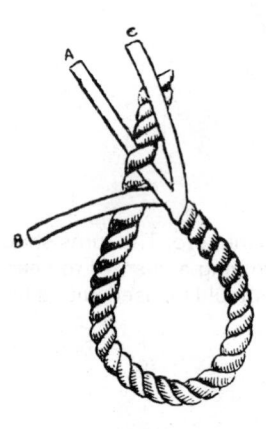

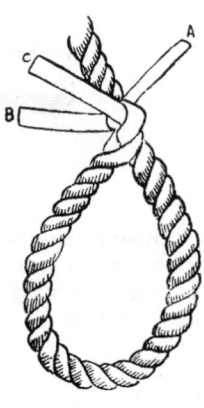

| Fig. 1 | Fig. 2 | Fig. 3 |

EYE SPLICE

(1) Unlay the three strands at the end of the rope enough to make at least three tucks — about one turn for each tuck — and form an eye by laying the opened strands on top of the standing part of the rope.

(2) Take the middle end (A, in Fig. 1) and tuck it, from right to left, underneath the nearest strand of the standing part.

(3) Pick up the left end (B, in Fig. 2) and tuck it — again from right to left — under the next strand to the left of the one under which (A) is tucked.

(4) Turn the whole splice over, then take the third end (C) and lead it over to the right of the third strand, so that the third tuck can, again, be made from right to left, as in Fig. 3.

(5) There should now be one end coming out from under each strand on the standing part. If two ends come from under the same strand the splice is wrong.

(6) Pull each end tight enough to make a tidy and snug fit. This completes the first round of tucks.

(7) For the second round, take each end over one strand and under the next towards the left. Pull each end tight.

(8) Repeat for the third round. Never use less than three rounds of tucks if the eye is to bear any strain.

(9) If desired, for neatness, the splice can be tapered by adding additional rounds of tucks, first with halved strands and then by halving again before the final round.

SHORT SPLICING

For joining two ropes of the same size together.

(1) Unlay the two ends to be joined — at least one turn for each round of tucks to be made.

(2) Marry these ends together, so that the strands of one rope lay alternately between the strands of the other.

(3) Hold firmly whilst making tucks. Tucks are made towards the left by passing each end, in turn, over one strand and under the next, in the same manner as described for the eye splice.

(4) If the rope is to bear any strain make at least three rounds of tucks each way.

LONG SPLICE

Seldom used in practice but very useful as a temporary measure — i.e. until the rope can be replaced with a new one — for rope which is required to run through a block because the splice does not thicken it.

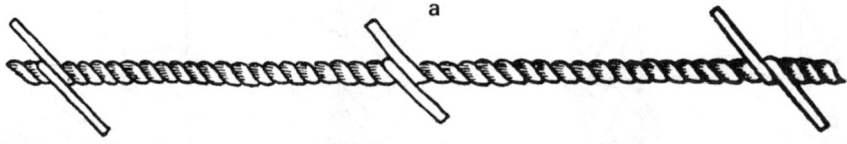

Fig. 4

(1) Unlay the ends of two ropes to at least four times the distance required for a short splice.

(2) Marry the ends together as though about to commence a short splice.

(3) Select two ends which cross one another from opposite sides, unlay one of them for some length and lay into its place the opposite strand from the other rope until only a short piece is left. Cut off surplus from the end which is unlaid.

(4) Repeat with two more strands but work in the opposite direction.

(5) The third pair of strands (at a in Fig. 4) are left in their original place, so that there are now three pairs of ends. Make an overhand knot with each pair so that the ends follow the lay of the rope and do not cross it.

(6) Pull very tight and then taper off by reducing the yarns in each strand.

BACK SPLICE

Where a rope is not required to run through a block — when whippings are preferable — a back splice may be used to prevent the strands unlaying.
After unlaying the strands for the estimated distance, form a crown by interlacing the strands at the ropes end. Then tuck the strands "over one and under one" backwards towards the standing part of the rope. This splice is really only of interest with natural fibre ropes. With man made fibres the rope ends can be fused together by heating.

EYE-SPLICE — MULTI-PLAIT ROPE

This double four-part rope is supple and simple to coil in either hand thus making it ideal for anchoring and mooring. The eye splice used is based upon the construction of the rope, which employs both "Z" or right-handed lay strands and "S" or left-handed strands. After whipping or stopping at the point of splice, divide the various Z and S strands as shown and tuck in two pairs front and back of the work. Thereafter the paired strands are divided and tucked separately. Finish by seizing ends as illustrated.

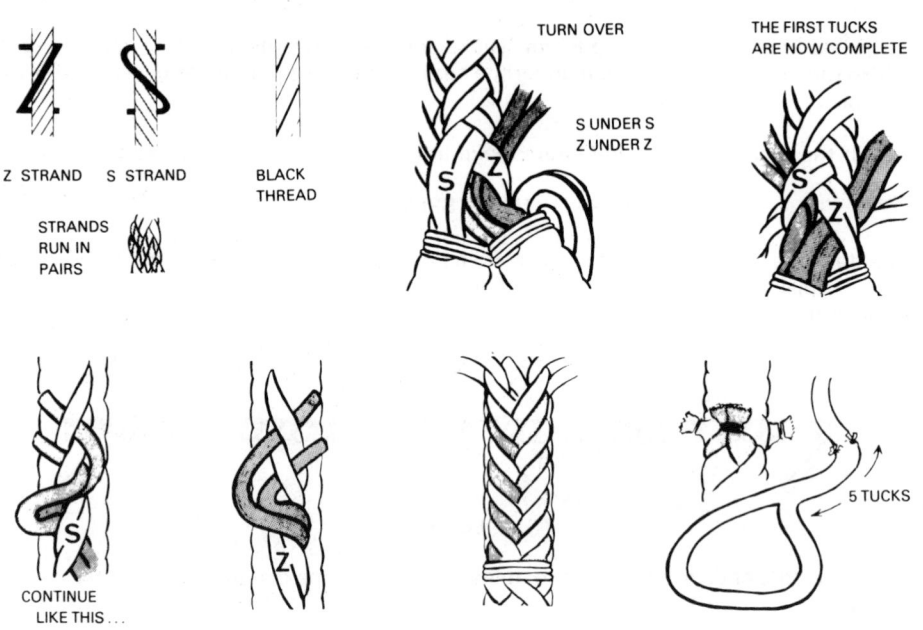

Z STRAND   S STRAND   BLACK THREAD

STRANDS RUN IN PAIRS

TURN OVER

THE FIRST TUCKS ARE NOW COMPLETE

S UNDER S
Z UNDER Z

CONTINUE LIKE THIS . . .

5 TUCKS

SEW AND SERVE EYE SPLICE — PLAITED ROPE

It is important that stoppings, sewing and finally serving are tight and neat otherwise the eye splice resulting will be loose and weak. Pass the sail needle right through the rope each time and tug stitch home tightly. Taper the unlaid rope yarns otherwise it will be impossible to apply a serving to the decreasing diameter of the splice. Set up taut before attempting to serve. Use No. 16 waxed whipping Polyester twine.

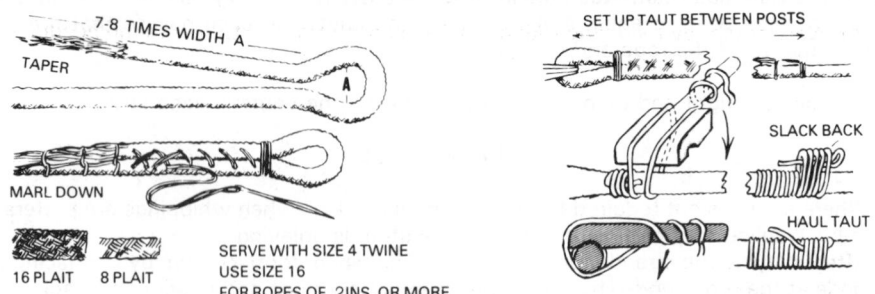

7-8 TIMES WIDTH A

TAPER

A

MARL DOWN

16 PLAIT   8 PLAIT

SERVE WITH SIZE 4 TWINE
USE SIZE 16
FOR ROPES OF 2INS. OR MORE

SET UP TAUT BETWEEN POSTS

SLACK BACK

HAUL TAUT

ROPE WHIPPINGS

Whippings are extensively used in connection with natural fibre ropes to secure the ends from unravelling but with modern man made fibres the ends of smaller ropes are usually fused together. There will always, however, be occasions when it is useful to be able to whip the end of a rope or seize an eye or thimble in the middle (e.g. double sheets).

Common Whipping. (1) Cut off a suitable length of twine and lay one end (D in Fig. 1) *along* the end of the rope.

(2) Then take half a dozen or more tight turns around the rope *and* the twine, working towards the end of rope and against the lay. Pull each turn tight as it is made.

(3) Now lay the other end of twine (BC in Fig. 2) along the rope and over the turns already made.

(4) With part A of the twine, continue to pass turns round over part B.

(5) When the loop remaining at E becomes too small to pass over the rope's end, pull tight on C and cut the end off (Fig. 3).

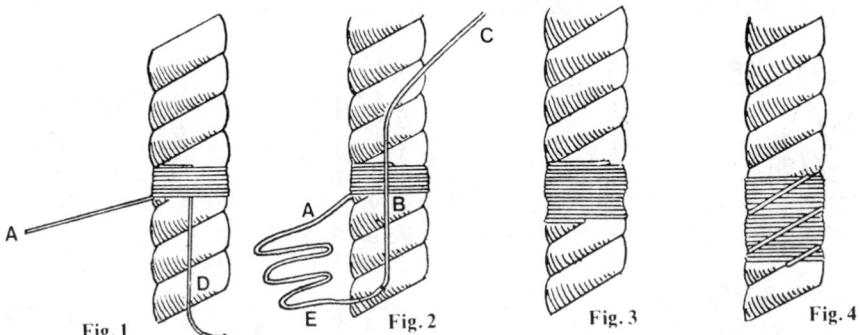

Fig. 1   Fig. 2   Fig. 3   Fig. 4

Palm and Needle Whipping. This is more secure than the common whipping and is very suitable for reef points and all mooring ropes.

(1) Thread a suitable length of twine through a sailmaker's needle.

(2) Pass the needle under one strand and draw through most of the twine.

(3) Take about a dozen or more turns of twine round the rope, working against the lay and pulling each turn well tight as it is made.

(4) Now stitch, by following round between each strand in turn with the needle, as in Fig. 4, and thus tightly frapping the turns in between each strand.

West Country Whipping. Useful when required to whip the bight of a rope.

(1) Place the middle of the twine against the rope, bring the two ends round in opposite directions and make a half-knot.

(2) Now bring the ends round (again, in opposite direction) to the opposite side and make another half-knot.

(3) Continue half-knotting the ends alternately on opposite sides of the rope.

(4) Finish with a reef knot when sufficient turns have been made.

KEEL BOATS — Sheets and Halyards Size Selector

Chart shows usual sail area in square feet for a given boat length in metres. If your boat is rigged with larger sails, use the rope size indicated for the sail area.

Overall Yacht Length m	6-8	9	10	11	12	14	16	18
Approx. Sail Area sq ft								
MAIN	90	144	171	198	252	405	540	720
GENOA/JIB	100	180	270	360	450	630	765	900
SPINNAKER	405	495	585	765	990	1260	1620	1980

SHEET SIZE mm dia								
MAIN	8	8	8	10	12	12	14	16
GENOA/JIB	10	10	12	12	14	14	16	16
SPINNAKER	8	10	10	10	12	12	12	14
SPINNAKER GUY	10	10	12	12	12	14	14	16

Suggested SHEET ropes: Marlowbraid, 16-plait matt, or KT3.

HALYARD SIZE mm dia								
MAIN	8	10	10	10	12	12	12	14
GENOA/JIB	8	10	10	12	12	12	14	16
SPINNAKER	8	8	10	10	12	12	12	14

Suggested HALYARD ropes: Marlowbraid, KT3 or super pre-stretched polyester.
Remember for KT3 Sheets or Halyards you can go down a size.

MOORING ROPES mm dia								
Displacement (approx.) tonnes	2	4	5	6.5	8	11	12	20
POLYESTER/NYLON	8-10	12	12	14	14	16	18	24
POLYPROPYLENE (Nelson)	10-12	14	16	18	20	20	24	28

Suggested MOORING ropes: 3-strand standard polyester, Multiplait nylon, Nelson or 3-strand nylon.

ANCHOR WARPS, PAINTER LINES								
NYLON	12	14	16	16	18	20	20	24
POLYESTER	14	16	18	18	20	24	24	24
NYLON (KEDGE)	8	8	10	10	10	12	12	12

Suggested ropes: Multiplait nylon, 3-strand nylon.

ANCHORS AND CHAINS								
BRUCE	5	7.5	10	10	15	20	20	30
DANFORTH & CQR	8	14	14	14	19	25	25	34
CHAIN	8	8	10	10	10	12	12	12

Bruce, Danforth and CQR anchor in kg. Other sizes are diameter in mm.

By courtesy of Marlow Ropes Limited

SIZES & BREAKING LOADS

16-plait matt polyester

Dia. mm	8	9	10	12	14	16	18	20
B/L kg.	1450	1900	2630	3470	4610	6200	7370	8300

Marlowbraid polyester

Dia. mm	6	8	9	10	12	14	16	18	20
B/L kg.	1000	1700	2000	2600	3600	4800	6300	8000	9800

KT3 100% Kevlar®/core

Dia. mm	3.5	4.5	5.5	6	8	10	12
B/L kg.	320	600	700	1200	2500	3840	5680

8-plait Marstron multifilament polypropylene

Dia. mm	5	6	8	10
B/L kg.	250	400	700	1000

3-strand super pre-stretched polyester

Dia. mm	3	4	5	6	7	8	9	10	12	14
B/L kg.	300	480	650	935	1235	1590	2010	2430	3360	4920

8-plait standard polyester

Dia. mm	1	1.5	2	3
B/L kg.	35	65	75	165

3 strand Hardyhemp polypropylene

Dia. mm	8	10	12	14	16
B/L kg.	650	1100	1600	2000	2500

3-strand standard polyester to BS 4928

Dia. mm	4	6	8	10	12	14	16	18	20	24
G.M.B.L.	400	780	1325	2025	2800	3450	4100	5100	6350	9140

3-strand Nelson spunstaple polypropylene* to BS 4928

Dia. mm	6	8	10	12	14	16	18	20	24
G.M.B.L.	550	960	1425	2030	2790	3500	4450	5370	7600

*available in multiplait

3-strand Blue Sturdee polypropylene to BS 4928

Dia. mm	4	6	8	10	12
G.M.B.L.	250	550	960	1425	2030

Multiplait nylon to BS 4928

Dia. mm	10	12	14	16	18	20	24
G.M.B.L.	2080	3000	4100	5300	6700	8300	12000

3-strand nylon to BS 4928

Dia. mm	8	10	12	14	16	18	20	24	28	32
G.M.B.L.	1350	2080	3000	4100	5300	6700	8300	12000	15800	20000

By courtesy of H&T Marlow Ltd.

GLOSSARY OF NAUTICAL TERMS

ABAFT	Towards the stern.
Abeam	At right angles to the line of the keel.
About	To go about, to change tack.
Aft	Towards the stern of the vessel.
Amidships	Midway between stem and stern.
Astern	Behind the vessel.
Athwart	From side to side.
Avast	To stop, to hold fast, *e.g.* avast heaving.
Awash	A vessel, wreck, or shoal so low that water constantly washes over.
Aweigh	Term to indicate that the anchor has broken out of the ground.
BACK	(a) Wind shifting anti clockwise (b) To assist an anchor by ''backing up'' with another anchor.
Backstay	Standing rigging from a masthead leading aft to take the strain of the mast.
Ballast	Iron, lead or stone placed in bottom of a ship to increase her stability.
Bar	A shoal in the approach to a harbour.
Battens	Thin pieces of wood or plastic set into the sail to preserve the shape.
Beacon	Aid to Navigation, lighted or unlighted, set on the shore or rocks.
Beam	(a) Extreme width of a vessel. (b) Athwartships timber on which the deck is laid.
Beam Bearing	Direction of some objects when abeam or at right angles to the fore and aft line.
Bearing	Direction of an object at sea expressed in Compass notation.
Bear up	To put the helm up, *i.e.* keep further away from the wind.
Beating	Sailing towards the direction of the wind by tacking.
Becket	Small rope circle, a simple eye.
Belay	To make a rope fast to a belaying pin or cleat.
Bend	Knot of various kinds.
Bight	Any part of a rope between the ends; also a curve or cove on a coastline.
Bilges	Bottom of vessel where water collects.
Binnacle	The box which houses the Mariner's Compass.
Bitter End	The last part of a cable left around the ''bitts'' when the rest is overboard.
Bitts	Pair of wooden or iron head vertical on deck with crosspiece for fastening cables.
Bluff	(a) Steep shore. (b) Full bowed vessel.
Bobstay	A stay for the bowsprit to prevent it lifting; lead from bowsprit end to stem at waterline.
Bollard	Heavy short post on a quay or deck to secure ship's mooring lines to.
Bolt rope	A strong rope sewn round the edge of sails to give strength and prevent tearing.
Boom	A spar for many purposes, such as to stretch out the foot of a fore and aft sail.
Boot-Topping	A band of paint at the waterline between ''wind and water''.
Bower	Main anchor carried forward in a vessel.

Bow	Forward part of a vessel.
Bowsprit	Heavy spar from deck leading forward from stem head to set head sails.
Breast Line	Ropes forward and aft at right angles to the ship to "breast" into jetty.
Bring up	To stop, as to come to anchor.
Broach to	To come up to the wind and get broadside into the trough of the sea.
Bulkheads	Partitions fore and aft or athwartships, forming separate compartments.
Bulwarks	A vessel's topsides that extend above the deck.
Buoy	A float, with distinguishing name, shape, colour or light.
Burgee	Pennant (pointed) shaped flag with design indicating the Yacht Club the vessel's owner belongs to.
By the head	Greater draught forward than aft.
By the lee	When running under sail, if the wind blows over the same side as the mainsail.
By the stern	Greater draught aft than forward.
CABLE	(a) $\frac{1}{10}$th Nautical mile, (b) Anchor chain.
Capstan	A vertical cylindrical machine for veering or hoisting the anchor chain.
Careen	To heel a vessel over on one side by tackles, to work on her bottom.
Carry way	To continue to move through the water.
Carvel	Edge to edge planking for a vessel's hull.
Caulk	To fill the side or deck seams with oakum or cotton to prevent leaking.
Chafe	Chafing gear, canvas, or the like wound round ropes and spars to prevent wear by rubbing.
Chain Plates	Metal strips fastened outside the hull to take the rigging strain.
Check	To slowly stop a vessel's movement or to slowly ease a rope.
Claw off	Working a vessel to windward off a lee shore.
Cleat	A two pronged device for making fast ropes.
Clew	The corner of the sail where the leech meets the foot.
Clinker	Planking when one edge overlaps the other lower plank.
Close-Hauled	Sailing close to the wind.
Companion	Ladder in a ship.
Cofferdam	A watertight space between two bulkheads.
Composite	A wooden vessel built with iron floors and frames.
Con	To give orders to the helmsman in narrow waters.
Counter	The overhanging portion of a stern.
Course	(a) The direction a vessel steers in. (b) The sail set from a lower yard.
Cradle	The frame erected round and under a vessel to support her out of the water.
Cringle	Rope round a thimble, worked into a sail clew.
Crown	(a) Where the arms of an anchor meet the shank. (b) The knot when the strands of a rope are interlocked to make a backsplice.
Crutch	(a) Metal fitting dropped into gunwale of a small boat often called row-locks. (b) A stanchion with half round upper end to support the boom (also Gallows).

DAVIT Iron crane for hoisting, lowering and holding boats in position in larger vessels.

Dead Reckoning The position found by calculation from course steered and distance run.

Deadweight Total weight of vessels carrying capacity in tons.

Deckhead Underside of a deck. The roof of a ship's cabin.

Deep (a) Unmarked soundings of the lead line. (b) Deep water channel between shoals.

Dolphin A built pile structure for mooring in harbour.

Downhaul Rope or tackle used to haul down sail or yard.

Down helm Order to helmsman to put tiller away from wind; up helm is towards wind.

Dowse (a) To extinguish a light. (b) Lower sail or spar quickly. (c) Spray with water.

Draught The depth of water occupied by a vessel at any time.

Drogue Sea anchor, normally of canvas, for vessel, to lie to in bad weather.

EARING Rope for bending sail or head cringle to a yard or clew cringle to a boom.

Ebb The period when the tide falls or flows from the land.

Eddy Circular motion of the water unconnected with general water movement.

Ensign The flag, always carried at the stern, that denotes a vessel's nationality.

FAIRLEAD A channel for leading a rope over an obstruction to avoid friction.

Fairway Shipping channel normally the centre of an approach channel.

Fathom Nautical measurement of depth of six feet or 1.83m.

Fender Soft rubber or other material to prevent chafe between vessels, or vessel and pier.

Fetch (a) To make, arrive at a desired point. (b) The distance the wind has from weather shore to ship.

Fiddle Wooden top, with divisions fitted to saloon table in rough weather.

Flare The overhang of a vessel's bow; also a light signal by pilots and fishermen.

Fix Obtained by taking accurate bearings or by astronomical observation.

Flashing Navigation light with duration of light less than dark, and single flash of regular intervals.

Foot The lower edge of a sail.

Fore and Aft In line with the keel—lengthways of the ship.

Forward Towards the bow.

Foul Opposite to clear, as "foul berth", "foul anchor", "foul bottom".

Frap To bind ropes together, or to bind a loose sail to prevent frapping.

Freeboard The distance from the waterline to the deck outboard edge.

Freshen Wind freshens when increasing

Full and Bye Close hauled but with the sails well filled.

Furl Gathering in sail and securing with gaskets to its spar.

GAFF	The spar to which the head of a fore and aft sail is bent.
Galley	The kitchen of a ship of any size.
Gallows	Frame of wood or metal with rounded top for supporting the boom.
Gimbals	Two concentric rings to hold the compass or stove horizontal at all times.
Go About	To tack.
Goose-neck	A metal fitting for securing a boom to a mast. Allows swing and topping.
Goose-winged	When running and the after mast sail is out on the side opposite to the fore sail.
Ground	(a) A ship touching bottom is said to ground. (b) Ground swell is the long coastal swell.
Gunter	A Sliding Gunter rig is when the gaff is hoisted vertically, reducing the necessity for a tall mast.
Gunwale	The heavy top rail of a boat.
Guy	A rope or wire used to steady a boat, derrick or spar.
Gybe	To allow a fore and aft sail to swing from one side to the other when running.
HALYARDS	Ropes or tackles used to hoist sails or flags.
Hanks	Strong clip hooks which attach head sails to the mast stays.
Hard	A place, often specially constructed, for beaching small vessels.
Hawse Pipes	Pipes leading down through the bows through which the anchor cables are led.
Hawser	A heavy rope used for mooring, kedging, warping, towing or as a temporary anchor warp.
Head	Forward in a ship, headsails are those set forward of the foremast.
Head Sea	Sea from ahead, beam sea is a wind blowing from abeam.
Head Sheets	A small platform at the forward end of a boat.
Heads	Toilets in a ship.
Heave the Lead	To take soundings.
Heave to	To stop, by sail or engine action to so reduce speed, when head into wind that vessel has as little forward motion as possible. Vessel is then "hove to".
Heaving Line	Light line, knotted on end to throw ashore when berthing as a messenger for a larger mooring line.
Heel	A list from the upright; the foot of a mast.
Helm	The tiller or wheel; the helmsman is he who steers a vessel.
Hitch	To make a rope fast to a spar or stay, but not to another rope.
Holding Ground	The type of bottom for anchor, *i.e.* good or bad holding ground.
Holiday	An unpainted or unvarnished spot in a vessel.
Horse	An iron bar parallel to the deck, running athwartship for a sail sheet to travel.
Hounds Band	A band around the top of the mast with securing eyes for attaching stays.
Hull	Structure of a vessel below deck level.
INBOARD	Towards midships.
Inshore	Towards the shore
Irons	A vessel is in irons when caught head to wind and unable to pay off on either tack.
Isophase	Navigation light where duration of light and dark are equal.

JACK-STAY	An iron rod, secured to a yard for bending sails to.
Jack Staff	Small staff in the bows from which the jack is flown.
Jib	The triangular sail set as the forward headsail.
Jury	After losing mast or rudder makeshift rig to get the vessel to safety.
KEDGE	A light weight anchor for kedging or warping.
Keel	The heavy backbone of any vessel, runs fore and aft on which the vessel sits when grounded.
King spoke	The spoke of the steering wheel which is upright when the wheel is amidships.
Knot	One nautical mile per hour.
LACING	The long line that secures the sail to a spar through eyelets.
Lash	To secure anything in a ship by binding tightly with small line.
Lashing	The rope used in lashing, *e.g.* two spars together.
Launch	To slide a vessel into the water. A small motor tender.
Lay	To go, *i.e.* lay aft or lay aloft, lay to (*i.e.* heave to) lay up, lay a course. The twisting of strands in a rope.
Lazy	An extra such as a lazy painter, *i.e.* an extra painter.
Leech	The after side of a fore and aft sail, and the outer sides of a square sail.
Lead	The lead weight at the end of the lead line used to find depth of water.
Lee Side	The side away from the wind direction.
Lee Tide	Tidal stream running with the wind.
Leeward (Loo'ard)	Towards the sheltered side.
Leeway	The sideways drift of a vessel from her course to leeward, due to wind pressure.
Life Line	Lines stretched fore and aft for crew to hold on to.
Lift	A rope or wire to support a spar as topping lift.
List	When a vessel heels through having greater weight on one side.
Log	An instrument for recording the distance run.
Log Book	The record of events on board a ship, especially navigational.
Loom	The reflection on the clouds when the Light is still below the horizon; also an oar handle.
Lubber Line	Line on the inside of a compass bowl indicating the ship's head.
Luff	To keep closer to the wind; forward edge of a sail.
MAKE	To attain, *i.e.* to make harbour. Make fast is to secure. Tides that make increases. Make sail is to set sail.
Man	Provide hands to do work such as man the boat, man the pumps etc.
Marline Spike	Pointed steel tool for opening strand of wire when splicing.
Marry	To bring two ropes together.
Messenger	Light line bent to a larger hawser and lead to the winch when the larger rope would be too heavy to do this.
Midships	Order to the helmsman to centralise the rudder.
Miss Stays	To stay up in the wind when tacking.
Moor	To Moor is to lie with two anchors down. Vessels are said to moor to a jetty when well made fast with several mooring lines.

NEAP TIDES When the tide does not rise or fall much, when the moon is in quadrature.

Neaped Of a grounded ship when the tide does not rise high enough to float her.

No Higher Not to come closer to the wind.

Nothing off Not to keep more off the wind.

OCCULTING Navigation light with duration of light more than dark and total eclipse at regular intervals.

Offing To seaward.

Overhaul To slack off a tackle.

PAY OUT To ease a chain or rope.

Pintle The vertical pin on which the rudder is shipped.

Pitching A ship's movement in a seaway in a fore and aft direction.

Pooped A term to indicate that a heavy sea has come inboard over the stern causing damage.

Port The left hand side of a ship looking forward.

Port Tack To sail with the wind on the port side before the beam.

RACON Beacon giving characteristic signal when triggered by ship's radar set.

Rake The inclination of the mast in the fore and aft line from the vertical.

Ratlines Horizontal ropes as steps affixed to the shrouds to facilitate climbing.

Reach The courses of a sailing vessel between being sailed close hauled and running.

Reefing To reduce sail area by taking in at the reefing points.

Rowlocks A space in the gunwale for working oars. Metal Crutches are now normally used for rowing.

Running Rigging That rigging which is not standing *e.g.*, halyards, gantlings, purchases, etc.

SAMSON POST Used to secure anchor or tow line.

Scantlings The dimensions of a ship's timbers.

Scuttles Round holes in the ship's side for ventilation and light.

Sheer The rise of a ship's deck towards the bow or stern from amidships.

Sheer Pole An iron bar seized to the shrouds just above the rigging screws to prevent the rigging unscrewing.

Sheer Strake The upper line of plating or planking on the hull.

Sheet Rope or chain at lower corner of sail for regulating its tension.

Shroud Set of ropes forming part of standing rigging and supporting mast or topmast.

Slack Water Stationary tidal stream.

Slack in Stays When a vessel is slow in coming about.

Sound To measure the depth of water by lead line or electronic means.

Spring A mooring rope. A back spring is a mooring rope led from forward aft or from aft forward.

Spring Tides Tides when moon is full or new, that is when range of tide is greatest.

Stand on	Maintain course.
Starboard	The right hand side of a ship facing forward.
Starboard Tack	With the wind on the starboard side forward of the beam.
Stem	The forward continuation of the keel to which the planking at the fore end of the boat is affixed.
Stern Sheets	The platform extending aft from the aftermost thwart.
Stern Post	The after continuation of the keel to which the planking at the after end is affixed, or in the case of boats with a transom, the transom.
Stiff	Not easily inclined and when inclined returns quickly to the vertical.
Surge	To hold a rope still on a capstan or drumhead whilst it is still revolving.
TABERNACLE	A box like structure on deck to hold the foot of the mast when this does not run through the deck. Usually opening aft to allow mast to be lowered.
Tackle	A purchase of ropes and blocks.
Taff rail	A rail around stern of vessel.
Take up	To tighten.
Taking a Round Turn	Turning a power vessel a full circle so as to avoid collision or to obey a Port Entry Signal against the vessel.
Thwarts	Planks placed across the boat to form seats.
Tiller	Lever for turning the rudder.
Toggle	A piece of wood for making fast an eye on its own part.
Transom	A board fitted on the after side of the stern post to which the after ends of the planking are fastened.
Trick	A period at the wheel.
Trim	Inclination of keel in fore/aft direction; to change set of sails.
Tumble Home	Where a ship's sides are inclined inwards above the water line.
Turning Short Round	Turning a vessel within as small a circle as possible.
UNDER WAY	When a vessel is not made fast to the ground.
Up and Down	Vertical, a term used in anchor work.
VANG	A guy for steadying a gaff.
Veer	To ease out a cable. A clockwise shift of the wind.
WARPING	Moving a vessel by means of a hawser.
Weather Side	The side upon which the wind is blowing.
Weather Tide	Where the tide is making against the wind.
Wear Ship	Turning a ship around before the wind, keeping the sails full (the opposite to tacking a square rigged vessel).
Weigh	To lift the anchor off the ground.
Wind Rode	Where an anchored vessel is lying to the wind rather than the tide.
YARD	A spar suspended from a mast, to spread the sails.
Yaw	When the ship's head is swung by the action of the waves.
Young Flood	The first movements in a Flood tide.

MOORING ALONGSIDE

Each year a large percentage of the total damage to yachts occurs when moored alongside a quay or jetty.

When approaching the berth, make sure it is clear of overhanging obstructions which can foul the rigging or other parts of the yacht. Look also to see if there are any warning notices on the quay side, or you may return from the shore later to find your stern well jacked up by a sewer pipe, and the tide still falling.

In general, when berthed alongside, the mooring ropes should be positioned as in the diagram below, but circumstances (depending on wind, range of tide, duration of stay, possible movements of other craft, etc.) may demand some modification. It is easier to make a seamanlike job if the function of each rope is understood.

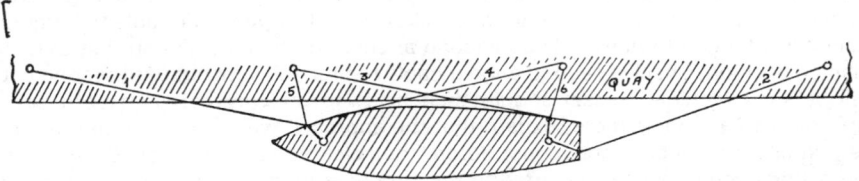

Head and Stern Ropes (1 and 2) should be strong enough to take the main load. They must also be of sufficient length to allow for the *range* of the tide. A rough rule for a range of 15 feet or less is to allow at least three times the range if the ship is berthed at half tide. If moored near High or Low Water the ropes should be adjusted later, as required. The head and stern ropes also position the ship alongside the jetty and, together with the Springs, assist in checking fore and aft surging.

The diagram showing one Head rope and one Stern is only illustrative and in practice, except for a brief stay at a wharf or pier, two ropes would always be used, normally one from each bow and one from either quarter. They need not necessarily be led to the same ring or bollard ashore. With larger vessels, heavier weights being involved — several mooring ropes would always be used and in yachts with bad weather this would generally be necessary, but certainly precautionary. But connect them before dark as it is always much easier, especially if wind increases during the night.

For'rd and After Springs (4 and 3) assist the head and stern ropes in keeping the ship alongside, prevent her from surging fore and aft, and keep the bow and stern from swinging in and out.

For'rd and After Breast Ropes (5 and 6). These are seldom necessary with small craft. They are used to hold the ship alongside the jetty when boarding or loading, or to limit its distance from the jetty. Never leave breast ropes unattended in tidal waters.

Ropes which require tending with the rise and fall of the tide should, whenever possible, be made fast so that each one can be tended without disturbing another.

Slip Ropes. Mooring lines are sometimes doubled so that they can be let go from on board. A slip rope is liable to jamb when letting go if it has not been passed correctly in the first place — when only ring-bolts are available ashore, it should be passed *down* through a ring which *hangs* at the quay side and *up* through one which *lies* horizontally on top of the quay. When pulling a slip rope on board after letting the end go, haul steadily, don't *jerk,* especially when the loose end is approaching the ring or bollard. A jerk can cause the end to flip round the hauling part and jamb. A "slip" rope is only to be used as a temporary measure.

Fenders. Place with the utmost care and, when adjusting for height, bear in mind that the swell from a passing vessel can cause fenders to be toppled inboard if the lanyards are too short.

ANCHORING

APPROACHING ANCHORAGE. Unlash anchor from stowed position and ensure that it is ready for letting go immediately it is required.

SELECTING BERTH. It is the duty of late arrivals to keep clear of vessels already anchored. Allow adequate clearance.

ONE OR TWO ANCHORS. A vessel moored with one anchor will swing over a much greater area than one moored with two (one upstream and one downstream) and should not be left unattended.

MAKING A STANDING OR RUNNING MOOR. Stem the tide and motor a little way past the selected berth, drop first anchor and fall back on tide veering double the amount of chain it is intended to ride to. Drop second anchor and then haul in on first until in the selected position. Shackle second anchor cable to first and veer out until second cable is well below waterline. Vessel should then be lying midway between both anchors. Similarly with a running moor, except that the approach will be made with the tide and the first anchor will be dropped just before the selected berth is reached. Alternatively the second anchor can be laid out with the dinghy — in this case the correct amount of chain is veered with the first anchor — not double the amount.

DEPTH OF WATER. Let out chain equivalent to at least three times maximum depth or five times if a warp is being used. If warp, ensure that it is connected to anchor by two fathoms of chain.

LAYING OUT KEDGE. Make fast end on board and then take the coil away in dinghy, paying out from there rather than paying out from the yacht. Much easier.

CLEARING A FOULED ANCHOR. Occasions arise when the anchor becomes fouled by some underwater obstruction, usually a cable or a mooring chain. If the anchor can be hauled up to the surface a rope can be passed under the obstruction to take the weight while the anchor is being freed, and then slipped. If this is not possible and assuming that the anchor has been properly buoyed with a buoy rope attached to the crown it should not prove difficult to trip the anchor by hauling on the buoy rope in the opposite direction to the lay of the main anchor cable. It is important that this main cable should be as slack as possible, possibly by using the vessel's auxiliary engine.

If the anchor has not been buoyed remedial action may be a little more difficult.

Considering first the stockless pattern such as the C.Q.R. it is a comparatively simple matter to slide a small loop of chain, attached to a warp, down the anchor cable when it will come to rest close to the crown of the anchor and the necessary pull can then be exerted.

If, however, it is a fisherman type anchor freeing may prove a little more difficult as the stock makes it difficult to get the 'retrieving' loop as far as the crown. If, however, the anchor cable is hove up as tightly as possible it will probably lift the stock off the ground and enable a chain or warp to be dragged under the stock up to the crown. A large bight of chain or weighted rope should be used, preferably towed by two dinghies spaced apart and starting from the downstream side. Once the loop has engaged with the anchor the main cable should be slacked away and tension applied by the warp in the opposite direction.

Alternatively a large bight of rope suitably weighted, 'middled' over the anchor cable and slid down to the anchor will probably engage the top arm and enable the anchor to be pulled clear provided that the angle of pull is as near horizontal as possible. In this case the main cable should not be hove in taut when the loop is slid down it.

RIDING TURN ON A WINCH

A problem which occurs sooner or later in most sailing craft is the "riding turn" on a winch. On a sheet winch the result may merely be embarrassing, on a halliard winch it creates a potentially dangerous situation with a sail that cannot be lowered. Fortunately riding turns seem to occur less frequently on halliard winches than on sheet winches.

The cause of the trouble is usually carelessness on the part of the winchman when winching in the sheet or, more likely, when "surging" it to free the sail a little.

When using the normal type of sheet winch about three turns are laid on the drum, the drum is rotated and as tension increases the winchman, who is probably also "tailing" the sheet inadvertently loses control and the sheet momentarily reverses direction. This causes the bottom turn (the one leading from the sail on to the drum) to ride down on to the skirt of the drum where it is then thrown back on to the other turns, jamming them. If the winchman does not spot this but continues winding, it will lock solid.

The first step in rectifying the situation is to heave to, thus allowing the crew to concentrate on the problem and also incidentally reducing the tension on the sheet a little. The object of the exercise is to relieve the tension on the sheet so that the riding turn can be sorted out with the aid of a large spike. This can be achieved in several ways, if the headsail is dropped it may be possible to unhank the tack of the sail thus giving sufficient slack. Assuming that this does not work it will be necessary to apply tension to the sheet or to the clew of the sail, the latter is usually the easiest alternative. A rope is bent on to the cringle in the clew of the sail and led via a snatchblock to another winch, or a purchase is used or possibly a Spanish windlass is rigged up. Once the tension has been reduced the riding turn is easily removed.

The halliard winch, however, presents a rather different problem as it will not be possible to attach a rope to the head of the sail to reduce tension in the halliard, and it is unlikely that the tack can be unclipped because of the tension in the sail. If a wire halliard is involved, fix a Crosbie clip on to the halliard several feet above the winch, place a strop above this, bend a rope on it and lead the rope via a snatchblock to another winch or a purchase. The Crosbie clip will prevent the strop sliding down the halliard as tension is applied. In the case of a rope halliard a strop made up of 4 or 5 feet of soft rope can be used. The rope is formed into a loop which is seized on to the halliard well above the winch and each side is passed round the halliard through the opposite side of the loop and back again. This process continues until all slack in the loop is used up when it is in effect plaited round the halliard. A purchase is attached to the bottom end of the strop and as the tension increases the strop grips the halliard. The rope used for the strop should be of smaller diameter than the halliard, otherwise it will not grip effectively.

GETTING ALOFT

At some time during his lifetime the average yachtsman may be faced with the problem of getting to the masthead in difficult circumstances. Perhaps past the first flush of youth, possibly overweight and with only his wife to assist him the situation looks difficult. Without mast steps (useful but expensive) or a rope ladder long enough to reach the masthead (unlikely to be part of the vessel's equipment) some form of mechanical assistance is required.

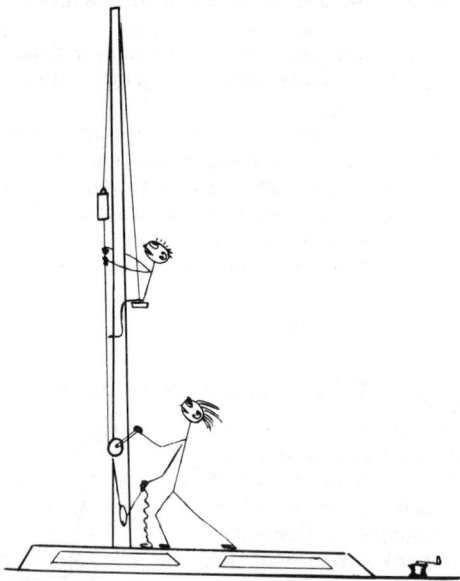

A counterweight is probably the most useful approach to the problem. As an example consider the use of 2 gallon water carriers which will probably be carried on board. Three, filled with water will weigh 60 lb. and will form a useful counterweight to a man weighing 140 lb. The carriers, or some other suitable weight, are attached to one end of the main halliard and the end of a spare halliard is also bent on. The weight is now hauled to the masthead and when it is up the man secures himself in a bosun's chair which is attached to the fall of the halliard. He now proceeds to haul himself up, aided by his wife on deck and the counterweight. His wife then firmly secures the halliard.

Cumbersome and slow perhaps but it offers the chance of getting aloft when no other assistance is available. It need hardly be mentioned that the person going aloft should be wearing a safety harness to clip on when working.

HEAVING TO

These few notes are not written for the experienced, long range cruising yachtsman who will already have evaluated the respective merits of heaving to, lying a'hull, towing warps and running under bare pole.

The weekend sailor, with a more modest cruising range and who prudently avoids going out in bad weather may not have contemplated the advantages of being able to leave his boat to look after itself for a short period, not necessarily in bad weather. It may be necessary to deal with a little domestic crisis below decks or merely have a peaceful meal in the cockpit and to do this, knowing that the vessel is quietly looking after itself, is greatly reassuring.

The object is to maintain a steady course at the lowest possible speed and ensure that the vessel's motion is as comfortable as possible and the principle is basically very simple.

The foresail is backed (hauled to windward), the mainsail eased slightly and the tiller lashed a little to leeward — the effect of this is that the main and foresail work against each other with the result that the vessel fore reaches slowly at probably 60°-65° off the wind and is thus under control, ie she does not sheer about but maintains a constant heading.

In practice, however, with modern hulls it may not be quite so simple particularly with the extreme design of light displacement hull with narrow fin keel and transom hung rudder. The average cruising yacht, however, should perform adequately once the owner has established the sail trim required. It is well worthwhile trying out the manoeuvre initially in light winds to see how the vessel performs and then in heavier winds.

Two important points to remember: always bear in mind that although the vessel may be moving very slowly through the water, due to tidal streams its speed over the ground may be quite appreciable so ensure that you have plenty of sea room and secondly to maintain a good look-out at regular intervals.

Remember Rule 5 of the Collision Regulations, the most important one of all.

TOWAGE — YACHTS

Towing or being towed is an eventuality which usually occurs at least once in a lifetime.

As with any emergency that is likely to occur at sea due consideration should be given to all the possibilities whilst the vessel is safely on her mooring and the owner is in a contemplative mood.

The ideal arrangement if one is being towed is to use the towed vessel's anchor cable, well secured to a strong cleat, the cable being passed to the towing vessel by means of a heaving line from either vessel. The chain must of course be secured below deck by a lashing and not shackled, in order that it can be slipped immediately if necessary. One of the advantages of using chain cable is that the weight in the bight reduces snubbing and also that being strongly secured below deck it may not be necessary to secure it to a cleat on deck. If it is not practicable to use the anchor chain and a warp is to be used, to what is it to be secured?

In general few modern yachts carry the equivalent of the old time samson post, and whilst the cleats provided are usually adequate for their particular purpose they may be woefully inadequate to deal with the strain of a tow rope. It is important therefore to consider where and how the towing line should be attached if there are no really adequate cleats or bollards suitably positioned.

Can the tow line be secured round the foot of the mast? If the latter is stepped through the deck the problem is solved. It is important to remember however that although the mast will take the direct strain, the warp should also be secured to the deck as close to the stem head as possible. If this is not done the vessel will sheer about in a surprising manner. With the modern mast stepped on deck the situation may be somewhat different unless it is mounted in a tabernacle when the strain can normally be applied at deck level. If however the mast is merely stepped in a shoe and held in position by the compression of the rigging further thought is needed. If perhaps due to damage, the rigging is slack this method should not be used as a severe jerk on the towline when the vessel is rolling could jerk the mast out of its shoe.

If the stanchions are of reasonable strength and through bolted then a warp secured round several of them and attached to the stem head could be used as the point of attachment for the tow line. This warp should be fixed in position before the tow line is secured.

Should the stanchions prove unsuitable it may be necessary to lead a warp even farther back perhaps to the after end of the cabin, remembering that wherever this warp leads from it must be secured to the stem head before the tow line is made fast.

Having considered these various aspects the prudent owner will probably come to the conclusion that the sensible course of action is to bolt a really stout cleat or bollard to the foredeck (with an adequate backing plate under the deck) during fitting out and thus eliminate the major problem if a tow is required.

A good point to consider when being towed is the tow line itself. The legal implications of towage are dealt with under "Notes on Towage and Salvage" in Section 13 — Shipmaster's Business and from this it will be obvious that one's own warp or anchor chain should be passed over to the towing vessel.

Consider now the other side of the picture — that of towing another vessel, and dealing with the point of tow first. If possible the attachment point of the tow line should not be at the stern, although on most yachts it will almost certainly be the only place to secure it. A tug for example has the towing point amidships, a position which permits complete manoeuvrability of the towing vessel.

The remarks about cleats on the towed vessel apply equally well to the towing vessel and although apparently not so important as the cleats at the forward end of the vessel, strong cleats or bitts on the quarters are vital when mooring up in a tidal harbour — the moral is have strong cleats sited wherever a heavy strain is likely to be imposed on the craft.

The towing situation can vary from pulling a vessel off a lee shore in heavy weather to quietly moving a vessel in harbour in calm conditions and obviously the procedure will vary considerably. Considering the first possibility the most important point is to ensure that the vessel rendering assistance is not herself endangered, either by getting a rope around her prop or running aground and thus creating yet another problem for the rescue authorities. When within a safe distance of the distressed vessel a line can be floated down attached to an empty water carrier, fender etc., and at this point it might be prudent for the rescuing vessel to drop her anchor in case for any reason she becomes unable to manoeuvre. Having transferred a line the remainder of the operation is a matter of good seamanship on both vessels, remembering that every situation is different.

If moving another vessel in calm water, especially in harbour, it is usually easier to carry this out with the second vessel lashed alongside the towing craft, properly secured with breast ropes and springs.

A final point in connection with being towed, the remarks under Salvage Notes may sound unduly alarming and induce the owner to refuse all offers of a tow in a difficult situation unless he is practically on the point of sinking. If however the vessel is adrift within the area of a harbour authority, assistance may be offered by one of the authority's launches, and this will almost certainly not be charged for, the tow will be to a place of safety but not necessarily where the owner would wish to go.

Distress & Rescue at Sea

15

THE RADIOTELEPHONE SILENCE PERIOD

All vessels MUST observe the RADIOTELEPHONE SILENCE PERIOD for 3 minutes, commencing at each hour and 30 minutes PAST each hour during which time transmissions on 2182 kHz other than DISTRESS, URGENCY or SAFETY transmissions must cease.

DISTRESS & EMERGENCY SIGNALS

EMERGENCY ACTION

RADIO TELEPHONE PROCEDURE
Set to International Distress Frequency 2182 kHz, or Ch. 16 (VHF).

First transmit alarm signal
(If equipment available) for 30 seconds to 1 minute.

THEN transmit distress call
(a) 'MAYDAY' spoken 3 times
(b) 'THIS IS (or DE spoken 'DELTA ECHO' if language difficulties)
(c) Name of ship spoken three times

THEN transmit distress message
(a) Distress signal 'MAYDAY'
(b) Name of ship
(c) Position
(d) Nature of emergency and assistance desired
(e) Any other information which might facilitate rescue

Acknowledgement will be
(a) Name of ship sending distress call — spoken three times
(b) 'THIS IS' (or 'DELTA ECHO')
(c) Name or identification of station acknowledging distress call

Visual signals
Full details of all distress signals are given in Annex IV of the Collision Regulations but the following ones are most likely to be of use on small vessels (assuming VHF is not available).

By night
(1) Parachute Flares
(2) Very Pistol (Red Flares)
(3) Hand held Red Flare

By 'Day
(1) Parachute Flares
(2) Orange Coloured Smoke Signal
(3) Slowly and repeatedly raising and lowering the arms outstretched to the sides.

Note: If a distress signal is not justified the appropriate International Code signal should be sent by Flag or Morse, i.e.
'V' I require assistance.
'W' I require medical assistance.

Anyone observing or hearing a ship, yacht or person in distress at sea should dial 999 and ask for COASTGUARD

RADIO TELEPHONE PROCEDURES
DISTRESS, EMERGENCY and SAFETY

All Distress and Emergency signals should be sent on 2182 kHz or 156.8 MHz (Channel 16 on VHF sets). However any other frequency may be used at any time if it appears probable that assistance may thereby be obtained more promptly.

The full description of all necessary procedures in connection with Radio Telephone and Radio Telegraphy operation is contained in the 'Handbook for Radio Operators' published by Lloyds of London Press Ltd for BTI Maritime but an abbreviated description sufficient for the operation of Radio Telephones in small craft is given below.

Certain of the larger types of radio telephone sets are equipped with an alarm signal which may be used to precede the actual distress message. It is a two tone alarm signal which activates the auto alarm fitted in the larger types of shipping.

It may also be used to precede an urgency Pan Pan signal in cases such as man overboard.

Silence Period — vessels fitted with equipment capable of receiving 2182 kHz should maintain a listening watch during the 3 minute silence period commencing at each hour and half hour.

Types of Priority Signals — There are three types of priority signals — Mayday, Pan Pan and Securité (pronounced SAY-CURE-E-TAY).

DISTRESS SIGNALS

A Mayday Call or a Distress Flare may be used only when there is grave and imminent danger to a ship, aircraft or person and, immediate assistance is required.

If for some reason there is an element of doubt about the necessity for sending a Mayday signal then an urgency Pan Pan signal (see on) should be sent. This will alert vessels in the vicinity and any coastal station or Coastguard Station within range. In the light of subsequent events the signal can either be cancelled or a Mayday call sent out. In this connection there are two important points to remember, firstly it is far better to give as much advance warning of trouble as possible to the Coast Radio Stations and secondly that if the situation becomes less urgent and help is no longer required then the Distress or Urgency signal must be immediately cancelled.

Mayday Relay Signals

Any vessel hearing a distress call must listen for a short period to see if it is acknowledged by a Coast Radio Station. If this does not occur then the vessel which has received the Mayday signal must re-transmit the signal but prefacing the distress call with the words Mayday Relay three times followed by the name or call sign of the vessel making the transmission three times.

Communications Control during the Distress Incident

In Coastal waters the primary responsibility for control of distress incidents lies with the Coastguards who initiate S.A.R. (Search and Rescue). The control of the distress traffic communications may lie either with the Coastguard Station or a Coast Radio Station who will impose silence on all vessels in the vicinity by transmitting the signal SEELONCE MAYDAY, followed by its own name or call-sign. (The signal will be transmitted on the frequency being used to control the incident.) When complete radio silence is no longer necessary the controlling station will transmit the following message:

MAYDAY
Hello all stations (repeated 3 times)
This is .... (name of control station)
Name of vessel in distress
PRUDONCE

Essential communications may then be resumed but it is essential to avoid interference with any signals relating to the MAYDAY incident. When all traffic relating to the incident is concluded the controlling station will send out a general signal SEELONCE FEENEE which permits resumption of normal working.

URGENCY SIGNALS

Pan Pan Signals

The words Pan Pan repeated three times are used where it is necessary to transmit a very urgent message concerning the safety of the ship or some person on board or within sight. It does not imply that the vessel herself is in immediate danger. Examples are cases of injury where urgent medical assistance or advice is required, man overboard when there is doubt about the ability of the vessel to rescue him. Pan Pan signals should where possible be addressed to a specific shore station or ship but if any doubt exists about the nearest shore station the urgency Pan Pan should be transmitted as a general call.

The Urgency Signal and message should normally be sent on 2182 kHz or Channel 16 but if the message itself is a long one the urgency signal should be transmitted on the Distress Frequency together with a statement that the message will be transmitted on a working frequency. Any vessel hearing an urgency signal must immediately cease transmitting and listen to check whether the urgency signal is acknowledged by a Coast Radio Station. After a short period of three minutes, if no acknowledgement is heard the listening vessel must endeavour to contact a shore station and relay the message.

SAFETY MESSAGES

Securité pronounced SAY-CURE-E-TAY repeated three times precedes any important navigational or meteorological warning. The safety signal is sent on a distress frequency, either 2182 kHz or Channel 16, together with an announcement giving the working channel on which the safety message will be broadcast. Any vessel hearing the safety message must at once cease working on the frequency chosen for the safety message and listen until they are satisfied that it does not concern them.

VHF Channel 67 is allocated for the exchange of safety messages between small craft and H.M. Coastguard when the message does not warrant the use of the Distress Channels. Small craft should contact the Coastguard station on Channel 16, stating they have safety traffic, when they will be instructed to change to Channel 67. Small craft should not endeavour to contact the Coastguard station initially on Channel 67 as they normally only maintain a listening watch on Channel 16.

Emergency Transmitters for Small Craft

Two types of emergency transmitters are available for small craft, the VHF Distress Beacon Buoy and the Distress Radio Telephone. The former is a buoyant battery operated automatic radio beacon transmitter giving continuous transmission for at least 48 hours on the Distress frequency and thus provides 'homing' facilities for aircraft engaged in the search. The transmitter can be operated from the deck of the vessel or in the sea, attached to the life raft by a small line. The Radio Telephone is also completely self contained and portable but is not submersible. As communication is by radio telephone it can be used for Pan Pan and Securité messages as well as distress calls.

PYROTECHNIC DISTRESS SIGNALS

All small craft should carry some means of indicating distress and preventing collision at night.

PYROTECHNIC SIGNALS

These are an internationally recognised way of doing this, using red flares or stars (hand held, projected, or parachute-suspended), or orange smokes (hand held or buoyant) for distress, and white flares for collision warning.

Distress flares should be used only when there is grave and imminent danger. If not in distress but needing assistance, signal "V" in morse (· · · –) or hoist flag "V". The distress signals you should carry depends not on the size of your boat, but on the distance from land you are likely to go.

Different types of distress flares are needed to raise the alarm and pin-point your position to rescuers. All craft sailing at night should carry white flares to attract the attention of larger vessels when there is risk of collision. Learn how to use your flares and teach your crew, so you will not be caught in distress, possibly at night, trying to read the labels.

INSHORE

Up to 3 miles from land or within sight of potential help carry 2 red handflares and 2 hand-held orange smoke signals.

To raise the alarm and later pin-point your position to rescuers use red handflares in conditions of poor visibility, high wind or darkness. In daylight with good visibility and a light wind hand-held orange smokes will be more distinctive.

COASTAL

Up to 7 miles from land or in conditions of low cloud carry 4 rockets discharging red stars, 4 red handflares and 2 hand-held orange smoke signals.

Beyond 3 miles hand-held signals may not be sighted, being below the visible horizon of potential help. Therefore, attract attention by firing flares which project red stars to 45m. These flares are particularly useful when low cloud might obscure a more powerful rocket. It is recommended that the first two signals be fired within 2 minutes. When rescuers are within visual range, use red handflares or hand-held orange smokes.

OFFSHORE

Over 7 miles from land carry 4 red parachute rockets, 4 red handflares and 2 buoyant orange smokes.

Beyond 7 miles, red star signals may not be sighted. Therefore fire rockets which project a very bright parachute-suspended flare to a height of over 300m. This is the most powerful type of flare. It is recommended that the first two rockets be fired within 2 minutes. When rescuers are within visual range but in conditions of poor visibility, high winds or darkness use red handflares. In daylight with good visibility and a light wind a 3 minute buoyant orange smoke will be more distinctive.

COLLISION WARNING

Carry 4 white handflares within easy reach from the cockpit. If a vessel is sighted on a collision course at night and shows no sign of seeing you, use a white handflare to draw attention to your position.

UK LIFE SAVING STATION SIGNALS

In the event of a ship being in distress off or stranded on the coast of the United Kingdom, the following signals should be used by life-saving stations when communicating with her, and by the ship when communicating with life-saving stations.

Reply to Distress Signals

Replies from life saving stations or maritime rescue unit to distress signals by ship or person:

SIGNALS	SIGNIFICATION
(a) By day — Orange smoke signal or combined light and sound signal (thunderlight) consisting of three single signals fired at approx. one minute intervals .... By night — White star rocket consisting of three single signals at approx. one minute intervals	'You are seen—assistance will be given as soon as possible.' (may be repeated)

If necessary the day signals may be given at night or the night signals by day.

Landing Signals (For guidance of small boats with crews or persons in distress.)

SIGNALS	SIGNIFICATION
(a) By day—Vertical motion of a white flag or the arms or green star signal or K (— · —) .... By night—Vertical motion of a white light or flare; a green star signal by day or night; or code letter K (— · —) by light or sound signal .... A lead (indication of direction) may be given by placing a steady white light or flare lower and in line with the observer*	'This is the best place to land.' *Line the two up and come in on this line of approach.
(b) By day—Horizontal motion of a white flag or arms extended horizontally .... By day or night—Horizontal motion of a white light or flare or firing of a red star signal or code letter S (- - -) by light or sound signal	'Landing here highly dangerous.
(c) By day—Horizontal motion of a white flag, followed by the placing of the white flag on the ground and the carrying of another white flag in the direction to be indicated .... By day or night—Horizontal motion of a white light or flare, followed by the placing of the white light or flare on the ground and the carrying of another white light or flare in the direction to be indicated or firing red star vertically and a white star in direction towards a better landing place or using Code letter S (- - -) followed by Code letter R (- — -) if better landing is more to the right or letter L (- — - -) if more to the left of approach line	'Landing here highly dangerous. A more favourable location to land is in the direction indicated.'

DISTRESS SIGNALS BY LIGHTHOUSES/VESSELS

Certain offshore light-stations are equipped with radio telephones to summon assistance for themselves or for vessels or aircraft they observe to be in distress. If unable to pass a radio message, they will use one or more of the following:

VISUAL DISTRESS SIGNALS

A rocket or rockets throwing red stars, each rocket preceded or accompanied by either a detonating signal, or sound rocket, repeated at regular intervals.

A square flag having above or below it a ball.

The International Code signal of distress indicated by NC or DZ.

A lighthouse or lightvessel, to indicate to a distressed vessel or aircraft that her plight has been seen, will by day or by night:

Lighthouse — fire a white star rocket.

Lightvessel — fire a detonating signal.

REPLY FROM THE SHORE (Coastguard or Lifesaving Station)

By day: Orange smoke signal.

By night: White star rocket.

Light-stations, which cover Scotland and the Isle of Man, have in addition to radiotelephones, *white* star rockets only to acknowledge a vessel's distress signal.

DANGER SIGNAL

When a vessel is seen to be standing into danger, the International Code signal NF, "You are running into danger," or signal flag U, "You are running into danger," will be hoisted and kept flying until answered. In addition, the lightvessel or lighthouse may fire a rocket sound signal, or detonating signal, and repeat it at short intervals until observed. The letter U in morse flashed by lamp or sounded on a horn may also be used.

In the case of lightvessels the signal PS, "You should not come any closer," may be used when a vessel is coming dangerously close.

CALL SIGNALS (NOT DISTRESS)

Lightvessels and lighthouses to attract the attention of passing vessels will:

By day: Hoist the appropriate International code signal.

By night: Make the call sign or letter K by morse lamp.

In the case of a lightvessel, a white flare may also be exhibited, and in fog or low visibility, when the signal cannot be used, the letter K may be made on the hand horn.

France. — Lights may also be exhibited by day in poor visibility.

Heights of structures are measured from focal plane of light to ground.

Lightvessels, when out of position, either drifted or on passage, discontinue their characteristic lights and fog signals. If they have drifted out of position they will show:

By day: Two black balls, one forward and one aft, and hoist International Code signal LO.

By night: Two red lights, one forward and one aft, also one red and one white light or flare shown simultaneously over the gunwale at least every 15 minutes.

A lightvessel under way shows the same lights, and makes the same sound signals as other vessels under way.

R.N.L.I. STATIONS WITH ALL-WEATHER LIFEBOATS
(arranged geographically around the coastline)

*North Sunderland	*Torbay	Tobermory
*Amble	Salcombe	Mallaig
*Blyth	Plymouth	Barra Island
*Tynemouth	Fowey	Stornoway (Lewis)
*Sunderland	*Falmouth	Lochinver
*Hartlepool	The Lizard	Longhope
Teesmouth	Penlee	Kirkwall
*Whitby	Sennen Cove	Stromness
*Scarborough	St. Mary's (Isles of Scilly)	Lerwick
*Filey	*St. Ives	Aith
Flamborough	Padstow (Trevose Head)	Thurso
*Bridlington	*Appledore	Wick
Humber	Ilfracombe	Invergordon
*Skegness	Barry Dock	Buckie
*Wells	*The Mumbles	Fraserburgh
Sheringham	*Tenby	Peterhead
*Cromer	Angle	*Aberdeen
*Gt. Yarmouth	St. David's	Montrose
& Gorleston	Fishguard	*Arbroath
Lowestoft	*New Quay	*Broughty Ferry (Dundee)
*Aldeburgh	*Barmouth	Anstruther
*Harwich	*Pwllheli	*Dunbar
Walton & Frinton	Porthdinllaen	Eyemouth
*Sheerness	*Holyhead	Portrush
*Margate	*Moelfre	Donaghadee
*Ramsgate	*Beaumaris	Newcastle Co. Down
Dover	*Llandudno (Orme's Head)	Clogher Head
Dungeness	*Rhyl	*Howth
*Hastings	Hoylake	*Dun Laoghaire
*Eastbourne	*Lytham-St. Anne's	Wicklow
Newhaven	*Fleetwood	Arklow
*Shoreham Harbour	*Barrow	Rosslare Harbour
*Selsey	Workington	Kilmore Quay
*Bembridge	Ramsey	Dunmore East
Yarmouth IoW	Douglas	Ballycotton
Calshot	*Port St. Mary	Courtmacsherry Harbour
Alderney	Port Erin	Baltimore
St. Helier	Portpatrick	Valentia
St. Peter Port	Girvan	Galway Bay
*Poole	Troon	Ballyglass
Swanage	Campbeltown	Arranmore
Weymouth	Oban	
*Exmouth	Islay	

R.N.L.I. STATIONS WITH INSHORE LIFEBOATS

Fast inflatable and rigid inflatable boats with speeds of 20-29 knots, for rapid launching and assistance inshore; mostly summer only. Stationed at the places marked with an asterisk (*) in the list above, and the following:

ABERDOVEY	CRIMDON DENE	MARAZION (St. Michael's	ST. ABBS
ABERSOCH	CULLERCOATS	Mount)	ST. AGNES
ABERYSTWYTH	FLINT	MINEHEAD	ST. BEES
ARRAN	HAPPISBURGH	MORECAMBE	ST. CATHERINE (Jersey)
ATLANTIC COLLEGE	HAYLING ISLAND	MUDEFORD	SILLOTH
(St. Donat's)	HELENSBURGH	NEWBIGGIN	SKERRIES
BANGOR (Co. Down)	HORTON & PORT EYNON	NEW BRIGHTON	SOUTHEND
BERWICK-UPON-TWEED	HUNSTANTON	NEWQUAY (Cornwall)	SOUTHWOLD
BLACKPOOL	KILKEEL	NORTH BERWICK	STAITHES & RUNSWICK
BORTH	KINGHORN	PEEL	STRANRAER
BRIGHTON	KIPPFORD	PENARTH	TEIGNMOUTH
BUDE	KIRKCUDBRIGHT	PORTAFERRY	TIGHNABRUAICH
BURNHAM-ON-CROUCH	LARGS	PORTHCAWL	TRAMORE
BURRY PORT	LITTLEHAMPTON	PORTSMOUTH	TREARDDUR BAY
CARDIGAN	LITTLESTONE-ON-SEA	(Langstone Harbour)	WALMER
CLACTON-ON-SEA	LITTLE AND BROADHAVEN	PORT ISAAC	WEST KIRBY
CLEETHORPES	LOUGH SWILLY	PORT TALBOT	WEST MERSEA
CLIFDEN	(Buncrana)	(Aberavon Beach)	WESTON-SUPER-MARE
CONWY	LYME REGIS	QUEENSFERRY	WHITSTABLE
COURTOWN	LYMINGTON	RED BAY	WITHERNSEA
CRASTER	MABLETHORPE	REDCAR	YOUGHAL
CRICCIETH	MACDUFF	RYE HARBOUR	

The R.N.L.I. is supported entirely by voluntary contributions, and all lifeboats are manned by volunteer crews except for a motor mechanic at each station and a full-time crew at Humber.

Subscriptions to the national membership scheme, donations, and legacies are gratefully received by The Director, Royal National Lifeboat Institution, West Quay Road, Poole, Dorset BH15 1HZ. Tel: 0202 671133.

SEARCH AND RESCUE PROCEDURE

General Arrangements

Around the coasts of the United Kingdom (and extending to Long. 30°W between Lat. 45°N and 61°N) it is the responsibility of HM Coastguard to initiate and coordinate the appropriate search and rescue procedure (SAR) for vessels in distress.

Coast Radio Stations, on receiving a distress message, either directly or relayed via another vessel, immediately alert the Coastguard and then transmit the Distress Signal on the distress frequencies 500 kHz and 2182 kHz (and Channel 16 after consultation with HM Coastguard) to vessels at sea, after which it ensures radio silence on the appropriate frequency by all vessels not involved in the emergency.

HM Coastguard through their Maritime Rescue Co-ordination and Sub-centres, have responsibility for and maintain 24 hour coverage on Channel 16 VHF. In addition there are Auxiliary Coastguard stations which can keep visual watch in periods of high casualty risk and which have a rescue capability.

When a vessel is in distress and the Coastguard have been informed, they will call upon the RNLI and or the RAF and RN depending on the nature and size of the emergency. The Air Rescue Coordination Centres at Edinburgh and Plymouth are responsible for providing rescue facilities for military and civil aircraft, but as far as service commitments permit, also assist ships in distress at the request of the appropriate Coastguard station. In addition the Royal Navy also provide helicopters when requested by the Coastguard, service commitments permitting, and if appropriate to the emergency Royal Navy surface vessels may assist. In the event of an emergency a considerable distance from land the Coastguard may request assistance from the Air Traffic Control centre covering the particular area, thus ensuring that any low flying aircraft in the vicinity of the incident keep watch for life rafts etc.

Distress signals re-transmitted or intercepted by satellites are relayed to Falmouth MRCC which takes appropriate action.

It will thus be seen that the resources available for SAR, including long range aircraft capable of operating up to 1000 miles from our shores are extensive, very effective and very rapidly brought into action.

The RNLI is the only part of the SAR organisation which is a private organisation supported entirely by voluntary contributions and which maintains lifeboats and inshore rescue boats round the shores of the United Kingdom, Irish Republic and the Channel Islands. The modern lifeboat fully equipped with radio telephone can keep in constant touch with the Coastguard, Coast Radio Stations and any rescue helicopters operating on the incident, thus permitting tight coordination of all rescue facilities. A lifeboat on a distress service will exhibit a quick flashing blue light at the masthead.

SEA RESCUE BY HELICOPTER

General Procedure

Once the helicopter has become airborne, how soon it locates the ship and how effective its work can be depends to a large extent on the ship herself.

LARGE VESSELS

From the air, especially if there is a lot of shipping in the area, it is very difficult for the pilot of a helicopter to pick out the particular ship he is looking for, from the many he can see, unless that ship uses a distinctive distress signal which can be clearly seen by him. One such signal is the daylight orange coloured smoke signal. This is very distinct from the air. A well-trained Aldis lamp can also be seen except in very bright sunlight. Display of these signals may mean all the difference between success and failure in the helicopter locating the casualty.

It is essential that the ship's position should be given as accurately as possible if the original distress signal is made by radio. The bearing (mag. or true) and distance from a fixed object, like a headland or lighthouse should be given if possible. The type of ship or yacht, colour of sails and hull should be included if time allows, along with brief details of lifesaving equipment, *e.g.*, liferaft.

Because of their operational limitations, helicopters should not be unnecessarily delayed at the scene of the rescue. Every effort should be made to provide a clear stretch of deck or hatchway and to mark this area with a large letter 'H' in white, prior to the arrival of the helicopter. A helicopter will approach the ship from astern and come to the hover over the cleared area, heading into wind. In order that the helicopter pilot and crewman may have as large an area of the ship as possible on which to operate consistent with the helicopter remaining heading into the wind, the ship should steam at a constant speed heading 30° to starboard of the prevailing wind direction. If this is not possible the ship should remain stationary head to wind. If these conditions are met the helicopter can lower on to or lift from the clear area, the maximum length of the winch cable being about 200ft. On no account should the strop on the end of the winch cable, when lowered to the vessel, be secured to any part of the vessel or allowed to become entangled in any rigging or fixtures. If the ship cannot comply with these conditions the helicopter may be able to lift a man from a boat towed astern on a long painter. If the vessel is on fire and making smoke it is of advantage to have the wind two points off the bow. In all cases an indication of wind direction is useful. Pennants and flags are acceptable for this purpose and possible smoke from the galley funnel, provided that there is not too much smoke.

Helicopters are well practised in rescuing survivors from either a deck or the sea and two methods are employed. These are:

(1)   The survivor, whether on deck or in the water, is rescued by means of the strop. The crewman is lowered from the helicopter together with the strop which is secured around the survivor's back and chest, and both are winched up into the helicopter.

(2)   If a survivor on a deck is injured to the extent that the use of a strop around his back and chest would aggravate the injury or cause suffering, a crewman is lowered on to the deck with a stretcher. The survivor is placed in the stretcher, strapped in in such a manner that it is impossible for him to slip or fall out, and both stretcher and crewman are winched up into the helicopter. If possible, the helicopter will be carrying a doctor who will be lowered to the deck and will assist the survivors as necessary.

If from the ship in trouble it is observed that the helicopter is going to pass by, or is on a course which will take it away, continued use should be made of visual distress signals, and at the same time, if fitted with radio, the fact reported to the Coastguard stating the present bearing and distance of the helicopter. The Coastguard will pass this information direct to the helicopter.

YACHTS AND SMALL VESSELS

A yacht in distress may not anticipate a helicopter rescue, particularly in view of the increasing number of inshore rescue boats, but it is always advantageous to be prepared for this type of operation. A yacht, particularly a small one, is not always easily identified from the air.

The necessary precautions to ensure easy identification should form part of the normal sea going equipment of every yacht, e.g. sail numbers should be clearly marked, canvas dodgers with the vessel's name clearly marked on them, and, if the dinghy is carried upside down on the deck, the name should be clearly painted on its bottom.

Failing these precautions a large strip of canvas with the vessels name on should be carried and in the event of an emergency it can be lashed on deck.

When the emergency occurs the use of a flare or smoke signal when the helicopter is sighted may materially speed up the rescue. **DO NOT FIRE PARACHUTE FLARES WHILST THE HELICOPTER IS EITHER DIRECTLY OVERHEAD OR CLOSE BY.** Once it is obvious that rescue is being carried out by this means a sea anchor, if available, should be streamed in order to reduce drift. Alternatively the main anchor and cable may be paid out to help reduce surface drift.

It is most important to remember that the helicopter crew will not under any circumstances risk the winching cable becoming entangled with the yacht's mast and rigging. A sailing yacht must therefore prepare for its crew to be picked up from the water a safe distance from the vessel. A life raft or inflatable dinghy should be made ready and on the approach of the helicopter it should be streamed, complete with crew, on the end of at least a 100ft warp firmly secured to the parent vessel (unless of course there is the danger of the latter foundering).

The winchman can then operate in safety, well clear of the yacht and her rigging. In the unfortunate event of the vessel having no life raft or inflatable dinghy it will be necessary for the crew to take to the water when the helicopter has located them. Again a long warp should be streamed, the crew with life jackets firmly secured can then drift to leeward attached to the warp in a bunch. In the unlikely event of some members of the crew having to be left in the water for a further period they will have means of returning to the yacht by means of the warp.

The 'pick up' problem does not arise in the case of the small sailing dinghy or the motor cruiser with no mast. In these cases the crew should remain on board unless otherwise instructed by the winchman. Finally, remember that a helicopter cannot remain airborne indefinitely, watch for and carry out the winchman's instructions exactly and immediately.

HIGH LINE TECHNIQUE

In very bad weather, it may not be possible to lower the crewman and strop directly on to the deck. In such a case, a rope extension of the winch line may be lowered to the ship. This should be handed by a member of the ship's crew and taken in as the helicopter pays out her wire. Coil down the line on deck clear of snags, *but do not make it fast.* The helicopter will pay out the full scope of wire and descend, while the ship's crew continue to take in the slack until the winch hook and strop are on board. The casualty will then be secured in the strop and, when he or another member of the ship's crew signifies that he is ready, the helicopter will ascend and take in the wire. Pay out the extension rope, keeping enough weight on it to keep it taut, until the end is reached, then cast the end clear of the ship's side; unless further evacuation of crew is intended when, if possible, the end of the line should be retained on board to make recovery of the strop for the next man easier — *but do not make the line fast.*

Rescue helicopters are fitted with marine VHF and may wish to communicate on Channel 6 (on scene co-ordination channel for SAR) during transfer. Yachts with VHF should however monitor Channel 16 (or other channel designated by HM Coastguard) and await instructions.

Remember — Keep clear of the main and tail rotors.

AIRCRAFT SEARCHES AND PATTERNS

Night Searches

In general night visual searches are dependant on the ability of the survivors to indicate their positions using Pyrotechnics, Lights, Fires, etc. The searching aircraft can only hope to illuminate an accurately defined area, i.e. on sighting red flares, or flashing lights.

There are several patterns of searches, but the ones most likely to be used for missing craft/persons are the following:

(1) **Expanding Square Search:** This procedure begins at a given point and expands in concentric squares, used to cover a limited area usually when survivors are known to be in a relatively small area. To execute a Square Search, the aircraft is flown in such a way as to make good the tracks shown in the diagram that follows.

EXPANDING SQUARE SEARCH

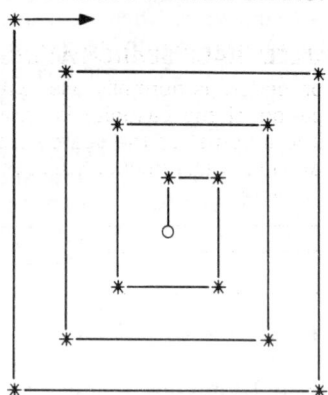

Note: The GREEN flares are used at night only by aircraft to indicate to the survivors that the aircraft is turning. Survivors should on seeing the flares, WAIT until the flare has died out and then fire a red flare to indicate the position of the casualty. When the aircraft fire the green flares the aircrews will not look out until the length of time it takes the flare to expire. This is to enable them to retain their night vision.

TRACK CRAWL SEARCH AT NIGHT

Track Crawl Search: the procedure for this search is to fly along the known course from the last known position towards the intended destination and return on a parallel track at the sweep width distance to one side of the original track; then to return parallel to the original track on the other side again at the sweep width distance.

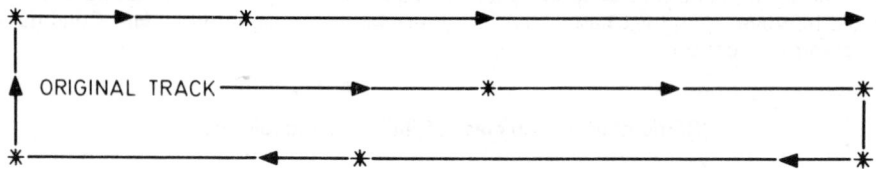

Note: Green Flares will be fired by the aircraft at each turning point and also if the legs are long at intervals of approximately five minutes. If the aircrew see a visual aid marking the survivors position several green flares will be fired in quick succession.

CREEPING LINE AHEAD SEARCH AT NIGHT

Creeping line ahead search: this procedure is used for search of a rectangular area by a single aircraft. The aircraft proceeds to a corner of the search area and flying at the allotted height sweeps the area maintaining parallel tracks.

(a) The search area is long and narrow.
(b) The search based on a first priority of the track.

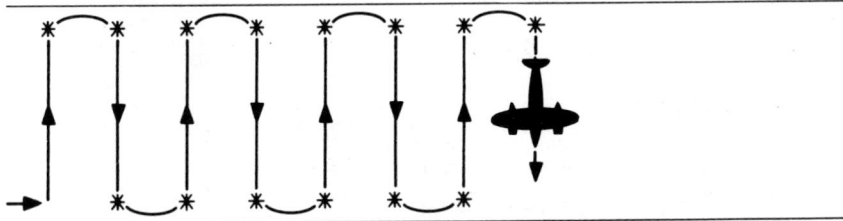

Note: Green flares will be fired by the aircraft at each turning point.

PARALLEL TRACK SEARCH AT NIGHT

Parallel Track Search: this procedure is normally used when the search area is large and only the approximate location of the casualty is known. A uniform coverage is desired. The aircraft proceeds to a corner of the search area and flying at the allotted height sweeps the area maintaining parallel tracks. Successive tracks are flown parallel to each other until the area is covered.

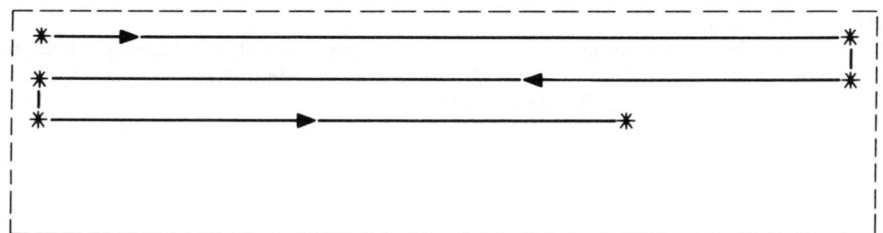

Note: Green flares will be fired along each leg at approximately five minute intervals and also at the turning point.

SIGNALS BY AIRCRAFT ON SEARCH AND RESCUE

DIRECTING SHIPS TOWARDS AN AIRCRAFT, SHIP OR PERSON IN DISTRESS

(A) **Procedures performed in sequence by an AIRCRAFT**

1. Aircraft circles the surface craft at least once.
2. Aircraft crosses the surface craft course close ahead at low altitude while rocking the wings, or by opening and closing the throttle or changing the propeller pitch.
3. Aircraft leads in the direction in which the surface craft is to be directed.

All three aircraft signals above mean: The aircraft is directing a surface craft towards an aircraft or surface craft in distress. (Repetition of signals have the same meaning.)

(B) Aircraft crossing the surface craft's wake close astern at low altitude while rocking the wings, or by opening and closing the throttle or changing propeller pitch.

The above signal means: The assistance of the surface craft is no longer required. (Repetition of such signals shall have the same meaning.)

H.M. COASTGUARD MARINE RESCUE CENTRES

DISTRICT	ADDRESS	TEL. NO.
Shetland	Lerwick, Shetland	0595 2976
Pentland	Kirkwall, Orkney	0856 3268
Aberdeen	Blaikies Quay, Aberdeen	0224 592334
Forth	Fifeness, Crail, Fife	0333 50666
Tyne/Tees	Tynemouth	091-257 2691
Humber	Bridlington	0262 672317
Yarmouth	Havenbridge House, Gt. Yarmouth, Norfolk	0493 851338
Thames	Hall Lane, Walton-on-Naze, Essex	0255 675518
Dover	Langdon Battery, Swingate, Dover, Kent	0304 210008
Solent	Solent	0705 552100
Portland	Grove Point, Portland, Dorset	0305 760439
Brixham	Brixham, Devon	0803 882704
Falmouth	Pendennis Point	0326 317575
Swansea	Mumbles, Swansea, West Glamorgan	0792 366534
Milford Haven	Castle Way, Dale, Haverfordwest, Dyfed	0646 636218
Holyhead	Holyhead, Anglesey	0407 762051
Liverpool	Crosby, Liverpool	051-931 3343
Belfast	Orlock Head	0247 883184
Clyde	Navy Buildings, Greenock	0475 29988
Oban	Boswell House, Argyll Square, Oban, Argyll	0631 63720
Stornoway	Stornoway, Isle of Lewis	0851 702013

VHF Maritime Radio

Coastguard Maritime Rescue Centres are on constant watch on Channel 16 — the distress and safety and calling channel (Other channels held include 10, 67, 73). CALLS SHOULD *ALWAYS* BE ON CH. 16.

SMALL CRAFT SAFETY

Every year, Coastguards are alerted to more than 1,000 small craft overdue or in distress. But often they do not have enough information (such as the appearance, equipment and sailing plans of the missing craft) to concentrate a search in the right area.

AS THE OWNER OR USER OF A SMALL CRAFT YOU CAN HELP THE COASTGUARD (AND YOURSELF) BY JOINING THE YACHT AND BOAT SAFETY SCHEME. It costs nothing, and one day might save your life as well as the lives of your family or friends.

The aims of the Yacht and Boat scheme are simple:

To provide your nearest Rescue Centre with the information needed to mount a successful search and rescue operation;

To promote closer links between the Coastguards and all small-craft owners and users.

YACHT AND BOAT SAFETY SCHEME

How do you join?

All you need to do is fill in a simple postcard. You can get one from Coastguard stations, marinas, yacht clubs, harbourmasters' offices and wherever you see the circular "Issuing Authority" sign. Describe your craft, its equipment and your normal sailing area, and then drop the card into a post-box. Remember to up-date the information whenever details change.

What information do the Coastguards need?

The following details will be helpful: the name of your club or association; type of craft or rig; name of craft, how and where displayed; colours of hull, topsides, sail; sailing/fishing number; speed and endurance under power; special identification features; life-raft and serial number; dinghy type and colour; lifejackets carried; radio — HF/MF trans/rec, VHF channels and call sign; type of distress signals carried; usual base, mooring, activity and sea areas; shore contact's name, address, telephone number; owner's name, address, telephone number; date.

Keeping in touch — VHF radio

You will sail more safely if your craft is fitted with VHF radio, so that you can pass distress, urgency and safety messages (including your latest position reports) direct to the Coastguards.

Pass distress and urgency messages on Channel 16. If you want to report your position, or change your plans, you should call up on Channel 16 and say you have "safety traffic". You will be asked to switch to Channel 67 (the small boat safety frequency) to pass your message.

When passing reports you should pass your vessel's name, call sign, departure and destination points and, if possible, your estimated time of arrival, the total number of persons on board and the Coastguard Rescue Centre which holds your safety scheme card.

Keeping in touch — MF radio

Yachts or boats fitted with MF radio transceivers only, or outside coastal VHF range, should contact the British Telecom Coast Radio Stations periodically to give their TR (position report); then, if it becomes necessary, Coastguards can use the last known TR to establish a search datum.

Passages outside coastal waters

If you intend to sail outside UK waters you are recommended to contact your nearest Coastguard station and give details. These can then be noted, and through their contact with overseas rescue organisations the Coastguards will be able to advise you of any measures which could improve your safety.

DEPARTMENT OF TRANSPORT

HM COASTGUARD

YACHT AND BOAT SAFETY SCHEME

Name of Craft	
How and where is the name displayed	

Details of Owner

Name

Address

Tel. No

Signature

Date

Details of Shore Contact

Name

Address

Tel. No.

Name of Club or Association

Type of Craft	Type of rig
Sailing or fishing number	Speed and endurance under power
Colours of craft	
Hull above water / below water	Details of radio
Topsides	HF MF Trans/Rec:
Sail	VHF Channels and call sign:
Spinnaker	Other Equipment:
Length feet metres	
Details of any special identification features	Type of distress signals carried
	Dinghy type
Usual base	colour
Usual mooring	Life raft type
Usual activity (eg fishing, racing, etc).	serial no.
Usual sea areas	Are life jackets carried

Form CG66

M336

VESSELS REPORTED MISSING OR OVERDUE

LLOYD'S SERVICES FOR DEEP-SEA YACHTSMEN

Reporting of yachts on overseas voyages

Yachtsmen intending to undertake overseas voyages and wishing to keep their relatives or families informed of their whereabouts should signal to passing merchant vessels with the International Code Signal ZD2 (Please report me to Lloyds, London) and are invited to contact the Intelligence Department, telephone No. 0260 772277, Ext. 2410 in order that the necessary arrangements can be made. Charges are made for any expenses incurred such as telephone calls, postage etc.

In addition, those relatives or friends who feel concerned for the safety of a yacht on an overseas voyage are advised to contact the above number at any time of the day or night.

If the yacht is considered to be outside the British Coastguard area of responsibility Lloyds will arrange for a general broadcast to shipping in the area or make inquiries of their agents along the vessel's route for later news. A person making an inquiry for an overdue yacht which is considered to be in the Coastguard area of responsibility will either be given the telephone number of the appropriate Coastguard Liaison Station to contact or Lloyds will pass the facts direct to that Station.

Reporting arrival of small vessels

If only yachtsmen (and others who put to sea) communicated with their relatives ashore, if only relatives could give worthwhile information about the vessels and their proposed itineraries — such lapses are all too typical when coastguards and others are asked to instigate inquiries.

It is very necessary in our crowded waterways to report to ports which vessels may enter and when delayed or stormbound always to telephone details to relatives or business. This may save endless trouble to overworked Lifeboat Crews, Coastguard, or harbour authorities.

ALWAYS REPORT ARRIVAL TO SOMEONE AFTER A PASSAGE

Fishing vessels reported missing or overdue

H.M. Coastguard are responsible for initiating search and rescue measures for overdue fishing vessels.

When a fishing vessel is considered to be missing, or overdue, a report should be made to the District Inspector of Fisheries who will notify the nearest Coastguard Rescue Centre giving the following information about the vessel:

Name of Port, letter and number — Description.
Whether fitted with R/T, W/T or both, give call sign and wave length.
Last known position. Date last seen, or heard on the air.
Probable fishing area. Any other relevant information.

If the D.I. of F. is not available, report direct to the Coastguard Rescue Centre. As soon as possible the report should be repeated to the District Inspector of Fisheries who will co-operate with the Coastguard in the rescue operation.

Do not delay in reporting any doubt concerning the safety of a vessel.

STATUTORY DUTIES OF MASTERS OF SHIPS TO RESCUE

Section 6 (1) of the Maritime Conventions Act, 1911, provides that the Master or person in charge of a vessel shall, so far as he can do so without serious danger to his own vessel, her crew and passengers (if any), render assistance to every person, even if such person be a subject of a foreign State at war with Her Majesty, who is found at sea in danger of being lost. If he fails to do so, he is guilty of a misdemeanour.

Section 22 of the Merchant Shipping (Safety Convention) Act, 1949, provides that the Master of a ship, on receiving at sea a distress signal or information from any source that a vessel or aircraft is in distress, must proceed with all speed to the assistance of the person in distress (informing them, if possible, that he is doing so), unless he is unable, or in the special circumstances of the case considers it unreasonable or unnecessary to do so, or unless he is released from this obligation under certain conditions. If the Master of any ship in distress requisitions any ship that has answered his call, it is the duty of the Master of the requisitioned ship to comply with the requisition by continuing to proceed with all speed to the assistance of the persons in distress.

A Master is released from the obligation to render assistance as soon as he is informed of the requisition of one or more ships other than his own and that the requisition is being complied with by the ship or ships requisitioned, or if he is informed by the Master of any ship that has reached the persons in distress that assistance is no longer required.

Section 22 (5) of the 1949 Act provides that if a Master of a British ship registered in the United Kingdom fails to act in accordance with these instructions he is guilty of a misdemeanour. Sections 22 (6) and 22 (7) provide that if the Master of a British ship registered in the United Kingdom receives at sea a signal of distress or information from any source that a vessel or aircraft is in distress, but is unable, or in the special circumstances of the case, considers it unreasonable or unnecessary, to go to the assistance of the persons in distress, he must forthwith cause a statement to be entered in the official log book, or if there is no official log book cause other record to be kept of his reasons for not going to the assistance. If he fails to do so he is liable to a fine.

On ships in which an official log is kept, the Master is required to enter or cause to be entered in the official log book every signal of distress or message that a vessel, aircraft or person is in distress at sea.

DUTIES OF MASTERS IN CASES OF COLLISION

These duties are prescribed in Section 422 and 423 of the Merchant Shipping Act:

"Section 422 — (1). In every case of collision between two vessels, it shall be the duty of the Master or person in charge of each vessel, if and so far as he can do so without danger to his own vessel, crew and passengers (if any) —

(a) to render to the other vessel, her Master, crew and passengers (if any) such assistance as may be practicable, and may be necessary to save them from any danger caused by the collision, and to stay by the other vessel until he has ascertained that she has no need of further assistance, and also

(b) to give to the Master or person in charge of the other vessel the name of his own vessel and of the port to which she belongs, and also the names of the ports from which she comes and to which she is bound.

"If the Master or person in charge fails without reasonable cause to comply with this section, he shall be guilty of a misdemeanour, and, if he is a certificated officer, an inquiry into his conduct may be held, and his certificate cancelled or suspended.

"Section 423 — (1). In every case of collision in which it is practicable so to do, the Master of every ship shall immediately after the occurrence cause a statement thereof, and of the circumstances under which the same occurred, to be entered in the official log book (if any), and the entry shall be signed by the Master, and also by the mate or one of the crew.

"(2) If the Master fails to comply with this section he shall for each offence be liable to a fine."

Safety at Sea

16

INTERNATIONAL REGULATIONS
for
PREVENTING COLLISIONS AT SEA – 1972

These are given fully in the Almanac in Section 8. A major contribution to SAFETY at SEA is for every person in charge of a vessel – both large and small – to understand his obligations under these most important Rules and act on them.

SAFETY AT SEA IN SMALL CRAFT

Safety at sea in small craft is not just a matter of carrying a packet of red flares — it is an attitude of mind and this fact should never be forgotten.

It starts with the knowledge that the ship is well found, with adequate gear and equipment and is suitable for the type of passage making that the owner contemplates. Following this should be the knowledge that the vessel is adequately provided with sufficient fuel for main or auxiliary engines and fitted with the necessary spares and equipment to deal with any situations that can be foreseen.

This — very basically deals with the vessel — what of the Skipper and crew?

The Skipper should have sufficient navigational knowledge to be aware of his position at all times and under all conditions, a basically simple requirement but one needing theoretical knowledge and the ability to put that knowledge to practical use.

He should, in addition, have sufficient knowledge of seamanship, weather forecasting, ship handling and the capabilities of his crew (and himself) to make sound judgements in difficult situations.

Having established that the ship is well found and the Skipper and crew are competent, consideration should be given to the provision of the accepted "safety equipment." Apart from obvious items such as personal buoyancy, safety harness, life rafts, etc, there is available an impressive range of equipment designed to assist, directly or indirectly, in avoiding or getting out of, the difficult situation. It is important to remember that all such equipment demands maintenance in some form or other, together with the necessary operating knowledge. In difficult circumstances at night, lack of knowledge of the whereabouts of white flares or how to operate them, may lead rapidly to a situation in which red rocket flares are needed!

Summing up therefore, safety at sea demands a well found ship and a competent Skipper and crew who do not exceed their limitations. A rescue operation for a small craft at sea is almost invariably due to an error of judgement somewhere along the line and is therefore, an admission of failure to perform adequately under conditions that should have been foreseen.

A final word — probably the greatest danger facing the small yacht at sea, is not being run down by a supertanker, but the everyday risk of man overboard — some ideas on dealing with this situation are included further on in this section.

DTp REQUIREMENTS FOR YACHTS

The Merchant Shipping (Life Saving Appliances) Rules 1965 and the Merchant Shipping (Fire Appliances) Rules 1965 came into force on May 6th, 1965 and Pleasure Yachts of 45 ft. in length or over are required to carry certain equipment as detailed below.

When satisfied that your vessel is equipped as required by the Rules, you may arrange for the DTp to carry out a full inspection and if satisfactory a certificate will be issued recording that the vessel is properly equipped as required under the appropriate rules. A charge is made for this service and details may be obtained from the nearest marine Survey Office.

Vessels of 13-21 metres in length

(a) If engaged on either a voyage to sea in the course of which it is more than 3 miles from the U.K. coast or a voyage to sea during the months of November to March inclusive:

(i) One or more inflatable liferafts of sufficient aggregate capacity to accommodate the total number of persons on board.

(ii) At least two lifebuoys one of which shall be fitted with a self-igniting light and self-activated smoke float.

(b) If a vessel which does not proceed to sea or which only proceeds to sea during the months of April to October, inclusive, on voyages in the course of which it is not more than 3 miles from the coast of the U.K.:

(i) Lifebuoys at least equal in number to half the total number of persons on board, but, in no case, less than two lifebuoys. One lifebuoy to be fitted with self igniting light and self-activated smoke float.

(c) A buoyant line at least 10 fathoms in length.

(d) One DTp approved lifejacket for every person on board.

(e) At least six pyrotechnic distress signals.

(f) In a position outside the machinery spaces, a hand pump with a permanent sea connection and a hose with a nozzle at least $\frac{1}{4}$in. in diameter capable of producing a jet of water having a throw of not less than 20ft which can be directed on any part of the ship. (In fully decked vessels of less than 50ft and open vessels of less than 70ft, two fire buckets may be substituted for this equipment.)

(g) A spray nozzle suitable for use with the hose in (f).

(h) If fitted with oil-fired boilers or internal combustion type engines, two portable fire extinguishers suitable for extinguishing oil fires.

Vessels of 21-26 metres in length
(a) At least two inflatable liferafts of sufficient aggregate capacity to accommodate twice the total number of persons on board.

(b) At least four lifebuoys. Two of these are to be fitted with self-igniting lights and self-activating smoke signals and the other two with 15 fathom lines.

(c) One DTp approved lifejacket for every person on board.

(d) A line-throwing appliance.

(e) At least one power-operated fire pump, a fire main, water service pipes and hydrants capable of supplying at least one jet of water which can reach any part of the ship.

(f) At least two fire hoses.

(g) At least three portable fire extinguishers or fire buckets (if fire buckets are provided at least one shall be fitted with a lanyard).

(h) If a fully decked ship, a fireman's axe.

(i) At least six pyrotechnic distress signals.

Additional requirements for vessels with oil-fired boilers or internal combustion type engines.
(j) If the source of power and the sea connection to the power operated pump required by (e) are not outside the boiler or machinery spaces, an additional fire pump and its source of power and sea connection shall be provided in a position outside these spaces. This additional pump may be manually operated but, in that case, it must be capable of producing a jet having a throw of not less than 20 ft through a hose and $\frac{3}{8}$in. diameter nozzle.

Vessels of 26 metres in length or over and vessels of any size of 150 tons gross or over
The Life Saving and Fire Appliance Rules call for comprehensive additional equipment to that laid down above. Advice on the requirements for these vessels will be given on request to the DTp.

Notes
(1) Where any equipment is required to be provided by the Rules, it should be approved equipment. It is in the Owners' interests to see that their suppliers supply the correct equipment.

(2) Lifejackets may be the Standard Kapok lifejackets or, if preferred, those complying

with British Standards specification No. B.S.3595: 1963, provided they do not depend wholly upon oral inflation.

(3) 4-man capacity inflatable liferafts are only permitted in vessels where the total number of persons aboard is 4 or less. If more than 4 persons are carried, the minimum capacity of any raft is to be 6.

(4) Certain items of liferaft equipment can be reduced and some omitted for vessels under 70 ft. in length. The supplier of the inflatable raft can advise.

(5) "Length" in relation to a registered ship means registered length, and in relation to an unregistered ship means the length from the fore part of the stem to the aft side of the head of the stern post or, if no stern post is fitted to take the rudder, to the fore side of the rudder stock at the point where the rudder passes out of the hull.

DTp RECOMMENDATIONS

Vessels 5.5 — 13.7 metres in length

The following recommendations are intended to guide owners and operators of seagoing pleasure craft on the safety equipment which should be carried. Needs in excess of this will vary according to the size and type of the craft and the conditions and area of the intended operations.

Owners and users must have equipped their craft as necessary with adequate navigation lights and means of giving sound signals to conform to the International Regulations for Preventing Collisions at Sea. It is assumed that the craft has been provided also with the usual equipment for its operation and safe navigation.

Because of the special considerations applicable to boats of less than 5.5 metres (18 feet) in length overall, namely their limited stowage space, fewer occupants and the wide diversity of types, the recommendations for craft in this category are shown separately from those of 5.5 metres (18 feet) to less than 13.7 metres (45 feet) in length overall.

In inland areas, the operations and equipment of craft may be subject to the requirements of local and water authorities. Other craft may be operating under organised club rules, which call for certain standards of equipment. Where these considerations do not apply or where they do not fully specify the safety equipment which should be carried, owners and users of pleasure craft operating in inland waters should also be guided by the following list of safety equipment. Needs will vary according to the size and type of the craft and the conditions and area of the intended operations. In very shallow water or on narrow canals with low banks, very little equipment may be needed.

Personal Safety Equipment

One lifejacket to BSI Specification should be carried for each person on board and should be worn at all times when there is a risk of being pitched or falling into the water. When not being worn the lifejacket should be kept in a safe but immediately accessible place.

One safety harness to BSI Specification 4224 should be carried for each person on board sailing yachts. (It may be advisable to carry one or more safety harnesses on other boats, depending on the circumstances.) It should be worn, appropriately adjusted, at all times when on deck in bad weather or at night, where there is a risk of falling overboard, except that it is inadvisable to wear it at speeds of 8 knots or more. Experience has shown that at such speeds it can be dangerous.

Sometimes it is advisable to wear both lifejacket and harness. When this is so, care should be taken to ensure that one does not interfere with the safe operation of the other.

Rescue Equipment

A minimum of 2 lifebuoys should be carried on each vessel for "man overboard" situations. If the vessel is proceeding by night, one of the lifebuoys should have an igniting light and a 30 metres (100 feet) buoyant line in reserve and it should be positioned within reach of the helmsman.

Other Flotation Equipment

Additional flotation equipment should be carried according to the following:

(i) **Up to 3 miles from land.**
Summer (1st April to 31st October inclusive) – 1 30 in. lifebuoy or buoyant seat of a pattern accepted by the DTp per 2 persons.

The lifebuoys specified above may be counted against this need, but if they are smaller than 30 in. each should be regarded as support for one person only. Alternatively the winter standard could be maintained.

Winter (1st November to 31 March inclusive) – 1 inflatable liferaft of DTp accepted type, or its equivalent, sufficient in size to carry all occupants, and which should be carried on deck, or in a locker opening directly to the deck. The liferaft should be serviced annually.

For craft in sheltered waters, the scale proposed for summer may usually be regarded as adequate in winter also. Liferafts may not be necessary on angling boats operating in organised groups each vessel of which is in continuous contact with another.

(ii) **Where the vessel is going beyond 3 miles from land.**
1 inflatable liferaft of DTp accepted type, or its equivalent, sufficient in size to carry all occupants, and which should be carried on deck, or in a locker opening directly to the deck. The liferaft should be serviced annually.

The following are acceptable alternatives to the inflatable liferaft of DTp accepted type or equivalent:

(i) A solid dinghy carried on deck. It may be a collapsible type but should be fitted with permanent, not inflatable, buoyancy and should have oars and rowlocks secured thereto.

(ii) An inflatable dinghy built with two compartments one of which is fully inflated or with one compartment which is fully inflated. It should be carried on deck, and should have oars and rowlocks secured.

(iii) An inflatable dinghy (with two compartments) which need not be carried on deck if the yacht has enough permanent buoyancy to float when swamped with 115 kilos (250 lb.) added weight.

In sheltered waters, the dinghy may be towed, provided the tow is secure.

Fire Fighting Appliances

Owners and builders will know that the degree of fire protection in a craft should not be limited to the fire appliances provided but can and should be considerably increased by avoiding any obvious fire hazards in the early stages of design and construction. Attention in this respect is drawn to the Home Office pamphlet 'Fire Precautions in Pleasure Craft.' Not withstanding such built-in precautions the following appliances are considered to be necessary:

For craft up to 9 m. (30 ft.) in length with cooking facilities only or with engines only, 1 fire extinguisher of not less than 1.4 kilos (3 lb.) in capacity (dry powder) is recommended. Craft having both cooking facilities and engines should carry an additional extinguisher of the same extinguishing capability. Carbon Dioxide (CO_2) or foam extinguishers of equivalent extinguishing capability are acceptable alternatives to dry powder appliances. BCF (bromo-chloro-difluoro-methane) or BTM (bromo-trifluoro-methane) extinguishers may be carried providing the owners are aware that the fumes given off are liable to be dangerous, especially in a confined space, and a notice to this effect should be prominently displayed at each such extinguisher.

For bigger craft and for those with more powerful engines requiring the carriage of large quantities of fuel, additional extinguishers of not less than 2.3 kilos (5 lb.) in capacity (dry powder) or equivalent and in some cases a fixed fire extinguishing installation, will be necessary.

Two buckets with lanyards should also be carried on all craft. A bag of sand, in addition, can be useful in containing and extinguishing burning spillages of oil or fuel.

Other Equipment

The following items are recommended for all craft:

2 Anchors, each with a warp or chain of appropriate size and length. Where warp is used at least 5.5 metres (3 fathoms) of chain should be used between anchor and warp.

1 Bilge pump.

Efficient compass and a spare.

Charts covering the intended area of operations.

6 Distress flares of which two should be of the rocket parachute type.

Daylight distress (smoke) signals.

An appropriate length of buoyant tow rope.

1 First Aid Box with anti-seasickness tablets.

1 Radio receiver for weather forecasts.

1 Water resistant torch.

1 Radar reflector capable of giving a consistent, identifiable echo during any movements within a band of at least ±20 degrees of heel, through the 360 degrees of azimuth. This should be mounted or hoisted where convenient to the working of the boat and, if possible, at a height of 4 metres or more above sea level.

Line which could be used as inboard lifelines in bad weather, if necessary.

1 suitable engine tool kit.

The name, number or generally recognised sail number of the boat should be painted in a prominent position on the vessel or on dodgers in letters or figures at least 22 centimetres (9 in.) high to facilitate identification.

Vessels of less than 5.5 metres in length

Care should be taken to avoid overloading the boat by carrying more persons or equipment than the boat was designed for, which will generally be shown on a plate affixed by the constructor. Sea angling vessels should be more restricted and the following scale is recommended:

Craft of 4.9 metres (16 feet) to less than 5.5 metres (18 feet) 4 persons.
Craft of 4.3 metres (14 feet) to less than 4.9 metres (16 feet) 3 persons.
Craft of 3.7 metres (12 feet) to less than 4.3 metres (14 feet) 2 persons.

Sea-angling from craft less than 3.7 metres (12 feet) in length is hazardous.

Owners of pleasure craft in this category who intend to proceed to the open sea more than 3 miles from base or whose craft are designed for cruising should, so far as is practicable having regard to the size and carrying capacity of the vessel, follow the recommendations for craft of 5.5 metres to 13.7 metres (18 feet-45 feet) when undertaking such voyages.

DTp CODE OF PRACTICE FOR SAIL TRAINING BOATS

This Code of Practice is designed to ensure maximum safety for the vessel and its crew and embodies many features which must of necessity be incorporated at the design and building stage. However, there are many other useful ideas which the average handyman owner of a cruising yacht can carry out himself.

No one will deny that a sail training boat should incorporate the maximum amount of safety features reasonable for its size.

However, the sail training boat will, in general, have a young, active crew and a professional skipper. Compare this to the average cruising yacht of comparable size with in all probability a weak family crew. In the latter case it is obvious that the vessel should be equally well equipped from a safety point of view.

Listed below are some suggestions which are in addition to the DTp recommendations for yachts listed elsewhere in this section.

1. Bower anchor, well secured, of appropriate size and kedge anchor.

	OA Length m.	Bower kg.	Kedge kg.
Suggested	9	15	8
weights	10	17	9
	11	20	10
	12	23	12
	13	26	13

2. Retaining pin in stem head fitting.
3. Companion Way – washboards 300mm. above deck level when open and when closed secured with catches that can be opened from inside as well as outside.
4. Harness attachment each side of companion way and each side of cockpit.
5. Jackstays to clip harnesses on when working on deck.
6. Dan buoy at least 6 ft. high.
7. Remote fuel and gas shut-off.
8. Gas cooker firmly secured with flame fail/safe device.
9. Hole in engine bulkhead to discharge fire extinguisher through.
10. Engine Box – flame retardant paint inside.
11. Drip tray under fuel filter.
12. Easy access to strum box.
13. Second bilge pump with long wandering pipe and strum box.
14. Locker lids so secured that they remain shut even when boat is inverted.

ROYAL YACHTING ASSOCIATION – TRAINING SCHEMES

The Royal Yachting Association designs and oversees a variety of training schemes for cruising yachtsmen – for both motor and sail. A beginner can move through his chosen scheme step by step, whilst of course gaining further practical experience along the way. Both practical and shore-based courses are included.

A training scheme can be entered at any appropriate level, and there is no compulsion to follow strictly the normal progression of courses. The beginner starts with an elementary course and may end the scheme, some enjoyable years later, passing the examination for Ocean Yachtmaster.

Certificates are awarded on successful completion of courses, both shore-based and practical. In the future it is possible that some form of certification will be required by people who wish to skipper a cruising boat. Even today, many countries require documentary evidence of ability. The RYA covers this by the award of the Helmsman's Overseas Certificate of Competence. This can be obtained, without further testing, by holders of a Day Skipper Practical Course Completion Certificate; others have to take a practical test at a recognised centre.

The information below covers, in outline, the training schemes for motor and sail.

RYA NATIONAL CRUISING SCHEME – MOTOR CRUISING COURSES

Course	Content	Ability after Course	Duration
Introduction to motor cruising	Safety and basic seamanship	Useful crew member	2 days
Helmsman's, practical	Safety, helmsmanship, boat handling, intro to engine maintenance.	Competent to handle a motor cruiser of specific type in sheltered waters	2 days
Day Skipper, shore-based	Basic seamanship and intro to navigation and meteorology		About 60 hours
Day Skipper, practical	Pilotage, boat handling, seamanship and navigation. Engine maintenance.	Competent to skipper a motor cruiser, by day, in familiar waters	4 days
Coastal Skipper/ Yachtmaster (Offshore), shore-based	Offshore and coastal navigation, pilotage, meterology		About 60 hours
Coastal Skipper, practical	Skippering techniques for coastal and offshore passages	Competent to skipper a motor cruiser on coastal passages by day and night	5 days

RYA NATIONAL CRUISING SCHEME – SAIL CRUISING COURSES

Course	Content	Ability after Course	Duration
Competent Crew, practical	Basic seamanship and helmsmanship. Safety	Useful crew member	5 days
Day Skipper, shore-based	Basic seamanship and intro to navigation and meterology		About 60 hours
Day Skipper, practical	Pilotage, boat handling, seamanship and navigation	Competent to skipper a small sailing yacht by day, in familiar waters	5 days
Coastal Skipper/ Yachtmaster (Offshore), shore-based	Offshore and coastal navigation, pilotage, meterology		About 60 hours
Coastal Skipper, practical	Skippering techniques for coastal and offshore passages	Competent to skipper a sailing yacht on coastal passages by day and night	5 days

Most readers of this Almanac will already be experienced sailors. We hope however, that these pages will help to inform beginners, as well as other sailors looking for more advanced training, what opportunities exist.

SAFETY IS A STATE OF MIND. TRAINING AND EXPERIENCE ENGENDER THE RIGHT STATE

Further information from:

The Royal Yachting Association,
RYA House,
Romsey Road,
Eastleigh,
Hampshire SO5 4YA.
Telephone: (0703) 629 962.

National Federation of Sea Schools,
Staddlestones,
Fletchwood Lane,
Totton, Southampton,
Hampshire SO4 2DZ.
Telephone: (0703) 869 956.

RUBBISH DUMPING AT SEA

In addition to it being an offence to discharge oil, oily waste or any noxious liquid into the sea or rivers (MARPOL 73/78 Annex I & II), it is now an offence to discharge any garbage into the sea or rivers. Plastic/synthetic materials are totally prohibited. Food wastes, paper, bottles, metal etc. 3M. from nearest land (baseline of territorial waters) if passed through a grinder, otherwise 11M. Dunnage, linings etc. which float — 25M. For most yachts coasting this will mean taking your rubbish back to the yacht club or home for disposal. (MARPOL 73/78 Annex V). Marinas and Port Authorities should provide facilities for disposal of rubbish.

NAVIGATION IN FOG

Basically there is no difference between navigating in fog or daylight but the sudden envelopment of a small craft in dense fog, preventing the navigator from seeing more than a few yards ahead, has a psychological effect which is quite surprising to those who have not experienced it before. The following checkpoints are suggested as a standard drill in the event of fog:

1. Immediately update the E.P. on the chart and then maintain an accurate check at say $\frac{1}{2}$ hour intervals.

2. If under power, immediately reduce speed in order that avoiding action is more easily taken if there appears to be imminent danger of collision.

3. If not already done, instruct all crew members to wear safety harness (and clip on). A man overboard situation in clear weather can be difficult, the same situation in dense fog could easily become catastrophic.

4. Remember to use your fog signal in accordance with the Collision Regulations.

Note: Power vessel making way through the water — 1 prolonged blast ev. 2 min. Power vessel under way but stopped — 2 prolonged blasts with 2 sec. intervals ev. 2 min. Sailing vessel — one prolonged and two short blasts ev. 2 min.

5. When coasting — if possible get out of the shipping lanes into shallow water where there is no possibility of being run down by a large vessel and if circumstances render it advisable anchor until it is safe to resume passage.

It is doubly important that a radar reflector is hoisted when in fog.

SEA EMERGENCIES

Emergencies inevitably occur at sea (as they do in every other context) but the prudent skipper will make every effort to see that they do not occur as a result of his own carelessness or unpreparedness. Every effort should be made to anticipate emergency situations and to plan how best to overcome them if they should occur. What sort of emergencies can happen? What action will be necessary? Are the right spares and equipment carried on board? Have the crew members been properly briefed? Do they know where the flares are stowed? (and do they know how to use them?)

These and many other questions should be given serious consideration — tragedies in yachts are fortunately rare, bearing in mind the numbers that put to sea — but those that do happen can usually be traced to carelessness or human error, perhaps even the simple one of neglecting to listen to the shipping forecast before departure.

Man overboard

This is one of the most difficult situations that can confront the small craft sailor and one which usually results from someone's carelessness. Every crew member should have a safety harness and it is the skipper's responsibility to ensure that they are worn when weather conditions demand it. Are there adequate attachment points on board and are the crew properly briefed on their location?

There is a general tendency for safety precautions to be rather more casual when rowing out in the dinghy than when underway at sea and it is salutary to reflect that amongst cruising people probably more drowning tragedies occur when rowing out to the parent vessel than when underway in her. Life jackets should always be worn (especially by children) if there is the slightest danger. (See on for man overboard drill.)

Collision at Sea

Fortunately a rare occurrence but nowadays a very real danger in those areas of high density of shipping such as the Straits of Dover. A sound knowledge of the Collision

Regulations is necessary to evaluate any possible close quarters situation which may arise — can the sound signals in restricted visibility be instantly remembered? Is the vessel on the correct course for crossing a shipping lane? And is the speed adequate? Remember Collision Regs. Rule No: 10 — 'a vessel of less than 20m in length or a sailing vessel shall not impede the safe passage of a power driven vessel following a traffic lane'. Even outside a traffic lane a large vessel operating in confined waters (which may not appear to be 'confined waters' to a small vessel) may be quite unable to take avoiding action and the responsibility for taking such action then lies squarely with the small vessel. It is important that such action should be taken in good time and is obvious to all vessels involved in the close quarters situation.

Severe Weather
The advent of rough weather should not necessarily be regarded as an emergency. Assuming that the vessel is well found and her crew are prepared, rough weather may pose problems in navigation but the situation unless it gets badly out of hand is not an emergency. The prudent skipper will have reefed down in adequate time, firmly secured all deck gear and have thermos flasks of hot water ready for the preparation of soup later, when conditions in the galley may become difficult. The navigator should ensure that his E.P. on the chart is up to date and consider whether it would be wise to alter course for an alternative destination, bearing in mind the probable conditions to be expected on arrival. For example, certain ports on the French and Belgian coasts can be dangerous for small craft with strong on shore winds.

In severe conditions the skipper may eventually be faced with the alternatives of heaving to, running under bare pole or lying a hull. He should have given careful consideration to these possibilities before the need arises and will certainly have practised heaving to in moderate conditions and assessed how his boat is likely to behave in more severe conditions. It is of course important to consider how much room there is to leeward when contemplating heaving to.

Finally remember to take action in good time. A dry, warm and well fed crew can deal much more easily with trouble than can the wet, cold and exhausted crew. (See Section 14 Seamanship.)

Gas Hazards
Gas explosions in small craft are fortunately rare and providing certain precautions are taken should never happen. The installation should be properly carried out and maintained; it is most important to regularly check all flexible connections and always to turn off gas at the cylinder when the cooker is not in use. Inevitably small quantities of gas escape each time the cooker is lit, and being heavier than air sinks down to the bilges where it accumulates. Pumping the bilges daily will evacuate any such accumulation.

Miscellaneous
Engine failure in a well found sailing yacht should not under normal circumstances be regarded as an emergency. If, however, it occurs for example when the vessel is entering a port with frequent fast moving cross channel ferries entering and leaving, then the situation may become difficult if there is insufficient wind to set sail. It is therefore important to regularly maintain the engine even if only occasionally used, filters should be changed at the appropriate intervals and if as sometimes happens no sediment trap is fitted in the fuel line, it would be wise to consider installing one.

Failure due to fuel line trouble should not therefore occur in well maintained craft. However, a blocked water inlet or worse, a rope round the propeller, can easily occur at any time particularly when in the vicinity of a large port and the prudent skipper will have considered how he would deal with the situation in the circumstances prevailing at the time.

On any passage at sea, the anchor if stowed on deck should be very firmly secured but should always be easily dropped when entering port.

Perhaps fire at sea is the worst emergency which can occur in small craft due to the incredible speed with which it can spread. Fortunately it is the most unusual disaster to occur but here again thought should be given to dealing with a fire in one's boat (see on for fire precautions). It need hardly be said that personal accidents which may occur ashore within easy reach of medical aid assume a very different complexion when the vessel is perhaps a day or more sailing distance away from medical aid. A working knowledge of first aid and the presence on board of an adequate first aid kit can be a very reassuring factor when dealing with accidents which may occur despite sensible precautions. (See First Aid Section 17.)

FIRE PRECAUTIONS IN SMALL VESSELS

Small vessels normally use Diesel or petrol in their main or auxiliary engines and paraffin or Calor gas for cooking purposes. Each fuel has its own particular hazards, but petrol and Calor gas must be treated with the greatest respect.

The flashpoint, ie the temperature at which a liquid gives off an inflammable gas, is much higher in Diesel and paraffin than it is with petrol, and the two former fuels are therefore, safer under normal working conditions. Both, however, are a fire risk if they come into contact with very hot metal, for example, an unlagged or uncooled exhaust pipe.

Considering first the engine installation, the fuel tank, especially if petrol, should be situated well away from the engine and exhaust pipe. Particular care should have been taken in the installation if, due to lack of space, it was necessary to place the tank close to the engine. The exhaust pipe should be well lagged and, if possible, fireproof thermal insulation placed between the engine and fuel tank to reduce the temperature rise in the fuel. The tank should have a vent pipe exhausting on deck to ensure that any fuel vapour is discharged well clear of the installation. The fuel pipe to the engine should be carefully installed and properly secured, the greatest danger in this connection is that of fracturing due to vibration. There is a great temptation in certain circumstances to use thin plastic piping for fuel pipe, mainly due to its flexibility and ease of installation in confined spaces. This should, of course, never be allowed. If a flexible connection is needed, it should be a proper armoured flexible pipe to British Standards Specification.

Apart from an actual spillage of petrol and the consequent possibility of fire, it will be appreciated that the great danger in small vessels is the accumulation of an explosive mixture in the bilges, caused by a mixture of air and either petrol vapour or Calor gas. There are various gas detecting devices on the market which will give adequate warning of a dangerous condition in the bilges. In addition, or perhaps as a substitute if no detector is carried, the bilges should be pumped daily. The average bilge pump, especially the diaphragm type, will pump air without the need for priming and will therefore, effectively evacuate any gases from the bilges.

The galley installation, particularly if a gas one, should be well designed and carefully maintained. Starting with the gas bottle, this should be installed in a separate compartment with a drain out through the ship's side so that any leakage from the valve or regulator is safely disposed of overside. As the gas is heavier than air, it will be appreciated that this compartment does not need a gas tight lid. This compartment should also accommodate the spare bottle if one is carried.

Pipework from the bottle to the cooker should be properly installed, being clipped at regular intervals to lessen the possibility of damage. Flexible connections to the cooker, particularly if the latter is in gimbals, should be inspected regularly for damage, slack nuts, etc. When the cooker is not in use, the gas should be turned off at the regulator, thus reducing the possibility of leaks.

Summarising, the following points should always be borne in mind:

1. Keep all compartments, where gas can accumulate, clear and well ventilated.

2. Maintain all installations, both gas and liquid fuel, in a good condition — this means regular inspection. It also means inspection of electrical equipment installed in a position where a spark could ignite an accumulation of gas.

3. When filling fuel tanks, ensure that there are no naked lights, smoking, etc and that the quantity required is known, thus reducing the risk of fuel overflowing.

4. Make sure that the fire extinguishers are in good order, properly positioned and everyone on board knows how to use them.

FIRE FIGHTING

The following points in connection with fire fighting are intended primarily for small vessels. An officer of a merchant ship is expected to have a good knowledge of fire drill in general and any particular precautions or methods of fire fighting required by a specific type of vessel or cargo.

In case of fire:

1. Alert all on board and tackle the fire, no matter how small as a major incident. A fire can get out of hand with astonishing rapidity. Extinguisher should be aimed at the base or centre of the fire where it will probably have the greatest hold.

2. Detail one crew member to alter course or stop the ship so that the wind is prevented from spreading the fire.

3. Close any hatches, ports, etc that will reduce the draught through the ship.

4. If you can transmit either by radio or visual signalling, inform the nearest ship or shore station of your predicament. It is better to cancel an alarm than to be too late to send one.

5. Launch the dinghy or life raft as soon as it is obvious that it will be required and if a dinghy, make sure that the 'survival kit', ie water, flares, etc, is placed aboard.

The above points may be dismissed as painfully obvious and indeed, they are, but they are intended to make the skipper of the small vessel consider his equipment and the general preparedness of himself and his crew to deal with a danger that may confront all of us at some time or other. Finally, again very obvious if water is used successfully to combat a fire – remember to pump the bilges as soon as possible.

MAN OVERBOARD

Sailing is probably one of the safest sports (certainly going to sea is safer than driving along the motorway) but there are certain risks which can be evaluated and provision made to deal with them. The greatest of these and one which in all probability will never happen in the life of the average yachtsman is "Man Overboard".

The rare chance of it happening and the rather awe inspiring problems tends to induce the "It won't happen to me" reaction in the average skipper. Probably it will not, but this is no excuse for neglecting seamanlike precautions – if it does happen it can easily prove fatal if the crew members have not practiced their drill – it is the Skipper's responsibility ultimately if an accident happens.

In many of the published articles on the subject the boats carrying out the exercise generally appear to be strongly crewed with three or four men on board. In the following notes it is assumed that the vessel concerned has a man and woman crew, perhaps with two small children – the real life family cruising situation. It is strongly recommended that a "Man Overboard" exercise should be carried out at reasonable intervals to familiarise all crew members with the problems and their solutions.

It is reasonable to assume that the vessel will have a reliable auxiliary engine and in all probability a VHF radio set, two items which can play an important part in the exercise.

There are three main stages in the M.O.B. Operation. First stop the vessel and return to the casualty, secondly secure him alongside and finally recover him aboard. All three stages must be carried out quickly and effectively. Mental concentration on these three stages will greatly help to discipline and steady the mind during the period when panic can rapidly develop and slow the whole operation down.

The immediate reaction to "Man Overboard" must be to release the danbuoy (with life buoy attached) from its position on the push pit in order to pin point the casualty's position. The vessel should then be turned to windward, foresail dropped or furled and having checked there are no ropes overside start the auxiliary engine and return to the scene of the incident. With the boat under control (mainsail freed off or dropped as necessary) a slow approach should be made, aiming to stop the vessel about 20 feet upwind of the casualty and allowing a slow drift down with the engine stopped. It must be appreciated that any boat will only remain stationary for a matter of seconds in a strong wind before it starts to fore reach or drift rapidly — even with no sail set. This particular point in the operation is the most crucial one from the boat handling angle. Previous exercises will have demonstrated how the vessel behaves in different wind and sea conditions, for example is it easier to approach from down wind of the casualty? The disadvantage of this method is that the auxiliary engine must be used up to the very last moment with the possibility of danger to the casualty.

This is one stage in fact where previous exercises in different wind strengths can literally mean the difference between life and death to the casualty.

After the immediate dropping of the danbuoy and with the vessel heading back to the casualty the opportunity should be taken to drop astern a 30 metre flotation line, attached to the vessel with a lifebuoy at the end. This may prove useful in getting a line to the casualty if difficulties arise when the vessel has been brought back to him.

The next stage on arrival at the casualty is to secure him alongside. There are various pieces of equipment now available to assist the operation. One type consists of a pole with a stiff plastic loop on the end which can be dropped over the head and shoulders of the casualty. When suitably positioned the loop can be tightened from the inboard end, thus enabling him to be firmly secured alongside. (The construction of a suitable piece of equipment, small enough to stow on board should be within the capability of the average handyman).

The third and final stage of the operation, getting the man aboard is undoubtedly the most difficult. A useful piece of equipment is a scrambling net as used by the R.N.L.I. This consists of a strong net six feet by eight feet with four or five inch mesh. This is suspended from the guard wire or stanchion bases and apart from providing a comparatively easy method of scrambling aboard it also enables the crew member to stand in the net and assist the casualty aboard. One occasionally hears references to transom hung boarding ladders being useful — nothing could be less useful. Whilst suitable as a bathing ladder in calm conditions, in anything of a seaway the transom will be rising and falling a matter of feet and anyone in the water underneath it would be in a dangerous position. Recovery must be effected amidships where the vessel's movement is at a minimum.

At this stage a decision must be made about the use of VHF if this is available. If the casualty is conscious and obviously able, with assistance, to scramble aboard — get him aboard. If however, he is unconscious or there is any doubt about getting him on board, immediately send out a Pan Pan signal giving the vessel's name, position and brief details of emergency, eg. "Pan Pan Yacht XYZ, Position six miles East of North Foreland, man overboard, request immediate assistance." It is far better to make a Pan Pan call in good time and then cancel it if recovery is successful than wait until it has proved impossible to recover the casualty.

Assuming that the person is unable to get back on board unaided some form of mechanical aid is essential. The use of a halliard winch single handed offers no chance of success — the average woman without someone to tail the fall would certainly not be able to lift a heavy weight. Additional power must be available and probably the easiest way of providing this is by means of a three fold purchase which can be hoisted up on the main halliard to a predetermined position and then used as a tackle to hoist the casualty aboard. This purchase consists of two treble blocks giving the very useful mechanical advantage of 4:1. The tackle should be suspended from the main halliard by means of a swivel snap shackle and the fall taken from the top block via a foresail sheet winch.

Two points to remember, firstly the point to which the tackle must be hoisted must be determined by trial and error and then carefully noted. Secondly the stowage of the tackle — inevitably a piece of equipment which may never be used will probably be stowed in some inaccessible position and when required will be found to be a tangled mass of blocks and rope — leading to delays. Probably the best way to stow the gear is in a tight polythene sleeve of sufficient length to allow the tackle to be stowed in it in the fully extended position with a block at each end of the sleeve. This will prevent the rope tangling and ensure that the tackle can be used immediately without having to overrun the turns. The bottom guard wire should always be set up with pelican hooks or lashings so that it can be quickly cut adrift without any trouble, thus enabling a casualty to be rolled aboard without having to be lifted over the top guard rail.

It is hoped that the foregoing notes may assist the family crew to work out their own approach to the problem, practice the drill and should it ever become necessary in real life, to successfully recover the man overboard.

ABANDONING SHIP

These notes apply to home waters in the Northern hemisphere where one is unlikely to be adrift for more than 5-7 days. All small vessels should have:
1. A simple list of 'Procedure on Abandoning Ship' on permanent display near the chart table/navigation area.
2. An Abandon Ship Waterproof Box/Bag near the liferaft or cabin entrance.

The following suggestions re: contents, may provide a useful guide:

BASIC SURVIVAL KIT
1. Container(s) of fresh water (with some air so they float) 2 litres per head.
2. Flares/rockets/smoke signals.
3. 'Space' Rescue blanket.
4. Glucose sweets — 500 grammes per head.
5. Torch.
6. Compass.
7. Plastic bucket — bailer.
8. 5 fathom warp.
9. Emergency radio.

If time allows
10. Extra warm clothing, sleeping bags, sweaters, etc.
11. First Aid Box.
12. Ship's Papers, money, passports — kept permanently in plastic folder.
13. Chart(s).
14. Rescue quoit with line.
15. Sheath knife and other tools.
16. Pencils and paper.
17. Food — bread, chocolate, canned food plus opener.

TWO CRAFT ARE BETTER THAN ONE — IF POSSIBLE TAKE LIFERAFT AND DINGHY.

PROCEDURE ON ABANDONING SHIP
Put on all possible waterproof clothing including gloves, headgear and lifejacket.
Collect survival kit.
Note present position.
Send out MAYDAY.
Launch liferaft — attached to ship.
Launch dinghy — attached to liferaft.
Try to enter liferaft direct (if impossible, use minimal swimming effort to get aboard).

IN THE LIFERAFT/DINGHY
Get a safe distance from the sinking vessel.
Collect all flotsam — the most unlikely articles can be adapted for use under survival conditions.
Keep warm — bodies together.
Remove all clothing from dead bodies and share between survivors.
Keep dry — especially feet.
Stream sea anchor.
Arrange lookout watches.
Use flares only on skipper's orders — when there is a real chance of being seen.
Arrange for collection of rain water.
Ration water to maximum $\frac{1}{2}$ litre per person per day — issued in small doses.
Do not drink sea water or urine.
If water in short supply only eat sweets from survival rations.

THE WIND CHILL FACTOR

The chart below shows the limitations imposed by winds at low temperatures. Although compiled primarily for use in arctic conditions, it will be of use for those sailing in areas covered by this almanac in winter months.

The point at which the temperature and wind speed intersect on the graph indicates the wind chill factor. The practical implications of the wind chill factors are given below the graph. It must be noted that 'proper clothing' means protecting all skin areas from direct wind with sufficient thickness to prevent undue coldness. If clothing becomes wet or frost forms on it, it should be dried as soon as possible.

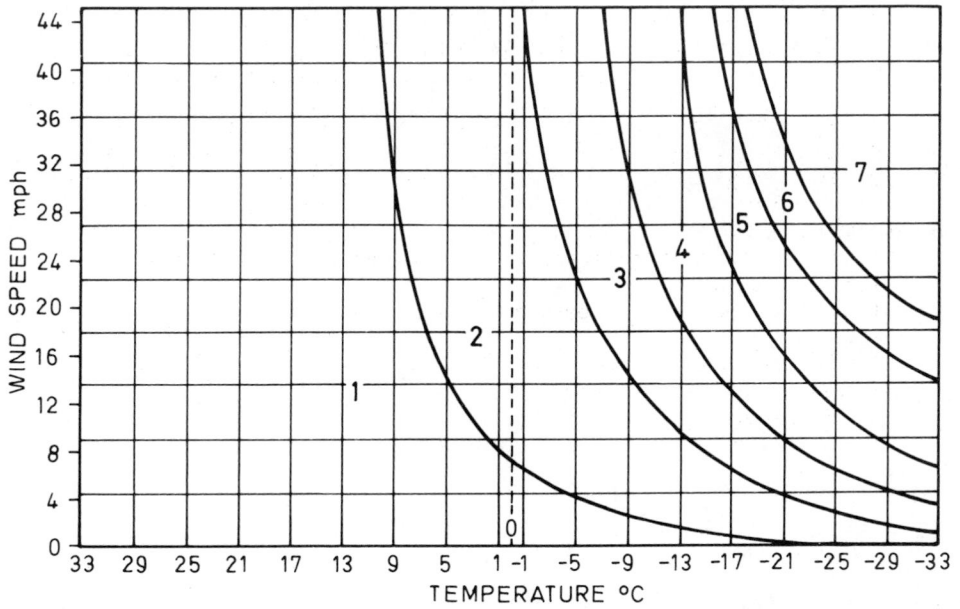

1. Comfortable with normal precautions.
2. Can become uncomfortable on overcast days unless properly clothed.
3. Heavy outer clothing necessary even on clear days.
4. Heavy clothing is mandatory. Unprotected skin will freeze over prolonged period of exposure.
5. Multiple layers of clothing mandatory, especially protection for the face.
6. Proper face protection becomes mandatory. One should not venture on deck alone, exposure must be controlled by careful scheduling.
7. Survival conditions. Crew can become easily fatigued and mutual observation of fellow crew members is mandatory.

PERSONAL NOTES

First Aid at Sea

MEDICAL ADVICE

In case of SERIOUS ILLNESS OR ACCIDENT AT SEA Masters of small vessels can get prompt medical advice by either:

1. RADIO—   Contact nearest shore station OR
                            Put out a call 'PAN PAN'

2. DIRECT SIGNALLING to other vessels by:

Flag W
OR   } = I require medical assistance
Morse W . — —

The principles of First Aid are to sustain life and prevent the condition becoming worse until expert help is available.

ALWAYS KEEP CALM AND REASSURE THE PATIENT.

FIRST AID BOX

The following suggestions apply to a vessel expecting to be at sea for not more than 72 hours. Dressings and drugs are preferably kept in separate polythene boxes with airtight lids.

DRESSINGS
Sterile non-adhesive dressings
  (Melolin—1 pack of 10 5cm × 5cm)
Gauze packs—6 large, 6 small
Cotton wool—30 grammes
Triangular bandage—2
Crepe bandage—1m × 7.5cm
Adhesive plaster—5m × 2.5cm
Blenderm (transparent waterproof
  adhesive tape) 5m × 5cm
Ambulance dressing No. 4—1
Wound dressing No. 8—3

OTHER ITEMS
Brook airway or
  Laerdal pocket mask
Scissors
Assorted safety pins
Disposable syringe and needle
  (13 gauge)
Reflective blanket
  ('Space' Rescue Blanket)
Clinical thermometer—Sub normal
and normal.
Splinter forceps

DRUGS

Indication	Drug
Seasickness	Kwells/Sealegs/Marzine/Avomine/Stugeron
Pain	Paracetamol
Indigestion	Magnesium Trisilicate
Diarrhoea	Lomotil
Constipation	Senokot
Stings, insect bites	Anthisan cream
Sunburn—Mild	Oily Calamine lotion

SUPPLEMENTARY MEDICAL KIT

Skin
50 Band Aid/Elastoplast
2 Fingerstalls

Cetrimide antiseptic solution
2 Locan (Anaesthetic) Cream
Athletes' Foot Cream or Powder
Sun Cream or Lotion

Injury
Hexalite Splint 2 18in × 3in
Hexalite Splint 2 18in × 6in

Eyes
Optrex

HYPOTHERMIA — EXPOSURE

Cold is dangerous — most people who die following immersion in Northern latitudes die from cold injury and not from drowning. Hypothermia is the medical name given to the condition which is often called 'exposure'.

TREATMENT OF SEVERE HYPOTHERMIA

IF ON RECOVERY FROM THE WATER A BODY FEELS ICE COLD:
1. If unconscious, open airway and check breathing. Complete the ABC of Resuscitation (described overleaf) if necessary, and place in Recovery Position (see p. 17:8.
2. Remove the outer clothing, and replace any wet clothing with dry.
3. Place casualty in sleeping bag, cover with blankets, etc.
4. Place a suitably covered hot-water bottle in left armpit or over breast bone — to warm 'core' circulation.
5. Give hot drinks and high energy food when conscious.
DO NOT place hot water bottles at extremities as this increases blood flow through the limbs and may result in a dangerous fall in 'core temperature'.
Note: Never presume that the casualty is dead simply because you cannot detect breathing or a pulse.
Note: It is best to rewarm a casualty at the speed cooling took place. Therefore, a person immersed in the sea should be rewarmed rapidly.

PREVENTION OF HYPOTHERMIA

ON BOARD THE EFFECTS OF COLD ARE INSIDIOUS AND MAY AFFECT ANY CREW MEMBER. They are more likely to occur at night and skippers should be aware of this risk if the temperature drops.

SYMPTOMS
Casualty's skin cold, pale and dry.
Body temperature below 35°C.
Slowing of physical and mental responses.
Irritability or unreasonable behaviour.
Cramps or shivering.
Unconsciousness may develop.
Difficulties with speech or vision.

NONE OF THESE WARNINGS SHOULD BE IGNORED.

SHOCK

This medical condition accompanies severe injury and illness. The blood circulation fails because blood pressure or volume of blood is reduced, thus failing to supply sufficient oxygen to the vital organs. The condition may prove fatal.

SIGNS AND SYMPTOMS
Skin becomes pale, cold and clammy.
Casualty may feel weak, faint or giddy.
Pulse is weak and rapid.
Breathing shallow and fast.
Possible unconsciousness.

TREATMENT
1. Treat any serious injury.
2. Lay him down, keep head low and turn to one side.
3. Raise legs, unless fracture of leg suspected.

4. Loosen tight clothing at neck, chest and waist.
5. Shelter from extremes of temperature — cover with blanket if cold.
6. Monitor condition of pulse, breathing, consciousness.
7. Arrange urgent removal to hospital.
   DO NOT give casualty anything to eat or drink.
   DO NOT use hot water bottles.

RESUSCITATION

When a casualty is not breathing and if the heart is not beating, it is vital to resuscitate the patient. The general rule is the ABC of resuscitation:
A — Airway
B — Breathing
C — Circulation

AIRWAY

When a casualty is unconscious the airway may be blocked or narrowed, making breathing noisy or impossible. Urgent action is needed to open the airway.
1. Lift the casualty's chin forward with the index and middle fingers of one hand while pressing the forehead backwards with the other hand. The patients jaw will lift the tongue forward, clear of the airway.
2. The casualty may start to breathe, if so, place in the recovery position.
3. Place your ear above the casualty's mouth and nose, look along chest to determine if breathing.
4. Clear the airway of any obstruction, such as food or vomit. Turn head to side, hook two fingers into mouth and sweep out any obstructions.
5. Check if casualty is breathing, if so, place in the recovery position.

BREATHING

Following checks of the airway, if the casualty is found not to be breathing, undertake mouth to mouth resuscitation.
1. Open your mouth and take a deep breath, pinch casualty's nostrils with your fingers and support the jaw.
2. Seal your lips around the patient's mouth and blow into the lungs. Watch the chest rise.
3. If chest does not rise, check airway not obstructed.
4. Remove your mouth well away from casualty's and watch his chest fall. Take a deep breath and repeat inflation.
5. After two inflations, check the carotid pulse. If pulse is beating, continue giving inflations at a rate of 12-16 times per minute, until natural breathing is restored.
6. When natural breathing returns, place casualty in the recovery position.

CIRCULATION

Check the carotid pulse after the first two inflations of the lungs. If it is not present, External Chest Compression must be performed in conjunction with mouth to mouth resuscitation.
1. Lay the casualty on his back on a firm surface. Kneel alongside the patient facing the chest, in line with the heart.
2. Find the junction of the rib margins at the bottom of the breastbone. Place the heel of one hand along the line of the breastbone, two fingers width above this point.
3. Cover this hand with the heel of the other hand and interlock fingers.
4. Keep arms straight and press down vertically on the lower half of the breastbone.
5. Press down about 4 to 5cm in the average adult, then release pressure. Complete 15 compressions at the rate of 80 compressions per minute.
6. Move to the patients mouth and give two breaths of mouth to mouth ventilation.

7. Continue with 15 compressions followed by two inflations.
8. Check the pulse after one minute, if pulse present then cease External Chest Compression, but continue mouth to mouth until breathing returns.
9. If no pulse present, continue with 15 compressions and two inflations. Check pulse every three minutes.

As soon as the pulse returns, stop compressions, but continue with mouth to mouth ventilation until the breathing is restored. Place casualty in recovery position.

RESUSCITATION FOR CHILDREN

The method and rate varies slightly from the adult cycle shown above.

BABIES AND CHILDREN UNDER TWO — For mouth to mouth ventilation, seal your lips around babies mouth and nose. Gently puff into lungs about 20 breaths per minute.

— For External Chest Compression, use two fingers only, at rate of 100 times per minute, pressing 1.5 to 2.5cm.

CHILDREN — For mouth to mouth ventilation, seal lips around mouth and nose, gently breathe at 20 times per minute.

— For External Compression, use one hand only, pressing 2.5 to 3.5cm at rate of 100 times per minute.

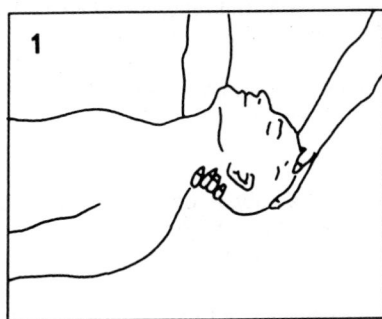

1 Neck is lifted

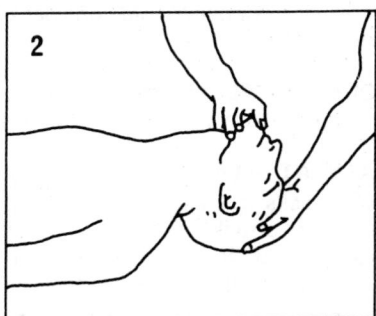

2 Head is tilted back

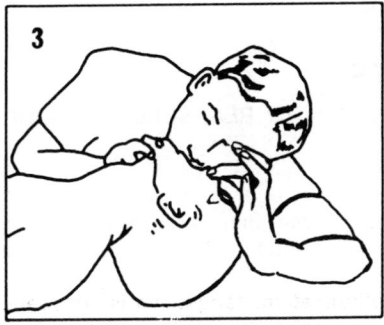

3 Lungs are inflated via nose or mouth
Chest should be seen to rise

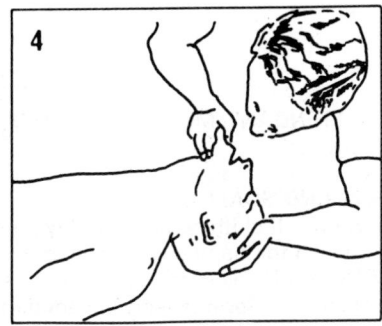

4 Victim exhales by himself, if necessary, through his mouth. Chest falls

Most people using this head-tilt oral method find in the excitement of the moment that it is not distasteful, but the few who are repulsed by the thought of physical contact with the patient can use a special mask, or a simple device known as the Resusciade. This has a nylon mouthpiece and valve set in a small plastic sheet. A Brook airway is considered the best appliance to use. Use of these devices should also reassure any persons worried about the risk of infection from direct mouth to mouth contact.

SEASICKNESS

PREVENTION IS MUCH BETTER AND EASIER THAN CURE.
AVOID LARGE MEALS AND ALCOHOL BEFORE SAILING. KEEP WARM AT ALL TIMES.

ANTI-SEASICKNESS PILLS — Take early — at least 1 hour before sailing or at the first indication of deteriorating weather conditions. The best preparations contain Hyoscine in a dose up to 0.6 mgm. (e.g. Kwells) which in excess causes a dry mouth. Some people prefer anti-histamines (e.g. Sea Legs, Dramamine, Marzine) but they are more likely to cause drowsiness. Avomine is helpful to calm an anxious passenger but is too likely to cause sleep to be of general use for active crew members. Many yachtsmen have found STUGERON (Cinnarizine) to be helpful. 1 tablet should be taken three times a day starting 24 hours before sailing.

Sailors should experiment. Small doses repeated every few hours are often more effective than large doses and cause less side effects.

Start treatment while still feeling 100%. All treatments are *much* less effective after symptoms have appeared.

RESPONSIBILITY of a job to do (e.g. taking the helm) will often prevent seasickness and an observant skipper should consider this when a member of the crew becomes pale or unusually quiet.

FREQUENT SMALL FEEDS — dry tack, dry bread, barley sugar, hot soup or other foods according to taste should be taken as appropriate with sips of water or tea.

TREATMENT — Prolonged sickness is dangerous.

Mild attacks will respond slowly to the measures outlined above under Prevention but more severe attacks will require sedation with Avomine (by injection if necessary).

Seasick crew should be kept warm in a bunk, if possible near fresh air, and given frequent sips of fluid when awake.

ANY PERSON VOMITING OVER THE SHIP'S SIDE MUST BE ATTACHED BY SAFETY HARNESS OR LINE.

ACCIDENTS

THE ATTENDANT MUST KEEP CALM AND CONSTANTLY REASSURE THE INJURED PERSON.

BURNS AND SCALDS

Principles — If clothing is alight, lay person down to prevent flames reaching facial area, and quench the flames with blanket or cold water. Continue cooling the damaged area for at least ten minutes with fresh or salt water.

Remove only loose clothing from burnt area. Do not attempt to pull off clothing stuck to skin. Cover lightly with sterile dressing. Keep patient warm. If burns severe, seek help.

Chemical Burns — Remove affected clothing and wash with water. If acid burn wash with diluted bicarbonate of soda if available. Dry and treat as above.

Electrical Burns — Switch off the current. If this is impossible stand on some dry insulating material such as wood or rubber and try to push the supply away from the patient, or the patient's limbs away from the supply with a piece of wood. If the patient is not breathing clear the airway and start artificial respiration and cardiac massage. Treat burn as above.

CUTS AND BLEEDING — a small quantity of blood can look excessive.

Most bleeding can easily be controlled by direct pressure and the majority of wounds will stop bleeding within 5 or 10 minutes. Apply pressure directly over the wound with a dressing and bandage firmly. Keep the patient lying down but if possible ELEVATE THE BLEEDING PART. If blood continues to soak through the dressing add gauze pads and bandage firmly. Repeat if necessary. Do not remove the original bandage.

FRACTURES

A fracture is a broken or cracked bone.

Damage to the surrounding tissues and organs may outweigh the importance of the fracture itself.

Symptoms

Pain.   **Swelling.**   **Deformity.**   **Loss of power.**   **Abnormal movement.**

In case of doubt always treat the condition as a fracture.

Bleeding into the surrounding tissues may be severe. If there is excessive swelling do not bandage too tightly as this can stop the circulation to the rest of the limb.

Treatment

Gently correct any deformity if the skin is tightly stretched over the bone or if there is evidence that the circulation is impeded.

Splint the limb using a Hexalite splint, by bandaging to the sound limb or to the trunk or support the limb in a comfortable position with cushions, rolled clothing, etc.

Loosen any clothing which might affect the circulation and watch for signs of constriction, e.g. —

If the hand or foot below the fracture becomes cold, blue and swollen — loosen the bandage.

Keep the limb raised above chest height.

Open Fracture

This is a severe injury in which part of a broken bone pierces the skin. The wound must be covered by a sterile dressing.

If a patient sustains a fracture when in an inaccessible position it is often better to let him move out of it under his own power if he can.

Once the legs are bandaged together movement of the patient may be very difficult.

SPRAINS

A sprain occurs when the ligaments supporting a joint are damaged, usually by a twist injury of the ankle, wrist or knee.

Treatment

Apply a pressure bandage by wrapping the joint and the area above and below in a good layer of cotton wool and then bandage firmly, preferably with a crepe bandage. If an arm joint is sprained support the arm in a sling.

IF IN DOUBT TREAT AS A FRACTURE.

HEAD INJURY

Keep the patient flat and quiet in his bunk if possible. Scalp wounds bleed profusely. Wash with plenty of water and then apply prolonged pressure with Melolyn covered by gauze.

Loss of consciousness following a blow on the head suggests concussion. Vomiting or increasing drowsiness are serious signs. Ensure complete rest in the recovery position shown overleaf until seen by a doctor.

Blood or straw-coloured fluid seeping from ear or nose may indicate a fractured skull. Place patient in recovery position with leaking side down to allow fluid to escape. Do not bandage or plug which could cause a build-up in the skull and pressure on the brain. Immobilise and maintain a check on patient's breathing.

WARNING
If a spinal injury is suspected do NOT place patient in recovery position. Use an airway to maintain respiration and as a means of giving mouth to mouth resuscitation. *Warn patient to lie still.* Soft, solid items such as luggage or padded objects can be placed to prevent movement of head or body.

SYMPTOMS SUGGESTING SERIOUS ILLNESS

MEDICAL HELP IS REQUIRED URGENTLY IN THE FOLLOWING SITUATIONS:

CONTINUOUS SEVERE PAIN IN THE CENTRE OF THE CHEST.
This suggests a heart attack. The patient should be rested and propped up in his bunk with three or four pillows.

CONTINUOUS SEVERE PAIN IN THE ABDOMEN.
If associated with vomiting and shock, this suggests a serious internal disorder such as a perforated bowel. Lay the patient down flat, if acceptable, or with one pillow if more comfortable. Give nothing by mouth. A pillow under the knees may help.

SICKNESS, PALLOR, SWEATING AND RAPID BREATHING.
This suggests internal bleeding. Confirmation of this may come from the patient vomiting blood or passing black motions. Keep him lying flat with no pillow and as quiet and comfortable as possible.

LOSS OF CONSCIOUSNESS — COMA.
This has many causes but is always serious. MAINTAIN A CLEAR AIRWAY.

Treatment
Remove dentures.
Clear the back of the mouth and throat with the finger and wipe away any liquid which has accumulated.
If patient not breathing start artificial respiration.
Once satisfied with the patient's breathing turn him onto his side with his uppermost knee drawn up to a right angle — RECOVERY POSITION.

The recovery position.

Keep patient's mouth downwards so that any liquid can run out.
Loosen all clothing and keep him warm.
Give nothing by mouth.
Someone should remain with patient to ensure the airway remains clear.

OTHER EMERGENCIES

HEATSTROKE
This is due to high temperature and high humidity.
The patient may collapse suddenly with a high temperature — 41°C (106°F) or more or appear confused and complain of headache or dizziness.

Treatment
Strip the patient. Cover him with sheets or towels soaked in cold water and keep them wet and cold till the patient's temperature is 39°C (102°F). Open all ventilators. Cool as rapidly as possible.

FITS, EPILEPSY
Try to prevent the patient injuring himself. Keep him horizontal.
After the attack, keep him quiet and resting for a few hours.

FAINTING
Either — with the patient sitting, hold his head between his knees.
Or — lay him down and raise legs.
In either case — loosen tight clothing and ensure he can breathe.

NOSE BLEEDS
SIT CASUALTY WITH HEAD WELL FORWARD.
Casualty to breathe through mouth, then pinch soft part of nose.
Bleeding should cease within 10 minutes, if not, continue pressure.
If bleeding persists, seek medical aid.

FOREIGN BODIES IN THE EYE
If the foreign body can be seen beneath the lower lids it can be removed with the moistened corner of a handkerchief. This can also be tried if it can be seen on the white of the eye.
Do not remove anything that adheres to the clear part of the eye.
If the foreign body cannot be seen, it is probably under the top lid.
In this case pulling the top lid over the bottom lid may cause the bottom lashes to sweep it clear.
The patient may try opening and closing his eye with his face in a bowl of clean water.
Should the eye be burned with splashes of caustic chemicals:
Lay the patient down.
Open the eye with your finger.
Wash the eye with large amounts of clean tepid water.

WEIL'S DISEASE — LEPTOSPIROSIS

This is caught through contact with water infected by animal urine. All those using waterways and river banks are at risk, since the disease can exist on wet vegetation and enters through cuts, grazes and the mucous membranes of the mouth, nose and eyes. Take the following simple precautions:
  1) Cover any cuts or grazes with waterproof dressings BEFORE sailing.
  2) If skin injury occurs during contact with untreated water wash with clean water, treat with antiseptic and cover.
  3) Avoid immersion and swallowing of untreated water.
  4) After water activity, wash hands thoroughly (or shower if immersed) before eating, drinking or smoking.
First symptoms can be confused with 'flu, e.g. fever, pain in joints or muscles. If you develop these symptoms after spending time in or by water, tell your doctor immediately. Antibiotics are effective in the early stages of infection, but if left more serious problems develop.

EMERGENCY CHILDBIRTH

Send for medical aid. If not available keep calm, and let nature take its course. Labour may begin with either: —

1. Backache and regular pains in the abdomen.
2. A ''show'' of blood-stained mucus.
3. A gush of water from the birth canal.

Reassure mother. Get basket or drawer and blanket ready for baby.

Boil a pair of scissors and three pieces of string about nine inches long, for about 15 minutes. These are to cut and tie the cord. Prepare a bed for the mother by covering the mattress with a plastic sheet or newspapers, then a clean sheet. Have a supply of hot water, jugs and basins available.

Scrub hands thoroughly and keep crew members with any infection well away.

The first stage of labour, during which the neck of the womb opens, usually lasts several hours. The abdominal pains are usually every 15 to 20 minutes, becoming more frequent as labour progresses.

In the second stage the baby's head descends the birth canal and it may be preceded by a gush of water.

Turn the mother onto her side with her knees drawn up, and cover the top half of her body with a blanket to keep her warm. Encourage her to relax as much as possible when the pains occur. Should a bowel movement appear, wipe it away and wipe from the birth canal.

The baby's head will appear, more of it becoming visible with each contraction. At this stage ask the mother not to bear down, but to try to relax and breathe through her mouth.

Once the baby's head is born, support it with one hand and gently feel if the cord is wrapped around the baby's neck. If it is, ease it gently over the baby's head or shoulders. If a membrane is over the face, remove it.

Do not pull on baby or the cord. The shoulders are usually born with the next pain: then gently lift baby under its armpits, towards mother's abdomen.

Immediately attend to the baby's breathing. Hold it upside down supporting it by the ankles and shoulders. It is slippery so preferably wrap a cloth around the ankles. Wipe the mouth out with a clean handkerchief over the little finger. If the baby does not cry begin gentle artificial respiration.

When the baby cries lay it down against its mother's legs, with the head down, to allow any fluid to drain from the mouth.

If there is excessive bleeding, massage of the lower abdomen will often stimulate the womb to contract.

The afterbirth will be expelled with a pain in about five to fifteen minutes. Then tie the cord, or tie it if the afterbirth has not been expelled in fifteen minutes. Tie one boiled piece of string tightly and firmly about six inches, and the second piece of string about eight inches, from the baby's navel.

Cut the cord between the ligatures. Cover the baby's end of the cord with a sterile dressing and do not apply any antiseptics, etc., to the cord.

Wrap the baby lightly in a blanket and place it in the temporary cot. Inspect the cord for bleeding ten minutes later and, if suspected, tie another piece of boiled string an inch below the first one.

If the afterbirth has not been expelled, cover the mother's end of the cord with a sterile dressing. Keep the afterbirth for the doctor to inspect.

Wash the mother. Replace the sheets and newspapers with dry ones. Give the mother a hot drink and biscuits, and then encourage her to sleep.

Weather Forecasting and Nautical Meteorology

18

RADIO WEATHER FORECASTS

Radio Weather Forecasts. The weather forecasts and gale warnings for shipping issued by the Meteorological Office and broadcast by the BBC and Coastal Radio stations, make a very important contribution towards the safety of all who sail the seas. The times of these broadcasts are given on pages 18:26-18:28 and on the loose card "Shipping Weather Forecast Areas". In addition to these routine issues, special forecasts for port areas are available — page 18:25.

This section includes details of all weather information broadcasts (for the area covered by the Almanac) which are contained in Admiralty List of Radio Signals, Vol.3. This information is not exhaustive and changes are inevitable. Mariners are therefore strongly advised to maintain a listening watch on VHF Chan. 16 and MF 2182 kHz. for announcements of weather information.

MARINE METEOROLOGY

Meteorology is the science of the atmosphere, embracing both weather and climate.

Marine meteorology deals with the cause and effect of changes in atmospheric conditions over the oceans.

Since 1854 when the Meteorological Office was first instituted, at that time as a Department of the Board of Trade under Admiral Fitzroy, British ships have voluntarily kept meteorological logs in all oceans covering the globe, and these data have added much to our knowledge of the climatology of the oceans.

In 1921 the selected ship scheme was introduced whereby observations are not only recorded in the logbooks, but coded and transmitted by radio to an appropriate shore station for synoptic purposes. Meanwhile ships' officers have themselves become accustomed to drawing their own weather maps from information contained in the Weather Bulletins. They are thereby better able to interpret radio forecasts.

It is important that the Navigator of a small craft should have some idea of what weather he may expect on a certain passage. On this will depend, whether it is prudent to undertake such a voyage and, in second, what course to take, but this course may have to be amended during the voyage, on a further forecast of the weather being obtained.

Generally speaking, it is imprudent to be badly "caught out" at sea when coasting — but if it is unavoidable, then a proper realisation of the likely weather will enable the vessel to be snugged down in plenty of time, and a proper offing obtained from any lee shore.

If it is decided to seek shelter of a harbour or some good anchorage, then an early recognition of the probable weather will enable this decision to be carried out in safety and before a shift of wind makes it an impossibility.

Weather is a most fascinating study, and happy is the man who makes wise use of the official forecast. To lie in a snug anchorage and hear the wind blowing, after having made a decision to seek shelter because of your information, is to have a feeling of mastery over the elements, and members of the crew — whether amateur or professional — will have renewed confidence in the Owner or Master, without which confidence there can never be a "happy ship".

It therefore behoves any Navigator who is unable to pick up the forecasts, to do his best to anticipate the probable weather for himself. He should keep a watch on the movement of the barometer; note any tendency to significant variations in the direction and force of the wind and, perhaps most important of all, keep a very wary eye open for changes in the appearance of the sky. Should he be able to take dry and wet bulb temperature readings, so much the better, as the information gained about the humidity of the air might be a useful guide to any impending change in visibility. The hints given in the following pages, used in conjunction with the observations made, should give some indication as to the kind of weather to expect in the next few hours but it is unlikely that the mariner, with only these means at his disposal, will become a "forecaster": this is a highly specialised job. Listen when possible to the official forecasts, and be guided by them.

SINGLE OBSERVER FORECASTING

The observer in temperate latitudes, who is unable to obtain an official forecast, should not expect much success with his own forecasts for periods longer than six hours. It is generally quite impossible from observations at a single place to say today what the weather will be like tomorrow.

Barometer and Barograph. The onset of a gale is often heralded by a fall of the barometer and by a backing of the wind, but sometimes it is associated with a rapidly rising barometer and veering wind. Both the barometer and the wind usually give significant indications of the change to come an appreciable time before the actual gale begins, but the time interval may vary widely.

The rate at which the barometer falls depends to some extent on the locality. Extremely rapid falls 10 mb. (0.3 in.) in three hours occasionally occur in the extreme north and west of the British Isles, but in the east and south they are very rare. Falls of 5 mb. (0.15 in.) in three hours may occur half a dozen times a month in stormy winters, but on the other hand a whole winter month may pass without such a fall.

In the British Isles a rapid rise or fall does not always bring a gale; in fact the wind will probably not actually reach gale force more than once out of every three occasions of rapid rise or fall. It is, however, not safe to conclude because a gale has not come with a rapidly falling barometer, that it will not come at all. Some of the worst gales come after the barometer has ceased falling or even when it has started rising. Another point worth remembering is that gales with a rapidly rising barometer are generally more squally than gales with a falling barometer. As the barograph may not give a long warning of an approaching gale, it should be looked at frequently.

In the southern districts of England and in the Irish Sea easterly gales often come on without much fall of barometer; so with a moderate easterly wind a slight fall of barometer should be looked on with suspicion, especially in late winter and early spring. In NE Scotland and Orkney and Shetland the same is true of southerly or south-easterly gales. As regards the direction from which a gale will come the barograph gives only a rough general indication, viz., S'ly gales are most likely with a falling barometer and NW'ly gales with a rising barometer. If the wind has been W'ly with alternations of good and bad weather and signs of an approaching gale are observed with a falling barometer, it is very probable that the gale will be from S or SW at first, veering to W or NW suddenly with the worst squalls as the cold front passes.

In addition to its usefulness in giving warning of approaching bad weather, the barograph is also of use in foretelling whether a quiet interval will last. If the pressure is above 1,020 mb. (30.12 in.) and steady or rising, quiet weather is likely to last for at least 24 hours. Strong winds may occur with a high barometer, but as they come on gradually, this increase acts as its own warning. In unsettled weather a rapid rise of barometer is often quickly followed by a fall, but if the rise reaches a comparatively high level, an improvement in the general conditions may be expected. The single observer has no means of foretelling whether the strongest winds will occur before or after the passage of a front. Generally the wind is strongest in the warm sector and decreases on passage of the cold front. On occasions however, the wind rises to a maximum shortly before or actually as the cold front passes, and continues for several hours to blow harder than it did in the warm sector.

The speed of the wind tends to increase near headlands and straits and the direction of the wind under these circumstances tends to follow the run of the coast.

Cloud. The single observer forecaster will probably derive more assistance from studying the trend of cloud development, than he will from any other single element on its own. Of all the cloud types, Ci and Cs are especially to be watched, as these often afford the first indications of the presence—possibly 500-600 miles away—of an advancing warm front or occlusion, with which bad weather is commonly associated. If fine cirrus is approaching from NW, increasing and thickening into a sheet and showing a halo, then it is fairly certain that bad weather will follow before long, especially if the barometer continues to fall and the wind backs and freshens. With these signs to guide him, the prudent mariner will take any necessary precautions to safeguard his craft.

The speed of the forerunning cirrus is not a good guide to the speed of approach of a depression, although slow moving cirrus is not usually found before a rapidly advancing depression. Upper clouds moving rapidly are not infrequently a sign of unsettled conditions.

Small or medium sized cumulus is a fair weather cloud forming over the land soon after sunrise and disappearing about sunset. Towering cumulus show that there is a large lapse-rate and so showers and squalls should be expected. Any clouds of Cu type observed over land at dawn are more likely to be Sc than true cumulus. At sea, as opposed to over the land, large, active cumulus may be found by night as well as by day, there being no appreciable diurnal range of temperature at the sea surface.

The increasing and thickening of high and medium cloud does not invariably indicate the approach of frontal weather, as it is not uncommon for the upper cloud associated with Cumulonimbus to spread over in advance of the main cloud mass. At times the undersurface of this type of cloud presents a rippled or mammillated appearance. Neither the barometer, which is often unsteady, nor the wind, can provide any useful indication of future trends in these conditions, but it is well to be prepared for showers and squalls and possibly thunder. The squalls may be quite severe and come from a direction quite different from that of the wind previously experienced.

In summer, the appearance in the sky of ragged looking Altocumulus or Ac. of the castellated variety is an almost certain indication that thunderstorms, more widespread than local, will follow before many hours have passed. This is especially the case in the English Channel area and the southern North Sea, as it is an indication that thundery troughs will move up from France, bringing storms which may be severe and possibly prolonged. If the sky clears after the passage of a cold front and the wind veers to NW, an interval of 6-12 hours of fair weather should follow. A close watch should however be kept on the barometer and wind. If the former begins to fall and the wind backs towards SW, with increasing upper cloud, renewed bad weather may be expected within a few hours.

The sun setting behind a bank of clouds may well mean the cloud of an advancing front. On the other hand a "low" sunset shows that there is no frontal cloud within many hours run. A "high" dawn may be due to the end of frontal cloud, but a "low" dawn has no special significance.

A heavy dew or hoar frost shows that the sky was clear during the night, but this, on its own, is not necessarily an indication of continued good weather throughout the day. A lot of haze in the lower layers shows the presence of an inversion at no great height, probably caused by subsidence in an anticyclone, and so is a sign of good weather. Unfortunately this prognostic is only valid in dry summer weather when it is already obviously fine. Clouds becoming lower indicate the approach of bad weather.

The popular prognostics of red sunrises and sunsets probably refer to the colour of clouds when the horizon is clear. Minute dust particles in the atmosphere, not amounting to haze, are responsible for the red colour. The tendency seems to be for a red sunrise to precede bad weather and a red sunset good weather, but the type of clouds should be studied in conjunction with the colour. If the redness in the morning is caused by high or medium clouds spreading from the west, but not quite extending to the eastern horizon the warning is emphasized. The season of the year is important as a sunset in winter reddening the south-western sky may be misleading, since the bad weather, if it comes, may come from the north; or again stray clouds in the north-west may be tinged with red at a summer sunset while the southern horizon is clouding over, due to a depression moving up from south. Cirrus dissolving indicates fine weather.

Temperature and Humidity of the Air. The temperature and humidity of the surface air over the land are not of great assistance to the single observer forecaster as they are so subject to local effects; but if full consideration is given to all existing circumstances the variation of temperature and humidity from the normal, at the place of observation, for the season and time of day may provide a clue to forthcoming changes in the weather. When the wind sets in from some cold or warm region the temperature does not generally reach its minimum or maximum respectively for a day or two.

Temperature of the Sea. Since it is only the surface of the sea which is in contact with the air, the temperature of the surface is of particular importance in meteorology. A comparison of sea and air temperatures is a useful guide in recognizing the type of air stream, air colder than sea meaning polar air and air warmer than sea tropical air. In a flat calm the actual surface of the sea may be several degrees warmer than the water at a depth of a couple of feet. This is particularly the case when the temperature is rising. Care therefore should be taken to collect water from as near the surface as possible when taking the sea temperature. At times the temperature is uniform from the surface downwards to a variable depth. This is particularly the case when there is interior mixing caused by waves or by tidal currents or when the temperature is falling, as at the end of the day or the end of the summer; cooling occurs by conduction to the air or radiation to the sky, and the surface water becomes denser and sinks.

The water used for taking the sea surface temperature should be drawn in a canvas or special rubber bucket from over the ship's side. The temperature of this water is taken by an ordinary thermometer. Some sea water thermometers have a small reservoir round the bulb so that if it is necessary to remove the thermometer from the bucket to read it, the bulb will remain immersed in water. The temperature should be read as soon as possible after the water has been drawn; many thermometers need to be in the water, provided that it is well stirred, for only about 30 seconds to read correctly.

Cold water from the depths, brought to the surface by shoals may cause a deterioration of visibility.

A long line of foam is often caused by the meeting of two currents, one of which sinks below the other. There is generally a difference in the temperature of the water on the two sides of the line.

Fog. Fog is forecast at sea whenever the temperature of the sea is equal to or below the dew-point of the air. This condition is most often found with a southerly or south-westerly wind. If the air is full of salt particles, fog may form before the air is cooled to its dew-point.

Occasionally fog is experienced with a westerly or north-westerly wind in the Channel Approaches. This is generally due to the existence of an anti-cyclone to the westward, round which a flow of tropical air reaches the British Isles after passing further north than usual. "Hazy" steaming lights often give a warning of the formation of fog.

A change in tidal stream or an ocean current often brings colder water to the surface and this may cool the air sufficiently to form fog.

An alteration in wind direction or speed may cause the fog to thin or thicken.

If the sky above a fog is free from cloud during the day, a clearance is more likely than if the sky is cloudy.

The clearance of a shallow fog has sometimes been successfully forecast when the top of the fog is observed to start breaking up into wisps. The periodical appearance of the masthead of a nearby ship can be a useful guide in these circumstances.

When sea fog clears, especially at night, it is often difficult to say whether the ship has run out of it or the fog has dispersed or blown away.

In general, fog in the open sea will not finally clear until the arrival of a cold front, though any increase in the sea temperature has a tendency to lift the fog.

Sea and Swell. Swell is often followed by strong winds or a gale from the direction of the swell, but it is far from being an infallible sign, as the depression causing the strong winds which are the cause of the swell may alter course or slow down and fill up. The most profitable use of swell is in showing the existence and rough position of a tropical revolving storm.

A heavy swell may be caused by strong winds at some distance or by moderate winds closer at hand, but a wave-period of ten seconds or a wave-length of 500 feet in the open sea shows that the wind producing the swell must at least have been of gale force.

TABLE OF SEA STATES

(1) SWELL WAVES — LENGTH

	metres
Short	0–100
Average	100–200
Long	over 200

(2) SWELL WAVES — HEIGHT

	metres
Low	0–2
Moderate	2–4
Heavy	over 4

(3) SEA WAVES — HEIGHT

Code	metres*
0 Calm — glassy	0
1 Calm — rippled	0–0.1
2 Smooth wavelets	0.1–0.5
3 Slight	0.5–1.25
4 Moderate	1.25–2.5
5 Rough	2.5–4
6 Very rough	4–6
7 High	6–9
8 Very high	9–14
9 Phenomenal	Over 14

NOTE: In each case the exact boundary of length or height is included in the lower category, e.g., a sea of four metres is described as "Rough".
*Average wave height.

CHANGE IN WAVE HEIGHT IN OPPOSING OR FOLLOWING CURRENTS

Following current with a velocity of 1/4 that of waves — wave height reduced by 25%.

Opposing current with a velocity of 1/10 that of waves — wave height increased by 21%.

Opposing current with a velocity of 1/4 that of waves — wave height increased by 300%.

Weather Forecasts from Daily Observations

SUNRISE

A low dawn (day breaking on or near the horizon) means FAIR weather.
A high dawn (day breaking above a cloud bank) means WIND.
A purple sky at dawn means BAD WEATHER (much wind or rain—stormy).
A red sunrise with clouds towering later means RAIN.

SUNSET

A rosy sky at sunset (whether cloudy or clear) means FAIR WEATHER.
A greenish-grey (or pale yellow) sky means RAIN.
A dark red or purple sky means RAIN.
A bright yellow (or copper coloured) sky means WIND.
A sickly looking grey or greenish orange (or copper sky) means WIND and RAIN.

MOON

A Full Moon, rising clear foretells FAIR WEATHER.
A Full Moon rising pale yellow brings RAIN.
In the WANE OF THE MOON a cloudy morning brings a FAIR afternoon.
A large RING around the Moon and HIGH CLOUDS foretells RAIN in several days.
A red MOON means WIND.

HALO (a large circle)

A Halo round the Sun or Moon—the larger the Halo the sooner the Rain. The open side of the Halo tells the quarter from which the rain will come.
A Halo round the Sun or Moon after fine weather means STORMY weather (wind or rain).

CORONA (a small circle)

A Corona round the Sun or Moon and growing larger indicates FAIR WEATHER.
A Corona round the Sun or Moon and growing smaller means RAIN.

RAINBOW

A Rainbow in the evening means Fair weather. A secondary bow—with colours reversed — may be seen frequently about 10° outside the main Rainbow.

WELL PROVED INDICATIONS FOR FORECASTING THE WEATHER

FAIR WEATHER. Barometer steady (near, 1012.5 mb. or 29.90 in.) or RISING at a steady rate. Mares Tail Clouds at great height or Cumulus clouds.

RAIN, Barometer falling slowly (about 0.14 mb. or 0.004 inches per hour). Strange hues of clouds with hard defined outlines. White distant watery looking clouds which increase and are followed by an overcast murky vapour that becomes cloudy—this is a certain sign of rain.

Wind

Barometer falling gradually (0.37 mb. or 0.011 inches per hour).
Hard edges on oily looking clouds.
High upper clouds crossing in a different direction from that of the lower clouds or surface wind. This, when visible, is a useful sign and foretells change of wind towards their direction. Generally the harder the clouds look the stronger the coming wind will be.

Wind and Rain together
Barometer falling moderately (say 0.51 mb. or 0.015 inches per hour).
Strong coloured clouds at low heights.

STORMY weather; Strong Winds (perhaps Rain)
Barometer falling or rising rapidly (say 1.35 mb. or 0.04 inches per hour).
If oily looking clouds overcast there will be Wind, but if watery looking clouds overcast there will be Rain.
Unusual hues of cloud with hard outlines. Green and black clouds foretell lightning and Storm.

SEAMEN'S RHYMES

These rhymes, which are familiar to all seamen, summarise rather neatly, and in a form which is easily remembered, a number of rules for the amateur weather forecaster. Experience has shown there to be a considerable degree of truth in them and on that account they are included here. It should be borne in mind, however, that the rhymes are neither infallible nor always true, and they should be accepted with caution.

THE BAROMETER.

Long foretold, long last,
Short notice, soon past,
Quick rise after low,
Sure sign of stronger blow.

When the glass falls low,
Prepare for a blow;
When it slowly rises high,
Lofty canvas you may fly.

At sea with low and falling glass,
Soundly sleeps a careless ass,
Only when it's high and rising,
Truly rests a careful wise one.

WIND AND WEATHER.

A red sky at night is a sailor's delight,
A red sky in the morning is a sailorman's warning.

The evening red and morning grey
Are sure signs of a fine day,
But the evening grey and the morning red,
Makes the sailor shake his head.

Mackerel sky and mare's tails,
Make lofty ships carry low sails.

When the wind shifts against the sun,
Trust it not, for back it will run.

When rain comes before the wind,
Halyards, sheets and braces mind,
But when wind comes before rain,
Soon you may make sail again.

If clouds are gathering thick and fast,
Keep sharp look out for sail and mast,
But if they slowly onward crawl,
Shoot your lines, nets and trawl.

WEATHER FORECASTS BY OBSERVATION
FORECASTING INSTRUMENTS

The BAROMETER and—to a much lesser extent—the THERMOMETER are the two most used instruments for forecasting the weather. In any vessel large enough to house it a BAROGRAPH—which is simply a recording barometer—is of the utmost value as the movements of the record—whether up or down on the scale—can be seen over any period of several days at a glance without any written recordings being necessary.

Many large vessels, and all meteorological voluntary recording vessels carry a Mercurial Barometer which houses a column of mercury and very accurate readings may be made by this standard barometer from which all other barometers may be set for comparison.

In any small vessel (and of course this is also used in larger vessels too) the Aneroid type barometer is always used. The word "ANEROID" means "no fluid" and relies for its movement on the pressure of the atmosphere and is therefore quite unlike the Mercurial Barometer. The Aneroid Barometer should occasionally be compared at sea level with the mercurial type and if the Aneroid requires adjusting this is done very simply by carefully turning the screw at the back of the instrument (using a thin ended screwdriver) thus turning the indicators on the face of the Aneroid to a higher or lower reading as required.

Forecasting Factors

The essential factors in forecasting the weather at sea are the following in their relationship one to the other;
(a)   The direction and force of the wind.
(b)   The pressure of the atmosphere (*i.e.* Barometer readings) and its heat (*i.e.* thermometer readings).
(c)   The formation and movement of cloud.

Expected weather cannot be forecast simply by reading the barometer and thermometer at any given time or place. It is very necessary that a record should be kept of their movements and in practice this means that the barometer and thermometer readings, Direction and force of the wind and cloud appearance should be entered continually in the Log Book so that a more or less constant record may be available.

On a passage in a vessel of any size watches must be kept and the watch on deck can find from the Log Book these observations made by previous watch keepers without rousing them from their sleep to ask them questions.

The mercury barometer. For purposes of comparison of different barometric readings, any variation from standard gravity has to be corrected by using a formula giving the gravity at the station in terms of the latitude and the height above sea level. Corrections must also be applied for any difference between the temperature of the instrument and the standard temperature, for the height above m.s.l.* (as it affects the height of atmosphere above the instrument) and for the instrumental errors given on the certificate which accompanies the barometer. When the three corrections for gravity, temperature and height of instrument above sea level have been made the resultant value can be directly compared with that of any other barometer similarly corrected. These corrections may be simply and rapidly-applied by the use of the Gold slide. When reading a barometer the eye should be exactly on a level with the top of the mercury column, thus eliminating parallax.

*m.s.l. = mean sea level. Allowances for change of barometric pressure due to height of tide are negligible as the atmospheric pressure near the surface decreases approximately one millibar for every 28 feet ascent.

TEMPERATURE CONVERSIONS

C°	F°	C°	F°	C°	F°	C°	F°	C°	F°
00	32.0								
01	33.8	21	69.8	41	105.8	61	141.8	81	177.8
02	35.6	22	71.6	42	107.6	62	143.6	82	179.6
03	37.4	23	73.4	43	109.4	63	145.4	83	181.4
04	39.2	24	75.2	44	111.2	64	147.2	84	183.2
05	41.0	25	77.0	45	113.0	65	149.0	85	185.0
06	42.8	26	78.8	46	114.8	66	150.8	86	186.8
07	44.6	27	80.6	47	116.6	67	152.6	87	188.6
08	46.4	28	82.4	48	118.4	68	154.4	88	190.4
09	48.2	29	84.2	49	120.2	69	156.2	89	192.2
10	50.0	30	86.0	50	122.0	70	158.0	90	194.0
11	51.8	31	87.8	51	123.8	71	159.8	91	195.8
12	53.6	32	89.6	52	125.6	72	161.6	92	197.6
13	55.4	33	91.4	53	127.4	73	163.4	93	199.4
14	57.2	34	93.2	54	129.2	74	165.2	94	201.2
15	59.0	35	95.0	55	131.0	75	167.0	95	203.0
16	60.8	36	96.8	56	132.8	76	168.8	96	204.8
17	62.6	37	98.6	57	134.6	77	170.6	97	206.6
18	64.4	38	100.4	58	136.4	78	172.4	98	208.4
19	66.2	39	102.2	59	138.2	79	174.2	99	210.2
20	68.0	40	104.0	60	140.0	80	176.0	100	212.0

CONVERTING BAROMETER READINGS — INCHES TO MILLIBARS

In.	Mill.	In.	Mill.	In.	Mill.	In.	Mill.
27.00	914.3						
27.05	916.0	28.05	949.9	29.05	983.8	30.05	1017.7
27.10	917.7	28.10	951.6	29.10	985.5	30.10	1019.4
27.15	919.4	28.15	953.2	29.15	987.2	30.15	1021.0
27.20	921.1	28.20	954.9	29.20	988.9	30.20	1022.7
27.25	922.8	28.25	956.6	29.25	990.6	30.25	1024.4
27.30	924.5	28.30	958.3	29.30	992.3	30.30	1026.1
27.35	926.2	28.35	960.0	29.35	994.0	30.35	1027.8
27.40	927.8	28.40	961.7	29.40	995.6	30.40	1029.5
27.45	929.5	28.45	963.4	29.45	997.3	30.45	1031.2
27.50	931.2	28.50	965.1	29.50	999.0	30.50	1032.9
27.55	932.9	28.55	966.8	29.55	1000.7	30.55	1034.6
27.60	934.6	28.60	968.5	29.60	1002.4	30.60	1036.3
27.65	936.3	28.65	970.2	29.65	1004.1	30.65	1038.0
27.70	938.0	28.70	971.9	29.70	1005.8	30.70	1039.7
27.75	939.7	28.75	973.6	29.75	1007.5	30.75	1041.4
27.80	941.4	28.80	975.3	29.80	1009.2	30.80	1043.1
27.85	943.1	28.85	977.0	29.85	1010.9	30.85	1044.8
27.90	944.8	28.90	978.6	29.90	1012.6	30.90	1046.4
27.95	946.5	28.95	980.3	29.95	1014.3	30.95	1048.1
28.00	948.2	29.00	982.1	30.00	1016.0	31.00	1049.8

BAROMETER INDICATIONS

Certain fundamental principles may be helpful to remember concerning weather.

GENERALLY

(a) **Low Pressure** shows unstable and changing conditions.
(b) **High Pressure** shows stable and continuing good conditions.
(c) **Steady Rise** shows good weather approaching.
(d) **Steady Fall** shows bad weather approaching.
(e) **Rapid Rise** shows better weather may not last.
(f) **Rapid Fall** shows stormy weather approaching rapidly.

The aneroid barometer also registers atmospheric pressure and consists fundamentally of a shallow box, made of thin corrugated metal, from which almost all the air has been removed. The pressure exerted by the atmosphere, on the outside of the box, is very great, while that inside is very small, and were it not for the presence of a spring placed between the faces of the box, the latter would be crushed. However, the spring allows a certain degree of controlled "collapse" to occur and the small relative movements of the faces due to the changes of pressure acting on the outside are magnified by a series of levers and made to actuate a pointer on a dial. For increased sensitivity a number of boxes are linked together. The aneriod needs no correction for temperature or for gravity — only for height above m.s.l.*

To guard against any loss of accuracy of reading, it should be checked fairly often against the corrected readings of a mercury barometer.

Barometer readings. Seldom does a single reading have important indications, it is the rate of change that counts, but directly we have two or more readings, separated by time or distance, or both, the observer is in a somewhat better position to deduce probable changes in weather conditions. How accurate these deductions will be depends on the correct interpretation of other factors and the intelligent application of known meteorological facts.

*m.s.l. = mean sea level. Allowances for change of barometric pressure due to height of tide are negligible as the atmospheric pressure near the surface decreases approximately one millibar for every 28 feet ascent.

THE HYGROMETER

Water Vapour. The atmosphere at all times has a certain amount of water vapour in it. When it holds the maximum quantity possible at any given temperature, the air is said to be saturated, and any fall in temperature will then cause the excess vapour to be condensed. As it is important to know what this water vapour content actually is, a hygrometer is used to measure it. This usually consists of two thermometers. One, known as the dry-bulb thermometer, indicates the temperature of the air. The other has its bulb wrapped in muslin, and is kept moist by being connected by a cotton wick to a small container of distilled water and is known as the wet-bulb thermometer. When evaporation takes place from the surface of the wet-bulb heat is abstracted from the bulb of the thermometer and its reading is less than that of the dry-bulb thermometer by an amount which indicates the humidity, or dampness of the air. When the air becomes saturated this so-called depression of the wet-bulb decreases to nothing because no evaporation is occurring at the wet-bulb. Hygrometer observations are important, as by means of a Dewpoint Table it is possible to find what fall in temperature will cause the formation of mist or fog in the local area. The lowest temperature to which air can be cooled without condensation is called the dew point. A Dewpoint (°C) Table appears on following page.

The two common types of instruments for measuring humidity are: (a) Mason's hygrometer, consisting of the wet and dry bulb thermometer side by side in a louvred screen—exposed on the weather side of the ship. (b) The "aspirated" psychrometer, in which a steady current of air is drawn past the two thermometers by means of a small electric, clockwork or hand operated fan.

DEWPOINT (°C) TABLE

Dry Bulb °C	Depression of Wet Bulb																		Dry Bulb °C
	0°	0.2°	0.4°	0.6°	0.8°	1.0°	2.0°	2.5°	3.0°	3.5°	4.0°	4.5°	5.0°	5.5°	6.0°	6.5°	7.0°	7.5°	
40	40	40	40	39	39	39	38	37	36	36	35	34	34	33	32	32	31	30	40
39	39	39	39	38	38	38	37	36	35	35	34	33	33	32	31	31	30	29	39
38	38	38	38	37	37	37	35	35	34	34	33	32	32	31	30	29	29	28	38
37	37	37	37	36	36	36	34	34	33	32	32	31	30	30	29	28	28	27	37
36	36	36	35	35	35	35	33	33	32	31	31	30	29	29	28	27	26	26	36
35	35	35	34	34	34	34	32	32	31	30	30	29	28	28	27	26	25	24	35
34	34	34	33	33	33	33	31	31	30	29	29	28	27	26	26	25	24	23	34
33	33	33	32	32	32	32	30	30	29	28	28	27	26	25	25	24	23	22	33
32	32	32	31	31	31	31	29	29	28	27	26	26	25	24	23	23	22	21	32
31	31	31	30	30	30	30	28	28	27	26	25	25	24	23	22	21	21	20	31
30	30	30	29	29	29	29	27	27	26	25	24	24	23	22	21	20	19	18	30
29	29	29	28	28	28	28	26	25	25	24	23	22	22	21	20	19	18	17	29
28	28	28	27	27	27	27	25	24	24	23	22	21	20	20	19	18	17	16	28
27	27	27	27	26	26	26	24	23	23	22	21	20	19	18	18	17	16	15	27
26	26	26	25	25	25	25	23	22	22	21	20	19	18	17	16	15	14	13	26
25	25	25	24	24	24	24	22	21	20	20	19	18	17	16	15	14	13	12	25
24	24	24	23	23	23	23	21	20	19	19	18	17	16	15	14	13	12	11	24
23	23	23	22	22	22	21	20	19	18	17	16	16	15	14	13	12	10	9	23
22	22	22	21	21	21	20	19	18	17	16	15	14	13	12	11	10	9	8	22
21	21	21	20	20	20	19	18	17	16	15	14	13	12	11	10	9	8	6	21
20	20	20	19	19	19	18	17	16	15	14	13	12	11	10	9	7	6	5	20
19	19	19	18	18	18	17	16	15	14	13	12	11	10	9	7	6	4	3	19
18	18	18	17	17	17	16	15	14	13	12	11	10	8	7	6	4	3	1	18
17	17	17	16	16	16	15	14	13	12	11	9	8	7	6	4	3	1	-0	17
16	16	16	15	15	15	14	12	11	10	9	8	7	6	4	3	1	0	-2	16
15	15	15	14	14	14	13	11	10	9	8	7	6	4	3	1	0	-2	-5	15
14	14	14	13	13	13	12	10	9	8	7	6	4	3	1	0	-2	-4	-7	14
13	13	13	12	12	11	11	9	8	7	6	4	3	1	0	-2	-4	-7	-9	13
12	12	12	11	11	10	10	8	7	6	4	3	1	0	-2	-4	-6	-9	-12	12
11	11	11	10	10	9	9	7	6	4	3	1	0	-2	-4	-6	-8	-12	-15	11
10	10	10	9	9	8	8	6	4	3	2	0	-2	-3	-6	-8	-11	-15	-19	10
9	9	9	8	8	7	7	4	3	2	0	-1	-3	-5	-8	-10	-14	-18		9
8	8	8	7	7	6	6	3	2	0	-1	-3	-5	-7	-10	-13	-17			8
7	7	7	6	6	5	5	2	1	-1	-3	-4	-7	-9	-12	-16				7
6	6	6	5	5	4	4	1	-0	-2	-4	-6	-9	-11	-15					6
5	5	5	4	4	3	2	0	-2	-4	-6	-8	-10	-14	-15					5
4	4	4	3	2	2	1	-1	-3	-5	-7	-10	-11	-14	-18					4
3	3	3	2	1	1	0	-3	-5	-7	-8	-11	-14	-17						3
2	2	2	1	0	0	-1	-4	-5	-8	-10	-13	-16							2
1	1	1	0	-1	-1	-2	-5	-7	-9	-12	-15	-19							1
0	0	-1	-1	-2	-2	-3	-7	-9	-11	-14	-18								0

In the table lines are ruled to draw attention to the fact that above the line evaporation is going on from a water surface, while below the line it is going on from ice surface. Owing to this, interpolation must not be made between figures on different sides of the lines.

CLOUDS

Clouds are aggregates of minute water drops or ice crystals or both held in suspension in the atmosphere. Cloud Atlases are available illustrating the many varieties of cloud forms. For practical purposes a classification into ten main types is adopted. This classification is as follows:

(1) High Clouds	(2) Middle Clouds	(3) Low Clouds	(4) Low Clouds of marked vertical extent
Cirrus (Ci)	Alto-cumulus (Ac)	Strato-cumulus (Sc)	Cumulus (Cu)
Cirro-cumulus (Cc)	Alto-stratus (As)	Stratus (St)	Cumulo-nimbus (Cb)
Cirro-stratus (Cs)	Nimbo-stratus (Ns)		

Brief descriptions of the different cloud types are given below:

Cirrus (Ci). Detached clouds composed of ice crystals, of delicate and fibrous appearance, without shading, generally white in colour, often of a silky appearance. Tufted cirrus clouds are popularly known as "Mares' Tails."

Cirro-cumulus (Cc). A cirriform layer or patch composed of small white flakes or of very small globular masses, without shadows, arranged in groups or lines, or more often in ripples resembling those of sand on the sea shore.

Cirro-stratus (Cs). A transparent whitish veil of fibrous or smooth appearance, composed of ice crystals, which totally or partially covers the sky and usually produces halo phenomena.

Alto-cumulus (Ac). A layer, or patches, composed of laminae or rather flattened globular masses, the smallest elements of the regularly arranged layer being fairly small and thin, with or without shading.

Alto-stratus (As). A striated or fibrous veil, more or less grey or bluish in colour. It does not give rise to halo phenomena.

Strato-cumulus (Sc). A layer, or patches, composed of globular masses or rolls; the smallest of the regularly arranged elements are fairly large; they are soft and grey with darker parts.

Stratus (St). A uniform layer of cloud, like fog, but not resting on the ground.

Nimbus-Stratus (Ns). A low, amorphous, and rainy layer, of a dark-grey colour and nearly uniform.

Cumulus (Cu). Thick clouds with vertical development; the upper surface is dome-shaped and exhibits protuberances, while the base is nearly horizontal.

Cumulo-nimbus (Cb). Heavy masses of cloud with great vertical development, whose cumuliform summits rise in the form of mountains or towers, the upper parts having a fibrous texture and often spreading out in the shape of an anvil.

The degree of cloudiness is normally expressed on a scale from 0 to 8, in which 0 represents a sky quite free from cloud and 8 an entirely overcast sky in which no patches of blue are visible. The estimation is one of "eighths of sky covered" (oktas).

The height of base cloud is a factor of great importance to aviation. During the daytime it may be measured by timing the ascent of a small balloon rising at a fixed rate. At night a ceiling light projector (cloud searchlight) may be used on large ships. As the use of balloons and searchlights is impracticable in most ships, cloud height is normally estimated at sea.

Approximate Heights of Cloud Bases.

High clouds above 18,000 ft; Middle clouds 8,000 to 18,000 ft; Low clouds below 8,000 ft.

These limits tend to be higher in low latitudes, and lower, especially for high clouds, in high latitudes.

HIGH CLOUD

Photo by R. K. Pilsbury.

(1) CIRRUS (Ci) (Mare's Tails). Cirrus increasing and thickening is a sign of unsettled weather.

HIGH CLOUD

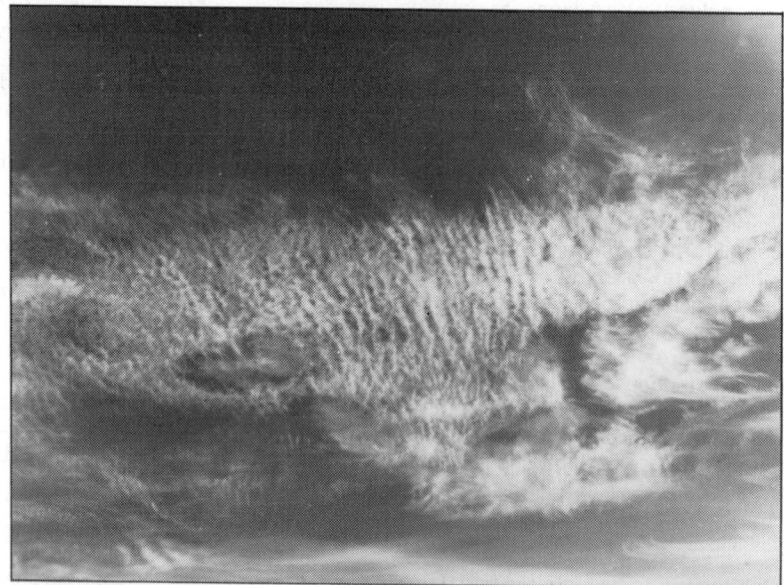

Photo by R. K. Pilsbury.

(2) CIRROCUMULUS (Cc) (Mackerel Sky).
When the above clouds move rapidly and become Cirrostratus unsettled weather is approaching.

HIGH CLOUD

Photo by R. K. Pilsbury.

(3) CIRROSTRATUS (Cs). A covering of this cloud with a Halo, as shown, is a sure sign of deteriorating weather approaching.

MIDDLE CLOUD

Photo by R. K. Pilsbury.

(4) ALTOCUMULUS (Ac). Similar to a Mackerel sky but with larger globules of cloud, often packed in tight lines. If these tend to join and become Altostratus, rain is on the way.
Altocumulus in lines with castellated tops, like the battlements on a castle wall, indicate thundery conditions.

MIDDLE CLOUD

(5) ALTOSTRATUS (As). A continuous layer of grey cloud from which rain will soon fall. It is then known as Nimbostratus (Ns) and its base may fall to only a few hundred feet above MSL.

LOW CLOUD

(6) CUMULONIMBUS (Cb). The Thunderstorm Cloud, often accompanied by sudden squalls and rapidly changing winds.

LOW CLOUD

Photo by R. K. Pilsbury.

(7) CUMULUS (Cu). Small Cumulus not increasing means fine weather, however if growing upwards like a 'Cauliflower', showers are likely.

LOW CLOUD

Photo by R. K. Pilsbury.

(8) STRATOCUMULUS (Sc). More frequent in the colder months especially near windward coasts.
STRATUS (St) (not illustrated) a grey featureless low cloud often shrouding cliff and hill tops on windward coasts. When broken by turbulence it is called FRACTOSTRATUS (FrSt).

WIND

WIND is the movement of air across the surface of the earth and basically it is caused by differences of temperature between one large area and another. This in turn gives rise to the pressure differences which are the direct cause of the air movements. The pressure difference over a unit distance is known as the pressure gradient and the steeper the gradient the stronger is the wind. (Air also moves upwards and downwards in the atmosphere and these movements are very largely responsible for the formation or dispersal of cloud; the occurence of precipitation, thunderstorms, etc.)

Buys Ballot's Law. A useful rule for the observer in the northern hemisphere to remember is, that when he faces the wind, the region of lowest barometric pressure will lie towards his right side and the highest towards his left. The reverse holds good in the southern hemisphere.

Permanent winds which blow in approximately the same direction throughout the year over large parts of the ocean are called "trade winds." Regular winds whose directions depend greatly on the sun's declination are termed seasonal winds. To this group belong the well-known monsoons of the Indian Ocean and China Sea. Similar periodic winds occur in many other localities, and in nearly all areas on the earth the "prevailing wind" depends more or less on the season and the consequent pressure distribution.

Rotational Effect of the Earth. When considering the motion of air over the earth's surface it is necessary to take into account the effect of the earth's rotation, which deflects moving air to the right in the Northern Hemisphere and to the left in the Southern Hemisphere. Near the surface of the earth the effect of friction is important and the air does not move exactly along the isobar but is inclined to it at an angle, inwards towards the low pressure.

Wind Direction and Speed. The direction of a wind is the true bearing of the point from which it blows. Wind force is estimated in the Beaufort scale. For use in synoptic weather messages, Beaufort force is converted into knots. It is generally estimated by the experienced observer with fairly reasonable accuracy, but only practice and careful observation can lead to proficiency in this. In modern, large, fast vessels the tendency is probably for an inexperienced observer to overestimate slightly the force of light winds and to underestimate the strong ones.

When determining wind direction, care should always be taken to eliminate the effect of the ship's speed and direction from the force and direction of the wind as observed. Tables are available for this purpose.

The effect of wind is always manifested on the surface of the sea. The probable appearance of waves in the open sea remote from land, which will be raised by different wind strengths is given in the table of Beaufort Wind Scale.

WHEN INTERPRETING WEATHER FORECASTS and deciding whether it is more prudent to remain (or seek shelter) in harbour until conditions moderate, be sure to consult the Beaufort Wind Scale and give careful consideration to the notes and WARNING at the bottom of the page.

CONVERSION TABLE FOR WIND SPEED

knots	metres per sec.	knots	metres per sec.
2	1	25	12.9
5	2.6	30	15.4
10	5.1	40	20.6
15	7.7	50	25.7
20	10.3	60	30.9

1 knot = 0.514 metres per sec.   1 metre per sec. = 1.943 knots.

BEAUFORT WIND SCALE

Beaufort Number	Mean Velocity		Descriptive Term	Deep Sea Criterion	Probable Height of Waves in metres *
	Knots	m/s			
0	Less than 1	0–0.2	Calm	Sea like a mirror	–
1	1–3	0.3–1.5	Light air	Ripples with the appearance of scales are formed but without foam crests.	0.1 (0.1)
2	4–6	1.6–3.3	Light breeze	Small wavelets, still short but more pronounced. Crests have a glassy appearance and do not break.	0.2 (0.3)
3	7–10	3.4–5.4	Gentle breeze	Large wavelets. Crests begin to break. Foam of glassy appearance. Perhaps scattered white horses.	0.6 (1)
4	11–16	5.5–7.9	Mod. Breeze	Small waves, becoming longer: fairly frequent horses.	1 (1.5)
5	17–21	8.0–10.7	Fresh breeze	Moderate waves, taking a more pronounced long form; many white horses are formed. (Chance of some spray).	2 (2.5)
6	22–27	10.8–13.8	Strong breeze	Large waves begin to form; the white foam crests are more extensive everywhere. (Probably some spray).	3 (4)
7	28–33	13.9–17.1	Near gale	Sea heaps up and white foam from breaking waves begins to be blown in streaks along the direction of the wind.	4 (5.5)
8	34–40	17.2–20.7	Gale	Moderately high waves of greater length; edges of crests begin to break into spindrift. The foam is blown in well-marked streaks along the direction of the wind.	5.5 (7.5)
9	41–47	20.8–24.4	Strong gale	High waves. Dense streaks of foam along the direction of the wind. Crests of waves begin to topple, tumble and roll over. Spray may affect visibility.	7 (10)
10	48–55	24.5–28.4	Storm	Very high waves with long overhanging crests. The resulting foam in great patches is blown in dense white streaks along the direction of the wind. On the whole the surface of the sea takes a white appearance. The tumbling of the sea becomes heavy and shocklike. Visibility affected.	9 (12.5)
11	56–63	28.5–32.6	Violent storm	Exceptionally high waves. (Small and medium-sized ships might be for a time lost to view behind the waves). The sea is completely covered with long white patches of foam lying along the direction of the wind. Everywhere the edges of the wave crests are blown into froth. Visibility affected.	11.5 (16)
12	64+	32.7+	Hurri-cane	The air is filled with foam and spray. Sea completely white with driving spray; visibility very seriously affected.	14 (–)

NOTES:
(1) It must be realised that it will be difficult at night to estimate wind force by the sea criterion.
(2) The lag effect between increase of wind and increase of sea should be borne in mind.
(3) Fetch, depth, swell, heavy rain and tide effects should be considered when estimating the wind force from the appearance of the sea.

*This table is intended only as a guide to show roughly what may be expected in the open sea, remote from land. In enclosed waters, or when near land with an off-shore wind, wave heights will be smaller, and the waves steeper. Figures in brackets indicate probable max. height of waves.

WARNING: FOR A GIVEN WIND FORCE, SEA CONDITIONS CAN BE MORE DANGEROUS NEAR LAND THAN IN THE OPEN SEA. IN MANY TIDAL WATERS WAVE HEIGHTS ARE LIABLE TO INCREASE CONSIDERABLY IN A MATTER OF MINUTES.

VISIBILITY SCALE = Specification for Use at Sea

The numbers 90 to 99 shown below are those used for reporting visibility observations in coded radio weather messages.

*90 — Visibility less than 55 yards.
*91 — Visibility 55-220 yards.
*92 — Visibility 220-550 yards.
*93 — Visibility 550-1,100 yards.
94 — Visibility 1,100-2,200 yards.
*Fog

95 — Visibility 2,200 yards-2.2 nautical miles.
96 — Visibility 2.2-5.4 nautical miles.
97 — Visibility 5.4-10.8 nautical miles.
98 — Visibility 10.8-27 nautical miles.
99 — Visibility 27 nautical miles or more.

Note: In a large vessel, the occasions on which the lowest numbers in the visibility scale, 90 and 91, are appropriate, can be determined by noting the distance at which objects on board become invisible in the fog.

If there is any obscurity or abnormal refraction the visible horizon may be very misleading as a means of judging distance, particularly when the height of the eye is great as in the case of an observer on the bridge of a large liner.

Visibility of less than 1,100 yards, however caused, is classed as fog (code figures 90-93 used). As a rough guide, poor visibility, but over 1,100 yards, is called mist if the humidity is 95% or higher, and haze if the humidity is less than 95%, *i.e.* the difference between mist and haze is simply one of damp air and dry air.

In the Beaufort notation describing weather, fog is represented by f, mist by m and haze by z. At night it is difficult to judge the density of fog with accuracy and the practice is to use the diffracted blur around the masthead light as a criterion.

Letters to indicate the state of the weather (Beaufort Notation).

"Beaufort Notation," a system of notation devised by Admiral Beaufort, consisting as a rule of the initial letter of the phenomenon to be indicated, has been in use for many years. It affords a simple and concise means of indicating by a group of letters either the actual state of the weather at the hour of observation, "present weather"; or a general summary of the conditions over the interval since the last observation was made, "past weather".

b	=	blue sky (0-2/8 clouded).	q	=	squally weather.
bc	=	sky partly clouded (3-5/8 clouded).	r	=	rain.
c	=	cloudy (6-8/8 clouded).	rs	=	sleet (rain and snow together).
d	=	drizzle.	s	=	snow.
e	=	wet air (without precipitation).	t	=	thunder.
f	=	fog.	tlr	=	thunderstsorm with rain.
g	=	gale.	tls	=	thunderstorm with snow.
h	=	hail.	u	=	ugly, threatening sky.
jp	=	precipitation in sight of ship or station.	v	=	unusual visibility.
kq	=	line squall.	w	=	dew.
ks	=	storm of drifting snow.	x	=	hoar frost.
kz	=	sandstorm or dust storm.	y	=	dry air.
l	=	lightning.	z	=	haze.
m	=	mist.			
o	=	overcast sky (the sky completely covered with a uniform layer of thick or heavy cloud).			

p, formerly used as a Beaufort letter, to denote "passing showers", is now only to be used as a prefix, denoting "passing showers of," *e.g.*, ph, passing showers of hail; phr, passing showers of mixed hail and rain.

The times of commencement and ending of heavy showers should be noted.

Capital letters indicate "intense"; the suffix$_0$ indicates "slight"; repetition of letters denotes continuity. The prefix i indicates "Intermittent." Thus R, indicates heavy rain; r_0 slight rain; rr, continuous rain; ir_0 intermittent slight rain.

g is used to indicate that a wind of at least Beaufort force 8 has persisted for not less than 10 minutes. If the wind in 10 minutes has not fallen below force 10, the capital letter G is used.

d, drizzle, is to be used for precipitation in which the drops are very small. If the drops are of appreciable size, although the rain is small in amount, r_0 is used.

DEPRESSIONS

The cyclonic systems of temperate latitudes are now usually referred to as depressions or "lows" to distinguish them from the tropical revolving storms which are often called cyclones or tropical cyclones.

The depression is a normal feature of temperature latitudes and is an integral part of the general circulation of the atmosphere, forming an essential link in the interchange of air between polar and equatorial regions.

Depressions in general move in both hemispheres in a more or less easterly direction, though considerable variations occur, including sometimes a reversal of direction for a time. More or less stationary and permanent areas of high pressure are to be found in the oceans between latitudes 20° and 40°N and S. In the North Atlantic, North and South Pacific and South Indian Oceans the tropical revolving storms progress round the equatorial sides of these areas and up their western sides in a poleward direction. Occasionally a tropical revolving storm will continue into temperate latitudes, gradually changing its character and becoming a depression. Such storms sometimes arrive in the neighbourhood of the British Isles.

The concept of the "frontal surface" is vital to the theory of the formation and development of depressions. Warm air masses of tropical origin meet the colder masses of polar origin along a sloping surface of discontinuity, the colder and therefore heavier air lying beneath the warmer lighter air in the form of a wedge of small angle. The sloping surface of discontinuity is called a "frontal surface." The depression is then envisaged as an unstable wave on the surface of discontinuity. Pictured in terms of development at the surface the cold air replaces the warm tropical air along the "cold front" while the warm air replaces the cold air at the "warm front." The movement of the depression as a whole is in the direction of the isobars in its warm sector. The cold front moves faster than the warm front and the warm sector becomes progressively more narrow. Eventually the cold front overtakes the warm front, at first near the centre of the depression but progressively further and further away from the centre, the warm air being lifted from the surface. This lifting of the warmer air is known as "occlusion." The depression is said to be "occluding," the line at the surface which now takes the place of the warm and cold fronts known as an "occlusion." Much of the bad weather in the temperate zones is associated with the fronts of depression. It is this fact which gives the "frontal theory" of depressions its great value as a forecasting tool.

THE WEATHER MAP

Wind

1) Blows along the isobars, anti clockwise round a low pressure area (a depression).
2) The closer the isobars the stronger the wind.
3) Shifts of wind and squalls are most likely to occur at fronts, particularly at cold fronts.

Rain

Most likely to occur at fronts: a) prolonged rain at warm fronts—defined by rounded modules
b) showers at cold fronts—defined by triangular modules.

Temperature and Humidity

Air flowing from, say, the SW across the British Isles will be warm and wet.
Air flowing from, say, Scandinavia in winter across the British Isles will be cold and dry.

Future Movement of Low

The "Low" will probably move in the direction of the isobars in the warm sector, *i.e.*, the isobars between the warm and cold fronts.

COASTAL WEATHER FORECASTS

The Meteorological Office provides routine weather information for vessels operating in the North Sea, the English Channel, the Irish Sea and the Eastern North Atlantic. Regular weather bulletins and gale warnings are issued by radio-telephony and radio-telegraphy from BTI coastal radio stations and broadcast by BBC Stations.

BBC INSHORE WATERS FORECAST REPORTING STATIONS

Gale warnings are issued for coastal sea areas when mean winds of at least force 8 or gusts reaching 43 to 51 knots are expected. The term 'severe gale' implies winds of Force 9 or gusts reaching 52 to 60 knots. 'Storm' implies a mean wind of Force 10 or gusts reaching 61 to 68 knots. 'Violent storm' implies a mean wind of Force 11 or gusts of 69 knots or more. 'Hurricane force' implies a mean wind of Force 12. The term 'hurricane' is used in conjunction with the word 'force' unless a true tropical cyclone is implied.

VISUAL STORM SIGNALS

Although official signals are now discontinued in Great Britain and Northern Ireland, this does not prevent organisations such as yacht clubs displaying gale warning cones on their own initiative.

PRESTEL FORECASTS

Shipping and Sailing Index, 2093 — Shipping Index, 20935 — Shipping Forecast, 20930 — Gale Warning Summary, 20931.

All forecasts are updated two or more times per day.

Oracle Shipping forecasts are available FREE on Oracle teletext. Forecasts are updated three times daily. General Index 301. Weather Map 302 — Marine Forecast 306.

SIGNIFICANCE OF TERMS USED IN FORECASTS

Gale Warnings. — The term *imminent* implies within six hours of the time of issue: *soon* implies between six and 12 hours: *later* implies more than 12 hours.

PRESSURE SYSTEMS

	Changes		Speed of Movements
Steady	Change less than 0.1 mb in 3 hours	Slowly	Up to 15 kts
Rising slowly or		Steadily	15–25 kts
Falling slowly	Change 0.1 to 1.5 mb in last 3 hours	Rather quickly	25–35 kts
Rising or Falling	Change 1.6 to 3.5 mb in last 3 hours	Rapidly	35–45 kts
Rising quickly or		Very rapidly	over 45 kts
Falling quickly	Change 3.6 to 6.0 mb in last 3 hours		
Rising or Falling			
Very rapidly	Change of more than 6.0 mb in last 3 hours		
Now Falling,	Change from rising to falling and vice		
now Rising	versa within last 3 hours		

VISIBILITY

GOOD: More than 5M.   **MODERATE**: 2–5M.
POOR: 1100yds.–2M.   **FOG**: Less than 1100yds.

MARINECALL

This telephone service provides details of the latest coastal weather conditions anywhere in the UK, 24 hours a day.

Simply dial 0898 500 and then the area code as shown on the map, for the relevant part of the coastline.

MARINECALL recorded forecasts are updated three times daily for areas 455 to 458 and 461 twice daily for all other areas, and give information for up to 12 miles off the coastline, including Irish Sea and Channel sea crossing routes.

The forecast starts at the beginning in every case and includes sea state information and relevant HW times. Also the time is provided on each call.

A 5 day weather outlook service is available by dialling 0898 500 450.

For the local inshore forecast for Shetland ring HM Coastguard at Lerwick 0595 2976.

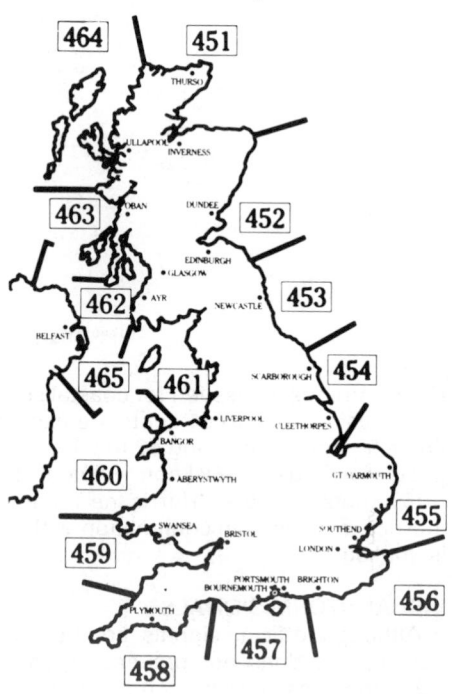

GIBRALTAR WEATHER FORECASTS

Twenty-four hour forecasts for Gibraltar and 50 miles radius. BFBS on Channel 1 (93.5, 97.8 MHz VHF), Weekdays 0745, 0845, 1230, 1715; Saturday and Sunday 0745, 0845, 1230.

G.B.C. on 1458 kHz 206m Medium Wave and 91.3, 92.6 and 100.5 MHz VHF at 0730, 0830, 0930, 1230, 1830.

All times local to Gibraltar (GMT + 2 hours April-October, GMT + 1 hour November to March).

RADIO TELEFIS EIREANN
Broadcasts on: (Radio 1) 567 kHz, 729 kHz. (Radio 2) 612 kHz, 1278 kHz.
Forecasts and gale warnings (Force 8 and greater) for waters within 30 nautical miles of the Irish coast and the Irish Sea are broadcast by meteorologists of the Central Analysis and Forecasting Office daily on Radio 1 at 0633, 1253, 1823 and 2355 Civil Time.
Gale warnings are repeated in news bulletins on Radio 1. Radio 2 broadcasts warnings on the first available programme junction after receipt from the Meteorological Service and repeats current warnings with news headlines on the hour throughout the 24 h.

SPECIAL FORECASTS FOR PORT AREAS

Forecasts of local weather conditions can be obtained from the appropriate forecasting centre by telephone. Enquirers should ask for 'Forecast Office'.

Area	Forecasting Centre	Telephone No.
NE Scotland	Sella Ness, Shetland Isles	(0806) 242069
	Kirkwall Airport, Orkney	(0856) 3802
N & E Scotland	Aberdeen Weather Centre	(0224) 210574
W & SE Scotland	Glasgow Weather Centre	041-248 3451
NE England	Newcastle Weather Centre	091-232 6453
NW England	Manchester Weather Centre	061-477 1060
E England	Leeds Weather Centre	(0532) 451990
	Norwich Weather Centre	(0603) 660779
Midlands	Nottingham Weather Centre	(0602) 384092
	Birmingham Weather Centre	021-717 0570
SE England	London Weather Centre	071-836 4311
S England	Southampton Weather Centre	(0703) 228844
SW England	Plymouth	(0752) 251860
W England	Bristol Weather Centre	(0272) 279298
Wales	Cardiff Weather Centre	(0222) 397020
N Ireland	Belfast (Aldergrove) Airport	(084 94) 22339

REPORTS OF PRESENT WEATHER From Meteorological Offices
Mariners requiring reports of actual weather conditions prevailing at specified places around the coast of the British Isles may obtain such reports by telephone from any of the Meteorological Office stations in the following list:

Name of Station	Telephone No.	Name of Station	Telephone No.
Kirkwall (Orkney)	(0856) 3802	Ronaldsway (Isle of Man)	(0624) 823311
Sella Ness*	(0806) 242069		(Night: 823313)
Wick	(0955) 2215	Carlisle*	(0228) 23422, Ext 440
Kinloss (Moray Firth)	(0309) 72161, Ext 674	Prestwick (Firth of Clyde)	(0292) 79800, Ext 2617
Shoeburyness*	(0702) 292271, Ext 3476	Tiree	(0879) 2456
Blackpool	(0253) 43061	Benbecula (Hebrides)	(0870) 2051
	(Night: 43063)	Stornoway	(0851) 702256
			(Night: 2282)

* Limited opening hours

H.M. Coastguard broadcasts inshore Small Craft warnings, Marinecall Weather Forecasts, etc. every 2 or 4 hours after an initial call on Chan. 16, changing to Chan. 67. They will also respond to a request for weather information at any time on Chan. 67. Broadcast times are shown for each station in Section 22.

Coastguard Stations and Lighthouses which make weather observations for the Meteorological Office may be prepared to respond to inquiries concerning actual weather conditions.

NAVTEX and **WEATHERFAX.** See Section 10.

UK WEATHER BULLETINS FOR SHIPPING

STATION	CALL SIGN	TYPE OF TRANS.	WORKING FREQ. kHz.	FORECAST TIMES GMT		FORECAST AND GALE WARNING AREAS
NITON 50°35'N 01°18'W		RT VHF	1834 Ch. 28	} 0733	1933	Portland, Wight, Dover
WEYMOUTH BAY 50°36'N 02°27'W		VHF	Ch. 05	0733	1933	Dover, Wight, Portland
START POINT 50°21'N 03°43'W		VHF	Ch. 26	0733	1933	Wight, Portland, Lundy, Sole, Plymouth, Biscay, Finisterre, Fastnet, Shannon
PENDENNIS 50°09'N 05°03'W		VHF	Ch. 62	0733	1933	Wight, Portland, Lundy, Sole, Plymouth, Biscay, Finisterre, Fastnet, Shannon
LANDS END 50°07'N 05°40'W	GLD	WT RT VHF	438, 464 2670 Ch. 27,64	0848 } 0733	2048 1933	Wight, Portland, Lundy, Sole, Plymouth, Biscay, Finisterre, Fastnet, Shannon
ILFRACOMBE 51°11'N 04°07'W		VHF	Ch. 05	0733	1933	Lundy, Fastnet
CELTIC RADIO 51°41'N 05°11'W		VHF	Ch. 24	0733	1933	Lundy, Fastnet
CARDIGAN BAY 52°50'N 04°38'W		VHF	Ch. 03	0703	1903	Irish Sea
ANGLESEY 53°24'N 04°18'W		VHF	Ch. 26	0703	1903	Irish Sea
MORECAMBE BAY 54°10'N 03°12'W		VHF	Ch. 04	0703	1903	Irish Sea
PORTPATRICK 54°51'N 05°07'W	GPK	WT RT VHF	458, 472 1883 Ch. 27	0830 } 0703	2030 1903	Irish Sea, Lundy, Malin, Hebrides,Rockall,Bailey }Irish Sea, Malin, }Lundy
CLYDE 55°55'N 04°48'W		VHF	Ch. 26	0703	1903	Lundy, Irish Sea, Malin
OBAN 56°25'N 05°35'W		VHF	Ch. 07	0703	1903	Lundy, Irish Sea, Malin Hebrides,Rockall,Bailey
ISLAY 55°46'N 06°27'W		VHF	Ch. 25	0703	1903	Lundy, Irish Sea, Malin
SKYE 57°28'N 06°41'W		VHF	Ch. 24	0703	1903	Malin, Hebrides, Bailey, Rockall
HEBRIDES 58°14'N 07°02'W		RT VHF	1866 Ch. 26	} 0703	1903	Malin, Hebrides, Bailey, Rockall
LEWIS 58°28'N 06°14'W		VHF	Ch. 05	0703	1903	Malin, Hebrides, Bailey, Rockall

Times of gale warnings–At end of next silent period after receipt, also at next of the following times: W/T 0818, 1218, 1618, 2018 GMT; R/T (VHF) 0303, 0903, 1503, 2103 GMT. Also on request.

STATION	CALL SIGN	TYPE OF TRANS.	WORKING FREQ. kHz.	FORECAST TIMES GMT		FORECAST AND GALE WARNING AREAS
WICK 58°26'N 03°06'W	GKR	WT RT	431, 458 1792 1824	0830 0703	2030 1903	SE Iceland, Faeroes, Fair Isle, Viking, Cromarty, Forties, N. & S. Utsire, plus Forth, Fisher, Hebrides, only on WT.
ORKNEY 58°47'N 02°57'W		VHF	Ch. 26	0703	1903	SE Iceland, Faeroes, Fair Isle, Viking, Cromarty, Forties, N. & S. Utsire
SHETLAND 60°09'N 01°12'W		VHF	Ch. 27	0703	1903	SE Iceland, Faeroes, Fair Isle, Viking, Cromarty, Forties, N. & S. Utsire
COLLAFIRTH 60°32'N 01°24'W		VHF	Ch. 24	0703	1903	SE Iceland, Faeroes, Fair Isle, Viking, Cromarty, Forties, N. & S. Utsire
CROMARTY 57°37'N 02°58'W		VHF	Ch. 28	0703	1903	SE Iceland, Faeroes, Fair Isle, Viking, Cromarty, Forties, N. & S. Utsire
BUCHAN 57°36'N 02°03'W		VHF	Ch. 25	0703	1903	South Utsire, Forth, Cromarty, Fisher, Forties
STONEHAVEN 56°57'N 02°13'W		RT VHF	2691 Ch. 26	} 0703	1903	Forth, Cromarty, Forties, Fisher, South Utsire
FORTH 55°57'N 02°27'W		VHF	Ch. 24	0703	1903	Forth, Cromarty, Fisher, Forties, South Utsire
CULLERCOATS 55°04'N 01°28'W	GCC	WT	458, 484	0830	2030	} Dogger, Tyne, Fisher, German Bight, Humber, Thames, Forth,
		RT VHF	2719 Ch. 26	} 0703	1903	} Dogger, Tyne, Fisher, Humber, German Bight
WHITBY 54°29'N 00°36'W		VHF	Ch. 25	0703	1903	Dogger, Tyne, Fisher, Humber, German Bight
GRIMSBY 54°34'N 00°05'W		VHF	Ch. 27	0733	1933	German Bight, Tyne, Humber, Thames, Dogger
HUMBER 53°20'N 00°17'E		RT VHF	1869 Ch. 26	0733	1933	German Bight, Humber, Thames, Tyne, Dogger
BACTON 52°51'N 01°28'E		VHF	Ch. 07	0733	1933	German Bight, Tyne, Humber, Thames, Dogger
ORFORDNESS 52°00'N 01°25'E		VHF	Ch. 62	0733	1933	Thames, Dover, Wight, Humber
THAMES 51°20'N 00°20'E		VHF	Ch. 02	0733	1933	Thames, Dover, Wight, Humber

UK WEATHER BULLETINS FOR SHIPPING

STATION	CALL SIGN	TYPE OF TRANS.	WORKING FREQ. kHz.	FORECAST TIMES GMT		FORECAST AND GALE WARNING AREAS
NORTH FORELAND 51°22'N 01°25'E	GNF	RT VHF	1848 Ch. 26	} 0733	1933	Thames, Dover, Wight, Humber, Plymouth, Portland, Sole, Biscay Finisterre, Fastnet
HASTINGS 50°52'N 00°37'E		VHF	Ch. 07	0733	1933	Thames, Dover, Wight, Humber
JERSEY 49°10.8'N 02°14.3'W		RT VHF	1726, Ch. 25, 82	} 0645 1245 2245	0745 1845	Ch. Isles S. of 50°N, E. of 03°W
DUBLIN 53°23'N 06°04'W		VHF	Ch. 83	0103 0703 1303 1903	0403 1003 1603 2203	Irish Sea and 30M. offshore.*
ROSSLARE 52°15'N 06°20'W		VHF	Ch. 23	0103 0703 1303 1903	0403 1003 1603 2203	Irish Sea and 30M. offshore.*
MINE HEAD 52°00'N 07°35'W		VHF	Ch. 83	0103 0703 1303 1903	0403 1003 1603 2203	Irish Sea and 30M. offshore.*
BANTRY 51°38'N 10°00'W		VHF	Ch. 23	0103 0703 1303 1903	0403 1003 1603 2203	Irish Sea and 30M. offshore.*
CORK 51°51'N 08°29'W		VHF	Ch. 26	0103 0703 1303 1903	0403 1003 1603 2203	Irish Sea and 30M. offshore.*
VALENTIA 51°56'N 10°21'W	EJK	WT RT VHF	429 1827 Ch. 24	0830 0833 (As Cork)	2030 2033	Fastnet Shannon
SHANNON 52°31'N 09°36'W		VHF	Ch. 28	0103 0703 1303 1903	0403 1003 1603 2203	Irish Sea and 30M. offshore.*
BELMULLET 54°06'N 10°03'W		VHF	Ch. 83	0103 0703 1303 1903	0403 1003 1603 2203	Irish Sea and 30M. offshore.*
GLEN HEAD 54°44'N 08°43'W		VHF	Ch. 24	0103 0703 1303 1903	0403 1003 1603 2203	Irish Sea and 30M. offshore.*
MALIN HEAD 55°22'N 07°20'W	EJM	VHF	Ch. 23	0103 0703 1303 1903	0403 1003 1603 2203	Irish Sea and 30M. offshore.*

Times of gale warnings–At end of next silent period after receipt, also at next of the following times: W/T 0818, 1218, 1618, 2018 GMT; R/T (VHF) 0303, 0903, 1503, 2103 GMT. Also on request. Also storm warnings at 0030, 0630, 1230, 1830. * 1 hr. earlier when DST in force.

B.B.C. RADIO WEATHER SERVICES

SHIPPING FORECASTS — RADIO 4 — 198kHz 1515m
Throughout the week: 0033, 0555, 1355, 1750 Longwave

GALE WARNINGS will be promulgated at programme junctions following their issue and following the next news-bulletin on the hour.

FORECAST FOR INSHORE WATERS

        RADIO 3 — 1215kHz 247m & FM 0655 throughout the week

        RADIO 4 — Longwave 0038 throughout the week

PRINCIPAL LAND WEATHER FORECASTS

RADIO 4 — Longwave & FM

Mon.-Fri.	Sat.	Sun.
0027*	0020*	0020*
0603*	0603*	0603*
0655	0655	0655
0755	0755	0755
0858*	0858	0855
1255	1255	1255
1755	1755	1755
2159	2159	2159
* approx.		

FM   **RADIO 1** 96-99MHz for Greenwich Time Signals.
          RADIO 2 88-91MHz for Greenwich Time Signals.
          RADIO 3 90.2-92.4MHz except Channel Islands: 94.75.
          RADIO 4 92-95MHz. and other frequencies in certain areas.

RUGBY TIME SIGNAL: MSF 2.5, 5.0 and 10.0MHz.

The signal is transmitted through 24 hours, alternating five minutes on with five minutes off, beginning at 00 hr. 00 min. GMT. A five millisec pulse ('pip') is radiated every second, and a 100 msec pulse ('beep') on each exact minute.

GREENWICH TIME SIGNALS

Mon.-Fri.	Radio	Sat.	Radio	Sun.	Radio
0000	2	0000	2	0000	2
0600	4	0600	4	0600	4
0700	1, 2, 3, 4	0700	2, 3, 4	0700	4
0800	1, 2, 4	0800	2, 4	0800	2, 4
0900	4	0900	4	0900	2, 4
1000	4	1000	4	1300	4
1100	4	1100	4	1600	4
1200	4	1300	1, 4	1700	1, 4
1300	2, 4	1400	4	2100	4
1400	4	1500	4		
1500	4				
1600	4 (Tue.-Fri.)				
1700	2, 4				
1900	2, 3, 4				
2200	4				

Signal normally consists of 6 pips. Start of first pip always occurs at second 55 and start of long, final pip marks the time.

The above information is correct at time of going to press but may be subject to variation.

FORECASTS FROM LOCAL RADIO STATIONS

STATION	FREQUENCY			TIMES Clock Time subject to variation
	kHz	Metres	MHz	
LBC CROWN FM LONDON TALKBACK	1152	261	97.3	Daily. After news bulletin, every hour.
ESSEX RADIO FM BREEZE AM	 1431 1359	 210 220	96.3 102.6	Weather: ev. hour + 3min. High Tide: 0700 0730 0800 0830 daily. Coastal Forecast 0600 0700 0800 0900 Sat.-Sun. Small craft and high wind warnings broadcast as required.
BBC RADIO KENT	1035 1602 774	290 187 388	96.7 104.2	Mon.-Fri. 0645 0745 0845 1705 1805 Sat. 0640 0745 0845 0945 1304 Sun. 0745 0845 0945 1304
BBC RADIO SUSSEX	1485 1161 1368	202 258 219	95.3 104.5 104	Sailing Forecast: Mon.-Fri. 0844 Sat. 0705 1015 Sun. 0905 Tide Times: Mon.-Fri. 0659 0759 1515 1615 1715 1745 Sat. 0705 1015 Sun. 0905 Small craft high wind warnings broadcast as required.
SOUTHERN SOUND FM South Coast Radio Brighton Newhaven Eastbourne Hastings	1323	227	 103.5 96.9 102.4 97.5	Daily. Every ½ h.
BBC RADIO SOLENT GALE and STRONG WIND warnings are broadcast regularly when in force.	999 1359	300 221	96.1	Mon.-Fri. 0604 0633* 0709 0733(L) 0745* 0809 0833(L) 0904 1004 1104 1204 1309 1404 1504 1604 1709 1733(L, tides, gunnery times) 1804 2204 2300(L). Sat. 0633*-0904 as above. Then 1000 1104 1204 1304 1404 1500(L) 1757(L) 1804. Sun. 0633* 0709 0733(L) 0745* 0809 0904(L) 1000 1104 1204 1304 1504(L). (L): Live *: Shipping forecast, coastguard report, tides, gunnery firing times, ship movements.
BOURNEMOUTH 2CR FM	828	362	102.3	On the hour, ev. hour 0600-1800
JERSEY RADIO	1026	292	88.8	Daily. 0645 0745 1245 1845 2245 Nav. Warnings: 0833 1633 2033 Gale Warnings: On receipt and (self-cancelling) 0907 1507 2107 All times GMT.
BBC RADIO GUERNSEY	1116	269	93.2	Mon.-Fri. 0732 0832 1732 Sat. 0832 0930 Sun. 0830

BBC RADIO
DEVON
  Exeter
  Plymouth
  N. Devon
  Torbay
 	
Shipping forecasts cover sea areas Portland,
Plymouth, Sole and Lundy.
Small craft warning service is also operated.
	
	990
	855
	801
	1458
		
		303
		351
		375
		206
			
			95.8
			103.4
			94.8
			103.4
				Weather (incl. inshore) Forecasts:
				Mon.-Fri. 0605 0633 0735 0833 1310
				              1735
				Sat. 0600 0632 0732 0832 1310
				Sun. 0658 0830 0930 1310
				Shipping Forecasts:
				Mon.-Fri. 0605 0833 1310 1733
				Sat. 0605 0633 0833 1310
				Sun. 0833 1310
				Storm warnings for area given on receipt or at
				first programme junction. Tidal information
				Mon.-Sat. 0733-0833. Sun. 0833

DEVONAIR RADIO Exeter Torbay E. Devon, S. Somerset W. Dorset	 666 954	 450 314	 96.4 97.0 103.0	Small craft warnings when given On the hour, ev. hour Mon.-Sun. 24 hours. Coastguard Report 0905 Mon.-Fri.

FORECASTS FROM LOCAL RADIO STATIONS

STATION	FREQUENCY			TIMES Clock Time subject to variation
	kHz	Metres	MHz	
PLYMOUTH Plymouth Sound	1152	261	97.0	0610 0706 0720 0806 0820 Between 0900-1700 on the hour 1745 2103 2203 Coastal Forecast: As and when available
BBC RADIO CORNWALL N. and E. Cornwall Mid and W. Cornwall: Isles of Scilly:	657 630	457 476	95.2 103.9 96.0	Mon.-Fri. 0605 0745 0845 1715 1745 Sat. 0715 0745 0815 0845 Sun. 0745 0815 0845 0915
BBC RADIO BRISTOL	1548	194	95.5 94.9 104.6	Weekdays: 0604 0632 0659 0707 0732 0759 0807 0832 0858 0904 1004 1104 1204 1233 1259 1307 1404 1504 1604 1632 1704 1750 1804 Sat. 0704 0804 0830 0904 1004 1204 1304 Sun. 0704 0804 0904 1004 1204 1304
BBC SOMERSET SOUND	1323	227		Weekdays: 0715, and after news bulletins every 30 minutes from 0700-0900, then 1200 1230 1300 1530 1600 1630 1700 1730 Sat. 0800 0830 0900 1000 Sun. 1200 1300 1400
RED DRAGON RADIO TOUCH AM	 1305 1359	 230 221	97.4 103.2	Incorporates coastal forecasts in their frequent general weather forecasts.
SWANSEA Swansea Sound	1170	257	96.4	On the hour, ev. hour Coastal Forecast: Mon.-Fri. 0725 0825 0925 (approx.) 1030 Sat.-Sun. 0825 1004
LIVERPOOL Radio City	1548	194	96.7	On the hour, ev. hour, 24 hr/day.
BBC RADIO MERSEYSIDE	1485	202	95.8	Mon.-Fri. on the hour + 0643 0743 1143 1750 1802 Sat.-Sun. On the hour 0600-midnight.
BBC RADIO LANCASHIRE	855 1557	351 193	103.9 95.5 104.5	Weekdays, hourly 0600-midnight 0630 0730 0830 1230 1330 1630 1730 Coastal report, forecast and tide times, 0635 0735 0835 1205
PRESTON & BLACKPOOL Red Rose Radio	999	301	97.4	On the hour, (24 hr/day)
BBC RADIO CUMBRIA	756 1458 837	397 206 358	95.6 96.1 104.2 95.2	Mon.-Fri. 0645 0740 0845 1710 1858 Sat.-Sun. 0820 0935 1115 Mon.-Fri. 0645 0734 0850 1710 1858 Sat.-Sun. 0820 0935 1115
AYR – West Sound DUMFRIES South West Sound	1035	290	96.7 97.5 97.2	Incorporates coastal forecasts from the Met office in their hourly or half hourly general weather forecasts.
BELFAST Downtown Radio Cool FM	1026	292	96.4 96.6 102.4 97.4	Incorporates coastal forecasts from the Met office in their hourly or half hourly general weather forecasts. As above.
GLASGOW Clyde One Clyde Two	 1152	 261	102.5	On the hour, 24 hr/day. Coastal Forecast: 0605 0705 0805 0915 1630

FORECASTS FROM LOCAL RADIO STATIONS

STATION	FREQUENCY			TIMES Clock Time subject to variation
	kHz	Metres	MHz	
MORAY FIRTH Inverness	1107	271	97.4	At end of news bulletin 0600-1700 Mon.-Sun. Also at 0630 0730 0830 1730 Mon.-Fri. Offshore forecast at variable times.
ABERDEEN North Sound Radio	1035	290	96.9	At end of news bulletin Mon.-Fri. 0900-1600 Sat. 0800 0900 1000 1200 1300 1400 Sun. 0900 1000 1200 1300 Also Mon.-Fri.0615 0645 0715 0815 0845 1720
DUNDEE/PERTH Radio Tay Dundee Perth	1161 1584	258 189	102.8 96.4	On the hour, ev. hour, half-hour at peak times Mon.-Fri. 0530-0100 Sat.-Sun. 0600-0100 Coastal Forecast: 3 times daily, as and when made available. Sat.-Sun. 5 times daily.
EDINBURGH Radio Forth RFM Max AM	 1548	 194	97.3	On the hour 0600-1900 On the hour 0600-1900
BBC RADIO NEWCASTLE	1458	206	95.4 96.0 104.4	Mon.-Fri. 0655 0755 0855 1155 1655 1755 Sat.-Sun. 0755 0855 0955
TYNE & WEAR METRO FM Great North Radio	 1152	 261	97.1	On the hour, 24 hr./day On the hour, 24 hr./day
BBC RADIO CLEVELAND	1548	194	95.0 95.8	Mon.-Fri. 0615 0715 0815 + every hr after news 0600-1800 Coastal 0645 0745 0845 1310 1645 Sat. 0700 0800 0900 1100 1300 Coastal 0745 0845 Sun. 0800 0900 1100 1300 Coastal 0745 0845 0945
TEESSIDE TFM Radio Great North Radio	 1170	 257	96.6	On the hour at 5 mins past (24 hr/day) updates at 35 mins past the hour. On the hour 24h./day.
BBC RADIO HUMBERSIDE	1485		95.9	Mon.-Fri. 0632 0732 0832 1632 1732 Sat.-Sun. 0730 0830 All week – hourly between 0800-1800
HUMBERSIDE Viking FM Classic Gold	 1161	 258	96.9 \	Mon.-Fri. 0600-0700 includes local weather. General weather reports on hour daily. As above but more detailed information.
BBC RADIO LINCOLNSHIRE	1368	219	94.9	Mon.-Fri. 0745 1145 1805 Sat. 0845 1145 1445 Sun. 1145
BBC RADIO NORFOLK North Coast Area East Coast Area	 873 855	 344 351	 104.4 95.1	Mon.-Fri. 0610 0710 0810 1100 1310 1500 1710 Also short forecast at 0630 0730 0830 then on the hour, ev. hour until 1800 Sat.-Sun. 0700 0800 0900 1100 1200 (Sun.) 1300 (Sat.) 1400 Coastguard Report live from Great Yarmouth at 0855 throughout the week. (Seven days)
GREAT YARMOUTH & NORWICH Radio Broadland	1152	260	102.4	On the hour ev. hour 0600-0000 Coastguard report at 0905 daily (Sunday 0903) Weather (two min. report) Mon.-Fri. 0715 1715 Sat. 0715 Sun. 0815
ORWELL FM SAXON FM	1170 1251		97.1 96.4	On the hour, ev. hour, 0600-0000 Coastal Forecast: 0800

FRENCH COAST METEOROLOGICAL STATIONS

Paris Tel: (45) 55.95.02. Rep: (45) 55.91.36.
Dunkerque Tel: (28) 66.45.25 Rep: (28) 63.44.44.
Boulogne Tel: (21) 31.52.23 Rep: (21) 33.82.55.
Le Touquet Tel: (21) 05.13.55.
Le Havre Tel: (35) 42.21.06 Rep: (35) 21.16.11.
Rouen Rep: (35) 80.11.44.
Caen Tel: (31) 26.28.11 Rep: (31) 75.14.14.
Deauville Rep: (31) 88.28.62.
Cherbourg Tel: (33) 22.91.77 Rep: (33) 43.20.40.
Granville Rep: (33) 50.10.00.
Dinard Tel: (99) 46.10.46 Rep: (99) 46.18.77.
Bréhat Rep: (96) 20.01.92.
*Morlaix Rep: (98) 88.34.04.
Brest Tel: (98) 84.60.64 Rep: (98) 84.82.83.
Brest Port Tel: (98) 84.60.64 Rep: (98) 94.82.83.
Quimper Tel: (98) 94.03.43 Rep: (98) 94.00.69.

Bénodet(1) Rep: (98) 94.00.57.
Lorient Tel: (97) 64.34.86 Rep: (97) 84.82.83.
Vannes Rep: (97) 42.49.49.
Rennes Tel: (99) 31.91.90 Rep: (99) 31.90.00.
Nantes Tel: (40) 84.80.19 Rep: (40) 04.15.15.
La Roche-s-Yon Tel: (51) 36.10.78
  Rep: (51) 62.45.99.
St-Nazaire(1) Tel: (40) 90.00.80 Rep: (40) 90.19.19.
La Rochelle Tel: (46) 41.29.14 Rep: (46) 50.62.32.
Biarritz Tel: (59) 23.84.15 Rep: (59) 22.03.30.
Royan Rep: (46) 38.39.20.
Bordeaux Tel: (56) 90.91.21.
*Bordeaux Centre Régional Météo
  Tel: (56) 34.20.11.
Arcachon Rep: (56) 83.84.85.

* Closed Sundays and holidays.   Rep: = Répondeurs automatiques.

FORECAST TERMS

Weather

Clair	Clear
Peu nuageux	Slightly cloudy ($^1/_4$ overcast)
Nuageux	Cloudy ($^1/_2$ overcast)
Très nuageux	Very cloudy ($^3/_4$ overcast)
Couvert	Overcast
Brume	Mist
Brouillard	Fog
Pluie	Rain
Ondée	Heavy showers
Grêle	Hail
Orage	Storm

Wind
Vitesse en noeuds Speed in knots

Sea state

0 Calme	Calm
1 Calme (Ridée)	Rippled Calm
2 Belle	Wavelets
3 Peu agitée	Large wavelets
4 Agitée	Small waves
5 Forte	Moderate waves
6 Très forte	Large waves
7 Grosse	High waves
8 Très grosse	Very high waves
9 Énorme	Enormous

Swell

Petite	Slight
Moderée	Moderate
Grande	Heavy

FORECAST ZONES

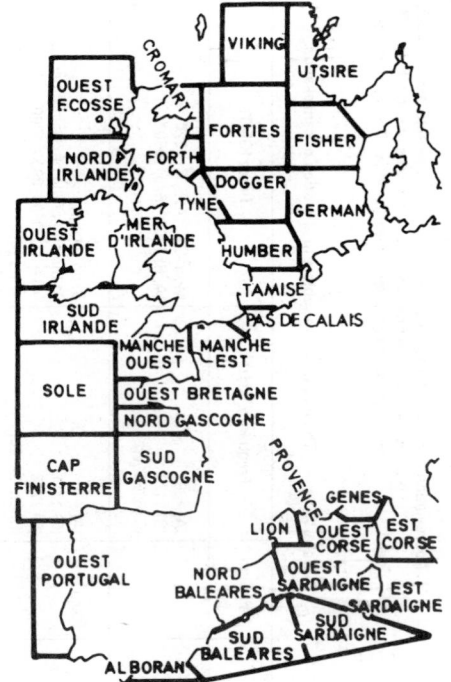

CONTINENTAL RADIO WEATHER SERVICES

Abbreviations: S. = Storm/Gale warnings.　F. = Forecasts, etc.　P. = After preliminary Call on 2,182 kHz.
H. + . . = Commencing at . . . minutes past the hour.　R. = On receipt and end of next silent period
* Broadcasts given 1h. earlier when DST (Daylight Saving Time) in force.

Note: The following are subject to alteration or cancellation

Station	Call Sign	Frequency (kHz)	Times (GMT)	Language	Details of Message	Sea Areas and Remarks
Sveriges Radio Swedish Broadcasting Corp.		(A) 189 (B) 1179 (C) 6065	Mon.-Sat. (A, B, C) 0520, (A, B) 1200, 1545, 2050　*	Swedish	F.	N & NW Europe Swedish Coastal Reports
Stockholm	SDJ	(A) 416 (C) 1771 (D) 1778 (E) Ch. 24, 28	S. on receipt At the end of the next silent period. (A) 0100, 0500, 0900, 1300, 1700, 2100 (C, D, E) 0133, 0533, 0933, 1333, 1733, 2133 At end of traffic lists. F. (C, D and E) 0933, 2133 on request. (A) 0900, 2100	(A) English (C, D, E) Swedish and English (C) English	S. F.	The Baltic The Baltic
Göteburg	SAG	(A) 450 (B) 1785 (C) Ch. 24, 26, 82	S. on receipt. At the end of the next silent period. (A) Every odd H+00. (B, C) 0233, 0633, 1033, 1433, 1833, 2233 At the end of the traffic lists. F. on request. (A) 0900, 2100. (B and C) 1033, 2233	(A) English (B, C) Swedish and English Swedish and English		Skaggerak and Kattegat
Kiel	DAO	2775	S. on receipt. At the end of the next silent period * 0233, 0633, 1033, 1433, 1833, 2233 F. 0750, 1950	German (English for local area only) German	S. F.	Baltic and Kattegat Baltic and Kattegat

CONTINENTAL RADIO WEATHER SERVICES

Station	Call Sign	Frequency (kHz)	Times (GMT)	Language	Details of Message	Sea Areas and Remarks
Deutsch-landfunk		(A) 153, (B) 207 (C) 549, (D) 756 (E) 810, (F) 1269 (G) 1539 (H) MHz 88.7 Hamburg 101.8 Aurich 101.9 Eutin 102.0 Lingen 102.2 Höhbeck 103.3 Flensburg	S. Frequently after news bulletins	German	S.	North Sea and Baltic coastal waters
			(F) 0005, 0540 (G) 0005 *	German	F.	North Sea, Skagerrak, Kattegat, South-west Baltic
Radio Mecklenburg-Vorpommern		558,729 88.5-91.5 MHz	0610 0445 (Mon-Fri) 0545, 0745, 1300 (after news)	German German	S. & F. S. & F.	South-west Baltic Weather information for small craft
Gdynia (Poland)	SPH (A) SPC (B)	(A) 447 (B) 2726 (C) Ch. 26	(A) 0100, 0700, 1300, 1900 (B, C) 0135, 0735, 1335, 1935	(A) English (B, C) English & Polish	Storm warnings Forecasts	Baltic Sea and Polish Coastal Waters
Danish Broadcast-ing Stations Kalundborg		(B) 1062 (A) 243	(A, B) 0450, 0750, 1050, 1650, 2150 *	Danish	Meteorological Institute Bulletins: Situation, forecasts and Storm warnings	Danish Islands, waters around Denmark, Sn. Baltic, North Sea and Faeroes.
Ronne		2586 Ch. 4	Sun. 0645, 2205 S. On receipt. F. On request.	S. Danish and English F. English.	Storm warnings Bulletins and forecasts	Danish Coastal waters, Skaggerak and North Sea. Kattegat, Skag-gerak and North Sea.
Skagen	OXP	S. 1701 Ch. 4, 1, 66, 64 F. 1701	S. On receipt. F. On request.	S. Danish and English F. English	Storm warnings Bulletins and forecasts	
Norwegian Broadcasting Service		155, 218, 629, 674, 701, 890, 1313, 1578, 6015	Mon.-Sat. 0500, 0600, 0700, 1020, 1100, 1400, 1730, 2100. Sun. 0600, 0800, 1130, 1730, 2100. *	Norwegian	Forecast	N. Atlantic, Eng. Ch., Bay of Biscay.
				Norwegian	F. & S.	Norwegian coastal waters

CONTINENTAL RADIO WEATHER SERVICES

Station	Call Sign	Frequency (kHz)	Times (GMT)	Language	Details of Message	Sea Areas and Remarks
Bergen (Norway)	LGN	(A) 416 (B) 1743 (C) Ch. 02, 05, 21, 24, 25	S. (A) (B) (C) on receipt and at end of next silent period. F. (A) (B) (C) on request.	S. Norwegian repeat English. F. Norwegian and English	Storm warnings Forecasts	S. Coastal waters of Wn. Norway. F. (A) Coastal waters of Wn. Norway. Lindnesnes — Krakenes. (B) Coastal waters Horda-land — Stadt and adjacent fishing banks.
Norddeich (Germany)	DAN	(A) 474, (B) 2614	S. On receipt. At the end of the next silent period. (A) 0900, 1300, 2100. (B) 0133, 0533, 0933, 1333, 1733, 2133. F. (A) 0800, 2000. (B) 0810, 2010 *	S. German and English F. English	Storm warnings Weather bulletins and forecasts	S. (B) Cromarty, Forties, Forth, Tyne, Dogger, Fisher, Humber, Dover, Thames, German Bight, Skaggerak (in German). German Bight (in English, (A) German Bight (in English). F. German Bight.
Norddeutscher Rundfunk		612, 702, 828, 972 88.9-104.5 MHz. (NDR 1) 87.6-98.7 MHz (NDR 2)	Every hour A detailed forecast at 2305 on 702 kHz *	German	F.	W. & Central Baltic and German Bight. W. & Central Baltic and German Bight.
Hamburg Cuxhaven Bremen		By telephone from meteorological office	F. Tel: 31 12 39 (Day 31 12 31) Tel: 3 64 00 Tel: 55 20 61/62			
Radio Bremen		936 89.3, 93.8 MHz	F. 0600, 1200, 1800 S. Synopsis and outlook 2205 *	German		German Bight, Skaggerak, Kattegat. W. Baltic Sea. Central North Sea.

CONTINENTAL RADIO WEATHER SERVICES

Station	Call Sign	Frequency (kHz)	Times (GMT)	Language	Details of Message	Sea Areas and Remarks
Scheveningen (Netherlands)	PCH	(A) 1862, (B) 1890, (C) 1939, (D) 2600, (E) 2824, (G) Ch. 23, 25, 27, 28, 83, 87	S. (A) (B) (C) (D) (G) on receipt (A) (B) at end of next silent period (G) on receipt and H+05 F. (B) (C) 0340, 0940, 1540, 2140 (E) 0340 (G) 0605, 1205, 1805, 2305 *	English & Dutch English & Dutch Dutch English & Dutch Dutch	S. Near gale and and strong breeze warnings F. Weather forecasts	Coastal waters North Sea Forecast Area Coastal waters North Sea Forecast Area
Belgium Radio & TV Service		926	0500, 0600, 0700, 0800, 1100, 1200, 1600, 1700, 1800, 2200 *	F. Dutch		Dover, Thames, Humber, Wight, Portland.
Ostende (Belgium)	OST/OSU	(A) 435 (C) 2761 (D) Ch. 27	S. (A, C, D) On receipt and end of next two silent periods F. (A, C, D) 0820, 1720	(A) English (C, D) English and Dutch	S. Storm warnings F. Weather forecasts	Belgian Coast Dover, Thames
FRANCE Radio France		162	0645, 2003 *	French	S. Storm warning F. Forecast	General covering NE Atlantic. A bulletin for small craft is provided Mar. 15-Oct. 31
Boulogne	FFB	(A) 450, (B) 1694 (C) 1771, (D) Ch. 23	S. (A, C) On receipt (A) 0018, 0418, 0818, 1218, 1618, 2018 (C) Every odd H + 03. F. (B) 0703, 1733. (D) 0633, 1133 *	French	S. Gale warnings F. General Summary, storm warnings, forecasts and further outlook	North Sea and English Channel

Note: The following stations give the local forecasts in French on VHF at 0633 and 1133 *Dunkerque Ch. 61, Calais Ch. 87, Boulogne Ch. 23, Dieppe Ch. 2, Le Havre Ch. 26, Port en Bessin Ch. 3, Cherbourg Ch. 2, Sain Malo Ch. 2, Paimpol Ch. 84, Plougasnou Ch. 83, Ouessant Ch. 82, Le Conquet Ch. 82, Pont l'Abbé Ch. 87, Sain Gilles Croix de Vie Ch. 27, Nantes Ch. 28, La Rochelle Ch. 21, Royan Ch. 23, Bayonne Ch. 24, Arcachon Ch. 82.

CONTINENTAL RADIO WEATHER SERVICES

Station	Call Sign	Frequency (kHz)	Times (GMT)	Language	Details of Message	Sea Areas and Remarks
Brest-Le Conquet	FFU	(A) 416, (B) 1673 (C) 1806, (D) 1876 (E) 2691, (G) Ch. 26	S. (A, C, E) On receipt and at end of next two silent periods. (A) 0018, 0418, 0818, 1218, 1618, 2018 (C, E) Every even H + 03 F. (B, D) 0600, (B, D, E) 0733, 1633, 2153, (G) 0633, 1133 *	French	S. Gale warnings F. Forecasts	English Channel, Biscay.
St. Naziare	FFO	(A) 1687 (B) 1722 (C) 2740 (D) Ch. 23	S. (A) On receipt and every odd H + 07 (D) On receipt and at end of next two silent periods. F. (B) (C) 0803, 1803 and on request. * (D) 0633, 1133		S. Gale warnings. F. General summary, storm warnings and forecasts. Report.	Seine Estuary to Vendee Coast.
Bordeaux-Arcachon	FFC	(A) 421, (B) 1820 (C) Ch. 82	S. (A) (B) On receipt and at end of next two silent periods. (A) 0018, 0418, 0818, 1218, 1618, 2018 (B) Every even H + 07 (C) On receipt and at end of next two silent periods. F. (B) 0703, 1703 * (C) 0633, 1133	French	S. Gale warnings. F. General summary, fore-casts and storm warnings. Reports	Charante Maritime to Spanish Border. VHF 1 hr. earlier in DST.
SPAIN Machichaco		(A) 1704	F. 1103, 1733	Spanish	F. Forecast	Biscay and Western Approaches.
Cabo Peñas	EAS	(A) 441, (B) 1757.5	(A) 1118, 1818, (B) 1103, 1733.	Spanish	S. Storm Warning F. Forecast.	Biscay and Northern Spain.
La Coruna (Elris)		1748	1103, 1733	Spanish	(A) Local weather reports (B) Storm warnings, general summary and forecasts for 12 and 24 hours for waters off N.W. Spain and Portugal.	

CONTINENTAL RADIO WEATHER SERVICES

Station	Call Sign	Frequency (kHz)	Times (GMT)	Language	Details of Message	Sea Areas and Remarks
Finisterre	EAF	(A) 472 (B) 1698	F. (A) 1118, 1818. F. (B) 1103, 1733.	Spanish Spanish	Repeats La Coruna reports. (A) Local weather; (B) Storm warnings. Repeats La Coruna reports. (A) Local weather; (B) Storm warnings.	
PORTUGAL Comandante Nunes Ribeiro	(A) CTV (B) CTV4 (C) CTW8 (D) CTU2 (E) CTV7	476 4232.5 8523.5 12999.5 17053.7	(A, B, C, D, E) 0800, 2000.	Portuguese repeated in English NB: All Transmissions are in morse code	Weather Messages	Coast of Portugal and Atlantic African Coast down to 30°N, including Madeira Isles
Portuguese State Radio	Faro Lisboa Azurara Porto Coimbra Lousa Lisboa Porto	558 666 720 1367 1449 87.9 MHz 95.7 MHz 96.7 MHz	F. 0705　*	Portuguese	24 hr. Forecast for Portuguese coastal waters and Madeira.	
Radio Nacional de Espana	Tenerife Bilbao La Coruna Sebastian Santander	621 639 639 774 855	F. 1000, 1300, 1700, 2100　*	Spanish	Weather messages	Spanish Coastal Waters and coastal waters of Islas Canarias
SPAIN Tarifa	EAC	(A) 484 (B) 1678	(A) 1118, 1818 (B) 1103, 1733	Spanish	Weather summary and general forecast for shipping for SW and Southern coasts of Spain.	
Gibraltar See page 18:24 for broadcasts by local radio stations	ZDK	Ch. 01, 04, 23, 25, 27, 86, 87	On request. 0000, 0600, 1200, 1800	English	Weather Message	Coastal waters within a radius of 50 miles

GLOSSARY OF TERMS USED IN MARINE METEOROLOGY

Air Mass. A mass of air which is largely homogeneous in a horizontal direction. Its physical properties are determined by the nature of the surface over which it forms and may be subsequently modified when the air mass moves over a different type of surface. Air masses are often separated from each other by frontal surfaces, which form discontinuities.

Anemometer. An instrument for measuring the speed of the wind.

Angle of Indraft. The angle between an isobar and the direction of the wind, near the earth's surface.

Anticyclone. A region characterised in the barometric pressure field by a system of closed isobars, with the highest pressure on the inside. It is also known as a "high."

Aurora. Bright streamers of light, ascending from the horizon towards the zenith, or luminous arcs, which are manifestations of electrical energy in the upper atmosphere. The aurora is seen in both hemispheres, in high and sometimes in medium or low latitudes. In the northern hemisphere it is known as Aurora Borealis, in the southern as Aurora Australis.

Backing. A change in the direction of the wind, in an anti-clockwise direction.

Blizzard. A high wind accompanied by great cold and drifting or falling snow.

Col. The saddle-backed region occurring between two anticyclones and two depressions, arranged alternately.

Cold Front. The boundary line between the advancing cold air at the rear of a depression and the warm sector. Line squalls may occur at the passage of this front, which was formerly called the squall line.

Cold Sector. The part of a depression associated with relatively cold air on the earth's surface.

Convection. In convection, heat is carried from one place to another by the bodily transfer of the matter containing it. In particular, this is the method by which heat raises the temperature of a fluid mass. The part in close contact with the heat rises, and the surrounding fluid moves in to take its place. This action in the atmosphere gives rise to convectional currents, which may produce cumulus or cumulonimbus cloud.

Convergence. Consider an area on the earth's surface. On the sides which face the wind, air will flow into the area, while on the other sides air will flow out. If, however, the wind is not uniform, more air may flow in than flows out, and the amount of air in the area will tend to increase. The air cannot, however, go on accumulating, and the excess will have to flow out over the top, thus leading to a rising air current, and perhaps to clouds and rain.

The contrary case, when more air flows out of the area than flows into it, is called **Divergence.** In this case there is a deficit of air, which is balanced by a descent of the upper air layers above the area. This descent is called **Subsidence.** The subsiding air warms up, its relative humidity falls, and fine weather is the usual accompaniment of subsidence, though fog may occur under certain conditions.

Corona(ae). A series of coloured rings round the sun or moon caused by diffraction of its light by water-drops, chiefly in alto-clouds.

Corposants. Luminous brush discharges of electricity, sometimes observed at the mastheads, and on projecting parts of ships during electrical storms. Also known as **St. Elmo's Fire.** Due to atmospheric electricity.

Cyclone. A name given to the tropical revolving storms of the Bay of Bengal and the Arabian Sea. Sometimes used as a general term for tropical revolving storms of all oceans, or in the form "Tropical Cyclone."

Cyclonic. Refers to wind circulating anti-clockwise round a low pressure area surrounded by an area of higher pressure in Northern latitudes — clockwise in Southern latitudes.

Dangerous Quadrant. The forward quadrant of the dangerous semi-circle of a cyclone, which before recurvature is nearer the pole (in both hemispheres).

Depression. A region characterised in the barometric pressure field by a system of closed isobars, having lowest pressure on the inside.

Dew. Water drops deposited by condensation of water vapour from the air, mainly on horizontal surfaces cooled by nocturnal radiation.

Dew Point. The lowest temperature to which air can be cooled without causing condensation.

Diurnal Variation. This term is used to indicate the changes, in the course of an average day, in the magnitude of a meteorological element. The most striking example of this is the diurnal variation of barometric pressure in the tropics, the chief component of which has a 12-hourly period. The maxima of this variation are about 10 a.m. and 10 p.m., the minima about 4 a.m. and 4 p.m., local time.

Doldrums. The equatorial oceanic regions of calms and light variable winds, accompanied by heavy rains, thunderstorms and squalls. These belts are variable in position and extent, and as a whole move north and south with the annual changes of the sun's declination.

Eye of Storm. The calm central area of a tropical cyclone. The most noticeable feature of this area is the sudden drop in wind from hurricane force to light unsteady breezes or even to a complete calm, with more or less cloudless sky and absence of rain. The sea in this area is, however, often very high and confused.

Front. The line of separation at or above the earth's surface between cold and warm air masses.

Frontogenesis. The development or marked intensification of a front.

Frontolysis. The disappearance or marked weakening of a front. Subsidence is the most important factor in causing frontolysis.

Gust. A comparatively rapid fluctuation in the strength of the wind, characteristic of winds near the surface of the earth. Gusts are mainly due to the turbulence or eddy motion arising from the friction offered by the ground to the flow of the current of air. (See **Squall**).

Hail. Hard pellets of ice, of various shapes and sizes, and more or less transparent, which fall from cumulonimbus clouds and are often associated with thunderstorms.

Halo. Halo phenomena constitute a large group of phenomena produced by the refraction or reflection of the light of the sun or moon by the ice crystals composing cirrus or cirrostratus cloud.

Hurricane. A name given to the tropical revolving storm of the West Indian region. Also applied to force 12 in the Beaufort scale, whatever its cause.

Inversion. An abbreviation for "inversion of temperature Gradient." The temperature of the air generally decreases with increasing height, but occasionally the reverse is the case; when the temperature thus increases with height there is said to be an inversion. When an inversion exists at the surface, fog often occurs.

Isallobars. Isallobars are lines drawn upon a chart through places at which equal changes of pressure have occurred in some period of time. Lines of equal change, or isallobars, are drawn to enclose regions of rising or of falling pressure.

Isobars. Lines drawn through positions having the same barometric pressure, when reduced to sea level.

Isotherms. Lines drawn through positions having the same temperatures.

Katabatic Wind. A wind that flows down slopes, usually at night. The air at the top of the slope is cooled to a greater amount by radiation than the air lower down, becomes heavier, and flows down the slope under the influence of gravity. The opposite of katabatic is anabatic, applied to a wind blowing up a slope, if it is caused by the convection of heated air.

Land and Sea Breezes. These are caused by the unequal heating and cooling of land and water under the influence of solar radiation by day and radiation to the sky at night, which produce a gradient of pressure near the coast. During the daytime the land is warmer than the sea and a breeze, the sea breeze, blows onshore; at night and in the early morning the land is cooler than the sea and the land breeze blows offshore. Land breeze is usually less developed than sea breeze.

Line Squall. A more or less violent squall, accompanying the passage of the cold front of a depression, distinguished by a sudden or rapid rise of wind strength, a change of wind direction, a rapid rise of the barometer and a fall of temperature. There is usually heavy rain or hail, sometimes a thunderstorm, or snow. The accompanying low black cloud forms a line or arch.

Local Winds. Winds prevalent in particular areas at particular times with special features, eg, the **Bora, Pampero, Mistral, Levanter, Sumatra.**

Mirage. The appearance of one or more images of a terrestrial object in the sky; also all forms of distortion of objects, due to abnormal refraction.

Occlusion, occluded depression. When the whole of the warm sector of a depression has been "pushed up" from the earth's surface by the advance of the cold front behind it, this is known as occlusion, and the depression in which it occurs is called an occluded depression.

Orographic Rain. Rain caused by the interference of rising land in the path of moisture laden air. A horizontal air current striking a mountain slope is deflected upwards, and the consequent dynamical cooling associated with the expansion of the air produces cloud and rain, if the air contains sufficient aqueous vapour.

Polar Front. The line of discontinuity, which is developed in suitable conditions between air originating in polar regions and air from low latitudes, and on which the majority of the depressions of temperate latitudes develop. It can sometimes be traced as a continuous wavy line thousands of miles in length, but it is interrupted when polar air breaks through to feed the trade winds, and is often replaced by a very complex series of fronts, or by a more gradual change of temperature.

Precipitation. Any aqueous deposit, in liquid or solid form, derived from the atmosphere. The precipitation at a given station during a given period includes not only the rainfall but also dew and the water equivalent of any solid deposits (snow, hail, or hoar frost) received in the rain gauge.

Recurvature of Storm. This expression refers to the recurvature of the track of a tropical cyclone. In the northern hemisphere a tropical cyclone, after proceeding in a more or less westerly direction, recurves and normally takes a north-easterly direction; in the southern hemisphere the final direction is normally south-easterly.

Ridge. An extension of an anticyclone or high pressure area shown on a pressure chart, corresponding to a ridge running out from the side of a mountain.

Roaring Forties. A nautical expression for the region of westerly winds in south temperate latitudes, which reach their greatest development south of 40°S. A general term for the prevailing westerly winds in the temperate latitudes of both hemispheres is **Brave West Winds.**

Scud. A word used by sailors to describe ragged fragments of cloud drifting rapidly in a strong wind, often underneath rain clouds. The meteorological term is fractostratus.

Secondary Depression or "Secondary." The isobars around a depression are frequently not quite symmetrical, they sometimes show bulges or distortions, which are accompanied by marked deflections in the general circulation of the wind in the depression; such distortions are called secondaries; they may appear merely as sinuosities in the isobars, but at other times they enclose separate centres of low pressure and show separate wind circulations from that of the parent depression.

Shower. In describing present or past weather, the following distinction is made between the use of the terms "showers" and "occasional precipitation." In general, showers are of short duration, and the fair periods between them are usually characterised by definite clearance of the sky. The clouds which give the showers are, therefore, isolated. The precipitation does not usually last more than fifteen minutes, though it may occasionally last for half an hour or more. Occasional precipitation, on the other hand, usually lasts for a longer time than the showers, and the sky in the periods between the precipitation is usually cloudy or overcast.

Sleet. Precipitation of snow and rain together, or of melting snow and rain.

Snow. Precipitation of ice crystals of feathery or needlelike structure.

Squall. A strong wind that increases suddenly, lasts for some minutes, and decreases again comparatively rapidly. It is frequently, but not necessarily, associated with a temporary change of direction. (See **Gust**).

Stratosphere. The region of the atmosphere immediately above the troposphere (q.v.). In the lower stratosphere temperature may continue to decrease with increase of height (but more slowly than in the troposphere) or may remain practically constant, or may increase with height. The transition from troposphere to stratosphere, judged by change of temperature with height, is not always abrupt.

At greater heights are other regions with special characteristics, e.g.:

(a) The ozonosphere, where the concentration of ozone gas is greatest, centred at a height of about 20 miles.

(b) The ionosphere, the highly electrically conducting region of ionised gases, extending upwards from the height of 50 or 60 miles. This region plays an important part in radio propagation. The main subdivisions of this region in order of increasing height are usually referred to as the D, E (or Kennelly-Heaviside), F (or Appleton) regions or layers.

Synoptic. An adjective derived from the noun "synopsis," a brief or condensed statement presenting a combined or general view of something. Thus a synoptic chart shows the weather conditions over a large area at a given instant of time.

Tendency of the Barometer. The amount of change in barometric pressure in the 3 hours preceding the time of observation. The characteristic of the tendency is the type of change during the same period, e.g. "rising," "falling at first then rising," "steady".

Thunder. The noise made by an electric discharge (lightning) from charged raindrops in a cloud to another cloud (or another part of the same cloud) or to the earth, or to the air surrounding the charged cloud. Sound travels 1 mile in about 5 seconds, while the lightning flash is seen as soon as it occurs, hence the interval of time between the two will give the distance from the observer.

Tornado. A violent and destructive whirl accompanying a thunderstorm.

Trade Winds. The name given to the winds which blow from the tropical high pressure belts towards the equatorial region of low pressure, from the N.E. in the northern hemisphere and from the S.E. in the southern hemisphere.

Troposphere. The lower region of the atmosphere, throughout which temperature in general decreases as height increases, and within which occur practically all clouds and the various other phenomena normally styled "weather." The upper boundary of the region is known as the tropopause. The height of the tropopause varies with latitude from an average of about $5\frac{1}{2}$ miles in polar regions to about 11 miles at the equator, but the height also varies from summer to winter and with the general meteorological situation. (See **Stratosphere**).

Trough. The trough line of a circular depression is the line, through the centre, perpendicular to the line of advance of the centre. During the passage of a depression over any given place the pressure at first falls and later rises; the trough line passes over the place during the period of transition from the falling to the rising barometer. The word trough is also used in a more general sense for any "valley" of low pressure, and is thus the opposite of a "ridge" of high pressure.

Typhoon. A name given to the tropical revolving storms of the China Sea and the west of the North Pacific Ocean.

Veering. A change in the direction of the wind, in a clockwise direction.

Vertex. The westernmost point in the track of a tropical revolving storm.

Vortex. Centre of tropical revolving storm, where barometric pressure is least.

Warm Sector, Warm Front. Most depressions in their earlier stages have an area of warm air on the side nearest the equator, known as the warm sector. The warm front is the boundary between the front of the warm sector, as the depression advances, and the colder air in front of it.

Waterspout. An air whirl, normally with a funnel shaped cloud projecting downwards from a cumulonimbus cloud, accompanied by an agitation of the sea surface beneath it, and the formation of a cloud of sprays. The waterspout is formed when the funnel shaped cloud has descended to join up with the cloud of spray; the spout then assumes the appearance of a column of water.

Wedge. An area of high pressure bounded by wedge shaped isobars. It is the converse of a V-shaped depression.

Radio and Satellite Aids to Navigation

19

RADIO AND SATELLITE AIDS TO NAVIGATION

Over the past few decades, electronic aids for yachtsmen have advanced dramatically in sophistication and ease of operation.

For years the most advanced aid for the navigation of small vessels was the RDF set, by means of which radio bearings were taken of fixed DF stations. This system is still in use but the advent of more accurate and advanced systems has led to declining importance from the yachtsman's point of view. Full information on its use, together with lists of the necessary DF stations, are still included for the benefit of those navigators who use the method.

Automatic position-fixing has been in use commercially for many years, using groups of shore stations. The advent of the microchip and miniaturisation generally, allowed the development to take place of very small, highly sophisticated units, which could easily be accommodated in small vessels. Thus Decca and Loran became practical possibilities for small craft. Omega, although having worldwide coverage, is of little interest to yachtsmen.

Satellite navigation has also been in use commercially for a number of years, but has only been available for small craft recently, for the same reasons that Decca etc. came into use, i.e. the development of very small sets.

The second-generation SatNav system, the Global Positioning System (GPS), was developed in the United States for military purposes, and is now made available for commercial purposes. This system can give a three-dimensional fix, i.e. it includes altitude as well as Latitude and Longitude. The third dimension is of little interest to yachtsmen, but is obviously of considerable use commercially.

Radio Direction Finding (RDF)

RDF bearings consist of two types:

(a) Bearings taken by the navigator of fixed stations.

(b) Bearings taken by a fixed station of a vessel which are then radioed to the vessel concerned, giving its position.

VHF EMERGENCY DF STATIONS

Certain Coastguard Stations will give a vessel its position using method (b) in an *emergency*, not as a normal check on navigational problems.

On request from a vessel in an emergency, the station will transmit the bearing of the vessel FROM the DF antenna. Watch is kept on Ch.16. Vessel transmits on Ch.16 (distress only) or Ch.67 (UK), Ch.67 (Guernsey), Ch.82 (Jersey), Ch.11 (France), in order that the station can determine its bearing which is transmitted on the same frequency.

The bearing given is only accurate to ±10°. No responsibility is accepted by H.M. Coastguard for any action taken by the master, based on information given.

In this Almanac stations appear in Sections 22 and 23 as appropriate. Consult General Index for page number.

Marine Directional Radiobeacons

Marine directional radiobeacons are designed and located mainly to enable vessels to enter a particular harbour in poor visibility or other adverse conditions. They are somewhat similar to air radio ranges, their special feature being that a bearing line is given as a line of approach (usually coinciding with the normal Leading Line). 'On beam' bearings and the terms 'to port' or 'to starboard' of the beam are given with reference to the ship steering towards the directional radiobeacon.

A central beam is signalled from the station and if the ship is 'on the beam' (i.e. on the correct line of approach), usually a steady continuous note is heard (or in some harbours, a certain Morse letter or letters). If for example, the vessel is to port of the approach beam, she might hear the letter A (· −) being transmitted continuously, but if to starboard of the beam she would then hear a succession of letter N's (− ·). Transmission of the A's and N's are so synchronised that when both are heard together on the central beam, they interlock, thus forming a continuous note. The same result is achieved at some stations by use of the letters E (·) and T (–) instead of A and N. Each station, of course, has different characteristics, and although Morse dots and dashes are used they are not necessarily given the normal Morse spacing. Station identification letters are usually non-directional.

Most directional radiobeacons also transmit non-directional signals for use with ship's D/F. Directional signals can be used with an ordinary radio receiver or with a D/F set with the aerial turned to the position of maximum reception.

Range

The range of radiobeacons, where known, is shown in nautical miles, in some cases, however, only the output (in kilowatts) is known. Where this is the case the following table will act as an approximate guide for converting to nautical miles.

Output	Range	Output	Range	Output	Range
0.025	45	0.3	155	1.5	280
0.05	80	0.4	170	2.0	300
0.1	100	0.5	180	3.0	330
0.2	130	1.0	240	5.0	400
				10.0	500

MARINE AND AERO RADIOBEACONS

Marine Radiobeacons

The automatic DF sets used by the majority of merchant ships require an uninterrupted carrier wave from the beacon to enable the set to 'lock on' when using automatic control rather than the interruption which occurs when the carrier is switched. Continuous carrier wave emission was introduced primarily for this purpose, but it also has considerable advantages for the small hand held DF set. Before the introduction of this type of emission the modulated carrier wave was switched so that nothing was radiated during the intervals between the Morse Code letters. With the A2A system the carrier wave is emitted continuously and the modulation is also switched on during the DF period. However, with aerobeacons the modulation is switched off during the DF period.

The following is a summary of radiobeacon emissions used by Marine and Aeronautical stations: former designations are given in parentheses.

A1A (A1)   Unmodulated carrier frequency during DF period; on-off keying of unmodulated carrier frequency during identification.

A2A (A2 & A2*)   Carrier frequency with modulating audio frequency during DF period; on-off keying of modulating audio frequency. Carrier frequency either continuous or keyed with audio frequency.

NON A2A   Unmodulated carrier frequency during DF period; continuous carrier
(AOA2)   frequency with on-off keying of modulating audio frequency during identification.

The composition of the Maritime Radiobeacon Characteristic Signal for Beacons situated North of Latitude 46°N has been standardised as follows:

(1) Identification Signal transmitted 3 to 6 times for (approx.)   22 sec.
(2) Long dash lasting for   25 sec.
(3) Identification Signal transmitted once or twice for (approx.)   8 sec.
(4) Silent period of at least   5 sec.

Total   60 sec. (1 min.)

(5) A prolonged silent period usually follows.

The Characteristic Signal for beacons situated South of Lat. 46°N is the same as above for Nos. 1, 2 and 4, but between Nos. 2 and 3 is given an additional Identification Signal (transmitted 4-8 times) for about 30 sec. with another long dash of 25 sec.; and a further 8 sec. Identification Signal.

Most marine radiobeacons are linked in groups from two to six with a common frequency which differs from any adjacent groups. Each beacon of the group transmits its call sign in turn, thus allowing the navigator to obtain several position lines in rapid succession. As each beacon transmits for one minute in a group of six, the complete group completes its cycle in 6 minutes, starting precisely on the hour (at 00 minutes) and repeating at 06 minutes, 12 minutes, etc., until the whole cycle starts again at the beginning of the next hour.

Aero Beacons

A glimpse at the list of aero beacons will show that these are few in number compared to Morse radiobeacons, bearing in mind that only those of use to surface vessels are included. These beacons, however, have the advantage that in general they are more powerful than the coastal marine beacons and also that they transmit continuously, unlike the morse beacons which transmit in sequence. The normal transmission consists of a long dash interrupted at approximately 15 second intervals with the call sign, although some may repeat the call sign continuously. The facility of being able to pick up a transmission at any moment without reference to a time sequence is often extremely useful, particularly when used in conjunction with a marine beacon.

The receiver should be used exactly as for marine beacons. However, in this case if the operator should forget to select DF/BFO position when he is taking his bearing, all he will hear is background noise. This once again illustrates the importance of developing an automatic procedure with respect to the operating controls of the particular set in use.

OPERATION OF RDF SETS

Various types of DF sets are available and it is particularly important that the manufacturer's instructions are followed correctly. Basically, the set should be tuned to the allocated frequency of the group, switched to the "ident" position for morse identification signal, and then to the appropriate DF position during the DF period, and by swinging the set from side to side, obtaining the null reading.

ERRORS AND CALIBRATION OF DF SETS

Quadrantal Error

The accuracy of an RDF set should not be relied upon until it has been checked for errors. The main error due to the vessel itself is quadrantal error which is caused by the re-radiation of radio waves from metal structures or rigging on the vessel. This re-radiated signal is picked up by the DF aerial and the set then indicates the resultant direction of the two waves. In the case of a sailing yacht the effect can be minimised by 'breaking' the closed loops of the rigging by inserting insulation but it is debatable whether this is really worth doing in most cases. It is much easier and more worthwhile to break the loops formed by steel life lines by using a rope seizing at one end of each line instead of a shackle. To calibrate for quadrantal error it is necessary to be within sight of a radio beacon or in a known position so that the magnetic bearing of the beacon can be accurately determined. The visual (magnetic) and the DF bearings are compared at regular intervals, say 10°, while the vessel is rotated through 360°. A curve can then be plotted of the quadrantal error for each 10° of relative bearing. Before plotting the curve it is important to remember to correct the compass bearings for deviation if any.

Night Effect

During the hours of darkness or more correctly between one hour before sunset to one hour after sunrise the radiobeacon signals are reflected back from the ionosphere and are picked up by the DF set slightly out of phase with the direct ground waves, resulting in a blurring of the null. The effect increases with distance from the beacon but close to the beacon, say within 15 miles, the effect is less noticeable. In areas where radiobeacons are numerous, it is found necessary to reduce the power output at night. In these cases the day and night ranges are both given, ie. 100/70. It is advisable to assume that MF beacons in general are not to be relied on at ranges of more than 70 miles in the presence of 'Night Effect', particularly around sunset and sunrise.

Coastal Refraction

Radio waves crossing a coast line at 90° are unaffected directionally but as the angle decreases refraction occurs, that is the radio wave is bent in towards the land. The error, however, is really only significant when the angle is small and will always give a fix closer to the coast line than the actual position. Similarly, aerobeacons situated well inland may have the path of their ground waves seriously 'bent' due to the presence of high ground.

Remember

1. A beacon selected should not be beyond its official range and not more than 25 miles at night whatever its range otherwise bearings may be unreliable.

2. Try to ensure that the ship's head is kept on a steady bearing during the operation. This is essential with the loop type aerial as the ship's heading will be needed at the instant the beacon bearing is taken.

3. The DF set bearing is corrected for deviation and quadrantal error if appropriate.

4. When choosing the beacon make sure that the bearing does not make a small angle with the coastline, that high ground does not intervene between the beacon and the vessel and that bearings should be as widely divergent as possible. As with visual bearings, considerable reliance can be placed on three well spaced bearings producing a small cocked hat.

5. Other aerial circuits near a loop aerial should be disconnected from their sets.

6. Radiobeacons may be suspended from operation without notice due to defects, maintenance, etc., particularly beacons situated in light vessels which may be removed from station for overhaul during the summer months.

SUPPRESSION OF ELECTRICAL APPARATUS

When any radio equipment is to be used on board it is important to ensure that any rotating electrical plant in the form of dynamos, alternators etc. is effectively suppressed. Normally, installations of this type are properly suppressed by the manufacturer, but if this has not been done or it has become defective it should be remedied if the best results are to be obtained from the radio equipment. It is incidentally worth bearing in mind that a very obtrusive static discharge can occur when the auxiliary of a sailing yacht is not in use but the propeller is allowed to rotate. A shaft brake should be fitted, alternatively a contact brush fitted on the shaft near the stern gland and suitably earthed will alleviate the trouble. All equipment should be earthed down to the engine bed plate and cathodic protection system.

REED'S RADIOBEACON MAPS

Marine Radiobeacons are indicated on the maps by a symbol with the relevant Reed's Station No. printed alongside it, thus: ●44. A firm line joins stations which are grouped together.

Aeronautical Radiobeacons. Those shown on the maps are each identified by a symbol and the appropriate Reed's Station No. ☉ A24. Note that the Station Nos. of the aeronautical radiobeacons are always prefixed by the letter A.

Calibration stations and Radar Beacons (Racons) are not shown on the maps.

Positions of Radiobeacons shown on the maps are diagrammatic only. Correct latitude and longitude of each station is given, to the nearest half minute.

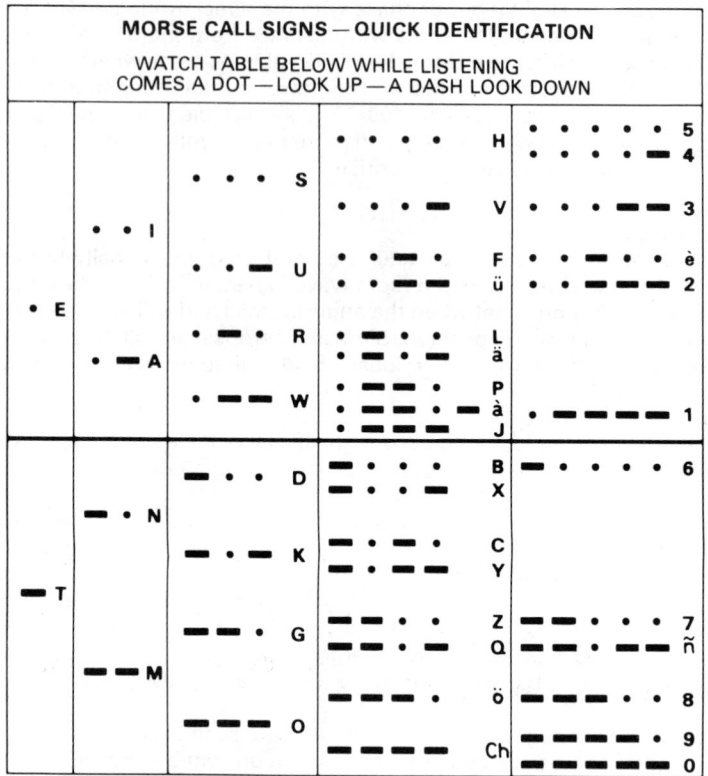

MORSE CALL SIGNS — QUICK IDENTIFICATION
WATCH TABLE BELOW WHILE LISTENING
COMES A DOT — LOOK UP — A DASH LOOK DOWN

RADIOBEACON CALIBRATION SERVICE

This service is operated by the Radiobeacon Stations listed below in **clear weather only** as follows:

GREAT BRITAIN, IRELAND, CHANNEL APPROACHES TO NOORD HINDER

STATION	LAT. North ° '	LONG. West ° '	RANGE AND FREQ.		MORSE IDENT.	MODE AND FOOTNOTES
Foreland Pt. Lt.	51 14.7	3 47.1	5	312.6	FP · · — · · — — ·	A2A	1
Point Lynas Lt.	53 25.0	4 17.3	5	310.3	PS · — — · · · ·	A2A	2
Cloch Pt. Lt.	55 56.5	4 52.7	8	308	CL — · — · · — · ·		3
Souter Pt. Lt.	54 58.2	1 21.8	5	312.6	PT · — — · —	A2A	1, 4
Ballycotton Lt.	51 49.5	7 59.0	5	312.6	BC — · · · — · — ·	A2A	5
Kish Bank Lt.	53 18.7	5 55.4	5	312.6	KH — · — · · · · ·	A2A	5
Mew Island Lt.	54 41.9	5 30.8	5	312.6	MC — — · — · — ·	A2A	5

FOOTNOTES:
1) Continuous from 1 hr. after sunrise to 1 hr. before sunset.
2) Continuous.
3) To Estuary Control VHF Ch. 16 or 12 at least 6 hr. in advance. Tel: Greenock (0475) 26221.
4) A fixed white light visible 230°-270° is shown during transmissions.
5) On request using the following procedure. Prior notice, date and time must be given to the Lighthouse Authority. On vessels arrival off Radio Beacon Station she should hoist a black ball (kept flying during calibration) and give three long followed by three short blasts to indicate readiness. Station acknowledges by hoisting her Ensign over Numeral Pennant 0. On ship completing calibration she lowers black ball and sounds three short sharp followed by three long blasts answered by the station by the Answering Pennant.

RADIOBEACON CALIBRATION SERVICE

NOORD HINDER TO BALTIC ENTRANCE

STATION	LAT. North ° ′	LONG. East ° ′	RANGE AND FREQ.	MORSE IDENT.	MODE AND FOOTNOTES	
Scheveningen Lt.	52 06.3	4 16.2	312.6	HO · · · · ‒ ‒ ‒	A2A	a
Ijmuiden Front Lt.	52 27.8	4 34.6	5　314.5	YC ‒ · ‒ ‒ ‒ · ‒ ·	A2A	b
Weser Pilot Vessels			313.5,	WB · ‒ ‒ ‒ · · ·	A2A	f
("Kapitan Konig" & "Gotthilf Hagen")			2168			
Wilhelmshaven....................	53 31.0	8 08.8	312.6,			
			2168	JB · ‒ ‒ ‒ ‒ · · ·	A2A	c
Bremerhaven......................	53 32.4	8 34.9	312.6,			
			2168	GB ‒ ‒ · ‒ · · ·	A2A	d
Hollerwettern Lt.	53 50.4	9 21.3	313.5,			
			2168	HB · · · · ‒ · · ·	A2A	e
Krautsand	53 45.6	9 22.6	312.6,			
			2168	KB ‒ · · ‒ ‒ · · ·	A2A	e
Svanemollevaerket	55 42.8	12 35.4	10　314.5,			
			2168	MU ‒ ‒ · · ‒	A1A	h
Friedrichsort Lt.	54 23.5	10 11.7	312.6,			
			2168	FB · ‒ · ‒ · · ·	A2A	j
Travemunde Lt.....................	53 57.8	10 53.0	312.6,			
			2168	UB · · ‒ ‒ · · ·	A2A	j
Timmendorf Pilot Stn.	53 59.6	11 22.7	311,			
			375,			
			485	02 ‒ ‒ ‒ · · ‒ ‒ ‒		k
Warnemunde Pilot Stn.	54 10.9	12 05.3	311,			
			485,			
			2200	LHD · ‒ · · · · · · ‒ · ·		l

FOOTNOTES:
a) To the Centrapos van DGSM at Hoek van Holland on VHF Ch. 01.
b) To Verkeersdienst Ijmuiden on VHF Ch. 12 (02550-19027 or through Scheveningen PCG-PCH.
c) To Waser-und Schiffahrtsant Wilhelmshaven, via Jade Revier on VHF Ch. 16, 20, 63.
d) To Waser-und Schiffahrtsant Bremerhaven through Bremerhaven Revier on VHF Ch. 05, 07.
e) To Revierzentrale Brunsbuttel or Tel: (04852) 8011-16 ext. 393 or (04852) 8400.
f) To Pilot vessel on duty in advance on Ch. 06 (Traffic managed on both frequencies).
h) Through Drogden Lt. Tel: (01) 53 05 88.
j) To Waser-und Schiffahrtsant Lubeck through Revierzentrale Travemunde Tel: (0452) 71117, Telex: 261419.
k) Through Pilot Stn. VHF Ch. 12 or Tel: 255.
l) To Warnemunde Pilot Stn. VHF Ch. 12 or Tel: 52358.

RADIOBEACON CALIBRATION SERVICE

SOUTHERN BALTIC

STATION	LAT. North ° '	LONG. East ° '	RANGE AND FREQ.	MORSE IDENT.	MODE AND FOOTNOTES	
Sassnitz..................................	54 30.7	13 38.7	311	SAZ ... ._ __..		a
			485			
			2200			
Swinoujscie Main Lt..............	53 55.1	14 17.2	306.5	OD ___ _..		
			2167			b
Kolobrzeg Lt	54 11.3	15 33.5	296.5	K _._	A1A, A2A	c
			2167			
Darlowo Lt................................	54 26.5	16 22.9	309	D _..	A1A, A2A	d
Ustka Lt...................................	54 35.4	16 51.4	306.5	U .._	A1A, A2A	e
Hel Lt......................................	54 36.1	18 48.9	306.5	H	A1A, A2A	f
			2167			
Gdynia.....................................	54 31.8	18 33.7	296.5	G __.	A1A, A2A	g

FOOTNOTES
a) To Sassnitz Hbr Master. 24 hours notice required.
b) To Swinoujscie Main Lt VHF Ch 12, 16.
c) To Kolobrzeg Lt VHF Ch 16.
d) To Darlowo Lt VHF Ch 16.
e) To Ustka Lt VHF Ch 16.
f) To Hel Lt VHF Ch 16.
g) On VHF Ch 16. A light is shown during transmissions.

RADIOBEACONS – UK AND IRELAND

In order to comply with internationally agreed regulations for medium frequency maritime radiobeacons, the General Lighthouse Authorities, Trinity House, the Northern-Lighthouse Board and the Commissioners of Irish Lights will be extensively re-organising their radiobeacon network from 1st April 1992. The alterations will give effect to an international requirement that radiobeacons be operated singly and continously rather than in groups on a time shared basis which has been the practice for many years; to achieve this it will be necessary for a number of radiobeacons to be discontinued.

Full details of the re-organisation were not available to us before going to press with this edition of Reed's, but final details, including information on the amended use of receivers to obtain most benefit from the service, will be available in yachting publications as well as in Notices to Mariners issued by the General Lighthouse Authorities and will also, of course, appear in our half-yearly supplement.

IDENTIFICATION SIGNALS OF
MARINE AND AERONAUTICAL RADIOBEACONS

GREAT BRITAIN & IRELAND, CHANNEL APPROACHES TO NOORD HINDER
See Diagrams 'A' and 'B'

Morse Ident.	Freq. kHz.	Reed's Station No.	Station	Morse Ident.	Freq. kHz.	Reed's Station No.	Station
AB	381	219	Akraberg (Sumbø)	FAW	370	A27	Fawley/Hythe
AH	294.2	246	Altacarry Head Lt. Ho.	FB	303.4	183	Flamborough Head
			(Rathlin East)	FD	289.6	179	Fidra
AL	310.3	108	Point d'Ailly	FE	305.7	45	Cap Frehel
ALD	383	A12	Alderney	FG	291.9	81	Pte. Barfleur
AP	370.5	A87	Aberporth	FN	287.3	285	Walney Island
				FOY	395	A67.5	Foynes
BC	287.3	54	Bloscon Roscoff	FP	303.4	198	Fife Ness.
BD	308	3	Barra Head	FS	305.7	120	Falls Lt. V.
BHD	318	A6	Berry Head				
BL	298.8	231	Butt of Lewis	GA	287.3	165	Outer Gabbard Lt. V.
BM	303.4	87	Brighton Marina	GD	310.3	195	Girdle Ness
BN	296.5	294	Ballycotton	GJ	294.2	60	St. Malo Grand Jardin
BNY	352	A67	Shannon/Bunratty	GL	308	9	Eagle Island
BPL	276.5	A81	Blackpool	GR	287.3	159	Goeree
BS	313.5	63	Port en Bessin	GUR	361	A15	Guernsey
BY	287.3	216	Bressay (Shetlands)	GY	285	42	Castle Breakwater, St. Peter
BY	414.5	A91	Brawdy				Port
CA	308	18	Pt. de Creach, Ushant	HB	275	A73	Belfast
CB	305.7	48	La Corbiere	HRN	401.5	A24	Bournemouth/Hurn
CDF	363.5	A96	Cardiff				
CH	303.4	84	Chichester Bar	IB	301.1	261	Bardsey
CM	287.3	168	Cromer	IW	276.5	A28	Bembridge
CN	301.1	267	Cregneish (I.O.M.)				
CP	291.9	69	St. Catherine's Point	JEY	367	A21	Jersey East
CR	287.3	39	Channel Lt. V.	JW	329	A18	Jersey West
CS	305.7	132	Calais				
CW	298.8	228	Cape Wrath	KD	291.9	204	Kinnairds Head
				KH	312.6	276	Kish Bank
DA	294.2	240	Pladda	KIN	374	A66	Kintyre
DD	352.5	A122	Ostend	KLY	378	A69	Killiney
DK	294.2	147	Dunkerque Lt. Buoy.	KS	370	A48	Kinloss
DO	364.5	A60	Dounreay/Thurso				
DO	294.2	57	Rosedo	LDV	324	A101	Landivisiau
DR	390	A106	Dinard	LG	294.2	255	Eilean Glas.
DU	310.3	117	Dungeness	LH	291.9	75	Le Havre
				LHO	346	A111	Le Havre/Octeville
EC	287.3	51	St. Helier	LK	298.8	237	Sule Skerry
EGT	328.5	A66.5	Londonderry	LN	345.5	A102	Lannion/Servel
éR	291.9	78	Pointe de Ver	LP	289.6	282	Loop Head
EX	337	A9	Exeter	LS	296.5	300	Lundy Island South
				LT	303.4	189	Longstone
				LT	358	A117	Le Touquet

GREAT BRITAIN & IRELAND, CHANNEL APPROACHES TO NOORD HINDER
See Diagrams 'A' and 'B'

Morse Ident.	Freq. kHz.	Reed's Station No.	Station	Morse Ident.	Freq. kHz.	Reed's Station No.	Station
LU	330	A42	Leuchars	RN	294.2	249	Rinns of Islay
LV	287.3	162	Dudgeon Lt. V.	RR	308	15	Round Island
LYX	397	A31	Lydd	RSH	326	A72	Dublin (Rush)
LZ	298.8	36	Lizard	RWY	359	A78	Ronaldsway (I.O.M.)
				RY	310.3	105	Royal Sovereign Lt. Tr.
MF	298.8	234	Muckle Fluga Lt.				
MK	275	A120	Calais/Dunkirk	SB	296.5	304	South Bishop Lt. Ho.
MW	294.2	243	Mew Island	SB	353	A105	Saint Brieuc
MY	337	225	Myggenaes (Faeroes)	SB	291.9	213	Sumburgh Head
MZ	308	12	Mizen Head	SHD	383	A45	Scotstown Head
				SJ	303.4	181	Souter Lt.
NB	312.6	96	Nab Tower	SK	287.3	156	Smiths Knoll Lt. V.
ND	397	A36	Great Yarmouth/N Denes	SM	356.5	A99	Saint Mawgan
NF	301.1	138	North Foreland	SN	289.6	279	Slyne Head
NH	303.4	90	Newhaven	SND	362.5	A33	Southend
NK	296.5	177	Inchkeith	SP	298.8	24	Start Point Lt. Ho.
NL	404	222	Nolso (Faeroes)	SR	301.1	258	Skerries
NP	296.5	153	Nieuwpoort W. Piet Lt.	SS	315.5	A57	Scatsa
NP	296.5	302	Nash Pt.	STM	321	A1	St. Marys (Isles of Scilly)
NR	291.9	207	North Ronaldsay (Orkneys)	STU	400	A90	Strumble
NR	287.3	171	Noord Hinder	SU	301.1	273	South Rock Lt. V.
				SUM	351	A54	Sumburgh (Shetlands)
OE	305.7	129	Ostend	SW	294.2	20	Ushant SW Lt. By.
OH	296.5	297	Old Head of Kinsale	SWN	320.5	A93	Swansea
OM	291.9	210	Stroma	SWY	669.5	A61	Stornoway
OO	375	A123	Ostend				
ONO	399.5	A124	Ostend	TI	291.9	72	Cap d'Antifer
OR	294.2	252	Hyskeir/Oigh-Sgeir	TR	296.5	306	Tuskar Rock
OTR	398.5	A39	Ottringham	TRN	355	A75	Turnberry
				TY	308	6	Tory Island
PB	291.9	66	Portland Bill				
PE	298.8	21	Penlee Pt.	UK	312.6	141	Sunk Lt.V.
PH	333	A3	Penzance Heliport				
PH	310.3	111	Cap d'Alprech Lt.	VG	298.8	33	Ile Vierge
PO	303.4	93	Poole Hbr.				
PS	287.3	288	Point Lynas	WH	305.7	126	West Hinder Lt. V.
PY	301.1	270	Point of Ayre (I.O.M.)	WIK	344	A51	Wick
PY	396.5	A3	Plymouth	WK	301.1	264	Wicklow Head
				WS	390.5	A97	Weston-super-Mare
QS	298.8	27	Casquets	WTD	368	A68	Waterford
RB	312.6	99	Cherbourg	ZB	296.5	150	Zeebrugge Mole Lt.Ho.
RD	298.8	30	Roches Douvres				

NOORD HINDER TO BALTIC ENTRANCE
See Diagram 'C'

Morse Ident.	Freq. kHz.	Reed's Station No.	Station	Morse Ident.	Freq. kHz.	Reed's Station No.	Station
AD	298.8	333	Ameland	KI	294.2	399	Kiel
AR	291.9	342	Alte Weser	KUL	344	435	Kullen
BE	298.8	336	Borkum Little	LA	296.5	360	Lista
BG	301.1	372	Hatteberget	LR	310.3	378	Laesø Rende
BH	296.5	363	Blaavandshuk Lt.				
				MR	294.2	405	Marineleuchte
DHE	397.2	351	Helgoland				
DB	308	324	Deutsche Bucht Lt.V.	NA	294.2	430	Nakke Hoved
DG	308	420	Drogden	NDO	372	A135	Nordholz
DON	355	A142	Donna, Dan Oilfield	NL	294.2	408	Neuland
EL	308	330	Elbe Lt. Float	RF	301.1	345	Rote Kliff, Sylt
ER	294.2	315	Eirland	RS	287.3	384	Rosnaes
FE	294.2	402	Fehmarnbelt	SG	287.3	387	Sjaellands Rev North Lt.Ho.
FK	414	375	Frederikshavn	SL	287.3	390	Sletterhage
FL	294.2	432	Fladen	SLT	286	A141	Sylt
FO	335	A154	Sterlene Lt.	SPY	381	A129	Amsterdam
FV	289.6	427	Falsterborev	ST	308	425	Stevns Klint
GR	303.4	417	Gedser	TD	301.1	411	Travemunde
GRE	277	A148	Grebbestad	TN	289.6	354	Thyborøn
GV	364	A126	Valken Burg	TP	283	A157	Sandefjord (Torp)
				TR	375	A143	Tor Oilfield
HB	310.3	381	Hals Barre	TU	301.1	373	Trubaduren
HE	308	423	Hestehoved				
HH	294.2	312	Hoek Van Holland	VS	301.1	348	Grosser Vogelsand
HK	308	327	Texel Lt.V.	VL	308	318	Vlieland
HM	296.5	357	Hanstholm				
HO	301.1	369	Hirsholm Main	WE	291.9	339	Wangerooge Lt.Ho.
				WN	303.4	414	Warnemunde
IR	406	366	Hirtshals Havn Front Lt.				
				YM	294.2	309	Ijmuiden

SOUTHERN BALTIC
See Diagram 'D'

Morse Ident.	Freq. kHz.	Station No.	Station	Morse Ident.	Freq. kHz.	Station No.	Station
AL	294.2	443.7	Almagrundet	HL	310.3	438.5	Hel
BN	301.1	444.3	Svenska Bjorn	JA	287.3	437.6	Jaroslawiec
FA	294.2	442.5	Faro	KB	287.3	437.3	Kolobrzeg
FAU	334	A439.0	Ronne	KM	310.3	438.7	Krynica Morska
				KO	296.5	444.9	Korso
GD	294.2	443.1	Gustav Dalen	KS	308	441.4	Stora Karslo
GS	294.2	444.0	Gotska Sandon	KT	294.2	442.8	Kungsgrundet

SOUTHERN BALTIC
See Diagram 'D'

Morse Ident.	Freq. kHz.	Reed's Station No.	Station	Morse Ident.	Freq. kHz.	Reed's Station No.	Station
LE	287.3	437.9	Leba	RO	287.3	438.2	Rozewie
LO	294.2	443.4	Landsort				
				SM	298.8	439.6	Sandhammaren
MN	298.8	439.3	Hammerodde	SO	308	441.1	Olands Sodra Udde
				SS	314.5	444.6	Simpnasklubb
NO	298.8	440.8	Olands Norra Udde				
				UK	298.8	439.9	Utklippan
OD	287.3	437.0	Swinoujscie				
OB	298.8	440.5	Hoburg	VY	406	442.0	Visby
OG	298.8	440.2	Olands Sodra Grund				
ON	305.7	441.7	Ostergarn	YM	294.2	309	Ijmuiden
OV	351	A442.3	Visby				

NORWAY & ICELAND
See Diagram 'C' and 'E'

Morse Ident.	Freq.	Reed's Station No.	Station	Morse Ident.	Freq.	Reed's Station No.	Station
ANY	343.5	A182	Andenes, Andoya	LN	289.6	453	Langoytangen
				LS	305.7	471	Hirtshals
BØ	289.6	585	Bokfjord Lt.	LL	305.7	474	Hallo
BU	308	537	Buholmrasa	LG	308	552	Landegode Lt.
BJ	301.1	534	Bjornsund				
				MA	303.4	588.7	Malarrif Lt.
DA	305.7	585.5	Dalatangi	MA	312.6	516	Marstein Lt.
DV	298.8	586	Djupivogur				
DY	287.3	447	Dyna Lt.	RK	355	A588.1	Reykjavik
				RN	291.9	587.5	Reykjanes
FH	287.3	573	Fruholmen Lt.	REK	379	A163	Reksten
FLV	374	A175	Fleinvaer	RSY	378	A160	Rennesøy (Stavanger N)
FN	312.6	519	Felstein				
FR	312.6	480	Faerder	SA	379	A588.4	Skagi
				SW	305.7	468	Skagen
GE	301.1	483	Skarvoy Lt.	SL	289.6	498	Slatteroy Lt.
GU	312.6	526	Geitungane	SY	296.5	510	Svinoy Lt.
				SK	289.6	543	Skomvaer Lt.
HG	294.2	501	Holmengra	SN	301.1	579	Sletnes Lt.
HD	308.0	507	Hendanes Lt.	SR	312.6	586.9	Skardhsfjara
HN	287.3	A586.3	Hornafjordhur	STT	317	A172	Stott
HA	294.2	531	Halten				
HO	310.3	546	Tennholmen	TAR	349	A169	Tarva
HK	303.4	564	Hekkingen Lt.	TN	301.1	495	Tresvikpynten
HS	308.0	576	Heines Lt.	TG	312.6	570	Torsvag Lt.
				TO	305.7	477	Torungen
IN	316	586.6	Ingolfshofdhi Lt.				
				UT	312.6	513	Utsira Lt.
KY	305.7	465	Oksoy	UTH	366	A166	Uthaug
KL	298.8	549	Sklinna				
KF	392	A587.8	Keflavik	VR	310.3	526	Utvaer
KN	291.9	558	Skrova	VD	294.2	582	Vardo Lt.
				VM	375	A587.2	Vestmannaeyjar
LEC	319	486	Stavanger				

USHANT TO GIBRALTAR (including AZORES)
See Diagram 'F'

Morse Ident.	Freq. kHz.	Reed's Station No.	Station	Morse Ident.	Freq. kHz.	Reed's Station No.	Station
ALV	262	A206	Alverca	MA	296.5	642	Cabo Machichaco
AOG	265	A210	Rota	MD	287.3	684	Cabo Mondego
AV	291.9	678	Aveiro Lt.	MGL	371	A256	Ponta Delgada
AVS	325	A199	Asturias	MIO	322	A206.5	Montijo
				MR	291.9	675	Montedor
B	289.6	714	Cabo Trafalgar	MRT	355	A208	Marateca
BA	301.1	654	Estaca de Bares	MT	398	A190	St. Nazaire/Montoir
BLO	370	A196	Bilboa	MTL	336	A203	Monte Real
BN	303.4	618	Les Baleines	MY	296.5	645	Cabo Mayor
BST	316	A184	Lanveoc				
C	305.7	660	Cabo Priorino	NZ	298.8	602	St. Nazaire, St. Gildas
CA	308	18	Pte de Creach, Ushant				
CP	389	A205	Caparica	O	289.6	717	Tarifa
CT	289.6	597	Pte de Combrit				
CV	287.3	687	Capo Carvoeiro	PI	308	696	Cabo Espichel
				POR	327	A201	Porto
D	289.6	711	Rota	PR	298.8	624	Ile du Piller
				PS	301.1	651	Cabo Penas
FAR	332	A209	Faro				
FI	310.3	666	Cabo Finisterre	RC	308	693	Cabo Roca
FIL	380	A265	Horta	RE	291.9	633	La Rochelle
FLO	270	A268	Flores	RO	310.3	669	Cabo Silleiro
FT	296.5	639	Cap Ferret				
				SM	289.6	594	Pte. St. Mathieu
GP	341	A259	Lajes	SM	303.4	705	Cabo de Santa Maria
GRA	283	A262	Graciosa	SMA	323	A253	Santa Maria
GX	301.1	600	Ile de Groix	SN	303.4	612	Ile de Sein N.W.
				SN	308	699	Cabo de Sines
HIG	328	A193	San Sebastian	SO	291.9	627	Les Sables d'Olonne
				STR	371	A204	Sintra
IA	301.1	648	Llanes				
IB	287.3	690	Ilha Berlenga	UH	289.6	589	Pte. de Penmarc'h Eckmuhl
L	305.7	657	Torres de Hercules	VC	303.4	702	Cape St. Vincent
LC	291.9	681	Leca	VI	310.3	663	Cabo Villano
LGS	364	A207	Lagos	VR	303.4	708	Vila Real de Sta. Antonio
LK	303.4	615	Pointe de la Coubre	VS	296.5	672	Cabo Estay
LOR	294.2	A187	Lorient				
				YE	312.6	621	Ile d'Yeu

RADIOBEACONS
CHANNEL APPROACHES TO NOORD HINDER

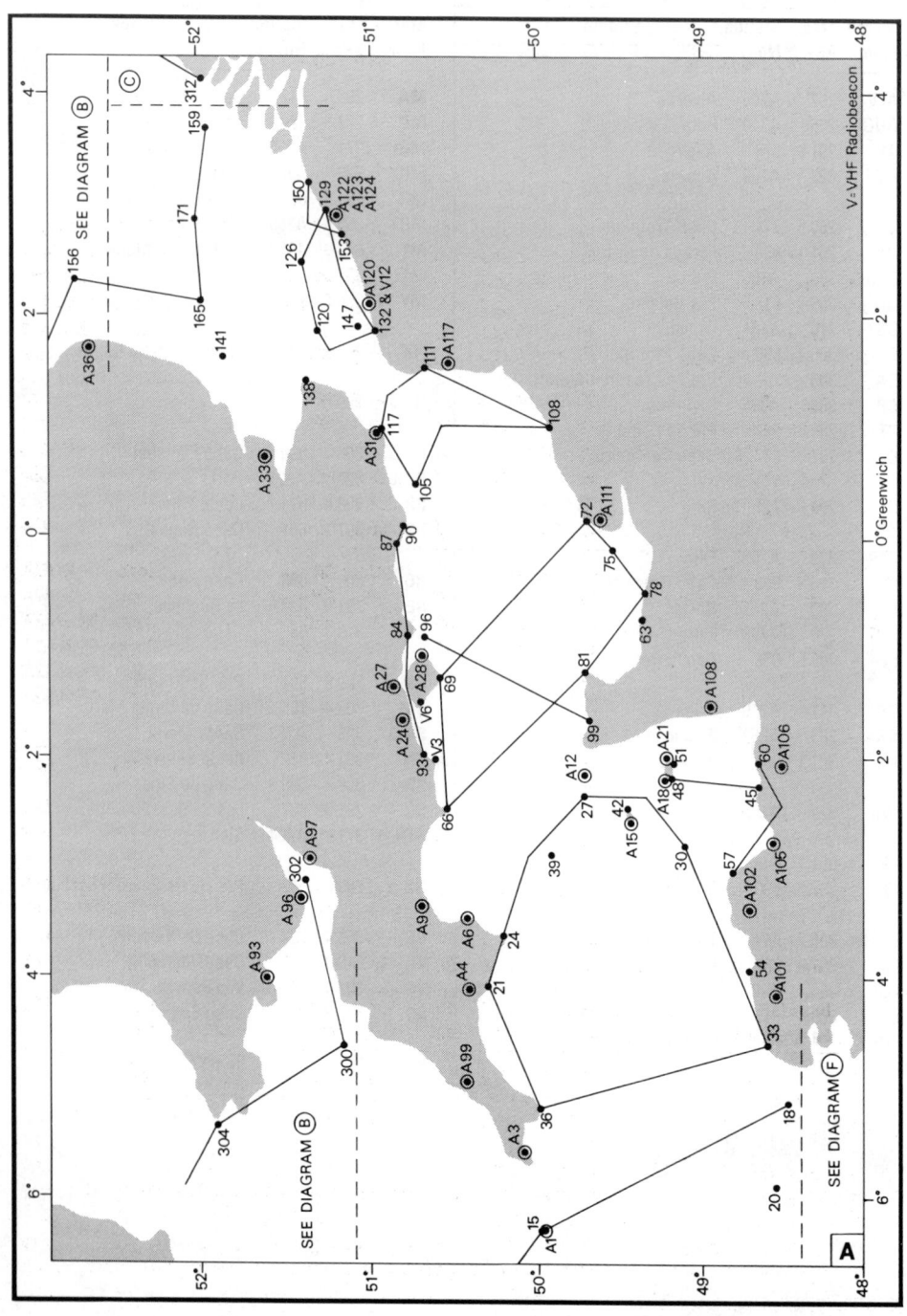

CHANNEL APPROACHES TO NOORD HINDER – See Diagram 'A'

REED'S STN. No.	STATION NAME AND GROUPING	LAT. North ° ′	LONG. West ° ′	RANGE AND FREQ.		MORSE IDENT.	TRANSMISSION Times/sequence Modes and FOOTNOTES	
3	Barra Head Lt. Ho. ……	56 47.1	7 39.2	$\frac{200}{70}$	308.0	BD – · · · – · ·	1	A2A
6	Tory Island Lt. ……	55 16.4	8 14.9	$\frac{100}{70}$	308.0	TY – – · – –	2	A2A
9	Eagle Island Lt. ……	54 17.0	10 05.5	$\frac{200}{100}$	308.0	GL – – · · – · ·	3	A2A
12	Mizen Head ……	51 27.1	9 48.8	$\frac{200}{100}$	308.0	MZ – – – – · ·	4	fR A2A
15	Round Island Lt. ……	49 58.7	6 19.3	$\frac{200}{100}$	308.0	RR · – · · – ·	5	A2A
18	Pte de Creach Lt, Ushant…	48 27.6	5 07.6	100	308.0	CA – · – · · – ·	6	R A2A
A1	St. Mary's, Isles of Scilly …	49 54.8	6 17.4	15	321	STM · · · – – –	Cont.	NON A2A
A3	Penzance Heliport ……	50 07.7	5 31.0	15	333	PH · – – · · · · ·	j	NON A2A
A4	Plymouth ……	50 25.4	4 06.7	20	396.5	PY · – – · – · – –	j	NON A2A
A6	Berry Head ……	50 23.9	3 29.6	25	318	BHD – · · · · · · · – · ·	Cont.	NON A2A
A9	Exeter ……	50 45.1	3 17.6	15	337	EX · – · · –	Cont.	NON A2A
20	Ushant SW Lanby ……	48 31.7	5 49.1	10	294.2	SW · · · · – –	Cont.	A2A
21	Penlee Pt. ……	50 19.1	4 11.3	50	298.8	PE · – – · ·	1	A2A
24	Start Point Lt. Ho. ……	50 13.3	3 38.5	70	298.8	SP · · · · – – ·	2	A2A
27	Casquets Lt. Ho. ……	49 43.4	2 22.6	50	298.8	QS – – · – · · ·	3	R A2A
30	Roches Douvres Lt. Ho. …	49 06.5	2 48.8	70	298.8	RD · – · – · ·	4	A2A
33	Ile Vierge Lt. ……	48 38.4	4 34.0	70	298.8	VG · · · – – – ·	5	A2A
36	Lizard Lt. Ho. ……	49 57.6	5 12.1	70	298.8	LZ · – · · – – · ·	6	A2A
39	Channel Lt. V. ……	49 54.4	2 53.7	10	287.3	CR – · – · · – ·	Cont.	R A2A
42	Castle Breakwater Lt. ……	49 27.4	2 31.4	10	285	GY – – · · – · –	Cont.	b A2A
A12	Alderney ……	49 42.6	2 11.9	50	383	ALD · – · – · · – · ·	Cont.	NON A2A
A15	Guernsey ……	49 26.1	2 38.3	30	361	GUR – – · · · – · – ·	Cont.	NON A2A
A18	Jersey West ……	49 12.4	2 13.3	25	329	JW · – – – · – –	Cont.	NON A2A
A21	Jersey East ……	49 13.2	2 02.2	75	367	JEY · – – – · · – · – –	Cont.	NON A2A
45	Cap Fréhel Lt. ……	48 41.1	2 19.1	20	305.7	FÉ · · – · · · – · ·	1, 3, 5	A2A
48	La Corbiere Lt. ……	49 10.9	2 14.9	20	305.7	CB – · – · – · · ·	2, 4, 6	a A2A
51	St. Helier Hbr. ……	49 10.6	2 07.5	10	287.3	EC · – · – · ·	Cont.	A2A
54	Roscoff-Bloscon Lt. ……	48 43.3	3 57.6	10	287.3	BC – · · · – · – ·	Cont.	A2A
A101	Landivisiau ……	48 32.8	4 08.2	–	324	LDV · – · · – · · · –	Cont.	A1A
A102	Lannion/Servel ……	48 43.3	3 18.5	50	345.5	LN · – · · – ·	Cont.	A1A
A105	Saint Brieuc ……	48 34.1	2 46.9	25	353	SB · · · – · · ·	Cont.	A1A
A106	Dinard ……	48 29.0	2 03.2		390	DR – · · · – ·	Cont.	A1A
A108	Granville ……	48 55.1	1 28.9	25	321	GV – – · · · · · –	Cont.	A1A
57	Rosedo Lt. Ile de Brehat …	48 51.5	3 00.3	10	294.2	DO – · · – – –	1, 5	A2A
60	Le Grande Jardin Lt. ……	48 40.3	2 04.9	10	294.2	GJ – – · · – – – –	2, 6	R A2A
63	Port en Bessin Lt. ……	49 21.0	0 45.6	5	313.5	BS – · · · · · ·	Cont.	A2A
66	Portland Bill Lt. Ho. ……	50 30.8	2 27.3	50	291.9	PB · – – · – · · ·	1	A2A
69	St. Catherine's Pt. Lt. ……	50 34.5	1 17.8	50	291.9	CP – · – · · – – ·	2	A2A
72	Cap d'Antifer Lt. Ho. ……	49 41.1	0 10.0E	50	291.9	TI – · ·	3	A2A
75	Le Havre Lanby ……	49 31.7	0 09.8	10	291.9	LH · – · · · · · ·	4	A2A
78	Pointe de Ver Lt. Ho. ……	49 20.5	0 31.2	20	291.9	éR · · – · · · · – ·	5	A2A
81	Pointe de Barfleur Lt. ……	49 41.9	1 15.9	70	291.9	FG · · – · – – ·	6	A2A

REED'S STN. No.	STATION NAME AND GROUPING	LAT. North ° ´	LONG. West ° ´	RANGE AND FREQ.		MORSE IDENT.		TRANSMISSION Times/sequence Modes and FOOTNOTES
A24	Bournemouth/Hurn	50 48.0	1 43.7	35	401.5	HRN · · · · · – · – ·	Cont.	NON A2A
A27	Fawley/Hythe	50 51.9	1 23.4	20	370	FAW · – · · – · – –	Cont.	NON A2A
A28	Bembridge	50 40.6	1 05.9		276.5	IW · · · – –	Cont.	NON A2A
84	Chichester Bar Bn.	50 45.9	0 56.4	10	303.4	CH – · – · · · · ·	1, 4	c A2A
87	Brighton Marina	50 48.7	0 06.0	10	303.4	BM – · · · – –	2, 5	A2A
90	Newhaven	50 46.9	0 03.5	10	303.4	NH – · · · · ·	3, 6	A2A
93	Poole Harbour	50 41.0	1 56.7	10	303.4	PO · – – · – – –	3, 6	A2A
96	Nab Lt.	50 40.1	0 57.1	10	312.6	NB – · – · · ·	1, 3, 5	A2A
99	Cherbourg (Fort de l'Ouest) Lt. Ho.	49 40.5	1 38.9	20	312.6	RB · – · – · · ·	2, 4, 6	A2A
			East					
A31	Lydd	50 58.2	0 57.3	15	397	LYX · – · · – · – – – · –	j	NON A2A
105	Royal Sovereign Lt.	50 43.4	0 26.1	50	310.3	RY · – · – · – –	2	A2A
108	Pointe d'Ailly	49 55.0	0 57.6	50	310.3	AL · – · – · ·	4	A2A
111	Cap d'Alprech Lt.	50 42.0	1 33.8	20	310.3	PH · – – · · · · ·	1, 3, 5	A2A
117	Dungeness Lt.	50 54.8	0 58.7	30	310.3	DU – · · · · · –	6	A2A
A111	Le Havre/Octeville	49 35.8	0 11.0	15	346	LHO · – · · · · · · · – –	Cont.	A2A
A117	Le Touquet	50 32.1	1 35.4	20	358	LT · – · · –	Cont.	A2A
A120	Calais/Dunkerque	50 59.9	2 03.3	15	275	MK – – – · –	Cont.	A1A
A122	Ostend	51 11.7	2 50.2	25	352.5	DD – · · – · ·	Cont.	A2A
A123	Ostend	51 12.3	2 54.0	25	375	OO – – – – – –	Cont.	A2A
A124	Ostend	51 13.1	2 59.9	50	399.5	ONO – – – – · – · · ·	Cont.	A2A
120	Falls Lt. V.	51 18.1	1 48.5	50	305.7	FS · · – · · · ·	1	A2A
126	West Hinder Lt. V.	51 23.0	2 26.3	20	305.7	WH · – – · · · ·	3	A2A
129	Ostend Rear Lt. Ho.	51 14.4	2 56.0	30	305.7	OE – – – ·	4	A2A
132	Calais Main Lt.	50 57.7	1 51.3	20	305.7	CS – · – · · · · ·	5	A2A
138	North Foreland Lt. Ho.	51 22.5	1 26.9	50	301.1	NF – · · · · – ·	Cont.	A2A
A33	Southend	51 34.6	0 42.1	20	362.5	SND · · · – · · – · ·	Cont.	NON A2A
141	Sunk Lt. F.	51 51.0	1 35.0	10	312.6	UK · · – – · –	Cont.	R A2A
147	Dunkerque Lanby	51 03.1	1 51.8	10	294.2	DK – · · – · –	Cont.	A2A
150	Zeebrugge Mole Lt. Ho.	51 20.9	3 12.3	5	296.5	ZB – – · · – – ·	1, 2	A2A
153	Nieuwpoort W. Pier Lt.	51 09.4	2 43.1	5	296.5	NP – · · – – ·	4, 5	A2A
156	Smiths Knoll Lt. V.	52 43.5	2 18.0	50	287.3	SK · · · – · –	1	R A2A
159	Goeree Lt. Tr.	51 55.5	3 40.2	50	287.3	GR – – · · – ·	2	A2A
162	Dudgeon Lt. V.	53 16.6	1 17.0	50	287.3	LV · – · · · · · –	3	R A2A
165	Outer Gabbard Lt. V.	51 59.4	2 04.6	50	287.3	GA – – · · – ·	4	A2A
168	Cromer Lt. Ho.	52 55.5	1 19.1	50	287.3	CM – · – · – –	5	A2A
171	Noord Hinder Lt. V.	52 00.2	2 51.2	50	287.3	NR – · · – ·	6	R A2A

GREAT BRITAIN AND IRELAND – See Diagram 'B'

REED'S STN. No.	STATION NAME AND GROUPING	LAT. North ° ′	LONG. West ° ′	RANGE AND FREQ.	MORSE IDENT.	TRANSMISSION Times/sequence Modes and FOOTNOTES
A36	Gt. Yarmouth/N. Denes ...	52 38.2	1 43.5	15	397	ND –· –··	Cont. NON A2A
A39	Ottringham	53 41.9	0 06.1	30	398.5	OTR –––– ·–·	Cont. NON A2A
177	Inchkeith Lt.	56 02.0	3 08.1	10	296.5	NK –· –·–	Cont. A2A
179	Fidra Lt.	56 04.4	2 47.0	10	289.6	FD ··–· –··	Cont. A2A
181	Souter Lt.	54 58.2	1 21.8	70	303.4	SJ ··· ·–––	1, 4 A2A
183	Flamborough Hd. Lt. Ho. ...	54 07.0	0 04.9	70	303.4	FB ··–· –···	2 A2A
189	Longstone Lt. Ho.	55 38.6	1 36.6	20	303.4	LT ·–·· –	5 A2A
198	Fife Ness Lt.	56 16.7	2 35.1	100⁄70	303.4	FP ··–· ·––·	6 A2A
A42	Leuchars	56 22.3	2 51.4	100	330	LU ·–·· ··–	Cont. NON A2A
195	Girdle Ness Lt.	57 08.3	2 02.8	50	310.3	GD ––· –··	Cont. A2A
A45	Scotstown Head	57 33.6	1 48.9	80	383	SHD ··· ···· –··	Cont. NON A2A
A48	Kinloss	57 39.0	3 34.8	50	370	KS –·– ···	Cont. NON A2A
A51	Wick	58 26.8	3 03.7	40	344	WIK ·–– ·· –·–	Cont. NON A2A
204	Kinnairds Head Lt. Ho.	57 41.9	2 00.1	100⁄70	291.9	KD –·– –···	1, 4 A2A
207	N. Ronaldsay Lt. Ho.	59 23.4	2 22.8	100⁄70	291.9	NR –·· ·–·	2 R A2A
210	Stroma-Swilkie Pt. Lt. Ho.	58 41.8	3 06.9	50	291.9	OM ––– ––	3, 6 A2A
213	Sumburgh Head..............	59 51.3	1 16.4	70	291.9	SB ··· –···	5 A2A
A54	Sumburgh	59 52.1	1 16.3	75	351	SUM ··· ··– –––	Cont. NON A2A
216	Bressay Lt. Ho. Shetlands	60 07.3	1 07.2	30	287.3	BY –··· –·––	Cont. A2A
A57	Scatsa	60 27.7	1 12.8	25	315.5	SS ·····	Cont. NON A2A
219	Akraberg Lt. (Faeroes)	61 23.6	6 40.3	100	381	AB ·– –···	Cont. g NON A2A
222	Nolsø Lt. (Faeroes)	61 57.5	6 36.3	100	404	NL –· ·–··	Cont. g A2A
225	Myggenaes (Faeroes)	62 06.4	7 35.1	100	337	MY –– –·––	Cont. g A2A
A60	Dounreay/Thurso	58 34.9	3 43.6	15	364.5	DO –·· –––	Cont. NON A2A
228	Cape Wrath Lt. Ho.	58 37.6	4 59.9	50	298.8	CW –·–· ·––	1 A2A
231	Butt of Lewis Lt. Ho.	58 30.9	6 15.7	150	298.8	BL –··· ·–··	2, 5 A2A
234	Muckle Flugga Lt. Ho. (N. Uist.)	60 51.3	0 53.0	150⁄70	298.8	MF –– ··–·	3, 6 A2A
237	Sule Skerry Lt. Ho.	59 05.1	4 24.3	100⁄70	298.8	LK ·–·· –·–	4 R A2A
A61	Stornoway	58 17.2	6 20.6	60	669.5	SWY ··· ·–– –·––	Cont. NON A2A
240	Pladda Lt., Arran I............	55 25.5	5 07.1	30	294.2	DA –·· ·–	1 A2A
243	Mew Island Lt. Ho.	54 41.9	5 30.8	50	294.2	MW –– ·––	2 A2A
246	Altacarry Head Lt. Ho. (Rathlin East)	55 18.1	6 10.2	50	294.2	AH ·– ····	3 A2A
249	Rinns of Islay	55 40.4	6 30.7	70	294.2	RN ·–· –·	4 A2A
252	Hyskeir Lt., Oigh Sgeir	56 58.1	6 40.8	50	294.2	OR ––– ·–·	5 A2A
255	Eileen Glas Lt. Ho............	57 51.4	6 38.5	50	294.2	LG ·–·· ––·	6 R A2A

FOOTNOTES – See page 19:22

RADIOBEACONS
GREAT BRITAIN AND IRELAND

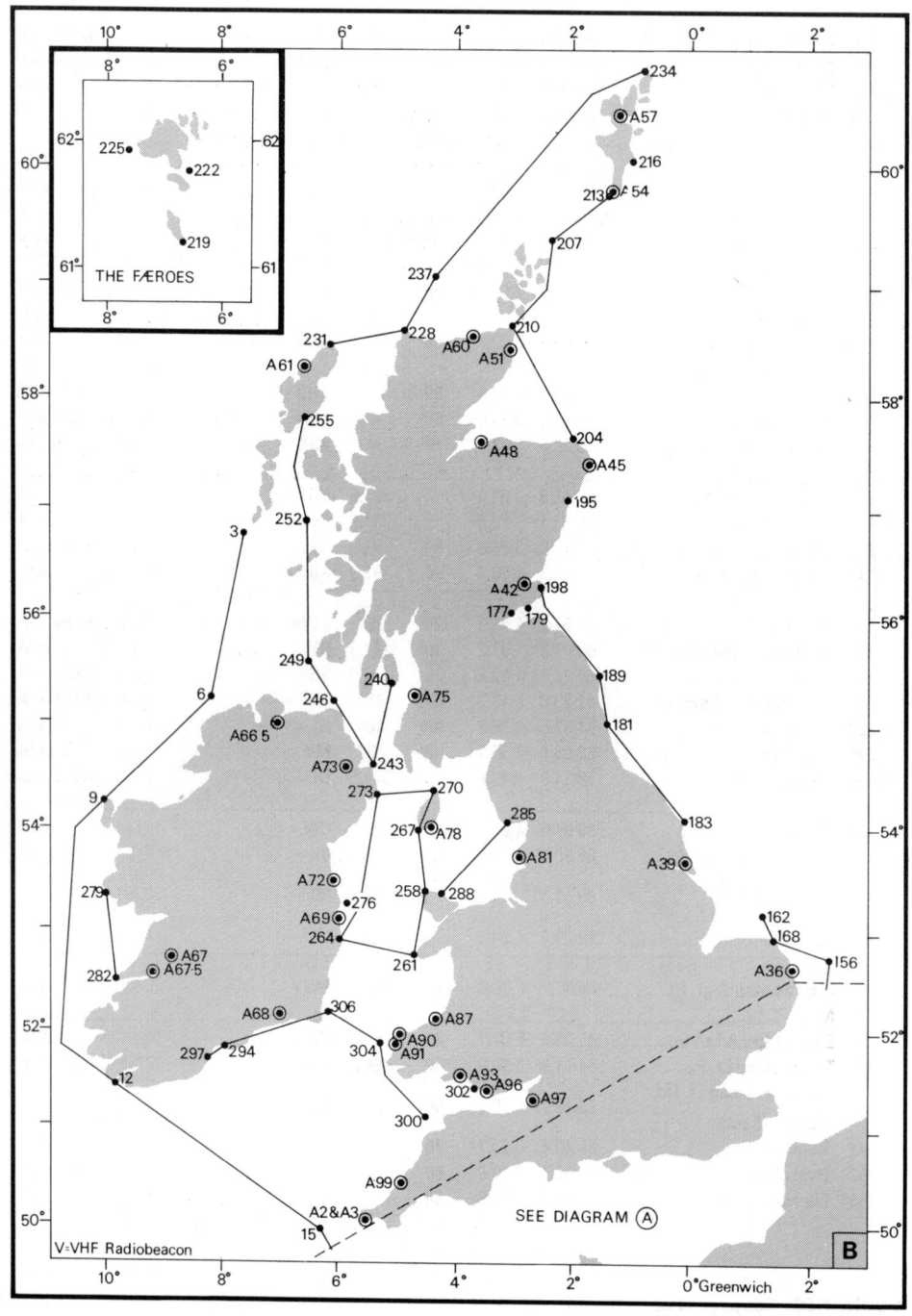

See Diagram 'B' – GREAT BRITAIN AND IRELAND Continued

REED'S STN. No.	STATION NAME AND GROUPING	LAT. North ° '	LONG. West ° '	RANGE AND FREQ.		MORSE IDENT.		TRANSMISSION Times/sequence Modes and FOOTNOTES
A66.5	Londonderry	55 02.7	7 09.3	25	328.5	EGT · --· -		j NON A2A
A67	Shannon/Bunratty	52 41.8	8 49.3	100	352	BNY -··· -· -·--	Cont.	NON A2A
A67.5	Foynes	52 34.0	9 11.7	50	395	FOY ··-· -----·--	Cont.	NON A2A
A68	Waterford	52 11.8	7 05.3	25	368	WTD ··-----··	Cont.	
A69	Killiney	53 16.2	6 06.3	50	378	KLY -·-··-·-·---	Cont.	NON A2A
A72	Dublin/Rush	53 30.7	6 06.6	30	326	RSH ·-··········	Cont.	A2A
A73	Belfast	54 37.0	5 52.9	15	275	HB ···· -···	Cont.	NON A2A
258	Skerries Lt. Ho.	53 25.3	4 36.5	50	301.1	SR ··· -·	1	A2A
261	Bardsey Lt.	52 45.0	4 47.9	30	301.1	IB ·· -···	2	A2A
264	Wicklow Head Lt.	52 57.9	5 59.8	70	301.1	WK ·-- -·-	3	A2A
267	Cregneish (I.o.M.)	54 03.9	4 45.9	50	301.1	CN -·-· -·	4	A2A
270	Point of Ayre Lt.	54 25.0	4 22.0	50	301.1	PY ·--· -·--	5	R A2A
273	South Rock Lt. V.	54 24.5	5 21.9	50	301.1	SU ···· ··-	6	A2A
276	Kish Bank Lt.	53 18.7	5 55.4	20	312.6	KH -·- ····	Cont.	R A2A
279	Slyne Head Lt.	53 24.0	10 14.0	50	289.6	SN ··· -·	1, 3, 5	A2A
282	Loop Head Lt.	52 33.7	9 55.9	50	289.6	LP ·-·· ·--·	2, 4, 6	A2A
A75	Turnberry	55 18.8	4 47.0	25	355	TRN - ··-· -··	Cont.	NON A2A
A78	Ronaldsway (I.o.M.)	54 05.2	4 36.5	20	359	RWY ·-· ·-- -·--		j NON A2A
A81	Blackpool	53 46.2	2 59.3	15	276.5	BPL -··· ·--· ·-··	Cont.	NON A2A
285	Walney Island Lt.	54 02.9	3 10.5	30	287.3	FN ··-· -·	1, 4	A2A
288	Point Lynas Lt.	53 25.0	4 17.3	40	287.3	PS ·--· ···	2, 5	A2A
A87	Aberporth	52 07.0	4 33.6	20	370.5	AP ·- ·--·	Cont.	NON A2A
A90	Strumble	52 00.5	5 01.0	40	400	STU ··· - ··-	Cont.	NON A2A
A91	Brawdy	51 53.4	5 07.3	30	414.5	BY -··· -·--		NON A2A
A93	Swansea	51 36.1	4 03.9	15	320.5	SWN ··· ·-- -·		j NON A2A
A96	Cardiff	51 23.6	3 20.2	20	363.5	CDF -·-· -·· ··-·	Cont.	NON A2A
A97	Weston Super Mare	51 20.3	2 56.3	15	390.5	WS ·-- ···		m NON A2A
A99	St. Mawgan	50 26.9	4 59.6	50	356.5	SM ··· --	Cont.	NON A2A
294	Ballycotton Lt.	51 49.6	7 59.1	50	296.5	BN -··· -·	1	A2A
297	Old Head of Kinsale Lt.	51 36.3	8 32.0	50	296.5	OH --- ····	2	A2A
300	Lundy I. South Lt. Ho.	51 09.7	4 39.3	50	296.5	LS ·-·· ···	3	e A2A
302	Nash Pt. Lt.	51 24.0	3 33.1	50	296.5	NP -· ·--·	4	A2A
304	South Bishop Lt. Ho.	51 51.2	5 24.7	50	296.5	SB ··· -···	5	A2A
306	Tuskar Rock Lt. Ho.	52 12.2	6 12.4	50	296.5	TR - ·-·	6	R A2A

FOOTNOTES – See page 19:22

REED'S STN. No.	STATION NAME AND GROUPING	LAT. North ° ′	LONG. East ° ′	RANGE AND FREQ.		MORSE IDENT.	TRANSMISSION Times/sequence Modes and FOOTNOTES	
A126	Valkenburg/Scheveningen	52 05.7	4 15.2	25	364	GV -- · ···-	Cont.	NON A2A
A129	Amsterdam/Spijkerboor ...	52 32.5	4 50.5	75	381	SPY ··· ·--· -·--	Cont.	NON A2A
309	Ijmuiden Front Lt.	52 27.8	4 34.6	20	294.2	YM -·-- --	1, 4	A2A
312	Hoek van Holland	51 58.9	4 06.8	20	294.2	HH ···· ····	2, 5	A2A
315	Eierland Lt. Ho.	53 11.0	4 51.4	20	294.2	ER · ·-·	3, 6	a A2A
318	Vlieland Lt.	53 17.8	5 03.6	70	308.0	VL ···- ·-··	1	A2A
324	Deutsche Bucht Lt. Float...	54 10.7	7 26.1	50	308.0	DB -·· -···	4	R A2A
327	Texel Lt. V.	52 47.1	4 06.6	50	308.0	HK ···· -·-	5	R A2A
330	Elbe Lt. Float	54 00.0	8 06.6	10	308.0	EL · ·-··	6	R A2A
333	Ameland Lt. Ho.	53 27.0	5 37.6	20	298.8	AD ·- -··	1, 3, 5	a A2A
336	Borkum Little Lt. Ho.	53 34.8	6 40.1	20	298.8	BE -··· ·	2, 4, 6	A2A
339	Wangerooge Lt. Ho.	53 47.5	7 51.5	30	291.9	WE ·-- ·	1, 3, 5	A2A
342	Alte Weser Lt.	53 51.9	8 07.7	10	291.9	AR ·- ·-·	2, 4, 6,	A2A
A135	Nordholz	53 47.2	8 48.5	30	372	NDO -· -·· ---	Cont.	NON A2A
345	Kampen Rote Kliff Lt. Ho. (Sylt)	54 56.9	8 20.5	20	301.1	RF ·-· ··-·	1, 3, 5	A2A
348	Grosser Vogelsand Lt.	53 59.8	8 28.7	10	301.1	VS ···- ···	2, 4, 6	A2A
A141	Westerland/Sylt.............	54 51.4	8 24.7	25	286	SLT ··· ·-·· -	Cont.	NON A2A
A142	Donna, Dan Oilfield	55 28.2	5 08.1	75	355	DON -·· --- -·	Cont.	NON A2A
A143	Tor Oilfield Ekofisk	56 38.5	3 19.8		375	TR - ·-·	Cont.	NON A2A
351	Helgoland Lt.	54 11.0	7 53.0	100	397.2	DHE -·· ···· ·	Cont.	f A1A
354	Thyboron Lt. Ho.	56 42.5	8 13.0	30	289.6	TN - -·	Cont.	A2A
357	Hanstholm Lt.	57 06.8	8 36.0	$\frac{100}{70}$	296.5	HM ···· --	1, 4	A2A
360	Lista Lt.	58 06.6	6 34.2	$\frac{100}{70}$	296.5	LA ·-·· ·-	2, 5	A2A
363	Blaavandshuk Lt.	55 33.5	8 05.1	$\frac{100}{70}$	296.5	BH -··· ····	3, 6	A2A
366	Hirtshals Havn Front Lt. ...	57 35.7	9 57.7	10	406	IR ·· ·-·	Cont.	A2A
369	Hirsholm Main Lt. Ho.	57 29.2	10 37.5	30	301.1	HO ···· ---	1, 4	A2A
372	Hatte Berget Lt.	57 51.8	11 27.7	30	301.1	BG -··· --·	2, 5	A2A
373	Trubaduren Lt.	57 35.7	11 38.1	30	301.1	TU - ··-	3, 6	fR A2A
375	Frederikshaven NE Breakwater Lt. Ho.	57 26.0	10 33.4	10	414	FK ··-· -·-		a A2A
378	Laesø Rende Lt.	57 13.2	10 40.4	30	310.3	LR ·-·· ·-·	1, 3, 5	R A2A
381	Hals Barre Lt.	56 57.3	10 25.6	50	310.3	HB ···· -···	2, 4, 6	R A2A

RADIOBEACONS
NOORD HINDER TO BALTIC ENTRANCE

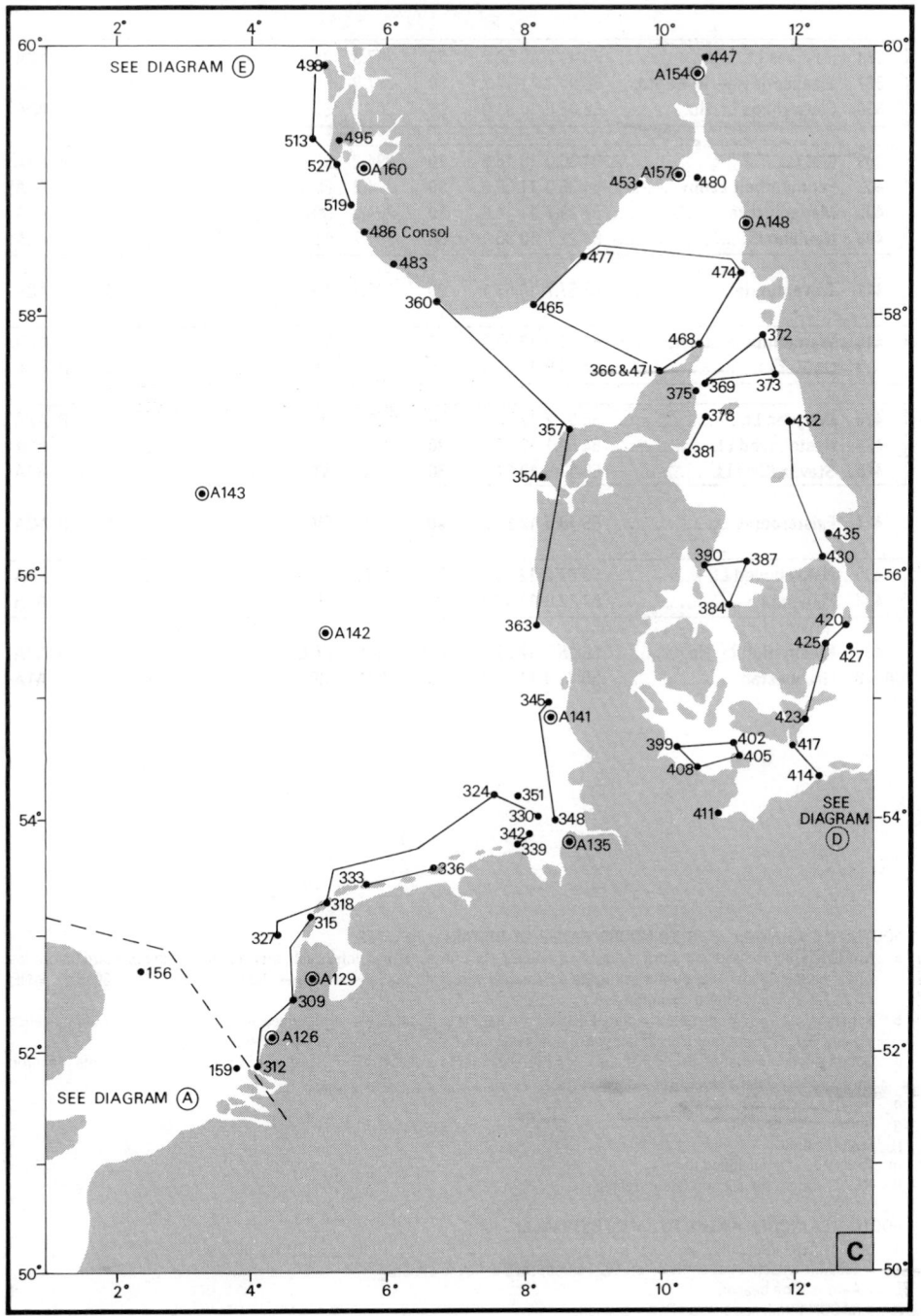

REED'S STN. No.	STATION NAME AND GROUPING	LAT. North ° '	LONG. East ° '	RANGE AND FREQ.	MORSE IDENT.	TRANSMISSION Times/sequence Modes and FOOTNOTES	
384	Rosnaes Lt.	55 44.7	10 52.2	30	287.3	RS · — · · · ·	1, 4	A2A
387	Sjaellands Rev. N. Lt. Ho.	56 06.1	11 12.2	30	287.3	SG · · · — — ·	2, 5	R A2A
390	Sletterhage Lt. Ho.	56 05.8	10 31.0	50	287.3	SL · · · · — · ·	3, 6	A2A
399	Kiel Lt.	54 30.0	10 16.5	10	294.2	KI — · — · ·	1, 4	R A2A
402	Fehmarnbelt Lanby	54 36.0	11 09.0	30	294.2	FE · · — · ·	2, 5	cR A2A
405	Marienluchte	54 29.7	11 14.3	30	294.2	MR — — · — ·	2, 5	c A2A
408	Neuland Lt.	54 21.7	10 36.1	30	294.2	NL — · · — · ·	3, 6	A2A
411	Travemunde	53 57.7	10 53.1	20	301.1	TD — · ·	1, 3, 5	A2A
414	Warnemunde Lt.	54 10.9	12 05.3	20	303.4	WN · — — — ·	1, 3, 5	A2A
417	Gedser Lt.	54 33.9	11 57.9	30	303.4	GR — — · · — ·	2, 4, 6	R A2A
420	Drogden Lt.	55 32.2	12 42.7	20	308	DG — · · — — ·	1, 4	R A2A
423	Hestehoved Lt.	54 50.1	12 10.1	30	308	HE · · · · ·	2	A2A
425	Stevns Klint Lt.	55 17.5	12 27.5	50	308	ST · · · —	5	A2A
427	Falsterborev Lt.	55 18.5	12 39.5	40	289.6	FV · · — · · · · —	2, 4, 6	R A2A
430	Nakkehoved Lt.	56 07.2	12 20.8	50	294.2	NA — · · —	1, 4	A2A
432	Fladen Lt.	57 12.9	11 49.8	30	294.2	FL · · — · · — · ·	2, 5	A2A
435	Kullen High Lt. Ho.	56 18.1	12 27.3	100	344	KUL — · — · · — · — · ·	Cont.	f A2A
A148	Grebbestad	58 41.9	11 14.7	50	277	GRE — — · · — · ·	Cont.	A1A

FOOTNOTES (CHANNEL APPR. TO NOORD HINDER/GT. BRITAIN & IRELAND)
a   No. 48 is synchronised with horn for distance finding. CB 4 times, 18 sec. long dash, then 13 pips. Each pip heard before fog signal equals 335m. Also during sequence 6 transmits wind information CB 4 times (500Hz) up to 8 dots (1000Hz) 1 = NE, 8 = N. Up to 8 dots (500Hz) Beaufort 1–8.
b   Synchro with horn for distance finding. Blast of horn begins simultaneously with 27 sec. long dash after 4 × GY identification signals. No. of secs. from start of long dash until blast heard (× 0.18) is distance from horn.
c   Coded Wind information Broadcast: CH × 4: 4 sec. Dash: up to 8 dashes (1 = NE to 8 = N): 4 sec. Dash: up to 8 dots (Beaufort 1 – 8): 12 sec. Dash: CH × 2: 5 sec. silence.
e   Reliable sector 234° – 216°.
g   Aero-marine beacon.
j   Daytime only.
m   Transmits at unspecified times.
R   RACON fitted, see section Radar Beacons.

FOOTNOTES (NOORD HINDER TO BALTIC ENTRANCE)
a   = Transmits in fog only.
c   = 405 Marienluchte transmits when 402 Fehmarnbelt Lanby is off air.
f   = Aero-marine beacon.
R   = RACON fitted, see section Radar Beacons.

RADIOBEACONS
SOUTHERN BALTIC

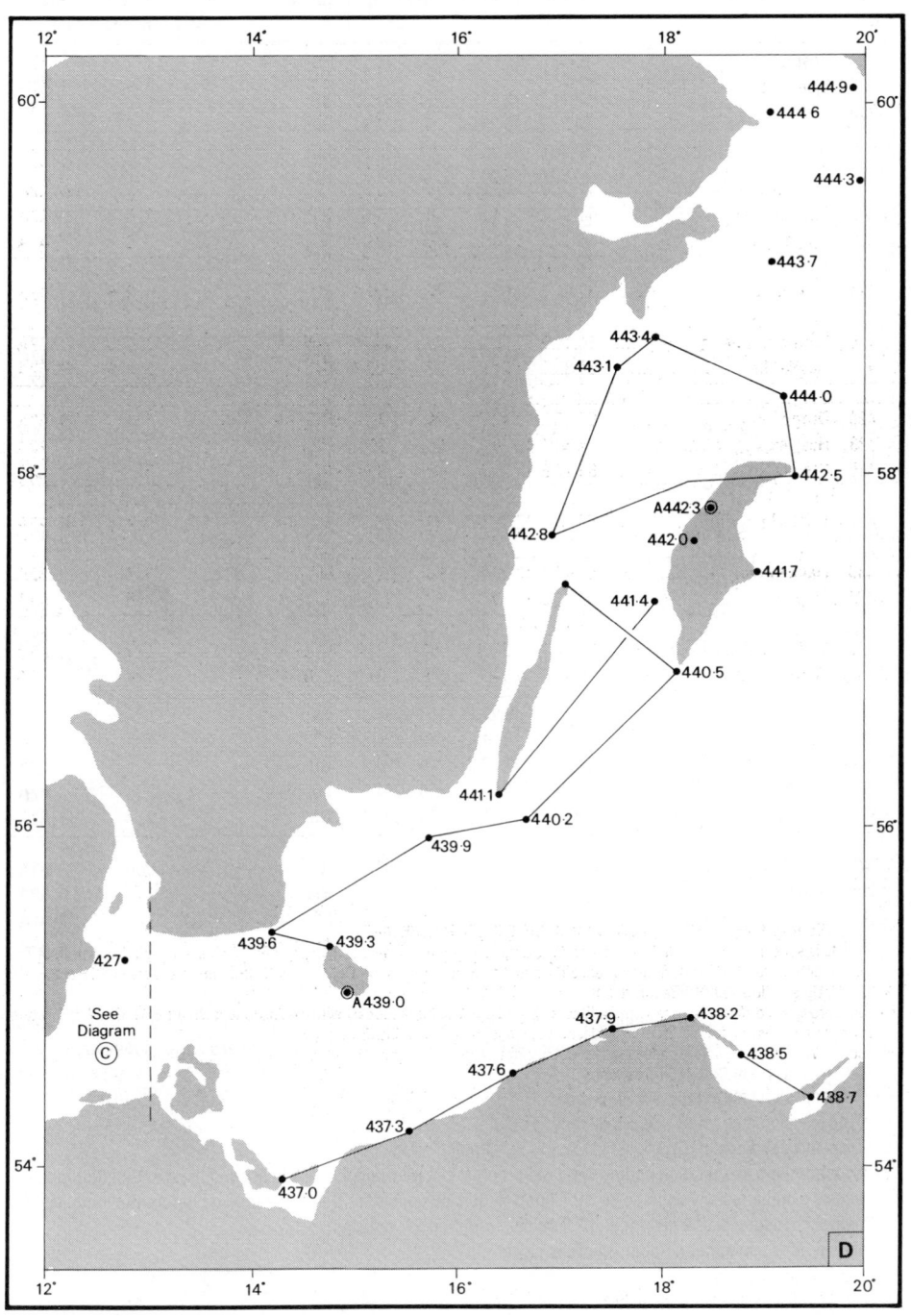

SOUTHERN BALTIC See Diagram 'D'

REEDS STN. No.	Station name and grouping	Lat. North ° ′	Long. East ° ′	Range and Freq.	Morse Ident.	Transmission times/sequence	modes & footnotes
437.0	Swinoujscie Main Lt	53 55.0	14 17.2	50 287.3	OD — — — —·	5	A2A
437.3	Kolobrzeg Lt	54 11.3	15 33.6	50 287.3	KB —·— —···	4	A2A
437.6	Jaroslawiec	54 32.7	16 33.0	50 287.3	JA ·——— ·—	3	A2A
437.9	Leba Rear Lt	54 46.0	17 33.3	50 287.3	LE ·—·· ·	2	A2A
438.2	Rozewie	54 50.0	18 20.1	50 287.3	RO ·—· ———	1	A2A
438.5	Hel Lt	54 36.1	18 48.9	50 310.3	HL ···· ·—··	5,6	ab, A2A
438.7	Krynica Morska Lt	54 23.2	19 27.2	50 310.3	KM —·— ——	3,4	c A2A
A 439.0	Ronne, Fauna	55 01.7	14 54.1	50 334	FAU ··—· ·— ··—	Cont	NON A2A
439.3	Hammerodde Lt, Bornholm	55 18.0	14 46.4	50 298.8	MN —— —·	3	A2A
439.6	Sandhammaren Lt	55 23.2	14 12.0	40 298.8	SM ··· ——	5	A2A
439.9	Utklippan Main Lt	55 57.2	15 42.3	50 298.8	UK ··— —·—	1	A2A
440.2	Olands Sodra Grund Lt	56 04.1	16 40.9	70 298.8	ÖG ———· ——·	6	R A2A
440.5	Hoburg Lt	56 55.4	18 09.2	70 298.8	OB ——— —···	4	A2A
440.8	Olands Norra Udde Lt	57 22.0	17 06.0	70 298.8	NO —· ———	2	A2A
441.1	Olands Sodra Udde Lt	56 11.8	16 24.0	20 308	SÖ ··· ———·	3,6	d, A2A
441.4	Stora Karlse Lt	57 17.4	17 57.8	40 308	KS —·— ···	1,4	c, A2A
441.7	Ostergarn East Lt	57 26.7	18 59.4	50 305.7	ÖN ———· —·	5,6	A2A
442.0	Visby Approach Lt	57 38.1	18 16.6	10 406	VY ···— —·——	Cont	A2A
A 442.3	Visby	57 43.9	18 23.9	25 351	OV ——— ···—	Cont	NON A2A
442.5	Faro	57 57.7	19 21.1	50 294.2	FA ··—· ·—	1	A2A
442.8	Kungsgrundet Lt	57 41.1	16 54.4	30 294.2	KT —·— —	4	A2A
443.1	Gustav Dalen Lt	58 35.7	17 28.3	40 294.2	GD ——· —··	3	A2A
443.4	Landsort South Lt	58 44.4	17 52.2	50 294.2	LO ·—·· ———	2	A2A
444.0	Gotska Sandon NW Lt	58 23.6	19 11.8	50 294.2	GS ——· ···	5	A2A
443.7	Almagrundet Lt	59 09.3	19 07.8	70 309	AL ·— ·—··	Cont	A1A
444.3	Svenska Bjorn Lt	59 32.9	20 01.5	50 301.1	BN —··· —·	3	R A2A
444.6	Simpnasklubb Lt	59 53.6	19 05.0	30 314.5	SS ··· ···	2,4,6	R A1A
444.9	Korso Front Lt	60 02.4	19 54.0	60 296.5	KO —·— ———	1,4	e, A2A

FOOTNOTES (SOUTHERN BALTIC)

a= Synchronised for distance finding. The nautophone begins simultaneously with the beginning of the group of 15 dashes of the radio beacon. Each dash received before the nautophone is heard corresponds to a distance of 2.5 cables from the station

b= Transmission times H+04, 10, 34, 40 only

c= Transmission times H+02, 08, 32, 38 only

d= Transmission times H+02, 05, 08, 11, 32, 35, 38, 41 only

e= Synchronised for distance finding with a nautophone at Marhallan Lt. The 6 second blast of the nautophone begins simultaneously with the 30 KO signals in quick time. Each KO signal, received before the long blast is heard corresponds to a distance of 2.5 cables from Marhallan Lt.

R= Racon fitted see section Radar Beacons

NORWAY & ICELAND – See Diagram 'C' and 'E'

REED'S STN. No.	STATION NAME AND GROUPING	LAT. North ° '	LONG. East ° '	RANGE AND FREQ.	MORSE IDENT.	TRANSMISSION Times/sequence Modes and FOOTNOTES
447	Dyna Lt. Oslofjord	59 53.7	10 41.4	10	287.3 DY –·· –·–	ab A2A
A154	Steilene NE Lt.	59 49.1	10 35.9	30	335 FO ··–· ·–·–	Cont. NON A2A
453	Langoytangen Lt.	58 59.6	9 45.5	20	289.6 LN ·–·· –·	Cont. A2A
A157	Sandefjord/Torp	59 04.7	10 15.9	50	283 TP – ·–––·	Cont. NON A2A
465	Oksoy Lt.	58 04.4	8 03.3	50	305.7 KY –·– –·––	1 A2A
468	Skagen W. Lt.	57 45.0	10 35.8	50	305.7 SW ··· ·––	2 A2A
471	Hirtshals Lt.	57 35.0	9 57.0	50	305.7 LS ·–·· ···	3 A2A
474	Hallo Lt.	58 20.2	11 13.2	50	305.7 LL ·–·· ·–··	4 A2A
477	Torungen Lt.	58 24.0	8 47.5	50	305.7 TO – –––	5 A2A
480	Faerder Lt.	59 01.6	10 31.6	50	312.6 FR ··–· ·–·	Cont. R A2A
483	Skarvoy Lt., Egersund	58 24.4	5 59.3	10	301.1 GE ––· ·	Cont. A2A
486	Stavanger Consol	58 37.6	5 37.7	1.5kW	319 LEC ·–·· · ––··	Cont. A1A
A160	Rennesoy	59 07.8	5 39.0		378 RSY ·–· ··· –·––	Cont. NON A2A
495	Tresvikpynten	59 16.4	5 19.8	10	301.1 TN – –·	Cont. A2A
498	Slatteroy Lt. Selbjornfjord	59 54.5	5 04.1	10	289.6 SL ··· ·–··	Cont. A2A
501	Holmengra Lt.	60 50.6	4 39.1	20	294.2 HG ···· ––·	Cont. R A2A
A163	Reksten	61 33.8	4 51.2	50	379 REK ·–· · –·–	Cont. NON A2A
507	Hendanes Lt. Vagsoy	61 57.9	5 02.2	10	308.0 HD ···· –··	Cont. A2A
510	Svinoy Lt.	62 19.7	5 16.4	$\frac{100}{70}$	296.5 SY ··· –·––	Cont. A2A
513	Utsira Lt.	59 18.5	4 52.3	$\frac{100}{70}$	312.6 UT ··– –	2 A2A
516	Marstein Lt.	60 07.9	5 00.7	50	312.6 MA –– ·–	3 A2A
519	Feistein	58 49.6	5 30.4	50	312.6 FN ··–· –·	4 R A2A
527	Geitungane	59 07.9	5 14.7	50	312.6 GU ––· ··–	6 A2A
526	Utvaer Lt.	61 02.2	4 30.9	$\frac{100}{70}$	310.3 VR ···– ·–·	Cont. A2A
531	Halten Lt.	64 10.3	9 24.9	50	294.2 HA ···· ·–	Cont. A2A
534	Bjornsund Lt.	62 53.8	6 49.0	50	301.1 BJ –··· ·–––	Cont. R A2A
A166	Uthaug	63 43.4	9 34.8	0.1kW	366 UTH ··– – ····	Cont. NON A2A
A169	Tarva	63 49.5	9 25.6		349 TAR – ·–· ·–·	Cont. NON A2A
537	Buholmrasa Lt.	64 24.2	10 27.7	20	308 BU –··· ··–	Cont. A2A
543	Skomvaer Lt. Rost	67 24.7	11 52.6	$\frac{100}{70}$	289.6 SK ··· –·–	Cont. A2A
546	Tennholmen Lt.	67 18.1	13 30.3	50	310.3 HO ···· –––	Cont. A2A
549	Sklinna Lt.	65 12.1	11 00.2	$\frac{100}{70}$	298.8 KL –·– ·–··	Cont. A2A
A172	Stott	66 55.8	13 27.0	0.1kW	317 STT ··· – –	Cont. NON A2A
A175	Fleinvaer	67 09.6	13 47.0		374 FLV ··–· ·–·· ···–	Cont. NON A2A
552	Landegode Lt.	67 26.9	14 23.2	10	308 LG ·–·· ––·	Cont. A2A
558	Skrova Lt.	68 09.3	14 39.5	$\frac{100}{70}$	291.9 KN –·– –·	Cont. ef A2A
564	Hekkingen Lt.	69 36.1	17 50.4	50	303.4 HK ···· –·–	Cont. A2A
A182	Andenes, Andoya	69 19.1	16 06.3		343.5 ANY ·– –· –·––	Cont. NON A2A

RADIOBEACONS
NORWAY & ICELAND

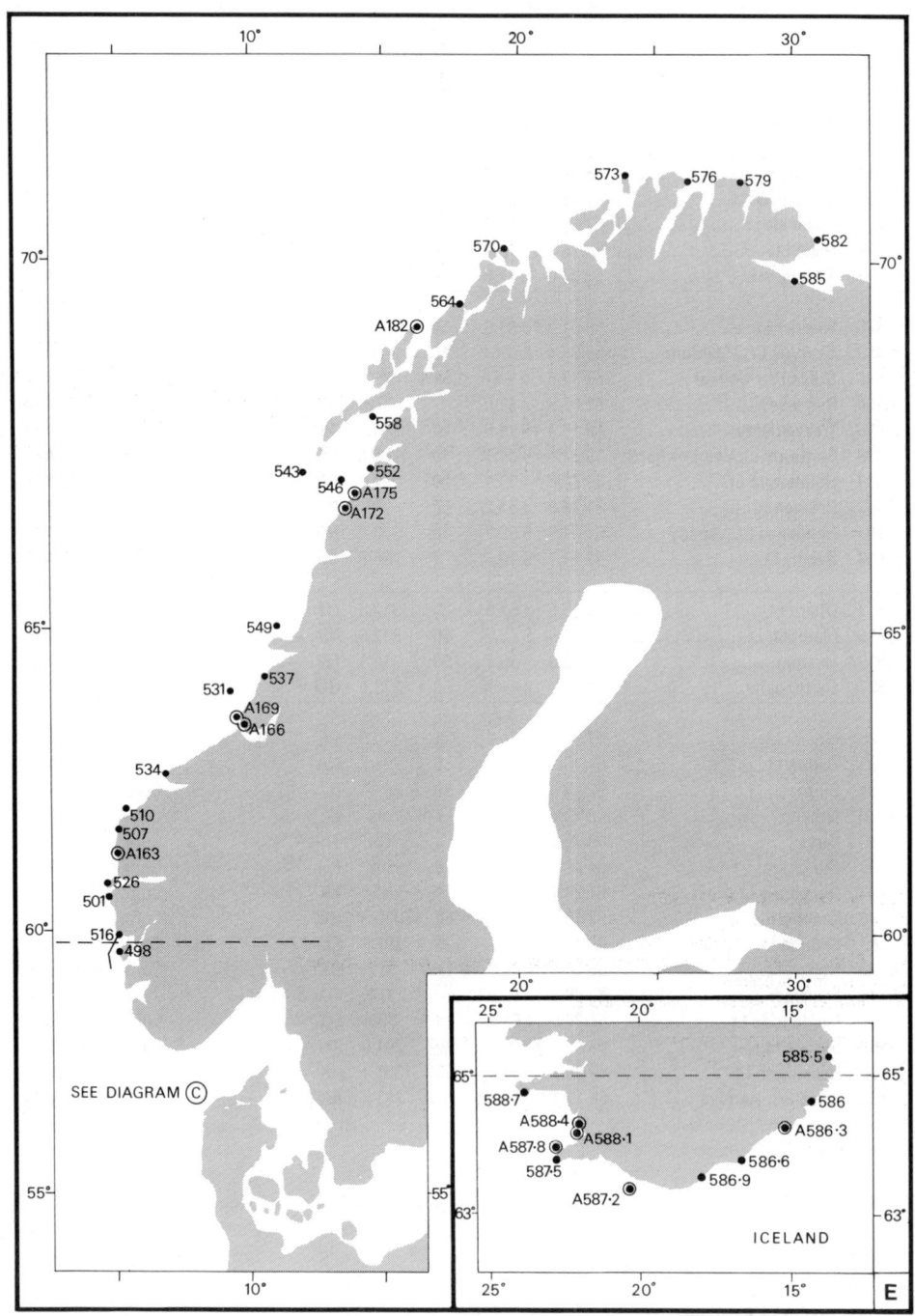

MARINE AND AERONAUTICAL RADIOBEACONS 19:27

NORWAY & ICELAND – See Diagrams 'C' and 'E'

REED'S STN. No.	STATION NAME AND GROUPING	LAT. North ° '	LONG. East ° '	RANGE AND FREQ.	MORSE IDENT.	TRANSMISSION Times/sequence Modes and FOOTNOTES
570	Torsvag Lt. Koja	70 14.7	19 30.6	50	312.6	TG – –– ·	Cont.	A2A
573	Fruholmen Lt.	71 05.6	23 59.5	50	287.3	FH · · –· ·· · ·	Cont.	A2A
576	Helnes Lt. Mageroy	71 03.7	26 13.4	50	308.0	HS · · · · · · ·	Cont.	f A2A
579	Sletnes Lt.	71 05.4	28 13.6	50	301.1	SN · · · –·	Cont.	f A2A
582	Vardo Lt. Hornoy	70 23.4	31 10.1	70	294.2	VD · · · – –· ·	Cont.	A2A
585	Bokfjord Lt. Hungerneset	69 52.6	30 10.7	50	289.6	BØ –· · · ––– ·	Cont.	A2A

ICELAND (South of 65°00'N)

West

		LAT. North	LONG. West			
585.5	Dalatangi Lt.	65 16.2	13 34.6	100	305.7	DA –· · · · –	Cont.	f A2A
586	Djupivogur	64 39.1	14 16.6	100/70	298.8	DV –· · · · · –	Cont.	f A2A
A586.3	Hornafjordhur	64 16.2	15 12.8	125	287.3	HN · · · · · –·	Cont.	A2A
586.6	Ingolfshofdhi Lt.	63 48.1	16 38.5	100	316	IN · · –·	Cont.	f A2A
586.9	Skardhsfjara Lt.	63 31.0	17 59.0	100	312.6	SR · · · · –·	Cont.	fR A2A
A587.2	Vestmannaeyjar	63 24.0	20 17.5	125	375	VM · · · ––	Cont.	A2A
587.5	Reykjanes	63 48.9	22 43.0	100	291.9	RN · –· –·	Cont.	f A2A
A587.8	Keflavik, Hvalsnes	63 59.1	22 43.9	150	392	KF –· –· · –·	Cont.	A2A
A588.1	Reykjavik	64 09.1	22 01.8	100	355	RK · –· –· –	Cont.	A2A
A588.4	Skagi	64 18.4	21 58.7	25	379	SA · · · · –·	Cont.	A2A
588.7	Malarrif Lt.	64 43.7	23 48.5	100	303.4	MA –– · –	Cont.	f A2A

FOOTNOTES (NORWAY & ICELAND)
a = Transmits in fog only.
b = In clear weather on request only.
e = Bearings to be used with caution as large and variable errors have been reported.
f = Aero-marine beacon.
R = RACON fitted, see section Radar Beacons.

FOOTNOTES (USHANT TO GIBRALTAR)
c = No: 642 – reliable sector 110°-220°.
d = No: 669 – reliable sector 020°-145°.
e = No: 672 – directional, Northward of beam N – · etc. On beam (width 4°) – continuous note. South-ward of beam A · – etc. Bearing line 069½° towards radiobeacon. The complementary signals, A and N, cannot be clearly distinguished within 7° of this bearing line. On beam range of 20 miles.
The beacon is synchronised with an air fog signal (nautophone located 90 ft. ENE of the light) for distance finding; the first blast of the nautophone begins at the same instant as the identification signal. The stop-watch time (in seconds) elapsing between the beginning of the radio identification signal and reception of the beginning of the first blast of the nautophone, when multiplied by the factor 0.18 gives the distance from the nautophone in nautical miles. Several observations are recommended.
f = Transmits in clear weather only at stated times.
g = Continuous at night or fog only.
R = RACON fitted see section Radar Beacons.

REED'S STN. No.	STATION NAME AND GROUPING	LAT. North ° '	LONG. West ° '	RANGE AND FREQ.	MORSE IDENT.	TRANSMISSION Times/sequence Modes and FOOTNOTES
589	Eckmuhl Lt. Ho. Pte. de Penmarc'h	47 48.0	4 22.4	50	289.6 ÜH · · — — · · · ·	1	A2A
594	Pte. de St. Mathieu Lt. Ho.	48 19.9	4 46.2	20	289.6 SM · · · — —	3	A2A
597	Pte. de Combrit	47 51.9	4 06.7	20	289.6 CT — · — · —	4	A2A
600	Ile de Groix-Pen Men Lt. Ho.	47 38.9	3 30.5	10	301.1 GX — — · — · · —	Cont.	A1A
A184	Lanveoc	48 17.1	4 26.0	80	316 BST — · · · · · · —	Cont.	A1A
A187	Lorient	47 45.8	3 26.4	80	294.2 LOR · — · · — — — · — ·	Cont.	A1A
A190	St. Nazaire/Montoir	47 20.0	2 02.6	50	398 MT — — —	Cont.	A1A
602	St. Nazaire Pte. de St. Gildas Lt.	47 08.1	2 14.7	10	298.8 NZ — · · — — ·	Cont.	A1A
612	Ile de Sein NW Lt.	48 02.7	4 52.0	100	303.4 SN · · · — ·	3	A2A
615	Pte. de la Coubre Lt.	45 41.9	1 13.9	100	303.4 LK · — · · — · —	4	A2A
618	Les Baleines Lt. Ho.	46 14.7	1 33.6	50	303.4 BN — · · · — ·	6	A2A
621	Ile D'Yeu Main Lt. Ho.	46 43.1	2 22.9	70	312.6 YE — · — — ·	3	A2A
624	Ile du Pilier Lt. Ho.	47 02.6	2 21.5	10	298.8 PR · — — · · — ·	Cont.	A2A
627	Les Sables d'Olonne (Tour de la Chaume Lt. Ho.)	46 29.7	1 47.8	5	291.9 SO · · · — — —	Cont.	A2A
633	La Rochelle, Tourelle Richelieu Lt. Ho.	46 09.0	1 10.3	5	291.9 RE · — · ·	Cont.	A1A
A193	San Sebastian	43 23.3	1 47.7	50	328 HIG · · · · — — ·	Cont.	A2A
A196	Bilbao	43 19.5	2 58.3	70	370 BLO — · · · — · — — —	Cont.	A2A
639	Cap Ferret Lt. Ho.	44 38.8	1 14.8	100	296.5 FT · · — · —	1, 2	A2A
642	Cabo Machicharo Lt. Ho.	43 27.5	2 45.1	100	296.5 MA — — · —	3, 4	c A2A
645	Cabo Mayor Lt. Ho.	43 29.5	3 47.4	50	296.5 MY — — — · —	5, 6	A2A
648	Llanes Lt. Ho.	43 25.2	4 44.9	50	301.1 IA · · · —	1, 2	A2A
651	Cabo Penas Lt. Ho.	43 39.4	5 50.8	50	301.1 PS · — — · · · ·	3, 4	A2A
654	Estaca de Bares Lt.	43 47.2	7 41.1	100	301.1 BA — · · · · —	5, 6	A2A
A199	Asturias	43 33.6	6 01.5	60	325 AVS · — · · · — · · ·	Cont.	NON A2A
657	Torre de Hercules Lt.	43 23.2	8 24.3	30	305.7 L · — · ·	1, 3, 5	A2A
660	Cabo Priorino	43 27.6	8 20.3	50	305.7 C — · — ·	2, 4, 6	A2A
663	Cabo Villano Lt. Ho.	43 09.7	9 12.6	100	310.3 VI · · · — · ·	1, 2	A2A
666	Cabo Finisterre Lt. Ho.	42 53.0	9 16.2	100	310.3 FI · · — · · ·	3, 4	A2A
669	Cabo Silleiro Lt. Ho.	42 06.3	8 53.7	200	310.3 RO · — · — — —	5, 6	d A2A
A201	Porto	41 19.0	8 42.0	250	327 POR · — — · — — — · — ·	Cont.	NON A2A
672	Cabo Estay, Ria de Vigo	42 11.2	8 48.7	7	296.5 VS · · · — · · ·	Cont.	eg A2A

FOOTNOTES – See page 19:27

RADIOBEACONS
USHANT TO GIBRALTAR
(including Azores)

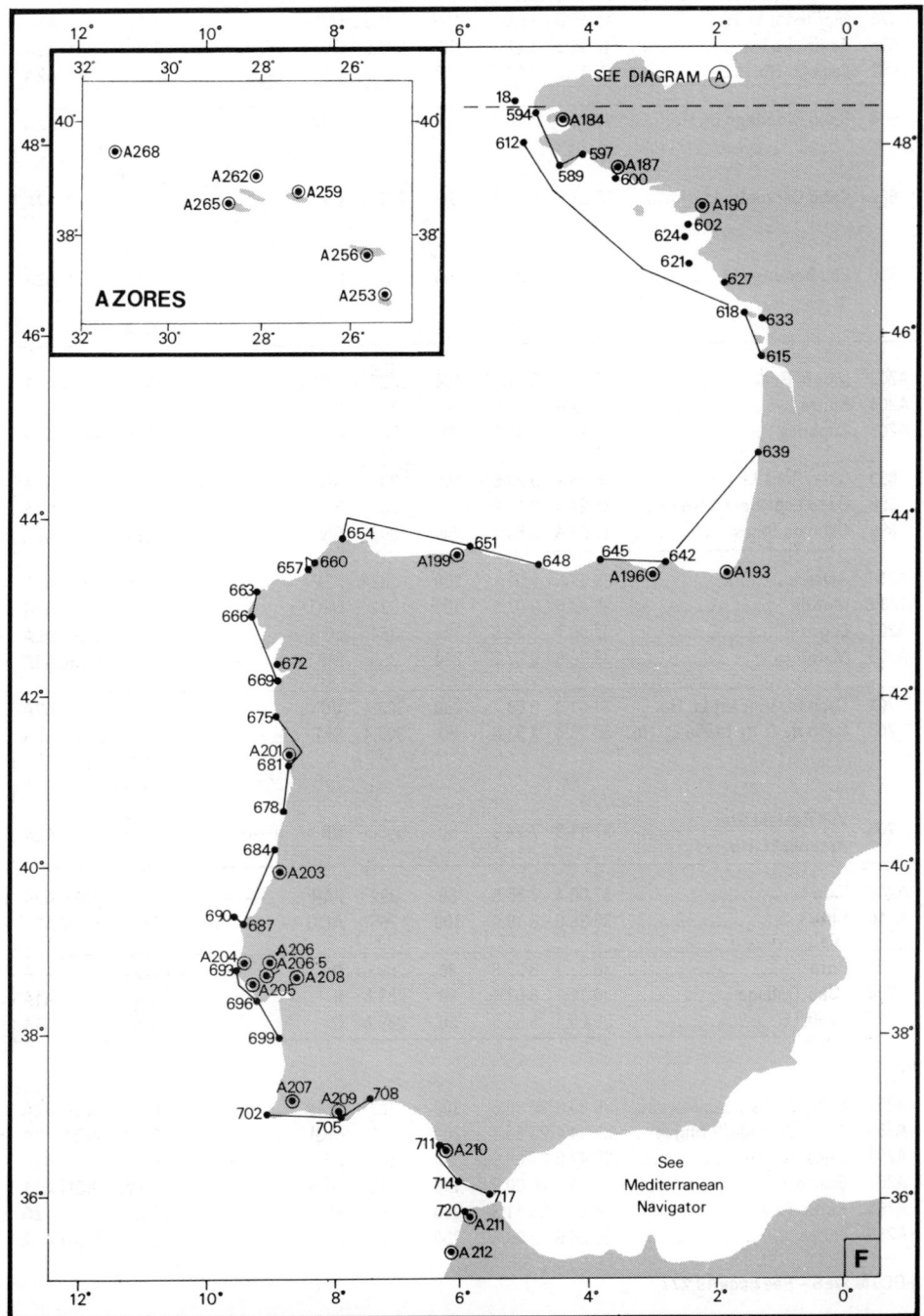

REED'S STN. No.	STATION NAME AND GROUPING	LAT. North ° ′	LONG. West ° ′	RANGE AND FREQ.		MORSE IDENT.	TRANSMISSION Times/sequence Modes and FOOTNOTES	
675	Montedor Lt. Ho.	41 45.0	8 52.4	150	291.9	MR — — · — ·	1, 2	A2A
678	Aveiro Lt. Ho.	40 38.5	8 44.8	50	291.9	AV · — · · · —	3, 4	A2A
681	Leca Lt. Ho.	41 12.0	8 42.7	100	291.9	LC · — · · — · — ·	5, 6	A2A
684	Cabo Mondego Lt. Ho.	40 11.4	8 54.2	100	287.3	MD — — — · ·	1, 2 H+00, 06, 30, 36	f A2A
687	Cabo Carvoeiro Lt. Ho.	39 21.5	9 24.4	50	287.3	CV — · — · · · · —	3, 4 H+02, 08, 32, 38	f A2A
690	Ilha Berlenga Lt.	39 24.8	9 30.5	200	287.3	IB · · — · · · ·	5, 6 H+04, 10, 34, 40	f A2A
A203	Monte Real	39 54.4	8 52.9	150	336	MTL — — · — · ·	Cont.	A2A
A204	Sintra	38 52.8	9 24.0	50	371	STR · · · — · — ·	Cont.	A2A
A205	Caparica	38 38.4	9 13.2	25	389	CP — · — · · — — ·	Cont.	NON A2A
693	Cabo Roca Lt. Ho.	38 46.7	9 29.8	100	308	RC · — · — · — ·	1, 2	A2A
696	Cabo Espichel Lt. Ho.	38 24.8	9 12.9	50	308	PI · — — · · ·	3, 4	A2A
699	Cabo de Sines.................	37 57.4	8 53.1	50	308	SN · · · — ·	5, 6	A2A
A206	Alverca	38 53.5	9 01.4	150	262	ALV · — · — · · — · · —	Cont.	NON A2A
A206.5	Montijo...........................	38 42.6	9 02.5	100	322	MIO — — · · — —	Cont.	A2A
A207	Lagos	37 09.7	8 36.8	100	364	LGS · — · · — — · · · ·	Cont.	NON A2A
A208	Marateca	39 39.8	8 37.2	200	355	MRT — — · — · —	Cont.	NON A1A
702	Cape St. Vincent Lt. Ho. ...	37 01.3	8 59.7	200	303.4	VC · · · — — · — ·	1, 2	A2A
705	Cabo de S. de Maria Lt. Ho.	36 58.4	7 51.8	50	303.4	SM · · · — —	3, 4 H+14, 20, 44, 50	fg A2A
708	Vila Real de Sta. Antonio Lt. Ho.	37 11.3	7 24.9	50	303.4	VR · · · — · — ·	5, 6	A2A
A209	Faro	37 00.4	7 55.5	50	332	FAR · · — · · — ·	Cont.	NON A2A
A210	Rota	36 38.6	6 19.0	100	265	AOG · — — — — — ·	Cont.	NON A2A
711	Rota	36 37.7	6 22.8	80	289.6	D — · ·	1, 2	A2A
714	Cabo Trafalgar	36 11.1	6 02.1	50	289.6	B — · · ·	3, 4	A1A
717	Tarifa Lt.	36 00.1	5 36.5	50	289.6	O — — —	5, 6	R A1A

AZORES

A253	Santa Maria.....................	36 59.8	25 10.6	300	323	SMA · · · — — · —	Cont.	NON A2A
A256	Ponta Delgada/S Miguel ...	37 44.4	25 35.1	200	371	MGL — — — — · · · — · ·	Cont.	NON A2A
A259	Lajes, Terceira.................	38 47.0	27 06.9	50	341	GP — — · · — — ·	Cont.	A2A
A262	Graciosa	39 04.8	28 00.9	100	283	GRA — — · · — · · —	Cont.	NON A2A
A265	Horta, Faial	38 31.3	28 41.3	250	380	FIL · · — · · · · — · ·	Cont.	A2A
A268	Flores	39 26.6	31 09.8	250	270	FLO · · — · · — · · — — —	Cont.	NON A2A

FOOTNOTES – See page 19:27

THE VHF RADIO LIGHTHOUSE

The VHF radio lighthouse is a rotating, directional, VHF radio beacon for use by the navigator. Apart from operating on VHF, it differs from the familiar MF radio beacon in that the latter radiates a uniform non-directional signal over 360°. The navigator then uses a special purpose direction finding radio receiver to determine his bearing from the beacon.

The VHF radio beacon radiates a signal which is directional in nature, from which the bearing can be obtained with any type of radio receiver capable of receiving the particular VHF channel used. It does this by radiating a signal which at one point in azimuth momentarily falls to zero. This 'null radial' is rotated electronically at a constant rate over the 120° arc of coverage of the beacon. At the end of its traverse it reverts instantaneously to its start position and commences another sweep, and so on.

A listener within the arc of coverage will thus hear a continuous signal which at some instant will fall off for a short instant of time before reverting to full strength. An identification start signal is transmitted when the null radial commences its sweep, and if the time between then and the instant when the null is heard is measured, then knowing the reference bearing of the start of the sweep and the speed of rotation, the bearing of the beacon can be deduced.

In practice, to make it easier to use, the transmitted signal is not a continuous tone but broken up into short 'beats' at the rate of 2 per second, to provide a simple timing clock. The user then only has to count the number of beats from the start signal to determine his bearing, there being 2 degrees per beat. With a simple table, or chart overlay, the bearing corresponding to any beat number can be read off. The bearing so obtained, because the information is contained in the transmitted signal, is not referenced to the ship's heading, and the accuracy of the bearing is unaffected by the ship's motion or by the proximity of metallic parts of the superstructure. The former is a particular advantage for small craft in violent seas compared with using a DF receiver.

In its basic form, with audible counting of beats, for which an 'entertainment' type of receiver can be used, the accuracy can be better than 2 degrees, depending on the sharpness of the null, the strength of the signal and the ability of the user to estimate the true null by interpolation between beats. The system is capable of development to give higher accuracy but this will require the use of a special receiver, incorporating electronic signal processing circuits.

As the system is on VHF, the range is horizon limited and will depend to a great extent on the relative heights of the transmitting antenna and receiver. However, 20 miles may be assumed to be a good average.

The system is similar to that of Consol, which is being phased out, but which is essentially a long range, long wave system.

VHF Radio beacons are shown on the radiobeacon diagram and prefixed with the letter V.

Transmission Sequence:
Pause 0.1s, Morse ident. 3.2s, Pause 1.0s, Digital Data 0.3s, Pause 1.0s, 70 beats 35.0s, Pause 1.0s, Morse ident. 3.2s, Pause 1.0s, Digital Data 0.1s, Pause 12.1s, Station Gap 2s.

The Digital Data transmissions have no navigational significance.

Transmitting Frequency: VHF Chan. 88 162.025 MHz.

Bearing of Lt Ho from seaward in Degrees

	Count of Beats	0	1	2	3	4	5	6	7	8	9
V3 Anvil Point Lt[1]	0	—	—	—	—	—	—	247	249	251
50°35'.5N, 1°57'.5W	10	253	255	257	259	261	263	265	267	269	271
Ident: AL (· – · – · · ·)	20	273	275	277	279	281	283	285	287	289	291
Sector: 247°-007°	30	293	295	297	299	301	303	305	307	309	311
Range: 14 miles	40	313	315	317	319	321	323	325	327	329	331
Alternate with	50	333	335	337	339	341	343	345	347	349	351
Scratchells Bay (V6)	60	353	355	357	359	001	003	005	007	—	—
V6 High Down Scratchells Bay[1]	0	—	—	—	—	—	—	—	337	339	341
50°39'.7N, 1°34'.6W	10	343	345	347	349	351	353	355	357	359	001
Ident: HD (· · · · – · ·)	20	003	005	007	009	011	013	015	017	019	021
Sector: 337°-097°	30	023	025	027	029	031	033	035	037	039	041
Range: 30 miles	40	043	045	047	049	051	053	055	057	059	061
Alternate with	50	063	065	067	069	071	073	075	077	079	081
Anvil Point Lt. (V3)	60	083	085	087	089	091	093	095	097	—	—
V12 Calais Main Lt.[1]	0	—	—	—	—	—	—	—	090	092	094
50°57'.7N, 1°51'.3E	10	096	098	100	102	104	106	108	110	112	114
Ident: CL (– · – · · – · ·)	20	116	118	120	122	124	126	128	130	132	134
Sector: 090°-210°	30	136	138	140	142	144	146	148	150	152	154
Range: 20 miles	40	156	158	160	162	164	166	168	170	172	174
	50	176	178	180	182	184	186	188	190	192	194
	60	196	198	200	202	204	206	208	210	—	—

[1] Beat numbers 10, 20, 30, 40, 50 and 60 are marked by a change in audio tone frequency.

RADAR BEACONS

GENERAL. Radar beacons can sometimes cause unwanted interference with the normal radar display, especially at close range. In the case of Racons, this interference may be reduced by the operation of the "differentiator" ("rain clutter") control on the ship's radar.

Under conditions of abnormal refraction a racon flash may be observed on the correct bearing at ranges far in excess of the given range, regardless of the range scale set on the ship's radar. **A racon flash should not be relied upon if the ship is believed to be beyond the quoted range of the beacon.**

A RACON is a radar responder beacon which gives a characteristic signal when triggered by the ship's radar set. The flash given by the Racon provides direct indication of range and bearing on the Plan Position Indicator.

Distance off is measured to the point at which the racon flash begins; the actual distance off will be a few hundred feet less than that indicated.

Frequency Coverage. All Radar Beacons operate throughout the 3 cm radar band unless otherwise stated. Racons operating throughout both 3 and 10 cm bands and those on a fixed frequency are mentioned in the footnotes.

Identification Signal. Except where otherwise stated the Racon flash appears as a single line or narrow sector extending radially towards the circumference of the screen. Some Racons display a morse flash often followed by a 'tail' ie Morse S, · · · – The overall length of the Racon flash (measured in miles) is shown in brackets after the morse identification signal ie (1.25).

Sweep Period. The time — period — taken by the Beacon to sweep over the whole range of frequencies covered. Where known it is shown in seconds.

Range. As this depends on the height and power of the Radar Beacon station as well as the power and range of the ship's Radar set, the Range at which the signal may be picked up is approximate only.

Azimuth Coverage. Except where otherwise stated, all Racons operate all round the horizon. Bearings quoted are those where signals may be received, and are towards the station.

WARNING: Radar Beacons are liable to suspend operation without notice, for varying periods, owing to maintenance work, etc.

Radar Beacons are also shown with Navigational Aids, Sections 22, 23, 24 and 25.

Radar Beacons are shown in the same geographical sequence as radiobeacons but do not appear on the diagrams.

STN. No.	STATION NAME	POSITION LAT.	LONG.	IDENTIFICATION SIGNAL	RANGE	SWEEP PERIOD	REMARKS

CHANNEL APPROACHES TO NOORD HINDER

		North	West			Seconds	
R5	Seven Stones Lt.V.	50 03.6	6 04.3	O – – –	15		b
R10	Bishop Rock Lt.	49 52.3	6 26.7	T –	18		bg
R12	Wolf Rock	49 56.7	5 48.5	T –	10		b
R15	Eddystone Lt.	50 10.8	4 15.9	T –	10		b
R20	West Bramble Lt.By.	50 47.2	1 18.6	T –	3	45	
R25	Nab Lt.	50 40.1	0 57.1	T –	10	90	
R30	EC1 Lt.By.	50 05.9	1 48.4	T –	10	90	
R35	EC2 Lt.By.	50 12.1	1 12.4	T –	10	90	
R40	EC3 Lt.By.	50 18.3	0 36.1	T –	10	90	
R45	Greenwich Lanby	50 24.5	0 00.0	T –	15		b
			East				
R50	Varne Lanby	51 01.3	1 24.0	T –	10		b
R52	Sandettie Lt. V.	51 09.4	1 47.2	T –	10		b
R55	East Goodwin Lt. V.	51 13.1	1 36.3	T –	10		b
R57	North East Goodwin Lt.By.	51 20.3	1 34.3	G – – ·	10		b
R60	Falls Lt. Float	51 18.1	1 48.5	O – – –	10		b
R65	Dover Strait TSS F3 Lanby	51 23.8	2 00.6	T –	10		b
R67	Outer Tongue Lt.By.	51 30.7	1 26.5	T –	10		b
R70	Thames Sea Reach Lt.By. 1	51 29.4	0 52.7	T –	10	90	
R75	Thames Sea Reach Lt.By. 7	51 30.1	0 37.2	T –	10	90	
R77	Thames Est. Barrow No. 3 Lt.By.	51 42.0	1 19.9	B – · · ·	10		b
R80	South Galloper Lt.By.	51 44.0	1 56.5	T –	10		
R85	Sunk Lt.V.	51 51.0	1 35.0	T –	10	90	
R88	Orfordness Lt.	52 05.0	1 34.6	T –	10		
R90	Harwich Channel Lt.By. 1 ...	51 56.1	1 26.9	T –	10		
			West				
R95	East Channel Lt. Float	49 58.7	2 28.9	T –	10	90	
R100	Channel Lt.V.	49 54.4	2 53.7	O – – –	15		b
R105	Casquets Lt.	49 43.4	2 22.6	T –	25		b
R110	Platte Fougère Lt.	49 30.9	2 29.1	P · – – ·			
R115	St Helier, Demi de Pas Lt. ...	49 09.1	2 06.1	T –	10	120	
R120	St. Helier, Mont Ubé Ldg. Lt.	49 10.4	2 03.5	T –	14	60	
			East				
R125	Maas Center Lt.By.	52 01.2	3 53.6	M – –	8	120	
R130	Goeree Lt.	51 55.5	3 40.2	T –	10		b
R135	Schouwenbank Lt.By.	51 45.0	3 14.4	O – – –	10	120	
R137	Zuid Vlije Lt.By. ZV15/SRK 28	51 38.2	4 14.5	K – · –			
R140	Noord Hinder Lt.By. NHR-SE	51 45.5	2 40.0	N – ·	10	120	
R145	Noord Hinder Lt.By. NHR-N	52 13.3	2 59.5	K – · –	10	120	
R150	Noord Hinder Lt.V.	52 00.2	2 51.2	T –	10		b
R160	Dunkerque Lanby	51 03.1	1 51.8				a
R170	Sangatte	50 57.2	1 46.6		11		f
R175	Vergoyer Lt.By. N.	50 39.7	1 22.3	C – · – ·	5-8	120-150	b
R180	Bassurelle Lt.By.	50 32.7	0 57.8	B – · · ·	6-10	120-150	
			West				
R183	Antifer App. Lt.By. A5	49 45.9	0 17.4	K – · –			
R185	Le Havre Lanby	49 31.7	0 09.8		8-10		ab
R188	St Médard Lt.	49 18.1	0 14.5				b
R190	Ouessant NE, Lt.By.	48 45.9	5 11.6	B – · · ·	20		
R195	Ouessant SW, Lanby	48 31.7	5 49.1	M – –	20		b
R200	Pte de Creach, Ile d'Ouessant	48 27.6	5 07.6	C – · – ·	20	120-150	c

FOOTNOTES:

a = The Racon signal appears as a series of 8 dots (or 8 groups of dots). The distance between each dot (or group of dots) corresponds to 0.3 miles.

b = 3 and 10 cm bands.

c = Sector 030-248 only.

f = The Racon signal appears as a series of 3 dots. The distance between each dot corresponds to 0.3 miles.

g = Sector 254°-215° only.

STN. No.	STATION NAME	POSITION LAT.	LONG.	IDENTIFICATION SIGNAL	RANGE	SWEEP PERIOD	REMARKS
GREAT BRITAIN AND IRELAND							
		North	East			Seconds	
R203	Outer Gabbard Lt.V.	51 59.4	2 04.6	T –	10		f
R205	Cross Sand Lt.By.	52 37.0	1 59.3	T –	10	90	
R210	Winterton Old Lt.Ho.	52 42.8	1 41.8	T –	10	90	
R215	Smiths Knoll Lt.V.	52 43.5	2 18.0	T –	10		f
R217	Newarp Lt.V.	52 48.4	1 55.8	O – – –	10		f
R220	North Haisbro Lt.By.	53 00.2	1 32.4	T –	10		f
R222	Cromer Lt.V.	52 55.5	1 19.1	C – . – .	25		f
R225	North Well Lt.By.	53 03.0	0 28.0	T –	10		
R233	Dudgeon Lt.V.	53 16.6	1 17.0	O – – –	10		f
R235	Inner Dowsing Lt.	53 19.7	0 34.0	T –	25		
R238	Dowsing Lt.V.	53 34.0	0 50.2	T –	10		f
R240	Spurn Lt. Float	53 33.5	0 14.3	M – –			f
R250	Humber Lt.By.	53 36.7	0 21.6	T –	7		f
			West				
R255	Tees Fairway By.	54 40.9	1 06.4	B – . . .			
R265	St. Abbs Head Lt.	55 55.0	2 08.2	T –	18	30	
R270	Inchkeith Fairway By.	56 03.5	3 00.0	T –	5	75	
R275	Firth of Forth North Channel Lt.By. 7	56 02.8	3 10.9	T –	5	60	
R280	Bell Rock Lt.	56 26.1	2 23.1	M – –	18		f
R285	Abertay Lt.By.	56 27.4	2 40.6	T – (1.0)	8	70	
R290	Scurdie Ness Lt.	56 42.1	2 26.2	T –	15	70	
R295	Girdle Ness Lt.	57 08.4	2 02.8	G – – .	25		df
R300	Aberdeen Fairway By.	57 09.3	2 01.9	T –	7	70	
R305	Buchan Ness Lt.	57 28.2	1 46.4	O – – –	25	72	e
R308	Rattray Head Lt.	57 36.6	1 48.8	M – –	15		af
R310	Cromarty Firth Fairway By.	57 40.0	3 54.1	M – –	5	75	
R315	Tarbat Ness Lt.	57 51.9	3 46.5	T –	12	70	
R320	Duncansby Head Lt.	58 38.7	3 01.4	T –	20	72	
R325	Lother Rock Lt.	58 43.8	2 58.6	M – –	10	70	
R330	North Ronaldsay Lt.	59 23.4	2 22.8	T –	10	75	
R335	Rumble Rock Bn.	60 28.2	1 07.1	O – – –	10	70	
R340	Ve Skerries Lt.	60 22.4	1 48.7	T –	15	70	
R345	Gruney Island Lt.	60 39.2	1 18.0	T –	18	70	
R350	Sule Skerry Lt.	59 05.1	4 24.3	T –	25	120	
R355	Eilean Glas Lt.	57 51.4	6 38.5	T –	12	70	
R360	Castlebay South By.	56 56.1	7 27.2	T –	7	70	
R365	Monach Lt.	57 31.6	7 41.6	T –	16	70	
R370	Kyleakin Lt.	57 16.7	5 44.5	T –	16	70	
R378	Dubh Sgeir Lt.	56 14.8	5 40.1	M – –	5	30	
R380	Sanda Lt.	55 16.5	5 34.9	T –	20	70	
R385	Point of Ayre Lt.	54 25.0	4 22.0	M – –	15	30	
R387	Lune Deep Lt.By.	53 55.8	3 11.0	T –	10		f
R390	Bar Lanby	53 32.0	3 20.9	T –	10	90	
R393	Skerries Lt.	53 25.3	4 36.5	T –	25		
R395	The Smalls Lt.	51 43.2	5 40.1	T –	25		f
R396	St. Gowan Lt.V.	51 30.5	4 59.8	T –	15		f
R397	West Helwick Lt.By.	51 31.4	4 23.6	T –	10		f
R398	Swansea Bay Lt.By.	51 28.3	3 55.5	T –	10		f
R400	Eng. and Welsh Grounds Lt. Buoy	51 26.9	3 00.1	O – – –	7		f
R405	Breaksea Lt. Float	51 19.9	3 19.0	T –	10		f
R410	Mizen Head Lt.	51 27.0	9 49.2	T –	24		f
R415	Cork Lt.By.	51 42.9	8 15.5	T –	7	72	

FOOTNOTES – See page 19:36

STN. No.	STATION NAME	POSITION LAT.	POSITION LONG.	IDENTIFICATION SIGNAL	RANGE	SWEEP PERIOD	REMARKS

GREAT BRITAIN AND IRELAND continued

		North	West			Seconds	
R420	Hook Head Lt.	52 07.4	6 55.7	K - · -	10		fg
R425	Coningbeg Lt.V.	52 02.4	6 39.5	M - -	13		
R430	Tuskar Rock Lt.	52 12.2	6 12.4	T -	18		
R435	Arklow Lanby	52 39.5	5 58.1	O - - -	10		
R440	Codling Lanby	53 03.0	5 40.7	G - - ·	10		
R445	Kish Bank Lt.	53 18.7	5 55.4	T -	15	120	
R450	South Rock Lt.V.	54 24.5	5 21.9	T -	13		
R455	Inishtrahull Lt.	55 25.9	7 14.6	T -	24		fh

FOOTNOTES:
a = Sector 110°-340° only.
d = Reduced coverage in sector 055°-165°.
e = Reduced coverage in sector 045°-155°.
f = 3 and 10 cm bands.
g = Sector 237°-177° only.
h = Sector 060°-310° only.

NOORD HINDER TO BALTIC ENTRANCE

		North	East			Seconds	
R457	Wandelaar Lt.	51 23.7	3 02.8	W · - -			d
R459	Bol Van Heist Lt.	51 23.4	3 12.0	H · · · ·			d
R460	Keeton Lt. By.	51 36.4	3 55.1	K - · -			d
R462	Rijn Field Platform P15-B	52 18.4	3 46.7	B - · · ·	10		bd
R465	Ijmuiden Lt.By.	52 28.7	4 23.9	Y - · - -			
R470	Texel Lt.V.	52 47.1	4 06.6	T -	10		d
R472	Logger Platform	53 00.9	4 13.1	X - · · -	10	120	ad
R474	Nam Field Platform K14-FA-1	53 16.2	3 37.7	7 - - · · ·			d
R475	Vlieland Lanby VL-CENTRE	53 27.0	4 40.0	C - · - ·	10		d
R477	Vlieland North Lt.By. VL-N	53 35.5	4 37.2	G - - ·	10	120	
R481	Placid Field Platform PL-K9C-PA	53 39.2	3 52.5	8 - - - · ·			d
R483	Terschelling Bank Platform 18-G	53 34.9	4 36.3	G - - ·	12-15		de
R486	DW Route Lt. By. FR/A	50 00.4	4 21.4	M - -		120	
R495	Westerems Lt.By.	53 37.2	6 19.5	G - - ·	8	48	
R500	Borkumriff Lt.By.	53 47.5	6 22.1	T -	8	48	
R505	TW/Ems Lt.By.	54 10.0	6 20.8	T -	6-10	55	
R510	Deutsche Bucht Lt.V.	54 10.7	7 26.1	T -	8	48	
R515	DB/Weser Lt.By.	54 02.4	7 43.1	K - · -	6	48	
R520	Weser Lt.By.	53 54.3	7 50.0	T -	7	72	
R525	Elbe Lt. Float	54 00.0	8 06.6	T -	6-8	48	
R530	Gorm Oilfield, Platform C	55 34.9	4 45.6	U · · - (1.5)	10	72	
R535	Tyra Gas Field East Platform	55 43.3	4 48.2	U · · - (1.5)	20	90	
R540	Tyra Gas Field West Platform	55 43.0	4 45.1	U · · - (1.5)	20	90	
R545	Gradyb Lt.By. No. 2	55 25.7	8 13.8	G - - · (1.0)	10		d
R550	Horns Rev W Lt.By.	55 34.5	7 26.2	NW - · · - - (1.0)	10		d
R555	Thyboren Approach Lt.By.	56 42.8	8 08.6	T - (1.5)	10	120	
R560	Skagen Lt.	57 44.2	10 37.9	G - - · (6.0)	20		d
R565	Skagens Rev Lt.By.	57 47.2	10 46.1	T - (1.5)	10	120	
R570	Laesø Trindel Lt.By. 3	57 28.0	11 25.0	K - · - (1.5)	10		ds
R575	Frederikshavn SPM By.	57 23.6	10 37.1	K - · - (1.5)	10	120	
R580	Laesø Rende Lt.	57 13.2	10 40.4	Q - - - · (6.0)	20		d
R585	Hals Barre Lt.	56 57.3	10 25.6	B - · · · (6.0)	15		d
R590	Svitringen Rende S. Lt.	56 51.1	10 36.4	G - - · (1.5)	5	120	
R595	Anholt Knob Lt.By. 6	56 45.4	11 53.1	T - (1.5)	10	120	
R600	Sjaellands Rev North Lt.	56 06.1	11 12.2	N - · (6.0)	20		cd
R605	Samso Baelt Lt.By. No. 16	55 55.2	10 57.2	T - (1.5)	10	120	
R610	Skanseodde Lt.	55 33.3	9 46.5	T - (1.5)	10	120	
R615	Romso Tue Lt.	55 33.5	10 49.3	T - (1.5)	10	120	

FOOTNOTES – See page 19:37

NOORD HINDER TO BALTIC ENTRANCE continued

STN. No.	STATION NAME	POSITION LAT. LONG.	IDENTIFICATION SIGNAL	RANGE	SWEEP PERIOD	REMARKS
		North East			Seconds	
R620	Halsskov Rev South Lt.	55 19.5 11 02.3	O – – – (1.0)	10		d
R625	Agerso Flak Lt	55 12.4 11 06.7	Z – – ·· (3.0)	10	120	d
R630	Bostrup East DW11 Lt.	55 02.7 10 59.3	K – · – (1.5)	10	120	
R635	Hojbjerg East Lt.	54 52.8 10 50.1	G – – · (1.5)	10	120	
R640	Landgelandsbaelt S. Lt.	54 48.1 10 50.3	O – – – (1.5)	10	120	
R645	Rodby Havn Approach Lt.By.	54 38.4 11 19.3	T – (1.5)	10	120	
R648	Rodsand Rende South Lt. ...	54 32.8 11 56.2	T – (1.5)	10	120	
R650	Gedser Lt.	54 33.9 11 57.9	G – – · (6.0)	20		d
R652	Kronlobets S Breakwater Lt.	55 42.5 12 36.8	T – 1.5)	10	120	
R655	Drogden Lt.	55 32.2 12 42.7	X – ·· – (6.0)	15		d
R660	Route T Lt.By. DW 79	54 46.1 12 44.0	Z – – ·· (1.0)	10		d
R665	Kadetrenden Lt.By. 71	54 27.7 12 12.3	T – (1.5)	10	120	
R667	Kalgrund Lt.	54 49.5 9 53.4	T –	8	72	
R670	Kiel Lt.	54 30.0 10 16.5	T –	8	60	
R673	Fehmarnsundbrucke Lt.	54 24.2 11 06.8	T –	2		d
R675	Kiel-Baltic Route Lt.By. 5 ...	54 35.5 11 01.1	M – –	8	60	
R680	Fehmarnbelt Lanby	54 36.0 11 09.0	T –	8	48	
R685	Trelleborg Lt.	55 21.4 13 09.1	T –	14		d
R690	Blenheim Lt. By.	55 16.5 12 52.8	B – ··· (1.1)			
R695	Falsterborev Lt.	55 18.5 12 39.5	M – – (1.8)	16		d
R700	Hollviken Lt.	55 30.7 12 51.0	N – · (0.6)	12		d
R705	Oskarsgrundet SW Lt.	55 34.7 12 49.1	O – – – 0.6)	5		d
R710	Kalkgrundet Lt.	55 37.0 12 54.0	K – · – (1.1)	11		d
R713	Pinhattan Lt.	55 45.3 12 52.1	T – (1.1)	13		d
R715	Knolen Lt.By.	55 51.2 12 44.5	K – · – (1.1)	6		d
R716	Grasrannan Lt.	55 51.7 12 48.0	G – – · (1.2)	8-10		d
R717	The Sound Lt.By. 'M4'	56 03.3 12 39.3	T – (0.4)			d
R720	Svinbadan Lt.	56 09.1 12 32.6	B – ··· (1.1)	15		d
R723	Morups Tange Lt.	56 55.5 12 21.8	M – – (0.9)	17		d
R725	Fladen Lt.	57 12.9 11 49.8	N – · (1.2)	15		d
R730	Trubaduren Lt.	57 35.7 11 38.1	T – (1.5)	14		d
R735	Trinda Brunskar	57 38.2 11 43.4	T – (0.1)	5		d
R740	Vasskarsgrund Lt.	57 39.2 11 43.5	B – ··· (0.5)	4		d
R745	Mavholmsbaden Lt	57 40.4 11 42.6	M – – – (0.9)	13	48	
R750	Buskars Knote Lt.	57 38.4 11 41.1	K – · – (0.5)	5		d
R755	Hatteberget Lt.	57 51.8 11 27.7	G – – · (1.1)	15		d
R760	Brofjorden Angoring Lt.By.	58 15.0 11 13.5	G – – · (1.0)			d
R765	Brandskarsflak Lt.	58 17.6 11 18.8	B – ··· (1.1)	15		d
R767	Vaderobod Lt.	58 32.6 11 02.0	C – ·– · (1.4)	18		d
R770	Ramskar Lt.	58 45.5 10 59.7	M – – (0.9)	13		d
R773	Klovningarna Lt.	58 56.0 10 59.5	K – · – (1.1)	12		d

FOOTNOTES:
a = Sector 060°-270° only.
b = Sector 030°-270° only
c = Sector 020°-280° only.
d = 3 and 10 cm bands.
e = Sector 000°-160° only.

STN. No.	STATION NAME	POSITION LAT. LONG.	IDENTIFICATION SIGNAL	RANGE	SWEEP PERIOD	REMARKS

SOUTHERN BALTIC

		North	East			Seconds	
R776.0	Prora Lt. Rugen.................	54 26.1	13 34.5	M – –	17		a
R776.3	Swinoujscie Lt. By. N-2	54 14.7	14 11.3	D – · ·	6-8	70	
R776.6	Swinoujscie Lt. By. N-4	54 07.5	14 13.2	M – –	6-8	70	
R776.9	Kullagrund Lt.	55 17.9	13 19.5	K – · – (1.1)	14		a
R777.2	Gasfeten Lt.	56 07.3	15 13.6	G – – · (1.1)	13		a
R777.5	Vastra Forsankingen Lt.	56 06.5	15 34.8	K – · – (1.1)	4		a
R777.8	Olands Sodra Grund Lt.	56 04.1	16 40.9	Ö – – – · (1.6)	17		a
R778.1	Utgrunden Lt.	56 22.5	16 15.6	N – · (0.6)			a
R778.4	Olandsbron	56 40.8	16 23.9		6		b
R778.7	Stotbotten Lt.	57 16.5	16 33.4	O – – – (0.8)	12		a
R779.0	Kungsgrundet Lt...............	57 41.1	16 54.4	K – · – (1.1)	17		a
R779.3	Vasterbaden Lt.	57 44.9	16 44.7	B – · · · (0.5)	12		a
R779.6	Gustav Dalen Lt.	58 35.7	17 28.3	G – – · (1.1)	16		a
R779.9	Norra Krankan Lt.	58 36.4	17 23.4	K – · – (1.1)	13		a
R780.2	Lillhammarsgrund Lt.	58 39.7	17 20.3	N – · (1.2)	11		a
R780.5	Bredgrund Lt., Landsort......	58 43.9	17 52.7	B – · · · (1.1)	14		a
R780.8	Almagrundet Lt.	59 09.3	19 07.8	G – – · (1.1)	16		a
R781.1	Revengegrundet Lt............	59 15.1	19 01.0	RT · – · – (3.7)	14		c
R781.4	Sandhamns Pilot Lookout...	59 17.3	18 54.9	T – (1.2)	17		cd
R781.7	Sandon	59 17.5	18 52.9	T – (0.4)			e
R782.0	Tistero Lt. By.	59 26.1	18 24.2	T – (0.1)	5		
R782.3	Svenska Bjorn Lt..............	59 32.9	20 01.5	B – · · · (1.1)	16		a
R782.6	Remmargrund Lt..............	59 45.6	19 19.2	M – – (0.9)	15		a
R782.9	Simpnasklubb Lt..............	59 53.6	19 05.0	N – · (0.6)	15		a

FOOTNOTES

a = 3 and 10 cm bands.
b = Racon appears as a succession of dots (Overall distance 0.5 miles).
c = R781.1 and R781.4 in line 305°.
d - Sector 215°-035° only.
e = On islet 0.6 miles west of Sandon.

STN. No.	STATION NAME	POSITION LAT.	LONG.	IDENTIFICATION SIGNAL	RANGE	SWEEP PERIOD	REMARKS
NORWAY & ICELAND		North	East			Seconds	
R785	Tor Oilfield	56 38.5	3 19.8	N – · (2.0)	16		b
R790	Eldfisk Oilfield	56 22.5	3 16.0	O – – – (2.0)	16		b
R795	Ling Bank Platform	58 11.3	2 28.4	G – – · (2.0)	16		b
R797	Oseberg A	60 29.5	2 46.6	K – · –			
R800	Svelvikrenna Sondra Lt.	59 35.9	10 25.4	T – (1.0)			
R802	Mefjordbaen Lt.	59 20.2	10 34.3	M – – (0.875)			b
R803	Hollenderbaen Lt.	59 09.6	10 37.7	O – – – (1.375)			b
R805	Faeder Lt.	59 01.6	10 31.6	T – (1.0)			bg
R810	Tresteinene Lt.	59 01.5	10 54.0	T – (1.0)		60	
R812	Svenner Lt.	58 58.2	10 09.0	N – · (1.25)			b
R814	Tvistein Lt.	58 56.3	9 56.3	M – – (0.875)			b
R815	Torungen Lt.	58 24.0	8 47.5	T – (1.0)			b
R816	Oksoy Lt.	58 04.4	8 03.3	O – – – (1.375)			b
R817	Ryvingen Lt.	57 58.1	7 29.5	M – –			b
R818	Lista Lt.	58 06.6	6 34.1	G – – · (1.125)			b
R820	Feistein Lt.	58 49.6	5 30.4	T – (1.0)			bc
R821	Arsgrunnen Lt.	59 08.3	5 26.4	M – – (0.875)			b
R822	Bragen Lt.	59 02.5	5 34.4	B – · · · (1.125)			b
R823	UMC By, E Frigg Gas Field...	59 54.3	2 22.1	C – · – ·			b
R824	Bollerflesi Lt.	60 43.6	4 42.4	N – · (1.25)			b
R825	Holmengra	60 50.6	4 39.1	T – (1.5)	10-20		bd
R826	Hellisloy Lt.	60 45.2	4 42.7	O – – – (1.375)			b
R827	Blana Lt.	61 24.7	4 50.0	B – · · · (1.125)			b
R828	Grimeskjaer Lt.	60 59.9	4 45.3	G – – · (1.125)			b
R829	Flavaer Lt.	62 18.9	5 35.2	O – – – (1.0)			
R830	Florauden Lt.	62 25.7	5 50.2	T – (1.0)			
R831	Flatflesa Lt.	62 50.3	6 41.5	M – –			b
R832	Kverna Lt.	62 35.4	6 14.8	T – (1.0)			
R833	Lyroddane	62 57.4	6 54.2	T – (1.0)			b
R835	Kvitholmen Lt.	63 01.4	7 14.2	O – – – (1.0)	8		b
R837	Hestskjer Lt.	63 05.1	7 29.6	K – · – (1.125)			b
R839	Grip Lt, Brattarskallen	63 14.0	7 36.7	G – – · (2.0)			ab
R840	Haugjegla Lt.	63 31.9	7 57.9	K – · –	12-14		b
R841	Valshalmskjaer Lt.	63 48.6	9 36.0	K – · – (1.375)			b
R842	Flesa Lt.	63 38.7	9 13.7	K – · – (1.125)			b
R843	Halten Lt.	64 10.3	9 24.9	T – (2.0)			b
R844	Buholmrasa Lt.	64 24.2	10 27.7	B – · · · (1.25)			b
R845	Langro Lt.	64 29.0	10 30.5	T – (1.0)			ab
R850	Gjeslingane Lt.	64 43.7	10 51.4	G – – · (1.0)	10-20		b
R852	Skomvaer Lt. Rost	67 24.7	11 52.6	T – (2.0)			b
R854	Landegode Lt., Eggeloysa ...	67 26.9	14 23.2	G – – · (1.125)			b
R856	Andersbakken Lt.	66 16.0	12 18.2	T – (1.0)			b
R858	Sortland Bridge	68 42.4	15 26.2	T – (0.5)			b
R859	Hadsel Bridge	68 34.3	15 00.3	T – (0.375)			b
R860	Maloy Skarholmen Lt.	67 46.1	14 24.5	M – – (0.875)			b
R861	Tromsø Bridge	69 39.1	18 58.8	T – (0.375)			b
R862	Gisundet Bridge	69 14.6	17 57.9	T – (0.375)			b
R863	Anda Lt.	69 03.9	15 10.7	T – (1.0)			b

FOOTNOTES – See page 19:40

STN. No.	STATION NAME	POSITION LAT.	LONG.	IDENTIFICATION SIGNAL	RANGE	SWEEP PERIOD	REMARKS

NORWAY & ICELAND continued

		North	East			Seconds	
R864	Hekkingen	69 36.1	17 50.2	M – –			b
R864.5	Sandnessundet Bridge	69 41.5	18 54.2	T – (0.375)			b
R865	Fruholmen Lt.	71 05.6	23 59.5	O – – – (1.375)			b
R866	Helnes Lt.	71 03.7	26 13.4	N – · (1.25)			b
R867	Slettnes Lt.	71 05.4	28 13.6	T – (1.0)			b
R868	Makkau Lt.	70 42.3	30 05.0	M – –			b
R869	Kjolnes Lt.	70 51.1	29 14.2	K – · – (0.875)			b
R870	Bokfjord Lt.	69 52.6	30 10.0	B – · · · (1.125)			b
		North	West				
R871	Hvanney Lt.	64 13.8	15 11.4	T –	11-20	90	
R872	Seley Lt.	64 58.7	13 31.2	M – –	10-15	90	
R873	Hrollaugseyjar Lt.	64 01.7	15 58.9	G – – ·	11-20	90	
R874	Skeldhararsandur	63 47.8	17 16.7	B – · · ·	10-15	90	
R876	Skaftaros Lt.	63 38.9	17 49.8	K – · –	10-15	90	
R878	Skardhsfjara Lt.	63 31.0	17 59.0	T –	10-15	120	
R879	Alvidruhamrar	63 27.4	18 18.5	G – – ·	10-15	60	
R880	Bakkafjara Lt.	63 32.2	20 09.3	N – ·	10-15	90	
R882	Knarraros Lt.	63 49.5	20 58.8	M – –	10-15	90	
R883	Selvogur Lt.	63 49.4	21 39.4	B – · · ·	11-20	60	
R884	Gardhskagi Lt.	64 04.9	22 41.6	G – – ·	11-20	60	
R885	Engey Lt.	64 10.5	21 55.5	T –	11-20	120	
R887	Thormodhssker Lt.	64 26.0	22 18.9	B – · · ·	11-20	60	
R888	Ondverdharness Lt.	64 53.1	24 02.9	C – · – ·	10	60	

FOOTNOTES:
a = Obscured in SW direction
b = 3 and 10 cm bands.
c = Sector 340°-220°.

d = Sector 000°-270°.
e = Sector 000°-240°.
g = Sector 225°-120°.

USHANT TO GIBRALTAR

		North	West			Seconds	
R890	Chausée de Sein Lt.By.	48 03.8	5 07.7	O – – –	10	120-150	
R895	St Nazaire La Couronnée ...	47 07.7	2 20.0		3-5		a
R897	St Nazaire Lt.By. SN1	47 00.0	2 40.0	Z – – · ·	3-8		
R900	BXA Lanby	45 37.6	1 28.6	B – · · ·		120-150	
R903	Puerto de Pasajes,						
	Pilot lookout	43 20.2	1 55.4	K – · –	20	72	
R905	Dique de Pta de Lucero	43 22.7	3 05.0	D – · ·	20	72	
R907	Punta Mera Front Lt.	43 23.1	8 21.5	M – –	22	72	c
R909	Cabo Vilano Lt.	43 09.7	9 12.6	M – –			e
R910	Cabo Torinana Lt.	43 03.3	9 17.7	T –			e
R911	Cabo Finistere Lt.	42 53.0	9 16.2	D – · ·			e
R912	Cabo Estay Front Ldg.Lt. ...	42 11.2	8 48.7	B – · · ·			
R915	Porto de Setubal Bn.2.........	38 27.1	8 58.4	H · · · ·	12	53	
R917	Dique de Contencion						
	de Arenas	37 06.6	6 49.9	K – · – (2.0)		72	
R920	Tarifa Lt.	36 00.1	5 36.5	D – · ·		80	

FOOTNOTES:
a = The Racon signal appears as a series of dots. The distance between each dot corresponds to 0.2 miles.

c = Sector 020°-196°.
d = Racon flash appears 2.0 miles long.
e = 3 and 10 cm bands.

NAVIGATION BY MEANS OF SHORE BASED STATIONS
Navigation by means of Shore Based Stations

There are three automatic position-fixing systems based on chains of shore stations transmitting on different wavelengths.

OMEGA

Omega is a long range hyperbolic fixing system operating in the very low frequency (VLF) band. Eight transmitting stations are sufficient to provide world-wide coverage.

Radio Frequency: The basic frequency is 10.2 kHz but signals of 11.33 kHz and 13.6 kHz are also transmitted. Each station transmits the same frequencies in turn, according to a schedule which repeats at 10-second intervals. The signals from individual stations are identified by the duration and sequence of the transmissions.

Principle: The phase of signals from pairs of stations are compared (as in the Decca system) and a number of possible hyperbolic position lines are defined by an observed phase difference.

Accuracy: Observations of phase difference must be corrected for the phase variations which may be predicted according to the time of the day, season of the year and geographical location. When these corrections are applied, fixing accuracy may be expected to be of the order of ± 1nm by day and ± 2nm by night (95 per cent probability).

Differential Omega: In the differential mode a fixed station monitors the unpredicted Omega propagation errors in a local area and broadcasts corrections which can be applied by ships in the general vicinity. This procedure has the potential for greatly increased accuracy.

The following radiobeacons transmit corrections:

Cap d'Alprech	50°52'N	1°35'E	Cabo Finisterre	42°53'N	9°16'W
Pointe de Créac'h	48°28'N	5°08'W	Lagos, Portugal	37°10'N	8°37'W
Ile d'Yeu	46°43'N	2°23'W	Horta	38°31'N	28°41'W

LORAN C

Loran C is a development from the less successful Loran A. The Radio Frequency is 100 kHz which is low enough to give a ground wave range of 800-1200nm. Also sky waves may be used at longer ranges.

Principle: A Loran C chain consists of a master transmitting station and two to four slaves designated W, X, Y, and Z. The time interval between reception of signals from master and slave pairs is measured coarsely by comparing pulse envelopes and then finely by comparing the phase of the radio frequency cycles within the envelopes. The measured time difference defines the observer's position as on a hyperbola which can be identified on the appropriate Loran C lattice chart. Two master-slave pairs are needed to obtain a fix. Each chain is identified by a unique group repetition interval (GRI) at which the complete pattern of signals is repeated.

Range: The ground wave coverage of 800-1200nm is increased to over 2000nm by the use of sky waves but with reduced accuracy.

Accuracy: Within ground wave coverage the fixing accuracy is usually better than ± 500 metres (95 per cent probability).

Coverage: Coverage is provided for areas in the N. Atlantic and the N. Pacific and also for the Mediterranean Sea.

NORWEGIAN SEA CHAIN

Ejde, Faeroes	62 18 N.	07 04 W.	7970 (SL3)
Sylt, Germany	54 48 N.	08 18 E.	7970-W
Bo, Norway	68 38 N.	14 28 E.	7970-X
Sandur, Iceland	64 54 N.	23 55 W.	7970-Y
Jan Mayen	70 55 N.	08 44 W.	7970-Z

ICELANDIC CHAIN

Sandur Iceland	64 54 N.	23 55 W.	9980 (SS2)
Angissoq, Greenland	59 59 N.	45 10 W.	9980-W
Ejde, Faeroes	62 18 N.	07 04 W.	9980-X

DECCA — COMMERCIAL SHIPPING

The Decca Navigator detects the radio position-line patterns laid down by a Chain of Decca transmitting stations ashore. There are usually three such patterns, numbered and overprinted on standard marine charts in Red, Green and Purple colours.

The receiver drives three position-line indicators called Decometers which automatically and continuously display at any instant the numbers of the Decca position-lines passing through the vessel. To distinguish them the Lanes in each pattern are numbered differently: Red 0-23, Green 30-47, Purple 50-79. These numbers recur in groups, referred to as 'Zones', denoted by letters of the alphabet. Once the Decometers have been set up, the position can be read off without operating any controls.

During daylight periods ranges of 400 nautical miles or more are obtained, at night the ranges may be expected to be 250 nautical miles under good reception conditions, or only 200 nautical miles under adverse conditions.

Fixed and variable errors for the different chains are published in the Decca Marine Data Sheet Handbook.

DECCA EQUIPMENT FOR SMALL CRAFT

Equipment manufactured for small craft does not utilise information received from the Decca chains in a similar manner to the so-called 'professional' receivers, resulting in differences in operation. The receivers give a direct reading of Latitude and Longitude, thus obviating the need for Lattice Charts and the updating occurs at 20 second intervals instead of continuously as in the commercial receiver. It is important to realize that the displayed latitude and longitude position is liable to fixed error and variable error. Fixed errors are caused by the bending of radio waves and are constant. Variable errors can arise from skywave effect, from self-generated interference and from thunderstorms. Whereas the sum of any errors offshore is unlikely to be important, IT IS VITAL FOR THE USER TO BE AWARE THAT THE DISPLAYED POSITION MUST BE REGARDED WITH CAUTION WHEN NAVIGATING IN NARROW CHANNELS OR CLOSE TO DANGERS. In short, this is not a substitute for established pilotage techniques.

An appraisal of the future of Decca and Loran C

Decca (DNS)

The existing contract for the maintenance of the Decca stations by Racal Decca Marine Navigation Ltd for the U.K. Government expires in 1994 with the possibility of extension to 1997. The 20 transmitters of the U.K. chain are approaching the end of their useful lives and would require expensive renewal or replacement in due course.

The Decca System has comparatively limited coverage in NW Europe and is not expanding elsewhere, in fact a number of countries are considering changing to Loran C.

Loran C

The U.S. Military Authorities will dispense with Loran C when the G.P.S. is fully operational, and will dispose of the Loran C stations to their "host" countries. The present coverage of Loran C is much greater than DNS and is currently expanding throughout the world, it being generally accepted that for civilian purposes a land-based navigational system, independent of U.S. Military satellite systems, is essential for the future. The Loran C system gives much greater coverage per station than DNS and provides equally satisfactory navigational facilities.

In some respects it is superior to DNS; for example, a range of 1000 miles enables coverage to be obtained in remote areas where it would be uneconomical to site DNS stations.

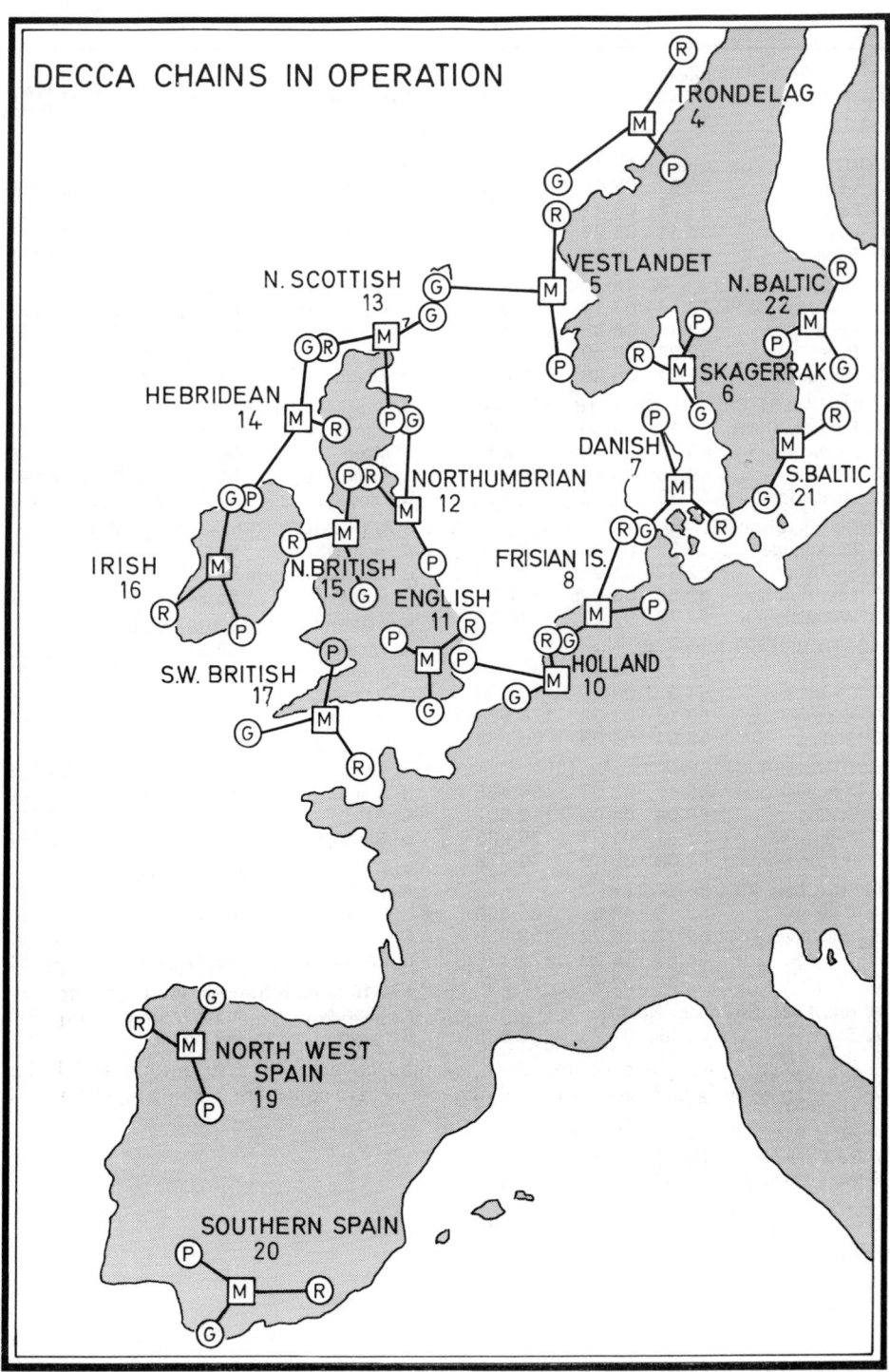

DECCA CHAINS IN OPERATION

Chain Name	Position N ° ' W ° '	Freq. (kHz)	Chain Name	Position N ° ' E ° '	Freq. (kHz)
SOUTH SPANISH (Chain 6A. No:20)			**HOLLAND** (Chain 2E. No:10)		
A Setenil	36 52 05 08	85.175	A Gilze-Rijen	51 37 04 56	84.550
B Padul	37 02 03 41	113.566	B Heiloo	52 35 04 45	112.733
C Los Barrios	36 11 05 29	127.762	C Sas van Gent	51 13 03 52	126.825
D Rociana	37 18 06 36	70.979	D Thorpeness	52 11 01 36	70.458
N.W. SPANISH (Chain 4C. No:19)			**FRISIAN ISLANDS** (Chain 9B. No:8)		
A San Juan de Rio	42 24 07 18	84.830	A Finsterwolde	53 12 07 06	85.720
B Noya	42 44 08 55	113.107	B Høyer	55 01 08 92	114.293
C Boal	43 27 06 49	127.245	C Heiloo	52 36 04 44	128.580
D Vitigudino	41 01 06 26	70.691	D Zeven	53 17 09 16	71.433
SOUTH-WEST BRITISH (Chain 1B. No:17)			**DANISH** (Chain 7B. No:7)		
A Bolberry Down	50 14 03 50	84.280	A Samsø	55 57 10 35	85.365
B Jersey	49 15 02 05	112.373	B Møen	54 57 12 28	113.820
C St. Mary's	49 56 06 18	126.420	C Eøjer	55 01 08 42	128.047
D Llancarfan	51 26 03 23	70.233	D Hjorring	57 27 10 03	71.138
ENGLISH (Chain 5B. No:11)			**SOUTH BALTIC** (Chain 0A. No:21)		
A Puckeridge	51 55 00 00E	85.00	A Holmsjö	56 27 15 40	84.100
B Shotisham	52 33 01 20E	113.33	B Sandhammaren	57 02 18 15	112.133
C East Hoathley	50 55 00 09E	127.50	C Burgsvik	55 24 14 11	126.150
D Wormleighton	52 12 01 22	70.83	**SKAGERRAK** (Chain 10B. No:6)		
NORTH BRITISH (Chain 3B. No:15)			A Fjällbacka	58 31 11 18	85.900
A Kidsdale	54 42 04 25	84.645	B Jomfruland	58 52 09 36	114.533
B Clanrolla	54 30 06 20	112.280	C Valda	57 29 11 57	128.850
C Neston	53 16 03 03	126.968	D Årjäng	59 21 12 11	71.583
D Stirling	56 04 04 03	70.538	**NORTH BALTIC** (Chain 4B. No:22)		
NORTHUMBRIAN (Chain 2A. No:12)			A Nynashamn	58 57 17 57	84.825
A AllerdeanGreens	55 42 02 02	84.455	B Åland	60 07 19 49	113.100
B Stirling	56 04 04 03	112.607	C Ar	57 55 18 57	127.238
C Peterhead	57 31 01 51	126.683	D Björkvik	58 51 16 34	70.688
D Burton Fleming	54 08 00 19	70.379	**VESTLANDET** (Chain 0E. No:5)		
IRISH (Chain 7D. No:16)			A Sotra	60 24 05 01	84.195
A Galway	53 15 08 59	85.450	B Statt	62 11 05 08	112.250
B Ballydavid	52 12 10 22	113.933	C Shetland Is.	60 03 01 15W	126.292
C Dungloe	54 53 08 23	128.175	D Jaren	58 47 05 33	70.162
D Youghal	51 57 07 45	71.208	**TRØNDELAG** (Chain 4E. No:4)		
HEBRIDEAN (Chain 8E. No:14)			A Skarsøy	63 20 08 27	84.915
A Barra	56 59 07 25	85.635	B Rørvik	64 55 11 10	113.220
B Kentra Moss	56 45 05 49	114.180	C Statt	62 12 05 08	127.373
C Butt of Lewis	58 30 06 16	128.452	D Berkak	62 50 10 03	70.763
D Dungloe	54 53 08 23	71.362			
NORTH SCOTTISH (Chain 6C. No:13)					
A Kirkwall	59 04 03 15	85.185			
B Butt of Lewis	58 30 06 15	113.580			
C Lerwick	60 10 01 11	127.778			
D Peterhead	57 31 01 51	70.988			

A Master   B Red Slave   C Green Slave   D Purple Slave

Satellite Navigation

U.S. Navy Navigation Satellite System (NNSS) (Transit or SatNav)

In the last decade satellite navigation for yachts has become a practical proposition and is now widely used. Originally developed for the U.S. Navy, SatNav consists of five satellites orbiting the Earth at a height of 1000km and transmitting data on frequencies of 400MHz and 150MHz.

The transmission frequency received by an observer decreases as the satellite passes overhead due to the Doppler effect. The rotation of the earth brings the receiver under each satellite orbit in turn, and as the receiver "sights" the satellite, it computes its position from the data transmitted.

The time between suitable satellite "passes" varies between 90 minutes in the low latitudes and 30 minutes in the high latitudes. The actual time of the satellite pass overhead varies between 10 and 15 minutes, during which time the receiver calculates the navigator's position.

SatNav does not provide continuous position-fixing like Decca and Loran C, and it is therefore necessary to maintain a D.R. Position on the chart between fixes. The accuracy of the system is basically good — of the order of ±100m — but correct input of the vessel's speed is necessary for this accuracy. The speed of the vessel will affect the Doppler effect and therefore the calculated position. This error can be of the order of ± 400 m for every knot of velocity error. In some sets speed and compass course can be keyed in manually and in the more sophisticated sets it can be done automatically by interfacing with automatic log and compass units.

Satellite fixes are based on the World Geodetic System (WGS72) Datum and for the best accuracy the receiver coordinates should be amended by the "shift" mentioned on the particular chart. For example, on Chart No. 1183 Thames Estuary, it states:

"Positions obtained from Satellite Navigation Systems are referred to WGS Datum: they should be moved 0.03 minutes Southwards and 0.12 minutes Eastwards to agree with the chart".

Global Positioning System (GPS)

GPS has been developed in the USA for military purposes by the Department of Defense, and by arrangement with the Department of Transportation a degraded version is utilized for civilian use. The system will eventually consist of 21 satellites with 3 spares in orbit at an altitude of 20,000km, each satellite rotating round the earth at 12-hour intervals. There are at least 4 satellites visible to a receiver at sea level at any one time, thus providing continuous position fixing.

The method of operation, basically is that each satellite broadcasts its exact position at an exact time, the receiver then notes the time taken for the transmission to reach it and converts that time into the distance from the satellite. This operation is carried out on 4 satellites and the receiver obtains 4 "position lines" or circles, the point of intersection being the navigator's position. The timing is of extreme importance and this is achieved by equipping the satellites with atomic clocks with an error of ± 1 second in 300,000 years.

Each satellite transmits data on two frequencies, the first designed for military purposes and not available for civilian use, giving extremely accurate position-fixing, probably of the order of 6 to 8 metres error. The transmission available to civilian users is deliberately degraded and the error will be of the order of ± 100m.

It should be noted that the position obtained by GPS should be amended for chart datum in exactly the same way as SatNav positions are amended.

RADIO BEARINGS CORRECTION TABLE

Radio bearings of a ship (Q.T.G.s) which have been taken by a distant radio station are great circle bearings and they are represented on a Mercator chart by curved lines, except when they coincide with a meridian or the equator. As meridians are shown as parallel straight lines on a Mercator chart, these great circle curves will cut each meridian at a different angle.

Convergency is the difference in the angles formed by the intersection of a great circle with two meridians. Its value between any two points on the Earth can be found from the approximate formulae:

Convergency = difference of longitude x sin. mean latitude.

If two places on the chart are joined, first by a great circle and then by a straight line, the latter makes an angle with the great circle at each end. Each of these two angles may, for all practical purposes, be regarded as being equal to the **Half Convergency.**

It is important to remember that the straight line bearing on the Mercator chart always lies on the equatorial side of the great circle bearing.

D/F bearings are all great circle bearings and must, therefore, be corrected for Half Convergency before they can be plotted on a Mercator chart.

Rule for applying Half Convergency

It is usual for the ship to take a Radio D/F bearing of the shore station: but in any case the following rule holds good even if the shore station has taken the bearings. **Always apply the Half Convergency TOWARDS THE EQUATOR.**

HALF CONVERGENCY CORRECTION TABLE

Mean Lat.	Longitude Difference between Radio Station and Ship												
	2°	4°	6°	8°	10°	12°	14°	16°	18°	20°	22°	24°	26°
3	0.1	0.1	0.2	0.2	0.3	0.3	0.4	0.4	0.5	0.5	0.6	0.6	0.7
6	0.1	0.2	0.3	0.4	0.5	0.6	0.7	0.8	0.9	1.0	1.1	1.2	1.3
9	0.2	0.3	0.5	0.6	0.9	0.9	1.1	1.2	1.4	1.5	1.7	1.8	2.0
12	0.2	0.4	0.6	0.8	1.1	1.2	1.5	1.6	1.9	2.0	2.3	2.5	2.7
15	0.3	0.5	0.8	1.0	1.3	1.6	1.9	2.0	2.3	2.5	2.8	3.1	3.3
18	0.3	0.6	1.0	1.2	1.6	1.9	2.2	2.4	2.8	3.0	3.4	3.7	4.0
21	0.3	0.7	1.1	1.4	1.9	2.2	2.5	2.8	3.2	3.5	3.9	4.3	4.6
24	0.4	0.8	1.2	1.6	2.1	2.5	2.9	3.2	3.6	4.0	4.4	4.8	5.2
27	0.4	0.9	1.3	1.8	2.3	2.8	3.2	3.6	4.0	4.5	5.0	5.4	5.9
30	0.5	1.0	1.4	2.0	2.5	3.0	3.5	4.0	4.5	5.0	5.5	6.0	6.5
33	0.5	1.1	1.5	2.2	2.7	3.3	3.8	4.4	4.9	5.4	6.0	6.5	7.1
36	0.6	1.2	1.7	2.4	2.9	3.5	4.1	4.7	5.3	5.9	6.5	7.0	7.6
39	0.6	1.3	1.8	2.6	3.1	3.8	4.4	5.0	5.6	6.3	7.0	7.5	8.1
42	0.7	1.4	1.9	2.8	3.3	4.0	4.7	5.3	6.0	6.7	7.5	8.0	8.7
45	0.7	1.5	2.0	2.9	3.5	4.2	5.0	5.6	6.3	7.1	7.9	8.5	9.2
48	0.7	1.5	2.1	3.0	3.7	4.5	5.3	5.9	6.7	7.4	8.2	8.9	9.6
51	0.8	1.6	2.3	3.2	3.9	4.7	5.5	6.2	7.0	7.8	8.5	9.3	10.0
54	0.8	1.6	2.4	3.4	4.1	4.9	5.7	6.5	7.3	8.1	8.9	9.7	10.5
57	0.8	1.7	2.5	3.5	4.3	5.1	5.9	6.8	7.6	8.4	9.2	10.0	10.9
60	0.9	1.8	2.6	3.6	4.4	5.2	6.1	7.0	7.9	8.7	9.5	10.3	11.2

Example: A vessel in Lat. 15° 20'N., Long. 50° 20'W. obtains a Radio D/F bearing from a Station in Lat. 53° 40'N., Long 5° 10'W. True bearing signalled as 070°.

Enter the above table with the mean latitude (53° 40' + 50° 20' = 104° 00' ÷ 2) = 52° 00', and the Diff. Long. (15° 20' – 5° 10') = 10° 10'W., and by inspection the approximate correction is found to be 4°. By the rule above this must be applied towards the Equator so 070° + 4° = 074°, which is the correct mercatorial bearing to lay off.

RADAR

Radar is probably the most useful of all the electronic navigation aids when coasting. It not only gives position but also indicates the dangers of collision or stranding.

Radar consists of four basic units: transmitter, aerial (scanner), receiver and display.

A very short pulse of powerful electromagnetic energy is transmitted from the aerial in a narrow, horizontal beam at the speed of light (300 million metres/sec.) at the same time a stream of electrons (the trace) is deflected from the centre of a cathode ray tube out towards the circumference of the tube face at a controlled rate, variable with the range scale in use. Only the outward trace is used.

Any object on the bearing of the transmitted pulse will re-radiate the energy in many directions and only a very small portion will return to the aerial.

REFLECTION

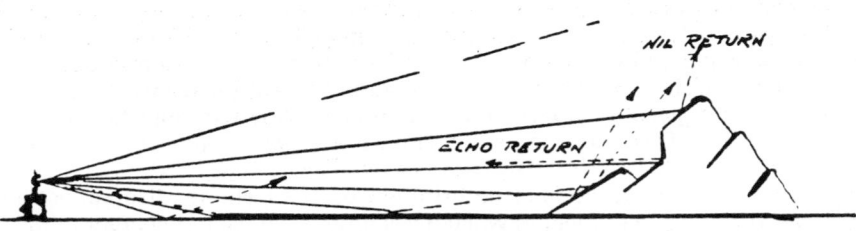

SPECULAR REFLECTION

SCATTERING

This signal once detected needs to be greatly amplified and changed to + D.C. - voltage. The D.C. pulse allows an increase in the flow of electrons to make a bright mark on the screen to record the 'echo'. This sequence takes place many times each second (Pulse Repetition Frequency), the space between is to allow a returned echo to be detected and displayed before the next transmission. PRFs vary with range and/or make of set. Between 500-2000 per second. The aerial is set to rotate at about 20 revs. per minute and the trace rotation is synchronised with the direction of the rotating aerial (scanner) so the direction of every echo from the observer is shown on the display. Even the smallest object will return several echoes before the beam moves on. This provides a storage effect of the returned energy to help display the weaker echoes.

A most important point of reference is the Heading Marker. To enable the radar to give direction, a switch device is placed at the aerial unit. When the aerial is pointing ahead a pulse is sent from the aerial to the radar display which causes a line to show on the screen which represents the ship's head so that any echo displayed on the screen can be referred to the ship's head and the bearing of the echo obtained. If the Heading Marker switch is not pointing exactly ahead, relative bearings will be in error. A quick check is to head towards a small prominent visible object and see if the echo is under the Heading Marker, noting any difference.

The narrow horizontal beam is determined by the size of the aerial. The larger the scanner the smaller is the horizontal beam. The 6m. shore scanners have 0.5° beams. Merchant ships must have less than 2°. These large scanners are not practicable on small craft and the usual yacht scanner of about 0.5m. has a 6° beam.

To allow for the motion at sea the vertical beam is about 20°. The transmitted pulse has to contain sufficient energy to travel many miles and produce a detectable echo return. If a peak power of 1.5 kW. is transmitted for 0.5 millionths of a second ($\frac{1}{2}$ microsecond) this produces a pulse 150m. long. The pulse is shorter on lower ranges (0.1sec. = 30m.)

This combined effect of pulse length and horizontal beam width will determine the picture resolution and ability to discriminate between objects close to each other. The beam distortion of echoes can be seen by apparently large echoes at the longer ranges, getting smaller as they near the centre. Small river or harbour entrances may not be detected, buoyed channels may close. Any objects within the beam at the same range will show on the radar at that bearing as a single echo.

The pulse length gives apparent length to an echo. Any two objects within the pulse appear as one. This is why the shortest pulse possible for detection is used on lower ranges.

The detection of objects is also determined by their shape, size aspect and material. Metal is a perfect reflector, while glass fibre is almost transparent to radar. This is why a metal reflector is a must for small glass fibre vessels (the metal reflectors may be set inside a fiberous material). Sea water is a very good re-radiator, most of the energy reflecting away but the scattered return from waves may give stronger echoes than objects within the waves. Sea clutter normally is more noticeable to windward, the backs of the lee waves giving less return to the aerial.

Small objects, buoy (A) boat (B) small fishing vessel (C) in an area of rough sea.

To remove this clutter around the centre of the display a special variable supression is provided which works outward from the centre decreasing to nil at about 3 miles. This control, 'Sea Clutter', is regarded as the most dangerous control on the set, as 'wanted' real echoes may be removed without the observer realising the extent of the 'hole' in the picture. This is worse for the small craft which may not be detected from a larger ship's radar display. 2(a) & 2(b)

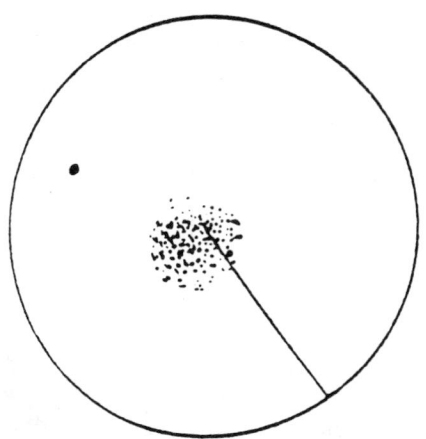
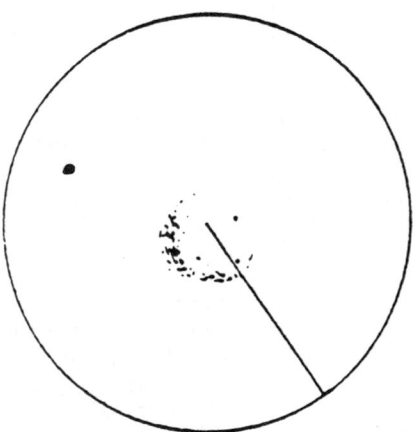

2(a) 'Sea Clutter masking echoes from A. B. and C.

2(b) Sea Clutter Suppression applied echoes A, B -not detected and C -just visible.

Navigating using Radar

Bearing in mind all the above limitations, radar is a most useful navigational aid. The presentation is a plan view of the locality which will relate to the chart in use. However, the picture will not be quite the same as the chart. Small insignificant objects may be enhanced while small prominent objects may not give a detectable return. Lower parts of the coast may be below the radar horizon and the coast on the radar will be inland from the charted coast.

Bearings are quite difficult to take on a small craft radar. The heading must be read at the instant the bearing is read and converted to a true bearing and unless the object is identified the bearing may be laid off from the wrong place. Lighthouses are not usually at the exact point of land. The ends of land will be displaced by half beam width. The best position is obtained by taking a visual bearing of an isolated object and the best radar only position is by taking 3 or more radar ranges from the land. This will produce a 'cocked hat'. Take the closest to danger to be your position. In fog always 'stand off' to seaward of you intended track.

To aid radar navigation, important objects such as lightships or fairway buoys are fitted with responder beacons, 'Racons', which produce a 'flash' away from the racon, usually about 2 miles long. The racon searches the whole marine radar X band and may only strike your frequency once or twice each 100 or so seconds.

Radar presentations not yet widely available to small craft radars are North up, where a compass heading is introduced. As the vessel yaws the Heading Marker moves while the picture is stable. Also true motion, where the centre spot is set to move across the screen at own vessel's course and speed.

Plenty of clear weather practice is essential to build confidence in your own ability, or attend a radar course where all these points will be amplified.

THE RADAR PLOT

In order to comply with the International Collision Regulations 'correct assessment' of a situation using radar can only be ascertained by carefully plotting the movement of an approaching vessel. Clear weather practice is essential before attempting radar navigation in fog.

The Relative Plot

The majority of small craft radars are only capable of a 'ships head up' display. This is where the heading marker is always at zero and any movement of the craft will show as lateral rotating movement of the radar picture. When plotting in this mode it is better to convert the relative bearings into compass bearings for plotting — (no need to apply variation or deviation) — the vessel's course steered is drawn on the plotting diagram. Continuity of the plot after course alterations by your own vessel will be preserved as the only thing to be altered is the heading line. If the plot were to be made 'head up' all echoes will have to be transferred each time the course is changed. This is a frequent cause of mistakes.

The relative plot is a reproduction of the radar picture and on it a forecast of future movement of echoes can be made.

Bearings of echoes should be taken with the cursor through the centre of the echo and the range taken using the inner edge of the range marker through the inner edge. At the moment of bearing the heading should be noted along with the time. The accuracy of the plot is only as good as the accuracy with which the ships head was noted. Without knowing the craft's heading at the moment of reading the bearing can be dangerous.

If our own vessel is stopped all ranges and bearings of echoes would produce a 'true motion picture'. All moving echoes would show their real direction while stationary objects would not move.

When your own vessel is moving, all stationary objects will show as movement in the opposite direction at your speed. The harbour entrance will 'come towards you' on the radar. All echoes which come from moving ships will move across the screen in a resultant direction of your own course and speed and the other's course and speed through the water. In order to decide upon a safe action, it is essential to know the other vessel's heading and speed. To do this we divide the movement into its known components to produce a triangle. By looking at the radar screen the afterglow from echo movement produces dim 'tails' behind the echo. This is only an indication of resultant movement, but useful in deciding which echoes may be closing.

To allow time to plot and assess which action to take the plot should start when the echo is some distance from the centre.

The triangle of motions is named in a standard form W. O. and A. A series of three ranges and bearings are taken in a time interval of 6 minutes (1/10th hour).

The first position is named O and the time noted. On 3 minutes a check position is taken. After the six minutes the range and bearing is taken and marked A. If the O→A line is reasonably straight it may be assumed the other vessel has probably not changed course during the plotting interval. This O→A line is projected past the centre to show the closest point of approach. A CPA of less than 1 mile should be

RADAR (HEAD UP)

6 MILE RANGE

Course 240°T. Speed 8 knots. Land to starboard.
Racon 'Flash' marks structure to port.
5 echoes detected. Echoes at 340° and and 130° visible beacons.
Echo at 240° vessel same course/speed.
Echo at 015° crossing clear.
Echo at 320° to be plotted.

RADAR PLOTTING SHEET

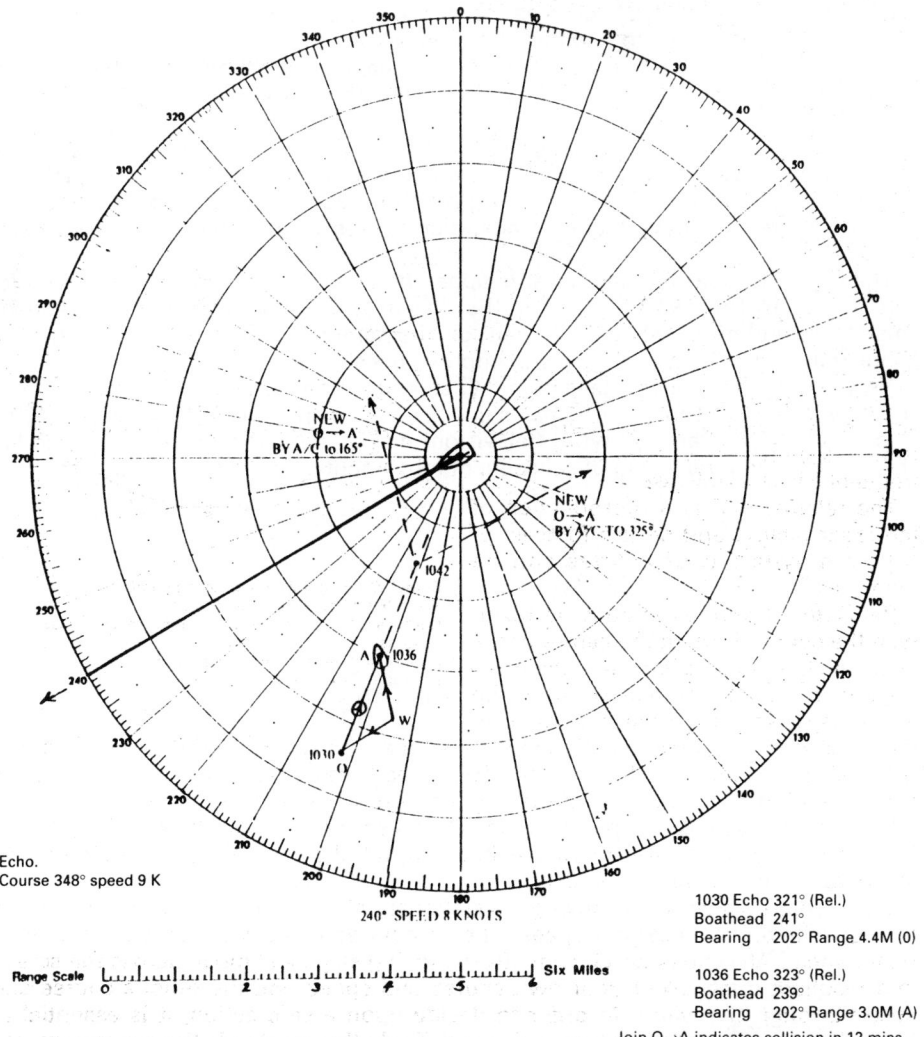

Echo.
Course 348° speed 9 K

240° SPEED 8 KNOTS

Range Scale ⌊ₗₗₗₗ|ₗₗₗₗ|ₗₗₗₗ|ₗₗₗₗ|ₗₗₗₗ|ₗₗₗₗ|ₗₗₗₗ|ₗₗₗₗ⌋ Six Miles
0 1 2 3 4 5 6

1030 Echo 321° (Rel.)
Boathead 241°
Bearing 202° Range 4.4M (0)

1036 Echo 323° (Rel.)
Boathead 239°
Bearing 202° Range 3.0M (A)

Join O→A indicates collision in 12 mins.

Assuming no significant changes in O→A. Plot the forecast position say in 6 min. at 1042. From this position lay off tangents to the chosen pass distance (1 mile ring). Take this line back to A on the plot. Rotate W—O about W to touch this new O-A line at O_1. W→O_1 is the new course. Repeat with the other O_1-A line.
Note: From the plot an alteration to starboard will mean running on a near parallel course for a long time. An alteration to port is not recommended as the other vessel may be altering to starboard as we alter to port—most dangerous. In this situation stopping own vessel before 1042 will allow the other to pass well ahead. Remember the craft on your port quarter will now overtake you.

considered potentially dangerous because of the small scale of the radar picture and the inaccuracy of radar bearings.

In the plotting interval of 6 minutes own vessel will have moved over a known course and distance (1/10th of the speed). This direction and distance is laid back from O and named W. W→O (Way of Own Ship). Join W to A. This represents the course and speed of the other vessel. W→A (Way of Another). Use arrows on each line to indicate direction.

With this information avoiding action can now be planned. Whatever action is decided this may be applied to the plot to see the possible effect before the alteration is made. Alternatively a safe distance can be decided on and taken back to the plot (a new O/A line) to find the alteration needed to achieve this.

To aid visual appreciation of the situation, sketch in a boat shape at the centre of the plot in the direction of your own heading and another shape at A in the Direction W   A, the other's heading.

With practice, and reasonable accuracy the radar plot gives a good general idea of the situation, assuming the other vessel has maintained course and speed. It is important to continue plotting an approaching echo until it is past and clear, especially after you have made an alteration, to see what effect has been made to the CPA.

The need for radar plotting became apparent soon after radar was introduced for use at sea in the 1940s. Many collisions in the early days were caused by misunderstanding of what was 'seen' on the screen. Since then technology and regulations have come a long way to improve the situation.

Very few of the modern developments extend to the small ships radar and most are only able to present the original 'ships head up' display. The information may be filtered to the 'Rasterscan' type (television) display. Guard rings are available but the plotting and forecasting of subsequent movements are left to the observer.

Radio Communications

20

RADIOTELEPHONY

The installation must be licensed by the Department of Trade and Industry (Marine Licensing Section), Waterloo Bridge House, Waterloo Road, London SE1 8UA. Details of examination, tuition, etc., can be obtained from the Royal Yachting Association, R.Y.A. House, Romsey Road, Eastleigh, Hants SO5 4YA.

Medium frequency in 1605-3800 kHz band has a range of approximately 200 miles.

Very High Frequency in 156-174 MHz band has a range of approximately 50 miles.

USE

Make sure you know how to use the set, the frequencies required, what you want to say, your position, and, if applicable, the nature of the problem. Speak clearly, at normal speed, don't shout. Don't use C.B. terms.

PROCEDURES

Coastguards

Call on Chan. 16; if for weather or other information they will tell you to go to Chan. 67. If for assistance or an emergency, they may shift to Chan. 67 or keep you on Chan. 16.

Port Stations

Call on Port's working frequency; depending on the enquiry they may ask you to go to their alternative frequency.

Marinas

VHF Chan. 80 is the prime working channel (with Chan. M for overload) of all U.K. Marinas.

To Make a Ship to Shore Telephone Call (VHF)

1. Listen to Working Frequencies of station required.

2. Free channel indicated by SILENCE. Pips, speech, etc., indicate channel occupied.

3. Call station 3 times, giving name of station, your vessel's name and call sign, for at least 5 seconds.

4. Pips will start when call is accepted. Operator will answer when he is ready.

5. Give number to be called, Account No. e.g. British Telecom GB14 with call sign, or method of payment, i.e. Yacht Telephone Debit (YTD) with telephone number to be debited.

6. Operator will try to connect call.

7. Proceed with call.

8. When completed, operator advises duration of call. Log the time for future reference.

For International calls arrange for billing with British Telecom International.

To Make a Ship to Shore Telephone Call (MF)
1. Follow the VHF procedure, using the paired frequencies shown. Call for up to 10 seconds.

2. Wait until answered, you will be "queued".

To Make a Shore to Ship Telephone Call
1. Dial 100, ask for Freephone Ship's Telephone Service, Portishead, OR Freephone 0800 378389, OR Phone Portishead (0278) 772200, normal charge apply.

2. Give name of vessel with call sign and type of vessel e.g. yacht.

3. Give coast station in whose area vessel currently lies (if known) and/or voyage details.

4. Give your telephone number (or number to be charged if different) and name.

5. Give name of person to be called.

PHONETIC ALPHABET

Letter	Word	Pronunciation	Letter	Word	Pronunciation
A	Alfa	<u>AL</u> FAH	N	November	NO <u>VEM</u> BER
B	Bravo	<u>BRAH</u> VOH	O	Oscar	<u>OSS</u> CAH
C	Charlie	<u>CHAR</u> LEE or	P	Papa	PAH <u>PAH</u>
		<u>SHAR</u> LEE	Q	Quebec	KEH <u>BECK</u>
D	Delta	<u>DELL</u> TAH	R	Romeo	<u>ROW</u> ME OH
E	Echo	<u>ECK</u> OH	S	Sierra	SEE <u>AIR</u> RAH
F	Foxtrot	<u>FOKS</u> TROT	T	Tango	<u>TANG</u> GO
G	Golf	GOLF	U	Uniform	<u>YOU</u> NEE FORM or
H	Hotel	HOH <u>TELL</u>			<u>OO</u> NEE FORM
I	India	<u>IN</u> DEE AH	V	Victor	<u>VIK</u> TAH
J	Juliett	<u>JEW</u> LEE <u>ETT</u>	W	Whiskey	<u>WISS</u> KEY
K	Kilo	<u>KEY</u> LOH	X	X-ray	<u>ECKS</u> RAY
L	Lima	<u>LEE</u> MAH	Y	Yankee	<u>YANG</u> KEY
M	Mike	MIKE	Z	Zulu	<u>ZOO</u> LOO

The syllables to be emphasised are underlined.

When necessary, a word or abbreviation can be spelt by the use of the prowords, 'I SPELL'. The word or abbreviation should be pronounced before being spelt, e.g.

SIGNAL 'I SPELL' — SIERRA INDIA GOLF NOVEMBER ALPHA LIMA — SIGNAL.

PROWORDS

Procedural words or short phrases used to facilitate the conduct of R/T communication.

PROWORD	USE OR MEANING
Affirmative	Yes, or permission granted.
Negative	No, or permission not granted or that is not correct.
All After	⎫ Used to identify part of a message and used in conjunction
All Before	⎭ with other appropriate prowords.
Call Sign	See paragraph on Figures.
Correct	You are correct.
Correction	Cancel the last word or phrase sent (or cancel word or phrase indicated) and substitute.
Figures	⎫
Grid Reference	⎬ See paragraph on Figures.
Read Back	Repeat back the whole message.
I read back	The following is my response to your instructions to read back.
I say again	Used by sender to emphasise or when conditions are bad to ensure that it is received. When giving repetitions requested by the receiver.
I spell	Used when spelling out a word or abbreviation.
Over*	My transmission is ended. I expect a reply or an acknowledgement from you.
Out*	My transmission is ended (I do not expect a reply.) Only one station need say "out" the other does not need to reply.
Roger	Message received and understood. Often used in U.K. waters. Other stations may use the proword "Received".
Say Again	Used by receiver requiring whole message to be repeated.
Seelonce	All stations maintain R/T silence and await directions. Used when receiving station requires time to consider the reply to a question, or when a base station controlling a number of mobiles requires one or more station to cease transmission. The proword in this case would be preceded by the Call Sign or Call Signs of the stations required to wait. Wait followed by a single digit indicates the appropriate period in minutes of waiting.

*The phrase 'over and out' is a contradiction of the definitions and is NEVER to be used.

FIGURES

Figures sent by R/T are predicted by the proword 'Figures' except Call Signs and Grid References. These should be preceded by the words 'Call Sign' or 'Grid Reference'. Each digit should be pronounced separately as shown below:

0	ZERO	
1	WUN	Emphasis on N.
2	TOO	Sharp T and long OO.
3	THUH-REE	Short U, rolling R and long E as in spree.
4	FOW-ER	Long O as in foe.
5	FIVE	Emphasis on the F with a long I.
6	SIX	Emphasis on the X.
7	SEVEN	Two distinct syllables.
8	ATE	With a long A.
9	NINER	Long I as in pie, emphasising each N.

NAVTEX

Navtex is an international single frequency (518 kHz) narrow band direct printing system which provides an edited series of coastal messages printed out on the bridge.

The subjects covered include navigational warnings, meteorological forecasts and gale warnings, ice information, electronic navigation aid warnings and initial distress messages.

A small dedicated receiver continually monitors the fixed frequency transmission. Messages pass through a filtering process and are printed out immediately for use by the watch keeper. For yachtsmen a special Navtex compact receiver is available.

Routine Broadcast Schedules

Identity Letter	Station			Transmission Times (G.M.T.)			
H	Härnösand	0000	0400	0800(W)	1200(I)	1600	2000(W)
B	Bodø	0018(W)	0418	0900	1218(W)	1618	2100
S	Niton	0018	0418(N)	0818(W)	1218	1618(N)	2018(W)
U	Tallin	0030	0430	0830(W)	1230(I)	1630	2030(W)
G	Cullercoats	0048	0448(N)	0848(W)	1248	1648(N)	2048(W)
O	Portpatrick	0130	0530(N)	0930(W)	1330	1730(N)	2130(W)
L	Rogaland	0148(W)	0548	0948(W)	1348(W)	1748	2148(W)
V	Vardø	0200	0500	0818	1100(W)	1700	2300(W)
T	Oostende	0248	0648(W)	1048	1448	1848(W)	2248
R	Reykjavik	0318	0718	1118	1518	1918	2318
J	Stockholm	0300	0730(W)	1130(I)	1500	1930(W)	2330
P	Scheveningen	0348	0748	1148(I)	1548	1948	2348
F	Brest-Le Conquet	0118	0518	0918	1318	1718	2118

I = Ice reports.   N = Navarea warnings.   W = Routine area weather forecasts.

Full area weather forecasts and Navarea (long term) warnings are only broadcast twice a day. The following subject indicator letters are used to show the category of message:

A. Coastal Navigation Warning.   E. Weather Message.
B. Gale Warning.   F. Pilot Service Message.
C. Ice Report.   G. Electronic Navaid Information.
D. Initial Distress Information.   L. Navarea Warning.
                    Z. QRU. (No Messages on Hand).

WEATHERFAX

Up to date weather forecasts are an important part of safety at sea, especially in small craft. Luckily, national forecasting services throughout the world are now able to give a series of forecasts for up to five days ahead, thanks to major advances in computing technology. These forecasts are surprisingly accurate and are available free of charge in graphical form to any yachtsman capable of receiving HF weather facsimile transmissions. Also available are current surface analysis maps (four times per day) so that the developing weather situation can be compared with the forecast, as well as sea state forecasts, ice coverage maps and the positions of ocean currents.

The information is transmitted from radio stations around the world according to published schedules. To receive a desired map, it is simply a matter of tuning a suitable radio receiver to the right frequency at the right time, provided you have the means to print out or display the resulting images.

If you already own an SSB receiver or transceiver (both of which are useful for receiving voice and morse weather forecasts), the add on equipment needed to print weather maps costs about the same as a good Decca or Loran set. If you need to start from scratch, the whole system costs about the same as a low cost radar. The decoding equipment can usually incorporate Naxtex reception at little extra cost, thus increasing the overall versatility of the system.

In most cases, weather maps for the mariner are greatly simplified. They are not designed just for the professional meteorologist, but for the layman. Forecasts maps generally show forecasted wind speed and direction for each area and the likely positions of developing weather fronts.

One U.K. manufacturer of weather facsimile systems is ICS Electronics Ltd. (telephone: 0903 731101), but there are also several other European, American and Japanese manufacturers who offer suitable equipment.

The definitive source of information about frequencies and transmission schedules is the Admiralty List of Radio Signals, Vol. 3. An abbreviated list of the main transmitting stations providing weather maps especially for the mariner in this area follows:

Station	Freq. (kHz)	Station	Freq. (kHz)
Northwood* (U.K.)	4247.85 6436.35 8494.85	Norkoeping (Sweden)	4037.5 6901 8077.5
Bracknell (U.K.)	3289.5 8040 11086.5 4782 9203 14436	Rota (Spain)	5785 9255
Offenbach (Germany)	134.2 3855 7880 13882.5	Moscow (U.S.S.R.)	5355 7750 10980

*Recommended. Note: The SSB receiver should normally be detuned from these frequencies by a small amount. See facsimile system manufacturer's handbook.

MARITIME VHF SERVICES

To contact any coast station by telephone ask Operator for Maritime Ships Telephone Service (Freephone) or ring Portishead radio (0278) 772200 who will re-direct the call.

Channel Numbers, Related Frequency in MHz as follows. Frequencies may be used for more than one purpose.

DISTRESS CALLING AND SAFETY: – Chan. 16. Coastguard Chan. 67. Digital Selective Calling Chan. 70.

INTERSHIP: – Chan. 6, 8, 10, 13, 9, 72, 73, 69, 67, 77, 15. Marinas and Yacht Harbours use Chan. 80 with Chan. 37 (M) as alternative. Yacht clubs use Chan. M2 (161.425 MHz) as Race Control.

PORT OPERATIONS; SIMPLEX: – Chan. ⎫ See stations details for frequencies
PORT OPERATIONS; DUPLEX: – Chan. ⎬ used. The first frequency given for a port
PUBLIC CORRESPONDENCE: – Chan. ⎭ is the WORKING FREQUENCY.

CHAN.	TRANSMITTER FREQUENCY MHz		CHAN.	TRANSMITTER FREQUENCY MHz		CHAN.	TRANSMITTER FREQUENCY MHz	
	SHIP	SHORE		SHIP	SHORE		SHIP	SHORE
1 60	156.025	160.625	11 70	156.525		80	157.025	161.625
	156.050	160.650		156.550				156.050
2 61	156.075	160.675	71	156.575		21	157.050	OR
	156.100	160.700						161.650
62	156.125	160.725	12	156.600		81	157.075	161.675
			72	156.625		22	157.100	161.700
3 63	156.150	160.750	13	156.650		82	157.125	161.725
	156.175	160.775	73	156.675				156.150
4	156.200	160.800	14	156.700		23	157.150	OR
								161.750
5 64	156.225	160.825	74	156.725				156.175
	156.250	160.850	15	156.750		83	157.175	OR
								161.775
6 65	156.275	160.875	75	156.7625	156.7875	24	157.200	161.800
	156.300		16	156.800	156.800	84	157.225	161.825
7 66	156.325	160.925	76	156.8125	156.8375	25	157.250	161.850
	156.350	160.950	17	156.850		85	157.275	161.875
8 67	156.375		77	156.875		26	157.300	161.900
	156.400		18	156.900	161.500	86	157.325	161.925
9 68	156.425		78	156.925	161.525	27	157.350	161.950
	156.450		19	156.950	161.550	87	157.375	161.975
10 69	156.475		79	156.975	161.575	28	157.400	162.000
	156.500		20	157.000	161.600	88	157.425	162.025

75 and 76 guard channels for 16.   Simplex channels are shown by the single frequency given.

HF TELEX SERVICES

For those yachtsmen wishing to keep in touch with the office over long distances, HF and MF telex links are possible via many coast radio stations. This extremely efficient method of communication allows virtually error free data transmission from a small lap portable computer on your boat, provided that you have a suitable radio transceiver and an ARQ telex modem.

The services provided by the coast station are fully automatic, allowing messages to be picked up or deposited when you call in. Database services are also offered, giving information ranging from weather forecasts to football results!

With many offices now devoid of telex and used only to facsimile, many coast stations now offer marine telex to Group III facsimile conversion facilities.

Assigned frequencies for this service are available on application to British Telecom, 43 Bartholomew Close, London EC1A 7HP. Tel: 071-583 9416.

INSHORE FISHING VESSELS
Recommended Frequency Usage for Intership Working

Area of Home Port	Primary Use kHz	Secondary Use kHz
Berwick to Fifeness	2306 3519	2226 2231 3373
Fifeness to Buchan Ness	2226 3373	2306 2231 3519
Buchan Ness to More Head	2231 3519	2226 2306 3373
More Head to Thurso	2226 3373	2231 2306 3519
Shetlands and Orkneys	2306 3519	2226 2231 3373
North Foreland to Cromer (including Lowestoft)	2226 3519	2231 2306 3373
Cromer to Humber (including Grimsby): (a) Trawlers (b) Seiners	2231 3519 2306 3373	2226 2306 3373 2226 2231 3519
Humber to Berwick (including Hull)	2226 3376	2231 2306 3519

In addition to using 2182 kHz, for distress, Fishing Vessels will also have exclusive use of 2381 kHz between 1700-0900 for intership and reporting to base.

UNITED KINGDOM SHIPS 2 MHz RADIOTELEPHONY SERVICE
Intership Frequency Arrangements

Class of vehicle	Area of use	Frequencies kHz
Fishing Vessels (all classes) ...	All Areas North Sea, Icelandic Sea and Norwegian Sea only	2226 2231 2306 3373 3519
Deep Sea Ships only	Atlantic 0°-60° N, South Atlantic, West, Central and Eastern Mediterranean	2421
Coasters, Yachts, etc., and Deep Sea Ships	All Areas	2241 2246 2301

UK COAST STATION RADIOTELEPHONY SERVICE

COAST STATION & TEL. NO.	CALL kHz	COAST STATION TRANS-MITS kHz	RECEIVES kHz	VHF WORK-ING CHAN-NEL	B'CAST FREQ. kHz	TRAFFIC LIST TIMES GMT			NAVIGA-TIONAL
NITON § 50° 34′ 42″N 01° 17′ 10″W (0983) 730 496 Telex 86167	2182	1834 2628† 2810	} 2009 2562	4* 28 81 64 85 87	1834 VHF 28	0233 0303 0633 0733	0903 1033 1433 1503	1833 1933 2103 2233	0233 1433 0633 1833 1033 2233
WEYMOUTH BAY § 50° 35′N 01° 18′W				5	VHF 5	AS FOR NITON			AS FOR NITON
START POINT § 50° 21′N 03° 43′W				26 60 65	VHF 26	AS FOR NITON			AS FOR NITON
PENDENNIS § 50° 09′N 05° 03′W				62 66	VHF 62	AS FOR NITON			AS FOR NITON
LAND'S END § 50° 07′ 04″N 05° 40′ 05″W (0736) 871364 Telex 45250 BT GLD G	2182	2670 2782† 3610†	} 2002 2120 64* 27	27 88 85	2670 VHF	AS FOR NITON			AS FOR NITON
ILFRACOMBE § 51° 10′ 42″N 04° 06′ 53″W				5 7*	VHF 5	AS FOR NITON			AS FOR NITON
CELTIC § 51° 41′N 05° 11′W				24	VHF 24	AS FOR NITON			AS FOR NITON
CARDIGAN BAY § 52° 50′N 04° 38′W				3 28	3	0203 0303 0603 0703	0903 1003 1403 1503	1803 1903 2103 2203	0203 1403 0603 1803 1003 2203
ANGLESEY § 53° 23′ 30″N 04° 17′ 49″W				26 28 61	VHF 26	AS FOR CARDIGAN BAY			AS FOR CARDIGAN BAY
MORECAMBE BAY § 54° 10′N 03° 12′W				4 82	VHF 4	AS FOR CARDIGAN BAY			AS FOR CARDIGAN BAY
PORTPATRICK § 54° 50′ 38″N 05° 07′ 24″W (077681) 312 Telex 777732	2182	1883 2607†	} 2104	27	1883 VHF 27	AS FOR CARDIGAN BAY			AS FOR CARDIGAN BAY

ALL UK STATIONS FITTED VHF CHAN. 16

NITON: VHF Chan. 4* for vessels in Brighton Area.
ILFRACOMBE: VHF Chan. 7* for vessels in Severn Area.
LAND'S END: VHF Chan. 64* for vessels in Scillies Area.

§ Direct calling station.
† Prime working channel.
Continued next page

UK COAST STATION RADIOTELEPHONY SERVICE

COAST STATION & TEL. NO.	CALL	TRANS-MITS kHz	RECEIVES kHz	VHF WORK-ING CHAN-NEL	B'CAST FREQ. kHz	TRAFFIC LIST TIMES GMT	ALL UK STATIONS FITTED VHF CHAN. 16 NAVIGA-TIONAL
		kHz					
CLYDE 55° 55'N 04° 48'W	§			26	VHF 26	AS FOR CARDIGAN BAY	AS FOR CARDIGAN BAY
OBAN 56° 27'N 05° 44'W				7	7	AS FOR CARDIGAN BAY	AS FOR CARDIGAN BAY
ISLAY 55° 46'N 06° 27'W	§			25 60	VHF 25	AS FOR CARDIGAN BAY	AS FOR CARDIGAN BAY
SKYE 57° 28'N 06° 41'W	§			24	VHF 24	AS FOR CARDIGAN BAY	AS FOR CARDIGAN BAY
HEBRIDES 58° 14'N 07° 02'W	§	2182	1866	2534 26	1866 VHF	AS FOR CARDIGAN BAY	AS FOR CARDIGAN BAY
LEWIS 58° 28'N 06° 14'W	§			5	VHF 5	AS FOR CARDIGAN BAY	AS FOR CARDIGAN BAY
WICK 58° 26'N 03° 06'W (0955) 2272 Telex 75284 BT GKR G		2182	2751† 1824 2840.6† 3538† 1792 2705† 1827† 2604† 2625†	}Ch.A 2006 Ch.B 2277 Ch.C 3335 Ch.D 3328 }Ch.E 2524 Ch.F 2548 Ch.G 2013 Ch.H 2381	1792 1824	0233 0903 1833 0303 1033 1903 0633 1433 2103 0703 1503 2233	0233 1433 0633 1833 1033 2233
ORKNEY 58° 47'N 02° 57'W	§			26	VHF 26	AS FOR WICK	AS FOR WICK
SHETLANDS 60° 08' 40"N 01° 12' 20"W	§			27	VHF 27	AS FOR WICK	AS FOR WICK
COLLAFIRTH 60° 32'N 01° 24'W	§			24	VHF 24	AS FOR WICK	AS FOR WICK
CROMARTY 57° 37'N 02° 58'W	§			84 28	VHF 28	AS FOR WICK	AS FOR WICK
BUCHAN 57° 36'N 02° 03'W	§			25 87	VHF 25	AS FOR WICK	AS FOR WICK

WICK/STONEHAVEN for UK F/Vls. Receives 2381 kHz, Transmits 1792 kHz 1700-0900.
§ Direct calling station.   † Prime working channel.

UK COAST STATION RADIOTELEPHONY SERVICE

ALL UK STATIONS FITTED VHF CHAN. 16

COAST STATION & TEL. NO.	CALL kHz	COAST STATION TRANS-MITS kHz	RECEIVES kHz		VHF WORK-ING CHAN-NEL	B'CAST FREQ. kHz	TRAFFIC LIST TIMES GMT	NAVIGA-TIONAL
STONEHAVEN § 56° 56′ 46″N 02° 12′ 39″W (0569) 62918 Telex 73159 BT GND G	2182	1856† 2691 1650 1946† 2779† 3617†	}Ch.I 2555 Ch.J 2552 Ch.K 2566 Ch.L 2146 Ch.M 3249		26	2691 VHF 26	AS FOR WICK	AS FOR WICK
FORTH § 55° 57′N 02° 27′W					24 62	VHF 24	AS FOR WICK	AS FOR WICK
CULLERCOATS § 55° 02′ 16″N 01° 25′ 39″W (091 297) 031 Telex 53345 BT GCC G	2182	1838† 2719 2828† 3750†	}Ch.N 2527 Ch.O 1953 Ch.P 2559		26	2719 VHF 26	AS FOR WICK	AS FOR WICK
WHITBY §					25 28	VHF 25	AS FOR WICK	AS FOR WICK
GRIMSBY §					4 27	VHF 27	0133 0903 1733 0303 0933 1933 0533 1333 2103 0733 1503 2133	0133 1333 0533 1733 0933 2133
HUMBER § 53° 19′ 43″N 00° 16′ 34″E (0521) 73448 Telex 56282	2182	1925† 1869 2684† 2810†	}Ch.Q 2569 Ch.R 2111 Ch.S 2562		26 24 85	1869 VHF 26	AS FOR GRIMSBY	AS FOR GRIMSBY
BACTON § 52° 51′N 01° 28′E					3 7 63 64	VHF 7	AS FOR GRIMSBY	AS FOR GRIMSBY
ORFORDNESS § 52° 00′N 01° 25′E					62 82	VHF 62	AS FOR GRIMSBY	AS FOR GRIMSBY
THAMES § 51° 19′ 43″N 00° 20′ 20″E					2 83	VHF 2	AS FOR GRIMSBY	AS FOR GRIMSBY
NORTH FORELAND§ 51° 21′ 37″N 01° 24′ 55″E (0843) 291984 Telex 96137 BT GNF G	2182	2698† 1848	}Ch.T 2016		5 26 66 65	1848 VHF 26	AS FOR GRIMSBY	AS FOR GRIMSBY
HASTINGS § 50° 52′N 00° 36′E					7 63	VHF 7	AS FOR GRIMSBY	AS FOR GRIMSBY

WICK/STONEHAVEN for UK F/Vls. Receives 2381 kHz, Transmits 1792 kHz 1700-0900.
HUMBER Transmits 1792 kHz. Receives 2381 kHz. 1700-0900 for UK F/Vls.
§ Direct calling station.   † Prime working channel.
Continued next page

UK COAST STATION RADIOTELEPHONY SERVICE

COAST STATION & TEL. NO.	CALL	COAST STATION		VHF WORK-ING CHAN-NEL	TRAFFIC LIST			ALL UK STATIONS FITTED VHF CHAN. 16	
		TRANS-MITS kHz	RECEIVES kHz		B'CAST FREQ. kHz	TIMES GMT		NAVIGA-TIONAL	
ST PETER PORT § 49° 07'N 02° 32'W (0481) 20085 Telex 4191488	2182	1662.5 } 1810 } 2182 }	1662.5 2049 2056 2182 2381	78 62‡	1810 VHF 78	0133 0933 1733 0533 1333 2133		0133 1333 0533 1733 0933 2133	
JERSEY § 49° 10.85'N 02° 14.3'W (0534) 41121	2182	1726	2049Foreign 2104 vls. 2534	25‡ 82 67*	1726 VHF 25 82	0645 1245 2245 0745 1845		0433 1633 0645 1845 0745 2033 0833 2245 1245	
DUBLIN § 53° 23'N 06° 04'W				83 67*	83	AS FOR MALIN HEAD		AS FOR MALIN HEAD	
ROSSLARE § 52° 15'N 06° 20'W				23 67*	23	AS FOR VALENTIA		AS FOR VALENTIA	
MINE HEAD § 52° 00'N 07° 35'W				83 67*	83	AS FOR VALENTIA		AS FOR VALENTIA	
BANTRY § 51° 38'N 10° 00'W				24 28 67*	24	AS FOR VALENTIA		AS FOR VALENTIA	
CORK § 51° 51'N 08° 29'W				26 67*	26	AS FOR VALENTIA		AS FOR VALENTIA	
VALENTIA § 51° 55' 48"N 10° 20' 54"W (353 667) 6109 Telex 73968 VALR EI	2182	1827 2614 2590	2049	24 28 67*	1827 24	0333 1333 1933 0733 1533 2133 0933 1733 2333 1133		0233 1433 0633 1833 1033 2233	
SHANNON § 52° 31'N 09° 36'W				24 28 67*	28	AS FOR VALENTIA		AS FOR VALENTIA	
BELMULLET § 54° 16'N 10° 03'W				83 67*	83	AS FOR MALIN HEAD		AS FOR MALIN HEAD	
GLEN HEAD § 54° 44'N 08° 43'W				24 67*	24	AS FOR MALIN HEAD		AS FOR MALIN HEAD	
MALIN HEAD § 55° 21' 45"N 07° 20' 30"W (353 77) 70103 Telex 42072 MALR EI	2182	1841 2593	2049	23 67* 85	1841 VHF 23	0103 1303 1903 0503 1503 2103 0903 1703 2303 1103		0033 1233 0433 1633 0833 2033	

ST PETER PORT 1662.5 kHz for SAR only.
* Safety traffic only · WX. Messages. B'Cast 1h earlier during daylight saving time.
§ Direct calling station.   ‡ Link Calls.

CONTINENTAL COAST STATION RADIOTELEPHONY SERVICE

H24 = continuous. H + = commencing at minutes past the hour. Ch. = channel. Frequency in bold type = prime frequency. (16) bracketed = transmits = transmits only. All VHF Channels H24 unless stated. Times quoted are GMT.

STATION	TRANSMITS kHz	RECEIVES kHz	HOURS OF SERVICE	VHF Channel	TRAFFIC LISTS Frequency & Times
BELGIUM **Ostend** 51° 11'N 2° 48'E Telex 81080Z OSRAD B	1817 1820 1905 / 1908 2087 2090 / 2170.5 2182 2253 / 2256 2373 2376 / 2481 2484 2758 / 2761 2814 2817* / 3629 3632* 3681 / 3684	2182 2484 2191 3178	H24 / H24 for Belgian V/ls / When 2182 on / Distress / *for Foreign V/ls	Vicinity 16 23 27 / 78 85 87 88 / La Panne 23 78 / Vicinity / Zeebrugge 27 87 / Vicinity / Ostend 27 85 88	2761 ev. H + 20 / Ch.16 27 ev. / H + 20
Antwerp 51° 17'N 4° 20'E Telex 32595Z ANRAD B			H24	Antwerpen 7 16 24 87 / 16 27 28 83 / Ghent 24 26 81 / Kortrijk 10 24 83 / Vilvoorde 16 24 28 / Ronquieres 10 24 25 / Mol 16 24 87 / Liege 16 24 27	Ch. 24 ev. / H + 05
HOLLAND **Scheveningen** 52° 10'N 5° 50'E Telex 73333 SCHR NL	1764 Ch B / 1862 Ch F / 1890 Ch I / 1939 Ch D / 2600 Ch C / 2824 Ch A / 3673 Ch E	2030 2160 / 2045 2051 2057 2513 / 1995 / 2520 3191 / 2048 2054	H24 / Mon.-Sat. 0700-2200 / Sun. 0800-2200 / 0700-2300 / Mon.-Sat. 0700-2200 / H24 As required	Goes 16 23 25 / Rotterdam 16 24 28 87 / Scheveningen 16 26 83 / Haarlem 16 23 25 / Wieringerwief 16 27 / Location L7 16 28 84 / Terschelling 16 25 78 / Nes 16 23 / Appingedam 16 27 / Lelystad 16 83 24	1862 2600 / ev. H + 05 / All VHF Ch. / except Ch.16 / ev. H + 05 / 2824 at 0105 / 0305 0505 2305
GERMANY **Norddeich** 53° 38'N 7° 12'E Telex 4127209 NDRDO D	1799 1911 2182 2614 2799 2848	2491 2541 2182 2023 2045† 2153 3161	H24 0600-2200	16 86 28 61	Ch. 28 ev. / H + 45 / 2614 ev. H + 45

† When 2182 kHz engaged in Distress working (only available 2200-0600 to German vessels).

STATION	TRANSMITS kHz	RECEIVES kHz	HOURS OF SERVICE	VHF Channel	TRAFFIC LISTS Frequency & Times
Bremen 53° 05'N 8° 48'E				25 28	Ch. 28 ev. H + 40
Helgoland 54° 11'N 7° 53'E				3 27 88	Ch. 27 ev. H + 20
Elbe-Weser 53° 50'N 8° 39'E Telex 232216 EWR D				1 23 24 / 26 28 62	Ch. 23 ev. H + 20 V/ls in Nord-Ostsee Canal Ch. 26 ev. H + 50
Hamburg 53° 33'N 9° 58'E				25 27 / 82 83	Ch. 27 ev. H + 40
Eiderstedt 54° 20'N 8° 47'E				25 64	Ch. 25 ev. H + 40
Nordfriesland 54° 55'N 8° 19'E				5 26	Ch. 26 ev. H + 50
DENMARK Blavand 55° 33'N 8° 07'E Telex 50377 BLRDO D	1713 1813 2170.5 2182 2593	2045 2059 / 2045 2076 / 2182 / 2045 3245	0600-2245 H24 H24 0600-2100 2045 used when Distress working	2 16 23 25	1813 ev. odd H + 05 VHF Ch. 2 23 ev. odd H + 05
Skagen 57° 44'N 10° 34'E Telex 67556 SGRDO DK	1701 2182	1988 2182 / 2049 2056 / 2049 2056 / 3259 2049	H24 H24 When 2182 on Distress on Request	16 1 2 3 / 4 64 / 83 19	1701 ev. odd H + 05 VHF Ch. 1, 64, 3, 4, 66 ev. odd H + 05
Ronne 55° 05'N 14° 44'E Telex 48158 RONNE DK	2182 **2586**	1995 2182 / 2049 2056 / 2049	H24 When 2182 on Distress	16 4 7 23	2586 ev. odd H + 05 VHF Ch. 4 ev. odd H + 05

STATION	TRANSMITS kHz	RECEIVES kHz	HOURS OF SERVICE	VHF Channel	TRAFFIC LISTS Frequency & Times
Lyngby 55°50'N 11°25'E Telex 37383 LYRDO DK	1687 2182* *2049 when 2182 on Distress	2069 2182 2049 2056	H24 When 2182 on Distress on request	Vejby 16 83 — Moen 2 16 64 84 — Roesnaes 2 4 16 26 23 — Kobenhavn 3 16 66 — Fornaes 5 16 — Langeland 5 16 — Als 7 16 — Anholt 7 16 — Hyldager 16 63 28 — Vejle 16 65	1687 ev. odd H + 05
GERMANY Flensburg 54°44'N 9°30'E				25 27 64	Ch. 27 ev. H + 25
Kiel 54°26'N 10°08'E Telex 299890 KLRDO D	1880 1915 2772 1883 1918 2182 2775	2143 2566 3158 2569 1627.5 3161 2182 2045 2146	H24 H24 H24 H24 H24	(16) 23 24 26 — 78 87	2775 ev. H + 25 — Ch. 24 ev. H + 25 — Ch. 26 ev. H + 26
Lubeck 54°13'N 10°43'E				(16) 24 27 — 82 83	Ch. 27 ev. H + 25
Rostock 54°10'N 12°06'E			H24	Buk 16 21 80 87 — Rostock 16 18 23 24 — 16 26 80 87 — Ahrenshoop 16 23 26 84	Ch. 21, 23, 26, 84 ev. even H + 20 in English and German
Rugen 54°35'N 13°37'E Telex 31535/6 RGRA DO	1719 2182	2191 2550 2182	H24	Arkona 1 5 16 62 — Gohren 1 5 16 66	1719 kHz at 0333 0733 1133 1533 1933 2333 Ch. 1.5 ev. odd H + 20 in English and German
POLAND Szczecin 53°28'N 14°35'E Telex 042251	1757 2090 2182 2191 2831	2090 2182 2191	H24	12 16 24 25 26 27	2831 kHz at 0105 0505 0905 1305 1705 2105 Ch. 27 at 0000 0400 0800 1200 1600 2000

STATION	TRANSMITS kHz	RECEIVES kHz	HOURS OF SERVICE	VHF Channel	TRAFFIC LISTS Frequency & Times
Witowo 54°33'N 16°32'E	2182 2191 2639 2719	2090 2182 2191	H24	16 12 25 26	2639 kHz at 0005 0405 0805 1205 1605 2005
Gdynia 54°33'N 18°32'E Telex 054291	1818 2182 2191 2726	2090 2182 2191	H24	12 16 25 26 27	2726 kHz and Ch. 26 at 0035 0435 0835 1235 1635 2035
SWEDEN **Harnosand** 62°43'N 18°08'E Telex 71069 HS DRDO S	1650 2182 2733	2216 2182 2216	H24	Kalix 16 28 Lulea 16 25 Skelleftea 16 23 Umea 16 26 Ornskoldsvik 16 28 Harnosand 16 23 Sundsvall 16 24 Hudiksvall 16 25 Gavle 16 23 Oregrund 16 24 Mjallom 16 64 Kramfors 16 84	1650, 2733 kHz at 0033 0433 0833 1233 1633 2033 Ch. 23, 24, 25, 26, 28, 84 as above
Stockholm 59°17'N 18°43'E Telex 13240 SDJ S	1771 1778 2182 2754	2477 1974 2182 2206	H24	Vaddo 16 28 27 Vasteras 16 25 Nacka (Stockholm) 3 16 23 Sodertalje 26 84 Hjalmaren 16 66 Toro 16 81 Norrkoping 16 24 Faro 16 27 Vasterik 16 28 85 Visby 16 23 Hoburgen 16 25 Emmaboda 16 24 Karlshamn 16 26 Olands Sodre Udde 16 25 Kivik 16 16 27 Smygehuk 16 28 24	1771, 1778 kHz at 0133 0533 0933 1333 1733 2133 Ch. 3, 23, 84, 85 (Vastervik) Ch. 87 (Vaddo) as above

STATION	TRANSMITS kHz	RECEIVES kHz	HOURS OF SERVICE	VHF Channel	TRAFFIC LISTS Frequency & Times
Tingstade 57°44'N 18°36'E Telex 4130 TDRS	2182 2768	2182 3289	H24	16	2768 kHz at ev. even H + 06
Karlskrona 56°11'N 15°33'E Telex 43049 KARS	2182 2789	2182 3185	H24	16	2789 kHz at ev. odd H + 54
Göteborg 57°28'N 11°56'E Telex 9290 GBGRDO S (For V/Ls fitted with maritex)	1785 1904 2182	2037 2221 2182	H24	Kristenhamn 16 28; Stromstad 16 20; Backefors 1 16; Tanum 16 78; Karlsborg 16 27; Uddevalla 16 27; Kungshamn 16 23; Jonkopping 16 23 84; Kode 16 81; Varberg 16 22; Göteborg 16 22; Halmstad 16 24 26; Hoganas 16 25; Baresback 16 27 82; Falsterbo 16 21	1785 kHz at 0233 0633 1033 1433 1833 2233 VHF all working channels as above

NORWAY – Notes: 1. Call sign for all MF *and* all VHF channels is the main station name.
2. 2049 kHz is used for calls *from* Foreign Vessels when 2182 kHz is engaged in Distress working.

STATION	TRANSMITS kHz	RECEIVES kHz	HOURS OF SERVICE	VHF Channel	TRAFFIC LISTS Frequency & Times
Tjøme 59°05'N 10°25'E Telex 70579 LGT N	1736 2182 2663 3631	2456 2049 2182 1632.5 2132 3203	H24	Halden 7 16 63; Tonsberg 81; Oslo 16 24 25 65; Drammen 16 27; Horten 79; Tjøme 2 16; Porgrunn 3 16 25; Risør 16 86 87	1736, 2649 kHz and all VHF Ch. except Ch. 16 at 0333 0733 1133 1533 1933 2333
Farsund 58°04'N 6°45'E Telex 21970 LGZ N	1750 2182 2635 2642 3645	2470 2049 2182 2118 2125 3217	H24	Arendal 5 88; Dolsveten 16 24 27; Kristiansand 24 27; Lindesnes 61; Kalåskniben 21; Farsund 7 25; Storefjell 7 16 25	1750, 2635 kHz and all VHF Ch. except Ch. 16 at 0133 0533 0933 1333 1733 2133

STATION	TRANSMITS kHz	RECEIVES kHz	HOURS OF SERVICE	VHF Channel	TRAFFIC LISTS Frequency & Times
Rogaland 58°39'N 5°36'E Telex 42360 LGO N	1729 2182 2656 3638	2449 2049 2182 2139 3210	H24	Haugesund 4 16 26; Bokn 3 16 28; Sand 25; Lifjell 18 20; Stavanger 16 23 27; Bjerkreim 5 16 24	1729 kHz and all VHF Ch. except Ch. 16 at 0333 0733 1133 1533 1933 2333
Bergen 60°25'N 5°22'E Telex 42144 LGN N	1743 2182 2670 3631	2463 2049 2090 3203 2182	H24	Stord 7 16 61 62; Ljoneshogda 19 16; Sotra 16 81 86; Odda 16; Inner Hardangerfjord 5 16 21; Bergen 2 25; 24 16; 18 22; Knarvik	1743 kHz and all VHF Ch. except Ch. 16 at 0133 0533 0933 1333 1733 2133
Florø 61°36'N 5°00'E Telex 42195 LGL N	1757 2182 2649 3645	2576 2049 2132 3217 2182	H24	Gulen 16 23 63; Ligtvor 18 28; Sogndal 16 16; Kinn 3 16; Storåsen 16 28; Bremanger 16 27; Sagtennene 16 24; Raudeberg 16 60	2649 kHz and all VHF Ch. except Ch. 16 at 0233 0633 1033 1433 1833 2133
Ålesund 62°28'N 6°12'E Telex 42395 LGA N	1722 2182 2663	2442 2049 1632.5 2182	H24	Nerlandshorn 5 16 62; Hjørunganes 16 61; Ålesund 16 24; Gamlemstveten 2 16 26; Moldeheia 7 16; Reinsfjell 16 25; Kristiansund 3 16; Gridsvagøy 16 85	1722 kHz and all VHF Ch. except Ch. 16 at 0333 0733 1133 1533 1933 2333
Ørlandet 63°41'N 9°36'E Telex 55295 LFO N	1743 2182 2635 1757 3631 3670 3627.9	2463 2182 2118 3203 2090 3199.9 2049 2576	H24	Trondheimsleden 2 16; Trondheims Fjord 16 28; Namsos 5 16; Kopparen 16 24 82; Yttevåg 3 16; Rørvik 16 23 26	2635, 1757 kHz and all VHF Ch. except Ch. 16 at 0133 0533 0933 1333 1733 2133

STATION	TRANSMITS kHz	RECEIVES kHz	HOURS OF SERVICE	VHF Channel			TRAFFIC LISTS Frequency & Times
Bodø 67° 16'N 14° 23'E Telex 65315 LGP N	1694 2182 2642 2656 2695 3645	2541 2182 2049 2125 1657.5 3217	H24	Vega Horva Mo Rana Traenfjord Rønvikfjell Fornesfjell Steigen Narvik Vaeroy Nesna Tysfjord Fredvang Hagskaret Lodingen Tjeldsundet	16 1 16 5 16 21 16 16 3 7 81 16 16 7 16	63 83 16 28 16 26 23 60 28 16 61 63	2656 kHz and all VHF Ch. except Ch. 16 at 0333 0733 1133 1533 1933 2333
Harstad 68° 48'N 16° 31'E Telex 65245 LGH N	1750 2182 2635 2663 3638	2470 2182 2049 2118 1632.5 3210	H24	Kvalnes Hadsel Stamnes Andenes Harstad Sørolines Kistefjell Tromsø Tønsnes Sandøy	16 16 16 16 1 19 16 16 7 2	88 24 64 27 16 28 26 16 25	1750 2635 kHz and all VHF Ch. except Ch. 16 at 0233 0633 1033 1433 1833 2233
Hammerfest 70° 41'N 23° 41'E Telex 65155 LGI N	1722 2182 2695 3652	2442 2182 2049 1657.5 3168	H24	Trolltind Helligfjell Fuglen Tyven Havøysund Honningsvagfjell Oksen	16 16 4 3 16 16 16 2	23 28 16 16 24 27 26 16	1722 kHz and all VHF Ch. 16 at 0133 0533 0933 1333 1733 2133
Vardø 70° 22'N 31° 06'E Telex 65135 LGV N	2182 2642 2656 3631	2049 2182 2125 2139 3203	H24	Mehamn Tana Berlevåg Båtsfjord Domen Vadsø Lyngberget	16 4 16 16 16 16 16	25 16 23 27 26 25 28	2656 kHz and all VHF Ch. except Ch. 16 at 0233 0633 1033 1433 1833 2233

STATION	TRANSMITS kHz	RECEIVES kHz	HOURS OF SERVICE	VHF Channel	TRAFFIC LISTS Frequency & Times
FRANCE **Dunkerque** 51°02'N 2°24'E				(16) 24 61	
Calais 50°55'N 1°43'E			H24 0600-2100	(16) 1 87	
Boulogne 50°43'N 1°37'E Telex 130289	1694 1771 2182 2747 3795	2182 2009 2049 2056 2083 2097 2153 2160 2167 2321 2421 2506 2527 2576 3168 2182	H24 H24 H24 H24 H24 H24 0600-2100	(16) 23 25	1771 ev. odd H + 03
Dieppe 49°55'N 1°04'E				(16) 2 24	
Fecamp 49°46'N 0°22'E			H24	16	
Le Havre 49°31'N 0°05'E			H24 0600-2100	16 26 28 23	
Rouen 49°27'N 1°02'E			H24 0600-2100	16 25 27	
Port en Bessin 49°20'N 0°42'W				(16) 3	
Cherbourg 49°38'N 1°36'W				(16) 27	
Jobourg 49°41'N 1°54'W			H24 0600-2100	16 21	

STATION	TRANSMITS kHz	RECEIVES kHz	HOURS OF SERVICE	VHF Channel	TRAFFIC LISTS Frequency & Times
St. Malo 48°38'N 2°02'W	1673 2182 **2691**	2182 2009 2049 / 2056 2083 2097 / 2153 2167 2463 / 2506 3168	H24 H24 H24 H24	(16) 2 1	
Paimpol 48°45'N 2°59'W				(16) 84	
Plougasnou 48°42'N 3°48'W				16 81	
Ouessant 48°27'N 5°05'W			H24	(16) 24 82	
Brest Le Conquet 48°20'N 4°44'W Telex 940176	1673 **1806** 2182 2726 / 3722	1.6-4 MHz. band / 2182	H24	(16) 26 28	1806 2691 ev. even H + 03
Quimperle 47°53'N 3°30'W	**1673** 1806 **1876** / 2182	2182 2009 2049 / 2056 2083 2097 / 2153 2160 2167 / 2463 2506 3168	H24 H24 H24 H24		
Pont L'Abbe 47°53'N 4°13'W			H24	16 86	
Belle Isle 47°21'N 3°09'W			H24 0600-2100	16 25 87	
St. Nazaire 47°21'N 2°06'W Telex 710045	**1687** 1722 2182 / 2740 3795	1995 2009 2049 / 2056 2083 2153 / 2160 2167 2182 / 2321 2491 2506 / 3168	H24 H24 H24 H24 H24 / 0600-2100	16	1687 ev. odd H + 07
Nantes St. Herblain 47°13'N 1°22'W			H24 0600-2100	23 24 / 16 28	

STATION	TRANSMITS kHz	RECEIVES kHz	HOURS OF SERVICE	VHF Channel	TRAFFIC LISTS Frequency & Times
Saint Hilaire De Riaz 46°43'N 1°57'W			H24 0600-2100	16 27	
Ile De Re 46°12'N 1°37'W			H24 0600-2100	16 28	
La Rochelle 46°14'N 1°33'W			H24 0600-2100	16 21 26	
Royan 45°34'N 0°58'W			H24 0600-2100	16 23 25	
Bordeaux 44°53'N 0°30'W			0600-2100	(16) 27. For vessels in Port	
Bordeaux-Arcachon 44°39'N 1°10'W Telex 560078	1820 **1862** 2182 2775 3722	2182 2009 2037 2049 2069 2153 2167 2321 2421 2506 2527 2541 3168	H24 H24 H24 H24 H24 0600-2100	16	1862 ev. even H + 07
Bayonne 43°16'N 1°24'W			H24 0600-2100	28 82 (16) 24	
SPAIN **Pasajes** 43°17'N 1°55'W			H24	16 26 27 20 25	Ch.27 0833 1633 0233 1033 1833 0633 1233 2233
Machichaco 43°27'N 2°45'W	**1704** 2191 2182 2586	2083 2191 2182 3283	H24	16 4 23 26 27	1704 ev. odd H + 33 0333-1933 Ch.23 0833 1633 0233 1033 1833 2333 0633 1233 2233
Bilbao 43°21'N 3°00'W			H24	16 20 27 25 26	Ch.26 0833 1633 0233 1033 1833 0633 1233 2233

STATION	TRANSMITS kHz	RECEIVES kHz	HOURS OF SERVICE	VHF Channel	TRAFFIC LISTS Frequency & Times
Santander 43° 25'N 3° 36'W			H24	16 26 27 / 24 28	Ch.24 0233 0633 / 0833 1033 1233 / 1633 1833 2233
Llanes 43° 26'N 4° 51'W			H24	16 21 23 25 83 / 24	Ch.25 0233 0633 / 0833 1033 1233 / 1633 1833 2233
Cabo de Penas 43° 39'N 5° 51'W	1757.5 2191 / 2182 / 2649	2013 2191 / 2182 / 3231	H24	16 24 25 26 / 27	1757.5 ev. odd / H + 33 2333 / 0333-1933 / Ch.26 0233 0633 / 0833 1033 1233 / 1633 1833 2233
Navia 43° 25'N 6° 56'W			H24	16 26 27 / 24 25	Ch.27 0233 0633 / 0833 1033 1233 / 1633 1833 2233
Cabo Ortegal 43° 43'N 7° 57'W			H24	16 25 65 / 84 86	Ch.25 0303 0703 / 0903 1103 1303 / 1703 1903 2203
Coruña 43° 20'N 8° 24'W	1748 2191 / 2182 / 2596	2122 (or 2049) 2191 / 2182 / 3290	H24	16 26 28 / 63 83	1748 ev. / odd H + 33 / (0333-1933) 2333 / Ch.26 0303 0703 / 0903 1103 1303 / 1703 1903 2303
Finisterre 42° 54'N 9° 16'W	1698 / 2182 / 2191 / 2806	2803 / 2182 / 2191 / 3283	H24	16 01 22 23 / 27 85	1698 ev. / odd H + 33 / (0333-1933) 2333 / Ch.01 0303 0703 / 0903 1103 1303 / 1703 1903 2303
Vigo 42° 16'N 8° 47'W			H24	16 21 22 86 / 26 62	Ch.26 0303 0703 / 0903 1103 1303 / 1703 1903 2303
La Guardia 41° 53'N 8° 52'W			H24	16 20 22 65 82	Ch.20 0303 0703 / 0903 1103 1303 / 1703 1903 2303

20:24 REED'S NAUTICAL ALMANAC

STATION	TRANSMITS kHz	RECEIVES kHz	HOURS OF SERVICE	VHF Channel	TRAFFIC LISTS Frequency & Times
PORTUGAL					
Arga 41°48'N 8°41'W			H24	16 23 24 25 26	
Arestal 40°46'N 8°21'W			H24	16 25 26 27 28	
Montejunto 39°10'N 9°03'W			H24	16 24 25 26 27	
Lisbon 38°44'N 9°14'W Telex 44802 LISRAD P	2182 2781 **2581** 3605 **2694**	2182	H24	16 23 25 26 / 28	2694 ev. even H + 05
Atalaia 38°10'N 8°38'W			H24	16 23 24 25 26	
Pico 37°18'N 8°39'W			H24	16 25 26 27 28	
Estoi 37°10'N 7°50'W			H24	16 23 25 26 28	
SPAIN					
Huelva 37°21'N 6°57'W			H24	16 24 25 26 27	Ch.26 0233 0833 1633 1033 1833 0633 1233 2233
Chipiona 36°42'N 6°25'W	1700 2182 2842 2191	2013 2182 3231 2191	H24		1700 ev. odd H + 33 0333-1933 2333
Cadiz 36°50'N 5°57'W			H24	16 20 25 26 27	Ch. 20 0233 0633 1233 2233 0833 1633 1033 1833

STATION	TRANSMITS kHz	RECEIVES kHz	HOURS OF SERVICE	VHF Channel	TRAFFIC LISTS Frequency & Times
Tarifa 36°03'N 5°33'W	**1678** 2182 2610 2191	2083 2182 3290 2191	H24	16 23 24 26 27	1678 ev. odd H+33 0333-1933 2333 Ch.27 0233 0633 0833 1033 1233 1633 1833 2233
Algeciras 36°09'N 5°27'W			H24	16 01 04 20 81	Ch.01 0233 0633 0833 1033 1233 1633 1833 2233
GIBRALTAR 36°07'N 5°22'W			Mon.-Sat. 0700-1900 Sun. 0700-1300	16 01 02 03 04 23 24 25 27 86 87	
Sao Miguel (Azores) 37°45'N 25°40'W	1663.5 2182 2742	2182	H24		2742 ev. odd H+35

Tides and
Tidal Streams

21

TIDAL INDEX FOR ALL PORTS ....SEE BACK OF ALMANAC

TIDAL HEIGHTS

All tidal heights in the British Isles are now above a Datum which is very close to L.A.T. Care should be taken to make allowances for the differences in Datum when reading Admiralty charts which are not yet to L.A.T. Generally speaking, the recent L.A.T. Datum is slightly lower than previous Datum, therefore the tide is apparently predicted higher.

There is no change in the case of foreign ports.

HEIGHTS OF ALL TIDAL PREDICTIONS SHOULD BE ADDED TO CHARTED DEPTHS AFTER REFERENCE TO THE DATUM OF THE CHART IN USE.

QUICK REFERENCE PAGE INDEX

TIDAL PREDICTIONS

TIDAL STREAM CHARTS

TIDAL DEFINITIONS

The Lunar Tide: The result of the tidal force arising from the gravitational effect of the Moon only. Due to the relative proximity of the moon it is the major tidal force.

The Solar Tide: The result of the tidal force arising from the gravitational effect of the Sun only. The solar tide generating forces are less than half of those caused by the Moon.

Spring Tides: When the Sun and Moon are in conjunction (New Moon) or in opposition (Full Moon) the two tide-generating forces are acting on the same meridians, so the height and range of the tide will be greater than at other periods. Spring high waters tend to occur at about the same time at any one place, e.g. London Bridge 0330 and 1530, Dover 0030 and 1230 and at approximately $1\frac{1}{2}$ days, after new and full Moon due to 'lag'.

Neap Tides: When the Sun and Moon are in quadrature, the two tide-generating forces are acting at right angles to each other, thus producing a tide which has a higher low water than average and a range which is smaller than at other periods. Neap high waters tend to occur at London Bridge at 0930 and 2130 and Dover at 0630 and 1830 and at approximately $1\frac{1}{2}$ days after the Moon's quarters, due to 'lag'.

Lag: This is the time interval which is required to overcome the inertia of the great masses of water in response to the tide generating forces.

Perigee Tides: The Moon's orbit is elliptical and so its distance from the Earth varies throughout the month. When it is nearest to the Earth the Moon is said to be in "Perigee", and when furthest away to be in "Apogee". The greatest attraction between Earth and Moon occurs at Perigee and, when this coincides with the time of New or Full Moon, the resulting spring tides are greater than average springs.
As one complete orbit takes approximately $27\frac{1}{2}$ days the Moon, will be *nearly* in Apogee when the next springs occur (about 15 days after the Perigee tides). In consequence these tides will be less than average springs.

Equinoctial Springs: The lunar and solar tide-generating forces are greater than average when the Moon and Sun have low declination and vice versa. This will occur when the Moon (new and full) has a low declination near the Equinoxes (21st March and 23rd September) when the Sun's declination is zero. Thus, at about these times of the year, greater than average spring tides can be expected.
The greatest spring tides will occur after a New or Full Moon which is in Perigee near the Equinox.

A Diagram of Specific Tidal Heights

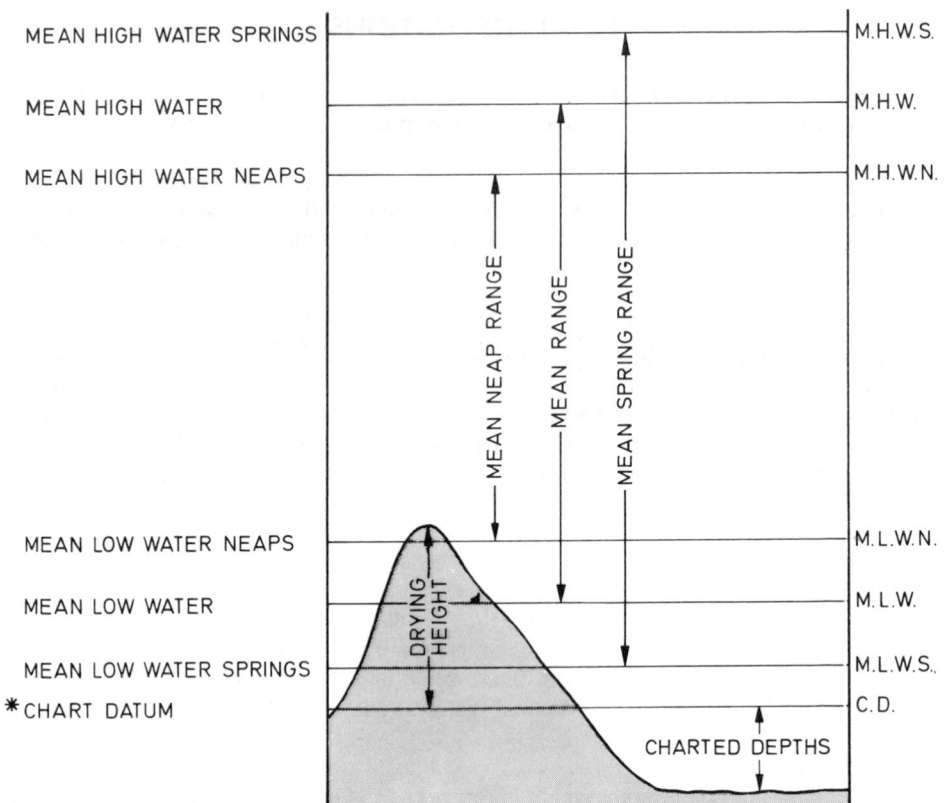

MEAN HIGH WATER SPRINGS — M.H.W.S.

MEAN HIGH WATER — M.H.W.

MEAN HIGH WATER NEAPS — M.H.W.N.

MEAN NEAP RANGE

MEAN RANGE

MEAN SPRING RANGE

MEAN LOW WATER NEAPS — M.L.W.N.

MEAN LOW WATER — M.L.W.

DRYING HEIGHT

MEAN LOW WATER SPRINGS — M.L.W.S.

＊CHART DATUM — C.D.

CHARTED DEPTHS

*Chart Datum is the plane from which the depths of all features, either permanently or nearly permanently covered by the sea, are measured. It is also the plane from which the heights of all features, periodically covered and uncovered by the sea, are measured. The former are known as charted depths, and the latter, which are distinguished on the chart from charted depths by an underline, are known as Drying Heights. It is a fixed level below which all charted depths on a chart are given and above which all heights of the tide are given in the tide tables.

By international agreement chart datum is at a level below which the tide seldom falls. On British charts this plane has been, in the past, usually near or below Mean Low Water Springs in the locality, but these datums are now adjusted to approximate to the level of the Lowest Astronomical Tide (L.A.T.).

The height of the tide is the vertical distance, at any moment, between the level of the sea surface and Chart Datum. Note that the tide tables give predicted heights which should not be confused with the depths of water. When the level of the sea surface is below chart datum the tabulated height is prefixed with a minus sign.

The rise of the tide is the difference between the height of the tide at any one time and the height of the preceding low water. It applies to flood tide only.

The range of the tide is the difference between the height of any high water and that of the preceding or succeeding low water.

Mean high water springs or neaps is the average level of high water at springs or neaps and is given above chart datum.

Mean low water springs or neaps is the average level of low water at springs or neaps.

Lowest astronomical tide (L.A.T.) is the lowest height which can be predicted to occur under (a) average meteorological conditions and (b) any combination of astronomical conditions. The level of L.A.T. is reached only occasionally and not every year. Lower levels than this can occur with particular meteorological conditions such, for example, as storm surges.

Charted depths are depths of water below the level of Chart Datum. They are given either in fathoms, fathoms and feet, feet or metres. Drying heights are always given in feet or metres, never in fathoms.

Drying heights on a chart are the heights above Chart Datum of all features which are periodically covered and uncovered by the sea (see diagram on p. 21:4). They are distinguished on the chart from charted depths by an underline.

The depth of water is the sum, at any moment, of the charted depth and the height of the tide (or the difference, at any moment, between the height of the tide and the charted drying height).

NOTE DIFFERENCE BETWEEN HEIGHT, DEPTH, AND RISE.

INSTRUCTIONS IN THE USE OF THE TIDE TABLES

General arrangement

The pages on Tides and Tidal Streams are arranged so that all the local information is given together; for example, pages for Portsmouth are next to Southampton; and all adjacent ports are on adjoining pages with the Solent Tidal Stream charts nearby. These pages are arranged anti-clockwise round the coasts of the British Isles commencing at Dover eastwards round England and Scotland down to Lands End; then eastwards round Ireland; the Channel Isles; and finally the Continental ports from Gibraltar to the Baltic Ports and Iceland.

Tidal pages also include tidal and navigational notes, Chart Datum and other ports for which the same predictions may be used without correction. This information is based on the most suitable port.

Standard Ports

In this Almanac, twice daily predictions are given of the Time (to the nearest minute) and the Height (to the nearest decimal of a metre) throughout the year for 48 Standard Ports, chosen for their general usefulness. Both High and Low Waters are given, and for Southampton the times and heights of both the First and Second High Waters and Low Water. Only Low Water predictions are given for Poole, as these can be predicted more accurately for this port. Tidal curves give predicted levels following low water.

Secondary Ports

Tidal information on these is given as Tidal Differences on Standard Ports.

The layout of data for secondary ports follows the system used in Admiralty Tide Tables except that the latitude and longitude columns are omitted and no mean level or seasonal changes are given. The differences for time and height should be applied to the standard port data to give the times and heights of high and low waters at secondary ports.

Time zones

The adjustment for time zones falls into two parts, the zone of the standard port and that of the secondary ports.

a. Standard ports

Where the zone is set at GMT there is no problem. Where the zone is set at −0100 one should subtract one hour from the printed times to arrive at GMT.

Example:
Cherbourg

Time zone −0100	Adjusted for GMT	Adjusted for BST
0235 4.9m	0135 4.9m	0235 4.9m
1505 4.7m	1405 4.7m	1505 4.7m

b. Secondary ports

Where the standard and secondary ports are both at the same time zone (in this case −0100) the differences should be directly applied and the result will be in the same time bracket as both the standard and secondary ports.

Example:

Omonville	Time zone −0100
Standard port Cherbourg	Time zone −0100

Standard port	Difference	Secondary port
0235 local time	−0015	0220 local Omonville time
0135 GMT		0120 GMT

Where the standard port is at GMT but the time difference is at −0100 the result will be in local **secondary port** time.

Example:

Corcubion (Spain)	Time zone −0100
Standard port Lisbon	Time zone GMT

Standard port	Difference	Secondary port
0820 GMT	+0055	0915 local Corcubion time
0820 GMT		0815 GMT

It follows that if the differences are applied exactly as they are printed the result will be in local time. 'Summer time' or 'daylight saving time' will require additional application.

It can be seen that secondary ports based on Lisbon are divided into GMT and −0100 zones. Those in Portugal keep GMT and those in Spain keep to −0100.

Note: All calculations based on differences are less accurate than Standard Port predictions since the differences given are average values.

To find the Time of High or Low Water

Find the page of the required port from the Tidal Index at the back of the Almanac.

Standard Ports are followed by an (S) and the time can be read off alongside the date on the appropriate page.

Secondary Ports are listed without the (S) and the page given is based on the nearest or most suitable port. The time differences should be applied to the data given for the appropriate standard port, interpolating as necessary.

To find the Height of High or Low Water

Find the correct page from the Tidal Index.

Heights for Standard Ports are given on the appropriate page in metres and decimetres.

Heights for Secondary Ports are found by applying the differences to the Standard Port data, interpolating between spring and neap tides where necessary.

Example:

Find the time and height of the afternoon H.W. and L.W. at ST. MARY'S (Isles of Scilly) on 14th January.

Note: The data used in this example do not refer to the year of these tables.

JANUARY

PLYMOUTH (DEVONPORT)

14 0309 1.0
0927 5.3
SA 1532 1.1
2149 5.0

PLACE	TIME DIFFERENCES				HEIGHT DIFFERENCES (Metres)			
	High Water		Low Water		MHWS	MHWN	MLWN	MLWS
PLYMOUTH .... (DEVONPORT) Isles of Scilly	0000 and 1200	0600 and 1800	0000 and 1200	0600 and 1800	5.5	4.4	2.2	0.8
St. Mary's	−0030	−0110	−0100	−0020	+0.2	−0.1	−0.2	−0.1

	TIME		HEIGHT	
	HW	LW	HW	LW
Standard Port	2149	1532	5.0	1.1
Differences	−0044	−0036	+0.1	−0.1
Secondary Port	2105	1456	5.1	1.0

The data for differences can be interpolated by the following graphic method or by the digital method shown on page 21:17. In the example the times and heights are shown on separate graphs, but by careful annotation of the graph lines, time and height can be drawn on the same sheet.

Height
  Choose a scale which will include the greatest differences shown (in this case from +0.2 to −0.2) and write the values along the top of the graph as appropriate.

  Choose a scale which will include the level of MHWS and that of MLWS (in this case 5.5 to 0.8) and write the values along this side of the graph as appropriate.

  Enter the data for the two high water points and join them with a straight line.

  Do the same with the low water points.

  Read off the difference values associated with the day in question (in this case predicted HW at Plymouth was 5.0 m and LW was 1.1 m).

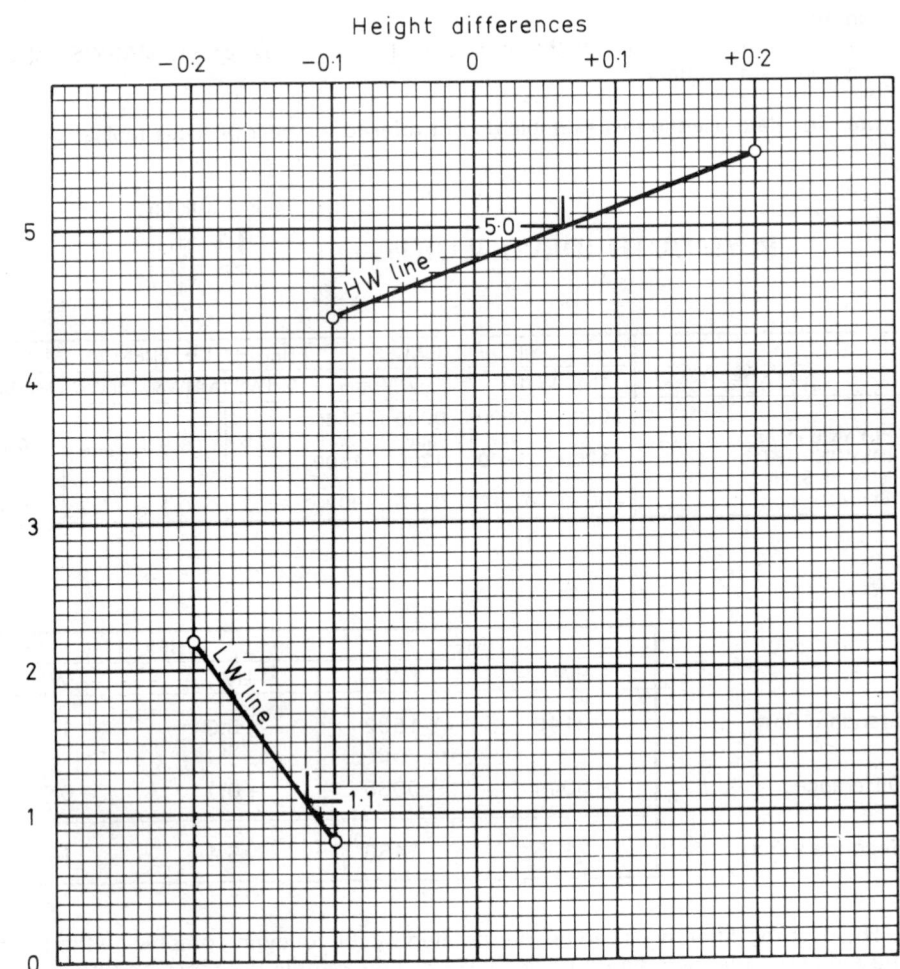

Height differences

Time

Along the top of the graph choose a suitable scale and enter the values which will include the greatest range of differences shown, in this case from –0020 to –0110.

The left hand edge of the graph is for HW times.

Enter a set of times down the left hand edge which covers the predicted time of HW at the standard port and also the two times at which the time differences are known, in this case 1800 and 0000 (2400).

The difference at 1800 is –0110 and at 0000 is –0030. Note these two points on the graph and join them with a straight line.

Where the predicted time of HW at the standard port cuts the straight line, the time difference can be read off the top of the graph at –0044 and applied:

2149
–0044
2105 = predicted time of HW at secondary port.

The right hand side is for LW times and the same process adopted for LW data.

Where there is a wide variation between the HW and LW time differences, the LW differences can be entered along the bottom of the graph in order to keep them separate.

In this example the HW and LW lines happen to be nearly parallel. This is quite by chance, and for another standard port may even cross if the data is so constructed. Where it appears to be too complex, plot HW and LW on different pieces of graph paper.

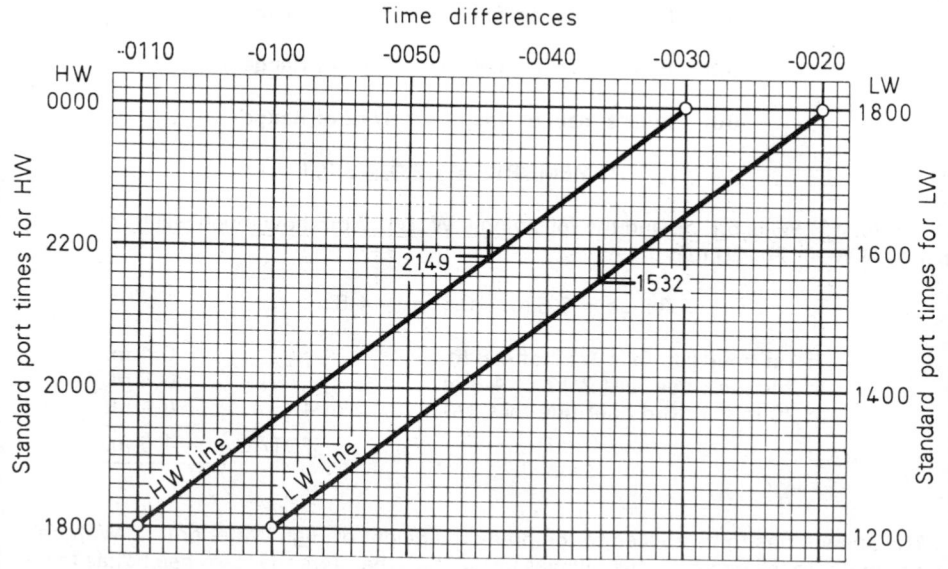

TIDE CURVES

INTERPOLATION

Interpolation between Springs and Neaps can be carried out either by calculation or more simply and quickly by eye. For most applications the latter method is quite adequate, especially when one bears in mind the variations which can occur as a result of meteorological conditions. Readers can make their own assessment of 'by eye' interpolation by comparing the results achieved with a calculated answer.

TO FIND THE HEIGHT OF THE TIDE AT ANY TIME

A. The 'Twelfths' Rule

The following calculations are all based upon the assumption that the tide rises and falls in the same pattern.

On an open coast facing on to deep water this is mainly true, but since most ports do not come within this category, the tidal curve at them is distorted (by shallow water effects in particular), the ebb tide more so than floodtide.

It follows that the answers to these calculations are approximate and should be treated with due caution.

TIDAL RISE OR FALL — THE 'TWELFTHS' RULE

The level of the water does not rise or fall at a constant rate throughout the duration of a rising or falling tide, but the amount by which it will do so in a given time from HW can be reckoned mentally by means of the following rough rule:

1st   hour's rise or fall   =   1/12 of Range

2nd   hour's rise or fall   =   2/12 of Range

3rd   hour's rise or fall   =   3/12 of Range

4th   hour's rise or fall   =   3/12 of Range

5th   hour's rise or fall   =   2/12 of Range

6th   hour's rise or fall   =   1/12 of Range

AID TO MEMORY: = 1,2,3,−3,2,1

Example: If H.W. is 5.5 m. and the following L.W. is 0.7 m., how much will this tide fall below H.W. in 2h. 20 min.:

Range = 5.5 m. − 0.7 m. = 4.8 m.

In 1st hour tide falls 1/12 of 4.8 m.	= 0.4 m.
In 2nd hour tide falls 2/12 of 4.8 m.	= 0.8 m.
In 20 min. of 3rd hour tide falls 1/3 × 3/12 of 4.8 m.	= 0.4 m.
TOTAL	= 1.6 m.

The answer has to be applied to the predicted height of High Water or Low Water as appropriate. In the example, the fall was calculated, therefore the H.W. height has to be used.

B. Admiralty curves

Basic Entry

Using the left hand half of the graph.

  a. Mark the predicted height of High Water along the top line

  b. Mark the predicted height of Low Water along the bottom line

  c. Join the two marks with a straight line

Using the right hand half of the graph

  d. Write in the predicted time of High Water in the H.W. box on the bottom line

  e. Write in the time values at one hour intervals as required along the bottom line

To find the height of tide at a given time

  f. Go to the required time along the bottom line

  g. Read vertically and note where it cuts the Spring or Neap curve, as appropriate

  h. Read horizontally from that point to where it cuts the sloping line which you have just drawn on the left

  i. Read vertically and note where it cuts on the top or bottom line

The result is in metres above Chart Datum.

For those tides falling between Spring and Neap, and where a significant difference in curves is seen, one should plot both and interpolate in the manner given under interpolation. Extrapolation is not permitted.

To find the time at which the tide reaches a certain height

Carry out the instructions (a) to (e) above.

  j. Find the height required on the top or bottom line (left hand half)

  k. Read vertically to the sloping line

  l. Read horizontally from that point to the Neap or Spring curve, as appropriate

  m. Read vertically down to see the time given along the bottom line in the right hand half.

Interpolation between Neap and Springs can be made where the difference in curves is significant. Extrapolation is not permitted.

Example A

To find the height of tide at Ullapool at 0400 h. on a given day

Predicted height of High Water	5.3m	Time 0745
Predicted height of Low Water	0.8m	
Range	4.5m	(a Spring tide)

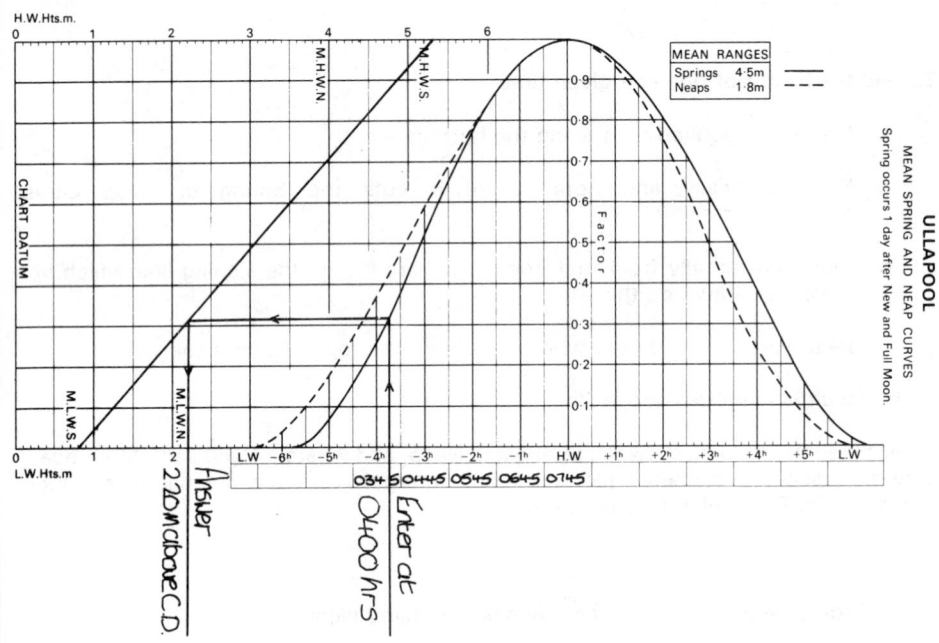

Answer: 2.20m above Chart Datum

Note. The answer is for a full Spring tide.

Example B

To find the height of tide at Ullapool at 0930 h. on a given day

Predicted height of High Water   3.9m   Time 1345
Predicted height of Low Water   2.1m

                Range   1.8m   (a Neap tide)

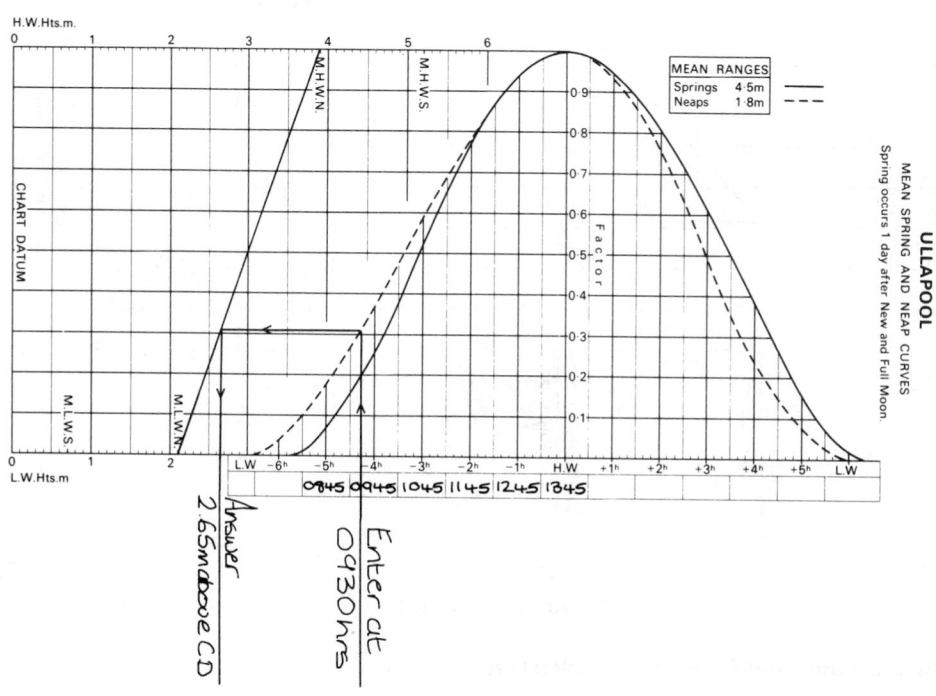

Answer: 2.65m above Chart Datum

Note. The answer is for a Neap tide.

Example C

To find the time at which the tide at Ullapool will reach 2.20m on a certain day

The exact reverse sequence used in example A is employed. The same basic data is used for ease of comparison.

Predicted height of High Water   5.3m   Time 0745
Predicted height of Low Water   0.8m

Range   4.5m   (a Spring tide)

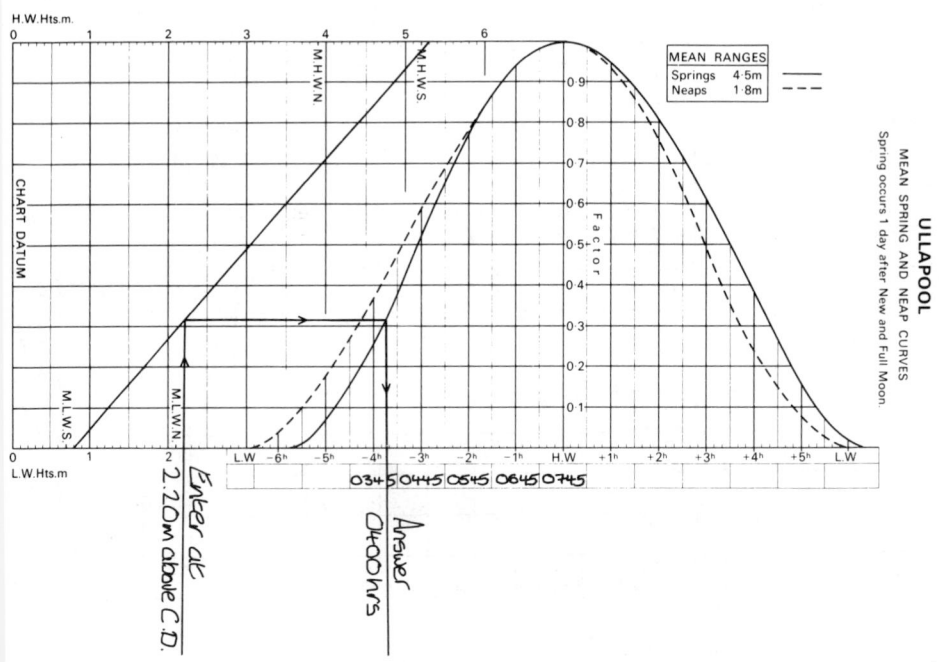

Answer: 0400 h.

Southampton and Swanage to Christchurch

Because of the complex nature of High Waters in the area, times are relative to Low Water. The procedure is otherwise identical.

Secondary Ports

Many secondary ports differ significantly from their standard port curve, therefore such curves should be used with great caution, particularly where the secondary port is not on the open coast.

On the left hand half of the graph the predicted heights of H.W. and L.W. at the secondary port should be plotted and the sloping line drawn. The choice of Spring or Neap curve and any interpolation between should be based upon the standard port data.

Interpolation by Reed's Method

Interpolation is made between Spring and Neap tides and falls into three groups.

a. When finding the height of tide predicted at a given time
b. When finding the time at which a given height will be reached
c. When applying time and height differences to calculate H.W. and L.W. at secondary ports.

The one format in the following examples will give an exact interpolation in all three cases. It may be used as an alternative to the system described on pages 21:6-21:9.

a. To find the predicted height of tide at Ullapool at 0700 on a given day

Predicted height of High Water   5.0m   Time 1045
Predicted height of Low Water   1.2m

                  Range   3.8m   (between Spring and Neap)

The sloping line is drawn on the left of the graph, as earlier described and the data is transferred to the boxes below as entitled or by simple calculation.

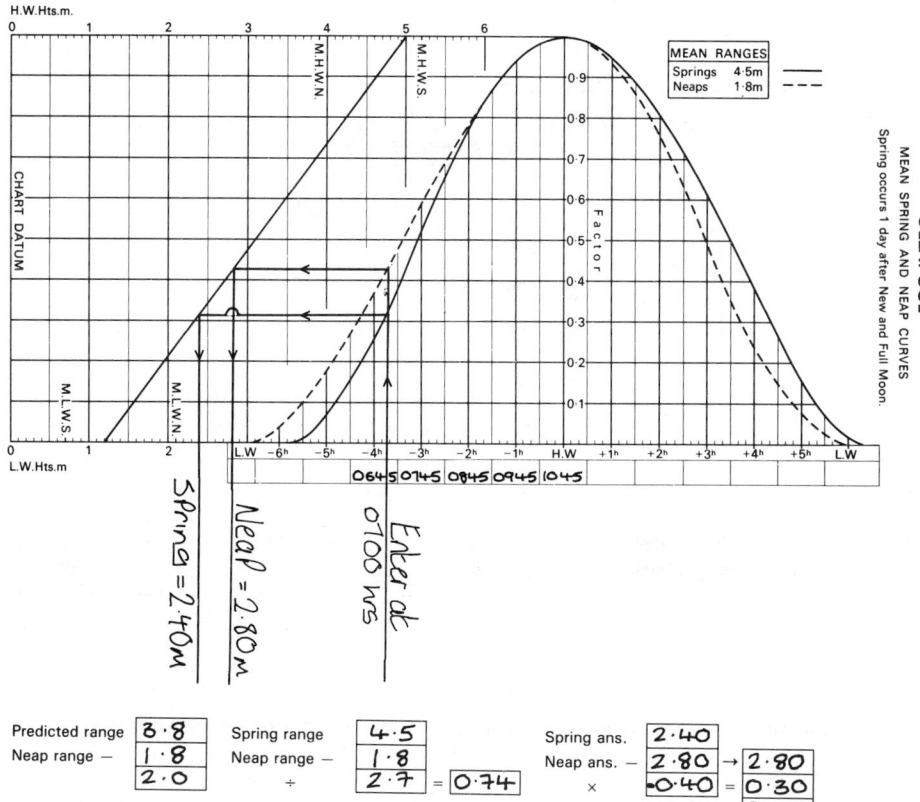

Predicted range | 3·8 | Spring range | 4·5 | Spring ans. | 2·40 |
Neap range − | 1·8 | Neap range − | 1·8 | Neap ans. − | 2·80 | → | 2·80 |
       | 2·0 | ÷ | 2·7 | = | 0·74 | × | 0·40 | = | 0·30 |
                                                        Ans. | 2·50 |

Note that the final answer must lie between the Spring and Neap answer.

b. To find the time at which the tide will reach 2.5m. at Ullapool.

Predicted height of High Water	5.0m	Time 1045
Predicted height of Low Water	1.2m	
Range	3.8m	(between Spring and Neap)

The sloping line is drawn on the left of the graph, as earlier described and the data is transferred to the boxes below, as entitled or by simple calculation.

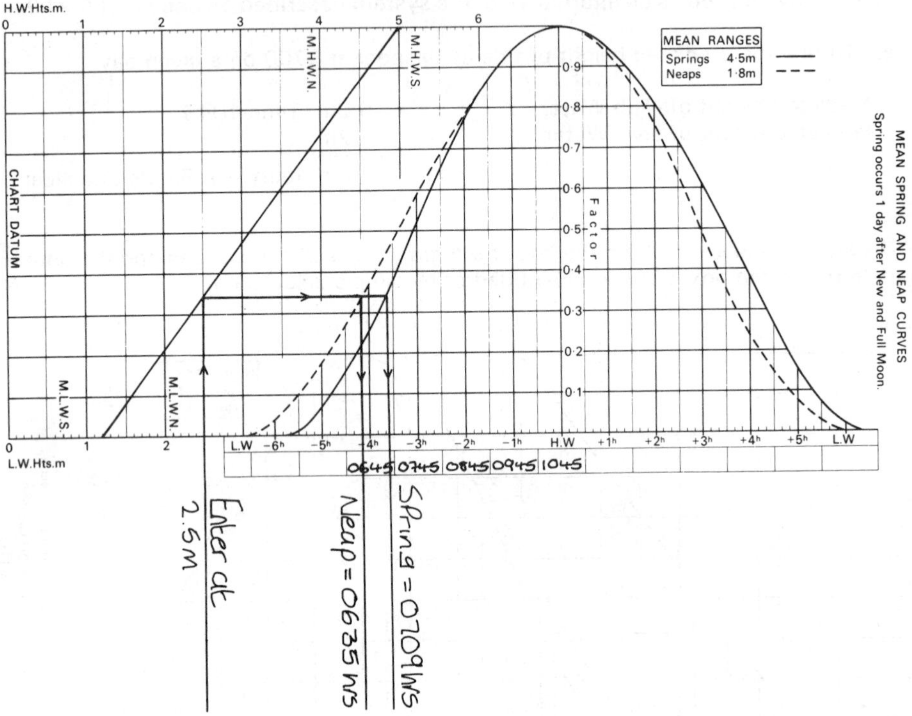

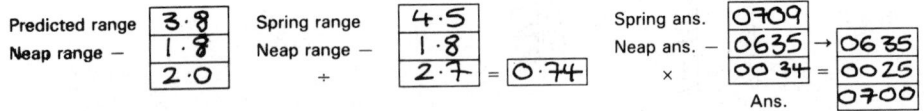

Predicted range	3·8	Spring range	4·5	Spring ans.	0709		
Neap range −	1·8	Neap range −	1·8	Neap ans. −	0635	→	0635
	2·0	÷	2·7 = 0·74	×	00 34	=	0025
					Ans.		0700

Note that the final answer must lie between the Spring and Neap answer.

c. To interpolate between the time differences given for High waters or Low waters for a secondary port (digital method).

This method is an alternative to the graphic system shown on Page 21:9. Its basis is that the left hand half of the format is designed to produce a factor or percentage. This shows how far between the two time differences the required time lies. For instance, a factor of 0.5 will show that the required time is halfway between.

Example: To find the HW time difference at Portnancon (see Differences on Ullapool) for a day when HW at Ullapool is predicted at 0300 hrs.

Copy of heading of Differences

	High Water	
	0100	0700
	and	and
	1300	1900
Portnancon	+0055	+0105

The required time of 0300 clearly lies between 0100 (the 'first time') and 0700 (the 'second time'), therefore the answer will lie between +0055 and +0105.

Enter the system of boxes thus:

Req'd time	0300	2nd time	0700	2nd time ans.	+0105		
1st time	0100	1st time	0100	1st time ans.	+0055	=	0065
	0200	−	0600	= 0·33	×	0010	0003
				(Factor)		Ans.	0058

IT IS SUGGESTED THAT USERS OF REED'S NAUTICAL ALMANAC DRAW UP FORMATS AT A USEFUL SIZE AND MAKE PHOTO-COPIES FOR READY USE.

The Multiplication Table

The multiplication table given on the following pages may be used where a calculator is not available. The table was originally designed for use in the older Admiralty system of tidal curve prediction which used factors (which are still shown in the curves as they are now drawn) but is clearly useful for other purposes.

The table allows the multiplication of numbers between 1.0 and 13.0 in steps of 0.02. Example:

5.8 (top line)
x0.78 (left or right edge)

Ans   4.5

Where the precise number figures required for multiplication are not given, interpolation may be made between adjacent values.

MULTIPLICATION TABLE

RANGE

FACTOR

1.00	1.4	1.8	2.2	2.6	3.0	3.4	3.8	4.2	4.6	5.0	5.4	5.8	6.2	6.6	7.0
.98	1.4	1.8	2.2	2.5	2.9	3.3	3.7	4.1	4.5	4.9	5.3	5.7	6.1	6.5	6.9
.96	1.3	1.7	2.1	2.5	2.9	3.3	3.6	4.0	4.4	4.8	5.2	5.6	6.0	6.3	6.7
.94	1.3	1.7	2.1	2.4	2.8	3.2	3.6	3.9	4.3	4.7	5.1	5.5	5.8	6.2	6.6
.92	1.3	1.7	2.0	2.4	2.8	3.1	3.5	3.9	4.2	4.6	5.0	5.3	5.7	6.1	6.4
.90	1.3	1.6	2.0	2.3	2.7	3.1	3.4	3.8	4.1	4.5	4.9	5.2	5.6	5.9	6.3
.88	1.2	1.6	1.9	2.3	2.6	3.0	3.3	3.7	4.0	4.4	4.8	5.1	5.5	5.8	6.2
.86	1.2	1.5	1.9	2.2	2.6	2.9	3.3	3.6	4.0	4.3	4.6	5.0	5.3	5.7	6.0
.84	1.2	1.5	1.8	2.2	2.5	2.9	3.2	3.5	3.9	4.2	4.5	4.9	5.2	5.5	5.9
.82	1.1	1.5	1.8	2.1	2.5	2.8	3.1	3.4	3.8	4.1	4.4	4.8	5.1	5.4	5.7
.80	1.1	1.4	1.8	2.1	2.4	2.7	3.0	3.4	3.7	4.0	4.3	4.6	5.0	5.3	5.6
.78	1.1	1.4	1.7	2.0	2.3	2.7	3.0	3.3	3.6	3.9	4.2	4.5	4.8	5.1	5.5
.76	1.1	1.4	1.7	2.0	2.3	2.6	2.9	3.2	3.5	3.8	4.1	4.4	4.7	5.0	5.3
.74	1.0	1.3	1.6	1.9	2.2	2.5	2.8	3.1	3.4	3.7	4.0	4.3	4.6	4.9	5.2
.72	1.0	1.3	1.6	1.9	2.2	2.4	2.7	3.0	3.3	3.6	3.9	4.2	4.5	4.8	5.0
.70	1.0	1.3	1.5	1.8	2.1	2.4	2.7	2.9	3.2	3.5	3.8	4.1	4.3	4.6	4.9
.68	1.0	1.2	1.5	1.8	2.0	2.3	2.6	2.9	3.1	3.4	3.7	3.9	4.2	4.5	4.8
.66	0.9	1.2	1.5	1.7	2.0	2.2	2.5	2.8	3.0	3.3	3.6	3.8	4.1	4.4	4.6
.64	0.9	1.1	1.4	1.7	1.9	2.2	2.4	2.7	2.9	3.2	3.5	3.7	4.0	4.2	4.5
.62	0.9	1.1	1.4	1.6	1.9	2.1	2.4	2.6	2.9	3.1	3.3	3.6	3.8	4.1	4.3
.60	0.8	1.1	1.3	1.6	1.8	2.0	2.3	2.5	2.8	3.0	3.2	3.5	3.7	4.0	4.2
.58	0.8	1.0	1.3	1.5	1.7	2.0	2.2	2.4	2.7	2.9	3.1	3.4	3.6	3.8	4.1
.56	0.8	1.0	1.2	1.5	1.7	1.9	2.1	2.4	2.6	2.8	3.0	3.2	3.5	3.7	3.9
.54	0.8	1.0	1.2	1.4	1.6	1.8	2.1	2.3	2.5	2.7	2.9	3.1	3.3	3.6	3.8
.52	0.7	0.9	1.1	1.4	1.6	1.8	2.0	2.2	2.4	2.6	2.8	3.0	3.2	3.4	3.6
.50	0.7	0.9	1.1	1.3	1.5	1.7	1.9	2.1	2.3	2.5	2.7	2.9	3.1	3.3	3.5
.48	0.7	0.9	1.1	1.2	1.4	1.6	1.8	2.0	2.2	2.4	2.6	2.8	3.0	3.2	3.4
.46	0.6	0.8	1.0	1.2	1.4	1.6	1.7	1.9	2.1	2.3	2.5	2.7	2.9	3.0	3.2
.44	0.6	0.8	1.0	1.1	1.3	1.5	1.7	1.8	2.0	2.2	2.4	2.6	2.7	2.9	3.1
.42	0.6	0.8	0.9	1.1	1.3	1.4	1.6	1.8	1.9	2.1	2.3	2.4	2.6	2.8	2.9
.40	0.6	0.7	0.9	1.0	1.2	1.4	1.5	1.7	1.8	2.0	2.2	2.3	2.5	2.6	2.8
.38	0.5	0.7	0.8	1.0	1.1	1.3	1.4	1.6	1.7	1.9	2.1	2.2	2.4	2.5	2.7
.36	0.5	0.6	0.8	0.9	1.1	1.2	1.4	1.5	1.7	1.8	1.9	2.1	2.2	2.4	2.5
.34	0.5	0.6	0.7	0.9	1.0	1.2	1.3	1.4	1.6	1.7	1.8	2.0	2.1	2.2	2.4
.32	0.4	0.6	0.7	0.8	1.0	1.1	1.2	1.3	1.5	1.6	1.7	1.9	2.0	2.1	2.2
.30	0.4	0.5	0.7	0.8	0.9	1.0	1.1	1.3	1.4	1.5	1.6	1.7	1.9	2.0	2.1
.28	0.4	0.5	0.6	0.7	0.8	1.0	1.1	1.2	1.3	1.4	1.5	1.6	1.7	1.8	2.0
.26	0.4	0.5	0.6	0.7	0.8	0.9	1.0	1.1	1.2	1.3	1.4	1.5	1.6	1.7	1.8
.24	0.3	0.4	0.5	0.6	0.7	0.8	0.9	1.0	1.1	1.2	1.3	1.4	1.5	1.6	1.7
.22	0.3	0.4	0.5	0.6	0.7	0.7	0.8	0.9	1.0	1.1	1.2	1.3	1.4	1.5	1.5
.20	0.3	0.4	0.4	0.5	0.6	0.7	0.8	0.8	0.9	1.0	1.1	1.2	1.2	1.3	1.4
.18	0.3	0.3	0.4	0.5	0.5	0.6	0.7	0.8	0.8	0.9	1.0	1.0	1.1	1.2	1.3
.16	0.2	0.3	0.4	0.4	0.5	0.5	0.6	0.7	0.7	0.8	0.9	0.9	1.0	1.1	1.1
.14	0.2	0.2	0.3	0.4	0.4	0.5	0.5	0.6	0.6	0.7	0.8	0.8	0.9	0.9	1.0
.12	0.2	0.2	0.3	0.3	0.4	0.4	0.5	0.5	0.6	0.6	0.6	0.7	0.7	0.8	0.8
.10	0.1	0.2	0.2	0.3	0.3	0.3	0.4	0.4	0.5	0.5	0.5	0.6	0.6	0.7	0.7
.08	0.1	0.1	0.2	0.2	0.2	0.3	0.3	0.3	0.4	0.4	0.4	0.5	0.5	0.5	0.6
.06	0.1	0.1	0.1	0.2	0.2	0.2	0.2	0.3	0.3	0.3	0.3	0.3	0.4	0.4	0.4
.04	0.1	0.1	0.1	0.1	0.1	0.1	0.2	0.2	0.2	0.2	0.2	0.2	0.2	0.3	0.3
.02	0.0	0.0	0.0	0.1	0.1	0.1	0.1	0.1	0.1	0.1	0.1	0.1	0.1	0.1	0.1

FACTOR

MULTIPLICATION TABLE
RANGE

FACTOR (left) | FACTOR (right)

7.4	7.8	8.2	8.6	9.0	9.4	9.8	10.2	10.6	11.0	11.4	11.8	12.2	12.6	13.0	1.00
7.3	7.6	8.0	8.4	8.8	9.2	9.6	10.0	10.4	10.8	11.2	11.6	12.0	12.4	12.7	.98
7.1	7.5	7.9	8.3	8.6	9.0	9.4	9.8	10.2	10.6	10.9	11.3	11.7	12.1	12.5	.96
7.0	7.3	7.7	8.1	8.5	8.8	9.2	9.6	10.0	10.3	10.7	11.1	11.5	11.8	12.2	.94
6.8	7.2	7.5	7.9	8.3	8.6	9.0	9.4	9.8	10.1	10.5	10.9	11.2	11.6	12.0	.92
6.7	7.0	7.4	7.7	8.1	8.5	8.8	9.2	9.6	9.9	10.3	10.6	11.0	11.3	11.7	.90
6.5	6.9	7.2	7.6	7.9	8.3	8.6	9.0	9.3	9.7	10.0	10.4	10.7	11.1	11.4	.88
6.4	6.7	7.1	7.4	7.7	8.1	8.4	8.8	9.1	9.5	9.8	10.1	10.5	10.8	11.2	.86
6.2	6.6	6.9	7.2	7.6	7.9	8.2	8.6	8.9	9.2	9.6	9.9	10.3	10.6	10.9	.84
6.1	6.4	6.7	7.1	7.4	7.7	8.0	8.4	8.7	9.0	9.3	9.7	10.0	10.3	10.7	.82
5.9	6.2	6.6	6.9	7.2	7.5	7.8	8.2	8.5	8.8	9.1	9.4	9.8	10.1	10.4	.80
5.8	6.1	6.4	6.7	7.0	7.3	7.6	8.0	8.3	8.6	8.9	9.2	9.5	9.8	10.1	.78
5.6	5.9	6.2	6.5	6.8	7.1	7.4	7.8	8.1	8.4	8.7	9.0	9.3	9.6	9.9	.76
5.5	5.8	6.1	6.4	6.8	7.0	7.3	7.5	7.8	8.1	8.4	8.7	9.0	9.3	9.6	.74
5.3	5.6	5.9	6.2	6.5	6.8	7.1	7.3	7.6	7.9	8.2	8.5	8.8	9.1	9.4	.72
5.2	5.5	5.7	6.0	6.3	6.6	6.9	7.1	7.4	7.7	8.0	8.3	8.5	8.8	9.1	.70
5.0	5.3	5.6	5.8	6.1	6.4	6.7	6.9	7.2	7.5	7.8	8.0	8.3	8.6	8.8	.68
4.9	5.1	5.4	5.7	5.9	6.2	6.5	6.7	7.0	7.3	7.5	7.8	8.1	8.3	8.6	.66
4.7	5.0	5.2	5.5	5.8	6.0	6.3	6.5	6.8	7.0	7.3	7.6	7.8	8.1	8.3	.64
4.6	4.8	5.1	5.3	5.6	5.8	6.1	6.3	6.6	6.8	7.1	7.3	7.6	7.8	8.1	.62
4.4	4.7	4.9	5.2	5.4	5.6	5.9	6.1	6.4	6.6	6.8	7.1	7.3	7.6	7.8	.60
4.3	4.5	4.8	5.0	5.2	5.5	5.7	5.9	6.1	6.4	6.6	6.8	7.1	7.3	7.5	.58
4.1	4.4	4.6	4.8	5.0	5.3	5.5	5.7	5.9	6.2	6.4	6.6	6.8	7.1	7.3	.56
4.0	4.2	4.4	4.6	4.9	5.1	5.3	5.5	5.7	5.9	6.2	6.4	6.6	6.8	7.0	.54
3.8	4.1	4.3	4.5	4.7	4.9	5.1	5.3	5.5	5.7	5.9	6.1	6.3	6.6	6.8	.52
3.7	3.9	4.1	4.3	4.5	4.7	4.9	5.1	5.3	5.5	5.7	5.9	6.1	6.3	6.5	.50
3.6	3.7	3.9	4.1	4.3	4.5	4.7	4.9	5.1	5.3	5.5	5.7	5.9	6.1	6.2	.48
3.4	3.6	3.8	4.0	4.1	4.3	4.5	4.7	4.9	5.1	5.2	5.4	5.6	5.8	6.0	.46
3.3	3.4	3.6	3.8	4.0	4.1	4.3	4.5	4.7	4.8	5.0	5.2	5.4	5.5	5.7	.44
3.1	3.3	3.4	3.6	3.8	3.9	4.1	4.3	4.5	4.6	4.8	5.0	5.1	5.3	5.5	.42
3.0	3.1	3.3	3.4	3.6	3.8	3.9	4.1	4.2	4.4	4.6	4.7	4.9	5.0	5.2	.40
2.8	3.0	3.1	3.3	3.4	3.6	3.7	3.9	4.0	4.2	4.3	4.5	4.6	4.8	4.9	.38
2.7	2.8	3.0	3.1	3.2	3.4	3.5	3.7	3.8	4.0	4.1	4.2	4.4	4.5	4.7	.36
2.5	2.7	2.8	2.9	3.1	3.2	3.3	3.5	3.6	3.7	3.9	4.0	4.2	4.3	4.4	.34
2.4	2.5	2.6	2.8	2.9	3.0	3.1	3.3	3.4	3.5	3.6	3.8	3.9	4.0	4.2	.32
2.2	2.3	2.5	2.6	2.7	2.8	2.9	3.1	3.2	3.3	3.4	3.5	3.7	3.8	3.9	.30
2.1	2.2	2.3	2.4	2.5	2.6	2.7	2.9	3.0	3.1	3.2	3.3	3.4	3.5	3.6	.28
1.9	2.0	2.1	2.2	2.3	2.4	2.5	2.7	2.8	2.9	3.0	3.1	3.2	3.3	3.4	.26
1.8	1.9	2.0	2.1	2.2	2.3	2.4	2.4	2.5	2.6	2.7	2.8	2.9	3.0	3.1	.24
1.6	1.7	1.8	1.9	2.0	2.1	2.2	2.2	2.3	2.4	2.5	2.6	2.7	2.8	2.9	.22
1.5	1.6	1.6	1.7	1.8	1.9	2.0	2.0	2.1	2.2	2.3	2.4	2.4	2.5	2.6	.20
1.3	1.4	1.5	1.5	1.6	1.7	1.8	1.8	1.9	2.0	2.1	2.1	2.2	2.3	2.3	.18
1.2	1.2	1.3	1.4	1.4	1.5	1.6	1.6	1.7	1.8	1.8	1.9	2.0	2.0	2.1	.16
1.0	1.1	1.1	1.2	1.2	1.3	1.4	1.4	1.5	1.5	1.6	1.7	1.7	1.8	1.8	.14
0.9	1.0	1.0	1.0	1.1	1.1	1.2	1.2	1.3	1.3	1.4	1.4	1.5	1.5	1.6	.12
0.7	0.8	0.8	0.9	0.9	0.9	1.0	1.0	1.1	1.1	1.1	1.2	1.2	1.3	1.3	.10
0.6	0.6	0.7	0.7	0.7	0.8	0.8	0.8	0.8	0.9	0.9	0.9	1.0	1.0	1.0	.08
0.4	0.5	0.5	0.5	0.5	0.6	0.6	0.6	0.6	0.7	0.7	0.7	0.7	0.8	0.8	.06
0.3	0.3	0.3	0.3	0.4	0.4	0.4	0.4	0.4	0.4	0.5	0.5	0.5	0.5	0.5	.04
0.1	0.2	0.2	0.2	0.2	0.2	0.2	0.2	0.2	0.2	0.2	0.2	0.2	0.3	0.3	.02

EFFECTS OF METEOROLOGICAL CONDITIONS UPON PREDICTED HEIGHTS OF THE TIDE

The Height of the Barometer: When the atmospheric pressure is increased, sea level is lowered and vice versa. A variation of one inch (approximately 34 millibars) in the height of the barometer causes a variation of about 0.3 metre in the height of sea level. (The mean barometric pressure in the south of England is 1016mb and in Scotland 1011mb.)

The Direction of the Wind: In some areas sea level is raised on the coast towards which the wind is blowing and vice versa. If steady wind conditions are established these conditions will remain static until there is a change in the force or direction of the wind.

Rain or melting snow: In relatively small land-locked seas in higher latitudes there is likely to be an appreciable rise in sea level following the melting of the snow. Generally speaking, rainfall will only affect the level of the rivers themselves at a distance inland from the mouth.

Storm surges: These are not infrequent occurences in the southern part of the North Sea, and may give rise to tides which rise or fall up to one metre above or below their predicted heights. Under more exceptional circumstances even greater variations may occur, particularly in the Helgoland Bight, on the coast of Holland, and in the Thames Estuary. These surges occur when conditions, which have caused a raising or lowering of sea level in one part of the North Sea, are replaced in a short space of time by conditions which have the reverse tendency. Such changes cause sea level to oscillate between a high and a low level, the oscillations gradually dying out as conditions become stable again. Surges are generally caused by a deep depression travelling eastwards past the northern entrance to the North Sea.

NOTES

It is important to remember the difference between Height, Rise and Range of tide, and Depth.

All tidal information is approximate so allow a good safety margin, particularly during and after periods of unsettled weather.

The loose Dover high water card has red lines drawn under each day, the length of which indicates the state of the tides. The longest red lines indicate spring tides. The shortest indicate neap tides.

The time of high water is approximately 50 minutes later each day.

Along the coast, the normal interval between successive high waters is 12 hours 25 minutes and between successive high and low waters is 6 hours 13 minutes.

As one goes further up a river or shorewards over large drying areas, the tide becomes distorted to give a shorter flood duration and a longer ebb duration. At London Bridge for example, the flood is of 5 hours 55 minutes duration and the ebb is of 6 hours 31 minutes.

Tidal streams run faster at springs and slower at neaps.

TIDAL STREAMS

Tidal streams are the horizontal movements of the water, occurring in response to the same forces as the vertical movements. In European waters, although not invariably the rule in other parts of the world, the tidal streams vary in magnitude with changing astronomical conditions in the same proportions as the range of the tide, so that the strongest streams occur at Spring tides and the weakest at Neap tides. In these circumstances the directions and rates of the tidal streams may be predicted by reference to the times of high water and the ranges of the tide at some suitable Standard Port. Thus, if in some channel the direction and rate of the stream, at one hour before high water at the Standard Port, is 040°, 3.0 knots, when the range of the tide at that port is 6 metres, then, at that interval from high water when the range is 3 metres, the direction and rate will be about 040°, $3 \times 3/6$ or 1.5 knots.

When the tidal streams are depicted simultaneously all round the British Isles, the Standard Port to which they are referred is Dover. When they are depicted in greater detail over a smaller area, they are referred to the nearest Standard Port.

Tidal streams are a horizontal oscillation of particles of water. In narrow channels and straits each particle travels in a more or less straight line, in the general direction of the channel; and then returns along the same path. There is no onward movement, simply an oscillation to and fro along the same track. The distance travelled in both directions varying from day to day with changes in the range of the tide. The periods for which the particles travel in the two directions may not be the same, but as the distance travelled in each direction is the same, the rate of travel will be greatest in the shorter period and vice versa.

The stream is said to be Slack at that instant when its direction of travel is reversed; but usually the expression is used to cover that period around the instant of reversal when the rate of the stream is a quarter of a knot or less. The tidal stream at most places attains its greatest rate roughly midway between successive occurrences of slack water. In rivers and estuaries, however, the greatest rate may be attained fairly soon after the stream has commenced to run in a particular direction.

In open waters the particles of water do not oscillate to and fro in a straight line, but travel in an ellipse. There is then no true slack water but a falling off in rate when the stream is running in directions at about right angles to those in which it flows at its greatest rates. The ellipse in which a particle travels will be largest at springs and smallest at neaps.

In the past the expressions "Flood" and "Ebb" were loosely employed to describe either the rising tide or the ingoing tidal stream and either the falling tide or the outgoing tidal stream. Such expressions can only legitimately be employed where the ingoing stream runs from low water to high water, and the outgoing stream from high water to low water. This is more or less what occurs in rivers and estuaries, but in open waters it is exceptional. The streams may be running at their greatest rates at the times of high and low water and in the old days seamen described such streams as "tide and a half", indicating that the stream which they described as the flood ran from three hours before to three hours after high water, and that described as the ebb from three hours before to three hours after low water. The streams are invariably described by the directions in which they are running, such as "ingoing", "outgoing", "eastgoing", "westgoing", etc.

Current is an onward horizontal movement of water, arising mainly from meteorological effects. The rate of movement is not affected by astronomical changes, but it may vary in direction and rate with meteorological conditions.

The horizontal movement of particles of water is the resultant of both tidal streams and current; this is described as "flow". Owing to the influence of the current the distance travelled by a particle in one direction will be greater than in the other, the duration and rate of flow will be increased in the former and correspondingly decreased in the latter. If the current is as strong as the tidal stream, then the flow will be constantly in one direction, varying from a maximum rate, when the tidal stream is running at its greatest rate, in the direction of the current, to zero when the tidal stream is running at its greatest rate in the opposite direction to the current. Generally the tidal streams around the British Isles are considerably stronger than the current, but in the eastern approaches to Dover Strait, at neap tides, during and after gales, the current may be strong enough to equalise the tidal streams, depending on meteorological conditions.

The tidal streams at any instant are described by their directions and rates.

CURRENTS OF THE WORLD

Few places other than the British Isles have Tides and Tidal Streams as explained; but all Oceans of the world have a movement of water as described above, generally setting in one direction. These are called ocean currents. It is necessary — as Coastal Navigators are advised to work the tides — for Ocean Navigators (if under sail or with low powered vessels) to use the ocean currents. Details of these currents are given on Ocean Charts; in Sailing Directions and *Ocean Passages for the World.*

RACES

A Race is caused generally when a headland protrudes into a fast moving tidal stream. A number of such Races exist on the coasts of the UK such as Portland, St. Catherine's, St. Albans, and Alderney. Races become more dangerous at Spring Tides and in rough weather, so use every endeavour to avoid them in these conditions.

OVERFALLS

Where the Tidal Stream crosses quickly shoaling water an Overfall occurs. This is really a "tumbling over" of the waters. In small boats keep clear of them or at least approach with caution.

TIDAL STREAMS and TIDAL STREAM CHARTS

STRENGTH OF THE TIDAL STREAM

The coasts of the United Kingdom, with its large volume of shipping, prevalence of fog and Tidal Streams, are probably the most difficult in the world to navigate. Although the average strength of the Tidal Streams is only 1 to 3 knots, in many places they run 3 to 5 knots, and in Pentland Firth and the Race of Alderney up to 9 and 10 knots during the height of the tidal stream.

Such streams cannot be ignored but with intelligence may be made use of and danger avoided.

The golden rule in low powered vessels is "Work Your Tidal Streams" — that is, use them to your advantage.

THE REQUIREMENTS OF THE NAVIGATOR

The Navigator requires to know at any hour which way the tidal stream is running, how long it will continue in that direction, and when it will turn and run in another direction, also when it is at maximum and when at minimum or Slack, so he can decide in advance if any allowance must be made to the Course to be steered.

Although the Sailing Directions contain much specialised information on local peculiarities, a greater understanding of the Streams generally can be obtained from a close study of the Tidal Stream Charts. With this in view over 100 chartlets of the UK waters are included in this Almanac.

The scale of those chartlets cannot show the peculiar movements of the Tidal Streams close to the coast, and frequently the Streams, close inshore, turn one or two hours earlier than the main channel streams. When crossing any Bay always allow for a set inshore.

INSET WARNING

Many strandings occur during foggy weather, and can frequently be attributed to the vessel having experienced an unusual inset.

Strong tidal insets are frequently unallowed for because they are unsuspected. It should be remembered however, that the stream will always set into a bay and thus towards the land.

Many Courses set on the coasts of the United Kingdom are towards a Headland, for example, approaching Flamborough Head from the South; the Longships from the North; Start Point and the Lizard from either direction. Generally there is deep water on the seaward side of such headlands and an offing of a mile or two extra is usually unimportant.

We strongly recommend that, in addition to allowances for Variation and Deviation of the Compass and Leeway, that an allowance for Inset should be carefully considered.

SET AND DRIFT

The effect of tidal streams upon a ship over a period of time is described by the "set" or direction in which they have carried the ship; and by the "drift" or distance to which they have carried the ship.

The seaman says, e.g., that during the previous 24 hours the Set and Drift has been 067° — 12 miles, meaning the vessel has been set 12 miles in an 067° direction. This is the exact opposite way in which we refer to the wind; as we speak of "a SW gale" meaning that it is coming from that direction.

HOW TO USE THE TIDAL STREAM CHARTS

(See also page 21:26)

The chartlets show the average direction of the main Tidal Streams around the coasts of the British Isles — at High Water Dover — and each hour before or after H.W. Dover (or the nearest Standard Port).

They enable the mariner to estimate the Set and Drift likely to be experienced over any period of time. Where two figures are given against the arrows, the smaller is the rate at neaps and the larger that at springs. Where no figures are given the rate generally will be less than 1 knot. Rates are either in knots or tenths of a knot as indicated, e.g. English & Bristol Channels Tidal Streams. Figures against arrows give mean neap and spring rates in tenths of a knot, thus: 11.19 indicates a mean neap rate of 1.1 knots and a mean spring rate of 1.9 knots.

These charts give a general idea of the tidal streams but, owing to their small scale, the inshore streams and detailed information of eddies and cross sets in the smaller channels and harbour entrances cannot be shown. The largest scale Chart or the Sailing Directions should always be consulted with regard to the tidal streams, when making harbour or when navigating in restricted waters.

If it is required to know how the Tidal Stream is setting at any time, first find the time of H.W. Dover (remember this is given in G.M.T.); then calculate how many hours before or after H.W. Dover the required time will be. On the corresponding chart will be shown the main direction of the stream in the desired locality.

Strong winds may prolong or retard Tidal Streams for even an hour or more.

Example:
Required to know the Set of the Tidal Stream and its Rate of Drift when leaving Poole to cross to Cherbourg at a certain time and date.

H.W. Dover is found to be 3 hours before this, therefore the Tidal Stream chartlets (H.W. Dover + 3 hours) should be consulted. These show the Tidal Stream setting down Channel about 260° (T) at 1½-3 knots (Neaps — Springs). Note how the height of tide is on your chosen day and decide whether this is a Neap or Spring tide or whereabouts in between and interpolate between the 1½-3 knots accordingly. See also page 21:26.

Page 21:39 shows that 2 hours later the stream is slackening and probably does not exceed 1 knot, but shows that there is still up to 2 knots three quarters of the way across. As the French Coast is approached, the Channel Islands Tidal Stream Charts should be consulted and the estimated stream allowed for as the land is approached.

COMPUTATION OF RATES

The loose card insert provided with this Almanac allows for easier and more accurate interpolation of current rates between spring and neap values.

Example
Required to predict the rate of the tidal stream off Ventnor (Isle of Wight) at 0400 when the tidal prediction for Dover for that day is:

LW	0521	0.1m	
			Range 5.7m
HW	1006	5.8m	
			Range 5.6m
LW	1737	0.2m	
			Range 5.5m
HW	2227	5.7m	

Mean range for day   5.6m

The appropriate chartlet is that for 6 hours before HW Dover which is the first of the English and Bristol Channel series in the Almanac.

On this it can be seen that the rates given off Ventnor are 13.23, that is to say 1.3kt at neaps and 2.3kt at springs.

On the computation card mark the points at which the neap and spring rates occur along the lower and upper dotted lines respectively and join the two points with a straight line. It can be seen that the tidal stream rate is given in tenths of a knot on the card.

Enter the table at the mean range (in this example 5.6m) on the left or right hand edge of the card and from the intersection of this level with the line which you have just drawn, follow the graph vertically to the scale of rates at the top or bottom of the card and read off the predicted rate, in this case 2.2kt.

If the predicted tidal range for the day is greater than that given for springs or less than neaps, the line is drawn in the same way and the rates taken off by extrapolation. For example, if the mean range for the day had been 6.6m the rate would have been 2.6kt.

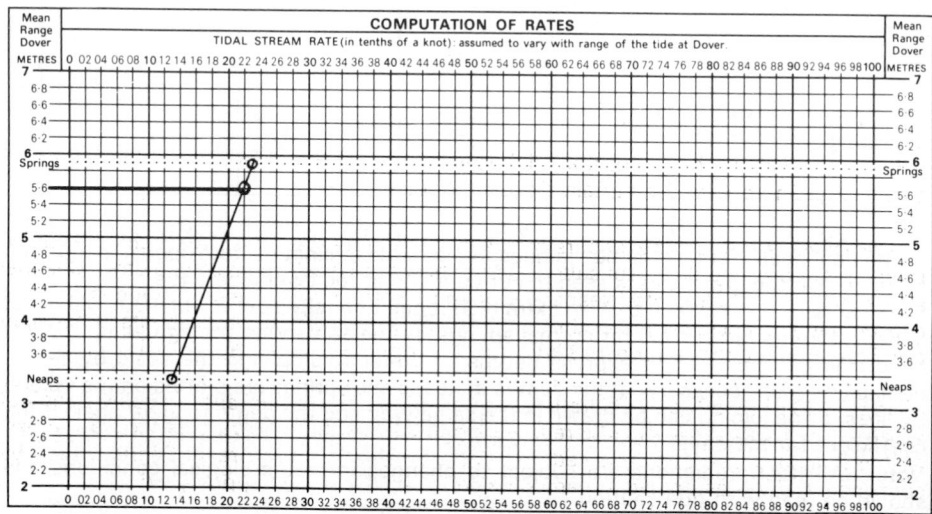

TIDAL COEFFICIENTS

The table opposite gives tidal coefficients for the year, based on Brest. They are designed principally to assist in the more accurate calculation of tidal stream velocities.

Explanation

The figures in the list of coefficients are based on the scale where:

45 is the coefficient for mean neap tides, 95 is the coefficient for mean spring tides

Therefore, if on a particular day the coefficient given is 70, the tide is half way between springs and neaps. If a figure in excess of 95 is given, then the range of that day's tide will be greater than mean springs and streams will run that much faster. If a number less than 45 is given, then a tidal range less than mean neaps is predicted.

Method of use

On the graph below, tidal stream speeds are set against tidal coefficients. The vertical lines pick out the neap and spring coefficients, *i.e.*, 45 and 95.

The neap and spring tidal stream rates for the tide in question are taken from the appropriate tidal stream chart and plotted on the 45 and 95 lines, and a straight line drawn across the two points, extending either side of them.

The coefficient of the day is noted and its position along the bottom of the graph pinpointed. Moving vertically upwards from this point, the line drawn earlier will be met and at this level the tidal stream speed can be read off.

Example

On page 21:37 it can be seen that the rate between Alderney and Guernsey is 2.1, 3.7. On the graph these points have been plotted on the 45 and 95 lines and a line drawn across.

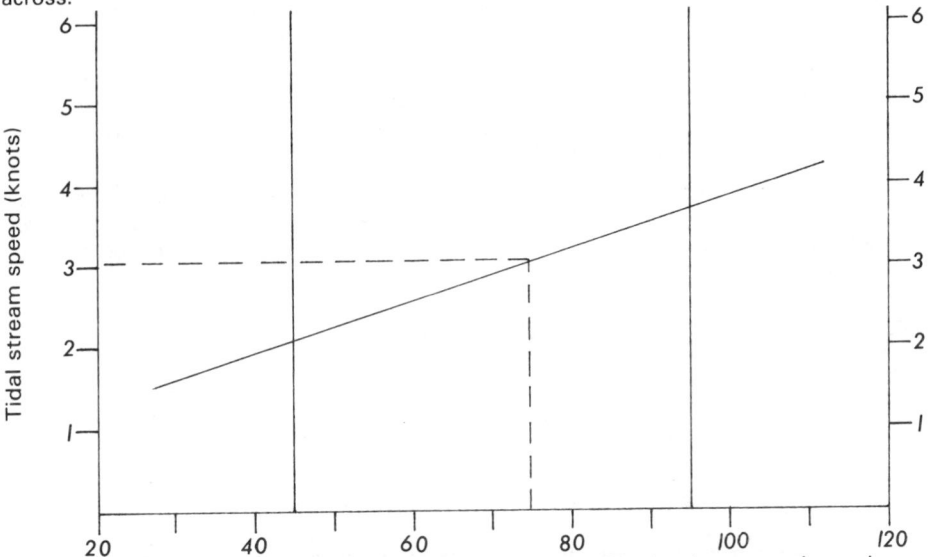

The tidal coefficient of the tide in question is found against its date opposite and seen to be 75. On the graph this is seen to cut your line at the level where the stream rate is 3.05 knots. It can be seen that an extra high range tide (say coefficient 100) will result in tidal streams faster than for normal springs. In the same way the figures up the left hand side can be used to express depths of water (multiplying the scale by ten or perhaps two, as necessary). If the depths at neaps and springs are plotted on the 45 and 95 lines, a line joining can be drawn in the same way and the depth read off against the coefficient for the day.

Note. All tidal predictions are subject to changes in meteorological conditions and should be read with due caution.

1992 TIDAL COEFFICIENTS BASED ON BREST

D. of M.	JAN am	JAN pm	FEB am	FEB pm	MAR am	MAR pm	APR am	APR pm	MAY am	MAY pm	JUNE am	JUNE pm	JULY am	JULY pm	AUG am	AUG pm	SEPT am	SEPT pm	OCT am	OCT pm	NOV am	NOV pm	DEC am	DEC pm	D. of M.
1	51	54	56	61	52	58	73	78	78	82	85	88	92	95	109	108	95	87	74	66	47	42	48	45	1
2	57	60	65	69	64	69	82	86	85	88	89	90	97	98	105	100	78	69	58	50	39	36	42	41	2
3	63	66	73	77	74	79	89	91	90	91	90	89	98	97	94	88	60	52	43	38	36	37	41	41	3
4	69	72	80	82	82	86	93	93	91	90	88	86	95	92	80	72	45	39	34	33	—	40	—	43	4
5	74	75	84	85	88	90	93	91	89	86	83	80	88	83	64	57	35	—	—	34	43	47	45	49	5
6	76	77	85	85	91	92	89	86	83	79	76	73	78	72	50	45	34	36	37	41	52	57	52	56	6
7	77	77	84	83	91	90	82	77	74	70	69	66	67	61	42	—	39	43	46	52	62	66	61	65	7
8	76	75	81	78	87	84	71	65	65	61	64	62	57	54	40	41	49	54	57	63	71	75	70	74	8
9	74	72	74	70	80	75	59	54	58	56	61	61	—	51	44	47	60	65	68	72	78	82	78	82	9
10	69	67	66	61	70	64	49	47	56	57	61	64	51	51	52	56	70	74	77	80	84	86	85	87	10
11	64	60	56	50	58	52	46	—	—	59	62	68	53	55	61	65	78	82	84	86	88	88	89	90	11
12	57	54	46	43	46	42	49	53	63	67	65	72	58	62	70	73	84	87	88	89	88	87	89	90	12
13	51	48	41	—	41	—	59	66	71	75	70	75	65	68	77	79	88	89	90	89	85	82	89	86	13
14	46	45	42	46	43	47	74	81	78	81	74	77	71	73	82	83	89	88	88	86	79	75	84	81	14
15	—	46	52	60	54	62	87	92	84	86	76	77	75	77	84	84	89	84	83	79	71	67	77	73	15
16	48	52	69	78	71	80	97	100	87	87	77	75	78	78	84	83	86	77	75	70	63	60	69	66	16
17	57	64	87	95	89	97	101	102	87	86	76	72	78	78	81	79	81	68	65	59	57	56	63	61	17
18	71	78	102	108	103	108	101	98	84	82	74	67	77	75	76	73	73	57	54	50	56	60	59	—	18
19	85	92	112	114	111	112	95	91	79	76	70	62	74	71	69	65	62	46	47	46	64	68	59	59	19
20	98	103	115	113	111	109	86	81	72	68	64	56	69	66	60	55	51	41	48	—	73	77	61	63	20
21	106	108	109	104	105	100	75	68	64	60	59	51	62	59	50	46	42	—	52	57	81	84	66	69	21
22	108	107	98	91	94	87	62	56	56	52	53	47	55	52	42	41	42	52	64	71	87	89	72	75	22
23	104	100	82	74	79	71	50	44	48	45	48	46	48	46	41	—	46	69	79	86	90	91	77	79	23
24	94	88	65	56	63	55	40	36	43	42	46	46	44	44	44	50	60	87	92	97	90	89	81	82	24
25	80	73	48	41	47	41	34	34	41	42	48	51	—	45	57	65	78	102	101	103	87	85	83	82	25
26	65	57	35	31	35	31	—	36	—	44	54	58	48	52	74	83	95	111	104	104	82	78	82	80	26
27	50	44	—	30	30	—	39	43	46	49	63	68	58	64	91	99	108	114	102	99	74	69	78	76	27
28	40	—	32	36	31	34	48	53	53	57	73	78	71	79	106	111	114	109	95	91	65	60	73	70	28
29	38	37	41	46	39	44	58	63	62	66	83	88	86	92	114	115	112	98	85	79	56	52	67	63	29
30	39	42	—	—	50	56	68	73	70	75	—	—	98	103	115	112	104	83	72	66	—	—	60	56	30
31	47	51	—	—	62	68	—	—	79	82	—	—	107	109	108	102	—	—	59	53	—	—	52	49	31

Extracted from Annuaire des Marées, Vol. 1, Ports of France 1992, by kind permission of Service Hydrographique et Océanographique de la Marine.

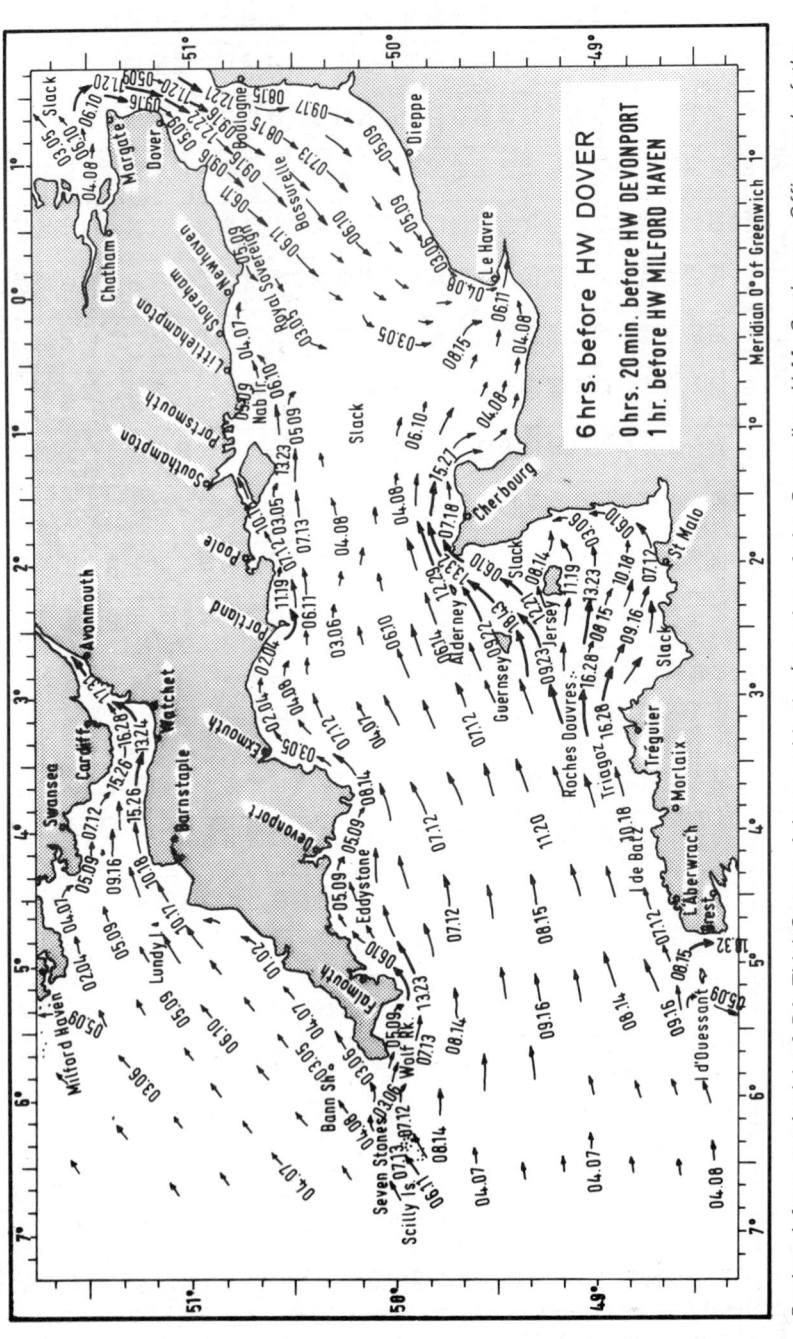

ENGLISH & BRISTOL CHANNELS TIDAL STREAMS

6 hrs. before HW DOVER
0 hrs. 20 min. before HW DEVONPORT
1 hr. before HW MILFORD HAVEN

Produced from portion(s) of BA Tidal Stream Atlases with the sanction of the Controller, H.M. Stationery Office and of the Hydrographer of the Navy.

ENGLISH & BRISTOL CHANNELS TIDAL STREAMS

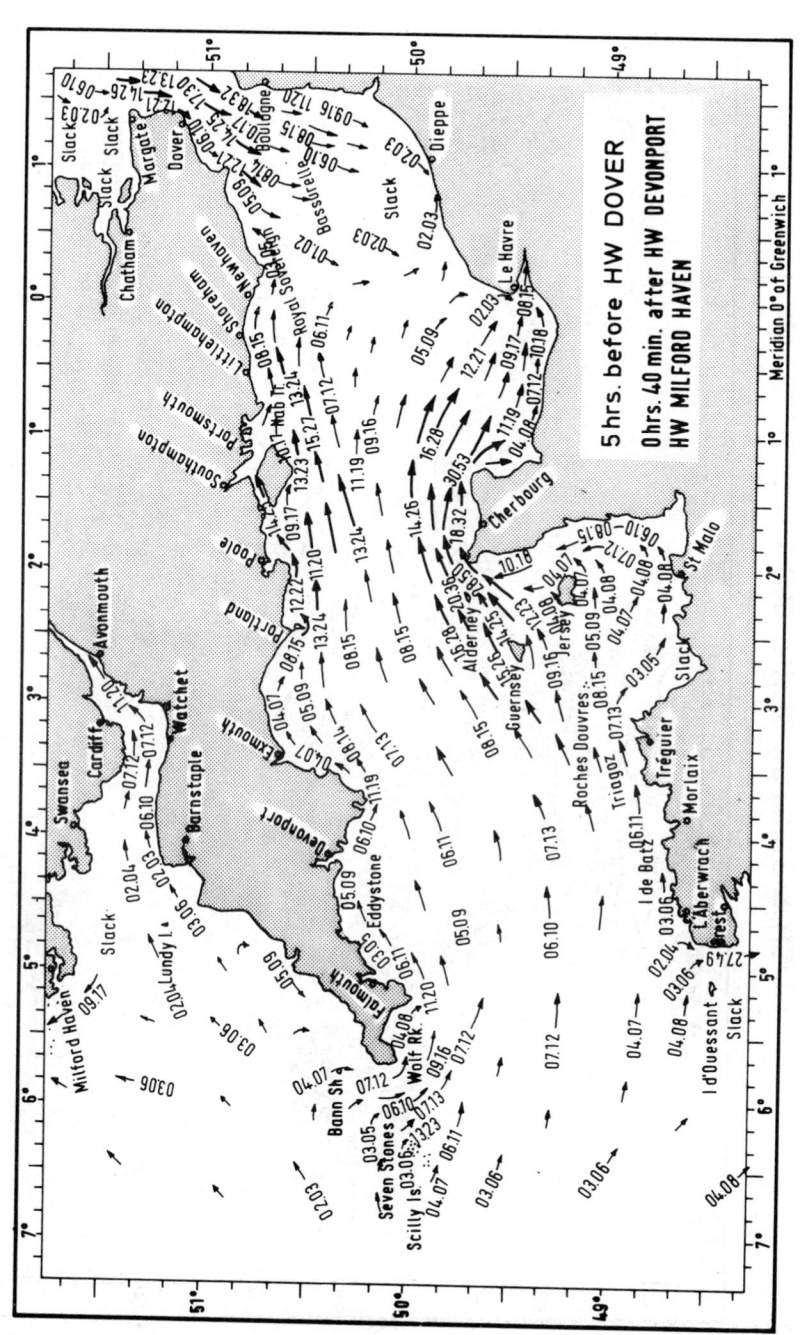

5 hrs. before HW DOVER

0 hrs. 40 min. after HW DEVONPORT
HW MILFORD HAVEN

Meridian 0° of Greenwich

ENGLISH & BRISTOL CHANNELS TIDAL STREAMS

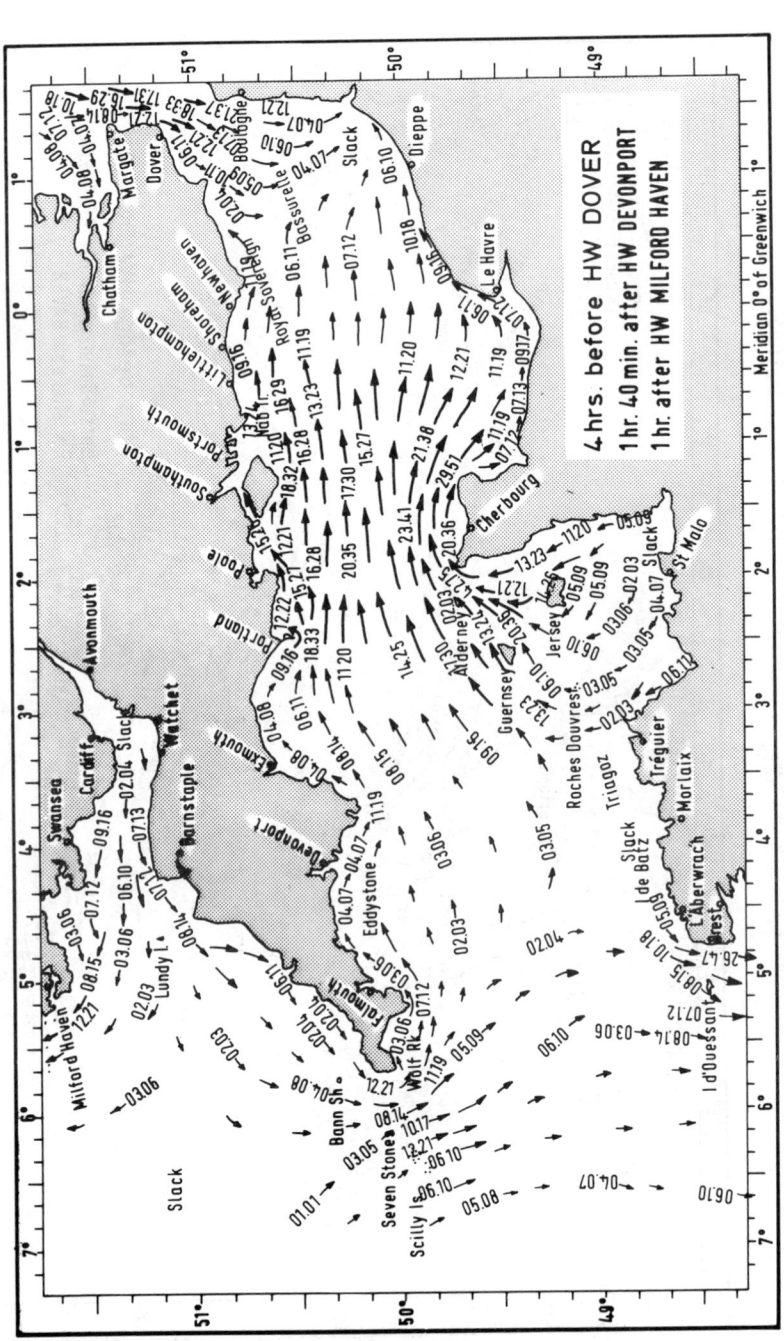

4 hrs. before HW DOVER
1 hr. 40 min. after HW DEVONPORT
1 hr. after HW MILFORD HAVEN

ENGLISH & BRISTOL CHANNELS TIDAL STREAMS

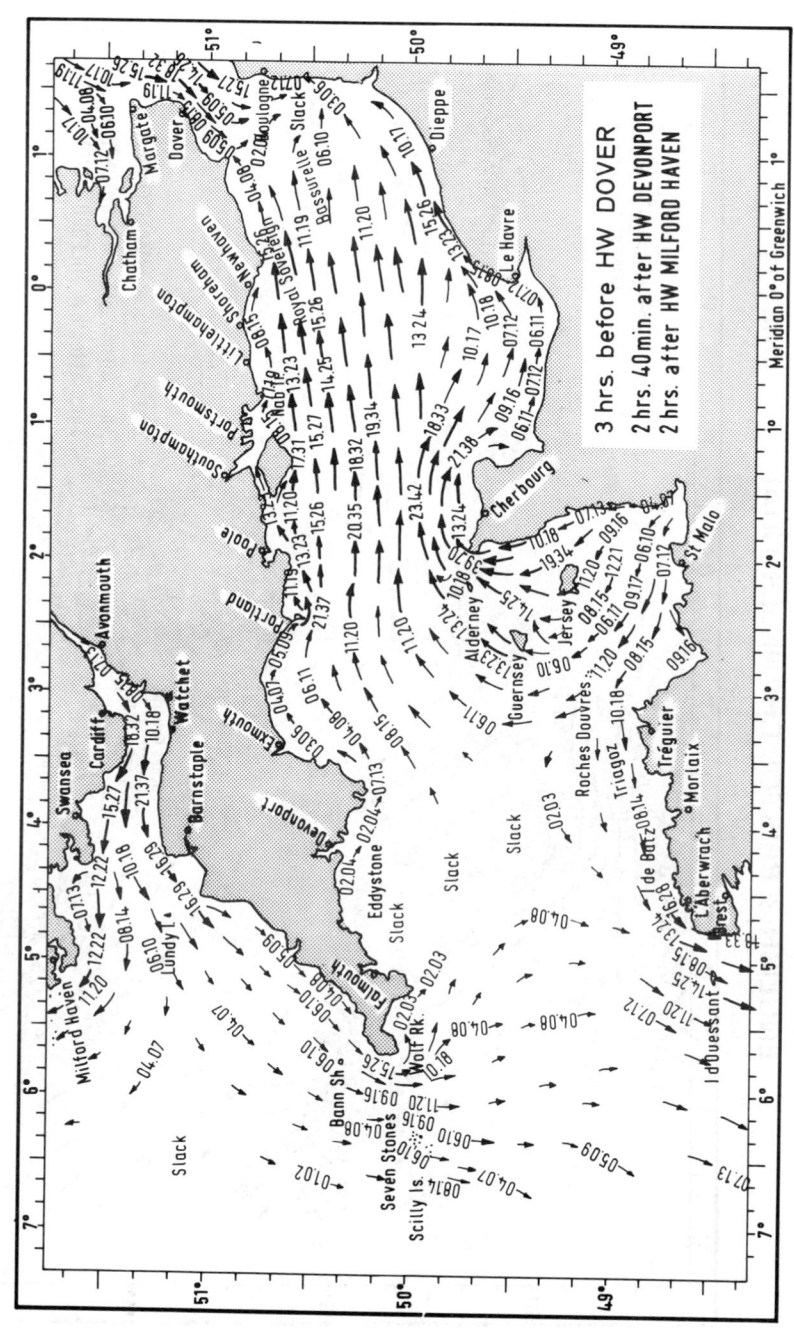

3 hrs. before HW DOVER
2 hrs. 40min. after HW DEVONPORT
2 hrs. after HW MILFORD HAVEN

ENGLISH & BRISTOL CHANNELS TIDAL STREAMS

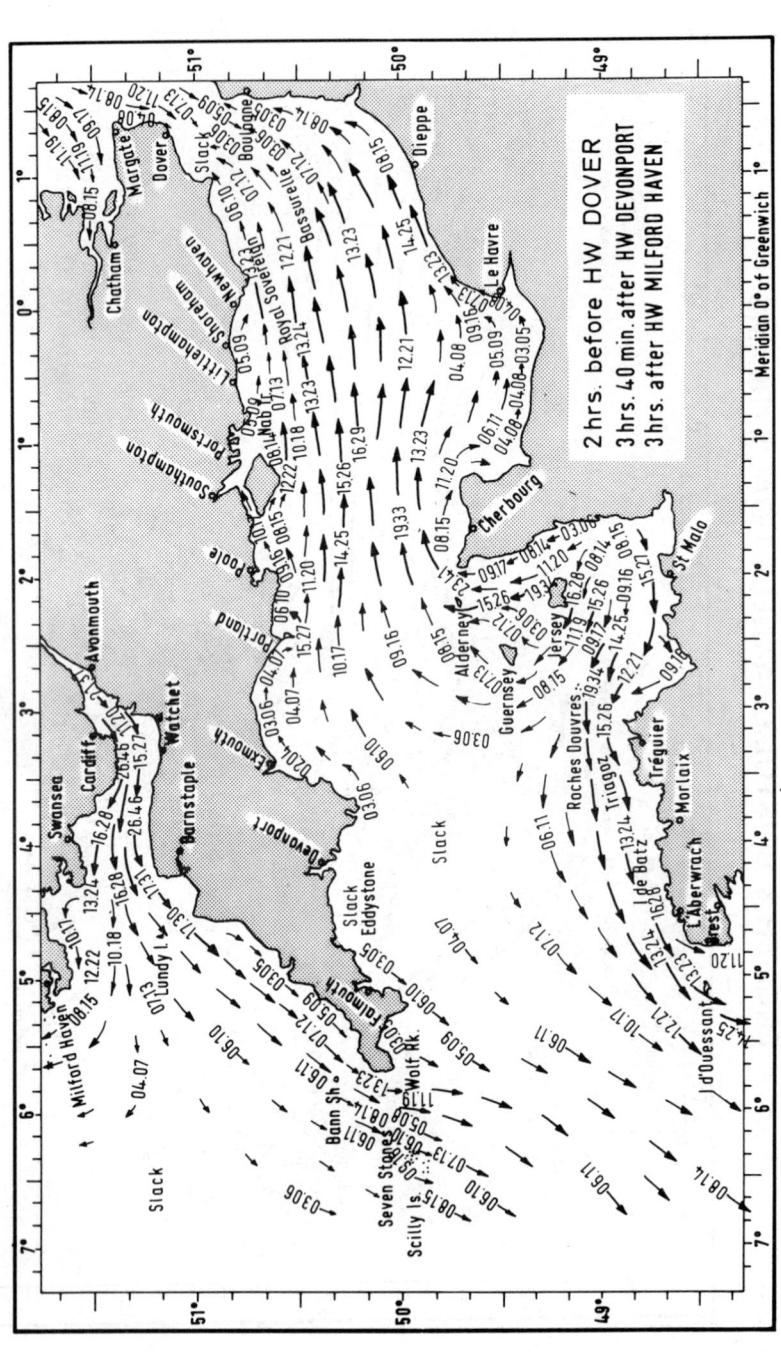

2 hrs. before HW DOVER
3 hrs. 40 min. after HW DEVONPORT
3 hrs. after HW MILFORD HAVEN

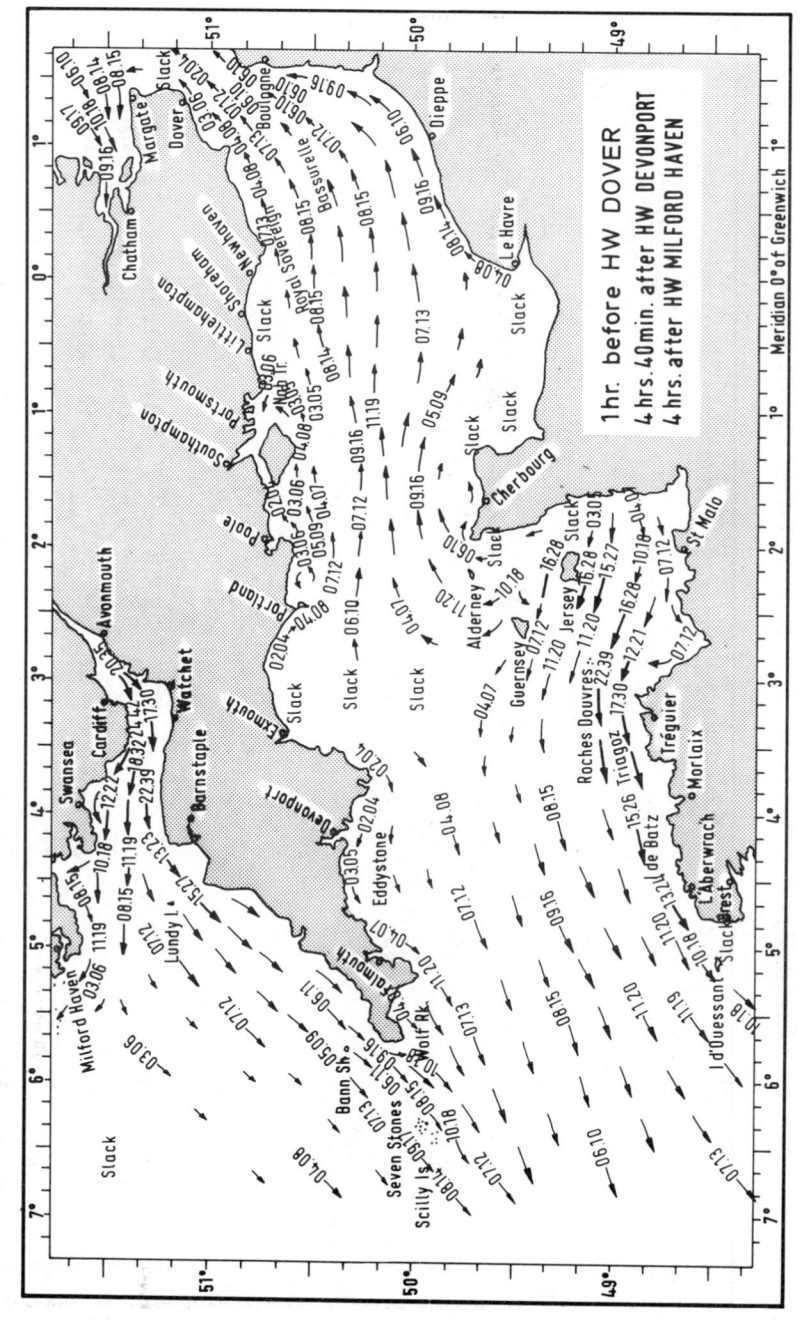

ENGLISH & BRISTOL CHANNELS TIDAL STREAMS

1hr. before HW DOVER
4 hrs. 40min. after HW DEVONPORT
4 hrs. after HW MILFORD HAVEN

ENGLISH & BRISTOL CHANNELS TIDAL STREAMS

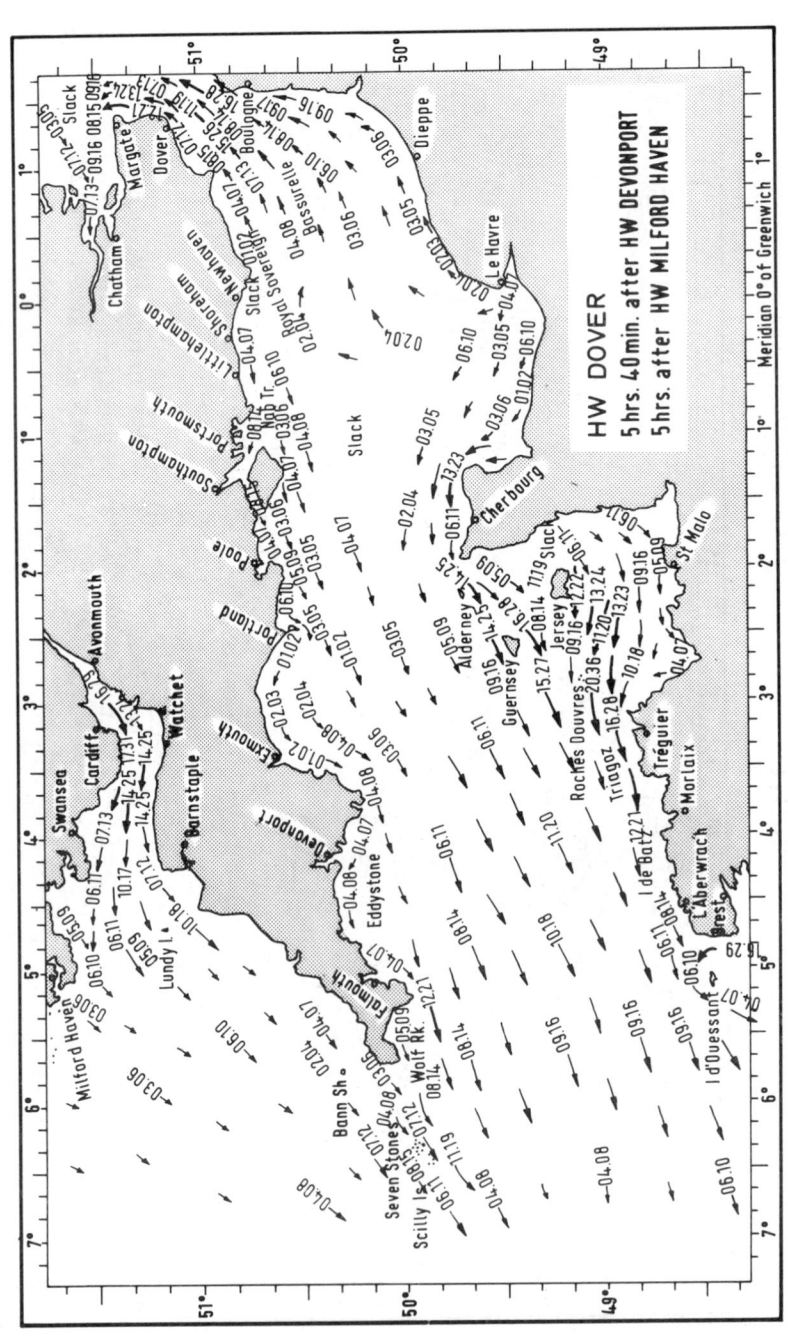

HW DOVER
5 hrs. 40 min. after HW DEVONPORT
5 hrs. after HW MILFORD HAVEN

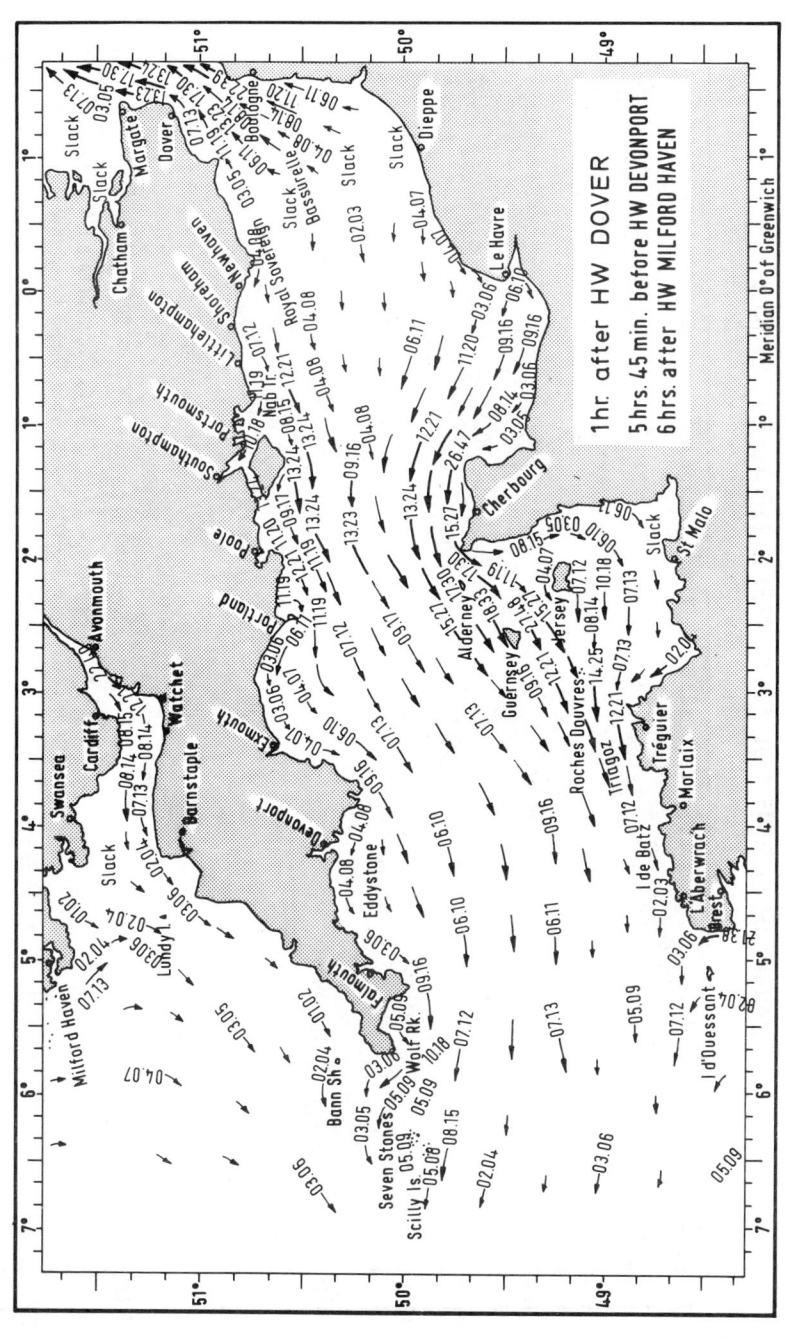

ENGLISH & BRISTOL CHANNELS TIDAL STREAMS

1hr. after HW DOVER
5 hrs. 45 min. before HW DEVONPORT
6 hrs. after HW MILFORD HAVEN

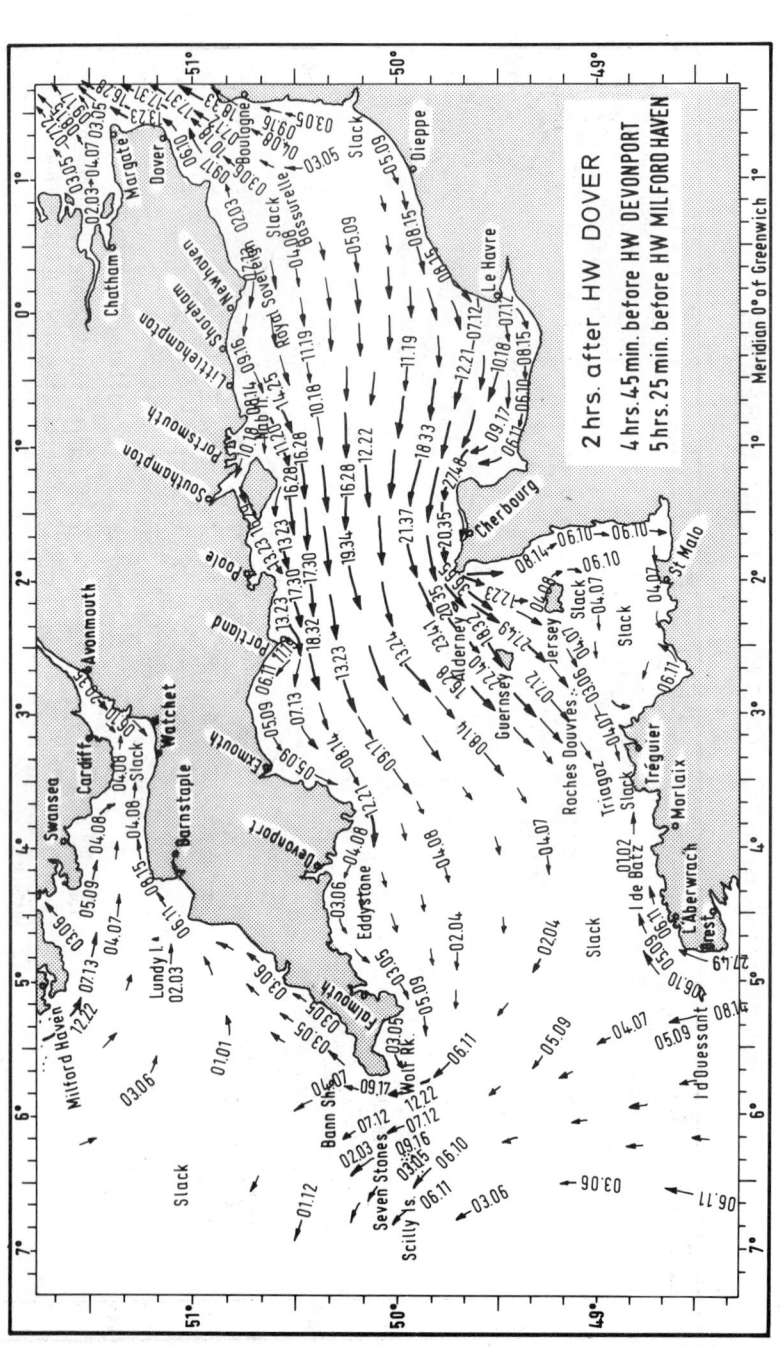

ENGLISH & BRISTOL CHANNELS TIDAL STREAMS

2 hrs. after HW DOVER
4 hrs.45min. before HW DEVONPORT
5 hrs.25min. before HW MILFORD HAVEN

ENGLISH & BRISTOL CHANNELS TIDAL STREAMS

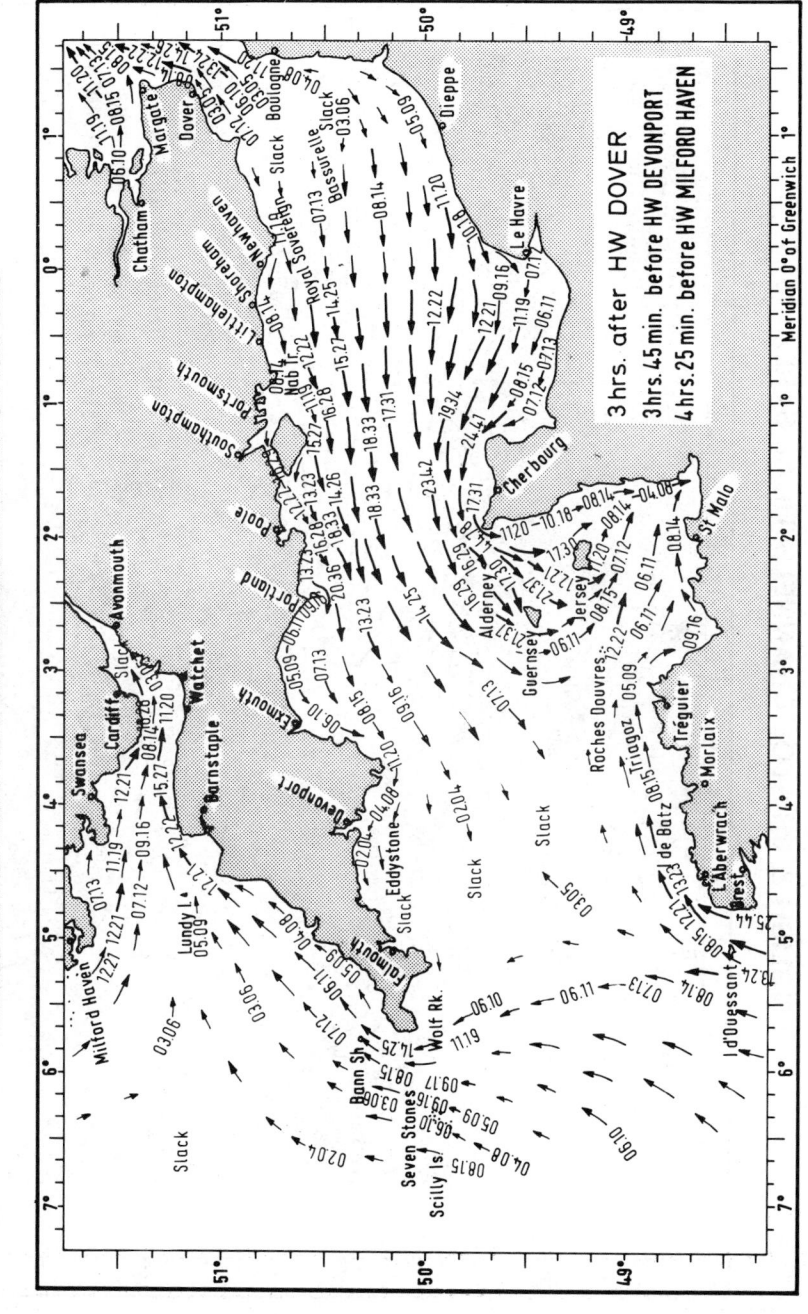

3 hrs. after HW DOVER
3 hrs. 45 min. before HW DEVONPORT
4 hrs. 25 min. before HW MILFORD HAVEN

ENGLISH & BRISTOL CHANNELS TIDAL STREAMS

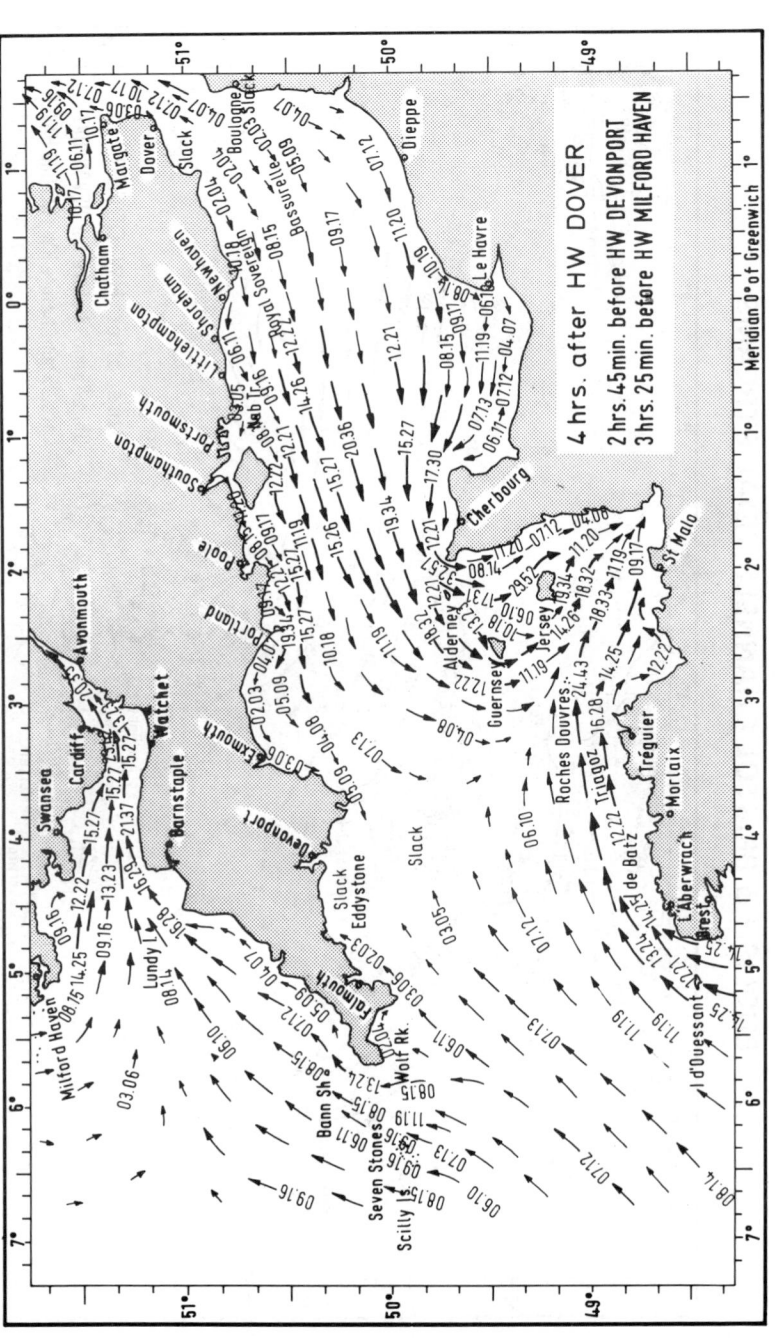

4 hrs. after HW DOVER

2 hrs. 45 min. before HW DEVONPORT
3 hrs. 25 min. before HW MILFORD HAVEN

ENGLISH & BRISTOL CHANNELS TIDAL STREAMS

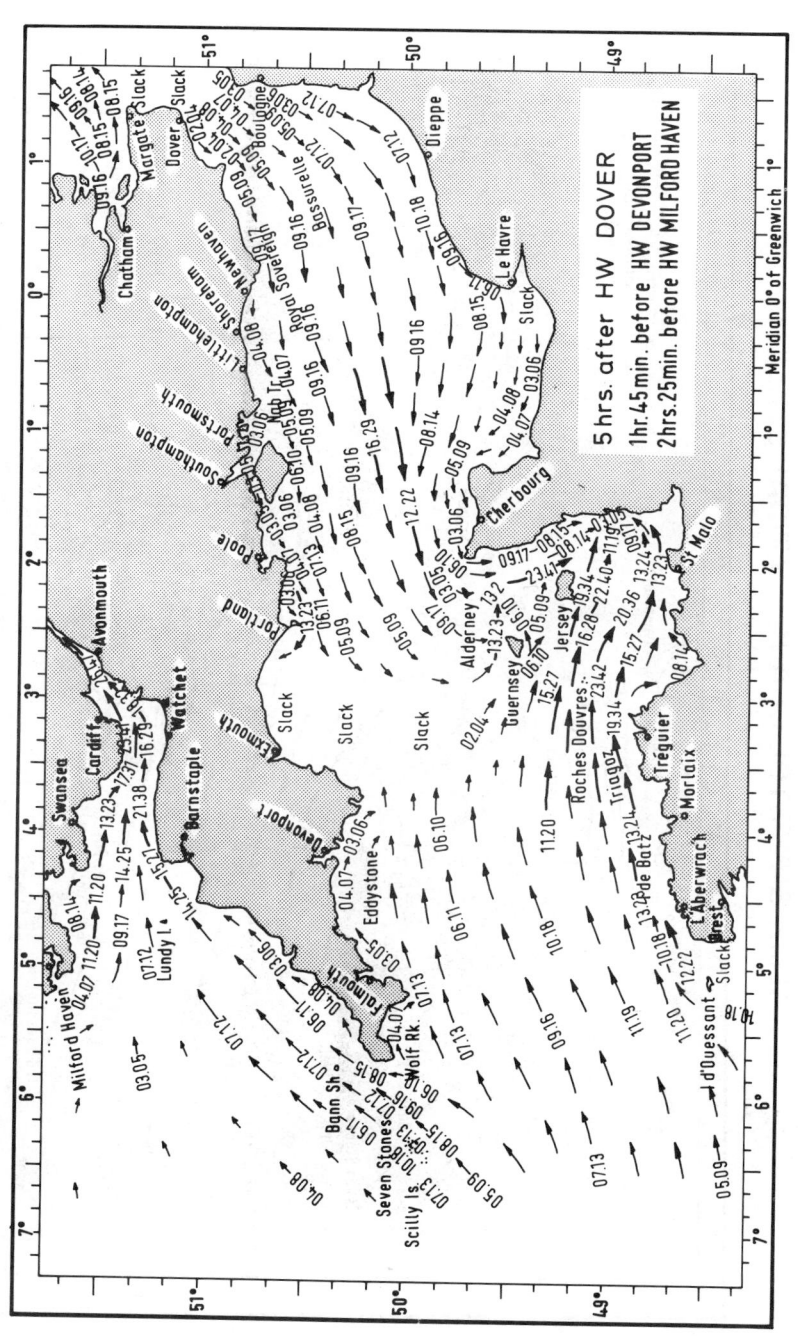

5 hrs. after HW DOVER
1hr.45min. before HW DEVONPORT
2hrs.25min. before HW MILFORD HAVEN

Meridian 0° of Greenwich

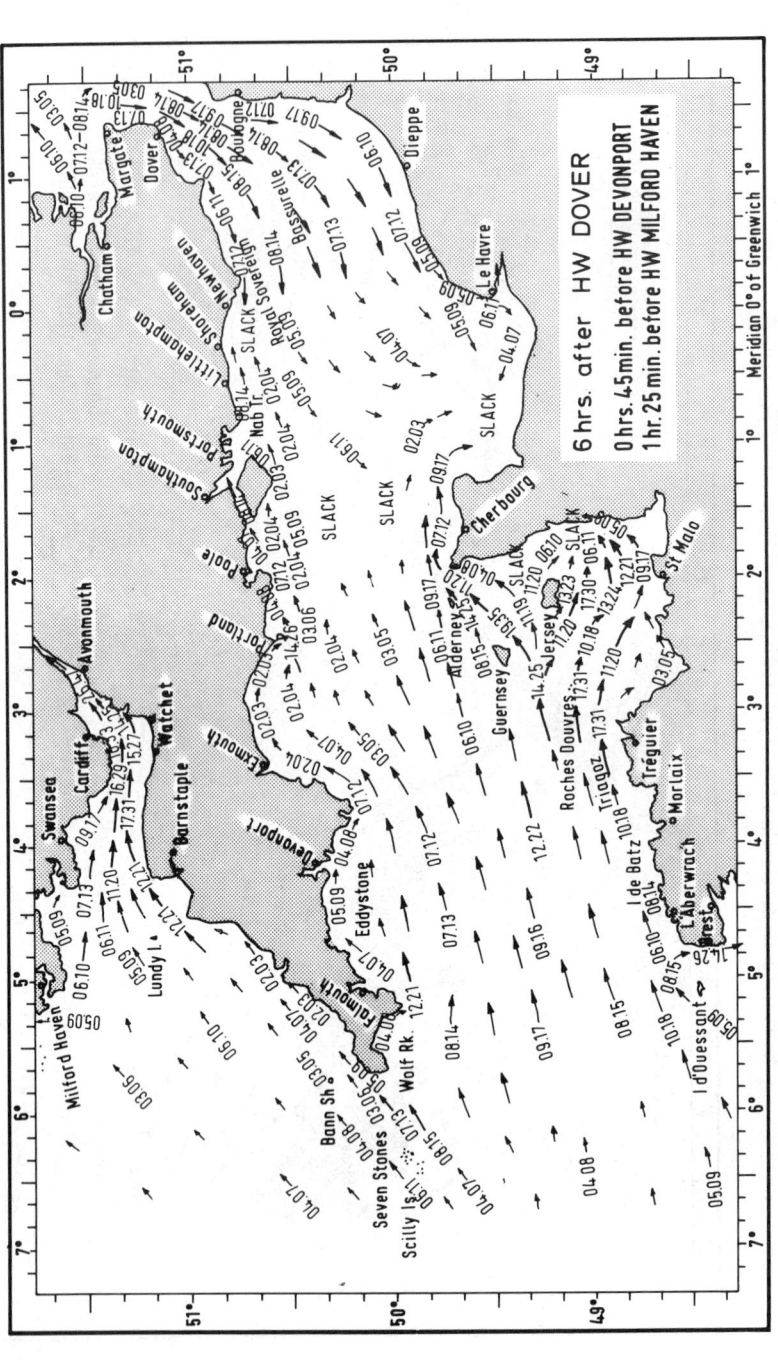

ENGLISH & BRISTOL CHANNELS TIDAL STREAMS

6 hrs. after HW DOVER

0 hrs. 45 min. before HW DEVONPORT
1 hr. 25 min. before HW MILFORD HAVEN

DOVER 21:41

Lat. 51°07′N. Long. 1°19′E.

GMT ADD 1 HOUR MARCH 29 — OCTOBER 25 FOR B.S.T.

HIGH & LOW WATER 1992

JANUARY

Days 1–15

Day	Time	m	Time	m	Time	m	Time	m
1 W	0303	1·9	0813	5·7	1538	1·7	2051	5·6
2 Th	0406	1·8	0912	5·8	1633	1·6	2142	5·8
3 F	0457	1·6	1002	6·0	1719	1·5	2226	6·1
4 Sa	0540	1·4	1045	6·1	1800	1·4	●2304	6·2
5 Su	0619	1·2	1123	6·2	1835	1·3	2340	6·3
6 M	0655	1·1	1157	6·2	1907	1·2		
7 Tu	0012	6·4	0728	1·1	1228	6·2	1938	1·2
8 W	0043	6·4	0801	1·1	1257	6·1	2009	1·2
9 Th	0114	6·4	0833	1·2	1327	6·1	2040	1·3
10 F	0145	6·3	0905	1·3	1358	6·0	2112	1·4
11 Sa	0218	6·2	0939	1·4	1433	5·8	2146	1·6
12 Su	0253	6·1	1013	1·6	1515	5·7	2224	1·8
13 M	0338	5·9	1055	1·8	1609	5·5	☽2315	2·0
14 Tu	0435	5·7	1156	2·0	1715	5·4		
15 W	0025	2·2	0546	5·6	1316	2·0	1829	5·4

Days 16–31

Day	Time	m	Time	m	Time	m	Time	m
16 Th	0154	2·1	0700	5·6	1439	1·8	1944	5·6
17 F	0317	1·8	0809	5·8	1555	1·5	2050	5·9
18 Sa	0426	1·4	0911	6·1	1658	1·2	2149	6·2
19 Su	0525	1·1	1007	6·4	1756	1·0	○2242	6·5
20 M	0619	0·8	1101	6·6	1850	0·8	2332	6·8
21 Tu	0710	0·5	1151	6·7	1940	0·6		
22 W	0018	6·9	0757	0·4	1238	6·7	2023	0·6
23 Th	0103	6·9	0842	0·4	1324	6·6	2103	0·7
24 F	0145	6·8	0922	0·6	1408	6·5	2139	0·9
25 Sa	0229	6·7	1003	0·8	1443	6·2	2216	1·2
26 Su	0315	6·4	1045	1·2	1542	5·9	☾2257	1·6
27 M	0406	6·0	1133	1·6	1638	5·5	2350	2·0
28 Tu	0509	5·6	1234	2·0	1751	5·2		
29 W	0102	2·2	0752	5·3	1349	2·1	1917	5·1
30 Th	0229	2·2	0752	5·3	1510	2·0	2033	5·3
31 F	0345	1·9	0900	5·5	1614	1·8	2128	5·6

FEBRUARY

Days 1–15

Day	Time	m	Time	m	Time	m	Time	m
1 Sa	0441	1·6	0952	5·7	1704	1·6	2212	5·9
2 Su	0526	1·4	1033	5·9	1746	1·4	2247	6·1
3 M	0605	1·2	1106	6·0	1821	1·2	●2319	6·3
4 Tu	0641	1·0	1137	6·2	1852	1·1	2350	6·4
5 W	0712	0·9	1204	6·2	1920	1·1		
6 Th	0019	6·5	0742	0·9	1232	6·3	1948	1·0
7 F	0048	6·5	0812	0·9	1259	6·3	2018	1·0
8 Sa	0116	6·5	0842	1·0	1327	6·2	2049	1·1
9 Su	0142	6·4	0912	1·2	1358	6·1	2118	1·3
10 M	0215	6·3	0942	1·4	1434	6·0	2150	1·6
11 Tu	0256	6·2	1016	1·6	1524	5·8	☽2234	1·8
12 W	0350	5·9	1108	1·9	1628	5·5	2339	2·1
13 Th	0504	5·6	1229	2·0	1751	5·3		
14 F	0113	2·1	0632	5·4	1408	1·9	1927	5·4
15 Sa	0251	1·8	0758	5·6	1535	1·6	2046	5·7

Days 16–29

Day	Time	m	Time	m	Time	m	Time	m
16 Su	0407	1·4	0907	6·0	1644	1·2	2143	6·2
17 M	0509	0·9	1002	6·3	1743	0·9	2233	6·5
18 Tu	0607	0·6	1051	6·6	1839	0·6	○2318	6·8
19 W	0657	0·4	1136	6·8	1927	0·5		
20 Th	0000	7·0	0744	0·3	1218	6·8	2005	0·5
21 F	0041	7·0	0823	0·3	1259	6·7	2039	0·6
22 Sa	0120	6·9	0900	0·5	1340	6·5	2111	0·8
23 Su	0159	6·7	0935	0·8	1420	6·3	2143	1·1
24 M	0242	6·4	1010	1·2	1505	5·9	2219	1·5
25 Tu	0329	6·0	1049	1·6	1557	5·5	☾2304	1·9
26 W	0428	5·5	1143	2·1	1706	5·1		
27 Th	0010	2·3	0553	5·0	1300	2·4	1845	4·9
28 F	0148	2·4	0731	5·0	1437	2·3	2009	5·1
29 Sa	0318	2·0	0843	5·3	1549	1·9	2105	5·5

MARCH

Days 1–15

Day	Time	m	Time	m	Time	m	Time	m
1 Su	0419	1·6	0934	5·6	1641	1·6	2148	5·8
2 M	0504	1·3	1012	5·8	1723	1·4	2221	6·1
3 Tu	0543	1·1	1041	6·0	1800	1·2	2252	6·3
4 W	0618	0·9	1108	6·2	1831	1·0	●2320	6·4
5 Th	0650	0·8	1134	6·3	1859	0·9	2350	6·5
6 F	0721	0·8	1201	6·4	1927	0·9		
7 Sa	0017	6·6	0751	0·8	1229	6·4	1957	0·9
8 Su	0043	6·6	0819	0·9	1259	6·4	2027	1·0
9 M	0113	6·5	0849	1·0	1330	6·3	2058	1·1
10 Tu	0147	6·4	0919	1·2	1408	6·1	2134	1·4
11 W	0227	6·2	0956	1·5	1457	5·9	2216	1·7
12 Th	0324	5·8	1048	1·8	1604	5·5	☽2320	1·9
13 F	0441	5·2	1207	2·0	1736	5·2		
14 Sa	0053	2·0	0624	5·3	1351	1·9	1921	5·4
15 Su	0233	1·7	0758	5·6	1518	1·5	2036	5·8

Days 16–31

Day	Time	m	Time	m	Time	m	Time	m
16 M	0349	1·2	0901	6·0	1626	1·2	2129	6·2
17 Tu	0451	0·9	0950	6·3	1725	0·9	2214	6·6
18 W	0547	0·6	1034	6·5	1818	0·7	○2257	6·8
19 Th	0638	0·4	1116	6·7	1902	0·5	2336	7·0
20 F	0720	0·3	1156	6·7	1937	0·5		
21 Sa	0015	7·0	0757	0·4	1234	6·7	2009	0·6
22 Su	0053	6·8	0832	0·6	1312	6·5	2043	0·8
23 M	0131	6·6	0905	0·9	1351	6·3	2115	1·1
24 Tu	0212	6·3	0939	1·2	1433	5·9	2150	1·4
25 W	0257	5·8	1016	1·7	1522	5·6	2231	1·8
26 Th	0353	5·3	1101	2·1	1626	5·1	☾2326	2·2
27 F	0518	4·9	1207	2·4	1800	4·9		
28 Sa	0050	2·4	0702	4·9	1342	2·4	1930	5·1
29 Su	0234	2·1	0812	5·2	1507	2·1	2029	5·4
30 M	0339	1·7	0901	5·6	1603	1·7	2111	5·7
31 Tu	0427	1·4	0936	5·7	1647	1·4	2145	6·0

APRIL

Days 1–15

Day	Time	m	Time	m	Time	m	Time	m
1 W	0509	1·1	1004	5·9	1725	1·2	2216	6·2
2 Th	0547	1·0	1031	6·2	1801	1·0	2247	6·4
3 F	0624	0·8	1101	6·3	1834	0·9	●2316	6·5
4 Sa	0656	0·8	1130	6·4	1906	0·8	2346	6·6
5 Su	0728	0·8	1203	6·5	1937	0·8		
6 M	0017	6·6	0758	0·8	1235	6·4	2011	0·9
7 Tu	0050	6·5	0830	1·0	1312	6·3	2046	1·0
8 W	0128	6·4	0905	1·1	1355	6·2	2125	1·2
9 Th	0216	6·1	0948	1·5	1450	5·9	2213	1·5
10 F	0318	5·7	1042	1·7	1602	5·5	☽2316	1·7
11 Sa	0442	5·4	1200	1·9	1733	5·4		
12 Su	0043	1·8	0625	5·4	1335	1·8	1907	5·5
13 M	0215	1·5	0747	5·7	1456	1·5	2015	5·9
14 Tu	0325	1·1	0844	6·0	1600	1·2	2105	6·2
15 W	0426	0·9	0929	6·2	1657	1·0	2149	6·5

Days 16–30

Day	Time	m	Time	m	Time	m	Time	m
16 Th	0520	0·7	1012	6·4	1747	0·8	2231	6·7
17 F	0608	0·6	1052	6·5	1829	0·7	○2312	6·8
18 Sa	0650	0·5	1133	6·6	1906	0·7	2353	6·8
19 Su	0728	0·6	1212	6·5	1942	0·7		
20 M	0031	6·6	0805	0·7	1250	6·4	2018	0·9
21 Tu	0109	6·4	0840	1·0	1328	6·2	2053	1·1
22 W	0149	6·1	0914	1·3	1411	6·0	2128	1·4
23 Th	0233	5·7	0948	1·7	1456	5·7	2206	1·7
24 F	0325	5·3	1027	2·0	1552	5·3	☾2254	2·0
25 Sa	0426	5·0	1120	2·3	1705	5·1	2357	2·2
26 Su	0607	4·9	1232	2·4	1829	5·1		
27 M	0119	2·1	0719	5·1	1354	2·2	1934	5·3
28 Tu	0236	1·9	0809	5·4	1501	1·9	2020	5·6
29 W	0334	1·6	0847	5·6	1555	1·6	2100	5·9
30 Th	0423	1·3	0919	5·9	1642	1·3	2135	6·1

TIDAL DIFFERENCES 21:44. TIDAL CURVE PAGE 21:45.

TIDAL STREAMS PAGES 21:28-21:40.

Datum of predictions: 3.67 m. below Ordnance Datum (Newlyn) or approx. L.A.T.

21:42 DOVER

HIGH & LOW WATER 1992 Lat. 51°07′N. Long. 1°19′E.

GMT ADD 1 HOUR MARCH 29 — OCTOBER 25 FOR B.S.T.

MAY

#	Time	m	#	Time	m
1 F	0509 / 0953 / 1726 / 2209	1·1 / 6·1 / 1·1 / 6·3	16 Sa ○	0540 / 1033 / 1800 / 2252	0·9 / 6·3 / 1·0 / 6·5
2 Sa ●	0551 / 1027 / 1808 / 2244	0·9 / 6·3 / 1·0 / 6·5	17 Su	0624 / 1116 / 1841 / 2336	0·9 / 6·4 / 0·9 / 6·5
3 Su	0632 / 1104 / 1846 / 2319	0·9 / 6·4 / 0·9 / 6·6	18 M	0703 / 1157 / 1920	0·9 / 6·4 / 0·9
4 M	0709 / 1140 / 1921 / 2356	0·8 / 6·5 / 1·0 / 6·6	19 Tu	0017 / 0740 / 1236 / 1957	6·4 / 1·0 / 6·3 / 1·0
5 Tu	0742 / 1221 / 1958	0·8 / 6·5 / 0·8	20 W	0055 / 0816 / 1314 / 2033	6·2 / 1·1 / 6·2 / 1·1
6 W	0038 / 0819 / 1307 / 2039	6·5 / 0·9 / 6·4 / 0·9	21 Th	0133 / 0850 / 1352 / 2108	6·0 / 1·3 / 6·1 / 1·3
7 Th	0124 / 0900 / 1359 / 2122	6·3 / 1·1 / 6·2 / 1·1	22 F	0213 / 0922 / 1433 / 2145	5·8 / 1·5 / 5·9 / 1·5
8 F	0220 / 0946 / 1458 / 2213	6·0 / 1·3 / 6·0 / 1·3	23 Sa	0258 / 0959 / 1519 / 2226	5·5 / 1·8 / 5·7 / 1·7
9 Sa ☽	0328 / 1041 / 1604 / 2315	5·8 / 1·5 / 5·8 / 1·4	24 Su ☾	0339 / 1042 / 1613 / 2315	5·3 / 2·0 / 5·4 / 1·9
10 Su	0445 / 1154 / 1720	5·6 / 1·7 / 5·7	25 M	0457 / 1137 / 1718	5·1 / 2·1 / 5·3
11 M	0032 / 0608 / 1316 / 1838	1·5 / 5·6 / 1·7 / 5·7	26 Tu	0014 / 0604 / 1242 / 1824	2·0 / 5·1 / 2·2 / 5·3
12 Tu	0151 / 0720 / 1427 / 1942	1·3 / 5·7 / 1·5 / 5·9	27 W	0124 / 0702 / 1352 / 1920	1·9 / 5·3 / 2·0 / 5·5
13 W	0258 / 0816 / 1529 / 2036	1·2 / 5·9 / 1·3 / 6·1	28 Th	0232 / 0751 / 1458 / 2009	1·7 / 5·5 / 1·8 / 5·7
14 Th	0357 / 0904 / 1626 / 2124	1·0 / 6·1 / 1·2 / 6·3	29 F	0334 / 0854 / 1559 / 2053	1·5 / 5·7 / 1·5 / 6·0
15 F	0452 / 0949 / 1715 / 2209	1·0 / 6·2 / 1·1 / 6·5	30 Sa	0440 / 0917 / 1654 / 2135	1·3 / 6·0 / 1·3 / 6·2
			31 Su	0522 / 0959 / 1743 / 2216	1·1 / 6·2 / 1·1 / 6·4

JUNE

#	Time	m	#	Time	m
1 M ●	0608 / 1042 / 1828 / 2259	1·0 / 6·4 / 0·9 / 6·5	16 Tu	0643 / 1144 / 1902	1·1 / 6·3 / 1·0
2 Tu	0652 / 1127 / 1910 / 2346	0·9 / 6·5 / 0·8 / 6·5	17 W	0005 / 0720 / 1222 / 1938	6·2 / 1·1 / 6·3 / 1·0
3 W	0733 / 1217 / 1952	0·8 / 6·5 / 0·8	18 Th	0042 / 0755 / 1257 / 2013	6·1 / 1·2 / 6·3 / 1·1
4 Th	0035 / 0813 / 1310 / 2034	6·5 / 0·9 / 6·5 / 0·8	19 F	0116 / 0826 / 1333 / 2047	6·0 / 1·3 / 6·2 / 1·2
5 F	0130 / 0857 / 1404 / 2121	6·4 / 0·9 / 6·4 / 0·8	20 Sa	0151 / 0858 / 1408 / 2121	5·9 / 1·4 / 6·1 / 1·3
6 Sa	0227 / 0945 / 1456 / 2212	6·2 / 1·1 / 6·3 / 1·0	21 Su	0227 / 0932 / 1444 / 2157	5·8 / 1·5 / 6·0 / 1·5
7 Su ☽	0325 / 1037 / 1550 / 2308	6·0 / 1·3 / 6·1 / 1·1	22 M	0307 / 1009 / 1527 / 2237	5·6 / 1·7 / 5·8 / 1·7
8 M	0427 / 1139 / 1652	5·8 / 1·5 / 6·0	23 Tu ☾	0355 / 1052 / 1616 / 2325	5·4 / 1·9 / 5·6 / 1·8
9 Tu	0012 / 0533 / 1246 / 1758	1·3 / 5·7 / 1·6 / 5·9	24 W	0451 / 1146 / 1713	5·3 / 2·0 / 5·5
10 W	0120 / 0641 / 1352 / 1904	1·3 / 5·7 / 1·6 / 5·9	25 Th	0025 / 0553 / 1252 / 1817	1·9 / 5·3 / 2·1 / 5·5
11 Th	0227 / 0747 / 1457 / 2006	1·4 / 5·7 / 1·6 / 5·9	26 F	0134 / 0655 / 1406 / 1919	1·9 / 5·4 / 2·0 / 5·6
12 F	0329 / 0842 / 1557 / 2101	1·3 / 5·8 / 1·5 / 6·0	27 Sa	0247 / 0752 / 1519 / 2015	1·7 / 5·6 / 1·8 / 5·8
13 Sa	0427 / 0932 / 1652 / 2152	1·3 / 6·0 / 1·3 / 6·1	28 Su	0355 / 0847 / 1624 / 2107	1·5 / 5·9 / 1·5 / 6·1
14 Su	0518 / 1020 / 1739 / 2240	1·2 / 6·1 / 1·2 / 6·2	29 M	0455 / 0939 / 1722 / 2157	1·3 / 6·1 / 1·2 / 6·3
15 M ○	0603 / 1104 / 1822 / 2323	1·2 / 6·2 / 1·1 / 6·3	30 Tu ●	0550 / 1030 / 1812 / 2248	1·0 / 6·4 / 0·9 / 6·5

JULY

#	Time	m	#	Time	m
1 W	0639 / 1120 / 1900 / 2339	0·9 / 6·6 / 0·7 / 6·6	16 Th	0703 / 1203 / 1921	1·2 / 6·4 / 1·0
2 Th	0727 / 1211 / 1947	0·8 / 6·7 / 0·6	17 F	0021 / 0734 / 1235 / 1954	6·2 / 1·2 / 6·4 / 1·0
3 F	0031 / 0811 / 1300 / 2032	6·6 / 0·7 / 6·7 / 0·5	18 Sa	0052 / 0804 / 1306 / 2026	6·2 / 1·2 / 6·4 / 1·1
4 Sa	0123 / 0856 / 1349 / 2117	6·6 / 0·8 / 6·7 / 0·6	19 Su	0121 / 0833 / 1337 / 2057	6·1 / 1·2 / 6·3 / 1·2
5 Su	0213 / 0939 / 1437 / 2203	6·4 / 0·9 / 6·6 / 0·7	20 M	0151 / 0904 / 1408 / 2129	6·0 / 1·3 / 6·2 / 1·3
6 M	0304 / 1024 / 1525 / 2251	6·3 / 1·1 / 6·4 / 1·0	21 Tu	0223 / 0938 / 1440 / 2203	5·9 / 1·5 / 6·1 / 1·5
7 Tu ☽	0355 / 1112 / 1619 / 2344	6·0 / 1·4 / 6·2 / 1·3	22 W	0300 / 1013 / 1519 / 2241	5·7 / 1·7 / 5·9 / 1·7
8 W	0452 / 1208 / 1719	5·7 / 1·6 / 5·9	23 Th	0346 / 1057 / 1612 / 2332	5·6 / 1·9 / 5·7 / 1·9
9 Th	0045 / 0600 / 1314 / 1828	1·5 / 5·5 / 1·8 / 5·7	24 F	0448 / 1158 / 1718	5·4 / 2·1 / 5·5
10 F	0154 / 0713 / 1426 / 1941	1·7 / 5·5 / 1·9 / 5·7	25 Sa	0042 / 0601 / 1319 / 1832	2·0 / 5·3 / 2·1 / 5·5
11 Sa	0304 / 0823 / 1536 / 2047	1·7 / 5·6 / 1·7 / 5·7	26 Su	0204 / 0719 / 1444 / 1945	1·9 / 5·4 / 1·9 / 5·7
12 Su	0409 / 0921 / 1635 / 2142	1·6 / 5·8 / 1·5 / 5·9	27 M	0325 / 0829 / 1600 / 2050	1·7 / 5·7 / 1·5 / 6·0
13 M	0502 / 1009 / 1702 / 2230	1·5 / 6·0 / 1·3 / 6·0	28 Tu	0433 / 0928 / 1702 / 2146	1·3 / 6·1 / 1·2 / 6·3
14 Tu ○	0549 / 1020 / 1808 / 2312	1·4 / 6·4 / 1·2 / 6·1	29 W ●	0532 / 1020 / 1757 / 2238	1·1 / 6·4 / 0·8 / 6·5
15 W	0628 / 1127 / 1848 / 2349	1·3 / 6·3 / 1·1 / 6·2	30 Th	0627 / 1109 / 1849 / 2327	0·8 / 6·7 / 0·6 / 6·7
			31 F	0719 / 1156 / 1938	0·7 / 6·9 / 0·4

AUGUST

#	Time	m	#	Time	m
1 Sa	0015 / 0804 / 1241 / 2023	6·8 / 0·6 / 6·9 / 0·4	16 Su	0021 / 0738 / 1235 / 2001	6·3 / 1·1 / 6·5 / 1·0
2 Su	0102 / 0846 / 1326 / 2105	6·7 / 0·6 / 6·9 / 0·5	17 M	0048 / 0808 / 1302 / 2032	6·3 / 1·1 / 6·5 / 1·1
3 M	0147 / 0922 / 1409 / 2146	6·6 / 0·8 / 6·8 / 0·7	18 Tu	0114 / 0837 / 1328 / 2101	6·2 / 1·2 / 6·4 / 1·2
4 Tu	0232 / 1000 / 1454 / 2227	6·4 / 1·0 / 6·5 / 1·0	19 W	0142 / 0908 / 1358 / 2132	6·1 / 1·4 / 6·3 / 1·4
5 W	0319 / 1040 / 1543 / 2312	6·1 / 1·4 / 6·2 / 1·4	20 Th	0216 / 0941 / 1433 / 2204	6·0 / 1·6 / 6·1 / 1·7
6 Th	0414 / 1129 / 1641	5·7 / 1·7 / 5·8	21 F ☾	0258 / 1020 / 1522 / 2249	5·8 / 1·9 / 5·9 / 1·9
7 F	0008 / 0520 / 1234 / 1756	1·8 / 5·4 / 2·1 / 5·5	22 Sa	0357 / 1118 / 1631	5·5 / 2·1 / 5·5
8 Sa	0119 / 0645 / 1357 / 1924	2·0 / 5·2 / 2·1 / 5·4	23 Su	0000 / 0519 / 1241 / 1800	2·1 / 5·3 / 2·2 / 5·4
9 Su	0240 / 0808 / 1518 / 2039	2·0 / 5·4 / 1·9 / 5·5	24 M	0131 / 0657 / 1418 / 1933	2·1 / 5·3 / 2·0 / 5·5
10 M	0352 / 0908 / 1621 / 2134	1·8 / 5·7 / 1·6 / 5·8	25 Tu	0301 / 0819 / 1538 / 2043	1·8 / 5·7 / 1·5 / 5·9
11 Tu	0447 / 0953 / 1711 / 2217	1·6 / 6·0 / 1·4 / 5·9	26 W	0412 / 0918 / 1641 / 2136	1·4 / 6·2 / 1·1 / 6·3
12 W	0533 / 1031 / 1754 / 2254	1·4 / 6·2 / 1·2 / 6·1	27 Th	0513 / 1006 / 1739 / 2224	1·0 / 6·5 / 0·8 / 6·6
13 Th ○	0612 / 1105 / 1831 / 2325	1·3 / 6·4 / 1·1 / 6·2	28 F ●	0610 / 1051 / 1832 / 2309	0·8 / 6·8 / 0·5 / 6·8
14 F	0643 / 1137 / 1902 / 2354	1·2 / 6·5 / 1·0 / 6·3	29 Sa	0700 / 1134 / 1920 / 2353	0·6 / 7·0 / 0·4 / 6·9
15 Sa	0712 / 1207 / 1931	1·1 / 6·5 / 1·0	30 Su	0744 / 1215 / 2004	0·6 / 7·1 / 0·4
			31 M	0035 / 0822 / 1256 / 2043	6·8 / 0·6 / 7·0 / 0·5

GENERAL — Eddies run off the mole head and turbulence occurs at the entrances. Sub-surface streams may differ appreciably from surface streams; caution is necessary.

WHEN TO ENTER — The best time is between –0200 and +0100 (Dover).

WHEN TO LEAVE — All times suitable, but caution required when meeting stream off ent.

DOVER 21:43

Lat. 51°07′N. Long. 1°19′E. HIGH & LOW WATER 1992

GMT ADD 1 HOUR MARCH 29 — OCTOBER 25 FOR B.S.T.

SEPTEMBER

Day	Time m	Time m	Time m	Time m	Day	Time m	Time m	Time m	Time m
1	0117 6.7	0856 0.8	Tu 1338 6.8	2121 0.7	16	0042 6.4	0813 1.2	W 1255 6.5	2034 1.2
2	0159 6.4	0931 1.1	W 1422 6.5	2157 1.1	17	0112 6.3	0846 1.3	Th 1326 6.4	2105 1.4
3	0246 6.1	1009 1.4	Th 1510 6.1	)) 2238 1.6	18	0145 6.2	0919 1.6	F 1402 6.2	2141 1.7
4	0338 5.7	1054 1.9	F 1607 5.7	2330 2.0	19	0229 6.0	1000 1.8	Sa 1451 5.9	((2227 1.9
5	0444 5.3	1156 2.2	Sa 1727 5.2		20	0329 5.6	1058 2.1	Su 1604 5.5	2336 2.2
6	0042 2.3	0617 5.1	Su 1324 2.3	1909 5.2	21	0458 5.3	1219 2.2	M 1746 5.3	
7	0212 2.3	0747 5.3	M 1456 2.1	2025 5.4	22	0110 2.1	0646 5.4	Tu 1357 1.9	1926 5.6
8	0328 2.0	0846 5.6	Tu 1559 1.7	2117 5.7	23	0242 1.8	0806 5.8	W 1515 1.4	2033 6.0
9	0424 1.7	0931 5.9	W 1648 1.4	2156 5.9	24	0330 1.4	0901 6.2	Th 1619 1.0	2122 6.4
10	0508 1.5	1006 6.2	Th 1729 1.2	2227 6.1	25	0449 1.1	0946 6.6	F 1715 0.8	2206 6.6
11	0546 1.3	1037 6.4	F 1804 1.1	2255 6.3	26	0544 0.8	1109 6.9	Sa 1807 0.6	● 2248 6.8
12	0617 1.2	1106 6.5	Sa 1836 1.0	○ 2320 6.4	27	0632 0.7	1109 7.1	Su 1855 0.5	2329 6.9
13	0645 1.1	1134 6.6	Su 1906 1.0	2347 6.4	28	0713 0.7	1150 7.1	M 1935 0.5	
14	0713 1.1	1201 6.6	M 1935 1.0		29	0010 6.8	0749 0.7	Tu 1229 7.0	2015 0.6
15	0014 6.4	0742 1.1	Tu 1228 6.6	2005 1.1	30	0049 6.7	0826 0.9	W 1310 6.8	2051 0.9

OCTOBER

Day	Time m	Time m	Time m	Time m	Day	Time m	Time m	Time m	Time m
1	0131 6.4	0903 1.2	Th 1352 6.4	2128 1.3	16	0050 6.4	0827 1.3	F 1304 6.4	2046 1.4
2	0216 6.1	0942 1.5	F 1440 6.0	2207 1.7	17	0130 6.3	0905 1.5	Sa 1347 6.2	2125 1.6
3	0307 5.8	1024 1.9	Sa 1538 5.5	)) 2254 2.1	18	0218 6.0	0950 1.7	Su 1442 5.9	2214 1.9
4	0409 5.4	1119 2.2	Su 1657 5.1	2358 2.5	19	0324 5.7	1048 1.9	M 1559 5.5	((2323 2.1
5	0534 5.1	1239 2.4	M 1839 5.1		20	0449 5.5	1205 2.0	Tu 1739 5.4	
6	0127 2.5	0707 5.2	Tu 1415 2.2	1954 5.3	21	0053 2.0	0627 5.6	W 1335 1.8	1910 5.7
7	0249 2.2	0811 5.6	W 1522 1.8	2046 5.6	22	0218 1.8	0741 5.9	Th 1451 1.4	2012 6.0
8	0345 1.9	0856 5.9	Th 1612 1.5	2124 5.9	23	0324 1.4	0834 6.3	F 1552 1.1	2100 6.3
9	0430 1.6	0932 6.1	F 1652 1.3	2153 6.1	24	0420 1.2	0921 6.6	Sa 1647 0.9	2143 6.5
10	0508 1.4	1003 6.3	Sa 1730 1.2	2219 6.2	25	0512 1.0	1003 6.8	Su 1737 0.8	● 2226 6.7
11	0543 1.3	1031 6.5	Su 1805 1.1	○ 2247 6.4	26	0558 0.9	1045 7.0	M 1824 0.7	2308 6.8
12	0615 1.1	1101 6.6	M 1838 1.0	2315 6.5	27	0641 0.8	1127 7.0	Tu 1906 0.7	2349 6.7
13	0648 1.1	1129 6.7	Tu 1910 1.0	2344 6.5	28	0721 0.9	1208 6.9	W 1947 0.9	
14	0720 1.1	1158 6.6	W 1941 1.1		29	0029 6.6	0801 1.0	Th 1249 6.6	2025 1.1
15	0017 6.5	0754 1.2	Th 1229 6.6	2012 1.2	30	0112 6.4	0840 1.2	F 1331 6.3	2101 1.4
					31	0154 6.2	0918 1.5	Sa 1416 6.0	2138 1.8

NOVEMBER

Day	Time m	Time m	Time m	Time m	Day	Time m	Time m	Time m	Time m
1	0240 5.9	0957 1.8	Su 1508 5.6	2219 2.1	16	0223 6.2	0945 1.4	M 1446 5.9	2207 1.7
2	0334 5.6	1045 2.1	M 1614 5.2	)) 2309 2.4	17	0324 6.0	1040 1.6	Tu 1557 5.7	((2311 1.9
3	0441 5.3	1146 2.3	Tu 1742 5.1		18	0434 5.8	1150 1.7	W 1718 5.6	
4	0018 2.5	0604 5.2	W 1304 2.3	1900 5.2	19	0031 1.9	0551 5.8	Th 1310 1.6	1836 5.7
5	0138 2.4	0716 5.4	Th 1422 2.1	1957 5.4	20	0148 1.8	0703 5.9	F 1422 1.4	1941 5.9
6	0246 2.1	0808 5.7	F 1519 1.8	2037 5.7	21	0254 1.6	0804 6.2	Sa 1524 1.2	2034 6.1
7	0332 1.8	0847 5.9	Sa 1607 1.5	2111 5.9	22	0352 1.4	0854 6.4	Su 1620 1.1	2122 6.3
8	0424 1.6	0922 6.2	Su 1651 1.3	2142 6.1	23	0445 1.2	0942 6.5	M 1712 1.0	2209 6.4
9	0508 1.4	1028 6.5	M 1732 1.2	2214 6.3	24	0533 1.1	1028 6.7	Tu 1758 1.0	● 2254 6.6
10	0528 1.2	1028 6.5	Tu 1811 1.1	2248 6.5	25	0618 1.0	1113 6.7	W 1842 1.0	2336 6.6
11	0627 1.1	1102 6.6	W 1848 1.1	2323 6.6	26	0700 1.0	1156 6.6	Th 1923 1.0	
12	0703 1.1	1137 6.6	Th 1921 1.1		27	0017 6.6	0741 1.1	F 1236 6.4	2001 1.2
13	0001 6.6	0738 1.1	F 1215 6.6	1957 1.2	28	0056 6.4	0819 1.2	Sa 1316 6.2	2037 1.4
14	0042 6.5	0816 1.2	Sa 1257 6.4	2034 1.3	29	0135 6.3	0856 1.4	Su 1357 6.0	2111 1.6
15	0128 6.4	0858 1.3	Su 1347 6.2	2117 1.4	30	0216 6.1	0932 1.6	M 1440 5.7	2145 1.9

DECEMBER

Day	Time m	Time m	Time m	Time m	Day	Time m	Time m	Time m	Time m
1	0300 5.9	1012 1.8	Tu 1528 5.5	2226 2.1	16	0312 6.3	1030 1.3	W 1541 6.0	2254 1.6
2	0349 5.6	1057 2.0	W 1627 5.2	)) 2315 2.3	17	0409 6.1	1130 1.4	Th 1644 5.8	2358 1.7
3	0449 5.4	1154 2.2	Th 1736 5.1		18	0512 6.0	1239 1.5	F 1753 5.7	
4	0018 2.4	0557 5.4	F 1302 2.2	1842 5.2	19	0112 1.8	0622 5.9	Sa 1349 1.5	1904 5.7
5	0128 2.3	0700 5.5	Sa 1411 2.0	1937 5.4	20	0220 1.8	0730 5.9	Su 1457 1.5	2011 5.8
6	0237 2.1	0754 5.6	Su 1515 1.8	2023 5.6	21	0327 1.6	0833 6.0	M 1559 1.4	2108 5.9
7	0339 1.8	0839 5.9	M 1612 1.5	2105 5.9	22	0426 1.5	0928 6.2	Tu 1655 1.3	2200 6.2
8	0434 1.5	0921 6.1	Tu 1702 1.3	2146 6.2	23	0518 1.3	1019 6.3	W 1743 1.2	2245 6.3
9	0523 1.3	1017 6.2	W 1749 1.2	○ 2227 6.4	24	0604 1.1	1105 6.4	Th 1827 1.1	● 2326 6.5
10	0608 1.0	1042 6.5	Th 1831 1.1	2309 6.5	25	0646 1.0	1147 6.4	F 1906 1.1	
11	0650 1.0	1125 6.6	F 1910 1.0	2354 6.6	26	0005 6.5	0724 1.0	Sa 1225 6.3	1941 1.2
12	0730 1.0	1210 6.6	Sa 1947 1.0		27	0041 6.5	0801 1.1	Su 1300 6.2	2013 1.3
13	0041 6.6	0809 0.9	Su 1257 6.5	2027 1.1	28	0116 6.4	0834 1.2	M 1333 6.1	2044 1.4
14	0130 6.6	0851 1.0	M 1348 6.4	2111 1.2	29	0149 6.3	0907 1.3	Tu 1408 5.9	2115 1.6
15	0220 6.5	0938 1.1	Tu 1443 6.2	2159 1.3	30	0226 6.2	0941 1.5	W 1444 5.7	2148 1.7
					31	0304 6.0	1016 1.7	Th 1527 5.5	2227 2.0

RATE AND SET — The streams in the entrance and harbour vary considerably. E. going stream begins −0210 (Dover). Sets 068°, 4 knots (Springs), 2½ knots (Neaps). W. going stream begins +0430 (Dover). Sets 224°. 2½ knots (Springs), 1½ knots (Neaps).

TIDAL DIFFERENCES ON DOVER

PLACE	TIME DIFFERENCES				HEIGHT DIFFERENCES (Metres)			
	High Water		Low Water		MHWS	MHWN	MLWN	MLWS
DOVER	0000 and 1200	0600 and 1800	0100 and 1300	0700 and 1900	6.7	5.3	2.0	0.8
Hastings	0000	−0010	−0030	−0030	+0.8	+0.5	+0.1	−0.1
Rye (Approaches)	+0005	−0010	−	−	+1.0	+0.7	−	−
Rye (Harbour)	+0005	−0010	−	−	−1.4	−1.7	Dries	Dries
Dungeness	−0010	−0015	−0020	−0010	+1.0	+0.6	+0.4	+0.1
Folkestone	−0020	−0005	−0010	−0010	+0.4	+0.4	0.0	−0.1
Deal	+0010	+0020	+0010	+0005	−0.6	−0.3	0.0	0.0
Richborough	+0015	+0015	+0030	+0030	−3.4	−2.6	−1.7	−0.7
Ramsgate	+0020	+0020	−0007	−0007	−1.8	−1.5	−0.8	−0.4

NOTE: Rye should be carefully considered. It dries out, tidal streams are strong and rough weather can make Rye Bay very dangerous for small vessels.
Folkestone is unsuitable except in emergency.
Ramsgate is an excellent harbour for all small yachts.
Refer to predictions on pages 21:41-21:43

TIDAL DIFFERENCES ON SHEERNESS

PLACE	TIME DIFFERENCES				HEIGHT DIFFERENCES (Metres)			
	High Water		Low Water		MHWS	MHWN	MLWN	MLWS
SHEERNESS	0200 and 1400	0800 and 2000	0200 and 1400	0700 and 1900	5.7	4.8	1.5	0.6
Broadstairs	−0052	−0035	−0006	−0024	−1.1	−1.1	−0.2	−0.2
Margate	−0034	−0027	−0013	−0034	−0.9	−0.9	−0.1	−0.1
Herne Bay	0000	−0005	+0002	+0002	−0.5	−0.5	−0.1	−0.1
Whitstable Approaches	+0008	+0002	−0013	+0016	−0.3	−0.3	0.0	−0.1
Hartyferry	−0010	−0005	0000	0000	−0.1	−0.1	0.0	0.0
River Swale								
Grovehurst Jetty	−0007	0000	0000	+0016	0.0	0.0	0.0	−0.1
River Medway								
Bee Ness	+0002	+0002	0000	+0005	+0.2	+0.1	0.0	0.0
Bartlett Creek	+0016	+0008	−	−	+0.1	0.0	−	−
Darnett Ness	+0004	+0004	0000	+0010	+0.2	+0.1	0.0	−0.1
Chatham (Lock Approaches)	+0010	+0012	+0012	+0018	+0.3	+0.1	−0.1	−0.2
Upnor	+0015	+0015	+0015	+0025	+0.2	+0.2	−0.1	−0.1
Rochester (Strood Pier).....	+0018	+0018	+0018	+0028	+0.2	+0.2	−0.2	−0.3
Wouldham	+0030	+0025	+0035	+0120	−0.2	−0.3	−1.0	−0.3
New Hythe	+0035	+0035	+0220	+0240	−1.6	−1.7	−1.2	−0.3
Allington Lock	+0050	+0035	−	−	−2.1	−2.2	−1.3	−0.4
River Thames								
Southend	−0005	−0005	−0005	−0005	0.0	0.0	−0.1	−0.1
Nore Sand	0000	0000	0000	0000	0.0	0.0	−0.2	−0.1
Yantlet Creek	0000	0000	0000	0000	0.0	0.0	−0.2	−0.2
Benfleet Creek	+0010	+0010	0000	+0010	+0.3	+0.3	0.1	−0.1
Thames Haven	+0010	+0010	0000	+0010	+0.5	+0.4	−0.1	−0.1
Cliffe Creek	+0015	+0015	+0010	+0010	+0.6	+0.5	−0.1	−0.1
SHEERNESS	0200 and 1400	0700 and 1900	0100 and 1300	0700 and 1900	5.7	4.8	1.5	0.6
Thames Estuary								
Shivering Sand Tower	−0025	−0019	−0008	−0026	−0.6	−0.6	−0.1	−0.1
Pan Sand Hole	−0035	−0035	−0035	−0035	−0.7	−0.7	−0.7	−0.7
S Shingles	−0040	−0040	−0040	−0040	−0.8	−0.8	−0.7	−0.7
SE Longsand Bn.	−0045	−0045	−0025	−0025	−0.9	−0.8	−0.1	−0.1
Havengore Creek	−0020	−0020	−0025	−0025	−0.3	−0.2	0.0	0.0

Refer to predictions on pages 21:46-21:48

DOVER
MEAN SPRING AND NEAP CURVES
Springs occur 2 days after New and Full Moon.

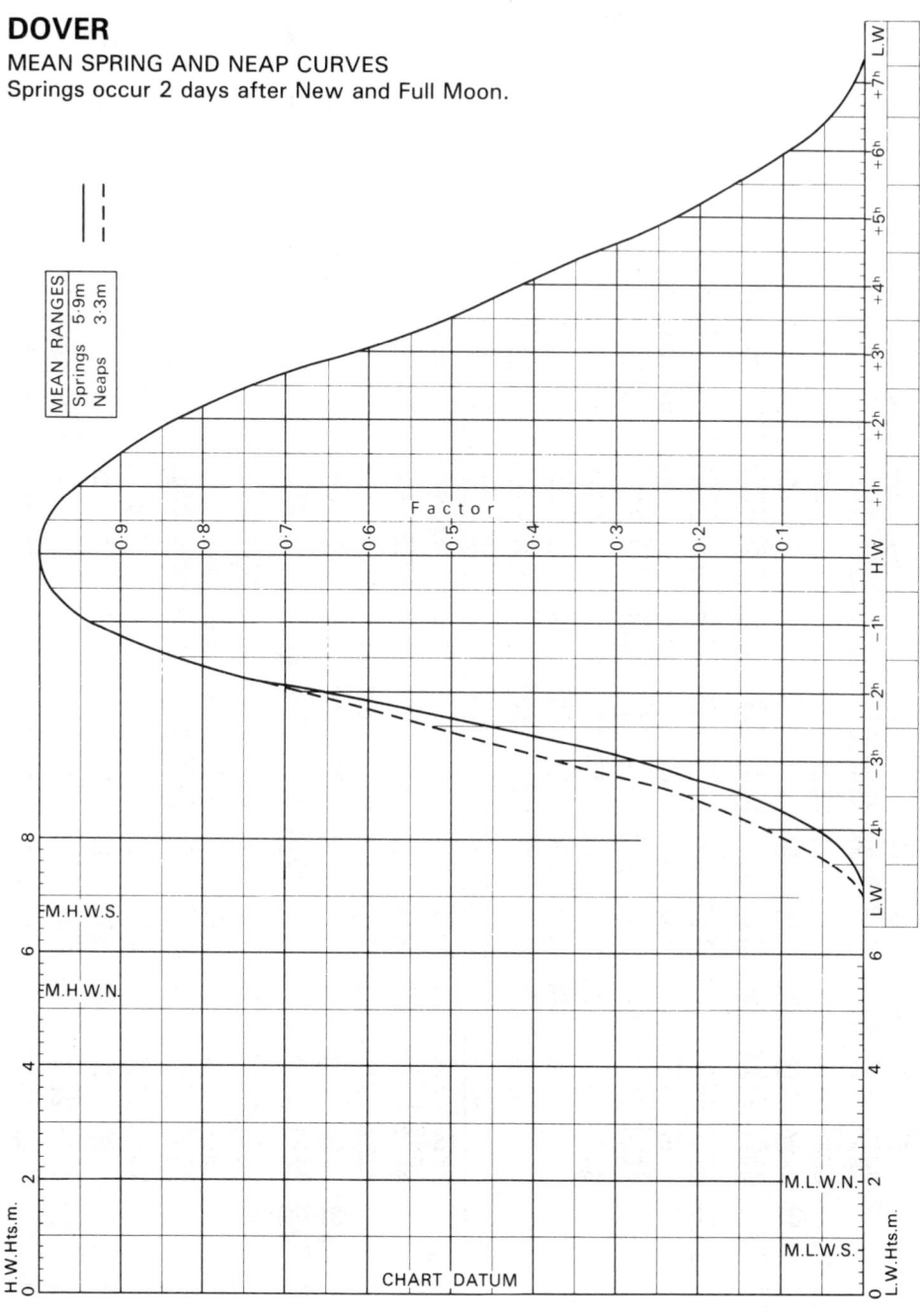

RIVER THAMES SHEERNESS

HIGH & LOW WATER 1992 Lat. 51°27′N. Long. 0°45′E.

ADD 1 HOUR MARCH 29 — OCTOBER 25 FOR B.S.T. GMT

JANUARY

Day	Time	m	Day	Time	m
1 W	0315 / 0943 / 1559 / 2219	1.5 / 5.0 / 1.2 / 5.1	16 Th	0206 / 0832 / 1456 / 2119	1.5 / 5.0 / 1.3 / 5.0
2 Th	0427 / 1045 / 1655 / 2312	1.3 / 5.1 / 1.2 / 5.2	17 F	0328 / 0946 / 1609 / 2226	1.3 / 5.2 / 1.1 / 5.2
3 F	0526 / 1137 / 1740 / 2358	1.1 / 5.2 / 1.2 / 5.3	18 Sa	0438 / 1054 / 1712 / 2326	1.1 / 5.4 / 1.0 / 5.5
4 Sa ●	0614 / 1222 / 1819	1.0 / 5.3 / 1.1	19 Su ○	0544 / 1153 / 1810	0.8 / 5.7 / 0.8
5 Su	0038 / 0655 / 1300 / 1853	5.4 / 0.9 / 5.4 / 1.1	20 M	0019 / 0646 / 1245 / 1900	5.6 / 0.5 / 5.9 / 0.7
6 M	0113 / 0730 / 1335 / 1926	5.4 / 0.9 / 5.4 / 1.0	21 Tu	0107 / 0740 / 1334 / 1947	5.8 / 0.3 / 6.0 / 0.7
7 Tu	0144 / 0802 / 1408 / 1957	5.5 / 0.8 / 5.5 / 1.0	22 W	0152 / 0827 / 1419 / 2030	5.9 / 0.2 / 6.1 / 0.6
8 W	0215 / 0833 / 1440 / 2029	5.5 / 0.8 / 5.5 / 0.9	23 Th	0236 / 0911 / 1504 / 2110	6.0 / 0.1 / 6.0 / 0.7
9 Th	0246 / 0904 / 1512 / 2103	5.5 / 0.8 / 5.5 / 1.0	24 F	0318 / 0952 / 1549 / 2148	6.0 / 0.2 / 5.9 / 0.8
10 F	0318 / 0936 / 1546 / 2136	5.5 / 0.8 / 5.4 / 1.1	25 Sa	0402 / 1030 / 1634 / 2226	5.9 / 0.4 / 5.6 / 0.9
11 Sa	0350 / 1009 / 1623 / 2209	5.4 / 0.9 / 5.3 / 1.2	26 Su	0447 / 1108 / 1722 / 2306	5.6 / 0.7 / 5.3 / 1.1
12 Su	0427 / 1041 / 1704 / 2247	5.3 / 1.0 / 5.1 / 1.3	27 M	0536 / 1149 / 1814 / 2357	5.3 / 1.0 / 5.0 / 1.4
13 M ☽	0509 / 1120 / 1751 / 2334	5.2 / 1.1 / 5.0 / 1.4	28 Tu	0636 / 1245 / 1919	5.0 / 1.3 / 4.7
14 Tu	0603 / 1214 / 1855	5.0 / 1.2 / 4.9	29 W	0107 / 0752 / 1405 / 2036	1.6 / 4.7 / 1.5 / 4.6
15 W	0042 / 0713 / 1330 / 2008	1.5 / 4.9 / 1.3 / 4.9	30 Th	0244 / 0919 / 1527 / 2153	1.6 / 4.7 / 1.5 / 4.8
			31 F	0412 / 1031 / 1633 / 2254	1.4 / 4.9 / 1.4 / 5.0

FEBRUARY

Day	Time	m	Day	Time	m
1 Sa	0515 / 1125 / 1723 / 2342	1.2 / 5.1 / 1.3 / 5.2	16 Su	0423 / 1041 / 1655 / 2311	1.0 / 5.3 / 1.1 / 5.3
2 Su	0603 / 1207 / 1803	1.0 / 5.3 / 1.1	17 M	0537 / 1142 / 1756	0.7 / 5.7 / 0.9
3 M ●	0021 / 0641 / 1243 / 1838	5.3 / 0.9 / 5.4 / 1.0	18 Tu ○	0004 / 0636 / 1232 / 1848	5.6 / 0.4 / 5.9 / 0.7
4 Tu	0055 / 0713 / 1316 / 1909	5.5 / 0.8 / 5.5 / 0.9	19 W	0050 / 0727 / 1319 / 1933	5.9 / 0.2 / 6.0 / 0.6
5 W	0126 / 0744 / 1347 / 1941	5.6 / 0.7 / 5.6 / 0.8	20 Th	0134 / 0811 / 1401 / 2013	6.0 / 0.1 / 6.1 / 0.5
6 Th	0155 / 0815 / 1416 / 2013	5.6 / 0.6 / 5.6 / 0.7	21 F	0215 / 0851 / 1443 / 2051	6.1 / 0.1 / 6.0 / 0.5
7 F	0225 / 0847 / 1447 / 2046	5.7 / 0.6 / 5.6 / 0.8	22 Sa	0256 / 0928 / 1524 / 2127	6.1 / 0.2 / 5.8 / 0.7
8 Sa	0256 / 0918 / 1519 / 2115	5.7 / 0.6 / 5.6 / 0.9	23 Su	0336 / 1000 / 1604 / 2200	5.9 / 0.5 / 5.6 / 0.8
9 Su	0327 / 0945 / 1553 / 2143	5.6 / 0.8 / 5.5 / 1.0	24 M	0419 / 1033 / 1645 / 2235	5.7 / 0.8 / 5.3 / 1.1
10 M	0359 / 1009 / 1630 / 2212	5.5 / 0.9 / 5.3 / 1.1	25 Tu	0504 / 1106 / 1730 / 2318	5.3 / 1.1 / 4.9 / 1.4
11 Tu ☽	0438 / 1037 / 1713 / 2252	5.4 / 1.0 / 5.1 / 1.2	26 W	0558 / 1154 / 1828	4.9 / 1.5 / 4.6
12 W	0526 / 1123 / 1810 / 2354	5.1 / 1.2 / 4.9 / 1.4	27 Th	0019 / 0713 / 1312 / 1947	1.6 / 4.5 / 1.8 / 4.4
13 Th	0634 / 1238 / 1926	4.9 / 1.4 / 4.7	28 F	0209 / 0850 / 1453 / 2121	1.7 / 4.5 / 1.8 / 4.5
14 F	0126 / 0801 / 1423 / 2049	1.5 / 4.8 / 1.5 / 4.8	29 Sa	0346 / 1007 / 1604 / 2227	1.5 / 4.8 / 1.5 / 4.8
15 Sa	0303 / 0927 / 1546 / 2206	1.3 / 5.0 / 1.3 / 5.0			

MARCH

Day	Time	m	Day	Time	m
1 Su	0449 / 1101 / 1657 / 2316	1.2 / 5.1 / 1.3 / 5.1	16 M	0412 / 1028 / 1638 / 2252	0.9 / 5.4 / 1.1 / 5.3
2 M	0536 / 1143 / 1739 / 2354	1.0 / 5.3 / 1.1 / 5.3	17 Tu	0523 / 1126 / 1737 / 2344	0.6 / 5.7 / 0.9 / 5.6
3 Tu ●	0614 / 1218 / 1814	0.8 / 5.5 / 0.9	18 W ○	0619 / 1214 / 1828	0.3 / 5.9 / 0.7
4 W	0028 / 0646 / 1249 / 1846	5.5 / 0.7 / 5.6 / 0.8	19 Th	0029 / 0706 / 1257 / 1912	5.9 / 0.2 / 6.0 / 0.5
5 Th	0059 / 0719 / 1320 / 1919	5.6 / 0.6 / 5.7 / 0.7	20 F	0112 / 0747 / 1338 / 1951	6.0 / 0.1 / 6.0 / 0.4
6 F	0128 / 0749 / 1349 / 1952	5.7 / 0.5 / 5.8 / 0.6	21 Sa	0151 / 0825 / 1418 / 2029	6.1 / 0.2 / 5.9 / 0.5
7 Sa	0159 / 0822 / 1420 / 2025	5.8 / 0.5 / 5.8 / 0.6	22 Su	0232 / 0858 / 1456 / 2105	6.1 / 0.4 / 5.8 / 0.6
8 Su	0229 / 0854 / 1453 / 2056	5.8 / 0.6 / 5.7 / 0.8	23 M	0311 / 0929 / 1534 / 2138	5.9 / 0.7 / 5.5 / 0.8
9 M	0301 / 0919 / 1527 / 2122	5.7 / 0.7 / 5.6 / 0.9	24 Tu	0352 / 0959 / 1612 / 2209	5.6 / 1.0 / 5.2 / 1.1
10 Tu	0336 / 0942 / 1602 / 2150	5.6 / 0.9 / 5.4 / 1.0	25 W	0435 / 1031 / 1652 / 2245	5.2 / 1.3 / 4.9 / 1.3
11 W ☽	0416 / 1010 / 1645 / 2231	5.4 / 1.0 / 5.1 / 1.1	26 Th	0526 / 1113 / 1742 / 2340	4.8 / 1.6 / 4.6 / 1.6
12 Th	0506 / 1058 / 1740 / 2333	5.2 / 1.3 / 4.9 / 1.3	27 F	0634 / 1219 / 1852	4.5 / 1.9 / 4.3
13 F	0615 / 1214 / 1856	4.9 / 1.5 / 4.7	28 Sa	0116 / 0802 / 1404 / 2025	1.7 / 4.4 / 1.9 / 4.2
14 Sa	0106 / 0744 / 1359 / 2025	1.4 / 4.8 / 1.6 / 4.7	29 Su	0301 / 0927 / 1522 / 2145	1.5 / 4.6 / 1.6 / 4.6
15 Su	0249 / 0914 / 1527 / 2148	1.3 / 5.0 / 1.4 / 5.0	30 M	0404 / 1024 / 1617 / 2237	1.2 / 5.0 / 1.3 / 5.0
			31 Tu	0454 / 1106 / 1702 / 2318	1.0 / 5.3 / 1.1 / 5.2

APRIL

Day	Time	m	Day	Time	m
1 W	0534 / 1143 / 1740 / 2354	0.8 / 5.5 / 0.9 / 5.5	16 Th	0556 / 1151 / 1804	0.4 / 5.8 / 0.7
2 Th	0611 / 1217 / 1817	0.6 / 5.6 / 0.8	17 F	0005 / 0639 / 1235 / 1848	5.8 / 0.3 / 5.8 / 0.6
3 F	0027 / 0645 / 1249 / 1852	5.6 / 0.6 / 5.7 / 0.7	18 Sa	0049 / 0719 / 1314 / 1930	5.9 / 0.3 / 5.9 / 0.5
4 Sa ●	0059 / 0720 / 1321 / 1928	5.7 / 0.5 / 5.8 / 0.6	19 Su	0130 / 0755 / 1354 / 2009	6.0 / 0.4 / 5.8 / 0.5
5 Su	0131 / 0755 / 1354 / 2005	5.8 / 0.5 / 5.8 / 0.6	20 M	0211 / 0829 / 1430 / 2046	5.9 / 0.6 / 5.7 / 0.7
6 M	0205 / 0827 / 1427 / 2039	5.8 / 0.6 / 5.7 / 0.7	21 Tu	0250 / 0901 / 1507 / 2118	5.7 / 0.8 / 5.4 / 0.9
7 Tu	0242 / 0857 / 1503 / 2110	5.8 / 0.6 / 5.6 / 0.8	22 W	0331 / 0931 / 1542 / 2149	5.4 / 1.1 / 5.2 / 1.1
8 W	0321 / 0925 / 1542 / 2143	5.6 / 0.9 / 5.4 / 0.9	23 Th	0412 / 1002 / 1620 / 2221	5.1 / 1.3 / 5.0 / 1.3
9 Th	0404 / 1002 / 1627 / 2230	5.5 / 1.1 / 5.2 / 1.0	24 F	0458 / 1041 / 1705 / 2309	4.9 / 1.6 / 4.7 / 1.4
10 F ☽	0459 / 1054 / 1725 / 2334	5.2 / 1.3 / 4.9 / 1.2	25 Sa	0546 / 1137 / 1804	4.6 / 1.8 / 4.5
11 Sa	0610 / 1208 / 1839	5.0 / 1.5 / 4.7	26 Su	0019 / 0703 / 1255 / 1919	1.5 / 4.5 / 1.8 / 4.4
12 Su	0103 / 0733 / 1341 / 2004	1.2 / 4.9 / 1.6 / 4.8	27 M	0155 / 0822 / 1423 / 2037	1.5 / 4.6 / 1.7 / 4.6
13 M	0234 / 0858 / 1503 / 2124	1.1 / 5.1 / 1.4 / 5.0	28 Tu	0305 / 0927 / 1525 / 2141	1.2 / 4.9 / 1.4 / 4.9
14 Tu	0353 / 1007 / 1613 / 2227	0.8 / 5.4 / 1.1 / 5.3	29 W	0400 / 1017 / 1616 / 2230	1.0 / 5.2 / 1.2 / 5.1
15 W	0501 / 1104 / 1713 / 2320	0.6 / 5.6 / 0.9 / 5.6	30 Th	0447 / 1101 / 1659 / 2312	0.8 / 5.4 / 1.0 / 5.4

To find H.W. Dover subtract 1h. 25min.

TIDAL DIFFERENCES PAGE 21:44. TIDAL CURVE PAGE 21:49.
TIDAL STREAMS PAGES 21:50-21:56.

Datum of predictions: 2.90 m. below Ordnance Datum (Newlyn) or approx. L.A.T.

SHEERNESS RIVER THAMES 21:47

Lat. 51°27′N. Long. 0°45′E.

GMT

HIGH & LOW WATER 1992

ADD 1 HOUR MARCH 29 — OCTOBER 25 FOR B.S.T.

MAY

Day	Time	m	Day	Time	m
1 F	0529 / 1139 / 1743 / 2351	0·7 / 5·6 / 0·8 / 5·6	16 Sa ○	0611 / 1214 / 1828	0·6 / 5·7 / 0·7
2 Sa ●	0610 / 1217 / 1824	0·6 / 5·7 / 0·7	17 Su	0029 / 0652 / 1255 / 1910	5·7 / 0·6 / 5·7 / 0·6
3 Su	0029 / 0650 / 1253 / 1906	5·7 / 0·6 / 5·8 / 0·6	18 M	0113 / 0728 / 1333 / 1951	5·7 / 0·7 / 5·7 / 0·6
4 M	0107 / 0728 / 1331 / 1947	5·8 / 0·6 / 5·8 / 0·6	19 Tu	0154 / 0804 / 1409 / 2029	5·7 / 0·8 / 5·6 / 0·7
5 Tu	0147 / 0806 / 1408 / 2027	5·8 / 0·7 / 5·7 / 0·6	20 W	0233 / 0836 / 1446 / 2103	5·6 / 1·0 / 5·4 / 0·9
6 W	0227 / 0842 / 1449 / 2107	5·8 / 0·8 / 5·6 / 0·7	21 Th	0312 / 0907 / 1519 / 2134	5·4 / 1·1 / 5·1 / 1·0
7 Th	0312 / 0919 / 1531 / 2150	5·7 / 1·0 / 5·4 / 0·8	22 F	0352 / 0938 / 1556 / 2206	5·2 / 1·3 / 5·1 / 1·1
8 F	0402 / 1002 / 1621 / 2241	5·5 / 1·1 / 5·3 / 0·9	23 Sa	0433 / 1016 / 1637 / 2247	5·0 / 1·4 / 5·0 / 1·2
9 Sa ☽	0459 / 1055 / 1718 / 2343	5·3 / 1·3 / 5·1 / 0·9	24 Su	0518 / 1102 / 1725 / 2339	4·9 / 1·5 / 4·8 / 1·2
10 Su	0604 / 1201 / 1825	5·2 / 5·0 / 5·0	25 M	0611 / 1200 / 1821	4·8 / 1·6 / 4·7
11 M	0056 / 0719 / 1317 / 1941	1·0 / 5·1 / 1·5 / 5·0	26 Tu	0043 / 0714 / 1309 / 1928	1·3 / 4·7 / 1·6 / 4·7
12 Tu	0213 / 0834 / 1433 / 2056	0·9 / 5·2 / 1·3 / 5·1	27 W	0155 / 0820 / 1420 / 2036	1·2 / 4·8 / 1·5 / 4·8
13 W	0327 / 0942 / 1542 / 2200	0·8 / 5·4 / 1·2 / 5·3	28 Th	0301 / 0921 / 1522 / 2136	1·1 / 5·1 / 1·3 / 5·1
14 Th	0433 / 1040 / 1645 / 2255	0·7 / 5·5 / 1·0 / 5·5	29 F	0357 / 1014 / 1617 / 2230	0·9 / 5·3 / 1·1 / 5·3
15 F	0526 / 1129 / 1740 / 2344	0·6 / 5·6 / 0·8 / 5·6	30 Sa	0448 / 1102 / 1708 / 2319	0·8 / 5·5 / 0·9 / 5·5
			31 Su	0537 / 1147 / 1758	0·8 / 5·6 / 0·8

JUNE

Day	Time	m	Day	Time	m
1 M ●	0005 / 0624 / 1231 / 1846	5·6 / 0·8 / 5·7 / 0·7	16 Tu	0102 / 0706 / 1319 / 1938	5·5 / 0·9 / 5·5 / 0·7
2 Tu	0049 / 0707 / 1313 / 1934	5·7 / 0·7 / 5·7 / 0·6	17 W	0141 / 0741 / 1354 / 2016	5·5 / 0·9 / 5·5 / 0·7
3 W	0134 / 0751 / 1357 / 2022	5·8 / 0·8 / 5·7 / 0·5	18 Th	0219 / 0815 / 1429 / 2050	5·5 / 1·0 / 5·5 / 0·8
4 Th	0220 / 0833 / 1440 / 2110	5·9 / 0·8 / 5·7 / 0·5	19 F	0254 / 0846 / 1501 / 2121	5·5 / 1·0 / 5·4 / 0·9
5 F	0308 / 0917 / 1527 / 2157	5·8 / 0·9 / 5·6 / 0·5	20 Sa	0329 / 0918 / 1535 / 2152	5·4 / 1·1 / 5·3 / 0·9
6 Sa	0359 / 1002 / 1616 / 2245	5·7 / 1·0 / 5·5 / 0·6	21 Su	0406 / 0953 / 1610 / 2226	5·3 / 1·2 / 5·2 / 0·9
7 Su	0452 / 1049 / 1708 / 2339	5·6 / 1·1 / 5·4 / 0·6	22 M	0444 / 1033 / 1649 / 2305	5·2 / 1·2 / 5·1 / 1·0
8 M	0551 / 1144 / 1807	5·4 / 1·2 / 5·3	23 Tu	0527 / 1116 / 1734 / 2353	5·1 / 1·4 / 5·0 / 1·1
9 Tu	0038 / 0656 / 1248 / 1914	0·7 / 5·3 / 1·3 / 5·2	24 W	0618 / 1210 / 1829	4·9 / 1·5 / 4·9
10 W	0144 / 0805 / 1359 / 2025	0·8 / 5·2 / 1·3 / 5·1	25 Th	0050 / 0720 / 1316 / 1937	1·2 / 4·9 / 1·5 / 4·9
11 Th	0254 / 0912 / 1511 / 2134	0·9 / 5·2 / 1·3 / 5·2	26 F	0201 / 0826 / 1429 / 2047	1·2 / 5·0 / 1·4 / 5·0
12 F	0400 / 1014 / 1621 / 2235	0·9 / 5·3 / 1·1 / 5·3	27 Sa	0310 / 0929 / 1536 / 2152	1·1 / 5·1 / 1·3 / 5·1
13 Sa	0459 / 1109 / 1722 / 2330	0·9 / 5·4 / 1·0 / 5·4	28 Su	0413 / 1028 / 1637 / 2251	1·0 / 5·3 / 1·1 / 5·4
14 Su	0547 / 1156 / 1812	0·9 / 5·5 / 0·8	29 M	0509 / 1123 / 1736 / 2346	0·9 / 5·5 / 0·9 / 5·6
15 M ○	0018 / 0628 / 1239 / 1857	5·5 / 0·9 / 5·5 / 0·7	30 Tu	0603 / 1214 / 1834	0·9 / 5·6 / 0·7

JULY

Day	Time	m	Day	Time	m
1 W	0036 / 0653 / 1300 / 1927	5·7 / 0·8 / 5·7 / 0·5	16 Th	0127 / 0721 / 1337 / 1959	5·5 / 1·0 / 5·5 / 0·7
2 Th	0126 / 0741 / 1347 / 2018	5·9 / 0·8 / 5·8 / 0·4	17 F	0201 / 0754 / 1409 / 2030	5·6 / 0·9 / 5·6 / 0·7
3 F	0212 / 0826 / 1432 / 2105	6·0 / 0·7 / 5·8 / 0·3	18 Sa	0233 / 0826 / 1440 / 2101	5·6 / 0·9 / 5·6 / 0·7
4 Sa	0300 / 0910 / 1517 / 2152	6·0 / 0·8 / 5·8 / 0·3	19 Su	0304 / 0858 / 1511 / 2132	5·6 / 0·9 / 5·6 / 0·7
5 Su	0348 / 0953 / 1602 / 2235	5·9 / 0·8 / 5·8 / 0·3	20 M	0338 / 0931 / 1543 / 2202	5·5 / 1·0 / 5·5 / 0·8
6 M	0437 / 1035 / 1651 / 2320	5·8 / 0·9 / 5·7 / 0·5	21 Tu	0412 / 1003 / 1617 / 2234	5·4 / 1·1 / 5·4 / 0·9
7 Tu	0529 / 1122 / 1743	5·5 / 1·1 / 5·5	22 W	0448 / 1038 / 1655 / 2308	5·3 / 1·2 / 5·2 / 1·1
8 W	0008 / 0627 / 1215 / 1843	0·7 / 5·3 / 1·3 / 5·3	23 Th	0532 / 1116 / 1742 / 2354	5·1 / 1·4 / 5·1 / 1·2
9 Th	0100 / 0730 / 1323 / 1955	1·0 / 5·1 / 1·4 / 5·1	24 F	0627 / 1217 / 1845	4·9 / 1·5 / 4·9
10 F	0218 / 0840 / 1443 / 2111	1·1 / 5·0 / 1·4 / 5·0	25 Sa	0100 / 0735 / 1335 / 2002	1·4 / 4·8 / 1·6 / 4·9
11 Sa	0331 / 0950 / 1603 / 2221	1·2 / 5·1 / 1·3 / 5·1	26 Su	0226 / 0850 / 1501 / 2119	1·4 / 4·9 / 1·4 / 5·0
12 Su	0435 / 1051 / 1711 / 2320	1·2 / 5·2 / 1·1 / 5·3	27 M	0342 / 1000 / 1613 / 2230	1·3 / 5·1 / 1·2 / 5·3
13 M	0527 / 1143 / 1804	1·1 / 5·3 / 0·9	28 Tu	0447 / 1102 / 1719 / 2330	1·1 / 5·4 / 0·9 / 5·6
14 Tu ○	0008 / 0611 / 1225 / 1848	5·4 / 1·1 / 5·4 / 0·8	29 W ●	0546 / 1157 / 1822	0·9 / 5·6 / 0·6
15 W	0050 / 0648 / 1303 / 1926	5·5 / 1·0 / 5·5 / 0·7	30 Th	0024 / 0639 / 1246 / 1919	5·8 / 0·8 / 5·8 / 0·4
			31 F	0113 / 0728 / 1331 / 2008	6·0 / 0·7 / 5·9 / 0·2

AUGUST

Day	Time	m	Day	Time	m
1 Sa	0159 / 0813 / 1415 / 2053	6·1 / 0·6 / 6·0 / 0·1	16 Su	0205 / 0804 / 1413 / 2034	5·7 / 0·8 / 5·7 / 0·6
2 Su	0243 / 0856 / 1458 / 2135	6·1 / 0·6 / 6·1 / 0·1	17 M	0236 / 0836 / 1443 / 2105	5·7 / 0·8 / 5·7 / 0·6
3 M	0328 / 0936 / 1542 / 2214	6·0 / 0·7 / 6·0 / 0·3	18 Tu	0307 / 0907 / 1514 / 2135	5·7 / 0·9 / 5·6 / 0·8
4 Tu	0413 / 1014 / 1627 / 2252	5·8 / 0·9 / 5·8 / 0·6	19 W	0339 / 0935 / 1546 / 2200	5·5 / 1·1 / 5·5 / 1·0
5 W	0459 / 1054 / 1715 / 2333	5·5 / 1·1 / 5·5 / 0·9	20 Th	0413 / 1002 / 1621 / 2226	5·4 / 1·2 / 5·4 / 1·1
6 Th	0551 / 1142 / 1812	5·2 / 1·3 / 5·2	21 F	0452 / 1037 / 1705 / 2304	5·2 / 1·3 / 5·2 / 1·3
7 F	0024 / 0652 / 1245 / 1926	1·2 / 4·9 / 1·5 / 4·9	22 Sa	0543 / 1130 / 1805	4·9 / 1·5 / 4·9
8 Sa	0137 / 0806 / 1418 / 2050	1·5 / 4·8 / 1·6 / 4·8	23 Su	0007 / 0652 / 1252 / 1927	1·5 / 4·8 / 1·6 / 4·8
9 Su ☽	0303 / 0927 / 1550 / 2207	1·6 / 4·8 / 1·4 / 5·0	24 M	0145 / 0813 / 1432 / 2056	1·6 / 4·8 / 1·5 / 4·9
10 M	0414 / 1033 / 1659 / 2306	1·4 / 5·1 / 1·1 / 5·3	25 Tu	0315 / 0934 / 1553 / 2213	1·4 / 5·0 / 1·2 / 5·3
11 Tu	0509 / 1125 / 1749 / 2353	1·3 / 5·3 / 0·9 / 5·4	26 W	0426 / 1042 / 1705 / 2315	1·2 / 5·3 / 0·8 / 5·6
12 W	0551 / 1207 / 1829	1·2 / 5·4 / 0·8	27 Th	0527 / 1139 / 1810	1·0 / 5·6 / 0·5
13 Th	0031 / 0627 / 1255 / 1903	5·5 / 1·0 / 5·5 / 0·7	28 F	0008 / 0622 / 1227 / 1902	5·9 / 0·8 / 5·9 / 0·3
14 F	0104 / 0659 / 1314 / 1934	5·6 / 0·9 / 5·6 / 0·6	29 Sa	0055 / 0710 / 1310 / 1948	6·1 / 0·7 / 6·1 / 0·1
15 Sa	0135 / 0731 / 1344 / 2005	5·7 / 0·8 / 5·7 / 0·6	30 Su	0138 / 0754 / 1352 / 2030	6·2 / 0·6 / 6·2 / 0·1
			31 M	0222 / 0834 / 1434 / 2110	6·1 / 0·6 / 6·2 / 0·2

GENERAL — When flooding — eddies form S. of Garrison Pt. Stream weak off dockyard. When ebbing — strong NE. stream with turbulence, landing difficult. Eddies NE. of Garrison Pt. Duration and rate of ebb increased by falling sea level. Heavy rain increases duration and rate of ebb and decreases flood.

21:48 RIVER THAMES **SHEERNESS**

HIGH & LOW WATER 1992 Lat. 51°27′N. Long. 0°45′E.

GMT ADD 1 HOUR MARCH 29 — OCTOBER 25 FOR B.S.T.

SEPTEMBER

Day	Time	m	Day	Time	m
1 Tu	0304 / 0914 / 1517 / 2146	6·0 / 0·7 / 6·0 / 0·5	16 W	0236 / 0842 / 1446 / 2104	5·8 / 0·9 / 5·7 / 0·9
2 W	0345 / 0950 / 1600 / 2220	5·7 / 0·9 / 5·8 / 0·8	17 Th	0308 / 0908 / 1518 / 2127	5·6 / 1·1 / 5·6 / 1·0
3 Th	0428 / 1027 / 1647 /)) 2255	5·4 / 1·1 / 5·5 / 1·2	18 F	0342 / 0935 / 1556 / 2150	5·4 / 1·2 / 5·4 / 1·2
4 F	0515 / 1109 / 1743 / 2340	5·1 / 1·4 / 5·1 / 1·5	19 Sa	0421 / 1009 / 1642 / ((2231	5·2 / 1·3 / 5·2 / 1·4
5 Sa	0611 / 1208 / 1853	4·8 / 1·6 / 4·7	20 Su	0511 / 1104 / 1743 / 2337	5·0 / 1·5 / 5·0 / 1·6
6 Su	0049 / 0724 / 1349 / 2023	1·8 / 4·6 / 1·7 / 4·7	21 M	0618 / 1228 / 1904	4·8 / 1·6 / 4·8
7 M	0229 / 0854 / 1527 / 2145	1·8 / 4·6 / 1·5 / 4·9	22 Tu	0117 / 0744 / 1412 / 2036	1·7 / 4·7 / 1·4 / 5·0
8 Tu	0345 / 1006 / 1633 / 2242	1·6 / 4·9 / 1·2 / 5·2	23 W	0250 / 0910 / 1535 / 2155	1·5 / 5·0 / 1·1 / 5·3
9 W	0440 / 1058 / 1720 / 2326	1·4 / 5·2 / 0·9 / 5·5	24 Th	0402 / 1019 / 1648 / 2255	1·3 / 5·4 / 0·7 / 5·7
10 Th	0522 / 1139 / 1758	1·2 / 5·4 / 0·8	25 F	0505 / 1115 / 1749 / 2347	1·0 / 5·7 / 0·5 / 5·9
11 F	0004 / 0558 / 1214 / 1831	5·6 / 1·0 / 5·6 / 0·7	26 Sa	0600 / 1203 / 1839 ●	0·8 / 5·9 / 0·3
12 Sa	0036 / 0631 / 1245 / O 1902	5·7 / 0·9 / 5·7 / 0·6	27 Su	0034 / 0648 / 1246 / 1924	6·1 / 0·7 / 6·1 / 0·2
13 Su	0106 / 0703 / 1314 / 1933	5·8 / 0·8 / 5·8 / 0·6	28 M	0116 / 0731 / 1328 / 2004	6·1 / 0·6 / 6·2 / 0·3
14 M	0135 / 0737 / 1344 / 2004	5·8 / 0·7 / 5·6 / 0·6	29 Tu	0157 / 0812 / 1411 / 2042	6·1 / 0·6 / 6·2 / 0·4
15 Tu	0205 / 0809 / 1415 / 2036	5·8 / 0·8 / 5·8 / 0·7	30 W	0237 / 0850 / 1453 / 2115	5·9 / 0·7 / 6·0 / 0·7

OCTOBER

Day	Time	m	Day	Time	m
1 Th	0317 / 0927 / 1536 / 2148	5·7 / 0·9 / 5·7 / 1·0	16 F	0242 / 0849 / 1458 / 2101	5·6 / 1·0 / 5·6 / 1·1
2 F	0357 / 1002 / 1621 / 2220	5·4 / 1·2 / 5·4 / 1·4	17 Sa	0318 / 0919 / 1541 / 2134	5·5 / 1·1 / 5·5 / 1·3
3 Sa	0440 / 1040 / 1713 /)) 2301	5·1 / 1·4 / 5·0 / 1·7	18 Su	0400 / 1000 / 1630 / 2219	5·3 / 1·2 / 5·3 / 1·4
4 Su	0530 / 1132 / 1818	4·8 / 1·6 / 4·7	19 M	0452 / 1058 / 1733 / ((2326	5·0 / 1·3 / 5·0 / 1·6
5 M	0000 / 0636 / 1300 / 1940	1·9 / 4·5 / 1·8 / 4·6	20 Tu	0558 / 1221 / 1850	4·9 / 1·4 / 4·9
6 Tu	0134 / 0801 / 1443 / 2104	2·0 / 4·5 / 1·6 / 4·8	21 W	0055 / 0720 / 1354 / 2016	1·7 / 4·8 / 1·3 / 5·1
7 W	0258 / 0921 / 1546 / 2204	1·8 / 4·8 / 1·3 / 5·1	22 Th	0222 / 0842 / 1514 / 2131	1·6 / 5·0 / 1·0 / 5·4
8 Th	0357 / 1017 / 1635 / 2249	1·5 / 5·1 / 1·0 / 5·4	23 F	0334 / 0952 / 1624 / 2231	1·3 / 5·4 / 0·7 / 5·7
9 F	0442 / 1101 / 1716 / 2327	1·2 / 5·4 / 0·8 / 5·5	24 Sa	0438 / 1048 / 1723 / 2323	1·1 / 5·6 / 0·5 / 5·8
10 Sa	0522 / 1137 / 1753	1·0 / 5·5 / 0·7	25 Su	0534 / 1137 / 1814 ●	0·9 / 5·9 / 0·4
11 Su	0001 / 0558 / 1211 / O 1825	5·7 / 0·9 / 5·7 / 0·7	26 M	0010 / 0624 / 1224 / 1856	5·9 / 0·7 / 6·0 / 0·4
12 M	0032 / 0634 / 1242 / 1859	5·8 / 0·8 / 5·8 / 0·6	27 Tu	0052 / 0709 / 1307 / 1935	6·0 / 0·6 / 6·1 / 0·5
13 Tu	0104 / 0709 / 1314 / 1933	5·8 / 0·8 / 5·8 / 0·7	28 W	0133 / 0751 / 1349 / 2012	5·9 / 0·6 / 6·0 / 0·7
14 W	0135 / 0744 / 1347 / 2005	5·9 / 0·8 / 5·8 / 0·8	29 Th	0212 / 0830 / 1433 / 2046	5·8 / 0·7 / 5·8 / 0·9
15 Th	0208 / 0818 / 1422 / 2034	5·8 / 0·9 / 5·8 / 0·9	30 F	0251 / 0907 / 1515 / 2117	5·6 / 0·9 / 5·6 / 1·2
			31 Sa	0329 / 0941 / 1559 / 2149	5·3 / 1·2 / 5·3 / 1·4

NOVEMBER

Day	Time	m	Day	Time	m
1 Su	0409 / 1014 / 1645 / 2226	5·1 / 1·3 / 5·0 / 1·6	16 M	0350 / 1007 / 1626 / 2217	5·4 / 1·0 / 5·4 / 1·3
2 M	0454 / 1058 / 1739 /)) 2316	4·9 / 1·5 / 4·8 / 1·8	17 Tu	0442 / 1104 / 1726 / ((2318	5·2 / 1·1 / 5·2 / 1·5
3 Tu	0549 / 1201 / 1843	4·7 / 1·6 / 4·6	18 W	0544 / 1212 / 1835	5·1 / 1·1 / 5·1
4 W	0025 / 0656 / 1331 / 1958	1·9 / 4·6 / 1·6 / 4·6	19 Th	0031 / 0656 / 1330 / 1951	1·6 / 5·0 / 1·1 / 5·1
5 Th	0154 / 0812 / 1447 / 2107	1·8 / 4·7 / 1·4 / 4·9	20 F	0149 / 0812 / 1446 / 2103	1·5 / 5·1 / 1·0 / 5·3
6 F	0303 / 0919 / 1542 / 2200	1·6 / 4·9 / 1·1 / 5·1	21 Sa	0303 / 0922 / 1555 / 2206	1·3 / 5·3 / 0·8 / 5·5
7 Sa	0356 / 1012 / 1628 / 2244	1·3 / 5·2 / 0·9 / 5·4	22 Su	0410 / 1024 / 1657 / 2301	1·2 / 5·5 / 0·7 / 5·6
8 Su	0441 / 1055 / 1709 / 2322	1·1 / 5·4 / 0·8 / 5·6	23 M	0511 / 1118 / 1747 / 2349	1·0 / 5·7 / 0·7 / 5·7
9 M	0522 / 1134 / 1749	1·0 / 5·6 / 0·8	24 Tu	0604 / 1207 / 1831 ●	0·8 / 5·8 / 0·7
10 Tu	0000 / 0603 / 1212 / O 1827	5·7 / 0·9 / 5·7 / 0·8	25 W	0034 / 0650 / 1252 / 1910	5·7 / 0·7 / 5·8 / 0·7
11 W	0035 / 0642 / 1249 / 1903	5·8 / 0·8 / 5·8 / 0·8	26 Th	0114 / 0730 / 1335 / 1947	5·7 / 0·7 / 5·8 / 0·8
12 Th	0110 / 0721 / 1327 / 1940	5·8 / 0·8 / 5·8 / 0·8	27 F	0154 / 0815 / 1418 / 2020	5·7 / 0·8 / 5·7 / 1·0
13 F	0147 / 0801 / 1405 / 2013	5·7 / 0·8 / 5·8 / 0·9	28 Sa	0232 / 0851 / 1455 / 2053	5·5 / 0·9 / 5·5 / 1·1
14 Sa	0225 / 0840 / 1447 / 2049	5·6 / 0·9 / 5·7 / 1·1	29 Su	0308 / 0924 / 1538 / 2122	5·4 / 1·0 / 5·3 / 1·3
15 Su	0305 / 0921 / 1534 / 2128	5·5 / 0·9 / 5·5 / 1·2	30 M	0343 / 0955 / 1617 / 2157	5·2 / 1·2 / 5·2 / 1·4

DECEMBER

Day	Time	m	Day	Time	m
1 Tu	0423 / 1028 / 1701 / 2238	5·1 / 1·2 / 5·0 / 1·5	16 W	0433 / 1102 / 1713 / ((2305	5·5 / 0·8 / 5·5 / 1·2
2 W	0506 / 1115 / 1750 /)) 2332	4·9 / 1·3 / 4·8 / 1·6	17 Th	0527 / 1156 / 1814	5·3 / 0·9 / 5·3
3 Th	0558 / 1214 / 1848	4·8 / 1·4 / 4·7	18 F	0004 / 0631 / 1259 / 1921	1·4 / 5·2 / 1·0 / 5·1
4 F	0035 / 0702 / 1326 / 1954	1·7 / 4·7 / 1·4 / 4·7	19 Sa	0113 / 0742 / 1411 / 2033	1·4 / 5·1 / 1·0 / 5·1
5 Sa	0151 / 0811 / 1437 / 2057	1·7 / 4·8 / 1·3 / 4·9	20 Su	0230 / 0856 / 1525 / 2141	1·4 / 5·2 / 1·0 / 5·2
6 Su	0300 / 0915 / 1536 / 2153	1·5 / 4·9 / 1·1 / 5·1	21 M	0346 / 1004 / 1631 / 2241	1·3 / 5·3 / 1·0 / 5·3
7 M	0356 / 1010 / 1628 / 2242	1·3 / 5·2 / 1·0 / 5·4	22 Tu	0455 / 1105 / 1726 / 2333	1·1 / 5·4 / 0·9 / 5·5
8 Tu	0447 / 1101 / 1715 / 2329	1·1 / 5·4 / 1·0 / 5·5	23 W	0553 / 1157 / 1811	0·9 / 5·5 / 0·9
9 W	0534 / 1146 / 1758	1·0 / 5·5 / 0·9	24 Th	0019 / 0641 / 1243 / 1850 ●	5·5 / 0·8 / 5·6 / 0·8
10 Th	0011 / 0621 / 1252 / 1841	5·6 / 0·9 / 5·7 / 0·9	25 F	0102 / 0723 / 1324 / 1926	5·6 / 0·7 / 5·6 / 0·9
11 F	0052 / 0707 / 1313 / 1921	5·7 / 0·8 / 5·8 / 0·9	26 Sa	0140 / 0802 / 1404 / 1959	5·6 / 0·7 / 5·6 / 0·9
12 Sa	0133 / 0752 / 1357 / 2002	5·7 / 0·7 / 5·8 / 0·9	27 Su	0215 / 0836 / 1440 / 2032	5·6 / 0·7 / 5·6 / 1·0
13 Su	0215 / 0840 / 1442 / 2044	5·7 / 0·6 / 5·8 / 0·9	28 M	0249 / 0907 / 1515 / 2101	5·5 / 0·8 / 5·5 / 1·0
14 M	0258 / 0927 / 1528 / 2128	5·6 / 0·6 / 5·7 / 1·0	29 Tu	0321 / 0935 / 1549 / 2134	5·4 / 0·9 / 5·4 / 1·1
15 Tu	0343 / 1013 / 1619 / 2214	5·6 / 0·7 / 5·6 / 1·1	30 W	0355 / 1004 / 1626 / 2207	5·3 / 0·9 / 5·2 / 1·2
			31 Th	0430 / 1040 / 1705 / 2248	5·2 / 1·0 / 5·1 / 1·3

RATE AND SET — Flood –0600 Sheerness, Spring rate 2½ kn. Ebb +0025 Sheerness, Spring rate 3 kn.

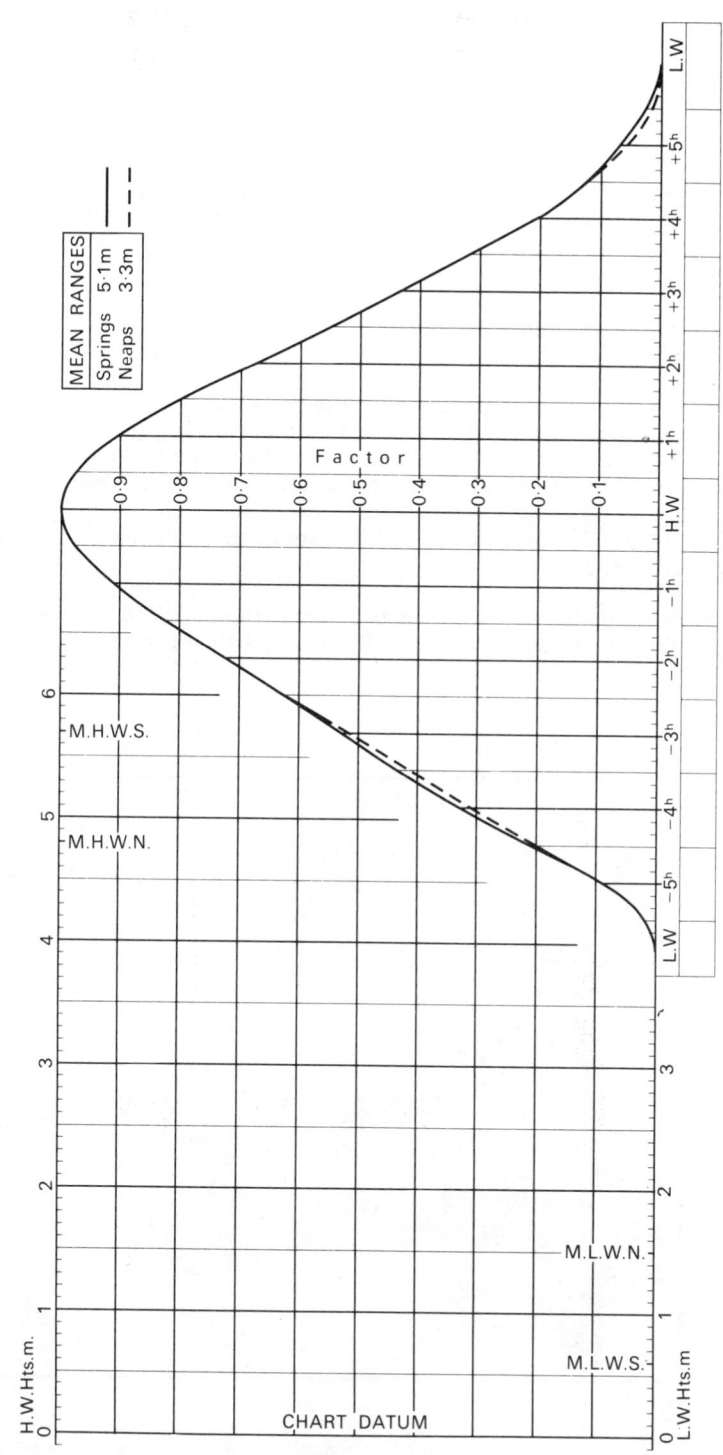

SHEERNESS

MEAN SPRING AND NEAP CURVES

Springs occur 2 days after New and Full Moon.

MEAN RANGES
Springs 5·1m
Neaps 3·3m

Factor

M.H.W.S.
M.H.W.N.

M.L.W.N.
M.L.W.S.

CHART DATUM

H.W.Hts.m.
L.W.Hts.m

L.W
H.W

RIVER THAMES ESTUARY TIDAL STREAMS

The 13 specially drawn Tidal Stream Charts of the Thames Estuary show the Direction and Rate of the Tidal Stream for each hour, both in relation to the time of High Water at Dover and also in relation to Sheerness.

For Sheerness High Water Times see p. 21:46-21:48 and for Dover High Water Times see p. 21:41-21:43.

The thicker the arrows the stronger Tidal Streams they indicate; the thinner arrows showing the times and position of weaker Streams. The figures shown for example as 1.6-3.0 indicate 1.6 knots at Neap Tides, and 3.0 knots at Spring Tides approximately. Arrows not numbered would indicate the rate as less than 1 knot.

Tidal Differences on Sheerness for Ports of the Thames Estuary and R. Medway are given on p. 21:44.

The following 13 charts are produced from portion(s) of BA Tidal Stream Atlases with the sanction of the Controller, H.M. Stationery Office and of the Hydrographer of the Navy.

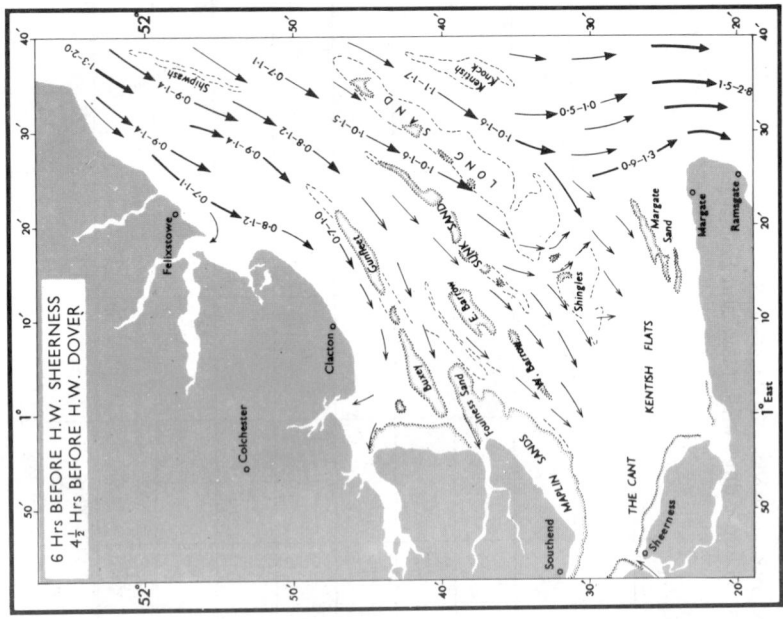

RIVER THAMES ESTUARY TIDAL STREAMS

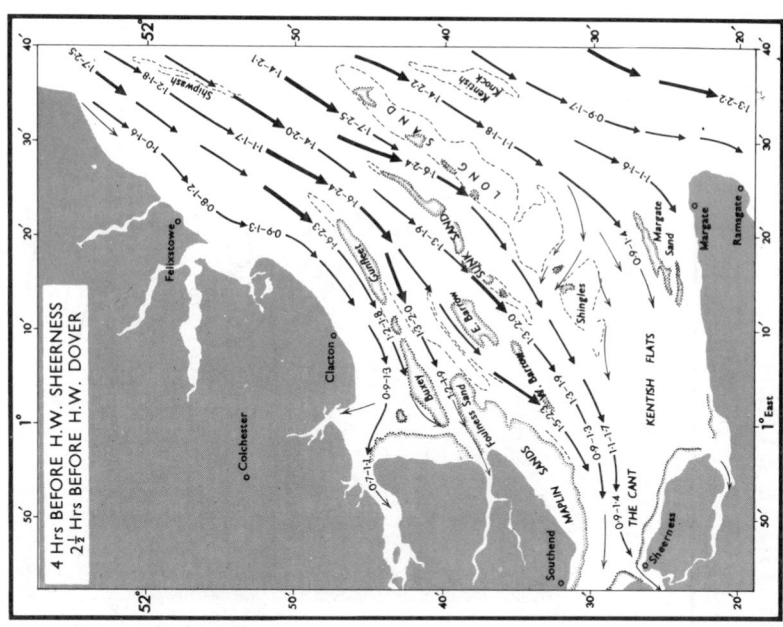

4 Hrs BEFORE H.W. SHEERNESS
2½ Hrs BEFORE H.W. DOVER

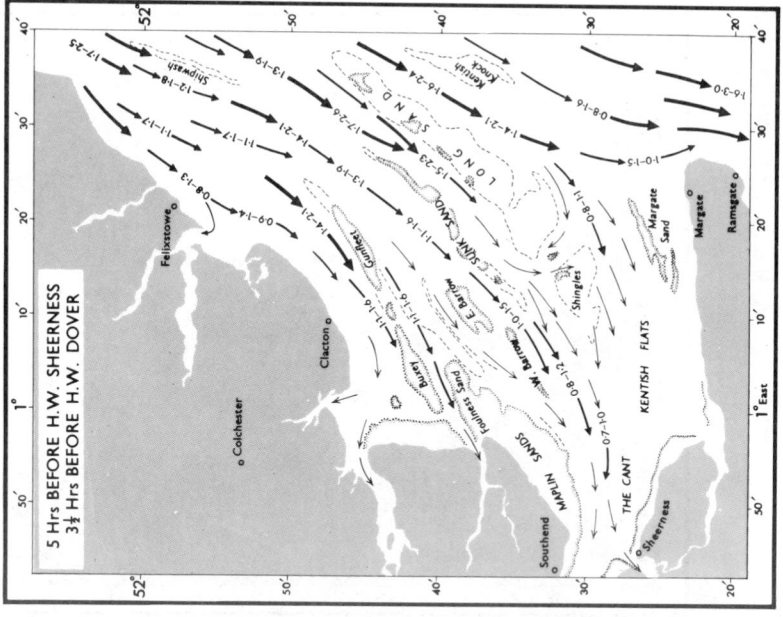

5 Hrs BEFORE H.W. SHEERNESS
3½ Hrs BEFORE H.W. DOVER

RIVER THAMES ESTUARY TIDAL STREAMS

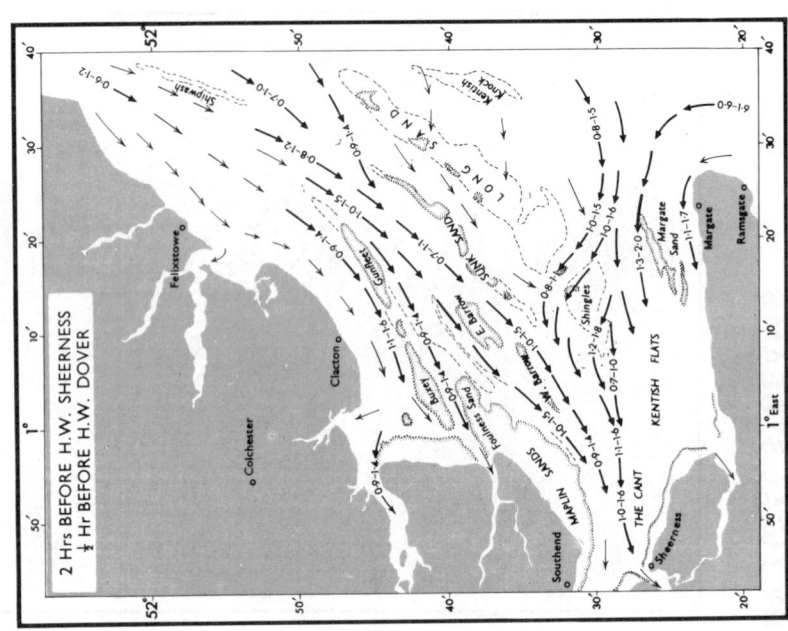

2 Hrs BEFORE H.W. SHEERNESS
¼ Hr BEFORE H.W. DOVER

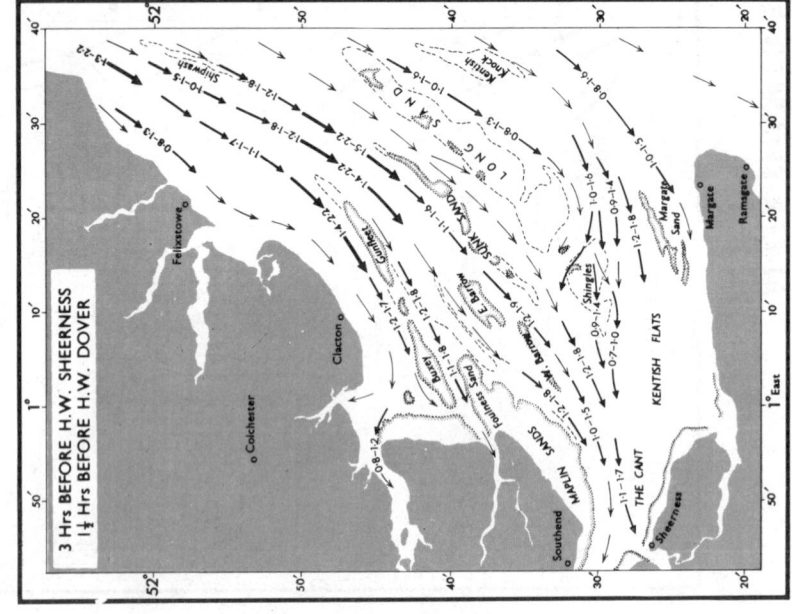

3 Hrs BEFORE H.W. SHEERNESS
1¼ Hrs BEFORE H.W. DOVER

RIVER THAMES ESTUARY TIDAL STREAMS

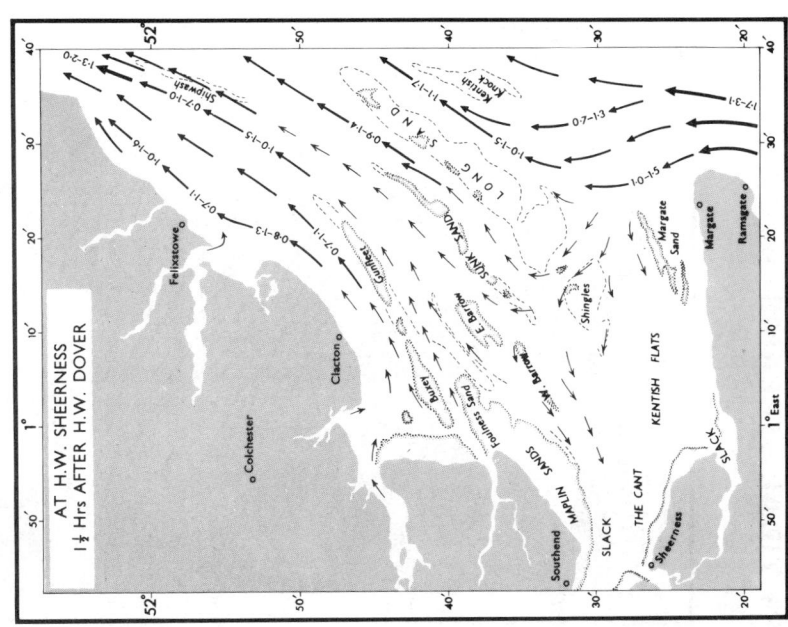

AT H.W. SHEERNESS
1¾ Hrs AFTER H.W. DOVER

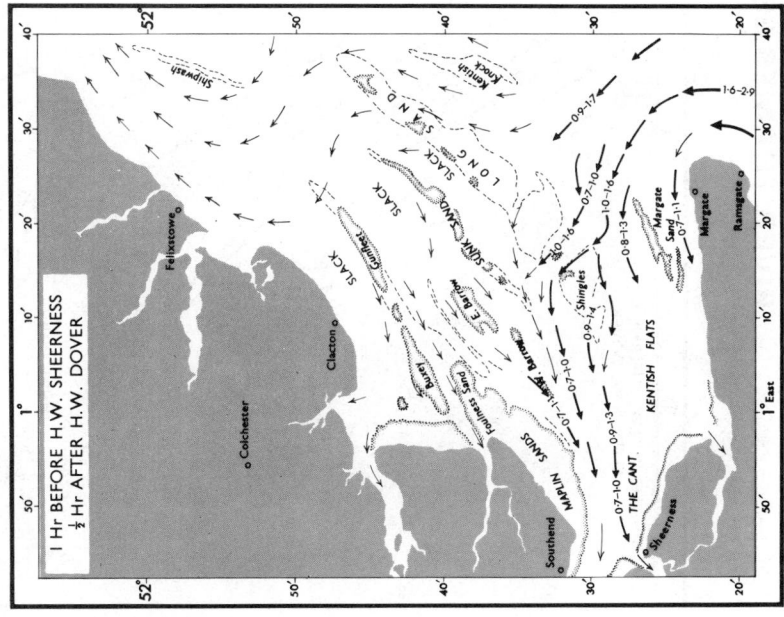

1 Hr BEFORE H.W. SHEERNESS
¾ Hr AFTER H.W. DOVER

RIVER THAMES ESTUARY TIDAL STREAMS

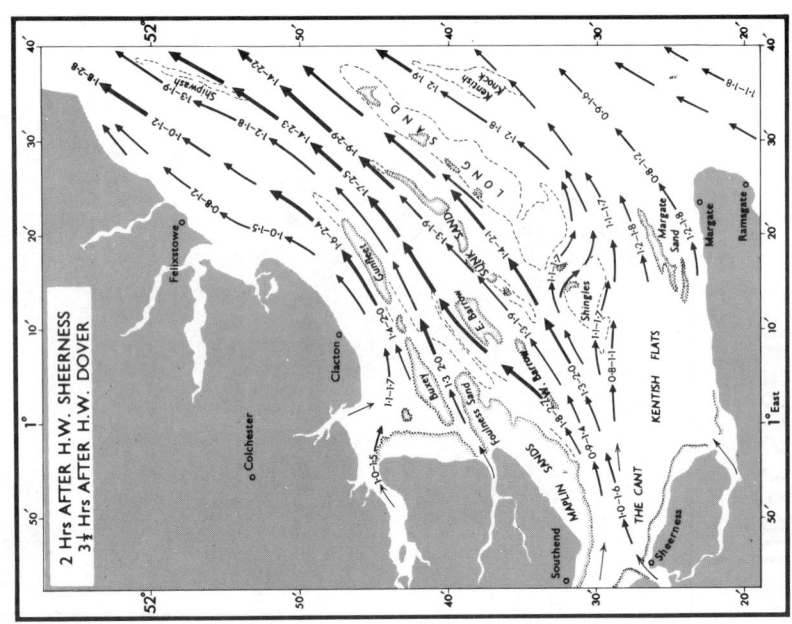

2 Hrs AFTER H.W. SHEERNESS
3½ Hrs AFTER H.W. DOVER

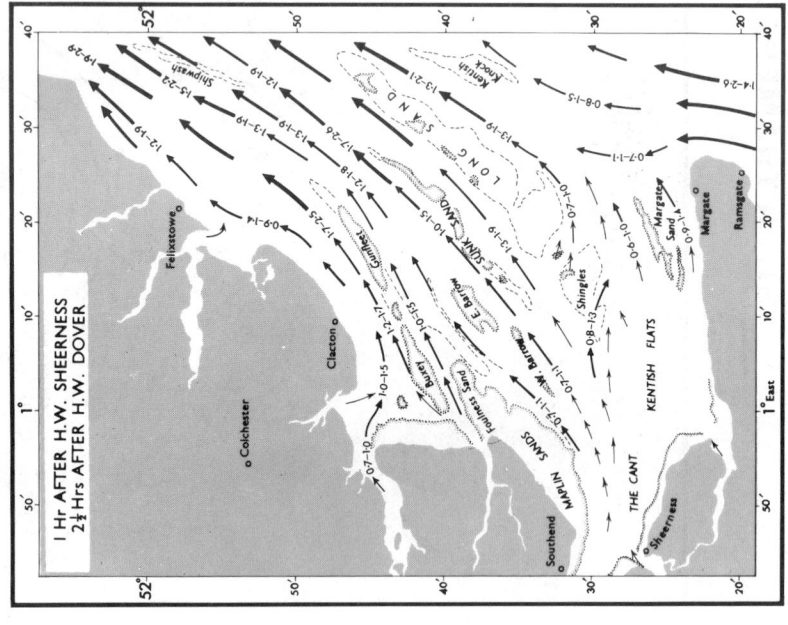

1 Hr AFTER H.W. SHEERNESS
2½ Hrs AFTER H.W. DOVER

RIVER THAMES ESTUARY TIDAL STREAMS

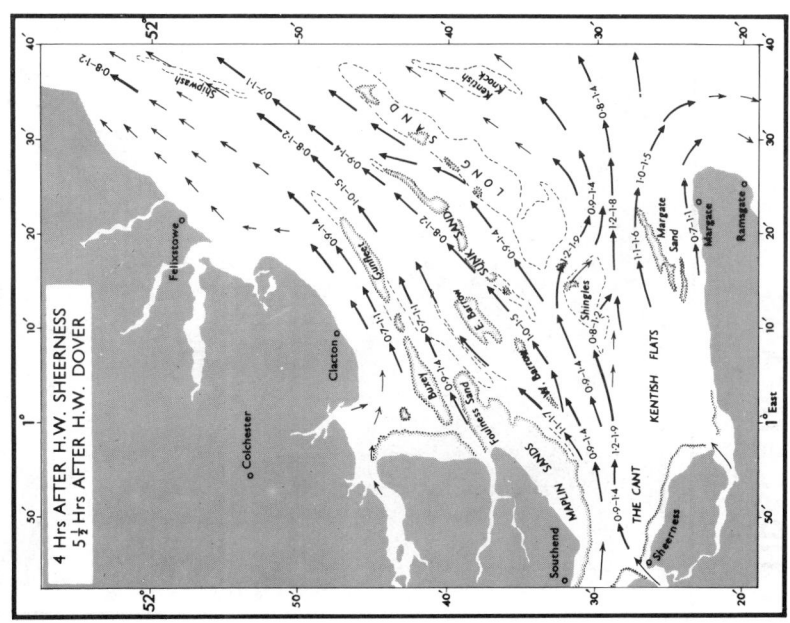

4 Hrs AFTER H.W. SHEERNESS
5½ Hrs AFTER H.W. DOVER

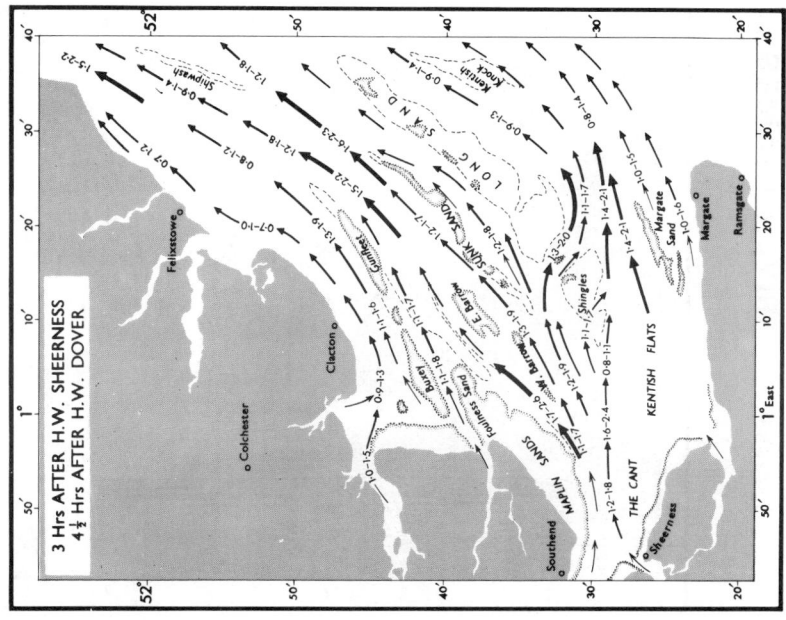

3 Hrs AFTER H.W. SHEERNESS
4½ Hrs AFTER H.W. DOVER

RIVER THAMES ESTUARY TIDAL STREAMS

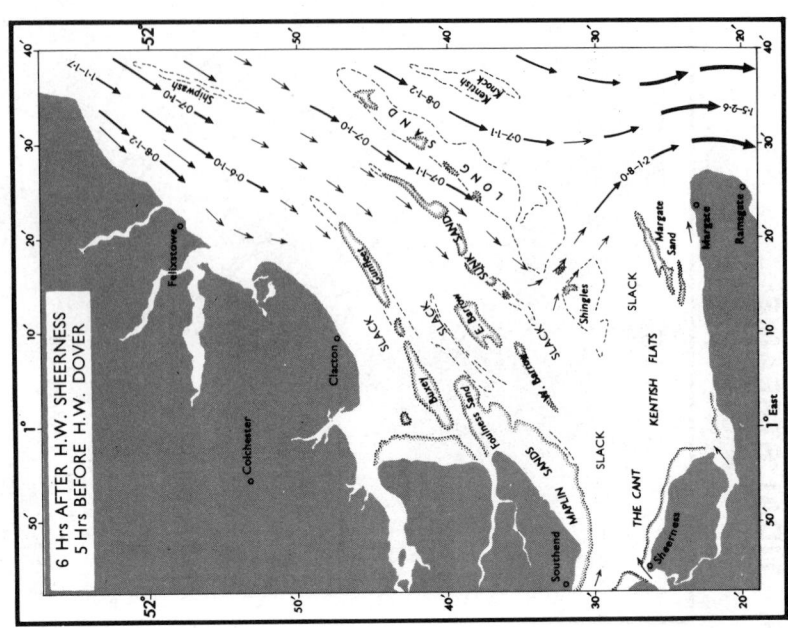

6 Hrs AFTER H.W. SHEERNESS
5 Hrs BEFORE H.W. DOVER

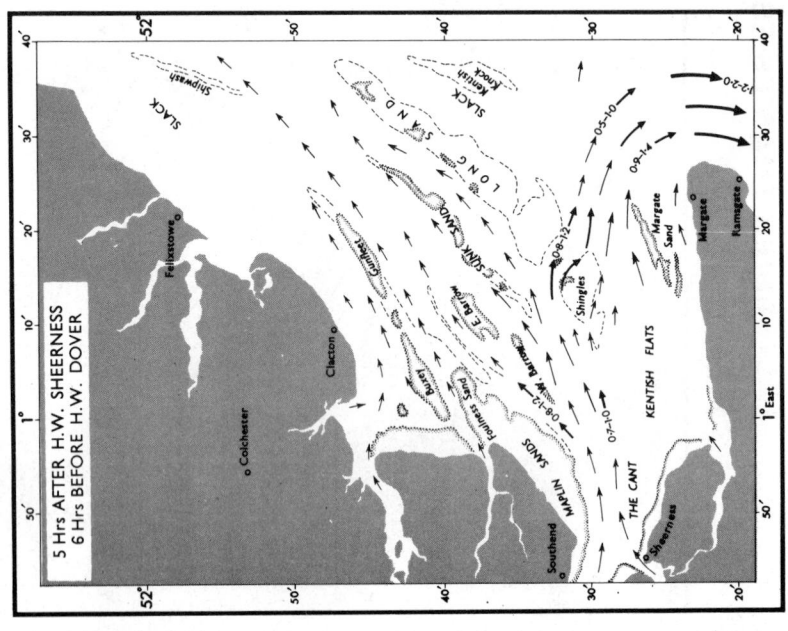

5 Hrs AFTER H.W. SHEERNESS
6 Hrs BEFORE H.W. DOVER

PLACE	TIME DIFFERENCES				HEIGHT DIFFERENCES (Metres)			
	High Water		Low Water		MHWS	MHWN	MLWN	MLWS
LONDON BRIDGE	0300 and 1500	0900 and 2100	0400 and 1600	1100 and 2300	7.1	5.8	1.6	0.5
Tilbury	−0055	−0040	−0045	−0110	−0.7	−0.5	0.0	0.0
Stoneness Lt.	−0045	−0035	−0040	−0102	−0.5	−0.3	0.0	0.0
Coldharbour Lt.	−0038	−0028	−0033	−0052	−0.3	−0.1	0.0	0.0
Crossness	−0025	−0025	−0030	−0045	−0.2	−0.1	0.0	0.0
Woolwich (Gallion's Point)	−0020	−0020	−0025	−0040	−0.1	−0.1	+0.1	0.0
India/Millwall Dock	−0010	−0010	−0015	−0030	0.0	+0.1	0.0	0.0
Greenwich Pier	−0005	−0005	−0015	−0015	0.0	+0.1	0.0	0.0
Surrey C. Docks (Greenland Ent.)	−0005	−0005	−0010	−0010	+0.1	+0.1	0.0	0.0
Westminster Br.	+0005	+0005	+0010	+0010	−0.3	−0.2	0.0	0.0
Chelsea Bridge	+0020	+0015	+0055	+0100	−0.8	−0.7	−0.6	−0.3
Hammersmith Br.	+0040	+0040	+0200	+0200	−1.4	−1.2	−0.2	−0.2
Barnes Bridge	+0045	+0040	+0220	+0210	−1.6	−1.7	−1.1	−0.5
Richmond Lock	+0100	+0055	+0325	+0305	−2.1	−2.2	−1.4	−0.3
Teddington Lock	+0100	+0100	—	—	−4.4	−4.3	—	—*

*Up river of Richmond lock the level is maintained at approximately half tide level.

Refer to predictions on pages 21:58-21:60

RIVER THAMES AND MEDWAY TIDAL STREAM NOTES

Streams set NNE-SSW across outer approaches. NE channels lie nearly in direction of main stream, therefore streams set along these channels. Eddies are formed at sides of channels and at entrances to swatchways. Most southern channels are swatchways, lie at an angle to main streams and in these the streams are more rotatory clockwise.

N.E. CHANNELS. E. Swin. Barrow Deep. Warp.
Ingoing: +0600; Sp. 2; set along channel.
Outgoing: −0025; Sp. 2; set along channel.

S.E. OF MAIN CHANNEL. Knock Deep. Black Deep, Irregular.
Ingoing: S.W. +0600; Sp. 1½-2; set along channel.
Outgoing: N.E. −0055; Sp. 1½-2; set along channel.

W. OF BARROW SANDS. Middle Deep, W. Swin, Barrow Swatchway, Wallet.
Ingoing: S.W. +0600; Sp. 1½-2; set along channel.
Outgoing: N.E. −0025; Sp. 1½-2; set along channel.
Barrow Swatchway lies across main stream; weak and irregular.

COLNE AND BLACKWATER.
Flood and Ebb across entrance.
Wivenhoe: Flood, −0600; Ebb, H.W.
Osea: Flood, −0610; Ebb, H.W.
Maldon: Flood, −0540; Ebb, +0010.

CROUCH.
Entrance: ¼ hr. after Gunfleet Spit.
Hullbridge: Flood, −0600; Ebb, H.W.

SWALE. Entrance from Medway.
Ingoing: −0555, slack, weak, −0525 set in from Medway. +0005, flows through to Estuary.
Outgoing: +0105, separates, runs to Medway.

SWALE. Entrance from Estuary.
Ingoing: −0555, slack, weak, −0525, set in from Estuary. +0005, flows through to Estuary.
Outgoing: +0105, separates, runs to Estuary.

SWALE. General Note.
Meeting of streams, is fairly constant, at Fowley Islands. **Parting,** varies—inequality in duration of streams—all streams strongest soon after beginning and then decrease. Sp. max. 3-4 kts.

SOUTHERN CHANNELS. S. Channel, Gore, Horse, Four Fathom, Princes.
Ingoing: +0600, Sp. mean 1½ kts.
Outgoing: H.W. Sp. mean 1½ kts.

CHANNELS. Queens, Edinburgh.
Rotatory clockwise streams, setting with channels when strongest; but when changing, setting towards shoals.

Times are given in relation to H.W. Sheerness and indicate beginning of streams. Rates are approx. in knots, maximum at Springs.

21:58 RIVER THAMES LONDON BRIDGE

HIGH & LOW WATER 1992 Lat. 51°30'N. Long. 0°05'W.

GMT ADD 1 HOUR MARCH 23 — OCTOBER 25 FOR B.S.T.

JANUARY

	Time	m		Time	m
1 W	0441 / 1105 / 1719 / 2339	1·4 / 6·2 / 1·1 / 6·4	16 Th	0327 / 0946 / 1616 / 2238	1·6 / 5·9 / 1·4 / 6·0
2 Th	0554 / 1208 / 1821	1·2 / 6·3 / 1·0	17 F	0458 / 1105 / 1736 / 2349	1·4 / 6·2 / 1·1 / 6·4
3 F	0034 / 0656 / 1259 / 1910	6·5 / 1·0 / 6·5 / 1·0	18 Sa	0615 / 1215 / 1850	1·0 / 6·6 / 0·9
4 Sa ●	0117 / 0744 / 1341 / 1952	6·6 / 0·9 / 6·6 / 0·9	19 Su	0050 / 0731 / 1316 / 1958	6·7 / 0·7 / 7·0 / 0·7
5 Su	0155 / 0826 / 1420 / 2032	6·7 / 0·6 / 6·7 / 0·9	20 M	0142 / 0833 / 1408 / 2053	7·0 / 0·3 / 7·3 / 0·6
6 M	0230 / 0904 / 1456 / 2110	6·8 / 0·7 / 6·8 / 0·8	21 Tu	0230 / 0927 / 1457 / 2142	7·2 / 0·0 / 7·6 / 0·5
7 Tu	0303 / 0939 / 1529 / 2145	6·8 / 0·7 / 6·9 / 0·9	22 W	0315 / 1014 / 1543 / 2226	7·4 / -0·2 / 7·7 / 0·4
8 W	0335 / 1012 / 1603 / 2219	6·9 / 0·7 / 6·9 / 0·9	23 Th	0359 / 1057 / 1628 / 2305	7·5 / -0·2 / 7·6 / 0·6
9 Th	0407 / 1042 / 1637 / 2251	6·8 / 0·8 / 6·8 / 1·0	24 F	0442 / 1136 / 1712 / 2339	7·4 / 0·0 / 7·4 / 0·8
10 F	0440 / 1112 / 1711 / 2320	6·7 / 0·8 / 6·7 / 1·1	25 Sa	0525 / 1210 / 1757	7·2 / 0·4 / 7·0
11 Sa	0512 / 1142 / 1744 / 2350	6·6 / 0·9 / 6·5 / 1·2	26 Su (	0010 / 0608 / 1239 / 1842	1·0 / 6·9 / 0·7 / 6·7
12 Su	0544 / 1211 / 1821	6·4 / 1·0 / 6·2	27 M	0042 / 0655 / 1314 / 1931	1·2 / 6·6 / 1·0 / 6·3
13 M)	0024 / 0622 / 1248 / 1906	1·3 / 6·2 / 1·1 / 6·0	28 Tu	0124 / 0752 / 1404 / 2030	1·4 / 6·2 / 1·2 / 6·0
14 Tu	0106 / 0710 / 1334 / 2005	1·5 / 6·0 / 1·2 / 5·8	29 W	0226 / 0901 / 1518 / 2142	1·6 / 5·9 / 1·5 / 5·9
15 W	0202 / 0820 / 1442 / 2122	1·6 / 5·8 / 1·4 / 5·8	30 Th	0359 / 1031 / 1637 / 2306	1·6 / 5·8 / 1·4 / 5·9
			31 F	0523 / 1147 / 1744	1·4 / 6·1 / 1·3

FEBRUARY

	Time	m		Time	m
1 Sa	0010 / 0635 / 1242 / 1843	6·2 / 1·1 / 6·3 / 1·1	16 Su	0600 / 1204 / 1835	1·0 / 6·6 / 1·0
2 Su	0057 / 0726 / 1324 / 1931	6·4 / 0·9 / 6·6 / 1·0	17 M	0035 / 0721 / 1304 / 1945	6·7 / 0·5 / 7·1 / 0·7
3 M ●	0137 / 0809 / 1402 / 2015	6·6 / 0·7 / 6·7 / 0·9	18 Tu	0128 / 0822 / 1357 / 2040	7·1 / 0·1 / 7·4 / 0·5
4 Tu	0212 / 0847 / 1436 / 2054	6·8 / 0·7 / 6·9 / 0·8	19 W	0215 / 0912 / 1442 / 2127	7·3 / -0·2 / 7·6 / 0·4
5 W	0244 / 0924 / 1508 / 2131	6·9 / 0·6 / 7·0 / 0·8	20 Th	0257 / 0957 / 1525 / 2207	7·5 / -0·3 / 7·7 / 0·4
6 Th	0315 / 0957 / 1539 / 2204	7·0 / 0·6 / 7·0 / 0·8	21 F	0339 / 1037 / 1607 / 2244	7·6 / -0·2 / 7·6 / 0·5
7 F	0346 / 1027 / 1610 / 2235	7·0 / 0·6 / 7·0 / 0·9	22 Sa	0419 / 1111 / 1647 / 2313	7·5 / 0·1 / 7·4 / 0·7
8 Sa	0416 / 1055 / 1642 / 2301	6·9 / 0·7 / 6·9 / 1·0	23 Su	0459 / 1137 / 1726 / 2339	7·3 / 0·5 / 7·0 / 0·9
9 Su	0447 / 1119 / 1713 / 2325	6·8 / 0·8 / 6·7 / 1·1	24 M	0539 / 1201 / 1804	7·0 / 0·8 / 6·6
10 M	0518 / 1142 / 1749 / 2351	6·6 / 0·9 / 6·5 / 1·1	25 Tu (	0007 / 0621 / 1229 / 1848	1·0 / 6·6 / 1·0 / 6·3
11 Tu	0553 / 1211 / 1828	6·4 / 1·0 / 6·2	26 W	0042 / 0714 / 1312 / 1940	1·2 / 6·2 / 1·3 / 5·9
12 W	0029 / 0638 / 1253 / 1920	1·2 / 6·2 / 1·1 / 5·9	27 Th	0131 / 0820 / 1413 / 2047	1·5 / 5·8 / 1·7 / 5·7
13 Th	0121 / 0744 / 1352 / 2039	1·4 / 5·9 / 1·4 / 5·7	28 F	0254 / 0948 / 1555 / 2220	1·8 / 5·6 / 1·8 / 5·6
14 F	0240 / 0901 / 1538 / 2206	1·6 / 5·8 / 1·6 / 5·9	29 Sa	0451 / 1122 / 1713 / 2342	1·6 / 5·9 / 1·5 / 5·9
15 Sa	0400 / 1045 / 1711 / 2329	1·4 / 6·1 / 1·3 / 6·3			

MARCH

	Time	m		Time	m
1 Su	0605 / 1218 / 1815	1·2 / 6·3 / 1·2	16 M	0546 / 1150 / 1817	0·8 / 6·7 / 1·0
2 M	0032 / 0659 / 1300 / 1906	6·3 / 0·9 / 6·6 / 1·0	17 Tu	0015 / 0707 / 1249 / 1927	6·8 / 0·4 / 7·2 / 0·7
3 Tu	0112 / 0742 / 1337 / 1951	6·6 / 0·7 / 6·7 / 0·9	18 W ○	0109 / 0805 / 1338 / 2020	7·1 / 0·0 / 7·4 / 0·5
4 W ●	0147 / 0822 / 1409 / 2032	6·8 / 0·6 / 6·9 / 0·8	19 Th	0155 / 0853 / 1422 / 2105	7·3 / -0·1 / 7·5 / 0·4
5 Th	0218 / 0858 / 1440 / 2108	7·0 / 0·6 / 7·0 / 0·7	20 F	0236 / 0934 / 1503 / 2145	7·5 / -0·1 / 7·6 / 0·4
6 F	0249 / 0932 / 1511 / 2143	7·1 / 0·5 / 7·1 / 0·7	21 Sa	0317 / 1010 / 1542 / 2217	7·5 / 0·1 / 7·5 / 0·5
7 Sa	0318 / 1004 / 1542 / 2214	7·1 / 0·6 / 7·1 / 0·8	22 Su	0355 / 1040 / 1619 / 2245	7·5 / 0·4 / 7·2 / 0·6
8 Su	0349 / 1033 / 1613 / 2240	7·1 / 0·6 / 7·1 / 0·9	23 M	0433 / 1102 / 1654 / 2309	7·2 / 0·7 / 6·9 / 0·8
9 M	0421 / 1055 / 1647 / 2302	7·0 / 0·8 / 6·9 / 0·9	24 Tu	0512 / 1126 / 1729 / 2336	6·9 / 0·9 / 6·6 / 0·9
10 Tu	0455 / 1115 / 1720 / 2329	6·8 / 0·9 / 6·6 / 1·0	25 W	0553 / 1157 / 1807	6·5 / 1·1 / 6·3
11 W	0534 / 1146 / 1801	6·6 / 1·0 / 6·3	26 Th (	0010 / 0642 / 1236 / 1855	1·1 / 6·1 / 1·3 / 5·9
12 Th)	0007 / 0622 / 1228 / 1853	1·1 / 6·2 / 1·2 / 5·9	27 F	0055 / 0744 / 1328 / 1959	1·3 / 5·8 / 1·7 / 5·6
13 F	0059 / 0731 / 1328 / 2012	1·3 / 5·9 / 1·5 / 5·7	28 Sa	0155 / 0903 / 1454 / 2121	1·7 / 5·6 / 2·0 / 5·5
14 Sa	0218 / 0901 / 1514 / 2143	1·5 / 5·9 / 1·7 / 5·8	29 Su	0407 / 1037 / 1637 / 2257	1·7 / 5·7 / 1·7 / 5·7
15 Su	0413 / 1033 / 1649 / 2309	1·3 / 6·2 / 1·4 / 6·3	30 M	0523 / 1142 / 1739 / 2356	1·3 / 6·1 / 1·4 / 6·1
			31 Tu	0619 / 1227 / 1832	1·0 / 6·5 / 1·1

APRIL

	Time	m		Time	m
1 W	0038 / 0706 / 1303 / 1919	6·4 / 0·8 / 6·7 / 0·9	16 Th	0046 / 0741 / 1317 / 1957	7·0 / 0·2 / 7·3 / 0·6
2 Th	0113 / 0748 / 1337 / 2001	6·7 / 0·7 / 6·8 / 0·8	17 F ○	0133 / 0826 / 1401 / 2040	7·1 / 0·2 / 7·3 / 0·6
3 F ●	0145 / 0827 / 1409 / 2040	6·9 / 0·6 / 7·0 / 0·7	18 Sa	0215 / 0905 / 1440 / 2118	7·2 / 0·3 / 7·3 / 0·5
4 Sa	0218 / 0904 / 1440 / 2118	7·0 / 0·6 / 7·1 / 0·7	19 Su	0254 / 0939 / 1517 / 2150	7·3 / 0·5 / 7·2 / 0·5
5 Su	0250 / 0938 / 1514 / 2152	7·1 / 0·6 / 7·2 / 0·7	20 M	0332 / 1007 / 1552 / 2219	7·3 / 0·6 / 7·1 / 0·6
6 M	0324 / 1009 / 1548 / 2221	7·2 / 0·6 / 7·1 / 0·7	21 Tu	0412 / 1031 / 1626 / 2245	7·1 / 0·8 / 6·8 / 0·8
7 Tu	0400 / 1035 / 1624 / 2248	7·2 / 0·7 / 7·0 / 0·8	22 W	0449 / 1058 / 1659 / 2313	6·8 / 1·0 / 6·6 / 0·9
8 W	0441 / 1059 / 1702 / 2319	7·0 / 0·9 / 6·7 / 0·9	23 Th	0530 / 1130 / 1736 / 2346	6·5 / 1·1 / 6·3 / 1·0
9 Th	0526 / 1133 / 1747	6·7 / 1·1 / 6·3	24 F (	0615 / 1210 / 1818	6·2 / 1·3 / 6·0
10 F)	0000 / 0621 / 1219 / 1843	1·0 / 6·3 / 1·3 / 6·0	25 Sa	0028 / 0710 / 1256 / 1916	1·2 / 5·9 / 1·6 / 5·7
11 Sa	0055 / 0730 / 1323 / 1958	1·2 / 6·0 / 1·6 / 5·8	26 Su	0120 / 0818 / 1358 / 2030	1·4 / 5·7 / 1·9 / 5·5
12 Su	0218 / 0851 / 1500 / 2122	1·3 / 6·1 / 1·7 / 6·0	27 M	0232 / 0932 / 1532 / 2150	1·6 / 5·7 / 1·9 / 5·6
13 M	0357 / 1016 / 1627 / 2245	1·0 / 6·4 / 1·4 / 6·4	28 Tu	0424 / 1042 / 1649 / 2259	1·5 / 5·9 / 1·6 / 5·9
14 Tu	0525 / 1129 / 1749 / 2351	0·7 / 6·8 / 1·1 / 6·8	29 W	0526 / 1137 / 1746 / 2350	1·2 / 6·2 / 1·3 / 6·2
15 W	0643 / 1228 / 1903	0·3 / 7·2 / 0·8	30 Th	0618 / 1221 / 1836	1·0 / 6·5 / 1·1

To find H.W. Dover subtract 1h. 40min.

TIDAL DIFFERENCES PAGE 21:57. TIDAL CURVE PAGE 21:61.
TIDAL STREAMS PAGES 21:50-21:56.
Datum of predictions: 3.20 m. below Ordnance Datum (Newlyn) or approx. L.A.T.

LONDON BRIDGE RIVER THAMES 21:59

Lat. 51°30′N. Long. 0°05′W. HIGH & LOW WATER 1992

GMT ADD 1 HOUR MARCH 29 — OCTOBER 25 FOR B.S.T.

MAY

Day	Time m	Time m	Time m	Time m
1 F	0032 6.5	0706 0.8	1259 6.7	1924 0.9
2 Sa	0110 6.7	0751 0.7	1335 6.9	● 2011 0.8
3 Su	0148 6.9	0833 0.7	1413 7.0	2053 0.7
4 M	0226 7.1	0914 0.6	1450 7.1	2134 0.6
5 Tu	0305 7.2	0950 0.6	1529 7.1	2212 0.5
6 W	0348 7.3	1026 0.7	1610 7.0	2248 0.6
7 Th	0434 7.1	1058 0.9	1654 6.8	2325 0.7
8 F	0525 6.9	1134 1.1	1743 6.5	
9 Sa	0008 0.9	0621 6.6	1222 1.4	☽ 1839 6.2
10 Su	0104 1.0	0726 6.4	1324 1.5	1947 6.1
11 M	0219 1.0	0836 6.4	1443 1.5	2100 6.2
12 Tu	0338 0.8	0950 6.6	1559 1.3	2216 6.4
13 W	0452 0.6	1102 6.8	1713 1.1	2325 6.6
14 Th	0610 0.5	1203 7.0	1831 1.0	
15 F	0022 6.8	0710 0.5	1255 7.0	1928 0.8
16 Sa	0112 6.8	0757 0.6	1338 7.0	○ 2015 0.7
17 Su	0155 6.9	0836 0.7	1418 6.9	2054 0.7
18 M	0236 7.0	0910 0.8	1454 6.9	2128 0.8
19 Tu	0315 7.0	0939 0.8	1529 6.9	2159 0.7
20 W	0353 7.0	1009 0.9	1603 6.8	2228 0.8
21 Th	0431 6.8	1038 1.0	1637 6.6	2257 0.9
22 F	0511 6.6	1111 1.1	1712 6.4	2329 1.0
23 Sa	0551 6.3	1147 1.3	1751 6.2	
24 Su	0008 1.0	0638 6.1	1229 1.4	☾ 1838 5.9
25 M	0052 1.2	0731 5.9	1319 1.6	1934 5.7
26 Tu	0145 1.3	0833 5.8	1418 1.7	2044 5.6
27 W	0251 1.4	0936 5.8	1531 1.7	2152 5.7
28 Th	0409 1.3	1035 6.0	1644 1.5	2252 5.9
29 F	0516 1.1	1130 6.3	1746 1.3	2346 6.2
30 Sa	0617 0.9	1219 6.5	1845 1.0	
31 Su	0035 6.5	0713 0.8	1306 6.7	1940 0.8

JUNE

Day	Time m	Time m	Time m	Time m
1 M	0121 6.7	0805 0.7	1351 6.9	● 2032 0.6
2 Tu	0208 7.0	0854 0.6	1434 7.0	2121 0.5
3 W	0254 7.2	0939 0.6	1518 7.1	2207 0.4
4 Th	0341 7.3	1023 0.7	1602 7.1	2252 0.3
5 F	0430 7.3	1104 0.8	1648 7.0	2336 0.4
6 Sa	0520 7.1	1143 1.0	1737 6.8	
7 Su	0019 0.6	0614 6.9	1205 1.2	☽ 1829 6.6
8 M	0107 0.7	0710 6.7	1314 1.3	1927 6.5
9 Tu	0204 0.7	0813 6.6	1416 1.4	2032 6.4
10 W	0307 0.7	0921 6.5	1525 1.3	2142 6.4
11 Th	0414 0.7	1030 6.6	1637 1.2	2257 6.4
12 F	0525 0.8	1136 6.6	1753 1.1	
13 Sa	0000 6.5	0632 0.8	1231 6.6	1900 1.0
14 Su	0053 6.5	0726 0.9	1319 6.6	1952 0.9
15 M	0140 6.6	0808 1.0	1359 6.7	○ 2034 0.8
16 Tu	0222 6.7	0844 0.9	1437 6.7	2112 0.7
17 W	0300 6.8	0918 0.9	1511 6.8	2146 0.7
18 Th	0338 6.9	0952 0.9	1545 6.7	2217 0.8
19 F	0413 6.8	1024 1.0	1619 6.7	2247 0.9
20 Sa	0449 6.7	1057 1.1	1652 6.6	2318 0.9
21 Su	0526 6.5	1129 1.1	1729 6.4	2350 0.9
22 M	0605 6.3	1205 1.2	1805 6.2	
23 Tu	0028 1.0	0646 6.1	1245 1.3	☾ 1846 6.0
24 W	0109 1.1	0734 5.9	1330 1.5	1937 5.8
25 Th	0158 1.2	0833 5.8	1426 1.6	2044 5.7
26 F	0301 1.3	0938 5.9	1539 1.6	2156 5.8
27 Sa	0421 1.2	1042 6.0	1658 1.4	2302 6.0
28 Su	0533 1.1	1144 6.3	1807 1.1	
29 M	0005 6.3	0641 0.9	1242 6.6	1914 0.8
30 Tu	0103 6.7	0744 0.7	1334 6.8	● 2016 0.6

JULY

Day	Time m	Time m	Time m	Time m
1 W	0157 7.0	0840 0.6	1422 7.0	2111 0.3
2 Th	0246 7.3	0931 0.5	1507 7.2	2202 0.1
3 F	0334 7.5	1017 0.5	1552 7.3	2249 0.0
4 Sa	0420 7.5	1059 0.6	1637 7.3	2333 0.1
5 Su	0508 7.4	1139 0.8	1723 7.1	
6 M	0012 0.3	0557 7.1	1215 1.0	1810 6.9
7 Tu	0052 0.5	0646 6.8	1253 1.1	☽ 1900 6.7
8 W	0133 0.7	0741 6.6	1340 1.2	1958 6.5
9 Th	0225 0.9	0843 6.4	1443 1.3	2107 6.3
10 F	0332 1.0	0952 6.3	1558 1.4	2224 6.2
11 Sa	0441 1.1	1105 6.3	1718 1.3	2339 6.2
12 Su	0551 1.1	1208 6.3	1838 1.1	
13 M	0038 6.4	0655 1.1	1300 6.4	1934 0.9
14 Tu	0126 6.5	0747 1.0	1342 6.5	○ 2019 0.8
15 W	0218 6.6	0825 1.0	1420 6.7	2057 0.7
16 Th	0244 6.8	0903 0.9	1454 6.8	2134 0.7
17 F	0319 6.9	0938 0.9	1527 6.8	2206 0.7
18 Sa	0352 6.9	1010 0.9	1557 6.8	2234 0.8
19 Su	0426 6.8	1041 0.9	1630 6.8	2302 0.8
20 M	0458 6.7	1111 1.0	1702 6.6	2330 0.8
21 Tu	0532 6.5	1140 1.1	1734 6.4	
22 W	0000 0.9	0607 6.3	1211 1.2	☾ 1810 6.2
23 Th	0034 1.0	0646 6.1	1249 1.3	1852 6.0
24 F	0114 1.0	0734 5.9	1335 1.4	1948 5.8
25 Sa	0208 1.3	0842 5.7	1443 1.6	2108 5.7
26 Su	0331 1.4	1001 5.8	1617 1.5	2228 5.9
27 M	0459 1.2	1115 6.1	1737 1.1	2344 6.3
28 Tu	0614 1.0	1222 6.5	1856 0.8	
29 W	0049 6.8	0726 0.8	1319 6.8	● 2005 0.4
30 Th	0144 7.2	0827 0.6	1406 7.1	2101 0.1
31 F	0233 7.5	0918 0.4	1451 7.4	2150 −0.1

AUGUST

Day	Time m	Time m	Time m	Time m
1 Sa	0319 7.6	1004 0.4	1535 7.5	2237 −0.2
2 Su	0404 7.6	1045 0.4	1619 7.5	2316 −0.1
3 M	0448 7.4	1122 0.6	1701 7.3	2353 0.2
4 Tu	0532 7.1	1154 0.9	1744 7.1	
5 W	0022 0.6	0617 6.8	1240 1.0	☽ 1831 6.7
6 Th	0055 0.8	0704 6.4	1302 1.2	1924 6.4
7 F	0135 1.1	0801 6.2	1410 1.4	2030 6.1
8 Sa	0240 1.3	0907 5.9	1517 1.5	2152 5.9
9 Su	0403 1.4	1031 5.9	1649 1.4	2319 6.1
10 M	0519 1.3	1146 6.1	1817 1.1	
11 Tu	0021 6.4	0627 1.1	1241 6.4	1914 0.8
12 W	0109 6.6	0720 0.9	1323 6.6	1958 0.7
13 Th	0148 6.8	0804 0.8	1359 6.8	○ 2037 0.6
14 F	0223 6.8	0842 0.8	1433 6.9	2112 0.6
15 Sa	0256 6.9	0918 0.8	1503 6.9	2143 0.7
16 Su	0325 6.9	0950 0.8	1532 7.0	2213 0.7
17 M	0356 6.9	1020 0.8	1602 6.9	2240 0.7
18 Tu	0427 6.8	1047 0.9	1633 6.8	2305 0.8
19 W	0458 6.7	1113 1.0	1705 6.6	2330 0.8
20 Th	0532 6.5	1140 1.1	1739 6.4	2358 0.9
21 F	0608 6.2	1214 1.1	1819 6.2	☾
22 Sa	0036 1.1	0653 5.9	1259 1.3	1916 5.9
23 Su	0127 1.4	0758 5.7	1401 1.5	2034 5.7
24 M	0249 1.6	0925 5.7	1545 1.5	2204 5.9
25 Tu	0433 1.4	1051 6.0	1716 1.1	2329 6.4
26 W	0551 1.0	1203 6.5	1842 0.7	
27 Th	0035 6.9	0709 0.7	1300 7.0	1951 0.2
28 F	0128 7.3	0811 0.5	1348 7.3	● 2046 −0.1
29 Sa	0215 7.6	0901 0.4	1432 7.5	2134 −0.2
30 Su	0300 7.6	0945 0.3	1514 7.6	2216 −0.2
31 M	0342 7.6	1024 0.4	1556 7.6	2252 0.0

Tidal Stream Rate (maximum). London Bridge: Flood — 2½ knots. Ebb — 3½ knots. Tidal Ebb and Flood (average). London Bridge: Ebb — 6 h. 32 min. Flood — 5 h. 55 min.

21:60 RIVER THAMES LONDON BRIDGE

HIGH & LOW WATER 1992 Lat. 51°30′N. Long. 0°05′W.

GMT ADD 1 HOUR MARCH 29 — OCTOBER 25 FOR B.S.T.

SEPTEMBER

Day	Time m	Time m	Time m	Time m
1 Tu	0424 7.4	1058 0.6	1637 7.4	2323 0.4
2 W	0505 7.0	1126 0.8	1719 7.1	2349 0.7
3 Th	0546 6.7	1154 1.0	1803 6.7)	
4 F	0017 1.0	0628 6.3	1227 1.1	1853 6.3
5 Sa	0055 1.2	0719 6.0	1312 1.4	1957 6.0
6 Su	0149 1.6	0822 5.7	1420 1.7	2115 5.7
7 M	0322 1.7	0948 5.6	1621 1.6	2252 5.9
8 Tu	0449 1.5	1118 6.0	1747 1.1	2357 6.4
9 W	0557 1.1	1214 6.4	1843 0.8	
10 Th	0043 6.7	0650 0.7	1257 6.7	1928 0.6
11 F	0123 6.8	0730 0.7	1334 6.9	2008 0.6
12 Sa	0157 6.9	0815 0.7	1405 7.0	2043 0.6 ○
13 Su	0226 6.9	0851 0.7	1439 7.0	2115 0.6
14 M	0256 7.0	0925 0.7	1503 7.1	2145 0.7
15 Tu	0325 7.0	0955 0.7	1534 7.1	2213 0.7
16 W	0356 7.0	1023 0.8	1604 7.0	2238 0.8
17 Th	0427 6.8	1048 0.9	1638 6.8	2302 0.8
18 F	0501 6.6	1115 0.9	1716 6.6	2332 1.0
19 Sa	0539 6.3	1149 1.1	1801 6.3 (	
20 Su	0010 1.2	0625 6.0	1235 1.2	1859 6.0
21 M	0102 1.4	0731 5.7	1338 1.5	2019 5.8
22 Tu	0225 1.7	0900 5.7	1527 1.4	2150 6.0
23 W	0410 1.5	1030 6.1	1659 1.0	2313 6.6
24 Th	0529 1.0	1142 6.6	1827 0.5	
25 F	0017 7.1	0649 0.7	1238 7.1	1933 0.1
26 Sa	0109 7.4	0749 0.5	1327 7.4	2025 0.0 ●
27 Su	0155 7.5	0839 0.4	1411 7.5	2110 0.0
28 M	0237 7.5	0922 0.4	1451 7.6	2149 0.1
29 Tu	0318 7.5	0959 0.4	1532 7.6	2223 0.3
30 W	0357 7.3	1031 0.5	1614 7.4	2251 0.6

OCTOBER

Day	Time m	Time m	Time m	Time m
1 Th	0437 7.0	1059 0.7	1655 7.1	2316 0.9
2 F	0515 6.6	1127 0.9	1739 6.7	2346 1.1
3 Sa	0554 6.2	1200 1.1	1827 6.2)	
4 Su	0022 1.4	0641 5.9	1241 1.4	1926 5.9
5 M	0112 1.7	0741 5.6	1337 1.7	2037 5.7
6 Tu	0227 1.9	0900 5.5	1542 1.7	2207 5.8
7 W	0413 1.7	1034 5.8	1705 1.3	2320 6.2
8 Th	0519 1.3	1139 6.2	1803 0.9	
9 F	0010 6.6	0614 0.9	1224 6.6	1849 0.7
10 Sa	0049 6.8	0700 0.8	1300 6.8	1930 0.6
11 Su	0123 6.9	0742 0.7	1333 6.9	2008 0.6 ○
12 M	0154 6.9	0820 0.7	1402 7.0	2043 0.6
13 Tu	0223 7.0	0857 0.7	1434 7.1	2117 0.6
14 W	0256 7.1	0931 0.7	1507 7.1	2149 0.6
15 Th	0329 7.1	1003 0.7	1542 7.1	2217 0.7
16 F	0403 6.9	1033 0.8	1620 7.0	2244 0.8
17 Sa	0441 6.7	1101 0.9	1704 6.8	2313 1.0
18 Su	0522 6.4	1137 1.0	1753 6.4	2354 1.3
19 M	0611 6.0	1225 1.2	1853 6.1 (	
20 Tu	0049 1.5	0719 5.8	1334 1.4	2011 6.0
21 W	0212 1.7	0842 5.9	1515 1.2	2135 6.3
22 Th	0348 1.4	1006 6.2	1640 0.8	2252 6.7
23 F	0502 1.1	1116 6.7	1801 0.4	2354 7.1
24 Sa	0621 0.6	1215 7.1	1909 0.2	
25 Su	0048 7.3	0724 0.6	1304 7.2	1959 0.2 ●
26 M	0134 7.3	0815 0.5	1349 7.3	2043 0.3
27 Tu	0216 7.3	0857 0.5	1432 7.4	2121 0.4
28 W	0256 7.2	0935 0.5	1512 7.4	2153 0.5
29 Th	0334 7.1	1007 0.5	1555 7.3	2221 0.7
30 F	0412 6.9	1037 0.7	1635 7.0	2249 0.9
31 Sa	0448 6.6	1106 0.9	1718 6.7	2320 1.1

NOVEMBER

Day	Time m	Time m	Time m	Time m
1 Su	0526 6.3	1137 1.1	1803 6.3	2357 1.4
2 M	0608 6.0	1215 1.3	1855 6.0)	
3 Tu	0042 1.6	0702 5.7	1304 1.5	1958 5.7
4 W	0138 1.9	0812 5.5	1413 1.7	2110 5.7
5 Th	0310 1.9	0931 5.6	1610 1.5	2223 5.9
6 F	0433 1.6	1044 5.9	1711 1.1	2322 6.2
7 Sa	0529 1.2	1137 6.3	1801 0.9	
8 Su	0007 6.5	0618 1.0	1219 6.5	1846 0.7
9 M	0045 6.7	0703 0.8	1256 6.7	1928 0.6
10 Tu	0120 6.9	0748 0.7	1331 6.9	2011 0.6 ○
11 W	0155 7.0	0830 0.6	1409 7.0	2051 0.6
12 Th	0232 7.1	0911 0.6	1447 7.2	2129 0.6
13 F	0310 7.1	0950 0.5	1528 7.2	2206 0.7
14 Sa	0349 7.0	1028 0.6	1612 7.2	2238 0.8
15 Su	0430 6.8	1104 0.8	1658 7.0	2312 1.1
16 M	0515 6.6	1143 0.9	1749 6.7	2351 1.3
17 Tu	0605 6.3	1231 1.1	1848 6.4 (	
18 W	0045 1.5	0706 6.1	1335 1.1	1957 6.3
19 Th	0158 1.6	0819 6.1	1457 1.0	2111 6.4
20 F	0319 1.4	0935 6.3	1612 0.7	2224 6.7
21 Sa	0433 1.1	1049 6.6	1727 0.6	2330 6.9
22 Su	0549 1.0	1151 6.8	1838 0.5	
23 M	0027 7.0	0635 0.8	1245 6.9	1933 0.5
24 Tu	0114 7.0	0752 0.7	1333 7.0	2016 0.6 ●
25 W	0158 7.0	0837 0.6	1416 7.1	2054 0.7
26 Th	0237 7.0	0915 0.6	1458 7.1	2128 0.7
27 F	0315 7.0	0950 0.6	1538 7.2	2159 0.8
28 Sa	0352 6.9	1021 0.7	1619 7.0	2230 0.9
29 Su	0427 6.7	1051 0.9	1658 6.8	2302 1.1
30 M	0504 6.5	1122 1.0	1739 6.5	2336 1.3

DECEMBER

Day	Time m	Time m	Time m	Time m
1 Tu	0542 6.2	1156 1.2	1822 6.2	
2 W	0015 1.5	0625 6.0	1238 1.3	1914 5.9)
3 Th	0100 1.6	0720 5.7	1327 1.4	2013 5.8
4 F	0155 1.8	0827 5.6	1429 1.5	2117 5.8
5 Sa	0307 1.8	0935 5.7	1553 1.4	2219 5.9
6 Su	0427 1.6	1035 5.9	1702 1.2	2313 6.2
7 M	0527 1.3	1129 6.2	1757 0.9	
8 Tu	0003 6.4	0622 1.0	1218 6.4	1849 0.8
9 W	0045 6.7	0716 0.8	1306 6.7	1941 0.6 ○
10 Th	0133 6.9	0808 0.6	1351 6.9	2030 0.6
11 F	0215 7.0	0858 0.5	1436 7.2	2117 0.5
12 Sa	0258 7.1	0945 0.4	1524 7.4	2200 0.6
13 Su	0341 7.2	1030 0.3	1606 7.4	2241 0.8
14 M	0423 7.1	1113 0.5	1652 7.2	2319 1.0
15 Tu	0508 6.9	1154 0.6	1742 7.0	2357 1.2
16 W	0556 6.7	1236 0.8	1835 6.7 (	
17 Th	0041 1.4	0649 6.5	1326 0.9	1934 6.5
18 F	0135 1.4	0751 6.4	1427 0.9	2042 6.4
19 Sa	0244 1.4	0903 6.4	1536 0.9	2153 6.5
20 Su	0359 1.3	1019 6.5	1647 0.8	2302 6.6
21 M	0515 1.1	1129 6.5	1801 0.8	
22 Tu	0004 6.7	0625 1.0	1229 6.6	1904 0.8
23 W	0057 6.7	0734 0.8	1320 6.7	1952 0.8
24 Th	0142 6.7	0820 0.7	1405 6.7	2033 0.9 ●
25 F	0223 6.8	0903 0.6	1446 7.0	2110 0.8
26 Sa	0300 6.9	0939 0.7	1524 7.1	2143 0.8
27 Su	0335 6.9	1012 0.7	1602 7.0	2216 0.9
28 M	0407 6.8	1040 0.8	1637 6.9	2245 1.0
29 Tu	0441 6.7	1108 0.9	1712 6.7	2316 1.1
30 W	0508 6.5	1150 1.0	1750 6.4	2350 1.2
31 Th	0553 6.3	1211 1.0	1829 6.2	

Dates when predicted H.W. height at London Bridge is 7.2 m. or more.

Jan. 20-25	Apr. 5-7, 15-20	July 2-5, 30-31	Oct. 25-29
Feb. 18-23	May 5-6	Aug. 1-3, 28-31	Nov. 12-14, 27
Mar. 17-23	June 3-5	Sept. 1, 26-30	Dec. 11-14

LONDON BRIDGE
MEAN SPRING AND NEAP CURVES
Springs occur 3 days after New and Full Moon.

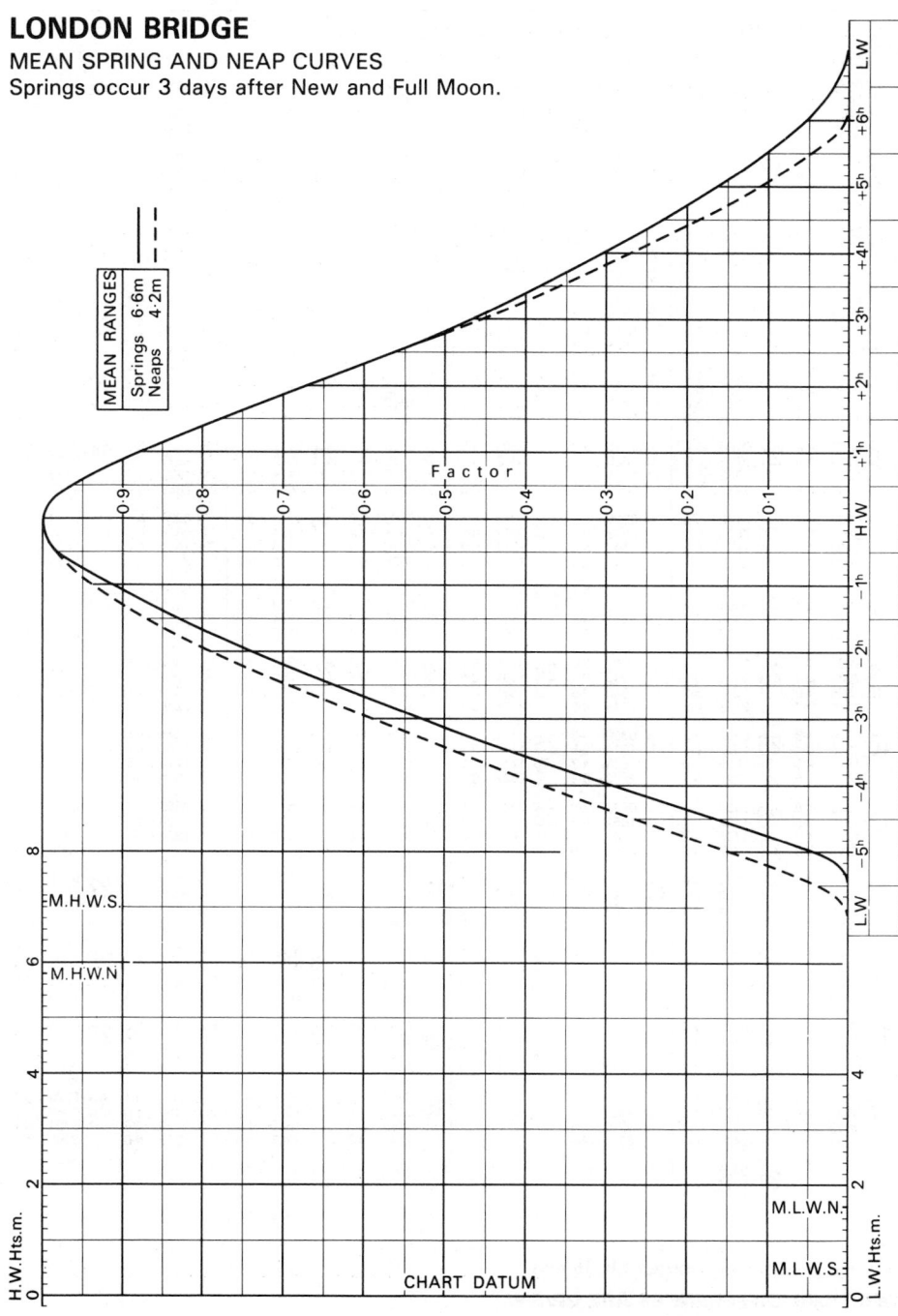

BURNHAM-ON-CROUCH

HIGH & LOW WATER 1992   Lat. 51°37'N. Long. 0°48'E.

GMT   ADD 1 HOUR MARCH 29 — OCTOBER 25 FOR B.S.T.

JANUARY

Date	Time m	Time m	Time m	Time m
1 W	0342 1.1	0933 4.5	1622 0.8	2213 4.5
2 Th	0453 0.9	1039 4.6	1716 0.8	2308 4.7
3 F	0548 0.8	1133 4.7	1802 0.8	2354 4.8
4 Sa ●	0631 0.6	1219 4.8	1838 0.8	
5 Su	0033 4.8	0706 0.6	1257 4.8	1910 0.8
6 M	0107 4.9	0739 0.5	1332 4.9	1939 0.8
7 Tu	0137 4.9	0809 0.5	1402 4.9	2009 0.7
8 W	0207 4.9	0838 0.4	1434 4.9	2039 0.7
9 Th	0238 4.9	0908 0.4	1504 4.9	2110 0.7
10 F	0308 4.9	0938 0.4	1536 4.8	2141 0.8
11 Sa	0340 4.9	1012 0.5	1610 4.7	2215 0.9
12 Su	0416 4.8	1048 0.6	1650 4.6	2255 1.0
13 M ☽	0459 4.7	1132 0.7	1738 4.5	2348 1.1
14 Tu	0552 4.5	1234 0.8	1838 4.3	
15 W	0059 1.1	0659 4.4	1352 0.9	1951 4.3
16 Th	0223 1.1	0818 4.4	1517 0.8	2111 4.4
17 F	0349 0.9	0939 4.6	1632 0.7	2221 4.6
18 Sa	0501 0.7	1050 4.8	1731 0.6	2322 4.8
19 Su ○	0600 0.4	1151 5.1	1821 0.5	
20 M	0016 5.0	0651 0.2	1244 5.3	1905 0.5
21 Tu	0104 5.2	0737 0.0	1332 5.4	1947 0.4
22 W	0148 5.3	0820 -0.1	1416 5.5	2027 0.4
23 Th	0229 5.4	0901 -0.2	1458 5.4	2104 0.5
24 F	0310 5.4	0941 -0.1	1540 5.2	2142 0.5
25 Sa	0350 5.3	1022 0.1	1622 5.0	2222 0.7
26 Su ☾	0434 5.1	1104 0.3	1705 4.7	2307 0.8
27 M	0521 4.8	1155 0.6	1755 4.4	
28 Tu	0003 1.0	0618 4.5	1303 0.9	1902 4.2
29 W	0128 1.2	0736 4.2	1433 1.1	2026 4.1
30 Th	0316 1.1	0907 4.2	1554 1.1	2147 4.2
31 F	0438 0.9	1023 4.3	1657 1.0	2248 4.4

FEBRUARY

Date	Time m	Time m	Time m	Time m
1 Sa	0535 0.7	1119 4.5	1745 0.9	2336 4.6
2 Su	0619 0.6	1202 4.7	1821 0.8	
3 M ●	0015 4.7	0653 0.5	1239 4.8	1851 0.7
4 Tu	0047 4.8	0723 0.4	1311 4.9	1921 0.6
5 W	0118 5.0	0754 0.4	1341 5.0	1950 0.5
6 Th	0148 5.0	0820 0.2	1411 5.0	2020 0.5
7 F	0218 5.1	0848 0.2	1441 5.0	2049 0.5
8 Sa	0247 5.1	0917 0.3	1511 5.0	2119 0.6
9 Su	0317 5.0	0945 0.4	1543 4.9	2148 0.6
10 M	0350 4.9	1014 0.5	1618 4.7	2222 0.8
11 Tu ☽	0428 4.8	1051 0.6	1701 4.5	2307 0.9
12 W	0517 4.6	1144 0.8	1755 4.3	
13 Th	0013 1.0	0622 4.4	1304 1.0	1907 4.2
14 F	0143 1.0	0746 4.3	1441 1.0	2037 4.2
15 Sa	0322 0.9	0904 4.4	1610 0.8	2201 4.4
16 Su	0447 0.6	1038 4.8	1715 0.7	2306 4.7
17 M	0550 0.3	1138 5.1	1807 0.5	
18 Tu ○	0000 5.0	0640 0.0	1230 5.3	1850 0.4
19 W	0047 5.2	0724 -0.2	1317 5.4	1930 0.3
20 Th	0129 5.4	0804 -0.3	1358 5.4	2009 0.3
21 F	0209 5.5	0842 -0.2	1438 5.3	2046 0.3
22 Sa	0248 5.5	0919 -0.1	1514 5.2	2122 0.4
23 Su	0327 5.3	0954 0.1	1553 4.9	2157 0.5
24 M	0408 5.1	1031 0.5	1631 4.6	2238 0.7
25 Tu ☾	0451 4.8	1114 0.8	1715 4.3	2327 0.9
26 W	0544 4.4	1210 1.1	1811 4.0	
27 Th	0042 1.1	0659 4.0	1343 1.3	1938 3.8
28 F	0243 1.1	0840 4.0	1520 1.3	2113 4.0
29 Sa	0412 0.9	0958 4.2	1629 1.1	2219 4.2

MARCH

Date	Time m	Time m	Time m	Time m
1 Su	0512 0.7	1054 4.4	1720 0.9	2307 4.5
2 M	0555 0.5	1137 4.7	1757 0.8	2347 4.7
3 Tu	0628 0.4	1213 4.8	1828 0.6	
4 W ●	0022 4.9	0657 0.3	1244 5.0	1858 0.5
5 Th	0053 5.0	0726 0.2	1317 5.1	1929 0.4
6 F	0125 5.1	0755 0.1	1346 5.1	1959 0.3
7 Sa	0155 5.2	0824 0.2	1416 5.1	2028 0.4
8 Su	0225 5.2	0853 0.2	1445 5.0	2058 0.4
9 M	0257 5.1	0919 0.3	1517 4.9	2127 0.5
10 Tu	0328 5.0	0947 0.5	1552 4.8	2200 0.6
11 W	0408 4.8	1022 0.7	1632 4.5	2244 0.7
12 Th ☽	0457 4.6	1115 0.9	1725 4.3	2349 0.9
13 F	0602 4.4	1235 1.1	1839 4.1	
14 Sa	0120 0.9	0729 4.3	1417 1.1	2012 4.1
15 Su	0307 0.7	0906 4.4	1550 0.9	2140 4.3
16 M	0432 0.4	1023 4.8	1657 0.7	2246 4.7
17 Tu	0534 0.2	1122 5.1	1748 0.5	2340 5.0
18 W ○	0623 0.0	1212 5.3	1831 0.4	
19 Th	0026 5.2	0705 -0.2	1255 5.3	1911 0.3
20 F	0108 5.4	0743 -0.2	1335 5.3	1950 0.2
21 Sa	0148 5.5	0820 -0.1	1414 5.2	2027 0.2
22 Su	0227 5.4	0854 -0.1	1450 5.1	2102 0.3
23 M	0304 5.3	0928 0.1	1524 4.9	2137 0.5
24 Tu	0343 5.0	1000 0.5	1559 4.6	2213 0.7
25 W	0425 4.6	1038 0.9	1639 4.3	2257 0.9
26 Th ☾	0514 4.3	1127 1.2	1727 4.0	
27 F	0001 1.1	0621 4.0	1242 1.4	1839 3.8
28 Sa	0149 1.1	0757 3.9	1429 1.4	2020 3.8
29 Su	0325 0.9	0920 4.1	1547 1.2	2135 4.1
30 M	0428 0.7	1017 4.4	1640 1.0	2227 4.4
31 Tu	0515 0.5	1101 4.6	1723 0.8	2310 4.6

APRIL

Date	Time m	Time m	Time m	Time m
1 W	0553 0.4	1138 4.8	1757 0.6	2347 4.9
2 Th	0626 0.3	1213 5.0	1831 0.5	
3 F ●	0023 5.0	0657 0.2	1247 5.1	1904 0.4
4 Sa	0057 5.1	0729 0.2	1319 5.2	1937 0.3
5 Su	0132 5.2	0759 0.2	1352 5.1	2008 0.3
6 M	0204 5.2	0829 0.3	1423 5.1	2039 0.4
7 Tu	0238 5.1	0858 0.4	1457 4.9	2112 0.4
8 W	0314 5.0	0929 0.6	1532 4.8	2150 0.5
9 Th	0357 4.8	1009 0.7	1615 4.5	2238 0.6
10 F ☽	0448 4.6	1104 0.9	1710 4.3	2344 0.7
11 Sa	0555 4.4	1220 1.1	1824 4.1	
12 Su	0111 0.7	0721 4.4	1353 1.1	1953 4.2
13 M	0250 0.5	0850 4.5	1524 0.9	2115 4.4
14 Tu	0412 0.3	1002 4.8	1632 0.8	2221 4.7
15 W	0512 0.1	1100 5.0	1726 0.6	2315 5.0
16 Th	0600 0.0	1150 5.1	1810 0.5	
17 F ○	0002 5.2	0642 0.0	1234 5.2	1851 0.3
18 Sa	0047 5.3	0721 0.0	1314 5.2	1931 0.3
19 Su	0128 5.3	0758 0.1	1352 5.1	2011 0.3
20 M	0207 5.3	0832 0.3	1425 5.0	2046 0.4
21 Tu	0245 5.1	0903 0.6	1458 4.8	2120 0.5
22 W	0323 4.8	0935 0.8	1532 4.6	2154 0.6
23 Th	0402 4.6	1007 1.0	1608 4.4	2235 0.8
24 F ☾	0447 4.3	1051 1.2	1651 4.2	2327 0.9
25 Sa	0541 4.1	1152 1.3	1748 4.0	
26 Su	0041 1.0	0654 3.9	1314 1.4	1906 3.9
27 M	0215 0.9	0819 4.0	1440 1.2	2030 4.0
28 Tu	0328 0.7	0924 4.3	1543 1.0	2135 4.3
29 W	0424 0.6	1013 4.6	1638 0.8	2224 4.6
30 Th	0509 0.4	1059 4.8	1721 0.7	2308 4.8

To find H.W. Dover subtract 1 h. 15 min.

NO TIDAL DIFFERENCES ARE GIVEN.

TIDAL STREAMS PAGES 21:50-21:56.

Datum of predictions: 2.35 m. below Ordnance Datum (Newlyn) or approx. L.A.T.

BURNHAM-ON-CROUCH 21:63

Lat. 51°37'N. Long. 0°48'E. HIGH & LOW WATER 1992

GMT ADD 1 HOUR MARCH 29 — OCTOBER 25 FOR B.S.T.

MAY

Day	Time	m	Time	m	Time	m	Time	m
1 F	0550	0·3	1138	5·0	1802	0·5	2350	5·0
2 Sa	0627	0·3	1216	5·1	1838	0·4	●	
3 Su	0030	5·1	0701	0·3	1253	5·1	1914	0·4
4 M	0108	5·2	0736	0·3	1331	5·1	1951	0·3
5 Tu	0146	5·2	0809	0·4	1405	5·1	2027	0·3
6 W	0225	5·1	0843	0·5	1442	4·9	2106	0·3
7 Th	0307	5·1	0920	0·6	1521	4·8	2148	0·3
8 F	0353	4·9	1004	0·8	1609	4·6	2240	0·4
9 Sa	0447	4·7	1058	0·9	1704	4·5	2342	0·5 ☽
10 Su	0551	4·6	1205	1·0	1811	4·4		
11 M	0100	0·5	0704	4·5	1325	1·1	1926	4·4
12 Tu	0226	0·4	0823	4·6	1449	1·0	2044	4·5
13 W	0343	0·3	0935	4·7	1602	0·9	2151	4·7
14 Th	0446	0·2	1035	4·9	1702	0·7	2250	4·9
15 F	0537	0·2	1126	5·0	1752	0·5	2343	5·0
16 Sa	0620	0·3	1213	5·0	1837	0·4	○	
17 Su	0029	5·1	0700	0·3	1254	5·0	1918	0·4
18 M	0112	5·1	0737	0·4	1332	5·0	1958	0·3
19 Tu	0152	5·0	0811	0·6	1405	4·9	2033	0·4
20 W	0229	4·9	0842	0·7	1438	4·8	2107	0·5
21 Th	0305	4·8	0913	0·9	1511	4·7	2140	0·6
22 F	0343	4·6	0945	1·0	1543	4·5	2215	0·6
23 Sa	0421	4·5	1023	1·1	1623	4·4	2257	0·7
24 Su	0504	4·3	1111	1·2	1708	4·3	2351	0·8
25 M	0555	4·2	1210	1·2	1804	4·2		
26 Tu	0057	0·8	0700	4·2	1323	1·2	1913	4·1
27 W	0214	0·7	0812	4·3	1438	1·1	2026	4·3
28 Th	0324	0·6	0917	4·5	1543	0·9	2131	4·5
29 F	0422	0·5	1012	4·7	1640	0·7	2227	4·7
30 Sa	0512	0·5	1101	4·9	1730	0·6	2318	4·9
31 Su	0556	0·5	1147	5·0	1814	0·5		

JUNE

Day	Time	m	Time	m	Time	m	Time	m
1 M	0004	5·0	0637	0·4	1230	5·1	1857	0·4 ●
2 Tu	0050	5·1	0716	0·5	1311	5·1	1939	0·3
3 W	0134	5·2	0753	0·5	1352	5·1	2020	0·2
4 Th	0218	5·2	0833	0·5	1434	5·0	2103	0·1
5 F	0303	5·2	0914	0·6	1517	5·0	2148	0·1
6 Sa	0350	5·1	0957	0·7	1603	4·9	2238	0·2
7 Su	0441	5·0	1047	0·8	1655	4·8	2332	0·2
8 M	0537	4·8	1144	0·9	1752	4·7		
9 Tu	0038	0·3	0639	4·7	1252	1·0	1856	4·6
10 W	0153	0·4	0751	4·6	1412	1·0	2010	4·6
11 Th	0311	0·4	0903	4·6	1532	0·9	2124	4·6
12 F	0420	0·5	1009	4·7	1642	0·8	2230	4·7
13 Sa	0515	0·5	1106	4·8	1738	0·6	2326	4·8
14 Su	0602	0·6	1154	4·9	1827	0·5		
15 M	0016	4·9	0639	0·6	1237	4·9	1910	0·4 ○
16 Tu	0100	4·9	0718	0·7	1315	4·9	1947	0·4
17 W	0138	4·9	0751	0·7	1349	4·9	2021	0·4
18 Th	0215	4·9	0823	0·8	1421	4·8	2053	0·4
19 F	0248	4·8	0853	0·8	1451	4·8	2123	0·4
20 Sa	0320	4·8	0925	0·8	1523	4·8	2154	0·5
21 Su	0354	4·7	0959	0·9	1557	4·7	2229	0·5
22 M	0429	4·6	1036	1·0	1635	4·6	2311	0·6
23 Tu	0512	4·5	1123	1·0	1719	4·5 ☽		
24 W	0002	0·7	0601	4·4	1219	1·1	1814	4·4
25 Th	0104	0·7	0702	4·3	1329	1·1	1919	4·3
26 F	0218	0·8	0812	4·4	1445	1·1	2033	4·4
27 Sa	0331	0·7	0923	4·5	1558	0·9	2146	4·5
28 Su	0435	0·7	1024	4·7	1701	0·7	2248	4·7
29 M	0528	0·6	1119	4·9	1755	0·6	2344	5·0
30 Tu	0617	0·6	1210	5·0	1844	0·4 ●		

JULY

Day	Time	m	Time	m	Time	m	Time	m
1 W	0036	5·1	0700	0·5	1257	5·1	1929	0·2
2 Th	0124	5·3	0742	0·5	1341	5·2	2012	0·0
3 F	0209	5·4	0823	0·5	1424	5·2	2057	-0·1
4 Sa	0255	5·4	0903	0·5	1508	5·2	2140	-0·1
5 Su	0340	5·3	0945	0·6	1552	5·2	2225	0·0
6 M	0425	5·1	1028	0·7	1636	5·1	2312	0·1
7 Tu	0514	4·9	1118	0·8	1727	4·9 ☽		
8 W	0008	0·3	0608	4·7	1215	1·0	1825	4·7
9 Th	0117	0·5	0713	4·6	1336	1·0	1938	4·5
10 F	0237	0·5	0830	4·4	1508	1·0	2059	4·5
11 Sa	0353	0·8	0944	4·5	1628	0·9	2213	4·6
12 Su	0457	0·8	1046	4·6	1731	0·7	2316	4·7
13 M	0548	0·8	1138	4·8	1820	0·6		
14 Th	0005	4·8	0627	0·8	1242	4·8	1900	0·5 ○
15 W	0047	4·9	0703	0·8	1258	4·9	1934	0·4
16 Th	0124	4·9	0733	0·7	1331	4·9	2004	0·4
17 F	0156	4·9	0802	0·7	1402	5·0	2033	0·3
18 Sa	0225	5·0	0833	0·7	1431	5·0	2102	0·3
19 Su	0257	5·2	0903	0·7	1500	5·0	2131	0·4
20 M	0327	4·9	0933	0·7	1530	4·9	2201	0·4
21 Tu	0358	4·8	1005	0·8	1603	4·8	2235	0·5
22 W	0434	4·7	1041	0·9	1642	4·7	2314	0·7
23 Th	0517	4·5	1128	1·0	1728	4·5		
24 F	0006	0·8	0609	4·4	1231	1·1	1829	4·4
25 Sa	0118	0·9	0717	4·3	1351	1·1	1945	4·3
26 Su	0243	0·9	0837	4·4	1517	1·0	2109	4·4
27 M	0402	0·8	0953	4·6	1636	0·8	2226	4·7
28 Tu	0506	0·7	1057	4·7	1738	0·5	2328	5·0
29 W	0600	0·6	1153	5·0	1831	0·3		
30 Th	0022	5·2	0647	0·5	1241	5·2	1918	0·1
31 F	0111	5·4	0727	0·5	1326	5·3	2001	-0·1

AUGUST

Day	Time	m	Time	m	Time	m	Time	m
1 Sa	0156	5·5	0808	0·4	1409	5·4	2043	-0·2
2 Su	0239	5·5	0848	0·4	1451	5·5	2123	-0·1
3 M	0320	5·4	0927	0·5	1532	5·4	2204	0·0
4 Tu	0402	5·2	1006	0·6	1614	5·3	2245	0·2
5 W	0445	4·9	1051	0·8	1701	5·0	2334	0·5
6 Th	0534	4·6	1144	1·0	1754	4·7		
7 F	0037	0·8	0633	4·4	1300	1·1	1907	4·4
8 Sa	0201	1·0	0754	4·2	1446	1·1	2038	4·3
9 Su	0328	1·1	0918	4·3	1614	0·9	2158	4·4
10 M	0438	1·0	1026	4·5	1718	0·7	2301	4·6
11 Tu	0530	0·9	1119	4·7	1806	0·6	2348	4·8
12 W	0609	0·9	1200	4·8	1842	0·5		
13 Th	0027	4·9	0641	0·8	1236	5·0	1911	0·4 ○
14 F	0101	5·0	0710	0·7	1308	5·1	1940	0·3
15 Sa	0132	5·1	0739	0·6	1337	5·1	2009	0·3
16 Su	0201	5·1	0811	0·5	1407	5·2	2037	0·3
17 M	0229	5·1	0839	0·6	1436	5·2	2106	0·3
18 Tu	0258	5·1	0908	0·6	1505	5·1	2132	0·5
19 W	0328	5·0	0937	0·7	1536	5·0	2200	0·6
20 Th	0400	4·8	1007	0·9	1611	4·8	2232	0·7
21 F	0439	4·7	1047	1·0	1655	4·7 ☽	2318	0·9
22 Sa	0528	4·5	1147	1·1	1753	4·4		
23 Su	0030	1·1	0633	4·3	1308	1·1	1911	4·3
24 M	0203	1·1	0758	4·3	1446	1·0	2044	4·4
25 Tu	0335	1·0	0925	4·5	1616	0·7	2208	4·7
26 W	0447	0·7	1036	4·7	1723	0·4	2312	5·1
27 Th	0541	0·7	1132	5·0	1816	0·2		
28 F	0004	5·3	0628	0·5	1222	5·3	1901	0·0 ●
29 Sa	0053	5·4	0710	0·4	1308	5·4	1943	-0·1
30 Su	0135	5·6	0750	0·4	1349	5·6	2023	-0·2
31 M	0218	5·5	0828	0·4	1429	5·6	2101	0·0

21:64 BURNHAM-ON-CROUCH

HIGH & LOW WATER 1992 Lat. 51°37'N. Long. 0°48'E.

GMT ADD 1 HOUR MARCH 29 — OCTOBER 25 FOR B.S.T.

SEPTEMBER

Day	Time	m		Time	m
1 Tu	0257	5.4	16 W	0231	5.2
	0906	0.5		0843	0.6
	1510	5.5		1441	5.2
	2138	0.2		2104	0.5
2 W	0336	5.1	17 Th	0300	5.0
	0944	0.6		0912	0.7
	1550	5.3		1512	5.1
	2215	0.5		2131	0.7
3 Th	0415	4.9	18 F	0332	4.9
	1025	0.8		0942	0.8
	1634	5.0		1547	4.9
) 2258		0.8		2201	0.9
4 F	0459	4.6	19 Sa	0409	4.7
	1115	1.0		1022	0.9
	1727	4.6		1632	4.7
	2354	1.1	(2245		1.0
5 Sa	0554	4.3	20 Su	0458	4.5
	1227	1.1		1118	1.0
	1838	4.3		1731	4.5
				2358	1.2
6 Su	0117	1.3	21 M	0604	4.3
	0711	4.1		1242	1.1
	1418	1.2		1850	4.4
	2011	4.2			
7 M	0254	1.3	22 Tu	0132	1.3
	0845	4.2		0729	4.2
	1549	1.0		1425	0.9
	2135	4.4		2025	4.5
8 Tu	0409	1.2	23 W	0308	1.1
	0955	4.4		0900	4.4
	1655	0.7		1557	0.6
	2235	4.6		2148	4.8
9 W	0502	1.0	24 Th	0422	0.9
	1049	4.7		1012	0.4
	1738	0.6		1703	0.4
	2321	4.8		2250	5.1
10 Th	0541	0.9	25 F	0520	0.7
	1130	4.9		1108	0.1
	1814	0.5		1756	0.1
	2358	5.0		2344	5.4
11 F	0614	0.8	26 Sa	0606	0.6
	1208	5.0		1158	5.4
	1844	0.4		1841	0.0
12 Sa	0032	5.1	27 Su	0032	5.5
	0645	0.6		0648	0.5
	1239	5.2		1244	5.5
O 1911		0.3		1921	0.0
13 Su	0102	5.2	28 M	0114	5.5
	0714	0.5		0729	0.4
	1311	5.3		1326	5.6
	1940	0.3		2000	0.0
14 M	0132	5.2	29 Tu	0155	5.4
	0745	0.5		0809	0.4
	1341	5.3		1407	5.6
	2011	0.3		2037	0.2
15 Tu	0202	5.2	30 W	0232	5.3
	0815	0.5		0846	0.5
	1411	5.3		1448	5.5
	2037	0.4		2112	0.5

OCTOBER

Day	Time	m		Time	m
1 Th	0310	5.1	16 F	0236	5.1
	0923	0.6		0854	0.6
	1528	5.2		1454	5.1
	2147	0.8		2108	0.8
2 F	0346	4.8	17 Sa	0310	4.9
	1003	0.8		0928	0.7
	1611	4.9		1533	4.9
	2225	1.1		2144	0.9
3 Sa	0426	4.5	18 Su	0349	4.7
	1048	1.0		1012	0.8
	1701	4.5		1621	4.8
) 2312		1.3		2231	1.1
4 Su	0515	4.3	19 M	0439	4.5
	1151	1.1		1110	0.9
	1804	4.2		1721	4.6
			(2339		1.3
5 M	0022	1.5	20 Tu	0545	4.3
	0622	4.1		1230	0.9
	1329	1.2		1838	4.5
	1931	4.1			
6 Tu	0200	1.5	21 W	0104	1.3
	0754	4.1		0706	4.3
	1504	1.0		1403	0.8
	2055	4.3		2004	4.6
7 W	0322	1.3	22 Th	0237	1.2
	0913	4.3		0830	4.5
	1609	0.8		1531	0.6
	2157	4.5		2124	4.8
8 Th	0421	1.1	23 F	0353	1.0
	1008	4.6		0944	4.8
	1658	0.6		1638	0.3
	2243	4.8		2227	5.1
9 F	0505	0.9	24 Sa	0454	0.8
	1053	4.8		1042	0.5
	1737	0.5		1731	0.2
	2323	5.0		2321	5.3
10 Sa	0541	0.8	25 Su	0545	0.6
	1130	5.0		1136	5.3
	1810	0.4		1817	0.1
	2358	5.1	●		
11 Su	0616	0.6	26 M	0009	5.4
	1208	5.2		0630	0.5
	1841	0.4		1222	5.5
				1858	0.2
12 M	0032	5.2	27 Tu	0051	5.4
	0648	0.6		0711	0.4
	1241	5.3		1307	5.5
	1911	0.4		1937	0.3
13 Tu	0102	5.3	28 W	0132	5.3
	0721	0.5		0752	0.4
	1315	5.3		1348	5.5
	1942	0.4		2014	0.4
14 W	0134	5.3	29 Th	0209	5.2
	0752	0.5		0830	0.5
	1346	5.3		1429	5.3
	2011	0.5		2048	0.7
15 Th	0205	5.2	30 F	0245	5.0
	0823	0.6		0908	0.6
	1421	5.2		1510	5.1
	2039	0.6		2120	0.9
			31 Sa	0320	4.8
				0945	0.7
				1550	4.8
				2154	1.1

NOVEMBER

Day	Time	m		Time	m
1 Su	0358	4.6	16 M	0340	4.8
	1025	0.9		1010	0.6
	1634	4.5		1616	4.9
	2236	1.3		2223	1.0
2 M	0441	4.4	17 Tu	0429	4.7
	1115	1.0		1107	0.6
	1725	4.3		1714	4.7
) 2331		1.4	(2323		1.2
3 Tu	0534	4.2	18 W	0530	4.5
	1222	1.1		1215	0.7
	1832	4.2		1821	4.6
4 W	0044	1.5	19 Th	0035	1.2
	0645	4.1		0640	4.5
	1351	1.0		1337	0.6
	1954	4.2		1938	4.6
5 Th	0212	1.4	20 F	0158	1.2
	0807	4.2		0758	4.6
	1508	0.9		1500	0.5
	2103	4.4		2055	4.7
6 F	0324	1.2	21 Sa	0320	1.0
	0914	4.4		0913	4.8
	1605	0.7		1610	0.4
	2157	4.6		2201	4.9
7 Sa	0420	1.0	22 Su	0428	0.9
	1006	4.7		1017	5.0
	1653	0.6		1708	0.4
	2241	4.9		2259	5.1
8 Su	0505	0.8	23 M	0524	0.7
	1050	4.9		1115	5.1
	1733	0.5		1757	0.4
	2321	5.0		2348	5.1
9 M	0545	0.7	24 Tu	0614	0.6
	1132	5.0		1206	5.2
	1810	0.5		1840	0.4
	2358	5.2	●		
10 Tu	0621	0.6	25 W	0033	5.2
	1212	5.2		0658	0.5
	1844	0.5		1251	5.3
O				1917	0.5
11 W	0036	5.2	26 Th	0114	5.2
	0657	0.6		0739	0.4
	1250	5.2		1334	5.2
	1916	0.5		1953	0.6
12 Th	0111	5.2	27 F	0151	5.1
	0733	0.5		0818	0.5
	1328	5.2		1414	5.1
	1949	0.6		2027	0.8
13 F	0145	5.2	28 Sa	0225	5.0
	0808	0.5		0853	0.5
	1404	5.2		1452	5.0
	2020	0.7		2058	0.9
14 Sa	0221	5.1	29 Su	0258	4.9
	0845	0.5		0928	0.6
	1444	5.1		1529	4.8
	2055	0.8		2131	1.0
15 Su	0258	5.0	30 M	0333	4.7
	0923	0.5		1003	0.7
	1527	5.0		1608	4.6
	2136	0.9		2206	1.1

DECEMBER

Day	Time	m		Time	m
1 Tu	0410	4.6	16 W	0422	4.9
	1041	0.8		1055	0.4
	1648	4.5		1701	4.9
	2249	1.2	(2304		1.0
2 W	0452	4.5	17 Th	0514	4.8
	1130	0.8		1155	0.4
	1735	4.3		1758	4.7
) 2342		1.3			
3 Th	0544	4.3	18 F	0005	1.1
	1231	0.9		0614	4.7
	1835	4.2		1304	0.5
				1904	4.6
4 F	0050	1.3	19 Sa	0120	1.1
	0646	4.3		0724	4.6
	1345	0.9		1426	0.6
	1945	4.2		2020	4.6
5 Sa	0207	1.3	20 Su	0246	1.1
	0800	4.3		0843	4.6
	1500	0.8		1543	0.6
	2055	4.4		2133	4.6
6 Su	0320	1.1	21 M	0407	0.9
	0909	4.4		0957	4.7
	1602	0.7		1648	0.6
	2151	4.6		2238	4.8
7 M	0421	1.0	22 Tu	0512	0.8
	1008	4.6		1100	4.9
	1654	0.7		1740	0.6
	2242	4.8		2332	4.9
8 Tu	0512	0.8	23 W	0606	0.6
	1059	4.8		1154	5.0
	1738	0.6		1824	0.6
	2328	5.0			
9 W	0556	0.7	24 Th	0019	5.0
	1146	5.0		0651	0.5
	1819	0.6		1241	5.0
O			● 1903		0.7
10 Th	0010	5.1	25 F	0058	5.0
	0638	0.6		0730	0.4
	1230	5.1		1322	5.1
	1856	0.6		1936	0.7
11 F	0051	5.1	26 Sa	0134	5.0
	0718	0.5		0806	0.4
	1312	5.2		1401	5.0
	1931	0.6		2008	0.7
12 Sa	0132	5.1	27 Su	0208	5.0
	0758	0.4		0838	0.4
	1355	5.2		1434	5.0
	2009	0.6		2038	0.8
13 Su	0211	5.1	28 M	0239	5.0
	0838	0.3		0910	0.4
	1438	5.2		1507	4.9
	2048	0.6		2110	0.8
14 M	0251	5.1	29 Tu	0311	4.9
	0920	0.3		0940	0.5
	1523	5.2		1540	4.8
	2128	0.7		2141	0.8
15 Tu	0334	5.0	30 W	0343	4.8
	1006	0.3		1012	0.5
	1609	5.0		1612	4.7
	2213	0.8		2215	0.9
			31 Th	0418	4.7
				1048	0.6
				1651	4.5
				2255	1.0

To find H.W. Dover subtract 1 h. 15 min.

NO TIDAL DIFFERENCES ARE GIVEN.

TIDAL STREAMS PAGES 21:50-21:56.

Datum of predictions: 2.35 m. below Ordnance Datum (Newlyn) or approx. L.A.T.

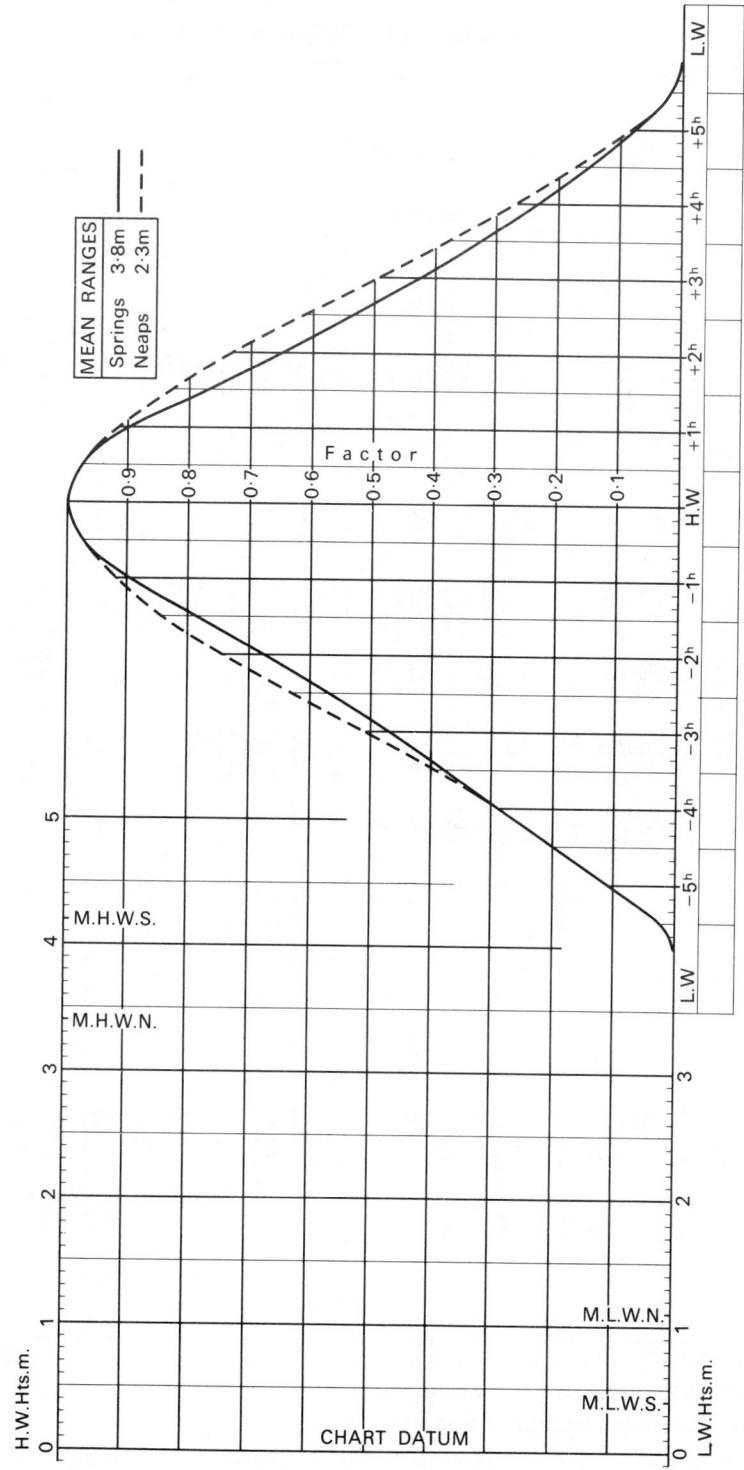

WALTON-ON-THE-NAZE
MEAN SPRING AND NEAP CURVES
Springs occur 2 days after New and Full Moon.

MEAN RANGES
Springs 3·8m
Neaps 2·3m

Factor

M.H.W.S.
M.H.W.N.

M.L.W.N.
M.L.W.S.

CHART DATUM

H.W.Hts.m.
LW.Hts.m.

WALTON-ON-THE-NAZE

HIGH & LOW WATER 1992   Lat. 51°51′N. Long. 1°16′E.

GMT   ADD 1 HOUR MARCH 29 — OCTOBER 25 FOR B.S.T.

JANUARY

Day	Time	m	Day	Time	m
1	0236	1·2	16	0124	1·2
	0851	3·6		0740	3·6
W	1512	0·9	Th	1413	0·9
	2129	3·7		2030	3·6
2	0341	1·0	17	0242	1·0
	0953	3·7		0857	3·7
Th	1603	0·9	F	1521	0·9
	2221	3·8		2136	3·7
3	0433	0·9	18	0348	0·8
	1045	3·8		1004	3·9
F	1647	0·9	Sa	1617	0·8
	2305	3·8		2234	3·9
4	0516	0·8	19	0445	0·6
	1129	3·9		1102	4·1
Sa	1723	0·9	Su	1706	0·7
●	2343	3·9	○	2326	4·0
5	0554	0·7	20	0537	0·4
	1207	3·9		1154	4·3
Su	1756	0·9	M	1751	0·6
6	0017	3·9	21	0014	4·2
	0628	0·7		0625	0·2
M	1242	3·9	Tu	1242	4·4
	1828	0·9		1836	0·6
7	0048	4·0	22	0059	4·3
	0700	0·6		0713	0·1
Tu	1314	3·9	W	1328	4·4
	1900	0·8		1920	0·6
8	0119	4·0	23	0142	4·3
	0733	0·6		0758	0·1
W	1347	4·0	Th	1413	4·3
	1934	0·8		2002	0·6
9	0151	4·0	24	0225	4·3
	0806	0·6		0843	0·1
Th	1419	3·9	F	1457	4·2
	2008	0·8		2044	0·7
10	0223	4·0	25	0308	4·3
	0840	0·6		0928	0·3
F	1453	3·9	Sa	1542	4·0
	2043	0·9		2128	0·8
11	0257	3·9	26	0355	4·1
	0917	0·7		1013	0·5
Sa	1529	3·8	Su	1628	3·8
	2121	1·0	(	2216	1·0
12	0336	3·9	27	0444	3·9
	0956	0·7		1105	0·8
Su	1612	3·7	M	1720	3·6
	2204	1·1		2313	1·1
13	0421	3·8	28	0543	3·6
	1042	0·8		1211	1·0
M	1702	3·6	Tu	1827	3·4
)	2258	1·2			
14	0516	3·6	29	0034	1·2
	1143	0·9		0700	3·4
Tu	1803	3·5	W	1333	1·1
				1948	3·3
15	0007	1·2	30	0212	1·2
	0624	3·6		0827	3·4
W	1256	1·0	Th	1447	1·2
	1914	3·5		2104	3·4
			31	0327	1·2
				0938	3·5
			F	1545	1·1
				2202	3·6

FEBRUARY

Day	Time	m	Day	Time	m
1	0421	0·9	16	0335	0·7
	1031	3·7		0952	3·8
Sa	1630	1·0	Su	1602	0·8
	2247	3·7		2219	3·8
2	0504	0·7	17	0435	0·5
	1113	3·8		1049	4·1
Su	1706	0·9	M	1652	0·7
	2325	3·8		2311	4·0
3	0539	0·7	18	0525	0·3
	1149	3·9		1140	4·3
M	1737	0·9	Tu	1736	0·6
●	2357	3·9	○	2357	4·2
4	0610	0·6	19	0611	0·1
	1221	4·0		1227	4·4
Tu	1808	0·8	W	1818	0·5
5	0028	4·0	20	0039	4·3
	0639	0·5		0655	0·0
W	1252	4·0	Th	1309	4·4
	1839	0·7		1900	0·5
6	0059	4·1	21	0121	4·4
	0712	0·4		0737	0·0
Th	1323	4·1	F	1351	4·3
	1913	0·6		1941	0·5
7	0130	4·1	22	0202	4·4
	0744	0·4		0818	0·1
F	1354	4·1	Sa	1430	4·2
	1945	0·6		2022	0·6
8	0201	4·1	23	0243	4·3
	0816	0·5		0858	0·4
Sa	1426	4·0	Su	1511	4·0
	2018	0·7		2101	0·7
9	0233	4·0	24	0327	4·1
	0847	0·6		0938	0·6
Su	1500	3·9	M	1552	3·7
	2051	0·8		2145	0·9
10	0308	4·0	25	0413	3·8
	0919	0·7		1023	0·9
M	1538	3·8	Tu	1638	3·5
	2128	0·9	(	2237	1·1
11	0349	3·9	26	0508	3·5
	0959	0·8		1120	1·2
Tu	1623	3·7	W	1736	3·3
)	2216	1·0		2351	1·2
12	0440	3·7	27	0624	3·3
	1054	0·9		1248	1·4
W	1720	3·5	Th	1902	3·1
	2323	1·1			
13	0547	3·6	28	0142	1·2
	1212	1·1		0801	3·2
Th	1832	3·4	F	1416	1·3
				2032	3·2
14	0048	1·1	29	0303	1·0
	0710	3·5		0915	3·4
F	1341	1·1	Sa	1519	1·2
	1958	3·4		2134	3·4
15	0218	1·0			
	0839	3·6			
Sa	1501	1·0			
	2117	3·6			

MARCH

Day	Time	m	Day	Time	m
1	0359	0·9	16	0321	0·6
	1007	3·6		0938	3·9
Su	1606	1·0	M	1545	0·9
	2220	3·6		2200	3·8
2	0440	0·7	17	0420	0·4
	1048	3·8		1034	4·1
M	1642	0·9	Tu	1633	0·7
	2258	3·8		2251	4·0
3	0513	0·6	18	0508	0·2
	1123	3·9		1122	4·2
Tu	1713	0·8	W	1716	0·6
	2332	3·9	○	2336	4·2
4	0543	0·5	19	0551	0·1
	1154	4·0		1205	4·3
W	1744	0·7	Th	1758	0·5
5	0003	4·1	20	0018	4·4
	0614	0·4		0632	0·1
Th	1227	4·1	F	1246	4·3
	1817	0·6		1839	0·4
6	0035	4·1	21	0059	4·4
	0645	0·4		0713	0·1
F	1257	4·1	Sa	1326	4·2
	1849	0·5		1920	0·4
7	0106	4·2	22	0140	4·4
	0717	0·4		0751	0·3
Sa	1328	4·1	Su	1404	4·1
	1921	0·6		1959	0·5
8	0138	4·2	23	0219	4·2
	0749	0·4		0829	0·5
Su	1359	4·1	M	1440	3·9
	1955	0·6		2039	0·7
9	0211	4·1	24	0301	4·0
	0819	0·5		0904	0·8
M	1433	4·0	Tu	1518	3·7
	2027	0·7		2118	0·8
10	0244	4·0	25	0345	3·8
	0850	0·7		0945	1·0
Tu	1510	3·8	W	1600	3·5
	2104	0·8		2206	1·0
11	0327	3·9	26	0437	3·5
	0928	0·8		1037	1·3
W	1553	3·7	Th	1651	3·3
	2152	0·9	(	2311	1·1
12	0419	3·7	27	0546	3·2
	1024	1·0		1151	1·4
Th	1649	3·5	F	1804	3·1
)	2259	1·0			
13	0527	3·5	28	0053	1·2
	1144	1·2		0720	3·1
F	1804	3·3	Sa	1330	1·4
				1942	3·1
14	0007	1·0	29	0220	1·0
	0653	3·4		0839	3·3
Sa	1319	1·2	Su	1440	1·3
	1935	3·3		2053	3·3
15	0204	0·9	30	0318	0·9
	0826	3·6		0932	3·5
Su	1443	1·0	M	1529	1·1
	2058	3·5		2142	3·5
			31	0402	0·9
				1014	3·7
			Tu	1609	0·9
				2223	3·7

APRIL

Day	Time	m	Day	Time	m
1	0438	0·6	16	0445	0·2
	1049	3·9		1101	4·1
W	1642	0·7	Th	1655	0·6
	2258	3·9		2313	4·2
2	0511	0·5	17	0527	0·2
	1123	4·0		1144	4·2
Th	1716	0·6	F	1737	0·5
	2333	4·1	○	2357	4·3
3	0543	0·4	18	0608	0·3
	1150	4·0		1224	4·2
F	1750	0·5	Sa	1819	0·5
●					
4	0007	4·2	19	0038	4·3
	0617	0·4		0648	0·5
Sa	1229	4·2	Su	1302	4·1
	1825	0·5		1902	0·5
5	0042	4·2	20	0119	4·2
	0649	0·4		0726	0·5
Su	1303	4·2	M	1338	4·0
	1859	0·5		1941	0·5
6	0116	4·2	21	0159	4·1
	0723	0·5		0801	0·7
M	1335	4·1	Tu	1413	3·9
	1934	0·5		2020	0·7
7	0151	4·1	22	0239	3·9
	0755	0·6		0836	0·9
Tu	1411	4·0	W	1449	3·7
	2011	0·6		2058	0·8
8	0229	4·0	23	0321	3·7
	0830	0·7		0912	1·1
W	1449	3·9	Th	1527	3·5
	2053	0·7		2142	0·9
9	0315	3·9	24	0409	3·5
	0914	0·8		1000	1·3
Th	1535	3·7	F	1613	3·4
	2145	0·7	(	2237	1·0
10	0410	3·7	25	0505	3·3
	1013	1·0		1102	1·4
F	1633	3·5	Sa	1712	3·2
	2254	0·8	)	2350	1·1
11	0520	3·6	26	0619	3·2
	1130	1·2		1221	1·4
Sa	1749	3·3	Su	1831	3·2
12	0018	0·8	27	0117	1·0
	0645	3·5		0741	3·3
Su	1257	1·2	M	1340	1·3
	1916	3·4		1952	3·3
13	0149	0·7	28	0223	0·9
	0811	3·7		0843	3·5
M	1419	1·1	Tu	1440	1·1
	2034	3·5		2053	3·5
14	0303	0·5	29	0314	0·7
	0918	3·9		0929	3·7
Tu	1521	0·9	W	1527	0·9
	2136	3·8		2139	3·7
15	0359	0·3	30	0356	0·6
	1013	4·0		1012	3·9
W	1612	0·7	Th	1607	0·8
	2227	4·0		2221	3·9

To find H.W. Dover subtract 0 h. 45 min. from above times.

TIDAL DIFFERENCES PAGE 21:69. TIDAL CURVE PAGE 21:65.

TIDAL STREAMS PAGES 21:50-21:56.

Datum of predictions: 2.16 m. below Ordnance Datum (Newlyn) or approx. L.A.T.

Lat. 51°51'N. Long. 1°16'E.   **HIGH & LOW WATER 1992**
GMT   **ADD 1 HOUR MARCH 29 — OCTOBER 25 FOR B.S.T.**

MAY

Day	Time	m		Day	Time	m
1 F	0435 1049 1647 2301	0·5 4·0 0·7 4·0		**16** Sa ○	0505 1123 1722 2339	0·4 4·1 0·6 4·1
2 Sa ●	0512 1126 1723 2340	0·5 4·1 0·6 4·1		**17** Su	0546 1204 1805	0·5 4·1 0·5
3 Su	0547 1203 1801	0·5 4·2 0·5		**18** M	0022 0625 1242 1848	4·1 0·6 4·0 0·5
4 M	0018 0624 1241 1841	4·2 0·5 4·1 0·5		**19** Tu	0103 0702 1317 1927	4·1 0·7 4·0 0·6
5 Tu	0057 0700 1317 1920	4·2 0·6 4·1 0·5		**20** W	0142 0737 1351 2005	4·0 0·9 3·9 0·6
6 W	0138 0738 1355 2004	4·2 0·7 4·0 0·5		**21** Th	0220 0812 1426 2042	3·9 1·0 3·8 0·7
7 Th	0222 0820 1437 2051	4·1 0·8 3·9 0·5		**22** F	0300 0847 1501 2121	3·7 1·1 3·7 0·8
8 F	0311 0908 1528 2148	4·0 0·9 3·7 0·6		**23** Sa	0341 0929 1543 2206	3·6 1·2 3·6 0·8
9 Sa ☽	0409 1007 1627 2252	3·8 1·0 3·6 0·6		**24** Su ○	0427 1020 1631 2301	3·5 1·2 3·5 0·9
10 Su	0515 1115 1736	3·7 1·1 3·5		**25** M	0520 1120 1729	3·4 1·3 3·4
11 M	0008 0629 1231 1850	0·6 3·7 1·1 3·6		**26** Tu	0005 0625 1229 1838	0·9 3·4 1·3 3·4
12 Tu	0127 0745 1348 2005	0·6 3·7 1·1 3·7		**27** W	0116 0735 1338 1948	0·9 3·4 1·2 3·4
13 W	0237 0853 1454 2108	0·5 3·8 0·9 3·8		**28** Th	0219 0836 1437 2049	0·8 3·6 1·0 3·6
14 Th	0334 0949 1549 2204	0·4 3·8 0·8 3·9		**29** F	0312 0928 1529 2142	0·7 3·8 0·9 3·8
15 F	0423 1038 1637 2254	0·4 4·0 0·7 4·1		**30** Sa	0359 1014 1616 2230	0·6 3·9 0·8 3·9
				31 Su	0441 1058 1659 2315	0·6 4·0 0·7 4·0

JUNE

Day	Time	m		Day	Time	m
1 M ●	0522 1140 1743	0·6 4·1 0·6		**16** Tu	0010 0605 1225 1836	4·0 0·8 4·0 0·6
2 Tu	0000 0603 1221 1827	4·1 0·6 4·1 0·5		**17** W	0049 0641 1300 1914	4·0 0·9 3·9 0·6
3 W	0045 0643 1303 1913	4·2 0·6 4·1 0·4		**18** Th	0127 0716 1333 1949	3·9 0·9 3·9 0·6
4 Th	0130 0727 1347 2001	4·2 0·7 4·1 0·3		**19** F	0202 0749 1405 2023	3·9 0·9 3·9 0·6
5 F	0218 0813 1433 2051	4·2 0·7 4·0 0·3		**20** Sa	0236 0825 1439 2058	3·8 1·0 3·8 0·6
6 Sa	0308 0901 1522 2145	4·1 0·8 3·9 0·4		**21** Su	0312 0903 1515 2136	3·8 1·0 3·8 0·7
7 Su ☽	0402 0955 1617 2242	3·9 0·9 3·9 0·4		**22** M	0350 0943 1556 2220	3·7 1·1 3·7 0·7
8 M	0501 1054 1716 2347	3·9 1·0 3·8 0·5		**23** Tu ☾	0435 1033 1642 2312	3·6 1·1 3·6 0·8
9 Tu	0604 1200 1821	3·8 1·1 3·7		**24** W	0526 1129 1739	3·5 1·2 3·5
10 W	0057 0714 1314 1933	0·6 3·7 1·1 3·7		**25** Th	0012 0627 1235 1843	0·9 3·5 1·2 3·5
11 Th	0208 0823 1427 2043	0·6 3·7 1·0 3·7		**26** F	0120 0735 1344 1955	0·9 3·5 1·1 3·5
12 F	0310 0925 1531 2145	0·6 3·8 0·9 3·8		**27** Sa	0226 0842 1450 2103	0·9 3·7 1·0 3·7
13 Sa	0402 1019 1624 2238	0·7 3·9 0·8 3·9		**28** Su	0324 0939 1548 2202	0·8 3·8 0·9 3·8
14 Su	0447 1105 1712 2326	0·7 3·9 0·7 4·0		**29** M	0414 1031 1640 2255	0·8 3·9 0·7 4·0
15 M ○	0527 1147 1756	0·8 3·9 0·6		**30** Tu ●	0502 1120 1729 2346	0·7 4·0 0·5 4·2

JULY

Day	Time	m		Day	Time	m
1 W	0546 1207 1817	0·7 4·1 0·4		**16** Th	0034 0621 1241 1855	4·0 0·9 4·0 0·5
2 Th	0034 0631 1252 1904	4·3 0·7 4·2 0·3		**17** F	0107 0653 1313 1927	4·0 0·8 4·0 0·5
3 F	0121 0716 1337 1954	4·3 0·6 4·2 0·2		**18** Sa	0138 0727 1344 1959	4·0 0·8 4·0 0·5
4 Sa	0209 0801 1423 2042	4·3 0·7 4·2 0·2		**19** Su	0211 0801 1415 2032	4·0 0·8 4·0 0·5
5 Su	0257 0847 1510 2131	4·3 0·7 4·2 0·2		**20** M	0243 0834 1447 2105	3·9 0·9 4·0 0·6
6 M	0345 0935 1557 2221	4·1 0·8 4·1 0·3		**21** Tu	0317 0910 1522 2142	3·9 0·9 3·9 0·7
7 Tu ☽	0437 1027 1651 2318	4·0 1·0 4·0 0·5		**22** W ☾	0355 0949 1603 2223	3·8 1·0 3·8 0·8
8 W	0533 1127 1750	3·8 1·1 3·8		**23** Th	0440 1038 1652 2316	3·7 1·1 3·7 0·9
9 Th	0024 0638 1241 1902	0·7 3·6 1·1 3·7		**24** F	0534 1140 1754	3·6 1·2 3·5
10 F	0137 0752 1405 2019	0·8 3·6 1·1 3·6		**25** Sa	0025 0642 1255 1909	1·0 3·5 1·2 3·5
11 Sa	0246 0901 1518 2129	0·9 3·6 1·0 3·7		**26** Su	0142 0756 1413 2029	1·0 3·5 1·1 3·6
12 Su	0345 1000 1617 2228	0·9 3·8 0·8 3·8		**27** M	0254 0910 1525 2141	1·0 3·7 0·9 3·8
13 M	0433 1058 1705 2316	0·9 3·8 0·7 3·9		**28** Tu	0353 1010 1624 2240	0·9 3·9 0·7 4·0
14 Tu ○	0512 1132 1746 2357	0·9 3·9 0·6 3·9		**29** W ●	0445 1104 1716 2332	0·8 4·0 0·5 4·2
15 W	0549 1208 1822	0·9 4·0 0·6		**30** Th	0532 1151 1805	0·7 4·2 0·3
				31 F	0021 0615 1236 1852	4·4 0·6 4·3 0·1

AUGUST

Day	Time	m		Day	Time	m
1 Sa	0107 0659 1321 1938	4·4 0·6 4·4 0·1		**16** Su	0112 0702 1319 1931	4·1 0·7 4·2 0·5
2 Su	0152 0744 1405 2023	4·4 0·6 4·4 0·1		**17** M	0142 0734 1349 2004	4·1 0·7 4·2 0·5
3 M	0236 0827 1449 2108	4·3 0·7 4·4 0·2		**18** Tu	0213 0806 1420 2033	4·1 0·8 4·1 0·6
4 Tu	0321 0911 1534 2153	4·2 0·8 4·3 0·4		**19** W	0244 0839 1453 2104	4·0 0·9 4·0 0·7
5 W ☽	0407 0959 1623 2244	4·0 0·9 4·1 0·7		**20** Th	0319 0912 1531 2139	3·9 1·0 3·9 0·9
6 Th	0458 1054 1719 2346	3·7 1·1 3·8 0·9		**21** F ☾	0400 0955 1617 2228	3·8 1·1 3·8 1·0
7 F	0558 1208 1832	3·5 1·2 3·6		**22** Sa	0452 1057 1718 2339	3·6 1·2 3·6 1·2
8 Sa	0104 0717 1345 1959	1·1 3·4 1·2 3·5		**23** Su	0558 1215 1836	3·5 1·2 3·5
9 Su	0223 0837 1505 2115	1·2 3·5 1·0 3·6		**24** M	0106 0721 1345 2005	1·2 3·4 1·1 3·6
10 M	0327 0941 1604 2214	1·1 3·7 0·8 3·8		**25** Tu	0229 0844 1507 2124	1·1 3·6 0·9 3·8
11 Tu	0416 1031 1651 2259	1·1 3·8 0·7 3·9		**26** W	0335 0950 1609 2224	1·0 3·8 0·6 4·1
12 W	0454 1111 1727 2337	1·0 3·9 0·6 4·0		**27** Th	0427 1044 1701 2315	0·8 4·1 0·4 4·3
13 Th ○	0526 1146 1758	0·9 4·0 0·6		**28** F ●	0513 1132 1747	0·7 4·3 0·2
14 F	0011 0557 1218 1829	4·0 0·8 4·1 0·5		**29** Sa	0003 0557 1217 1832	4·4 0·6 4·4 0·1
15 Sa	0042 0628 1248 1900	4·1 0·7 4·2 0·5		**30** Su	0046 0639 1300 1916	4·5 0·6 4·5 0·1
				31 M	0130 0721 1342 1958	4·4 0·6 4·5 0·2

WALTON-ON-THE-NAZE

HIGH & LOW WATER 1992 — Lat. 51°51′N. Long. 1°16′E.

GMT — ADD 1 HOUR MARCH 29 — OCTOBER 25 FOR B.S.T.

SEPTEMBER

Day	Time m	Day	Time m
1 Tu	0211 4.3 / 0804 0.6 / 1425 4.5 / 2040 0.4	16 W	0144 4.2 / 0738 0.7 / 1354 4.2 / 2002 0.7
2 W	0253 4.1 / 0846 0.8 / 1508 4.3 / 2121 0.7	17 Th	0215 4.1 / 0811 0.8 / 1427 4.1 / 2032 0.8
3 Th	0335 3.9 / 0931 0.9 / 1555 4.0 / 2207 0.9	18 F	0249 4.0 / 0844 0.9 / 1505 4.0 / 2105 1.0
4 F	0421 3.7 / 1024 1.1 / 1651 3.7 / 2304 1.2	19 Sa	0328 3.8 / 0928 1.0 / 1553 3.8 / 2153 1.1
5 Sa	0519 3.5 / 1136 1.2 / 1803 3.5	20 Su	0420 3.6 / 1028 1.1 / 1655 3.6 / 2308 1.3
6 Su	0024 1.4 / 0636 3.3 / 1320 1.2 / 1934 3.4	21 M	0529 3.5 / 1151 1.2 / 1815 3.5
7 M	0152 1.4 / 0806 3.4 / 1442 1.1 / 2053 3.5	22 Tu	0038 1.3 / 0653 3.4 / 1326 1.0 / 1947 3.6
8 Tu	0300 1.3 / 0912 3.6 / 1541 0.9 / 2149 3.7	23 W	0205 1.2 / 0820 3.6 / 1449 0.8 / 2105 3.9
9 W	0349 1.1 / 1003 3.8 / 1624 0.7 / 2233 3.9	24 Th	0312 1.0 / 0928 3.9 / 1550 0.5 / 2204 4.1
10 Th	0427 1.0 / 1042 3.9 / 1659 0.7 / 2309 4.0	25 F	0406 0.9 / 1021 4.1 / 1641 0.3 / 2255 4.3
11 F	0459 0.9 / 1118 4.1 / 1729 0.6 / 2342 4.1	26 Sa	0451 0.7 / 1109 4.3 / 1726 0.2 / ● 2342 4.4
12 Sa	0530 0.8 / 1149 4.2 / 1758 0.5 / ○	27 Su	0534 0.6 / 1154 4.5 / 1808 0.2
13 Su	0012 4.2 / 0601 0.7 / 1221 4.2 / 1829 0.5	28 M	0024 4.4 / 0617 0.6 / 1236 4.6 / 1850 0.2
14 M	0043 4.2 / 0634 0.7 / 1252 4.3 / 1902 0.5	29 Tu	0106 4.4 / 0700 0.6 / 1319 4.5 / 1931 0.4
15 Tu	0113 4.2 / 0707 0.7 / 1323 4.2 / 1931 0.6	30 W	0145 4.3 / 0742 0.6 / 1402 4.4 / 2011 0.6

OCTOBER

Day	Time m	Day	Time m
1 Th	0225 4.1 / 0823 0.8 / 1444 4.2 / 2050 0.9	16 F	0149 4.1 / 0751 0.8 / 1408 4.1 / 2006 0.9
2 F	0304 3.9 / 0907 0.9 / 1531 3.9 / 2131 1.2	17 Sa	0225 4.0 / 0829 0.8 / 1450 4.0 / 2046 1.0
3 Sa	0346 3.7 / 0956 1.1 / 1623 3.7 / 2221 1.4	18 Su	0307 3.8 / 0917 0.9 / 1541 3.8 / 2138 1.2
4 Su	0438 3.5 / 1101 1.2 / 1729 3.4 / 2332 1.5	19 M	0400 3.7 / 1019 1.0 / 1644 3.7 / 2249 1.3
5 M	0547 3.3 / 1235 1.2 / 1855 3.3	20 Tu	0509 3.5 / 1139 1.0 / 1803 3.6
6 Tu	0103 1.5 / 0717 3.3 / 1401 1.1 / 2015 3.5	21 W	0012 1.4 / 0631 3.5 / 1306 0.9 / 1927 3.7
7 W	0218 1.4 / 0832 3.5 / 1500 0.9 / 2114 3.7	22 Th	0137 1.3 / 0752 3.6 / 1426 0.7 / 2043 3.9
8 Th	0311 1.2 / 0924 3.7 / 1546 0.8 / 2157 3.9	23 F	0246 1.1 / 0901 3.9 / 1527 0.5 / 2142 4.1
9 F	0352 1.0 / 1006 3.9 / 1623 0.7 / 2235 4.0	24 Sa	0342 0.9 / 0956 4.1 / 1617 0.4 / 2233 4.3
10 Sa	0427 0.9 / 1042 4.1 / 1655 0.6 / 2309 4.1	25 Su	0430 0.8 / 1047 4.3 / 1702 0.3 / ● 2319 4.3
11 Su	0501 0.8 / 1118 4.2 / 1726 0.6 / ○ 2342 4.2	26 M	0515 0.7 / 1132 4.4 / 1744 0.4
12 M	0534 0.7 / 1151 4.3 / 1758 0.6	27 Tu	0001 4.3 / 0558 0.6 / 1217 4.5 / 1825 0.5
13 Tu	0012 4.3 / 0608 0.7 / 1225 4.3 / 1831 0.6	28 W	0042 4.3 / 0642 0.6 / 1259 4.4 / 1906 0.6
14 W	0045 4.3 / 0642 0.7 / 1257 4.3 / 1902 0.7	29 Th	0121 4.2 / 0724 0.6 / 1342 4.3 / 1944 0.8
15 Th	0117 4.2 / 0716 0.7 / 1333 4.2 / 1934 0.8	30 F	0159 4.0 / 0806 0.7 / 1425 4.1 / 2020 1.0
		31 Sa	0236 3.9 / 0847 0.9 / 1508 3.9 / 2058 1.2

NOVEMBER

Day	Time m	Day	Time m
1 Su	0317 3.7 / 0931 1.0 / 1555 3.7 / 2143 1.4	16 M	0257 3.9 / 0915 0.7 / 1536 3.9 / 2129 1.1
2 M	0402 3.6 / 1024 1.1 / 1649 3.5 / 2241 1.5	17 Tu	0350 3.8 / 1016 0.8 / 1637 3.8 / 2233 1.2
3 Tu	0458 3.4 / 1132 1.2 / 1757 3.4 / 2353 1.5	18 W	0454 3.7 / 1125 0.8 / 1746 3.7 / 2344 1.3
4 W	0610 3.3 / 1255 1.1 / 1917 3.4	19 Th	0605 3.6 / 1242 0.8 / 1902 3.7
5 Th	0114 1.5 / 0730 3.4 / 1405 1.0 / 2023 3.6	20 F	0102 1.3 / 0721 3.7 / 1358 0.7 / 2015 3.8
6 F	0219 1.3 / 0833 3.6 / 1457 0.9 / 2114 3.7	21 Sa	0216 1.1 / 0832 3.9 / 1501 0.6 / 2117 4.0
7 Sa	0310 1.1 / 0922 3.8 / 1541 0.8 / 2155 3.9	22 Su	0318 1.0 / 0932 4.0 / 1555 0.5 / 2212 4.1
8 Su	0352 1.0 / 1004 3.9 / 1619 0.7 / 2233 4.1	23 M	0410 0.9 / 1027 4.1 / 1642 0.5 / 2259 4.2
9 M	0430 0.9 / 1044 4.1 / 1655 0.7 / 2309 4.2	24 Tu	0459 0.7 / 1115 4.2 / 1725 0.6 / ● 2343 4.2
10 Tu	0506 0.8 / 1122 4.2 / 1729 0.7 / ○ 2346 4.2	25 W	0544 0.6 / 1201 4.3 / 1804 0.7
11 W	0543 0.7 / 1200 4.2 / 1803 0.7	26 Th	0024 4.2 / 0628 0.6 / 1245 4.2 / 1843 0.8
12 Th	0021 4.2 / 0621 0.7 / 1238 4.2 / 1838 0.7	27 F	0102 4.1 / 0710 0.6 / 1326 4.2 / 1920 0.9
13 F	0056 4.2 / 0659 0.7 / 1316 4.2 / 1913 0.8	28 Sa	0138 4.0 / 0749 0.7 / 1406 4.0 / 1955 1.0
14 Sa	0133 4.1 / 0740 0.7 / 1358 4.1 / 1952 0.9	29 Su	0213 3.9 / 0829 0.8 / 1446 3.9 / 2032 1.1
15 Su	0212 4.0 / 0823 0.7 / 1443 4.1 / 2037 1.0	30 M	0250 3.8 / 0907 0.8 / 1527 3.8 / 2111 1.2

DECEMBER

Day	Time m	Day	Time m
1 Tu	0329 3.7 / 0949 0.9 / 1610 3.6 / 2157 1.3	16 W	0342 4.0 / 1004 0.5 / 1623 3.9 / 2213 1.1
2 W	0414 3.6 / 1040 1.0 / 1659 3.5 / 2252 1.4	17 Th	0437 3.9 / 1105 0.6 / 1723 3.8 / 2315 1.2
3 Th	0508 3.5 / 1140 1.0 / 1800 3.4 / 2358 1.4	18 F	0539 3.8 / 1212 0.7 / 1829 3.7
4 F	0611 3.4 / 1250 1.0 / 1909 3.4	19 Sa	0027 1.2 / 0648 3.7 / 1327 0.7 / 1942 3.7
5 Sa	0110 1.3 / 0723 3.5 / 1358 1.0 / 2015 3.6	20 Su	0145 1.2 / 0804 3.7 / 1437 0.7 / 2051 3.8
6 Su	0216 1.2 / 0829 3.6 / 1454 0.9 / 2108 3.7	21 M	0258 1.0 / 0914 3.8 / 1536 0.7 / 2152 3.9
7 M	0311 1.1 / 0924 3.7 / 1542 0.8 / 2156 3.9	22 Tu	0359 0.9 / 1013 3.9 / 1626 0.8 / 2244 4.0
8 Tu	0359 0.9 / 1012 3.9 / 1624 0.8 / 2240 4.0	23 W	0451 0.8 / 1105 4.0 / 1709 0.8 / 2329 4.0
9 W	0441 0.8 / 1057 0.8 / 1704 0.8 / ○ 2320 4.1	24 Th	0537 0.6 / 1151 4.1 / 1749 0.8 / ●
10 Th	0523 0.8 / 1140 4.1 / 1742 0.8	25 F	0008 4.0 / 0618 0.6 / 1232 4.1 / 1824 0.8
11 F	0001 4.1 / 0605 0.6 / 1222 4.2 / 1819 0.7	26 Sa	0045 4.0 / 0657 0.6 / 1312 4.1 / 1859 0.9
12 Sa	0042 4.1 / 0648 0.5 / 1306 4.2 / 1900 0.7	27 Su	0120 4.0 / 0733 0.6 / 1347 4.0 / 1933 0.9
13 Su	0123 4.1 / 0733 0.5 / 1351 4.2 / 1944 0.8	28 M	0152 4.0 / 0808 0.6 / 1422 4.0 / 2008 0.9
14 M	0205 4.1 / 0820 0.5 / 1439 4.2 / 2029 0.9	29 Tu	0226 4.0 / 0842 0.6 / 1457 3.9 / 2043 1.0
15 Tu	0251 4.0 / 0911 0.5 / 1528 4.1 / 2118 1.0	30 W	0300 3.9 / 0917 0.7 / 1532 3.8 / 2121 1.0
		31 Th	0338 3.8 / 0956 0.8 / 1613 3.7 / 2204 1.1

To find H.W. Dover subtract 0 h. 45 min. from above times.

TIDAL DIFFERENCES PAGE 21:69. TIDAL CURVE PAGE 21:65.

TIDAL STREAMS PAGES 21:50-21:56.

Datum of predictions: 2.16 m. below Ordnance Datum (Newlyn) or approx. L.A.T.

PLACE	TIME DIFFERENCES				HEIGHT DIFFERENCES (Metres)			
	High Water		Low Water		MHWS	MHWN	MLWN	MLWS
WALTON-ON-THE-NAZE ..	0000 and 1200	0600 and 1800	0500 and 1700	1100 and 2300	4.2	3.4	1.1	0.4
Whitaker Beacon	+0022	+0024	+0033	+0027	+0.6	+0.5	+0.2	+0.1
Holliwell Point	+0034	+0037	+0100	+0037	+1.1	+0.9	+0.3	+0.1
River Roach								
Rochford	+0050	+0040	Dries	Dries	−0.8	−1.1	Dries	Dries
River Crouch								
North Fambridge	+0115	+0050	+0130	+0100	+1.1	+0.8	0.0	−0.1
Hullbridge	+0115	+0050	+0135	+0105	+1.1	+0.8	0.0	−0.1
Battlesbridge	+0120	+0110	Dries	Dries	−1.8	−2.0	Dries	Dries
River Blackwater								
Bradwell-on-Sea	+0035	+0023	+0047	+0004	+1.1	+0.8	+0.2	+0.1
Osea Island	+0057	+0045	+0050	+0007	+1.1	+0.9	+0.1	0.0
Maldon	+0107	+0055	−	−	−1.3	−1.1	−	−
West Mersea.................	+0035	+0015	+0055	+0010	+0.9	+0.4	+0.1	+0.1
River Colne								
Brightlingsea	+0025	+0021	+0046	+0004	+0.8	+0.4	+0.1	0.0
Wivenhoe	+0030	+0023	−	−	+0.4	0.0	Dries	Dries
Colchester	+0035	+0025	Dries	Dries	0.0	−0.3	Dries	Dries
Clacton-on-Sea	+0012	+0010	+0025	+0008	+0.3	+0.1	0.0	0.0
Bramble Creek	+0010	−0007	−0005	+0010	+0.3	+0.3	+0.3	+0.3
Sunk Head Tower	0000	+0002	−0002	+0002	−0.3	−0.3	−0.1	−0.1
Harwich	+0007	+0002	−0010	−0012	−0.2	0.0	0.0	0.0
River Stour								
Mistley	+0032	+0027	−0010	−0012	0.0	0.0	−0.1	−0.1
Wrabness	+0017	+0015	−0010	−0012	−0.1	0.0	0.0	0.0
River Orwell								
Ipswich	+0022	+0027	0000	−0012	0.0	0.0	−0.1	−0.1
Pin Mill	+0012	+0015	−0008	−0012	−0.1	0.0	0.0	0.0
WALTON-ON-THE-NAZE ..	0100 and 1300	0700 and 1900	0100 and 1300	0700 and 1900	4.2	3.4	1.1	0.4
Felixstowe Pier	−0005	−0007	−0018	−0020	−0.5	−0.4	0.0	0.0
River Deben								
Woodbridge Haven	0000	−0005	−0020	−0025	−0.5	−0.5	−0.1	+0.1
Woodbridge	+0045	+0025	+0025	−0020	−0.2	−0.3	−0.2	0.0
Bawdsey	−0010	−0012	−0028	−0032	−0.8	−0.7	−0.2	−0.2
Orford Haven								
Bar	−0015	−0017	−0038	−0042	−1.0	−0.8	−0.2	−0.1
Orford Quay	+0040	+0040	+0055	+0055	−1.6	−1.3	+0.2	0.0
Slaughden	+0100	+0100	+0115	+0115	−1.3	−1.0	+0.2	0.0
Iken Cliff	+0130	+0130	+0155	+0155	−1.3	−1.0	+0.2	0.0
Snape	+0200	+2000	−	−	−1.3	−1.0	−0.3	+0.4

Refer to predictions on pages 21:66-21:68

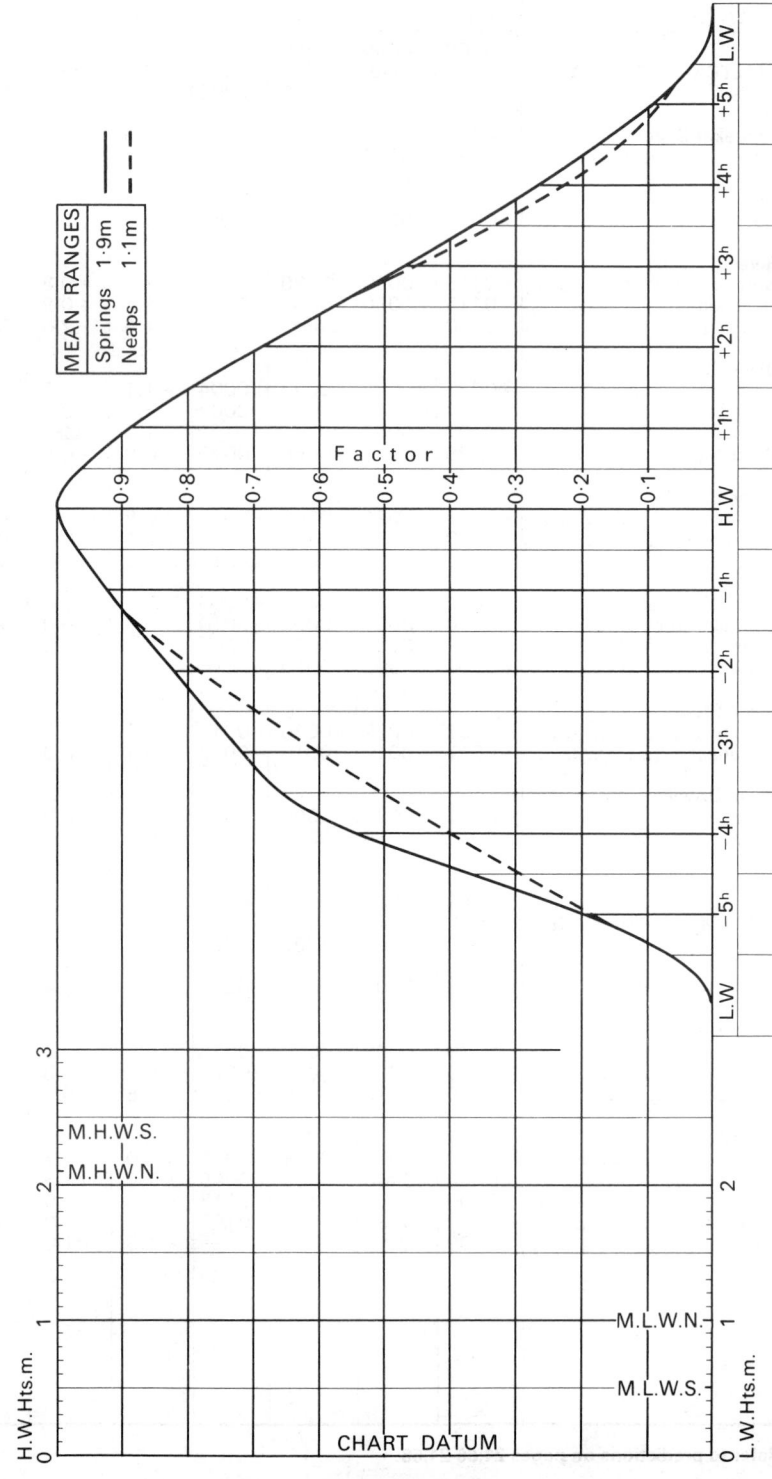

LOWESTOFT

MEAN SPRING AND NEAP CURVES

Springs occur 2 days after New and Full Moon.

MEAN RANGES
Springs 1·9m
Neaps 1·1m

LOWESTOFT 21:71

Lat. 52°28′N. Long. 1°45′E. **HIGH & LOW WATER 1992**

GMT ADD 1 HOUR MARCH 29 — OCTOBER 25 FOR B.S.T.

JANUARY

Day	Time	m	Time	m	Time	m	Time	m
1 W	0018	1.1	0633	2.2	1252	0.9	1920	2.2
2 Th	0130	1.0	0743	2.2	1345	0.9	2005	2.3
3 F	0224	0.9	0835	2.2	1430	0.9	2043	2.3
4 Sa	0309	0.8	0920	2.2	● 2116	2.4		
5 Su	0348	0.7	1001	2.2	1537	0.9	2146	2.4
6 M	0424	0.6	1037	2.2	1603	0.9	2216	2.5
7 Tu	0458	0.6	1111	2.2	1631	0.9	2248	2.5
8 W	0530	0.6	1145	2.2	1703	0.8	2320	2.5
9 Th	0603	0.6	1216	2.1	1739	0.9	2356	2.4
10 F	0637	0.6	1250	2.1	1816	0.9		
11 Sa	0033	2.4	0711	0.6	1330	2.1	1858	0.9
12 Su	0113	2.4	0750	0.7	1416	2.0	1943	1.0
13 M	0158	2.3	0837	0.8	1516	2.0	) 2037	1.1
14 Tu	0256	2.2	0937	0.8	1624	2.0	2146	1.2
15 W	0430	2.2	1050	0.9	1726	2.1	2315	1.1
16 Th	0531	2.2	1158	0.8	1822	2.1		
17 F	0026	1.0	0637	2.2	1254	0.8	1913	2.2
18 Sa	0131	0.8	0739	2.3	1350	0.7	2003	2.3
19 Su	0237	0.6	0839	2.4	1446	0.7	2050	2.5
20 M	0331	0.3	0935	2.4	1541	0.6	2137	2.6
21 Tu	0422	0.1	1026	2.5	1628	0.6	2224	2.7
22 W	0507	0.0	1113	2.4	1713	0.6	2309	2.7
23 Th	0552	0.0	1200	2.3	1754	0.6	2354	2.7
24 F	0635	0.0	1246	2.2	1835	0.7		
25 Sa	0041	2.6	0718	0.2	1331	2.1	1916	0.8
26 Su	0130	2.5	0805	0.5	1426	2.0	(2001	0.9
27 M	0226	2.4	0856	0.7	1528	2.0	2058	1.0
28 Tu	0333	2.2	1000	0.9	1635	2.0	2218	1.1
29 W	0456	2.1	1120	1.0	1746	2.0		
30 Th	0009	1.1	0630	2.1	1235	1.1	1854	2.1
31 F	0124	0.9	0743	2.1	1333	1.0	1946	2.2

FEBRUARY

Day	Time	m	Time	m	Time	m	Time	m
1 Sa	0215	0.8	0833	2.1	1416	1.0	2026	2.2
2 Su	0254	0.7	0913	2.2	1450	0.9	2100	2.3
3 M	0330	0.6	0948	2.2	1518	0.9	● 2130	2.4
4 Tu	0403	0.5	1020	2.2	1545	0.8	2158	2.4
5 W	0435	0.4	1050	2.2	1615	0.7	2230	2.5
6 Th	0505	0.4	1118	2.2	1646	0.7	2301	2.5
7 F	0537	0.4	1145	2.2	1720	0.7	2335	2.5
8 Sa	0607	0.5	1215	2.1	1752	0.7		
9 Su	0009	2.4	0637	0.5	1248	2.1	1828	0.8
10 M	0045	2.4	0713	0.6	1330	2.0	1909	0.9
11 Tu	0128	2.3	0754	0.7	1420	2.0	(2000	0.9
12 W	0224	2.2	0850	0.8	1528	2.0	2105	1.0
13 Th	0348	2.1	1007	0.9	1643	2.0	2241	1.0
14 F	0513	2.1	1130	0.9	1748	2.0		
15 Sa	0009	0.9	0626	2.1	1237	0.9	1846	2.1
16 Su	0122	0.6	0733	2.2	1339	0.8	1941	2.3
17 M	0226	0.4	0833	2.3	1435	0.7	2033	2.4
18 Tu	0316	0.1	0924	2.4	1524	0.6	○ 2120	2.6
19 W	0403	0.0	1011	2.4	1609	0.5	2207	2.7
20 Th	0446	-0.1	1052	2.4	1652	0.5	2250	2.7
21 F	0530	0.0	1135	2.3	1731	0.5	2335	2.7
22 Sa	0611	0.1	1216	2.2	1809	0.5		
23 Su	0018	2.6	0650	0.3	1258	2.1	1848	0.7
24 M	0105	2.5	0730	0.6	1343	2.1	1931	0.8
25 Tu	0200	2.3	0815	0.9	1435	2.0	2024	0.9
26 W	0309	2.1	0911	1.1	1539	2.0	2143	1.1
27 Th	0437	2.0	1045	1.2	1654	2.0	2352	1.0
28 F	0616	2.0	1218	1.2	1813	2.0		
29 Sa	0103	0.9	0726	2.0	1315	1.1	1916	2.1

MARCH

Day	Time	m	Time	m	Time	m	Time	m
1 Su	0150	0.7	0815	2.1	1354	1.0	2001	2.1
2 M	0228	0.6	0852	2.1	1424	0.9	2033	2.2
3 Tu	0301	0.5	0926	2.2	1450	0.8	2103	2.3
4 W	0333	0.4	0954	2.2	1520	0.7	● 2133	2.4
5 Th	0405	0.4	1022	2.2	1552	0.6	2207	2.4
6 F	0435	0.4	1046	2.2	1626	0.6	2239	2.5
7 Sa	0507	0.4	1115	2.2	1658	0.6	2313	2.4
8 Su	0535	0.5	1145	2.2	1731	0.6	2346	2.4
9 M	0603	0.5	1216	2.2	1805	0.7		
10 Tu	0024	2.3	0637	0.6	1254	2.1	1846	0.9
11 W	0109	2.2	0718	0.8	1341	2.0	) 1937	0.8
12 Th	0211	2.1	0816	0.9	1443	2.0	2048	0.9
13 F	0337	2.0	0937	1.0	1601	2.0	2224	0.8
14 Sa	0503	2.0	1109	1.0	1716	2.0	2354	0.7
15 Su	0620	2.1	1222	0.9	1820	2.1		
16 M	0105	0.5	0728	2.2	1322	0.8	1920	2.3
17 Tu	0205	0.2	0822	2.3	1415	0.7	2013	2.4
18 W	0256	0.1	0907	2.3	1503	0.5	○ 2101	2.6
19 Th	0341	0.0	0948	2.4	1546	0.4	2146	2.7
20 F	0424	0.0	1028	2.4	1628	0.4	2231	2.7
21 Sa	0503	0.1	1107	2.3	1709	0.4	2315	2.6
22 Su	0543	0.3	1145	2.3	1748	0.5	2358	2.5
23 M	0618	0.5	1224	2.2	1828	0.6		
24 Tu	0045	2.3	0654	0.8	1303	2.1	1909	0.7
25 W	0139	2.2	0733	1.0	1350	2.1	2000	0.9
26 Th	0245	2.0	0820	1.2	1445	2.0	(2107	1.0
27 F	0411	1.9	0937	1.3	1552	1.9	2309	0.9
28 Sa	0539	1.9	1141	1.3	1703	1.9		
29 Su	0022	0.8	0652	2.0	1237	1.2	1818	2.0
30 M	0111	0.7	0743	2.1	1315	1.0	1915	2.1
31 Tu	0150	0.6	0822	2.1	1345	0.9	1956	2.2

APRIL

Day	Time	m	Time	m	Time	m	Time	m
1 W	0224	0.5	0854	2.2	1416	0.8	2030	2.3
2 Th	0256	0.4	0922	2.2	1450	0.7	2103	2.4
3 F	0330	0.4	0948	2.2	1526	0.6	● 2139	2.4
4 Sa	0401	0.4	1015	2.3	1603	0.5	2215	2.4
5 Su	0433	0.4	1045	2.3	1639	0.5	2252	2.4
6 M	0505	0.5	1116	2.3	1715	0.6	2330	2.4
7 Tu	0535	0.6	1152	2.3	1752	0.6		
8 W	0011	2.3	0611	0.7	1231	2.2	1839	0.6
9 Th	0101	2.2	0658	0.8	1316	2.1	1937	0.7
10 F	0209	2.1	0800	1.0	1416	2.1	) 2048	0.7
11 Sa	0335	2.0	0918	1.1	1530	2.0	2213	0.7
12 Su	0458	2.1	1046	1.1	1646	2.1	2333	0.5
13 M	0611	2.1	1158	1.0	1754	2.2		
14 Tu	0041	0.4	0713	2.2	1258	0.9	1856	2.3
15 W	0139	0.3	0801	2.2	1350	0.7	1952	2.4
16 Th	0230	0.2	0845	2.3	1439	0.6	2041	2.5
17 F	0315	0.2	0924	2.4	1524	0.5	2128	2.6
18 Sa	0358	0.2	1001	2.4	1609	0.5	2213	2.6
19 Su	0437	0.4	1039	2.4	1650	0.5	2256	2.5
20 M	0515	0.6	1116	2.3	1731	0.5	2341	2.4
21 Tu	0548	0.8	1150	2.3	1811	0.6		
22 W	0028	2.2	0618	0.9	1228	2.2	1852	0.7
23 Th	0118	2.1	0652	1.1	1309	2.2	1939	0.8
24 F	0222	2.0	0705	1.2	1358	2.1	(2035	0.8
25 Sa	0305	2.0	0835	1.3	1458	2.0	2152	0.9
26 Su	0446	2.0	1003	1.3	1601	2.0	2318	0.8
27 M	0556	2.0	1133	1.2	1707	2.0		
28 Tu	0015	0.7	0654	2.0	1220	1.1	1809	2.1
29 W	0100	0.6	0737	2.1	1301	1.0	1903	2.1
30 Th	0137	0.6	0813	2.2	1339	0.9	1950	2.2

To find H.W. Dover add 1 h. 40 min.

TIDAL DIFFERENCES PAGE 21:74. TIDAL CURVE PAGE 21:70.

Datum of predictions: 1.50 m. below Ordnance Datum (Newlyn) or approx. L.A.T.

LOWESTOFT

HIGH & LOW WATER 1992 Lat. 52°28'N. Long. 1°45'E.
GMT   ADD 1 HOUR MARCH 29 — OCTOBER 25 FOR B.S.T.

MAY

Day	Time	m	Time	m	Time	m	Time	m
1 F	0215	0·5	0843	2·2	1420	0·7	2031	2·3
2 Sa	0250	0·5	0911	2·3	1501	0·6	● 2113	2·4
3 Su	0328	0·5	0943	2·3	1543	0·6	2154	2·4
4 M	0403	0·5	1018	2·4	1626	0·5	2235	2·4
5 Tu	0439	0·6	1054	2·4	1709	0·5	2318	2·4
6 W	0518	0·7	1133	2·4	1756	0·5		
7 Th	0005	2·3	0601	0·8	1215	2·3	1848	0·5
8 F	0101	2·2	0652	0·9	1301	2·3	1945	0·5
9 Sa	0211	2·1	0752	1·0	1358	2·2	☽ 2046	0·5
10 Su	0330	2·1	0900	1·1	1505	2·2	2156	0·5
11 M	0445	2·1	1015	1·1	1616	2·2	2307	0·4
12 Tu	0548	2·1	1126	1·0	1728	2·2		
13 W	0011	0·4	0648	2·2	1228	0·9	1831	2·3
14 Th	0109	0·4	0737	2·2	1326	0·8	1931	2·4
15 F	0201	0·4	0820	2·3	1418	0·7	2024	2·4
16 Sa	0248	0·4	0900	2·4	1509	0·6	○ 2113	2·4
17 Su	0331	0·5	0939	2·4	1556	0·5	2200	2·4
18 M	0411	0·6	1015	2·4	1639	0·5	2245	2·3
19 Tu	0446	0·8	1050	2·4	1720	0·5	2328	2·2
20 W	0518	0·9	1131	2·4	1758	0·6		
21 Th	0013	2·2	0546	1·0	1158	2·3	1837	0·6
22 F	0101	2·1	0620	1·0	1235	2·3	1918	0·7
23 Sa	0152	2·0	0701	1·1	1320	2·2	2003	0·7
24 Su	0250	2·0	0752	1·2	1411	2·1	☾ 2056	0·8
25 M	0350	2·0	0852	1·2	1509	2·1	2200	0·8
26 Tu	0452	2·0	1005	1·2	1613	2·1	2309	0·8
27 W	0548	2·0	1120	1·2	1716	2·1		
28 Th	0003	0·7	0641	2·1	1216	1·1	1816	2·1
29 F	0050	0·7	0722	2·2	1305	1·0	1911	2·2
30 Sa	0131	0·6	0752	2·3	1352	0·8	2000	2·3
31 Su	0215	0·6	0837	2·3	1439	0·7	2048	2·3

JUNE

Day	Time	m	Time	m	Time	m	Time	m
1 M	0256	0·6	0915	2·4	1530	0·6	● 2135	2·4
2 Tu	0341	0·6	0954	2·4	1620	0·5	2224	2·4
3 W	0426	0·6	1035	2·5	1709	0·4	2313	2·4
4 Th	0513	0·7	1118	2·5	1758	0·3		
5 F	0003	2·3	0601	0·8	1203	2·5	1846	0·2
6 Sa	0100	2·2	0650	0·9	1250	2·4	1937	0·3
7 Su	0201	2·2	0741	0·9	1343	2·4	☽ 2031	0·3
8 M	0309	2·1	0837	1·0	1443	2·3	2130	0·4
9 Tu	0416	2·1	0939	1·1	1550	2·3	2235	0·5
10 W	0520	2·1	1050	1·1	1701	2·3	2341	0·5
11 Th	0618	2·1	1200	1·0	1811	2·3		
12 F	0041	0·6	0713	2·2	1307	0·9	1916	2·3
13 Sa	0137	0·6	0800	2·3	1409	0·8	2016	2·3
14 Su	0228	0·7	0841	2·3	1501	0·7	2107	2·3
15 M	0311	0·8	0918	2·4	1546	0·6	○ 2154	2·3
16 Tu	0350	0·8	0954	2·4	1630	0·5	2237	2·2
17 W	0424	0·9	1028	2·4	1707	0·5	2318	2·2
18 Th	0454	0·9	1101	2·4	1743	0·5		
19 F	0000	2·2	0524	0·9	1135	2·4	1818	0·5
20 Sa	0039	2·1	0556	0·9	1211	2·4	1854	0·6
21 Su	0120	2·1	0635	1·0	1250	2·3	1931	0·6
22 M	0205	2·0	0718	1·0	1333	2·3	2013	0·7
23 Tu	0256	2·0	0807	1·1	1424	2·2	☾ 2101	0·7
24 W	0352	2·0	0903	1·1	1522	2·1	2201	0·8
25 Th	0450	2·0	1015	1·2	1631	2·1	2309	0·8
26 F	0546	2·1	1130	1·1	1739	2·1		
27 Sa	0007	0·8	0635	2·1	1231	1·0	1839	2·1
28 Su	0056	0·7	0722	2·2	1328	0·9	1935	2·2
29 M	0145	0·7	0807	2·3	1426	0·7	2030	2·3
30 Tu	0235	0·7	0850	2·4	1522	0·5	● 2124	2·3

JULY

Day	Time	m	Time	m	Time	m	Time	m
1 W	0326	0·6	0935	2·5	1613	0·3	2215	2·4
2 Th	0418	0·6	1020	2·6	1701	0·2	2305	2·4
3 F	0507	0·6	1103	2·6	1748	0·1	2356	2·4
4 Sa	0552	0·7	1150	2·6	1833	0·1		
5 Su	0046	2·3	0635	0·7	1237	2·6	1920	0·1
6 M	0139	2·2	0720	0·8	1326	2·5	2007	0·3
7 Tu	0235	2·1	0809	0·9	1422	2·4	☽ 2101	0·4
8 W	0339	2·1	0905	1·0	1528	2·3	2201	0·6
9 Th	0445	2·1	1016	1·0	1641	2·2	2311	0·7
10 F	0546	2·1	1141	1·0	1800	2·2		
11 Sa	0018	0·8	0646	2·2	1303	0·9	1916	2·2
12 Su	0120	0·9	0739	2·2	1405	0·8	2018	2·2
13 M	0213	0·9	0824	2·3	1454	0·7	2107	2·2
14 Tu	0256	0·9	0901	2·4	1535	0·6	○ 2150	2·2
15 W	0333	0·9	0937	2·4	1613	0·5	2228	2·2
16 Th	0403	0·9	1011	2·4	1648	0·4	2303	2·2
17 F	0433	0·8	1043	2·5	1722	0·4	2337	2·2
18 Sa	0501	0·8	1115	2·5	1754	0·5		
19 Su	0011	2·2	0533	0·8	1146	2·4	1826	0·5
20 M	0043	2·1	0609	0·8	1222	2·4	1858	0·6
21 Tu	0118	2·1	0646	0·9	1300	2·3	1933	0·6
22 W	0200	2·0	0728	1·0	1345	2·3	☾ 2015	0·7
23 Th	0252	2·0	0818	1·1	1439	2·2	2107	0·8
24 F	0356	2·0	0920	1·1	1550	2·1	2215	0·9
25 Sa	0458	2·0	1045	1·1	1707	2·1	2328	0·9
26 Su	0556	2·1	1203	1·0	1815	2·1		
27 M	0030	0·8	0648	2·2	1311	0·8	1916	2·2
28 Tu	0124	0·8	0739	2·3	1413	0·6	2018	2·3
29 W	0220	0·7	0828	2·4	1509	0·4	● 2115	2·4
30 Th	0315	0·6	0916	2·5	1600	0·1	2203	2·4
31 F	0405	0·6	1001	2·7	1645	0·0	2250	2·4

AUGUST

Day	Time	m	Time	m	Time	m	Time	m
1 Sa	0450	0·5	1048	2·7	1730	−0·1	2337	2·4
2 Su	0533	0·6	1133	2·7	1813	0·0		
3 M	0022	2·3	0615	0·6	1218	2·7	1856	0·1
4 Tu	0109	2·2	0658	0·7	1307	2·6	1941	0·3
5 W	0158	2·1	0743	0·8	1401	2·4	☽ 2030	0·6
6 Th	0256	2·1	0835	0·9	1505	2·3	2126	0·8
7 F	0401	2·1	0946	1·0	1626	2·2	2241	1·0
8 Sa	0511	2·1	1131	1·0	1756	2·1		
9 Su	0003	1·0	0620	2·1	1258	0·9	1918	2·1
10 M	0109	1·0	0720	2·2	1354	0·7	2015	2·2
11 Tu	0200	1·0	0807	2·3	1437	0·6	2058	2·2
12 W	0239	1·0	0845	2·3	1516	0·5	2135	2·4
13 Th	0311	0·9	0918	2·4	1550	0·5	○ 2209	2·2
14 F	0339	0·8	0948	2·5	1622	0·4	2241	2·2
15 Sa	0407	0·8	1020	2·5	1654	0·4	2309	2·2
16 Su	0437	0·7	1050	2·5	1724	0·4	2337	2·2
17 M	0509	0·7	1122	2·5	1752	0·5		
18 Tu	0005	2·2	0541	0·8	1156	2·4	1822	0·6
19 W	0035	2·1	0616	0·8	1231	2·4	1854	0·7
20 Th	0113	2·1	0656	0·9	1313	2·3	1931	0·8
21 F	0200	2·1	0743	1·0	1405	2·2	☾ 2020	0·9
22 Sa	0300	2·0	0843	1·0	1520	2·1	2130	1·0
23 Su	0411	2·0	1009	1·0	1645	2·1	2256	1·0
24 M	0518	2·1	1141	0·9	1758	2·1		
25 Tu	0007	1·0	0618	2·2	1252	0·7	1905	2·2
26 W	0107	0·9	0713	2·5	1356	0·5	2007	2·3
27 Th	0203	0·7	0805	2·5	1450	0·2	2100	2·4
28 F	0256	0·6	0856	2·6	1539	0·1	● 2146	2·4
29 Sa	0345	0·5	0943	2·7	1624	0·0	2230	2·5
30 Su	0428	0·5	1028	2·8	1707	0·0	2311	2·4
31 M	0511	0·5	1113	2·8	1748	0·1	2354	2·4

GENERAL — Changes in sands and channels frequent. Streams run in direction of coast. Streams run across shoals and channels not parallel with coast. S. going set towards shoals on SW. N. going set towards shoals on NE. N. gales, during N. going, seas break heavily.
RATE AND SET — Position. Winterton Ness; S. going, Strong at Local H.W., N. going. Strong at Local L.W., N. Chan: S. going +0545 Dover, Sp. 2¼ kn.: N. going −0030 Dover, Sp. 2¼ kn.

LOWESTOFT 21:73

Lat. 52°28'N. Long. 1°45'E. **HIGH & LOW WATER 1992**

GMT **ADD 1 HOUR MARCH 29 — OCTOBER 25 FOR B.S.T.**

SEPTEMBER

Date	Time m	Time m	Time m	Time m
1 Tu	0552 0·5	1158 2·7	1830 0·3	
2 W	0035 2·3	0633 0·6	1246 2·6	1911 0·6
3 Th	0122 2·2	0718 0·8	1341 2·4	1956 0·8
4 F	0213 2·1	0811 0·9	1446 2·2	2048 1·1
5 Sa	0315 2·1	0922 1·0	1613 2·1	2207 1·2
6 Su	0424 2·1	1115 1·0	1746 2·1	2345 1·2
7 M	0541 2·1	1235 0·9	1901 2·1	
8 Tu	0050 1·2	0650 2·2	1330 0·7	1954 2·2
9 W	0135 1·1	0741 2·2	1411 0·6	2035 2·2
10 Th	0211 1·0	0818 2·2	1446 0·6	2109 2·2
11 F	0239 0·9	0850 2·2	1518 0·5	2141 2·3
12 Sa	0307 0·8	0922 2·5	1550 0·5	○ 2209 2·3
13 Su	0337 0·7	0952 2·5	1620 0·5	2237 2·3
14 M	0411 0·7	1024 2·5	1650 0·5	2301 2·3
15 Tu	0443 0·7	1058 2·5	1718 0·6	2330 2·3
16 W	0516 0·7	1131 2·4	1745 0·7	
17 Th	0001 2·3	0550 0·8	1209 2·4	1816 0·7
18 F	0037 2·2	0630 0·8	1250 2·3	1854 0·8
19 Sa	0120 2·2	0718 0·9	1346 2·2	1946 1·0
20 Su	0216 2·1	0824 0·9	1503 2·1	2058 1·1
21 M	0328 2·1	0948 0·9	1631 2·1	2228 1·1
22 Tu	0443 2·1	1118 0·8	1746 2·2	2346 1·0
23 W	0548 2·2	1231 0·6	1852 2·2	
24 Th	0046 0·9	0648 2·4	1331 0·4	1950 2·3
25 F	0141 0·8	0743 2·5	1426 0·2	2039 2·4
26 Sa	0231 0·7	0833 2·7	1515 0·1	● 2122 2·5
27 Su	0320 0·6	0922 2·8	1558 0·1	2203 2·5
28 M	0405 0·5	1007 2·8	1641 0·2	2245 2·5
29 Tu	0448 0·5	1052 2·8	1722 0·3	2324 2·4
30 W	0531 0·5	1139 2·7	1801 0·6	

OCTOBER

Date	Time m	Time m	Time m	Time m
1 Th	0003 2·4	0615 0·6	1226 2·5	1841 0·8
2 F	0046 2·3	0700 0·7	1320 2·3	1920 1·0
3 Sa	0133 2·2	0750 0·9	1428 2·2	) 2009 1·2
4 Su	0228 2·2	0856 1·0	1550 2·1	2115 1·4
5 M	0331 2·1	1035 1·0	1713 2·1	2305 1·4
6 Tu	0443 2·1	1156 0·9	1826 2·1	
7 W	0013 1·3	0554 2·2	1250 0·8	1920 2·2
8 Th	0056 1·2	0656 2·2	1333 0·7	2003 2·2
9 F	0131 1·1	0739 2·3	1409 0·6	2037 2·3
10 Sa	0201 0·9	0815 2·4	1441 0·6	2109 2·3
11 Su	0233 0·8	0848 2·4	1513 0·6	○ 2135 2·4
12 M	0309 0·8	0922 2·5	1543 0·6	2200 2·4
13 Tu	0345 0·7	0958 2·5	1613 0·6	2228 2·4
14 W	0420 0·7	1033 2·5	1643 0·7	2300 2·4
15 Th	0458 0·7	1111 2·4	1713 0·7	2333 2·4
16 F	0535 0·7	1150 2·4	1746 0·8	
17 Sa	0011 2·4	0618 0·7	1237 2·3	1828 0·9
18 Su	0054 2·3	0715 0·8	1337 2·2	1924 1·1
19 M	0146 2·2	0820 0·8	1456 2·1	(2037 1·2
20 Tu	0252 2·2	0935 0·8	1620 2·1	2200 1·2
21 W	0407 2·2	1056 0·7	1731 2·2	2318 1·1
22 Th	0518 2·3	1203 0·5	1835 2·3	
23 F	0020 1·0	0620 2·4	1303 0·4	1928 2·3
24 Sa	0115 0·9	0718 2·5	1358 0·3	2015 2·4
25 Su	0207 0·8	0811 2·7	1446 0·2	● 2058 2·5
26 M	0258 0·7	0901 2·8	1533 0·3	2139 2·5
27 Tu	0346 0·6	0948 2·7	1616 0·4	2218 2·5
28 W	0431 0·6	1035 2·7	1656 0·6	2256 2·5
29 Th	0516 0·6	1122 2·5	1733 0·8	2335 2·5
30 F	0600 0·6	1211 2·4	1809 1·0	
31 Sa	0015 2·4	0645 0·7	1303 2·3	1846 1·1

NOVEMBER

Date	Time m	Time m	Time m	Time m
1 Su	0056 2·4	0731 0·8	1403 2·1	1928 1·3
2 M	0145 2·3	0824 0·9	1513 2·1	) 2020 1·3
3 Tu	0243 2·2	0931 0·9	1624 2·1	2133 1·4
4 W	0345 2·2	1056 0·9	1731 2·1	2305 1·3
5 Th	0448 2·2	1158 0·8	1831 2·2	2348 1·1
6 F	0001 1·2	0550 2·2	1243 0·8	1920 2·2
7 Sa	0045 1·1	0645 2·3	1322 0·7	2000 2·3
8 Su	0122 1·0	0731 2·3	1358 0·7	2030 2·3
9 M	0201 0·9	0813 2·4	1431 0·7	2056 2·4
10 Tu	0241 0·8	0854 2·4	1505 0·7	○ 2126 2·4
11 W	0324 0·8	0933 2·5	1541 0·7	2200 2·5
12 Th	0405 0·7	1015 2·5	1615 0·7	2235 2·5
13 F	0448 0·7	1056 2·4	1652 0·8	2313 2·5
14 Sa	0535 0·6	1141 2·4	1731 0·9	2352 2·5
15 Su	0624 0·6	1231 2·3	1818 1·0	
16 M	0037 2·4	0716 0·6	1333 2·2	1916 1·1
17 Tu	0128 2·4	0815 0·6	1445 2·2	(2018 1·1
18 W	0228 2·3	0918 0·6	1601 2·1	2130 1·2
19 Th	0337 2·3	1028 0·6	1709 2·2	2243 1·2
20 F	0448 2·4	1133 0·5	1811 2·2	
21 Sa	0556 2·4	1235 0·5	1903 2·3	
22 Su	0048 1·0	0658 2·5	1330 0·5	1952 2·4
23 M	0148 0·8	0741 2·6	1422 0·5	2035 2·5
24 Tu	0255 0·7	0846 2·6	1509 0·6	● 2115 2·5
25 W	0335 0·6	0937 2·5	1552 0·7	2154 2·5
26 Th	0422 0·6	1024 2·5	1633 0·8	2231 2·5
27 F	0505 0·6	1111 2·4	1709 0·9	2309 2·5
28 Sa	0546 0·6	1156 2·3	1741 1·0	2346 2·5
29 Su	0628 0·6	1245 2·2	1813 1·1	
30 M	0024 2·4	0707 0·7	1333 2·1	1850 1·2

DECEMBER

Date	Time m	Time m	Time m	Time m
1 Tu	0107 2·4	0750 0·8	1428 2·1	1935 1·2
2 W	0156 2·3	0839 0·8	1528 2·1	) 2028 1·3
3 Th	0250 2·2	0937 0·9	1630 2·1	2131 1·3
4 F	0352 2·2	1046 0·9	1730 2·1	2250 1·3
5 Sa	0456 2·2	1146 0·9	1824 2·1	2356 1·2
6 Su	0556 2·2	1233 0·8	1907 2·2	
7 M	0046 1·1	0652 2·2	1315 0·8	1945 2·3
8 Tu	0133 1·0	0741 2·3	1354 0·8	2020 2·4
9 W	0220 0·9	0828 2·3	1435 0·7	2056 2·4
10 Th	0309 0·7	0915 2·4	1516 0·7	○ 2135 2·5
11 F	0400 0·6	1001 2·4	1600 0·7	2215 2·6
12 Sa	0448 0·5	1048 2·4	1645 0·7	2256 2·6
13 Su	0535 0·4	1135 2·4	1731 0·8	2339 2·6
14 M	0622 0·4	1228 2·3	1818 0·9	
15 Tu	0024 2·5	0709 0·4	1322 2·2	1907 0·9
16 W	0113 2·5	0800 0·4	1424 2·2	(2000 1·0
17 Th	0207 2·4	0854 0·5	1531 2·1	2056 1·1
18 F	0311 2·4	0956 0·6	1639 2·1	2205 1·1
19 Sa	0424 2·4	1103 0·6	1741 2·2	2318 1·1
20 Su	0535 2·4	1207 0·7	1839 2·2	
21 M	0031 1·0	0643 2·4	1309 0·7	1930 2·3
22 Tu	0141 0·9	0748 2·4	1403 0·8	2016 2·4
23 W	0239 0·7	0845 2·4	1452 0·8	2058 2·4
24 Th	0328 0·6	0933 2·5	1535 0·8	● 2135 2·5
25 F	0413 0·5	1018 2·3	1613 0·9	2213 2·5
26 Sa	0452 0·5	1101 2·3	1646 0·9	2248 2·5
27 Su	0530 0·5	1141 2·2	1716 0·9	2324 2·5
28 M	0605 0·5	1220 2·2	1746 0·9	2358 2·5
29 Tu	0641 0·6	1300 2·1	1818 1·0	
30 W	0035 2·4	0715 0·7	1341 2·1	1858 1·0
31 Th	0115 2·4	0754 0·7	1428 2·0	1941 1·1

Position S. Chan, S. going –0610. Sp. 2¼ kn.; N. going +0010, Sp. 2¼ kn. In narrow chan. between N.W. side of Lowestoft Bank and harbour ent. 4 kn. may be exceeded at Springs. Position Brush Quay. Ingoing, +0545 Dover, 3¼-4 kn.; Outgoing, –0030 Dover, 3¼-4 kn. Ingoing stream corresponds approximately with S. going. Outgoing stream corresponds approximately with N. going.

TIDAL DIFFERENCES ON LOWESTOFT

PLACE	TIME DIFFERENCES				HEIGHT DIFFERENCES (Metres)			
	High Water		Low Water		MHWS	MHWN	MLWN	MLWS
LOWESTOFT	0300 and 1500	0900 and 2100	0200 and 1400	0800 and 2000	2.4	2.1	1.0	0.5
Orfordness	+0135	+0135	+0135	+0125	+0.4	+0.6	−0.1	0.0
Aldeburgh	+0120	+0120	+0120	+0110	+0.4	+0.6	0.0	0.0
Sizewell	+0047	+0047	+0032	+0032	0.0	−0.1	−0.2	−0.2
Southwold	+0035	+0035	+0040	+0030	+0.1	+0.1	−0.1	−0.1
Great Yarmouth								
Gorleston	−0035	−0035	−0030	−0030	0.0	−0.1	0.0	0.0
Caister-on-Sea	−0130	−0130	−0100	−0100	0.0	−0.1	0.0	0.0
Winterton-on-Sea	−0225	−0215	−0135	−0135	+0.8	+0.5	+0.2	+0.1

Low Water Yarmouth Yacht Station is 0 h. 25 min. after L.W. Lowestoft giving max. headroom under bridges for vessels leaving R. Bure.
Between Winterton and Gt Yarmouth rise of tide occurs mainly during $3\frac{1}{2}$ hrs. following L.W. at WINTERTON, level is within 0.3 m. of predicted H.W. height 4 hrs. before H.W. at Lowestoft till 1 hr. before H.W. at Lowestoft. At CAISTER where double high waters sometimes occur, and at GT. YARMOUTH level within 0.3 m. of H.W. height from 3 hrs. before H.W. until H.W. at Lowestoft.

Refer to predictions on pages 21:71-21:73

THE WASH

The Wash is not necessarily a difficult place to navigate, especially with local knowledge. It is an important bight of coast for small coasting vessels giving access to the thriving ports of Boston and King's Lynn as well as inland navigation through the River Nene, Wisbech, River Welland, and River Witham.

The periphery of the Wash area is encumbered with sandbanks that dry for some considerable way from the shore. Tidal streams run quite fast (2 knots at Springs) **and it is sensible to use the largest scale charts available.** The land is low lying with frequent poor visibility so care is necessary in this whole area. Tidal streams however set roughly straight in and out of the Wash Channels.

In thick weather with shallow water surrounding soundings should never be neglected.

Anchorage may be found anywhere in good weather in the entrance to the Wash but tidal rise and fall must be borne in mind.

RIVER HUMBER

The River Humber serves the main ports of Grimsby, Immingham, Hull and Goole. The River at Trent Falls (near Burton Stather) marks the meeting of the R. Trent and R. Ouse. The R. Trent is navigable for small vessels to Keadby and Gainsborough and runs up to Newark.

The River Ouse runs from Trent Falls to Goole, 9 miles, to Selby 25$\frac{1}{2}$ miles and to York 44 miles. The Aire and Calder Navigation is entered at Goole, the Aire running 34 miles to Leeds and the Leeds and Liverpool Canal.

FLOOD AND EBB STREAMS

The flood and ebb streams vary considerably in the Estuary. In the Lower Reaches the out going stream may reach speeds in excess of 5 knots at half spring ebb.

The Ouse and Trent have a much shorter period of flood, reaching speeds of 4 to 6 knots at Springs.

Due allowance for set is necessary in the upper reaches where the channel crosses the river athwart the tide.

TRENT AEGRE OR BORE

During spring tides the AEGRE forms on the first of flood, reaching various heights. May exceed 1.5m between Keadby and Gainsborough. Dangerous to small craft.

NAVIGATION

Below Hull the channel is relatively stable and 6 metre draught vessels may navigate at all states of tide. Chart published annually by Associated British Ports.

Above Hull the river is subject to very rapid changes. Bi-monthly Chart published.

A steep sea called "Hessle Whelps" develops when a W. wind meets the flood between Hessle and Barton. Dangerous to small craft.

The deeper water in the Trent and Ouse runs on the outside of the bights. Stone training walls present a danger when submerged. Cover about $\frac{1}{2}$ tide.

ANCHORAGES

Shelter for small craft against all winds but SSW to NW can be found just inside the point at Spurn. Hawke Anchorage offers protection to shipping from Northerly gales.

IMMINGHAM
MEAN SPRING AND NEAP CURVES
Springs occur 2 days after New and Full Moon.

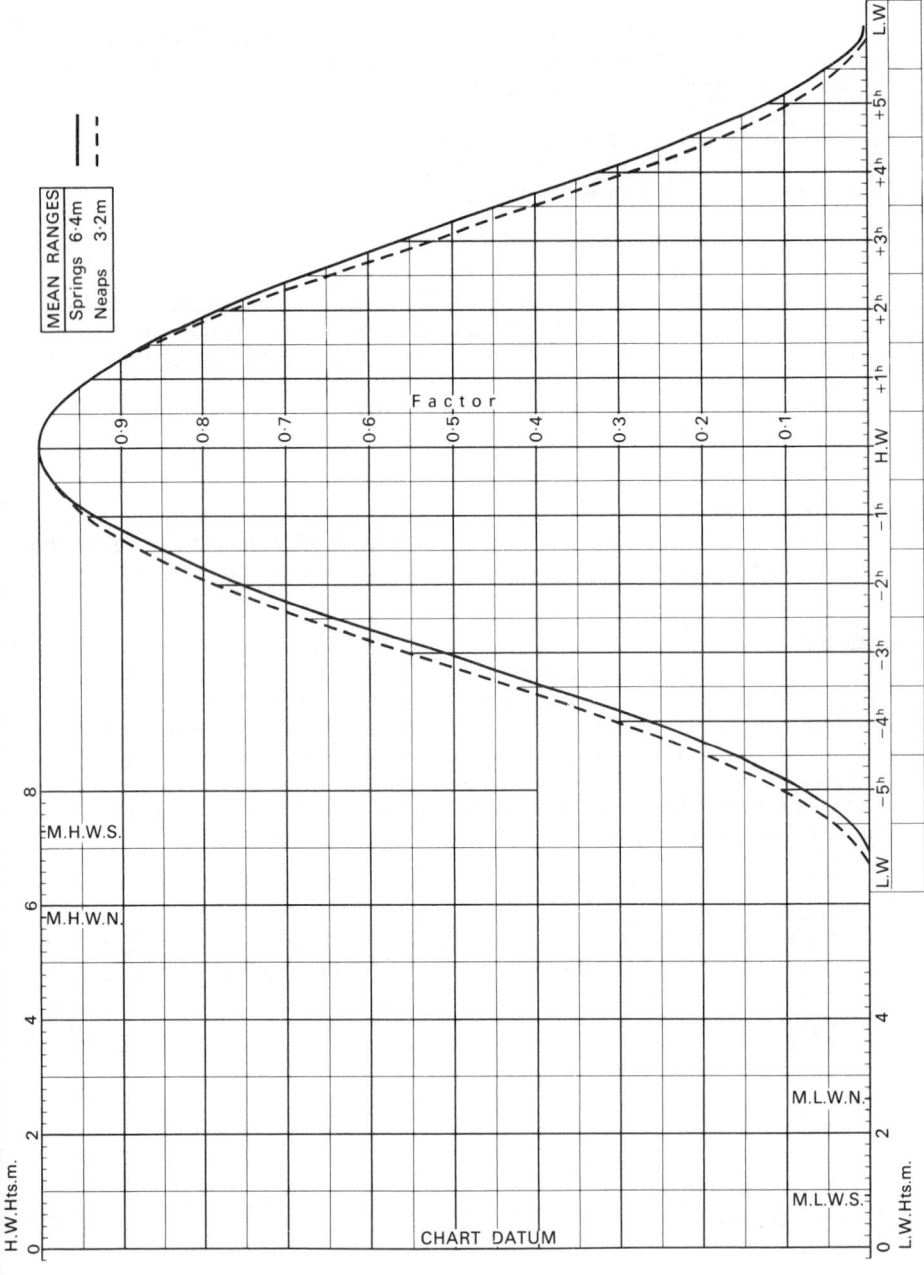

IMMINGHAM RIVER HUMBER 21:77

Lat. 53°38'N. Long. 0°11'W. **HIGH & LOW WATER 1992**

GMT **ADD 1 HOUR MARCH 29 — OCTOBER 25 FOR B.S.T.**

Moon symbols: ● new moon · ○ full moon · ☽ first quarter · ☾ last quarter

JANUARY

Day		Times (Time, m)
1	W	0301 6.1 · 0917 2.2 · 1536 6.1 · 2145 2.3
2	Th	0403 6.2 · 1012 2.1 · 1624 6.3 · 2238 2.1
3	F	0454 6.3 · 1057 2.0 · 1704 6.6 · 2323 1.8
4	Sa	0536 6.5 · 1137 1.9 · 1740 6.8 ●
5	Su	0004 1.6 · 0615 6.6 · 1215 1.8 · 1815 6.9
6	M	0039 1.5 · 0650 6.7 · 1249 1.7 · 1848 7.0
7	Tu	0113 1.4 · 0723 6.7 · 1323 1.7 · 1920 7.0
8	W	0145 1.4 · 0755 6.6 · 1354 1.7 · 1951 7.0
9	Th	0216 1.4 · 0827 6.6 · 1425 1.8 · 2023 6.9
10	F	0247 1.5 · 0900 6.4 · 1456 2.0 · 2056 6.7
11	Sa	0319 1.6 · 0932 6.2 · 1528 2.1 · 2131 6.5
12	Su	0353 1.8 · 1009 6.0 · 1604 2.3 · 2212 6.3
13	M	0435 2.0 · 1055 5.9 · 1654 2.5 · 2304 6.1 ☽
14	Tu	0530 2.2 · 1157 5.7 · 1801 2.7
15	W	0017 5.9 · 0646 2.4 · 1317 5.7 · 1930 2.6
16	Th	0144 5.9 · 0809 2.3 · 1434 6.0 · 2051 2.3
17	F	0304 6.2 · 0924 2.1 · 1541 6.4 · 2202 1.9
18	Sa	0413 6.5 · 1028 1.8 · 1637 6.8 · 2304 1.4
19	Su	0513 6.9 · 1126 1.5 · 1727 7.1 ○
20	M	0000 1.0 · 0607 7.2 · 1218 1.2 · 1815 7.4
21	Tu	0052 0.6 · 0656 7.4 · 1306 1.1 · 1900 7.6
22	W	0140 0.4 · 0742 7.4 · 1349 1.0 · 1944 7.7
23	Th	0223 0.4 · 0827 7.3 · 1432 1.1 · 2027 7.6
24	F	0305 0.6 · 0911 7.0 · 1510 1.3 · 2110 7.3
25	Sa	0345 1.0 · 0952 6.7 · 1549 1.6 · 2153 7.0
26	Su	0424 1.4 · 1035 6.3 · 1630 2.0 · 2242 6.5 ☾
27	M	0508 1.9 · 1125 5.9 · 1720 2.4 · 2342 6.0
28	Tu	0605 2.4 · 1229 5.6 · 1832 2.7
29	W	0104 5.7 · 0713 2.7 · 1349 5.6 · 2005 2.8
30	Th	0237 5.6 · 0844 2.7 · 1507 5.8 · 2127 2.5
31	F	0350 5.8 · 0949 2.5 · 1603 6.1 · 2224 2.2

FEBRUARY

Day		Times (Time, m)
1	Sa	0444 6.1 · 1040 2.2 · 1648 6.4 · 2311 1.8
2	Su	0526 6.4 · 1120 2.0 · 1725 6.7 · 2349 1.6
3	M	0601 6.6 · 1158 1.7 · 1758 6.9 ●
4	Tu	0024 1.4 · 0634 6.7 · 1232 1.6 · 1829 7.0
5	W	0056 1.2 · 0704 6.8 · 1304 1.5 · 1900 7.1
6	Th	0127 1.2 · 0733 6.8 · 1335 1.4 · 1931 7.1
7	F	0157 1.2 · 0802 6.8 · 1405 1.5 · 2001 7.1
8	Sa	0226 1.2 · 0832 6.6 · 1433 1.6 · 2032 6.9
9	Su	0254 1.4 · 0901 6.5 · 1503 1.7 · 2103 6.8
10	M	0322 1.6 · 0932 6.3 · 1535 1.9 · 2139 6.5
11	Tu	0357 1.8 · 1010 6.1 · 1617 2.2 · 2227 6.2 ☽
12	W	0447 2.1 · 1105 5.8 · 1720 2.5 · 2339 5.9
13	Th	0600 2.5 · 1229 5.7 · 1853 2.6
14	F	0119 5.7 · 0737 2.5 · 1406 5.8 · 2032 2.3
15	Sa	0237 6.0 · 0905 2.2 · 1522 6.2 · 2150 1.8
16	Su	0407 6.4 · 1016 1.9 · 1624 6.7 · 2255 1.2
17	M	0506 6.9 · 1115 1.4 · 1715 7.1 · 2350 0.8
18	Tu	0557 7.2 · 1205 1.1 · 1801 7.5 ○
19	W	0039 0.4 · 0642 7.4 · 1250 0.9 · 1843 7.7
20	Th	0123 0.3 · 0724 7.5 · 1331 0.8 · 1926 7.8
21	F	0204 0.3 · 0804 7.3 · 1409 0.9 · 2005 7.7
22	Sa	0240 0.6 · 0842 7.1 · 1444 1.1 · 2044 7.4
23	Su	0314 1.0 · 0918 6.7 · 1519 1.4 · 2125 7.0
24	M	0348 1.5 · 0955 6.4 · 1555 1.8 · 2207 6.4
25	Tu	0424 2.0 · 1035 6.0 · 1640 2.3 · 2301 5.9 ☾
26	W	0513 2.5 · 1132 5.6 · 1744 2.7
27	Th	0025 5.4 · 0632 2.9 · 1259 5.4 · 1928 2.9
28	F	0211 5.4 · 0811 3.0 · 1430 5.6 · 2101 2.6
29	Sa	0329 5.7 · 0924 2.7 · 1536 5.9 · 2202 2.2

MARCH

Day		Times (Time, m)
1	Su	0423 6.0 · 1016 2.3 · 1623 6.3 · 2247 1.8
2	M	0504 6.3 · 1058 2.0 · 1702 6.6 · 2325 1.5
3	Tu	0539 6.5 · 1134 1.7 · 1736 6.8
4	W	0000 1.3 · 0610 6.7 · 1217 1.1 · 1807 7.0 ●
5	Th	0032 1.1 · 0638 6.8 · 1241 1.3 · 1836 7.1
6	F	0103 1.0 · 0707 6.9 · 1312 1.2 · 1907 7.2
7	Sa	0133 1.0 · 0735 6.9 · 1342 1.2 · 1938 7.1
8	Su	0202 1.1 · 0805 6.8 · 1412 1.3 · 2009 7.0
9	M	0234 1.3 · 0834 6.7 · 1443 1.5 · 2043 6.8
10	Tu	0258 1.5 · 0905 6.5 · 1515 1.7 · 2121 6.5
11	W	0334 1.8 · 0943 6.2 · 1557 2.0 · 2212 6.2 ☽
12	Th	0421 2.2 · 1038 5.9 · 1702 2.3 · 2327 5.8
13	F	0536 2.5 · 1205 5.7 · 1839 2.4
14	Sa	0113 5.7 · 0720 2.6 · 1347 5.8 · 2019 2.1
15	Su	0247 6.0 · 0850 2.3 · 1507 6.2 · 2138 1.6
16	M	0357 6.5 · 1000 1.9 · 1607 6.7 · 2240 1.1
17	Tu	0452 6.9 · 1057 1.4 · 1658 7.1 · 2333 0.7
18	W	0540 7.2 · 1146 1.1 · 1742 7.4 ○
19	Th	0019 0.4 · 0621 7.3 · 1228 0.9 · 1824 7.6
20	F	0100 0.3 · 0659 7.4 · 1307 0.7 · 1903 7.7
21	Sa	0138 0.5 · 0735 7.3 · 1345 0.8 · 1942 7.5
22	Su	0212 0.8 · 0811 7.1 · 1419 1.0 · 2020 7.2
23	M	0243 1.2 · 0844 6.8 · 1451 1.3 · 2058 6.8
24	Tu	0314 1.6 · 0918 6.5 · 1527 1.7 · 2141 6.3
25	W	0348 2.1 · 0956 6.1 · 1607 2.1 · 2231 5.8
26	Th	0433 2.6 · 1047 5.7 · 1706 2.6 · 2349 5.4 ☾
27	F	0543 2.9 · 1207 5.4 · 1843 2.8
28	Sa	0128 5.3 · 0726 3.1 · 1342 5.5 · 2019 2.6
29	Su	0250 5.5 · 0844 2.8 · 1454 5.8 · 2122 2.2
30	M	0345 5.9 · 0941 2.4 · 1546 6.1 · 2210 1.8
31	Tu	0428 6.2 · 1024 2.1 · 1627 6.4 · 2251 1.5

APRIL

Day		Times (Time, m)
1	W	0504 6.5 · 1102 1.7 · 1704 6.7 · 2327 1.3
2	Th	0537 6.7 · 1139 1.5 · 1737 6.9
3	F	0003 1.1 · 0608 6.8 · 1214 1.3 · 1810 7.1 ●
4	Sa	0035 1.0 · 0638 6.9 · 1248 1.1 · 1842 7.1
5	Su	0107 1.0 · 0709 7.0 · 1321 1.1 · 1916 7.1
6	M	0140 1.1 · 0741 6.9 · 1354 1.2 · 1952 7.0
7	Tu	0211 1.3 · 0813 6.8 · 1429 1.3 · 2032 6.8
8	W	0243 1.5 · 0850 6.5 · 1507 1.5 · 2117 6.5
9	Th	0322 1.8 · 0932 6.3 · 1553 1.8 · 2214 6.1
10	F	0413 2.2 · 1031 6.0 · 1701 2.1 · 2333 5.8
11	Sa	0530 2.5 · 1156 5.8 · 1835 2.1 ☽
12	Su	0107 5.8 · 0706 2.6 · 1327 6.0 · 2004 1.8
13	M	0232 6.1 · 0829 2.3 · 1444 6.3 · 2117 1.4
14	Tu	0338 6.5 · 0936 1.9 · 1545 6.7 · 2217 1.1
15	W	0431 6.8 · 1033 1.5 · 1635 7.0 · 2308 0.8
16	Th	0516 7.0 · 1120 1.2 · 1719 7.2 · 2353 0.7
17	F	0556 7.1 · 1204 1.0 · 1801 7.4 ○
18	Sa	0034 0.7 · 0632 7.2 · 1243 0.9 · 1841 7.4
19	Su	0110 0.8 · 0707 7.2 · 1320 1.0 · 1921 7.2
20	M	0144 1.1 · 0741 7.0 · 1355 1.1 · 2001 6.9
21	Tu	0216 1.4 · 0816 6.8 · 1429 1.4 · 2040 6.6
22	W	0247 1.8 · 0850 6.6 · 1504 1.7 · 2121 6.2
23	Th	0321 2.2 · 0927 6.3 · 1543 2.0 · 2209 5.8
24	F	0402 2.5 · 1013 5.9 · 1637 2.3 · 2313 5.5 ☾
25	Sa	0501 2.9 · 1119 5.6 · 1753 2.5
26	Su	0034 5.4 · 0625 3.0 · 1242 5.5 · 1919 2.5
27	M	0151 5.5 · 0748 2.9 · 1357 5.7 · 2026 2.2
28	Tu	0251 5.7 · 0850 2.6 · 1456 6.0 · 2119 1.9
29	W	0341 6.0 · 0939 2.2 · 1543 6.3 · 2206 1.7
30	Th	0423 6.3 · 1024 1.9 · 1626 6.5 · 2249 1.4

To find H.W. Dover add 5 h. 00 min.

TIDAL DIFFERENCES PAGE 21:80. TIDAL CURVE PAGE 21:76.

Datum of predictions: 3.90 m. below Ordnance Datum (Newlyn) or approx. L.A.T.

21:78 RIVER HUMBER **IMMINGHAM**

HIGH & LOW WATER 1992 Lat. 53°38′N. Long. 0°11′W.

GMT ADD 1 HOUR MARCH 29 — OCTOBER 25 FOR B.S.T.

MAY

Day	Time	m	Day	Time	m
1 F	0501 1105 1705 2329	6·6 1·6 6·7 1·3	**16** ○	0529 1140 1742	6·9 1·3 7·0
2 Sa ●	0534 1144 1742	6·8 1·4 6·9	**17** Su	0007 0605 1222 1824	1·1 7·0 1·2 7·0
3 Su	0007 0610 1224 1819	1·2 6·9 1·2 7·0	**18** M	0045 0642 1300 1906	1·2 7·0 1·2 6·9
4 M	0043 0643 1302 1859	1·1 7·0 1·1 7·1	**19** Tu	0120 0717 1338 1947	1·4 7·0 1·3 6·7
5 Tu	0120 0720 1341 1942	1·2 7·0 1·1 7·0	**20** W	0154 0752 1412 2026	1·6 6·8 1·4 6·5
6 W	0157 0759 1422 2029	1·3 7·0 1·2 6·8	**21** Th	0225 0827 1447 2105	1·8 6·7 1·6 6·2
7 Th	0236 0842 1507 2121	1·6 6·8 1·3 6·6	**22** F	0300 0904 1525 2148	2·1 6·5 1·8 6·0
8 F	0321 0931 1559 2221	1·8 6·6 1·5 6·3	**23** Sa	0338 0946 1610 2237	2·4 6·2 2·0 5·7
9 Sa)	0416 1030 1705 2333	2·1 6·3 1·7 6·1	**24** Su	0424 1037 1705 2337	2·6 6·0 2·2 5·6
10 Su	0525 1143 1822	2·4 6·2 1·7	**25** M	0525 1140 1812	2·8 5·8 2·3
11	0050 0643 1302 1938	6·0 2·4 6·2 1·6	**26** Tu	0043 0636 1249 1920	5·5 2·9 5·7 2·3
12 Tu	0205 0759 1415 2047	6·2 2·2 6·4 1·4	**27** W	0147 0747 1355 2022	5·6 2·7 5·9 2·1
13 W	0310 0905 1517 2148	6·4 2·0 6·6 1·3	**28** Th	0246 0847 1453 2118	5·8 2·5 6·1 1·9
14 Th	0403 1003 1610 2240	6·6 1·7 6·8 1·2	**29** F	0336 0941 1545 2207	6·1 2·1 6·3 1·7
15 F	0448 1055 1658 2325	6·7 1·5 6·9 1·1	**30** Sa	0421 1031 1633 2255	6·4 1·8 6·5 1·5
			31 Su	0504 1118 1718 2340	6·7 1·5 6·8 1·3

JUNE

Day	Time	m	Day	Time	m
1 M ●	0543 1203 1803	6·9 1·2 6·9	**16** Tu	0024 0622 1246 1856	1·5 6·9 1·4 6·7
2 Tu	0024 0624 1249 1849	1·3 7·1 1·1 7·0	**17** W	0100 0659 1324 1934	1·6 6·9 1·3 6·6
3 W	0107 0706 1334 1938	1·2 7·1 1·0 7·0	**18** Th	0135 0734 1359 2011	1·7 6·9 1·4 6·5
4 Th	0151 0751 1422 2029	1·3 7·2 0·9 7·0	**19** F	0209 0808 1432 2047	1·8 6·8 1·5 6·4
5 F	0234 0836 1510 2121	1·5 7·1 1·0 6·8	**20** Sa	0242 0843 1507 2122	1·9 6·7 1·6 6·2
6 Sa	0321 0927 1600 2217	1·7 6·9 1·2 6·6	**21** Su	0315 0919 1542 2200	2·1 6·5 1·7 6·0
7 Su)	0412 1021 1657 2318	1·9 6·7 1·3 6·3	**22** M	0352 1000 1623 2244	2·3 6·3 1·9 5·8
8 M	0509 1122 1758	2·1 6·5 1·5	**23** Tu (	0434 1045 1712 2336	2·5 6·1 2·1 5·7
9 Tu	0022 0612 1229 1904	6·2 2·2 6·4 1·6	**24** W	0527 1142 1811	2·7 5·9 2·3
10 W	0130 0723 2012	6·1 2·3 1·7	**25** Th	0038 0636 1249 1919	5·6 2·7 5·8 2·3
11 Th	0236 0833 1449 2115	6·1 2·2 6·4 1·7	**26** F	0145 0751 1401 2027	5·7 2·6 5·9 2·2
12 F	0334 0936 1550 2212	6·3 2·0 6·4 1·6	**27** Sa	0250 0858 1507 2129	5·9 2·3 6·1 2·0
13 Sa	0424 1033 1644 2301	6·4 1·8 6·5 1·6	**28** Su	0346 1000 1606 2226	6·2 2·0 6·4 1·7
14 Su	0506 1122 1732 2344	6·6 1·6 6·6 1·5	**29** M	0437 1055 1701 2319	6·6 1·6 6·7 1·5
15 M ○	0546 1207 1814	6·8 1·4 6·7	**30** Tu ●	0523 1149 1753	6·9 1·2 6·9

JULY

Day	Time	m	Day	Time	m
1 W	0010 0608 1241 1843	1·3 7·1 0·9 7·1	**16** Th	0043 0642 1309 1919	1·6 7·0 1·3 6·7
2 Th	0057 0655 1330 1934	1·2 7·3 0·7 7·2	**17** F	0117 0714 1341 1951	1·6 7·0 1·3 6·7
3 F	0144 0740 1418 2022	1·1 7·4 0·6 7·2	**18** Sa	0149 0747 1412 2022	1·6 7·0 1·3 6·6
4 Sa	0229 0826 1504 2111	1·2 7·4 0·7 7·0	**19** Su	0220 0819 1443 2053	1·7 6·9 1·4 6·4
5 Su	0312 0914 1549 2200	1·3 7·3 0·8 6·8	**20** M	0250 0851 1514 2125	1·8 6·7 1·6 6·3
6 M	0356 1002 1635 2251	1·6 7·1 1·1 6·5	**21** Tu	0321 0925 1545 2159	2·0 6·5 1·7 6·1
7 Tu)	0444 1055 1726 2346	1·8 6·8 1·5 6·2	**22** W	0355 1002 1621 2238	2·2 6·3 2·0 5·9
8 W	0537 1156 1827	2·1 6·4 1·8	**23** Th	0435 1048 1709 2332	2·4 6·0 2·2 5·7
9 Th	0049 0643 1307 1935	6·0 2·3 6·2 2·1	**24** F	0534 1153 1817	2·6 5·8 2·4
10 F	0159 0801 1427 2046	5·9 2·4 6·1 2·1	**25** Sa	0046 0657 1316 1940	5·6 2·7 5·8 2·4
11 Sa	0307 0917 1539 2149	6·0 2·2 6·1 2·1	**26** Su	0208 0825 1439 2057	5·8 2·5 6·0 2·2
12 Su	0404 1019 1637 2241	6·2 2·0 6·3 1·9	**27** M	0317 0936 1550 2204	6·1 2·0 6·3 1·9
13 M	0451 1111 1735 2326	6·5 1·7 6·5 1·8	**28** Tu	0416 1040 1651 2304	6·5 1·6 6·7 1·6
14 Tu ○	0530 1156 1807	6·7 1·5 6·6	**29** W ●	0508 1137 1746 2357	6·9 1·1 7·0 1·3
15 W	0007 0607 1234 1843	1·7 6·9 1·4 6·6	**30** Th	0556 1231 1835	7·3 0·7 7·3
			31 F	0045 0641 1319 1921	1·0 7·5 0·5 7·4

AUGUST

Day	Time	m	Day	Time	m
1 Sa	0130 0724 1405 2006	0·9 7·7 0·4 7·4	**16** Su	0126 0723 1348 1952	1·4 7·1 1·2 6·8
2 Su	0213 0809 1447 2050	0·9 7·7 0·5 7·2	**17** M	0155 0752 1416 2022	1·4 7·1 1·3 6·6
3 M	0253 0853 1528 2134	1·1 7·5 0·8 6·9	**18** Tu	0225 0823 1444 2050	1·6 6·9 1·5 6·5
4 Tu	0332 0938 1607 2217	1·3 7·2 1·2 6·5	**19** W	0253 0854 1511 2119	1·8 6·7 1·7 6·3
5 W	0413 1024 1651 2305	1·7 6·8 1·6 6·2	**20** Th	0322 0928 1542 2153	2·0 6·4 1·9 6·1
6 Th	0502 1122 1744	2·1 6·3 2·1	**21** F (	0400 1010 1624 2241	2·2 6·1 2·2 5·8
7 F	0005 0605 1238 1856	5·8 2·5 5·9 2·5	**22** Sa	0454 1115 1729 2357	2·5 5·8 2·6 5·6
8 Sa	0123 0734 1411 2019	5·7 2·6 5·8 2·6	**23** Su	0621 1249 1904	2·7 5·7 2·7
9 Su	0243 0901 1529 2131	5·8 2·4 6·0 2·4	**24** M	0135 0801 1423 2034	5·7 2·5 5·9 2·4
10 M	0346 1007 1628 2224	6·1 2·1 6·2 2·2	**25** Tu	0256 0921 1539 2148	6·1 2·0 6·4 2·0
11 Tu	0434 1058 1713 2309	6·4 1·8 6·4 1·9	**26** W	0357 1027 1640 2247	6·6 1·4 6·8 1·6
12 W	0513 1139 1751 2347	6·6 1·5 6·6 1·7	**27** Th	0451 1123 1732 2340	7·0 0·9 7·2 1·2
13 Th ○	0549 1215 1824	6·9 1·4 6·7	**28** F	0537 1214 1818	7·4 0·6 7·4
14 F	0022 0621 1248 1855	1·5 7·0 1·3 6·8	**29** Sa	0027 0621 1300 1900	0·9 7·7 0·3 7·5
15 Sa	0055 0652 1319 1924	1·4 7·0 1·2 6·8	**30** Su	0110 0704 1342 1942	0·8 7·8 0·3 7·5
			31 M	0151 0747 1422 2022	0·8 7·8 0·5 7·3

GENERAL — Tidal streams run generally in direction of channel. The stream in main channel is irregular and constantly changes.

RATE AND SET — Hull Roads — Ingoing stream begins +0220 Dover, Sp. rate 5 kn. Outgoing stream begins –0450 Dover, Sp. rate 4 kn.

IMMINGHAM RIVER HUMBER 21:79

Lat. 53°38'N. Long. 0°11'W.   HIGH & LOW WATER 1992

GMT   ADD 1 HOUR MARCH 29 — OCTOBER 25 FOR B.S.T.

SEPTEMBER

Day	Time	m	Day	Time	m
1 Tu	0229 / 0829 / 1500 / 2101	1·0 / 7·6 / 0·9 / 7·0	**16** W	0159 / 0757 / 1415 / 2018	1·4 / 7·0 / 1·5 / 6·7
2 W	0305 / 0911 / 1535 / 2141	1·3 / 7·2 / 1·4 / 6·6	**17** Th	0227 / 0829 / 1443 / 2047	1·6 / 6·8 / 1·7 / 6·5
3 Th	0343 / 0956 / 1613 / 2223	1·6 / 6·7 / 1·9 / 6·2	**18** F	0258 / 0904 / 1514 / 2122	1·8 / 6·5 / 2·0 / 6·3
4 F	0428 / 1051 / 1702 / 2319	2·1 / 6·1 / 2·5 / 5·8	**19** Sa	0338 / 0950 / 1557 / 2210	2·1 / 6·2 / 2·3 / 6·0
5 Sa	0530 / 1211 / 1817	2·5 / 5·7 / 2·9	**20** Su	0433 / 1059 / 1702 / 2327	2·4 / 5·8 / 2·7 / 5·7
6 Su	0041 / 0707 / 1351 / 1951	5·6 / 2·7 / 5·6 / 2·9	**21** M	0601 / 1238 / 1841	2·6 / 5·7 / 2·8
7 M	0212 / 0842 / 1511 / 2107	5·7 / 2·5 / 5·9 / 2·7	**22** Tu	0110 / 0744 / 1412 / 2015	5·8 / 2·3 / 6·0 / 2·5
8 Tu	0319 / 0946 / 1607 / 2202	6·0 / 2·1 / 6·2 / 2·3	**23** W	0233 / 0903 / 1524 / 2128	6·2 / 1·8 / 6·5 / 2·1
9 W	0409 / 1033 / 1649 / 2244	6·4 / 1·8 / 6·5 / 2·0	**24** Th	0338 / 1007 / 1623 / 2227	6·6 / 1·3 / 6·9 / 1·6
10 Th	0448 / 1112 / 1725 / 2322	6·6 / 1·6 / 6·6 / 1·7	**25** F	0430 / 1104 / 1712 / 2318	7·1 / 0·9 / 7·2 / 1·2
11 F	0523 / 1147 / 1756 / 2356	6·9 / 1·4 / 6·8 / 1·5	**26** Sa ●	0516 / 1151 / 1754	7·5 / 0·6 / 7·4
12 Sa ○	0554 / 1218 / 1825	7·0 / 1·2 / 6·9	**27** Su	0004 / 0558 / 1236 / 1835	0·9 / 7·7 / 0·5 / 7·5
13 Su	0028 / 0625 / 1249 / 1853	1·4 / 7·1 / 1·2 / 6·9	**28** M	0046 / 0641 / 1316 / 1914	0·8 / 7·7 / 0·5 / 7·5
14 M	0059 / 0655 / 1319 / 1921	1·3 / 7·1 / 1·2 / 6·9	**29** Tu	0126 / 0723 / 1354 / 1951	0·8 / 7·7 / 0·8 / 7·3
15 Tu	0128 / 0726 / 1348 / 1949	1·3 / 7·1 / 1·3 / 6·8	**30** W	0204 / 0804 / 1429 / 2029	1·0 / 7·4 / 1·2 / 7·0

OCTOBER

Day	Time	m	Day	Time	m
1 Th	0239 / 0846 / 1503 / 2105	1·3 / 7·0 / 1·7 / 6·7	**16** F	0209 / 0812 / 1422 / 2026	1·5 / 6·8 / 1·8 / 6·7
2 F	0317 / 0931 / 1539 / 2145	1·7 / 6·5 / 2·2 / 6·3	**17** Sa	0246 / 0854 / 1458 / 2105	1·7 / 6·6 / 2·0 / 6·5
3 Sa	0359 / 1024 / 1624 / 2235	2·1 / 6·0 / 2·7 / 5·9	**18** Su	0328 / 0946 / 1543 / 2157	1·9 / 6·2 / 2·4 / 6·2
4 Su	0457 / 1140 / 1732 / 2353	2·5 / 5·6 / 3·1 / 5·6	**19** M	0427 / 1057 / 1651 / 2313	2·2 / 6·0 / 2·7 / 6·0
5 M	0628 / 1313 / 1909	2·7 / 5·5 / 3·2	**20** Tu	0553 / 1228 / 1822	2·3 / 5·9 / 2·8
6 Tu	0124 / 0802 / 1433 / 2029	5·6 / 2·6 / 5·7 / 2·9	**21** W	0046 / 0724 / 1352 / 1951	6·0 / 2·1 / 6·1 / 2·5
7 W	0237 / 0907 / 1529 / 2125	5·9 / 2·2 / 6·1 / 2·5	**22** Th	0206 / 0839 / 1501 / 2101	6·3 / 1·7 / 6·5 / 2·1
8 Th	0331 / 0955 / 1613 / 2209	6·2 / 1·9 / 6·4 / 2·2	**23** F	0311 / 0942 / 1559 / 2200	6·7 / 1·3 / 6·8 / 1·7
9 F	0413 / 1039 / 1649 / 2248	6·5 / 1·7 / 6·6 / 1·9	**24** Sa	0404 / 1037 / 1647 / 2252	7·0 / 1·0 / 7·1 / 1·4
10 Sa	0449 / 1111 / 1729 / 2323	6·8 / 1·5 / 6·8 / 1·6	**25** Su	0452 / 1126 / 1729 / 2339	7·3 / 0·8 / 7·3 / 1·1
11 Su ○	0523 / 1146 / 1751 / 2357	7·0 / 1·3 / 6·9 / 1·4	**26** M	0537 / 1210 / 1808	7·5 / 0·8 / 7·4
12 M	0556 / 1218 / 1821	7·1 / 1·3 / 7·0	**27** Tu	0021 / 0619 / 1249 / 1846	1·0 / 7·6 / 0·9 / 7·4
13 Tu	0031 / 0627 / 1249 / 1850	1·3 / 7·1 / 1·3 / 7·0	**28** W	0102 / 0702 / 1327 / 1923	1·0 / 7·4 / 1·1 / 7·3
14 W	0103 / 0700 / 1320 / 1921	1·3 / 7·1 / 1·4 / 7·0	**29** Th	0141 / 0744 / 1402 / 1959	1·1 / 7·2 / 1·5 / 7·0
15 Th	0137 / 0734 / 1351 / 1952	1·4 / 7·0 / 1·6 / 6·9	**30** F	0218 / 0827 / 1436 / 2036	1·4 / 6·8 / 1·9 / 6·8
			31 Sa	0254 / 0911 / 1511 / 2114	1·7 / 6·4 / 2·3 / 6·5

NOVEMBER

Day	Time	m	Day	Time	m
1 Su	0334 / 0959 / 1552 / 2159	2·0 / 6·0 / 2·6 / 6·1	**16** M	0328 / 0948 / 1542 / 2152	1·7 / 6·4 / 2·2 / 6·5
2 M	0424 / 1101 / 1647 / 2301	2·4 / 5·7 / 3·0 / 5·8	**17** Tu	0427 / 1052 / 1644 / 2259	1·8 / 6·2 / 2·5 / 6·3
3 Tu	0534 / 1217 / 1805	2·6 / 5·5 / 3·2	**18** W	0539 / 1207 / 1758	1·9 / 6·1 / 2·6
4 W	0021 / 0659 / 1333 / 1928	5·7 / 2·6 / 5·6 / 3·1	**19** Th	0017 / 0655 / 1323 / 1917	6·2 / 1·9 / 6·2 / 2·5
5 Th	0137 / 0809 / 1434 / 2033	5·8 / 2·4 / 5·8 / 2·8	**20** F	0133 / 0808 / 1432 / 2029	6·4 / 1·7 / 6·4 / 2·2
6 F	0239 / 0904 / 1525 / 2124	6·0 / 2·2 / 6·1 / 2·5	**21** Sa	0242 / 0912 / 1531 / 2132	6·6 / 1·5 / 6·6 / 1·9
7 Sa	0329 / 0949 / 1607 / 2209	6·3 / 1·9 / 6·4 / 2·1	**22** Su	0341 / 1009 / 1621 / 2227	6·8 / 1·4 / 6·8 / 1·6
8 Su	0412 / 1031 / 1644 / 2248	6·5 / 1·7 / 6·6 / 1·8	**23** M	0433 / 1059 / 1705 / 2316	7·0 / 1·3 / 7·0 / 1·4
9 M	0451 / 1111 / 1718 / 2327	6·8 / 1·5 / 6·8 / 1·6	**24** Tu ●	0520 / 1144 / 1744	7·1 / 1·2 / 7·2
10 Tu	0527 / 1147 / 1751	6·9 / 1·4 / 7·0	**25** W	0001 / 0604 / 1225 / 1822	1·2 / 7·2 / 1·3 / 7·2
11 W	0005 / 0603 / 1222 / 1824	1·4 / 7·0 / 1·4 / 7·1	**26** Th	0043 / 0648 / 1304 / 1859	1·2 / 7·1 / 1·4 / 7·2
12 Th	0042 / 0641 / 1259 / 1859	1·3 / 7·0 / 1·5 / 7·1	**27** F	0123 / 0731 / 1340 / 1935	1·3 / 7·0 / 1·7 / 7·1
13 F	0120 / 0721 / 1334 / 1935	1·3 / 7·0 / 1·6 / 7·1	**28** Sa	0201 / 0812 / 1413 / 2012	1·4 / 6·7 / 1·9 / 6·9
14 Sa	0159 / 0805 / 1412 / 2015	1·4 / 6·9 / 1·7 / 6·9	**29** Su	0236 / 0851 / 1447 / 2049	1·6 / 6·5 / 2·2 / 6·7
15 Su	0242 / 0853 / 1453 / 2100	1·5 / 6·7 / 2·0 / 6·7	**30** M	0312 / 0934 / 1524 / 2128	1·8 / 6·2 / 2·4 / 6·4

DECEMBER

Day	Time	m	Day	Time	m
1 Tu	0353 / 1019 / 1607 / 2216	2·1 / 5·9 / 2·7 / 6·2	**16** W	0419 / 1037 / 1630 / ☾2240	1·4 / 6·5 / 2·1 / 6·7
2 W	0442 / 1113 / 1701 / 2313	2·3 / 5·7 / 2·9 / 5·9	**17** Th	0516 / 1137 / 1729 / 2344	1·6 / 6·3 / 2·3 / 6·5
3 Th ☽	0544 / 1217 / 1808	2·5 / 5·6 / 3·0	**18** F	0619 / 1246 / 1838	1·8 / 6·1 / 2·4
4 F	0022 / 0655 / 1324 / 1923	5·8 / 2·5 / 5·6 / 3·0	**19** Sa	0056 / 0730 / 1357 / 1954	6·3 / 1·9 / 6·1 / 2·4
5 Sa	0133 / 0801 / 1426 / 2029	5·8 / 2·4 / 5·8 / 2·7	**20** Su	0212 / 0840 / 1501 / 2105	6·3 / 1·9 / 6·3 / 2·2
6 Su	0236 / 0858 / 1519 / 2124	6·0 / 2·2 / 6·1 / 2·4	**21** M	0321 / 0943 / 1557 / 2207	6·5 / 1·8 / 6·5 / 1·9
7 M	0329 / 0949 / 1604 / 2214	6·2 / 2·0 / 6·4 / 2·1	**22** Tu	0421 / 1037 / 1645 / 2302	6·6 / 1·7 / 6·7 / 1·7
8 Tu	0419 / 1035 / 1647 / 2259	6·5 / 1·8 / 6·7 / 1·7	**23** W	0512 / 1125 / 1727 / 2350	6·7 / 1·6 / 6·9 / 1·4
9 W ○	0502 / 1119 / 1725 / 2343	6·7 / 1·6 / 6·9 / 1·5	**24** Th ●	0558 / 1207 / 1805	6·8 / 1·6 / 7·1
10 Th	0546 / 1201 / 1803	6·9 / 1·5 / 7·1	**25** F	0032 / 0641 / 1246 / 1842	1·3 / 6·9 / 1·6 / 7·1
11 F	0027 / 0628 / 1243 / 1842	1·3 / 7·0 / 1·6 / 7·2	**26** Sa	0110 / 0720 / 1323 / 1917	1·3 / 6·8 / 1·6 / 7·1
12 Sa	0110 / 0714 / 1326 / 1923	1·1 / 7·1 / 1·4 / 7·3	**27** Su	0145 / 0755 / 1355 / 1951	1·3 / 6·7 / 1·8 / 7·0
13 Su	0155 / 0801 / 1408 / 2006	1·1 / 7·1 / 1·5 / 7·2	**28** M	0219 / 0830 / 1427 / 2026	1·4 / 6·6 / 1·9 / 6·9
14 M	0240 / 0850 / 1451 / 2053	1·1 / 6·9 / 1·5 / 7·1	**29** Tu	0250 / 0904 / 1458 / 2100	1·6 / 6·4 / 2·0 / 6·7
15 Tu	0328 / 0941 / 1538 / 2143	1·2 / 6·9 / 1·9 / 6·9	**30** W	0324 / 0939 / 1532 / 2136	1·7 / 6·2 / 2·2 / 6·5
			31 Th	0400 / 1017 / 1610 / 2219	1·9 / 6·0 / 2·5 / 6·2

For further information on Upper Humber, see p. 21:75.

TIDAL DIFFERENCES ON IMMINGHAM

PLACE	TIME DIFFERENCES				HEIGHT DIFFERENCES (Metres)			
	High Water		Low Water		MHWS	MHWN	MLWN	MLWS
IMMINGHAM	0100 and 1300	0700 and 1900	0100 and 1300	0700 and 1900	7.3	5.8	2.6	0.9
Cromer	+0050	+0030	+0050	+0130	-2.1	-1.7	-0.5	-0.1
Blakeney Bar	+0035	+0025	+0030	+0040	-1.6	-1.3	-	-
Blakeney....................	+0115	+0055	+0130	+0130	-3.9	-3.8	-	-
Wells Bar	+0020	+0020	+0020	+0020	-1.3	-1.0	-	-
Wells	+0035	+0045	+0340	+0310	-3.8	-3.8	-	-
Burnham (Overy Staithe)	+0045	+0055	-	-	-5.0	-4.9	-	-
Brancaster Bar	+0030	+0030	-	-	-0.6	-0.6	-	-
The Wash								
Hunstanton	+0010	+0020	+0105	+0025	+0.1	-0.2	-0.1	0.0
Old Lynn Road	+0020	+0020	-	-	-0.1	-0.1	-	-
West Stones	+0025	+0025	+0115	+0040	-0.3	-0.4	-0.3	+0.2
Kings Lynn	+0030	+0030	+0305	+0140	-0.5	-0.8	-0.8	+0.1
Wisbech Cut	+0020	+0025	+0200	+0030	-0.3	-0.7	-0.4	-
Lawyers Sluice	+0010	+0020	-	-	-0.3	-0.6	-	-
Tabs Head	0000	+0005	+0125	+0020	+0.2	-0.2	-0.2	-0.2
Boston......................	0000	+0010	+0140	+0050	-0.5	-1.0	-0.9	-0.5
Clay Hole	+0010	+0010	+0025	+0025	-0.2	-0.2	-1.7	-1.7
Skegness	+0010	+0015	+0030	+0020	-0.4	-0.5	-0.1	0.0
Inner Dowsing Lt. Tower	0000	0000	+0010	+0010	-0.9	-0.7	-0.1	+0.3
Humber								
Bull Sand Fort	-0020	-0030	-0035	-0015	-0.4	-0.3	+0.1	+0.2
Grimsby	-0003	-0011	-0015	-0002	-0.3	-0.2	0.0	+0.1
N. Killingham	+0005	+0005	+0010	+0010	0.0	0.0	0.0	0.0
Paull........................	+0010	+0010	+0015	+0015	+0.1	+0.1	-0.1	-0.1
Kingston upon Hull	+0005	+0015	+0010	+0020	+0.2	0.0	-0.2	-0.2
Humber Bridge...........	+0020	+0020	+0040	+0040	0.0	0.0	-0.4	-0.4
Brough	+0035	+0035	+0110	+0110	-0.5	-0.5	-0.9	-0.9
River Trent								
Burton Stather	+0105	+0045	+0335	+0305	-2.1	-2.3	-2.3	Dries
Keadby	+0135	+0125	+0415	+0355	-2.7	-3.1	Dries	Dries
Owston Ferry	+0155	+0145	-	-	-3.5	-3.9	Dries	Dries
Gainsborough	+0230	+0230	-	-	-	-	Dries	Dries
River Ouse								
Blacktoft...................	+0055	+0050	+0310	+0255	-1.5	-1.8	-1.9	-0.8
Goole	+0130	+0115	+0355	+0350	-1.6	-2.1	-1.9	-0.6

Refer to predictions on pages 21:77-21:79
The Trent and Ouse and Humber above Hessle are liable to frequent change. Beware half tide training walls along R. Trent. Beware tidal bore (max. height 1.5m.) on first flood on Trent.

TIDAL DIFFERENCES ON MIDDLESBROUGH (RIVER TEES ENT).

PLACE	TIME DIFFERENCES				HEIGHT DIFFERENCES (Metres)			
	High Water		Low Water		MHWS	MHWN	MLWN	MLWS
RIVER TEES ENTRANCE	0000 and 1200	0600 and 1800	0000 and 1200	0600 and 1800	5.5	4.3	2.0	0.9
Bridlington.................	+0100	+0050	+0055	+0050	+0.6	+0.4	+0.3	+0.2
Flamborough Head	+0056	+0048	+0053	+0046	+0.5	+0.4	+0.3	+0.2
Filey Bay....................	+0042	+0042	+0047	+0034	+0.3	+0.6	+0.4	+0.1
Scarborough	+0040	+0040	+0030	+0030	+0.2	+0.3	+0.3	0.0
Whitby	+0014	+0014	+0011	+0011	+0.1	0.0	-0.1	-0.1
Staithes	+0010	+0010	+0006	+0006	-0.1	0.0	0.0	0.0
River Tees								
Middlesbrough (Dock Ent.)	0000	+0002	0000	-0003	+0.1	+0.2	+0.1	-0.1
Tees Bridge (Newport)	-0002	+0004	+0005	-0003	+0.1	+0.2	0.0	-0.1
Hartlepool	-0004	-0004	-0006	-0006	-0.1	-0.1	-0.2	-0.1
Seaham	-0015	-0015	-0015	-0015	-0.3	-0.2	0.0	-0.2
Sunderland	-0017	-0017	-0016	-0016	-0.3	-0.1	0.0	-0.1

Refer to predictions on pages 21:82-21:84.

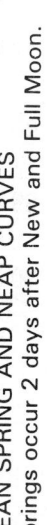

RIVER TEES ENTRANCE

MEAN SPRING AND NEAP CURVES

Springs occur 2 days after New and Full Moon.

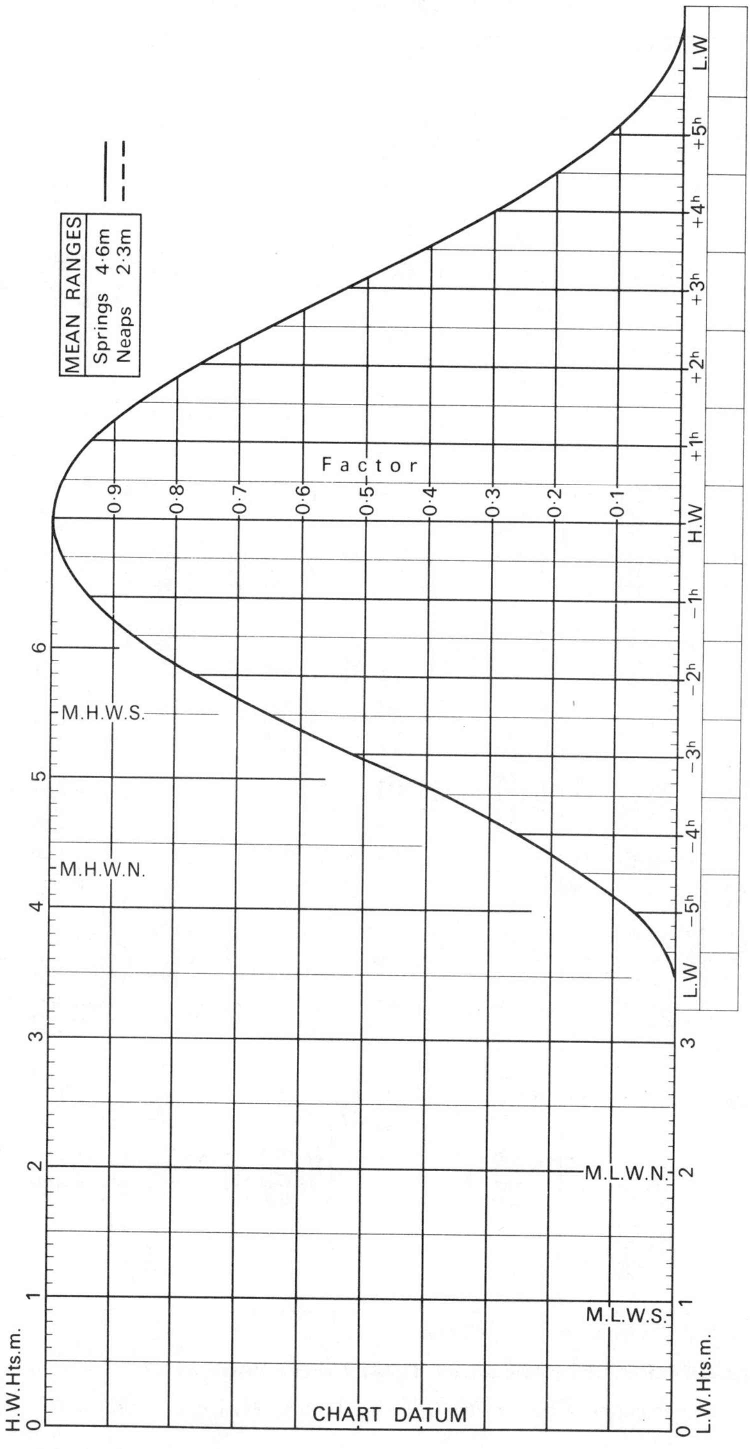
MEAN RANGES
Springs 4·6m
Neaps 2·3m
H.W.Hts.m.
L.W.Hts.m.
CHART DATUM
M.H.W.S.
M.H.W.N.
M.L.W.N.
M.L.W.S.
Factor
0·9 0·8 0·7 0·6 0·5 0·4 0·3 0·2 0·1
L.W −5h −4h −3h −2h −1h H.W +1h +2h +3h +4h +5h L.W
0 1 2 3 4 5 6

21:82 RIVER TEES MIDDLESBROUGH

HIGH & LOW WATER 1992   Lat. 54°35′N. Long. 1°13′W.

GMT   ADD 1 HOUR MARCH 29 — OCTOBER 25 FOR B.S.T.

	JANUARY				FEBRUARY				MARCH				APRIL		
	Time	m	Time	m	Time	m	Time	m	Time	m	Time	m	Time	m	Time	m

JANUARY

1 W — 0041 4·7, 0703 1·8, 1313 4·7, 1938 1·9 | 16 Th — 0607 2·0, 1224 4·7, 1845 2·0
2 Th — 0140 4·8, 0756 1·8, 1405 4·9, 2028 1·7 | 17 F — 0050 4·8, 0720 1·8, 1327 4·9, 1955 1·5
3 F — 0233 4·9, 0841 1·7, 1450 5·0, 2113 1·4 | 18 Sa — 0157 5·1, 0821 1·4, 1424 5·2, 2052 1·0
4 Sa — 0318 5·0, 0920 1·6, 1528 5·2, ● 2151 1·2 | 19 Su — 0255 5·4, 0913 1·1, 1515 5·5, ○ 2144 0·5
5 Su — 0356 5·0, 0955 1·5, 1604 5·3, 2227 1·1 | 20 M — 0346 5·6, 1001 0·8, 1602 5·8, 2231 0·1
6 M — 0432 5·1, 1028 1·4, 1636 5·3, 2259 1·0 | 21 Tu — 0435 5·8, 1045 0·7, 1646 5·9, 2318 −0·1
7 Tu — 0504 5·1, 1101 1·4, 1707 5·3, 2332 1·0 | 22 W — 0520 5·8, 1129 0·7, 1729 5·9
8 W — 0538 5·0, 1134 1·4, 1741 5·3 | 23 Th — 0003 −0·1, 0605 5·7, 1211 0·8, 1814 5·8
9 Th — 0004 1·1, 0612 5·0, 1208 1·5, 1814 5·2 | 24 F — 0046 0·1, 0650 5·5, 1255 1·0, 1859 5·6
10 F — 0038 1·2, 0647 4·9, 1243 1·6, 1851 5·1 | 25 Sa — 0131 0·5, 0737 5·2, 1337 1·4, 1947 5·3
11 Sa — 0114 1·3, 0726 4·7, 1321 1·8, 1930 5·0 | 26 Su — 0218 1·0, 0826 4·9, 1425 1·7, ◐ 2041 5·0
12 Su — 0153 1·5, 0810 4·6, 1401 2·0, 2014 4·8 | 27 M — 0308 1·5, 0920 4·7, 1520 2·1, 2144 4·7
13 M — 0239 1·7, 0902 4·5, 1453 2·2, ◐ 2112 4·7 | 28 Tu — 0407 1·9, 1023 4·5, 1632 2·3, 2258 4·5
14 Tu — 0334 1·9, 1003 4·4, 1600 2·3, 2220 4·6 | 29 W — 0519 2·2, 1134 4·4, 1804 2·4
15 W — 0445 2·1, 1113 4·5, 1722 2·3, 2336 4·6 | 30 Th — 0017 4·4, 0638 2·3, 1246 4·5, 1924 2·1
31 F — 0127 4·5, 0742 2·2, 1347 4·7, 2020 1·8

FEBRUARY

1 Sa — 0223 4·7, 0830 1·9, 1435 4·9, 2103 1·5 | 16 Su — 0145 5·0, 0809 1·5, 1409 5·2, 2040 0·8
2 Su — 0306 4·8, 0907 1·7, 1513 5·1, 2138 1·2 | 17 M — 0244 5·3, 0900 1·1, 1459 5·5, 2130 0·3
3 M — 0343 4·9, 0941 1·5, 1547 5·2, ● 2211 1·0 | 18 Tu — 0332 5·6, 0945 0·7, 1544 5·8, ○ 2215 −0·1
4 Tu — 0416 5·0, 1012 1·3, 1618 5·3, 2241 0·8 | 19 W — 0418 5·7, 1028 0·5, 1629 6·0, 2258 −0·2
5 W — 0444 5·1, 1044 1·1, 1647 5·4, 2311 0·7 | 20 Th — 0500 5·8, 1109 0·5, 1710 6·0, 2340 −0·1
6 Th — 0513 5·1, 1115 1·1, 1715 5·4, 2342 0·8 | 21 F — 0541 5·7, 1149 0·6, 1751 5·9
7 F — 0542 5·1, 1144 1·1, 1746 5·4 | 22 Sa — 0021 0·1, 0620 5·5, 1228 0·8, 1833 5·7
8 Sa — 0012 0·8, 0614 5·0, 1217 1·2, 1819 5·3 | 23 Su — 0102 0·6, 0701 5·3, 1307 1·2, 1916 5·3
9 Su — 0045 1·0, 0650 4·9, 1250 1·4, 1855 5·1 | 24 M — 0140 1·1, 0744 5·0, 1348 1·6, 2005 5·0
10 M — 0120 1·2, 0729 4·8, 1328 1·6, 1937 4·9 | 25 Tu — 0224 1·7, 0833 4·7, 1436 2·0, ◐ 2105 4·6
11 Tu — 0200 1·5, 0816 4·6, 1415 1·8, ◐ 2033 4·7 | 26 W — 0315 2·2, 0932 4·4, 1540 2·3, 2219 4·3
12 W — 0253 1·8, 0918 4·5, 1517 2·1, 2144 4·5 | 27 Th — 0424 2·6, 1044 4·3, 1719 2·5, 2346 4·2
13 Th — 0404 2·1, 1031 4·4, 1644 2·2, 2309 4·5 | 28 F — 0600 2·6, 1205 4·3, 1857 2·3
14 F — 0536 2·2, 1153 4·5, 1824 1·9 | 29 Sa — 0103 4·3, 0718 2·4, 1314 4·5, 1955 1·9
15 Sa — 0035 4·7, 0704 1·9, 1307 4·8, 1942 1·4

MARCH

1 Su — 0159 4·5, 0804 2·1, 1406 4·8, 2035 1·5 | 16 M — 0128 5·0, 0747 1·6, 1344 5·1, 2018 0·7
2 M — 0243 4·7, 0842 1·8, 1445 5·0, 2110 1·2 | 17 Tu — 0224 5·3, 0838 1·1, 1437 5·4, 2107 0·3
3 Tu — 0318 4·9, 0916 1·5, 1519 5·2, 2141 1·0 | 18 W — 0311 5·5, 0923 0·8, 1522 5·7, ○ 2151 0·0
4 W — 0347 5·0, 0947 1·2, 1549 5·3, ● 2212 0·8 | 19 Th — 0353 5·6, 1005 0·6, 1605 5·8, 2233 0·0
5 Th — 0416 5·1, 1018 1·0, 1619 5·4, 2242 0·6 | 20 F — 0433 5·7, 1045 0·5, 1644 5·9, 2312 0·1
6 F — 0443 5·2, 1049 0·9, 1647 5·4, 2313 0·6 | 21 Sa — 0510 5·6, 1123 0·6, 1725 5·7, 2350 0·5
7 Sa — 0513 5·2, 1120 0·9, 1718 5·4, 2344 0·7 | 22 Su — 0548 5·5, 1200 0·8, 1806 5·5
8 Su — 0544 5·2, 1153 0·9, 1752 5·4 | 23 M — 0028 0·9, 0626 5·2, 1238 1·1, 1850 5·2
9 M — 0018 0·9, 0619 5·1, 1228 1·1, 1831 5·2 | 24 Tu — 0104 1·4, 0706 5·0, 1319 1·5, 1937 4·9
10 Tu — 0055 1·1, 0659 4·9, 1309 1·3, 1918 5·0 | 25 W — 0144 1·9, 0753 4·7, 1404 1·9, ◐ 2034 4·6
11 W — 0136 1·5, 0749 4·7, 1357 1·6, 2014 4·7 | 26 Th — 0231 2·3, 0848 4·5, 1502 2·2, ◐ 2143 4·3
12 Th — 0231 1·8, 0850 4·5, 1501 1·8, ◐ 2129 4·5 | 27 F — 0333 2·7, 0957 4·4, 1621 2·4, 2302 4·2
13 F — 0341 2·2, 1003 4·4, 1625 1·9, 2254 4·5 | 28 Sa — 0459 2·8, 1112 4·4, 1757 2·3
14 Sa — 0515 2·2, 1126 4·5, 1804 1·7 | 29 Su — 0018 4·3, 0624 2·6, 1222 4·5, 1903 2·0
15 Su — 0019 4·7, 0645 2·0, 1242 4·8, 1920 1·2 | 30 M — 0116 4·5, 0720 2·3, 1319 4·7, 1949 1·7
31 Tu — 0159 4·7, 0803 1·9, 1403 4·9, 2027 1·3

APRIL

1 W — 0238 4·9, 0840 1·6, 1440 5·1, 2103 1·1 | 16 Th — 0243 5·4, 0855 1·0, 1455 5·5, 2123 0·4
2 Th — 0311 5·1, 0916 1·3, 1513 5·3, 2137 0·9 | 17 F — 0323 5·5, 0938 0·8, 1539 5·6, ○ 2203 0·5
3 F — 0340 5·2, 0949 1·1, 1546 5·4, ● 2211 0·7 | 18 Sa — 0404 5·5, 1019 0·7, 1621 5·6, 2242 0·6
4 Sa — 0412 5·3, 1022 0·9, 1619 5·4, 2244 0·7 | 19 Su — 0440 5·5, 1058 0·8, 1701 5·5, 2319 0·9
5 Su — 0443 5·3, 1057 0·8, 1654 5·4, 2319 0·8 | 20 M — 0517 5·4, 1136 1·0, 1744 5·3, 2356 1·3
6 M — 0518 5·3, 1133 0·9, 1734 5·4, 2356 1·0 | 21 Tu — 0555 5·2, 1214 1·2, 1827 5·1
7 Tu — 0556 5·2, 1212 1·0, 1819 5·2 | 22 W — 0034 1·6, 0637 5·1, 1256 1·5, 1916 4·9
8 W — 0036 1·2, 0641 5·1, 1259 1·1, 1911 5·0 | 23 Th — 0113 2·0, 0723 4·9, 1340 1·7, 2010 4·6
9 Th — 0124 1·6, 0733 4·9, 1351 1·4, 2013 4·8 | 24 F — 0200 2·3, 0817 4·7, 1435 2·0, ◐ 2111 4·4
10 F — 0221 1·9, 0835 4·7, 1457 1·6, 2126 4·6 | 25 Sa — 0257 2·6, 0905 4·5, 1539 2·1, 2217 4·4
11 Sa — 0330 2·1, 0947 4·6, 1617 1·6, 2244 4·6 | 26 Su — 0407 2·7, 1024 4·5, 1651 2·1, 2322 4·4
12 Su — 0455 2·2, 1104 4·7, 1741 1·4, 2358 4·8 | 27 M — 0520 2·6, 1127 4·6, 1758 2·0
13 M — 0616 2·0, 1214 4·9, 1852 1·1 | 28 Tu — 0019 4·6, 0625 2·4, 1225 4·7, 1853 1·8
14 Tu — 0103 5·0, 0718 1·6, 1316 5·1, 1949 0·8 | 29 W — 0109 4·7, 0716 2·1, 1314 4·9, 1939 1·5
15 W — 0155 5·2, 0810 1·3, 1409 5·4, 2037 0·5 | 30 Th — 0151 4·9, 0800 1·7, 1358 5·0, 2021 1·3

To find H.W. Dover subtract 4 h. 45 min.

TIDAL DIFFERENCES PAGE 21:80. TIDAL CURVE PAGE 21:81.

Datum of predictions: 2.85 m. below Ordnance Datum (Newlyn) or approx. L.A.T.

MIDDLESBROUGH RIVER TEES 21:83

Lat. 54°35′N. Long. 1°13′W.   HIGH & LOW WATER 1992

GMT   ADD 1 HOUR MARCH 29 — OCTOBER 25 FOR B.S.T.

MAY

Date	Time	m	Time	m	Time	m	Time	m
1 F	0231	5.1	0841	1.4	1438	5.2	2102	1.1
2 Sa ●	0306	5.2	0920	1.2	1516	5.3	2140	0.9
3 Su	0342	5.3	0959	1.0	1556	5.4	2218	0.9
4 M	0421	5.4	1040	0.9	1639	5.4	2259	1.0
5 Tu	0500	5.4	1120	0.8	1724	5.4	2342	1.1
6 W	0544	5.3	1207	0.9	1814	5.2		
7 Th	0027	1.3	0631	5.0	1256	1.0	1911	5.1
8 F	0117	1.6	0726	5.0	1351	1.1	2012	4.9
9 Sa)	0214	1.8	0826	4.9			2119	4.8
10 Su	0319	2.0	0933	4.8	1604	1.3	2227	4.8
11 M	0431	2.0	1040	4.9	1715	1.2	2333	4.9
12 Tu	0544	1.9	1147	4.9	1821	1.1		
13 W	0034	5.0	0647	1.6	1248	5.1	1917	1.0
14 Th	0126	5.1	0742	1.5	1342	5.2	2009	0.9
15 F	0214	5.3	0831	1.2	1433	5.3	2054	0.9
16 Sa ○	0257	5.3	0916	1.1	1518	5.4	2135	1.0
17 Su	0337	5.3	0958	1.0	1602	5.4	2215	1.1
18 M	0416	5.3	1038	1.0	1644	5.3	2252	1.3
19 Tu	0454	5.3	1118	1.1	1727	5.2	2330	1.5
20 W	0532	5.2	1157	1.2	1810	5.0		
21 Th	0008	1.7	0614	5.1	1238	1.4	1857	4.9
22 F	0049	1.9	0701	5.0	1321	1.6	1946	4.7
23 Sa	0134	2.1	0750	4.9	1410	1.7	2037	4.6
24 Su (	0225	2.3	0843	4.7	1502	1.9	2133	4.5
25 M	0322	2.4	0940	4.8	1600	2.0	2230	4.5
26 Tu	0424	2.5	1038	4.6	1659	1.9	2326	4.6
27 W	0527	2.4	1134	4.7	1758	1.8		
28 Th	0019	4.7	0626	2.2	1228	4.8	1852	1.7
29 F	0109	4.9	0720	1.9	1319	5.0	1943	1.5
30 Sa	0154	5.0	0809	1.6	1407	5.1	2030	1.3
31 Su	0238	5.2	0855	1.3	1455	5.3	2116	1.1

JUNE

Date	Time	m	Time	m	Time	m	Time	m
1 M ●	0320	5.3	0941	1.0	1542	5.4	2201	1.0
2 Tu	0404	5.4	1028	0.8	1630	5.4	2247	1.0
3 W	0449	5.5	1115	0.7	1720	5.4	2332	1.1
4 Th	0535	5.5	1203	0.6	1812	5.4		
5 F	0019	1.2	0624	5.4	1255	0.6	1906	5.3
6 Sa	0110	1.4	0716	5.3	1347	0.7	2002	5.1
7 Su)	0203	1.6	0813	5.2	1445	0.9	2102	5.0
8 M	0301	1.8	0913	5.1	1544	1.1	2203	4.9
9 Tu	0404	1.9	1016	5.0	1648	1.2	2304	4.8
10 W	0510	1.9	1120	4.9	1751	1.3	2333	4.6
11 Th	0004	4.9	0618	1.8	1224	5.0	1850	1.3
12 F	0100	4.9	0718	1.7	1323	5.0	1945	1.3
13 Sa	0151	5.0	0813	1.5	1417	5.1	2032	1.3
14 Su	0238	5.1	0902	1.3	1505	5.1	2117	1.3
15 M ○	0320	5.2	0945	1.2	1550	5.1	2156	1.4
16 Tu	0400	5.3	1027	1.1	1632	5.1	2234	1.4
17 W	0439	5.3	1105	1.1	1713	5.1	2311	1.5
18 Th	0517	5.3	1142	1.1	1752	5.0	2347	1.5
19 F	0556	5.2	1219	1.2	1831	4.9		
20 Sa	0025	1.7	0637	5.1	1259	1.3	1914	4.8
21 Su	0106	1.8	0719	5.0	1339	1.5	2000	4.7
22 M	0148	2.0	0805	4.9	1424	1.6	2047	4.6
23 Tu (	0236	2.2	0854	4.8	1512	1.8	2139	4.5
24 W	0329	2.3	0949	4.7	1607	1.9	2234	4.5
25 Th	0430	2.3	1047	4.6	1706	1.9	2333	4.6
26 F	0537	2.3	1147	4.7	1811	1.9		
27 Sa	0031	4.7	0643	2.0	1248	4.8	1913	1.7
28 Su	0126	4.9	0745	1.7	1345	5.0	2009	1.5
29 M	0217	5.1	0838	1.3	1440	5.2	2102	1.2
30 Tu ●	0305	5.4	0931	0.9	1532	5.4	2149	1.0

JULY

Date	Time	m	Time	m	Time	m	Time	m
1 W	0351	5.5	1019	0.6	1622	5.5	2237	0.9
2 Th	0437	5.7	1108	0.3	1711	5.6	2322	0.9
3 F	0524	5.7	1156	0.2	1800	5.6		
4 Sa	0008	0.9	0610	5.7	1243	0.3	1850	5.4
5 Su	0055	1.1	0659	5.6	1333	0.4	1942	5.3
6 M	0143	1.3	0753	5.4	1424	0.7	2034	5.1
7 Tu)	0235	1.6	0848	5.2	1517	1.0	2132	4.9
8 W	0332	1.8	0950	5.0	1618	1.4	2233	4.7
9 Th	0438	2.0	1057	4.8	1723	1.6	2336	4.7
10 F	0553	2.0	1205	4.8	1829	1.7		
11 Sa	0039	4.7	0703	1.9	1310	4.8	1928	1.7
12 Su	0137	4.8	0804	1.6	1409	4.9	2021	1.6
13 M	0227	5.0	0858	1.4	1458	5.0	2104	1.5
14 Tu ○	0311	5.1	0937	1.2	1542	5.1	2142	1.4
15 W	0349	5.2	1015	1.0	1619	5.1	2218	1.3
16 Th	0425	5.3	1049	0.9	1654	5.1	2252	1.3
17 F	0459	5.3	1123	0.9	1728	5.0	2326	1.3
18 Sa	0532	5.3	1157	1.0	1802	5.0		
19 Su	0000	1.3	0606	5.3	1231	1.1	1837	4.9
20 M	0035	1.5	0659	5.2	1306	1.2	1916	4.8
21 Tu	0112	1.6	0722	5.0	1343	1.5	1959	4.7
22 W (	0151	1.9	0805	4.8	1426	1.7	2047	4.5
23 Th	0239	2.1	0858	4.7	1516	1.9	2143	4.5
24 F	0337	2.2	1000	4.6	1619	2.1	2248	4.5
25 Sa	0451	2.3	1111	4.6	1734	2.1	2356	4.6
26 Su	0612	2.1	1224	4.7	1850	1.9		
27 M	0100	4.8	0725	1.7	1330	4.9	1955	1.6
28 Tu	0158	5.1	0827	1.2	1428	5.2	2048	1.2
29 W	0250	5.4	0918	0.7	1520	5.5	2137	0.9
30 Th ●	0337	5.7	1006	0.3	1609	5.7	2222	0.7
31 F	0422	5.9	1054	0.0	1654	5.7	2306	0.6

AUGUST

Date	Time	m	Time	m	Time	m	Time	m
1 Sa	0506	5.9	1139	-0.1	1739	5.7	2349	0.6
2 Su	0551	5.9	1224	0.0	1824	5.6		
3 M	0032	0.8	0636	5.8	1309	0.3	1912	5.4
4 Tu	0116	1.1	0725	5.5	1354	0.8	2001	5.1
5 W)	0203	1.4	0817	5.2	1446	1.2	2054	4.8
6 Th	0257	1.8	0919	4.9	1543	1.7	2156	4.6
7 F	0405	2.1	1030	4.8	1651	2.0	2305	4.5
8 Sa	0530	2.2	1149	4.8	1809	2.2		
9 Su	0018	4.6	0654	2.0	1302	4.6	1917	2.1
10 M	0121	4.7	0756	1.7	1359	4.7	2009	1.9
11 Tu	0213	4.9	0842	1.4	1447	4.9	2049	1.7
12 W	0255	5.1	0921	1.1	1526	5.0	2126	1.4
13 Th ○	0330	5.3	0955	0.9	1600	5.1	2158	1.3
14 F	0404	5.4	1027	0.8	1630	5.1	2230	1.1
15 Sa	0433	5.4	1057	0.8	1659	5.1	2301	1.1
16 Su	0503	5.4	1127	0.8	1728	5.1	2332	1.1
17 M	0532	5.4	1158	0.9	1759	5.0		
18 Tu	0003	1.2	0606	5.3	1231	0.9	1834	4.9
19 W	0038	1.4	0641	5.3	1304	1.3	1912	4.8
20 Th	0114	1.6	0723	5.0	1344	1.6	2000	4.6
21 F (	0200	1.9	0814	4.7	1433	1.9	2057	4.5
22 Sa	0259	2.1	0923	4.5	1540	2.2	2207	4.4
23 Su	0417	2.2	1042	4.5	1705	2.3	2325	4.5
24 M	0550	2.0	1205	4.6	1832	2.1		
25 Tu	0036	4.7	0710	1.7	1316	4.9	1939	1.7
26 W	0137	5.1	0810	1.2	1414	5.2	2031	1.3
27 Th	0230	5.5	0902	0.4	1504	5.5	2118	0.9
28 F ●	0315	5.8	0949	0.0	1549	5.7	2201	0.6
29 Sa	0358	6.0	1031	-0.3	1632	5.8	2244	0.5
30 Su	0442	6.0	1115	-0.2	1713	5.8	2325	0.5
31 M	0524	6.0	1156	-0.1	1755	5.6		

GENERAL — Streams set in direction of the channel. Turbulence at entrance especially with E. and NE. gales. Turbulence off Fifth Buoy during outgoing stream. Heavy rain increases duration and rate of outgoing stream. Heavy rain decreases duration and rate of ingoing stream.
WHEN TO ENTER — Between half flood and H.W. in bad weather. Great caution during NW., SE. and E. gales.

21:84 RIVER TEES MIDDLESBROUGH

Lat. 54°35'N. Long. 1°13'W. HIGH & LOW WATER 1992

GMT ADD 1 HOUR MARCH 29 — OCTOBER 25 FOR B.S.T.

SEPTEMBER

Day	Time	m	Day	Time	m
1	0005	0.7	16	0532	5.3
	0607	5.8		1157	1.0
Tu	1238	0.5	W	1758	5.1
	1837	5.4			
2	0048	1.0	17	0008	1.3
	0655	5.5		0609	5.2
W	1321	1.0	Th	1232	1.3
	1923	5.1		1837	4.9
3	0133	1.4	18	0048	1.5
	0747	5.1		0654	4.9
Th	1407	1.6	F	1313	1.6
)	2013	4.8		1923	4.7
4	0224	1.9	19	0135	1.7
	0848	4.7		0750	4.7
F	1501	2.1	Sa	1403	2.0
	2115	4.6	(	2023	4.5
5	0330	2.2	20	0236	2.0
	1003	4.5		0901	4.5
Sa	1612	2.5	Su	1510	2.3
	2227	4.4		2137	4.5
6	0503	2.3	21	0357	2.1
	1129	4.4		1024	4.5
Su	1743	2.6	M	1638	2.4
	2347	4.5		2257	4.5
7	0636	2.1	22	0530	1.9
	1245	4.5		1149	4.6
M	1856	2.4	Tu	1809	2.2
8	0055	4.7	23	0011	4.8
	0735	1.8		0649	1.4
Tu	1341	4.7	W	1257	4.9
	1947	2.1		1916	1.7
9	0145	4.9	24	0113	5.1
	0817	1.5		0747	0.9
W	1426	4.8	Th	1352	5.0
	2025	1.8		2009	1.3
10	0227	5.1	25	0205	5.5
	0852	1.2		0837	0.4
Th	1501	5.0	F	1441	5.6
	2059	1.5		2054	0.9
11	0302	5.3	26	0251	5.8
	0924	0.9		0903	0.1
F	1532	5.1	Sa	1523	5.7
	2131	1.3	●	2137	0.6
12	0333	5.4	27	0335	6.0
	0955	0.8		1005	0.0
Sa	1558	5.2	Su	1605	5.8
○	2201	1.1		2218	0.5
13	0402	5.4	28	0418	6.0
	1026	0.7		1047	0.1
Su	1628	5.2	M	1644	5.8
	2233	1.0		2259	0.6
14	0430	5.5	29	0459	5.9
	1055	0.7		1126	0.4
M	1654	5.2	Tu	1724	5.7
	2302	1.0		2339	0.8
15	0500	5.4	30	0542	5.7
	1125	0.9		1205	0.8
Tu	1724	5.2	W	1805	5.4
	2334	1.1			

OCTOBER

Day	Time	m	Day	Time	m
1	0019	1.1	16	0551	5.2
	0627	5.4		1208	1.4
Th	1246	1.3	F	1813	5.1
	1847	5.2			
2	0104	1.5	17	0031	1.4
	0719	5.0		0638	5.0
F	1330	1.9	Sa	1252	1.7
	1936	4.9		1902	4.9
3	0154	1.9	18	0123	1.6
	0819	4.7		0739	4.8
Sa	1419	2.4	Su	1344	2.0
)	2035	4.6		2002	4.7
4	0257	2.2	19	0225	1.8
	0932	4.4		0850	4.6
Su	1526	2.7	M	1453	2.3
	2146	4.5	(	2113	4.6
5	0423	2.4	20	0343	1.8
	1046	4.3		1009	4.6
M	1654	2.8	Tu	1615	2.4
	2302	4.5		2230	4.7
6	0554	2.2	21	0508	1.6
	1210	4.4		1127	4.7
Tu	1815	2.6	W	1740	2.2
				2343	4.9
7	0011	4.6	22	0621	1.3
	0654	1.9		1234	5.0
W	1306	4.6	Th	1847	1.8
	1909	2.3			
8	0106	4.9	23	0045	5.2
	0738	1.6		0720	0.9
Th	1348	4.8	F	1327	5.2
	1950	2.0		1942	1.4
9	0148	5.1	24	0140	5.5
	0814	1.3		0810	0.6
F	1426	5.0	Sa	1416	5.5
	2025	1.7		2030	1.1
10	0227	5.2	25	0228	5.7
	0847	1.1		0855	0.4
Sa	1457	5.1	Su	1459	5.6
	2100	1.4	●	2114	0.8
11	0259	5.4	26	0313	5.8
	0920	0.9		0938	0.4
Su	1526	5.3	M	1539	5.7
○	2133	1.2		2155	0.7
12	0330	5.4	27	0356	5.8
	0951	0.8		1019	0.5
M	1554	5.3	Tu	1619	5.7
	2203	1.1		2237	0.8
13	0400	5.5	28	0439	5.7
	1024	0.8		1059	0.8
Tu	1625	5.3	W	1657	5.6
	2237	1.0		2318	0.9
14	0433	5.4	29	0522	5.5
	1057	0.9		1137	1.1
W	1656	5.3	Th	1736	5.4
	2311	1.1		2358	1.2
15	0510	5.4	30	0607	5.3
	1130	1.1		1215	1.6
Th	1732	5.2	F	1819	5.2
	2349	1.2			
			31	0042	1.5
				0657	5.0
			Sa	1247	2.0
				1906	5.0

NOVEMBER

Day	Time	m	Day	Time	m
1	0130	1.8	16	0119	1.2
	0753	4.7		0733	4.9
Su	1344	2.4	M	1335	1.9
	2001	4.8		1949	5.0
2	0225	2.1	17	0218	1.4
	0857	4.5		0838	4.8
M	1442	2.7	Tu	1438	2.1
)	2104	4.6	(	2054	4.9
3	0333	2.3	18	0326	1.5
	1006	4.4		0950	4.7
Tu	1554	2.8	W	1550	2.2
	2212	4.6		2203	4.9
4	0448	2.3	19	0439	1.4
	1115	4.4		1059	4.8
W	1712	2.8	Th	1706	2.1
	2319	4.6		2315	4.9
5	0555	2.1	20	0551	1.3
	1214	4.6		1204	4.9
Th	1816	2.5	F	1816	1.9
6	0017	4.8	21	0019	5.1
	0647	1.9		0652	1.1
F	1303	4.8	Sa	1302	5.1
	1906	2.2		1916	1.6
7	0106	4.9	22	0117	5.3
	0730	1.6		0746	0.9
Sa	1344	4.9	Su	1352	5.3
	1949	1.9		2009	1.3
8	0148	5.1	23	0210	5.5
	0810	1.4		0834	0.8
Su	1421	5.1	M	1438	5.4
	2028	1.6		2055	1.1
9	0227	5.2	24	0258	5.5
	0847	1.2		0918	0.8
M	1455	5.3	Tu	1520	5.5
	2106	1.4	●	2141	0.9
10	0304	5.4	25	0343	5.6
	0923	1.1		0958	0.9
Tu	1529	5.4	W	1600	5.6
○	2141	1.2		2222	0.9
11	0339	5.4	26	0428	5.5
	0958	1.0		1038	1.1
W	1602	5.4	Th	1639	5.5
	2218	1.1		2304	1.0
12	0418	5.4	27	0510	5.4
	1035	1.0		1115	1.3
Th	1637	5.4	F	1718	5.4
	2258	1.0		2343	1.1
13	0459	5.4	28	0552	5.2
	1113	1.2		1153	1.6
F	1717	5.4	Sa	1758	5.3
	2339	1.0			
14	0544	5.3	29	0024	1.3
	1156	1.3		0637	5.0
Sa	1800	5.3	Su	1232	1.9
				1841	5.1
15	0025	1.1	30	0106	1.6
	0636	5.1		0725	4.8
Su	1242	1.6	M	1314	2.2
	1851	5.1		1929	5.0

DECEMBER

Day	Time	m	Day	Time	m
1	0151	1.8	16	0205	1.0
	0816	4.6		0820	5.0
Tu	1401	2.4	W	1418	1.8
	2021	4.8	(	2031	5.1
2	0245	2.0	17	0305	1.2
	0912	4.5		0922	4.9
W	1457	2.6	Th	1520	2.0
)	2120	4.7		2137	5.0
3	0341	2.2	18	0410	1.3
	1013	4.4		1027	4.8
Th	1602	2.7	F	1631	2.0
	2221	4.6		2247	4.9
4	0445	2.2	19	0519	1.4
	1113	4.5		1134	4.7
F	1710	2.6	Sa	1747	2.0
	2322	4.6		2357	4.9
5	0547	2.1	20	0626	1.4
	1211	4.6		1238	4.9
Sa	1815	2.4	Su	1856	1.8
6	0019	4.7	21	0102	5.0
	0643	1.9		0725	1.4
Su	1302	4.8	M	1334	5.0
	1910	2.2		1956	1.5
7	0112	4.9	22	0202	5.1
	0732	1.7		0818	1.3
M	1347	5.0	Tu	1426	5.2
	1959	1.8		2048	1.2
8	0158	5.1	23	0252	5.2
	0818	1.5		0906	1.2
Tu	1428	5.2	W	1509	5.3
	2042	1.5		2134	1.0
9	0243	5.2	24	0337	5.3
	0900	1.3		0947	1.2
W	1508	5.3	Th	1550	5.4
○	2126	1.2		2215	0.9
10	0326	5.4	25	0421	5.3
	0942	1.1		1024	1.3
Th	1546	5.5	F	1628	5.4
	2208	0.9		2254	0.9
11	0409	5.5	26	0459	5.2
	1024	1.1		1109	1.3
F	1626	5.5	Sa	1703	5.4
	2251	0.8		2330	1.0
12	0454	5.5	27	0536	5.2
	1105	1.1		1133	1.4
Sa	1708	5.6	Su	1739	5.4
	2336	0.7			
13	0541	5.4	28	0005	1.1
	1149	1.1		0613	5.0
Su	1752	5.5	M	1208	1.6
				1816	5.3
14	0022	0.7	29	0041	1.2
	0630	5.3		0652	4.9
M	1235	1.3	Tu	1245	1.7
	1840	5.4		1855	5.1
15	0113	0.8	30	0119	1.5
	0723	5.2		0733	4.7
Tu	1324	1.5	W	1324	2.0
	1933	5.3		1939	4.9
			31	0158	1.7
				0819	4.6
			Th	1407	2.2
				2024	4.8

RATE AND SET — Off Entrance to R. Tees — SE. going begins +0150 Dover, Sp. rate 1½ kn. NW. going begins –0420 Dover, Sp. rate 1½ kn. In entrance — ingoing begins –0025 Dover, Sp. rate 2-3 kn. Outgoing begins +0530 Dover. Sp. rate 2-3 kn.

NORTH SEA — TIDAL STREAMS

Produced from portion(s) of BA Tidal Stream Atlases with the santion of the Controller, H.M. Stationery Office and of the Hydrographer of the Navy.

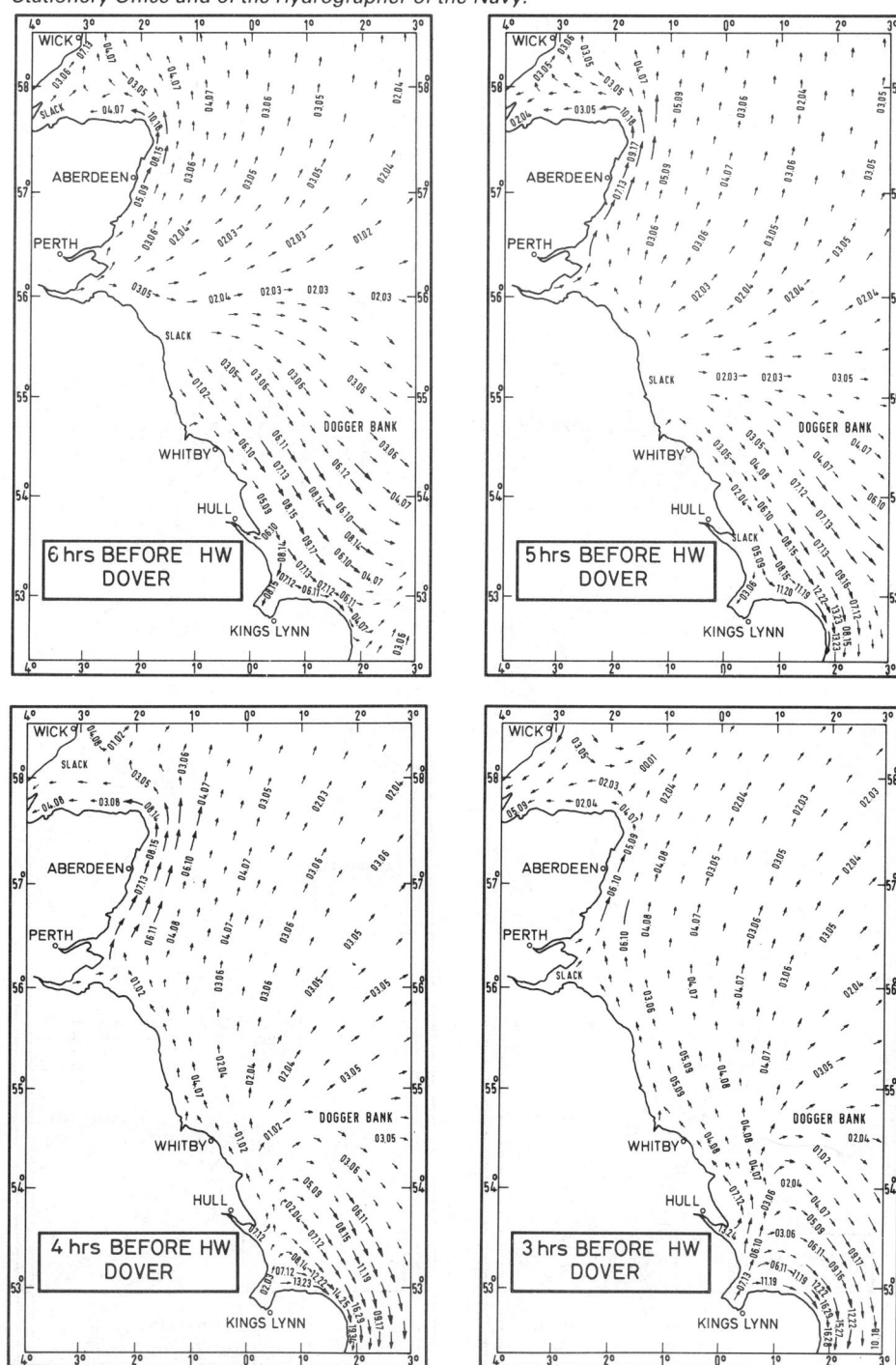

NORTH SEA — TIDAL STREAMS

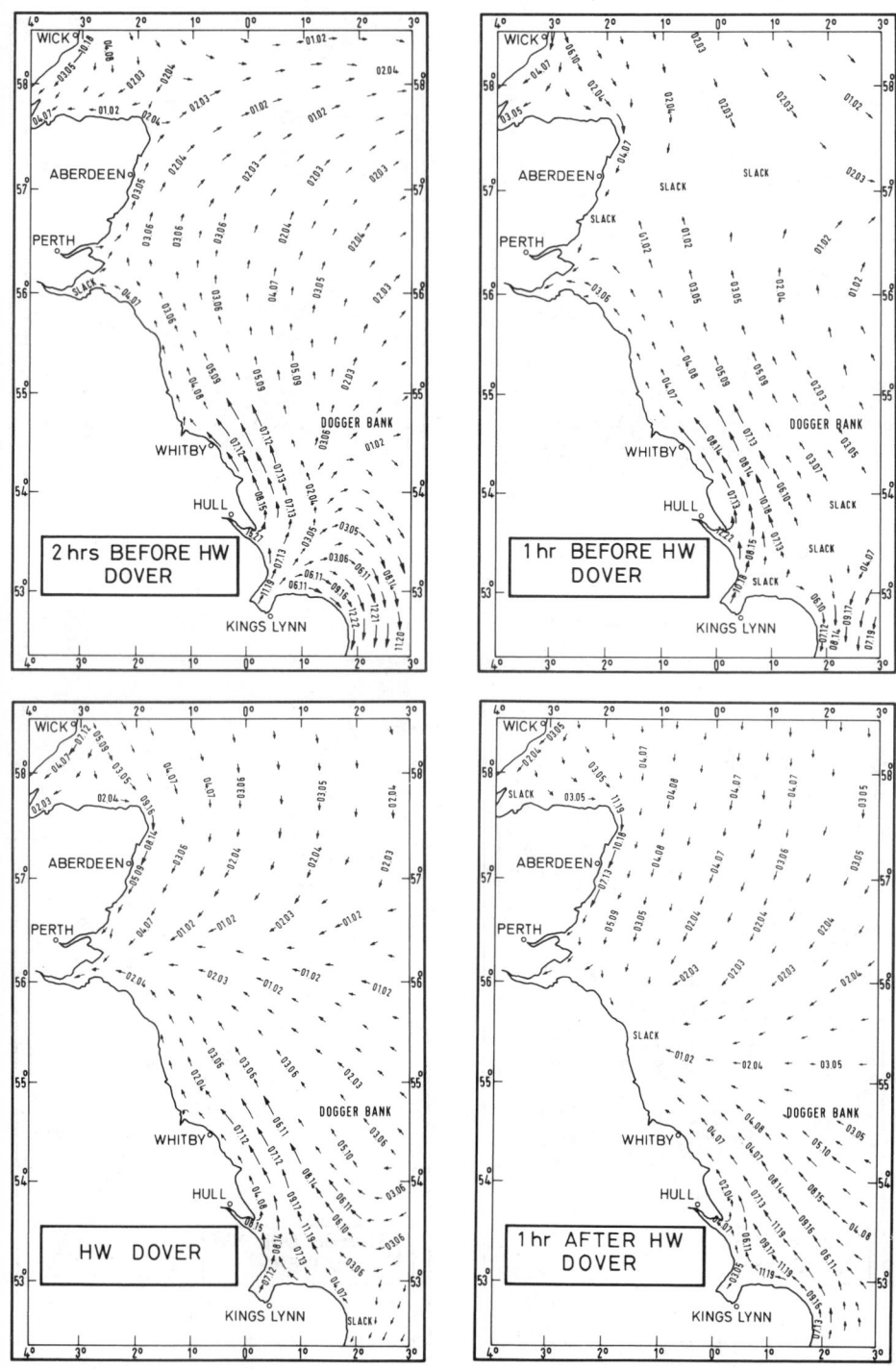

NORTH SEA — TIDAL STREAMS

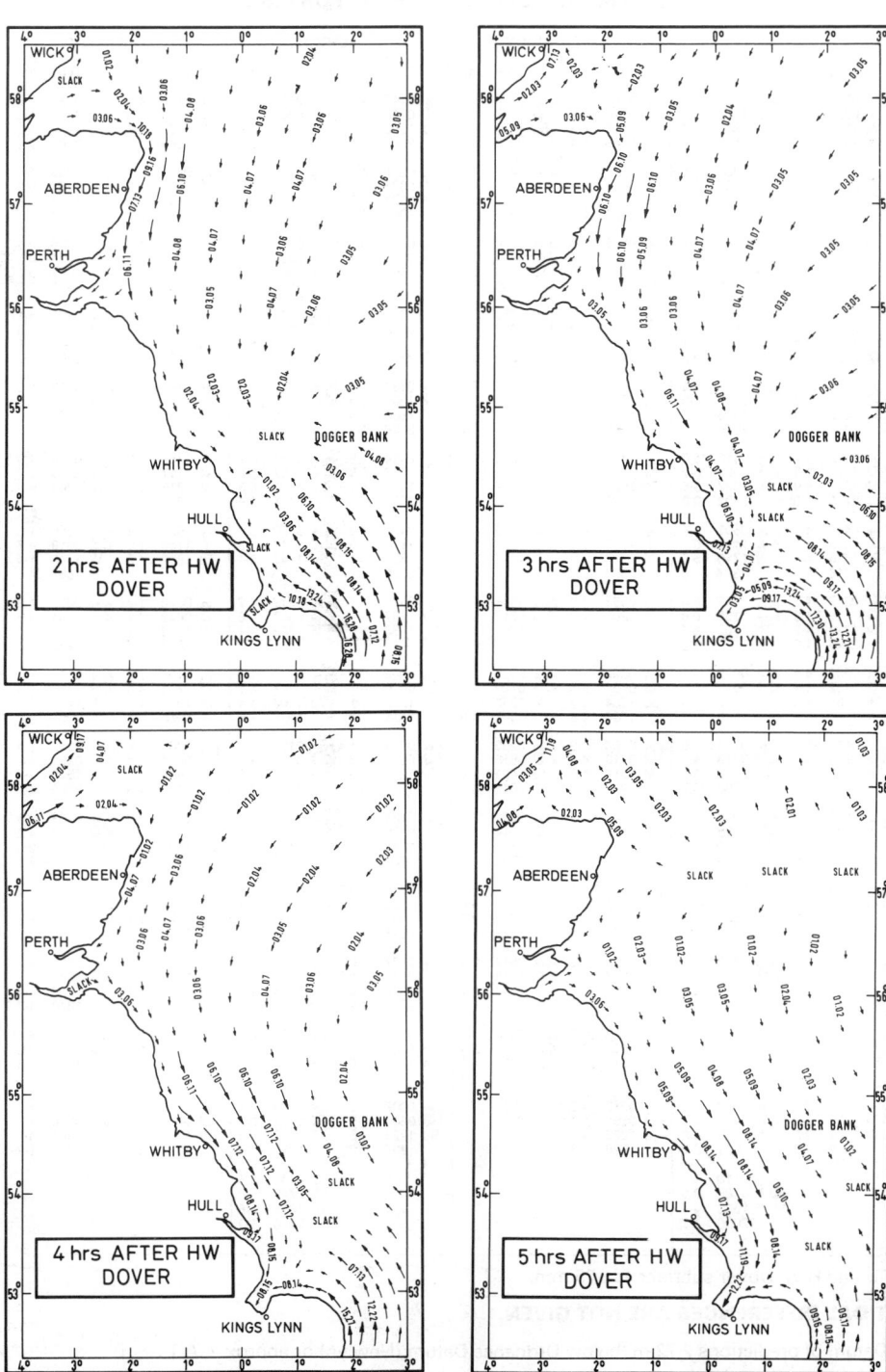

21:88   SUNDERLAND

HIGH & LOW WATER 1992   Lat. 54°55'N. Long. 1°21'W.

GMT   ADD 1 HOUR MARCH 29 — OCTOBER 25 FOR B.S.T.

JANUARY

Day	Time m / Time m / Time m / Time m	Day	Time m / Time m / Time m / Time m
1 W	0024 4.4 / 0650 1.7 / 1256 4.4 / 1924 1.8	16	0554 1.9 / 1207 4.3 / Th 1832 1.9
2 Th	0123 4.5 / 0742 1.7 / 1347 4.6 / 2014 1.6	17	0033 4.5 / 0707 1.7 / F 1310 4.6 / 1941 1.5
3 F	0215 4.6 / 0827 1.6 / 1432 4.7 / 2058 1.4	18	0140 4.7 / 0807 1.4 / Sa 1406 4.9 / 2038 1.0
4 Sa	0300 4.6 / 0905 1.5 / 1510 4.8 / ● 2136 1.2	19	0237 5.0 / 0858 1.1 / Su 1457 5.1 / ○ 2129 0.5
5 Su	0338 4.7 / 0940 1.4 / 1545 4.9 / 2211 1.1	20	0328 5.2 / 0946 0.8 / M 1543 5.4 / 2215 0.2
6 M	0413 4.7 / 1012 1.3 / 1617 4.9 / 2243 1.0	21	0416 5.3 / 1029 0.7 / Tu 1627 5.5 / 2302 0.0
7 Tu	0445 4.7 / 1045 1.3 / 1648 4.9 / 2316 1.0	22	0501 5.4 / 1113 0.7 / W 1710 5.5 / 2347 0.0
8 W	0519 4.7 / 1118 1.3 / 1722 4.9 / 2348 1.0	23	0546 5.3 / 1155 0.8 / Th 1755 5.4
9 Th	0553 4.6 / 1152 1.4 / 1755 4.8	24	0030 0.2 / 0631 5.1 / F 1239 1.0 / 1840 5.2
10 F	0022 1.1 / 0628 4.5 / 1227 1.5 / 1832 4.7	25	0115 0.5 / 0718 4.9 / Sa 1322 1.3 / 1928 5.0
11 Sa	0058 1.3 / 0707 4.4 / 1305 1.7 / 1911 4.6	26	0203 1.0 / 0808 4.6 / Su 1410 1.7 / (2023 4.7
12 Su	0138 1.5 / 0752 4.3 / 1346 1.9 / 1956 4.5	27	0254 1.4 / 0902 4.3 / M 1506 2.0 / 2126 4.4
13 M	0224 1.7 / 0844 4.2 / 1438 2.1 /) 2054 4.3	28	0353 1.9 / 1006 4.2 / Tu 1619 2.2 / 2241 4.2
14 Tu	0320 1.9 / 0946 4.1 / 1546 2.2 / 2203 4.3	29	0506 2.1 / 1117 4.1 / W 1751 2.2
15 W	0432 2.0 / 1056 4.2 / 1709 2.2 / 2319 4.3	30	0000 4.1 / 0625 2.2 / Th 1229 4.2 / 1911 2.0
		31	0110 4.2 / 0728 2.0 / F 1330 4.4 / 2006 1.7

FEBRUARY

Day	Time m / Time m / Time m / Time m	Day	Time m / Time m / Time m / Time m
1 Sa	0205 4.4 / 0816 1.9 / 1417 4.5 / 2048 1.4	16	0128 4.6 / 0755 1.4 / Su 1351 4.8 / 2026 0.8
2 Su	0248 4.5 / 0852 1.6 / 1455 4.7 / 2123 1.2	17	0226 4.9 / 0845 1.1 / M 1441 5.1 / 2115 0.3
3 M	0325 4.6 / 0926 1.4 / 1529 4.9 / ● 2156 1.0	18	0314 5.2 / 0930 0.8 / Tu 1526 5.4 / ○ 2200 0.0
4 Tu	0357 4.7 / 0957 1.2 / 1559 4.9 / 2225 0.8	19	0359 5.3 / 1012 0.6 / W 1610 5.5 / 2242 -0.1
5 W	0425 4.7 / 1028 1.1 / 1628 5.0 / 2255 0.8	20	0441 5.4 / 1053 0.5 / Th 1651 5.5 / 2324 -0.1
6 Th	0454 4.7 / 1059 1.1 / 1656 5.0 / 2326 0.8	21	0522 5.3 / 1133 0.6 / F 1732 5.5
7 F	0523 4.7 / 1128 1.1 / 1727 5.0 / 2356 0.8	22	0005 0.2 / 0601 5.1 / Sa 1212 0.8 / 1814 5.2
8 Sa	0555 4.7 / 1201 1.2 / 1800 4.9	23	0046 0.6 / 0642 4.9 / Su 1251 1.1 / 1857 5.0
9 Su	0029 1.0 / 0631 4.6 / 1234 1.3 / 1836 4.8	24	0125 1.1 / 0725 4.6 / M 1333 1.5 / 1947 4.6
10 M	0104 1.2 / 0710 4.4 / 1312 1.5 / 1918 4.6	25	0209 1.6 / 0815 4.3 / Tu 1421 1.9 / ● 2047 4.3
11 Tu	0145 1.5 / 0758 4.3 / 1400 1.8 / 2015 4.4	26	0301 2.1 / 0914 4.1 / W 1526 2.2 / 2202 4.0
12 W	0238 1.8 / 0900 4.2 / 1503 2.0 / 2126 4.2	27	0411 2.4 / 1027 4.0 / Th 1706 2.3 / 2329 4.0
13 Th	0350 2.0 / 1014 4.1 / 1631 2.1 / 2252 4.2	28	0547 2.5 / 1148 4.0 / F 1844 2.1
14 F	0523 2.1 / 1136 4.2 / 1811 1.8	29	0046 4.1 / 0703 2.3 / Sa 1257 4.2 / 1941 1.8
15 Sa	0018 4.3 / 0651 1.8 / 1250 4.5 / 1928 1.3		

MARCH

Day	Time m / Time m / Time m / Time m	Day	Time m / Time m / Time m / Time m
1 Su	0142 4.2 / 0750 2.0 / 1348 4.4 / 2021 1.5	16	0111 4.6 / 0733 1.5 / M 1327 4.8 / 2004 0.7
2 M	0225 4.4 / 0828 1.7 / 1427 4.6 / 2055 1.2	17	0206 4.9 / 0824 1.1 / Tu 1419 5.1 / 2052 0.3
3 Tu	0300 4.6 / 0901 1.4 / 1501 4.8 / 2126 0.9	18	0253 5.1 / 0908 0.8 / W 1504 5.3 / ○ 2136 0.1
4 W	0329 4.7 / 0932 1.2 / 1531 4.9 / 2157 0.8	19	0335 5.2 / 0950 0.6 / Th 1546 5.4 / 2217 0.1
5 Th	0357 4.8 / 1003 1.0 / 1600 5.0 / 2226 0.7	20	0414 5.3 / 1029 0.6 / F 1625 5.4 / 2256 0.2
6 F	0424 4.8 / 1033 0.9 / 1628 5.1 / 2257 0.6	21	0451 5.2 / 1107 0.6 / Sa 1706 5.3 / 2334 0.5
7 Sa	0454 4.8 / 1104 0.9 / 1659 5.1 / 2328 0.7	22	0529 5.1 / 1144 0.8 / Su 1747 5.1
8 Su	0525 4.8 / 1137 0.9 / 1733 5.0	23	0012 0.9 / 0607 4.9 / M 1222 1.1 / 1831 4.9
9 M	0002 0.9 / 0600 4.7 / 1212 1.1 / 1812 4.8	24	0048 1.4 / 0647 4.6 / Tu 1303 1.4 / 1918 4.6
10 Tu	0039 1.1 / 0640 4.6 / 1253 1.3 / 1859 4.7	25	0129 1.8 / 0734 4.4 / W 1349 1.8 / 2016 4.3
11 W	0121 1.4 / 0730 4.4 / 1342 1.5 / 1956 4.4	26	0216 2.2 / 0830 4.2 / Th 1448 2.1 / ○ 2125 4.0
12 Th	0208 1.8 / 0832 4.2 / 1447 1.8 / 2111 4.2	27	0319 2.5 / 0939 4.1 / F 1608 2.3 / 2245 4.0
13 F	0327 2.0 / 0946 4.1 / 1612 1.8 / 2237 4.2	28	0446 2.6 / 1055 4.1 / Sa 1744 2.2
14 Sa	0502 2.1 / 1109 4.2 / 1751 1.6	29	0001 4.0 / 0611 2.5 / Su 1205 4.2 / 1850 1.9
15 Su	0002 4.3 / 0632 1.9 / 1225 4.5 / 1907 1.2	30	0059 4.2 / 0707 2.2 / M 1302 4.4 / 1935 1.6
		31	0142 4.4 / 0749 1.8 / Tu 1345 4.6 / 2013 1.3

APRIL

Day	Time m / Time m / Time m / Time m	Day	Time m / Time m / Time m / Time m
1 W	0220 4.6 / 0826 1.5 / 1422 4.7 / 2048 1.0	16	0225 5.0 / 0841 1.0 / Th 1437 5.1 / 2108 0.4
2 Th	0253 4.7 / 0901 1.3 / 1455 4.9 / 2122 0.9	17	0305 5.1 / 0923 0.8 / F 1521 5.2 / ○ 2148 0.5
3 F	0322 4.8 / 0934 1.0 / 1528 5.0 / ● 2156 0.7	18	0345 5.1 / 1004 0.8 / Sa 1602 5.2 / 2226 0.6
4 Sa	0353 4.9 / 1007 0.9 / 1600 5.1 / 2228 0.7	19	0421 5.1 / 1042 0.8 / Su 1642 5.1 / 2303 0.9
5 Su	0424 4.9 / 1041 0.8 / 1635 5.1 / 2303 0.8	20	0458 5.0 / 1120 0.9 / M 1725 5.0 / 2340 1.2
6 M	0459 4.9 / 1117 0.9 / 1715 5.0 / 2340 1.0	21	0536 4.9 / 1158 1.2 / Tu 1808 4.8
7 Tu	0537 4.8 / 1156 1.0 / 1800 4.9	22	0018 1.6 / 0618 4.7 / W 1240 1.4 / 1857 4.5
8 W	0020 1.2 / 0622 4.7 / 1243 1.1 / 1852 4.7	23	0057 1.9 / 0704 4.5 / Th 1325 1.7 / 1952 4.3
9 Th	0108 1.5 / 0714 4.5 / 1336 1.3 / 1955 4.5	24	0145 2.2 / 0759 4.4 / F 1420 1.9 / (2053 4.2
10 F	0206 1.8 / 0817 4.4 / 1442 1.5 / 2108 4.3	25	0242 2.4 / 0901 4.2 / Sa 1525 2.0 / 2200 4.1
11 Sa	0316 2.0 / 0929 4.3 / 1603 1.5 / 2227 4.3	26	0353 2.5 / 1007 4.2 / Su 1638 2.0 / 2305 4.1
12 Su	0442 2.1 / 1047 4.3 / 1728 1.4 / 2341 4.4	27	0507 2.5 / 1110 4.3 / M 1745 1.9
13 M	0603 1.9 / 1157 4.5 / 1839 1.1	28	0002 4.3 / 0612 2.2 / Tu 1208 4.4 / 1840 1.7
14 Tu	0046 4.6 / 0705 1.6 / 1259 4.8 / 1935 0.8	29	0052 4.4 / 0703 2.0 / W 1257 4.5 / 1925 1.4
15 W	0138 4.8 / 0756 1.2 / 1351 5.0 / 2023 0.5	30	0134 4.6 / 0746 1.7 / Th 1341 4.7 / 2007 1.2

To find H.W. Dover subtract 4 h. 25 min.

TIDAL DIFFERENCES ARE NOT GIVEN.

Datum of predictions 2.72 m. below Ordnance Datum (Newlyn) or approx. L.A.T.

SUNDERLAND 21:89

Lat. 54°55'N. Long. 1°21'W. **HIGH & LOW WATER 1992**

GMT ADD 1 HOUR MARCH 29 — OCTOBER 25 FOR B.S.T.

MAY

Day	Time m	Time m	Time m	Time m
1 F	0213 4·7	0827 1·4	1420 4·8	2047 1·0
2 Sa ●	0248 4·9	0905 1·2	1458 5·0	2125 0·9
3 Su	0324 5·0	0944 1·0	1538 5·0	2203 0·9
4 M	0402 5·0	1024 0·9	1620 5·0	2243 1·0
5 Tu	0441 5·0	1104 0·8	1705 5·0	2326 1·1
6 W	0525 4·9	1151 0·9	1755 4·9	
7 Th	0011 1·3	0612 4·8	1852 4·7	
8 F	0101 1·5	0707 4·7	1336 1·1	1954 4·6
9 Sa)	0159 1·8	0808 4·6	1440 1·2	2101 4·5
10 Su	0305 1·9	0915 4·5	1550 1·2	2210 4·5
11 M	0418 2·0	1023 4·5	1702 1·2	2316 4·5
12 Tu	0531 1·8	1130 4·6	1808 1·1	
13 W	0017 4·6	0634 1·6	1231 4·7	1904 1·0
14 Th	0109 4·8	0728 1·4	1325 4·9	1955 0·9
15 F	0156 4·9	0817 1·2	1415 4·9	2040 0·9
16	0239 4·9	0901 1·1	1500 5·0	○ 2120 0·9
17 Su	0319 5·0	0943 1·0	1543 5·0	2200 1·1
18 M	0357 5·0	1022 1·0	1625 4·9	2236 1·2
19 Tu	0435 4·9	1102 1·0	1708 4·8	2314 1·4
20 W	0513 4·9	1141 1·2	1751 4·7	2352 1·6
21 Th	0555 4·8	1222 1·3	1838 4·5	
22 F	0033 1·8	0642 4·6	1305 1·5	1927 4·4
23 Sa	0118 2·0	0731 4·5	1355 1·7	2019 4·3
24 Su	0210 2·2	0825 4·4	1448 1·8	☾ 2115 4·2
25 M	0308 2·3	0922 4·3	1546 1·9	2213 4·2
26 Tu	0411 2·3	1021 4·3	1646 1·9	2309 4·3
27 W	0514 2·3	1117 4·4	1745 1·8	
28 Th	0002 4·4	0613 2·1	1210 4·5	1839 1·6
29 F	0052 4·5	0707 1·8	1255 4·6	1929 1·4
30 Sa	0137 4·7	0755 1·5	1349 4·8	2016 1·2
31 Su	0220 4·8	0841 1·3	1437 4·9	2101 1·1

JUNE

Day	Time m	Time m	Time m	Time m
1 M ●	0302 5·0	0926 1·0	1524 5·0	2146 1·0
2 Tu	0345 5·1	1012 0·8	1611 5·1	2231 1·0
3 W	0430 5·1	1059 0·7	1701 5·1	2316 1·1
4 Th	0516 5·1	1147 0·6	1753 5·0	
5 F	0003 1·2	0605 5·0	1239 0·7	1847 4·9
6 Sa	0054 1·4	0657 4·9	1332 0·8	1944 4·8
7 Su)	0148 1·5	0755 4·8	1430 0·9	2044 4·6
8 M	0247 1·7	0855 4·7	1530 1·0	2146 4·6
9 Tu	0350 1·8	0959 4·6	1635 1·2	2247 4·5
10 W	0457 1·8	1103 4·6	1738 1·2	2347 4·5
11 Th	0605 1·7	1207 4·6	1837 1·3	
12 F	0043 4·6	0705 1·6	1306 4·7	1931 1·3
13 Sa	0134 4·7	0759 1·4	1359 4·7	2018 1·3
14 Su	0220 4·8	0847 1·2	1447 4·8	2102 1·3
15 M	0302 4·9	0930 1·1	1532 4·8	○ 2141 1·3
16 Tu	0342 4·9	1011 1·1	1613 4·8	2218 1·4
17 W	0420 4·9	1049 1·0	1654 4·7	2255 1·4
18 Th	0458 4·9	1126 1·1	1733 4·7	2331 1·5
19 F	0537 4·9	1203 1·2	1812 4·6	
20 Sa	0009 1·6	0618 4·8	1243 1·3	1855 4·5
21 Su	0050 1·7	0700 4·7	1324 1·4	1941 4·4
22 M	0133 1·9	0747 4·6	1409 1·6	2029 4·3
23 Tu	0221 2·0	0836 4·4	1458 1·7	☾ 2121 4·2
24 W	0315 2·2	0931 4·3	1553 1·8	2217 4·2
25 Th	0417 2·2	1030 4·3	1653 1·8	2316 4·3
26 F	0524 2·1	1130 4·4	1758 1·8	
27 Sa	0014 4·4	0630 1·9	1231 4·5	1900 1·6
28 Su	0109 4·6	0731 1·6	1328 4·7	1955 1·4
29 M	0159 4·8	0824 1·3	1422 4·9	2047 1·2
30 Tu	0247 5·0	0916 0·9	1514 5·0	● 2134 1·0

JULY

Day	Time m	Time m	Time m	Time m
1 W	0333 5·1	1004 0·6	1603 5·1	2221 0·9
2 Th	0418 5·3	1052 0·4	1652 5·2	2306 0·9
3 F	0505 5·3	1140 0·3	1741 5·2	2352 0·9
4 Sa	0551 5·3	1227 0·3	1831 5·1	
5 Su	0039 1·1	1317 0·5	1923 4·9	
6 M	0128 1·3	0734 5·0	1409 0·7	2016 4·7
7 Tu	0220 1·5	0830 4·8	1503 1·0	2114 4·5
8 W	0318 1·7	0932 4·6	1604 1·3	2216 4·4
9 Th	0425 1·9	1040 4·5	1710 1·5	2319 4·4
10 F	0540 1·9	1148 4·4	1816 1·6	
11 Sa	0022 4·4	0650 1·8	1253 4·5	1915 1·6
12 Su	0120 4·5	0750 1·6	1351 4·5	2007 1·6
13 M	0209 4·6	0840 1·3	1440 4·6	2049 1·5
14 Tu	0253 4·8	0922 1·1	1524 4·7	○ 2127 1·4
15 W	0331 4·9	1000 1·0	1600 4·7	2203 1·3
16 Th	0406 4·9	1033 0·9	1635 4·7	2236 1·2
17 F	0440 5·0	1107 0·9	1709 4·7	2310 1·2
18 Sa	0513 5·0	1141 1·0	1743 4·6	2344 1·3
19 Su	0547 4·9	1215 1·1	1818 4·6	
20 M	0019 1·4	0624 4·8	1250 1·2	1857 4·5
21 Tu	0056 1·6	0703 4·7	1328 1·4	1940 4·4
22 W	0136 1·8	0748 4·5	1411 1·6	☾ 2029 4·2
23 Th	0224 2·0	0840 4·4	1502 1·8	2125 4·2
24 F	0323 2·1	0942 4·3	1605 2·0	2231 4·2
25 Sa	0438 2·2	1054 4·3	1721 2·0	2339 4·3
26 Su	0559 2·0	1207 4·4	1837 1·8	
27 M	0043 4·5	0712 1·6	1313 4·6	1941 1·5
28 Tu	0141 4·7	0813 1·2	1410 4·9	2034 1·2
29 W	0232 5·0	0903 0·7	1502 5·1	● 2122 0·9
30 Th	0318 5·3	0951 0·3	1550 5·3	2207 0·7
31 F	0403 5·4	1038 0·1	1635 5·3	2250 0·6

AUGUST

Day	Time m	Time m	Time m	Time m
1 Sa	0447 5·5	1123 0·0	1720 5·3	2333 0·7
2 Su	0532 5·5	1208 0·1	1805 5·2	
3 M	0016 0·8	0617 5·3	1253 0·4	1853 5·0
4 Tu	0100 1·1	0706 5·1	1339 0·8	1942 4·7
5 W	0148 1·4	0759 4·8	1431 1·2	2036 4·5
6 Th	0242 1·7	0901 4·5	1529 1·6	2138 4·3
7 F	0351 2·0	1013 4·3	1638 1·9	2248 4·2
8 Sa	0517 2·1	1132 4·2	1756 2·1	2308 4·2
9 Su	0001 4·3	0641 1·9	1245 4·3	1904 2·0
10 M	0104 4·4	0742 1·6	1342 4·5	1955 1·8
11 Tu	0155 4·6	0828 1·3	1429 4·5	2035 1·6
12 W	0237 4·8	0906 1·1	1508 4·6	2111 1·4
13 Th	0312 4·9	0940 0·9	1542 4·7	○ 2143 1·2
14 F	0345 5·0	1011 0·8	1611 4·8	2214 1·1
15 Sa	0414 5·0	1041 0·8	1640 4·8	2245 1·0
16 Su	0444 5·0	1111 0·8	1709 4·7	2316 1·1
17 M	0513 5·0	1142 0·9	1740 4·7	2347 1·2
18 Tu	0547 4·9	1215 1·1	1815 4·6	
19 W	0022 1·3	0622 4·7	1248 1·3	1853 4·4
20 Th	0058 1·6	0704 4·5	1329 1·6	1941 4·3
21 F	0145 1·8	0756 4·4	1418 1·8	☾ 2039 4·2
22 Sa	0244 2·0	0905 4·2	1523 2·1	2150 4·1
23 Su	0403 2·1	1025 4·2	1652 2·1	2308 4·2
24 M	0537 2·0	1148 4·3	1819 2·0	
25 Tu	0019 4·4	0657 1·6	1259 4·6	1925 1·6
26 W	0120 4·7	0758 1·0	1356 4·9	2017 1·2
27 Th	0212 5·1	0847 0·5	1446 5·1	2103 0·9
28 F	0257 5·4	0932 0·1	1531 5·3	● 2146 0·6
29 Sa	0340 5·5	1017 -0·1	1613 5·4	2228 0·5
30 Su	0423 5·6	1059 -0·1	1654 5·4	2309 0·5
31 M	0505 5·5	1140 0·1	1736 5·2	2349 0·7

GENERAL — Streams at entrance are weak. Gales from ENE. to ESE. send heavy seas into outer harbour. Winds between WNW. and NNE. increase height of sea level. Winds between SSW. and SSE decrease height of sea level. Winds between SE. and S. reduce rate. Streams generally run in direction of channel inside entrance. Streams generally run in direction of coast outside entrance.

SUNDERLAND

HIGH & LOW WATER 1992 Lat. 54°55'N. Long. 1°21'W.

GMT ADD 1 HOUR MARCH 29 — OCTOBER 25 FOR B.S.T.

SEPTEMBER

Day	Time	m	Day	Time	m
1 Tu	0548 / 1222 / 1818	5.4 / 0.5 / 5.0	16 W	0513 / 1141 / 1739 / 2352	5.0 / 1.0 / 4.7 / 1.2
2 W	0032 / 0636 / 1305 / 1904	1.0 / 5.1 / 1.0 / 4.8	17 Th	0550 / 1216 / 1818	4.8 / 1.3 / 4.6
3 Th	0117 / 0728 / 1352 / 1955 ☽	1.4 / 4.7 / 1.5 / 4.5	18 F	0032 / 0635 / 1257 / 1904	1.4 / 4.6 / 1.6 / 4.4
4 F	0209 / 0830 / 1447 / 2057	1.8 / 4.4 / 2.0 / 4.3	19 Sa	0119 / 0731 / 1348 / 2005 ☾	1.7 / 4.4 / 1.8 / 4.2
5 Sa	0316 / 0946 / 1558 / 2210	2.1 / 4.3 / 2.3 / 4.1	20 Su	0221 / 0843 / 1456 / 2119	1.9 / 4.2 / 2.2 / 4.2
6 Su	0450 / 1112 / 1730 / 2330	2.2 / 4.1 / 2.4 / 4.2	21 M	0343 / 1007 / 1625 / 2240	2.0 / 4.2 / 2.3 / 4.2
7 M	0623 / 1228 / 1843	2.0 / 4.2 / 2.3	22 Tu	0517 / 1132 / 1756 / 2354	1.8 / 4.3 / 2.0 / 4.5
8 Tu	0038 / 0721 / 1324 / 1933	4.3 / 1.7 / 4.4 / 2.0	23 W	0636 / 1240 / 1903	1.4 / 4.6 / 1.7
9 W	0128 / 0803 / 1408 / 2011	4.6 / 1.4 / 4.5 / 1.7	24 Th	0056 / 0733 / 1335 / 1955	4.8 / 0.9 / 4.9 / 1.3
10 Th	0209 / 0838 / 1443 / 2044	4.7 / 1.1 / 4.7 / 1.5	25 F	0147 / 0823 / 1423 / 2040	5.1 / 0.4 / 5.2 / 0.9
11 F	0244 / 0909 / 1514 / 2116	4.9 / 1.0 / 4.8 / 1.2	26 Sa	0233 / 0905 / 1505 / ● 2122	5.4 / 0.1 / 5.3 / 0.7
12 Sa	0315 / 0940 / 1540 / ○ 2146	5.0 / 0.8 / 4.8 / 1.1	27 Su	0317 / 0950 / 1546 / 2203	5.5 / 0.0 / 5.4 / 0.6
13 Su	0343 / 1010 / 1609 / 2217	5.1 / 0.7 / 4.9 / 1.0	28 M	0359 / 1031 / 1625 / 2243	5.6 / 0.1 / 5.4 / 0.6
14 M	0411 / 1039 / 1635 / 2246	5.1 / 0.8 / 4.9 / 1.0	29 Tu	0440 / 1110 / 1705 / 2323	5.5 / 0.4 / 5.2 / 0.8
15 Tu	0441 / 1109 / 1705 / 2318	5.0 / 0.9 / 4.8 / 1.1	30 W	0523 / 1149 / 1746	5.3 / 0.8 / 5.1

OCTOBER

Day	Time	m	Day	Time	m
1 Th	0003 / 0608 / 1230 / 1828	1.1 / 5.0 / 1.3 / 4.8	16 F	0532 / 1152 / 1754	4.8 / 1.3 / 4.7
2 F	0048 / 0700 / 1314 / 1917	1.4 / 4.7 / 1.8 / 4.5	17 Sa	0015 / 0619 / 1236 / 1843	1.3 / 4.6 / 1.6 / 4.6
3 Sa	0139 / 0801 / 1404 / 2017 ☽	1.8 / 4.3 / 2.2 / 4.3	18 Su	0107 / 0720 / 1329 / 1944	1.5 / 4.4 / 1.9 / 4.4
4 Su	0242 / 0914 / 1512 / 2128	2.1 / 4.1 / 2.6 / 4.2	19 M	0210 / 0832 / 1438 / 2055 ☾	1.7 / 4.3 / 2.2 / 4.3
5 M	0410 / 1037 / 1641 / 2245	2.2 / 4.1 / 2.7 / 4.2	20 Tu	0329 / 0952 / 1601 / 2213	1.7 / 4.3 / 2.2 / 4.4
6 Tu	0541 / 1153 / 1802 / 2354	2.1 / 4.1 / 2.5 / 4.3	21 W	0455 / 1110 / 1727 / 2326	1.6 / 4.4 / 2.1 / 4.6
7 W	0641 / 1249 / 1856	1.8 / 4.3 / 2.2	22 Th	0608 / 1217 / 1834	1.2 / 4.6 / 1.7
8 Th	0049 / 0724 / 1331 / 1936	4.5 / 1.6 / 4.5 / 1.9	23 F	0028 / 0707 / 1310 / 1928	4.8 / 0.9 / 4.9 / 1.4
9 F	0131 / 0800 / 1408 / 2011	4.7 / 1.3 / 4.7 / 1.6	24 Sa	0123 / 0756 / 1358 / 2016	5.1 / 0.6 / 5.1 / 1.1
10 Sa	0209 / 0833 / 1439 / 2045	4.9 / 1.1 / 4.8 / 1.4	25 Su	0210 / 0841 / 1441 / ● 2059	5.3 / 0.4 / 5.2 / 0.8
11 Su	0241 / 0905 / 1508 / ○ 2118	5.0 / 0.9 / 4.9 / 1.2	26 M	0255 / 0923 / 1521 / 2140	5.4 / 0.4 / 5.3 / 0.7
12 M	0312 / 0936 / 1536 / 2148	5.0 / 0.8 / 4.9 / 1.1	27 Tu	0338 / 1004 / 1600 / 2221	5.4 / 0.5 / 5.3 / 0.8
13 Tu	0342 / 1008 / 1606 / 2221	5.1 / 0.8 / 5.0 / 1.0	28 W	0420 / 1043 / 1638 / 2302	5.3 / 0.8 / 5.2 / 0.9
14 W	0414 / 1041 / 1637 / 2255	5.1 / 0.9 / 4.9 / 1.1	29 Th	0503 / 1121 / 1717 / 2342	5.1 / 1.1 / 5.1 / 1.1
15 Th	0451 / 1114 / 1713 / 2333	5.0 / 1.1 / 4.9 / 1.2	30 F	0548 / 1159 / 1800	4.9 / 1.5 / 4.9
			31 Sa	0026 / 0638 / 1241 / 1847	1.4 / 4.6 / 1.9 / 4.7

NOVEMBER

Day	Time	m	Day	Time	m
1 Su	0114 / 0734 / 1329 / 1942	1.7 / 4.4 / 2.3 / 4.5	16 M	0103 / 0714 / 1319 / 1930	1.2 / 4.6 / 1.8 / 4.6
2 M	0210 / 0839 / 1427 / 2046 ☽	2.0 / 4.2 / 2.5 / 4.3	17 Tu	0203 / 0820 / 1423 / ☾ 2036	1.3 / 4.5 / 2.0 / 4.5
3 Tu	0319 / 0949 / 1540 / 2155	2.1 / 4.1 / 2.7 / 4.3	18 W	0312 / 0932 / 1536 / 2146	1.4 / 4.4 / 2.1 / 4.5
4 W	0435 / 1058 / 1659 / 2302	2.2 / 4.1 / 2.6 / 4.3	19 Th	0426 / 1042 / 1653 / 2258	1.4 / 4.5 / 2.0 / 4.6
5 Th	0542 / 1157 / 1803	2.0 / 4.3 / 2.4	20 F	0538 / 1147 / 1803	1.2 / 4.6 / 1.8
6 F	0000 / 0634 / 1246 / 1853	4.4 / 1.8 / 4.4 / 2.1	21 Sa	0002 / 0639 / 1245 / 1903	4.8 / 1.1 / 4.8 / 1.5
7 Sa	0049 / 0717 / 1327 / 1935	4.6 / 1.6 / 4.6 / 1.8	22 Su	0100 / 0732 / 1335 / 1955	4.9 / 0.9 / 4.9 / 1.2
8 Su	0131 / 0756 / 1403 / 2014	4.7 / 1.3 / 4.8 / 1.6	23 M	0152 / 0820 / 1420 / 2041	5.1 / 0.8 / 5.1 / 1.0
9 M	0209 / 0833 / 1437 / 2051	4.9 / 1.2 / 4.9 / 1.3	24 Tu	0240 / 0903 / 1502 / ● 2126	5.2 / 0.8 / 5.1 / 0.9
10 Tu	0246 / 0908 / 1511 / ○ 2126	5.0 / 1.0 / 5.0 / 1.2	25 W	0325 / 0943 / 1542 / 2207	5.2 / 0.9 / 5.2 / 0.9
11 W	0321 / 0943 / 1543 / 2203	5.0 / 1.0 / 5.0 / 1.0	26 Th	0409 / 1022 / 1620 / 2248	5.1 / 1.1 / 5.1 / 0.9
12 Th	0359 / 1019 / 1618 / 2242	5.1 / 1.0 / 5.0 / 1.0	27 F	0451 / 1059 / 1659 / 2327	5.0 / 1.3 / 5.1 / 1.1
13 F	0440 / 1057 / 1658 / 2323	5.0 / 1.1 / 5.0 / 1.0	28 Sa	0533 / 1137 / 1739	4.8 / 1.5 / 4.9
14 Sa	0525 / 1140 / 1741	4.9 / 1.3 / 4.9	29 Su	0008 / 0618 / 1216 / 1822	1.3 / 4.6 / 1.8 / 4.8
15 Su	0009 / 0617 / 1226 / 1832	1.1 / 4.8 / 1.5 / 4.8	30 M	0050 / 0706 / 1258 / 1910	1.5 / 4.5 / 2.0 / 4.6

DECEMBER

Day	Time	m	Day	Time	m
1 Tu	0136 / 0758 / 1346 / 2003	1.7 / 4.3 / 2.3 / 4.5	16 W	0150 / 0802 / 1403 / 2013	0.9 / 4.7 / 1.7 / 4.8
2 W	0230 / 0854 / 1442 / 2102 ☽	1.9 / 4.2 / 2.5 / 4.3	17 Th	0251 / 0904 / 1506 / 2119	1.1 / 4.5 / 1.9 / 4.6
3 Th	0327 / 0956 / 1548 / 2204	2.1 / 4.1 / 2.5 / 4.3	18 F	0356 / 1010 / 1618 / 2230	1.3 / 4.5 / 2.0 / 4.6
4 F	0432 / 1056 / 1657 / 2305	2.1 / 4.2 / 2.5 / 4.3	19 Sa	0506 / 1117 / 1734 / 2340	1.4 / 4.5 / 1.9 / 4.6
5 Sa	0534 / 1154 / 1802	2.0 / 4.3 / 2.3	20 Su	0613 / 1221 / 1843	1.4 / 4.6 / 1.7
6 Su	0002 / 0630 / 1245 / 1857	4.4 / 1.8 / 4.5 / 2.1	21 M	0045 / 0712 / 1317 / 1942	4.7 / 1.5 / 4.7 / 1.5
7 M	0055 / 0719 / 1330 / 1945	4.6 / 1.6 / 4.6 / 1.8	22 Tu	0144 / 0804 / 1408 / 2034	4.8 / 1.3 / 4.8 / 1.2
8 Tu	0141 / 0804 / 1410 / 2028	4.7 / 1.4 / 4.8 / 1.5	23 W	0234 / 0851 / 1451 / 2119	4.9 / 1.2 / 4.9 / 1.0
9 W	0225 / 0845 / 1450 / ○ 2111	4.9 / 1.2 / 4.9 / 1.2	24 Th	0319 / 0932 / 1532 / ● 2200	4.9 / 1.2 / 5.0 / 0.9
10 Th	0308 / 0927 / 1528 / 2153	5.0 / 1.1 / 5.1 / 0.9	25 F	0402 / 1008 / 1609 / 2238	4.9 / 1.2 / 5.1 / 0.9
11 F	0350 / 1008 / 1607 / 2235	5.1 / 1.0 / 5.1 / 0.8	26 Sa	0440 / 1043 / 1644 / 2314	4.9 / 1.3 / 5.0 / 0.9
12 Sa	0435 / 1049 / 1649 / 2320	5.1 / 1.0 / 5.2 / 0.7	27 Su	0517 / 1117 / 1720 / 2349	4.8 / 1.4 / 5.0 / 1.1
13 Su	0522 / 1133 / 1733	5.1 / 1.1 / 5.1	28 M	0554 / 1152 / 1757	4.7 / 1.5 / 4.9
14 M	0006 / 0611 / 1219 / 1821	0.7 / 5.0 / 1.3 / 5.0	29 Tu	0025 / 0633 / 1229 / 1836	1.2 / 4.6 / 1.7 / 4.8
15 Tu	0057 / 0704 / 1308 / 1914	0.8 / 4.8 / 1.5 / 4.9	30 W	0103 / 0714 / 1308 / 1920	1.4 / 4.6 / 1.9 / 4.6
			31 Th	0143 / 0801 / 1352 / 2006	1.6 / 4.3 / 2.1 / 4.4

RATE AND SET — Off Sunderland — S. going begins –0100 Dover. N. going begins +0500 Dover.
In River Wear — Ingoing begins –0135 Dover. Outgoing begins +0425 Dover.

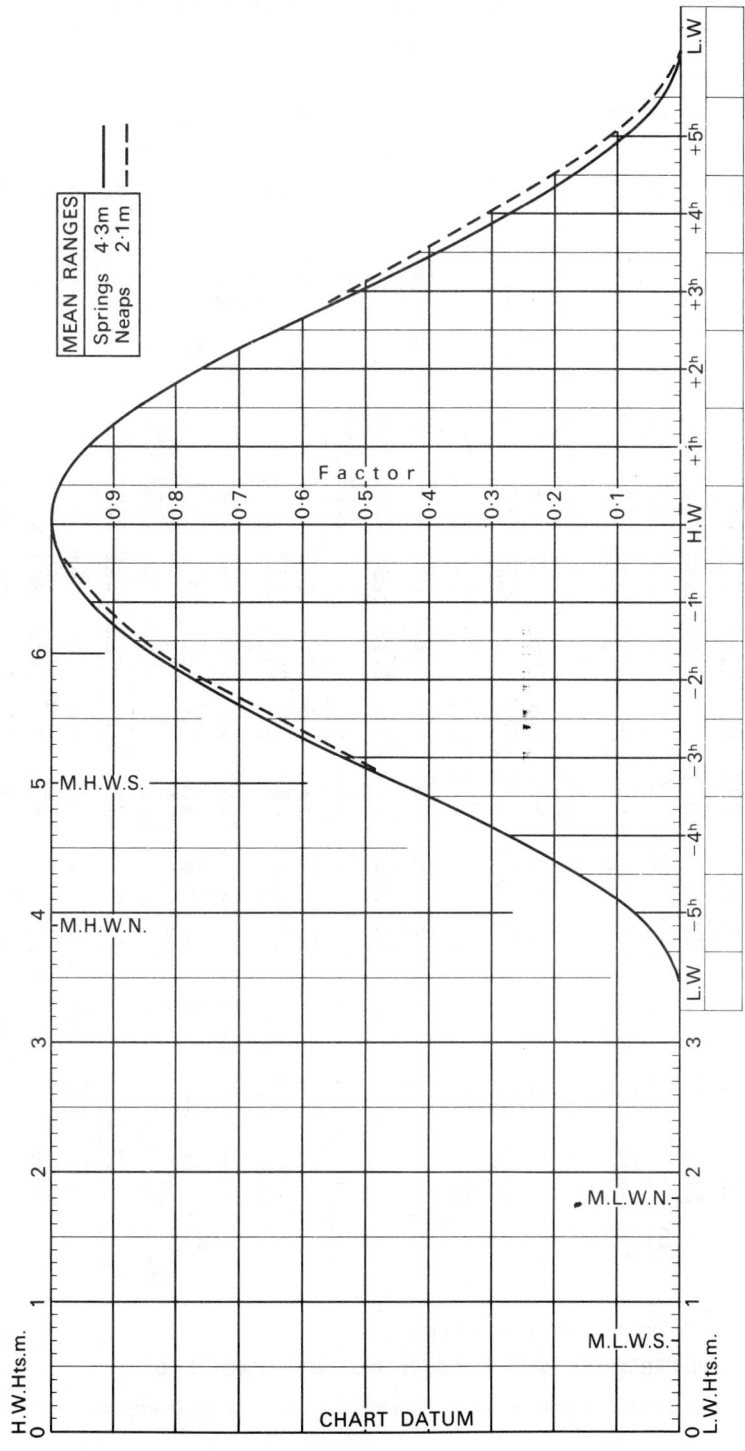

RIVER TYNE (NORTH SHIELDS)
MEAN SPRING AND NEAP CURVES
Springs occur 2 days after New and Full Moon.

MEAN RANGES
Springs 4·3m
Neaps 2·1m

Factor

M.H.W.S.

M.H.W.N.

M.L.W.N.

M.L.W.S.

CHART DATUM

H.W.Hts.m.

L.W.Hts.m.

NORTH SHIELDS RIVER TYNE

HIGH & LOW WATER 1992 Lat. 55°00′N. Long. 1°27′W.

GMT ADD 1 HOUR MARCH 29 — OCTOBER 25 FOR B.S.T.

JANUARY

Day	Time	m	Day	Time	m
1 W	0031 / 0657 / 1304 / 1931	4·3 / 1·6 / 4·3 / 1·6	16 Th	0544 / 1157 / 1825	1·7 / 4·2 / 1·7
2 Th	0130 / 0749 / 1354 / 2020	4·4 / 1·6 / 4·5 / 1·5	17 F	0029 / 0659 / 1303 / 1933	4·4 / 1·6 / 4·4 / 1·4
3 F	0219 / 0833 / 1434 / 2101	4·5 / 1·5 / 4·6 / 1·3	18 Sa	0135 / 0801 / 1359 / 2032	4·7 / 1·4 / 4·7 / 1·0
4 Sa	0301 / 0910 / 1510 / 2138 ●	4·6 / 1·4 / 4·7 / 1·2	19 Su	0233 / 0854 / 1449 / 2125 ○	4·9 / 1·2 / 5·0 / 0·7
5 Su	0338 / 0943 / 1543 / 2212	4·7 / 1·3 / 4·8 / 1·1	20 M	0325 / 0942 / 1535 / 2216	5·1 / 1·0 / 5·2 / 0·4
6 M	0413 / 1014 / 1614 / 2244	4·7 / 1·3 / 4·8 / 1·0	21 Tu	0413 / 1027 / 1621 / 2304	5·2 / 0·8 / 5·4 / 0·3
7 Tu	0445 / 1045 / 1644 / 2315	4·7 / 1·2 / 4·8 / 0·9	22 W	0459 / 1111 / 1706 / 2349	5·2 / 0·8 / 5·5 / 0·3
8 W	0519 / 1116 / 1716 / 2347	4·6 / 1·2 / 4·8 / 1·0	23 Th	0546 / 1153 / 1753	5·1 / 0·8 / 5·4
9 Th	0551 / 1149 / 1749	4·5 / 1·3 / 4·7	24 F	0034 / 0632 / 1235 / 1841	0·4 / 4·9 / 1·0 / 5·2
10 F	0019 / 0627 / 1222 / 1824	1·0 / 4·4 / 1·3 / 4·6	25 Sa	0117 / 0719 / 1319 / 1931	0·6 / 4·6 / 1·2 / 4·9
11 Sa	0053 / 0703 / 1300 / 1904	1·1 / 4·3 / 1·5 / 4·5	26 Su	0204 / 0809 / 1411 / 2027 ☾	1·0 / 4·4 / 1·5 / 4·6
12 Su	0131 / 0747 / 1342 / 1952	1·3 / 4·2 / 1·7 / 4·4	27 M	0256 / 0904 / 1514 / 2131	1·4 / 4·2 / 1·8 / 4·2
13 M	0216 / 0836 / 1437 / 2049 ☽	1·4 / 4·1 / 1·8 / 4·3	28 Tu	0359 / 1010 / 1638 / 2248	1·8 / 4·0 / 2·0 / 4·0
14 Tu	0312 / 0935 / 1545 / 2156	1·6 / 4·1 / 1·9 / 4·2	29 W	0519 / 1129 / 1808	2·0 / 4·0 / 2·0
15 W	0423 / 1044 / 1706 / 2312	1·7 / 4·1 / 1·9 / 4·2	30 Th	0012 / 0635 / 1243 / 1917	4·0 / 1·9 / 4·1 / 1·8
			31 F	0120 / 0733 / 1338 / 2008	4·1 / 1·8 / 4·2 / 1·5

FEBRUARY

Day	Time	m	Day	Time	m
1 Sa	0211 / 0818 / 1419 / 2050	4·3 / 1·6 / 4·4 / 1·3	16 Su	0130 / 0751 / 1348 / 2023	4·5 / 1·4 / 4·6 / 0·9
2 Su	0250 / 0854 / 1454 / 2125	4·4 / 1·4 / 4·6 / 1·1	17 M	0225 / 0843 / 1437 / 2115	4·8 / 1·1 / 5·0 / 0·5
3 M	0324 / 0927 / 1525 / 2157 ●	4·5 / 1·2 / 4·7 / 0·9	18 Tu	0314 / 0929 / 1521 / 2203 ○	5·0 / 0·8 / 5·3 / 0·2
4 Tu	0356 / 0957 / 1555 / 2228	4·6 / 1·1 / 4·8 / 0·8	19 W	0357 / 1012 / 1604 / 2247	5·1 / 0·6 / 5·5 / 0·1
5 W	0426 / 1027 / 1623 / 2257	4·6 / 1·0 / 4·9 / 0·8	20 Th	0440 / 1052 / 1648 / 2329	5·2 / 0·6 / 5·5 / 0·2
6 Th	0455 / 1057 / 1652 / 2325	4·6 / 1·0 / 4·9 / 0·8	21 F	0522 / 1130 / 1732	5·1 / 0·6 / 5·4
7 F	0525 / 1126 / 2354	4·6 / 1·0 / 0·8	22 Sa	0008 / 0604 / 1210 / 1817	0·4 / 4·9 / 0·8 / 5·2
8 Sa	0556 / 1157 / 1756	4·5 / 1·1 / 4·8	23 Su	0046 / 0646 / 1249 / 1903	0·7 / 4·7 / 1·1 / 4·9
9 Su	0025 / 0629 / 1231 / 1834	0·9 / 4·5 / 1·2 / 4·7	24 M	0126 / 0731 / 1334 / 1955	1·1 / 4·4 / 1·4 / 4·5
10 M	0059 / 0707 / 1310 / 1919	1·1 / 4·4 / 1·4 / 4·5	25 Tu	0211 / 0820 / 1430 / 2054	1·6 / 4·1 / 1·8 / 4·1
11 Tu	0140 / 0754 / 1358 / 2015	1·3 / 4·2 / 1·6 / 4·3	26 W	0308 / 0921 / 1553 / 2214	2·0 / 3·9 / 2·0 / 3·8
12 W	0232 / 0851 / 1504 / 2124	1·6 / 4·1 / 1·8 / 4·2	27 Th	0438 / 1044 / 1740 / 2351	2·2 / 3·8 / 2·0 / 3·8
13 Th	0346 / 1004 / 1633 / 2248	1·8 / 4·0 / 1·9 / 4·1	28 F	0610 / 1212 / 1853	2·1 / 3·8 / 1·8
14 F	0522 / 1132 / 1808	1·9 / 4·0 / 1·7	29 Sa	0103 / 0710 / 1313 / 1945	3·9 / 1·9 / 4·0 / 1·5
15 Sa	0019 / 0648 / 1249 / 1924	4·2 / 1·7 / 4·3 / 1·3			

MARCH

Day	Time	m	Day	Time	m
1 Su	0152 / 0755 / 1355 / 2027	4·1 / 1·6 / 4·3 / 1·2	16 M	0119 / 0735 / 1330 / 2008	4·4 / 1·3 / 4·7 / 0·7
2 M	0229 / 0832 / 1430 / 2103	4·3 / 1·4 / 4·5 / 1·0	17 Tu	0211 / 0825 / 1418 / 2058	4·7 / 1·0 / 5·0 / 0·4
3 Tu	0301 / 0904 / 1500 / 2134	4·4 / 1·2 / 4·7 / 0·8	18 W	0256 / 0910 / 1501 / 2143 ○	5·0 / 0·7 / 5·3 / 0·2
4 W	0332 / 0934 / 1529 / 2203	4·6 / 1·0 / 4·8 / 0·7	19 Th	0336 / 0950 / 1543 / 2224	5·1 / 0·6 / 5·4 / 0·2
5 Th	0400 / 1004 / 1557 / 2231	4·6 / 0·9 / 4·9 / 0·7	20 F	0416 / 1030 / 1626 / 2302	5·1 / 0·5 / 5·4 / 0·3
6 F	0428 / 1034 / 1626 / 2259	4·7 / 0·8 / 5·0 / 0·7	21 Sa	0455 / 1108 / 1709 / 2339	5·1 / 0·6 / 5·3 / 0·6
7 Sa	0457 / 1105 / 1657 / 2327	4·7 / 0·8 / 5·0 / 0·7	22 Su	0534 / 1146 / 1753	4·9 / 0·8 / 5·1
8 Su	0526 / 1136 / 1732 / 2358	4·7 / 0·9 / 4·9 / 0·9	23 M	0014 / 0614 / 1224 / 1839	0·9 / 4·7 / 1·0 / 4·7
9 M	0600 / 1210 / 1811	4·6 / 1·1 / 4·8	24 Tu	0049 / 0655 / 1306 / 1927	1·3 / 4·4 / 1·3 / 4·4
10 Tu	0032 / 0638 / 1249 / 1859	1·1 / 4·5 / 1·3 / 4·6	25 W	0130 / 0740 / 1355 / 2023	1·7 / 4·2 / 1·6 / 4·0
11 W	0114 / 0726 / 1338 / 1957	1·4 / 4·3 / 1·5 / 4·3	26 Th	0222 / 0834 / 1507 / 2136 ☾	2·0 / 3·9 / 1·9 / 3·7
12 Th	0208 / 0825 / 1446 / 2108	1·7 / 4·1 / 1·7 / 4·1	27 F	0342 / 0948 / 1649 / 2312	2·2 / 3·7 / 1·9 / 3·6
13 F	0327 / 0942 / 1621 / 2240	1·9 / 3·9 / 1·8 / 4·0	28 Sa	0525 / 1120 / 1811	2·2 / 3·7 / 1·7
14 Sa	0511 / 1115 / 1758	1·9 / 4·0 / 1·5	29 Su	0028 / 0632 / 1229 / 1906	3·8 / 2·0 / 3·9 / 1·4
15 Su	0012 / 0635 / 1234 / 1910	4·1 / 1·7 / 4·3 / 1·1	30 M	0119 / 0719 / 1316 / 1948	4·0 / 1·7 / 4·1 / 1·2
			31 Tu	0157 / 0758 / 1352 / 2025	4·2 / 1·4 / 4·3 / 1·0

APRIL

Day	Time	m	Day	Time	m
1 W	0230 / 0833 / 1426 / 2058	4·4 / 1·2 / 4·5 / 0·8	16 Th	0232 / 0847 / 1440 / 2117	4·9 / 0·8 / 5·1 / 0·4
2 Th	0300 / 0905 / 1457 / 2129	4·5 / 1·0 / 4·7 / 0·7	17 F	0312 / 0929 / 1522 / 2157 ○	5·0 / 0·7 / 5·2 / 0·5
3 F	0328 / 0938 / 1528 / 2200	4·7 / 0·9 / 4·9 / 0·7	18 Sa	0350 / 1009 / 1606 / 2234	5·0 / 0·7 / 5·2 / 0·6
4 Sa	0357 / 1010 / 1600 / 2231	4·8 / 0·8 / 4·9 / 0·7	19 Su	0428 / 1047 / 1648 / 2309	5·0 / 0·7 / 5·1 / 0·9
5 Su	0427 / 1044 / 1635 / 2302	4·8 / 0·8 / 5·0 / 0·8	20 M	0505 / 1123 / 1732 / 2343	4·9 / 0·8 / 4·9 / 1·1
6 M	0459 / 1118 / 1715 / 2336	4·8 / 0·8 / 4·9 / 1·0	21 Tu	0543 / 1201 / 1817	4·7 / 1·0 / 4·6
7 Tu	0536 / 1156 / 1800	4·7 / 1·0 / 4·8	22 W	0018 / 0622 / 1242 / 1903	1·4 / 4·5 / 1·2 / 4·3
8 W	0014 / 0618 / 1239 / 1852	1·2 / 4·6 / 1·1 / 4·5	23 Th	0057 / 0706 / 1328 / 1955	1·7 / 4·2 / 1·4 / 4·0
9 Th	0100 / 0709 / 1334 / 1952	1·5 / 4·4 / 1·3 / 4·3	24 F	0144 / 0754 / 1426 / 2056	2·0 / 4·0 / 1·6 / 3·8
10 F	0159 / 0811 / 1446 / 2105	1·7 / 4·2 / 1·5 / 4·1	25 Sa	0246 / 0854 / 1543 / 2213	2·1 / 3·8 / 1·7 / 3·6
11 Sa	0319 / 0928 / 1616 / 2234	1·9 / 4·0 / 1·5 / 4·0	26 Su	0412 / 1010 / 1704 / 2330	2·2 / 3·7 / 1·6 / 3·7
12 Su	0455 / 1055 / 1740 / 2356	1·9 / 4·1 / 1·3 / 4·2	27 M	0552 / 1125 / 1807	2·0 / 3·8 / 1·5
13 M	0612 / 1208 / 1848	1·6 / 4·4 / 1·0	28 Tu	0028 / 0628 / 1221 / 1855	3·9 / 1·8 / 4·0 / 1·3
14 Tu	0057 / 0712 / 1306 / 1944	4·4 / 1·3 / 4·7 / 0·7	29 W	0112 / 0714 / 1306 / 1937	4·1 / 1·5 / 4·2 / 1·1
15 W	0148 / 0802 / 1355 / 2033	4·7 / 1·0 / 4·9 / 0·5	30 Th	0143 / 0755 / 1345 / 2015	4·3 / 1·3 / 4·4 / 1·0

To find H.W. Dover subtract 4 h. 30 min.

TIDAL DIFFERENCES PAGE 21:95. TIDAL CURVE PAGE 21:91.

Datum of predictions: 2.60 m. below Ordnance Datum (Newlyn) or approx. L.A.T.

RIVER TYNE NORTH SHIELDS — 21:93

Lat. 55°00'N. Long. 1°27'W. HIGH & LOW WATER 1992

GMT ADD 1 HOUR MARCH 29 — OCTOBER 25 FOR B.S.T.

MAY

Day	Time	m	Time	m	Day	Time	m	Time	m
1 F	0220	4·5	1422	4·6	16	0249	4·8	1505	4·9
	0833	1·1	2051	0·9		0911	0·9	2132	0·9
2 Sa	0253	4·7	1458	4·8	17 Su	0327	4·9	1549	4·9
	0910	0·9	2128	0·9		0950	0·9	2209	1·0
3 Su	0325	4·8	1538	4·9	18 M	0404	4·9	1631	4·8
	0948	0·8	2204	0·9		1028	0·9	2244	1·1
4 M	0400	4·9	1620	4·9	19 Tu	0441	4·8	1713	4·7
	1026	0·8	2242	0·9		1105	0·9	2318	1·3
5 Tu	0438	4·9	1705	4·9	20 W	0518	4·7	1756	4·5
	1106	0·8	2322	1·1		1143	1·0	2353	1·4
6 W	0519	4·8	1756	4·8	21 Th	0556	4·5	1838	4·3
	1150	0·8				1221	1·1		
7 Th	0005	1·2	1239	1·0	22	0029	1·6	1303	1·2
	0607	4·7	1850	4·6		0635	4·4	1924	4·1
8 F	0055	1·4	1337	1·1	23 Sa	0112	1·7	1351	1·4
	0700	4·5	1951	4·3		0720	4·2	2013	3·9
9 Sa	0154	1·7	1444	1·2	24 Su	0201	1·9	1446	1·5
	0802	4·4	2100	4·2		0809	4·0	2111	3·7
10 Su	0307	1·8	1600	1·2	25 M	0301	2·0	1548	1·5
	0914	4·3	2216	4·1		0908	3·9	2216	3·7
11 M	0427	1·8	1713	1·1	26 Tu	0413	2·0	1651	1·5
	1030	4·3	2327	4·2		1013	3·8	2318	3·8
12 Tu	0540	1·6	1818	1·0	27 W	0522	1·9	1749	1·5
	1139	4·4				1116	3·9		
13 W	0029	4·4	1238	4·6	28 Th	0011	4·0	1212	4·1
	0643	1·4	1914	0·9		0621	1·7	1842	1·4
14 Th	0120	4·6	1331	4·8	29 F	0057	4·2	1303	4·3
	0737	1·2	2005	0·8		0712	1·5	1930	1·2
15 F	0206	4·7	1419	4·9	30 Sa	0138	4·5	1349	4·5
	0826	1·0	2050	0·8		0758	1·3	2015	1·1
					31 Su	0219	4·7	1436	4·7
						0843	1·1	2100	1·0

JUNE

Day	Time	m	Time	m	Day	Time	m	Time	m
1 M	0258	4·8	1522	4·9	16	0348	4·8	1617	4·7
	0927	0·9	2143	1·0		1016	1·0	2224	1·2
2 Tu	0339	4·9	1610	4·9	17 W	0423	4·7	1655	4·6
	1012	0·8	2228	1·0		1051	1·0	2257	1·3
3 W	0423	5·0	1659	4·9	18 Th	0457	4·7	1733	4·5
	1058	0·7	2312	1·1		1126	1·0	2330	1·3
4 Th	0509	5·0	1750	4·8	19 F	0532	4·6	1811	4·4
	1146	0·7	2358	1·1		1201	1·0		
5 F	0558	4·9	1843	4·7	20 Sa	0004	1·4	1238	1·1
	1238	0·7				0608	4·5	1850	4·2
6 Sa	0048	1·3	1333	0·8	21 Su	0041	1·5	1316	1·2
	0652	4·8	1941	4·5		0646	4·4	1933	4·1
7 Su	0142	1·4	1432	0·9	22 M	0121	1·6	1358	1·3
	0749	4·7	2042	4·3		0730	4·3	2018	3·9
8 M	0244	1·6	1535	1·0	23 Tu	0209	1·8	1446	1·4
	0853	4·6	2146	4·2		0818	4·1	2108	3·9
9 Tu	0353	1·7	1640	1·1	24 W	0307	1·9	1541	1·6
	1000	4·5	2252	4·2		0914	4·0	2206	3·9
10 W	0506	1·6	1746	1·2	25 Th	0413	1·9	1642	1·6
	1108	4·4	2357	4·3		1016	4·0	2306	4·0
11 Th	0615	1·6	1846	1·2	26 F	0523	1·8	1749	1·6
	1212	4·4				1122	4·1		
12 F	0055	4·4	1313	4·5	27 Sa	0007	4·2	1225	4·3
	0716	1·4	1941	1·2		0629	1·7	1852	1·5
13 Sa	0145	4·5	1406	4·6	28 Su	0102	4·4	1324	4·5
	0809	1·3	2029	1·2		0727	1·4	1948	1·3
14 Su	0229	4·7	1454	4·6	29 M	0151	4·6	1419	4·7
	0856	1·2	2111	1·2		0820	1·2	2042	1·2
15 M	0310	4·7	1536	4·7	30 Tu	0239	4·8	1511	4·9
	0938	1·1	2149	1·2		0911	0·9	2131	1·1

JULY

Day	Time	m	Time	m	Day	Time	m	Time	m
1 W	0325	5·0	1600	5·0	16	0403	4·8	1637	4·6
	1002	0·7	2217	1·0		1037	0·9	2237	1·2
2 Th	0410	5·1	1649	5·0	17 F	0435	4·8	1709	4·6
	1051	0·5	2302	0·9		1108	0·9	2308	1·1
3 F	0457	5·2	1739	5·0	18 Sa	0506	4·8	1743	4·5
	1139	0·4	2347	0·9		1139	0·9	2339	1·2
4 Sa	0546	5·2	1829	4·8	19 Su	0539	4·7	1817	4·4
	1228	0·4				1210	0·9		
5 Su	0034	1·0	1317	0·5	20 M	0012	1·3	1242	1·0
	0636	5·1	1920	4·7		0614	4·6	1852	4·3
6 M	0121	1·2	1408	0·8	21 Tu	0048	1·4	1317	1·2
	0730	5·0	2015	4·5		0652	4·5	1931	4·2
7 Tu	0215	1·4	1503	1·0	22 W	0127	1·6	1358	1·4
	0827	4·7	2112	4·3		0735	4·4	2015	4·1
8 W	0318	1·6	1604	1·3	23 Th	0216	1·7	1446	1·6
	0931	4·5	2216	4·2		0827	4·2	2108	4·0
9 Th	0433	1·8	1713	1·5	24 F	0317	1·9	1549	1·8
	1040	4·3	2325	4·2		0928	4·1	2212	4·0
10 F	0551	1·8	1822	1·6	25 Sa	0433	1·9	1708	1·8
	1154	4·2				1041	4·1	2323	4·1
11 Sa	0032	4·2	1302	4·2	26 Su	0554	1·8	1827	1·7
	0702	1·6	1924	1·6		1158	4·2		
12 Su	0130	4·4	1359	4·4	27 M	0034	4·3	1310	4·4
	0759	1·5	2015	1·5		0704	1·5	1933	1·5
13 M	0216	4·5	1446	4·5	28 Tu	0133	4·5	1409	4·7
	0847	1·3	2057	1·4		0805	1·2	2027	1·2
14 Tu	0257	4·6	1527	4·7	29 W	0223	4·8	1500	4·9
	0928	1·1	2134	1·3		0900	0·8	2118	1·0
15 W	0331	4·7	1602	4·6	30 Th	0311	5·0	1548	5·1
	1003	1·0	2206	1·2		0950	0·5	2203	0·8
					31 F	0356	5·3	1634	5·1
						1038	0·3	2247	0·7

AUGUST

Day	Time	m	Time	m	Day	Time	m	Time	m
1 Sa	0441	5·5	1720	5·1	16	0440	4·9	1712	4·6
	1125	0·2	2330	0·7		1112	0·8	2313	1·1
2 Su	0527	5·5	1807	5·0	17 M	0509	4·9	1742	4·6
	1210	0·3				1140	0·9	2344	1·1
3 M	0012	0·8	1253	0·5	18 Tu	0542	4·8	1814	4·5
	0615	5·3	1853	4·8		1210	1·0		
4 Tu	0056	1·1	1338	0·8	19 W	0017	1·3	1241	1·2
	0706	5·1	1942	4·6		0618	4·7	1849	4·4
5 W	0145	1·3	1427	1·3	20 Th	0055	1·5	1319	1·4
	0801	4·7	2036	4·3		0700	4·5	1933	4·3
6 Th	0244	1·6	1527	1·6	21 F	0138	1·7	1406	1·7
	0901	4·4	2138	4·1		0752	4·3	2025	4·1
7 F	0402	1·9	1644	1·9	22 Sa	0237	1·9	1511	1·9
	1016	4·1	2252	4·0		0856	4·1	2132	4·0
8 Sa	0534	1·9	1805	2·0	23 Su	0359	1·9	1641	2·0
	1140	4·0				1014	4·0	2254	4·0
9 Su	0012	4·1	1256	4·1	24 M	0533	1·8	1811	1·8
	0652	1·8	1910	1·8		1146	4·1		
10 M	0114	4·3	1352	4·3	25 Tu	0015	4·2	1300	4·4
	0748	1·5	2001	1·7		0652	1·5	1919	1·5
11 Tu	0202	4·4	1434	4·4	26 W	0117	4·6	1358	4·7
	0834	1·3	2040	1·5		0752	1·0	2013	1·2
12 W	0239	4·6	1511	4·5	27 Th	0208	5·0	1446	5·0
	0912	1·1	2115	1·3		0846	0·6	2101	0·9
13 Th	0311	4·7	1543	4·6	28 F	0253	5·3	1531	5·2
	0946	0·9	2145	1·1		0935	0·3	2145	0·7
14 F	0342	4·8	1614	4·7	29 Sa	0336	5·5	1614	5·3
	1016	0·8	2214	1·1		1020	0·2	2227	0·6
15 Sa	0410	4·9	1644	4·6	30 Su	0420	5·6	1657	5·2
	1045	0·8	2244	1·0		1102	0·2	2308	0·6
					31 M	0505	5·6	1739	5·1
						1144	0·3	2349	0·8

GENERAL — Streams run in direction of channel inside entrance and run in direction of coast outside entrance. Heavy rains increase duration and rate of outgoing stream, and decrease duration and rate of ingoing stream. Turbulence at entrance during outgoing stream, especially with NE gales.

WHEN TO ENTER — Before ingoing stream has ceased — especially during NNE. gales. Beware of tidal stream.

NORTH SHIELDS **RIVER TYNE**

HIGH & LOW WATER 1992 **Lat. 55°00′N. Long. 1°27′W.**

GMT **ADD 1 HOUR MARCH 29 — OCTOBER 25 FOR B.S.T.**

SEPTEMBER

Day	Time	m	Day	Time	m
1 Tu	0551 1224 1822	5·4 0·7 4·9	16 W	0513 1139 1740 2353	4·9 1·0 4·7 1·2
2 W	0031 0641 1304 1909	1·0 5·1 1·1 4·7	17 Th	0551 1211 1815	4·8 1·2 4·6
3 Th ☽	0117 0734 1351 1959	1·3 4·7 1·5 4·4	18 F	0029 0635 1249 1900	1·4 4·6 1·5 4·4
4 F	0213 0834 1447 2058	1·7 4·3 1·9 4·1	19 Sa ☾	0114 0730 1338 1955	1·6 4·4 1·8 4·2
5 Sa	0332 0950 1610 2217	2·0 4·0 2·2 3·9	20 Su	0216 0837 1449 2107	1·8 4·2 2·0 4·1
6 Su	0515 1126 1744 2347	2·0 3·9 2·2 4·0	21 M	0342 1002 1624 2234	1·9 4·0 2·1 4·1
7 M	0632 1242 1850	1·8 4·0 2·0	22 Tu	0520 1134 1756 2356	1·7 4·2 1·9 4·3
8 Tu	0052 0728 1334 1938	4·2 1·5 4·2 1·7	23 W	0636 1246 1900	1·3 4·5 1·6
9 W	0137 0811 1415 2016	4·4 1·2 4·4 1·5	24 Th	0057 0735 1340 1954	4·7 0·9 4·8 1·2
10 Th	0213 0847 1449 2050	4·6 1·0 4·5 1·3	25 F	0147 0826 1426 2040	5·1 0·6 5·1 0·9
11 F	0246 0919 1518 2119	4·8 0·9 4·7 1·1	26 Sa ●	0232 0912 1508 2124	5·4 0·3 5·2 0·7
12 Sa ○	0314 0948 1546 2150	4·9 0·8 4·7 1·0	27 Su	0315 0956 1549 2204	5·6 0·3 5·3 0·6
13 Su	0342 1016 1614 2220	5·0 0·8 4·8 1·0	28 M	0359 1037 1630 2245	5·6 0·4 5·3 0·7
14 M	0412 1042 1641 2249	5·0 0·8 4·8 1·0	29 Tu	0444 1116 1711 2325	5·5 0·6 5·2 0·8
15 Tu	0441 1111 1709 2319	5·0 0·9 4·8 1·1	30 W	0529 1154 1751	5·3 0·9 5·0

OCTOBER

Day	Time	m	Day	Time	m
1 Th	0005 0617 1232 1835	1·1 5·0 1·3 4·7	16 F	0534 1150 1753	4·9 1·3 4·7
2 F	0050 0709 1314 1923	1·4 4·6 1·7 4·4	17 Sa	0015 0624 1232 1839	1·3 4·7 1·5 4·6
3 Sa ☽	0144 0806 1406 2019	1·7 4·2 2·1 4·1	18 Su	0106 0720 1324 1938	1·5 4·4 1·8 4·4
4 Su	0256 0918 1524 2132	1·9 3·9 2·3 3·9	19 M ☾	0211 0827 1434 2050	1·6 4·2 2·0 4·2
5 M	0435 1051 1705 2301	1·9 3·8 2·3 3·9	20 Tu	0334 0950 1606 2213	1·7 4·1 2·0 4·2
6 Tu	0556 1210 1814	1·8 3·9 2·1	21 W	0501 1116 1732 2332	1·5 4·2 1·9 4·5
7 W	0011 0650 1303 1903	4·1 1·5 4·1 1·8	22 Th	0612 1224 1836	1·2 4·5 1·6
8 Th	0100 0734 1342 1944	4·3 1·3 4·3 1·6	23 F	0032 0710 1317 1930	4·8 0·9 4·8 1·3
9 F	0138 0811 1416 2018	4·5 1·1 4·5 1·4	24 Sa	0124 0802 1404 2018	5·1 0·7 5·0 1·0
10 Sa	0212 0843 1446 2051	4·7 1·0 4·7 1·2	25 Su ●	0212 0849 1446 2103	5·3 0·6 5·2 0·9
11 Su ○	0243 0914 1514 2122	4·8 0·9 4·8 1·1	26 M	0256 0932 1525 2145	5·5 0·6 5·3 0·8
12 M	0314 0943 1542 2155	5·0 0·9 4·9 1·0	27 Tu	0341 1012 1604 2226	5·5 0·7 5·2 0·8
13 Tu	0345 1013 1610 2226	5·0 0·9 5·0 1·0	28 W	0426 1049 1644 2305	5·4 0·9 5·1 0·9
14 W	0417 1042 1640 2259	5·0 1·0 4·9 1·0	29 Th	0511 1126 1723 2344	5·1 1·2 5·0 1·1
15 Th	0454 1115 1713 2334	5·0 1·1 4·9 1·1	30 F	0557 1203 1805	4·9 1·5 4·8
			31 Sa	0028 0645 1242 1849	1·3 4·6 1·8 4·5

NOVEMBER

Day	Time	m	Day	Time	m
1 Su	0114 0737 1328 1940	1·5 4·2 2·0 4·2	16 M	0103 0714 1317 1926	1·2 4·5 1·7 4·6
2 M ☽	0213 0837 1429 2040	1·7 4·0 2·2 4·0	17 Tu ☾	0205 0818 1422 2033	1·3 4·3 1·8 4·5
3 Tu	0329 0953 1553 2155	1·8 3·8 2·3 3·9	18 W	0317 0931 1539 2148	1·4 4·2 1·9 4·5
4 W	0451 1113 1715 2311	1·8 3·8 2·2 4·0	19 Th	0433 1045 1658 2301	1·3 4·3 1·8 4·6
5 Th	0556 1214 1814	1·7 4·0 2·0	20 F	0542 1153 1807	1·2 4·4 1·6
6 F	0010 0645 1259 1902	4·1 1·5 4·2 1·7	21 Sa	0005 0643 1250 1906	4·7 1·1 4·7 1·4
7 Sa	0056 0726 1337 1941	4·3 1·3 4·4 1·5	22 Su	0103 0737 1340 1959	4·9 1·0 4·9 1·2
8 Su	0135 0802 1409 2019	4·5 1·2 4·6 1·3	23 M	0155 0826 1425 2046	5·1 1·0 5·0 1·1
9 M	0211 0837 1440 2056	4·7 1·1 4·8 1·1	24 Tu ●	0243 0911 1505 2129	5·2 1·0 5·1 1·0
10 Tu ○	0247 0911 1511 2131	4·9 1·1 4·9 1·0	25 W	0328 0950 1545 2212	5·2 1·1 5·1 0·9
11 W	0322 0946 1543 2207	5·0 1·1 5·0 1·0	26 Th	0413 1028 1624 2249	5·1 1·2 5·0 1·0
12 Th	0402 1021 1617 2245	5·1 1·1 5·0 1·0	27 F	0455 1104 1701 2329	5·0 1·3 4·9 1·1
13 F	0442 1059 1655 2325	5·0 1·2 5·0 1·0	28 Sa	0537 1139 1740	4·8 1·4 4·8
14 Sa	0527 1139 1739	4·9 1·3 4·9	29 Su	0007 0619 1215 1819	1·2 4·6 1·6 4·6
15 Su	0011 0618 1224 1828	1·1 4·7 1·5 4·7	30 M	0049 0704 1255 1903	1·3 4·3 1·8 4·4

DECEMBER

Day	Time	m	Day	Time	m
1 Tu	0134 0754 1341 1952	1·5 4·1 2·0 4·2	16 W ☾	0152 0801 1402 2012	1·0 4·5 1·6 4·7
2 W ☽	0226 0850 1439 2050	1·6 3·9 2·1 4·0	17 Th	0253 0903 1507 2119	1·1 4·4 1·7 4·6
3 Th	0328 0955 1550 2156	1·7 3·8 2·2 3·9	18 F	0359 1010 1623 2230	1·3 4·3 1·8 4·5
4 F	0435 1101 1705 2304	1·8 3·9 2·1 4·0	19 Sa	0508 1119 1739 2342	1·4 4·3 1·7 4·5
5 Sa	0537 1200 1808	1·7 4·0 1·9	20 Su	0617 1224 1848	1·4 4·4 1·6
6 Su	0004 0632 1248 1900	4·1 1·6 4·3 1·7	21 M	0046 0717 1321 1947	4·6 1·4 4·6 1·4
7 M	0055 0720 1328 1947	4·3 1·5 4·5 1·5	22 Tu	0145 0811 1411 2037	4·7 1·3 4·8 1·2
8 Tu	0141 0804 1408 2029	4·6 1·4 4·7 1·3	23 W	0236 0856 1453 2122	4·8 1·3 4·9 1·1
9 W ○	0225 0846 1444 2110	4·8 1·2 4·9 1·1	24 Th ●	0321 0936 1532 2203	4·9 1·2 4·9 1·0
10 Th	0307 0927 1522 2152	4·9 1·1 5·0 0·9	25 F	0402 1013 1609 2240	4·9 1·2 5·0 1·0
11 F	0349 1007 1602 2235	5·0 1·1 5·1 0·8	26 Sa	0441 1045 1642 2315	4·9 1·2 4·9 0·9
12 Sa	0434 1048 1644 2320	5·1 1·1 5·1 0·8	27 Su	0518 1118 1718 2349	4·8 1·3 4·9 1·0
13 Su	0520 1132 1729	5·0 1·1 5·1	28 M	0554 1150 1753	4·6 1·3 4·7
14 M	0007 0610 1217 1818	0·8 4·9 1·2 5·0	29 Tu	0022 0632 1225 1829	1·1 4·4 1·5 4·6
15 Tu	0057 0703 1306 1912	0·8 4·7 1·4 4·9	30 W	0059 0713 1303 1912	1·2 4·2 1·6 4·4
			31 Th	0138 0755 1347 1957	1·4 4·1 1·8 4·2

RATE AND SET — Off ent. S. going begins −0100 Dover, Sp. rate 2¼ kn. N. going begins +0500 Dover. Sp. rate 2½ kn. In ent. Ingoing begins −0100 Dover, Sp. rate 2¼ kn. Outgoing begins +0510 Dover. Sp. rate 2½ kn.

TIDAL DIFFERENCES ON RIVER TYNE (NORTH SHIELDS)   21:95

PLACE	TIME DIFFERENCES				HEIGHT DIFFERENCES (Metres)			
	High Water		Low Water		MHWS	MHWN	MLWN	MLWS
RIVER TYNE .... (NORTH SHIELDS)	0200 and 1400	0800 and 2000	0100 and 1300	0800 and 2000	5.0	3.9	1.8	0.7
River Tyne								
Entrance	+0005	+0005	−0005	−0005	+0.1	0.0	0.0	+0.1
Newcastle-upon-Tyne	+0003	+0003	+0008	+0008	+0.3	+0.2	+0.1	+0.1
Blyth	+0005	−0007	−0001	+0009	0.0	0.0	−0.1	+0.1
Coquet Road	−0010	−0010	−0020	−0020	+0.1	+0.1	0.0	+0.1
Amble	−0023	−0015	−0023	−0014	0.0	+0.2	+0.2	+0.1
Alnmouth	−0030	−0022	−0032	−0026	0.0	+0.1	+0.1	+0.1
Craster	−0035	−0030	−0040	−0038	−0.1	0.0	0.0	0.0
North Sunderland (Northumberland)	−0048	−0044	−0058	−0102	−0.2	−0.2	−0.2	0.0
Holy Island	−0043	−0039	−0105	−0110	−0.2	−0.2	−0.3	−0.1
Berwick	−0053	−0053	−0109	−0109	−0.3	−0.1	−0.5	−0.1

Refer to predictions on pages 21:92-21:94

TIDAL DIFFERENCES ON LEITH

PLACE	TIME DIFFERENCES				HEIGHT DIFFERENCES (Metres)			
	High Water		Low Water		MHWS	MHWN	MLWN	MLWS
LEITH	0300 and 1500	0900 and 2100	0300 and 1500	0900 and 2100	5.6	4.5	2.1	0.8
SCOTLAND								
Eyemouth	−0015	−0025	−0014	−0004	−0.9	−0.8	−	−
Cove Harbour	−0010	−0015	0000	+0010	−0.6	−0.5	−	−
Dunbar	−0005	−0010	+0010	+0017	−0.4	−0.3	−0.1	−0.1
Fidra	−0005	−0005	−0010	−0010	−0.4	−0.1	0.0	−0.2
Cockenzie	−0007	−0015	−0013	−0005	−0.2	0.0	−	−
Granton	0000	0000	0000	0000	0.0	0.0	0.0	0.0
Firth of Forth								
Aberdour	+0004	0000	−0002	−0007	+0.1	+0.1	0.0	0.0
Burntisland	+0002	−0002	−0002	−0004	0.0	0.0	0.0	0.0
Dysart	−0002	−0007	−0004	−0003	0.0	0.0	0.0	0.0
Methil	−0006	−0012	−0007	−0001	−0.1	−0.1	−0.1	−0.1
Lower Largo	−0007	−0018	−0010	−0006	−0.1	−0.1	−0.1	−0.1
St Monance	−0009	−0030	−0017	−0015	−0.1	−0.1	−0.1	−0.1
Anstruther Easter	−0010	−0035	−0020	−0020	−0.1	−0.1	−0.1	−0.1
Crail	−0011	−0040	−0023	−0025	−0.1	−0.1	−0.1	−0.1
River Forth								
Rosyth	+0007	+0003	−0001	−0011	+0.2	+0.2	+0.1	0.0
Grangemouth	+0032	+0013	−0053	−0026	+0.1	0.0	−0.2	−0.3
Kincardine	+0022	+0033	−0029	−0041	+0.2	0.0	−0.4	−0.3
Alloa	+0047	+0043	+0024	+0014	0.0	−0.3	−	−0.7
Stirling	+0108	+0114	+0437	+0427	−3.1	−2.9	−2.2	−0.7

Refer to predictions on pages 21:97-21:99

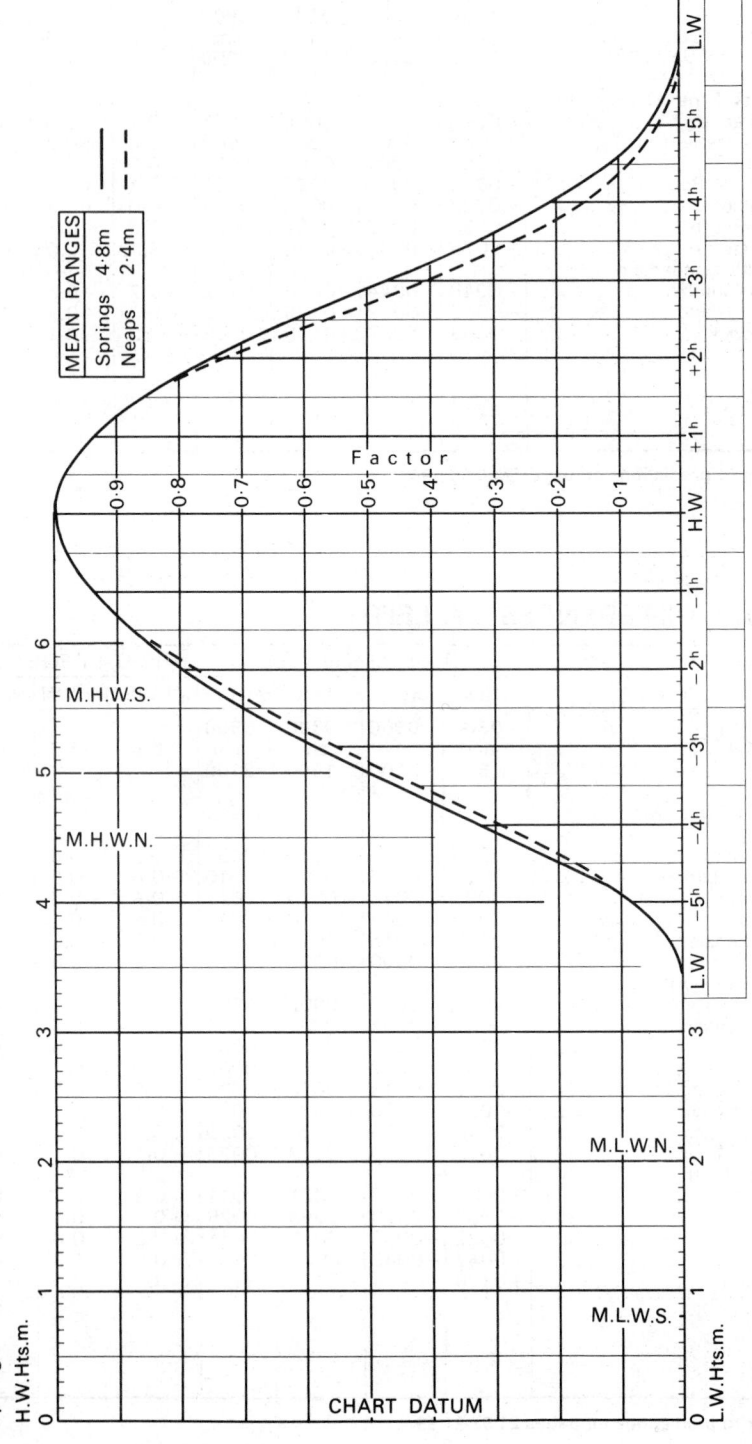

LEITH

MEAN SPRING AND NEAP CURVES

Springs occur 2 days after New and Full Moon.

LEITH FIRTH OF FORTH 21:97

Lat. 55°59'N. Long. 3°10'W. **HIGH & LOW WATER 1992**

GMT **ADD 1 HOUR MARCH 29 — OCTOBER 25 FOR B.S.T.**

JANUARY

Day	Time	m	Time	m	Time	m	Time	m
1 W	0541	1·9	1200	4·7	1807	1·8		
2 Th	0035	4·9	0633	1·8	1254	4·9	1901	1·6
3 F	0128	4·9	0715	1·7	1341	5·0	1946	1·4
4 Sa ●	0213	5·0	0750	1·6	1420	5·1	2022	1·3
5 Su	0250	5·1	0820	1·5	1452	5·2	2056	1·2
6 M	0324	5·1	0850	1·4	1522	5·3	2126	1·1
7 Tu	0358	5·1	0920	1·4	1552	5·2	2156	1·1
8 W	0430	5·1	0952	1·3	1622	5·2	2226	1·1
9 Th	0505	5·0	1026	1·4	1658	5·2	2258	1·2
10 F	0545	4·9	1100	1·5	1735	5·1	2331	1·3
11 Sa	0626	4·8	1135	1·6	1820	4·9		
12 Su	0007	1·5	0713	4·6	1215	1·8	1913	4·8
13 M ☽	0052	1·7	0805	4·4	1305	2·1	2011	4·6
14 Tu	0154	1·9	0901	4·4	1422	2·2	2116	4·6
15 W	0322	2·0	1001	4·4	1558	2·1	2222	4·6
16 Th	0441	1·9	1103	4·6	1715	1·9	2331	4·8
17 F	0545	1·7	1205	4·8	1818	1·5		
18 Sa	0037	5·1	0643	1·4	1303	5·2	1916	1·1
19 Su ○	0137	5·4	0735	1·1	1308	5·5	2011	0·7
20 M	0233	5·7	0824	0·9	1450	5·8	2101	0·4
21 Tu	0326	5·9	0911	0·7	1541	5·9	2146	0·2
22 W	0415	5·9	0954	0·7	1631	6·0	2231	0·2
23 Th	0503	5·8	1033	0·7	1718	5·9	2313	0·4
24 F	0550	5·6	1113	0·9	1807	5·7	2354	0·7
25 Sa	0637	5·3	1152	1·2	1856	5·4		
26 Su ☾	0039	1·2	0726	5·0	1239	1·6	1946	5·1
27 M	0131	1·6	0816	4·7	1341	1·9	2043	4·8
28 Tu	0241	2·0	0913	4·4	1507	2·2	2146	4·5
29 W	0401	2·2	1016	4·4	1637	2·1	2301	4·4
30 Th	0516	2·2	1126	4·4	1756	1·9		
31 F	0016	4·5	0616	2·1	1233	4·6	1854	1·7

FEBRUARY

Day	Time	m	Time	m	Time	m	Time	m
1 Sa	0115	4·7	0701	1·9	1322	4·8	1937	1·4
2 Su	0158	4·9	0737	1·7	1401	5·0	2011	1·2
3 M ●	0233	5·1	0807	1·4	1433	5·2	2041	1·1
4 Tu	0305	5·2	0835	1·3	1501	5·3	2109	0·9
5 W	0335	5·2	0905	1·1	1531	5·4	2137	0·8
6 Th	0407	5·2	0935	1·0	1603	5·4	2205	0·8
7 F	0441	5·2	1005	1·0	1635	5·3	2231	0·9
8 Sa	0516	5·0	1033	1·1	1711	5·2	2300	1·0
9 Su	0554	4·8	1105	1·3	1750	5·1	2330	1·2
10 M	0635	4·7	1139	1·5	1837	4·8		
11 Tu ☽	0005	1·5	0722	4·5	1222	1·7	1937	4·6
12 W	0054	1·8	0820	4·3	1324	2·0	2045	4·5
13 Th	0215	2·1	0926	4·3	1518	2·1	2158	4·5
14 F	0409	2·1	1035	4·5	1658	1·8	2315	4·7
15 Sa	0530	1·8	1145	4·8	1811	1·4		
16 Su	0026	5·0	0631	1·4	1248	5·2	1909	0·9
17 M	0126	5·4	0726	1·0	1345	5·6	2001	0·5
18 Tu ○	0220	5·7	0813	0·7	1437	5·9	2046	0·2
19 W	0309	5·9	0854	0·5	1524	6·1	2130	0·0
20 Th	0354	5·9	0933	0·5	1611	6·1	2209	0·1
21 F	0439	5·8	1009	0·5	1656	6·0	2245	0·3
22 Sa	0522	5·6	1043	0·7	1741	5·7	2320	0·7
23 Su	0605	5·3	1118	1·0	1826	5·4	2354	1·2
24 M	0649	4·9	1158	1·4	1913	5·0		
25 Tu ☾	0035	1·7	0735	4·6	1250	1·8	2007	4·6
26 W	0137	2·2	0828	4·3	1420	2·2	2109	4·3
27 Th	0315	2·5	0931	4·2	1609	2·2	2226	4·2
28 F	0446	2·4	1045	4·2	1733	2·0	2348	4·3
29 Sa	0552	2·2	1158	4·4	1830	1·7		

MARCH

Day	Time	m	Time	m	Time	m	Time	m
1 Su	0050	4·6	0637	1·9	1254	4·7	1911	1·4
2 M	0131	4·8	0711	1·6	1333	4·9	1943	1·1
3 Tu	0205	5·0	0743	1·3	1405	5·1	2015	0·9
4 W ●	0237	5·2	0813	1·1	1435	5·3	2043	0·7
5 Th	0309	5·3	0843	0·9	1507	5·4	2111	0·6
6 F	0341	5·3	0913	0·9	1539	5·4	2137	0·6
7 Sa	0415	5·2	0941	0·8	1609	5·4	2203	0·7
8 Su	0448	5·1	1009	0·9	1648	5·3	2230	0·8
9 M	0524	4·9	1041	1·0	1730	5·1	2300	1·1
10 Tu	0603	4·7	1115	1·2	1818	4·8	2335	1·4
11 W	0650	4·6	1158	1·5	1920	4·6		
12 Th ☽	0022	1·7	0752	4·4	1303	1·8	2028	4·4
13 F	0141	2·1	0900	4·4	1505	2·0	2143	4·4
14 Sa	0348	2·1	1015	4·5	1646	1·7	2300	4·6
15 Su	0518	1·8	1126	4·8	1756	1·2		
16 M	0011	5·0	0616	1·4	1231	5·2	1854	0·8
17 Tu	0111	5·4	0707	1·0	1328	5·6	1943	0·4
18 W ○	0201	5·6	0750	0·7	1416	5·9	2026	0·2
19 Th	0246	5·8	0831	0·5	1503	6·0	2103	0·1
20 F	0330	5·8	0907	0·4	1546	6·0	2139	0·2
21 Sa	0413	5·7	0941	0·5	1631	5·8	2213	0·5
22 Su	0452	5·4	1015	0·7	1713	5·5	2243	0·9
23 M	0531	5·2	1048	1·0	1756	5·2	2313	1·3
24 Tu	0611	4·8	1126	1·3	1841	4·8	2346	1·8
25 W	0654	4·5	1213	1·8	1931	4·4		
26 Th ☾	0035	2·2	0745	4·3	1333	2·1	2031	4·2
27 F	0215	2·6	0845	4·1	1530	2·2	2141	4·1
28 Sa	0400	2·5	0954	4·1	1648	2·0	2258	4·2
29 Su	0509	2·3	1107	4·3	1746	1·7		
30 M	0005	4·5	0558	1·9	1205	4·5	1830	1·4
31 Tu	0050	4·7	0635	1·6	1250	4·8	1905	1·1

APRIL

Day	Time	m	Time	m	Time	m	Time	m
1 W	0128	5·0	0711	1·3	1328	5·0	1939	0·9
2 Th	0203	5·1	0745	1·1	1403	5·2	2011	0·7
3 F ●	0237	5·2	0816	0·9	1437	5·3	2039	0·6
4 Sa	0311	5·2	0846	0·8	1515	5·4	2109	0·6
5 Su	0345	5·2	0918	0·7	1552	5·3	2135	0·7
6 M	0420	5·1	0950	0·8	1633	5·2	2205	0·8
7 Tu	0458	5·0	1024	0·9	1720	5·1	2239	1·1
8 W	0541	4·9	1103	1·1	1815	4·9	2318	1·4
9 Th	0633	4·7	1154	1·4	1913	4·7		
10 F ☽	0011	1·8	0735	4·6	1309	1·6	2020	4·5
11 Sa	0137	2·1	0845	4·5	1501	1·7	2131	4·5
12 Su	0333	2·1	0956	4·6	1628	1·5	2245	4·7
13 M	0452	1·8	1107	4·9	1733	1·1	2350	5·0
14 Tu	0552	1·4	1209	5·2	1828	0·8		
15 W	0048	5·3	0643	1·1	1305	5·5	1916	0·5
16 Th	0137	5·5	0726	0·8	1354	5·7	1958	0·4
17 F ○	0222	5·6	0805	0·7	1441	5·7	2037	0·4
18 Sa	0305	5·6	0843	0·6	1526	5·7	2109	0·6
19 Su	0345	5·4	0918	0·7	1609	5·5	2139	0·8
20 M	0424	5·3	0952	0·8	1650	5·3	2209	1·1
21 Tu	0500	5·1	1026	1·0	1731	5·0	2239	1·4
22 W	0535	4·8	1103	1·3	1813	4·7	2313	1·8
23 Th	0615	4·6	1148	1·6	1900	4·4	2358	2·1
24 F ☾	0701	4·4	1252	1·9	1954	4·2		
25 Sa	0111	2·4	0800	4·2	1431	2·1	2056	4·2
26 Su	0258	2·5	0903	4·2	1552	2·0	2201	4·2
27 M	0415	2·3	1009	4·3	1652	1·8	2305	4·3
28 Tu	0509	2·0	1111	4·5	1741	1·5		
29 W	0000	4·6	0556	1·7	1201	4·7	1824	1·2
30 Th	0045	4·8	0635	1·4	1246	4·9	1901	1·0

To find H.W. Dover subtract 3 h. 45 min.

TIDAL DIFFERENCES PAGE 21:95. TIDAL CURVE PAGE 21:96.

Datum of predictions: 2.90 m. below Ordnance Datum (Newlyn) or approx. L.A.T.

FIRTH OF FORTH **LEITH**

HIGH & LOW WATER 1992   Lat. 55°59'N. Long. 3°10'W.

GMT   ADD 1 HOUR MARCH 29 — OCTOBER 25 FOR B.S.T.

MAY

Day	Time	m	Day	Time	m
1 F	0124	5·0	16 Sa	0200	5·3
	0713	1·2		0746	0·9
	1330	5·1		1424	5·4
	1935	0·9		○ 2011	0·9
2 Sa ●	0201	5·1	17 Su	0241	5·3
	0748	1·0		0826	0·9
	1411	5·2		1509	5·4
	2009	0·8		2045	1·0
3 Su	0239	5·2	18 M	0320	5·3
	0824	0·8		0903	0·9
	1452	5·3		1550	5·2
	2041	0·8		2115	1·2
4 M	0318	5·2	19 Tu	0358	5·2
	0900	0·7		0937	1·0
	1537	5·3		1630	5·1
	2115	0·8		2143	1·3
5 Tu	0358	5·2	20 W	0431	5·0
	0937	0·7		1013	1·1
	1626	5·2		1709	5·0
	2150	0·9		2216	1·5
6 W	0441	5·1	21 Th	0503	4·9
	1018	0·8		1048	1·3
	1716	5·1		1746	4·7
	2230	1·1		2252	1·7
7 Th	0530	5·0	22 F	0541	4·8
	1105	0·9		1130	1·5
	1811	5·0		1830	4·6
	2316	1·4		2335	1·9
8 F	0626	4·9	23 Sa	0624	4·6
	1203	1·2		1220	1·7
	1907	4·9		1918	4·4
9 Sa ☽	0015	1·7	24 Su ☾	0030	2·1
	0726	4·8		0716	4·4
	1320	1·4		1328	1·9
	2009	4·8		2013	4·3
10 Su	0137	1·9	25 M	0148	2·3
	0830	4·7		0816	4·3
	1445	1·4		1446	1·9
	2115	4·7		2111	4·3
11 M	0309	1·9	26 Tu	0311	2·3
	0935	4·8		0918	4·3
	1600	1·3		1554	1·8
	2220	4·8		2211	4·4
12 Tu	0422	1·8	27 W	0416	2·1
	1043	4·9		1018	4·4
	1703	1·2		1652	1·6
	2324	4·9		2307	4·5
13 W	0524	1·5	28 Th	0511	1·9
	1145	5·1		1115	4·6
	1800	1·0		1741	1·5
				2358	4·7
14 Th	0022	5·1	29 F	0558	1·6
	0616	1·3		1207	4·8
	1243	5·3		1824	1·3
	1850	0·9			
15 F	0113	5·2	30 Sa	0045	4·8
	0703	1·1		0641	1·3
	1335	5·4		1258	4·9
	1933	0·9		1903	1·1
			31 Su	0128	5·0
				0724	1·1
				1346	5·1
				1943	1·0

JUNE

Day	Time	m	Day	Time	m
1 M	0211	5·1	16 Tu	0301	5·2
	0807	0·9		0856	1·0
	1435	5·2		1535	5·1
	● 2022	0·9		2056	1·4
2 Tu	0254	5·3	17 W	0335	5·1
	0850	0·7		0930	1·0
	1526	5·3		1611	5·0
	2101	0·9		2126	1·4
3 W	0341	5·3	18 Th	0407	5·1
	0935	0·6		1001	1·1
	1616	5·4		1646	5·0
	2145	1·0		2200	1·4
4 Th	0430	5·3	19 F	0437	5·0
	1022	0·6		1033	1·2
	1709	5·4		1720	4·9
	2230	1·1		2233	1·5
5 F	0522	5·3	20 Sa	0511	4·9
	1113	0·7		1109	1·3
	1801	5·3		1800	4·8
	2318	1·3		2313	1·6
6 Sa	0616	5·2	21 Su	0552	4·8
	1207	0·9		1148	1·4
	1856	5·2		1843	4·6
				2354	1·8
7 Su ☽	0015	1·5	22 M	0639	4·7
	0713	5·1		1233	1·6
	1309	1·1		1931	4·5
	1952	5·0			
8 M	0120	1·7	23 Tu ☾	0045	2·0
	0811	5·0		0733	4·5
	1416	1·3		1331	1·8
	2052	4·9		2026	4·4
9 Tu	0235	1·8	24 W	0152	2·2
	0913	4·9		0831	4·4
	1526	1·4		1445	1·9
	2152	4·8		2122	4·3
10 W	0346	1·8	25 Th	0313	2·2
	1016	4·9		0933	4·4
	1633	1·4		1556	1·9
	2254	4·8		2220	4·4
11 Th	0454	1·7	26 F	0424	2·0
	1120	4·9		1033	4·5
	1733	1·4		1656	1·7
	2354	4·9		2315	4·5
12 F	0554	1·5	27 Sa	0522	1·8
	1224	5·0		1133	4·6
	1826	1·4		1748	1·6
13 Sa	0048	5·0	28 Su	0007	4·7
	0648	1·3		0615	1·5
	1320	5·1		1231	4·8
	1913	1·3		1837	1·4
14 Su	0139	5·1	29 M	0058	5·0
	0737	1·2		0705	1·2
	1411	5·1		1328	5·1
	1952	1·3		1924	1·2
15 M ○	0222	5·2	30 Tu ●	0146	5·2
	0818	1·1		0756	0·8
	1454	5·1		1422	5·3
	2026	1·4		2009	1·0

JULY

Day	Time	m	Day	Time	m
1 W	0237	5·4	16 Th	0315	5·2
	0845	0·6		0918	1·0
	1515	5·5		1550	5·1
	2056	0·9		2111	1·3
2 Th	0328	5·6	17 F	0343	5·2
	0933	0·4		0946	1·0
	1605	5·6		1620	5·1
	2141	0·8		2141	1·3
3 F	0418	5·7	18 Sa	0411	5·2
	1020	0·3		1015	1·0
	1656	5·6		1654	5·0
	2226	0·8		2213	1·3
4 Sa	0511	5·7	19 Su	0443	5·2
	1105	0·4		1045	1·0
	1746	5·6		1730	4·9
	2309	1·0		2246	1·4
5 Su	0601	5·6	20 M	0520	5·0
	1154	0·6		1115	1·1
	1837	5·4		1809	4·8
	2356	1·2		2320	1·5
6 M	0654	5·4	21 Tu	0603	4·9
	1245	0·9		1150	1·3
	1930	5·1		1854	4·6
				2358	1·7
7 Tu ☽	0050	1·5	22 W	0652	4·7
	0748	5·2		1228	1·6
	1343	1·2		1943	4·4
	2024	4·9			
8 W	0154	1·7	23 Th	0043	2·0
	0846	5·0		0748	4·5
	1448	1·6		1320	1·9
	2120	4·7		2037	4·3
9 Th	0311	1·9	24 F	0150	2·2
	0948	4·9		0852	4·4
	1600	1·8		1443	2·0
	2222	4·6		2135	4·3
10 F	0430	1·9	25 Sa	0331	2·2
	1058	4·7		0958	4·4
	1709	1·8		1611	2·0
	2326	4·6		2237	4·4
11 Sa	0543	1·7	26 Su	0452	1·9
	1207	4·7		1105	4·5
	1811	1·8		1720	1·8
				2337	4·7
12 Su	0030	4·8	27 M	0558	1·6
	0645	1·5		1211	4·8
	1309	4·9		1816	1·5
	1900	1·7			
13 M	0122	4·9	28 Tu	0035	5·0
	0733	1·3		0654	1·1
	1400	5·0		1311	5·1
	1941	1·6		1909	1·2
14 Tu	0205	5·1	29 W	0130	5·3
	0815	1·2		0746	0·7
	1441	5·1		1407	5·5
	2013	1·5		1958	0·9
15 W ○	0243	5·2	30 Th	0222	5·6
	0848	1·1		0835	0·4
	1516	5·1		1500	5·7
	2041	1·4		2045	0·7
			31 F	0313	5·9
				0922	0·1
				1548	5·8
				2128	0·6

AUGUST

Day	Time	m	Day	Time	m
1 Sa	0401	6·0	16 Su	0345	5·4
	1005	0·1		0948	0·8
	1637	5·8		1626	5·2
	2209	0·6		2148	1·1
2 Su	0450	6·0	17 M	0416	5·3
	1046	0·2		1015	0·8
	1724	5·7		1700	5·1
	2248	0·7		2218	1·2
3 M	0541	5·8	18 Tu	0450	5·2
	1128	0·5		1043	1·0
	1813	5·5		1735	4·9
	2330	1·0		2248	1·3
4 Tu	0630	5·6	19 W	0530	5·0
	1211	0·9		1111	1·2
	1901	5·2		1816	4·7
				2322	1·5
5 W	0015	1·4	20 Th	0615	4·8
	0722	5·2		1143	1·5
	1301	1·4		1901	4·5
	☽ 1952	4·9			
6 Th	0113	1·7	21 F	0000	1·8
	0818	4·9		0713	4·6
	1405	1·8		1226	1·8
	2046	4·6		☾ 1956	4·4
7 F	0235	2·0	22 Sa	0054	2·1
	0920	4·6		0820	4·4
	1528	2·1		1330	2·1
	2150	4·5		2100	4·3
8 Sa	0411	2·1	23 Su	0245	2·2
	1033	4·5		0931	4·4
	1650	2·2		1531	2·2
	2300	4·5		2205	4·5
9 Su	0535	1·9	24 M	0431	2·0
	1152	4·5		1043	4·5
	1758	2·1		1658	2·0
				2313	4·7
10 M	0009	4·6	25 Tu	0554	1·5
	0637	1·6		1154	4·8
	1256	4·7		1801	1·6
	1846	1·9			
11 Tu	0103	4·9	26 W	0015	5·1
	0722	1·4		0641	1·0
	1343	4·9		1256	5·2
	1924	1·7		1854	1·2
12 W	0146	5·1	27 Th	0111	5·5
	0800	1·2		0731	0·6
	1420	5·1		1350	5·6
	1954	1·5		1941	0·8
13 Th	0220	5·2	28 F	0203	5·8
	0828	1·0		0818	0·2
	1452	5·2		1439	5·8
	2022	1·3		● 2026	0·5
14 F	0248	5·3	29 Sa	0252	6·1
	0856	0·9		0901	0·0
	1522	5·2		1526	5·9
	2050	1·2		2105	0·5
15 Sa ○	0316	5·4	30 Su	0341	6·1
	0920	0·8		0941	0·0
	1554	5·2		1613	5·9
	2118	1·1		2145	0·5
			31 M	0428	6·1
				1020	0·2
				1658	5·7
				2222	0·6

GENERAL — Stream near entrance weak, increases inwards.

LEITH FIRTH OF FORTH

21:99

Lat. 55°59′N. Long. 3°10′W. **HIGH & LOW WATER 1992**

GMT **ADD 1 HOUR MARCH 29 — OCTOBER 25 FOR B.S.T.**

SEPTEMBER

Day	Time	m	Time	m	Time	m	Time	m
1 Tu	0515	5·9	1056	0·6	1743	5·5	2300	0·9
2 W	0603	5·5	1133	1·0	1830	5·1	2341	1·3
3 Th)	0654	5·1	1215	1·6	1918	4·8		
4 F	0033	1·8	0748	4·7	1313	2·1	2011	4·5
5 Sa	0201	2·1	0852	4·4	1450	2·5	2115	4·3
6 Su	0352	2·2	1005	4·3	1626	2·5	2226	4·4
7 M	0516	2·0	1128	4·4	1733	2·3	2339	4·5
8 Tu	0613	1·7	1231	4·7	1820	2·0		
9 W	0035	4·8	0654	1·4	1316	4·9	1856	1·7
10 Th	0116	5·0	0728	1·2	1350	5·1	1926	1·5
11 F	0148	5·2	0758	1·0	1422	5·2	1956	1·2
12 Sa O	0218	5·4	0824	0·8	1452	5·3	2024	1·1
13 Su	0246	5·4	0852	0·7	1522	5·3	2054	1·0
14 M	0318	5·4	0918	0·7	1556	5·3	2124	1·0
15 Tu	0350	5·4	0945	0·8	1628	5·1	2152	1·1
16 W	0426	5·3	1011	0·9	1701	5·0	2222	1·2
17 Th	0505	5·1	1039	1·1	1739	4·8	2256	1·4
18 F	0554	4·8	1111	1·4	1826	4·6	2335	1·6
19 Sa (	0652	4·6	1154	1·8	1924	4·5		
20 Su	0031	1·9	0801	4·5	1256	2·1	2031	4·5
21 M	0224	2·1	0913	4·4	1501	2·3	2141	4·6
22 Tu	0413	1·9	1026	4·6	1637	2·0	2250	4·8
23 W	0524	1·4	1135	5·0	1741	1·6	2354	5·2
24 Th	0620	1·0	1237	5·3	1833	1·2		
25 F	0052	5·6	0711	0·6	1330	5·7	1920	0·9
26 Sa ●	0143	5·9	0754	0·3	1416	5·9	2001	0·6
27 Su	0231	6·1	0835	0·2	1501	5·9	2041	0·5
28 M	0318	6·1	0915	0·2	1545	5·9	2120	0·5
29 Tu	0405	6·0	0950	0·5	1630	5·7	2156	0·7
30 W	0452	5·7	1024	0·8	1713	5·4	2233	1·0

OCTOBER

Day	Time	m	Time	m	Time	m	Time	m
1 Th	0539	5·4	1056	1·3	1756	5·1	2313	1·3
2 F	0628	5·0	1131	1·8	1841	4·8		
3 Sa)	0003	1·8	0720	4·6	1220	2·3	1933	4·5
4 Su	0126	2·1	0820	4·4	1354	2·6	2033	4·3
5 M	0315	2·2	0928	4·3	1541	2·7	2141	4·3
6 Tu	0433	2·1	1043	4·4	1652	2·4	2250	4·5
7 W	0530	1·8	1148	4·6	1741	2·1	2350	4·7
8 Th	0613	1·5	1235	4·9	1818	1·8		
9 F	0035	4·8	0648	1·3	1313	5·1	1854	1·5
10 Sa	0111	5·2	0720	1·0	1346	5·3	1928	1·3
11 Su O	0145	5·3	0752	0·9	1420	5·3	1958	1·1
12 M	0218	5·4	0820	0·8	1452	5·4	2030	1·0
13 Tu	0254	5·4	0848	0·8	1526	5·3	2101	1·0
14 W	0330	5·4	0916	0·9	1558	5·2	2131	1·0
15 Th	0411	5·3	0945	1·0	1633	5·1	2205	1·1
16 F	0456	5·1	1016	1·2	1715	5·0	2243	1·3
17 Sa	0546	4·9	1054	1·5	1803	4·8	2328	1·5
18 Su	0645	4·7	1139	1·8	1903	4·7		
19 M (	0031	1·8	0750	4·6	1246	2·1	2011	4·7
20 Tu	0216	1·9	0858	4·6	1441	2·3	2120	4·7
21 W	0350	1·7	1009	4·8	1613	2·0	2230	5·0
22 Th	0500	1·4	1115	5·0	1716	1·7	2333	5·3
23 F	0556	1·0	1213	5·3	1809	1·3		
24 Sa	0030	5·6	0645	0·7	1305	5·6	1856	1·0
25 Su ●	0122	5·8	0730	0·5	1354	5·7	1941	0·8
26 M	0211	5·9	0811	0·5	1439	5·8	2020	0·7
27 Tu	0300	5·9	0848	0·6	1522	5·7	2100	0·7
28 W	0346	5·8	0922	0·8	1603	5·6	2137	0·9
29 Th	0431	5·5	0954	1·1	1645	5·4	2215	1·1
30 F	0516	5·3	1026	1·5	1724	5·1	2254	1·4
31 Sa	0601	5·0	1101	1·9	1805	4·9	2341	1·7

NOVEMBER

Day	Time	m	Time	m	Time	m	Time	m
1 Su	0650	4·7	1145	2·2	1852	4·6		
2 M)	0045	2·0	0743	4·4	1250	2·5	1948	4·5
3 Tu	0216	2·2	0843	4·3	1433	2·6	2050	4·4
4 W	0335	2·1	0946	4·4	1554	2·5	2154	4·4
5 Th	0435	1·9	1050	4·5	1652	2·2	2254	4·6
6 F	0524	1·7	1145	4·8	1739	1·9	2346	4·8
7 Sa	0607	1·4	1230	5·0	1820	1·7		
8 Su	0031	5·0	0645	1·2	1309	5·1	1858	1·4
9 M	0113	5·2	0718	1·1	1346	5·3	1933	1·2
10 Tu O	0154	5·3	0752	1·0	1422	5·3	2009	1·1
11 W	0233	5·3	0824	1·0	1458	5·3	2045	1·0
12 Th	0316	5·3	0856	1·0	1535	5·3	2120	1·0
13 F	0401	5·3	0930	1·1	1616	5·3	2200	1·0
14 Sa	0450	5·2	1005	1·2	1701	5·2	2243	1·1
15 Su	0541	5·1	1048	1·5	1754	5·1	2333	1·3
16 M	0637	5·0	1139	1·7	1852	5·0		
17 Tu (	0037	1·5	0737	4·9	1245	2·0	1956	4·9
18 W	0200	1·6	0841	4·8	1415	2·1	2100	4·9
19 Th	0318	1·5	0945	4·9	1539	2·0	2205	5·0
20 F	0428	1·4	1048	5·0	1646	1·8	2309	5·2
21 Sa	0528	1·2	1148	5·2	1745	1·5		
22 Su	0009	5·4	0620	1·1	1243	5·4	1837	1·2
23 M	0105	5·6	0707	1·0	1333	5·5	1924	1·1
24 Tu ●	0158	5·6	0750	1·0	1418	5·6	2009	1·0
25 W	0246	5·6	0830	1·0	1501	5·6	2050	0·9
26 Th	0331	5·5	0903	1·2	1543	5·5	2130	1·0
27 F	0415	5·4	0935	1·4	1620	5·3	2205	1·1
28 Sa	0456	5·2	1005	1·6	1656	5·2	2241	1·3
29 Su	0537	5·0	1041	1·8	1731	5·0	2320	1·5
30 M	0618	4·8	1120	2·0	1813	4·8		

DECEMBER

Day	Time	m	Time	m	Time	m	Time	m
1 Tu	0005	1·8	0703	4·6	1209	2·2	1901	4·7
2 W	0105	1·9	0754	4·5	1316	2·4	2000	4·5
3 Th	0222	2·1	0852	4·4	1441	2·4	2100	4·5
4 F	0333	2·0	0952	4·5	1554	2·3	2200	4·5
5 Sa	0433	1·9	1050	4·6	1654	2·1	2258	4·6
6 Su	0524	1·7	1143	4·7	1745	1·9	2352	4·8
7 M	0609	1·5	1230	4·9	1830	1·6		
8 Tu	0043	5·0	0650	1·4	1313	5·1	1911	1·4
9 W O	0130	5·1	0728	1·2	1354	5·2	1952	1·1
10 Th	0216	5·3	0805	1·1	1435	5·4	2033	0·9
11 F	0303	5·4	0845	1·1	1518	5·5	2116	0·8
12 Sa	0352	5·4	0924	1·1	1605	5·5	2200	0·8
13 Su	0443	5·5	1005	1·1	1654	5·5	2246	0·8
14 M	0533	5·4	1048	1·2	1745	5·4	2335	0·9
15 Tu	0626	5·3	1137	1·4	1839	5·3		
16 W (	0030	1·1	0720	5·1	1233	1·6	1937	5·2
17 Th	0133	1·3	0816	5·0	1341	1·9	2037	5·1
18 F	0243	1·5	0916	4·9	1500	1·9	2139	5·0
19 Sa	0354	1·6	1018	4·9	1616	1·9	2245	5·0
20 Su	0501	1·5	1122	4·9	1724	1·7	2352	5·1
21 M	0601	1·5	1222	5·1	1826	1·5		
22 Tu	0054	5·2	0654	1·4	1316	5·2	1920	1·3
23 W	0148	5·3	0739	1·4	1405	5·3	2007	1·1
24 Th ●	0237	5·4	0818	1·4	1448	5·4	2050	1·1
25 F	0320	5·4	0850	1·4	1526	5·4	2126	1·1
26 Sa	0400	5·3	0920	1·4	1600	5·4	2156	1·1
27 Su	0435	5·2	0950	1·4	1631	5·3	2226	1·2
28 M	0509	5·1	1022	1·5	1701	5·2	2258	1·3
29 Tu	0545	5·0	1056	1·6	1737	5·1	2331	1·4
30 W	0624	4·8	1135	1·8	1820	4·9		
31 Th	0013	1·6	0711	4·6	1220	2·0	1911	4·7

RATE AND SET — Position 3¾ M., 270°, Isle of May; Ingoing, 240°, −0155 Dover, Sp. 1 kn.; Outgoing, 060°, +0415 Dover, Sp. 1 kn. Streams ½ h. later on N. side than on S. side. Position 4 M 052°. Inchkeith Lt. Ho.; Ingoing −0215 Dover begins S. ends W. Outgoing, +0400 Dover begins N. ends E. Position near Oxcars Lt. Ho.: Ingoing, −0215 Dover, Sp. 1½ kn.; Outgoing +0445 Dover, Sp. 1¾ kn.

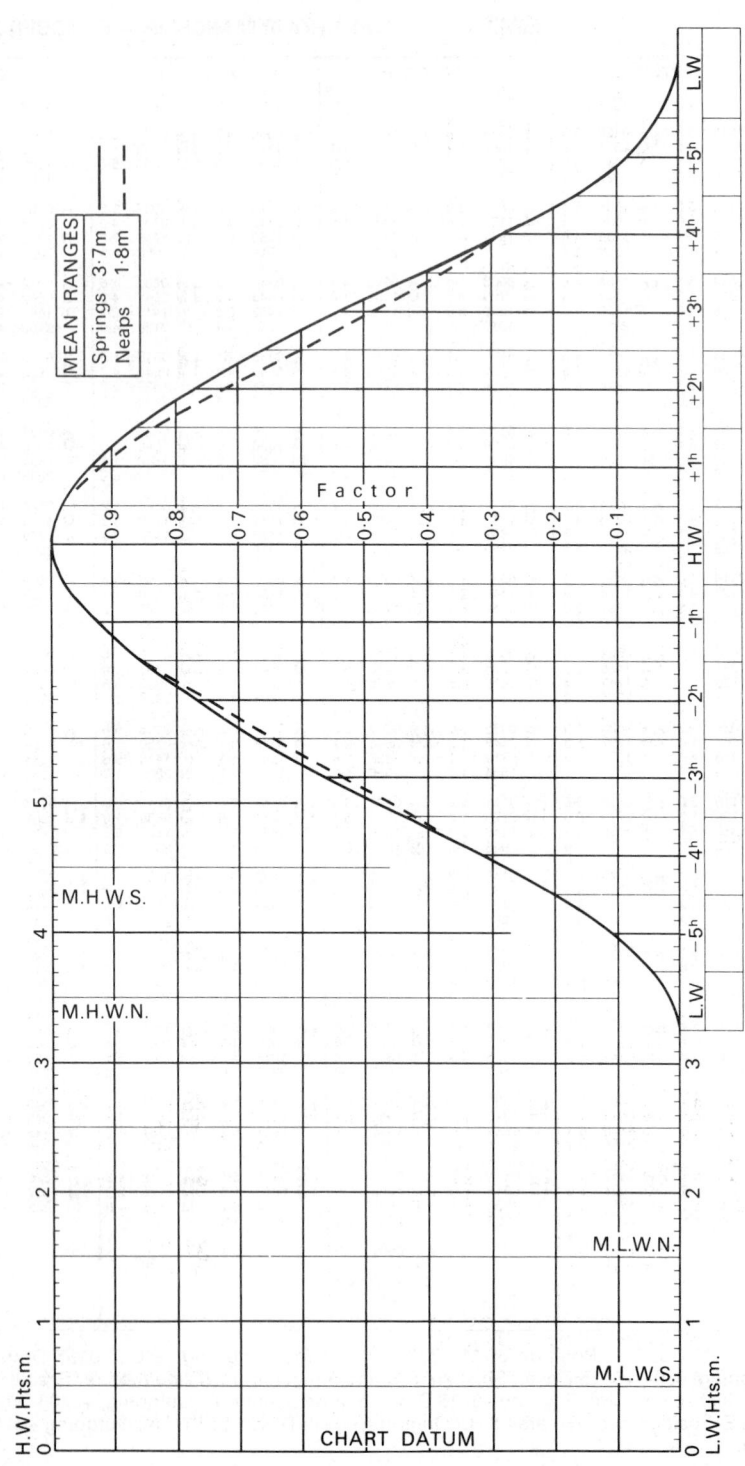

ABERDEEN
MEAN SPRING AND NEAP CURVES
Springs occur 2 days after New and Full Moon.

MEAN RANGES
Springs 3·7m ——
Neaps 1·8m - - -

Factor

0·9 0·8 0·7 0·6 0·5 0·4 0·3 0·2 0·1

H.W.Hts.m.

M.H.W.S.

M.H.W.N.

CHART DATUM

M.L.W.N.

M.L.W.S.

L.W.Hts.m.

L.W +5h +4h +3h +2h +1h H.W -1h -2h -3h -4h -5h L.W

ABERDEEN 21:101

HIGH & LOW WATER 1992 Lat. 57°09′N. Long. 2°04′W.

GMT ADD 1 HOUR MARCH 29 — OCTOBER 25 FOR B.S.T.

JANUARY

Time	m		Time	m
1 W 0434/1054/1705/2319	1.4/3.6/1.4/3.6	**16** Th	0327/0956/1604/2219	1.5/3.6/1.6/3.7
2 Th 0525/1142/1754	1.3/3.8/1.2	**17** F	0435/1055/1709/2323	1.4/3.9/1.3/3.9
3 F 0008/0607/1221/1838	3.7/1.3/3.9/1.1	**18** Sa	0534/1149/1805	1.2/4.1/0.9
4 Sa 0052/0645/1257/●1914	3.8/1.3/4.1/1.0	**19** Su	0021/0625/1236/○1856	4.2/1.0/4.4/0.6
5 Su 0130/0720/1330/1948	3.9/1.2/4.1/0.9	**20** M	0113/0713/1323/1944	4.4/0.8/4.6/0.3
6 M 0205/0752/1401/2020	4.0/1.2/4.2/0.9	**21** Tu	0202/0758/1409/2030	4.5/0.7/4.7/0.2
7 Tu 0240/0825/1432/2053	4.0/1.2/4.2/0.8	**22** W	0250/0842/1454/2117	4.5/0.7/4.7/0.2
8 W 0314/0857/1504/2127	4.0/1.2/4.2/0.9	**23** Th	0338/0924/1541/2202	4.4/0.8/4.7/0.3
9 Th 0349/0931/1538/2200	3.9/1.3/4.1/0.9	**24** F	0423/1007/1628/2248	4.2/0.9/4.5/0.6
10 F 0424/1006/1614/2237	3.8/1.4/4.1/1.1	**25** Sa	0509/1052/1718/2337	3.9/1.1/4.2/0.9
11 Sa 0504/1044/1655/2318	3.7/1.5/3.9/1.2	**26** Su	0558/1142/1814/☾	3.6/1.3/3.9
12 Su 0546/1127/1742	3.5/1.6/3.8	**27** M	0031/0655/1242/1919	1.3/3.4/1.6/3.6
13 M 0005/0638/1221/☽1839	1.4/3.4/1.7/3.6	**28** Tu	0137/0739/1404/2037	1.6/3.3/1.7/3.4
14 Tu 0103/0740/1328/1948	1.5/3.4/1.8/3.5	**29** W	0256/0917/1538/2159	1.7/3.3/1.7/3.3
15 W 0212/0849/1449/2104	1.6/3.4/1.8/3.5	**30** Th	0412/1026/1651/2306	1.7/3.4/1.5/3.4
		31 F	0509/1120/1743/2357	1.6/3.6/1.3/3.6

FEBRUARY

Time	m		Time	m
1 Sa 0554/1203/1824	1.4/3.8/1.1	**16** Su	0523/1132/1753	1.2/4.0/0.7
2 Su 0038/0631/1239/1859	3.7/1.3/3.9/0.9	**17** M	0011/0614/1221/1842	4.1/0.9/4.3/0.4
3 M 0113/0704/1312/●1930	3.9/1.2/4.1/0.8	**18** Tu	0100/0659/1307/○1928	4.4/0.7/4.6/0.2
4 Tu 0145/0735/1342/2001	4.0/1.1/4.2/0.7	**19** W	0145/0740/1351/2011	4.5/0.6/4.7/0.1
5 W 0218/0805/1412/2030	4.1/1.0/4.2/0.7	**20** Th	0227/0820/1434/2053	4.4/0.5/4.8/0.1
6 Th 0249/0836/1442/2101	4.0/1.0/4.3/0.7	**21** F	0310/0900/1518/2135	4.3/0.5/4.7/0.3
7 F 0319/0905/1514/2132	4.0/1.0/4.2/0.8	**22** Sa	0350/0939/1602/2216	4.1/0.7/4.4/0.6
8 Sa 0350/0938/1546/2204	3.9/1.1/4.2/0.9	**23** Su	0431/1020/1648/2257	3.9/0.9/4.1/1.0
9 Su 0424/1013/1623/2241	3.8/1.2/4.0/1.1	**24** M	0515/1105/1739/2342	3.6/1.2/3.7/1.4
10 M 0502/1052/1706/2323	3.7/1.3/3.8/1.3	**25** Tu	0604/1158/1839/☾	3.4/1.5/3.4
11 Tu 0549/1142/1803/☽	3.5/1.5/3.6	**26** W	0038/0704/1314/1959	1.7/3.2/1.7/3.2
12 W 0015/0649/1246/1914	1.5/3.4/1.7/3.5	**27** Th	0204/0825/1507/2132	1.9/3.1/1.7/3.1
13 Th 0127/0805/1412/2042	1.6/3.4/1.7/3.4	**28** F	0345/0948/1628/2245	1.9/3.2/1.6/3.3
14 F 0257/0924/1543/2204	1.7/3.5/1.5/3.6	**29** Sa	0449/1051/1720/2336	1.7/3.4/1.3/3.5
15 Sa 0420/1034/1657/2315	1.5/3.7/1.1/3.9			

MARCH

Time	m		Time	m
1 Su 0533/1137/1800	1.5/3.6/1.1	**16** M	0508/1113/1736/2356	1.2/4.0/0.6/4.1
2 M 0015/0610/1215/1834	3.7/1.3/3.8/0.9	**17** Tu	0556/1203/1824	0.9/4.3/0.3
3 Tu 0049/0642/1248/1904	3.9/1.1/4.0/0.7	**18** W	0042/0639/1249/○1907	4.2/0.6/4.5/0.1
4 W 0121/0712/1319/●1934	4.0/1.0/4.1/0.6	**19** Th	0124/0719/1331/1948	4.3/0.5/4.6/0.1
5 Th 0151/0741/1348/2004	4.0/0.9/4.2/0.6	**20** F	0204/0758/1413/2027	4.3/0.4/4.6/0.2
6 F 0220/0811/1418/2033	4.1/0.8/4.2/0.6	**21** Sa	0243/0837/1456/2105	4.2/0.5/4.5/0.4
7 Sa 0250/0842/1450/2104	4.0/0.8/4.2/0.7	**22** Su	0319/0915/1538/2143	4.1/0.6/4.2/0.8
8 Su 0319/0914/1524/2136	4.0/0.9/4.2/0.8	**23** M	0357/0955/1623/2220	3.9/0.8/3.9/1.1
9 M 0352/0949/1612/2212	3.9/1.0/4.0/1.0	**24** Tu	0437/1038/1711/2259	3.7/1.1/3.6/1.5
10 Tu 0430/1030/1648/2254	3.8/1.1/3.8/1.3	**25** W	0520/1127/1808/2349	3.5/1.4/3.3/1.8
11 W 0516/1120/1747/2347	3.6/1.3/3.6/1.5	**26** Th	0614/1234/1921/☾	3.3/1.6/3.1
12 Th 0618/1227/1904	3.4/1.5/3.4	**27** F	0104/0726/1419/2053	2.0/3.1/1.7/3.1
13 F 0103/0737/1357/2033	1.7/3.4/1.5/3.4	**28** Sa	0300/0854/1548/2209	2.0/3.1/1.5/3.2
14 Sa 0244/0901/1531/2157	1.7/3.4/1.3/3.6	**29** Su	0414/1009/1642/2302	1.8/3.2/1.3/3.4
15 Su 0409/1014/1641/2304	1.5/3.7/1.0/3.8	**30** M	0501/1101/1725/2343	1.5/3.4/1.1/3.6
		31 Tu	0539/1142/1800	1.3/3.7/0.9

APRIL

Time	m		Time	m
1 W 0018/0612/1217/1832	3.8/1.1/3.8/0.8	**16** Th	0019/0617/1229/1845	4.1/0.7/4.3/0.3
2 Th 0050/0643/1249/1903	3.9/0.9/4.0/0.7	**17** F	0102/0657/1313/○1926	4.1/0.5/4.4/0.3
3 F 0121/0714/1321/1934	4.0/0.8/4.1/0.6	**18** Sa	0140/0738/1355/2004	4.2/0.5/4.3/0.5
4 Sa 0151/0745/1354/2005	4.0/0.8/4.2/0.6	**19** Su	0218/0818/1437/2040	4.1/0.5/4.2/0.7
5 Su 0222/0819/1429/2037	4.1/0.7/4.2/0.7	**20** M	0254/0857/1519/2115	4.0/0.7/4.0/0.9
6 M 0254/0854/1507/2112	4.0/0.8/4.1/0.9	**21** Tu	0329/0936/1603/2150	3.9/0.8/3.8/1.2
7 Tu 0329/0934/1552/2152	4.0/0.9/4.0/1.1	**22** W	0406/1017/1649/2230	3.7/1.0/3.5/1.5
8 W 0410/1019/1644/2240	3.9/1.0/3.8/1.3	**23** Th	0447/1104/1742/2315	3.6/1.2/3.3/1.7
9 Th 0501/1113/1749/2337	3.7/1.2/3.6/1.6	**24** F	0536/1201/1843/☾	3.4/1.4/3.2
10 F 0604/1224/1904	3.5/1.3/3.5	**25** Sa	0018/0636/1320/1958	1.9/3.2/1.5/3.1
11 Sa 0056/0721/1351/2027	1.7/3.4/1.3/3.5	**26** Su	0148/0752/1446/2112	2.0/3.2/1.5/3.2
12 Su 0232/0842/1515/2143	1.8/3.5/1.1/3.6	**27** M	0314/0910/1552/2213	1.8/3.2/1.4/3.3
13 M 0348/0953/1621/2245	1.5/3.7/0.8/3.8	**28** Tu	0413/1012/1640/2301	1.6/3.4/1.2/3.5
14 Tu 0445/1052/1715/2336	1.2/3.9/0.6/3.9	**29** W	0457/1059/1720/2340	1.4/3.5/1.0/3.6
15 W 0533/1143/1803	0.9/4.1/0.4	**30** Th	0534/1140/1757	1.2/3.7/0.9

To find H.W. Dover subtract 2 h. 20 min.

TIDAL DIFFERENCES PAGES 21:104-21:105. TIDAL CURVE PAGE 21:100.

Datum of predictions: 2.25 m. below Ordnance Datum (Newlyn) or approx. L.A.T.

ABERDEEN

Lat. 57°09′N. Long. 2°04′W. **HIGH & LOW WATER 1992**

GMT **ADD 1 HOUR MARCH 29 — OCTOBER 25 FOR B.S.T.**

MAY

Day	Time	m	Time	m	Time	m	Time	m
1 F	0015	3.8	0611	1.0	1217	3.9	1831	0.8
2 Sa ●	0049	3.9	0646	0.9	1255	4.0	1904	0.7
3 Su	0123	4.0	0723	0.8	1333	4.1	1940	0.7
4 M	0157	4.1	0801	0.7	1413	4.1	2018	0.8
5 Tu	0234	4.1	0842	0.7	1458	4.1	2058	0.9
6 W	0315	4.1	0927	0.7	1549	4.0	2143	1.1
7 Th	0402	4.0	1016	0.8	1645	3.9	2234	1.3
8 F	0455	3.8	1113	0.9	1749	3.7	2334	1.5
9 Sa ☽	0557	3.7	1221	1.0	1857	3.6		
10 Su	0046	1.6	0707	3.6	1338	1.1	2009	3.5
11 M	0206	1.6	0820	3.6	1453	1.0	2118	3.6
12 Tu	0318	1.4	0929	3.7	1557	0.8	2219	3.6
13 W	0417	1.2	1030	3.9	1652	0.7	2312	3.8
14 Th	0509	1.0	1123	4.0	1740	0.6	2357	3.9
15 F	0556	0.8	1212	4.1	1824	0.6		
16 Sa ○	0039	4.0	0641	0.7	1257	4.1	1903	0.6
17 Su	0119	4.0	0723	0.7	1341	4.0	1941	0.8
18 M	0155	4.0	0802	0.7	1423	4.0	2018	0.9
19 Tu	0230	4.0	0842	0.7	1504	3.8	2053	1.1
20 W	0305	3.9	0921	0.8	1546	3.7	2129	1.3
21 Th	0342	3.8	1000	1.0	1628	3.6	2207	1.4
22 F	0421	3.7	1042	1.1	1715	3.4	2249	1.6
23 Sa	0505	3.6	1130	1.2	1805	3.3	2342	1.7
24 Su (	0557	3.4	1228	1.4	1903	3.2		
25 M	0043	1.8	0657	3.3	1335	1.4	2008	3.2
26 Tu	0157	1.8	0805	3.3	1444	1.4	2111	3.2
27 W	0307	1.7	0911	3.3	1543	1.3	2207	3.4
28 Th	0403	1.5	1009	3.5	1634	1.2	2255	3.5
29 F	0452	1.4	1059	3.6	1718	1.1	2337	3.7
30 Sa	0537	1.2	1144	3.8	1758	0.9		
31 Su	0017	3.9	0619	1.0	1229	3.9	1839	0.9

JUNE

Day	Time	m	Time	m	Time	m	Time	m
1 M ●	0056	4.0	0702	0.8	1316	4.1	1920	0.8
2 Tu	0135	4.2	0747	0.7	1402	4.1	2004	0.8
3 W	0218	4.2	0832	0.6	1453	4.2	2049	0.9
4 Th	0304	4.2	0919	0.6	1545	4.1	2136	1.0
5 F	0352	4.2	1012	0.6	1640	4.0	2227	1.1
6 Sa	0445	4.1	1106	0.7	1737	3.9	2322	1.3
7 Su ☽	0543	4.0	1207	0.8	1836	3.7		
8 M	0024	1.4	0646	3.8	1313	0.9	1941	3.6
9 Tu	0131	1.4	0754	3.7	1422	1.0	2046	3.5
10 W	0242	1.4	0903	3.7	1528	1.0	2149	3.5
11 Th	0349	1.3	1007	3.7	1627	1.0	2245	3.6
12 F	0448	1.1	1106	3.8	1719	1.0	2336	3.7
13 Sa	0542	1.0	1158	3.8	1805	1.0		
14 Su	0019	3.8	0628	0.9	1246	3.8	1846	1.0
15 M ○	0059	3.9	0712	0.8	1330	3.9	1924	1.0
16 Tu	0135	4.0	0751	0.8	1411	3.9	2001	1.1
17 W	0211	4.0	0827	0.8	1449	3.8	2034	1.1
18 Th	0244	4.0	0903	0.8	1527	3.8	2110	1.2
19 F	0318	3.9	0939	0.8	1604	3.7	2145	1.3
20 Sa	0355	3.9	1016	0.9	1644	3.6	2223	1.4
21 Su	0435	3.8	1057	1.1	1726	3.5	2305	1.5
22 M (	0519	3.6	1142	1.2	1812	3.4	2353	1.6
23 Tu	0610	3.5	1234	1.3	1906	3.3		
24 W	0050	1.7	0707	3.4	1333	1.4	2006	3.2
25 Th	0157	1.7	0811	3.4	1437	1.4	2108	3.3
26 F	0305	1.6	0917	3.4	1541	1.4	2206	3.4
27 Sa	0410	1.5	1020	3.5	1637	1.3	2258	3.6
28 Su	0506	1.3	1118	3.7	1729	1.1	2346	3.9
29 M	0557	1.0	1211	3.9	1818	1.0		
30 Tu	0032	4.1	0646	0.8	1302	4.1	1904	0.9

JULY

Day	Time	m	Time	m	Time	m	Time	m
1 W	0116	4.3	0734	0.5	1352	4.3	1951	0.8
2 Th	0202	4.4	0820	0.4	1442	4.3	2037	0.8
3 F	0249	4.4	0908	0.3	1532	4.3	2122	0.8
4 Sa	0338	4.4	0957	0.3	1623	4.2	2209	0.9
5 Su	0427	4.3	1048	0.5	1713	4.0	2258	1.0
6 M	0520	4.2	1142	0.7	1807	3.8	2351	1.2
7 Tu ☽	0619	4.0	1241	0.9	1904	3.5		
8 W	0053	1.4	0723	3.8	1345	1.2	2009	3.4
9 Th	0205	1.4	0834	3.6	1456	1.3	2115	3.4
10 F	0322	1.4	0948	3.5	1603	1.4	2220	3.5
11 Sa	0433	1.3	1054	3.5	1702	1.3	2315	3.6
12 Su	0532	1.1	1150	3.6	1750	1.3		
13 M	0001	3.7	0619	1.0	1236	3.7	1832	1.2
14 Tu ○	0041	3.9	0700	0.9	1317	3.8	1909	1.1
15 W	0117	4.0	0735	0.8	1354	3.9	1942	1.1
16 Th	0149	4.0	0809	0.7	1429	3.9	2015	1.1
17 F	0222	4.1	0842	0.7	1503	3.9	2047	1.1
18 Sa	0254	4.1	0914	0.7	1536	3.9	2119	1.1
19 Su	0328	4.0	0948	0.8	1610	3.8	2153	1.2
20 M	0403	4.0	1021	0.9	1647	3.7	2230	1.3
21 Tu	0441	3.9	1059	1.1	1726	3.5	2311	1.4
22 W (	0525	3.7	1142	1.3	1812	3.4	2358	1.6
23 Th	0618	3.5	1232	1.4	1909	3.3		
24 F	0059	1.7	0721	3.4	1337	1.6	2013	3.3
25 Sa	0215	1.7	0834	3.4	1451	1.6	2121	3.4
26 Su	0334	1.6	0950	3.5	1604	1.5	2224	3.6
27 M	0442	1.3	1058	3.7	1708	1.3	2320	3.9
28 Tu	0540	1.0	1156	4.0	1801	1.1		
29 W ●	0011	4.2	0631	0.6	1248	4.2	1849	0.9
30 Th	0057	4.4	0719	0.4	1337	4.4	1934	0.7
31 F	0144	4.6	0805	0.2	1425	4.4	2018	0.6

AUGUST

Day	Time	m	Time	m	Time	m	Time	m
1 Sa	0229	4.7	0850	0.1	1511	4.4	2101	0.6
2 Su	0315	4.7	0936	0.2	1556	4.3	2145	0.7
3 M	0403	4.5	1021	0.4	1644	4.0	2230	0.9
4 Tu	0454	4.3	1111	0.7	1732	3.8	2318	1.1
5 W ☽	0549	4.0	1203	1.1	1827	3.5	2322	1.5
6 Th	0015	1.4	0652	3.7	1303	1.4	1928	3.4
7 F	0130	1.5	0806	3.4	1420	1.6	2042	3.3
8 Sa	0303	1.6	0929	3.3	1542	1.7	2155	3.4
9 Su	0424	1.4	1042	3.4	1647	1.6	2255	3.5
10 M	0522	1.2	1139	3.5	1736	1.5	2343	3.7
11 Tu	0605	1.1	1222	3.7	1815	1.3		
12 W	0021	3.9	0642	0.9	1259	3.8	1849	1.2
13 Th	0056	4.1	0714	0.8	1331	4.0	1921	1.1
14 F ●	0127	4.1	0745	0.7	1404	4.0	1951	1.0
15 Sa	0158	4.2	0816	0.6	1434	4.0	2022	1.0
16 Su	0227	4.2	0846	0.7	1505	4.0	2053	1.0
17 M	0258	4.2	0917	0.7	1536	3.9	2124	1.1
18 Tu	0332	4.1	0948	0.9	1609	3.8	2157	1.2
19 W	0407	4.0	1021	1.1	1645	3.7	2235	1.3
20 Th	0448	4.5	1101	1.3	1727	3.6	2322	1.5
21 F (	0540	3.6	1149	1.5	1822	3.4		
22 Sa	0021	1.6	0648	3.4	1252	1.7	1931	3.4
23 Su	0140	1.7	0804	3.4	1418	1.7	2049	3.5
24 M	0311	1.6	0932	3.5	1546	1.6	2200	3.7
25 Tu	0427	1.3	1044	3.7	1651	1.4	2259	4.0
26 W	0525	0.9	1142	4.0	1744	1.1	2351	4.3
27 Th	0615	0.5	1231	4.3	1831	0.8		
28 F ○	0038	4.5	0700	0.3	1317	4.4	1914	0.6
29 Sa	0123	4.7	0745	0.1	1401	4.5	1955	0.5
30 Su	0208	4.8	0827	0.1	1444	4.4	2036	0.5
31 M	0253	4.7	0911	0.2	1528	4.3	2118	0.6

GENERAL — Heavy rains increase duration and rate of ebb. Eddies form in entrance between Point Law and Pocre Quay.

WHEN TO ENTER — At most times — caution against possible heavy streams. In S. or SE gales — caution against N. set round N. pier.

ABERDEEN 21:103

HIGH & LOW WATER 1992 Lat. 57°09'N. Long. 2°04'W.

GMT ADD 1 HOUR MARCH 29 — OCTOBER 25 FOR B.S.T.

SEPTEMBER

Day	Time	m	Day	Time	m
1 Tu	0338	4·6	16	0305	4·2
	0953	0·5		0917	0·9
	1612	4·0	W	1535	3·9
	2202	0·8		2131	1·1
2 W	0427	4·3	17	0342	4·0
	1037	0·9		0950	1·1
	1657	3·8	Th	1610	3·8
	2248	1·1		2210	1·3
3 Th	0520	3·9	18	0426	3·8
	1123	1·3		1030	1·3
	1747	3·6	F	1654	3·7
)	2343	1·4		2257	1·4
4 F	0622	3·5	19	0520	3·6
	1219	1·7		1119	1·6
	1848	3·4	Sa	1751	3·6
			(	2358	1·6
5 Sa	0057	1·6	20	0634	3·5
	0740	3·3		1228	1·8
	1340	1·9	Su	1904	3·5
	2004	3·3			
6 Su	0243	1·7	21	0123	1·6
	0910	3·2		0757	3·4
	1518	1·9	M	1359	1·8
	2125	3·3		2026	3·5
7 M	0407	1·5	22	0256	1·5
	1024	3·3		0921	3·6
	1627	1·8	Tu	1529	1·7
	2230	3·5		2139	3·7
8 Tu	0502	1·3	23	0410	1·2
	1118	3·5		1030	3·8
	1713	1·6	W	1634	1·4
	2318	3·7		2241	4·0
9 W	0543	1·1	24	0506	0·8
	1158	3·7		1125	4·1
	1751	1·3	Th	1725	1·1
	2357	3·9		2332	4·3
10 Th	0617	0·9	25	0556	0·5
	1232	3·9		1211	4·3
	1824	1·2	F	1810	0·8
11 F	0031	4·0	26	0018	4·6
	0649	0·8		0639	0·2
	1304	4·0	Sa	1256	4·4
	1855	1·0	●	1852	0·6
12 Sa	0102	4·1	27	0103	4·7
	0719	0·7		0723	0·2
	1335	4·1	Su	1337	4·4
○	1926	1·0		1933	0·5
13 Su	0131	4·2	28	0147	4·8
	0748	0·7		0804	0·2
	1405	4·1	M	1419	4·4
	1955	0·9		2013	0·5
14 M	0201	4·2	29	0232	4·7
	0816	0·7		0847	0·4
	1434	4·1	Tu	1458	4·3
	2025	1·0		2054	0·7
15 Tu	0232	4·2	30	0317	4·4
	0846	0·8		0924	0·7
	1504	4·0	W	1539	4·1
	2057	1·0		2138	0·9

OCTOBER

Day	Time	m	Day	Time	m
1 Th	0404	4·1	16	0328	4·1
	1004	1·1		0929	1·2
	1621	3·9	F	1546	4·0
	2223	1·1		2156	1·2
2 F	0455	3·8	17	0417	3·9
	1047	1·5		1013	1·4
	1709	3·6	Sa	1634	3·9
	2316	1·4		2247	1·3
3 Sa	0556	3·5	18	0518	3·7
	1137	1·8		1106	1·7
	1805	3·4	Su	1733	3·7
)				2351	1·5
4 Su	0027	1·7	19	0629	3·6
	0709	3·3		1217	1·8
	1217	2·1	M	1846	3·6
	1917	3·3	(		
5 M	0206	1·7	20	0113	1·5
	0834	3·2		0748	3·6
	1437	2·1	Tu	1347	1·9
	2042	3·3		2006	3·7
6 Tu	0331	1·6	21	0239	1·3
	0949	3·3		0905	3·7
	1552	1·9	W	1508	1·7
	2152	3·4		2118	3·8
7 W	0427	1·4	22	0348	1·1
	1044	3·5		1010	3·9
	1641	1·6	Th	1612	1·4
	2244	3·6		2220	4·1
8 Th	0509	1·2	23	0444	0·8
	1125	3·7		1104	4·1
	1720	1·4	F	1702	1·1
	2326	3·8		2312	4·3
9 F	0546	1·0	24	0533	0·6
	1201	3·9		1151	4·2
	1754	1·2	Sa	1749	0·9
10 Sa	0001	4·0	25	0000	4·5
	0618	0·9		0618	0·4
	1235	4·0	Su	1234	4·3
	1827	1·1	●	1832	0·7
11 Su	0034	4·1	26	0046	4·6
	0649	0·8		0700	0·4
	1306	4·1	M	1316	4·4
○	1857	1·0		1914	0·6
12 M	0106	4·2	27	0131	4·6
	0719	0·8		0741	0·5
	1335	4·1	Tu	1355	4·4
	1928	1·0		1957	0·6
13 Tu	0137	4·2	28	0215	4·5
	0748	0·8		0820	0·7
	1405	4·1	W	1433	4·3
	2001	1·0		2037	0·7
14 W	0211	4·2	29	0300	4·3
	0816	0·9		0858	1·0
	1436	4·1	Th	1512	4·1
	2036	1·0		2121	0·9
15 Th	0247	4·2	30	0346	4·0
	0853	1·0		0936	1·3
	1508	4·1	F	1552	4·0
	2114	1·1		2204	1·1
			31	0435	3·8
				1017	1·6
			Sa	1634	3·8
				2252	1·3

NOVEMBER

Day	Time	m	Day	Time	m
1 Su	0529	3·5	16	0515	3·9
	1104	1·9		1059	1·6
	1725	3·6	M	1722	3·9
	2351	1·5		2344	1·2
2 M	0631	3·4	17	0619	3·8
	1204	2·0		1204	1·7
	1825	3·4	Tu	1828	3·8
)			(		
3 Tu	0107	1·7	18	0057	1·2
	0742	3·3		0730	3·7
	1330	2·1	W	1321	1·8
	1940	3·4		1941	3·8
4 W	0230	1·6	19	0212	1·2
	0856	3·3		0842	3·7
	1454	2·0	Th	1437	1·7
	2056	3·4		2053	3·9
5 Th	0336	1·5	20	0321	1·1
	0956	3·5		0945	3·8
	1556	1·8	F	1543	1·5
	2157	3·5		2156	4·0
6 F	0426	1·4	21	0420	0·9
	1045	3·6		1041	3·9
	1641	1·6	Sa	1640	1·2
	2247	3·7		2254	4·2
7 Sa	0506	1·2	22	0512	0·8
	1126	3·8		1130	4·1
	1722	1·4	Su	1730	1·0
	2327	3·9		2346	4·3
8 Su	0543	1·1	23	0558	0·7
	1201	3·9		1215	4·2
	1757	1·2	M	1818	0·9
9 M	0004	4·0	24	0034	4·3
	0617	1·0		0642	0·8
	1235	4·1	Tu	1256	4·3
	1832	1·1	●	1902	0·8
10 Tu	0041	4·1	25	0120	4·3
	0649	1·0		0723	0·8
	1307	4·2	W	1335	4·3
○	1907	1·0		1945	0·7
11 W	0117	4·2	26	0205	4·2
	0723	1·0		0801	1·0
	1340	4·2	Th	1413	4·3
	1942	1·0		2026	0·8
12 Th	0155	4·2	27	0247	4·1
	0758	1·0		0837	1·2
	1413	4·3	F	1450	4·2
	2022	0·9		2107	0·9
13 F	0237	4·2	28	0331	4·0
	0836	1·1		0914	1·4
	1450	4·3	Sa	1527	4·1
	2104	0·9		2146	1·0
14 Sa	0324	4·1	29	0413	3·8
	0918	1·3		0952	1·5
	1534	4·2	Su	1604	4·0
	2150	1·0		2228	1·2
15 Su	0416	4·0	30	0458	3·7
	1004	1·4		1034	1·7
	1623	4·1	M	1648	3·8
	2242	1·1		2315	1·3

DECEMBER

Day	Time	m	Day	Time	m
1 Tu	0549	3·5	16	0600	3·9
	1122	1·8		1143	1·5
	1737	3·6	W	1805	4·1
(			(		
2 W	0008	1·5	17	0032	1·0
	0645	3·4		0702	3·7
	1221	2·0	Th	1248	1·6
)	1836	3·5		1912	3·9
3 Th	0114	1·6	18	0140	1·1
	0748	3·3		0809	3·6
	1334	2·0	F	1401	1·6
	1944	3·4		2023	3·9
4 F	0225	1·6	19	0250	1·2
	0856	3·4		0915	3·7
	1449	1·9	Sa	1514	1·5
	2054	3·4		2134	3·8
5 Sa	0328	1·5	20	0356	1·2
	0955	3·5		1017	3·7
	1552	1·8	Su	1621	1·4
	2156	3·5		2238	3·9
6 Su	0420	1·4	21	0454	1·1
	1044	3·6		1112	3·9
	1642	1·6	M	1719	1·2
	2248	3·7		2336	4·0
7 M	0504	1·3	22	0543	1·1
	1126	3·8		1200	4·0
	1727	1·4	Tu	1810	1·0
	2333	3·8			
8 Tu	0544	1·2	23	0027	4·0
	1204	4·0		0628	1·1
	1808	1·2	W	1242	4·2
				1855	0·9
9 W	0017	4·0	24	0113	4·1
	0624	1·1		0707	1·1
	1241	4·2	Th	1320	4·2
○	1849	1·0	●	1937	0·8
10 Th	0059	4·1	25	0154	4·1
	0702	1·0		0745	1·1
	1317	4·3	F	1355	4·3
	1930	0·9		2015	0·8
11 F	0142	4·2	26	0233	4·0
	0742	1·0		0820	1·2
	1357	4·4	Sa	1430	4·3
	2012	0·8		2050	0·8
12 Sa	0229	4·3	27	0311	4·0
	0825	1·1		0854	1·2
	1437	4·5	Su	1504	4·2
	2056	0·7		2125	0·9
13 Su	0317	4·3	28	0348	3·9
	0908	1·1		0929	1·3
	1522	4·4	M	1538	4·1
	2143	0·7		2202	1·0
14 M	0407	4·2	29	0426	3·8
	0955	1·2		1004	1·4
	1612	4·3	Tu	1616	4·0
	2234	0·8		2238	1·1
15 Tu	0502	4·1	30	0506	3·7
	1045	1·4		1044	1·6
	1705	4·2	W	1657	3·9
	2330	0·9		2320	1·3
			31	0551	3·5
				1129	1·7
			Th	1744	3·7

RATE AND SET — Across entrance SE.-NW., Spring rate 1 kn. in River Dee; Ingoing begins –0340 Dover, not very strong. Outgoing begins +0245 Dover, not very strong.

TIDAL DIFFERENCES ON ABERDEEN

PLACE	TIME DIFFERENCES				HEIGHT DIFFERENCES (Metres)			
	High Water		Low Water		MHWS	MHWN	MLWN	MLWS
ABERDEEN	0000 and 1200	0600 and 1800	0100 and 1300	0700 and 1900	4.3	3.4	1.6	0.6
River Tay								
Bar	+0100	+0100	+0050	+0110	+0.9	+0.8	+0.3	+0.1
Dundee	+0140	+0120	+0055	+0145	+1.1	+0.9	+0.3	+0.1
Newburgh	+0215	+0200	+0250	+0335	−0.2	−0.4	−1.1	−0.5
Perth	+0220	+0225	+0510	+0530	−0.9	−1.4	−1.2	−0.3
Monifeith	+0123	+0115	+0110	+0135	+0.9	+0.9	+0.3	+0.1
Arbroath	+0056	+0037	+0034	+0055	+0.7	+0.7	+0.2	+0.1
Montrose	+0100	+0100	+0030	+0040	+0.5	+0.5	+0.3	+0.1
Inverbervie	+0035	+0035	+0022	+0025	+0.4	+0.4	+0.2	+0.1
Stonehaven	+0013	+0008	+0013	+0009	+0.2	+0.2	+0.1	0.0
Peterhead	−0035	−0045	−0035	−0040	−0.5	−0.3	−0.1	−0.1
Fraserburgh	−0105	−0115	−0120	−0110	−0.6	−0.5	−0.2	0.0
ABERDEEN	0200 and 1400	0900 and 2100	0400 and 1600	0900 and 2100	4.3	3.4	1.6	0.6
Gardenstown	−0055	−0135	−0135	−0048	−0.7	−0.5	−0.4	−0.1
Banff	−0100	−0150	−0150	−0050	−0.8	−0.6	−0.5	−0.2
Whitehills	−0122	−0137	−0117	−0127	−0.4	−0.3	+0.1	+0.1
Cullen	−0126	−0140	−0120	−0133	−0.3	−0.2	0.0	+0.1
Buckie	−0130	−0145	−0125	−0140	−0.2	−0.2	0.0	+0.1
Lossiemouth	−0125	−0200	−0130	−0130	−0.2	−0.2	0.0	0.0
Burghead	−0120	−0150	−0135	−0120	−0.2	−0.2	0.0	0.0
Findhorn	−0120	−0150	−0135	−0123	−0.1	−0.2	0.0	0.0
Nairn	−0120	−0150	−0135	−0130	0.0	−0.1	0.0	+0.1
McDermott Base	−0110	−0140	−0120	−0115	−0.1	−0.1	+0.1	+0.3
ABERDEEN	0300 and 1500	1000 and 2200	0000 and 1200	0700 and 1900	4.3	3.4	1.6	0.6
Inverness Firth								
Fortrose.................	−0125	−0125	−0125	−0125	0.0	0.0	−	−
Inverness	−0050	−0150	−0200	−0105	+0.5	+0.3	+0.2	+0.1
Cromarty Firth								
Cromarty	−0120	−0155	−0155	−0120	0.0	0.0	+0.1	+0.2
Invergordon	−0105	−0200	−0200	−0110	+0.1	+0.1	+0.1	+0.1
Dingwall	−0045	−0145	−	−	+0.1	+0.2	−	−
ABERDEEN	0300 and 1500	0800 and 2000	0200 and 1400	0800 and 2000	4.3	3.4	1.6	0.6
Balintore	−0120	−0205	−0145	−0115	−0.1	0.0	+0.1	+0.2
Dornoch Firth								
Portmahomack	−0120	−0210	−0140	−0110	−0.2	−0.1	+0.1	+0.1
Meikle Ferry	−0100	−0140	−0120	−0055	+0.1	0.0	−0.1	0.0
Golspie	−0130	−0215	−0155	−0130	−0.3	−0.3	−0.1	0.0
Helmsdale	−0140	−0200	−0150	−0135	−0.5	−0.4	−0.1	−0.1
Lybster	−0150	−0220	−0205	−0210	−0.8	−0.9	−0.2	−0.1
Wick	−0155	−0220	−0210	−0220	−0.9	−0.7	−0.2	−0.1
Duncansby Head	−0320	−0320	−0320	−0320	−1.2	−1.0	−	−

Refer to predictions on pages 21:101-21:103

TIDAL DIFFERENCES ON ABERDEEN

PLACE	TIME DIFFERENCES				HEIGHT DIFFERENCES (Metres)			
	High Water		Low Water		MHWS	MHWN	MLWN	MLWS
ABERDEEN	0300 and 1500	1100 and 2300	0200 and 1400	0900 and 2100	**4.3**	**3.4**	**1.6**	**0.6**
Orkney Islands								
Muckle Skerry	−0230	−0230	−0230	−0230	−1.7	−1.4	−0.6	−0.2
Burrayness	−0200	−0200	−0155	−0155	−1.0	−0.9	−0.3	0.0
Deer Sound	−0245	−0245	−0245	−0245	−1.1	−0.9	−0.3	0.0
Kirkwall	−0305	−0245	−0305	−0250	−1.4	−1.2	−0.5	−0.2
Kettletoft Pier	−0230	−0230	−0225	−0225	−1.1	−0.9	−0.3	0.0
Pierowall	−0355	−0355	−0355	−0355	−0.6	−0.6	−0.2	0.0
Tingwall Jetty	−0355	−0345	−0355	−0340	−1.2	−1.0	−0.3	−0.1
Stromness	−0430	−0355	−0415	−0420	−0.7	−0.8	−0.1	−0.1
Widewall Bay	−0400	−0400	−0400	−0400	−0.7	−0.7	−0.3	−0.2
ABERDEEN	0300 and 1500	1000 and 2200	0100 and 1300	0800 and 2000	**4.3**	**3.4**	**1.6**	**0.6**
Stroma	−0320	−0320	−0320	−0320	−1.2	−1.1	−0.3	−0.1
Scrabster	−0455	−0510	−0500	−0445	+0.7	+0.3	+0.5	+0.2

Refer to predictions on pages 21:101-21:103

TIDAL DIFFERENCES ON LERWICK

PLACE	TIME DIFFERENCES				HEIGHT DIFFERENCES (Metres)			
	High Water		Low Water		MHWS	MHWN	MLWN	MLWS
LERWICK	0000 and 1200	0600 and 1800	0100 and 1300	0800 and 2000	**2.2**	**1.6**	**0.9**	**0.5**
Fair Isle	−0020	−0025	−0020	−0035	0.0	+0.1	0.0	−0.1
Shetland Islands								
Sumburgh..................	+0002	+0002	+0005	+0005	−0.5	−0.3	−0.2	−0.2
Dury Voe	−0015	−0015	−0010	−0010	+0.1	+0.2	0.0	0.0
Out Skerries	−0025	−0025	−0010	−0010	+0.1	+0.1	0.0	0.0
Toft Pier	−0105	−0100	−0125	−0115	+0.1	+0.1	−0.2	−0.2
Burra Voe (Yell Sound)	−0025	−0025	−0025	−0025	+0.2	+0.2	0.0	0.0
Mid Yell	−0030	−0020	−0035	−0025	+0.2	+0.2	+0.1	0.0
Balta Sound	−0055	−0055	−0045	−0045	+0.1	+0.2	0.0	−0.1
Burra Firth.................	−0110	−0110	−0115	−0115	+0.3	+0.3	0.0	0.0
Bluemull Sound	−0135	−0135	−0155	−0155	+0.4	+0.3	+0.1	0.0
Sullom Voe	−0135	−0125	−0135	−0120	+0.1	+0.3	0.0	−0.2
Hillswick	−0220	−0220	−0200	−0200	0.0	0.0	−0.1	0.0
Scalloway	−0150	−0150	−0150	−0150	−0.6	−0.3	−0.3	0.0
Quendale Bay	−0025	−0025	−0030	−0030	−0.4	−0.1	−0.2	0.0
Foula	−0140	−0130	−0140	−0120	−0.2	−0.1	−0.1	−0.1

Refer to predictions on pages 21:109-21:111

21:106

MORAY FIRTH INVERNESS

Lat. 57°30′N. Long. 4°15′W. HIGH & LOW WATER 1992

GMT ADD 1 HOUR MARCH 29 — OCTOBER 25 FOR B.S.T.

JANUARY

Day	Time	m	Time	m	Time	m	Time	m
1 W	0314	1·6	0909	4·0	1550	1·6	2139	4·0
16 Th	0154	1·7	0806	4·0	1438	1·8	2030	4·1
2 Th	0413	1·5	1008	4·2	1646	1·4	2241	4·1
17 F	0315	1·5	0910	4·3	1555	1·4	2144	4·3
3 F	0500	1·5	1058	4·4	1733	1·3	2339	4·2
18 Sa	0424	1·3	1017	4·6	1658	1·0	2258	4·6
4 Sa	0540	1·4	1145	4·5	1809	1·1		
19 Su	0519	1·1	1118	4·9	1751	0·7		
5 Su	0028	4·3	0614	1·4	1228	4·6	1840	1·0
20 M	0006	4·9	0608	0·9	1219	5·1	1836	0·4
6 M	0110	4·4	0643	1·4	1305	4·7	1906	1·0
21 Tu	0107	5·0	0648	0·9	1315	5·3	1914	0·3
7 Tu	0149	4·4	0710	1·4	1341	4·7	1931	1·0
22 W	0200	5·0	0723	0·8	1404	5·3	1948	0·3
8 W	0224	4·4	0734	1·4	1414	4·7	1955	1·0
23 Th	0245	4·9	0753	0·9	1450	5·2	2020	0·4
9 Th	0257	4·3	0758	1·6	1447	4·6	2019	1·1
24 F	0327	4·6	0824	1·0	1532	5·0	2055	0·7
10 F	0328	4·2	0823	1·6	1520	4·5	2047	1·2
25 Sa	0406	4·3	0859	1·3	1613	4·7	2138	1·1
11 Sa	0402	4·0	0852	1·7	1555	4·3	2121	1·4
26 Su	0445	4·0	0942	1·5	1658	4·3	2232	1·4
12 Su	0436	3·9	0929	1·8	1633	4·1	2205	1·5
27 M	0529	3·7	1043	1·8	1748	3·9	2344	1·7
13 M	0516	3·7	1021	1·9	1717	4·0	2306	1·7
28 Tu	0623	3·6	1215	1·9	1853	3·6		
14 Tu	0605	3·7	1134	2·0	1811	3·9		
29 W	0117	1·9	0729	3·6	1407	1·9	2009	3·6
15 W	0024	1·7	0703	3·8	1308	2·0	1917	3·9
30 Th	0248	1·9	0837	3·7	1534	1·7	2123	3·7
31 F	0355	1·8	0940	3·9	1634	1·5	2227	3·9

FEBRUARY

Day	Time	m	Time	m	Time	m	Time	m
1 Sa	0446	1·6	1035	4·2	1718	1·3	2321	4·1
16 Su	0411	1·4	0955	4·5	1645	0·9	2245	4·6
2 Su	0525	1·5	1122	4·4	1754	1·1		
17 M	0507	1·1	1058	4·8	1737	0·5	2349	4·9
3 M	0006	4·3	0559	1·3	1205	4·5	1824	0·9
18 Tu	0554	0·8	1158	5·1	1822	0·2		
4 Tu	0046	4·4	0628	1·2	1243	4·6	1851	0·8
19 W	0046	5·0	0633	0·7	1254	5·3	1859	0·1
5 W	0125	4·5	0706	1·2	1318	4·7	1914	0·8
20 Th	0135	5·0	0706	0·6	1343	5·4	1931	0·2
6 Th	0159	4·5	0718	1·1	1351	4·7	1937	0·8
21 F	0220	4·8	0736	0·6	1428	5·2	2001	0·4
7 F	0229	4·4	0740	1·2	1424	4·7	1959	0·9
22 Sa	0258	4·6	0804	0·8	1509	5·0	2031	0·7
8 Sa	0258	4·3	0803	1·2	1454	4·6	2022	1·0
23 Su	0334	4·3	0834	1·0	1549	4·6	2103	1·1
9 Su	0328	4·2	0829	1·3	1527	4·5	2050	1·2
24 M	0411	4·0	0909	1·3	1630	4·1	2142	1·6
10 M	0400	4·0	0859	1·5	1604	4·2	2125	1·4
25 Tu	0450	3·7	0958	1·7	1717	3·7	2239	1·9
11 Tu	0438	3·8	0942	1·7	1649	4·0	2215	1·7
26 W	0536	3·5	1058	1·9	1820	3·4		
12 W	0525	3·7	1025	1·9	1744	3·8	2333	1·8
27 Th	0015	2·2	0642	3·4	1330	1·9	1943	3·4
13 Th	0625	3·7	1224	1·9	1857	3·8		
28 F	0216	2·1	0758	3·5	1507	1·7	2058	3·5
14 F	0118	1·9	0735	3·8	1413	1·7	2014	3·9
29 Sa	0332	1·9	0905	3·7	1608	1·5	2200	3·8
15 Sa	0258	1·7	0846	4·1	1541	1·3	2134	4·3

MARCH

Day	Time	m	Time	m	Time	m	Time	m
1 Su	0422	1·7	1001	3·9	1652	1·2	2250	4·1
16 M	0354	1·4	0931	4·4	1626	0·7	2226	4·5
2 M	0503	1·4	1050	4·2	1728	1·0	2335	4·3
17 Tu	0448	1·0	1035	4·7	1718	0·4	2326	4·7
3 Tu	0537	1·2	1134	4·4	1759	0·9		
18 W	0534	0·7	1135	5·0	1802	0·2		
4 W	0016	4·4	0607	1·1	1214	4·5	1827	0·7
19 Th	0020	4·8	0613	0·6	1229	5·2	1840	0·1
5 Th	0054	4·5	0634	1·0	1250	4·7	1853	0·7
20 F	0109	4·8	0648	0·5	1319	5·2	1911	0·3
6 F	0127	4·5	0659	0·9	1325	4·7	1916	0·7
21 Sa	0153	4·7	0719	0·5	1406	5·0	1940	0·5
7 Sa	0200	4·5	0723	0·9	1400	4·7	1939	0·8
22 Su	0229	4·5	0747	0·7	1447	4·7	2007	0·9
8 Su	0229	4·4	0746	1·0	1434	4·6	2002	0·9
23 M	0304	4·3	0815	0·9	1527	4·3	2034	1·3
9 M	0300	4·3	0811	1·1	1509	4·4	2028	1·2
24 Tu	0339	4·0	0848	1·2	1608	3·9	2104	1·7
10 Tu	0333	4·1	0841	1·3	1549	4·2	2100	1·4
25 W	0415	3·8	0929	1·5	1653	3·6	2149	2·0
11 W	0412	4·0	0922	1·5	1636	3·9	2147	1·7
26 Th	0458	3·5	1035	1·8	1750	3·3	2307	2·3
12 Th	0501	3·8	1020	1·7	1736	3·7	2306	1·9
27 F	0554	3·3	1233	1·9	1907	3·3		
13 F	0603	3·7	1207	1·7	1849	3·7		
28 Sa	0121	2·2	0708	3·3	1419	1·7	2019	3·5
14 Sa	0102	2·0	0743	3·7	1359	1·5	2007	3·9
29 Su	0250	2·0	0819	3·5	1524	1·5	2118	3·7
15 Su	0244	1·7	0824	4·0	1522	1·1	2120	4·2
30 M	0346	1·7	0917	3·8	1613	1·3	2209	4·0
31 Tu	0429	1·5	1008	4·0	1652	1·0	2254	4·2

APRIL

Day	Time	m	Time	m	Time	m	Time	m
1 W	0505	1·2	1053	4·2	1726	0·9	2336	4·3
16 Th	0511	0·8	1109	4·8	1740	0·4	2352	4·6
2 Th	0538	1·1	1135	4·4	1758	0·8		
17 F	0552	0·6	1206	4·9	1820	0·4		
3 F	0016	4·4	0609	0·9	1216	4·6	1827	0·7
18 Sa	0040	4·6	0631	0·6	1258	4·8	1853	0·5
4 Sa	0054	4·5	0637	0·9	1257	4·6	1854	0·7
19 Su	0125	4·6	0704	0·6	1346	4·7	1921	0·8
5 Su	0130	4·5	0705	0·9	1337	4·6	1919	0·8
20 M	0204	4·5	0734	0·8	1429	4·4	1947	1·1
6 M	0204	4·5	0732	0·9	1417	4·5	1945	1·0
21 Tu	0238	4·3	0802	0·9	1510	4·1	2012	1·4
7 Tu	0238	4·4	0800	0·9	1500	4·4	2013	1·2
22 W	0312	4·1	0832	1·2	1550	3·8	2041	1·7
8 W	0316	4·3	0833	1·1	1545	4·2	2049	1·5
23 Th	0348	3·9	0909	1·4	1633	3·6	2118	2·0
9 Th	0400	4·1	0916	1·3	1638	3·9	2138	1·8
24 F	0428	3·7	1001	1·6	1720	3·4	2218	2·2
10 F	0450	3·9	1024	1·4	1736	3·8	2258	2·0
25 Sa	0515	3·5	1125	1·7	1820	3·3	2356	2·2
11 Sa	0550	3·8	1200	1·4	1844	3·8		
26 Su	0615	3·4	1305	1·7	1924	3·4		
12 Su	0048	1·9	0657	3·8	1339	1·2	1953	3·9
27 M	0138	2·1	0722	3·5	1424	1·5	2023	3·6
13 M	0219	1·7	0803	4·0	1459	0·9	2058	4·2
28 Tu	0249	1·8	0822	3·7	1521	1·3	2117	3·8
14 Tu	0327	1·3	0906	4·3	1602	0·7	2200	4·4
29 W	0341	1·6	0915	3·9	1608	1·2	2205	4·0
15 W	0422	1·0	1009	4·6	1656	0·5	2256	4·5
30 Th	0424	1·4	1005	4·1	1649	1·0	2250	4·2

To find H.W. Dover subtract 1 h. 15 min.

TIDAL DIFFERENCES ARE NOT GIVEN.

Datum of predictions 2.25 m below Ordnance Datum (Newlyn) or approx. L.A.T.

INVERNESS MORAY FIRTH 21:107

Lat. 57°30′N. Long. 2°04′W.   HIGH & LOW WATER 1992

GMT   ADD 1 HOUR MARCH 29 — OCTOBER 25 FOR B.S.T.

MAY

Day	Tide 1	Tide 2	Tide 3	Tide 4
1 F	0504 1.2	1053 4.3	1725 0.9	2335 4.3
16	0536 0.8	1145 4.5	1758 0.8 ○	
2 Sa	0541 1.0	1143 4.4	1759 0.8 ●	
17	0014 4.5	0617 0.8	1241 4.5	1834 0.9
3 Su	0019 4.5	0617 0.9	1231 4.5	1833 0.8
18	0058 4.5	0651 0.8	1331 4.4	1904 1.0
4 M	0101 4.5	0651 0.8	1319 4.6	1904 0.9
19	0139 4.4	0723 0.8	1414 4.2	1931 1.2
5 Tu	0143 4.6	0723 0.8	1408 4.5	1935 1.0
20	0215 4.4	0751 1.0	1454 4.1	1957 1.4
6 W	0225 4.5	0755 0.9	1457 4.4	2007 1.2
21	0251 4.2	0819 1.1	1532 3.9	2024 1.6
7 Th	0309 4.4	0831 1.0	1546 4.3	2044 1.5
22	0326 4.1	0851 1.2	1611 3.8	2056 1.8
8 F	0355 4.2	0916 1.1	1638 4.1	2135 1.7
23	0403 3.9	0931 1.4	1651 3.6	2142 1.9
9 Sa	0444 4.1	1021 1.2	1731 3.9	2248 1.8 ☾
24	0444 3.7	1029 1.5	1736 3.5	2244 2.0
10 Su	0539 4.0	1145 1.2	1829 3.9	
25	0531 3.6	1142 1.6	1828 3.4	
11 M	0017 1.8	0638 4.0	1313 1.1	1929 3.9
26	0007 2.0	0625 3.6	1302 1.6	1923 3.5
12 Tu	0143 1.6	0740 4.1	1430 1.0	2030 4.0
27	0130 1.9	0723 3.6	1413 1.5	2017 3.6
13 W	0254 1.4	0841 4.3	2130 4.1	
28	0237 1.7	0819 3.8	1514 1.3	2110 3.8
14 Th	0355 1.1	0944 4.4	1630 0.7	2227 4.3
29	0335 1.5	0915 4.0	1605 1.2	2201 4.1
15 F	0448 0.9	1046 4.5	1718 0.7	2322 4.4
30	0427 1.3	1010 4.2	1650 1.1	2253 4.3
31 Su	0513 1.1	1109 4.3	1734 1.0	2344 4.5

JUNE

Day	Tide 1	Tide 2	Tide 3	Tide 4
1 M	0557 0.9	1210 4.5	1814 0.9	
16	0034 4.4	0642 0.9	1317 4.3	1851 1.2
2 Tu	0034 4.6	0639 0.8	1307 4.6	1853 1.0
17	0117 4.4	0711 0.9	1359 4.2	1917 1.3
3 W	0125 4.7	0715 0.7	1403 4.6	1928 1.0
18	0154 4.4	0738 0.9	1436 4.2	1943 1.4
4 Th	0214 4.7	0750 0.6	1453 4.6	2002 1.2
19	0228 4.4	0804 1.0	1511 4.1	2008 1.5
5 F	0300 4.7	0828 0.7	1542 4.5	2039 1.3
20	0302 4.3	0831 1.1	1545 4.0	2036 1.6
6 Sa	0346 4.5	0910 0.8	1629 4.3	2124 1.5
21	0338 4.1	0903 1.2	1620 3.8	2109 1.7
7 Su	0433 4.4	1007 0.9	1715 4.1	2224 1.6 ☾
22	0414 4.0	0942 1.4	1656 3.7	2153 1.8
8 M	0522 4.2	1117 1.1	1806 3.9	2337 1.6
23	0454 3.8	1035 1.5	1738 3.6	2252 1.9 ☽
9 Tu	0616 4.1	1236 1.1	1900 3.8	
24	0539 3.7	1139 1.6	1826 3.5	
10 W	0100 1.6	0716 4.1	1355 1.1	1959 3.8
25	0007 1.9	0630 3.7	1254 1.6	1920 3.6
11 Th	0220 1.5	0817 4.1	1506 1.1	2058 3.9
26	0127 1.8	0729 3.7	1411 1.6	2016 3.7
12 F	0331 1.3	0923 4.1	1607 1.1	2200 4.1
27	0246 1.7	0831 3.9	1518 1.4	2113 4.0
13 Sa	0432 1.1	1028 4.2	1658 1.1	2256 4.2
28	0352 1.4	0937 4.1	1618 1.3	2213 4.3
14 Su	0522 1.0	1131 4.2	1741 1.1	2348 4.3
29	0449 1.2	1045 4.3	1712 1.1	2313 4.5
15 M	0607 0.9	1228 4.3	1818 1.2 ○	
30	0541 0.9	1152 4.6	1759 1.0 ●	

JULY

Day	Tide 1	Tide 2	Tide 3	Tide 4
1 W	0010 4.7	0627 0.6	1255 4.7	1842 0.9
16	0051 4.5	0657 0.8	1337 4.3	1902 1.2
2 Th	0107 4.9	0706 0.5	1351 4.8	1919 0.9
17	0130 4.5	0723 0.8	1413 4.3	1926 1.2
3 F	0159 5.0	0742 0.4	1441 4.8	1952 0.9
18	0204 4.5	0746 0.8	1445 4.3	1950 1.3
4 Sa	0247 5.0	0817 0.4	1527 4.6	2026 1.0
19	0237 4.5	0810 0.9	1516 4.2	2014 1.4
5 Su	0331 4.9	0855 0.6	1609 4.4	2104 1.2
20	0310 4.4	0835 1.1	1548 4.0	2041 1.5
6 M	0415 4.7	0942 0.8	1652 4.1	2151 1.4
21	0343 4.2	0904 1.2	1620 3.9	2115 1.6
7 Tu	0501 4.4	1042 1.1	1736 3.9	2255 1.5 ☾
22	0419 4.0	0942 1.4	1656 3.7	2158 1.8 ☽
8 W	0551 4.1	1153 1.3	1829 3.7	
23	0501 3.9	1033 1.6	1740 3.6	2302 1.9
9 Th	0016 1.6	0650 3.9	1317 1.5	1927 3.7
24	0550 3.7	1144 1.7	1832 3.6	
10 F	0148 1.6	0758 3.8	1437 1.5	2031 3.8
25	0028 1.9	0650 3.7	1311 1.8	1932 3.7
11 Sa	0313 1.5	0909 3.9	1547 1.5	2134 3.9
26	0202 1.8	0800 3.8	1438 1.7	2035 4.0
12 Su	0421 1.3	1018 4.0	1641 1.4	2232 4.1
27	0324 1.5	0913 4.1	1554 1.5	2140 4.3
13 M	0513 1.1	1118 4.1	1726 1.4	2324 4.3
28	0430 1.1	1026 4.4	1653 1.3	2245 4.6
14 Tu	0555 1.0	1211 4.2	1804 1.3 ○	
29	0525 0.7	1134 4.7	1744 1.0	2345 4.9 ●
15 W	0011 4.4	0628 0.9	1257 4.3	1834 1.3
30	0613 0.4	1236 4.9	1827 0.8	
31 F	0045 5.1	0654 0.2	1333 5.0	1904 0.7

AUGUST

Day	Tide 1	Tide 2	Tide 3	Tide 4
1 Sa	0137 5.3	0729 0.2	1421 4.9	1937 0.7
16	0135 4.7	0726 0.8	1415 4.4	1931 1.1
2 Su	0225 5.2	0802 0.2	1503 4.7	2008 0.8
17	0208 4.6	0748 0.9	1445 4.3	1953 1.2
3 M	0310 5.1	0835 0.5	1545 4.5	2041 1.0
18	0241 4.5	0810 1.0	1515 4.2	2017 1.3
4 Tu	0354 4.8	0915 0.8	1625 4.2	2121 1.3
19	0313 4.4	0835 1.2	1546 4.0	2045 1.5
5 W	0438 4.4	1003 1.2	1708 3.9	2215 1.5 ☾
20	0349 4.2	0906 1.4	1621 3.9	2124 1.7
6 Th	0527 4.0	1106 1.6	1755 3.7	2336 1.7
21	0431 3.9	0949 1.7	1704 3.8	2221 1.9 ☽
7 F	0626 3.7	1234 1.8	1857 3.6	
22	0524 3.7	1054 1.9	1758 3.7	2347 1.9
8 Sa	0125 1.8	0740 3.6	1412 1.9	2005 3.7
23	0629 3.7	1231 2.0	1903 3.8	
9 Su	0302 1.6	0855 3.7	1529 1.8	2110 3.9
24	0135 1.8	0743 3.8	1416 1.8	2010 4.0
10 M	0410 1.4	1004 3.9	1626 1.6	2209 4.1
25	0306 1.4	0857 4.1	1534 1.5	2115 4.4
11 Tu	0458 1.2	1059 4.0	1708 1.5	2258 4.3
26	0413 1.0	1008 4.5	1635 1.2	2219 4.8
12 W	0537 1.0	1148 4.2	1744 1.3	2344 4.4
27	0508 0.6	1111 4.8	1725 0.9	2321 5.1
13 Th	0609 0.9	1229 4.4	1815 1.2 ○	
28	0555 0.3	1211 5.0	1809 0.7 ●	
14 F	0024 4.5	0637 0.8	1309 4.4	1842 1.1
29	0019 5.3	0643 0.1	1305 5.0	1846 0.6
15 Sa	0102 4.6	0703 0.8	1343 4.5	1907 1.1
30	0114 5.4	0711 0.1	1354 4.9	1918 0.6
31 M	0203 5.3	0744 0.3	1437 4.8	1949 0.7

GENERAL — Streams run in direction of channels. Turbulence at many points, e.g., Craigton Pt., Kessock Ferry, Inverness Beacon, Fort George. N. and NE. gales form considerable sea.
Melting snow and heavy rain increase both duration and rate of outgoing stream; ingoing stream decreased. For safe passage, study tides and tidal streams.

MORAY FIRTH INVERNESS

HIGH & LOW WATER 1992 Lat. 57°30′N. Long. 4°15′W.

GMT ADD 1 HOUR MARCH 29 — OCTOBER 25 FOR B.S.T.

SEPTEMBER

Day	Time m	Time m	Time m	Time m		Day	Time m	Time m	Time m	Time m
1 Tu	0247 5·1	0814 0·6	1518 4·5	2020 1·0		16 W	0215 4·6	0748 1·1	1444 4·3	1958 1·3
2 W	0331 4·8	0847 1·0	1556 4·2	2055 1·3		17 Th	0251 4·5	0812 1·3	1516 4·2	2026 1·4
3 Th	0415 4·3	0925 1·5	1636 3·9	☽ 2143 1·6		18 F	0330 4·2	0841 1·5	1554 4·1	2103 1·6
4 F	0504 3·9	1019 1·9	1724 3·7	2259 1·8		19 Sa	0415 4·0	0921 1·8	1640 3·9	☾ 2158 1·8
5 Sa	0605 3·6	1147 2·1	1825 3·5			20 Su	0513 3·8	1029 2·0	1736 3·8	2328 1·9
6 Su	0101 1·9	0722 3·5	1343 2·2	1936 3·6		21 M	0619 3·7	1209 2·1	1843 3·9	
7 M	0242 1·7	0835 3·6	1506 2·0	2041 3·8		22 Tu	0117 1·7	0732 3·9	1356 1·9	1949 4·1
8 Tu	0347 1·5	0937 3·8	1600 1·8	2137 4·0		23 W	0246 1·3	0831 4·2	1514 1·6	2054 4·5
9 W	0434 1·3	1028 4·1	1642 1·5	2227 4·3		24 Th	0352 0·9	0946 4·5	1613 1·2	2155 4·9
10 Th	0511 1·1	1113 4·3	1718 1·3	2311 4·4		25 F	0448 0·5	1045 4·8	1703 0·9	2254 5·2
11 F	0544 0·9	1154 4·4	1750 1·2	2352 4·6		26 Sa	0534 0·3	1144 4·9	1747 0·7	● 2353 5·3
12 Sa	0613 0·8	1234 4·5	1820 1·1	○		27 Su	0617 0·2	1236 5·0	1826 0·6	
13 Su	0029 4·7	0640 0·8	1310 4·5	1846 1·1		28 M	0049 5·4	0653 0·3	1326 4·9	1900 0·6
14 M	0105 4·7	0703 0·8	1343 4·5	1910 1·1		29 Tu	0141 5·3	0724 0·5	1408 4·7	1932 0·8
15 Tu	0141 4·7	0726 0·9	1414 4·4	1934 1·2		30 W	0227 5·0	0753 0·9	1448 4·5	2003 1·0

OCTOBER

Day	Time m	Time m	Time m	Time m		Day	Time m	Time m	Time m	Time m
1 Th	0311 4·6	0822 1·3	1526 4·3	2036 1·3		16 F	0237 4·5	0757 1·4	1454 4·4	2016 1·3
2 F	0355 4·2	0855 1·7	1606 4·0	2119 1·6		17 Sa	0322 4·3	0829 1·6	1537 4·3	2055 1·5
3 Sa	0444 3·8	0938 2·1	1651 3·8	2228 1·9		18 Su	0413 4·1	0910 1·9	1625 4·1	2151 1·6
4 Su	0540 3·5	1054 2·3	1747 3·6			19 M	0509 3·9	1017 2·1	1722 4·0	☾ 2317 1·7
5 M	0017 1·9	0650 3·5	1254 2·3	1857 3·6		20 Tu	0611 3·9	1155 2·1	1826 4·0	
6 Tu	0159 1·8	0759 3·6	1424 2·1	2002 3·7		21 W	0056 1·5	0718 4·0	1331 1·9	1929 4·2
7 W	0306 1·6	0857 3·8	1448 1·8	2057 4·0		22 Th	0219 1·2	0820 4·3	1448 1·6	2031 4·5
8 Th	0355 1·4	0946 4·1	1608 1·6	2147 4·2		23 F	0326 0·9	0920 4·5	1547 1·3	2130 4·8
9 F	0437 1·2	1032 4·3	1646 1·4	2232 4·4		24 Sa	0422 0·7	1019 4·7	1640 1·0	2231 5·0
10 Sa	0512 1·0	1117 4·4	1721 1·2	2315 4·6		25 Su	0512 0·5	1115 4·8	1726 0·8	2331 5·2
11 Su	0544 0·9	1157 4·5	1752 1·1	○ 2357 4·7		26 M	0555 0·5	1210 4·9	1809 0·7	
12 M	0613 0·9	1234 4·6	1822 1·1			27 Tu	0029 5·1	0634 0·6	1258 4·9	1847 0·7
13 Tu	0036 4·7	0640 0·9	1301 4·6	1851 1·1		28 W	0122 5·0	0706 0·8	1342 4·8	1919 0·8
14 W	0117 4·7	0705 1·0	1345 4·6	1918 1·1		29 Th	0210 4·8	0735 1·1	1422 4·6	1951 1·0
15 Th	0157 4·6	0731 1·2	1418 4·5	1946 1·2		30 F	0254 4·5	0802 1·5	1500 4·4	2022 1·3
						31 Sa	0338 4·1	0832 1·8	1537 4·2	2059 1·5

NOVEMBER

Day	Time m	Time m	Time m	Time m		Day	Time m	Time m	Time m	Time m
1 Su	0422 3·9	0909 2·1	1619 3·9	2151 1·7		16 M	0411 4·3	0904 1·8	1617 4·4	2144 1·4
2 M	0511 3·6	1004 2·3	1706 3·7	☽ 2310 1·9		17 Tu	0501 4·1	1004 2·0	1708 4·2	☾ 2259 1·4
3 Tu	0607 3·6	1136 2·3	1805 3·7			18 W	0557 4·1	1126 2·0	1806 4·2	
4 W	0046 1·9	0709 3·6	1314 2·2	1909 3·7		19 Th	0024 1·4	0657 4·1	1254 1·9	1907 4·3
5 Th	0205 1·7	0806 3·8	1429 2·0	2007 3·9		20 F	0147 1·2	0755 4·2	1413 1·6	2006 4·5
6 F	0305 1·5	0858 4·0	1522 1·8	2101 4·1		21 Sa	0258 1·0	0854 4·4	1521 1·4	2109 4·6
7 Sa	0352 1·4	0947 4·2	1611 1·6	2149 4·3		22 Su	0359 0·9	0952 4·5	1619 1·2	2213 4·8
8 Su	0434 1·2	1032 4·4	1649 1·4	2236 4·4		23 M	0450 0·8	1050 4·7	1712 1·0	2315 4·8
9 M	0511 1·1	1117 4·5	1726 1·3	2324 4·4		24 Tu	0537 0·9	1144 4·8	1757 0·9	●
10 Tu	0544 1·1	1158 4·6	1802 1·2			25 W	0015 4·8	0617 1·0	1234 4·8	1837 0·9
11 W	0011 4·7	0617 1·1	1240 4·7	1834 1·1		26 Th	0110 4·7	0651 1·1	1319 4·8	1911 0·9
12 Th	0058 4·7	0648 1·2	1319 4·8	1907 1·1		27 F	0157 4·6	0719 1·3	1400 4·7	1941 1·0
13 F	0146 4·6	0718 1·3	1400 4·7	1939 1·1		28 Sa	0240 4·4	0746 1·5	1436 4·6	2009 1·2
14 Sa	0234 4·6	0749 1·4	1443 4·6	2012 1·2		29 Su	0319 4·2	0813 1·7	1511 4·4	2040 1·3
15 Su	0321 4·4	0822 1·6	1527 4·5	2051 1·3		30 M	0357 4·0	0844 1·9	1549 4·2	2118 1·5

DECEMBER

Day	Time m	Time m	Time m	Time m		Day	Time m	Time m	Time m	Time m
1 Tu	0438 3·8	0924 2·1	1629 4·0	2208 1·7		16 W	0447 4·3	0943 1·7	1651 4·5	☾ 2233 1·2
2 W	0522 3·7	1021 2·2	1715 3·8	☽ 2318 1·8		17 Th	0535 4·1	1050 1·8	1743 4·4	2347 1·3
3 Th	0611 3·6	1141 2·2	1808 3·7			18 F	0629 4·0	1212 1·8	1841 4·3	
4 F	0040 1·8	0709 3·7	1308 2·2	1908 3·8		19 Sa	0109 1·3	0727 4·0	1338 1·7	1945 4·2
5 Sa	0155 1·7	0805 3·8	1424 2·0	2006 3·9		20 Su	0229 1·3	0827 4·1	1459 1·5	2050 4·3
6 Su	0258 1·6	0857 3·9	1524 1·8	2102 4·0		21 M	0338 1·3	0930 4·3	1607 1·3	2200 4·4
7 M	0349 1·5	0947 4·2	1616 1·6	2156 4·2		22 Tu	0434 1·2	1031 4·5	1703 1·1	2306 4·5
8 Tu	0435 1·4	1036 4·4	1701 1·4	2253 4·4		23 W	0522 1·2	1126 4·6	1750 1·0	
9 W	0518 1·3	1124 4·7	1744 1·2	2348 4·6		24 Th	0006 4·5	0602 1·2	1215 4·7	● 1830 0·9
10 Th	0557 1·2	1211 4·8	1824 1·0			25 F	0057 4·5	0637 1·3	1258 4·8	1902 0·9
11 F	0043 4·7	0634 1·2	1301 4·9	1900 0·9		26 Sa	0142 4·5	0706 1·3	1339 4·8	1929 0·9
12 Sa	0137 4·8	0710 1·2	1346 5·0	1933 0·8		27 Su	0221 4·4	0732 1·4	1414 4·7	1954 1·0
13 Su	0227 4·8	0742 1·3	1432 5·0	2007 0·8		28 M	0256 4·3	0757 1·5	1447 4·6	2020 1·1
14 M	0313 4·7	0815 1·4	1518 4·9	2044 0·9		29 Tu	0330 4·2	0822 1·6	1521 4·4	2048 1·3
15 Tu	0400 4·5	0853 1·5	1603 4·7	2131 1·0		30 W	0404 4·0	0852 1·8	1556 4·3	2122 1·4
						31 Th	0440 3·8	0930 1·9	1634 4·0	2208 1·6

RATE AND SET — Off Cromarty Lt. Ho. — WSW. going –0555 Dover, Sp. rate ¾ kn.; ENE. going +0030 Dover. Sp. rate 1 kn. off Covesea Lt. Ho. — SW. going –0420 Dover, Sp. rate ½ kn.; NE. going +0200 Dover, Sp. rate ½ kn.

LERWICK SHETLAND ISLANDS

Lat. 60°09'N. Long. 1°08'W.   HIGH & LOW WATER 1992

GMT   ADD 1 HOUR MARCH 29 — OCTOBER 25 FOR B.S.T.

JANUARY

Day	Time	m	Day	Time	m
1 W	0208 / 0820 / 1441 / 2052	0.9 / 1.8 / 0.8 / 1.8	**16** TH	0101 / 0731 / 1344 / 2001	0.9 / 1.8 / 0.9 / 1.8
2 TH	0256 / 0906 / 1529 / 2139	0.9 / 1.9 / 0.8 / 1.9	**17** F	0211 / 0832 / 1446 / 2104	0.9 / 2.0 / 0.7 / 2.0
3 F	0337 / 0947 / 1611 / 2220	0.9 / 2.0 / 0.7 / 1.9	**18** SA	0307 / 0924 / 1539 / 2157	0.8 / 2.1 / 0.5 / 2.1
4 SA	0414 / 1025 / 1649 / ●2258	0.8 / 2.1 / 0.6 / 1.9	**19** SU	0357 / 1011 / 1628 / ○2246	0.7 / 2.2 / 0.4 / 2.2
5 SU	0449 / 1101 / 1724 / 2335	0.8 / 2.1 / 0.6 / 2.0	**20** M	0444 / 1057 / 1715 / 2332	0.6 / 2.4 / 0.2 / 2.2
6 M	0522 / 1136 / 1757	0.8 / 2.2 / 0.6	**21** TU	0528 / 1141 / 1801	0.5 / 2.4 / 0.2
7 TU	0009 / 0554 / 1210 / 1829	2.0 / 0.8 / 2.2 / 0.6	**22** W	0017 / 0611 / 1226 / 1847	2.2 / 0.5 / 2.4 / 0.2
8 W	0044 / 0627 / 1244 / 1901	1.9 / 0.8 / 2.1 / 0.6	**23** TH	0102 / 0655 / 1311 / 1933	2.1 / 0.5 / 2.4 / 0.2
9 TH	0119 / 0700 / 1318 / 1933	1.9 / 0.9 / 2.1 / 0.6	**24** F	0146 / 0739 / 1356 / 2020	2.0 / 0.6 / 2.2 / 0.4
10 F	0154 / 0734 / 1353 / 2008	1.8 / 0.8 / 2.0 / 0.7	**25** SA	0230 / 0825 / 1444 / 2110	1.9 / 0.7 / 2.1 / 0.6
11 SA	0231 / 0811 / 1431 / 2045	1.8 / 0.9 / 1.9 / 0.7	**26** SU	0317 / 0916 / 1536 / 2205	1.8 / 0.8 / 1.9 / 0.7
12 SU	0312 / 0854 / 1513 / 2129	1.7 / 1.0 / 1.9 / 0.8	**27** M	0411 / 1022 / 1641 / 2316	1.7 / 0.9 / 1.7 / 0.9
13 M	0359 / 0947 / 1604 / 2224	1.7 / 1.0 / 1.8 / 0.9	**28** TU	0520 / 1158 / 1811	1.6 / 1.0 / 1.6
14 TU	0458 / 1057 / 1711 / 2337	1.7 / 1.0 / 1.7 / 0.9	**29** W	0039 / 0646 / 1328 / 1939	1.0 / 1.6 / 0.9 / 1.6
15 W	0614 / 1224 / 1839	1.7 / 1.0 / 1.7	**30** TH	0148 / 0756 / 1432 / 2042	1.0 / 1.7 / 0.9 / 1.7
			31 F	0240 / 0848 / 1520 / 2011	1.0 / 1.8 / 0.8 / 1.7

FEBRUARY

Day	Time	m	Day	Time	m
1 SA	0323 / 0931 / 1559 / 2207	0.9 / 1.9 / 0.7 / 1.8	**16** SU	0255 / 0906 / 1526 / 2145	0.8 / 2.0 / 0.4 / 2.0
2 SU	0359 / 1008 / 1634 / 2242	0.8 / 2.0 / 0.6 / 1.9	**17** M	0344 / 0955 / 1614 / 2231	0.6 / 2.2 / 0.2 / 2.1
3 M	0433 / 1042 / 1705 / ●2315	0.8 / 2.1 / 0.5 / 1.9	**18** TU	0428 / 1040 / 1659 / ○2314	0.5 / 2.3 / 0.1 / 2.2
4 TU	0504 / 1115 / 1735 / 2347	0.7 / 2.1 / 0.5 / 2.0	**19** W	0511 / 1124 / 1743 / 2356	0.4 / 2.4 / 0.1 / 2.2
5 W	0534 / 1148 / 1804	0.7 / 2.2 / 0.5	**20** TH	0552 / 1207 / 1825	0.4 / 2.4 / 0.1
6 TH	0018 / 0604 / 1220 / 1832	2.0 / 0.6 / 2.2 / 0.5	**21** F	0036 / 0633 / 1250 / 1907	2.1 / 0.4 / 2.3 / 0.3
7 F	0050 / 0635 / 1253 / 1902	2.0 / 0.7 / 2.1 / 0.5	**22** SA	0117 / 0714 / 1334 / 1949	2.0 / 0.5 / 2.2 / 0.4
8 SA	0123 / 0708 / 1327 / 1934	1.9 / 0.7 / 2.1 / 0.6	**23** SU	0157 / 0756 / 1418 / 2031	1.9 / 0.6 / 2.0 / 0.6
9 SU	0157 / 0742 / 1403 / 2009	1.9 / 0.8 / 2.0 / 0.7	**24** M	0239 / 0842 / 1506 / 2116	1.8 / 0.7 / 1.8 / 0.8
10 M	0235 / 0822 / 1443 / 2049	1.8 / 0.8 / 1.9 / 0.8	**25** TU	0324 / 0940 / 1603 / 2215	1.7 / 0.9 / 1.6 / 1.0
11 TU	0318 / 0911 / 1533 / 2141	1.8 / 0.9 / 1.8 / 0.9	**26** W	0422 / 1118 / 1733 / 2355	1.6 / 1.0 / 1.5 / 1.1
12 W	0413 / 1018 / 1640 / 2255	1.7 / 1.0 / 1.7 / 1.0	**27** TH	0554 / 1308 / 1921	1.6 / 0.9 / 1.5
13 TH	0529 / 1153 / 1816	1.7 / 1.0 / 1.7	**28** F	0124 / 0727 / 1414 / 2026	1.1 / 1.6 / 0.8 / 1.6
14 F	0036 / 0700 / 1327 / 1949	1.0 / 1.7 / 0.8 / 1.8	**29** SA	0221 / 0825 / 1501 / 2110	1.0 / 1.7 / 0.7 / 1.7
15 SA	0157 / 0811 / 1433 / 2053	0.9 / 1.9 / 0.6 / 1.9			

MARCH

Day	Time	m	Day	Time	m
1 SU	0303 / 0908 / 1537 / 2146	0.9 / 1.8 / 0.6 / 1.8	**16** M	0239 / 0847 / 1510 / 2128	0.7 / 2.0 / 0.3 / 2.0
2 M	0338 / 0944 / 1608 / 2218	0.8 / 1.9 / 0.5 / 1.9	**17** TU	0326 / 0936 / 1556 / 2211	0.6 / 2.2 / 0.2 / 2.0
3 TU	0410 / 1018 / 1637 / 2249	0.7 / 2.0 / 0.5 / 1.9	**18** W	0409 / 1021 / 1639 / ○2252	0.4 / 2.3 / 0.1 / 2.1
4 W	0440 / 1050 / 1705 / ●2319	0.6 / 2.1 / 0.4 / 2.0	**19** TH	0450 / 1105 / 1721 / 2332	0.4 / 2.3 / 0.1 / 2.1
5 TH	0510 / 1122 / 1734 / 2350	0.6 / 2.1 / 0.4 / 2.0	**20** F	0531 / 1147 / 1801	0.3 / 2.3 / 0.2
6 F	0540 / 1155 / 1803	0.5 / 2.1 / 0.4	**21** SA	0010 / 0611 / 1230 / 1839	2.1 / 0.3 / 2.2 / 0.3
7 SA	0021 / 0611 / 1229 / 1833	2.0 / 0.6 / 2.1 / 0.5	**22** SU	0048 / 0651 / 1312 / 1917	2.0 / 0.4 / 2.1 / 0.5
8 SU	0054 / 0644 / 1304 / 1905	2.0 / 0.6 / 2.1 / 0.6	**23** M	0126 / 0732 / 1354 / 1954	2.0 / 0.5 / 1.9 / 0.7
9 M	0129 / 1342 / 1941	1.9 / 2.0 / 0.7	**24** TU	0205 / 0816 / 1439 / 2034	1.8 / 0.7 / 1.7 / 0.8
10 TU	0207 / 0801 / 1425 / 2023	1.9 / 0.7 / 1.9 / 0.8	**25** W	0247 / 0909 / 1533 / 2122	1.7 / 0.8 / 1.6 / 1.0
11 W	0250 / 0852 / 1518 / 2117	1.8 / 0.8 / 1.8 / 0.9	**26** TH	0338 / 1032 / 1651 / 2247	1.6 / 0.9 / 1.4 / 1.1
12 TH	0345 / 1001 / 1629 / 2235	1.7 / 0.9 / 1.7 / 1.0	**27** F	0451 / 1232 / 1847	1.5 / 0.9 / 1.4
13 F	0500 / 1138 / 1807	1.7 / 0.8 / 1.6	**28** SA	0046 / 0637 / 1341 / 1955	1.1 / 1.6 / 0.8 / 1.5
14 SA	0022 / 0633 / 1312 / 1938	1.0 / 1.7 / 0.7 / 1.7	**29** SU	0149 / 0747 / 1427 / 2039	1.0 / 1.6 / 0.7 / 1.6
15 SU	0143 / 0749 / 1417 / 2039	0.9 / 1.8 / 0.5 / 1.8	**30** M	0233 / 0834 / 1503 / 2115	0.9 / 1.7 / 0.6 / 1.7
			31 TU	0308 / 0912 / 1534 / 2146	0.8 / 1.8 / 0.5 / 1.8

APRIL

Day	Time	m	Day	Time	m
1 W	0340 / 0947 / 1603 / 2217	0.7 / 1.9 / 0.5 / 1.9	**16** TH	0349 / 1002 / 1617 / 2228	0.4 / 2.2 / 0.2 / 2.0
2 TH	0411 / 1021 / 1632 / 2248	0.6 / 2.0 / 0.4 / 2.0	**17** F	0431 / 1046 / 1657 / ○2307	0.4 / 2.2 / 0.3 / 2.1
3 F	0442 / 1055 / 1702 / ●2320	0.5 / 2.1 / 0.4 / 2.0	**18** SA	0511 / 1128 / 1735 / 2345	0.3 / 2.2 / 0.4 / 2.1
4 SA	0515 / 1130 / 1734 / 2354	0.5 / 2.1 / 0.4 / 2.1	**19** SU	0552 / 1210 / 1812	0.3 / 2.1 / 0.5
5 SU	0549 / 1207 / 1808	0.5 / 2.1 / 0.5	**20** M	0022 / 0632 / 1252 / 1848	2.0 / 0.4 / 2.0 / 0.6
6 M	0029 / 0626 / 1246 / 1844	2.0 / 0.5 / 2.0 / 0.6	**21** TU	0100 / 0713 / 1334 / 1924	2.0 / 0.5 / 1.8 / 0.7
7 TU	0107 / 0706 / 1328 / 1924	2.0 / 0.5 / 2.0 / 0.7	**22** W	0139 / 0757 / 1418 / 2002	1.9 / 0.6 / 1.7 / 0.8
8 W	0148 / 0752 / 1417 / 2010	1.9 / 0.6 / 1.9 / 0.8	**23** TH	0220 / 0846 / 1507 / 2047	1.8 / 0.7 / 1.5 / 0.9
9 TH	0234 / 0847 / 1514 / 2108	1.8 / 0.7 / 1.7 / 0.9	**24** F	0306 / 0949 / 1610 / 2148	1.7 / 0.8 / 1.4 / 1.0
10 F	0330 / 0958 / 1626 / 2226	1.7 / 0.7 / 1.6 / 1.0	**25** SA	0403 / 1125 / 1741 / 2330	1.6 / 0.8 / 1.4 / 1.0
11 SA	0442 / 1128 / 1757	1.7 / 0.7 / 1.6	**26** SU	0520 / 1245 / 1903	1.5 / 0.8 / 1.5
12 SU	0004 / 0607 / 1253 / 1919	1.0 / 1.7 / 0.6 / 1.7	**27** M	0056 / 0644 / 1337 / 1954	1.0 / 1.6 / 0.7 / 1.6
13 M	0122 / 0724 / 1357 / 2018	0.8 / 1.8 / 0.4 / 1.8	**28** TU	0148 / 0744 / 1416 / 2034	0.9 / 1.6 / 0.5 / 1.7
14 TU	0218 / 0824 / 1449 / 2106	0.7 / 1.9 / 0.3 / 1.9	**29** W	0228 / 0830 / 1451 / 2109	0.8 / 1.7 / 0.6 / 1.8
15 W	0305 / 0915 / 1534 / 2148	0.6 / 2.1 / 0.2 / 2.0	**30** TH	0304 / 0911 / 1523 / 2142	0.7 / 1.8 / 0.5 / 1.9

To find H.W. Dover add 0 h. 08 min.

TIDAL DIFFERENCES PAGE 21:105. TIDAL STREAMS PAGES 21:112-21:119.

Datum of predictions: 1.22 m. below Ordnance Datum (Newlyn) or approx. L.A.T.

SHETLAND ISLANDS **LERWICK**

HIGH & LOW WATER 1992   Lat. 60°09'N. Long. 1°08'W.

GMT   ADD 1 HOUR MARCH 29 — OCTOBER 25 FOR B.S.T.

MAY

Day	Time	m	Day	Time	m
1	0339	0.6	**16**	0414	0.4
	0950	1.9		1029	2.0
F	1557	0.5	SA	1634	0.5
	2217	2.0	O	2244	2.0
2	0415	0.5	**17**	0456	0.4
	1028	2.0		1112	2.0
SA	1632	0.5	SU	1712	0.5
●	2252	2.0		2322	2.0
3	0452	0.5	**18**	0537	0.4
	1108	2.1		1154	1.9
SU	1709	0.5	M	1749	0.6
	2330	2.1			
4	0532	0.4	**19**	0000	2.0
	1150	2.1		0618	0.4
M	1748	0.5	TU	1235	1.9
				1824	0.7
5	0009	2.1	**20**	0039	2.0
	0613	0.4		0658	0.5
TU	1234	2.0	W	1316	1.8
	1829	0.6		1900	0.7
6	0050	2.1	**21**	0117	1.9
	0658	0.4		0739	0.6
W	1321	2.0	TH	1358	1.7
	1914	0.7		1938	0.8
7	0135	2.0	**22**	0157	1.8
	0748	0.5		0823	0.6
TH	1412	1.9	F	1442	1.6
	2004	0.8		2020	0.9
8	0223	1.9	**23**	0239	1.7
	0845	0.5		0910	0.7
F	1509	1.7	SA	1531	1.5
	2102	0.8		2108	0.9
9	0318	1.8	**24**	0325	1.7
	0952	0.5		1006	0.7
SA	1616	1.6	SU	1630	1.5
	2213	0.9		2209	1.0
10	0423	1.8	**25**	0419	1.6
	1110	0.5		1113	0.8
SU	1734	1.6	M	1740	1.5
	2337	0.9		2325	1.0
11	0540	1.7	**26**	0524	1.6
	1227	0.5		1220	0.8
M	1851	1.6	TU	1848	1.5
12	0052	0.8	**27**	0040	0.9
	0656	1.8		0636	1.6
TU	1332	0.4	W	1315	0.7
	1951	1.7		1941	1.6
13	0153	0.7	**28**	0137	0.9
	0800	1.9		0739	1.7
W	1425	0.4	TH	1400	0.7
	2040	1.8		2026	1.7
14	0244	0.6	**29**	0224	0.8
	0855	1.9		0832	1.8
TH	1512	0.4	F	1443	0.6
	2124	1.9		2107	1.9
15	0330	0.5	**30**	0308	0.7
	0944	2.0		0920	1.9
F	1554	0.4	SA	1524	0.6
	2205	1.9		2147	2.0
			31	0351	0.6
				1005	1.9
			SU	1606	0.5
				2228	2.1

JUNE

Day	Time	m	Day	Time	m
1	0434	0.5	**16**	0526	0.4
	1051	2.0		1139	1.9
M	1649	0.5	TU	1729	0.7
●	2310	2.1		2342	2.0
2	0518	0.4	**17**	0605	0.5
	1136	2.1		1218	1.8
TU	1733	0.5	W	1805	0.7
	2352	2.1			
3	0604	0.3	**18**	0019	2.0
	1223	2.0		0641	0.5
W	1819	0.6	TH	1256	1.8
				1840	0.7
4	0036	2.1	**19**	0056	2.0
	0651	0.3		0718	0.5
TH	1312	2.0	F	1334	1.7
	1905	0.6		1915	0.7
5	0122	2.1	**20**	0133	1.9
	0742	0.3		0754	0.6
F	1403	1.9	SA	1413	1.6
	1955	0.7		1952	0.8
6	0211	2.0	**21**	0210	1.9
	0837	0.3		0832	0.6
SA	1456	1.8	SU	1453	1.6
	2049	0.7		2032	0.8
7	0303	1.9	**22**	0250	1.8
	0937	0.4		0913	0.7
SU	1555	1.7	M	1537	1.6
	2150	0.8		2118	0.9
8	0402	1.8	**23**	0334	1.7
	1045	0.5		0959	0.7
M	1702	1.6	TU	1627	1.5
	2302	0.8		2213	0.9
9	0511	1.8	**24**	0425	1.6
	1157	0.5		1054	0.8
TU	1813	1.6	W	1727	1.6
				2321	1.0
10	0019	0.8	**25**	0528	1.6
	0627	1.8		1159	0.8
W	1304	0.5	TH	1836	1.6
	1919	1.6			
11	0128	0.7	**26**	0038	0.9
	0738	1.8		0644	1.6
TH	1401	0.6	F	1307	0.8
	2014	1.7		1940	1.7
12	0226	0.6	**27**	0145	0.8
	0838	1.8		0756	1.7
F	1450	0.6	SA	1406	0.8
	2102	1.8		2033	1.8
13	0316	0.6	**28**	0241	0.7
	0930	1.8		0855	1.8
SA	1533	0.6	SU	1459	0.7
	2145	1.9		2122	2.0
14	0402	0.5	**29**	0331	0.6
	1016	1.9		0947	1.9
SU	1615	0.6	M	1547	0.6
	2225	2.0		2207	2.1
15	0445	0.5	**30**	0418	0.4
	1059	1.9		1036	2.0
M	1653	0.6	TU	1634	0.6
O	2304	2.0	●	2252	2.2

JULY

Day	Time	m	Day	Time	m
1	0505	0.3	**16**	0546	0.5
	1124	2.1		1157	1.9
W	1720	0.5	TH	1745	0.7
	2336	2.2		2358	2.1
2	0552	0.2	**17**	0619	0.5
	1210	2.1		1232	1.9
TH	1806	0.5	F	1817	0.7
3	0021	2.3	**18**	0032	2.1
	0639	0.2		0650	0.5
F	1258	2.1	SA	1306	1.8
	1851	0.5		1849	0.7
4	0107	2.2	**19**	0107	2.0
	0728	0.2		0722	0.5
SA	1345	2.0	SU	1341	1.8
	1938	0.6		1923	0.7
5	0154	2.2	**20**	0141	2.0
	0819	0.3		0754	0.6
SU	1434	1.9	M	1416	1.8
	2027	0.6		1958	0.8
6	0243	2.1	**21**	0218	1.9
	0913	0.4		0829	0.7
M	1526	1.8	TU	1454	1.7
	2122	0.7		2038	0.9
7	0338	1.9	**22**	0257	1.8
	1013	0.5		0909	0.8
TU	1623	1.7	W	1537	1.7
	2227	0.8		2125	0.9
8	0442	1.8	**23**	0343	1.7
	1122	0.6		0957	0.8
W	1731	1.6	TH	1628	1.6
	2347	0.8		2226	1.0
9	0600	1.7	**24**	0441	1.7
	1234	0.7		1059	0.9
TH	1844	1.6	F	1735	1.7
				2347	1.0
10	0107	0.8	**25**	0600	1.6
	0720	1.7		1221	0.9
F	1339	0.8	SA	1856	1.7
	1949	1.7			
11	0214	0.7	**26**	0113	0.7
	0826	0.8		0729	1.7
SA	1433	0.8	SU	1339	0.9
	2042	1.8		2004	1.8
12	0308	0.7	**27**	0220	0.8
	0920	1.7		0838	1.8
SU	1518	0.8	M	1440	0.8
	2128	1.9		2059	2.0
13	0354	0.6	**28**	0314	0.6
	1005	1.8		0933	2.0
M	1559	0.8	TU	1532	0.7
	2209	2.0		2148	2.1
14	0435	0.5	**29**	0403	0.4
	1045	1.8		1022	2.1
TU	1636	0.7	W	1619	0.6
O	2247	2.0	●	2234	2.3
15	0512	0.5	**30**	0450	0.2
	1122	1.9		1108	2.2
W	1711	0.7	TH	1704	0.5
	2323	2.1		2318	2.4
			31	0536	0.1
				1153	2.2
			F	1748	0.5

AUGUST

Day	Time	m	Day	Time	m
1	0003	2.4	**16**	0006	2.1
	0621	0.1		0619	0.5
SA	1238	2.2	SU	1236	2.0
	1831	0.5		1822	0.7
2	0048	2.4	**17**	0039	2.1
	0707	0.2		0648	0.6
SU	1322	2.1	M	1308	1.9
	1916	0.5		1854	0.7
3	0134	2.3	**18**	0113	2.1
	0754	0.3		0718	0.6
M	1406	2.0	TU	1341	1.9
	2002	0.6		1928	0.8
4	0221	2.1	**19**	0148	2.0
	0843	0.5		0751	0.7
TU	1453	1.8	W	1417	1.9
	2052	0.7		2005	0.8
5	0313	2.0	**20**	0227	1.9
	0937	0.7		0829	0.8
W	1544	1.7	TH	1457	1.8
	2153	0.8		2051	0.9
6	0413	1.8	**21**	0313	1.8
	1042	0.8		0915	0.9
TH	1645	1.7	F	1547	1.7
	2317	0.9		2151	1.0
7	0534	1.7	**22**	0412	1.7
	1203	0.9		1019	1.0
F	1806	1.6	SA	1653	1.7
				2315	1.0
8	0053	0.9	**23**	0536	1.6
	0707	1.6		1151	1.1
SA	1320	1.0	SU	1820	1.7
	1926	1.7			
9	0205	0.8	**24**	0051	0.9
	0818	1.7		0713	1.7
SU	1418	0.9	M	1322	1.0
	2025	1.8		1939	1.9
10	0258	0.7	**25**	0203	0.7
	0909	1.7		0823	1.9
M	1504	0.9	TU	1425	0.9
	2111	1.9		2038	2.0
11	0341	0.7	**26**	0257	0.5
	0950	1.8		0917	2.0
TU	1543	0.8	W	1516	0.7
	2151	2.0		2128	2.2
12	0418	0.6	**27**	0346	0.4
	1026	1.9		1004	2.1
W	1618	0.8	TH	1601	0.6
	2227	2.1		2214	2.3
13	0450	0.5	**28**	0432	0.2
	1100	1.9		1048	2.2
TH	1650	0.7	F	1645	0.5
O	2301	2.1	●	2259	2.4
14	0521	0.5	**29**	0516	0.2
	1132	2.0		1131	2.2
F	1721	0.7	SA	1727	0.4
	2334	2.2		2343	2.5
15	0550	0.5	**30**	0600	0.2
	1204	2.0		1213	2.2
SA	1752	0.6	SU	1810	0.4
			31	0027	2.4
				0643	0.3
			M	1255	2.2
				1852	0.5

LERWICK SHETLAND ISLANDS 21:111

Lat. 60°09′N. Long. 1°08′W.

HIGH & LOW WATER 1992

GMT   ADD 1 HOUR MARCH 29 — OCTOBER 25 FOR B.S.T.

SEPTEMBER

Day	Time	m	Day	Time	m
1 TU	0113 / 0726 / 1336 / 1937	2.3 / 0.4 / 2.1 / 0.6	16 W	0048 / 0647 / 1311 / 1903	2.1 / 0.7 / 2.0 / 0.8
2 W	0159 / 0811 / 1419 / 2025	2.2 / 0.6 / 1.9 / 0.7	17 TH	0125 / 0721 / 1347 / 1943	2.1 / 0.8 / 2.0 / 0.8
3 TH	0248 / 0859 / 1506 / 2123	2.0 / 0.8 / 1.8 / 0.8	18 F	0206 / 0800 / 1429 / 2030	2.0 / 0.9 / 1.9 / 0.9
4 F	0346 / 0958 / 1603 / 2250	1.8 / 1.0 / 1.7 / 0.9	19 SA	0256 / 0849 / 1519 / 2133	1.9 / 1.0 / 1.8 / 1.0
5 SA	0508 / 1128 / 1723	1.6 / 1.1 / 1.7	20 SU	0359 / 0958 / 1626 / 2258	1.8 / 1.1 / 1.8 / 1.0
6 SU	0037 / 0652 / 1259 / 1857	1.0 / 1.6 / 1.1 / 1.7	21 M	0525 / 1135 / 1752	1.7 / 1.1 / 1.8
7 M	0149 / 0803 / 1359 / 2002	0.9 / 1.7 / 1.0 / 1.8	22 TU	0033 / 0659 / 1306 / 1913	0.9 / 1.8 / 1.0 / 1.9
8 TU	0239 / 0850 / 1444 / 2048	0.8 / 1.7 / 1.0 / 1.9	23 W	0144 / 0806 / 1407 / 2015	0.7 / 1.9 / 0.9 / 2.1
9 W	0318 / 0928 / 1521 / 2127	0.7 / 1.8 / 0.9 / 2.0	24 TH	0238 / 0858 / 1457 / 2107	0.5 / 2.0 / 0.7 / 2.2
10 TH	0351 / 1001 / 1554 / 2202	0.6 / 1.9 / 0.8 / 2.1	25 F	0326 / 0943 / 1542 / 2154	0.4 / 2.2 / 0.6 / 2.4
11 F	0421 / 1032 / 1625 / 2235	0.6 / 1.9 / 0.7 / 2.1	26 SA	0411 / 1026 / 1624 / 2239	0.3 / 2.2 / 0.5 / 2.4
12 SA	0450 / 1103 / 1655 / 2307	0.5 / 1.9 / 0.7 / 2.2	27 SU	0454 / 1107 / 1707 / 2323	0.3 / 2.3 / 0.4 / 2.5
13 SU	0518 / 1133 / 1725 / 2339	0.5 / 2.1 / 0.7 / 2.2	28 M	0536 / 1147 / 1749	0.4 / 2.3 / 0.4
14 M	0546 / 1204 / 1756	0.6 / 2.1 / 0.7	29 TU	0007 / 0617 / 1227 / 1831	2.4 / 0.4 / 2.2 / 0.5
15 TU	0013 / 0615 / 1237 / 1828	2.2 / 0.6 / 2.1 / 0.7	30 W	0052 / 0657 / 1308 / 1915	2.3 / 0.6 / 2.1 / 0.6

OCTOBER

Day	Time	m	Day	Time	m
1 TH	0137 / 0739 / 1349 / 2002	2.1 / 0.8 / 2.0 / 0.7	16 F	0109 / 0700 / 1326 / 1930	2.1 / 0.8 / 2.1 / 0.8
2 F	0226 / 0822 / 1434 / 2059	1.9 / 0.9 / 1.9 / 0.9	17 SA	0154 / 0744 / 1410 / 2022	2.0 / 0.9 / 2.0 / 0.8
3 SA	0321 / 0915 / 1525 / 2219	1.8 / 1.1 / 1.8 / 1.0	18 SU	0247 / 0837 / 1502 / 2125	1.9 / 1.0 / 1.9 / 0.9
4 SU	0436 / 1036 / 1635	1.6 / 1.2 / 1.7	19 M	0352 / 0946 / 1606 / 2245	1.8 / 1.1 / 1.7 / 0.8
5 M	0007 / 0620 / 1224 / 1811	1.0 / 1.6 / 1.2 / 1.7	20 TU	0512 / 1116 / 1725	1.8 / 1.1 / 1.9
6 TU	0119 / 0733 / 1329 / 1925	0.9 / 1.7 / 1.1 / 1.8	21 W	0011 / 0638 / 1242 / 1845	0.8 / 1.8 / 1.0 / 1.9
7 W	0207 / 0820 / 1415 / 2015	0.8 / 1.7 / 1.0 / 1.9	22 TH	0121 / 0744 / 1345 / 1951	0.6 / 1.9 / 0.9 / 2.1
8 TH	0245 / 0857 / 1452 / 2055	0.8 / 1.8 / 0.9 / 2.0	23 F	0217 / 0836 / 1436 / 2046	0.5 / 2.0 / 0.7 / 2.2
9 F	0318 / 0930 / 1525 / 2131	0.7 / 1.9 / 0.8 / 2.1	24 SA	0305 / 0921 / 1522 / 2135	0.4 / 2.1 / 0.6 / 2.3
10 SA	0347 / 1003 / 1556 / 2205	0.6 / 2.0 / 0.7 / 2.1	25 SU	0350 / 1003 / 1606 / ● 2221	0.4 / 2.2 / 0.5 / 2.4
11 SU	0416 / 1032 / 1627 / ○ 2239	0.6 / 2.1 / 0.7 / 2.2	26 M	0432 / 1043 / 1649 / 2306	0.4 / 2.3 / 0.5 / 2.4
12 M	0445 / 1103 / 1659 / 2314	0.6 / 2.2 / 0.7 / 2.2	27 TU	0513 / 1123 / 1731 / 2350	0.5 / 2.3 / 0.5 / 2.3
13 TU	0516 / 1136 / 1733 / 2350	0.6 / 2.2 / 0.7 / 2.2	28 W	0553 / 1203 / 1814	0.6 / 2.3 / 0.5
14 W	0548 / 1210 / 1808	0.7 / 2.2 / 0.7	29 TH	0034 / 0631 / 1243 / 1858	2.2 / 0.7 / 2.2 / 0.6
15 TH	0027 / 0622 / 1247 / 1847	2.2 / 0.8 / 2.1 / 0.7	30 F	0118 / 0710 / 1324 / 1944	2.0 / 0.9 / 2.1 / 0.7
			31 SA	0204 / 0751 / 1406 / 2035	1.9 / 1.0 / 2.0 / 0.8

NOVEMBER

Day	Time	m	Day	Time	m
1 SU	0255 / 0837 / 1453 / 2138	1.8 / 1.1 / 1.9 / 0.9	16 M	0239 / 0828 / 1448 / 2116	1.9 / 1.0 / 2.0 / 0.7
2 M	0356 / 0938 / 1549 / 2305	1.6 / 1.2 / 1.8 / 1.0	17 TU	0339 / 0931 / 1547 / 2226	1.8 / 1.0 / 2.0 / 0.7
3 TU	0518 / 1112 / 1701	1.6 / 1.2 / 1.7	18 W	0450 / 1048 / 1657 / 2344	1.8 / 1.1 / 1.9 / 0.7
4 W	0026 / 0641 / 1239 / 1824	0.9 / 1.6 / 1.1 / 1.7	19 TH	0607 / 1210 / 1815	1.8 / 1.0 / 1.9
5 TH	0121 / 0737 / 1334 / 1928	0.9 / 1.7 / 1.1 / 1.8	20 F	0055 / 0715 / 1319 / 1926	0.6 / 1.9 / 0.9 / 2.0
6 F	0202 / 0818 / 1416 / 2016	0.8 / 1.8 / 1.0 / 1.9	21 SA	0154 / 0811 / 1415 / 2027	0.6 / 1.9 / 0.8 / 2.1
7 SA	0238 / 0854 / 1452 / 2057	0.8 / 1.9 / 0.9 / 2.0	22 SU	0245 / 0858 / 1505 / 2119	0.6 / 2.0 / 0.7 / 2.2
8 SU	0310 / 0928 / 1527 / 2136	0.7 / 2.0 / 0.8 / 2.1	23 M	0330 / 0942 / 1552 / 2207	0.6 / 2.1 / 0.6 / 2.2
9 M	0342 / 1002 / 1601 / 2213	0.7 / 2.1 / 0.7 / 2.1	24 TU	0413 / 1023 / 1636 / 2252	0.6 / 2.2 / 0.5 / 2.2
10 TU	0415 / 1036 / 1637 / ○ 2252	0.7 / 2.2 / 0.7 / 2.2	25 W	0453 / 1104 / 1719 / 2336	0.6 / 2.2 / 0.5 / 2.2
11 W	0450 / 1112 / 1715 / 2331	0.7 / 2.2 / 0.6 / 2.2	26 TH	0532 / 1143 / 1802	0.7 / 2.2 / 0.5
12 TH	0527 / 1149 / 1754	0.7 / 2.3 / 0.6	27 F	0018 / 0609 / 1223 / 1843	2.1 / 0.8 / 2.2 / 0.6
13 F	0013 / 0606 / 1229 / 1836	2.2 / 0.8 / 2.2 / 0.6	28 SA	0100 / 0647 / 1304 / 1926	2.0 / 0.8 / 2.1 / 0.7
14 SA	0058 / 0649 / 1311 / 1923	2.1 / 0.9 / 2.2 / 0.6	29 SU	0142 / 0725 / 1342 / 2009	1.9 / 0.9 / 2.1 / 0.7
15 SU	0146 / 0735 / 1357 / 2015	2.0 / 0.9 / 2.1 / 0.7	30 M	0226 / 0806 / 1423 / 2055	1.8 / 1.0 / 2.0 / 0.8

DECEMBER

Day	Time	m	Day	Time	m
1 TU	0313 / 0852 / 1508 / 2148	1.7 / 1.1 / 1.9 / 0.9	16 W	0318 / 0910 / 1526 / 2201	1.9 / 0.9 / 2.0 / 0.6
2 W	0408 / 0948 / 1559 / 2252	1.6 / 1.1 / 1.8 / 0.9	17 TH	0419 / 1015 / 1630 / 2312	1.8 / 0.9 / 2.0 / 0.7
3 TH	0515 / 1103 / 1702	1.6 / 1.1 / 1.7	18 F	0529 / 1134 / 1745	1.8 / 1.0 / 1.9
4 F	0004 / 0629 / 1226 / 1817	0.9 / 1.7 / 1.1 / 1.7	19 SA	0026 / 0642 / 1253 / 1904	0.7 / 1.8 / 0.9 / 1.9
5 SA	0103 / 0727 / 1328 / 1926	0.9 / 1.7 / 1.0 / 1.8	20 SU	0132 / 0745 / 1359 / 2012	0.7 / 1.9 / 0.8 / 1.9
6 SU	0150 / 0814 / 1415 / 2020	0.9 / 1.8 / 1.0 / 1.9	21 M	0227 / 0839 / 1454 / 2109	0.7 / 1.9 / 0.7 / 2.0
7 M	0232 / 0854 / 1458 / 2107	0.8 / 2.0 / 0.9 / 2.0	22 TU	0315 / 0925 / 1544 / 2158	0.7 / 2.0 / 0.6 / 2.0
8 TU	0311 / 0933 / 1538 / 2151	0.8 / 2.1 / 0.8 / 2.0	23 W	0358 / 1008 / 1628 / 2242	0.7 / 2.1 / 0.6 / 2.0
9 W	0351 / 1012 / 1619 / ○ 2234	0.8 / 2.2 / 0.7 / 2.1	24 TH	0438 / 1048 / 1710 / ● 2323	0.7 / 2.2 / 0.5 / 2.0
10 TH	0431 / 1053 / 1700 / 2317	0.7 / 2.3 / 0.6 / 2.2	25 F	0515 / 1127 / 1750	0.7 / 2.2 / 0.5
11 F	0512 / 1132 / 1743	0.7 / 2.3 / 0.5	26 SA	0002 / 0551 / 1205 / 1827	2.0 / 0.7 / 2.2 / 0.5
12 SA	0001 / 0554 / 1214 / 1827	2.2 / 0.7 / 2.3 / 0.5	27 SU	0040 / 0626 / 1242 / 1903	2.0 / 0.8 / 2.2 / 0.6
13 SU	0047 / 0639 / 1258 / 1914	2.2 / 0.7 / 2.3 / 0.4	28 M	0118 / 0701 / 1318 / 1938	1.9 / 0.8 / 2.1 / 0.6
14 M	0134 / 0725 / 1343 / 2004	2.1 / 0.8 / 2.2 / 0.5	29 TU	0155 / 0736 / 1354 / 2014	1.8 / 0.9 / 2.0 / 0.7
15 TU	0224 / 0813 / 1432 / 2059	2.0 / 0.8 / 2.1 / 0.5	30 W	0233 / 0813 / 1432 / 2052	1.8 / 0.9 / 1.9 / 0.8
			31 TH	0315 / 0855 / 1513 / 2134	1.7 / 0.8 / 1.8 / 0.9

To find H.W. Dover add 0 h. 08 min.

TIDAL DIFFERENCES PAGE 211:105. TIDAL STREAMS PAGES 21:112-21:119.

Datum of predictions: 1.22 m. below Ordnance Datum (Newlyn) or approx. L.A.T.

PENTLAND FIRTH

SPECIAL CAUTION

The Pentland Firth probably represents the most difficult navigational passage on the Coasts of the United Kingdom, normally used by vessels of all sizes. Owing to the great strength of the Tidal Stream (more than the speed of the average small vessel) at times, the utmost care should be used, especially in thick weather or uncertain visibility. Study the Tidal Stream Charts given on pages 21:113-21:119 for safety's sake.

NOTES ON THE TIDAL STREAMS

1. **GENERAL.** The streams in the approaches are more or less rotatory clockwise, with maximum Spring rate in the east of $1\frac{1}{2}$ kts. and in the west of 1 kt. As the land is approached the streams begin earlier, run more in the direction of the coast and into the channels. The rates increase as streams narrow in channels; direction changes quickly with low rate, and slowly with high rate. Close westward of Pentland Skerries the S.E. going stream is said to attain a Spring rate of $10\frac{1}{2}$ kts. The land formations cause changes in set and rate of streams, and form many eddies, races, overfalls.

2. **KIRKWALL. Eastern Approaches.**
(a) **Spurness Sound:** Strong stream, N.E. Sp. $3\frac{1}{2}$ kts. − S.W. Sp. $4\frac{1}{4}$ kts.

(b) **Stronsay Firth:** Strong and regular in mid-channel, eddies on both sides. A race forms off Mull Head during S.E. going stream—violent in S. and S.E. gales.

3. **KIRKWALL. Western Approaches.**
(a) **Westray Firth:** Rotatory clockwise. S.E. going, − 0530, Sp. 3 kts. N.W. going, + 0040, Sp. 3 kts.

(b) **Eynhallow Sound.**
S.E. going, − 0545, Sp. 2-3 kts. N.W. going, + 0015, Sp. 2-3 kts.

The rate increases from the entrances to a maximum of 7 kts. Sp. Turbulence is found where the N.W. going stream meets the Atlantic Swell. Dangerous race in Westray between Faraclett Head and Wart Holm.

4. **SCAPA FLOW. Eastern Approaches.**
Holm and Water Sound: Closed by breakwaters, Probably no regular streams.

5. **SCAPA FLOW. Western Approaches.**
Hoy Sound. Unreliable. Spring rate reaches 7 kts. in the narrows. Dangerous overfalls in W. gales at mouth. Eddies form both sides of stream.

6. **SCAPA FLOW. Southern Approaches.**
Hoxa Sound: Main stream.
Ingoing: + 0340. Outgoing: − 0120
Stream is affected by eddies, rate varies 2-4.

7. **SCAPA FLOW. General.** An inland sea with very weak and variable streams. There is a fetch from side to side which is very strong in gales.

8. **PENTLAND FIRTH. General.** The streams run very strongly, vary considerably, and may differ appreciably from information available. The greatest care is therefore required when navigating these channels.

9. **PENTLAND FIRTH. Eddies and races.** A number of very dangerous races, eddies and overfalls form under different conditions. Fullest possible information should be obtained concerning this area.

10. **PENTLAND FIRTH. Main Channel.**
(a) E. going: − 0450, 105°, Sp. $3\frac{1}{2}$ kts. rate increases to 9 kts. between Stroma and Swona.

(b) W. going: H.W. Sp. 8 kts. rate increases to 9 kts. between Stroma and Swona. Rate decreases off Dunnet Head.

N.B.—**Times are given in relation to H.W. Dover,** and indicate the beginning of the streams. Rates are approx. maximum at Springs, in knots.

PENTLAND FIRTH TIDAL STREAMS

The 13 charts for the Pentland Firth area show tidal streams at hourly intervals commencing 6h. before and ending 6h. after H.W. Dover. For Dover High Water times see pages 21:41-21:43. The thicker the arrows the stronger tidal streams they indicate; the thinner arrows show rates and position of weaker streams. The figures shown against the arrows, e.g. 19, 34 indicate a mean neap rate of 1.9 knots and a mean spring rate of 3.4 knots approximately.

Important Note. Eddies may occur in some areas due to the very strong rate of tidal streams. Where possible these have been indicated.

The following charts are produced from portion(s) of BA Tidal Stream Atlases with the sanction of the Controller, H.M .Stationery Office and of the Hydrographer of the Navy.

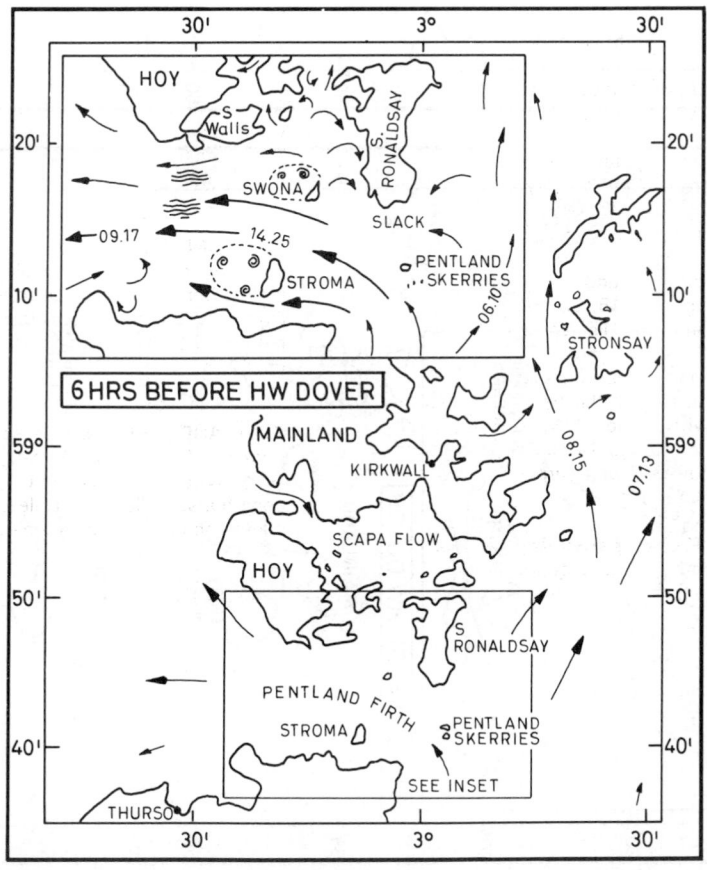

PENTLAND FIRTH TIDAL STREAMS

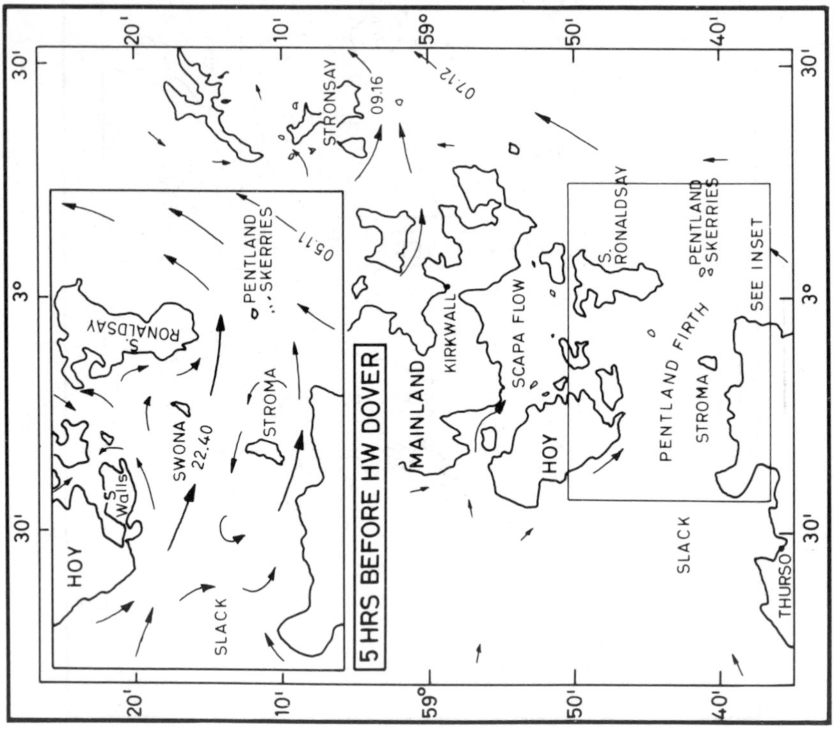

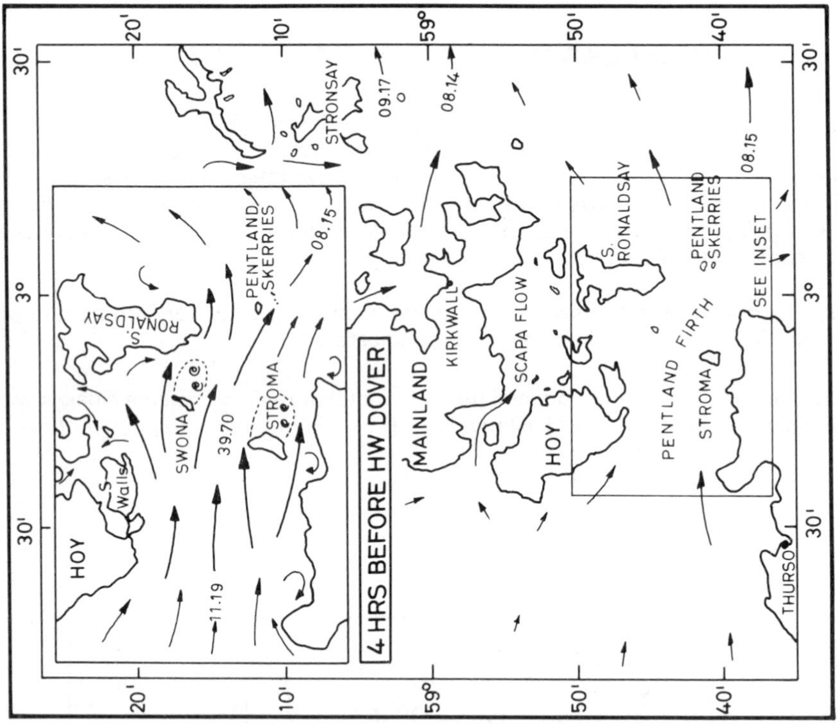

4 HRS BEFORE HW DOVER

5 HRS BEFORE HW DOVER

PENTLAND FIRTH TIDAL STREAMS

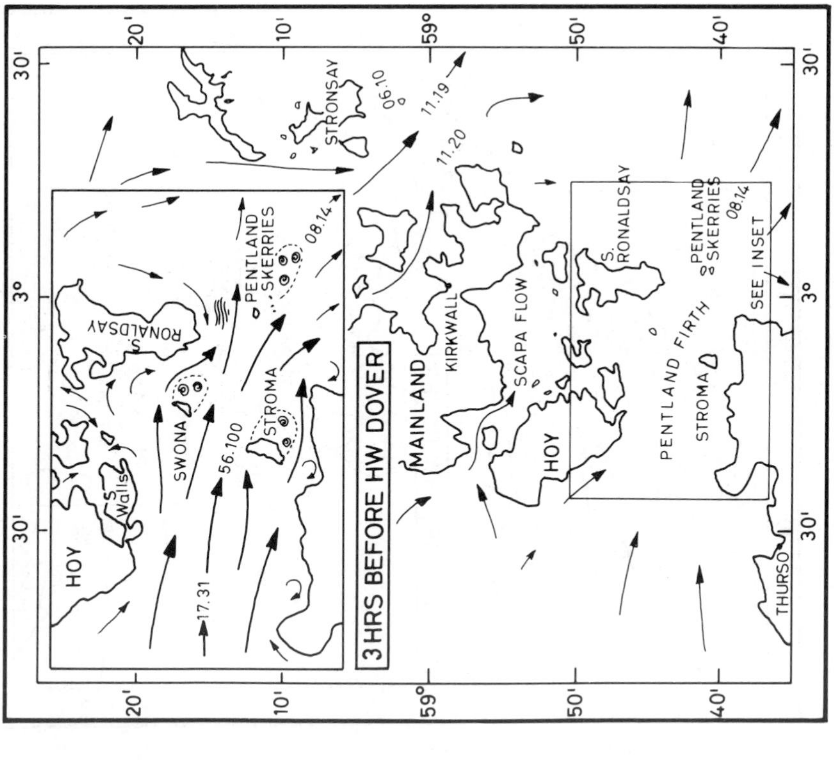

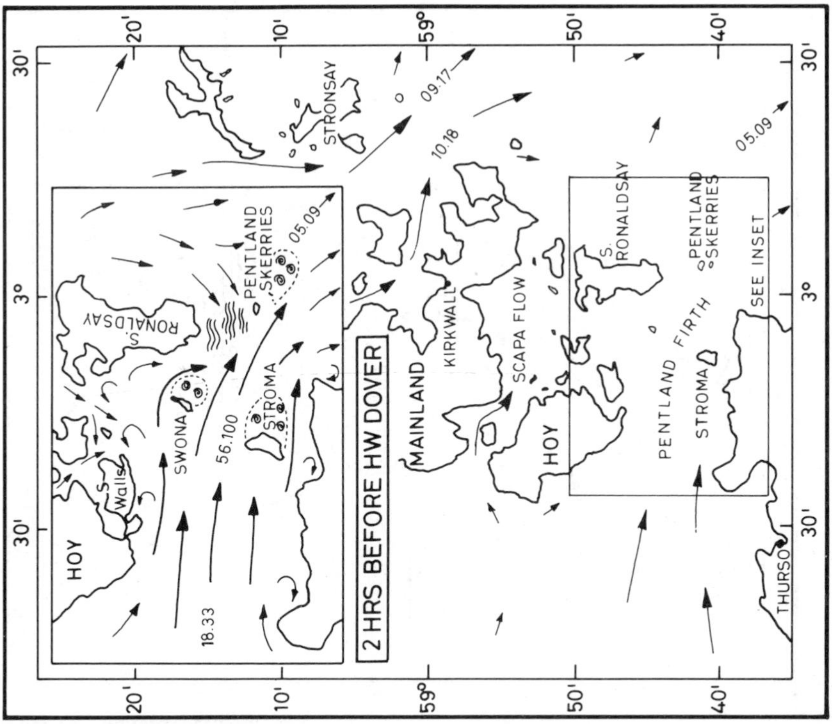

2 HRS BEFORE HW DOVER

3 HRS BEFORE HW DOVER

PENTLAND FIRTH TIDAL STREAMS

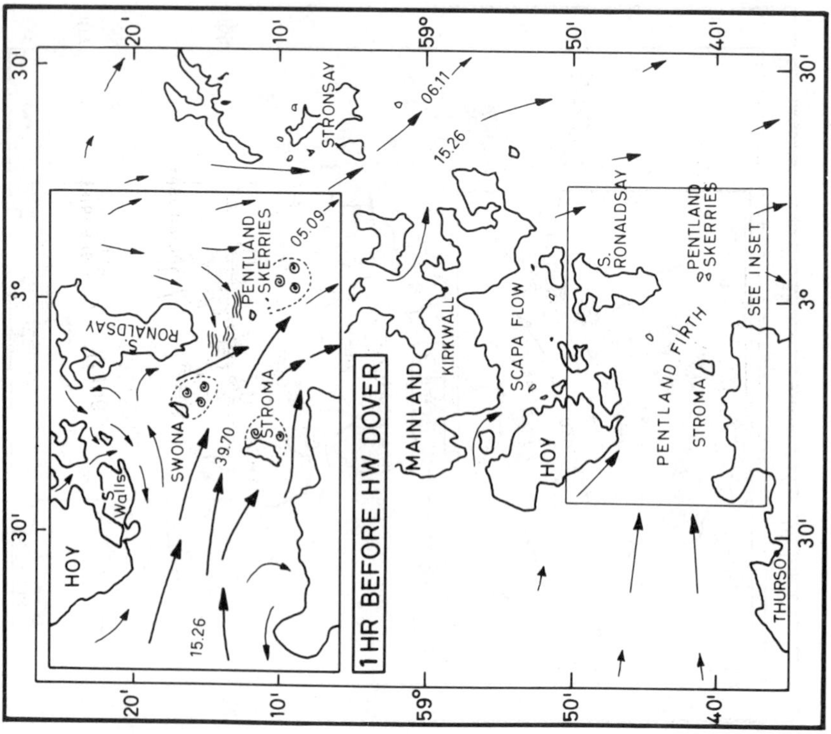

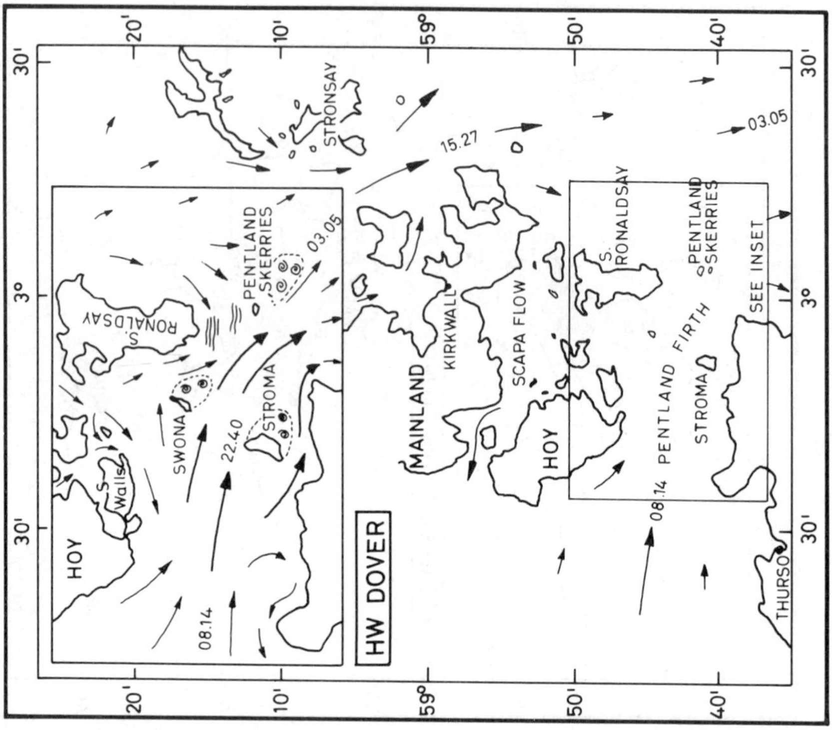

PENTLAND FIRTH TIDAL STREAMS

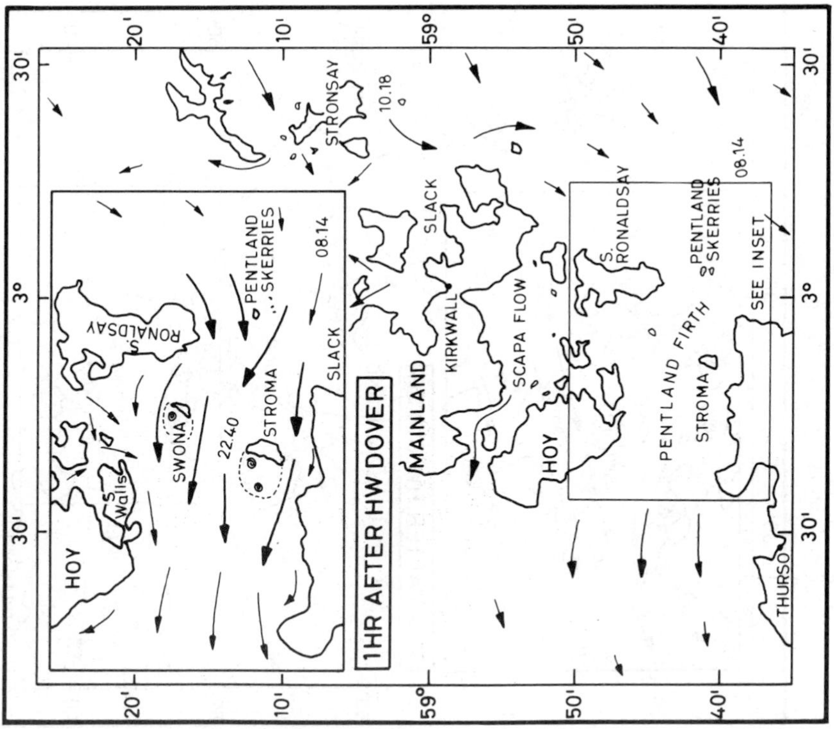

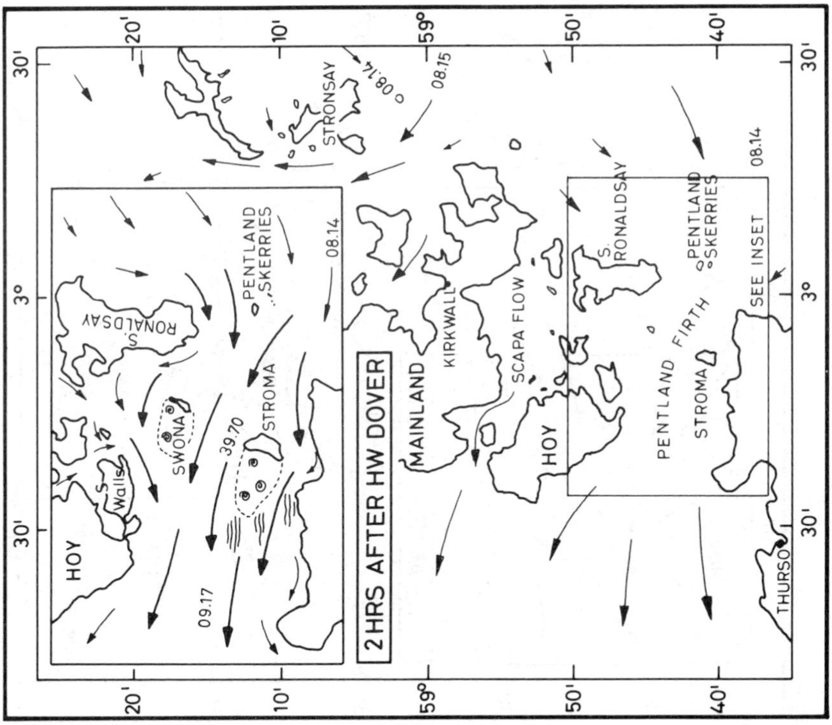

PENTLAND FIRTH TIDAL STREAMS

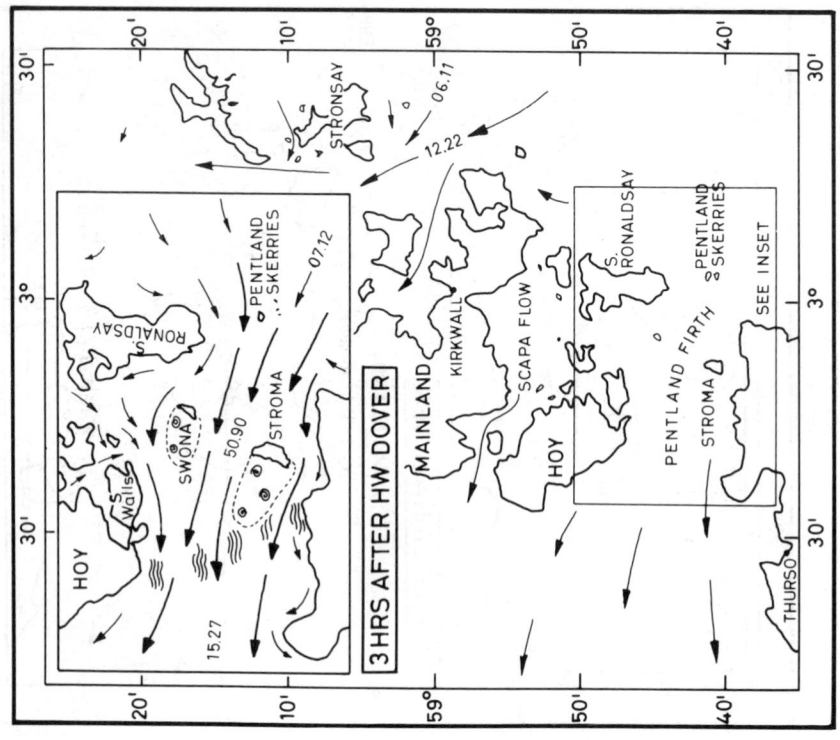

PENTLAND FIRTH TIDAL STREAMS

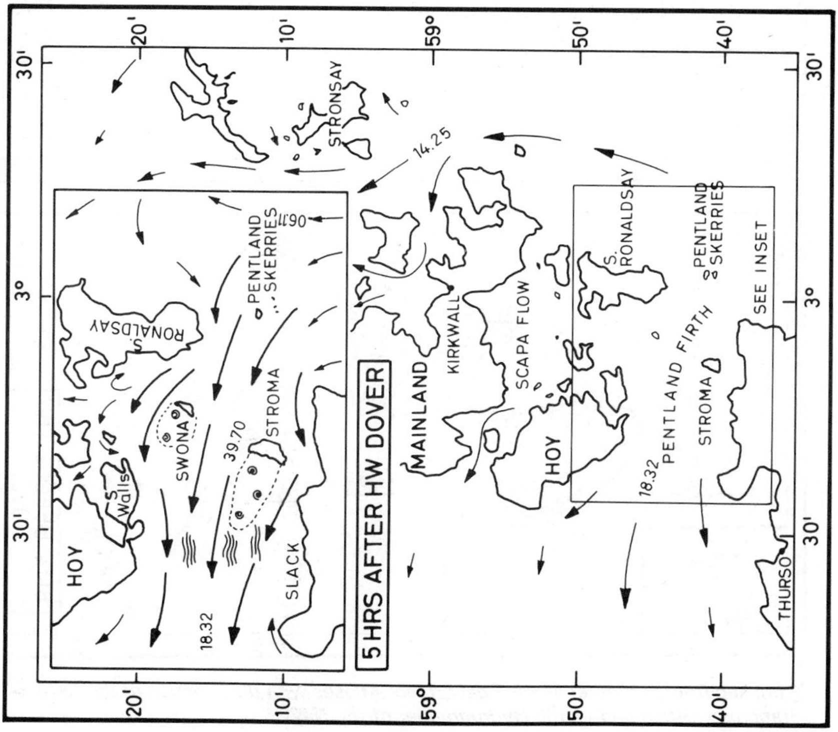

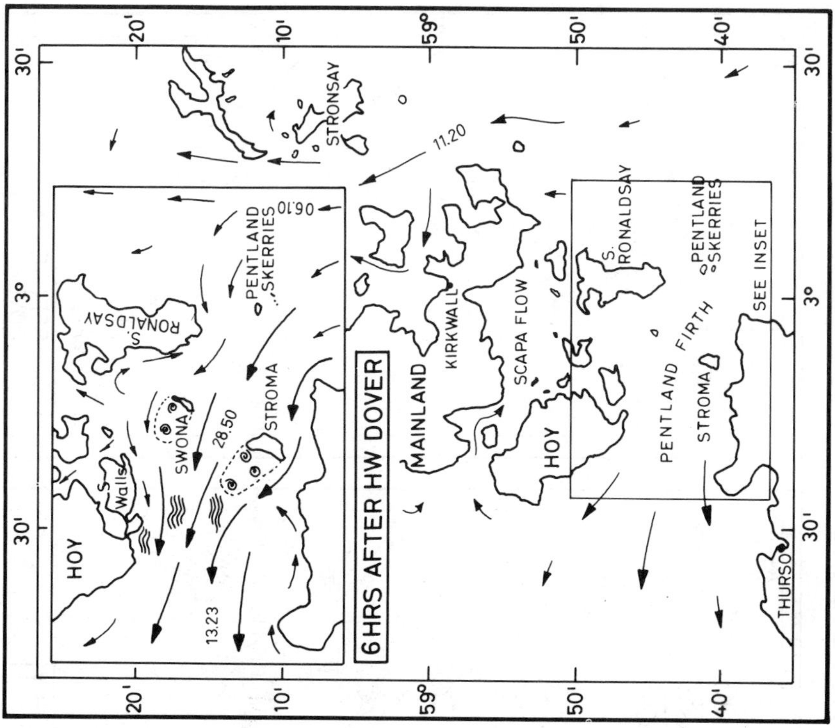

WEST COAST OF SCOTLAND

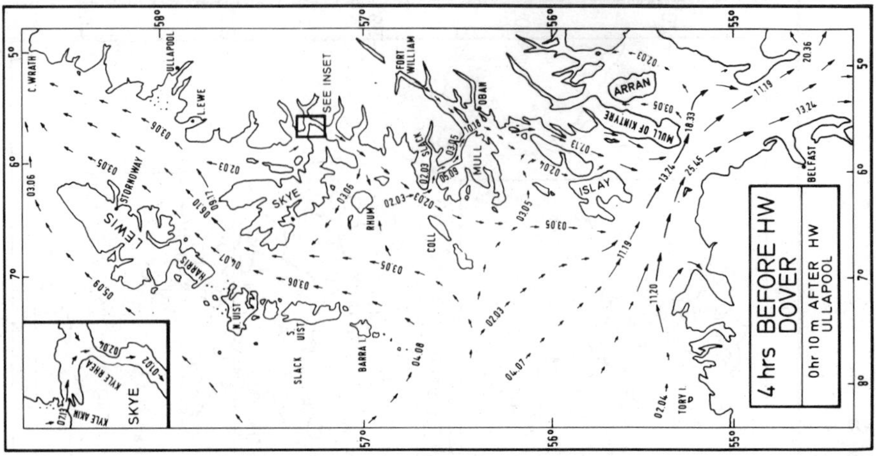

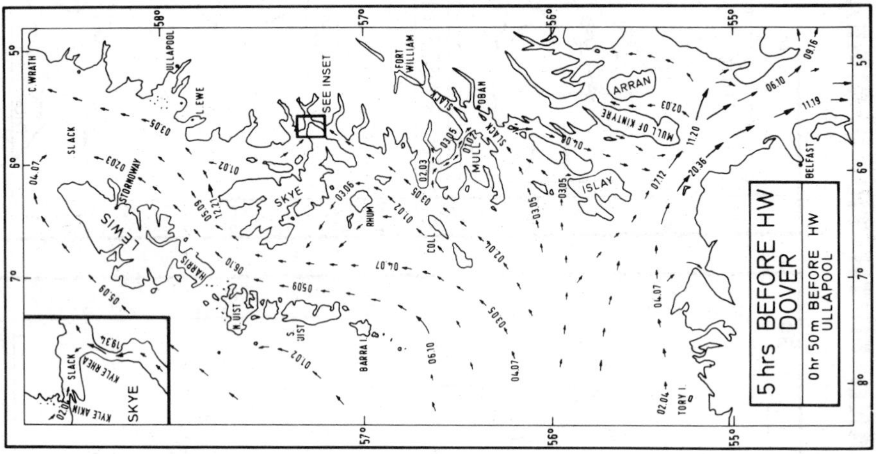

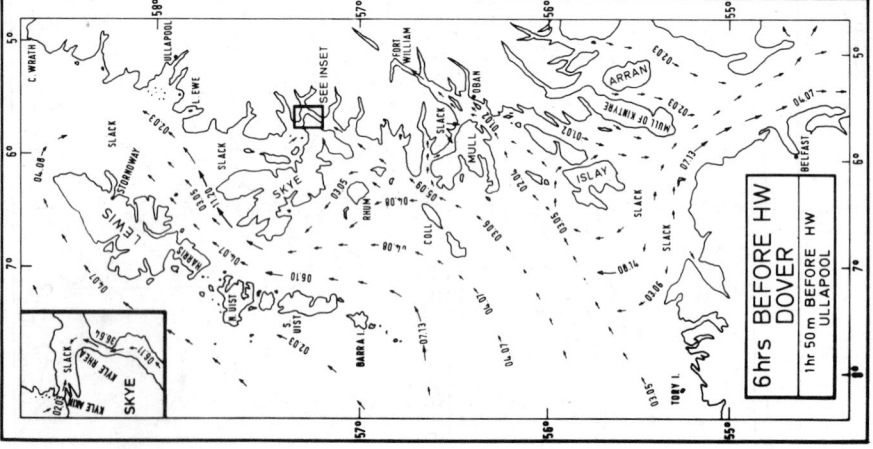

Produced from portion(s) of BA Tidal Stream Atlases with the sanction of the Controller, H.M. Stationery Office and of the Hydrographer of the Navy.

WEST COAST OF SCOTLAND

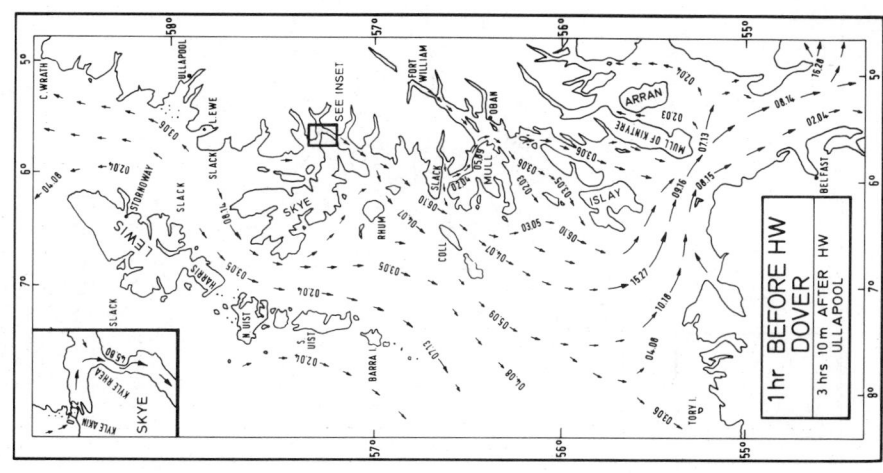

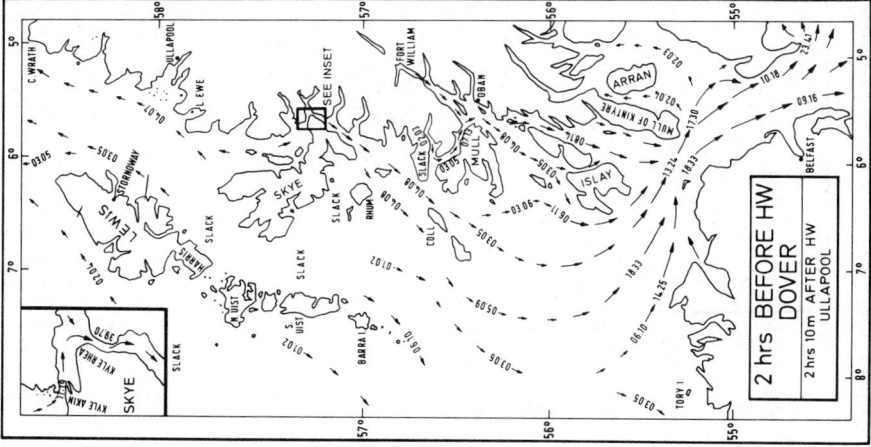

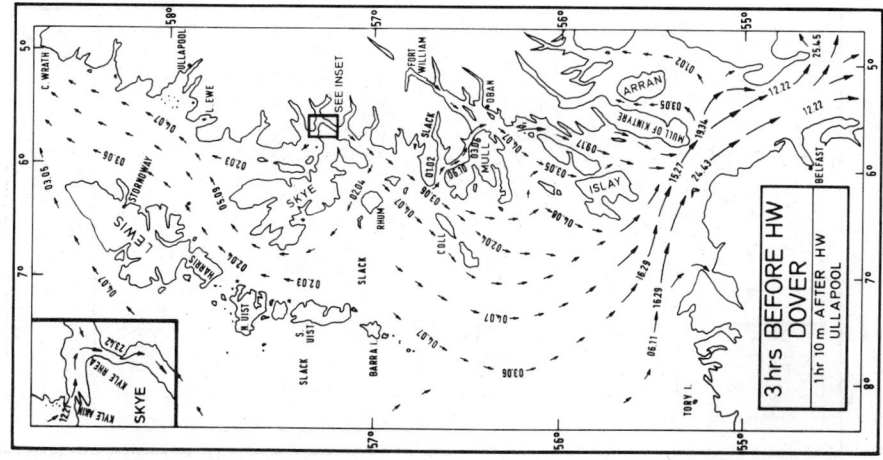

WEST COAST OF SCOTLAND

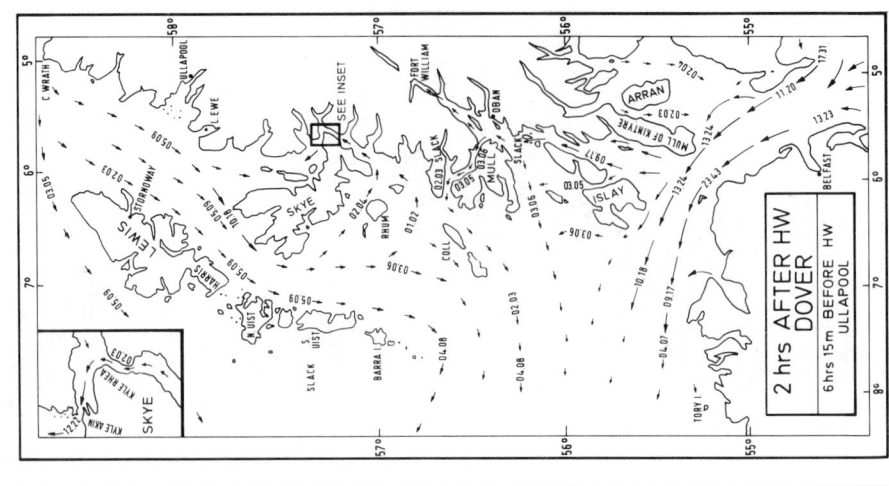

2 hrs AFTER HW DOVER
6 hrs 15m BEFORE HW ULLAPOOL

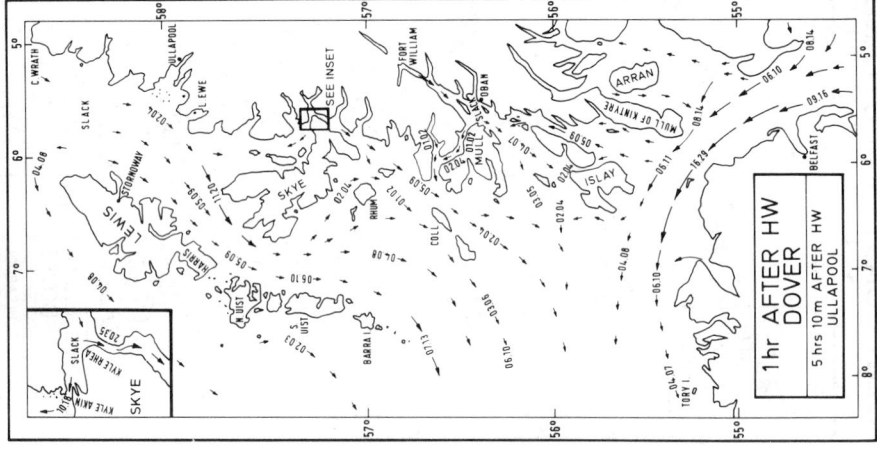

1hr AFTER HW DOVER
5 hrs 10m AFTER HW ULLAPOOL

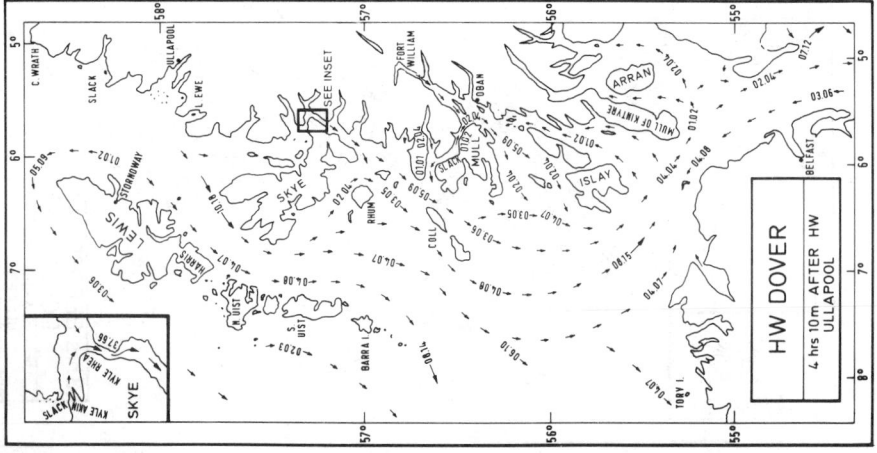

HW DOVER
4 hrs 10m AFTER HW ULLAPOOL

WEST COAST OF SCOTLAND

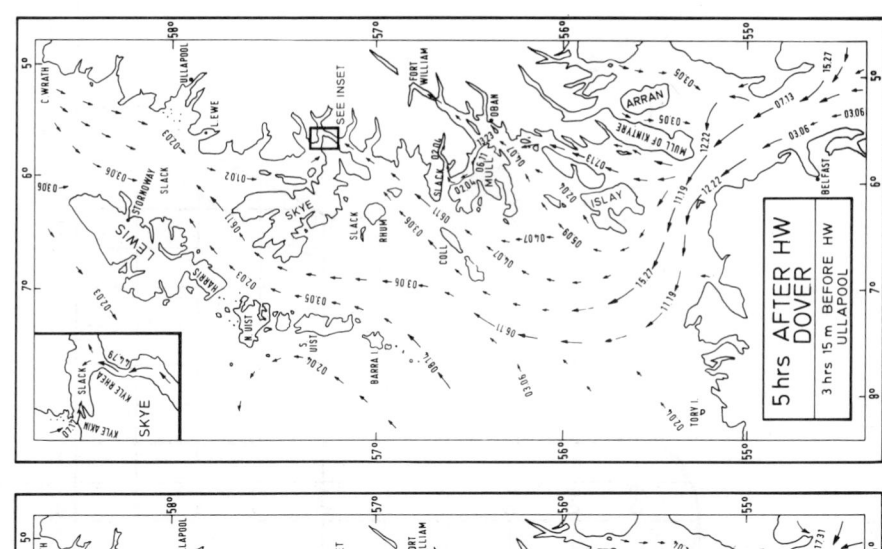

5 hrs AFTER HW DOVER

3 hrs 15 m BEFORE HW ULLAPOOL

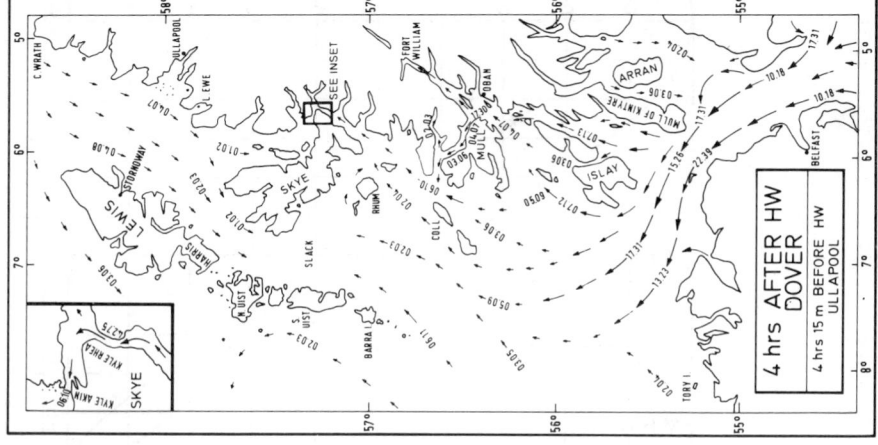

4 hrs AFTER HW DOVER

4 hrs 15 m BEFORE HW ULLAPOOL

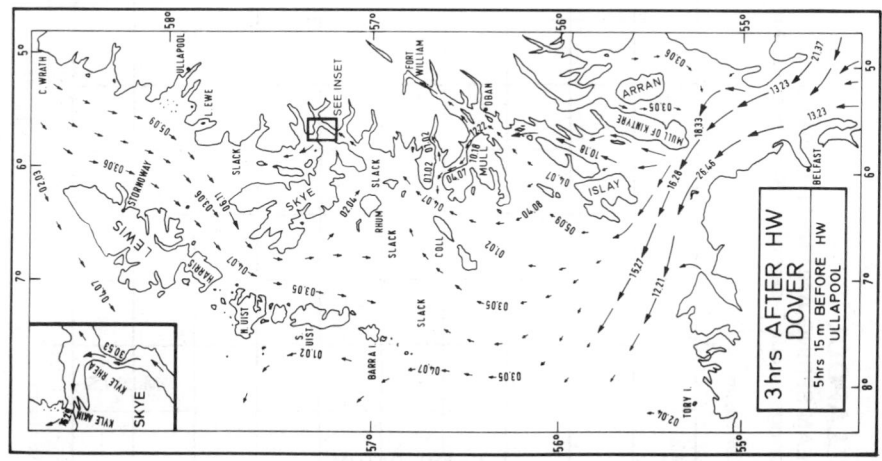

3 hrs AFTER HW DOVER

5 hrs 15 m BEFORE HW ULLAPOOL

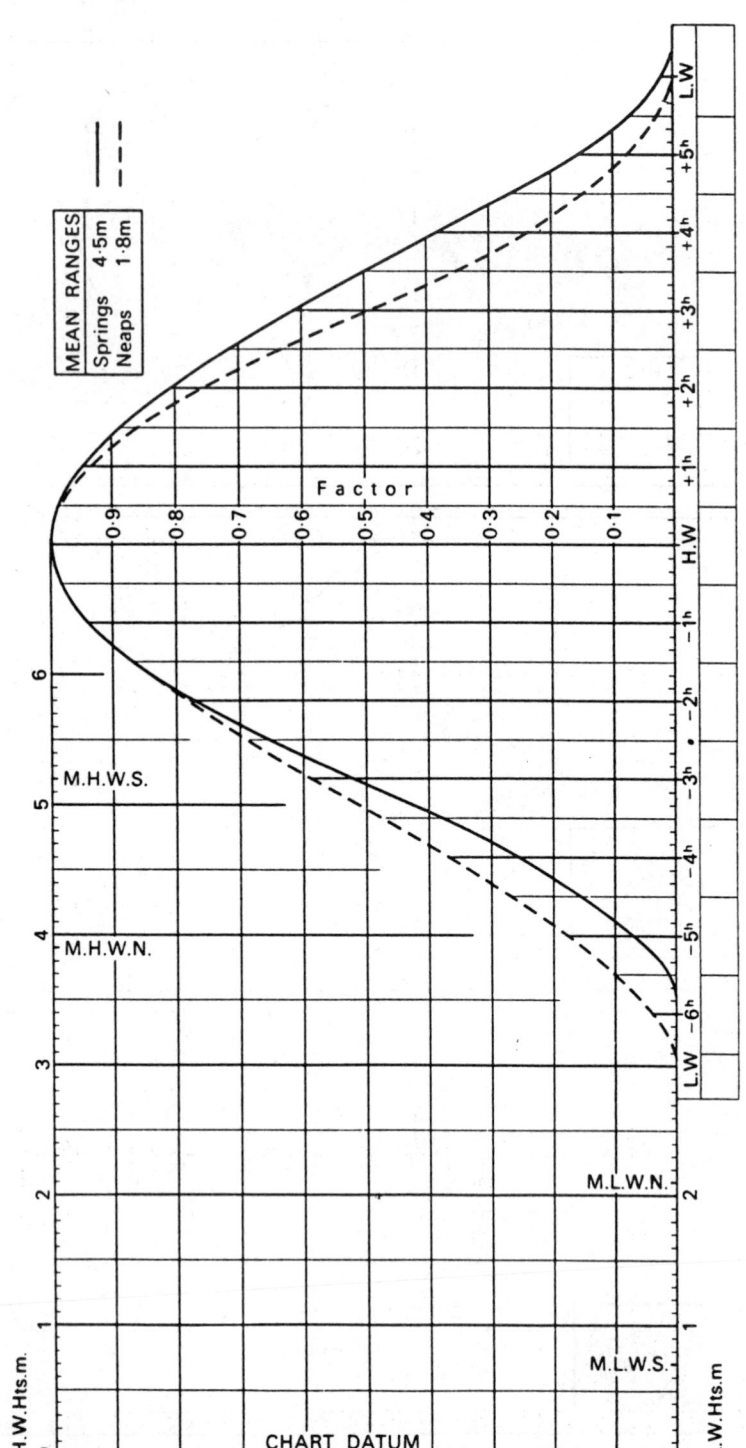

ULLAPOOL

MEAN SPRING AND NEAP CURVES

Springs occur 1 day after New and Full Moon.

MEAN RANGES

Springs	4·5m
Neaps	1·8m

ULLAPOOL WESTERN ISLES 21:125

Lat. 57°54′N. Long. 5°10′W. HIGH & LOW WATER 1992

GMT   ADD 1 HOUR MARCH 29 — OCTOBER 25 FOR B.S.T.

JANUARY

Day	Time	m	Day	Time	m
1 W	0435 / 1049 / 1704 / 2315	4.2 / 1.9 / 4.2 / 1.7	**16** TH	0342 / 1000 / 1608 / 2223	4.2 / 2.0 / 4.4 / 1.7
2 TH	0521 / 1141 / 1748 / 2358	4.4 / 1.7 / 4.2 / 1.6	**17** F	0439 / 1106 / 1705 / 2322	4.5 / 1.6 / 4.6 / 1.4
3 F	0600 / 1223 / 1826	4.6 / 1.5 / 4.3	**18** SA	0529 / 1200 / 1756	4.9 / 1.1 / 4.9
4 SA	0036 / 0635 / 1301 / ● 1858	1.5 / 4.7 / 1.4 / 4.4	**19** SU	0013 / 0615 / 1249 / O 1843	1.1 / 5.2 / 0.7 / 5.1
5 SU	0112 / 0708 / 1336 / 1930	1.4 / 4.9 / 1.3 / 4.5	**20** M	0101 / 0700 / 1335 / 1929	0.8 / 5.4 / 0.4 / 5.2
6 M	0146 / 0741 / 1410 / 2002	1.3 / 5.0 / 1.2 / 4.5	**21** TU	0146 / 0744 / 1419 / 2015	0.6 / 5.6 / 0.2 / 5.3
7 TU	0219 / 0813 / 1444 / 2035	1.3 / 5.0 / 1.1 / 4.5	**22** W	0229 / 0828 / 1503 / 2100	0.5 / 5.5 / 0.2 / 5.1
8 W	0253 / 0847 / 1517 / 2108	1.5 / 5.0 / 1.2 / 4.5	**23** TH	0313 / 0912 / 1547 / 2146	0.6 / 5.4 / 0.3 / 4.9
9 TH	0327 / 0920 / 1552 / 2143	1.4 / 4.8 / 1.2 / 4.4	**24** F	0356 / 0957 / 1632 / 2234	0.8 / 5.1 / 0.6 / 4.6
10 F	0402 / 0956 / 1628 / 2221	1.5 / 4.7 / 1.4 / 4.2	**25** SA	0441 / 1046 / 1719 / 2330	1.1 / 4.7 / 1.0 / 4.3
11 SA	0440 / 1034 / 1707 / 2304	1.7 / 4.5 / 1.5 / 4.1	**26** SU	0528 / 1146 / 1809	1.4 / 4.3 / 1.4
12 SU	0521 / 1120 / 1751 / 2358	1.9 / 4.3 / 1.7 / 4.0	**27** M	0038 / 0620 / 1310 / 1909	4.0 / 1.8 / 4.0 / 1.8
13 M	0610 / 1221 / 1844	2.1 / 4.1 / 1.9	**28** TU	0159 / 0729 / 1440 / 2028	3.9 / 2.1 / 3.8 / 2.1
14 TU	0111 / 0712 / 1341 / 1949	3.9 / 2.2 / 4.1 / 2.0	**29** W	0313 / 0911 / 1553 / 2156	3.9 / 2.0 / 3.8 / 2.1
15 W	0233 / 0834 / 1501 / 2109	4.0 / 2.2 / 4.1 / 1.9	**30** TH	0414 / 1041 / 1651 / 2301	4.0 / 2.0 / 3.9 / 2.0
			31 F	0503 / 1136 / 1736 / 2346	4.2 / 1.9 / 4.0 / 1.8

FEBRUARY

Day	Time	m	Day	Time	m
1 SA	0543 / 1215 / 1812	4.4 / 1.6 / 4.2	**16** SU	0513 / 1149 / 1743	4.8 / 1.0 / 4.8
2 SU	0023 / 0617 / 1249 / 1843	1.6 / 4.7 / 1.4 / 4.4	**17** M	0000 / 0559 / 1236 / 1828	1.1 / 5.2 / 0.5 / 5.1
3 M	0057 / 0649 / 1320 / ● 1912	1.4 / 4.9 / 1.2 / 4.5	**18** TU	0046 / 0643 / 1319 / O 1911	0.7 / 5.4 / 0.2 / 5.3
4 TU	0128 / 0719 / 1350 / 1941	1.2 / 5.0 / 1.0 / 4.6	**19** W	0129 / 0725 / 1400 / 1953	0.4 / 5.6 / 0.0 / 5.3
5 W	0159 / 0749 / 1420 / 2010	1.1 / 5.1 / 0.9 / 4.7	**20** TH	0210 / 0806 / 1441 / 2034	0.3 / 5.5 / 0.0 / 5.2
6 TH	0230 / 0819 / 1451 / 2039	1.1 / 5.1 / 0.9 / 4.7	**21** F	0251 / 0846 / 1522 / 2115	0.4 / 5.3 / 0.2 / 5.0
7 F	0302 / 0850 / 1523 / 2110	1.2 / 5.0 / 0.9 / 4.6	**22** SA	0331 / 0927 / 1602 / 2157	0.6 / 5.0 / 0.6 / 4.7
8 SA	0335 / 0922 / 1556 / 2142	1.2 / 4.9 / 1.1 / 4.5	**23** SU	0412 / 1010 / 1644 / 2243	0.9 / 4.6 / 1.0 / 4.3
9 SU	0410 / 0956 / 1632 / 2218	1.4 / 4.7 / 1.3 / 4.3	**24** M	0455 / 1059 / 1728 / 2343	1.3 / 4.2 / 1.5 / 4.0
10 M	0448 / 1037 / 1713 / 2303	1.6 / 4.4 / 1.5 / 4.1	**25** TU	0543 / 1223 / 1819	1.8 / 3.8 / 2.0
11 TU	0533 / 1132 / 1801	1.9 / 4.2 / 1.8	**26** W	0113 / 0645 / 1412 / 1935	3.8 / 2.2 / 3.6 / 2.3
12 W	0012 / 0631 / 1304 / 1903	4.0 / 2.1 / 4.0 / 2.0	**27** TH	0238 / 0840 / 1530 / 2129	3.8 / 2.4 / 3.6 / 2.3
13 TH	0156 / 0756 / 1442 / 2031	3.9 / 2.2 / 4.0 / 2.1	**28** F	0345 / 1029 / 1630 / 2243	3.9 / 2.2 / 3.7 / 2.1
14 F	0319 / 0941 / 1555 / 2204	4.1 / 2.0 / 4.2 / 1.9	**29** SA	0437 / 1120 / 1715 / 2327	4.1 / 1.9 / 3.9 / 1.9
15 SA	0421 / 1055 / 1653 / 2309	4.5 / 1.5 / 4.5 / 1.5			

MARCH

Day	Time	m	Day	Time	m
1 SU	0517 / 1155 / 1749	4.4 / 1.6 / 4.2	**16** M	0454 / 1131 / 1725 / 2343	4.8 / 0.8 / 4.8 / 1.0
2 M	0002 / 0551 / 1225 / 1818	1.6 / 4.6 / 1.3 / 4.4	**17** TU	0540 / 1215 / 1808	5.1 / 0.4 / 5.0
3 TU	0034 / 0622 / 1254 / 1845	1.3 / 4.8 / 1.0 / 4.6	**18** W	0026 / 0622 / 1257 / O 1849	0.6 / 5.3 / 0.2 / 5.2
4 W	0104 / 0651 / 1322 / 1912	1.1 / 5.0 / 0.9 / 4.7	**19** TH	0108 / 0703 / 1337 / 1928	0.4 / 5.4 / 0.1 / 5.2
5 TH	0133 / 0720 / 1351 / 1940	1.0 / 5.1 / 0.7 / 4.8	**20** F	0148 / 0742 / 1416 / 2006	0.3 / 5.3 / 0.1 / 5.1
6 F	0204 / 0750 / 1421 / 2008	0.9 / 5.1 / 0.7 / 4.8	**21** SA	0227 / 0821 / 1454 / 2044	0.4 / 5.1 / 0.4 / 4.9
7 SA	0235 / 0820 / 1453 / 2038	0.9 / 5.0 / 0.8 / 4.8	**22** SU	0306 / 0859 / 1532 / 2123	0.6 / 4.8 / 0.7 / 4.7
8 SU	0309 / 0852 / 1527 / 2109	1.0 / 4.9 / 0.9 / 4.7	**23** M	0346 / 0939 / 1611 / 2204	0.9 / 4.4 / 1.2 / 4.4
9 M	0344 / 0927 / 1603 / 2145	1.2 / 4.7 / 1.2 / 4.5	**24** TU	0427 / 1025 / 1651 / 2257	1.3 / 4.0 / 1.6 / 4.0
10 TU	0424 / 1010 / 1644 / 2229	1.4 / 4.4 / 1.5 / 4.3	**25** W	0513 / 1141 / 1739	1.8 / 3.7 / 2.0
11 W	0510 / 1111 / 1733 / 2340	1.7 / 4.1 / 1.8 / 4.0	**26** TH	0022 / 0612 / 1335 / 1846	3.8 / 2.1 / 3.5 / 2.4
12 TH	0610 / 1256 / 1837	1.9 / 3.9 / 2.1	**27** F	0154 / 0756 / 1455 / 2044	3.7 / 2.3 / 3.5 / 2.4
13 F	0135 / 0740 / 1432 / 2011	3.9 / 2.0 / 4.0 / 2.1	**28** SA	0304 / 0951 / 1555 / 2208	3.8 / 2.1 / 3.7 / 2.2
14 SA	0300 / 0928 / 1541 / 2148	4.1 / 1.8 / 4.2 / 1.9	**29** SU	0358 / 1044 / 1640 / 2255	4.0 / 1.9 / 3.9 / 1.9
15 SU	0402 / 1039 / 1636 / 2253	4.4 / 1.3 / 4.5 / 1.5	**30** M	0441 / 1120 / 1715 / 2331	4.2 / 1.6 / 4.1 / 1.6
			31 TU	0517 / 1150 / 1745	4.5 / 1.3 / 4.4

APRIL

Day	Time	m	Day	Time	m
1 W	0003 / 0548 / 1220 / 1812	1.4 / 4.7 / 1.0 / 4.6	**16** TH	0005 / 0602 / 1234 / 1826	0.7 / 5.0 / 0.4 / 5.0
2 TH	0034 / 0619 / 1249 / 1841	1.1 / 4.8 / 0.8 / 4.8	**17** F	0046 / 0642 / 1313 / O 1904	0.6 / 5.1 / 0.3 / 5.0
3 F	0105 / 0650 / 1320 / ● 1910	1.0 / 5.0 / 0.7 / 4.9	**18** SA	0126 / 0721 / 1351 / 1941	0.5 / 5.0 / 0.4 / 5.0
4 SA	0137 / 0722 / 1352 / 1940	0.9 / 5.0 / 0.7 / 4.9	**19** SU	0205 / 0800 / 1428 / 2018	0.6 / 4.8 / 0.7 / 4.9
5 SU	0211 / 0755 / 1426 / 2012	0.9 / 5.0 / 0.8 / 4.9	**20** M	0244 / 0838 / 1506 / 2057	0.8 / 4.6 / 1.0 / 4.7
6 M	0247 / 0832 / 1502 / 2047	0.9 / 4.9 / 0.9 / 4.8	**21** TU	0324 / 0918 / 1543 / 2138	1.0 / 4.3 / 1.3 / 4.4
7 TU	0325 / 0912 / 1542 / 2127	1.1 / 4.6 / 1.2 / 4.6	**22** W	0405 / 1005 / 1624 / 2227	1.4 / 4.0 / 1.7 / 4.2
8 W	0409 / 1003 / 1626 / 2217	1.3 / 4.4 / 1.5 / 4.3	**23** TH	0451 / 1111 / 1709 / 2335	1.7 / 3.7 / 2.0 / 3.9
9 TH	0500 / 1117 / 1718 / 2337	1.5 / 4.1 / 1.8 / 4.1	**24** F	0546 / 1243 / 1809	2.0 / 3.5 / 2.2
10 F	0604 / 1254 / 1825	1.7 / 3.9 / 2.0	**25** SA	0058 / 0703 / 1402 / 1936	3.8 / 2.1 / 3.5 / 2.4
11 SA	0119 / 0732 / 1416 / 1955	4.0 / 1.8 / 4.0 / 2.0	**26** SU	0210 / 0838 / 1504 / 2108	3.8 / 2.1 / 3.7 / 2.2
12 SU	0237 / 0906 / 1521 / 2125	4.2 / 1.6 / 4.2 / 1.8	**27** M	0308 / 0946 / 1552 / 2207	3.9 / 1.9 / 3.8 / 2.0
13 M	0339 / 1015 / 1616 / 2230	4.4 / 1.2 / 4.4 / 1.4	**28** TU	0355 / 1031 / 1632 / 2250	4.1 / 1.6 / 4.1 / 1.7
14 TU	0432 / 1107 / 1703 / 2320	4.7 / 0.8 / 4.7 / 1.0	**29** W	0436 / 1107 / 1706 / 2326	4.3 / 1.4 / 4.3 / 1.5
15 W	0519 / 1152 / 1746	4.9 / 0.5 / 4.9	**30** TH	0512 / 1141 / 1738	4.5 / 1.2 / 4.5

To find H.W. Dover add 4 h. 10 min.

TIDAL DIFFERENCES PAGE 21:128. TIDAL CURVE PAGE 21:124.

Datum of predictions: 2.75 m. below Ordnance Datum (Newlyn) or approx. L.A.T.

WESTERN ISLES **ULLAPOOL**

HIGH & LOW WATER 1992   Lat. 57°54'N. Long. 5°10'W.

GMT   ADD 1 HOUR MARCH 29 — OCTOBER 25 FOR B.S.T.

MAY

Day	Time	m		Day	Time	m
1	0001	1.3		**16**	0027	0.9
	0547	4.7			0628	4.7
F	1216	1.0			1251	0.7
	1810	4.7		O	1845	4.8
2	0036	1.1		**17**	0109	0.8
	0623	4.8			0707	4.7
SA	1250	0.9		SU	1330	0.8
●	1843	4.9			1923	4.9
3	0113	0.9		**18**	0149	0.8
	0700	4.9			0746	4.6
SU	1327	0.8		M	1407	1.0
	1918	5.0			2000	4.8
4	0151	0.8		**19**	0228	0.9
	0739	4.9			0825	4.4
M	1405	0.8		TU	1445	1.1
	1955	5.0			2039	4.7
5	0231	0.8		**20**	0308	1.1
	0822	4.8			0905	4.2
TU	1445	0.9		W	1523	1.4
	2036	4.9			2119	4.5
6	0315	0.9		**21**	0348	1.3
	0911	4.7			0949	4.0
W	1529	1.1		TH	1602	1.6
	2123	4.7			2204	4.4
7	0402	1.1		**22**	0431	1.5
	1008	4.4			1040	3.9
TH	1617	1.4		F	1645	1.8
	2220	4.5			2256	4.2
8	0456	1.2		**23**	0519	1.7
	1120	4.2			1142	3.7
F	1711	1.6		SA	1734	2.0
	2334	4.3			2356	4.0
9	0600	1.4		**24**	0613	1.9
	1239	4.1			1251	3.6
SA	1815	1.8		SU	1834	2.2
10	0056	4.2		**25**	0102	3.9
	0715	1.5			0717	1.9
SU	1352	4.1		M	1357	3.7
	1932	1.8			1946	2.2
11	0211	4.2		**26**	0206	3.9
	0835	1.4			0826	1.9
M	1456	4.2		TU	1454	3.8
	2053	1.7			2058	2.1
12	0315	4.4		**27**	0302	4.0
	0944	1.2			0927	1.8
TU	1552	4.3		W	1543	4.0
	2201	1.5			2157	1.9
13	0411	4.5		**28**	0352	4.2
	1040	1.0			1018	1.6
W	1642	4.5		TH	1626	4.2
	2256	1.2			2246	1.7
14	0501	4.6		**29**	0437	4.3
	1128	0.8			1102	1.4
TH	1726	4.7		F	1706	4.4
	2344	1.0			2330	1.5
15	0546	4.7		**30**	0520	4.5
	1211	0.7			1144	1.2
F	1807	4.8		SA	1745	4.7
				31	0012	1.2
					0603	4.7
				SU	1226	1.0
					1824	4.9

JUNE

Day	Time	m		Day	Time	m
1	0054	1.0		**16**	0137	1.0
	0646	4.9			0737	4.4
M	1308	0.9		TU	1352	1.2
●	1904	5.0			1947	4.8
2	0137	0.8		**17**	0215	1.0
	0731	4.9			0812	4.4
TU	1350	0.9		W	1428	1.2
	1947	5.1			2023	4.8
3	0221	0.7		**18**	0253	1.1
	0818	4.9			0848	4.4
W	1434	0.9		TH	1504	1.3
	2032	5.1			2059	4.7
4	0307	0.7		**19**	0330	1.1
	0909	4.8			0925	4.3
TH	1520	1.0		F	1541	1.4
	2120	5.0			2137	4.6
5	0356	0.7		**20**	0407	1.3
	1003	4.6			1004	4.1
F	1608	1.1		SA	1619	1.5
	2214	4.8			2218	4.4
6	0448	0.9		**21**	0446	1.4
	1104	4.4			1047	4.0
SA	1700	1.3		SU	1659	1.7
	2316	4.6			2302	4.3
7	0544	1.0		**22**	0528	1.6
	1210	4.3			1137	3.9
SU	1757	1.5		M	1744	1.9
					2353	4.1
8	0026	4.4		**23**	0615	1.8
	0646	1.2			1236	3.8
M	1320	4.1		TU	1836	2.1
	1901	1.6				
9	0140	4.2		**24**	0054	4.0
	0756	1.3			0709	1.9
TU	1426	4.1		W	1343	3.8
	2014	1.7			1939	2.2
10	0250	4.2		**25**	0203	3.9
	0908	1.4			0813	1.9
W	1528	4.2		TH	1449	3.9
	2129	1.7			2054	2.1
11	0353	4.2		**26**	0308	4.0
	1012	1.3			0923	1.9
TH	1622	4.3		F	1547	4.1
	2234	1.5			2205	2.0
12	0449	4.3		**27**	0407	4.2
	1107	1.3			1026	1.7
F	1711	4.4		SA	1638	4.3
	2328	1.3			2303	1.7
13	0538	4.4		**28**	0500	4.4
	1153	1.2			1119	1.5
SA	1754	4.6		SU	1725	4.6
					2354	1.3
14	0015	1.2		**29**	0550	4.7
	0621	4.4			1208	1.2
SU	1236	1.2		M	1810	4.9
	1833	4.7				
15	0058	1.1		**30**	0041	1.0
	0700	4.4			0636	4.9
M	1315	1.1		TU	1254	1.0
O	1911	4.8		●	1853	5.1

JULY

Day	Time	m		Day	Time	m
1	0126	0.7		**16**	0200	1.0
	0722	5.1			0754	4.5
W	1339	0.8		TH	1410	1.1
	1937	5.3			2003	4.9
2	0211	0.5		**17**	0233	1.0
	0809	5.1			0824	4.6
TH	1423	0.7		F	1443	1.1
	2022	5.3			2035	4.9
3	0256	0.3		**18**	0305	1.0
	0856	5.1			0855	4.5
F	1508	0.7		SA	1516	1.2
	2108	5.3			2107	4.9
4	0342	0.4		**19**	0338	1.0
	0944	4.9			0927	4.5
SA	1553	0.8		SU	1549	1.3
	2156	5.1			2141	4.7
5	0430	0.5		**20**	0411	1.2
	1036	4.7			1001	4.3
SU	1640	1.0		M	1624	1.5
	2248	4.8			2216	4.5
6	0519	0.8		**21**	0447	1.4
	1133	4.4			1038	4.2
M	1730	1.2		TU	1701	1.7
	2349	4.5			2256	4.3
7	0613	1.1		**22**	0526	1.6
	1239	4.2			1122	4.0
TU	1826	1.5		W	1744	1.9
					2347	4.1
8	0104	4.2		**23**	0612	1.8
	0715	1.5			1224	3.9
W	1353	4.0		TH	1838	2.1
	1933	1.8				
9	0226	4.0		**24**	0102	3.9
	0829	1.7			0710	2.0
TH	1504	4.0		F	1352	3.8
	2056	1.9			1952	2.3
10	0340	4.0		**25**	0232	3.9
	0947	1.8			0829	2.1
F	1607	4.1		SA	1515	4.0
	2220	1.8			2128	2.1
11	0443	4.0		**26**	0346	4.1
	1051	1.7			0956	2.0
SA	1700	4.2		SU	1618	4.3
	2323	1.7			2245	1.8
12	0534	4.1		**27**	0446	4.4
	1144	1.6			1102	1.7
SU	1745	4.4		M	1709	4.6
					2341	1.3
13	0011	1.5		**28**	0537	4.7
	0616	4.3			1155	1.3
M	1226	1.4		TU	1756	5.0
	1823	4.6				
14	0051	1.3		**29**	0029	0.9
	0652	4.4			0623	5.0
TU	1303	1.3		W	1241	0.9
O	1858	4.8		●	1839	5.3
15	0127	1.1		**30**	0113	0.5
	0723	4.9			0707	5.2
W	1337	1.2		TH	1325	0.6
	1931	4.9			1922	5.5
				31	0157	0.2
					0751	5.3
				F	1408	0.4
					2004	5.6

AUGUST

Day	Time	m		Day	Time	m
1	0239	0.1		**16**	0236	0.8
	0834	5.3			0823	4.8
SA	1450	0.4		SU	1448	1.0
	2047	5.5			2036	5.0
2	0322	0.1		**17**	0306	0.9
	0917	5.1			0852	4.7
SU	1532	0.5		M	1519	1.1
	2131	5.3			2106	4.9
3	0405	0.4		**18**	0338	1.0
	1003	4.9			0921	4.6
M	1616	0.7		TU	1551	1.3
	2217	4.9			2137	4.7
4	0450	0.8		**19**	0411	1.3
	1052	4.5			0953	4.6
TU	1701	1.1		W	1626	1.5
	2310	4.5			2212	4.5
5	0538	1.2		**20**	0447	1.5
	1153	4.2			1029	4.2
W	1751	1.5		TH	1706	1.8
					2257	4.2
6	0025	4.1		**21**	0530	1.8
	0632	1.7			1121	4.0
TH	1315	3.9		F	1756	2.1
	1851	1.9				
7	0205	3.8		**22**	0014	3.9
	0746	2.0			0625	2.1
F	1440	3.8		SA	1302	3.8
	2025	2.2			1909	2.3
8	0329	3.8		**23**	0209	3.9
	0927	2.2			0747	2.3
SA	1551	3.9		SU	1450	4.0
	2217	2.1			2104	2.2
9	0435	3.9		**24**	0331	4.1
	1046	2.0			0934	2.1
SU	1647	4.1		M	1559	4.3
	2322	1.8			2231	1.8
10	0526	4.0		**25**	0431	4.4
	1136	1.8			1047	1.7
M	1732	4.4		TU	1652	4.7
					2327	1.2
11	0004	1.6		**26**	0521	4.8
	0604	4.8			1139	1.2
TU	1214	1.6		W	1738	5.1
	1808	4.6				
12	0038	1.3		**27**	0013	0.7
	0635	4.8			0605	5.1
W	1247	1.3		TH	1225	0.8
	1839	4.8			1821	5.4
13	0109	1.1		**28**	0056	0.3
	0702	4.6			0647	5.6
TH	1318	1.1		F	1307	0.4
O	1908	5.0		●	1902	5.6
14	0138	0.9		**29**	0137	0.0
	0729	4.7			0728	5.5
F	1348	1.0		SA	1348	0.2
	1937	5.1			1943	5.7
15	0207	0.8		**30**	0217	0.0
	0756	4.8			0808	5.4
SA	1417	1.0		SU	1428	0.2
	2006	5.1			2023	5.6
				31	0257	0.1
					0849	5.3
				M	1508	0.4
					2104	5.3

ULLAPOOL WESTERN ISLES 21:127

Lat. 57°54′N. Long. 5°10′W.

HIGH & LOW WATER 1992

GMT   ADD 1 HOUR MARCH 29 — OCTOBER 25 FOR B.S.T.

	SEPTEMBER				OCTOBER				NOVEMBER				DECEMBER		
	Time	m	Time	m	Time	m	Time	m	Time	m	Time	m	Time	m	Time	m
1 TU	0338 0930 1549 2146	0.4 5.0 0.7 4.9	**16** W	0307 0849 1524 2107	1.0 4.8 1.2 4.8	**1** TH	0351 0942 1607 2205	1.1 4.7 1.2 4.3	**16** F	0319 0902 1544 2133	1.3 4.8 1.4 4.6	**1** SU	0452 1108 1727	2.0 4.2 2.0	**16** M	0439 1045 1723 2348	1.6 4.5 1.5 4.2	**1** TU	0514 1128 1752	2.0 4.2 1.9	**16** W	0521 1137 1808	1.5 4.6 1.3
2 W	0419 1013 1632 2233	0.9 4.6 1.1 4.4	**17** TH	0341 0920 1600 2144	1.2 4.6 1.5 4.6	**2** F	0432 1031 1653 2309	1.5 4.3 1.7 3.9	**17** SA	0400 0944 1630 2230	1.5 4.6 1.6 4.3	**2** M	0008 0547 1230 1837	3.7 2.3 4.0 2.2	**17** TU	0537 1204 1831	1.8 4.4 1.6	**2** W	0019 0608 1235 1853	3.7 2.2 4.0 2.1	**17** TH	0034 0620 1253 1914	4.3 1.7 4.4 1.5
3 TH	0503 1107 1718 2343	1.4 4.2 1.6 4.0	**18** F	0418 0956 1641 2231	1.5 4.4 1.7 4.3	**3** SA	0519 1147 1749	2.0 4.0 2.1	**18** SU	0447 1044 1727 2359	1.8 4.3 1.9 4.1	**3** TU	0139 0706 1350 2014	3.6 2.5 3.9 2.3	**18** W	0107 0646 1328 1950	4.2 2.0 4.3 1.6	**3** TH	0134 0716 1345 2003	3.7 2.3 4.0 2.1	**18** F	0148 0730 1411 2028	4.2 1.8 4.3 1.5
4 F	0553 1232 1816	1.9 3.9 2.1	**19** SA	0502 1048 1734 2358	1.9 4.1 2.0 4.0	**4** SU	0104 0622 1329 1922	3.6 2.4 3.8 2.4	**19** M	0546 1224 1844	2.1 4.1 2.0	**4** W	0250 0844 1455 2132	3.7 2.4 4.0 2.1	**19** TH	0220 0807 1440 2107	4.2 1.9 4.4 1.5	**4** F	0241 0835 1448 2111	3.8 2.3 4.0 2.0	**19** SA	0256 0849 1522 2140	4.2 1.8 4.3 1.5
5 SA	0141 0703 1411 1956	3.7 2.3 3.8 2.4	**20** SU	0559 1235 1851	2.2 3.9 2.2	**5** M	0236 0816 1449 2132	3.6 2.5 3.9 2.3	**20** TU	0135 0707 1400 2023	4.0 2.2 4.2 1.9	**5** TH	0344 0952 1547 2221	3.9 2.2 4.1 1.9	**20** F	0322 0925 1542 2211	4.4 1.7 4.6 1.2	**5** SA	0335 0943 1542 2206	4.0 2.2 4.2 1.9	**20** SU	0357 1003 1623 2241	4.4 1.7 4.4 1.4
6 SU	0311 0904 1527 2210	3.7 2.4 3.9 2.2	**21** M	0154 0723 1427 2047	3.9 2.3 4.0 2.1	**6** TU	0343 0953 1549 2233	3.7 2.3 4.1 2.0	**21** W	0249 0844 1510 2143	4.2 2.1 4.4 1.5	**6** F	0426 1038 1629 2258	4.1 2.0 4.4 1.6	**21** SA	0416 1027 1637 2303	4.6 1.5 4.8 1.0	**6** SU	0420 1035 1629 2251	4.2 2.0 4.4 1.7	**21** M	0450 1105 1717 2333	4.5 1.5 4.5 1.3
7 M	0418 1031 1625 2309	3.8 2.2 4.1 1.9	**22** TU	0312 0913 1536 2212	4.1 2.2 4.3 1.7	**7** W	0432 1044 1634 2310	4.0 2.0 4.3 1.7	**22** TH	0348 0959 1606 2240	4.5 1.7 4.7 1.1	**7** SA	0501 1116 1706 2332	4.3 1.7 4.6 1.4	**22** SU	0505 1120 1725 2349	4.8 1.2 4.9 0.9	**7** M	0500 1119 1711 2332	4.4 1.7 4.6 1.5	**22** TU	0537 1156 1803	4.7 1.3 4.6
8 TU	0506 1118 1709 2345	4.0 1.9 4.4 1.6	**23** W	0411 1027 1630 2307	4.5 1.7 4.7 1.1	**8** TH	0508 1121 1710 2341	4.2 1.8 4.5 1.4	**23** F	0438 1054 1656 2328	4.8 1.3 5.0 0.8	**8** SU	0532 1150 1740	4.6 1.5 4.8	**23** M	0548 1206 1810	5.0 0.9 5.0	**8** TU	0537 1159 1752	4.6 1.5 4.8	**23** W	0018 0618 1242 1844	1.2 4.9 1.1 4.6
9 W	0541 1153 1744	4.2 1.6 4.6	**24** TH	0500 1119 1718 2352	4.8 1.2 5.1 0.7	**9** F	0537 1152 1741	4.4 1.5 4.7	**24** SA	0523 1141 1741	5.0 0.9 5.2	**9** M	0004 0602 1224 1813	1.2 4.8 1.3 4.9	**24** TU	0032 0629 1250 1851	0.8 5.1 0.9 5.0	**9** W	0011 0613 1235 1831	1.3 4.9 1.3 4.9	**24** TH	0059 0656 1323 1922	1.1 5.0 1.1 4.6
10 TH	0014 0609 1223 1813	1.4 4.4 1.4 4.8	**25** F	0544 1203 1801	5.1 0.8 5.4	**10** SA	0009 0604 1222 1810	1.2 4.7 1.3 4.9	**25** SU	0010 0604 1224 1822	0.5 5.1 0.7 5.3	**10** TU	0037 0633 1258 1847	1.1 5.0 1.0 5.0	**25** W	0112 0708 1332 1931	0.8 5.1 0.8 4.9	**10** TH	0051 0650 1320 1913	1.1 5.0 1.1 5.0	**25** F	0137 0733 1402 1957	1.1 5.0 1.0 4.6
11 F	0042 0634 1252 1841	1.1 4.6 1.1 5.0	**26** SA	0033 0625 1245 1841	0.3 5.3 0.5 5.6	**11** SU	0037 0630 1252 1840	1.0 4.8 1.1 5.1	**26** M	0051 0644 1305 1903	0.4 5.1 0.5 5.3	**11** W	0111 0705 1334 1923	1.0 5.1 1.1 5.1	**26** TH	0151 0746 1412 2010	0.9 5.1 0.9 4.7	**11** F	0131 0729 1402 1955	1.0 5.1 0.9 5.1	**26** SA	0214 0808 1439 2032	1.1 5.0 1.0 4.5
12 SA	0110 0700 1321 1909	0.9 4.8 1.0 5.1	**27** SU	0014 0705 1326 1921	0.1 5.5 0.3 5.6	**12** M	0106 0657 1322 1909	0.9 5.0 1.0 5.1	**27** TU	0131 0723 1346 1942	0.5 5.3 0.5 5.2	**12** TH	0147 0739 1412 2002	1.0 5.1 1.0 5.0	**27** F	0230 0825 1453 2049	1.1 5.0 1.1 4.5	**12** SA	0213 0809 1445 2040	1.0 5.0 0.8 5.0	**27** SU	0250 0844 1516 2107	1.2 5.0 1.1 4.4
13 SU	0137 0726 1350 1937	0.8 4.9 0.9 5.2	**28** M	0153 0744 1405 2000	0.1 5.4 0.5 5.5	**13** TU	0137 0725 1354 1941	0.9 5.0 1.0 5.1	**28** W	0210 0801 1426 2022	0.6 5.2 0.7 5.0	**13** F	0225 0816 1452 2045	1.1 5.0 1.1 4.9	**28** SA	0308 0904 1534 2130	1.3 4.9 1.3 4.3	**13** SU	0256 0852 1530 2129	1.0 5.2 0.8 4.9	**28** M	0326 0920 1553 2144	1.3 4.8 1.2 4.3
14 M	0206 0752 1419 2006	0.8 5.0 0.9 5.1	**29** TU	0232 0822 1445 2040	0.3 5.3 0.5 5.2	**14** W	0208 0755 1428 2014	0.9 5.0 1.0 5.0	**29** TH	0248 0840 1507 2102	0.9 5.0 1.0 4.6	**14** SA	0305 0857 1537 2134	1.2 4.9 1.3 4.7	**29** SU	0347 0946 1616 2215	1.5 4.6 1.5 4.1	**14** M	0341 0940 1618 2223	1.1 5.0 0.9 4.6	**29** TU	0402 0958 1630 2224	1.5 4.7 1.4 4.1
15 TU	0236 0820 1451 2035	0.9 4.9 1.0 5.0	**30** W	0311 0902 1526 2120	0.6 5.0 0.8 4.8	**15** TH	0242 0827 1504 2050	1.0 5.0 1.2 4.9	**30** F	0327 0921 1549 2146	1.2 4.7 1.3 4.3	**15** SU	0349 0945 1626 2233	1.4 4.8 1.4 4.4	**30** M	0428 1033 1701 2310	1.8 4.4 1.7 3.9	**15** TU	0429 1034 1710 2324	1.3 4.8 1.1 4.4	**30** W	0441 1033 1710 2310	1.7 4.5 1.6 4.0
							31 SA	0408 1007 1634 2243	1.6 4.5 1.7 3.9							**31** TH	0523 1127 1754	1.9 4.2 1.8

To find H.W. Dover add 4 h. 10 min.

TIDAL DIFFERENCES PAGE 21:128. TIDAL CURVE PAGE 21:124.

Datum of predictions: 2.75 m. below Ordnance Datum (Newlyn) or approx. L.A.T.

PLACE	TIME DIFFERENCES				HEIGHT DIFFERENCES (Metres)			
	High Water		Low Water		MHWS	MHWN	MLWN	MLWS
ULLAPOOL...............	0100 and 1300	0700 and 1900	0300 and 1500	0900 and 2100	5.2	3.9	2.1	0.7
Sule Skerry	+0100	+0120	+0110	+0100	−1.2	−0.9	−0.4	−0.1
Loch Eriboll								
Portnancon	+0055	+0105	+0055	+0100	0.0	+0.1	+0.1	+0.2
Kyle of Durness	+0030	+0030	+0050	+0050	−0.6	−0.4	−0.3	−0.1
Rona	+0010	+0030	+0010	+0030	−1.8	−1.4	−0.8	−0.3
Outer Hebrides								
Stornoway	−0010	−0010	−0010	−0010	−0.4	−0.2	−0.1	0.0
Loch Shell	−0023	−0010	−0010	−0027	−0.4	−0.3	−0.2	0.0
E Loch Tarbert	−0035	−0020	−0020	−0030	−0.2	−0.2	0.0	+0.1
Loch Maddy	−0054	−0024	−0026	−0040	−0.4	−0.3	−0.2	0.0
Loch Carnan	−0100	−0020	−0030	−0050	−0.7	−0.7	−0.2	−0.1
Loch Skiport	−0110	−0035	−0034	−0034	−0.6	−0.6	−0.4	−0.2
Loch Boisdale	−0105	−0040	−0030	−0050	−1.1	−0.9	−0.4	−0.2
Barra (North Bay)	−0113	−0041	−0044	−0058	−1.0	−0.7	−0.3	−0.1
Castle Bay	−0125	−0050	−0055	−0110	−0.9	−0.8	−0.4	−0.1
Barra Head	−0125	−0050	−0055	−0105	−1.2	−0.9	−0.3	+0.1
Shillay	−0113	−0053	−0057	−0117	−1.0	−0.9	−0.8	−0.3
Balivanich	−0113	−0027	−0041	−0055	−1.1	−0.8	−0.6	−0.2
Scolpaig	−0046	−0046	−0049	−0049	−1.3	−0.9	−0.5	0.0
Leverburgh	−0051	−0030	−0025	−0035	−0.6	−0.4	−0.2	−0.1
W Loch Tarbert	−0103	−0043	−0024	−0044	−1.0	−0.7	−0.8	−0.3
Little Bernera	−0031	−0021	−0027	−0037	−0.9	−0.8	−0.5	−0.2
Carloway	−0050	+0010	−0045	−0025	−1.0	−0.7	−0.5	−0.1
ULLAPOOL................	0000 and 1200	0600 and 1800	0300 and 1500	0900 and 2100	5.2	3.9	2.1	0.7
Village Bay (St Kilda) ...	−0110	−0040	−0100	−0100	−1.9	−1.4	−0.9	−0.3
Flannan Isles	−0036	−0026	−0026	−0036	−1.3	−0.9	−0.7	−0.2
Rockall	−0115	−0115	−0125	−0125	−2.4	−1.8	−1.0	−0.3
Loch Bervie	+0030	+0010	+0010	+0020	−0.3	−0.3	−0.2	0.0
Loch Laxford	+0015	+0015	+0005	+0005	−0.3	−0.4	−0.2	0.0
Eddrachillis Bay								
Badcall Bay	+0005	+0005	+0005	+0005	−0.7	−0.5	−0.5	+0.2
Loch Inver	−0005	−0005	−0005	−0005	−0.2	0.0	0.0	+0.1
Summer Isles								
Tanera Mor	−0005	−0005	−0010	−0010	−0.1	+0.1	0.0	+0.1
Loch Gairloch								
Gairloch	−0020	−0020	−0010	−0010	0.0	+0.1	−0.3	−0.1
Loch Torridon								
Sheildag	−0020	−0020	−0015	−0015	+0.4	+0.3	+0.1	0.0
Inner Sound								
Applecross	−0020	−0015	−0005	−0025	+0.1	+0.1	+0.1	0.0
Loch Carron								
Plockton	−0020	−0020	−0010	−0010	+0.5	+0.5	+0.5	+0.2
Rona								
Loch a'Bhraige	−0020	0000	−0010	0000	−0.1	−0.1	−0.1	−0.2
Skye								
Broadford Bay	−0035	−0020	−0025	−0030	+0.3	+0.2	+0.1	−0.1
Portree	−0025	−0025	−0025	−0025	+0.1	−0.2	−0.2	0.0
Loch Snizort (Uig Bay)	−0045	−0020	−0005	−0025	+0.1	−0.4	−0.2	0.0
Loch Harport	−0115	−0035	−0020	−0100	−0.1	−0.1	0.0	+0.1
Soay								
Camus nan Gall	−0055	−0025	−0025	−0045	−0.4	−0.2	−	−
Loch Alsh								
Kyle of Lochalsh	−0040	−0020	−0005	−0025	+0.1	0.0	+0.1	+0.1
Dornie Bridge	−0040	−0010	−0005	−0020	+0.1	−0.1	0.0	0.0
Kyle Rhea								
Glenelg Bay	−0105	−0034	−0034	−0054	−0.4	−0.4	−0.9	−0.1
Loch Hourn	−0125	−0050	−0040	−0110	−0.2	−0.1	−0.1	+0.1

Refer to predictions on pages 21:125-21:127

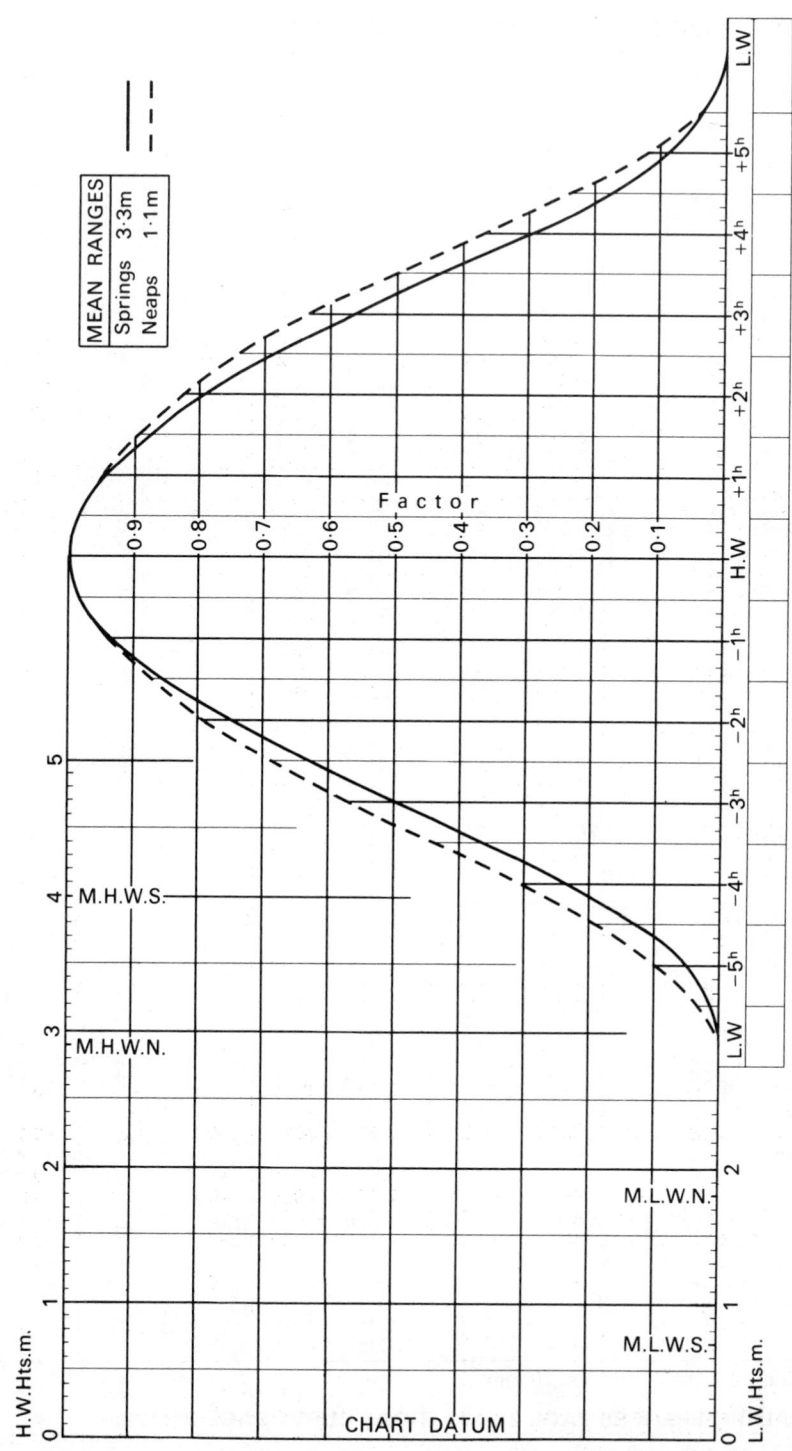

OBAN

MEAN SPRING AND NEAP CURVES

Springs occur 2 days after New and Full Moon.

MEAN RANGES
Springs 3·3m
Neaps 1·1m

WEST COAST OF SCOTLAND OBAN

HIGH & LOW WATER 1992   Lat. 56°25'N. Long. 5°29'W.

GMT   ADD 1 HOUR MARCH 29 — OCTOBER 25 FOR B.S.T.

JANUARY

Day	Time	m	Day	Time	m
1 W	0328	3.3	**16**	0159	3.1
	0908	1.7		0825	1.7
	1605	3.2	TH	1512	3.3
	2156	1.7		2054	1.5
2 TH	0415	3.4	**17**	0321	3.3
	1008	1.6		0942	1.4
	1641	3.3	F	1612	3.5
	2239	1.5		2156	1.2
3 F	0453	3.6	**18**	0419	3.6
	1056	1.5		1042	1.1
	1711	3.5	SA	1701	3.7
	2318	1.4		2249	0.9
4 SA	0527	3.8	**19**	0507	3.9
	1137	1.4		1133	0.9
	1741	3.6	SU	1745	3.9
●	2354	1.2	O	2338	0.6
5 SU	0600	3.9	**20**	0552	4.2
	1214	1.4		1219	0.6
	1812	3.7	M	1827	4.1
6 M	0030	1.2	**21**	0023	0.4
	0633	4.0		0634	4.3
	1250	1.3	TU	1304	0.6
	1844	3.8		1907	4.1
7 TU	0105	1.2	**22**	0108	0.3
	0707	4.0		0714	4.3
	1324	1.3	W	1347	0.6
	1915	3.8		1946	4.0
8 W	0139	1.2	**23**	0152	0.4
	0739	4.0		0755	4.2
	1357	1.4	TH	1429	0.7
	1945	3.7		2025	3.9
9 TH	0210	1.3	**24**	0236	0.5
	0811	3.9		0834	4.0
	1428	1.5	F	1512	1.0
	2014	3.6		2104	3.7
10 F	0240	1.4	**25**	0321	0.8
	0841	3.8		0914	3.7
	1500	1.5	SA	1557	1.2
	2042	3.5		2146	3.4
11 SA	0310	1.5	**26**	0408	1.1
	0913	3.6		0957	3.4
	1536	1.6	SU	1646	1.5
	2114	3.4		2235	3.2
12 SU	0345	1.6	**27**	0500	1.4
	0950	3.4		1047	3.1
	1619	1.7	M	1745	1.8
	2154	3.2		2345	3.0
13 M	0429	1.8	**28**	0603	1.7
				1212	2.9
	1714	1.8	TU	1858	1.9
	2248	3.1			
14 TU	0531	1.8	**29**	0139	2.9
	1157	3.1		0721	1.9
	1824	1.8	W	1504	2.8
				2024	1.9
15 W	0011	3.0	**30**	0313	3.1
	0654	1.9		0852	1.9
	1350	3.1	TH	1605	3.0
	1942	1.7		2137	1.8
			31	0408	3.3
				1006	1.8
			F	1641	3.2
				2227	1.6

FEBRUARY

Day	Time	m	Day	Time	m
1	0446	3.5	**16**	0414	3.6
	1053	1.6		1039	1.0
SA	1708	3.4	SU	1653	3.6
	2306	1.4		2236	0.7
2	0517	3.7	**17**	0500	3.9
	1129	1.4		1126	0.7
SU	1734	3.5	M	1733	3.9
	2341	1.2		2324	0.4
3	0547	3.9	**18**	0541	4.1
	1201	1.3		1207	0.5
M	1802	3.7	TU	1811	4.0
●			O		
4	0014	1.1	**19**	0008	0.2
	0617	4.0		0619	4.3
TU	1233	1.2	W	1247	0.4
	1829	3.8		1847	4.1
5	0046	1.0	**20**	0050	0.1
	0647	4.0		0656	4.3
W	1302	1.1	TH	1326	0.4
	1856	3.8		1922	4.1
6	0116	1.0	**21**	0131	0.2
	0716	4.0		0732	4.2
TH	1331	1.1	F	1404	0.6
	1922	3.8		1956	3.9
7	0144	1.0	**22**	0212	0.4
	0743	4.0		0807	3.9
F	1359	1.1	SA	1443	0.8
	1947	3.7		2031	3.7
8	0210	1.1	**23**	0254	0.7
	0810	3.8		0842	3.6
SA	1428	1.2	SU	1522	1.1
	2012	3.6		2108	3.5
9	0238	1.2	**24**	0337	1.0
	0839	3.7		0918	3.3
SU	1502	1.3	M	1606	1.4
	2041	3.5		2150	3.2
10	0310	1.5	**25**	0426	1.4
	0912	3.5		0958	3.0
M	1542	1.5	TU	1659	1.7
	2117	3.3		2248	2.9
11	0352	1.5	**26**	0526	1.8
	0954	3.2		1100	2.7
TU	1634	1.6	W	1811	1.9
	2205	3.1			
12	0452	1.7	**27**	0043	2.8
	1102	3.0		0648	2.0
W	1744	1.7	TH	1444	2.6
	2320	2.9		1944	1.9
13	0621	1.8	**28**	0251	2.9
	1334	2.9		0838	2.0
TH	1910	1.7	F	1548	2.8
				2113	1.8
14	0133	2.9	**29**	0349	3.1
	0811	1.9		0958	1.8
F	1509	3.1	SA	1622	3.1
	2033	1.5		2207	1.6
15	0316	3.2			
	0941	1.4			
SA	1607	3.3			
	2141	1.1			

MARCH

Day	Time	m	Day	Time	m
1	0425	3.4	**16**	0402	3.5
	1037	1.5		1026	0.9
SU	1647	3.3	M	1635	3.5
	2246	1.3		2217	0.6
2	0454	3.6	**17**	0445	3.8
	1108	1.3		1109	0.6
M	1712	3.5	TU	1713	3.8
	2319	1.1		2303	0.4
3	0523	3.8	**18**	0523	4.0
	1137	1.1		1147	0.4
TU	1738	3.7	W	1748	4.0
	2350	1.0	O	2346	0.2
4	0552	3.9	**19**	0558	4.1
	1205	1.0		1224	0.4
W	1804	3.8	TH	1821	4.0
●					
5	0019	0.9	**20**	0027	0.1
	0620	4.0		0632	4.0
TH	1234	0.9	F	1300	0.4
	1829	3.8		1854	4.0
6	0047	0.8	**21**	0108	0.2
	0647	4.0		0705	4.0
F	1301	0.9	SA	1336	0.6
	1853	3.8		1927	3.9
7	0114	0.8	**22**	0147	0.4
	0714	4.0		0738	3.8
SA	1330	0.9	SU	1413	0.8
	1917	3.8		2002	3.7
8	0141	0.9	**23**	0227	0.7
	0742	3.8		0811	3.5
SU	1401	0.9	M	1451	1.1
	1944	3.7		2038	3.5
9	0211	1.0	**24**	0309	1.1
	0811	3.6		0845	3.2
M	1436	1.1	TU	1533	1.3
	2016	3.5		2119	3.2
10	0247	1.2	**25**	0356	1.5
	0846	3.4		0923	2.9
TU	1518	1.2	W	1625	1.6
	2054	3.3		2215	3.0
11	0332	1.4	**26**	0455	1.8
	0929	3.1		1019	2.7
W	1611	1.4	TH	1734	1.8
	2143	3.1		2356	2.8
12	0435	1.6	**27**	0615	2.0
	1043	2.8		1326	2.6
TH	1722	1.6	F	1902	1.9
	2302	2.9			
13	0610	1.7	**28**	0201	2.9
	1333	2.7		0759	2.0
F	1848	1.5	SA	1502	2.7
				2030	1.8
14	0130	2.9	**29**	0307	3.1
	0809	1.6		0920	1.8
SA	1457	3.0	SU	1541	3.0
	2013	1.3		2130	1.6
15	0308	3.2	**30**	0347	3.3
	0934	1.2		1001	1.5
SU	1551	3.3	M	1611	3.2
	2122	1.0		2211	1.3
			31	0419	3.5
				1033	1.3
			TU	1638	3.4
				2245	1.1

APRIL

Day	Time	m	Day	Time	m
1	0450	3.7	**16**	0500	3.9
	1102	1.1		1122	0.6
W	1705	3.6	TH	1722	3.8
	2317	1.0		2322	0.4
2	0520	3.9	**17**	0534	3.9
	1131	0.9		1158	0.5
TH	1731	3.7	F	1755	3.9
	2346	0.8	O		
3	0549	3.9	**18**	0003	0.4
	1201	0.8		0606	3.9
F	1757	3.8	SA	1234	0.6
●				1828	3.9
4	0015	0.8	**19**	0044	0.5
	0618	4.0		0639	3.8
SA	1231	0.7	SU	1310	0.7
	1823	3.8		1902	3.8
5	0045	0.8	**20**	0123	0.7
	0648	3.9		0712	3.6
SU	1303	0.7	M	1347	0.9
	1851	3.8		1938	3.7
6	0117	0.8	**21**	0204	0.9
	0719	3.8		0746	3.4
M	1338	0.8	TU	1426	1.1
	1923	3.7		2016	3.5
7	0153	0.9	**22**	0246	1.2
	0753	3.6		0821	3.2
TU	1418	0.9	W	1508	1.3
	1959	3.6		2100	3.3
8	0235	1.1	**23**	0332	1.5
	0833	3.3		0902	3.0
W	1504	1.1	TH	1558	1.5
	2043	3.4		2154	3.1
9	0326	1.3	**24**	0427	1.8
	0924	3.0		0957	2.8
TH	1600	1.3	F	1700	1.7
	2139	3.1		2315	2.9
10	0435	1.5	**25**	0538	1.9
	1054	2.7		1146	2.6
F	1709	1.4	SA	1815	1.8
	2305	2.9			
11	0608	1.6	**26**	0052	2.9
	1315	2.7		0701	2.0
SA	1828	1.4	SU	1341	2.7
				1932	1.8
12	0121	3.0	**27**	0206	3.0
	0756	1.5		0816	1.8
SU	1432	2.9	M	1441	2.9
	1948	1.2		2036	1.7
13	0248	3.2	**28**	0256	3.2
	0913	1.2		0908	1.6
M	1526	3.2	TU	1522	3.1
	2056	1.0		2124	1.5
14	0342	3.5	**29**	0336	3.4
	1003	0.9		0947	1.4
TU	1610	3.4	W	1556	3.3
	2151	0.7		2203	1.3
15	0424	3.7	**30**	0412	3.6
	1045	0.7		1022	1.2
W	1647	3.7	TH	1626	3.5
	2239	0.5		2238	1.1

To find H.W. Dover add 5 h. 20 min.

TIDAL DIFFERENCES PAGE 21:133. TIDAL CURVE PAGE 21:129.

Datum of predictions: 2.10 m. below Ordnance Datum (Newlyn) or approx. L.A.T.

OBAN WEST COAST OF SCOTLAND 21:131

Lat. 56°25′N. Long. 5°29′W. HIGH & LOW WATER 1992

GMT ADD 1 HOUR MARCH 29 — OCTOBER 25 FOR B.S.T.

MAY

Day	Time	m		Time	m
1 F	0446	3.8	16	0513	3.7
	1055	1.0		1133	0.8
	1656	3.6	SA	1733	3.7
	2311	0.9	O	2342	0.7
2 SA	0520	3.8	17	0545	3.7
	1129	0.8		1210	0.8
	1727	3.7	SU	1808	3.8
●	2346	0.8			
3 SU	0553	3.9	18	0023	0.8
	1204	0.7		0618	3.6
	1759	3.8	M	1248	0.9
				1844	3.8
4 M	0021	0.8	19	0104	1.0
	0628	3.8		0653	3.5
	1242	0.7	TU	1326	0.9
	1833	3.8		1922	3.7
5 TU	0101	0.8	20	0145	1.1
	0705	3.7		0729	3.4
	1322	0.7	W	1406	1.1
	1911	3.7		2002	3.6
6 W	0143	0.9	21	0226	1.3
	0746	3.6		0806	3.3
	1406	0.8	TH	1448	1.3
	1954	3.6		2045	3.4
7 TH	0232	1.0	22	0310	1.6
	0833	3.3		0847	3.1
	1455	0.9	F	1533	1.5
	2043	3.5		2133	3.3
8 F	0328	1.2	23	0359	1.7
	0931	3.1		0934	3.0
	1551	1.1	SA	1623	1.6
	2143	3.3		2232	3.1
9 SA	0435	1.4	24	0455	1.9
	1055	2.9		1037	2.8
	1655	1.2	SU	1721	1.8
	2303	3.1		2342	3.1
10 SU	0557	1.5	25	0558	1.9
	1238	2.8		1201	2.8
	1805	1.2	M	1825	1.8
11 M	0051	3.1	26	0055	3.1
	0725	1.6		0704	1.9
	1356	2.9	TU	1321	2.8
	1917	1.2		1928	1.8
12 TU	0219	3.2	27	0158	3.2
	0839	1.3		0804	1.7
	1455	3.1	W	1421	3.0
	2024	1.0		2025	1.6
13 W	0317	3.4	28	0249	3.3
	0934	1.1		0854	1.5
	1542	3.3	TH	1507	3.1
	2123	0.9		2114	1.5
14 TH	0402	3.5	29	0334	3.5
	1018	1.0		0939	1.3
	1622	3.5	F	1547	3.3
	2213	0.8		2159	1.3
15 F	0439	3.6	30	0416	3.6
	1057	0.9		1020	1.1
	1658	3.6	SA	1625	3.5
	2259	0.7		2241	1.1
			31	0456	3.7
				1101	0.9
			SU	1703	3.7
				2324	0.9

JUNE

Day	Time	m		Time	m
1 M	0537	3.8	16	0009	1.1
	1143	0.7		0607	3.5
	1743	3.8	TU	1232	1.0
●				1833	3.8
2 TU	0007	0.8	17	0050	1.2
	0617	3.8		0641	3.5
	1226	0.6	W	1310	1.0
	1824	3.9		1910	3.8
3 W	0053	0.8	18	0129	1.2
	0700	3.7		0716	3.5
	1311	0.6	TH	1348	1.1
	1907	3.9		1948	3.7
4 TH	0140	0.8	19	0208	1.4
	0745	3.6		0752	3.4
	1357	0.6	F	1426	1.2
	1953	3.8		2026	3.6
5 F	0230	0.9	20	0247	1.5
	0833	3.4		0828	3.3
	1446	0.7	SA	1504	1.3
	2043	3.7		2105	3.5
6 SA	0325	1.1	21	0326	1.6
	0927	3.3		0904	3.2
	1538	0.8	SU	1542	1.5
	2139	3.5		2146	3.4
7 SU	0425	1.3	22	0408	1.7
	1031	3.1		0943	3.1
	1635	1.0	M	1623	1.6
	2244	3.3		2234	3.2
8 M	0532	1.4	23	0457	1.8
	1148	3.0		1031	3.0
	1737	1.1	TU	1711	1.8
				2333	3.1
9 TU	0007	3.2	24	0553	1.8
	0645	1.5		1135	2.9
	1310	3.0	W	1810	1.8
	1843	1.2			
10 W	0141	3.2	25	0047	3.1
	0758	1.5		0657	1.8
	1420	3.0	TH	1258	2.9
	1951	1.2		1918	1.8
11 TH	0254	3.2	26	0201	3.2
	0915	1.4		0801	1.7
	1517	3.2	F	1414	3.0
	2055	1.2		2026	1.7
12 F	0346	3.3	27	0303	3.3
	0952	1.3		0859	1.5
	1604	3.3	SA	1514	3.2
	2153	1.2		2128	1.5
13 SA	0427	3.4	28	0356	3.5
	1035	1.2		0952	1.2
	1644	3.5	SU	1604	3.4
	2243	1.1		2223	1.2
14 SU	0501	3.4	29	0444	3.6
	1115	1.1		1040	0.9
	1721	3.6	M	1651	3.7
	2328	1.1		2313	1.0
15 M	0534	3.5	30	0528	3.8
	1153	1.0		1127	0.7
	1757	3.7	TU	1735	3.9
●					

JULY

Day	Time	m		Time	m
1 W	0001	0.8	16	0037	1.2
	0611	3.8		0629	3.6
	1213	0.5	TH	1252	0.9
	1819	4.0		1854	3.9
2 TH	0048	0.7	17	0112	1.2
	0654	3.9		0701	3.7
	1259	0.4	F	1327	1.0
	1903	4.1		1927	3.9
3 F	0135	0.7	18	0145	1.2
	0737	3.8		0732	3.6
	1344	0.4	SA	1400	1.1
	1947	4.0		2000	3.8
4 SA	0222	0.8	19	0218	1.3
	0821	3.7		0802	3.5
	1431	0.5	SU	1431	1.2
	2033	3.9		2031	3.7
5 SU	0311	0.9	20	0250	1.4
	0907	3.5		0830	3.4
	1519	0.6	M	1500	1.4
	2120	3.7		2103	3.5
6 M	0402	1.1	21	0324	1.5
	0957	3.3		0900	3.3
	1611	0.9	TU	1531	1.5
	2213	3.4		2136	3.4
7 TU	0459	1.3	22	0404	1.6
	1056	3.1		0935	3.1
	1706	1.1	W	1609	1.7
	2316	3.2		2218	3.2
8 W	0602	1.5	23	0453	1.7
	1214	3.0		1021	3.0
	1809	1.3	TH	1702	1.8
				2324	3.0
9 TH	0050	3.0	24	0558	1.8
	0713	1.6		1133	2.9
	1345	2.9	F	1818	1.8
	1919	1.5			
10 F	0238	3.0	25	0115	3.0
	0827	1.6		0713	1.7
	1501	3.0	SA	1323	2.9
	2034	1.5		1950	1.8
11 SA	0344	3.1	26	0245	3.1
	0931	1.5		0827	1.5
	1558	3.2	SU	1455	3.1
	2143	1.5		2113	1.5
12 SU	0428	3.2	27	0347	3.3
	1021	1.4		0930	1.2
	1641	3.4	M	1555	3.4
	2237	1.4		2216	1.2
13 M	0501	3.3	28	0436	3.6
	1102	1.2		1024	0.9
	1716	3.6	TU	1644	3.7
	2322	1.3		2307	0.9
14 TU	0530	3.4	29	0520	3.8
	1140	1.1		1112	0.6
	1749	3.7	W	1736	4.0
O			●	2354	0.7
15 W	0000	1.2	30	0601	3.9
	0558	3.5		1158	0.3
	1217	1.0	TH	1810	4.2
	1821	3.8			
			31	0038	0.5
				0641	4.0
			F	1243	0.2
				1850	4.3

AUGUST

Day	Time	m		Time	m
1 SA	0121	0.5	16	0117	1.1
	0720	4.0		0706	3.8
	1327	0.2	SU	1329	1.0
	1931	4.2		1929	4.0
2 SU	0204	0.6	17	0146	1.1
	0759	3.9		0732	3.7
	1411	0.3	M	1356	1.1
	2011	4.1		1956	3.8
3 M	0248	0.7	18	0215	1.2
	0839	3.7		0757	3.6
	1456	0.5	TU	1422	1.2
	2052	3.8		2023	3.7
4 TU	0333	1.0	19	0246	1.3
	0921	3.5		0824	3.5
	1543	0.8	W	1451	1.4
	2136	3.5		2053	3.5
5 W	0423	1.3	20	0323	1.5
	1010	3.2		0857	3.2
	1635	1.2	TH	1527	1.6
	2226	3.1		2129	3.2
6 TH	0520	1.6	21	0410	1.6
	1117	3.0		0940	3.1
	1736	1.5	F	1619	1.7
	2343	2.9		2224	3.0
7 F	0631	1.7	22	0515	1.7
	1312	2.9		1045	2.9
	1852	1.7	SA	1741	1.9
8 SA	0233	2.8	23	0045	2.8
	0754	1.8		0637	1.7
	1454	3.0	SU	1251	2.9
	2023	1.8		1933	1.8
9 SU	0344	2.9	24	0238	3.0
	0913	1.7		0801	1.5
	1554	3.2	M	1447	3.1
	2146	1.7		2109	1.5
10 M	0426	3.1	25	0338	3.2
	1008	1.5		0910	1.2
	1634	3.4	TU	1547	3.5
	2237	1.5		2211	1.2
11 TU	0454	3.3	26	0425	3.5
	1048	1.3		1006	0.8
	1705	3.6	W	1633	3.8
	2314	1.4		2258	0.8
12 W	0519	3.5	27	0506	3.8
	1124	1.2		1055	0.5
	1733	3.8	TH	1714	4.1
	2346	1.2		2340	0.5
13 TH	0544	3.6	28	0544	4.0
	1157	1.0		1140	0.2
	1802	3.9	F	1753	4.3
O					
14 F	0017	1.1	29	0020	0.4
	0611	3.7		0620	4.1
	1230	0.9	SA	1223	0.1
	1831	4.0		1831	4.4
15 SA	0047	1.1	30	0100	0.4
	0639	3.8		0657	4.1
	1300	0.9	SU	1305	0.1
	1900	4.0		1908	4.3
			31	0140	0.5
				0733	0.4
			M	1348	0.3
				1945	4.1

Streams run with channel in Sound of Kerrera. Eddies at side of channel. Weak in Oban Bay. In Sound of Jura and adjoining lochs between Gigha and Crinan, rise of tide occurs mainly during 3½ h. after L.W. and fall occurs mainly during 3½ h. after H.W. Between initial fall and L.W. there are periods when changes in level are small and irregular.

WEST COAST OF SCOTLAND **OBAN**

Lat. 56°25′N. Long. 5°29′W. **HIGH & LOW WATER 1992**

GMT **ADD 1 HOUR MARCH 29 — OCTOBER 25 FOR B.S.T.**

SEPTEMBER

Day	Time	m	Time	m	Time	m	Time	m
1 TU	0220	0.7	0810	3.8	1431	0.6	2021	3.8
2 W	0302	1.0	0849	3.6	1516	0.9	2059	3.4
3 TH	0347	1.3	0933	3.3	1606	1.3	2142	3.1
4 F	0441	1.6	1033	3.0	1707	1.7	2243	2.8
5 SA	0550	1.8	1232	2.9	1827	1.9		
6 SU	0219	2.7	0719	1.9	1438	3.0	2017	2.0
7 M	0329	2.9	0847	1.8	1536	3.2	2143	1.8
8 TU	0407	3.1	0945	1.6	1612	3.4	2223	1.6
9 W	0433	3.3	1025	1.3	1640	3.7	2253	1.4
10 TH	0456	3.5	1059	1.2	1706	3.9	2321	1.2
11 F	0520	3.7	1131	1.0	1734	4.0	2349	1.1
12 SA	0546	3.8	1201	1.0	1803	4.1	O	
13 SU	0017	1.0	0612	3.9	1231	0.9	1830	4.1
14 M	0046	0.9	0637	3.9	1258	1.0	1857	4.0
15 TU	0114	1.0	0702	3.9	1324	1.1	1924	3.9
16 W	0143	1.0	0728	3.7	1351	1.2	1951	3.7
17 TH	0216	1.2	0757	3.6	1423	1.3	2022	3.5
18 F	0254	1.3	0832	3.4	1504	1.5	2100	3.2
19 SA	0343	1.5	0917	3.2	1600	1.7	2156	2.9
20 SU	0448	1.6	1025	3.0	1728	1.8		
21 M	0037	2.8	0610	1.7	1236	3.0	1926	1.8
22 TU	0224	2.9	0735	1.5	1432	3.2	2101	1.5
23 W	0321	3.2	0847	1.2	1531	3.6	2157	1.1
24 TH	0406	3.5	0945	0.8	1615	3.9	2240	0.8
25 F	0446	3.8	1033	0.5	1655	4.1	2320	0.6
26 SA	0522	4.0	1118	0.3	1732	4.3	● 2358	0.4
27 SU	0558	4.2	1201	0.2	1808	4.3		
28 M	0035	0.4	0632	4.2	1243	0.3	1843	4.2
29 TU	0114	0.5	0707	4.1	1325	0.7	1918	4.0
30 W	0152	0.7	0744	3.9	1407	1.1	1953	3.7

OCTOBER

Day	Time	m	Time	m	Time	m	Time	m
1 TH	0232	1.0	0822	3.7	1451	1.1	2029	3.4
2 F	0316	1.3	0905	3.4	1540	1.5	2108	3.1
3 SA	0407	1.6	1001	3.2	1639	1.8	2202	2.8
4 SU	0512	1.8	1139	3.0	1758	2.1		
5 M	0111	2.7	0635	2.0	1349	3.0	1942	2.1
6 TU	0250	2.8	0803	1.9	1454	3.2	2106	1.9
7 W	0330	3.1	0908	1.7	1533	3.4	2147	1.7
8 TH	0358	3.3	0952	1.5	1604	3.7	2218	1.5
9 F	0424	3.5	1028	1.3	1633	3.8	2247	1.3
10 SA	0450	3.7	1100	1.2	1703	4.0	2316	1.1
11 SU	0517	3.8	1131	1.1	1733	4.1	O 2345	1.0
12 M	0543	3.9	1200	1.0	1802	4.1		
13 TU	0015	0.9	0609	4.0	1229	1.0	1830	4.0
14 W	0046	0.9	0636	3.9	1259	1.1	1859	3.9
15 TH	0118	1.0	0706	3.9	1331	1.2	1931	3.7
16 F	0155	1.1	0739	3.8	1409	1.3	2006	3.5
17 SA	0237	1.2	0819	3.6	1456	1.5	2050	3.2
18 SU	0328	1.4	0909	3.4	1557	1.7	2156	3.0
19 M	0431	1.5	1019	3.2	1722	1.8		
20 TU	0014	2.8	0546	1.6	1213	3.2	1907	1.7
21 W	0155	3.0	0706	1.5	1404	3.3	2035	1.5
22 TH	0256	3.2	0819	1.2	1507	3.6	2132	1.2
23 F	0343	3.5	0919	1.0	1554	3.8	2217	0.9
24 SA	0423	3.8	1011	0.7	1634	4.0	2256	0.8
25 SU	0500	4.0	1057	0.6	1711	4.1	● 2334	0.6
26 M	0536	4.1	1140	0.5	1746	4.1		
27 TU	0012	0.6	0610	4.1	1223	0.6	1821	4.0
28 W	0050	0.7	0646	4.1	1305	0.7	1855	3.9
29 TH	0128	0.9	0723	4.0	1347	1.0	1931	3.7
30 F	0208	1.1	0802	3.8	1430	1.2	2007	3.4
31 SA	0251	1.3	0845	3.6	1517	1.6	2047	3.2

NOVEMBER

Day	Time	m	Time	m	Time	m	Time	m
1 SU	0338	1.6	0937	3.4	1612	1.9	2138	3.0
2 M	0436	1.8	1048	3.2	1718	2.1	2306	2.8
3 TU	0546	2.0	1222	3.1	1838	2.1		
4 W	0117	2.9	0704	2.0	1345	3.2	1956	2.0
5 TH	0228	3.0	0814	1.9	1439	3.4	2052	1.9
6 F	0311	3.2	0908	1.8	1521	3.6	2133	1.7
7 SA	0345	3.4	0950	1.6	1558	3.7	2209	1.4
8 SU	0417	3.6	1027	1.4	1632	3.9	2242	1.3
9 M	0447	3.8	1101	1.3	1706	4.0	O 2315	1.1
10 TU	0516	3.9	1134	1.2	1739	4.0	2348	1.0
11 W	0546	4.0	1207	1.1	1812	4.0		
12 TH	0023	0.9	0618	4.0	1243	1.1	1846	3.9
13 F	0101	0.9	0653	4.0	1322	1.2	1924	3.8
14 SA	0142	1.0	0732	3.9	1406	1.3	2005	3.6
15 SU	0226	1.1	0816	3.8	1456	1.4	2054	3.3
16 M	0317	1.2	0907	3.6	1555	1.6	2158	3.1
17 TU	0416	1.4	1012	3.4	1708	1.7	2332	3.0
18 W	0522	1.4	1139	3.3	1833	1.7		
19 TH	0111	3.1	0634	1.4	1323	3.4	1955	1.6
20 F	0222	3.2	0747	1.3	1440	3.5	2100	1.4
21 SA	0317	3.4	0852	1.2	1535	3.7	2151	1.2
22 SU	0402	3.7	0949	1.0	1619	3.8	2234	1.1
23 M	0443	3.8	1039	0.9	1657	3.9	2314	0.9
24 TU	0520	4.0	1125	0.9	1733	3.9	● 2353	0.9
25 W	0556	4.1	1208	0.9	1807	3.9		
26 TH	0031	0.9	0632	4.1	1250	1.0	1842	3.8
27 F	0110	1.0	0709	4.0	1331	1.2	1917	3.7
28 SA	0149	1.1	0748	3.8	1413	1.4	1954	3.5
29 SU	0230	1.3	0829	3.7	1456	1.6	2033	3.4
30 M	0313	1.5	0913	3.6	1542	1.8	2115	3.2

DECEMBER

Day	Time	m	Time	m	Time	m	Time	m
1 TU	0400	1.7	1003	3.4	1633	2.0	2208	3.1
2 W	0454	1.9	1105	3.3	1732	2.1	2321	3.0
3 TH	0557	2.0	1220	3.2	1838	2.1		
4 F	0051	3.0	0705	2.0	1333	3.3	1943	2.0
5 SA	0205	3.1	0811	2.0	1433	3.4	2039	1.8
6 SU	0259	3.3	0906	1.9	1523	3.5	2126	1.6
7 M	0341	3.4	0953	1.7	1606	3.7	2208	1.4
8 TU	0419	3.6	1035	1.5	1647	3.8	2248	1.2
9 W	0455	3.8	1115	1.3	1726	3.9	O 2327	1.0
10 TH	0531	4.0	1155	1.2	1804	4.0		
11 F	0007	0.9	0608	4.1	1236	1.1	1843	3.9
12 SA	0049	0.8	0648	4.1	1319	1.1	1923	3.9
13 SU	0132	0.8	0729	4.1	1404	1.1	2005	3.7
14 M	0217	0.9	0813	4.0	1452	1.2	2052	3.6
15 TU	0306	1.0	0901	3.8	1545	1.3	2144	3.4
16 W	0358	1.1	0956	3.6	1644	1.5	2249	3.2
17 TH	0457	1.3	1102	3.4	1753	1.6		
18 F	0013	3.1	0602	1.4	1231	3.3	1909	1.7
19 SA	0142	3.2	0713	1.5	1415	3.3	2024	1.5
20 SU	0253	3.3	0827	1.5	1527	3.4	2126	1.5
21 M	0349	3.5	0933	1.4	1618	3.5	2217	1.3
22 TU	0434	3.7	1030	1.3	1658	3.6	2300	1.1
23 W	0514	3.8	1117	1.2	1732	3.6	2340	1.1
24 TH	0549	3.9	1200	1.2	1803 ●	3.7		
25 F	0018	1.0	0623	4.0	1240	1.2	1834	3.7
26 SA	0056	1.0	0658	4.1	1318	1.1	1907	3.7
27 SU	0133	1.1	0733	4.0	1355	1.3	1941	3.7
28 M	0210	1.2	0809	3.9	1432	1.5	2014	3.6
29 TU	0247	1.4	0845	3.8	1509	1.6	2049	3.5
30 W	0325	1.6	0923	3.6	1548	1.8	2124	3.3
31 TH	0403	1.7	1004	3.4	1631	1.9	2204	3.2

RATE AND SET — Sound of Kerrera, mid-channel — NE. –0100 Dover Sp., 1-1½ kn. SW. +0500 Dover Sp., 1-1½ kn. Ferry rocks, Sp., 1½-2 kn. Dunollie Lt. Tower, Sp., 2-2½ kn.
To find H.W. Dover add 5 h. 20 min.

TIDAL DIFFERENCES PAGE 21:133. TIDAL CURVE PAGE 21:129.

Datum of predictions: 2.10 m. below Ordnance Datum (Newlyn) or approx. L.A.T.

PLACE	TIME DIFFERENCES				HEIGHT DIFFERENCES (Metres)			
	High Water		Low Water		MHWS	MHWN	MLWN	MLWS
OBAN	0000 and 1200	0600 and 1800	0100 and 1300	0700 and 1900	4.0	2.9	1.8	0.7
Loch Nevis								
Inverie Bay	+0030	+0020	+0035	+0020	+1.0	+0.9	+0.2	0.0
Mallaig	+0040	+0020	+0035	+0030	+1.0	+0.9	+0.3	0.0
Eigg								
Bay of Laig	+0015	+0030	+0040	+0005	+0.7	+0.6	−0.2	−0.2
Loch Moidart	+0015	+0015	+0040	+0020	+0.8	+0.6	−0.2	−0.2
Coll								
Loch Eatharna	+0025	+0010	+0015	+0025	+0.4	+0.3	−	−
Tiree								
Gott Bay	0000	+0010	+0005	+0010	0.0	+0.1	0.0	0.0
OBAN	0100 and 1300	0700 and 1900	0100 and 1300	0800 and 2000	4.0	2.9	1.8	0.7
Mull								
Carsaig Bay	−0015	−0005	−0030	+0020	+0.1	+0.2	0.0	−0.1
Iona	−0010	−0005	−0020	+0015	0.0	+0.1	−0.3	−0.2
Bunessan	−0015	−0015	−0010	−0015	+0.3	+0.1	0.0	−0.1
Ulva Sound	−0010	−0015	0000	−0005	+0.4	+0.3	0.0	−0.1
Loch Sunart								
Salen	−0015	+0015	+0010	+0005	+0.6	+0.5	−0.1	−0.1
Sound of Mull								
Tobermoray	+0025	+0010	+0015	+0025	+0.4	+0.4	0.0	0.0
Salen	+0045	+0015	+0020	+0030	+0.2	+0.2	−0.1	0.0
Loch Aline	−	+0012	+0012	−	+0.5	+0.3	−	−
Craignure	+0030	+0005	+0010	+0015	0.0	+0.1	−0.1	−0.1
Loch Linnhe								
Corran	+0007	+0007	+0004	+0004	+0.4	+0.4	−0.1	0.0
Corpach	0000	+0020	+0040	0000	0.0	0.0	−0.2	−0.2
Loch Eil Head	+0025	+0045	+0105	+0025	−	−	−	−
Loch Leven Head	+0045	+0045	+0045	+0045	−	−	−	−
Port Appin	−0005	−0005	−0030	0000	+0.2	+0.2	+0.1	+0.1
Loch Creran								
Barcaldine Pier	+0010	+0020	+0040	+0015	+0.1	+0.1	0.0	+0.1
Loch Creran Head	+0015	+0025	+0120	+0020	−0.3	−0.3	−0.4	−0.3
Loch Etive								
Dunstaffnage Bay	+0005	0000	0000	+0005	+0.1	+0.1	+0.1	+0.1
Connel	+0020	+0005	+0010	+0015	−0.3	−0.2	−0.1	+0.1
Bonawe	+0150	+0205	+0240	+0210	−2.0	−1.7	−1.3	−0.5
Seil Sound	−0035	−0015	−0040	−0015	−1.3	−0.9	−0.7	−0.3
Colonsay								
Scalasaig	−0020	−0005	−0015	+0005	−0.1	−0.2	−0.2	−0.2
Jura								
Glengarrisdale Bay	−0020	0000	−0010	0000	−0.4	−0.2	0.0	−0.2
Islay								
Rubha A'Mhail	−0020	0000	+0005	−0015	−0.3	−0.1	−0.3	−0.1
Ardnave Point	−0035	+0010	0000	−0025	−0.4	−0.2	−0.3	−0.1
Orsay	−0110	−0110	−0040	−0040	−1.4	−0.6	−0.5	−0.2
Bruichladdich	−0100	−0005	−0110	−0040	−1.7	−1.4	−0.4	+0.1
Port Ellen	−0530	−0050	−0045	−0530	−3.1	−2.1	−1.3	−0.4
Port Askaig	−0110	−0030	−0020	−0020	−1.9	−1.4	−0.8	−0.3
Sound of Jura								
Craighouse	−0430	−0130	−0050	−0500	−2.8	−2.0	−1.4	−0.4
Loch Melfort	−0055	−0025	−0040	−0035	−1.2	−0.8	−0.5	−0.1
Loch Beag	−0110	−0045	−0035	−0045	−1.6	−1.2	−0.8	−0.4
Carsaig Bay	−0105	−0040	−0050	−0050	−2.1	−1.6	−1.0	−0.4
Sound of Gigha	−0450	−0210	−0130	−0410	−2.5	−1.6	−1.0	−0.1
Machrihanish	−0520	−0350	−0340	−0540	Mean range 0.5 metres			

Refer to predictions on pages 21:130-21:132

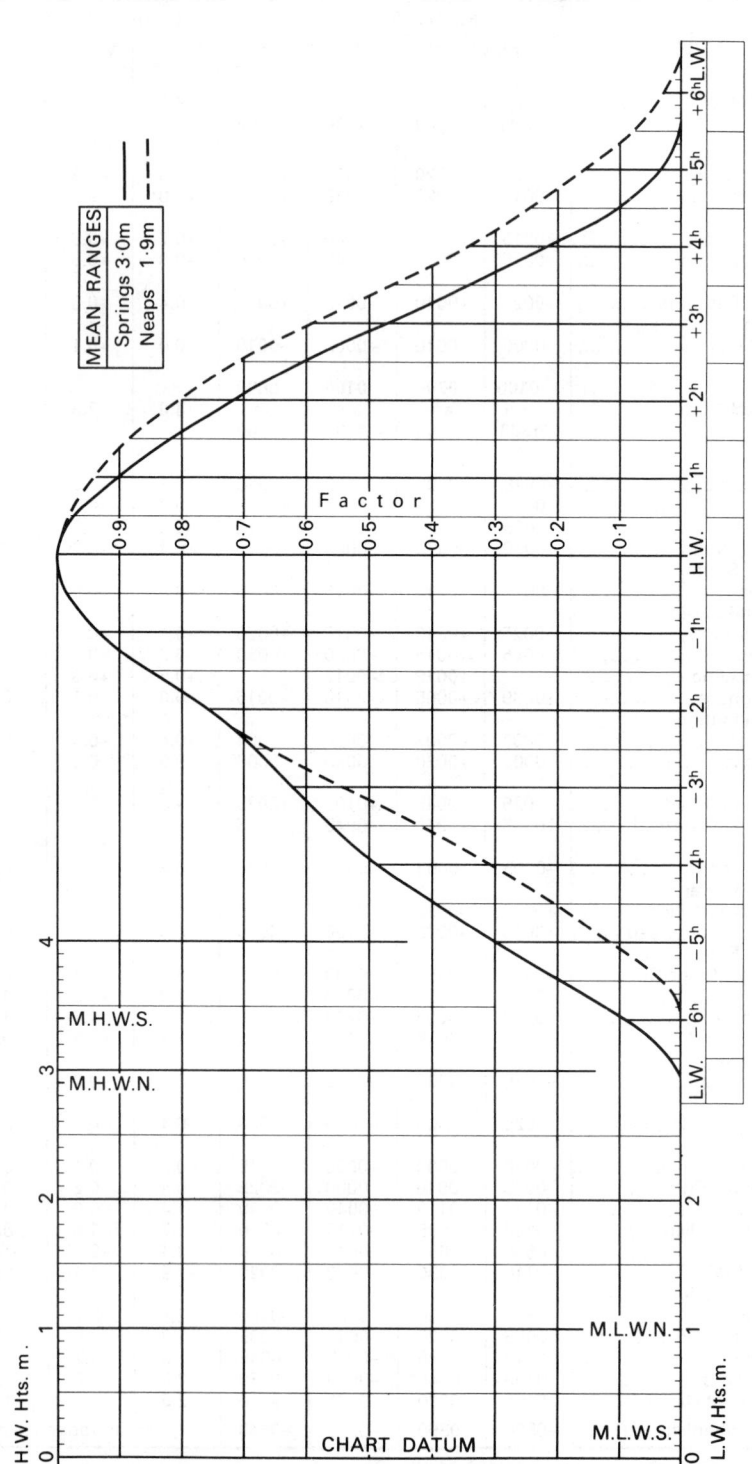

GREENOCK

MEAN SPRING AND NEAP CURVES
Springs occur 2 days after New and Full Moon.

MEAN RANGES
Springs 3·0m
Neaps 1·9m

Factor

M.H.W.S.
M.H.W.N.

M.L.W.N.
M.L.W.S.

CHART DATUM

H.W. Hts. m.
L.W.Hts.m.

Lat. 55°57'N. Long. 4°46'W. **HIGH & LOW WATER 1992**

GMT ADD 1 HOUR MARCH 29 — OCTOBER 25 FOR B.S.T.

JANUARY

Day	Time	m	Day	Time	m
1 W	0300 / 0946 / 1528 / 2157	1.0 / 3.1 / 0.9 / 3.0	16 TH	0218 / 0837 / 1437 / 2121	0.8 / 2.9 / 0.9 / 2.9
2 TH	0354 / 1042 / 1619 / 2258	1.0 / 3.2 / 0.8 / 3.0	17 F	0321 / 0950 / 1539 / 2238	0.7 / 3.1 / 0.7 / 3.0
3 F	0440 / 1129 / 1705 / 2348	0.9 / 3.3 / 0.7 / 3.0	18 SA	0415 / 1051 / 1633 / 2337	0.6 / 3.3 / 0.5 / 3.2
4 SA ●	0522 / 1211 / 1747	0.9 / 3.4 / 0.7	19 SU ○	0503 / 1143 / 1722	0.4 / 3.5 / 0.2
5 SU	0030 / 0558 / 1249 / 1824	3.0 / 0.9 / 3.4 / 0.6	20 M	0028 / 0549 / 1231 / 1808	3.4 / 0.3 / 3.8 / 0.1
6 M	0107 / 0632 / 1323 / 1858	3.0 / 1.0 / 3.4 / 0.6	21 TU	0114 / 0634 / 1316 / 1854	3.5 / 0.3 / 3.9 / 0.0
7 TU	0140 / 0703 / 1355 / 1931	3.1 / 1.0 / 3.4 / 0.6	22 W	0158 / 0718 / 1400 / 1939	3.6 / 0.3 / 4.1 / 0.0
8 W	0212 / 0734 / 1427 / 2004	3.1 / 0.9 / 3.4 / 0.6	23 TH	0241 / 0802 / 1443 / 2024	3.6 / 0.3 / 4.1 / 0.1
9 TH	0245 / 0807 / 1459 / 2040	3.2 / 0.9 / 3.4 / 0.6	24 F	0323 / 0847 / 1526 / 2110	3.5 / 0.4 / 4.0 / 0.2
10 F	0320 / 0844 / 1534 / 2118	3.2 / 0.9 / 3.4 / 0.6	25 SA	0406 / 0934 / 1610 / 2158	3.4 / 0.5 / 3.8 / 0.5
11 SA	0359 / 0924 / 1611 / 2202	3.2 / 1.0 / 3.3 / 0.7	26 SU	0451 / 1025 / 1655 / 2251	3.3 / 0.7 / 3.6 / 0.8
12 SU	0441 / 1010 / 1653 / 2252	3.1 / 1.0 / 3.2 / 0.8	27 M	0539 / 1113 / 1744 / 2357	3.1 / 0.9 / 3.3 / 1.0
13 M	0528 / 1102 / 1739 / 2351	3.1 / 1.1 / 3.1 / 0.8	28 TU	0634 / 1244 / 1840	2.9 / 1.0 / 3.0
14 TU	0621 / 1206 / 1833	3.0 / 1.1 / 2.9	29 W	0130 / 0749 / 1410 / 2000	1.2 / 2.8 / 1.0 / 2.8
15 W	0103 / 0722 / 1323 / 1945	0.9 / 2.9 / 1.1 / 2.8	30 TH	0248 / 0916 / 1523 / 2143	1.1 / 2.9 / 0.9 / 2.7
			31 F	0343 / 1023 / 1606 / 2253	1.1 / 3.0 / 0.8 / 2.8

FEBRUARY

Day	Time	m	Day	Time	m
1 SA	0429 / 1115 / 1651 / 2342	1.0 / 3.1 / 0.7 / 2.9	16 SU	0357 / 1031 / 1617 / 2327	0.6 / 3.2 / 0.4 / 3.1
2 SU	0508 / 1158 / 1730	1.0 / 3.2 / 0.7	17 M	0445 / 1126 / 1705	0.4 / 3.5 / 0.1
3 M ●	0021 / 0542 / 1235 / 1804	2.9 / 0.9 / 3.3 / 0.6	18 TU ○	0014 / 0530 / 1214 / 1750	3.3 / 0.3 / 3.7 / 0.0
4 TU	0054 / 0613 / 1308 / 1835	3.0 / 0.9 / 3.4 / 0.6	19 W	0058 / 0613 / 1258 / 1833	3.5 / 0.1 / 3.9 / -0.1
5 W	0124 / 0642 / 1339 / 1906	3.1 / 0.8 / 3.4 / 0.5	20 TH	0138 / 0655 / 1340 / 1916	3.5 / 0.1 / 4.0 / -0.1
6 TH	0154 / 0711 / 1408 / 1937	3.2 / 0.7 / 3.4 / 0.4	21 F	0218 / 0737 / 1421 / 1958	3.5 / 0.1 / 3.9 / 0.0
7 F	0224 / 0743 / 1439 / 2010	3.2 / 0.6 / 3.4 / 0.4	22 SA	0256 / 0820 / 1502 / 2040	3.5 / 0.2 / 3.8 / 0.2
8 SA	0257 / 0817 / 1511 / 2047	3.2 / 0.6 / 3.3 / 0.4	23 SU	0335 / 0903 / 1543 / 2123	3.3 / 0.4 / 3.6 / 0.5
9 SU	0333 / 0855 / 1546 / 2127	3.2 / 0.6 / 3.3 / 0.4	24 M	0415 / 0950 / 1624 / 2210	3.2 / 0.5 / 3.3 / 0.8
10 M	0412 / 0937 / 1624 / 2213	3.1 / 0.7 / 3.2 / 0.6	25 TU	0457 / 1045 / 1708 / 2306	3.0 / 0.8 / 3.0 / 1.1
11 TU	0454 / 1025 / 1706 / 2309	3.1 / 0.8 / 3.0 / 0.7	26 W	0544 / 1203 / 1756	2.8 / 1.0 / 2.7
12 W	0541 / 1125 / 1754	3.0 / 0.9 / 2.9	27 TH	0056 / 0645 / 1347 / 1903	1.3 / 2.7 / 1.0 / 2.5
13 TH	0024 / 0635 / 1246 / 1857	0.9 / 2.9 / 1.0 / 2.7	28 F	0228 / 0836 / 1453 / 2126	1.3 / 2.6 / 0.9 / 2.5
14 F	0154 / 0747 / 1416 / 2059	0.9 / 2.8 / 0.9 / 2.7	29 SA	0322 / 0958 / 1544 / 2237	1.2 / 2.8 / 0.8 / 2.6
15 SA	0303 / 0920 / 1523 / 2228	0.8 / 3.0 / 0.6 / 2.9			

MARCH

Day	Time	m	Day	Time	m
1 SU	0406 / 1053 / 1626 / 2323	1.0 / 3.0 / 0.7 / 2.8	16 M	0336 / 1008 / 1556 / 2309	0.6 / 3.2 / 0.3 / 3.1
2 M	0443 / 1136 / 1703 / 2359	0.9 / 3.1 / 0.6 / 2.9	17 TU	0423 / 1104 / 1644 / 2354	0.4 / 3.4 / 0.1 / 3.3
3 TU ○	0516 / 1212 / 1736	0.8 / 3.2 / 0.6	18 W	0507 / 1152 / 1728	0.2 / 3.6 / 0.0
4 W ●	0030 / 0545 / 1245 / 1806	3.0 / 0.7 / 3.3 / 0.5	19 TH	0035 / 0550 / 1236 / 1810	3.4 / 0.1 / 3.7 / -0.1
5 TH	0059 / 0614 / 1315 / 1836	3.1 / 0.6 / 3.3 / 0.4	20 F	0114 / 0631 / 1318 / 1851	3.4 / 0.0 / 3.8 / 0.0
6 F	0128 / 0644 / 1345 / 1908	3.2 / 0.5 / 3.3 / 0.3	21 SA	0151 / 0712 / 1357 / 1931	3.4 / 0.0 / 3.7 / 0.1
7 SA	0159 / 0716 / 1415 / 1941	3.2 / 0.4 / 3.3 / 0.2	22 SU	0228 / 0753 / 1436 / 2011	3.3 / 0.1 / 3.5 / 0.3
8 SU	0232 / 0751 / 1448 / 2018	3.2 / 0.3 / 3.2 / 0.2	23 M	0304 / 0835 / 1515 / 2050	3.2 / 0.2 / 3.3 / 0.5
9 M	0307 / 0829 / 1523 / 2059	3.2 / 0.3 / 3.2 / 0.3	24 TU	0341 / 0920 / 1554 / 2132	3.1 / 0.4 / 3.1 / 0.8
10 TU	0345 / 0911 / 1601 / 2145	3.2 / 0.4 / 3.1 / 0.5	25 W	0420 / 1011 / 1635 / 2221	2.9 / 0.7 / 2.8 / 1.1
11 W	0426 / 0959 / 1643 / 2240	3.1 / 0.5 / 2.9 / 0.7	26 TH	0502 / 1122 / 1720 / 2349	2.8 / 0.9 / 2.6 / 1.3
12 TH	0511 / 1059 / 1730 / 2359	2.9 / 0.7 / 2.8 / 0.9	27 F	0554 / 1307 / 1817	2.7 / 1.0 / 2.4
13 F	0602 / 1224 / 1833	2.9 / 0.8 / 2.6	28 SA	0149 / 0724 / 1418 / 2037	1.3 / 2.6 / 1.0 / 2.4
14 SA	0134 / 0710 / 1358 / 2052	0.9 / 2.8 / 0.7 / 2.6	29 SU	0246 / 0914 / 1508 / 2158	1.2 / 2.7 / 0.9 / 2.5
15 SU	0243 / 0853 / 1504 / 2214	0.8 / 2.9 / 0.5 / 2.8	30 M	0330 / 1015 / 1550 / 2245	1.1 / 2.8 / 0.7 / 2.7
			31 TU	0408 / 1101 / 1627 / 2323	0.9 / 3.0 / 0.6 / 2.9

APRIL

Day	Time	m	Day	Time	m
1 W	0441 / 1139 / 1701 / 2356	0.8 / 3.1 / 0.5 / 3.0	16 TH	0444 / 1128 / 1704	0.2 / 3.5 / 0.1
2 TH	0512 / 1214 / 1733	0.6 / 3.1 / 0.4	17 F ○	0009 / 0527 / 1213 / 1746	3.3 / 0.1 / 3.5 / 0.1
3 F	0027 / 0543 / 1247 / 1806	3.1 / 0.5 / 3.2 / 0.3	18 SA ●	0048 / 0609 / 1255 / 1827	3.3 / 0.0 / 3.5 / 0.1
4 SA	0059 / 0616 / 1319 / 1840	3.2 / 0.3 / 3.2 / 0.2	19 SU	0125 / 0650 / 1335 / 1906	3.3 / 0.0 / 3.4 / 0.3
5 SU	0132 / 0651 / 1352 / 1917	3.2 / 0.2 / 3.2 / 0.1	20 M	0201 / 0731 / 1413 / 1945	3.2 / 0.1 / 3.2 / 0.4
6 M	0207 / 0729 / 1427 / 1956	3.2 / 0.2 / 3.1 / 0.2	21 TU	0236 / 0813 / 1450 / 2023	3.2 / 0.2 / 3.1 / 0.7
7 TU	0244 / 0809 / 1505 / 2039	3.2 / 0.2 / 3.1 / 0.3	22 W	0312 / 0857 / 1529 / 2103	3.1 / 0.4 / 2.9 / 0.9
8 W	0323 / 0854 / 1546 / 2127	3.2 / 0.2 / 3.0 / 0.5	23 TH	0350 / 0946 / 1608 / 2149	3.0 / 0.6 / 2.8 / 1.1
9 TH	0404 / 0946 / 1630 / 2226	3.2 / 0.4 / 2.9 / 0.7	24 F	0431 / 1047 / 1653 / 2253	2.9 / 0.9 / 2.6 / 1.3
10 F	0450 / 1049 / 1723 / 2345	3.1 / 0.6 / 2.8 / 0.9	25 SA	0518 / 1208 / 1747	2.8 / 1.0 / 2.5
11 SA	0542 / 1212 / 1838	3.0 / 0.7 / 2.6	26 SU	0037 / 0621 / 1324 / 1911	1.4 / 2.7 / 1.0 / 2.5
12 SU	0111 / 0649 / 1337 / 2037	0.9 / 3.0 / 0.6 / 2.7	27 M	0151 / 0757 / 1419 / 2051	1.3 / 2.6 / 0.9 / 2.5
13 M	0217 / 0824 / 1440 / 2150	0.8 / 3.0 / 0.4 / 2.9	28 TU	0241 / 0909 / 1505 / 2151	1.1 / 2.7 / 0.7 / 2.7
14 TU	0310 / 0941 / 1532 / 2243	0.6 / 3.2 / 0.3 / 3.1	29 W	0323 / 1014 / 1546 / 2237	1.0 / 2.8 / 0.6 / 2.9
15 W	0359 / 1039 / 1620 / 2328	0.4 / 3.3 / 0.1 / 3.2	30 TH	0401 / 1059 / 1624 / 2316	0.8 / 2.9 / 0.5 / 3.0

To find H.W. Dover subtract 1 h. 15 min.

TIDAL DIFFERENCES PAGE 21:138. TIDAL CURVE PAGE 21:134.

Datum of predictions: 1.62 m. below Ordnance Datum (Newlyn) or approx. L.A.T.

21:136 — FIRTH OF CLYDE GREENOCK

HIGH & LOW WATER 1992 Lat. 55°57′N. Long. 4°46′W.

GMT ADD 1 HOUR MARCH 29 — OCTOBER 25 FOR B.S.T.

MAY

Date	Time	m	Date	Time	m
1 F	0437 / 1139 / 1701 / 2353	0.6 / 3.0 / 0.3 / 3.1	16	0508 / 1152 / 1727 (O)	0.2 / 3.2 / 0.3
2 SA	0514 / 1217 / 1738 (•)	0.4 / 3.1 / 0.2	17 SU	0024 / 0551 / 1236 / 1808	3.2 / 0.1 / 3.2 / 0.4
3 SU	0030 / 0551 / 1255 / 1817	3.2 / 0.2 / 3.1 / 0.2	18 M	0102 / 0634 / 1316 / 1847	3.2 / 0.1 / 3.1 / 0.5
4 M	0107 / 0631 / 1333 / 1857	3.2 / 0.1 / 3.1 / 0.2	19 TU	0139 / 0715 / 1355 / 1926	3.2 / 0.2 / 3.0 / 0.6
5 TU	0145 / 0712 / 1412 / 1940	3.3 / 0.0 / 3.1 / 0.2	20 W	0215 / 0757 / 1432 / 2003	3.2 / 0.3 / 2.9 / 0.8
6 W	0225 / 0757 / 1454 / 2027	3.2 / 0.1 / 3.1 / 0.4	21	0251 / 0839 / 1510 / 2042	3.1 / 0.5 / 2.9 / 0.9
7 TH	0306 / 0845 / 1539 / 2118	3.4 / 0.1 / 3.0 / 0.6	22 F	0328 / 0923 / 1549 / 2125	3.1 / 0.6 / 2.8 / 1.1
8 F	0350 / 0939 / 1628 / 2217	3.4 / 0.1 / 3.0 / 0.7	23 SA	0407 / 1013 / 1632 / 2217	3.0 / 0.8 / 2.8 / 1.2
9 SA	0438 / 1042 / 1726 / 2328	3.3 / 0.4 / 2.9 / 0.8	24 SU	0451 / 1110 / 1722 / 2320	2.9 / 0.9 / 2.7 / 1.3
10 SU	0531 / 1155 / 1841	3.2 / 0.5 / 2.8	25 M	0543 / 1214 / 1821	2.9 / 0.9 / 2.7
11 M	0042 / 0635 / 1309 / 2006	0.8 / 3.2 / 0.5 / 2.9	26	0032 / 0645 / 1317 / 1933	1.2 / 2.8 / 0.9 / 2.9
12 TU	0147 / 0754 / 1413 / 2116	0.7 / 3.1 / 0.4 / 3.0	27 W	0137 / 0727 / 1413 / 2045	1.1 / 2.7 / 0.8 / 2.7
13 W	0244 / 0909 / 1508 / 2212	0.6 / 3.2 / 0.3 / 3.1	28 TH	0232 / 0803 / 1503 / 2144	1.0 / 2.7 / 0.6 / 2.8
14 TH	0335 / 1011 / 1557 / 2300	0.4 / 3.2 / 0.3 / 3.2	29 F	0320 / 1013 / 1549 / 2235	0.8 / 2.8 / 0.5 / 2.9
15 F	0423 / 1104 / 1643 / 2344	0.3 / 3.3 / 0.3 / 3.2	30 SA	0404 / 1104 / 1633 / 2320	0.6 / 2.9 / 0.4 / 3.1
			31 SU	0448 / 1150 / 1716	0.4 / 3.0 / 0.3

JUNE

Date	Time	m	Date	Time	m
1 M	0003 / 0531 / 1235 / 1759 (•)	3.2 / 0.2 / 3.1 / 0.3	16 TU	0047 / 0621 / 1305 / 1834	3.2 / 0.3 / 3.0 / 0.7
2 TU	0045 / 0615 / 1319 / 1843	3.3 / 0.1 / 3.1 / 0.3	17 W	0124 / 0702 / 1343 / 1911	3.2 / 0.4 / 2.9 / 0.8
3 W	0127 / 0700 / 1403 / 1929	3.4 / 0.0 / 3.2 / 0.3	18 TH	0200 / 0741 / 1419 / 1947	3.2 / 0.4 / 2.9 / 0.9
4 TH	0210 / 0747 / 1448 / 2016	3.5 / 0.0 / 3.2 / 0.4	19 F	0235 / 0818 / 1454 / 2023	3.2 / 0.5 / 3.0 / 0.9
5 F	0254 / 0837 / 1535 / 2107	3.6 / 0.0 / 3.2 / 0.5	20 SA	0310 / 0857 / 1531 / 2100	3.2 / 0.6 / 3.0 / 1.0
6 SA	0339 / 0929 / 1625 / 2202	3.6 / 0.1 / 3.2 / 0.6	21 SU	0347 / 0938 / 1610 / 2142	3.2 / 0.7 / 3.0 / 1.0
7 SU	0427 / 1026 / 1719 / 2302	3.6 / 0.3 / 3.1 / 0.7	22 M	0426 / 1023 / 1654 / 2230	3.1 / 0.7 / 2.9 / 1.1
8 M	0519 / 1129 / 1819	3.5 / 0.4 / 3.0	23 TU	0509 / 1114 / 1742 / 2325	3.0 / 0.8 / 2.9 / 1.1
9 TU	0008 / 0616 / 1238 / 1928	0.8 / 3.4 / 0.5 / 3.0	24 W	0558 / 1213 / 1837	2.9 / 0.8 / 2.8
10 W	0115 / 0722 / 1345 / 2037	0.7 / 3.2 / 0.5 / 3.0	25 TH	0029 / 0655 / 1319 / 1939	1.1 / 2.8 / 0.8 / 2.8
11 TH	0218 / 0835 / 1445 / 2139	0.7 / 3.1 / 0.6 / 3.0	26 F	0137 / 0806 / 1422 / 2048	1.0 / 2.7 / 0.7 / 2.8
12 F	0314 / 0944 / 1539 / 2234	0.5 / 3.1 / 0.6 / 3.1	27 SA	0240 / 0925 / 1519 / 2153	0.9 / 2.7 / 0.6 / 2.9
13 SA	0406 / 1045 / 1628 / 2322	0.4 / 3.0 / 0.6 / 3.1	28 SU	0335 / 1033 / 1610 / 2249	0.7 / 2.8 / 0.5 / 3.1
14 SU	0454 / 1137 / 1713	0.4 / 3.0 / 0.6	29 M	0426 / 1130 / 1658 / 2340	0.5 / 3.0 / 0.4 / 3.2
15 M	0006 / 0539 / 1224 / 1755 (•)	3.2 / 0.3 / 3.0 / 0.7	30 TU	0515 / 1220 / 1745	0.3 / 3.1 / 0.3

JULY

Date	Time	m	Date	Time	m
1 W	0027 / 0601 / 1308 / 1830	3.4 / 0.1 / 3.3 / 0.3	16 TH	0112 / 0645 / 1331 / 1854	3.3 / 0.5 / 3.0 / 0.8
2 TH	0112 / 0648 / 1353 / 1915	3.6 / 0.0 / 3.4 / 0.3	17 F	0146 / 0719 / 1403 / 1926	3.3 / 0.5 / 3.1 / 0.8
3 F	0156 / 0734 / 1438 / 2001	3.7 / 0.0 / 3.4 / 0.3	18 SA	0218 / 0752 / 1435 / 1958	3.3 / 0.5 / 3.1 / 0.8
4 SA	0241 / 0822 / 1523 / 2048	3.8 / 0.0 / 3.4 / 0.4	19 SU	0250 / 0826 / 1508 / 2031	3.3 / 0.6 / 3.1 / 0.8
5 SU	0326 / 0910 / 1609 / 2138	3.8 / 0.1 / 3.4 / 0.5	20 M	0323 / 0902 / 1544 / 2108	3.3 / 0.6 / 3.1 / 0.8
6 M	0412 / 1002 / 1656 / 2232	3.8 / 0.3 / 3.3 / 0.6	21 TU	0358 / 0941 / 1623 / 2150	3.2 / 0.6 / 3.1 / 0.9
7 TU	0500 / 1058 / 1748 / 2332	3.6 / 0.5 / 3.2 / 0.7	22 W	0437 / 1026 / 1705 / 2237	3.1 / 0.7 / 3.0 / 0.9
8 W	0551 / 1202 / 1846	3.4 / 0.7 / 3.0	23 TH	0519 / 1120 / 1753 / 2334	3.0 / 0.8 / 2.9 / 1.0
9 TH	0041 / 0649 / 1317 / 1954	0.8 / 3.2 / 0.8 / 3.0	24 F	0607 / 1227 / 1847	2.9 / 0.9 / 2.9
10 F	0154 / 0800 / 1428 / 2107	0.8 / 3.0 / 0.8 / 3.0	25 SA	0045 / 0706 / 1346 / 1953	1.0 / 2.8 / 0.9 / 2.8
11 SA	0259 / 0922 / 1528 / 2211	0.7 / 2.9 / 0.8 / 3.0	26 SU	0205 / 0837 / 1455 / 2112	0.9 / 2.7 / 0.8 / 2.9
12 SU	0354 / 1034 / 1619 / 2306	0.6 / 2.9 / 0.7 / 3.1	27 M	0313 / 1010 / 1552 / 2223	0.8 / 2.8 / 0.7 / 3.1
13 M	0443 / 1131 / 1704 / 2353	0.5 / 2.9 / 0.8 / 3.2	28 TU	0409 / 1115 / 1641 / 2319	0.5 / 3.0 / 0.5 / 3.3
14 TU	0528 / 1217 / 1744	0.3 / 2.9 / 0.8	29 W	0458 / 1207 / 1727	0.3 / 3.2 / 0.4
15 W	0034 / 0607 / 1257 / 1821	3.3 / 0.5 / 3.0 / 0.8	30 TH	0009 / 0545 / 1254 / 1811	3.6 / 0.1 / 3.4 / 0.3
			31 F	0055 / 0630 / 1337 / 1855	3.8 / 0.0 / 3.5 / 0.2

AUGUST

Date	Time	m	Date	Time	m
1 SA	0139 / 0715 / 1420 / 1939	3.9 / -0.1 / 3.6 / 0.2	16 SU	0156 / 0721 / 1410 / 1929	3.4 / 0.6 / 3.2 / 0.7
2 SU	0223 / 0800 / 1501 / 2024	4.0 / 0.0 / 3.6 / 0.2	17 M	0226 / 0753 / 1441 / 2001	3.3 / 0.5 / 3.3 / 0.7
3 M	0306 / 0845 / 1544 / 2110	4.0 / 0.1 / 3.5 / 0.4	18 TU	0257 / 0827 / 1515 / 2036	3.3 / 0.5 / 3.3 / 0.7
4 TU	0350 / 0933 / 1627 / 2200	3.9 / 0.3 / 3.4 / 0.5	19 W	0330 / 0905 / 1552 / 2115	3.2 / 0.6 / 3.2 / 0.7
5 W	0435 / 1023 / 1712 / 2256	3.6 / 0.6 / 3.3 / 0.7	20 TH	0406 / 0948 / 1632 / 2201	3.2 / 0.7 / 3.2 / 0.8
6 TH	0522 / 1124 / 1803	3.4 / 0.9 / 3.1	21 F	0447 / 1039 / 1716 / 2255	3.0 / 0.8 / 3.1 / 0.9
7 F	0007 / 0614 / 1249 / 1906	0.9 / 3.2 / 1.1 / 2.9	22 SA	0531 / 1145 / 1806	2.9 / 1.0 / 3.0
8 SA	0134 / 0723 / 1417 / 2034	0.9 / 2.9 / 1.1 / 2.9	23 SU	0006 / 0625 / 1317 / 1906	1.0 / 2.8 / 1.1 / 2.9
9 SU	0246 / 0908 / 1518 / 2152	0.9 / 2.8 / 1.1 / 3.0	24 M	0139 / 0801 / 1435 / 2034	1.0 / 2.8 / 1.0 / 3.0
10 M	0341 / 1028 / 1607 / 2251	0.8 / 2.8 / 1.0 / 3.1	25 TU	0253 / 0957 / 1532 / 2158	0.8 / 2.9 / 0.8 / 3.2
11 TU	0428 / 1123 / 1649 / 2339	0.7 / 2.9 / 1.0 / 3.2	26 W	0350 / 1100 / 1621 / 2258	0.5 / 3.1 / 0.6 / 3.4
12 W	0510 / 1205 / 1727	0.6 / 3.0 / 0.9	27 TH	0439 / 1150 / 1706 / 2348	0.3 / 3.3 / 0.4 / 3.7
13 TH	0019 / 0547 / 1241 / 1800 (O)	3.3 / 0.6 / 3.1 / 0.9	28 F	0525 / 1234 / 1750 (•)	0.1 / 3.5 / 0.3
14 F	0055 / 0620 / 1312 / 1830	3.4 / 0.6 / 3.2 / 0.8	29 SA	0034 / 0609 / 1316 / 1832	3.9 / 0.0 / 3.6 / 0.2
15 SA	0126 / 0651 / 1341 / 1859	3.4 / 0.6 / 3.2 / 0.8	30 SU	0118 / 0652 / 1355 / 1915	4.0 / 0.0 / 3.7 / 0.1
			31 M	0200 / 0735 / 1435 / 1958	4.0 / 0.1 / 3.6 / 0.2

GENERAL — Duration and rate of ebb increased and decreased by: snow; heavy rain; strong and persistent N. and E. winds. Duration and rate of flood increased and ebb decreased by: strong and persistent S. and SW. winds.

GREENOCK FIRTH OF CLYDE 21:137

Lat. 55°57'N. Long. 4°46'W.   HIGH & LOW WATER 1992

GMT   ADD 1 HOUR MARCH 29 — OCTOBER 25 FOR B.S.T.

SEPTEMBER

Day	DoW	Time	m	Time	m	Time	m	Time	m
1	TU	0242	3.9	0817	0.2	1514	3.5	2042	0.3
2	W	0324	3.8	0901	0.5	1555	3.4	2129	0.5
3	TH	0407	3.5	0948	0.8	1637	3.3	2223	0.7
4	F	0451	3.3	1043	1.1	1723	3.1	2335	1.0
5	SA	0541	3.0	1213	1.4	1819	2.9		
6	SU	0113	1.1	0645	2.7	1358	1.4	1952	2.9
7	M	0226	1.0	0854	2.7	1458	1.3	2126	3.0
8	TU	0320	0.9	1013	2.8	1544	1.2	2228	3.1
9	W	0405	0.8	1103	3.0	1625	1.1	2315	3.3
10	TH	0444	0.8	1142	3.1	1700	1.0	2354	3.4
11	F	0519	0.7	1214	3.2	1732	0.9		
12	SA ○	0028	3.4	0550	0.6	1244	3.3	1800	0.8
13	SU	0100	3.4	0620	0.6	1313	3.3	1829	0.7
14	M	0129	3.4	0650	0.5	1342	3.4	1900	0.6
15	TU	0159	3.3	0722	0.5	1413	3.4	1933	0.6
16	W	0230	3.3	0757	0.5	1447	3.4	2009	0.5
17	TH	0304	3.2	0835	0.6	1524	3.4	2049	0.6
18	F	0341	3.2	0918	0.7	1604	3.3	2135	0.7
19	SA	0422	3.1	1010	0.9	1647	3.2	2231	0.9
20	SU	0508	3.0	1118	1.1	1735	3.2	2345	1.0
21	M	0604	2.8	1253	1.2	1834	3.1		
22	TU	0120	1.0	0757	2.8	1411	1.1	2002	3.1
23	W	0233	0.8	0941	3.0	1508	0.9	2131	3.3
24	TH	0328	0.5	1040	3.2	1557	0.7	2233	3.6
25	F	0417	0.3	1128	3.5	1642	0.5	2324	3.8
26	SA •	0502	0.1	1210	3.6	1726	0.3		
27	SU	0010	3.9	0545	0.1	1250	3.7	1808	0.2
28	M	0054	4.0	0627	0.1	1329	3.7	1851	0.1
29	TU	0136	3.9	0709	0.2	1407	3.7	1933	0.2
30	W	0217	3.8	0750	0.4	1445	3.6	2017	0.3

OCTOBER

Day	DoW	Time	m	Time	m	Time	m	Time	m
1	TH	0258	3.6	0832	0.7	1524	3.5	2103	0.5
2	F	0339	3.4	0916	1.0	1604	3.3	2156	0.8
3	SA	0422	3.1	1006	1.3	1648	3.2	2304	1.0
4	SU	0510	2.9	1123	1.5	1739	3.1		
5	M	0039	1.2	0610	2.7	1319	1.6	1856	3.0
6	TU	0154	1.1	0813	2.7	1423	1.5	2042	3.0
7	W	0248	1.0	0937	2.8	1511	1.4	2150	3.1
8	TH	0332	0.9	1027	3.0	1552	1.2	2239	3.2
9	F	0411	0.8	1106	3.2	1627	1.1	2320	3.3
10	SA	0446	0.7	1140	3.3	1659	1.0	2356	3.4
11	SU ○	0518	0.7	1211	3.4	1730	0.8		
12	M	0029	3.4	0549	0.6	1243	3.4	1801	0.7
13	TU	0101	3.3	0622	0.5	1314	3.5	1834	0.6
14	W	0134	3.3	0656	0.5	1348	3.5	1910	0.5
15	TH	0208	3.3	0734	0.5	1423	3.5	1949	0.5
16	F	0244	3.2	0814	0.6	1501	3.5	2032	0.5
17	SA	0324	3.2	0900	0.8	1542	3.5	2121	0.6
18	SU	0408	3.1	0954	1.0	1626	3.4	2219	0.8
19	M	0458	3.0	1103	1.2	1715	3.4	2333	0.9
20	TU	0603	2.9	1229	1.3	1815	3.3		
21	W	0058	0.9	0751	2.9	1343	1.1	1936	3.3
22	TH	0208	0.7	0915	3.1	1441	1.0	2101	3.4
23	F	0304	0.5	1013	3.3	1532	0.7	2205	3.6
24	SA	0353	0.4	1101	3.5	1619	0.5	2259	3.7
25	SU •	0440	0.3	1145	3.6	1704	0.4	2346	3.8
26	M	0523	0.2	1225	3.7	1748	0.3		
27	TU	0031	3.8	0605	0.3	1304	3.7	1830	0.2
28	W	0114	3.7	0647	0.4	1342	3.7	1913	0.3
29	TH	0154	3.6	0727	0.6	1420	3.6	1957	0.4
30	F	0235	3.4	0808	0.8	1458	3.5	2043	0.6
31	SA	0315	3.2	0850	1.1	1537	3.4	2133	0.8

NOVEMBER

Day	DoW	Time	m	Time	m	Time	m	Time	m
1	SU	0357	3.1	0936	1.3	1619	3.3	2232	1.0
2	M	0444	2.9	1036	1.5	1706	3.2	2347	1.2
3	TU	0539	2.8	1206	1.7	1806	3.1		
4	W	0103	1.2	0659	2.8	1328	1.6	1932	3.0
5	TH	0203	1.1	0832	2.9	1424	1.5	2053	3.1
6	F	0251	1.0	0934	3.0	1510	1.3	2152	3.1
7	SA	0333	0.9	1021	3.1	1549	1.2	2240	3.2
8	SU	0411	0.8	1101	3.2	1625	1.0	2321	3.3
9	M •	0447	0.7	1138	3.4	1700	0.8		
10	TU ○	0000	3.3	0522	0.6	1214	3.5	1736	0.7
11	W	0037	3.3	0559	0.5	1249	3.5	1814	0.5
12	TH	0114	3.3	0637	0.4	1326	3.6	1853	0.4
13	F	0152	3.3	0718	0.6	1404	3.7	1936	0.4
14	SA	0233	3.2	0802	0.7	1444	3.7	2022	0.4
15	SU	0316	3.1	0850	0.8	1527	3.7	2113	0.5
16	M	0403	3.2	0944	1.0	1613	3.7	2210	0.6
17	TU	0457	3.2	1047	1.1	1703	3.6	2317	0.7
18	W	0602	3.1	1159	1.2	1801	3.5		
19	TH	0030	0.8	0724	3.1	1311	1.1	1911	3.5
20	F	0139	0.7	0841	3.2	1413	1.0	2028	3.5
21	SA	0239	0.6	0943	3.3	1508	0.8	2137	3.5
22	SU	0332	0.5	1034	3.5	1558	0.6	2235	3.5
23	M	0420	0.5	1121	3.5	1646	0.5	2327	3.5
24	TU	0506	0.5	1203	3.6	1732	0.4		
25	W	0013	3.5	0549	0.5	1244	3.6	1815	0.4
26	TH	0057	3.5	0630	0.6	1323	3.6	1859	0.4
27	F	0138	3.4	0710	0.8	1402	3.6	1942	0.5
28	SA	0218	3.3	0750	0.9	1438	3.6	2025	0.6
29	SU	0257	3.2	0829	1.1	1515	3.5	2110	0.8
30	M	0337	3.1	0911	1.3	1555	3.4	2158	0.9

DECEMBER

Day	DoW	Time	m	Time	m	Time	m	Time	m
1	TU	0420	3.0	0958	1.4	1637	3.3	2252	1.1
2	W	0508	3.0	1054	1.5	1726	3.2	2353	1.2
3	TH	0604	2.9	1203	1.6	1824	3.1		
4	F	0058	1.2	0711	2.9	1315	1.5	1936	3.0
5	SA	0158	1.1	0824	2.9	1416	1.4	2051	3.0
6	SU	0250	1.0	0927	3.0	1507	1.2	2155	3.0
7	M	0336	0.8	1019	3.2	1552	1.0	2247	3.1
8	TU	0419	0.7	1105	3.3	1634	0.8	2334	3.1
9	W ○	0501	0.6	1147	3.4	1716	0.6		
10	TH	0018	3.2	0542	0.5	1228	3.6	1758	0.5
11	F	0100	3.3	0624	0.5	1309	3.7	1841	0.3
12	SA	0143	3.4	0707	0.5	1350	3.8	1926	0.3
13	SU	0226	3.4	0752	0.6	1432	3.9	2012	0.3
14	M	0310	3.4	0839	0.7	1515	3.9	2101	0.3
15	TU	0357	3.4	0929	0.8	1601	3.9	2154	0.4
16	W	0448	3.3	1025	0.9	1650	3.8	2252	0.6
17	TH	0544	3.2	1127	1.0	1743	3.6	2357	0.7
18	F	0648	3.2	1236	1.0	1844	3.5		
19	SA	0108	0.7	0800	3.2	1345	0.9	1955	3.4
20	SU	0216	0.8	0909	3.2	1447	0.8	2110	3.3
21	M	0315	0.7	1009	3.3	1543	0.7	2218	3.3
22	TU	0407	0.7	1101	3.4	1634	0.5	2315	3.3
23	W	0454	0.7	1147	3.5	1721	0.5		
24	TH	0005	3.3	0538	0.7	1230	3.5	1804	0.4
25	F	0049	3.3	0618	0.8	1309	3.6	1846	0.5
26	SA	0129	3.2	0657	0.8	1346	3.6	1926	0.5
27	SU	0205	3.2	0733	0.9	1422	3.6	2004	0.6
28	M	0241	3.2	0809	1.0	1456	3.5	2042	0.7
29	TU	0316	3.2	0844	1.1	1532	3.5	2121	0.8
30	W	0354	3.1	0922	1.1	1609	3.4	2203	0.9
31	TH	0435	3.1	1005	1.2	1649	3.2	2250	1.0

RATE AND SET — All streams are weak, irregular, unreliable — being much affected by weather conditions. Off Whiteforeland Point: Ingoing −0430 Dover, Spring rate 1-1½ kn.; Outgoing +0130 Dover, Spring rate 1-1½ kn.

TIDAL DIFFERENCES ON GREENOCK

PLACE	TIME DIFFERENCES				HEIGHT DIFFERENCES (Metres)			
	High Water		Low Water		MHWS	MHWN	MLWN	MLWS
GREENOCK	0000 and 1200	0600 and 1800	0000 and 1200	0600 and 1800	3.4	2.9	1.0	0.4
Firth of Clyde								
Southend, Kintyre	−0020	−0040	−0040	+0035	−1.3	−1.2	−0.5	−0.2
Sanda Island	−0040	−0040	−	−	−1.0	−0.9	−	−
Campbeltown	+0010	+0005	+0005	+0020	−0.5	−0.3	+0.1	+0.2
Carradale	0000	+0010	0000	+0010	−0.3	−0.2	+0.1	+0.1
Loch Ranza	−0015	−0005	−0005	−0010	−0.4	−0.3	−0.1	0.0
Loch Fyne								
East Loch Tarbert	+0005	+0005	−0020	+0015	0.0	0.0	+0.1	−0.1
Lochgilphead	+0008	+0008	+0005	+0022	0.0	0.0	−0.2	−0.1
Inverary	+0011	+0011	+0034	+0034	−0.1	+0.1	−0.5	−0.2
Kyles of Bute								
Rubha Bodach	−0020	−0010	−0007	−0007	−0.2	−0.1	+0.2	+0.2
Tighnabruich	+0007	−0010	−0002	−0015	0.0	+0.2	+0.4	+0.5
Firth of Clyde (Cont)								
Millport	−0005	−0025	−0025	−0005	0.0	−0.1	0.0	+0.1
Rothesay Bay	−0020	−0015	−0010	−0002	+0.2	+0.2	+0.2	+0.2
Wemyss Bay	−0005	−0005	−0005	−0005	0.0	0.0	+0.1	+0.1
Loch Long								
Coulport	−0005	−0005	−0005	−0005	0.0	0.0	−0.1	−0.1
Lochgoilhead	+0015	0000	−0005	−0005	−0.2	−0.3	−0.3	−0.3
Arrochar	−0005	−0005	−0005	−0005	0.0	0.0	−0.1	−0.1
Gare Loch								
Rosneath (Rhu Pier)	−0005	−0005	−0005	−0005	0.0	−0.1	0.0	0.0
Shandon	−0005	−0005	−0005	−0005	0.0	0.0	0.0	−0.1
Garelochhead	0000	0000	0000	0000	0.0	0.0	0.0	−0.1
River Clyde								
Helensburgh	0000	0000	0000	0000	0.0	0.0	0.0	0.0
Port Glasgow	+0010	+0005	+0010	+0020	+0.2	+0.1	0.0	0.0
Bowling	+0020	+0010	+0030	+0055	+0.6	+0.5	+0.3	+0.1
Renfrew	+0025	+0015	+0035	+0100	+0.9	+0.8	+0.5	+0.2
Glasgow	+0025	+0015	+0035	+0105	+1.3	+1.2	+0.6	+0.4
Firth of Clyde (Cont.)								
Brodick Bay	0000	0000	+0005	+0005	−0.2	−0.2	0.0	0.0
Lamlash	−0016	−0036	−0024	−0004	−0.2	−0.2	−	−
Ardrossan	−0020	−0010	−0010	−0010	−0.2	−0.2	+0.1	+0.1
Irvine	−0020	−0020	−0030	−0010	−0.3	−0.3	−0.1	0.0
Troon	−0025	−0025	−0020	−0020	−0.2	−0.2	0.0	0.0
Ayr	−0025	−0025	−0030	−0015	−0.4	−0.3	+0.1	+0.1
Girvan	−0025	−0040	−0035	−0010	−0.3	−0.3	−0.1	0.0
Ballantrae	−0025	−0030	−0025	−0015	−0.3	−0.3	−0.2	−0.1
Loch Ryan								
Stranraer	−0020	−0020	−0017	−0017	−0.4	−0.4	−0.4	−0.2

Refer to predictions on pages 21:135-21:137

LIVERPOOL MERSEY 21:139

HIGH & LOW WATER 1992
Lat. 53°25'N. Long. 3°00'W.

GMT ADD 1 HOUR MARCH 29 — OCTOBER 25 FOR B.S.T.

	JANUARY				FEBRUARY				MARCH				APRIL		
	Time m		Time m		Time m		Time m		Time m		Time m		Time m		Time m
1	0246 2.5	**16**	0138 2.7	**1**	0414 2.4	**16**	0341 1.9	**1**	0352 2.6	**16**	0325 1.9	**1**	0433 1.8	**16**	0448 0.9
W	0830 7.9	Th	0727 7.7		0956 8.3		0925 8.7		0932 8.1		0908 8.7		1012 8.8		1024 9.5
	1514 2.6		1420 2.7	Sa	1644 2.1	Su	1620 1.3	Su	1620 2.2	M	1604 1.2	W	1654 1.5	Th	1719 0.5
	2058 8.0		2001 8.0		2221 8.2		2156 8.9		2159 8.1		2141 8.9		2231 8.7		2248 9.5
2	0342 2.3	**17**	0251 2.3	**2**	0457 2.1	**17**	0440 1.3	**2**	0433 2.1	**17**	0423 1.2	**2**	0508 1.5	**17**	0532 0.7
	0924 8.3		0837 8.2		1035 8.7		1019 9.3		1012 8.6		1000 9.3		1045 9.0		1106 9.6
Th	1610 2.3	F	1529 2.1	Su	1723 1.8	M	1716 0.6	M	1658 1.8	Tu	1658 0.5	Th	1727 1.2	F	1800 0.5
	2150 8.2		2107 8.5		2258 8.5		2247 9.5		2234 8.5		2228 9.4		2302 9.0		○ 2327 9.6
3	0430 2.1	**18**	0355 1.8	**3**	0530 1.8	**18**	0530 0.7	**3**	0508 1.7	**18**	0512 0.7	**3**	0542 1.2	**18**	0612 0.6
	1010 8.6		0936 8.8		1111 9.0		1106 9.8		1045 8.9		1047 9.8		1118 9.2		1147 9.6
F	1657 2.1	Sa	1631 1.5	M	1756 1.6	Tu	1805 0.1	Tu	1730 1.4	W	1744 0.2	F	1801 1.0	Sa	1836 0.6
	2235 8.4		2206 9.0		● 2330 8.7		○ 2332 9.8		2305 8.8		○ 2312 9.7		● 2333 9.1		
4	0511 2.0	**19**	0451 1.3	**4**	0603 1.6	**19**	0617 0.4	**4**	0539 1.4	**19**	0556 0.4	**4**	0615 1.0	**19**	0005 9.5
	1051 8.8		1030 9.3		1143 9.1		1151 10.1		1118 9.2		1130 10.0		1150 9.4		0650 0.7
Sa	1736 1.9	Su	1727 0.9	Tu	1827 1.4	W	1849 −0.1	W	1800 1.2	Th	1827 0.0	Sa	1835 1.0	Su	1227 9.4
	● 2313 8.6		○ 2258 9.4						● 2334 9.0		2353 9.8				1913 0.9
5	0546 1.8	**20**	0543 0.9	**5**	0001 8.8	**20**	0015 9.9	**5**	0608 1.2	**20**	0636 0.3	**5**	0005 9.2	**20**	0043 9.3
	1127 9.0		1120 9.7		0632 1.4		0659 0.2		1149 9.3		1211 10.0		0650 1.0		0728 1.0
Su	1812 1.7	M	1818 0.4	W	1215 9.2	Th	1234 10.2	Th	1831 1.0	F	1904 0.1	Su	1224 9.4	M	1304 9.0
	2349 8.7		2347 9.7		1856 1.3		1931 −0.1						1909 1.0		1947 1.4
6	0618 1.8	**21**	0631 0.6	**6**	0031 8.9	**21**	0056 9.8	**6**	0004 9.1	**21**	0031 9.7	**6**	0039 9.2	**21**	0120 9.0
	1201 9.1		1207 10.0		0702 1.3		0738 0.3		0641 1.1		0714 0.4		0726 1.1		0805 1.4
M	1845 1.6	Tu	1907 0.1	Th	1245 9.2	F	1314 10.0	F	1218 9.4	Sa	1250 9.8	M	1259 9.3	Tu	1341 8.6
					1926 1.2		2009 0.2		1902 1.0		1941 0.5		1941 1.2		2019 1.9
7	0021 8.7	**22**	0034 9.8	**7**	0100 8.9	**22**	0135 9.6	**7**	0034 9.1	**22**	0109 9.5	**7**	0114 9.1	**22**	0157 8.6
	0649 1.7		0716 0.5		0734 1.4		0816 0.6		0712 1.1		0751 0.7		0801 1.3		0840 1.9
Tu	1235 9.1	W	1253 10.1	F	1316 9.2	Sa	1355 9.7	Sa	1249 9.3	Su	1328 9.4	Tu	1337 9.0	W	1420 8.1
	1916 1.6		1952 0.1		1957 1.3		2046 0.8		1931 1.1		2015 1.0		2016 1.6		2053 2.4
8	0052 8.7	**23**	0119 9.7	**8**	0130 8.8	**23**	0215 9.1	**8**	0103 9.1	**23**	0145 9.1	**8**	0152 8.8	**23**	0237 8.2
	0720 1.7		0759 0.6		0805 1.5		0854 1.2		0744 1.2		0827 1.2		0840 1.8		0919 2.4
W	1307 9.0	Th	1337 10.0	Sa	1345 9.0	Su	1434 9.1	Su	1320 9.2	M	1405 8.9	W	1420 8.7	Th	1505 7.6
	1947 1.6		2034 0.3		2027 1.5		2122 1.5		2002 1.3		2049 1.7		2056 2.0		2131 3.0
9	0124 8.6	**24**	0202 9.4	**9**	0159 8.6	**24**	0254 8.6	**9**	0134 8.9	**24**	0222 8.6	**9**	0239 8.5	**24**	0327 7.7
	0752 1.8		0840 0.9		0837 1.8		0934 1.8		0816 1.5		0904 1.9		0928 2.0		1007 2.8
Th	1340 8.9	F	1420 9.6	Su	1418 8.8	M	1517 8.4	M	1354 9.0	Tu	1446 8.2	Th	1514 8.2	F	1602 7.1
	2019 1.7		2117 0.8		2100 1.8		2202 2.2		2033 1.6		2124 2.4		2146 2.4		(2226 3.4
10	0157 8.4	**25**	0246 9.0	**10**	0233 8.4	**25**	0339 8.0	**10**	0209 8.7	**25**	0304 8.1	**10**	0338 8.0	**25**	0430 7.3
	0827 2.0		0922 1.4		0912 2.1		1019 2.5		0851 1.8		0945 2.5		1030 2.4		1115 3.1
F	1412 8.7	Sa	1504 9.2	M	1454 8.5	Tu	1606 7.6	Tu	1432 8.7	W	1532 7.5	F	1623 7.7	Sa	1715 6.8
	2054 1.9		2157 1.4		2135 2.2		(2251 3.0		2108 2.0		2206 3.1		) 2255 2.8		2349 3.6
11	0229 8.2	**26**	0331 8.5	**11**	0315 8.1	**26**	0435 7.4	**11**	0250 8.3	**26**	0357 7.5	**11**	0457 7.7	**26**	0546 7.1
	0903 2.3		1006 1.9		0953 2.5		1120 3.1		0934 2.3		1041 3.1		1154 2.7		1236 3.1
Sa	1447 8.5	Su	1552 8.5	Tu	1542 8.1	W	1716 7.0	W	1521 8.2	Th	1637 6.9	Sa	1750 7.6	Su	1839 6.9
	2131 2.2		(2244 2.1		) 2221 2.6				2156 2.5		(2312 3.6				
12	0307 8.0	**27**	0421 8.0	**12**	0409 7.8	**27**	0005 3.5	**12**	0345 7.9	**27**	0512 7.0	**12**	0027 2.8	**27**	0114 3.4
	0943 2.6		1058 2.5		1052 2.9		0557 7.0		1033 2.7		1207 3.4		0624 7.8		0700 7.3
Su	1529 8.2	M	1648 7.9	W	1645 7.7	Th	1255 3.4	Th	1627 7.7	F	1811 6.7	Su	1324 2.2	M	1347 2.8
	2213 2.5		2342 2.7		2329 2.9		1856 6.8		) 2304 2.9				1914 7.8		1947 7.3
13	0353 7.8	**28**	0525 7.5	**13**	0526 7.4	**28**	0144 3.5	**13**	0505 7.5	**28**	0056 3.7	**13**	0152 2.5	**28**	0218 3.0
	1031 2.9		1207 3.0		1219 3.0		0733 7.1		1201 2.9		0645 7.0		0741 8.2		0809 7.6
M	1620 7.9	Tu	1800 7.3	Th	1814 7.5	F	1427 3.2	F	1758 7.4	Sa	1341 3.2	M	1439 1.7	Tu	1443 2.4
	) 2305 2.7						2022 7.1				1942 6.9		2022 8.3		2036 7.7
14	0452 7.6	**29**	0056 3.1	**14**	0103 3.0	**29**	0258 3.1	**14**	0042 3.0	**29**	0218 3.3	**14**	0301 1.9	**29**	0308 2.5
	1134 3.1		0643 7.3		0659 7.5		0843 7.6		0641 7.5		0801 7.4		0844 8.7		0850 8.1
Tu	1726 7.7	W	1333 3.2	F	1357 2.7	Sa	1532 2.7	Sa	1341 2.5	Su	1449 2.8	Tu	1541 1.2	W	1531 2.0
			1928 7.3		1944 7.7		2118 7.6		1931 7.7		2042 7.5		2118 8.9		2117 8.2
15	0017 2.9	**30**	0216 3.1	**15**	0232 2.6			**15**	0213 2.6	**30**	0314 2.8	**15**	0359 1.4	**30**	0352 2.1
	0608 7.5		0805 7.5		0820 8.0				0804 8.0		0854 7.9		0938 9.2		0931 8.5
W	1259 3.0	Th	1454 2.9	Sa	1515 2.1			Su	1501 1.9	M	1539 2.3	W	1633 0.7	Th	1613 1.7
	1845 7.7		2043 7.4		2057 8.3				2043 8.3		2124 8.0		2204 9.2		2153 8.6
		31	0324 2.8							**31**	0356 2.3				
			0907 7.9								0935 8.4				
		F	1557 2.5							Tu	1619 1.8				
			2139 7.8								2200 8.4				

To find H.W. Dover subtract 0 h. 15 min.

TIDAL DIFFERENCES PAGES 21:143-21:144. TIDAL CURVE PAGE 21:142.

TIDAL STREAMS PAGES 21:148-21:153.

Datum of predictions: 4.93 m. below Ordnance Datum (Newlyn) or approx. L.A.T.

MERSEY **LIVERPOOL**

HIGH & LOW WATER 1992   Lat. 53°25'N. Long. 3°00'W.

GMT   ADD 1 HOUR MARCH 29 — OCTOBER 25 FOR B.S.T.

	MAY				JUNE				JULY				AUGUST		
	Time	m		Time	m		Time	m		Time	m		Time	m	

MAY

	Time	m		Time	m
1 F	0433 1009 1652 2228	1·7 8·8 1·4 8·9	**16** ○	0509 1045 Sa 1733 2305	1·2 9·1 1·1 9·2
2 Sa ●	0512 1045 1732 2304	1·3 9·1 1·2 9·1	**17** Su	0551 1127 1811 2344	1·1 9·1 1·2 9·2
3 Su	0551 1123 1810 2342	1·1 9·3 1·1 9·3	**18** M	0631 1207 1848	1·1 8·9 1·4
4 M	0632 1203 1848	1·0 9·3 1·1	**19** Tu	0022 0709 1245 1921	9·1 1·3 8·7 1·6
5 Tu	0019 0712 1243 1926	9·3 1·0 9·3 1·2	**20** W	0059 0745 1323 1955	8·9 1·6 8·5 1·9
6 W	0102 0754 1328 2006	9·2 1·1 9·1 1·5	**21** Th	0137 0820 1401 2029	8·7 1·9 8·2 2·3
7 Th	0147 0839 1418 2050	9·0 1·4 8·7 1·8	**22** F	0216 0857 1442 2105	8·4 2·2 7·8 2·6
8 F	0237 0931 1512 2143	8·7 1·7 8·3 2·2	**23** Sa	0300 0939 1528 2150	8·0 2·4 7·5 3·0
9 Sa ☽	0336 1033 1620 2249	8·3 1·9 8·0 2·5	**24** Su ☾	0350 1028 1624 2248	7·7 2·7 7·2 3·2
10 Su	0447 1144 1733	8·1 2·0 7·9	**25** M	0449 1130 1729 2358	7·5 2·8 7·1 3·3
11 M	0007 0601 1259 1848	2·5 8·1 1·9 8·0	**26** Tu	0554 1236 1836	7·4 2·8 7·2
12 Tu	0123 0713 1409 1954	2·3 8·3 1·7 8·3	**27** W	0110 0657 1341 1937	3·1 7·6 2·6 7·5
13 W	0232 0816 1451 2050	2·0 8·6 1·4 8·6	**28** Th	0212 0755 1439 2027	2·8 7·9 1·9 8·0
14 Th	0331 0911 1604 2139	1·6 8·8 1·2 8·9	**29** F	0307 0846 1531 2114	2·3 8·3 1·9 8·4
15 F	0423 1000 1651 2224	1·4 9·0 1·1 9·1	**30** Sa	0357 0932 1619 2156	1·9 8·6 1·6 8·8
			31 Su	0445 1017 1705 2240	1·5 8·9 1·4 9·1

JUNE

	Time	m		Time	m
1 M	0532 1102 1749 2323	1·2 9·2 1·2 9·3	**16** Tu	0617 1153 1828	1·5 8·7 1·6
2 Tu	0617 1147 1832	1·0 9·3 1·1	**17** W	0007 0655 1229 1902	9·0 1·5 8·6 1·7
3 W	0007 0703 1234 1916	9·4 0·8 9·3 1·1	**18** Th	0043 0730 1304 1934	9·0 1·6 8·5 1·8
4 Th	0053 0751 1323 2001	9·4 0·8 9·2 1·2	**19** F	0119 0802 1340 2006	8·8 1·7 8·4 2·0
5 F	0142 0839 1413 2047	9·3 0·9 9·0 1·5	**20** Sa	0155 0836 1416 2042	8·7 1·8 8·2 2·2
6 Sa	0233 0929 1507 2139	9·1 1·1 8·7 1·7	**21** Su	0232 0911 1454 2119	8·4 2·0 7·9 2·5
7 Su ☽	0328 1024 1604 2235	8·8 1·4 8·4 2·0	**22** M	0312 0950 1536 2204	8·2 2·3 7·7 2·8
8 M	0427 1123 1706 2340	8·6 1·6 8·1 2·2	**23** Tu	0357 1037 1626 2258	7·9 2·5 7·5 3·0
9 Tu	0532 1228 1814	8·3 1·8 8·0	**24** W ☾	0451 1133 1726	7·7 2·7 7·3
10 W	0049 0641 1335 1921	2·3 8·2 1·9 8·1	**25** Th	0004 0554 1241 1834	3·1 7·6 2·7 7·4
11 Th	0159 0748 1440 2023	2·2 8·2 1·9 8·3	**26** F	0117 0702 1351 1940	3·0 7·7 2·6 7·7
12 F	0304 0849 1538 2117	2·1 8·3 1·8 8·5	**27** Sa	0226 0805 1453 2039	2·6 8·0 2·3 8·2
13 Sa	0402 0942 1628 2206	1·7 8·5 1·7 8·7	**28** Su	0327 0903 1550 2131	2·0 8·4 1·9 8·6
14 Su	0452 1030 1712 2249	1·7 8·6 1·6 8·9	**29** M	0423 0956 1642 2221	1·7 8·8 1·5 9·0
15 M ○	0537 1113 1751 2329	1·5 8·7 1·6 9·0	**30** Tu ●	0516 1047 1733 2309	1·2 9·1 1·2 9·4

JULY

	Time	m		Time	m
1 W	0607 1136 1821 2357	0·8 9·4 0·9 9·6	**16** Th	0639 1212 1843	1·5 8·7 1·6
2 Th	0656 1225 1907	0·5 9·5 0·8	**17** F	0025 0710 1245 1914	9·1 1·4 8·7 1·6
3 F	0045 0744 1313 1954	9·8 0·4 9·5 0·8	**18** Sa	0057 0740 1316 1945	9·1 1·4 8·6 1·7
4 Sa	0133 0830 1401 2039	9·7 0·4 9·4 1·0	**19** Su	0130 0811 1347 2018	8·9 1·5 8·5 1·8
5 Su	0219 0917 1449 2124	9·6 0·7 9·1 1·3	**20** M	0202 0843 1419 2051	8·8 1·7 8·3 2·1
6 M	0308 1003 1539 2213	9·2 1·1 8·7 1·7	**21** Tu	0236 0917 1454 2129	8·5 2·0 8·1 2·4
7 Tu	0400 1055 1634 2308	8·8 1·5 8·3 2·1	**22** W	0314 0955 1535 2213	8·2 2·3 7·8 2·8
8 W	0458 1153 1737	8·3 2·0 7·9	**23** Th	0359 1042 1627 2309	7·9 2·6 7·6 3·0
9 Th	0014 0605 1300 1848	2·5 7·9 2·3 7·8	**24** F	0458 1144 1737	7·6 2·9 7·4
10 F	0128 0721 1412 1958	2·6 7·8 2·4 7·9	**25** Sa	0027 0614 1306 1857	3·1 7·5 2·9 7·5
11 Sa	0243 0832 1517 2100	2·5 7·8 2·3 8·1	**26** Su	0151 0734 1422 2011	2·8 7·7 2·6 8·0
12 Su	0349 0931 1612 2152	2·2 8·3 2·1 8·5	**27** M	0303 0843 1528 2112	2·3 8·2 2·1 8·5
13 M	0442 1020 1658 2237	2·0 8·8 1·9 8·9	**28** Tu	0406 0942 1626 2206	1·7 8·7 1·6 9·1
14 Tu ○	0526 1101 1737 2315	1·7 8·5 1·8 9·0	**29** W	0504 1034 1719 2257	1·1 9·2 1·1 9·6
15 W	0604 1139 1811 2351	1·6 9·1 1·7 9·1	**30** Th	0556 1123 1808 2343	0·6 9·6 0·7 9·9
			31 F	0643 1210 1855	0·2 9·8 0·5

AUGUST

	Time	m		Time	m
1 Sa	0029 0730 1256 1938	10·1 0·0 9·8 0·5	**16** ○	0032 0713 1248 1920	9·3 1·2 8·9 1·4
2 Su ☽	0114 0812 1340 2020	10·1 0·1 9·6 0·7	**17**	0103 0742 1317 1952	9·2 1·3 8·8 1·6
3 M	0158 0854 1423 2101	9·8 0·5 9·3 1·0	**18** Tu	0133 0813 1347 2025	9·0 1·5 8·6 1·9
4 Tu	0242 0936 1508 2145	9·4 1·0 8·8 1·6	**19** W	0202 0844 1418 2058	8·8 1·9 8·4 2·2
5 W ☽	0328 1021 1557 2235	8·8 1·7 8·3 2·2	**20**	0237 0919 1456 2138	8·5 2·2 8·1 2·6
6	0423 1115 1657 2339	8·2 2·4 7·8 2·7	**21** ☾	0319 1002 1545 2231	8·1 2·6 7·8 3·0
7 F	0532 1224 1812	7·6 2·9 7·5	**22** Sa	0417 1101 1654 2349	7·7 3·0 7·5 3·2
8 Sa	0103 0657 1347 1935	3·0 7·3 3·0 7·5	**23** Su	0540 1228 1825	7·4 3·1 7·4
9 Su	0227 0819 1500 2044	2·8 7·5 2·8 7·9	**24** M	0124 0712 1358 1949	2·9 7·6 2·8 7·9
10 M	0336 0919 1557 2138	2·5 7·9 2·4 8·4	**25** Tu	0244 0827 1510 2056	2·3 8·1 2·2 8·6
11 Tu	0430 1006 1642 2220	2·1 8·2 2·1 8·8	**26** W	0350 0928 1610 2150	1·6 8·8 1·5 9·2
12 W ○	0511 1044 1719 2257	1·7 8·5 1·8 9·0	**27** Th	0448 1019 1702 2240	0·9 9·3 1·0 9·8
13 Th ○	0546 1118 1751 2330	1·5 8·7 1·6 9·2	**28** F	0539 1106 1750 2325	0·4 9·8 0·6 10·1
14 F	0617 1149 1821	1·4 8·9 1·5	**29** Sa	0624 1150 1835	0·0 10·0 0·3
15	0001 0645 1219 1850	9·3 1·3 8·9 1·4	**30** Su	0008 0707 1232 1916	10·3 -0·1 9·9 0·3
			31 M	0050 0748 1314 1957	10·2 0·2 9·7 0·6

GENERAL — Duration of flood decreases as river is ascended; Duration of flood at Widnes 2½ h.; at Warrington 1¾ h. Streams run generally in direction of channel when banks are dry; across channel directly to and from entrance when banks are covered; Considerable swell on bar during strong NW. winds.

Lat. 53°25'N. Long. 3°00'W. **HIGH & LOW WATER 1992**

GMT   ADD 1 HOUR MARCH 29 — OCTOBER 25 FOR B.S.T.

SEPTEMBER

Day	Time	m	Time	m	Time	m	Time	m
1 Tu	0133	9.9	0826	0.6	1354	9.4	2036	1.0
2 W	0213	9.3	0904	1.3	1436	8.9	2118	1.7
3 Th	0258	8.7	0946	2.0	1521	8.3	2204	2.4
4 F	0349	7.9	1035	2.8	1619	7.7	2308	3.0
5 Sa	0458	7.2	1147	3.3	1736	7.3		
6 Su	0036	3.3	0634	7.0	1321	3.4	1909	7.3
7 M	0206	3.0	0801	7.2	1437	3.1	2022	7.8
8 Tu	0314	2.6	0900	7.8	1534	2.6	2114	8.3
9 W	0403	2.1	0943	8.2	1617	2.2	2155	8.7
10 Th	0442	1.8	1019	8.6	1652	1.8	2230	9.0
11 F	0516	1.5	1051	8.8	1725	1.6	2302	9.2
12 Sa	0546	1.3	1120	9.0	1754	1.4	○2333	9.4
13 Su	0615	1.2	1150	9.1	1824	1.3		
14 M	0003	9.4	0645	1.2	1218	9.1	1856	1.3
15 Tu	0034	9.3	0714	1.3	1246	9.0	1927	1.5
16 W	0103	9.1	0745	1.5	1317	8.9	2001	1.8
17 Th	0134	8.9	0816	1.8	1349	8.7	2034	2.1
18 F	0211	8.6	0850	2.2	1427	8.3	2114	2.5
19 Sa	0256	8.1	0932	2.7	1518	7.9	☽2209	2.9
20 Su	0356	7.7	1034	3.1	1630	7.6	2329	3.1
21 M	0520	7.4	1203	3.2	1804	7.5		
22 Tu	0106	2.8	0655	7.6	1337	2.9	1928	8.0
23 W	0226	2.2	0811	8.2	1450	2.2	2036	8.7
24 Th	0332	1.5	0910	8.9	1549	1.6	2129	9.3
25 F	0427	0.8	0959	9.4	1641	1.0	2217	9.8
26 Sa	0516	0.4	1044	9.8	1727	0.6	●2302	10.1
27 Su	0600	0.2	1126	10.0	1811	0.4	2344	10.2
28 M	0641	0.2	1207	9.9	1852	0.5		
29 Tu	0027	10.0	0720	0.5	1248	9.7	1933	0.7
30 W	0107	9.7	0757	1.0	1327	9.4	2012	1.2

OCTOBER

Day	Time	m	Time	m	Time	m	Time	m
1 Th	0148	9.1	0834	1.6	1406	8.9	2053	1.8
2 F	0230	8.5	0912	2.3	1450	8.3	2138	2.5
3 Sa	0319	7.8	0959	3.0	1545	7.8	☽2237	3.1
4 Su	0423	7.2	1106	3.5	1657	7.3		
5 M	0000	3.3	0553	6.9	1241	3.7	1825	7.3
6 Tu	0127	3.2	0723	7.1	1359	3.3	1942	7.6
7 W	0233	2.8	0825	7.6	1456	2.9	2037	8.1
8 Th	0324	2.3	0910	8.1	1541	2.4	2119	8.6
9 F	0403	1.9	0946	8.5	1619	2.0	2156	8.9
10 Sa	0438	1.6	1019	8.8	1652	1.7	2230	9.1
11 Su	0511	1.4	1048	9.0	1725	1.5	○2302	9.3
12 M	0543	1.3	1118	9.2	1757	1.4	2333	9.3
13 Tu	0615	1.2	1149	9.2	1832	1.4		
14 W	0005	9.3	0648	1.3	1221	9.2	1906	1.5
15 Th	0039	9.2	0721	1.5	1253	9.1	1942	1.7
16 F	0114	9.0	0755	1.8	1330	8.9	2020	2.0
17 Sa	0155	8.6	0832	2.2	1413	8.5	2104	2.3
18 Su	0244	8.2	0918	2.6	1507	8.1	2202	2.6
19 M	0346	7.8	1020	3.0	1617	7.8	☽2319	2.8
20 Tu	0508	7.6	1144	3.1	1743	7.6		
21 W	0046	2.5	0634	7.8	1312	2.8	1903	8.2
22 Th	0202	2.0	0747	8.3	1425	2.2	2009	8.7
23 F	0305	1.5	0846	8.8	1524	1.7	2105	9.2
24 Sa	0402	1.0	0935	9.3	1617	1.2	2155	9.6
25 Su	0449	0.7	1020	9.6	1705	0.9	●2240	9.8
26 M	0534	0.6	1104	9.8	1749	0.8	2323	9.9
27 Tu	0615	0.7	1144	9.7	1831	0.8		
28 W	0005	9.7	0653	0.9	1224	9.6	1912	1.0
29 Th	0046	9.3	0731	1.3	1303	9.3	1951	1.4
30 F	0126	8.9	0808	1.8	1342	8.9	2032	1.9
31 Sa	0206	8.4	0844	2.4	1425	8.4	2114	2.4

NOVEMBER

Day	Time	m	Time	m	Time	m	Time	m
1 Su	0253	7.8	0925	3.0	1514	8.0	2204	2.9
2 M	0348	7.3	1020	3.4	1614	7.6	☽2311	3.2
3 Tu	0458	7.0	1137	3.7	1726	7.3		
4 W	0025	3.2	0621	7.0	1259	3.6	1842	7.5
5 Th	0134	3.0	0731	7.3	1402	3.2	1945	7.9
6 F	0229	2.6	0823	7.8	1453	2.8	2034	8.2
7 Sa	0315	2.2	0904	8.2	1536	2.3	2117	8.6
8 Su	0357	1.9	0941	8.6	1616	2.0	2155	8.9
9 M	0435	1.7	1014	8.9	1654	1.7	2230	9.1
10 Tu	0512	1.5	1048	9.1	1733	1.5	○2306	9.2
11 W	0549	1.4	1123	9.3	1811	1.4	2343	9.3
12 Th	0627	1.3	1200	9.3	1850	1.4		
13 F	0022	9.3	0703	1.4	1239	9.3	1931	1.5
14 Sa	0103	9.1	0742	1.7	1321	9.1	2015	1.7
15 Su	0148	8.8	0823	2.0	1408	8.8	2103	1.9
16 M	0240	8.5	0912	2.3	1501	8.5	2159	2.1
17 Tu	0341	8.1	1012	2.6	1606	8.3	☽2305	2.3
18 W	0451	7.9	1123	2.7	1718	8.2		
19 Th	0019	2.2	0605	7.9	1241	2.6	1832	8.3
20 F	0131	2.0	0716	8.2	1352	2.3	1940	8.6
21 Sa	0236	1.7	0818	8.6	1457	1.9	2040	8.9
22 Su	0334	1.4	0911	8.9	1553	1.6	2134	9.2
23 M	0426	1.2	1000	9.2	1644	1.3	2221	9.3
24 Tu	0511	1.1	1044	9.4	1730	1.2	●2306	9.3
25 W	0553	1.1	1126	9.5	1814	1.2	2349	9.2
26 Th	0632	1.3	1207	9.4	1855	1.3		
27 F	0029	9.0	0709	1.5	1245	9.2	1934	1.5
28 Sa	0109	8.8	0745	1.8	1324	9.0	2012	1.8
29 Su	0147	8.4	0819	2.3	1402	8.7	2050	2.2
30 M	0227	8.1	0856	2.6	1446	8.3	2131	2.5

DECEMBER

Day	Time	m	Time	m	Time	m	Time	m
1 Tu	0311	7.7	0936	3.0	1532	7.9	2216	2.8
2 W	0403	7.4	1028	3.3	1628	7.6	☽2312	3.0
3 Th	0505	7.1	1136	3.5	1730	7.5		
4 F	0018	3.1	0614	7.1	1250	3.4	1838	7.5
5 Sa	0124	2.9	0720	7.4	1355	3.1	1940	7.8
6 Su	0222	2.6	0815	7.8	1450	2.7	2032	8.1
7 M	0314	2.3	0901	8.2	1541	2.3	2118	8.5
8 Tu	0400	2.0	0943	8.6	1627	1.9	2202	8.8
9 W	0445	1.7	1024	9.0	1712	1.6	2244	9.1
10 Th	0527	1.4	1105	9.3	1756	1.3	2327	9.3
11 F	0610	1.3	1146	9.5	1841	1.1		
12 Sa	0011	9.4	0652	1.2	1229	9.5	1926	1.1
13 Su	0056	9.3	0735	1.3	1314	9.5	2012	1.1
14 M	0142	9.2	0819	1.5	1402	9.3	2058	1.3
15 Tu	0232	8.9	0905	1.7	1453	9.1	2149	1.5
16 W	0325	8.6	0957	2.0	1548	8.8	☽2244	1.8
17 Th	0424	8.3	1057	2.3	1649	8.5	2347	2.0
18 F	0532	8.0	1205	2.5	1758	8.3		
19 Sa	0056	2.1	0642	8.0	1320	2.5	1910	8.2
20 Su	0206	2.1	0751	8.2	1432	2.3	2018	8.4
21 M	0310	1.9	0851	8.5	1535	2.0	2118	8.6
22 Tu	0406	1.8	0945	8.8	1631	1.7	2210	8.8
23 W	0455	1.6	1031	9.1	1720	1.5	2257	8.9
24 Th	0537	1.5	1115	9.2	1804	1.4	●2339	8.9
25 F	0617	1.5	1154	9.3	1843	1.4		
26 Sa	0017	8.9	0652	1.6	1231	9.2	1920	1.5
27 Su	0052	8.8	0726	1.7	1306	9.1	1952	1.6
28 M	0126	8.6	0757	1.9	1341	8.9	2025	1.8
29 Tu	0201	8.4	0827	2.2	1416	8.7	2057	2.0
30 W	0236	8.1	0903	2.5	1454	8.4	2132	2.3
31 Th	0315	7.8	0941	2.8	1536	8.0	2213	2.6

RATE AND SET — 2 M. outside Queen's Chan. ent. E. going, sets ESE, begins –0540 Dover, 2½ kn.; W. going, sets WNW, begins H.W. Dover 2 kn. Spring rate increases to 4½-5 kn. off Rock Lt. Twr.

LIVERPOOL

MEAN SPRING AND NEAP CURVES
Springs occur 2 days after New and Full Moon.

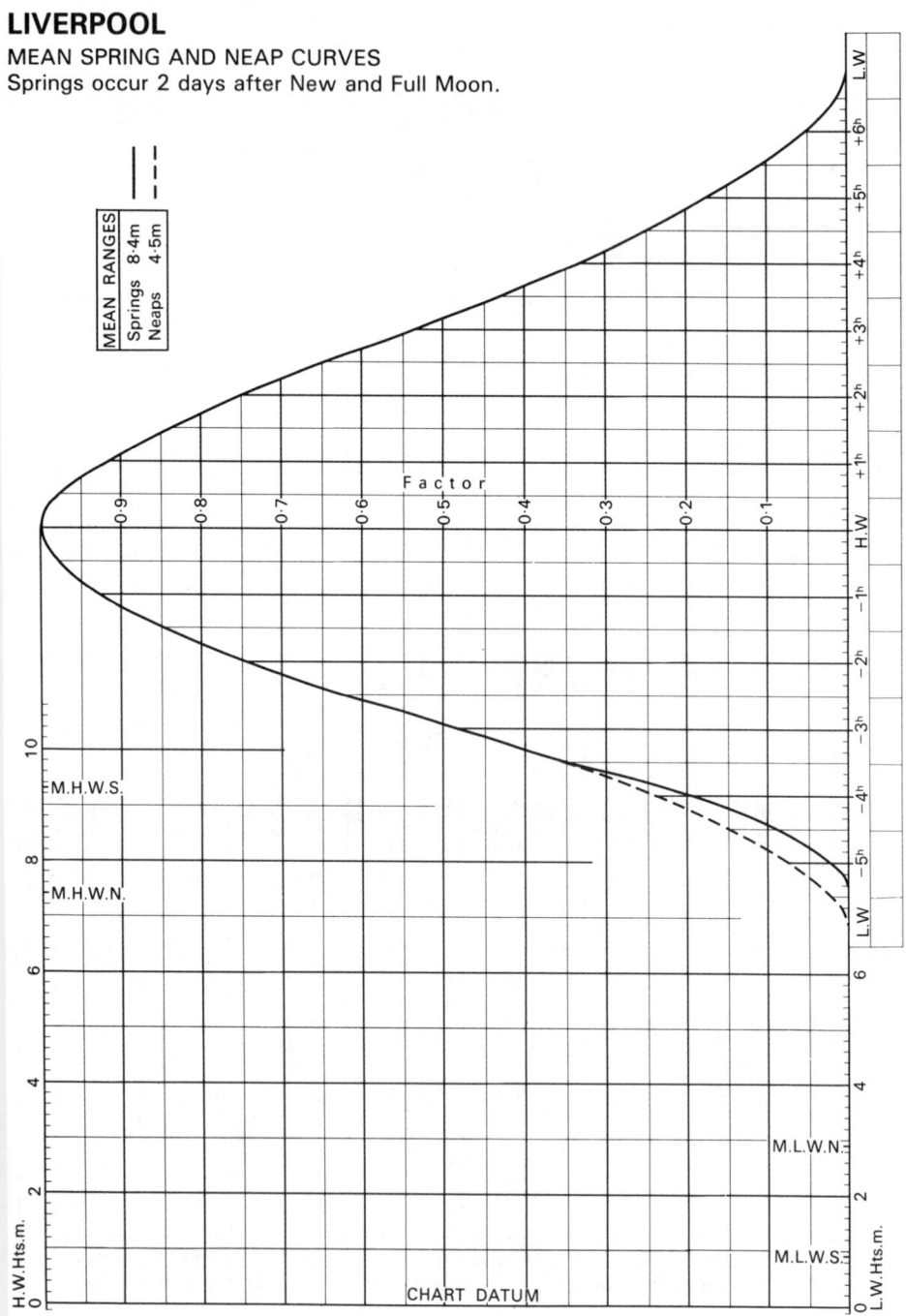

PLACE	TIME DIFFERENCES				HEIGHT DIFFERENCES (Metres)			
	High Water		Low Water		MHWS	MHWN	MLWN	MLWS
LIVERPOOL	0000 and 1200	0600 and 1800	0200 and 1400	0800 and 2000	**9.3**	**7.4**	**2.9**	**0.9**
Portpatrick	+0018	+0026	0000	−0035	−5.5	−4.4	−2.0	−0.6
Wigtown Bay								
Drummore	+0030	+0040	+0015	+0020	−3.4	−2.5	−0.9	−0.3
Port William	+0030	+0030	+0025	0000	−2.9	−2.2	−0.8	−
Isle of Whithorn	+0020	+0025	+0025	+0005	−2.4	−2.0	−0.8	−0.2
Garliestown	+0025	+0035	+0030	+0005	−2.3	−1.7	−0.5	−
Solway Firth								
Kirkcudbright Bay	+0015	+0015	+0010	0000	−1.8	−1.5	−0.5	−0.1
Hestan Islet	+0025	+0025	+0020	+0025	−1.0	−1.1	−0.5	0.0
Southerness Point	+0030	+0030	+0030	+0010	−0.7	−0.7	−	−
Annan Waterfoot	+0050	+0105	+0220	+0310	−2.2	−2.6	−2.7	†
Torduff Point	+0105	+0140	+0520	+0410	−4.1	−4.9	†	†
Redkirk	+0110	+0215	+0715	+0445	−5.5	−6.2	†	†
ENGLAND								
Silloth	+0030	+0040	+0045	+0055	−0.1	−0.3	−0.6	−0.1
Maryport	+0017	+0032	+0020	+0005	−0.7	−0.8	−0.4	0.0
Workington	+0020	+0020	+0020	+0010	−1.1	−1.0	−0.1	+0.3
Whitehaven	+0005	+0015	+0010	+0005	−1.3	−1.1	−0.5	+0.1
LIVERPOOL	0000 and 1200	0600 and 1800	0200 and 1400	0700 and 1900	**9.3**	**7.4**	**2.9**	**0.9**
Tarn Point	+0005	+0005	+0010	0000	−1.0	−1.0	−0.4	0.0
Duddon Bar	+0003	+0003	+0008	+0002	−0.8	−0.8	−0.3	0.0
Morecambe Bay								
Barrow (Ramsden Dock)	+0015	+0015	+0015	+0015	−0.2	−0.3	−0.1	+0.1
Haws Point	+0010	+0010	+0010	+0010	−0.1	−0.3	−0.1	+0.1
Ulverston	+0020	+0040	−	−	0.0	−0.1	−	−
Arnside	+0100	+0135	−	−	+0.5	+0.2	−	−
Morecambe	+0005	+0010	+0030	+0015	+0.2	0.0	0.0	+0.2
Heysham	+0005	+0005	+0015	0000	+0.1	0.0	0.0	+0.2
River Lune								
Glasson Dock	+0020	+0030	+0220	+0240	−2.7	−3.0	−	−
Lancaster	+0110	+0030	−	−	−5.0	−4.9	Dries	Dries
River Wyre								
Wyre Lighthouse	−0010	−0010	+0005	0000	−0.1	−0.1	−	−
Fleetwood	0000	0000	+0005	0000	−0.1	−0.1	+0.1	+0.3
Blackpool	−0015	−0005	−0005	−0015	−0.4	−0.4	−0.1	+0.1
River Ribble								
Preston	+0010	+0010	+0335	+0310	−4.0	−4.1	−2.8	−0.8
Liverpool Bay								
Southport	−0020	−0010	−	−	−0.3	−0.3	−	−
Formby	−0015	−0010	−0020	−0020	−0.3	−0.1	0.0	+0.1
Rock Channel	−0030	−0030	−0030	−0030	−0.4	−0.2	−0.2	0.0
New Brighton	−0008	−0008	−0006	−0006	−0.1	−0.3	+0.1	+0.2
River Mersey								
Eastham	+0003	+0006	+0015	+0030	+0.4	+0.3	−0.1	−0.1
Hale Head	+0030	+0025	−	−	−2.4	−2.5	−	−
Widnes	+0040	+0045	+0400	+0345	−4.2	−4.4	−2.5	−0.3
Fiddler's Ferry	+0100	+0115	+0540	+0450	−5.9	−6.3	−2.4	−0.4

Refer to predictions on pages 21:139-21:141
† Tide does not usually fall below chart datum.

TIDAL DIFFERENCES ON LIVERPOOL

PLACE	TIME DIFFERENCES				HEIGHT DIFFERENCES (Metres)			
	High Water		Low Water		MHWS	MHWN	MLWN	MLWS
LIVERPOOL	0000 and 1200	0600 and 1800	0200 and 1400	0700 and 1900	9.3	7.4	2.9	0.9
River Dee								
Hilbre Island	− 0015	− 0012	− 0010	− 0015	− 0.3	− 0.2	+ 0.2	+ 0.4
Mostyn Quay	− 0020	− 0015	− 0020	− 0020	− 0.8	− 0.7	−	−
Connah's Quay	0000	+ 0015	+ 0355	+ 0340	− 4.6	− 4.4	Dries	Dries
Chester	+ 0105	+ 0105	+ 0500	+ 0500	− 5.3	− 5.4	Dries	Dries
Isle of Man								
Peel	− 0015	+ 0010	0000	− 0010	− 4.0	− 3.2	− 1.4	− 0.4
Ramsey	− 0003	+ 0012	0000	− 0015	− 2.1	− 1.7	− 0.3	+ 0.1
Douglas	− 0004	− 0004	− 0022	− 0032	− 2.4	− 2.0	− 0.5	− 0.1
Port St. Mary	+ 0005	+ 0015	− 0010	− 0030	− 3.4	− 2.7	− 1.2	− 0.3
Calf Sound	+ 0005	+ 0005	− 0015	− 0025	− 3.2	− 2.6	− 0.9	− 0.3
Port Erin	− 0005	+ 0015	− 0010	− 0050	− 4.1	− 3.2	− 1.3	− 0.5
WALES								
Colwyn Bay	− 0035	− 0025	−	−	− 1.5	− 1.3	−	−
Llandudno	− 0035	− 0025	− 0025	− 0035	− 1.9	− 1.5	− 0.5	− 0.2

Refer to predictions on pages 21:139-21:141

TIDAL DIFFERENCES ON HOLYHEAD

PLACE	TIME DIFFERENCES				HEIGHT DIFFERENCES (Metres)			
	High Water		Low Water		MHWS	MHWN	MLWN	MLWS
HOLYHEAD	0000 and 1200	0600 and 1800	0500 and 1700	1100 and 2300	5.7	4.5	2.0	0.7
Conwy	+ 0020	+ 0020	−	+ 0050	+ 2.1	+ 1.6	+ 0.3	−
Menai Strait								
Beaumaris	+ 0025	+ 0010	+ 0055	+ 0035	+ 2.0	+ 1.6	+ 0.5	+ 0.1
Menai Bridge	+ 0030	+ 0010	+ 0100	+ 0035	+ 1.7	+ 1.4	+ 0.3	0.0
Port Dinorwic	− 0015	− 0025	+ 0030	0000	0.0	0.0	0.0	+ 0.1
Caernarfon	− 0030	− 0030	+ 0015	− 0005	− 0.4	− 0.4	− 0.1	− 0.1
Fort Belan	− 0040	− 0015	− 0025	− 0005	− 1.0	− 0.9	− 0.2	− 0.1
Trwyn Dinmor	+ 0025	+ 0015	+ 0050	+ 0035	+ 1.9	+ 1.5	+ 0.5	+ 0.2
Moelfre	+ 0025	+ 0020	+ 0050	+ 0035	+ 1.9	+ 1.4	+ 0.5	+ 0.2
Amlwch	+ 0020	+ 0010	+ 0035	+ 0025	+ 1.6	+ 1.3	+ 0.5	+ 0.2
Cemaes Bay	+ 0020	+ 0025	+ 0040	+ 0035	+ 1.0	+ 0.7	+ 0.3	+ 0.1
Trearddur Bay	− 0045	− 0025	− 0015	− 0015	− 0.4	− 0.4	0.0	+ 0.1
Porth Trecastell	− 0045	− 0025	− 0005	− 0015	− 0.6	− 0.6	0.0	0.0
Llanddwyn Island	− 0115	− 0055	− 0030	− 0020	− 0.7	− 0.5	− 0.1	0.0
Trefor	− 0115	− 0100	− 0030	− 0020	− 0.8	− 0.9	− 0.2	− 0.1
Porth Dinllaen	− 0120	− 0105	− 0035	− 0025	− 1.0	− 1.0	− 0.2	− 0.2
Porth Ysgaden	− 0125	− 0110	− 0040	− 0035	− 1.1	− 1.0	− 0.1	− 0.1
Bardsey Island	− 0220	− 0240	− 0145	− 0140	− 1.2	− 1.2	− 0.5	− 0.1

Refer to predictions on pages 21:145-21:147

Lat. 53°18'N. Long. 4°38'W. HIGH & LOW WATER 1992

GMT ADD 1 HOUR MARCH 29 — OCTOBER 25 FOR B.S.T.

JANUARY

Day	Time m	Time m	Time m	Time m
1 W	0130 1.7	0749 4.8	1359 1.7	2016 4.8
16 Th	0022 1.8	0650 4.6	1302 1.8	1917 4.8
2 Th	0225 1.6	0839 5.0	1453 1.5	2104 4.9
17 F	0128 1.6	0754 4.9	1405 1.4	2020 5.1
3 F	0310 1.5	0919 5.1	1536 1.4	2145 5.0
18 Sa	0227 1.3	0847 5.3	1501 1.0	2114 5.3
4 Sa	0349 1.4	0957 5.3	1614 1.2	● 2221 5.1
19 Su	0318 1.0	0935 5.6	1552 0.6	○ 2202 5.6
5 Su	0424 1.3	1031 5.4	1649 1.1	2255 5.1
20 M	0407 0.7	1020 5.9	1640 0.3	2248 5.8
6 M	0458 1.2	1105 5.5	1723 1.1	2329 5.1
21 Tu	0454 0.5	1105 6.1	1727 0.1	2334 5.8
7 Tu	0530 1.2	1137 5.5	1756 1.1	
22 W	0539 0.4	1150 6.1	1812 0.1	
8 W	0001 5.1	0603 1.2	1211 5.4	1828 1.1
23 Th	0019 5.7	0642 0.3	1236 6.0	1859 0.3
9 Th	0034 5.0	0636 1.3	1245 5.4	1902 1.2
24 F	0106 5.5	0710 0.7	1321 5.8	1945 0.6
10 F	0107 4.9	0712 1.6	1320 5.2	1937 1.3
25 Sa	0152 5.2	0757 1.0	1409 5.4	2034 1.0
11 Sa	0144 4.8	0749 1.6	1358 5.1	2016 1.5
26 Su	0242 4.9	0847 1.4	1503 5.0	☾ 2128 1.4
12 Su	0225 4.7	0832 1.8	1442 4.9	2101 1.6
27 M	0339 4.6	0948 1.7	1607 4.7	2234 1.8
13 M	0314 4.6	0924 2.0	1535 4.7	☽ 2156 1.8
28 Tu	0449 4.4	1104 2.0	1729 4.4	2351 2.0
14 Tu	0417 4.5	1028 2.1	1645 4.6	2306 1.9
29 W	0612 4.4	1229 2.1	1859 4.3	
15 W	0536 4.5	1147 2.0	1805 4.6	
30 Th	0107 2.0	0730 4.5	1345 1.9	2009 4.5
31 F	0211 1.9	0826 4.8	1443 1.7	2058 4.7

FEBRUARY

Day	Time m	Time m	Time m	Time m
1 Sa	0257 1.7	0908 5.0	1525 1.4	2136 4.8
16 Su	0215 1.4	0833 5.2	1450 0.9	2104 5.3
2 Su	0336 1.4	0943 5.2	1600 1.2	2207 5.0
17 M	0307 0.9	0921 5.6	1539 0.5	2149 5.6
3 M	0409 1.2	1016 5.4	1631 1.0	● 2238 5.1
18 Tu	0353 0.6	1004 5.9	1624 0.2	○ 2231 5.8
4 Tu	0440 1.1	1045 5.5	1708 0.9	2306 5.2
19 W	0435 0.3	1047 6.1	1708 0.0	2313 5.8
5 W	0509 1.0	1116 5.5	1732 0.9	2336 5.2
20 Th	0519 0.2	1130 6.2	1750 0.1	2356 5.8
6 Th	0540 1.0	1147 5.5	1801 0.9	
21 F	0601 0.3	1212 6.0	1832 0.3	
7 F	0005 5.2	0611 1.0	1218 5.5	1832 0.9
22 Sa	0036 5.6	0643 0.5	1256 5.8	1914 0.6
8 Sa	0038 5.2	0642 1.1	1252 5.4	1903 1.1
23 Su	0119 5.3	0727 0.8	1340 5.4	1958 1.1
9 Su	0117 5.1	0717 1.3	1326 5.3	1938 1.2
24 M	0204 5.0	0813 1.2	1427 4.9	2047 1.6
10 M	0147 4.9	0755 1.5	1405 5.1	2019 1.4
25 Tu	0253 4.7	0908 1.7	1525 4.5	☾ 2148 2.0
11 Tu	0229 4.8	0843 1.7	1453 4.8	☽ 2111 1.7
26 W	0356 4.4	1023 2.1	1648 4.2	2311 2.3
12 W	0325 4.5	0946 1.9	1602 4.6	2221 1.9
27 Th	0526 4.2	1157 2.2	1836 4.1	
13 Th	0448 4.4	1112 2.0	1734 4.5	2353 2.0
28 F	0038 2.3	0702 4.3	1321 2.0	1952 4.3
14 F	0622 4.5	1241 1.8	1903 4.6	
29 Sa	0148 2.1	0802 4.6	1420 1.7	2039 4.5
15 Sa	0112 1.7	0737 4.8	1352 1.4	2011 5.0

MARCH

Day	Time m	Time m	Time m	Time m
1 Su	0236 1.8	0846 4.9	1501 1.4	2115 4.8
16 M	0158 1.3	0815 5.2	1432 0.8	2047 5.3
2 M	0314 1.5	0919 5.1	1535 1.2	2145 5.0
17 Tu	0249 0.9	0901 5.6	1519 0.4	2129 5.5
3 Tu	0345 1.2	0950 5.3	1604 1.0	2212 5.1
18 W	0334 0.6	0945 5.9	1603 0.2	○ 2209 5.7
4 W	0414 1.0	1020 5.4	1633 0.8	● 2238 5.3
19 Th	0414 0.3	1026 6.0	1644 0.1	2249 5.8
5 Th	0442 0.9	1049 5.5	1701 0.8	2306 5.3
20 F	0457 0.2	1108 6.0	1725 0.2	2329 5.7
6 F	0512 0.8	1119 5.6	1730 0.7	2337 5.4
21 Sa	0537 0.3	1150 5.8	1805 0.4	
7 Sa	0543 0.8	1151 5.6	1801 0.8	
22 Su	0010 5.6	0619 0.5	1232 5.6	1845 0.8
8 Su	0008 5.3	0615 0.9	1224 5.5	1834 0.9
23 M	0050 5.3	0702 0.8	1314 5.2	1927 1.2
9 M	0042 5.2	0650 1.0	1300 5.3	1909 1.1
24 Tu	0131 5.1	0747 1.2	1359 4.8	2011 1.6
10 Tu	0119 5.1	0731 1.2	1341 5.1	1951 1.4
25 W	0216 4.7	0839 1.6	1453 4.4	2105 2.1
11 W	0201 4.9	0820 1.5	1432 4.8	2044 1.7
26 Th	0312 4.4	0945 2.0	1607 4.1	☾ 2223 2.4
12 Th	0250 4.6	0925 1.7	1542 4.5	☽ 2157 2.0
27 F	0431 4.2	1113 2.1	1753 4.0	2356 2.4
13 F	0421 4.4	1054 1.8	1714 4.4	2333 2.0
28 Sa	0610 4.2	1238 2.0	1914 4.2	
14 Sa	0601 4.5	1224 1.6	1852 4.6	
29 Su	0109 2.2	0721 4.1	1340 1.8	2005 4.4
15 Su	0056 1.7	0719 4.8	1335 1.2	1957 4.9
30 M	0159 1.9	0808 4.7	1423 1.5	2042 4.7
31 Tu	0239 1.6	0844 5.0	1457 1.2	2111 4.9

APRIL

Day	Time m	Time m	Time m	Time m
1 W	0311 1.3	0917 5.2	1528 1.0	2139 5.1
16 Th	0311 0.7	0922 5.7	1539 0.4	2146 5.6
2 Th	0342 1.0	0948 5.3	1557 0.9	2207 5.3
17 F	0353 0.5	1004 5.7	1620 0.4	○ 2226 5.6
3 F	0413 0.9	1019 5.5	1628 0.7	● 2237 5.4
18 Sa	0435 0.4	1047 5.7	1701 0.5	2306 5.4
4 Sa	0444 0.8	1051 5.5	1659 0.7	2308 5.4
19 Su	0518 0.5	1129 5.5	1740 0.7	2346 5.5
5 Su	0518 0.7	1125 5.5	1733 0.7	2342 5.4
20 M	0600 0.7	1211 5.3	1819 1.0	
6 M	0553 0.8	1203 5.5	1808 0.9	
21 Tu	0027 5.3	0642 0.9	1253 5.0	1900 1.3
7 Tu	0019 5.4	0634 0.9	1242 5.3	*1849 1.1
22 W	0106 5.1	0726 1.2	1337 4.7	1942 1.7
8 W	0100 5.2	0719 1.1	1330 5.1	1935 1.4
23 Th	0148 4.8	0813 1.5	1426 4.4	2032 2.0
9 Th	0148 5.0	0812 1.3	1426 4.8	2033 1.7
24 F	0239 4.6	0910 1.8	1527 4.2	☾ 2135 2.3
10 F	0249 4.8	0919 1.5	1539 4.5	☽ 2149 1.9
25 Sa	0341 4.4	1020 2.0	1648 4.0	2255 2.4
11 Sa	0409 4.6	1044 1.6	1712 4.5	2316 1.9
26 Su	0501 4.3	1136 2.0	1811 4.1	
12 Su	0540 4.7	1205 1.4	1834 4.6	
27 M	0010 2.3	0617 4.4	1241 1.8	1912 4.3
13 M	0034 1.7	0655 4.9	1313 1.1	1935 4.9
28 Tu	0107 2.0	0714 4.6	1331 1.6	1955 4.6
14 Tu	0135 1.3	0759 5.2	1409 0.8	2025 5.2
29 W	0152 1.7	0759 4.8	1411 1.4	2030 4.8
15 W	0226 1.0	0839 5.5	1457 0.5	2107 5.4
30 Th	0232 1.4	0837 5.0	1447 1.1	2103 5.0

To find H.W. Dover add 0h. 50 min.

TIDAL DIFFERENCES PAGE 21:144.

TIDAL STREAMS PAGES 21:148-21:153.

Datum of predictions: 3.05 m. below Ordnance Datum (Newlyn) or approx. L.A.T.

ANGLESEY **HOLYHEAD**

HIGH & LOW WATER 1992 Lat. 53°18'N. Long. 4°38'W.

GMT ADD 1 HOUR MARCH 29 — OCTOBER 25 FOR B.S.T.

MAY

Time	m		Time	m
1 F 0307 0912 1521 2134	1·2 5·2 1·0 5·2	**16** Sa	0336 0948 2207 ○	0·8 5·4 5·4
2 Sa ● 0342 0948 1556 2207	1·0 5·4 0·8 5·4	**17** Su	0420 1031 1640 2247	0·7 5·4 0·8 5·5
3 Su 0419 1026 1633 2244	0·8 5·5 0·8 5·5	**18** M	0504 1113 1720 2327	0·7 5·3 1·0 5·4
4 M 0457 1105 1711 2323	0·7 5·5 0·8 5·5	**19** Tu	0544 1154 1800	0·8 5·1 1·1
5 Tu 0539 1147 1753	0·7 5·4 0·9	**20** W	0007 0625 1235 1838	5·3 1·0 4·9 1·3
6 W 0005 0624 1234 1839	5·5 0·8 5·3 1·0	**21** Th	0045 0706 1316 1919	5·2 1·2 4·7 1·6
7 Th 0052 0714 1326 1930	5·3 0·9 5·1 1·3	**22** F	0126 0748 1359 2002	5·0 1·4 4·5 1·8
8 F 0144 0811 1425 2029	5·2 1·1 4·8 1·5	**23** Sa	0209 0836 1449 2053	4·8 1·6 4·3 2·0
9 Sa) 0244 0915 1535 2139	5·0 1·2 4·7 1·7	**24** Su	0300 0928 1548 2152	4·6 1·7 4·2 2·2
10 Su 0356 1028 1655 2254	4·8 1·3 4·6 1·7	**25** M	0400 1028 1655 2259	4·5 1·8 4·2 2·2
11 M 0515 1142 1807	4·8 1·2 4·7	**26** Tu	0508 1133 1801	4·4 1·8 4·3
12 Tu 0005 0625 1246 1907	1·6 5·0 1·1 4·9	**27** W	0004 0612 1231 1857	2·1 4·5 1·7 4·5
13 W 0109 0726 1344 1959	1·4 5·1 0·9 5·0	**28** Th	0100 0707 1321 1944	1·9 4·7 1·6 4·7
14 Th 0204 0816 1433 2044	1·1 5·3 0·8 5·2	**29** F	0148 0757 1406 2026	1·6 4·9 1·3 4·9
15 F 0251 0904 1518 2127	0·9 5·3 0·8 5·3	**30** Sa	0233 0840 1449 2105	1·3 5·1 1·1 5·2
		31 Su	0315 0922 1529 2145	1·1 5·2 1·0 5·4

JUNE

Time	m		Time	m
1 M ● 0357 1006 1612 2226	0·9 5·4 0·8 5·5	**16** Tu	0452 1101 1705 2312	0·9 5·1 1·1 5·4
2 Tu 0442 1049 1657 2309	0·7 5·5 0·8 5·6	**17** W	0532 1139 1742 2349	1·0 5·0 1·2 5·3
3 W 0529 1137 1743 2356	0·6 5·5 0·8 5·6	**18** Th	0608 1217 1818	1·0 4·9 1·3
4 Th 0618 1228 1832	0·6 5·4 0·9	**19** F	0025 0645 1252 1855	5·3 1·1 4·8 1·4
5 F 0045 0709 1320 1924	5·6 0·6 5·2 1·0	**20** Sa	0100 0721 1330 1933	5·2 1·2 4·7 1·5
6 Sa 0137 0804 1416 2019	5·4 0·8 5·0 1·2	**21** Su	0140 0801 1411 2013	5·0 1·4 4·6 1·7
7 Su 0233 0901 1518 2119	5·3 0·9 4·8 1·4	**22** M	0222 0843 1456 2100	4·9 1·5 4·5 1·9
8 M 0335 1004 1626 2226	5·1 1·1 4·7 1·5	**23** Tu	0310 0931 1549 2155 (	4·7 1·7 4·4 2·0
9 Tu 0445 1112 1734 2334	5·0 1·2 4·7 1·4	**24** W	0406 1027 1654 2258	4·6 1·8 4·3 2·1
10 W 0556 1218 1839	4·9 1·2 4·7	**25** Th	0512 1130 1800	4·5 1·8 4·4
11 Th 0042 0700 1319 1937	1·5 4·9 1·2 4·9	**26** F	0007 0618 1234 1900	2·0 4·6 1·7 4·6
12 F 0144 0759 1413 2027	1·4 4·9 1·2 5·0	**27** Sa	0109 0720 1331 1954	1·8 4·7 1·5 4·8
13 Sa 0239 0851 1501 2112	1·2 5·0 1·1 5·2	**28** Su	0204 0813 1422 2042	1·5 4·9 1·3 5·1
14 Su 0327 0938 1545 2155	1·1 5·1 1·1 5·3	**29** M	0254 0904 1510 2127	1·2 5·1 1·1 5·3
15 M 0412 1020 1626 2234 ○	1·0 5·1 1·1 5·4	**30** Tu	0342 0952 1557 2212 ●	0·9 5·3 0·8 5·6

JULY

Time	m		Time	m
1 W 0430 1038 1644 2257	0·6 5·5 0·7 5·8	**16** Th	0513 1119 1722 2329	1·0 5·1 1·1 5·4
2 Th 0519 1126 1732 2344	0·4 5·6 0·6 5·9	**17** F	0547 1151 1754	0·9 5·0 1·1
3 F 0607 1215 1819	0·3 5·6 0·6	**18** Sa	0001 0619 1224 1827	5·4 1·0 5·0 1·2
4 Sa 0031 0656 1304 1907	5·8 0·3 5·4 0·7	**19** Su	0035 0652 1257 1900	5·3 1·1 4·9 1·3
5 Su 0120 0745 1355 1958	5·7 0·5 5·2 0·9	**20** M	0109 0726 1333 1937	5·2 1·2 4·8 1·5
6 M 0212 0837 1450 2051	5·5 0·8 5·0 1·2	**21** Tu	0145 0802 1411 2016	5·1 1·3 4·7 1·7
7 Tu 0308 0935 1550 2152	5·2 1·1 4·8 1·5	**22** W	0225 0843 1454 2103	4·9 1·5 4·6 1·9
8 W 0413 1038 1658 2302	4·9 1·3 4·6 1·7	**23** Th	0314 0932 1550 2202	4·7 1·7 4·4 2·0
9 Th 0525 1149 1810	4·7 1·5 4·6	**24** F	0416 1035 1704 2316	4·5 1·9 4·4 2·1
10 F 0018 0642 1257 1919	1·7 4·6 1·6 4·7	**25** Sa	0534 1151 1821	4·5 1·9 4·5
11 Sa 0130 0751 1359 2016	1·7 4·7 1·6 4·8	**26** Su	0035 0650 1302 1928	1·9 4·6 1·7 4·7
12 Su 0230 0846 1451 2104	1·5 4·8 1·5 5·0	**27** M	0141 0757 1402 2025	1·6 4·8 1·4 5·1
13 M 0321 0932 1535 2143	1·3 4·9 1·3 5·2	**28** Tu	0239 0851 1456 2112	1·2 5·1 1·3 5·4
14 Tu 0403 1012 1613 2220 ○	1·1 5·0 1·2 5·3	**29** W	0329 0939 1543 2157 ●	0·8 5·4 0·8 5·7
15 W 0440 1047 1648 2255	1·0 5·0 1·1 5·4	**30** Th	0416 1024 1628 2241	0·4 5·6 0·5 6·0
		31 F	0502 1109 1713 2326	0·2 5·7 0·4 6·1

AUGUST

Time	m		Time	m
1 Sa 0549 1154 1800	0·1 5·7 0·4	**16** Su	0549 1153 1757	0·9 5·2 1·0
2 Su 0011 0634 1241 1845	6·1 0·2 5·6 0·5	**17** M	0004 0618 1224 1829	5·5 1·0 5·1 1·1
3 M 0057 0720 1327 1933	5·9 0·4 5·4 0·8	**18** Tu	0036 0649 1256 1902	5·4 1·1 5·0 1·3
4 Tu 0145 0808 1416 2022	5·6 0·8 5·1 1·1	**19** W	0110 0723 1331 1940	5·2 1·3 4·9 1·5
5 W 0237 0901 1511 2119	5·2 1·2 4·8 1·5	**20** Th	0148 0801 1412 2023	5·0 1·5 4·8 1·7
6 Th 0339 1003 1619 2231	4·8 1·6 4·6 1·8	**21** F	0233 0849 1503 2121	4·8 1·7 4·6 2·0
7 F 0457 1119 1740 2357	4·5 1·9 4·5 2·0	**22** Sa	0334 0952 1609 2240	4·5 2·0 4·4 2·1
8 Sa 0628 1238 1902	4·4 2·0 4·6	**23** Su	0501 1118 1750	4·4 2·1 4·5
9 Su 0119 0745 1347 2005	1·9 4·5 1·8 4·8	**24** M	0010 0631 1241 1907	1·9 4·5 1·9 4·8
10 M 0222 0840 1439 2051	1·6 4·6 1·6 5·0	**25** Tu	0123 0742 1345 2006	1·5 4·8 1·5 5·1
11 Tu 0308 0921 1521 2128	1·4 4·8 1·4 5·2	**26** W	0222 0836 1439 2054	1·1 5·2 1·1 5·5
12 W 0346 0955 1555 2202	1·2 5·0 1·2 5·3	**27** Th	0312 0922 1525 2138	0·6 5·5 0·7 5·9
13 Th 0419 1026 1627 2233 ○	1·0 5·1 1·1 5·5	**28** F	0357 1004 1609 2220	0·3 5·7 0·4 6·1
14 F 0449 1054 1657 2302	0·9 5·1 1·0 5·5	**29** Sa	0441 1047 1652 2304	0·1 5·8 0·3 6·2
15 Sa 0519 1123 1726 2333	0·9 5·2 1·0 5·5	**30** Su	0525 1129 1736 2347	0·0 5·8 0·3 6·1
		31 M	0607 1212 1819	0·2 5·7 0·4

GENERAL — Strong tide rips — flood and ebb — off Langdon ridge.

HIGH & LOW WATER 1992 Lat. 53°18'N. Long. 4°38'W.

GMT ADD 1 HOUR MARCH 29 — OCTOBER 25 FOR B.S.T.

SEPTEMBER

Day	Time	m	Time	m	Day	Time	m	Time	m
1 Tu	0032	5.9	1257	5.5	16 W	0007	5.4	1225	5.2
	0652	0.5	1906	0.7		0615	1.1	1834	1.2
2 W	0119	5.6	1344	5.2	17 Th	0041	5.3	1300	5.1
	0737	0.9	1954	1.1		0650	1.2	1912	1.4
3 Th	0209	5.1	1436	4.9	18 F	0120	5.1	1341	4.9
	0827	1.4	》2050	1.6		0730	1.5	1958	1.7
4 F	0308	4.7	1539	4.6	19 Sa	0208	4.8	1434	4.7
	0928	1.9	2203	1.9		0819	1.8	☾2058	1.9
5 Sa	0428	4.3	1706	4.4	20 Su	0312	4.5	1549	4.5
	1047	2.2	2333	2.1		0925	2.0	2220	2.0
6 Su	0611	4.2	1838	4.5	21 M	0442	4.4	1725	4.6
	1212	2.2				1055	2.1	2350	1.8
7 M	0059	2.0	1324	2.1	22 Tu	0617	4.6	1846	4.9
	0730	4.4	1942	4.7		1219	1.9		
8 Tu	0201	1.7	1418	1.8	23 W	0104	1.4	1326	1.5
	0822	4.6	2027	5.0		0726	4.9	1945	5.3
9 W	0246	1.5	1457	1.5	24 Th	0202	1.0	1418	1.1
	0858	4.8	2104	5.2		0818	5.2	2033	5.6
10 Th	0319	1.2	1529	1.3	25 F	0250	0.6	1504	0.7
	0929	5.0	2135	5.4		0901	5.5	2117	5.9
11 F	0350	1.1	1559	1.1	26 Sa	0334	0.3	1546	0.5
	0957	5.1	2204	5.5		0942	5.8	●2157	6.1
12 Sa	0419	0.9	1627	1.0	27 Su	0417	0.2	1628	0.3
	1024	5.2	○2233	5.6		1023	5.9	2241	6.2
13 Su	0445	0.9	1657	1.0	28 M	0458	0.2	1712	0.4
	1052	5.3	2304	5.6		1104	5.9	2325	6.0
14 M	0515	0.9	1727	1.0	29 Tu	0542	0.4	1757	0.5
	1120	5.3	2334	5.5		1147	5.7		
15 Tu	0544	0.9	1758	1.1	30 W	0010	5.8	1229	5.5
	1151	5.3				0624	0.7	1842	0.8

OCTOBER

Day	Time	m	Time	m	Day	Time	m	Time	m
1 Th	0055	5.4	1314	5.3	16 F	0021	5.3	1239	5.3
	0709	1.1	1931	1.2		0627	1.2	1856	1.3
2 F	0144	5.0	1404	4.9	17 Sa	0104	5.1	1324	5.1
	0757	1.6	2025	1.6		0710	1.5	1945	1.5
3 Sa	0240	4.6	1503	4.6	18 Su	0157	4.9	1420	4.9
	0853	2.0	》2132	2.0		0804	1.8	2049	1.7
4 Su	0356	4.2	1621	4.4	19 M	0304	4.6	1532	4.7
	1007	2.3	2258	2.1		0911	2.0	☾2206	1.8
5 M	0536	4.1	1754	4.4	20 Tu	0431	4.5	1702	4.8
	1134	2.4				1035	2.1	2329	1.6
6 Tu	0019	2.1	1248	2.2	21 W	0556	4.7	1818	5.0
	0656	4.3	1903	4.6		1156	1.9		
7 W	0123	1.8	1341	2.0	22 Th	0039	1.3	1300	1.5
	0748	4.5	1952	4.9		0702	4.9	1919	5.3
8 Th	0208	1.6	1422	1.7	23 F	0137	1.0	1354	1.2
	0826	4.8	2029	5.1		0754	5.2	2009	5.6
9 F	0243	1.4	1456	1.4	24 Sa	0226	0.7	1442	0.9
	0857	5.0	2101	5.3		0839	5.5	2054	5.8
10 Sa	0314	1.2	1527	1.2	25 Su	0311	0.5	1527	0.6
	0921	5.2	2132	5.4		0921	5.7	●2138	5.9
11 Su	0343	1.0	1556	1.1	26 M	0353	0.4	1610	0.5
	0952	5.3	○2202	5.5		1002	5.8	2221	5.9
12 M	0412	0.9	1627	1.0	27 Tu	0435	0.5	1654	0.6
	1021	5.4	2234	5.6		1042	5.8	2305	5.8
13 Tu	0442	0.9	1659	1.0	28 W	0518	0.7	1739	0.7
	1051	5.5	2306	5.6		1125	5.7	2350	5.5
14 W	0515	1.0	1734	1.0	29 Th	0608	1.0	1824	1.0
	1125	5.5	2342	5.5		1208	5.5		
15 Th	0549	1.1	1812	1.2	30 F	0035	5.2	1250	5.3
	1200	5.4				0643	1.3	1910	1.3
					31 Sa	0121	4.9	1335	5.1
						0728	1.7	2001	1.6

NOVEMBER

Day	Time	m	Time	m	Day	Time	m	Time	m
1 Su	0213	4.6	1426	4.8	16 M	0151	5.0	1411	5.1
	0819	2.0	2057	1.9		0755	1.6	2040	1.5
2 M	0314	4.3	1529	4.6	17 Tu	0254	4.8	1517	5.0
	0921	2.3	》2206	2.1		0858	1.8	☾2149	1.5
3 Tu	0434	4.2	1647	4.5	18 W	0410	4.7	1633	5.0
	1037	2.4	2322	2.1		1012	1.9	2302	1.4
4 W	0554	4.2	1801	4.5	19 Th	0527	4.7	1747	5.0
	1151	2.4				1126	1.8		
5 Th	0027	2.0	1256	2.2	20 F	0011	1.3	1232	1.6
	0656	4.4	1900	4.7		0634	4.9	1852	5.2
6 F	0119	1.8	1338	1.9	21 Sa	0112	1.1	1331	1.3
	0741	4.7	1945	4.9		0730	5.1	1948	5.4
7 Sa	0159	1.5	1418	1.6	22 Su	0205	1.0	1423	1.1
	0818	4.9	2023	5.1		0823	5.3	2037	5.5
8 Su	0234	1.3	1453	1.4	23 M	0253	0.9	1512	0.9
	0850	5.1	2058	5.3		0903	5.5	●2124	5.6
9 M	0308	1.2	1528	1.2	24 Tu	0336	0.8	1557	0.8
	0921	5.3	○2134	5.4		0945	5.6	2209	5.6
10 Tu	0341	1.1	1603	1.1	25 W	0420	0.8	1642	0.8
	0953	5.4	2209	5.5		1027	5.7	2252	5.5
11 W	0416	1.0	1640	1.0	26 Th	0501	1.0	1726	0.9
	1027	5.5	2245	5.5		1109	5.7	2336	5.3
12 Th	0451	1.0	1718	1.0	27 F	0543	1.1	1810	1.0
	1104	5.6	2326	5.5		1150	5.6		
13 F	0530	1.0	1801	1.0	28 Sa	0019	5.1	1231	5.4
	1143	5.6				0624	1.3	1852	1.2
14 Sa	0010	5.4	1228	5.5	29 Su	0100	4.9	1310	5.2
	0614	1.2	1848	1.1		0704	1.6	1934	1.4
15 Su	0057	5.2	1316	5.3	30 M	0144	4.7	1354	5.0
	0702	1.4	1941	1.3		0747	1.8	2020	1.7

DECEMBER

Day	Time	m	Time	m	Day	Time	m	Time	m
1 Tu	0230	4.5	1442	4.8	16 W	0236	5.0	1454	5.3
	0834	2.0	2111	1.9		0839	1.4	☾2124	1.2
2 W	0327	4.3	1539	4.6	17 Th	0341	4.8	1600	5.1
	0931	2.2	》2210	2.0		0942	1.6	2230	1.3
3 Th	0433	4.3	1647	4.5	18 F	0451	4.7	1715	5.0
	1037	2.3	2315	2.0		1052	1.7	2340	1.4
4 F	0542	4.3	1754	4.6	19 Sa	0601	4.8	1827	5.0
	1146	2.3				1204	1.7		
5 Sa	0017	1.9	1246	2.1	20 Su	0046	1.4	1312	1.6
	0643	4.5	1853	4.7		0706	4.9	1931	5.0
6 Su	0109	1.8	1337	1.9	21 M	0147	1.3	1412	1.4
	0733	4.7	1944	4.9		0804	5.1	2029	5.1
7 M	0155	1.6	1420	1.6	22 Tu	0240	1.2	1505	1.2
	0815	4.9	2029	5.1		0853	5.3	2118	5.2
8 Tu	0236	1.4	1503	1.4	23 W	0327	1.1	1553	1.0
	0854	5.2	2110	5.2		0936	5.4	●2203	5.3
9 W	0315	1.2	1543	1.1	24 Th	0409	1.1	1635	0.9
	0931	5.4	○2149	5.4		1017	5.5	2244	5.3
10 Th	0355	1.0	1624	0.9	25 F	0449	1.1	1716	0.9
	1009	5.5	2231	5.5		1057	5.6	2323	5.2
11 F	0435	0.8	1708	0.8	26 Sa	0527	1.1	1754	1.0
	1049	5.7	2315	5.5		1134	5.6		
12 Sa	0519	0.7	1753	0.7	27 Su	0000	5.2	1210	5.5
	1132	5.7				0604	1.2	1831	1.1
13 Su	0000	5.5	1218	5.7	28 M	0036	5.0	1245	5.4
	0604	0.9	1841	0.8		0639	1.3	1906	1.2
14 M	0049	5.4	1306	5.6	29 Tu	0112	4.9	1321	5.2
	0653	1.1	1931	0.9		0716	1.5	1942	1.4
15 Tu	0140	5.2	1357	5.5	30 W	0149	4.8	1401	5.0
	0744	1.2	2025	1.0		0754	1.7	2023	1.6
					31 Th	0232	4.6	1446	4.8
						0837	1.9	2108	1.8

RATE AND SET — Streams in the bay weak. NNE-SSW. between N. Stack, Skerries and Carmel Head. Close N. of breakwater no perceptible E. stream but W. going between −0330 and +0530 (Dover) for 9 h. Between Skerries and Carmel Head NE. going begins +0500 Dover, Spring rate 5-6 kn.; SW. going begins −0100 Dover, Spring rate 5-6 kn. Variation in rate and set.

N.W. ENGLAND AND WALES
NOTES ON THE TIDAL STREAMS

1. **GENERAL.** Streams near entrance to St. George's Channel differ from those in approaches. Main flood off entrance +0600 (Dover) Spring 2½ kts. Time of ebb, H.W. (Dover). Branches of the main stream flow into the bays, etc., and are divided by islands and headlands, especially by the Isle of Man. A possible W. set occurs during ingoing stream S.W. and W. of Calf of Man. All streams fairly strong—Sp. 2½ kts.—except S.W. and W. of Calf of Man, where they are weak and irregular.

2. **CARDIGAN BAY.**
(a) Weak in bay.
(b) Strong between Cardigan Isle and coast.
(c) **Afon Teifl.**
i. Flood +0235
ii. Ebb −0420.
(d) **Afon Dyfl.**
i. N. going +0430. Sp. ¾ kts.
ii. S. going −0130, Sp. ¾ kts.
(e) **Barmouth.**
i. Flood +0425. Sp. 3-4 kts.
ii. Ebb −0250. Sp. 3-4 kts.
(f) **Tremadoc Bay.**
i. Entered by branch of Cardigan stream.
ii. Generally weak in Bay.
(g) **Portmadoc.**
i. Flood +0425, fairly strong.
ii. Ebb −0300, fairly strong.
(h) **Coast near Bardsey Isle.**
i. W. going, +0300 Dover, strong.
ii. E. going, −0300 Dover, strong.
iii. Further off shore—N.W. and S.E.

3. **CAERNARVON BAY.**
(a) N. and S. across entrance.
(b) N. going +0610, Sp. 2½ kts.
(c) S. going −0010, Sp. 2 kts.
(d) Further East—stream follows coast.

4. **MENAI STRAIT.**
(a) Maximum rate 7-8 kts.
(b) **N.E. entrance—off Beaumaris.**
i. Tide 1 hr. later than S.W. Ent.
ii. Sp. Range 9 ft. greater than S.W.
iii. S.W. going −0425, Sp. 5 kts.
iv. N.E. going +0135, Sp. 5 kts.
(c) **S.W. entrance.**
i. E. going +0440, Sp. 5 kts.
ii. W. going −0130, Sp. 5 kts.
(d) Bar and depths constantly change.
(e) Streams sometimes flow right through, sometimes from both entrances and meet in Strait, sometimes separate and flow out of both entrances.

5. **ANGLESEY.**
(a) **Holyhead Bay.**
i. Streams weak.
ii. N.N.E. and S.S.W.

5. (b) **Skerries. 1m N.W.**
i. N.E. going −0555, Sp. 4½ kts.
ii. S.W. going +0030, Sp. 4½ kts.
iii. Eddies probably E. and S.W.
(c) **N. Coast.**
i. E. and S.E. going +0530, Sp. 3-5 kts.
ii. W. and N.W. going −0030, Sp. 3-5 kts.

6. **LIVERPOOL AND APPROACHES.**
(a) **Great Ormes Head.**
i. E. going −0610, Sp. 3 kts.
ii. W. going H.W., Sp. 3 kts.
(b) **R. Dee—Entrance.**
i. Flood, −0445, runs for 5 hrs.
(c) **Liverpool Bay—Queens Chan.**
i. E.S.E. going −0540, Sp. 2½ kts.
ii. W.N.W. going H.W. Sp. 2 kts.

7. **MORECAMBE BAY.**
(a) **Mersey to Morecambe.**
i. E. onshore −0545, weak.
ii. W. offshore +0005, weak.
(b) **Lune Deep.**
i. Ingoing 060° −0500, Sp. 2½ kts.
ii. Outgoing 240° +0035, Sp. 2 kts.
(c) **Morecambe Bay towards St. Bees Head.**
i. Weak and uncertain.
ii. With coast near land.
iii. S.S.E. going −0145, Sp. 1 kt.
iv. Approx. diff. further N.−1 hr.

8. **SOLWAY FIRTH.**
(a) **Three Fms. Bank.**
i. Ingoing −0500, Sp. 2 kts.
ii. Outgoing +0045, Sp. 2 kts.

9. **ISLE OF MAN.**
(a) During Ingoing St. George.
i. N.E. going off N. part of N.W. coast.
ii. S.W. going off S. part of N.W. coast.
iii. N.E. going off S. part of S.E. coast.
iv. S. going off N. part of S.E. coast.
(b) During outgoing St. Georges — opposite.
(c) Affected by local conditions.

N.B.—Times are given in relation to H.W. Dover and indicate the beginnings of streams. Rates are approx. maximum at Springs in knots. For general details see chartlets on p. 21:149-21:153.

N.W. ENGLAND AND WALES

TIDAL STREAMS

The 13 charts for this area show tidal streams at hourly intervals commencing 6 hours before H.W. Dover and ending 6 hours after H.W. Dover. For Dover H.W. times see pages 21:41-21:43.

Directions of the tidal streams is shown by arrows. The thicker the arrows the stronger the tidal streams they indicate; the thinner arrows show rates and position of weaker streams.

The figures shown against the arrows, as for example 19.34, indicate 1.9 knots at Neap Tides and 3.4 knots at Spring Tides approx.

The following charts are produced from portion(s) of BA Tidal Stream Atlases with the sanction of the Controller H.M. Stationery Office and of the Hydrographer of the Navy.

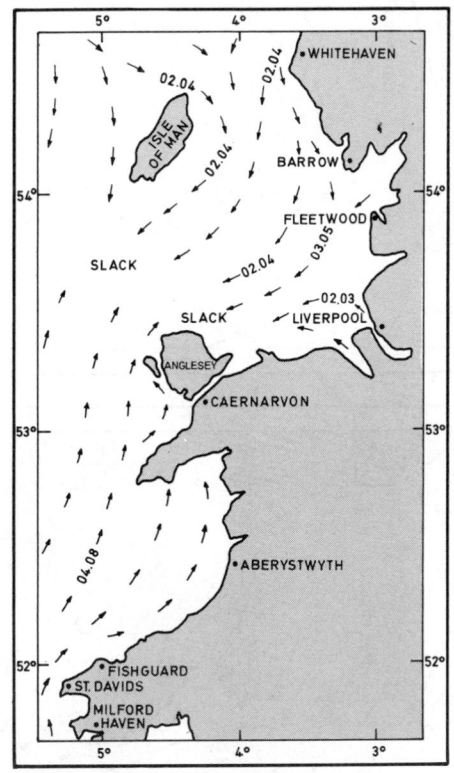

6 hrs BEFORE HW DOVER
6 hrs 15 m BEFORE /AFTER HW LIVERPOOL
1 hr BEFORE HW MILFORD HAVEN

N.W. ENGLAND AND WALES TIDAL STREAMS

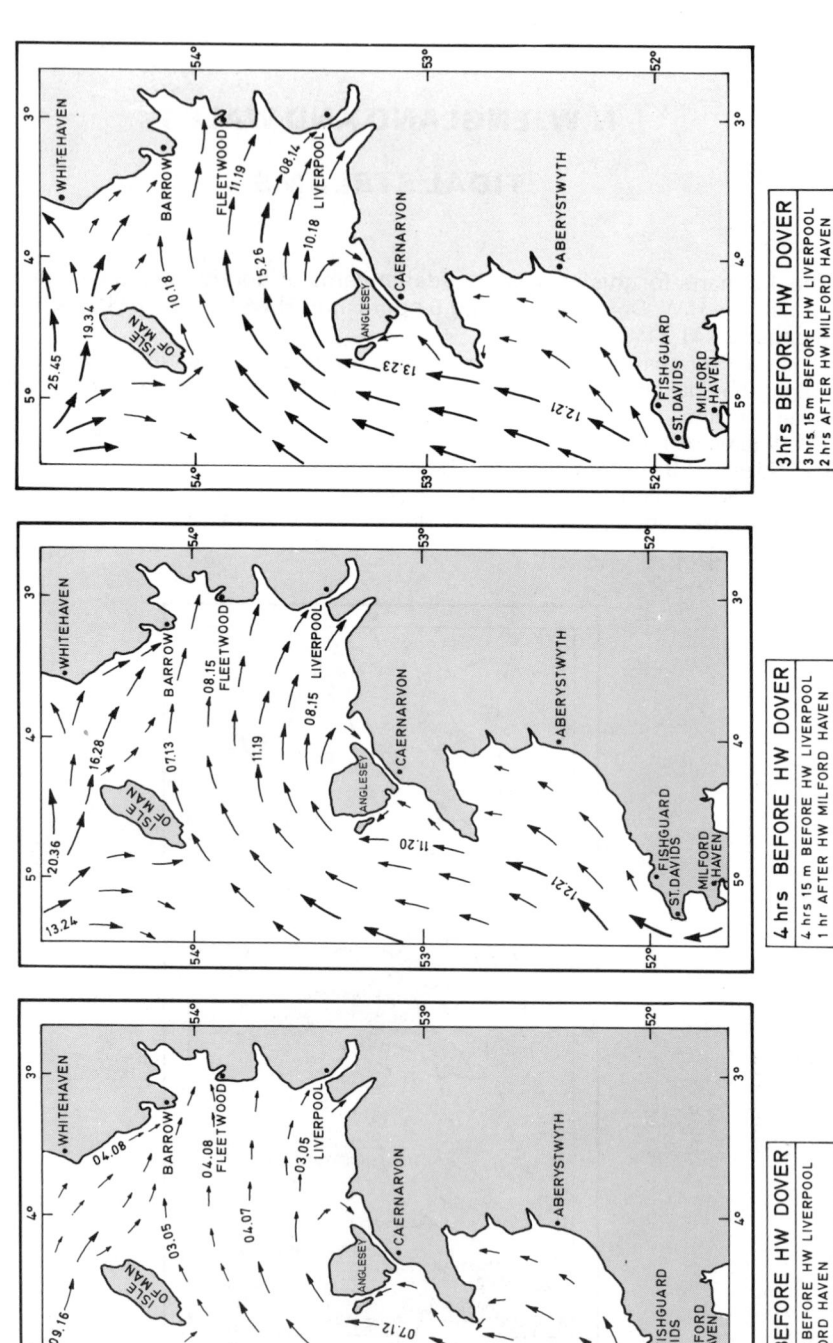

3 hrs BEFORE HW DOVER
3 hrs 15 m BEFORE HW LIVERPOOL
2 hrs AFTER HW MILFORD HAVEN

4 hrs BEFORE HW DOVER
4 hrs 15 m BEFORE HW LIVERPOOL
1 hr AFTER HW MILFORD HAVEN

5 hrs BEFORE HW DOVER
5 hrs 15 m BEFORE HW LIVERPOOL
HW MILFORD HAVEN

N.W. ENGLAND AND WALES TIDAL STREAMS

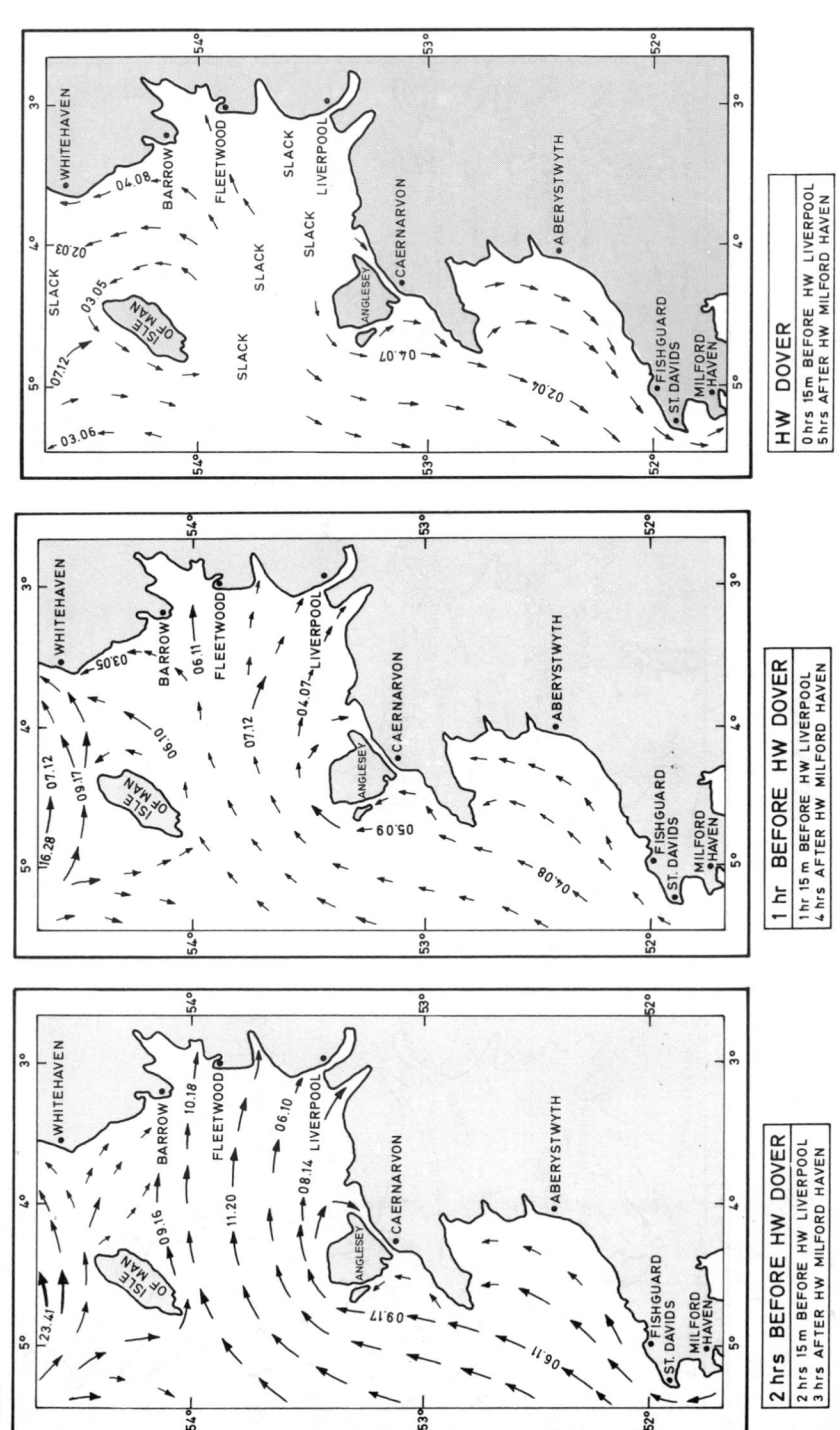

HW DOVER

0 hrs 15m BEFORE HW LIVERPOOL
5 hrs AFTER HW MILFORD HAVEN

1 hr BEFORE HW DOVER

1 hr 15 m BEFORE HW LIVERPOOL
4 hrs AFTER HW MILFORD HAVEN

2 hrs BEFORE HW DOVER

2 hrs 15m BEFORE HW LIVERPOOL
3 hrs AFTER HW MILFORD HAVEN

N.W. ENGLAND AND WALES TIDAL STREAMS

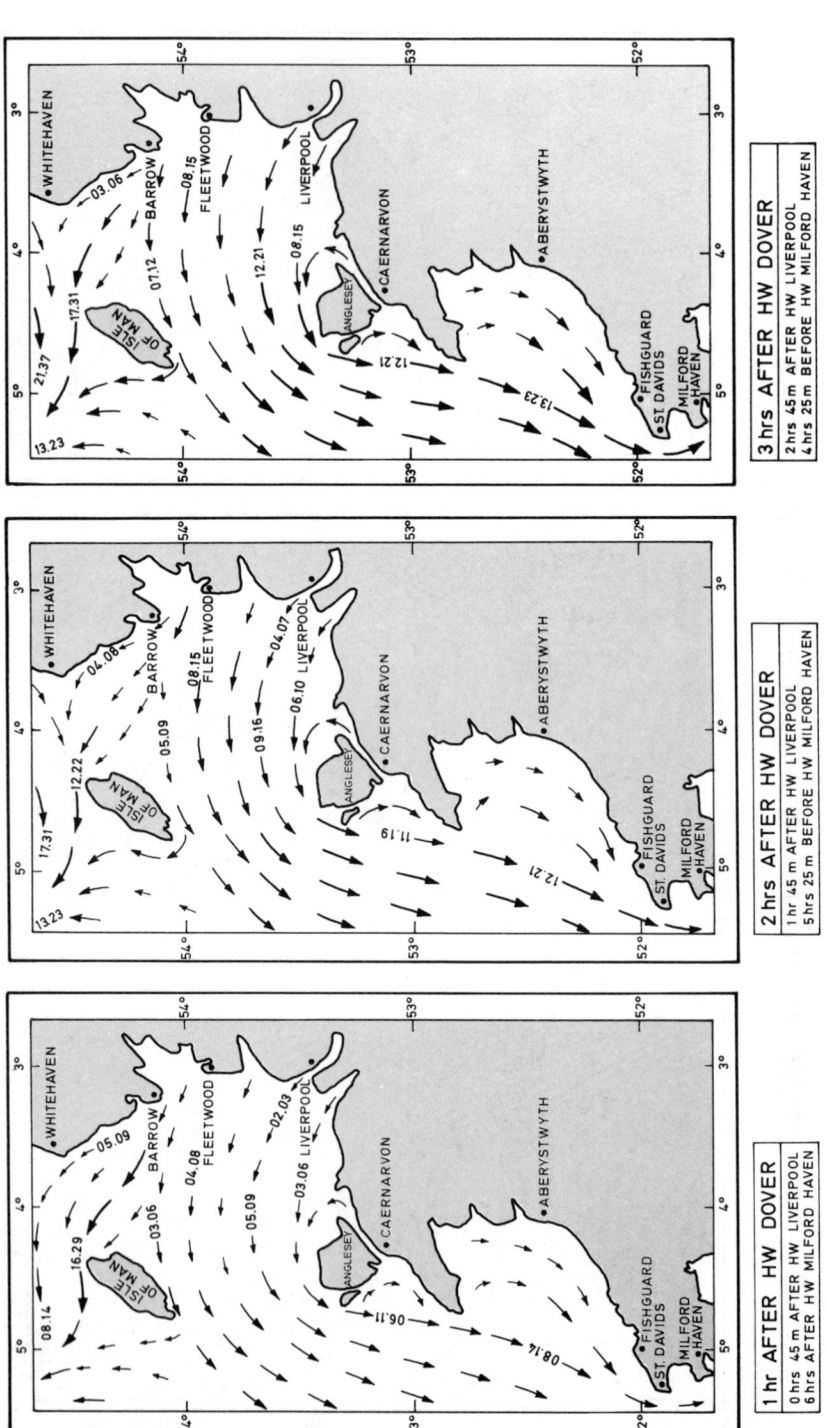

1 hr AFTER HW DOVER
0 hrs 45 m AFTER HW LIVERPOOL
6 hrs AFTER HW MILFORD HAVEN

2 hrs AFTER HW DOVER
1 hr 45 m AFTER HW LIVERPOOL
5 hrs 25m BEFORE HW MILFORD HAVEN

3 hrs AFTER HW DOVER
2 hrs 45 m AFTER HW LIVERPOOL
4 hrs 25m BEFORE HW MILFORD HAVEN

N.W. ENGLAND AND WALES TIDAL STREAMS

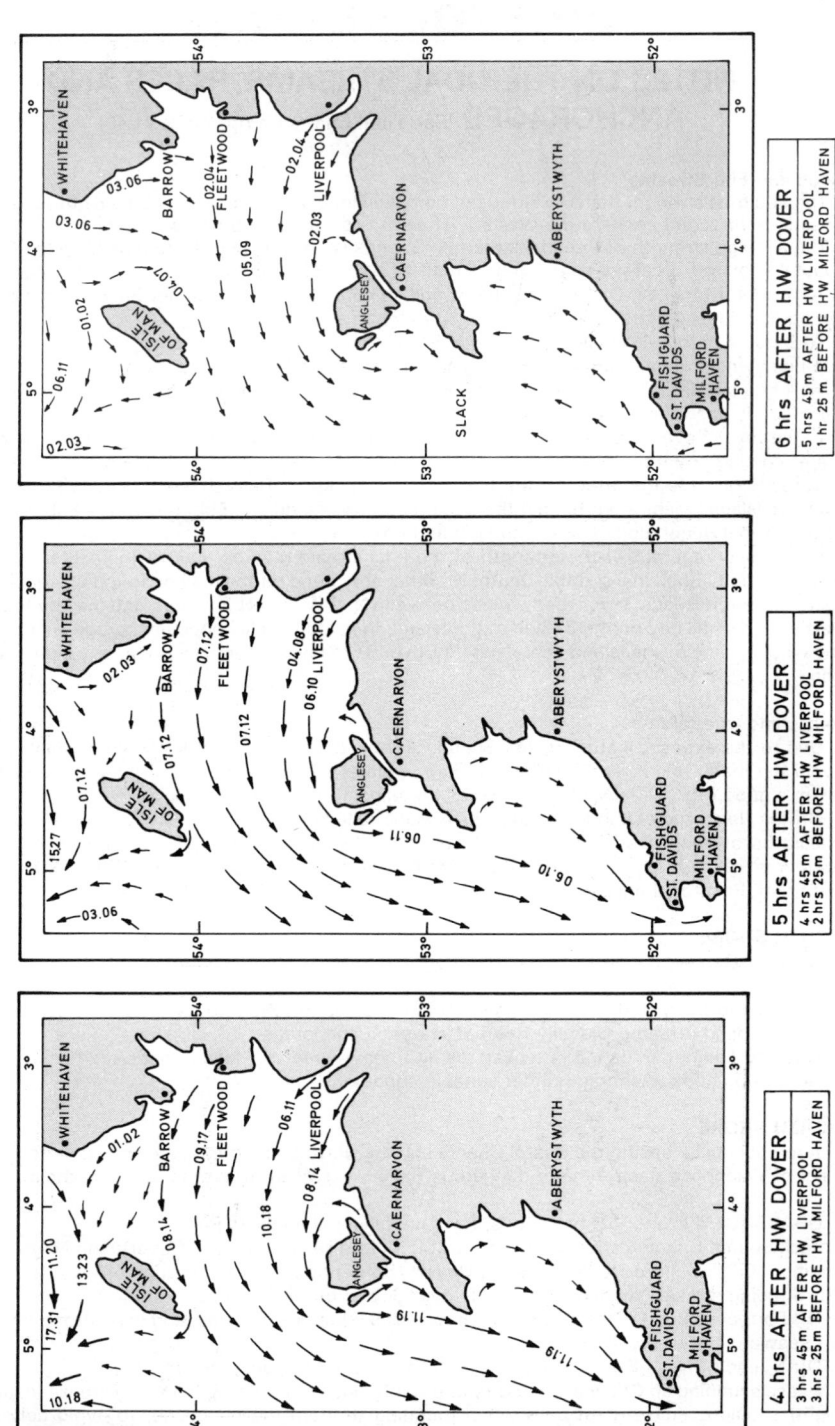

6 hrs AFTER HW DOVER
5 hrs 45 m AFTER HW LIVERPOOL
1 hr 25 m BEFORE HW MILFORD HAVEN

5 hrs AFTER HW DOVER
4 hrs 45 m AFTER HW LIVERPOOL
2 hrs 25 m BEFORE HW MILFORD HAVEN

4 hrs AFTER HW DOVER
3 hrs 45 m AFTER HW LIVERPOOL
3 hrs 25 m BEFORE HW MILFORD HAVEN

BRISTOL CHANNEL

NOTES ON THE TIDAL STREAMS, RACES AND
ANCHORAGES (See Tidal Charts on pp. 21:28-21:40)

Flood and Ebb Streams

The Ebb runs stronger than the Flood but both the Flood and the Ebb run about 6 hours each, except close in to Ilfracombe where the Westerly stream runs for about 9 hours.

The average strength of the tidal stream at Springs is 3 knots, increasing higher up the Channel to about 4 knots off Breaksea Lanby and 5 knots off Lavernock Point.

At 1 hour after H.W. Dover the Ebb has still an hour to run in the Upper Bristol Channel, but the young Flood has just commenced in the entrance to the Bristol Channel.

At 5 hours before H.W. Dover the Flood is still running in the Upper Bristol Channel, but the Ebb has commenced along both shores from Mumbles Head to The Foreland.

At 4 hours before H.W. Dover the Ebb is now running everywhere except above Newport where the Flood is nearly finished.

In the River Severn above Inward Rock the height of Low Water is much affected by the fresh water coming down river.

In the River Wye the effect of the tide is felt as far as St. Briavel.

Lundy Island will be seen to split the tide on both the Flood and Ebb, but on the Ebb the tide runs strongest between Lundy Island and Hartland Point.

Good anchorage out of the strength of the tidal stream may be had off the eastern side of the Island in Lundy Road in a suitable depth. No other very good refuge may be found up channel before Barry or Cardiff Roads. In northerly winds between N.N.W. and N.E. anchorage may be found in the Rattler — a small bay on the S. side of the Island. In Easterly gales good anchorage is obtainable on the western side of the Island near Jenny's Cove. Be ready to weigh anchor at any sign of a shift of wind.

Races and Overfalls

Due to the exposed nature of the Bristol Channel great care must be taken in small vessels to avoid the many Races and Overfalls. In bad weather all headlands and offlying shoals should be given a good offing. Many of these Races are dangerous to small vessels.

Off the North end of Lundy Island a heavy Race called the White Horses is particularly violent and should be avoided. During the strength of the E. going stream this Race ends about one mile northward of the N. point of the Island, extending over Stanley Bank. A strong Race extends also off the South Point of the Island.

SOUTH SHORE

A Race extends off Hartland Point for about two miles north westward during the strength of the stream.

In Barnstaple Bay both ingoing and outgoing streams run 3-3½ knots at Springs across Bideford Bar. With wind offshore Clovelly Road offers good anchorage.

Foreland Ledge has dangerous overfalls and heavy breaking seas in bad weather. Blue Anchor Road affords good anchorage under suitable conditions.

NORTH SHORE

Approaching or leaving the Bristol Channel by the North Shore great care should be taken to keep clear of Wildgoose Race—a very dangerous Race—just West of Skomar and Skokholm Island.

GRASSHOLM Island, off both ends, has Overfalls and a strong Race.

Jack Sound, S. going stream begins +0200 Milford Haven (−0300 Dover); and N. going stream begins −0425 Milford Haven (+0300 Dover). Spring rate in each direction of channel 6-7 knots, but S. going stream has dangerous eddy near S. end of Midland Isle.

Off Porthcawl Breakwater, W. going stream runs 6 knots at Springs, and very strong Race occurs off seaward end of breakwater.

Off S. end of Nash Passage heavy Overfalls occur on E. going stream.

Vessels running up Channel into Barry or other Roads with a strong following breeze (especially at night) should exercise great care when rounding to stem the flood tide, to avoid collision with anchored vessels and loss of ground tackle.

BRISTOL CHANNEL NOTES continued

1. **GENERAL.** Streams are generally E. and W. in direction of the main channel. The main ingoing stream is formed by streams from St. George's Channel and from Land's End. Outgoing, the main stream divides into S. and N. going streams. From +0030 to −0530 Dover St. George's and Land's End streams flow into Bristol Channel. From −0530 to +0030 Dover, the streams from Bristol Channel separate to St. George's and Land's End. Brief irregularity at periods of change.

2. **ENTRANCE.**
   (a) E. going, +0030, 2 kts.
   (b) W. going, −0530, 2 kts.
   (c) Usually a swell from W.
   (d) Ebb stronger than flood.
   (e) Stream generally weak.

3. **LUNDY.**
   (a) Streams increase towards island.
   (b) Between Lundy and Hartland Pt. 3 kts.
   (c) Streams meet and divide 3 M. off N. and S. ends of island, 5 kts.
   (d) Dangerous Race-Stanley Bank.
   (e) Races off N. and S. during E. and W. streams.
   (f) E.N.E. +0030, 2 kts.
   (g) W.S.W. −0530, 2 kts.

4. **S. SHORE.**
   (a) **Off Ilfracombe.**
   i. E. going, +0050, 3 kts.
   ii. W. going, −0520, 3 kts.
   (b) **Off Foreland Point.**
   i. E. going, +0100, 5 kts.
   ii. W. going, −0500, 5 kts.
   (c) **Between Steep Holm and Flat Holm.**
   i. E. going, +0200, 3 kts.
   ii. W. going, −0400, 4 kts.
   (d) Dangerous Race off Morte Point.
   (e) Eddies, confused seas off most headlands.
   (f) **Avonmouth Docks**
   Spring stream sets across entrance at 5 knots.

5. **N.W. APPROACH.**
   (a) Give headlands good offing.
   (b) Eddies and confused seas off most headlands.
   (c) **Near Smalls.**
   i. S. going, +0015, 5 kts.
   ii. N. going, −0545, 5 kts.
   (d) Race and eddies—Grassholm
   (e) Wildgoose Race − W. of Skomer − dangerous.
   (f) Overfalls, shoals and rocks off islands.

6. **N. SHORE.**
   (a) **Off Milford Haven.**
   i. E × S −0005, 2-3 kts.
   ii. W × N +0600, 2-3 kts.
   (b) Often confused seas at entrance.
   (c) Race off St Gowans Hd.
   (d) Weak set into Carmarthen Bay.
   (e) **Off Worms Hd.**
   i. E going, $2\frac{1}{4}$ kts. +0100.
   ii. W going, $2\frac{1}{2}$ kts. −0510.
   (f) **Approach Swansea.**
   i. E. going, 2 kts. −0100.
   ii. W. going, 2 kts. −0510.
   (g) **Scarweather.** Variable and confused.
   (h) Eddies near sands and shoals.
   (i) Between Nash and Breaksea Point.
   i. E. going, +0120, 3 kts.
   ii. W. going, −0450, 3 kts.
   (j) Possible Race off Breaksea Point.
   (k) **Between Breaksea and Lavernock Point.**
   i. Streams in direction of coast—4-5 kts.
   ii. May be overfalls off Lavernock.

N.B.—Times are given in relation to H.W. Dover and indicate the beginning of the streams. Rates are approx, max. at springs in knots. Further details may be found as footnotes to individual ports.

RIVERS TAW and TORRIDGE

Meteorological conditions considerably affect the heights of high and low water.
At **Fremington** the Spring Low Water stand, which lasts for 2 to $2\frac{1}{2}$ hours commences half an hour after L.W. time. At Neaps there is no stand.
At **Barnstaple** the Low Water stand lasts until 1 hour 45 minutes before H.W.
At **Bideford** the Low Water stand may last 2 to 3 hours at Springs.

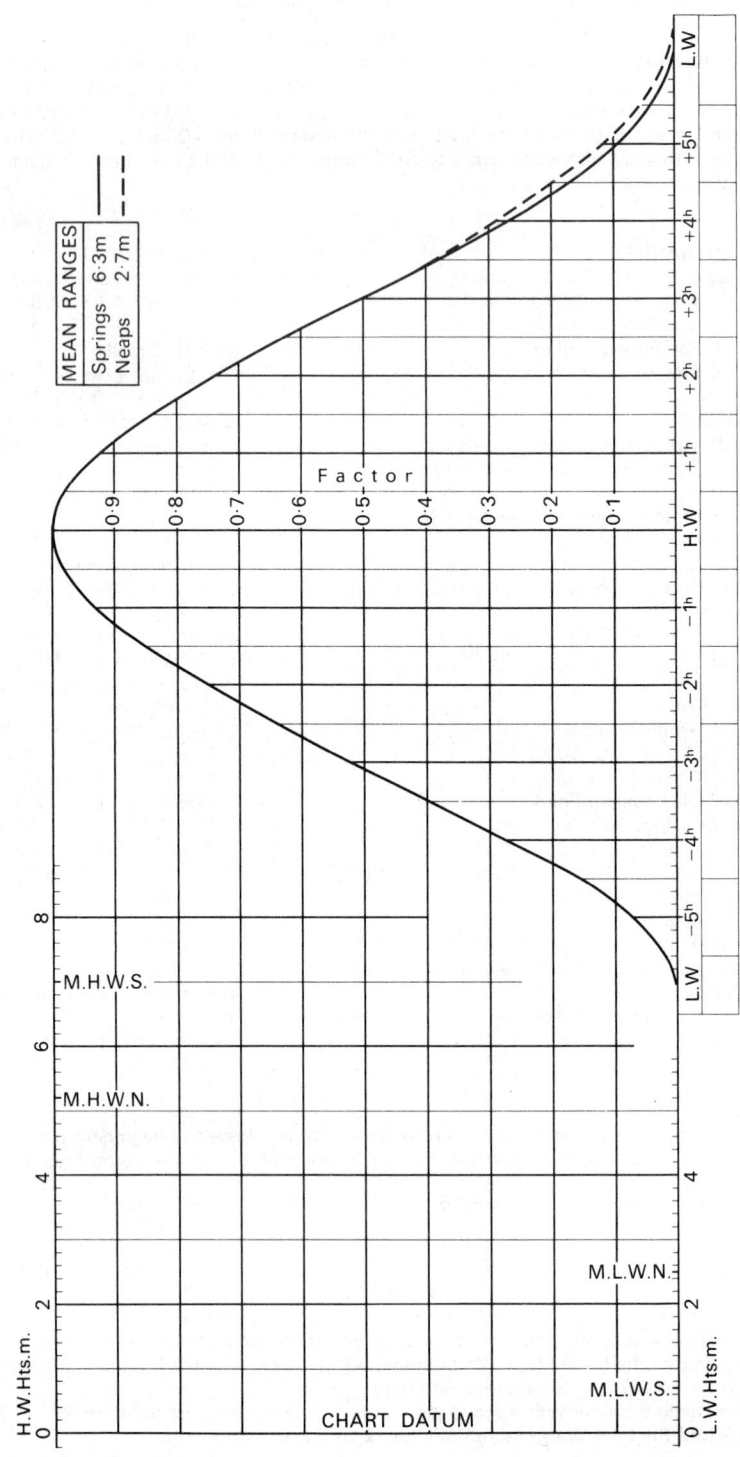

MILFORD HAVEN

MEAN SPRING AND NEAP CURVES

Springs occur 2 days after New and Full Moon.

MEAN RANGES

Springs 6·3m

Neaps 2·7m

Factor

M.H.W.S.

M.H.W.N.

M.L.W.N.

M.L.W.S.

CHART DATUM

H.W.Hts.m.

L.W.Hts.m.

TIDAL DIFFERENCES ON MILFORD HAVEN

PLACE	TIME DIFFERENCES				HEIGHT DIFFERENCES (Metres)			
	High Water		Low Water		MHWS	MHWN	MLWN	MLWS
MILFORD HAVEN	0100 and 1300	0800 and 2000	0100 and 1300	0700 and 1900	**7.0**	**5.2**	**2.5**	**0.7**
Cardigan Bay								
Aberdaron	+0210	+0200	+0240	+0310	-2.4	-1.9	-0.6	-0.2
St. Tudwal's Roads	+0155	+0145	+0240	+0310	-2.2	-1.9	-0.7	-0.2
Pwllheli	+0210	+0150	+0245	+0320	-2.0	-1.8	-0.6	-0.2
Criccieth	+0210	+0155	+0255	+0320	-2.0	-1.8	-0.7	-0.3
Barmouth	+0215	+0205	+0310	+0320	-2.0	-1.7	-0.7	0.0
Aberdovey	+0215	+0200	+0230	+0305	-2.0	-1.7	-0.5	0.0
Aberystwyth	+0145	+0130	+0210	+0245	-2.0	-1.7	-0.7	0.0
Aberaeron	+0150	+0125	+0200	+0235	-2.1	-1.8	-0.6	-0.1
New Quay	+0150	+0125	+0155	+0230	-2.1	-1.8	-0.6	-0.1
Aberporth	+0135	+0120	+0150	+0220	-2.1	-1.8	-0.6	-0.1
Port Cardigan	+0140	+0120	+0220	+0130	-2.3	-1.8	-0.5	0.0
Fishguard	+0115	+0100	+0110	+0135	-2.2	-1.8	-0.5	+0.1
Porthgain	+0055	+0045	+0045	+0100	-2.5	-1.8	-0.6	0.0
Ramsey Sound	+0030	+0030	+0030	+0030	-1.9	-1.3	-0.3	0.0
Solva	+0015	+0010	+0035	+0015	-1.5	-1.0	-0.2	0.0
Little Haven	+0010	+0010	+0025	+0015	-1.1	-0.8	-0.2	0.0
Martin's Haven	+0010	+0010	+0015	+0015	-0.8	-0.5	+0.1	+0.1
Skomer Island	-0005	-0005	+0005	+0005	-0.4	-0.1	0.0	0.0
Dale Roads	-0005	-0005	-0008	-0008	0.0	0.0	0.0	-0.1
Cleddau River								
Neyland	+0002	+0010	0000	0000	0.0	0.0	0.0	0.0
Black Tar	+0010	+0020	+0005	0000	+0.1	+0.1	0.0	-0.1
Haverfordwest	+0010	+0025	—	—	-4.8	-4.9	Dries	Dries
Stackpole Quay	-0005	+0025	-0010	-0010	+0.9	+0.7	+0.2	+0.3
Tenby	-0015	-0010	-0015	-0020	+1.4	+1.1	+0.5	+0.2
Towy River								
Ferryside	0000	-0010	+0220	0000	-0.3	-0.7	-1.7	-0.6
Carmarthen	+0010	0000	—	—	-4.4	-4.8	Dries	Dries
Burry Inlet								
Burry Port	+0003	+0003	+0007	+0007	+1.6	+1.4	+0.5	+0.4
Mumbles	+0005	+0010	-0020	-0015	+2.3	+1.7	+0.6	+0.2
Swansea	+0004	+0007	-0005	-0005	+2.6	+2.1	+0.7	+0.3
Port Talbot	-0005	+0005	-0015	-0030	+2.6	+2.1	+0.8	+0.3
Porthcawl	0000	0000	0000	-0015	+2.9	+2.3	+0.8	+0.3
MILFORD HAVEN	0100 and 1300	0700 and 1900	0100 and 1300	0700 and 1900	**7.0**	**5.2**	**2.5**	**0.7**
Ilfracombe	-0030	-0015	-0035	-0055	+2.2	+1.7	+0.5	0.0
Rivers Taw and Torridge								
Appledore	-0020	-0025	+0015	-0045	+0.5	0.0	-0.9	-0.5
Yelland Marsh	-0010	-0015	+0100	-0015	-0.4	-0.9	-1.7	-1.1
Fremington	-0010	-0015	+0030	-0030	-0.5	-1.2	-1.6	+0.1
Barnstaple	0000	-0015	-0155	-0245	-2.9	-3.8	-2.2	-0.4
Bideford	-0020	-0025	0000	0000	-1.1	-1.6	-2.5	-0.7
Clovelly	-0030	-0030	-0020	-0040	+1.3	+1.1	+0.2	+0.2
Lundy Island	-0030	-0030	-0020	-0040	+1.0	+0.7	+0.2	+0.1
Bude	-0040	-0040	-0035	-0045	+0.7	+0.6	—	—
Boscastle	-0045	-0010	-0110	-0100	+0.3	+0.4	+0.2	+0.2
Port Isaac	-0100	-0100	-0100	-0100	+0.5	+0.6	0.0	+0.2
Padstow	-0055	-0050	-0040	-0050	+0.3	+0.4	+0.1	+0.1
Wadebridge	-0052	-0052	+0235	+0245	-3.8	-3.8	-2.5	-0.4
Newquay	-0100	-0110	-0105	-0050	0.0	+0.1	0.0	-0.1
Perranporth	-0100	-0110	-0110	-0050	-0.1	0.0	0.0	+0.1
Portreath	-0055	-0112	-0107	-0045	-0.2	-0.1	0.0	+0.1
St. Ives	-0050	-0115	-0105	-0040	-0.4	-0.3	-0.1	+0.1
Cape Cornwall	-0130	-0145	-0120	-0120	-1.0	-0.9	-0.5	-0.1
Sennen Cove	-0130	-0145	-0125	-0125	-0.9	-0.4	—	—

Refer to predictions on pages 21:158-21:160

MILFORD HAVEN

HIGH & LOW WATER 1992   Lat. 51°42'N. Long. 5°01'W.

GMT   ADD 1 HOUR MARCH 29 — OCTOBER 25 FOR B.S.T.

	JANUARY				FEBRUARY				MARCH				APRIL		
	Time	m		Time	m		Time	m		Time	m		Time	m	
1 W	0324 0950 1552 2220	5·7 2·1 5·7 2·0	**16** Th	0208 0842 1450 2119	5·5 2·3 5·7 2·0	**1** Sa	0449 1116 1712 2332	6·0 1·8 5·9 1·6	**16** Su	0416 1048 1649 2311	6·3 1·2 6·5 1·1	**1** Su	0424 1051 1648 2308	5·9 1·8 5·8 1·7	**16** M	0400 1033 1633 2252	6·3 1·1 6·5 1·0	**1** W	0508 1126 1726 2342	6·4 1·1 6·4 1·1	**16** Th	0518 1144 1742	7·0 0·5 7·0
2 Th	0420 1045 1644 2308	6·0 1·9 5·9 1·8	**17** F	0325 0956 1602 2226	5·8 1·8 6·1 1·6	**2** Su	0530 1153 1750	6·3 1·5 6·2	**17** M	0511 1142 1740	6·9 0·7 7·0	**2** M	0505 1127 1725 2342	6·2 1·4 6·2 1·3	**17** Tu	0454 1123 1722 2340	6·9 0·6 6·9 0·5	**2** Th	0542 1200 1758	6·7 0·9 6·6	**17** F	0001 0601 1225 1822	0·5 7·2 0·4 7·2
3 F	0506 1130 1729 2349	6·2 1·6 6·1 1·6	**18** Sa	0430 1058 1701 2322	6·4 1·3 6·5 1·1	**3** M	0007 0607 1227 1825	1·4 6·6 1·2 6·4	**18** Tu	0000 0600 1229 1827	0·6 7·3 0·3 7·3	**3** Tu	0540 1200 1758	6·5 1·1 6·4	**18** W	0540 1208 1805	7·3 0·3 7·3	**3** F	0014 0615 1231 1831	0·9 6·9 0·7 6·8	**18** Sa	0042 0642 1304 1902	0·4 7·2 0·5 7·2
4 Sa	0549 1210 1808	6·4 1·5 6·3	**19** Su	0525 1153 1754	6·8 0·8 6·9	**4** Tu	0039 0641 1257 1856	1·2 6·7 1·1 6·6	**19** W	0046 0646 1313 1910	0·2 7·6 0·0 7·5	**4** W	0014 0614 1231 1831	1·1 6·7 0·9 6·7	**19** Th	0024 0624 1250 1848	0·2 7·5 0·1 7·4	**4** Sa	0046 0648 1303 1903	0·7 7·0 0·6 6·9	**19** Su	0121 0721 1341 1940	0·5 7·0 0·7 7·0
5 Su	0025 0625 1245 1843	1·4 6·6 1·3 6·4	**20** M	0014 0615 1243 1843	0·7 7·3 0·5 7·2	**5** W	0110 0713 1327 1927	1·0 6·8 0·9 6·6	**20** Th	0128 0728 1355 1951	0·1 7·7 0·0 7·5	**5** Th	0043 0645 1300 1900	0·9 6·9 0·7 6·8	**20** F	0106 0706 1330 1926	0·1 7·6 0·1 7·4	**5** Su	0119 0721 1335 1935	0·7 7·0 0·7 6·9	**20** M	0158 0758 1415 2016	0·7 6·8 1·0 6·7
6 M	0057 0700 1319 1917	1·3 6·7 1·2 6·4	**21** Tu	0102 0703 1331 1930	0·4 7·5 0·2 7·4	**6** Th	0138 0742 1358 1957	1·0 6·9 0·9 6·6	**21** F	0209 0811 1434 2030	0·2 7·6 0·3 7·2	**6** F	0113 0716 1330 1930	0·8 7·0 0·7 6·8	**21** Sa	0144 0745 1406 2004	0·2 7·4 0·4 7·2	**6** M	0151 0755 1409 2011	0·8 6·9 0·9 6·8	**21** Tu	0234 0836 1450 2054	1·1 6·4 1·4 6·4
7 Tu	0130 0734 1349 1949	1·3 6·7 1·4 6·4	**22** W	0148 0749 1416 2013	0·3 7·6 0·2 7·3	**7** F	0208 0813 1427 2026	1·0 6·8 1·0 6·6	**22** Sa	0249 0850 1512 2110	0·4 7·2 0·7 6·9	**7** Sa	0142 0747 1401 1959	0·8 6·9 0·8 6·8	**22** Su	0222 0822 1442 2040	0·5 7·1 0·8 6·8	**7** Tu	0227 0832 1444 2049	1·0 6·6 1·1 6·5	**22** W	0311 0912 1524 2134	1·5 6·0 1·7 6·0
8 W	0201 0806 1422 2022	1·3 6·6 1·2 6·4	**23** Th	0232 0833 1500 2057	0·4 7·5 0·4 7·1	**8** Sa	0239 0843 1458 2057	1·1 6·7 1·2 6·4	**23** Su	0327 0928 1549 2148	0·9 6·7 1·2 6·4	**8** Su	0213 0818 1430 2030	0·9 6·8 0·9 6·7	**23** M	0258 0900 1515 2118	0·9 6·6 1·3 6·4	**8** W	0305 0912 1525 2131	1·3 6·3 1·4 6·2	**23** Th	0349 0953 1602 2217	1·8 5·5 2·1 5·6
9 Th	0232 0839 1453 2053	1·3 6·5 1·4 6·2	**24** F	0314 0917 1542 2139	0·6 7·2 0·8 6·7	**9** Su	0308 0915 1529 2129	1·4 6·5 1·4 6·2	**24** M	0404 1009 1626 2230	1·4 6·2 1·8 5·9	**9** M	0244 0850 1503 2104	1·1 6·6 1·2 6·4	**24** Tu	0334 0936 1549 2157	1·4 6·1 1·8 5·9	**9** Th	0352 1002 1614 2224	1·6 5·9 1·8 5·8	**24** F	0435 1041 1651 2315	2·2 5·2 2·5 5·2
10 F	0304 0911 1527 2127	1·5 6·4 1·5 6·1	**25** Sa	0356 1000 1624 2223	1·0 6·8 1·2 6·3	**10** M	0341 0950 1604 2207	1·6 6·2 1·7 6·0	**25** Tu	0445 1052 1708 2320	1·9 5·6 2·3 5·4	**10** Tu	0318 0927 1538 2142	1·4 6·3 1·5 6·1	**25** W	0413 1019 1627 2244	1·9 5·5 2·2 5·4	**10** F	0452 1104 1723 2337	1·9 5·5 2·2 5·5	**25** Sa	0537 1147 1805	2·5 4·9 2·7
11 Sa	0336 0946 1602 2202	1·7 6·1 1·8 5·9	**26** Su	0440 1045 1709 2311	1·5 6·2 1·8 5·8	**11** Tu	0419 1031 1647 2254	1·9 5·8 2·0 5·6	**26** W	0539 1150 1810	2·5 5·1 2·7	**11** W	0357 1009 1621 2231	1·7 5·9 1·9 5·7	**26** Th	0501 1110 1723 2350	2·4 5·0 2·7 5·0	**11** Sa	0617 1228 1855	2·1 5·2 2·3	**26** Su	0031 0700 1314 1938	5·1 2·6 4·8 2·6
12 Su	0414 1024 1642 2244	2·0 6·0 2·0 5·7	**27** M	0527 1134 1800	2·0 5·7 2·2	**12** W	0512 1127 1750	2·3 5·5 2·3	**27** Th	0034 0704 1323 2002	5·0 2·9 4·8 2·9	**12** Th	0451 1106 1726 2340	2·1 5·5 2·3 5·4	**27** F	0607 1232 1900	2·7 4·7 2·9	**12** Su	0109 0754 1402 2026	5·5 2·0 5·4 2·0	**27** M	0154 0822 1433 2053	5·2 2·3 5·1 2·3
13 M	0458 1111 1733 2337	2·2 5·7 2·2 5·5	**28** Tu	0007 0629 1239 1913	5·4 2·4 5·4 2·6	**13** Th	0001 0634 1249 1923	5·4 2·5 5·3 2·5	**28** F	0219 0900 1505 2135	5·0 2·6 5·0 2·5	**13** F	0617 1232 1903	2·4 5·2 2·5	**28** Sa	0128 0808 1420 2049	4·9 2·7 4·8 2·6	**13** M	0234 0911 1515 2135	5·8 1·6 5·9 1·5	**28** Tu	0257 0921 1527 2145	5·5 2·0 5·5 1·9
14 Tu	0558 1211 1841	2·4 5·5 2·4	**29** W	0126 0758 1409 2049	5·2 2·6 5·1 2·6	**14** F	0134 0816 1429 2100	5·3 2·4 5·4 2·2	**29** Sa	0335 1006 1604 2227	5·4 2·2 5·4 2·1	**14** Sa	0119 0805 1418 2046	5·3 2·3 5·3 2·2	**29** Su	0254 0925 1528 2149	5·3 2·3 5·2 2·2	**14** Tu	0338 1011 1610 2230	6·3 1·0 6·4 1·0	**29** W	0346 1007 1610 2227	5·9 1·6 5·9 1·6
15 W	0046 0717 1327 2002	5·3 2·5 5·5 2·3	**30** Th	0256 0929 1531 2202	5·3 2·5 5·3 2·3	**15** Sa	0307 0943 1549 2213	5·7 1·9 5·9 1·6				**15** Su	0254 0932 1536 2159	5·7 1·7 5·9 1·6	**30** M	0357 1013 1613 2231	5·8 1·8 5·7 1·7	**15** W	0430 1058 1658 2318	6·8 0·7 6·8 0·7	**30** Th	0427 1047 1648 2306	6·2 1·3 6·2 1·3
			31 F	0400 1030 1628 2252	5·6 2·1 5·6 2·0												**31** Tu	0430 1051 1651 2308	6·1 1·4 6·1 1·4					

To find H.W. Dover add 5h. 00 min.

TIDAL DIFFERENCES PAGE 21:157. TIDAL CURVE PAGE 21:156.

TIDAL STREAMS PAGES 21:28-21:40 and 21:154-21:155.

Datum of predictions: 3.71 m. below Ordnance Datum (Newlyn) or approx. L.A.T.

MILFORD HAVEN   21:159

Lat. 51°42′N. Long. 5°01′W.   **HIGH & LOW WATER 1992**

GMT   **ADD 1 HOUR MARCH 29 — OCTOBER 25 FOR B.S.T.**

MAY

Day	Time	m	Time	m	Time	m	Time	m
1 F	0506	6.5	1125	1.1	1725	6.5	2343	1.0
2 Sa ●	0543	6.7	1201	0.9	1801	6.8		
3 Su	0019	0.8	0621	6.9	1236	0.7	1838	6.9
4 M	0056	0.8	0659	6.9	1314	0.7	1916	6.9
5 Tu	0135	0.8	0740	6.8	1354	0.8	1957	6.8
6 W	0218	0.9	0823	6.6	1436	1.1	2042	6.6
7 Th	0304	1.1	0910	6.3	1524	1.3	2129	6.4
8 F	0356	1.4	1002	6.0	1617	1.6	2226	6.1
9 Sa ☽	0458	1.6	1104	5.7	1722	1.9	2333	5.8
10 Su	0611	1.8	1217	5.5	1839	2.0		
11 M	0049	5.8	0728	1.8	1335	5.6	1957	1.9
12 Tu	0205	5.9	0842	1.6	1446	5.9	2105	1.6
13 W	0310	6.2	0941	1.3	1542	6.2	2203	1.3
14 Th	0404	6.4	1033	1.1	1633	6.5	2252	1.0
15 F	0454	6.6	1119	0.9	1718	6.7	2339	0.9
16 Sa ○	0539	6.7	1203	0.9	1801	6.8		
17 Su	0022	0.8	0621	6.7	1242	0.9	1841	6.8
18 M	0102	0.9	0702	6.6	1319	1.0	1920	6.8
19 Tu	0140	1.0	0740	6.5	1355	1.2	1958	6.6
20 W	0216	1.2	0816	6.2	1429	1.4	2034	6.4
21 Th	0253	1.4	0854	6.0	1504	1.6	2114	6.1
22 F	0331	1.7	0932	5.7	1542	1.9	2155	5.8
23 Sa	0412	1.9	1014	5.4	1624	2.2	2241	5.6
24 Su	0501	2.2	1105	5.2	1719	2.4	2337	5.3
25 M	0601	2.3	1207	5.1	1828	2.5		
26 Tu	0042	5.3	0709	2.3	1317	5.1	1941	2.4
27 W	0149	5.4	0816	2.2	1425	5.3	2046	2.2
28 Th	0250	5.6	0914	1.9	1519	5.6	2139	1.9
29 F	0342	5.9	1003	1.6	1607	6.0	2227	1.6
30 Sa	0428	6.2	1048	1.3	1651	6.3	2312	1.3
31 Su	0513	6.5	1132	1.1	1734	6.6	2356	1.0

JUNE

Day	Time	m	Time	m	Time	m	Time	m
1 M ●	0558	6.7	1215	0.9	1818	6.9		
2 Tu	0041	0.8	0643	6.8	1259	0.8	1903	7.0
3 W	0127	0.7	0730	6.8	1345	0.8	1948	7.0
4 Th	0213	0.7	0816	6.7	1432	0.9	2036	6.9
5 F	0304	0.8	0905	6.6	1521	1.1	2127	6.7
6 Sa	0356	1.0	0957	6.3	1613	1.3	2220	6.4
7 Su ☽	0451	1.3	1052	6.0	1709	1.5	2318	6.2
8 M	0550	1.5	1153	5.8	1812	1.7		
9 Tu	0021	6.0	0656	1.7	1300	5.7	1921	1.8
10 W	0130	5.9	0804	1.7	1409	5.7	2032	1.8
11 Th	0237	5.9	0910	1.7	1514	5.9	2136	1.7
12 F	0339	6.0	1009	1.5	1609	6.1	2233	1.5
13 Sa	0434	6.2	1059	1.4	1659	6.3	2322	1.3
14 Su	0522	6.3	1144	1.3	1744	6.5		
15 M ○	0007	1.2	0605	6.3	1225	1.2	1825	6.6
16 Tu	0046	1.1	0645	6.4	1302	1.2	1903	6.6
17 W	0124	1.1	0723	6.3	1337	1.2	1941	6.6
18 Th	0159	1.2	0758	6.3	1411	1.3	2016	6.5
19 F	0233	1.3	0833	6.1	1444	1.4	2051	6.3
20 Sa	0308	1.4	0908	6.0	1518	1.6	2128	6.1
21 Su	0345	1.6	0945	5.8	1556	1.8	2206	5.9
22 M	0424	1.8	1026	5.6	1637	2.1	2249	5.7
23 Tu	0509	2.1	1111	5.4	1727	2.3	2339	5.5
24 W	0604	2.2	1207	5.2	1829	2.4		
25 Th	0039	5.4	0709	2.3	1313	5.2	1940	2.4
26 F	0147	5.4	0816	2.2	1422	5.4	2049	2.2
27 Sa	0254	5.6	0919	1.9	1525	5.8	2150	1.8
28 Su	0355	6.0	1017	1.6	1621	6.2	2247	1.4
29 M	0449	6.3	1109	1.2	1713	6.6	2339	1.1
30 Tu	0542	6.6	1200	0.9	1803	6.9		

JULY

Day	Time	m	Time	m	Time	m	Time	m
1 W	0029	0.7	0631	6.9	1248	0.7	1850	7.1
2 Th	0119	0.5	0719	7.0	1335	0.6	1938	7.2
3 F	0206	0.4	0806	7.0	1423	0.6	2026	7.2
4 Sa	0254	0.5	0853	6.9	1510	0.7	2114	7.1
5 Su	0342	0.7	0941	6.6	1557	0.9	2202	6.8
6 M	0430	1.0	1028	6.3	1647	1.3	2251	6.4
7 Tu ☽	0520	1.4	1120	6.0	1740	1.6	2346	6.0
8 W	0617	1.8	1219	5.7	1842	1.9		
9 Th	0050	5.7	0724	2.0	1331	5.5	1957	2.1
10 F	0205	5.5	0840	2.1	1447	5.6	2114	2.1
11 Sa	0319	5.6	0949	2.0	1552	5.8	2219	1.9
12 Su	0430	5.8	1044	1.8	1658	6.1	2311	1.6
13 M	0509	6.0	1130	1.5	1730	6.3	2354	1.4
14 Tu ○	0551	6.2	1210	1.4	1810	6.5		
15 W	0032	1.2	0629	6.3	1245	1.2	1846	6.6
16 Th	0106	1.1	0704	6.4	1319	1.2	1921	6.6
17 F	0138	1.1	0737	6.4	1349	1.1	1954	6.6
18 Sa	0209	1.1	0809	6.3	1420	1.2	2026	6.5
19 Su	0242	1.2	0842	6.2	1453	1.3	2058	6.4
20 M	0314	1.4	0912	6.1	1524	1.5	2131	6.2
21 Tu	0346	1.6	0946	5.9	1557	1.8	2206	5.9
22 W	0423	1.8	1024	5.7	1637	2.1	2248	5.7
23 Th	0508	2.1	1111	5.4	1729	2.3	2340	5.5
24 F	0607	2.3	1212	5.3	1841	2.5		
25 Sa	0050	5.3	0723	2.4	1331	5.3	2006	2.4
26 Su	0215	5.4	0844	2.2	1453	5.6	2125	2.0
27 M	0331	5.8	0955	1.8	1600	6.1	2230	1.5
28 Tu	0433	6.2	1054	1.3	1657	6.6	2325	1.0
29 W ●	0527	6.7	1146	0.8	1749	7.0		
30 Th	0017	0.6	0617	7.0	1235	0.5	1836	7.4
31 F	0104	0.3	0703	7.3	1321	0.3	1923	7.6

AUGUST

Day	Time	m	Time	m	Time	m	Time	m
1 Sa	0151	0.1	0748	7.3	1406	0.2	2008	7.5
2 Su	0234	0.2	0832	7.2	1450	0.4	2051	7.3
3 M	0318	0.5	0915	6.9	1534	0.7	2136	6.9
4 Tu	0402	0.9	0959	6.5	1617	1.2	2221	6.5
5 W	0445	1.4	1047	6.0	1705	1.7	2311	5.9
6 Th	0536	2.0	1140	5.6	1803	2.1		
7 F	0011	5.4	0641	2.4	1252	5.3	1923	2.4
8 Sa	0134	5.1	0812	2.5	1423	5.3	2058	2.4
9 Su	0303	5.2	0935	2.3	1536	5.6	2207	2.1
10 M	0406	5.5	1031	1.9	1630	6.0	2258	1.7
11 Tu	0454	5.9	1115	1.6	1712	6.3	2337	1.4
12 W	0533	6.1	1151	1.4	1750	6.5		
13 Th ○	0011	1.2	0608	6.3	1225	1.2	1825	6.7
14 F	0043	1.1	0641	6.5	1255	1.0	1857	6.8
15 Sa	0113	1.1	0712	6.6	1324	1.0	1928	6.8
16 Su	0142	0.9	0742	6.6	1352	1.0	1958	6.7
17 M	0212	1.0	0811	6.5	1422	1.1	2027	6.6
18 Tu	0242	1.2	0840	6.4	1451	1.4	2058	6.4
19 W	0312	1.4	0911	6.2	1524	1.6	2131	6.1
20 Th	0345	1.7	0946	5.9	1557	1.9	2209	5.8
21 F ☽	0423	2.0	1030	5.6	1644	2.2	2259	5.5
22 Sa	0519	2.3	1129	5.3	1758	2.5		
23 Su	0012	5.2	0645	2.5	1256	5.2	1938	2.5
24 M	0149	5.2	0822	2.3	1432	5.5	2110	2.0
25 Tu	0317	5.7	0941	1.8	1545	6.1	2217	1.4
26 W	0419	6.3	1040	1.2	1641	6.7	2311	0.9
27 Th	0511	6.8	1130	0.7	1732	7.2		
28 F ●	0000	0.4	0558	7.2	1217	0.3	1818	7.6
29 Sa	0045	0.1	0643	7.5	1302	0.1	1903	7.7
30 Su	0128	0.0	0726	7.6	1344	0.1	1945	7.7
31 M	0211	0.2	0808	7.3	1426	0.3	2027	7.4

GENERAL — Inside entrance streams are ingoing and outgoing. Outside streams run across entrance E. x S., W. x N. As streams meet there is often a confused sea. Outside — stream follows coast. Race off St. Gowan's Head, overfalls on St. Gowan's Shoals.

MILFORD HAVEN

HIGH & LOW WATER 1992 Lat. 51°42'N. Long. 5°01'W.

GMT ADD 1 HOUR MARCH 29 — OCTOBER 25 FOR B.S.T.

SEPTEMBER

Day	Time	m	Day	Time	m
1 Tu	0250 / 0849 / 1507 / 2108	0·5 / 7·0 / 0·7 / 6·9	16 W	0212 / 0812 / 1425 / 2030	1·1 / 6·6 / 1·3 / 6·5
2 W	0331 / 0929 / 1548 / 2150	1·0 / 6·6 / 1·2 / 6·4	17 Th	0243 / 0844 / 1457 / 2104	1·3 / 6·4 / 1·5 / 6·2
3 Th 〗	0410 / 1013 / 1633 / 2237	1·6 / 6·0 / 1·8 / 5·7	18 F	0317 / 0919 / 1534 / 2145	1·7 / 6·1 / 1·8 / 5·9
4 F	0457 / 1104 / 1727 / 2333	2·2 / 5·5 / 2·3 / 5·2	19 〖	0356 / 1004 / 1623 / 2237	2·0 / 5·7 / 2·2 / 5·5
5 Sa	0558 / 1215 / 1849	2·6 / 5·1 / 2·7	20 Su	0454 / 1108 / 1742 / 2354	2·4 / 5·4 / 2·5 / 5·2
6 Su	0100 / 0741 / 1357 / 2039	4·9 / 2·8 / 5·1 / 2·6	21 M	0625 / 1239 / 1927	2·6 / 5·3 / 2·4
7 M	0243 / 0915 / 1515 / 2148	5·0 / 2·5 / 5·5 / 2·2	22 Tu	0137 / 0808 / 1418 / 2057	5·2 / 2·3 / 5·6 / 2·0
8 Tu	0346 / 1010 / 1606 / 2234	5·4 / 2·1 / 5·9 / 1·8	23 W	0303 / 0925 / 1528 / 2202	5·7 / 1·8 / 6·2 / 1·3
9 W	0430 / 1051 / 1648 / 2312	5·9 / 1·7 / 6·3 / 1·4	24 Th	0402 / 1021 / 1623 / 2252	6·3 / 1·2 / 6·8 / 0·8
10 Th	0508 / 1126 / 1725 / 2344	6·2 / 1·4 / 6·6 / 1·2	25 F	0452 / 1111 / 1732 / 2339	6·9 / 0·7 / 7·3 / 0·4
11 F ●	0542 / 1158 / 1757	6·4 / 1·1 / 6·7	26 Sa	0537 / 1156 / 1757	7·3 / 0·3 / 7·6
12 Sa ○	0015 / 0614 / 1228 / 1829	1·0 / 6·6 / 1·0 / 6·9	27 Su	0022 / 0621 / 1239 / 1841	0·2 / 7·5 / 0·2 / 7·7
13 Su	0045 / 0645 / 1300 / 1900	0·9 / 6·7 / 0·9 / 6·9	28 M	0104 / 0702 / 1321 / 1921	0·2 / 7·5 / 0·2 / 7·6
14 M	0113 / 0713 / 1326 / 1930	0·8 / 6·8 / 0·9 / 6·9	29 Tu	0145 / 0742 / 1402 / 2002	0·4 / 7·4 / 0·5 / 7·2
15 Tu	0142 / 0742 / 1355 / 1959	0·9 / 6·7 / 1·0 / 6·7	30 W	0223 / 0822 / 1442 / 2043	0·7 / 7·0 / 0·9 / 6·8

OCTOBER

Day	Time	m	Day	Time	m
1 Th	0301 / 0903 / 1522 / 2124	1·2 / 6·6 / 1·4 / 6·2	16 F	0223 / 0826 / 1443 / 2050	1·3 / 6·5 / 1·5 / 6·3
2 F	0341 / 0945 / 1604 / 2207	1·8 / 6·1 / 1·9 / 5·7	17 Sa	0301 / 0907 / 1527 / 2135	1·6 / 6·2 / 1·8 / 6·0
3 Sa 〗	0423 / 1034 / 1657 / 2302	2·3 / 5·6 / 2·4 / 5·2	18 Su	0348 / 0956 / 1623 / 2233	1·9 / 5·9 / 2·1 / 5·6
4 Su	0519 / 1140 / 1811	2·7 / 5·2 / 2·7	19 M	0449 / 1102 / 1740 / 2349	2·3 / 5·6 / 2·3 / 5·3
5 M	0021 / 0653 / 1313 / 1957	4·8 / 2·9 / 5·1 / 2·7	20 Tu	0615 / 1228 / 1914	2·4 / 5·5 / 2·2
6 Tu	0204 / 0836 / 1437 / 2111	4·9 / 2·7 / 5·4 / 2·3	21 W	0121 / 0748 / 1357 / 2036	5·4 / 2·2 / 5·8 / 1·8
7 W	0312 / 0935 / 1532 / 2159	5·3 / 2·2 / 5·8 / 1·9	22 Th	0242 / 0903 / 1505 / 2139	5·8 / 1·8 / 6·3 / 1·4
8 Th	0359 / 1019 / 1616 / 2237	5·8 / 1·8 / 6·2 / 1·6	23 F	0339 / 0959 / 1600 / 2230	6·3 / 1·3 / 6·7 / 0·9
9 F	0437 / 1054 / 1652 / 2312	6·1 / 1·5 / 6·5 / 1·3	24 Sa	0430 / 1049 / 1649 / 2316	6·8 / 0·9 / 7·1 / 0·7
10 Sa	0511 / 1127 / 1727 / 2344	6·4 / 1·2 / 6·7 / 1·1	25 Su ○	0515 / 1134 / 1736	7·1 / 0·6 / 7·3
11 Su	0544 / 1158 / 1800	6·6 / 1·1 / 6·9	26 M	0001 / 0558 / 1219 / 1819	0·5 / 7·3 / 0·5 / 7·4
12 M	0015 / 0615 / 1229 / 1832	0·9 / 6·8 / 1·0 / 6·9	27 Tu	0042 / 0641 / 1302 / 1902	0·5 / 7·3 / 0·5 / 7·3
13 Tu	0046 / 0646 / 1300 / 1903	0·9 / 6·9 / 0·9 / 6·9	28 W	0123 / 0721 / 1341 / 1941	0·7 / 7·2 / 0·7 / 7·0
14 W	0117 / 0717 / 1333 / 1937	0·9 / 6·8 / 1·0 / 6·8	29 Th	0201 / 0801 / 1422 / 2022	1·0 / 6·9 / 1·0 / 6·6
15 Th	0148 / 0751 / 1406 / 2012	1·1 / 6·7 / 1·2 / 6·6	30 F	0239 / 0842 / 1501 / 2101	1·4 / 6·6 / 1·5 / 6·2
			31 Sa	0315 / 0922 / 1542 / 2145	1·8 / 6·2 / 1·9 / 5·7

NOVEMBER

Day	Time	m	Day	Time	m
1 Su	0356 / 1009 / 1630 / 2233	2·2 / 5·8 / 2·3 / 5·3	16 M	0348 / 0956 / 1626 / 2231	1·7 / 6·2 / 1·7 / 5·9
2 M	0445 / 1104 / 1729 / 2334	2·5 / 5·4 / 2·6 / 5·0	17 Tu 〖	0448 / 1058 / 1733 / 2337	2·0 / 6·0 / 1·9 / 5·6
3 Tu	0554 / 1215 / 1848	2·8 / 5·2 / 2·7	18 W	0600 / 1210 / 1849	2·1 / 5·9 / 2·0
4 W	0057 / 0726 / 1338 / 2009	5·0 / 2·8 / 5·3 / 2·5	19 Th	0055 / 0719 / 1326 / 2005	5·6 / 2·1 / 5·9 / 1·8
5 Th	0218 / 0842 / 1444 / 2110	5·2 / 2·5 / 5·6 / 2·2	20 F	0209 / 0832 / 1436 / 2111	5·8 / 1·8 / 6·2 / 1·6
6 F	0314 / 0934 / 1534 / 2156	5·6 / 2·1 / 5·9 / 1·8	21 Sa	0312 / 0934 / 1536 / 2206	6·2 / 1·5 / 6·5 / 1·3
7 Sa	0357 / 1016 / 1616 / 2235	5·9 / 1·8 / 6·2 / 1·5	22 Su	0407 / 1027 / 1630 / 2257	6·5 / 1·2 / 6·7 / 1·1
8 Su	0437 / 1054 / 1654 / 2312	6·2 / 1·5 / 6·5 / 1·3	23 M	0455 / 1118 / 1718 / 2342	6·8 / 1·0 / 6·9 / 0·9
9 M	0512 / 1130 / 1730 / 2347	6·5 / 1·3 / 6·7 / 1·1	24 Tu ●	0542 / 1203 / 1803	7·0 / 0·9 / 6·9
10 Tu ○	0547 / 1205 / 1807	6·7 / 1·1 / 6·8	25 W	0025 / 0624 / 1246 / 1845	0·9 / 7·1 / 0·9 / 6·9
11 W	0021 / 0622 / 1241 / 1842	1·0 / 6·9 / 1·0 / 6·9	26 Th	0106 / 0704 / 1327 / 1926	1·0 / 7·0 / 1·0 / 6·8
12 Th	0056 / 0659 / 1317 / 1920	1·0 / 6·9 / 1·0 / 6·8	27 F	0144 / 0745 / 1406 / 2005	1·1 / 6·9 / 1·2 / 6·5
13 F	0134 / 0737 / 1357 / 2001	1·1 / 6·9 / 1·1 / 6·7	28 Sa	0220 / 0823 / 1444 / 2043	1·4 / 6·6 / 1·4 / 6·2
14 Sa	0213 / 0818 / 1440 / 2044	1·2 / 6·7 / 1·3 / 6·4	29 Su	0256 / 0903 / 1521 / 2122	1·6 / 6·4 / 1·7 / 5·9
15 Su	0257 / 0904 / 1529 / 2134	1·4 / 6·5 / 1·5 / 6·2	30 M	0332 / 0943 / 1602 / 2203	1·9 / 6·1 / 2·0 / 5·6

DECEMBER

Day	Time	m	Day	Time	m
1 Tu	0413 / 1028 / 1647 / 2251	2·2 / 5·8 / 2·2 / 5·4	16 W 〖	0435 / 1042 / 1713 / 2316	1·5 / 6·4 / 1·5 / 6·0
2 W	0504 / 1120 / 1743 / 2347	2·5 / 5·5 / 2·5 / 5·2	17 Th	0534 / 1143 / 1817	1·8 / 6·1 / 1·8
3 Th	0607 / 1215 / 1849	2·6 / 5·3 / 2·5	18 F	0019 / 0642 / 1249 / 1926	5·8 / 2·0 / 6·0 / 1·9
4 F	0057 / 0723 / 1333 / 2001	5·1 / 2·7 / 5·4 / 2·4	19 Sa	0131 / 0755 / 1402 / 2039	5·7 / 2·0 / 5·9 / 1·9
5 Sa	0209 / 0833 / 1437 / 2103	5·3 / 2·5 / 5·6 / 2·2	20 Su	0243 / 0908 / 1512 / 2145	5·9 / 1·9 / 6·0 / 1·7
6 Su	0310 / 0931 / 1532 / 2153	5·6 / 2·2 / 5·8 / 1·9	21 M	0346 / 1012 / 1613 / 2241	6·1 / 1·6 / 6·2 / 1·5
7 M	0357 / 1019 / 1619 / 2238	5·9 / 1·9 / 6·1 / 1·6	22 Tu	0441 / 1105 / 1705 / 2329	6·4 / 1·4 / 6·4 / 1·3
8 Tu	0441 / 1102 / 1702 / 2320	6·3 / 1·6 / 6·4 / 1·4	23 W	0529 / 1153 / 1751	6·7 / 1·2 / 6·6
9 W ○	0522 / 1143 / 1744	6·6 / 1·3 / 6·7	24 Th ●	0012 / 0612 / 1236 / 1834	1·2 / 6·8 / 1·1 / 6·6
10 Th	0001 / 0603 / 1225 / 1827	1·1 / 6·8 / 1·0 / 6·8	25 F	0052 / 0652 / 1314 / 1912	1·1 / 6·9 / 1·1 / 6·6
11 F	0042 / 0645 / 1307 / 1910	1·0 / 7·0 / 0·9 / 6·9	26 Sa	0128 / 0730 / 1351 / 1948	1·1 / 6·9 / 1·1 / 6·5
12 Sa	0124 / 0728 / 1352 / 1954	0·9 / 7·1 / 0·8 / 6·9	27 Su	0202 / 0806 / 1425 / 2023	1·2 / 6·8 / 1·2 / 6·4
13 Su	0209 / 0813 / 1439 / 2040	0·9 / 7·0 / 0·9 / 6·8	28 M	0234 / 0842 / 1457 / 2057	1·4 / 6·6 / 1·4 / 6·2
14 M	0254 / 0900 / 1527 / 2128	1·1 / 6·9 / 1·1 / 6·5	29 Tu	0308 / 0915 / 1531 / 2132	1·6 / 6·4 / 1·6 / 6·0
15 Tu	0343 / 0949 / 1619 / 2219	1·3 / 6·7 / 1·3 / 6·3	30 W	0342 / 0952 / 1607 / 2209	1·8 / 6·1 / 1·9 / 5·7
			31 Th	0420 / 1031 / 1648 / 2249	2·1 / 5·8 / 2·1 / 5·5

RATE AND SET — Ent. Flood begins +0130 Dover, Spring rate 1½ kn.; Ebb begins −0430 Dover, Spring rate 1¾ kn. 1 M. off ent.; E. x S. begins −0005 Dover, Spring rate 2-3 kn.; W. x N. begins +0600 Dover, Spring rate 2-3 kn. 2 M. off St. Gowan's Head: ENE, begins −0100 Dover, Spring rate 3 kn.; WSW. begins +0500 Dover.

AVONMOUTH

MEAN SPRING AND NEAP CURVES
Springs occur 2 days after New and Full Moon.

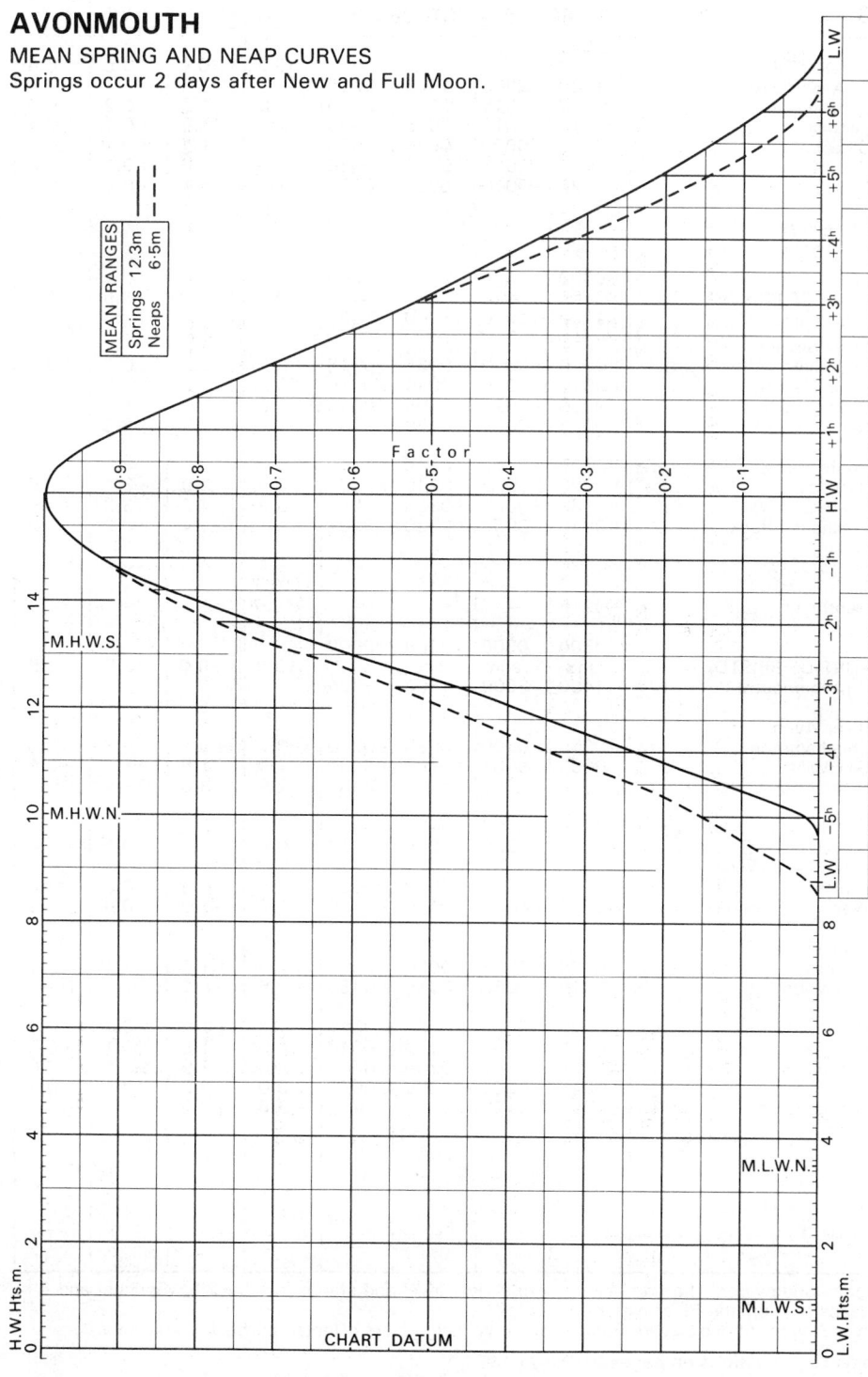

TIDAL DIFFERENCES ON BRISTOL (AVONMOUTH)

PLACE	TIME DIFFERENCES				HEIGHT DIFFERENCES (Metres)			
	High Water		Low Water		MHWS	MHWN	MLWN	MLWS
PORT OF BRISTOL .... (Avonmouth)	0600 and 1800	1100 and 2300	0300 and 1500	0800 and 2000	13.2	10.0	3.5	0.9
Barry	− 0030	− 0015	− 0125	− 0030	− 1.8	− 1.3	+ 0.2	0.0
Flatholm	− 0015	− 0015	− 0045	− 0045	− 1.4	− 1.2	+ 0.2	+ 0.1
Steepholm	− 0020	− 0020	− 0050	− 0050	− 1.6	− 1.4	+ 0.1	− 0.1
Cardiff	− 0015	− 0015	− 0100	− 0030	− 1.0	− 0.6	+ 0.1	0.0
Newport	− 0020	− 0010	0000	− 0020	− 1.1	− 1.0	− 0.6	− 0.7
River Wye								
Chepstow	+ 0020	+ 0020	−	−	−	−	−	−
PORT OF BRISTOL .... (Avonmouth)	0000 and 1200	0600 and 1800	0000 and 1200	0700 and 1900	13.2	10.0	3.5	0.9
River Severn								
Sudbrook	+ 0010	+ 0010	+ 0025	+ 0015	+ 0.2	+ 0.1	− 0.1	+ 0.1
Beachley (Aust.)	+ 0010	+ 0015	+ 0040	+ 0025	− 0.2	− 0.2	− 0.5	− 0.3
Inward Rocks	+ 0020	+ 0020	+ 0105	+ 0045	− 1.0	− 1.1	− 1.4	− 0.6
Narlwood Rocks	+ 0025	+ 0025	+ 0120	+ 0100	− 1.9	− 2.0	− 2.3	− 0.8
White House	+ 0025	+ 0025	+ 0145	+ 0120	− 3.0	− 3.1	− 3.6	− 1.0
Berkeley	+ 0030	+ 0045	+ 0245	+ 0220	− 3.8	− 3.9	− 3.4	− 0.5
Sharpness Dock	+ 0035	+ 0050	+ 0305	+ 0245	− 3.9	− 4.2	− 3.3	− 0.4
Wellhouse Rock	+ 0040	+ 0055	+ 0320	+ 0305	− 4.1	− 4.4	− 3.1	− 0.2
Epney	+ 0130	−	−	−	− 9.4	−	−	−
Minsterworth	+ 0140	−	−	−	− 10.1	−	−	−
Llanthony	+ 0215	−	−	−	− 10.7	−	−	−
PORT OF BRISTOL .... (Avonmouth)	0200 and 1400	0800 and 2000	0300 and 1500	0800 and 2000	13.2	10.0	3.5	0.9
River Avon								
Shirehampton	0000	0000	+ 0035	+ 0010	− 0.7	− 0.7	− 0.8	0.0
Sea Mills	+ 0005	+ 0005	+ 0105	+ 0030	− 1.4	− 1.5	− 1.7	− 0.1
Bristol (Cumberland Basin)	+ 0010	+ 0010	Dries	Dries	− 2.9	− 3.0	Dries	Dries
Portishead	− 0002	0000	−	−	− 0.1	− 0.1	−	−
Clevedon	− 0010	− 0020	− 0025	− 0015	− 0.4	− 0.2	+ 0.2	0.0
English and Welsh Grounds	− 0008	− 0008	− 0030	− 0030	− 0.5	− 0.8	− 0.3	0.0
Weston-super-Mare	− 0020	− 0030	− 0130	− 0030	− 1.2	− 1.0	− 0.8	− 0.2
River Parrett								
Burnham	− 0020	− 0025	− 0030	0000	− 2.3	− 1.9	− 1.4	− 1.1
Bridgwater	− 0015	− 0030	+ 0305	+ 0455	− 8.6	− 8.1	Dries	Dries
Hinkley Point	− 0020	− 0025	− 0100	− 0040	− 1.7	− 1.6	+ 0.1	− 0.1
Watchet	− 0035	− 0050	− 0145	− 0040	− 1.9	− 1.5	+ 0.1	+ 0.1
Minehead	− 0035	− 0045	− 0100	− 0100	− 2.6	− 1.9	− 0.1	0.0
Porlock Bay	− 0045	− 0055	− 0205	− 0050	− 3.0	− 2.2	− 0.1	− 0.1
Lynmouth	− 0055	− 0115	−	−	− 3.6	− 2.7	−	−

Notes. Bridgwater. The tide falls to normal river level and stands low for 2 h. (Springs) and 8 h. (Neaps).   Bristol. River water only at L.W.
River Severn. Above Severn Road Bridge L.W. heights are affected by fresh water flow.

Refer to predictions on pages 21:163-21:165

AVONMOUTH PORT OF BRISTOL 21:163

Lat. 51°30′N. Long. 2°43′W. HIGH & LOW WATER 1992

GMT ADD 1 HOUR MARCH 29 — OCTOBER 25 FOR B.S.T.

Each entry is given as Time (GMT) and height (m). Moon‑phase symbols: ● new, ○ full,) first quarter, (last quarter.

JANUARY

Day				
1 W	0407 10.7	1034 3.2	1638 10.8	2308 3.0
16 Th	0256 10.5	0932 3.5	1541 10.9	2219 3.0
2 Th	0511 11.2	1142 2.7	1737 11.3	
17 F	0413 11.2	1054 2.7	1652 11.7	2332 2.3
3 F	0011 2.6	0603 11.7	1236 2.3	1827 11.7
18 Sa	0522 12.1	1211 2.1	1758 12.4	
4 Sa ●	0100 2.2	0648 12.1	1324 1.8	1910 12.0
19 Su ○	0048 1.7	0624 12.9	1324 1.4	1857 13.1
5 Su	0144 1.9	0728 12.4	1405 1.8	1947 12.1
20 M	0151 1.1	0719 13.6	1422 0.8	1948 13.7
6 M	0223 1.8	0804 12.5	1443 1.8	2020 12.2
21 Tu	0244 0.6	0806 14.0	1511 0.5	2034 13.9
7 Tu	0258 1.8	0834 12.5	1517 1.7	2050 12.2
22 W	0331 0.4	0851 14.2	1555 0.4	2117 13.9
8 W	0328 1.8	0904 12.5	1548 1.8	2119 12.2
23 Th	0410 0.5	0934 14.1	1631 0.6	2159 13.6
9 Th	0357 1.9	0935 12.3	1616 1.8	2150 12.0
24 F	0445 0.8	1016 13.6	1705 1.1	2240 12.9
10 F	0424 2.0	1007 12.0	1645 2.0	2223 11.7
25 Sa	0518 1.4	1057 12.8	1734 1.7	2320 12.1
11 Sa	0452 2.2	1041 11.6	1713 2.3	2255 11.3 (
26 Su	0547 2.0	1137 11.9	1804 2.4 (	
12 Su	0520 2.5	1115 11.2	1743 2.6	2330 10.8
27 M	0001 11.2	0619 2.7	1221 11.0	1838 3.1
13 M)	0554 2.9	1154 10.7	1821 3.0	
28 Tu	0048 10.3	0700 3.5	1317 10.1	1926 3.8
14 Tu	0017 10.4	1252 10.3	1913 3.4	
29 W	0158 9.7	0813 4.1	1437 9.7	2105 4.2
15 W	0126 10.2	0744 3.7	1419 10.3	2040 3.5
30 Th	0327 9.8	0957 3.8	1607 10.0	2234 3.6
31 F	0445 10.5	1111 3.1	1716 10.7	2340 2.8

FEBRUARY

Day				
1 Sa	0543 11.4	1210 2.4	1808 11.4	
16 Su	0506 11.9	1158 2.1	1747 12.3	
2 Su	0035 2.2	0629 12.0	1300 1.9	1852 11.9
17 M	0036 1.7	0611 12.9	1314 1.2	1845 13.2
3 M ●	0123 1.8	0709 12.4	1345 1.6	1928 12.3
18 Tu	0141 0.9	0704 13.7	1411 0.5	1934 13.8
4 Tu	0205 1.5	0744 12.6	1425 1.4	2001 12.5
19 W	0232 0.3	0751 14.2	1457 0.1	2016 14.2
5 W	0240 1.4	0813 12.8	1500 1.3	2029 12.7
20 Th	0314 0.0	0832 14.4	1536 0.1	2056 14.2
6 Th	0312 1.3	0843 12.9	1531 1.3	2057 12.8
21 F	0352 0.2	0911 14.2	1610 0.4	2134 13.8
7 F	0342 1.4	0912 12.9	1600 1.3	2127 12.6
22 Sa	0423 0.6	0950 13.7	1638 1.0	2212 13.1
8 Sa	0410 1.5	0943 12.6	1627 1.5	2157 12.3
23 Su	0449 1.2	1028 12.6	1702 1.6	2247 12.2
9 Su	0434 1.9	1014 12.2	1651 1.8	2227 11.9
24 M	0515 1.9	1104 11.8	1726 2.3	2320 11.2
10 M	0458 2.1	1044 11.7	1715 2.2	2257 11.4
25 Tu	0540 2.6	1137 10.8	1753 3.1	2357 10.7 (
11 Tu	0525 2.4	1118 11.1	1746 2.6	2334 10.8)
26 W	0612 3.4	1244 9.7	1831 3.9	
12 W	0603 2.9	1207 10.5	1831 3.1	
27 Th	0100 9.3	0706 4.2	1348 9.1	1942 4.6
13 Th	0038 10.3	0659 3.5	1334 10.1	1945 3.6
28 F	0246 9.2	0924 4.3	1534 9.4	2206 4.0
14 F	0218 10.2	0853 3.7	1512 10.4	2149 3.3
29 Sa	0417 10.1	1041 3.3	1648 10.3	2311 3.0
15 Sa	0349 10.9	1031 2.9	1635 11.3	2312 2.4

MARCH

Day				
1 Su	0515 11.1	1139 2.4	1742 11.2	
16 M	0452 11.9	1144 1.9	1732 12.3	
2 M	0007 2.2	0603 11.9	1232 1.8	1825 11.9
17 Tu	0021 1.6	0556 12.9	1257 1.1	1827 13.1
3 Tu	0056 1.6	0642 12.4	1320 1.4	1902 12.3
18 W	0123 0.8	0646 13.6	1351 0.5	1914 13.7
4 W ●	0140 1.3	0717 12.7	1401 1.1	1934 12.7
19 Th	0212 0.3	0730 14.0	1436 0.2	1954 14.0
5 Th	0218 1.1	0748 13.0	1437 1.0	2002 12.9
20 F	0253 0.2	0809 14.1	1512 0.3	2032 14.0
6 F	0251 1.0	0816 13.1	1510 1.0	2030 13.1
21 Sa	0327 0.4	0847 14.0	1543 0.7	2107 13.7
7 Sa	0322 1.0	0847 13.1	1539 1.0	2101 13.0
22 Su	0356 0.8	0924 13.4	1609 1.2	2143 13.0
8 Su	0350 1.2	0918 12.9	1606 1.2	2132 12.7
23 M	0421 1.3	1000 12.6	1631 1.8	2217 12.1
9 M	0416 1.4	0950 12.5	1628 1.5	2203 12.2
24 Tu	0445 1.9	1033 11.6	1654 2.4	2248 11.1
10 Tu	0437 1.8	1023 11.9	1652 1.9	2234 11.7
25 W	0509 2.6	1105 10.6	1719 3.0	2320 10.2
11 W	0504 2.1	1058 11.3	1722 2.3	2315 11.0
26 Th	0540 3.3	1144 9.6	1753 3.7 (	
12 Th	0542 2.7	1150 10.5	1808 3.0)	
27 F	0015 9.3	0627 4.1	1302 8.9	1850 4.5
13 F	0019 10.3	0639 3.4	1317 10.0	1924 3.6
28 Sa	0159 9.0	0815 4.5	1444 9.1	2124 4.4
14 Sa	0158 10.1	0834 3.6	1456 10.3	2129 3.3
29 Su	0332 9.7	1004 3.5	1606 10.0	2233 3.2
15 Su	0334 10.8	1014 2.8	1623 11.3	2255 2.4
30 M	0435 10.7	1101 2.5	1702 10.9	2327 2.4
31 Tu	0525 11.6	1154 1.9	1747 11.7	

APRIL

Day				
1 W	0021 1.8	0607 12.2	1245 1.5	1827 12.2
16 Th	0057 1.1	0624 13.1	1326 0.9	1849 13.2
2 Th	0107 1.4	0643 12.6	1330 1.2	1900 12.6
17 F	0145 0.8	0707 13.4	1409 0.8	1930 13.5
3 F	0148 1.1	0717 12.9	1408 1.0	1933 13.0
18 Sa	0226 0.7	0747 13.5	1446 0.9	2006 13.5
4 Sa	0225 1.0	0749 13.1	1443 0.9	2004 13.2
19 Su	0300 0.9	0823 13.3	1515 1.2	2043 13.3
5 Su	0258 1.0	0822 13.2	1517 1.0	2037 13.1
20 M	0329 1.2	0900 12.9	1542 1.5	2118 12.7
6 M	0331 1.1	0857 13.0	1546 1.1	2111 12.9
21 Tu	0356 1.6	0936 12.2	1606 2.0	2153 11.9
7 Tu	0359 1.3	0934 12.6	1613 1.4	2146 12.4
22 W	0421 2.0	1009 11.3	1630 2.4	2224 11.1
8 W	0424 1.6	1012 12.0	1638 1.8	2226 11.8
23 Th	0447 2.5	1042 10.5	1655 2.9	2258 10.3
9 Th	0455 2.0	1055 11.3	1713 2.3	2313 11.1
24 F	0518 3.1	1120 9.8	1729 3.4	2346 9.6 (
10 F	0537 2.6	1153 10.6	1803 2.9)	
25 Sa	0601 3.6	1221 9.2	1818 4.0	
11 Sa	0021 10.5	0642 3.1	1313 10.2	1926 3.4
26 Su	0107 9.2	0706 4.0	1348 9.2	1937 4.3
12 Su	0148 10.4	0826 3.2	1442 10.5	2111 3.0
27 M	0233 9.6	0903 3.7	1507 9.7	2136 3.7
13 M	0317 11.1	0953 2.5	1603 11.3	2231 2.3
28 Tu	0341 10.4	1012 2.9	1610 10.5	2238 2.9
14 Tu	0433 11.9	1118 1.9	1709 12.2	2354 1.7
29 W	0434 11.1	1106 2.3	1658 11.3	2333 2.3
15 W	0533 12.6	1232 1.3	1804 12.8	
30 Th	0520 11.8	1200 1.8	1743 11.9	

To find H.W. Dover add 4 h. 00 min. to above times.

TIDAL DIFFERENCES PAGE 21:162. TIDAL CURVE PAGE 21:161.

TIDAL STREAMS PAGES 21:28-21:40 and 21:154-21:155.

Datum or predictions: 6.50 m. below Ordnance Datum (Newlyn) or approx. L.A.T.

21:164   PORT OF BRISTOL AVONMOUTH

HIGH & LOW WATER 1992   Lat. 51°30'N. Long. 2°43'W.

GMT   ADD 1 HOUR MARCH 29 — OCTOBER 25 FOR B.S.T.

MAY

Day	Time	m	Time	m	Time	m	Time	m
1 F	0025	1.8	0604	12.3	1250	1.5	1824	12.4
2 Sa	0113	1.4	0643	12.7	1335	1.2	● 1902	12.8
3 Su	0157	1.2	0723	12.9	1418	1.0	1940	13.1
4 M	0236	1.1	0802	13.0	1456	1.0	2018	13.1
5 Tu	0314	1.1	0843	13.0	1532	1.2	2058	13.0
6 W	0350	1.3	0925	12.6	1606	1.4	2141	12.6
7 Th	0424	1.6	1010	12.2	1640	1.8	2227	12.1
8 F	0501	1.9	1059	11.6	1719	2.2	2319	11.6
9 Sa	0547	2.3	1157	11.0	1811	2.6	)	
10 Su	0022	11.1	0650	2.7	1304	10.7	1924	2.9
11 M	0134	11.0	0809	2.9	1420	10.9	2046	2.7
12 Tu	0251	11.3	0924	2.4	1535	11.3	2159	2.3
13 W	0403	11.7	1038	2.1	1632	11.9	2316	2.1
14 Th	0505	12.1	1156	1.9	1736	12.2		
15 F	0025	1.8	0558	12.4	1253	1.7	1824	12.5
16 Sa	0117	1.5	0643	12.5	1340	1.6	○ 1906	12.8
17 Su	0159	1.4	0726	12.6	1418	1.6	1945	12.9
18 M	0236	1.5	0804	12.6	1451	1.6	2023	12.7
19 Tu	0308	1.6	0842	12.3	1521	1.8	2100	12.4
20 W	0338	1.8	0918	11.9	1549	2.1	2134	11.9
21 Th	0406	2.1	0952	11.4	1614	2.4	2207	11.3
22 F	0434	2.4	1024	10.9	1641	2.7	2242	10.8
23 Sa	0504	2.7	1102	10.4	1713	3.0	2323	10.3
24 Su	0542	3.0	1147	9.9	1754	3.3	(	
25 M	0018	9.9	0629	3.3	1246	9.7	1848	3.6
26 Tu	0127	9.8	0731	3.5	1358	9.8	1958	3.7
27 W	0237	10.1	0853	3.3	1505	10.2	2128	3.4
28 Th	0338	10.7	1007	2.8	1603	10.9	2237	2.8
29 F	0433	11.3	1109	2.3	1657	11.5	2337	2.2
30 Sa	0523	11.9	1207	1.9	1747	12.2		
31 Su	0035	1.8	0612	12.4	1303	1.5	1834	12.7

JUNE

Day	Time	m	Time	m	Time	m	Time	m
1 M	0128	1.4	0700	12.7	1354	1.3	● 1920	13.0
2 Tu	0218	1.2	0747	13.0	1440	1.1	2005	13.2
3 W	0304	1.1	0833	13.0	1525	1.2	2051	13.2
4 Th	0348	1.2	0921	12.9	1606	1.3	2138	13.0
5 F	0430	1.3	1007	12.6	1647	1.5	2226	12.7
6 Sa	0511	1.6	1057	12.2	1727	1.8	2316	12.3
7 Su	0554	1.8	1147	11.7	1814	2.1	)	
8 M	0010	11.8	0642	2.2	1245	11.3	1907	2.4
9 Tu	0110	11.4	0740	2.4	1348	11.0	2011	2.7
10 W	0219	11.2	0846	2.6	1458	11.0	2121	2.7
11 Th	0328	11.2	0956	2.6	1606	11.2	2234	2.6
12 F	0434	11.4	1111	2.6	1706	11.5	2347	2.4
13 Sa	0533	11.6	1219	2.4	1800	11.9		
14 Su	0046	2.2	0624	11.6	1312	2.2	1846	12.2
15 M	0134	2.0	0712	12.0	1354	2.0	○ 1928	12.4
16 Tu	0215	1.9	0749	12.1	1432	1.9	2008	12.4
17 W	0251	1.8	0827	12.1	1505	2.0	2044	12.3
18 Th	0324	1.9	0903	11.9	1536	2.1	2117	12.1
19 F	0355	2.0	0934	11.7	1604	2.2	2149	11.8
20 Sa	0423	2.1	1006	11.5	1631	2.4	2223	11.5
21 Su	0452	2.2	1040	11.1	1659	2.5	2258	11.1
22 M	0523	2.4	1115	10.7	1733	2.8	2337	10.7
23 Tu	0600	2.7	1156	10.3	1811	3.1	(	
24 W	0024	10.3	0642	3.1	1246	10.1	1900	3.4
25 Th	0124	10.1	0737	3.3	1355	10.1	2006	3.4
26 F	0239	10.3	0900	3.3	1510	10.5	2142	3.3
27 Sa	0346	10.8	1021	2.8	1614	11.2	2254	2.6
28 Su	0448	11.5	1127	2.2	1715	11.9		
29 M	0000	2.1	0549	12.1	1234	1.8	1812	12.5
30 Tu	0106	1.7	0645	12.6	1335	1.4	● 1906	13.0

JULY

Day	Time	m	Time	m	Time	m	Time	m
1 W	0206	1.3	0737	13.0	1430	1.1	1955	13.4
2 Th	0258	1.1	0825	13.3	1519	0.9	2043	13.6
3 F	0345	0.8	0911	13.4	1604	0.9	2128	13.6
4 Sa	0428	0.9	0956	13.2	1644	1.0	2214	13.3
5 Su	0506	1.1	1042	12.8	1722	1.3	2259	12.9
6 M	0543	1.4	1127	12.2	1758	1.8	2347	12.2
7 Tu	0619	2.0	1215	11.6	1839	2.3	)	
8 W	0038	11.5	0702	2.5	1309	10.9	1927	2.9
9 Th	0138	10.8	0758	3.1	1415	10.5	2037	3.3
10 F	0249	10.5	0914	3.4	1529	10.5	2157	3.3
11 Sa	0404	10.6	1034	3.2	1641	10.9	2313	2.9
12 Su	0512	11.0	1146	2.8	1740	11.5		
13 M	0018	2.5	0607	11.4	1245	2.4	1831	11.9
14 Tu	0110	2.1	0655	11.8	1333	2.1	○ 1914	12.2
15 W	0155	1.9	0735	12.0	1413	1.9	1952	12.4
16 Th	0234	1.8	0812	12.2	1450	1.8	2026	12.5
17 F	0308	1.7	0843	12.2	1522	1.9	2057	12.5
18 Sa	0339	1.7	0912	12.2	1550	1.9	2127	12.4
19 Su	0407	1.7	0942	12.1	1617	2.0	2157	12.1
20 M	0435	1.9	1012	11.8	1642	2.1	2230	11.7
21 Tu	0502	2.1	1042	11.3	1709	2.4	2301	11.2
22 W	0529	2.4	1115	10.9	1739	2.8	2334	10.7
23 Th	0601	2.8	1151	10.4	1815	3.2	(	
24 F	0021	10.3	0642	3.3	1249	10.1	1909	3.6
25 Sa	0135	10.0	0751	3.6	1421	10.1	2044	3.7
26 Su	0305	10.4	0931	3.3	1539	10.8	2221	3.0
27 M	0421	11.2	1058	2.6	1651	11.8	2334	2.3
28 Tu	0530	12.0	1211	2.0	1756	12.5		
29 W	0052	1.8	0631	12.7	1324	1.4	● 1853	13.2
30 Th	0157	1.2	0735	13.3	1422	0.9	1942	13.8
31 F	0250	0.6	0812	13.7	1510	0.5	2029	14.1

AUGUST

Day	Time	m	Time	m	Time	m	Time	m
1 Sa	0335	0.4	0856	13.9	1552	0.5	2111	14.1
2 Su	0414	0.5	0938	13.7	1630	0.7	2155	13.8
3 M	0449	0.9	1019	13.2	1704	1.1	2237	13.1
4 Tu	0520	1.4	1101	12.5	1733	1.7	2318	12.3
5 W	0549	2.1	1142	11.6	1804	2.4	)	
6 Th	0001	11.3	0621	2.8	1227	10.7	1842	3.2
7 F	0053	10.4	0703	3.6	1330	10.2	1941	3.9
8 Sa	0208	9.8	0826	4.1	1456	9.9	2128	3.9
9 Su	0338	9.9	1003	3.7	1620	10.5	2248	3.2
10 M	0454	10.7	1120	2.9	1722	11.5	2351	2.5
11 Tu	0550	11.4	1219	2.3	1812	12.0		
12 W	0046	2.0	0636	11.9	1309	1.9	1855	12.4
13 Th	0133	1.7	0716	12.3	1352	1.6	○ 1931	12.7
14 F	0212	1.5	0749	12.5	1433	1.5	2004	12.8
15 Sa	0247	1.4	0819	12.6	1501	1.5	2032	12.8
16 Su	0319	1.4	0846	12.6	1531	1.6	2100	12.8
17 M	0348	1.5	0914	12.5	1557	1.7	2129	12.5
18 Tu	0413	1.6	0942	12.2	1621	1.9	2159	12.1
19 W	0437	1.9	1012	11.7	1645	2.3	2228	11.5
20 Th	0501	2.3	1040	11.2	1709	2.7	2258	11.0
21 F	0527	2.7	1112	10.7	1742	3.1	2339	10.4
22 Sa	0605	3.2	1204	10.2	1831	3.6	(	
23 Su	0050	9.9	0706	3.7	1335	9.9	1957	3.9
24 M	0234	10.0	0907	3.7	1514	10.6	2156	3.3
25 Tu	0402	10.9	1034	2.8	1634	11.6	2315	2.4
26 W	0515	12.0	1156	2.0	1742	12.6		
27 Th	0041	1.6	0617	12.9	1310	1.3	1838	13.5
28 F	0144	0.9	0707	13.6	1406	0.6	● 1926	14.1
29 Sa	0233	0.4	0752	14.0	1453	0.3	2009	14.4
30 Su	0317	0.2	0833	14.2	1534	0.3	2050	14.3
31 M	0353	0.5	0912	13.9	1607	0.7	2129	13.9

GENERAL — Caution is necessary owing to Bore, shifting sands, and rapidity of streams. Tidal streams generally run in the direction of the channels when banks are uncovered. They run directly in and out of estuary and rivers when banks are covered. Bar of the Severn is N. of Avonmouth.

WHEN TO ENTER — Average period of admission is 2½ h. before until 1½ h. after H.W.

AVONMOUTH PORT OF BRISTOL. 21:165

Lat. 51°30'N. Long. 2°43'W. HIGH & LOW WATER 1992

GMT ADD 1 HOUR MARCH 29 — OCTOBER 25 FOR B.S.T.

Moon phases:) first quarter, ○ full moon, (last quarter, ● new moon. Times are Time (HHMM) and height m.

SEPTEMBER

Day	Time m	Time m	Time m	Time m
1 Tu	0424 1·0	0952 13·3	1638 1·2	2210 13·1
2 W	0451 1·6	1031 12·5	1705 1·9	2248 12·1
3 Th)	0516 2·3	1109 11·5	2327 11·0	
4 F	0544 3·1	1149 10·5	1804 3·4	
5 Sa	0014 9·9	0621 3·9	1249 9·6	1853 4·2
6 Su	0131 9·2	0724 4·6	1423 9·4	2101 4·4
7 M	0311 9·4	0943 4·2	1556 10·2	2223 3·4
8 Tu	0430 10·4	1052 3·1	1658 11·3	2322 2·4
9 W	0525 11·4	1149 2·2	1746 12·1	
10 Th	0015 1·8	0610 12·0	1239 1·7	1828 12·5
11 F	0103 1·5	0649 12·4	1324 1·5	1904 12·8
12 Sa ○	0145 1·3	0721 12·6	1402 1·4	1935 12·9
13 Su	0222 1·2	0749 12·8	1436 1·3	2002 13·0
14 M	0253 1·2	0816 12·9	1507 1·4	2032 13·0
15 Tu	0322 1·3	0844 12·8	1535 1·6	2101 12·7
16 W	0350 1·6	0914 12·5	1600 1·8	2132 12·3
17 Th	0413 1·9	0945 12·1	1623 2·2	2203 11·7
18 F	0435 2·2	1014 11·5	1647 2·5	2235 11·1
19 Sa (	0504 2·6	1049 11·0	1720 3·0	2319 10·5
20 Su	0543 3·2	1144 10·3	1810 3·6	
21 M	0035 9·9	0646 3·7	1317 10·0	1941 3·9
22 Tu	0216 10·0	0844 3·7	1456 10·6	2136 3·2
23 W	0346 11·0	1014 2·8	1617 11·7	2258 2·3
24 Th	0458 12·1	1137 2·0	1723 12·7	
25 F	0022 1·5	0557 13·0	1252 1·2	1818 13·5
26 Sa ●	0123 0·8	0646 13·6	1345 0·6	1904 14·0
27 Su	0212 0·4	0730 14·0	1430 0·4	1947 14·2
28 M	0253 0·4	0809 14·1	1508 0·5	2026 14·1
29 Tu	0328 0·7	0847 13·9	1542 0·9	2105 13·7
30 W	0357 1·2	0927 13·3	1612 1·4	2145 12·9

OCTOBER

Day	Time m	Time m	Time m	Time m
1 Th	0423 1·9	1004 12·4	1637 2·1	2223 11·8
2 F	0448 2·5	1041 11·4	1704 2·8	2259 10·8
3 Sa)	0515 3·2	1119 10·4	1736 3·5	2343 9·8
4 Su	0547 3·9	1215 9·5	1819 4·2	
5 M	0053 9·1	0641 4·6	1345 9·2	1959 4·6
6 Tu	0229 9·2	0905 4·5	1515 9·9	2148 3·7
7 W	0350 10·1	1017 3·4	1621 10·9	2244 2·7
8 Th	0448 11·0	1111 2·5	1711 11·7	2337 2·0
9 F	0533 11·8	1203 2·0	1753 12·3	
10 Sa	0027 1·6	0614 12·6	1249 1·6	1831 12·6
11 Su ○	0112 1·4	0648 12·6	1330 1·4	1903 12·8
12 M	0149 1·3	0717 12·8	1406 1·3	1933 13·0
13 Tu	0225 1·2	0747 13·0	1440 1·4	2005 13·0
14 W	0257 1·3	0817 13·0	1512 1·5	2037 12·8
15 Th	0328 1·5	0851 12·7	1542 1·8	2112 12·4
16 F	0356 1·8	0927 12·3	1607 2·1	2149 11·9
17 Sa	0421 2·2	1003 11·8	1635 2·4	2230 11·3
18 Su	0451 2·6	1045 11·2	1713 2·9	2320 10·6
19 M (	0534 3·1	1146 10·6	1808 3·4	
20 Tu	0034 10·2	0643 3·6	1309 10·3	1938 3·6
21 W	0201 10·3	0826 3·5	1437 10·8	2114 3·0
22 Th	0325 11·1	0950 2·7	1556 11·8	2233 2·3
23 F	0435 12·0	1111 2·0	1659 12·6	2354 1·7
24 Sa	0533 12·8	1225 1·5	1754 13·2	
25 Su ●	0056 1·2	0624 13·3	1320 1·0	1842 13·5
26 M	0145 0·9	0707 13·6	1405 0·8	1924 13·7
27 Tu	0226 0·9	0747 13·7	1444 0·9	2005 13·6
28 W	0301 1·2	0825 13·6	1518 1·2	2044 13·3
29 Th	0332 1·6	0904 13·1	1548 1·6	2124 12·6
30 F	0400 2·1	0942 12·3	1616 2·2	2202 11·7
31 Sa	0426 2·6	1020 11·4	1644 2·8	2238 10·8

NOVEMBER

Day	Time m	Time m	Time m	Time m
1 Su	0452 3·2	1057 10·6	1715 3·3	2319 10·0
2 M)	0525 3·7	1144 9·8	1754 3·9	
3 Tu	0014 9·4	0608 4·2	1255 9·4	1853 4·2
4 W	0130 9·2	0720 4·5	1416 9·6	2046 4·0
5 Th	0249 9·7	0922 4·0	1525 10·3	2156 3·3
6 F	0353 10·4	1023 3·2	1621 11·1	2249 2·6
7 Sa	0445 11·2	1116 2·5	1708 11·7	2342 2·1
8 Su	0529 11·8	1205 2·1	1750 12·2	
9 M	0031 1·7	0608 12·3	1252 1·7	1828 12·5
10 Tu ○	0116 1·5	0645 12·7	1335 1·5	1906 12·8
11 W	0157 1·3	0721 12·9	1415 1·4	1942 12·9
12 Th	0234 1·3	0758 13·0	1454 1·5	2022 12·9
13 F	0312 1·5	0837 12·9	1531 1·6	2103 12·7
14 Sa	0348 1·7	0918 12·7	1606 1·9	2145 12·3
15 Su	0420 2·0	1002 12·3	1641 2·2	2231 11·8
16 M	0457 2·4	1049 11·8	1722 2·5	2323 11·2
17 Tu (	0543 2·8	1147 11·3	1817 2·9	
18 W	0025 10·8	0645 3·1	1255 11·0	1927 3·0
19 Th	0138 10·7	0802 3·1	1412 11·1	2044 2·8
20 F	0256 11·1	0919 2·8	1527 11·6	2157 2·5
21 Sa	0406 11·7	1035 2·4	1633 12·1	2316 2·2
22 Su	0506 12·2	1151 2·0	1730 12·5	
23 M	0025 1·8	0558 12·7	1252 1·6	1821 12·8
24 Tu ●	0117 1·6	0645 13·0	1340 1·4	1906 13·0
25 W	0201 1·5	0727 13·2	1420 1·4	1948 13·0
26 Th	0240 1·5	0808 13·2	1457 1·5	2029 12·8
27 F	0312 1·8	0847 12·9	1531 1·8	2107 12·4
28 Sa	0343 2·1	0925 12·4	1600 2·1	2145 11·8
29 Su	0410 2·5	1000 11·8	1630 2·5	2219 11·2
30 M	0437 2·9	1035 11·1	1658 2·9	2254 10·7

DECEMBER

Day	Time m	Time m	Time m	Time m
1 Tu	0506 3·2	1115 10·6	1732 3·2	2334 10·2
2 W)	0542 3·5	1201 10·1	1814 3·5	
3 Th	0027 9·8	0628 3·9	1303 9·8	1907 3·8
4 F	0133 9·6	0730 4·1	1415 9·9	2026 3·8
5 Sa	0243 9·9	0905 3·9	1519 10·3	2152 3·4
6 Su	0346 10·5	1021 3·3	1616 10·9	2251 2·7
7 M	0440 11·2	1118 2·6	1708 11·6	2347 2·2
8 Tu	0530 11·9	1212 2·1	1756 12·2	
9 W ○	0039 1·7	0617 12·5	1306 1·7	1842 12·6
10 Th	0131 1·4	0702 12·9	1355 1·5	1927 12·9
11 F	0219 1·3	0745 13·2	1443 1·3	2012 13·1
12 Sa	0304 1·3	0829 13·3	1527 1·3	2057 13·1
13 Su	0346 1·4	0912 13·2	1609 1·4	2142 12·9
14 M	0426 1·5	0959 13·0	1649 1·6	2227 12·6
15 Tu	0505 1·8	1045 12·6	1729 1·9	2316 12·1
16 W (	0546 2·1	1136 12·1	1812 2·2	
17 Th	0008 11·5	0634 2·5	1232 11·6	1903 2·6
18 F	0107 11·1	0730 2·8	1338 11·2	2005 2·9
19 Sa	0218 10·9	0842 3·0	1450 11·1	2119 3·0
20 Su	0331 11·0	0957 2·9	1602 11·3	2237 2·8
21 M	0438 11·5	1116 2·6	1706 11·7	2353 2·5
22 Tu	0537 12·0	1224 2·2	1803 12·0	
23 W	0052 2·1	0628 12·4	1317 1·8	1852 12·3
24 Th ●	0140 1·8	0713 12·7	1402 1·7	1935 12·5
25 F	0222 1·7	0755 12·9	1442 1·6	2016 12·6
26 Sa	0257 1·7	0833 12·8	1517 1·7	2051 12·5
27 Su	0329 1·9	0908 12·6	1548 1·9	2125 12·2
28 M	0357 2·1	0941 12·3	1616 2·0	2156 11·9
29 Tu	0423 2·3	1012 11·9	1641 2·2	2227 11·5
30 W	0449 2·5	1044 11·4	1709 2·5	2259 11·0
31 Th	0518 2·8	1119 10·9	1742 2·8	2334 10·5

RATE AND SET — Off ent. to Avon: Flood begins –0508 Avonmouth, Spring rate 5 kn.; Ebb begins +0032 Avonmouth. Spring rate is 4 kn. Flood stream sets towards bank NE. of dock ent. Ebb stream sets towards bank between Avonmouth and Portishead. Greatest rate in R. Severn is in the Shoots 8 kn. THE BORE — High tides greater than 12.8 m. give appreciable bores. Starts 2 M. above Sharpness, forms a front 1.2-1.5 m. high. Rate 4 kns. becoming 14 kns. at Rosemary. No danger if taken head on in middle and deep water. Beware floating branches, etc.

FALMOUTH

HIGH & LOW WATER 1992   Lat. 50°09'N. Long. 5°03'W.

GMT   **ADD 1 HOUR MARCH 29 — OCTOBER 25 FOR B.S.T.**

JANUARY

Day	Time	m		Time	m
1	0204	4.5	**16**	0105	4.3
	0842	1.7		0753	1.8
W	1431	4.4	TH	1343	4.3
	2110	1.5		2034	1.6
2	0303	4.6	**17**	0228	4.5
	0942	1.5		0914	1.4
TH	1530	4.5	F	1506	1.5
	2205	1.4		2145	1.3
3	0355	4.8	**18**	0339	4.9
	1033	1.3		1018	1.1
F	1621	4.7	SA	1615	4.8
	2251	1.3		2242	0.9
4	0441	5.0	**19**	0439	5.2
	1118	1.2		1112	0.7
SA	1705	4.8	SU	1711	5.1
●	2333	1.2	O	2333	0.6
5	0522	5.1	**20**	0531	5.5
	1158	1.1		1200	0.3
SU	1744	4.8	M	1802	5.3
6	0011	1.1	**21**	0019	0.3
	0558	5.1		0618	5.6
M	1234	1.0	TU	1246	0.1
	1819	4.8		1847	5.4
7	0046	1.1	**22**	0104	0.2
	0631	5.1		0702	5.7
TU	1307	1.0	W	1330	0.1
	1850	4.8		1930	5.3
8	0119	1.1	**23**	0147	0.3
	0701	5.1		0744	5.6
W	1339	1.1	TH	1412	0.2
	1919	4.7		2011	5.2
9	0150	1.2	**24**	0229	0.4
	0728	5.0		0824	5.4
TH	1410	1.1	F	1454	0.5
	1945	4.6		2050	5.0
10	0221	1.3	**25**	0311	0.7
	0744	1.2		0903	5.1
F	1442	1.2	SA	1536	0.8
	2012	4.6		2130	4.7
11	0254	1.3	**26**	0353	1.1
	0822	4.7		0943	4.8
SA	1517	1.3	SU	1619	1.2
	2044	4.5		2213	4.5
12	0332	1.4	**27**	0439	1.4
	0857	4.6		1029	4.5
SU	1557	1.4	M	1706	1.5
	2126	4.4		2303	4.4
13	0416	1.6	**28**	0532	1.7
	0946	4.5		1126	4.2
M	1646	1.5	TU	1803	1.8
	2226	4.3			
14	0511	1.7	**29**	0004	4.2
	1053	4.3		0641	2.0
TU	1748	1.7	W	1235	4.1
	2341	4.2		1921	2.0
15	0623	1.8	**30**	0116	4.2
	1215	4.3		0811	2.0
W	1908	1.7	TH	1353	4.1
				2044	1.9
			31	0229	4.4
				0925	1.7
			F	1505	4.2
				2147	1.6

FEBRUARY

Day	Time	m		Time	m
1	0331	4.6	**16**	0327	4.8
	1018	1.4		1007	1.0
SA	1603	4.5	SU	1606	4.8
	2235	1.3		2230	0.9
2	0422	4.8	**17**	0427	5.2
	1102	1.2		1059	0.5
SU	1650	4.7	M	1700	5.1
	2316	1.2		2318	0.4
3	0505	5.0	**18**	0518	5.5
	1140	1.0		1145	0.1
M	1729	4.8	TU	1747	5.4
●	2353	1.0	O		
4	0542	5.1	**19**	0003	0.1
	1215	0.8		0603	5.7
TU	1804	4.9	W	1228	0.0
				1829	5.5
5	0027	0.9	**20**	0046	0.0
	0615	5.2		0644	5.7
W	1247	0.8	TH	1309	0.0
	1835	4.9		1909	5.4
6	0059	0.8	**21**	0126	0.1
	0645	5.1		0723	5.6
TH	1317	0.8	F	1349	0.1
	1903	4.9		1946	5.3
7	0129	0.9	**22**	0205	0.3
	0711	5.0		0759	5.3
F	1347	0.8	SA	1427	0.4
	1926	4.8		2020	5.0
8	0159	0.9	**23**	0244	0.6
	0732	4.9		0833	5.0
SA	1418	0.9	SU	1504	0.8
	1946	4.7		2052	4.8
9	0231	1.1	**24**	0322	1.0
	0753	4.8		0906	4.7
SU	1450	1.1	M	1542	1.3
	2008	4.6		2128	4.5
10	0305	1.2	**25**	0401	1.4
	0820	4.7		0946	4.4
M	1527	1.3	TU	1622	1.6
	2043	4.5		2214	4.3
11	0345	1.3	**26**	0447	1.8
	0902	4.5		1039	4.1
TU	1611	1.4	W	1711	1.9
	2139	4.3		2314	4.1
12	0436	1.6	**27**	0551	2.1
	1010	4.2		1149	3.9
W	1708	1.7	TH	1829	2.2
	2301	4.2			
13	0546	1.8	**28**	0028	4.1
	1143	4.1		0738	2.1
TH	1831	1.9	F	1314	3.9
				2018	2.1
14	0034	4.2	**29**	0150	4.2
	0727	1.9		0904	1.8
F	1326	4.1	SA	1438	4.1
	2015	1.7		2125	1.7
15	0209	4.4			
	0903	1.5			
SA	1458	4.4			
	2133	1.3			

MARCH

Day	Time	m		Time	m
1	0301	4.4	**16**	0310	4.8
	0956	1.5		0949	0.9
SU	1540	4.4	M	1550	4.8
	2213	1.4		2211	0.8
2	0356	4.7	**17**	0409	5.2
	1038	1.2		1039	0.4
M	1627	4.6	TU	1641	5.1
	2252	1.1		2258	0.4
3	0440	5.0	**18**	0458	5.5
	1114	0.9		1123	0.1
TU	1706	4.9	W	1726	5.4
	2328	0.9	O	2341	0.1
4	0519	5.1	**19**	0542	5.6
	1147	0.7		1205	0.0
W	1742	5.0	TH	1807	5.5
●					
5	0001	0.7	**20**	0023	0.0
	0553	5.2		0622	5.6
TH	1220	0.6	F	1245	0.0
	1813	5.0		1843	5.4
6	0033	0.6	**21**	0103	0.1
	0624	5.2		0658	5.5
F	1251	0.6	SA	1323	0.2
	1841	5.0		1917	5.3
7	0105	0.6	**22**	0140	0.3
	0651	5.1		0732	5.2
SA	1322	0.6	SU	1359	0.5
	1906	4.9		1948	5.1
8	0136	0.7	**23**	0217	0.7
	0714	4.9		0802	4.9
SU	1354	0.8	M	1434	0.9
	1925	4.8		2017	4.8
9	0209	0.9	**24**	0252	1.1
	0733	4.8		0833	4.6
M	1427	1.0	TU	1508	1.3
	1946	4.7		2050	4.6
10	0244	1.1	**25**	0329	1.4
	0758	4.6		0910	4.3
TU	1504	1.2	W	1544	1.6
	2019	4.5		2133	4.3
11	0325	1.3	**26**	0410	1.8
	0841	4.4		1002	4.0
W	1548	1.4	TH	1629	2.0
	2117	4.3		2231	4.1
12	0416	1.5	**27**	0508	2.0
	0956	4.2		1109	3.8
TH	1646	1.7	F	1739	2.2
	2242	4.2		2342	4.0
13	0528	1.8	**28**	0648	2.1
	1135	4.0		1231	3.8
F	1813	1.9	SA	1933	2.2
14	0018	4.2	**29**	0102	4.1
	0715	1.8		0824	1.9
SA	1319	4.0	SU	1355	4.0
	2002	1.7		2049	1.8
15	0154	4.4	**30**	0217	4.3
	0849	1.4		0919	1.5
SU	1447	4.4	M	1501	4.3
	2116	1.3		2138	1.4
			31	0317	4.6
				1002	1.2
			TU	1551	4.6
				2219	1.2

APRIL

Day	Time	m		Time	m
1	0405	4.9	**16**	0432	5.3
	1039	0.9		1057	0.3
W	1633	4.9	TH	1659	5.3
	2256	0.9		2317	0.3
2	0447	5.0	**17**	0516	5.4
	1115	0.7		1139	0.2
TH	1711	5.0	F	1740	5.4
	2331	0.7	O	2359	0.2
3	0525	5.1	**18**	0556	5.4
	1149	0.5		1220	0.3
F	1746	5.1	SA	1816	5.3
4	0006	0.6	**19**	0039	0.3
	0559	5.1		0633	5.2
SA	1224	0.5	SU	1257	0.5
	1817	5.1		1849	5.2
5	0040	0.6	**20**	0117	0.6
	0631	5.1		0706	5.0
SU	1258	0.6	M	1333	0.8
	1846	5.0		1919	5.0
6	0115	0.6	**21**	0153	0.9
	0700	4.9		0736	4.7
M	1333	0.7	TU	1407	1.1
	1913	4.9		1948	4.8
7	0152	0.8	**22**	0228	1.2
	0728	4.7		0807	4.5
TU	1410	0.9	W	1441	1.3
	1941	4.8		2021	4.6
8	0231	1.0	**23**	0303	1.4
	0801	4.5		0843	4.2
W	1450	1.2	TH	1516	1.6
	2020	4.6		2102	4.4
9	0315	1.3	**24**	0343	1.7
	0853	4.3		0931	4.0
TH	1538	1.4	F	1558	1.9
	2121	4.4		2155	4.2
10	0410	1.5	**25**	0435	1.9
	1007	4.1		1032	3.9
F	1639	1.7	SA	1658	2.1
	2238	4.3		2258	4.1
11	0524	1.7	**26**	0548	2.0
	1134	4.0		1142	3.9
SA	1804	1.8	SU	1824	2.1
12	0004	4.3	**27**	0008	4.1
	0700	1.6		0717	1.9
SU	1306	4.1	M	1257	4.0
	1939	1.6		1949	1.9
13	0131	4.4	**28**	0119	4.3
	0822	1.3		0824	1.6
M	1424	4.4	TU	1406	4.2
	2050	1.3		2049	1.6
14	0244	4.7	**29**	0225	4.5
	0922	0.9		0915	1.3
TU	1525	4.8	W	1503	4.5
	2145	0.9		2136	1.3
15	0343	5.1	**30**	0320	4.7
	1012	0.5		0958	1.1
W	1615	5.1	TH	1552	4.8
	2233	0.5		2219	1.0

To find H.W. Dover add 6 h. 00 min. to above times.

TIDAL DIFFERENCES ARE NOT GIVEN.

Datum of predictions: 2.91 m. below Ordnance Datum (Newlyn) or approx. L.A.T.

FALMOUTH

Lat. 50°09'N. Long. 5°03'W.

HIGH & LOW WATER 1992

GMT ADD 1 HOUR MARCH 29 — OCTOBER 25 FOR B.S.T.

MAY

Day	Time	m	Day	Time	m
1 F	0409 1039 1636 2259	4.9 0.8 5.0 0.8	16 SA	0450 1114 1712 O 2336	5.1 0.6 5.2 0.6
2 SA	0453 1119 1716 ● 2339	5.0 0.6 5.1 0.6	17 SU	0532 1156 1751	5.0 0.6 5.2
3 SU	0535 1158 1754	5.0 0.6 5.1	18 M	0018 0610 1235 1825	0.6 5.0 0.8 5.1
4 M	0018 0614 1237 1831	0.6 5.0 0.6 5.1	19 TU	0057 0645 1312 1857	0.8 4.8 1.0 5.0
5 TU	0059 0652 1317 1907	0.6 4.9 0.7 5.0	20 W	0134 0717 1347 1928	1.0 4.6 1.2 4.8
6 W	0140 0732 1359 1946	0.7 4.7 0.9 4.9	21 TH	0209 0748 1421 2000	1.2 4.5 1.3 4.7
7 TH	0224 0816 1444 2032	0.9 4.6 1.1 4.7	22 F	0244 0823 1456 2037	1.3 4.3 1.5 4.5
8 F	0313 0909 1535 2127	1.1 4.4 1.3 4.6	23 SA	0321 0904 1535 2122	1.5 4.2 1.7 4.4
9 SA	0408 1012 1634 2232	1.3 4.2 1.5 4.5	24 SU	0404 0954 1622 2214	1.6 4.1 1.8 4.3
10 SU	0515 1123 1746 2344	1.4 4.2 1.6 4.4	25 M	0457 1052 1722 2313	1.7 4.0 1.9 4.2
11 M	0631 1238 1905	1.4 4.3 1.5	26 TU	0602 1155 1833	1.7 4.1 1.9
12 TU	0059 0746 1349 2015	4.5 1.3 4.4 1.3	27 W	0017 0712 1302 1944	4.3 1.6 4.2 1.7
13 W	0209 0849 1450 2114	4.7 1.1 4.7 1.1	28 TH	0124 0818 1407 2047	4.3 1.4 4.4 1.5
14 TH	0310 0942 1543 2206	4.8 0.8 4.9 0.8	29 F	0229 0914 1506 2141	4.5 1.3 4.6 1.3
15 F	0403 1030 1630 2253	5.0 0.7 5.1 0.6	30 SA	0329 1005 1559 2230	4.7 1.0 4.8 1.0
			31 SU	0423 1052 1649 2316	4.8 0.8 5.0 0.7

JUNE

Day	Time	m	Day	Time	m
1 M	0513 1137 1735 ●	4.9 0.7 5.1	16 TU	0002 0553 1218 1807	0.9 4.8 1.0 5.0
2 TU	0002 0600 1222 1819	0.6 5.0 0.6 5.2	17 W	0042 0629 1256 1841	0.9 4.7 1.0 5.0
3 W	0047 0647 1307 1903	0.5 4.9 0.6 5.2	18 TH	0118 0702 1331 1912	1.0 4.6 1.1 4.9
4 TH	0133 0732 1352 1947	0.5 4.9 0.7 5.1	19 F	0152 0733 1404 1943	1.1 4.5 1.2 4.8
5 F	0219 0819 1438 2033	0.6 4.7 0.8 5.0	20 SA	0225 0803 1436 2014	1.2 4.5 1.3 4.7
6 SA	0307 0908 1527 2122	0.8 4.6 1.0 4.8	21 SU	0258 0836 1510 2049	1.3 4.4 1.4 4.6
7 SU	0358 1001 1620 2217	1.0 4.5 1.2 4.7	22 M	0334 0915 1549 2130	1.3 4.3 1.5 4.5
8 M	0454 1058 1719 2316	1.2 4.4 1.3 4.6	23 TU	0415 1001 1634 2219	1.4 4.2 1.6 4.4
9 TU	0556 1200 1825	1.3 4.3 1.4	24 W	0505 1056 1730 2318	1.5 4.2 1.7 4.3
10 W	0021 0703 1306 1935	4.5 1.3 4.4 1.4	25 TH	0605 1200 1837	1.6 4.2 1.7
11 TH	0129 0810 1410 2041	4.5 1.3 4.5 1.3	26 F	0025 0716 1310 1953	4.2 1.6 4.3 1.6
12 F	0234 0911 1509 2139	4.6 1.2 4.7 1.2	27 SA	0139 0830 1421 2105	4.3 1.4 4.4 1.4
13 SA	0334 1004 1601 2231	4.6 1.1 4.8 1.0	28 SU	0252 0935 1528 2207	4.4 1.3 4.7 1.2
14 SU	0426 1053 1648 2318	4.7 1.0 4.9 0.9	29 M	0359 1032 1627 2300	4.6 1.0 4.9 0.8
15 M	0512 1137 1730 O	4.8 0.9 5.0	30 TU	0458 1123 1720 ● 2350	4.8 0.7 5.1 0.5

JULY

Day	Time	m	Day	Time	m
1 W	0550 1211 1809	5.0 0.5 5.3	16 TH	0025 0614 1239 1826	0.9 4.7 0.9 5.0
2 TH	0037 0639 1257 1855	0.3 5.1 0.4 5.4	17 F	0100 0646 1312 1857	0.9 4.7 0.9 5.0
3 F	0123 0725 1342 1940	0.2 5.1 0.4 5.3	18 SA	0132 0715 1343 1925	0.9 4.7 1.0 4.9
4 SA	0208 0809 1426 2023	0.3 5.0 0.5 5.2	19 SU	0202 0742 1413 1951	1.0 4.6 1.1 4.8
5 SU	0253 0853 1511 2107	0.4 4.9 0.6 5.1	20 M	0232 0808 1443 2017	1.0 4.6 1.2 4.7
6 M	0338 0938 1558 2153	0.7 4.7 0.9 4.8	21 TU	0303 0836 1517 2048	1.1 4.5 1.3 4.6
7 TU	0426 1026 1648 2244	1.0 4.5 1.2 4.6	22 W	0339 0911 1555 2128	1.3 4.4 1.4 4.4
8 W	0518 1119 1744 2341	1.3 4.4 1.4 4.4	23 TH	0420 0959 1642 2223	1.4 4.3 1.5 4.3
9 TH	0618 1220 1851	1.4 4.3 1.6	24 F	0513 1104 1743 2335	1.6 4.2 1.7 4.2
10 F	0047 0729 1327 2007	4.3 1.6 4.3 1.6	25 SA	0622 1222 1905	1.7 4.2 1.8
11 SA	0159 0842 1435 2118	4.2 1.5 4.4 1.5	26 SU	0059 0752 1345 2039	4.1 1.7 4.3 1.6
12 SU	0308 0945 1536 2216	4.3 1.4 4.6 1.3	27 M	0228 0915 1505 2151	4.3 1.4 4.6 1.3
13 M	0407 1037 1628 2305	4.4 1.3 4.8 1.1	28 TU	0345 1017 1612 2248	4.5 1.1 4.9 0.8
14 TU	0456 1122 1713 2347	4.6 1.1 4.9 0.9	29 W	0446 1110 1707 O 2337	4.9 0.6 5.2 0.4
15 W	0538 1202 1752	4.7 1.0 5.0	30 TH	0539 1157 1757	5.1 0.3 5.5
31 F	0023 0625 1242 1842	0.1 5.3 0.1 5.6			

AUGUST

Day	Time	m	Day	Time	m
1 SA	0107 0709 1325 1924	0.0 5.3 0.0 5.6	16 SU	0106 0653 1318 1903	0.7 4.9 0.8 5.0
2 SU	0150 0750 1407 2005	0.0 5.2 0.2 5.4	17 M	0135 0718 1347 1927	0.8 4.8 0.9 4.9
3 M	0232 0830 1449 2045	0.2 5.1 0.4 5.2	18 TU	0204 0740 1416 1947	0.9 4.7 1.0 4.8
4 TU	0313 0909 1526 2125	0.5 4.8 0.7 4.9	19 W	0234 0800 1448 2010	1.0 4.6 1.1 4.7
5 W	0356 0951 1616 2209	0.9 4.6 1.1 4.6	20 TH	0307 0827 1524 2043	1.2 4.5 1.3 4.5
6 TH	0441 1038 1705 2302	1.3 4.4 1.4 4.3	21 F	0346 0911 1608 2137	1.3 4.4 1.5 4.3
7 F	0535 1136 1809	1.6 4.2 1.8	22 SA	0435 1020 1706 2259	1.6 4.2 1.7 4.1
8 SA	0007 0647 1246 1937	4.1 1.9 4.1 1.9	23 SU	0057 1148 1834	1.8 4.1 1.9
9 SU	0127 0818 1404 2102	4.0 1.9 4.2 1.7	24 M	0036 0727 1332 2023	4.0 1.9 4.2 1.7
10 M	0247 0929 1514 2202	4.1 1.6 4.4 1.4	25 TU	0215 0900 1449 2138	4.2 1.5 4.6 1.3
11 TU	0350 1021 1609 2248	4.3 1.3 4.7 1.2	26 W	0333 1003 1557 2233	4.6 1.1 5.0 0.7
12 W	0439 1104 1654 2328	4.6 1.1 4.9 1.0	27 TH	0432 1053 1651 2320	5.0 0.6 5.4 0.3
13 TH	0519 1142 1732 O	4.8 0.9 5.1	28 F	0521 1139 1739 ●	5.3 0.2 5.6
14 F	0003 0554 1216 1806	0.8 4.9 0.8 5.1	29 SA	0004 0606 1223 1822	0.0 5.5 0.0 5.7
15 SA	0036 0625 1248 1836	0.7 4.9 0.7 5.1	30 SU	0047 0647 1304 1903	0.0 5.5 0.0 5.7
			31 M	0127 0726 1345 1942	0.0 5.4 0.1 5.7

GENERAL — Streams run generally in direction of channel. During freshes — outgoing stream increases in rate and duration.

RATE AND SET — In channel: Ingoing begins +0015 Dover, Spring rate 1½ kn.; Outgoing begins –0605 Dover, Spring rate 1½ kn.

FALMOUTH

Lat. 50°09'N. Long. 5°03'W. **HIGH & LOW WATER 1992**

GMT   ADD 1 HOUR MARCH 29 — OCTOBER 25 FOR B.S.T.

SEPTEMBER

Day	Time	m	Day	Time	m
1 TU	0207	0.2	16 W	0137	0.8
	0802	5.2		0715	4.9
	1424	0.4		1352	0.9
	2018	5.2		1924	4.8
2 W	0246	0.6	17 TH	0209	1.0
	0838	4.9		0734	4.8
	1504	0.8		1425	1.1
	2054	4.8		1943	4.7
3 TH	0325	1.1	18 F	0243	1.2
	0914	4.7		0759	4.6
	1545	1.3		1502	1.3
	2134	4.5		2016	4.5
4 F	0406	1.4	19 SA	0323	1.4
	0958	4.4		0844	4.4
	1630	1.6		1547	1.5
	2224	4.2		2115	4.2
5 SA	0454	1.8	20 SU	0413	1.7
	1054	4.2		0958	4.3
	1730	2.0		1648	1.8
	2330	3.9		2245	4.0
6 SU	0606	2.1	21 M	0525	1.9
	1206	4.1		1129	4.2
	1908	2.1		1820	1.9
7 M	0054	3.9	22 TU	0025	4.0
	0752	2.1		0711	1.9
	1329	4.2		1305	4.3
	2042	1.9		2007	1.7
8 TU	0220	4.0	23 W	0202	4.3
	0907	1.4		0841	1.5
	1444	4.4		1431	4.6
	2139	1.5		2118	1.2
9 W	0324	4.3	24 TH	0315	4.7
	0957	1.4		0941	1.1
	1541	4.7		1536	5.1
	2222	1.3		2211	0.7
10 TH	0412	4.6	25 F	0411	5.1
	1038	1.2		1031	0.6
	1626	4.9		1630	5.4
	2259	1.0		2257	0.3
11 F	0451	4.9	26	0459	5.4
	1114	0.9		1117	0.2
	1705	5.1	●	2341	0.0
	2333	0.7			
12 SA	0527	5.0	27 SU	0542	5.5
	1147	0.7		1159	0.0
	1740	5.2		1800	5.7
O					
13 SU	0005	0.6	28 M	0022	0.0
	0559	5.1		0622	5.6
	1220	0.7		1241	0.0
	1811	5.2		1839	5.6
14 M	0037	0.6	29 TU	0103	0.1
	0628	5.1		0659	5.5
	1250	0.7		1321	0.2
	1839	5.1		1916	5.4
15 TU	0107	0.7	30 W	0141	0.4
	0654	5.0		0734	5.3
	1321	0.8		1400	0.6
	1904	5.0		1951	5.1

OCTOBER

Day	Time	m	Day	Time	m
1 TH	0219	0.8	16 F	0149	1.0
	0806	5.0		0722	4.9
	1438	1.0		1409	1.1
	2024	4.8		1937	4.7
2 F	0256	1.3	17 SA	0227	1.3
	0840	4.7		0753	4.7
	1517	1.3		1450	1.3
	2101	4.4		2016	4.5
3 SA	0334	1.6	18 SU	0311	1.4
	0921	4.5		0841	4.6
	1600	1.7		1539	1.5
	2148	4.1		2118	4.3
4 SU	0419	2.0	19 M	0404	1.7
	1015	4.3		0952	4.4
	1656	2.0		1642	1.7
	2252	3.9		2242	4.1
5 M	0525	2.2	20 TU	0517	1.9
	1123	4.1		1115	4.3
	1825	2.2		1808	1.8
6 TU	0011	3.9	21 W	0013	4.2
	0708	2.2		0649	1.8
	1242	4.2		1244	4.5
	2001	2.0		1940	1.6
7 W	0135	4.0	22 TH	0140	4.4
	0828	2.0		0812	1.5
	1359	4.4		1405	4.7
	2101	1.7		2049	1.2
8 TH	0242	4.3	23 F	0249	4.7
	0920	1.6		0914	1.2
	1500	4.6		1510	5.0
	2145	1.3		2144	0.8
9 F	0333	4.6	24 SA	0345	5.1
	1002	1.3		1006	0.7
	1548	4.9		1604	5.3
	2224	1.1		2232	0.5
10 SA	0416	4.9	25 SU	0433	5.3
	1040	1.0		1053	0.4
	1630	5.1		1652	5.5
	2259	0.8	●	2316	0.3
11 SU	0454	5.1	26 M	0517	5.5
	1115	0.8		1136	0.3
	1709	5.2		1735	5.5
O	2333	0.7		2358	0.3
12 M	0529	5.2	27 TU	0556	5.5
	1149	0.7		1219	0.3
	1744	5.2		1815	5.5
13 TU	0007	0.7	28 W	0039	0.4
	0601	5.2		0633	5.4
	1224	0.7		1259	0.5
	1815	5.2		1852	5.3
14 W	0041	0.7	29 TH	0118	0.7
	0631	5.1		0708	5.3
	1257	0.8		1338	0.8
	1845	5.0		1926	5.0
15 TH	0114	0.8	30 F	0155	1.1
	0657	5.0		0739	5.0
	1332	0.9		1416	1.1
	1911	4.9		1958	4.7
31 SA				0231	1.3
				0811	4.8
				1454	1.4
				2033	4.4

NOVEMBER

Day	Time	m	Day	Time	m
1 SU	0308	1.6	16 M	0305	1.3
	0849	4.6		0847	4.8
	1535	1.7		1536	1.3
	2116	4.2		2126	4.4
2 M	0350	1.9	17 TU	0359	1.5
	0938	4.4		0947	4.6
	1624	1.9		1635	1.4
	2212	4.1		2234	4.3
3 TU	0445	2.1	18 W	0503	1.7
	1038	4.3		1058	4.6
	1730	2.1		1746	1.5
	2320	4.0		2350	4.3
4 W	0601	2.2	19 TH	0619	1.7
	1146	4.3		1215	4.6
	1853	2.0		1903	1.5
5 TH	0034	4.1	20 F	0108	4.5
	0725	2.1		0736	1.5
	1258	4.4		1331	4.7
	2003	1.8		2014	1.3
6 F	0145	4.3	21 SA	0216	4.7
	0828	1.8		0842	1.3
	1405	4.5		1439	4.9
	2056	1.5		2114	1.1
7 SA	0244	4.6	22 SU	0315	5.0
	0918	1.5		0939	1.0
	1502	4.8		1537	5.1
	2141	1.3		2206	0.8
8 SU	0333	4.8	23 M	0407	5.2
	1002	1.3		1030	0.8
	1551	5.0		1628	5.2
	2222	1.1		2253	0.7
9 M	0418	5.1	24 TU	0452	5.3
	1042	1.0		1116	0.7
	1635	5.1		1714	5.3
	2302	0.9	●	2337	0.7
10 TU	0458	5.2	25 W	0534	5.4
	1121	0.9		1200	0.7
	1716	5.2		1755	5.2
O	2340	0.8			
11 W	0536	5.3	26 TH	0019	0.8
	1200	0.8		0612	5.4
	1755	5.1		1242	0.8
				1833	5.1
12 TH	0018	0.8	27 F	0059	0.9
	0601	5.2		0646	5.2
	1239	0.8		1321	1.0
	1831	5.1		1907	4.9
13 F	0057	0.8	28 SA	0136	1.1
	0646	5.2		0718	5.1
	1319	0.9		1359	1.2
	1907	4.9		1938	4.7
14 SA	0137	1.0	29 SU	0212	1.3
	0721	5.1		0749	4.9
	1400	1.0		1435	1.3
	1945	4.8		2010	4.5
15 SU	0219	1.2	30 M	0247	1.5
	0759	4.9		0823	4.8
	1445	1.2		1511	1.5
	2029	4.6		2047	4.4

DECEMBER

Day	Time	m	Day	Time	m
1 TU	0324	1.7	16 W	0347	1.2
	0903	4.6		0936	4.9
	1552	1.7		1619	1.2
	2133	4.3		2216	4.5
2 W	0407	1.9	17 TH	0442	1.3
	0952	4.5		1035	4.7
	1639	1.8		1717	1.3
	2228	4.2		2320	4.4
3 TH	0500	2.0	18 F	0545	1.5
	1050	4.4		1142	4.6
	1738	1.9		1824	1.4
	2332	4.2			
4 F	0606	2.0	19 SA	0029	4.4
	1155	4.4		0656	1.6
	1846	1.9		1255	4.6
				1935	1.4
5 SA	0040	4.3	20 SU	0140	4.5
	0719	2.0		0809	1.5
	1303	4.4		1407	4.6
	1955	1.7		2043	1.3
6 SU	0147	4.4	21 M	0245	4.7
	0825	1.7		0915	1.3
	1409	4.5		1512	4.7
	2054	1.5		2143	1.3
7 M	0247	4.7	22 TU	0343	4.9
	0922	1.5		1011	1.2
	1510	4.7		1609	4.9
	2146	1.3		2234	1.1
8 TU	0341	4.9	23 W	0432	5.1
	1012	1.3		1101	1.0
	1604	4.9		1657	4.9
	2233	1.1		2321	1.0
9 W	0430	5.1	24 TH	0517	5.2
	1058	1.0		1146	0.9
	1653	5.0		1740	5.0
	2318	0.9	●		
10 TH	0515	5.2	25 F	0003	0.9
	1142	0.8		0555	5.3
	1739	5.1		1228	0.9
O				1818	5.0
11 F	0002	0.8	26 SA	0043	1.0
	0557	5.3		0630	5.2
	1226	0.7		1306	0.9
	1822	5.1		1851	4.9
12 SA	0045	0.7	27 SU	0119	1.1
	0638	5.3		0701	5.1
	1310	0.7		1341	1.0
	1905	5.0		1921	4.8
13 SU	0128	0.9	28 M	0153	1.2
	0719	5.3		0730	5.0
	1354	0.7		1414	1.2
	1947	4.9		1949	4.7
14 M	0212	0.9	29 TU	0225	1.3
	0801	5.2		0759	4.9
	1439	0.8		1446	1.3
	2031	4.8		2019	4.6
15 TU	0258	1.0	30 W	0257	1.4
	0845	5.0		0831	4.8
	1527	1.0		1519	1.4
	2120	4.6		2054	4.5
31 TH				0332	1.5
				0909	4.6
				1556	1.5
				2138	4.4

To find H.W. Dover add 6 h. 00 min. to above times.

TIDAL DIFFERENCES ARE NOT GIVEN.

Datum of predictions: 2.91 m. below Ordnance Datum (Newlyn) or approx. L.A.T.

DEVONPORT

MEAN SPRING AND NEAP CURVES
Springs occur 2 days after New and Full Moon.

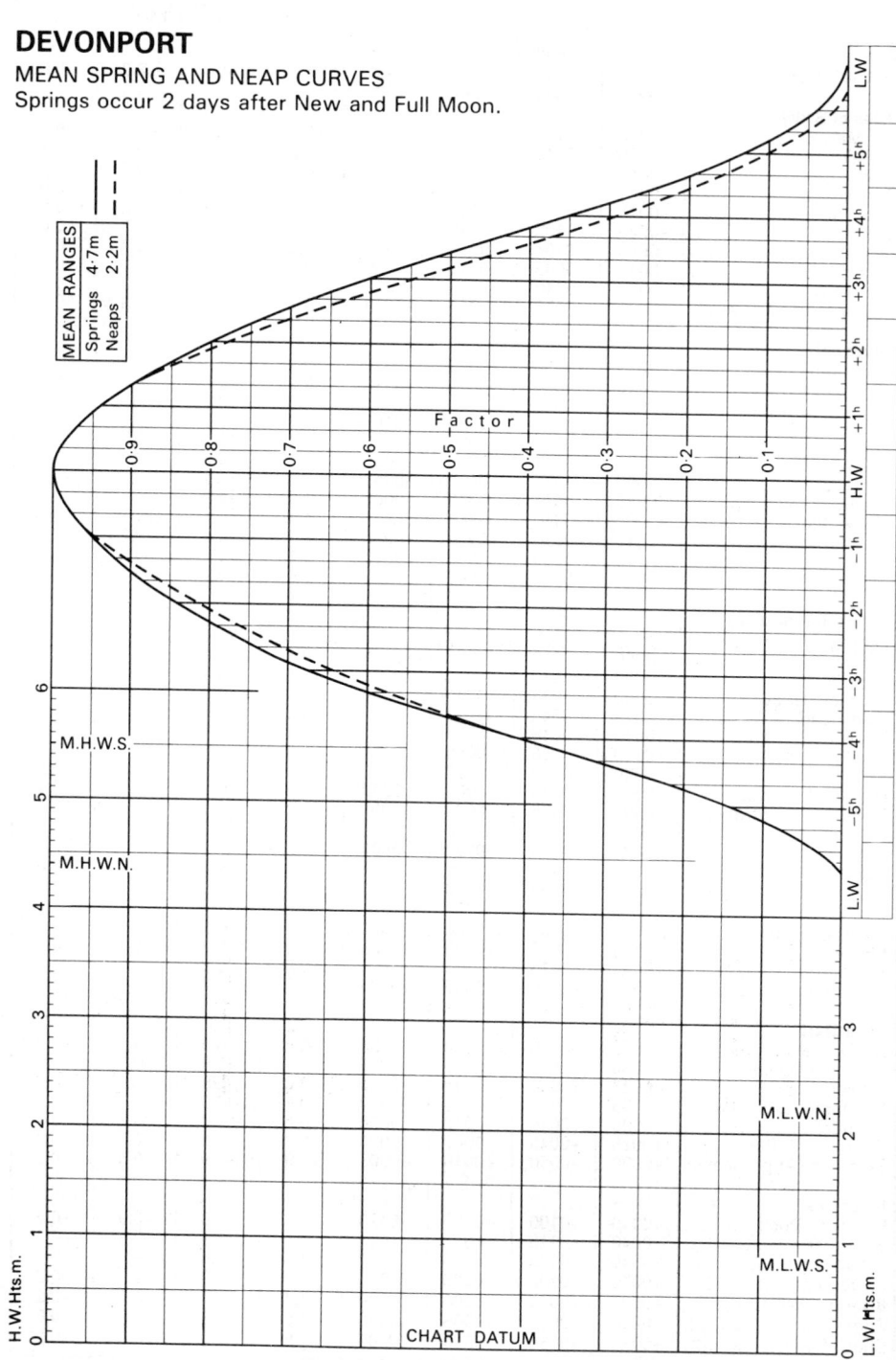

TIDAL DIFFERENCES ON PLYMOUTH

PLACE	TIME DIFFERENCES				HEIGHT DIFFERENCES (Metres)			
	High Water		Low Water		MHWS	MHWN	MLWN	MLWS
PLYMOUTH	0000 and 1200	0600 and 1800	0000 and 1200	0600 and 1800	5.5	4.4	2.2	0.8
Isles of Scilly								
St. Marys	−0030	−0110	−0100	−0020	+0.2	−0.1	−0.2	−0.1
Tresco	−0030	−0110	−0100	−0020	+0.2	−0.1	−0.2	−0.1
Lands End	−0040	−0105	−0045	−0020	+0.1	0.0	−0.2	0.0
Mousehole	−0040	−0105	−0045	−0020	+0.1	0.0	−0.2	0.0
Newlyn	−0040	−0105	−0045	−0020	+0.1	0.0	−0.2	0.0
Penzance	−0040	−0105	−0045	−0020	+0.1	0.0	−0.2	0.0
Porthleven	−0045	−0105	−0035	−0025	0.0	−0.1	−0.2	0.0
Lizard Point	−0045	−0055	−0040	−0030	−0.2	−0.2	−0.3	−0.2
Coverack	−0030	−0040	−0020	−0010	−0.2	−0.2	−0.3	−0.2
Helford River Entrance	−0030	−0035	−0015	−0010	−0.2	−0.2	−0.3	−0.2
River Fal								
Falmouth	−0030	−0030	−0010	−0010	−0.2	−0.2	−0.3	−0.2
St. Mawes	−0030	−0030	−0010	−0010	−0.2	−0.2	−0.3	−0.2
Truro	−0020	−0025	−	−	−2.0	−2.0	Dries	Dries
Mevagissey	−0010	−0015	−0005	+0005	−0.1	−0.1	−0.2	−0.1
Pentewan	−0010	−0015	−0005	+0005	−0.1	−0.1	−0.2	−0.1
Charlestown	−0005	−0015	0000	−0005	−0.2	−0.2	−0.3	−0.2
Par	−0005	−0015	0000	−0010	−0.4	−0.4	−0.4	−0.2
Fowey	−0010	−0015	−0010	−0005	−0.1	−0.1	−0.2	−0.2
Lostwithiel	+0005	−0010	−	−	−4.1	−4.1	Dries	Dries
Polperro	−0010	−0010	−0005	−0005	−0.1	−0.2	−0.2	−0.2
Looe	−0010	−0010	−0005	−0005	−0.1	−0.2	−0.2	−0.2
Whitesand Bay	0000	0000	0000	0000	0.0	+0.1	−0.1	+0.2
Rivers Tamar, Tavy & Lynher								
Saltash	0000	+0010	0000	−0005	+0.1	+0.1	+0.1	+0.1
Cargreen	0000	+0010	+0020	+0020	0.0	0.0	−0.1	0.0
Cotehele Quay	0000	+0020	+0045	+0045	−0.9	−0.9	−0.8	−0.4
Weir Head	+0045	+0045	−	−	−3.5	−3.5	−	−
Maristow	+0015	+0015	−	−	−2.1	−2.1	−	−
Jupiter Point	+0010	+0005	0000	−0005	0.0	0.0	+0.1	0.0
St. Germans	0000	0000	+0020	+0020	−0.3	−0.1	0.0	+0.2
Bovisand	0000	−0020	0000	−0010	−0.2	−0.1	0.0	+0.1
River Yealm Entrance	+0006	+0006	+0002	+0002	−0.1	−0.1	−0.1	−0.1
PLYMOUTH	0100 and 1300	0600 and 1800	0100 and 1300	0600 and 1800	5.5	4.4	2.2	0.8
River Avon Bar	+0005	+0005	0000	0000	−0.1	−0.1	−0.1	−0.1
Salcombe	0000	+0010	+0005	−0005	−0.2	−0.3	−0.1	−0.1
Kingsbridge	+0015	+0015	−	−	−0.8	−0.8	−	−
Start Point	+0005	+0030	−0005	+0005	−0.2	−0.4	−0.1	−0.1
River Dart								
Dartmouth	+0015	+0025	0000	−0005	−0.6	−0.6	−0.2	−0.2
Greenway Quay	+0030	+0045	+0025	+0005	−0.6	−0.6	−0.2	−0.2
Totnes	+0025	+0040	+0115	+0030	−2.0	−2.1	Dries	Dries
Brixham	+0025	+0040	+0015	0000	−0.7	−0.6	−0.1	−0.1
Torquay	+0025	+0045	+0010	0000	−0.6	−0.7	−0.2	−0.1
Teignmouth Bar	+0025	+0040	0000	0000	−0.7	−0.8	−0.3	−0.2
Exmouth (Approaches)	+0030	+0050	+0015	+0005	−0.9	−1.0	−0.5	−0.3
River Exe								
Exmouth Dock	+0040	+0100	+0050	+0020	−1.5	−1.6	−0.9	−0.6
Starcross	+0040	+0110	−	−	−1.4	−1.5	−0.8	−0.1
Topsham	+0045	+0105	−	−	−1.5	−1.6	−	−
Lyme Regis	+0040	+0100	+0005	−0005	−1.2	−1.3	−0.5	−0.2
Bridport (West Bay)	+0025	+0040	0000	0000	−1.4	−1.4	−0.6	−0.2
Chesil Beach	+0040	+0055	−0005	+0010	−1.6	−1.5	−0.5	0.0
Chesil Cove	+0035	+0050	−0010	+0005	−1.5	−1.6	−0.5	−0.2

Refer to predictions on pages 21:171-21:173

PLYMOUTH (DEVONPORT) 21:171

Lat. 50°22′N. Long. 4°11′W. **HIGH & LOW WATER 1992**

GMT ADD 1 HOUR MARCH 29 — OCTOBER 25 FOR B.S.T.

JANUARY

Day	Time	m	Time	m
1 W	0234 / 0852 / 1501 / 2120	4.7 / 2.0 / 4.6 / 1.8	**16** TH 0135 / 0803 / 1413 / 2044	4.5 / 2.1 / 4.5 / 1.9
2 TH	0333 / 0952 / 1600 / 2215	4.8 / 1.8 / 4.7 / 1.7	**17** F 0258 / 0924 / 1536 / 2155	4.7 / 1.7 / 4.7 / 1.5
3 F	0425 / 1043 / 1651 / 2301	5.0 / 1.6 / 4.9 / 1.5	**18** SA 0409 / 1028 / 1645 / 2252	5.1 / 1.3 / 5.0 / 1.1
4 SA	0511 / 1128 / 1735 / ●2343	5.2 / 1.4 / 5.0 / 1.4	**19** SU 0509 / 1122 / 1741 / O2343	5.4 / 0.9 / 5.3 / 0.8
5 SU	0552 / 1208 / 1814	5.3 / 1.3 / 5.0	**20** M 0601 / 1210 / 1832	5.7 / 0.5 / 5.5
6 M	0021 / 0628 / 1244 / 1849	1.3 / 5.3 / 1.2 / 5.0	**21** TU 0029 / 0648 / 1256 / 1917	0.5 / 5.8 / 0.3 / 5.6
7 TU	0056 / 0701 / 1317 / 1920	1.3 / 5.3 / 1.2 / 5.0	**22** W 0114 / 0732 / 1340 / 2000	0.4 / 5.9 / 0.3 / 5.5
8 W	0129 / 0731 / 1349 / 1949	1.3 / 5.3 / 1.3 / 4.9	**23** TH 0157 / 0818 / 1422 / 2041	0.5 / 5.8 / 0.4 / 5.4
9 TH	0200 / 0758 / 1420 / 2015	1.4 / 5.2 / 1.3 / 4.8	**24** F 0239 / 0854 / 1504 / 2120	0.6 / 5.4 / 0.7 / 5.2
10 F	0231 / 0824 / 1452 / 2042	1.5 / 5.0 / 1.4 / 4.8	**25** SA 0321 / 0933 / 1546 / 2200	0.9 / 5.3 / 1.0 / 4.9
11 SA	0304 / 0852 / 1527 / 2114	1.6 / 4.9 / 1.5 / 4.7	**26** SU 0403 / 1013 / 1629 / 2243	1.3 / 5.0 / 1.4 / 4.7
12 SU	0342 / 0927 / 1607 / 2156	1.7 / 4.8 / 1.7 / 4.6	**27** M 0449 / 1100 / 1716 / 2333	1.7 / 4.7 / 1.8 / 4.5
13 M	0426 / 1016 / 1656 / 2256	1.9 / 4.7 / 1.8 / 4.5	**28** TU 0542 / 1156 / 1813	2.0 / 4.4 / 2.1
14 TU	0521 / 1123 / 1758	2.0 / 4.5 / 2.0	**29** W 0034 / 0651 / 1305 / 1931	4.4 / 2.3 / 4.3 / 2.3
15 W	0011 / 0633 / 1245 / 1918	4.4 / 2.1 / 4.5 / 2.0	**30** TH 0146 / 0821 / 1423 / 2054	4.4 / 2.3 / 4.3 / 2.2
			31 F 0259 / 0935 / 1535 / 2157	4.6 / 2.0 / 4.4 / 1.9

FEBRUARY

Day	Time	m	Time	m
1 SA	0401 / 1028 / 1633 / 2245	4.8 / 1.7 / 4.7 / 1.6	**16** SU 0357 / 1017 / 1636 / 2240	5.0 / 1.2 / 5.0 / 1.1
2 SU	0452 / 1112 / 1720 / 2326	5.0 / 1.4 / 4.9 / 1.4	**17** M 0457 / 1109 / 1730 / 2328	5.4 / 0.7 / 5.3 / 0.6
3 M	0535 / 1150 / 1759	5.2 / 1.2 / 5.0	**18** TU 0548 / 1155 / 1817	5.7 / 0.3 / 5.6
4 TU	0003 / 0623 / 1225 / 1834	1.2 / 5.3 / 1.0 / 5.1	**19** W 0013 / 0633 / 1238 / 1859	0.3 / 5.9 / 0.1 / 5.7
5 W	0037 / 0645 / 1257 / 1905	1.1 / 5.4 / 1.0 / 5.1	**20** TH 0056 / 0714 / 1319 / 1939	0.2 / 5.9 / 0.1 / 5.6
6 TH	0109 / 0715 / 1327 / 1933	1.0 / 5.3 / 1.0 / 5.1	**21** F 0136 / 0753 / 1359 / 2016	0.3 / 5.8 / 0.3 / 5.5
7 F	0139 / 0741 / 1357 / 1956	1.1 / 5.2 / 1.0 / 5.0	**22** SA 0215 / 0829 / 1437 / 2050	0.5 / 5.5 / 0.6 / 5.2
8 SA	0209 / 0802 / 1428 / 2016	1.1 / 5.1 / 1.1 / 4.9	**23** SU 0254 / 0903 / 1514 / 2122	0.8 / 5.2 / 1.0 / 5.0
9 SU	0241 / 0823 / 1500 / 2038	1.3 / 5.0 / 1.3 / 4.8	**24** M 0332 / 0936 / 1552 / 2158	1.2 / 4.9 / 1.5 / 4.7
10 M	0315 / 0850 / 1537 / 2113	1.4 / 4.9 / 1.5 / 4.7	**25** TU 0411 / 1016 / 1632 / 2244	1.7 / 4.6 / 1.9 / 4.5
11 TU	0355 / 0932 / 1621 / 2209	1.6 / 4.7 / 1.7 / 4.5	**26** W 0457 / 1109 / 1721 / 2344	2.1 / 4.3 / 2.2 / 4.3
12 W	0446 / 1044 / 1718 / 2331	1.9 / 4.4 / 2.0 / 4.4	**27** TH 0601 / 1219 / 1839	2.4 / 4.1 / 2.5
13 TH	0556 / 1213 / 1841	2.1 / 4.3 / 2.2	**28** F 0058 / 0748 / 1344 / 2028	4.3 / 2.4 / 4.1 / 2.4
14 F	0104 / 0737 / 1356 / 2025	4.4 / 2.2 / 4.3 / 2.0	**29** SA 0220 / 0914 / 1508 / 2135	4.4 / 2.1 / 4.3 / 2.0
15 SA	0239 / 0821 / 1528 / 2143	4.6 / 1.8 / 4.6 / 1.6		

MARCH

Day	Time	m	Time	m
1 SU	0331 / 1006 / 1610 / 2223	4.6 / 1.8 / 4.6 / 1.7	**16** M 0340 / 0959 / 1620 / 2221	5.0 / 1.1 / 5.0 / 1.0
2 M	0426 / 1048 / 1657 / 2302	4.9 / 1.4 / 4.8 / 1.3	**17** TU 0439 / 1049 / 1711 / 2308	5.4 / 0.6 / 5.3 / 0.6
3 TU	0510 / 1124 / 1736 / 2338	5.2 / 1.1 / 5.1 / 1.1	**18** W 0528 / 1133 / 1756 / 2351	5.7 / 0.3 / 5.6 / 0.3
4 W	0549 / 1157 / 1812	5.3 / 0.9 / 5.2	**19** TH 0612 / 1215 / 1837	5.8 / 0.1 / 5.7
5 TH	0011 / 0623 / 1230 / 1843	0.9 / 5.4 / 0.8 / 5.2	**20** F 0033 / 0652 / 1255 / 1913	0.2 / 5.8 / 0.2 / 5.6
6 F	0043 / 0654 / 1301 / 1911	0.8 / 5.4 / 0.8 / 5.2	**21** SA 0113 / 0728 / 1333 / 1947	0.3 / 5.7 / 0.4 / 5.5
7 SA	0115 / 0721 / 1332 / 1936	0.8 / 5.3 / 0.8 / 5.1	**22** SU 0150 / 0802 / 1409 / 2018	0.5 / 5.4 / 0.7 / 5.3
8 SU	0146 / 0748 / 1404 / 1955	0.9 / 5.1 / 1.0 / 5.0	**23** M 0227 / 0832 / 1444 / 2047	0.9 / 5.1 / 1.1 / 5.0
9 M	0219 / 0803 / 1437 / 2016	1.1 / 5.0 / 1.2 / 4.9	**24** TU 0302 / 0903 / 1518 / 2120	1.3 / 4.8 / 1.6 / 4.8
10 TU	0254 / 0828 / 1514 / 2049	1.3 / 4.8 / 1.4 / 4.7	**25** W 0339 / 0940 / 1554 / 2203	1.7 / 4.5 / 1.9 / 4.5
11 W	0335 / 0911 / 1558 / 2147	1.6 / 4.6 / 1.7 / 4.5	**26** TH 0420 / 1032 / 1639 / 2301	2.1 / 4.2 / 2.3 / 4.3
12 TH	0426 / 1026 / 1656 / 2312	1.8 / 4.3 / 2.0 / 4.4	**27** F 0518 / 1139 / 1749	2.3 / 4.0 / 2.5
13 F	0538 / 1205 / 1823	2.1 / 4.2 / 2.2	**28** SA 0012 / 0658 / 1301 / 1943	4.2 / 2.4 / 4.0 / 2.5
14 SA	0048 / 0725 / 1349 / 2012	4.5 / 2.1 / 4.2 / 2.0	**29** SU 0132 / 0834 / 1425 / 2059	4.3 / 2.2 / 4.2 / 2.1
15 SU	0224 / 0859 / 1517 / 2126	4.6 / 1.7 / 4.6 / 1.5	**30** M 0247 / 0929 / 1531 / 2148	4.5 / 1.8 / 4.5 / 1.7
			31 TU 0347 / 1012 / 1621 / 2229	4.8 / 1.4 / 4.8 / 1.4

APRIL

Day	Time	m	Time	m
1 W	0435 / 1049 / 1703 / 2306	5.1 / 1.1 / 5.1 / 1.1	**16** TH 0502 / 1107 / 1729 / 2327	5.5 / 0.5 / 5.5 / 0.5
2 TH	0517 / 1125 / 1741 / 2341	5.2 / 0.9 / 5.2 / 0.9 O	**17** F 0546 / 1149 / 1810	5.6 / 0.4 / 5.6
3 F	0555 / 1159 / 1816	5.3 / 0.7 / 5.3	**18** SA 0009 / 0626 / 1230 / 1846	0.4 / 5.6 / 0.5 / 5.5
4 SA	0016 / 0629 / 1234 / 1847	0.8 / 5.3 / 0.7 / 5.3	**19** SU 0049 / 0703 / 1307 / 1919	0.5 / 5.4 / 0.7 / 5.4
5 SU	0050 / 0701 / 1308 / 1916	0.8 / 5.3 / 0.8 / 5.2	**20** M 0127 / 0736 / 1343 / 1949	0.8 / 5.2 / 1.0 / 5.2
6 M	0125 / 0730 / 1343 / 1943	0.8 / 5.1 / 0.9 / 5.1	**21** TU 0203 / 0806 / 1417 / 2018	1.1 / 4.9 / 1.3 / 5.0
7 TU	0202 / 0758 / 1420 / 2011	1.1 / 4.9 / 1.1 / 5.0	**22** W 0238 / 0837 / 1451 / 2051	1.4 / 4.7 / 1.6 / 4.8
8 W	0241 / 0831 / 1500 / 2050	1.2 / 4.7 / 1.4 / 4.8	**23** TH 0313 / 0911 / 1526 / 2132	1.7 / 4.4 / 1.9 / 4.6
9 TH	0325 / 0923 / 1548 / 2151	1.5 / 4.5 / 1.7 / 4.6	**24** F 0353 / 1001 / 1608 / 2225	2.0 / 4.2 / 2.2 / 4.4
10 F	0420 / 1037 / 1649 / 2308	1.8 / 4.3 / 2.0 / 4.5	**25** SA 0445 / 1102 / 1708 / 2328	2.2 / 4.1 / 2.4 / 4.3
11 SA	0534 / 1204 / 1814	2.0 / 4.2 / 2.1	**26** SU 0558 / 1212 / 1834	2.3 / 4.1 / 2.4
12 SU	0034 / 0710 / 1336 / 1949	4.5 / 1.9 / 4.3 / 1.9	**27** M 0038 / 0710 / 1327 / 1959	4.3 / 2.2 / 4.2 / 2.2
13 M	0201 / 0832 / 1454 / 2100	4.6 / 1.6 / 4.6 / 1.5	**28** TU 0149 / 0834 / 1436 / 2059	4.5 / 1.9 / 4.4 / 1.9
14 TU	0314 / 0932 / 1555 / 2155	5.0 / 1.1 / 5.0 / 1.1	**29** W 0255 / 0925 / 1533 / 2146	4.7 / 1.6 / 4.7 / 1.5
15 W	0413 / 1022 / 1645 / 2243	5.3 / 0.7 / 5.3 / 0.7	**30** TH 0350 / 1008 / 1622 / 2229	4.9 / 1.3 / 5.0 / 1.2

To find H.W. Dover add 5 h. 40 min.

TIDAL DIFFERENCES PAGE 21:170. TIDAL CURVE PAGE 21:169.

TIDAL STREAMS PAGES 21:28-21:40.

Datum of predictions: 3.22 m. below Ordnance Datum (Newlyn) or approx. L.A.T.

(DEVONPORT) PLYMOUTH

HIGH & LOW WATER 1992 — Lat. 50°22′N. Long. 4°11′W.

GMT   ADD 1 HOUR MARCH 29 — OCTOBER 25 FOR B.S.T.

MAY

Day	Time	m	Day	Time	m
1 F	0439 / 1049 / 1706 / 2309	5.1 / 1.0 / 5.2 / 1.0	**16** O	0520 / 1124 / 1742 / 2346	5.3 / 0.8 / 5.4 / 0.8
2 SA ●	0523 / 1129 / 1746 / 2349	5.2 / 0.8 / 5.3 / 0.8	**17** SU	0602 / 1206 / 1821	5.2 / 0.8 / 5.4
3 SU	0605 / 1208 / 1824	5.2 / 0.8 / 5.3	**18** M	0028 / 0640 / 1245 / 1855	0.8 / 5.2 / 1.0 / 5.3
4 M	0028 / 0644 / 1247 / 1901	0.8 / 5.2 / 0.8 / 5.3	**19** TU	0107 / 0715 / 1322 / 1927	1.0 / 5.0 / 1.2 / 5.2
5 TU	0109 / 0722 / 1327 / 1937	0.8 / 5.1 / 0.9 / 5.2	**20** W	0144 / 0747 / 1357 / 1958	1.2 / 4.8 / 1.4 / 5.0
6 W	0150 / 0802 / 1409 / 2016	0.9 / 4.9 / 1.1 / 5.1	**21** TH	0219 / 0818 / 1431 / 2030	1.4 / 4.7 / 1.6 / 4.9
7 TH	0234 / 0846 / 1454 / 2102	1.1 / 4.8 / 1.3 / 4.9	**22** F	0254 / 0853 / 1506 / 2107	1.6 / 4.5 / 1.8 / 4.7
8 F	0323 / 0939 / 1545 / 2157	1.3 / 4.6 / 1.6 / 4.8	**23** SA	0331 / 0934 / 1545 / 2152	1.8 / 4.4 / 2.0 / 4.6
9 SA	0418 / 1042 / 1644 / 2302	1.5 / 4.4 / 1.8 / 4.7	**24** SU	0414 / 1024 / 1632 / 2244	1.9 / 4.3 / 2.1 / 4.5
10 SU	0525 / 1153 / 1756	1.7 / 4.4 / 1.9	**25** M	0507 / 1122 / 1732 / 2343	2.0 / 4.2 / 2.2 / 4.4
11 M	0014 / 0641 / 1308 / 1915	4.6 / 1.7 / 4.5 / 1.8	**26** TU	0612 / 1225 / 1843	2.0 / 4.3 / 2.2
12 TU	0129 / 0756 / 1419 / 2025	4.7 / 1.5 / 4.6 / 1.6	**27** W	0047 / 0722 / 1332 / 1954	4.5 / 1.9 / 4.4 / 2.0
13 W	0239 / 0859 / 1520 / 2124	4.9 / 1.3 / 4.9 / 1.3	**28** TH	0154 / 0828 / 1437 / 2057	4.5 / 1.7 / 4.6 / 1.8
14 TH	0340 / 0952 / 1613 / 2216	5.0 / 1.0 / 5.1 / 1.0	**29** F	0259 / 0924 / 1536 / 2151	4.7 / 1.5 / 4.8 / 1.5
15 F	0433 / 1040 / 1700 / 2303	5.2 / 0.9 / 5.3 / 0.8	**30** SA	0359 / 1015 / 1629 / 2240	4.9 / 1.2 / 5.0 / 1.2
			31 SU	0453 / 1102 / 1719 / 2326	5.0 / 1.0 / 5.2 / 0.9

JUNE

Day	Time	m	Day	Time	m
1 M ●	0543 / 1147 / 1805	5.1 / 0.9 / 5.3	**16**	0012 / 0623 / 1228 / 1837	1.1 / 5.0 / 1.2 / 5.2
2 TU	0012 / 0630 / 1232 / 1849	0.8 / 5.2 / 0.8 / 5.4	**17** W	0052 / 0659 / 1306 / 1911	1.1 / 4.9 / 1.2 / 5.2
3 W	0057 / 0717 / 1317 / 1933	0.7 / 5.1 / 0.8 / 5.4	**18** TH	0128 / 0732 / 1341 / 1942	1.2 / 4.8 / 1.3 / 5.1
4 TH	0143 / 0802 / 1402 / 2017	0.7 / 5.1 / 0.9 / 5.3	**19** F	0202 / 0803 / 1414 / 2013	1.3 / 4.7 / 1.4 / 5.0
5 F	0229 / 0849 / 1448 / 2103	0.8 / 4.9 / 1.0 / 5.2	**20** SA	0235 / 0833 / 1446 / 2044	1.4 / 4.7 / 1.6 / 4.9
6 SA	0317 / 0938 / 1537 / 2152	1.0 / 4.8 / 1.2 / 5.0	**21** SU	0308 / 0906 / 1520 / 2119	1.5 / 4.6 / 1.7 / 4.8
7 SU	0408 / 1031 / 1630 / 2247	1.2 / 4.7 / 1.4 / 4.9	**22** M	0344 / 0945 / 1559 / 2200	1.6 / 4.5 / 1.8 / 4.7
8 M	0504 / 1128 / 1729 / 2346	1.4 / 4.6 / 1.6 / 4.8	**23** TU	0425 / 1031 / 1644 / 2249	1.7 / 4.4 / 1.9 / 4.6
9 TU	0606 / 1230 / 1835	1.5 / 4.5 / 1.7	**24** W	0515 / 1126 / 1740 / 2348	1.8 / 4.4 / 2.0 / 4.5
10 W	0051 / 0713 / 1336 / 1945	4.7 / 1.6 / 4.6 / 1.7	**25** TH	0615 / 1230 / 1847	1.9 / 4.4 / 2.0
11 TH	0159 / 0820 / 1440 / 2051	4.7 / 1.5 / 4.7 / 1.6	**26** F	0055 / 0726 / 1340 / 2003	4.4 / 1.9 / 4.4 / 1.9
12 F	0304 / 0921 / 1539 / 2149	4.7 / 1.4 / 4.9 / 1.4	**27** SA	0209 / 0840 / 1451 / 2115	4.5 / 1.7 / 4.6 / 1.7
13 SA	0404 / 1014 / 1631 / 2241	4.8 / 1.3 / 5.0 / 1.2	**28** SU	0322 / 0945 / 1558 / 2217	4.6 / 1.5 / 4.9 / 1.4
14 SU	0456 / 1103 / 1718 / 2328	4.9 / 1.2 / 5.1 / 1.1	**29** M	0429 / 1042 / 1657 / 2310	4.8 / 1.2 / 5.1 / 1.0
15 M ○	0542 / 1147 / 1800	5.0 / 1.1 / 5.2	**30** TU	0528 / 1133 / 1750	5.0 / 0.9 / 5.3

JULY

Day	Time	m	Day	Time	m
1 W	0000 / 0620 / 1221 / 1839	0.7 / 5.2 / 0.7 / 5.5	**16**	0035 / 0644 / 1249 / 1856	1.1 / 4.9 / 1.1 / 5.2
2 TH	0047 / 0709 / 1307 / 1925	0.5 / 5.3 / 0.6 / 5.6	**17** F	0110 / 0716 / 1322 / 1927	1.1 / 4.9 / 1.1 / 5.2
3 F	0133 / 0755 / 1352 / 2010	0.4 / 5.3 / 0.6 / 5.5	**18** SA	0142 / 0745 / 1353 / 1955	1.1 / 4.8 / 1.2 / 5.1
4 SA	0218 / 0839 / 1436 / 2053	0.5 / 5.2 / 0.7 / 5.4	**19** SU	0212 / 0812 / 1423 / 2021	1.2 / 4.8 / 1.3 / 5.0
5 SU	0303 / 0923 / 1521 / 2137	0.6 / 5.1 / 0.8 / 5.3	**20** M	0242 / 0838 / 1453 / 2047	1.2 / 4.8 / 1.4 / 4.9
6 M	0348 / 1008 / 1608 / 2223	0.9 / 4.9 / 1.1 / 5.0	**21** TU	0313 / 0906 / 1527 / 2118	1.3 / 4.7 / 1.5 / 4.8
7 TU	0436 / 1056 / 1658 / 2314	1.2 / 4.7 / 1.4 / 4.8	**22** W	0349 / 0941 / 1605 / 2158	1.5 / 4.6 / 1.7 / 4.6
8 W	0528 / 1149 / 1754	1.5 / 4.6 / 1.7	**23** TH	0430 / 1029 / 1652 / 2253	1.7 / 4.5 / 1.8 / 4.5
9 TH	0011 / 0628 / 1250 / 1901	4.6 / 1.7 / 4.5 / 1.9	**24** F	0523 / 1134 / 1753	1.9 / 4.4 / 2.0
10 F	0117 / 0739 / 1357 / 2017	4.5 / 1.9 / 4.5 / 1.9	**25** SA	0005 / 0632 / 1252 / 1915	4.4 / 2.0 / 4.4 / 2.1
11 SA	0229 / 0852 / 1505 / 2128	4.6 / 1.8 / 4.6 / 1.8	**26** SU	0129 / 0802 / 1415 / 2049	4.3 / 2.0 / 4.5 / 1.9
12 SU	0338 / 0955 / 1606 / 2226	4.5 / 1.7 / 4.8 / 1.6	**27** M	0258 / 0925 / 1535 / 2201	4.5 / 1.7 / 4.8 / 1.5
13 M	0437 / 1047 / 1658 / 2315	4.6 / 1.5 / 5.0 / 1.3	**28** TU	0415 / 1027 / 1642 / 2258	4.7 / 1.3 / 5.1 / 1.0
14 TU ○	0526 / 1132 / 1743 / 2357	4.8 / 1.3 / 5.1 / 1.2	**29** W ●	0516 / 1120 / 1737 / 2347	5.1 / 0.8 / 5.4 / 0.6
15 W	0608 / 1212 / 1822	4.9 / 1.2 / 5.2	**30** TH	0609 / 1207 / 1827	5.3 / 0.5 / 5.7
			31 F	0033 / 0655 / 1252 / 1912	0.3 / 5.5 / 0.3 / 5.8

AUGUST

Day	Time	m	Day	Time	m
1 SA	0117 / 0739 / 1335 / 1954	0.2 / 5.5 / 0.2 / 5.8	**16**	0116 / 0723 / 1328 / 1933	0.9 / 5.1 / 1.0 / 5.2
2 SU	0200 / 0820 / 1417 / 2035	0.2 / 5.4 / 0.4 / 5.6	**17** M	0145 / 0748 / 1357 / 1957	1.0 / 5.0 / 1.1 / 5.1
3 M	0242 / 0900 / 1459 / 2115	0.4 / 5.3 / 0.6 / 5.4	**18** TU	0214 / 0810 / 1426 / 2017	1.1 / 4.9 / 1.2 / 5.0
4 TU	0323 / 0939 / 1541 / 2155	0.7 / 5.0 / 0.9 / 5.1	**19** W	0244 / 0830 / 1458 / 2040	1.2 / 4.8 / 1.3 / 4.9
5 W	0406 / 1021 / 1626 / 2239	1.1 / 4.8 / 1.3 / 4.8	**20** TH	0317 / 0857 / 1534 / 2113	1.4 / 4.7 / 1.5 / 4.7
6 TH	0451 / 1108 / 1715 / 2332	1.5 / 4.6 / 1.7 / 4.5	**21** F	0356 / 0941 / 1618 / 2207	1.6 / 4.6 / 1.8 / 4.5
7 F	0545 / 1206 / 1819	1.9 / 4.4 / 2.1	**22** SA	0445 / 1050 / 1716 / 2329	1.9 / 4.4 / 2.0 / 4.3
8 SA	0037 / 0657 / 1316 / 1947	4.3 / 2.2 / 4.3 / 2.2	**23** SU	0555 / 1218 / 1844	2.1 / 4.3 / 2.2
9 SU	0157 / 0828 / 1434 / 2112	4.2 / 2.2 / 4.4 / 2.0	**24** M	0106 / 0737 / 1352 / 2033	4.2 / 2.2 / 4.4 / 2.0
10 M	0317 / 0939 / 1544 / 2212	4.3 / 1.9 / 4.6 / 1.7	**25** TU	0245 / 0910 / 1519 / 2148	4.4 / 1.8 / 4.8 / 1.5
11 TU	0420 / 1031 / 1639 / 2258	4.5 / 1.6 / 4.9 / 1.4	**26** W	0403 / 1013 / 1627 / 2243	4.8 / 1.3 / 5.2 / 0.9
12 W	0509 / 1114 / 1724 / 2338	4.8 / 1.3 / 5.1 / 1.2	**27** TH	0502 / 1112 / 1721 / 2330	5.2 / 0.8 / 5.6 / 0.5
13 TH ○	0549 / 1152 / 1802	5.0 / 1.1 / 5.3	**28** F ●	0551 / 1149 / 1809	5.5 / 0.4 / 5.8
14 F	0013 / 0624 / 1226 / 1836	1.0 / 5.1 / 1.0 / 5.3	**29** SA	0014 / 0636 / 1233 / 1852	0.2 / 5.7 / 0.1 / 5.9
15 SA	0046 / 0655 / 1258 / 1906	0.9 / 5.1 / 0.9 / 5.3	**30** SU	0057 / 0717 / 1314 / 1933	0.1 / 5.7 / 0.1 / 5.9
			31 M	0137 / 0756 / 1355 / 2012	0.2 / 5.6 / 0.3 / 5.7

GENERAL — Strong N. winds, heavy rains, increase rate and duration of ebb. Strong S. winds increase rate and duration of flood.

RATE AND SET — Entrance: Flood begins +0100 Dover, Spring rate 1½ kn.; Ebb begins −0525 Dover. Spring rate 1½ kn. 3 cables N. of Breakwater Fort — stream is irregular.

PLYMOUTH (DEVONPORT) 21:173

Lat. 50°22'N. Long. 4°11'W.

HIGH & LOW WATER 1992

GMT   ADD 1 HOUR MARCH 29 — OCTOBER 25 FOR B.S.T

SEPTEMBER

Day	Time	m		Day	Time	m
1 TU	0217	0.4	**16** W	0147	1.0
	0832	5.4		0745	5.1
	1434	0.6		1402	1.1
	2048	5.4		1954	5.0
2 W	0256	0.8	**17** TH	0219	1.2
	0908	5.1		0804	5.0
	1514	1.0		1435	1.3
	2124	5.0		2013	4.9
3 TH	0335	1.3	**18** F	0253	1.4
	0944	4.9		0829	4.8
	1555	1.5		1512	1.5
	2204	4.7		2046	4.7
4 F	0416	1.7	**19** SA	0333	1.7
	1028	4.6		0914	4.6
	1640	1.9		1557	1.8
	2254	4.4		2145	4.4
5 SA	0504	2.1	**20** SU	0423	2.0
	1124	4.4		1028	4.5
	1740	2.3		1658	2.1
				2315	4.2
6 SU	0000	4.1	**21** M	0535	2.2
	0616	2.4		1159	4.4
	1236	4.3		1830	2.2
	1918	2.4			
7 M	0124	4.1	**22** TU	0055	4.2
	0802	2.4		0721	2.2
	1359	4.4		1335	4.5
	2052	2.2		2017	2.0
8 TU	0250	4.2	**23** W	0232	4.5
	0917	2.1		0851	1.8
	1514	4.6		1501	4.8
	2149	1.8		2128	1.4
9 W	0354	4.5	**24** TH	0345	4.9
	1007	1.7		0951	1.3
	1611	4.9		1606	5.3
	2232	1.5		2221	0.9
10 TH	0442	4.8	**25** F	0441	5.3
	1048	1.4		1041	0.8
	1656	5.1		1700	5.6
	2309	1.2		2307	0.5
11 F	0521	5.1	**26** SA	0529	5.6
	1124	1.1		1127	0.4
	1735	5.3		1747	5.8
	2343	0.9		● 2351	0.2
12 SA	0557	5.2	**27** SU	0612	5.7
	1157	0.9		1209	0.2
	1810	5.4		1830	5.9
O					
13 SU	0015	0.8	**28** M	0032	0.2
	0629	5.3		0652	5.8
	1230	0.9		1251	0.2
	1841	5.4		1909	5.8
14 M	0047	0.8	**29** TU	0113	0.3
	0658	5.3		0729	5.7
	1300	0.9		1331	0.4
	1909	5.3		1946	5.6
15 TU	0117	0.9	**30** W	0151	0.6
	0724	5.2		0804	5.5
	1331	1.0		1410	0.8
	1934	5.2		2021	5.3

OCTOBER

Day	Time	m		Day	Time	m
1 TH	0229	1.0	**16** F	0159	1.2
	0836	5.2		0752	5.1
	1448	1.2		1419	1.3
	2054	5.0		2007	4.9
2 F	0306	1.5	**17** SA	0237	1.5
	0910	4.9		0823	4.9
	1527	1.6		1500	1.5
	2131	4.6		2046	4.7
3 SA	0344	1.9	**18** SU	0321	1.7
	0951	4.7		0911	4.8
	1610	2.0		1549	1.8
	2218	4.3		2148	4.5
4 SU	0429	2.3	**19** M	0414	2.0
	1045	4.5		1022	4.6
	1706	2.3		1652	2.0
	2322	4.1		2312	4.3
5 M	0535	2.5	**20** TU	0527	2.2
	1153	4.3		1145	4.5
	1835	2.5		1818	2.1
6 TU	0041	4.1	**21** W	0043	4.4
	0718	2.5		0659	2.1
	1312	4.4		1314	4.7
	2011	2.3		1950	1.9
7 W	0205	4.2	**22** TH	0210	4.6
	0838	2.3		0822	1.8
	1429	4.6		1435	4.9
	2111	2.0		2059	1.4
8 TH	0312	4.5	**23** F	0319	4.9
	0924	1.9		0924	1.4
	1530	4.8		1540	5.2
	2155	1.6		2154	1.0
9 F	0403	4.8	**24** SA	0415	5.3
	1012	1.5		1016	0.9
	1618	5.1		1634	5.5
	2234	1.3		2242	0.7
10 SA	0446	5.1	**25** SU	0503	5.5
	1050	1.2		1103	0.6
	1700	5.3		1722	5.7
	2309	1.0		2326	0.5
11 SU	0524	5.3	**26** M	0547	5.7
	1125	1.0		1146	0.5
	1739	5.4		1805	5.7
O 2343	0.9				
12 M	0559	5.4	**27** TU	0008	0.5
	1159	0.9		0626	5.7
	1814	5.4		1229	0.5
				1845	5.7
13 TU	0017	0.9	**28** W	0049	0.6
	0631	5.4		0703	5.6
	1234	0.9		1309	0.7
	1845	5.4		1922	5.5
14 W	0051	0.9	**29** TH	0128	0.9
	0701	5.3		0738	5.5
	1307	1.0		1348	1.0
	1915	5.2		1956	5.2
15 TH	0124	1.0	**30** F	0205	1.3
	0727	5.2		0809	5.2
	1342	1.1		1426	1.3
	1941	5.1		2028	4.9
			31 SA	0241	1.6
				0841	5.0
				1504	1.7
				2103	4.6

NOVEMBER

Day	Time	m		Day	Time	m
1 SU	0318	1.9	**16** M	0315	1.6
	0919	4.8		0917	5.0
	1545	2.0		1546	1.6
	2146	4.4		2156	4.6
2 M	0400	2.2	**17** TU	0409	1.8
	1008	4.6		1017	4.8
	1634	2.2		1645	1.7
	2242	4.3		2304	4.5
3 TU	0455	2.4	**18** W	0513	2.0
	1108	4.5		1128	4.8
	1740	2.4		1756	1.8
	2350	4.2			
4 W	0611	2.5	**19** TH	0020	4.5
	1216	4.5		0629	2.0
	1903	2.3		1245	4.8
				1913	1.8
5 TH	0104	4.3	**20** F	0138	4.7
	0735	2.4		0746	1.8
	1328	4.6		1401	4.9
	2013	2.1		2024	1.6
6 F	0215	4.5	**21** SA	0246	4.9
	0838	2.1		0852	1.5
	1435	4.7		1509	5.1
	2106	1.8		2124	1.3
7 SA	0314	4.8	**22** SU	0345	5.2
	0928	1.8		0949	1.2
	1532	5.0		1607	5.3
	2151	1.5		2216	1.0
8 SU	0403	5.0	**23** M	0437	5.4
	1012	1.5		1040	1.0
	1621	5.2		1658	5.4
	2232	1.3		2303	0.9
9 M	0448	5.3	**24** TU	0522	5.5
	1052	1.2		1126	0.9
	1705	5.3		1744	5.5
	2312	1.1	● 2347	0.9
10 TU	0528	5.4	**25** W	0604	5.6
	1131	1.0		1210	0.9
	1746	5.4		1825	5.4
O 2350	1.0				
11 W	0606	5.5	**26** TH	0029	1.0
	1210	1.0		0642	5.6
	1825	5.3		1252	1.0
				1903	5.3
12 TH	0028	1.0	**27** F	0109	1.1
	0642	5.4		0716	5.4
	1249	1.0		1331	1.2
	1901	5.3		1937	5.1
13 F	0107	1.0	**28** SA	0146	1.3
	0716	5.4		0748	5.3
	1329	1.1		1409	1.4
	1937	5.1		2008	4.9
14 SA	0147	1.2	**29** SU	0222	1.6
	0751	5.3		0819	5.1
	1410	1.2		1445	1.6
	2015	5.0		2040	4.7
15 SU	0229	1.4	**30** M	0257	1.8
	0829	5.1		0853	5.0
	1455	1.4		1521	1.8
	2059	4.8		2117	4.6

DECEMBER

Day	Time	m		Day	Time	m
1 TU	0334	2.0	**16** W	0357	1.4
	0933	4.8		1006	5.1
	1602	2.0		1629	1.4
	2203	4.5		2246	4.7
2 W	0417	2.2	**17** TH	0452	1.6
	1022	4.7		1105	4.9
	1649	2.1		1727	1.6
	2258	4.4		2350	4.6
3 TH	0510	2.3	**18** F	0555	1.8
	1120	4.6		1212	4.8
	1748	2.2		1834	1.7
4 F	0002	4.4	**19** SA	0059	4.6
	0616	2.3		0706	1.9
	1225	4.6		1325	4.8
	1856	2.2		1945	1.7
5 SA	0110	4.5	**20** SU	0210	4.7
	0729	2.3		0819	1.8
	1333	4.6		1437	4.8
	2005	2.0		2053	1.6
6 SU	0217	4.6	**21** M	0315	4.9
	0835	2.0		0925	1.6
	1439	4.7		1542	4.9
	2104	1.8		2153	1.5
7 M	0317	4.9	**22** TU	0413	5.1
	0932	1.8		1021	1.4
	1540	4.9		1639	5.0
	2156	1.5		2244	1.3
8 TU	0411	5.1	**23** W	0502	5.3
	1022	1.5		1111	1.2
	1634	5.1		1727	5.1
	2243	1.3		2331	1.2
9 W	0500	5.3	**24** TH	0547	5.4
	1108	1.2		1156	1.1
	1723	5.2		1810	5.2
O 2328	1.1	●		
10 TH	0545	5.4	**25** F	0013	1.1
	1152	1.0		0625	5.5
	1809	5.3		1238	1.1
				1848	5.2
11 F	0012	1.0	**26** SA	0053	1.2
	0627	5.5		0700	5.4
	1236	0.9		1316	1.1
	1852	5.3		1921	5.1
12 SA	0055	0.9	**27** SU	0129	1.3
	0708	5.5		0731	5.3
	1320	0.9		1351	1.2
	1935	5.2		1951	5.0
13 SU	0138	1.0	**28** M	0203	1.4
	0749	5.5		0800	5.2
	1404	0.9		1424	1.4
	2017	5.1		2019	4.9
14 M	0222	1.1	**29** TU	0235	1.5
	0831	5.4		0829	5.1
	1449	1.0		1516	1.5
	2101	5.0		2049	4.8
15 TU	0308	1.2	**30** W	0307	1.7
	0915	5.2		0901	5.0
	1539	1.2		1529	1.7
	2150	4.8		2124	4.7
			31 TH	0342	1.8
				0939	4.8
				1606	1.8
				2208	4.6

To find H.W. Dover add 5h. 40 min.

TIDAL DIFFERENCES PAGE 21:170. TIDAL CURVE PAGE 21:169.

TIDAL STREAMS PAGES 21:28-21:40.

Datum of predictions: 3.22 m. below Ordnance Datum (Newlyn) or approx. L.A.T.

21:174 (TORBAY PORTS) DARTMOUTH

HIGH & LOW WATER 1992 Lat. 50°21'N. Long. 3°34'W.

GMT ADD 1 HOUR MARCH 29 — OCTOBER 25 FOR B.S.T.

JANUARY

Day	Time	m	Day	Time	m
1 W	0252 / 0849 / 1520 / 2117	4.1 / 1.8 / 4.0 / 1.6	16 TH	0151 / 0759 / 1430 / 2041	3.9 / 1.9 / 3.9 / 1.7
2 TH	0353 / 0950 / 1621 / 2213	4.2 / 1.6 / 4.1 / 1.5	17 F	0317 / 0921 / 1556 / 2153	4.1 / 1.5 / 4.1 / 1.3
3 F	0447 / 1042 / 1714 / 2300	4.4 / 1.4 / 4.3 / 1.3	18 SA	0430 / 1026 / 1708 / 2251	4.5 / 1.1 / 4.4 / 0.9
4 SA	0534 / 1127 / 1759 / ● 2342	4.6 / 1.2 / 4.4 / 1.2	19 SU	0532 / 1121 / 1815 / O 2342	4.8 / 0.7 / 4.7 / 0.6
5 SU	0617 / 1207 / 1839	4.7 / 1.1 / 4.4	20 M	0626 / 1209 / 1856	5.1 / 0.3 / 4.9
6 M	0020 / 0653 / 1244 / 1913	1.1 / 4.7 / 1.0 / 4.4	21 TU	0028 / 0712 / 1256 / 1940	0.3 / 5.2 / 0.1 / 5.0
7 TU	0056 / 0725 / 1317 / 1943	1.1 / 4.7 / 1.0 / 4.4	22 W	0114 / 0755 / 1339 / 2022	0.2 / 5.3 / 0.1 / 4.9
8 W	0129 / 0754 / 1348 / 2011	1.1 / 4.7 / 1.1 / 4.3	23 TH	0156 / 0836 / 1421 / 2102	0.3 / 5.2 / 0.2 / 4.8
9 TH	0159 / 0820 / 1419 / 2037	1.2 / 4.6 / 1.1 / 4.2	24 F	0237 / 0915 / 1502 / 2140	0.4 / 5.0 / 0.5 / 4.6
10 F	0229 / 0846 / 1450 / 2103	1.3 / 4.4 / 1.2 / 4.2	25 SA	0319 / 0953 / 1543 / 2219	0.7 / 4.7 / 0.8 / 4.3
11 SA	0302 / 0913 / 1525 / 2135	1.4 / 4.3 / 1.3 / 4.1	26 SU	0400 / 1032 / 1626 / 2301	1.1 / 4.4 / 1.2 / 4.1
12 SU	0339 / 0947 / 1604 / 2215	1.5 / 4.2 / 1.5 / 4.0	27 M	0445 / 1117 / 1712 / 2350	1.5 / 4.1 / 1.6 / 3.9
13 M	0423 / 1035 / 1652 / 2314	1.7 / 4.1 / 1.6 / 3.9	28 TU	0537 / 1212 / 1808	1.8 / 3.8 / 1.9
14 TU	0517 / 1140 / 1753	1.8 / 3.9 / 1.8	29 W	0049 / 0647 / 1320 / 1927	3.8 / 2.1 / 3.7 / 2.1
15 W	0027 / 0629 / 1300 / 1914	3.8 / 1.9 / 3.8 / 1.8	30 TH	0203 / 0817 / 1441 / 2051	3.8 / 2.1 / 3.7 / 2.0
			31 F	0318 / 0933 / 1555 / 2155	4.0 / 1.8 / 3.8 / 1.7

FEBRUARY

Day	Time	m	Day	Time	m
1 SA	0422 / 1026 / 1655 / 2244	4.2 / 1.5 / 4.1 / 1.4	16 SU	0418 / 1015 / 1658 / 2239	4.4 / 1.0 / 4.4 / 0.9
2 SU	0515 / 1111 / 1744 / 2325	4.4 / 1.2 / 4.3 / 1.2	17 M	0520 / 1108 / 1754 / 2327	4.8 / 0.5 / 4.7 / 0.4
3 M	0559 / 1149 / 1824 / ●	4.6 / 1.0 / 4.4	18 TU	0613 / 1154 / 1842 / O	5.1 / 0.1 / 5.0
4 TU	0002 / 0637 / 1224 / 1858	1.0 / 4.7 / 0.8 / 4.5	19 W	0012 / 0657 / 1238 / 1923	0.1 / 5.3 / -0.1 / 5.1
5 W	0037 / 0709 / 1257 / 1929	0.9 / 4.8 / 0.8 / 4.5	20 TH	0056 / 0738 / 1319 / 2002	0.0 / 5.3 / -0.1 / 5.0
6 TH	0109 / 0739 / 1327 / 1956	0.8 / 4.7 / 0.8 / 4.5	21 F	0135 / 0815 / 1358 / 2038	0.1 / 5.2 / 0.1 / 4.9
7 F	0138 / 0804 / 1356 / 2018	0.9 / 4.6 / 0.8 / 4.4	22 SA	0214 / 0851 / 1435 / 2111	0.3 / 4.9 / 0.4 / 4.6
8 SA	0208 / 0824 / 1427 / 2038	0.9 / 4.5 / 0.9 / 4.3	23 SU	0252 / 0924 / 1512 / 2142	0.6 / 4.6 / 0.8 / 4.4
9 SU	0239 / 0845 / 1458 / 2059	1.1 / 4.4 / 1.1 / 4.2	24 M	0329 / 0956 / 1549 / 2217	1.0 / 4.3 / 1.3 / 4.1
10 M	0313 / 0911 / 1534 / 2134	1.2 / 4.3 / 1.3 / 4.1	25 TU	0408 / 1035 / 1628 / 2302	1.5 / 4.0 / 1.7 / 3.9
11 TU	0352 / 0952 / 1618 / 2228	1.4 / 4.1 / 1.5 / 3.9	26 W	0453 / 1127 / 1717	1.9 / 3.7 / 2.0
12 W	0442 / 1058 / 1714 / 2348	1.7 / 3.8 / 1.8 / 3.8	27 TH	0001 / 0556 / 1235 / 1835	3.7 / 2.2 / 3.5 / 2.3
13 TH	0551 / 1229 / 1837	1.9 / 3.7 / 2.0	28 F	0113 / 0744 / 1400 / 2024	3.7 / 2.2 / 3.5 / 2.2
14 F	0119 / 0733 / 1413 / 2021	3.8 / 2.0 / 3.7 / 1.8	29 SA	0238 / 0911 / 1527 / 2133	3.8 / 1.9 / 3.7 / 1.8
15 SA	0257 / 0910 / 1548 / 2141	4.0 / 1.6 / 4.0 / 1.4			

MARCH

Day	Time	m	Day	Time	m
1 SU	0351 / 1004 / 1631 / 2221	4.0 / 1.6 / 4.0 / 1.5	16 M	0400 / 0957 / 1642 / 2219	4.4 / 0.9 / 4.4 / 0.8
2 M	0448 / 1047 / 1720 / 2301	4.3 / 1.2 / 4.2 / 1.1	17 TU	0501 / 1048 / 1734 / 2307	4.8 / 0.4 / 4.7 / 0.0
3 TU	0533 / 1123 / 1800 / 2337	4.6 / 0.9 / 4.5 / 0.9	18 W	0552 / 1132 / 1821 / 2350	5.1 / 0.1 / 5.0 / 0.1
4 W	0614 / 1156 / 1837	4.7 / 0.7 / 4.6	19 TH	0637 / 1214 / 1901	5.2 / -0.1 / 5.1
5 TH	0010 / 0648 / 1230 / 1907	0.7 / 4.8 / 0.6 / 4.6	20 F	0033 / 0716 / 1255 / 1937	0.0 / 5.2 / 0.0 / 5.0
6 F	0043 / 0718 / 1301 / 1935	0.6 / 4.8 / 0.6 / 4.6	21 SA	0113 / 0751 / 1332 / 2009	0.1 / 5.1 / 0.2 / 4.9
7 SA	0115 / 0744 / 1331 / 1959	0.6 / 4.7 / 0.6 / 4.5	22 SU	0149 / 0824 / 1408 / 2040	0.3 / 4.8 / 0.5 / 4.7
8 SU	0145 / 0807 / 1403 / 2017	0.7 / 4.5 / 0.8 / 4.4	23 M	0226 / 0853 / 1442 / 2108	0.7 / 4.5 / 0.9 / 4.4
9 M	0218 / 0825 / 1435 / 2038	0.9 / 4.4 / 1.0 / 4.3	24 TU	0300 / 0924 / 1516 / 2140	1.1 / 4.2 / 1.4 / 4.2
10 TU	0252 / 0850 / 1512 / 2110	1.1 / 4.2 / 1.2 / 4.1	25 W	0336 / 1000 / 1551 / 2222	1.5 / 3.9 / 1.7 / 3.9
11 W	0332 / 0932 / 1555 / 2206	1.3 / 4.0 / 1.5 / 3.9	26 TH	0417 / 1050 / 1635 / 2319	1.9 / 3.6 / 2.1 / 3.7
12 TH	0423 / 1045 / 1652 / 2330	1.6 / 3.7 / 1.8 / 3.8	27 F	0514 / 1156 / 1744	2.1 / 3.4 / 2.3
13 F	0533 / 1221 / 1818	1.9 / 3.6 / 2.0	28 SA	0028 / 0654 / 1316 / 1939	3.6 / 2.2 / 3.4 / 2.3
14 SA	0103 / 0721 / 1406 / 2008	3.8 / 1.9 / 3.6 / 1.8	29 SU	0148 / 0831 / 1443 / 2056	3.7 / 2.0 / 3.6 / 1.9
15 SU	0242 / 0856 / 1537 / 2123	4.0 / 1.5 / 4.0 / 1.3	30 M	0306 / 0926 / 1551 / 2146	3.9 / 1.6 / 3.9 / 1.5
			31 TU	0408 / 1010 / 1643 / 2227	4.2 / 1.2 / 4.2 / 1.2

APRIL

Day	Time	m	Day	Time	m
1 W	0457 / 1048 / 1726 / 2305	4.5 / 0.9 / 4.5 / 0.9	16 TH	0525 / 1106 / 1753 / 2326	4.9 / 0.3 / 4.9 / 0.3
2 TH	0541 / 1124 / 1805 / 2340	4.6 / 0.7 / 4.6 / 0.7	17 F	0611 / 1148 / 1835 / O	5.0 / 0.2 / 5.0
3 F	0620 / 1158 / 1841 / ●	-4.7 / 0.5 / 4.7	18 SA	0008 / 0651 / 1230 / 1910	0.2 / 5.0 / 0.3 / 4.9
4 SA	0015 / 0654 / 1234 / 1911	0.6 / 4.7 / 0.5 / 4.7	19 SU	0049 / 0727 / 1307 / 1942	0.3 / 4.8 / 0.5 / 4.8
5 SU	0050 / 0725 / 1308 / 1939	0.6 / 4.7 / 0.6 / 4.6	20 M	0127 / 0759 / 1342 / 2011	0.6 / 4.6 / 0.8 / 4.6
6 M	0125 / 0753 / 1342 / 2006	0.6 / 4.5 / 0.7 / 4.5	21 TU	0202 / 0828 / 1416 / 2040	0.9 / 4.3 / 1.1 / 4.4
7 TU	0201 / 0820 / 1419 / 2033	0.8 / 4.3 / 0.9 / 4.4	22 W	0236 / 0858 / 1449 / 2112	1.2 / 4.1 / 1.4 / 4.2
8 W	0239 / 0852 / 1458 / 2111	1.0 / 4.1 / 1.2 / 4.2	23 TH	0311 / 0934 / 1524 / 2152	1.5 / 3.8 / 1.7 / 4.0
9 TH	0323 / 0943 / 1545 / 2210	1.3 / 3.9 / 1.5 / 4.0	24 F	0350 / 1020 / 1605 / 2244	1.8 / 3.6 / 2.0 / 3.8
10 F	0417 / 1055 / 1645 / 2326	1.6 / 3.7 / 1.8 / 3.9	25 SA	0441 / 1120 / 1704 / 2345	2.0 / 3.5 / 2.2 / 3.7
11 SA	0529 / 1220 / 1809	1.8 / 3.6 / 1.9	26 SU	0553 / 1228 / 1830	2.1 / 3.5 / 2.2
12 SU	0049 / 0706 / 1352 / 1945	3.9 / 2.0 / 3.7 / 1.7	27 M	0053 / 0723 / 1343 / 1955	3.7 / 2.0 / 3.6 / 2.0
13 M	0218 / 0829 / 1513 / 2057	4.0 / 1.4 / 4.0 / 1.3	28 TU	0206 / 0831 / 1454 / 2056	3.9 / 1.7 / 3.8 / 1.7
14 TU	0333 / 0930 / 1616 / 2153	4.3 / 0.9 / 4.4 / 0.9	29 W	0314 / 0922 / 1553 / 2144	4.1 / 1.4 / 4.1 / 1.3
15 W	0434 / 1020 / 1708 / 2242	4.7 / 0.5 / 4.7 / 0.5	30 TH	0411 / 1006 / 1644 / 2227	4.3 / 1.1 / 4.4 / 1.0

To find H.W. Dover add 5 h. 10 min.

NO TIDAL DIFFERENCES ARE GIVEN.

See note on tides between Dartmouth and Portland p. 21:186.

Datum of predictions: 2.62 m. below Ordnance Datum (Newlyn) or approx. L.A.T.

DARTMOUTH (TORBAY PORTS) 21:175

Lat. 50°21'N. Long. 3°34'W. **HIGH & LOW WATER 1992**

GMT ADD 1 HOUR MARCH 29 — OCTOBER 25 FOR B.S.T.

MAY

Day	Time	m	Day	Time	m
1 F	0501	4.5	16 SA	0544	4.7
	1048	0.8		1123	0.6
	1729	4.6		1806	4.8
	2308	0.8		O 2345	
2 SA	0547	4.6	17 SU	0627	4.6
	1128	0.6		1205	0.6
	1811	4.7		1846	4.8
	● 2348	0.6			
3 SU	0630	4.6	18 M	0027	0.6
	1207	0.6		0704	4.6
	1849	4.7		1245	0.8
				1919	4.7
4 M	0027	0.6	19 TU	0107	0.8
	0708	4.6		0739	4.4
	1247	0.6		1322	1.0
	1925	4.7		1950	4.6
5 TU	0109	0.6	20 W	0143	1.0
	0745	4.5		0809	4.2
	1327	0.7		1356	1.2
	2000	4.6		2020	4.4
6 W	0149	0.7	21 TH	0218	1.2
	0824	4.3		0840	4.1
	1408	0.9		1429	1.4
	2038	4.5		2052	4.3
7 TH	0232	0.9	22 F	0252	1.4
	0907	4.2		0914	3.9
	1452	1.1		1504	1.6
	2123	4.3		2128	4.1
8 F	0321	1.1	23 SA	0328	1.6
	0959	4.0		0954	3.8
	1542	1.4		1542	1.8
	2216	4.2		2211	4.0
9 SA	0415	1.3	24 SU	0411	1.7
	1100	3.8		1043	3.7
	1640	1.6		1628	1.9
	2320	4.1		2302	3.9
10 SU	0521	1.5	25 M	0503	1.8
	1209	3.8		1139	3.6
	1751	1.7		1727	2.0
11 M	0030	4.0	26 TU	0000	3.8
	0637	1.5		0607	1.8
	1323	3.9		1241	3.7
	1911	1.6		1839	2.0
12 TU	0145	4.1	27 W	0102	3.9
	0752	1.3		0718	1.7
	1437	4.0		1348	3.8
	2021	1.4		1950	1.8
13 W	0257	4.3	28 TH	0211	3.9
	0856	1.1		0824	1.5
	1540	4.3		1455	4.0
	2121	1.1		2054	1.6
14 TH	0400	4.4	29 F	0318	4.1
	0950	0.8		0921	1.3
	1634	4.5		1556	4.2
	2214	0.8		2149	1.3
15 F	0455	4.6	30 SA	0420	4.3
	1039	0.7		1013	1.0
	1723	4.7		1651	4.4
	2302	0.6		2239	1.0
			31 SU	0516	4.4
				1101	0.8
				1743	4.6
				2325	0.7

JUNE

Day	Time	m	Day	Time	m
1 M	0607	4.5	16 TU	0011	0.9
	1146	0.7		0648	4.5
	1830	4.7		1227	1.0
	●			1901	4.6
2 TU	0011	0.6	17 W	0052	0.9
	0655	4.6		0723	4.3
	1232	0.6		1306	1.0
	1913	4.8		1935	4.6
3 W	0057	0.5	18 TH	0128	1.0
	0740	4.5		0755	4.2
	1317	0.6		1340	1.1
	1956	4.8		2005	4.5
4 TH	0142	0.5	19 F	0201	1.1
	0824	4.5		0825	4.1
	1401	0.7		1413	1.2
	2039	4.7		2035	4.4
5 F	0228	0.6	20 SA	0233	1.2
	0910	4.3		0854	4.1
	1446	0.8		1444	1.4
	2124	4.6		2105	4.3
6 SA	0315	0.8	21 SU	0306	1.3
	0958	4.2		0927	4.0
	1534	1.0		1518	1.5
	2211	4.4		2139	4.2
7 SU	0405	1.0	22 M	0341	1.4
	1049	4.1		1005	3.9
	1627	1.2		1556	1.6
	2305	4.3		2219	4.1
8 M	0500	1.2	23 TU	0422	1.5
	1145	4.0		1049	3.8
	1725	1.4		1640	1.7
				2307	4.0
9 TU	0002	4.2	24 W	0511	1.6
	0601	1.3		1143	3.8
	1246	3.9		1735	1.8
	1831	1.5			
10 W	0106	4.1	25 TH	0004	3.9
	0709	1.4		0610	1.7
	1352	4.0		1246	3.8
	1941	1.5		1843	1.8
11 TH	0216	4.1	26 F	0110	3.8
	0806	1.3		0722	1.7
	1458	4.1		1356	3.9
	2048	1.4		1959	1.7
12 F	0323	4.1	27 SA	0226	3.9
	0918	1.2		0837	1.5
	1559	4.3		1510	4.0
	2147	1.2		2112	1.5
13 SA	0425	4.2	28 SU	0342	4.0
	1012	1.1		0943	1.3
	1653	4.4		1619	4.3
	2240	1.0		2215	1.2
14 SU	0519	4.3	29 M	0451	4.2
	1102	1.0		1041	1.0
	1742	4.5		1720	4.5
	2327	0.9		2309	0.8
15 M	0606	4.4	30 TU	0552	4.4
	1146	0.9		1132	0.7
	1825	4.6		1815	4.7
	○			● 2359	0.5

JULY

Day	Time	m	Day	Time	m
1 W	0645	4.6	16 TH	0035	0.9
	1220	0.5		0708	4.3
	1903	4.9		1249	0.9
				1920	4.6
2 TH	0047	0.3	17 F	0110	0.9
	0733	4.7		0739	4.3
	1307	0.4		1322	0.9
	1948	5.0		1950	4.6
3 F	0132	0.2	18 SA	0141	0.9
	0817	4.7		0808	4.3
	1351	0.4		1352	1.0
	2032	4.9		2017	4.5
4 SA	0217	0.3	19 SU	0211	1.0
	0900	4.6		0834	4.2
	1434	0.5		1422	1.1
	2114	4.8		2043	4.4
5 SU	0301	0.4	20 M	0240	1.0
	0943	4.5		0859	4.2
	1519	0.6		1451	1.2
	2157	4.7		2108	4.3
6 M	0345	0.7	21 TU	0311	1.1
	1027	4.3		0927	4.1
	1605	0.9		1525	1.3
	2242	4.4		2138	4.2
7 TU	0432	1.0	22 W	0346	1.3
	1114	4.1		1001	4.0
	1654	1.1		1602	1.5
	2332	4.2		2217	4.0
8 W	0524	1.3	23 TH	0427	1.5
	1205	4.0		1048	3.9
	1749	1.5		1648	1.6
				2311	3.9
9 TH	0027	4.0	24 F	0519	1.7
	0623	1.5		1151	3.8
	1305	3.9		1748	1.8
	1857	1.7			
10 F	0133	3.9	25 SA	0021	3.8
	0735	1.7		0628	1.8
	1414	3.9		1307	3.8
	2013	1.7		1911	1.9
11 SA	0247	3.8	26 SU	0145	3.7
	0849	1.6		0758	1.8
	1524	4.0		1433	3.9
	2125	1.6		2046	1.7
12 SU	0358	3.9	27 M	0317	3.9
	0953	1.5		0922	1.5
	1627	4.2		1555	4.2
	2224	1.4		2159	1.3
13 M	0459	4.0	28 TU	0437	4.1
	1046	1.3		1025	1.1
	1728	4.4		1704	4.5
	2314	1.1		2257	1.0
14 TU	0550	4.2	29 W	0540	4.5
	1131	1.1		1119	0.6
	1801	4.8		1801	4.8
	○ 2356	1.0		2346	0.4
15 W	0633	4.3	30 TH	0634	4.7
	1211	1.0		1206	0.3
	1847	4.6		1852	5.1
			31 F	0033	0.1
				0719	4.9
				1252	0.1
				1936	5.2

AUGUST

Day	Time	m	Day	Time	m
1 SA	0117	0.0	16 SU	0116	0.7
	0802	4.9		0746	4.5
	1334	0.0		1328	0.8
	2016	5.2		1956	4.6
2 SU	0159	0.0	17 M	0144	0.8
	0842	4.8		0810	4.4
	1416	0.2		1356	0.9
	2056	5.0		2019	4.5
3 M	0240	0.2	18 TU	0213	0.9
	0921	4.7		0832	4.3
	1457	0.4		1425	1.0
	2136	4.8		2039	4.4
4 TU	0321	0.5	19 W	0242	1.0
	0959	4.4		0852	4.2
	1538	0.7		1456	1.1
	2214	4.5		2101	4.3
5 W	0403	0.9	20 TH	0315	1.2
	1040	4.2		0918	4.1
	1623	1.1		1531	1.3
	2257	4.2		2134	4.1
6 TH	0447	1.3	21 F	0353	1.4
	1126	4.0		1001	4.0
	1711	1.5		1615	1.6
	2349	3.9		2226	3.9
7 F	0540	1.7	22 SA	0441	1.7
	1222	3.8		1108	3.8
	1814	1.9		1712	1.8
				2346	3.7
8 SA	0052	3.7	23 SU	0550	1.9
	0653	2.0		1234	3.7
	1332	3.7		1840	2.0
	1943	2.0			
9 SU	0214	3.6	24 M	0121	3.6
	0824	2.0		0733	2.0
	1452	3.8		1409	3.8
	2109	1.8		2030	1.8
10 M	0337	3.7	25 TU	0304	3.8
	0937	1.7		0907	1.6
	1604	4.0		1539	4.2
	2210	1.5		2146	1.3
11 TU	0442	3.9	26 W	0424	4.2
	1030	1.4		1011	1.1
	1701	4.3		1649	4.6
	2257	1.2		2242	0.7
12 W	0532	4.2	27 TH	0525	4.6
	1113	1.1		1102	0.6
	1748	4.5		1745	5.0
	2337	1.0		2329	0.3
13 TH	0614	4.4	28 F	0616	4.9
	1151	0.9		1148	0.2
	1827	4.7		1834	5.2
	O				
14 F	0012	0.8	29 SA	0013	0.0
	0649	4.5		0700	5.1
	1225	0.8		1233	-0.1
	1900	4.7		1916	5.3
15 SA	0046	0.7	30 SU	0057	-0.1
	0719	4.5		0740	5.1
	1258	0.7		1314	-0.1
	1930	4.7		1956	5.3
			31 M	0136	0.0
				0818	5.0
				1354	0.1
				2034	5.1

GENERAL — Little stream, but open to winds from SE. to SSW.

RATE AND SET — Coastal, off Dartmouth; NE. begins +0540 Dover; SW begins –0100 Dover. Entrance — Dartmouth; Ingoing begins +0055 Dover; Outgoing begins –0515 Dover. Off entrance a possible SW. set during flood and NE. set during ebb. Flood stream weak off West shore of entrance, but increases inwards to 3½ kn. in narrows.

21:176 (TORBAY PORTS) DARTMOUTH

HIGH & LOW WATER 1992 Lat. 50°21'N. Long. 3°34'W.

GMT ADD 1 HOUR MARCH 29 — OCTOBER 25 FOR B.S.T.

SEPTEMBER

Day	Time	m	Day	Time	m
1 TU	0216	0.2	**16**	0146	0.8
	0853	4.8		0808	4.5
	1432	0.4		1401	0.9
	2109	4.8		2016	4.4
2 W	0254	0.6	**17**	0218	1.0
	0929	4.5		0826	4.4
	1512	0.8	TH	1433	1.1
	2144	4.4		2035	4.3
3 TH	0332	1.1	**18**	0251	1.2
	1004	4.3		0851	4.2
	1552	1.3	F	1510	1.3
	2223	4.1		2107	4.1
4 F	0413	1.5	**19**	0330	1.5
	1047	4.0		0935	4.0
	1636	1.7	SA	1554	1.6
	2312	3.8		2205	3.8
5 SA	0500	1.9	**20**	0420	1.8
	1141	3.8		1047	3.9
	1735	2.1	SU	1654	1.9
				2333	3.6
6 SU	0016	3.5	**21**	0530	2.0
	0611	2.2		1215	3.8
	1251	3.7	M	1826	2.0
	1914	2.2			
7 M	0140	3.5	**22**	0110	3.6
	0758	2.2		0717	2.0
	1416	3.8	TU	1351	3.9
	2049	2.2		2013	1.8
8 TU	0309	3.6	**23**	0250	3.9
	0914	1.9		0848	1.6
	1533	4.0	W	1520	4.2
	2147	1.6		2125	1.2
9 W	0415	3.9	**24**	0406	4.3
	1005	1.5		0949	1.1
	1632	4.3	TH	1627	4.7
	2231	1.3		2219	0.7
10 TH	0504	4.2	**25**	0503	4.7
	1047	1.2		1040	0.6
	1719	4.5	F	1723	5.0
	2308	1.0		2306	0.3
11 F	0545	4.5	**26**	0553	5.0
	1123	0.9		1126	0.2
	1759	4.7	SA	1812	5.2
	2342	0.7		2350	0.0
12 SA	0622	4.6	**27**	0637	5.1
	1156	0.7		1208	0.0
	1835	4.8	SU	1855	5.3
O					
13 SU	0014	0.6	**28**	0032	0.0
	0654	4.7		0716	5.2
	1230	0.7	M	1251	0.0
	1905	4.8		1933	5.2
14 M	0047	0.6	**29**	0113	0.1
	0722	4.7		0752	5.1
	1300	0.7		1330	0.2
	1933	4.7		2008	5.0
15 TU	0117	0.7	**30**	0150	0.4
	0747	4.6		0826	4.9
	1330	0.8	W	1409	0.6
	1957	4.6		2043	4.7

OCTOBER

Day	Time	m	Day	Time	m
1	0228	0.8	**16**	0158	1.0
	0857	4.6		0814	4.5
TH	1446	1.0	F	1418	1.1
	2115	4.4		2029	4.3
2	0304	1.3	**17**	0235	1.3
	0931	4.3		0845	4.3
F	1525	1.4	SA	1458	1.3
	2151	4.0		2107	4.1
3	0341	1.7	**18**	0319	1.5
	1010	4.1		0932	4.2
SA	1607	1.8	SU	1546	1.6
	2237	3.7		2207	3.9
4	0426	2.1	**19**	0411	1.8
	1103	3.9		1041	4.0
SU	1702	2.1	M	1648	1.8
	2339	3.5		2330	3.7
5	0530	2.3	**20**	0523	2.0
	1209	3.7		1202	3.9
M	1831		TU	1813	1.9
6	0056	3.5	**21**	0058	3.8
	0714	2.3		0655	1.9
TU	1327	3.8	W	1329	4.1
	2007	2.1		1946	1.7
7	0222	3.6	**22**	0227	4.0
	0835	2.1		0818	1.6
W	1447	4.0	TH	1453	4.3
	2108	1.8		2056	1.2
8	0331	3.9	**23**	0339	4.3
	0928	1.7		0921	1.2
TH	1550	4.2	F	1600	4.6
	2153	1.4		2152	0.8
9	0424	4.2	**24**	0437	4.7
	1010	1.3		1014	0.7
F	1640	4.5	SA	1656	4.9
	2233	1.1		2241	0.5
10	0509	4.5	**25**	0526	4.9
	1049	1.0		1102	0.4
SA	1723	4.7	SU	1746	5.1
	2308	0.8	●	2325	0.3
11	0548	4.7	**26**	0612	5.1
	1124	0.8		1145	0.3
SU	1803	4.8	M	1830	5.1
O	2342	0.7			
12	0624	4.8	**27**	0007	0.3
	1158	0.7		0651	5.1
M	1839	4.8	TU	1228	0.3
				1909	5.1
13	0016	0.7	**28**	0049	0.4
	0655	4.8		0727	5.0
TU	1234	0.7	W	1309	0.5
	1909	4.8		1945	4.9
14	0051	0.7	**29**	0128	0.7
	0725	4.7		0801	4.9
W	1307	0.8	TH	1347	0.8
	1939	4.6		2018	4.6
15	0124	0.8	**30**	0204	1.1
	0750	4.6		0831	4.6
TH	1341	0.9	F	1425	1.1
	2004	4.5		2050	4.3
			31	0239	1.4
				0902	4.4
			SA	1502	1.5
				2124	4.0

NOVEMBER

Day	Time	m	Day	Time	m
1	0316	1.7	**16**	0313	1.4
	0939	4.2		0937	4.4
SU	1542	1.8	M	1543	1.4
	2205	3.8		2215	4.0
2	0357	2.0	**17**	0406	1.6
	1027	4.0		1036	4.2
M	1630	2.0	TU	1641	1.5
	2300	3.7		2322	3.9
3	0451	2.2	**18**	0509	1.8
	1126	3.9		1145	4.2
TU	1735	2.2	W	1751	1.6
4	0006	3.6	**19**	0036	3.9
	0606	2.3		0624	1.8
W	1232	3.9	TH	1300	4.2
	1859	2.1		1909	1.6
5	0119	3.7	**20**	0154	4.1
	0731	2.2		0742	1.6
TH	1344	4.0	F	1418	4.3
	2009	1.9		2020	1.4
6	0233	3.9	**21**	0305	4.3
	0835	1.9		0849	1.3
F	1453	4.1	SA	1528	4.5
	2103	1.6		2121	1.1
7	0333	4.2	**22**	0406	4.6
	0925	1.6		0947	1.0
SA	1552	4.4	SU	1628	4.7
	2149	1.3		2214	0.8
8	0424	4.4	**23**	0459	4.8
	1010	1.3		1039	0.8
SU	1643	4.6	M	1721	4.8
	2231	1.1		2302	0.7
9	0511	4.7	**24**	0546	4.9
	1051	1.0		1125	0.7
M	1728	4.7	TU	1808	4.9
	2311	0.9	●	2346	0.7
10	0552	4.8	**25**	0629	5.0
	1130	0.9		1209	0.7
TU	1811	4.8	W	1850	4.8
O	2349	0.8			
11	0631	4.9	**26**	0028	0.8
	1209	0.8		0706	5.0
W	1850	4.7	TH	1252	0.8
				1927	4.7
12	0027	0.8	**27**	0109	0.9
	0706	4.9		0739	4.8
TH	1249	0.8	F	1330	1.0
	1925	4.7		2000	4.5
13	0107	0.8	**28**	0145	1.1
	0739	4.9		0810	4.7
F	1329	0.9	SA	1408	1.2
	2000	4.5		2030	4.3
14	0146	1.0	**29**	0221	1.4
	0813	4.7		0841	4.5
SA	1409	1.0	SU	1443	1.4
	2037	4.4		2101	4.1
15	0228	1.2	**30**	0255	1.6
	0851	4.3		0914	4.4
SU	1453	1.2	M	1519	1.6
	2120	4.2		2137	4.0

DECEMBER

Day	Time	m	Day	Time	m
1	0331	1.8	**16**	0354	1.2
	0953	4.2		1025	4.5
TU	1559	1.8	W	1626	1.2
	2222	3.9		2304	4.1
2	0414	2.0	**17**	0448	1.4
	1041	4.1		1123	4.3
W	1645	1.9	TH	1723	1.4
	2316	3.8			
3	0506	2.1	**18**	0006	4.0
	1137	4.0		0550	1.6
TH	1743	2.0	F	1228	4.2
				1830	1.5
4	0018	3.8	**19**	0114	4.0
	0611	2.1		0702	1.7
F	1241	4.0	SA	1341	4.2
	1852	2.0		1941	1.5
5	0125	3.9	**20**	0227	4.1
	0725	2.1		0815	1.6
SA	1349	4.0	SU	1455	4.2
	2001	1.8		2050	1.4
6	0235	4.0	**21**	0335	4.3
	0832	1.8		0922	1.4
SU	1457	4.1	M	1602	4.3
	2101	1.6		2151	1.3
7	0337	4.3	**22**	0434	4.5
	0930	1.6		1019	1.2
M	1600	4.3	TU	1701	4.5
	2154	1.3		2243	1.1
8	0432	4.5	**23**	0525	4.7
	1020	1.3		1110	1.0
TU	1656	4.5	W	1751	4.5
	2242	1.1		2330	1.0
9	0523	4.8	**24**	0612	4.8
	1107	1.0		1155	0.9
W	1747	4.6	TH	1835	4.6
O	2327	0.9	●		
10	0610	4.8	**25**	0012	0.9
	1151	0.8		0650	4.9
TH	1834	4.7	F	1232	0.9
				1912	4.6
11	0011	0.8	**26**	0053	1.0
	0652	4.9		0724	4.8
F	1236	0.7	SA	1316	0.9
	1916	4.7		1944	4.5
12	0055	0.7	**27**	0129	1.1
	0732	4.9		0754	4.7
SA	1320	0.7	SU	1350	1.0
	1958	4.6		2013	4.4
13	0137	0.8	**28**	0202	1.2
	0811	4.9		0822	4.6
SU	1403	0.7	M	1423	1.2
	2039	4.5		2041	4.3
14	0221	0.9	**29**	0233	1.3
	0852	4.8		0851	4.5
M	1447	0.8	TU	1454	1.3
	2122	4.4		2110	4.2
15	0306	1.0	**30**	0305	1.5
	0936	4.6		0922	4.4
TU	1534	1.0	W	1527	1.5
	2209	4.2		2144	4.1
			31	0339	1.6
				0959	4.2
			TH	1603	1.6
				2227	4.0

To find H.W. Dover add 5 h. 10 min.

NO TIDAL DIFFERENCES ARE GIVEN.

See note on tides between Dartmouth and Portland p. 21:186.

Datum of predictions: 2.62 m. below Ordnance Datum (Newlyn) or approx. L.A.T.

APPROACHES TO PORTLAND
TIDAL STREAMS

These thirteen charts show tidal streams at hourly intervals commencing 6h. before and ending 6h. after H.W. Devonport see pages 21:171-21:173. Times before and after H.W. Dover are also indicated. For Dover H.W. Times see pages 21:41-21:43.

Figures shown against the arrows give mean neap and spring rates in tenths of a knot, for example 28.57 indicates a mean neap rate of 2.8 knots and a mean spring rate of 5.7 knots.

The approximate extent of Portland Race is indicated by a dotted line. Although it is prudent to avoid the Race altogether and pass outside, under normal conditions small vessels can pass 'inside the Race' where there is generally a channel within about $\frac{1}{4}$ mile of the Bill.

If possible arrive at slack water. Bound West inside the Race (unless with full power) round the Bill from about $\frac{1}{2}$ hour before H.W. Dover to $2\frac{1}{2}$h. after H.W. Dover. Bound East, round Bill from about $4\frac{1}{2}$h. after H.W. Dover to 5h. before H.W. Dover. Study the chartlets carefully.

Produced from portion(s) of BA Tidal Stream Atlases with the sanction of the Controller, H.M. Stationery Office and of the Hydrographer of the Navy.

0h. 45min. after HW DOVER

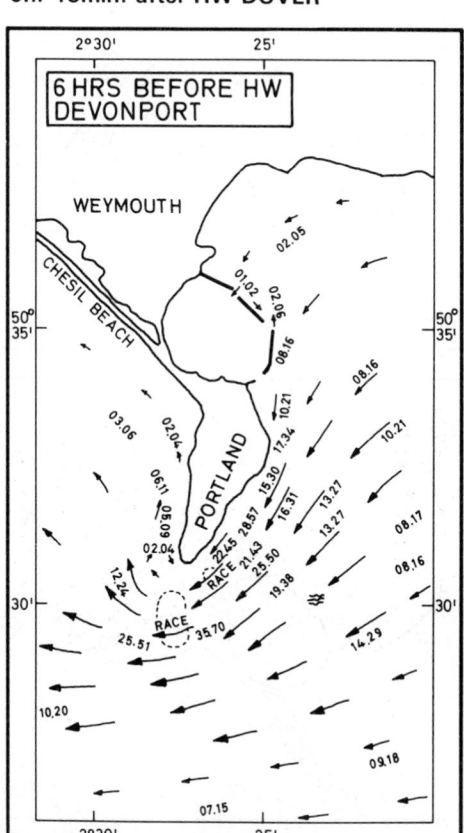

APPROACHES TO PORTLAND TIDAL STREAMS

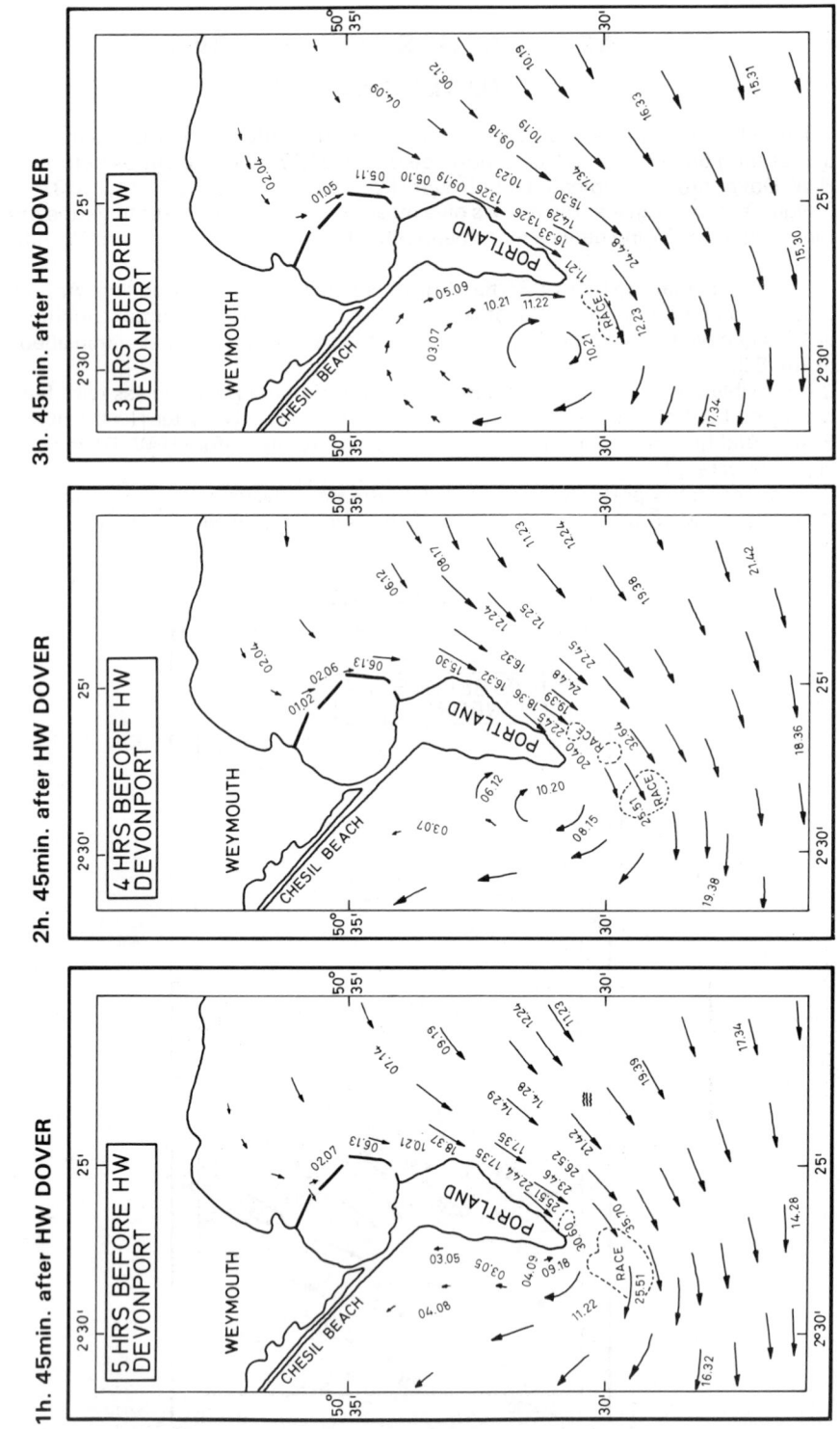

APPROACHES TO PORTLAND TIDAL STREAMS

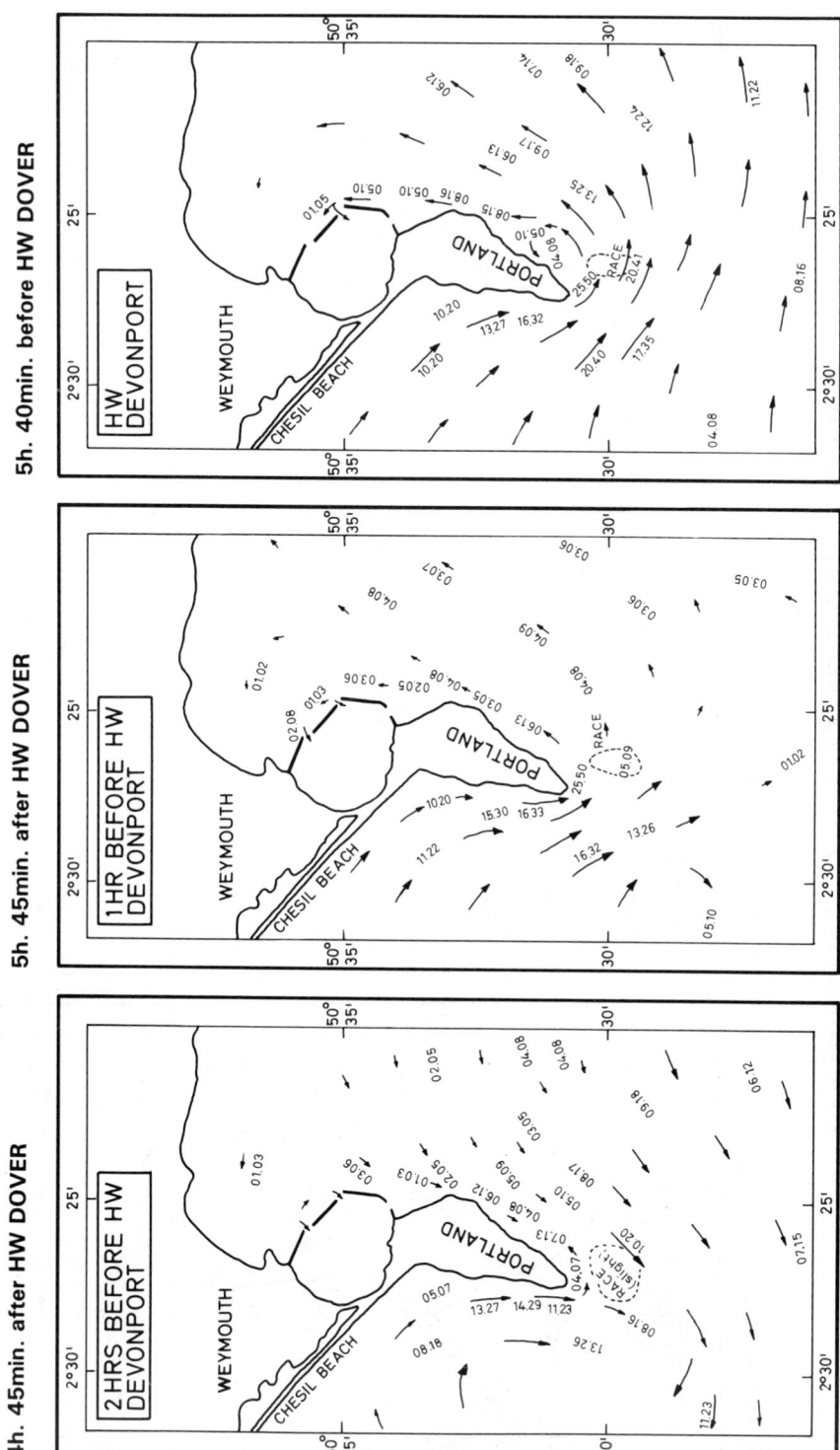

APPROACHES TO PORTLAND TIDAL STREAMS

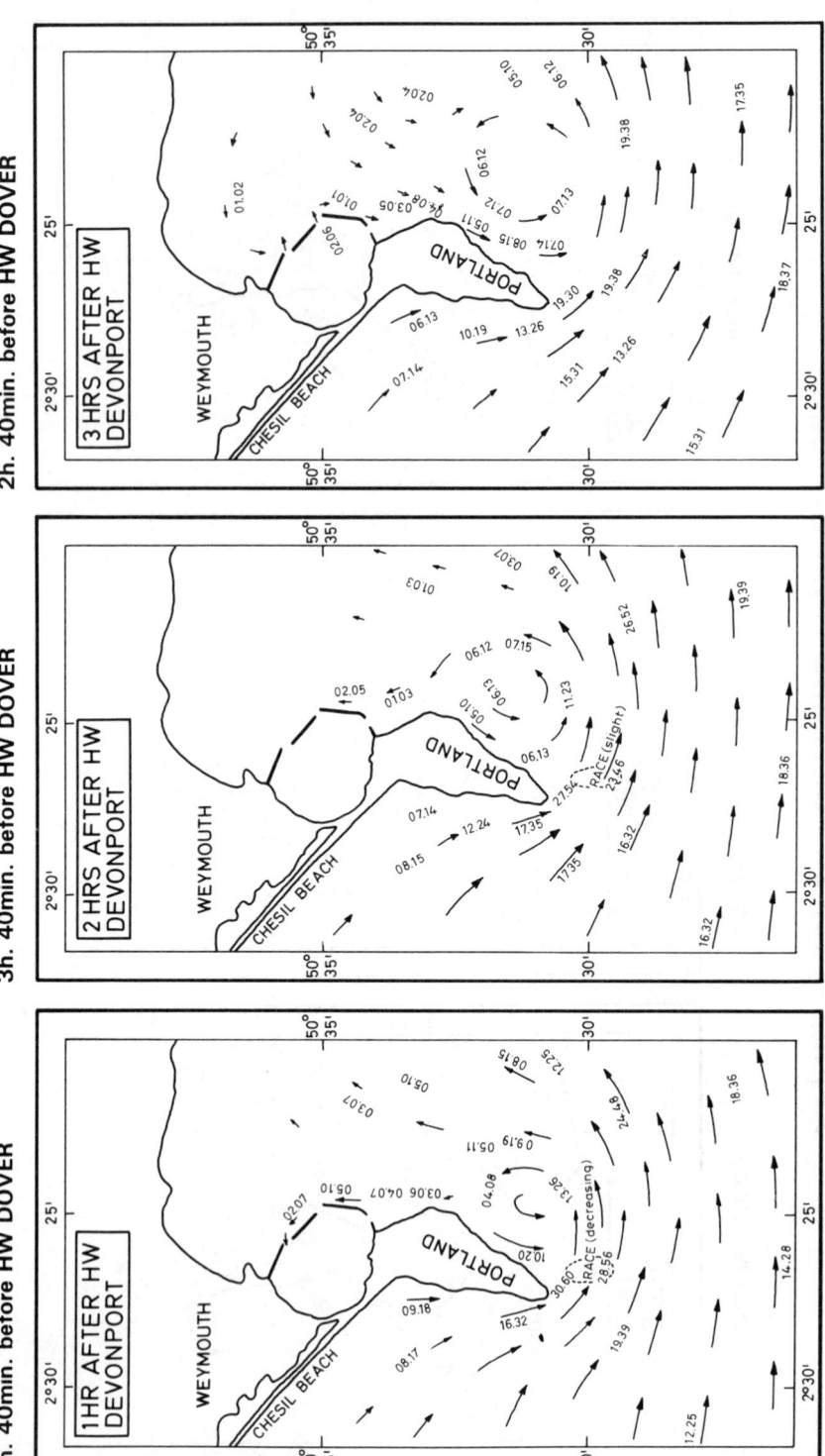

APPROACHES TO PORTLAND TIDAL STREAMS

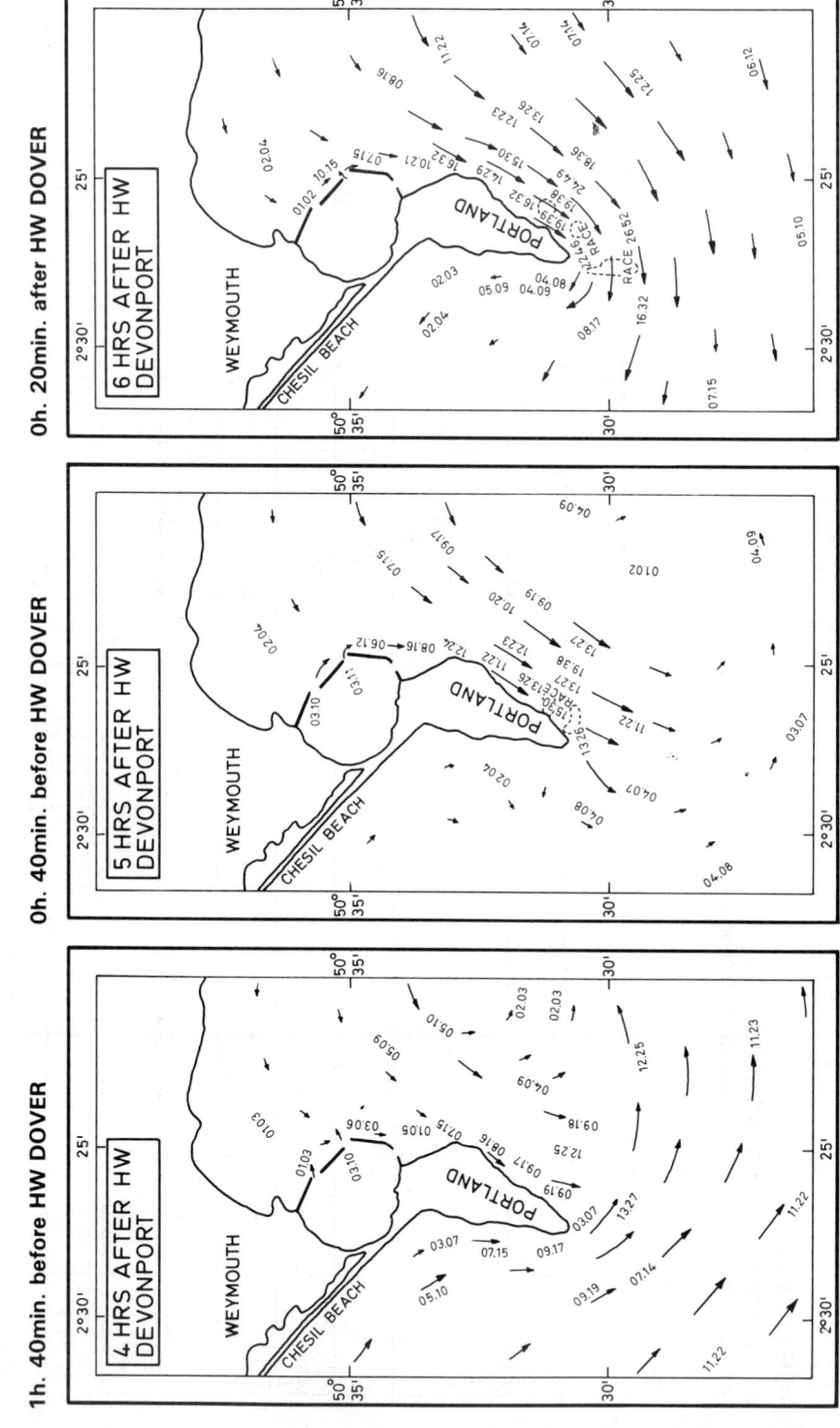

1h. 40min. before HW DOVER

4 HRS AFTER HW DEVONPORT

Oh. 40min. before HW DOVER

5 HRS AFTER HW DEVONPORT

Oh. 20min. after HW DOVER

6 HRS AFTER HW DEVONPORT

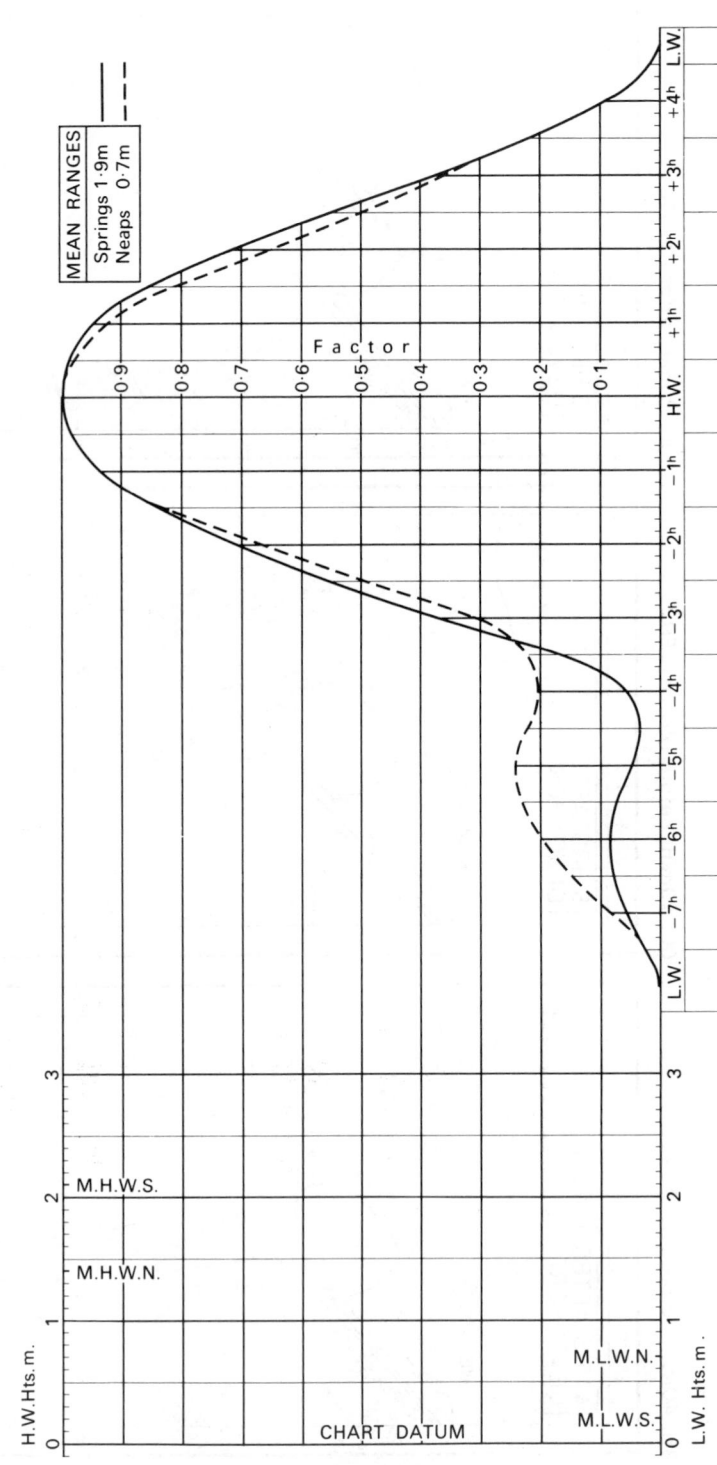

PORTLAND
MEAN SPRING AND NEAP CURVES
Springs occur 2 days after New and Full Moon.

MEAN RANGES
Springs 1·9m
Neaps 0·7m

Factor

0·9 0·8 0·7 0·6 0·5 0·4 0·3 0·2 0·1

L.W. +4ʰ +3ʰ +2ʰ +1ʰ H.W. −1ʰ −2ʰ −3ʰ −4ʰ −5ʰ −6ʰ −7ʰ L.W.

H.W.Hts.m.

M.H.W.S.

M.H.W.N.

M.L.W.N.

M.L.W.S.

CHART DATUM

L.W. Hts. m.

Lat. 50°34'N. Long. 2°26'W. **HIGH & LOW WATER 1992**

GMT   ADD 1 HOUR MARCH 29 — OCTOBER 25 FOR B.S.T.

JANUARY

Day	Time	m	Day	Time	m
1 W	0336 / 0840 / 1613 / 2102	1.7 / 0.8 / 1.5 / 0.7	16 TH	0228 / 0735 / 1518 / 2013	1.5 / 0.9 / 1.5 / 0.7
2 TH	0441 / 0944 / 1718 / 2200	1.8 / 0.7 / 1.6 / 0.7	17 F	0352 / 0853 / 1642 / 2125	1.7 / 0.7 / 1.7 / 0.6
3 F	0539 / 1037 / 1812 / 2249	1.9 / 0.6 / 1.7 / 0.6	18 SA	0505 / 0957 / 1753 / 2226	1.9 / 0.6 / 1.9 / 0.4
4 SA	0630 / 1119 / 1855 / ●2327	2.0 / 0.5 / 1.8 / 0.5	19 SU	0609 / 1049 / 1853 / O 2317	2.2 / 0.4 / 2.1 / 0.3
5 SU	0712 / 1153 / 1931 / 2359	2.1 / 0.4 / 1.8 / 0.4	20 M	0704 / 1137 / 1946	2.4 / 0.3 / 2.2
6 M	0745 / 1223 / 2001	2.1 / 0.4 / 1.8	21 TU	0002 / 0749 / 1221 / 2032	0.3 / 2.5 / 0.2 / 2.3
7 TU	0027 / 0812 / 1252 / 2030	0.4 / 2.1 / 0.3 / 1.8	22 W	0042 / 0829 / 1304 / 2112	0.3 / 2.6 / 0.2 / 2.3
8 W	0054 / 0837 / 1321 / 2058	0.4 / 2.0 / 0.3 / 1.8	23 TH	0121 / 0905 / 1348 / 2148	0.3 / 2.5 / 0.2 / 2.2
9 TH	0122 / 0902 / 1351 / 2127	0.4 / 2.0 / 0.4 / 1.7	24 F	0201 / 0942 / 1431 / 2222	0.3 / 2.3 / 0.2 / 2.0
10 F	0149 / 0927 / 1421 / 2153	0.4 / 1.9 / 0.4 / 1.7	25 SA	0241 / 1021 / 1513 / 2256	0.3 / 2.1 / 0.3 / 1.8
11 SA	0218 / 0956 / 1454 / 2222	0.5 / 1.8 / 0.5 / 1.6	26 SU	0321 / 1100 / 1554 / 2329	0.4 / 1.8 / 0.5 / 1.6
12 SU	0251 / 1029 / 1530 / 2255	0.6 / 1.7 / 0.6 / 1.6	27 M	0403 / 1141 / 1636	0.6 / 1.6 / 0.6
13 M	0332 / 1111 / 1616 / 2345	0.7 / 1.6 / 0.7 / 1.5	28 TU	0011 / 0457 / 1234 / 1732	1.4 / 0.7 / 1.4 / 0.8
14 TU	0432 / 1213 / 1721	0.9 / 1.5 / 0.8	29 W	0115 / 0604 / 1359 / 1856	1.4 / 0.8 / 1.3 / 0.8
15 W	0059 / 0559 / 1340 / 1847	1.5 / 0.9 / 1.5 / 0.8	30 TH	0249 / 0813 / 1547 / 2031	1.4 / 0.8 / 1.3 / 0.8
			31 F	0413 / 0929 / 1702 / 2141	1.6 / 0.7 / 1.4 / 0.7

FEBRUARY

Day	Time	m	Day	Time	m
1 SA	0517 / 1021 / 1754 / 2232	1.7 / 0.6 / 1.6 / 0.5	16 SU	0444 / 0938 / 1740 / 2210	1.9 / 0.4 / 1.8 / 0.4
2 SU	0610 / 1101 / 1836 / 2311	1.9 / 0.4 / 1.7 / 0.4	17 M	0549 / 1033 / 1841 / 2301	2.1 / 0.2 / 2.0 / 0.2
3 M	0653 / 1134 / 1913 / ●2343	2.0 / 0.3 / 1.8 / 0.3	18 TU	0645 / 1120 / 1932 / O 2344	2.4 / 0.1 / 2.2 / 0.2
4 TU	0727 / 1202 / 1945	2.1 / 0.2 / 1.9	19 W	0731 / 1204 / 2015	2.5 / 0.1 / 2.3
5 W	0008 / 0754 / 1228 / 2013	0.3 / 2.1 / 0.2 / 1.9	20 TH	0022 / 0811 / 1244 / 2049	0.1 / 2.6 / 0.1 / 2.3
6 TH	0032 / 0817 / 1256 / 2041	0.2 / 2.1 / 0.2 / 1.9	21 F	0100 / 0847 / 1325 / 2121	0.1 / 2.5 / 0.1 / 2.3
7 F	0058 / 0842 / 1326 / 2108	0.2 / 2.0 / 0.2 / 1.9	22 SA	0137 / 0922 / 1405 / 2151	0.2 / 2.3 / 0.2 / 2.1
8 SA	0127 / 0909 / 1357 / 2134	0.2 / 2.0 / 0.2 / 1.8	23 SU	0215 / 0957 / 1444 / 2219	0.2 / 2.0 / 0.3 / 1.8
9 SU	0155 / 0938 / 1426 / 2158	0.3 / 1.9 / 0.3 / 1.7	24 M	0252 / 1030 / 1515 / 2245	0.3 / 1.7 / 0.4 / 1.6
10 M	0226 / 1007 / 1456 / 2224	0.4 / 1.7 / 0.4 / 1.6	25 TU	0325 / 1058 / 1542 / 2312	0.5 / 1.5 / 0.6 / 1.4
11 TU	0259 / 1041 / 1531 / 2300	0.6 / 1.6 / 0.6 / 1.5	26 W	0402 / 1130 / 1613 / 2354	0.6 / 1.2 / 0.7 / 1.3
12 W	0347 / 1130 / 1627	0.7 / 1.4 / 0.7	27 TH	0513 / 1249 / 1732	0.8 / 1.1 / 0.8
13 TH	0006 / 0512 / 1301 / 1803	1.4 / 0.9 / 1.3 / 0.8	28 F	0146 / 0745 / 1534 / 2004	1.3 / 0.8 / 1.2 / 0.8
14 F	0151 / 0709 / 1501 / 1949	1.4 / 0.8 / 1.4 / 0.7	29 SA	0345 / 0906 / 1641 / 2118	1.4 / 0.7 / 1.3 / 0.7
15 SA	0328 / 0834 / 1629 / 2107	1.6 / 0.6 / 1.5 / 0.5			

MARCH

Day	Time	m	Day	Time	m
1 SU	0449 / 0952 / 1725 / 2205	1.6 / 0.5 / 1.5 / 0.5	16 M	0420 / 0917 / 1721 / 2148	1.8 / 0.3 / 1.7 / 0.3
2 M	0538 / 1031 / 1808 / 2245	1.8 / 0.3 / 1.7 / 0.4	17 TU	0526 / 1013 / 1823 / 2240	2.1 / 0.1 / 2.0 / 0.1
3 TU	0620 / 1105 / 1848 / 2318	2.0 / 0.2 / 1.8 / 0.3	18 W	0623 / 1102 / 1913 / O 2324	2.3 / 0.0 / 2.2 / 0.1
4 W	0657 / 1135 / 1923 / ●2344	2.0 / 0.2 / 1.9 / 0.2	19 TH	0712 / 1145 / 1953	2.4 / 0.0 / 2.3
5 TH	0727 / 1202 / 1952	2.1 / 0.1 / 2.0	20 F	0003 / 0752 / 1223 / 2024	0.0 / 2.4 / 0.0 / 2.3
6 F	0009 / 0755 / 1230 / 2020	0.1 / 2.1 / 0.1 / 2.0	21 SA	0039 / 0828 / 1301 / 2051	0.0 / 2.3 / 0.1 / 2.3
7 SA	0035 / 0824 / 1300 / 2047	0.1 / 2.0 / 0.2 / 2.0	22 SU	0116 / 0902 / 1337 / 2118	0.1 / 2.2 / 0.2 / 2.1
8 SU	0105 / 0855 / 1332 / 2114	0.1 / 2.0 / 0.1 / 1.9	23 M	0152 / 0933 / 1412 / 2146	0.2 / 1.9 / 0.3 / 1.9
9 M	0136 / 0925 / 1404 / 2139	0.2 / 1.9 / 0.2 / 1.7	24 TU	0227 / 1001 / 1441 / 2211	0.3 / 1.6 / 0.4 / 1.6
10 TU	0207 / 0954 / 1433 / 2205	0.3 / 1.7 / 0.3 / 1.6	25 W	0256 / 1023 / 1500 / 2233	0.5 / 1.4 / 0.6 / 1.4
11 W	0239 / 1024 / 1505 / 2239	0.4 / 1.5 / 0.5 / 1.5	26 TH	0327 / 1048 / 1519 / 2304	0.6 / 1.2 / 0.7 / 1.3
12 TH	0326 / 1112 / 1558 / 2341	0.6 / 1.4 / 0.7 / 1.4	27 F	0424 / 1158 / 1614	0.7 / 1.1 / 0.8
13 F	0454 / 1253 / 1744	0.7 / 1.2 / 0.8	28 SA	0032 / 0648 / 1456 / 1916	1.3 / 0.7 / 1.1 / 0.8
14 SA	0132 / 0651 / 1452 / 1933	1.4 / 0.7 / 1.3 / 0.7	29 SU	0252 / 0816 / 1556 / 2035	1.4 / 0.6 / 1.3 / 0.7
15 SU	0307 / 0813 / 1613 / 2048	1.6 / 0.5 / 1.6 / 0.5	30 M	0401 / 0905 / 1643 / 2124	1.6 / 0.5 / 1.5 / 0.5
			31 TU	0451 / 0949 / 1729 / 2206	1.7 / 0.5 / 1.7 / 0.4

APRIL

Day	Time	m	Day	Time	m
1 W	0537 / 1029 / 1814 / 2243	1.9 / 0.2 / 1.9 / 0.3	16 TH	0559 / 1042 / 1848 / 2305	2.1 / 0.1 / 2.1 / 0.1
2 TH	0618 / 1104 / 1853 / 2316	2.0 / 0.1 / 2.0 / 0.2	17 F	0651 / 1125 / 1927 / O 2345	2.2 / 0.1 / 2.2 / 0.0
3 F	0657 / 1134 / 1927 / ●2345	2.0 / 0.2 / 2.1 / 0.2	18 SA	0733 / 1202 / 1958	2.2 / 0.2 / 2.2
4 SA	0732 / 1204 / 1957	2.1 / 0.1 / 2.1	19 SU	0022 / 0810 / 1236 / 2024	0.1 / 2.1 / 0.2 / 2.2
5 SU	0015 / 0808 / 1236 / 2026	0.2 / 2.0 / 0.2 / 2.0	20 M	0057 / 0842 / 1310 / 2052	0.1 / 2.0 / 0.3 / 2.1
6 M	0047 / 0843 / 1311 / 2057	0.1 / 2.0 / 0.2 / 1.9	21 TU	0132 / 0912 / 1343 / 2121	0.2 / 1.8 / 0.3 / 1.9
7 TU	0122 / 0918 / 1346 / 2128	0.2 / 1.8 / 0.2 / 1.8	22 W	0207 / 0938 / 1413 / 2149	0.3 / 1.6 / 0.4 / 1.7
8 W	0156 / 0950 / 1421 / 2159	0.3 / 1.7 / 0.3 / 1.7	23 TH	0237 / 0958 / 1435· / 2215	0.4 / 1.4 / 0.5 / 1.5
9 TH	0234 / 1025 / 1458 / 2239	0.4 / 1.5 / 0.4 / 1.5	24 F	0311 / 1032 / 1459 / 2247	0.6 / 1.2 / 0.6 / 1.4
10 F	0327 / 1121 / 1558 / 2342	0.5 / 1.3 / 0.6 / 1.4	25 SA	0401 / 1134 / 1552 / 2350	0.6 / 1.1 / 0.7 / 1.3
11 SA	0451 / 1257 / 1736	0.6 / 1.3 / 0.7	26 SU	0531 / 1328 / 1754	0.7 / 1.2 / 0.8
12 SU	0116 / 0629 / 1433 / 1910	1.5 / 0.5 / 1.4 / 0.6	27 M	0135 / 0700 / 1448 / 1927	1.4 / 0.6 / 1.3 / 0.7
13 M	0242 / 0745 / 1547 / 2021	1.6 / 0.4 / 1.6 / 0.5	28 TU	0254 / 0804 / 1544 / 2029	1.5 / 0.5 / 1.5 / 0.6
14 TU	0353 / 0851 / 1655 / 2123	1.8 / 0.2 / 1.7 / 0.3	29 W	0353 / 0857 / 1640 / 2119	1.6 / 0.4 / 1.7 / 0.5
15 W	0458 / 0951 / 1757 / 2218	2.0 / 0.1 / 1.9 / 0.2	30 TH	0447 / 0946 / 1732 / 2205	1.7 / 0.3 / 1.8 / 0.4

To find H.W. Dover add 4 h. 40 min.

TIDAL DIFFERENCES PAGE 21:186. TIDAL CURVE PAGE 21:182.

TIDAL STREAMS PAGES 21:177-21:181.

NOTE. Double low waters occur at Portland. Predictions are for the 1st low water.

Datum of predictions: 0.93 m. below Ordnance Datum (Newlyn) or approx. L.A.T.

PORTLAND

HIGH & LOW WATER 1992   Lat. 50°34′N. Long. 2°26′W.

GMT   ADD 1 HOUR MARCH 29 — OCTOBER 25 FOR B.S.T.

MAY

Day	Time	m	Day	Time	m
1 F	0537 / 1028 / 1817 / 2245	1.9 / 0.2 / 2.0 / 0.3	**16** SA O	0630 / 1103 / 1901 / 2330	1.9 / 0.2 / 2.1 / 0.2
2 SA ●	0624 / 1105 / 1857 / 2322	2.0 / 0.2 / 2.1 / 0.2	**17** SU	0714 / 1142 / 1936	1.9 / 0.2 / 2.1
3 SU	0709 / 1139 / 1933 / 2357	2.0 / 0.2 / 2.1 / 0.2	**18** M	0008 / 0752 / 1215 / 2007	0.1 / 1.9 / 0.2 / 2.1
4 M	0754 / 1216 / 2009	2.0 / 0.2 / 2.1	**19** TU	0044 / 0824 / 1249 / 2037	0.1 / 1.8 / 0.3 / 2.0
5 TU	0035 / 0835 / 1256 / 2047	0.2 / 2.0 / 0.2 / 2.0	**20** W	0117 / 0854 / 1323 / 2106	0.2 / 1.7 / 0.3 / 1.9
6 W	0114 / 0915 / 1337 / 2124	0.2 / 1.9 / 0.2 / 1.9	**21** TH	0151 / 0922 / 1355 / 2136	0.3 / 1.5 / 0.4 / 1.7
7 TH	0154 / 0954 / 1418 / 2203	0.2 / 1.9 / 0.3 / 1.8	**22** F	0224 / 0950 / 1424 / 2205	0.4 / 1.4 / 0.5 / 1.6
8 F	0238 / 1037 / 1503 / 2246	0.3 / 1.5 / 0.4 / 1.7	**23** SA	0257 / 1023 / 1454 / 2237	0.5 / 1.3 / 0.6 / 1.5
9 SA	0332 / 1132 / 1601 / 2342	0.3 / 1.4 / 0.5 / 0.2	**24** SU	0338 / 1107 / 1537 / 2320	0.5 / 1.2 / 0.7 / 1.4
10 SU	0441 / 1246 / 1718	0.4 / 1.4 / 0.6	**25** M	0433 / 1212 / 1646	0.6 / 1.3 / 0.7
11 M	0055 / 0559 / 1403 / 1839	1.6 / 1.6 / 1.4 / 0.6	**26** TU	0024 / 0542 / 1326 / 1809	1.4 / 0.6 / 1.3 / 0.7
12 TU	0211 / 0714 / 1514 / 1951	1.6 / 1.6 / 1.6 / 0.5	**27** W	0139 / 0652 / 1436 / 1924	1.4 / 0.5 / 1.5 / 0.7
13 W	0324 / 0823 / 1620 / 2056	1.7 / 1.8 / 1.7 / 0.4	**28** TH	0251 / 0757 / 1540 / 2029	1.5 / 0.5 / 1.6 / 0.6
14 TH	0432 / 0925 / 1723 / 2154	1.8 / 0.2 / 1.9 / 0.3	**29** F	0356 / 0857 / 1642 / 2125	1.6 / 0.4 / 1.7 / 0.5
15 F	0535 / 1019 / 1817 / 2247	1.9 / 0.2 / 2.0 / 0.2	**30** SA	0458 / 0949 / 1738 / 2215	1.7 / 0.3 / 1.9 / 0.4
			31 SU	0556 / 1036 / 1828 / 2301	1.8 / 0.3 / 2.0 / 0.3

JUNE

Day	Time	m	Day	Time	m
1 M ●	0650 / 1119 / 1915 / 2343	1.9 / 0.3 / 2.1 / 0.3	**16** TU	0737 / 1202 / 1957	1.7 / 0.3 / 2.0
2 TU	0741 / 1202 / 1958	2.0 / 0.3 / 2.2	**17** W	0032 / 0809 / 1235 / 2027	0.2 / 1.7 / 0.3 / 2.0
3 W	0025 / 0829 / 1246 / 2041	0.3 / 2.0 / 0.3 / 2.1	**18** TH	0104 / 0840 / 1307 / 2056	0.2 / 1.7 / 0.3 / 1.9
4 TH	0107 / 0915 / 1331 / 2121	0.2 / 1.9 / 0.3 / 2.1	**19** F	0136 / 0909 / 1339 / 2122	0.3 / 1.6 / 0.3 / 1.8
5 F	0151 / 0957 / 1416 / 2201	0.2 / 1.8 / 0.3 / 2.0	**20** SA	0207 / 0937 / 1409 / 2150	0.3 / 1.5 / 0.4 / 1.7
6 SA	0238 / 1040 / 1501 / 2244	0.2 / 1.7 / 0.3 / 1.9	**21** SU	0238 / 1006 / 1440 / 2219	0.3 / 1.5 / 0.5 / 1.6
7 SU	0327 / 1127 / 1552 / 2332	0.2 / 1.5 / 0.4 / 1.7	**22** M	0311 / 1039 / 1513 / 2252	0.4 / 1.4 / 0.6 / 1.6
8 M	0424 / 1222 / 1653	0.3 / 1.5 / 0.5	**23** TU	0349 / 1120 / 1559 / 2336	0.5 / 1.4 / 0.6 / 1.5
9 TU	0030 / 0529 / 1326 / 1804	1.6 / 0.3 / 1.5 / 0.5	**24** W	0440 / 1216 / 1701	0.5 / 1.4 / 0.7
10 W	0140 / 0640 / 1434 / 1919	1.6 / 0.4 / 1.5 / 0.6	**25** TH	0035 / 0543 / 1324 / 1819	1.4 / 0.6 / 1.4 / 0.7
11 TH	0254 / 0750 / 1541 / 2031	1.5 / 0.4 / 1.6 / 0.5	**26** F	0151 / 0655 / 1439 / 1939	1.4 / 0.6 / 1.5 / 0.7
12 F	0406 / 0855 / 1646 / 2135	1.6 / 0.4 / 1.7 / 0.4	**27** SA	0309 / 0808 / 1554 / 2050	1.5 / 0.5 / 1.6 / 0.6
13 SA	0513 / 0953 / 1745 / 2232	1.6 / 0.4 / 1.9 / 0.4	**28** SU	0425 / 0915 / 1702 / 2151	1.6 / 0.4 / 1.8 / 0.5
14 SU	0610 / 1044 / 1838 / 2319	1.7 / 0.3 / 1.9 / 0.3	**29** M	0534 / 1014 / 1805 / 2244	1.7 / 0.4 / 2.0 / 0.4
15 M ○	0658 / 1126 / 1922 / 2358	1.7 / 0.3 / 2.0 / 0.2	**30** TU ●	0636 / 1105 / 1901 / 2331	1.9 / 0.3 / 2.2 / 0.4

JULY

Day	Time	m	Day	Time	m
1 W	0731 / 1152 / 1950	2.0 / 0.2 / 2.3	**16** TH	0018 / 0754 / 1222 / 2015	0.2 / 1.7 / 0.2 / 2.0
2 TH	0015 / 0821 / 1237 / 2033	0.3 / 2.1 / 0.2 / 2.4	**17** F	0047 / 0823 / 1250 / 2040	0.2 / 1.7 / 0.2 / 2.0
3 F	0059 / 0907 / 1320 / 2112	0.2 / 2.1 / 0.2 / 2.3	**18** SA	0115 / 0851 / 1318 / 2104	0.2 / 1.7 / 0.3 / 1.9
4 SA	0143 / 0949 / 1404 / 2150	0.1 / 2.0 / 0.2 / 2.2	**19** SU	0144 / 0918 / 1347 / 2129	0.2 / 1.7 / 0.3 / 1.9
5 SU	0228 / 1030 / 1447 / 2231	0.1 / 1.9 / 0.2 / 2.0	**20** M	0214 / 0946 / 1417 / 2156	0.3 / 1.7 / 0.4 / 1.8
6 M	0315 / 1109 / 1533 / 2315	0.1 / 1.7 / 0.3 / 1.8	**21** TU	0244 / 1012 / 1448 / 2225	0.3 / 1.6 / 0.5 / 1.7
7 TU	0402 / 1153 / 1625	0.3 / 1.6 / 0.4	**22** W	0314 / 1042 / 1522 / 2259	0.4 / 1.5 / 0.6 / 1.6
8 W	0005 / 0457 / 1245 / 1726	1.6 / 0.4 / 1.5 / 0.5	**23** TH	0351 / 1121 / 1610 / 2346	0.6 / 1.5 / 0.7 / 1.4
9 TH	0106 / 0600 / 1349 / 1844	1.6 / 0.5 / 1.5 / 0.6	**24** F	0443 / 1222 / 1722	0.7 / 1.4 / 0.8
10 F	0220 / 0712 / 1502 / 2007	1.4 / 0.6 / 1.5 / 0.6	**25** SA	0058 / 0600 / 1347 / 1857	1.4 / 0.7 / 1.4 / 0.8
11 SA	0341 / 0825 / 1614 / 2120	1.4 / 0.6 / 1.6 / 0.6	**26** SU	0233 / 0730 / 1517 / 2024	1.4 / 0.7 / 1.6 / 0.7
12 SU	0454 / 0933 / 1721 / 2220	1.4 / 0.5 / 1.8 / 0.5	**27** M	0350 / 0850 / 1636 / 2132	1.5 / 0.5 / 1.8 / 0.5
13 M	0554 / 1029 / 1820 / 2308	1.5 / 0.4 / 1.9 / 0.4	**28** TU	0518 / 0957 / 1745 / 2229	1.7 / 0.4 / 2.0 / 0.4
14 TU ○	0642 / 1115 / 1909 / 2346	1.6 / 0.3 / 2.0 / 0.3	**29** W ●	0624 / 1053 / 1909 / 2317	1.9 / 0.3 / 2.3 / 0.3
15 W	0721 / 1152 / 1946	1.7 / 0.3 / 2.0	**30** TH	0721 / 1141 / 1935	2.1 / 0.3 / 2.5
			31 F	0002 / 0809 / 1224 / 2018	0.2 / 2.2 / 0.2 / 2.5

AUGUST

Day	Time	m	Day	Time	m
1 SA	0045 / 0852 / 1304 / 2057	0.2 / 2.3 / 0.2 / 2.5	**16** SU	0051 / 0829 / 1255 / 2042	0.2 / 1.9 / 0.2 / 2.0
2 SU	0129 / 0931 / 1345 / 2136	0.1 / 2.2 / 0.2 / 2.4	**17** M	0118 / 0855 / 1322 / 2108	0.2 / 1.9 / 0.2 / 2.0
3 M	0213 / 1008 / 1428 / 2215	0.2 / 2.1 / 0.2 / 2.2	**18** TU	0148 / 0922 / 1353 / 2135	0.3 / 1.9 / 0.3 / 1.9
4 TU	0256 / 1043 / 1511 / 2255	0.2 / 1.9 / 0.3 / 1.9	**19** W	0217 / 0947 / 1423 / 2202	0.3 / 1.8 / 0.4 / 1.8
5 W	0339 / 1119 / 1556 / 2337	0.4 / 1.7 / 0.4 / 1.6	**20** TH	0244 / 1012 / 1453 / 2231	0.4 / 1.7 / 0.6 / 1.6
6 TH	0421 / 1200 / 1648	0.5 / 1.5 / 0.6	**21** F	0314 / 1044 / 1533 / 2310	0.6 / 1.5 / 0.7 / 1.5
7 F	0026 / 0513 / 1258 / 1805	1.4 / 0.7 / 1.4 / 0.7	**22** SA	0358 / 1136 / 1642	0.7 / 1.4 / 0.9
8 SA	0142 / 0631 / 1424 / 1949	1.3 / 0.8 / 1.4 / 0.8	**23** SU	0023 / 0520 / 1311 / 1833	1.4 / 0.8 / 1.4 / 0.9
9 SU	0324 / 0803 / 1553 / 2111	1.3 / 0.8 / 1.6 / 0.7	**24** M	0218 / 0709 / 1454 / 2007	1.4 / 0.8 / 1.6 / 0.7
10 M	0442 / 0919 / 1702 / 2207	1.4 / 0.7 / 1.7 / 0.6	**25** TU	0352 / 0834 / 1614 / 2115	1.5 / 0.6 / 1.9 / 0.5
11 TU	0537 / 1014 / 1800 / 2251	1.5 / 0.5 / 1.9 / 0.4	**26** W	0506 / 0940 / 1723 / 2212	1.7 / 0.5 / 2.1 / 0.3
12 W	0622 / 1100 / 1847 / 2327	1.7 / 0.4 / 2.0 / 0.3	**27** TH	0610 / 1036 / 1824 / 2302	2.0 / 0.3 / 2.4 / 0.2
13 TH ○	0701 / 1135 / 1925 / 2357	1.8 / 0.3 / 2.1 / 0.2	**28** F ●	0707 / 1124 / 1916 / 2347	2.2 / 0.2 / 2.6 / 0.2
14 F	0734 / 1203 / 1953	1.9 / 0.2 / 2.1	**29** SA	0753 / 1206 / 2001	2.4 / 0.2 / 2.5
15 SA	0024 / 0803 / 1228 / 2018	0.2 / 1.9 / 0.2 / 2.1	**30** SU	0029 / 0832 / 1246 / 2040	0.2 / 2.4 / 0.2 / 2.6
			31 M	0110 / 0905 / 1325 / 2118	0.2 / 0.2 / 0.2 / 2.5

GENERAL — PENINSULA: Tides off Bill, strong. Eddies in E. and W. Bay. At end of E. going stream eddy fills the E. Bay. **PORTLAND HARBOUR:** In Ship Channel, Spring rate 1 kn.; irregular; eddies off heads of breakwater.

PORTLAND   21:185

Lat. 50°34′N. Long. 2°26′W.

HIGH & LOW WATER 1992

GMT   ADD 1 HOUR MARCH 29 — OCTOBER 25 FOR B.S.T.

SEPTEMBER

Date	Time	m	Time	m	Time	m	Time	m
1 TU	0151	0.3	0938	0.2	1408	0.2	2156	2.2
2 W	0232	0.3	1010	2.0	1449	0.4	2232	1.9
3 TH	0310	0.5	1042	1.8	1528	0.5	2306	1.6
4 F	0342	0.7	1115	1.6	1612	0.7	2343	1.4
5 SA	0420	0.8	1202	1.4	1724	0.8		
6 SU	0103	1.2	0540	0.9	1342	1.4	1931	0.9
7 M	0317	1.3	0749	0.9	1530	1.6	2052	0.7
8 TU	0423	1.4	0901	0.8	1635	1.8	2141	0.6
9 W	0509	1.6	0951	0.6	1727	1.9	2223	0.4
10 TH	0551	1.8	1032	0.5	1812	2.1	2259	0.4
11 F	0633	1.9	1109	0.4	1851	2.2	2332	0.3
12 SA	0708	2.0	1138	0.3	1923	2.2	○ 2358	0.3
13 SU	0738	2.1	1204	0.3	1952	2.2		
14 M	0024	0.3	0805	2.1	1230	0.2	2020	2.1
15 TU	0051	0.3	0830	2.1	1259	0.3	2049	2.1
16 W	0121	0.3	0857	2.0	1330	0.3	2119	2.0
17 TH	0151	0.4	0924	1.9	1401	0.4	2146	1.8
18 F	0219	0.5	0951	1.8	1433	0.6	2213	1.7
19 SA	0249	0.6	1022	1.6	1513	0.8	2252	1.5
20 SU	0332	0.8	1114	1.5	1627	0.9		
21 M	0016	1.4	0503	0.9	1254	1.5	1820	0.9
22 TU	0213	1.4	0657	0.9	1434	1.7	1947	0.7
23 W	0337	1.6	0815	0.7	1550	2.0	2053	0.5
24 TH	0446	1.8	0919	0.6	1657	2.2	2152	0.4
25 F	0551	2.1	1015	0.4	1759	2.4	2245	0.3
26 SA	0646	2.3	1104	0.3	1854	2.5	● 2330	0.2
27 SU	0730	2.4	1147	0.2	1940	2.6		
28 M	0010	0.3	0806	2.5	1227	0.2	2022	2.6
29 TU	0049	0.3	0835	2.5	1306	0.3	2059	2.4
30 W	0127	0.4	0906	2.4	1346	0.4	2134	2.2

OCTOBER

Date	Time	m	Time	m	Time	m	Time	m
1 TH	0205	0.5	0937	2.1	1426	0.5	2206	1.9
2 F	0239	0.6	1009	1.9	1503	0.6	2234	1.6
3 SA	0307	0.7	1039	1.7	1542	0.8	2307	1.4
4 SU	0335	0.9	1118	1.5	1647	0.9		
5 M	0027	1.3	0443	1.0	1244	1.5	1846	0.9
6 TU	0245	1.3	0709	1.0	1443	1.6	2008	0.8
7 W	0343	1.5	0822	0.9	1549	1.8	2058	0.7
8 TH	0426	1.7	0911	0.6	1640	1.9	2143	0.5
9 F	0512	1.9	0955	0.6	1727	2.1	2224	0.5
10 SA	0556	2.0	1034	0.5	1809	2.1	2259	0.4
11 SU	0636	2.1	1108	0.4	1848	2.2	○ 2329	0.4
12 M	0708	2.2	1138	0.3	1924	2.2	2357	0.4
13 TU	0737	2.2	1207	0.4	1959	2.2		
14 W	0025	0.4	0806	2.2	1239	0.4	2033	2.1
15 TH	0057	0.4	0837	2.1	1313	0.6	2106	2.0
16 F	0131	0.5	0908	2.0	1348	0.5	2138	1.9
17 SA	0204	0.5	0940	1.9	1423	0.6	2210	1.7
18 SU	0239	0.7	1017	1.8	1510	0.7	2257	1.6
19 M	0330	0.8	1112	1.7	1624	0.8		
20 TU	0019	1.5	0456	0.9	1238	1.7	1759	0.8
21 W	0156	1.6	0634	0.9	1406	1.8	1919	0.7
22 TH	0312	1.7	0749	0.8	1520	2.0	2027	0.5
23 F	0419	1.9	0853	0.6	1630	2.1	2129	0.4
24 SA	0523	2.1	0951	0.5	1734	2.3	2224	0.4
25 SU	0618	2.3	1043	0.4	1832	2.4	● 2311	0.3
26 M	0704	2.4	1129	0.3	1921	2.4	2350	0.4
27 TU	0739	2.5	1209	0.3	2002	2.4		
28 W	0025	0.4	0810	2.5	1248	0.4	2039	2.3
29 TH	0102	0.5	0840	2.4	1328	0.4	2111	2.1
30 F	0137	0.6	0911	2.2	1406	0.6	2141	1.9
31 SA	0211	0.7	0944	2.0	1442	0.7	2210	1.6

NOVEMBER

Date	Time	m	Time	m	Time	m	Time	m
1 SU	0240	0.8	1015	1.8	1520	0.8	2243	1.5
2 M	0309	0.9	1051	1.7	1610	0.9	2341	1.3
3 TU	0359	1.0	1148	1.6	1730	0.9		
4 W	0118	1.4	0542	1.0	1320	1.6	1854	0.8
5 TH	0235	1.5	0715	1.0	1441	1.7	1957	0.8
6 F	0329	1.7	0815	0.9	1541	1.8	2051	0.7
7 SA	0420	1.9	0907	0.8	1635	1.9	2139	0.6
8 SU	0509	2.0	0953	0.6	1725	2.0	2220	0.5
9 M	0554	2.1	1034	0.6	1812	2.1	2257	0.5
10 TU	0635	2.2	1112	0.5	1857	2.2	○ 2329	0.4
11 W	0711	2.3	1147	0.5	1939	2.2		
12 TH	0003	0.4	0746	2.3	1223	0.5	2019	2.2
13 F	0040	0.5	0823	2.2	1300	0.5	2059	2.1
14 SA	0118	0.5	0900	2.1	1339	0.5	2137	1.9
15 SU	0157	0.5	0937	2.1	1420	0.5	2217	1.8
16 M	0239	0.6	1017	2.0	1510	0.6	2304	1.7
17 TU	0328	0.7	1107	1.9	1612	0.6		
18 W	0008	1.6	0437	0.8	1215	1.8	1728	0.7
19 TH	0124	1.6	0559	0.9	1333	1.8	1845	0.7
20 F	0237	1.7	0716	0.8	1450	1.9	1957	0.6
21 SA	0344	1.9	0825	0.7	1603	2.0	2102	0.6
22 SU	0448	2.0	0928	0.6	1710	2.0	2200	0.5
23 M	0546	2.2	1024	0.5	1811	2.1	2249	0.4
24 TU	0635	2.3	1112	0.4	1901	2.2	● 2330	0.4
25 W	0717	2.3	1155	0.4	1943	2.2		
26 TH	0007	0.5	0751	2.4	1233	0.4	2019	2.1
27 F	0041	0.5	0823	2.3	1310	0.4	2051	2.0
28 SA	0115	0.6	0854	2.2	1346	0.5	2120	1.9
29 SU	0149	0.6	0925	2.1	1421	0.6	2149	1.7
30 M	0220	0.7	0954	1.9	1456	0.7	2219	1.6

DECEMBER

Date	Time	m	Time	m	Time	m	Time	m
1 TU	0249	0.8	1026	1.8	1534	0.7	2257	1.5
2 W	0325	0.9	1104	1.7	1622	0.8	2350	1.4
3 TH	0420	1.0	1200	1.6	1725	0.8		
4 F	0100	1.5	0541	1.0	1836	0.8		
5 SA	0211	1.6	0702	1.0	1944	0.8		
6 SU	0316	1.7	0811	0.9	1539	1.7	2044	0.7
7 M	0415	1.9	0909	0.8	1641	1.8	2137	0.6
8 TU	0511	2.0	1001	0.7	1739	2.0	2224	0.5
9 W	0603	2.1	1046	0.6	1832	2.1	2307	0.5
10 TH	0649	2.2	1128	0.5	1922	2.2	2347	0.5
11 F	0733	2.3	1207	0.5	2009	2.2		
12 SA	0026	0.5	0823	2.3	1248	0.5	2053	2.1
13 SU	0107	0.5	0852	2.3	1330	0.4	2135	2.0
14 M	0148	0.5	0930	2.2	1413	0.4	2216	1.9
15 TU	0231	0.5	1010	2.1	1459	0.4	2257	1.8
16 W	0315	0.6	1054	2.0	1552	0.5	2345	1.7
17 TH	0409	0.7	1148	1.8	1654	0.6		
18 F	0045	1.6	0519	0.8	1257	1.7	1805	0.7
19 SA	0154	1.6	0638	0.8	1416	1.7	1920	0.7
20 SU	0305	1.7	0757	0.8	1537	1.7	2031	0.7
21 M	0412	1.8	0907	0.7	1649	1.8	2135	0.6
22 TU	0516	2.0	1009	0.6	1752	1.8	2230	0.5
23 W	0613	2.1	1100	0.5	1844	1.9	2315	0.5
24 TH	0701	2.2	1143	0.4	1927	2.0	● 2354	0.4
25 F	0740	2.2	1219	0.4	2002	2.0		
26 SA	0027	0.4	0812	2.2	1252	0.4	2032	1.9
27 SU	0058	0.4	0839	2.2	1325	0.3	2100	1.9
28 M	0127	0.5	0905	2.1	1356	0.4	2128	1.8
29 TU	0155	0.5	0932	2.0	1427	0.5	2154	1.7
30 W	0224	0.6	0958	1.9	1459	0.5	2221	1.6
31 TH	0253	0.7	1028	1.7	1531	0.6	2253	1.5

RATE AND SET — 5 M. S. of Bill: E. going begins +0545 Dover. 3½ kn. W. going begins −0020 Dover, 2-3 kn. increasing to 5 kn. or more off eastern side of peninsula. In harbour streams imperceptible.

See notes on Race on page 21:186.

PLACE	TIME DIFFERENCES				HEIGHT DIFFERENCES (Metres)			
	High Water		Low Water		MHWS	MHWN	MLWN	MLWS
PORTLAND	0100 and 1300	0700 and 1900	0100 and 1300	0700 and 1900	2.1	1.4	0.7	0.2
Lulworth Cove	−0015	−0005	−0005	+0005	+0.2	+0.1	+0.2	+0.1

At Spring tides there are double low waters between Portland and Lulworth.

TIDAL NOTES

Between Dartmouth and Portland the tidal curve gradually becomes more and more distorted, especially on the rising tide; the rise is relatively fast for the first hour after low water and there is then a noticeable slackening in the rate of rise for the next $1\frac{1}{2}$ hours, after which the rapid rate of rise is resumed. There is often a 'stand' at high water which, while not very noticeable at Dartmouth, lasts for about an hour at Torquay and for $1\frac{1}{2}$ hours at Lyme Regis.

THE RACE—Cause—strong S. going stream both sides of Bill, meeting E. and W. going streams off the Bill. Varies in position and extent. Extends off Bill—SE. during E. going stream. Extends off Bill—SW. during W. going stream. Furthest off Bill—2 M.—during strong N. winds. Passage $\frac{1}{2}$-$\frac{3}{4}$ M. wide—smooth—usually between Race and Bill—depth 5.5-16.4 m. Stream strong near Race 6-8 kn., but not in Race. Race is an area of overfalls, steep, heavy, breaking seas. Strongest when—streams are strongest—wind against stream—E. gale and E. going stream. CAUTION—Before approaching this area, study condition of all streams.

Refer to predictions on pages 21:183-21:185

TIDAL DIFFERENCES ON POOLE (TOWN QUAY)

PLACE	TIME DIFFERENCES				HEIGHT DIFFERENCES (Metres)			
	High Water		Low Water		MHWS	MHWN	MLWN	MLWS
POOLE (TOWN QUAY)	1000 and 2200	0400 and 1600	0500 and 1700	1100 and 2300	2.1	1.6	1.1	0.4
Harbour Entrance	−0030	−0035	−0045	−0025	−0.1	0.0	0.0	−0.1
Pottery Pier	+0020	+0020	+0005	+0005	−0.1	+0.1	+0.1	+0.2
Wareham	+0030	+0025	+0125	+0040	+0.1	+0.1	0.0	+0.3
Cleavel Point	−0010	−0010	−0010	−0010	0.0	−0.1	0.0	−0.1

Refer to predictions on pages 21:187-21:189

POOLE (TOWN QUAY)   21:187

Lat. 50°43′N. Long. 1°59′W.   HIGH & LOW WATER 1992

GMT   ADD 1 HOUR MARCH 29 — OCTOBER 25 FOR B.S.T.

	JANUARY				FEBRUARY				MARCH				APRIL		
	Time	m	Time	m	Time	m	Time	m	Time	m	Time	m	Time	m	Time	m
1 W	0129 1405	1.1 1.9 1.0 1.8	**16** TH 1316	0026 1.1 1.8 1.0 1.7	**1** SA 1522	0259 1.1 1.8 0.9 1.9	**16** SU 1503	0232 0.9 1.9 0.6 2.0	**1** SU 1501	0240 1.1 1.7 0.9 1.8	**16** M 1445	0218 0.8 1.9 0.6 2.0	**1** W 1535	0322 0.8 1.9 2.0	**16** TH 1550	0329 0.5 2.2 0.3 2.2
2 TH 1454	0224 1.0 1.9 0.9 1.9	**17** F 1420	0139 1.0 1.9 0.9 1.9	**2** SU 1600	0340 1.0 1.9 0.8 1.9	**17** M 1550	0323 0.6 2.1 0.4 2.2	**2** M 1536	0319 0.9 1.8 0.8 1.9	**17** TU 1531	0308 0.6 2.0 0.3 2.2	**2** TH 1605	0354 0.6 1.9 0.6 2.0	**17** F 1630	0409 0.3 2.2 0.3 2.2
3 F 1537	0313 1.0 1.9 0.9 1.9	**18** SA 1515	0241 0.9 2.0 0.7 2.0	**3** M 1632	0416 0.9 1.8 0.6	**18** TU 1632	0409 0.5 2.2 0.2 2.3	**3** TU 1607	0354 0.8 1.9 0.6 2.0	**18** W 1613	0352 0.4 2.2 0.2 2.3	**3** F 1635	0423 0.5 2.0 0.5	**18** SA 1709	0448 0.3 2.2 0.3
4 SA 1615	0355 0.9 2.0 0.8 2.0	**19** SU 1603	0335 0.7 2.1 0.5 2.2	**4** TU 1703	0448 0.8 1.9 0.6	**19** W 1715	0452 0.3 2.3 0.2	**4** W 1636	0424 0.6 1.9 0.5 2.0	**19** TH 1652	0431 0.3 2.3 0.2 2.3	**4** SA 1706	0452 0.5 2.0 0.5	**19** SU 1747	0526 2.2 0.4 2.2 0.5
5 SU 1650	0432 0.9 2.0 0.7 2.0	**20** M 1648	0423 0.5 2.2 0.3 2.3	**5** W 1732	2.0 0.7 0.5	**20** TH 1755	0535 2.3 0.2 0.2	**5** TH 1705	0452 0.6 2.0 0.5	**20** F 1733	0512 0.2 2.2 0.2	**5** SU 1739	2.0 0.5 0.5	**20** M 1827	0605 2.1 0.5 2.0 0.6
6 M 1724	0508 0.8 2.0 0.7	**21** TU 1734	0509 0.4 2.3 0.2	**6** TH 1800	2.0 0.6 0.5	**21** F 1836	0616 2.3 0.3 2.2 0.2	**6** F 1733	2.0 0.5 0.5	**21** SA 1811	0551 2.3 0.3 2.2 0.3	**6** M 1815	2.0 0.5 0.6	**21** TU 1907	0644 2.0 0.6 1.9 0.8
7 TU 1755	2.0 0.8 2.0 0.7	**22** W 1816	0555 2.3 0.4 2.3 0.2	**7** F 1830	2.0 0.6 1.9 0.6	**22** SA 1918	0658 2.2 0.4 2.1 0.4	**7** SA 1802	2.0 0.5 2.0 0.5	**22** SU 1850	0631 2.2 0.4 2.0 0.5	**7** TU 1855	0634 2.0 0.6 1.9 0.7	**22** W 1952	0726 1.9 0.8 1.8 1.0
8 W 1827	2.0 0.8 1.9 0.7	**23** TH 1900	0640 2.3 0.4 2.2 0.3	**8** SA 1901	2.0 0.7 1.9 0.6	**23** SU 2001	0742 2.1 0.6 1.9 0.6	**8** SU 1835	2.0 0.5 2.0 0.6	**23** M 1932	0711 2.0 0.6 1.9 0.8	**8** W 1944	0717 1.9 0.7 1.9 0.9	**23** TH 2046	0812 1.7 1.0 1.7 1.2
9 TH 1858	2.0 0.8 1.9 0.7	**24** F 1946	0726 2.2 0.5 2.1 0.5	**9** SU 1938	1.9 0.8 1.9 0.8	**24** M 2051	0829 1.9 0.8 1.8 0.9	**9** M 1912	1.9 0.6 1.9 0.7	**24** TU 2019	0754 1.9 0.8 1.8 1.0	**9** TH 2047	0810 1.8 0.9 1.8 1.0	**24** F 2155	0909 1.6 1.2 1.6 1.3
10 F 1932	2.0 0.9 1.9 0.8	**25** SA 2034	0814 2.2 0.6 1.9 0.6	**10** M 2021	1.9 0.8 1.8 0.9	**25** TU 2154	0925 1.8 1.0 1.7 1.2	**10** TU 1956	1.9 0.8 1.8 0.9	**25** W 2118	0845 1.7 1.0 1.7 1.2	**10** F 2212	1.7 1.0 1.7 1.2	**25** SA 2315	1024 1.5 1.2 1.3 1.3
11 SA 2011	1.9 0.9 1.8 0.9	**26** SU 2129	0907 2.0 0.8 1.8 0.9	**11** TU 2114	1.8 1.0 1.7 1.0	**26** W 2319	1038 1.7 1.2 1.5 1.3	**11** W 2053	1.8 0.9 1.7 1.0	**26** TH 2243	0952 1.6 1.2 1.5 1.3	**11** SA 2345	1055 1.6 1.0 1.7 1.1	**26** SU 1141	1.5 1.6
12 SU 2057	1.9 1.0 1.8 0.9	**27** M 2234	1007 1.9 1.0 1.7 1.0	**12** W 2230	0957 1.8 1.1 1.6 1.2	**27** TH 1206	1.5 1.2	**12** TH 2215	0930 1.7 1.0 1.6 1.2	**27** F 1122	1.5 1.3 1.5	**12** SU 1222	1.7 1.0 1.8	**27** M 1245	0024 1.3 1.5 1.2 1.7
13 M 2153	1.8 1.1 1.7 1.0	**28** TU 2350	1121 1.8 1.1 1.6 1.2	**13** TH 1127	1.7 1.2 1.6	**28** F 1322	0044 1.3 1.5 1.2 1.6	**13** F 2358	1109 1.6 1.1 1.6 1.2	**28** SA 1242	0010 1.3 1.4 1.2 1.5	**13** M 1329	0100 1.0 1.8 0.8 1.9	**28** TU 1336	0120 1.2 1.6 1.0 1.8
14 TU 2306	1042 1.8 1.2 1.7 1.1	**29** W 1238	1.7 1.2 1.6	**14** F 1259	0006 1.2 1.7 1.0 1.7	**29** SA 1417	0150 1.2 1.6 1.0 1.7	**14** SA 1244	1.6 1.0 1.7	**29** SU 1340	0118 1.3 1.5 1.1 1.7	**14** TU 1422	0158 0.8 1.9 0.6 2.0	**29** W 1418	0205 1.0 1.7 0.9 1.9
15 W 1159	1.8 1.2 1.7	**30** TH 1345	0106 1.2 1.7 1.1 1.7	**15** SA 1407	0129 1.0 1.8 0.9 1.8					**15** SU 1352	0119 1.0 1.8 0.8 1.9	**30** M 1425	0208 1.1 1.6 0.9 1.8	**15** W 1509	0246 0.6 2.0 0.5 2.2	**30** TH 1456	0243 0.9 1.8 0.8 2.0
			31 F 1439	0208 1.2 1.8 1.0 1.8							**31** TU 1502	0248 0.9 1.8 0.8 1.9				

TIDAL DIFFERENCES PAGE 21:186.
Special TIDAL CURVES for Poole pages 21:190-21:191.
Datum of predictions: 1.4 m. below Ordnance Datum (Newlyn) or approx. L.A.T.
CAUTION — Meterological effects can be significant at Neap tides in particular. The variations in the tide between Portland and Portsmouth are complicated. Tidal curves for individual ports in the Solent appear on pages 21:199-21:201.

(TOWN QUAY) POOLE

HIGH & LOW WATER 1992 Lat. 50°43′N. Long. 1°59′W.

GMT   ADD 1 HOUR MARCH 29 — OCTOBER 25 FOR B.S.T.

MAY

Day	Time	m		Day	Time	m
1 F	0318 / 1532	0.7 1.9 / 0.6 2.0		16 SA	0349 / 1608	0.5 2.1 / 0.5 2.2 ○
2 SA	0353 / 1607 ●	0.6 2.0 / 0.6 2.1		17 SU	0429 / 1647	0.5 2.1 / 0.6 2.1
3 SU	0427 / 1642	0.5 2.0 / 0.6 2.1		18 M	0508 / 1727	0.5 2.0 / 0.6
4 M	0503 / 1721	0.5 2.1 / 0.6 2.0		19 TU	0546 / 1806	0.6 2.0 / 0.8
5 TU	0541 / 1802	2.0 2.0 / 0.6		20 W	0625 / 1846	2.0 0.7 / 0.9
6 W	0623 / 1848	2.0 0.6 / 0.8		21 TH	0704 / 1928	1.9 0.8 / 1.0
7 TH	0711 / 1941	1.9 0.7 / 0.9		22 F	0745 / 2014	1.8 0.9 / 1.1
8 F	0807 / 2044	1.8 0.8 / 1.0		23 SA	0831 / 2107	1.7 1.0 / 1.2
9 SA	0914 / 2159	1.8 0.9 / 1.0		24 SU	0926 / 2209	1.7 1.1 / 1.3
10 SU	1034 / 2319	1.7 0.9 / 1.0		25 M	1029 / 2315	1.6 1.2 / 1.3
11 M	1151	1.7 0.9 / 1.9		26 TU	1134	1.5 1.2 / 1.7
12 TU	0030 / 1258	1.0 1.8 / 0.8 1.9		27 W	0017 / 1234	1.2 1.6 / 1.2 1.8
13 W	0130 / 1354	0.8 2.0 / 0.7		28 TH	0112 / 1328	1.1 1.7 / 1.1 1.8
14 TH	0221 / 1442	0.7 2.1 / 0.6		29 F	0200 / 1415	1.0 1.8 / 0.9
15 F	0307 / 1527	0.6 2.2 / 0.6		30 SA	0244 / 1500	0.8 1.9 / 0.8 2.0
				31 SU	0326 / 1543	0.7 2.0 / 0.7 2.1

JUNE

Day	Time	m		Day	Time	m
1 M	0407 / 1625 ●	0.6 2.0 / 0.6 2.1		16 TU	0453 / 1712	0.7 2.0 / 0.8
2 TU	0448 / 1709	0.5 2.1 / 0.6		17 W	0530 / 1750	0.7 2.0 / 0.8
3 W	0532 / 1755	0.5 2.1 / 0.6		18 TH	0607 / 1827	0.7 1.9 / 0.8
4 TH	0618 / 1843	0.5 2.1 / 0.6		19 F	0643 / 1904	0.8 1.9 / 0.9
5 F	0707 / 1936	2.0 0.6 / 0.7		20 SA	0719 / 1942	1.9 0.8 / 1.0
6 SA	0800 / 2032	2.0 0.6 / 0.8		21 SU	0756 / 2023	1.8 0.9 / 1.0
7 SU	0859 / 2136	1.9 0.8 / 0.9		22 M	0838 / 2109	1.8 0.9 / 1.1
8 M	1005 / 2246	1.9 0.8 / 1.0		23 TU	0925 / 2204	1.7 1.0 / 1.2
9 TU	1115 / 2354	1.9 0.9 / 1.0		24 W	1023 / 2308	1.7 1.1 / 1.2
10 W	1223	1.8 0.9		25 TH	1128	1.7 1.1
11 TH	0059 / 1325	0.9 1.8 / 0.9 1.9		26 F	0014 / 1235	1.2 1.7 / 1.1 1.8
12 F	0156 / 1419	0.9 1.9 / 0.8 2.0		27 SA	0117 / 1337	1.0 1.7 / 1.0 1.9
13 SA	0246 / 1508	0.8 2.0 / 0.8 2.0		28 SU	0214 / 1434	0.9 1.8 / 0.9 2.0
14 SU	0332 / 1552	0.8 2.0 / 0.8		29 M	0306 / 1524	0.8 1.9 / 0.8 2.0
15 M	0414 / 1632 ○	0.7 2.0 / 0.8		30 TU	0353 / 1612 ●	0.7 2.0 / 0.6 2.1

JULY

Day	Time	m		Day	Time	m
1 W	0438 / 1658	0.5 2.2 / 0.5		16 TH	0515 / 1733	0.6 2.0 / 0.8
2 TH	0523 / 1746	0.4 2.2 / 0.5		17 F	0548 / 1805	0.6 2.0 / 0.8
3 F	0609 / 1833	0.3 2.2 / 0.5		18 SA	0620 / 1838	0.6 1.9 / 0.8
4 SA	0655 / 1921	0.4 2.2 / 0.5		19 SU	0650 / 1910	0.7 1.9 / 0.9
5 SU	0745 / 2013	0.5 2.1 / 0.6		20 M	0722 / 1945	0.8 1.9 / 0.9
6 M	0837 / 2108	0.6 2.0 / 0.8		21 TU	0757 / 2023	0.8 1.9 / 0.9
7 TU	0933 / 2210	0.9 1.9 / 0.9		22 W	0838 / 2108	0.9 1.8 / 1.0
8 W	1038 / 2318	0.9 1.9 / 1.0		23 TH	0927 / 2206	1.0 1.7 / 1.1
9 TH	1147	1.8 1.0		24 F	1031 / 2320	1.1 1.7 / 1.2
10 F	0028 / 1258	1.0 1.7 / 1.0 1.8		25 SA	1150	1.2 1.7
11 SA	0135 / 1400	1.0 1.8 / 1.0 1.8		26 SU	0040 / 1309	1.1 1.7 / 1.1 1.8
12 SU	0232 / 1453	0.9 1.9 / 1.0 1.9		27 M	0151 / 1415	1.0 1.8 / 1.0 1.9
13 M	0320 / 1540	0.9 1.9 / 0.9		28 TU	0249 / 1512	0.8 1.9 / 0.8 2.0
14 TU	0402 / 1620 ○	0.8 1.9 / 0.8		29 W	0340 / 1601	0.6 2.0 / 0.6 2.1
15 W	0439 / 1657	0.7 2.0 / 0.8		30 TH	0426 / 1646	0.4 2.2 / 0.5 2.1
				31 F	0511 / 1733	0.3 2.3 / 0.3

AUGUST

Day	Time	m		Day	Time	m
1 SA	0554 / 1816	2.3 0.2 / 2.3		16 SU	0552 / 1809	2.0 0.6 / 0.6
2 SU	0638 / 1901	2.2 0.2 / 2.3		17 M	0621 / 1839	2.0 0.6 / 2.0
3 M	0722 / 1948	2.2 0.3 / 2.2		18 TU	0650 / 1910	1.9 0.6 / 0.7
4 TU	0810 / 2038	2.0 0.5 / 0.7		19 W	0723 / 1946	1.9 0.8 / 0.8
5 W	0901 / 2134	1.9 0.8 / 0.9		20 TH	0801 / 2028	1.9 0.9 / 0.9
6 TH	1002 / 2242	1.8 1.0 / 1.0		21 F	0849 / 2123	1.8 1.0 / 1.0
7 F	1116 / 2359	1.7 1.1 / 1.2		22 SA	0952 / 2240	1.7 1.2 / 1.2
8 SA	1235	1.7 1.2		23 SU	1121	1.6 1.2
9 SU	0114 / 1345	1.1 1.7 / 1.2 1.7		24 M	0013 / 1251	1.2 1.7 / 1.2 1.7
10 M	0216 / 1441	1.0 1.8 / 1.1 1.8		25 TU	0132 / 1401	1.0 1.8 / 1.0 1.8
11 TU	0306 / 1527	0.9 1.9 / 1.0		26 W	0233 / 1457	0.8 1.9 / 0.8 2.0
12 W	0347 / 1605	0.8 1.9 / 0.9		27 TH	0323 / 1545	0.5 2.1 / 0.5 2.2
13 TH	0422 / 1638 ○	0.7 2.0 / 0.8		28 F	0409 / 1630 ●	0.3 2.3 / 0.3
14 F	0453 / 1711	0.6 2.0 / 0.7		29 SA	0451 / 1713	0.2 2.3 / 0.3
15 SA	0523 / 1741	2.0 0.6 / 0.6		30 SU	0534 / 1755	2.3 0.2 / 2.3
				31 M	0615 / 1838	2.3 0.2 / 0.3

Sea level is above mean tide level from 2 h. after L.W. to 2 h. before the next L.W. and H.W. will occur between 5 h. after L.W. and 3 h. before the next L.W.

GENERAL — Streams are much affected by shallow waters, and at springs cause double H.W. Small tide range but strong tidal streams. Streams vary with local tides. In the harbour main flood is for 5 h. Two periods of ebb occur, separated by slack or even weak flood for approx. 7½ h.

POOLE (TOWN QUAY) 21:189

Lat. 50°43'N. Long. 1°59'W. HIGH & LOW WATER 1992

GMT ADD 1 HOUR MARCH 29 — OCTOBER 25 FOR B.S.T

SEPTEMBER

Date	Day	Time	m	Time	m
1	TU	0658	2.2 / 0.3	1921	2.2 / 0.5
16	W	0623	2.0 / 0.6	1841	2.0 / 0.7
2	W	0743	2.1 / 0.6	2008	2.1 / 0.7
17	TH	0657	2.0 / 0.8	1917	2.0 / 0.8
3	TH	0832	1.9 / 0.8	2101	1.9 / 0.9
18	F	0737	1.9 / 0.9	2001	1.9 / 0.9
4	F	0931	1.8 / 1.0	2206	1.8 / 1.1
19	SA	0826	1.8 / 1.0	2057	1.8 / 1.0
5	SA	1048	1.7 / 1.4	2329	1.7 / 1.2
20	SU	0933	1.7 / 1.2	2216	1.7 / 1.1
6	SU	1212	1.6 / 1.6		
21	M	1106	1.7 / 1.2	2352	1.7 / 1.1
7	M	0049	1.2 / 1.7	1325	1.3 / 1.6
22	TU	1233	1.7 / 1.2		
8	TU	0154	1.1 / 1.7	1421	1.2 / 1.7
23	W	0111	1.0 / 1.8	1342	1.0 / 1.9
9	W	0242	1.0 / 1.8	1505	1.0 / 1.8
24	TH	0212	0.8 / 2.0	1437	0.8 / 2.0
10	TH	0322	0.9 / 1.9	1542	0.9 / 1.9
25	F	0303	0.5 / 2.2	1525	0.5 / 2.2
11	F	0357	0.8 / 2.0	1613	0.8 / 1.9
26	SA	0348	0.3 / 2.3	1608	0.3 / 2.3
12	SA	0427	0.6 / 2.0	1642	0.6 / 2.0 ○
27	SU	0430	0.3 / 2.3	1650	0.3 / 2.3
13	SU	0455	0.6 / 2.1	1712	0.6
28	M	0511	0.3 / 2.3	1733	0.3
14	M	0523	2.0 / 0.6	1740	0.6
29	TU	0553	2.3 / 0.3	1813	0.4
15	TU	0552	2.0 / 0.6	1809	0.6
30	W	0635	2.2 / 0.5	1855	0.5

OCTOBER

Date	Day	Time	m	Time	m
1	TH	0718	2.1 / 0.7	1941	2.0 / 0.8
16	F	0639	2.0 / 0.8	1858	2.0 / 0.8
2	F	0806	1.9 / 0.9	2030	1.9 / 0.9
17	SA	0723	2.0 / 0.9	1946	1.9 / 0.9
3	SA	0902	1.8 / 1.2	2132	1.8 / 1.2
18	SU	0816	1.9 / 1.0	2045	1.8 / 1.0
4	SU	1015	1.7 / 1.3	2251	1.6 / 1.3
19	M	0925	1.8 / 1.2	2201	1.8 / 1.0
5	M	1137	1.6 / 1.4	2329	1.5 / 1.0
20	TU	1051	1.8 / 1.2	2329	1.7 / 1.0
6	TU	0009	1.3 / 1.7	1250	1.3 / 1.5
21	W	1211	1.8 / 1.1		1.8
7	W	0114	1.2 / 1.7	1346	1.2 / 1.7
22	TH	0044	0.9 / 1.9	1318	0.9 / 1.8
8	TH	0205	1.0 / 1.8	1431	1.1 / 1.8
23	F	0146	0.8 / 2.0	1413	0.8 / 2.0
9	F	0246	0.9 / 1.9	1508	0.9 / 1.9
24	SA	0237	0.6 / 2.2	1502	0.6 / 2.2
10	SA	0321	0.8 / 2.0	1542	0.8 / 1.9
25	SU	0324	0.5 / 2.3	1547	0.5 / 2.2 ●
11	SU	0355	0.7 / 2.0	1612	0.7 / 2.0 ○
26	M	0407	0.4 / 2.3	1629	0.4 / 2.3
12	M	0425	0.6 / 2.1	1641	0.6 / 2.0
27	TU	0449	0.4 / 2.3	1710	0.5 / 2.3
13	TU	0455	0.6 / 2.1	1712	0.6 / 2.2
28	W	0532	2.3 / 0.5	1752	2.2 / 0.5
14	W	0526	2.1 / 0.6	1744	2.2 / 0.6
29	TH	0613	2.2 / 0.6	1833	2.2 / 0.6
15	TH	0601	2.1 / 0.7	1820	2.0 / 0.7
30	F	0656	2.1 / 0.8	1916	2.0 / 0.8
31	SA	0742	2.0 / 1.0	2003	1.9 / 1.0

NOVEMBER

Date	Day	Time	m	Time	m
1	SU	0833	1.9 / 1.2	2056	1.8 / 1.1
16	M	0811	2.0 / 0.9	2037	1.9 / 0.9
2	M	0935	1.8 / 1.3	2200	1.7 / 1.2
17	TU	0914	1.9 / 1.1	2144	1.8 / 0.9
3	TU	1047	1.7 / 1.4	2311	1.6 / 1.3
18	W	1028	1.8 / 1.1	2301	1.8 / 1.0
4	W	1155	1.7 / 1.3		1.5
19	TH	1141	1.9 / 1.0		1.8
5	TH	0017	1.2 / 1.7	1256	1.3 / 1.6
20	F	0012	0.9 / 1.9	1250	1.0 / 1.9
6	F	0113	1.2 / 1.8	1345	1.2 / 1.7
21	SA	0117	0.9 / 2.0	1348	0.9 / 2.0
7	SA	0200	1.0 / 1.9	1428	1.0 / 1.8
22	SU	0212	0.8 / 2.1	1440	0.8 / 2.1
8	SU	0241	0.9 / 2.0	1506	0.9 / 1.9
23	M	0302	0.7 / 2.2	1527	0.6 / 2.2
9	M	0319	0.8 / 2.0	1541	0.8 / 2.0
24	TU	0348	0.6 / 2.2	1611	0.6 / 2.2 ●
10	TU	0355	0.8 / 2.1	1615	0.7 / 2.1 ○
25	W	0431	0.6 / 2.2	1652	0.6 / 2.2
11	W	0430	0.7 / 2.2	1649	0.6 / 2.1
26	TH	0513	0.6 / 2.2	1735	0.6 / 2.2
12	TH	0507	0.7 / 2.2	1726	0.6 / 2.1
27	F	0555	2.2 / 0.6	1814	2.1 / 0.7
13	F	0546	2.1 / 0.7	1805	2.0 / 0.6
28	SA	0636	2.0 / 0.8	1854	2.0 / 0.8
14	SA	0629	2.1 / 0.8	1849	2.0 / 0.7
29	SU	0718	1.9 / 0.9	1936	1.9 / 0.9
15	SU	0716	2.0 / 0.9	1939	1.9 / 0.8
30	M	0802	1.9 / 1.1	2019	1.8 / 1.0

DECEMBER

Date	Day	Time	m	Time	m
1	TU	0851	1.8 / 1.2	2107	1.7 / 1.1
16	W	0855	2.0 / 0.9	2120	1.9 / 0.8
2	W	0947	1.8 / 1.3	2203	1.7 / 1.2
17	TH	0959	2.0 / 1.0	2227	1.8 / 0.9
3	TH	1050	1.8 / 1.3	2307	1.6 / 1.2
18	F	1110	1.9 / 1.0	2339	1.8 / 1.0
4	F	1152	1.8 / 1.3		1.6
19	SA	1221	1.9 / 1.0		1.8
5	SA	0008	1.2 / 1.8	1252	1.2 / 1.7
20	SU	0048	1.0 / 2.0	1326	0.9 / 1.9
6	SU	0107	1.2 / 1.9	1344	1.1 / 1.8
21	M	0151	0.9 / 2.0	1424	0.9 / 2.0
7	M	0159	1.0 / 1.9	1431	1.0 / 1.9
22	TU	0245	1.0 / 2.0	1514	0.8 / 2.0
8	TU	0245	0.9 / 2.0	1514	0.9 / 2.0
23	W	0334	0.8 / 2.1	1559	0.7 / 2.1
9	W	0328	0.9 / 2.0	1554	0.8 / 2.0 ○
24	TH	0418	0.8 / 2.1	1639	0.6 / 2.1 ●
10	TH	0410	0.8 / 2.2	1633	0.6 / 2.1
25	F	0458	0.8 / 2.1	1719	0.6 / 2.0
11	F	0451	0.7 / 2.2	1714	0.6 / 2.0
26	SA	0538	2.0 / 0.8	1756	2.0 / 0.6
12	SA	0535	2.2 / 0.8	1756	2.0 / 0.5
27	SU	0615	2.0 / 0.8	1831	2.0 / 0.7
13	SU	0620	2.2 / 0.6	1841	2.1 / 0.5
28	M	0652	2.0 / 0.9	1906	1.9 / 0.8
14	M	0707	2.2 / 0.7	1928	2.0 / 0.6
29	TU	0729	2.0 / 0.7	1942	1.9 / 0.9
15	TU	0758	2.1 / 0.8	2021	2.0 / 0.7
30	W	0809	1.9 / 1.0	2020	1.8 / 0.9
31	TH	0851	1.9 / 1.1	2102	1.7 / 1.0

At Springs: streams are strong. At Neaps: streams are weak and uncertain. Intervals between H.W.'s shorter at ent. than at Bridge. H.W. at ent. ½ h. (approx.) earlier than at Bridge.

RATE AND SET — Springs: Position, outside Bar; E. going coastal 025°-345°, +0500 Portsmouth Sp. 1½ kn.; W. going coastal 160°-180° –0050 Portsmouth, Sp. 1¼ kn. Position — ent. chan.: Ingoing +0550 Portsmouth, Sp. 2½-3 kn.; outgoing –0150 Portsmouth, Sp. 4-4¾ kn.

POOLE Tidal Curve

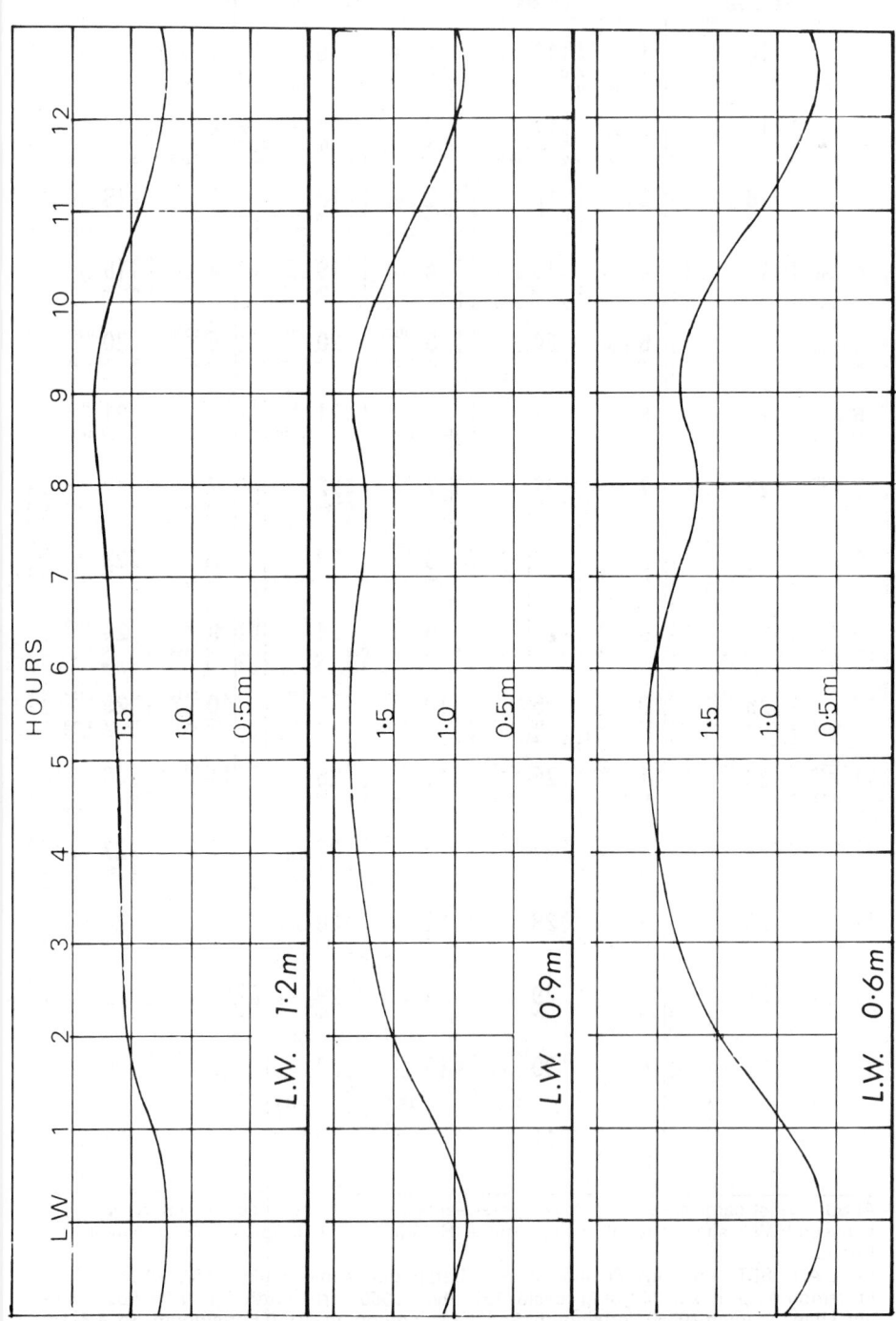

POOLE Tidal Curve

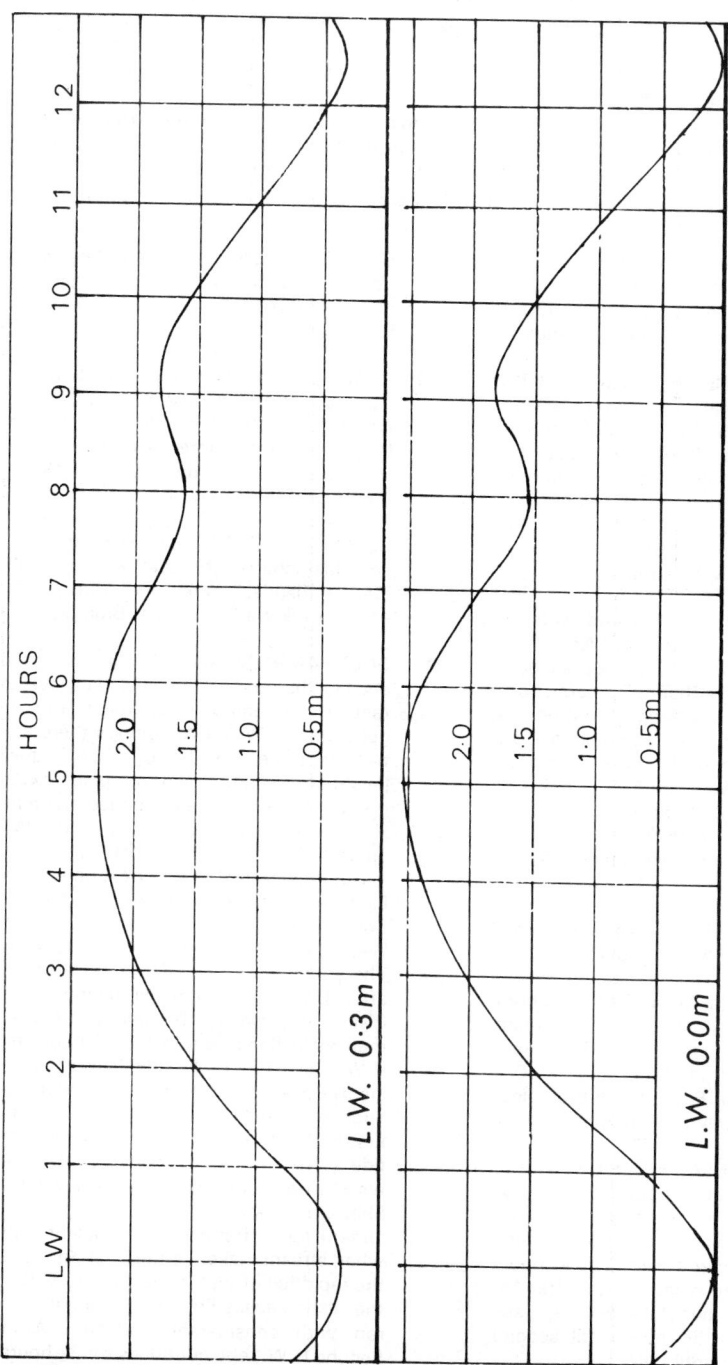

POOLE BRIDGE — Predicted tidal curve

Instructions
1. Find predicted time and height of L.W. from pages 21:187-21:189
2. Select the curve whose L.W. height is closest to that predicted.
3. Read off the predicted height at the required period after L.W.
   All heights are in metres above chart datum.

TIDAL STREAMS
SOLENT AND ADJACENT WATERS

1. **GENERAL.** Western approach to the English Channel streams are rotatory, clockwise. N.E. and E.N.E. +0400; S.E. −0500; W.S.W. −0100; N.W. +0100. East of Portland streams in a straight line. At no times are the streams running in one direction in the English Channel. Where streams meet and separate—weak, irregular or slack, with the greatest rate between two such areas. Rates greatest in narrowest parts—max. 4-5 kts. Storm surges, usually raise, sometimes depress sea level.

2. Between Swanage and Christchurch there is a stand of the Tide from the time of High Water at Portsmouth until two hours later. When the range of the tide is large there may be a second high water during this stand; at neaps the only high water occurs during it.

3. **In Freshwater Bay,** the Needles Channel and the Solent there is a stand of the tide from one hour before to one hour after High Water at Portsmouth.

4. **NEEDLES CHANNEL APPROACH.** 1¼ M. 273° Needles Lt. Ho. (a) E. going +0530 2½ kts.; (b) W. going −0030 3 kts.; (c) Streams strong across Shingles.

5. **NEEDLES CHANNEL between Hurst Pt. and Albert Fort.** (a) N.E. +0505 4 kts.; (b) S.W. −0055 4½ kts.; (c) Strong, disturbed seas on Bridge, Shingles; (d) Set − to and from Shingles; (e) Overfalls − S.E. Shingles during N.E. stream; (f) Turbulence − S. and S.E. Hurst Pt. during N.E. stream; (g) Strong E. eddy S. Hurst Pt. during S.W. stream.

6. **NORTH CHANNEL.** (a) Flood sets in deepest water. Sp. 3-3½ kts.; Np. 2 kts; increases as Hurst Pt. is approached; joins main Needles Channel stream about 2 cables S. of Pt. causing violent eddies 4-5 knots. (b) Ebb, main ebb branches off at Hurst Pt. (causing strong inshore eddy), through N. channel. Sp. 4 kts.; Np. 3 kts. (c) E. & W. streams run about 6 hours each. Stream slackens as narrows are left and ebb diminishes into Christchurch Bay.

7. **HURST.** An uncomfortable anchorage, eddies are strong and irregular.

8. **WEST SOLENT.** (a) Main stream − about direction of channels; (b) W. stream stronger than E. stream; (c) E. stream +0505 2½-3 kts.; (d) W. stream −0100, 3½ kts.; (e) W. of Egypt Pt. & Brambles, streams turn nearly at same time.

9. **YARMOUTH. I.O.W.** (a) Outer roads. Sp. 2½-3 kts.; (b) Last of flood eddies to W. towards Sconce Pt. where it turns out and rejoins E. going stream; (c) Outside Black Rock, Fiddler's Race eddy should be avoided in bad weather. (d) After 1st H.W. Yarmouth tide falls a little, rises again at H.W. +30 min. until second H.W., then ebbs until L.W.

10. **COWES ROADS.** E. stream begins at about +0515. W. stream begins at about −0030. Maximum rate 3-4 kts. at Prince Consort By.

11. **COWES.** (a) Floods for 6½ hours; Ebbs for 4¾ hours strong at maximum at Sp.; (b) At Springs after 1st H.W. tide falls a little; then rises more to make second H.W. one hour later; then ebbs to L.W. At Neaps one H.W. only.

12. **CALSHOT Lt.F.** (a) Streams rotatory − see tidal charts; (b) Last 2 hours ebb stream divides here and runs both eastward & westward past Brambles.

13. **SOUTHAMPTON WATER.** (a) NE. gale and high barometer may lower sea level 2 feet. (b) Streams in approach run in general E. & W. (c) At Springs there are two separate H.W.'s of about equal height with an interval of up to approx. 2 hrs. (d) At Neaps one prolonged stand at H.W. − ebb approx. 3¼ hrs. and L.W. approx. 5½ hrs. after 1st H.W. (e) Flood in Southampton Water corresponds with East going Solent stream. (f) Ebb in Southampton Water corresponds with West going Solent stream. (g) Flood (i) The young Flood rises for about 2 hours after L.W.; then remains nearly slack (rising very slowly) for about 2 hours; then main flood sets in for 2¾ hours till H.W.; (ii) After H.W. tide falls about 9 ins. for one hour; then rises for about 1¼ hours making second H.W. same level as first H.W. (or even higher). (iii) At Neaps tide stands for long time near H.W. − with no observable difference in level. (h) Ebb; Little tidal fall occurs as long as W. stream runs strongly in the Solent; but when stream makes to the E. at Spithead the rapid fall of water everywhere within the Island causes Ebb at Southampton to run with considerable velocity. After Second H.W., ebb continues for 3¼ hours

falling most rapidly 2 hours after it, at which time the stream runs strongest in the fairway.

14. HYTHE PIER. Rate and set W. side of dredged channel: (i) 1st flood +0515, Portsmouth, Sp. rate $\frac{1}{2}$ kt.; (ii) True flood +0330, Portsmouth, Sp. rate 1 kt.; (iii) 1st ebb, −0015, Portsmouth, Sp. rate very weak; (iv) True ebb, +0145, Portsmouth, Sp. rate 2kts. Portsmouth times see pp. 21:210-21:212.

15. EAST SOLENT. (a) Streams generally in direction of Solent; (b) E. going, +0435; (c) W. going, −0115; (d) Rates vary considerably; (e) W. going stronger than E. going; (f) Eastwards the streams begin earlier.

16. ISLE OF WIGHT — South Coast. 4$\frac{1}{2}$M. 205° Needles. (a) E. going +0545, 040°*, 2 kts.; (b) W. going, −0015, 265°, 2$\frac{1}{4}$ kts. (c) Streams nearly in a straight line. (d) Race off St. Catherine's Hd. violent with wind against stream, and at Springs during W. gale during W. stream; (e) Main E. going stream joins E. going Solent and flows on to Selsey Bill, similarly W. going streams part and join again. (f) Flood or E. going stream sets dangerously towards Brook and Atherfield Ledges (especially with strong W'ly winds). Strong indraft on same stream between I.O.W. and OWERS must be allowed for. Stream makes earlier off the E. coast of I.O.W. than further West. (g) Ebb or W. going stream makes earliest off W. part of I.O.W. coast. Both streams turn earlier inshore than offshore.

17. SPITHEAD. E. APPROACH. (a) Streams rotatory anti-clockwise — see tidal charts; (b) **Caution.** E. stream sets for 5 hours towards Chichester Harbour entrance and Bracklesham Bay — so be cautious — especially in thick weather; (c) Guard against the E. stream at times setting towards and over the Horse and Dean Elbow shoals.

18. SPITHEAD. (a) At Spithead and towards the Brambles the W. stream runs for approx. 5 hours for about 2$\frac{1}{2}$ hours before until 2$\frac{1}{2}$ hours after H.W.

Portsmouth; (b) E. stream runs for about 7 hours with no slack water at the turn of the streams.

19. PORTSMOUTH HARBOUR APPROACH. Off entrance. (a) Ingoing, +0545, Strong; (b) Outgoing, +0030 Strong. Spithead. (c) E. going, +0345; (d) W. going, −0145; (e) Off Spit Refuge Buoy, stream sets across Portsmouth channel for first 4 hours flood and first two hours ebb. Flood sets for four hours across the channel towards LANGSTON; then for 1 hour towards Southsea Castle and then slowly towards the Harbour; Ebb sets W. and SW. and then SE. for the last 3 hours at 2$\frac{1}{2}$-3 knots.

20. PORTSMOUTH OUTER. (a) Flood, duration about 7 hours. Tide rises slowly for the first 4 hours flood (slack period between 2nd and 3rd hour). Rises faster for the next 3 hours, running strongest between the 5th and 7th hour. At times a small stream runs in for about a quarter of an hour after H.W. (b) Ebb, duration about 5 hours, starts shortly after H.W. but falls slowly until E. stream makes at Spithead, the latter part of ebb being far the stronger, being about 4$\frac{1}{2}$ kts. at Sp. between the 3rd and 4th hour ebb.

21. PORTSMOUTH INNER (a) Flood in two periods, +0530, 1-3$\frac{1}{2}$ kts.; (b) Ebb in one period, +0040, 5 kts.; (c) Inwards — ebb and flood decrease. (d) Eddies — both sides of harbour entrance; (e) Portchester — ebb begins +0050, ceases +0515, approx. 3 hrs. or more slack — then flood.

22. LANGSTON HARBOUR. Streams run very fast in entrance; Ebb runs fastest when shoals uncover at last part of ebb. Flood and Ebb both make about quarter of an hour after L. & H. Water by the shore.

23. CHICHESTER HARBOUR. Flood about 7 hours, ebb about 5 hours. Ebb runs fast 6 knots at top Springs; Flood about 3 knots. Do not enter in bad weather except at H.W.; otherwise between half flood and High Water. Consult Tidal Stream charts but W. going stream commences about 2 hours before H.W. Portsmouth and E. going about 3 hours after H.W. Portsmouth.

N.B.–Times are given in relation in H.W. Dover unless stated otherwise, and indicate the beginning of the stream. Rates are approx. maximum at Springs in knots. Tidal streams in relation to Portsmouth see pages 21:194-21:198.
*Changes very quickly to 080°.

THE SOLENT AND ADJACENT WATERS TIDAL STREAMS

Thirteen charts are given showing tidal streams at hourly intervals commencing 6 hours before H.W. Portsmouth and ending 6 hours after H.W. Portsmouth. For Portsmouth H.W. Times see pages 21:210-21:212.

Tidal stream direction is shown by arrows. The thicker the arrows, the stronger the tidal streams they indicate; the thinner arrows show rates and position of weaker streams.

Figures shown against the arrows, e.g. 19.34, indicate a mean Neap rate of 1.9 knots and a mean Spring rate of 3.4 knots approx.

The following charts are produced from portion(s) of BA Tidal Stream Atlases with the sanction of the Controller, H.M. Stationery Office and of the Hydrographer of the Navy.

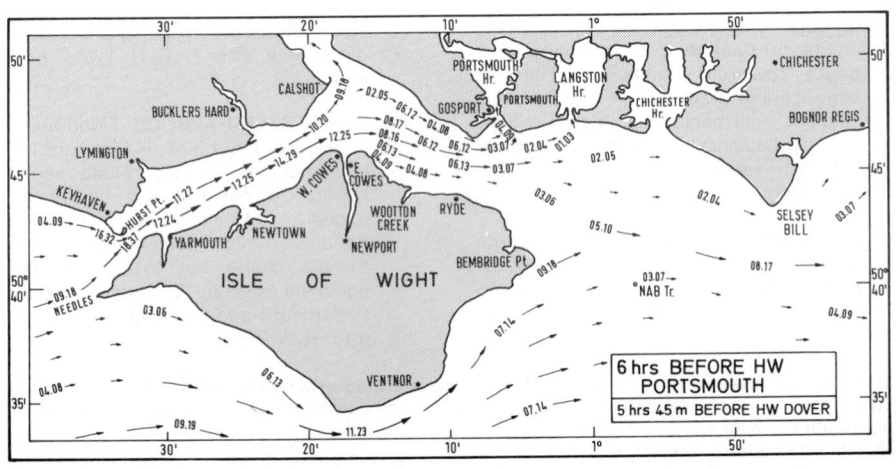

THE SOLENT AND ADJACENT WATERS
TIDAL STREAMS

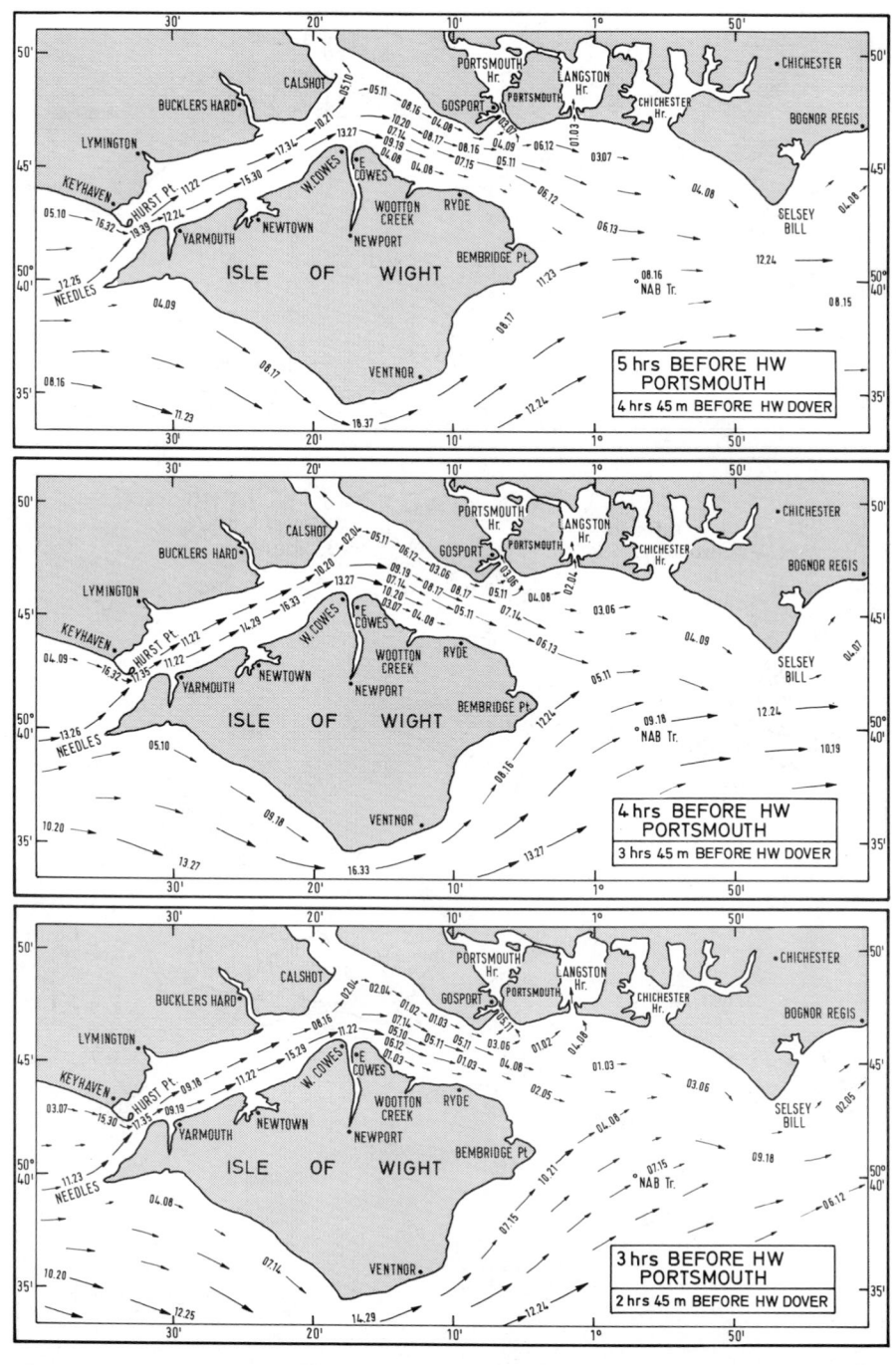

THE SOLENT AND ADJACENT WATERS
TIDAL STREAMS

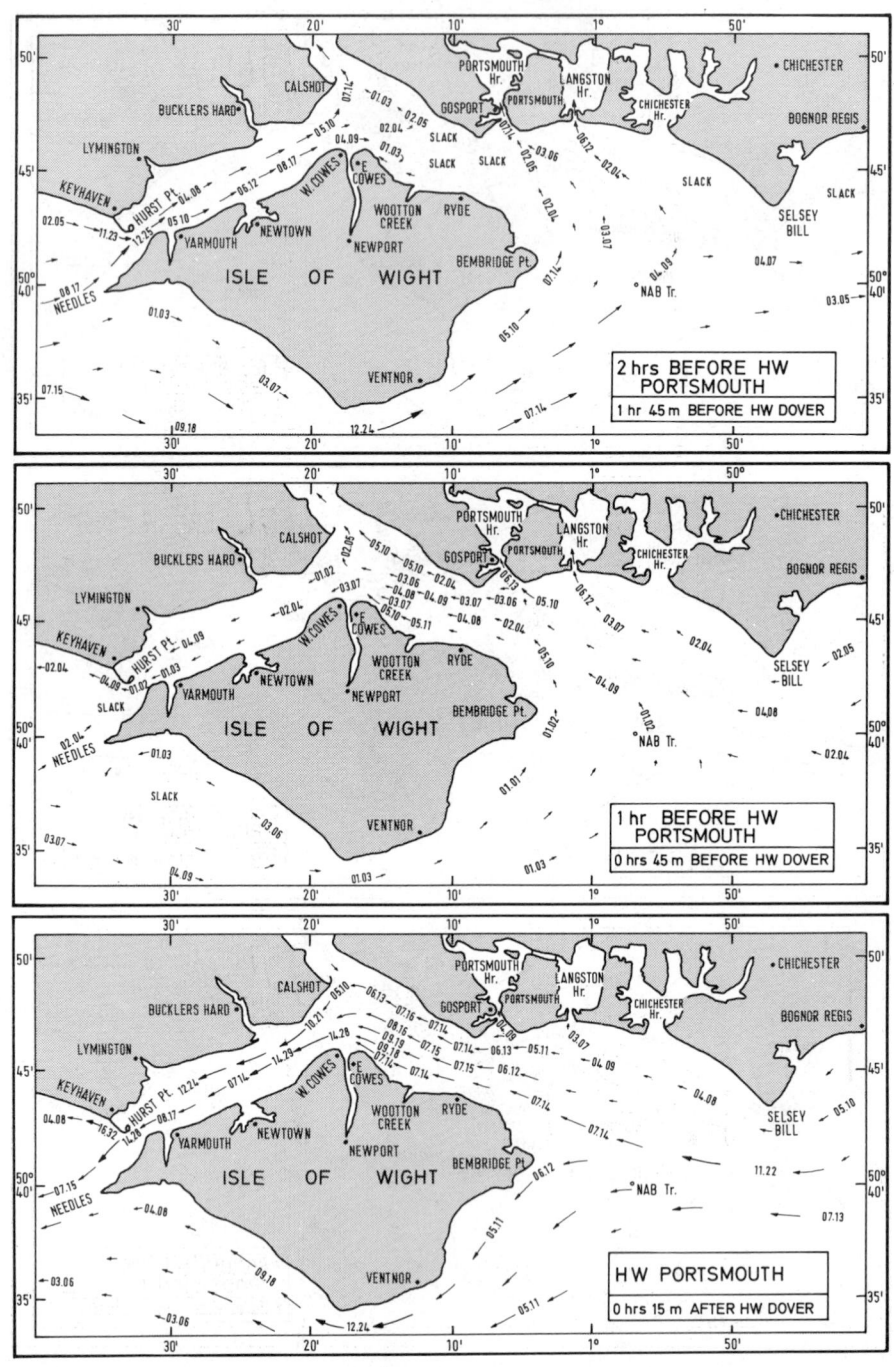

THE SOLENT AND ADJACENT WATERS
TIDAL STREAMS

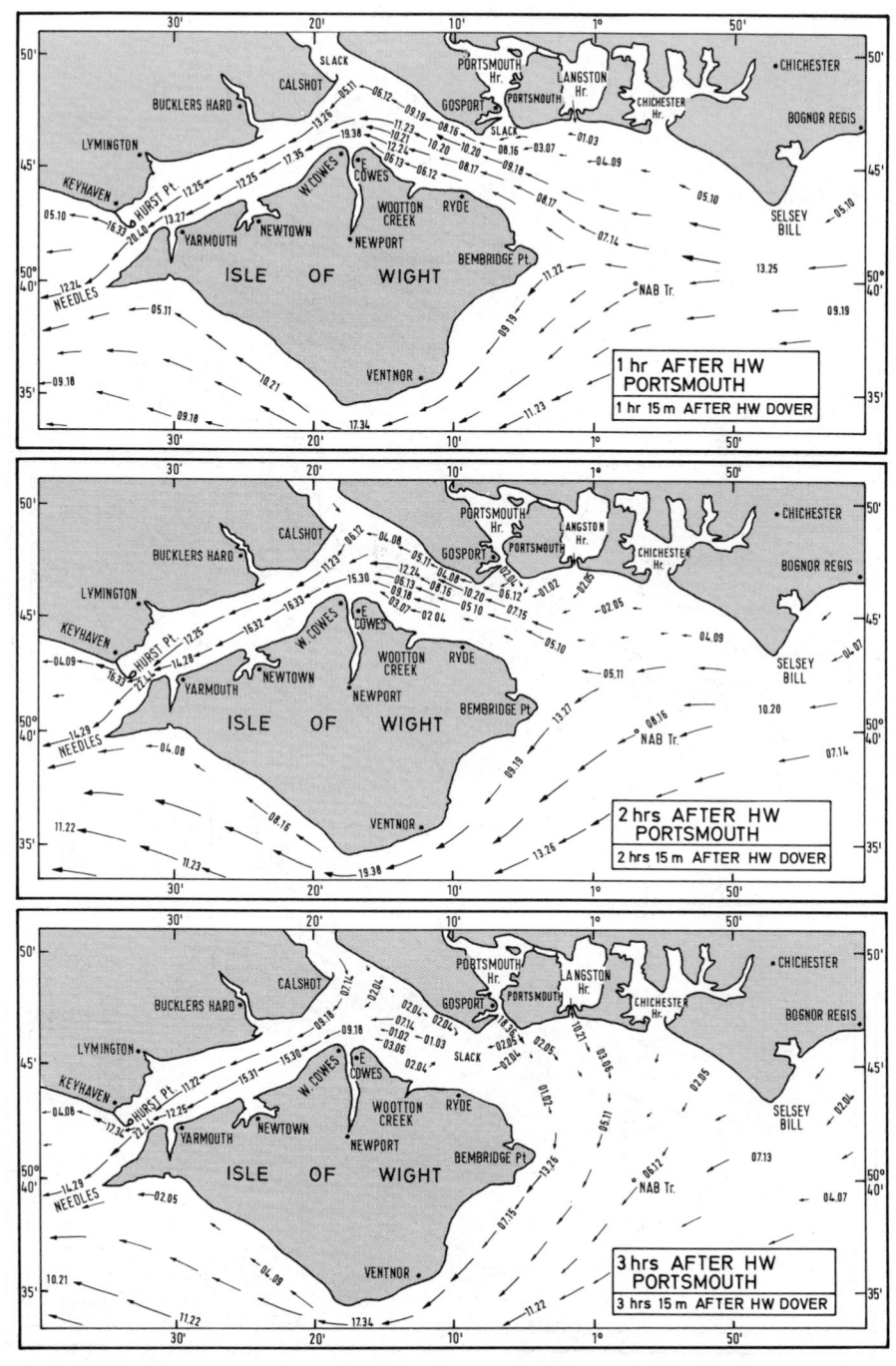

THE SOLENT AND ADJACENT WATERS
TIDAL STREAMS

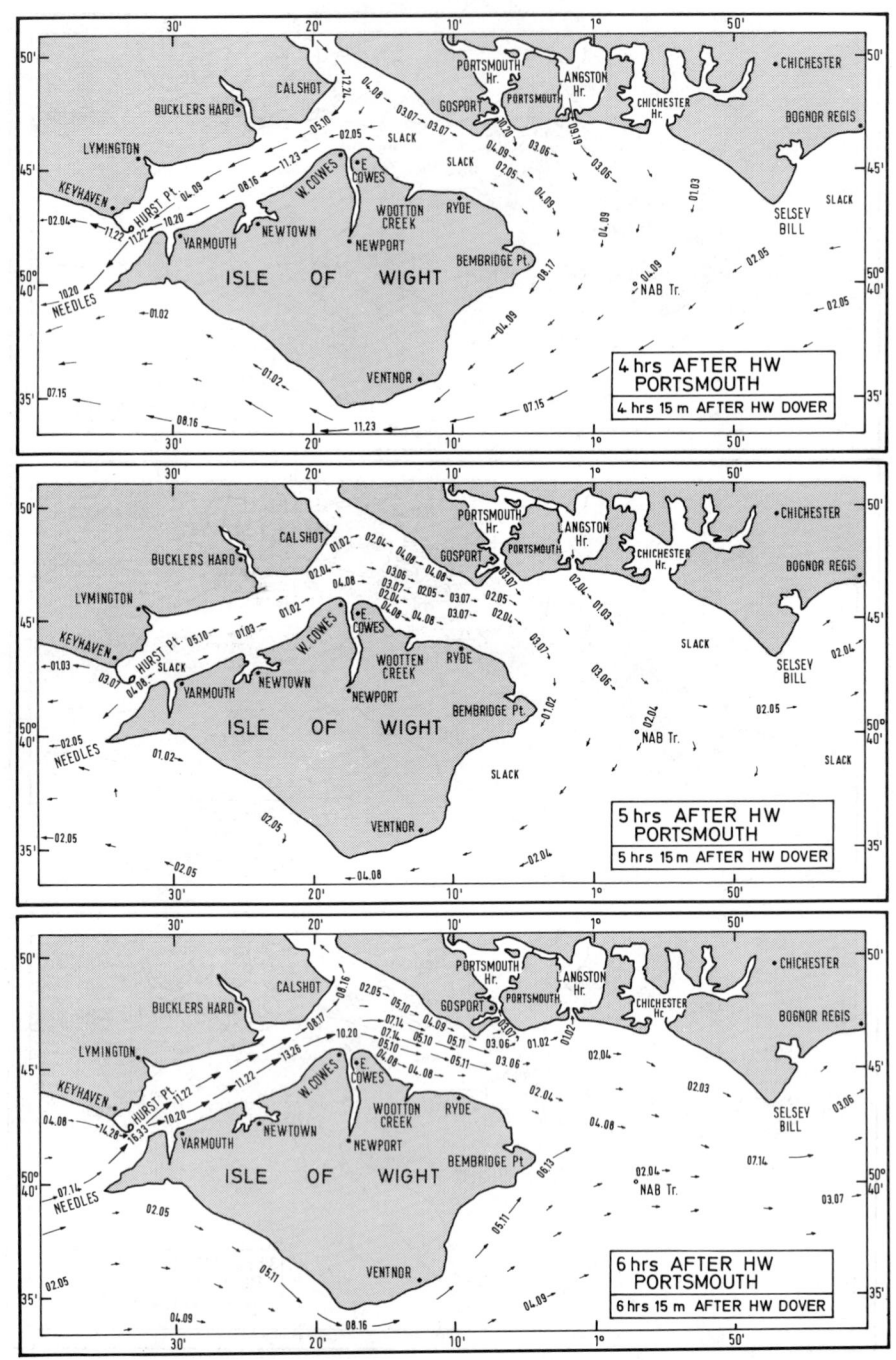

TIDAL CURVES — SWANAGE TO CHRISTCHURCH

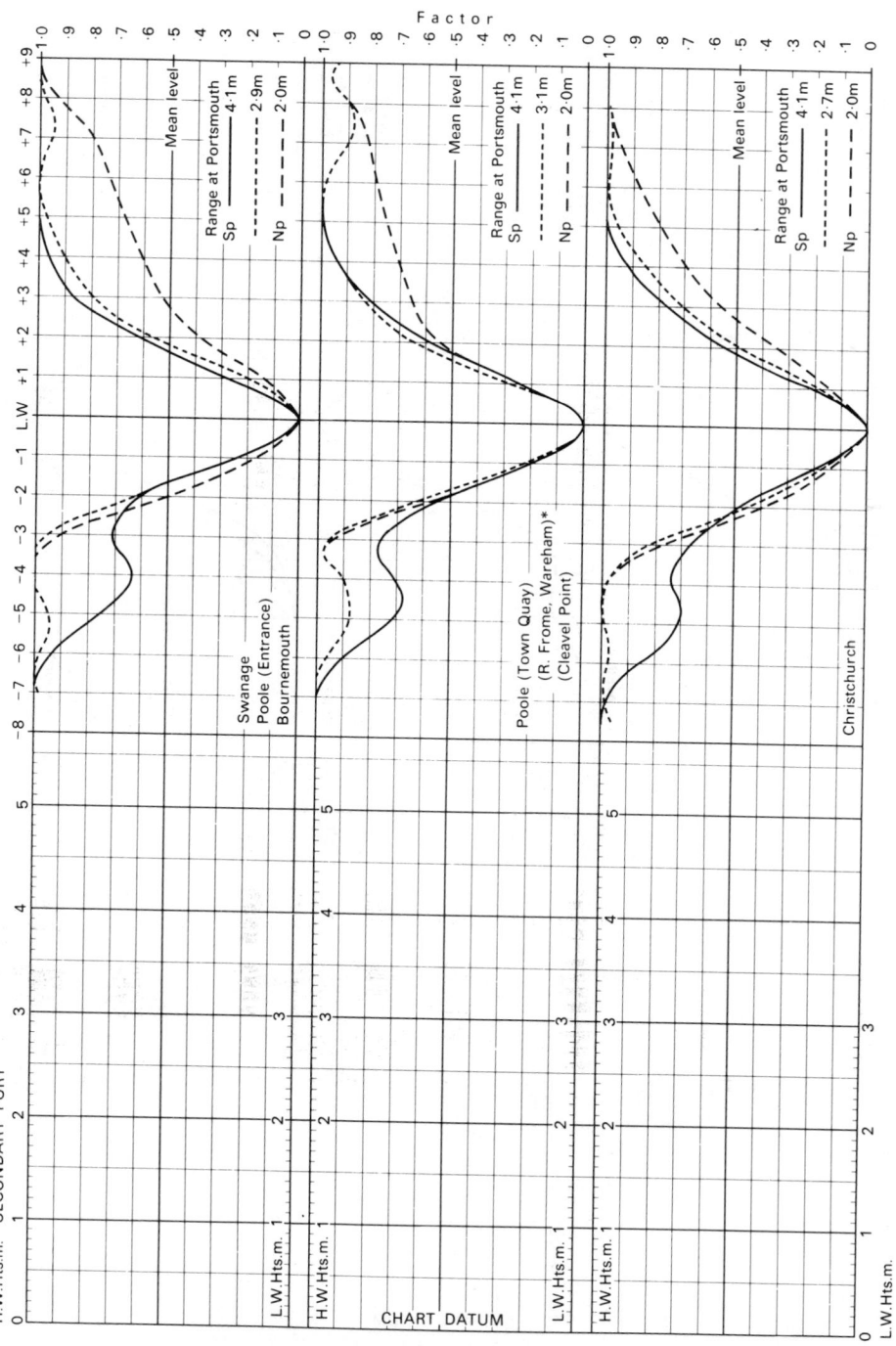

TIDAL CURVES — LYMINGTON TO COWES

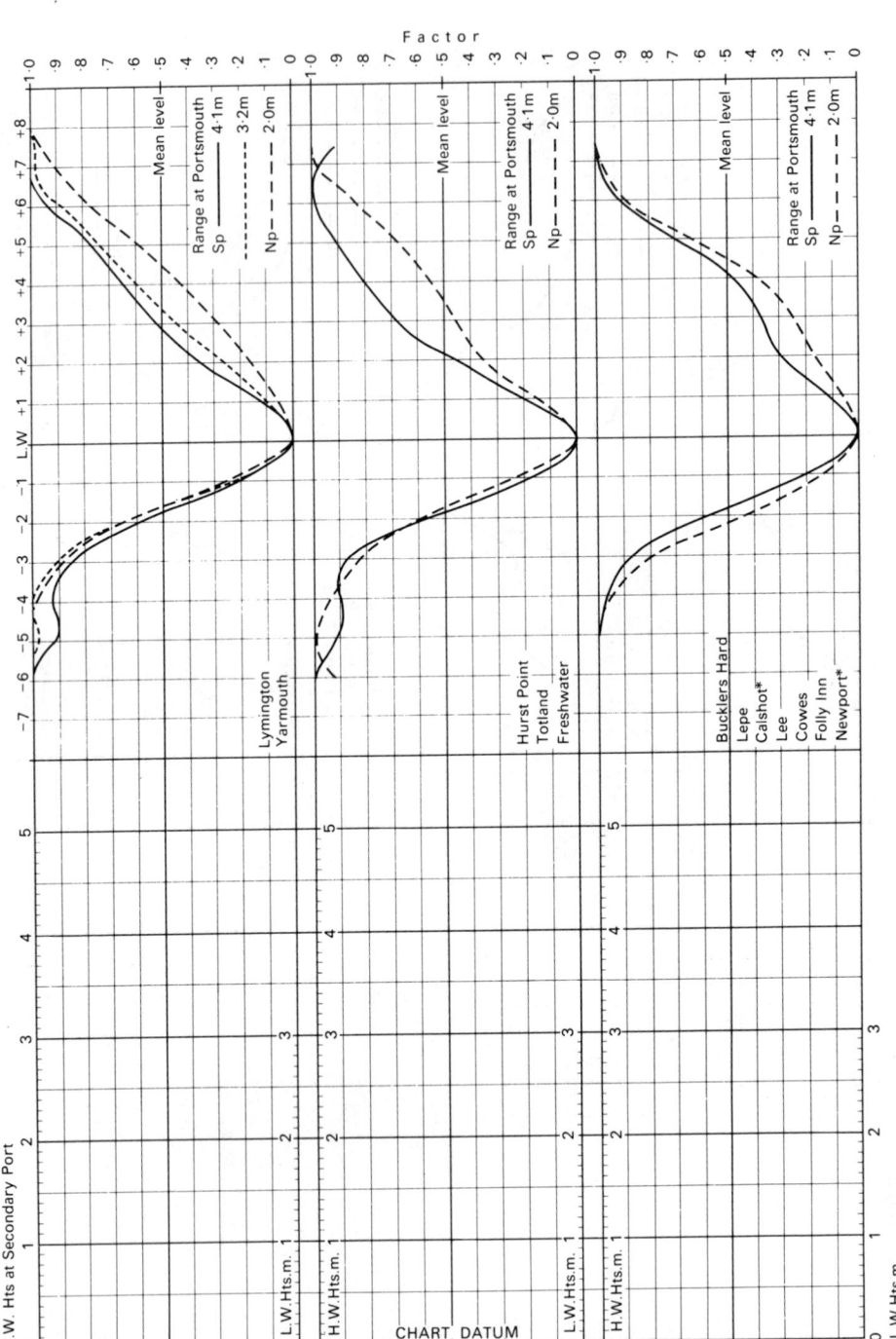

TIDAL CURVES — RYDE TO SELSEY

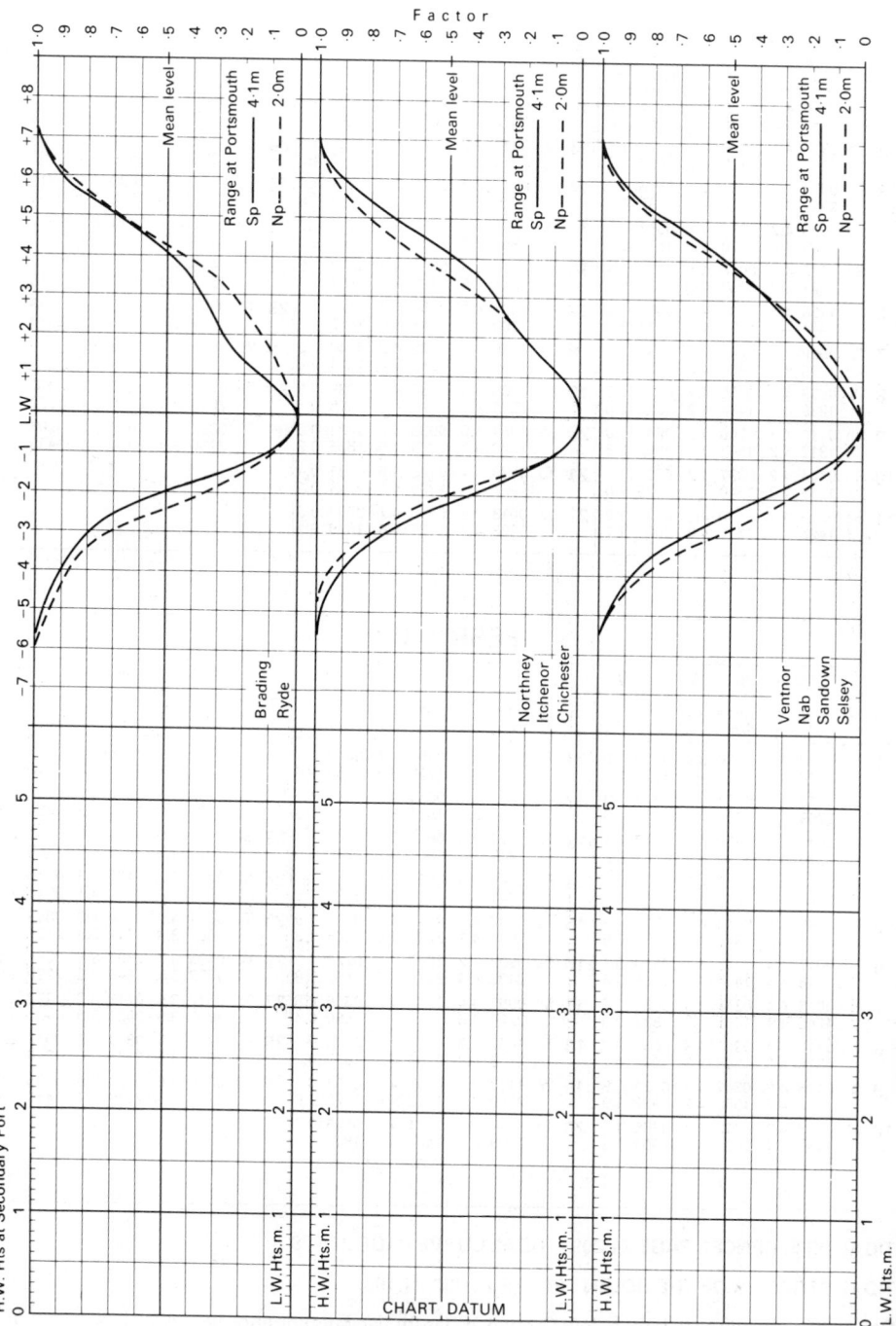

SOUTHAMPTON

1st and 2nd HIGH and LOW WATER 1992

GMT ADD 1 HOUR MARCH 29–OCTOBER 25 FOR B.S.T.

JANUARY

Date	Day	1st H.W. Time Ht.	2nd H.W. Time Ht.	L.W Time Ht.
1	W	0820 4.0 / 2057 4.0	0955 3.9 / 2235 3.9	0125 1.6 / 1358 1.4
2	Th	0910 4.1 / 2146 4.1	1051 4.0 / 2329 4.0	0226 1.5 / 1453 1.3
3	F	0951 4.1 / 2227 4.2	1137 4.0 / — —	0316 1.4 / 1538 1.1
4	Sa	1029 4.2 / 2303 4.2	0015 4.1 / 1220 4.1	0357 1.2 / 1616 0.9
5	Su	1103 4.3 / 2337 4.3	0055 4.1 / 1257 4.1	0435 1.1 / 1651 0.8
6	M	1136 4.3 / — —	0131 4.2 / 1331 4.2	0507 1.0 / 1721 0.8
7	Tu	0009 4.3 / 1208 4.3	0204 4.2 / 1403 4.2	0538 1.0 / 1753 0.8
8	W	0039 4.3 / 1239 4.3	0235 4.2 / 1434 4.2	0610 1.0 / 1822 0.8
9	Th	0111 4.3 / 1312 4.2	0306 4.2 / 1507 4.2	0642 1.0 / 1852 0.9
10	F	0144 4.2 / 1349 4.2	0337 4.2 / 1540 4.1	0714 1.1 / 1925 1.0
11	Sa	0221 4.2 / 1428 4.1	0410 4.1 / 1615 4.0	0749 1.2 / 2001 1.2
12	Su	0303 4.1 / 1515 3.9	0447 4.1 / 1656 3.9	0830 1.4 / 2044 1.4
13	M	0353 4.0 / 1612 3.8	0531 4.0 / 1747 3.8	0921 1.6 / 2142 1.7
14	Tu	0454 3.9 / 1722 3.7	0628 3.9 / 1855 3.7	1027 1.8 / 2253 1.8
15	W	0605 3.8 / 1842 3.7	0738 3.8 / 2016 3.7	1144 1.7 / — —
16	Th	0716 3.9 / 1957 3.9	0852 3.9 / 2135 3.8	0017 1.8 / 1303 1.5
17	F	0821 4.1 / 2100 4.1	1002 4.0 / 2243 4.0	0134 1.5 / 1412 1.2
18	Sa	0916 4.3 / 2154 4.3	1102 4.2 / 2343 4.2	0240 1.2 / 1511 0.9
19	Su	1006 4.4 / 2241 4.5	1157 4.3 / — —	0339 0.9 / 1605 0.5
20	M	1054 4.6 / 2328 4.7	0035 4.4 / 1249 4.5	0431 0.6 / 1655 0.3
21	Tu	1139 4.7 / — —	0125 4.6 / 1339 4.5	0521 0.4 / 1744 0.1
22	W	0013 4.8 / 1225 4.7	0213 4.7 / 1427 4.6	0608 0.3 / 1829 0.1
23	Th	0058 4.8 / 1311 4.6	0300 4.7 / 1513 4.6	0652 0.3 / 1912 0.2
24	F	0144 4.7 / 1358 4.6	0346 4.7 / 1558 4.5	0733 0.5 / 1950 0.4
25	Sa	0231 4.6 / 1447 4.3	0428 4.5 / 1641 4.3	0812 0.7 / 2030 0.7
26	Su	0322 4.3 / 1544 4.1	0511 4.3 / 1728 4.1	0854 1.0 / 2116 1.1
27	M	0419 4.1 / 1647 3.8	0558 4.1 / 1822 3.9	0944 1.4 / 2213 1.6
28	Tu	0523 3.8 / 1805 3.7	0655 3.9 / 1934 3.7	1049 1.7 / 2328 1.9
29	W	0638 3.7 / 1931 3.6	0806 3.7 / 2059 3.6	— — / 1210 1.8
30	Th	0752 3.7 / 2043 3.8	0922 3.7 / 2215 3.7	0052 1.9 / 1330 1.8
31	F	0852 3.8 / 2136 3.9	1027 3.8 / 2314 3.8	0204 1.8 / 1435 1.6

FEBRUARY

Date	Day	1st H.W. Time Ht.	2nd H.W. Time Ht.	L.W Time Ht.
1	Sa	0939 4.0 / 2216 4.1	1120 3.9 / — —	0259 1.6 / 1524 1.3
2	Su	1016 4.1 / 2249 4.2	0001 4.0 / 1203 4.0	0343 1.3 / 1601 1.0
3	M	1049 4.2 / 2320 4.3	0038 4.1 / 1240 4.1	0417 1.1 / 1634 0.8
4	Tu	1119 4.4 / 2349 4.4	0113 4.2 / 1312 4.2	0449 0.9 / 1703 0.7
5	W	1149 4.4 / — —	0144 4.3 / 1345 4.3	0519 0.8 / 1734 0.6
6	Th	0017 4.4 / 1218 4.4	0214 4.3 / 1417 4.3	0550 0.7 / 1804 0.6
7	F	0045 4.4 / 1248 4.4	0244 4.3 / 1448 4.3	0621 0.7 / 1833 0.6
8	Sa	0113 4.4 / 1320 4.3	0313 4.3 / 1518 4.3	0651 0.7 / 1901 0.7
9	Su	0146 4.3 / 1356 4.2	0342 4.3 / 1550 4.2	0721 0.9 / 1932 1.0
10	M	0223 4.2 / 1439 4.1	0413 4.2 / 1624 4.1	0756 1.1 / 2008 1.3
11	Tu	0309 4.1 / 1533 3.9	0450 4.1 / 1710 3.9	0840 1.4 / 2058 1.6
12	W	0407 3.9 / 1642 3.7	0541 4.0 / 1814 3.8	0940 1.7 / 2212 1.8
13	Th	0520 3.8 / 1813 3.7	0652 3.8 / 1945 3.7	1103 1.8 / 2346 1.9
14	F	0646 3.8 / 1941 3.8	0820 3.8 / 2117 3.8	— — / 1237 1.6
15	Sa	0802 4.0 / 2047 4.1	0941 3.9 / 2230 4.0	0117 1.6 / 1356 1.3
16	Su	0902 4.2 / 2139 4.4	1048 4.1 / 2328 4.3	0228 1.2 / 1457 0.8
17	M	0951 4.4 / 2226 4.6	1143 4.3 / — —	0326 0.8 / 1550 0.4
18	Tu	1037 4.6 / 2308 4.8	0020 4.5 / 1234 4.5	0416 0.5 / 1639 0.2
19	W	1122 4.7 / 2352 4.9	0107 4.7 / 1322 4.6	0504 0.3 / 1725 0.0
20	Th	— — / 1205 4.7	0154 4.7 / 1408 4.6	0548 0.2 / 1808 0.0
21	F	0033 4.9 / 1249 4.7	0238 4.8 / 1454 4.6	0630 0.2 / 1848 0.1
22	Sa	0115 4.7 / 1332 4.5	0320 4.7 / 1535 4.5	0707 0.3 / 1924 0.3
23	Su	0159 4.5 / 1418 4.3	0359 4.5 / 1615 4.3	0742 0.6 / 1958 0.7
24	M	0243 4.3 / 1508 4.0	0435 4.3 / 1654 4.1	0816 0.9 / 2037 1.2
25	Tu	0334 4.0 / 1607 3.8	0514 4.0 / 1742 3.8	0858 1.4 / 2127 1.7
26	W	0433 3.7 / 1722 3.5	0603 3.8 / 1848 3.6	0956 1.8 / 2239 2.0
27	Th	0547 3.5 / 1857 3.5	0711 3.6 / 2021 3.5	1122 2.0 / — —
28	F	0715 3.5 / 2018 3.6	0840 3.5 / 2146 3.6	0012 2.2 / 1256 2.0
29	Sa	0826 3.6 / 2115 3.8	0957 3.6 / 2249 3.7	0135 2.0 / 1410 1.7

TIDAL DIFFERENCES PAGE 21:209   TIDAL CURVE PAGE 21:208.

TIDAL STREAMS OF THE SOLENT PAGES 21:192-21:198.

Datum of predictions 2.74m. below Ordnance Datum (Newlyn) or approx. L.A.T.

Lat. 50° 54'N, Long. 1°24'W

1st and 2nd HIGH and LOW WATER 1992

MARCH

Date	Day	1st H.W. Time	Ht.	2nd H.W. Time	Ht.	L.W. Time	Ht.
1	Su	0916	3.8	1054	3.7	0236	1.7
		2153	4.0	2335	3.9	1500	1.4
2	M	0954	4.0	1138	3.9	0318	1.4
		2226	4.2	——		1537	1.1
3	Tu	1026	4.2	0012	4.1	0352	1.0
		2253	4.3	1215	4.1	1609	0.8
4	W	1055	4.3	0044	4.2	0424	0.8
		2321	4.4	1247	4.2	1639	0.6
5	Th	1125	4.4	0115	4.3	0455	0.6
		2349	4.5	1320	4.3	1710	0.5
6	F	1154	4.5	0147	4.4	0528	0.5
		——		1354	4.3	1741	0.5
7	Sa	0016	4.5	0217	4.4	0559	0.5
		1223	4.5	1425	4.3	1811	0.5
8	Su	0044	4.5	0247	4.4	0629	0.6
		1255	4.4	1456	4.3	1841	0.6
9	M	0116	4.4	0315	4.4	0659	0.7
		1332	4.3	1528	4.3	1911	0.8
10	Tu	0154	4.3	0347	4.3	0732	1.0
		1416	4.1	1603	4.2	1947	1.2
11	W	0241	4.1	0423	4.2	0814	1.3
		1511	4.0	1649	4.0	2039	1.5
12	Th	0339	4.0	0513	4.0	0915	1.6
		1624	3.8	1756	3.8	2153	1.8
13	F	0456	3.8	0627	3.8	1041	1.7
		1758	3.8	1929	3.8	2332	1.9
14	Sa	0627	3.8	0800	3.8	——	
		1927	3.9	2102	3.9	1219	1.6
15	Su	0747	4.0	0926	3.9	0104	1.6
		2032	4.2	2213	4.1	1338	1.2
16	M	0846	4.2	1031	4.1	0212	1.2
		2120	4.4	2309	4.4	1439	0.8
17	Tu	0934	4.4	1125	4.3	0306	0.7
		2204	4.6	2358	4.5	1530	0.4
18	W	1018	4.6	——		0355	0.4
		2245	4.8	1214	4.4	1616	0.2
19	Th	1101	4.7	0043	4.6	0439	0.2
		2326	4.8	1301	4.5	1700	0.1
20	F	1142	4.7	0128	4.7	0522	0.1
		——		1346	4.6	1743	0.1
21	Sa	0006	4.8	0211	4.7	0602	0.2
		1225	4.6	1430	4.5	1822	0.2
22	Su	0047	4.6	0252	4.6	0639	0.3
		1306	4.5	1510	4.5	1857	0.5
23	M	0126	4.4	0327	4.4	0711	0.6
		1351	4.3	1548	4.3	1929	0.8
24	Tu	0209	4.2	0401	4.2	0744	0.9
		1438	4.0	1624	4.1	2003	1.3
25	W	0256	3.9	0436	4.0	0820	1.4
		1534	3.7	1708	3.8	2049	1.7
26	Th	0349	3.7	0519	3.7	0913	1.8
		1642	3.5	1808	3.6	2155	2.1
27	F	0458	3.5	0621	3.5	1030	2.0
		1811	3.4	1933	3.5	2324	2.2
28	Sa	0624	3.4	0747	3.4	——	
		1935	3.5	2100	3.5	1207	2.0
29	Su	0743	3.5	0910	3.5	0052	2.1
		2034	3.7	2205	3.7	1325	1.8
30	M	0839	3.7	1014	3.7	0154	1.7
		2115	3.9	2253	3.9	1420	1.5
31	Tu	0919	3.9	1100	3.8	0241	1.4
		2149	4.1	2332	4.0	1500	1.1

APRIL

Date	Day	1st H.W. Time	Ht.	2nd H.W. Time	Ht.	L.W. Time	Ht.
1	W	0954	4.1	1139	4.0	0319	1.0
		2219	4.3	——		1534	0.8
2	Th	1025	4.3	0007	4.2	0351	0.8
		2249	4.4	1215	4.1	1607	0.6
3	F	1057	4.4	0040	4.3	0426	0.6
		2318	4.5	1251	4.2	1641	0.5
4	Sa	1130	4.4	0113	4.4	0501	0.5
		2347	4.5	1327	4.3	1715	0.5
5	Su	——		0146	4.4	0536	0.4
		1202	4.4	1403	4.3	1751	0.5
6	M	0019	4.5	0220	4.4	0610	0.5
		1237	4.4	1438	4.3	1824	0.6
7	Tu	0054	4.4	0253	4.4	0644	0.6
		1317	4.3	1513	4.3	1859	0.8
8	W	0135	4.3	0327	4.3	0719	0.8
		1404	4.2	1553	4.2	1940	1.1
9	Th	0225	4.1	0408	4.2	0804	1.1
		1505	4.0	1644	4.0	2034	1.5
10	F	0327	4.0	0502	4.0	0907	1.4
		1619	3.9	1752	3.9	2150	1.7
11	Sa	0445	3.8	0616	3.8	1029	1.6
		1747	3.9	1918	3.9	2320	1.7
12	Su	0612	3.8	0744	3.8	1159	1.5
		1908	4.1	2041	4.0	——	
13	M	0727	4.0	0904	3.9	0043	1.5
		2009	4.3	2148	4.2	1314	1.1
14	Tu	0826	4.2	1009	4.1	0149	1.1
		2057	4.5	2243	4.4	1415	0.8
15	W	0914	4.4	1102	4.3	0242	0.7
		2140	4.6	2331	4.5	1504	0.5
16	Th	0958	4.5	1151	4.4	0328	0.4
		2220	4.7	——		1549	0.3
17	F	1041	4.5	0016	4.6	0412	0.3
		2301	4.7	1238	4.4	1634	0.3
18	Sa	1122	4.5	0100	4.5	0455	0.2
		2340	4.6	1322	4.4	1716	0.3
19	Su	——		0142	4.5	0535	0.3
		1204	4.5	1406	4.4	1755	0.5
20	M	0019	4.5	0221	4.4	0611	0.4
		1245	4.3	1446	4.3	1831	0.7
21	Tu	0059	4.3	0257	4.3	0644	0.7
		1328	4.2	1523	4.2	1903	1.0
22	W	0139	4.1	0329	4.1	0716	1.0
		1414	4.0	1600	4.0	1937	1.3
23	Th	0223	3.9	0403	3.9	0752	1.3
		1506	3.8	1642	3.8	2021	1.7
24	F	0314	3.7	0445	3.7	0839	1.6
		1607	3.6	1734	3.7	2119	2.0
25	Sa	0415	3.5	0539	3.6	0945	1.9
		1720	3.5	1843	3.6	2234	2.1
26	Su	0529	3.5	0652	3.5	1106	1.9
		1836	3.6	2000	3.6	2353	2.0
27	M	0645	3.5	0811	3.5	——	
		1938	3.7	2107	3.7	1223	1.8
28	Tu	0747	3.7	0918	3.6	0101	1.7
		2025	3.9	2159	3.8	1325	1.5
29	W	0836	3.8	1012	3.8	0153	1.4
		2014	4.1	2243	4.0	1411	1.2
30	Th	0915	4.0	1056	3.9	0236	1.1
		2139	4.2	2322	4.2	1452	1.0

CAUTION. The variations in the tide between Portland and Portsmouth are complicated. Tidal curves for individual ports in the Solent area appear on pages 21:199-21:201.

SOUTHAMPTON

1st and 2nd HIGH and LOW WATER 1992
GMT   ADD 1 HOUR MARCH 29–OCTOBER 25 FOR B.S.T.

MAY

Date	Day	1st H.W. Time h.min.	Ht. m.	2nd H.W. Time h.min.	Ht. m.	L.W Time h.min.	Ht. m.
1	F	0953	4.2	1138	4.1	0314	0.8
		2213	4.4	—	—	1530	0.8
2	Sa	1029	4.3	0000	4.3	0352	0.6
		2247	4.5	1218	4.2	1609	0.6
3	Su	1106	4.4	0038	4.3	0434	0.5
		2322	4.5	1259	4.3	1651	0.6
4	M	1144	4.4	0117	4.4	0513	0.4
		2359	4.5	1340	4.3	1731	0.6
5	Tu	—	—	0157	4.4	0554	0.5
		1225	4.4	1422	4.3	1813	0.7
6	W	0040	4.4	0236	4.4	0633	0.5
		1311	4.3	1505	4.3	1855	0.8
7	Th	0126	4.3	0317	4.3	0716	0.7
		1403	4.2	1552	4.2	1941	1.1
8	F	0218	4.2	0403	4.2	0804	0.9
		1503	4.1	1644	4.2	2036	1.3
9	Sa	0321	4.0	0459	4.0	0904	1.2
		1613	4.1	1748	4.1	2144	1.5
10	Su	0433	3.9	0606	3.9	1015	1.3
		1730	4.1	1902	4.1	2300	1.5
11	M	0552	3.9	0723	3.9	1132	1.3
		1840	4.2	2013	4.1	—	—
12	Tu	0703	4.0	0837	4.0	0013	1.3
		1941	4.3	2117	4.2	1242	1.1
13	W	0803	4.1	0941	4.1	0118	1.1
		2032	4.4	2213	4.3	1343	0.9
14	Th	0854	4.3	1037	4.2	0213	0.8
		2116	4.5	2302	4.4	1436	0.7
15	F	0940	4.3	1128	4.3	0302	0.6
		2159	4.5	2349	4.4	1525	0.6
16	Sa	1023	4.4	—	—	0347	0.5
		2239	4.5	1215	4.3	1610	0.6
17	Su	1107	4.4	0033	4.4	0430	0.5
		2318	4.4	1302	4.3	1652	0.7
18	M	1149	4.3	0114	4.3	0510	0.5
		2357	4.3	1345	4.3	1732	0.8
19	Tu	—	—	0154	4.2	0547	0.6
		1230	4.2	1426	4.2	1808	0.9
20	W	0035	4.2	0229	4.2	0621	0.8
		1311	4.1	1503	4.1	1841	1.1
21	Th	0114	4.0	0303	4.1	0653	1.0
		1353	4.0	1539	4.0	1915	1.3
22	F	0155	3.9	0337	3.9	0728	1.2
		1439	3.8	1617	3.9	1955	1.5
23	Sa	0242	3.8	0417	3.8	0809	1.4
		1530	3.7	1702	3.8	2045	1.7
24	Su	0335	3.6	0504	3.7	0902	1.6
		1628	3.7	1755	3.7	2144	1.8
25	M	0437	3.6	0603	3.6	1005	1.7
		1731	3.7	1857	3.7	2252	1.8
26	Tu	0544	3.6	0711	3.6	1115	1.7
		1834	3.7	2001	3.7	2358	1.7
27	W	0649	3.6	0818	3.6	—	—
		1929	3.9	2059	3.8	1221	1.6
28	Th	0746	3.8	0918	3.7	0058	1.5
		2015	4.0	2149	4.0	1318	1.4
29	F	0836	3.9	1012	3.9	0150	1.2
		2058	4.2	2236	4.1	1408	1.2
30	Sa	0920	4.1	1100	4.0	0236	1.0
		2139	4.3	2321	4.2	1455	1.0
31	Su	1004	4.2	1148	4.1	0323	0.7
		2220	4.4	—	—	1542	0.8

JUNE

Date	Day	1st H.W. Time h.min.	Ht. m.	2nd H.W. Time h.min.	Ht. m.	L.W Time h.min.	Ht. m.
1	M	1047	4.3	0007	4.3	0409	0.6
		2300	4.4	1235	4.2	1630	0.7
2	Tu	1131	4.4	0050	4.3	0455	0.5
		2343	4.5	1323	4.3	1718	0.7
3	W	—	—	0137	4.4	0542	0.4
		1217	4.4	1411	4.3	1806	0.7
4	Th	0029	4.4	0223	4.4	0628	0.4
		1306	4.4	1459	4.4	1853	0.7
5	F	0117	4.4	0309	4.3	0713	0.5
		1357	4.4	1548	4.4	1939	0.8
6	Sa	0210	4.3	0358	4.3	0800	0.7
		1454	4.4	1639	4.3	2030	1.0
7	Su	0308	4.2	0450	4.2	0852	0.9
		1555	4.3	1734	4.3	2127	1.2
8	M	0414	4.1	0550	4.0	0953	1.1
		1702	4.2	1835	4.2	2231	1.3
9	Tu	0525	4.0	0657	4.0	1059	1.2
		1809	4.2	1940	4.2	2339	1.3
10	W	0636	4.0	0806	4.0	—	—
		1912	4.2	2043	4.2	1208	1.2
11	Th	0742	4.0	0914	4.0	0045	1.2
		2008	4.2	2142	4.2	1313	1.2
12	F	0837	4.1	1013	4.1	0145	1.1
		2057	4.3	2236	4.2	1412	1.1
13	Sa	0928	4.2	1109	4.1	0240	0.9
		2141	4.3	2325	4.2	1503	1.0
14	Su	1013	4.2	—	—	0328	0.8
		2222	4.3	1200	4.1	1551	0.9
15	M	1056	4.3	0010	4.2	0412	0.7
		2301	4.3	1246	4.2	1634	0.9
16	Tu	1137	4.2	0052	4.2	0452	0.7
		2340	4.2	1329	4.2	1713	0.9
17	W	—	—	0132	4.1	0528	0.7
		1216	4.2	1408	4.2	1748	1.0
18	Th	0016	4.2	0207	4.1	0602	0.8
		1253	4.2	1443	4.1	1821	1.1
19	F	0052	4.1	0241	4.1	0632	0.9
		1329	4.1	1517	4.1	1854	1.2
20	Sa	0129	4.0	0315	4.0	0706	1.0
		1407	4.0	1551	4.0	1929	1.3
21	Su	0209	3.9	0350	3.9	0741	1.2
		1449	3.9	1628	3.9	2010	1.4
22	M	0255	3.8	0430	3.8	0823	1.4
		1536	3.9	1709	3.9	2056	1.6
23	Tu	0347	3.7	0518	3.8	0912	1.5
		1629	3.8	1759	3.8	2152	1.7
24	W	0445	3.7	0613	3.7	1011	1.7
		1730	3.8	1857	3.8	2256	1.7
25	Th	0551	3.6	0718	3.7	1119	1.7
		1831	3.8	1958	3.8	—	—
26	F	0658	3.7	0827	3.7	0003	1.6
		1930	3.9	2100	3.9	1227	1.6
27	Sa	0800	3.8	0931	3.8	0106	1.4
		2023	4.1	2157	4.1	1330	1.4
28	Su	0854	4.0	1030	4.0	0205	1.2
		2112	4.2	2250	4.2	1428	1.2
29	M	0945	4.2	1126	4.1	0259	0.9
		2159	4.3	2342	4.3	1522	1.0
30	Tu	1032	4.3	—	—	0351	0.6
		2244	4.4	1217	4.2	1615	0.8

TIDAL DIFFERENCES PAGE 21:209   TIDAL CURVE PAGE 21:208.

TIDAL STREAMS OF THE SOLENT PAGES 21:192-21:198.

Datum of predictions 2.74m. below Ordnance Datum (Newlyn) or approx. L.A.T.

SOUTHAMPTON

Lat. 50° 54'N, Long. 1°24'W
1st and 2nd HIGH and LOW WATER 1992

JULY

Date	Day	1st H.W. Time h.min.	Ht. m.	2nd H.W. Time h.min.	Ht. m.	L.W. Time h.min.	Ht. m.
1	W	1119	4.5	0032	4.3	0441	0.4
		2330	4.5			1707	0.6
2	Th	—	—	0121	4.4	0531	0.3
		1206	4.6	1358	4.5	1757	0.5
3	F	0016	4.5	0210	4.4	0619	0.3
		1254	4.6	1448	4.5	1844	0.5
4	Sa	0104	4.5	0258	4.4	0705	0.3
		1342	4.6	1536	4.5	1930	0.6
5	Su	0154	4.4	0347	4.4	0748	0.4
		1434	4.5	1624	4.5	2015	0.7
6	M	0248	4.3	0435	4.3	0834	0.7
		1528	4.4	1712	4.4	2103	0.9
7	Tu	0347	4.1	0527	4.1	0925	0.9
		1628	4.3	1804	4.3	2158	1.2
8	W	0454	4.0	0627	4.0	1024	1.2
		1734	4.1	1903	4.1	2301	1.4
9	Th	0608	3.9	0735	3.9	1133	1.4
		1842	4.0	2009	4.0	—	—
10	F	0722	3.9	0848	3.9	0014	1.5
		1947	4.0	2115	4.0	1245	1.5
11	Sa	0828	4.0	0957	3.9	0123	1.4
		2044	4.1	2215	4.0	1353	1.5
12	Su	0922	4.1	1057	4.0	0224	1.3
		2130	4.1	2308	4.0	1451	1.4
13	M	1008	4.1	1149	4.1	0316	1.1
		2213	4.2	2356	4.1	1539	1.2
14	Tu	1048	4.2	—	—	0400	0.9
		2249	4.2	1233	4.1	1619	1.1
15	W	1125	4.2	0036	4.1	0438	0.8
		2324	4.2	1313	4.2	1655	1.0
16	Th	1158	4.3	0113	4.1	0510	0.7
		2357	4.2	1348	4.2	1728	1.0
17	F	—	—	0147	4.1	0541	0.7
		1230	4.3	1420	4.2	1800	1.0
18	Sa	0028	4.2	0219	4.1	0611	0.8
		1301	4.2	1452	4.2	1830	1.0
19	Su	0101	4.2	0252	4.1	0642	0.8
		1334	4.2	1523	4.1	1902	1.1
20	M	0136	4.1	0324	4.1	0712	1.0
		1408	4.1	1554	4.1	1935	1.2
21	Tu	0215	4.0	0358	4.0	0746	1.1
		1448	4.0	1628	4.0	2013	1.3
22	W	0300	3.9	0437	3.9	0826	1.4
		1536	3.9	1709	4.0	2101	1.6
23	Th	0353	3.8	0523	3.8	0917	1.6
		1632	3.9	1759	3.9	2159	1.7
24	F	0500	3.7	0626	3.7	1024	1.8
		1739	3.8	1904	3.9	2314	1.8
25	Sa	0615	3.7	0741	3.7	1144	1.8
		1849	3.9	2016	3.9	—	—
26	Su	0732	3.8	0900	3.8	0032	1.6
		1956	4.0	2127	4.0	1302	1.7
27	M	0836	4.0	1010	3.9	0142	1.3
		2051	4.2	2228	4.1	1410	1.4
28	Tu	0930	4.2	1110	4.1	0244	1.0
		2142	4.3	2324	4.3	1510	1.0
29	W	1018	4.4	—	—	0337	0.6
		2228	4.5	1203	4.3	1603	0.7
30	Th	1103	4.6	0016	4.4	0428	0.4
		2313	4.6	1253	4.5	1654	0.5
31	F	1149	4.7	0105	4.5	0517	0.2
		2359	4.6	1342	4.6	1741	0.4

AUGUST

Date	Day	1st H.W. Time h.min.	Ht. m.	2nd H.W. Time h.min.	Ht. m.	L.W. Time h.min.	Ht. m.
1	Sa	—	—	0155	4.5	0604	0.1
		1233	4.8	1429	4.7	1828	0.3
2	Su	0045	4.6	0243	4.5	0648	0.1
		1318	4.8	1516	4.7	1911	0.4
3	M	0131	4.6	0328	4.5	0729	0.3
		1405	4.6	1600	4.6	1952	0.6
4	Tu	0222	4.4	0414	4.4	0809	0.6
		1455	4.4	1644	4.4	2034	0.8
5	W	0318	4.2	0501	4.2	0853	1.0
		1551	4.2	1730	4.2	2121	1.2
6	Th	0421	3.9	0554	4.0	0948	1.4
		1656	4.0	1825	4.0	2224	1.5
7	F	0538	3.8	0703	3.8	1100	1.7
		1811	3.8	1934	3.8	2343	1.7
8	Sa	0705	3.7	0827	3.7	—	—
		1927	3.8	2049	3.8	1222	1.9
9	Su	0821	3.8	0945	3.8	0105	1.7
		2032	3.9	2159	3.8	1340	1.8
10	M	0917	4.0	1047	3.9	0214	1.5
		2122	4.0	2255	3.9	1441	1.6
11	Tu	1001	4.1	1138	4.0	0306	1.3
		2200	4.1	2341	4.0	1527	1.4
12	W	1035	4.2	—	—	0348	1.0
		2235	4.2	1218	4.1	1603	1.1
13	Th	1105	4.3	0020	4.1	0420	0.8
		2305	4.3	1252	4.2	1636	1.0
14	F	1134	4.4	0053	4.2	0450	0.7
		2334	4.3	1324	4.2	1705	0.9
15	Sa	—	—	0125	4.2	0520	0.7
		1202	4.4	1354	4.3	1736	0.8
16	Su	0003	4.3	0156	4.2	0548	0.7
		1230	4.4	1424	4.3	1805	0.8
17	M	0033	4.3	0228	4.2	0617	0.7
		1258	4.4	1453	4.3	1836	0.8
18	Tu	0105	4.3	0259	4.2	0645	0.8
		1330	4.3	1523	4.3	1906	1.0
19	W	0139	4.2	0329	4.1	0715	1.0
		1406	4.2	1552	4.2	1939	1.2
20	Th	0222	4.0	0404	4.0	0750	1.3
		1450	4.1	1627	4.1	2020	1.5
21	F	0313	3.9	0446	3.9	0837	1.6
		1545	3.9	1714	4.0	2116	1.7
22	Sa	0419	3.7	0546	3.8	0946	1.9
		1654	3.8	1820	3.8	2235	1.9
23	Su	0546	3.7	0711	3.7	1116	2.0
		1818	3.8	1945	3.8	—	—
24	M	0714	3.8	0842	3.8	0006	1.8
		1935	4.0	2106	3.9	1247	1.8
25	Tu	0822	4.1	0957	4.0	0127	1.4
		2035	4.2	2213	4.1	1358	1.4
26	W	0915	4.3	1056	4.2	0231	1.0
		2126	4.4	2310	4.3	1457	1.0
27	Th	1000	4.6	1147	4.5	0322	0.6
		2211	4.6	—	—	1548	0.6
28	F	1043	4.7	0000	4.4	0411	0.3
		2254	4.7	1234	4.6	1635	0.4
29	Sa	1124	4.9	0048	4.6	0457	0.1
		2338	4.7	1320	4.7	1722	0.2
30	Su	—	—	0136	4.6	0542	0.0
		1207	4.9	1407	4.8	1806	0.2
31	M	0022	4.7	0223	4.6	0626	0.1
		1249	4.8	1451	4.7	1847	0.3

CAUTION. The variations in the tide between Portland and Portsmouth are complicated. Tidal curves for individual ports in the Solent area appear on pages 21:199-21:201.

SOUTHAMPTON

1st and 2nd HIGH and LOW WATER 1992

GMT   ADD 1 HOUR MARCH 29–OCTOBER 25 FOR B.S.T.

SEPTEMBER

Date	Day	1st H.W. Time h.min.	Ht. m.	2nd H.W. Time h.min.	Ht. m.	L.W Time h.min.	Ht. m.
1	Tu	0107 / 1335	4.6 / 4.6	0308 / 1534	4.5 / 4.6	0706 / 1925	0.3 / 0.5
2	W	0155 / 1421	4.4 / 4.4	0351 / 1613	4.4 / 4.4	0744 / 2003	0.6 / 0.8
3	Th	0248 / 1514	4.1 / 4.1	0435 / 1655	4.2 / 4.2	0823 / 2045	1.1 / 1.3
4	F	0350 / 1617	3.9 / 3.8	0525 / 1746	3.9 / 3.9	0915 / 2145	1.6 / 1.7
5	Sa	0508 / 1735	3.7 / 3.6	0633 / 1857	3.7 / 3.7	1026 / 2309	2.0 / 2.0
6	Su	0642 / 1903	3.6 / 3.6	0802 / 2022	3.6 / 3.6	1158 / — —	2.1 /
7	M	0805 / 2014	3.7 / 3.7	0927 / 2138	3.7 / 3.7	0043 / 1321	2.0 / 2.0
8	Tu	0901 / 2104	3.9 / 3.9	1029 / 2224	3.8 / 3.8	0156 / 1421	1.7 / 1.8
9	W	0940 / 2141	4.1 / 4.1	1116 / 2320	4.0 / 4.0	0247 / 1507	1.4 / 1.4
10	Th	1011 / 2212	4.2 / 4.2	1153 / 2356	4.1 / 4.1	0326 / 1541	1.1 / 1.1
11	F	1039 / 2241	4.3 / 4.3	— — / 1225	/ 4.2	0356 / 1610	0.9 / 0.9
12	Sa	1106 / 2310	4.4 / 4.4	0029 / 1255	4.2 / 4.3	0425 / 1639	0.7 / 0.7
13	Su	1133 / 2338	4.5 / 4.5	0101 / 1326	4.3 / 4.4	0454 / 1710	0.6 / 0.7
14	M	— — / 1200	/ 4.5	0133 / 1356	4.3 / 4.4	0524 / 1742	0.6 / 0.6
15	Tu	0007 / 1226	4.4 / 4.5	0204 / 1425	4.3 / 4.4	0554 / 1812	0.6 / 0.7
16	W	0038 / 1257	4.4 / 4.4	0236 / 1454	4.3 / 4.4	0623 / 1842	0.7 / 0.8
17	Th	0113 / 1334	4.3 / 4.3	0307 / 1524	4.2 / 4.3	0652 / 1913	1.0 / 1.1
18	F	0155 / 1417	4.1 / 4.1	0341 / 1558	4.1 / 4.2	0728 / 1954	1.3 / 1.4
19	Sa	0246 / 1512	3.9 / 4.0	0423 / 1645	4.0 / 4.0	0814 / 2048	1.6 / 1.7
20	Su	0355 / 1625	3.8 / 3.8	0525 / 1753	3.8 / 3.8	0925 / 2211	1.9 / 1.9
21	M	0526 / 1756	3.7 / 3.8	0654 / 1924	3.7 / 3.8	1100 / 2347	2.0 / 1.8
22	Tu	0657 / 1917	3.9 / 3.9	0827 / 2050	3.8 / 3.9	1232 / — —	1.8 /
23	W	0804 / 2019	4.2 / 4.2	0940 / 2158	4.1 / 4.1	0109 / 1344	1.4 / 1.4
24	Th	0854 / 2107	4.4 / 4.4	1037 / 2253	4.3 / 4.3	0212 / 1439	1.0 / 0.9
25	F	0937 / 2151	4.7 / 4.6	1126 / 2342	4.5 / 4.5	0303 / 1527	0.6 / 0.5
26	Sa	1019 / 2233	4.8 / 4.7	— — / 1212	/ 4.7	0349 / 1613	0.3 / 0.3
27	Su	1059 / 2317	4.9 / 4.8	0028 / 1256	4.6 / 4.7	0435 / 1658	0.1 / 0.2
28	M	1140 / — —	4.9 /	0116 / 1341	4.6 / 4.7	0520 / 1741	0.1 / 0.2
29	Tu	0000 / 1223	4.7 / 4.8	0202 / 1426	4.6 / 4.7	0602 / 1822	0.2 / 0.3
30	W	0045 / 1306	4.6 / 4.6	0247 / 1506	4.5 / 4.5	0641 / 1858	0.5 / 0.5

OCTOBER

Date	Day	1st H.W. Time h.min.	Ht. m.	2nd H.W. Time h.min.	Ht. m.	L.W Time h.min.	Ht. m.
1	Th	0130 / 1351	4.4 / 4.3	0328 / 1544	4.4 / 4.3	0717 / 1933	0.8 / 0.9
2	F	0222 / 1439	4.1 / 4.0	0410 / 1622	4.2 / 4.1	0755 / 2014	1.2 / 1.3
3	Sa	0320 / 1537	3.8 / 3.7	0457 / 1708	3.9 / 3.8	0843 / 2107	1.7 / 1.7
4	Su	0433 / 1651	3.6 / 3.5	0559 / 1814	3.7 / 3.6	0949 / 2227	2.1 / 2.0
5	M	0604 / 1819	3.5 / 3.5	0725 / 1940	3.6 / 3.5	1118 / — —	2.2 /
6	Tu	0728 / 1937	3.6 / 3.6	0850 / 2101	3.6 / 3.6	0001 / 1243	2.1 / 2.1
7	W	0826 / 2031	3.8 / 3.8	0953 / 2201	3.7 / 3.7	0118 / 1346	1.9 / 1.9
8	Th	0906 / 2111	4.0 / 4.0	1040 / 2248	3.9 / 3.9	0212 / 1432	1.6 / 1.5
9	F	0938 / 2143	4.2 / 4.2	1118 / 2326	4.1 / 4.0	0251 / 1507	1.2 / 1.2
10	Sa	1006 / 2214	4.3 / 4.3	1151 / — —	4.2 /	0323 / 1540	1.0 / 0.9
11	Su	1034 / 2243	4.5 / 4.4	0000 / 1222	4.2 / 4.3	0354 / 1611	0.8 / 0.7
12	M	1102 / 2314	4.5 / 4.5	0033 / 1254	4.3 / 4.4	0425 / 1644	0.7 / 0.6
13	Tu	1132 / 2345	4.6 / 4.5	0108 / 1327	4.3 / 4.4	0458 / 1717	0.6 / 0.6
14	W	— — / 1201	/ 4.6	0142 / 1400	4.4 / 4.4	0532 / 1751	0.7 / 0.6
15	Th	0018 / 1234	4.4 / 4.5	0217 / 1432	4.3 / 4.4	0605 / 1824	0.8 / 0.7
16	F	0057 / 1313	4.3 / 4.3	0252 / 1505	4.3 / 4.3	0640 / 1859	0.9 / 0.9
17	Sa	0140 / 1357	4.2 / 4.2	0330 / 1543	4.2 / 4.2	0718 / 1941	1.2 / 1.2
18	Su	0235 / 1455	4.0 / 4.0	0416 / 1633	4.0 / 4.0	0807 / 2037	1.5 / 1.5
19	M	0344 / 1606	3.9 / 3.9	0518 / 1739	3.9 / 3.9	0916 / 2154	1.8 / 1.7
20	Tu	0509 / 1733	3.9 / 3.8	0641 / 1905	3.9 / 3.8	1043 / 2324	1.9 / 1.7
21	W	0633 / 1855	4.0 / 4.0	0806 / 2029	4.0 / 3.9	1209 / — —	1.7 /
22	Th	0740 / 1957	4.2 / 4.2	0916 / 2137	4.2 / 4.1	0043 / 1319	1.4 / 1.3
23	F	0830 / 2047	4.5 / 4.4	1012 / 2233	4.4 / 4.3	0147 / 1415	1.0 / 0.9
24	Sa	0915 / 2132	4.6 / 4.5	1103 / 2323	4.5 / 4.4	0238 / 1503	0.7 / 0.6
25	Su	0956 / 2215	4.7 / 4.6	1149 / — —	4.6 /	0326 / 1549	0.4 / 0.4
26	M	1036 / 2258	4.8 / 4.7	0010 / 1233	4.5 / 4.7	0411 / 1634	0.3 / 0.3
27	Tu	1118 / 2342	4.7 / 4.6	0057 / 1318	4.6 / 4.6	0456 / 1717	0.3 / 0.3
28	W	1159 / — —	4.6 /	0143 / 1401	4.6 / 4.6	0539 / 1758	0.5 / 0.4
29	Th	0026 / 1240	4.5 / 4.4	0228 / 1440	4.5 / 4.4	0619 / 1833	0.7 / 0.6
30	F	0111 / 1323	4.3 / 4.2	0308 / 1517	4.3 / 4.2	0654 / 1908	1.0 / 0.9
31	Sa	0159 / 1409	4.1 / 4.0	0340 / 1554	4.1 / 4.0	0731 / 1946	1.3 / 1.3

TIDAL DIFFERENCES PAGE 21:209   **TIDAL CURVE PAGE 21:208.**

TIDAL STREAMS OF THE SOLENT PAGES 21:192-21:198.

Datum of predictions 2.74m. below Ordnance Datum (Newlyn) or approx. L.A.T.

Lat. 50° 54'N, Long. 1°24'W

1st and 2nd HIGH and LOW WATER 1992

NOVEMBER

Date	Day	1st H.W. Time	Ht.	2nd H.W. Time	Ht.	L.W Time	Ht.
1	Su	0252	3.9	0432	3.9	0814	1.7
		1500	3.8	1636	3.8	2032	1.6
2	M	0353	3.7	0525	3.7	0908	2.0
		1601	3.6	1729	3.6	2134	1.9
3	Tu	0506	3.6	0632	3.6	1021	2.2
		1716	3.5	1841	3.5	2254	2.0
4	W	0622	3.6	0747	3.6	1140	2.1
		1833	3.5	1959	3.5	—	—
5	Th	0727	3.7	0855	3.7	0014	2.0
		1938	3.7	2108	3.6	1249	1.9
6	F	0816	3.9	0949	3.8	0117	1.7
		2027	3.8	2203	3.8	1343	1.6
7	Sa	0855	4.1	1033	4.0	0204	1.4
		2107	4.0	2248	4.0	1426	1.3
8	Su	0929	4.2	1112	4.2	0244	1.2
		2143	4.2	2327	4.1	1504	1.0
9	M	1022	4.4	1148	4.3	0320	1.0
		2218	4.4	—	—	1541	0.8
10	Tu	1034	4.5	0006	4.2	0357	0.8
		2253	4.4	1224	4.4	1618	0.7
11	W	1108	4.6	0045	4.3	0435	0.7
		2328	4.5	1302	4.4	1658	0.6
12	Th	1142	4.6	0124	4.4	0514	0.7
		—	—	1339	4.4	1736	0.6
13	F	0007	4.5	0204	4.4	0554	0.8
		1219	4.5	1416	4.4	1815	0.6
14	Sa	0047	4.4	0244	4.3	0634	0.9
		1300	4.4	1455	4.3	1853	0.8
15	Su	0134	4.3	0327	4.3	0717	1.1
		1348	4.3	1538	4.2	1937	1.0
16	M	0229	4.2	0416	4.2	0807	1.3
		1443	4.1	1627	4.1	2031	1.2
17	Tu	0331	4.1	0512	4.1	0907	1.5
		1550	4.0	1728	4.0	2136	1.4
18	W	0444	4.1	0621	4.1	1019	1.6
		1706	3.9	1842	3.9	2252	1.5
19	Th	0601	4.1	0736	4.1	1136	1.5
		1824	4.0	2000	3.9	—	—
20	F	0708	4.2	0845	4.2	0008	1.3
		1932	4.1	2111	4.1	1246	1.3
21	Sa	0804	4.4	0945	4.3	0115	1.1
		2028	4.3	2211	4.2	1347	1.0
22	Su	0852	4.5	1038	4.4	0211	0.9
		2117	4.4	2305	4.3	1440	0.8
23	M	0937	4.6	1128	4.5	0303	0.7
		2203	4.5	2355	4.4	1528	0.6
24	Tu	1018	4.6	—	—	0351	0.6
		2247	4.5	1213	4.5	1614	0.5
25	W	1101	4.6	0044	4.4	0437	0.6
		2330	4.5	1259	4.5	1658	0.5
26	Th	1142	4.5	0130	4.4	0520	0.7
		—	—	1341	4.4	1737	0.6
27	F	0014	4.4	0214	4.4	0558	0.8
		1222	4.4	1421	4.3	1813	0.7
28	Sa	0057	4.3	0254	4.3	0634	1.0
		1301	4.2	1456	4.2	1847	0.9
29	Su	0138	4.2	0330	4.2	0709	1.2
		1341	4.0	1530	4.1	1921	1.2
30	M	0223	4.0	0409	4.0	0746	1.5
		1426	3.9	1608	3.9	1958	1.4

DECEMBER

Date	Day	1st H.W. Time	Ht.	2nd H.W. Time	Ht.	L.W Time	Ht.
1	Tu	0310	3.8	0449	3.9	0828	1.7
		1515	3.7	1650	3.8	2045	1.7
2	W	0404	3.7	0537	3.7	0922	1.9
		1612	3.6	1743	3.6	2143	1.8
3	Th	0506	3.6	0636	3.7	1027	2.0
		1719	3.5	1849	3.5	2253	1.9
4	F	0612	3.7	0742	3.7	1136	1.9
		1829	3.6	2000	3.6	—	—
5	Sa	0713	3.8	0845	3.7	0004	1.8
		1933	3.7	2107	3.7	1242	1.7
6	Su	0805	3.9	0904	3.9	0105	1.7
		2026	3.9	2203	3.8	1339	1.5
7	M	0849	4.1	1029	4.1	0159	1.4
		2113	4.1	2254	4.0	1427	1.2
8	Tu	0931	4.3	1114	4.2	0246	1.2
		2154	4.2	2340	4.1	1512	1.0
9	W	1009	4.4	1157	4.3	0332	1.0
		2235	4.4	—	—	1556	0.8
10	Th	1048	4.5	0025	4.3	0416	0.8
		2316	4.5	1240	4.4	1641	0.6
11	F	1127	4.5	0109	4.3	0502	0.7
		2357	4.5	1322	4.4	1724	0.5
12	Sa	—	—	0154	4.4	0547	0.7
		1207	4.5	1405	4.4	1807	0.5
13	Su	0040	4.5	0238	4.4	0630	0.7
		1251	4.5	1448	4.4	1850	0.5
14	M	0126	4.5	0323	4.4	0713	0.8
		1338	4.4	1533	4.4	1933	0.6
15	Tu	0217	4.5	0410	4.4	0759	1.0
		1429	4.3	1620	4.3	2019	0.8
16	W	0312	4.4	0459	4.3	0849	1.1
		1529	4.2	1714	4.1	2113	1.1
17	Th	0415	4.3	0557	4.2	0948	1.3
		1636	4.0	1816	4.0	2216	1.3
18	F	0523	4.2	0701	4.2	1057	1.4
		1750	4.0	1927	3.9	2329	1.4
19	Sa	0634	4.2	0810	4.1	—	—
		1906	4.0	2042	4.0	1209	1.4
20	Su	0739	4.2	0916	4.2	0041	1.4
		2011	4.1	2150	4.1	1317	1.3
21	M	0834	4.3	1015	4.2	0148	1.2
		2108	4.2	2252	4.2	1419	1.1
22	Tu	0923	4.4	1110	4.3	0246	1.1
		2157	4.3	2346	4.2	1512	0.9
23	W	1009	4.4	—	—	0339	1.0
		2241	4.4	1200	4.3	1602	0.7
24	Th	1050	4.4	0035	4.3	0424	0.9
		2324	4.4	1246	4.3	1644	0.7
25	F	1129	4.4	0120	4.3	0505	0.9
		—	—	1326	4.3	1723	0.6
26	Sa	0004	4.4	0201	4.3	0541	0.9
		1205	4.3	1403	4.3	1756	0.7
27	Su	0040	4.3	0237	4.3	0614	1.0
		1241	4.3	1437	4.2	1827	0.8
28	M	0115	4.3	0310	4.2	0645	1.1
		1316	4.2	1510	4.1	1857	0.9
29	Tu	0150	4.2	0342	4.1	0717	1.2
		1353	4.1	1543	4.1	1929	1.1
30	W	0227	4.0	0414	4.0	0751	1.4
		1433	3.9	1617	3.9	2003	1.3
31	Th	0310	3.9	0451	3.9	0830	1.5
		1518	3.8	1657	3.8	2045	1.5

CAUTION. The variations in the tide between Portland and Portsmouth are complicated. Tidal curves for individual ports in the Solent area appear on pages 21:199-21:201.

SOUTHAMPTON

MEAN SPRING AND NEAP CURVES
Springs occur 2 days after New and Full Moon.

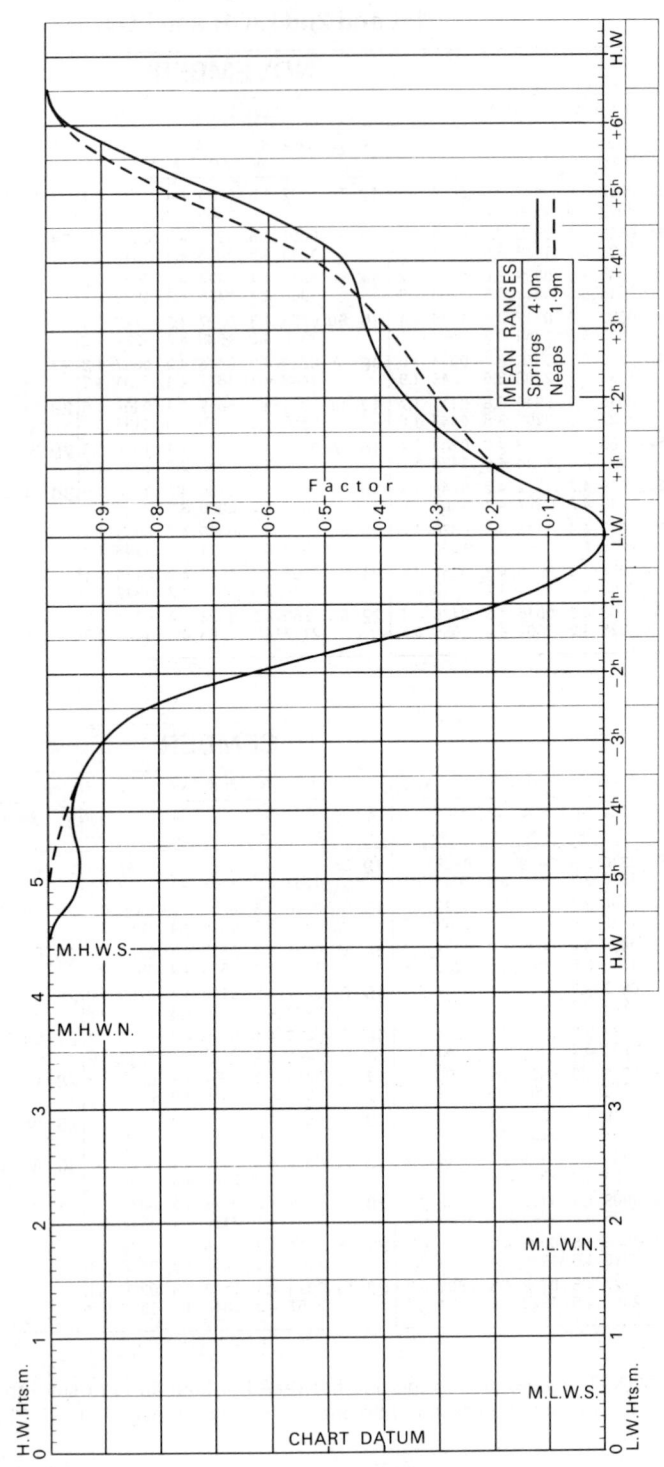

PLACE	TIME DIFFERENCES				HEIGHT DIFFERENCES (Metres)			
	High Water		Low Water		MHWS	MHWN	MLWN	MLWS
PORTSMOUTH	0000 and 1200	0600 and 1800	0500 and 1700	1100 and 2300	4.7	3.8	1.8	0.6
Swanage	−0250	+0105	−0105	−0105	−2.7	−2.2	−0.7	−0.3
Bournemouth	−0240	+0055	−0050	−0030	−2.7	−2.2	−0.8	−0.3
Christchurch (Entrance)	−0230	+0030	−0035	−0035	−2.9	−2.4	−1.2	−0.2
Christchurch (Tuckton)	−0205	+0110	+0110	+0105	−3.0	−2.5	−1.0	+0.1
Hurst Point	−0115	−0005	−0030	−0025	−2.0	−1.5	−0.5	−0.1
Lymington	−0110	+0005	−0020	−0020	−1.7	−1.2	−0.5	−0.1
Bucklers Hard	−0040	−0010	+0010	−0010	−1.0	−0.8	−0.2	−0.3
Stansore Point	−0050	−0010	−0005	−0010	−0.9	−0.6	−0.2	0.0
Isle of Wight								
Yarmouth	−0105	+0005	−0025	−0030	−1.6	−1.3	−0.4	0.0
Totland Bay	−0130	−0045	−0040	−0040	−2.0	−1.5	−0.5	−0.1
Freshwater	−0210	+0025	−0040	−0020	−2.1	−1.5	−0.4	0.0
Ventnor	−0025	−0030	−0025	−0030	−0.8	−0.6	−0.2	+0.2
Sandown	0000	+0005	+0010	+0025	−0.6	−0.5	−0.2	0.0
Foreland	−0010	0000	+0005	+0010	−0.1	−0.1	0.0	+0.1
Bembridge Harbour ...	−0010	+0005	+0020	0000	−1.6	−1.5	−1.4	−0.6
Ryde	−0010	+0010	−0005	−0010	−0.2	−0.1	0.0	+0.1
Medina River								
Cowes	−0015	+0015	0000	−0020	−0.5	−0.3	−0.1	0.0
Folly Inn	−0015	+0015	0000	−0020	−0.6	−0.4	−0.1	+0.2
Newport	−	−	−	−	−0.6	−0.4	+0.1	+0.8
PORTSMOUTH	0500 and 1700	1000 and 2200	0000 and 1200	0600 and 1800	4.7	3.8	1.8	0.6
Lee-on-the-Solent	−0005	+0005	−0015	−0010	−0.2	−0.1	+0.1	+0.2
Chichester Harbour								
Entrance	−0010	+0005	+0015	+0020	+0.2	+0.2	0.0	+0.1
Northney	+0010	+0015	+0015	+0025	+0.2	0.0	−0.2	−0.3
Bosham	0000	+0010	−	−	+0.2	+0.1	−	−
Itchenor	−0005	+0005	+0005	+0025	+0.1	0.0	−0.2	−0.2
Dell Quay	+0005	+0015	−	−	+0.2	+0.1	−	−
Selsey Bill	−0005	−0005	+0035	+0035	+0.6	+0.6	0.0	0.0
Nab Tower	+0015	0000	+0015	+0015	−0.2	0.0	+0.2	0.0

The first H.W. of spring tides is shown.

Refer to predictions on pages 21:210-21:212

TIDAL DIFFERENCES ON SOUTHAMPTON

PLACE	TIME DIFFERENCES				HEIGHT DIFFERENCES (Metres)			
	High Water		Low Water		MHWS	MHWN	MLWN	MLWS
SOUTHAMPTON	0400 and 1600	1100 and 2300	0000 and 1200	0600 and 1800	4.5	3.7	1.8	0.5
Calshot Castle	+0015	+0030	+0015	+0005	0.0	0.0	+0.2	+0.3
Redbridge	−0020	+0005	0000	−0005	−0.1	−0.1	−0.1	−0.1
River Hamble								
Warsash	+0020	+0010	+0010	0000	0.0	+0.1	+0.1	+0.3
Bursledon	+0020	+0020	+0010	+0010	+0.1	+0.1	+0.2	+0.2

Refer to predictions on pages 21:202-21:207

PORTSMOUTH

HIGH & LOW WATER 1992 Lat. 50°48′N. Long. 1°07′W.

GMT ADD 1 HOUR MARCH 29 — OCTOBER 25 FOR B.S.T.

JANUARY

Day	Time	m	Day	Time	m
1 W	0138 / 0819 / 1415 / 2057	1.8 / 4.3 / 1.7 / 4.2	**16** TH	0034 / 0721 / 1325 / 2005	1.8 / 4.2 / 1.7 / 4.0
2 TH	0235 / 0914 / 1506 / 2150	1.7 / 4.4 / 1.5 / 4.3	**17** F	0149 / 0833 / 1431 / 2116	1.7 / 4.3 / 1.4 / 4.3
3 F	0325 / 1002 / 1550 / 2236	1.6 / 4.4 / 1.4 / 4.4	**18** SA	0253 / 0937 / 1527 / 2216	1.4 / 4.5 / 1.1 / 4.5
4 SA	0408 / 1043 / 1629 / 2315 ●	1.5 / 4.5 / 1.3 / 4.5	**19** SU	0348 / 1032 / 1617 / 2308 ○	1.1 / 4.7 / 0.7 / 4.8
5 SU	0447 / 1120 / 1705 / 2351	1.4 / 4.5 / 1.1 / 4.5	**20** M	0437 / 1122 / 1703 / 2356	0.8 / 4.9 / 0.5 / 5.0
6 M	0522 / 1154 / 1738	1.3 / 4.5 / 1.1	**21** TU	0523 / 1209 / 1747	0.6 / 5.0 / 0.3
7 TU	0024 / 0555 / 1226 / 1808	4.6 / 1.3 / 4.5 / 1.1	**22** W	0042 / 0608 / 1255 / 1829	5.1 / 0.6 / 5.0 / 0.3
8 W	0057 / 0627 / 1258 / 1839	4.5 / 1.3 / 4.4 / 1.1	**23** TH	0126 / 0652 / 1339 / 1912	5.1 / 0.6 / 4.8 / 0.4
9 TH	0129 / 0659 / 1330 / 1910	4.5 / 1.3 / 4.4 / 1.1	**24** F	0210 / 0737 / 1424 / 1956	4.9 / 0.8 / 4.7 / 0.7
10 F	0202 / 0732 / 1404 / 1943	4.5 / 1.2 / 4.3 / 1.2	**25** SA	0255 / 0823 / 1511 / 2043	4.8 / 1.0 / 4.4 / 1.0
11 SA	0237 / 0808 / 1442 / 2020	4.4 / 1.5 / 4.2 / 1.4	**26** SU	0342 / 0915 / 1601 / 2136	4.6 / 1.3 / 4.2 / 1.4
12 SU	0317 / 0850 / 1525 / 2105	4.3 / 1.6 / 4.0 / 1.5	**27** M	0432 / 1014 / ‡240	4.3 / 1.6 / 1.7
13 M	0403 / 0942 / 1619 / 2200	4.2 / 1.8 / 4.0 / 1.7	**28** TU	0529 / 1127 / 1807 / 2357	4.1 / 1.8 / 3.8 / 2.0
14 TU	0500 / 1047 / 1726 / 2311	4.2 / 1.9 / 3.9 / 1.8	**29** W	0635 / 1246 / 1926	4.0 / 1.9 / 3.8
15 W	0607 / 1206 / 1845	4.1 / 1.9 / 3.9	**30** TH	0114 / 0747 / 1355 / 2039	2.0 / 4.0 / 1.8 / 3.9
			31 F	0219 / 0853 / 1451 / 2136	1.9 / 4.1 / 1.6 / 4.1

FEBRUARY

Day	Time	m	Day	Time	m
1 SA	0311 / 0945 / 1535 / 2221	1.8 / 4.2 / 1.4 / 4.3	**16** SU	0243 / 0925 / 1515 / 2205	1.4 / 4.4 / 1.0 / 4.5
2 SU	0353 / 1027 / 1613 / 2259	1.6 / 4.4 / 1.2 / 4.4	**17** M	0336 / 1021 / 1603 / 2254	1.0 / 4.7 / 0.6 / 4.8
3 M	0430 / 1103 / 1647 / 2332 ●	1.4 / 4.4 / 1.0 / 4.5	**18** TU	0423 / 1109 / 1647 / 2339 ○	0.7 / 4.9 / 0.3 / 5.0
4 TU	0503 / 1136 / 1717	1.2 / 4.4 / 0.9	**19** W	0507 / 1153 / 1729	0.4 / 5.0 / 0.2
5 W	0004 / 0533 / 1208 / 1745	4.6 / 1.1 / 4.5 / 0.8	**20** TH	0022 / 0548 / 1236 / 1808	5.1 / 0.3 / 5.0 / 0.2
6 TH	0035 / 0602 / 1239 / 1813	4.6 / 1.0 / 4.5 / 0.8	**21** F	0103 / 0629 / 1318 / 1848	5.1 / 0.4 / 4.9 / 0.3
7 F	0105 / 0631 / 1310 / 1842	4.6 / 1.0 / 4.4 / 0.9	**22** SA	0143 / 0710 / 1359 / 1929	4.9 / 0.6 / 4.7 / 0.6
8 SA	0135 / 0701 / 1342 / 1913	4.5 / 1.1 / 4.4 / 1.0	**23** SU	0223 / 0752 / 1441 / 2011	4.7 / 0.9 / 4.4 / 1.0
9 SU	0208 / 0735 / 1417 / 1948	4.4 / 1.2 / 4.3 / 1.2	**24** M	0305 / 0838 / 1527 / 2059	4.4 / 1.3 / 4.1 / 1.5
10 M	0243 / 0813 / 1457 / 2030	4.3 / 1.3 / 4.1 / 1.4	**25** TU	0350 / 0932 / 1620 / 2201	4.2 / 1.6 / 3.9 / 1.9
11 TU	0326 / 0900 / 1549 / 2122	4.2 / 1.6 / 4.0 / 1.7	**26** W	0442 / 1044 / 1727 / 2325	3.9 / 1.9 / 3.7 / 2.1
12 W	0421 / 1004 / 1657 / 2236	4.1 / 1.8 / 3.8 / 1.9	**27** TH	0550 / 1213 / 1853	3.7 / 2.0 / 3.7
13 TH	0532 / 1133 / 1823	4.0 / 1.9 / 3.8	**28** F	0052 / 0713 / 1331 / 2017	2.2 / 3.7 / 1.9 / 3.8
14 F	0013 / 0656 / 1307 / 1952	1.9 / 3.9 / 1.7 / 3.9	**29** SA	0200 / 0830 / 1428 / 2116	2.0 / 3.8 / 1.7 / 4.0
15 SA	0138 / 0818 / 1418 / 2106	1.7 / 4.1 / 1.4 / 4.2			

MARCH

Day	Time	m	Day	Time	m
1 SU	0252 / 0924 / 1513 / 2158	1.8 / 4.0 / 1.5 / 4.2	**16** M	0229 / 0912 / 1457 / 2147	1.3 / 4.4 / 0.9 / 4.6
2 M	0332 / 1005 / 1549 / 2233	1.5 / 4.2 / 1.2 / 4.4	**17** TU	0320 / 1005 / 1544 / 2234	0.9 / 4.6 / 0.5 / 4.9
3 TU	0407 / 1040 / 1621 / 2306	1.3 / 4.3 / 1.0 / 4.5	**18** W	0405 / 1051 / 1627 / 2317 ○	0.6 / 4.9 / 0.3 / 5.0
4 W	0438 / 1113 / 1651 / 2337 ●	1.0 / 4.4 / 0.8 / 4.6	**19** TH	0446 / 1134 / 1707 / 2358	0.4 / 5.0 / 0.2 / 5.0
5 TH	0507 / 1145 / 1719	0.9 / 4.5 / 0.7	**20** F	0526 / 1214 / 1746	0.3 / 4.9 / 0.3
6 F	0007 / 0535 / 1217 / 1746	4.6 / 0.8 / 4.5 / 0.7	**21** SA	0036 / 0604 / 1254 / 1824	5.0 / 0.4 / 4.8 / 0.5
7 SA	0038 / 0603 / 1249 / 1815	4.6 / 0.8 / 4.5 / 0.8	**22** SU	0114 / 0643 / 1333 / 1902	4.8 / 0.6 / 4.6 / 0.8
8 SU	0109 / 0633 / 1321 / 1847	4.5 / 0.8 / 4.5 / 0.9	**23** M	0151 / 0722 / 1413 / 1943	4.6 / 0.9 / 4.4 / 1.2
9 M	0141 / 0707 / 1357 / 1923	4.4 / 1.0 / 4.3 / 1.1	**24** TU	0229 / 0804 / 1455 / 2028	4.3 / 1.3 / 4.1 / 1.6
10 TU	0217 / 0745 / 1439 / 2006	4.3 / 1.2 / 4.2 / 1.4	**25** W	0309 / 0853 / 1544 / 2126	4.0 / 1.7 / 3.9 / 2.0
11 W	0300 / 0833 / 1533 / 2101	4.1 / 1.6 / 4.0 / 1.7	**26** TH	0357 / 0959 / 1646 / 2248	3.8 / 2.0 / 3.7 / 2.2
12 TH	0357 / 0937 / 1644 / 2221	4.0 / 1.7 / 3.8 / 1.9	**27** F	0500 / 1128 / 1809	3.6 / 2.1 / 3.6
13 F	0513 / 1114 / 1813 / 2017	3.8 / 1.8 / 3.8 / 3.8	**28** SA	0017 / 0624 / 1250 / 1935	2.2 / 3.5 / 2.0 / 3.7
14 SA	0005 / 0643 / 1252 / 1941	1.9 / 3.8 / 1.7 / 4.0	**29** SU	0127 / 0750 / 1350 / 2037	2.1 / 3.6 / 1.8 / 3.9
15 SU	0128 / 0807 / 1402 / 2052	1.7 / 4.1 / 1.3 / 4.3	**30** M	0219 / 0848 / 1436 / 2121	1.8 / 3.8 / 1.5 / 4.2
			31 TU	0300 / 0931 / 1514 / 2158	1.5 / 4.1 / 1.3 / 4.4

APRIL

Day	Time	m	Day	Time	m
1 W	0335 / 1009 / 1548 / 2232	1.3 / 4.3 / 1.0 / 4.5	**16** TH	0342 / 1029 / 1603 / 2252	0.7 / 4.8 / 0.5 / 4.9
2 TH	0407 / 1044 / 1619 / 2305	1.0 / 4.4 / 0.9 / 4.6	**17** F	0423 / 1111 / 1644 / 2332 ○	0.5 / 4.9 / 0.5 / 4.9
3 F	0437 / 1118 / 1650 / 2338 ●	0.8 / 4.5 / 0.8 / 4.7	**18** SA	0503 / 1152 / 1723	0.5 / 4.9 / 0.5
4 SA	0507 / 1153 / 1720	0.8 / 4.6 / 0.7	**19** SU	0010 / 0540 / 1231 / 1800	4.9 / 0.6 / 4.8 / 0.7
5 SU	0011 / 0537 / 1228 / 1752	4.6 / 0.8 / 4.6 / 0.8	**20** M	0046 / 0618 / 1309 / 1839	4.7 / 0.8 / 4.6 / 1.0
6 M	0045 / 0610 / 1304 / 1828	4.6 / 0.8 / 4.5 / 0.9	**21** TU	0122 / 0656 / 1347 / 1918	4.5 / 1.0 / 4.4 / 1.3
7 TU	0120 / 0646 / 1344 / 1907	4.5 / 0.9 / 4.4 / 1.1	**22** W	0157 / 0737 / 1427 / 2002	4.3 / 1.3 / 4.2 / 1.7
8 W	0200 / 0728 / 1431 / 1954	4.3 / 1.1 / 4.3 / 1.4	**23** TH	0234 / 0821 / 1512 / 2054	4.0 / 1.6 / 4.0 / 2.0
9 TH	0247 / 0819 / 1528 / 2055	4.1 / 1.4 / 4.1 / 1.7	**24** F	0318 / 0917 / 1606 / 2202	3.8 / 1.9 / 3.8 / 2.2
10 F	0347 / 0928 / 1639 / 2218	3.9 / 1.8 / 3.9 / 1.9	**25** SA	0413 / 1030 / 1713 / 2321	3.7 / 2.0 / 3.5 / 2.2
11 SA	0504 / 1100 / 1802 / 2352	3.8 / 1.7 / 3.9 / 1.8	**26** SU	0523 / 1148 / 1828	3.6 / 2.0 / 3.8
12 SU	0630 / 1229 / 1922	3.9 / 1.6 / 4.1	**27** M	0032 / 0641 / 1253 / 1935	2.1 / 3.6 / 1.9 / 3.9
13 M	0108 / 0748 / 1338 / 2028	1.6 / 4.0 / 1.3 / 4.4	**28** TU	0129 / 0749 / 1345 / 2029	1.9 / 3.8 / 1.7 / 4.1
14 TU	0208 / 0851 / 1433 / 2122	1.2 / 4.0 / 0.9 / 4.6	**29** W	0215 / 0843 / 1429 / 2113	1.6 / 4.0 / 1.4 / 4.3
15 W	0258 / 0943 / 1521 / 2209	0.9 / 4.6 / 0.7 / 4.8	**30** TH	0255 / 0928 / 1508 / 2153	1.4 / 4.2 / 1.2 / 4.5

To find H.W. Dover (approx.) subtract 0 h. 20 min.

TIDAL DIFFERENCES PAGE 21:209. TIDAL CURVE PAGE 21:213.

TIDAL STREAMS PAGES 21:192-21:198 AND 21:28-21:40.

Datum of predictions: 2.7 m. below Ordnance Datum (Newlyn) or approx. L.A.T.

PORTSMOUTH

21:211

Lat. 50°48′N. Long. 1°07′W. **HIGH & LOW WATER 1992**

GMT   ADD 1 HOUR MARCH 29 — OCTOBER 25 FOR B.S.T.

MAY

	Time	m		Time	m
1 F	0331 1010 1545 2232	1.1 4.4 1.0 4.6	**16** SA O	0402 1050 1622 2308	0.8 4.7 0.8 4.8
2 SA ●	0406 1050 1621 2309	1.0 4.5 0.9 4.7	**17** SU	0443 1131 1702 2346	0.8 4.7 0.9 4.7
3 SU	0441 1129 1657 2347	0.8 4.6 0.9 4.7	**18** M	0522 1210 1741	0.8 4.6 1.0
4 M	0517 1209 1735	0.8 4.7 0.9	**19** TU	0022 0559 1249 1819	4.6 1.0 4.5 1.2
5 TU	0026 0554 1252 1815	4.6 0.8 4.6 1.0	**20** W	0057 0637 1326 1858	4.5 1.1 4.4 1.4
6 W	0107 0635 1337 1900	4.5 0.9 4.5 1.2	**21** TH	0131 0715 1404 1939	4.3 1.3 4.2 1.6
7 TH	0151 0722 1427 1951	4.4 1.1 4.4 1.4	**22** F	0207 0755 1444 2023	4.1 1.5 4.1 1.8
8 F	0242 0816 1524 2052	4.2 1.3 4.3 1.6	**23** SA	0247 0840 1530 2115	4.0 1.7 4.0 2.0
9 SA	0341 0922 1630 2206	4.1 1.4 4.2 1.7	**24** SU	0333 0933 1622 2215	3.9 1.8 3.9 2.1
10 SU	0450 1040 1741 2325	4.0 1.5 4.2 1.7	**25** M	0428 1035 1721 2321	3.8 1.9 3.9 2.1
11 M	0606 1158 1853	4.0 1.5 4.3	**26** TU	0531 1140 1824	3.7 1.9 4.0
12 TU	0038 0718 1306 1957	1.6 4.1 1.3 4.4	**27** W	0024 0639 1242 1925	2.0 3.8 1.8 4.1
13 W	0139 0822 1404 2053	1.4 4.3 1.1 4.6	**28** TH	0121 0744 1337 2021	1.8 3.9 1.6 4.2
14 TH	0232 0917 1454 2142	1.1 4.5 1.0 4.7	**29** F	0210 0843 1426 2111	1.6 4.1 1.4 4.4
15 F	0319 1005 1540 2226	0.9 4.6 0.9 4.8	**30** SA	0256 0935 1512 2159	1.3 4.3 1.2 4.6
			31 SU	0339 1023 1556 2244	1.1 4.5 1.1 4.7

JUNE

	Time	m		Time	m
1 M ●	0421 1110 1639 2328	0.9 4.6 1.0 4.7	**16** TU	0508 1155 1726	1.1 4.5 1.2
2 TU	0503 1156 1723	0.8 4.7 0.9	**17** W	0004 0544 1233 1803	4.5 1.1 4.5 1.3
3 W	0012 0545 1243 1808	4.7 0.8 4.7 0.9	**18** TH	0038 0620 1308 1839	4.4 1.1 4.4 1.3
4 TH	0058 0630 1331 1855	4.7 0.8 4.7 1.0	**19** F	0112 0655 1343 1915	4.4 1.2 4.4 1.4
5 F	0145 0716 1421 1946	4.6 0.9 4.6 1.1	**20** SA	0145 0730 1418 1952	4.3 1.3 4.3 1.6
6 SA	0235 0810 1514 2041	4.5 1.0 4.5 1.3	**21** SU	0220 0806 1456 2032	4.2 1.4 4.2 1.7
7 SU	0329 0907 1611 2143	4.3 1.2 4.4 1.5	**22** M	0259 0846 1538 2117	4.1 1.5 4.2 1.8
8 M	0429 1012 1712 2251	4.2 1.3 4.4 1.6	**23** TU	0344 0932 1625 2211	4.0 1.7 4.1 1.9
9 TU	0535 1121 1817	4.1 1.4 4.3	**24** W	0436 1029 1720 2313	3.9 1.8 4.1 1.9
10 W	0001 0643 1231 1920	1.6 4.1 1.4 4.4	**25** TH	0538 1134 1822	3.9 1.8 4.1
11 TH	0107 0749 1334 2020	1.5 4.2 1.4 4.4	**26** F	0021 0648 1243 1927	1.9 3.9 1.8 4.2
12 F	0206 0850 1430 2115	1.4 4.3 1.3 4.5	**27** SA	0126 0759 1347 2031	1.7 4.0 1.6 4.3
13 SA	0258 0944 1520 2204	1.3 4.4 1.3 4.6	**28** SU	0225 0905 1445 2130	1.5 4.2 1.4 4.5
14 SU	0345 1032 1605 2248	1.2 4.5 1.2 4.6	**29** M	0318 1003 1537 2224	1.2 4.4 1.2 4.6
15 M O	0428 1116 1647 2327	1.1 4.5 1.2 4.6	**30** TU ●	0406 1056 1626 2313	1.0 4.6 1.0 4.7

JULY

	Time	m		Time	m
1 W	0453 1146 1713	0.7 4.8 0.8	**16** TH	0529 1216 1746	1.0 4.5 1.2
2 TH	0001 0537 1234 1759	4.8 0.6 4.9 0.7	**17** F	0021 0601 1249 1818	4.5 1.0 4.5 1.2
3 F	0048 0622 1321 1845	4.8 0.5 4.9 0.7	**18** SA	0053 0632 1320 1850	4.4 1.0 4.5 1.2
4 SA	0134 0707 1407 1932	4.8 0.6 4.9 0.8	**19** SU	0124 0702 1351 1921	4.4 1.1 4.4 1.3
5 SU	0222 0755 1455 2022	4.7 0.7 4.8 1.0	**20** M	0156 0733 1424 1955	4.3 1.2 4.4 1.4
6 M	0311 0845 1546 2116	4.5 0.9 4.6 1.2	**21** TU	0230 0807 1459 2032	4.3 1.3 4.3 1.5
7 TU	0404 0940 1639 2216	4.4 1.2 4.5 1.4	**22** W	0309 0846 1540 2116	4.2 1.4 4.2 1.7
8 W	0502 1044 1738 2324	4.2 1.4 4.3 1.6	**23** TH	0355 0934 1629 2213	4.0 1.7 4.1 1.8
9 TH	0607 1154 1842	4.1 1.6 4.2	**24** F	0453 1037 1730 2326	3.9 1.8 4.1 1.9
10 F	0036 0718 1306 1948	1.7 4.0 1.7 4.2	**25** SA	0604 1157 1841	3.9 1.9 4.0
11 SA	0144 0828 1410 2051	1.6 4.1 1.7 4.2	**26** SU	0048 0726 1318 1958	1.8 3.9 1.8 4.1
12 SU	0243 0929 1505 2146	1.5 4.2 1.6 4.3	**27** M	0201 0844 1426 2109	1.6 4.1 1.6 4.3
13 M	0333 1020 1553 2233	1.4 4.3 1.5 4.4	**28** TU	0301 0950 1524 2209	1.3 4.3 1.2 4.5
14 TU	0416 1104 1634 2313	1.2 4.4 1.3 4.4	**29** W ●	0353 1045 1614 2301	0.9 4.6 0.9 4.7
15 W	0454 1142 1712 2348	1.1 4.5 1.2 4.5	**30** TH	0440 1133 1701 2349	0.6 4.9 0.7 4.9
			31 F	0525 1219 1746	0.4 5.0 0.5

AUGUST

	Time	m		Time	m
1 SA	0034 0607 1304 1829	5.0 0.3 5.1 0.5	**16** SU	0032 0605 1255 1822	4.5 0.9 4.6 1.0
2 SU	0119 0650 1347 1913	4.9 0.3 5.0 0.6	**17** M	0102 0633 1324 1851	4.5 0.9 4.5 1.0
3 M	0203 0733 1431 1958	4.8 0.5 4.9 0.8	**18** TU	0133 0702 1354 1921	4.4 1.0 4.5 1.1
4 TU	0248 0819 1516 2046	4.6 0.8 4.7 1.1	**19** W	0205 0734 1427 1956	4.4 1.2 4.4 1 3
5 W	0337 0909 1604 2141	4.4 1.2 4.4 1.4	**20** TH	0242 0811 1504 2037	4.3 1.4 4.3 1.5
6 TH	0430 1009 1658 2247	4.2 1.6 4.2 1.7	**21** F	0326 0857 1551 2130	4.1 1.6 4.2 1.7
7 F	0534 1122 1802	4.0 1.8 4.0	**22** SA	0422 0959 1651 2245	4.0 1.8 4.0 1.9
8 SA	0006 0649 1243 1916	1.9 3.9 2.0 3.9	**23** SU	0537 1127 1809	3.8 2.0 3.9
9 SU	0123 0810 1355 2031	1.8 3.9 1.9 4.0	**24** M	0020 0706 1259 1935	1.9 3.9 1.9 4.0
10 M	0227 0917 1453 2131	1.7 4.1 1.8 4.1	**25** TU	0141 0830 1411 2053	1.6 4.1 1.6 4.2
11 TU	0318 1007 1540 2218	1.5 4.3 1.6 4.2	**26** W	0244 0936 1509 2154	1.2 4.4 1.2 4.5
12 W	0400 1048 1619 2256	1.3 4.4 1.4 4.3	**27** TH	0336 1029 1558 2245	0.8 4.7 0.8 4.8
13 TH O	0436 1123 1653 2330	1.1 4.5 1.2 4.4	**28** F ●	0423 1116 1644 2332	0.5 5.0 0.5 5.0
14 F	0508 1155 1725	1.0 4.6 1.1	**29** SA	0506 1200 1727	0.3 5.1 0.4
15 SA	0001 0537 1225 1754	4.5 0.9 4.6 1.0	**30** SU	0016 0547 1242 1808	5.0 0.2 5.1 0.4
			31 M	0059 0628 1323 1850	5.0 0.3 5.1 0.5

GENERAL — At most times the entrance and the Spithead streams run in opposite directions, thus causing confused seas in some parts. Eddies off both sides of the harbour entrance and the piers and jetties. Streams to and from various channels meet and divide near N. Corner jetty.

PORTSMOUTH

HIGH & LOW WATER 1992 Lat. 50°48'N. Long. 1°07'W.

GMT ADD 1 HOUR MARCH 29 — OCTOBER 25 FOR B.S.T.

SEPTEMBER

Day	Time	m	Time	m		Time	m	Time	m
1 TU	0141	4.9	1404	4.9	16	0110	4.6	1328	4.6
	0710	0.5	1932	0.7		0635	1.0	1853	1.1
2 W	0224	4.7	1446	4.7	17	0144	4.5	TH 1401	4.5
	0753	0.9	2017	1.1		0709	1.2	1928	1.2
3 TH	0309	4.4	1530	4.4	18	0222	4.4	F 1439	4.3
	0841	1.3	2109	1.4		0747	1.4	2011	1.4
4 F	0400	4.2	1620	4.1	19	0308	4.2	SA 1526	4.2
	0938	1.7	2213	1.8		0835	1.7	2105	1.7
5 SA	0502	3.9	1722	3.9	20	0406	4.0	SU 1629	4.0
	1053	2.0	2335	2.0		0940	1.9	2222	1.8
6 SU	0620	3.8	1842	3.8	21	0523	3.9	M 1750	3.9
	1219	2.2				1111	2.0	2359	1.8
7 M	0057	2.0	1334	2.1	22	0651	4.0	TU 1918	4.0
	0748	3.9	2006	3.8		1241	1.9		
8 TU	0204	1.8	1432	1.9	23	0120	1.6	W 1352	1.6
	0856	4.0	2109	4.0		0812	4.2	2035	4.3
9 W	0254	1.6	1517	1.7	24	0223	1.2	TH 1449	1.2
	0944	4.2	2154	4.1		0915	4.5	2135	4.5
10 TH	0335	1.4	1555	1.4	25	0315	0.8	F 1538	0.8
	1022	4.4	2231	4.3		1007	4.8	2225	4.8
11 F	0410	1.2	1627	1.2	26	0401	0.5	SA 1622	0.6
	1055	4.5	2304	4.4		1053	5.0	• 2311	5.0
12 SA	0441	1.0	1657	1.0	27	0444	0.4	SU 1705	0.4
	1127	4.6	O 2336	4.5		1136	5.1	2354	5.1
13 SU	0510	0.9	1726	1.0	28	0525	0.3	M 1746	0.4
	1157	4.7				1217	5.1		
14 M	0007	4.6	1227	4.7	29	0036	5.0	TU 1258	5.0
	0537	0.9	1753	0.9		0606	0.5	1826	0.6
15 TU	0039	4.6	1257	4.6	30	0118	4.9	W 1337	4.9
	0605	0.9	1822	1.0		0647	0.7	1907	0.8

OCTOBER

Day	Time	m	Time	m		Time	m	Time	m
1 TH	0200	4.7	1417	4.6	16	0128	4.6	F 1342	4.5
	0729	1.1	1951	1.2		0651	1.2	1910	1.2
2 F	0243	4.4	1458	4.3	17	0210	4.5	SA 1424	4.4
	0815	1.5	2039	1.5		0734	1.4	1956	1.4
3 SA	0331	4.2	1544	4.1	18	0259	4.3	SU 1514	4.2
	0910	1.9	2139	1.9		0825	1.7	2053	1.6
4 SU	0429	4.0	1641	3.8	19	0359	4.2	M 1618	4.1
	1021	2.2	2256	2.1		0932	1.9	2208	1.7
5 M	0541	3.8	1755	3.7	20	0512	4.1	TU 1735	4.0
	1143	2.3				1056	1.9	2335	1.7
6 TU	0016	2.1	1258	2.2	21	0632	4.1	W 1858	4.1
	0705	3.9	1921	3.7		1218	1.8		
7 W	0123	2.0	1356	2.0	22	0052	1.5	TH 1327	1.5
	0814	4.0	2028	3.9		0734	4.3	2010	4.3
8 TH	0215	1.7	1442	1.8	23	0156	1.2	F 1424	1.2
	0904	4.2	2116	4.1		0848	4.6	2110	4.6
9 F	0258	1.5	1520	1.5	24	0249	1.0	SA 1514	1.0
	0944	4.4	2156	4.3		0941	4.8	2202	4.8
10 SA	0334	1.3	1555	1.3	25	0337	0.7	SU 1600	0.7
	1019	4.5	2232	4.4		1028	5.0	• 2249	4.9
11 SU	0408	1.1	1643	1.1	26	0421	0.6	M 1643	0.6
	1053	4.6	O 2306	4.6		1111	5.1	2333	5.0
12 M	0439	1.0	1656	1.0	27	0504	0.6	TU 1724	0.7
	1127	4.7	2340	4.6		1153	5.1		
13 TU	0510	1.0	1726	1.0	28	0015	5.0	W 1233	4.9
	1157	4.7				0545	0.8	1805	0.8
14 W	0015	4.7	1232	4.7	29	0057	4.8	TH 1311	4.8
	0540	1.0	1757	1.0		0626	1.0	1845	1.0
15 TH	0051	4.7	1306	4.6	30	0137	4.7	F 1349	4.6
	0614	1.1	1832	1.1		0708	1.3	1927	1.3
					31	0219	4.5	SA 1428	4.3
						0752	1.6	2013	1.6

NOVEMBER

Day	Time	m	Time	m		Time	m	Time	m
1 SU	0304	4.3	1510	4.1	16	0254	4.5	M 1507	4.3
	0842	1.9	2104	1.8		0820	1.5	2045	1.4
2 M	0354	4.1	1559	3.9	17	0351	4.4	TU 1607	4.2
	0942	2.1	2207	2.0		0922	1.7	2151	1.5
3 TU	0453	4.0	1700	3.8	18	0456	4.3	W 1716	4.1
	1052	2.3	2317	2.1		1034	1.8	2306	1.6
4 W	0601	3.9	1812	3.7	19	0605	4.3	TH 1831	4.2
	1202	2.2				1148	1.7		
5 TH	0024	2.0	1304	2.1	20	0019	1.5	F 1258	1.6
	0708	4.0	1923	3.8		0714	4.4	1941	4.3
6 F	0122	1.9	1355	1.9	21	0126	1.4	SA 1358	1.4
	0806	4.2	2022	4.0		0817	4.6	2044	4.5
7 SA	0210	1.7	1439	1.7	22	0223	1.2	SU 1452	1.2
	0854	4.3	2111	4.2		0913	4.7	2139	4.7
8 SU	0253	1.5	1518	1.5	23	0314	1.1	M 1540	1.0
	0937	4.5	2154	4.4		1003	4.9	2229	4.8
9 M	0332	1.3	1554	1.3	24	0401	1.0	TU 1625	0.9
	1016	4.6	2235	4.5		1048	4.9	• 2314	4.8
10 TU	0408	1.2	1629	1.1	25	0445	1.0	W 1707	0.9
	1054	4.7	O 2315	4.7		1131	4.9	2357	4.7
11 W	0444	1.1	1704	1.0	26	0527	1.0	TH 1748	0.9
	1132	4.8	2355	4.7		1210	4.8		
12 TH	0521	1.1	1740	1.0	27	0038	4.8	F 1248	4.7
	1210	4.8				0608	1.2	1827	1.1
13 F	0035	4.7	1249	4.7	28	0118	4.7	SA 1324	4.5
	0559	1.1	1818	1.0		0648	1.3	1906	1.2
14 SA	0118	4.7	1330	4.6	29	0156	4.5	SU 1400	4.4
	0641	1.2	1901	1.1		0729	1.5	1946	1.4
15 SU	0203	4.6	1415	4.5	30	0236	4.4	M 1438	4.2
	0727	1.4	1949	1.2		0812	1.8	2028	1.6

DECEMBER

Day	Time	m	Time	m		Time	m	Time	m
1 TU	0317	4.2	1520	4.0	16	0335	4.6	W 1551	4.4
	0859	1.9	2115	1.8		0903	1.4	2128	1.3
2 W	0404	4.1	1608	3.9	17	0432	4.5	TH 1653	4.2
	0954	2.1	2210	1.9		1006	1.6	2233	1.4
3 TH	0457	4.1	1706	3.8	18	0535	4.4	F 1801	4.2
	1055	2.2	2312	2.0		1116	1.6	2345	1.6
4 F	0556	4.1	1812	3.8	19	0641	4.4	SA 1913	4.2
	1159	2.1				1228	1.6		
5 SA	0015	2.0	1300	2.0	20	0056	1.6	SU 1335	1.5
	0658	4.1	1920	3.9		0746	4.5	2021	4.3
6 SU	0115	1.9	1354	1.8	21	0201	1.5	M 1435	1.4
	0757	4.3	2022	4.1		0847	4.5	2121	4.5
7 M	0209	1.7	1442	1.6	22	0257	1.4	TU 1526	1.2
	0851	4.4	2118	4.3		0941	4.6	2214	4.6
8 TU	0257	1.5	1526	1.4	23	0347	1.3	W 1612	1.1
	0940	4.5	2207	4.5		1030	4.7	2301	4.7
9 W	0341	1.4	1607	1.2	24	0432	1.2	TH 1654	1.0
	1026	4.7	O 2254	4.6		1113	4.7	• 2344	4.7
10 TH	0424	1.2	1648	1.0	25	0513	1.2	F 1733	1.0
	1109	4.8	2339	4.7		1152	4.7		
11 F	0506	1.1	1728	0.9	26	0023	4.7	SA 1229	4.6
	1152	4.8				0551	1.2	1809	1.0
12 SA	0023	4.8	1236	4.8	27	0059	4.6	SU 1302	4.5
	0548	1.0	1809	0.8		0628	1.3	1843	1.1
13 SU	0108	4.8	1320	4.7	28	0133	4.5	M 1335	4.4
	0632	1.0	1853	0.8		0704	1.4	1917	1.2
14 M	0155	4.8	1406	4.6	29	0207	4.5	TU 1408	4.3
	0718	1.1	1939	0.9		0740	1.5	1952	1.3
15 TU	0243	4.7	1456	4.5	30	0242	4.4	W 1444	4.2
	0808	1.2	2030	1.1		0818	1.7	2029	1.5
					31	0320	4.3	TH 1525	4.0
						0859	1.8	2110	1.7

RATE AND SET — Position: mid-chan., off ent., ingoing, +0530 Portsmouth; outgoing, +0015 Portsmouth, Position: Spithead; E. going, +0330 Portsmouth; W. going, –0200 Portsmouth. Position: in ent. Flood, +0515 Portsmouth in two periods. Ebb. +0025 Portsmouth, inwards the streams become later and weaker.

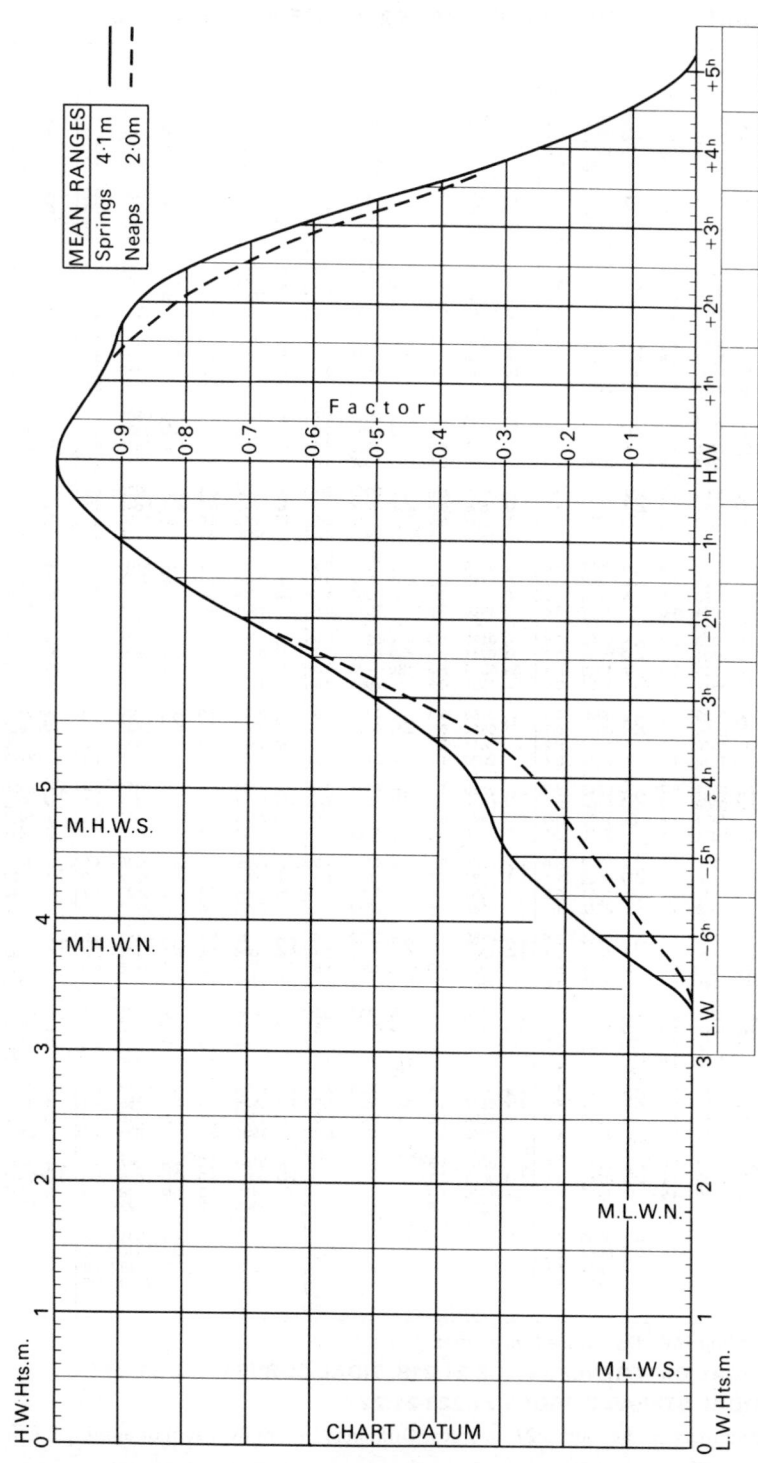

PORTSMOUTH
MEAN SPRING AND NEAP CURVES
Springs occur 2 days after New and Full Moon.

SOUTH COAST SHOREHAM

HIGH & LOW WATER 1992   Lat. 50°50'N. Long. 0°15'W.

GMT   ADD 1 HOUR MARCH 29 — OCTOBER 25 FOR B.S.T.

JANUARY

Day	Time	m	Day	Time	m
1 W	0217	1.6	16 Th	0105	1.7
	0815	5.3		0715	5.2
	1450	1.5		1350	1.5
	2056	5.2		1958	5.2
2 Th	0315	1.5	17 F	0221	1.4
	0912	5.4		0827	5.5
	1542	1.3		1459	1.2
	2149	5.4		2105	5.6
3 F	0405	1.3	18 Sa	0326	1.1
	1000	5.6		0928	5.9
	1627	1.1		1559	0.9
	2233	5.6		2205	6.0
4 Sa	0446	1.2	19 Su	0422	0.9
	1042	5.8		1023	6.2
	1705	1.0		1653	0.7
	● 2312	5.8		○ 2259	6.3
5 Su	0523	1.2	20 M	0514	0.8
	1118	5.9		1115	6.4
	1741	1.0		1743	0.6
	2347	5.9		2350	6.5
6 M	0556	1.2	21 Tu	0603	0.7
	1151	5.9		1204	6.5
	1812	1.0		1830	0.6
7 Tu	0020	5.9	22 W	0037	6.6
	0629	1.2		0649	0.7
	1223	5.9		1252	6.5
	1844	1.0		1917	0.6
8 W	0050	5.9	23 Th	0123	6.6
	0701	1.2		0738	0.7
	1255	5.8		1338	6.4
	1917	1.0		2001	0.6
9 Th	0120	5.8	24 F	0206	6.5
	0734	1.2		0820	0.7
	1329	5.7		1424	6.2
	1949	1.1		2044	0.7
10 F	0151	5.7	25 Sa	0245	6.3
	0809	1.3		0904	0.9
	1404	5.6		1507	5.9
	2024	1.1		2126	0.9
11 Sa	0224	5.6	26 Su	0326	6.0
	0844	1.3		0949	1.1
	1441	5.4		1551	5.5
	2059	1.3		© 2212	1.2
12 Su	0259	5.4	27 M	0411	5.5
	0924	1.4		1042	1.4
	1522	5.2		1645	5.1
	2141	1.5		2310	1.6
13 M	0345	5.2	28 Tu	0511	5.1
	1012	1.6		1149	1.7
	1612	5.0		1758	4.7
	) 2234	1.6			
14 Tu	0442	5.0	29 W	0026	1.9
	1116	1.7		0627	4.9
	1719	4.9		1310	1.9
	2344	1.7		1922	4.7
15 W	0557	5.0	30 Th	0146	1.9
	1233	1.7		0746	4.8
	1840	4.9		1425	1.8
				2036	4.9
			31 F	0255	1.8
				0854	5.0
				1524	1.6
				2135	5.2

FEBRUARY

Day	Time	m	Day	Time	m
1 Sa	0349	1.6	16 Su	0316	1.2
	0947	5.3		0919	5.8
	1611	1.3		1548	0.9
	2222	5.5		2155	6.1
2 Su	0432	1.3	17 M	0412	0.8
	1030	5.6		1013	6.2
	1651	1.1		1640	0.6
	2259	5.8		2247	6.4
3 M	0508	1.2	18 Tu	0501	0.6
	1105	5.8		1101	6.5
	1724	0.9		1729	0.5
	● 2332	5.9		○ 2333	6.6
4 Tu	0539	1.1	19 W	0547	0.5
	1136	5.9		1146	6.6
	1754	0.9		1813	0.4
5 W	0002	6.0	20 Th	0017	6.7
	0609	1.0		0631	0.5
	1206	5.9		1232	6.6
	1825	0.8		1856	0.4
6 Th	0039	6.0	21 F	0059	6.7
	0639	0.9		0714	0.5
	1236	5.9		1316	6.5
	1856	0.8		1936	0.4
7 F	0058	6.0	22 Sa	0138	6.5
	0710	0.9		0754	0.6
	1308	5.9		1356	6.3
	1926	0.8		2015	0.6
8 Sa	0125	5.9	23 Su	0212	6.3
	0741	0.9		0833	0.7
	1339	5.8		1433	6.0
	1957	0.8		2052	0.8
9 Su	0153	5.8	24 M	0246	6.0
	0814	0.9		0911	1.0
	1411	5.7		1512	5.5
	2030	1.0		2133	1.2
10 M	0225	5.7	25 Tu	0324	5.5
	0849	1.1		0957	1.4
	1446	5.4		1559	5.0
	2106	1.2		© 2224	1.7
11 Tu	0303	5.4	26 W	0418	4.9
	0932	1.3		1058	1.9
	1531	5.1		1709	4.6
	) 2155	1.5		2339	2.1
12 W	0351	5.1	27 Th	0539	4.6
	1031	1.6		1223	2.1
	1636	4.9		1844	4.5
	2305	1.7			
13 Th	0516	4.9	28 F	0111	2.2
	1155	1.7		0713	4.5
	1808	4.8		1351	2.1
				2010	4.7
14 F	0038	1.8	29 Sa	0229	2.1
	0650	5.0		0831	4.8
	1328	1.6		1457	1.8
	1943	5.1		2113	5.0
15 Sa	0206	1.5			
	0813	5.3			
	1446	1.3			
	2057	5.6			

MARCH

Day	Time	m	Day	Time	m
1 Su	0325	1.8	16 M	0302	1.1
	0930	5.1		0908	5.7
	1546	1.5		1531	0.9
	2159	5.4		2140	6.1
2 M	0407	1.4	17 Tu	0356	0.8
	1011	5.5		0958	6.0
	1624	1.1		1622	0.6
	2236	5.7		2227	6.4
3 Tu	0442	1.1	18 W	0443	0.5
	1044	5.8		1043	6.4
	1658	0.9		1706	0.4
	2307	5.9		○ 2310	6.6
4 W	0513	0.9	19 Th	0527	0.4
	1113	5.9		1126	6.5
	1728	0.8		1750	0.4
	● 2335	6.0		2351	6.6
5 Th	0543	0.8	20 F	0609	0.4
	1142	6.0		1208	6.5
	1759	0.7		1830	0.4
6 F	0002	6.1	21 Sa	0030	6.6
	0613	0.7		0648	0.5
	1212	6.0		1250	6.4
	1830	0.7		1908	0.5
7 Sa	0031	6.1	22 Su	0105	6.4
	0644	0.7		0725	0.6
	1244	6.0		1328	6.0
	1901	0.7		1944	0.7
8 Su	0059	6.1	23 M	0138	6.2
	0715	0.7		0800	0.9
	1315	6.0		1403	5.9
	1932	0.7		2020	0.9
9 M	0128	6.0	24 Tu	0209	5.8
	0748	0.7		0836	1.1
	1348	5.8		1439	5.5
	2005	0.9		2058	1.3
10 Tu	0200	5.8	25 W	0246	5.4
	0823	1.0		0916	1.5
	1423	5.6		1522	5.1
	2044	1.1		2146	1.8
11 W	0239	5.4	26 Th	0336	4.9
	0907	1.2		1013	1.9
	1509	5.3		1627	4.7
	2133	1.5		© 2257	2.2
12 Th	0333	5.1	27 F	0452	4.5
	1006	1.6		1131	2.2
	1616	5.0		1758	4.5
	) 2247	1.7			
13 F	0455	4.8	28 Sa	0026	2.4
	1132	1.7		0630	4.4
	1754	4.9		1304	2.2
				1929	4.6
14 Sa	0024	1.8	29 Su	0148	2.2
	0635	5.0		0755	4.8
	1312	1.6		1416	2.0
	1931	5.2		2035	5.0
15 Su	0153	1.5	30 M	0247	1.9
	0802	5.3		0856	5.0
	1431	1.3		1508	1.6
	2045	5.7		2123	5.4
			31 Tu	0331	1.5
				0940	5.4
				1549	1.3
				2200	5.7

APRIL

Day	Time	m	Day	Time	m
1 W	0407	1.1	16 Th	0422	0.6
	1013	5.7		1021	6.2
	1623	0.9		1643	0.5
	2232	5.9		2243	6.4
2 Th	0439	0.9	17 F	0505	0.5
	1042	5.9		1102	6.3
	1656	0.8		1725	0.5
	2301	6.0		○ 2324	6.4
3 F	0511	0.7	18 Sa	0544	0.5
	1112	6.0		1143	6.3
	1729	0.7		1804	0.6
	2332	6.1			
4 Sa	0544	0.7	19 Su	0000	6.3
	1145	6.0		0622	0.6
	1801	0.7		1224	6.2
				1841	0.7
5 Su	0002	6.1	20 M	0035	6.2
	0617	0.6		0657	0.7
	1220	6.1		1302	6.0
	1836	0.7		1917	0.9
6 M	0035	6.1	21 Tu	0109	6.0
	0653	0.6		0731	0.9
	1257	6.0		1338	5.8
	1911	0.8		1953	1.1
7 Tu	0109	6.0	22 W	0142	5.7
	0729	0.8		0807	1.1
	1334	5.9		1415	5.5
	1949	0.9		2031	1.5
8 W	0145	5.8	23 Th	0218	5.3
	0810	0.9		0846	1.5
	1415	5.7		1458	5.1
	2033	1.2		2118	1.8
9 Th	0229	5.5	24 F	0307	4.9
	0857	1.2		0937	1.8
	1506	5.4		1554	4.8
	2128	1.5		(2220	2.2
10 F	0329	5.1	25 Sa	0412	4.5
	0958	1.5		1043	2.1
	1615	5.1		1709	4.6
	) 2241	1.7		2335	2.3
11 Sa	0447	4.9	26 Su	0535	4.4
	1122	1.7		1203	2.2
	1748	5.1		1830	4.7
12 Su	0013	1.7	27 M	0053	2.2
	0623	4.9		0701	4.5
	1253	1.5		1317	2.1
	1916	5.4		1940	4.9
13 M	0136	1.4	28 Tu	0155	2.0
	0746	5.2		0806	4.8
	1409	1.2		1416	1.8
	2024	5.7		2035	5.2
14 Tu	0241	1.1	29 W	0244	1.6
	0848	5.6		0855	5.1
	1508	0.9		1502	1.4
	2117	6.1		2116	5.5
15 W	0335	0.8	30 Th	0326	1.2
	0937	6.0		0931	5.5
	1557	0.6		1542	1.1
	2203	6.3		2151	5.8

To find H.W. Dover use these times.

TIDAL DIFFERENCES PAGE 21:218. TIDAL CURVE PAGE 21:217.

TIDAL STREAMS PAGES 21:223-21:227.

Datum of predictions: 3:27 m. below Ordnance Datum (Newlyn) or approx. L.A.T.

SHOREHAM SOUTH COAST 21:215

Lat. 50°50′N. Long. 0°15′W. **HIGH & LOW WATER 1992**

GMT ADD 1 HOUR MARCH 29 — OCTOBER 25 FOR B.S.T.

MAY

Day	Time	m	Time	m	Time	m	Time	m
1 F	0403	1.0	1006	5.7	1620	0.9	2225	5.9
2 Sa ●	0439	0.8	1042	5.9	1657	0.8	2301	6.0
3 Su	0517	0.7	1121	6.0	1736	0.8	2338	6.1
4 M	0556	0.7	1203	6.1	1815	0.9		
5 Tu	0017	6.1	0637	0.8	1246	6.1	1857	0.9
6 W	0058	6.1	0719	0.9	1330	6.0	1942	1.1
7 Th	0141	5.9	0805	1.0	1417	5.7	2032	1.2
8 F	0231	5.6	0856	1.2	1511	5.6	2128	1.4
9 Sa ☽	0330	5.3	0957	1.4	1617	5.4	2236	1.5
10 Su	0442	5.1	1109	1.5	1732	5.4	2354	1.5
11 M	0603	5.1	1228	1.4	1848	5.5		
12 Tu	0110	1.4	0719	5.2	1340	1.3	1955	5.7
13 W	0215	1.1	0822	5.5	1440	1.0	2048	5.9
14 Th	0310	0.9	0913	5.7	1532	0.9	2136	6.0
15 F	0359	0.8	0959	5.9	1620	0.8	2219	6.1
16 Sa ○	0442	0.7	1042	6.0	1702	0.8	2259	6.1
17 Su	0522	0.7	1125	6.0	1743	0.8	2337	6.1
18 M	0601	0.8	1205	5.9	1819	1.0		
19 Tu	0012	6.0	0635	0.9	1244	5.9	1856	1.1
20 W	0046	5.9	0710	1.0	1321	5.7	1932	1.3
21 Th	0121	5.7	0746	1.2	1357	5.6	2010	1.5
22 F	0200	5.4	0825	1.4	1437	5.3	2055	1.7
23 Sa	0243	5.1	0909	1.7	1523	5.1	2145	2.0
24 Su ☾	0336	4.8	1001	1.9	1620	4.9	2243	2.1
25 M	0442	4.6	1102	2.0	1726	4.8	2348	2.1
26 Tu	0552	4.5	1209	2.0	1833	4.9		
27 W	0052	2.0	0700	4.4	1313	1.9	1932	5.1
28 Th	0150	1.7	0758	5.0	1409	1.6	2024	5.3
29 F	0240	1.4	0845	5.3	1459	1.3	2108	5.6
30 Sa	0325	1.1	0930	5.6	1545	1.1	2152	5.8
31 Su	0410	0.9	1015	5.8	1630	1.0	2235	6.0

JUNE

Day	Time	m	Time	m	Time	m	Time	m
1 M ●	0455	0.8	1101	6.0	1716	1.0	2318	6.1
2 Tu	0540	0.6	1151	6.1	1802	1.0		
3 W	0005	6.2	0627	0.9	1240	6.2	1849	1.0
4 Th	0051	6.1	0716	0.9	1329	6.2	1938	1.1
5 F	0140	6.0	0804	1.0	1419	6.1	2030	1.1
6 Sa	0231	5.9	0855	1.0	1510	6.0	2123	1.2
7 Su ☽	0327	5.6	0948	1.1	1605	5.8	2222	1.3
8 M	0426	5.4	1049	1.3	1707	5.6	2328	1.4
9 Tu	0534	5.2	1156	1.4	1813	5.5		
10 W	0039	1.4	0646	5.1	1306	1.4	1920	5.5
11 Th	0147	1.3	0752	5.2	1412	1.3	2019	5.6
12 F	0246	1.2	0849	5.3	1509	1.2	2111	5.7
13 Sa	0339	1.1	0941	5.5	1600	1.1	2158	5.8
14 Su	0425	1.0	1028	5.7	1645	1.1	2243	5.8
15 M ○	0507	1.0	1111	5.8	1727	1.1	2321	5.9
16 Tu	0544	1.0	1153	5.8	1804	1.2	2357	5.9
17 W	0620	1.0	1231	5.8	1839	1.3		
18 Th	0031	5.8	0654	1.1	1305	5.8	1915	1.3
19 F	0106	5.7	0729	1.2	1340	5.7	1950	1.4
20 Sa	0142	5.5	0805	1.3	1415	5.5	2029	1.5
21 Su	0221	5.3	0843	1.4	1452	5.4	2110	1.7
22 M	0303	5.1	0923	1.6	1535	5.2	2155	1.8
23 Tu ☾	0350	4.8	1010	1.8	1624	5.0	2246	1.9
24 W	0446	4.7	1104	1.9	1722	4.9	2348	1.9
25 Th	0550	4.7	1209	1.9	1828	4.9		
26 F	0053	1.8	0657	4.8	1317	1.8	1932	5.1
27 Sa	0157	1.6	0801	5.1	1420	1.6	2031	5.4
28 Su	0255	1.3	0900	5.4	1518	1.3	2126	5.7
29 M	0348	1.1	0955	5.7	1611	1.1	2215	5.9
30 Tu	0440	0.9	1047	6.0	1701	1.0	2304	6.1

JULY

Day	Time	m	Time	m	Time	m	Time	m
1 W	0530	0.9	1140	6.2	1752	1.0	2354	6.3
2 Th	0618	0.8	1232	6.3	1841	1.0		
3 F	0044	6.3	0707	0.8	1321	6.4	1931	0.9
4 Sa	0134	6.3	0756	0.8	1410	6.4	2020	0.9
5 Su	0222	6.1	0844	0.8	1457	6.3	2109	1.0
6 M	0310	5.9	0932	0.9	1543	6.0	2200	1.1
7 Tu ☽	0402	5.6	1022	1.1	1632	5.7	2257	1.3
8 W	0458	5.2	1121	1.4	1732	5.4		
9 Th	0002	1.5	0606	5.0	1230	1.6	1840	5.2
10 F	0114	1.6	0720	4.9	1344	1.7	1949	5.2
11 Sa	0223	1.6	0828	5.0	1450	1.6	2051	5.3
12 Su	0322	1.4	0927	5.2	1546	1.5	2146	5.4
13 M	0412	1.3	1019	5.5	1634	1.4	2232	5.6
14 Tu ○	0454	1.1	1101	5.7	1713	1.3	2310	5.8
15 W	0531	1.1	1140	5.8	1749	1.2	2345	5.8
16 Th	0603	1.1	1215	5.8	1822	1.2		
17 F	0016	5.8	0637	1.1	1247	5.8	1854	1.2
18 Sa	0048	5.8	0709	1.1	1318	5.8	1928	1.2
19 Su	0121	5.7	0742	1.1	1348	5.7	2001	1.3
20 M	0153	5.5	0814	1.2	1419	5.6	2035	1.3
21 Tu	0228	5.3	0849	1.3	1452	5.4	2111	1.5
22 W ☾	0305	5.1	0926	1.5	1530	5.2	2154	1.7
23 Th	0342	4.9	1012	1.8	1622	5.0	2249	1.8
24 F	0447	4.7	1114	1.9	1729	4.8	2359	1.9
25 Sa	0604	4.7	1231	1.9	1848	4.9		
26 Su	0119	1.8	0726	4.9	1350	1.7	2002	5.2
27 M	0231	1.5	0839	5.3	1459	1.4	2107	5.6
28 Tu	0332	1.2	0939	5.8	1557	1.2	2201	6.0
29 W	0427	0.9	1035	6.1	1650	1.0	2251	6.3
30 Th ●	0518	0.8	1126	6.4	1739	0.9	2341	6.4
31 F	0606	0.7	1216	6.5	1828	0.8		

AUGUST

Day	Time	m	Time	m	Time	m	Time	m
1 Sa	0030	6.5	0654	0.7	1303	6.6	1916	0.7
2 Su	0117	6.4	0740	0.7	1349	6.6	2001	0.7
3 M	0203	6.3	0824	0.7	1431	6.4	2046	0.8
4 Tu	0246	6.0	0906	0.8	1510	6.1	2131	1.0
5 W ☽	0329	5.7	0951	1.1	1554	5.7	2213	1.3
6 Th	0418	5.2	1044	1.5	1648	5.3	2322	1.7
7 F	0524	4.8	1154	1.9	1800	4.9		
8 Sa	0039	1.9	0648	4.7	1316	2.0	1922	4.8
9 Su	0158	1.9	0808	4.8	1422	2.0	2035	5.0
10 M	0303	1.7	0912	5.1	1531	1.8	2133	5.2
11 Tu	0355	1.5	1004	5.4	1618	1.5	2220	5.5
12 W	0436	1.3	1045	5.7	1655	1.3	2255	5.8
13 Th ○	0511	1.1	1121	5.9	1729	1.2	2326	5.9
14 F	0544	1.0	1151	5.9	1759	1.1	2355	5.9
15 Sa	0614	1.0	1221	5.9	1830	1.1		
16 Su	0025	5.9	0645	1.0	1249	5.9	1900	1.0
17 M	0056	5.8	0715	0.9	1316	5.9	1930	1.0
18 Tu	0124	5.7	0744	1.0	1344	5.8	2002	1.1
19 W	0154	5.6	0815	1.2	1414	5.6	2035	1.2
20 Th	0227	5.4	0849	1.4	1450	5.3	2114	1.5
21 F ☾	0306	5.1	0933	1.7	1537	5.0	2205	1.8
22 Sa	0403	4.8	1036	1.9	1647	4.8	2320	1.9
23 Su	0528	4.7	1201	2.0	1817	4.8		
24 M	0050	1.9	0703	4.9	1331	1.8	1944	5.1
25 Tu	0212	1.6	0823	5.4	1444	1.5	2053	5.6
26 W	0316	1.2	0925	5.9	1542	1.1	2148	6.1
27 Th	0412	0.9	1018	6.3	1633	0.8	2235	6.4
28 F ●	0501	0.7	1107	6.5	1722	0.7	2321	6.4
29 Sa	0547	0.6	1153	6.7	1808	0.6		
30 Su	0008	6.6	0633	0.6	1238	6.7	1853	0.6
31 M	0053	6.5	0715	0.6	1320	6.6	1936	0.6

GENERAL — Off harbour W. going stream begins about 2 h. before local H.W. and flows for about 6 h. The effect of E. Breakwater on this stream is to direct a south-westerly stream across and into the entrance which can attain a rate of 2 knots at Springs; that part of this stream which is caught by W. Breakwater and deflected into the harbour is then diverted NE. from the head of W. Pier towards the head of E. Pier, causing a marked set between the pier heads which is strongest from 1 h. before H.W. until H.W. slack, after which it decreases in strength until it is finally overcome by the ebb stream about 1 h. after H.W. Within harbour flood stream sets almost entirely up Western Arm with little change in rate except at the bottleneck off Soldier's Point (about 3 cables NNW. of the head of W. Pier), where it

SHOREHAM SOUTH COAST

HIGH & LOW WATER 1992 Lat. 50°50'N. Long. 0°15'W.

GMT ADD 1 HOUR MARCH 29 — OCTOBER 25 FOR B.S.T.

SEPTEMBER

Day	Time	m	Time	m	Time	m	Time	m
1 Tu	0136	6.4	0756	0.7	1359	6.4	2017	0.8
16 W	0056	5.9	0716	1.0	1313	5.9	1931	1.0
2 W	0216	6.1	0836	0.9	1435	6.1	2057	1.0
17 Th	0127	5.8	0747	1.1	1344	5.7	2005	1.1
3 Th	0255	5.7	0918	1.3	1514	5.7	2142	1.4
18 F	0200	5.6	0824	1.4	1421	5.5	2046	1.4
4 F	0341	5.2	1007	1.7	1605	5.1	2240	1.8
19 Sa	0242	5.3	0909	1.7	1511	5.1	2139	1.7
5 Sa	0444	4.8	1117	2.1	1719	4.7		
20 Su	0342	5.0	1013	1.9	1623	4.9	2255	1.9
6 Su	0000	2.1	0613	4.6	1246	2.3	1850	4.6
21 M	0509	4.9	1142	2.0	1757	4.9		
7 M	0127	2.2	0741	4.7	1407	2.2	2012	4.8
22 Tu	0030	1.9	0647	5.1	1314	1.8	1928	5.2
8 Tu	0237	2.0	0848	5.0	1507	2.0	2113	5.1
23 W	0154	1.5	0805	5.5	1426	1.4	2036	5.6
9 W	0329	1.7	0939	5.4	1552	1.6	2158	5.5
24 Th	0258	1.1	0905	6.0	1525	1.0	2129	6.1
10 Th	0409	1.4	1019	5.7	1629	1.3	2233	5.8
25 F	0350	0.8	0955	6.4	1614	0.7	2214	6.4
11 F	0444	1.1	1052	5.9	1701	1.1	2302	5.9
26 Sa	0438	0.6	1041	6.6	1701	0.6	2257	6.5
12 Sa	0516	1.0	1121	6.0	1730	1.0	2329	6.0
27 Su	0524	0.5	1123	6.7	1745	0.5	2343	6.6
13 Su	0545	0.9	1149	6.0	1800	0.9	2357	6.0
28 M	0606	0.5	1206	6.6	1828	0.6		
14 M	0615	0.9	1216	6.0	1830	0.9		
29 Tu	0026	6.5	0648	0.6	1246	6.5	1907	0.7
15 Tu	0027	5.9	0645	0.9	1245	6.0	1900	0.9
30 W	0107	6.3	0727	0.8	1324	6.3	1947	0.8

OCTOBER

Day	Time	m	Time	m	Time	m	Time	m
1 Th	0147	6.1	0805	1.1	1359	6.0	2025	1.1
16 F	0110	5.9	0727	1.2	1326	5.8	1947	1.1
2 F	0223	5.7	0846	1.4	1438	5.6	2106	1.5
17 Sa	0147	5.7	0809	1.4	1407	5.6	2033	1.3
3 Sa	0307	5.3	0935	1.8	1527	5.1	2200	1.9
18 Su	0235	5.5	0859	1.6	1501	5.3	2128	1.6
4 Su	0408	4.9	1040	2.2	1638	4.7	2315	2.2
19 M	0336	5.3	1005	1.8	1612	5.0	2242	1.8
5 M	0532	4.6	1205	2.4	1810	4.5		
20 Tu	0459	5.1	1129	1.9	1741	5.0		
6 Tu	0043	2.3	0700	4.7	1327	2.4	1936	4.6
21 W	0009	1.7	0628	5.3	1254	1.7	1907	5.2
7 W	0157	2.1	0809	5.0	1430	2.1	2041	5.0
22 Th	0129	1.5	0742	5.7	1404	1.3	2014	5.6
8 Th	0251	1.8	0901	5.3	1517	1.7	2126	5.4
23 F	0233	1.1	0839	6.0	1501	0.9	2107	6.0
9 F	0334	1.5	0942	5.7	1554	1.3	2200	5.7
24 Sa	0326	0.8	0929	6.3	1553	0.7	2152	6.3
10 Sa	0410	1.2	1015	5.9	1627	1.1	2229	5.9
25 Su	0414	0.6	1014	6.5	1638	0.6	2235	6.4
11 Su	0442	1.0	1045	6.0	1659	0.9	2257	6.0
26 M	0500	0.6	1056	6.5	1723	0.6	2318	6.4
12 M	0513	0.9	1115	6.0	1730	0.8	2328	6.0
27 Tu	0542	0.7	1137	6.5	1803	0.6		
13 Tu	0544	0.9	1145	6.0	1801	0.8		
28 W	0002	6.3	0622	0.8	1217	6.4	1841	0.8
14 W	0001	6.0	0618	1.0	1216	6.0	1835	0.9
29 Th	0043	6.2	0700	1.0	1254	6.2	1918	0.9
15 Th	0034	6.0	0651	1.0	1250	6.0	1910	1.0
30 F	0121	6.0	0739	1.2	1330	5.9	1955	1.2
31 Sa	0159	5.7	0819	1.5	1409	5.6	2037	1.5

NOVEMBER

Day	Time	m	Time	m	Time	m	Time	m
1 Su	0242	5.4	0906	1.8	1456	5.2	2127	1.8
16 M	0236	5.8	0856	1.4	1459	5.6	2124	1.3
2 M	0335	5.1	1004	2.2	1558	4.8	2228	2.1
17 Tu	0333	5.6	0957	1.6	1604	5.3	2229	1.5
3 Tu	0444	4.8	1115	2.4	1717	4.6	2345	2.2
18 W	0443	5.5	1110	1.6	1719	5.2	2343	1.5
4 W	0603	4.8	1232	2.3	1840	4.6		
19 Th	0559	5.5	1227	1.5	1838	5.3		
5 Th	0059	2.2	0715	4.9	1338	2.1	1950	4.8
20 F	0059	1.4	0711	5.7	1338	1.3	1946	5.5
6 F	0200	1.9	0812	5.2	1430	1.8	2041	5.2
21 Sa	0205	1.2	0811	5.9	1438	1.0	2043	5.7
7 Sa	0249	1.6	0856	5.5	1512	1.4	2120	5.5
22 Su	0303	1.0	0902	6.1	1531	0.8	2131	6.0
8 Su	0329	1.3	0935	5.7	1551	1.1	2153	5.7
23 M	0353	0.8	0949	6.2	1620	0.7	2216	6.1
9 M	0406	1.1	1008	5.9	1626	1.0	2226	5.9
24 Tu	0439	0.8	1034	6.2	1704	0.7	2301	6.1
10 Tu	0442	1.0	1042	6.0	1702	0.9	2302	6.0
25 W	0522	0.8	1115	6.2	1743	0.8	2345	6.1
11 W	0518	1.0	1117	6.1	1737	0.8	2340	6.1
26 Th	0603	1.0	1155	6.2	1821	0.9		
12 Th	0555	1.0	1155	6.1	1817	0.9		
27 F	0025	6.1	0640	1.1	1232	6.1	1857	1.0
13 F	0020	6.1	0634	1.1	1234	6.1	1856	1.0
28 Sa	0103	6.0	0717	1.3	1309	5.9	1934	1.2
14 Sa	0103	6.1	0717	1.2	1318	6.0	1940	1.1
29 Su	0140	5.8	0756	1.5	1347	5.6	2013	1.4
15 Su	0146	6.0	0803	1.3	1404	5.8	2028	1.2
30 M	0219	5.6	0839	1.7	1432	5.3	2056	1.6

DECEMBER

Day	Time	m	Time	m	Time	m	Time	m
1 Tu	0302	5.3	0927	1.9	1521	5.0	2145	1.8
16 W	0323	6.0	0943	1.2	1549	5.6	2211	1.1
2 W	0354	5.1	1022	2.1	1621	4.8	2243	2.0
17 Th	0420	5.8	1045	1.3	1651	5.4	2313	1.3
3 Th	0457	4.9	1126	2.2	1731	4.6	2349	2.1
18 F	0524	5.6	1155	1.4	1803	5.2		
4 F	0604	4.9	1233	2.1	1842	4.7		
19 Sa	0025	1.4	0633	5.5	1307	1.4	1916	5.2
5 Sa	0057	2.0	0708	5.0	1334	1.9	1943	4.9
20 Su	0137	1.3	0740	5.6	1414	1.2	2021	5.4
6 Su	0156	1.8	0803	5.2	1427	1.6	2033	5.2
21 M	0241	1.2	0840	5.7	1514	1.1	2116	5.6
7 M	0246	1.5	0851	5.5	1513	1.3	2118	5.5
22 Tu	0338	1.1	0933	5.8	1606	1.0	2206	5.8
8 Tu	0332	1.3	0935	5.7	1557	1.1	2159	5.8
23 W	0427	1.0	1021	5.9	1650	0.9	2253	5.9
9 W	0414	1.1	1016	5.9	1639	0.9	2242	6.0
24 Th	0510	1.0	1102	6.0	1731	0.9	2335	6.0
10 Th	0456	1.0	1057	6.1	1721	0.9	2327	6.1
25 F	0549	1.1	1142	6.1	1807	0.9		
11 F	0540	1.0	1141	6.2	1805	0.9		
26 Sa	0013	6.0	0625	1.1	1218	6.0	1841	1.0
12 Sa	0011	6.2	0624	1.0	1226	6.2	1850	0.9
27 Su	0048	6.0	0700	1.2	1253	5.9	1915	1.0
13 Su	0058	6.3	0711	1.1	1313	6.2	1936	0.9
28 M	0121	5.9	0735	1.3	1329	5.8	1951	1.1
14 M	0145	6.2	0758	1.1	1403	6.1	2025	0.9
29 Tu	0154	5.8	0813	1.4	1406	5.5	2028	1.2
15 Tu	0232	6.1	0849	1.1	1453	5.9	2115	1.0
30 W	0229	5.6	0851	1.5	1446	5.3	2106	1.4
31 Th	0308	5.4	0933	1.7	1530	5.0	2149	1.7

attains a rate of 4 knots at Springs. Above Soldier's Pt. the flood and ebb streams set along the axis of the channel. The ebb stream combined with the river current can attain a rate of 5 knots off Soldier's Pt. at Springs, but owing to the increased depth and width of the harbour entrance, the maximum rate there is not more than 3 knots at Springs; from 1½ hours after H.W. until 1 h. before L..W. this ebb stream from the harbour overcomes the last of the W. going and the beginning of the E. going Channel streams which are therefore, not felt until well clear of the Harbour. In Eastern Arm of harbour there is practically no tidal stream at any time, even at the height of the flood.

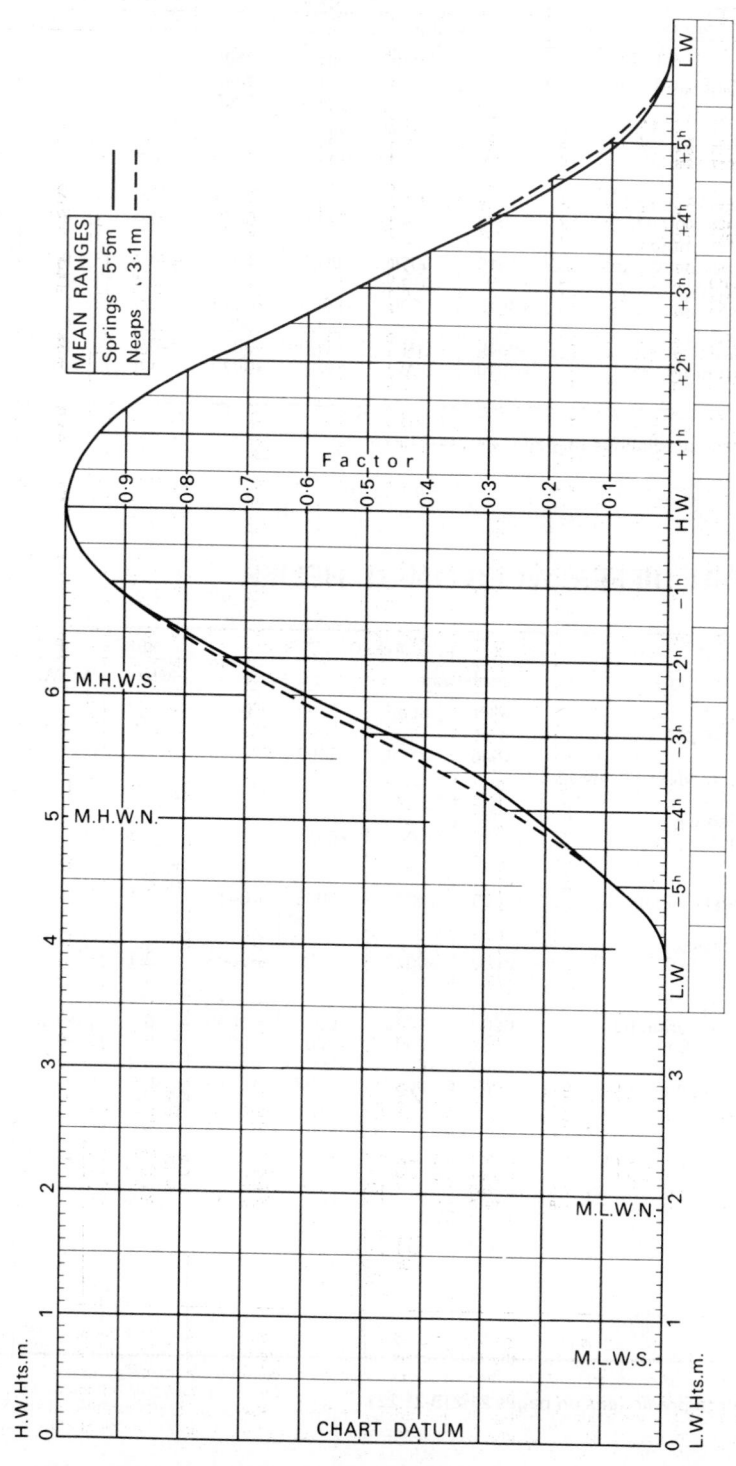

SHOREHAM
MEAN SPRING AND NEAP CURVES
Springs occur 2 days after New and Full Moon.

MEAN RANGES
Springs 5·5m
Neaps , 3·1m

Factor

M.H.W.S.
M.H.W.N.
M.L.W.N.
M.L.W.S.

H.W.Hts.m.
L.W.Hts.m.

CHART DATUM

TIDAL DIFFERENCES ON SHOREHAM

PLACE	TIME DIFFERENCES				HEIGHT DIFFERENCES (Metres)			
	High Water		Low Water		MHWS	MHWN	MLWN	MLWS
SHOREHAM	0500 and 1700	1000 and 2200	0000 and 1200	0600 and 1800	6.2	5.0	1.9	0.7
Pagham	+0015	0000	−0015	−0025	−0.7	−0.5	−0.1	−0.1
Bognor Regis	+0010	−0005	−0005	−0020	−0.6	−0.5	−0.2	−0.1
River Arun								
Littlehampton (Entrance)	+0010	0000	−0005	−0010	−0.4	−0.4	−0.2	−0.2
Littlehampton (Norfolk Wharf)	+0015	+0005	0000	+0045	−0.7	−0.7	−0.3	+0.2
Arundel	−	+0120	−	−	−3.1	−2.8	−	−
Worthing	+0010	0000	−0005	−0010	−0.1	−0.2	0.0	0.0
Brighton	−0010	−0005	−0005	−0005	+0.3	+0.1	0.0	−0.1
Newhaven	−0015	−0010	0000	0000	+0.4	+0.2	0.0	−0.2
Eastbourne	−0010	−0005	+0015	+0020	+1.1	+0.6	+0.2	+0.1

Refer to predictions on pages 21:214-21:216

TIDAL DIFFERENCES ON ST. HELIER

PLACE	TIME DIFFERENCES				HEIGHT DIFFERENCES (Metres)			
	High Water		Low Water		MHWS	MHWN	MLWN	MLWS
ST. HELIER .... CHANNEL ISLANDS	0300 and 1500	0900 and 2100	0200 and 1400	0900 and 2100	11.1	8.1	4.1	1.3
Alderney Braye	+0050	+0040	+0025	+0105	−4.8	−3.4	−1.5	−0.5
Sark Maseline Pier	+0005	+0015	+0005	+0010	−2.1	−1.5	−0.6	−0.3
Guernsey St. Peter Port	0000	+0012	−0008	+0002	−2.1	−1.4	−0.6	−0.3
Jersey St. Catherine Bay	0000	+0010	+0010	+0010	0.0	−0.1	0.0	+0.1
Bouley Bay	+0002	+0002	+0004	+0004	−0.3	−0.3	−0.1	−0.1
Les Ecrehou	+0004	+0012	+0010	+0020	−0.2	+0.3	−0.3	0.0
Les Minquiers	+0007	0000	−0008	+0013	+0.5	+0.8	−0.1	+0.1

Refer to predictions on pages 21:219-21:221

ST. HELIER, JERSEY

Lat. 49°11′N. Long. 2°07′W.

HIGH & LOW WATER 1992

GMT **ADD 1 HOUR MARCH 29 — OCTOBER 25 FOR B.S.T.**

JANUARY

Day				
1 W	0325 8.9	1003 3.6	1555 8.9	2231 3.5
16 Th	0215 8.5	0901 3.9	1504 8.5	2139 3.6
2 Th	0423 9.2	1102 3.3	1649 9.2	2325 3.2
17 F	0341 9.0	1027 3.3	1623 9.2	2257 3.0
3 F	0511 9.6	1151 2.8	1736 9.6	
18 Sa	0448 9.8	1136 2.5	1723 10.0	2358 2.2
4 Sa	0008 2.8	0554 10.0	1234 2.4	1818 9.9
19 Su	0543 10.6	1234 1.6	1815 10.7	
5 Su	0049 2.5	0634 10.3	1313 2.1	1856 10.1
20 M	0053 1.4	0634 11.0	1323 0.9	1903 11.3
6 M	0126 2.3	0712 10.4	1348 2.0	1933 10.1
21 Tu	0141 1.0	0720 11.8	1409 0.6	1948 11.6
7 Tu	0159 2.2	0747 10.4	1420 2.0	2006 10.0
22 W	0226 0.8	0804 11.9	1453 0.6	2032 11.5
8 W	0230 2.3	0819 10.2	1450 2.1	2037 9.8
23 Th	0310 0.9	0847 11.7	1534 0.9	2114 11.2
9 Th	0300 2.4	0850 10.0	1519 2.4	2107 9.6
24 F	0350 1.3	0929 11.2	1614 1.4	2156 10.6
10 F	0328 2.7	0918 9.5	1546 2.6	2136 9.4
25 Sa	0431 1.9	1012 10.5	1654 2.2	2238 10.0
11 Sa	0356 3.0	0948 9.5	1617 2.9	2207 9.2
26 Su	0512 2.7	1054 9.8	1736 3.0	2323 9.3
12 Su	0430 3.3	1021 9.2	1654 3.2	2245 8.9
27 M	0557 3.4	1143 9.0	1824 3.7	
13 M	0512 3.6	1105 9.1	1743 3.5	2334 8.6
28 Tu	0017 8.6	0650 4.0	1243 8.3	1923 4.2
14 Tu	0610 3.9	1205 9.5	1848 3.8	
29 W	0127 8.2	0759 4.3	1406 8.0	2039 4.4
15 W	0045 8.4	0728 4.1	1328 8.3	2011 3.9
30 Th	0250 8.2	0924 4.3	1531 8.1	2200 4.2
31 F	0402 8.6	1040 3.8	1634 8.6	2305 3.7

FEBRUARY

Day				
1 Sa	0457 9.1	1136 3.1	1723 9.2	2354 3.0
16 Su	0440 9.6	1126 2.3	1716 9.9	2350 2.0
2 Su	0540 9.7	1221 2.5	1803 9.7	
17 M	0534 10.6	1222 1.3	1805 10.8	
3 M	0036 2.4	0619 10.2	1259 2.0	1841 10.1
18 Tu	0042 1.1	0622 11.4	1310 0.6	1850 11.5
4 Tu	0112 2.0	0655 10.6	1333 1.6	1914 10.4
19 W	0128 0.5	0706 12.0	1354 0.2	1933 11.8
5 W	0144 1.8	0728 10.7	1404 1.5	1947 10.5
20 Th	0211 0.3	0748 12.1	1434 0.2	2012 11.8
6 Th	0213 1.8	0801 10.7	1432 1.6	2016 10.4
21 F	0250 0.5	0827 11.9	1512 0.6	2051 11.4
7 F	0242 1.9	0829 10.5	1457 1.8	2043 10.2
22 Sa	0328 1.0	0907 11.3	1548 1.3	2128 10.8
8 Sa	0307 2.1	0855 10.3	1522 2.1	2108 10.0
23 Su	0403 1.7	0943 10.6	1621 2.1	2204 10.0
9 Su	0332 2.4	0921 10.0	1549 2.4	2136 9.7
24 M	0438 2.5	1020 9.7	1657 3.0	2242 9.2
10 M	0400 2.8	0952 9.7	1621 2.8	2210 9.4
25 Tu	0516 3.3	1101 8.8	1736 3.8	2325 8.5
11 Tu	0438 3.2	1030 9.2	1705 3.3	2254 9.0
26 W	0603 4.0	1151 8.0	1829 4.4	
12 W	0532 3.7	1122 8.6	1808 3.8	2357 8.4
27 Th	0031 7.9	0709 4.5	1320 7.5	1947 4.7
13 Th	0650 4.0	1246 8.0	1935 4.1	
28 F	0215 7.7	0840 4.6	1508 7.7	2125 4.6
14 F	0140 8.1	0832 4.0	1449 8.1	2117 3.8
29 Sa	0341 8.1	1014 4.1	1616 8.3	2244 3.9
15 Sa	0328 8.6	1013 3.4	1616 8.9	2245 3.0

MARCH

Day				
1 Su	0437 8.8	1115 3.3	1702 9.0	2336 3.1
16 M	0426 9.6	1111 2.1	1659 10.0	2334 1.8
2 M	0519 9.5	1158 2.5	1740 9.7	
17 Tu	0518 10.6	1205 1.2	1747 10.9	
3 Tu	0015 2.4	0557 10.2	1236 1.9	1815 10.2
18 W	0025 1.0	0604 11.4	1250 0.5	1829 11.5
4 W	0052 1.8	0632 10.6	1309 1.5	1849 10.6
19 Th	0109 0.4	0646 11.8	1333 0.2	1910 11.8
5 Th	0123 1.5	0704 10.9	1340 1.3	1920 10.8
20 F	0149 0.3	0727 11.9	1411 0.3	1948 11.7
6 F	0152 1.4	0735 11.0	1408 1.3	1949 10.7
21 Sa	0227 0.5	0805 11.6	1446 0.8	2025 11.3
7 Sa	0220 1.5	0804 10.8	1435 1.5	2016 10.6
22 Su	0303 1.0	0842 11.1	1519 1.5	2100 10.7
8 Su	0246 1.8	0832 10.6	1500 1.8	2043 10.4
23 M	0335 1.7	0917 10.3	1550 2.3	2132 9.9
9 M	0313 2.1	0858 10.3	1528 2.2	2111 10.1
24 Tu	0407 2.5	0950 9.5	1623 3.1	2206 9.2
10 Tu	0343 2.5	0929 9.9	1602 2.7	2146 9.7
25 W	0442 3.3	1026 8.7	1659 3.8	2244 8.5
11 W	0423 3.0	1009 9.3	1648 3.2	2230 9.1
26 Th	0526 3.9	1112 7.9	1749 4.4	2340 7.8
12 Th	0518 3.5	1102 8.5	1753 3.8	2333 8.4
27 F	0628 4.4	1234 7.4	1859 4.8	
13 F	0636 3.9	1234 7.9	1920 4.0	
28 Sa	0127 7.5	0752 4.6	1427 7.5	2037 4.7
14 Sa	0127 8.1	0818 3.9	1443 8.0	2103 3.8
29 Su	0303 7.9	0929 4.2	1539 8.1	2204 4.1
15 Su	0317 8.6	0959 3.2	1603 8.9	2231 2.9
30 M	0402 8.5	1037 3.5	1627 8.8	2302 3.3
31 Tu	0447 9.3	1125 2.7	1706 9.5	2344 2.6

APRIL

Day				
1 W	0525 10.0	1203 2.1	1743 10.1	
16 Th	0000 1.2	0539 11.0	1225 0.9	1804 11.2
2 Th	0021 2.0	0600 10.5	1238 1.6	1817 10.6
17 F	0045 0.8	0622 11.3	1307 0.7	1843 11.4
3 F	0055 1.6	0634 10.8	1310 1.4	1849 10.9
18 Sa	0126 0.7	0703 11.4	1345 0.9	1923 11.3
4 Sa	0127 1.4	0707 11.0	1341 1.3	1920 10.9
19 Su	0202 0.9	0741 11.1	1420 1.3	1958 10.9
5 Su	0158 1.5	0738 10.9	1412 1.5	1951 10.9
20 M	0237 1.3	0818 10.6	1453 1.8	2033 10.4
6 M	0229 1.6	0809 10.7	1443 1.8	2022 10.6
21 Tu	0311 1.9	0853 10.0	1524 2.5	2105 9.8
7 Tu	0301 1.9	0842 10.4	1517 2.2	2056 10.3
22 W	0343 2.6	0927 9.3	1556 3.1	2139 9.2
8 W	0336 2.3	0918 9.8	1556 2.6	2135 9.8
23 Th	0419 3.2	1002 8.6	1631 3.7	2216 8.6
9 Th	0421 2.6	1003 9.3	1647 3.2	2224 8.9
24 F	0459 3.7	1045 8.1	1718 4.1	2306 8.1
10 F	0519 3.2	1104 8.6	1751 3.8	2334 8.6
25 Sa	0553 4.1	1151 7.6	1817 4.5	
11 Sa	0634 3.6	1239 8.1	1913 3.8	
26 Su	0027 7.7	0702 4.3	1324 7.5	1934 4.5
12 Su	0119 8.3	0804 3.5	1425 8.3	2046 3.5
27 M	0201 7.8	0822 4.1	1442 7.9	2100 4.2
13 M	0253 8.8	0935 2.9	1539 9.1	2207 2.8
28 Tu	0308 8.3	0936 3.7	1538 8.5	2209 3.6
14 Tu	0400 9.6	1045 2.1	1634 9.9	2311 1.9
29 W	0400 8.9	1034 3.1	1623 9.2	2301 3.0
15 W	0452 10.4	1140 1.4	1720 10.7	
30 Th	0444 9.5	1119 2.5	1704 9.8	2344 2.4

To find H.W. Dover add 4 h. 45 min.

TIDAL DIFFERENCES PAGE 21:218. TIDAL CURVE PAGE 21:222.

TIDAL STREAMS PAGES 21:28-21:40.

Datum of predictions: 5.88 m. below Local Ordnance Datum or approx. L.A.T.

ST. HELIER, JERSEY

HIGH & LOW WATER 1992   **CHANNEL ISLANDS**

GMT   **ADD 1 HOUR MARCH 29 — OCTOBER 25 FOR B.S.T.**

MAY

Day	Time m	Time m	Day	Time m	Time m
1 F	0523 10.1	1201 2.0	16 Sa	0019 1.5	0557 10.6
		1742 10.3		1241 1.5	1818 10.7
2 Sa	0024 1.9	0601 10.6	17 Su	0102 1.3	0639 10.6
	1239 1.7	● 1817 10.7		1320 1.6	1857 10.7
3 Su	0102 1.7	0639 10.8	18 M	0140 1.4	0720 10.5
	1316 1.5	1853 10.9		1357 1.8	1935 10.5
4 M	0138 1.5	0716 10.9	19 Tu	0216 1.7	0758 10.1
	1354 1.6	1930 11.0		1430 2.1	2012 10.2
5 Tu	0216 1.6	0754 10.8	20 W	0251 2.0	0833 9.7
	1432 1.8	2008 10.8		1503 2.5	2047 9.7
6 W	0256 1.8	0833 10.5	21 Th	0324 2.5	0910 9.2
	1512 2.1	2049 10.5		1536 2.9	2121 9.3
7 Th	0338 2.1	0918 10.0	22 F	0359 2.9	0945 8.8
	1559 2.4	2134 10.0		1610 3.3	2157 8.8
8 F	0427 2.4	1009 9.4	23 Sa	0435 3.3	1024 8.4
	1649 2.9	2228 9.5		1649 3.7	2240 8.4
9 Sa	0522 2.8	1112 8.9	24 Su	0519 3.6	1112 8.1
	1750 3.2	》 2336 9.0		1736 4.0	《 2333 8.1
10 Su	0628 3.1	1231 8.6	25 M	0611 3.8	1212 7.9
	1900 3.4			1834 4.1	
11 M	0059 8.8	0742 3.1	26 Tu	0042 8.0	0712 3.9
	1354 8.7	2018 3.3		1324 8.0	1944 4.1
12 Tu	0219 9.0	0903 2.9	27 W	0155 8.1	0820 3.8
	1504 9.1	2135 2.9		1430 8.3	2057 3.9
13 W	0327 9.4	1012 2.4	28 Th	0300 8.5	0929 3.5
	1602 9.7	2238 2.4		1528 8.8	2204 3.4
14 Th	0423 9.9	1108 2.0	29 F	0355 9.1	1028 3.1
	1652 10.2	2333 1.8		1619 9.4	2301 2.9
15 F	0512 10.3	1157 1.6	30 Sa	0444 9.6	1122 2.5
	1736 10.5			1705 10.0	2351 2.3
			31 Su	0530 10.1	1210 2.1
				1750 10.5	

JUNE

Day	Time m	Time m	Day	Time m	Time m
1 M	0038 1.9	0615 10.6	16 Tu	0121 1.8	0703 10.0
	1256 1.7	● 1834 10.9		1337 2.1	1919 10.3
2 Tu	0123 1.5	0700 10.8	17 W	0159 1.8	0741 9.9
	1341 1.6	1917 11.1		1412 2.2	1957 10.1
3 W	0208 1.4	0745 10.8	18 Th	0234 2.0	0818 9.8
	1425 1.6	2001 11.1		1446 2.3	2032 9.9
4 Th	0251 1.4	0830 10.7	19 F	0307 2.2	0853 9.5
	1510 1.7	2046 10.9		1517 2.6	2105 9.6
5 F	0338 1.5	0918 10.4	20 Sa	0338 2.5	0927 9.2
	1557 2.0	2134 10.5		1548 2.9	2138 9.3
6 Sa	0424 1.8	1009 10.0	21 Su	0410 2.8	0959 8.9
	1647 2.3	2226 10.1		1620 3.1	2212 9.0
7 Su	0516 2.2	1105 9.5	22 M	0444 3.0	1034 8.6
	1740 2.7	》 2325 9.6		1657 3.4	2249 8.7
8 M	0612 2.6	1207 9.2	23 Sa	0523 3.3	1115 8.4
	1839 3.0			1742 3.7	《 2336 8.4
9 Tu	0029 9.2	0714 2.9	24 W	0612 3.6	1208 8.3
	1316 9.0	1945 3.2		1838 3.9	
10 W	0141 9.0	0823 3.0	25 Th	0036 8.3	0714 3.7
	1425 9.0	2056 3.1		1314 8.3	1947 4.0
11 Th	0250 9.1	0932 3.0	26 F	0151 8.3	0823 3.7
	1527 9.2	2203 2.9		1427 8.5	2105 3.8
12 F	0353 9.3	1035 2.8	27 Sa	0305 8.6	0939 3.4
	1623 9.5	2304 2.6		1536 9.0	2221 3.3
13 Sa	0448 9.6	1129 2.5	28 Su	0412 9.1	1048 2.9
	1712 9.9	2356 2.2		1637 9.6	2325 2.6
14 Su	0537 9.8	1217 2.3	29 M	0509 9.8	1147 2.3
	1757 10.1			1730 10.3	
15 M	0041 2.0	0621 10.0	30 Tu	0021 2.0	0601 10.4
	1259 2.1	○ 1839 10.3		1241 1.8	● 1821 10.9

JULY

Day	Time m	Time m	Day	Time m	Time m
1 W	0112 1.4	0650 10.8	16 Th	0142 1.8	0724 10.1
	1330 1.3	1907 11.3		1355 2.0	1938 10.4
2 Th	0158 1.0	0738 11.1	17 F	0215 1.7	0759 10.1
	1418 1.1	1954 11.5		1426 2.0	2012 10.3
3 F	0244 0.8	0825 11.2	18 Sa	0246 1.8	0832 9.9
	1503 1.1	2040 11.4		1456 2.1	2044 10.1
4 Sa	0329 0.9	0910 11.0	19 Su	0314 2.0	0901 9.7
	1548 1.3	2125 11.1		1522 2.4	2112 9.8
5 Su	0413 1.3	0956 10.6	20 M	0341 2.3	0929 9.4
	1633 1.8	2212 10.6		1550 2.7	2141 9.5
6 M	0459 1.8	1044 10.1	21 Tu	0409 2.6	0956 9.2
	1720 2.3	2301 10.0		1620 3.0	2210 9.2
7 Tu	0547 2.4	1136 9.5	22 W	0441 3.0	1028 9.0
	1811 2.8	》 2356 9.4		1658 3.4	《 2247 8.9
8 W	0641 3.0	1235 9.0	23 Th	0523 3.3	1111 8.7
	1909 3.3			1747 3.7	2336 8.5
9 Th	0100 8.8	0741 3.4	24 F	0619 3.7	1210 8.4
	1342 8.7	2015 3.6		1855 4.0	
10 F	0213 8.6	0851 3.6	25 Sa	0049 8.2	0733 3.9
	1454 8.7	2129 3.6		1333 8.3	2020 4.0
11 Sa	0328 8.6	1004 3.5	26 Su	0226 8.2	0900 3.8
	1559 8.9	2240 3.3		1507 8.6	2150 3.6
12 Su	0430 8.9	1106 3.2	27 M	0353 8.7	1024 3.2
	1654 9.3	2337 2.8		1621 9.3	2306 2.7
13 M	0522 9.3	1158 2.8	28 Tu	0458 9.6	1132 2.4
	1742 9.7			1719 10.2	
14 Tu	0025 2.4	0607 9.8	29 W	0007 1.8	0551 10.4
	1242 2.4	○ 1824 10.1		1228 1.6	● 1810 11.0
15 W	0106 2.0	0646 9.9	30 Th	0059 1.1	0641 11.0
	1320 2.1	1902 10.3		1319 1.0	1857 11.6
			31 F	0147 0.5	0726 11.5
				1405 0.6	1942 11.9

AUGUST

Day	Time m	Time m	Day	Time m	Time m
1 Sa	0230 0.4	0809 11.7	16 Su	0219 1.5	0805 10.4
	1449 0.6	2025 11.9		1430 1.9	2018 10.5
2 Su	0312 0.5	0853 11.5	17 M	0246 1.8	0832 10.2
	1531 0.9	2108 11.5		1456 2.1	2044 10.2
3 M	0353 1.0	0935 11.0	18 Tu	0311 2.1	0857 9.9
	1612 1.5	2150 10.9		1521 2.4	2108 9.9
4 Tu	0435 1.7	1017 10.3	19 W	0336 2.4	0922 9.7
	1654 2.2	2234 10.1		1549 2.8	2136 9.6
5 W	0518 2.5	1102 9.6	20 Th	0407 2.8	0950 9.4
	1739 2.9	》 2320 9.3		1623 3.2	2210 9.2
6 Th	0604 3.3	1153 8.9	21 F	0447 3.3	1030 9.0
	1832 3.6			1711 3.6	《 2255 8.6
7 F	0019 8.5	0702 3.9	22 Sa	0543 3.7	1125 8.5
	1300 8.3	1937 4.0		1821 4.0	
8 Sa	0140 8.0	0813 4.3	23 Su	0007 8.1	0702 4.1
	1426 8.2	2058 4.1		1255 8.1	1954 4.1
9 Su	0310 8.1	0938 4.2	24 M	0206 7.9	0837 4.0
	1542 8.5	2220 3.8		1451 8.4	2132 3.6
10 M	0419 8.5	1049 3.7	25 Tu	0345 8.6	1009 3.3
	1640 9.0	2322 3.1		1610 9.3	2252 2.7
11 Tu	0508 9.1	1142 3.1	26 W	0448 9.6	1119 2.3
	1725 9.6			1706 10.3	2353 1.6
12 W	0007 2.5	0549 9.6	27 Th	0539 10.6	1214 1.4
	1224 2.5	1805 10.1		1756 11.3	
13 Th	0046 2.0	0627 10.1	28 F	0043 0.8	0624 11.4
	1300 2.0	1842 10.5		1302 0.7	1841 11.9
14 F	0120 1.6	0702 10.4	29 Sa	0128 0.3	0707 11.9
	1333 1.7	1916 10.7		1345 0.3	1923 12.2
15 Sa	0151 1.5	0734 10.5	30 Su	0211 0.2	0748 11.9
	1404 1.7	1948 10.7		1427 0.4	2005 12.1
			31 M	0250 0.5	0829 11.7
				1507 0.8	2044 11.6

GENERAL — Streams rotatory, counter clockwise and strong. When strong, set along channels and coast. When weak, may set across channels and onshore. Coastal streams considerably different from main channels. Islands and rocks break the streams, causing eddies and variation in rate and set.

CAUTION — Local streams should be studied in detail. Dangerous to enter 1 h. before H.W.

RATE AND SET — Ent.; ingoing begins about +0200 Dover 3 kn. Outgoing –0500 Dover 2 kn.

ST. HELIER, JERSEY 21:221

Lat. 49°11'N. Long. 2°07'W. HIGH & LOW WATER 1992

GMT ADD 1 HOUR MARCH 29 — OCTOBER 25 FOR B.S.T.

SEPTEMBER

#	Time	m	#	Time	m
1 Tu	0328 / 0907 / 1546 / 2124	1.1 / 11.1 / 1.5 / 10.9	16 W	0243 / 0826 / 1456 / 2042	2.0 / 10.3 / 2.3 / 10.2
2 W	0406 / 0946 / 1624 / 2203	1.9 / 10.4 / 2.3 / 10.0	17 Th	0311 / 0853 / 1525 / 2110	2.4 / 10.0 / 2.7 / 9.8
3 Th	0445 / 1026 / 1706 /) 2247	2.8 / 9.5 / 3.1 / 9.1	18 F	0342 / 0924 / 1600 / 2145	2.9 / 9.7 / 3.1 / 9.3
4 F	0527 / 1112 / 1756 / 2340	3.7 / 8.7 / 3.9 / 8.2	19 Sa	0424 / 1004 / 1652 / (2233	3.4 / 9.2 / 3.6 / 8.6
5 Sa	0622 / 1218 / 1902	4.3 / 8.0 / 4.4	20 Su	0525 / 1102 / 1805 / 2351	3.9 / 8.6 / 4.0 / 8.0
6 Su	0109 / 0738 / 1358 / 2027	7.7 / 4.7 / 7.8 / 4.5	21 M	0646 / 1239 / 1938	4.2 / 8.1 / 4.0
7 M	0253 / 0911 / 1524 / 2157	7.8 / 4.5 / 8.1 / 4.1	22 Tu	0159 / 0823 / 1437 / 2117	8.0 / 4.0 / 8.5 / 3.5
8 Tu	0359 / 1027 / 1619 / 2258	8.3 / 3.9 / 8.9 / 3.3	23 W	0331 / 0952 / 1553 / 2234	8.8 / 3.2 / 9.4 / 2.5
9 W	0445 / 1119 / 1702 / 2342	9.0 / 3.2 / 9.6 / 2.6	24 Th	0430 / 1101 / 1648 / 2333	9.8 / 2.2 / 10.4 / 1.6
10 Th	0523 / 1158 / 1739	9.7 / 2.5 / 10.2	25 F	0518 / 1154 / 1734	10.8 / 1.3 / 11.3
11 F	0019 / 0558 / 1235 / 1814	2.0 / 10.3 / 2.0 / 10.7	26 Sa	0021 / 0601 / 1241 / ● 1819	0.8 / 11.5 / 0.7 / 11.9
12 Sa	0052 / 0632 / 1306 / ○ 1848	1.6 / 10.6 / 1.7 / 10.9	27 Su	0104 / 0643 / 1323 / 1900	0.5 / 11.9 / 0.4 / 12.1
13 Su	0123 / 0703 / 1335 / 1920	1.4 / 10.8 / 1.6 / 11.0	28 M	0145 / 0723 / 1404 / 1941	0.5 / 11.9 / 0.6 / 11.9
14 M	0151 / 0734 / 1404 / 1948	1.5 / 10.8 / 1.7 / 10.8	29 Tu	0225 / 0802 / 1442 / 2020	0.8 / 11.6 / 1.0 / 11.3
15 Tu	0218 / 0801 / 1430 / 2015	1.7 / 10.6 / 1.9 / 10.5	30 W	0301 / 0839 / 1519 / 2057	1.5 / 11.0 / 1.7 / 10.6

OCTOBER

#	Time	m	#	Time	m
1 Th	0336 / 0915 / 1556 / 2135	2.3 / 10.2 / 2.5 / 9.7	16 F	0254 / 0833 / 1514 / 2054	2.5 / 10.3 / 2.6 / 9.9
2 F	0413 / 0952 / 1635 / 2214	3.1 / 9.4 / 3.3 / 8.9	17 Sa	0332 / 0908 / 1555 / 2135	2.9 / 9.9 / 3.0 / 9.4
3 Sa	0454 / 1034 / 1722 /) 2306	3.9 / 8.6 / 4.0 / 8.1	18 Su	0419 / 0955 / 1649 / 2230	3.4 / 9.4 / 3.5 / 8.7
4 Su	0546 / 1136 / 1825	4.5 / 8.0 / 4.5	19 M	0519 / 1057 / 1800 / (2351	3.8 / 8.8 / 3.8 / 8.2
5 M	0031 / 0657 / 1317 / 1948	7.6 / 4.8 / 7.7 / 4.6	20 Tu	0636 / 1231 / 1924	4.0 / 8.4 / 3.8
6 Tu	0216 / 0829 / 1447 / 2115	7.7 / 4.7 / 8.1 / 4.2	21 W	0141 / 0805 / 1413 / 2053	8.3 / 3.8 / 8.7 / 3.3
7 W	0324 / 0949 / 1545 / 2219	8.2 / 4.2 / 8.7 / 3.6	22 Th	0304 / 0928 / 1527 / 2207	9.0 / 3.2 / 9.5 / 2.6
8 Th	0410 / 1042 / 1628 / 2305	8.9 / 3.4 / 9.4 / 2.9	23 F	0403 / 1035 / 1623 / 2306	9.8 / 2.4 / 10.3 / 1.8
9 F	0449 / 1125 / 1706 / 2343	9.6 / 2.8 / 10.1 / 2.3	24 Sa	0452 / 1129 / 1711 / 2356	10.6 / 1.6 / 11.0 / 1.3
10 Sa	0525 / 1201 / 1742	10.2 / 2.2 / 10.6	25 Su	0536 / 1217 / 1756 / ●	11.2 / 1.1 / 11.4
11 Su	0018 / 0558 / 1235 / ○ 1817	1.9 / 10.7 / 1.9 / 10.9	26 M	0039 / 0618 / 1300 / 1838	1.0 / 11.5 / 0.9 / 11.6
12 M	0050 / 0631 / 1307 / 1849	1.7 / 10.9 / 1.7 / 11.0	27 Tu	0120 / 0657 / 1340 / 1919	1.1 / 11.5 / 1.0 / 11.4
13 Tu	0121 / 0702 / 1338 / 1920	1.6 / 11.0 / 1.8 / 10.9	28 W	0159 / 0737 / 1419 / 1957	1.4 / 11.3 / 1.4 / 10.9
14 W	0152 / 0731 / 1409 / 1949	1.8 / 10.9 / 1.9 / 10.7	29 Th	0236 / 0813 / 1456 / 2034	1.9 / 10.8 / 2.0 / 10.3
15 Th	0222 / 0801 / 1440 / 2020	2.1 / 10.6 / 2.2 / 10.4	30 F	0311 / 0850 / 1531 / 2112	2.6 / 10.1 / 2.6 / 9.6
			31 Sa	0346 / 0927 / 1609 / 2150	3.2 / 9.5 / 3.3 / 8.9

NOVEMBER

#	Time	m	#	Time	m
1 Su	0424 / 1006 / 1652 / 2238	3.8 / 8.8 / 3.8 / 8.3	16 M	0417 / 0955 / 1648 / 2233	3.1 / 9.8 / 3.0 / 9.2
2 M	0511 / 1058 / 1746 /) 2343	4.3 / 8.2 / 4.3 / 7.9	17 Tu	0515 / 1055 / 1750 / (2344	3.4 / 9.3 / 3.3 / 8.8
3 Tu	0610 / 1215 / 1853	4.7 / 7.9 / 4.5	18 W	0621 / 1211 / 1902	3.6 / 8.9 / 3.4
4 W	0110 / 0726 / 1344 / 2009	7.8 / 4.7 / 8.0 / 4.3	19 Th	0109 / 0737 / 1335 / 2019	8.7 / 3.6 / 9.0 / 3.3
5 Th	0226 / 0846 / 1453 / 2119	8.1 / 4.4 / 8.4 / 3.9	20 F	0226 / 0854 / 1451 / 2134	9.1 / 3.3 / 9.3 / 2.9
6 F	0321 / 0950 / 1543 / 2214	8.7 / 3.9 / 9.0 / 3.4	21 Sa	0331 / 1004 / 1553 / 2235	9.6 / 2.8 / 9.9 / 2.4
7 Sa	0406 / 1041 / 1627 / 2259	9.3 / 3.3 / 9.6 / 2.8	22 Su	0424 / 1102 / 1645 / 2329	10.2 / 2.2 / 10.4 / 2.0
8 Su	0445 / 1123 / 1706 / 2340	9.9 / 2.7 / 10.1 / 2.4	23 M	0512 / 1153 / 1733	10.6 / 1.8 / 10.7
9 M	0523 / 1203 / 1743 / ●	10.4 / 2.3 / 10.6	24 Tu	0015 / 0556 / 1238 / 1818	1.8 / 10.9 / 1.5 / 10.8
10 Tu	0018 / 0558 / 1241 / ○ 1819	2.1 / 10.7 / 2.0 / 10.8	25 W	0057 / 0636 / 1320 / 1859	1.7 / 11.0 / 1.5 / 10.9
11 W	0055 / 0634 / 1317 / 1856	1.9 / 11.0 / 1.9 / 10.9	26 Th	0137 / 0717 / 1359 / 1940	1.8 / 10.9 / 1.7 / 10.5
12 Th	0131 / 0709 / 1354 / 1933	1.9 / 11.0 / 1.9 / 10.8	27 F	0215 / 0755 / 1436 / 2018	2.1 / 10.6 / 2.0 / 10.1
13 F	0209 / 0745 / 1432 / 2009	2.1 / 10.9 / 2.1 / 10.5	28 Sa	0250 / 0832 / 1511 / 2056	2.6 / 10.2 / 2.5 / 9.6
14 Sa	0247 / 0823 / 1511 / 2051	2.3 / 10.6 / 2.3 / 10.2	29 Su	0324 / 0908 / 1546 / 2134	3.0 / 9.7 / 2.9 / 9.2
15 Su	0309 / 0905 / 1556 / 2138	2.7 / 10.3 / 2.6 / 9.7	30 M	0359 / 0946 / 1623 / 2213	3.4 / 9.2 / 3.4 / 8.7

DECEMBER

#	Time	m	#	Time	m
1 Tu	0437 / 1027 / 1705 / 2258	3.8 / 8.7 / 3.9 / 8.3	16 W	0502 / 1044 / 1732 / (2323	2.8 / 9.9 / 2.7 / 9.4
2 W	0522 / 1118 / 1754 /) 2354	4.2 / 8.2 / 4.0 / 8.1	17 Th	0558 / 1144 / 1832	3.2 / 9.4 / 3.1
3 Th	0618 / 1221 / 1853	4.4 / 8.1 / 4.2	18 F	0029 / 0703 / 1255 / 1940	9.1 / 3.4 / 9.1 / 3.3
4 F	0103 / 0724 / 1334 / 2002	8.1 / 4.5 / 8.1 / 4.1	19 Sa	0142 / 0815 / 1412 / 2054	9.0 / 3.5 / 9.0 / 3.3
5 Sa	0211 / 0837 / 1442 / 2108	8.3 / 4.3 / 8.5 / 3.9	20 Su	0254 / 0929 / 1522 / 2204	9.1 / 3.3 / 9.2 / 3.1
6 Su	0311 / 0945 / 1539 / 2209	8.7 / 3.9 / 8.9 / 3.4	21 M	0357 / 1037 / 1624 / 2305	9.5 / 2.9 / 9.5 / 2.8
7 M	0402 / 1042 / 1628 / 2302	9.3 / 3.3 / 9.5 / 3.0	22 Tu	0451 / 1133 / 1718 / 2356	9.9 / 2.5 / 9.9 / 2.4
8 Tu	0448 / 1132 / 1713 / 2350	9.9 / 2.8 / 10.0 / 2.5	23 W	0539 / 1222 / 1804	10.3 / 2.1 / 10.2
9 W	0532 / 1218 / 1757 / ○	10.4 / 2.3 / 10.5	24 Th	0042 / 0622 / 1306 / 1846	2.2 / 10.5 / 1.9 / 10.3
10 Th	0035 / 0614 / 1302 / 1839	2.1 / 10.8 / 1.9 / 10.8	25 F	0121 / 0703 / 1345 / 1926	2.1 / 10.6 / 1.8 / 10.3
11 F	0117 / 0655 / 1344 / 1923	1.9 / 11.1 / 1.7 / 10.9	26 Sa	0159 / 0741 / 1420 / 2004	2.1 / 10.6 / 1.9 / 10.2
12 Sa	0159 / 0737 / 1426 / 2005	1.9 / 11.2 / 1.6 / 10.9	27 Su	0233 / 0818 / 1454 / 2040	2.2 / 10.4 / 2.1 / 9.9
13 Su	0243 / 0819 / 1508 / 2049	1.9 / 11.1 / 1.7 / 10.6	28 M	0304 / 0853 / 1525 / 2114	2.5 / 10.0 / 2.4 / 9.6
14 M	0327 / 0904 / 1552 / 2136	2.1 / 10.8 / 2.0 / 10.3	29 Tu	0335 / 0925 / 1555 / 2145	2.8 / 9.6 / 2.8 / 9.2
15 Tu	0413 / 0952 / 1640 / 2226	2.4 / 10.4 / 2.3 / 9.8	30 W	0404 / 0957 / 1626 / 2217	3.2 / 9.3 / 3.1 / 8.9
			31 Th	0438 / 1031 / 1702 / 2254	3.5 / 8.9 / 3.5 / 8.6

RACE OF ALDERNEY — Between Alderney and coast of France. Streams SW. and NE. SW. begins −0050 Dover max. rate +0200 Dover. NE. begins +0520 Dover max. rate −0420 Dover. Little slack water in Race.

Max. Spring rate 7-9½ kn. Neap rate 5½ kn.

ST. HELIER

MEAN SPRING AND NEAP CURVES
Springs occur 2 days after New and Full Moon.

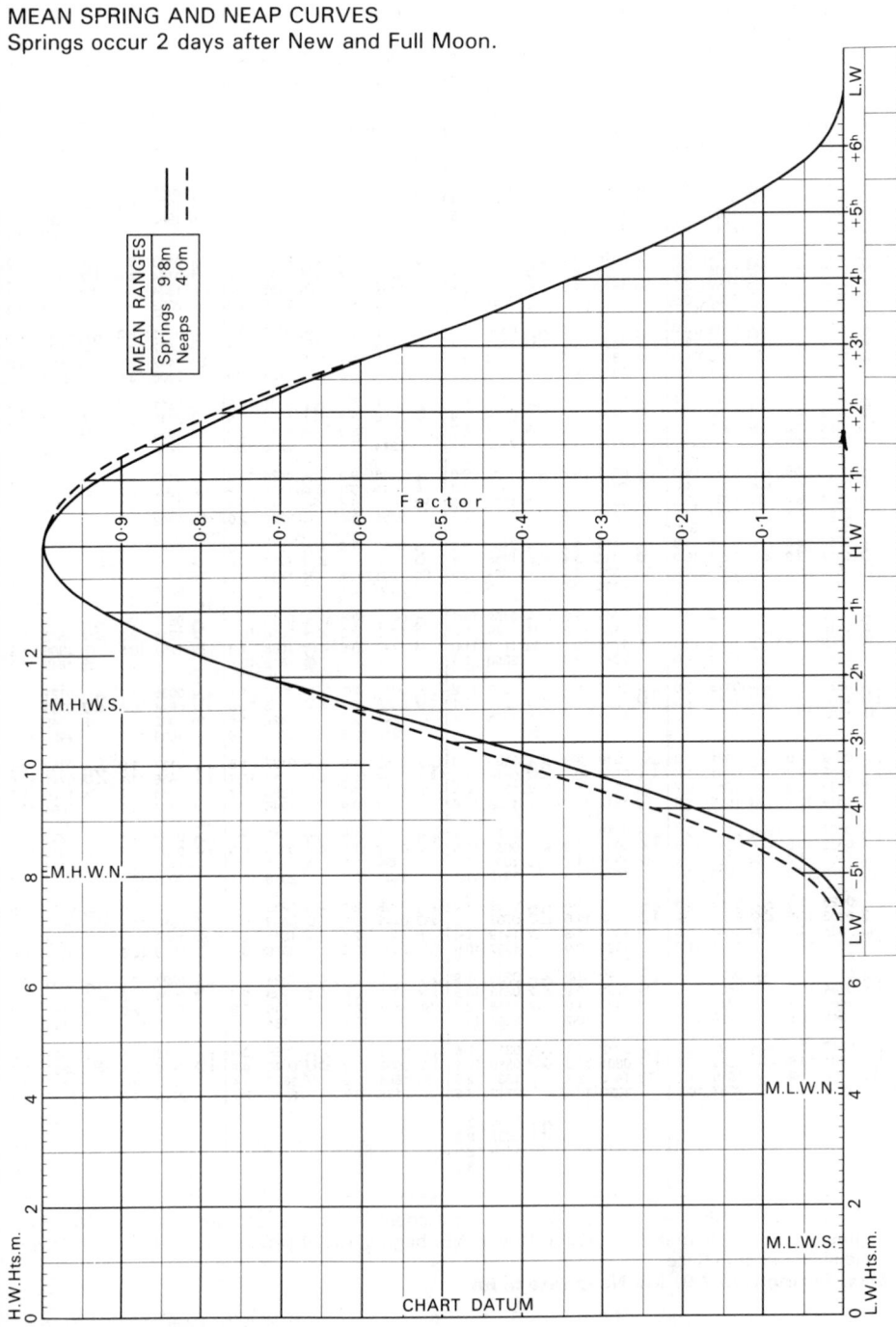

CHANNEL ISLANDS NOTES ON THE TIDAL STREAMS

1. GENERAL
(a) Tides—great rise and fall.
(b) Tidal Streams—rates high.
(c) Gales from S.W. and N.W. send in heaviest seas.
(d) Worst period—from 3 h. before to 3 h. after H.W. at the shore.
(e) Generally rotatory anti-clockwise.
(f) At max. rate streams set up and'down channel and shore.
(g) At low rate streams set across channel and onshore.
(h) Big differences in nearby localities.
(i) Many eddies formed by islands across main streams.
(j) Streams near islands and coast, considerably different from those in open seas.

2. CAP DE LA HAGUE (Northward).
i. E. going, +0600, Sp. 6 kts.
ii. W. going, −0015, Sp. 7 kts.
iii. Inshore off Cherbourg.
  W. going from −0300 to +0400.

3. CASQUETS.
(a) 3 M. North.
i. E. going, +0600, Sp. 4 kts.
ii. W. going, −0010, Sp. 4 kts.

(b) S.W. of Casquets, strong, eddy—2 M. wide-during S.W. stream.

(c) N.E. of Casquets, eddy during N.E. stream.

4. ALDERNEY
(a) Between Alderney and Cap de la Hague.
i. N.E. going, +0520, Sp. 6-8 kts.
ii. S.W. going, −0050, Sp. 6-8 kts.

(b) Wind against tide—breaking seas, heavy overfalls.

(c) S. of Alderney—eddy during S.W. stream.

(d) N. of Alderney—eddy during N.E. stream.

(e) Difficult and dangerous to enter harbour at H.W.

(f) Alderney Race—see pages 21:224-21:227

5. GUERNSEY.
(a) Divides the streams, forms eddies.
(b) Off S.W. point.
i. E. going along S. coast and N.E. going along N.W. coast, +0215.
ii. W. going along S. coast and S.W. going along N.W. coast, presumed about −0400.

6. HERM.
(a) Between Herm and Jethou.
i. S.E. going, +0200.
ii. N.W. going, −0125.

7. SARK.
(a) Off S.W. coast—rotatory anti-clockwise.
i. S.W. going, +0120.
ii. N.E. going, −0455.
(b) Eddies formed.
(c) Off S.E. coast.
i. S.W. going, −0210.
ii. N.E. going, +0245.

8. JERSEY.
(a) Southwards during rising tide.
(b) Northwards during first 3 h. of ebb.
(c) Generally rotatory.
(d) N. coast and S. coast
i. E. going, +0200, Sp. 4 kts.
ii. W. going, −0440, Sp. 4 kts.
(e) W. coast and E. coast.
i. S. going, −0215, Sp. 4½ kts.
ii. N. going, +0500, Sp. 4½ kts.

N.B.—Times are given in relation to H.W. Dover and indicate beginning of streams. Rates are approx. at Springs in knots. Further details may be found as footnotes in individual ports. See also Channel Islands notes in Visual Navigational Aids Section.

CHANNEL ISLANDS – TIDAL STREAMS CHARTS
Pages 21:224-21:227 show the Direction and Rate of the Tidal Stream for each hour before and after High Water Dover, and also St. Helier. The weight of the arrows (i.e. very heavy arrows) show where the stream is strongest, and the arrow head indicates the direction in which it turns. Strengths of the Tidal Stream are written in figures alongside the arrows the smallest figures show the Rate (strength) at average Neap Tides, and the greater figures indicate the Rate at SPRING Tides. Figures are now given in knots and decimals of a knot.

TIDAL STREAMS
for
CHANNEL ISLANDS
and adjacent coasts of
FRANCE

These 13 charts show tidal streams at hourly intervals commencing 6 h. before and, ending 6 h. after H.W. Dover. For Dover H.W. Times see pages 21:41-21:43. Times before and after H.W. St. Helier are also indicated. For St. Helier H.W. Times see pages 21:219-21:221.

A thick arrow indicates a strong stream and a thin arrow where it is weaker. Strengths of the tidal stream are written in figures alongside the arrows, the smaller figures showing the rate (strength) at average Neap tides and the greater figures indicating the rate at Spring tides.

CAUTION: Due to the very strong rates of the tidal streams in some of the areas covered, many eddies may occur.

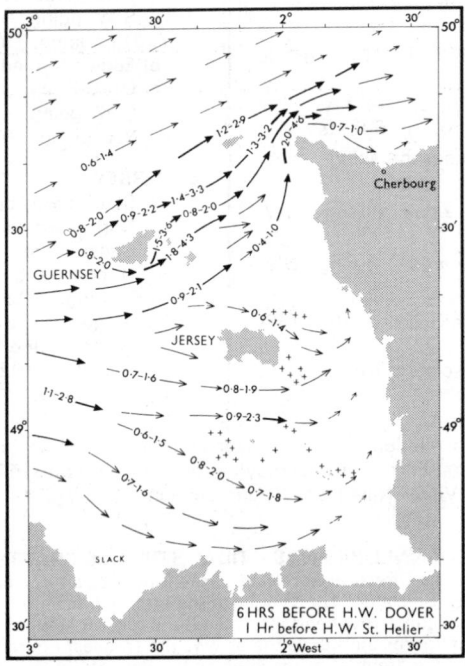

Produced from portion(s) of BA Tidal Stream Atlases with the sanction of the Controller, H.M. Stationery Office and of the Hydrographer of the Navy.

CHANNEL ISLANDS and adjacent coasts of FRANCE

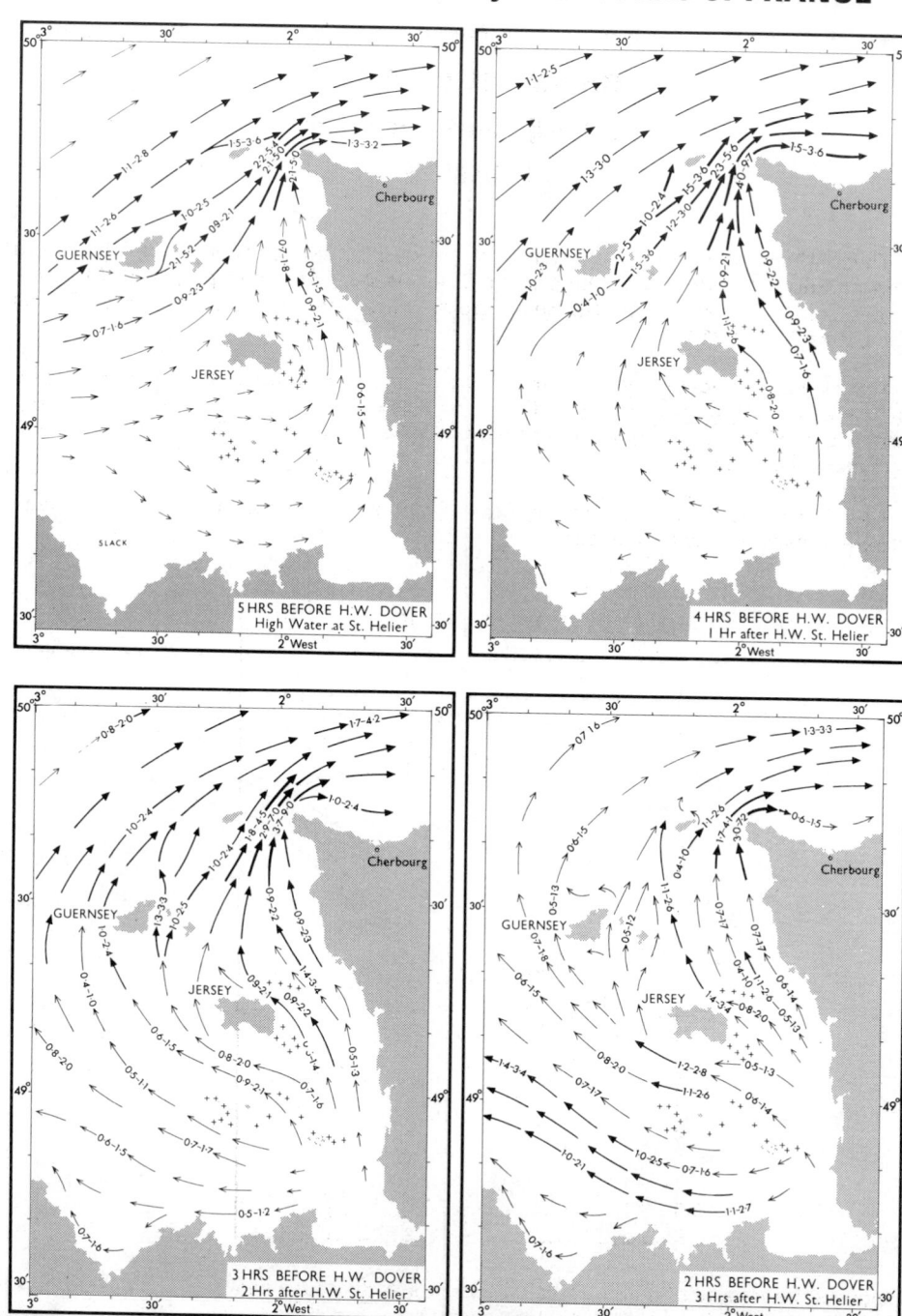

CHANNEL ISLANDS and adjacent coasts of FRANCE

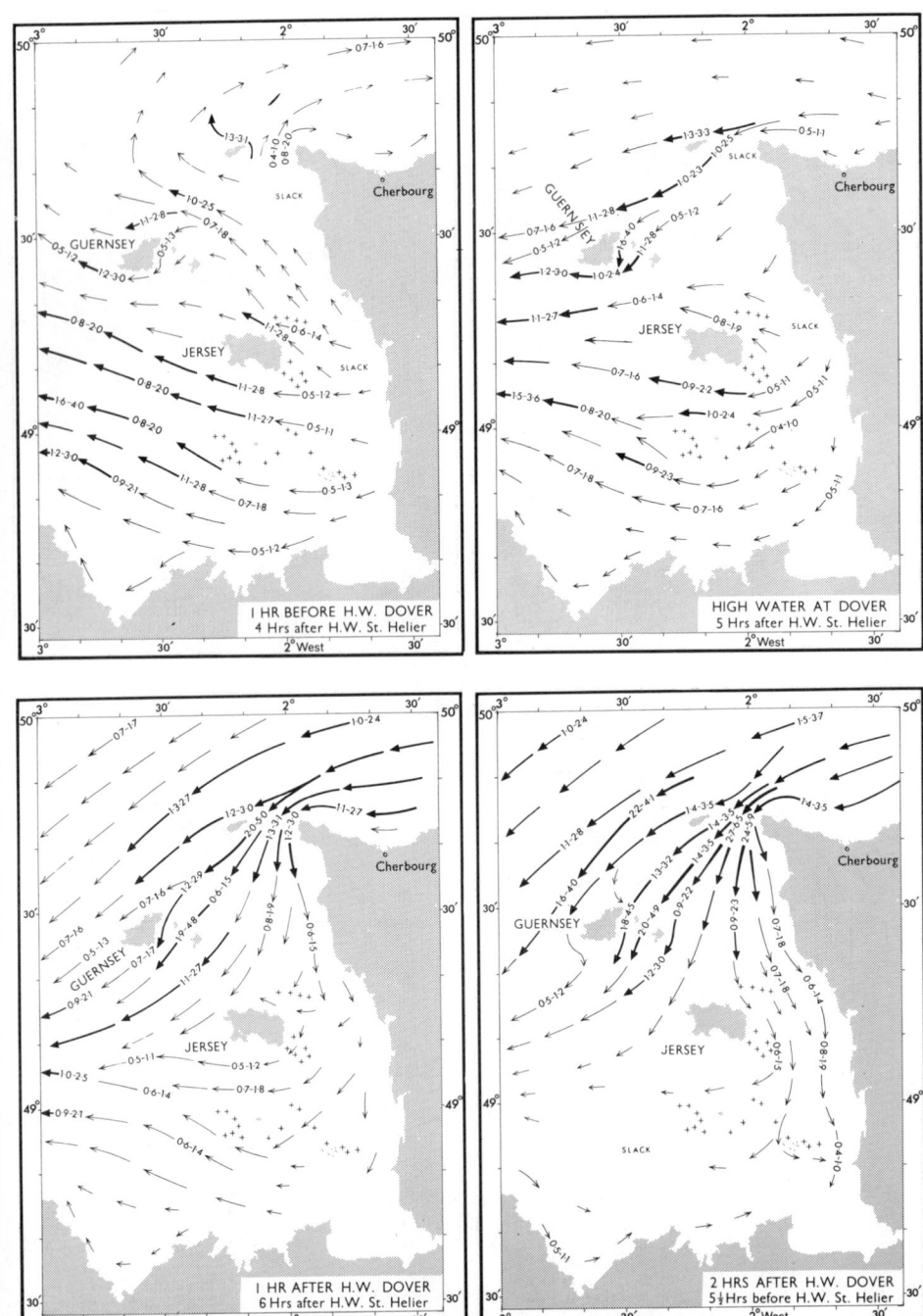

CHANNEL ISLANDS and adjacent coasts of FRANCE

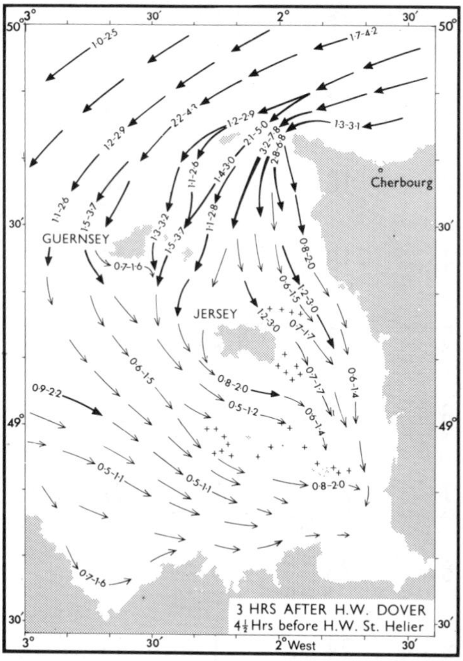

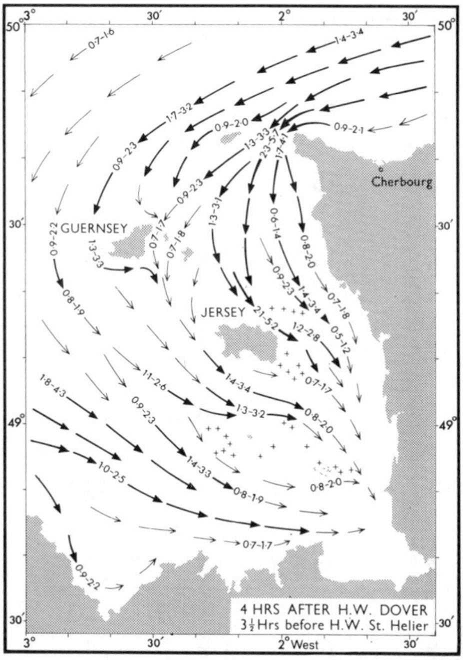

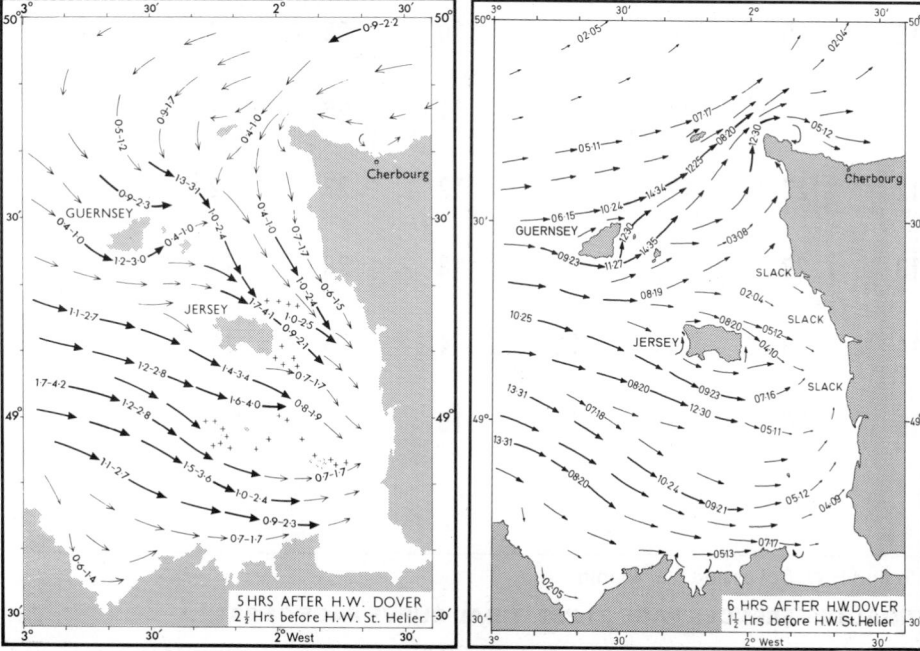

COBH IRELAND (SOUTH COAST)

HIGH & LOW WATER 1992 Lat. 51°50'N. Long. 8°19'W.

GMT   ADD 1 HOUR MARCH 29 — OCTOBER 25 FOR B.S.T.

JANUARY

Day	Time	m	Day	Time	m
1 W	0219 / 0851 / 1452 / 2121	3.6 / 1.0 / 3.6 / 1.0	16 TH	0121 / 0802 / 1401 / 2035	3.5 / 1.3 / 3.6 / 1.2
2 TH	0319 / 0948 / 1546 / 2213	3.7 / 1.0 / 3.7 / 0.9	17 F	0237 / 0912 / 1510 / 2141	3.7 / 1.1 / 3.7 / 1.0
3 F	0410 / 1036 / 1631 / 2258	3.8 / 0.9 / 3.8 / 0.9	18 SA	0342 / 1014 / 1609 / 2239	3.9 / 0.8 / 4.0 / 0.7
4 SA	0453 / 1118 / 1711 / ●2337	3.9 / 0.9 / 3.8 / 0.8	19 SU	0437 / 1108 / 1700 / O2330	4.1 / 0.6 / 4.2 / 0.4
5 SU	0532 / 1154 / 1746	3.9 / 0.9 / 3.9	20 M	0526 / 1157 / 1747	4.3 / 0.4 / 4.3
6 M	0012 / 0606 / 1227 / 1817	0.8 / 4.0 / 0.9 / 3.9	21 TU	0017 / 0612 / 1244 / 1831	0.2 / 4.5 / 0.2 / 4.4
7 TU	0043 / 0638 / 1257 / 1848	0.8 / 4.0 / 0.9 / 3.9	22 W	0103 / 0656 / 1329 / 1914	0.1 / 4.5 / 0.2 / 4.4
8 W	0113 / 0710 / 1327 / 1918	0.8 / 4.0 / 0.9 / 3.9	23 TH	0148 / 0740 / 1413 / 1958	0.1 / 4.4 / 0.3 / 4.3
9 TH	0143 / 0742 / 1359 / 1951	0.9 / 4.0 / 1.0 / 3.9	24 F	0233 / 0824 / 1458 / 2042	0.3 / 4.3 / 0.5 / 4.1
10 F	0216 / 0816 / 1435 / 2027	0.9 / 3.9 / 1.0 / 3.8	25 SA	0319 / 0910 / 1545 / 2130	0.4 / 4.0 / 0.7 / 3.9
11 SA	0254 / 0855 / 1516 / 2108	1.0 / 3.8 / 1.1 / 3.7	26 SU	0408 / 0959 / 1636 / 2222	0.7 / 3.8 / 0.9 / 3.7
12 SU	0338 / 0939 / 1605 / 2156	1.1 / 3.7 / 1.2 / 3.6	27 M	0501 / 1054 / 1732 / 2322	0.9 / 3.5 / 1.1 / 3.4
13 M	0432 / 1031 / 1703 / 2255	1.2 / 3.6 / 1.3 / 3.5	28 TU	0601 / 1158 / 1836	1.2 / 3.3 / 1.3
14 TU	0536 / 1134 / 1810	1.3 / 3.5 / 1.4	29 W	0032 / 0710 / 1312 / 1947	3.3 / 1.3 / 3.2 / 1.3
15 W	0004 / 0647 / 1246 / 1922	3.5 / 1.4 / 3.5 / 1.4	30 TH	0150 / 0823 / 1428 / 2057	3.3 / 1.3 / 3.3 / 1.3
			31 F	0300 / 0928 / 1529 / 2155	3.4 / 1.2 / 3.4 / 1.1

FEBRUARY

Day	Time	m	Day	Time	m
1 SA	0355 / 1019 / 1617 / 2242	3.6 / 1.1 / 3.6 / 1.0	16 SU	0328 / 1001 / 1555 / 2225	3.8 / 0.8 / 3.9 / 0.6
2 SU	0438 / 1101 / 1656 / 2320	3.8 / 0.9 / 3.8 / 0.8	17 M	0424 / 1054 / 1646 / 2316	4.1 / 0.4 / 4.1 / 0.3
3 M	0515 / 1136 / 1730 / ●2354	3.9 / 0.8 / 3.9 / 0.7	18 TU	0512 / 1142 / 1731 O	4.3 / 0.2 / 4.3
4 TU	0548 / 1208 / 1800	4.0 / 0.8 / 4.0	19 W	0002 / 0555 / 1226 / 1813	0.1 / 4.5 / 0.1 / 4.4
5 W	0024 / 0618 / 1238 / 1828	0.7 / 4.1 / 0.7 / 4.0	20 TH	0045 / 0637 / 1308 / 1854	0.0 / 4.5 / 0.1 / 4.4
6 TH	0053 / 0647 / 1307 / 1857	0.7 / 4.1 / 0.7 / 4.0	21 F	0127 / 0718 / 1350 / 1935	0.0 / 4.4 / 0.2 / 4.3
7 F	0122 / 0717 / 1336 / 1927	0.7 / 4.1 / 0.8 / 4.0	22 SA	0208 / 0758 / 1430 / 2015	0.2 / 4.3 / 0.4 / 4.1
8 SA	0152 / 0748 / 1408 / 1959	0.8 / 4.1 / 0.9 / 4.0	23 SU	0250 / 0839 / 1512 / 2058	0.4 / 4.0 / 0.6 / 3.9
9 SU	0225 / 0822 / 1443 / 2035	0.9 / 4.0 / 1.0 / 3.9	24 M	0333 / 0922 / 1557 / 2144	0.7 / 3.7 / 0.9 / 3.6
10 M	0303 / 0901 / 1525 / 2119	1.0 / 3.8 / 1.1 / 3.7	25 TU	0421 / 1011 / 1649 / 2240	1.0 / 3.4 / 1.2 / 3.3
11 TU	0352 / 0950 / 1620 / 2213	1.2 / 3.6 / 1.3 / 3.6	26 W	0518 / 1112 / 1751 / 2350	1.3 / 3.1 / 1.4 / 3.1
12 W	0456 / 1051 / 1729 / 2324	1.3 / 3.5 / 1.4 / 3.4	27 TH	0627 / 1229 / 1908	1.5 / 3.0 / 1.5
13 TH	0612 / 1208 / 1849	1.4 / 3.3 / 1.4	28 F	0115 / 0748 / 1358 / 2028	3.1 / 1.5 / 3.1 / 1.4
14 F	0049 / 0735 / 1314 / 2012	3.4 / 1.3 / 3.4 / 1.2	29 SA	0235 / 0901 / 1507 / 2131	3.4 / 1.3 / 3.3 / 1.2
15 SA	0216 / 0855 / 1453 / 2126	3.5 / 1.1 / 3.6 / 0.9			

MARCH

Day	Time	m	Day	Time	m
1 SU	0332 / 0954 / 1555 / 2217	3.5 / 1.1 / 3.5 / 1.0	16 M	0310 / 0943 / 1537 / 2207	3.7 / 0.6 / 3.8 / 0.5
2 M	0415 / 1035 / 1633 / 2255	3.7 / 0.9 / 3.7 / 0.8	17 TU	0405 / 1035 / 1627 / 2257	4.0 / 0.3 / 4.1 / 0.2
3 TU	0451 / 1110 / 1706 / 2329	3.9 / 0.8 / 3.9 / 0.7	18 W	0452 / 1121 / 1711 / 2342	4.3 / 0.1 / 4.3 / 0.0
4 W	0523 / 1143 / 1737 ●	4.0 / 0.7 / 4.0	19 TH	0535 / 1204 / 1753	4.4 / 0.0 / 4.4
5 TH	0000 / 0553 / 1214 / 1805	0.6 / 4.1 / 0.6 / 4.1	20 F	0024 / 0614 / 1245 / 1832	-0.1 / 4.4 / 0.0 / 4.4
6 F	0031 / 0623 / 1244 / 1834	0.6 / 4.2 / 0.6 / 4.1	21 SA	0105 / 0653 / 1324 / 1910	0.0 / 4.3 / 0.2 / 4.3
7 SA	0101 / 0652 / 1314 / 1903	0.6 / 4.2 / 0.6 / 4.1	22 SU	0144 / 0731 / 1403 / 1949	0.2 / 4.1 / 0.4 / 4.1
8 SU	0131 / 0722 / 1345 / 1935	0.7 / 4.1 / 0.7 / 4.0	23 M	0222 / 0808 / 1441 / 2028	0.5 / 3.9 / 0.6 / 3.8
9 M	0203 / 0756 / 1419 / 2010	0.8 / 4.0 / 0.9 / 3.9	24 TU	0301 / 0848 / 1521 / 2111	0.8 / 3.6 / 0.9 / 3.5
10 TU	0241 / 0834 / 1500 / 2053	0.9 / 3.8 / 1.0 / 3.7	25 W	0344 / 0932 / 1607 / 2203	1.1 / 3.3 / 1.2 / 3.3
11 W	0329 / 0922 / 1554 / 2149	1.1 / 3.6 / 1.2 / 3.5	26 TH	0435 / 1028 / 1706 / 2308	1.3 / 3.1 / 1.4 / 3.1
12 TH	0433 / 1024 / 1705 / 2301	1.3 / 3.4 / 1.3 / 3.3	27 F	0540 / 1141 / 1820	1.5 / 2.9 / 1.5
13 F	0551 / 1143 / 1827	1.5 / 3.2 / 1.3	28 SA	0030 / 0658 / 1311 / 1942	3.0 / 1.5 / 2.9 / 1.4
14 SA	0029 / 0717 / 1314 / 1954	3.3 / 1.2 / 3.2 / 1.2	29 SU	0152 / 0815 / 1426 / 2050	3.1 / 1.3 / 3.1 / 1.2
15 SU	0159 / 0839 / 1435 / 2109	3.4 / 1.0 / 3.5 / 0.8	30 M	0253 / 0913 / 1518 / 2140	3.3 / 1.1 / 3.4 / 1.0
			31 TU	0339 / 0958 / 1559 / 2221	3.6 / 0.9 / 3.6 / 0.8

APRIL

Day	Time	m	Day	Time	m
1 W	0418 / 1037 / 1635 / 2258	3.8 / 0.7 / 3.8 / 0.6	16 TH	0428 / 1058 / 1648 / 2319	4.1 / 0.1 / 4.1 / 0.1
2 TH	0452 / 1113 / 1708 / 2332	4.0 / 0.6 / 4.0 / 0.5	17 F	0511 / 1141 / 1730 / O	4.2 / 0.1 / 4.2
3 F	0525 / 1147 / 1740 ●	4.1 / 0.5 / 4.1	18 SA	0002 / 0551 / 1222 / 1810	0.1 / 4.2 / 0.1 / 4.2
4 SA	0006 / 0557 / 1221 / 1811	0.5 / 4.1 / 0.5 / 4.1	19 SU	0042 / 0630 / 1301 / 1848	0.2 / 4.1 / 0.3 / 4.1
5 SU	0040 / 0629 / 1255 / 1843	0.5 / 4.1 / 0.6 / 4.1	20 M	0120 / 0707 / 1338 / 1926	0.3 / 3.9 / 0.5 / 3.9
6 M	0115 / 0702 / 1329 / 1918	0.6 / 4.0 / 0.7 / 4.0	21 TU	0157 / 0743 / 1414 / 2004	0.6 / 3.7 / 0.7 / 3.7
7 TU	0151 / 0738 / 1406 / 1957	0.7 / 3.9 / 0.8 / 3.9	22 W	0233 / 0820 / 1451 / 2045	0.8 / 3.5 / 0.9 / 3.5
8 W	0233 / 0819 / 1451 / 2043	0.8 / 3.7 / 0.9 / 3.7	23 TH	0312 / 0901 / 1533 / 2132	1.0 / 3.3 / 1.1 / 3.3
9 TH	0323 / 0910 / 1546 / 2140	1.0 / 3.5 / 1.1 / 3.5	24 F	0358 / 0951 / 1625 / 2229	1.2 / 3.1 / 1.2 / 3.1
10 F	0426 / 1013 / 1654 / 2251	1.3 / 3.3 / 1.3 / 3.3	25 SA	0455 / 1054 / 1728 / 2337	1.3 / 3.0 / 1.3 / 3.0
11 SA	0539 / 1129 / 1812	1.2 / 3.2 / 1.1	26 SU	0601 / 1208 / 1840	1.3 / 3.0 / 1.3
12 SU	0013 / 0658 / 1253 / 1933	3.3 / 1.1 / 3.2 / 1.0	27 M	0051 / 0712 / 1323 / 1950	3.1 / 1.3 / 3.1 / 1.2
13 M	0136 / 0815 / 1410 / 2045	3.4 / 0.8 / 3.4 / 0.7	28 TU	0157 / 0816 / 1425 / 2049	3.3 / 1.1 / 3.3 / 1.0
14 TU	0245 / 0918 / 1511 / 2143	3.7 / 0.5 / 3.7 / 0.4	29 W	0251 / 0910 / 1514 / 2138	3.5 / 0.9 / 3.5 / 0.9
15 W	0340 / 1011 / 1603 / 2234	3.9 / 0.3 / 4.0 / 0.2	30 TH	0337 / 0957 / 1557 / 2222	3.7 / 0.7 / 3.7 / 0.7

To find H.W. Dover add 5 h. 46 min.

TIDAL DIFFERENCES PAGE 21:232. TIDAL CURVE PAGE 21:231.

Datum of predictions: 0.13 m. above Ordnance Datum (Dublin) or approx. L.A.T.

COBH IRELAND (SOUTH COAST) 21:229

Lat. 51°50'N. Long. 8°19'W.

HIGH & LOW WATER 1992

GMT — **ADD 1 HOUR MARCH 29 — OCTOBER 25 FOR B.S.T.**

MAY

Day	Time m	Time m	Time m	Time m	Day	Time m	Time m	Time m	Time m
1 F	0418 3.8	1039 0.6	1637 3.9	2303 0.6	16 SA	0449 3.9	1119 0.3	1710 4.0	2341 0.3
2 SA	0456 3.9	1120 0.5	1714 4.0	● 2342 0.5	17 SU	0531 3.9	1201 0.3	1752 4.0	
3 SU	0533 4.0	1159 0.5	1751 4.0		18 M	0022 0.4	0610 3.8	1241 0.4	1830 3.9
4 M	0022 0.5	0610 4.0	1238 0.5	1828 4.0	19 TU	0101 0.5	0647 3.7	1318 0.5	1908 3.8
5 TU	0102 0.5	0648 3.9	1319 0.6	1908 4.0	20	0136 0.6	0722 3.6	1352 0.7	1945 3.6
6 W	0144 0.6	0729 3.8	1401 0.6	1952 3.9	21 TH	0210 0.8	0758 3.5	1427 0.8	2023 3.5
7 TH	0230 0.7	0814 3.7	1449 0.7	2041 3.7	22 F	0246 0.9	0836 3.3	1505 0.9	2105 3.4
8 F	0321 0.8	0906 3.5	1543 0.8	2137 3.6	23 SA	0326 1.0	0920 3.2	1549 1.0	2152 3.3
9 SA	0420 0.9	1006 3.4	1645 0.8	2242 3.4	24 SU	0414 1.1	1011 3.2	1642 1.1	2247 3.2
10 SU	0525 0.9	1113 3.3	1754 0.8	2353 3.4	25 M	0509 1.1	1109 3.1	1742 1.1	2347 3.2
11 M	0635 0.8	1226 3.3	1906 0.8		26 TU	0611 1.1	1214 3.1	1846 1.1	
12 TU	0106 3.4	0744 0.7	1338 3.4	2014 0.8	27 W	0051 3.2	0715 1.1	1320 3.2	1950 1.1
13 W	0213 3.6	0847 0.5	1441 3.6	2115 0.4	28 TH	0154 3.3	0817 1.0	1421 3.4	2050 0.9
14 TH	0312 3.7	0943 0.4	1536 3.8	2209 0.3	29 F	0250 3.5	0914 0.9	1516 3.6	2144 0.8
15 F	0403 3.8	1033 0.3	1625 3.9	2257 0.3	30 SA	0341 3.6	1006 0.7	1605 3.7	2234 0.7
					31 SU	0428 3.8	1054 0.6	1651 3.9	2321 0.5

JUNE

Day	Time m	Time m	Time m	Time m	Day	Time m	Time m	Time m	Time m
1 M	0512 3.9	1140 0.5	1734 4.0	●	16 TU	0006 0.5	0555 3.6	1225 0.5	1816 3.8
2 TU	0006 0.5	0555 3.9	1225 0.4	1817 4.0	17 W	0044 0.6	0631 3.6	1301 0.6	1852 3.7
3 W	0052 0.5	0638 3.9	1310 0.4	1901 4.0	18 TH	0117 0.7	0704 3.6	1333 0.6	1926 3.7
4 TH	0137 0.4	0722 3.9	1356 0.4	1947 4.0	19 F	0149 0.7	0737 3.5	1405 0.7	2000 3.6
5 F	0224 0.4	0808 3.8	1444 0.4	2036 3.9	20 SA	0220 0.8	0811 3.5	1438 0.8	2037 3.6
6 SA	0314 0.5	0858 3.7	1535 0.5	2128 3.7	21 SU	0256 0.8	0849 3.5	1515 0.8	2116 3.5
7 SU	0407 0.6	0952 3.6	1630 0.5	2225 3.6	22 M	0336 0.9	0931 3.4	1600 0.9	2201 3.4
8 M	0504 0.6	1051 3.5	1731 0.6	2327 3.5	23 TU	0424 1.0	1019 3.3	1651 1.0	2252 3.3
9 TU	0605 0.7	1155 3.4	1835 0.6		24 W	0518 1.0	1115 3.3	1750 1.1	2351 3.3
10 W	0032 3.4	0709 0.7	1303 3.4	1941 0.6	25 TH	0619 1.1	1219 3.3	1855 1.1	
11 TH	0139 3.4	0814 0.7	1409 3.5	2045 0.6	26 F	0056 3.3	0725 1.1	1327 3.3	2002 1.0
12 F	0243 3.5	0915 0.6	1510 3.6	2144 0.5	27 SA	0203 3.4	0832 1.0	1435 3.4	2108 0.9
13 SA	0340 3.6	1011 0.5	1605 3.7	2237 0.5	28 SU	0307 3.5	0935 0.8	1536 3.6	2208 0.7
14 SU	0430 3.6	1100 0.5	1653 3.7	2324 0.5	29 M	0404 3.6	1032 0.7	1631 3.8	2302 0.5
15 M	0515 3.6	1147 0.5	1737 3.8	○	30 TU	0455 3.8	1124 0.5	1720 3.9	● 2352 0.4

JULY

Day	Time m	Time m	Time m	Time m	Day	Time m	Time m	Time m	Time m
1 W	0542 3.9	1212 0.3	1807 4.1		16 TH	0025 0.6	0614 3.6	1242 0.6	1833 3.8
2 TH	0039 0.2	0627 4.0	1259 0.2	1851 4.1	17 F	0056 0.6	0644 3.7	1312 0.6	1904 3.8
3 F	0126 0.2	0711 4.0	1345 0.1	1937 4.1	18 SA	0125 0.6	0714 3.7	1340 0.6	1934 3.8
4 SA	0211 0.2	0756 4.0	1431 0.1	2022 4.1	19 SU	0154 0.7	0744 3.7	1410 0.7	2006 3.7
5 SU	0258 0.2	0842 3.9	1518 0.2	2110 3.9	20 M	0225 0.7	0817 3.7	1443 0.7	2041 3.7
6 M	0346 0.4	0931 3.8	1609 0.3	2201 3.7	21 TU	0301 0.8	0854 3.6	1521 0.8	2120 3.6
7 TU	0438 0.5	1024 3.6	1703 0.5	2256 3.5	22 W	0343 0.9	0936 3.5	1607 0.9	2206 3.5
8 W	0534 0.7	1123 3.4	1802 0.7	2358 3.4	23 TH	0433 1.0	1027 3.4	1703 1.1	2300 3.4
9 TH	0635 0.8	1228 3.3	1908 0.8		24 F	0533 1.1	1128 3.3	1809 1.2	
10 F	0105 3.3	0742 0.9	1339 3.3	2016 0.8	25 SA	0007 3.3	0641 1.2	1247 3.2	1922 1.2
11 SA	0216 3.2	0850 0.9	1449 3.4	2123 0.8	26 SU	0122 3.2	0756 1.1	1400 3.3	2038 1.0
12 SU	0321 3.3	0952 0.8	1549 3.5	2220 0.7	27 M	0238 3.4	0910 0.9	1513 3.5	2147 0.8
13 M	0416 3.4	1045 0.7	1640 3.6	2309 0.7	28 TU	0344 3.6	1013 0.7	1613 3.8	2245 0.5
14 TU	0501 3.5	1129 0.6	1725 3.7 ○	2350 0.6	29 W	0438 3.8	1108 0.4	1705 4.0 ●	2336 0.3
15 W	0540 3.6	1208 0.6	1800 3.7		30 TH	0527 4.0	1156 0.2	1751 4.2	
					31 F	0023 0.1	0611 4.1	1243 0.0	1835 4.3

AUGUST

Day	Time m	Time m	Time m	Time m	Day	Time m	Time m	Time m	Time m
1 SA	0108 0.0	0654 4.2	1327 -0.1	1918 4.3	16 SU	0058 0.6	0648 3.8	1313 0.6	1906 3.9
2 SU	0152 0.0	0737 4.2	1411 0.0	2001 4.2	17 M	0126 0.6	0716 3.9	1342 0.6	1935 3.9
3 M	0236 0.1	0820 4.1	1456 0.1	2046 4.0	18 TU	0156 0.7	0747 3.8	1412 0.7	2007 3.8
4 TU	0321 0.3	0906 3.9	1542 0.3	2132 3.8	19 W	0229 0.8	0821 3.8	1448 0.8	2044 3.7
5 W	0409 0.5	0955 3.7	1633 0.6	2224 3.5	20 TH	0307 0.9	0900 3.7	1531 1.0	2127 3.6
6 TH	0502 0.8	1051 3.4	1730 0.8	2323 3.3	21 F	0355 1.1	0949 3.5	1627 1.1	2221 3.4
7 F	0602 1.0	1156 3.2	1835 1.0		22 SA	0456 1.2	1051 3.3	1736 1.3	2330 3.2
8 SA	0034 3.1	0712 1.1	1313 3.1	1950 1.1	23 SU	0609 1.3	1209 3.2	1854 1.3	
9 SU	0153 3.1	0828 1.1	1431 3.2	2104 1.0	24 M	0052 3.2	0730 1.2	1336 3.3	2017 1.1
10 M	0306 3.2	0935 1.0	1534 3.4	2203 0.9	25 TU	0215 3.3	0850 1.0	1454 3.5	2129 0.8
11 TU	0401 3.3	1027 0.8	1623 3.5	2250 0.8	26 W	0324 3.6	0955 0.6	1555 3.8	2227 0.5
12 W	0444 3.5	1110 0.7	1703 3.7	2328 0.7	27 TH	0419 3.9	1049 0.3	1646 4.1	2316 0.2
13 TH	0520 3.6	1146 0.6	1738 3.8 ○		28 F	0507 4.1	1137 0.1	1731 4.3 ●	
14 F	0000 0.6	0551 3.7	1217 0.5	1808 3.9	29 SA	0002 0.0	0550 4.3	1222 -0.1	1814 4.4
15 SA	0030 0.6	0620 3.8	1246 0.5	1837 3.9	30 SU	0046 -0.1	0632 4.4	1305 -0.1	1855 4.3
					31 M	0128 0.0	0713 4.3	1347 0.0	1936 4.3

GENERAL — In Cork Harbour flood stream is irregular with eddies and counter-streams. Strong, persistent S. winds increase duration and rate of flood. Strong, persistent N. winds increase duration and rate of ebb. In position 1½ M. ESE. Daunt Rock the streams are rotatory clockwise, but are very much affected by the wind.

COBH IRELAND (SOUTH COAST)

HIGH & LOW WATER 1992   Lat. 51°50'N. Long. 8°19'W.

GMT   ADD 1 HOUR MARCH 29 — OCTOBER 25 FOR B.S.T.

SEPTEMBER

Day	Time	m	Day	Time	m
1 TU	0210 / 0755 / 1430 W / 2018	0.1 / 4.2 / 0.2 / 4.0	16	0130 / 0720 / 1347 / 1939	0.7 / 4.0 / 0.8 / 3.9
2 W	0253 / 0838 / 1515 TH / 2102	0.4 / 3.9 / 0.5 / 3.8	17	0203 / 0754 / 1423 / 2015	0.8 / 3.9 / 0.9 / 3.8
3 TH	0339 / 0926 / 1603 F / 2151	0.7 / 3.7 / 0.8 / 3.5	18	0241 / 0834 / 1507 / 2059	1.0 / 3.7 / 1.1 / 3.6
4 F	0430 / 1020 / 1658 SA / 2249	0.9 / 3.4 / 1.1 / 3.2	19	0330 / 0924 / 1605 / 2155	1.1 / 3.5 / 1.2 / 3.4
5 SA	0530 / 1126 / 1804 SU	1.2 / 3.2 / 1.3	20	0434 / 1030 / 1716 SU / 2307	1.3 / 3.4 / 1.3 / 3.2
6 SU	0002 / 0642 / 1247 M / 1922	3.0 / 1.3 / 3.1 / 1.3	21	0549 / 1150 / 1836 M	1.3 / 3.3 / 1.3
7 M	0128 / 0803 / 1409 TU / 2039	3.0 / 1.2 / 3.2 / 1.2	22	0031 / 0712 / 1317 / 1958	3.2 / 1.2 / 3.4 / 1.1
8 TU	0243 / 0910 / 1511 W / 2136	3.1 / 1.1 / 3.4 / 1.0	23	0154 / 0830 / 1433 W / 2108	3.4 / 0.9 / 3.6 / 0.8
9 W	0336 / 1000 / 1558 TH / 2221	3.6 / 0.9 / 3.6 / 0.9	24	0302 / 0934 / 1533 TH / 2204	3.7 / 0.6 / 3.9 / 0.4
10 TH	0417 / 1041 / 1636 F / 2257	3.6 / 0.7 / 3.8 / 0.2	25	0356 / 1026 / 1623 F / 2253	4.0 / 0.3 / 4.2 / 0.2
11 F	0452 / 1115 / 1709 / 2330 ●	3.7 / 0.6 / 3.9 / 0.6	26	0443 / 1114 / 1708 / 2338	4.2 / 0.1 / 4.4 / 0.0
12 SA	0523 / 1147 / 1740 ○	3.9 / 0.6 / 4.0	27	0527 / 1158 / 1750 SU	4.4 / 0.0 / 4.4
13 SU	0000 / 0552 / 1217 M / 1808	0.6 / 4.0 / 0.6 / 4.0	28	0021 / 0608 M / 1241 / 1831	0.0 / 4.4 / 0.0 / 4.4
14 M	0030 / 0620 / 1246 TU / 1837	0.6 / 4.0 / 0.6 / 4.1	29	0103 / 0649 TU / 1323 / 1911	0.1 / 4.3 / 0.1 / 4.2
15 TU	0059 / 0649 / 1316 W / 1907	4.0 / 4.0 / 0.7 / 4.0	30	0144 / 0730 W / 1404 / 1951	0.3 / 4.2 / 0.4 / 4.0

OCTOBER

Day	Time	m	Day	Time	m
1 TH	0226 / 0813 / 1447 F / 2033	0.5 / 3.9 / 0.7 / 3.7	16	0146 / 0737 / 1409 / 1957	0.9 / 3.9 / 1.0 / 3.8
2 F	0310 / 0858 / 1533 SA / 2120	0.8 / 3.7 / 1.0 / 3.4	17	0228 / 0820 / 1457 / 2044	1.0 / 3.8 / 1.1 / 3.7
3 SA	0359 / 0951 / 1626 SU / 2215	1.1 / 3.4 / 1.2 / 3.2	18	0319 / 0913 / 1555 SU / 2142	1.1 / 3.6 / 1.2 / 3.5
4 SU	0457 / 1055 / 1730 M / 2326	1.3 / 3.2 / 1.4 / 3.0	19	0422 / 1019 / 1704 M / 2252	1.2 / 3.5 / 1.3 / 3.3
5 M	0607 / 1213 / 1844 TU	1.4 / 3.1 / 1.4	20	0535 / 1135 / 1820 TU	1.2 / 3.4 / 1.2
6 TU	0049 / 0724 / 1332 W / 1958	3.0 / 1.3 / 3.2 / 1.3	21	0011 / 0653 / 1256 / 1936	3.3 / 1.1 / 3.5 / 1.0
7 W	0204 / 0830 / 1434 TH / 2056	3.2 / 1.2 / 3.4 / 1.2	22	0129 / 0806 / 1408 TH / 2042	3.5 / 0.9 / 3.7 / 0.8
8 TH	0258 / 0921 / 1521 F / 2141	3.4 / 1.0 / 3.6 / 1.0	23	0235 / 0908 / 1507 F / 2139	3.8 / 0.6 / 4.0 / 0.5
9 F	0341 / 1003 / 1600 SA / 2220	3.6 / 0.8 / 3.8 / 0.8	24	0330 / 1002 / 1558 SA / 2229	4.0 / 0.3 / 4.2 / 0.3
10 SA	0418 / 1040 / 1636 SU / 2255	3.8 / 0.7 / 4.0 / 0.7	25	0419 / 1050 / 1644 ● / 2314	4.2 / 0.2 / 4.3 / 0.2
11 SU	0451 / 1114 / 1709 ○ / 2329	4.0 / 0.6 / 4.1 / 0.6	26	0504 / 1136 / 1727 / 2358	4.3 / 0.2 / 4.4 / 0.2
12 M	0523 / 1148 / 1740 TU	4.1 / 0.6 / 4.1	27	0547 / 1219 / 1808 TU	4.4 / 0.2 / 4.3
13 TU	0002 / 0554 / 1221 W / 1811	0.6 / 4.1 / 0.7 / 4.1	28	0040 / 0628 / 1301 W / 1848	0.3 / 4.3 / 0.4 / 4.1
14 W	0036 / 0626 / 1255 TH / 1843	0.7 / 4.1 / 0.7 / 4.1	29	0121 / 0709 / 1341 TH / 1927	0.5 / 4.1 / 0.6 / 3.9
15 TH	0110 / 0700 / 1330 F / 1918	0.8 / 4.0 / 0.8 / 4.0	30	0201 / 0750 / 1422 F / 2007	0.7 / 3.9 / 0.9 / 3.7
			31 SA	0243 / 0834 / 1504 / 2050	0.9 / 3.7 / 1.1 / 3.5

NOVEMBER

Day	Time	m	Day	Time	m
1 SU	0328 / 0923 / 1552 M / 2141	1.1 / 3.5 / 1.3 / 3.3	16	0313 / 0907 / 1547 M / 2131	1.0 / 3.8 / 1.1 / 3.6
2 M	0420 / 1020 / 1648 TU / 2242	1.3 / 3.3 / 1.4 / 3.1	17	0412 / 1008 / 1651 TU / 2236	1.0 / 3.7 / 1.1 / 3.5
3 TU	0521 / 1126 / 1753 W / 2353	1.4 / 3.2 / 1.5 / 3.1	18	0518 / 1116 / 1759 W / 2347	1.0 / 3.6 / 1.1 / 3.5
4 W	0629 / 1236 / 1900 TH	1.4 / 3.3 / 1.4	19	0629 / 1228 / 1908 TH	1.0 / 3.6 / 1.0
5 TH	0105 / 0734 / 1341 F / 2001	3.2 / 1.3 / 3.4 / 1.3	20	0059 / 0737 / 1338 / 2013	3.6 / 0.8 / 3.7 / 0.8
6 F	0206 / 0830 / 1434 SA / 2053	3.4 / 1.2 / 3.6 / 1.1	21	0206 / 0841 / 1444 SA / 2112	3.8 / 0.7 / 3.9 / 0.6
7 SA	0257 / 0919 / 1519 SU / 2139	3.6 / 1.0 / 3.8 / 0.9	22	0305 / 0924 / 1534 SU / 2205	4.0 / 0.5 / 4.1 / 0.5
8 SU	0340 / 1002 / 1600 M / 2220	3.8 / 0.9 / 4.0 / 0.8	23	0358 / 1029 / 1623 M / 2254	4.1 / 0.4 / 4.2 / 0.4
9 M	0419 / 1042 / 1638 TU / 2300	4.0 / 0.8 / 4.1 / 0.7	24	0446 / 1116 / 1708 ● / 2319	4.2 / 0.4 / 4.2 / 0.4
10 TU	0457 / 1121 / 1715 W / 2339	4.1 / 0.7 / 4.2 / 0.7	25	0530 / 1201 / 1750 ○	4.2 / 0.5 / 4.1
11 W	0533 / 1200 / 1751	4.1 / 0.7 / 4.2	26	0021 / 0612 / 1242 TH / 1829	0.5 / 4.2 / 0.6 / 4.0
12 TH	0017 / 0612 / 1239 / 1827	0.7 / 4.0 / 0.8 / 4.1	27	0102 / 0652 / 1321 F / 1907	0.6 / 4.1 / 0.7 / 3.9
13 F	0056 / 0648 / 1319 / 1905	0.8 / 4.1 / 0.8 / 4.0	28	0140 / 0731 / 1359 SA / 1944	0.7 / 3.9 / 0.9 / 3.7
14 SA	0132 / 0728 / 1403 SU / 1947	0.8 / 4.0 / 0.9 / 3.9	29	0217 / 0811 / 1436 SU / 2023	0.9 / 3.8 / 1.1 / 3.6
15 SU	0221 / 0814 / 1452 / 2035	0.9 / 3.9 / 1.0 / 3.8	30	0255 / 0853 / 1516 M / 2105	1.1 / 3.6 / 1.2 / 3.5

DECEMBER

Day	Time	m	Day	Time	m
1 TU	0339 / 0939 / 1602 W / 2154	1.2 / 3.5 / 1.3 / 3.4	16	0356 / 0950 / 1630 W / 2214	0.8 / 3.9 / 0.9 / 3.7
2 W	0429 / 1032 / 1656 TH / 2252	1.3 / 3.4 / 1.4 / 3.3	17	0456 / 1051 / 1732 TH / 2318	0.9 / 3.8 / 1.0 / 3.6
3 TH	0527 / 1132 / 1756 F / 2356	1.4 / 3.4 / 1.4 / 3.3	18	0600 / 1156 / 1837 F	0.9 / 3.7 / 1.0
4 F	0630 / 1236 / 1859 SA	1.4 / 3.5 / 1.4	19	0026 / 0707 / 1306 SA / 1943	3.6 / 0.9 / 3.7 / 1.0
5 SA	0103 / 0732 / 1338 SU / 2000	3.4 / 1.3 / 3.5 / 1.3	20	0137 / 0814 / 1413 SU / 2048	3.7 / 0.9 / 3.7 / 0.8
6 SU	0205 / 0831 / 1434 M / 2056	3.5 / 1.2 / 3.7 / 1.1	21	0242 / 0916 / 1514 M / 2146	3.8 / 0.8 / 3.8 / 0.7
7 M	0300 / 0924 / 1525 TU / 2147	3.7 / 1.1 / 3.9 / 1.0	22	0341 / 1012 / 1608 TU / 2238	3.9 / 0.7 / 3.9 / 0.6
8 TU	0348 / 1013 / 1610 W / 2234	3.9 / 0.9 / 4.0 / 0.9	23	0432 / 1102 / 1655 W / 2325	4.0 / 0.6 / 4.0 / 0.6
9 W	0433 / 1059 / 1653 TH / 2319 ○	4.1 / 0.8 / 4.1 / 0.7	24	0518 / 1147 / 1737 ●	4.1 / 0.6 / 4.0
10 TH	0515 / 1143 / 1734 F	4.2 / 0.7 / 4.2	25	0007 / 0559 / 1228 F / 1815	0.6 / 4.1 / 0.7 / 4.0
11 F	0002 / 0556 / 1227 SA / 1814	0.7 / 4.2 / 0.7 / 4.2	26	0046 / 0637 / 1303 SA / 1849	0.6 / 4.1 / 0.8 / 3.9
12 SA	0045 / 0638 / 1310 SU / 1856	0.6 / 4.2 / 0.7 / 4.1	27	0120 / 0712 / 1336 SU / 1922	0.7 / 4.0 / 0.9 / 3.8
13 SU	0128 / 0721 / 1355 M / 1939	0.6 / 4.2 / 0.7 / 4.1	28	0152 / 0746 / 1406 M / 1955	0.8 / 3.9 / 1.0 / 3.8
14 M	0214 / 0806 / 1442 TU / 2026	0.7 / 4.1 / 0.8 / 4.0	29	0223 / 0821 / 1439 TU / 2031	0.9 / 3.8 / 1.1 / 3.7
15 TU	0303 / 0856 / 1534 W / 2117	0.8 / 4.0 / 0.9 / 3.8	30	0258 / 0859 / 1517 W / 2157	1.0 / 3.7 / 1.2 / 3.5
			31 TH	0340 / 0941 / 1603 / 2157	1.2 / 3.6 / 1.3 / 3.5

RATE AND SET — Off Cobh. Flood begins 5½ h. before H.W. runs for 5¾ h., Ebb begins ¼ h. after H.W. runs for 6¾ h. Off Monkstown. Flood begins 5 h. before H.W. runs for 5½ h., Ebb begins ¾ h. after H.W. runs for 7 h.

COBH

MEAN SPRING AND NEAP CURVES

Springs occur 2 days after New and Full Moon.

H.W.Hts.m.

MEAN RANGES	
Springs	3·6m
Neaps	2·0m

Factor

0·9 0·8 0·7 0·6 0·5 0·4 0·3 0·2 0·1

M.H.W.S.

M.H.W.N.

M.L.W.N.

M.L.W.S.

CHART DATUM

L.W.Hts.m.

L.W +6h +5h +4h +3h +2h +1h H.W −1h −2h −3h −4h −5h L.W

TIDAL DIFFERENCES ON COBH

PLACE	TIME DIFFERENCES				HEIGHT DIFFERENCES (Metres)			
	High Water		Low Water		MHWS	MHWN	MLWN	MLWS
COBH	0500 and 1700	1100 and 2300	0500 and 1700	1100 and 2300	4.2	3.2	1.3	0.4
Tralee Bay								
Fenit Pier	−0057	−0017	−0029	−0109	+0.5	+0.2	+0.3	+0.1
Smerwick Harbour	−0107	−0027	−0041	−0121	−0.3	−0.4	−	−
Dingle Harbour...........	−0111	−0041	−0049	−0119	−0.3	−0.4	0.0	0.0
Castlemaine Harbour								
Cromane Point	−0026	−0006	−0017	−0037	+0.4	+0.2	+0.4	+0.2
Valentia Harbour								
Knights Town	−0118	−0038	−0056	−0136	−0.6	−0.4	−0.1	0.0
Ballinskelligs Bay								
Castle	−0119	−0039	−0054	−0134	−0.5	−0.5	−0.1	0.0
Kenmare River								
West Cove	−0113	−0033	−0049	−0129	−0.6	−0.5	−0.1	0.0
Dunkerron Harbour	−0117	−0027	−0050	−0140	−0.2	−0.3	+0.1	0.0
Coulagh Bay								
Ballycrovane Harbour...	−0116	−0036	−0053	−0133	−0.6	−0.5	−0.1	0.0
Black Ball Harbour	−0115	−0035	−0047	−0127	−0.7	−0.6	−0.1	+0.1
Bantry Bay								
Castletown Bearhaven	−0048	−0012	−0025	−0101	−0.9	−0.6	−0.1	0.0
Bantry.......................	−0045	−0025	−0040	−0105	−0.9	−0.8	−0.2	0.0
Dunmanus Bay								
Dunbeacon Harbour ...	−0057	−0025	−0032	−0104	−0.8	−0.7	−0.3	−0.1
Dunmanus Harbour......	−0107	−0031	−0044	−0120	−0.7	−0.6	−0.2	0.0
Crookhaven	−0057	−0033	−0048	−0112	−0.8	−0.6	−0.4	−0.1
Skull........................	−0040	−0015	−0015	−0110	−0.9	−0.6	−0.2	0.0
Baltimore	−0025	−0005	−0010	−0050	−0.6	−0.3	+0.1	+0.2
Castletownshend........	−0020	−0030	−0020	−0050	−0.4	−0.2	+0.1	+0.3
Clonakilty Bay	−0033	−0011	−0019	−0041	−0.3	−0.2	−	−
Courtmacsherry	−0029	−0007	+0005	−0017	−0.4	−0.3	−0.2	−0.1
Kinsale	−0019	−0005	−0009	−0023	−0.2	0.0	+0.1	+0.2
Cork Harbour								
Marino Point	0000	+0010	0000	+0010	+0.1	+0.1	0.0	0.0
Cork City...................	+0005	+0010	+0020	+0010	+0.4	+0.4	+0.3	+0.2
Ringaskiddy	+0005	+0020	+0007	+0013	+0.1	+0.1	+0.1	+0.1
Ballycotton...............	−0011	+0001	+0003	−0009	0.0	0.0	−0.1	0.0
Youghal	0000	+0010	+0010	0000	−0.2	−0.1	−0.1	−0.1
Dungarvan Harbour ...	+0004	+0012	+0007	−0001	0.0	+0.1	−0.2	0.0
Waterford Harbour								
Dunmore East	+0013	+0013	+0001	+0001	0.0	0.0	−0.2	0.0
Cheekpoint................	+0022	+0022	+0022	+0022	+0.2	+0.2	+0.2	+0.1
Waterford	+0057	+0057	+0046	+0046	+0.4	+0.3	−0.1	0.1
New Ross	+0100	+0030	+0055	+0130	+0.3	+0.4	+0.3	+0.4
Baginbun Head...........	+0003	+0003	−0008	−0008	−0.2	−0.1	+0.2	+0.2
Great Saltee	+0019	+0009	−0004	+0006	−0.3	−0.4	−	−
Carnsore Point	+0029	+0019	−0002	+0008	−1.1	−1.0	−	−

Refer to predictions on pages 21:228-21:230

DUBLIN NORTH WALL 21:233

Lat. 53°21'N. Long. 6°13'W.
GMT

HIGH & LOW WATER 1992
ADD 1 HOUR MARCH 29 — OCTOBER 25 FOR B.S.T.

JANUARY

Day	Time	m	Day	Time	m
1 W	0220 / 0904 / 1456 / 2129	1.3 / 3.7 / 1.4 / 3.7	16 Th	0117 / 0806 / 1351 / 2032	1.3 / 3.5 / 1.3 / 3.7
2 Th	0311 / 0952 / 1545 / 2219	1.3 / 3.8 / 1.2 / 3.8	17 F	0219 / 0905 / 1451 / 2131	1.2 / 3.8 / 1.0 / 3.9
3 F	0355 / 1034 / 1628 / 2259	1.2 / 4.0 / 1.1 / 3.8	18 Sa	0315 / 0959 / 1546 / 2226	1.0 / 4.0 / 0.7 / 4.1
4 Sa	0434 / 1112 / 1706 / 2337	1.1 / 4.1 / 1.0 / 3.8	19 Su	0406 / 1048 / 1637 / 2316	0.8 / 4.3 / 0.5 / 4.2
5 Su	0512 / 1147 / 1743	1.0 / 4.1 / 0.9	20 M	0452 / 1136 / 1726	0.7 / 4.5 / 0.3
6 M	0012 / 0549 / 1222 / 1817	3.8 / 1.0 / 4.1 / 0.9	21 Tu	0005 / 0539 / 1222 / 1812	4.3 / 0.6 / 4.6 / 0.2
7 Tu	0046 / 0624 / 1256 / 1853	3.7 / 0.9 / 4.1 / 0.9	22 W	0052 / 0624 / 1309 / 1900	4.2 / 0.6 / 4.6 / 0.2
8 W	0120 / 0700 / 1330 / 1928	3.7 / 1.0 / 4.0 / 0.9	23 Th	0138 / 0710 / 1355 / 1948	4.1 / 0.6 / 4.5 / 0.4
9 Th	0154 / 0735 / 1405 / 2002	3.6 / 1.0 / 3.9 / 1.0	24 F	0225 / 0757 / 1444 / 2036	4.0 / 0.8 / 4.3 / 0.6
10 F	0230 / 0811 / 1444 / 2037	3.6 / 1.1 / 3.8 / 1.1	25 Sa	0314 / 0846 / 1536 / 2128	3.8 / 1.0 / 4.1 / 0.9
11 Sa	0311 / 0849 / 1528 / 2117	3.5 / 1.3 / 3.6 / 1.2	26 Su	0406 / 0942 / 1637 / 2226	3.6 / 1.2 / 3.9 / 1.2
12 Su	0357 / 0934 / 1617 / 2203	3.4 / 1.4 / 3.5 / 1.3	27 M	0508 / 1047 / 1746 / 2330	3.5 / 1.5 / 3.7 / 1.5
13 M	0451 / 1027 / 1712 / 2301	3.3 / 1.5 / 3.5 / 1.4	28 Tu	0617 / 1203 / 1859	3.4 / 1.6 / 3.5
14 Tu	0553 / 1132 / 1817	3.3 / 1.6 / 3.5	29 W	0042 / 0727 / 1327 / 2009	1.6 / 3.5 / 1.6 / 3.5
15 W	0008 / 0702 / 1242 / 1926	1.4 / 3.4 / 1.5 / 3.6	30 Th	0152 / 0833 / 1437 / 2112	1.6 / 3.6 / 1.5 / 3.6
			31 F	0250 / 0929 / 1531 / 2204	1.5 / 3.8 / 1.3 / 3.6

FEBRUARY

Day	Time	m	Day	Time	m
1 Sa	0338 / 1017 / 1613 / 2248	1.3 / 3.9 / 1.1 / 3.7	16 Su	0305 / 0946 / 1538 / 2217	1.1 / 4.0 / 0.7 / 4.1
2 Su	0419 / 1058 / 1649 / 2323	1.1 / 4.0 / 1.0 / 3.7	17 M	0356 / 1037 / 1627 / 2306	0.8 / 4.3 / 0.4 / 4.2
3 M	0455 / 1133 / 1723 / 2356	1.0 / 4.0 / 0.9 / 3.7	18 Tu	0441 / 1123 / 1712 / 2350	0.6 / 4.5 / 0.2 / 4.3
4 Tu	0529 / 1205 / 1754	0.9 / 4.0 / 0.8	19 W	0525 / 1207 / 1756	0.5 / 4.6 / 0.2
5 W	0025 / 0601 / 1235 / 1825	3.7 / 0.8 / 4.0 / 0.8	20 Th	0031 / 0605 / 1249 / 1839	4.2 / 0.5 / 4.6 / 0.2
6 Th	0052 / 0632 / 1302 / 1853	3.7 / 0.8 / 4.0 / 0.8	21 F	0110 / 0648 / 1331 / 1920	4.2 / 0.5 / 4.5 / 0.4
7 F	0119 / 0702 / 1333 / 1923	3.7 / 0.8 / 3.9 / 0.8	22 Sa	0149 / 0728 / 1415 / 2004	4.0 / 0.7 / 4.3 / 0.7
8 Sa	0151 / 0733 / 1408 / 1954	3.7 / 0.9 / 3.8 / 0.9	23 Su	0232 / 0813 / 1504 / 2049	3.9 / 0.9 / 4.1 / 1.0
9 Su	0229 / 0808 / 1450 / 2032	3.6 / 1.0 / 3.8 / 1.0	24 M	0319 / 0904 / 1600 / 2141	3.7 / 1.1 / 3.8 / 1.3
10 M	0314 / 0850 / 1539 / 2117	3.5 / 1.1 / 3.7 / 1.2	25 Tu	0416 / 1007 / 1711 / 2244	3.5 / 1.4 / 3.5 / 1.6
11 Tu	0406 / 0942 / 1637 / 2214	3.4 / 1.3 / 3.6 / 1.3	26 W	0527 / 1125 / 1828	3.4 / 1.6 / 3.4
12 W	0509 / 1049 / 1746 / 2330	3.3 / 1.4 / 3.5 / 1.5	27 Th	0001 / 0646 / 1256 / 1944	1.8 / 3.4 / 1.6 / 3.4
13 Th	0627 / 1214 / 1904	3.4 / 1.4 / 3.5	28 F	0123 / 0801 / 1415 / 2051	1.7 / 3.5 / 1.5 / 3.4
14 F	0055 / 0744 / 1334 / 2018	1.5 / 3.5 / 1.3 / 3.7	29 Sa	0229 / 0905 / 1510 / 2146	1.5 / 3.7 / 1.3 / 3.5
15 Sa	0206 / 0850 / 1442 / 2121	1.3 / 3.7 / 1.0 / 3.9			

MARCH

Day	Time	m	Day	Time	m
1 Su	0318 / 0956 / 1550 / 2228	1.3 / 3.8 / 1.1 / 3.6	16 M	0253 / 0932 / 1524 / 2206	1.1 / 4.0 / 0.6 / 4.0
2 M	0357 / 1037 / 1626 / 2302	1.1 / 3.9 / 1.0 / 3.7	17 Tu	0342 / 1023 / 1612 / 2251	0.8 / 4.3 / 0.4 / 4.1
3 Tu	0433 / 1111 / 1657 / 2332	1.0 / 3.9 / 0.9 / 3.7	18 W	0426 / 1108 / 1655 / 2332	0.7 / 4.4 / 0.3 / 4.2
4 W	0505 / 1140 / 1725 / 2357	0.9 / 3.9 / 0.8 / 3.8	19 Th	0506 / 1149 / 1736	0.5 / 4.5 / 0.3
5 Th	0533 / 1207 / 1751	0.8 / 3.9 / 0.7	20 F	0008 / 0546 / 1228 / 1815	4.2 / 0.5 / 4.5 / 0.4
6 F	0021 / 0600 / 1232 / 1818	3.8 / 0.7 / 3.9 / 0.7	21 Sa	0042 / 0625 / 1307 / 1853	4.1 / 0.5 / 4.4 / 0.6
7 Sa	0048 / 0628 / 1303 / 1846	3.8 / 0.7 / 3.9 / 0.7	22 Su	0117 / 0704 / 1349 / 1933	4.0 / 0.6 / 4.2 / 0.8
8 Su	0119 / 0700 / 1340 / 1920	3.8 / 0.7 / 3.9 / 0.8	23 M	0157 / 0748 / 1436 / 2015	3.9 / 0.8 / 3.9 / 1.1
9 M	0157 / 0737 / 1422 / 2001	3.8 / 0.8 / 3.8 / 0.9	24 Tu	0242 / 0837 / 1531 / 2104	3.8 / 1.1 / 3.7 / 1.4
10 Tu	0242 / 0822 / 1514 / 2047	3.7 / 1.0 / 3.7 / 1.1	25 W	0335 / 0938 / 1638 / 2206	3.6 / 1.3 / 3.4 / 1.6
11 W	0335 / 0917 / 1616 / 2148	3.5 / 1.1 / 3.6 / 1.4	26 Th	0445 / 1057 / 1757 / 2325	3.4 / 1.5 / 3.3 / 1.8
12 Th	0442 / 1030 / 1730 / 2312	3.4 / 1.3 / 3.5 / 1.5	27 F	0610 / 1219 / 1912	3.4 / 1.5 / 3.3
13 F	0607 / 1203 / 1853	3.3 / 1.3 / 3.5	28 Sa	0046 / 0726 / 1337 / 2020	1.7 / 3.4 / 1.4 / 3.4
14 Sa	0041 / 0727 / 1323 / 2008	1.5 / 3.5 / 1.1 / 3.6	29 Su	0157 / 0832 / 1434 / 2117	1.6 / 3.5 / 1.3 / 3.5
15 Su	0154 / 0834 / 1429 / 2111	1.3 / 3.8 / 0.9 / 3.8	30 M	0247 / 0925 / 1517 / 2159	1.4 / 3.6 / 1.1 / 3.6
			31 Tu	0328 / 1006 / 1550 / 2233	1.2 / 3.7 / 1.0 / 3.6

APRIL

Day	Time	m	Day	Time	m
1 W	0403 / 1041 / 1621 / 2259	1.0 / 3.8 / 0.9 / 3.7	16 Th	0406 / 1051 / 1634 / 2312	0.7 / 4.3 / 0.4 / 4.1
2 Th	0433 / 1109 / 1648 / 2325	0.9 / 3.8 / 0.8 / 3.7	17 F	0447 / 1132 / 1713 / 2346	0.6 / 4.3 / 0.5 / 4.1
3 F	0501 / 1136 / 1715 / 2350	0.8 / 3.9 / 0.7 / 3.8	18 Sa	0526 / 1210 / 1751	0.6 / 4.3 / 0.6
4 Sa	0529 / 1205 / 1744	0.7 / 3.9 / 0.7	19 Su	0018 / 0605 / 1248 / 1829	4.1 / 0.6 / 4.2 / 0.8
5 Su	0019 / 0600 / 1239 / 1817	3.9 / 0.6 / 4.0 / 0.7	20 M	0052 / 0646 / 1328 / 1907	4.1 / 0.7 / 4.0 / 0.9
6 M	0055 / 0636 / 1319 / 1856	3.9 / 0.6 / 3.9 / 0.7	21 Tu	0131 / 0730 / 1415 / 1949	4.0 / 0.8 / 3.8 / 1.2
7 Tu	0135 / 0719 / 1407 / 1940	3.9 / 0.7 / 3.9 / 0.9	22 W	0216 / 0819 / 1507 / 2039	3.9 / 1.0 / 3.6 / 1.4
8 W	0223 / 0808 / 1501 / 2030	3.8 / 0.8 / 3.7 / 1.1	23 Th	0308 / 0917 / 1610 / 2138	3.7 / 1.2 / 3.4 / 1.5
9 Th	0321 / 0908 / 1606 / 2136	3.7 / 1.0 / 3.6 / 1.3	24 F	0413 / 1024 / 1720 / 2248	3.5 / 1.3 / 3.3 / 1.7
10 F	0431 / 1028 / 1723 / 2301	3.6 / 1.1 / 3.5 / 1.5	25 Sa	0529 / 1136 / 1831	3.4 / 1.4 / 3.2
11 Sa	0553 / 1151 / 1842	3.5 / 1.1 / 3.5	26 Su	0000 / 0642 / 1243 / 1935	1.7 / 3.4 / 1.4 / 3.3
12 Su	0022 / 0709 / 1307 / 1954	1.5 / 3.6 / 1.0 / 3.6	27 M	0107 / 0747 / 1342 / 2030	1.6 / 3.4 / 1.3 / 3.4
13 M	0133 / 0816 / 1411 / 2056	1.3 / 3.8 / 0.8 / 3.8	28 Tu	0202 / 0842 / 1429 / 2117	1.4 / 3.4 / 1.2 / 3.4
14 Tu	0232 / 0914 / 1505 / 2149	1.1 / 4.0 / 0.6 / 3.9	29 W	0247 / 0925 / 1507 / 2152	1.3 / 3.5 / 1.1 / 3.5
15 W	0321 / 1004 / 1552 / 2234	0.9 / 4.2 / 0.5 / 4.0	30 Th	0324 / 1002 / 1539 / 2223	1.1 / 3.6 / 1.0 / 3.6

To find H.W. Dover subtract 0 h. 35 min.

TIDAL DIFFERENCES PAGE 21:237. TIDAL CURVE PAGE 21:236.

TIDAL STREAMS PAGES 21:238-21:242.

Datum of predictions: 0.20 m. above Ordnance Datum (Dublin) or approx. L.A.T.

NORTH WALL DUBLIN

HIGH & LOW WATER 1992
Lat. 53°21'N. Long. 6°13'W.

GMT   ADD 1 HOUR MARCH 29 — OCTOBER 25 FOR B.S.T.

MAY

Day	Time m	Time m	Time m	Time m		Day	Time m	Time m	Time m	Time m
1 F	0356 1.0	1034 3.7	1610 0.9	2252 3.7		16 Sa	0430 0.8	1115 4.1	1654 0.7	○ 2327 4.0
2 Sa	0427 0.9	1106 3.8	1641 0.8	● 2323 3.9		17 Su	0512 0.8	1154 4.0	1732 0.8	
3 Su	0501 0.7	1143 3.9	1716 0.7			18 M	0001 4.0	0553 0.8	1234 4.0	1810 0.9
4 M	0000 4.0	0539 0.6	1224 4.0	1756 0.7		19 Tu	0036 4.0	0634 0.8	1314 4.0	1849 1.0
5 Tu	0039 4.0	0621 0.5	1309 4.0	1839 0.7		20 W	0114 4.0	0717 0.9	1358 3.7	1931 1.1
6 W	0124 4.0	0709 0.6	1359 3.9	1927 0.9		21 Th	0158 3.9	0804 1.0	1446 3.6	2018 1.2
7 Th	0216 4.0	0804 0.7	1456 3.8	2022 1.0		22 F	0247 3.8	0856 1.1	1539 3.4	2110 1.4
8 F	0314 3.9	0908 0.8	1600 3.7	2128 1.2		23 Sa	0341 3.6	0950 1.2	1637 3.3	2207 1.5
9 Sa	0420 3.8	1020 0.9	1711 3.6	☽ 2242 1.4		24 Su	0441 3.4	1049 1.3	1739 3.2	☾ 2309 1.5
10 Su	0533 3.7	1133 0.9	1822 3.5	2354 1.4		25 M	0547 3.3	1147 1.3	1838 3.2	
11 M	0645 3.8	1242 0.9	1931 3.6			26 Tu	0010 1.5	0649 3.3	1242 1.3	1934 3.3
12 Tu	0103 1.3	0751 3.8	1345 0.8	2033 3.7		27 W	0104 1.5	0745 3.3	1333 1.2	2023 3.3
13 W	0205 1.2	0851 4.0	1440 0.7	2127 3.8		28 Th	0155 1.4	0834 3.4	1418 1.2	2105 3.4
14 Th	0258 1.0	0945 4.0	1528 0.7	2212 3.9		29 F	0239 1.3	0918 3.5	1457 1.1	2143 3.6
15 F	0346 0.9	1033 4.1	1613 0.7	2252 4.0		30 Sa	0318 1.1	1000 3.6	1535 0.9	2221 3.7
						31 Su	0357 0.9	1042 3.8	1614 0.8	2301 3.9

JUNE

Day	Time m	Time m	Time m	Time m		Day	Time m	Time m	Time m	Time m
1 M	0440 0.7	1126 3.9	1655 0.7	● 2343 4.0		16 Tu	0543 0.9	1221 3.8	1754 0.9	
2 Tu	0523 0.5	1211 4.0	1740 0.7			17 W	0027 4.1	0622 0.8	1300 3.8	1832 0.9
3 W	0028 4.2	0611 0.4	1300 4.0	1827 0.7		18 Th	0103 4.0	0703 0.8	1340 3.7	1913 1.0
4 Th	0116 4.2	0703 0.4	1352 4.0	1917 0.8		19 F	0142 4.0	0744 0.9	1420 3.6	1954 1.0
5 F	0206 4.2	0758 0.4	1447 3.9	2012 0.9		20 Sa	0222 3.9	0826 0.9	1503 3.5	2037 1.1
6 Sa	0301 4.1	0857 0.5	1545 3.8	2111 1.1		21 Su	0305 3.7	0911 1.0	1548 3.4	2124 1.3
7 Su	0402 4.0	1000 0.7	1648 3.6	☽ 2216 1.2		22 M	0350 3.5	0957 1.1	1637 3.3	2213 1.4
8 M	0506 3.9	1105 0.8	1754 3.6	2322 1.3		23 Tu	0440 3.4	1047 1.2	1729 3.2	☾ 2306 1.5
9 Tu	0615 3.8	1210 0.9	1900 3.6			24 W	0536 3.3	1140 1.3	1825 3.2	
10 W	0029 1.3	0723 3.8	1314 0.9	2002 3.6		25 Th	0003 1.5	0636 3.3	1235 1.3	1923 3.3
11 Th	0135 1.3	0826 3.8	1412 1.0	2100 3.7		26 F	0100 1.5	0738 3.3	1328 1.3	2016 3.4
12 F	0237 1.2	0925 3.8	1505 1.0	2149 3.8		27 Sa	0155 1.4	0837 3.4	1419 1.2	2107 3.5
13 Sa	0331 1.1	1016 3.9	1552 1.0	2234 3.9		28 Su	0247 1.2	0931 3.6	1508 1.1	2155 3.7
14 Su	0419 1.0	1102 3.9	1635 1.0	2313 4.0		29 M	0336 0.9	1023 3.8	1555 0.9	2241 4.0
15 M	0502 0.9	1143 3.8	1715 0.9	○ 2350 4.0		30 Tu	0426 0.7	1112 3.9	1641 0.8	● 2327 4.2

JULY

Day	Time m	Time m	Time m	Time m		Day	Time m	Time m	Time m	Time m
1 W	0513 0.5	1200 4.1	1727 0.7			16 Th	0012 4.1	0607 0.8	1242 3.7	1814 0.9
2 Th	0015 4.3	0603 0.3	1249 4.1	1815 0.6		17 F	0048 4.1	0642 0.8	1316 3.7	1849 0.9
3 F	0102 4.4	0652 0.2	1338 4.1	1903 0.6		18 Sa	0120 4.0	0716 0.8	1348 3.7	1924 0.9
4 Sa	0151 4.4	0744 0.3	1427 4.0	1954 0.7		19 Su	0152 3.9	0751 0.9	1423 3.6	2001 1.0
5 Su	0242 4.3	0837 0.4	1521 3.9	2046 0.9		20 M	0227 3.8	0826 0.9	1500 3.5	2036 1.1
6 M	0335 4.2	0932 0.6	1616 3.7	2143 1.1		21 Tu	0307 3.7	0903 1.0	1542 3.4	2117 1.2
7 Tu	0434 4.0	1033 0.8	1716 3.6	☽ 2245 1.3		22 W	0350 3.5	0945 1.2	1628 3.4	☾ 2204 1.4
8 W	0540 3.8	1134 1.0	1821 3.5	2354 1.4		23 Th	0441 3.4	1035 1.3	1723 3.3	2302 1.5
9 Th	0652 3.7	1241 1.2	1927 3.5			24 F	0542 3.3	1139 1.4	1827 3.3	
10 F	0107 1.5	0801 3.6	1345 1.3	2030 3.6		25 Sa	0012 1.5	0652 3.3	1248 1.4	1934 3.4
11 Sa	0219 1.4	0907 3.6	1443 1.2	2128 3.7		26 Su	0121 1.4	0806 3.4	1354 1.3	2037 3.6
12 Su	0319 1.3	1004 3.7	1534 1.2	2217 3.9		27 M	0226 1.2	0911 3.6	1450 1.2	2134 3.8
13 M	0409 1.1	1052 3.7	1619 1.1	2259 4.0		28 Tu	0322 0.9	1007 3.8	1542 1.0	2224 4.0
14 Tu	0452 1.0	1132 3.7	1659 1.0	○ 2337 4.0		29 W	0414 0.6	1059 4.0	1630 0.8	● 2312 4.3
15 W	0530 0.9	1208 3.7	1737 0.9			30 Th	0503 0.3	1147 4.1	1715 0.6	2358 4.5
						31 F	0550 0.2	1232 4.2	1800 0.5	

AUGUST

Day	Time m	Time m	Time m	Time m		Day	Time m	Time m	Time m	Time m
1 Sa	0043 4.6	0635 0.1	1317 4.2	1843 0.5		16 Su	0052 4.0	0642 0.8	1314 3.7	1852 0.8
2 Su	0128 4.6	0723 0.2	1402 4.1	1930 0.6		17 M	0119 3.9	0712 0.8	1344 3.7	1923 0.9
3 M	0216 4.5	0811 0.4	1449 4.0	2018 0.8		18 Tu	0151 3.9	0741 0.9	1419 3.7	1955 1.0
4 Tu	0305 4.3	0900 0.7	1538 3.8	2111 1.0		19 W	0230 3.8	0815 1.0	1500 3.6	2033 1.1
5 W	0400 4.0	0956 1.0	1634 3.7	2212 1.3		20 Th	0314 3.7	0857 1.1	1548 3.5	2121 1.3
6 Th	0506 3.7	1058 1.3	1739 3.6	2323 1.5		21 F	0406 3.5	0948 1.3	1642 3.4	☾ 2221 1.4
7 F	0622 3.5	1207 1.5	1849 3.5			22 Sa	0508 3.4	1057 1.5	1749 3.4	2342 1.5
8 Sa	0045 1.6	0738 3.5	1320 1.5	1959 3.6		23 Su	0625 3.4	1222 1.5	1904 3.4	
9 Su	0205 1.5	0853 3.5	1425 1.5	2105 3.7		24 M	0103 1.4	0747 3.5	1337 1.4	2015 3.6
10 M	0308 1.3	0955 3.5	1517 1.3	2200 3.9		25 Tu	0212 1.1	0857 3.7	1437 1.2	2115 3.9
11 Tu	0357 1.2	1041 3.6	1602 1.2	2244 4.0		26 W	0310 0.8	0955 3.9	1529 1.0	2207 4.1
12 W	0437 1.0	1119 3.7	1641 1.0	2320 4.0		27 Th	0400 0.5	1045 4.1	1616 0.7	2255 4.4
13 Th	0512 0.9	1150 3.7	1716 0.9	○ 2353 4.1		28 F	0447 0.3	1130 4.2	1658 0.6	● 2339 4.5
14 F	0543 0.8	1219 3.7	1750 0.8			29 Sa	0532 0.2	1212 4.3	1740 0.5	
15 Sa	0024 4.0	0612 0.8	1248 3.7	1821 0.8		30 Su	0022 4.6	0614 0.2	1253 4.3	1822 0.5
						31 M	0104 4.6	0657 0.3	1333 4.2	1906 0.5

GENERAL — Streams set roughly N. and S. through Dublin Bay. Streams set across the ent. to Liffey. In Port of Dublin streams are weak. Heavy rains increase ebb sometimes overcome ingoing flood stream. S. gales cause high tides in Liffey, and N. gales low tides. Streams in St. George's Channel turn about 1½ h. later than those inshore.

DUBLIN NORTH WALL 21:235

Lat. 53°21′N. Long. 6°13′W.

GMT

HIGH & LOW WATER 1992

ADD 1 HOUR MARCH 29 — OCTOBER 25 FOR B.S.T.

SEPTEMBER

Day	Time	m	Time	m		Day	Time	m	Time	m
1 Tu	0149	4.5	0741	0.5		16 W	0121	3.9	0704	0.8
	1415	4.1	1951	0.7			1347	3.8	1924	0.9
2 W	0236	4.2	0827	0.8		17 Th	0201	3.8	0741	1.0
	1501	3.9	2042	1.0			1427	3.7	2005	1.0
3 Th	0329	3.9	0919	1.2		18 F	0247	3.7	0825	1.1
	1553	3.8	☽ 2142	1.3			1517	3.6	2054	1.2
4 F	0435	3.6	1021	1.5		19 Sa	0343	3.6	0918	1.4
	1658	3.6	2258	1.5			1533	3.5	(2159	1.3
5 Sa	0556	3.4	1136	1.6		20	0451	3.4	1033	1.6
	1814	3.5					1726	3.5	2327	1.4
6 Su	0025	1.6	0717	3.3		21 M	0612	3.4	1204	1.6
	1255	1.7	1928	3.6			1843	3.5		
7 M	0148	1.5	0836	3.4		22 Tu	0049	1.2	0734	3.5
	1404	1.6	2039	3.7			1320	1.5	1955	3.7
8 Tu	0250	1.3	0936	3.5		23 W	0157	1.0	0842	3.7
	1457	1.4	2136	3.8			1422	1.2	2056	4.0
9 W	0336	1.1	1023	3.6		24 Th	0254	0.7	0939	3.9
	1541	1.2	2220	3.9			1512	1.0	2149	4.2
10 Th	0413	1.0	1058	3.7		25 F	0343	0.5	1027	4.1
	1617	1.1	2255	4.0			1557	0.8	2235	4.4
11 F	0444	0.9	1125	3.7		26 Sa	0428	0.3	1111	4.2
	1651	0.9	2326	4.0			1641	0.6	● 2319	4.5
12 Sa	0512	0.9	1150	3.8		27 Su	0511	0.3	1150	4.3
	1722	0.9	○ 2354	4.0			1722	0.5		
13 Su	0540	0.8	1215	3.8		28 M	0001	4.6	0551	0.3
	1751	0.8					1227	4.3	1803	0.5
14 M	0019	4.0	0605	0.8		29 Tu	0042	4.5	0632	0.5
	1241	3.8	1819	0.8			1304	4.2	1845	0.6
15 Tu	0048	4.0	0634	0.8		30 W	0124	4.3	0713	0.7
	1310	3.8	1849	0.8			1344	4.1	1930	0.8

OCTOBER

Day	Time	m	Time	m		Day	Time	m	Time	m
1 Th	0212	4.1	0757	1.0		16 F	0142	3.9	0717	1.0
	1429	4.0	2019	1.0			1406	3.9	1947	0.9
2 F	0304	3.8	0847	1.3		17 Sa	0233	3.7	0804	1.1
	1519	3.8	2119	1.3			1458	3.8	2042	1.1
3 Sa	0410	3.5	0948	1.6		18 Su	0332	3.6	0901	1.4
	1623	3.7	☽ 2234	1.5			1559	3.7	2153	1.2
4 Su	0529	3.4	1104	1.8		19 M	0442	3.5	1019	1.5
	1739	3.6	2357	1.5			1709	3.6	(2315	1.2
5 M	0649	3.3	1222	1.8		20 Tu	0601	3.5	1144	1.6
	1853	3.6					1825	3.7		
6 Tu	0114	1.4	0805	3.4		21 W	0031	1.1	0717	3.6
	1334	1.7	2002	3.6			1257	1.5	1934	3.8
7 W	0216	1.3	0905	3.5		22 Th	0137	0.9	0823	3.7
	1429	1.5	2100	3.7			1359	1.3	2036	4.0
8 Th	0303	1.2	0950	3.6		23 F	0233	0.7	0918	3.9
	1512	1.3	2146	3.8			1453	1.1	2129	4.2
9 F	0339	1.1	1026	3.7		24 Sa	0232	0.5	1007	4.1
	1549	1.1	2223	3.8			1539	0.9	2217	4.4
10 Sa	0410	1.0	1054	3.7		25 Su	0407	0.5	1049	4.2
	1621	1.0	2254	3.9			1623	0.7	● 2302	4.4
11 Su	0437	0.9	1118	3.8		26 M	0449	0.5	1129	4.2
	1651	0.9	○ 2322	3.9			1705	0.6	2343	4.4
12 M	0505	0.9	1143	3.9		27 Tu	0530	0.5	1204	4.3
	1720	0.9	2350	3.9			1747	0.6		
13 Tu	0532	0.8	1211	3.9		28 W	0024	4.3	0610	0.7
	1751	0.8					1241	4.3	1829	0.7
14 W	0021	3.9	0601	0.8		29 Th	0106	4.2	0650	0.9
	1243	4.0	1824	0.8			1320	4.2	1914	0.8
15 Th	0059	3.9	0636	0.8		30 F	0152	4.0	0734	1.1
	1321	3.9	1903	0.8			1404	4.1	2004	1.0
						31 Sa	0243	3.7	0822	1.4
							1454	3.9	2101	1.2

NOVEMBER

Day	Time	m	Time	m		Day	Time	m	Time	m
1 Su	0345	3.5	0919	1.6		16 M	0324	3.7	0850	1.3
	1553	3.8	2206	1.4			1545	3.9	2142	0.9
2 M	0454	3.3	1027	1.7		17 Tu	0430	3.6	1000	1.4
	1702	3.6	☽ 2316	1.4			1651	3.9	(2254	1.0
3 Tu	0607	3.3	1139	1.7		18 W	0542	3.6	1116	1.5
	1812	3.5					1801	3.9		
4 W	0025	1.4	0717	3.3		19 Th	0003	1.0	0653	3.6
	1248	1.7	1919	3.5			1211	1.4	1910	3.9
5 Th	0127	1.4	0818	3.4		20 F	0109	0.9	0758	3.7
	1347	1.6	2016	3.6			1333	1.3	2012	4.0
6 F	0216	1.3	0905	3.5		21 Sa	0208	0.8	0854	3.9
	1434	1.4	2104	3.6			1432	1.2	2110	4.1
7 Sa	0256	1.2	0945	3.6		22 Su	0300	0.7	0945	4.0
	1514	1.3	2143	3.7			1522	1.0	2200	4.2
8 Su	0331	1.1	1016	3.7		23 M	0346	0.7	1030	4.1
	1549	1.1	2219	3.8			1610	0.9	2248	4.2
9 M	0402	1.0	1044	3.8		24 Tu	0431	0.7	1111	4.2
	1621	1.0	2251	3.8			1654	0.8	● 2330	4.2
10 Tu	0431	0.9	1113	3.9		25 W	0512	0.8	1147	4.2
	1654	0.9	○ 2325	3.9			1736	0.8		
11 W	0502	0.9	1146	4.0		26 Th	0011	4.1	0553	0.9
	1727	0.8					1224	4.3	1819	0.8
12 Th	0003	4.0	0539	0.8		27 F	0052	4.0	0632	1.0
	1224	4.1	1807	0.7			1303	4.2	1902	0.9
13 F	0045	4.0	0618	0.8		28 Sa	0135	3.9	0714	1.1
	1249	4.1	1849	0.7			1344	4.1	1948	1.0
14 Sa	0131	3.9	0702	0.9		29 Su	0222	3.7	0759	1.2
	1352	4.1	1938	0.8			1430	4.0	2036	1.1
15 Su	0223	3.8	0751	1.1		30 M	0312	3.5	0849	1.4
	1444	4.0	2036	0.8			1522	3.8	2129	1.2

DECEMBER

Day	Time	m	Time	m		Day	Time	m	Time	m
1 Tu	0410	3.4	0945	1.5		16 W	0406	3.7	0935	1.2
	1619	3.7	2227	1.3			1627	4.0	(2224	0.9
2 W	0513	3.3	1047	1.6		17 Th	0512	3.6	1042	1.7
	1722	3.5	☽ 2326	1.4			1733	3.9	2330	1.0
3 Th	0617	3.3	1150	1.7		18 F	0621	3.6	1153	1.7
	1825	3.4					1843	3.9		
4 F	0025	1.4	0719	3.3		19 Sa	0038	1.0	0727	3.7
	1250	1.6	1924	3.4			1304	1.4	1949	3.9
5 Sa	0120	1.4	0812	3.4		20 Su	0141	1.0	0829	3.8
	1345	1.5	2016	3.5			1411	1.3	2051	4.0
6 Su	0208	1.3	0857	3.5		21 M	0239	1.0	0924	3.9
	1433	1.4	2103	3.6			1510	1.2	2148	4.0
7 M	0250	1.2	0936	3.6		22 Tu	0329	1.0	1013	4.0
	1514	1.3	2143	3.7			1600	1.0	2237	4.0
8 Tu	0328	1.1	1012	3.8		23 W	0416	1.0	1055	4.1
	1553	1.1	2224	3.8			1645	0.9	2322	4.0
9 W	0404	1.0	1048	3.9		24 Th	0458	0.9	1134	4.2
	1631	0.9	○ 2305	3.9			1727	0.9	●	
10 Th	0441	1.0	1126	4.1		25 F	0001	4.0	0537	0.9
	1711	0.7	2347	4.0			1211	4.2	1807	0.8
11 F	0522	0.9	1207	4.2		26 Sa	0039	3.9	0617	0.9
	1753	0.6					1249	4.2	1846	0.8
12 Sa	0032	4.0	0604	0.8		27 Su	0116	3.8	0655	1.0
	1252	4.3	1839	0.5			1326	4.1	1926	0.9
13 Su	0120	4.0	0649	0.8		28 M	0155	3.7	0734	1.1
	1338	4.3	1928	0.5			1405	4.0	2006	1.0
14 M	0211	3.9	0738	0.9		29 Tu	0236	3.6	0815	1.2
	1430	4.2	2022	0.6			1447	3.9	2049	1.1
15 Tu	0307	3.8	0833	1.1		30 W	0321	3.5	0900	1.3
	1525	4.1	2121	0.7			1534	3.7	2134	1.2
						31 Th	0410	3.4	0950	1.5
							1624	3.5	2224	1.4

RATE AND SET — Outside Dublin Bay; N. set –0600 until H.W. Dublin; maximum 3¼ kn. S. set H.W. until +0600 Dublin; maximum 4¼ kn. Inside Dublin Bay; round Dalkey Isle, S. shore; between Rosebeg bank and N. shore — only part into Liffey. Position ¾ M. NNE. of Kish Lt. Ho., S. going begins –0105 Dublin, Spring rate 2 kn.; N. going begins +0505 Dublin, Spring rate 2 kn.

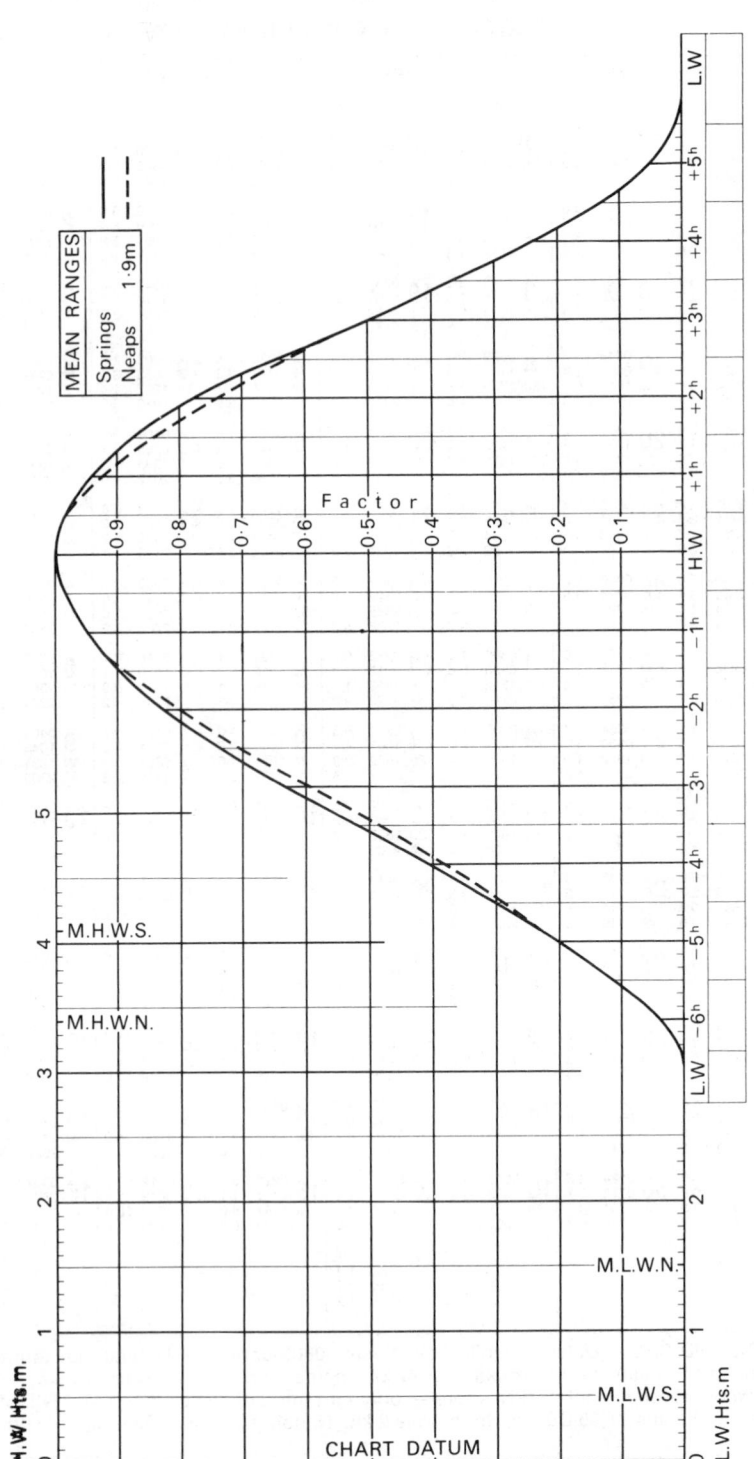

DUBLIN

MEAN SPRING AND NEAP CURVES

Springs occur 1 day after New and Full Moon.

MEAN RANGES
Springs
Neaps 1·9m

Factor

0·9 0·8 0·7 0·6 0·5 0·4 0·3 0·2 0·1

M.H.W.S.
M.H.W.N.
M.L.W.N.
M.L.W.S.

CHART DATUM

H.W.Hts.m.
L.W.Hts.m.

PLACE	TIME DIFFERENCES				HEIGHT DIFFERENCES (Metres)			
	High Water		Low Water		MHWS	MHWN	MLWN	MLWS
DUBLIN (NORTH WALL)	0000 and 1200	0700 and 1900	0000 and 1200	0500 and 1700	4.1	3.4	1.5	0.5
IRELAND								
Tuskar Rock	−0457	−0627	−0601	−0517	−1.5	−1.4	–	–
Rosslare Harbour	−0440	−0710	−0710	−0440	−2.2	−2.0	−0.7	−0.3
*Wexford Harbour	−0350	−0720	−0725	−0325	−2.4	−2.0	−1.0	−0.3
Blackwater Head	−0441	−0601	−0540	−0500	−2.5	−2.2	–	–
Pollduff	−0321	−0431	−0414	−0340	−2.9	−2.6	–	–
Courtown	−0300	−0400	−0345	−0315	−3.0	−2.8	–	–
Arklow.......................	−0215	−0255	−0245	−0225	−2.4	−2.0	−0.3	+0.1
Mizen Head	−0123	−0151	−0144	−0130	−2.0	−1.7	–	–
Wicklow....................	−0035	−0047	−0044	−0038	−1.4	−1.1	−0.6	0.0
Greystones	−0008	−0008	−0008	−0008	−0.5	−0.4	–	–
Dun Laoghaire	−0006	−0001	−0002	−0003	0.0	0.0	0.0	+0.1
Dublin Bar	−0006	−0001	−0002	−0003	0.0	0.0	0.0	+0.1
Howth	−0005	−0015	−0005	+0005	0.0	0.0	−0.3	0.0
Malahide	−0019	−0013	+0014	+0006	+0.1	+0.1	0.0	0.0
Balbriggan	−0021	−0015	+0010	+0002	+0.3	+0.2	–	–
River Boyne								
Bar	−0025	−0015	+0110	0000	+0.4	+0.3	–	–
Dunany Point	−0028	−0018	−0008	−0006	+0.7	+0.9	–	–
Dunalk								
Soldiers Point	−0010	−0010	0000	+0045	+1.0	+0.8	+0.1	−0.1
NORTHERN IRELAND								
Carlingford Lough								
Cranfield Point	−0027	+0011	+0017	−0007	+0.7	+0.9	+0.3	+0.2
Warrenpoint	−0020	−0010	+0040	+0040	+0.1	+0.9	+0.1	+0.2
Newry (Victoria Lock) ...	−0010	−0010	+0040	Dries	+1.1	+1.0	+0.1	Dries

*Wexford. Bar and channel marked. Pilots essential. Phone Wexford 33205

Refer to predictions on pages 21:233-21:235

TIDAL STREAMS
FOR
NORTH AND SOUTH IRELAND

These 13 charts show tidal streams at hourly intervals commencing 6 h. before and ending 6 h. after H.W. Dover. For Dover H.W. Times see pages 21:41-21:43.

The thicker the arrows the stronger tidal streams they indicate; the thinner arrows show rates and position of weaker streams. The figures shown against the arrows, e.g. 19.34 indicate a mean neap rate of 1.9 knots and a mean spring rate of 3.4 knots approximately.

The following charts are produced from portion(s) of BA Tidal Stream Atlases with the sanction of the Controller, H.M. Stationery Office and of the Hydrographer of the Navy.

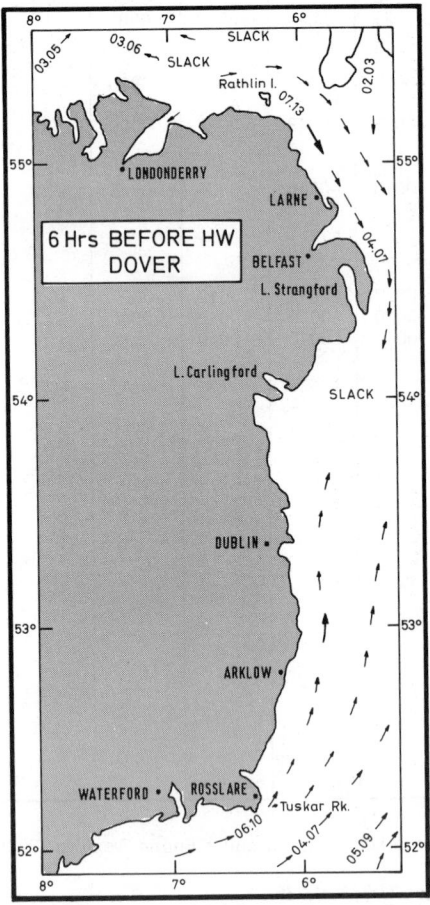

NORTH AND SOUTH IRELAND TIDAL STREAM CHARTS

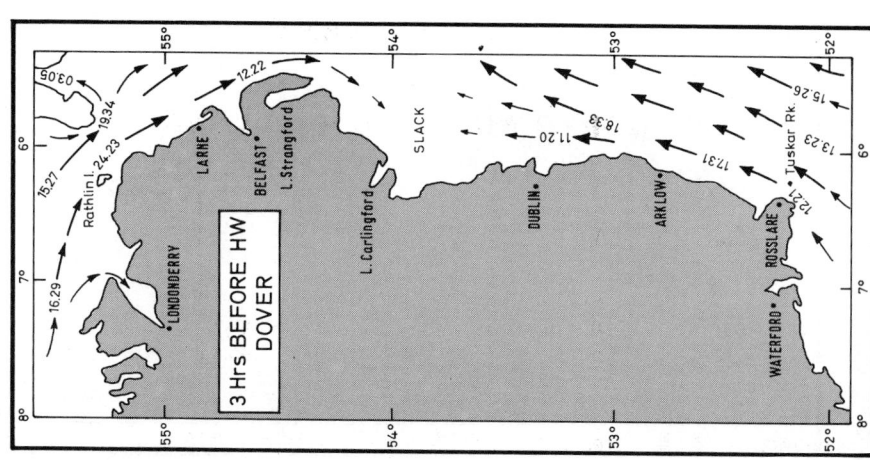

3 Hrs BEFORE HW DOVER

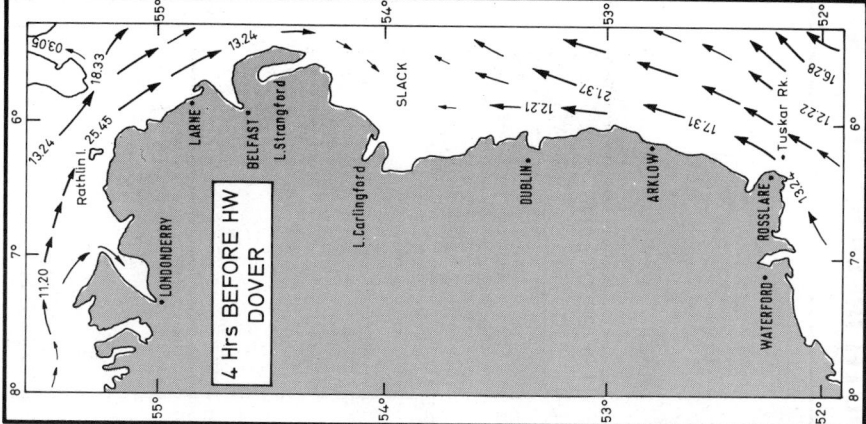

4 Hrs BEFORE HW DOVER

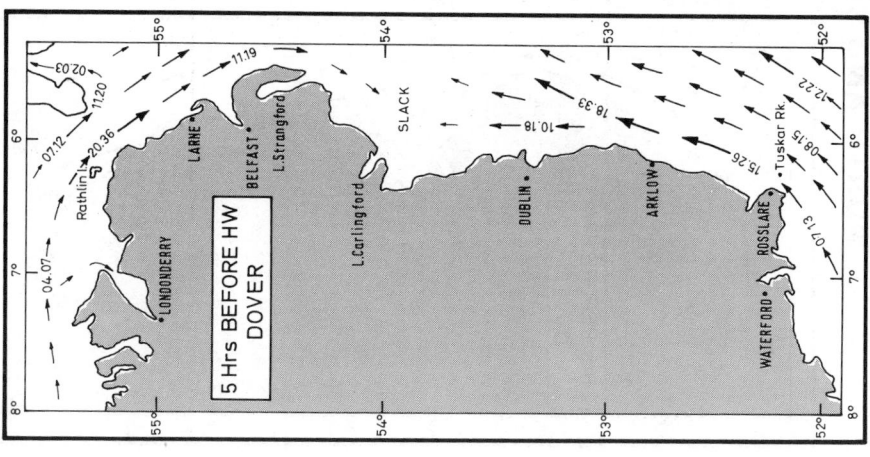

5 Hrs BEFORE HW DOVER

NORTH AND SOUTH IRELAND TIDAL STREAM CHARTS

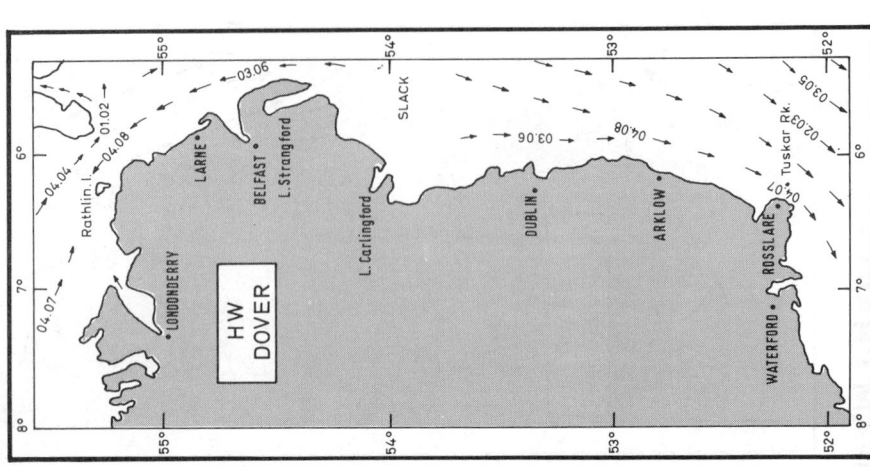

HW DOVER

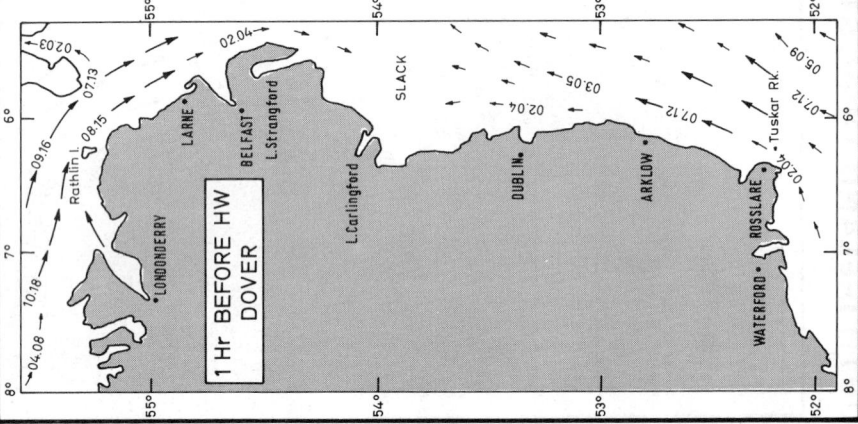

1 Hr BEFORE HW DOVER

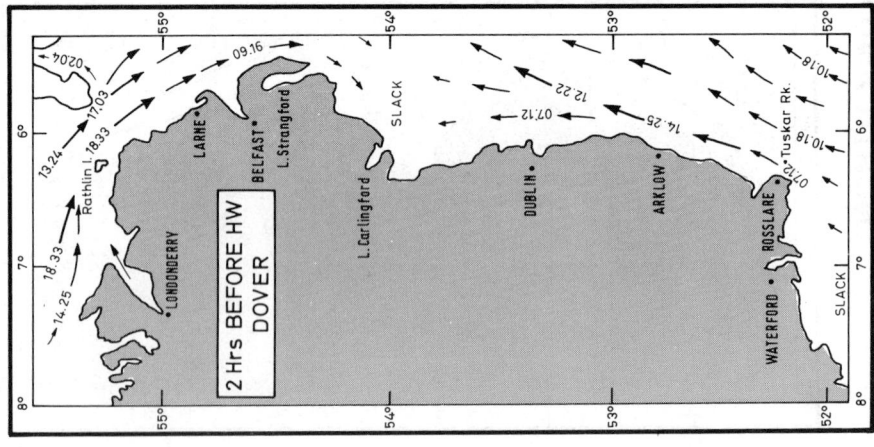

2 Hrs BEFORE HW DOVER

NORTH AND SOUTH IRELAND TIDAL STREAM CHARTS

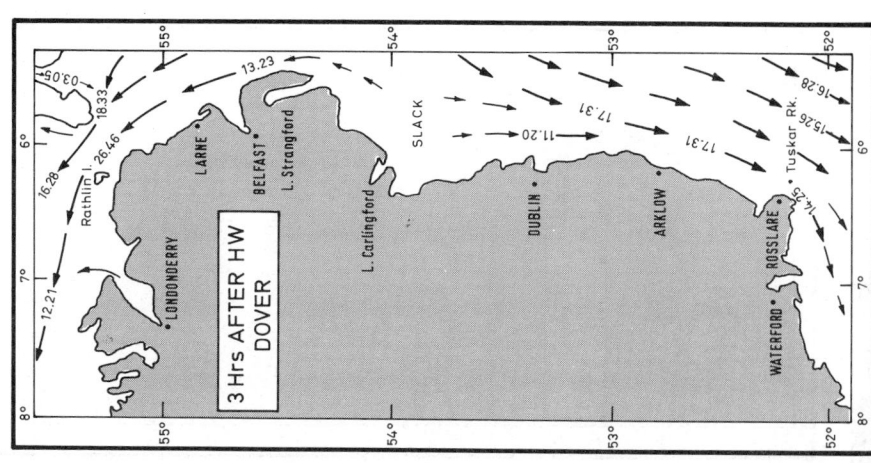

3 Hrs AFTER HW DOVER

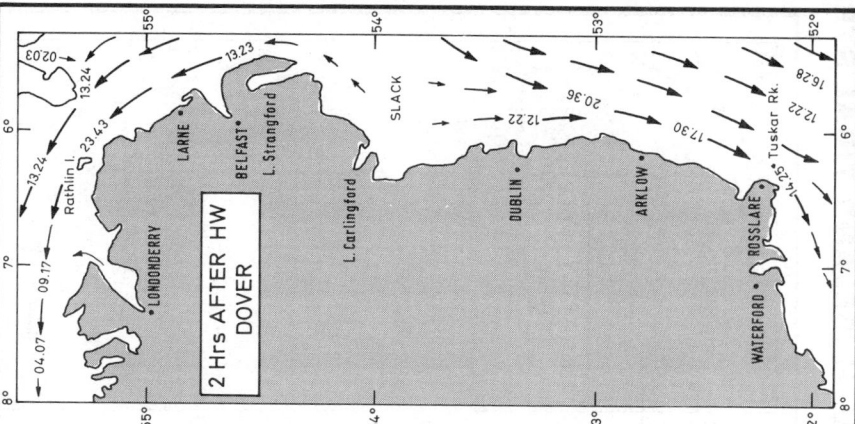

2 Hrs AFTER HW DOVER

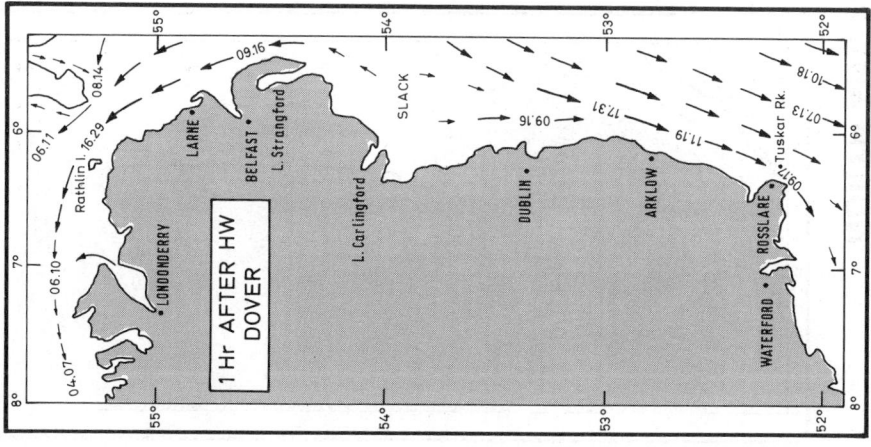

1 Hr AFTER HW DOVER

NORTH AND SOUTH IRELAND TIDAL STREAM CHARTS

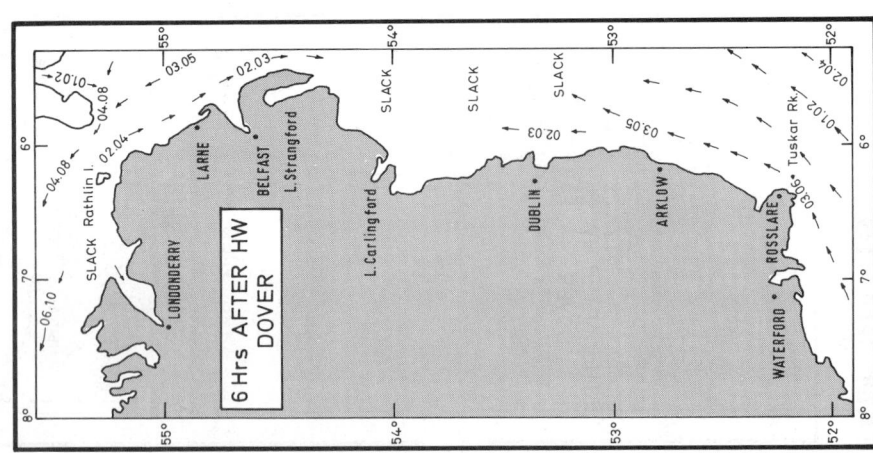

6 Hrs AFTER HW DOVER

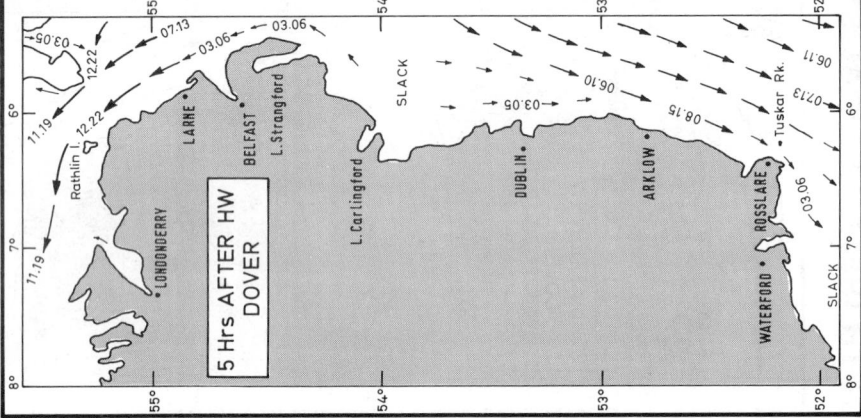

5 Hrs AFTER HW DOVER

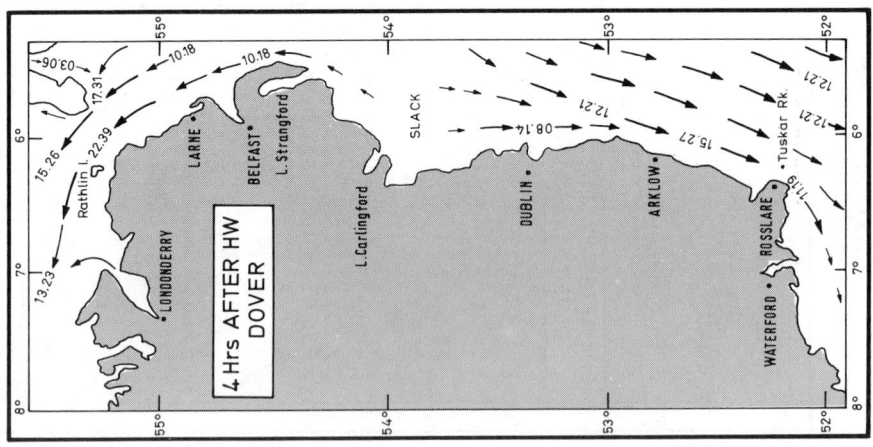

4 Hrs AFTER HW DOVER

BELFAST IRELAND (North East)   21:243

HIGH & LOW WATER 1992   Lat. 54°36′N. Long. 5°55′W.

GMT   ADD 1 HOUR MARCH 29 — OCTOBER 25 FOR B.S.T.

JANUARY

	Time	m		Time	m
1 W	0206 0825 1440 2043	0·8 3·1 0·8 3·2	16 Th	0104 0717 1335 1947	1·0 3·1 1·1 3·1
2 Th	0258 0912 1531 2134	0·9 3·2 0·8 3·2	17 F	0213 0825 1444 2056	1·0 3·2 0·9 3·2
3 F	0345 0956 1616 2219	0·9 3·3 0·7 3·2	18 Sa	0315 0924 1543 2157	0·8 3·4 0·7 3·3
4 Sa	0424 1037 1657 ● 2258	0·8 0·7 0·7 3·2	19 Su	0410 1017 1637 ○ 2252	0·7 3·6 0·5 3·4
5 Su	0501 1113 1733 2334	0·8 3·5 0·6 3·2	20 M	0501 1108 1726 2343	0·6 3·7 0·3 3·4
6 M	0533 1147 1807	0·8 3·5 0·6	21 Tu	0549 1156 1812	0·5 3·8 0·1
7 Tu	0008 0604 1219 1838	3·2 3·5 3·5 0·6	22 W	0031 0720 1242 1859	3·4 0·4 3·9 0·1
8 W	0041 0635 1252 1910	3·2 3·5 3·5 0·6	23 Th	0117 0720 1328 1945	3·3 0·4 3·8 0·1
9 Th	0114 0710 1324 1945	3·2 0·7 3·5 0·6	24 F	0204 0806 1416 2033	3·2 0·5 3·7 0·3
10 F	0149 0747 1359 2023	3·2 0·6 3·5 0·7	25 Sa	0251 0854 1508 2122	3·1 0·6 3·5 0·5
11 Sa	0229 0827 1439 2105	3·2 0·7 3·4 0·7	26 Su	0343 0949 1603 ☾ 2219	3·0 0·8 3·4 0·7
12 Su	0312 0914 1524 2153	3·1 0·9 3·3 0·8	27 M	0442 1051 1706 2323	2·9 0·9 3·2 0·9
13 M	0402 1006 1616 ☽ 2248	3·1 1·1 3·2 0·9	28 Tu	0547 1204 1814	2·9 1·0 3·0
14 Tu	0459 1108 1719 2353	3·0 1·2 3·1 1·0	29 W	0034 0653 1317 1920	1·0 2·9 1·0 3·0
15 W	0607 1219 1831	3·0 1·2 3·1	30 Th	0142 0754 1422 2022	1·0 3·0 0·9 3·0
			31 F	0240 0849 1515 2115	1·0 3·1 0·8 3·0

FEBRUARY

	Time	m		Time	m
1 Sa	0328 0936 1602 2202	0·9 3·2 0·7 3·0	16 Su	0303 0908 1529 2149	0·9 3·4 0·6 3·2
2 Su	0409 1019 1641 2242	0·9 3·3 0·6 3·1	17 M	0357 1002 1621 2242	0·7 3·6 0·4 3·4
3 M	0444 1057 1716 ● 2316	0·8 3·4 0·5 3·1	18 Tu	0445 1051 1708 ○ 2329	0·5 3·7 0·2 3·4
4 Tu	0515 1129 1746 2347	0·7 3·4 0·5 3·2	19 W	0530 1137 1753	0·4 3·8 0·1
5 W	0543 1158 1814	0·6 3·4 0·5	20 Th	0012 0614 1222 1835	3·4 0·4 3·9 0·1
6 Th	0017 0612 1227 1843	3·2 0·6 3·5 0·5	21 F	0043 0656 1306 1919	3·4 0·4 3·8 0·2
7 F	0046 0626 1256 1914	3·2 0·6 3·5 0·5	22 Sa	0134 0738 1351 2001	3·3 0·4 3·7 0·4
8 Sa	0119 0720 1330 1949	3·3 0·6 3·5 0·5	23 Su	0216 0822 1439 2046	3·2 0·6 3·5 0·6
9 Su	0155 0758 1408 2029	3·3 0·7 3·4 0·6	24 M	0303 0911 1531 2136	3·1 0·7 3·3 0·8
10 M	0236 0840 1451 2115	3·2 0·8 3·3 0·8	25 Tu	0355 1010 1631 ☾ 2237	3·0 0·9 3·1 1·1
11 Tu	0324 0931 1543 2209	3·1 0·9 3·2 0·9	26 W	0458 1125 1740 2353	2·9 1·0 2·9 1·2
12 W	0420 1031 1648 2316	3·1 1·1 3·1 1·1	27 Th	0610 1246 1852	2·8 1·0 2·8
13 Th	0530 1149 1808	3·0 1·2 3·0	28 F	0110 0719 1357 1957	1·2 2·9 0·9 2·8
14 F	0039 0653 1316 1934	1·2 3·0 1·1 3·0	29 Sa	0213 0819 1453 2053	1·1 3·0 0·8 2·9
15 Sa	0158 0805 1430 2049	1·1 3·2 0·9 3·1			

MARCH

	Time	m		Time	m
1 Su	0304 0910 1538 2139	1·0 3·1 0·7 2·9	16 M	0247 0847 1511 2135	0·9 3·3 0·5 3·2
2 M	0345 0955 1617 2219	0·9 3·2 0·6 3·0	17 Tu	0339 0942 1600 2224	0·7 3·5 0·3 3·3
3 Tu	0419 1031 1649 2252	0·7 3·2 0·5 3·1	18 W	0426 1030 1645 ○ 2308	0·5 3·7 0·2 3·4
4 W	0449 1104 1718 ● 2322	0·6 3·3 0·5 3·1	19 Th	0508 1116 1729 2347	0·4 3·8 0·1 3·5
5 Th	0519 1132 1746 2349	0·6 3·3 0·4 3·2	20 F	0550 1158 1810	0·3 3·8 0·2
6 F	0549 1158 1814	0·5 3·4 0·4	21 Sa	0025 0631 1242 1849	3·4 0·4 3·7 0·3
7 Sa	0018 0619 1229 1845	3·3 0·5 3·4 0·4	22 Su	0103 0712 1324 1930	3·4 0·4 3·6 0·5
8 Su	0050 0655 1303 1920	3·3 0·5 3·4 0·5	23 M	0142 0754 1411 2012	3·3 0·5 3·4 0·7
9 M	0127 0733 1342 2001	3·3 0·6 3·3 0·6	24 Tu	0226 0840 1500 2058	3·2 0·7 3·2 1·0
10 Tu	0208 0816 1429 2046	3·3 0·7 3·3 0·8	25 W	0315 0935 1557 2153	3·1 0·9 3·0 1·2
11 W	0257 0907 1524 2142	3·2 0·8 3·1 1·0	26 Th	0414 1045 1705 ☾ 2305	3·0 1·0 2·8 1·3
12 Th	0356 1010 1633 ☽ 2254	3·1 1·0 3·0 1·1	27 F	0523 1207 1815	2·9 1·0 2·7
13 F	0508 1133 1758	3·0 1·0 2·9	28 Sa	0025 0635 1319 1921	1·3 2·9 1·0 2·7
14 Sa	0025 0629 1303 1926	1·2 3·0 1·0 2·9	29 Su	0133 0738 1415 2018	1·2 2·9 0·8 2·8
15 Su	0144 0745 1413 2037	1·1 3·2 0·7 3·1	30 M	0226 0833 1501 2105	1·0 3·0 0·7 2·9
			31 Tu	0308 0918 1539 2145	0·9 3·0 0·6 3·0

APRIL

	Time	m		Time	m
1 W	0345 0957 1614 2219	0·8 3·1 0·5 3·0	16 Th	0403 1007 1621 2242	0·5 3·6 0·3 3·4
2 Th	0419 1030 1645 2251	0·7 3·2 0·5 3·1	17 F	0445 1054 1704 ○ 2322	0·4 3·7 0·3 3·4
3 F	0451 1101 1715 ● 2320	0·6 3·2 0·4 3·2	18 Sa	0527 1136 1743 2358	0·4 3·6 0·4 3·5
4 Sa	0522 1132 1746 2351	0·5 3·3 0·4 3·3	19 Su	0608 1218 1822	0·4 3·6 0·5
5 Su	0557 1205 1819	0·5 3·3 0·4	20 M	0036 0648 1302 1902	3·5 0·5 3·4 0·7
6 M	0027 0634 1243 1857	3·3 0·4 3·3 0·5	21 Tu	0114 0730 1345 1942	3·4 0·6 3·3 0·8
7 Tu	0106 0716 1327 1940	3·3 0·4 3·3 0·6	22 W	0157 0815 1433 2025	3·3 0·7 3·1 1·0
8 W	0149 0802 1418 2029	3·3 0·5 3·2 0·8	23 Th	0244 0907 1527 2115	3·2 0·8 2·9 1·1
9 Th	0242 0857 1517 2129	3·1 0·7 3·0 1·0	24 F	0338 1007 1626 2216	3·1 0·9 2·7 1·2
10 F	0342 1003 1628 ☽ 2245	3·1 0·8 2·9 1·1	25 Sa	0438 1116 1730 2326	3·0 1·0 2·7 1·3
11 Sa	0454 1125 1754	3·1 0·8 2·8	26 Su	0543 1224 1834	2·9 0·9 2·7
12 Su	0012 0611 1246 1914	1·1 3·1 0·7 2·9	27 M	0035 0646 1321 1930	1·2 2·9 0·9 2·7
13 M	0126 0723 1352 2020	1·0 3·2 0·6 3·0	28 Tu	0133 0742 1411 2019	1·1 2·9 0·9 2·8
14 Tu	0225 0825 1447 2115	0·8 3·3 0·4 3·2	29 W	0222 0830 1453 2103	1·0 2·9 0·7 2·9
15 W	0317 0918 1536 2202	0·7 3·5 0·3 3·3	30 Th	0304 0914 1532 2141	0·9 3·0 0·6 3·0

To find H.W. Dover use above times.

TIDAL DIFFERENCES PAGE 21:247. TIDAL CURVE PAGE 21:246.

TIDAL STREAMS PAGES 21:238-21:242.

Datum of predictions: 2.01 m. below Ordnance Datum (Belfast) or approx. L.A.T.

IRELAND (North East) BELFAST

HIGH & LOW WATER 1992 Lat. 54°36′N. Long. 5°55′W.

GMT ADD 1 HOUR MARCH 29 — OCTOBER 25 FOR B.S.T.

MAY

Day	Time	m	Time	m	Time	m	Time	m
1 F	0343	0·7	0952	3·1	1609	0·5	2217	3·2
2 Sa ●	0421	0·6	1030	3·2	1645	0·5	2252	3·3
3 Su	0459	0·5	1108	3·2	1722	0·5	2329	3·3
4 M	0539	0·4	1149	3·3	1801	0·5		
5 Tu	0008	3·4	0621	0·4	1232	3·2	1843	0·5
6 W	0052	3·4	0707	0·4	1320	3·2	1930	0·6
7 Th	0141	3·4	0758	0·4	1413	3·1	2023	0·8
8 F	0234	3·3	0854	0·5	1515	3·0	2125	0·9
9 Sa ☽	0335	3·2	1000	0·6	1627	2·9	2238	1·0
10 Su	0441	3·2	1113	0·6	1744	2·8	2354	1·0
11 M	0551	3·2	1224	0·5	1855	2·9		
12 Tu	0102	0·9	0659	3·2	1327	0·5	1957	3·0
13 W	0201	0·8	0759	3·3	1422	0·4	2050	3·1
14 Th	0253	0·7	0856	3·4	1512	0·4	2136	3·3
15 F	0342	0·6	0946	3·5	1559	0·5	2219	3·4
16 Sa ○	0427	0·5	1033	3·5	1641	0·5	2258	3·4
17 Su	0509	0·5	1118	3·4	1722	0·6	2336	3·5
18 M	0550	0·5	1200	3·4	1800	0·7		
19 Tu	0014	3·5	0631	0·5	1241	3·3	1838	0·8
20 W	0053	3·5	0712	0·6	1323	3·2	1916	0·9
21 Th	0133	3·4	0754	0·7	1406	3·1	1957	1·0
22 F	0216	3·3	0839	0·7	1453	2·9	2042	1·0
23 Sa	0301	3·2	0928	0·8	1543	2·9	2132	1·1
24 Su ☾	0352	3·1	1023	0·9	1638	2·8	2228	1·2
25 M	0447	3·0	1119	0·9	1734	2·8	2329	1·2
26 Tu	0543	2·9	1217	0·9	1831	2·8		
27 W	0031	1·1	0641	2·9	1312	0·8	1926	2·9
28 Th	0128	1·1	0735	2·9	1402	0·8	2015	3·0
29 F	0220	1·0	0827	3·0	1450	0·7	2101	3·1
30 Sa	0310	0·8	0917	3·1	1535	0·6	2146	3·2
31 Su	0356	0·7	1003	3·1	1620	0·6	2228	3·3

JUNE

Day	Time	m	Time	m	Time	m	Time	m
1 M ●	0441	0·5	1051	3·2	1704	0·5	2312	3·4
2 Tu	0527	0·4	1137	3·2	1749	0·5	2357	3·5
3 W	0614	0·3	1227	3·2	1835	0·5		
4 Th	0043	3·5	0702	0·3	1317	3·2	1924	0·6
5 F	0133	3·5	0754	0·3	1411	3·1	2018	0·6
6 Sa	0226	3·5	0849	0·3	1510	3·0	2117	0·7
7 Su ☽	0324	3·4	0948	0·3	1614	2·9	2220	0·8
8 M	0424	3·3	1051	0·4	1722	2·9	2327	0·8
9 Tu	0533	3·3	1157	0·5	1828	2·9		
10 W	0034	0·8	0634	3·3	1300	0·5	1928	3·0
11 Th	0135	0·8	0737	3·3	1358	0·6	2023	3·1
12 F	0232	0·7	0834	3·3	1451	0·6	2112	3·2
13 Sa	0324	0·6	0928	3·3	1539	0·7	2157	3·3
14 Su	0412	0·6	1017	3·3	1624	0·7	2238	3·4
15 M ○	0455	0·5	1101	3·3	1704	0·7	2318	3·4
16 Tu	0537	0·5	1143	3·2	1742	0·8	2356	3·5
17 W	0615	0·6	1222	3·2	1817	0·8		
18 Th	0032	3·5	0652	0·6	1300	3·1	1852	0·8
19 F	0109	3·5	0730	0·6	1338	3·1	1928	0·9
20 Sa	0147	3·4	0808	0·6	1418	3·0	2008	0·9
21 Su	0226	3·3	0849	0·7	1500	3·0	2051	0·9
22 M	0308	3·2	0934	0·8	1545	2·9	2139	1·0
23 Tu ☾	0353	3·1	1021	0·8	1635	2·9	2233	1·1
24 W	0445	3·1	1116	0·9	1732	2·9	2332	1·1
25 Th	0543	3·0	1214	0·9	1829	2·9		
26 F	0036	1·1	0645	3·0	1314	0·9	1928	3·0
27 Sa	0140	1·0	0747	3·0	1412	0·8	2025	3·1
28 Su	0240	0·9	0847	3·1	1508	0·8	2118	3·2
29 M	0335	0·7	0945	3·1	1600	0·7	2209	3·4
30 Tu ●	0427	0·5	1037	3·2	1649	0·6	2258	3·5

JULY

Day	Time	m	Time	m	Time	m	Time	m
1 W	0516	0·4	1129	3·2	1737	0·5	2344	3·6
2 Th	0604	0·2	1218	3·3	1825	0·5		
3 F	0032	3·7	0652	0·1	1309	3·2	1913	0·5
4 Sa	0121	3·7	0741	0·1	1359	3·2	2004	0·5
5 Su	0211	3·6	0832	0·2	1451	3·1	2056	0·6
6 M	0304	3·5	0925	0·3	1549	3·0	2153	0·7
7 Tu ☽	0402	3·4	1023	0·4	1649	2·9	2255	0·8
8 W	0504	3·3	1125	0·6	1754	2·9		
9 Th	0004	0·8	0610	3·2	1231	0·7	1857	3·0
10 F	0112	0·8	0714	3·1	1335	0·8	1955	3·0
11 Sa	0213	0·8	0816	3·1	1433	0·8	2049	3·1
12 Su	0310	0·7	0912	3·1	1524	0·8	2136	3·2
13 M	0359	0·6	1002	3·1	1609	0·8	2220	3·3
14 Tu ○	0446	0·6	1045	3·1	1648	0·6	2259	3·4
15 W	0522	0·5	1125	3·1	1723	0·8	2336	3·5
16 Th	0557	0·5	1200	3·1	1756	0·8		
17 F	0010	3·5	0629	0·5	1234	3·1	1827	0·7
18 Sa	0042	3·5	0700	0·5	1306	3·1	1859	0·7
19 Su	0114	3·4	0734	0·6	1340	3·1	1935	0·7
20 M	0148	3·4	0809	0·6	1418	3·1	2015	0·8
21 Tu	0226	3·3	0849	0·7	1458	3·1	2057	0·9
22 W ☾	0308	3·3	0934	0·8	1545	3·1	2146	1·0
23 Th	0357	3·2	1024	0·9	1638	3·0	2242	1·1
24 F	0455	3·1	1123	1·0	1740	3·0	2350	1·2
25 Sa	0604	3·0	1232	1·0	1848	3·0		
26 Su	0106	1·1	0717	3·0	1342	1·0	1954	3·1
27 M	0216	1·0	0827	3·1	1446	0·9	2056	3·3
28 Tu	0317	0·7	0929	3·2	1543	0·8	2149	3·4
29 W ●	0410	0·5	1024	3·2	1634	0·6	2240	3·6
30 Th	0459	0·3	1115	3·3	1722	0·5	2327	3·7
31 F	0547	0·1	1203	3·3	1808	0·4		

AUGUST

Day	Time	m	Time	m	Time	m	Time	m
1 Sa	0014	3·8	0632	0·0	1249	3·3	1853	0·4
2 Su	0102	3·8	0719	0·1	1335	3·3	1940	0·4
3 M	0149	3·7	0805	0·2	1423	3·2	2027	0·5
4 Tu	0240	3·6	0854	0·3	1514	3·1	2121	0·7
5 W ☽	0335	3·4	0948	0·6	1612	3·0	2221	0·8
6 Th	0435	3·2	1049	0·6	1715	2·9	2333	0·9
7 F	0544	3·1	1201	0·9	1822	2·9		
8 Sa	0048	0·9	0653	3·0	1313	1·0	1926	3·0
9 Su	0157	0·9	0758	3·0	1415	1·0	2023	3·1
10 M	0254	0·8	0856	3·0	1507	0·9	2114	3·2
11 Tu	0343	0·7	0943	3·0	1550	0·9	2159	3·3
12 W	0424	0·6	1026	3·1	1628	0·8	2238	3·4
13 Th ○	0501	0·5	1102	3·1	1701	0·8	2313	3·4
14 F	0532	0·5	1134	3·1	1729	0·7	2344	3·4
15 Sa	0600	0·5	1203	3·2	1758	0·7		
16 Su	0012	3·4	0628	0·5	1232	3·2	1829	0·6
17 M	0042	3·4	0659	0·5	1303	3·2	1903	0·6
18 Tu	0113	3·4	0733	0·6	1338	3·3	1940	0·7
19 W	0151	3·4	0811	0·6	1419	3·3	2022	0·7
20 Th	0232	3·3	0853	0·8	1504	3·2	2108	0·9
21 F ☾	0322	3·2	0942	0·9	1557	3·1	2204	1·1
22 Sa	0421	3·1	1044	1·1	1701	3·1	2316	1·2
23 Su	0534	3·0	1200	1·2	1814	3·1		
24 M	0039	1·1	0656	3·0	1320	1·1	1927	3·2
25 Tu	0155	0·9	0811	3·1	1427	1·0	2032	3·3
26 W	0257	0·7	0914	3·2	1524	0·9	2128	3·5
27 Th	0350	0·4	1007	3·3	1614	0·6	2219	3·7
28 F ●	0438	0·2	1057	3·4	1701	0·5	2306	3·8
29 Sa	0523	0·1	1140	3·4	1744	0·4	2351	3·9
30 Su	0607	0·1	1224	3·4	1828	0·4		
31 M	0036	3·9	0650	0·2	1306	3·4	1913	0·4

GENERAL — Entrance to Belfast Lough at right angles to main stream. Strong streams across entrance. Weak streams inside.

RATE AND SET — At head of Lough. Flood, 160°-260° — little strength; Ebb 330°-080° — 1½-2 kn. Off entrance: N. and S. approx. 3 kn.

BELFAST IRELAND (North East)

Lat. 54°36′N. Long. 5°55′W.   **HIGH & LOW WATER 1992**

GMT   ADD 1 HOUR MARCH 29 — OCTOBER 25 FOR B.S.T.

SEPTEMBER

#	Day	Time m	Time m	Time m	Time m
1	Tu	0123 3.8	0735 0.3	1349 3.3	1958 0.5
16	W	0043 3.4	0659 0.6	1307 3.4	1912 0.7
2	W	0212 3.6	0820 0.5	1437 3.2	2049 0.7
17	Th	0121 3.4	0737 0.7	1347 3.4	1954 0.7
3	Th	0305 3.4	0911 0.8	1531 3.1	) 2146 0.9
18	F	0205 3.3	0820 0.8	1433 3.3	2042 0.9
4	F	0407 3.1	1012 1.0	1634 3.0	2301 1.0
19	Sa	0256 3.2	0911 1.0	1528 3.2	(2139 1.0
5	Sa	0518 3.0	1127 1.0	1744 2.9	
20	Su	0359 3.0	1016 1.2	1633 3.1	2254 1.1
6	Su	0022 1.0	0629 2.9	1246 1.2	1853 3.0
21	M	0516 2.9	1139 1.2	1749 3.1	
7	M	0133 0.9	0735 2.9	1351 1.1	1955 3.0
22	Tu	0019 1.0	0641 3.0	1302 1.2	1903 3.2
8	Tu	0230 0.8	0832 2.9	1442 1.0	2047 3.1
23	W	0134 0.9	0755 3.1	1408 1.0	2008 3.4
9	W	0318 0.7	0919 3.0	1525 0.9	2132 3.2
24	Th	0234 0.8	0856 3.2	1503 0.8	2104 3.6
10	Th	0357 0.6	0959 3.0	1600 0.8	2212 3.3
25	F	0327 0.4	0948 3.4	1552 0.6	2156 3.7
11	F	0431 0.6	1034 3.1	1633 0.7	2244 3.3
26	Sa	0414 0.3	1033 3.5	1638 0.5	● 2242 3.8
12	Sa	0501 0.5	1104 3.2	1702 0.7	○ 2313 3.4
27	Su	0458 0.2	1115 3.5	1722 0.4	2327 3.9
13	Su	0529 0.5	1132 3.2	1730 0.6	2342 3.4
28	M	0542 0.2	1156 3.5	1804 0.4	
14	M	0556 0.5	1801 0.6		
29	Tu	0012 3.8	0624 0.3	1236 3.5	1846 0.5
15	Tu	0010 3.4	0625 0.5	1232 3.4	1835 0.6
30	W	0059 3.7	0706 0.5	1319 3.5	1931 0.6

OCTOBER

#	Day	Time m	Time m	Time m	Time m
1	Th	0147 3.5	0749 0.7	1404 3.4	2020 0.7
16	F	0102 3.3	0714 0.7	1326 3.4	1937 0.7
2	F	0239 3.3	0837 1.0	1456 3.2	2117 0.9
17	Sa	0148 3.2	0759 0.8	1413 3.4	2027 0.8
3	Sa	0338 3.1	0934 1.2	1555 3.1	) 2226 1.0
18	Su	0242 3.1	0854 1.0	1510 3.3	2128 0.9
4	Su	0445 2.9	1044 1.3	1704 3.0	2346 1.0
19	M	0346 3.0	1002 1.2	1614 3.2	(2241 0.9
5	M	0556 2.8	1204 1.3	1812 3.0	
20	Tu	0504 2.9	1122 1.2	1727 3.2	
6	Tu	0057 1.0	0702 2.8	1312 1.3	1916 3.0
21	W	0001 0.9	0625 3.0	1241 1.1	1839 3.3
7	W	0155 0.9	0758 2.9	1405 1.1	2011 3.1
22	Th	0112 0.7	0737 3.1	1345 1.0	1944 3.4
8	Th	0242 0.8	0846 2.9	1449 1.0	2057 3.2
23	F	0211 0.6	0834 3.2	1442 0.8	2042 3.6
9	F	0321 0.7	0925 3.0	1527 0.9	2138 3.2
24	Sa	0303 0.4	0925 3.4	1531 0.7	2134 3.7
10	Sa	0356 0.6	1000 3.1	1600 0.8	2212 3.3
25	Su	0350 0.4	1010 3.5	1616 0.6	● 2221 3.8
11	Su	0427 0.6	1033 3.2	1633 0.7	○ 2242 3.3
26	M	0435 0.4	1052 3.6	1701 0.5	2308 3.8
12	M	0457 0.6	1102 3.3	1704 0.6	2312 3.3
27	Tu	0518 0.4	1132 3.6	1743 0.5	2353 3.7
13	Tu	0526 0.5	1132 3.4	1736 0.6	2344 3.4
28	W	0600 0.6	1212 3.6	1827 0.5	
14	W	0558 0.6	1205 3.4	1812 0.6	
29	Th	0038 3.6	0641 0.7	1253 3.6	1910 0.6
15	Th	0019 3.4	0634 0.6	1243 3.5	1852 0.6
30	F	0124 3.4	0723 0.9	1337 3.5	1957 0.7
31	Sa	0212 3.2	0808 1.0	1425 3.4	2049 0.9

NOVEMBER

#	Day	Time m	Time m	Time m	Time m
1	Su	0307 3.0	0857 1.2	1518 3.2	2149 1.0
16	M	0234 3.1	0846 0.9	1457 3.4	2119 0.6
2	M	0406 2.9	0956 1.3	1619 3.1	) 2257 1.0
17	Tu	0338 3.0	0950 1.0	1559 3.4	(2227 0.7
3	Tu	0511 2.8	1105 1.4	1723 3.0	
18	W	0449 2.8	1104 1.1	1706 3.3	2339 0.7
4	W	0004 1.0	0614 2.8	1214 1.3	1827 3.0
19	Th	0605 3.0	1217 1.1	1815 3.4	
5	Th	0103 1.0	0712 2.8	1313 1.2	1923 3.0
20	F	0046 0.7	0714 3.1	1321 1.0	1921 3.4
6	F	0154 0.9	0801 2.9	1404 1.1	2013 3.1
21	Sa	0147 0.6	0813 3.2	1419 0.8	2020 3.5
7	Sa	0237 0.8	0846 3.0	1447 1.0	2057 3.1
22	Su	0242 0.6	0905 3.3	1511 0.7	2115 3.6
8	Su	0317 0.7	0924 3.1	1527 0.9	2136 3.2
23	M	0331 0.5	0950 3.5	1600 0.6	2206 3.6
9	M	0352 0.7	1000 3.3	1604 0.8	2213 3.2
24	Tu	0417 0.6	1034 3.6	1645 0.6	○ 2252 3.6
10	Tu	0427 0.6	1035 3.4	1641 0.7	○ 2248 3.3
25	W	0501 0.6	1115 3.6	1729 0.6	2337 3.5
11	W	0502 0.6	1111 3.4	1719 0.6	2326 3.3
26	Th	0542 0.7	1156 3.6	1812 0.6	
12	Th	0539 0.6	1147 3.5	1758 0.6	
27	F	0021 3.5	0621 0.8	1235 3.6	1855 0.6
13	F	0007 3.3	0618 0.6	1228 3.5	1842 0.5
28	Sa	0104 3.3	0700 0.9	1316 3.6	1937 0.7
14	Sa	0050 3.3	0641 0.7	1301 3.5	1928 0.5
29	Su	0148 3.2	0741 1.0	1358 3.5	2022 0.8
15	Su	0140 3.2	0749 0.8	1402 3.5	2020 0.6
30	M	0230 3.1	0823 1.1	1444 3.4	2110 0.9

DECEMBER

#	Day	Time m	Time m	Time m	Time m
1	Tu	0322 3.0	0911 1.2	1534 3.2	2202 1.0
16	W	0324 3.0	0934 0.8	1542 3.5	2206 0.5
2	W	0416 2.9	1004 1.2	1627 3.1	) 2259 1.0
17	Th	0428 3.0	1038 0.9	1645 3.4	2312 0.6
3	Th	0513 2.8	1105 1.3	1725 3.0	2358 1.0
18	F	0539 3.0	1149 1.0	1753 3.3	
4	F	0611 2.9	1208 1.3	1824 3.0	
19	Sa	0019 0.7	0648 3.0	1257 0.9	1900 3.3
5	Sa	0055 1.0	0707 2.9	1309 1.2	1921 3.0
20	Su	0124 0.7	0751 3.1	1401 0.9	2005 3.4
6	Su	0147 0.9	0759 3.0	1404 1.1	2013 3.1
21	M	0223 0.7	0846 3.2	1458 0.8	2103 3.4
7	M	0234 0.9	0847 3.1	1454 1.0	2103 3.1
22	Tu	0317 0.7	0935 3.4	1549 0.7	2155 3.4
8	Tu	0319 0.8	0931 3.2	1541 0.8	2148 3.2
23	W	0404 0.7	1020 3.5	1637 0.6	2242 3.4
9	W	0403 0.7	1013 3.4	1624 0.7	○ 2231 3.3
24	Th	0448 0.8	1102 3.6	1719 0.6	2326 3.4
10	Th	0444 0.6	1054 3.5	1706 0.6	2315 3.3
25	F	0527 0.8	1140 3.6	1800 0.6	
11	F	0526 0.6	1134 3.6	1750 0.5	
26	Sa	0005 3.3	0604 0.8	1218 3.6	1838 0.6
12	Sa	0000 3.3	0610 0.6	1218 3.6	1835 0.4
27	Su	0043 3.3	0639 0.8	1255 3.6	1914 0.6
13	Su	0045 3.3	0655 0.6	1303 3.6	1923 0.3
28	M	0120 3.2	0714 0.9	1331 3.5	1951 0.7
14	M	0133 3.2	0742 0.6	1352 3.6	2012 0.3
29	Tu	0158 3.1	0751 0.9	1409 3.5	2030 0.7
15	Tu	0226 3.1	0836 0.6	1444 3.6	2107 0.4
30	W	0239 3.1	0832 1.0	1450 3.4	2112 0.8
31	Th	0322 3.0	0917 1.0	1534 3.2	2159 0.9

To find H.W. Dover use above times.

TIDAL DIFFERENCES PAGE 21:247. TIDAL CURVE PAGE 21:246.

TIDAL STREAMS PAGES 21:238-21:242.

Datum of predictions: 2.01 m. below Ordnance Datum (Belfast) or approx. L.A.T.

BELFAST

MEAN SPRING AND NEAP CURVES

Springs occur 2 days after New and Full Moon.

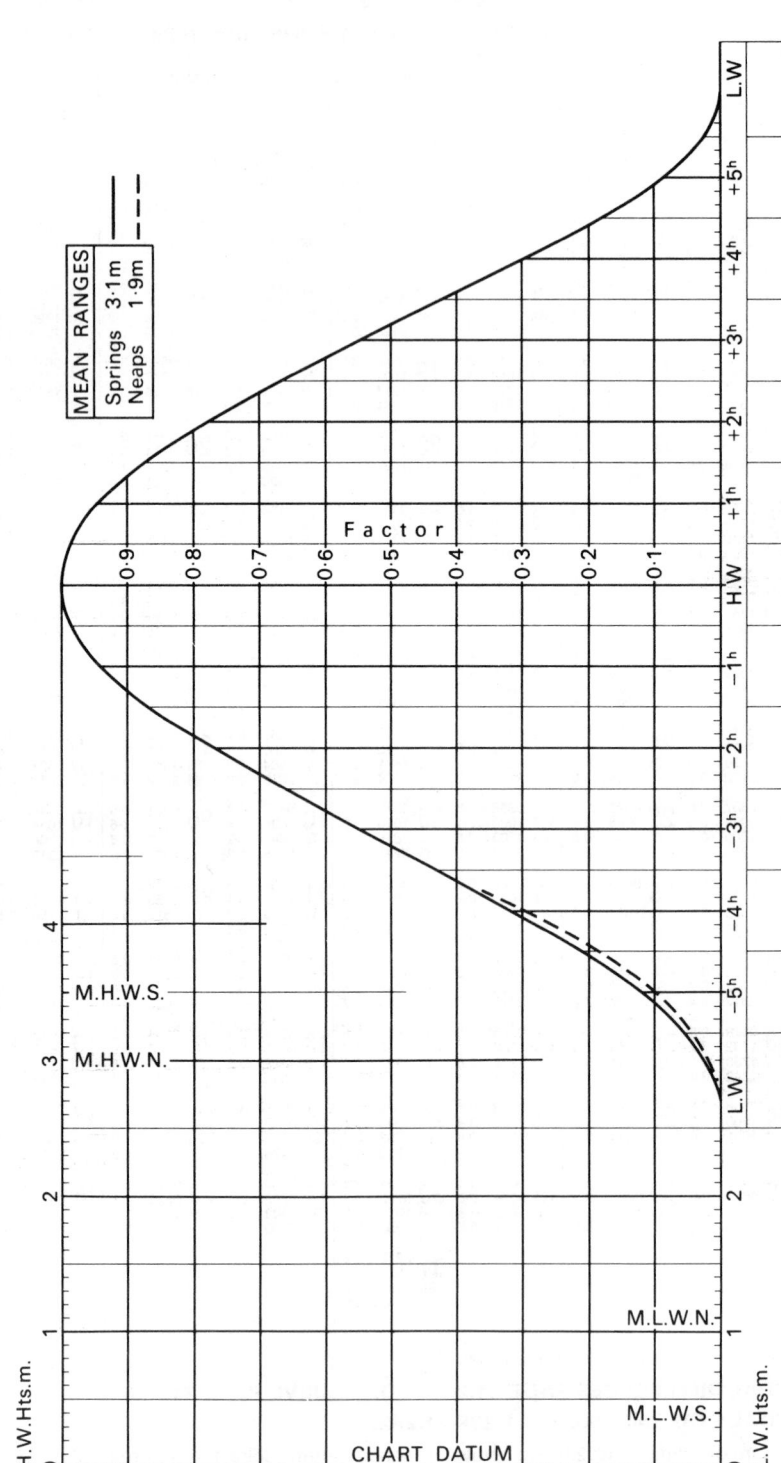

MEAN RANGES
Springs 3·1m
Neaps 1·9m

TIDAL DIFFERENCES ON BELFAST

PLACE	TIME DIFFERENCES				HEIGHT DIFFERENCES (Metres)			
	High Water		Low Water		MHWS	MHWN	MLWN	MLWS
BELFAST	0100 and 1300	0700 and 1900	0000 and 1200	0600 and 1800	3.5	3.0	1.1	0.4
Kilkeel	+0010	+0010	0000	0000	+0.8	+1.4	+0.8	+0.3
Dundrum Bay								
Newcastle	+0025	+0035	+0020	+0040	+1.6	+1.1	+0.4	+0.1
Killough Harbour	0000	+0020	–	–	+1.8	+1.6	–	–
Strangford Lough								
Killard Point	+0011	+0021	+0005	+0025	+1.0	+0.8	+0.1	+0.1
Strangford	+0147	+0157	+0148	+0208	+0.1	+0.1	–0.2	0.0
Quoile Barrier	+0150	+0200	+0150	+0300	+0.2	+0.2	–0.3	–0.1
Killyleagh	+0157	+0207	+0211	+0231	+0.3	+0.3	–	–
South Rock	+0023	+0023	+0025	+0025	+1.0	+0.8	+0.1	+0.1
Portavogie	+0010	+0020	+0010	+0020	+1.2	+0.9	+0.3	+0.2
Donaghadee	+0020	+0020	+0023	+0023	+0.5	+0.4	0.0	+0.1
Carrickfergus	+0005	+0005	+0005	+0005	–0.3	–0.3	–0.2	–0.1
Larne	+0005	0000	+0010	–0005	–0.7	–0.5	–0.3	0.0
Red Bay	+0022	–0010	+0007	–0017	–1.9	–1.5	–0.8	–0.2
Cushendun	+0010	–0030	0000	–0025	–1.7	–1.5	–0.6	–0.2

Refer to predictions on pages 21:243-21:245

TIDAL DIFFERENCES ON LONDONDERRY

PLACE	TIME DIFFERENCES				HEIGHT DIFFERENCES (Metres)			
	High Water		Low Water		MHWS	MHWN	MLWN	MLWS
LONDONDERRY	0200 and 1400	0900 and 2100	0300 and 1500	0700 and 1900	2.7	2.1	1.2	0.5
Ballycastle Bay	+0053	–0147	–0125	+0056	–1.5	–1.0	–0.5	–0.2
LONDONDERRY	0200 and 1400	0800 and 2000	0500 and 1700	1100 and 2300	2.7	2.1	1.2	0.5
Portrush	–0105	–0105	–0105	–0105	–0.8	–0.7	–0.4	–0.1
Coleraine	–0030	–0130	–0110	–0020	–0.5	–0.3	–0.3	–0.1
Lough Foyle								
Warren Point	–0121	–0139	–0156	–0132	–0.4	–0.2	–	–
Moville	–0046	–0058	–0108	–0052	–0.4	–0.2	–0.2	–0.1
Quigley's Point	–0025	–0040	–0025	–0040	–0.4	–0.3	–0.3	–0.2
Culmore Point	–0010	–0030	–0020	–0040	–0.3	–0.3	–0.2	–0.1
Culdaff Bay	–0136	–0156	–0206	–0146	+0.1	+0.2	–	–

Refer to predictions on pages 21:248-21:250

LONDONDERRY

HIGH & LOW WATER 1992 Lat. 55°00'N. Long. 7°19'W.

GMT ADD 1 HOUR MARCH 29 — OCTOBER 25 FOR B.S.T.

JANUARY

Day	Time	m	Time	m	Time	m	Time	m
1 W	0543	2.5	1144	1.1	1804	2.4		
2 Th	0027	1.0	0628	2.6	1238	1.1	1849	2.4
3 F	0106	1.0	0710	2.7	1323	1.0	1928	2.5
4 Sa ●	0141	0.9	0747	2.8	1401	1.0	2004	2.5
5 Su	0215	0.9	0822	2.9	1434	1.0	2036	2.5
6 M	0246	0.9	0853	2.9	1507	1.0	2104	2.5
7 Tu	0314	0.9	0924	2.9	1538	1.0	2134	2.5
8 W	0343	0.9	0955	2.9	1612	1.0	2204	2.5
9 Th	0416	0.9	1027	2.8	1647	1.0	2240	2.5
10 F	0452	0.9	1104	2.8	1727	1.0	2318	2.4
11 Sa	0532	1.0	1143	2.7	1811	1.1		
12 Su	0003	2.3	0618	1.0	1231	2.6	1902	1.2
13 M ☽	0056	2.2	0713	1.1	1330	2.5	2002	1.2
14 Tu	0205	2.1	0822	1.2	1446	2.4	2112	1.2
15 W	0336	2.1	0946	1.2	1612	2.4	2230	1.1
16 Th	0459	2.3	1113	1.1	1725	2.5	2339	1.0
17 F	0601	2.5	1224	0.9	1825	2.7		
18 Sa	0035	0.8	0653	2.7	1323	0.8	1917	2.8
19 Su ○	0124	0.7	0740	2.9	1415	0.6	2005	2.9
20 M	0209	0.5	0825	3.1	1504	0.6	2051	2.9
21 Tu	0254	0.5	0907	3.2	1550	0.6	2136	2.9
22 W	0338	0.4	0948	3.2	1635	0.6	2220	2.8
23 Th	0421	0.5	1030	3.1	1720	0.7	2305	2.7
24 F	0505	0.6	1112	2.9	1807	0.9	2350	2.5
25 Sa	0551	0.7	1157	2.7	1855	1.0		
26 Su ☾	0041	2.3	0641	0.9	1249	2.5	1951	1.2
27 M	0142	2.2	0737	1.1	1359	2.2	2058	1.2
28 Tu	0304	2.1	0850	1.2	1550	2.1	2217	1.2
29 W	0427	2.2	1024	1.3	1715	2.4	2323	1.2
30 Th	0530	2.3	1810	2.2				
31 F	0015	1.0	0619	2.5	1243	1.1	1852	2.3

FEBRUARY

Day	Time	m	Time	m	Time	m	Time	m
1 Sa	0059	0.9	0702	2.6	1326	1.0	1930	2.4
2 Su	0137	0.8	0738	2.7	1401	0.9	2002	2.5
3 M ●	0211	0.8	0813	2.8	1433	0.9	2030	2.5
4 Tu	0242	0.7	0843	2.9	1501	0.9	2057	2.5
5 W	0308	0.7	0911	2.9	1529	0.9	2122	2.6
6 Th	0335	0.7	0939	2.8	1559	0.8	2149	2.5
7 F	0403	0.7	1007	2.8	1630	0.8	2219	2.5
8 Sa	0435	0.8	1040	2.7	1705	0.9	2252	2.4
9 Su	0512	0.8	1116	2.6	1744	0.9	2330	2.3
10 M	0554	0.9	1200	2.5	1829	1.0		
11 Tu ☽	0015	2.2	0646	1.0	1256	2.3	1924	1.1
12 W	0117	2.0	0751	1.1	1415	2.2	2032	1.2
13 Th	0256	2.0	0928	1.2	1607	2.2	2202	1.2
14 F	0457	2.1	1235	1.1	1729	2.3	2327	1.0
15 Sa	0600	2.4	1235	0.9	1825	2.5		
16 Su	0027	0.8	0648	2.7	1327	0.7	1913	2.7
17 M	0116	0.6	0731	2.9	1413	0.5	1958	2.8
18 Tu ○	0201	0.4	0812	3.1	1456	0.4	2040	2.9
19 W	0243	0.3	0853	3.2	1536	0.4	2119	2.8
20 Th	0325	0.3	0931	3.1	1616	0.5	2200	2.8
21 F	0406	0.4	1010	3.0	1655	0.6	2238	2.6
22 Sa	0447	0.5	1048	2.8	1733	0.7	2319	2.5
23 Su	0529	0.6	1129	2.5	1814	0.9		
24 M	0001	2.3	0612	0.8	1214	2.3	1900	1.1
25 Tu ☾	0055	2.2	0704	1.0	1319	2.0	2002	1.2
26 W	0216	2.0	0818	1.2	1552	1.9	2134	1.2
27 Th	0403	2.1	1027	1.3	1712	2.0	2258	1.2
28 F	0512	2.2	1156	1.1	1801	2.1	2357	1.0
29 Sa	0601	2.4	1242	1.0	1841	2.2		

MARCH

Day	Time	m	Time	m	Time	m	Time	m
1 Su	0041	0.9	0642	2.6	1316	0.9	1914	2.4
2 M	0119	0.8	0719	2.7	1347	0.8	1945	2.4
3 Tu	0154	0.7	0752	2.8	1416	0.7	2013	2.5
4 W ●	0225	0.6	0822	2.8	1444	0.6	2039	2.5
5 Th	0253	0.6	0850	2.8	1512	0.6	2104	2.5
6 F	0321	0.6	0918	2.8	1541	0.6	2131	2.5
7 Sa	0350	0.6	0948	2.7	1610	0.6	2200	2.5
8 Su	0423	0.6	1020	2.6	1644	0.7	2233	2.4
9 M	0459	0.7	1058	2.5	1723	0.8	2311	2.3
10 Tu	0543	0.8	1143	2.4	1807	0.9	2356	2.2
11 W ☽	0635	1.0	1242	2.2	1900	1.0		
12 Th	0056	2.0	0742	1.1	1411	2.0	2005	1.1
13 F	0237	2.0	0957	1.2	1617	2.1	2136	1.1
14 Sa	0452	2.2	1142	0.9	1726	2.2	2312	1.0
15 Su	0547	2.5	1235	0.7	1817	2.4		
16 M	0012	0.8	0632	2.7	1320	0.5	1900	2.6
17 Tu	0100	0.6	0713	2.9	1401	0.4	1942	2.7
18 W	0145	0.4	0752	3.0	1439	0.3	2022	2.8
19 Th ○	0227	0.3	0830	3.0	1515	0.3	2100	2.7
20 F	0307	0.3	0908	2.9	1550	0.4	2136	2.7
21 Sa	0346	0.3	0946	2.8	1624	0.5	2212	2.6
22 Su	0426	0.4	1023	2.6	1658	0.6	2248	2.5
23 M	0505	0.6	1102	2.3	1733	0.8	2327	2.3
24 Tu	0547	0.6	1144	2.1	1815	0.9		
25 W ☾	0015	2.2	0635	1.0	1242	1.9	1907	1.1
26 Th	0123	2.1	0741	1.2	1519	1.7	2023	1.2
27 F	0311	2.0	1002	1.2	1642	1.8	2207	1.2
28 Sa	0431	2.2	1130	1.1	1730	2.0	2316	1.1
29 Su	0523	2.3	1212	1.0	1810	2.1		
30 M	0005	0.9	0605	2.5	1245	0.8	1842	2.3
31 Tu	0046	0.8	0643	2.6	1316	0.7	1913	2.4

APRIL

Day	Time	m	Time	m	Time	m	Time	m
1 W	0121	0.6	0719	2.7	1345	0.6	1942	2.4
2 Th	0155	0.6	0751	2.7	1415	0.5	2012	2.5
3 F ●	0227	0.5	0822	2.8	1446	0.5	2040	2.5
4 Sa	0300	0.5	0853	2.7	1515	0.5	2110	2.5
5 Su	0334	0.5	0927	2.6	1548	0.5	2142	2.5
6 M	0412	0.5	1003	2.5	1624	0.5	2217	2.4
7 Tu	0452	0.6	1047	2.4	1704	0.6	2258	2.3
8 W	0539	0.8	1136	2.2	1749	0.7	2346	2.3
9 Th	0634	0.9	1241	2.1	1842	0.9		
10 F ☽	0046	2.2	0751	1.0	1416	2.0	1945	1.0
11 Sa	0222	2.1	1012	1.0	1600	2.0	2108	1.0
12 Su	0417	2.3	1126	0.8	1705	2.2	2240	0.9
13 M	0518	2.5	1217	0.6	1804	2.5	2344	0.7
14 Tu	0604	2.6	1300	0.5	1839	2.5		
15 W	0036	0.6	0646	2.7	1338	0.4	1920	2.6
16 Th	0123	0.5	0727	2.8	1413	0.4	1959	2.6
17 F ○	0205	0.4	0805	2.8	1447	0.4	2036	2.6
18 Sa	0246	0.4	0843	2.7	1519	0.4	2111	2.6
19 Su	0325	0.4	0921	2.5	1550	0.5	2145	2.4
20 M	0403	0.5	0959	2.4	1623	0.6	2221	2.5
21 Tu	0441	0.7	1037	2.2	1657	0.7	2259	2.4
22 W	0520	0.8	1119	2.0	1736	0.9	2344	2.3
23 Th	0607	0.9	1211	1.8	1822	1.0		
24 F ☾	0039	2.2	0702	1.1	1337	1.7	1920	1.1
25 Sa	0154	2.2	0820	1.1	1528	1.8	2039	1.2
26 Su	0318	2.2	1003	1.1	1630	1.9	2203	1.1
27 M	0423	2.2	1106	1.0	1715	2.0	2306	1.0
28 Tu	0513	2.3	1150	0.9	1754	2.1	2356	0.9
29 W	0556	2.4	1228	0.7	1831	2.3		
30 Th	0038	0.7	0636	2.5	1304	0.6	1906	2.4

To find H.W. Dover add 2 h. 50 min.

TIDAL DIFFERENCES PAGE 21:247. TIDAL CURVE PAGE 21:251.

TIDAL STREAMS PAGES 21:238-21:242.

Datum of predictions: 1.61 m. below Ordnance Datum (Belfast) or approx. L.A.T.

LONDONDERRY IRELAND (North)

Lat. 55°00'N. Long. 7°19'W.

HIGH & LOW WATER 1992

GMT   ADD 1 HOUR MARCH 29 — OCTOBER 25 FOR B.S.T.

MAY

Day	Time	m	Day	Time	m
1 F	0119 / 0714 / 1340 / 1941	0·6 / 2·6 / 0·5 / 2·4	16	0144 / 0742 / ○ 2012	0·6 / 2·5 / 2·5
2 Sa ●	0158 / 0751 / 1415 / 2015	0·5 / 2·6 / 0·5 / 2·5	17 Su	0226 / 0823 / 1450 / 2049	0·6 / 2·4 / 0·5 / 2·6
3 Su	0237 / 0829 / 1450 / 2050	0·5 / 2·6 / 0·4 / 2·5	18 M	0305 / 0901 / 1521 / 2122	0·6 / 2·3 / 0·6 / 2·6
4 M	0318 / 0910 / 1527 / 2127	0·5 / 2·6 / 0·4 / 2·6	19 Tu	0342 / 0938 / 1553 / 2157	0·6 / 2·2 / 0·6 / 2·5
5 Tu	0402 / 0952 / 1604 / 2206	0·5 / 2·5 / 0·4 / 2·5	20 W	0419 / 1016 / 1627 / 2235	0·7 / 2·1 / 0·7 / 2·5
6 W	0447 / 1040 / 1647 / 2249	0·6 / 2·4 / 0·5 / 2·5	21 Th	0457 / 1055 / 1704 / 2316	0·8 / 2·1 / 0·8 / 2·5
7 Th	0537 / 1133 / 1734 / 2339	0·7 / 2·3 / 0·6 / 2·4	22 F	0537 / 1139 / 1746	0·9 / 2·0 / 0·9
8 F	0636 / 1238 / 1827	0·8 / 2·1 / 0·7	23 Sa	0003 / 0624 / 1232 / 1834	2·4 / 1·0 / 1·9 / 1·0
9 Sa ☽	0039 / 0754 / 1358 / 1926	2·4 / 0·9 / 2·1 / 0·8	24 Su	0056 / 0719 / 1300 / ☾ 1930	2·3 / 1·0 / 1·8 / 1·0
10 Su	0155 / 0934 / 1522 / 2037	2·3 / 0·9 / 2·1 / 0·9	25 M	0158 / 0825 / 1434 / 2037	2·2 / 1·1 / 1·8 / 1·1
11 M	0325 / 1048 / 1628 / 2157	2·3 / 0·8 / 2·2 / 0·9	26 Tu	0305 / 0936 / 1600 / 2149	2·2 / 1·0 / 1·9 / 1·0
12 Tu	0434 / 1143 / 1723 / 2309	2·4 / 0·7 / 2·3 / 0·8	27 W	0409 / 1041 / 1655 / 2255	2·2 / 1·0 / 2·0 / 1·0
13 W	0529 / 1229 / 1811	2·5 / 0·6 / 2·4	28 Th	0504 / 1134 / 1743 / 2351	2·3 / 0·8 / 2·1 / 0·8
14 Th	0007 / 0617 / 1307 / 1855	0·7 / 2·5 / 0·5 / 2·4	29 F	0553 / 1221 / 1828	2·4 / 0·7 / 2·3
15 F	0057 / 0702 / 1344 / 1935	0·6 / 2·5 / 0·5 / 2·5	30 Sa	0042 / 0641 / 1303 / 1912	0·7 / 2·5 / 0·6 / 2·4
			31 Su	0131 / 0726 / 1345 / 1952	0·6 / 2·5 / 0·5 / 2·5

JUNE

Day	Time	m	Day	Time	m
1 M ●	0219 / 0811 / 1426 / 2034	0·5 / 2·6 / 0·4 / 2·6	16	0250 / 0849 / 1501 / 2107	0·7 / 2·3 / 0·5 / 2·6
2 Tu	0305 / 0856 / 1507 / 2115	0·5 / 2·6 / 0·4 / 2·7	17 W	0325 / 0924 / 1532 / 2141	0·7 / 2·2 / 0·7 / 2·6
3 W	0353 / 0943 / 1549 / 2157	0·5 / 2·6 / 0·4 / 2·7	18 Th	0359 / 0956 / 1604 / 2214	0·8 / 2·2 / 0·7 / 2·6
4 Th	0442 / 1033 / 1634 / 2242	0·5 / 2·5 / 0·4 / 2·7	19 F	0433 / 1030 / 1638 / 2249	0·8 / 2·2 / 0·7 / 2·6
5 F	0534 / 1125 / 1720 / 2330	0·6 / 2·4 / 0·5 / 2·7	20 Sa	0509 / 1106 / 1715 / 2329	0·8 / 2·1 / 0·8 / 2·5
6 Sa	0629 / 1222 / 1811	0·7 / 2·3 / 0·6	21 Su	0550 / 1146 / 1754	0·9 / 2·1 / 0·9
7 Su ☽	0024 / 0733 / 1327 / ☽ 1906	2·6 / 0·8 / 2·2 / 0·7	22 M	0011 / 0634 / 1232 / 1841	2·4 / 0·9 / 2·0 / 0·9
8 M	0124 / 0844 / 1437 / 2008	2·5 / 0·9 / 2·1 / 0·8	23 Tu ☾	0057 / 0724 / 1328 / ☾ 1934	2·4 / 1·0 / 1·9 / 1·0
9 Tu	0237 / 0959 / 1548 / 2118	2·4 / 0·9 / 2·1 / 0·9	24 W	0155 / 0823 / 1436 / 2037	2·3 / 1·0 / 1·9 / 1·0
10 W	0353 / 1102 / 1649 / 2233	2·3 / 0·8 / 2·2 / 0·9	25 Th	0303 / 0931 / 1552 / 2153	2·2 / 1·0 / 1·9 / 1·0
11 Th	0459 / 1154 / 1744 / 2340	2·3 / 0·8 / 2·2 / 0·9	26 F	0413 / 1040 / 1659 / 2308	2·2 / 1·0 / 2·0 / 0·9
12 F	0557 / 1238 / 1832	2·3 / 0·7 / 2·3	27 Sa	0519 / 1140 / 1757	2·3 / 0·9 / 2·2
13 Sa	0038 / 0646 / 1319 / 1916	0·8 / 2·3 / 0·7 / 2·4	28 Su	0014 / 0617 / 1234 / 1849	0·8 / 2·4 / 0·7 / 2·4
14 Su	0127 / 0731 / 1355 / 1955	0·8 / 2·3 / 0·7 / 2·5	29 M	0112 / 0709 / 1321 / 1935	0·7 / 2·5 / 0·6 / 2·6
15 M ○	0212 / 0811 / 1429 / ○ 2032	0·7 / 2·3 / 0·7 / 2·6	30 Tu ●	0205 / 0758 / 1408 / ● 2020	0·6 / 2·6 / 0·5 / 2·7

JULY

Day	Time	m	Day	Time	m
1 W	0256 / 0846 / 1451 / 2104	0·5 / 2·7 / 0·4 / 2·9	16	0311 / 0908 / 1517 / 2122	0·8 / 2·3 / 0·7 / 2·7
2 Th	0345 / 0932 / 1535 / 2146	0·4 / 2·7 / 0·3 / 2·9	17 F	0341 / 0935 / 1545 / 2152	0·8 / 2·3 / 0·7 / 2·7
3 F	0433 / 1019 / 1620 / 2230	0·5 / 2·6 / 0·3 / 2·9	18 Sa	0409 / 1003 / 1614 / 2223	0·8 / 2·3 / 0·7 / 2·7
4 Sa	0520 / 1106 / 1705 / 2315	0·5 / 2·5 / 0·4 / 2·8	19 Su	0441 / 1033 / 1645 / 2255	0·8 / 2·3 / 0·7 / 2·6
5 Su	0610 / 1157 / 1753	0·6 / 2·4 / 0·5	20 M	0516 / 1106 / 1722 / 2332	0·8 / 2·2 / 0·8 / 2·5
6 M	0003 / 0703 / 1252 / 1843	2·7 / 0·8 / 2·3 / 0·6	21 Tu	0556 / 1144 / 1801	0·9 / 2·2 / 0·8
7 Tu ☽	0055 / 0801 / 1354 / ☽ 1940	2·5 / 0·9 / 2·1 / 0·8	22 W	0012 / 0639 / 1229 / ☾ 1849	2·4 / 0·9 / 2·1 / 0·9
8 W	0158 / 0908 / 1507 / 2046	2·3 / 1·0 / 2·1 / 0·9	23 Th	0102 / 0731 / 1326 / 1948	2·3 / 1·0 / 2·0 / 1·0
9 Th	0322 / 1020 / 1620 / 2206	2·2 / 1·0 / 2·1 / 1·0	24 F	0208 / 0834 / 1446 / 2105	2·2 / 1·1 / 1·9 / 1·1
10 F	0447 / 1123 / 1723 / 2326	2·1 / 0·9 / 2·2 / 1·0	25 Sa	0335 / 0950 / 1624 / 2240	2·1 / 1·0 / 2·0 / 1·0
11 Sa	0553 / 1215 / 1817	2·1 / 0·9 / 2·3	26 Su	0459 / 1108 / 1739	2·2 / 0·9 / 2·2
12 Su	0031 / 0643 / 1300 / 1902	1·0 / 2·2 / 0·8 / 2·4	27 M	0001 / 0604 / 1211 / 1834	0·9 / 2·4 / 0·8 / 2·4
13 M	0121 / 0727 / 1341 / 1941	0·9 / 2·2 / 0·8 / 2·5	28 Tu	0103 / 0657 / 1303 / 1921	0·7 / 2·5 / 0·6 / 2·7
14 Tu ○	0204 / 0805 / 1415 / ○ 2018	0·8 / 2·3 / 0·7 / 2·6	29 W	0157 / 0745 / 1351 / ● 2005	0·5 / 2·7 / 0·4 / 2·9
15 W	0240 / 0839 / 1447 / 2051	0·8 / 2·3 / 0·7 / 2·7	30 Th	0244 / 0832 / 1436 / 2047	0·4 / 2·7 / 0·3 / 3·0
			31 F	0329 / 0915 / 1519 / 2129	0·4 / 2·8 / 0·3 / 3·1

AUGUST

Day	Time	m	Day	Time	m
1 Sa	0414 / 0959 / 1603 / 2210	0·4 / 2·7 / 0·3 / 3·0	16	0343 / 0935 / 1550 / 2153	0·7 / 2·4 / 0·6 / 2·7
2 Su	0458 / 1042 / 1647 / 2252	0·5 / 2·6 / 0·3 / 2·9	17 M	0413 / 1002 / 1620 / 2223	0·7 / 2·4 / 0·7 / 2·6
3 M	0542 / 1126 / 1732 / 2334	0·6 / 2·5 / 0·5 / 2·7	18 Tu	0445 / 1034 / 1654 / 2258	0·7 / 2·3 / 0·7 / 2·5
4 Tu	0628 / 1214 / 1818	0·8 / 2·3 / 0·7	19 W	0522 / 1109 / 1733 / 2337	0·8 / 2·3 / 0·8 / 2·4
5 W	0024 / 0719 / 1310 / ☽ 1912	2·4 / 0·9 / 2·1 / 0·9	20 Th	0605 / 1150 / 1821	0·9 / 2·1 / 0·9
6 Th	0124 / 0820 / 1426 / 2019	2·2 / 1·0 / 2·0 / 1·0	21 F ☾	0028 / 0655 / 1243 / ☾ 1920	2·3 / 1·0 / 2·0 / 1·1
7 F	0310 / 0941 / 1557 / 2153	2·0 / 1·1 / 2·1 / 1·1	22 Sa	0117 / 0755 / 1401 / 2040	2·1 / 1·1 / 2·0 / 1·1
8 Sa	0452 / 1058 / 1709 / 2329	2·0 / 1·1 / 2·2 / 1·1	23 Su	0321 / 0912 / 1604 / 2238	2·1 / 1·1 / 2·1 / 1·1
9 Su	0551 / 1156 / 1801	2·1 / 1·0 / 2·3	24 M	0455 / 1042 / 1725	2·2 / 1·0 / 2·3
10 M	0032 / 0638 / 1242 / 1845	1·0 / 2·2 / 0·9 / 2·5	25 Tu	0001 / 0556 / 1151 / 1817	0·9 / 2·4 / 0·8 / 2·6
11 Tu	0116 / 0716 / 1321 / 1923	0·9 / 2·3 / 0·8 / 2·6	26 W	0056 / 0645 / 1245 / 1902	0·7 / 2·6 / 0·6 / 2·9
12 W	0151 / 0749 / 1358 / 1958	0·8 / 2·4 / 0·7 / 2·7	27 Th	0151 / 0730 / 1331 / 1944	0·5 / 2·7 / 0·4 / 3·0
13 Th	0222 / 0819 / 1429 / 2029	0·8 / 2·4 / 0·6 / 2·8	28 F	0226 / 0812 / 1416 / 2025	0·4 / 2·8 / 0·3 / 3·1
14 F	0250 / 0846 / 1457 / 2058	0·7 / 2·4 / 0·6 / 2·8	29 Sa ●	0308 / 0853 / 1458 / ● 2104	0·3 / 2·9 / 0·2 / 3·1
15 Sa	0317 / 0910 / 1524 / 2125	0·7 / 2·5 / 0·6 / 2·8	30 Su	0348 / 0934 / 1541 / 2143	0·4 / 2·8 / 0·3 / 3·0
			31 M	0427 / 1013 / 1623 / 2223	0·5 / 2·7 / 0·4 / 2·8

GENERAL — Greater part of Lough Foyle — shoals. Streams in direction of main channels. Sets to outer sides of bend. Streams at one side are earlier. Rates of stream increase off salient points.

21:250 IRELAND (North) LONDONDERRY

Lat. 55°00'N. Long. 7°19'W. HIGH & LOW WATER 1992

GMT ADD 1 HOUR MARCH 29 — OCTOBER 25 FOR B.S.T.

SEPTEMBER

Day	Time	m	Time	m	Time	m	Time	m
1 Tu	0506	0.6	1054	2.5	1706	0.5	2305	2.6
16 W	0416	0.7	1006	2.5	1633	0.7	2230	2.6
2 W	0547	0.8	1136	2.4	1751	0.7	2350	2.3
17 Th	0452	0.8	1041	2.4	1713	0.9	2313	2.4
3 Th)	0634	1.0	1227	2.2	1843	1.0		
18 F	0536	0.9	1125	2.3	1804	1.0		
4 F	0050	2.0	0730	1.1	1340	2.1	1952	1.2
19 Sa	0008	2.2	0628	1.0	1219	2.2	(1906	1.1
5 Sa	0311	1.9	0853	1.2	1529	2.1	2155	1.2
20 Su	0124	2.1	0728	1.1	1338	2.1	2036	1.2
6 Su	0444	2.0	1024	1.2	1644	2.3	2329	1.1
21 M	0319	2.1	0844	1.1	1542	2.2	2249	1.1
7 M	0536	2.1	1127	1.0	1736	2.4	2354	0.9
22 Tu	0445	2.3	1014	1.0	1702	2.5		
8 Tu	0018	1.0	0617	2.2	1215	0.9	1817	2.6
23 W	0540	2.5	1126	0.8	1751	2.7		
9 W	0053	0.9	0652	2.4	1255	0.8	1855	2.7
24 Th	0041	0.6	0625	2.7	1221	0.6	1835	3.0
10 Th	0124	0.8	0723	2.5	1330	0.7	1927	2.8
25 F	0123	0.5	0707	2.8	1307	0.5	1916	3.1
11 F	0152	0.7	0751	2.5	1401	0.6	1958	2.8
26 Sa	0202	0.4	0748	2.9	1352	0.3	1957	3.1
12 Sa	0219	0.7	0816	2.6	O 1430	0.6	2026	2.8
27 Su	0239	0.4	0827	2.9	1434	0.3	2036	3.1
13 Su	0246	0.6	0840	2.6	1457	0.6	2054	2.8
28 M	0315	0.4	0905	2.9	1515	0.4	2114	3.0
14 M	0312	0.6	0905	2.6	1525	0.6	2122	2.7
29 Tu	0352	0.5	0942	2.8	1557	0.5	2153	2.7
15 Tu	0342	0.6	0934	2.6	1556	0.7	2155	2.7
30 W	0427	0.7	1020	2.6	1638	0.7	2233	2.5

OCTOBER

Day	Time	m	Time	m	Time	m	Time	m
1 Th	0504	0.8	1059	2.5	1722	0.9	2316	2.4
16 F	0428	0.8	1021	2.6	1701	0.9	2259	2.4
2 F	0546	1.0	1147	2.4	1812	1.1		
17 Sa	0513	0.9	1108	2.5	1754	1.1	2358	2.3
3 Sa	0014	2.0	0638	1.2	1250	2.3	) 1919	1.3
18 Su	0605	1.0	1204	2.4	1900	1.2		
4 Su	0225	1.9	0749	1.3	1432	2.2	2121	1.3
19 M	0117	2.2	0706	1.1	1320	2.4	(2042	1.2
5 M	0410	2.0	0927	1.3	1559	2.3	2257	1.2
20 Tu	0303	2.2	0818	1.1	1504	2.4	2234	1.1
6 Tu	0502	2.1	1041	1.2	1654	2.5	2340	1.1
21 W	0421	2.3	0942	1.1	1626	2.6	2332	0.9
7 W	0542	2.3	1133	1.0	1737	2.6		
22 Th	0515	2.5	1055	0.9	1719	2.8		
8 Th	0014	0.9	0615	2.4	1215	0.9	1815	2.7
23 F	0017	0.7	0601	2.7	1153	0.7	1805	3.0
9 F	0043	0.8	0652	2.5	1252	0.8	1849	2.8
24 Sa	0056	0.6	0643	2.8	1242	0.6	1848	3.0
10 Sa	0113	0.7	0716	2.6	1326	0.7	1921	2.9
25 Su	0133	0.5	0723	2.9	1327	0.5	● 1930	3.0
11 Su	0142	0.6	0744	2.7	1358	0.6	1952	2.9
26 M	0208	0.5	0801	2.9	1411	0.5	2009	3.0
12 M	0212	0.6	0811	2.7	1430	0.6	2023	2.8
27 Tu	0243	0.6	0837	2.9	1451	0.6	2047	2.8
13 Tu	0242	0.6	0839	2.7	1503	0.7	2056	2.8
28 W	0315	0.7	0914	2.8	1531	0.7	2125	2.6
14 W	0314	0.6	0910	2.7	1538	0.7	2131	2.7
29 Th	0349	0.8	0950	2.8	1612	0.8	2204	2.4
15 Th	0348	0.7	0943	2.6	1616	0.8	2212	2.6
30 F	0424	0.9	1028	2.7	1652	1.0	2247	2.3
31 Sa	0505	1.0	1113	2.6	1740	1.1	2337	2.1

NOVEMBER

Day	Time	m	Time	m	Time	m	Time	m
1 Su	0551	1.2	1208	2.5	1836	1.3		
16 M	0547	0.9	1151	2.7	1856	1.2		
2 M	0055	2.0	0652	1.3	1320	2.4	) 1954	1.4
17 Tu	0103	2.3	0646	1.0	1259	2.6	(2023	1.2
3 Tu	0249	2.0	0808	1.3	1444	2.4	2128	1.3
18 W	0227	2.3	0752	1.1	1422	2.6	2156	1.1
4 W	0400	2.1	0931	1.3	1553	2.5	2233	1.2
19 Th	0345	2.4	0908	1.1	1545	2.7	2259	1.0
5 Th	0448	2.2	1035	1.2	1645	2.6	2318	1.1
20 F	0445	2.5	1023	1.0	1648	2.7	2347	0.9
6 F	0527	2.4	1126	1.0	1729	2.7	2356	0.9
21 Sa	0536	2.6	1126	0.9	1740	2.8		
7 Sa	0603	2.5	1210	0.9	1808	2.8		
22 Su	0028	0.8	0619	2.7	1219	0.8	1827	2.8
8 Su	0032	0.8	0638	2.6	1249	0.8	1846	2.8
23 M	0106	0.7	0702	2.8	1307	0.7	1909	2.8
9 M	0106	0.7	0712	2.7	1327	0.7	1921	2.8
24 Tu	0141	0.7	0740	2.9	● 1351	0.7	1949	2.8
10 Tu	0140	0.7	0744	2.8	1405	0.7	O 1958	2.9
25 W	0215	0.7	0818	2.9	1432	0.8	2029	2.7
11 W	0213	0.6	0818	2.8	1443	0.7	2036	2.8
26 Th	0249	0.8	0853	2.9	1511	0.8	2107	2.6
12 Th	0250	0.6	0851	2.8	1524	0.8	2115	2.8
27 F	0322	0.8	0929	2.9	1549	0.9	2145	2.5
13 F	0328	0.7	0928	2.8	1607	0.8	2200	2.7
28 Sa	0356	0.9	1006	2.8	1627	1.0	2223	2.3
14 Sa	0409	0.7	1009	2.8	1655	0.9	2251	2.5
29 Su	0434	1.0	1047	2.8	1709	1.1	2306	2.2
15 Su	0455	0.8	1057	2.7	1750	1.1	2350	2.4
30 M	0516	1.1	1133	2.7	1757	1.2	2358	2.2

DECEMBER

Day	Time	m	Time	m	Time	m	Time	m
1 Tu	0605	1.2	1228	2.6	1853	1.3		
16 W	0039	2.4	0628	0.9	1238	2.7	(1952	1.1
2 W	0104	2.1	0704	1.3	1331	2.5	) 1959	1.3
17 Th	0149	2.4	0728	1.0	1347	2.6	2110	1.1
3 Th	0223	2.1	0813	1.3	1442	2.5	2111	1.3
18 F	0305	2.3	0837	1.1	1508	2.6	2223	1.1
4 F	0335	2.2	0925	1.3	1546	2.5	2214	1.2
19 Sa	0416	2.4	0953	1.1	1624	2.6	2320	1.0
5 Sa	0431	2.3	1030	1.2	1642	2.6	2306	1.1
20 Su	0515	2.5	1105	1.1	1726	2.6		
6 Su	0520	2.4	1126	1.1	1732	2.6	2353	1.0
21 M	0008	0.9	0604	2.6	1207	1.0	1818	2.6
7 M	0604	2.5	1215	0.9	1817	2.7		
22 Tu	0049	0.9	0649	2.7	1259	0.9	1904	2.6
8 Tu	0035	0.8	0645	2.7	1303	0.8	1859	2.8
23 W	0127	0.9	0730	2.8	1344	0.9	1947	2.6
9 W	0114	0.7	0724	2.8	1348	0.8	O 1941	2.8
24 Th	0204	0.8	0806	2.9	● 1425	0.9	2025	2.6
10 Th	0154	0.7	0804	2.9	1433	0.7	2025	2.9
25 F	0236	0.8	0843	2.9	1501	0.9	2100	2.5
11 F	0233	0.6	0842	3.0	1518	0.7	2108	2.8
26 Sa	0308	0.9	0917	2.9	1535	1.0	2132	2.5
12 Sa	0314	0.6	0922	3.0	1604	0.8	2155	2.8
27 Su	0341	0.9	0950	2.9	1609	1.0	2204	2.5
13 Su	0357	0.6	1004	3.0	1652	0.9	2244	2.7
28 M	0414	0.9	1027	2.9	1644	1.1	2240	2.4
14 M	0444	0.7	1049	3.0	1746	1.0	2339	2.6
29 Tu	0449	1.0	1105	2.8	1725	1.1	2318	2.3
15 Tu	0533	0.8	1140	2.9	1843	1.1		
30 W	0530	1.1	1146	2.7	1808	1.2		
31 Th	0003	2.2	0617	1.1	1234	2.6	1900	1.2

WHEN TO ENTER — Lough Foyle easily entered at all states of the tide.

RATE AND SET — Clear of entrance to Lough; W. going, +0245, Londonderry, E. going, –0345, Londonderry, in entrance; Flood, +0600 (Lon.), Sp. 3½ kn.; Ebb, –0030 (Lon.), Sp. 3¼ kn. Off Redcastle: Flood, +0600 (Lon.), Sp. 1¼ kn.; Ebb, –0010 L(Lon.), Sp. 1½ kn.

LONDONDERRY

MEAN SPRING AND NEAP CURVES

Springs occur 1 day after New and Full Moon.

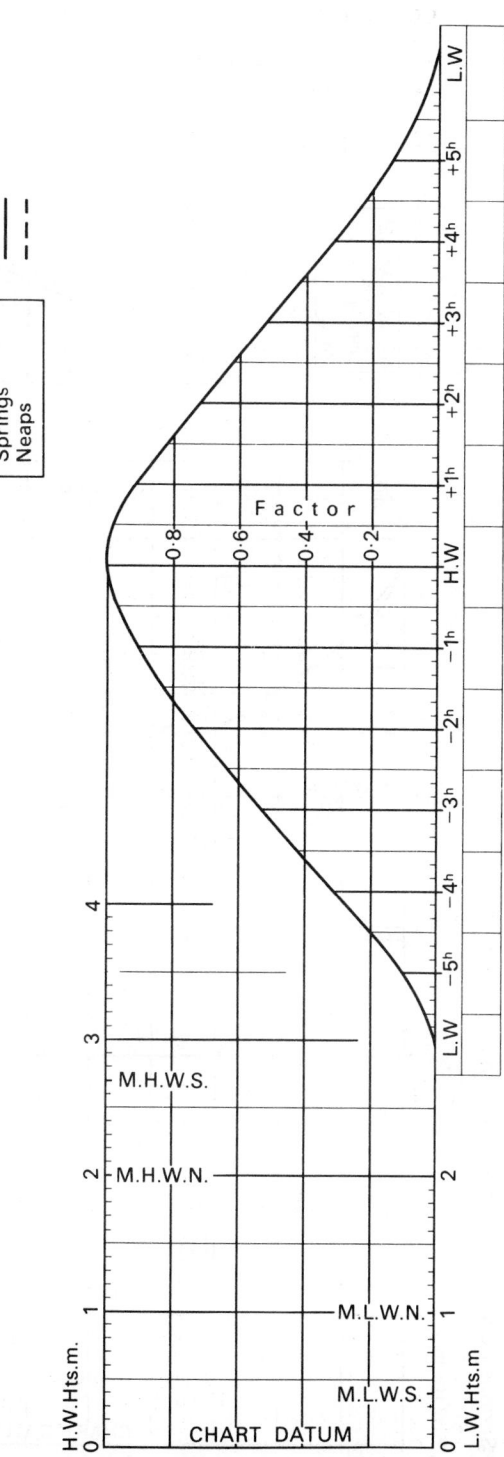

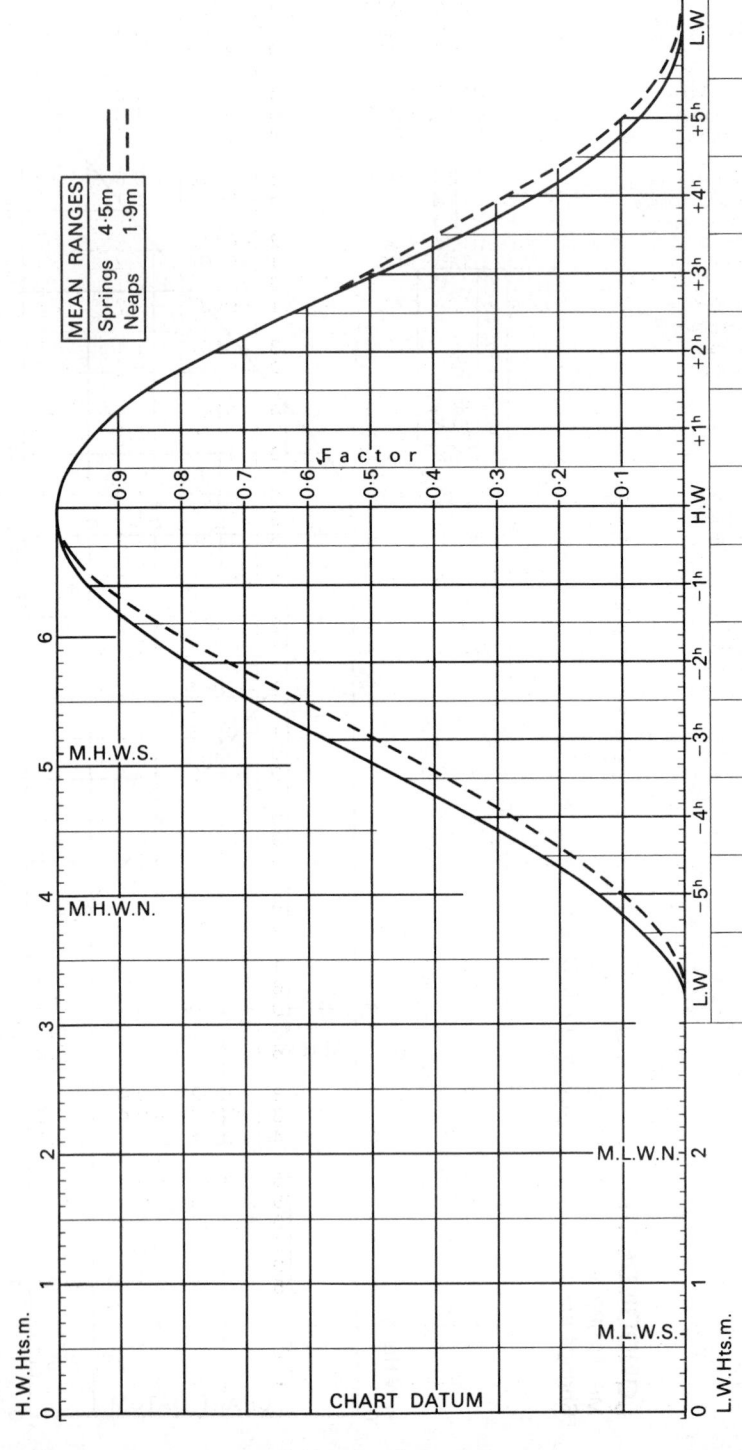

GALWAY

MEAN SPRING AND NEAP CURVES

Springs occur 1 day after New and Full Moon.

H.W.Hts.m.

L.W.Hts.m.

MEAN RANGES
Springs 4·5m
Neaps 1·9m

Factor

M.H.W.S.

M.H.W.N.

M.L.W.N.

M.L.W.S.

CHART DATUM

PLACE	TIME DIFFERENCES				HEIGHT DIFFERENCES (Metres)			
	High Water		Low Water		MHWS	MHWN	MLWN	MLWS
GALWAY	0200 and 1400	0900 and 2100	0200 and 1400	0800 and 2000	5.1	3.9	2.0	0.6
Inistrahull	+0100	+0100	+0115	+0200	−1.8	−1.4	−0.4	−0.2
Portmore	+0120	+0120	+0135	+0135	−1.3	−1.1	−0.4	−0.1
Trawbreaga Bay	+0115	+0059	+0109	+0125	−1.1	−0.8	−	−
Lough Swilly								
Rathmullan	+0125	+0050	+0126	+0118	−0.8	−0.7	−0.1	−0.1
Fanad Head	+0115	+0040	+0125	+0120	−1.1	−0.9	−0.5	−0.1
Mulroy Bay								
Bar	+0108	+0052	+0102	+0118	−1.2	−1.0	−	−
Fanny's Bay	+0145	+0129	+0151	+0207	−2.2	−1.7	−	−
Seamount Bay	+0210	+0154	+0226	+0242	−3.1	−2.3	−	−
Cranford Bay	+0329	+0313	+0351	+0407	−3.7	−2.8	−	−
Sheephaven								
Downies Bay	+0057	+0043	+0053	+0107	−1.1	−0.9	−	−
Inishbofin Bay	+0040	+0026	+0032	+0046	−1.2	−0.9	−	−
GALWAY	0600 and 1800	1100 and 2300	0000 and 1200	0700 and 1900	5.1	3.9	2.0	0.6
Gweedore Harbour	+0048	+0100	+0055	+0107	−1.3	−1.0	−0.5	−0.1
Burtonport	+0042	+0055	+0115	+0055	−1.2	−1.0	−0.6	−0.1
Loughros More Bay	+0042	+0054	+0046	+0058	−1.1	−0.9	−	−
Donegal Bay								
Killybegs	+0040	+0050	+0055	+0035	−1.0	−0.9	−0.5	0.0
Donegal Harbour (Salt Hill Quay)	+0038	+0050	+0052	+0104	−1.2	−0.9	−	−
Mullaghmore	+0036	+0048	+0047	+0059	−1.4	−1.0	−0.4	−0.2
Sligo Harbour (Oyster Island)	+0043	+0055	+0042	+0054	−1.0	−0.9	−0.5	−0.1
Ballysadare Bay (Culleenamore)	+0059	+0111	+0111	+0123	−1.2	−0.9	−	−
Killala Bay (Inishcrone)	+0035	+0055	+0030	+0050	−1.3	−1.2	−0.7	−0.2
Broadhaven	+0040	+0050	+0040	+0050	−1.4	−1.1	−0.4	−0.1
Blacksod Bay								
Blacksod Quay	+0025	+0035	+0040	+0040	−1.2	−1.0	−0.6	−0.2
Bull's Mouth	+0101	+0057	+0109	+0105	−1.5	−1.0	−0.6	−0.1
Clare Island	+0019	+0013	+0029	+0023	−1.0	−0.7	−0.4	−0.1
Westport Bay								
Inishraher	+0030	+0012	+0058	+0026	−0.6	−0.5	−0.3	−0.1
Killary Harbour	+0021	+0015	+0035	+0029	−1.0	−0.8	−0.4	−0.1
Inishbofin								
Bofin Harbour	+0013	+0009	+0021	+0017	−1.0	−0.8	−0.4	−0.1
Clifden Bay	+0005	+0005	+0016	+0016	−0.7	−0.5	−	−
Slyne Head	+0002	+0002	+0010	+0010	−0.7	−0.5	−	−
Roundstone Bay	+0003	+0003	+0008	+0008	−0.7	−0.5	−0.3	−0.1
Kilkieran Cove	+0005	+0005	+0016	+0016	−0.3	−0.2	−0.1	0.0
Aran Islands								
Killeany Bay	−0008	−0008	+0003	+0003	−0.4	−0.3	−0.2	−0.1
Liscannor	−0003	−0007	+0006	+0002	−0.4	−0.3	−	−
Seafield Point	−0006	−0014	+0004	−0004	−0.5	−0.4	−	−
River Shannon								
Kilbaha Bay	−0010	+0005	−0025	+0040	−0.8	−0.6	−0.5	−0.4
Carrigaholt	+0005	−0010	+0005	+0005	0.0	0.0	−0.1	−0.1
Kilrush	+0025	+0020	+0030	+0030	−0.1	−0.2	−0.3	−0.1
Foynes Island	+0105	+0055	+0055	+0055	+0.1	+0.1	−0.2	−0.3
Mellon Point	+0130	+0115	+0100	+0215	+0.8	+0.6	−0.1	−0.2
Limerick Dock	+0135	+0150	+0125	+0235	+0.8	+0.6	−0.8	−0.2
River Fergus								
Coney Island	+0125	+0115	+0050	+0205	+0.1	0.0	−	−

Refer to predictions on pages 21::254-21:256

IRELAND (West) GALWAY

HIGH & LOW WATER 1992   Lat. 53°16′N. Long. 9°03′W.

GMT   ADD 1 HOUR MARCH 29 — OCTOBER 25 FOR B.S.T.

JANUARY

Day	Time	m	Time	m	Time	m	Time	m
1 W	0216	4.4	0827	1.8	1449	4.2	2049	1.8
2 Th	0307	4.5	0918	1.6	1538	4.4	2135	1.7
3 F	0352	4.7	1003	1.4	1623	4.5	2217	1.5
4 Sa	0433	4.8	1044	1.2	1702	4.6	●2255	1.4
5 Su	0512	4.9	1122	1.1	1740	4.6	2333	1.3
6 M	0550	5.0	1157	1.0	1817	4.7		
7 Tu	0008	1.2	0627	4.9	1230	1.0	1853	4.7
8 W	0042	1.3	0702	4.9	1306	1.0	1927	4.6
9 Th	0117	1.3	0735	4.8	1340	1.1	2001	4.5
10 F	0152	1.4	0811	4.6	1415	1.3	2036	4.4
11 Sa	0229	1.6	0849	4.5	1453	1.4	2114	4.2
12 Su	0310	1.8	0929	4.3	1535	1.6	2159	4.1
13 M	0400	2.0	1019	4.1	1627	1.8	☽2254	4.0
14 Tu	0504	2.1	1123	4.0	1734	1.9		
15 W	0005	4.0	0624	2.0	1241	4.0	1850	1.9
16 Th	0120	4.1	0740	1.8	1355	4.2	2002	1.7
17 F	0226	4.4	0844	1.5	1458	4.5	2101	1.4
18 Sa	0321	4.7	0939	1.0	1553	4.8	2153	1.1
19 Su	0413	5.1	1028	0.6	1644	5.1	○2241	0.7
20 M	0501	5.4	1115	0.3	1732	5.3	2326	0.5
21 Tu	0547	5.6	1158	0.1	1817	5.4		
22 W	0010	0.4	0632	5.6	1242	0.2	1902	5.3
23 Th	0053	0.5	0719	5.5	1324	0.3	1947	5.2
24 F	0137	0.7	0804	5.2	1409	0.7	2032	4.9
25 Sa	0223	1.0	0850	4.9	1456	1.1	2119	4.6
26 Su	0312	1.4	0940	4.5	1548	1.5	ℂ2213	4.3
27 M	0401	1.7	1041	4.1	1649	1.9	2316	4.0
28 Tu	0525	2.0	1200	3.8	1812	2.1		
29 W	0036	3.9	0700	2.1	1330	3.8	1938	2.1
30 Th	0154	4.0	0819	1.9	1443	3.9	2043	2.0
31 F	0254	4.1	0914	1.7	1534	4.1	2129	1.7

FEBRUARY

Day	Time	m	Time	m	Time	m	Time	m
1 Sa	0342	4.4	0956	1.4	1616	4.3	2209	1.5
2 Su	0421	4.6	1033	1.2	1652	4.5	2245	1.2
3 M	0459	4.7	1106	0.9	1726	4.6	●2318	1.0
4 Tu	0533	4.9	1139	0.8	1758	4.7	2350	0.9
5 W	0607	4.9	1210	0.7	1829	4.7		
6 Th	0021	0.9	0638	4.9	1239	0.7	1900	4.7
7 F	0050	0.9	0710	4.9	1309	0.8	1930	4.6
8 Sa	0123	1.0	0742	4.7	1340	0.9	2002	4.5
9 Su	0155	1.2	0816	4.6	1413	1.1	2036	4.4
10 M	0232	1.4	0856	4.4	1453	1.4	2117	4.2
11 Tu	0317	1.6	0942	4.1	1542	1.6	☽2207	4.0
12 W	0416	1.9	1044	3.9	1648	1.9	2318	3.8
13 Th	0543	2.0	1208	3.8	1819	2.0		
14 F	0048	3.9	0721	1.8	1338	4.0	1948	1.8
15 Sa	0209	4.2	0834	1.4	1450	4.3	2053	1.4
16 Su	0311	4.6	0931	0.9	1545	4.7	2145	0.9
17 M	0402	5.0	1016	0.4	1633	5.0	2228	0.5
18 Tu	0448	5.3	1058	0.1	1716	5.3	○2311	0.1
19 W	0532	5.5	1139	−0.1	1758	5.4	2351	0.1
20 Th	0614	5.6	1219	0.0	1839	5.4		
21 F	0031	0.2	0656	5.5	1259	0.2	1920	5.2
22 Sa	0112	0.4	0740	5.2	1340	0.6	2002	4.9
23 Su	0155	0.8	0823	4.8	1422	1.0	2047	4.6
24 M	0240	1.2	0910	4.4	1510	1.5	2135	4.2
25 Tu	0332	1.6	1004	3.9	1607	2.0	ℂ2233	3.8
26 W	0442	2.0	1119	3.6	1733	2.2	2353	3.6
27 Th	0628	2.2	1306	3.5	1920	2.2		
28 F	0128	3.7	0801	2.0	1429	3.7	2027	2.0
29 Sa	0237	3.9	0856	1.7	1519	3.9	2114	1.7

MARCH

Day	Time	m	Time	m	Time	m	Time	m
1 Su	0324	4.1	0936	1.4	1557	4.2	2150	1.4
2 M	0403	4.4	1012	1.1	1631	4.4	2224	1.1
3 Tu	0437	4.6	1042	0.8	1702	4.6	2255	0.9
4 W	0509	4.8	1112	0.6	1732	4.7	●2325	0.7
5 Th	0540	4.9			1801	4.8	2353	0.6
6 F	0611	4.9	1208	0.5	1829	4.8		
7 Sa	0022	0.6	0642	4.9	1238	0.6	1859	4.8
8 Su	0053	0.7	0714	4.8	1309	0.7	1931	4.7
9 M	0127	1.0	0749	4.6	1342	1.0	2006	4.5
10 Tu	0205	1.1	0830	4.4	1423	1.3	2047	4.3
11 W	0250	1.4	0919	4.1	1512	1.6	2139	4.0
12 Th	0352	1.7	1023	3.9	1623	1.9	☽2251	3.8
13 F	0501	1.9	1151	3.8	1804	2.0		
14 Sa	0028	3.8	0707	1.6	1327	3.9	1937	1.7
15 Su	0154	4.1	0820	1.2	1437	4.3	2039	1.3
16 M	0256	4.5	0912	0.7	1528	4.7	2127	0.8
17 Tu	0343	4.9	0956	0.3	1613	5.0	2209	0.4
18 W	0428	5.2	1035	0.1	1654	5.2	○2249	0.2
19 Th	0511	5.4	1115	0.0	1734	5.3	2329	0.1
20 F	0551	5.4	1153	0.0	1814	5.3		
21 Sa	0008	0.2	0634	5.3	1232	0.3	1855	5.1
22 Su	0048	0.5	0714	5.0	1312	0.7	1935	4.9
23 M	0130	0.7	0758	4.7	1352	1.1	2018	4.5
24 Tu	0213	1.2	0843	4.2	1437	1.6	2103	4.2
25 W	0304	1.6	0935	3.9	1531	2.0	2156	3.8
26 Th	0409	1.9	1041	3.5	1651	2.3	ℂ2308	3.6
27 F	0543	2.1	1221	3.4	1836	2.3		
28 Sa	0042	3.6	0717	2.0	1354	3.6	1951	2.1
29 Su	0159	3.7	0818	1.7	1447	3.8	2042	1.8
30 M	0251	4.0	0901	1.4	1527	4.1	2119	1.4
31 Tu	0331	4.2	0936	1.1	1600	4.3	2153	1.1

APRIL

Day	Time	m	Time	m	Time	m	Time	m
1 W	0406	4.4	1009	0.9	1630	4.5	2224	0.9
2 Th	0438	4.6	1038	0.7	1659	4.7	2254	0.7
3 F	0509	4.8	1106	0.6	1727	4.8	●2323	0.6
4 Sa	0542	4.9	1136	0.6	1757	4.9	2356	0.5
5 Su	0614	4.9	1208	0.6	1829	4.9		
6 M	0028	0.6	0650	4.8	1242	0.8	1904	4.8
7 Tu	0106	0.8	0730	4.7	1320	1.0	1944	4.6
8 W	0148	1.0	0815	4.5	1405	1.3	2030	4.4
9 Th	0239	1.3	0908	4.2	1500	1.6	2127	4.1
10 F	0345	1.5	1014	4.0	1613	1.9	☽2238	3.9
11 Sa	0513	1.6	1139	3.9	1749	1.9		
12 Su	0008	3.9	0646	1.5	1307	4.0	1914	1.7
13 M	0131	4.2	0754	1.1	1413	4.3	2015	1.3
14 Tu	0232	4.5	0846	0.8	1504	4.5	2103	0.9
15 W	0321	4.8	0929	0.5	1548	4.9	2145	0.6
16 Th	0404	5.0	1010	0.3	1630	5.1	2226	0.4
17 F	0447	5.2	1049	0.3	1709	5.2	○2306	0.3
18 Sa	0529	5.2	1127	0.4	1749	5.2	2346	0.4
19 Su	0611	5.0	1207	0.6	1829	5.1		
20 M	0027	0.6	0653	4.8	1246	0.9	1910	4.9
21 Tu	0109	0.9	0735	4.5	1327	1.3	1952	4.6
22 W	0154	1.2	0820	4.2	1412	1.6	2036	4.3
23 Th	0243	1.5	0910	3.9	1504	2.0	2125	4.0
24 F	0341	1.8	1007	3.7	1610	2.2	ℂ2226	3.8
25 Sa	0454	1.9	1122	3.5	1734	2.2	2342	3.7
26 Su	0614	1.9	1250	3.6	1855	2.1		
27 M	0100	3.7	0720	1.8	1355	3.8	1954	1.9
28 Tu	0201	3.9	0812	1.6	1442	4.0	2039	1.6
29 W	0247	4.1	0851	1.3	1518	4.2	2115	1.3
30 Th	0325	4.3	0927	1.1	1552	4.3	2149	1.1

To find H.W. Dover subtract 6 h. 20 min.

TIDAL DIFFERENCES PAGE 21:253. TIDAL CURVE PAGE 21:252.

Datum of predictions: 0.20 m. below Ordnance Datum (Dublin) or approx. L.A.T.

GALWAY IRELAND (West)   21:255

Lat. 53°16′N. Long. 9°03′W.

GMT   ADD 1 HOUR MARCH 29 — OCTOBER 25 FOR B.S.T.

HIGH & LOW WATER 1992

MAY

Day	Time m	Day	Time m
1 F	0402 4·5, 1000 0·9, 1623 4·6, 2223 0·9	16 Sa	0427 4·8, 1026 0·8, 1647 5·0, ○ 2248 0·7
2 Sa	0437 4·7, 1033 0·8, 1654 4·8, ● 2255 0·7	17 Su	0511 4·8, 1106 0·8, 1727 5·0, 2329 0·7
3 Su	0512 4·8, 1108 0·7, 1729 4·9, 2332 0·6	18 M	0553 4·8, 1147 1·0, 1808 5·0
4 M	0551 4·9, 1144 0·7, 1805 5·0	19 Tu	0011 0·8, 0635 4·6, 1227 1·1, 1849 4·8
5 Tu	0010 0·6, 0632 4·9, 1224 0·8, 1846 4·9	20 W	0053 1·0, 0719 4·5, 1309 1·4, 1931 4·6
6 W	0052 0·7, 0717 4·8, 1307 1·0, 1931 4·8	21 Th	0137 1·2, 0802 4·3, 1351 1·6, 2013 4·4
7 Th	0140 0·9, 0806 4·6, 1357 1·3, 2022 4·6	22 F	0222 1·4, 0847 4·1, 1439 1·8, 2058 4·2
8 F	0234 1·1, 0901 4·4, 1454 1·5, 2119 4·4	23 Sa	0311 1·6, 0935 3·9, 1532 2·0, 2148 4·0
9 Sa	0339 1·3, 1006 4·2, 1603 1·7,) 2227 4·2	24 Su	0406 1·7, 1030 3·8, 1634 2·1, 2244 3·8
10 Su	0455 1·4, 1119 4·1, 1723 1·8, 2344 4·1	25 M	0506 1·8, 1134 3·7, 1744 2·1, 2349 3·8
11 M	0612 1·4, 1236 4·2, 1842 1·6	26 Tu	0610 1·8, 1245 3·8, 1852 2·0
12 Tu	0100 4·2, 0720 1·2, 1342 4·4, 1945 1·2	27 W	0056 3·8, 0709 1·7, 1342 3·9, 1947 1·8
13 W	0204 4·4, 0815 1·0, 1436 4·6, 2037 1·1	28 Th	0152 4·0, 0759 1·5, 1429 4·1, 2032 1·6
14 Th	0256 4·6, 0901 0·9, 1522 4·8, 2122 0·9	29 F	0242 4·2, 0843 1·3, 1508 4·3, 2114 1·3
15 F	0342 4·7, 0945 0·8, 1604 4·9, 2206 0·7	30 Sa	0325 4·4, 0924 1·2, 1546 4·6, 2153 1·0
		31 Su	0407 4·6, 1004 1·0, 1624 4·8, 2233 0·8

JUNE

Day	Time m	Day	Time m
1 M	0449 4·8, 1045 0·9, 1705 5·0, ● 2315 0·6	16 Tu	0540 4·6, 1132 1·1, 1751 4·9, 2358 0·9
2 Tu	0534 4·9, 1127 0·8, 1749 5·1, 2358 0·5	17 W	0621 4·5, 1211 1·2, 1831 4·8
3 W	0619 4·9, 1212 0·8, 1834 5·1	18 Th	0039 0·9, 0702 4·5, 1252 1·3, 1912 4·7
4 Th	0045 0·5, 0709 4·9, 1259 0·9, 1923 5·0	19 F	0119 1·0, 0741 4·4, 1331 1·4, 1951 4·6
5 F	0134 0·7, 0758 4·8, 1349 1·1, 2013 4·9	20 Sa	0158 1·1, 0820 4·2, 1411 1·5, 2030 4·4
6 Sa	0227 0·8, 0851 4·6, 1443 1·3, 2108 4·7	21 Su	0237 1·3, 0901 4·1, 1454 1·7, 2111 4·2
7 Su	0324 1·0, 0948 4·4, 1541 1·5,) 2207 4·4	22 M	0319 1·5, 0943 4·0, 1541 1·8, 2156 4·0
8 M	0427 1·2, 1051 4·3, 1651 1·6, 2315 4·3	23 Tu	0407 1·6, 1031 3·9, 1635 2·0, (2247 3·9
9 Tu	0534 1·4, 1129 4·2, 1805 1·6	24 W	0501 1·7, 1129 3·8, 1740 2·0, 2349 3·8
10 W	0028 4·2, 0643 1·4, 1309 4·3, 1914 1·6	25 Th	0601 1·7, 1234 3·8, 1848 1·9
11 Th	0135 4·2, 0745 1·4, 1408 4·4, 2013 1·4	26 F	0056 3·8, 0704 1·7, 1335 4·0, 1949 1·7
12 F	0234 4·3, 0837 1·3, 1458 4·6, 2105 1·2	27 Sa	0159 4·0, 0802 1·6, 1429 4·2, 2043 1·4
13 Sa	0325 4·4, 0925 1·2, 1545 4·7, 2152 1·1	28 Su	0254 4·2, 0856 1·4, 1517 4·5, 2131 1·1
14 Su	0413 4·5, 1009 1·2, 1628 4·8, 2235 0·9	29 M	0345 4·5, 0943 1·1, 1603 4·8, 2219 0·8
15 M	0457 4·6, 1051 1·2, 1709 4·9, ○ 2318 0·9	30 Tu	0434 4·7, 1030 0·9, 1649 5·0, ● 2304 0·5

JULY

Day	Time m	Day	Time m
1 W	0522 4·9, 1116 0·7, 1736 5·2, 2349 0·3	16 Th	0604 4·5, 1154 1·0, 1812 4·8
2 Th	0608 5·1, 1201 0·6, 1824 5·3	17 F	0019 0·8, 0641 4·5, 1231 1·0, 1849 4·8
3 F	0035 0·3, 0656 5·1, 1248 0·6, 1912 5·3	18 Sa	0053 0·8, 0716 4·5, 1306 1·1, 1924 4·7
4 Sa	0121 0·3, 0744 5·0, 1334 0·7, 1959 5·1	19 Su	0127 0·9, 0751 4·4, 1340 1·2, 1959 4·5
5 Su	0209 0·5, 0832 4·8, 1423 0·9, 2050 4·9	20 M	0201 1·0, 0825 4·3, 1416 1·4, 2034 4·4
6 M	0258 0·8, 0924 4·6, 1517 1·2, 2143 4·6	21 Tu	0237 1·2, 0901 4·1, 1456 1·6, 2114 4·2
7 Tu	0353 1·1, 1019 4·4, 1617 1·5,) 2244 4·3	22 W	0317 1·4, 0941 4·0, 1541 1·8,) 2159 4·0
8 W	0457 1·4, 1123 4·2, 1729 1·7, 2356 4·0	23 Th	0403 1·6, 1030 3·9, 1638 1·9, 2257 3·8
9 Th	0610 1·6, 1235 4·1, 1848 1·7	24 F	0504 1·8, 1133 3·8, 1753 2·0
10 F	0113 4·0, 0721 1·7, 1344 4·2, 1959 1·6	25 Sa	0010 3·7, 0618 1·8, 1249 3·8, 1913 1·9
11 Sa	0222 4·0, 0833 1·7, 1442 4·3, 2057 1·4	26 Su	0127 3·9, 0733 1·7, 1358 4·1, 2022 1·5
12 Su	0318 4·1, 0915 1·5, 1531 4·5, 2145 1·2	27 M	0234 4·1, 0837 1·4, 1457 4·4, 2118 1·1
13 M	0404 4·3, 1000 1·4, 1614 4·6, 2227 1·0	28 Tu	0331 4·4, 0931 1·1, 1548 4·8, 2206 0·6
14 Tu	0448 4·4, 1040 1·2, 1657 4·7, ○ 2306 0·9	29 W	0421 4·8, 1019 0·7, 1635 5·1, ● 2251 0·3
15 W	0527 4·5, 1119 1·1, 1734 4·8, 2344 0·8	30 Th	0508 5·0, 1102 0·5, 1722 5·4, 2334 0·0
		31 F	0553 5·2, 1146 0·3, 1807 5·5

AUGUST

Day	Time m	Day	Time m
1 Sa	0017 0·0, 0638 5·3, 1229 0·3, 1853 5·4	16 Su	0024 0·6, 0646 4·6, 1236 0·9, 1855 4·8
2 Su	0100 0·1, 0721 5·2, 1313 0·4, 1938 5·3	17 M	0053 0·7, 0717 4·6, 1307 1·0, 1927 4·6
3 M	0144 0·3, 0806 5·0, 1358 0·7, 2026 4·9	18 Tu	0124 0·9, 0748 4·4, 1340 1·2, 2001 4·5
4 Tu	0229 0·7, 0854 4·7, 1447 1·1, 2115 4·6	19 W	0157 1·1, 0822 4·3, 1415 1·4, 2037 4·3
5 W	0319 1·2, 0946 4·4, 1543 1·5,) 2213 4·2	20 Th	0233 1·3, 0900 4·1, 1457 1·6, 2122 4·0
6 Th	0420 1·6, 1048 4·1, 1655 1·8, 2326 3·8	21 F	0318 1·6, 0946 3·9, 1553 1·9, (2219 3·8
7 F	0539 1·9, 1204 3·9, 1829 1·9	22 Sa	0420 1·9, 1051 3·8, 1713 2·0, 2337 3·7
8 Sa	0057 3·7, 0709 2·0, 1326 3·9, 1954 1·8	23 Su	0546 2·0, 1215 3·8, 1852 1·8
9 Su	0216 3·8, 0818 2·0, 1429 4·1, 2051 1·6	24 M	0106 3·8, 0716 1·9, 1337 4·1, 2008 1·4
10 M	0312 4·0, 0908 1·7, 1519 4·3, 2136 1·3	25 Tu	0220 4·1, 0823 1·5, 1442 4·5, 2104 1·0
11 Tu	0356 4·2, 0949 1·4, 1602 4·5, 2214 1·1	26 W	0317 4·5, 0917 1·0, 1532 4·9, 2150 0·5
12 W	0433 4·4, 1026 1·2, 1640 4·7, 2248 0·8	27 Th	0404 4·9, 1002 0·5, 1619 5·3, 2233 0·1
13 Th	0508 4·5, 1059 1·0, 1715 4·8, ○ 2322 0·7	28 F	0449 5·2, 1044 0·3, 1704 5·5, ● 2313 −0·1
14 F	0542 4·6, 1133 0·9, 1749 4·8, 2353 0·6	29 Sa	0532 5·4, 1125 0·1, 1747 5·6, 2353 −0·1
15 Sa	0614 4·6, 1204 0·8, 1822 4·8	30 Su	0614 5·4, 1207 0·1, 1831 5·5
		31 M	0034 0·0, 0656 5·3, 1248 0·3, 1914 5·3

GENERAL — Little stream off Aran.

RATE AND SET — Narrow abreast of Chapel Rock — Sp. 2 kn. in Bay — general rate Sp. 1-1½ kn. — much affected by W. winds which increase rise and delay turn.

IRELAND (West) GALWAY

HIGH & LOW WATER 1992 Lat. 53°16′N. Long. 9°03′W.

GMT ADD 1 HOUR MARCH 29 — OCTOBER 25 FOR B.S.T.

SEPTEMBER

Day	Time m	Time m	Time m	Time m
1 Tu	0116 0.4	0740 5.0	1331 0.7	1959 4.9
16 W	0049 0.9	0713 4.7	1309 1.1	1930 4.6
2 W	0159 0.9	0825 4.7	1447 1.1	2049 4.5
17 Th	0123 1.1	0747 4.5	1345 1.3	2009 4.4
3 Th)	0247 1.4	0915 4.4	1514 1.5	2145 4.1
18 F	0201 1.4	0827 4.3	1429 1.6	2056 4.2
4 F	0346 1.8	1014 4.0	1626 1.9	2259 3.7
19 Sa (	0247 1.7	0917 4.1	1527 1.8	2156 3.9
5 Sa	0511 2.2	1133 3.8	1811 2.0	
20 Su	0353 2.0	1024 3.9	1654 2.0	2318 3.8
6 Su	0042 3.6	0655 2.2	1304 3.8	1941 1.9
21 M	0526 2.1	1836 1.8		
7 M	0206 3.8	0804 2.0	1412 4.0	2034 1.6
22 Tu	0052 3.9	0700 1.9	1319 4.2	1949 1.4
8 Tu	0257 4.0	0850 1.7	1500 4.2	2115 1.4
23 W	0205 4.3	0806 1.5	1422 4.6	2043 0.9
9 W	0336 4.2	0928 1.5	1539 4.5	2149 1.1
24 Th	0258 4.7	0857 1.0	1512 5.0	2127 0.5
10 Th	0410 4.4	1002 1.2	1616 4.7	2221 1.0
25 F	0341 5.0	0941 0.6	1557 5.3	2209 0.2
11 F	0442 4.6	1034 1.0	1648 4.8	2252 0.7
26 Sa ●	0426 5.3	1021 0.3	2248 0.0	
12 Sa	0513 4.7	1106 0.8	1720 4.9	○ 2322 0.6
27 Su	0508 5.5	1102 0.2	1723 5.6	2327 0.1
13 Su	0543 4.8	1136 0.8	1753 4.9	2350 0.6
28 M	0549 5.5	1143 0.2	1807 5.5	
14 M	0612 4.8	1205 0.8	1824 4.9	
29 Tu	0007 0.3	0631 5.4	1225 0.4	1850 5.2
15 Tu	0019 0.7	0642 4.7	1236 0.9	1856 4.8
30 W	0048 0.7	0713 5.1	1309 0.8	1935 4.9

OCTOBER

Day	Time m	Time m	Time m	Time m
1 Th	0131 1.1	0758 4.8	1355 1.2	2025 4.5
16 F	0057 1.2	0721 4.8	1326 1.3	1951 4.6
2 F	0218 1.6	0846 4.4	1449 1.6	2119 4.1
17 Sa	0140 1.5	0806 4.6	1413 1.5	2042 4.3
3 Sa	0315 2.0	0943 4.1	1557 2.0	) 2228 3.8
18 Su	0232 1.8	0900 4.3	1517 1.7	2145 4.1
4 Su	0434 2.3	1057 3.9	1733 2.1	
19 M	0339 2.0	1007 4.2	1638 1.8	(2304 4.0
5 M	0005 3.7	0617 2.3	1225 3.9	1902 2.0
20 Tu	0508 2.1	1130 4.2	1810 1.7	
6 Tu	0134 3.8	0728 2.2	1337 4.0	1958 1.8
21 W	0031 4.2	0635 1.9	1253 4.4	1921 1.4
7 W	0226 4.0	0819 1.9	1429 4.2	2040 1.5
22 Th	0141 4.5	0741 1.6	1358 4.7	2015 1.0
8 Th	0305 4.2	0858 1.6	1510 4.4	2117 1.3
23 F	0234 4.8	0833 1.2	1449 5.0	2101 0.7
9 F	0339 4.5	0934 1.3	1545 4.6	2149 1.1
24 Sa	0319 5.1	0918 0.8	1535 5.3	2143 0.5
10 Sa	0412 4.7	1006 1.1	1619 4.8	2219 0.9
25 Su ●	0402 5.4	1000 0.6	1620 5.4	2224 0.4
11 Su	0441 4.8	1037 1.0	1649 4.9	2248 0.8
26 M	0444 5.5	1041 0.5	1702 5.4	2304 0.5
12 M	0511 4.9	1106 0.9	1720 4.9	2318 0.8
27 Tu	0525 5.5	1123 0.5	1746 5.3	2344 0.7
13 Tu	0540 5.0	1137 0.9	1754 4.9	2349 0.9
28 W	0607 5.4	1205 0.7	1831 5.1	
14 W	0610 5.0	1210 0.9	1829 4.9	
29 Th	0025 1.0	0649 5.2	1249 1.0	1916 4.8
15 Th	0021 1.0	0643 4.9	1245 1.1	1907 4.7
30 F	0107 1.4	0734 4.9	1335 1.3	2004 4.5
31 Sa	0154 1.8	0820 4.6	1427 1.7	2056 4.2

NOVEMBER

Day	Time m	Time m	Time m	Time m
1 Su	0247 2.1	0912 4.3	1528 1.9	2155 3.9
16 M	0223 1.7	0849 4.7	1507 1.5	2132 4.4
2 M	0353 2.3	1013 4.1	1640 2.1	) 2308 3.8
17 Tu	0327 1.9	0952 4.5	1617 1.6	2241 4.3
3 Tu	0513 2.4	1126 4.0	1757 2.1	
18 W	0441 2.0	1104 4.4	1733 1.6	2357 4.4
4 W	0032 3.8	0634 2.3	1241 4.0	1903 2.0
19 Th	0600 1.9	1221 4.5	1845 1.5	
5 Th	0138 4.0	0734 2.1	1341 4.1	1954 1.8
20 F	0109 4.5	0710 1.7	1328 4.6	1944 1.3
6 F	0225 4.2	0820 1.9	1429 4.3	2034 1.6
21 Sa	0206 4.8	0808 1.4	1426 4.8	2034 1.1
7 Sa	0303 4.5	0900 1.6	1508 4.5	2111 1.4
22 Su	0256 5.0	0857 1.2	1515 5.0	2119 1.0
8 Su	0336 4.7	0935 1.4	1545 4.7	2143 1.2
23 M	0341 5.2	0942 1.0	1602 5.1	2203 0.9
9 M	0407 4.8	1007 1.2	1620 4.8	2216 1.1
24 Tu	0423 5.3	1026 0.8	1647 5.2	2245 0.9
10 Tu	0438 5.0	1040 1.0	1654 4.9	○ 2249 1.0
25 W	0506 5.4	1109 0.8	1732 5.1	2327 1.0
11 W	0511 5.1	1115 1.0	1732 5.0	2325 1.0
26 Th	0549 5.3	1153 0.9	1815 5.0	
12 Th	0546 5.1	1151 0.9	1811 5.0	
27 F	0008 1.2	0631 5.2	1236 1.0	1900 4.8
13 F	0001 1.1	0624 5.1	1231 1.0	1853 4.9
28 Sa	0050 1.4	0714 5.0	1320 1.3	1944 4.6
14 Sa	0043 1.3	0707 5.0	1316 1.1	1940 4.8
29 Su	0134 1.7	0758 4.8	1406 1.5	2030 4.4
15 Su	0130 1.5	0755 4.9	1408 1.3	2033 4.6
30 M	0220 1.9	0843 4.5	1454 1.7	2118 4.2

DECEMBER

Day	Time m	Time m	Time m	Time m
1 Tu	0312 2.1	0932 4.3	1548 1.9	2213 4.0
16 W	0307 1.5	0932 4.8	1548 1.3	(2213 4.6
2 W	0412 2.3	1027 4.1	1647 2.0	) 2315 3.9
17 Th	0409 1.7	1034 4.5	1654 1.5	2319 4.4
3 Th	0520 2.3	1130 4.0	1750 2.0	
18 F	0520 1.8	1146 4.4	1805 1.6	
4 F	0027 4.0	0632 2.3	1238 4.0	1852 2.0
19 Sa	0031 4.4	0638 1.8	1300 4.4	1914 1.6
5 Sa	0128 4.1	0733 2.1	1338 4.1	1945 1.8
20 Su	0138 4.6	0745 1.7	1406 4.5	2013 1.5
6 Su	0218 4.3	0820 1.9	1427 4.3	2030 1.7
21 M	0234 4.7	0843 1.5	1503 4.6	2105 1.4
7 M	0258 4.5	0903 1.8	1511 4.5	2111 1.5
22 Tu	0324 4.9	0932 1.3	1553 4.7	2152 1.3
8 Tu	0335 4.7	0942 1.4	1553 4.7	2150 1.3
23 W	0410 5.1	1019 1.1	1638 4.8	2234 1.2
9 W	0410 4.9	1020 1.2	1633 4.9	○ 2228 1.2
24 Th	0452 5.2	1101 1.0	1722 4.9	2316 1.2
10 Th	0448 5.1	1059 1.0	1715 5.0	2309 1.1
25 F	0534 5.2	1143 0.9	1804 4.9	2356 1.2
11 F	0529 5.2	1140 0.8	1758 5.1	2351 1.0
26 Sa	0615 5.1	1222 0.9	1845 4.8	
12 Sa	0611 5.3	1226 0.8	1843 5.1	
27 Su	0035 1.3	0656 5.1	1302 1.0	1924 4.7
13 Su	0035 1.1	0657 5.3	1309 0.8	1931 5.0
28 M	0114 1.4	0735 4.9	1341 1.2	2004 4.5
14 M	0121 1.2	0745 5.2	1358 0.9	2020 4.9
29 Tu	0154 1.5	0815 4.7	1420 1.4	2043 4.4
15 Tu	0212 1.3	0837 5.0	1450 1.1	2114 4.7
30 W	0234 1.7	0854 4.5	1500 1.6	2124 4.2
31 Th	0318 1.9	0936 4.3	1545 1.8	2209 4.0

To find H.W. Dover subtract 6 h. 20 min.

TIDAL DIFFERENCES PAGE 21:253. TIDAL CURVE PAGE 21:252.

Datum of predictions: 0.20 m. below Ordnance Datum (Dublin) or approx. L.A.T.

GIBRALTAR 21:257

Lat. 36°08′N. Long. 5°21′W. **HIGH & LOW WATER 1992**

TIME ZONE –0100 SUBTRACT 1 HOUR FROM TIMES SHOWN FOR GMT

JANUARY

Day	Time	m	Time	m	Time	m	Time	m
1 W	0027	0.7	0615	0.3	1250	0.8	1849	0.2
2 TH	0120	0.8	0702	0.2	1340	0.8	1932	0.2
3 F	0206	0.8	0743	0.2	1423	0.8	2011	0.1
4 SA	0246	0.8	0822	0.2	1502	0.8	● 2049	0.1
5 SU	0324	0.9	0859	0.2	1537	0.8	2125	0.1
6 M	0359	0.9	0934	0.2	1611	0.8	2159	0.1
7 TU	0433	0.9	1009	0.1	1645	0.8	2233	0.1
8 W	0507	0.9	1044	0.1	1718	0.8	2306	0.1
9 TH	0540	0.8	1118	0.2	1753	0.8	2340	0.1
10 F	0615	0.8	1154	0.2	1831	0.8		
11 SA	0015	0.2	0653	0.8	1235	0.2	1914	0.7
12 SU	0056	0.2	0736	0.8	1322	0.2	2006	0.7
13 M	0146	0.2	0827	0.7	1421	0.2	2109	0.7
14 TU	0250	0.3	0930	0.7	1539	0.2	2224	0.7
15 W	0410	0.3	1043	0.7	1704	0.2	2341	0.7
16 TH	0528	0.2	1156	0.8	1814	0.1		
17 F	0047	0.8	0632	0.2	1302	0.8	1910	0.1
18 SA	0145	0.8	0727	0.1	1400	0.9	1959	0.0
19 SU	0236	0.9	0817	0.0	1452	0.9	O 2045	0.0
20 M	0324	1.0	0903	0.0	1541	1.0	2128	-0.1
21 TU	0410	1.0	0948	0.0	1627	1.0	2211	-0.1
22 W	0455	1.0	1033	0.0	1713	1.0	2253	0.0
23 TH	0540	1.0	1117	0.0	1759	0.9	2335	0.0
24 F	0625	0.9	1202	0.0	1846	0.8		
25 SA	0018	0.1	0711	0.9	1249	0.1	1934	0.8
26 SU	0104	0.1	0801	0.8	1342	0.2	2027	0.7
27 M	0157	0.2	0856	0.7	1449	0.2	2130	0.6
28 TU	0308	0.3	1002	0.7	1620	0.2	2243	0.6
29 W	0442	0.3	1118	0.6	1739	0.2	2358	0.6
30 TH	0557	0.2	1228	0.6	1836	0.2		
31 F	0059	0.7	0650	0.2	1324	0.7	1920	0.1

FEBRUARY

Day	Time	m	Time	m	Time	m	Time	m
1 SA	0148	0.7	0732	0.2	1409	0.7	1959	0.1
2 SU	0229	0.7	0810	0.1	1446	0.7	2034	0.0
3 M	0304	0.8	0845	0.1	1520	0.8	● 2108	0.0
4 TU	0338	0.8	0917	0.0	1552	0.8	2139	0.0
5 W	0409	0.8	0949	0.0	1624	0.8	2210	0.0
6 TH	0441	0.8	1020	0.0	1655	0.8	2240	0.0
7 F	0512	0.8	1052	0.0	1728	0.8	2310	0.0
8 SA	0545	0.8	1124	0.0	1804	0.8	2342	0.1
9 SU	0620	0.8	1200	0.2	1844	0.7		
10 M	0019	0.1	0700	0.7	1242	0.1	1931	0.7
11 TU	0104	0.1	0749	0.7	1335	0.2	2032	0.6
12 W	0204	0.2	0852	0.7	1453	0.2	2151	0.6
13 TH	0334	0.2	1014	0.6	1643	0.2	2318	0.6
14 F	0513	0.2	1140	0.7	1804	0.1		
15 SA	0031	0.7	0623	0.1	1252	0.7	1900	0.0
16 SU	0131	0.8	0718	0.0	1350	0.8	1948	0.0
17 M	0222	0.9	0806	0.0	1441	0.9	2031	-0.1
18 TU	0308	0.9	0850	-0.1	1527	0.9	O 2111	-0.1
19 W	0352	1.0	0932	-0.1	1611	0.9	2151	-0.1
20 TH	0435	1.0	1012	-0.1	1654	0.9	2229	-0.1
21 F	0516	0.9	1053	-0.1	1736	0.9	2307	0.0
22 SA	0558	0.9	1133	0.0	1819	0.8	2346	0.0
23 SU	0640	0.8	1214	0.0	1903	0.7		
24 M	0026	0.1	0723	0.7	1300	0.1	1951	0.7
25 TU	0112	0.2	0813	0.6	1357	0.2	2048	0.6
26 W	0214	0.2	0916	0.6	1532	0.2	2202	0.6
27 TH	0405	0.3	1040	0.5	1713	0.2	2324	0.6
28 F	0538	0.2	1204	0.6	1814	0.2		
29 SA	0032	0.6	0632	0.2	1304	0.6	1858	0.1

MARCH

Day	Time	m	Time	m	Time	m	Time	m
1 SU	0123	0.7	0714	0.1	1348	0.7	1936	0.1
2 M	0203	0.7	0749	0.1	1424	0.7	2010	0.0
3 TU	0237	0.8	0822	0.0	1457	0.8	2041	0.0
4 W	0309	0.8	0853	0.0	1528	0.8	● 2111	0.0
5 TH	0340	0.8	0923	0.0	1559	0.8	2140	0.0
6 F	0411	0.8	0953	0.0	1631	0.8	2210	0.0
7 SA	0442	0.8	1024	0.0	1704	0.8	2240	0.0
8 SU	0516	0.8	1057	0.0	1741	0.8	2313	0.0
9 M	0552	0.8	1132	0.0	1822	0.7	2351	0.1
10 TU	0634	0.7	1214	0.1	1911	0.7		
11 W	0037	0.1	0724	0.7	1306	0.1	2012	0.6
12 TH	0139	0.2	0830	0.6	1427	0.2	2132	0.6
13 F	0320	0.2	0957	0.6	1631	0.2	2259	0.6
14 SA	0505	0.2	1127	0.6	1749	0.1		
15 SU	0013	0.7	0611	0.1	1239	0.7	1843	0.0
16 M	0112	0.8	0703	0.0	1336	0.8	1928	0.0
17 TU	0202	0.9	0748	-0.1	1425	0.9	2009	-0.1
18 W	0247	0.9	0830	-0.1	1510	0.9	O 2048	-0.1
19 TH	0330	1.0	0910	-0.1	1552	0.9	2126	-0.1
20 F	0411	1.0	0948	-0.1	1633	0.9	2203	-0.1
21 SA	0451	0.9	1026	-0.1	1713	0.9	2239	0.0
22 SU	0530	0.9	1104	0.0	1753	0.8	2316	0.1
23 M	0609	0.8	1143	0.1	1835	0.7	2354	0.1
24 TU	0649	0.7	1225	0.1	1920	0.7		
25 W	0038	0.2	0734	0.6	1316	0.2	2013	0.6
26 TH	0136	0.3	0833	0.6	1441	0.3	2121	0.6
27 F	0321	0.3	0955	0.5	1630	0.3	2240	0.6
28 SA	0504	0.3	1135	0.5	1736	0.3	2351	0.6
29 SU	0601	0.2	1230	0.6	1824	0.2		
30 M	0044	0.7	0643	0.1	1316	0.6	1902	0.1
31 TU	0125	0.7	0719	0.1	1353	0.7	1936	0.1

APRIL

Day	Time	m	Time	m	Time	m	Time	m
1 W	0201	0.8	0751	0.0	1426	0.8	2008	0.0
2 TH	0234	0.8	0823	0.0	1459	0.8	2038	0.0
3 F	0307	0.8	0854	0.0	1532	0.8	● 2109	0.0
4 SA	0340	0.9	0926	0.0	1607	0.8	2141	0.0
5 SU	0415	0.9	0959	0.0	1644	0.8	2214	0.0
6 M	0452	0.9	1034	0.0	1724	0.8	2251	0.1
7 TU	0532	0.8	1113	0.0	1808	0.8	2333	0.1
8 W	0617	0.8	1157	0.1	1900	0.7		
9 TH	0023	0.2	0711	0.7	1254	0.2	2002	0.7
10 F	0132	0.2	0820	0.7	1419	0.2	2117	0.7
11 SA	0315	0.2	0944	0.7	1610	0.2	2237	0.7
12 SU	0448	0.2	1109	0.7	1723	0.2	2349	0.8
13 M	0552	0.1	1219	0.7	1818	0.1		
14 TU	0048	0.8	0642	0.0	1316	0.8	1903	0.0
15 W	0139	0.9	0727	0.0	1405	0.9	1944	0.0
16 TH	0224	0.9	0808	0.0	1449	0.9	2023	0.0
17 F	0306	0.9	0847	-0.1	1531	0.9	O 2100	0.0
18 SA	0347	0.9	0925	0.0	1611	0.9	2137	0.0
19 SU	0425	0.9	1002	0.0	1650	0.9	2213	0.1
20 M	0503	0.9	1040	0.0	1729	0.8	2251	0.1
21 TU	0541	0.9	1118	0.1	1810	0.8	2330	0.2
22 W	0620	0.7	1159	0.2	1853	0.7		
23 TH	0013	0.2	0702	0.7	1248	0.2	1941	0.7
24 F	0108	0.3	0754	0.6	1355	0.3	2039	0.6
25 SA	0230	0.3	0903	0.6	1526	0.3	2146	0.6
26 SU	0405	0.3	1024	0.6	1640	0.3	2253	0.6
27 M	0512	0.3	1135	0.6	1734	0.2	2350	0.7
28 TU	0600	0.2	1229	0.7	1818	0.2		
29 W	0037	0.7	0640	0.1	1313	0.7	1855	0.2
30 TH	0119	0.8	0716	0.1	1352	0.8	1930	0.1

Datum of predictions: 0.1 m. below M.L.W.S. and 0.1 m. above L.A.T.

In Gibraltar Bay the tidal streams off Europa Point are more or less rotatory, changing from E.-going to SW.-going, through S. between 4 and 5 h. after H.W. at Gibraltar, and from SW.-going to E.-going, also through S., between 1 h. before and ½ h. after H.W. at Gibraltar.

21:258 GIBRALTAR

HIGH & LOW WATER 1992 Lat. 36°08′N. Long. 5°21′W.

TIME ZONE –0100 SUBTRACT 1 HOUR FROM TIMES SHOWN FOR GMT

MAY

Day	Time/m	Time/m	Time/m	Time/m
1 F	0157 0.8	0751 0.1	1429 0.8	2005 0.1
2 SA	0235 0.9	0826 0.0	1507 0.9	● 2040 0.1
3 SU	0313 0.9	0902 0.0	1546 0.9	2117 0.1
4 M	0353 0.9	0939 0.0	1628 0.9	2156 0.1
5 TU	0435 0.9	1019 0.0	1711 0.9	2238 0.1
6 W	0520 0.9	1102 0.1	1759 0.9	2325 0.2
7 TH	0609 0.9	1151 0.1	1852 0.8	
8 F	0020 0.2	0705 0.8	1250 0.2	1951 0.8
9 SA	0129 0.2	0810 0.8	1406 0.2	2058 0.8
10 SU	0256 0.2	0925 0.7	1535 0.2	2210 0.8
11 M	0420 0.2	1042 0.7	1649 0.2	2319 0.8
12 TU	0526 0.2	1152 0.8	1747 0.2	
13 W	0020 0.8	0618 0.1	1252 0.8	1835 0.1
14 TH	0114 0.9	0705 0.1	1343 0.8	1919 0.1
15 F	0201 0.9	0747 0.1	1428 0.9	1959 0.1
16 SA	0244 0.9	0827 0.0	1510 0.9	O 2038 0.1
17 SU	0325 0.9	0905 0.1	1550 0.9	2116 0.1
18 M	0404 0.9	0943 0.1	1629 0.9	2153 0.2
19 TU	0441 0.9	1021 0.1	1708 0.9	2232 0.2
20 W	0518 0.9	1059 0.1	1746 0.8	2311 0.2
21 TH	0555 0.8	1139 0.2	1826 0.8	2353 0.3
22 F	0635 0.7	1223 0.2	1909 0.8	
23 SA	0041 0.3	0719 0.7	1314 0.2	1956 0.7
24 SU	0139 0.3	0813 0.7	1417 0.3	2049 0.7
25 M	0251 0.3	0918 0.6	1526 0.3	2148 0.7
26 TU	0404 0.3	1028 0.6	1631 0.3	2248 0.7
27 W	0506 0.3	1133 0.7	1725 0.3	2344 0.7
28 TH	0557 0.2	1228 0.7	1812 0.2	
29 F	0035 0.8	0642 0.2	1317 0.8	1855 0.2
30 SA	0123 0.8	0724 0.1	1402 0.8	1937 0.2
31 SU	0208 0.9	0805 0.1	1446 0.9	2019 0.1

JUNE

Day	Time/m	Time/m	Time/m	Time/m
1 M	0253 0.9	0846 0.1	1530 0.9	● 2101 0.1
2 TU	0338 1.0	0928 0.1	1615 1.0	2145 0.1
3 W	0424 1.0	1011 0.1	1701 1.0	2231 0.1
4 TH	0512 1.0	1057 0.1	1749 0.9	2320 0.1
5 F	0602 0.9	1145 0.2	1840 0.9	
6 SA	0013 0.2	0655 0.9	1239 0.2	1934 0.9
7 SU	0114 0.2	0754 0.8	1341 0.2	2033 0.8
8 M	0225 0.2	0859 0.8	1452 0.2	2138 0.8
9 TU	0343 0.2	1010 0.7	1608 0.2	2246 0.8
10 W	0456 0.2	1122 0.8	1715 0.2	2351 0.8
11 TH	0556 0.2	1226 0.8	1812 0.2	
12 F	0049 0.8	0647 0.2	1321 0.8	1859 0.2
13 SA	0141 0.9	0732 0.1	1409 0.8	1943 0.2
14 SU	0226 0.9	0813 0.1	1452 0.9	2023 0.2
15 M	0307 0.9	0851 0.9	1532 0.9	O 2101 0.2
16 TU	0346 0.9	0929 0.1	1610 0.9	2139 0.2
17 W	0422 0.9	1005 0.1	1646 0.9	2216 0.2
18 TH	0457 0.9	1042 0.1	1722 0.9	2253 0.2
19 F	0531 0.8	1118 0.2	1758 0.8	2331 0.2
20 SA	0607 0.8	1155 0.2	1834 0.8	
21 SU	0010 0.2	0645 0.8	1235 0.2	1913 0.8
22 M	0054 0.3	0729 0.7	1319 0.3	1957 0.7
23 TU	0145 0.3	0822 0.7	1412 0.3	2048 0.7
24 W	0249 0.3	0926 0.7	1517 0.3	2148 0.7
25 TH	0403 0.3	1038 0.7	1628 0.3	2253 0.7
26 F	0514 0.3	1147 0.7	1733 0.3	2358 0.7
27 SA	0614 0.2	1247 0.8	1829 0.2	
28 SU	0056 0.8	0705 0.1	1341 0.8	1919 0.2
29 M	0150 0.9	0751 0.1	1429 0.9	2006 0.1
30 TU	0239 1.0	0835 0.1	1516 1.0	● 2052 0.1

JULY

Day	Time/m	Time/m	Time/m	Time/m
1 W	0327 1.0	0919 0.0	1601 1.0	2137 0.1
2 TH	0414 1.0	1002 0.0	1647 1.0	2223 0.1
3 F	0501 1.0	1045 0.0	1733 1.0	2309 0.1
4 SA	0549 1.0	1130 0.1	1821 1.0	2357 0.1
5 SU	0639 0.9	1216 0.2	1910 0.9	
6 M	0048 0.2	0731 0.9	1308 0.2	2003 0.9
7 TU	0148 0.2	0829 0.8	1407 0.2	2103 0.8
8 W	0300 0.3	0936 0.7	1521 0.3	2211 0.8
9 TH	0426 0.3	1051 0.7	1645 0.3	2323 0.8
10 F	0541 0.3	1203 0.7	1756 0.3	
11 SA	0029 0.8	0637 0.2	1304 0.8	1849 0.3
12 SU	0125 0.8	0722 0.2	1353 0.8	1933 0.2
13 M	0212 0.8	0802 0.1	1436 0.9	2012 0.2
14 TU	0252 0.9	0838 0.1	1514 0.9	O 2048 0.2
15 W	0328 0.9	0913 0.1	1549 0.9	2123 0.2
16 TH	0401 0.9	0947 0.1	1622 0.9	2157 0.1
17 F	0434 0.9	1019 0.1	1654 0.9	2230 0.1
18 SA	0505 0.9	1051 0.1	1726 0.9	2303 0.1
19 SU	0537 0.8	1123 0.1	1758 0.9	2337 0.2
20 M	0612 0.8	1155 0.2	1832 0.8	
21 TU	0013 0.2	0650 0.8	1231 0.2	1911 0.8
22 W	0055 0.2	0737 0.7	1314 0.3	1958 0.8
23 TH	0147 0.3	0837 0.7	1411 0.3	2057 0.7
24 F	0302 0.3	0954 0.7	1534 0.3	2212 0.7
25 SA	0441 0.3	1116 0.7	1705 0.3	2330 0.8
26 SU	0558 0.2	1226 0.8	1814 0.3	
27 M	0038 0.8	0653 0.2	1324 0.9	1908 0.2
28 TU	0136 0.9	0740 0.1	1414 0.9	1956 0.1
29 W	0227 1.0	0823 0.0	1500 1.0	● 2041 0.1
30 TH	0314 1.0	0904 0.0	1545 1.1	2124 0.0
31 F	0400 1.1	0945 0.0	1628 1.1	2207 0.0

AUGUST

Day	Time/m	Time/m	Time/m	Time/m
1 SA	0445 1.0	1025 0.0	1712 1.1	2249 0.0
2 SU	0530 1.0	1106 0.0	1757 1.0	2333 0.1
3 M	0616 1.0	1148 0.1	1843 1.0	
4 TU	0019 0.1	0705 0.9	1232 0.2	1932 0.9
5 W	0110 0.2	0759 0.8	1323 0.3	2028 0.8
6 TH	0216 0.3	0904 0.7	1431 0.3	2137 0.8
7 F	0400 0.3	1022 0.7	1622 0.4	2258 0.7
8 SA	0531 0.3	1143 0.7	1749 0.4	
9 SU	0013 0.7	0627 0.3	1248 0.8	1842 0.3
10 M	0111 0.8	0710 0.2	1337 0.8	1923 0.3
11 TU	0156 0.9	0746 0.1	1419 0.9	1958 0.2
12 W	0233 0.9	0819 0.1	1451 0.9	2031 0.2
13 TH	0306 0.9	0851 0.1	1523 0.9	O 2102 0.1
14 F	0337 1.0	0922 0.1	1554 1.0	2133 0.1
15 SA	0407 1.0	0951 0.1	1623 1.0	2203 0.1
16 SU	0436 0.9	1020 0.1	1653 0.9	2233 0.1
17 M	0507 0.9	1049 0.1	1723 0.9	2304 0.2
18 TU	0540 0.9	1119 0.1	1755 0.9	2337 0.2
19 W	0617 0.8	1152 0.2	1832 0.9	
20 TH	0015 0.2	0702 0.8	1232 0.3	1918 0.8
21 F	0103 0.3	0802 0.7	1325 0.3	2019 0.8
22 SA	0215 0.3	0924 0.7	1453 0.4	2142 0.7
23 SU	0422 0.3	1054 0.7	1651 0.4	2312 0.8
24 M	0546 0.3	1208 0.8	1804 0.3	
25 TU	0025 0.9	0639 0.2	1307 0.9	1856 0.2
26 W	0123 0.9	0724 0.1	1356 1.0	1942 0.1
27 TH	0212 1.0	0805 0.0	1441 1.1	2024 0.0
28 F	0258 1.1	0844 0.0	1524 1.1	● 2105 0.0
29 SA	0342 1.1	0923 0.0	1606 1.1	2146 0.0
30 SU	0425 1.0	1001 0.0	1648 1.1	2226 0.0
31 M	0508 1.0	1039 0.1	1730 1.1	2306 0.1

Tidal streams and currents in the anchorage off Gibraltar set approx. parallel with Detached Mole. In calm weather there is usually a S.-going current with a rate of about a quarter of a knot. Strong W. winds strengthen this and strong E. winds reverse the current to N.-going. In these conditions the current may attain a rate of 1 knot or more.

GIBRALTAR

Lat. 36°08′N. Long. 5°21′W.

21:259

HIGH & LOW WATER 1992

TIME ZONE –0100 SUBTRACT 1 HOUR FROM TIMES SHOWN FOR GMT

SEPTEMBER

Day	Time	m	Day	Time	m
1 TU	0552 / 1118 / 1814 W / 2348	1.0 / 0.1 / 1.0 / 0.2	**16**	0514 / 1047 / 1725 / 2307	0.9 / 0.2 / 1.0 / 0.2
2 W	0638 / 1158 / 1900 TH	0.9 / 0.2 / 0.9	**17**	0552 / 1122 / 1803 / 2345	0.9 / 0.3 / 0.9 / 0.3
3 TH	0034 / 0729 / 1244 F / 1953	0.3 / 0.8 / 0.3 / 0.8	**18**	0640 / 1203 / 1852	0.8 / 0.3 / 0.9
4 F	0134 / 0832 / 1347 SA / 2103	0.3 / 0.8 / 0.4 / 0.8	**19**	0033 / 0741 / 1259 / 1956	0.3 / 0.8 / 0.4 / 0.8
5 SA	0330 / 0953 / 1602 SU / 2232	0.4 / 0.7 / 0.4 / 0.7	**20**	0147 / 0904 / 1436 / 2125	0.4 / 0.8 / 0.4 / 0.8
6 SU	0513 / 1119 / 1738 M / 2354	0.4 / 0.7 / 0.4 / 0.7	**21**	0407 / 1033 / 1639 / 2257	0.4 / 0.8 / 0.4 / 0.8
7 M	0608 / 1225 / 1827 TU	0.3 / 0.8 / 0.3	**22**	0528 / 1147 / 1748	0.3 / 0.9 / 0.3
8 TU	0051 / 0648 / 1312 W / 1903	0.8 / 0.3 / 0.8 / 0.3	**23**	0009 / 0619 / 1245 / 1838	0.9 / 0.2 / 1.0 / 0.2
9 W	0133 / 0722 / 1350 TH / 1935	0.8 / 0.2 / 0.9 / 0.2	**24**	0106 / 0702 / 1334 / 1922	1.0 / 0.1 / 1.0 / 0.1
10 TH	0208 / 0753 / 1422 F / 2006	0.9 / 0.2 / 0.9 / 0.2	**25**	0154 / 0742 / 1419 / 2004	1.0 / 0.1 / 1.1 / 0.1
11 F	0239 / 0823 / 1452 SA / 2036	0.9 / 0.1 / 1.0 / 0.1	**26**	0239 / 0821 / 1501 / ● 2043	1.1 / 0.1 / 1.1 / 0.0
12 SA	0309 / 0852 / 1522 SU / O 2105	1.0 / 0.1 / 1.0 / 0.1	**27**	0322 / 0858 / 1543 / 2122	1.1 / 0.1 / 1.2 / 0.0
13 SU	0338 / 0920 / 1550 M / 2134	1.0 / 0.1 / 1.0 / 0.1	**28**	0404 / 0935 / 1624 / 2201	1.1 / 0.1 / 1.1 / 0.1
14 M	0408 / 0948 / 1620 TU / 2203	1.0 / 0.1 / 1.0 / 0.1	**29**	0446 / 1013 / 1705 / 2240	1.1 / 0.1 / 1.1 / 0.1
15 TU	0439 / 1017 / 1651 W / 2233	1.0 / 0.2 / 1.0 / 0.2	**30**	0528 / 1050 / 1746 / 2320	1.0 / 0.2 / 1.0 / 0.2

OCTOBER

Day	Time	m	Day	Time	m
1 TH	0613 / 1130 / 1831 F	0.9 / 0.3 / 0.9	**16**	0537 / 1103 / 1747 / 2327	0.9 / 0.3 / 1.0 / 0.3
2 F	0004 / 0702 / 1214 SA / 1921	0.3 / 0.9 / 0.4 / 0.8	**17**	0627 / 1149 / 1839	0.9 / 0.3 / 0.9
3 SA	0059 / 0801 / 1314 SU / 2028	0.4 / 0.8 / 0.5 / 0.8	**18**	0019 / 0729 / 1251 / 1946	0.4 / 0.9 / 0.4 / 0.9
4 SU	0239 / 0916 / 1518 M / 2155	0.4 / 0.8 / 0.5 / 0.7	**19**	0136 / 0845 / 1429 / 2110	0.4 / 0.8 / 0.4 / 0.8
5 M	0433 / 1038 / 1704 TU / 2320	0.4 / 0.8 / 0.5 / 0.8	**20**	0337 / 1007 / 1616 / 2235	0.4 / 0.9 / 0.4 / 0.9
6 TU	0532 / 1146 / 1755 W	0.4 / 0.8 / 0.4	**21**	0457 / 1118 / 1724 / 2346	0.3 / 0.9 / 0.3 / 0.9
7 W	0019 / 0614 / 1235 TH / 1832	0.8 / 0.3 / 0.9 / 0.3	**22**	0552 / 1218 / 1816	0.3 / 1.0 / 0.2
8 TH	0101 / 0649 / 1313 F / 1905	0.9 / 0.3 / 0.9 / 0.3	**23**	0044 / 0637 / 1309 / 1900	1.0 / 0.2 / 1.1 / 0.2
9 F	0136 / 0721 / 1346 SA / 1936	0.9 / 0.2 / 1.0 / 0.2	**24**	0134 / 0718 / 1356 / 1942	1.0 / 0.2 / 1.1 / 0.1
10 SA	0208 / 0751 / 1417 SU / 2006	0.9 / 0.2 / 1.0 / 0.2	**25**	0219 / 0757 / 1439 / ● 2022	1.1 / 0.1 / 1.1 / 0.1
11 SU	0239 / 0820 / 1448 M / O 2035	1.0 / 0.2 / 1.0 / 0.2	**26**	0302 / 0835 / 1521 / 2101	1.1 / 0.1 / 1.1 / 0.1
12 M	0310 / 0857 / 1519 TU / 2105	1.0 / 0.2 / 1.0 / 0.2	**27**	0344 / 0913 / 1602 / 2139	1.1 / 0.2 / 1.1 / 0.1
13 TU	0342 / 0929 / 1551 W / 2136	1.0 / 0.2 / 1.0 / 0.2	**28**	0425 / 0951 / 1642 / 2218	1.1 / 0.2 / 1.1 / 0.2
14 W	0417 / 0950 / 1625 TH / 2209	1.0 / 0.2 / 1.0 / 0.2	**29**	0507 / 1029 / 1723 / 2258	1.0 / 0.3 / 1.0 / 0.3
15 TH	0455 / 1024 / 1703 F / 2245	1.0 / 0.2 / 1.0 / 0.2	**30**	0550 / 1109 / 1806 / 2341	1.0 / 0.3 / 0.9 / 0.3
			31 SA	0637 / 1154 / 1853	0.9 / 0.4 / 0.8

NOVEMBER

Day	Time	m	Day	Time	m
1 SU	0031 / 0729 / 1250 M / 1951	0.4 / 0.8 / 0.5 / 0.8	**16**	0015 / 0718 / 1250 / 1937	0.3 / 0.9 / 0.3 / 0.9
2 M	0143 / 0830 / 1414 TU / 2103	0.4 / 0.8 / 0.5 / 0.8	**17**	0125 / 0823 / 1411 / 2050	0.4 / 0.9 / 0.4 / 0.9
3 TU	0319 / 0939 / 1555 W / 2221	0.5 / 0.8 / 0.5 / 0.7	**18**	0253 / 0934 / 1540 / 2206	0.4 / 0.9 / 0.3 / 0.9
4 W	0434 / 1045 / 1702 TH / 2327	0.4 / 0.8 / 0.4 / 0.8	**19**	0416 / 1044 / 1653 / 2318	0.3 / 0.9 / 0.3 / 0.9
5 TH	0526 / 1140 / 1749 F	0.4 / 0.8 / 0.4	**20**	0518 / 1147 / 1750	0.3 / 1.0 / 0.2
6 F	0016 / 0606 / 1225 SA / 1827	0.8 / 0.3 / 0.9 / 0.3	**21**	0019 / 0609 / 1244 / 1838	0.9 / 0.3 / 1.0 / 0.2
7 SA	0057 / 0642 / 1304 SU / 1901	0.9 / 0.3 / 0.9 / 0.2	**22**	0113 / 0655 / 1333 / 1923	1.0 / 0.2 / 1.0 / 0.2
8 SU	0134 / 0716 / 1340 M / 1935	0.9 / 0.3 / 1.0 / 0.2	**23**	0201 / 0737 / 1419 / 2004	1.0 / 0.2 / 1.0 / 0.1
9 M	0209 / 0749 / 1415 TU / 2008	1.0 / 0.2 / 1.0 / 0.2	**24**	0245 / 0817 / 1503 / ● 2044	1.0 / 0.2 / 1.0 / 0.1
10 TU	0245 / 0822 / 1451 W / O 2042	1.0 / 0.2 / 1.0 / 0.2	**25**	0328 / 0857 / 1544 / 2123	1.0 / 0.2 / 1.0 / 0.2
11 W	0322 / 0856 / 1529 TH / 2117	1.0 / 0.2 / 1.0 / 0.2	**26**	0409 / 0936 / 1625 / 2203	1.0 / 0.2 / 1.0 / 0.2
12 TH	0401 / 0933 / 1609 F / 2154	1.0 / 0.2 / 1.0 / 0.2	**27**	0450 / 1015 / 1704 / 2242	1.0 / 0.3 / 0.9 / 0.2
13 F	0443 / 1012 / 1652 SA / 2235	1.0 / 0.2 / 1.0 / 0.2	**28**	0530 / 1055 / 1745 / 2323	0.9 / 0.3 / 0.9 / 0.3
14 SA	0525 / 1056 / 1740 SU / 2321	1.0 / 0.3 / 1.0 / 0.3	**29**	0612 / 1138 / 1827	0.9 / 0.3 / 0.8
15 SU	0620 / 1147 / 1834 M	1.0 / 0.3 / 0.9	**30**	0008 / 0655 / 1226 / 1913	0.3 / 0.9 / 0.4 / 0.8

DECEMBER

Day	Time	m	Day	Time	m
1 TU	0059 / 0743 / 1323 W / 2007	0.4 / 0.8 / 0.4 / 0.7	**16**	0104 / 0758 / 1344 / 2024	0.2 / 0.9 / 0.3 / 0.8
2 W	0200 / 0836 / 1431 TH / 2109	0.4 / 0.8 / 0.4 / 0.7	**17**	0210 / 0901 / 1459 / 2133	0.3 / 0.9 / 0.3 / 0.8
3 TH	0310 / 0933 / 1546 F / 2215	0.4 / 0.8 / 0.4 / 0.7	**18**	0327 / 1008 / 1617 / 2244	0.3 / 0.9 / 0.3 / 0.8
4 F	0417 / 1032 / 1650 SA / 2317	0.4 / 0.8 / 0.3 / 0.7	**19**	0441 / 1116 / 1725 / 2352	0.3 / 0.9 / 0.2 / 0.8
5 SA	0512 / 1127 / 1742 SU	0.3 / 0.8 / 0.3	**20**	0544 / 1219 / 1822	0.3 / 0.9 / 0.2
6 SU	0011 / 0559 / 1218 M / 1826	0.8 / 0.3 / 0.8 / 0.2	**21**	0052 / 0637 / 1315 / 1910	0.8 / 0.2 / 0.9 / 0.2
7 M	0059 / 0641 / 1304 TU / 1907	0.8 / 0.3 / 0.9 / 0.2	**22**	0145 / 0723 / 1405 / 1953	0.9 / 0.2 / 0.9 / 0.1
8 TU	0142 / 0722 / 1348 W / 1947	0.9 / 0.2 / 0.9 / 0.2	**23**	0231 / 0806 / 1450 / 2034	0.9 / 0.2 / 0.9 / 0.1
9 W	0225 / 0802 / 1431 TH / O 2026	0.9 / 0.2 / 1.0 / 0.1	**24**	0314 / 0846 / 1531 / ● 2113	0.9 / 0.2 / 0.9 / 0.1
10 TH	0307 / 0842 / 1515 F / 2106	1.0 / 0.2 / 1.0 / 0.1	**25**	0354 / 0925 / 1610 / 2150	0.9 / 0.2 / 0.9 / 0.1
11 F	0350 / 0924 / 1600 SA / 2147	1.0 / 0.2 / 1.0 / 0.1	**26**	0432 / 1003 / 1647 / 2228	0.9 / 0.2 / 0.9 / 0.1
12 SA	0434 / 1007 / 1646 SU / 2231	1.0 / 0.2 / 1.0 / 0.1	**27**	0509 / 1040 / 1723 / 2305	0.9 / 0.2 / 0.9 / 0.2
13 SU	0521 / 1054 / 1735 M / 2317	1.0 / 0.2 / 1.0 / 0.2	**28**	0545 / 1118 / 1800 / 2342	0.9 / 0.2 / 0.8 / 0.2
14 M	0610 / 1144 / 1827 TU	1.0 / 0.2 / 0.9	**29**	0622 / 1157 / 1838	0.8 / 0.2 / 0.8
15 TU	0007 / 0702 / 1239 W / 1922	0.2 / 0.9 / 0.2 / 0.9	**30**	0021 / 0659 / 1240 / 1919	0.2 / 0.8 / 0.2 / 0.7
			31 TH	0104 / 0741 / 1327 / 2007	0.3 / 0.9 / 0.3 / 0.7

PORTUGAL **LISBON**

Lat. 38°42'N. Long. 9°08'W. **HIGH & LOW WATER 1992**

GMT (LOCAL TIME FACTORS SHOULD BE APPLIED)

JANUARY

Day	Time	m	Day	Time	m
1	0025	3.3	16	0522	1.3
	0617	1.3		1200	3.1
W	1253	3.2	TH	1748	1.1
	1832	1.2			
2	0116	3.4	17	0034	3.3
	0702	1.1		0625	1.0
TH	1342	3.3	F	1308	3.3
	1913	1.1		1845	0.9
3	0200	3.5	18	0133	3.6
	0743	1.0		0720	0.7
F	1424	3.3	SA	1404	3.5
	1949	1.1		1937	0.7
4	0240	3.6	19	0225	3.8
	0819	0.9		0811	0.5
SA	1503	3.4	SU	1454	3.7
●	2025	1.0	○	2026	0.5
5	0317	3.7	20	0312	4.1
	0854	0.9		0859	0.3
SU	1540	3.4	M	1540	3.9
	2059	0.9		2113	0.4
6	0353	3.7	21	0358	4.2
	0928	0.8		0945	0.3
M	1614	3.4	TU	1625	3.9
	2133	0.9		2158	0.4
7	0426	3.7	22	0443	4.2
	1001	0.8		1030	0.3
TU	1647	3.4	W	1709	3.9
	2207	0.9		2242	0.5
8	0458	3.6	23	0527	4.1
	1034	0.8		1114	0.5
W	1718	3.4	TH	1752	3.8
	2241	0.9		2327	0.7
9	0529	3.6	24	0611	3.9
	1108	0.9		1159	0.7
TH	1749	3.3	F	1837	3.6
	2316	1.0			
10	0559	3.5	25	0013	0.9
	1143	1.0		0657	3.7
F	1820	3.2	SA	1246	1.0
	2354	1.1		1937	3.4
11	0632	3.3	26	0105	1.2
	1222	1.1		0748	3.4
SA	1856	3.1	SU	1340	1.3
				2018	3.2
12	0037	1.2	27	0208	1.4
	0710	3.2		0848	3.1
SU	1310	1.2	M	1448	1.5
	1940	3.0		2126	3.0
13	0132	1.4	28	0331	1.6
	0800	3.1		1005	2.9
M	1410	1.4	TU	1608	1.6
	2039	3.0		2246	3.0
14	0245	1.5	29	0456	1.5
	0908	3.0		1129	2.9
TU	1525	1.4	W	1721	1.5
	2156	3.0			
15	0407	1.4	30	0001	3.1
	1035	3.0		0602	1.4
W	1642	1.3	TH	1237	3.0
	2321	3.1		1815	1.4
			31	0059	3.2
				0652	1.3
			F	1328	3.1
				1858	1.3

FEBRUARY

Day	Time	m	Day	Time	m
1	0144	3.4	16	0119	3.6
	0731	1.1		0709	0.7
SA	1409	3.2	SU	1351	3.5
	1935	1.1		1926	0.7
2	0223	3.5	17	0210	3.9
	0805	0.9		0758	0.5
SU	1446	3.4	M	1438	3.8
	2010	0.9		2013	0.5
3	0259	3.6	18	0256	4.1
	0837	0.8		0843	0.3
M	1520	3.4	TU	1522	3.9
●	2042	0.8	○	2057	0.4
4	0332	3.7	19	0340	4.2
	0908	0.7		0926	0.2
TU	1552	3.5	W	1604	4.0
	2115	0.7		2140	0.3
5	0404	3.7	20	0422	4.3
	0938	0.7		1007	0.3
W	1622	3.5	TH	1645	4.0
	2146	0.7		2221	0.4
6	0433	3.7	21	0504	4.1
	1009	0.7		1047	0.5
TH	1650	3.5	F	1725	3.9
	2218	0.7		2301	0.6
7	0501	3.7	22	0545	3.9
	1040	0.7		1126	0.7
F	1718	3.5	SA	1806	3.7
	2250	0.8		2342	0.8
8	0529	3.6	23	0627	3.6
	1112	0.8		1206	1.0
SA	1746	3.4	SU	1849	3.4
	2325	0.9			
9	0558	3.5	24	0026	1.1
	1148	0.9		0713	3.3
SU	1818	3.3	M	1251	1.3
				1937	3.2
10	0005	1.0	25	0120	1.4
	0633	3.3		0808	3.0
M	1230	1.1	TU	1348	1.6
	1857	3.2		2039	3.0
11	0054	1.2	26	0239	1.6
	0720	3.1		0923	2.8
TU	1325	1.3	W	1514	1.7
	1953	3.0		2203	2.9
12	0202	1.4	27	0424	1.6
	0829	2.9		1058	2.7
W	1441	1.4	TH	1649	1.7
	2115	2.9		2331	2.9
13	0335	1.4	28	0543	1.5
	1008	2.8		1213	2.8
TH	1613	1.4	F	1754	1.5
	2256	3.0			
14	0504	1.3	29	0033	3.1
	1146	3.0		0632	1.3
F	1732	1.2	SA	1305	3.0
				1838	1.3
15	0018	3.3			
	0613	1.0			
SA	1257	3.3			
	1833	1.0			

MARCH

Day	Time	m	Day	Time	m
1	0120	3.3	16	0100	3.6
	0709	1.1		0653	0.7
SU	1345	3.2	M	1332	3.6
	1915	1.1		1910	0.7
2	0159	3.5	17	0150	3.9
	0741	0.9		0740	0.5
M	1421	3.4	TU	1417	3.8
	1948	0.9		1955	0.5
3	0233	3.6	18	0236	4.1
	0811	0.8		0822	0.3
TU	1453	3.5	W	1500	4.0
	2019	0.8	○	2037	0.4
4	0306	3.7	19	0319	4.2
	0841	0.7		0902	0.3
W	1524	3.6	TH	1540	4.0
●	2051	0.7		2118	0.4
5	0337	3.8	20	0400	4.2
	0911	0.6		0940	0.4
TH	1554	3.6	F	1620	4.0
	2122	0.6		2157	0.4
6	0406	3.7	21	0440	4.0
	0941	0.6		1017	0.6
F	1622	3.6	SA	1659	3.9
	2154	0.6		2235	0.6
7	0435	3.7	22	0520	3.8
	1013	0.6		1053	0.8
SA	1650	3.6	SU	1738	3.7
	2227	0.7		2314	0.8
8	0504	3.6	23	0600	3.5
	1046	0.7		1130	1.0
SU	1719	3.5	M	1818	3.5
	2302	0.8		2354	1.1
9	0535	3.5	24	0644	3.2
	1122	0.9		1209	1.3
M	1753	3.4	TU	1903	3.2
	2343	0.9			
10	0613	3.3	25	0043	1.4
	1203	1.0		0735	2.9
TU	1835	3.2	W	1259	1.5
				1959	3.0
11	0032	1.1	26	0151	1.6
	0704	3.1		0843	2.7
W	1257	1.3	TH	1415	1.7
	1933	3.1		2116	2.8
12	0141	1.3	27	0335	1.7
	0817	2.9		1013	2.6
TH	1415	1.5	F	1601	1.7
	2058	3.0		2244	2.9
13	0318	1.4	28	0503	1.5
	0958	2.8		1134	2.8
F	1555	1.5	SA	1717	1.6
	2239	3.0		2354	3.0
14	0452	1.2	29	0555	1.4
	1133	3.0		1229	3.0
SA	1718	1.2	SU	1805	1.4
15	0000	3.3	30	0044	3.2
	0600	1.0		0633	1.2
SU	1240	3.3	M	1311	3.2
	1819	1.0		1843	1.2
			31	0125	3.4
				0706	1.0
			TU	1347	3.4
				1917	1.0

APRIL

Day	Time	m	Day	Time	m
1	0201	3.5	16	0213	4.0
	0738	0.8		0757	0.5
W	1421	3.5	TH	1436	3.9
	1950	0.8		2015	0.5
2	0234	3.6	17	0257	4.0
	0809	0.7		0836	0.5
TH	1453	3.6	F	1517	4.0
	2023	0.7	○	2055	0.5
3	0307	3.7	18	0338	3.9
	0841	0.6		0913	0.6
F	1524	3.7	SA	1556	3.9
●	2057	0.6		2133	0.6
4	0339	3.7	19	0418	3.8
	0914	0.6		0949	0.7
SA	1556	3.7	SU	1635	3.8
	2131	0.6		2211	0.7
5	0412	3.7	20	0458	3.6
	0948	0.6		1024	0.9
SU	1628	3.7	M	1714	3.7
	2207	0.6		2249	0.9
6	0446	3.6	21	0538	3.4
	1024	0.7		1100	1.1
M	1702	3.6	TU	1753	3.5
	2246	0.7		2329	1.1
7	0524	3.5	22	0620	3.2
	1103	0.8		1139	1.3
TU	1741	3.5	W	1836	3.3
	2330	0.9			
8	0609	3.3	23	0015	1.3
	1148	1.0		0700	2.9
W	1829	3.3	TH	1225	1.5
				1926	3.1
9	0023	1.1	24	0113	1.5
	0705	3.1		0806	2.8
TH	1245	1.3	F	1327	1.6
	1931	3.2		2029	2.9
10	0135	1.2	25	0213	1.6
	0819	2.9		0918	2.7
F	1404	1.4	SA	1455	1.7
	2051	3.1		2143	2.9
11	0308	1.3	26	0359	1.5
	0948	2.9		1034	2.8
SA	1541	1.4	SU	1619	1.6
	2219	3.2		2255	3.0
12	0436	1.2	27	0500	1.4
	1111	3.1		1137	2.9
SU	1701	1.2	M	1717	1.5
	2335	3.4		2353	3.1
13	0541	1.0	28	0546	1.2
	1215	3.3		1226	3.1
M	1800	1.0	TU	1802	1.3
14	0036	3.6	29	0040	3.3
	0632	0.7		0624	1.1
TU	1308	3.6	W	1307	3.3
	1849	0.8		1840	1.1
15	0127	3.8	30	0122	3.4
	0716	0.6		0700	0.9
W	1354	3.8	TH	1344	3.5
	1934	0.6		1918	0.9

TIDAL DIFFERENCES PAGES 21:264-21:265. TIDAL CURVE PAGE 21:263.

Datum of predictions: 0.5 m. below M.L.W.S. and at L.A.T.

LISBON PORTUGAL

Lat. 38°42'N. Long. 9°08'W.   HIGH & LOW WATER 1992

GMT   (LOCAL TIME FACTORS SHOULD BE APPLIED)

	MAY Time	m	Time	m		JUNE Time	m	Time	m		JULY Time	m	Time	m		AUGUST Time	m	Time	m
1	0200	3.5	0237	3.7	**1**	0258	3.6	0344	3.5	**1**	0331	3.7	0402	3.4	**1**	0444	3.9	0437	3.5
	0736	0.8 **16**	0811	0.8		0829	0.7 **16**	0904	0.9		0901	0.6 **16**	0921	0.9		1017	0.4 **16**	1003	0.7
F	1421	3.6 SA	1456	3.8	M	1517	3.8 TU	1559	3.7		1549	4.0 TH	1615	3.7	SA	1702	4.2 SU	1649	3.6
	1955	0.8 O	2034	0.7	●	2058	0.6	2134	0.9		2133	0.4	2149	0.8		2248	0.4	2224	0.7
2	0238	3.6	0319	3.7	**2**	0343	3.6	0422	3.4	**2**	0417	3.8	0435	3.4	**2**	0528	3.9	0506	3.4
	0812	0.7 **17**	0848	0.8		0913	0.7 **17**	0940	1.0		0947	0.5 **17**	0955	0.9		1102	0.5 **17**	1035	0.8
SA	1457	3.7 SU	1536	3.8	TU	1601	3.8 W	1636	3.7	TH	1635	4.0 F	1648	3.7	SU	1747	4.0 M	1717	3.5
●	2033	0.7	2113	0.7		2143	0.6	2211	0.9		2220	0.4	2222	0.8		2333	0.6	2256	0.8
3	0316	3.6	0400	3.6	**3**	0429	3.6	0459	3.4	**3**	0504	3.8	0508	3.4	**3**	0613	3.7	0534	3.4
	0849	0.6 **18**	0924	0.9		0958	0.7 **18**	1016	1.0		1034	0.6 **18**	1029	0.9		1149	0.7 **18**	1109	0.9
SU	1534	3.7 M	1615	3.8	W	1647	3.9 TH	1712	3.6	F	1721	4.0 SA	1719	3.6	M	1834	3.8 TU	1746	3.4
	2112	0.6	2151	0.8		2231	0.6	2247	1.0		2309	0.5	2255	0.9				2330	0.9
4	0355	3.6	0440	3.5	**4**	0516	3.6	0535	3.3	**4**	0550	3.7	0539	3.3	**4**	0020	0.8	0604	3.3
	0928	0.6 **19**	1000	0.9		1045	0.8 **19**	1053	1.1		1122	0.7 **19**	1103	1.0		0700	3.5 **19**	1147	1.0
M	1612	3.8 TU	1654	3.7	TH	1734	3.8 F	1748	3.5	SA	1809	3.9 SU	1750	3.5	TU	1240	1.0 W	1820	3.2
	2153	0.6	2229	0.9		2321	0.7	2324	1.0		2358	0.7	2329	1.0		1924	3.5		
5	0436	3.6	0519	3.3	**5**	0606	3.5	0612	3.2	**5**	0639	3.6	0611	3.3	**5**	0114	1.1	0009	1.1
	1009	0.7 **20**	1037	1.1		1135	0.9 **20**	1131	1.2		1214	0.9 **20**	1140	1.1		0753	3.3 **20**	0641	3.1
TU	1653	3.9 W	1733	3.5	F	1824	3.7 SA	1824	3.4	SU	1858	3.8 M	1822	3.4	W	1341	1.3 TH	1233	1.2
	2237	0.7	2308	1.0												2023	3.2	1902	3.0
6	0521	3.5	0559	3.2	**6**	0015	0.8	0004	1.1	**6**	0052	0.9	0006	1.1	**6**	0219	1.4	0059	1.3
	1053	0.8 **21**	1115	1.2		0658	3.4 **21**	0649	3.1		0730	3.5 **21**	0644	3.2		0857	3.1 **21**	0731	3.0
W	1739	3.6 TH	1813	3.4	SA	1232	1.0 SU	1214	1.3	M	1311	1.1 TU	1221	1.2	TH	1500	1.4 F	1334	1.4
	2325	0.8	2350	1.2		1918	3.6	1902	3.2		1952	3.6	1857	3.2		2135	3.0	2003	2.9
7	0611	3.3	0641	3.0	**7**	0117	1.0	0049	1.3	**7**	0153	1.1	0050	1.2	**7**	0339	1.5	0209	1.4
	1142	1.1 **22**	1158	1.3		0756	3.3 **22**	0731	3.0		0827	3.3 **22**	0724	3.1		1014	3.0 **22**	0844	2.9
TH	1830	3.5 F	1856	3.2	SU	1337	1.2 M	1303	1.4	TU	1418	1.3 W	1311	1.4	F	1628	1.5 SA	1500	1.4
						2018	3.5	1945	3.1		2054	3.4	1941	3.1		2258	2.9	2132	2.8
8	0021	1.0	0038	1.3	**8**	0228	1.1	0141	1.4	**8**	0303	1.3	0144	1.4	**8**	0456	1.5	0338	1.4
	0707	3.2 **23**	0728	2.9		0859	3.2 **23**	0820	3.0		0933	3.2 **23**	0816	3.0		1132	3.1 **23**	1017	3.0
F	1241	1.2 SA	1249	1.5	M	1452	1.3 TU	1403	1.5	W	1535	1.4 TH	1416	1.5	SA	1740	1.4 SU	1631	1.3
	1929	3.4	1945	3.1		2125	3.4	2037	3.0		2205	3.2	2041	2.9				2308	2.9
9	0131	1.1	0137	1.4	**9**	0340	1.2	0244	1.4	**9**	0413	1.3	0253	1.4	**9**	0010	3.0	0459	1.3
	0813	3.1 **24**	0823	2.8		1008	3.2 **24**	0918	2.9		1044	3.2 **24**	0924	2.9		0555	1.4 **24**	1142	3.2
SA	1355	1.3 SL	1354	1.6	TU	1607	1.3 W	1513	1.5	TH	1648	1.4 F	1536	1.5	SU	1235	3.2 M	1742	1.1
	2039	3.3	2041	3.0		2235	3.4	2139	3.0		2319	3.2	2200	2.9		1833	1.2		
10	0253	1.2	0246	1.5	**10**	0445	1.2	0350	1.4	**10**	0517	1.3	0410	1.4	**10**	0106	3.1	0022	3.1
	0928	3.1 **25**	0925	2.8		1115	3.3 **25**	1024	3.0		1153	3.3 **25**	1047	3.0		0641	1.2 **25**	0602	1.0
SU	1521	1.4 M	1509	1.6	W	1712	1.2 TH	1623	1.5	F	1751	1.3 SA	1653	1.3	M	1324	3.4 TU	1246	3.5
	2154	3.3	2145	3.0		2343	3.4	2250	3.0				2327	3.0		1914	1.1	1838	0.8
11	0412	1.1	0353	1.4	**11**	0541	1.1	0452	1.3	**11**	0025	3.2	0519	1.2	**11**	0150	3.2	0119	3.4
	1042	3.2 **26**	1030	2.9		1216	3.4 **26**	1131	3.1		0610	1.3 **26**	1203	3.2		0719	1.1 **26**	0656	0.7
M	1636	1.2 TU	1617	1.5	TH	1807	1.1 F	1724	1.3	SA	1252	3.4 SU	1758	1.1	TU	1405	3.5 W	1339	3.8
	2306	3.4	2249	3.0				2358	3.1		1842	1.2				1949	0.9	1928	0.5
12	0515	1.0	0450	1.3	**12**	0042	3.4	0547	1.2	**12**	0121	3.3	0038	3.2	**12**	0228	3.3	0208	3.7
	1146	3.4 **27**	1129	3.0		0628	1.1 **27**	1231	3.3		0656	1.2 **27**	0618	1.0		0754	1.0 **27**	0744	0.5
TU	1737	1.1 W	1713	1.4	F	1309	3.5 SA	1819	1.1	SU	1341	3.5 M	1305	3.4	W	1442	3.6 TH	1427	4.0
			2347	3.1		1854	1.0				1926	1.1	1853	0.8		2021	0.8	2014	0.3
13	0009	3.6	0538	1.2	**13**	0134	3.5	0058	3.3	**13**	0207	3.3	0137	3.4	**13**	0303	3.4	0253	3.9
	0606	0.9 **28**	1220	3.2		0711	1.0 **28**	0638	1.0		0734	1.1 **28**	0711	0.8		0827	0.9 **28**	0829	0.3
W	1242	3.5 TH	1802	1.2	SA	1356	3.6 SU	1325	3.5	M	1424	3.6 TU	1358	3.7	TH	1516	3.7 F	1512	4.2
	1827	0.9				1938	0.9	1909	0.9		2005	1.0	1944	0.6		2052	0.7 O	2058	0.2
14	0104	3.7	0039	3.3	**14**	0221	3.5	0153	3.4	**14**	0248	3.4	0227	3.6	**14**	0336	3.5	0337	4.0
	0651	0.8 **29**	0622	1.0		0750	1.0 **29**	0726	0.8		0811	1.0 **29**	0800	0.6		0859	0.9 **29**	0913	0.3
TH	1330	3.7 F	1306	3.4	SU	1439	3.7 M	1415	3.7	TU	1503	3.7 W	1446	3.9	F	1549	3.7 SA	1556	4.2
	1912	0.8	1846	1.0		2018	0.9	1958	0.7		2041	0.9 ●	2032	0.4		2122	0.7	2140	0.2
15	0152	3.7	0127	3.4	**15**	0304	3.5	0243	3.6	**15**	0326	3.4	0314	3.8	**15**	0407	3.5	0420	4.0
	0732	0.8 **30**	0704	0.9		0828	1.0 **30**	0814	0.7		0846	0.9 **30**	0847	0.4		0931	0.7 **30**	0956	0.3
F	1414	3.8 SA	1350	3.5	M	1520	3.7 TU	1502	3.9	W	1540	3.7 TH	1532	4.1	SA	1620	3.7 SU	1640	4.1
	1954	0.7	1930	0.8		2057	0.9 ●	2046	0.5		2116	0.8	2118	0.3		2153	0.7	2222	0.4
			0212	3.5									0359	3.9				0502	3.9
	31		0747	0.8							**31**		0932	0.4		**31**		1039	0.5
		SU	1433	3.7								F	1618	4.2			M	1723	4.0
			2013	0.7									2203	0.3				2304	0.6

GENERAL — Some danger in entering Rio Tejo is caused by the tidal streams. In the middle of Barra Grande they set directly through, but on either side of the middle they set towards Cachopo do Norte and Cachopo do Sul. Streams set strongly towards the bank extending NW. from Forte Bugio, and eddies occur. In ordinary weather max. rate of ingoing stream on the bar is about 3 kn., and outgoing 4 kn. After heavy rains the outgoing may attain a rate of about 5 kn.

PORTUGAL LISBON

HIGH & LOW WATER 1992   Lat. 38°42′N. Long. 9°08′W.

GMT   (LOCAL TIME FACTORS SHOULD BE APPLIED)

SEPTEMBER

Day	Time	m		Time	m
1	0545 / 1122 / TU 1808 / 2346	3.8 / 0.7 / 3.7 / 0.9	**16**	0504 / 1044 / W 1719 / 2301	3.4 / 0.8 / 3.4 / 0.9
2	0630 / 1209 / W 1857	3.5 / 1.0 / 3.4	**17**	0535 / 1122 / TH 1755 / 2341	3.3 / 0.9 / 3.2 / 1.0
3	0033 / 0721 / TH 1305 / 1953	1.2 / 3.3 / 1.3 / 3.1	**18**	0615 / 1208 / F 1842	3.2 / 1.1 / 3.0
4	0132 / 0822 / F 1423 / 2105	1.5 / 3.0 / 1.5 / 2.8	**19**	0030 / 0708 / SA 1310 / 1948	1.2 / 3.0 / 1.3 / 2.8
5	0258 / 0941 / SA 1606 / 2233	1.6 / 2.9 / 1.5 / 2.8	**20**	0140 / 0824 / SU 1439 / 2119	1.4 / 2.9 / 1.4 / 2.8
6	0433 / 1104 / SU 1725 / 2349	1.6 / 3.0 / 1.4 / 2.9	**21**	0315 / 0957 / M 1614 / 2252	1.4 / 3.0 / 1.2 / 2.9
7	0538 / 1210 / M 1815	1.5 / 3.1 / 1.2	**22**	0442 / 1120 / TU 1726	1.3 / 3.2 / 1.0
8	0043 / 0622 / TU 1259 / 1852	3.0 / 1.3 / 3.3 / 1.1	**23**	0003 / 0546 / W 1225 / 1820	3.2 / 1.0 / 3.5 / 0.7
9	0125 / 0658 / W 1339 / 1923	3.2 / 1.1 / 3.4 / 0.9	**24**	0058 / 0638 / TH 1317 / 1908	3.5 / 0.7 / 3.8 / 0.5
10	0201 / 0731 / TH 1415 / 1953	3.3 / 0.9 / 3.6 / 0.8	**25**	0146 / 0725 / F 1405 / 1952	3.7 / 0.5 / 4.0 / 0.3
11	0235 / 0802 / F 1448 / 2023	3.5 / 0.8 / 3.6 / 0.7	**26**	0230 / 0809 / SA 1450 / ● 2034	3.9 / 0.3 / 4.1 / 0.3
12	0306 / 0833 / SA 1520 / O 2053	3.5 / 0.7 / 3.7 / 0.6	**27**	0313 / 0852 / SU 1534 / 2115	4.0 / 0.3 / 4.1 / 0.3
13	0337 / 0905 / SU 1550 / 2123	3.6 / 0.6 / 3.7 / 0.6	**28**	0355 / 0933 / M 1617 / 2155	4.0 / 0.3 / 4.0 / 0.4
14	0406 / 0937 / M 1620 / 2154	3.6 / 0.6 / 3.6 / 0.7	**29**	0437 / 1015 / TU 1700 / 2234	3.9 / 0.5 / 3.8 / 0.7
15	0435 / 1009 / TU 1649 / 2226	3.5 / 0.7 / 3.5 / 0.7	**30**	0519 / 1056 / W 1744 / 2314	3.7 / 0.7 / 3.6 / 0.9

OCTOBER

Day	Time	m		Time	m
1	0603 / 1140 / TH 1831 / 2356	3.5 / 1.0 / 3.3 / 1.2	**16**	0520 / 1107 / F 1746 / 2323	3.4 / 0.8 / 3.2 / 1.0
2	0651 / 1231 / F 1925	3.3 / 1.2 / 3.0	**17**	0605 / 1156 / SA 1838	3.3 / 1.0 / 3.0
3	0048 / 0749 / SA 1342 / 2032	1.5 / 3.0 / 1.5 / 2.8	**18**	0015 / 0701 / SU 1259 / 1945	1.2 / 3.2 / 1.2 / 2.9
4	0205 / 0901 / SU 1525 / 2155	1.6 / 2.9 / 1.6 / 2.7	**19**	0125 / 0813 / M 1424 / 2106	1.3 / 3.1 / 1.3 / 2.9
5	0349 / 1023 / M 1649 / 2311	1.7 / 2.9 / 1.5 / 2.8	**20**	0256 / 0936 / TU 1554 / 2229	1.4 / 3.1 / 1.2 / 3.0
6	0503 / 1132 / TU 1741	1.5 / 3.0 / 1.3	**21**	0421 / 1055 / W 1704 / 2338	1.2 / 3.3 / 1.0 / 3.2
7	0008 / 0550 / W 1224 / 1818	3.0 / 1.3 / 3.2 / 1.1	**22**	0526 / 1200 / TH 1759	1.0 / 3.5 / 0.7
8	0052 / 0628 / TH 1306 / 1850	3.2 / 1.1 / 3.3 / 1.0	**23**	0034 / 0618 / F 1255 / 1846	3.5 / 0.8 / 3.7 / 0.6
9	0129 / 0701 / F 1342 / 1921	3.3 / 1.0 / 3.5 / 0.8	**24**	0123 / 0705 / SA 1344 / 1930	3.7 / 0.6 / 3.9 / 0.5
10	0203 / 0734 / SA 1417 / 1952	3.5 / 0.8 / 3.6 / 0.7	**25**	0208 / 0749 / SU 1430 / ● 2011	3.9 / 0.5 / 4.0 / 0.4
11	0236 / 0806 / SU 1450 / O 2023	3.6 / 0.7 / 3.6 / 0.6	**26**	0252 / 0832 / M 1514 / 2051	4.0 / 0.4 / 3.9 / 0.5
12	0307 / 0839 / M 1523 / 2055	3.6 / 0.6 / 3.6 / 0.6	**27**	0334 / 0913 / TU 1558 / 2129	4.0 / 0.5 / 3.8 / 0.6
13	0339 / 0913 / TU 1555 / 2128	3.6 / 0.6 / 3.6 / 0.6	**28**	0416 / 0954 / W 1640 / 2208	3.9 / 0.6 / 3.7 / 0.8
14	0410 / 0948 / W 1628 / 2203	3.6 / 0.6 / 3.5 / 0.7	**29**	0457 / 1034 / TH 1723 / 2246	3.7 / 0.8 / 3.4 / 1.0
15	0443 / 1026 / TH 1704 / 2241	3.6 / 0.7 / 3.4 / 0.8	**30**	0540 / 1117 / F 1808 / 2314	3.5 / 1.0 / 3.2 / 0.9
31	0625 / 1203 / SA 1857	3.3 / 1.2 / 3.0			

NOVEMBER

Day	Time	m		Time	m
1	0013 / 0715 / SU 1301 / 1954	1.4 / 3.1 / 1.4 / 2.8	**16**	0006 / 0655 / M 1251 / 1935	1.1 / 3.4 / 1.0 / 3.1
2	0114 / 0816 / M 1419 / 2102	1.6 / 3.0 / 1.5 / 2.7	**17**	0112 / 0759 / TU 1405 / 2044	1.2 / 3.3 / 1.1 / 3.1
3	0239 / 0926 / TU 1544 / 2214	1.7 / 2.9 / 1.5 / 2.8	**18**	0232 / 0911 / W 1526 / 2158	1.3 / 3.3 / 1.1 / 3.1
4	0404 / 1036 / W 1646 / 2318	1.6 / 3.0 / 1.4 / 2.9	**19**	0354 / 1025 / TH 1637 / 2308	1.3 / 3.3 / 1.0 / 3.3
5	0503 / 1136 / TH 1732	1.4 / 3.1 / 1.2	**20**	0502 / 1134 / F 1735	1.1 / 3.5 / 0.9
6	0008 / 0548 / F 1225 / 1810	3.1 / 1.3 / 3.2 / 1.1	**21**	0009 / 0558 / SA 1233 / 1824	3.5 / 0.9 / 3.6 / 0.8
7	0051 / 0627 / SA 1306 / 1845	3.3 / 1.1 / 3.3 / 0.9	**22**	0102 / 0647 / SU 1326 / 1909	3.6 / 0.8 / 3.7 / 0.7
8	0129 / 0704 / SU 1345 / 1920	3.4 / 0.9 / 3.4 / 0.8	**23**	0150 / 0733 / M 1414 / 1951	3.8 / 0.7 / 3.7 / 0.7
9	0205 / 0740 / M 1422 / 1955	3.5 / 0.8 / 3.5 / 0.7	**24**	0235 / 0816 / TU 1459 / ● 2031	3.8 / 0.6 / 3.7 / 0.7
10	0241 / 0816 / TU 1500 / O 2031	3.6 / 0.7 / 3.5 / 0.7	**25**	0318 / 0857 / W 1543 / 2109	3.9 / 0.6 / 3.7 / 0.8
11	0317 / 0854 / W 1537 / 2108	3.7 / 0.6 / 3.5 / 0.7	**26**	0359 / 0937 / TH 1624 / 2147	3.8 / 0.7 / 3.5 / 0.8
12	0354 / 0933 / TH 1616 / 2147	3.7 / 0.6 / 3.4 / 0.7	**27**	0440 / 1017 / F 1705 / 2224	3.7 / 0.8 / 3.4 / 1.0
13	0432 / 1015 / F 1658 / 2228	3.7 / 0.6 / 3.4 / 0.8	**28**	0520 / 1056 / SA 1746 / 2303	3.6 / 0.9 / 3.3 / 1.1
14	0514 / 1059 / SA 1744 / 2314	3.6 / 0.7 / 3.3 / 0.9	**29**	0600 / 1137 / SU 1828 / 2344	3.4 / 1.1 / 3.1 / 1.2
15	0601 / 1150 / SU 1836	3.5 / 0.9 / 3.2	**30**	0642 / 1222 / M 1913	3.3 / 1.2 / 3.0

DECEMBER

Day	Time	m		Time	m
1	0031 / 0729 / TU 1316 / 2004	1.4 / 3.1 / 1.4 / 2.9	**16**	0054 / 0738 / W 1339 / 2017	1.1 / 3.5 / 1.0 / 3.3
2	0131 / 0823 / W 1421 / 2104	1.5 / 3.0 / 1.5 / 2.8	**17**	0203 / 0842 / TH 1452 / 2124	1.2 / 3.4 / 1.2 / 3.2
3	0244 / 0925 / TH 1531 / 2210	1.6 / 2.9 / 1.5 / 2.9	**18**	0321 / 0954 / F 1605 / 2237	1.3 / 3.3 / 1.2 / 3.2
4	0358 / 1031 / F 1633 / 2313	1.6 / 3.0 / 1.4 / 3.0	**19**	0436 / 1108 / SA 1710 / 2345	1.3 / 3.3 / 1.1 / 3.3
5	0459 / 1133 / SA 1724	1.4 / 3.0 / 1.3	**20**	0540 / 1215 / SU 1806	1.1 / 3.4 / 1.1
6	0007 / 0548 / SU 1227 / 1808	3.1 / 1.3 / 3.1 / 1.1	**21**	0045 / 0634 / M 1313 / 1853	3.5 / 1.0 / 3.5 / 1.0
7	0055 / 0633 / M 1315 / 1850	3.3 / 1.1 / 3.3 / 1.0	**22**	0137 / 0722 / TU 1403 / 1936	3.6 / 0.9 / 3.5 / 0.9
8	0138 / 0715 / TU 1359 / 1931	3.4 / 0.9 / 3.4 / 0.8	**23**	0223 / 0805 / W 1448 / 2016	3.7 / 0.8 / 3.5 / 0.9
9	0219 / 0757 / W 1442 / O 2012	3.6 / 0.7 / 3.5 / 0.7	**24**	0305 / 0845 / TH 1530 / ● 2053	3.8 / 0.8 / 3.5 / 0.8
10	0300 / 0840 / TH 1524 / 2053	3.7 / 0.6 / 3.6 / 0.6	**25**	0345 / 0923 / F 1608 / 2129	3.8 / 0.8 / 3.5 / 0.8
11	0342 / 0922 / F 1607 / 2136	3.8 / 0.5 / 3.6 / 0.6	**26**	0422 / 0959 / SA 1645 / 2205	3.8 / 0.8 / 3.5 / 0.9
12	0424 / 1007 / SA 1651 / 2220	3.8 / 0.5 / 3.6 / 0.6	**27**	0459 / 1035 / SU 1721 / 2240	3.7 / 0.8 / 3.4 / 0.9
13	0507 / 1052 / SU 1736 / 2306	3.8 / 0.6 / 3.5 / 0.7	**28**	0534 / 1110 / M 1756 / 2317	3.6 / 0.9 / 3.3 / 1.0
14	0553 / 1141 / M 1825 / 2356	3.8 / 0.7 / 3.5 / 0.9	**29**	0609 / 1147 / TU 1832 / 2355	3.5 / 1.1 / 3.2 / 1.2
15	0643 / 1236 / TU 1917	3.7 / 0.9 / 3.3	**30**	0645 / 1227 / W 1911	3.3 / 1.2 / 3.1
			31	0039 / 0725 / TH 1314 / 1956	1.3 / 3.1 / 1.3 / 3.0

TIDAL DIFFERENCES PAGES 21:264-21:265. TIDAL CURVE PAGE 21:263.

Datum of predictions: 0.5 m. below M.L.W.S.. and at L.A.T.

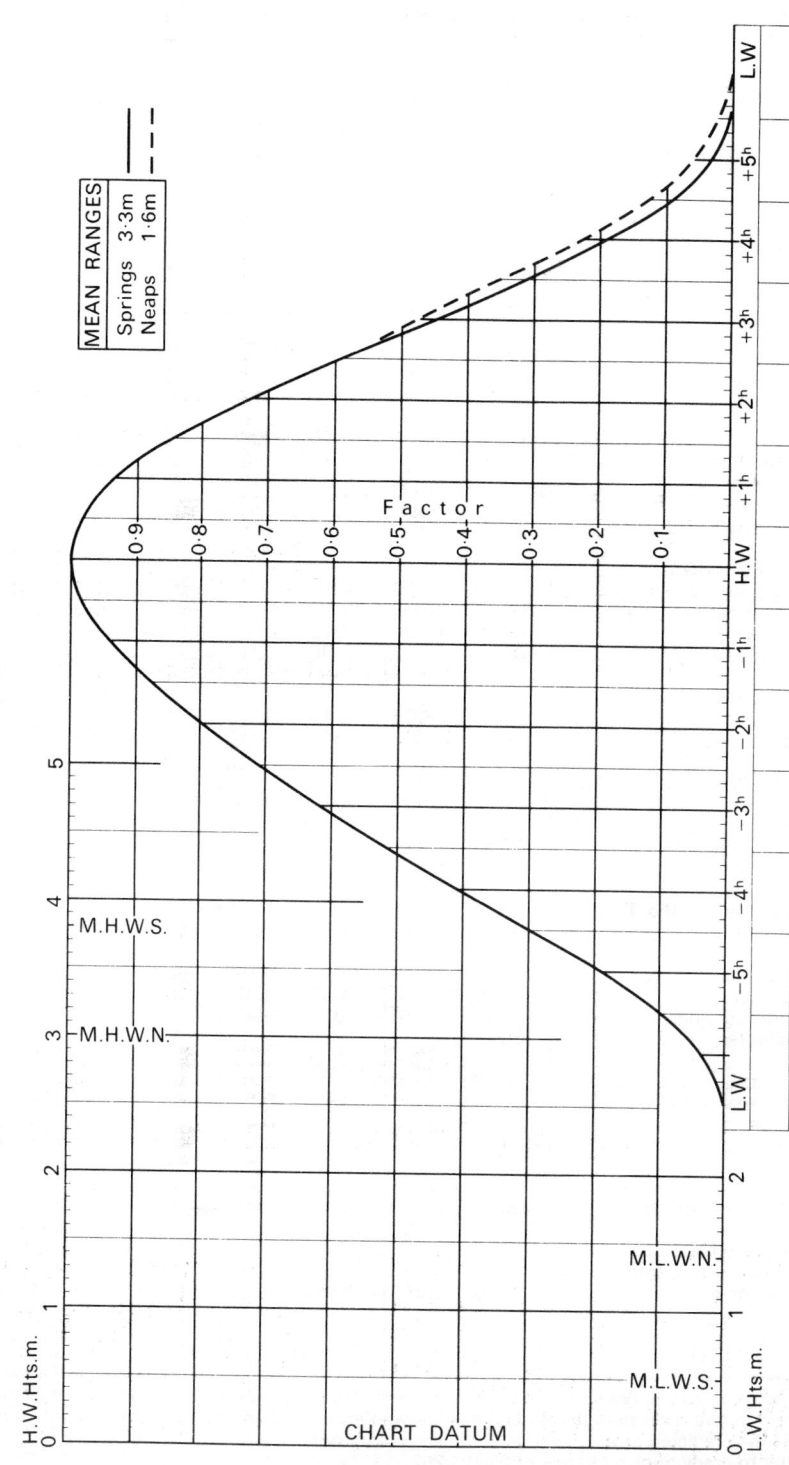

LISBON

MEAN SPRING AND NEAP CURVES

Springs occur 1 day after New and Full Moon.

MEAN RANGES

Springs 3·3m
Neaps 1·6m

Factor

TIDAL DIFFERENCES ON LISBON

PLACE	TIME DIFFERENCES				HEIGHT DIFFERENCES (Metres)			
	High Water		Low Water		MHWS	MHWN	MLWN	MLWS
(Zone −0100)								
LISBON	0500 and 1700	1000 and 2200	0300 and 1500	0800 and 2000	3.8	3.0	1.4	0.5
Corcubion	+0055	+0110	+0120	+0135	−0.4	−0.4	−0.2	−0.2
Muros	+0050	+0105	+0115	+0130	−0.3	−0.3	−0.1	−0.1
Ria de Arosa								
Villagarcia	+0040	+0100	+0110	+0120	−0.2	−0.2	0.0	0.0
Ria de Pontevedra								
Marin	+0050	+0110	+0120	+0130	−0.4	−0.4	−0.1	0.0
Vigo	+0040	+0100	+0105	+0125	−0.3	−0.3	−0.1	−0.1
Bayona	+0035	+0050	+0100	+0115	−0.3	−0.3	−0.1	−0.1
La Guardia	+0040	+0055	+0105	+0120	−0.5	−0.5	−0.2	−0.2
LISBON	0400 and 1600	0900 and 2100	0400 and 1600	0900 and 2100	3.8	3.0	1.4	0.5
(Zone GMT)								
PORTUGAL								
Viana do Castelo	−0020	0000	+0010	+0015	−0.3	−0.3	0.0	0.0
Esposende	−0020	0000	+0010	+0015	−0.6	−0.5	−0.1	0.0
Povoa de Varzim	−0020	0000	+0010	+0015	−0.3	−0.3	0.0	0.0
Porto de Leixoes	−0025	−0010	0000	+0010	−0.3	−0.3	−0.1	0.0
Rio Douro								
Entrance	−0010	+0005	+0015	+0025	−0.6	−0.5	−0.1	0.0
Oporto (Porto)	+0002	+0002	+0040	+0040	−0.5	−0.4	−0.1	+0.1
Barra de Aveiro	+0005	+0010	+0010	+0015	−0.6	−0.4	0.0	+0.2
Figueira da Foz	−0015	0000	+0010	+0020	−0.4	−0.4	0.0	+0.1
Enseada da Nazare (Pederneira)	−0030	−0015	−0005	+0005	−0.6	−0.5	−0.1	0.0
Peniche	−0035	−0015	−0005	0000	−0.3	−0.4	−0.1	+0.1
River Tagus (Rio Tejo)								
Cascais	−0040	−0025	−0015	−0010	−0.3	−0.3	+0.1	+0.2
Sesimbra	−0045	−0030	−0020	−0010	−0.4	−0.4	0.0	+0.1
Setubal	−0020	−0015	−0005	+0005	−0.4	−0.3	−0.1	0.0
Porto de Sines	−0050	−0030	−0020	−0010	−0.4	−0.4	0.0	+0.1
Milfontes	−0040	−0030	—	—	−0.1	−0.1	+0.1	+0.2
Arrifana	−0030	−0020	—	—	−0.1	0.0	0.0	+0.2
Enseada de Belixe	−0050	−0030	−0020	−0015	+0.3	+0.2	+0.3	+0.3
Lagos	−0100	−0040	−0030	−0025	−0.4	−0.4	0.0	+0.1
Ponta do Altar	−0100	−0040	−0030	−0025	−0.3	−0.3	0.0	+0.1
Enseada de Albufeira	−0035	+0015	−0005	0000	−0.2	−0.2	+0.1	+0.2
Cabo de Santa Maria	−0050	−0030	−0015	+0005	−0.4	−0.4	0.0	+0.1
Rio Guadiana								
Vila Real de Santo António	−0050	−0015	−0010	0000	−0.4	−0.3	0.0	+0.2

Note: Time zones. Predictions for the standard port are based on GMT. Where a secondary port lies in a different time zone the differences shown can be applied without further correction in order to give the predicted *local zone* time at the secondary port.
Refer to predictions on pages 21:260-21:262

PLACE	TIME DIFFERENCES				HEIGHT DIFFERENCES (Metres)			
	High Water		Low Water		MHWS	MHWN	MLWN	MLWS
LISBON	0500 and 1700	1000 and 2200	0500 and 1700	1100 and 2300	**3.8**	**3.0**	**1.4**	**0.5**
(Zone −0100)								
SPAIN								
Ayamonte	+0005	+0015	+0025	+0045	−0.7	−0.6	−0.4	−0.2
Ria de Huelva								
Bar	0000	+0015	+0035	+0030	−0.5	−0.5	−0.2	−0.2
Huelva, Muelle de Fabrica	+0010	+0025	+0045	+0040	−0.3	−0.3	−0.2	−0.2
Rio Guadalquivir								
Bar	−0005	+0005	+0020	+0030	−0.5	−0.5	−0.2	−0.1
Bonanza	+0025	+0040	+0100	+0120	−0.8	−0.6	−0.3	−0.1
Corta de los Jerónimos	+0210	+0230	+0255	+0345	−1.1	−0.9	−0.4	−0.1
Sevilla	+0400	+0430	+0510	+0545	−1.7	−1.2	−0.6	0.0
Rota	−0010	+0010	+0025	+0015	−0.8	−0.7	−0.3	−0.1
Cadiz								
Puerto	0000	+0020	+0040	+0025	−0.5	−0.5	−0.2	−0.1
La Carraca	+0020	+0050	+0100	+0040	−0.4	−0.4	−0.2	0.0
Rio Barbate	+0016	+0016	+0045	+0045	−1.9	−1.5	−0.4	+0.1

Note: Time zones. Predictions for the standard port are based on GMT. Where a secondary port lies in a different time zone the differences shown can be applied without further correction in order to give the predicted *local zone* time at the secondary port.
Refer to predictions on pages 21:260-21:262

PLACE	TIME DIFFERENCES				HEIGHT DIFFERENCES (Metres)			
	High Water		Low Water		MHWS	MHWN	MLWN	MLWS
POINTE DE GRAVE	0000 and 1200	0600 and 1800	0500 and 1700	1200 and 2400	5.3	4.3	2.1	1.0
Ile de Re								
St. Martin	−0025	−0045	−0005	−0005	+0.8	+0.4	+0.1	−0.3
La Pallice	+0005	−0035	−0020	−0015	+0.8	+0.6	+0.4	0.0
La Rochelle	+0005	−0035	−0020	−0015	+0.8	+0.6	+0.4	0.0
Ile d'Aix	−0005	−0035	−0025	−0015	+0.9	+0.7	+0.4	0.0
La Charente								
Rochefort	+0015	−0020	+0045	+0120	+1.1	+0.8	+0.1	+0.4
La Cayenne	−0015	−0035	−0020	0000	+0.5	+0.3	+0.3	+0.1
La Gironde								
Royan	0000	−0020	−0010	−0005	−0.2	−0.2	−0.2	−0.1
Richard	+0015	+0020	+0025	+0030	0.0	0.0	−0.2	−0.2
Lamena	+0035	+0045	+0100	+0130	+0.2	+0.1	−0.4	−0.3
Pauillac	+0045	+0110	+0140	+0220	+0.2	0.0	−0.8	−0.5
La Reuille	+0120	+0155	+0230	+0320	−0.2	−0.4	−1.4	−0.9
La Garonne								
Le Marquis................	+0130	+0205	+0250	+0340	−0.2	−0.4	−1.6	−1.0
Bordeaux	+0155	+0235	+0330	+0425	−0.1	−0.3	−1.7	−1.0
La Dordogne								
Libourne....................	+0245	+0315	+0525	+0600	−0.6	−0.8	−2.0	−0.4
Bassin d'Arcachon								
Cap Ferret	−0015	0000	+0005	+0015	−1.2	−1.0	−0.7	−0.6
Arcachon	+0005	+0030	+0015	+0040	−1.1	−1.1	−1.0	−0.8
L'Adour								
Boucau	−0035	−0030	−0010	−0030	−1.0	−0.9	−0.3	−0.2
St. Jean de Luz								
Socoa	−0050	−0045	−0025	−0040	−1.0	−1.0	−0.5	−0.5
SPAIN								
Pasajes	−0050	−0030	−0015	−0045	−1.1	−1.2	−0.5	−0.5
San Sebastian	−0110	−0030	−0020	−0040	−1.1	−0.9	−0.5	−0.2
Guetaria....................	−0110	−0030	−0020	−0040	−0.9	−0.7	−0.5	−0.2
Lequeitio	−0115	−0035	−0025	−0045	1.1	−0.9	−0.5	−0.2
Bermeo	−0055	−0015	−0005	−0025	−0.6	−0.5	−0.4	−0.1
Abra de Bilbao	−0125	−0045	−0035	−0055	−1.1	−0.9	−0.5	−0.2
Portugalete	−0100	−0020	−0010	−0030	−1.1	−1.0	−0.5	−0.2
Castro Urdiales..........	−0040	−0120	−0020	−0110	−0.9	−0.9	−0.2	−0.2
Ria de Santona	−0005	−0045	+0015	−0035	−0.8	−0.9	−0.2	−0.2
Santander	−0020	−0100	0000	−0050	−0.8	−0.8	−0.2	−0.2
Ria de Suances..........	0000	−0030	+0020	−0020	−0.9	−1.0	−0.2	−0.2
San Vicente de la Barquera	−0020	−0100	0000	−0050	−0.9	−1.0	−0.2	−0.2
Ria de Tina Mayor	−0020	−0100	0000	−0050	−0.9	−0.9	−0.2	−0.2
Ribadesella	+0005	−0020	+0020	−0020	−1.3	−1.2	−0.6	−0.4
Gijon	−0005	−0030	+0010	−0030	−1.3	−1.2	−0.6	−0.4
Luanco	−0010	−0035	+0005	−0035	−1.3	−1.2	−0.6	−0.4
Aviles	−0100	−0040	−0015	−0050	−1.4	−1.3	−0.7	−0.5
San Esteban de Pravia	−0005	−0030	+0010	−0030	−1.3	−1.2	−0.6	−0.4
Luarca......................	+0010	−0015	+0025	−0015	−1.1	−1.0	−0.5	−0.3
Ribadeo	+0010	−0015	+0025	−0015	−1.3	−1.2	−0.6	−0.4
Ria de Vivero..............	+0010	−0015	+0025	−0015	−1.3	−1.2	−0.6	−0.4
Santa Marta de Ortigueira	−0020	0000	+0020	−0010	−1.2	−1.1	−0.6	−0.4
El Ferrol del Caudillo ...	−0045	−0110	−0010	−0105	−1.5	−1.3	−0.7	−0.4
La Coruna	−0110	−0050	−0030	−0100	−1.5	−1.5	−0.6	−0.5
Ria de Corme	−0025	−0005	+0015	−0015	−1.6	−1.5	−0.6	−0.5
Ria de Camarinas........	−0120	−0055	−0030	−0100	−1.5	−1.5	−0.6	−0.5

Note: Time zone. The predictions for the standard port are on the same time zone as the differences shown. No further adjustment is necessary.   **Refer to predictions on pages 21:267-21:269.**

POINTE DE GRAVE 21:267

NW. FRANCE. **HIGH & LOW WATER 1992**

TIME ZONE-0100 SUBTRACT 1 HOUR FROM TIMES SHOWN FOR GMT

JANUARY

Day	Time	m	Time	m	Time	m	Time	m
1 W	0247	4.5	0827	1.8	1512	4.5	2048	1.8
2 TH	0333	4.6	0921	1.7	1556	4.6	2138	1.7
3 F	0413	4.8	1008	1.5	1633	4.7	2221	1.6
4 SA	0448	4.9	1049	1.4	1708	4.8	● 2259	1.5
5 SU	0521	5.0	1125	1.4	1740	4.9	2333	1.5
6 M	0552	5.0	1158	1.3	1811	4.9		
7 TU	0005	1.4	0623	5.0	1229	1.3	1841	4.9
8 W	0037	1.4	0652	5.0	1301	1.4	1912	4.8
9 TH	0109	1.5	0723	4.9	1333	1.4	1944	4.7
10 F	0143	1.5	0756	4.8	1408	1.6	2019	4.6
11 SA	0220	1.6	0833	4.7	1445	1.7	2101	4.5
12 SU	0301	1.8	0914	4.5	1529	1.9	2153	4.3
13 M	0350	1.9	1019	4.3	1622	2.0	2302	4.2
14 TU	0451	2.0	1136	4.2	1728	2.1		
15 W	0020	4.3	0603	2.0	1256	4.3	1841	2.1
16 TH	0133	4.4	0717	1.9	1408	4.5	1952	1.9
17 F	0237	4.7	0825	1.6	1510	4.7	2056	1.6
18 SA	0334	5.0	0927	1.3	1606	5.0	2155	1.3
19 SU	0427	5.3	1023	1.0	1658	5.2	○ 2248	1.1
20 M	0517	5.6	1114	0.8	1747	5.4	2337	0.9
21 TU	0604	5.7	1202	0.7	1833	5.4		
22 W	0023	0.8	0651	5.7	1248	0.7	1918	5.4
23 TH	0107	0.8	0736	5.6	1331	0.8	2001	5.2
24 F	0151	0.9	0820	5.3	1415	1.0	2042	5.0
25 SA	0235	1.2	0904	5.0	1500	1.3	2125	4.7
26 SU	0323	1.5	0954	4.6	1549	1.7	2215	4.4
27 M	0419	1.8	1059	4.3	1648	2.0	2333	4.1
28 TU	0530	2.1	1233	4.1	1800	2.2		
29 W	0114	4.1	0650	2.1	1355	4.1	1917	2.2
30 TH	0225	4.3	0804	2.0	1454	4.3	2024	2.1
31 F	0316	4.5	0902	1.8	1539	4.4	2117	1.9

FEBRUARY

Day	Time	m	Time	m	Time	m	Time	m
1 SA	0356	4.7	0948	1.6	1615	4.6	2201	1.7
2 SU	0430	4.9	1026	1.5	1647	4.8	2237	1.5
3 M	0501	5.0	1101	1.3	1718	4.9	● 2310	1.4
4 TU	0530	5.1	1132	1.2	1747	5.0	2342	1.3
5 W	0559	5.2	1203	1.2	1816	5.0		
6 TH	0013	1.2	0626	5.2	1234	1.2	1844	5.0
7 F	0044	1.2	0654	5.1	1305	1.2	1912	5.0
8 SA	0116	1.3	0723	5.0	1336	1.4	1943	4.9
9 SU	0149	1.4	0752	4.9	1410	1.5	2019	4.7
10 M	0227	1.5	0834	4.7	1449	1.7	2103	4.5
11 TU	0311	1.7	0926	4.4	1537	1.9	2205	4.3
12 W	0407	1.9	1049	4.2	1640	2.1	2334	4.2
13 TH	0521	2.0	1225	4.2	1800	2.2		
14 F	0104	4.4	0647	1.9	1347	4.4	1925	2.0
15 SA	0217	4.7	0806	1.7	1455	4.7	2039	1.7
16 SU	0319	5.0	0911	1.3	1553	5.0	2140	1.3
17 M	0412	5.4	1007	1.0	1644	5.3	2232	1.0
18 TU	0501	5.6	1057	0.7	1730	5.5	○ 2319	0.8
19 W	0546	5.8	1142	0.6	1813	5.5		
20 TH	0003	0.6	0629	5.7	1225	0.6	1853	5.5
21 F	0045	0.7	0710	5.6	1306	0.8	1930	5.3
22 SA	0125	0.8	0749	5.3	1346	1.0	2004	5.0
23 SU	0206	1.1	0827	5.0	1427	1.3	2038	4.7
24 M	0250	1.4	0909	4.6	1512	1.7	2117	4.4
25 TU	0341	1.8	1005	4.2	1605	2.1	2215	4.1
26 W	0448	2.2	1143	3.9	1715	2.4		
27 TH	0023	3.9	0614	2.3	1321	3.9	1839	2.4
28 F	0153	4.1	0801	2.2	1425	4.1	1954	2.3
29 SA	0249	4.3	0834	1.9	1511	4.3	2050	2.0

MARCH

Day	Time	m	Time	m	Time	m	Time	m
1 SU	0330	4.6	0919	1.7	1548	4.6	2133	1.8
2 M	0404	4.8	0956	1.5	1620	4.8	2210	1.5
3 TU	0434	5.0	1030	1.3	1650	5.0	2244	1.3
4 W	0504	5.1	1103	1.2	1720	5.1	● 2316	1.2
5 TH	0532	5.2	1135	1.1	1749	5.1	2348	1.1
6 F	0600	5.2	1206	1.1	1817	5.1		
7 SA	0020	1.1	0652	5.2	1238	1.1	1846	5.1
8 SU	0051	1.1	0656	5.1	1309	1.2	1916	5.0
9 M	0125	1.2	0727	4.9	1343	1.4	1951	4.9
10 TU	0202	1.3	0808	4.7	1422	1.6	2035	4.7
11 W	0245	1.5	0900	4.4	1509	1.8	2138	4.4
12 TH	0341	1.8	1042	4.2	1612	2.1	2310	4.3
13 F	0457	2.0	1209	4.2	1737	2.2		
14 SA	0044	4.4	0630	1.9	1332	4.4	1909	2.0
15 SU	0200	4.7	0751	1.6	1440	4.7	2023	1.7
16 M	0302	5.0	0854	1.3	1536	5.0	2122	1.3
17 TU	0355	5.3	0947	1.0	1625	5.3	2212	1.0
18 W	0442	5.5	1035	0.8	1709	5.4	○ 2258	0.7
19 TH	0525	5.6	1119	0.7	1749	5.5	2341	0.6
20 F	0606	5.6	1201	0.7	1827	5.4		
21 SA	0022	0.7	0644	5.4	1241	0.9	1901	5.3
22 SU	0101	0.9	0721	5.2	1319	1.1	1933	5.0
23 M	0140	1.1	0758	4.8	1358	1.4	2005	4.7
24 TU	0221	1.5	0838	4.5	1439	1.8	2043	4.4
25 W	0308	1.8	0930	4.1	1528	2.1	2135	4.1
26 TH	0410	2.1	1053	3.9	1632	2.4	2317	3.9
27 F	0532	2.3	1231	3.9	1753	2.4		
28 SA	0104	4.0	0653	2.2	1340	4.0	1910	2.3
29 SU	0208	4.2	0754	2.0	1431	4.3	2010	2.1
30 M	0253	4.5	0840	1.7	1512	4.5	2057	1.8
31 TU	0330	4.7	0920	1.5	1547	4.7	2136	1.5

APRIL

Day	Time	m	Time	m	Time	m	Time	m
1 W	0403	4.9	0957	1.3	1620	4.9	2213	1.3
2 TH	0434	5.0	1032	1.2	1651	5.1	2248	1.1
3 F	0505	5.1	1106	1.1	1723	5.1	● 2322	1.0
4 SA	0536	5.1	1140	1.1	1754	5.2	2356	1.0
5 SU	0607	5.1	1214	1.1	1826	5.1		
6 M	0031	1.0	0640	5.0	1248	1.2	1900	5.1
7 TU	0107	1.1	0717	4.9	1324	1.4	1939	4.9
8 W	0146	1.2	0804	4.6	1406	1.6	2029	4.7
9 TH	0232	1.5	0908	4.4	1457	1.8	2136	4.5
10 F	0331	1.7	1031	4.2	1603	2.0	2301	4.4
11 SA	0450	1.9	1158	4.2	1729	2.1		
12 SU	0027	4.5	0619	1.8	1316	4.4	1854	1.9
13 M	0141	4.7	0733	1.6	1421	4.7	2004	1.6
14 TU	0243	5.0	0833	1.3	1516	4.9	2100	1.3
15 W	0335	5.2	0924	1.0	1603	5.1	2150	1.0
16 TH	0422	5.3	1012	0.9	1646	5.3	2236	0.8
17 F	0504	5.4	1056	0.9	1726	5.3	○ 2320	0.8
18 SA	0544	5.3	1137	0.9	1802	5.2		
19 SU	0000	0.8	0623	5.2	1217	1.1	1837	5.1
20 M	0040	1.0	0659	4.9	1255	1.3	1910	4.9
21 TU	0118	1.2	0736	4.7	1333	1.5	1944	4.7
22 W	0158	1.5	0817	4.4	1412	1.8	2024	4.5
23 TH	0242	1.8	0906	4.2	1457	2.0	2113	4.2
24 F	0336	2.0	1010	4.0	1553	2.2	2226	4.1
25 SA	0444	2.2	1130	3.9	1703	2.3	2359	4.0
26 SU	0558	2.2	1244	4.0	1816	2.3		
27 M	0112	4.1	0702	2.0	1342	4.2	1921	2.1
28 TU	0206	4.3	0754	1.8	1429	4.4	2013	1.9
29 W	0249	4.5	0839	1.6	1509	4.6	2058	1.6
30 TH	0327	4.7	0920	1.4	1546	4.8	2139	1.4

TIDAL DIFFERENCES PAGE 21:266.

Datum of predictions: 1.0 m. below M.L.W.S. and 0.5 m. below L.A.T.

POINTE DE GRAVE

HIGH & LOW WATER 1992   Lat. 45°34'N. Long. 1°04'W.

TIME ZONE-0100 SUBTRACT 1 HOUR FROM TIMES SHOWN FOR GMT

MAY

Day	Time	m	Day	Time	m
1 F	0402 / 0959 / 1622 / 2219	4.9 / 1.3 / 5.0 / 1.2	**16** O	0446 / 1035 / 1705 / 2302	5.0 / 1.1 / 5.1 / 1.0
2 SA ●	0438 / 1037 / 1658 / 2257	5.0 / 1.2 / 5.1 / 1.0	**17** SU	0526 / 1117 / 1743 / 2343	5.0 / 1.2 / 5.1 / 1.1
3 SU	0514 / 1115 / 1735 / 2336	5.0 / 1.1 / 5.2 / 1.0	**18** M	0605 / 1156 / 1818	4.9 / 1.2 / 5.0
4 M	0552 / 1154 / 1813	5.0 / 1.1 / 5.2	**19** TU	0023 / 0642 / 1234 / 1852	1.1 / 4.8 / 1.4 / 4.9
5 TU	0015 / 0633 / 1233 / 1854	1.0 / 5.0 / 1.2 / 5.1	**20** W	0101 / 0718 / 1310 / 1927	1.3 / 4.6 / 1.5 / 4.8
6 W	0056 / 0719 / 1314 / 1940	1.0 / 4.8 / 1.3 / 5.0	**21** TH	0138 / 0756 / 1348 / 2006	1.5 / 4.5 / 1.7 / 4.6
7 TH	0140 / 0812 / 1400 / 2034	1.2 / 4.6 / 1.5 / 4.8	**22** F	0218 / 0839 / 1428 / 2050	1.6 / 4.3 / 1.8 / 4.4
8 F	0230 / 0915 / 1455 / 2138	1.4 / 4.5 / 1.7 / 4.7	**23** SA	0302 / 0929 / 1515 / 2143	1.8 / 4.2 / 2.0 / 4.3
9 SA	0330 / 1027 / 1600 / 2251	1.6 / 4.4 / 1.8 / 4.6	**24** SU	0355 / 1029 / 1611 / 2249	1.9 / 4.1 / 2.1 / 4.1
10 SU	0442 / 1141 / 1716	1.7 / 4.4 / 1.9	**25** M	0457 / 1137 / 1717	2.0 / 4.1 / 2.2
11 M	0006 / 0559 / 1253 / 1832	4.6 / 1.7 / 4.5 / 1.8	**26** TU	0002 / 0601 / 1242 / 1823	4.1 / 2.0 / 4.1 / 2.1
12 TU	0117 / 0708 / 1357 / 1939	4.7 / 1.5 / 4.6 / 1.6	**27** W	0106 / 0701 / 1338 / 1923	4.2 / 1.9 / 4.3 / 1.9
13 W	0220 / 0808 / 1453 / 2037	4.8 / 1.4 / 4.8 / 1.3	**28** TH	0200 / 0754 / 1426 / 2016	4.3 / 1.7 / 4.5 / 1.7
14 TH	0315 / 0901 / 1542 / 2129	4.9 / 1.2 / 4.9 / 1.2	**29** F	0246 / 0841 / 1510 / 2104	4.5 / 1.6 / 4.7 / 1.5
15 F	0402 / 0949 / 1625 / 2217	5.0 / 1.1 / 5.0 / 1.1	**30** SA	0330 / 0926 / 1552 / 2149	4.7 / 1.4 / 4.9 / 1.3
			31 SU	0413 / 1010 / 1635 / 2233	4.8 / 1.3 / 5.1 / 1.1

JUNE

Day	Time	m	Day	Time	m
1 M ●	0457 / 1054 / 1718 / 2318	5.0 / 1.2 / 5.2 / 1.0	**16** TU	0548 / 1138 / 1801	4.8 / 1.4 / 5.0
2 TU	0542 / 1138 / 1803	5.0 / 1.1 / 5.3	**17** W	0006 / 0623 / 1214 / 1834	1.2 / 4.7 / 1.4 / 4.9
3 W	0003 / 0629 / 1223 / 1850	0.9 / 5.0 / 1.1 / 5.3	**18** TH	0041 / 0656 / 1248 / 1907	1.3 / 4.7 / 1.4 / 4.9
4 TH	0049 / 0719 / 1308 / 1939	0.9 / 4.9 / 1.2 / 5.2	**19** F	0116 / 0730 / 1323 / 1941	1.4 / 4.6 / 1.5 / 4.8
5 F	0136 / 0812 / 1357 / 2032	1.0 / 4.8 / 1.3 / 5.1	**20** SA	0150 / 0806 / 1359 / 2019	1.5 / 4.5 / 1.6 / 4.6
6 SA	0226 / 0908 / 1449 / 2129	1.2 / 4.7 / 1.4 / 4.9	**21** SU	0228 / 0847 / 1438 / 2100	1.6 / 4.4 / 1.7 / 4.5
7 SU	0321 / 1009 / 1547 / 2231	1.3 / 4.6 / 1.6 / 4.7	**22** M	0309 / 0933 / 1524 / 2150	1.7 / 4.3 / 1.9 / 4.3
8 M	0422 / 1114 / 1652 / 2339	1.5 / 4.5 / 1.7 / 4.6	**23** TU	0358 / 1029 / 1618 / 2249	1.9 / 4.2 / 2.0 / 4.2
9 TU	0528 / 1223 / 1802	1.6 / 4.4 / 1.7	**24** W	0455 / 1133 / 1720 / 2357	2.0 / 4.1 / 2.1 / 4.2
10 W	0050 / 0637 / 1331 / 1912	4.6 / 1.6 / 4.5 / 1.6	**25** TH	0559 / 1239 / 1827	2.0 / 4.2 / 2.0
11 TH	0158 / 0740 / 1431 / 2014	4.6 / 1.6 / 4.6 / 1.5	**26** F	0104 / 0702 / 1340 / 1930	4.2 / 1.9 / 4.4 / 1.9
12 F	0256 / 0838 / 1523 / 2111	4.6 / 1.5 / 4.7 / 1.4	**27** SA	0205 / 0800 / 1435 / 2027	4.4 / 1.8 / 4.6 / 1.6
13 SA	0347 / 0930 / 1608 / 2201	4.7 / 1.4 / 4.8 / 1.3	**28** SU	0300 / 0854 / 1525 / 2121	4.6 / 1.6 / 4.8 / 1.4
14 SU	0431 / 1017 / 1648 / 2247	4.7 / 1.4 / 4.9 / 1.2	**29** M	0351 / 0945 / 1614 / 2212	4.8 / 1.4 / 5.1 / 1.1
15 M	0511 / 1059 / 1726 / 2328	4.8 / 1.3 / 4.9 / 1.2	**30** TU ●	0442 / 1035 / 1703 / 2302	4.9 / 1.2 / 5.3 / 0.9

JULY

Day	Time	m	Day	Time	m
1 W	0531 / 1124 / 1751 / 2351	5.1 / 1.0 / 5.4 / 0.8	**16** TH	0559 / 1152 / 1811	4.8 / 1.3 / 5.0
2 TH	0621 / 1212 / 1840	5.1 / 1.0 / 5.5	**17** F	0017 / 0629 / 1224 / 1840	1.2 / 4.8 / 1.3 / 5.0
3 F	0039 / 0710 / 1258 / 1928	0.8 / 5.1 / 0.9 / 5.4	**18** SA	0048 / 0659 / 1256 / 1911	1.3 / 4.8 / 1.3 / 4.9
4 SA	0125 / 0759 / 1344 / 2018	0.8 / 5.1 / 1.0 / 5.3	**19** SU	0120 / 0731 / 1329 / 1942	1.3 / 4.7 / 1.4 / 4.8
5 SU	0212 / 0848 / 1432 / 2109	1.0 / 4.9 / 1.2 / 5.1	**20** M	0153 / 0805 / 1404 / 2017	1.4 / 4.6 / 1.5 / 4.7
6 M	0300 / 0940 / 1524 / 2203	1.2 / 4.7 / 1.3 / 4.8	**21** TU	0229 / 0843 / 1442 / 2057	1.6 / 4.5 / 1.7 / 4.5
7 TU	0353 / 1037 / 1622 / 2306	1.4 / 4.5 / 1.6 / 4.6	**22** W	0309 / 0930 / 1527 / 2149	1.7 / 4.3 / 1.8 / 4.3
8 W	0454 / 1146 / 1730	1.6 / 4.3 / 1.8	**23** TH	0357 / 1030 / 1623 / 2257	1.9 / 4.2 / 2.0 / 4.2
9 TH	0021 / 0602 / 1304 / 1844	4.4 / 1.8 / 4.3 / 1.8	**24** F	0457 / 1144 / 1731	2.0 / 4.2 / 2.1
10 F	0138 / 0713 / 1413 / 1954	4.3 / 1.8 / 4.4 / 1.8	**25** SA	0017 / 0608 / 1259 / 1846	4.1 / 2.1 / 4.3 / 2.0
11 SA	0242 / 0817 / 1509 / 2055	4.4 / 1.8 / 4.5 / 1.6	**26** SU	0131 / 0720 / 1405 / 1955	4.3 / 1.9 / 4.5 / 1.7
12 SU	0334 / 0913 / 1555 / 2147	4.5 / 1.7 / 4.7 / 1.5	**27** M	0236 / 0825 / 1503 / 2057	4.5 / 1.7 / 4.8 / 1.5
13 M	0416 / 1000 / 1633 / 2231	4.6 / 1.5 / 4.8 / 1.4	**28** TU	0333 / 0920 / 1556 / 2154	4.8 / 1.4 / 5.1 / 1.1
14 TU O	0453 / 1042 / 1708 / 2310	4.7 / 1.5 / 4.9 / 1.3	**29** W	0427 / 1018 / 1647 / 2246	5.0 / 1.1 / 5.4 / 0.9
15 W	0527 / 1118 / 1740 / 2345	4.7 / 1.4 / 5.0 / 1.3	**30** TH	0517 / 1109 / 1736 / 2336	5.2 / 0.9 / 5.6 / 0.7
			31 F	0606 / 1156 / 1823	5.3 / 0.8 / 5.7

AUGUST

Day	Time	m	Day	Time	m
1 SA	0022 / 0652 / 1241 / 1910	0.6 / 5.3 / 0.7 / 5.6	**16** SU	0019 / 0629 / 1229 / 1839	1.2 / 4.9 / 1.2 / 5.0
2 SU	0106 / 0736 / 1325 / 1955	0.7 / 5.2 / 0.8 / 5.4	**17** M	0050 / 0658 / 1300 / 1907	1.2 / 4.9 / 1.3 / 4.9
3 M	0150 / 0820 / 1409 / 2042	0.9 / 5.0 / 1.0 / 5.1	**18** TU	0121 / 0728 / 1333 / 1937	1.3 / 4.8 / 1.4 / 4.8
4 TU	0234 / 0905 / 1456 / 2132	1.1 / 4.8 / 1.3 / 4.8	**19** W	0154 / 0802 / 1408 / 2012	1.5 / 4.7 / 1.5 / 4.6
5 W	0323 / 0955 / 1550 / 2232	1.4 / 4.5 / 1.6 / 4.4	**20** TH	0230 / 0843 / 1449 / 2101	1.7 / 4.5 / 1.7 / 4.4
6 TH	0419 / 1102 / 1657 / 2354	1.8 / 4.2 / 1.9 / 4.2	**21** F	0314 / 0940 / 1540 / 2215	1.9 / 4.3 / 1.9 / 4.2
7 F	0528 / 1237 / 1818	2.0 / 4.1 / 2.0	**22** SA	0410 / 1103 / 1648 / 2348	2.1 / 4.2 / 2.1 / 4.1
8 SA	0121 / 0646 / 1357 / 1936	4.1 / 2.1 / 4.2 / 2.0	**23** SU	0525 / 1230 / 1812	2.1 / 4.3 / 2.0
9 SU	0227 / 0757 / 1455 / 2039	4.2 / 2.0 / 4.4 / 1.8	**24** M	0111 / 0649 / 1344 / 1933	4.3 / 2.0 / 4.6 / 1.8
10 M	0317 / 0854 / 1538 / 2128	4.4 / 1.8 / 4.6 / 1.6	**25** TU	0219 / 0804 / 1445 / 2040	4.5 / 1.8 / 4.9 / 1.4
11 TU	0357 / 0941 / 1614 / 2209	4.5 / 1.7 / 4.8 / 1.5	**26** W	0318 / 0907 / 1540 / 2137	4.8 / 1.4 / 5.2 / 1.1
12 W	0430 / 1020 / 1645 / 2245	4.7 / 1.5 / 5.0 / 1.3	**27** TH	0411 / 1001 / 1630 / 2228	5.1 / 1.1 / 5.5 / 0.8
13 TH O	0502 / 1055 / 1715 / 2318	4.8 / 1.4 / 5.1 / 1.2	**28** F ●	0500 / 1051 / 1718 / 2316	5.3 / 0.8 / 5.7 / 0.7
14 F	0531 / 1127 / 1744 / 2349	4.9 / 1.3 / 5.1 / 1.2	**29** SA	0545 / 1136 / 1803	5.4 / 0.7 / 5.7
15 SA	0600 / 1158 / 1812	4.9 / 1.2 / 5.1	**30** SU	0000 / 0629 / 1220 / 1847	0.6 / 5.4 / 0.6 / 5.6
			31 M	0043 / 0710 / 1302 / 1930	0.7 / 5.3 / 0.8 / 5.4

GENERAL — Rade de Royan flood SE. begins +0030, ebb NW. +0600. Sp. 3.8 kn. — eddies. Port Bloc nearly ½ M. S. of Pointe de Grave is well sheltered. Very strong streams and currents are encountered between the point and the harbour.

POINTE DE GRAVE 21:269

NW. FRANCE. HIGH & LOW WATER 1992

TIME ZONE -0100 SUBTRACT 1 HOUR FROM TIMES SHOWN FOR GMT

SEPTEMBER

Day	Time	m	Time	m	Time	m	Time	m
1 TU	0125	0.9	0750	5.1	1345	1.0	2014	5.1
16 W	0053	1.3	0659	4.9	1307	1.3	1907	4.8
2 W	0208	1.2	0830	4.8	1430	1.3	2101	4.7
17 TH	0126	1.5	0732	4.8	1342	1.5	1945	4.6
3 TH	0253	1.6	0916	4.5	1521	1.7	2200	4.3
18 F	0202	1.7	0814	4.6	1423	1.6	2035	4.4
4 F	0347	1.9	1020	4.2	1627	2.0	2328	4.0
19 .	0246	1.9	0913	4.4	1514	1.9	2159	4.2
5 SA	0454	2.2	1208	4.0	1752	2.2		
20 SU	0343	2.1	1042	4.3	1623	2.0	2336	4.1
6 SU	0058	4.0	0616	2.3	1334	4.2	1914	2.1
21 M	0501	2.2	1212	4.4	1753	2.0		
7 M	0203	4.1	0732	2.2	1431	4.4	2016	1.9
22 TU	0057	4.3	0631	2.1	1326	4.6	1917	1.8
8 TU	0252	4.3	0830	2.0	1514	4.6	2102	1.7
23 W	0204	4.6	0748	1.8	1429	5.0	2023	1.4
9 W	0330	4.5	0915	1.7	1548	4.8	2141	1.5
24 TH	0301	4.9	0849	1.4	1523	5.3	2117	1.1
10 TH	0403	4.7	0954	1.5	1619	5.0	2216	1.3
25 F	0353	5.2	0942	1.0	1612	5.5	2207	0.9
11 F	0434	4.9	1028	1.4	1648	5.0	2248	1.2
26 SA	0440	5.4	1031	0.8	1658	5.7	2254	0.7
12 SA	0504	5.0	1100	1.2	1716	5.1	2320	1.2
27 SU	0524	5.5	1116	0.7	1742	5.6	2338	0.7
13 SU	0533	5.0	1132	1.2	1744	5.1	2351	1.2
28 M	0606	5.4	1159	0.7	1825	5.5		
14 M	0602	5.0	1203	1.2	1811	5.1		
29 TU	0020	0.9	0646	5.3	1242	0.8	1907	5.3
15 TU	0022	1.2	0630	5.0	1235	1.2	1839	5.0
30 W	0102	1.1	0724	5.1	1324	1.1	1950	4.9

OCTOBER

Day	Time	m	Time	m	Time	m	Time	m
1 TH	0144	1.4	0803	4.8	1407	1.4	2036	4.6
16 F	0107	1.5	0719	4.8	1326	1.4	1939	4.6
2 F	0228	1.7	0847	4.5	1457	1.8	2133	4.2
17 SA	0146	1.7	0806	4.7	1410	1.6	2038	4.4
3 SA	0318	2.0	0948	4.2	1559	2.1	2254	4.0
18 SU	0232	1.9	0910	4.5	1503	1.8	2159	4.2
4 SU	0422	2.3	1125	4.1	1718	2.3		
19 M	0332	2.0	1032	4.4	1613	2.0	2325	4.2
5 M	0019	4.0	0539	2.4	1253	4.1	1838	2.2
20 TU	0449	2.1	1155	4.5	1739	1.9		
6 TU	0125	4.1	0655	2.3	1354	4.3	1940	2.0
21 W	0041	4.4	0615	2.0	1308	4.7	1859	1.7
7 W	0215	4.3	0755	2.1	1439	4.5	2027	1.8
22 TH	0146	4.7	0729	1.7	1410	5.0	2002	1.4
8 TH	0256	4.5	0842	1.8	1517	4.7	2107	1.6
23 F	0243	4.9	0829	1.4	1505	5.2	2056	1.2
9 F	0332	4.7	0922	1.6	1549	4.9	2143	1.4
24 SA	0334	5.1	0922	1.1	1555	5.4	2146	1.0
10 SA	0405	4.9	0959	1.4	1620	5.0	2218	1.3
25 SU	0420	5.3	1011	0.9	1641	5.5	2233	0.9
11 SU	0437	5.0	1033	1.3	1650	5.1	2252	1.2
26 M	0504	5.4	1057	0.8	1725	5.4	2317	0.9
12 M	0508	5.1	1107	1.2	1720	5.1	2325	1.2
27 TU	0545	5.3	1141	0.9	1807	5.3		
13 TU	0539	5.1	1140	1.2	1750	5.0	2358	1.3
28 W	0000	1.0	0625	5.2	1224	1.0	1849	5.1
14 W	0610	5.0	1214	1.2	1821	4.9		
29 TH	0041	1.2	0703	5.0	1306	1.2	1930	4.8
15 TH	0032	1.4	0642	5.0	1249	1.3	1856	4.8
30 F	0122	1.5	0742	4.8	1349	1.5	2013	4.5
31 SA	0205	1.7	0824	4.6	1435	1.8	2103	4.3

NOVEMBER

Day	Time	m	Time	m	Time	m	Time	m
1 SU	0251	2.0	0917	4.3	1529	2.0	2206	4.1
16 M	0228	1.7	0908	4.7	1459	1.6	2151	4.4
2 M	0345	2.2	1030	4.2	1633	2.2	2322	4.0
17 TU	0326	1.8	1018	4.6	1604	1.8	2305	4.4
3 TU	0451	2.3	1154	4.1	1743	2.2		
18 W	0436	1.9	1132	4.6	1718	1.8		
4 W	0032	4.1	0602	2.3	1302	4.2	1848	2.1
19 TH	0017	4.5	0552	1.9	1244	4.7	1832	1.7
5 TH	0130	4.2	0706	2.1	1350	4.4	1942	1.9
20 F	0124	4.6	0704	1.7	1350	4.9	1937	1.5
6 F	0218	4.4	0800	1.9	1440	4.6	2028	1.7
21 SA	0224	4.8	0807	1.5	1448	5.0	2034	1.4
7 SA	0259	4.6	0846	1.7	1518	4.7	2109	1.5
22 SU	0316	5.0	0903	1.3	1540	5.1	2126	1.2
8 SU	0335	4.8	0926	1.5	1552	4.9	2147	1.4
23 M	0404	5.1	0955	1.1	1627	5.2	2215	1.2
9 M	0410	4.9	1005	1.4	1626	5.0	2224	1.3
24 TU	0448	5.2	1042	1.1	1711	5.2	● 2300	1.2
10 TU	0444	5.0	1042	1.2	1700	5.0	2301	1.3
25 W	0529	5.2	1128	1.1	1753	5.1	2343	1.2
11 W	0519	5.1	1120	1.2	1736	5.0	2338	1.3
26 TH	0609	5.1	1210	1.1	1832	5.0		
12 TH	0556	5.1	1157	1.2	1813	4.9		
27 F	0024	1.3	0646	5.0	1251	1.3	1910	4.8
13 F	0016	1.4	0634	5.1	1237	1.2	1855	4.8
28 SA	0103	1.5	0722	4.9	1330	1.4	1947	4.6
14 SA	0057	1.4	0717	5.0	1318	1.3	1943	4.7
29 SU	0141	1.6	0759	4.7	1410	1.6	2028	4.5
15 SU	0138	1.6	0807	4.9	1405	1.5	2042	4.5
30 M	0221	1.8	0842	4.5	1453	1.8	2114	4.3

DECEMBER

Day	Time	m	Time	m	Time	m	Time	m
1 TU	0305	2.0	0933	4.4	1542	2.0	2212	4.2
16 W	0313	1.5	0956	4.9	1544	1.5	2234	4.6
2 W	0357	2.1	1038	4.2	1639	2.1	2321	4.1
17 TH	0413	1.7	1102	4.7	1648	1.7	2344	4.5
3 TH	0459	2.2	1153	4.2	1742	2.1		
18 F	0522	1.8	1215	4.6	1758	1.8		
4 F	0030	4.1	0605	2.2	1301	4.2	1845	2.1
19 SA	0057	4.5	0635	1.8	1329	4.6	1908	1.7
5 SA	0130	4.3	0708	2.1	1356	4.3	1941	1.9
20 SU	0205	4.6	0745	1.7	1434	4.7	2012	1.6
6 SU	0220	4.5	0803	1.9	1442	4.5	2030	1.8
21 M	0303	4.8	0847	1.5	1529	4.8	2109	1.5
7 M	0303	4.6	0851	1.7	1523	4.6	2115	1.6
22 TU	0352	4.9	0942	1.4	1617	4.9	2200	1.4
8 TU	0343	4.8	0936	1.5	1603	4.8	2158	1.5
23 W	0436	5.0	1031	1.2	1659	5.0	2246	1.3
9 W	0422	4.9	1019	1.3	1643	5.0	○ 2240	1.3
24 TH	0516	5.1	1115	1.2	1738	5.0	● 2328	1.3
10 TH	0502	5.2	1101	1.2	1724	5.0	2322	1.3
25 F	0553	5.2	1155	1.2	1814	5.0		
11 F	0543	5.3	1144	1.1	1807	5.1		
26 SA	0006	1.3	0626	5.1	1232	1.2	1846	4.9
12 SA	0004	1.2	0627	5.3	1228	1.1	1852	5.0
27 SU	0041	1.4	0658	5.0	1306	1.3	1918	4.8
13 SU	0047	1.2	0712	5.3	1312	1.1	1941	5.0
28 M	0115	1.5	0730	4.9	1340	1.4	1951	4.7
14 M	0132	1.3	0802	5.2	1359	1.2	2033	4.8
29 TU	0149	1.6	0804	4.8	1415	1.6	2027	4.6
15 TU	0220	1.4	0856	5.0	1449	1.4	2130	4.7
30 W	0226	1.7	0842	4.6	1453	1.8	2200	4.2
31 TH	0307	1.9	0927	4.4	1538	1.9	2200	4.2

TIDAL DIFFERENCES PAGE 21:266.

Datum of predictions: 1.0 m. below M.L.W.S. and 0.5 m. below L.A.T.

TIDAL STREAMS
from
ÎLE D'OUESSANT
to
ÎLE DE NOIRMOUTIER

The following 13 charts show tidal streams at hourly intervals commencing 6h. before and ending 6h. after H.W. Brest. For Brest H.W. Times see pages 21:277-21:279. Times before and after H.W. Dover are also given. For Dover H.W. Times see pages 21:41-21:43.

Tidal stream direction is shown by arrows. Thin arrows show rates and position of weak streams and thick arrows, indicate stronger streams.

CAUTION: Due to the very strong rates of the tidal stream in some of the areas covered, many eddies may occur.

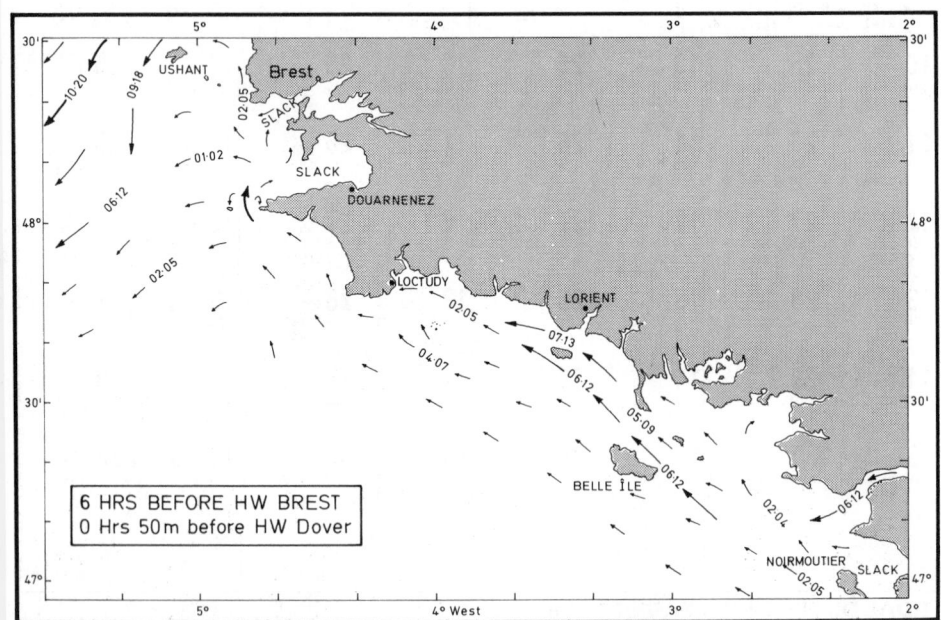

6 HRS BEFORE HW BREST
0 Hrs 50m before HW Dover

Produced from portion(s) of BA Tidal Stream Atlases with the sanction of the Controller, H.M. Stationery Office and of the Hydrographer of the Navy.

ÎLE D'OUESSANT to ÎLE DE NOIRMOUTIER

5 HRS BEFORE HW BREST
0 Hrs 10m after HW Dover

4 HRS BEFORE HW BREST
1 Hr 10m after HW Dover

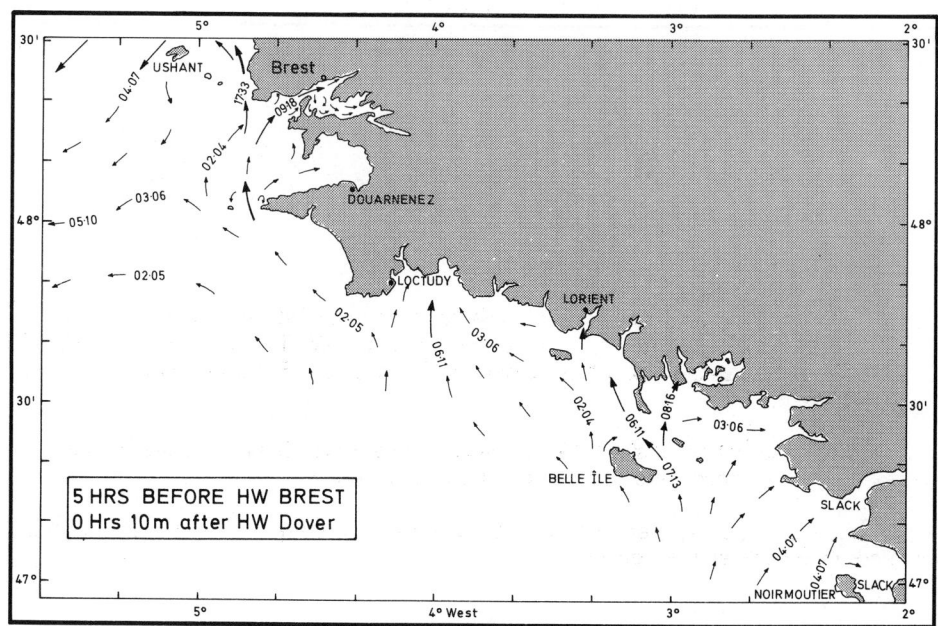

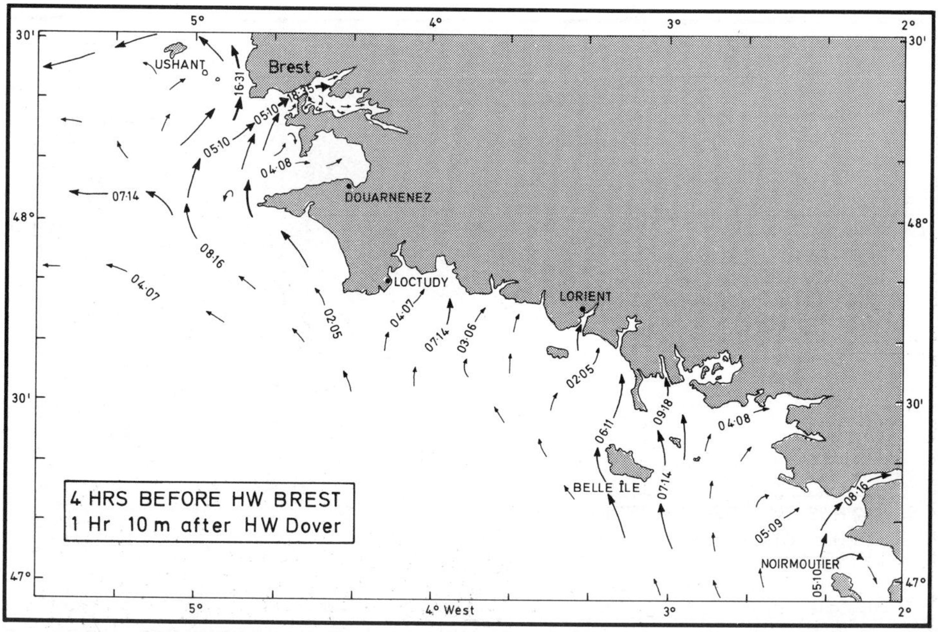

ÎLE D'OUESSANT to ÎLE DE NOIRMOUTIER

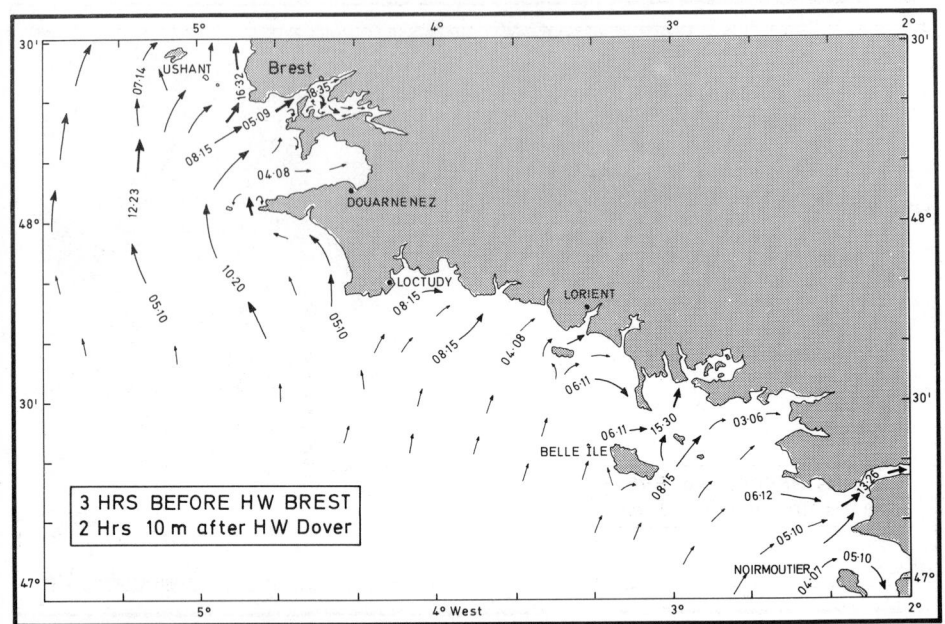

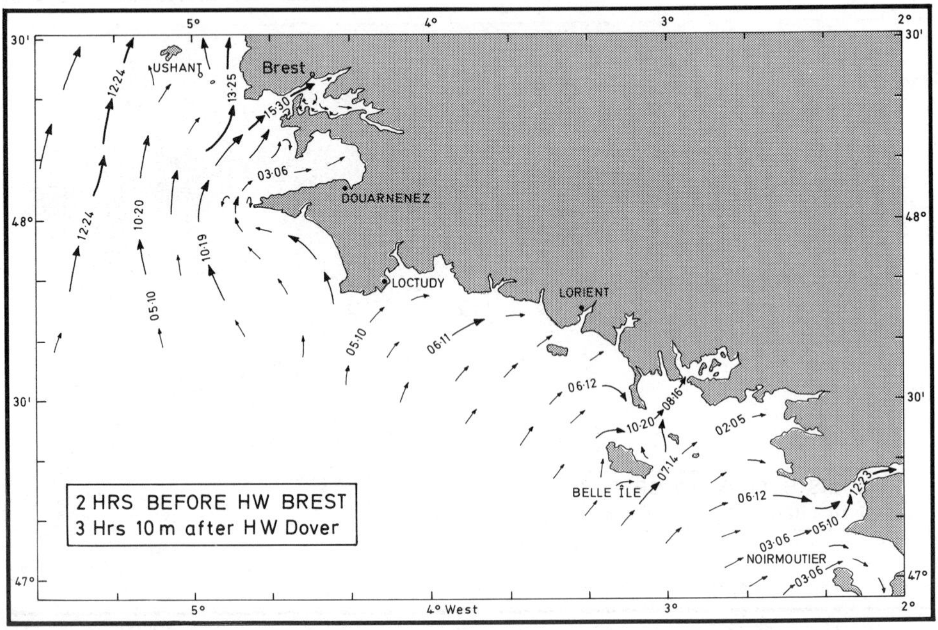

ÎLE D'OUESSANT to ÎLE DE NOIRMOUTIER

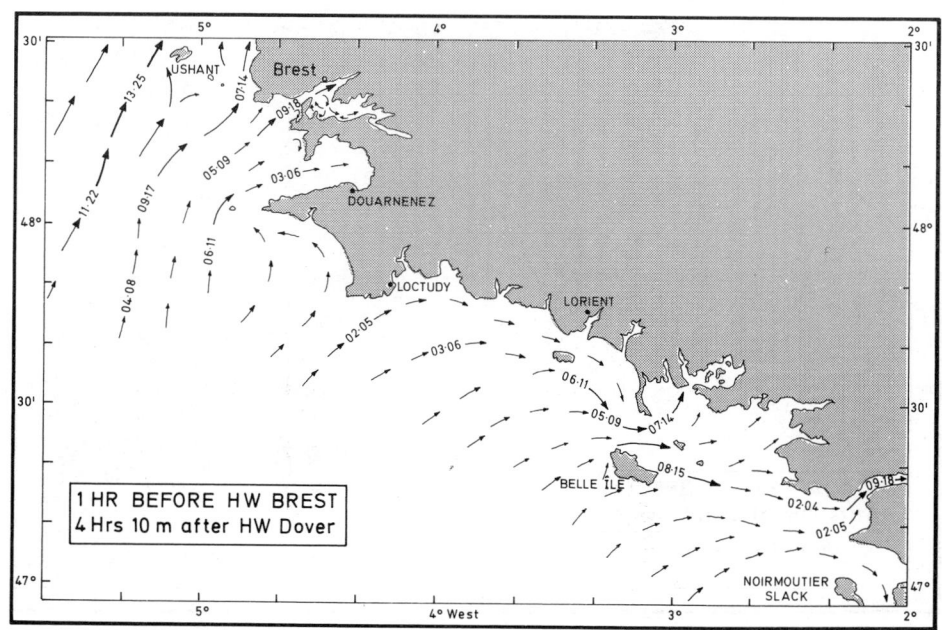

1 HR BEFORE HW BREST
4 Hrs 10 m after HW Dover

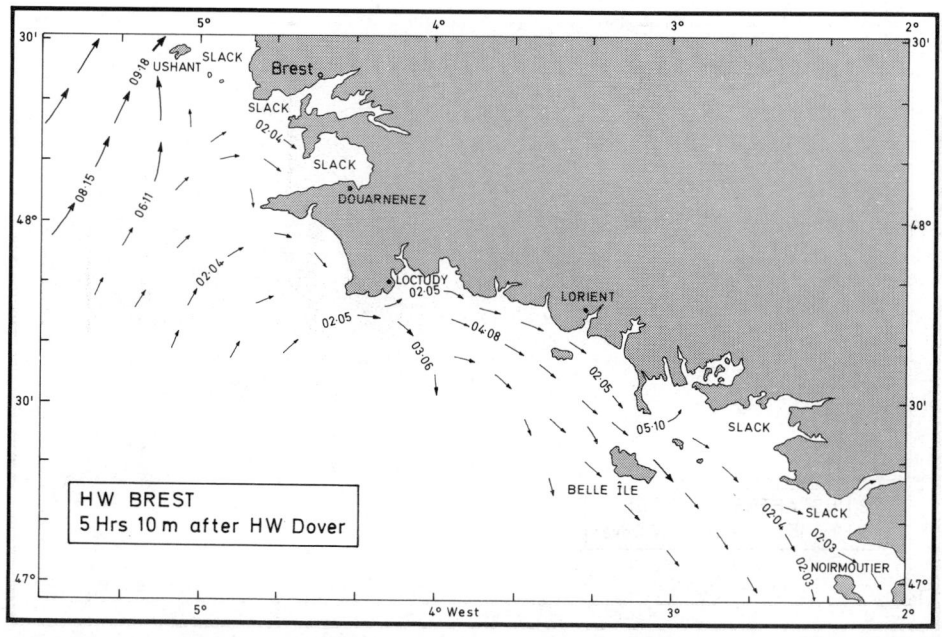

HW BREST
5 Hrs 10 m after HW Dover

ÎLE D'OUESSANT to ÎLE DE NOIRMOUTIER

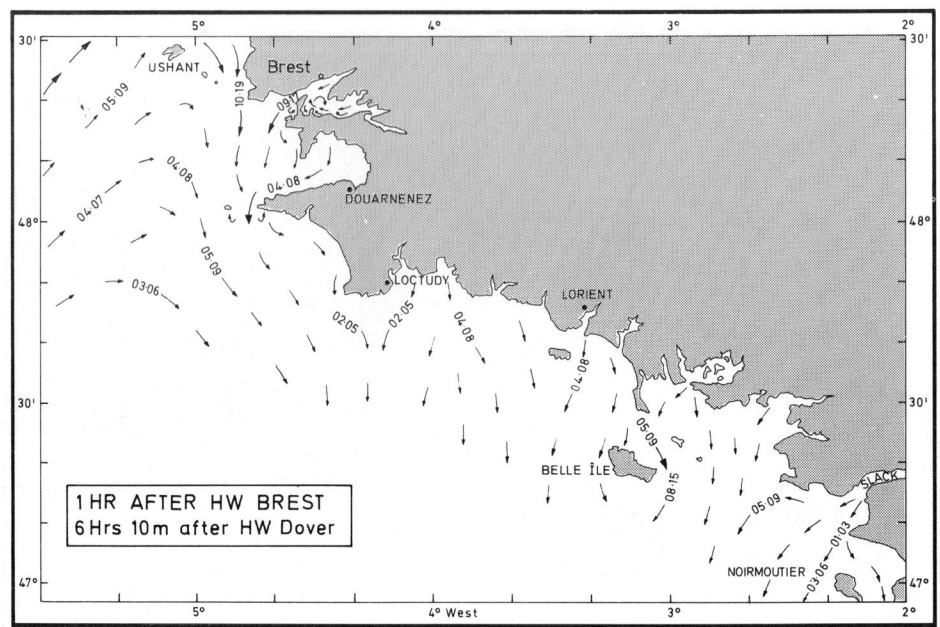

1 HR AFTER HW BREST
6 Hrs 10m after HW Dover

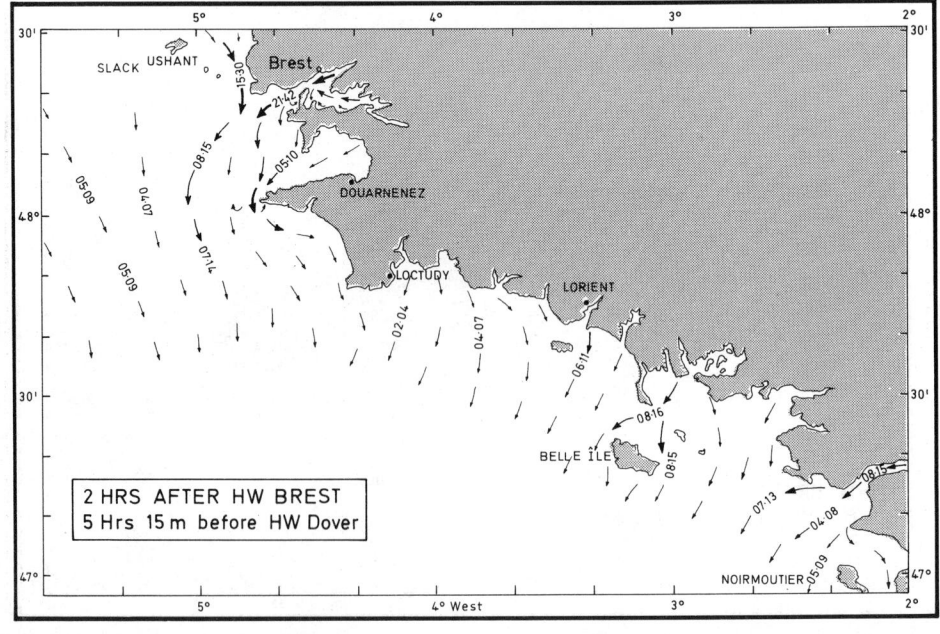

2 HRS AFTER HW BREST
5 Hrs 15m before HW Dover

ÎLE D'OUESSANT to ÎLE DE NOIRMOUTIER

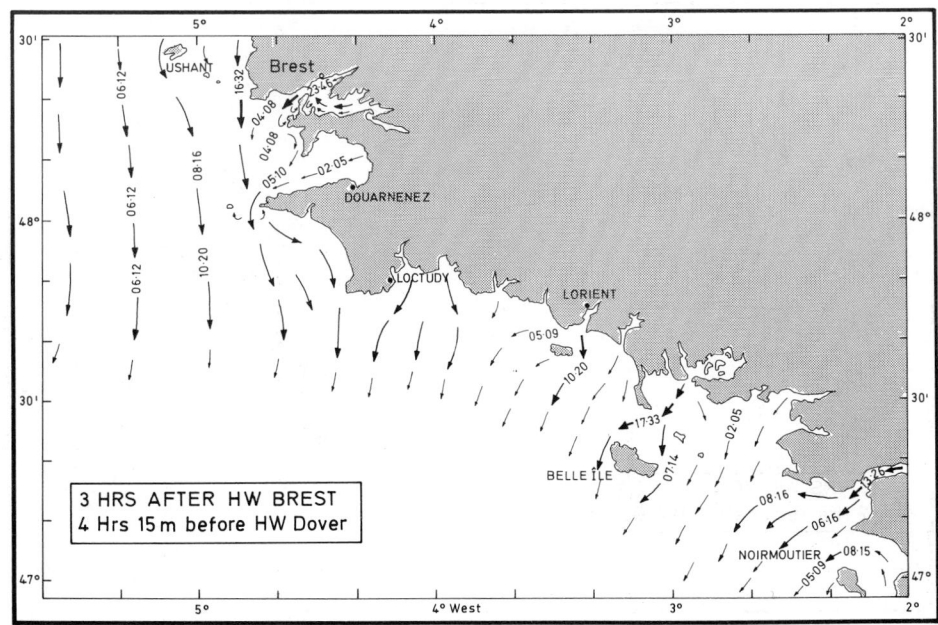

3 HRS AFTER HW BREST
4 Hrs 15m before HW Dover

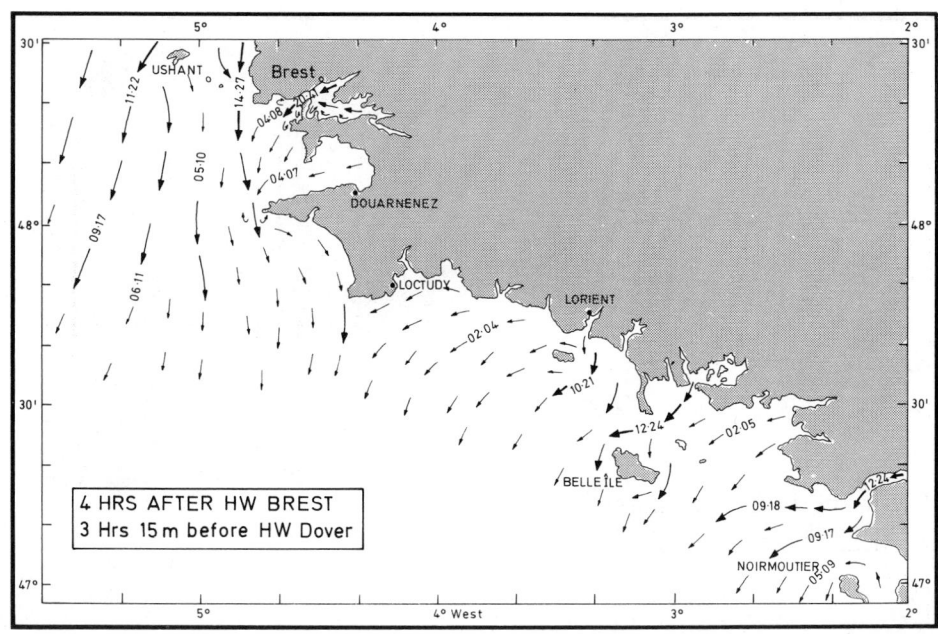

4 HRS AFTER HW BREST
3 Hrs 15m before HW Dover

ÎLE D'OUESSANT to ÎLE DE NOIRMOUTIER

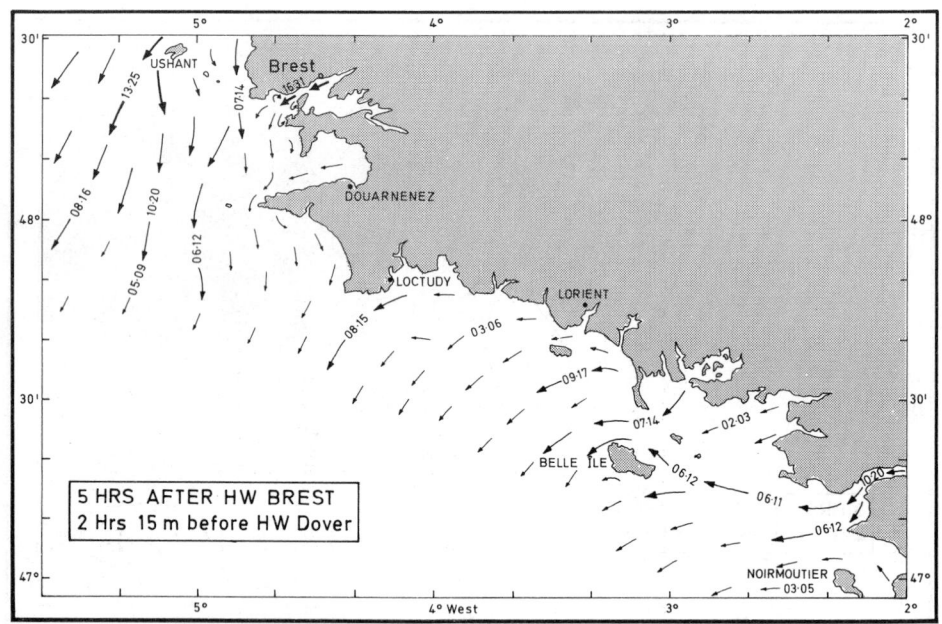

5 HRS AFTER HW BREST
2 Hrs 15 m before HW Dover

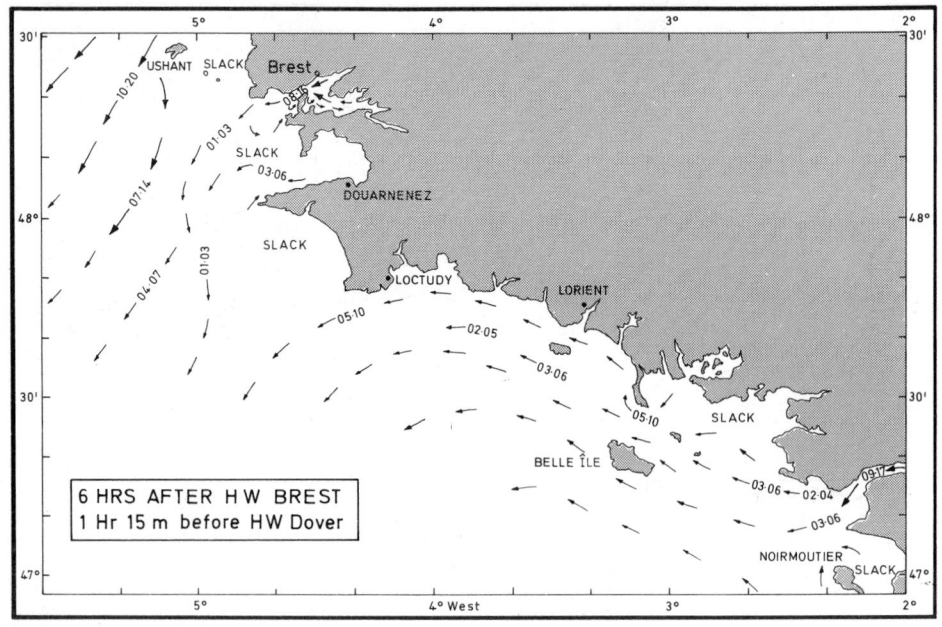

6 HRS AFTER HW BREST
1 Hr 15 m before HW Dover

BREST 21:277

Lat. 48°23′N. Long. 4°29′W. **HIGH & LOW WATER 1992**

TIME ZONE-0100 SUBTRACT 1 HOUR FROM TIMES SHOWN FOR GMT

JANUARY

Day	Time	m	Time	m	Time	m	Time	m
1 W	0212	6.1	0835	2.7	1442	6.1	2103	2.7
16 TH	0100	6.0	0728	2.8	1339	6.1	2004	2.7
2 TH	0309	6.3	0930	2.5	1534	6.3	2154	2.5
17 F	0214	6.3	0839	2.4	1447	6.4	2110	2.3
3 F	0357	6.6	1016	2.3	1619	6.5	2237	2.3
18 SA	0318	6.7	0940	2.0	1546	6.8	2208	1.8
4 SA	0439	6.8	1056	2.1	1657	6.6	● 2314	2.2
19 SU	0413	7.2	1034	1.5	1639	7.2	O 2259	1.4
5 SU	0515	6.9	1132	2.0	1733	6.7	2349	2.1
20 M	0504	7.6	1124	1.1	1728	7.5	2348	1.1
6 M	0550	7.0	1206	1.9	1806	6.8		
21 TU	0552	7.9	1211	0.8	1815	7.7		
7 TU	0023	2.0	0623	7.0	1239	1.9	1839	6.8
22 W	0034	1.0	0638	8.0	1257	0.8	1900	7.6
8 W	0055	2.0	0655	7.0	1311	1.9	1911	6.7
23 TH	0120	1.0	0722	7.9	1342	1.0	1943	7.4
9 TH	0128	2.1	0727	6.9	1345	2.0	1943	6.6
24 F	0203	1.3	0803	7.5	1425	1.4	2025	7.1
10 F	0202	2.2	0800	6.7	1419	2.2	2017	6.4
25 SA	0247	1.7	0846	7.1	1510	1.9	2108	6.6
11 SA	0238	2.3	0835	6.5	1457	2.4	2055	6.3
26 SU	0333	2.2	0932	6.5	1558	2.4	2158	6.2
12 SU	0318	2.5	0915	6.3	1540	2.6	2139	6.1
27 M	0425	2.7	1026	6.0	1655	2.9	2300	5.8
13 M	0404	2.7	1004	6.1	1632	2.8	2234	5.9
28 TU	0529	3.0	1137	5.7	1808	3.2		
14 TU	0502	2.9	1107	5.9	1735	3.0	2343	5.9
29 W	0019	5.6	0650	3.2	1302	5.6	1932	3.2
15 W	0612	2.9	1221	5.9	1850	2.9		
30 TH	0145	5.7	0811	3.1	1422	5.7	2046	3.0
31 F	0254	6.0	0916	2.8	1522	5.9	2142	2.7

FEBRUARY

Day	Time	m	Time	m	Time	m	Time	m
1 SA	0346	6.3	1004	2.5	1607	6.2	2225	2.4
16 SU	0307	6.6	0930	1.9	1536	6.7	2157	1.7
2 SU	0426	6.6	1043	2.1	1644	6.5	2301	2.1
17 M	0403	7.2	1023	1.3	1627	7.2	2247	1.2
3 M	0501	6.8	1117	1.9	1717	6.7	2333	1.9
18 TU	0451	7.7	1110	0.9	1713	7.6	O 2332	0.8
4 TU	0533	7.0	1149	1.7	1748	6.9		
19 W	0535	8.0	1154	0.6	1756	7.8		
5 W	0004	1.8	0603	7.2	1219	1.6	1818	7.0
20 TH	0015	0.7	0617	8.1	1235	0.6	1838	7.8
6 TH	0034	1.7	0633	7.2	1248	1.6	1848	7.0
21 F	0056	0.8	0658	7.9	1315	0.8	1916	7.6
7 F	0103	1.7	0703	7.2	1318	1.6	1917	6.9
22 SA	0135	1.1	0735	7.6	1355	1.3	1955	7.2
8 SA	0134	1.8	0731	7.0	1349	1.8	1947	6.8
23 SU	0215	1.6	0814	7.0	1435	1.8	2033	6.7
9 SU	0206	1.9	0803	6.8	1423	2.0	2021	6.6
24 M	0256	2.1	0854	6.4	1518	2.4	2116	6.1
10 M	0241	2.2	0839	6.5	1501	2.3	2058	6.3
25 TU	0342	2.7	0942	5.9	1610	3.0	2211	5.7
11 TU	0323	2.5	0921	6.2	1548	2.7	2148	6.0
26 W	0442	3.1	1048	5.4	1721	3.3	2332	5.4
12 W	0416	2.8	1018	5.8	1650	3.0	2256	5.8
27 TH	0607	3.3	1222	5.3	1856	3.4		
13 TH	0529	3.0	1140	5.7	1813	3.1		
28 F	0112	5.5	0742	3.2	1356	5.4	2022	3.2
14 F	0027	5.8	0700	2.9	1315	5.8	1944	2.8
29 SA	0232	5.7	0854	2.9	1501	5.7	2121	2.8
15 SA	0157	6.1	0824	2.5	1435	6.2	2059	2.3

MARCH

Day	Time	m	Time	m	Time	m	Time	m
1 SU	0325	6.1	0943	2.5	1546	6.1	2203	2.4
16 M	0254	6.7	0915	1.8	1521	6.8	2141	1.6
2 M	0404	6.5	1021	2.1	1621	6.4	2237	2.1
17 TU	0346	7.2	1006	1.2	1609	7.3	2228	1.1
3 TU	0438	6.8	1053	1.8	1653	6.7	2308	1.8
18 W	0431	7.7	1050	0.8	1652	7.6	O 2310	0.8
4 W	0508	7.0	1123	1.6	1722	7.0	● 2338	1.6
19 TH	0513	7.9	1131	0.7	1733	7.8	2350	0.7
5 TH	0537	7.2	1152	1.4	1751	7.1		
20 F	0552	8.0	1210	0.7	1811	7.7		
6 F	0006	1.4	0605	7.3	1221	1.3	1820	7.2
21 SA	0029	0.9	0631	7.7	1248	1.0	1850	7.5
7 SA	0035	1.4	0635	7.3	1250	1.4	1850	7.1
22 SU	0107	1.2	0707	7.4	1326	1.4	1926	7.1
8 SU	0106	1.5	0704	7.2	1321	1.5	1921	7.0
23 M	0145	1.6	0745	6.9	1405	1.9	2003	6.6
9 M	0138	1.7	0736	6.9	1355	1.8	1954	6.7
24 TU	0225	2.2	0824	6.3	1446	2.5	2045	6.1
10 TU	0214	2.0	0813	6.6	1434	2.2	2033	6.4
25 W	0309	2.7	0908	5.8	1535	3.0	2136	5.7
11 W	0257	2.4	0856	6.2	1522	2.6	2123	6.0
26 TH	0405	3.1	1009	5.4	1641	3.3	2249	5.4
12 TH	0352	2.7	0955	5.8	1627	3.0	2235	5.7
27 F	0524	3.3	1138	5.2	1812	3.4		
13 F	0510	3.0	1121	5.6	1758	3.1		
28 SA	0028	5.4	0659	3.3	1314	5.3	1940	3.2
14 SA	0014	5.8	0647	2.9	1302	5.7	1933	2.8
29 SU	0151	5.6	0815	2.9	1422	5.6	2043	2.8
15 SU	0146	6.1	0812	2.4	1422	6.2	2046	2.2
30 M	0247	6.0	0906	2.6	1509	6.0	2127	2.5
31 TU	0328	6.4	0945	2.2	1546	6.4	2203	2.1

APRIL

Day	Time	m	Time	m	Time	m	Time	m
1 W	0403	6.7	1019	1.9	1619	6.7	2235	1.8
16 TH	0407	7.5	1025	1.1	1628	7.4	2246	1.1
2 TH	0434	7.0	1050	1.6	1650	7.0	2305	1.5
17 F	0448	7.6	1106	1.0	1708	7.5	O 2326	1.1
3 F	0505	7.2	1120	1.4	1720	7.2	● 2336	1.4
18 SA	0528	7.6	1145	1.1	1747	7.5		
4 SA	0536	7.3	1151	1.3	1751	7.3		
19 SU	0005	1.2	0606	7.4	1224	1.4	1825	7.3
5 SU	0007	1.3	0607	7.3	1224	1.4	1824	7.3
20 M	0043	1.5	0644	7.1	1302	1.7	1904	7.0
6 M	0041	1.4	0641	7.2	1258	1.5	1859	7.1
21 TU	0121	1.8	0722	6.7	1341	2.1	1941	6.6
7 TU	0117	1.6	0717	6.9	1336	1.8	1936	6.8
22 W	0201	2.2	0800	6.3	1422	2.5	2022	6.2
8 W	0157	1.9	0758	6.6	1420	2.2	2021	6.5
23 TH	0245	2.6	0845	5.8	1510	2.9	2110	5.9
9 TH	0245	2.3	0846	6.2	1513	2.6	2116	6.1
24 F	0337	2.9	0939	5.5	1609	3.2	2212	5.6
10 F	0346	2.6	0951	5.8	1624	2.8	2232	5.9
25 SA	0444	3.2	1051	5.3	1723	3.3	2333	5.5
11 SA	0506	2.8	1117	5.7	1751	2.9		
26 SU	0603	3.2	1214	5.4	1841	3.2		
12 SU	0005	6.0	0636	2.6	1248	5.9	1917	2.5
27 M	0051	5.6	0716	3.0	1324	5.6	1947	2.9
13 M	0128	6.3	0753	2.2	1402	6.3	2024	2.1
28 TU	0153	5.9	0813	2.7	1418	6.0	2037	2.6
14 TU	0231	6.7	0852	1.8	1458	6.8	2118	1.6
29 W	0240	6.2	0858	2.3	1501	6.3	2118	2.2
15 W	0322	7.2	0942	1.4	1545	7.2	2204	1.3
30 TH	0320	6.5	0937	2.0	1538	6.6	2155	1.9

TIDAL DIFFERENCES PAGES 21:281-21:282. TIDAL CURVE PAGE 21:280.

TIDAL STREAMS PAGES 21:28-21:40 AND 21:270-21:276.

Datum of predictions: 1.4 m. below M.L.W.S. and 0.5 m. below L.A.T.

BREST

HIGH & LOW WATER 1992   Lat. 48°23'N. Long. 4°29'W.

TIME ZONE-0100 SUBTRACT 1 HOUR FROM TIMES SHOWN FOR GMT

MAY

Day	Time	m	Time	m	Time	m	Time	m
1 F	0356	6.8	1013	1.8	1614	6.9	2231	1.6
16 SA	0427	7.1	1045	1.6	1648	7.2	2306	1.5
2 SA	0431	7.1	1048	1.6	1649	7.2	2306	1.5
17 SU	0508	7.1	1126	1.6	1728	7.2	2346	1.6
3 SU	0507	7.2	1124	1.5	1725	7.3	2343	1.4
18 M	0548	7.0	1205	1.7	1807	7.1		
4 M	0544	7.2	1202	1.5	1804	7.3		
19 TU	0025	1.7	0626	6.8	1244	1.9	1846	6.9
5 TU	0022	1.4	0624	7.1	1242	1.6	1845	7.2
20 W	0103	1.9	0704	6.6	1323	2.2	1924	6.7
6 W	0104	1.6	0706	6.9	1326	1.8	1929	7.0
21 TH	0143	2.2	0743	6.3	1403	2.4	2003	6.4
7 TH	0150	1.8	0752	6.6	1416	2.1	2018	6.7
22 F	0224	2.4	0824	6.0	1447	2.7	2046	6.1
8 F	0243	2.1	0846	6.3	1513	2.4	2116	6.4
23 SA	0311	2.5	0910	5.8	1536	2.9	2136	5.9
9 SA	0346	2.4	0950	6.1	1621	2.6	2226	6.2
24 SU	0404	2.9	1005	5.6	1633	3.0	2236	5.8
10 SU	0459	2.5	1107	6.0	1737	2.6	2346	6.2
25 M	0504	3.0	1109	5.6	1736	3.0	2343	5.7
11 M	0615	2.4	1224	6.1	1850	2.4		
26 TU	0609	2.9	1216	5.7	1840	2.9		
12 TU	0059	6.4	0724	2.2	1332	6.4	1955	2.1
27 W	0047	5.9	0710	2.8	1317	5.9	1938	2.7
13 W	0202	6.7	0824	2.0	1429	6.7	2050	1.9
28 TH	0144	6.1	0804	2.6	1409	6.2	2029	2.4
14 TH	0255	6.9	0915	1.7	1520	6.9	2139	1.7
29 F	0233	6.3	0852	2.3	1456	6.5	2115	2.1
15 F	0343	7.0	1002	1.6	1605	7.1	2224	1.5
30 SA	0318	6.6	0937	2.0	1540	6.8	2158	1.9
31 SU	0401	6.8	1020	1.8	1622	7.0	2241	1.6

JUNE

Day	Time	m	Time	m	Time	m	Time	m
1 M	0444	7.0	1103	1.6	1705	7.2	2324	1.5
16 TU	0534	6.7	1152	2.0	1753	7.0		
2 TU	0527	7.1	1147	1.5	1750	7.3		
17 W	0011	1.8	0612	6.7	1229	2.0	1830	6.9
3 W	0009	1.4	0613	7.1	1232	1.5	1836	7.3
18 TH	0048	1.9	0649	6.6	1306	2.1	1906	6.8
4 TH	0056	1.4	0700	7.0	1321	1.6	1924	7.2
19 F	0124	2.0	0724	6.5	1343	2.2	1942	6.6
5 F	0146	1.6	0749	6.9	1412	1.8	2014	7.0
20 SA	0201	2.2	0800	6.3	1420	2.4	2019	6.4
6 SA	0239	1.8	0841	6.6	1507	2.0	2108	6.8
21 SU	0240	2.4	0838	6.1	1501	2.6	2059	6.2
7 SU	0336	2.0	0938	6.4	1607	2.2	2209	6.6
22 M	0323	2.6	0921	6.0	1546	2.7	2145	6.0
8 M	0438	2.2	1042	6.3	1710	2.4	2316	6.4
23 TU	0410	2.7	1010	5.8	1637	2.8	2238	5.9
9 TU	0544	2.3	1150	6.2	1817	2.4		
24 W	0505	2.8	1108	5.8	1734	2.9	2340	5.8
10 W	0025	6.3	0650	2.4	1257	6.2	1922	2.4
25 TH	0606	2.9	1212	5.8	1837	2.8		
11 TH	0130	6.4	0754	2.3	1401	6.4	2023	2.3
26 F	0044	5.9	0709	2.8	1317	6.0	1940	2.7
12 F	0230	6.5	0852	2.2	1457	6.5	2118	2.1
27 SA	0147	6.1	0810	2.6	1417	6.3	2039	2.4
13 SA	0323	6.6	0943	2.1	1548	6.7	2207	2.0
28 SU	0245	6.3	0906	2.3	1512	6.6	2132	2.1
14 SU	0411	6.7	1030	2.0	1633	6.9	2251	1.9
29 M	0337	6.5	0958	2.0	1603	7.0	2223	1.7
15 M	0454	6.7	1112	2.0	1714	6.9	2332	1.8
30 TU	0427	6.7	1047	1.7	1651	7.3	2311	1.4

JULY

Day	Time	m	Time	m	Time	m	Time	m
1 W	0515	7.2	1135	1.4	1739	7.5	2359	1.2
16 TH	0555	6.7	1212	1.9	1812	7.0		
2 TH	0603	7.3	1223	1.3	1827	7.6		
17 F	0028	1.8	0629	6.7	1245	1.9	1845	7.0
3 F	0047	1.1	0651	7.3	1311	1.3	1914	7.6
18 SA	0101	1.8	0701	6.7	1317	2.0	1917	6.9
4 SA	0136	1.2	0738	7.2	1400	1.4	2001	7.4
19 SU	0134	1.9	0732	6.6	1350	2.1	1949	6.7
5 SU	0224	1.4	0826	7.0	1449	1.6	2050	7.1
20 M	0207	2.0	0805	6.5	1425	2.2	2023	6.5
6 M	0315	1.7	0915	6.7	1541	2.0	2141	6.7
21 TU	0243	2.3	0840	6.3	1502	2.4	2059	6.3
7 TU	0408	2.1	1009	6.4	1637	2.3	2240	6.4
22 W	0323	2.5	0921	6.1	1545	2.7	2144	6.0
8 W	0507	2.4	1112	6.1	1740	2.6	2347	6.1
23 TH	0410	2.7	1010	5.9	1638	2.8	2241	5.8
9 TH	0614	2.7	1223	6.0	1850	2.7		
24 F	0509	2.9	1114	5.8	1743	3.0	2351	5.8
10 F	0059	6.0	0726	2.8	1336	6.0	2001	2.7
25 SA	0620	2.9	1230	5.8	1858	2.9		
11 SA	0210	6.0	0833	2.7	1441	6.2	2103	2.5
26 SU	0110	5.9	0736	2.8	1346	6.1	2012	2.6
12 SU	0310	6.2	0931	2.5	1536	6.4	2156	2.3
27 M	0221	6.1	0844	2.5	1452	6.5	2115	2.1
13 M	0400	6.4	1019	2.3	1622	6.7	2240	2.1
28 TU	0321	6.6	0943	2.0	1549	7.0	2210	1.6
14 TU	0443	6.5	1100	1.9	1702	6.8	2319	1.9
29 W	0414	7.0	1035	1.5	1639	7.4	2259	1.2
15 W	0520	6.9	1137	1.5	1738	6.9	2355	1.8
30 TH	0503	7.4	1123	1.2	1727	7.8	2346	0.9
31 F	0550	7.6	1209	0.9	1813	7.9		

AUGUST

Day	Time	m	Time	m	Time	m	Time	m
1 SA	0032	0.7	0635	7.7	1254	0.9	1857	7.9
16 SU	0034	1.6	0633	7.0	1248	1.7	1848	7.1
2 SU	0117	0.8	0719	7.5	1339	1.1	1940	7.7
17 M	0103	1.7	0703	6.9	1318	1.8	1917	7.0
3 M	0201	1.1	0801	7.2	1423	1.5	2023	7.3
18 TU	0134	1.8	0732	6.7	1350	2.0	1948	6.7
4 TU	0246	1.6	0845	6.8	1509	1.9	2108	6.7
19 W	0206	2.1	0804	6.5	1424	2.2	2022	6.5
5 W	0334	2.1	0934	6.4	1601	2.4	2202	6.2
20 TH	0243	2.4	0841	6.3	1504	2.5	2102	6.1
6 TH	0430	2.7	1033	6.0	1703	2.8	2309	5.8
21 F	0328	2.7	0927	6.0	1555	2.8	2156	5.8
7 F	0539	3.0	1149	5.7	1820	3.0		
22 SA	0426	3.0	1031	5.8	1703	3.0	2312	5.6
8 SA	0032	5.6	0652	3.1	1315	5.8	1942	3.0
23 SU	0545	3.1	1157	5.7	1830	3.0		
9 SU	0154	5.7	0819	3.0	1429	6.0	2052	2.7
24 M	0044	5.7	0714	2.9	1327	6.0	1954	2.6
10 M	0258	5.9	0919	2.7	1524	6.3	2144	2.4
25 TU	0205	6.1	0830	2.5	1438	6.5	2101	2.1
11 TU	0347	6.2	1006	2.4	1608	6.6	2226	2.1
26 W	0308	6.6	0929	1.9	1535	7.1	2155	1.5
12 W	0427	6.5	1044	2.1	1645	6.8	2301	1.9
27 TH	0400	7.2	1020	1.3	1623	7.6	2243	1.0
13 TH	0502	6.7	1118	1.8	1718	7.0	2334	1.7
28 F	0446	7.6	1105	0.9	1708	8.0	2327	0.6
14 F	0533	6.9	1149	1.8	1748	7.1		
29 SA	0533	7.9	1149	0.7	1751	8.1		
15 SA	0004	1.6	0603	6.9	1219	1.7	1818	7.1
30 SU	0010	0.6	0612	7.9	1231	0.7	1833	8.0
31 M	0052	0.8	0654	7.7	1312	1.0	1914	7.7

RATE AND SET — Between Le Trepied By. and middle of W. ent. to Goulet de Brest. ENE., –0030, Dover, Sp. 3 kn.; WSW. +0545, Dover, Sp. 3 kn. Ent. to Anse de Berthaume; E., –0145, Dover, Sp. 2 kn.; W., +0430, Dover, Sp. 2 kn. Anch. in Grande Rade: E., –0045, Dover, Sp. 2½ kn., W., +0530, Dover, Sp. 2½ kn. Raz Sein (Chan.), NE., –0130, Dover, Sp. 7 kn. max.; SW., +0445, Dover, Sp. 6 kn. max.

BREST

Lat. 48°23′N. Long. 4°29′W.

HIGH & LOW WATER 1992

TIME ZONE-0100 SUBTRACT 1 HOUR FROM TIMES SHOWN FOR GMT.

SEPTEMBER

	Time	m		Time	m
1 TU	0133 / 0733 / 1354 / 1954	1.2 / 7.3 / 1.5 / 7.2	**16** W	0103 / 0703 / 1319 / 1918	1.7 / 7.0 / 1.8 / 6.9
2 W	0215 / 0815 / 1437 / 2037	1.7 / 6.8 / 2.0 / 6.6	**17** TH	0136 / 0735 / 1354 / 1954	2.0 / 6.7 / 2.1 / 6.6
3 TH	0301 / 0900 / 1526 / 2127	2.3 / 6.3 / 2.6 / 6.0	**18** F	0214 / 0813 / 1435 / 2035	2.3 / 6.4 / 2.5 / 6.2
4 F	0355 / 0957 / 1627 / 2233	2.9 / 5.9 / 3.0 / 5.6	**19** SA	0300 / 0900 / 1528 / 2131	2.7 / 6.1 / 2.8 / 5.8
5 SA	0506 / 1116 / 1750	3.3 / 5.6 / 3.3	**20** SU	0402 / 1007 / 1641 / 2251	3.0 / 5.8 / 3.0 / 5.6
6 SU	0004 / 0637 / 1251 / 1921	5.4 / 3.3 / 5.6 / 3.2	**21** M	0527 / 1140 / 1814	3.1 / 5.8 / 3.0
7 M	0135 / 0800 / 1410 / 2033	5.5 / 3.1 / 5.9 / 2.9	**22** TU	0029 / 0659 / 1313 / 1939	5.8 / 2.9 / 6.1 / 2.5
8 TU	0240 / 0900 / 1505 / 2123	5.9 / 2.8 / 6.2 / 2.5	**23** W	0150 / 0814 / 1422 / 2044	6.2 / 2.4 / 6.7 / 2.0
9 W	0326 / 0944 / 1546 / 2202	6.2 / 2.4 / 6.5 / 2.2	**24** TH	0250 / 0911 / 1516 / 2136	6.8 / 1.8 / 7.2 / 1.4
10 TH	0403 / 1019 / 1620 / 2236	6.5 / 2.1 / 6.8 / 1.9	**25** F	0340 / 0959 / 1602 / 2221	7.3 / 1.2 / 7.7 / 0.9
11 F	0435 / 1051 / 1651 / 2306	6.8 / 1.8 / 7.1 / 1.7	**26** SA	0424 / 1043 / 1646 / 2304	7.7 / 0.9 / 8.0 / 0.7
12 SA	0505 / 1120 / 1720 / 2335	7.0 / 1.7 / 7.2 / 1.5	**27** SU	0506 / 1125 / 1727 / 2345	7.9 / 0.7 / 8.1 / 0.7
13 SU	0534 / 1149 / 1748	7.1 / 1.6 / 7.3	**28** M	0547 / 1205 / 1808	7.9 / 0.9 / 7.9
14 M	0003 / 0603 / 1218 / 1817	1.5 / 7.2 / 1.6 / 7.1	**29** TU	0026 / 0628 / 1246 / 1848	1.0 / 7.7 / 1.2 / 7.6
15 TU	0033 / 0632 / 1248 / 1847	1.6 / 7.1 / 1.7 / 7.1	**30** W	0106 / 0707 / 1327 / 1928	1.4 / 7.3 / 1.6 / 7.1

OCTOBER

	Time	m		Time	m
1 TH	0147 / 0748 / 1409 / 2009	1.9 / 6.8 / 2.1 / 6.5	**16** F	0115 / 0716 / 1335 / 1935	2.0 / 6.9 / 2.1 / 6.6
2 F	0232 / 0832 / 1456 / 2057	2.5 / 6.3 / 2.7 / 6.0	**17** SA	0157 / 0758 / 1420 / 2022	2.3 / 6.6 / 2.4 / 6.3
3 SA	0324 / 0926 / 1556 / 2200	3.0 / 5.9 / 3.1 / 5.5	**18** SU	0247 / 0849 / 1517 / 2120	2.7 / 6.3 / 2.7 / 6.0
4 SU	0432 / 1040 / 1715 / 2327	3.3 / 5.6 / 3.3 / 5.4	**19** M	0352 / 0958 / 1632 / 2241	2.9 / 6.0 / 2.9 / 5.8
5 M	0601 / 1215 / 1845	3.4 / 5.6 / 3.2	**20** TU	0515 / 1126 / 1759	3.0 / 6.0 / 2.8
6 TU	0058 / 0725 / 1335 / 1958	5.5 / 3.2 / 5.8 / 3.0	**21** W	0011 / 0640 / 1251 / 1918	6.0 / 2.7 / 6.3 / 2.4
7 W	0205 / 0825 / 1430 / 2049	5.8 / 2.9 / 6.1 / 2.6	**22** TH	0127 / 0751 / 1358 / 2020	6.4 / 2.3 / 6.6 / 1.9
8 TH	0252 / 0910 / 1512 / 2129	6.2 / 2.5 / 6.5 / 2.3	**23** F	0226 / 0847 / 1452 / 2112	6.9 / 1.8 / 7.2 / 1.5
9 F	0330 / 0946 / 1546 / 2202	6.5 / 2.2 / 6.8 / 2.0	**24** SA	0316 / 0935 / 1558 / 2158	7.3 / 1.4 / 7.6 / 1.2
10 SA	0402 / 1018 / 1618 / 2233	6.9 / 1.9 / 7.0 / 1.8	**25** SU	0401 / 1020 / 1622 / 2241	7.6 / 1.1 / 7.8 / 1.1
11 SU	0433 / 1049 / 1648 / 2304	7.1 / 1.7 / 7.1 / 1.6	**26** M	0444 / 1102 / 1702 / 2323	7.8 / 1.1 / 7.8 / 1.1
12 M	0503 / 1119 / 1718 / 2334	7.2 / 1.6 / 7.3 / 1.5	**27** TU	0525 / 1143 / 1745	7.7 / 1.2 / 7.6
13 TU	0534 / 1150 / 1749	7.3 / 1.5 / 7.3	**28** W	0004 / 0606 / 1224 / 1826	1.3 / 7.6 / 1.4 / 7.3
14 W	0005 / 0605 / 1222 / 1822	1.6 / 7.3 / 1.6 / 7.2	**29** TH	0044 / 0646 / 1305 / 1906	1.7 / 7.2 / 1.8 / 6.9
15 TH	0039 / 0639 / 1256 / 1857	1.7 / 7.1 / 1.8 / 6.9	**30** F	0125 / 0727 / 1347 / 1947	2.1 / 6.9 / 2.2 / 6.5
			31 SA	0209 / 0809 / 1432 / 2032	2.5 / 6.4 / 2.6 / 6.0

NOVEMBER

	Time	m		Time	m
1 SU	0258 / 0858 / 1525 / 2127	2.9 / 6.1 / 3.0 / 5.7	**16** M	0242 / 0845 / 1512 / 2115	2.4 / 6.6 / 2.4 / 6.2
2 M	0357 / 1000 / 1632 / 2238	3.2 / 5.8 / 3.2 / 5.5	**17** TU	0345 / 0949 / 1620 / 2225	2.6 / 6.1 / 2.6 / 6.1
3 TU	0509 / 1118 / 1749 / 2358	3.3 / 5.7 / 3.2 / 5.5	**18** W	0457 / 1105 / 1734 / 2343	2.7 / 6.3 / 2.6 / 6.2
4 W	0626 / 1236 / 1901	3.3 / 5.8 / 3.1	**19** TH	0612 / 1221 / 1847	2.6 / 6.5 / 2.4
5 TH	0109 / 0732 / 1338 / 1959	5.8 / 3.0 / 6.0 / 2.8	**20** F	0055 / 0720 / 1328 / 1951	6.4 / 2.3 / 6.7 / 2.2
6 F	0203 / 0823 / 1426 / 2044	6.1 / 2.7 / 6.3 / 2.5	**21** SA	0158 / 0820 / 1426 / 2047	6.7 / 2.1 / 6.9 / 1.9
7 SA	0247 / 0905 / 1506 / 2123	6.4 / 2.4 / 6.6 / 2.2	**22** SU	0252 / 0912 / 1517 / 2137	7.0 / 1.8 / 7.2 / 1.7
8 SU	0325 / 0941 / 1542 / 2159	6.6 / 2.1 / 6.9 / 2.0	**23** M	0341 / 1000 / 1604 / 2223	7.3 / 1.6 / 7.3 / 1.6
9 M	0400 / 1016 / 1617 / 2234	7.0 / 1.9 / 7.1 / 1.8	**24** TU	0426 / 1045 / 1648 / 2307	7.4 / 1.5 / 7.3 / 1.6
10 TU	0434 / 1051 / 1652 / 2308	7.2 / 1.7 / 7.2 / 1.7	**25** W	0509 / 1128 / 1730 / 2348	7.4 / 1.5 / 7.3 / 1.7
11 W	0509 / 1126 / 1727 / 2344	7.3 / 1.6 / 7.2 / 1.7	**26** TH	0550 / 1209 / 1811	7.4 / 1.6 / 7.1
12 TH	0546 / 1203 / 1805	7.3 / 1.6 / 7.2	**27** F	0029 / 0631 / 1249 / 1851	1.9 / 7.2 / 1.8 / 6.8
13 F	0022 / 0624 / 1243 / 1845	1.8 / 7.2 / 1.7 / 7.0	**28** SA	0109 / 0710 / 1329 / 1930	2.1 / 7.0 / 2.1 / 6.6
14 SA	0104 / 0705 / 1326 / 1928	1.9 / 7.1 / 1.9 / 6.8	**29** SU	0149 / 0749 / 1410 / 2010	2.4 / 6.7 / 2.4 / 6.3
15 SU	0150 / 0752 / 1415 / 2017	2.2 / 6.8 / 2.2 / 6.5	**30** M	0232 / 0831 / 1455 / 2054	2.7 / 6.4 / 2.7 / 6.0

DECEMBER

	Time	m		Time	m
1 TU	0319 / 0919 / 1545 / 2146	2.9 / 6.1 / 2.9 / 5.8	**16** W	0329 / 0931 / 1559 / 2201	2.2 / 6.8 / 2.2 / 6.4
2 W	0413 / 1015 / 1643 / 2247	3.1 / 5.9 / 3.1 / 5.7	**17** TH	0430 / 1034 / 1702 / 2308	2.4 / 6.5 / 2.4 / 6.3
3 TH	0515 / 1120 / 1748 / 2354	3.2 / 5.8 / 3.1 / 5.7	**18** F	0536 / 1143 / 1811	2.5 / 6.4 / 2.5
4 F	0621 / 1228 / 1852	3.1 / 5.9 / 3.0	**19** SA	0019 / 0646 / 1254 / 1920	6.3 / 2.6 / 6.4 / 2.5
5 SA	0058 / 0722 / 1328 / 1950	5.9 / 3.0 / 6.0 / 2.8	**20** SU	0129 / 0753 / 1402 / 2025	6.4 / 2.4 / 6.5 / 2.4
6 SU	0155 / 0816 / 1420 / 2040	6.1 / 2.7 / 6.3 / 2.6	**21** M	0232 / 0854 / 1501 / 2122	6.6 / 2.3 / 6.6 / 2.2
7 M	0244 / 0903 / 1506 / 2125	6.4 / 2.4 / 6.5 / 2.3	**22** TU	0328 / 0948 / 1553 / 2212	6.8 / 2.1 / 6.8 / 2.1
8 TU	0328 / 0946 / 1549 / 2207	6.7 / 2.1 / 6.8 / 2.1	**23** W	0416 / 1035 / 1638 / 2257	7.0 / 1.9 / 6.9 / 1.9
9 W	0409 / 1028 / 1630 / 2248	7.0 / 1.9 / 7.0 / 1.8	**24** TH	0500 / 1118 / 1720 / 2338	7.2 / 1.8 / 7.0 / 1.9
10 TH	0450 / 1109 / 1711 / 2330	7.3 / 1.6 / 7.2 / 1.7	**25** F	0540 / 1157 / 1759	7.2 / 1.7 / 7.0
11 F	0532 / 1151 / 1753	7.4 / 1.5 / 7.2	**26** SA	0016 / 0617 / 1234 / 1836	1.9 / 7.2 / 1.8 / 6.9
12 SA	0012 / 0615 / 1234 / 1837	1.6 / 7.5 / 1.5 / 7.2	**27** SU	0053 / 0654 / 1311 / 1910	2.0 / 7.1 / 1.9 / 6.7
13 SU	0057 / 0700 / 1320 / 1923	1.6 / 7.4 / 1.5 / 7.1	**28** M	0128 / 0728 / 1346 / 1945	2.1 / 6.9 / 2.1 / 6.6
14 M	0144 / 0746 / 1409 / 2010	1.8 / 7.2 / 1.7 / 6.9	**29** TU	0204 / 0802 / 1423 / 2021	2.3 / 6.7 / 2.3 / 6.3
15 TU	0235 / 0836 / 1501 / 2102	2.0 / 7.0 / 1.9 / 6.6	**30** W	0242 / 0840 / 1502 / 2059	2.5 / 6.4 / 2.5 / 6.1
			31 TH	0323 / 0921 / 1545 / 2144	2.7 / 6.2 / 2.7 / 5.9

Le Four Channel: NNW., −0045, Dover, Sp. 6 kn. max.; SSW., +0600, Dover, (+0530 at S. end), Sp. 6 kn. max.

TIDAL DIFFERENCES PAGES 21:281-21:282. TIDAL CURVE PAGE 21:280. ·

TIDAL STREAMS PAGES 21:28-21:40 AND 21:270-21:276.

Datum of predictions: 1.4 m. below M.L.W.S. and 0.5 m. below L.A.T.

BREST

MEAN SPRING AND NEAP CURVES
Springs occur 2 days after New and Full Moon.

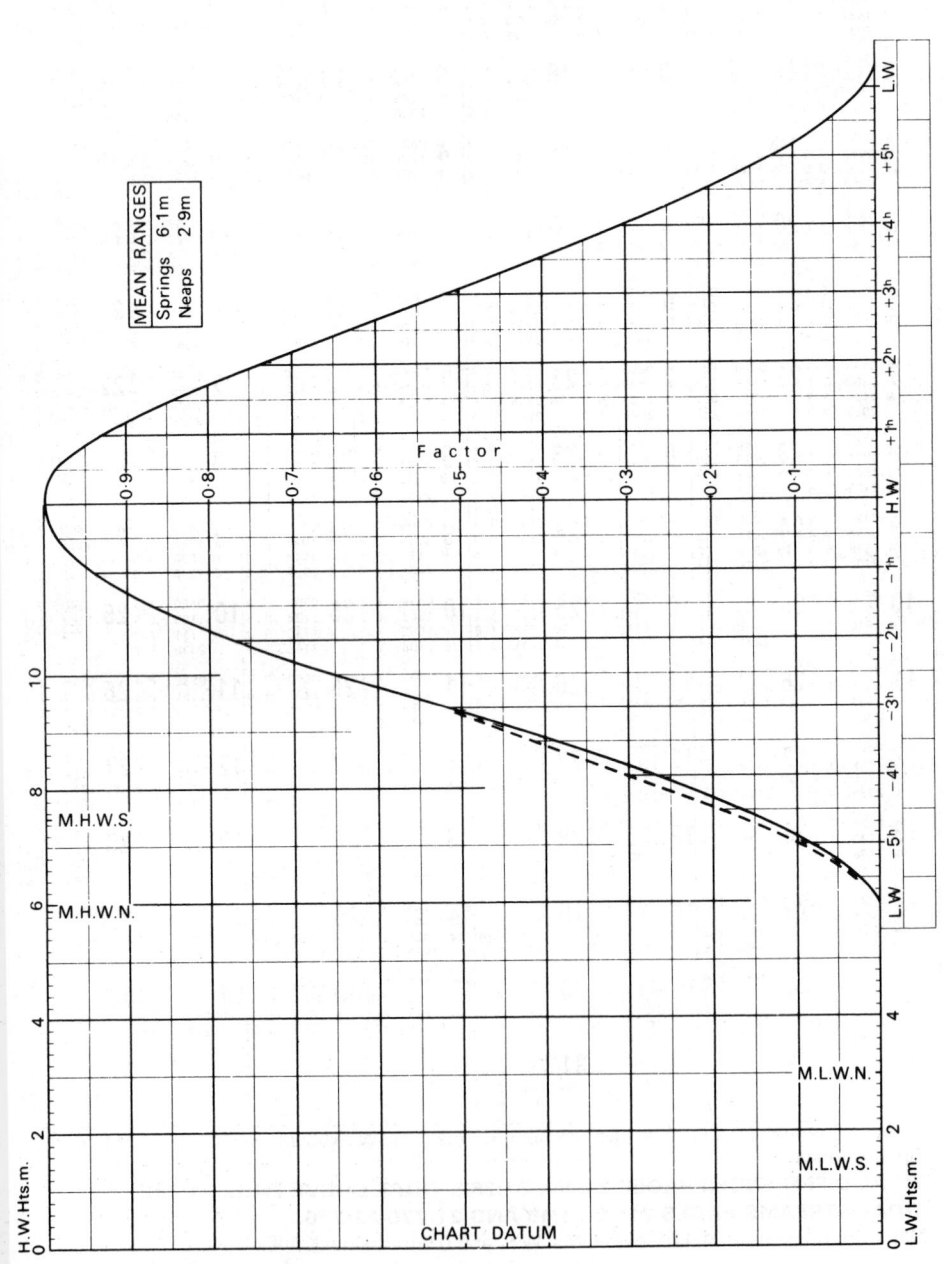

TIDAL DIFFERENCES ON BREST

PLACE	TIME DIFFERENCES				HEIGHT DIFFERENCES (Metres)			
	High Water		Low Water		MHWS	MHWN	MLWN	MLWS
BREST..................	0000 and 1200	0600 and 1800	0000 and 1200	0600 and 1800	7.5	5.9	3.0	1.4
Trebeurden	+0105	+0110	+0120	+0100	+1.6	+1.3	+0.5	−0.1
Anse de Primel..........	+0100	+0110	+0115	+0055	+1.7	+1.3	+0.6	0.0
Rade de Morlaix								
Morlaix								
(Chateau du Taureau)	+0100	+0115	+0115	+0050	+1.5	+1.1	+0.5	−0.1
Roscoff	+0055	+0105	+0115	+0050	+1.4	+1.1	+0.4	−0.1
Ile de Batz	+0045	+0100	+0105	+0050	+1.4	+1.1	+0.5	0.0
L'Aber Vrac'h								
Ile Cézon...................	+0020	+0030	+0035	+0020	+0.4	+0.2	−0.1	−0.3
L'Aber Benoit.............	+0020	+0020	+0035	+0035	+0.6	+0.5	0.0	−0.2
Portsall	+0020	+0020	+0020	+0010	+0.1	0.0	−0.2	−0.4
Ushant (Ouessant)								
Baie de Lampaul	0000	+0005	−0005	−0005	0.0	−0.1	0.0	+0.1
Molene	+0010	+0010	+0015	+0015	0.0	+0.1	−0.1	−0.2
Le Conquet	0000	0000	+0010	0000	−0.3	−0.3	−0.1	0.0
La Penfeld	−0005	−0005	0000	−0005	+0.1	0.0	+0.2	+0.2
Camaret	−0015	−0015	−0015	−0020	−0.5	−0.5	−0.2	−0.1
Morgat	−0010	−0010	−0015	−0015	−0.5	−0.5	−0.2	0.0
Dourarnenez	−0015	−0010	−0015	−0020	−0.5	−0.5	−0.2	0.0
Ile de Sein	−0010	−0010	−0010	−0015	−1.1	−0.9	−0.5	−0.3
Audierne..................	−0020	−0040	−0040	−0020	−2.3	−1.9	−0.9	−0.5
Guilvinec	−0010	−0035	−0035	−0020	−2.4	−1.9	−1.0	−0.5
Pont l'Abbe River								
Loctudy	−0010	−0030	−0030	−0025	−2.6	−2.1	−1.3	−0.9
Odet River								
Benodet	−0010	−0025	−0040	−0015	−2.6	−2.2	−1.3	−0.8
Corniguel	+0015	+0010	−0015	−0010	−2.6	−2.1	−1.4	−1.1
Concarneau	−0005	−0035	−0030	−0020	−2.5	−2.0	−1.0	−0.6
Iles de Glenan								
Ile de Penfret..............	−0010	−0025	−0030	−0020	−2.5	−2.0	−1.2	−0.6
Port Louis	−0010	−0025	−0020	−0020	−2.4	−1.9	−0.9	−0.5
Lorient.......................	+0005	−0025	−0025	−0015	−2.4	−1.9	−1.0	−0.5
Ile de Groix								
Port Tudy	−0005	−0035	−0030	−0025	−2.4	−1.9	−0.9	−0.5
Port-Haliguen	0000	−0020	−0025	−0015	−2.3	−1.9	−1.0	−0.8
Belle-Ile								
Le Palais....................	−0015	−0030	−0030	−0025	−2.3	−1.9	−1.0	−0.6
Crac'h River								
La Trinite....................	+0010	−0020	−0025	−0015	−2.1	−1.7	−0.9	−0.7
Morbihan								
Port-Navalo	+0025	−0005	−0010	−0005	−2.5	−2.0	−1.1	−0.7
Auray	+0025	−0005	+0025	−0005	−2.6	−2.0	−1.1	−0.6
Vannes	+0145	+0155	+0200	+0105	−4.1	−3.2	−2.0	−1.0
Ile de Hoedic	−0005	−0025	−0030	−0020	−2.3	−1.9	−1.1	−0.8
Pénerf	−0010	−0020	−0025	−0020	−2.0	−1.7	−1.0	−0.7
Le Croisic	+0030	−0030	−0015	0010	−2.3	−1.8	−1.1	−0.8

Differences continued on page 21: 282

Note: Time zone. The predictions for the standard port are on the same time zone as the diffferences shown. No further adjustment is necessary. **Refer to predictions on pages 21:277-21:279**

TIDAL DIFFERENCES ON BREST

PLACE	TIME DIFFERENCES				HEIGHT DIFFERENCES (Metres)			
	High Water		Low Water		MHWS	MHWN	MLWN	MLWS
BREST	0000 and 1200	0600 and 1800	0000 and 1200	0600 and 1800	7.5	5.9	3.0	1.4
La Loire								
Le Pouliguen	+0015	−0040	0000	−0020	−2.2	−1.8	−1.2	−0.9
Le Grand-Charpentier	+0010	−0030	−0020	−0020	−2.2	−2.0	−1.3	−0.9
St. Nazaire	+0030	−0025	−0025	−0010	−2.0	−1.7	−1.1	−0.8
Paimboeuf	+0015	−0005	+0120	+0030	−1.9	−1.6	−1.3	−0.5
Le Pellerin	+0140	+0100	+0300	+0210	−1.7	−1.4	−1.2	+0.1
Nantes(Chantenay)	+0155	+0140	+0330	+0245	−1.7	−1.3	−1.1	+0.1
BREST	0500 and 1700	1100 and 2300	0500 and 1700	1100 and 2300	7.5	5.9	3.0	1.4
Pornic	−0035	−0015	+0005	+0005	−2.1	−1.9	−1.4	−1.1
Ile de Noirmoutier								
Bois de la Chaise	−0030	−0020	0000	−0005	−2.1	−1.9	−1.4	−1.0
Fromentine	−0025	−0020	−0005	+0015	−2.2	−1.9	−1.3	−0.9
Ile d'Yeu								
Port Joinville	−0035	−0010	−0035	−0035	−2.2	−1.8	−0.9	−0.6
St. Gilles-sur-Vie	−0030	−0015	−0030	−0035	−2.2	−1.7	−0.9	−0.6
Les Sables d'Olonne	−0030	+0015	−0035	−0030	−2.2	−1.7	−0.9	−0.6

Note: Time zone. The predictions for the standard port are on the same time zone as the differences shown. No further adjustment is necessary. **Refer to predictions on pages 21:277-21:279**

TIDAL DIFFERENCES ON ST. MALO

PLACE	TIME DIFFERENCES				HEIGHT DIFFERENCES (Metres)			
	High Water		Low Water		MHWS	MHWN	MLWN	MLWS
ST. MALO	0100 and 1300	0800 and 2000	0300 and 1500	0800 and 2000	12.2	9.2	4.4	1.5
Iles Chausey	+0010	+0010	+0015	+0010	+0.8	+0.7	+0.5	+0.5
Dielette	+0040	+0035	+0010	+0030	−2.5	−1.8	−0.8	−0.2
Carteret	+0025	+0025	+0020	+0025	−1.0	−0.7	−0.4	0.0
Le Sénéquet	+0015	+0020	+0025	+0025	−0.3	−0.2	−0.1	−0.1
Granville	+0005	+0005	+0010	+0005	+0.8	+0.6	+0.2	−0.1
Cancale	0000	+0005	+0010	+0010	+1.3	+1.1	+0.7	+0.6
St. Cast	0000	0000	−0020	−0005	−0.1	−0.1	0.0	0.0
Erquy	−0005	−0005	−0030	−0015	−0.8	−0.5	−0.4	−0.1
Dahouet	−0005	−0005	−0035	−0010	−0.9	−0.5	−0.5	−0.2
Le Légué	−0005	0000	−0030	−0020	−0.8	−0.5	−0.3	−0.1
Binic	−0005	0000	−0030	−0020	−0.8	−0.5	−0.3	−0.1
Portrieux	−0005	−0005	−0030	−0020	−0.8	−0.6	−0.3	−0.1
Paimpol	−0010	−0005	−0035	−0035	−1.3	−0.9	−0.5	−0.1
Ile de Bréhat	−0015	−0005	−0050	−0045	−1.7	−1.2	−0.7	−0.3
Les Heaux de Brehát	−0005	−0015	−0115	−0020	−2.3	−1.6	−1.0	−0.4
Lezardrieux	−0010	−0010	−0050	−0030	−1.7	−1.2	−0.6	−0.2
Plougrescant	−0040	−0040	−0120	−0055	−2.5	−1.7	−0.9	−0.1
Tréguier	−0035	−0035	−0130	−0050	−2.4	−1.7	−1.1	−0.4
Perros-Guirec	−0035	−0045	−0125	−0105	−2.8	−1.9	−0.9	−0.2
Ploumanac'h	−0035	−0040	−0130	−0105	−3.2	−2.1	−1.0	−0.4

Note: Time zone. The predictions for the standard port are on the same time zone as the diferences shown. No further adjustment is necessary. **Refer to predictions on pages 21:283-21:285.**

ST. MALO
21:283

Lat. 48°38'N. Long. 2°02'W.   **HIGH & LOW WATER 1992**

JANUARY

Day	Time	m	#	Time	m
1 W	0415 / 1102 / 1643 / 2335	9.7 / 3.8 / 9.7 / 3.7	16 TH	0303 / 0956 / 1546 / 2235	9.3 / 4.0 / 9.5 / 3.7
2 TH	0514 / 1202 / 1739	10.1 / 3.4 / 10.1	17 F	0421 / 1115 / 1659 / 2348	9.9 / 3.3 / 10.2 / 2.9
3 F	0029 / 0602 / 1252 / 1826	3.3 / 10.6 / 3.0 / 10.4	18 SA	0526 / 1223 / 1802	10.7 / 2.4 / 11.0
4 SA ●	0113 / 0644 / 1335 / 1907	3.0 / 10.9 / 2.7 / 10.7	19 SU O	0051 / 0623 / 1324 / 1856	2.2 / 11.6 / 1.6 / 11.7
5 SU	0152 / 0721 / 1413 / 1942	2.7 / 11.2 / 2.5 / 10.9	20 M	0149 / 0715 / 1421 / 1946	1.5 / 12.3 / 1.4 / 12.2
6 M	0227 / 0755 / 1447 / 2015	2.6 / 11.3 / 2.3 / 11.0	21 TU	0242 / 0803 / 1512 / 2032	1.0 / 12.7 / 0.6 / 12.5
7 TU	0300 / 0826 / 1520 / 2045	2.5 / 11.4 / 2.3 / 11.1	22 W	0330 / 0848 / 1557 / 2115	0.8 / 12.9 / 0.5 / 12.5
8 W	0331 / 0857 / 1550 / 2115	2.5 / 11.3 / 2.3 / 11.0	23 TH	0413 / 0929 / 1639 / 2155	0.9 / 12.7 / 0.8 / 12.2
9 TH	0400 / 0927 / 1620 / 2145	2.6 / 11.2 / 2.5 / 10.9	24 F	0452 / 1008 / 1716 / 2232	1.3 / 12.3 / 1.4 / 11.6
10 F	0429 / 0957 / 1649 / 2216	2.8 / 10.9 / 2.8 / 10.6	25 SA	0528 / 1046 / 1750 / 2309	1.9 / 11.6 / 2.2 / 10.9
11 SA	0458 / 1029 / 1720 / 2249	3.1 / 10.6 / 3.1 / 10.2	26 SU	0603 / 1125 / 1826 / 2351	2.7 / 10.7 / 3.1 / 10.0
12 SU	0531 / 1104 / 1756 / 2328	3.5 / 10.1 / 3.5 / 9.8	27 M	0644 / 1212 / 1910	3.5 / 9.7 / 3.9
13 M	0613 / 1149 / 1843	3.9 / 9.6 / 3.9	28 TU	0047 / 0739 / 1321 / 2014	9.2 / 4.3 / 8.9 / 4.4
14 TU	0020 / 0709 / 1252 / 1946	9.4 / 4.2 / 9.2 / 4.2	29 W	0215 / 0901 / 1501 / 2148	8.7 / 4.7 / 8.5 / 4.8
15 W	0135 / 0826 / 1419 / 2110	9.1 / 4.3 / 9.1 / 4.1	30 TH	0352 / 1034 / 1601 / 2313	8.9 / 4.5 / 8.9 / 4.3
			31 F	0500 / 1145 / 1729	9.4 / 3.9 / 9.5

FEBRUARY

Day	Time	m	#	Time	m
1 SA	0013 / 0549 / 1236 / 1813	3.7 / 10.1 / 3.2 / 10.1	16 SU	0516 / 1208 / 1753	10.4 / 2.5 / 10.8
2 SU	0058 / 0629 / 1319 / 1851	3.1 / 10.7 / 2.7 / 10.6	17 M	0037 / 0612 / 1311 / 1844	2.1 / 11.5 / 1.5 / 11.7
3 M ●	0137 / 0704 / 1356 / 1924	2.7 / 11.1 / 2.3 / 11.0	18 TU O	0135 / 0702 / 1406 / 1931	1.3 / 12.4 / 0.7 / 12.4
4 TU	0212 / 0737 / 1430 / 1955	2.3 / 11.4 / 2.0 / 11.3	19 W	0226 / 0747 / 1454 / 2013	0.7 / 12.9 / 0.3 / 12.8
5 W	0243 / 0807 / 1501 / 2024	2.1 / 11.7 / 1.8 / 11.5	20 TH	0311 / 0829 / 1536 / 2053	0.4 / 13.1 / 0.2 / 12.8
6 TH	0313 / 0836 / 1531 / 2052	1.9 / 11.8 / 1.7 / 11.6	21 F	0351 / 0908 / 1614 / 2129	0.5 / 13.0 / 0.6 / 12.5
7 F	0341 / 0904 / 1559 / 2121	1.9 / 11.8 / 1.8 / 11.5	22 SA	0426 / 0943 / 1646 / 2203	0.9 / 12.4 / 1.2 / 11.8
8 SA	0409 / 0932 / 1627 / 2149	2.0 / 11.6 / 2.0 / 11.3	23 SU	0457 / 1017 / 1715 / 2235	1.6 / 11.6 / 2.1 / 11.0
9 SU	0436 / 1001 / 1655 / 2219	2.4 / 11.3 / 2.4 / 10.9	24 M	0526 / 1050 / 1743 / 2309	2.6 / 10.6 / 3.1 / 10.1
10 M	0506 / 1032 / 1725 / 2252	2.8 / 10.6 / 3.0 / 10.3	25 TU	0559 / 1128 / 1817 / 2353	3.5 / 9.5 / 4.1 / 9.1
11 TU	0541 / 1110 / 1805 / 2334	3.4 / 10.0 / 3.6 / 9.7	26 W	0645 / 1223 / 1911	4.4 / 8.5 / 4.9
12 W	0629 / 1203 / 1902	3.9 / 9.3 / 4.1	27 TH	0117 / 0803 / 1420 / 2056	8.3 / 5.1 / 7.9 / 5.3
13 TH	0039 / 0741 / 1331 / 2029	9.1 / 4.3 / 8.8 / 4.4	28 F	0321 / 0957 / 1609 / 2244	8.2 / 4.9 / 8.3 / 4.9
14 F	0223 / 0924 / 1526 / 2210	8.9 / 4.2 / 8.9 / 4.0	29 SA	0437 / 1117 / 1708 / 2346	8.9 / 4.2 / 9.1 / 4.0
15 SA	0404 / 1056 / 1651 / 2331	9.4 / 3.5 / 9.8 / 3.1			

MARCH

Day	Time	m	#	Time	m
1 SU	0524 / 1208 / 1748	9.7 / 3.4 / 9.9	16 M	0458 / 1151 / 1734	10.4 / 2.4 / 10.8
2 M	0031 / 0602 / 1250 / 1823	3.3 / 10.4 / 2.7 / 10.6	17 TU	0017 / 0552 / 1250 / 1823	2.1 / 11.5 / 1.5 / 11.7
3 TU	0109 / 0637 / 1328 / 1856	2.6 / 11.0 / 2.2 / 11.1	18 W O	0113 / 0640 / 1343 / 1907	1.3 / 12.3 / 0.8 / 12.4
4 W ●	0144 / 0710 / 1402 / 1927	2.2 / 11.5 / 1.8 / 11.5	19 TH	0202 / 0724 / 1429 / 1948	0.7 / 12.8 / 0.5 / 12.7
5 TH	0217 / 0741 / 1435 / 1957	1.8 / 11.8 / 1.5 / 11.8	20 F	0246 / 0805 / 1509 / 2026	0.5 / 12.9 / 0.5 / 12.7
6 F	0247 / 0810 / 1505 / 2026	1.6 / 12.0 / 1.4 / 11.9	21 SA	0324 / 0842 / 1544 / 2102	0.6 / 12.7 / 0.9 / 12.3
7 SA	0318 / 0839 / 1535 / 2054	1.5 / 12.0 / 1.4 / 11.9	22 SU	0357 / 0917 / 1614 / 2134	1.1 / 12.1 / 1.5 / 11.7
8 SU	0347 / 0908 / 1603 / 2124	1.6 / 11.8 / 1.7 / 11.7	23 M	0426 / 0949 / 1641 / 2205	1.8 / 11.3 / 2.3 / 10.9
9 M	0416 / 0938 / 1631 / 2154	2.0 / 11.4 / 2.2 / 11.3	24 TU	0454 / 1021 / 1706 / 2237	2.6 / 10.4 / 3.3 / 10.0
10 TU	0446 / 1010 / 1702 / 2227	2.5 / 10.8 / 2.8 / 10.4	25 W	0524 / 1055 / 1736 / 2315	3.6 / 9.4 / 4.2 / 9.1
11 W	0520 / 1048 / 1741 / 2309	3.1 / 10.1 / 3.5 / 9.9	26 TH	0603 / 1142 / 1822	4.4 / 8.4 / 5.0
12 TH	0607 / 1140 / 1838	3.8 / 9.2 / 4.2	27 F	0023 / 0709 / 1324 / 1955	8.2 / 5.1 / 7.8 / 5.5
13 F	0013 / 0719 / 1311 / 2007	9.1 / 4.3 / 8.6 / 4.5	28 SA	0224 / 0900 / 1518 / 2153	8.0 / 5.1 / 8.1 / 5.2
14 SA	0202 / 0904 / 1515 / 2152	8.8 / 4.3 / 8.8 / 4.1	29 SU	0348 / 1027 / 1623 / 2300	8.5 / 4.5 / 8.8 / 4.4
15 SU	0348 / 1039 / 1637 / 2313	9.4 / 3.5 / 9.8 / 3.2	30 M	0440 / 1123 / 1706 / 2348	9.3 / 3.7 / 9.6 / 3.5
			31 TU	0522 / 1209 / 1744	10.1 / 3.0 / 10.4

APRIL

Day	Time	m	#	Time	m
1 W	0029 / 0600 / 1250 / 1820	2.8 / 10.8 / 2.4 / 11.0	16 TH	0047 / 0614 / 1316 / 1841	1.6 / 11.9 / 1.3 / 12.1
2 TH	0108 / 0636 / 1328 / 1854	2.3 / 11.4 / 1.9 / 11.5	17 F O	0136 / 0659 / 1401 / 1922	1.2 / 12.2 / 1.1 / 12.3
3 F ●	0144 / 0710 / 1404 / 1927	1.8 / 11.7 / 1.6 / 11.8	18 SA	0219 / 0740 / 1441 / 2001	1.1 / 12.3 / 1.2 / 12.2
4 SA	0220 / 0743 / 1438 / 1959	1.6 / 11.9 / 1.4 / 12.0	19 SU	0257 / 0819 / 1515 / 2037	1.2 / 12.1 / 1.5 / 12.0
5 SU	0254 / 0815 / 1511 / 2031	1.5 / 12.0 / 1.5 / 12.0	20 M	0331 / 0855 / 1546 / 2111	1.6 / 11.6 / 2.0 / 11.5
6 M	0327 / 0848 / 1543 / 2103	1.6 / 11.8 / 1.7 / 11.8	21 TU	0402 / 0928 / 1614 / 2143	2.1 / 11.0 / 2.7 / 10.8
7 TU	0400 / 0923 / 1615 / 2138	1.9 / 11.4 / 2.2 / 11.4	22 W	0431 / 1002 / 1642 / 2217	2.8 / 10.2 / 3.4 / 10.0
8 W	0434 / 1000 / 1650 / 2216	2.4 / 10.8 / 2.8 / 10.7	23 TH	0502 / 1037 / 1712 / 2255	3.6 / 9.4 / 4.2 / 9.3
9 TH	0513 / 1043 / 1734 / 2304	3.0 / 10.1 / 3.5 / 10.0	24 F	0539 / 1123 / 1753 / 2351	4.3 / 8.7 / 4.8 / 8.6
10 F	0604 / 1143 / 1834	3.6 / 9.3 / 4.1	25 SA	0632 / 1233 / 1902	4.8 / 8.3 / 5.2
11 SA	0014 / 0717 / 1314 / 2001	9.3 / 4.1 / 8.9 / 4.4	26 SU	0114 / 0754 / 1401 / 2042	8.3 / 5.0 / 8.3 / 5.2
12 SU	0154 / 0852 / 1458 / 2134	9.1 / 4.0 / 9.1 / 4.0	27 M	0236 / 0920 / 1515 / 2157	8.6 / 4.6 / 8.7 / 4.6
13 M	0325 / 1018 / 1612 / 2250	9.6 / 3.4 / 9.9 / 3.2	28 TU	0340 / 1025 / 1611 / 2254	9.1 / 4.0 / 9.4 / 3.9
14 TU	0432 / 1127 / 1708 / 2352	10.5 / 2.5 / 10.8 / 2.3	29 W	0431 / 1119 / 1657 / 2343	9.8 / 3.3 / 10.2 / 3.2
15 W	0526 / 1225 / 1757	11.3 / 1.8 / 11.6	30 TH	0516 / 1207 / 1740	10.5 / 2.7 / 10.8

TIDAL DIFFERENCES PAGE 21:282.

Chart Datum: 6.6 m. below Lallemand System.

ST. MALO

HIGH & LOW WATER 1992   Lat. 48°38′N. Long.2°02′W.

TIME ZONE-0100 SUBTRACT 1 HOUR FROM TIMES SHOWN FOR GMT

YEAR 1992

MAY

Date	Time m	Time m	Time m	Time m		Date	Time m	Time m	Time m	Time m
1 F	0028 2.6	0559 11.1	1251 2.2	1820 11.3		16	0111 1.9	0637 11.5	1336 1.9	1900 11.7 O
2 SA	0112 2.1	0639 11.4	1333 1.9	1858 11.7 ●		17 SU	0155 1.8	0721 11.5	1417 2.0	1941 11.7
3 SU	0154 1.8	0718 11.7	1414 1.7	1935 11.9		18 M	0235 1.9	0802 11.4	1453 2.1	2019 11.6
4 M	0234 1.6	0757 11.8	1452 1.7	2013 12.0		19 TU	0311 2.1	0840 11.1	1526 2.4	2055 11.3
5 TU	0314 1.7	0836 11.7	1531 1.9	2052 11.8		20 W	0358 2.4	0916 10.8	1558 2.8	2130 10.8
6 W	0353 1.9	0918 11.4	1610 2.2	2133 11.5		21 TH	0418 2.8	0951 10.3	1629 3.3	2205 10.3
7 TH	0434 2.2	1002 10.9	1652 2.7	2219 10.9		22 F	0451 3.3	1026 9.8	1701 3.9	2241 9.8
8 F	0520 2.8	1052 10.3	1740 3.3	2312 10.3		23 SA	0525 3.8	1118 9.3	1737 4.3	2324 9.3
9 SA	0613 3.3	1152 9.7	1840 3.8			24 SU	0546 4.2	1153 9.0	1826 4.7	
10 SU	0018 9.9	0719 3.6	1307 9.4	1953 3.9		25 M	0018 9.0	0701 4.4	1253 8.8	1932 4.8
11 M	0136 9.7	0834 3.6	1428 9.6	2110 3.7		26 TU	0124 8.9	0809 4.4	1402 8.9	2046 4.6
12 TU	0253 9.9	0949 3.3	1539 10.1	2221 3.2		27 W	0232 9.1	0920 4.2	1509 9.3	2154 4.1
13 W	0400 10.4	1057 2.8	1638 10.7	2324 2.7		28 TH	0335 9.6	1024 3.7	1608 9.9	2254 3.6
14 TH	0457 10.9	1157 2.4	1729 11.2			29 F	0432 10.1	1122 3.2	1700 10.5	2349 3.0
15 F	0020 2.2	0549 11.3	1250 2.1	1816 11.6		30 SA	0523 10.6	1216 2.7	1748 11.1	
						31 SU	0041 2.5	0612 11.1	1306 2.3	1833 11.5

JUNE

Date	Time m	Time m	Time m	Time m		Date	Time m	Time m	Time m	Time m
1 M	0131 2.0	0659 11.4	1354 2.0	1918 11.8		16 TU	0220 2.3	0750 11.0	1438 2.5	2006 11.4 ●
2 TU	0219 1.8	0745 11.7	1441 1.8	2003 12.0		17 W	0258 2.3	0828 11.0	1513 2.6	2041 11.3
3 W	0307 1.6	0831 11.7	1526 1.8	2048 12.0		18 TH	0333 2.4	0902 10.9	1546 2.7	2115 11.1
4 TH	0353 1.6	0918 11.6	1611 1.9	2134 11.8		19 F	0406 2.6	0935 10.7	1617 3.0	2147 10.8
5 F	0439 1.8	1004 11.3	1657 2.3	2221 11.5		20 SA	0437 2.9	1007 10.4	1648 3.3	2220 10.4
6 SA	0526 2.2	1053 10.9	1744 2.7	2310 11.0		21 SU	0508 3.2	1040 10.1	1719 3.6	2254 10.1
7 SU	0615 2.6	1144 10.5	1836 3.1			22 M	0541 3.6	1116 9.8	1754 4.0	2333 9.7
8 M	0004 10.6	0708 3.0	1243 10.1	1934 3.4		23 TU	0620 3.9	1159 9.4	1839 4.2	
9 TU	0106 10.2	0807 3.3	1351 9.9	2039 3.5		24 W	0022 9.4	0710 4.1	1255 9.2	1939 4.4
10 W	0216 10.0	0915 3.4	1510 10.0	2148 3.5		25 TH	0126 9.2	0814 4.2	1405 9.2	2053 4.3
11 TH	0327 10.1	1025 3.3	1608 10.3	2256 3.2		26 F	0239 9.3	0928 4.1	1517 9.5	2207 4.0
12 F	0432 10.3	1130 3.1	1707 10.6	2356 2.9		27 SA	0350 9.6	1039 3.6	1623 10.0	2314 3.4
13 SA	0530 10.6	1227 2.8	1759 11.0			28 SU	0453 10.1	1143 3.1	1721 10.7	
14 SU	0050 2.6	0622 10.8	1316 2.6	1846 11.2		29 M	0014 2.7	0551 10.7	1242 2.5	1815 11.3
15 M	0138 2.4	0709 10.9	1359 2.5	1928 11.4		30 TU	0112 2.1	0645 11.3	1338 2.0	1906 11.8 ●

JULY

Date	Time m	Time m	Time m	Time m		Date	Time m	Time m	Time m	Time m
1 W	0207 1.6	0736 11.7	1431 1.6	1954 12.2		16 TH	0241 2.3	0810 11.1	1456 2.4	2022 11.5
2 TH	0300 1.3	0825 12.0	1520 1.4	2041 12.5		17 F	0315 2.2	0841 11.2	1528 2.4	2052 11.5
3 F	0349 1.1	0911 12.1	1607 1.3	2127 12.4		18 SA	0345 2.2	0910 11.2	1557 2.4	2121 11.3
4 SA	0435 1.1	0956 12.0	1651 1.5	2210 12.2		19 SU	0415 2.4	0939 11.0	1625 2.6	2151 11.1
5 SU	0518 1.4	1039 11.6	1734 1.9	2254 11.7		20 M	0443 2.6	1008 10.8	1652 3.0	2220 10.7
6 M	0600 2.0	1122 11.1	1817 2.5	2339 11.1		21 TU	0511 3.0	1039 10.4	1722 3.4	2252 10.2
7 TU	0644 2.6	1210 10.5	1905 3.1			22 W	0543 3.4	1113 10.0	1758 3.8	2331 9.7
8 W	0031 10.4	0734 3.3	1308 9.9	2003 3.6		23 TH	0623 3.8	1157 9.5	1847 4.2	
9 TH	0137 9.8	0836 3.6	1422 9.6	2114 3.9		24 F	0025 9.2	0718 4.2	1301 9.2	1956 4.5
10 F	0256 9.5	0952 4.0	1542 9.7	2230 3.8		25 SA	0143 9.0	0835 4.4	1427 9.1	2124 4.3
11 SA	0414 9.6	1106 3.8	1652 10.0	2338 3.4		26 SU	0313 9.1	1001 4.1	1551 9.6	2244 3.7
12 SU	0520 10.0	1209 3.4	1748 10.5			27 M	0431 9.7	1116 3.4	1701 10.3	2352 2.8
13 M	0035 3.0	0613 10.4	1301 3.0	1834 10.9		28 TU	0536 10.5	1222 2.6	1800 11.2	
14 TU	0123 2.7	0657 10.7	1344 2.7	1914 11.0		29 W	0054 2.0	0632 11.3	1322 1.8	1852 12.0 ●
15 W	0205 2.4	0736 10.9	1422 2.5	1950 11.4		30 TH	0153 1.3	0723 12.0	1416 1.2	1941 12.6
						31 F	0246 0.8	0810 12.4	1506 0.8	2026 13.0

AUGUST

Date	Time m	Time m	Time m	Time m		Date	Time m	Time m	Time m	Time m
1 SA	0334 0.6	0854 12.6	1552 0.7	2109 13.0		16 SU	0317 1.9	0839 11.5	1529 2.0	2051 11.7
2 SU	0418 0.6	0935 12.5	1633 1.0	2150 12.7		17 M	0345 2.0	0907 11.5	1556 2.2	2119 11.5
3 M	0457 1.1	1014 12.0	1711 1.5	2229 12.0		18 TU	0412 2.2	0935 11.3	1623 2.5	2147 11.1
4 TU	0534 1.8	1052 11.4	1748 2.3	2308 11.2		19 W	0439 2.6	1003 10.9	1651 2.9	2216 10.6
5 W	0611 2.7	1134 10.6	1829 3.1	2354 10.2		20 TH	0507 3.1	1034 10.4	1723 3.5	2250 10.0
6 TH	0653 3.6	1225 9.7	1922 3.9			21 F	0543 3.7	1112 9.8	1806 4.1	2338 9.3
7 F	0056 9.3	0753 4.3	1343 9.1	2038 4.4		22 SA	0634 4.3	1209 9.2	1912 4.5	
8 SA	0228 8.8	0920 4.6	1522 9.0	2208 4.4		23 SU	0056 8.8	0753 4.6	1343 8.9	2048 4.5
9 SU	0402 9.0	1047 4.3	1639 9.5	2322 3.8		24 M	0247 8.8	0933 4.3	1528 9.3	2221 3.8
10 M	0509 9.5	1152 3.8	1733 10.2			25 TU	0416 9.5	1055 3.5	1644 10.2	2333 2.8
11 TU	0017 3.2	0557 10.1	1241 3.2	1815 10.8		26 W	0520 10.5	1202 2.5	1742 11.2	
12 W	0102 2.7	0636 10.6	1322 2.7	1851 11.2		27 TH	0035 1.9	0624 11.5	1301 1.7	1833 12.2
13 TH	0141 2.4	0711 11.0	1358 2.4	1924 11.5		28 F	0132 1.1	0700 12.3	1356 1.0	1920 12.9
14 F	0215 2.1	0742 11.3	1430 2.2	1955 11.7		29 SA	0224 0.6	0747 12.7	1444 0.6	2004 13.2
15 SA	0247 2.0	0811 11.5	1500 2.0	2024 11.8		30 SU	0310 0.4	0829 12.9	1528 0.5	2045 13.1
						31 M	0351 0.6	0908 12.7	1606 0.9	2124 12.7

ST. MALO
Lat. 48°38′N. Long. 2°02′W.

21:285

HIGH & LOW WATER 1992

TIME ZONE-0100 SUBTRACT 1 HOUR FROM TIMES SHOWN FOR GMT

SEPTEMBER

Day	Time	m	Day	Time	m
1 TU	0428 / 0945 / 1641 W / 2200	1.2 / 12.1 / 1.5 / 11.9	16	0342 / 0903 / 1556 / 2118	2.1 / 11.6 / 2.3 / 11.3
2 W	0500 / 1020 / 1714 TH / 2237	2.0 / 11.4 / 2.4 / 11.0	17	0410 / 0932 / 1625 / 2148	2.5 / 11.2 / 2.7 / 10.8
3 TH	0532 / 1058 / 1750 F / 2317	3.0 / 10.4 / 3.4 / 9.9	18	0439 / 1004 / 1657 / 2223	3.0 / 10.6 / 3.3 / 10.1
4 F	0609 / 1145 SA / 1838	4.0 / 9.5 / 4.3	19	0515 / 1043 / 1741 / 2312	3.7 / 10.0 / 4.0 / 9.3
5 SA	0015 / 0704 SU / 1304 / 1957	8.9 / 4.8 / 8.7 / 4.9	20	0607 / 1141 / 1846	4.3 / 9.2 / 4.5
6 SU	0159 / 0844 M / 1457 / 2143	8.3 / 5.2 / 8.6 / 4.9	21	0033 / 0729 / 1321 / 2025	8.7 / 4.7 / 8.9 / 4.5
7 M	0344 / 1024 TU / 1616 / 2258	8.5 / 4.8 / 9.1 / 4.2	22	0232 / 0912 / 1508 / 2201	8.8 / 4.4 / 9.3 / 3.8
8 TU	0447 / 1126 W / 1706 / 2349	9.2 / 4.1 / 9.9 / 3.5	23	0358 / 1035 / 1622 / 2313	9.6 / 3.5 / 10.3 / 2.8
9 W	0529 / 1211 TH / 1745	10.0 / 3.4 / 10.5	24	0459 / 1140 / 1719	10.6 / 2.5 / 11.3
10 TH	0030 / 0604 F / 1250 / 1819	2.9 / 10.6 / 2.8 / 11.1	25	0013 / 0549 / 1238 / 1808	1.8 / 11.6 / 1.6 / 12.2
11 F	0107 / 0637 SA / 1325 / 1852 ●	2.4 / 11.1 / 2.4 / 11.5	26	0108 / 0636 / 1330 / 1854	1.1 / 12.3 / 1.0 / 12.8
12 SA	0142 / 0708 SU / 1357 / 1923 ○	2.1 / 11.5 / 2.1 / 11.8	27	0158 / 0720 / 1418 / 1938	0.7 / 12.7 / 0.7 / 13.0
13 SU	0214 / 0738 M / 1428 / 1952	1.9 / 11.7 / 1.9 / 11.9	28	0242 / 0801 / 1500 / 2019	0.7 / 12.8 / 0.8 / 12.9
14 M	0244 / 0806 TU / 1458 / 2020	1.8 / 11.8 / 1.9 / 11.9	29	0322 / 0840 / 1538 / 2057	1.6 / 12.5 / 1.2 / 12.4
15 TU	0314 / 0835 W / 1527 / 2049	1.8 / 11.8 / 2.0 / 11.7	30	0356 / 0916 / 1611 / 2133	1.6 / 12.0 / 1.8 / 11.6

OCTOBER

Day	Time	m	Day	Time	m
1 TH	0427 / 0951 / 1643 F / 2209	2.4 / 11.2 / 2.7 / 10.7	16	0350 / 0913 / 1610 / 2134	2.5 / 11.4 / 2.7 / 10.8
2 F	0456 / 1027 / 1716 SA / 2247	3.3 / 10.3 / 3.6 / 9.6	17	0424 / 0950 / 1647 / 2215	3.0 / 10.8 / 3.2 / 10.2
3 SA	0529 / 1111 / 1759 SU / 2341	4.2 / 9.3 / 4.5 / 8.7	18	0505 / 1035 / 1734 / 2309	3.7 / 10.1 / 3.8 / 9.4
4 SU	0617 / 1223 M / 1908	5.0 / 8.5 / 5.1	19	0600 / 1138 / 1840	4.3 / 9.5 / 4.3
5 M	0117 / 0752 TU / 1410 / 2055	8.1 / 5.5 / 8.3 / 5.2	20	0032 / 0719 / 1310 / 2010	9.0 / 4.6 / 9.2 / 4.3
6 TU	0301 / 0940 W / 1228 / 2214	8.3 / 5.2 / 8.8 / 4.6	21	0214 / 0852 / 1444 / 2139	9.1 / 4.3 / 9.6 / 3.7
7 W	0405 / 1044 TH / 1623 / 2307	9.0 / 4.4 / 9.5 / 3.8	22	0333 / 1011 / 1554 / 2249	9.8 / 3.5 / 10.4 / 2.9
8 TH	0447 / 1129 F / 1704 / 2350	9.7 / 3.7 / 10.2 / 3.1	23	0432 / 1116 / 1651 / 2349	10.7 / 2.6 / 11.3 / 2.1
9 F	0523 / 1209 SA / 1740	10.5 / 3.0 / 10.9	24	0523 / 1213 / 1742	11.5 / 1.9 / 12.0
10 SA	0029 / 0558 SU / 1247 / 1815	2.6 / 11.0 / 2.5 / 11.4	25	0043 / 0609 / 1305 / 1829 ●	1.5 / 12.1 / 1.4 / 12.4
11 SU	0106 / 0632 M / 1323 / 1849 ○	2.2 / 11.5 / 2.2 / 11.7	26	0132 / 0654 / 1352 / 1914	1.3 / 12.4 / 1.2 / 12.5
12 M	0141 / 0705 TU / 1357 / 1922	2.0 / 11.7 / 2.0 / 11.9	27	0216 / 0735 / 1435 / 1956	1.3 / 12.4 / 1.3 / 12.3
13 TU	0214 / 0736 W / 1431 / 1953	1.9 / 11.9 / 1.9 / 11.9	28	0255 / 0815 / 1513 / 2035	1.6 / 12.2 / 1.6 / 11.9
14 W	0247 / 0807 TH / 1504 / 2025	1.9 / 11.9 / 2.0 / 11.7	29	0329 / 0853 / 1548 / 2113	2.1 / 11.7 / 2.2 / 11.2
15 TH	0318 / 0839 F / 1536 / 2058	2.1 / 11.7 / 2.2 / 11.4	30	0401 / 0929 / 1620 / 2149	2.7 / 11.0 / 2.9 / 10.5
			31 SA	0431 / 1006 / 1654 / 2228	3.5 / 10.3 / 3.6 / 9.6

NOVEMBER

Day	Time	m	Day	Time	m
1 SU	0503 / 1047 / 1731 M / 2314	4.2 / 9.5 / 4.3 / 8.9	16	0509 / 1039 / 1740 / 2315	3.4 / 10.5 / 3.3 / 9.9
2 M	0544 / 1142 / 1824	4.9 / 8.8 / 4.9	17	0603 / 1138 TU / 1840	3.8 / 10.0 / 3.7
3 TU	0020 / 0650 / 1259 / 1943	8.4 / 5.3 / 8.5 / 5.1	18	0023 / 0710 / 1251 W / 1951	9.5 / 4.1 / 9.8 / 3.8
4 W	0144 / 0825 / 1420 / 2106	8.3 / 5.3 / 8.6 / 4.8	19	0144 / 0826 / 1411 TH / 2108	9.5 / 4.0 / 9.9 / 3.6
5 TH	0257 / 0941 / 1523 / 2210	8.8 / 4.8 / 9.2 / 4.2	20	0300 / 0942 / 1523 F / 2221	9.9 / 3.6 / 10.3 / 3.1
6 F	0352 / 1037 / 1613 / 2302	9.4 / 4.1 / 9.8 / 3.6	21	0403 / 1049 / 1624 SA / 2324	10.5 / 3.0 / 10.9 / 2.6
7 SA	0437 / 1131 / 1658 / 2348	10.1 / 3.4 / 10.5 / 3.0	22	0457 / 1149 / 1719 SU	11.1 / 2.4 / 11.3
8 SU	0519 / 1213 / 1739	10.8 / 2.9 / 11.0	23	0020 / 0547 / 1243 M / 1810	2.2 / 11.6 / 2.0 / 11.7
9 M	0030 / 0558 / 1251 / 1819	2.4 / 11.3 / 2.4 / 11.4	24	0110 / 0634 / 1332 TU / 1857 ●	2.0 / 11.9 / 1.8 / 11.3
10 TU	0110 / 0636 / 1331 / 1856	2.2 / 11.6 / 2.2 / 11.6	25	0155 / 0718 / 1416 W / 1941	1.9 / 11.9 / 1.8 / 11.7
11 W	0149 / 0712 / 1410 / 1934	2.1 / 11.8 / 2.0 / 11.7	26	0235 / 0759 / 1456 TH / 2022	2.1 / 11.8 / 2.0 / 11.4
12 TH	0227 / 0749 / 1449 / 2011	2.1 / 11.9 / 2.0 / 11.6	27	0311 / 0838 / 1533 F / 2100	2.3 / 11.5 / 2.3 / 11.1
13 F	0304 / 0826 / 1528 / 2051	2.2 / 11.8 / 2.2 / 11.4	28	0345 / 0914 / 1607 SA / 2136	2.8 / 11.1 / 2.7 / 10.6
14 SA	0342 / 0906 / 1607 / 2133	2.5 / 11.5 / 2.5 / 11.0	29	0417 / 0950 / 1640 SU / 2211	3.2 / 10.8 / 3.3 / 10.1
15 SU	0423 / 0949 / 1651 / 2220	2.9 / 11.1 / 2.9 / 10.5	30	0448 / 1026 / 1713 M / 2248	3.8 / 10.0 / 3.8 / 9.5

DECEMBER

Day	Time	m	Day	Time	m
1 TU	0522 / 1105 / 1750 W / 2331	4.3 / 9.5 / 4.2 / 9.1	16	0559 / 1126 / 1829	3.0 / 10.8 / 2.9
2 W	0604 / 1154 / 1839	4.7 / 9.1 / 4.6	17	0001 / 0652 / 1223 TH / 1925	10.2 / 3.4 / 10.3 / 3.3
3 TH	0026 / 0703 / 1256 / 1944	8.8 / 4.9 / 8.9 / 4.7	18	0105 / 0754 / 1332 F / 2031	9.9 / 3.7 / 10.0 / 3.6
4 F	0135 / 0818 / 1408 / 2057	8.8 / 4.9 / 9.0 / 4.5	19	0220 / 0907 / 1448 SA / 2147	9.8 / 3.7 / 9.9 / 3.6
5 SA	0246 / 0931 / 1516 / 2205	9.1 / 4.5 / 9.4 / 4.1	20	0333 / 1022 / 1600 SU / 2259	10.0 / 3.4 / 10.2 / 3.3
6 SU	0348 / 1035 / 1614 / 2304	9.6 / 4.0 / 9.9 / 3.5	21	0438 / 1130 / 1704 M	10.5 / 3.0 / 10.5
7 M	0441 / 1131 / 1706 / 2356	10.3 / 3.3 / 10.4 / 3.0	22	0002 / 0534 / 1229 TU / 1800	2.9 / 10.9 / 2.6 / 10.9
8 TU	0528 / 1221 / 1753	10.9 / 2.8 / 10.9	23	0056 / 0624 / 1320 W / 1849	2.6 / 11.3 / 2.3 / 11.1
9 W	0044 / 0612 / 1309 / 1838 ○	2.6 / 11.3 / 2.3 / 11.3	24	0142 / 0708 / 1405 TH / 1932 ●	2.4 / 11.5 / 2.1 / 11.3
10 TH	0130 / 0655 / 1355 / 1922	2.3 / 11.7 / 2.0 / 11.6	25	0223 / 0749 / 1445 F / 2011	2.3 / 11.6 / 2.1 / 11.3
11 F	0215 / 0738 / 1441 / 2005	2.5 / 11.9 / 1.8 / 11.7	26	0300 / 0825 / 1521 SA / 2046	2.3 / 11.6 / 2.2 / 11.2
12 SA	0259 / 0821 / 1526 / 2049	1.9 / 12.0 / 1.8 / 11.7	27	0333 / 0859 / 1553 SU / 2118	2.5 / 11.4 / 2.3 / 11.0
13 SU	0343 / 0904 / 1611 / 2133	2.0 / 12.0 / 1.9 / 11.5	28	0404 / 0930 / 1624 M / 2149	2.7 / 11.1 / 2.6 / 10.7
14 M	0427 / 0949 / 1655 / 2219	2.3 / 11.7 / 2.1 / 11.1	29	0432 / 1001 / 1652 TU / 2219	3.0 / 10.7 / 3.0 / 10.3
15 TU	0512 / 1036 / 1741 / 2307	2.6 / 11.3 / 2.5 / 10.7	30	0459 / 1032 / 1720 W / 2251	3.4 / 10.3 / 3.4 / 9.9
			31 TH	0529 / 1106 / 1753 / 2329	3.8 / 9.8 / 9.9 / 9.5

TIDAL DIFFERENCES PAGE 21:282.

Chart Datum: 6.6 m. below Lallemand System.

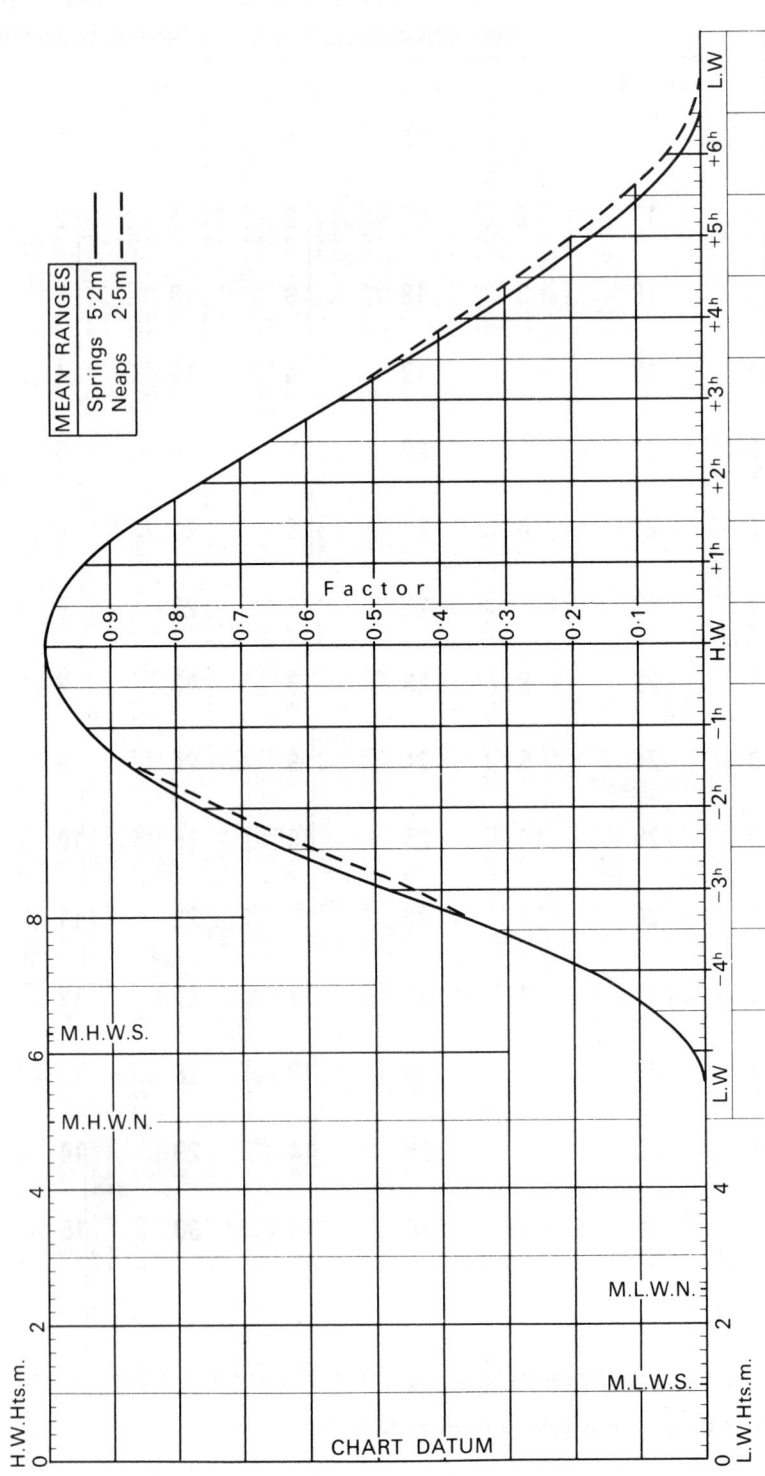

CHERBOURG

MEAN SPRING AND NEAP CURVES

Springs occur 2 days after New and Full Moon.

CHERBOURG

Lat. 49°39′N. Long. 1°38′W.

HIGH & LOW WATER 1992

TIME ZONE-0100 SUBTRACT 1 HOUR FROM TIMES SHOWN FOR GMT

JANUARY

Day	Time	m	Time	m	Time	m	Time	m
1 W	0022	2.4	0602	5.3	1255	2.3	1834	5.2
2 TH	0121	2.3	0658	5.5	1349	2.1	1929	5.4
3 F	0210	2.1	0744	5.7	1434	1.9	2013	5.6
4 SA	0252	1.9	0825	5.9	1514	1.7	●2051	5.8
5 SU	0330	1.8	0901	6.0	1551	1.5	2126	5.9
6 M	0407	1.7	0936	6.0	1625	1.5	2158	5.9
7 TU	0439	1.7	1008	6.0	1657	1.4	2229	5.9
8 W	0511	1.7	1039	6.0	1729	1.5	2300	5.8
9 TH	0542	1.8	1111	5.9	1800	1.6	2331	5.7
10 F	0613	1.9	1143	5.8	1831	1.7		
11 SA	0004	5.6	0647	2.1	1217	5.6	1906	1.9
12 SU	0040	5.4	0726	2.4	1255	5.4	1947	2.1
13 M	0122	5.2	0813	2.8	1343	5.1	2037	2.3
14 TU	0217	5.1	0914	2.6	1448	5.0	2144	2.5
15 W	0329	5.0	1032	2.6	1611	5.0	2304	2.5
16 TH	0453	5.1	1153	2.4	1735	5.2		
17 F	0022	2.2	0606	5.5	1303	2.0	1845	5.5
18 SA	0128	1.9	0708	5.9	1405	1.5	1944	5.9
19 SU	0227	1.5	0803	6.3	1501	1.1	○2038	6.3
20 M	0320	1.2	0855	6.6	1552	0.7	2129	6.5
21 TU	0410	0.9	0944	6.8	1639	0.6	2217	6.6
22 W	0458	0.8	1032	6.8	1724	0.5	2303	6.6
23 TH	0542	0.9	1116	6.7	1808	0.7	2345	6.4
24 F	0626	1.1	1158	6.5	1850	1.0		
25 SA	0025	6.1	0708	1.5	1237	6.1	1931	1.5
26 SU	0105	5.7	0751	1.9	1319	5.6	2014	2.0
27 M	0149	5.3	0840	2.3	1408	5.1	2106	2.5
28 TU	0247	5.0	0944	2.7	1520	4.8	2219	2.8
29 W	0409	4.8	1109	2.8	1656	4.7	2348	2.8
30 TH	0534	4.9	1231	2.6	1820	4.9		
31 F	0101	2.6	0640	5.2	1333	2.3	1917	5.2

FEBRUARY

Day	Time	m	Time	m	Time	m	Time	m
1 SA	0156	2.3	0729	5.5	1421	2.0	1959	5.5
2 SU	0239	2.0	0810	5.8	1500	1.7	2036	5.7
3 M	0316	1.8	0846	6.0	1535	1.5	●2109	5.9
4 TU	0350	1.6	0919	6.1	1607	1.3	2140	6.0
5 W	0421	1.5	0950	6.2	1637	1.2	2209	6.0
6 TH	0451	1.4	1020	6.2	1707	1.2	2237	6.0
7 F	0520	1.4	1050	6.2	1736	1.2	2307	6.0
8 SA	0550	1.5	1120	6.0	1805	1.4	2336	5.8
9 SU	0621	1.6	1149	5.8	1836	1.6		
10 M	0006	5.7	0655	1.9	1221	5.6	1913	1.9
11 TU	0040	5.4	0737	2.1	1301	5.3	1958	2.2
12 W	0127	5.2	0832	2.4	1401	5.0	2100	2.5
13 TH	0238	5.2	0949	2.6	1536	4.8	2228	2.6
14 F	0421	4.9	1124	2.4	1719	5.0		
15 SA	0001	2.4	0550	5.3	1254	2.0	1835	5.4
16 SU	0116	2.0	0656	5.8	1353	1.5	1935	5.9
17 M	0216	1.5	0753	6.2	1447	1.0	2028	6.3
18 TU	0309	1.0	0844	6.6	1533	0.6	○2116	6.6
19 W	0356	0.8	0932	6.9	1623	0.4	2201	6.7
20 TH	0441	0.6	1015	6.9	1705	0.4	2242	6.7
21 F	0522	0.7	1056	6.8	1744	0.6	2319	6.5
22 SA	0600	0.9	1133	6.5	1820	1.0	2353	6.2
23 SU	0637	1.3	1207	6.1	1856	1.5		
24 M	0026	5.8	0714	1.8	1242	5.6	1932	2.0
25 TU	0102	5.4	0756	2.2	1324	5.0	2016	2.6
26 W	0152	4.9	0838	2.7	1430	4.6	2123	3.0
27 TH	0318	4.6	1018	2.9	1624	4.4	2311	3.0
28 F	0503	4.7	1159	2.7	1801	4.7		
29 SA	0038	2.8	0617	5.0	1308	2.4	1856	5.0

MARCH

Day	Time	m	Time	m	Time	m	Time	m
1 SU	0135	2.4	0706	5.3	1357	2.0	1935	5.4
2 M	0218	2.0	0746	5.7	1436	1.7	2010	5.7
3 TU	0257	1.7	0822	5.9	1510	1.4	2043	5.9
4 W	0326	1.5	0856	6.1	1541	1.2	2114	6.0
5 TH	0357	1.3	0927	6.2	1611	1.1	2144	6.1
6 F	0426	1.3	0957	6.3	1641	1.0	2212	6.2
7 SA	0456	1.2	1027	6.3	1710	1.1	2241	6.1
8 SU	0526	1.2	1058	6.2	1740	1.2	2311	6.0
9 M	0558	1.4	1128	5.9	1812	1.4	2340	5.8
10 TU	0633	1.6	1201	5.7	1848	1.8		
11 W	0015	5.6	0706	1.9	1242	5.3	1935	2.2
12 TH	0102	5.2	0809	2.3	1344	4.9	2039	2.5
13 F	0215	4.9	0928	2.5	1525	4.8	2210	2.7
14 SA	0405	4.9	1107	2.4	1654	5.0	2348	2.4
15 SU	0537	5.2	1235	1.9	1824	5.4		
16 M	0102	1.9	0642	5.7	1336	1.4	1920	5.9
17 TU	0200	1.4	0737	6.2	1429	0.9	2010	6.3
18 W	0251	1.0	0827	6.6	1517	0.6	○2055	6.6
19 TH	0337	0.7	0912	6.8	1600	0.5	2137	6.7
20 F	0418	0.6	0953	6.8	1640	0.6	2215	6.6
21 SA	0457	0.7	1031	6.6	1716	0.8	2250	6.5
22 SU	0533	0.9	1106	6.3	1750	1.2	2322	6.2
23 M	0608	1.3	1139	5.9	1824	1.6	2353	5.8
24 TU	0643	1.7	1213	5.5	1858	2.1		
25 W	0027	5.4	0722	2.1	1252	5.0	1940	2.6
26 TH	0112	5.0	0802	2.6	1352	4.6	2041	3.0
27 F	0229	4.6	0929	2.8	1541	4.4	2234	3.1
28 SA	0417	4.6	1110	2.8	1718	4.6	2355	2.8
29 SU	0535	4.8	1224	2.5	1816	4.9		
30 M	0056	2.5	0628	5.1	1317	2.1	1858	5.3
31 TU	0141	2.1	0711	5.5	1358	1.8	1935	5.6

APRIL

Day	Time	m	Time	m	Time	m	Time	m
1 W	0219	1.8	0750	5.8	1434	1.5	2010	5.9
2 TH	0254	1.5	0826	6.0	1507	1.2	2043	6.1
3 F	0326	1.3	0900	6.2	1540	1.1	●2115	6.2
4 SA	0359	1.1	0932	6.3	1613	1.0	2146	6.3
5 SU	0432	1.1	1005	6.3	1645	1.1	2218	6.2
6 M	0506	1.1	1040	6.2	1719	1.2	2251	6.1
7 TU	0541	1.2	1115	6.0	1754	1.4	2326	5.9
8 W	0619	1.5	1154	5.7	1835	1.8		
9 TH	0007	5.7	0705	1.8	1242	5.3	1926	2.4
10 F	0059	5.3	0803	2.1	1348	5.0	2035	2.5
11 SA	0213	5.0	0922	2.3	1525	4.9	2205	2.5
12 SU	0353	5.0	1053	2.3	1657	5.1	2333	2.3
13 M	0517	5.3	1212	1.8	1803	5.5		
14 TU	0042	1.9	0621	5.7	1313	1.4	1858	5.9
15 W	0139	1.4	0715	6.1	1406	1.1	1946	6.2
16 TH	0229	1.1	0804	6.4	1453	0.9	2030	6.4
17 F	0314	0.9	0849	6.5	1535	0.8	○2110	6.5
18 SA	0355	0.9	0930	6.5	1613	0.9	2147	6.4
19 SU	0433	1.1	1007	6.3	1649	1.1	2222	6.3
20 M	0509	1.1	1043	6.0	1724	1.4	2255	6.1
21 TU	0543	1.3	1117	5.8	1758	1.8	2328	5.8
22 W	0619	1.7	1153	5.4	1834	2.1		
23 TH	0004	5.4	0657	2.0	1232	5.1	1915	2.4
24 F	0048	5.1	0744	2.4	1325	4.8	2010	2.8
25 SA	0149	4.6	0847	2.6	1445	4.6	2128	3.0
26 SU	0316	4.6	1008	2.7	1613	4.6	2300	2.9
27 M	0435	4.7	1123	2.5	1719	4.8		
28 TU	0000	2.8	0535	5.0	1221	2.2	1809	5.2
29 W	0052	2.2	0625	5.3	1309	1.9	1851	5.5
30 TH	0136	1.9	0709	5.6	1351	1.6	1931	5.8

TIDAL DIFFERENCES PAGE 21:290. TIDAL CURVE PAGE 21:286.

TIDAL STREAMS PAGES 21:28-21:40 AND 21:223-21:227.

Datum of predictions: 1.1 m. below M.L.W.S. and 0.5 m. below L.A.T.

CHERBOURG

HIGH & LOW WATER 1992   Lat. 49°39'N. Long. 1°38'W.

TIME ZONE-0100 SUBTRACT 1 HOUR FROM TIMES SHOWN FOR GMT

MAY

Day	Time	m	Day	Time	m
1 F	0217	1.6	**16**	0251	1.3
	0750	5.8		0827	6.1
	1430	1.4		1510	1.3
	2008	6.0	O	2046	6.2
2 SA	0254	1.4	**17**	0333	1.2
	0830	6.0		0910	6.1
	1508	1.2	SU	1550	1.3
●	2045	6.2		2124	6.2
3 SU	0332	1.2	**18**	0412	1.2
	0908	6.2		0948	6.0
	1546	1.1	M	1627	1.4
	2121	6.3		2200	6.1
4 M	0411	1.1	**19**	0449	1.3
	0946	6.2		1025	5.9
	1624	1.2	TU	1703	1.6
	2159	6.3		2235	6.0
5 TU	0450	1.0	**20**	0525	1.4
	1026	6.2		1101	5.7
	1704	1.3	W	1739	1.8
	2238	6.2		2311	5.8
6 W	0530	1.1	**21**	0601	1.6
	1108	6.0		1137	5.5
	1746	1.5	TH	1816	2.1
	2320	6.0		2348	5.6
7 TH	0614	1.3	**22**	0639	1.9
	1154	5.8		1215	5.3
	1832	1.7	F	1855	2.3
8 F	0007	5.8	**23**	0028	5.3
	0705	1.6		0720	2.1
	1246	5.5	SA	1259	5.0
	1928	2.0		1941	2.5
9 SA	0102	5.5	**24**	0115	5.0
	0804	1.8		0809	2.3
	1351	5.2	SU	1352	4.8
	2035	2.3		2038	2.7
10 SU	0201	5.3	**25**	0214	4.9
	0915	2.0		0907	2.4
	1511	5.1	M	1457	4.8
	2153	2.3		2145	2.7
11 M	0332	5.2	**26**	0322	4.8
	1032	1.9		1013	2.4
	1629	5.3	TU	1605	4.8
	2308	2.2		2253	2.6
12 TU	0447	5.4	**27**	0428	4.9
	1144	1.8		1117	2.3
	1733	5.5	W	1707	5.0
				2354	2.4
13 W	0015	1.9	**28**	0529	5.1
	0552	5.8		1214	2.1
	1245	1.6	TH	1801	5.3
	1829	5.8			
14 TH	0113	1.6	**29**	0048	2.1
	0649	5.9		0624	5.3
	1339	1.4	F	1306	1.9
	1919	6.0		1849	5.6
15 F	0205	1.4	**30**	0137	1.8
	0741	6.0		0714	5.6
	1427	1.3	SA	1354	1.6
	2005	6.1		1934	5.9
			31 SU	0223	1.5
				0801	5.8
				1440	1.4
				2018	6.1

JUNE

Day	Time	m	Day	Time	m
1	0309	1.3	**16**	0356	1.4
	0847	6.0		0934	5.8
M	1525	1.3	TU	1612	1.6
●	2101	6.2		2144	6.0
2	0354	1.1	**17**	0434	1.4
	0932	6.2		1010	5.8
TU	1609	1.2	W	1648	1.7
	2145	6.3		2220	6.0
3	0439	1.0	**18**	0510	1.4
	1017	6.2		1045	5.7
W	1655	1.2	TH	1723	1.8
	2230	6.3		2255	5.9
4	0525	1.0	**19**	0545	1.5
	1104	6.1		1119	5.6
TH	1742	1.3	F	1758	1.9
	2317	6.2		2330	5.7
5	0613	1.0	**20**	0619	1.6
	1152	6.0		1153	5.5
F	1832	1.5	SA	1833	2.0
6	0006	6.1	**21**	0005	5.5
	0703	1.2		0654	1.8
SA	1244	5.8	SU	1229	5.3
	1926	1.7		1910	2.2
7	0058	5.9	**22**	0043	5.3
	0758	1.5		0732	2.0
SU	1340	5.5	M	1309	5.1
	2025	1.9		1953	2.4
8	0156	5.6	**23**	0125	5.1
	0857	1.7		0815	2.2
M	1443	5.4	TU	1355	5.0
	2129	2.1		2044	2.5
9	0302	5.4	**24**	0217	5.0
	1003	1.9		0909	2.3
TU	1551	5.3	W	1452	4.9
	2237	2.1		2147	2.6
10	0411	5.3	**25**	0320	4.9
	1111	1.9		1012	2.4
W	1658	5.4	TH	1558	5.0
	2345	2.1		2256	2.5
11	0520	5.3	**26**	0430	4.9
	1215	1.9		1121	2.3
TH	1759	5.5	F	1707	5.1
12	0047	1.9	**27**	0003	2.3
	0624	5.5		0540	5.1
F	1313	1.8	SA	1225	2.1
	1854	5.7		1810	5.4
13	0143	1.8	**28**	0103	2.0
	0722	5.8		0643	5.4
SA	1405	1.8	SU	1323	1.9
	1943	5.8		1905	5.7
14	0232	1.6	**29**	0158	1.6
	0812	5.9		0739	5.7
SU	1451	1.7	M	1417	1.6
	2027	5.9		1957	6.0
15	0316	1.5	**30**	0250	1.3
	0856	5.8		0830	5.8
M	1532	1.6	TU	1509	1.3
O	2107	6.1	●	2046	6.3

JULY

Day	Time	m	Day	Time	m
1	0340	1.0	**16**	0418	1.4
	0920	6.2		0954	5.8
W	1558	1.2	TH	1634	1.6
	2134	6.4		2203	6.0
2	0429	0.8	**17**	0452	1.3
	1009	6.3		1026	5.8
TH	1647	1.1	F	1704	1.6
	2223	6.5		2235	6.0
3	0517	0.7	**18**	0523	1.4
	1057	6.3		1056	5.8
F	1735	1.1	SA	1735	1.7
	2310	6.5		2306	5.9
4	0604	0.7	**19**	0553	1.4
	1144	6.3		1126	5.7
SA	1823	1.2	SU	1805	1.8
	2358	6.4		2337	5.8
5	0651	0.9	**20**	0623	1.6
	1230	6.1		1156	5.6
SU	1912	1.4	M	1837	1.9
6	0044	6.1	**21**	0009	5.6
	0739	1.2		0655	1.8
M	1317	5.8	TU	1229	5.4
	2002	1.7		1912	2.1
7	0132	5.8	**22**	0044	5.4
	0830	1.6		0731	2.0
TU	1408	5.5	W	1306	5.2
	2058	2.0		1955	2.3
8	0227	5.4	**23**	0126	5.1
	0927	2.0		0811	2.2
W	1508	5.3	TH	1353	5.1
	2202	2.2		2050	2.5
9	0333	5.1	**24**	0222	4.9
	1033	2.2		0915	2.5
TH	1618	5.2	F	1456	4.9
	2314	2.3		2203	2.6
10	0451	5.0	**25**	0338	4.8
	1146	2.3		1033	2.5
F	1731	5.2	SA	1619	5.0
				2324	2.5
11	0024	2.2	**26**	0507	4.9
	0607	5.1		1153	2.4
SA	1252	2.3	SU	1740	5.2
	1835	5.4			
12	0126	2.0	**27**	0037	2.1
	0711	5.3		0622	5.2
SU	1349	2.1	M	1301	2.0
	1929	5.6		1845	5.6
13	0219	1.8	**28**	0140	1.7
	0802	5.5		0722	5.7
M	1437	1.9	TU	1401	1.7
	2014	5.8		1941	6.0
14	0303	1.6	**29**	0237	1.2
	0844	5.7		0817	6.0
TU	1519	1.6	W	1455	1.3
O	2054	5.9	●	2033	6.4
15	0342	1.5	**30**	0309	0.9
	0921	5.8		0908	6.3
W	1557	1.7	TH	1546	1.0
	2130	6.0		2123	6.6
			31 F	0417	0.6
				0957	6.5
				1634	0.8
				2211	6.8

AUGUST

Day	Time	m	Day	Time	m
1	0503	0.5	**16**	0456	1.3
	1042	6.6		1028	6.0
SA	1720	0.8	SU	1708	1.5
	2256	6.8		2239	6.1
2	0547	0.5	**17**	0524	1.3
	1126	6.5		1055	5.9
SU	1804	0.9	M	1736	1.6
	2340	6.6		2308	6.0
3	0630	0.8	**18**	0552	1.4
	1207	6.3		1123	5.8
M	1848	1.2	TU	1805	1.7
				2337	5.8
4	0021	6.2	**19**	0621	1.6
	0712	1.2		1152	5.7
TU	1247	5.9	W	1838	1.9
	1932	1.6			
5	0108	5.8	**20**	0008	5.5
	0756	1.7		0654	1.9
W	1329	5.6	TH	1224	5.4
	2022	2.1		1916	2.2
6	0150	5.3	**21**	0045	5.2
	0847	2.2		0736	2.2
TH	1422	5.2	F	1306	5.2
	2123	2.4		2007	2.5
7	0256	4.9	**22**	0138	4.9
	0955	2.6		0832	2.5
F	1539	4.9	SA	1409	4.9
	2243	2.6		2120	2.6
8	0428	4.7	**23**	0302	4.7
	1120	2.7		0955	2.7
SA	1707	4.9	SU	1543	4.9
				2254	2.6
9	0005	2.5	**24**	0448	4.8
	0559	4.8		1130	2.5
SU	1236	2.6	M	1720	5.1
	1821	5.2			
10	0122	2.2	**25**	0018	2.2
	0703	5.1		0608	5.2
M	1336	2.3	TU	1246	2.1
	1915	5.5		1829	5.6
11	0204	1.9	**26**	0126	1.6
	0748	5.4		0708	5.7
TU	1420	2.0	W	1346	1.6
	1958	5.8		1925	6.1
12	0246	1.7	**27**	0220	1.1
	0826	5.7		0801	6.2
W	1502	1.8	TH	1440	1.2
	2035	6.0		2017	6.5
13	0323	1.5	**28**	0310	0.7
	0859	5.9		0851	6.5
TH	1537	1.6	F	1529	0.9
O	2109	6.1	●	2106	6.8
14	0356	1.3	**29**	0357	0.5
	0931	5.9		0937	6.7
F	1610	1.5	SA	1615	0.7
	2141	6.2		2152	6.9
15	0427	1.3	**30**	0441	0.4
	1000	6.0		1020	6.7
SA	1639	1.5	SU	1658	0.7
	2211	6.2		2235	6.9
			31 M	0522	0.6
				1100	6.6
				1739	0.8
				2315	6.6

GENERAL — Tidal streams in entrance — strong.

RATE AND SET — 5-10 M. N. of Cherbourg. E. going –0600 Dover, Sp. 4½ kn.; W. going –0015 Dover, Sp. 3½ kn. Between Cap de la Hague and Cherbourg outside all offshore dangers;

CHERBOURG 21:289

Lat. 49°39′N. Long. 1°38′W.

HIGH & LOW WATER 1992

TIME ZONE-0100 SUBTRACT 1 HOUR FROM TIMES SHOWN FOR GMT

SEPTEMBER

Day	Time	m		Time	m
1 TU	0602 / 1137 / 1819 / 2353	0.9 / 6.4 / 1.2 / 6.2	**16**	0522 / 1052 / W 1738 / 2310	1.4 / 6.0 / 1.6 / 5.9
2 W	0640 / 1213 / 1859	1.4 / 6.0 / 1.6	**17**	0552 / 1121 / TH 1811 / 2342	1.6 / 5.8 / 1.8 / 5.6
3 TH	0031 / 0720 / 1250 / 1944	5.7 / 1.9 / 5.6 / 2.1	**18**	0626 / 1154 / F 1849	1.9 / 5.6 / 2.1
4 F	0115 / 0806 / 1339 / 2042	5.2 / 2.5 / 5.1 / 2.6	**19**	0020 / 0709 / SA 1237 / 1940	5.3 / 2.3 / 5.3 / 2.4
5 SA	0220 / 0914 / 1458 / 2209	4.7 / 2.9 / 4.8 / 2.8	**20**	0117 / 0807 / SU 1343 / 2055	5.0 / 2.6 / 5.0 / 2.6
6 SU	0406 / 1054 / 1642 / 2342	4.6 / 3.0 / 4.8 / 2.7	**21**	0248 / 0935 / M 1524 / 2234	4.8 / 2.8 / 4.9 / 2.5
7 M	0544 / 1216 / 1759	4.7 / 2.8 / 5.0	**22**	0437 / 1114 / TU 1702	4.9 / 2.6 / 5.2
8 TU	0049 / 0642 / 1314 / 1851	2.4 / 5.1 / 2.4 / 5.4	**23**	0007 / 0552 / W 1229 / 1810	2.1 / 5.4 / 2.1 / 5.7
9 W	0139 / 0722 / 1359 / 1932	2.0 / 5.4 / 2.0 / 5.7	**24**	0105 / 0649 / TH 1328 / 1906	1.6 / 5.8 / 1.6 / 6.2
10 TH	0219 / 0757 / 1437 / 2008	1.7 / 5.7 / 1.8 / 6.0	**25**	0158 / 0740 / F 1420 / 1956	1.1 / 6.3 / 1.1 / 6.6
11 F	0255 / 0830 / 1510 / 2042	1.5 / 5.9 / 1.6 / 6.1	**26**	0247 / 0827 / SA 1507 / ● 2044	0.8 / 6.6 / 0.8 / 6.8
12 SA	0326 / 0901 / 1542 / O 2113	1.3 / 6.1 / 1.5 / 6.2	**27**	0333 / 0911 / SU 1552 / 2128	0.6 / 6.7 / 0.7 / 6.9
13 SU	0356 / 0930 / 1610 / 2142	1.3 / 6.1 / 1.4 / 6.2	**28**	0415 / 0952 / M 1633 / 2210	0.6 / 6.7 / 0.7 / 6.8
14 M	0425 / 0957 / 1639 / 2210	1.2 / 6.1 / 1.4 / 6.2	**29**	0455 / 1030 / TU 1713 / 2249	0.8 / 6.6 / 0.9 / 6.5
15 TU	0454 / 1024 / 1708 / 2240	1.3 / 6.1 / 1.4 / 6.1	**30**	0533 / 1106 / W 1751 / 2326	1.2 / 6.3 / 1.3 / 6.1

OCTOBER

Day	Time	m		Time	m
1 TH	0610 / 1140 / 1829	1.6 / 6.0 / 1.7	**16**	0532 / 1103 / F 1754 / 2330	1.7 / 6.0 / 1.7 / 5.7
2 F	0003 / 0647 / 1217 / 1910	5.6 / 2.1 / 5.6 / 2.2	**17**	0610 / 1141 / SA 1836	2.0 / 5.7 / 1.9
3 SA	0046 / 0731 / 1304 / 2003	5.2 / 2.6 / 5.1 / 2.6	**18**	0015 / 0657 / SU 1230 / 1930	5.4 / 2.3 / 5.4 / 2.2
4 SU	0147 / 0834 / 1417 / 2124	4.8 / 3.0 / 4.8 / 2.9	**19**	0115 / 0759 / M 1337 / 2043	5.1 / 2.6 / 5.2 / 2.4
5 M	0328 / 1017 / 1559 / 2300	4.6 / 3.1 / 4.7 / 2.8	**20**	0242 / 0924 / TU 1508 / 2215	4.9 / 2.7 / 5.1 / 2.4
6 TU	0503 / 1139 / 1718	4.7 / 2.9 / 4.9	**21**	0418 / 1055 / W 1638 / 2342	5.1 / 2.5 / 5.3 / 2.0
7 W	0010 / 0601 / 1238 / 1813	2.5 / 5.0 / 2.3 / 5.3	**22**	0529 / 1207 / TH 1746	5.5 / 2.1 / 5.7
8 TH	0101 / 0643 / 1324 / 1855	2.2 / 5.4 / 2.2 / 5.6	**23**	0040 / 0625 / F 1305 / 1842	1.6 / 5.9 / 1.6 / 6.1
9 F	0142 / 0719 / 1402 / 1933	1.9 / 5.7 / 1.9 / 5.9	**24**	0134 / 0715 / SA 1357 / 1933	1.2 / 6.3 / 1.3 / 6.5
10 SA	0218 / 0754 / 1436 / 2009	1.6 / 5.9 / 1.7 / 6.1	**25**	0223 / 0802 / SU 1445 / ● 2020	1.0 / 6.5 / 1.0 / 6.6
11 SU	0251 / 0827 / 1509 / 2042	1.4 / 6.1 / 1.5 / 6.2	**26**	0308 / 0845 / M 1529 / 2105	0.9 / 6.6 / 0.9 / 6.6
12 M	0323 / 0857 / 1540 / 2113	1.3 / 6.2 / 1.4 / 6.3	**27**	0350 / 0925 / TU 1610 / 2146	1.0 / 6.6 / 1.0 / 6.5
13 TU	0355 / 0926 / 1612 / 2145	1.3 / 6.2 / 1.3 / 6.2	**28**	0430 / 1002 / W 1649 / 2225	1.2 / 6.5 / 1.1 / 6.3
14 W	0426 / 0957 / 1645 / 2217	1.3 / 6.2 / 1.4 / 6.2	**29**	0507 / 1038 / TH 1727 / 2302	1.4 / 6.3 / 1.4 / 6.0
15 TH	0458 / 1028 / 1718 / 2252	1.5 / 6.1 / 1.5 / 6.0	**30**	0544 / 1114 / F 1804 / 2340	1.8 / 6.0 / 1.7 / 5.6
			31	0622 / 1152 / SA 1844	2.2 / 5.6 / 2.1

NOVEMBER

Day	Time	m		Time	m
1 SU	0022 / 0704 / 1237 / 1931	5.3 / 2.6 / 5.3 / 2.5	**16**	0014 / 0655 / M 1229 / 1928	5.6 / 2.1 / 5.7 / 1.9
2 M	0115 / 0757 / 1336 / 2033	4.9 / 2.9 / 4.9 / 2.7	**17**	0113 / 0756 / TU 1330 / 2033	5.4 / 2.4 / 5.4 / 2.1
3 TU	0230 / 0913 / 1457 / 2154	4.7 / 3.1 / 4.8 / 2.8	**18**	0226 / 0909 / W 1446 / 2150	5.2 / 2.5 / 5.3 / 2.2
4 W	0355 / 1042 / 1616 / 2310	4.7 / 3.0 / 4.8 / 2.7	**19**	0347 / 1027 / TH 1606 / 2310	5.3 / 2.4 / 5.4 / 2.0
5 TH	0502 / 1146 / 1719	4.9 / 2.7 / 5.1	**20**	0457 / 1139 / F 1715	5.5 / 2.1 / 5.6
6 F	0009 / 0553 / 1238 / 1809	2.4 / 5.2 / 2.4 / 5.4	**21**	0013 / 0556 / SA 1241 / 1816	1.8 / 5.8 / 1.8 / 5.9
7 SA	0056 / 0635 / 1321 / 1853	2.1 / 5.5 / 2.1 / 5.6	**22**	0109 / 0649 / SU 1335 / 1911	1.6 / 6.1 / 1.5 / 6.1
8 SU	0137 / 0714 / 1401 / 1933	1.9 / 5.8 / 1.8 / 5.9	**23**	0201 / 0737 / M 1425 / 2001	1.4 / 6.3 / 1.3 / 6.2
9 M	0214 / 0751 / 1437 / 2011	1.7 / 6.0 / 1.6 / 6.1	**24**	0247 / 0822 / TU 1510 / ● 2046	1.3 / 6.4 / 1.2 / 6.3
10 TU	0251 / 0826 / 1513 / O 2047	1.5 / 6.2 / 1.4 / 6.2	**25**	0329 / 0903 / W 1552 / 2128	1.4 / 6.4 / 1.2 / 6.2
11 W	0328 / 0900 / 1550 / 2124	1.4 / 6.3 / 1.3 / 6.2	**26**	0410 / 0941 / TH 1631 / 2207	1.5 / 6.4 / 1.3 / 6.1
12 TH	0404 / 0936 / 1627 / 2201	1.4 / 6.3 / 1.3 / 6.2	**27**	0448 / 1019 / F 1709 / 2244	1.6 / 6.2 / 1.4 / 6.0
13 F	0442 / 1013 / 1706 / 2242	1.5 / 6.3 / 1.3 / 6.1	**28**	0525 / 1048 / SA 1746 / 2322	1.8 / 6.0 / 1.6 / 5.7
14 SA	0521 / 1053 / 1747 / 2325	1.6 / 6.1 / 1.5 / 5.9	**29**	0602 / 1133 / SU 1823	2.1 / 5.8 / 1.9
15 SU	0605 / 1138 / 1833	1.9 / 5.9 / 1.7	**30**	0000 / 0641 / M 1212 / 1903	5.5 / 2.3 / 5.5 / 2.2

DECEMBER

Day	Time	m		Time	m
1 TU	0042 / 0724 / 1257 / 1948	5.2 / 2.6 / 5.2 / 2.4	**16**	0102 / 0745 / W 1316 / 2016	5.7 / 1.9 / 5.8 / 1.8
2 W	0132 / 0815 / 1351 / 2043	5.0 / 2.8 / 5.0 / 2.6	**17**	0200 / 0845 / TH 1417 / 2119	5.5 / 2.2 / 5.5 / 2.0
3 TH	0233 / 0919 / 1457 / 2149	4.8 / 2.9 / 4.9 / 2.7	**18**	0308 / 0953 / F 1528 / 2230	5.4 / 2.3 / 5.4 / 2.1
4 F	0342 / 1031 / 1607 / 2258	4.9 / 2.9 / 4.9 / 2.6	**19**	0419 / 1106 / SA 1643 / 2343	5.4 / 2.3 / 5.4 / 2.1
5 SA	0447 / 1139 / 1711	5.0 / 2.7 / 5.1	**20**	0526 / 1216 / SU 1753	5.5 / 2.1 / 5.5
6 SU	0000 / 0544 / 1238 / 1808	2.4 / 5.3 / 2.4 / 5.3	**21**	0047 / 0626 / M 1317 / 1855	2.0 / 5.7 / 1.9 / 5.7
7 M	0052 / 0633 / 1324 / 1858	2.2 / 5.6 / 2.1 / 5.6	**22**	0143 / 0720 / TU 1410 / 1949	1.8 / 5.9 / 1.7 / 5.8
8 TU	0139 / 0717 / 1407 / 1943	1.9 / 5.8 / 1.7 / 5.9	**23**	0232 / 0807 / W 1457 / 2035	1.7 / 6.1 / 1.5 / 6.0
9 W	0223 / 0759 / 1450 / O 2026	1.7 / 6.0 / 1.5 / 6.1	**24**	0316 / 0849 / TH 1539 / ● 2116	1.6 / 6.2 / 1.4 / 6.0
10 TH	0306 / 0840 / 1533 / 2108	1.5 / 6.3 / 1.3 / 6.2	**25**	0357 / 0928 / F 1618 / 2153	1.6 / 6.2 / 1.3 / 6.0
11 F	0349 / 0921 / 1616 / 2151	1.4 / 6.4 / 1.1 / 6.3	**26**	0435 / 1004 / SA 1654 / 2228	1.6 / 6.2 / 1.4 / 6.0
12 SA	0432 / 1004 / 1659 / 2235	1.4 / 6.4 / 1.1 / 6.2	**27**	0510 / 1039 / SU 1729 / 2302	1.7 / 6.1 / 1.5 / 5.9
13 SU	0516 / 1048 / 1744 / 2321	1.4 / 6.4 / 1.1 / 6.1	**28**	0544 / 1114 / M 1802 / 2336	1.8 / 6.0 / 1.6 / 5.7
14 M	0603 / 1133 / 1830	1.5 / 6.3 / 1.3	**29**	0617 / 1147 / TU 1835	2.0 / 5.8 / 1.8
15 TU	0010 / 0652 / 1223 / 1920	5.9 / 1.7 / 6.0 / 1.5	**30**	0009 / 0651 / W 1221 / 1910	5.5 / 2.2 / 5.5 / 2.0
			31	0044 / 0729 / TH 1259 / 1949	5.3 / 2.4 / 5.3 / 2.3

ESE. going. +0545 Dover, Sp. 4 kn.; WNW. going –0100 Dover, Sp. 4 kn. Grande Rade: SE. going +0415 Dover, Sp. 1½ kn.; WNW. going –0230 Dover. Sp. 1½ kn.
Counter current between Fort des Flamands and Port Militaire during SE. stream; W. going — Commercial Harbour; N. going — Port Militaire; SE. going — Digue du Homet.

TIDAL DIFFERENCES ON CHERBOURG

PLACE	TIME DIFFERENCES				HEIGHT DIFFERENCES (Metres)			
	High Water		Low Water		MHWS	MHWN	MLWN	MLWS
CHERBOURG	0300 and 1500	1000 and 2200	0400 and 1600	1000 and 2200	6.3	5.0	2.5	1.1
Rade de la Capelle	+0110	+0055	+0125	+0115	+0.9	+0.9	+0.2	+0.2
St. Vaast	+0105	+0055	+0120	+0100	+0.3	+0.4	−0.2	−0.2
Barfleur	+0100	+0100	+0050	−0040	+0.3	+0.3	+0.1	+0.1
Omonville	−0015	−0010	−0020	−0025	−0.1	0.0	+0.1	+0.0
Goury	−0100	−0045	−0110	−0120	+1.6	+1.5	+1.0	+0.1

Note: Time zone. The predictions for the standard port are on the same time zone as the differences shown. No further adjustment is necessary.

Refer to predictions on pages 21:287-21:289

TIDAL DIFFERENCES ON LE HAVRE

PLACE	TIME DIFFERENCES				HEIGHT DIFFERENCES (Metres)			
	High Water		Low Water		MHWS	MHWN	MLWN	MLWS
LE HAVRE	0000 and 1200	0500 and 1700	0000 and 1200	0700 and 1900	7.9	6.6	3.0	1.2
La Seine								
Honfleur	−0140	−0135	+0005	+0040	−0.1	−0.2	−0.1	+0.2
Tancarville	−0105	−0100	+0105	+0140	−0.1	−0.1	−0.2	+1.0
Quillebeouf	−0045	−0050	+0120	+0200	0.0	0.0	0.0	+1.4
Vatteville...................	+0005	−0020	+0225	+0250	0.0	−0.1	+0.6	+2.3
Caudebec	+0020	−0015	+0230	+0300	−0.3	−0.2	+0.7	+2.4
Heurteauville.............	+0110	+0030	+0310	+0330	−0.5	−0.2	+0.9	+2.7
Duclair......................	+0225	+0150	+0355	+0410	−0.4	−0.3	+1.2	+3.3
Rouen	+0440	+0415	+0525	+0525	−0.2	−0.1	+1.4	+3.6
Trouville	−0035	−0015	0000	−0010	−0.2	−0.2	−0.2	−0.1
Dives	−0055	−	−	−0115	−0.5	−0.5	−0.6	−0.4
Ouistreham	−0020	−0010	−0005	−0010	−0.3	−0.3	·−0.3	−0.2
Courseulles	−0030	−	−	−0020	−0.8	−1.0	−0.7	−0.3
Port-en-Bessen...........	−0045	−0040	−0040	−0045	−0.7	−0.6	−0.3	−0.1

In La Seine double high waters occur near Springs in the river below Duclair. The time differences refer to the first high water. The second high water occurs about 2h. 20 min. later.
Note: Time zone. The predictions for the standard port are on the same time zone as the differences shown. No further adjustment is necessary.

Refer to predictions on pages 21:292-21:294

LE HAVRE

MEAN SPRING AND NEAP CURVES
Springs occur 2 days after New and Full Moon.

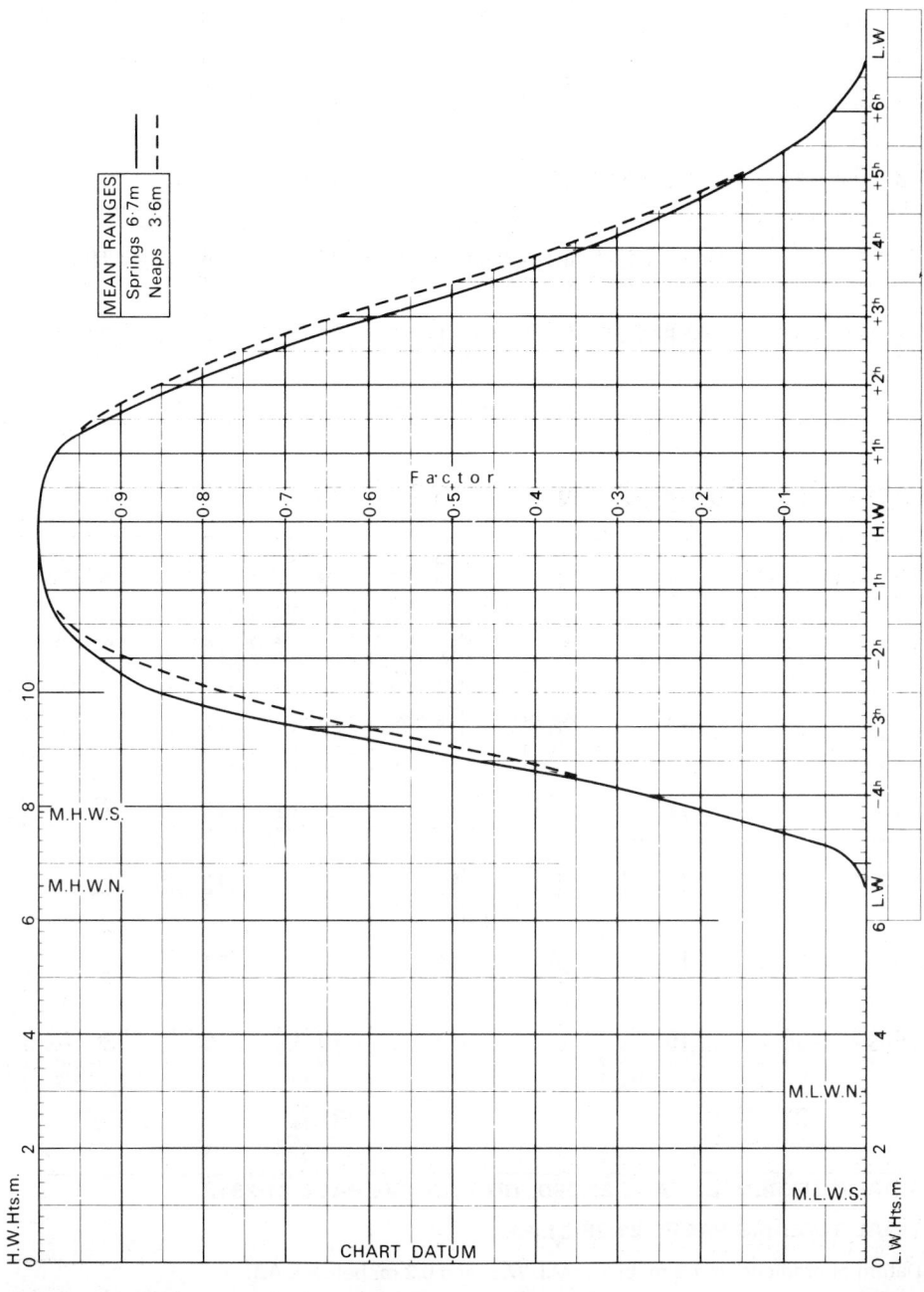

21:292 FRANCE, NORTH COAST LE HAVRE

HIGH & LOW WATER 1992 Lat. 49°29'N. Long. 0°07'E.

TIME ZONE-0100 SUBTRACT 1 HOUR FROM TIMES SHOWN FOR GMT

(Note: ● = new moon, O = full moon. Times in hours; m = height in metres.)

JANUARY

Days 1–15

Day	Time	m	Time	m		Time	m	Time	m
1	0224	2.8	0808	6.9	W	1459	2.6	2042	6.8
2	0325	2.6	0902	7.1	TH	1555	2.4	2132	7.0
3	0416	2.4	0946	7.3	F	1642	2.1	2214	7.2
4	0500	2.2	1024	7.4	SA	1723	1.9	● 2251	7.3
5	0540	2.0	1058	7.5	SU	1801	1.7	2323	7.4
6	0618	1.9	1131	7.6	M	1838	1.6	2356	7.4
7	0653	1.9	1204	7.6	TU	1911	1.6		
8	0028	7.4	0725	1.9	W	1236	7.5	1942	1.7
9	0100	7.4	0756	2.0	TH	1308	7.5	2012	1.8
10	0131	7.3	0826	2.1	F	1341	7.3	2042	2.0
11	0205	7.2	0857	2.3	SA	1416	7.2	2113	2.2
12	0241	7.0	0933	2.5	SU	1456	6.9	2150	2.5
13	0324	6.8	1016	2.8	M	1544	6.7	2237	2.7
14	0417	6.7	1112	2.9	TU	1647	6.6	2339	2.9
15	0530	6.6	1224	3.0	W	1814	6.5		

Days 16–31

Day	Time	m	Time	m		Time	m	Time	m
16	0059	2.9	0656	6.7	TH	1353	2.7	1936	6.7
17	0229	2.6	0806	7.0	F	1511	2.2	2044	7.1
18	0340	2.1	0906	7.4	SA	1616	1.7	2142	7.5
19	0442	1.7	1000	7.7	SU	1717	1.2	O 2234	7.8
20	0542	1.3	1051	8.0	M	1815	0.9	2324	8.0
21	0637	1.0	1139	8.1	TU	1906	0.6		
22	0011	8.1	0726	0.9	W	1226	8.2	1952	0.6
23	0057	8.1	0810	0.9	TH	1311	8.1	2033	0.8
24	0141	7.9	0849	1.2	F	1354	7.9	2110	1.2
25	0223	7.6	0926	1.6	SA	1437	7.5	2145	1.7
26	0305	7.3	1003	2.1	SU	1521	7.1	2221	2.3
27	0352	6.9	1044	2.6	M	1615	6.7	2307	2.8
28	0453	6.6	1136	3.0	TU	1729	6.3		
29	0014	3.2	0615	6.4	W	1300	3.2	1909	6.2
30	0142	3.3	0743	6.5	TH	1426	3.0	2026	6.4
31	0259	3.0	0845	6.7	F	1534	2.6	2119	6.7

FEBRUARY

Days 1–15

Day	Time	m	Time	m		Time	m	Time	m
1	0400	2.6	0931	7.0	SA	1627	2.2	2159	7.0
2	0448	2.2	1008	7.3	SU	1710	1.9	2233	7.3
3	0528	1.9	1040	7.5	M	1748	1.6	● 2303	7.4
4	0605	1.7	1111	7.6	TU	1823	1.5	2334	7.5
5	0638	1.6	1143	7.7	W	1854	1.4		
6	0005	7.6	0708	1.5	TH	1215	7.7	1923	1.4
7	0035	7.6	0736	1.6	F	1246	7.7	1952	1.4
8	0106	7.5	0805	1.7	SA	1317	7.6	2020	1.6
9	0138	7.4	0835	1.8	SU	1351	7.4	2049	1.8
10	0210	7.2	0907	2.1	M	1426	7.2	2121	2.4
11	0246	7.0	0942	2.4	TU	1506	6.9	2200	2.5
12	0333	6.8	1028	2.7	W	1607	6.5	2258	2.9
13	0444	6.5	1144	3.0	TH	1743	6.4		
14	0022	3.1	0627	6.5	F	1323	2.8	1919	6.6
15	0207	2.8	0749	6.8	SA	1452	2.3	2032	7.0

Days 16–29

Day	Time	m	Time	m		Time	m	Time	m
16	0325	2.2	0854	7.5	SU	1603	1.7	2131	7.5
17	0433	1.6	0949	7.7	M	1708	1.1	2222	7.8
18	0534	1.1	1038	8.0	TU	1804	0.7	O 2308	8.1
19	0625	0.8	1123	8.2	W	1851	0.4	2352	8.2
20	0710	0.6	1207	8.3	TH	1932	0.4		
21	0034	8.1	0749	0.7	F	1249	8.2	2009	0.7
22	0114	8.0	0824	1.0	SA	1329	7.9	2042	1.1
23	0152	7.7	0856	1.4	SU	1407	7.5	2111	1.7
24	0228	7.3	0926	2.0	M	1446	7.1	2140	2.3
25	0307	6.9	1000	2.5	TU	1533	6.6	2219	2.9
26	0401	6.5	1049	3.0	W	1643	6.1	2321	3.4
27	0525	6.1	1207	3.4	TH	1833	6.0		
28	0059	3.6	0709	6.1	F	1347	3.3	2001	6.2
29	0230	3.2	0820	6.6	SA	1505	2.8	2056	6.6

MARCH

Days 1–15

Day	Time	m	Time	m		Time	m	Time	m
1	0337	2.7	0907	6.8	SU	1602	2.3	2134	6.9
2	0427	2.2	0942	7.1	M	1647	1.9	2206	7.2
3	0507	1.8	1014	7.4	TU	1726	1.6	2236	7.4
4	0543	1.6	1046	7.6	W	1800	1.4	● 2307	7.6
5	0615	1.4	1118	7.7	TH	1830	1.3	2338	7.7
6	0644	1.3	1150	7.8	F	1859	1.2		
7	0009	7.7	0713	1.3	SA	1223	7.8	1928	1.2
8	0041	7.7	0744	1.3	SU	1256	7.7	1958	1.4
9	0113	7.6	0815	1.5	M	1331	7.5	2028	1.7
10	0147	7.4	0847	1.8	TU	1408	7.2	2100	2.1
11	0223	7.2	0922	2.2	W	1452	6.8	2139	2.5
12	0311	6.8	1011	2.6	TH	1554	6.5	2238	2.9
13	0426	6.5	1124	2.9	F	1735	6.4		
14	0007	3.1	0613	6.5	SA	1306	2.7	1907	6.6
15	0153	2.7	0734	6.8	SU	1436	2.2	2018	7.1

Days 16–31

Day	Time	m	Time	m		Time	m	Time	m
16	0312	2.1	0839	7.3	M	1549	1.6	2115	7.5
17	0419	1.5	0932	7.7	TU	1652	1.1	2202	7.8
18	0517	1.0	1019	8.0	W	1744	0.7	O 2246	8.0
19	0605	0.8	1102	8.1	TH	1828	0.5	2328	8.1
20	0647	0.7	1144	8.1	F	1907	0.6		
21	0008	8.1	0723	0.8	SA	1225	8.0	1941	0.9
22	0046	7.9	0756	1.0	SU	1304	7.8	2011	1.3
23	0122	7.7	0827	1.4	M	1341	7.4	2039	1.8
24	0157	7.3	0855	1.9	TU	1419	7.0	2106	2.4
25	0234	6.9	0926	2.4	W	1503	6.5	2143	2.9
26	0322	6.4	1010	2.9	TH	1606	6.1	2242	3.4
27	0439	6.1	1122	3.3	F	1744	5.9		
28	0014	3.6	0618	6.0	SA	1258	3.3	1913	6.1
29	0146	3.3	0735	6.2	SU	1417	2.9	2014	6.5
30	0254	2.8	0828	6.6	M	1518	2.4	2056	6.9
31	0347	2.3	0907	7.0	TU	1608	2.0	2130	7.2

APRIL

Days 1–15

Day	Time	m	Time	m		Time	m	Time	m
1	0431	1.9	0942	7.3	W	1650	1.6	2203	7.4
2	0510	1.6	1016	7.5	TH	1727	1.4	2236	7.6
3	0544	1.4	1051	7.7	F	1759	1.3	● 2309	7.7
4	0616	1.3	1125	7.7	SA	1831	1.2	2342	7.7
5	0649	1.2	1200	7.8	SU	1904	1.2		
6	0016	7.7	0723	1.2	M	1237	7.7	1938	1.4
7	0052	7.6	0758	1.4	TU	1316	7.5	2012	1.6
8	0131	7.4	0833	1.6	W	1359	7.2	2047	2.0
9	0213	7.2	0912	2.0	TH	1448	6.9	2131	2.4
10	0306	6.9	1003	2.4	F	1555	6.6	2233	2.8
11	0423	6.6	1118	2.6	SA	1729	6.6		
12	0003	2.9	0558	6.6	SU	1254	2.5	1850	6.8
13	0136	2.5	0714	6.9	M	1416	2.1	1957	7.2
14	0251	2.0	0817	7.3	TU	1525	1.6	2052	7.5
15	0355	1.6	0910	7.6	W	1626	1.2	2139	7.7

Days 16–30

Day	Time	m	Time	m		Time	m	Time	m
16	0451	1.2	0957	7.8	TH	1717	1.0	2222	7.9
17	0539	1.0	1040	7.9	F	1759	0.9	O 2303	7.9
18	0619	0.9	1122	7.9	SA	1837	1.0	2342	7.9
19	0655	1.0	1203	7.8	SU	1911	1.2		
20	0019	7.8	0729	1.2	M	1242	7.6	1942	1.5
21	0056	7.6	0759	1.5	TU	1320	7.3	2012	1.9
22	0132	7.3	0829	1.9	W	1358	7.0	2042	2.4
23	0209	6.9	0901	2.3	TH	1440	6.6	2118	2.8
24	0253	6.5	0943	2.7	F	1534	6.3	2212	3.2
25	0354	6.2	1044	3.1	SA	1651	6.1	2329	3.4
26	0520	6.1	1203	3.1	SU	1811	6.2		
27	0048	3.3	0635	6.2	M	1317	2.9	1916	6.4
28	0156	2.9	0735	6.5	TU	1421	2.5	2007	6.8
29	0254	2.5	0823	6.8	W	1515	2.2	2048	7.1
30	0344	2.1	0905	7.1	TH	1603	1.9	2127	7.3

TIDAL DIFFERENCES PAGE 21:290. TIDAL CURVE PAGE 21:291.

TIDAL STREAMS PAGES 21:28-21:40.

Datum of predictions: 1.2 m. below M.L.W.S. and 0.3 m. below L.A.T.

LE HAVRE FRANCE, NORTH COAST 21:293

Lat. 49°29'N. Long. 0°07'E. HIGH & LOW WATER 1992

TIME ZONE-0100 SUBTRACT 1 HOUR FROM TIMES SHOWN FOR GMT

MAY

Day	Time	m	Day	Time	m
1 F	0428	1.8	16	0509	1.4
	0944	7.4	SA	1022	7.6
	1646	1.6		1729	1.4
	2203	7.5	O	2241	7.7
2 SA	0509	1.5	17	0551	1.3
	1022	7.5	SU	1104	7.6
	1725	1.5		1808	1.5
●	2240	7.6		2320	7.7
3 SU	0547	1.3	18	0628	1.3
	1101	7.6	M	1145	7.6
	1804	1.3		1844	1.6
	2317	7.7		2358	7.6
4 M	0627	1.2	19	0704	1.4
	1140	7.7		1223	7.5
	1843	1.3	TU	1918	1.7
	2356	7.7			
5 TU	0706	1.1	20	0035	7.5
	1222	7.7		0737	1.5
	1922	1.4	W	1302	7.3
				1951	2.0
6 W	0037	7.7	21	0111	7.3
	0746	1.2		0810	1.8
	1306	7.5	TH	1340	7.1
	2002	1.6		2025	2.3
7 TH	0121	7.5	22	0149	7.0
	0826	1.5		0843	2.1
	1354	7.3	F	1418	6.8
	2044	1.9		2101	2.6
8 F	0208	7.3	23	0228	6.8
	0911	1.8		0920	2.4
	1447	7.1	SA	1501	6.6
	2133	2.2		2144	2.9
9 SA	0304	7.1	24	0313	6.5
	1006	2.1		1006	2.7
	1554	6.9	SU	1553	6.4
	2236	2.5		2239	3.1
10 SU	0416	6.8	25	0412	6.3
	1116	2.3		1105	2.9
	1712	6.8	M	1701	6.3
	2354	2.5		2343	3.1
11 M	0535	6.8	26	0524	6.3
	1233	2.2		1209	2.9
	1824	7.0	TU	1810	6.4
12 TU	0111	2.4	27	0048	3.0
	0645	6.9		0613	6.4
	1346	2.0	W	1313	2.7
	1928	7.2		1910	6.7
13 W	0221	2.1	28	0151	2.7
	0750	7.2		0731	6.7
	1453	1.8	TH	1415	2.5
	2025	7.4		2001	6.9
14 TH	0324	1.8	29	0250	2.4
	0846	7.3		0823	6.9
	1553	1.6	F	1512	2.2
	2115	7.6		2047	7.2
15 F	0421	1.5	30	0344	2.0
	0936	7.5		0910	7.2
	1645	1.5	SA	1605	1.9
	2159	7.7		2131	7.4
			31	0434	1.7
				0955	7.4
			SU	1654	1.7
				2213	7.6

JUNE

Day	Time	m	Day	Time	m
1 M	0522	1.4	16	0605	1.6
	1040	7.5		1130	7.4
	1741	1.5	TU	1822	1.8
●	2256	7.7		2340	7.5
2 TU	0609	1.2	17	0643	1.5
	1125	7.7		1207	7.4
	1828	1.4	W	1859	1.8
	2340	7.8			
3 W	0655	1.1	18	0016	7.5
	1212	7.7		0719	1.6
	1914	1.3	TH	1243	7.3
				1935	1.9
4 TH	0026	7.8	19	0051	7.4
	0742	1.1		0753	1.7
	1259	7.7	F	1318	7.2
	2001	1.4		2008	2.1
5 F	0114	7.7	20	0126	7.2
	0828	1.2		0826	1.9
	1349	7.5	SA	1353	7.1
	2048	1.6		2042	2.3
6 SA	0204	7.5	21	0201	7.1
	0916	1.4		0858	2.1
	1442	7.4	SU	1428	6.9
	2138	1.8		2115	2.5
7 SU	0257	7.3	22	0237	6.9
	1006	1.7		0932	2.3
	1540	7.2	M	1506	6.8
	2232	2.1		2154	2.7
8 M	0358	7.1	23	0320	6.7
	1102	1.9		1012	2.5
	1644	7.0	TU	1552	6.6
	2332	2.3		2242	2.8
9 TU	0504	6.9	24	0412	6.5
	1204	2.1		1103	2.7
	1749	7.0	W	1650	6.6
				2340	2.9
10 W	0038	2.3	25	0517	6.5
	0612	6.9		1205	2.8
	1311	2.2	TH	1800	6.6
	1855	7.1			
11 TH	0146	2.3	26	0046	2.9
	0722	6.9		0632	6.5
	1418	2.2	F	1315	2.7
	1958	7.2		1909	6.7
12 F	0251	2.1	27	0159	2.6
	0826	7.0		0741	6.7
	1519	2.1	SA	1427	2.5
	2053	7.3		2009	7.0
13 SA	0350	2.0	28	0306	2.2
	0921	7.2		0840	7.0
	1614	2.0	SU	1531	2.2
	2141	7.4		2102	7.2
14 SU	0441	1.8	29	0405	1.8
	1009	7.3		0934	7.3
	1701	1.9	M	1629	1.8
	2224	7.5		2152	7.5
15 M	0525	1.7	30	0501	1.4
	1052	7.4		1024	7.5
	1743	1.8	TU	1724	1.5
O	2303	7.5	●	2240	7.7

JULY

Day	Time	m	Day	Time	m
1 W	0556	1.1	16	0627	1.5
	1113	7.7		1147	7.4
	1819	1.3	TH	1844	1.7
	2328	7.9		2355	7.6
2 TH	0649	0.9	17	0702	1.5
	1202	7.8		1219	7.4
	1911	1.1	F	1917	1.7
3 F	0017	7.9	18	0028	7.5
	0739	0.8		0734	1.5
	1250	7.9	SA	1252	7.4
	2000	1.1		1948	1.8
4 SA	0105	7.9	19	0101	7.5
	0826	0.8		0804	1.6
	1338	7.8	SU	1324	7.3
	2045	1.2		2017	1.9
5 SU	0152	7.8	20	0132	7.3
	0910	1.0		0832	1.8
	1426	7.7	M	1355	7.2
	2129	1.4		2046	2.1
6 M	0240	7.6	21	0205	7.2
	0953	1.4		0900	2.0
	1515	7.4	TU	1428	7.1
	2213	1.8		2118	2.3
7 TU	0331	7.3	22	0242	7.0
	1037	1.8		0933	2.3
	1608	7.1	W	1507	6.9
	2302	2.1		2156	2.6
8 W	0428	7.0	23	0325	6.7
	1128	2.2		1014	2.6
	1708	6.9	TH	1554	6.7
				2246	2.8
9 TH	0000	2.5	24	0421	6.5
	0533	6.7		1109	2.9
	1232	2.6	F	1656	6.6
	1819	6.8		2352	3.0
10 F	0110	2.6	25	0539	6.4
	0656	6.6		1223	3.0
	1344	2.7	SA	1821	6.6
	1934	6.8			
11 SA	0222	2.5	26	0117	2.8
	0813	6.7		0708	6.5
	1451	2.6	SU	1353	2.8
	2037	7.0		1939	6.8
12 SU	0325	2.3	27	0238	2.4
	0918	6.9		0818	6.9
	1550	2.4	M	1509	2.3
	2128	7.2		2041	7.2
13 M	0420	2.1	28	0345	1.9
	0959	7.1		0918	7.3
	1642	2.2	TU	1612	1.8
	2211	7.3		2136	7.5
14 TU	0508	1.9	29	0447	1.4
	1039	7.3		1010	7.6
	1713	2.0	W	1713	1.4
O	2248	7.5	●	2227	7.8
15 W	0549	1.7	30	0547	1.0
	1114	7.4		1100	7.9
	1807	1.8	TH	1810	1.1
	2322	7.5		2315	8.1
			31	0641	0.7
				1147	8.0
			F	1902	0.9

AUGUST

Day	Time	m	Day	Time	m
1 SA	0002	8.2	16	0002	7.7
	0728	0.5		0710	1.4
	1233	8.1	SU	1223	7.5
	1948	0.8		1923	1.6
2 SU	0048	8.1	17	0033	7.6
	0811	0.6		0737	1.5
	1318	8.0	M	1253	7.5
	2029	0.9		1951	1.7
3 M	0133	8.0	18	0104	7.5
	0851	0.9		0805	1.6
	1402	7.8	TU	1323	7.4
	2108	1.3		2019	1.9
4 TU	0217	7.7	19	0136	7.3
	0928	1.3		0833	1.9
	1445	7.5	W	1355	7.2
	2146	1.7		2050	2.1
5 W	0301	7.3	20	0211	7.1
	1005	1.9		0905	2.2
	1530	7.1	TH	1431	7.0
	2227	2.2		2124	2.4
6 TH	0352	6.9	21	0251	6.8
	1048	2.5		0939	2.6
	1626	6.8	F	1514	6.7
	2320	2.7		2200	2.7
7 F	0501	6.5	22	0345	6.5
	1150	3.0		1030	2.9
	1742	6.5	SA	1615	6.5
				2311	3.0
8 SA	0034	3.0	23	0507	6.3
	0635	6.3		1145	3.1
	1313	3.1	SU	1749	6.4
	1913	6.5			
9 SU	0157	2.9	24	0046	3.0
	0801	6.5		0648	6.4
	1430	3.0	M	1330	3.0
	2023	6.7		1918	6.7
10 M	0307	2.6	25	0219	2.5
	0900	6.7		0802	6.9
	1536	2.6	TU	1453	2.4
	2114	7.0		2025	7.2
11 TU	0406	2.2	26	0329	1.8
	0944	7.0		0903	7.4
	1630	2.3	W	1558	1.8
	2154	7.3		2121	7.6
12 W	0454	1.9	27	0433	1.3
	1020	7.3		0954	7.8
	1713	2.0	TH	1700	1.3
	2228	7.5		2210	8.0
13 TH	0533	1.6	28	0532	0.8
	1051	7.4		1041	8.0
	1750	1.7	F	1756	0.9
O	2259	7.6	●	2257	8.2
14 F	0608	1.5	29	0624	0.5
	1121	7.5		1127	8.2
	1824	1.6	SA	1844	0.7
	2330	7.7		2342	8.3
15 SA	0641	1.4	30	0708	0.4
	1152	7.5		1210	8.2
	1855	1.6	SU	1927	0.7
			31	0026	8.2
				0748	0.6
			M	1253	8.1
				2006	0.9

At Le Havre there is a stand of about 2 h. around H.W. In the R. Seine below Rouen double High Waters occur; and in the R. Seine Estuary a stand of about 2 h. occurs and generally the fall of tide for about the first 2 h. after H.W. is barely discernible.

GENERAL — At Springs: double H.W. with fall and rise between period 2 h. At Neaps: prolonged stand 3 h. Max. fall in 2¾ h. after H.W. approx. 8 in. Stream in Seine decreases inwards.

21:294 FRANCE, NORTH COAST **LE HAVRE**

HIGH & LOW WATER 1992   Lat. 49°29′N. Long. 0°07′E.

TIME ZONE-0100 SUBTRACT 1 HOUR FROM TIMES SHOWN FOR GMT

SEPTEMBER

	Time	m		Time	m
1 TU	0109 0324 1333 2041	8.0 1.0 7.9 1.3	**16** W	0037 0739 1254 1955	7.6 1.6 7.5 1.7
2 W	0150 0858 1413 2115	7.7 1.5 7.5 1.8	**17** TH	0111 0809 1327 2027	7.4 1.9 7.3 2.0
3 TH	0232 0930 1454 2151	7.2 2.1 7.1 2.4	**18** F	0148 0840 1404 2101	7.1 2.2 7.1 2.3
4 F	0320 1009 1546 2239	6.8 2.8 6.7 2.9	**19** SA	0231 0916 1449 2141	6.8 2.6 6.8 2.7
5 SA	0428 1110 1705 2356	6.3 3.3 6.3 3.2	**20** SU	0327 1007 1554 2249	6.5 3.0 6.6 3.0
6 SU	0610 1243 1846	6.1 3.5 6.3	**21** M	0455 1127 1733	6.4 3.2 6.5
7 M	0129 0741 1408 2001	3.1 6.3 3.2 6.5	**22** TU	0028 0633 1316 1900	2.9 6.6 2.9 6.8
8 TU	0243 0840 1515 2052	2.7 6.7 2.7 6.9	**23** W	0202 0745 1436 2006	2.4 7.0 2.3 7.2
9 W	0341 0920 1606 2129	2.3 7.0 2.2 7.2	**24** TH	0312 0843 1541 2101	1.8 7.5 1.7 7.2
10 TH	0427 0953 1647 2201	1.9 7.3 7.5	**25** F	0414 0933 1640 2150	1.2 7.9 1.2 8.0
11 F	0506 1022 1725 2231	1.6 7.5 1.7 7.6	**26** SA	0510 1019 1734 ● 2236	0.8 8.1 0.9 8.2
12 SA	0542 1052 1758 ○ 2302	1.5 7.6 1.5 7.7	**27** SU	0559 1102 1820 2320	0.6 8.2 0.8 8.3
13 SU	0613 1122 1827 2334	1.4 7.6 1.5 7.8	**28** M	0642 1145 1902	0.7 8.2 0.8
14 M	0641 1153 1856	1.4 7.7 1.5	**29** TU	0003 0721 1226 1939	8.2 0.9 8.1 1.4
15 TU	0005 0709 1223 1925	7.7 1.4 7.6 1.6	**30** W	0045 0756 1305 2013	8.0 1.2 7.8 1.4

OCTOBER

	Time	m		Time	m
1 TH	0126 0828 1343 2045	7.6 1.8 7.5 1.9	**16** F	0053 0750 1307 2011	7.5 1.9 7.4 1.9
2 F	0207 0859 1423 2119	7.2 2.3 7.1 2.4	**17** SA	0135 0825 1349 2048	7.3 2.2 7.2 2.2
3 SA	0253 0936 1513 2204	6.7 2.9 6.6 2.9	**18** SU	0222 0906 1439 2134	7.0 2.6 6.9 2.5
4 SU	0356 1034 1626 2315	6.3 3.4 6.3 3.3	**19** M	0321 1000 1544 2240	6.7 2.9 6.7 2.8
5 M	0529 1204 1800	6.1 3.6 6.2	**20** TU	0447 1120 1717	6.6 3.1 6.6
6 TU	0047 0658 1330 1920	3.3 6.5 3.3 6.4	**21** W	0013 0614 1257 1837	2.8 6.8 2.8 6.9
7 W	0202 0801 1435 2014	2.9 6.6 2.8 6.7	**22** TH	0140 0722 1414 1942	2.3 7.1 2.3 7.3
8 TH	0259 0843 1527 2054	2.5 7.0 2.4 7.1	**23** F	0249 0820 1518 2038	1.8 7.5 1.8 7.6
9 F	0348 0917 1612 2128	2.1 7.3 2.0 7.4	**24** SA	0349 0910 1616 2128	1.4 7.9 1.4 7.9
10 SA	0431 0948 1651 2201	1.8 7.5 1.7 7.6	**25** SU	0444 0955 1708 ● 2215	1.1 8.0 1.1 8.0
11 SU	0508 1020 1726 ○ 2234	1.6 7.6 1.6 7.7	**26** M	0532 1039 1754 2259	1.0 8.1 1.1 8.1
12 M	0541 1052 1758 2307	1.5 7.7 1.5 7.7	**27** TU	0614 1120 1835 2342	1.1 8.0 1.1 8.0
13 TU	0611 1123 1829 2341	1.5 7.7 1.5 7.7	**28** W	0652 1201 1912	1.2 8.0 1.2
14 W	0643 1156 1902	1.5 7.7 1.5	**29** TH	0024 0728 1240 1947	7.8 1.5 7.8 1.5
15 TH	0015 0716 1230 1936	7.7 1.6 7.6 1.6	**30** F	0105 0801 1318 2020	7.5 1.9 7.5 1.9
			31 SA	0146 0834 1358 2054	7.2 2.4 7.1 2.4

NOVEMBER

	Time	m		Time	m
1 SU	0230 0912 1443 2135	6.8 2.9 6.7 2.8	**16** M	0217 0905 1432 2133	7.2 2.3 7.2 2.2
2 M	0323 1003 1543 2232	6.5 3.3 6.4 3.1	**17** TU	0316 1000 1535 2236	7.0 2.6 7.0 2.4
3 TU	0435 1113 1701 2347	6.3 3.5 6.2 3.3	**18** W	0430 1111 1653 2351	6.9 2.7 6.9 2.5
4 W	0554 1232 1817	6.3 3.4 6.3	**19** TH	0545 1229 1807	7.0 2.6 7.0
5 TH	0102 0700 1341 1920	3.1 6.5 3.1 6.5	**20** F	0109 0652 1345 1914	2.3 7.2 2.3 7.2
6 F	0207 0752 1439 2009	2.8 6.8 2.7 6.9	**21** SA	0219 0753 1451 2015	2.0 7.4 2.0 7.4
7 SA	0301 0834 1529 2051	2.4 7.1 2.3 7.2	**22** SU	0321 0846 1550 2110	1.8 7.7 1.7 7.6
8 SU	0348 0911 1613 2129	2.1 7.4 2.0 7.4	**23** M	0416 0934 1643 2159	1.6 7.8 1.5 7.7
9 M	0430 0947 1652 2206	1.9 7.6 1.8 7.6	**24** TU	0505 1019 ● 2244	1.5 7.9 1.4 7.8
10 TU	0507 1022 1729 ○ 2243	1.7 7.7 1.6 7.7	**25** W	0548 1101 1811 2327	1.5 7.9 1.3 7.8
11 W	0544 1057 1806 2320	1.6 7.7 1.5 7.7	**26** TH	0628 1141 1850	1.6 7.8 1.4
12 TH	0621 1134 1844 2359	1.6 7.8 1.4 7.7	**27** F	0008 0705 1220 1926	7.7 1.7 7.7 1.6
13 F	0700 1213 1923	1.6 7.7 1.5	**28** SA	0046 0741 1258 2000	7.5 2.0 7.5 1.8
14 SA	0041 0739 1255 2003	7.6 1.8 7.6 1.7	**29** SU	0126 0816 1336 2034	7.3 2.3 7.3 2.1
15 SU	0127 0819 1341 2045	7.4 2.1 7.4 1.9	**30** M	0205 0852 1415 2110	7.0 2.6 7.0 2.5

DECEMBER

	Time	m		Time	m
1 TU	0246 0932 1458 2152	6.7 2.9 6.7 2.8	**16** W	0303 0956 1518 2224	7.3 2.1 7.3 2.0
2 W	0335 1020 1552 2243	6.5 3.2 6.4 3.0	**17** TH	0402 1051 1622 2321	7.1 2.4 7.1 2.3
3 TH	0438 1119 1701 2344	6.4 3.3 6.3 3.1	**18** F	0509 1154 1732	7.0 2.5 6.9
4 F	0549 1224 1813	6.4 3.3 6.4	**19** SA	0030 0617 1308 1845	2.4 7.0 2.5 6.9
5 SA	0051 0652 1332 1916	3.1 6.6 3.1 6.6	**20** SU	0145 0725 1422 1956	2.4 7.1 2.4 7.0
6 SU	0159 0746 1436 2010	2.8 6.8 2.7 6.8	**21** M	0254 0827 1527 2058	2.3 7.3 2.1 7.2
7 M	0259 0833 1531 2057	2.5 7.1 2.3 7.1	**22** TU	0353 0920 1623 2150	2.1 7.5 1.9 7.4
8 TU	0351 0916 1619 2140	2.2 7.4 2.0 7.4	**23** W	0445 1006 1711 2235	1.9 7.6 1.7 7.5
9 W	0437 1001 1704 ○ 2222	1.9 7.6 1.7 7.5	**24** TH	0530 1048 1754 ● 2316	1.9 7.7 1.5 7.5
10 TH	0522 1037 1748 2305	1.8 7.7 1.4 7.6	**25** F	0610 1126 1833 2353	1.8 7.7 1.3 7.6
11 F	0606 1118 1833 2348	1.6 7.8 1.3 7.7	**26** SA	0648 1202 1909	1.8 7.7 1.5
12 SA	0651 1201 1918	1.5 7.9 1.2	**27** SU	0029 0724 1238 1943	7.5 1.9 7.6 1.6
13 SU	0033 0736 1247 2003	7.7 1.5 7.8 1.3	**28** M	0103 0758 1313 2015	7.4 2.0 7.5 1.8
14 M	0120 0821 1334 2048	7.6 1.7 7.7 1.5	**29** TU	0137 0830 1346 2045	7.2 2.2 7.3 2.1
15 TU	0209 0907 1424 2134	7.5 1.9 7.5 1.7	**30** W	0211 0901 1419 2115	7.1 2.5 7.1 2.4
			31 TH	0244 0935 1456 2150	6.9 2.7 6.8 2.6

RATE AND SET — E. going stronger and longer than W. at harbour entrance. Flood from 4½ h. before 1st H.W. Havre; Ebb from ¾ h. before 1st H.W. to 5 h. before following 1st H.W. Off Honfleur; E. going –0430, Dover Sp. 5 kn.; W. going –0130, Dover, Sp. 5 kn.

There is a stand of about 2 hours around H.W.

SOUTHERN NORTH SEA TIDAL STREAMS

The 13 specially drawn Tidal Stream Charts of the Southern North Sea show the direction and rate of the tidal stream for each hour in relation to the time of H.W. Dover. For Dover High Water times see pages 21:41-21:43. The thicker the arrows the stronger tidal streams they indicate; the thinner arrows show rates and position of weaker streams. The figures shown against the arrows, as for example 19:34, indicate 1.9 knots at Neap Tide and 3.4 knots at Spring Tides approximately.

The following charts are produced from portion(s) of BA Tidal Stream Atlases with the sanction of the Controller, H.M. Stationery Office and of the Hydrographer of the Navy.

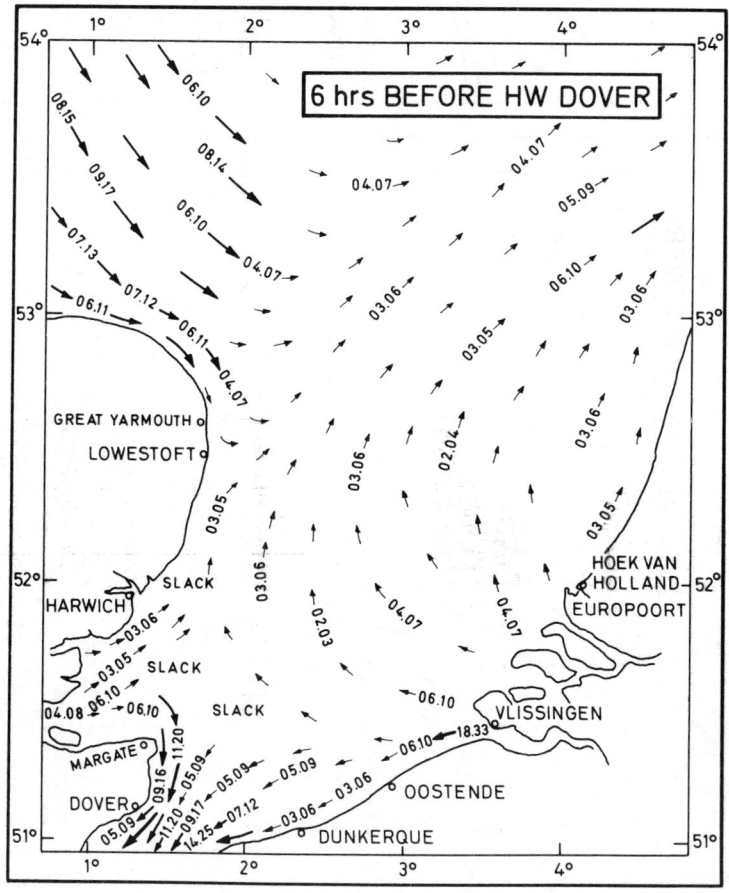

6 hrs BEFORE HW DOVER

SOUTHERN NORTH SEA TIDAL STREAMS

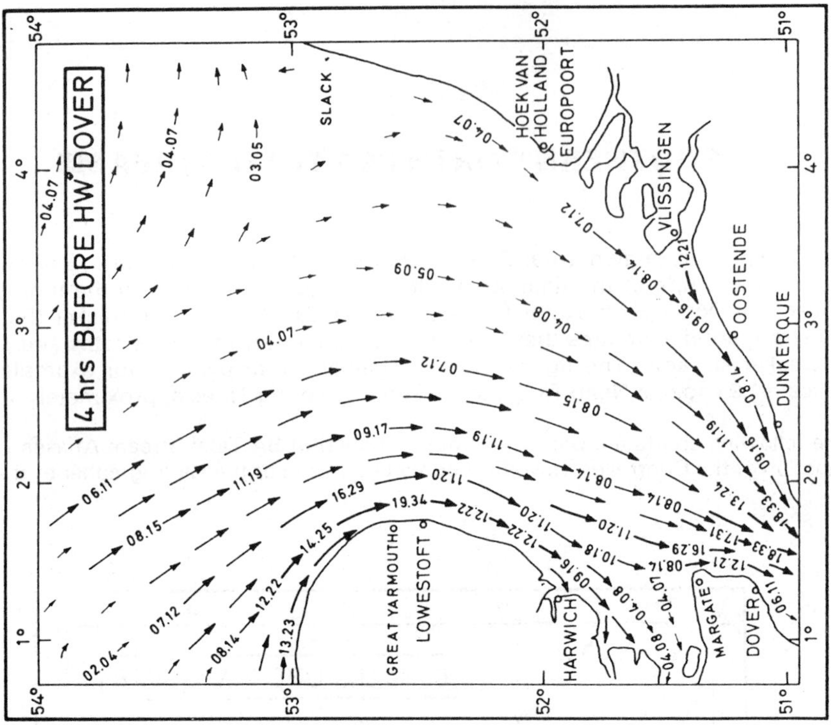

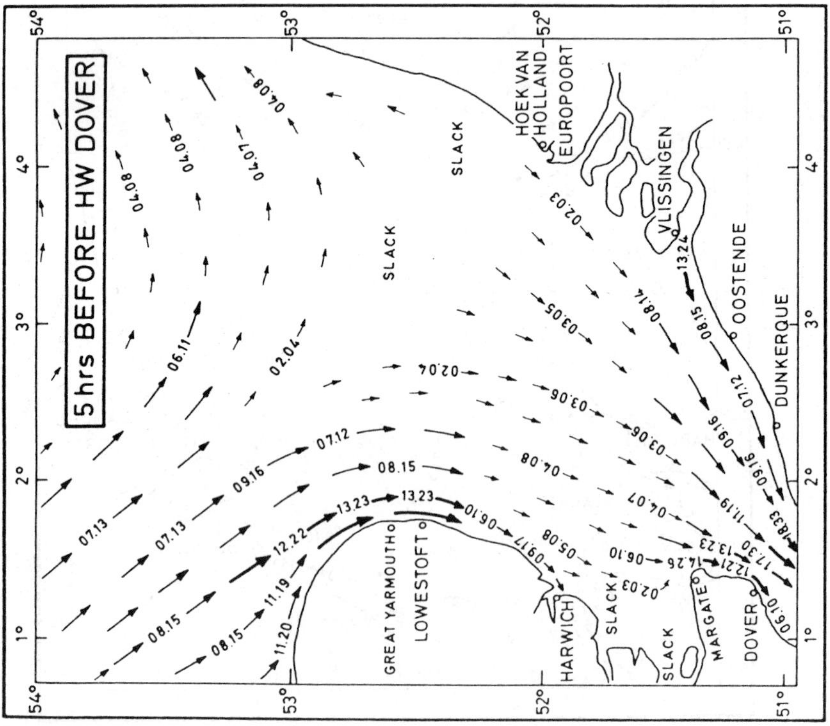

4 hrs BEFORE HW DOVER

5 hrs BEFORE HW DOVER

SOUTHERN NORTH SEA TIDAL STREAMS

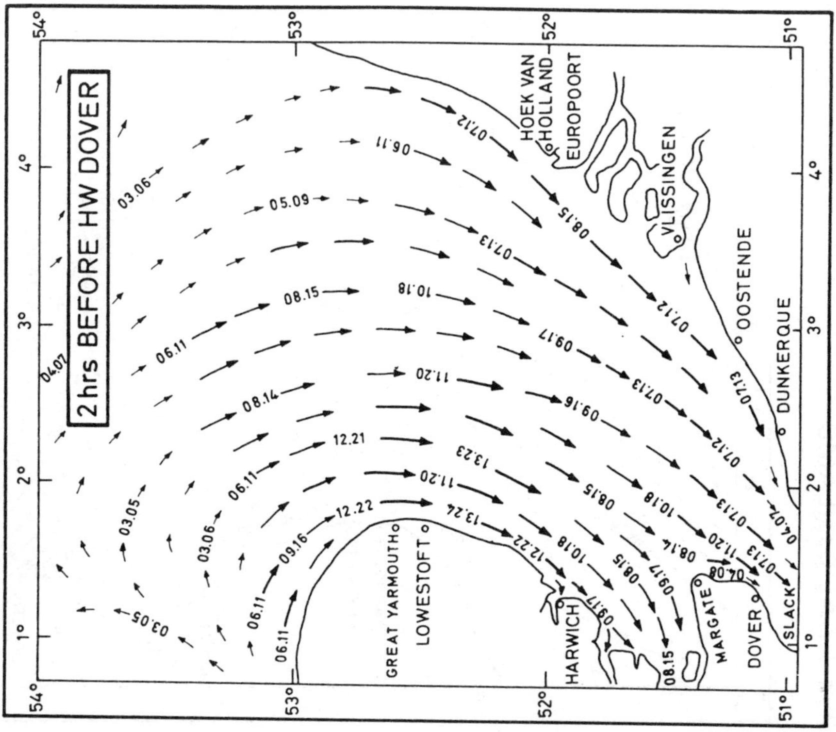

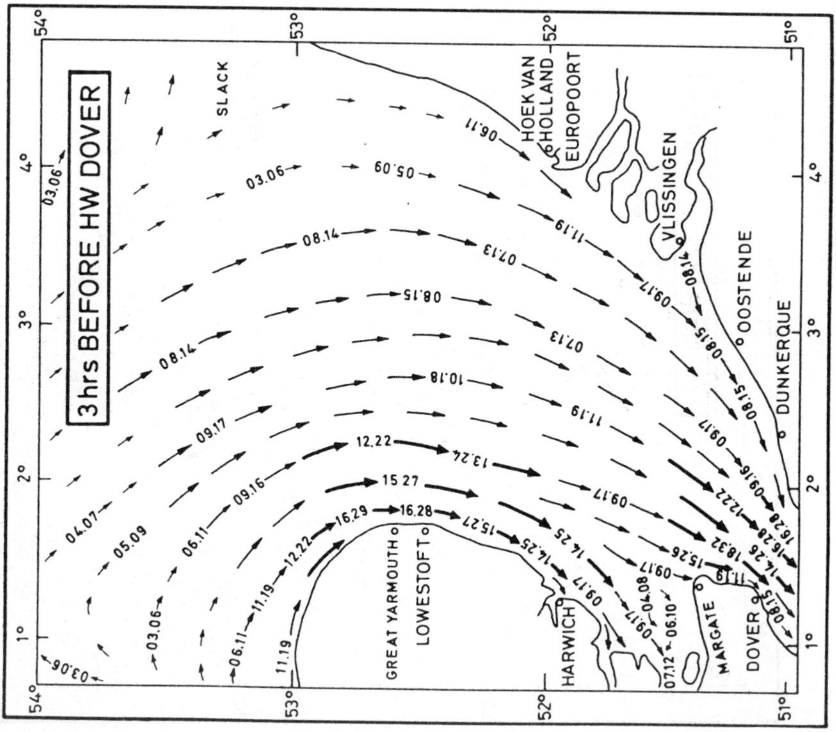

2 hrs BEFORE HW DOVER

3 hrs BEFORE HW DOVER

SOUTHERN NORTH SEA TIDAL STREAMS

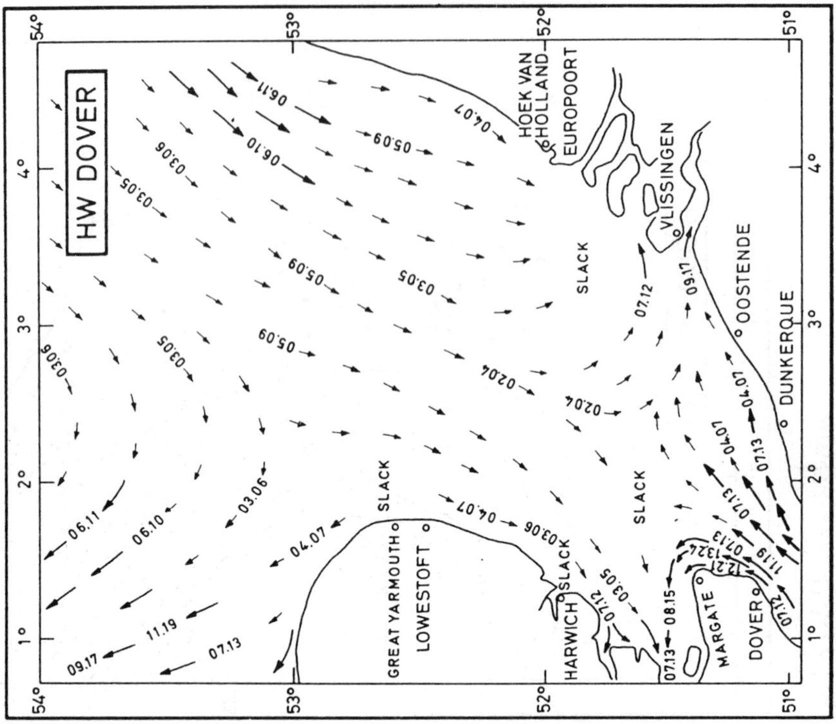

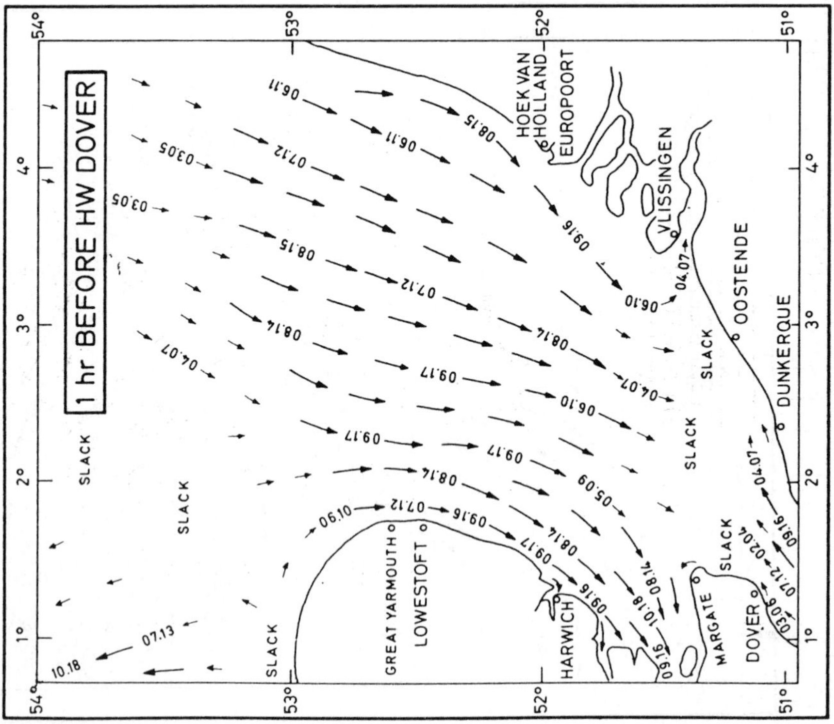

HW DOVER

1 hr BEFORE HW DOVER

SOUTHERN NORTH SEA TIDAL STREAMS

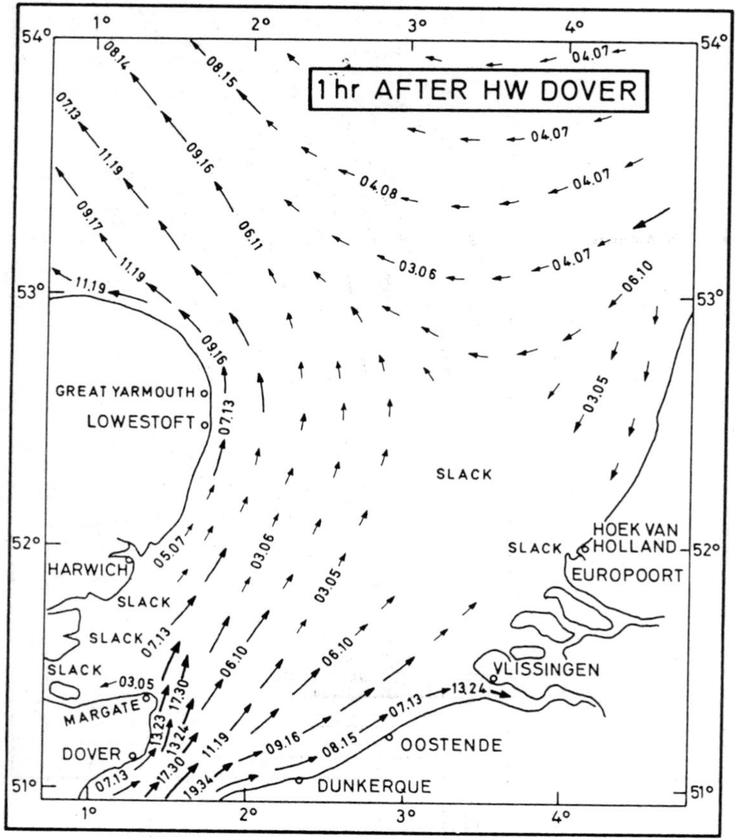

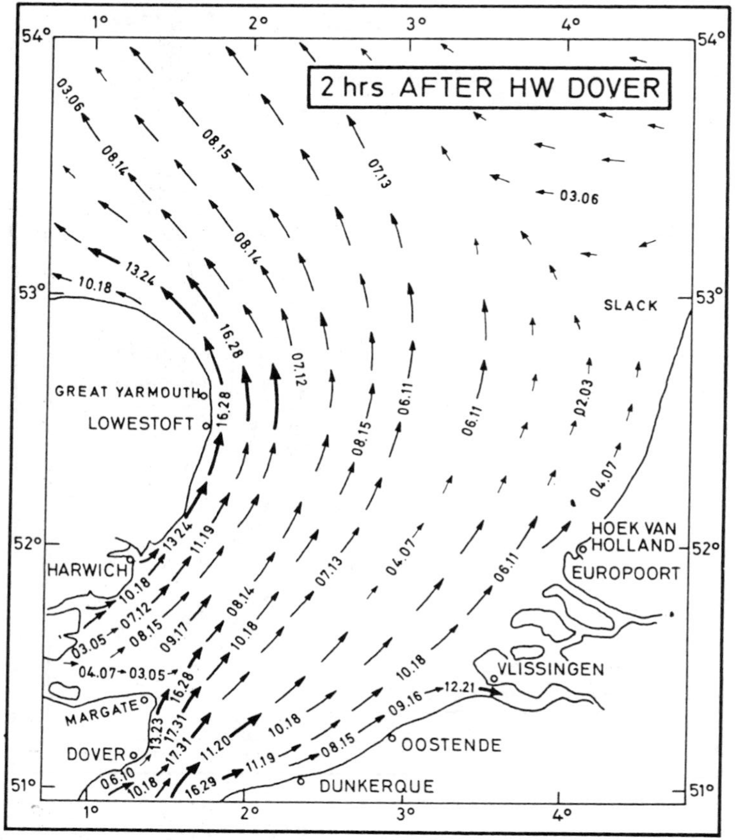

SOUTHERN NORTH SEA TIDAL STREAMS

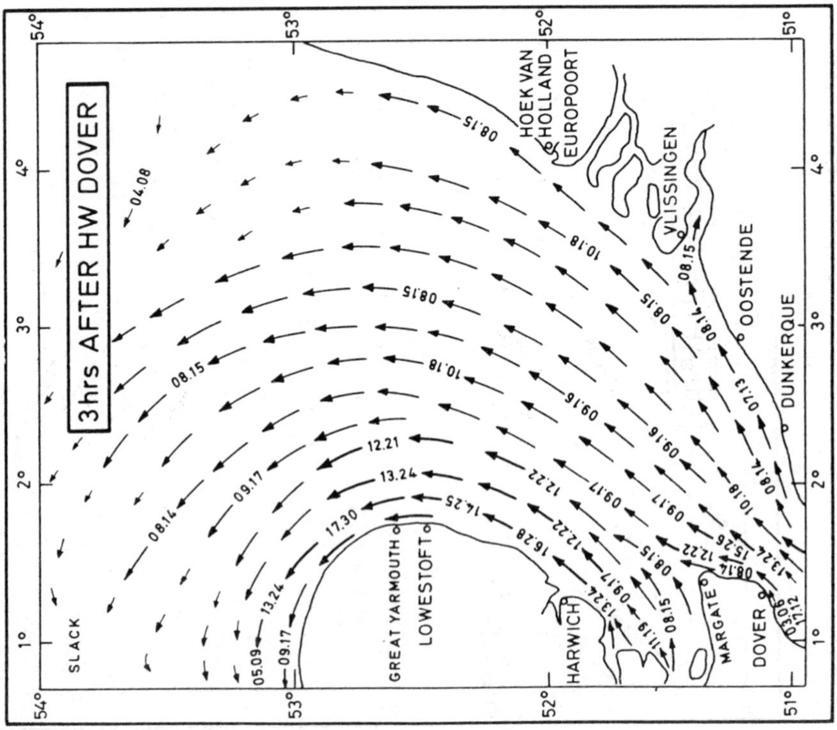

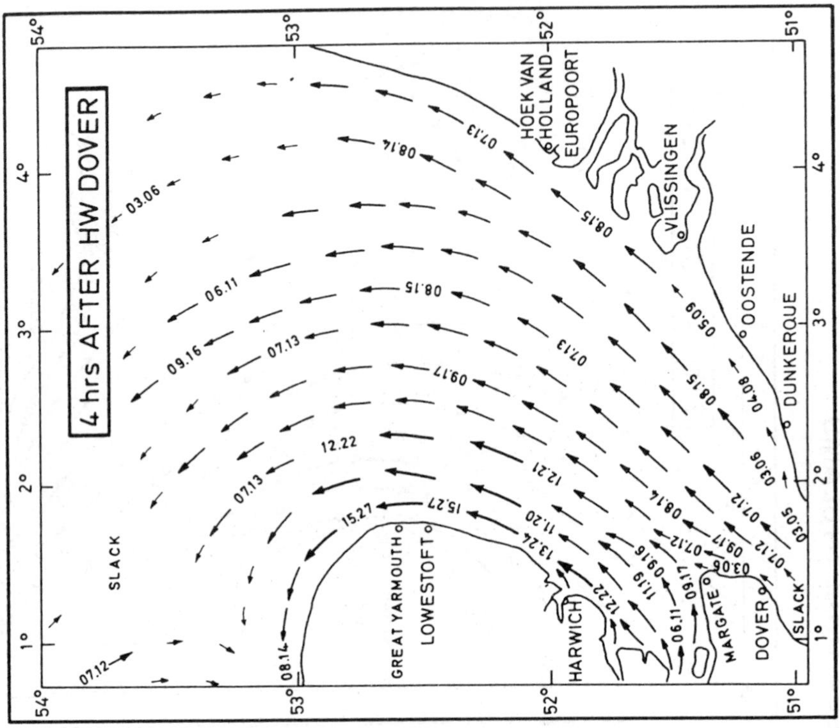

4 hrs AFTER HW DOVER

3 hrs AFTER HW DOVER

SOUTHERN NORTH SEA TIDAL STREAMS

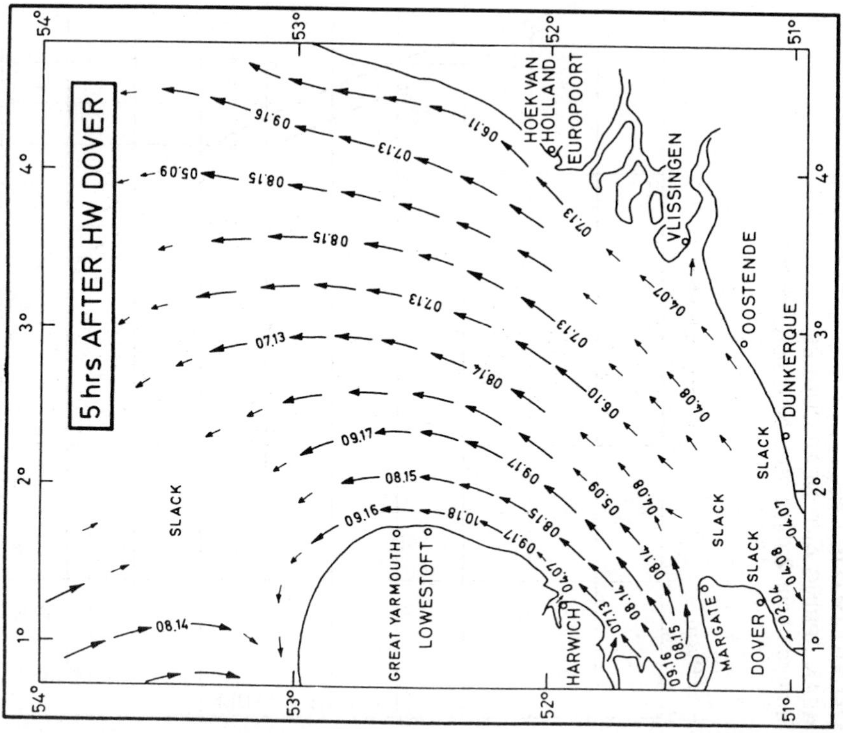

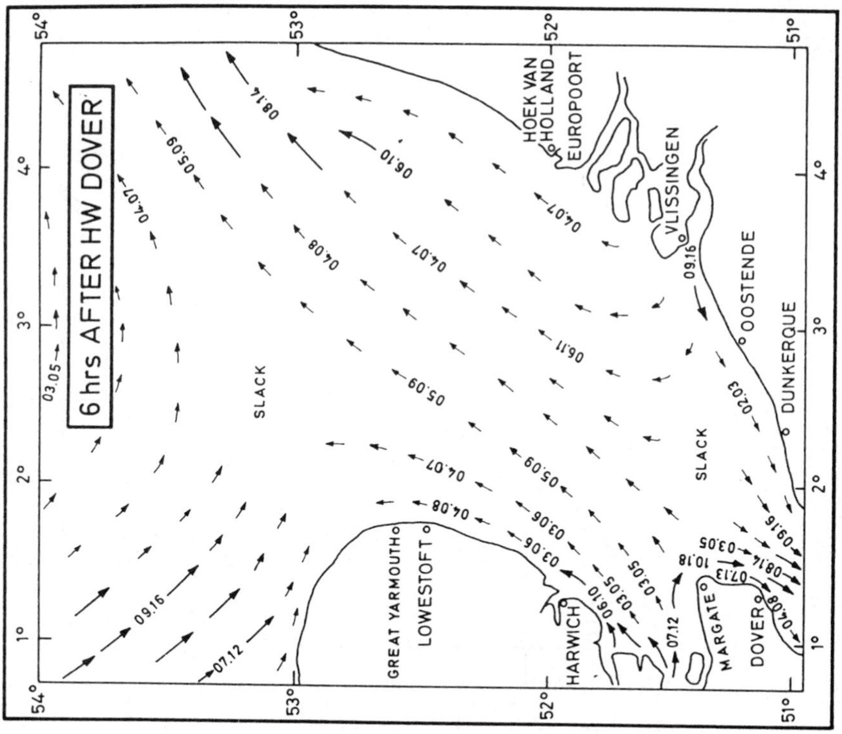

6 hrs AFTER HW DOVER

5 hrs AFTER HW DOVER

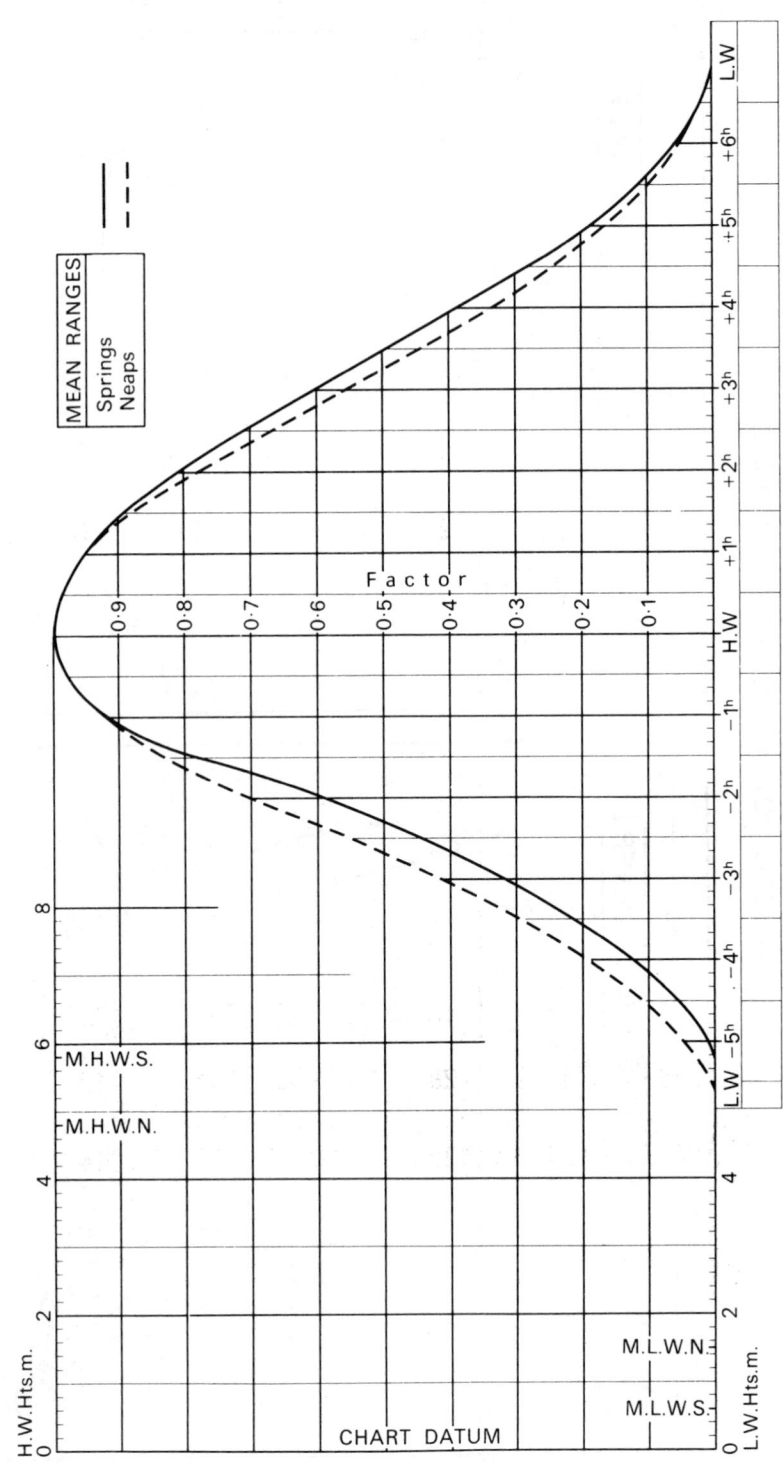

DUNKERQUE
MEAN SPRING AND NEAP CURVES
Springs occur 2 days after New and Full Moon.

DUNKERQUE

Lat. 51°03'N. Long. 2°22'E.

HIGH & LOW WATER 1992

TIME ZONE -0100 SUBTRACT 1 HOUR FROM TIMES SHOWN FOR GMT

JANUARY

Day	Time	m	Time	m	Time	m	Time	m		Day	Time	m	Time	m	Time	m	Time	m
1 W	0435	1.6	1005	5.2	1716	1.4	2243	5.1		16 TH	0321	1.6	0853	5.0	1603	1.4	2134	5.1
2 TH	0539	1.4	1103	5.3	1811	1.3	2337	5.3		17 F	0438	1.4	1010	5.3	1713	1.2	2245	5.3
3 F	0629	1.3	1153	5.4	1855	1.2				18 SA	0545	1.1	1114	5.6	1815	0.9	2341	5.6
4 SA ●	0022	5.4	0710	1.1	1237	5.6	1932	1.2		19 SU ○	0643	0.8	1206	5.9	1908	0.7		
5 SU	0100	5.5	0748	1.0	1315	5.7	2006	1.1		20	0030	5.8	0733	0.6	1255	6.1	1957	0.6
6 M	0135	5.6	0823	0.9	1350	5.7	2039	1.1		21	0117	6.0	0821	0.4	1342	6.3	2043	0.5
7 TU	0206	5.7	0856	0.9	1422	5.7	2111	1.1		22	0201	6.1	0908	0.3	1430	6.3	2128	0.5
8 W	0235	5.7	0929	0.9	1452	5.7	2142	1.1		23	0246	6.1	0954	0.3	1517	6.2	2212	0.7
9 TH	0304	5.6	1000	0.9	1525	5.6	2211	1.1		24	0330	6.1	1039	0.4	1603	6.0	2255	0.9
10 F	0336	5.6	1031	0.9	1558	5.5	2242	1.2		25 SA	0414	5.9	1124	0.6	1649	5.7	2339	1.1
11 SA	0408	5.5	1105	1.0	1634	5.4	2318	1.3		26 SU	0500	5.7	1210	0.9	1737	5.4		
12 SU	0443	5.3	1145	1.1	1715	5.3				27 M	0026	1.3	0552	5.4	1301	1.2	1835	5.1
13 M	0000	1.4	0530	5.2	1232	1.2	1808	5.1		28 TU	0122	1.6	0659	5.1	1402	1.6	1949	4.8
14 TU	0051	1.5	0632	5.1	1331	1.4	1911	5.0		29 W	0230	1.8	0822	4.8	1521	1.8	2108	4.6
15 W	0158	1.6	0740	5.0	1445	1.5	2018	5.0		30 TH	0359	1.8	0941	4.8	1653	1.7	2221	4.7
										31 F	0520	1.6	1050	5.0	1754	1.5	2323	5.0

FEBRUARY

Day	Time	m	Time	m	Time	m	Time	m		Day	Time	m	Time	m	Time	m	Time	m
1 SA	0614	1.3	1144	5.2	1839	1.3				16 SU	0532	1.0	1107	5.5	1804	0.9	2334	5.5
2 SU	0008	5.2	0655	1.1	1224	5.4	1915	1.1		17 M	0631	0.6	1158	5.9	1856	0.6		
3 M ●	0044	5.5	0730	0.9	1259	5.6	1947	1.0		18 TU ○	0019	5.8	0721	0.4	1243	6.1	1942	0.5
4 TU	0115	5.6	0802	0.8	1330	5.7	2017	0.9		19 W	0100	6.0	0806	0.2	1326	6.3	2025	0.4
5 W	0144	5.7	0834	0.9	1358	5.8	2048	0.9		20 TH	0141	6.2	0850	0.1	1409	6.3	2107	0.5
6 TH	0210	5.8	0906	0.7	1426	5.9	2118	0.8		21 F	0221	6.2	0932	0.2	1451	6.2	2147	0.6
7 F	0237	5.8	0936	0.7	1454	5.8	2147	0.9		22 SA	0302	6.2	1013	0.3	1533	6.0	2226	0.7
8 SA	0304	5.8	1006	0.7	1522	5.8	2216	0.9		23 SU	0342	6.0	1052	0.6	1613	5.8	2305	0.9
9 SU	0330	5.7	1037	0.7	1550	5.7	2248	1.0		24 M	0425	5.8	1133	0.9	1656	5.4	2346	1.2
10 M	0401	5.6	1113	0.9	1626	5.5	2326	1.1		25 TU	0512	5.4	1217	1.3	1747	5.0		
11 TU	0441	5.5	1155	1.0	1715	5.3				26 W	0036	1.5	0614	5.0	1314	1.7	1858	4.6
12 W	0012	1.3	0540	5.2	1248	1.3	1822	5.0		27 TH	0142	1.8	0743	4.6	1433	2.0	2030	4.4
13 TH	0114	1.5	0642	4.9	1401	1.5	1941	4.8		28 F	0317	1.9	0915	4.4	1618	1.9	2155	4.5
14 F	0241	1.6	0826	4.9	1532	1.5	2114	4.8		29 SA	0451	1.6	1030	4.8	1728	1.6	2259	4.8
15 SA	0414	1.4	1000	5.1	1656	1.2	2237	5.1										

MARCH

Day	Time	m	Time	m	Time	m	Time	m		Day	Time	m	Time	m	Time	m	Time	m
1 SU	0548	1.3	1122	5.1	1814	1.3	2343	5.2		16 M	0516	0.9	1055	5.5	1747	0.8	2319	5.5
2 M	0630	1.0	1201	5.4	1849	1.1				17 TU	0614	0.5	1144	5.9	1837	0.6		
3 TU	0018	5.4	0704	0.8	1234	5.6	1919	0.9		18 W ○	0000	5.8	0701	0.3	1226	6.1	1921	0.5
4 W	0049	5.7	0734	0.7	1304	5.8	1949	0.8		19 TH	0038	6.0	0745	0.2	1305	6.2	2003	0.5
5 TH	0117	5.8	0806	0.6	1331	5.9	2020	0.7		20 F	0116	6.2	0827	0.2	1344	6.2	2042	0.5
6 F	0142	5.9	0838	0.6	1358	5.9	2051	0.7		21 SA	0156	6.2	0907	0.3	1424	6.1	2121	0.6
7 SA	0208	5.9	0910	0.5	1425	5.9	2121	0.7		22 SU	0236	6.2	0946	0.4	1504	5.9	2158	0.7
8 SU	0234	5.9	0941	0.6	1452	5.9	2152	0.7		23 M	0316	6.0	1023	0.7	1543	5.7	2235	0.8
9 M	0302	5.9	1013	0.6	1521	5.8	2224	0.8		24 TU	0358	5.7	1101	1.0	1624	5.4	2315	1.1
10 TU	0334	5.8	1048	0.8	1558	5.6	2302	0.9		25 W	0444	5.4	1143	1.3	1711	5.0		
11 W	0417	5.6	1129	1.0	1647	5.3	2349	1.1		26 TH	0003	1.4	0542	4.9	1235	1.7	1815	4.6
12 TH	0517	5.2	1224	1.2	1757	5.0				27 F	0105	1.7	0701	4.5	1348	2.0	1944	4.3
13 F	0053	1.4	0642	4.9	1340	1.5	1924	4.7		28 SA	0233	1.8	0837	4.4	1527	2.0	2115	4.4
14 SA	0225	1.5	0817	4.9	1515	1.5	2108	4.8		29 SU	0405	1.6	0954	4.7	1644	1.7	2220	4.7
15 SU	0359	1.3	0952	5.1	1641	1.2	2226	5.1		30 M	0507	1.3	1047	5.0	1735	1.3	2307	5.1
										31 TU	0552	1.0	1128	5.3	1813	1.1	2345	5.4

APRIL

Day	Time	m	Time	m	Time	m	Time	m		Day	Time	m	Time	m	Time	m	Time	m
1 W	0628	0.9	1202	5.6	1845	0.9				16 TH	0639	0.4	1205	5.9	1858	0.6		
2 TH	0018	5.6	0701	0.7	1233	5.7	1916	0.8		17 F ○	0014	5.9	0722	0.4	1243	6.0	1939	0.6
3 F ●	0046	5.8	0734	0.6	1301	5.9	1949	0.7		18 SA	0053	6.1	0804	0.4	1322	6.0	2018	0.6
4 SA	0112	5.9	0802	0.7	1329	5.9	2022	0.7		19 SU	0134	6.1	0843	0.5	1402	5.9	2057	0.6
5 SU	0140	6.0	0843	0.5	1358	5.9	2057	0.7		20 M	0215	6.0	0922	0.7	1443	5.8	2135	0.7
6 M	0210	6.0	0918	0.6	1429	5.9	2131	0.7		21 TU	0257	5.9	0959	0.9	1522	5.6	2213	0.8
7 TU	0244	5.9	0954	0.6	1505	5.8	2208	0.8		22 W	0340	5.6	1036	1.1	1603	5.3	2253	1.0
8 W	0323	5.8	1032	0.8	1546	5.6	2250	0.9		23 TH	0426	5.3	1116	1.4	1648	5.0	2338	1.3
9 TH	0412	5.5	1118	1.0	1642	5.2	2342	1.1		24 F	0519	4.9	1204	1.6	1744	4.7		
10 F	0521	5.2	1216	1.3	1756	4.9				25 SA	0034	1.5	0622	4.6	1307	1.9	1851	4.5
11 SA	0052	1.3	0641	5.0	1335	1.4	1918	4.7		26 SU	0147	1.6	0738	4.5	1431	1.9	2014	4.5
12 SU	0220	1.3	0810	5.0	1514	1.4	2055	4.9		27 M	0308	1.6	0859	4.6	1546	1.7	2129	4.7
13 M	0343	1.1	0935	5.2	1621	1.1	2205	5.2		28 TU	0413	1.3	1000	4.9	1643	1.4	2223	5.0
14 TU	0454	0.8	1036	5.5	1723	0.9	2256	5.5		29 W	0504	1.1	1046	5.2	1728	1.2	2306	5.3
15 W	0550	0.5	1124	5.8	1814	0.7	2337	5.8		30 TH	0546	0.9	1125	5.4	1806	1.0	2342	5.5

TIDAL DIFFERENCES PAGE 21:306. TIDAL CURVES PAGE 21:302.

TIDAL STREAMS PAGES 21:28-21:40.

Datum of predictions: 0.6 m. below M.L.W.S. and 0.2 m below L.A.T.

DUNKERQUE

HIGH & LOW WATER 1992

Lat. 51°03′N. Long. 2°22′E.

TIME ZONE-0100 SUBTRACT 1 HOUR FROM TIMES SHOWN FOR GMT

MAY

Day	Time	m	Day	Time	m
1 F	0624 / 1158 / 1842	0.8 / 5.6 / 0.9 ○	16 SA	0702 / 1225 / 1918	0.7 / 5.7 / 0.8
2 SA	0013 / 0701 / 1229 / 1918 ●	5.7 / 0.7 / 5.7 / 0.8	17 SU	0036 / 0744 / 1306 / 1959	5.8 / 0.7 / 5.8 / 0.7
3 SU	0042 / 0739 / 1301 / 1956	5.8 / 0.6 / 5.8 / 0.7	18 M	0120 / 0824 / 1348 / 2039	5.9 / 0.8 / 5.7 / 0.7
4 M	0116 / 0819 / 1337 / 2036	5.9 / 0.6 / 5.9 / 0.7	19 TU	0204 / 0903 / 1429 / 2119	5.8 / 0.9 / 5.6 / 0.8
5 TU	0154 / 0859 / 1416 / 2117	6.0 / 0.6 / 5.8 / 0.6	20 W	0247 / 0940 / 1509 / 2157	5.7 / 1.0 / 5.5 / 0.8
6 W	0237 / 0941 / 1500 / 2201	5.9 / 0.7 / 5.7 / 0.7	21 TH	0328 / 1016 / 1547 / 2236	5.5 / 1.1 / 5.3 / 1.0
7 TH	0326 / 1026 / 1551 / 2250	5.8 / 0.8 / 5.5 / 0.8	22 F	0410 / 1054 / 1627 / 2316	5.3 / 1.3 / 5.2 / 1.1
8 F	0423 / 1117 / 1649 / 2346	5.6 / 1.0 / 5.3 / 0.9	23 SA	0455 / 1135 / 1714	5.1 / 1.5 / 5.0
9 SA	0526 / 1218 / 1753	5.4 / 1.2 / 5.1	24 SU	0002 / 0545 / 1224 / 1807	1.3 / 4.9 / 1.6 / 4.8
10 SU	0055 / 0634 / 1331 / 1905	1.0 / 5.2 / 1.3 / 5.0	25 M	0057 / 0641 / 1327 / 1908	1.4 / 4.8 / 1.7 / 4.7
11 M	0210 / 0753 / 1445 / 2028	1.0 / 5.2 / 1.3 / 5.0	26 TU	0204 / 0744 / 1441 / 2015	1.4 / 4.8 / 1.6 / 4.7
12 TU	0320 / 0910 / 1554 / 2135	0.9 / 5.3 / 1.1 / 5.3	27 W	0312 / 0851 / 1545 / 2122	1.3 / 4.9 / 1.5 / 4.9
13 W	0426 / 1010 / 1655 / 2228	0.8 / 5.5 / 1.0 / 5.5	28 TH	0410 / 0951 / 1639 / 2217	1.2 / 5.0 / 1.3 / 5.1
14 TH	0525 / 1100 / 1748 / 2313	0.7 / 5.6 / 0.9 / 5.6	29 F	0501 / 1039 / 1726 / 2301	1.1 / 5.2 / 1.1 / 5.3
15 F	0616 / 1144 / 1835 / 2355	0.7 / 5.7 / 0.8 / 5.8	30 SA	0547 / 1120 / 1809 / 2339	1.0 / 5.4 / 1.0 / 5.5
			31 SU	0631 / 1159 / 1852	0.8 / 5.6 / 0.9

JUNE

Day	Time	m	Day	Time	m
1 M	0017 / 0715 / 1238 / 1935 ●	5.7 / 0.7 / 5.7 / 0.7	16 TU	0113 / 0810 / 1339 / 2027	5.7 / 1.0 / 5.6 / 0.8
2 TU	0059 / 0759 / 1321 / 2021	5.9 / 0.7 / 5.8 / 0.6	17 W	0156 / 0847 / 1417 / 2105	5.7 / 1.0 / 5.6 / 0.8
3 W	0144 / 0845 / 1408 / 2108	6.0 / 0.6 / 5.8 / 0.5	18 TH	0236 / 0923 / 1453 / 2141	5.6 / 1.0 / 5.5 / 0.8
4 TH	0234 / 0933 / 1457 / 2158	6.0 / 0.6 / 5.8 / 0.5	19 F	0313 / 0957 / 1526 / 2217	5.5 / 1.1 / 5.5 / 0.9
5 F	0326 / 1022 / 1548 / 2249	5.9 / 0.7 / 5.7 / 0.6	20 SA	0348 / 1031 / 1601 / 2251	5.4 / 1.2 / 5.4 / 0.9
6 SA	0420 / 1113 / 1641 / 2344	5.8 / 0.9 / 5.5 / 0.6	21 SU	0426 / 1105 / 1640 / 2328	5.3 / 1.3 / 5.2 / 1.0
7 SU	0516 / 1210 / 1737	5.6 / 1.0 / 5.4	22 M	0508 / 1144 / 1725	5.2 / 1.4 / 5.1
8 M	0044 / 0616 / 1312 / 1840	0.7 / 5.4 / 1.2 / 5.3	23 TU	0011 / 0554 / 1230 / 1816	1.1 / 5.1 / 1.5 / 5.0
9 TU	0147 / 0725 / 1417 / 1951	0.8 / 5.3 / 1.2 / 5.2	24 W	0101 / 0646 / 1327 / 1912	1.2 / 5.0 / 1.5 / 4.9
10 W	0251 / 0836 / 1522 / 2059	0.9 / 5.3 / 1.2 / 5.2	25 TH	0203 / 0743 / 1437 / 2013	1.3 / 4.9 / 1.6 / 4.9
11 TH	0356 / 0939 / 1626 / 2159	0.9 / 5.3 / 1.2 / 5.3	26 F	0312 / 0845 / 1545 / 2118	1.3 / 4.9 / 1.5 / 5.0
12 F	0500 / 1036 / 1726 / 2253	1.0 / 5.4 / 1.1 / 5.4	27 SA	0415 / 0948 / 1644 / 2219	1.3 / 5.0 / 1.3 / 5.1
13 SA	0558 / 1127 / 1818 / 2342	1.0 / 5.4 / 1.0 / 5.5	28 SU	0513 / 1045 / 1741 / 2312	1.1 / 5.2 / 1.1 / 5.4
14 SU	0647 / 1214 / 1904	1.0 / 5.5 / 0.9	29 M	0606 / 1135 / 1832	1.0 / 5.5 / 0.9
15 M	0029 / 0730 / 1258 / 1947 ○	5.6 / 1.0 / 5.5 / 0.8	30 TU	0000 / 0656 / 1222 / 1921 ●	5.7 / 0.8 / 5.7 / 0.7

JULY

Day	Time	m	Day	Time	m
1 W	0046 / 0745 / 1309 / 2010	5.9 / 0.7 / 5.8 / 0.5	16 TH	0143 / 0829 / 1359 / 2047	5.6 / 1.0 / 5.6 / 0.7
2 TH	0134 / 0833 / 1356 / 2059	6.1 / 0.6 / 5.9 / 0.4	17 F	0217 / 0902 / 1429 / 2121	5.7 / 1.0 / 5.7 / 0.7
3 F	0224 / 0921 / 1444 / 2148	6.1 / 0.6 / 5.9 / 0.3	18 SA	0248 / 0934 / 1458 / 2153	5.7 / 1.0 / 5.6 / 0.7
4 SA	0314 / 1009 / 1532 / 2237	6.1 / 0.6 / 5.9 / 0.3	19 SU	0318 / 1004 / 1529 / 2223	5.6 / 1.0 / 5.6 / 0.8
5 SU	0405 / 1058 / 1620 / 2327	6.0 / 0.7 / 5.8 / 0.4	20 M	0350 / 1034 / 1601 / 2255	5.5 / 1.1 / 5.5 / 0.8
6 M	0456 / 1148 / 1710	5.8 / 0.9 / 5.7	21 TU	0425 / 1106 / 1636 / 2331	5.4 / 1.2 / 5.3 / 0.9
7 TU	0020 / 0549 / 1242 / 1805	0.6 / 5.6 / 1.1 / 5.5	22 W	0503 / 1145 / 1717	5.3 / 1.3 / 5.2
8 W	0116 / 0648 / 1341 / 1910	0.8 / 5.3 / 1.3 / 5.3	23 TH	0013 / 0549 / 1232 / 1812	1.1 / 5.1 / 1.4 / 5.0
9 TH	0217 / 0757 / 1445 / 2023	1.1 / 5.1 / 1.4 / 5.1	24 F	0106 / 0646 / 1333 / 1917	1.3 / 5.0 / 1.5 / 4.9
10 F	0324 / 0908 / 1557 / 2135	1.3 / 5.0 / 1.4 / 5.1	25 SA	0215 / 0751 / 1452 / 2028	1.4 / 4.9 / 1.6 / 4.9
11 SA	0440 / 1015 / 1709 / 2240	1.3 / 5.0 / 1.3 / 5.2	26 SU	0332 / 0905 / 1611 / 2148	1.4 / 4.9 / 1.4 / 5.0
12 SU	0545 / 1116 / 1807 / 2337	1.3 / 5.1 / 1.1 / 5.3	27 M	0445 / 1021 / 1720 / 2255	1.2 / 5.1 / 1.1 / 5.3
13 M	0635 / 1207 / 1853	1.2 / 5.3 / 1.0	28 TU	0549 / 1121 / 1819 / 2347	1.0 / 5.3 / 0.8 / 5.7
14 TU	0025 / 0717 / 1249 / 1934 ○	5.5 / 1.1 / 5.5 / 0.8	29 W	0643 / 1209 / 1910 ●	0.8 / 5.7 / 0.5
15 W	0105 / 0754 / 1325 / 2012	5.6 / 1.0 / 5.6 / 0.8	30 TH	0034 / 0732 / 1254 / 1957	5.6 / 0.6 / 5.9 / 0.3
			31 F	0120 / 0818 / 1338 / 2044	6.2 / 0.5 / 6.1 / 0.2

AUGUST

Day	Time	m	Day	Time	m
1 SA	0206 / 0904 / 1422 / 2130	6.2 / 0.5 / 6.1 / 0.1	16 SU	0217 / 0906 / 1427 / 2124	5.8 / 0.9 / 5.8 / 0.7
2 SU	0253 / 0949 / 1506 / 2216	6.2 / 0.6 / 6.1 / 0.2	17 M	0244 / 0935 / 1453 / 2153	5.8 / 0.9 / 5.8 / 0.7
3 M	0340 / 1034 / 1551 / 2302	6.1 / 0.7 / 6.0 / 0.4	18 TU	0312 / 1002 / 1520 / 2223	5.7 / 0.9 / 5.7 / 0.8
4 TU	0426 / 1118 / 1638 / 2348	5.9 / 0.9 / 5.9 / 0.6	19 W	0339 / 1033 / 1548 / 2256	5.6 / 1.0 / 5.6 / 0.9
5 W	0514 / 1206 / 1729	5.6 / 1.1 / 5.6	20 TH	0409 / 1108 / 1622 / 2335	5.5 / 1.1 / 5.4 / 1.1
6 TH	0039 / 0609 / 1300 / 1831	1.0 / 5.3 / 1.3 / 5.3	21 F	0451 / 1152 / 1714	5.3 / 1.3 / 5.2
7 F	0138 / 0717 / 1407 / 1951	1.3 / 4.9 / 1.6 / 5.0	22 SA	0025 / 0553 / 1249 / 1832	1.5 / 5.0 / 1.5 / 4.9
8 SA	0252 / 0838 / 1530 / 2115	1.6 / 4.7 / 1.6 / 4.9	23 SU	0131 / 0711 / 1411 / 1957	1.6 / 4.8 / 1.6 / 4.8
9 SU	0421 / 0957 / 1653 / 2230	1.6 / 4.8 / 1.4 / 5.0	24 M	0259 / 0838 / 1544 / 2129	1.6 / 4.8 / 1.6 / 5.0
10 M	0530 / 1105 / 1752 / 2329	1.5 / 5.0 / 1.2 / 5.2	25 TU	0424 / 1007 / 1702 / 2242	1.3 / 5.0 / 1.1 / 5.4
11 TU	0619 / 1154 / 1837	1.3 / 5.3 / 1.0	26 W	0534 / 1108 / 1804 / 2334	1.0 / 5.4 / 0.7 / 5.8
12 W	0012 / 0659 / 1231 / 1915	5.4 / 1.1 / 5.5 / 0.8	27 TH	0628 / 1154 / 1854	0.7 / 5.8 / 0.4
13 TH	0047 / 0733 / 1303 / 1949 ○	5.6 / 0.7 / 5.6 / 0.7	28 F	0019 / 0715 / 1235 / 1940 ●	6.1 / 0.6 / 6.0 / 0.2
14 F	0120 / 0804 / 1334 / 2021	5.7 / 0.9 / 5.7 / 0.7	29 SA	0101 / 0759 / 1315 / 2024	6.2 / 0.5 / 6.2 / 0.2
15 SA	0150 / 0835 / 1401 / 2053	5.8 / 0.9 / 5.8 / 0.7	30 SU	0143 / 0842 / 1356 / 2107	6.3 / 0.5 / 6.3 / 0.2
			31 M	0226 / 0924 / 1438 / 2150	6.3 / 0.6 / 6.3 / 0.3

RATE AND SET — Dunkerque Roads. ENE. –0130, Dover, Sp. 3 kn.: WSW. +0415 Dover, Sp. 3 kn. Heads of jetties. ENE. –0200 Dover, Sp. 3 kn..; WSW. +0315 Dover, Sp. 2½ kn. Max. rate of ENE. stream occurs at H.W.

DUNKERQUE 21:305

Lat. 51°03′N. Long. 2°22′E.   HIGH & LOW WATER 1992

TIME ZONE-0100 SUBTRACT 1 HOUR FROM TIMES SHOWN FOR GMT

SEPTEMBER

Day	Time	m	Time	m	Day	Time	m	Time	m
1 TU	0310	6.1	1005	0.7	16	0238	5.8	0934	0.9
	1521	6.2	2233	0.5	W	1447	5.8	2155	0.8
2 W	0354	5.9	1047	0.9	17	0305	5.7	1005	1.0
	1607	5.9	2315	0.8	TH	1517	5.7	2228	0.9
3 TH	0439	5.6	1130	1.1	18	0336	5.6	1041	1.1
	1656	5.6			F	1554	5.5	2307	1.1
4 F	0002	1.2	0531	5.2	19	0419	5.3	1125	1.3
	1221	1.4	1758	5.2	SA	1646	5.3	2357	1.4
5 SA	0059	1.6	0638	4.8	20	0522	5.0	1225	1.5
	1328	1.7	1920	4.8	SU	1812	5.0		
6 SU	0217	1.9	0806	4.5	21	0106	1.6	0651	4.8
	1500	1.8	2052	4.7	M	1350	1.6	1941	4.9
7 M	0355	1.9	0934	4.6	22	0238	1.6	0822	4.8
	1629	1.5	2211	4.9	TU	1525	1.4	2114	5.1
8 TU	0506	1.6	1042	4.9	23	0406	1.3	0951	5.1
	1729	1.2	2308	5.2	W	1643	1.0	2225	5.5
9 W	0555	1.3	1128	5.2	24	0515	1.0	1049	5.5
	1813	1.0	2348	5.4	TH	1744	0.6	2316	5.9
10 TH	0633	1.1	1204	5.5	25	0608	0.7	1133	5.8
	1849	0.8			F	1833	0.4	2359	6.1
11 F	0021	5.6	0705	1.0	26	0654	0.6	1212	6.1
	1236	5.7	1920	0.8	SA	1918	0.3		
12 SA	0052	5.8	0734	0.9	27	0039	6.3	0736	0.6
	1305	5.8	1951	0.7	SU	1250	6.3	2001	0.3
13 SU	0119	5.9	0804	0.9	28	0119	6.3	0818	0.6
	1330	5.9	2022	0.7	M	1331	6.3	2043	0.3
14 M	0145	5.9	0835	0.9	29	0208	6.2	0858	0.7
	1355	5.9	2054	0.7	TU	1413	6.3	2124	0.5
15 TU	0211	5.9	0905	0.9	30	0242	6.1	0938	0.8
	1420	5.9	2124	0.7	W	1456	6.2	2205	0.7

OCTOBER

Day	Time	m	Time	m	Day	Time	m	Time	m
1 TH	0326	5.8	1019	0.9	16	0244	5.8	0946	1.0
	1542	5.9	2245	1.0	F	1502	5.8	2209	1.0
2 F	0410	5.5	1101	1.2	17	0322	5.6	1026	1.1
	1631	5.5	2329	1.4	SA	1546	5.6	2251	1.2
3 SA	0500	5.1	1149	1.4	18	0410	5.3	1114	1.2
	1731	5.1			SU	1647	5.3	2344	1.4
4 SU	0022	1.8	0602	4.8	19	0519	5.1	1217	1.4
	1253	1.7	1846	4.8	M	1807	5.1		
5 M	0136	2.0	0724	4.5	20	0054	1.6	0639	4.9
	1421	1.8	2017	4.6	TU	1339	1.5	1926	5.0
6 TU	0312	2.0	0854	4.6	21	0222	1.6	0804	4.9
	1548	1.6	2135	4.8	W	1506	1.3	2053	5.2
7 W	0426	1.8	1002	4.9	22	0344	1.4	0927	5.2
	1651	1.3	2230	5.1	TH	1619	0.9	2202	5.6
8 TH	0519	1.4	1051	5.2	23	0450	1.1	1024	5.6
	1737	1.1	2313	5.4	F	1719	0.7	2254	5.9
9 F	0559	1.2	1130	5.5	24	0544	0.9	1109	5.8
	1814	0.9	2348	5.6	SA	1811	0.5	2337	6.1
10 SA	0631	1.1	1203	5.7	25	0631	0.8	1148	6.1
	1847	0.9			SU	1857	0.5		
11 SU	0019	5.8	0701	1.0	26	0017	6.1	0714	0.7
	1233	5.8	1918	0.8	M	1228	6.2	1940	0.5
12 M	0047	5.9	0732	0.9	27	0057	6.2	0756	0.7
	1259	5.9	1951	0.8	TU	1310	6.2	2022	0.6
13 TU	0114	5.9	0805	0.9	28	0139	6.1	0836	0.8
	1325	6.0	2025	0.8	W	1354	6.2	2102	0.7
14 W	0142	5.9	0838	0.9	29	0222	5.9	0917	0.9
	1354	6.0	2059	0.8	TH	1438	6.1	2142	0.9
15 TH	0212	5.9	0911	0.9	30	0305	5.7	0957	1.0
	1426	5.9	2133	0.9	F	1525	5.8	2221	1.2
					31	0349	5.5	1038	1.2
					SA	1613	5.5	2301	1.5

NOVEMBER

Day	Time	m	Time	m	Day	Time	m	Time	m
1 SU	0434	5.2	1124	1.4	16	0413	5.4	1113	1.1
	1706	5.2	2348	1.8	M	1651	5.5	2339	1.3
2 M	0527	4.9	1218	1.6	17	0514	5.3	1214	1.2
	1806	4.9			TU	1755	5.3		
3 TU	0049	2.0	0631	4.7	18	0045	1.5	0621	5.1
	1330	1.7	1919	4.7	W	1326	1.2	1906	5.3
4 W	0212	2.1	0751	4.6	19	0201	1.5	0735	5.1
	1451	1.7	2039	4.8	TH	1441	1.2	2024	5.3
5 TH	0328	1.9	0907	4.8	20	0315	1.4	0852	5.3
	1557	1.5	2141	5.0	F	1550	1.0	2133	5.5
6 F	0428	1.6	1004	5.1	21	0421	1.2	0954	5.5
	1650	1.3	2229	5.2	SA	1653	0.9	2229	5.7
7 SA	0515	1.4	1049	5.3	22	0520	1.1	1044	5.7
	1733	1.1	2309	5.5	SU	1749	0.8	2318	5.8
8 SU	0553	1.2	1127	5.6	23	0611	1.0	1129	5.9
	1811	1.0	2344	5.6	M	1839	0.8		
9 M	0628	1.1	1200	5.7	24	0001	5.9	0657	0.9
	1846	0.9			TU	1213	6.0	● 1924	0.8
10 TU	0016	5.8	0703	1.0	25	0043	5.9	0740	0.8
	1230	5.9	1923	0.9	W	1257	6.0	2006	0.8
	O 1923	0.9							
11 W	0046	5.9	0739	1.0	26	0126	5.9	0822	0.8
	1301	6.0	2000	0.8	TH	1343	6.0	2046	0.9
12 TH	0119	5.9	0817	0.9	27	0209	5.8	0902	0.9
	1336	6.0	2038	0.8	F	1428	5.9	2124	1.0
13 F	0156	5.9	0856	0.9	28	0251	5.7	0942	0.9
	1415	6.0	2118	0.9	SA	1512	5.7	2201	1.2
14 SA	0236	5.8	0937	0.9	29	0330	5.5	1020	1.1
	1500	5.9	2200	1.0	SU	1554	5.5	2238	1.4
15 SU	0320	5.7	1022	1.0	30	0409	5.4	1100	1.2
	1551	5.7	2246	1.2	M	1637	5.3	2317	1.6

DECEMBER

Day	Time	m	Time	m	Day	Time	m	Time	m
1 TU	0452	5.2	1144	1.4	16	0457	5.6	1203	0.9
	1724	5.1			W	1735	5.6		
2 W	0002	1.8	0542	5.0	17	0027	1.3	0555	5.4
	1235	1.5	1817	4.9	TH	1304	1.0	1837	5.4
3 TH	0059	1.9	0640	4.8	18	0131	1.4	0700	5.3
	1339	1.6	1919	4.8	F	1410	1.1	1948	5.3
4 F	0213	1.9	0748	4.8	19	0240	1.5	0813	5.3
	1450	1.6	2027	4.9	SA	1518	1.2	2101	5.3
5 SA	0323	1.8	0859	4.9	20	0349	1.4	0924	5.3
	1553	1.5	2131	5.0	SU	1628	1.1	2205	5.4
6 SU	0422	1.6	0959	5.1	21	0457	1.3	1025	5.5
	1647	1.4	2223	5.2	M	1734	1.1	2303	5.5
7 M	0512	1.4	1047	5.3	22	0557	1.2	1119	5.6
	1734	1.2	2308	5.4	TU	1828	1.0	2354	5.6
8 TU	0556	1.3	1128	5.5	23	0647	1.0	1208	5.7
	1817	1.1	2347	5.6	W	1914	1.0		
9 W	0638	1.1	1205	5.7	24	0038	5.7	0731	0.9
	1859	0.9	O		TH	1253	5.8	● 1955	0.9
10 TH	0024	5.8	0719	1.0	25	0120	5.7	0812	0.8
	1243	5.9	1941	0.8	F	1337	5.9	2033	1.0
11 F	0102	5.9	0802	0.8	26	0159	5.8	0851	0.8
	1324	6.1	2024	0.8	SA	1417	5.8	2109	1.0
12 SA	0144	5.9	0846	0.7	27	0235	5.7	0927	0.8
	1408	6.1	2108	0.8	SU	1455	5.8	2142	1.1
13 SU	0228	5.9	0932	0.7	28	0308	5.7	1002	0.9
	1455	6.1	2153	0.8	M	1530	5.6	2215	1.2
14 M	0314	5.8	1019	0.7	29	0340	5.6	1035	1.0
	1545	5.9	2240	1.0	TU	1604	5.5	2247	1.3
15 TU	0404	5.7	1109	0.8	30	0416	5.4	1109	1.1
	1638	5.8	2330	1.1	W	1642	5.3	2321	1.4
					31	0457	5.3	1147	1.2
					TH	1726	5.2		

TIDAL DIFFERENCES PAGE 21:306. TIDAL CURVE PAGE 21:302.

TIDAL STREAMS PAGES 21:28-21:40.

Datum of predictions: 0.6 m. below M.L.W.S. and 0.2 m. below L.A.T.

TIDAL DIFFERENCES ON DUNKERQUE

PLACE	TIME DIFFERENCES				HEIGHT DIFFERENCES (Metres)			
	High Water		Low Water		MHWS	MHWN	MLWN	MLWS
DUNKERQUE	0200 and 1400	0800 and 2000	0200 and 1400	0900 and 2100	5.8	4.8	1.4	0.6
Gravelines	−0010	−0010	−0020	0000	+0.2	+0.1	−0.1	−0.1
Calais	−0017	−0024	−0016	−0012	+1.3	+1.1	+0.5	+0.3
Wissant	−0030	–	–	–	+1.7	+1.5	+0.7	+0.6
Boulogne	−0045	−0055	−0045	−0031	+3.1	+2.4	+1.3	+0.5
Le Touquet, Etaples	−0048	–	–	–	+3.2	+2.4	+1.3	+0.4
Berck	−0052	–	–	–	+3.5	+2.5	+1.4	+0.4
La Somme								
Le Hourdel	−0039	−0055	–	–	+4.2	+3.1	–	–
St. Valéry	−0032	−0041	–	–	+4.2	+3.2	–	–
Cayeux	−0053	−0111	−0130	−0055	+4.4	+3.1	+3.1	+0.4
Le Treport	−0110	−0116	−0117	−0057	+3.6	+2.6	+0.1	+0.1
Dieppe	−0100	−0122	−0122	−0108	+3.5	+2.4	+1.1	+0.1
St. Valery-en-Caux	−0118	−0137	−0129	−0121	+3.1	+2.3	+1.0	+0.4
Fecamp	−0122	−0139	−0156	−0051	+2.1	+1.7	+1.1	+0.2
Antifer	−0146	−0201	−0213	−0208	+2.2	+1.8	+1.5	+0.6

Note: Time zone. The predictions for the standard port are on the same time zone as the differences shown. No further sdjustment is necessary.

Refer to predictions on pages 21:303-21:305

TIDAL DIFFERENCES ON ANTWERP

PLACE	TIME DIFFERENCES				HEIGHT DIFFERENCES (Metres)			
	High Water		Low Water		MHWS	MHWN	MLWN	MLWS
ANTWERP (PROSPERPOLDER)	0000 and 1200	0500 and 1700	0000 and 1200	0600 and 1800	5.8	4.8	0.8	0.3
Boudewijnsluis	+0013	+0005	+0025	+0020	0.0	+0.1	0.0	0.0
Royersluis	+0030	+0015	+0045	+0041	+0.2	+0.3	0.0	0.0
Boom	+0125	+0110	+0155	+0150	−0.2	0.0	−0.4	+0.2
Gentbrugge	+0430	+0415	+0630	+0600	−3.9	−3.3	−1.1	−0.4

Note: Time zone. The predictions for the standard port are on the same time zone as the differences shown. No further adjustment is necessary.

Refer to predictions on pages 21:312-21:314

VLISSINGEN (FLUSHING) 21:307

Lat. 51°27'N. Long. 3°36'E.

HIGH & LOW WATER 1992

TIME ZONE-0100 SUBTRACT 1 HOUR FROM TIMES SHOWN FOR GMT

JANUARY

Day	Time	m	Day	Time	m
1 W	0535 / 1129 / 1806	0.9 / 4.0 / 0.8	**16** TH	0404 / 1036 / 1650 / 2309	1.0 / 4.0 / 0.7 / 4.1
2 TH	0005 / 0625 / 1225 / 1845	4.1 / 0.8 / 4.1 / 0.8	**17** F	0526 / 1137 / 1755	0.8 / 4.2 / 0.6
3 F	0055 / 0715 / 1320 / 1925	4.2 / 0.7 / 4.3 / 0.8	**18** SA	0008 / 0636 / 1235 / 1858	4.3 / 0.6 / 4.4 / 0.5
4 SA	0146 / 0755 / 1354 / ●2006	4.3 / 0.6 / 4.3 / 0.8	**19** SU	0102 / 0726 / 1322 / ○1948	4.5 / 0.4 / 4.7 / 0.4
5 SU	0220 / 0829 / 1436 / 2036	4.3 / 0.5 / 4.4 / 0.7	**20** M	0149 / 0820 / 1409 / 2036	4.7 / 0.1 / 4.9 / 0.3
6 M	0252 / 0905 / 1505 / 2110	4.4 / 0.4 / 4.5 / 0.7	**21** TU	0235 / 0908 / 1453 / 2122	4.8 / 0.0 / 5.0 / 0.3
7 TU	0326 / 0946 / 1539 / 2145	4.5 / 0.3 / 4.6 / 0.7	**22** W	0318 / 0956 / 1540 / 2208	4.9 / -0.1 / 5.1 / 0.3
8 W	0356 / 1019 / 1610 / 2225	4.5 / 0.3 / 4.6 / 0.7	**23** TH	0405 / 1046 / 1626 / 2251	4.9 / -0.1 / 5.0 / 0.4
9 TH	0428 / 1056 / 1645 / 2255	4.5 / 0.3 / 4.5 / 0.7	**24** F	0450 / 1128 / 1716 / 2336	4.8 / 0.0 / 4.8 / 0.5
10 F	0502 / 1130 / 1719 / 2325	4.4 / 0.4 / 4.4 / 0.8	**25** SA	0537 / 1216 / 1807	4.7 / 0.1 / 4.6
11 SA	0535 / 1154 / 1756	4.3 / 0.4 / 4.3	**26** SU	0019 / 0629 / 1255 / 1901	0.6 / 4.5 / 0.3 / 4.3
12 SU	0006 / 0616 / 1235 / 1835	0.8 / 4.2 / 0.5 / 4.2	**27** M	0110 / 0725 / 1350 / 1959	0.7 / 4.2 / 0.5 / 4.0
13 M	0045 / 0655 / 1326 / 1935	0.8 / 4.1 / 0.6 / 4.0	**28** TU	0210 / 0825 / 1456 / 2116	0.9 / 3.9 / 0.8 / 3.7
14 TU	0140 / 0806 / 1426 / 2051	0.9 / 3.9 / 0.7 / 4.0	**29** W	0336 / 0950 / 1615 / 2235	1.0 / 3.7 / 0.9 / 3.7
15 W	0244 / 0921 / 1541 / 2200	1.0 / 3.9 / 0.8 / 3.9	**30** TH	0500 / 1110 / 1724 / 2346	1.0 / 3.8 / 0.9 / 3.8
			31 F	0610 / 1215 / 1830	0.8 / 4.0 / 0.9

FEBRUARY

Day	Time	m	Day	Time	m
1 SA	0046 / 0659 / 1310 / 1909	4.0 / 0.7 / 4.2 / 0.8	**16** SU	0620 / 1218 / 1846	0.5 / 4.4 / 0.5
2 SU	0125 / 0745 / 1350 / 1945	4.2 / 0.5 / 4.3 / 0.7	**17** M	0047 / 0716 / 1312 / 1935	4.4 / 0.3 / 4.7 / 0.4
3 M	0205 / 0816 / 1415 / ●2020	4.3 / 0.4 / 4.4 / 0.7	**18** TU	0136 / 0808 / 1356 / ○2022	4.6 / 0.0 / 4.9 / 0.3
4 TU	0231 / 0849 / 1447 / 2056	4.4 / 0.3 / 4.6 / 0.6	**19** W	0216 / 0856 / 1436 / 2106	4.8 / -0.1 / 5.0 / 0.2
5 W	0301 / 0926 / 1517 / 2128	4.6 / 0.2 / 4.6 / 0.5	**20** TH	0258 / 0938 / 1518 / 2148	4.9 / -0.2 / 5.0 / 0.2
6 TH	0331 / 1000 / 1549 / 2159	4.6 / 0.2 / 4.7 / 0.5	**21** F	0343 / 1019 / 1605 / 2229	5.0 / -0.2 / 5.0 / 0.3
7 F	0402 / 1032 / 1618 / 2236	4.6 / 0.2 / 4.6 / 0.5	**22** SA	0425 / 1106 / 1649 / 2309	4.9 / 0.0 / 4.8 / 0.4
8 SA	0432 / 1106 / 1649 / 2306	4.6 / 0.2 / 4.6 / 0.6	**23** SU	0506 / 1142 / 1735 / 2352	4.8 / 0.1 / 4.5 / 0.5
9 SU	0506 / 1136 / 1721 / 2335	4.5 / 0.3 / 4.5 / 0.6	**24** M	0555 / 1222 / 1825	4.5 / 0.4 / 4.2
10 M	0537 / 1211 / 1758	4.5 / 0.4 / 4.4	**25** TU	0036 / 0646 / 1305 / 1915	0.6 / 4.2 / 0.6 / 3.9
11 TU	0016 / 0617 / 1250 / 1848	0.6 / 4.3 / 0.4 / 4.2	**26** W	0124 / 0745 / 1410 / 2014	0.8 / 3.9 / 0.9 / 3.5
12 W	0059 / 0716 / 1345 / 2006	0.7 / 4.1 / 0.6 / 3.9	**27** TH	0225 / 0916 / 1524 / 2206	1.0 / 3.5 / 1.1 / 3.4
13 TH	0210 / 0836 / 1500 / 2125	0.9 / 3.9 / 0.8 / 3.8	**28** F	0415 / 1046 / 1655 / 2326	1.0 / 3.6 / 1.1 / 3.6
14 F	0335 / 1006 / 1626 / 2246	0.9 / 3.9 / 0.8 / 3.8	**29** SA	0535 / 1155 / 1754	0.8 / 3.8 / 0.9
15 SA	0506 / 1118 / 1746 / 2358	0.8 / 4.1 / 0.7 / 4.1			

MARCH

Day	Time	m	Day	Time	m
1 SU	0015 / 0636 / 1245 / 1844	3.9 / 0.6 / 4.1 / 0.8	**16** M	0605 / 1208 / 1832	0.4 / 4.4 / 0.5
2 M	0106 / 0726 / 1321 / 1925	4.1 / 0.4 / 4.3 / 0.6	**17** TU	0031 / 0706 / 1252 / 1922	4.3 / 0.2 / 4.7 / 0.3
3 TU	0138 / 0756 / 1355 / 1956	4.3 / 0.3 / 4.5 / 0.6	**18** W	0116 / 0749 / 1335 / ○2006	4.6 / 0.0 / 4.8 / 0.2
4 W	0206 / 0825 / 1421 / ●2030	4.5 / 0.2 / 4.6 / 0.5	**19** TH	0156 / 0836 / 1416 / 2047	4.8 / -0.1 / 4.9 / 0.2
5 TH	0235 / 0858 / 1448 / 2102	4.6 / 0.1 / 4.7 / 0.4	**20** F	0236 / 0915 / 1455 / 2128	4.9 / -0.1 / 4.9 / 0.2
6 F	0302 / 0932 / 1517 / 2136	4.7 / 0.1 / 4.7 / 0.4	**21** SA	0317 / 0955 / 1540 / 2208	4.9 / -0.1 / 4.8 / 0.2
7 SA	0336 / 1005 / 1549 / 2210	4.7 / 0.1 / 4.7 / 0.4	**22** SU	0358 / 1035 / 1623 / 2248	4.9 / 0.1 / 4.7 / 0.3
8 SU	0403 / 1036 / 1620 / 2239	4.7 / 0.2 / 4.6 / 0.4	**23** M	0443 / 1116 / 1705 / 2325	4.7 / 0.3 / 4.4 / 0.4
9 M	0435 / 1111 / 1656 / 2309	4.7 / 0.2 / 4.6 / 0.4	**24** TU	0526 / 1150 / 1750	4.5 / 0.5 / 4.2
10 TU	0513 / 1146 / 1735 / 2356	4.6 / 0.3 / 4.4 / 0.5	**25** W	0006 / 0609 / 1230 / 1835	0.5 / 4.2 / 0.7 / 3.8
11 W	0556 / 1226 / 1822	4.5 / 0.4 / 4.2	**26** TH	0055 / 0706 / 1330 / 1936	0.7 / 3.8 / 1.0 / 3.5
12 TH	0046 / 0648 / 1326 / 1936	0.6 / 4.2 / 0.6 / 3.9	**27** F	0215 / 0826 / 1444 / 2054	0.9 / 3.5 / 1.1 / 3.3
13 F	0149 / 0810 / 1440 / 2100	0.7 / 3.9 / 0.8 / 3.7	**28** SA	0336 / 1006 / 1604 / 2246	0.9 / 3.5 / 1.1 / 3.4
14 SA	0314 / 0945 / 1605 / 2225	0.9 / 3.9 / 0.8 / 3.7	**29** SU	0450 / 1121 / 1714 / 2345	0.8 / 3.7 / 0.9 / 3.7
15 SU	0455 / 1105 / 1736 / 2339	0.7 / 4.1 / 0.7 / 4.0	**30** M	0606 / 1210 / 1816	0.6 / 4.0 / 0.7
			31 TU	0025 / 0646 / 1248 / 1855	4.0 / 0.4 / 4.3 / 0.6

APRIL

Day	Time	m	Day	Time	m
1 W	0101 / 0722 / 1319 / 1926	4.3 / 0.3 / 4.5 / 0.5	**16** TH	0053 / 0729 / 1316 / 1945	4.5 / 0.0 / 4.7 / 0.3
2 TH	0131 / 0756 / 1349 / 1959	4.4 / 0.2 / 4.6 / 0.4	**17** F	0135 / 0812 / 1356 / ○2026	4.7 / 0.0 / 4.8 / 0.2
3 F	0159 / 0825 / 1417 / ●2035	4.6 / 0.1 / 4.7 / 0.3	**18** SA	0215 / 0852 / 1436 / 2106	4.8 / 0.0 / 4.7 / 0.2
4 SA	0230 / 0902 / 1449 / 2110	4.7 / 0.1 / 4.7 / 0.3	**19** SU	0256 / 0930 / 1519 / 2145	4.8 / 0.1 / 4.7 / 0.2
5 SU	0305 / 0935 / 1522 / 2145	4.8 / 0.1 / 4.7 / 0.3	**20** M	0336 / 1008 / 1601 / 2226	4.8 / 0.2 / 4.5 / 0.2
6 M	0336 / 1012 / 1556 / 2222	4.8 / 0.2 / 4.7 / 0.3	**21** TU	0420 / 1045 / 1638 / 2302	4.6 / 0.4 / 4.3 / 0.3
7 TU	0413 / 1048 / 1636 / 2306	4.8 / 0.2 / 4.6 / 0.3	**22** W	0458 / 1119 / 1718 / 2345	4.4 / 0.6 / 4.1 / 0.4
8 W	0452 / 1126 / 1717 / 2346	4.7 / 0.3 / 4.4 / 0.3	**23** TH	0545 / 1200 / 1805	4.2 / 0.7 / 3.9
9 TH	0537 / 1212 / 1809	4.5 / 0.4 / 4.1	**24** F	0036 / 0636 / 1256 / 1856	0.6 / 3.9 / 0.9 / 3.7
10 F	0035 / 0635 / 1304 / 1926	0.4 / 4.2 / 0.6 / 3.9	**25** SA	0146 / 0746 / 1416 / 2000	0.7 / 3.7 / 1.1 / 3.5
11 SA	0145 / 0806 / 1426 / 2048	0.6 / 4.0 / 0.8 / 3.7	**26** SU	0255 / 0906 / 1526 / 2124	0.8 / 3.5 / 1.0 / 3.4
12 SU	0315 / 0930 / 1555 / 2205	0.6 / 4.0 / 0.8 / 3.8	**27** M	0355 / 1026 / 1630 / 2256	0.7 / 3.7 / 0.9 / 3.6
13 M	0440 / 1048 / 1726 / 2318	0.5 / 4.0 / 0.7 / 4.0	**28** TU	0506 / 1122 / 1725 / 2342	0.6 / 3.9 / 0.8 / 3.9
14 TU	0556 / 1145 / 1818	0.3 / 4.4 / 0.5	**29** W	0606 / 1205 / 1816	0.5 / 4.2 / 0.6
15 W	0009 / 0645 / 1235 / 1902	4.3 / 0.1 / 4.6 / 0.3	**30** TH	0020 / 0646 / 1239 / 1856	4.2 / 0.3 / 4.4 / 0.5

TIDAL DIFFERENCES PAGE 21:311. TIDAL CURVE PAGE 21:310.

TIDAL STREAMS PAGES 21:295-21:301.

Datum of predictions: 0.3 m below M.L.W.S. and 0.2 m. above L.A.T.

(FLUSHING) VLISSINGEN

HIGH & LOW WATER 1992 — Lat. 51°27′N. Long. 3°36′E.

TIME ZONE-0100 SUBTRACT 1 HOUR FROM TIMES SHOWN FOR GMT

MAY

Day	Time	m	Time	m	Time	m	Time	m
1 F	0055	4.4	0716	0.3	1315	4.6	1928	0.4
16 SA O	0115	4.5	0751	0.2	1340	4.5	2005	0.3
2 SA ●	0127	4.5	0756	0.2	1347	4.7	2006	0.3
17 SU	0157	4.6	0825	0.2	1426	4.5	2048	0.2
3 SU	0202	4.7	0830	0.2	1422	4.7	2046	0.3
18 M	0239	4.6	0906	0.3	1506	4.5	2126	0.2
4 M	0236	4.8	0908	0.2	1459	4.7	2125	0.2
19 TU	0321	4.6	0942	0.4	1542	4.4	2206	0.2
5 TU	0315	4.8	0951	0.2	1538	4.6	2208	0.2
20 W	0401	4.6	1020	0.5	1625	4.3	2248	0.3
6 W	0355	4.8	1030	0.3	1620	4.5	2255	0.2
21 TH	0441	4.4	1056	0.6	1658	4.2	2330	0.3
7 TH	0441	4.7	1112	0.3	1707	4.4	2342	0.2
22 F	0528	4.3	1136	0.7	1742	4.1		
8 F	0530	4.6	1206	0.5	1806	4.1		
23 SA	0004	0.4	0616	4.1	1214	0.9	1831	3.9
9 SA	0040	0.3	0635	4.3	1259	0.6	1916	4.0
24 SU	0111	0.5	0706	3.9	1315	1.0	1926	3.7
10 SU	0146	0.3	0755	4.2	1416	0.7	2030	3.9
25 M	0216	0.6	0806	3.8	1446	1.0	2025	3.6
11 M	0255	0.4	0910	4.2	1541	0.7	2142	3.9
26 TU	0310	0.6	0909	3.8	1506	0.9	2135	3.7
12 TU	0415	0.3	1025	4.3	1649	0.6	2250	4.1
27 W	0405	0.6	1020	3.9	1638	0.8	2246	3.8
13 W	0530	0.3	1121	4.4	1756	0.5	2345	4.3
28 TH	0505	0.5	1115	4.1	1726	0.7	2336	4.0
14 TH	0622	0.2	1215	4.5	1842	0.4		
29 F	0556	0.5	1200	4.3	1809	0.6		
15 F	0030	4.4	0708	0.2	1257	4.5	1926	0.3
30 SA	0017	4.3	0641	0.4	1238	4.5	1856	0.5
31 SU	0057	4.5	0720	0.3	1322	4.6	1940	0.4

JUNE

Day	Time	m	Time	m	Time	m	Time	m
1 M ●	0135	4.6	0802	0.2	1401	4.7	2026	0.3
16 TU	0231	4.5	0841	0.5	1451	4.4	2109	0.3
2 TU	0216	4.7	0847	0.2	1443	4.7	2112	0.2
17 W	0311	4.5	0919	0.6	1529	4.4	2156	0.2
3 W	0300	4.8	0932	0.3	1526	4.6	2158	0.1
18 TH	0347	4.5	0956	0.6	1605	4.4	2230	0.2
4 TH	0345	4.8	1016	0.3	1613	4.6	2248	0.1
19 F	0426	4.5	1035	0.6	1641	4.4	2316	0.2
5 F	0433	4.8	1106	0.4	1702	4.5	2335	0.1
20 SA	0505	4.4	1116	0.7	1719	4.3	2350	0.3
6 SA	0525	4.7	1155	0.5	1759	4.3		
21 SU	0545	4.3	1144	0.8	1800	4.2		
7 SU	0036	0.1	0629	4.5	1244	0.5	1902	4.2
22 M	0025	0.4	0625	4.1	1229	0.8	1845	4.0
8 M	0129	0.1	0738	4.4	1355	0.6	2005	4.1
23 TU	0105	0.5	0716	4.0	1314	0.9	1936	3.9
9 TU	0235	0.2	0816	4.3	1506	0.7	2109	4.1
24 W	0205	0.6	0816	3.9	1425	1.0	2041	3.8
10 W	0346	0.3	0949	4.3	1620	0.7	2218	4.1
25 TH	0316	0.6	0916	3.9	1535	0.9	2139	3.8
11 TH	0455	0.4	1058	4.3	1726	0.6	2319	4.2
26 F	0405	0.6	1020	4.0	1646	0.9	2246	3.9
12 F	0558	0.4	1151	4.3	1819	0.5		
27 SA	0505	0.6	1120	4.1	1735	0.7	2346	4.1
13 SA	0016	4.3	0646	0.4	1246	4.3	1905	0.4
28 SU	0559	0.5	1211	4.3	1831	0.6		
14 SU	0104	4.4	0728	0.4	1328	4.4	1949	0.4
29 M	0033	4.4	0656	0.5	1259	4.5	1920	0.4
15 M	0149	4.6	0805	0.3	1416	4.6	2032	0.3
30 TU ●	0118	4.6	0742	0.3	1346	4.6	2010	0.2

JULY

Day	Time	m	Time	m	Time	m	Time	m
1 W	0203	4.8	0828	0.3	1428	4.7	2058	0.1
16 TH	0256	4.5	0900	0.6	1511	4.5	2132	0.2
2 TH	0248	4.9	0917	0.3	1516	4.7	2150	0.0
17 F	0332	4.6	0936	0.6	1545	4.5	2209	0.2
3 F	0336	5.0	1003	0.3	1558	4.7	2236	-0.1
18 SA	0406	4.6	1012	0.6	1617	4.5	2246	0.2
4 SA	0422	4.9	1049	0.4	1617	4.7	2328	-0.1
19 SU	0439	4.6	1045	0.6	1656	4.5	2322	0.3
5 SU	0512	4.9	1140	0.4	1739	4.6		
20 M	0515	4.5	1119	0.7	1726	4.4	2356	0.4
6 M	0018	-0.1	0609	4.7	1230	0.5	1835	4.5
21 TU	0545	4.5	1156	0.7	1758	4.3		
7 TU	0111	0.1	0707	4.5	1322	0.6	1935	4.3
22 W	0026	0.4	0626	4.2	1224	0.8	1839	4.1
8 W	0206	0.2	0809	4.3	1426	0.7	2036	4.2
23 TH	0106	0.5	0716	4.1	1315	0.9	1936	4.0
9 TH	0306	0.4	0915	4.1	1535	0.8	2145	4.0
24 F	0155	0.7	0806	4.0	1420	0.9	2051	3.9
10 F	0425	0.6	1030	4.1	1655	0.8	2300	4.0
25 SA	0305	0.8	0929	3.9	1535	1.0	2206	3.9
11 SA	0536	0.6	1138	4.1	1800	0.7	2311	4.0
26 SU	0426	0.8	1046	4.0	1700	0.7	2311	4.0
12 SU	0001	4.1	0625	0.6	1236	4.2	1855	0.5
27 M	0535	0.7	1148	4.2	1806	0.6		
13 M	0059	4.3	0715	0.7	1326	4.3	1939	0.4
28 TU	0016	4.3	0636	0.5	1245	4.4	1906	0.4
14 TU	0146	4.4	0749	0.7	1406	4.3	2020	0.4
29 W ●	0105	4.6	0726	0.4	1329	4.6	1955	0.2
15 W	0225	4.5	0825	0.7	1440	4.4	2055	0.3
30 TH	0146	4.9	0816	0.3	1413	4.8	2046	0.0
31 F	0233	5.0	0900	0.3	1456	4.9	2136	-0.1

AUGUST

Day	Time	m	Time	m	Time	m	Time	m
1 SA	0316	5.1	0946	0.3	1543	4.9	2219	-0.1
16 SU	0338	4.7	0946	0.6	1549	4.7	2220	0.2
2 SU	0403	5.1	1032	0.3	1625	4.9	2308	-0.1
17 M	0407	4.7	1026	0.6	1618	4.6	2249	0.3
3 M	0448	5.0	1115	0.4	1712	4.8	2349	0.0
18 TU	0438	4.6	1049	0.6	1649	4.6	2320	0.4
4 TU	0541	4.8	1159	0.5	1802	4.6		
19 W	0506	4.5	1115	0.7	1719	4.5	2351	0.5
5 W	0038	0.2	0636	4.5	1245	0.6	1858	4.4
20 TH	0538	4.4	1156	0.7	1757	4.4		
6 TH	0125	0.4	0736	4.2	1345	0.8	2000	4.1
21 F	0025	0.5	0621	4.3	1241	0.8	1845	4.2
7 F	0226	0.7	0840	3.9	1500	0.9	2115	3.9
22 SA	0116	0.7	0725	4.0	1335	0.9	1949	3.9
8 SA	0346	0.9	1003	3.8	1625	0.9	2240	3.8
23 SU	0226	0.9	0845	3.8	1500	1.0	2126	3.8
9 SU	0511	0.9	1125	3.9	1746	0.8	2351	4.0
24 M	0350	0.9	1016	3.8	1636	0.9	2250	4.0
10 M	0616	0.9	1225	4.1	1846	0.6		
25 TU	0515	0.8	1128	4.0	1745	0.7	2355	4.3
11 TU	0050	4.3	0655	0.8	1309	4.3	1931	0.5
26 W	0618	0.6	1225	4.4	1850	0.4		
12 W	0136	4.4	0735	0.8	1348	4.4	2006	0.4
27 TH	0047	4.7	0710	0.5	1309	4.6	1946	0.2
13 TH O	0208	4.5	0808	0.7	1419	4.5	2038	0.3
28 F ●	0130	4.9	0757	0.4	1353	4.8	2025	0.0
14 F	0238	4.6	0838	0.6	1447	4.6	2110	0.2
29 SA	0215	5.1	0842	0.3	1434	5.0	2113	-0.1
15 SA	0305	4.7	0916	0.6	1519	4.7	2145	0.2
30 SU	0256	5.1	0927	0.3	1515	5.1	2158	-0.1
31 M	0337	5.1	1008	0.3	1558	5.0	2239	0.0

GENERAL — Tidal streams, rotatory anti-clockwise near entrance. Strong SW., NW. and E. winds affect tides and streams. Inland the rotatory character disappears.

RATE AND SET — Flushing Roads — flood continues 1¾ h. after H.W. at average rate — 1¾ kn. Flushing Roads — ebb 3½-5 kn. — deep water. South of Westkapelle: SE. going –0500, Dover; NW. going, +0030, Dover. Deurloo Channel — general set across fairway.

VLISSINGEN (FLUSHING) 21:309

Lat. 51°27′N. Long. 3°36′E. HIGH & LOW WATER 1992

TIME ZONE -0100 SUBTRACT 1 HOUR FROM TIMES SHOWN FOR GMT

SEPTEMBER

Day	Time	m	Day	Time	m
1 TU	0423 / 1052 / 1646 / 2322	4.9 / 0.4 / 4.9 / 0.2	**16** W	0406 / 1026 / 1616 / 2245	4.7 / 0.6 / 4.7 / 0.4
2 W	0509 / 1135 / 1727	4.7 / 0.5 / 4.7	**17** TH	0437 / 1056 / 1652 / 2321	4.6 / 0.6 / 4.7 / 0.5
3 TH	0005 / 0559 / 1216 / 1819	0.4 / 4.4 / 0.7 / 4.4	**18** F	0511 / 1126 / 1728 / 2356	4.5 / 0.6 / 4.6 / 0.6
4 F	0045 / 0656 / 1304 / 1920	0.7 / 4.1 / 0.8 / 4.1	**19** SA	0556 / 1212 / 1815	4.3 / 0.7 / 4.4
5 SA	0145 / 0800 / 1425 / 2040	0.9 / 3.8 / 1.0 / 3.8	**20** SU	0048 / 0649 / 1316 / 1922	0.7 / 4.0 / 0.8 / 4.0
6 SU	0305 / 0924 / 1556 / 2215	1.1 / 3.5 / 1.0 / 3.7	**21** M	0156 / 0821 / 1440 / 2106	1.0 / 3.8 / 0.9 / 3.9
7 M	0445 / 1055 / 1726 / 2336	1.2 / 3.7 / 0.9 / 3.9	**22** TU	0336 / 0945 / 1610 / 2230	1.0 / 3.8 / 0.9 / 4.1
8 TU	0545 / 1200 / 1826	1.0 / 4.0 / 0.7	**23** W	0444 / 1105 / 1736 / 2335	0.9 / 4.0 / 0.6 / 4.4
9 W	0025 / 0636 / 1245 / 1906	4.2 / 0.9 / 4.2 / 0.5	**24** TH	0606 / 1201 / 1835	0.7 / 4.3 / 0.4
10 TH	0108 / 0709 / 1326 / 1940	4.4 / 0.8 / 4.4 / 0.4	**25** F	0025 / 0655 / 1247 / 1926	4.7 / 0.5 / 4.6 / 0.2
11 F	0139 / 0746 / 1356 / 2012	4.6 / 0.7 / 4.5 / 0.3	**26** SA	0109 / 0738 / 1329 / ● 2008	4.9 / 0.4 / 4.8 / 0.1
12 SA	0210 / 0811 / 1419 / O 2046	4.6 / 0.6 / 4.6 / 0.3	**27** SU	0151 / 0822 / 1411 / 2050	5.0 / 0.4 / 5.0 / 0.0
13 SU	0237 / 0846 / 1447 / 2116	4.7 / 0.6 / 4.7 / 0.3	**28** M	0233 / 0903 / 1454 / 2132	5.1 / 0.3 / 5.1 / 0.1
14 M	0306 / 0921 / 1517 / 2148	4.7 / 0.5 / 4.8 / 0.3	**29** TU	0316 / 0945 / 1535 / 2216	5.0 / 0.4 / 5.0 / 0.2
15 TU	0335 / 0956 / 1547 / 2218	4.8 / 0.6 / 4.7 / 0.4	**30** W	0359 / 1025 / 1616 / 2252	4.8 / 0.4 / 4.9 / 0.4

OCTOBER

Day	Time	m	Day	Time	m
1 TH	0442 / 1108 / 1702 / 2330	4.6 / 0.5 / 4.7 / 0.6	**16** F	0413 / 1035 / 1629 / 2256	4.6 / 0.6 / 4.8 / 0.6
2 F	0529 / 1150 / 1749	4.3 / 0.7 / 4.4	**17** SA	0455 / 1116 / 1712 / 2341	4.5 / 0.6 / 4.6 / 0.7
3 SA	0009 / 0618 / 1235 / 1846	0.9 / 4.0 / 0.8 / 4.0	**18** SU	0537 / 1206 / 1801	4.3 / 0.6 / 4.4
4 SU	0106 / 0716 / 1344 / 2000	1.1 / 3.7 / 1.0 / 3.7	**19** M	0030 / 0638 / 1306 / 1916	0.8 / 4.0 / 0.7 / 4.1
5 M	0225 / 0835 / 1504 / 2146	1.3 / 3.5 / 1.1 / 3.6	**20** TU	0146 / 0759 / 1425 / 2046	1.0 / 3.8 / 0.8 / 4.0
6 TU	0350 / 1026 / 1630 / 2255	1.3 / 3.5 / 1.0 / 3.8	**21** W	0316 / 0929 / 1544 / 2205	1.1 / 3.8 / 0.8 / 4.2
7 W	0506 / 1125 / 1734 / 2355	1.2 / 3.8 / 0.8 / 4.1	**22** TH	0436 / 1040 / 1716 / 2311	1.0 / 4.0 / 0.6 / 4.4
8 TH	0600 / 1209 / 1824	1.0 / 4.1 / 0.6	**23** F	0540 / 1138 / 1815	0.8 / 4.3 / 0.4
9 F	0035 / 0640 / 1246 / 1906	4.4 / 0.8 / 4.3 / 0.5	**24** SA	0006 / 0636 / 1225 / 1902	4.6 / 0.6 / 4.6 / 0.3
10 SA	0105 / 0716 / 1317 / 1935	4.5 / 0.7 / 4.5 / 0.4	**25** SU	0048 / 0715 / 1308 / ● 1947	4.8 / 0.5 / 4.8 / 0.2
11 SU	0136 / 0746 / 1345 / O 2010	4.6 / 0.6 / 4.6 / 0.4	**26** M	0132 / 0800 / 1349 / 2026	4.9 / 0.4 / 4.9 / 0.2
12 M	0202 / 0815 / 1416 / 2039	4.7 / 0.6 / 4.7 / 0.4	**27** TU	0213 / 0846 / 1432 / 2107	4.9 / 0.4 / 4.9 / 0.3
13 TU	0235 / 0850 / 1446 / 2116	4.8 / 0.5 / 4.8 / 0.4	**28** W	0256 / 0925 / 1516 / 2146	4.8 / 0.4 / 4.9 / 0.4
14 W	0306 / 0926 / 1519 / 2151	4.8 / 0.5 / 4.8 / 0.4	**29** TH	0339 / 1006 / 1557 / 2225	4.7 / 0.4 / 4.8 / 0.6
15 TH	0338 / 1000 / 1553 / 2226	4.7 / 0.6 / 4.8 / 0.5	**30** F	0422 / 1046 / 1641 / 2302	4.5 / 0.5 / 4.6 / 0.8
			31 SA	0502 / 1125 / 1728 / 2346	4.3 / 0.6 / 4.4 / 1.0

NOVEMBER

Day	Time	m	Day	Time	m
1 SU	0550 / 1216 / 1820	4.1 / 0.8 / 4.1	**16** M	0531 / 1202 / 1758	4.3 / 0.5 / 4.5
2 M	0030 / 0640 / 1315 / 1915	1.1 / 3.8 / 0.9 / 3.8	**17** TU	0022 / 0635 / 1305 / 1905	0.8 / 4.1 / 0.6 / 4.3
3 TU	0146 / 0735 / 1425 / 2024	1.3 / 3.6 / 1.0 / 3.7	**18** W	0125 / 0745 / 1416 / 2026	0.9 / 4.0 / 0.6 / 4.2
4 W	0255 / 0900 / 1536 / 2200	1.3 / 3.5 / 0.9 / 3.7	**19** TH	0239 / 0858 / 1530 / . 2135	1.0 / 4.0 / 0.6 / 4.2
5 TH	0406 / 1036 / 1644 / 2301	1.2 / 3.7 / 0.9 / 3.9	**20** F	0400 / 1005 / 1646 / 2245	1.0 / 4.1 / 0.6 / 4.3
6 F	0516 / 1126 / 1745 / 2350	1.1 / 3.9 / 0.7 / 4.2	**21** SA	0516 / 1107 / 1756 / 2346	0.9 / 4.2 / 0.5 / 4.5
7 SA	0555 / 1206 / 1826	0.9 / 4.1 / 0.6	**22** SU	0616 / 1201 / 1840	0.7 / 4.4 / 0.4
8 SU	0025 / 0635 / 1239 / 1905	4.4 / 0.8 / 4.3 / 0.5	**23** M	0031 / 0701 / 1247 / 1926	4.6 / 0.6 / 4.6 / 0.4
9 M	0058 / 0709 / 1312 / 1936	4.5 / 0.7 / 4.5 / 0.5	**24** TU	0117 / 0746 / 1335 / ● 2006	4.6 / 0.5 / 4.7 / 0.4
10 TU	0132 / 0746 / 1347 / O 2011	4.7 / 0.6 / 4.7 / 0.4	**25** W	0200 / 0828 / 1418 / 2046	4.6 / 0.4 / 4.7 / 0.5
11 W	0207 / 0826 / 1420 / 2045	4.7 / 0.6 / 4.8 / 0.4	**26** TH	0242 / 0908 / 1501 / 2126	4.6 / 0.4 / 4.7 / 0.6
12 TH	0243 / 0905 / 1458 / 2122	4.7 / 0.5 / 4.8 / 0.5	**27** F	0326 / 0948 / 1542 / 2159	4.5 / 0.4 / 4.7 / 0.7
13 F	0319 / 0945 / 1536 / 2202	4.7 / 0.5 / 4.8 / 0.5	**28** SA	0406 / 1030 / 1626 / 2235	4.5 / 0.4 / 4.6 / 0.8
14 SA	0358 / 1025 / 1616 / 2246	4.6 / 0.5 / 4.8 / 0.6	**29** SU	0445 / 1110 / 1709 / 2315	4.3 / 0.5 / 4.4 / 0.9
15 SU	0443 / 1109 / 1702 / 2330	4.5 / 0.5 / 4.7 / 0.7	**30** M	0525 / 1156 / 1756	4.2 / 0.6 / 4.2

DECEMBER

Day	Time	m	Day	Time	m
1 TU	0000 / 0610 / 1247 / 1842	1.0 / 4.1 / 0.7 / 4.0	**16** W	0012 / 0619 / 1255 / 1856	0.7 / 4.3 / 0.3 / 4.5
2 W	0056 / 0700 / 1346 / 1940	1.1 / 3.9 / 0.8 / 3.9	**17** TH	0110 / 0726 / 1356 / 2002	0.8 / 4.2 / 0.4 / 4.4
3 TH	0205 / 0756 / 1434 / 2034	1.2 / 3.7 / 0.9 / 3.8	**18** F	0216 / 0826 / 1456 / 2106	0.9 / 4.1 / 0.5 / 4.2
4 F	0310 / 0859 / 1539 / 2155	1.2 / 3.7 / 0.9 / 3.8	**19** SA	0326 / 0935 / 1604 / 2215	0.9 / 4.1 / 0.6 / 4.2
5 SA	0404 / 1016 / 1639 / 2255	1.2 / 3.7 / 0.8 / 4.0	**20** SU	0446 / 1041 / 1726 / 2321	0.9 / 4.1 / 0.6 / 4.2
6 SU	0506 / 1115 / 1736 / 2346	1.0 / 3.9 / 0.8 / 4.2	**21** M	0550 / 1142 / 1820	0.7 / 4.2 / 0.6
7 M	0555 / 1159 / 1826	0.9 / 4.1 / 0.7	**22** TU	0019 / 0645 / 1239 / 1905	4.3 / 0.7 / 4.3 / 0.6
8 TU	0025 / 0634 / 1241 / 1906	4.3 / 0.8 / 4.3 / 0.6	**23** W	0107 / 0729 / 1325 / 1951	4.4 / 0.5 / 4.4 / 0.6
9 W	0106 / 0726 / 1321 / O 1942	4.5 / 0.7 / 4.5 / 0.5	**24** TH	0156 / 0815 / 1410 / ● 2025	4.4 / 0.5 / 4.5 / 0.7
10 TH	0145 / 0805 / 1400 / 2026	4.6 / 0.5 / 4.7 / 0.5	**25** F	0236 / 0856 / 1452 / 2106	4.4 / 0.4 / 4.6 / 0.7
11 F	0226 / 0845 / 1442 / 2109	4.7 / 0.4 / 4.8 / 0.5	**26** SA	0316 / 0935 / 1531 / 2140	4.5 / 0.3 / 4.6 / 0.7
12 SA	0305 / 0933 / 1523 / 2150	4.7 / 0.3 / 4.9 / 0.5	**27** SU	0348 / 1011 / 1608 / 2216	4.5 / 0.3 / 4.6 / 0.7
13 SU	0348 / 1026 / 1611 / 2238	4.7 / 0.3 / 4.9 / 0.5	**28** M	0428 / 1049 / 1647 / 2256	4.5 / 0.3 / 4.5 / 0.8
14 M	0435 / 1124 / 1655 / 2325	4.6 / 0.4 / 4.8 / 0.6	**29** TU	0505 / 1124 / 1726 / 2330	4.4 / 0.4 / 4.4 / 0.8
15 TU	0526 / 1159 / 1752	4.5 / 0.3 / 4.6	**30** W	0542 / 1206 / 1808	4.4 / 0.5 / 4.2
			31 TH	0005 / 0619 / 1246 / 1849	0.9 / 4.2 / 0.6 / 4.1

TIDAL DIFFERENCES PAGE 21:311. TIDAL CURVE PAGE 21:310.

TIDAL STREAMS PAGES 21:295-21:301.

Datum of predictions: 0.3 m. below M.L.W.S.. and 0.2 m. above L.A.T.

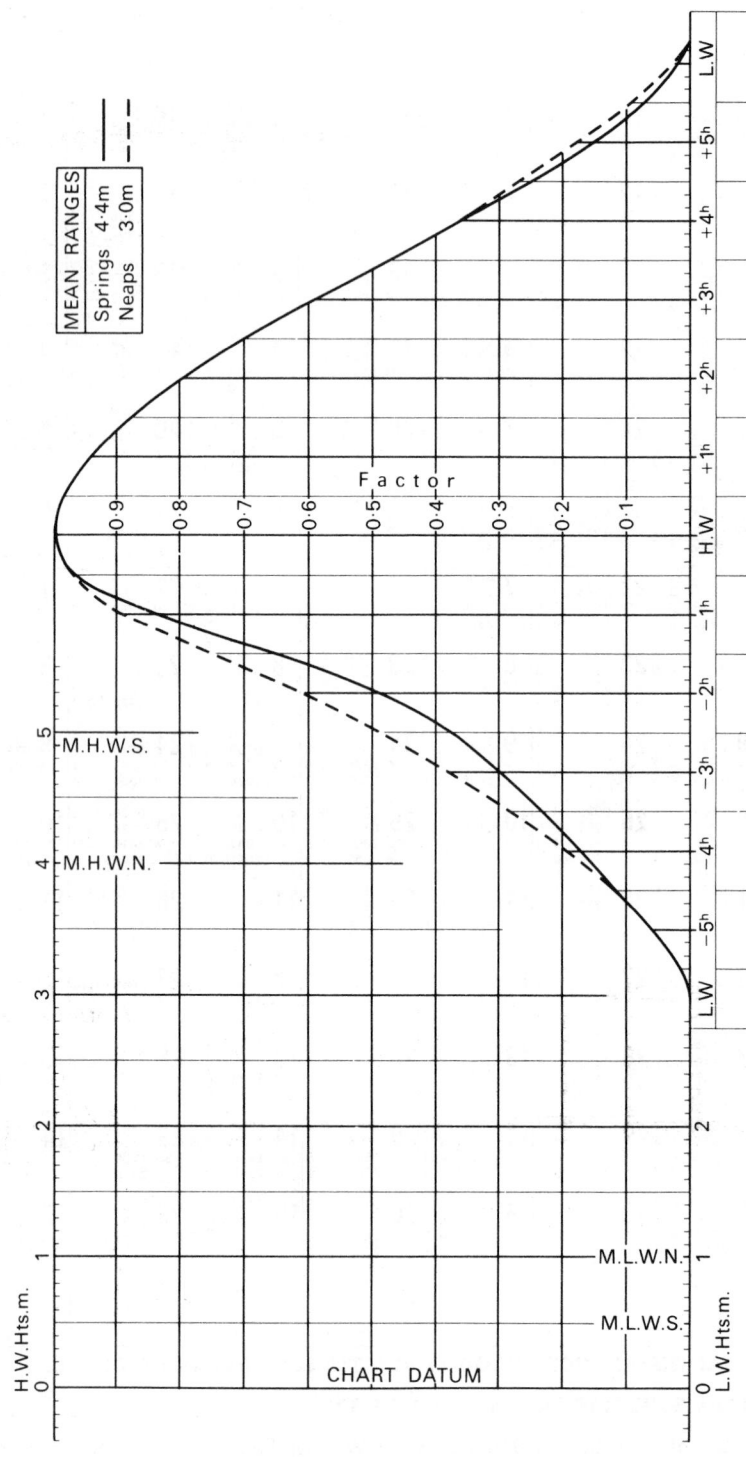

VLISSINGEN (FLUSHING)
MEAN SPRING AND NEAP CURVES
Springs occur 2 days after New and Full Moon.

PLACE	TIME DIFFERENCES				HEIGHT DIFFERENCES (Metres)			
	High Water		Low Water		MHWS	MHWN	MLWN	MLWS
VLISSINGEN (FLUSHING)	0300 and 1500	0900 and 2100	0400 and 1600	1000 and 2200	4.7	3.9	0.8	0.3
IJmuiden	+0145	+0143	+0304	+0321	−2.7	−2.2	−0.6	−0.1
Scheveningen	+0105	+0102	+0226	+0246	−2.6	−2.2	−0.6	−0.1
Eurogeul Entrance								
Platform	+0012	0000	−0028	−0059	−2.7	−2.2	−0.5	−0.1
Nieuwe Waterweg								
Maassluis	+0201	+0136	+0040	0000	−2.8	−2.2	−0.6	0.0
Nieuwe Maas								
Vlaardingen	+0157	+0143	+0115	+0035	−2.7	−2.2	−0.6	0.0
Rotterdam	+0202	+0156	+0313	+0400	−2.7	−2.2	−0.6	−0.1
Lek								
Krimpen	+0246	+0227	+0351	+0438	−2.9	−2.3	−0.4	+0.1
Streefkerk	+0323	+0302	+0431	+0521	−3.0	−2.3	−0.3	+0.2
Schoonhoven	+0409	+0345	+0517	+0600	−2.9	−2.2	−0.2	+0.4
Oude Maas								
Spijkenisse...............	+0208	+0150	+0258	+0337	−2.9	−2.3	−0.6	−0.1
Goidschalxoord	+0244	+0221	+0314	+0410	−3.2	−2.6	−0.5	+0.1
Puttershoek	+0250	+0230	+0400	+0445	−3.4	−2.8	−0.5	0.0
De Noord								
Alblasserdam	+0235	+0220	+0350	+0450	−3.1	−2.6	−0.4	+0.1
De Kil								
's-Gravendeel	+0231	+0225	+0448	+0529	−3.8	−3.0	−0.5	+0.1
Merwede								
Dordrecht	+0234	+0229	+0432	+0518	−3.5	−2.8	−0.5	+0.1
Sliedrecht	+0410	+0355	+0600	+0615	−3.6	−2.9	−0.4	+0.2
Gorinchem...............	+0445	+0435	+0705	+0725	−3.7	−3.1	−0.3	+0.3
Haringvlietsluizen	+0016	+0014	+0006	−0026	−1.8	−1.7	−0.5	0.0
Oster Schelde								
Roompot...................	+0115	+0115	+0115	+0115	−	−	−	−
Wemeldinge	+0145	+0145	+0125	+0125	−	−	−	−
Lodijkse Gat.	+0145	+0145	+0125	+0125	−	−	−	−
Zijpe								
Philipsdam (West)	+0135	+0135	+0125	+0125	−	−	−	−
Walcheren								
Oostkapelle								
(Oosterhodfd)........	+0005	+0005	−0005	−0020	−1.1	−0.9	−0.2	0.0
Westkapelle	−0024	−0014	−0012	−0023	−0.6	−0.5	−0.1	0.0
Wester Schelde								
Breskens....................	−0005	−0005	−0002	−0002	+0.1	0.0	0.0	0.0
Terneuzen	+0021	+0022	+0022	+0033	+0.3	+0.3	0.0	0.0
Hansweert	+0114	+0054	+0040	+0100	+0.5	_0.6	0.0	−0.1
Bath	+0126	+0117	+0117	+0144	+0.8	+0.9	0.0	0.0
Cadzand								
(Wielingen Sluis) ..	−0030	−0025	−0020	−0025	−0.1	−0.2	+0.1	0.0
Zeebrugge	−0035	−0015	−0020	−0035	+0.1	0.0	+0.3	+0.1
Oostende	−0055	−0040	−0030	−0045	+0.3	+0.3	+0.3	+0.1
Nieuwpoort	−0110	−0050	−0035	−0045	+0.6	+0.4	+0.4	+0.1

Note: Time zone. The predictions for the standard port are on the same time zone as the differences shown. No further adjustment is necessary.
Refer to predictions on pages 21:307-21:309

PROSPERPOLDER ANTWERP

HIGH & LOW WATER 1992   Lat. 51°21'N. Long. 4°14'E.

TIME ZONE –0100 SUBTRACT 1 HOUR FROM TIMES SHOWN FOR GMT

JANUARY

Day	Time	m	Time	m	Day	Time	m	Time	m
1 W	0021	5.0	0657	0.9	16 Th	0527	1.0	1139	5.0
	1248	5.0	1926	0.6		1811	0.9		
2 Th	0119	5.1	0801	0.8	17 F	0021	5.1	0645	0.9
	1344	5.2	2019	0.6		1250	5.2	1924	0.7
3 F	0211	5.3	0849	0.6	18 Sa	0127	5.4	0757	0.7
	1432	5.4	2101	0.6		1354	5.6	2029	0.6
4 Sa	0256	5.4	0931	0.6	19 Su	0225	5.6	0901	0.5
	1515	5.5	2139	0.7		1449	5.9	2127	0.5
5 Su	0335	5.5	1010	0.5	20 M	0315	5.9	0959	0.2
	1553	5.7	● 2214	0.7		1538	6.2	2219	0.4
6 M	0410	5.6	1045	0.5	21 Tu	0403	6.0	1051	0.0
	1628	5.7	2248	0.7		1626	6.3	2308	0.4
7 Tu	0444	5.7	1119	0.5	22 W	0449	6.1	1140	-0.2
	1701	5.7	2320	0.7		1712	6.4	2354	0.4
8 W	0516	5.8	1151	0.4	23 Th	0534	6.2	1227	-0.3
	1733	5.8	2353	0.6		1758	6.3		
9 Th	0549	5.6	1222	0.4	24 F	0038	0.5	0619	6.1
	1807	5.8				1310	-0.3	1846	6.1
10 F	0027	0.6	0622	5.7	25 Sa	0119	0.5	0706	5.9
	1252	0.4	1841	5.7		1351	-0.1	1934	5.8
11 Sa	0100	0.7	0656	5.5	26 Su	0201	0.6	0754	5.6
	1324	0.5	1917	5.5		1433	0.1	(2023	5.4
12 Su	0137	0.7	0733	5.4	27 M	0243	0.7	0846	5.3
	1401	0.6	1958	5.3		1517	0.3	2119	5.0
13 M	0218	0.8	0818	5.2	28 Tu	0334	0.8	0948	4.9
	1442	0.6	) 2051	5.1		1610	0.6	2228	4.7
14 Tu	0305	0.9	0915	5.0	29 W	0438	1.0	1106	4.6
	1535	0.8	2157	5.0		1718	0.9	2349	4.6
15 W	0407	1.0	1027	4.9	30 Th	0610	1.0	1222	4.7
	1647	0.9	2309	5.0		1848	0.9		
					31 F	0056	4.8	0735	0.8
						1324	5.0	1952	0.7

FEBRUARY

Day	Time	m	Time	m	Day	Time	m	Time	m
1 Sa	0152	5.1	0829	0.5	16 Su	0113	5.1	0742	0.5
	1416	5.3	2040	0.6		1342	5.5	2018	0.5
2 Su	0239	5.4	0912	0.4	17 M	0213	5.4	0851	0.2
	1500	5.6	2119	0.5		1437	5.9	2117	0.4
3 M	0319	5.6	0950	0.3	18 Tu	0303	5.8	0948	-0.1
	1538	5.7	● 2156	0.5		1525	6.2	2207	0.3
4 Tu	0353	5.7	1027	0.3	19 W	0348	6.0	1037	-0.4
	1610	5.8	2230	0.5		1610	6.4	2254	0.2
5 W	0426	5.8	1059	0.2	20 Th	0430	6.2	1123	-0.5
	1641	5.9	2302	0.5		1654	6.4	2337	0.2
6 Th	0457	5.9	1132	0.2	21 F	0512	6.2	1205	-0.5
	1712	6.0	2334	0.4		1736	6.3		
7 F	0526	5.9	1201	0.2	22 Sa	0018	0.2	0554	6.1
	1743	6.0				1246	-0.4	1818	6.0
8 Sa	0008	0.4	0557	5.9	23 Su	0055	0.3	0636	5.9
	1232	0.3	1814	5.8		1321	-0.1	1900	5.7
9 Su	0042	0.5	0628	5.7	24 M	0131	0.4	0720	5.6
	1303	0.4	1848	5.7		1357	0.2	1944	5.3
10 M	0114	0.6	0703	5.6	25 Tu	0208	0.5	0805	5.2
	1334	0.4	1927	5.5		1434	0.4	(2030	4.9
11 Tu	0151	0.6	0744	5.4	26 W	0251	0.7	0900	4.8
	1412	0.5	) 2013	5.3		1522	0.7	2132	4.5
12 W	0234	0.7	0836	5.2	27 Th	0352	0.9	1019	4.4
	1500	0.7	2117	5.0		1630	1.0	2305	4.2
13 Th	0332	0.8	0946	4.9	28 F	0518	1.0	1153	4.5
	1610	0.9	2231	4.8		1800	1.0		
14 F	0455	0.9	1106	4.8	29 Sa	0027	4.5	0657	0.8
	1743	0.9	2354	4.8		1300	4.9	1920	0.7
15 Sa	0621	0.8	1234	5.0					
	1906	0.7							

MARCH

Day	Time	m	Time	m	Day	Time	m	Time	m
1 Su	0127	4.9	0759	0.4	16 M	0059	5.0	0731	0.3
	1352	5.3	2012	0.5		1330	5.5	2006	0.5
2 M	0215	5.3	0846	0.2	17 Tu	0157	5.4	0839	0.0
	1436	5.6	2056	0.3		1422	5.9	2103	0.3
3 Tu	0254	5.6	0925	0.1	18 W	0243	5.7	0931	-0.3
	1512	5.8	2134	0.3		1507	6.2	2150	0.2
4 W	0328	5.7	1002	0.1	19 Th	0327	6.0	1017	-0.5
	● 2207	0.3				1549	6.3	2234	0.1
5 Th	0359	5.9	1034	0.1	20 F	0406	6.1	1101	-0.5
	1614	6.0	2240	0.3		1630	6.2	2315	0.1
6 F	0428	6.0	1105	0.1	21 Sa	0447	6.2	1140	-0.4
	1642	6.1	2313	0.3		1709	6.1	2353	0.1
7 Sa	0458	6.0	1137	0.1	22 Su	0527	6.1	1217	-0.2
	1713	6.0	2347	0.3		1749	5.9		
8 Su	0529	6.0	1210	0.2	23 M	0029	0.2	0607	5.9
	1746	5.9				1249	0.1	1828	5.5
9 M	0021	0.3	0601	5.8	24 Tu	0102	0.3	0646	5.5
	1241	0.3	1821	5.8		1321	0.3	1906	5.2
10 Tu	0055	0.4	0638	5.7	25 W	0137	0.5	0727	5.2
	1313	0.4	1900	5.6		1355	0.6	1947	4.8
11 W	0130	0.5	0719	5.5	26 Th	0215	0.6	0816	4.8
	1348	0.5	1948	5.3		1437	0.8	(2040	4.5
12 Th	0205	0.5	0811	5.3	27 F	0307	0.8	0928	4.4
	1436	0.6	) 2049	4.9		1542	1.0	2203	4.2
13 F	0311	0.7	0921	5.0	28 Sa	0431	1.0	1106	4.4
	1549	0.9	2206	4.7		1716	1.1	2344	4.3
14 Sa	0435	0.7	1047	4.8	29 Su	0604	0.8	1224	4.8
	1726	0.9	2337	4.6		1838	0.8		
15 Su	0604	0.6	1222	5.1	30 M	0050	4.8	0716	0.5
	1855	0.7				1319	5.3	1937	0.4
					31 Tu	0140	5.2	0809	0.2
						1404	5.6	2025	0.3

APRIL

Day	Time	m	Time	m	Day	Time	m	Time	m
1 W	0220	5.5	0853	0.1	16 Th	0220	5.7	0910	-0.3
	1440	5.8	2104	0.2		1444	6.0	2129	0.2
2 Th	0256	5.7	0929	0.1	17 F	0303	5.9	0955	-0.3
	1512	5.9	2138	0.2		1525	6.0	○ 2212	0.1
3 F	0327	5.9	1002	0.1	18 Sa	0342	6.0	1035	-0.2
	1542	6.0	● 2212	0.2		1604	6.0	2251	0.1
4 Sa	0356	6.0	1035	0.2	19 Su	0423	6.1	1112	-0.1
	1613	6.1	2248	0.2		1644	5.9	2329	0.1
5 Su	0428	6.1	1109	0.2	20 M	0502	6.0	1146	0.1
	1647	6.1	2325	0.2		1722	5.7		
6 M	0502	6.1	1146	0.2	21 Tu	0003	0.2	0542	5.8
	1722	6.0				1218	0.3	1758	5.5
7 Tu	0003	0.3	0537	6.0	22 W	0036	0.4	0619	5.5
	1221	0.3	1800	5.8		1249	0.5	1835	5.2
8 W	0039	0.3	0617	5.9	23 Th	0109	0.5	0659	5.3
	1255	0.4	1842	5.6		1321	0.6	1914	5.0
9 Th	0117	0.4	0702	5.7	24 F	0144	0.6	0744	5.0
	1334	0.5	1931	5.3		1401	0.8	(2005	4.7
10 F	0202	0.5	0758	5.4	25 Sa	0227	0.7	0846	4.7
	1425	0.6	) 2034	4.9		1451	0.9	2115	4.4
11 Sa	0304	0.5	0910	5.1	26 Su	0332	0.8	1002	4.6
	1541	0.8	2152	4.7		1619	1.0	2237	4.4
12 Su	0427	0.5	1038	5.0	27 M	0508	0.8	1126	4.8
	1712	0.8	2322	4.7		1746	0.8	2357	4.7
13 M	0550	0.4	1207	5.2	28 Tu	0622	0.6	1231	5.1
	1838	0.6				1852	0.6		
14 Tu	0038	5.0	0714	0.1	29 W	0055	5.1	0723	0.4
	1310	5.6	1948	0.4		1320	5.5	1944	0.4
15 W	0134	5.4	0818	-0.2	30 Th	0140	5.4	0811	0.3
	1401	5.9	2043	0.2		1359	5.7	2026	0.3

TIDAL DIFFERENCES PAGE 21:306.

TIDAL STREAMS PAGES 21:295-21:301.

Datum of predictions = Chart Datum: 0.45 m. below TAW.

Lat. 51°21'N. Long. 4°14'E. **HIGH & LOW WATER 1992**

TIME ZONE –0100 SUBTRACT 1 HOUR FROM TIMES SHOWN FOR GMT

MAY

Day	Time	m		Day	Time	m
1 F	0218 0850 1434 2104	5.6 0.3 5.8 0.3		16 Sa ○	0240 0929 1503 2149	5.7 0.0 5.8 0.3
2 Sa ●	0251 0927 1510 2142	5.8 0.3 6.0 0.3		17 Su	0321 1009 1543 2228	5.8 0.1 5.8 0.3
3 Su	0327 1003 1545 2221	6.0 0.3 6.1 0.2		18 M	0402 1044 1623 2306	5.9 0.3 5.7 0.3
4 M	0402 1044 1623 2304	6.1 0.3 6.1 0.2		19 Tu	0442 1118 1701 2342	5.8 0.4 5.6 0.3
5 Tu	0440 1123 1702 2346	6.1 0.3 6.0 0.2		20 W	0520 1150 1737	5.7 0.5 5.5
6 W	0520 1204 1744	6.1 0.4 5.9		21 Th	0015 0558 1222 1814	0.4 5.6 0.6 5.4
7 Th	0028 0604 1243 1831	0.3 6.0 0.5 5.7		22 F	0048 0638 1255 1853	0.5 5.5 0.7 5.2
8 F	0112 0653 1327 1924	0.3 5.8 0.5 5.4		23 Sa	0120 0720 1331 1938	0.5 5.3 0.7 5.1
9 Sa ☽	0202 0754 1422 2027	0.3 5.6 0.6 5.1		24 Su ☾	0158 0811 1415 2034	0.5 5.1 0.8 4.9
10 Su	0304 0904 1532 2139	0.3 5.4 0.7 5.0		25 M	0244 0912 1510 2139	0.6 5.0 0.9 4.8
11 M	0416 1023 1651 2257	0.2 5.3 0.7 5.0		26 Tu	0346 1017 1628 2247	0.7 5.0 0.9 4.8
12 Tu	0529 1142 1811	0.2 5.4 0.6		27 W	0511 1125 1747 2353	0.7 5.1 0.8 5.0
13 W	0010 0648 1243 1923	5.1 0.1 5.6 0.5		28 Th	0618 1225 1848	0.6 5.3 0.6
14 Th	0107 0754 1335 2019	5.4 0.1 5.7 0.3		29 F	0049 0716 1314 1938	5.3 0.3 5.5 0.5
15 F	0155 0844 1422 2107	5.6 -0.1 5.8 0.3		30 Sa	0135 0805 1359 2026	5.5 0.5 5.7 0.4
				31 Su	0219 0850 1442 2112	5.8 0.4 5.9 0.4

JUNE

Day	Time	m		Day	Time	m
1 M ●	0300 0935 1522 2159	6.0 0.4 6.0 0.3		16 Tu	0349 1020 1609 2248	5.7 0.6 5.6 0.4
2 Tu	0342 1021 1606 2247	6.1 0.4 6.1 0.3		17 W	0428 1054 1647 2325	5.7 0.6 5.7 0.4
3 W	0424 1106 1649 2334	6.2 0.4 6.1 0.2		18 Th	0506 1127 1723 2358	5.8 0.6 5.7 0.4
4 Th	0509 1151 1734	6.2 0.4 6.0		19 F	0543 1200 1758	5.8 0.6 5.6
5 F	0021 0557 1236 1824	0.1 6.2 0.5 5.8		20 Sa	0031 0618 1234 1834	0.4 5.7 0.6 5.6
6 Sa	0110 0649 1324 1917	0.1 6.1 0.5 5.7		21 Su	0100 0656 1307 1913	0.4 5.6 0.6 5.5
7 Su ☽	0201 0747 1416 2015	0.0 5.9 0.6 5.5		22 M	0134 0737 1347 1957	0.4 5.5 0.6 5.3
8 M	0256 0850 1515 2118	0.0 5.7 0.6 5.3		23 Tu	0212 0825 1430 ☾ 2047	0.4 5.3 0.7 5.2
9 Tu	0356 0959 1620 2227	0.0 5.5 0.7 5.2		24 W	0257 0921 1522 2146	0.5 5.2 0.8 5.0
10 W	0459 1111 1732 2339	0.1 5.4 0.7 5.2		25 Th	0353 1023 1630 2251	0.6 5.1 0.9 5.0
11 Th	0614 1215 1853	0.2 5.4 0.6		26 F	0508 1127 1746 2356	0.7 5.2 0.8 5.1
12 F	0041 0724 1312 1955	5.3 0.2 5.5 0.5		27 Sa	0619 1231 1852	0.7 5.3 0.7
13 Sa	0134 0819 1402 2046	5.4 0.3 5.5 0.4		28 Su	0057 0723 1327 1951	5.4 0.6 5.6 0.6
14 Su	0223 0905 1447 2131	5.5 0.4 5.5 0.4		29 M	0151 0819 1419 2049	5.6 0.6 5.8 0.5
15 M ○	0307 0943 1529 2210	5.6 0.5 5.6 0.4		30 Tu ●	0240 0912 1507 2142	5.9 0.5 6.0 0.4

JULY

Day	Time	m		Day	Time	m
1 W	0328 1004 1553 2235	6.1 0.5 6.1 0.2		16 Th	0416 1034 1633 2306	5.8 0.6 5.8 0.3
2 Th	0414 1054 1638 2326	6.3 0.4 6.1 0.1		17 F	0449 1108 1705 2340	5.9 0.6 5.9 0.3
3 F	0501 1142 1725	6.4 0.4 6.1		18 Sa	0523 1142 1737	6.0 0.5 5.9
4 Sa	0015 0549 1229 1812	-0.1 6.4 0.5 6.1		19 Su	0011 0556 1214 1810	0.2 6.0 0.5 5.9
5 Su	0103 0638 1316 1902	-0.2 6.3 0.5 6.0		20 M	0041 0629 1246 1843	0.3 5.9 0.5 5.8
6 M	0149 0731 1402 1954	-0.2 6.1 0.5 5.8		21 Tu	0110 0703 1321 1919	0.3 5.7 0.6 5.6
7 Tu ☽	0237 0827 1451 2051	-0.1 5.8 0.6 5.6		22 W	0144 0742 1359 ☾ 1959	0.4 5.5 0.6 5.4
8 W	0328 0929 1546 2155	0.0 5.5 0.7 5.3		23 Th	0223 0829 1444 2050	0.5 5.3 0.7 5.2
9 Th	0424 1037 1649 2306	0.2 5.2 0.8 5.1		24 F	0310 0928 1541 2156	0.7 5.1 0.8 5.0
10 F	0533 1146 1817	0.4 5.1 0.8		25 Sa	0416 1037 1657 2308	0.8 5.0 0.9 5.0
11 Sa	0015 0655 1249 1933	5.1 0.6 5.1 0.7		26 Su	0539 1150 1814	0.9 5.1 0.9
12 Su	0117 0755 1347 2029	5.2 0.6 5.3 0.5		27 M	0024 0650 1302 1923	5.2 0.8 5.3 0.7
13 M	0211 0843 1436 2114	5.4 0.6 5.4 0.5		28 Tu	0131 0757 1402 2030	5.5 0.6 5.6 0.5
14 Tu ○	0257 0924 1518 2155	5.5 0.6 5.5 0.4		29 W	0226 0858 1453 ● 2131	5.9 0.5 5.9 0.3
15 W	0339 0959 1557 2231	5.7 0.7 5.7 0.4		30 Th	0315 0953 1539 2224	6.2 0.5 6.1 0.1
				31 F	0402 1042 1624 2315	6.4 0.4 6.2 -0.2

AUGUST

Day	Time	m		Day	Time	m
1 Sa	0447 1130 1708	6.5 0.4 6.3		16 Su	0458 1120 1712 2347	6.1 0.4 6.1 0.2
2 Su	0003 0532 1215 1753	-0.3 6.5 0.4 6.3		17 M	0527 1153 1742	6.1 0.4 6.1
3 M	0046 0618 1259 1839	-0.3 6.3 0.4 6.1		18 Tu	0017 0558 1225 1814	0.3 6.0 0.5 5.9
4 Tu	0130 0706 1340 1927	-0.2 6.0 0.5 5.9		19 W	0046 0632 1257 1846	0.4 5.8 0.5 5.7
5 W ☽	0211 0757 1422 2019	0.0 5.7 0.6 5.5		20 Th	0117 0707 1333 1924	0.5 5.6 0.6 5.6
6 Th	0254 0853 1510 2119	0.2 5.3 0.7 5.2		21 F	0152 0749 1413 ☾ 2011	0.6 5.4 0.7 5.3
7 F	0343 0959 1609 2233	0.5 4.9 0.9 4.9		22 Sa	0236 0844 1505 2112	0.8 5.1 0.8 5.1
8 Sa	0449 1115 1734 2351	0.8 4.7 1.0 4.8		23 Su	0338 0955 1619 2230	1.0 4.8 1.0 4.9
9 Su	0619 1228 1909	0.9 4.8 0.8		24 M	0506 1116 1744 2358	1.0 4.8 0.9 5.0
10 M	0100 0731 1328 2008	5.0 0.8 5.1 0.6		25 Tu	0627 1243 1902	0.9 5.0 0.7
11 Tu	0155 0820 1419 2054	5.3 0.6 5.4 0.4		26 W	0116 0742 1347 2018	5.5 0.7 5.6 0.4
12 W	0242 0903 1501 2134	5.6 0.6 5.6 0.3		27 Th	0212 0847 1437 2119	5.9 0.5 5.8 0.1
13 Th	0321 0939 1538 ○ 2210	5.8 0.6 5.8 0.3		28 F	0300 0941 1521 ● 2210	6.2 0.4 6.1 -0.1
14 F	0356 1014 1612 2244	5.9 0.5 5.9 0.2		29 Sa	0343 1028 1604 2258	6.4 0.3 6.2 -0.3
15 Sa	0427 1048 1641 2316	6.0 0.5 6.0 0.2		30 Su	0427 1115 1647 2343	6.5 0.3 6.3 -0.3
				31 M	0509 1157 1729	6.4 0.3 6.3

PROSPERPOLDER ANTWERP

Lat. 51°21'N. Long. 4°14'E. HIGH & LOW WATER 1992

TIME ZONE –0100 SUBTRACT 1 HOUR FROM TIMES SHOWN FOR GMT

SEPTEMBER

Day	Time	m	Day	Time	m
1 Tu	0025	-0.2	16 W	0529	6.0
	0553	6.2		1203	0.5
	1236	0.4		1744	6.0
	1812	6.1			
2 W	0103	0.0	17 Th	0022	0.5
	0636	5.8		0603	5.8
	1314	0.5		1236	0.6
	1857	5.8		1818	5.8
3 Th	0140	0.3	18 F	0053	0.7
	0723	5.4		0639	5.6
	1351	0.6		1310	0.7
	1945	5.4		1857	5.7
4 F	0216	0.6	19 Sa	0127	0.8
	0812	5.0		0721	5.4
	1433	0.6		1348	0.8
	2042	5.0		1942	5.4
5 Sa	0301	0.9	20 Su	0209	0.9
	0914	4.6		0815	5.0
	2155	4.6		1440	0.9
				2043	5.1
6 Su	0404	1.1	21 M	0312	1.1
	1035	4.3		0925	4.6
	1651	1.1		1555	1.0
	2322	4.6		2203	4.9
7 M	0536	1.2	22 Tu	0442	1.1
	1200	4.5		1052	4.6
	1832	1.0		1722	0.9
				2342	5.0
8 Tu	0035	4.9	23 W	0610	1.0
	0657	0.9		1225	4.9
	1304	4.9		1846	0.7
	1937	0.6			
9 W	0131	5.3	24 Th	0059	5.5
	0752	0.6		0731	0.7
	1355	5.3		1327	5.3
	2025	0.4		2005	0.3
10 Th	0218	5.7	25 F	0152	5.9
	0836	0.4		0833	0.5
	1437	5.6		1416	5.7
	2107	0.2		2103	0.0
11 F	0257	5.9	26 Sa	0239	6.2
	0915	0.4		0924	0.4
	1512	5.8		1500	6.0
	2143	0.2		2152	-0.2
12 Sa	0329	6.0	27 Su	0322	6.3
	0950	0.4		1010	0.3
	1545	6.0		1541	6.2
	2217	0.2		2237	-0.2
13 Su	0359	6.1	28 M	0403	6.3
	1024	0.4		1054	0.3
	1613	6.1		1623	6.3
	2248	0.2		2319	-0.2
14 M	0427	6.1	29 Tu	0445	6.2
	1057	0.4		1134	0.3
	1642	6.0		1704	6.2
	2319	0.3		2358	0.0
15 Tu	0458	6.1	30 W	0526	6.0
	1129	0.4		1212	0.4
	1712	6.1		1746	6.0
	2350	0.4			

OCTOBER

Day	Time	m	Day	Time	m
1 Th	0034	0.3	16 F	0000	0.7
	0608	5.6		0540	5.8
	1248	0.6		1218	0.6
	1828	5.7		1757	5.9
2 F	0106	0.6	17 Sa	0034	0.8
	0650	5.2		0618	5.6
	1323	0.7		1255	0.7
	1913	5.3		1838	5.7
3 Sa	0140	0.9	18 Su	0110	0.9
	0734	4.9		0703	5.4
	1401	0.9		1335	0.8
	2004	4.9		1926	5.5
4 Su	0220	1.1	19 M	0154	1.0
	0829	4.5		0758	5.0
	1449	1.1		1429	0.8
	2111	4.6		2027	5.2
5 M	0317	1.3	20 Tu	0258	1.1
	0943	4.3		0908	4.8
	1606	1.2		1543	0.9
	2235	4.5		2149	5.0
6 Tu	0448	1.3	21 W	0423	1.1
	1115	4.3		1034	4.4
	1739	1.1		1705	0.8
	2358	4.8		2323	5.1
7 W	0612	1.0	22 Th	0550	1.0
	1228	4.7		1200	4.9
	1853	0.7		1829	0.6
8 Th	0059	5.2	23 F	0036	5.5
	0714	0.7		0713	0.8
	1321	5.2		1302	5.3
	1948	0.4		1945	0.3
9 F	0145	5.6	24 Sa	0130	5.8
	0804	0.4		0813	0.6
	1405	5.6		1351	5.6
	2033	0.3		2043	0.0
10 Sa	0225	5.9	25 Su	0216	6.0
	0846	0.3		0904	0.4
	1442	5.8		1436	5.9
	2112	0.3		2131	0.0
11 Su	0258	6.0	26 M	0300	6.1
	0922	0.3		0949	0.4
	1512	6.0		1518	6.1
	2146	0.3		2214	0.0
12 M	0328	6.0	27 Tu	0341	6.1
	0956	0.4		1033	0.4
	1542	6.1		1600	6.1
	2217	0.4		2254	0.1
13 Tu	0357	6.1	28 W	0423	6.0
	1030	0.4		1112	0.4
	1613	6.1		1641	6.1
	2249	0.5		2330	0.4
14 W	0430	6.1	29 Th	0504	5.8
	1105	0.5		1149	0.5
	1645	6.0		1723	5.9
	2325	0.5			
15 Th	0504	6.0	30 F	0004	0.6
	1142	0.5		0544	5.6
	1720	6.0		1224	0.7
				1805	5.6
			31 Sa	0035	0.8
				0624	5.2
				1257	0.8
				1848	5.3

NOVEMBER

Day	Time	m	Day	Time	m
1 Su	0109	1.0	16 M	0102	0.9
	0706	5.0		0653	5.5
	1333	0.9		1335	0.7
	1934	5.0		1919	5.7
2 M	0145	1.1	17 Tu	0149	0.9
	0754	4.7		0749	5.2
	1413	1.0		1429	0.7
	2030	4.8		2020	5.4
3 Tu	0232	1.2	18 W	0250	1.0
	0856	4.6		0856	5.0
	1512	1.1		1535	0.6
	2136	4.7		2136	5.3
4 W	0348	1.3	19 Th	0403	1.1
	1007	4.5		1012	4.9
	1644	1.1		1645	0.5
	2257	4.7		2258	5.3
5 Th	0519	1.1	20 F	0520	1.0
	1130	4.6		1129	5.0
	1758	0.9		1805	0.5
6 F	0010	5.0	21 Sa	0008	5.4
	0628	0.8		0646	0.9
	1236	5.0		1234	5.3
	1900	0.6		1921	0.3
7 Sa	0104	5.4	22 Su	0106	5.6
	0724	0.6		0751	0.7
	1324	5.4		1327	5.5
	1952	0.5		2020	0.2
8 Su	0147	5.7	23 M	0155	5.7
	0811	0.5		0844	0.5
	1405	5.7		1415	5.7
	2036	0.4		2108	0.2
9 M	0223	5.8	24 Tu	0242	5.7
	0856	0.5		0931	0.5
	1439	5.8		1500	5.8
	2111	0.5		2150	0.3
10 Tu	0257	5.9	25 W	0324	5.8
	0925	0.5		1013	0.5
	1512	6.0		1543	5.9
	2146	0.6		2230	0.4
11 W	0331	6.0	26 Th	0406	5.7
	1003	0.5		1052	0.5
	1548	6.1		1626	5.9
	2223	0.6		2305	0.6
12 Th	0406	6.0	27 F	0447	5.6
	1044	0.6		1130	0.6
	1623	6.1		1708	5.8
	2302	0.7		2337	0.8
13 F	0444	6.0	28 Sa	0527	5.5
	1125	0.6		1205	0.7
	1701	6.1		1749	5.6
	2342	0.7			
14 Sa	0523	5.9	29 Su	0010	0.9
	1207	0.6		0607	5.4
	1742	6.0		1239	0.7
				1828	5.5
15 Su	0021	0.8	30 M	0043	0.9
	0605	5.7		0645	5.3
	1249	0.7		1312	0.8
	1827	5.9		1909	5.3

DECEMBER

Day	Time	m	Day	Time	m
1 Tu	0117	0.9	16 W	0145	0.8
	0727	5.1		0738	5.6
	1347	0.8		1425	0.3
	1955	5.2		2011	5.7
2 W	0157	1.0	17 Th	0239	0.8
	0816	5.0		0837	5.4
	1427	0.8		1519	0.3
	2049	5.0		2117	5.5
3 Th	0246	1.0	18 F	0339	0.9
	0914	4.9		0945	5.2
	1524	0.9		1620	0.3
	2149	4.9		2228	5.3
4 F	0359	1.1	19 Sa	0447	0.9
	1017	4.8		1058	5.1
	1651	0.9		1733	0.3
	2257	4.9		2340	5.3
5 Sa	0527	1.0	20 Su	0614	0.9
	1127	4.9		1207	5.2
	1803	0.8		1855	0.4
6 Su	0005	5.1	21 M	0042	5.3
	0631	0.9		0730	0.8
	1232	5.1		1307	5.3
	1902	0.7		1958	0.4
7 M	0102	5.3	22 Tu	0138	5.4
	0724	0.8		0826	0.6
	1323	5.4		1401	5.4
	1951	0.7		2047	0.4
8 Tu	0148	5.5	23 W	0229	5.5
	0812	0.7		0915	0.5
	1406	5.6		1450	5.6
	2034	0.7		2131	0.5
9 W	0229	5.7	24 Th	0314	5.5
	0856	0.7		0957	0.5
	1447	5.8		1535	5.7
	2118	0.7		2209	0.6
10 Th	0310	5.8	25 F	0356	5.6
	0941	0.6		1038	0.5
	1527	6.0		1616	5.7
	2200	0.7		2244	0.7
11 F	0349	5.9	26 Sa	0437	5.6
	1026	0.6		1115	0.5
	1607	6.1		1657	5.7
	2244	0.7		2318	0.7
12 Sa	0431	6.0	27 Su	0513	5.7
	1113	0.5		1150	0.5
	1649	6.1		1733	5.7
	2329	0.7		2350	0.7
13 Su	0513	6.0	28 M	0550	5.7
	1200	0.4		1222	0.5
	1733	6.1		1808	5.7
14 M	0014	0.7	29 Tu	0022	0.7
	0557	5.9		0624	5.6
	1246	0.4		1253	0.5
	1819	6.1		1843	5.6
15 Tu	0059	0.7	30 W	0055	0.7
	0645	5.7		0700	5.5
	1334	0.3		1321	0.5
	1912	5.9		1921	5.5
			31 Th	0130	0.8
				0738	5.4
				1354	0.5
				2004	5.3

TIDAL DIFFERENCES PAGE 21:306.

TIDAL STREAMS PAGES 21:295-21:301.

Datum of predictions = Chart Datum: 0.45 m. below TAW.

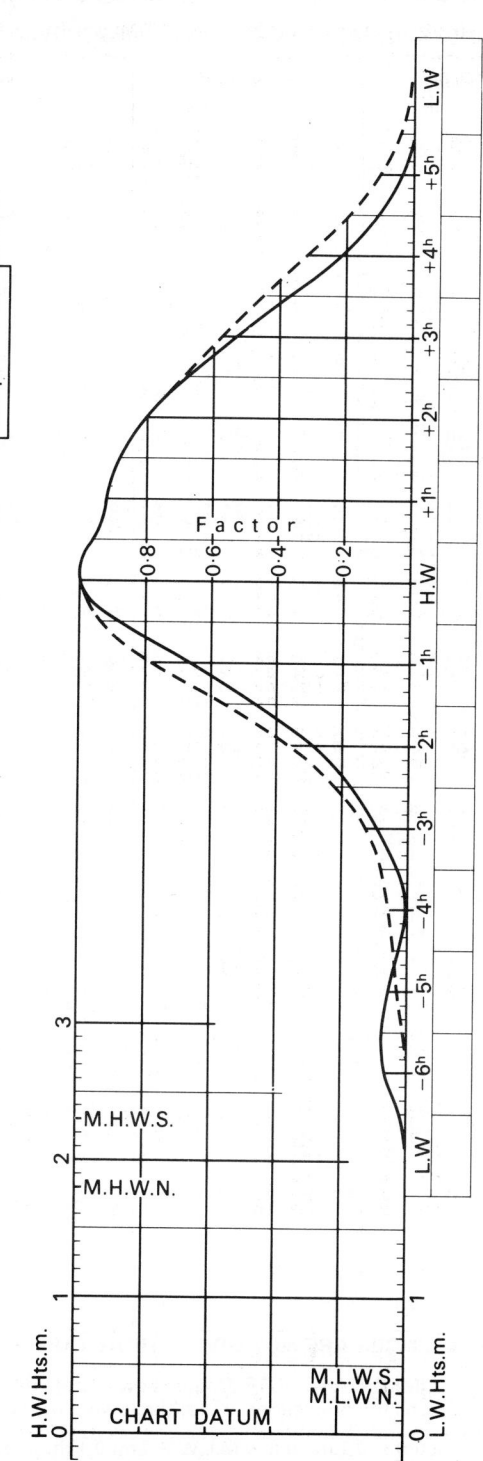

HOEK VAN HOLLAND
MEAN SPRING AND NEAP CURVES
Springs occur 3 days after New and Full Moon.

HOEK VAN HOLLAND

HIGH & LOW WATER 1992   Lat. 51°59′N. Long. 4°07′E.

TIME ZONE -0100 SUBTRACT 1 HOUR FROM TIMES SHOWN FOR GMT

JANUARY

Day	Time / m	Day	Time / m
1	0740 0.4 / 1158 1.8 / W 1946 0.3	16	0450 0.4 / 1109 1.8 / TH 1654 0.2 / 2345 1.8
2	0039 1.9 / 0905 0.3 / TH 1253 1.9 / 2117 0.4	17	0534 0.4 / 1215 1.9 / F 1753 0.3
3	0134 1.9 / 0934 0.3 / F 1348 1.9 / 1935 0.4	18	0045 1.9 / 0625 0.3 / SA 1304 2.0 / 1843 0.3
4	0213 1.9 / 1020 0.3 / SA 1434 1.9 / ● 2015 0.5	19	0134 1.9 / 0705 0.2 / SU 1354 2.1 / O 1929 0.3
5	0314 1.9 / 0824 0.3 / SU 1503 2.0 / 2055 0.5	20	0224 2.0 / 0745 0.2 / M 1436 2.2 / 2245 0.4
6	0339 1.9 / 0854 0.2 / M 1538 2.1 / 2156 0.5	21	0307 2.0 / 0825 0.1 / TU 1525 2.3 / 2346 0.4
7	0353 2.0 / 0914 0.1 / TU 1615 2.1 / 2330 0.5	22	0355 2.0 / 0901 0.0 / W 1607 2.3
8	0434 2.0 / 0944 0.1 / W 1644 2.1	23	0030 0.4 / 0437 2.1 / TH 0949 0.0 / 1654 2.3
9	0010 0.4 / 0502 2.0 / TH 1025 0.1 / 1725 2.1	24	0126 0.4 / 0525 2.0 / F 1355 0.0 / 1741 2.2
10	0045 0.4 / 0533 1.9 / F 1105 0.1 / 1754 2.0	25	0204 0.4 / 0614 2.0 / SA 1444 0.0 / 1837 2.1
11	0135 0.4 / 0608 1.9 / SA 1145 0.1 / 1828 2.0	26	0305 0.4 / 0704 2.0 / SU 1244 0.1 / 1935 2.0
12	0157 0.4 / 0643 1.9 / SU 1225 0.1 / 1914 2.0	27	0145 0.4 / 0758 1.9 / M 1354 0.1 / 2035 1.8
13	0204 0.4 / 0738 1.8 / M 1325 0.1 / 2019 1.9	28	0235 0.4 / 0905 1.8 / TU 1504 0.2 / 2144 1.7
14	0235 0.4 / 0844 1.8 / TU 1434 0.1 / 2135 1.8	29	0355 0.4 / 1024 1.7 / W 1624 0.3 / 2319 1.6
15	0325 0.4 / 0959 1.7 / W 1535 0.2 / 2245 1.8	30	0505 0.3 / 1133 1.7 / TH 1745 0.3
		31	0024 1.7 / 0604 0.3 / F 1249 1.8 / 1850 0.4

FEBRUARY

Day	Time / m	Day	Time / m
1	0125 1.8 / 0930 0.2 / SA 1338 1.9 / 2145 0.4	16	0035 1.7 / 0554 0.2 / SU 1255 2.0 / 2107 0.3
2	0208 1.9 / 1004 0.2 / SU 1418 2.0 / 2230 0.4	17	0124 1.8 / 0646 0.2 / M 1337 2.1 / 2145 0.3
3	0256 1.9 / 0810 0.2 / M 1443 2.0 / ● 2047 0.4	18	0203 1.9 / 0725 0.1 / TU 1425 2.2 / O 2235 0.3
4	0313 1.9 / 0834 0.1 / TU 1513 2.1 / 2147 0.4	19	0250 2.0 / 0759 0.0 / W 1506 2.3 / 2315 0.3
5	0355 2.0 / 0855 0.1 / W 1554 2.1 / 2310 0.4	20	0335 2.0 / 0838 0.0 / TH 1548 2.3
6	0410 2.0 / 1144 0.1 / TH 1624 2.1 / 2345 0.4	21	0016 0.4 / 0414 2.1 / F 1250 0.0 / 1635 2.2
7	0437 2.0 / 1235 0.0 / F 1654 2.1	22	0106 0.3 / 0456 2.1 / SA 1346 0.0 / 1718 2.1
8	0046 0.3 / 0508 2.0 / SA 1316 0.0 / 1724 2.1	23	0156 0.3 / 0545 2.1 / SU 1425 0.0 / 1804 2.0
9	0115 0.3 / 0538 2.0 / SU 1059 0.0 / 1754 2.0	24	0224 0.3 / 0624 2.0 / M 1250 0.1 / 1854 1.9
10	0135 0.4 / 0614 2.0 / M 1145 0.0 / 1839 2.0	25	0107 0.3 / 0713 1.9 / TU 1335 0.1 / 1943 1.7
11	0004 0.3 / 0654 1.9 / TU 1234 0.0 / 1924 1.9	26	0210 0.2 / 0819 1.8 / W 1445 0.2 / 2054 1.5
12	0150 0.3 / 0755 1.9 / W 1415 0.1 / 2045 1.8	27	0325 0.3 / 0939 1.6 / TH 1604 0.3 / 2254 1.4
13	0245 0.3 / 0914 1.8 / TH 1530 0.2 / 2153 1.7	28	0445 0.2 / 1119 1.6 / F 1715 0.3
14	0404 0.3 / 1033 1.7 / F 1644 0.2 / 2325 1.6	29	0005 1.5 / 0540 0.2 / SA 1224 1.7 / 1815 0.3
15	0520 0.3 / 1155 1.8 / SA 1744 0.3		

MARCH

Day	Time / m	Day	Time / m
1	0053 1.7 / 0624 0.2 / SU 1314 1.8 / 2117 0.3	16	0019 1.6 / 0826 0.1 / M 1238 2.0 / 2045 0.2
2	0144 1.8 / M 1355 1.9 / 2155 0.3	17	0103 1.7 / 0926 0.1 / TU 1325 2.1 / 2125 0.2
3	0218 1.9 / 1014 0.1 / TU 1425 2.0 / 2225 0.3	18	0155 1.9 / 0655 0.0 / W 1405 2.1 / 2210 0.3
4	0243 1.9 / 0804 0.1 / W 1454 2.1 / ● 2217 0.3	19	0230 2.0 / 0738 0.0 / TH 1445 2.2 / 2256 0.3
5	0314 2.0 / 1047 0.1 / TH 1520 2.1 / 2250 0.3	20	0310 2.0 / 0819 0.0 / F 1524 2.2 / 2339 0.2
6	0344 2.0 / 1124 0.1 / F 1549 2.1 / 2324 0.3	21	0350 2.1 / 1226 0.0 / SA 1608 2.1
7	0407 2.0 / 1216 0.0 / SA 1625 2.1 / 2355 0.3	22	0036 0.2 / 0434 2.1 / SU 1316 0.0 / 1651 2.0
8	0440 2.0 / 0951 0.1 / SU 1657 2.1 / 2215 0.3	23	0126 0.2 / 0545 2.1 / M 1355 0.1 / 1734 1.9
9	0510 2.0 / 1029 0.1 / M 1730 2.0 / 2244 0.2	24	0205 0.2 / 0554 2.0 / TU 1430 0.2 / 1818 1.8
10	0547 2.1 / 1115 0.0 / TU 1815 2.0 / 2335 0.2	25	0027 0.2 / 0644 1.9 / W 1340 0.2 / 1903 1.6
11	0628 2.0 / 1204 0.1 / W 1858 1.8	26	0140 0.1 / 0739 1.7 / TH 1440 0.2 / 2003 1.5
12	0050 0.2 / 0743 1.9 / TH 1415 0.1 / 2004 1.7	27	0305 0.1 / 0854 1.6 / F 1545 0.3 / 2129 1.3
13	0236 0.2 / 0854 1.8 / F 1514 0.2 / 2145 1.5	28	0420 0.1 / 1044 1.5 / SA 1654 0.3 / 2323 1.4
14	0335 0.2 / 1013 1.7 / SA 1640 0.2 / 2315 1.5	29	0515 0.1 / 1143 1.7 / SU 1744 0.3
15	0444 0.2 / 1133 1.8 / SU 1950 0.2	30	0024 1.6 / 0604 0.1 / M 1233 1.8 / 2020 0.3
		31	0103 1.7 / 0644 0.1 / TU 1319 1.9 / 2124 0.2

APRIL

Day	Time / m	Day	Time / m
1	0144 1.8 / 0930 0.1 / W 1348 2.0 / 2210 0.2	16	0128 1.8 / 0940 0.0 / TH 1344 2.1 / 2145 0.2
2	0208 1.9 / 1010 0.1 / TH 1418 2.0 / 2240 0.3	17	0207 1.9 / 0715 0.1 / F 1425 2.0 / O 2236 0.2
3	0234 1.9 / 1040 0.1 / F 1447 2.1 / ● 2240 0.3	18	0246 2.0 / 1100 0.1 / SA 1504 2.0 / 2326 0.2
4	0305 2.0 / 0819 0.1 / SA 1520 2.1 / 2314 0.2	19	0327 2.1 / 1155 0.1 / SU 1546 2.0
5	0337 2.0 / 1144 0.1 / SU 1557 2.1 / 2114 0.2	20	0017 0.1 / 0408 2.1 / M 1246 0.1 / 1627 1.9
6	0411 2.1 / 0925 0.1 / M 1630 2.0 / 2145 0.2	21	0101 0.1 / 0450 2.1 / TU 1325 0.1 / 1710 1.8
7	0446 2.1 / 1009 0.1 / TU 1711 2.0 / 2229 0.1	22	0145 0.1 / 0535 2.0 / W 1405 0.2 / 1755 1.7
8	0527 2.1 / 1055 0.1 / W 1754 1.9 / 2314 0.1	23	0000 0.1 / 0614 1.9 / TH 1330 0.3 / 1832 1.6
9	0610 2.1 / 1330 0.1 / TH 1845 1.7	24	0108 0.0 / 0703 1.8 / F 1420 0.3 / 1929 1.5
10	0035 0.1 / 0704 1.9 / F 1410 0.1 / 2005 1.6	25	0240 0.0 / 0820 1.6 / SA 1535 0.3 / 2034 1.4
11	0155 0.1 / 0822 1.8 / SA 1505 0.2 / 2134 1.5	26	0355 0.0 / 0923 1.6 / SU 1624 0.3 / 2159 1.3
12	0304 0.1 / 1015 1.8 / SU 1800 0.2 / 2243 1.5	27	0445 0.0 / 1053 1.6 / M 1714 0.3 / 2334 1.5
13	0415 0.1 / 1330 0.2 / M 1930 0.2 / 2354 1.6	28	0534 0.0 / 1154 1.8 / TU 1930 0.2
14	0744 0.1 / 1214 0.2 / TU 2027 0.2	29	0019 1.6 / 0647 0.1 / W 1234 1.9 / 2055 0.2
15	0044 1.7 / 0844 0.0 / W 1300 2.0 / 2110 0.2	30	0052 1.7 / 0845 0.1 / TH 1315 1.9 / 2135 0.2

TIDAL DIFFERENCES ARE NOT GIVEN. TIDAL CURVE PAGE 21:315

LOW WATER — IMPORTANT NOTE. Double Low Waters often occur at Hoek Van Holland. On these occasions the predictions are for the lower Low Water which is usually the second.

Datum of predictions: 0.2 m. below M.L.W.S. and 0.1 m. above L.A.T.

HOEK VAN HOLLAND 21:317

Lat. 51°59'N. Long. 4°07'E. HIGH & LOW WATER 1992

TIME ZONE-0100 SUBTRACT 1 HOUR FROM TIMES SHOWN FOR GMT

MAY

Day	Time	m	Day	Time	m
1 F	0128	1.8	16	0144	1.9
	0946	0.1		0950	0.2
	1345	2.0	SA	1407	1.9
	2225	0.2	O	2155	0.2
2 SA	0200	1.9	17	0227	2.0
	1025	0.1		1030	0.2
	1414	2.0	SU	1455	1.9
●	2235	0.2		2255	0.2
3 SU	0235	2.0	18	0310	2.0
	0756	0.1		1117	0.2
	1451	2.1	M	1534	1.8
	2023	0.2		2355	0.1
4 M	0314	2.1	19	0350	2.0
	0835	0.2		1204	0.2
	1535	2.0	TU	1615	1.8
	2055	0.2			
5 TU	0348	2.1	20	0036	0.0
	0909	0.2		0435	2.0
	1611	2.0	W	1301	0.3
	2129	0.1		1655	1.8
6 W	0428	2.1	21	0104	0.0
	1235	0.2		0515	2.0
	1654	1.9	TH	1335	0.3
	2213	0.1		1730	1.7
7 TH	0514	2.1	22	0137	0.0
	1320	0.2		0559	1.9
	1740	1.8	F	1330	0.3
	2309	0.0		1814	1.7
8 F	0600	2.1	23	0020	0.0
	1346	0.2		0644	1.8
	1834	1.7	SA	1400	0.3
				1905	1.6
9 SA	0024	0.0	24	0120	0.0
	0700	2.0		0745	1.8
	1436	0.2	SU	1445	0.3
	1959	1.6		1959	1.5
10 SU	0134	0.0	25	0325	0.0
	0823	1.9		0833	1.7
	1607	0.2	M	1555	0.3
	2102	1.5		2059	1.5
11 M	0245	0.2	26	0414	0.0
	0945	1.9		0955	1.7
	1744	0.2	TU	1634	0.3
	2213	1.6		2204	1.5
12 TU	0614	0.0	27	0505	0.1
	1054	1.9		1055	1.7
	1904	0.2	W	1735	0.2
	2324	1.6		2314	1.6
13 W	0736	0.0	28	0616	0.1
	1154	2.0		1144	1.8
	2004	0.2	TH	1950	0.2
14 TH	0018	1.7	29	0015	1.7
	0836	0.0		0805	0.1
	1237	2.0	F	1228	1.9
	2055	0.2		2106	0.2
15 F	0105	1.8	30	0048	1.8
	0910	0.1		0905	0.1
	1325	2.0	SA	1315	2.0
	2115	0.2		2156	0.2
			31	0128	1.9
				0654	0.2
			SU	1355	2.0
				1929	0.2

JUNE

Day	Time	m	Day	Time	m
1	0211	2.0	16	0257	2.0
	0740	0.2		0930	0.4
M	1434	2.0	TU	1528	1.8
●	2005	0.2		2044	0.1
2	0250	2.1	17	0337	2.0
	0815	0.2		1150	0.4
TU	1515	2.0	W	1604	1.8
	2035	0.1		2124	0.1
3	0334	2.1	18	0414	2.0
	1206	0.2		1235	0.4
W	1556	1.9	TH	1645	1.8
	2120	0.1		2154	0.0
4	0417	2.2	19	0458	2.0
	1235	0.2		1250	0.4
TH	1644	1.8	F	1719	1.8
	2201	0.0		2244	0.0
5	0505	2.2	20	0534	2.0
	1325	0.2		1320	0.4
F	1734	1.8	SA	1755	1.8
	2255	0.0		2340	0.0
6	0554	2.1	21	0613	1.9
	1405	0.2		1337	0.3
SA	1833	1.7	SU	1823	1.7
7	0005	0.0	22	0025	0.0
	0659	2.1		0653	1.9
SU	1500	0.2	M	1420	0.3
	1945	1.7		1924	1.7
8	0105	0.0	23	0115	0.0
	0802	2.0		0708	1.8
M	1557	0.3	TU	1510	0.3
	2045	1.7		2020	1.6
9	0214	0.0	24	0205	0.0
	0914	2.0		0854	1.8
TU	1715	0.2	W	1600	0.3
	2149	1.7		2115	1.6
10	0325	0.0	25	0255	0.1
	1025	1.9		0943	1.8
W	1825	0.2	TH	1654	0.3
	2254	1.7		2225	1.6
11	0655	0.1	26	0410	0.2
	1135	1.9		1043	1.8
TH	1927	0.2	F	1737	0.3
	2354	1.8		2313	1.7
12	0745	0.1	27	0514	0.2
	1224	1.9		1148	1.9
F	2030	0.2	SA	1820	0.3
13	0044	1.8	28	0015	1.8
	0854	0.2		0554	0.2
SA	1310	1.9	SU	1245	1.9
	2120	0.2		1835	0.2
14	0135	1.9	29	0104	1.9
	0838	0.3		0645	0.2
SU	1405	1.8	M	1334	1.9
	2205	0.2		1903	0.2
15	0213	1.9	30	0148	2.0
	0827	0.3		0725	0.2
M	1443	1.8	TU	1414	1.9
	2005	0.2	●	1945	0.1

JULY

Day	Time	m	Day	Time	m
1	0234	2.1	16	0323	2.0
	0805	0.3		0916	0.5
W	1504	1.9	TH	1554	1.9
	2019	0.1		2054	0.1
2	0316	2.2	17	0358	2.1
	1124	0.3		1128	0.5
TH	1544	1.9	F	1624	1.9
	2105	0.0		2129	0.0
3	0401	2.2	18	0434	2.1
	1214	0.3		1220	0.4
F	1629	1.9	SA	1654	1.9
	2145	0.0		2204	0.0
4	0450	2.2	19	0508	2.1
	1316	0.3		1250	0.4
SA	1724	1.9	SU	1723	1.9
	2236	0.0		2254	0.0
5	0540	2.2	20	0544	2.0
	1355	0.3		1325	0.4
SU	1814	1.9	M	1758	1.9
	2336	0.0		2325	0.1
6	0634	2.1	21	0619	2.0
	1455	0.3		1347	0.4
M	1915	1.8	TU	1834	1.8
7	0035	0.0	22	0020	0.1
	0734	2.1		0655	1.9
TU	1540	0.3	W	1400	0.4
	2008	1.8		1904	1.8
8	0145	0.0	23	0105	0.1
	0833	2.0		0744	1.9
W	1655	0.3	TH	1415	0.4
	2115	1.8		2014	1.7
9	0300	0.1	24	0205	0.1
	0949	1.9		0904	1.8
TH	1755	0.3	F	1505	0.4
	2224	1.7		2135	1.7
10	0404	0.2	25	0325	0.2
	1105	1.8		1004	1.8
F	1844	0.3	SA	1615	0.4
	2329	1.7		2233	1.7
11	0700	0.2	26	0435	0.2
	1208	1.8		1115	1.8
SA	2007	0.3	SU	1736	0.3
				2355	1.8
12	0028	1.8	27	0545	0.3
	0905	0.3		1218	1.8
SU	1309	1.8	M	1804	0.3
	2126	0.2			
13	0128	1.9	28	0044	1.9
	1005	0.4		0626	0.3
M	1353	1.8	TU	1315	1.9
	1915	0.2		1845	0.2
14	0213	1.9	29	0134	2.1
	0755	0.4		0704	0.3
TU	1449	1.8	W	1405	1.9
O	1953	0.1	●	1925	0.1
15	0254	2.0	30	0216	2.2
	0840	0.5		0745	0.4
W	1535	1.9	TH	1444	2.0
	2035	0.1		1959	0.1
			31	0259	2.3
				1115	0.4
			F	1528	2.0
				2037	0.0

AUGUST

Day	Time	m	Day	Time	m
1	0345	2.3	16	0408	2.2
	1155	0.4		1140	0.5
SA	1615	2.0	SU	1624	2.0
	2121	0.0		2136	0.1
2	0430	2.3	17	0438	2.1
	1250	0.4		1225	0.4
SU	1656	2.0	M	1654	2.0
	2209	0.0		2205	0.1
3	0514	2.3	18	0508	2.1
	1334	0.4		1254	0.4
M	1745	2.0	TU	1725	2.0
	2258	0.1		2246	0.1
4	0606	2.2	19	0538	2.1
	1424	0.4		1327	0.4
TU	1834	2.0	W	1754	2.0
				2319	0.1
5	0004	0.1	20	0614	2.0
	0704	2.0		1145	0.4
W	1520	0.4	TH	1834	2.0
	1928	1.9		2354	0.1
6	0124	0.1	21	0654	2.0
	0805	1.9		1235	0.4
TH	1415	0.4	F	1914	1.9
	2023	1.8			
7	0234	0.2	22	0127	0.2
	0904	1.7		0754	1.8
F	1524	0.3	SA	1414	0.4
	2149	1.7		2035	1.8
8	0344	0.3	23	0254	0.3
	1039	1.6		0914	1.7
SA	1640	0.3	SU	1525	0.4
	2309	1.7		2204	1.7
9	0505	0.4	24	0414	0.3
	1159	1.7		1044	1.7
SU	1740	0.3	M	1650	0.4
				2324	1.8
10	0018	1.8	25	0525	0.4
	0627	0.4		1205	1.7
M	1259	1.8	TU	1745	0.3
	1825	0.2			
11	0124	1.9	26	0029	2.0
	0944	0.4		0609	0.4
TU	1343	1.8	W	1254	1.8
	2144	0.2		1819	0.2
12	0204	2.0	27	0117	2.1
	1030	0.4		0935	0.4
W	1435	1.9	TH	1346	1.9
	1934	0.2		1855	0.1
13	0233	2.0	28	0157	2.3
	1005	0.5		0725	0.4
TH	1505	1.9	F	1425	2.0
O	2005	0.1	●	1938	0.1
14	0304	2.1	29	0239	2.3
	0835	0.5		0806	0.4
F	1528	2.0	SA	1506	2.1
	2029	0.1		2015	0.0
15	0354	2.1	30	0322	2.4
	0854	0.5		1140	0.4
SA	1559	2.0	SU	1546	2.1
	2105	0.1		2058	0.0
			31	0405	2.3
				1236	0.4
			M	1644	2.2
				2141	0.1

GENERAL — L.W. stand approx. 3 h. Sometimes develops into double H.W. Wind and up river levels affect tides. Double Low Waters occur in R. Maas ent. (and W. Coast of Holland generally) about the time of Spring Tides.

21:318 HOEK VAN HOLLAND

HIGH & LOW WATER 1992　　　Lat. 51°59′N. Long. 4°07′E.

TIME ZONE-0100 SUBTRACT 1 HOUR FROM TIMES SHOWN FOR GMT

SEPTEMBER

	Time	m		Time	m
1 TU	0455 1325 1714	2.2 0.4 2.1	**16** W	0436 0955 1650 2210	2.2 0.4 2.1 0.2
2 W	0200 0534 1404 1800	0.2 2.1 0.4 2.1	**17** TH	0511 1030 1724 2245	2.1 0.4 2.1 0.2
3 TH	0250 0624 1227 1848	0.2 2.0 0.4 2.0	**18** F	0547 1104 1805 2335	2.1 0.3 2.1 0.2
4 F	0107 0714 1340 1948	0.3 1.8 0.4 1.9	**19** SA	0628 1200 1848	2.0 0.3 2.1
5 SA	0214 0823 1445 2103	0.3 1.6 0.3 1.7	**20** SU	0106 0724 1340 1948	0.3 1.8 0.3 1.9
6 SU	0340 1014 1614 2254	0.4 1.5 0.3 1.7	**21** M	0234 0849 1455 2133	0.4 1.7 0.3 1.8
7 M	0449 1134 1715	0.5 1.6 0.3	**22** TU	0344 1025 1604 2315	0.4 1.6 0.3 1.9
8 TU	0003 0555 1234 1754	1.8 0.5 1.7 0.3	**23** W	0657 1145 1705	0.4 1.7 0.3
9 W	0052 0920 1325 2124	1.9 0.4 1.8 0.2	**24** TH	0008 0815 1238 1749	2.0 0.4 1.8 0.2
10 TH	0133 0954 1404 1915	2.0 0.4 1.9 0.2	**25** F	0054 0905 1320 1829	2.2 0.4 1.9 0.2
11 F	0203 1015 1435 1944	2.1 0.5 2.0 0.2	**26** SA	0136 0950 1401 1915	2.3 0.4 2.1 0.1
12 SA	0238 0815 1458 2005	2.1 0.5 2.1 0.2	**27** SU	0218 0738 1442 1951	2.3 0.5 2.2 0.1
13 SU	0304 0829 1525 2024	2.2 0.5 2.1 0.2	**28** M	0301 0815 1524 2035	2.3 0.5 2.2 0.2
14 M	0337 0855 1554 2105	2.2 0.5 2.1 0.2	**29** TU	0344 1210 1606 2119	2.3 0.4 2.2 0.2
15 TU	0404 1145 1625 2131	2.2 0.4 2.1 0.2	**30** W	0426 1306 1648	2.2 0.4 2.2

OCTOBER

	Time	m		Time	m
1 TH	0135 0510 1351 1730	0.3 2.1 0.4 2.2	**16** F	0446 1010 1704 2230	2.1 0.3 2.2 0.3
2 F	0205 0554 1140 1818	0.4 1.9 0.4 2.1	**17** SA	0524 1056 1745 2325	2.0 0.3 2.2 0.3
3 SA	0045 0642 1254 1914	0.4 1.8 0.3 1.9	**18** SU	0614 1144 1835	1.9 0.2 2.1
4 SU	0154 0738 1418 2023	0.5 1.6 0.3 1.7	**19** M	0130 0709 1310 1933	0.4 1.8 0.3 2.0
5 M	0305 0853 1550 2219	0.5 1.5 0.3 1.7	**20** TU	0230 0834 1430 2125	0.4 1.6 0.3 1.9
6 TU	0430 1114 1644 2344	0.5 1.5 0.3 1.8	**21** W	0335 0953 1535 2233	0.5 1.6 0.3 1.9
7 W	0525 1205 1734	0.5 1.7 0.3	**22** TH	0647 1114 1914 2345	0.4 1.7 0.3 2.1
8 TH	0024 0820 1254 1830	1.9 0.5 1.8 0.2	**23** F	0810 1210 2025	0.4 1.8 0.2
9 F	0104 0915 1323 1854	2.0 0.4 1.9 0.3	**24** SA	0034 0855 1258 1809	2.2 0.4 1.9 0.2
10 SA	0134 0955 1354 1930	2.1 0.4 2.0 0.3	**25** SU	0116 0915 1340 1852	2.2 0.4 2.1 0.2
11 SU	0205 1035 1425 1933	2.1 0.5 2.0 0.3	**26** M	0200 1005 1421 1936	2.2 0.5 2.1 0.2
12 M	0234 0754 1450 2006	2.2 0.5 2.1 0.3	**27** TU	0245 0755 1505 2020	2.2 0.4 2.2 0.3
13 TU	0304 0824 1520 2036	2.2 0.4 2.2 0.3	**28** W	0324 1151 1544	2.2 0.4 2.2
14 W	0338 0854 1555 2110	2.2 0.4 2.2 0.3	**29** TH	0021 0406 1235 1626	0.4 2.1 0.4 2.2
15 TH	0415 0930 1629 2145	2.2 0.4 2.2 0.3	**30** F	0105 0450 1326 1714	0.4 2.0 0.3 2.2
			31 SA	0155 0534 1109 1759	0.5 1.9 0.3 2.1

NOVEMBER

	Time	m		Time	m
1 SU	0040 0618 1215 1843	0.5 1.8 0.2 1.9	**16** M	0120 0605 1139 1827	0.4 1.9 0.2 2.1
2 M	0130 0715 1324 1955	0.5 1.7 0.2 1.8	**17** TU	0137 0709 1244 1932	0.5 1.8 0.2 2.0
3 TU	0235 0803 1520 2054	0.6 1.6 0.2 1.7	**18** W	0230 0834 1406 2059	0.5 1.7 0.2 2.0
4 W	0354 0913 1614 2244	0.6 1.5 0.2 1.7	**19** TH	0500 1459 2208	0.5 1.9 0.2 2.0
5 TH	0500 1104 1715 2333	0.5 1.6 0.2 1.9	**20** F	0630 1045 1901 2314	0.5 1.7 0.2 2.0
6 F	0707 1204 1810	0.5 1.7 0.3	**21** SA	0735 1145 1944	0.4 1.8 0.2
7 SA	0025 0815 1238 2007	2.0 0.4 1.8 0.3	**22** SU	0015 0824 2055	2.1 0.4 1.9 0.3
8 SU	0053 0914 1315 2114	2.0 0.4 1.9 0.3	**23** M	0104 0904 1320 1846	2.1 0.4 2.0 0.3
9 M	0130 0954 1344 1914	2.1 0.4 2.0 0.3	**24** TU	0147 0950 1407 1924	2.1 0.4 2.1 0.4
10 TU	0204 1040 1417 1945	2.2 0.4 2.1 0.3	**25** W	0227 1046 1447 2015	2.1 0.4 2.1 0.4
11 W	0236 0809 1455 2015	2.2 0.4 2.2 0.3	**26** TH	0311 1135 1530 2355	2.0 0.3 2.2 0.5
12 TH	0314 0840 1530 2049	2.2 0.4 2.2 0.3	**27** F	0354 1226 1614	2.0 0.4 2.2
13 F	0354 1608 2135	2.1 0.3 2.2 0.4	**28** SA	0034 0428 1300 1654	0.5 1.9 0.4 2.1
14 SA	0434 0956 1651 2219	2.1 0.2 2.2 0.4	**29** SU	0125 0956 1045 1733	0.5 1.9 0.2 2.1
15 SU	0517 1039 1736	2.0 0.2 2.0	**30** M	0017 0558 1144 1829	0.6 1.9 0.1 2.0

DECEMBER

	Time	m		Time	m
1 TU	0110 0645 1244 1914	0.5 1.8 0.1 1.9	**16** W	0214 0653 1236 1925	0.4 1.8 0.1 2.1
2 W	0157 0745 1350 2014	0.5 1.7 0.2 1.8	**17** TH	0258 0805 1335 2035	0.5 1.8 0.1 2.0
3 TH	0314 0829 1555 2114	0.5 1.7 0.2 1.8	**18** F	0300 1434 2144	0.5 1.8 0.1 2.0
4 F	0414 0923 1635 2223	0.5 1.6 0.2 1.8	**19** SA	0547 1014 1545 2243	0.5 1.9 0.2 1.9
5 SA	0505 1043 1740 2329	0.5 1.6 0.3 1.9	**20** SU	0655 1119 1924 2355	0.6 1.8 0.2 1.9
6 SU	0607 1149 1910	0.5 1.7 0.3	**21** M	0807 1214 2034	0.4 1.9 0.3
7 M	0014 0846 1325 2034	1.9 0.4 1.8 0.3	**22** TU	0048 0855 1308 2130	1.9 0.4 1.9 0.4
8 TU	0059 0914 1315 2146	2.0 0.4 1.9 0.3	**23** W	0137 0944 1353 1950	1.9 0.3 2.0 0.4
9 W	0138 1010 1355 1925	2.1 0.4 2.0 0.4	**24** TH	0234 1036 1444 2046	1.9 0.3 2.1 0.5
10 TH	0216 0744 1434 2006	2.1 0.4 2.1 0.4	**25** F	0312 0829 1520 2330	1.9 0.2 2.1 0.5
11 F	0256 0826 1514 2035	2.1 0.3 2.2 0.4	**26** SA	0405 0910 1604	1.9 0.2 2.1
12 SA	0337 0859 1555 2126	2.1 0.2 2.3 0.4	**27** SU	0004 0423 0944 1644	0.5 2.0 0.1 2.1
13 SU	0425 0939 1637	2.0 0.2 2.3	**28** M	0106 0505 1024 1725	0.5 2.0 0.1 2.1
14 M	0044 0507 1025 1726	0.4 2.0 0.1 2.0	**29** TU	0120 0538 1105 1804	0.5 1.9 0.1 2.0
15 TU	0124 0557 1125 1820	0.4 2.0 0.1 2.2	**30** W	0057 0652 1204 1834	0.5 1.9 0.1 2.0
			31 TH	0130 0652 1254 1923	0.5 1.8 0.1 1.9

RATE AND SET — Near ent. to New Waterway NE. stream sets E. on to N. mole. Stream runs in to New Waterway for 4¾ h. (–0230 to +0215 Hoek). Stream runs out for 8 h. Ingoing: Commence same time as outside NE., Max. rate Sp. 4 kn. –0100. Hoek. Outgoing: Commences while outside still NE. and continues while outside set SW.; Max. rate Sp. 5 kn. +0500 Hoek.

HARLINGEN

Lat. 53° 10'N Long. 5° 24'E

HIGH and LOW WATER 1992

TIME ZONE –0100 SUBTRACT 1 HOUR FROM TIMES SHOWN FOR G.M.T.

JANUARY

Day		Time Ht.	Time Ht.	Time Ht.	Time Ht.
1	W	0118 0.4	0604 2.1	1359 0.4	1844 2.0
2	Th	0233 0.4	0705 2.1	1509 0.4	1944 2.1
3	F	0339 0.3	0804 2.1	1559 0.3	2034 2.2
4	Sa	0428 0.3	0855 2.1	1644 0.4	2125 2.3
5	Su	0513 0.4	0934 2.0	1715 0.4	2205 2.4
6	M	0552 0.4	1015 2.0	1749 0.4	2240 2.4
7	Tu	0624 0.4	1045 2.1	1824 0.3	2316 2.4
8	W	0653 0.4	1114 2.1	1854 0.3	2355 2.4
9	Th	0729 0.4	1144 2.1	1929 0.3	
10	F	0014 2.4	0759 0.4	1224 2.0	2000 0.3
11	Sa	0055 2.3	0829 0.4	1300 2.0	2029 0.3
12	Su	0125 2.3	0909 0.4	1314 1.9	2109 0.3
13	M	0144 2.2	0938 0.4	1355 2.0	2158 0.3
14	Tu	0234 2.2	1029 0.5	1444 2.0	2248 0.4
15	W	0340 2.2	1138 0.5	1555 2.0	
16	Th	0010 0.4	0450 2.1	1249 0.5	1725 2.0
17	F	0129 0.4	0604 2.1	1357 0.4	1855 2.2
18	Sa	0249 0.3	0734 2.1	1519 0.4	2014 2.2
19	Su	0358 0.2	0905 2.1	1624 0.3	2114 2.3
20	M	0509 0.2	1010 2.2	1719 0.3	2227 2.4
21	Tu	0600 0.1	1105 2.1	1812 0.2	2316 2.5
22	W	0648 0.1	1156 2.1	1859 0.1	2356 2.5
23	Th	0734 0.1	1230 2.1	1939 0.1	
24	F	0041 2.5	0812 0.1	1316 2.0	2024 0.0
25	Sa	0126 2.4	0853 0.1	1345 2.0	2058 0.1
26	Su	0155 2.3	0929 0.2	1420 2.0	2144 0.1
27	M	0224 2.2	1009 0.3	1420 1.9	2217 0.3
28	Tu	0305 2.1	1048 0.4	1520 1.9	
29	W	0415 1.9	1137 0.5	1644 1.9	
30	Th	0038 0.5	0524 1.9	1257 0.5	1804 1.9
31	F	0158 0.4	0634 1.9	1418 0.4	1920 2.1

FEBRUARY

Day		Time Ht.	Time Ht.	Time Ht.	Time Ht.
1	Sa	0307 0.3	0745 2.0	1534 0.3	2025 2.2
2	Su	0408 0.3	0845 2.0	1629 0.2	2115 2.3
3	M	0452 0.3	0935 2.0	1658 0.2	2150 2.3
4	Tu	0533 0.3	1005 2.0	1740 0.3	2225 2.3
5	W	0609 0.3	1024 2.0	1809 0.2	2255 2.4
6	Th	0639 0.3	1115 2.1	1844 0.2	2336 2.4
7	F	0708 0.3	1134 2.1	1919 0.2	
8	Sa	0006 2.4	0739 0.3	1226 2.0	1944 0.2
9	Su	0046 2.3	0803 0.3	1235 2.0	2014 0.2
10	M	0116 2.2	0833 0.3	1254 2.0	2048 0.2
11	Tu	0135 2.2	0909 0.3	1314 2.0	2129 0.2
12	W	0205 2.1	0937 0.4	1405 2.0	2219 0.3
13	Th	0254 2.0	1049 0.4	1514 1.9	2329 0.4
14	F	0414 1.9	1157 0.5	1654 1.9	
15	Sa	0108 0.4	0615 1.9	1339 0.4	1835 2.0
16	Su	0240 0.3	0756 2.0	1509 0.3	2010 2.2
17	M	0359 0.1	0906 2.1	1608 0.2	2116 2.3
18	Tu	0455 0.1	1006 2.1	1709 0.1	2206 2.4
19	W	0545 0.0	1046 2.1	1759 0.1	2249 2.5
20	Th	0631 0.0	1130 2.1	1841 0.0	2341 2.5
21	F	0711 0.0	1216 2.1	1921 0.1	
22	Sa	0020 2.4	0749 0.1	1240 2.1	2002 0.1
23	Su	0106 2.3	0824 0.1	1310 2.0	2039 0.0
24	M	0136 2.2	0859 0.2	1314 2.0	2108 0.1
25	Tu	0155 2.1	0918 0.3	1356 2.0	2137 0.2
26	W	0230 1.9	0954 0.4	1424 1.9	2218 0.4
27	Th	0314 1.8	1039 0.5	1545 1.8	2317 0.5
28	F	0444 1.7	1143 0.5	1736 1.9	
29	Sa	0058 0.5	0604 1.7	1337 0.5	1835 2.0

MARCH

Day		Time Ht.	Time Ht.	Time Ht.	Time Ht.
1	Su	0248 0.3	0715 1.8	1459 0.3	2000 2.1
2	M	0349 0.2	0830 1.9	1553 0.2	2044 2.2
3	Tu	0429 0.1	0915 1.9	1635 0.1	2136 2.2
4	W	0503 0.1	0944 2.0	1713 0.1	2205 2.3
5	Th	0539 0.2	1014 2.0	1751 0.1	2235 2.3
6	F	0619 0.2	1055 2.0	1823 0.1	2310 2.3
7	Sa	0648 0.2	1115 2.1	1859 0.1	2346 2.3
8	Su	0718 0.2	1154 2.1	1928 0.1	
9	M	0014 2.2	0743 0.2	1236 2.0	1959 0.1
10	Tu	0050 2.1	0809 0.3	1234 2.0	2009 0.1
11	W	0104 2.0	0838 0.3	1254 2.0	2109 0.2
12	Th	0135 2.0	0918 0.3	1356 2.0	2209 0.2
13	F	0235 1.8	1018 0.4	1454 1.9	2319 0.3
14	Sa	0430 1.7	1127 0.4	1645 1.9	
15	Su	0038 0.3	0614 1.8	1319 0.4	1835 2.0
16	M	0218 0.1	0745 1.9	1448 0.2	1956 2.2
17	Tu	0339 0.0	0835 2.0	1553 0.1	2056 2.3
18	W	0439 0.0	0935 2.0	1649 0.0	2142 2.4
19	Th	0525 0.0	1026 2.1	1739 0.0	2230 2.4
20	F	0609 0.0	1100 2.1	1818 -0.1	2316 2.4
21	Sa	0645 0.1	1135 2.1	1859 -0.1	2344 2.3
22	Su	0719 0.1	1216 2.1	1935 -0.1	
23	M	0030 2.2	0749 0.1	1235 2.1	2008 0.0
24	Tu	0106 2.1	0813 0.2	1254 2.1	2039 0.1
25	W	0136 1.9	0838 0.2	1314 2.0	2109 0.1
26	Th	0155 1.8	0909 0.3	1354 2.0	2149 0.3
27	F	0245 1.6	0938 0.4	1454 1.9	2233 0.4
28	Sa	0404 1.6	1038 0.4	1640 1.8	2348 0.5
29	Su	0524 1.6	1213 0.5	1804 1.9	
30	M	0143 0.3	0644 1.7	1358 0.3	1914 2.0
31	Tu	0253 0.2	0745 1.8	1519 0.2	2015 2.1

APRIL

Day		Time Ht.	Time Ht.	Time Ht.	Time Ht.
1	W	0349 0.1	0845 1.9	1559 0.1	2054 2.2
2	Th	0430 0.0	0936 2.0	1644 0.1	2146 2.2
3	F	0509 0.0	1024 2.0	1719 0.0	2210 2.2
4	Sa	0543 0.1	1024 2.0	1802 0.0	2245 2.2
5	Su	0619 0.1	1105 2.1	1839 0.0	2326 2.2
6	M	0648 0.1	1134 2.1	1909 0.0	
7	Tu	0006 2.1	0718 0.2	1204 2.1	1944 0.1
8	W	0040 2.0	0749 0.2	1234 2.0	2019 0.1
9	Th	0115 1.9	0829 0.2	1255 2.0	2109 0.1
10	F	0150 1.8	0909 0.2	1335 2.0	2200 0.2
11	Sa	0300 1.7	1009 0.3	1507 2.0	2309 0.2
12	Su	0444 1.7	1123 0.3	1645 2.0	
13	M	0039 0.1	0806 1.8	1259 0.2	1820 2.1
14	Tu	0159 0.0	0726 1.9	1429 0.1	1925 2.0
15	W	0313 -0.1	0826 1.9	1529 0.0	2036 2.3
16	Th	0408 -0.1	0917 2.0	1629 0.0	2126 2.3
17	F	0458 0.0	0956 2.1	1719 0.0	2206 2.2
18	Sa	0542 0.1	1035 2.1	1759 0.0	2246 2.2
19	Su	0613 0.1	1106 2.1	1839 0.0	2314 2.2
20	M	0648 0.1	1145 2.2	1908 0.0	
21	Tu	0000 2.1	0719 0.1	1216 2.2	1939 0.0
22	W	0030 2.0	0738 0.1	1240 2.2	2008 0.1
23	Th	0106 1.8	0808 0.2	1305 2.1	2049 0.2
24	F	0124 1.7	0844 0.2	1340 2.0	2119 0.3
25	Sa	0155 1.6	0919 0.2	1435 1.9	2157 0.3
26	Su	0320 1.5	1019 0.3	1534 1.9	2308 0.4
27	M	0450 1.6	1119 0.3	1705 1.9	
28	Tu	0049 0.3	0554 1.7	1247 0.3	1825 2.0
29	W	0200 0.2	0704 1.8	1420 0.2	1915 2.1
30	Th	0253 0.0	0805 1.9	1514 0.1	2015 2.1

TIDAL DIFFERENCES PAGE 21:322

Heights are referred to Chart Datum

HARLINGEN

HIGH and LOW WATER 1992 Lat. 53° 10'N Long. 5° 24'E

TIME ZONE –0100 SUBTRACT 1 HOUR FROM TIMES SHOWN FOR G.M.T.

MAY

Day	Time	Ht. m.	Day	Time	Ht. m.
1	0343	0.0	16	0429	0.0
	0855	2.0		0926	2.1
F	1604	0.0	Sa	1655	0.0
	2100	2.1		2145	2.1
2	0434	0.0	17	0514	0.1
	0935	2.0		1006	2.1
Sa	1649	0.0	Su	1735	0.1
	2124	2.1		2220	2.1
3	0514	0.0	18	0549	0.2
	1016	2.0		1045	2.2
Su	1734	0.0	M	1813	0.1
	2226	2.1		2255	2.1
4	0554	0.1	19	0619	0.2
	1034	2.1		1104	2.3
M	1819	0.0	Tu	1849	0.1
	2305	2.1		2336	2.0
5	0628	0.1	20	0649	0.1
	1120	2.1		1156	2.3
Tu	1859	0.0	W	1919	0.1
	2351	2.1		2355	1.9
6	0709	0.1	21	0718	0.1
	1206	2.1		1225	2.3
W	1933	0.0	Th	1953	0.2
7	0035	2.0	22	0034	1.8
	0739	0.1		0749	0.1
Th	1240	2.2	F	1244	2.2
	2019	0.1		2029	0.2
8	0120	1.9	23	0055	1.7
	0820	0.1		0823	0.1
F	1325	2.1	Sa	1335	2.1
	2104	0.1		2109	0.3
9	0214	1.8	24	0140	1.6
	0910	0.1		0858	0.2
Sa	1415	2.1	Su	1404	2.0
	2158	0.1		2143	0.3
10	0324	1.7	25	0227	1.6
	1009	0.2		0949	0.2
Su	1514	2.1	M	1454	2.0
	2303	0.1		2233	0.3
11	0434	1.7	26	0340	1.6
	1113	0.2		1043	0.2
M	1640	2.1	Tu	1554	2.0
				2349	0.3
12	0019	0.0	27	0445	1.6
	0556	1.8		1138	0.3
Tu	1227	0.1	W	1654	2.0
	1756	2.2			
13	0139	0.0	28	0059	0.2
	0650	1.8		0555	1.7
W	1348	0.1	Th	1308	0.2
	1855	2.2		1754	2.0
14	0239	-0.1	29	0203	0.1
	0756	1.9		0715	1.8
Th	1509	0.0	F	1418	0.2
	1955	2.2		1904	2.1
15	0339	0.0	30	0304	0.0
	0846	2.0		0810	1.9
F	1604	0.0	Sa	1529	0.1
	2056	2.2		2004	2.1
			31	0354	0.0
				0900	2.0
			Su	1619	0.1
				2055	2.1

JUNE

Day	Time	Ht. m.	Day	Time	Ht. m.
1	0444	0.0	16	0529	0.2
	0945	2.1		1015	2.3
M	1708	0.0	Tu	1759	0.2
	2145	2.1		2235	1.9
2	0530	0.1	17	0559	0.2
	1025	2.1		1056	2.3
Tu	1800	0.0	W	1828	0.2
	2256	2.0		2316	1.9
3	0608	0.1	18	0629	0.2
	1105	2.2		1130	2.3
W	1845	0.0	Th	1903	0.2
	2334	2.0		2335	1.9
4	0658	0.1	19	0704	0.1
	1155	2.3		1217	2.3
Th	1934	0.0	F	1939	0.2
5	0024	1.9	20	0014	1.9
	0739	0.1		0738	0.1
F	1247	2.3	Sa	1245	2.3
	2022	0.0		2013	0.2
6	0125	1.9	21	0054	1.8
	0825	0.1		0809	0.1
Sa	1325	2.3	Su	1314	2.2
	2105	0.0		2049	0.2
7	0220	1.8	22	0135	1.7
	0909	0.1		0843	0.1
Su	1426	2.3	M	1334	2.1
	2159	0.0		2118	0.2
8	0304	1.8	23	0145	1.7
	1004	0.0		0923	0.1
M	1515	2.2	Tu	1414	2.1
	2254	0.0		2158	0.3
9	0404	1.8	24	0225	1.7
	1059	0.1		1008	0.2
Tu	1625	2.2	W	1516	2.1
	2354	0.0		2248	0.3
10	0504	1.8	25	0324	1.7
	1209	0.1		1103	0.2
W	1714	2.2	Th	1605	2.1
				2348	0.3
11	0059	0.0	26	0424	1.8
	0615	1.8		1219	0.3
Th	1324	0.1	F	1655	2.1
	1825	2.1			
12	0203	0.0	27	0109	0.2
	0716	1.9		0550	1.8
F	1433	0.1	Sa	1340	0.3
	1919	2.1		1815	2.1
13	0309	0.1	28	0219	0.2
	0754	2.0		0710	1.9
Sa	1539	0.1	Su	1450	0.2
	2014	2.1		1924	2.1
14	0403	0.1	29	0319	0.1
	0845	2.1		0814	2.1
Su	1633	0.1	M	1554	0.1
	2104	2.0		2034	2.1
15	0449	0.2	30	0420	0.1
	0935	2.2		0914	2.2
M	1719	0.1	Tu	1649	0.1
	2206	2.0		2144	2.1

JULY

Day	Time	Ht. m.	Day	Time	Ht. m.
1	0515	0.1	16	0549	0.2
	1015	2.2		1035	2.4
W	1749	0.1	Th	1819	0.3
	2250	2.0		2256	1.9
2	0559	0.1	17	0619	0.2
	1100	2.3		1104	2.4
Th	1839	0.0	F	1848	0.3
	2346	2.0		2314	2.0
3	0649	0.1	18	0649	0.2
	1156	2.4		1156	2.4
F	1926	0.0	Sa	1929	0.3
				2354	2.0
4	0037	2.0	19	0718	0.1
	0739	0.1		1225	2.4
Sa	1236	2.4	Su	1959	0.2
	2013	0.0			
5	0127	2.0	20	0025	1.9
	0819	0.0		0753	0.1
Su	1326	2.4	M	1306	2.3
	2059	0.0		2029	0.3
6	0205	1.9	21	0054	1.9
	0904	0.0		0823	0.2
M	1405	2.4	Tu	1330	2.2
	2144	0.0		2053	0.3
7	0244	1.8	22	0135	1.8
	0948	0.0		0859	0.2
Tu	1455	2.3	W	1344	2.1
	2222	0.1		2128	0.3
8	0335	1.8	23	0144	1.8
	1038	0.1		0939	0.2
W	1540	2.2	Th	1425	2.1
	2319	0.1		2203	0.3
9	0417	1.8	24	0224	1.9
	1138	0.1		1017	0.3
Th	1634	2.1	F	1505	2.1
				2259	0.4
10	0018	0.2	25	0346	1.9
	0525	1.9		1118	0.3
F	1248	0.2	Sa	1614	2.1
	1756	2.0			
11	0123	0.2	26	0008	0.4
	0615	1.9		0455	1.9
Sa	1403	0.2	Su	1248	0.4
	1855	2.0		1734	2.0
12	0240	0.2	27	0139	0.4
	0725	2.1		0615	2.0
Su	1518	0.2	M	1413	0.3
	1954	2.0		1904	2.0
13	0339	0.2	28	0249	0.3
	0824	2.2		0744	2.1
M	1619	0.1	Tu	1528	0.2
	2054	2.0		2040	2.0
14	0429	0.2	29	0353	0.2
	0926	2.3		0854	2.3
Tu	1703	0.2	W	1642	0.1
	2145	2.0		2145	2.1
15	0514	0.2	30	0459	0.2
	1006	2.3		1000	2.4
W	1743	0.2	Th	1739	0.1
	2220	1.9		2245	2.1
			31	0552	0.1
				1050	2.4
			F	1829	0.0
				2335	2.1

AUGUST

Day	Time	Ht. m.	Day	Time	Ht. m.
1	0639	0.1	16	0634	0.2
	1145	2.5		1120	2.4
Sa	1913	0.0	Su	1902	0.3
				2324	2.1
2	0016	2.1	17	0708	0.2
	0724	0.0		1205	2.4
Su	1225	2.5	M	1934	0.3
	1955	0.0			
3	0106	2.0	18	0016	2.1
	0805	-0.1		0739	0.2
M	1306	2.5	Tu	1236	2.3
	2035	0.0		1959	0.3
4	0146	2.0	19	0035	2.0
	0849	0.0		0809	0.2
Tu	1350	2.4	W	1306	2.2
	2113	0.1		2024	0.4
5	0210	1.9	20	0045	2.0
	0929	0.0		0839	0.3
W	1425	2.3	Th	1325	2.2
	2148	0.2		2054	0.4
6	0230	1.9	21	0110	2.0
	1009	0.2		0909	0.3
Th	1516	2.1	F	1334	2.1
	2234	0.3		2129	0.4
7	0310	1.9	22	0145	2.0
	1059	0.3		1000	0.3
F	1600	2.0	Sa	1425	2.1
	2329	0.4		2213	0.4
8	0424	1.9	23	0244	2.0
	1209	0.4		1053	0.4
Sa	1704	1.9	Su	1544	2.0
				2317	0.5
9	0039	0.4	24	0420	2.0
	0544	2.0		1207	0.4
Su	1334	0.4	M	1735	1.9
	1814	1.9			
10	0210	0.4	25	0059	0.5
	0654	2.1		0555	2.1
M	1500	0.3	Tu	1348	0.4
	1940	1.9		1904	2.0
11	0319	0.3	26	0218	0.4
	0755	2.2		0725	2.2
Tu	1509	0.2	W	1513	0.2
	2044	2.0		2036	2.1
12	0409	0.2	27	0339	0.3
	0900	2.3		0835	2.4
W	1645	0.2	Th	1625	0.2
	2124	2.0		2137	2.1
13	0454	0.2	28	0442	0.2
	0946	2.4		0934	2.5
Th	1729	0.3	F	1719	0.1
	2145	2.0		2214	2.2
14	0529	0.2	29	0531	0.2
	1025	2.4		1036	2.5
F	1758	0.3	Sa	1808	0.1
	2236	2.0		2316	2.1
15	0558	0.2	30	0621	0.1
	1056	2.4		1115	2.5
Sa	1829	0.3	Su	1848	0.1
	2254	2.0		2350	2.1
			31	0701	0.0
				1206	2.5
			M	1928	0.1

TIDAL DIFFERENCES PAGE 21:322

Heights are referred to Chart Datum

HARLINGEN

Lat. 53° 10'N Long. 5° 24'E
HIGH and LOW WATER 1992
TIME ZONE –0100 SUBTRACT 1 HOUR FROM TIMES SHOWN FOR G.M.T.

SEPTEMBER

Time h.min.	Ht. m.		Time h.min.	Ht. m.
1 0030	2.1	**16** 0708		0.3
0744	0.0	1207		2.3
Tu 1240	2.5	W 1929		0.4
2009	0.2			
2 0106	2.1	**17** 0005		2.1
0824	0.1	0739		0.3
W 1326	2.3	Th 1236		2.3
2039	0.3	1949		0.4
3 0115	2.1	**18** 0036		2.1
0858	0.2	0809		0.3
Th 1355	2.2	F 1306		2.2
2108	0.4	2029		0.4
4 0140	2.1	**19** 0034		2.1
0939	0.3	0850		0.4
F 1415	2.0	Sa 1305		2.1
2149	0.5	2047		0.4
5 0220	2.0	**20** 0015		2.2
1013	0.4	0934		0.4
Sa 1510	1.9	Su 1354		2.0
2223	0.5	2138		0.5
6 0334	2.0	**21** 0214		2.1
1119	0.6	1033		0.5
Su 1625	1.8	M 1530		1.9
2323	0.6	2253		0.5
7 0510	2.0	**22** 0405		2.1
1237	0.6	1158		0.5
M 1745	1.8	Tu 1725		1.9
8 0118	0.6	**23** 0023		0.5
0624	2.1	0535		2.2
Tu 1418	0.4	1339		0.4
1855	1.9	1854		2.0
9 0239	0.4	**24** 0153		0.4
0734	2.3	0715		2.3
W 1530	0.3	Th 1452		0.3
2025	2.0	2016		2.1
10 0333	0.3	**25** 0313		0.3
0824	2.4	0820		2.4
Th 1613	0.2	F 1558		0.2
2054	2.1	2105		2.2
11 0424	0.2	**26** 0419		0.3
0920	2.4	0916		2.5
F 1654	0.3	Sa 1655		0.2
2124	2.1	2156		2.2
12 0501	0.3	**27** 0509		0.2
0956	2.4	1006		2.5
Sa 1729	0.3	Su 1744		0.2
2154	2.1	2240		2.2
13 0539	0.3	**28** 0559		0.2
1014	2.4	1050		2.5
Su 1759	0.3	M 1824		0.3
2224	2.1	2316		2.2
14 0608	0.3	**29** 0639		0.2
1050	2.4	1135		2.5
M 1829	0.3	Tu 1859		0.3
2305	2.2	2356		2.3
15 0644	0.3	**30** 0718		0.1
1125	2.4	1217		2.4
Tu 1901	0.4	W 1934		0.3
2335	2.2			

OCTOBER

Time h.min.	Ht. m.		Time h.min.	Ht. m.
1 0020	2.3	**16** 0719		0.4
0753	0.2	1216		2.2
Th 1245	2.2	F 1928		0.5
2004	0.5			
2 0034	2.2	**17** 0015		2.3
0829	0.3	0754		0.4
F 1305	2.1	Sa 1234		2.1
2029	0.5	1959		0.5
3 0104	2.2	**18** 0034		2.3
0858	0.4	0834		0.4
Sa 1334	1.9	Su 1304		2.0
2059	0.5	2027		0.5
4 0145	2.1	**19** 0110		2.3
0939	0.5	0929		0.4
Su 1420	1.8	M 1345		1.9
2139	0.6	2133		0.5
5 0244	2.1	**20** 0204		2.2
1029	0.6	1029		0.5
M 1535	1.7	1550		1.8
2229	0.6	2244		0.5
6 0420	2.0	**21** 0405		2.2
1143	0.7	1149		0.4
Tu 1704	1.8	W 1736		1.9
2347	0.6			
7 0556	2.1	**22** 0009		0.5
1308	0.6	0535		2.3
W 1815	1.9	Th 1318		0.4
		1834		2.0
8 0143	0.5	**23** 0133		0.4
0655	2.2	0656		2.4
Th 1428	0.4	F 1434		0.3
1924	2.0	1946		2.1
9 0249	0.4	**24** 0249		0.3
0750	2.3	0750		2.4
F 1529	0.3	Sa 1539		0.2
2014	2.1	2035		2.2
10 0339	0.3	**25** 0354		0.3
0846	2.4	0845		2.5
Sa 1609	0.3	Su 1629		0.3
2105	2.1	2126		2.2
11 0423	0.3	**26** 0449		0.3
0926	2.4	0936		2.5
Su 1649	0.3	M 1715		0.4
2124	2.2	2206		2.3
12 0504	0.3	**27** 0536		0.3
0952	2.4	1014		2.4
M 1723	0.3	Tu 1754		0.4
2155	2.2	2240		2.3
13 0539	0.3	**28** 0619		0.3
1015	2.4	1054		2.4
Tu 1758	0.4	W 1829		0.4
2224	2.2	2316		2.4
14 0619	0.3	**29** 0654		0.3
1056	2.4	1135		2.3
W 1828	0.4	Th 1859		0.4
2305	2.3	2350		2.4
15 0649	0.3	**30** 0730		0.3
1124	2.3	1210		2.2
Th 1859	0.4	F 1929		0.4
2345	2.3			
		31 0025		2.4
		0809		0.4
		Sa 1234		2.0
		1958		0.4

NOVEMBER

Time h.min.	Ht. m.		Time h.min.	Ht. m.
1 0034	2.3	**16** 0034		2.4
0838	0.5	0829		0.4
Su 1254	1.9	M 1317		2.0
2039	0.5	2028		0.4
2 0114	2.3	**17** 0130		2.3
0908	0.6	0924		0.4
M 1340	1.8	Tu 1420		1.9
2109	0.5	2129		0.4
3 0210	2.2	**18** 0230		2.3
0959	0.6	1017		0.4
Tu 1435	1.8	W 1544		1.9
2159	0.5	2233		0.4
4 0320	2.1	**19** 0344		2.3
1038	0.7	1138		0.4
W 1614	1.8	Th 1654		1.9
2259	0.6	2337		0.4
5 0435	2.1	**20** 0505		2.3
1126	0.6	1248		0.3
Th 1725	1.8	F 1816		2.0
6 0008	0.6	**21** 0108		0.4
0545	2.2	0604		2.3
F 1329	0.5	Sa 1359		0.3
1834	2.0	1910		2.0
7 0148	0.5	**22** 0229		0.3
0644	2.2	0715		2.3
Sa 1429	0.4	Su 1509		0.3
1935	2.1	1954		2.1
8 0252	0.4	**23** 0329		0.3
0744	2.3	0815		2.3
Su 1524	0.4	M 1559		0.3
2015	2.1	2050		2.2
9 0339	0.4	**24** 0429		0.3
0824	2.3	0915		2.3
M 1610	0.4	Tu 1652		0.4
2055	2.2	2136		2.3
10 0429	0.3	**25** 0515		0.3
0904	2.3	0956		2.3
Tu 1652	0.3	W 1729		0.5
2134	2.2	2216		2.4
11 0512	0.3	**26** 0559		0.4
0934	2.3	1024		2.2
W 1728	0.4	Th 1804		0.5
2205	2.3	2256		2.4
12 0554	0.3	**27** 0638		0.4
1020	2.3	1104		2.2
Th 1809	0.4	F 1828		0.4
2234	2.3	2326		2.5
13 0634	0.4	**28** 0709		0.4
1055	2.3	1134		2.1
F 1839	0.4	Sa 1909		0.4
2314	2.4	2355		2.5
14 0709	0.4	**29** 0744		0.5
1155	2.2	1210		2.0
Sa 1919	0.5	Su 1939		0.4
2354	2.4			
15 0749	0.4	**30** 0030		2.4
1234	2.1	0819		0.5
Su 1943	0.4	M 1224		1.9
		2008		0.4

DECEMBER

Time h.min.	Ht. m.		Time h.min.	Ht. m.
1 0105	2.3	**16** 0140		2.4
0849	0.5	0929		0.3
Tu 1254	1.9	W 1425		1.9
2037	0.4	2129		0.3
2 0134	2.3	**17** 0230		2.4
0929	0.6	1013		0.3
W 1350	1.8	Th 1507		1.9
2128	0.4	2223		0.3
3 0224	2.2	**18** 0336		2.3
1019	0.6	1113		0.3
Th 1450	1.8	F 1605		1.9
2218	0.5	2329		0.3
4 0324	2.1	**19** 0424		2.3
1113	0.6	1219		0.4
F 1600	1.8	Sa 1715		1.9
2319	0.5			
5 0424	2.1	**20** 0044		0.3
1229	0.5	0525		2.2
Sa 1705	1.9	Su 1328		0.4
		1825		2.0
6 0039	0.5	**21** 0159		0.3
0530	2.2	0634		2.2
Su 1339	0.5	M 1433		0.4
1830	2.0	1915		2.1
7 0200	0.5	**22** 0309		0.3
0630	2.2	0750		2.2
M 1433	0.4	Tu 1539		0.4
1930	2.1	2025		2.2
8 0253	0.4	**23** 0414		0.3
0730	2.2	0855		2.2
Tu 1529	0.3	W 1629		0.4
2017	2.2	2104		2.3
9 0348	0.3	**24** 0504		0.3
0815	2.3	0925		2.1
W 1619	0.3	Th 1714		0.4
2104	2.4	2145		2.4
10 0444	0.3	**25** 0545		0.4
0905	2.3	1015		2.1
Th 1709	0.4	F 1749		0.4
2150	2.3	2224		2.4
11 0539	0.3	**26** 0624		0.4
1004	2.2	1044		2.1
F 1749	0.4	Sa 1819		0.4
2225	2.4	2305		2.5
12 0619	0.3	**27** 0653		0.4
1106	2.2	1114		2.0
Sa 1829	0.4	Su 1859		0.3
2316	2.4	2335		2.5
13 0709	0.3	**28** 0729		0.4
1144	2.1	1155		2.0
Su 1909	0.4	M 1929		0.3
14 0000	2.4	**29** 0020		2.4
0759	0.3	0759		0.4
M 1234	2.1	Tu 1214		2.0
1959	0.4	1959		0.3
15 0056	2.4	**30** 0055		2.4
0840	0.3	0828		0.4
Tu 1324	2.0	W 1255		2.0
2038	0.3	2029		0.3
		31 0115		2.3
		0858		0.5
		Th 1304		1.9
		2103		0.3

TIDAL DIFFERENCES PAGE 21:322

Heights are referred to Chart Datum

TIDAL DIFFERENCES ON CUXHAVEN

PLACE	TIME DIFFERENCES				HEIGHT DIFFERENCES (Metres)			
	High Water		Low Water		MHWS	MHWN	MLWN	MLWS
CUXHAVEN	0200 and 1400	0800 and 2000	0200 and 1400	0900 and 2100	3.4	2.9	0.4	0.0
River Elbe								
Scharhörn	−0045	−0048	−0056	−0057	−0.1	−0.1	+0.1	0.0
Brunsbüttel	+0057	+0057	+0112	+0113	−0.3	−0.2	−0.2	0.0
Glückstadt	+0200	+0204	+0212	+0210	−0.3	−0.2	−0.2	0.0
Stadersand	+0237	+0240	+0257	+0252	−0.2	0.0	−0.2	0.0
Schulau	+0258	+0310	+0333	+0316	−0.1	+0.1	−0.2	0.0
Nienstedten	+0317	+0326	+0400	+0342	+0.1	+0.3	−0.3	+0.1
Hamburg	+0333	+0342	+0421	+0403	+0.2	+0.3	−0.3	0.0
Harburg	+0341	+0347	+0429	+0413	+0.2	+0.4	−0.3	0.0
Schöpfstelle	+0346	+0353	+0443	+0426	+0.2	+0.4	−0.3	0.0
Bunthaus	+0356	+0402	+0501	+0444	−0.1	+0.1	−0.3	0.0
Zollenspieker	+0422	+0430	+0555	+0533	−0.3	−0.1	+0.2	+0.5
River Weser								
Alte Weser Lighthouse	−0102	−0102	−0120	−0105	−0.1	−0.2	0.0	0.0
Bremerhaven	+0020	+0020	−0010	−0005	+0.7	+0.6	0.0	0.0
Nordenham	+0037	+0037	+0015	+0015	+0.7	+0.6	−0.2	−0.1
Brake	+0110	+0110	+0105	+0105	+0.6	+0.5	−0.3	−0.2
Elsfleth	+0120	+0120	+0120	+0120	+0.7	+0.6	−0.2	0.0
Vegesack	+0150	+0150	+0205	+0205	+0.6	+0.5	−0.4	−0.1
Bremen	+0158	+0158	+0225	+0225	+0.7	+0.6	−0.5	−0.2
River Jade								
Wangerooge Ost	−0110	−0110	−0123	−0123	0.0	0.0	+0.1	0.0
Wangerooge West	−0115	−0115	−0135	−0135	−0.1	−0.3	0.0	0.0
Schillighörn	−0040	−0040	−0103	−0103	+0.2	+0.2	+0.1	0.0
Hooksiel	−0027	−0027	−0058	−0058	+0.4	+0.4	+0.2	−
Wilhelmshaven	−0010	−0010	−0050	−0050	+0.9	+0.8	+0.2	0.0
Schweiburger Tief	0000	0000	−0040	−0040	+0.9	+0.8	+0.2	0.0

Note: Time zone. The predictions for the standard port are on the same time zone as the differences shown. No further adjustment is necessary.
Refer to predictions on pages 21:323-21:325

TIDAL DIFFERENCES ON HARLINGEN

PLACE	TIME DIFFERENCES				HEIGHT DIFFERENCES (Metres)			
	High Water		Low Water		MHWS	MHWN	MLWN	MLWS
HARLINGEN	1100 and 2300	0500 and 1700	0000 and 1200	0600 and 1800	2.3	1.9	0.3	0.2
Lauwersoog	+0013	+0047	−0050	−0113	+0.1	+0.1	−0.2	−0.5
Nes	+0011	+0054	−0039	−0056	+0.1	+0.1	−0.2	−0.4
West Terschelling	−0032	−0008	−0138	−0149	−0.2	−0.1	0.0	−0.2
Vlieland	−0106	−0041	−0200	−0212	−0.1	−0.1	0.0	−0.2
Kornwerderzand	−0011	−0025	−0058	−0025	−0.1	−0.1	0.0	0.0
Den Oever	−0058	−0135	−0201	−0147	−0.3	−0.2	+0.1	0.0
Den Helder	−0203	−0115	−0321	−0309	−0.4	−0.3	+0.2	+0.1

Note: Time zone. The predictions for the standard port are on the same time zone as the differences shown. No further adjustment is necessary.
Refer to predictions on pages 21:319-21:321

CUXHAVEN 21:323

Lat. 53°52'N. Long. 8°43'E. HIGH & LOW WATER 1992

TIME ZONE-0100 SUBTRACT 1 HOUR FROM TIMES SHOWN FOR GMT

JANUARY

Day	Time	m	Time	m	Time	m	Time	m
1 W	0412	0.5	1000	3.2	1649	0.4	2235	3.1
2 TH	0521	0.4	1106	3.2	1751	0.4	2332	3.2
3 F	0622	0.4	1203	3.2	1844	0.4		
4 SA	0021	3.3	0714	0.3	1329	3.2	1929 ●	0.4
5 SU	0103	3.4	0758	0.2			2009	0.3
6 M	0140	3.4	0836	0.2	1406	3.2	2044	0.2
7 TU	0214	3.4	0911	0.1	1441	3.2	2117	0.2
8 W	0248	3.5	0943	0.1	1513	3.1	2147	0.2
9 TH	0318	3.5	1013	0.2	1542	3.1	2215	0.2
10 F	0348	3.4	1042	0.2	1612	3.1	2243	0.2
11 SA	0421	3.4	1114	0.2	1645	3.0	2314	0.2
12 SU	0457	3.3	1145	0.2	1719	3.0	2347	0.3
13 M	0534	3.2	1217	0.3	1759	3.0		
14 TU	0028	0.4	0620	3.1	1301	0.4	1853	2.9
15 W	0129	0.5	0724	3.0	1407	0.4	2004	2.9
16 TH	0249	0.5	0842	3.0	1528	0.4	2123	3.0
17 F	0416	0.4	1001	3.1	1651	0.3	2240	3.2
18 SA	0536	0.3	1114	3.2	1805	0.2	2345	3.3
19 SU	0646	0.1	1219	3.2	1909 O	0.1		
20 M	0042	3.5	0747	0.0	1316	3.3	2004	0.1
21 TU	0134	3.5	0842	-0.1	1410	3.3	2057	0.0
22 W	0225	3.6	0935	-0.1	1502	3.3	2146	-0.1
23 TH	0314	3.6	1023	-0.1	1549	3.3	2230	-0.1
24 F	0357	3.6	1104	-0.1	1630	3.2	2308	0.0
25 SA	0439	3.6	1140	0.0	1711	3.2	2344	0.1
26 SU	0522	3.5	1215	0.2	1752	3.1		
27 M	0021	0.2	0606	3.4	1252	0.3	1834	3.0
28 TU	0104	0.3	0656	3.2	1337	0.4	1927	2.9
29 W	0202	0.4	0800	3.0	1440	0.5	2036	2.9
30 TH	0320	0.4	0918	2.9	1559	0.4	2155	3.0
31 F	0446	0.3	1038	2.9	1718	0.4	2307	3.1

FEBRUARY

Day	Time	m	Time	m	Time	m	Time	m
1 SA	0600	0.2	1145	3.0	1822	0.3		
2 SU	0003	3.2	0657	0.1	1235	3.0	1911	0.2
3 M	0046	3.2	0741	0.0	1314	3.0	1952 ●	0.1
4 TU	0124	3.3	0820	0.0	1350	3.1	2029	0.0
5 W	0158	3.4	0854	0.0	1424	3.1	2101	0.0
6 TH	0230	3.4	0924	0.0	1453	3.1	2129	0.0
7 F	0258	3.4	0951	0.0	1519	3.1	2156	0.0
8 SA	0327	3.4	1019	0.0	1547	3.1	2225	0.0
9 SU	0359	3.3	1050	0.0	1619	3.0	2256	0.0
10 M	0434	3.3	1120	0.1	1650	3.0	2325	0.1
11 TU	0506	3.2	1144	0.2	1722	3.0	2354	0.2
12 W	0543	3.1	1217	0.3	1807	2.9		
13 TH	0044	0.3	0640	2.9	1318	0.4	1917	2.9
14 F	0205	0.3	0804	2.8	1447	0.3	2047	2.9
15 SA	0345	0.2	0938	2.9	1625	0.2	2217	3.1
16 SU	0519	0.1	1102	3.0	1750	0.1	2332	3.2
17 M	0636	0.0	1211	3.1	1859	0.0		
18 TU	0032	3.4	0737	-0.2	1308	3.2	1955 O	-0.1
19 W	0123	3.5	0830	-0.3	1357	3.2	2044	-0.2
20 TH	0211	3.5	0918	-0.3	1443	3.2	2129	-0.2
21 F	0256	3.5	1001	-0.3	1526	3.2	2211	-0.2
22 SA	0338	3.5	1040	-0.2	1605	3.2	2247	-0.2
23 SU	0417	3.5	1113	-0.1	1641	3.2	2319	-0.1
24 M	0455	3.4	1142	0.1	1715	3.1		
25 TU	0533	3.2	1210	0.2	1751	3.0		
26 W	0024	0.1	0615	3.0	1245	0.3	1837	2.9
27 TH	0114	0.2	0714	2.8	1342	0.4	1945	2.8
28 F	0231	0.3	0836	2.6	1507	0.4	2113	2.8
29 SA	0406	0.2	1005	2.6	1640	0.3	2238	2.9

MARCH

Day	Time	m	Time	m	Time	m	Time	m
1 SU	0532	0.1	1121	2.8	1756	0.2	2340	3.0
2 M	0634	0.0	1214	2.9	1849	0.1		
3 TU	0024	3.1	0718	-0.1	1252	3.0	1929	0.0
4 W	0100	3.2	0754	-0.1	1326	3.0	2005 ●	-0.1
5 TH	0134	3.2	0828	-0.2	1358	3.0	2038	-0.2
6 F	0206	3.3	0857	-0.2	1427	3.1	2106	-0.2
7 SA	0235	3.3	0924	-0.1	1453	3.1	2134	-0.2
8 SU	0305	3.3	0954	-0.1	1522	3.1	2206	-0.1
9 M	0339	3.2	1027	0.0	1555	3.1	2239	-0.1
10 TU	0414	3.2	1058	0.0	1628	3.1	2310	-0.1
11 W	0449	3.1	1124	0.1	1700	3.0	2339	0.0
12 TH	0526	3.0	1156	0.2	1744	2.9		
13 F	0026	0.1	0623	2.8	1255	0.3	1854	2.9
14 SA	0146	0.1	0748	2.6	1427	0.3	2028	2.9
15 SU	0329	0.1	0926	2.8	1610	0.2	2203	3.0
16 M	0507	-0.1	1052	2.9	1737	0.0	2320	3.2
17 TU	0622	-0.2	1159	3.0	1844	-0.1		
18 W	0017	3.3	0720	-0.3	1252	3.1	1938	-0.2
19 TH	0106	3.4	0809	-0.3	1337	3.2	2025 O	-0.3
20 F	0152	3.4	0853	-0.3	1419	3.2	2106	-0.3
21 SA	0235	3.4	0933	-0.2	1458	3.2	2145	-0.3
22 SU	0316	3.4	1009	-0.2	1536	3.3	2221	-0.2
23 M	0354	3.4	1041	-0.1	1610	3.2	2254	-0.1
24 TU	0430	3.3	1110	0.0	1642	3.2	2324	-0.1
25 W	0505	3.1	1135	0.1	1716	3.0	2355	0.0
26 TH	0543	2.8	1205	0.2	1759	2.9		
27 F	0039	0.1	0636	2.6	1256	0.3	1902	2.8
28 SA	0148	0.2	0753	2.5	1416	0.3	2028	2.7
29 SU	0320	0.2	0923	2.5	1552	0.2	2156	2.8
30 M	0450	0.1	1043	2.7	1715	0.1	2304	3.0
31 TU	0557	0.0	1138	2.8	1812	0.0	2349	3.1

APRIL

Day	Time	m	Time	m	Time	m	Time	m
1 W	0641	-0.1	1217	2.9	1853	-0.1		
2 TH	0026	3.1	0717	-0.2	1251	3.0	1931	-0.2
3 F	0102	3.2	0752	-0.2	1325	3.0	2007 ●	-0.2
4 SA	0136	3.2	0824	-0.2	1357	3.1	2039	-0.2
5 SU	0209	3.2	0856	-0.2	1427	3.1	2112	-0.2
6 M	0244	3.2	0929	-0.1	1459	3.2	2148	-0.2
7 TU	0320	3.2	1005	-0.1	1536	3.2	2225	-0.2
8 W	0400	3.1	1040	-0.1	1613	3.1	2302	-0.2
9 TH	0441	3.0	1113	0.0	1651	3.1	2339	-0.1
10 F	0526	2.9	1153	0.1	1740	3.0		
11 SA	0030	0.0	0625	2.8	1254	0.2	1851	3.0
12 SU	0147	0.1	0746	2.8	1422	0.2	2021	3.1
13 M	0323	0.0	0918	2.8	1558	0.1	2149	3.2
14 TU	0452	-0.1	1038	3.0	1719	0.0	2300	3.3
15 W	0600	-0.2	1138	3.1	1821	-0.1	2355	3.3
16 TH	0651	-0.3	1227	3.1	1912	-0.2		
17 F	0043	3.3	0739	-0.3	1312	3.2	2000	-0.2
18 SA	0130	3.4	0825	-0.3	1354	3.3	2042	-0.2
19 SU	0214	3.4	0903	-0.1	1431	3.3	2120	-0.2
20 M	0253	3.4	0937	0.0	1507	3.3	2156	-0.1
21 TU	0330	3.3	1010	0.0	1542	3.3	2231	-0.1
22 W	0406	3.1	1040	0.0	1615	3.2	2303	-0.1
23 TH	0442	3.0	1108	0.1	1650	3.1	2336	0.0
24 F	0520	2.8	1138	0.2	1732	3.0		
25 SA	0015	0.1	0607	2.6	1222	0.2	1826	2.9
26 SU	0112	0.2	0712	2.6	1329	0.3	1939	2.9
27 M	0229	0.2	0830	2.6	1454	0.3	2100	2.9
28 TU	0352	0.3	0946	2.7	1616	0.2	2210	3.0
29 W	0501	0.0	1045	2.8	1719	0.1	2301	3.1
30 TH	0550	-0.1	1130	3.0	1807	0.0	2343	3.1

TIDAL DIFFERENCES PAGE 21:322.

Datum of predictions: at M.L.W.S. and 0.5 m. above L.A.T.

CUXHAVEN

HIGH & LOW WATER 1992   **Lat. 51°52′N. Long. 8°43′E.**

TIME ZONE-0100 SUBTRACT 1 HOUR FROM TIMES SHOWN FOR GMT

MAY

#	Time	m	#	Time	m
1 F	0631 / 1210 / 1851	-0.2 / 3.0 / -0.1	16 SA	0019 / 0707 / 1245 / O 1933	3.3 / -0.1 / 3.3 / -0.1
2 SA	0024 / 0711 / 1249 / ● 1933	3.2 / -0.2 / 3.1 / -0.1	17 SU	0109 / 0756 / 1330 / 2019	3.3 / 0.0 / 3.4 / -0.1
3 SU	0104 / 0750 / 1327 / 2012	3.2 / -0.2 / 3.2 / -0.2	18 M	0154 / 0836 / 1408 / 2058	3.4 / 0.0 / 3.4 / -0.1
4 M	0143 / 0828 / 1403 / 2051	3.2 / -0.1 / 3.3 / -0.2	19 TU	0232 / 0910 / 1443 / 2135	3.3 / 0.1 / 3.4 / -0.1
5 TU	0224 / 0908 / 1441 / 2134	3.2 / -0.1 / 3.3 / -0.2	20 W	0309 / 0943 / 1518 / 2211	3.2 / 0.0 / 3.4 / -0.1
6 W	0308 / 0950 / 1522 / 2218	3.2 / -0.1 / 3.3 / -0.2	21 TH	0345 / 1016 / 1554 / 2246	3.1 / 0.0 / 3.3 / 0.0
7 TH	0353 / 1030 / 1605 / 2301	3.1 / -0.1 / 3.3 / -0.2	22 F	0423 / 1048 / 1629 / 2320	3.0 / 0.1 / 3.2 / 0.0
8 F	0439 / 1111 / 1651 / 2346	3.0 / 0.0 / 3.2 / -0.2	23 SA	0500 / 1119 / 1709 / 2356	2.8 / 0.1 / 3.2 / 0.1
9 SA	0531 / 1159 / 1745	2.9 / 0.1 / 3.2	24 SU	0541 / 1156 / 1754	2.8 / 0.2 / 3.1
10 SU	0040 / 0632 / 1300 / 1853	0.0 / 2.9 / 0.2 / 3.3	25 M	0041 / 0630 / 1247 / 1850	0.2 / 2.7 / 0.3 / 3.0
11 M	0150 / 0744 / 1417 / 2011	0.1 / 2.9 / 0.3 / 3.3	26 TU	0137 / 0731 / 1353 / 1957	0.2 / 2.7 / 0.3 / 3.0
12 TU	0311 / 0903 / 1539 / 2128	0.1 / 3.0 / 0.2 / 3.3	27 W	0244 / 0838 / 1507 / 2105	0.2 / 2.8 / 0.3 / 3.0
13 W	0428 / 1013 / 1652 / 2233	0.0 / 3.1 / 0.1 / 3.3	28 TH	0352 / 0942 / 1617 / 2206	0.1 / 2.9 / 0.2 / 3.1
14 TH	0529 / 1109 / 1750 / 2328	-0.1 / 3.1 / 0.0 / 3.3	29 F	0451 / 1038 / 1716 / 2257	0.0 / 3.0 / 0.1 / 3.1
15 F	0618 / 1158 / 1842	-0.1 / 3.2 / -0.1	30 SA	0543 / 1128 / 1810 / 2346	0.0 / 3.1 / 0.0 / 3.2
			31 SU	0632 / 1214 / 1901	0.0 / 3.2 / 0.0

JUNE

#	Time	m	#	Time	m
1 M	0034 / 0720 / 1259 / ● 1948	3.3 / 0.0 / 3.3 / -0.1	16 TU	0136 / 0814 / 1349 / 2041	3.3 / 0.1 / 3.5 / 0.0
2 TU	0121 / 0806 / 1343 / 2036	3.3 / 0.0 / 3.4 / -0.1	17 W	0215 / 0850 / 1425 / 2118	3.2 / 0.1 / 3.4 / 0.0
3 W	0210 / 0853 / 1428 / 2125	3.3 / 0.0 / 3.4 / -0.2	18 TH	0251 / 0925 / 1501 / 2154	3.2 / 0.0 / 3.4 / 0.0
4 TH	0301 / 0941 / 1514 / 2215	3.2 / -0.1 / 3.5 / -0.2	19 F	0328 / 0958 / 1535 / 2228	3.1 / 0.0 / 3.4 / 0.0
5 F	0350 / 1025 / 1600 / 2302	3.2 / -0.1 / 3.5 / -0.2	20 SA	0403 / 1029 / 1609 / 2301	3.0 / 0.1 / 3.4 / 0.1
6 SA	0438 / 1110 / 1649 / 2349	3.1 / 0.0 / 3.4 / -0.1	21 SU	0437 / 1100 / 1645 / 2335	3.0 / 0.1 / 3.3 / 0.1
7 SU	0530 / 1200 / 1743	3.1 / 0.1 / 3.4	22 M	0513 / 1133 / 1724	2.9 / 0.2 / 3.3
8 M	0042 / 0628 / 1257 / 1845	0.0 / 3.1 / 0.2 / 3.5	23 TU	0011 / 0551 / 1211 / 1806	0.2 / 2.9 / 0.3 / 3.2
9 TU	0141 / 0730 / 1401 / 1951	0.1 / 3.2 / 0.3 / 3.4	24 W	0050 / 0636 / 1259 / 1858	0.1 / 2.9 / 0.3 / 3.1
10 W	0246 / 0835 / 1509 / 2058	0.1 / 3.1 / 0.2 / 3.4	25 TH	0139 / 0732 / 1401 / 2000	0.2 / 2.9 / 0.4 / 3.0
11 TH	0352 / 0940 / 1617 / 2202	0.1 / 3.1 / 0.2 / 3.3	26 F	0242 / 0837 / 1513 / 2108	0.2 / 2.9 / 0.3 / 3.1
12 F	0453 / 1038 / 1719 / 2303	0.1 / 3.2 / 0.1 / 3.3	27 SA	0350 / 0944 / 1626 / 2213	0.2 / 3.0 / 0.2 / 3.1
13 SA	0548 / 1131 / 1816 / 2359	0.1 / 3.2 / 0.1 / 3.3	28 SU	0457 / 1048 / 1733 / 2313	0.2 / 3.2 / 0.2 / 3.2
14 SU	0640 / 1222 / 1911	0.3 / 3.3 / 0.1	29 M	0600 / 1145 / 1835	0.2 / 3.3 / 0.1
15 M	0051 / 0730 / 1308 / O 2000	3.3 / 0.1 / 3.4 / 0.0	30 TU	0011 / 0658 / 1237 / ● 1932	3.3 / 0.1 / 3.4 / 0.0

JULY

#	Time	m	#	Time	m
1 W	0106 / 0751 / 1328 / 2026	3.3 / 0.0 / 3.5 / -0.1	16 TH	0159 / 0835 / 1409 / 2103	3.2 / 0.0 / 3.4 / 0.0
2 TH	0200 / 0844 / 1418 / 2120	3.3 / 0.0 / 3.5 / -0.1	17 F	0236 / 0910 / 1444 / 2137	3.2 / 0.0 / 3.4 / 0.0
3 F	0254 / 0935 / 1507 / 2212	3.3 / -0.1 / 3.6 / -0.2	18 SA	0309 / 0941 / 1515 / 2207	3.1 / 0.0 / 3.4 / 0.0
4 SA	0344 / 1021 / 1553 / 2257	3.3 / -0.1 / 3.6 / -0.2	19 SU	0339 / 1009 / 1545 / 2236	3.1 / 0.1 / 3.4 / 0.1
5 SU	0430 / 1104 / 1640 / 2341	3.2 / 0.0 / 3.6 / -0.1	20 M	0409 / 1038 / 1618 / 2308	3.1 / 0.1 / 3.4 / 0.1
6 M	0517 / 1149 / 1730	3.2 / 0.1 / 3.5	21 TU	0442 / 1110 / 1654 / 2340	3.0 / 0.2 / 3.3 / 0.2
7 TU	0027 / 0609 / 1239 / 1824	0.0 / 3.2 / 0.2 / 3.5	22 W	0516 / 1143 / 1730	3.0 / 0.2 / 3.3
8 W	0117 / 0701 / 1331 / 1920	0.2 / 3.1 / 0.3 / 3.4	23 TH	0010 / 0551 / 1218 / 1810	0.2 / 3.0 / 0.3 / 3.2
9 TH	0209 / 0756 / 1430 / 2022	0.3 / 3.1 / 0.3 / 3.3	24 F	0045 / 0636 / 1306 / 1904	0.3 / 3.0 / 0.4 / 3.1
10 F	0309 / 0859 / 1539 / 2131	0.3 / 3.1 / 0.3 / 3.2	25 SA	0140 / 0738 / 1417 / 2016	0.4 / 2.9 / 0.4 / 3.0
11 SA	0416 / 1007 / 1652 / 2241	0.3 / 3.1 / 0.3 / 3.1	26 SU	0256 / 0855 / 1543 / 2135	0.4 / 3.0 / 0.3 / 3.0
12 SU	0522 / 1110 / 1758 / 2345	0.3 / 3.2 / 0.2 / 3.2	27 M	0420 / 1014 / 1706 / 2250	0.3 / 3.1 / 0.2 / 3.1
13 M	0621 / 1204 / 1854	0.2 / 3.3 / 0.1	28 TU	0537 / 1124 / 1819 / 2357	0.2 / 3.3 / 0.1 / 3.2
14 TU	0037 / 0712 / 1251 / O 1944	3.2 / 0.2 / 3.4 / 0.1	29 W	0644 / 1223 / 1922 ●	0.1 / 3.4 / 0.0
15 W	0121 / 0756 / 1332 / 2026	3.3 / 0.1 / 3.4 / 0.0	30 TH	0056 / 0742 / 1316 / 2019	3.3 / 0.1 / 3.6 / -0.1
			31 F	0151 / 0835 / 1407 / 2111	3.3 / 0.0 / 3.6 / -0.1

AUGUST

#	Time	m	#	Time	m
1 SA	0242 / 0925 / 1455 / 2200	3.3 / -0.1 / 3.6 / -0.2	16 SU	0244 / 0920 / 1452 / 2141	3.2 / 0.0 / 3.4 / 0.1
2 SU	0329 / 1010 / 1539 / 2243	3.3 / -0.1 / 3.6 / -0.1	17 M	0311 / 0946 / 1520 / 2207	3.2 / 0.0 / 3.4 / 0.1
3 M	0412 / 1050 / 1623 / 2322	3.3 / -0.1 / 3.6 / 0.0	18 TU	0338 / 1014 / 1551 / 2238	3.1 / 0.1 / 3.4 / 0.2
4 TU	0454 / 1130 / 1708	3.3 / 0.0 / 3.5	19 W	0411 / 1047 / 1626 / 2310	3.1 / 0.2 / 3.3 / 0.2
5 W	0001 / 0538 / 1211 / 1755	0.1 / 3.2 / 0.1 / 3.4	20 TH	0444 / 1118 / 1700 / 2337	3.1 / 0.2 / 3.3 / 0.3
6 TH	0041 / 0623 / 1254 / 1844	0.2 / 3.1 / 0.3 / 3.3	21 F	0515 / 1148 / 1734	3.1 / 0.3 / 3.1
7 F	0124 / 0712 / 1347 / 1943	0.4 / 3.1 / 0.4 / 3.1	22 SA	0006 / 0553 / 1228 / 1823	0.4 / 3.0 / 0.4 / 3.0
8 SA	0221 / 0816 / 1458 / 2058	0.5 / 3.0 / 0.4 / 3.0	23 SU	0055 / 0654 / 1338 / 1938	0.5 / 2.9 / 0.4 / 2.9
9 SU	0336 / 0934 / 1624 / 2220	0.5 / 3.0 / 0.4 / 2.9	24 M	0217 / 0818 / 1513 / 2110	0.5 / 2.9 / 0.4 / 2.9
10 M	0457 / 1050 / 1743 / 2332	0.4 / 3.1 / 0.2 / 3.0	25 TU	0353 / 0949 / 1649 / 2236	0.4 / 3.1 / 0.2 / 3.0
11 TU	0606 / 1151 / 1842	0.3 / 3.2 / 0.1	26 W	0522 / 1108 / 1808 / 2347	0.3 / 3.3 / 0.1 / 3.1
12 W	0026 / 0658 / 1236 / 1928	3.1 / 0.2 / 3.3 / 0.1	27 TH	0633 / 1210 / 1912	0.2 / 3.4 / 0.0
13 TH	0105 / 0740 / 1314 / O 2008	3.1 / 0.1 / 3.4 / 0.0	28 F	0045 / 0732 / 1302 / ● 2006	3.3 / 0.1 / 3.6 / -0.1
14 F	0140 / 0818 / 1350 / 2043	3.3 / 0.1 / 3.4 / 0.0	29 SA	0135 / 0822 / 1350 / 2054	3.3 / 0.0 / 3.6 / -0.1
15 SA	0214 / 0852 / 1422 / 2114	3.2 / 0.0 / 3.4 / 0.0	30 SU	0222 / 0908 / 1436 / 2139	3.4 / -0.1 / 3.6 / -0.1
			31 M	0305 / 0951 / 1519 / 2219	3.3 / -0.1 / 3.6 / -0.1

CUXHAVEN 21:325

Lat. 53°52′N. Long. 8°43′E.   HIGH & LOW WATER 1992

TIME ZONE −0100 SUBTRACT 1 HOUR FROM TIMES SHOWN FOR GMT

Heights in metres. O = Full Moon, ● = New Moon.

SEPTEMBER

Day	Time	m	Time	m	Time	m	Time	m
1 TU	0346	3.3	1030	0.0	1601	3.6	2256	0.1
2 W	0425	3.3	1106	0.1	1643	3.5	2330	0.2
3 TH	0503	3.3	1141	0.2	1724	3.3		
4 F	0003	0.4	0542	3.2	1218	0.3	1808	3.1
5 SA	0040	0.5	0628	3.0	1307	0.4	1904	2.9
6 SU	0133	0.6	0732	2.9	1418	0.5	2021	2.7
7 M	0252	0.6	0857	2.9	1550	0.4	2151	2.7
8 TU	0425	0.5	1024	3.0	1720	0.3	2311	2.9
9 W	0545	0.4	1132	3.2	1824	0.2		
10 TH	0007	3.0	0639	0.3	1215	3.3	1906	0.1
11 F	0042	3.1	0716	0.2	1248	3.3	1940	0.1
12 SA	0113	3.1	0751	0.2	1322	3.3	O 2013	0.1
13 SU	0144	3.1	0825	0.1	1354	3.3	2043	0.1
14 M	0214	3.2	0855	0.2	1425	3.3	2111	0.1
15 TU	0241	3.2	0922	0.0	1455	3.3	2139	0.2
16 W	0309	3.2	0952	0.1	1526	3.3	2210	0.3
17 TH	0341	3.2	1025	0.2	1601	3.3	2242	0.3
18 F	0415	3.2	1058	0.2	1636	3.2	2311	0.3
19 SA	0448	3.2	1128	0.3	1712	3.1	2341	0.4
20 SU	0527	3.1	1209	0.4	1802	2.9		
21 M	0032	0.5	0629	3.0	1319	0.4	1918	2.8
22 TU	0155	0.5	0756	3.0	1456	0.4	2054	2.8
23 W	0336	0.5	0931	3.1	1636	0.3	2223	3.0
24 TH	0508	0.4	1052	3.3	1755	0.1	2333	3.2
25 F	0618	0.2	1152	3.4	1854	0.0		
26 SA	0026	3.3	0713	0.1	1241	3.5	● 1943	0.0
27 SU	0113	3.3	0801	0.1	1328	3.6	2030	0.0
28 M	0156	3.4	0845	0.0	1413	3.6	2112	0.0
29 TU	0238	3.4	0926	0.1	1457	3.6	2151	0.1
30 W	0318	3.4	1006	0.1	1538	3.5	2227	0.2

OCTOBER

Day	Time	m	Time	m	Time	m	Time	m
1 TH	0355	3.4	1042	0.1	1617	3.4	2259	0.3
2 F	0430	3.3	1115	0.2	1655	3.2	2328	0.4
3 SA	0506	3.2	1149	0.3	1736	3.0		
4 SU	0001	0.5	0550	3.1	1233	0.4	1828	2.8
5 M	0049	0.6	0650	2.9	1338	0.5	1941	2.6
6 TU	0204	0.7	0812	2.9	1506	0.5	2109	2.6
7 W	0338	0.6	0942	3.0	1638	0.4	2231	2.8
8 TH	0505	0.5	1054	3.1	1747	0.3	2329	3.0
9 F	0604	0.4	1140	3.2	1830	0.2		
10 SA	0006	3.1	0642	0.3	1213	3.3	1902	0.2
11 SU	0036	3.1	0717	0.2	1247	3.3	O 1935	0.1
12 M	0109	3.2	0753	0.2	1322	3.3	2009	0.1
13 TU	0142	3.2	0827	0.1	1356	3.3	2041	0.2
14 W	0212	3.3	0859	0.1	1429	3.3	2113	0.3
15 TH	0243	3.3	0932	0.2	1504	3.3	2147	0.3
16 F	0317	3.4	1008	0.2	1541	3.3	2220	0.3
17 SA	0353	3.3	1044	0.2	1619	3.1	2253	0.4
18 SU	0430	3.2	1120	0.2	1702	3.0	2330	0.4
19 M	0515	3.2	1205	0.3	1756	2.9		
20 TU	0024	0.5	0619	3.1	1314	0.4	1909	2.9
21 W	0144	0.6	0742	3.2	1445	0.4	2039	2.9
22 TH	0319	0.6	0912	3.2	1618	0.3	2204	3.0
23 F	0447	0.4	1051	3.3	1732	0.2	2309	3.2
24 SA	0554	0.3	1127	3.4	1827	0.1		
25 SU	0000	3.3	0647	0.2	1216	3.5	● 1915	0.1
26 M	0047	3.3	0736	0.2	1304	3.5	2002	0.2
27 TU	0130	3.4	0821	0.2	1351	3.5	2044	0.2
28 W	0211	3.5	0902	0.2	1434	3.5	2122	0.3
29 TH	0249	3.5	0941	0.2	1514	3.5	2157	0.3
30 F	0326	3.5	1019	0.2	1552	3.3	2230	0.4
31 SA	0401	3.4	1054	0.3	1630	3.1	2300	0.4

NOVEMBER

Day	Time	m	Time	m	Time	m	Time	m
1 SU	0437	3.3	1127	0.3	1708	2.9	2331	0.5
2 M	0519	3.2	1206	0.4	1755	2.8		
3 TU	0013	0.6	0612	3.1	1300	0.5	1856	2.7
4 W	0115	0.7	0720	3.0	1412	0.6	2011	2.7
5 TH	0236	0.7	0840	3.0	1534	0.5	2127	2.8
6 F	0400	0.6	0954	3.1	1646	0.4	2230	2.9
7 SA	0507	0.5	1049	3.2	1737	0.4	2316	3.1
8 SU	0556	0.4	1130	3.2	1816	0.3	2355	3.2
9 M	0637	0.3	1208	3.2	1855	0.2		
10 TU	0033	3.2	0719	0.2	1248	3.3	O 1934	0.2
11 W	0110	3.3	0758	0.2	1326	3.3	2012	0.2
12 TH	0146	3.3	0834	0.2	1406	3.3	2051	0.3
13 F	0222	3.4	0911	0.2	1448	3.3	2130	0.3
14 SA	0259	3.4	0959	0.2	1530	3.2	2208	0.3
15 SU	0339	3.4	1038	0.2	1612	3.2	2245	0.3
16 M	0421	3.4	1119	0.2	1658	3.1	2328	0.4
17 TU	0510	3.3	1207	0.3	1753	3.0		
18 W	0023	0.5	0612	3.3	1310	0.4	1900	3.0
19 TH	0133	0.6	0726	3.4	1427	0.4	2017	3.0
20 F	0255	0.6	0845	3.4	1548	0.4	2133	3.1
21 SA	0415	0.5	0956	3.4	1658	0.3	2237	3.2
22 SU	0521	0.4	1057	3.4	1754	0.2	2331	3.2
23 M	0618	0.3	1152	3.4	1845	0.3		
24 TU	0020	3.3	0711	0.3	1244	3.4	● 1935	0.3
25 W	0106	3.4	0800	0.3	1331	3.5	2019	0.4
26 TH	0147	3.5	0841	0.3	1413	3.4	2057	0.4
27 F	0224	3.6	0920	0.3	1452	3.4	2132	0.4
28 SA	0302	3.5	0959	0.2	1530	3.2	2207	0.3
29 SU	0338	3.5	1035	0.2	1607	3.1	2238	0.3
30 M	0414	3.4	1108	0.3	1644	3.0	2308	0.4

DECEMBER

Day	Time	m	Time	m	Time	m	Time	m
1 TU	0451	3.3	1143	0.3	1723	2.9	2342	0.5
2 W	0534	3.2	1223	0.4	1808	2.8		
3 TH	0027	0.6	0626	3.1	1314	0.5	1905	2.8
4 F	0128	0.6	0730	3.0	1417	0.5	2010	2.8
5 SA	0242	0.6	0840	3.0	1527	0.5	2117	2.9
6 SU	0356	0.6	0945	3.1	1631	0.4	2218	3.1
7 M	0500	0.5	1040	3.2	1725	0.4	2310	3.2
8 TU	0556	0.4	1129	3.2	1815	0.3	2357	3.3
9 W	0646	0.3	1216	3.2	1903	0.3	O	
10 TH	0041	3.4	0733	0.2	1301	3.3	1948	0.2
11 F	0123	3.4	0819	0.2	1348	3.3	2034	0.2
12 SA	0206	3.5	0906	0.1	1436	3.3	2120	0.2
13 SU	0249	3.5	0954	0.1	1523	3.3	2203	0.2
14 M	0331	3.6	1037	0.1	1607	3.2	2242	0.2
15 TU	0415	3.5	1118	0.1	1653	3.2	2325	0.3
16 W	0503	3.5	1204	0.2	1745	3.1		
17 TH	0016	0.4	0559	3.5	1257	0.3	1842	3.1
18 F	0114	0.5	0702	3.4	1359	0.4	1945	3.1
19 SA	0220	0.5	0810	3.4	1506	0.4	2053	3.1
20 SU	0333	0.5	0920	3.3	1616	0.4	2200	3.1
21 M	0446	0.4	1028	3.3	1721	0.3	2302	3.2
22 TU	0551	0.3	1131	3.3	1819	0.3	2358	3.3
23 W	0650	0.3	1228	3.3	1913	0.3		
24 TH	0047	3.4	0742	0.2	1315	3.3	● 1959	0.3
25 F	0129	3.5	0825	0.2	1356	3.3	2037	0.3
26 SA	0206	3.5	0904	0.2	1434	3.2	2113	0.2
27 SU	0243	3.5	0941	0.2	1511	3.2	2148	0.2
28 M	0318	3.5	1016	0.2	1546	3.1	2218	0.2
29 TU	0351	3.4	1047	0.2	1618	3.1	2246	0.3
30 W	0424	3.4	1117	0.3	1650	3.0	2314	0.3
31 TH	0500	3.3	1148	0.3	1724	2.9	2347	0.4

TIDAL DIFFERENCES PAGE 21:322.

Datum of predictions: at M.L.W.S. and 0.5 m. above L.A.T.

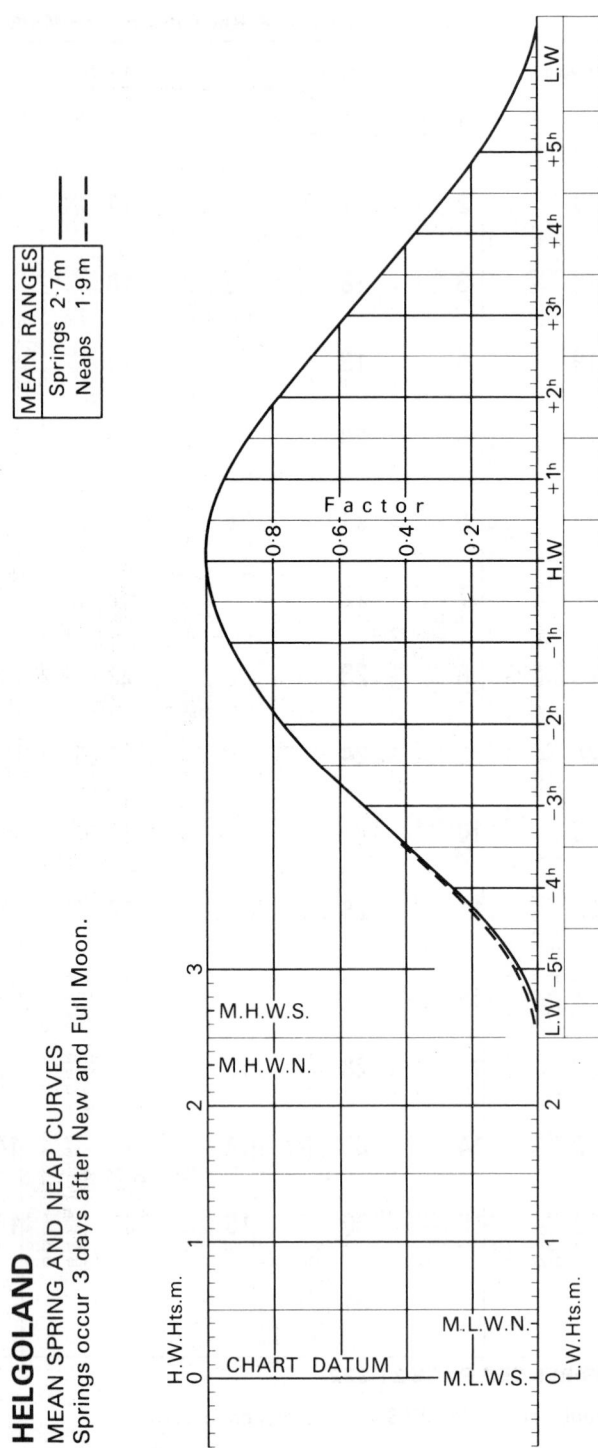

HELGOLAND

MEAN SPRING AND NEAP CURVES
Springs occur 3 days after New and Full Moon.

MEAN RANGES
Springs 2·7m ———
Neaps 1·9m – – –

HELGOLAND

Lat. 54°11′N. Long. 7°53′E.

HIGH & LOW WATER 1992

TIME ZONE-0100 SUBTRACT 1 HOUR FROM TIMES SHOWN FOR GMT

JANUARY

Day	Time	m		Day	Time	m
1 W	0301 0850 1534 2122	0.4 2.5 0.4 2.5		16 TH	0139 0732 1417 2012	0.5 2.4 0.4 2.4
2 TH	0409 0954 1633 2219	0.4 2.5 0.4 2.6		17 F	0302 0852 1536 2127	0.4 2.5 0.4 2.5
3 F	0506 1050 1724 2309	0.4 2.6 0.4 2.7		18 SA	0418 1005 1647 2232	0.3 2.5 0.2 2.7
4 SA	0556 1137 1809 ● 2352	0.3 2.6 0.4 2.7		19 SU	0526 1108 1749 O 2328	0.1 2.6 0.1 2.8
5 SU	0640 1217 1847	0.2 2.5 0.3		20 M	0626 1203 1844	0.0 2.6 0.1
6 M	0029 0717 1252 1922	2.8 0.2 2.5 0.2		21 TU	0020 0721 1253 1935	2.8 -0.1 2.6 0.0
7 TU	0103 0751 1326 1954	2.8 0.1 2.5 0.2		22 W	0111 0812 1343 2024	2.9 -0.2 2.6 -0.1
8 W	0137 0822 1359 2024	2.8 0.1 2.5 0.2		23 TH	0200 0859 1429 2107	2.9 -0.2 2.6 -0.1
9 TH	0208 0851 1428 2053	2.8 0.2 2.5 0.2		24 F	0243 0939 1512 2146	2.9 -0.1 2.6 0.0
10 F	0237 0921 1459 2124	2.7 0.2 2.4 0.2		25 SA	0323 1017 1553 2225	2.9 0.0 2.5 0.1
11 SA	0310 0954 1533 2157	2.7 0.2 2.4 0.2		26 SU	0406 1055 1635 2307	2.8 0.1 2.5 0.2
12 SU	0346 1027 1608 2233	2.6 0.2 2.4 0.3		27 M	0452 1135 1720 2354	2.7 0.3 2.4 0.3
13 M	0423 1102 1649 2317	2.6 0.3 2.3 0.4		28 TU	0544 1225 1815	2.5 0.4 2.3
14 TU	0510 1149 1744	2.5 0.4 2.3		29 W	0056 0650 1332 1925	0.4 2.3 0.5 2.3
15 W	0020 0614 1258 1854	0.5 2.4 0.4 2.3		30 TH	0217 0809 1453 2045	0.4 2.3 0.4 2.3
				31 F	0341 0927 1608 2156	0.3 2.3 0.4 2.4

FEBRUARY

Day	Time	m		Day	Time	m
1 SA	0451 1032 1708 2251	0.2 2.3 0.3 2.5		16 SU	0406 0951 1636 2218	0.1 2.3 0.1 2.6
2 SU	0543 1122 1754 2335	0.1 2.4 0.2 2.6		17 M	0519 1059 1741 2318	-0.1 2.4 0.0 2.7
3 M	0625 1201 1833 ●	0.1 2.4 0.1		18 TU	0618 1153 1835 O	-0.2 2.5 -0.1
4 TU	0013 0702 1235 1908	2.6 0.0 2.4 0.0		19 W	0008 0710 1239 1923	2.8 -0.3 2.5 -0.2
5 W	0046 0735 1307 1939	2.7 0.0 2.4 0.0		20 TH	0055 0756 1322 2008	2.8 -0.3 2.5 -0.2
6 TH	0117 0804 1337 2006	2.7 0.0 2.5 0.0		21 F	0140 0838 1405 2049	2.8 -0.3 2.5 -0.2
7 F	0146 0830 1404 2034	2.7 0.0 2.5 0.0		22 SA	0221 0915 1445 2125	2.8 -0.2 2.5 -0.1
8 SA	0214 0858 1432 2105	2.7 0.0 2.4 0.0		23 SU	0259 0950 1522 2200	2.8 -0.1 2.5 -0.1
9 SU	0245 0930 1505 2138	2.6 0.0 2.4 0.0		24 M	0337 1021 1558 2235	2.7 0.1 2.5 0.0
10 M	0319 1001 1537 2208	2.6 0.1 2.4 0.1		25 TU	0417 1054 1637 2315	2.5 0.2 2.4 0.1
11 TU	0352 1028 1610 2243	2.5 0.2 2.4 0.2		26 W	0502 1136 1725	2.3 0.4 2.3
12 W	0431 1106 1655 2338	2.4 0.3 2.3 0.3		27 TH	0012 0603 1241 1835	0.3 2.1 0.4 2.2
13 TH	0531 1212 1806	2.3 0.4 2.2		28 F	0133 0725 1408 2002	0.3 2.0 0.4 2.2
14 F	0101 0655 1342 1936	0.3 2.2 0.4 2.3		29 SA	0308 0854 1538 2126	0.2 2.0 0.3 2.3
15 SA	0237 0828 1516 2104	0.2 2.2 0.3 2.4				

MARCH

Day	Time	m		Day	Time	m
1 SU	0428 1009 1647 2228	0.1 2.1 0.2 2.4		16 M	0357 0939 1625 2204	-0.1 2.3 0.1 2.5
2 M	0523 1101 1735 2312	0.0 2.3 0.1 2.5		17 TU	0507 1044 1727 2302	-0.2 2.4 -0.1 2.6
3 TU	0603 1138 1812 2348	-0.1 2.3 0.0 2.5		18 W	0602 1135 1819 2350	-0.3 2.4 -0.2 2.7
4 W	0638 1210 1846 ●	-0.1 2.4 -0.1		19 TH	0650 1218 1905	-0.3 2.5 -0.3
5 TH	0020 0709 1240 1917	2.6 -0.2 2.4 -0.2		20 F	0034 0732 1258 1947	2.7 -0.3 2.5 -0.3
6 F	0050 0738 1308 1945	2.6 -0.2 2.4 -0.2		21 SA	0116 0811 1337 2026	2.7 -0.3 2.5 -0.3
7 SA	0119 0805 1336 2014	2.6 -0.2 2.4 -0.2		22 SU	0156 0847 1415 2102	2.7 -0.2 2.6 -0.2
8 SU	0149 0834 1406 2047	2.6 -0.1 2.5 -0.1		23 M	0235 0919 1451 2135	2.7 -0.1 2.6 -0.1
9 M	0222 0907 1439 2121	2.6 0.0 2.5 -0.1		24 TU	0311 0950 1526 2209	2.6 0.1 2.5 0.0
10 TU	0257 0939 1513 2154	2.5 0.0 2.4 -0.1		25 W	0348 1020 1602 2247	2.4 0.2 2.4 0.0
11 W	0332 1008 1545 2228	2.4 0.1 2.4 0.0		26 TH	0429 1058 1647 2337	2.2 0.3 2.3 0.1
12 TH	0412 1045 1630 2322	2.3 0.2 2.3 0.1		27 F	0523 1156 1751	2.0 0.4 2.2
13 F	0512 1151 1741	2.2 0.3 2.2		28 SA	0051 0641 1321 1916	0.2 1.9 0.4 2.1
14 SA	0046 0638 1325 1915	0.1 2.1 0.3 2.3		29 SU	0223 0811 1454 2043	0.2 1.9 0.3 2.2
15 SU	0226 0815 1504 2048	0.1 2.1 0.2 2.4		30 M	0348 0930 1610 2150	0.1 2.1 0.2 2.3
				31 TU	0447 1025 1701 2235	0.0 2.2 0.0 2.4

APRIL

Day	Time	m		Day	Time	m
1 W	0526 1102 1739 2312	-0.1 2.3 0.0 2.5		16 TH	0534 1108 1755 2326	-0.3 2.4 -0.2 2.6
2 TH	0601 1134 1814 2346	-0.2 2.3 -0.1 2.5		17 F	0621 1153 1842 O	-0.3 2.5 -0.2
3 F	0635 1206 1849 ●	-0.2 2.4 -0.2		18 SA	0012 0705 1233 1924	2.7 -0.2 2.6 -0.2
4 SA	0019 0706 1237 1921	2.5 -0.2 2.4 -0.2		19 SU	0054 0743 1311 2001	2.7 -0.1 2.6 -0.2
5 SU	0051 0736 1318 1954	2.5 -0.2 2.5 -0.2		20 M	0133 0817 1348 2038	2.7 0.0 2.6 -0.1
6 M	0126 0810 1342 2030	2.6 -0.1 2.5 -0.1		21 TU	0211 0850 1424 2113	2.6 0.0 2.6 -0.1
7 TU	0202 0846 1418 2109	2.5 -0.1 2.5 -0.2		22 W	0248 0922 1459 2148	2.5 0.1 2.5 -0.1
8 W	0241 0923 1455 2147	2.5 0.0 2.5 -0.2		23 TH	0325 0954 1536 2225	2.3 0.1 2.4 0.0
9 TH	0323 0959 1535 2229	2.4 0.0 2.4 -0.1		24 F	0405 1030 1618 2310	2.1 0.2 2.4 0.1
10 F	0410 1043 1625 2326	2.3 0.1 2.4 0.0		25 SA	0453 1120 1714	2.0 0.3 2.3
11 SA	0512 1149 1736	2.0 0.2 2.4		26 SU	0011 0558 1231 1826	0.2 1.9 0.3 2.2
12 SU	0046 0634 1318 1905	0.1 2.1 0.3 2.4		27 M	0129 0717 1356 1946	0.2 2.0 0.3 2.2
13 M	0219 0804 1452 2033	0.0 2.2 0.2 2.5		28 TU	0249 0834 1513 2055	0.1 2.1 0.2 2.3
14 TU	0343 0921 1608 2143	-0.1 2.3 0.0 2.6		29 W	0352 0932 1611 2146	0.0 2.2 0.1 2.4
15 W	0445 1020 1705 2238	-0.2 2.4 -0.1 2.6		30 TH	0437 1015 1655 2228	-0.1 2.3 0.0 2.5

TIDAL DIFFERENCES PAGE 21:330. TIDAL CURVE PAGE 21:326.

Datum of predictions: at M.L.W.S. and 0.5 m. above L.A.T.

HELGOLAND

HIGH & LOW WATER 1992   **Lat. 54°11'N. Long. 7°53'E.**

TIME ZONE-0100 SUBTRACT 1 HOUR FROM TIMES SHOWN FOR GMT

MAY

Day	Time	m	Day	Time	m
1 F	0516 / 1053 / 1736 / 2308	-0.1 / 2.4 / -0.1 / 2.5	**16** SA O	0551 / 1126 / 1818 / 2351	-0.1 / 2.6 / -0.1 / 2.6
2 SA ●	0555 / 1129 / 1816 / 2347	-0.2 / 2.5 / -0.1 / 2.5	**17** SU	0637 / 1211 / 1902	0.0 / 2.6 / -0.1
3 SU	0632 / 1205 / 1855	-0.2 / 2.5 / -0.2	**18** M	0034 / 0717 / 1249 / 1941	2.7 / 0.1 / -0.1 / -0.1
4 M	0025 / 0709 / 1242 / 1935	2.6 / -0.1 / 2.6 / -0.2	**19** TU	0112 / 0752 / 1325 / 2017	2.6 / 0.1 / 2.7 / -0.1
5 TU	0106 / 0750 / 1323 / 2018	2.6 / -0.2 / 2.6 / -0.2	**20** W	0150 / 0825 / 1402 / 2054	2.5 / 0.1 / 2.7 / 0.0
6 W	0149 / 0832 / 1404 / 2102	2.5 / -0.1 / 2.6 / -0.2	**21** TH	0227 / 0859 / 1438 / 2130	2.4 / 0.1 / 2.6 / 0.0
7 TH	0233 / 0914 / 1447 / 2147	2.5 / 0.0 / 2.6 / -0.2	**22** F	0305 / 0933 / 1515 / 2206	2.3 / 0.1 / 2.6 / 0.0
8 F	0320 / 0957 / 1533 / 2235	2.4 / 0.0 / 2.6 / -0.2	**23** SA	0343 / 1008 / 1555 / 2245	2.2 / 0.2 / 2.5 / 0.1
9 SA	0413 / 1048 / 1628 / 2333	2.3 / 0.1 / 2.5 / -0.1	**24** SU	0426 / 1050 / 1641 / 2332	2.1 / 0.2 / 2.5 / 0.2
10 SU	0515 / 1151 / 1735	2.2 / 0.2 / 2.6	**25** M	0516 / 1144 / 1736	2.1 / 0.3 / 2.4
11 M	0044 / 0628 / 1309 / 1854	0.0 / 2.3 / 0.3 / 2.6	**26** TU	0031 / 0617 / 1251 / 1842	0.2 / 2.1 / 0.3 / 2.3
12 TU	0204 / 0745 / 1431 / 2011	0.0 / 2.3 / 0.2 / 2.6	**27** W	0138 / 0725 / 1405 / 1950	0.2 / 2.1 / 0.3 / 2.4
13 W	0316 / 0846 / 1541 / 2116	0.0 / 2.4 / 0.1 / 2.6	**28** TH	0244 / 0808 / 1510 / 2049	0.1 / 2.2 / 0.2 / 2.4
14 TH	0414 / 0949 / 1636 / 2210	-0.1 / 2.4 / 0.0 / 2.6	**29** F	0339 / 0922 / 1605 / 2141	0.1 / 2.4 / 0.1 / 2.5
15 F	0502 / 1038 / 1727 / 2302	-0.1 / 2.5 / -0.1 / 2.6	**30** SA	0428 / 1010 / 1656 / 2230	0.0 / 2.5 / 0.1 / 2.5
			31 SU	0516 / 1055 / 1744 / 2318	0.0 / 2.6 / 0.0 / 2.6

JUNE

Day	Time	m	Day	Time	m
1 M ●	0602 / 1138 / 1831	0.0 / 2.6 / -0.1	**16** TU	0017 / 0656 / 1232 / 1924	2.6 / 0.1 / 2.7 / 0.0
2 TU	0004 / 0647 / 1222 / 1919	2.6 / 0.0 / 2.7 / -0.1	**17** W	0055 / 0732 / 1308 / 2000	2.6 / 0.1 / 2.7 / 0.0
3 W	0052 / 0735 / 1309 / 2009	2.6 / 0.0 / 2.7 / -0.2	**18** TH	0132 / 0806 / 1345 / 2036	2.5 / 0.1 / 2.7 / 0.0
4 TH	0141 / 0824 / 1357 / 2058	2.5 / -0.1 / 2.7 / -0.2	**19** F	0209 / 0840 / 1420 / 2109	2.4 / 0.0 / 2.7 / 0.0
5 F	0228 / 0909 / 1443 / 2145	2.5 / 0.0 / 2.7 / -0.2	**20** SA	0244 / 0912 / 1454 / 2142	2.4 / 0.1 / 2.7 / 0.1
6 SA	0316 / 0955 / 1531 / 2235	2.4 / 0.0 / 2.7 / -0.1	**21** SU	0319 / 0945 / 1530 / 2218	2.3 / 0.1 / 2.6 / 0.1
7 SU	0409 / 1046 / 1626 / 2329	2.4 / 0.1 / 2.7 / 0.0	**22** M	0356 / 1021 / 1609 / 2256	2.3 / 0.2 / 2.6 / 0.2
8 M	0508 / 1144 / 1727	2.4 / 0.2 / 2.7	**23** TU	0436 / 1101 / 1651 / 2337	2.3 / 0.3 / 2.5 / 0.2
9 TU	0030 / 0621 / 1249 / 1833	0.1 / 2.4 / 0.3 / 2.7	**24** W	0521 / 1152 / 1742	2.3 / 0.4 / 2.5
10 W	0134 / 0716 / 1359 / 1941	0.1 / 2.4 / 0.2 / 2.6	**25** TH	0029 / 0617 / 1256 / 1844	0.3 / 2.3 / 0.4 / 2.4
11 TH	0240 / 0820 / 1507 / ~2045	0.1 / 2.4 / 0.2 / 2.6	**26** F	0133 / 0722 / 1407 / 1951	0.3 / 2.3 / 0.3 / 2.4
12 F	0339 / 0918 / 1608 / 2144	0.1 / 2.5 / 0.1 / 2.6	**27** SA	0239 / 0828 / 1516 / 2056	0.2 / 2.4 / 0.3 / 2.5
13 SA	0433 / 1003 / 1703 / 2241	0.1 / 2.5 / 0.1 / 2.6	**28** SU	0343 / 0929 / 1619 / 2158	0.2 / 2.5 / 0.2 / 2.5
14 SU	0525 / 1103 / 1757 / 2333	0.1 / 2.6 / 0.1 / 2.6	**29** M	0443 / 1026 / 1719 / 2256	0.1 / 2.6 / 0.1 / 2.6
15 M O	0614 / 1151 / 1844	0.1 / 2.7 / 0.0	**30** TU ●	0540 / 1118 / 1815 / 2350	0.1 / 2.7 / 0.0 / 2.6

JULY

Day	Time	m	Day	Time	m
1 W	0633 / 1208 / 1909	0.0 / 2.8 / -0.1	**16** TH	0040 / 0716 / 1253 / 1944	2.5 / 0.1 / 2.7 / 0.0
2 TH	0041 / 0724 / 1259 / 2002	2.6 / 0.0 / 2.8 / -0.2	**17** F	0115 / 0750 / 1328 / 2016	2.5 / 0.0 / 2.7 / 0.0
3 F	0132 / 0815 / 1349 / 2052	2.6 / -0.1 / 2.8 / -0.2	**18** SA	0149 / 0820 / 1400 / 2046	2.5 / 0.0 / 2.7 / 0.0
4 SA	0220 / 0901 / 1435 / 2137	2.6 / -0.1 / 2.9 / -0.2	**19** SU	0219 / 0849 / 1429 / 2114	2.5 / 0.1 / 2.7 / 0.1
5 SU	0306 / 0945 / 1520 / 2222	2.5 / 0.0 / 2.9 / -0.1	**20** M	0250 / 0920 / 1501 / 2147	2.4 / 0.1 / 2.7 / 0.1
6 M	0354 / 1032 / 1610 / 2310	2.5 / 0.0 / 2.8 / 0.0	**21** TU	0324 / 0953 / 1537 / 2221	2.4 / 0.2 / 2.7 / 0.2
7 TU	0446 / 1123 / 1705	2.5 / 0.2 / 2.8	**22** W	0359 / 1027 / 1613 / 2253	2.4 / 0.2 / 2.6 / 0.3
8 W	0000 / 0540 / 1217 / 1802	0.1 / 2.5 / 0.3 / 2.7	**23** TH	0435 / 1104 / 1652 / 2331	2.4 / 0.3 / 2.5 / 0.3
9 TH	0054 / 0636 / 1318 / 1905	0.2 / 2.4 / 0.3 / 2.6	**24** F	0519 / 1157 / 1747	2.4 / 0.4 / 2.4
10 F	0156 / 0740 / 1429 / 2014	0.3 / 2.4 / 0.3 / 2.5	**25** SA	0030 / 0622 / 1310 / 1859	0.4 / 2.3 / 0.4 / 2.4
11 SA	0304 / 0847 / 1542 / 2123	0.3 / 2.5 / 0.2 / 2.5	**26** SU	0147 / 0738 / 1433 / 2019	0.4 / 2.4 / 0.3 / 2.4
12 SU	0409 / 0950 / 1647 / 2225	0.2 / 2.6 / 0.2 / 2.5	**27** M	0307 / 0855 / 1552 / 2134	0.3 / 2.5 / 0.2 / 2.5
13 M	0506 / 1046 / 1742 / 2318	0.3 / 2.6 / 0.1 / 2.5	**28** TU	0421 / 1005 / 1702 / 2241	0.2 / 2.6 / 0.1 / 2.5
14 TU O	0556 / 1134 / 1829	0.2 / 2.7 / 0.1	**29** W ●	0525 / 1104 / 1804 / 2339	0.1 / 2.7 / 0.0 / 2.6
15 W	0003 / 0639 / 1216 / 1909	2.6 / 0.1 / 2.7 / 0.0	**30** TH	0622 / 1157 / 1859	0.1 / 2.8 / -0.1
			31 F	0030 / 0713 / 1247 / 1950	2.6 / 0.0 / 2.9 / -0.2

AUGUST

Day	Time	m	Day	Time	m
1 SA	0118 / 0802 / 1336 / 2037	2.6 / -0.1 / 2.9 / -0.2	**16** SU	0124 / 0757 / 1335 / 2017	2.5 / 0.0 / 2.7 / 0.0
2 SU	0204 / 0847 / 1420 / 2119	2.6 / -0.1 / 2.9 / -0.2	**17** M	0151 / 0824 / 1403 / 2044	2.5 / 0.0 / 2.7 / 0.1
3 M	0247 / 0928 / 1502 / 2159	2.6 / -0.1 / 2.9 / -0.1	**18** TU	0219 / 0854 / 1433 / 2115	2.5 / 0.1 / 2.7 / 0.2
4 TU	0329 / 1009 / 1546 / 2240	2.6 / 0.0 / 2.8 / 0.1	**19** W	0251 / 0927 / 1507 / 2147	2.5 / 0.1 / 2.7 / 0.2
5 W	0414 / 1053 / 1635 / 2322	2.5 / 0.1 / 2.7 / 0.2	**20** TH	0326 / 0959 / 1541 / 2217	2.5 / 0.2 / 2.6 / 0.3
6 TH	0501 / 1139 / 1726	2.5 / 0.3 / 2.6	**21** F	0358 / 1031 / 1616 / 2249	2.5 / 0.3 / 2.5 / 0.4
7 F	0008 / 0553 / 1235 / 1826	0.4 / 2.4 / 0.4 / 2.5	**22** SA	0436 / 1117 / 1707 / 2344	2.5 / 0.4 / 2.4 / 0.5
8 SA	0110 / 0658 / 1351 / 1941	0.5 / 2.4 / 0.4 / 2.3	**23** SU	0537 / 1231 / 1823	2.4 / 0.4 / 2.3
9 SU	0228 / 0816 / 1517 / 2102	0.5 / 2.4 / 0.3 / 2.3	**24** M	0108 / 0701 / 1405 / 1954	0.5 / 2.4 / 2.3 / 2.3
10 M	0348 / 0932 / 1633 / 2212	0.4 / 2.5 / 0.2 / 2.4	**25** TU	0242 / 0831 / 1536 / 2119	0.4 / 2.5 / 0.2 / 2.4
11 TU	0453 / 1032 / 1729 / 2306	0.3 / 2.6 / 0.1 / 2.4	**26** W	0405 / 0949 / 1651 / 2229	0.3 / 2.6 / 0.1 / 2.5
12 W	0541 / 1118 / 1812 / 2347	0.2 / 2.7 / 0.1 / 2.5	**27** TH	0513 / 1051 / 1751 / 2326	0.2 / 2.8 / 0.0 / 2.6
13 TH O	0621 / 1157 / 1849	0.2 / 2.7 / 0.0	**28** F ●	0608 / 1143 / 1843	0.1 / 2.9 / -0.1
14 F	0022 / 0657 / 1233 / 1922	2.5 / 0.1 / 2.7 / 0.0	**29** SA	0014 / 0657 / 1230 / 1930	2.7 / 0.0 / 2.9 / -0.1
15 SA	0054 / 0729 / 1305 / 1951	2.5 / 0.0 / 2.7 / 0.0	**30** SU	0058 / 0743 / 1315 / 2013	2.7 / -0.1 / 2.9 / -0.2
			31 M	0141 / 0826 / 1359 / 2053	2.7 / -0.1 / 2.9 / -0.1

RATE AND SET — Flood. W. of Helgoland, sets SE, rate 1½ kn. S. of Helgoland, sets E. rate 1½ kn. Hog Stean, sets E. rate 1½ kn. Ebb: Generally opposite to flood; W. of Helgoland — rate less; Between Islands — rate greater.

HELGOLAND

Lat. 54°11'N. Long. 7°53'E.   HIGH & LOW WATER 1992

TIME ZONE-0100 SUBTRACT 1 HOUR FROM TIMES SHOWN FOR GMT

SEPTEMBER

#	Day	Time	m	Time	m	Time	m	Time	m		#	Day	Time	m	Time	m	Time	m	Time	m
1	TU	0222	2.7	0905	-0.1	1439	2.9	2131	0.0		16	W	0150	2.6	0830	0.1	1407	2.7	2044	0.2
2	W	0301	2.7	0943	0.0	1520	2.8	2207	0.2		17	TH	0222	2.6	0904	0.2	1441	2.7	2117	0.3
3	TH	0341	2.6	1021	0.1	1604	2.7	2243	0.3		18	F	0256	2.6	0937	0.2	1516	2.6	2149	0.3
4	F	0422	2.5	1103	0.3	1651	2.5	2324	0.5		19	SA	0330	2.6	1011	0.3	1554	2.5	2224	0.4
5	SA	0511	2.4	1157	0.4	1749	2.3				20	SU	0410	2.5	1057	0.4	1646	2.3	2320	0.5
6	SU	0024	0.6	0616	2.4	1313	0.4	1906	2.2		21	M	0512	2.4	1211	0.4	1804	2.2		
7	M	0148	0.6	0741	2.3	1446	0.4	2035	2.2		22	TU	0046	0.5	0640	2.4	1348	0.4	1938	2.3
8	TU	0318	0.5	0907	2.4	1611	0.3	2153	2.3		23	W	0225	0.5	0814	2.5	1522	0.2	2106	2.4
9	W	0432	0.4	1013	2.6	1709	0.2	2248	2.4		24	TH	0350	0.4	0933	2.7	1635	0.1	2214	2.5
10	TH	0521	0.3	1057	2.7	1747	0.1	2324	2.5		25	F	0456	0.2	1033	2.8	1731	0.0	2306	2.6
11	F	0556	0.2	1131	2.7	1820	0.1	2354	2.5		26	SA	0548	0.1	1123	2.9	1819	-0.1	● 2352	2.7
12	SA	0629	0.1	1204	2.7	1852	0.0	O			27	SU	0636	0.0	1209	2.9	1904	-0.1		
13	SU	0024	2.5	0702	0.0	1236	2.7	1920	0.0		28	M	0034	2.7	0719	0.0	1253	2.9	1945	0.0
14	M	0053	2.5	0731	0.0	1306	2.7	1946	0.1		29	TU	0114	2.7	0801	0.0	1336	2.9	2024	0.1
15	TU	0121	2.6	0759	0.0	1336	2.7	2013	0.1		30	W	0155	2.8	0841	0.0	1417	2.8	2100	0.2

OCTOBER

#	Day	Time	m	Time	m	Time	m	Time	m		#	Day	Time	m	Time	m	Time	m	Time	m
1	TH	0234	2.8	0918	0.1	1456	2.8	2134	0.3		16	F	0159	2.7	0846	0.2	1422	2.6	2056	0.3
2	F	0310	2.7	0954	0.2	1536	2.6	2208	0.4		17	SA	0235	2.7	0923	0.2	1501	2.5	2132	0.3
3	SA	0349	2.6	1034	0.3	1619	2.4	2247	0.5		18	SU	0314	2.6	1003	0.2	1545	2.4	2214	0.4
4	SU	0435	2.5	1124	0.4	1714	2.2	2342	0.6		19	M	0400	2.6	1053	0.3	1641	2.3	2312	0.5
5	M	0537	2.4	1233	0.5	1827	2.1				20	TU	0503	2.5	1205	0.4	1756	2.3		
6	TU	0101	0.7	0658	2.3	1401	0.5	1955	2.1		21	W	0033	0.6	0627	2.6	1334	0.4	1924	2.3
7	W	0230	0.6	0826	2.4	1528	0.4	2116	2.2		22	TH	0207	0.5	0756	2.6	1502	0.3	2047	2.4
8	TH	0352	0.5	0937	2.5	1611	0.3	2213	2.4		23	F	0329	0.4	0911	2.7	1611	0.2	2150	2.6
9	F	0445	0.4	1023	2.6	1709	0.2	2249	2.5		24	SA	0431	0.3	1009	2.8	1704	0.1	2240	2.6
10	SA	0521	0.3	1056	2.7	1741	0.1	2319	2.5		25	SU	0523	0.2	1100	2.8	1750	0.1	● 2326	2.7
11	SU	0555	0.2	1129	2.7	1814	0.1	O 2350	2.5		26	M	0611	0.1	1148	2.8	1836	0.1		
12	M	0630	0.1	1203	2.7	1845	0.1				27	TU	0010	2.8	0656	0.1	1232	2.9	1917	0.2
13	TU	0021	2.6	0703	0.1	1237	2.7	1915	0.1		28	W	0050	2.8	0737	0.2	1314	2.9	1955	0.3
14	W	0053	2.6	0735	0.1	1311	2.7	1947	0.2		29	TH	0130	2.9	0817	0.2	1355	2.8	2031	0.3
15	TH	0125	2.7	0809	0.1	1346	2.7	2020	0.3		30	F	0209	2.8	0855	0.2	1434	2.7	2105	0.4
											31	SA	0246	2.8	0932	0.2	1512	2.5	2139	0.4

NOVEMBER

#	Day	Time	m	Time	m	Time	m	Time	m		#	Day	Time	m	Time	m	Time	m	Time	m
1	SU	0323	2.7	1010	0.3	1553	2.3	2217	0.5		16	M	0306	2.7	1001	0.2	1542	2.5	2211	0.4
2	M	0406	2.5	1054	0.4	1642	2.2	2305	0.6		17	TU	0356	2.7	1053	0.2	1639	2.4	2308	0.5
3	TU	0500	2.5	1151	0.5	1744	2.1				18	W	0458	2.7	1158	0.3	1746	2.4		
4	W	0010	0.7	0609	2.4	1304	0.5	1859	2.1		19	TH	0020	0.6	0612	2.7	1314	0.4	1902	2.4
5	TH	0131	0.7	0728	2.4	1423	0.5	2016	2.2		20	F	0142	0.5	0730	2.7	1431	0.3	2016	2.5
6	F	0250	0.6	0840	2.5	1530	0.4	2118	2.4		21	SA	0258	0.4	0842	2.7	1537	0.2	2119	2.5
7	SA	0352	0.5	0934	2.6	1617	0.4	2202	2.5		22	SU	0402	0.3	0942	2.7	1631	0.2	2212	2.6
8	SU	0437	0.4	1015	2.6	1655	0.3	2238	2.6		23	M	0456	0.3	1037	2.7	1721	0.2	2302	2.7
9	M	0516	0.3	1053	2.6	1733	0.2	2315	2.6		24	TU	0549	0.2	1129	2.8	1810	0.3	● 2349	2.8
10	TU	0556	0.2	1131	2.6	1811	0.2	O 2351	2.7		25	W	0637	0.2	1215	2.8	1854	0.3		
11	W	0635	0.2	1210	2.7	1847	0.2				26	TH	0031	2.9	0718	0.2	1256	2.8	1931	0.4
12	TH	0027	2.7	0714	0.2	1250	2.7	1926	0.2		27	F	0109	2.9	0757	0.2	1335	2.7	2007	0.3
13	F	0106	2.8	0754	0.2	1331	2.7	2006	0.3		28	SA	0148	2.9	0836	0.2	1414	2.6	2042	0.3
14	SA	0145	2.8	0836	0.2	1413	2.6	2044	0.3		29	SU	0226	2.8	0913	0.2	1452	2.5	2117	0.3
15	SU	0224	2.8	0917	0.2	1455	2.5	2124	0.3		30	M	0302	2.7	0948	0.3	1530	2.4	2151	0.4

DECEMBER

#	Day	Time	m	Time	m	Time	m	Time	m		#	Day	Time	m	Time	m	Time	m	Time	m
1	TU	0341	2.7	1026	0.3	1611	2.3	2230	0.5		16	W	0350	2.8	1046	0.2	1629	2.5	2300	0.4
2	W	0425	2.6	1110	0.4	1658	2.2	2319	0.6		17	TH	0446	2.8	1142	0.3	1728	2.5		
3	TH	0517	2.5	1202	0.5	1755	2.2				18	F	0000	0.5	0549	2.8	1243	0.3	1830	2.4
4	F	0021	0.6	0620	2.4	1306	0.5	1901	2.2		19	SA	0108	0.5	0657	2.7	1351	0.4	1938	2.5
5	SA	0134	0.6	0729	2.4	1413	0.5	2008	2.3		20	SU	0221	0.4	0808	2.6	1459	0.3	2045	2.5
6	SU	0244	0.6	0833	2.5	1514	0.5	2106	2.5		21	M	0331	0.4	0915	2.6	1602	0.3	2146	2.6
7	M	0344	0.5	0928	2.6	1606	0.4	2156	2.6		22	TU	0435	0.3	1017	2.6	1659	0.3	2242	2.6
8	TU	0436	0.4	1016	2.6	1655	0.3	2241	2.6		23	W	0532	0.3	1114	2.6	1751	0.3	2333	2.7
9	W	0524	0.3	1103	2.6	1741	0.2	O 2324	2.7		24	TH	0622	0.2	1201	2.6	1836	0.3		
10	TH	0611	0.2	1148	2.6	1826	0.2				25	F	0016	2.8	0704	0.2	1241	2.6	1914	0.3
11	F	0006	2.8	0657	0.1	1233	2.6	1911	0.2		26	SA	0054	2.8	0742	0.2	1319	2.6	1949	0.3
12	SA	0051	2.8	0744	0.2	1321	2.6	1957	0.2		27	SU	0131	2.8	0820	0.2	1356	2.5	2023	0.2
13	SU	0137	2.8	0831	0.1	1406	2.6	2040	0.2		28	M	0208	2.8	0854	0.2	1432	2.5	2056	0.2
14	M	0219	2.9	0914	0.1	1450	2.6	2121	0.2		29	TU	0241	2.8	0925	0.2	1504	2.4	2127	0.2
15	TU	0302	2.8	0958	0.1	1536	2.5	2206	0.3		30	W	0315	2.7	0957	0.3	1538	2.3	2159	0.3
											31	TH	0350	2.6	1031	0.3	1614	2.3	2235	0.4

TIDAL DIFFERENCES PAGE 21:330. TIDAL CURVE PAGE 21:326.

Datum of predictions: at M.L.W.S.. and 0.5 m. above L.A.T.

TIDAL DIFFERENCES ON HELGOLAND

PLACE	TIME DIFFERENCES				HEIGHT DIFFERENCES (Metres)			
	High Water		Low Water		MHWS	MHWN	MLWN	MLWS
HELGOLAND	0100 and 1300	0600 and 1800	0100 and 1300	0800 and 2000	2.7	2.3	0.4	0.0
GERMANY								
Lister Tief								
Landfall Buoy	+0150	+0150	–	–	–	–	–	–
List	+0256	+0246	+0207	+0213	–0.8	–0.6	–0.2	0.0
Hörnum	+0225	+0221	+0134	+0143	–0.5	–0.3	–0.2	0.0
Amrum–Hafen	+0144	+0140	+0129	+0140	+0.2	+0.3	–0.1	0.0
Dagebüll	+0230	+0222	+0217	+0231	+0.5	+0.6	–0.1	0.0
Schmal–Tief Buoy	+0045	+0045	–	–	–	–	–	–
Suderoogsand	+0116	+0102	+0038	+0122	+0.3	+0.3	+0.1	0.0
Hever								
Husum	+0213	+0159	+0128	+0212	+1.1	+1.1	+0.1	0.0
Ausseneider Buoy	+0029	+0024	–	–	–	–	–	–
Süderhöft	+0101	+0052	+0037	+0102	+0.8	+0.8	+0.1	0.0
Norder Piep Buoy	+0036	+0031	–	–	–	–	–	–
Büsum	+0054	+0049	+0000	+0028	+1.0	+0.9	+0.1	0.0
HELGOLAND	0200 and 1400	0700 and 1900	0200 and 1400	0800 and 2000	2.7	2.3	0.4	0.0
East Frisian islands and coast								
Weser Light–Vessel	–0010	–0010	–	–	–	–	–	–
Spiekeroog Reede	+0001	+0005	–0031	–0013	+0.4	+0.4	+0.1	0.0
Neuharlingersiel	+0019	+0012	–	–	+0.5	+0.5	0.0	0.0
Langeoog Ostmole	+0003	–0002	–0036	–0019	+0.3	+0.3	0.0	0.0
Norderney (Riffgat)	–0023	–0030	–0059	–0046	+0.1	+0.1	0.0	0.0
Norddeich Hafen	–0015	–0018	–0032	–0010	+0.2	+0.2	0.0	0.0
River Ems								
Memmert	–0030	–0037	–0113	–0100	0.0	+0.1	0.0	0.0
Borkum (Fischerbalje)	–0045	–0049	–0123	–0105	0.0	+0.1	0.0	0.0
Emshorn	–0033	–0041	–0106	–0042	+0.1	+0.2	0.0	0.0
Knock	+0019	+0007	–0027	+0003	+0.6	+0.6	0.0	0.0
Emden	+0041	+0026	–0014	+0022	+0.8	+0.8	0.0	0.0
NETHERLANDS								
Nieuwe Statenzul	+0045	+0045	–	–	+0.9	+1.0	–	–
Delfzijl	+0020	–0005	–0035	+0005	+0.8	+0.9	+0.1	+0.2
Eemshaven	–0025	–0045	–0115	–0035	+0.3	+0.4	+0.2	+0.2
Schiermonnikoog	–0120	–0140	–0230	–0220	+0.1	+0.2	+0.2	+0.2
Noordwinning (Platform K13–A)	–0421	–0402	–0447	–0445	–1.0	–1.0	+0.1	+0.1

Note: Time zone. The predictions for the standard port are on the same time zone as the differences shown. No further adjustment is necessary.
Refer to predictions on pages 21:327-21:329

ESBJERG 21:331

Lat. 55°28'N. Long. 8°26'E. **HIGH & LOW WATER 1992**

TIME ZONE-0100 SUBTRACT 1 HOUR FROM TIMES SHOWN FOR GMT

JANUARY

Day	Time	m	Day	Time	m
1 W	0539 / 1211 / 1811	0.2 / 1.6 / 0.2	16 TH	0430 / 1048 / 1712 / 2338	0.4 / 1.6 / 0.4 / 1.5
2 TH	0041 / 0639 / 1305 / 1901	1.6 / 0.2 / 1.6 / 0.2	17 F	0549 / 1211 / 1821	0.3 / 1.5 / 0.3
3 F	0130 / 0731 / 1351 / 1945	1.6 / 0.1 / 1.5 / 0.1	18 SA	0049 / 0655 / 1321 / 1918	1.5 / 0.2 / 1.5 / 0.2
4 SA	0212 / 0816 / 1433 / ●2025	1.6 / 0.1 / 1.4 / 0.1	19 SU	0150 / 0752 / 1422 / O 2010	1.6 / 0.1 / 1.5 / 0.1
5 SU	0250 / 0857 / 1510 / 2101	1.6 / 0.0 / 1.4 / 0.1	20 M	0244 / 0843 / 1517 / 2058	1.7 / 0.0 / 1.5 / 0.0
6 M	0324 / 0935 / 1545 / 2136	1.6 / 0.1 / 1.4 / 0.1	21 TU	0334 / 0932 / 1608 / 2144	1.7 / -0.1 / 1.5 / 0.0
7 TU	0356 / 1010 / 1618 / 2209	1.7 / 0.1 / 1.4 / 0.1	22 W	0422 / 1018 / 1655 / 2229	1.8 / -0.1 / 1.5 / 0.0
8 W	0427 / 1044 / 1649 / 2242	1.7 / 0.1 / 1.4 / 0.2	23 TH	0507 / 1104 / 1739 / 2313	1.8 / -0.1 / 1.5 / 0.0
9 TH	0458 / 1117 / 1722 / 2315	1.8 / 0.1 / 1.5 / 0.2	24 F	0552 / 1149 / 1822 / 2359	1.9 / 0.0 / 1.5 / 0.0
10 F	0531 / 1150 / 1755 / 2351	1.8 / 0.2 / 1.5 / 0.2	25 SA	0638 / 1235 / 1906	1.9 / 0.1 / 1.5
11 SA	0606 / 1226 / 1831	1.9 / 0.2 / 1.5	26 SU	0047 / 0726 / 1323 / 1956	0.1 / 1.8 / 0.1 / 1.5
12 SU	0031 / 0644 / 1307 / 1911	0.2 / 1.9 / 0.3 / 1.5	27 M	0139 / 0821 / 1417 / 2055	0.1 / 1.7 / 0.3 / 1.5
13 M	0115 / 0729 / 1353 / 1959	0.3 / 1.8 / 0.3 / 1.5	28 TU	0240 / 0926 / 1519 / 2202	0.2 / 1.6 / 0.3 / 1.5
14 TU	0207 / 0821 / 1448 / 2059	0.4 / 1.7 / 0.4 / 1.5	29 W	0353 / 1035 / 1632 / 2310	0.3 / 1.5 / 0.4 / 1.5
15 W	0311 / 0927 / 1556 / 2215	0.4 / 1.6 / 0.4 / 1.5	30 TH	0512 / 1141 / 1740	0.3 / 1.5 / 0.3
			31 F	0011 / 0618 / 1239 / 1836	1.5 / 0.2 / 1.4 / 0.3

FEBRUARY

Day	Time	m	Day	Time	m
1 SA	0104 / 0712 / 1330 / 1923	1.6 / 0.1 / 1.4 / 0.2	16 SU	0023 / 0638 / 1304 / 1859	1.5 / 0.1 / 1.5 / 0.2
2 SU	0150 / 0758 / 1414 / 2004	1.6 / 0.1 / 1.4 / 0.1	17 M	0129 / 0736 / 1407 / 1952	1.6 / 0.0 / 1.5 / 0.0
3 M	0230 / 0838 / 1453 / ●2041	1.7 / 0.1 / 1.4 / 0.1	18 TU	0226 / 0828 / 1501 / O 2040	1.7 / -0.1 / 1.5 / -0.1
4 TU	0306 / 0915 / 1529 / 2115	1.7 / 0.0 / 1.4 / 0.1	19 W	0318 / 0915 / 1550 / 2126	1.8 / -0.2 / 1.5 / -0.1
5 W	0339 / 0948 / 1603 / 2148	1.7 / 0.1 / 1.5 / 0.1	20 TH	0405 / 1000 / 1633 / 2210	1.8 / -0.2 / 1.5 / -0.1
6 TH	0411 / 1020 / 1634 / 2220	1.8 / 0.1 / 1.5 / 0.1	21 F	0449 / 1043 / 1713 / 2254	1.8 / -0.1 / 1.6 / -0.1
7 F	0442 / 1051 / 1703 / 2253	1.8 / 0.1 / 1.5 / 0.1	22 SA	0531 / 1125 / 1752 / 2337	1.8 / -0.1 / 1.6 / -0.1
8 SA	0513 / 1123 / 1733 / 2328	1.8 / 0.1 / 1.5 / 0.1	23 SU	0613 / 1206 / 1832	1.8 / 0.0 / 1.6
9 SU	0545 / 1157 / 1805	1.8 / 0.2 / 1.6	24 M	0022 / 0655 / 1250 / 1914	0.0 / 1.7 / 0.1 / 1.5
10 M	0006 / 0620 / 1235 / 1840	0.2 / 1.8 / 0.2 / 1.6	25 TU	0111 / 0743 / 1336 / 2005	0.1 / 1.6 / 0.2 / 1.5
11 TU	0048 / 0700 / 1318 / 1923	0.2 / 1.8 / 0.3 / 1.5	26 W	0205 / 0839 / 1431 / 2109	0.2 / 1.4 / 0.3 / 1.4
12 W	0136 / 0750 / 1409 / 2018	0.3 / 1.7 / 0.4 / 1.5	27 TH	0313 / 0949 / 1542 / 2223	0.3 / 1.3 / 0.4 / 1.4
13 TH	0236 / 0853 / 1514 / 2130	0.3 / 1.5 / 0.4 / 1.4	28 F	0438 / 1104 / 1701 / 2333	0.3 / 1.3 / 0.4 / 1.4
14 F	0356 / 1017 / 1637 / 2300	0.4 / 1.3 / 0.4 / 1.4	29 SA	0551 / 1209 / 1806	0.2 / 1.3 / 0.3
15 SA	0526 / 1148 / 1756	0.3 / 1.4 / 0.3			

MARCH

Day	Time	m	Day	Time	m
1 SU	0032 / 0647 / 1305 / 1857	1.5 / 0.2 / 1.4 / 0.2	16 M	0000 / 0621 / 1249 / 1839	1.5 / 0.1 / 1.4 / 0.1
2 M	0122 / 0734 / 1352 / 1939	1.6 / 0.1 / 1.4 / 0.1	17 TU	0110 / 0719 / 1350 / 1933	1.6 / -0.1 / 1.5 / 0.0
3 TU	0205 / 0813 / 1433 / 2017	1.6 / 0.0 / 1.5 / 0.1	18 W	0208 / 0809 / 1442 / O 2021	1.7 / -0.2 / 1.5 / -0.1
4 W	0244 / 0849 / 1510 / ●2052	1.7 / 0.0 / 1.5 / 0.1	19 TH	0259 / 0855 / 1527 / 2107	1.8 / -0.2 / 1.5 / -0.2
5 TH	0319 / 0922 / 1545 / 2125	1.7 / 0.0 / 1.5 / 0.1	20 F	0345 / 0937 / 1608 / 2150	1.8 / -0.2 / 1.5 / -0.2
6 F	0353 / 0954 / 1616 / 2158	1.8 / 0.0 / 1.5 / 0.1	21 SA	0427 / 1018 / 1645 / 2233	1.7 / -0.1 / 1.5 / -0.2
7 SA	0425 / 1025 / 1645 / 2232	1.8 / 0.1 / 1.5 / 0.1	22 SU	0507 / 1058 / 1721 / 2315	1.7 / -0.1 / 1.5 / -0.2
8 SU	0456 / 1057 / 1714 / 2307	1.7 / 0.1 / 1.5 / 0.1	23 M	0544 / 1137 / 1757 / 2358	1.6 / 0.0 / 1.5 / -0.1
9 M	0528 / 1131 / 1744 / 2345	1.7 / 0.1 / 1.5 / 0.1	24 TU	0622 / 1217 / 1835	1.5 / 0.1 / 1.5
10 TU	0602 / 1208 / 1818	1.7 / 0.1 / 1.5	25 W	0042 / 0702 / 1259 / 1917	0.0 / 1.4 / 0.1 / 1.4
11 W	0026 / 0641 / 1251 / 1859	0.1 / 1.6 / 0.2 / 1.5	26 TH	0132 / 0750 / 1346 / 2010	0.1 / 1.3 / 0.2 / 1.4
12 TH	0115 / 0731 / 1341 / 1952	0.1 / 1.5 / 0.2 / 1.5	27 F	0232 / 0851 / 1445 / 2119	0.2 / 1.2 / 0.3 / 1.4
13 F	0214 / 0834 / 1445 / 2104	0.2 / 1.4 / 0.3 / 1.4	28 SA	0351 / 1012 / 1606 / 2240	0.3 / 1.2 / 0.4 / 1.4
14 SA	0335 / 0959 / 1609 / 2234	0.3 / 1.3 / 0.3 / 1.4	29 SU	0512 / 1130 / 1723 / 2350	0.2 / 1.2 / 0.3 / 1.4
15 SU	0507 / 1132 / 1734	0.2 / 1.3 / 0.3	30 M	0613 / 1231 / 1821	0.2 / 1.3 / 0.2
			31 TU	0046 / 0701 / 1322 / 1906	1.5 / 0.1 / 1.4 / 0.2

APRIL

Day	Time	m	Day	Time	m
1 W	0133 / 0742 / 1406 / 1946	1.6 / 0.0 / 1.4 / 0.1	16 TH	0148 / 0747 / 1418 / 2001	1.7 / -0.2 / 1.5 / -0.2
2 TH	0216 / 0818 / 1445 / 2024	1.7 / 0.0 / 1.5 / 0.0	17 F	0238 / 0832 / 1502 / O 2047	1.7 / -0.2 / 1.5 / -0.3
3 F	0255 / 0853 / 1522 / ●2100	1.7 / 0.0 / 1.5 / 0.0	18 SA	0323 / 0914 / 1542 / 2131	1.6 / -0.2 / 1.5 / -0.3
4 SA	0332 / 0926 / 1556 / 2136	1.7 / 0.0 / 1.5 / 0.0	19 SU	0404 / 0954 / 1618 / 2213	1.6 / -0.1 / 1.5 / -0.3
5 SU	0407 / 0959 / 1628 / 2212	1.6 / 0.0 / 1.5 / 0.0	20 M	0441 / 1032 / 1653 / 2254	1.5 / -0.1 / 1.5 / -0.2
6 M	0441 / 1034 / 1658 / 2250	1.6 / 0.0 / 1.5 / 0.0	21 TU	0516 / 1109 / 1726 / 2335	1.4 / -0.1 / 1.4 / -0.1
7 TU	0515 / 1110 / 1730 / 2329	1.5 / 0.0 / 1.5 / 0.0	22 W	0550 / 1147 / 1801	1.3 / 0.0 / 1.4
8 W	0551 / 1149 / 1805	1.5 / 0.0 / 1.5	23 TH	0017 / 0625 / 1226 / 1838	-0.1 / 1.3 / 0.0 / 1.4
9 TH	0012 / 0632 / 1233 / 1847	0.0 / 1.4 / 0.1 / 1.5	24 F	0102 / 0707 / 1308 / 1922	0.0 / 1.2 / 0.1 / 1.4
10 F	0103 / 0723 / 1323 / 1941	0.0 / 1.4 / 0.2 / 1.4	25 SA	0153 / 0758 / 1357 / 2016	0.1 / 1.2 / 0.2 / 1.4
11 SA	0203 / 0826 / 1426 / 2051	0.1 / 1.3 / 0.2 / 1.4	26 SU	0256 / 0904 / 1501 / 2126	0.2 / 1.1 / 0.3 / 1.4
12 SU	0320 / 0947 / 1547 / 2217	0.2 / 1.2 / 0.3 / 1.4	27 M	0414 / 1029 / 1620 / 2247	0.2 / 1.2 / 0.3 / 1.4
13 M	0448 / 1116 / 1709 / 2341	0.1 / 1.3 / 0.2 / 1.5	28 TU	0524 / 1144 / 1730 / 2357	0.2 / 1.2 / 0.3 / 1.5
14 TU	0600 / 1229 / 1817	0.0 / 1.4 / 0.0	29 W	0618 / 1241 / 1825	0.1 / 1.3 / 0.2
15 W	0050 / 0658 / 1328 / 1912	1.6 / -0.1 / 1.4 / -0.1	30 TH	0052 / 0703 / 1330 / 1911	1.5 / 0.0 / 1.4 / 0.1

TIDAL DIFFERENCES PAGE 21:334.

Datum of predictions: 0.1 m. above M.L.W.S. and 0.4 m. above L.A.T.

ESBJERG

HIGH & LOW WATER 1992   Lat. 55°28′N. Long. 8°26′E.

TIME ZONE-0100 SUBTRACT 1 HOUR FROM TIMES SHOWN FOR GMT

MAY

Day	Time	m	Day	Time	m
1 F	0141 / 0743 / 1414 / 1953	1.6 / 0.0 / 1.4 / 0.0	**16** SA	0217 / 0809 / 1437 / 2028	1.6 / -0.2 / 1.4 / -0.3
2 SA	0226 / 0821 / 1455 / 2034 ●	1.6 / -0.1 / 1.4 / 0.0	**17** SU	0301 / 0851 / 1518 / 2113	1.5 / -0.1 / 1.4 / -0.3
3 SU	0308 / 0858 / 1533 / 2114	1.6 / -0.1 / 1.4 / -0.1	**18** M	0341 / 0930 / 1554 / 2155	1.4 / -0.1 / 1.4 / -0.2
4 M	0348 / 0936 / 1610 / 2154	1.5 / -0.1 / 1.4 / -0.1	**19** TU	0417 / 1008 / 1628 / 2235	1.3 / -0.1 / 1.4 / -0.2
5 TU	0427 / 1014 / 1645 / 2235	1.4 / 0.0 / 1.4 / -0.1	**20** W	0450 / 1045 / 1700 / 2315	1.2 / -0.1 / 1.4 / -0.1
6 W	0506 / 1053 / 1721 / 2318	1.4 / 0.0 / 1.4 / -0.1	**21** TH	0522 / 1121 / 1733 / 2354	1.2 / 0.0 / 1.4 / -0.1
7 TH	0546 / 1135 / 1800	1.4 / 0.0 / 1.4	**22** F	0556 / 1157 / 1808	1.2 / 0.0 / 1.5
8 F	0004 / 0629 / 1221 / 1844	-0.1 / 1.3 / 0.0 / 1.5	**23** SA	0034 / 0634 / 1237 / 1848	0.0 / 1.2 / 0.0 / 1.5
9 SA	0055 / 0720 / 1312 / 1937	0.0 / 1.3 / 0.1 / 1.5	**24** SU	0117 / 0717 / 1320 / 1934	0.1 / 1.2 / 0.1 / 1.5
10 SU	0154 / 0821 / 1412 / 2043	0.0 / 1.3 / 0.1 / 1.5	**25** M	0207 / 0809 / 1411 / 2028	0.1 / 1.2 / 0.2 / 1.5
11 M	0305 / 0935 / 1525 / 2202	0.1 / 1.2 / 0.1 / 1.5	**26** TU	0306 / 0912 / 1513 / 2134	0.2 / 1.2 / 0.3 / 1.4
12 TU	0424 / 1055 / 1643 / 2321	0.1 / 1.3 / 0.1 / 1.6	**27** W	0416 / 1031 / 1626 / 2251	0.2 / 1.2 / 0.3 / 1.5
13 W	0535 / 1204 / 1752	0.0 / 1.3 / 0.0	**28** TH	0522 / 1145 / 1734	0.2 / 1.3 / 0.2
14 TH	0028 / 0633 / 1303 / 1850	1.6 / -0.1 / 1.4 / -0.1	**29** F	0001 / 0617 / 1246 / 1831	1.5 / 0.1 / 1.3 / 0.1
15 F	0126 / 0724 / 1353 / 1941	1.6 / -0.1 / 1.4 / -0.2	**30** SA	0101 / 0705 / 1337 / 1922	1.5 / 0.0 / 1.4 / 0.0
			31 SU	0154 / 0749 / 1425 / 2009	1.5 / 0.0 / 1.4 / -0.1

JUNE

Day	Time	m	Day	Time	m
1 M	0243 / 0832 / 1509 / 2054 ●	1.4 / -0.1 / 1.4 / -0.1	**16** TU	0320 / 0910 / 1534 / 2138	1.2 / -0.1 / 1.4 / -0.2
2 TU	0330 / 0914 / 1552 / 2139	1.4 / -0.1 / 1.4 / -0.1	**17** W	0356 / 0947 / 1607 / 2217	1.2 / -0.1 / 1.4 / -0.2
3 W	0415 / 0957 / 1633 / 2223	1.4 / -0.1 / 1.4 / -0.2	**18** TH	0428 / 1023 / 1639 / 2254	1.2 / -0.1 / 1.4 / -0.1
4 TH	0458 / 1039 / 1713 / 2309	1.3 / -0.1 / 1.4 / -0.2	**19** F	0500 / 1058 / 1711 / 2330	1.2 / -0.1 / 1.4 / -0.1
5 F	0542 / 1123 / 1755 / 2356	1.3 / -0.1 / 1.5 / -0.2	**20** SA	0532 / 1132 / 1744	1.2 / 0.0 / 1.5
6 SA	0626 / 1209 / 1841	1.3 / -0.1 / 1.5	**21** SU	0006 / 0607 / 1209 / 1820	0.0 / 1.3 / 0.0 / 1.5
7 SU	0046 / 0714 / 1300 / 1932	-0.1 / 1.3 / 0.0 / 1.6	**22** M	0044 / 0645 / 1248 / 1901	0.0 / 1.3 / 0.0 / 1.6
8 M	0141 / 0810 / 1356 / 2034	-0.1 / 1.3 / 0.0 / 1.6	**23** TU	0125 / 0727 / 1332 / 1947	0.1 / 1.3 / 0.1 / 1.6
9 TU	0244 / 0916 / 1501 / 2145	0.0 / 1.3 / 0.0 / 1.5	**24** W	0213 / 0817 / 1424 / 2042	0.1 / 1.3 / 0.2 / 1.5
10 W	0354 / 1028 / 1615 / 2259	0.0 / 1.3 / 0.0 / 1.5	**25** TH	0309 / 0918 / 1527 / 2147	0.2 / 1.3 / 0.2 / 1.4
11 TH	0505 / 1136 / 1726	0.0 / 1.3 / 0.0	**26** F	0416 / 1033 / 1640 / 2304	0.2 / 1.2 / 0.2 / 1.4
12 F	0006 / 0607 / 1236 / 1829	1.5 / 0.0 / 1.4 / -0.1	**27** SA	0526 / 1150 / 1751	0.2 / 1.3 / 0.1
13 SA	0104 / 0700 / 1328 / 1923	1.5 / -0.1 / 1.4 / -0.2	**28** SU	0018 / 0626 / 1256 / 1852	1.4 / 0.1 / 1.3 / 0.0
14 SU	0155 / 0747 / 1415 / 2012	1.4 / -0.1 / 1.4 / -0.2	**29** M	0122 / 0720 / 1352 / 1946	1.4 / 0.0 / 1.4 / -0.1
15 M	0240 / 0830 / 1456 / 2057 ●	1.3 / -0.1 / 1.4 / -0.2	**30** TU	0218 / 0809 / 1444 / 2036 ●	1.4 / -0.1 / 1.4 / -0.2

JULY

Day	Time	m	Day	Time	m
1 W	0311 / 0855 / 1532 / 2124	1.3 / -0.1 / 1.4 / -0.2	**16** TH	0337 / 0927 / 1548 / 2157	1.2 / -0.1 / 1.4 / -0.1
2 TH	0401 / 0940 / 1618 / 2210	1.3 / -0.1 / 1.4 / -0.2	**17** F	0410 / 1002 / 1620 / 2232	1.2 / -0.1 / 1.4 / -0.1
3 F	0448 / 1025 / 1702 / 2256	1.3 / -0.2 / 1.5 / -0.2	**18** SA	0441 / 1035 / 1650 / 2305	1.2 / -0.1 / 1.5 / -0.1
4 SA	0532 / 1109 / 1747 / 2343	1.3 / -0.2 / 1.6 / -0.2	**19** SU	0512 / 1108 / 1722 / 2338	1.3 / -0.1 / 1.5 / -0.1
5 SU	0616 / 1155 / 1832	1.3 / -0.2 / 1.6	**20** M	0543 / 1142 / 1756	1.3 / -0.1 / 1.6
6 M	0030 / 0701 / 1244 / 1922	-0.2 / 1.3 / -0.2 / 1.6	**21** TU	0012 / 0616 / 1219 / 1833	0.0 / 1.4 / 0.0 / 1.6
7 TU	0121 / 0751 / 1336 / 2018	-0.1 / 1.3 / -0.1 / 1.6	**22** W	0049 / 0653 / 1300 / 1915	0.0 / 1.4 / 0.0 / 1.6
8 W	0217 / 0849 / 1436 / 2124	0.0 / 1.3 / -0.1 / 1.5	**23** TH	0131 / 0736 / 1346 / 2003	0.1 / 1.4 / 0.1 / 1.5
9 TH	0320 / 0956 / 1546 / 2234	0.1 / 1.3 / 0.0 / 1.5	**24** F	0220 / 0827 / 1442 / 2102	0.2 / 1.3 / 0.1 / 1.4
10 F	0432 / 1104 / 1701 / 2341	0.1 / 1.3 / 0.0 / 1.4	**25** SA	0321 / 0933 / 1553 / 2215	0.2 / 1.3 / 0.2 / 1.3
11 SA	0540 / 1207 / 1809	0.1 / 1.3 / -0.1	**26** SU	0436 / 1053 / 1714 / 2338	0.2 / 1.3 / 0.1 / 1.3
12 SU	0042 / 0637 / 1304 / 1906	1.4 / 0.0 / 1.4 / -0.1	**27** M	0551 / 1213 / 1826	0.1 / 1.3 / 0.0
13 M	0135 / 0727 / 1353 / 1956	1.3 / 0.0 / 1.4 / -0.2	**28** TU	0052 / 0653 / 1321 / 1925	1.3 / 0.0 / 1.3 / -0.1
14 TU	0221 / 0811 / 1436 / 2040	1.3 / -0.1 / 1.4 / -0.2	**29** W	0156 / 0747 / 1418 / 2018	1.3 / -0.1 / 1.4 / -0.2
15 W	0301 / 0851 / 1514 / 2120	1.2 / -0.1 / 1.4 / -0.2	**30** TH	0252 / 0836 / 1511 / 2107	1.3 / -0.2 / 1.5 / -0.3
			31 F	0344 / 0922 / 1600 / 2153	1.4 / -0.2 / 1.5 / -0.3

AUGUST

Day	Time	m	Day	Time	m
1 SA	0431 / 1008 / 1647 / 2239	1.4 / -0.2 / 1.6 / -0.3	**16** SU	0422 / 1011 / 1631 / 2237	1.3 / -0.1 / 1.5 / -0.1
2 SU	0515 / 1052 / 1732 / 2323	1.4 / -0.3 / 1.6 / -0.2	**17** M	0451 / 1044 / 1702 / 2309	1.3 / -0.1 / 1.5 / -0.1
3 M	0556 / 1137 / 1817	1.4 / -0.3 / 1.6	**18** TU	0520 / 1117 / 1735 / 2341	1.4 / -0.1 / 1.6 / 0.0
4 TU	0008 / 0638 / 1224 / 1904	-0.2 / 1.4 / -0.3 / 1.6	**19** W	0551 / 1153 / 1809	1.4 / -0.1 / 1.6
5 W	0056 / 0724 / 1314 / 1957	-0.1 / 1.4 / -0.2 / 1.5	**20** TH	0016 / 0624 / 1233 / 1848	0.0 / 1.4 / 0.0 / 1.5
6 TH	0146 / 0817 / 1410 / 2058	0.0 / 1.4 / -0.1 / 1.4	**21** F	0057 / 0703 / 1317 / 1934	0.1 / 1.4 / 0.0 / 1.5
7 F	0244 / 0920 / 1517 / 2206	0.1 / 1.3 / 0.0 / 1.3	**22** SA	0143 / 0751 / 1410 / 2030	0.1 / 1.4 / 0.1 / 1.4
8 SA	0354 / 1030 / 1632 / 2316	0.2 / 1.3 / 0.0 / 1.3	**23** SU	0241 / 0852 / 1519 / 2142	0.2 / 1.3 / 0.1 / 1.3
9 SU	0509 / 1138 / 1749	0.2 / 1.3 / 0.0	**24** M	0356 / 1011 / 1645 / 2308	0.2 / 1.3 / 0.1 / 1.3
10 M	0018 / 0613 / 1238 / 1848	1.2 / 0.1 / 1.3 / -0.1	**25** TU	0520 / 1137 / 1803	0.2 / 1.3 / 0.0
11 TU	0114 / 0705 / 1330 / 1937	1.2 / 0.0 / 1.4 / -0.1	**26** W	0028 / 0629 / 1252 / 1905	1.3 / 0.1 / 1.4 / -0.1
12 W	0201 / 0750 / 1414 / 2020	1.2 / 0.0 / 1.4 / -0.2	**27** TH	0135 / 0725 / 1354 / 1958	1.3 / -0.1 / 1.5 / -0.3
13 TH	0242 / 0829 / 1452 / 2059	1.2 / -0.1 / 1.4 / -0.2	**28** F	0231 / 0816 / 1448 / 2047 ●	1.4 / -0.2 / 1.5 / -0.3
14 F	0318 / 0905 / 1527 / 2134	1.3 / -0.1 / 1.4 / -0.1	**29** SA	0322 / 0903 / 1539 / 2133	1.4 / -0.3 / 1.6 / -0.3
15 SA	0351 / 0939 / 1600 / 2206	1.3 / -0.1 / 1.5 / -0.1	**30** SU	0408 / 0948 / 1626 / 2217	1.4 / -0.3 / 1.6 / -0.3
			31 M	0450 / 1032 / 1712 / 2300	1.4 / -0.3 / 1.6 / -0.2

Lat. 55°28′N. Long. 8°26′E.   **HIGH & LOW WATER 1992**

TIME ZONE-0100 SUBTRACT 1 HOUR FROM TIMES SHOWN FOR GMT

SEPTEMBER

Day	Time	m	Day	Time	m
1 TU	0530 / 1117 / 1756 / 2343	1.4 / -0.3 / 1.6 / -0.2	16 W	0500 / 1054 / 1715 / 2313	1.4 / -0.1 / 1.5 / 0.0
2 W	0611 / 1203 / 1841	1.4 / -0.3 / 1.5	17 TH	0530 / 1131 / 1750 / 2349	1.4 / -0.1 / 1.5 / 0.0
3 TH	0027 / 0653 / 1251 / 1930	-0.1 / 1.4 / -0.2 / 1.4	18 F	0602 / 1210 / 1828	1.4 / -0.1 / 1.4
4 F	0114 / 0741 / 1344 / 2026	0.0 / 1.4 / -0.1 / 1.3	19 SA	0029 / 0640 / 1255 / 1913	0.1 / 1.4 / 0.0 / 1.4
5 SA	0206 / 0840 / 1448 / 2133	0.1 / 1.3 / 0.0 / 1.2	20 SU	0115 / 0727 / 1349 / 2010	0.1 / 1.4 / 0.0 / 1.3
6 SU	0313 / 0951 / 1607 / 2246	0.2 / 1.3 / 0.0 / 1.2	21 M	0212 / 0827 / 1457 / 2122	0.2 / 1.4 / 0.1 / 1.3
7 M	0433 / 1104 / 1724 / 2352	0.2 / 1.3 / 0.0 / 1.2	22 TU	0327 / 0943 / 1622 / 2248	0.2 / 1.3 / 0.1 / 1.2
8 TU	0544 / 1207 / 1824	0.2 / 1.3 / 0.0	23 W	0453 / 1110 / 1742	0.2 / 1.4 / 0.0
9 W	0048 / 0638 / 1301 / 1913	1.2 / 0.1 / 1.4 / -0.1	24 TH	0008 / 0605 / 1227 / 1844	1.3 / 0.1 / 1.5 / -0.1
10 TH	0136 / 0724 / 1346 / 1954	1.3 / 0.0 / 1.4 / -0.1	25 F	0114 / 0703 / 1330 / 1937	1.4 / -0.1 / 1.6 / -0.2
11 F	0218 / 0804 / 1426 / 2031	1.3 / 0.0 / 1.5 / -0.2	26 SA	0209 / 0754 / 1426 / ● 2025	1.5 / -0.2 / 1.6 / -0.3
12 SA	0255 / 0840 / 1503 / ○ 2105	1.4 / 0.0 / 1.5 / -0.1	27 SU	0257 / 0842 / 1516 / 2110	1.5 / -0.3 / 1.6 / -0.3
13 SU	0329 / 0914 / 1537 / 2137	1.4 / -0.1 / 1.5 / -0.1	28 M	0341 / 0927 / 1603 / 2153	1.5 / -0.3 / 1.6 / -0.2
14 M	0401 / 0947 / 1610 / 2209	1.4 / -0.1 / 1.5 / -0.1	29 TU	0422 / 1012 / 1648 / 2235	1.5 / -0.1 / 1.5 / -0.2
15 TU	0431 / 1020 / 1643 / 2240	1.4 / -0.1 / 1.5 / 0.0	30 W	0502 / 1056 / 1731 / 2316	1.5 / -0.3 / 1.5 / -0.1

OCTOBER

Day	Time	m	Day	Time	m
1 TH	0540 / 1141 / 1813 / 2358	1.5 / -0.3 / 1.4 / 0.0	16 F	0513 / 1113 / 1736 / 2327	1.5 / 0.0 / 1.4 / 0.1
2 F	0620 / 1228 / 1858	1.4 / -0.2 / 1.4	17 SA	0547 / 1154 / 1815	1.5 / 0.0 / 1.4
3 SA	0041 / 0704 / 1319 / 1948	0.1 / 1.4 / -0.1 / 1.2	18 SU	0009 / 0625 / 1241 / 1901	0.1 / 1.5 / 0.0 / 1.3
4 SU	0130 / 0756 / 1417 / 2051	0.2 / 1.4 / 0.0 / 1.1	19 M	0056 / 0713 / 1335 / 1958	0.1 / 1.5 / 0.1 / 1.3
5 M	0229 / 0901 / 1531 / 2206	0.3 / 1.3 / 0.1 / 1.1	20 TU	0153 / 0812 / 1442 / 2108	0.2 / 1.5 / 0.1 / 1.3
6 TU	0345 / 1017 / 1648 / 2317	0.3 / 1.3 / 0.1 / 1.2	21 W	0304 / 0926 / 1602 / 2231	0.3 / 1.5 / 0.1 / 1.3
7 W	0503 / 1127 / 1751	0.3 / 1.4 / 0.0	22 TH	0426 / 1049 / 1719 / 2348	0.2 / 1.5 / 0.0 / 1.4
8 TH	0016 / 0603 / 1224 / 1840	1.3 / 0.2 / 1.4 / 0.0	23 F	0540 / 1205 / 1822	0.1 / 1.6 / -0.1
9 F	0106 / 0651 / 1312 / 1922	1.4 / 0.1 / 1.5 / -0.1	24 SA	0051 / 0640 / 1309 / 1915	1.5 / 0.0 / 1.7 / -0.2
10 SA	0149 / 0733 / 1355 / 2000	1.4 / 0.1 / 1.6 / -0.1	25 SU	0145 / 0733 / 1404 / ○ 2002	1.6 / -0.2 / 1.7 / -0.2
11 SU	0228 / 0811 / 1435 / ○ 2034	1.5 / 0.0 / 1.6 / -0.1	26 M	0233 / 0822 / 1454 / 2047	1.6 / -0.2 / 1.6 / -0.2
12 M	0304 / 0847 / 1513 / 2108	1.5 / 0.0 / 1.6 / -0.1	27 TU	0316 / 0908 / 1540 / 2129	1.6 / -0.3 / 1.5 / -0.1
13 TU	0338 / 0922 / 1549 / 2141	1.5 / 0.0 / 1.5 / 0.0	28 W	0356 / 0953 / 1623 / 2210	1.5 / -0.3 / 1.4 / -0.1
14 W	0411 / 0958 / 1624 / 2214	1.5 / 0.0 / 1.5 / 0.0	29 TH	0435 / 1037 / 1704 / 2250	1.5 / -0.2 / 1.4 / 0.0
15 TH	0442 / 1035 / 1659 / 2250	1.5 / 0.0 / 1.4 / 0.0	30 F	0512 / 1121 / 1743 / 2330	1.5 / -0.2 / 1.3 / 0.0
			31 SA	0549 / 1205 / 1823	1.5 / -0.1 / 1.2

NOVEMBER

Day	Time	m	Day	Time	m
1 SU	0011 / 0628 / 1252 / 1907	0.1 / 1.5 / 0.0 / 1.2	16 M	0618 / 1230 / 1854	1.6 / 0.0 / 1.4
2 M	0056 / 0712 / 1344 / 1959	0.2 / 1.5 / 0.1 / 1.2	17 TU	0042 / 0705 / 1324 / 1948	0.2 / 1.6 / 0.1 / 1.4
3 TU	0146 / 0805 / 1445 / 2107	0.3 / 1.4 / 0.2 / 1.2	18 W	0138 / 0802 / 1426 / 2055	0.2 / 1.6 / 0.1 / 1.4
4 W	0249 / 0911 / 1556 / 2225	0.4 / 1.4 / 0.2 / 1.2	19 TH	0244 / 0912 / 1539 / 2211	0.3 / 1.6 / 0.1 / 1.4
5 TH	0404 / 1028 / 1704 / 2332	0.4 / 1.5 / 0.2 / 1.3	20 F	0400 / 1031 / 1653 / 2325	0.3 / 1.7 / 0.1 / 1.5
6 F	0515 / 1135 / 1759	0.4 / 1.5 / 0.1	21 SA	0515 / 1146 / 1758	0.2 / 1.7 / 0.0
7 SA	0026 / 0610 / 1231 / 1844	1.4 / 0.3 / 1.6 / 0.1	22 SU	0028 / 0619 / 1250 / 1852	1.5 / 0.2 / 1.7 / 0.0
8 SU	0114 / 0657 / 1320 / 1924	1.5 / 0.2 / 1.6 / 0.0	23 M	0123 / 0714 / 1345 / 1941	1.6 / -0.1 / 1.7 / -0.1
9 M	0156 / 0739 / 1405 / 2002	1.6 / 0.1 / 1.6 / 0.0	24 TU	0211 / 0805 / 1435 / ● 2026	1.6 / -0.1 / 1.6 / -0.1
10 TU	0236 / 0820 / 1447 / ○ 2039	1.6 / 0.0 / 1.6 / 0.0	25 W	0254 / 0852 / 1520 / 2108	1.6 / -0.2 / 1.5 / 0.0
11 W	0314 / 0859 / 1528 / 2115	1.6 / 0.0 / 1.5 / 0.0	26 TH	0335 / 0937 / 1601 / 2148	1.6 / -0.1 / 1.4 / 0.0
12 TH	0351 / 0938 / 1608 / 2153	1.5 / 0.0 / 1.5 / 0.0	27 F	0412 / 1020 / 1639 / 2227	1.6 / -0.1 / 1.3 / 0.1
13 F	0426 / 1018 / 1647 / 2231	1.5 / 0.0 / 1.4 / 0.1	28 SA	0447 / 1102 / 1715 / 2306	1.6 / 0.0 / 1.3 / 0.1
14 SA	0501 / 1059 / 1726 / 2311	1.5 / 0.0 / 1.4 / 0.1	29 SU	0521 / 1143 / 1750 / 2344	1.6 / 0.0 / 1.3 / 0.1
15 SU	0537 / 1143 / 1808 / 2354	1.4 / 0.0 / 1.4 / 0.1	30 M	0557 / 1224 / 1829	1.6 / 0.1 / 1.3

DECEMBER

Day	Time	m	Day	Time	m
1 TU	0024 / 0635 / 1308 / 1911	0.2 / 1.6 / 0.2 / 1.3	16 W	0029 / 0657 / 1309 / 1936	0.1 / 1.8 / 0.1 / 1.5
2 W	0108 / 0719 / 1356 / 2003	0.3 / 1.6 / 0.2 / 1.3	17 TH	0122 / 0752 / 1406 / 2036	0.2 / 1.8 / 0.2 / 1.5
3 TH	0157 / 0810 / 1452 / 2108	0.4 / 1.6 / 0.3 / 1.3	18 F	0222 / 0857 / 1511 / 2147	0.2 / 1.7 / 0.2 / 1.5
4 F	0257 / 0914 / 1557 / 2225	0.4 / 1.6 / 0.3 / 1.4	19 SA	0333 / 1013 / 1624 / 2300	0.3 / 1.7 / 0.2 / 1.5
5 SA	0408 / 1029 / 1702 / 2334	0.5 / 1.6 / 0.3 / 1.4	20 SU	0449 / 1127 / 1732	0.2 / 1.7 / 0.2
6 SU	0519 / 1140 / 1758	0.4 / 1.6 / 0.2	21 M	0005 / 0559 / 1232 / 1831	1.6 / 0.1 / 1.7 / 0.1
7 M	0031 / 0617 / 1240 / 1846	1.5 / 0.3 / 1.6 / 0.2	22 TU	0102 / 0658 / 1329 / 1922	1.6 / 0.0 / 1.6 / 0.1
8 TU	0121 / 0708 / 1333 / 1930	1.6 / 0.2 / 1.6 / 0.1	23 W	0152 / 0751 / 1419 / 2008	1.7 / 0.0 / 1.5 / 0.1
9 W	0207 / 0754 / 1422 / ○ 2012	1.6 / 0.1 / 1.6 / 0.1	24 TH	0237 / 0838 / 1503 / ● 2050	1.7 / -0.1 / 1.4 / 0.1
10 TH	0250 / 0838 / 1508 / 2053	1.6 / 0.1 / 1.5 / 0.1	25 F	0317 / 0922 / 1543 / 2129	1.6 / 0.0 / 1.4 / 0.1
11 F	0331 / 0921 / 1553 / 2134	1.6 / 0.0 / 1.5 / 0.1	26 SA	0354 / 1003 / 1618 / 2207	1.6 / 0.0 / 1.3 / 0.1
12 SA	0411 / 1004 / 1635 / 2215	1.6 / 0.0 / 1.5 / 0.1	27 SU	0427 / 1042 / 1650 / 2243	1.6 / 0.0 / 1.3 / 0.1
13 SU	0450 / 1047 / 1717 / 2258	1.6 / 0.0 / 1.4 / 0.1	28 M	0458 / 1119 / 1722 / 2319	1.7 / 0.1 / 1.4 / 0.2
14 M	0529 / 1132 / 1800 / 2342	1.7 / 0.0 / 1.4 / 0.1	29 TU	0530 / 1155 / 1756 / 2355	1.7 / 0.1 / 1.4 / 0.2
15 TU	0611 / 1218 / 1845	1.7 / 0.0 / 1.5	30 W	0604 / 1232 / 1833	1.8 / 0.2 / 1.4
			31 TH	0033 / 0642 / 1312 / 1914	0.3 / 1.8 / 0.2 / 1.5

TIDAL DIFFERENCES PAGE 21:334.

Datum of predictions: 0.1 m. above M.L.W.S. and 0.4 m. above L.A.T.

TIDAL DIFFERENCES ON ESBJERG

PLACE	TIME DIFFERENCES				HEIGHT DIFFERENCES (Metres)			
	High Water		Low Water		MHWS	MHWN	MLWN	MLWS
ESBJERG	0300 and 1500	0700 and 1900	0100 and 1300	0800 and 2000	1.6	1.4	0.2	-0.1
Hirtshals....................	+0055	+0320	+0340	+0100	-1.3	-1.1	-0.1	+0.1
Hanstholm..................	+0100	+0340	+0340	+0130	-1.3	-1.1	-0.1	+0.1
Thyboron	+0120	+0230	+0410	+0210	-1.2	-1.1	-0.1	+0.1
Torsminde	+0030	+0050	-0040	-0010	-0.7	-0.7	-0.1	+0.1
Blavandshuk	-0120	-0110	-0050	-0100	+0.2	0.0	+0.1	+0.1
Gradyb Bar	-0130	-0115	–	–	-0.1	-0.2	+0.1	+0.1
Rømø Havn	-0040	-0005	0000	-0020	+0.3	+0.2	+0.1	+0.1
Højer	-0020	+0015	–	–	+0.8	+0.7	+0.2	+0.1

Refer to predictions on pages 21:331-21:333

TIDAL DIFFERENCES ON BERGEN

PLACE	TIME DIFFERENCES				HEIGHT DIFFERENCES (Metres)			
	High Water		Low Water		MHWS	MHWN	MLWN	MLWS
BERGEN....................	0500 and 1700	1000 and 2200	0300 and 1500	1100 and 2300	1.5	1.1	0.6	0.2
Vatlestraumen	-0012	-0012	-0012	-0012	0.0	+0.1	+0.2	0.0
Samnangerfjord								
Tysse	-0018	-0018	-0018	-0018	-0.2	0.0	0.0	0.0
Hardangerfjord								
Lokksund	+0007	+0007	+0007	+0007	-0.3	-0.1	0.0	0.0
Norheimsund	+0020	+0020	+0020	+0020	0.0	+0.1	+0.2	0.0
Sørfjord, Odda	+0024	+0024	+0024	+0024	0.0	+0.1	0.0	0.0
Eidfjord	+0019	+0019	+0019	+0019	0.0	+0.1	+0.2	0.0
Stolem	-0016	-0016	-0016	-0016	-0.2	-0.1	0.0	0.0
Engesund	-0010	-0010	-0010	-0010	–	–	–	–
Bømlafjord								
Leirvik......................	+0010	+0010	+0010	+0010	-0.4	-0.3	-0.2	0.0
Akrafjord								
Fjaera	+0020	+0020	+0020	+0020	–	–	–	–
Ølen.........................	+0005	+0010	+0005	+0010	-0.3	-0.1	0.0	0.0

Refer to predictions on pages 21:336-21:338

TIDAL DIFFERENCES ON BERGEN 21:335

PLACE	TIME DIFFERENCES				HEIGHT DIFFERENCES (Metres)			
	High Water		Low Water		MHWS	MHWN	MLWN	MLWS
BERGEN	0500 and 1700	1000 and 2200	0300 and 1500	1100 and 2300	1.5	1.1	0.6	0.2
Bømlo								
Espevaer	−0020	−0015	−0025	−0010	−0.5	−0.3	−0.1	0.0
Karmsund								
Haugesund	−0030	−0015	−0010	−0130	−0.7	−0.5	−0.3	−0.1
Utsira	−0020	0000	0000	−0120	−0.7	−0.6	−0.3	−0.1
Saudafjord...............	−0030	−0010	−0010	−0130	−0.9	−0.6	−0.3	−0.1
Jøsenfjord	−0040	−0015	−0015	−0135	−0.9	−0.6	−0.3	−0.1
Lysebotn.................	−0030	−0005	−0005	−0125	−0.8	−0.6	−0.3	−0.1
Stavanger	−0040	−0015	−0015	−0135	−0.9	−0.7	−0.3	−0.1
Kvassheim.................	−0110	−0045	−0100	−0220	−1.1	−0.9	−0.4	−0.2
Egersund	−0025	0000	+0025	−0055	−1.2	−0.9	−0.5	−0.2
Tregde......................	−	−	−	−	−1.2	−0.8	−0.5	−0.1
Arendal	−	−	−	−	−1.2	−0.9	−0.5	−0.1
Nevlunghamn	−	−	−	−	−1.2	−0.8	−0.5	−0.1
Helgeroa...................	−	−	−	−	−1.1	−0.8	−0.4	−0.1
Horten......................	−	−	−	−	−1.1	−0.8	−0.4	−0.1
South Kaholmen	−	−	−	−	−1.0	−0.7	−0.4	−0.1
Oslo...........................	−	−	−	−	−1.0	−0.7	−0.3	−0.1
Baltic Sea	See footnotes							
Denmark								
Kobenhavn	−	−	−	−	−1.3	−1.1	−0.5	−0.3
Hornbaek	−	−	−	−	−1.3	−1.1	−0.5	−0.3
Korsor......................	−	−	−	−	−1.3	−1.0	−0.6	−0.3
Gedser	−	−	−	−	−1.3	−1.1	−0.5	−0.3
Slipshavn	−	−	−	−	−1.2	−1.0	−0.6	−0.4
Fredericia	−	−	−	−	−1.2	−1.0	−0.6	−0.4
Arhus	−	−	−	−	−1.2	−1.0	−0.6	−0.4
Fredrikshavn..............	−	−	−	−	−1.1	−0.8	−0.4	−0.2

Refer to predictions on pages 21:336-21:338

Tides in the Baltic Sea: In the Kattegat and Baltic Sea the tidal range is largely insignificant, the principal changes in sea level being caused by meteorological conditions.

In the Kattegat some heights of High and Low water are given, but not times since the curve is so flat as to make the crest and trough poorly defined with regard to time. As a rough guide, the time of High Water along the south coast of Norway occurs at the time of Low Water at Bergen, and vice versa.

BERGEN

HIGH & LOW WATER 1992   Lat. 60°24′N. Long. 5°18′E.

TIME ZONE-0100 SUBTRACT 1 HOUR FROM TIMES SHOWN FOR GMT

JANUARY

	Time	m		Time	m
1 W	0205 0814 1429 2049	0.6 1.3 0.6 1.3	**16** TH	0051 0716 1332 1948	0.5 1.2 0.6 1.3
2 TH	0253 0913 1521 2137	0.6 1.4 0.5 1.4	**17** F	0203 0825 1440 2056	0.5 1.3 0.5 1.3
3 F	0342 0954 1609 2225	0.5 1.4 0.5 1.4	**18** SA	0308 0924 1539 2155	0.4 1.4 0.3 1.4
4 SA	0420 1028 1647 ●2303	0.5 1.5 0.5 1.4	**19** SU	0356 1015 1627 ○2243	0.3 1.5 0.2 1.5
5 SU	0455 1107 1722 2338	0.4 1.5 0.4 1.4	**20** M	0444 1100 1715 2334	0.3 1.6 0.1 1.6
6 M	0526 1141 1757	0.5 1.5 0.4	**21** TU	0530 1149 1804	0.2 1.6 0.1
7 TU	0013 0557 1216 1828	1.4 0.4 1.5 0.4	**22** W	0020 0612 1234 1850	1.6 0.2 1.6 0.1
8 W	0047 0628 1247 1856	1.4 0.4 1.5 0.4	**23** TH	0109 0654 1322 1934	1.5 0.2 1.6 0.1
9 TH	0119 0656 1325 1929	1.4 0.4 1.5 0.4	**24** F	0157 0738 1410 2019	1.5 0.3 1.5 0.2
10 F	0155 0732 1401 2002	1.4 0.5 1.4 0.4	**25** SA	0242 0822 1458 2107	1.4 0.4 1.4 0.3
11 SA	0234 0809 1438 2043	1.3 0.5 1.4 0.5	**26** SU	0330 0907 1546 2202	1.2 0.4 1.4 0.4
12 SU	0315 0846 1526 2127	1.3 0.5 1.3 0.5	**27** M	0421 1006 1642 2301	1.2 0.5 1.3 0.5
13 M	0359 0933 1613 2221	1.2 0.6 1.3 0.5	**28** TU	0513 1121 1746	1.2 0.6 1.2
14 TU	0501 1045 1714 2333	1.2 0.6 1.2 0.6	**29** W	0019 0624 1256 1912	0.6 1.1 0.6 1.1
15 W	0602 1210 1826	1.2 0.6 1.2	**30** TH	0140 0749 1418 2030	0.6 1.2 0.6 1.2
			31 F	0242 0850 1519 2124	0.6 1.2 0.5 1.2

FEBRUARY

	Time	m		Time	m
1 SA	0325 0937 1556 2212	0.5 1.3 0.4 1.3	**16** SU	0254 0909 1525 2140	0.4 1.3 0.2 1.3
2 SU	0407 1019 1634 2250	0.5 1.4 0.4 1.3	**17** M	0345 0957 1616 2228	0.2 1.4 0.1 1.4
3 M	0438 1050 1709 ●2318	0.4 1.4 0.3 1.4	**18** TU	0430 1045 1701 ○2316	0.1 1.5 0.0 1.5
4 TU	0509 1125 1733 2349	0.3 1.4 0.3 1.4	**19** W	0512 1131 1743	0.1 1.6 0.0
5 W	0540 1152 1804	0.3 1.5 0.2	**20** TH	0002 0554 1213 1828	1.5 0.1 1.6 0.0
6 TH	0020 0604 1224 1832	1.4 0.3 1.4 0.2	**21** F	0044 0632 1301 1906	1.5 0.1 1.5 0.0
7 F	0051 0632 1257 1855	1.4 0.3 1.4 0.2	**22** SA	0128 0709 1342 1946	1.4 0.2 1.5 0.1
8 SA	0124 0708 1327 1932	1.3 0.3 1.4 0.3	**23** SU	0208 0752 1428 2027	1.3 0.2 1.4 0.3
9 SU	0157 0738 1403 1958	1.3 0.3 1.3 0.3	**24** M	0252 0833 1516 2108	1.3 0.4 1.3 0.4
10 M	0238 0809 1449 2044	1.2 0.4 1.3 0.4	**25** TU	0340 0921 1604 2209	1.2 0.5 1.2 0.5
11 TU	0324 0857 1540 2132	1.2 0.5 1.2 0.5	**26** W	0428 1040 1709 2325	1.1 0.6 1.1 0.6
12 W	0415 1007 1639 2244	1.1 0.5 1.2 0.5	**27** TH	0533 1237 1841	1.1 0.6 1.0
13 TH	0524 1143 1758	1.1 0.6 1.1	**28** F	0110 0711 1358 2017	0.6 1.1 0.5 1.0
14 F	0020 0649 1318 1930	0.5 1.1 0.5 1.2	**29** SA	0222 0831 1450 2109	0.6 1.1 0.5 1.1
15 SA	0149 0804 1430 2045	0.5 1.2 0.4 1.2			

MARCH

	Time	m		Time	m
1 SU	0301 0916 1535 2144	0.5 1.2 0.4 1.2	**16** M	0238 0853 1512 2124	0.3 1.3 0.1 1.3
2 M	0346 0955 1610 2219	0.4 1.3 0.3 1.3	**17** TU	0326 0941 1600 2212	0.2 1.4 0.0 1.4
3 TU	0414 1029 1638 2253	0.3 1.3 0.2 1.3	**18** W	0411 1027 1639 ○2254	0.1 1.5 0.0 1.4
4 W	0441 1057 1705 ●2321	0.2 1.4 0.2 1.3	**19** TH	0450 1109 1724 2336	0.0 1.5 -0.1 1.4
5 TH	0509 1125 1733 2352	0.2 1.4 0.1 1.3	**20** F	0532 1154 1803	0.0 1.5 0.0
6 F	0540 1156 1757	0.2 1.4 0.1	**21** SA	0018 0610 1239 1838	1.4 0.1 1.5 0.1
7 SA	0022 0610 1229 1832	1.3 0.2 1.4 0.1	**22** SU	0057 0645 1321 1916	1.4 0.1 1.4 0.2
8 SU	0051 0643 1302 1857	1.3 0.2 1.4 0.2	**23** M	0139 0727 1403 1951	1.3 0.2 1.3 0.3
9 M	0126 0710 1339 1934	1.3 0.2 1.3 0.2	**24** TU	0216 0804 1447 2028	1.3 0.3 1.2 0.4
10 TU	0210 0747 1427 2011	1.2 0.3 1.2 0.3	**25** W	0300 0856 1535 2120	1.2 0.4 1.1 0.5
11 W	0251 0835 1526 2110	1.2 0.4 1.2 0.4	**26** TH	0352 1008 1633 2234	1.1 0.5 1.0 0.6
12 TH	0350 0945 1628 2220	1.1 0.5 1.1 0.5	**27** F	0450 1153 1754	1.0 0.6 1.0
13 F	0459 1128 1747	1.1 0.5 1.1	**28** SA	0027 0631 1326 1930	0.6 1.0 0.5 1.0
14 SA	0006 0622 1302 1917	0.5 1.1 0.4 1.1	**29** SU	0139 0754 1414 2033	0.6 1.1 0.4 1.1
15 SU	0136 0748 1414 2029	0.4 1.1 0.3 1.2	**30** M	0235 0844 1459 2118	0.5 1.1 0.3 1.1
			31 TU	0306 0918 1530 2146	0.4 1.2 0.3 1.2

APRIL

	Time	m		Time	m
1 W	0341 0957 1602 2221	0.3 1.3 0.2 1.3	**16** TH	0348 1004 1616 2235	0.1 1.4 0.0 1.4
2 TH	0412 1024 1633 2248	0.2 1.3 0.1 1.3	**17** F	0430 1046 1654 O 2310	0.1 1.5 0.0 1.4
3 F	0444 1059 1700 ●2320	0.2 1.4 0.1 1.3	**18** SA	0512 1132 1733 2352	0.1 1.5 0.1 1.4
4 SA	0511 1130 1732 2354	0.1 1.4 0.1 1.3	**19** SU	0551 1214 1809	0.1 1.4 0.2
5 SU	0546 1209 1800	0.1 1.4 0.1	**20** M	0032 0627 1259 1844	1.4 0.2 1.4 0.3
6 M	0033 0624 1244 1839	1.3 0.2 1.4 0.2	**21** TU	0109 0704 1340 1917	1.3 0.3 1.3 0.4
7 TU	0108 0703 1332 1916	1.3 0.2 1.3 0.2	**22** W	0146 0747 1427 1958	1.3 0.3 1.2 0.5
8 W	0152 0740 1420 2004	1.3 0.3 1.2 0.3	**23** TH	0230 0839 1507 2041	1.2 0.4 1.1 0.5
9 TH	0240 0839 1515 2052	1.2 0.3 1.2 0.4	**24** F	0317 0936 1601 2149	1.1 0.5 1.0 0.6
10 F	0332 0951 1600 2215	1.1 0.4 1.1 0.5	**25** SA	0415 1054 1710 2318	1.1 0.5 1.0 0.6
11 SA	0444 1123 1732 2351	1.0 0.4 1.1 0.5	**26** SU	0527 1219 1831	1.0 0.5 1.0
12 SU	0606 1246 1858	1.1 0.3 1.1	**27** M	0040 0648 1317 1936	0.6 1.0 0.4 1.0
13 M	0117 0722 1351 2010	0.4 1.1 0.2 1.2	**28** TU	0141 0746 1405 2024	0.5 1.1 0.4 1.1
14 TU	0215 0827 1446 2101	0.3 1.2 0.1 1.3	**29** W	0223 0835 1443 2110	0.4 1.2 0.3 1.2
15 W	0303 0922 1530 2149	0.2 1.3 0.1 1.3	**30** TH	0301 0913 1522 2145	0.3 1.2 0.2 1.2

TIDAL DIFFERENCES PAGES 21:334-21:335.

Datum of predictions: 0.2 m. below M.L.W.S. and 0.1 m. above L.A.T.

BERGEN 21:337

Lat. 60°24'N. Long. 5°18'E. HIGH & LOW WATER 1992

TIME ZONE-0100 SUBTRACT 1 HOUR FROM TIMES SHOWN FOR GMT

MAY

Day	Time	m	Day	Time	m
1	0336	0.3	16	0410	0.2
	0952	1.3		1029	1.4
F	1553	0.2	SA	1634	0.2
	2216	1.3	O 2249		1.4
2	0411	0.2	17	0454	0.2
	1030	1.3		1113	1.4
SA	1629	0.2	SU	1712	0.2
● 2252		1.3		2328	1.4
3	0451	0.2	18	0532	0.2
	1106	1.4		1159	1.4
SU	1705	0.2	M	1747	0.3
	2331	1.4			
4	0527	0.1	19	0006	1.4
	1149	1.4		0614	0.2
M	1741	0.2	TU	1240	1.3
				1824	0.3
5	0010	1.4	20	0043	1.4
	0605	0.2		0652	0.3
TU	1234	1.4	W	1320	1.3
	1825	0.2		1901	0.4
6	0051	1.4	21	0128	1.3
	0652	0.2		0732	0.3
W	1321	1.3	TH	1401	1.2
	1905	0.3		1936	0.4
7	0141	1.3	22	0205	1.2
	0739	0.2		0813	0.4
TH	1415	1.3	F	1442	1.1
	1952	0.3		2019	0.5
8	0231	1.3	23	0251	1.2
	0840	0.2		0900	0.4
F	1508	1.2	SA	1532	1.1
	2049	0.4		2109	0.5
9	0329	1.2	24	0338	1.2
	0952	0.3		0957	0.5
SA	1611	1.1	SU	1623	1.1
	2202	0.4		2211	0.6
10	0431	1.2	25	0430	1.1
	1104	0.3		1106	0.5
SU	1723	1.1	M	1725	1.0
	2328	0.4		2323	0.6
11	0547	1.1	26	0531	1.1
	1219	0.3		1211	0.4
M	1835	1.1	TU	1830	1.0
12	0043	0.4	27	0038	0.5
	0659	1.2		0802	1.1
TU	1328	0.2	W	1305	0.4
	1940	1.2		1931	1.1
13	0144	0.3	28	0130	0.5
	0800	1.2		0738	1.1
W	1419	0.2	TH	1357	0.4
	2038	1.2		2020	1.1
14	0240	0.3	29	0219	0.4
	0859	1.3		0831	1.2
TH	1507	0.2	F	1439	0.3
	2123	1.3		2102	1.2
15	0328	0.2	30	0307	0.3
	0947	1.3		0915	1.2
F	1552	0.2	SA	1524	0.3
	2211	1.4		2147	1.3
			31	0348	0.2
				1003	1.3
			SU	1605	0.2
				2224	1.4

JUNE

Day	Time	m	Day	Time	m
1	0432	0.2	16	0525	0.2
	1048	1.4		1144	1.3
			TU	1732	0.3
● 2309		1.4		2348	1.4
2	0518	0.1	17	0603	0.3
	1133	1.4		1219	1.3
TU	1729	0.2	W	1807	0.3
	2355	1.4			
3	0600	0.1	18	0026	1.4
	1225	1.4		0638	0.3
W	1813	0.2	TH	1301	1.3
				1842	0.4
4	0038	1.4	19	0101	1.3
	0647	0.1		0713	0.3
TH	1315	1.4	F	1338	1.2
	1900	0.2		1912	0.4
5	0129	1.4	20	0140	1.3
	0737	0.1		0749	0.3
F	1406	1.3	SA	1418	1.2
	1946	0.3		1949	0.4
6	0219	1.3	21	0218	1.2
	0834	0.2		0826	0.3
SA	1500	1.3	SU	1455	1.2
	2044	0.3		2032	0.4
7	0316	1.3	22	0257	1.2
	0936	0.2		0909	0.4
SU	1558	1.2	M	1542	1.1
	2146	0.4		2116	0.5
8	0415	1.2	23	0345	1.1
	1040	0.3		0954	0.4
M	1656	1.1	TU	1626	1.1
	2255	0.4		2214	0.5
9	0518	1.2	24	0437	1.1
	1146	0.3		1053	0.4
TU	1802	1.1	W	1725	1.0
				2320	0.5
10	0010	0.4	25	0539	1.1
	0622	1.2		1155	0.4
W	1251	0.3	TH	1827	1.1
	1907	1.1			
11	0115	0.4	26	0032	0.5
	0731	1.2		0644	1.1
TH	1350	0.3	F	1303	0.4
	2006	1.2		1929	1.1
12	0218	0.3	27	0141	0.4
	0830	1.2		0749	1.1
F	1445	0.3	SA	1405	0.4
	2104	1.3		2024	1.2
13	0313	0.3	28	0239	0.4
	0928	1.3		0848	1.2
SA	1530	0.3	SU	1456	0.3
	2145	1.3		2116	1.3
14	0401	0.3	29	0331	0.3
	1016	1.3		0943	1.3
SU	1615	0.3	M	1544	0.3
	2231	1.4		2207	1.4
15	0439	0.3	30	0416	0.2
	1058	1.3		1035	1.4
M	1654	0.3	TU	1634	0.2
O 2309		1.4	● 2253		1.4

JULY

Day	Time	m	Day	Time	m
1	0505	0.1	16	0543	0.2
	1120	1.4		1202	1.3
W	1719	0.2	TH	1747	0.3
	2339	1.5			
2	0551	0.0	17	0002	1.4
	1213	1.4		0618	0.2
TH	1805	0.1	F	1237	1.3
				1818	0.3
3	0024	1.5	18	0037	1.4
	0640	0.0		0645	0.2
F	1303	1.4	SA	1308	1.3
	1847	0.2		1849	0.3
4	0112	1.5	19	0112	1.3
	0728	0.0		0717	0.2
SA	1351	1.4	SU	1342	1.2
	1935	0.2		1919	0.3
5	0204	1.5	20	0148	1.3
	0816	0.1		0743	0.3
SU	1441	1.3	M	1419	1.2
	2026	0.3		1958	0.4
6	0258	1.3	21	0223	1.2
	0910	0.2		0822	0.3
M	1533	1.2	TU	1458	1.2
	2117	0.3		2036	0.4
7	0350	1.3	22	0305	1.2
	1003	0.3		0900	0.4
TU	1628	1.2	W	1540	1.1
	2220	0.4		2113	0.5
8	0448	1.2	23	0353	1.1
	1111	0.3		0948	0.4
W	1723	1.1	TH	1631	1.1
	2328	0.4		2216	0.5
9	0554	1.2	24	0445	1.1
	1220	0.4		1104	0.5
TH	1828	1.1	F	1733	1.1
				2337	0.5
10	0047	0.5	25	0557	1.1
	0707	1.1		1216	0.5
F	1329	0.4	SA	1845	1.1
	1938	1.1			
11	0203	0.4	26	0107	0.5
	0819	1.2		0716	1.1
SA	1427	0.4	SU	1335	0.4
	2039	1.2		1954	1.2
12	0305	0.4	27	0217	0.4
	0921	1.2		0833	1.2
SU	1516	0.4	M	1437	0.4
	2135	1.3		2057	1.3
13	0355	0.3	28	0312	0.3
	1003	1.2		0928	1.3
M	1602	0.4	TU	1529	0.3
	2214	1.3		2148	1.4
14	0433	0.3	29	0404	0.1
	1045	1.3		1020	1.4
TU	1637	0.4	W	1618	0.2
O 2252		1.4	● 2234		1.5
15	0512	0.3	30	0450	0.0
	1131	1.3		1109	1.4
W	1715	0.3	TH	1704	0.1
	2331	1.4		2320	1.5
			31	0535	0.0
				1155	1.5
			F	1750	0.1

AUGUST

Day	Time	m	Day	Time	m
1	0005	1.5	16	0011	1.4
	0621	0.0		0616	0.2
SA	1244	1.5	SU	1238	1.3
	1828	0.1		1819	0.3
2	0053	1.5	17	0039	1.4
	0705	0.0		0643	0.2
SU	1328	1.4	M	1309	1.3
	1913	0.1		1846	0.3
3	0141	1.5	18	0115	1.4
	0753	0.1		0710	0.3
M	1416	1.4	TU	1342	1.3
	1957	0.2		1923	0.3
4	0233	1.4	19	0152	1.3
	0838	0.2		0743	0.3
TU	1503	1.3	W	1419	1.2
	2048	0.3		1951	0.4
5	0324	1.3	20	0230	1.3
	0925	0.3		0815	0.4
W	1554	1.2	TH	1458	1.2
	2145	0.4		2039	0.5
6	0418	1.2	21	0322	1.2
	1026	0.4		0906	0.5
TH	1649	1.2	F	1546	1.1
	2257	0.5		2141	0.5
7	0524	1.1	22	0414	1.1
	1143	0.5		1009	0.5
F	1751	1.1	SA	1648	1.1
				2308	0.6
8	0031	0.5	23	0527	1.1
	0639	1.1		1146	0.6
SA	1308	0.6	SU	1809	1.1
	1913	1.1			
9	0156	0.5	24	0045	0.5
	0804	1.1		0653	1.1
SU	1420	0.5	M	1320	0.5
	2025	1.2		1935	1.2
10	0257	0.4	25	0204	0.4
	0913	1.2		0816	1.2
M	1508	0.5	TU	1421	0.4
	2117	1.3		2037	1.3
11	0339	0.4	26	0303	0.3
	0951	1.2		0915	1.3
TU	1547	0.4	W	1516	0.3
	2155	1.3		2128	1.4
12	0418	0.3	27	0347	0.1
	1030	1.3		1003	1.4
W	1625	0.4	TH	1602	0.2
	2233	1.4		2217	1.5
13	0453	0.3	28	0433	0.0
	1105	1.3		1049	1.5
TH	1653	0.3	F	1644	0.1
O 2308		1.4	● 2303		1.6
14	0520	0.2	29	0515	0.0
	1136	1.4		1134	1.5
F	1724	0.3	SA	1726	0.1
	2340	1.4		2345	1.6
15	0548	0.2	30	0557	0.0
	1207	1.4		1220	1.5
SA	1755	0.3	SU	1808	0.1
			31	0033	1.6
				0638	0.0
			M	1303	1.5
				1848	0.2

BERGEN

HIGH & LOW WATER 1992   Lat. 60°24′N. Long. 5°18′E.

TIME ZONE-0100 SUBTRACT 1 HOUR FROM TIMES SHOWN FOR GMT

SEPTEMBER

Day	Time	m	Day	Time	m
1 TU	0120 / 0721 / 1346 / 1931	1.5 / 0.1 / 1.4 / 0.3	16 W	0042 / 0638 / 1306 / 1851	1.4 / 0.3 / 1.4 / 0.4
2 W	0207 / 0802 / 1431 / 2015	1.5 / 0.3 / 1.4 / 0.4	17 TH	0120 / 0711 / 1344 / 1928	1.4 / 0.4 / 1.4 / 0.4
3 TH	0255 / 0847 / 1519 / 2111	1.3 / 0.4 / 1.3 / 0.5	18 F	0208 / 0748 / 1435 / 2016	1.3 / 0.4 / 1.3 / 0.5
4 F	0350 / 0942 / 1611 / 2226	1.2 / 0.6 / 1.2 / 0.6	19 SA	0259 / 0830 / 1523 / 2119	1.3 / 0.5 / 1.2 / 0.6
5 SA	0451 / 1100 / 1715	1.1 / 0.7 / 1.2	20 SU	0358 / 0943 / 1626 / 2255	1.2 / 0.6 / 1.2 / 0.6
6 SU	0012 / 0617 / 1245 / 1841	0.6 / 1.1 / 0.7 / 1.1	21 M	0514 / 1122 / 1747	1.2 / 0.6 / 1.2
7 M	0144 / 0753 / 1357 / 2006	0.6 / 1.1 / 0.6 / 1.2	22 TU	0034 / 0643 / 1302 / 1910	0.5 / 1.2 / 0.6 / 1.3
8 TU	0235 / 0854 / 1449 / 2054	0.5 / 1.2 / 0.6 / 1.3	23 W	0143 / 0758 / 1407 / 2019	0.4 / 1.3 / 0.5 / 1.4
9 W	0313 / 0932 / 1528 / 2132	0.4 / 1.3 / 0.5 / 1.4	24 TH	0238 / 0857 / 1456 / 2112	0.3 / 1.4 / 0.4 / 1.5
10 TH	0352 / 1004 / 1555 / 2211	0.4 / 1.3 / 0.4 / 1.4	25 F	0327 / 0943 / 1542 / 2157	0.2 / 1.5 / 0.3 / 1.6
11 F	0419 / 1035 / 1630 / 2239	0.3 / 1.4 / 0.3 / 1.5	26 SA	0409 / 1028 / 1628 / ● 2239	0.1 / 1.6 / 0.2 / 1.6
12 SA	0447 / 1058 / 1658 / ○ 2310	0.3 / 1.4 / 0.3 / 1.5	27 SU	0455 / 1111 / 1706 / 2325	0.1 / 1.6 / 0.2 / 1.7
13 SU	0515 / 1137 / 1722 / 2341	0.2 / 1.4 / 0.3 / 1.5	28 M	0533 / 1153 / 1744	0.3 / 1.6 / 0.2
14 M	0542 / 1205 / 1753	0.2 / 1.4 / 0.3	29 TU	0009 / 0614 / 1233 / 1825	1.7 / 0.2 / 1.6 / 0.2
15 TU	0009 / 0610 / 1235 / 1823	1.5 / 0.3 / 1.4 / 0.3	30 W	0054 / 0649 / 1318 / 1909	1.6 / 0.3 / 1.5 / 0.3

OCTOBER

Day	Time	m	Day	Time	m
1 TH	0142 / 0730 / 1359 / 1954	1.5 / 0.4 / 1.5 / 0.5	16 F	0102 / 0653 / 1326 / 1921	1.5 / 0.4 / 1.5 / 0.5
2 F	0230 / 0807 / 1447 / 2042	1.4 / 0.6 / 1.4 / 0.6	17 SA	0150 / 0734 / 1414 / 2013	1.4 / 0.5 / 1.4 / 0.5
3 SA	0322 / 0902 / 1538 / 2154	1.3 / 0.7 / 1.3 / 0.7	18 SU	0249 / 0824 / 1507 / 2119	1.4 / 0.6 / 1.4 / 0.6
4 SU	0419 / 1022 / 1637 / 2337	1.2 / 0.8 / 1.2 / 0.7	19 M	0344 / 0936 / 1608 / 2244	1.3 / 0.7 / 1.3 / 0.6
5 M	0542 / 1201 / 1806	1.1 / 0.8 / 1.2	20 TU	0456 / 1104 / 1727	1.3 / 0.7 / 1.3
6 TU	0113 / 0718 / 1327 / 1931	0.7 / 1.2 / 0.7 / 1.3	21 W	0007 / 0619 / 1235 / 1847	0.5 / 1.3 / 0.6 / 1.3
7 W	0200 / 0819 / 1415 / 2019	0.6 / 1.2 / 0.6 / 1.3	22 TH	0119 / 0738 / 1339 / 1951	0.5 / 1.3 / 0.5 / 1.4
8 TH	0239 / 0858 / 1453 / 2101	0.5 / 1.3 / 0.6 / 1.4	23 F	0214 / 0830 / 1435 / 2047	0.4 / 1.4 / 0.4 / 1.5
9 F	0317 / 0936 / 1524 / 2140	0.4 / 1.3 / 0.5 / 1.5	24 SA	0302 / 0921 / 1520 / 2136	0.3 / 1.5 / 0.4 / 1.6
10 SA	0345 / 1004 / 1559 / 2208	0.4 / 1.5 / 0.4 / 1.5	25 SU	0352 / 1004 / 1605 / ● 2220	0.2 / 1.6 / 0.3 / 1.7
11 SU	0416 / 1035 / 1627 / ○ 2242	0.3 / 1.5 / 0.4 / 1.5	26 M	0429 / 1048 / 1647 / 2306	0.2 / 1.7 / 0.3 / 1.7
12 M	0444 / 1106 / 1658 / 2314	0.3 / 1.5 / 0.4 / 1.6	27 TU	0511 / 1130 / 1729 / 2352	0.3 / 1.7 / 0.3 / 1.7
13 TU	0513 / 1135 / 1727 / 2346	0.3 / 1.5 / 0.4 / 1.6	28 W	0551 / 1210 / 1809	0.3 / 1.7 / 0.4
14 W	0541 / 1207 / 1805	0.3 / 1.5 / 0.4	29 TH	0034 / 0625 / 1251 / 1853	1.6 / 0.4 / 1.6 / 0.4
15 TH	0025 / 0616 / 1245 / 1840	1.5 / 0.4 / 1.5 / 0.4	30 F	0118 / 0703 / 1335 / 1934	1.5 / 0.5 / 1.5 / 0.5
			31 SA	0210 / 0745 / 1417 / 2026	1.4 / 0.6 / 1.5 / 0.6

NOVEMBER

Day	Time	m	Day	Time	m
1 SU	0258 / 0826 / 1502 / 2124	1.3 / 0.7 / 1.4 / 0.7	16 M	0239 / 0817 / 1456 / 2112	1.4 / 0.6 / 1.4 / 0.5
2 M	0350 / 0927 / 1559 / 2246	1.3 / 0.8 / 1.3 / 0.7	17 TU	0341 / 0918 / 1557 / 2226	1.4 / 0.7 / 1.4 / 0.5
3 TU	0458 / 1059 / 1708	1.2 / 0.8 / 1.3	18 W	0445 / 1041 / 1700 / 2340	1.3 / 0.7 / 1.4 / 0.5
4 W	0008 / 0612 / 1221 / 1826	0.7 / 1.2 / 0.8 / 1.3	19 TH	0555 / 1200 / 1816	1.3 / 0.7 / 1.4
5 TH	0109 / 0728 / 1323 / 1928	0.7 / 1.3 / 0.7 / 1.3	20 F	0048 / 0704 / 1312 / 1924	0.5 / 1.4 / 0.6 / 1.5
6 F	0157 / 0816 / 1411 / 2020	0.6 / 1.3 / 0.7 / 1.4	21 SA	0149 / 0805 / 1413 / 2022	0.4 / 1.4 / 0.5 / 1.5
7 SA	0235 / 0855 / 1450 / 2058	0.5 / 1.4 / 0.6 / 1.5	22 SU	0241 / 0856 / 1501 / 2117	0.4 / 1.5 / 0.5 / 1.6
8 SU	0307 / 0933 / 1525 / 2137	0.5 / 1.5 / 0.5 / 1.5	23 M	0329 / 0945 / 1549 / 2205	0.4 / 1.6 / 0.4 / 1.6
9 M	0341 / 1004 / 1600 / 2215	0.4 / 1.5 / 0.5 / 1.6	24 TU	0410 / 1029 / 1634 / ● 2249	0.4 / 1.6 / 0.4 / 1.6
10 TU	0414 / 1037 / 1634 / ○ 2248	0.4 / 1.6 / 0.5 / 1.6	25 W	0454 / 1110 / 1718 / 2337	0.4 / 1.7 / 0.4 / 1.6
11 W	0449 / 1112 / 1710 / 2330	0.4 / 1.6 / 0.4 / 1.6	26 TH	0529 / 1152 / 1757	0.4 / 1.7 / 0.4
12 TH	0525 / 1148 / 1749	0.4 / 1.6 / 0.4	27 F	0020 / 0608 / 1234 / 1839	1.6 / 0.5 / 1.6 / 0.5
13 F	0008 / 0603 / 1229 / 1830	1.6 / 0.4 / 1.6 / 0.4	28 SA	0104 / 0645 / 1310 / 1918	1.5 / 0.5 / 1.6 / 0.5
14 SA	0055 / 0639 / 1312 / 1913	1.5 / 0.5 / 1.6 / 0.5	29 SU	0144 / 0724 / 1353 / 2005	1.5 / 0.6 / 1.5 / 0.6
15 SU	0145 / 0726 / 1359 / 2011	1.5 / 0.5 / 1.5 / 0.5	30 M	0230 / 0802 / 1438 / 2050	1.4 / 0.7 / 1.5 / 0.6

DECEMBER

Day	Time	m	Day	Time	m
1 TU	0315 / 0850 / 1518 / 2147	1.3 / 0.7 / 1.5 / 0.7	16 W	0322 / 0902 / 1535 / 2158	1.4 / 0.5 / 1.5 / 0.4
2 W	0406 / 0947 / 1616 / 2245	1.3 / 0.8 / 1.4 / 0.7	17 TH	0420 / 1005 / 1637 / 2306	1.4 / 0.6 / 1.4 / 0.5
3 TH	0500 / 1059 / 1711 / 2351	1.2 / 0.8 / 1.3 / 0.7	18 F	0522 / 1119 / 1745	1.3 / 0.6 / 1.4
4 F	0607 / 1211 / 1820	1.2 / 0.8 / 1.3	19 SA	0017 / 0633 / 1237 / 1853	0.5 / 1.3 / 0.6 / 1.4
5 SA	0049 / 0714 / 1311 / 1923	0.7 / 1.3 / 0.7 / 1.3	20 SU	0125 / 0734 / 1349 / 2001	0.5 / 1.3 / 0.6 / 1.4
6 SU	0146 / 0809 / 1404 / 2016	0.6 / 1.3 / 0.7 / 1.4	21 M	0221 / 0836 / 1445 / 2100	0.5 / 1.4 / 0.5 / 1.5
7 M	0228 / 0857 / 1452 / 2108	0.6 / 1.4 / 0.6 / 1.4	22 TU	0316 / 0928 / 1540 / 2155	0.5 / 1.5 / 0.5 / 1.5
8 TU	0309 / 0934 / 1539 / 2148	0.5 / 1.5 / 0.5 / 1.5	23 W	0357 / 1012 / 1628 / 2240	0.5 / 1.5 / 0.4 / 1.5
9 W	0349 / 1012 / 1616 / ○ 2232	0.5 / 1.5 / 0.5 / 1.5	24 TH	0442 / 1058 / 1706 / ● 2326	0.5 / 1.6 / 0.4 / 1.5
10 TH	0431 / 1050 / 1658 / 2318	0.4 / 1.6 / 0.4 / 1.6	25 F	0517 / 1136 / 1748	0.5 / 1.6 / 0.4
11 F	0509 / 1132 / 1740	0.4 / 1.6 / 0.4	26 SA	0008 / 0556 / 1215 / 1827	1.5 / 0.5 / 1.6 / 0.4
12 SA	0000 / 0555 / 1214 / 1826	1.6 / 0.4 / 1.6 / 0.3	27 SU	0046 / 0630 / 1250 / 1902	1.5 / 0.5 / 1.6 / 0.4
13 SU	0049 / 0637 / 1300 / 1912	1.6 / 0.4 / 1.6 / 0.3	28 M	0121 / 0702 / 1327 / 1939	1.4 / 0.5 / 1.5 / 0.5
14 M	0137 / 0718 / 1350 / 1959	1.5 / 0.4 / 1.6 / 0.4	29 TU	0202 / 0733 / 1405 / 2010	1.4 / 0.5 / 1.5 / 0.5
15 TU	0227 / 0808 / 1441 / 2056	1.5 / 0.5 / 1.5 / 0.4	30 W	0239 / 0814 / 1443 / 2051	1.3 / 0.6 / 1.4 / 0.5
			31 TH	0320 / 0855 / 1527 / 2132	1.3 / 0.6 / 1.3 / 0.6

TIDAL DIFFERENCES PAGES 21:334-21:335.

Datum of predictions: 0.2 m. below M.L.W.S. and 0.1 m. above L.A.T.

REYKJAVIK ICELAND 21:339

Lat. 64°09′N. Long. 21°56′W.

GMT

HIGH & LOW WATER 1992

JANUARY

Day	Time	m		Day	Time	m
1 W	0357 / 1019 / 1619 / 2228	3·4 / 1·2 / 3·2 / 1·2		16 Th	0251 / 0918 / 1521 / 2139	3·3 / 1·4 / 3·1 / 1·2
2 Th	0449 / 1108 / 1708 / 2315	3·6 / 1·1 / 3·3 / 1·0		17 F	0359 / 1027 / 1627 / 2241	3·6 / 1·1 / 3·3 / 0·9
3 F	0532 / 1150 / 1749 / 2353	3·7 / 0·9 / 3·4 / 0·6		18 Sa	0457 / 1122 / 1723 / 2333	3·9 / 0·8 / 3·6 / 0·6
4 Sa	0610 / 1227 / 1825 / ●	3·9 / 0·8 / 3·5		19 Su	0546 / 1210 / 1812 / ○	4·2 / 0·4 / 3·9
5 Su	0029 / 0643 / 1300 / 1859	0·8 / 4·0 / 0·7 / 3·6		20 M	0021 / 0634 / 1256 / 1859	0·3 / 4·5 / 0·2 / 4·0
6 M	0102 / 0717 / 1333 / 1931	0·7 / 4·0 / 0·7 / 3·6		21 Tu	0106 / 0719 / 1340 / 1945	0·1 / 4·6 / 0·1 / 4·2
7 Tu	0134 / 0748 / 1405 / 2004	0·7 / 4·0 / 0·6 / 3·6		22 W	0151 / 0804 / 1423 / 2030	0·1 / 4·6 / 0·0 / 4·2
8 W	0206 / 0819 / 1437 / 2036	0·7 / 4·0 / 0·7 / 3·6		23 Th	0236 / 0851 / 1505 / 2117	0·1 / 4·5 / 0·2 / 4·1
9 Th	0237 / 0851 / 1510 / 2110	0·8 / 3·9 / 0·7 / 3·6		24 F	0321 / 0936 / 1549 / 2204	0·4 / 4·2 / 0·4 / 3·9
10 F	0311 / 0924 / 1543 / 2145	0·9 / 3·8 / 0·9 / 3·5		25 Sa	0409 / 1024 / 1634 / 2255	0·7 / 3·9 / 0·7 / 3·7
11 Sa	0348 / 1000 / 1621 / 2227	1·0 / 3·6 / 1·0 / 3·4		26 Su	0502 / 1115 / 1725 / (2351	1·0 / 3·5 / 1·1 / 3·4
12 Su	0430 / 1044 / 1705 / 2318	1·2 / 3·4 / 1·2 / 3·3		27 M	0603 / 1214 / 1822	1·3 / 3·2 / 1·4
13 M	0525 / 1139 / 1800 /)	1·4 / 3·2 / 1·3		28 Tu	0057 / 0719 / 1324 / 1938	3·2 / 1·6 / 2·9 / 1·6
14 Tu	0022 / 0634 / 1246 / 1907	3·2 / 1·5 / 3·1 / 1·4		29 W	0218 / 0849 / 1447 / 2107	3·1 / 1·6 / 2·9 / 1·6
15 W	0135 / 0755 / 1404 / 2023	3·2 / 1·5 / 3·0 / 1·3		30 Th	0338 / 1009 / 1606 / 2217	3·2 / 1·5 / 3·0 / 1·4
				31 F	0438 / 1101 / 1659 / 2305	3·4 / 1·3 / 3·2 / 1·2

FEBRUARY

Day	Time	m		Day	Time	m
1 Sa	0520 / 1139 / 1739 / 2343	3·6 / 1·1 / 3·3 / 1·0		16 Su	0444 / 1111 / 1713 / 2322	3·9 / 0·7 / 3·6 / 0·5
2 Su	0556 / 1212 / 1811	3·8 / 0·9 / 3·5		17 M	0533 / 1156 / 1800	4·2 / 0·4 / 4·0
3 M	0015 / 0628 / 1243 / ● 1842	0·8 / 4·0 / 0·7 / 3·7		18 Tu	0008 / 0618 / 1238 / ○ 1843	0·2 / 4·5 / 0·1 / 4·2
4 Tu	0046 / 0657 / 1313 / 1912	0·7 / 4·1 / 0·6 / 3·8		19 W	0050 / 0700 / 1319 / 1926	0·0 / 4·6 / 0·0 / 4·4
5 W	0116 / 0726 / 1341 / 1941	0·6 / 4·1 / 0·5 / 3·9		20 Th	0133 / 0742 / 1358 / 2006	0·0 / 4·6 / 0·0 / 4·4
6 Th	0145 / 0754 / 1409 / 2009	0·6 / 4·1 / 0·5 / 3·9		21 F	0215 / 0825 / 1437 / 2049	0·0 / 4·4 / 0·1 / 4·3
7 F	0215 / 0822 / 1439 / 2039	0·6 / 4·0 / 0·6 / 3·9		22 Sa	0257 / 0907 / 1515 / 2131	0·3 / 4·2 / 0·4 / 4·0
8 Sa	0244 / 0851 / 1508 / 2110	0·7 / 3·9 / 0·7 / 3·8		23 Su	0339 / 0950 / 1556 / 2216	0·6 / 3·8 / 0·7 / 3·8
9 Su	0317 / 0922 / 1544 / 2145	0·8 / 3·8 / 0·8 / 3·6		24 M	0427 / 1037 / 1638 / 2309	1·0 / 3·4 / 1·1 / 3·4
10 M	0355 / 1000 / 1619 / 2230	1·0 / 3·5 / 1·0 / 3·5		25 Tu	0522 / 1133 / 1733 / (	1·4 / 3·1 / 1·5
11 Tu	0442 / 1049 / 1709 /) 2333	1·3 / 3·3 / 1·2 / 3·3		26 W	0014 / 0634 / 1242 / 1849	3·1 / 1·7 / 2·8 / 1·7
12 W	0550 / 1201 / 1819	1·5 / 3·0 / 1·4		27 Th	0135 / 0813 / 1413 / 2037	3·0 / 1·7 / 2·7 / 1·7
13 Th	0056 / 0719 / 1331 / 1951	3·2 / 1·6 / 2·9 / 1·5		28 F	0310 / 0949 / 1545 / 2202	3·1 / 1·6 / 2·8 / 1·5
14 F	0223 / 0858 / 1503 / 2122	3·3 / 1·5 / 3·0 / 1·3		29 Sa	0417 / 1041 / 1641 / 2248	3·3 / 1·3 / 3·1 / 1·3
15 Sa	0343 / 1016 / 1619 / 2230	3·5 / 1·1 / 3·3 / 0·9				

MARCH

Day	Time	m		Day	Time	m
1 Su	0459 / 1118 / 1719 / 2323	3·5 / 1·1 / 3·3 / 1·0		16 M	0427 / 1051 / 1658 / 2306	3·8 / 0·6 / 3·7 / 0·5
2 M	0533 / 1149 / 1750 / 2354	3·7 / 0·8 / 3·6 / 0·8		17 Tu	0515 / 1134 / 1742 / 2350	4·1 / 0·3 / 4·0 / 0·2
3 Tu	0604 / 1217 / 1818	3·9 / 0·7 / 3·8		18 W	0558 / 1214 / 1822 / ○	4·4 / 0·1 / 4·3
4 W	0024 / 0632 / 1245 / 1846	0·6 / 4·0 / 0·5 / 3·9		19 Th	0032 / 0639 / 1253 / 1902	0·0 / 4·4 / 0·0 / 4·4
5 Th	0053 / 0659 / 1312 / 1913	0·5 / 4·1 / 0·4 / 4·0		20 F	0113 / 0719 / 1330 / 1941	0·0 / 4·4 / 0·0 / 4·4
6 F	0121 / 0726 / 1340 / 1941	0·5 / 4·1 / 0·4 / 4·1		21 Sa	0152 / 0759 / 1408 / 2020	0·1 / 4·2 / 0·2 / 4·3
7 Sa	0149 / 0754 / 1408 / 2009	0·5 / 4·1 / 0·4 / 4·0		22 Su	0233 / 0840 / 1444 / 2100	0·3 / 4·0 / 0·4 / 4·0
8 Su	0220 / 0823 / 1439 / 2040	0·5 / 4·0 / 0·5 / 4·0		23 M	0314 / 0921 / 1522 / 2143	0·6 / 3·7 / 0·8 / 3·7
9 M	0254 / 0856 / 1511 / 2117	0·7 / 3·8 / 0·7 / 3·8		24 Tu	0357 / 1006 / 1603 / 2234	1·0 / 3·3 / 1·2 / 3·4
10 Tu	0332 / 0934 / 1549 / 2203	0·9 / 3·5 / 0·9 / 3·6		25 W	0448 / 1059 / 1654 / 2334	1·3 / 3·0 / 1·4 / 3·1
11 W	0421 / 1026 / 1640 / 2309	1·1 / 3·2 / 1·2 / 3·3		26 Th	0554 / 1205 / 1805 / (	1·6 / 2·8 / 1·7
12 Th	0530 / 1144 / 1756 /)	1·4 / 3·0 / 1·4		27 F	0050 / 0723 / 1328 / 1949	2·9 / 1·7 / 2·7 / 1·7
13 F	0036 / 0703 / 1317 / 1934	3·2 / 1·5 / 2·8 / 1·5		28 Sa	0220 / 0903 / 1503 / 2124	3·0 / 1·6 / 2·8 / 1·6
14 Sa	0206 / 0844 / 1451 / 2108	3·2 / 1·4 / 3·0 / 1·2		29 Su	0335 / 1002 / 1604 / 2216	3·1 / 1·3 / 3·0 / 1·3
15 Su	0327 / 0959 / 1604 / 2216	3·5 / 1·0 / 3·3 / 0·9		30 M	0423 / 1041 / 1645 / 2254	3·3 / 1·1 / 3·3 / 1·1
				31 Tu	0459 / 1113 / 1716 / 2326	3·6 / 0·9 / 3·5 / 0·8

APRIL

Day	Time	m		Day	Time	m
1 W	0530 / 1143 / 1747 / 2356	3·7 / 0·7 / 3·8 / 0·6		16 Th	0534 / 1147 / 1758	4·1 / 0·2 / 4·2
2 Th	0600 / 1212 / 1815	3·9 / 0·5 / 3·9		17 F	0011 / 0615 / 1227 / ○ 1838	0·1 / 4·1 / 0·2 / 4·3
3 F	0025 / 0629 / 1241 / ● 1843	0·5 / 4·0 / 0·4 / 4·1		18 Sa	0052 / 0656 / 1304 / 1917	0·1 / 4·0 / 0·2 / 4·3
4 Sa	0056 / 0659 / 1310 / 1913	0·4 / 4·0 / 0·3 / 4·1		19 Su	0133 / 0737 / 1341 / 1957	0·2 / 3·9 / 0·3 / 4·1
5 Su	0127 / 0728 / 1341 / 1945	0·4 / 3·9 / 0·4 / 4·1		20 M	0212 / 0816 / 1419 / 2036	0·4 / 3·7 / 0·5 / 3·9
6 M	0201 / 0802 / 1415 / 2022	0·4 / 3·8 / 0·5 / 4·0		21 Tu	0253 / 0858 / 1457 / 2119	0·6 / 3·5 / 0·8 / 3·7
7 Tu	0239 / 0840 / 1453 / 2103	0·6 / 3·7 / 0·6 / 3·8		22 W	0335 / 0942 / 1538 / 2207	0·9 / 3·2 / 1·0 / 3·4
8 W	0324 / 0927 / 1536 / 2157	0·8 / 3·4 / 0·8 / 3·6		23 Th	0423 / 1033 / 1626 / 2302	1·1 / 3·0 / 1·3 / 3·2
9 Th	0419 / 1028 / 1634 / 2306	1·0 / 3·1 / 1·1 / 3·4		24 F	0520 / 1132 / 1727 / (	1·4 / 2·8 / 1·5
10 F	0530 / 1146 / 1753 /)	1·2 / 2·9 / 1·3		25 Sa	0005 / 0629 / 1241 / 1848	3·0 / 1·5 / 2·7 / 1·6
11 Sa	0027 / 0655 / 1310 / 1924	3·2 / 1·3 / 2·9 / 1·3		26 Su	0119 / 0749 / 1358 / 2018	2·9 / 1·5 / 2·8 / 1·5
12 Su	0148 / 0822 / 1434 / 2050	3·3 / 1·2 / 3·1 / 1·1		27 M	0232 / 0900 / 1508 / 2125	3·0 / 1·3 / 3·0 / 1·4
13 M	0303 / 0932 / 1543 / 2155	3·5 / 0·9 / 3·4 / 0·8		28 Tu	0329 / 0949 / 1557 / 2212	3·1 / 1·1 / 3·1 / 1·1
14 Tu	0402 / 1024 / 1634 / 2245	3·7 / 0·6 / 3·7 / 0·5		29 W	0414 / 1028 / 1637 / 2248	3·3 / 0·9 / 3·4 / 0·9
15 W	0451 / 1108 / 1718 / 2330	3·9 / 0·4 / 4·0 / 0·3		30 Th	0451 / 1104 / 1711 / 2323	3·5 / 0·7 / 3·7 / 0·7

TIDAL DIFFERENCES PAGE 21:342.

Heights are referred to Chart Datum (approx. M.L.W.S.).

ICELAND REYKJAVIK

HIGH & LOW WATER 1992   Lat. 64°09'N. Long. 21°56'W.

GMT

MAY

Day	Time	m	Day	Time	m
1 F	0525 / 1137 / 1743 / 2357	3·6 / 0·6 / 3·8 / 0·5	**16** Sa ○	0556 / 1204 / 1818	3·7 / 0·4 / 4·0
2 Sa ●	0558 / 1210 / 1815	3·7 / 0·4 / 4·0	**17** Su	0035 / 0638 / 1243 / 1857	0·3 / 3·7 / 0·4 / 4·0
3 Su	0032 / 0634 / 1245 / 1850	0·4 / 3·8 / 0·3 / 4·1	**18** M	0116 / 0719 / 1321 / 1938	0·4 / 3·6 / 0·4 / 3·9
4 M	0109 / 0710 / 1321 / 1930	0·3 / 3·8 / 0·3 / 4·1	**19** Tu	0155 / 0758 / 1359 / 2018	0·5 / 3·5 / 0·6 / 3·8
5 Tu	0149 / 0751 / 1401 / 2012	0·4 / 3·7 / 0·4 / 4·0	**20** W	0234 / 0839 / 1437 / 2058	0·6 / 3·4 / 0·7 / 3·6
6 W	0233 / 0837 / 1444 / 2101	0·5 / 3·5 / 0·5 / 3·9	**21** Th	0315 / 0921 / 1517 / 2142	0·8 / 3·2 / 0·9 / 3·4
7 Th	0324 / 0931 / 1535 / 2159	0·6 / 3·4 / 0·7 / 3·7	**22** F	0359 / 1006 / 1600 / 2228	0·9 / 3·1 / 1·1 / 3·3
8 F	0421 / 1033 / 1635 / 2304	0·8 / 3·2 / 0·9 / 3·5	**23** Sa	0447 / 1055 / 1651 / 2320	1·1 / 2·9 / 1·2 / 3·1
9 Sa ☽	0527 / 1142 / 1747	0·9 / 3·0 / 1·1	**24** Su ☾	0540 / 1151 / 1751	1·2 / 2·8 / 1·4
10 Su	0012 / 0639 / 1255 / 1906	3·4 / 1·0 / 3·0 / 1·1	**25** M	0018 / 0806 / 1255 / 1903	3·0 / 1·3 / 2·8 / 1·4
11 M	0124 / 0751 / 1409 / 2023	3·3 / 1·0 / 3·1 / 1·0	**26** Tu	0121 / 0744 / 1359 / 2015	2·9 / 1·2 / 2·9 / 1·4
12 Tu	0233 / 0857 / 1514 / 2128	3·4 / 0·8 / 3·4 / 0·8	**27** W	0222 / 0844 / 1458 / 2115	3·0 / 1·2 / 3·1 / 1·2
13 W	0334 / 0952 / 1609 / 2223	3·5 / 0·7 / 3·6 / 0·6	**28** Th	0318 / 0935 / 1549 / 2206	3·1 / 1·0 / 3·3 / 1·0
14 Th	0426 / 1040 / 1655 / 2311	3·6 / 0·5 / 3·8 / 0·5	**29** F	0407 / 1021 / 1631 / 2249	3·2 / 0·8 / 3·5 / 0·8
15 F	0512 / 1123 / 1737 / 2354	3·7 / 0·4 / 3·9 / 0·4	**30** Sa	0449 / 1102 / 1712 / 2332	3·4 / 0·6 / 3·7 / 0·6
			31 Su	0532 / 1143 / 1753	3·5 / 0·5 / 3·9

JUNE

Day	Time	m	Day	Time	m
1 M ●	0012 / 0614 / 1225 / 1835	0·4 / 3·6 / 0·3 / 4·0	**16** Tu	0102 / 0703 / 1306 / 1923	0·5 / 3·4 / 0·5 / 3·8
2 Tu	0056 / 0657 / 1307 / 1919	0·3 / 3·6 / 0·2 / 4·1	**17** W	0140 / 0741 / 1342 / 1959	0·5 / 3·4 / 0·5 / 3·7
3 W	0141 / 0745 / 1352 / 2006	0·2 / 3·6 / 0·2 / 4·0	**18** Th	0216 / 0818 / 1419 / 2036	0·5 / 3·3 / 0·6 / 3·6
4 Th	0229 / 0834 / 1439 / 2057	0·2 / 3·5 / 0·3 / 4·0	**19** F	0253 / 0856 / 1454 / 2114	0·6 / 3·3 / 0·7 / 3·5
5 F	0319 / 0928 / 1531 / 2152	0·3 / 3·5 / 0·4 / 3·8	**20** Sa	0331 / 0934 / 1532 / 2152	0·7 / 3·2 / 0·8 / 3·4
6 Sa	0413 / 1026 / 1628 / 2251	0·4 / 3·3 / 0·6 / 3·6	**21** Su	0409 / 1016 / 1613 / 2234	0·8 / 3·1 / 1·0 / 3·2
7 Su ☽	0511 / 1126 / 1732 / 2351	0·6 / 3·2 / 0·8 / 3·5	**22** M	0451 / 1102 / 1701 / 2322	0·9 / 3·0 / 1·1 / 3·1
8 M	0611 / 1231 / 1841	0·7 / 3·2 / 0·9	**23** Tu ☾	0539 / 1154 / 1758	1·0 / 2·9 / 1·3
9 Tu	0055 / 0716 / 1337 / 1952	3·3 / 0·8 / 3·2 / 1·0	**24** W	0017 / 0634 / 1253 / 1904	2·9 / 1·1 / 2·9 / 1·3
10 W	0159 / 0820 / 1443 / 2101	3·2 / 0·9 / 3·3 / 1·0	**25** Th	0117 / 0735 / 1357 / 2013	2·9 / 1·1 / 2·9 / 1·3
11 Th	0304 / 0921 / 1543 / 2202	3·2 / 0·8 / 3·4 / 0·8	**26** F	0220 / 0839 / 1500 / 2121	2·9 / 1·1 / 3·1 / 1·1
12 F	0403 / 1016 / 1635 / 2255	3·2 / 0·8 / 3·5 / 0·7	**27** Sa	0324 / 0941 / 1557 / 2220	3·0 / 0·9 / 3·3 / 0·9
13 Sa	0455 / 1105 / 1722 / 2340	3·3 / 0·7 / 3·7 / 0·6	**28** Su	0420 / 1034 / 1648 / 2311	3·1 / 0·7 / 3·5 / 0·7
14 Su	0542 / 1149 / 1804	3·3 / 0·6 / 3·7	**29** M	0511 / 1123 / 1736 / 2358	3·3 / 0·5 / 3·8 / 0·4
15 M ○	0022 / 0624 / 1228 / 1845	0·5 / 3·4 / 0·5 / 3·8	**30** Tu ●	0600 / 1210 / 1822	3·4 / 0·3 / 4·0

JULY

Day	Time	m	Day	Time	m
1 W	0045 / 0648 / 1256 / 1909	0·2 / 3·6 / 0·1 / 4·1	**16** Th	0121 / 0720 / 1324 / 1938	0·4 / 3·4 / 0·4 / 3·7
2 Th	0131 / 0734 / 1341 / 1957	0·0 / 3·7 / 0·0 / 4·2	**17** F	0154 / 0754 / 1357 / 2009	0·4 / 3·4 / 0·4 / 3·7
3 F	0218 / 0823 / 1429 / 2044	0·0 / 3·7 / 0·0 / 4·1	**18** Sa	0225 / 0826 / 1429 / 2042	0·4 / 3·4 / 0·5 / 3·6
4 Sa	0304 / 0914 / 1518 / 2135	0·0 / 3·7 / 0·1 / 4·0	**19** Su	0257 / 0858 / 1501 / 2114	0·5 / 3·4 / 0·6 / 3·5
5 Su	0353 / 1006 / 1610 / 2228	0·2 / 3·6 / 0·3 / 3·7	**20** M	0329 / 0932 / 1536 / 2148	0·6 / 3·3 / 0·7 / 3·3
6 M	0444 / 1101 / 1706 / 2323	0·4 / 3·4 / 0·6 / 3·5	**21** Tu	0404 / 1012 / 1616 / 2228	0·7 / 3·2 / 0·9 / 3·2
7 Tu ☽	0537 / 1158 / 1810	0·6 / 3·3 / 0·8	**22** W ☾	0445 / 1058 / 1704 / 2318	0·9 / 3·0 / 1·1 / 3·0
8 W	0022 / 0636 / 1303 / 1919	3·2 / 0·8 / 3·1 / 1·0	**23** Th	0534 / 1156 / 1805	1·0 / 2·9 / 1·2
9 Th	0127 / 0742 / 1412 / 2034	3·0 / 1·0 / 3·1 / 1·1	**24** F	0019 / 0636 / 1304 / 1921	2·8 / 1·1 / 2·9 / 1·3
10 F	0239 / 0854 / 1522 / 2146	2·9 / 1·0 / 3·1 / 1·0	**25** Sa	0133 / 0751 / 1419 / 2044	2·7 / 1·2 / 3·0 / 1·2
11 Sa	0348 / 1000 / 1623 / 2245	2·9 / 1·0 / 3·3 / 0·9	**26** Su	0249 / 0908 / 1531 / 2157	2·8 / 1·0 / 3·2 / 1·0
12 Su	0445 / 1055 / 1712 / 2332	3·0 / 0·8 / 3·4 / 0·7	**27** M	0359 / 1014 / 1630 / 2257	2·9 / 0·7 / 3·5 / 0·6
13 M	0532 / 1137 / 1754 / 2346	3·1 / 0·7 / 3·6 / 0·3	**28** Tu	0457 / 1109 / 1720 / 2346	3·2 / 0·4 / 3·8 / 0·3
14 Tu ○	0011 / 0611 / 1217 / 1831	0·6 / 3·2 / 0·5 / 3·7	**29** W ●	0546 / 1157 / 1808	3·5 / 0·1 / 4·0
15 W	0048 / 0646 / 1252 / 1904	0·5 / 3·3 / 0·4 / 3·7	**30** Th	0031 / 0632 / 1242 / 1853	0·0 / 3·7 / -0·1 / 4·2
			31 F	0114 / 0719 / 1326 / 1938	-0·2 / 3·9 / -0·2 / 4·3

AUGUST

Day	Time	m	Day	Time	m
1 Sa	0157 / 0804 / 1411 / 2023	-0·2 / 3·9 / -0·2 / 4·2	**16** Su	0154 / 0754 / 1401 / 2008	0·3 / 3·6 / 0·3 / 3·7
2 Su	0240 / 0849 / 1457 / 2110	-0·2 / 3·9 / -0·1 / 4·0	**17** M	0223 / 0822 / 1430 / 2036	0·3 / 3·6 / 0·4 / 3·6
3 M	0324 / 0938 / 1545 / 2159	0·0 / 3·8 / 0·0 / 3·7	**18** Tu	0251 / 0853 / 1503 / 2107	0·4 / 3·5 / 0·6 / 3·4
4 Tu	0410 / 1028 / 1637 / 2252	0·3 / 3·5 / 0·5 / 3·4	**19** W	0324 / 0927 / 1538 / 2142	0·6 / 3·3 / 0·7 / 3·2
5 W	0459 / 1125 / 1736 / 2350	0·6 / 3·3 / 0·9 / 3·0	**20** Th	0400 / 1009 / 1621 / 2228	0·8 / 3·2 / 1·0 / 3·0
6 Th	0557 / 1229 / 1846	0·9 / 3·0 / 1·1	**21** F ☾	0447 / 1109 / 1723 / 2336	1·0 / 3·0 / 1·2 / 2·8
7 F	0057 / 0707 / 1344 / 2011	2·8 / 1·2 / 2·9 / 1·3	**22** Sa	0551 / 1227 / 1846	1·2 / 2·9 / 1·3
8 Sa	0215 / 0834 / 1507 / 2138	2·6 / 1·2 / 2·9 / 1·2	**23** Su	0102 / 0719 / 1352 / 2020	2·6 / 1·2 / 2·9 / 1·3
9 Su	0336 / 0953 / 1613 / 2237	2·7 / 1·1 / 3·1 / 1·0	**24** M	0229 / 0849 / 1511 / 2142	2·7 / 1·1 / 3·1 / 1·0
10 M	0437 / 1045 / 1701 / 2319	2·9 / 0·9 / 3·3 / 0·8	**25** Tu	0345 / 1000 / 1614 / 2241	2·9 / 0·7 / 3·5 / 0·6
11 Tu	0519 / 1126 / 1739 / 2354	3·1 / 0·7 / 3·5 / 0·6	**26** W	0442 / 1054 / 1705 / 2327	3·3 / 0·4 / 3·8 / 0·2
12 W	0554 / 1200 / 1811	3·2 / 0·5 / 3·6	**27** Th	0530 / 1140 / 1750	3·6 / 0·0 / 4·1
13 Th ○	0027 / 0627 / 1232 / 1842	0·4 / 3·4 / 0·4 / 3·7	**28** F ●	0010 / 0614 / 1224 / 1832	-0·1 / 3·9 / -0·2 / 4·3
14 F	0056 / 0656 / 1302 / 1912	0·3 / 3·5 / 0·3 / 3·8	**29** Sa	0050 / 0656 / 1306 / 1914	-0·3 / 4·1 / -0·3 / 4·3
15 Sa	0126 / 0724 / 1331 / 1940	0·3 / 3·6 / 0·3 / 3·8	**30** Su	0131 / 0738 / 1349 / 1958	-0·3 / 4·2 / -0·3 / 4·2
			31 M	0211 / 0822 / 1432 / 2042	-0·2 / 4·1 / -0·1 / 4·0

REYKJAVIK ICELAND

Lat. 64°09'N. Long. 21°56'W.

GMT

HIGH & LOW WATER 1992

SEPTEMBER

	Time	m		Time	m
1 Tu	0253 0905 1518 2129	0·0 3·9 0·2 3·7	**16** W	0219 0820 1434 2034	0·4 3·7 0·5 3·5
2 W	0335 0955 1607 2220	0·3 3·6 0·6 3·3	**17** Th	0251 0856 1511 2111	0·5 3·5 0·7 3·3
3 Th	0421 1051 1704 2318	0·7 3·3 0·9 2·9	**18** F	0328 0938 1556 2159	0·7 3·3 0·9 3·0
4 F	0519 1157 1815	1·1 3·0 1·3	**19** Sa	0414 1041 1701 2315	1·0 3·1 1·2 2·7
5 Sa	0028 0634 1316 1947	2·6 1·3 2·8 1·4	**20** Su	0526 1205 1829	1·2 2·9 1·3
6 Su	0152 0813 1444 2121	2·5 1·4 2·9 1·3	**21** M	0045 0700 1333 2005	2·6 1·3 3·0 1·2
7 M	0321 0939 1555 2219	2·6 1·2 3·0 1·0	**22** Tu	0215 0833 1451 2124	2·7 1·1 3·2 0·9
8 Tu	0420 1028 1640 2257	2·9 1·0 3·3 0·8	**23** W	0329 0943 1553 2220	3·0 0·7 3·5 0·5
9 W	0459 1106 1715 2329	3·1 0·7 3·5 0·6	**24** Th	0424 1035 1644 2304	3·4 0·4 3·9 0·2
10 Th	0530 1137 1746 2358	3·3 0·5 3·6 0·4	**25** F	0511 1127 1727 2346	3·8 0·0 4·1 −0·1
11 F	0600 1207 1814	3·5 0·4 3·7	**26** Sa	0553 1204 1810 ●	4·1 −0·2 4·2
12 Sa	0027 0628 1236 1842 ○	0·3 3·7 0·3 3·8	**27** Su	0025 0632 1246 1852	−0·2 4·2 −0·3 4·2
13 Su	0055 0655 1304 1909	0·2 3·7 0·3 3·8	**28** M	0104 0713 1327 1933	−0·2 4·3 −0·2 4·1
14 M	0121 0723 1333 1935	0·2 3·8 0·3 3·7	**29** Tu	0144 0753 1409 2016	−0·1 4·2 0·0 3·9
15 Tu	0149 0751 1402 2005	0·3 3·8 0·4 3·6	**30** W	0223 0839 1453 2101	0·1 3·9 0·3 3·6

OCTOBER

	Time	m		Time	m
1 Th	0304 0925 1541 2150	0·5 3·6 0·7 3·2	**16** F	0229 0839 1458 2058	0·5 3·7 0·7 3·3
2 F	0349 1020 1635 2248	0·8 3·3 1·0 2·9	**17** Sa	0311 0928 1549 2153	0·7 3·5 0·9 3·0
3 Sa	0444 1123 1743 2356	1·2 3·0 1·3 2·7	**18** Su	0403 1033 1657 2311	1·0 3·3 1·1 2·8
4 Su	0557 1239 1909	1·4 2·8 1·4	**19** M	0516 1151 1818	1·2 3·1 1·2
5 M	0116 0734 1404 2042	2·6 1·5 2·8 1·3	**20** Tu	0034 0645 1312 1942	2·8 1·2 3·1 1·1
6 Tu	0244 0904 1517 2142	2·7 1·3 3·0 1·1	**21** W	0157 0812 1426 2056	2·9 1·1 3·3 0·9
7 W	0346 0957 1606 2223	2·9 1·1 3·2 0·9	**22** Th	0308 0921 1529 2152	3·2 0·8 3·6 0·6
8 Th	0427 1037 1642 2255	3·2 0·9 3·4 0·7	**23** F	0403 1014 1620 2238	3·6 0·5 3·8 0·3
9 F	0501 1109 1715 2326	3·4 0·7 3·6 0·5	**24** Sa	0449 1102 1706 2320	3·9 0·2 4·0 0·1
10 Sa	0530 1140 1744 2354	3·6 0·5 3·7 0·4	**25** Su	0532 1146 1749 ●	4·1 0·0 4·1
11 Su	0558 1210 1812 ○	3·8 0·4 3·8	**26** M	0001 0612 1227 1831	0·0 4·3 0·0 4·0
12 M	0024 0627 1239 1841	0·3 3·9 0·3 3·8	**27** Tu	0041 0653 1309 1913	0·0 4·3 0·0 3·9
13 Tu	0052 0656 1309 1910	0·3 3·9 0·3 3·7	**28** W	0120 0734 1351 1955	0·1 4·2 0·2 3·7
14 W	0123 0728 1341 1941	0·3 3·9 0·4 3·7	**29** Th	0159 0818 1434 2039	0·3 4·0 0·5 3·5
15 Th	0154 0759 1418 2016	0·4 3·8 0·5 3·5	**30** F	0240 0903 1519 2127	0·6 3·7 0·7 3·2
			31 Sa	0324 0952 1610 2219	0·9 3·4 1·0 3·0

NOVEMBER

	Time	m		Time	m
1 Su	0413 1048 1708 2318	1·2 3·2 1·2 2·8	**16** M	0400 1026 1649 2302	0·9 3·6 0·9 3·1
2 M	0515 1153 1815)	1·4 3·0 1·4	**17** Tu	0506 1134 1758 (	1·1 3·4 1·0
3 Tu	0028 0634 1304 1934	2·7 1·5 2·9 1·4	**18** W	0015 0624 1245 1912	3·0 1·1 3·4 1·0
4 W	0144 0802 1416 2043	2·8 1·5 3·0 1·3	**19** Th	0130 0742 1355 2020	3·1 1·1 3·4 0·9
5 Th	0254 0910 1515 2135	2·9 1·3 3·1 1·1	**20** F	0239 0854 1500 2121	3·3 0·9 3·5 0·8
6 F	0345 0957 1600 2214	3·2 1·1 3·2 0·9	**21** Sa	0338 0953 1556 2213	3·6 0·7 3·6 0·6
7 Sa	0424 1037 1638 2249	3·4 0·9 3·4 0·7	**22** Su	0428 1044 1647 2259	3·8 0·5 3·7 0·5
8 Su	0458 1111 1712 2323	3·6 0·8 3·6 0·6	**23** M	0515 1130 1733 2343	4·0 0·4 3·8 0·4
9 M	0530 1144 1747 2356	3·8 0·6 3·7 0·5	**24** Tu	0557 1214 1817	4·1 0·3 3·8
10 Tu	0601 1217 1818 ○	3·9 0·5 3·7	**25** W	0024 0639 1256 1859	0·3 4·2 0·3 3·8
11 W	0028 0635 1252 1852	0·4 4·0 0·4 3·7	**26** Th	0104 0720 1338 1940	0·4 4·1 0·4 3·7
12 Th	0102 0710 1328 1928	0·4 4·0 0·4 3·7	**27** F	0144 0801 1419 2022	0·5 4·0 0·6 3·5
13 F	0138 0749 1409 2011	0·4 4·0 0·5 3·6	**28** Sa	0222 0843 1500 2103	0·6 3·8 0·7 3·4
14 Sa	0219 0833 1456 2058	0·5 4·0 0·6 3·4	**29** Su	0303 0925 1542 2148	0·8 3·6 0·9 3·2
15 Su	0305 0925 1548 2155	0·7 3·7 0·8 3·2	**30** M	0343 1010 1628 2237	1·0 3·4 1·1 3·1

DECEMBER

	Time	m		Time	m
1 Tu	0433 1101 1720 2332	1·3 3·2 1·3 3·0	**16** W	0449 1111 1730 (	0·9 3·7 0·8 3·4
2 W	0530 1158 1818)	1·5 3·1 1·4	**17** Th	0557 1214 1834	1·1 3·5 1·0
3 Th	0035 0642 1302 1924	2·9 1·6 3·0 1·4	**18** F	0056 0709 1321 1941	3·3 1·2 3·4 1·1
4 F	0142 0757 1406 2027	3·0 1·6 2·9 1·3	**19** Sa	0206 0825 1430 2049	3·4 1·2 3·3 1·0
5 Sa	0247 0904 1507 2124	3·1 1·4 2·9 1·2	**20** Su	0314 0934 1536 2152	3·5 1·1 3·3 1·0
6 Su	0341 0957 1557 2210	3·3 1·3 3·0 1·0	**21** M	0413 1033 1634 2245	3·7 0·9 3·4 0·8
7 M	0424 1041 1641 2252	3·5 1·2 3·4 0·8	**22** Tu	0504 1123 1725 2332	3·9 0·7 3·5 0·7
8 Tu	0504 1120 1720 2330	3·7 1·0 3·5 0·7	**23** W	0549 1207 1808	4·0 0·6 3·6
9 W	0542 1200 1800	3·9 0·7 3·6	**24** Th	0014 0629 1248 1849	0·6 4·1 0·5 3·7
10 Th	0010 0619 1239 1839	0·5 4·1 0·5 3·7	**25** F	0052 0709 1326 1927	0·6 4·1 0·5 3·7
11 F	0049 0700 1320 1921	0·4 4·2 0·4 3·8	**26** Sa	0130 0745 1402 2002	0·6 4·1 0·6 3·7
12 Sa	0130 0742 1404 2006	0·4 4·2 0·4 3·7	**27** Su	0205 0820 1437 2039	0·6 4·0 0·6 3·6
13 Su	0213 0827 1450 2054	0·4 4·2 0·4 3·7	**28** M	0240 0857 1512 2115	0·7 3·9 0·8 3·5
14 M	0300 0917 1539 2148	0·5 4·1 0·5 3·6	**29** Tu	0315 0932 1549 2155	0·9 3·7 0·9 3·4
15 Tu	0350 1012 1633 2245	0·7 3·9 0·7 3·5	**30** W	0353 1012 1628 2237	3·5 1·1 1·1 3·3
			31 Th	0437 1055 1713 2329	1·3 3·3 1·2 3·1

TIDAL DIFFERENCES PAGE 21:342.

Heights are referred to Chart Datum (approx. M.L.W.S.).

PLACE	TIME DIFFERENCES				HEIGHT DIFFERENCES (Metres)			
AND POSITION	High Water		Low Water		MHWS	MHWN	MLWN	MLWS
REYKJAVIK	0300 and 1500	0800 and 2000	0200 and 1400	0700 and 1900	4.0	2.9	1.3	0.2
FAEROE ISLANDS **Bordoy** Klaksvik .... (62°14′N 06°35′W)	+0345	+0345	+0345	+0345	−2.6	−2.1	−0.8	−0.2
Streymoy Torshavn.................. (62°00′N 06°45′W)	−0035	−0035	+0149	+0149	−3.7	−2.7	−1.2	−0.2
Vestmanna................ (62°09′N 07°10′W)	+0145	+0145	+0145	+0145	−2.0	−1.5	−0.7	−0.2
Sandoy Sandur .... (61°50′N 06°48′W)	+0100	+0100	+0100	+0100	−1.8	−1.5	−0.5	−0.2
Suduroy Vagur .... (61°28′N 06°48′W)	+0050	+0050	+0050	+0050	−3.0	−2.3	−0.9	−0.2
ICELAND **Vestmannaejyar** Heimaey................... (63°27′N 20°15′W)	−0044	−0044	−0044	−0044	−1.4	−1.0	−0.4	−0.1
Thorlakshofn............. (63°51′N 21°22′W)	−0032	−0032	−0032	−0032	−1.1	−0.9	−0.4	−0.1
Faxaflot Hafnarfjördhur .... (64°04′N 21°57′W)	+0004	+0004	+0004	+0004	0.0	−0.2	–	–
Hvammsvik .... (64°22′N 21°35′W)	+0001	+0001	−0003	−0003	+0.3	+0.3	+0.1	−0.1
Akranes .... (64°19′N 22°06′W)	+0002	+0002	−0001	−0001	0.0	0.0	−0.1	0.0
Breidafjördhur Stykkisholmur .... (65°05′N 22°42′W)	+0037	+0037	+0037	+0037	+0.6	+0.5	+0.3	0.0
Arnarfjördhur Bildudalur .... (65°41′N 23°36′W)	+0132	+0132	+0132	+0132	−1.0	−0.7	–	–
Sugandafjördhur Sudhureyri................ (66°08′N 23°32′W)	+0159	+0159	+0159	+0159	−1.3	−0.9	–	–
Eyjarfjördhur Akureyri .... (65°41′N 18°05′W)	+0415	+0415	+0405	+0405	−2.5	−1.7	−0.7	0.0
Husavik .... (66°02′N 17°21′W)	+0458	+0458	+0458	+0458	−2.4	−1.7	–	–
Thorshofn .... (66°12′N 15°20′W)	+0524	+0524	+0524	+0524	−2.7	−1.9	–	–
Borgafjördhur Bakkagerdi................ (65°31′N 13°49′W)	−0555	−0555	−0555	−0555	−2.4	−1.7	−0.6	−0.1
Seydisfjördhur Skalanes.................. (65°18′N 13°43′W)	−0500	−0500	−0500	−0500	–	–	–	–
Berufjördhur Djupivogur................ (64°39′N 14°18′W)	−0255	−0255	−0255	−0255	−2.1	−1.5	−0.7	−0.1
Ingolfshodfdi.............. (63°48′N 16°38′W)	+0005	+0005	+0005	+0005	–	–	–	–

Refer to predictions on pages 21:339-21:341

Visual Navigational Aids and Port Information

22

United Kingdom & Ireland

IMPORTANT — BEFORE USING THIS SECTION, CONSULT SECTION 1 AT FRONT OF ALMANAC, WHICH GIVES LATEST CORRECTIONS UP TO TIME OF GOING TO PRESS.

VISUAL NAVIGATIONAL AIDS IN REED'S

Aids are shown in geographical order, commencing at Lands End and proceeding anti-clockwise round England and Scotland, down the West Coast of England and Wales, and the Bristol Channel back to Lands End. Aids on the Irish Coast follow in the same anti-clockwise setting, commencing in the South at Fastnet. Then Europe, South to the Azores and North to the Baltic. The A-Z Index of Ports at the back of the Almanac enables the page number to be found at once for any particular place.

Each section has been compiled whenever possible in the order that the Navigator would find the Aids when approaching from seaward. Channels are laid out in number/name order starting from seaward, i.e. Fairway Buoy . . . No: 1 By . . . No: 2 By . . . Nonsuch By . . . etc. etc.

Reed's Nautical Almanac uses Admiralty List of Lights and Fog Signals as the prime source document. It may not be appreciated that ALLFS, rather than the charts give the latest known details of lights. ALLFS is corrected for all changes of lights of any significance more quickly than chart correcting notices.

Only those changes to lights which are both significant and permanent are promulgated by Notices to Mariners and charts may not be corrected for minor changes until the next New Edition or Revised Print. It is possible therefore that a change may be in Reed's which is not on your chart.

As we no longer publish details of general buoyage for the Continent, it is essential that you use the latest fully corrected charts for this purpose. This is especially the case in the inshore areas and in the Baltic where the geography is very complex.

How the information is arranged
The name of the light or buoy is given first – bold type for all lights – large bold type for lights of long nominal (luminous)

range such as lighthouses – medium type for unlit buoys. This is followed by the characteristic and colour of the light – all lights are white unless otherwise stated. The nominal (or luminous) range of the light is then given and the description of the structure and elevation in metres. Lastly come arcs of visibility, for and other signals, together with any other useful information.

e.g. **CAVA**
58°53′N 3°10′W Lt.Ho. Fl.W.R. 3 sec. W.10M. R.8M white octagonal Tr. 12m. W.351°-113°; R.113°-143°; W.143°-251°; R.251°-271°; W.271°-298°. Dia(4) 90 sec.

Interpretation
Lighthouse flashing white and red sectors every 3 seconds. White light visible 10 sea miles. Red light visible 8 sea miles. Structure white octagonal tower. Elevation of light 12 metres. Arc of visibility: white light 351°-113°; red light 113°-143°; white light 143°-251°; red light 251°-271°; white light 271°-298°. Fog horn diaphone 4 blasts every 90 seconds.

INTERNATIONAL SIGNALS FOR A PILOT
The following signals are to be made by any vessel requiring a Pilot:
By Day – The International Code flag G signifying 'I require a Pilot'.
At night – The International Code Signal G (– – •) by flashing or Sound.
This signal when displayed shall be deemed a signal for a pilot, and must only be used by vessels when a pilot is required.

UNIFIED SYSTEM OF PORT TRAFFIC SIGNALS
Mariners are reminded that a unified system of port traffic signals will be progressively introduced worldwide as and when new or revised signals are needed by a Port Authority. For fuller details see front of this Almanac.

IALA MARITIME BUOYAGE SYSTEM 'A'
(See colour plates at front of this Almanac)

The system

The system of buoyage provides the five types of marks described below which may be used in combination:

The significance of any mark depends upon one or more of the following features:

> By night — colour and rhythm of light.

> By day — colour, shape, topmark.

Lateral marks used in conjunction with a conventional direction of buoyage, generally used for well defined channels. These marks indicate the port and starboard sides of the route to be followed. Where a channel divides, a modified lateral mark may be used to indicate the preferred route.

Cardinal marks used in conjunction with the mariner's compass, indicate where the mariner may find navigable water.

Isolated Danger marks indicate isolated dangers of limited size that have navigable water all around them.

Safe Water marks indicate that there is navigable water all around their position, e.g. mid-channel marks.

Special marks not primarily intended to assist navigation but indicating an area or feature referred to in nautical documents.

NOTE. Trinity House buoys will change from acetylene to electric power. They will be fitted with solar panels which appear as dark patches.

CONVENTIONAL DIRECTION OF BUOYAGE

The conventional direction of buoyage may be defined in one of two ways:

The general direction taken by the mariner when approaching a harbour, river, estuary or other waterway from seaward, or

In other areas it is determined by the appropriate authority. In principle, it follows a clockwise direction around land masses.

The conventional direction is indicated in appropriate nautical documents

CONVENTIONAL

DIRECTION OF BUOYAGE

AROUND THE UK

The Direction of Buoyage in rivers and estuaries is from seaward inwards.

LATERAL MARKS

Port hand Marks		**Starboard hand Marks**	
Colour :	Red	Colour :	Green
Shape (Buoys) :	Cylindrical (can), pillar or spar	Shape (Buoys) :	Conical, pillar or spar
Topmark (if any) :	Single red cylinder (can)	Topmark (if any) :	Single green cone, point upward
Light (when fitted) :	Red, any other than composite group flashing (2+1)	Light (when fitted) :	Green, any other than composite group flashing (2+1)

At the point where a channel divides, when proceeding in the conventional direction of buoyage, a preferred channel may be indicated by modifying Port or Starboard lateral marks as follows:

Preferred channel to Starboard :		**Preferred channel to Port :**	
Colour :	Red with one broad green horizontal band	Colour :	Green with one broad red horizontal band
Shape (Buoys) :	Cylindrical (can), pillar or spar	Shape (Buoys) :	Conical, pillar or spar
Topmark (if any) :	Single red cylinder (can)	Topmark (if any) :	Single green cone, point upward
Light (when fitted) :	Red, Composite group flashing (2+1)	Light when fitted :	Green, Composite group flashing (2+1)

CARDINAL MARKS

The four quadrants (North, East, South and West) are bounded by the true bearings NW-NE, NE-SE, SE-SW, SW-NW, taken from the point of interest. A cardinal mark is named after the quadrant in which it is placed. The name of a cardinal mark indicates that it should be passed to the named side of the mark. It may be used:

to indicate that the deepest water in that area is on the named side of the mark

to indicate the safe side on which to pass a danger

to draw attention to a feature in a channel such as a bend, a junction, a bifurcation, or the end of a shoal

NORTH CARDINAL MARK:

Topmark :	2 black cones, one above the other, points upward.
Colour :	Black above yellow.
Shape :	Pillar or spar.
Light (when fitted) :	White, V.Qk.Fl. or Qk.Fl.

EAST CARDINAL MARK:

Topmark :	2 black cones, one above the other, base to base.
Colour :	Black with a single broad horizontal yellow band.
Shape :	Pillar or spar.
Light (when fitted) :	White, V.Qk.Fl.(3) every 5s or Qk.Fl.(3) every 10s

SOUTH CARDINAL MARK:

Topmark :	2 black cones, one above the other, points downward.
Colour :	Yellow above black.
Shape :	Pillar or spar.
Light (when fitted) :	White, V.Qk.Fl.(6) + long flash every 10s or Qk.Fl.(6) + long flash every 15s

WEST CARDINAL MARK:

Topmark :	2 black cones, one above the other, point to point.
Colour :	Yellow with a single broad horizontal black band.
Shape :	Pillar or spar.
Light (when fitted) :	White, V.Qk.Fl.(9) every 10s or Qk.Fl.(9) every 15s

ISOLATED DANGER MARK is a mark over an isolated danger which has navigable water all around it.

Topmark :	2 black spheres, one above the other.
Colour :	Black with one or more broad horizontal red bands.
Shape :	Pillar or spar preferred.
Light (when fitted) :	White, Gp.Fl.(2).

SAFE WATER MARKS indicate that there is navigable water all round the mark; these include centre line marks and mid-channel marks. Such a mark may also be used as an alternative to a cardinal or a lateral mark to indicate a landfall.

Colour :	Red and white vertical stripes.
Shape :	Spherical, pillar with spherical topmark or spar.
Topmark (if any) :	Single red sphere.
Light (when fitted) :	White, Isophase, occulting, one long flash every 10s or Morse A.

SPECIAL MARKS

Marks not primarily intended to assist navigation but which indicate a special area or feature referred to in appropriate nautical documents, e.g.

Ocean Data Acquisition Systems (ODAS) marks; Traffic Separation marks where use of conventional channel marking may cause confusion; Spoil Ground marks; Military Exercise Zone marks; Cable or pipe line marks; Recreation Zone marks.

Colour :	Yellow
Shape :	Optional but not conflicting with navigational marks (e.g. a yellow can buoy will not be used in a 'starboard' situation in region A).
Topmark (if any) :	Single yellow 'X' shape.
Light (when fitted) :	Yellow

NEW DANGERS

Used to describe newly discovered hazards not yet shown on charts, including naturally occurring obstructions such as sandbanks or rocks or man-made dangers such as wrecks.

New Dangers will be marked in accordance with these rules. In the case of an especially grave danger, one of the marks may be duplicated.

Any lighted mark used for this purpose shall have an appropriate cardinal or lateral V.Qk.Fl. or Qk.Fl. light character.

A duplicate mark will be identical to its partner in all respects. A duplicate mark may carry a racon, coded Morse D. The duplicate mark will be removed when the new danger has been sufficiently promulgated.

LIGHT CHARACTERISTICS

Abb.	Old Abb.		Period shown
F		FIXED a continuous steady light.	
		OCCULTING total duration of light more than dark and total eclipse at regular intervals.	
Oc.	Occ.	SINGLE OCCULTING steady light with eclipse regularly repeated.	
Oc.(2)	Gp.Occ.(2)	GROUP OCCULTING two or more eclipses in a group, regularly repeated.	
Oc.(2+3)	Gp.Occ. (2+3)	COMPOSITE GROUP OCCULTING in which successive groups in a period have different number of eclipses.	
Iso.		ISOPHASE a light where duration of light and darkness are equal.	
		FLASHING single flash at regular intervals. Duration of light less than dark.	
Fl.		SINGLE FLASHING light in which flash is regularly repeated at less than 50 flashes per minute.	
L.Fl.		LONG FLASHING a flash of 2 or more seconds, regularly repeated.	
Fl.(3)	Gp.Fl.(3)	GROUP FLASHING successive groups, specified in number, regularly repeated.	
Fl.(2+1)	Gp.Fl. (2+1)	COMPOSITE GROUP FLASHING in which successive groups in a period have different number of flashes.	

QUICK usually 50 or 60 flashes per minute.

Q.	Qk.Fl.	CONTINUOUS QUICK in which a flash is regularly repeated.
Q.(3)	Qk.Fl.(3)	GROUP QUICK in which a specified group of flashes is regularly repeated.
IQ	Int.Qk.Fl.	INTERRUPTED QUICK sequence of flashes interrupted by regularly repeated eclipses of constant and long duration.

VERY QUICK usually either 100 or 120 flashes per minute

VQ.	V.Qk.Fl.	CONTINUOUS VERY QUICK flash is regularly repeated.
VQ.(3)	V.Qk.(3)	GROUP VERY QUICK specified group of flashes regularly repeated.
IVQ.	Int.V.Qk.Fl.	INTERRUPTED VERY QUICK FLASH in groups with total eclipse at regular intervals of constant and long duration.

ULTRA QUICK usually 240 to 300 flashes per minute.

UQ.		CONTINUOUS ULTRA QUICK in which flash is regularly repeated.
IUQ.		INTERRUPTED ULTRA QUICK in groups with total eclipse at intervals of long duration.
Mo.(K)		MORSE CODE in which appearances of light of two clearly different durations are grouped to represent a character(s) in the Morse Code.
F.Fl.		FIXED AND FLASHING steady light with one brilliant flash at regular intervals.
Al.WR.	Alt.WR.	ALTERNATING a light which alters in colour in successive flashes.

SEA TRAFFIC SEPARATION ROUTES

The observance of these Traffic Separation Schemes, which are included in the International Collision Regulations is mandatory for British ships and any infringement renders Masters and Owners liable to prosecution. The following points should be noted: *(i) ships navigating in a traffic lane must proceed in the general direction of traffic flow for that lane; (ii) if they are crossing a lane then they must do so as nearly as practicable at right-angles to the general direction of traffic flow; (iii) they should not navigate in a separation zone except to cross it at right-angles; (iv) in connection with Deep Water Routes fishing vessels are reminded of the requirements of Rule 10(i) ('A vessel engaged in fishing shall not impede the passage of any vessel following a traffic lane'). Pleasure craft are reminded of Rule 10(j) i.e. 'A vessel of less than 20m in length or a sailing vessel shall not impede the safe passage of a power driven vessel following a traffic lane'.*

Ships proceeding in the proper fashion along a traffic lane do not have priority over crossing traffic, unless there are special local rules. The Steering and Sailing Rules covering encounters between vessels operate within a traffic separation scheme just as elsewhere. Thus, for example, if a crossing vessel has a through vessel on her starboard, the crossing vessel must give way, but in the reverse situation the crossing vessel should always stand on and the through ship give way.

If a ship needs to cross a lane she should always cross it at right-angles. Only where there are special circumstances which make it not reasonable practicable to cross at right-angles, such as for example the need to obey the Steering and Sailing Rules or very bad weather conditions, may a ship cross otherwise than at right-angles. Crossing at right-angles *(i) keeps the time the crossing vessel is in the lane to a minimum; (ii) leads to a clear encounter situation with through vessels..*

If the special circumstances of the case compel a ship to cross other than at right-angles, a master must judge the course to steer very carefully keeping in mind the density of traffic, speed in clearing the lanes, and clarity of encounter situation with through vessels.

Vessels entering and leaving traffic lanes should normally enter and leave the lanes at the extremities but where it is necessary to enter from the side this should be done at as small an angle as practicable.

Sailing craft with an auxiliary engine should use their engine if due to light or adverse winds they cannot otherwise comply with proper sailing procedures.

There are no special local rules modifying Collision Regulations in the Schemes described in this section. However, sailing vessels and other craft under 20m have unrestricted use of the inshore Traffic Zones. **ATTENTION IS DRAWN TO RULE 10.**

The routeing diagrams shown are intended only for rapid reference and illustrative purposes. For accurate details and changes that may have taken place since this Almanac went to press it is essential to consult the latest updated Admiralty chart.

FOG SIGNALS

Due to various factors, both atmospheric and mechanical fog signals cannot and should not be relied upon implicitly.

Most fog signals are now of the Horn (Electric) type although compressed air diaphone, siren, reed, explosive, morse letter combination i.e. • – (A) etc. will be found, also bells, gongs, and whistles which are mainly on buoys or pier heads.

Fog detector Lts, show over a specified arc and are usually F. or Fl.Blue.

LIGHT VESSELS

When out of position will show:
By day: Flag L.O. and B. Ball each end
By night: R.Lt. each end and if possible R/W Lts. or flares.
In fog: Signal for vessel at anchor will be given.
The number of manned Lt.V's is diminishing rapidly.

BEARINGS OF LIGHTS

BEARINGS OF LIGHTS ARE TRUE FROM SEAWARD.
ALL LIGHTS ARE WHITE UNLESS OTHERWISE STATED.
ALL HEIGHTS ARE GIVEN ABOVE HIGH WATER.

Range of lights see page 7:24.

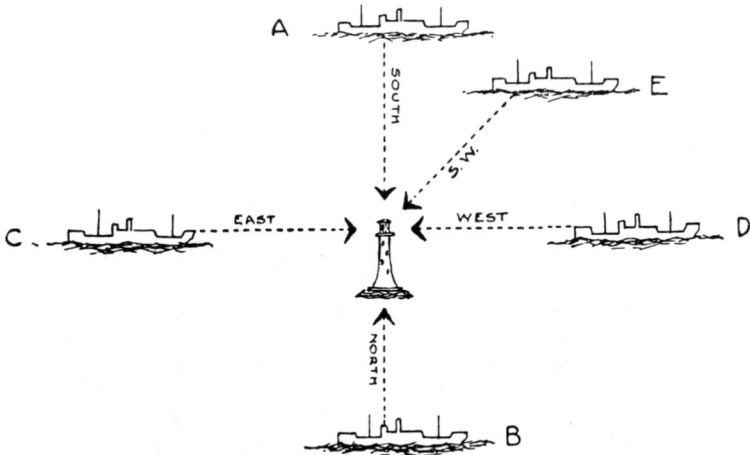

A shows a vessel from which a lighthouse bears S.
B shows a vessel from which a lighthouse bears N.
C shows a vessel from which a lighthouse bears E.
D shows a vessel from which a lighthouse bears W.
E shows a vessel from which a lighthouse bears S.W.

Remember the Bearing is always from the Ship
This sketch illustrates a lighthouse showing red sectors over off-lying rocks.

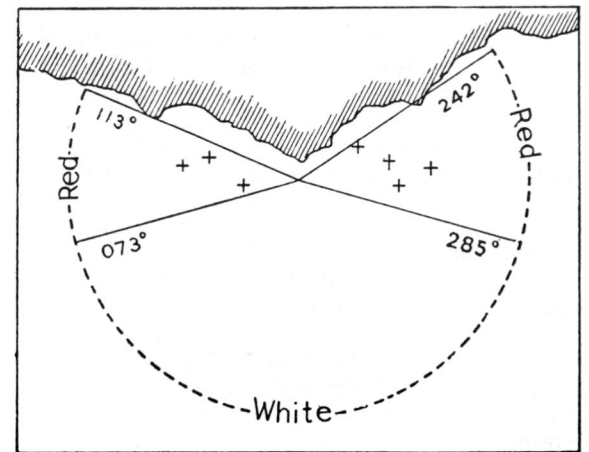

Shows Red 242° to 285°

Shows White 285°
through North to 073°

Shows Red 073° to 113°

EXERCISE AREAS

Naval Exercise Areas are marked on the charts. Extreme caution is necessary when proceeding through or near these areas, used for minelaying, clearing exercises etc.

Firing Practice Ranges and Exercise Areas are not shown on Navigational Charts. A general area is shown on a special series of 6 PEXA charts. Area indicated by DZ buoys or other marks, flags etc., also Fl.R. or F.R. Lts. Area may be patrolled by Range Safety Craft when in use.

Historic Wreck Sites – no one may enter, anchor, dive on or interfere in anyway unless specifically licensed.

Marine Farms which may be floating or fixed structures, and their associated moorings should be avoided. The charted positions of the farms are approximate, and further farms may be established without notice. The farms are generally marked by buoys or beacons, which may be lit.

WAYPOINTS

Reed's have devised a system of waypoints to assist the yachtsman in maximising the use of his position fixing system.

A series of offshore waypoints link to provide a ring road around the British Isles and the Continent; Inshore Waypoints (linked together with the Offshore Waypoints) bring the Mariner to within a short distance of the harbour; Harbour Waypoints are at/near the harbour/channel entrance.

Generally, we have endeavoured to give a clear course between all positions. Exceptionally the complexity of the coast line makes this difficult and the vessel will need to proceed "as safe nagivation permits" between some places/ positions.

The suggested routes are not necessarily the shortest route and the navigator may find one more to his liking. In the final analysis only the navigator can decide on the best and safest route to take.

The routes run from headland to headland, thence into bays, and in/out of ports and rejoin the main route. In some instances the offshore waypoint may coincide with the inshore/harbour waypoint where the harbour lies close to the main route.

Offshore waypoints appear near the main feature in the vicinity i.e. Land's End offshore waypoint will be close to Longships Lt. and Lizard offshore waypoint close to Lizard Lt. etc. Inshore waypoints are inserted where appropriate and in blocks together if this makes them clearer. Harbour waypoints are shown under the harbour heading.

The schematic diagram illustrates the principle, plotting all the points on your charts will fully illustrate the system.

Finally: CHECK BEFORE USING, only you can decide which waypoints suit your current/future requirements.

BRITISH & CONTINENTAL
WAYPOINTS SYSTEM

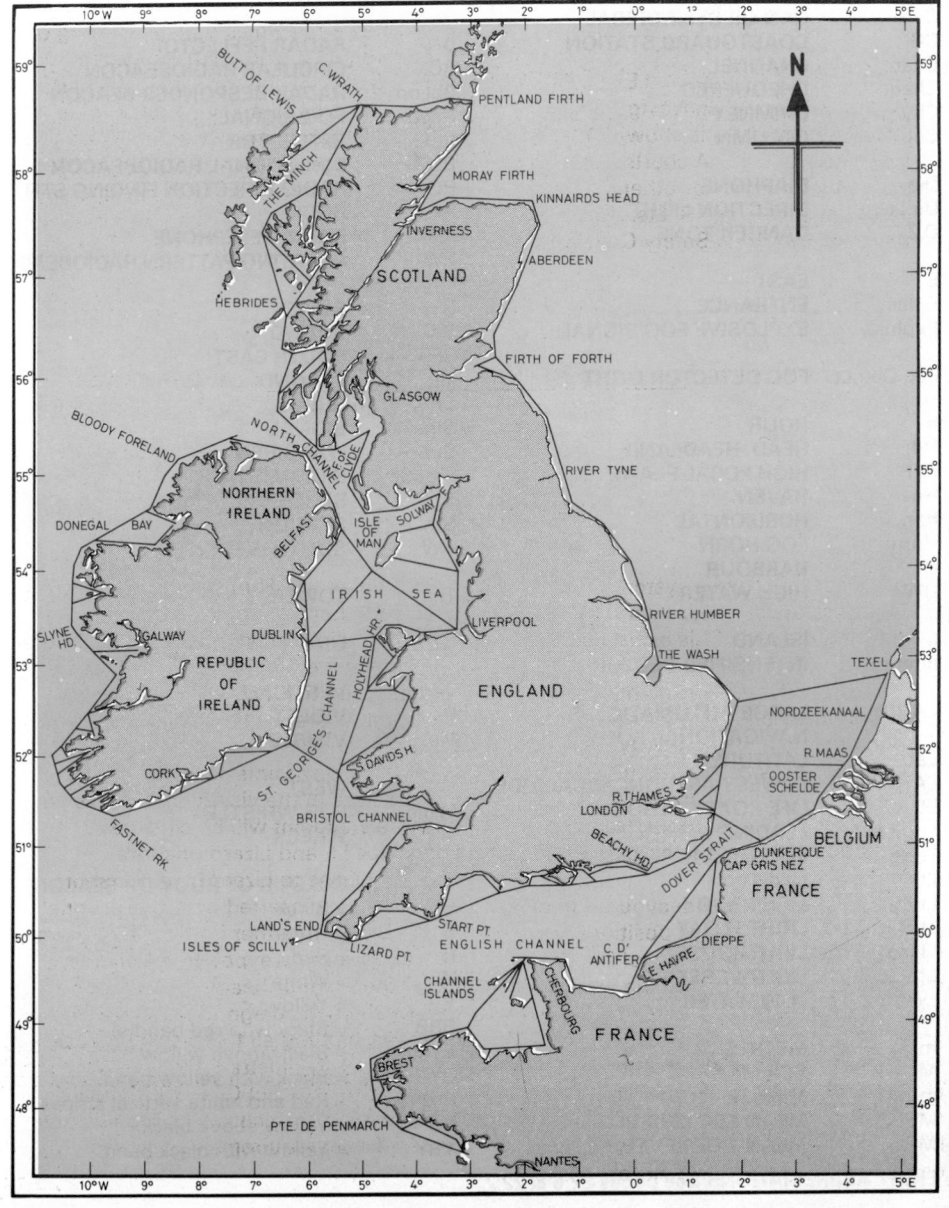

ABBREVIATIONS

Anche.	ANCHORAGE	N	NORTH
Apprs.	APPROACHES	NE	NORTH EAST
		NW	NORTH WEST
Bell ( ) sec.	AUTOMATIC BELL BUOY		
Bell w.a.	FOG BELL (WAVE ACTUATED)	obsc.	OBSCURED
Bk.	BANK	Occas.	OCCASIONAL
Bl. or Bu.	BLUE	Or.	ORANGE, AMBER OR YELLOW
Bn.	BEACON		
By.	BUOY	Pass.	PASSAGE
		Pt.	POINT
Can	CAN OR CYLINDRICAL		
CG	COASTGUARD STATION	ᴠᴜᴠ	RADAR REFLECTOR
Chan.	CHANNEL	RC.	CIRCULAR RADIOBEACON
Cheq.	CHEQUERED	Racon	RADAR RESPONDER BEACON
Chy.	CHIMNEY	Reed	FOG SIGNAL
Col.	COLUMN	Refl.	REFLECTOR
		RD	DIRECTIONAL RADIOBEACON
Dia.	DIAPHONE	RG	RADIO DIRECTION FINDING STN.
Dir.Lt.	DIRECTION LIGHT	Rk.	ROCK
D.Z.	DANGER ZONE	R/T	RADIO TELEPHONE
		RW	ROTATING PATTERN RADIOBEACON
E	EAST		
Entce.	ENTRANCE	S	SOUTH
Explos.	EXPLOSIVE FOG SIGNAL	Sd.	SOUND
		SE	SOUTH EAST
Fog Detr.Lt.	FOG DETECTOR LIGHT	sec.	SECOND
		Sh.	SHOAL
h	HOUR	Sig.	SIGNAL
Hd.	HEAD, HEADLAND	Siren	FOG SIREN
HFP	HIGH FOCAL PLANE	Sig. Stn.	SIGNAL STATION
Hn.	HAVEN	Sph.	SPHERICAL
hor.	HORIZONTAL	Stn.	STATION
Horn	FOG HORN	SW	SOUTH WEST
Hr.	HARBOUR		
HW	HIGH WATER	Tr.	TOWER
I.	ISLAND	(U)	UNWATCHED
Intens.	INTENSIFIED SECTOR		
		vert.	VERTICAL
LANBY	LARGE AUTOMATIC	Vi.	VIOLET
	NAVIGATIONAL BUOY	vis.	VISIBLE
Lat.	LATITUDE		
LAT	LOWEST ASTRONOMICAL TIDE	W	WEST
LB	LIFE BOAT STATION	Whis.	FOG WHISTLE
Ldg.Lts.	LEADING LIGHTS	Wk.	WRECK
Long.	LONGITUDE		
Lt.	LIGHT		COLOUR OF BUOY OR BEACON
Lt.By.	LIGHT BUOY	B	= Black
Lt.F.	LIGHT FLOAT	G	= Green
Lt.Ho.	LIGHTHOUSE	R	= Red
Lt.V.	LIGHT-VESSEL	W	= White
LW	LOW WATER	Y	= Yellow
		BRB	= Black with red band(s).
m	METRES	BY	= Black above yellow.
M	SEA MILE	BYB	= Black with yellow band.
min	MINUTE	RWVS	= Red and white vertical stripes.
MSL	MEAN SEA LEVEL	YB	= Yellow above black.
MTL	MEAN TIDE LEVEL	YBY	= Yellow with black band.

LIGHT ABBREVIATIONS See pages 22:6 & 22:7

NAVIGATIONAL AIDS AND PORT INFORMATION

ALL BEARINGS ARE TRUE FROM SEAWARD

GENERAL DOCUMENTATION RECOMMENDATIONS

Customs Form C.1328 (3 parts). H.M. Customs & Excise Notice No. 8. Part 1 Registry — Registrar of Shipping — Over 24m. Small Ships Register — RYA — Less than 24m. International Certificate of Pleasure Navigation. Certificate of Competence. Marine Insurance Certificate. Eurocheque Card. Passports. Vaccination Certificates. Charts, Almanacs, etc.

UNITED KINGDOM

Fly Flag 'Q' and report to Customs Office or request visit by telephone. Assistance may be possible via Port Radio (Harbour Master). Registration Document. Passports.

Entry by Road:

Ensure both craft and car are fully insured — incl. craft when in the water! Customs Form C1329 for temp. importation (up to 12 months). Speed limit when towing 50 mph (80 kmph) on open roads, 30 mph (50 kmph) in built up areas. Before using Inland Waterways contact Inland Waterways Assoc. for Information Tel: 071-586 2556.

ANIMALS — RABIES

It is not an offence to have a pet aboard a yacht or vessel, provided you do not take it outside U.K. waters.
If however you do so for even a very brief period, whether or not the animal is allowed to land, then it is an offence to land the animal or permit it to land without a license issued by M.A.F.F.
The animal must be securely confined in a locked/enclosed part of the vessel. The presence of the animal must be reported to the Port Health Authority and HM Customs BEFORE arrival.
Failure to comply with the regulations can result in heavy fines, imprisonment and destruction of the animal.

INLAND WATERWAYS

Most locks operate 0800-1700 winter, and 0800-1900 summer. Some especially sea or river locks operate 0600-2200 **BUT** these are approximate times only. Full particulars must be obtained from British Waterways (0923) 226422 or other authorities. Particular attention must be paid to meal times when Lock Keepers will not be available. One can assume that if the lock is fitted with VHF (when fitted use VHF Chan 16 & 74) then it is manned by a Lock Keeper. Otherwise "do it yourself".

SOUTH COAST OF ENGLAND

BISHOP ROCK 49°52.3'N, 6°26.7'W. Lt. Fl.(2) 15 sec. 29M. Granite Tr. 44m. Horn (N) 90 sec. Racon.
ROUND ROCK By. Pillar B.Y. Topmark N.
GUNNERS By. Pillar Y.B. Topmark S.
OLD WRECK By. Pillar B.Y. Topmark N.
Lt.By. Fl.(5) Y. 20 sec. Pillar 49°55'N, 6°40'W.
HISTORIC WRECK SITES
TEARING LEDGE. 49°52.2'N, 6°26.5'W. 200m radius.
ST. MARY'S SOUND. 49°54.26'N, 6°19.83'W. 100m radius.

ST. MARY'S (ISLES OF SCILLY) **R.G. STN.** 49°55.69'N, 6°18.17'W. Controlled by MRCC Falmouth. VHF Chan. 16, 67.

ST. MARY'S 49°54'N, 6°18'W. HM. Tel: (0720) 22768. Pilots: (0720) 22570.
HARBOUR WAYPOINT. 49°54.0'N, 6°17.0'W.
Radio — Port: VHF Chan. 16, 14. Summer 0800-1700: Winter Mon.-Fri. 0800-1700. Sat. 0800-1200.
P/Station: S of Penninis Lt.Ho. or W of Bishop Rock.
Anchorages: St. Mary's Pool, New Grimsby, Tresco Channel, Porthcouger, Watermill Cove, Porthcressa.
No visitors moorings available. 180 yachts may lie in St. Mary's Pool (Charge made). Berthing at Quay at HM direction only.

PENNINIS HEAD. Lt.Ho. Fl.20 sec. 20M. vis. 231° to 117°. Circular white metal Tr. 36m.

Lt. 2 F.R. Hor. on wind generator 1.3M. NE.
SPANISH LEDGE By. Pillar B.Y.B. Topmark E.
WOOLPACK Bn. Topmark S off St. Mary's
Island. N side St. Mary's Sound 7m.
BARTHOLOMEW LEDGES By. Can.R.

ST. MARY'S POOL Pier Lt. F.G. 3M. vis. 072°
to 192°, end of Pier.
ST. AGNES ISLAND Bn. Disused Lt.Ho.Tr.
23m.
HATS By. Pillar Y.B. Topmark S.
CROW ROCK Bn. Topmark Is. D. In Crow
Sound. 6m.

ROUND ISLAND 49°58.7'N, 6°19.3'W. Lt.
Fl. 10 sec. 24M. vis. 021° to 288° and between
islands. Circular white Tr. 55m. Horn (4) 60
sec. Radio Bn.
ST. MARTIN'S ISLAND Daymark Bn. R.W.Hor.
bands. Cylindrical with conical top on St.
Martin's Head. 56m.

SEVEN STONES 50°03.58'N, 6°04.28'W.
Lt.V. Fl.(3) 30 sec. 25M. Lt.Tr. amidships, name
in white on sides. 12m. Horn (3) 60 sec.
Racon.

WOLF ROCK 49°56.7'N, 5°48.4'W. Lt. Fl. 15
sec. 23M. Circular granite Tr. 34m. H24.
Racon.
Distress Sig. Nauto. 30 sec. Two mooring Bys.
2½ and 1 cable 059° from Lt.Ho.

OFFSHORE WAYPOINT LAND'S END.
50°03.0´N, 5°45.0´W.

LONGSHIPS 50°04'N, 5°44.8'W. Lt.
Iso.W.R. 10 sec. W.19M. R.18M. R.15M.
W.327°-189°, R.189°-327°. H24. Circular
granite Tr. 35m. highest Rk. off Land's End.
Horn 10 sec.

OFFSHORE WAYPOINT RUNNELSTONE.
50°00.0´N, 5°40.0´W.

RUNNELSTONE Lt.By. Q.(6) + L.Fl. 15 sec.
Pillar Y.B. Topmark S. Bell. Whis.
RUNNELSTONE LOW Bn. Conical R. On
Gwennap Head. Storm Sig. Stn. 6m.
RUNNELSTONE HIGH Bn. B.W. On Gwennap
Head. Square base cone top. 10m.

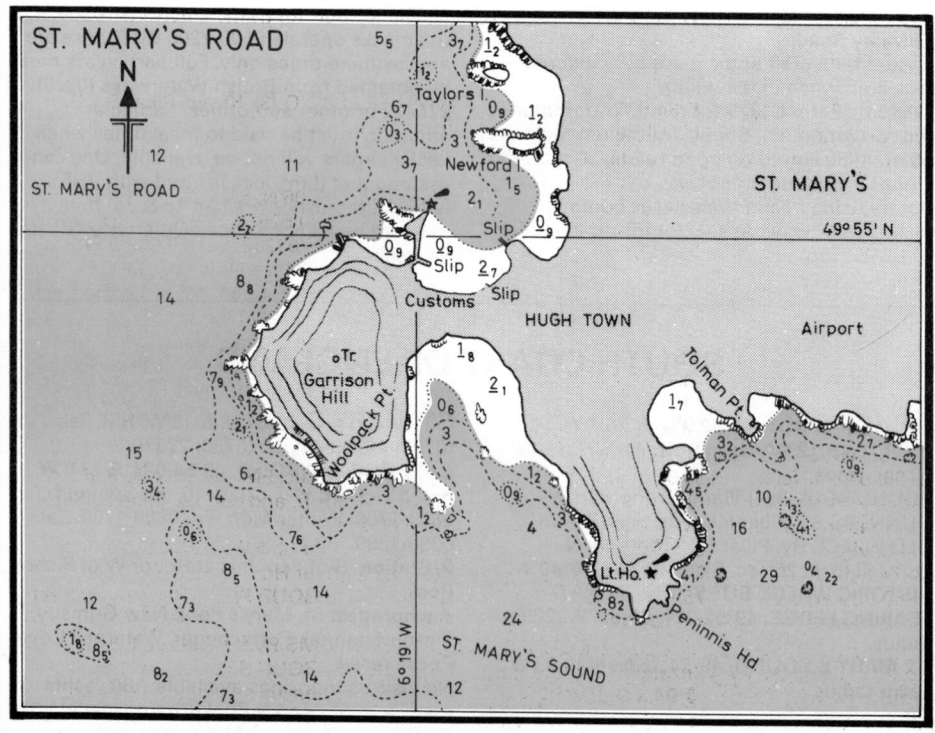

SEA TRAFFIC SEPARATION ROUTES

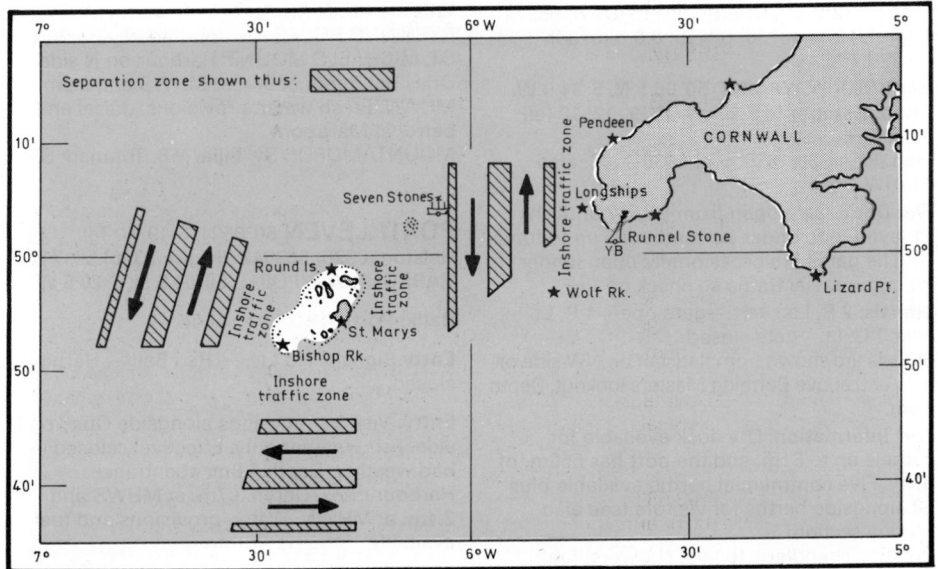

OFF LAND'S END, SOUTH AND WEST OF THE ISLES OF SCILLY. All traffic lanes 3M. wide.

TATER-DU 50°03.1′N, 5°34.6′W. Lt. Fl.(3) 15 sec. 23M. vis. 241° to 074°. White round Tr. 34m. Horn(2) 30 sec.
Same structure F.R. 14M. vis. 060° to 074° over Runnelstone and in places 074° to 077° within 4M.

MOUNTS BAY

Pilotage (for Newlyn, Penzance etc.) Office. Tel: (0736) 66113, 62523, 0900-1700; (0736) 61119, 61017 O.O.H. Fax: (0736) 51614.
Boarding Service: (0736) 60055, (0860) 500756, 0900-1700; (0736) 740025 O.O.H. Fax: (0736) 67024. Telex: 45530 JHB G.
Radio — Pilots: VHF Chan. 16, 9, 12. Information provided on vessel movements and navigational matters.
HISTORIC WRECK SITES
(1) 50°03.4′N, 5°17.1′W. 75m. radius. (2) 50°02.33′N, 5°16.4′W. 75m. radius.

MOUSEHOLE. Tel: Penzance 731511.
HARBOUR WAYPOINT. 50°04.5′N, 5°31.0′W.
Entry: Enter from westward. Hr. dries out at LW Springs. Depths 2.7m. at MHWS & 1.8m. at MHWN. Rocks at back of both piers.
PIER. Lts. 2 F.G.vert. on N Pier Head. 4M. 6m. and 5m. R.Lt. shown instead when Hr. closed.

LOW LEE Lt.By. Q.(3) 10 sec. Pillar B.Y.B. Topmark E.

NEWLYN 50°06′N, 5°32′W. Tel: H.M. Penzance (0736) 62523, 61017 O.O.H. Berthing Master: (0736) 763362. Fax: (0736) 51614. Lookout Stn. (0736) 61146.
Radio — Port: VHF Chan. 16, 9, 12. Mon.-Fri. 0800-1700. Sat. 0800-1200.
Visitors moorings: o'night only on W side centre jetty, clear of fishing vessels. Depth 3m. at LW Springs. Approaches dredged to 2.4m.

S.Pier Lt. Fl. 5 sec. 9M. vis. 253° to 336°. Circular white Tr. and cupola. Base R. 10m. Siren 60 sec.
NEWLYN N Pier Lt. F.W.G. 2M. G. 238° to 248°. White over Hr.
NEWLYN HARBOUR PIER F.R. on old (inner) Pier Head.
MARY WILLIAMS PIER HEAD Lt. 2 F.R.
NEWLYN HARBOUR Slipway for repair of vessels commences at base of S Pier and extends for distance of 122m. in an approximate NE'ly direction.
NEWLYN HARBOUR By. Spar. R.
GEAR ROCK Bn. Topmark Is. D. 12m. W side apprs. Penzance.

PENZANCE 50°07'N, 5°32'W. Tel: Harbour Master: Penzance (0736) 66113. (Day) 61119 (Night): Berthing Master: 66113 (Day), 65974 (Night).Pilots: (0736) 67415: 0.0 h (0736) 796829.

HARBOUR WAYPOINT. 50°06.5'N, 5°31.0'W. Radio: Harbour VHF Chan. 16, 9, 12, 10 (oil pollution)
Mon.-Fri. 0830-1630. Sat. 0830-1230. also 2 h-HW-1 h.

Wet Dock: Gate open from HW –2 until HW +1, every tide under all conditions up to force 10. The gates are occasionally open longer for commercial traffic so check on VHF.

Signals: 2 R. Lts. vert.—gate open. 1 R. Lt. over 1 G. Lt.—gate closed.
Signals are shown from flagstaff on NW side of gate ent. above Berthing Masters lookout. Depth 4.5m.

Port Information: Dry dock available for vessels up to 61m. and the port has 550m. of quay. Five commercial berths available plus 50 alongside berths for visitors (see also Marina section).
Repairs, chandlery, toilets, showers, fuel (2 h-HW) and office hrs. available.

Anchorage: (Fair weather) E of Albert Pier.

PENZANCE BAY. Anchorages 3c. SE of Newlyn. S Pier in 7m. or 7c. E of Newlyn. S Pier in 15m. or 3c. SE of The Gear in 12.5m.

SOUTH PIER HEAD. Fl. W.R. 5 sec. W.17M. R.12M. 11m. R.159°-268°; W.268°-344½°; R.344½°-shore. White circular Tr. with B. base

ALBERT PIER HEAD. 2 F.G. vert. 2M. R.Col. 11m.
WET DOCK, N ARM. Lt. 2 F.R. vert. 2M. Col.
RYEMOND ROCKS Bn. Topmark S.
ST. MICHAELS MOUNT: Harbour on N side. Dries but depth of 3m. at MHWS and 2.0m. at MHWN. Fresh water, provisions, diesel and petrol at Marazion.
MOUNTAMOPUS By. Pillar Y.B. Topmark S.

PORTHLEVEN 50°05'N, 5°19'W. Tel: Helston (0326) 563042. (Night (0326) 561710).
HARBOUR WAYPOINT. 50°04.5'N, 5°20.5'W.

Radio Port: VHF Chan. 16 occas.

Entry Signals: No Lts. — Red Ball — Harbour closed.

Entry: Visitors moorings alongside Quay on E side. Fair weather only. Effectively closed in bad weather. Depth 1.8m. at entrance. Harbour dries. Depth 3.7m. at MHWS and 2.4m. at MHWN. Water, provisions and fuel available.

S. Pier Lt. F.G. 4M. G.Col. 10m. shown when inner Hbr. open.

Inner Harbour Lt. F.G. 4M. on Stonewall 10m. 033°-067° shown when required for vessels entering.

OFFSHORE WAYPOINT LIZARD. 49°55.0'N, 5°12.0'W.

HISTORIC WRECK SITE. 49°58.5'N, 5°14.45'W. 100m. radius.

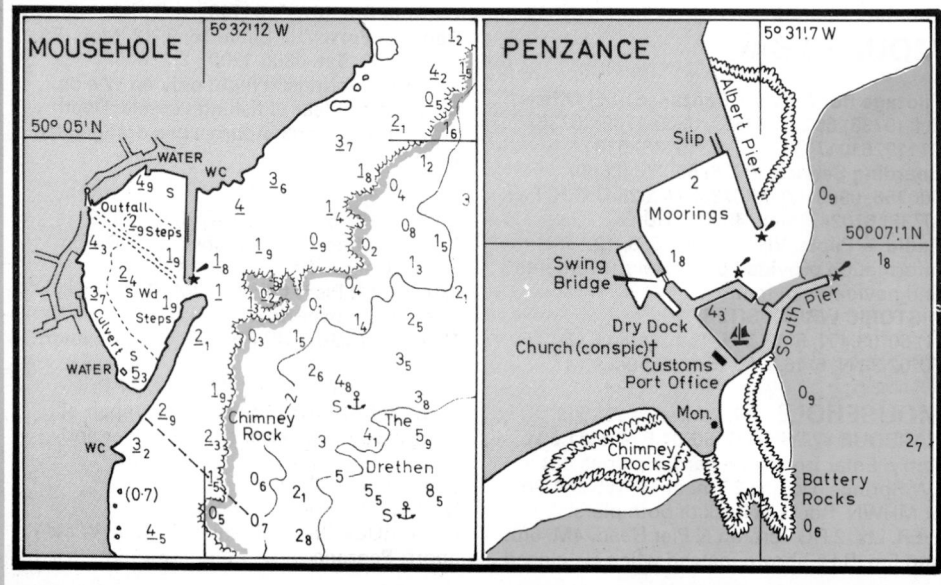

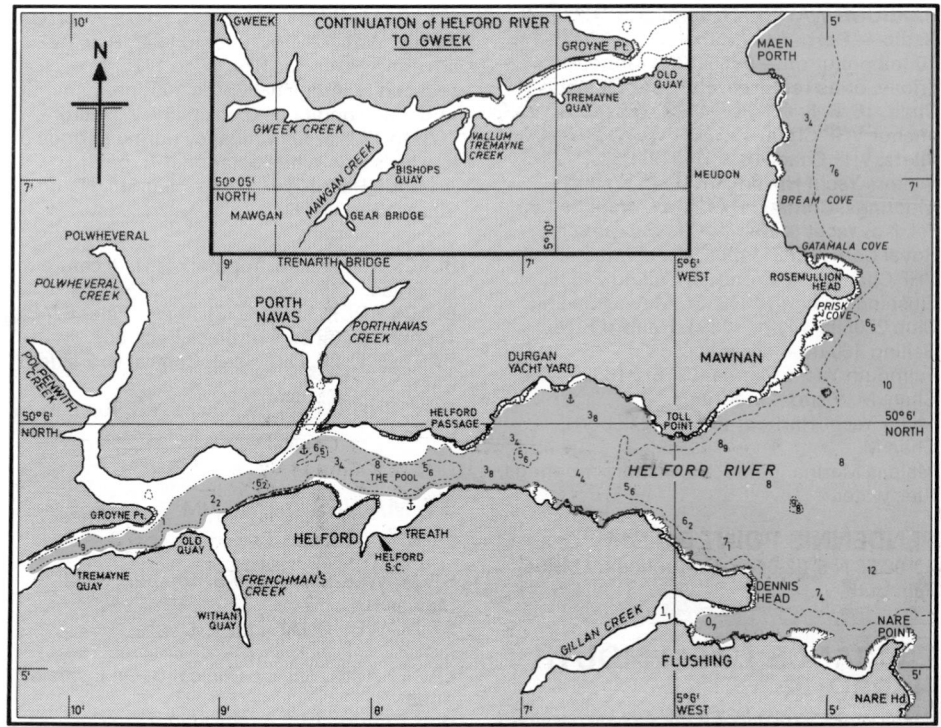

LIZARD 49°57.6′N, 5°12.1′W.

Lt.Ho. Fl. 3 sec. 29M. Octagonal white Tr. ½M. E Lizard Head, on cliff. 70m. Lloyd's Sig.Stn. Siren Mo(N) 60 sec. Calibration Stn. R.C.

VROGUE, N Bn. R.W. vert. stripes. Oblong, on Bass Point Lizard.

VROGUE, S Bn. R.W. vert. stripes. Oblong, Storm Sig.Stn. 2m.

INSHORE WAYPOINT OFF MANACLES RK. 50°02.75′N, 5°01.5′W.

MANACLES. Lt.By. Q.(3) 10 sec. Pillar B.Y.B. Topmark E. Outside Rk. off Manacle Point ↯ Bell w.a.

CULDROSE TIP. Lt.By. Fl.Y. 10 sec. Sph. Y. Bell. SE of Manacles.

LOWLAND POINT. Lt.By. Fl.(2)R. 10 sec. SE of Manacles. Bell ↯.

AUGUST ROCK Lt.By. Fl.G. 5 sec.

INSHORE WAYPOINT OFF HELFORD RIVER. 50°05.75′N, 5°01.5′W.

HELSTON Lt.By. Fl.Y. 2½ sec. 091° distant 2-6 miles from Nare East Point. Conical Y.

HELFORD RIVER

HARBOUR WAYPOINT. 50°05.75′N, 5°05.0′W.
Entry: Bar. One mile inside river Bar stretches halfway across channel from Passage Pt. indicated by telegraph cable notice board on North shore, leaving 2-7m. in the narrow channel along the South side. Harbour is available at all times. 3.6-11m. inside Bar. Vessels awaiting tide to cross Bar can anchor off Durgan, a good berth according to wind. Tidal stream runs 1 h after H. and L.W. Visitors moorings: Durgan, Helford, Port Navas, Gweek.
Approach. To clear the Gedges keep Pennance Pt. well open of Rosemullion Pt. until Poshan Pt. on South side of ent. is well open of Mawnan Chair on North side, then stand in.
DENNIS HEAD. By. Pillar B.Y.B. Topmark W.
THE VOOSE. By. Pillar B.Y. Topmark N.
THE POOLE. By. Conical G.

MRCC FALMOUTH (0326) 317575. Weather broadcast ev. 4 h from 0140.

FALMOUTH 50°08′N 5°01′W. Tel: Falmouth
(0326) 312285 & 314379. Telex: 45349
FALHAR G. Pilots: (0326) 211376 Mon./Fri. 9-5: (0836) 661668 other times.

HARBOUR WAYPOINT. 50°08.5′N, 5°01.5′W.
Radio — Port: VHF Chan. 16, 11, 12, 13, 14, 10 (oil pollution)—0900-1700 Monday to Friday, or as required. Harbour Launch VHF Chan. 16, 6, 8, 10, 12, 14, 73. Vessels at anchor VHF Chan. 16.
Pilots: VHF Chan. 16, 9, 11, 12. H24.
Visitors Yacht Haven and Deep Water Moorings. Contact: H.M. Max. draught 1.8m. Tel. No. Yacht Clubs:
Royal Cornwall 311105. Launch meets visitors VHF Chan M. Restronquet Sailing 74536. Flushing Sailing 74043. St. Mawes Sailing Club 270686. Mylor 74391. Helford River Sailing 460 (Manaccan).
Falmouth Yacht Marina (0326) 316620. VHF Chan. M. Visitors moorings.
Mylor Yacht Harbour (0326) 72121. VHF Chan M.
Malpas Marina, pontoons, visitors moorings, fuel, water.

PENDENNIS POINT RG Stn.
50°08.68′N 5°02.66′W. Controlled by MRCC Falmouth.

ENTRANCE TO FALMOUTH HARBOUR
INSHORE WAYPOINT SE OF ST. ANTHONY HEAD. 50°06.5′N, 4°56.0′W.

ST. ANTHONY 50°08.4′N, 5°00.9′W. Lt. Oc. 15 sec. W.R. 22M. W. 295° to 004°, R. to 022°, covering Manacles Rks. W. to 172°. W. sector reduced in intensity 022° to 100° permanently under all conditions of visibility. W. sector 100° to 172° at full brilliancy during periods of low visibility. White octagonal Tr. on St. Anthony Head. 22m. Lloyd's Sig.Stn. Nauto 30 sec. Shown H24.

BLACK ROCK Bn.B. Topmark Is.D. in centre of Hr. Entce.
BLACK ROCK. Lt.By. Q.(3) 10 sec. Pillar B.Y.B. Topmark E. Close E of Black Rock Bn.
CASTLE. Lt.By. Fl.G. 1sec. Conical G. E side of Chan.
GOVERNOR (THE) By. Pillar B.Y.B. Topmark E.

ST. MAWES. Tel. No. HM. St. Mawes 270553.

ST. MAWES By. Pillar Y.B. Topmark S. Off St. Mawes Hr.
ST. MAWES QUAY. Lt. 2 F.R. vert.

EAST NARROWS By. Conical G. On E side of Chan
WEST NARROWS Lt.By. Fl.(2)R. 10 sec. Can.R. On W side of Chan.

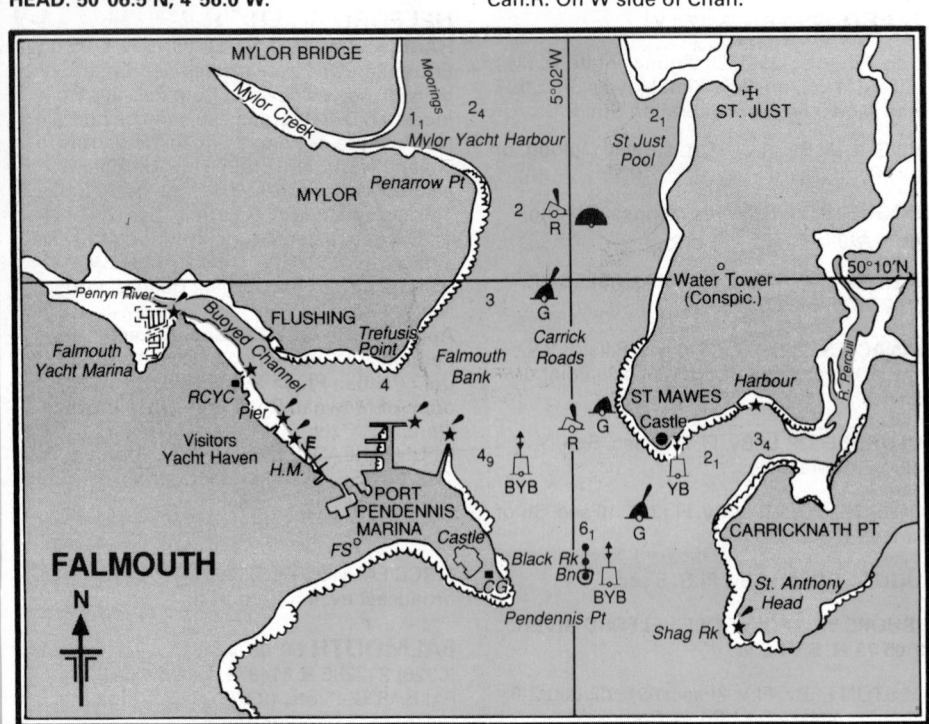

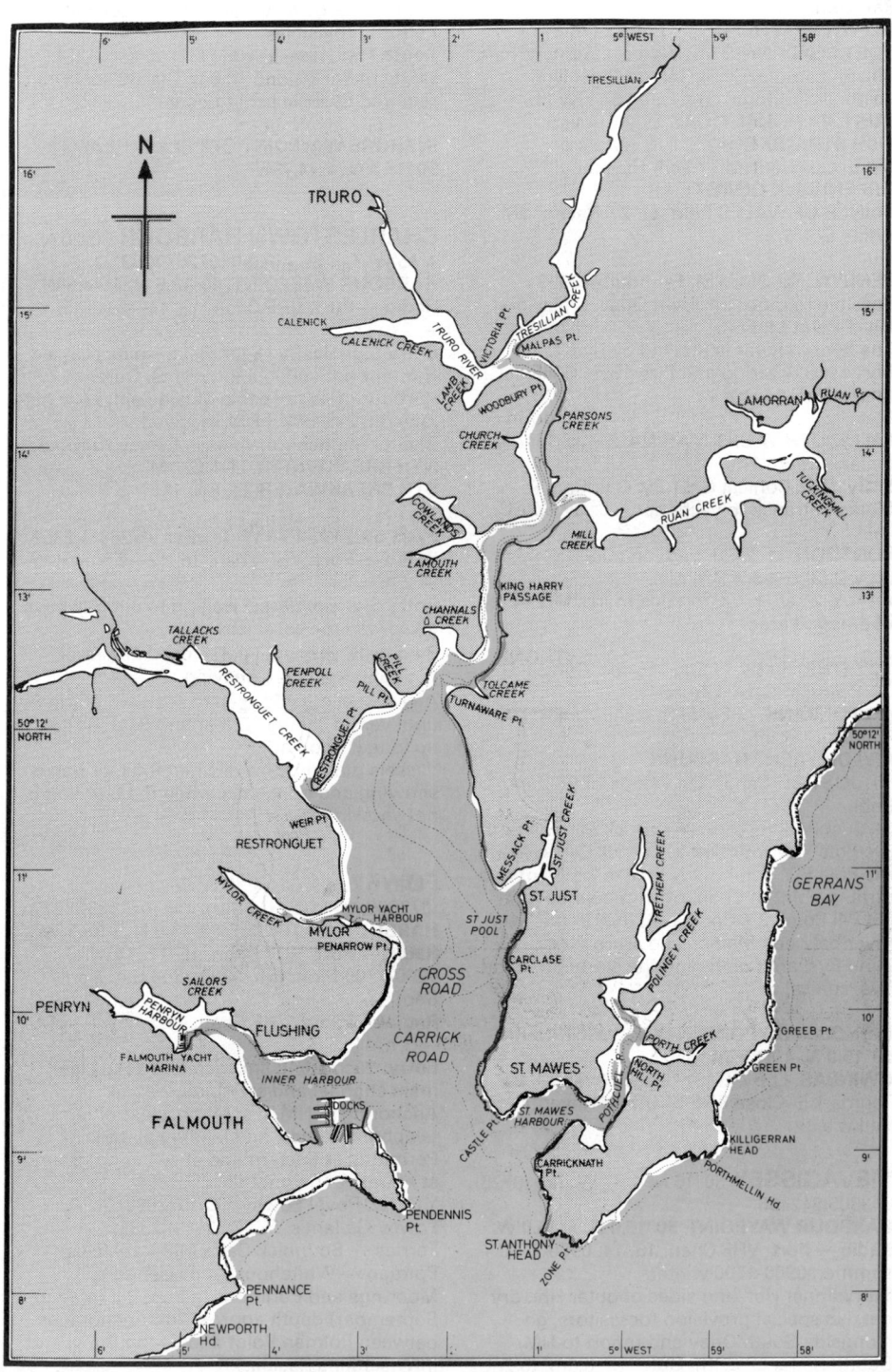

EAST BREAKWATER HEAD. Lt. Fl.R. 2 sec. 3M. 20m.
NORTH ARM HEAD. Lt. Q. 3M. 20m.
PORT PENDENNIS MARINA at County Wharf. Village complex with 70 moorings. No visitors moorings. Lock open 3h-HW-3h.
CUSTOM HOUSE QUAY. Lt. 2 F.R. vert.
FISH STRAND QUAY. 2 F.R. vert. North Quay. Visitors Yacht Haven.
GREENBANK QUAY. Lt. F.R.
PRINCE OF WALES PIER. Lt. 2 F.R. vert. 3M. White Col. 6m.

PENRYN. Tel. No. HM. Falmouth 73352. Possible to moor on Town Quay. Check first.
No. 1 Point Lt. Fl.R.
The Penryn River is marked by Bys. Can.R. on port hand entering and three Bys. Conical G. on starboard hand.

FALMOUTH YACHT MARINA above Boyers Cellars. Depth 2m.
Lt.By. Q.G. Conical G. **Lt.By.** Q.R. Can. R. Marks Entrance to yacht hbr.

PONTOON. Lt. 2 F.R. vert. on pile.
Lt. V.Q.(3) 5 sec. ⊕ B.Y. pile.
Lt. Fl.Y. 2 sec. Y. "X" on pile marks NW limit of dredged area.

VILT (THE). Lt.By. Fl.(3)G. 15 sec. Conical G. On E side of Carrick Road.
NORTH BANK. Lt.By. Fl.R. 4 sec. Can.R. Off Penarrow Point.
MYLOR YACHT HARBOUR.
ST. JUST By. Can.R. On W side of St. Just Pool.
St. Just Pool to Truro — Carrick Carlys South Bn. Pole Y.B. Topmark S. Carrick Carlys North Bn. Pole B.Y. Topmark N. marks E side of and turning point of Chan. off Turnaware Point. Off Pill Point. 3 × Conical G. Bys. In the Truro River between Malpas and Truro the port hand Bys. are Can.R. and the starboard hand Bys. conical G.

INSHORE WAYPOINT NE OF GWINEAS RK.
50°15.0′N, 4°44.0′W.
GWINEAS. Lt.By. Q.(3) 10 sec. Pillar B.Y.B. Topmark E. Close ENE of Goran Haven. ⌇⌇ Bell w.a.

MEVAGISSEY 50°16′N, 4°47′W. Tel: (0726) 843305/842496.
HARBOUR WAYPOINT. 50°16.0′N, 4°46.0′W.
Radio — Port: VHF Chan. 16, 14. 0900-2100 summer, 0900-1700 winter.
Entry: Inner Hbr. and sides of outer Hbr. dry out. No special provision for visitors, go alongside South Quay and report to HM. Depth: Entrance 2.1m. Outer Hr. 0.5m. to 2m.

with 4.3m. at MHWS, 3m. at MHWN at centre of inner Harbour. Water, Fuel (Diesel and Petrol), provisions.
South Pier Head. Lt.Ho. Fl.(2) 10 sec. 12M. White metal 8-sided Tr. 9m. Dia. 30 sec. when required by local fishing boats.

INSHORE WAYPOINT OFF BLACKHEAD.
50°17.5′N, 4°44.75′W.

CHARLESTOWN HARBOUR 50°20′N, 4°45′W. Tel: St. Austell (0726) 73331/2.
HARBOUR WAYPOINT. 50°19.5′N, 4°44.5′W.
Radio — Port: VHF Chan. 16, 14—2 h — H.W. — 2 h.
Entry Signals: By Night: R. Lt.—gates closed. Harbour not suitable for yachts. Outer Harbour dries to ½ cable outside ent. Lock gate lowered 2 h.-HW if ETA received. Shelter in onshore winds in Fowey Harbour.
NTH BREAKWATER. Lt. F.G. 1M.
STH BREAKWATER. Lt. F.R. 1M.

PAR 50°21′N 4°43′W. Tel: Par (072681) 2281.
Radio — Port: VHF Chan. 16, 12—2 h — H.W. — 2 h.
Entry Signals: Vessel waiting to enter always gives way to vessel leaving.
By day: R. shape ⎫ port closed or vessel
By night: R. Lt. ⎰ leaving
Any vessel outside keep to seaward of the By. until vessel sailing is clear and R. Lt. or flag no longer shown.
Vessels may only leave when R. Lt. or flag is showing and only enter when R. Lt. or flag is not showing.

FOWEY 50°20′N 4°39′W. Tel: Fowey (072683) 2471/2. HM Customs (072683) 3777.
HARBOUR WAYPOINT. 50°19.0′N, 4°38.5′W.
Radio — Port: VHF Chan. 16, 12, 14. Hrs. 0900-1700 Mon.-Fri., 0900-1200 Sat. April-Sept.
Radio — Pilots: VHF Chan. 16, 9. 2 h. — ETA — 1 h.
Entry: Yachts and small craft to keep clear main channel and swinging ground. Anchoring at HM. discretion, clear of fairway, telephone cables, and landing places. Permitted at Eastern end of swinging ground at entrance to Pont Pill.
Y.C. Tel: Royal Fowey Y.C. (072683) 3573. Fowey Gallant's Y.C. (072683) 2335.
Ferries — Bodnnick-Caffa Mill = vehicles; Polruan — Whitehouse = passengers. Moorings and Pontoons in Pont Pill (May to September) depth approx. 2m. Anchorages between Polman Point and Swing Buoy, and in Wisemans Reach.

Landing at Fowey and Polruan Town Quays. Water available at both quays also on pontoon at Albert Quay.

Main channel dredged to 7m. as far as Mixtow. Beyond Wisemans Reach river is tidal and dries at LW. Visitors moorings on pontoons opposite Albert Quay and at Pont Pill. Also on buoys at Pont Pill and Penleath Point. Marked FHC visitor and painted Y. or W. Fuel by can from garages or by hose from Polruan Quay (Tidal). Refuse skip at head of Pont Pill. Tidal stream about 3 kts. at mid ebb. Speed limits 6 knots. Fuel — barge Fowey Refueller available 0900-1800 daily (Mon-Fri. in winter). VHF Chan. 16. Tel. 0836 519341. An out of hours service is possible by prior arrangement (Polruan 697 for out of hours emergencies).

FOWEY. Lt.Ho. Fl. 5 sec. W.R. W.11M. R.9M. White octagonal Tr. R. lantern. W entce. to Hr. 28m. R.284°-295°; W.295°-028°; R.028°-054°.
WHITEHOUSE POINT. Lt.Iso.W.R.G. 3 sec. W.11M. R.8M. G.8M. G.017°-022°; W.022°-032°; R. 032°-037°. Conspicuous R. iron Col. 11m.
N. PIER HEAD. Lt. 2 F.R. vert. 8M. R.Col. 4m. Ferry slip breakwater.
CAIRN ROCK By. Can.R. marks Port side Chan. SE of Lower Cairn Point.
UDDER ROCK By. Pillar Y.B. Topmark S. Rock dries 0.6m at L.W. Bell w.a.
GRIBBIN HEAD Daymark R.W. bands Tr. on Gribbin Head W of Fowey. 104m.
CANNIS. Lt.By. V.Q.(6) + L.Fl. 10 sec. Pillar Y.B. Topmark S. ⌇⌇ Cannis Rk. dries 4.3m. Bell w.a.

INSHORE WAYPOINT OFF CANNIS RK.
50°18.0′N, 4°39.5′W.
INSHORE WAYPOINT OFF POLPERRO.
50°18.75′N, 4°32.0′W.

POLPERRO 50°20′N, 4°31′W. Tel: (0503) 72417
HARBOUR WAYPOINT. 50°19.5′N, 4°31.0′W.
Entry Signals:

By day: 1 B. ball ⎫ harbour closed in bad
By night: 1 R. Lt. ⎬ weather. Storm gates put
⎭ across

Harbour dries. Depth MHWS 3.4m. MHWN 1.5m. In SE/S winds, hr. is closed by gate to protect it from the swell.
Anchorage: Outside piers.
Fuel and water available inside hr.
Measured Distance: 1 mile (a) front bn. 54.5m; rear bn. 101m. (b) front 91m. rear 103m. W. with B. vert. stripe. Course 096°—276° (Mag.). Lts. shown occasionally from these bns. between Polperro and Looe.

W. pair close E of Talland Ch; E pair ½ mile NW of Hannanfore Pt.
R. fixed Lts. shown from batteries nr. Bovisand when night firing taking place.
W. PIER HEAD. Lt. F.W. or R. 4M. Stone structure Bl. top Head of tidal basin. 4m.

INSHORE WAYPOINT OFF LOOE. 50°18.75′N, 4°28.0′W.

LOOE 50°21′N, 4°27′W. Tel: Looe 2839 (Night: 2647).
HARBOUR WAYPOINT. 50°20.0′N, 4°25.5′W.
Entry: Visitors moorings on Quay on Port side. Harbour dries. Speed limit 5 kts. – Tide can reach 5 kts. at Springs.
Maximum draught 2.9m. Depth at West Quay 2.6 to 3.5m. at MHWS; 1.4 to 2.3m. MHWN. At East Quay 3.4 to 4.0m. at MHWS: 2.3 to 2.8m. MHWN.
Provisions, water, fuel (diesel and petrol) available.
R. Flag displayed from jetty when conditions outside hr. unsuitable for boats or when tide ebbing.
PIER Lt. Oc.W.R. 3 sec. W. 15M. R. 12M. W.013°-207°; R.207°-267°; W.267°-313°; R.313°-332°. R. iron Col. 8m.
NAIZLEE POINT. Fog Sig. Siren(2) 30 sec.
MIDMAIN Lt.Bn. Fl.(3) 10 sec. 2M. B.Y.B. Topmark E.
James Eagan Layne Wreck By. Can. R.

EDDYSTONE ROCK 50°10.8′N, 4°15.9′W. Lt. Fl.(2) 10 sec. 24M. Granite Tr. with R. lantern 41m. Helo. Platform. Aux. Lt. F.R. 13M. 28m 112°-129°. Fog signal. Horn. (3) 60 sec. Racon.
Lt.By. Fl.R. 10 sec. Pillar R.Y. vert. stripes 50°07′N, 4°30′W. 10M. ⌇⌇ SW of Eddystone Rks.

INSHORE WAYPOINT OFF RAME HD.
50°18.0′N, 4°13.5′W.

RAME HEAD R.G. STN. 50°19.0′N 4°13.1′W. Controlled by MRSC Brixham.

INSHORE WAYPOINT OFF PLYMOUTH SOUND. 50°18.0′N, 4°09.0′W.
HISTORIC WRECK SITE. RAME HEAD.
50°18.96′N, 4°11.57′W. 150m. radius.
HMS CAMBRIDGE (WEMBURY POINT GUNNERY RANGE) 50°19′N, 4°06′W. Tel: Range Officer (0752) 553740 Ext. Cambridge 412. 0900-1700 Mon.-Fri. Quartermaster (0752) 553740 Ext. Cambridge 406 other times.

Radio: VHF Chan. 16, 10, 11 when range operating. Information given on firing. Give vessels name and position.

WESTERN ENTRANCE TO PLYMOUTH SOUND

WEMBURY POINT. Lt. Oc.Y. 10 sec. 45m. Occas.
SHAGSTONE. Lt. Fl.(2) 15 sec.
WHIDBEY Lt. Oc.(2) G.10 sec. 3M. W. ▽ Or. stripe. Col. 29m. Vis. 000°-160°. Q.Y. indicates mains power failure.
D.G. RAMEHEAD SOUTH Lt.By. Fl.(4)Y. 15 sec. Can. Y.
D.G. RAMEHEAD (N). Lt. By. Fl.(4)Y. 15 sec. Can. Y.
D.G. Lt.By. Fl.(2)Y. 15 sec. Can. Y.
D.G. PENLEE (W). Lt.By. Fl.Y. 15 sec.
D.G. PENLEE (E). Lt.By. Fl.Y. 10 sec.
OSR NORTH Lt.By. Fl.Y. 2 sec. Can. Y. 50°18.97'N 4°09.86'W.
OSR SOUTH Lt.By. Fl.Y. 2 sec. Can. Y. 50°18.83'N 4°10.04'.W.
DRAYSTONE. Lt.By. Fl.(2)R. 5 sec. Can. R. off Penlee Point.
KNAP. Lt.By. Fl.G. 5 sec. W of Knap Shoal. Conical G.
MAKER POINT. Lt.Bn. Fl.(2)W.R.G. 10 sec. W.11M. R.6M. G.6M. White metal framework Tr. 15m. White Sector leads towards W Chan. Q.Y. indicates mains power failure.
PANTHER By. Spar B.Y. Topmark N.
D.G. INNER By. Can. Y.

PLYMOUTH 50°20'N 4°09'W. Tel: Sutton Hbr. (0752) 664186 (Night (0752) 362322): Long Room Port Control (0752) 552411, 552412, 663225: Millbay Docks (0752) 662191. Fax: (0752) 222070. Devonport Dockyard & Hamoaze. (0752) 552413/553005. Cattewater Hbr. (0752) 665934. Pilots (0752) 662708 Fax: (0752) 669691. M.O.D. Pilots (0752) 553874 & 552411.
HARBOUR WAYPOINT. 50°19.5´N, 4°09.0´W.
Radio — Port: Long Room Port Control VHF Chan. 16, 8, 12, 14. H24.
Sutton Harbour & Marina Radio. VHF Chan. 16, M, 80 (on request). H24.
Devonport Dockyard Radio. VHF Chan. 13, 73. H24.
Millbay Docks Radio. VHF Chan. 16, 14 when ferries operating only.
Cattewater Hbr. Radio. VHF Chan. 16, 12—0900-1700.
Radio — Pilots: VHF Chan. 13, 14, 16; 08, 11, 12.

Mayflower Marina (0752) 556633. VHF Chan. M.
Queen Anne's Battery. Tel: (0752) 671142. Marina VHF Chan. M.
Anchorages: In Cawsand, Kingsand outside breakwater and off Millbrook and St. Johns Lake inside. Good protection from SW gales.
Entry: Signals to control all movements of vessels over 20m which use or cross recommended tracks for deep draught channels are shown from Drakes Island for Sound and, Flagstaff Port Control Signal station (PCS) for Hamoaze as follows:

No signal	= No restriction unless passed on VHF Chan. 13 or 14.
3 R. Fl. Lts.	= Serious Emergency. No movements unless directed by PCS.
1 R. over 2 G. Oc. Lt.	= Outgoing traffic only on track. Crossing traffic only with PCS approval.
2 G. over 1 R. Oc. Lt.	= Incoming traffic only on track. Crossing traffic only with PCS approval.
2 G. over 1 W. Oc. Lt.	= Proceed in either direction. H.M. vessels given wide berth.

Mandatory for all vessels over 20m in length to report when passing 50°22.16'N 4°11.30'W and maintain listening watch on VHF Chan. 13, 14 or 16. Report when berthed. Obtain permission at least 1hr. 5min. before departure. Report at above position, the breakwater, and line Penlee Point/Shagstone.
Measured Distance: R. Tamar (E Side). For motor boats and small craft. One mile. 2 pairs of B.W.V.S. bns. close N of R. Albert Br. and on Warren Pt. A pair of bns. with diamonds B.W.V.S. situated on St. Budeaux Wharf and above Bull Pt. lead along the running line on a 193° (Mag.) course.

WEST ENTRANCE
PLYMOUTH BREAKWATER W END. Lt. Fl.W.R. 10 sec. W.15M. R.12M. Grey Twr. 19m. W.262°-208°; R.208°-262°. Same structure Lt. Iso. 4 sec. 12M. 12m. Vis. 031°-039°. Bell 15 sec.
Lt. F.R. on tower on fort 700m. E when diving taking place. Traffic Signals 1.3M NNE on Drakes Island.
E. HEAD Lt. Iso W.R. 5 sec, 8M. 9m. R.190°-353°; W.353°-001°; R.001°-018°; W.018°-190°.
QUEENS GROUND Lt.By. Fl.(2)R. 10 sec. Can. R.
NEW GROUNDS Lt.By. Fl.R. 2 sec. Can. R.
C Lt.By. Fl.Y. 2.5 sec. Mooring buoy inside B'water.

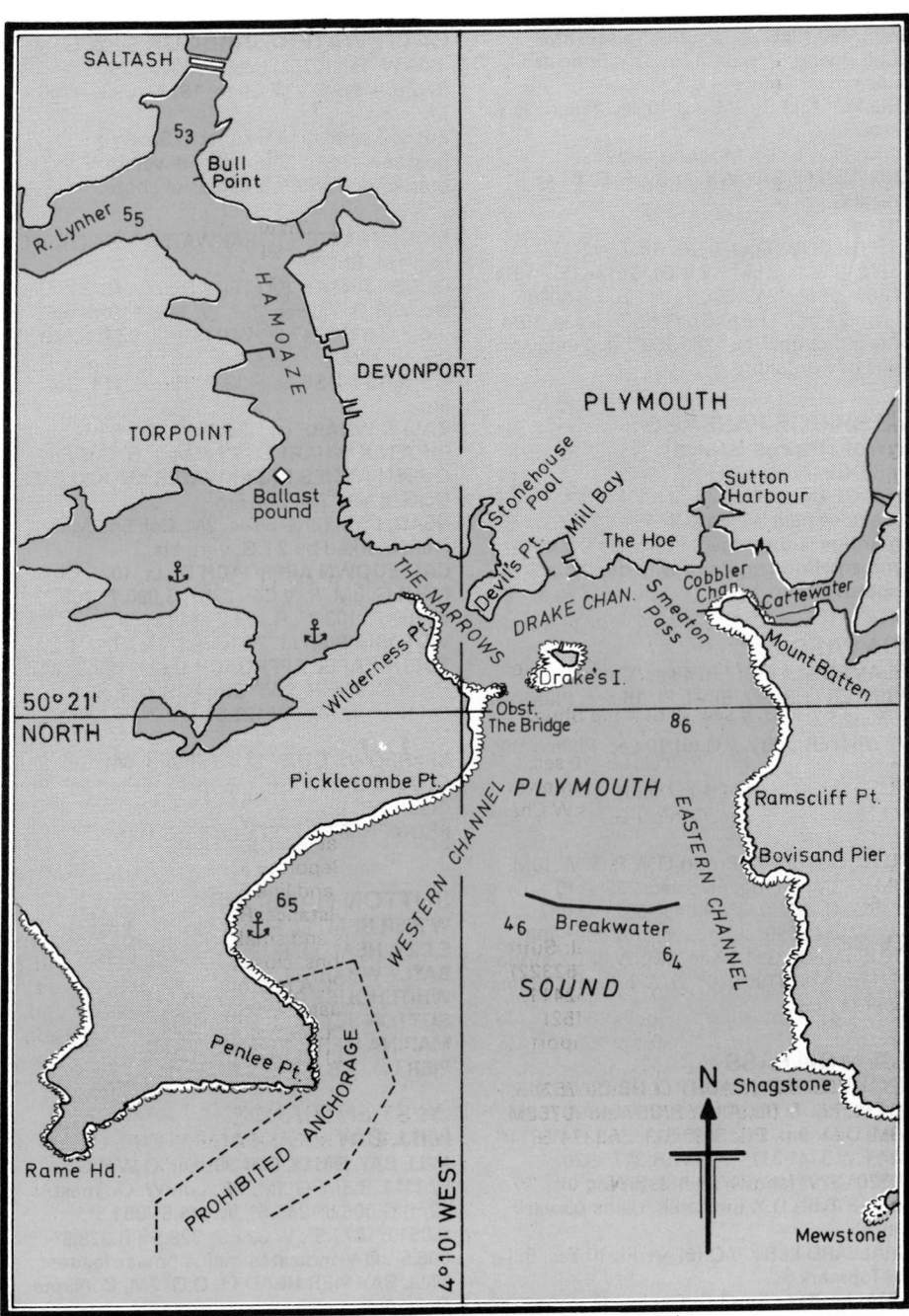

D Lt.By. Fl.Y. 10 sec. Mooring buoy inside B'water.

EAST ENTRANCE
RENNEY POINT Bn. B.W. ◊ 11m.

W TINKER Lt.By. Q.(9) 15 sec. Pillar Y.B.Y. Topmark W.
E TINKER Lt.By. Q.R. Can. R.

PLYMOUTH BREAKWATER E END Bn. ○ on B.Col. 10m.

BOVISAND PIER Lt. Oc.(2)G. 15 sec. 3M. W.Col. Diving Signals. 17m. Q.Y. indicates mains power failure.
DUKE ROCK Lt.By. V.Q.(9) 10 sec. Pillar Y.B.Y. Topmark W.
F Lt.By. Fl.Y. 5 sec. Mooring buoy.
JENNYCLIFFE BAY WK. Lt.By. Fl.G. 6 sec. Conical G.

WITHYHEDGE Dir.Lt. 070°. Dir. F.W.R.G. W.13M. R.5M. G.5M. W ▽ Or. Stripe Col. 13m. F.G.060°-065°; F.W.069°-071°; F.R.075°-080° (shown 24 hr.). Lt.Bn. Gp.Fl.(2)Bl. 5 sec. 10M. Same structure. Vis. 120°-160°. Q.Y. indicates mains power failure.

THE BRIDGE PASSAGE
(SW of Drakes Island)
W BRIDGE By. Can. R.
E BRIDGE By. Conical G.
Steer close past By. Can. R.
The Bridge (submerged) connects Drake Island and Redding Point with depths at LW of approx. 0.5 to 1m.

ASIA PASS
MELAMPUS Lt.By. Fl.R. 4 sec. Can. R.
S WINTER Lt.By. Q.(6) + L.Fl. 15 sec. Pillar Y.B. Topmark S.
NW WINTER Lt.By. V.Q.(9) 10 sec. Pillar Y.B.Y. Topmark W.
ASIA Lt.By. Fl.(2) R. 5 sec. Can.R.
ASH Lt.By. Fl.G. 3 sec. Conical G.
Ldg. Lts. 349°
MALLARD SHOAL (Front) Q.W.R.G. W.10M. R.3M. G.3M. (in fog. Fl. 5 sec. 232°-110°). Or ▽ Col. 5m. G.233°-043°; R.043°-067°; G.067°-087°; W.087°-099°. Ldg. Sector R.099°-108°.
HOE (Rear) Oc.G. 1.3 sec. 3M. W. ▽ Or. stripe. Col. 11m. Vis. 310°-040°. Q.Y. indicates mains power failure.

SMEATON PASS
ROYAL WESTERN YACHT CLUB Dir.Lt. 315.5°. Dir. F.W.R.G. & Dir. Alt.W.R.G. W.13M. R.5M. G.5M. Or. ▽ 9m. F.G. 309°-311°. Alt G.W.311°-314°; F.W.314°-317°; Alt. W.R.317°-320°; F.R.320°-329° (shown 24 hr.). (In fog vis. 313.5°-316.5°) Q.Y. indicates mains power failure.
S MALLARD Lt.By. V.Q.(6) + L.Fl. 10 sec. Pillar Y.B. Topmark S.
W MALLARD Lt.By. Q.G. Conical G.
NE WINTER Lt.By. Q.R. Can.R.
Lt.By. Fl.(2)G. 10 sec. Conical G.
Lt.By. Fl.R. 5 sec. Can.R.
Lt.By. Fl.(2)R. 10 sec. Can.R.

HISTORIC WRECK SITE CATTEWATER. 50°21.7'N, 4°07.61'W. 50m. radius.

CATTEWATER HARBOUR 50°20'N
4°09'W. Tel: (0752) 665934 0900-1700.
Radio — Port: VHF Chan. 16, 12. 0900-1700 Mon.-Fri.
Entry: Speed limit 8 knots in Smeaton Passage, Drake Channel and waters N and W thereof and within 2 cables of shore.

MOUNTBATTEN BREAKWATER Lt. Fl.(3)G.10 sec. 4M. Col. 7m.
QUEEN ANNES BATTERY Dir.Lt. 048°30'. Dir. Oc. W.R.G. 7.5 sec. 3M. W. Twr. R. roof on bldg. G.038°-047.2°; W.047.2°-049.7°; R.049.7°-060.5°. H24.
FISHERS NOSE Lt. Fl.(3)R. 10 sec. 4M. Col. 6m.
BALTIC WHARF Lt. 2 F.R.Vert. 5M. 8m.
PHOENIX WHARF Lt. 2 F.R.Vert. G. Col. 6m.
QUEEN ANNES BREAKWATER KNUCKLE. Lt. Oc.G. 8 sec. 2M. Col. 5m.
HEAD. Lt. Fl.(2)G. 5 sec. 2M. Col. 5m. Marina Piers marked by 2 F.G. vert. Lts.
CATTEDOWN APPROACH Dir.Lt. 102°. Dir. F.W.R.G. 8M. R. ▽ Col. 27m. G.090.7°-100.7°; W.100.7°-103.2°; R.103.2°-113.2°.
VICTORIA PIER Lt. 2 F.R.Vert. 4M. R. Col. 8m.
TURNCHAPEL APPROACH Dir.Lt. 128.5°. Dir. F.W.R.G. 8M. R. ▽ W. Stripe. R.W. Col. G.117.8°-127.8°; W.127.8°-129.2°; R.129.2°-139.2°.
SPARROWS QUAY Lt. 2 F.R.Vert. 6M. Col. 8m.
CLOVELLY BAY Ldg.Lts. 198°. (Front) F.R. Bn. (Rear) F.R. Bn.
PROMPHLETT JETTY Lt. 2 F.G.Vert.

SUTTON HARBOUR
W PIER HEAD Lt. Fl.R. 3 sec. 2M. Post 5m.
E PIER HEAD Lt. Fl.G. 3 sec. 2M. Post 5m.
BAYLY WHARF Lt. 2 F.G.Vert.
WHITEHOUSE PIER Lt. 2 F.R.Vert.
SUTTON JETTY Lt. 2 F.R.Vert.
MARINA PIER F. SE END Lt. Q.R.
PIER Lts. A.B.C.D.E. 2 F.R.Vert.

MILL BAY
MILL BAY. Dir. Lt. 048°30'. Dir. Q.W.R.G. W.11M. R.3M. G.3M. W. △ on W. Or. mast. 12m. G.006.5°-045.5°; W.045.5°-051.5°; R.051.5°-071.5°; W.321.5°-329.5°; R.329.5°-006.5°. Q.Y. indicates mains power failure.
MILL BAY PIER HEAD Lt. Q.G. 2M. Concrete Col. 10m.
CAMBER JETTY HEAD Lt. Q.R. 2M. Metal Col. 5m.
N. SIDE. Lt. Oc. G. 3 sec.
MARINA WAVESCREEN. S. END Lt. Oc. R. 3 sec.
TRINITY PIER HEAD Lt. 2 F.G.Vert.
RO/RO FERRY TERM. HEAD Lt. 2 F.R.Vert.

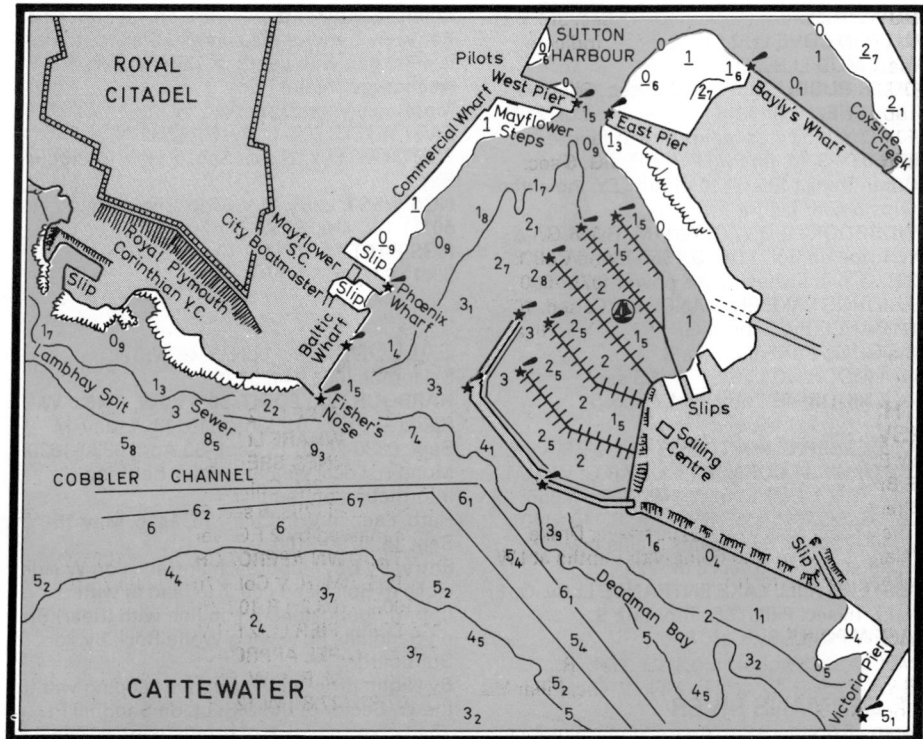

DRAKES CHANNEL

EASTERN KINGS Lt. (in fog) Fl. 5 sec. Roof of D.G.Stn. 259°-062°. Q.Y. indicates mains power failure.

WESTERN KINGS Dir.Lt. 271°. Dir. F.W.R.G. W.13M. R.5M. G.5M. W ▽ Or. Stripe Col. 14m. F.G.264°-266°; F.W.270°-272°; F.R.276°-284° (shown 24 hr.). Q.Y. indicates mains power failure.

RAVENNESS POINT Dir.Lt. 225°. Dir. F.W.R.G. & Dir. Al. W.R.G. W.13M. R.5M. G.5M. W. ▽ Or. Stripe Col. 11m. F.G.217°-221°; Al. W.G.221°-224°; F.W.224°-226°; Alt. W.R.226°-229°; F.R.229°-237° (shown 24 hr.). In fog Fl.(2) 15 sec. 160°-305°. Q.Y. indicates mains power failure.

N DRAKES Lt.By. Fl.R 4 sec. Can. R.

NW DRAKES IS. Lt.By. Fl.(2)R. 10 sec. Can. R.

E VANGUARD Lt.By. Q.G. Conical G.

BRIDGE Lt. Fl.(2)Bl. 5 sec. 3M. W. ▽ Or. Stripe Col. 5m. Vis. 140°-210°. Q.Y. indicates mains power failure.

W VANGUARD Lt.By. Fl.G. 3 sec. Conical B.

THE NARROWS

C-IN-C's PIER Dir.Lt. 343°. Dir. F.W.R.G. & Dir. Al. W.R.G. W.13M. R.5M. G.5M. W. ▽ Or. Stripe. W. Hut. 7m. F.G.331°-338°; Al.

W.G.338°-342°; F.W.342°-344°; Al. W.R.344°-348°; F.R.348°-351° (shown 24 hr.). In fog F. 314.5°-344.5°. Q.Y. indicates mains power failure.

DEVILS POINT Lt. Q.G. 3M. Or/W. Col. (In fog Fl. 5 sec.). Q.Y. indicates mains power failure.

BATTERY Lt.By. Fl.R. 2 sec. Can. R.

CREMYLL Lt.Bn. Fl.R. 4 sec. R.W. Bn. 5m. (In fog Fl.(2) 15 sec. 097°-338°). Q.Y. indicates mains power failure.

OCEANS COURT POORMANS POINT Dir.Lt. 085°. Dir. Q.W.R.G. W.11M. R.3M. G.3M. Or. ▽ W. Col. 15m. G.010°-080°; W.080°-090°; R.090°-100°. (In fog Fl. 5 sec. 270°-100°).

OCEAN QUAY MARINA S Lt. 2 F.R.Vert. Q.Y. indicates mains power failure.

MARINA PONTOON E Lt. 2 F.R.Vert.

PONTOON B Lt. 2 F.R.Vert.

CREMYLL Lt.By. Fl.R. 2 sec. Can. R.

TORPOINT. Tel: (0752) 813658.
Radio: VHF Chan. 16. M. c/s Firebrace. Moorings in Ballast Pound (Dries).

DEVONPORT DOCKYARD & HAMOAZE. Tel: (0752) 552413/553005.
Radio: VHF Chan. 13, 73. H24. C/S: Flag. Controls movements N. of the Narrows.

HAMOAZE

MUTTON COVE Lt. 2 F.G.Vert.
WEST MUD Lt.By. Q.R. Can. R.
SOUTH RUBBLE Lt.By. Fl.G. 3 sec. Conical G.
SLIP JTY E. Lt. (In fog) Fl. 5 sec. W. Col. 270°-110°. Q.Y. indicates mains power failure.
No. 1 JTY S. Lt. (In fog) Fl.(3) 15 sec. SW Corner Transit Shed 310°-190°. Q.Y. indicates mains power failure.
MILLBROOK Lt. Q.W.G. W.11M. G.3M. W. Δ Or. Stripe on Col. 11m. G.165°-180°; W.180°-230°. Q.Y. indicates mains power failure.
ST. JOHNS LAKE ENTRANCE By. Can. R.
ENTRANCE By. Conical G.
ST. JOHNS LAKE By. Can. R.
No. 1 MOORING Lt.By. Fl.Y. 2.5 sec.
No. 2 MOORING Lt.By. Fl.Y. 5 sec.

YONDERBERRY POINT JETTY Lt. 2 F.R. vert.
NORTH WEST CORNER Lt. Q.W.R.G. W.11M. R.3M. G.3M. Col. 12m. W.340°-355°; R.355°-025°; G.025°-055°; W.055°-110°; R.110°-140°; W.140°-230°. Q.Y. indicates mains power failure. In fog Fl. 5 sec. 318°-220°.
WESTERN MILL LAKE ENTRANCE Lt.By. Q.(6) + L.Fl. 15 sec. Pillar Y.B. Topmark S.
CAREW POINT By. Can. R.

ST. GERMANS RIVER

Depths 5.5m. to 8.3m. up to Jupiter Point. River navigable to St. Germans Quay. Tideford can be reached at MHWS with draught of 2m.
LYNHER Lt.By. Q.R. Can. R.
FOUL GROUND marked by Lynher Lt.By. and 3 × Sph. Y. Bys. — obst. 2.5m. above sea bed.
BEGGERS ISLAND. By. Can. R.
SANDACRE POINT. Lt.By. Fl.G. 5 sec. Conical G.
Channel continues to Lynher River, Sconner Lake, Polbathick Lake, River Tiddy. Viaduct across River Tiddy and Lynher River clearance 21m above MHWS.

RIVER TAMAR

BULL POINT JETTY Lt. 2 F.G.Vert.
TOWN QUAY Lt. 2 F.R.Vert.
SALTASH PIER Lt. 2 F.R.vert.
SOUTH TAMAR Lt.By. Q.G. Conical G.
NORTH TAMAR Lt.By. Q.G. Conical G.
ERNESETTLE PIER Lt. 2 F.G.Vert.

RIVER YEALM Tel: HM (0752) 872533.

HARBOUR WAYPOINT. 50°18.0´N, 4°05.5´W.
Ldg. Bns. leading 089° into Cellar Bay, thence round Misery Point. Opposite Misery Point is Bn. G.W. Topmark W. □ Δ. Spit By. Can. R. marks spit inside harbour. Many mooring Bys. for yachts between Warren and Madge

Points. Sand Bar dries 0.1m. on 1st Ldg. Line. Between S end of the spit and S shore there is 40m. gap with depth of 1.5m. at LW.
Anchorage: Yealm Pool.
Moorings: Visitors marked "V".
EAST RUTTS D.Z. Lt.By. 50°12´42″N, 3°59´08″W. Fl.Y. 2½ sec. Sph. Y. ∿ in Bigbury Bay.
NGS WEST. Lt.By. Fl.Y. 5sec. Conical Y. 50°11.1´N, 4°00.8´W.
NGS EAST. Lt.By. Fl.Y. 10sec. Conical Y. 50°11.2´N, 3°59.0´W.

SALCOMBE 50°14´N, 3°46´W. Tel:

Salcombe (054 844) 3791.
HARBOUR WAYPOINT. 50°11.0´N, 3°46.0´W.
Radio — Port: VHF Chan. 16, 14. 1 May-14 Sept. 0830-2030, 15 Sept.-30 April 0830-1630 Mon-Fri. Local weather, tides, berthing information on request.
Harb. Launch VHF Chan. 16, 14, 6. May 15-Sept 15. 0700-2100.
Entry: By Day—approach entrance on W side close to Bolt Head 000°T to lead in with (Front) Poundstone Bn. in line with (Rear) Bn. on Sandhills Pt. leaving Wolfe Rock By. to Starboard.
By Night: proceed in as above keeping within the W. Sector of the DIR. Lt. on Sandhill Pt. The G. Sector lies E of proper course. The R. Sector to W'ward. On approaching Wolfe Rock By. the Lt. on Blackstone Lt.Bn. will be seen (R. Sector). When this changes to W. alter course to starboard to pick up the inner Ldg. Lts. 042½T. In rough weather especially on ebb tide approach Bar with caution. Fuel Barge 2c. from Scroble Pt.
Salcombe: Speed limit 8 knots. Draught 5.5m.
Anchorage: Baston Lake in 8m., The Bag, Mabel shoal.
Launching Hard: Batson Creek.
Moorings: Numerous for visitors.
Facilities: Provisions, water, fuel (diesel and petrol), barge at Middle Ground.
STAREHOLE By. Sph. Y. (May-Sept.).
GARA By. Sph.Y. (May-Sept.).
GAMMON By. Sph.Y. (May-Sept.).
SANDHILL POINT. Dir.Lt. 000° Dir. Fl.W.R.G. 2 sec. W.10M. R.7M. G.7M. R.W. ◊ on W. mast 27m. R.002.5°-182.5°; G.182.5°-357.5°; W.357.5°-002.5°.
Ldg.Bns. 000° (Front) Poundstone Bn. (Rear) Sandhill Point Lt.Bn.
BLACKSTONE ROCK. Lt. Q.W.R. 2M. Bn. 4m. R.218°-048°; W.048°-218°.
WOLFE ROCK By. Conical G.
Ldg.Lts. 042°30´ (Front) Q. 5m. Mast 8m. (Rear) 8M. Stone Col. 45m.
Landing Stage Lt. F.R. 3M. White Col. 4m.
HISTORIC WRECK SITE PRAWLE POINT. 50°12.7´N, 3°44.33´W. 300m. radius.

EAST PRAWLE RG STN. 50°13.10′N, 3°42.48′W. Coastguard Emergency. DF STN VHF Chan 16 & 67. Controlled by MRSC Brixham.

OFFSHORE WAYPOINT START POINT. 50°10.0′N, 3°38.0′W.

START POINT. 50°13.3′N, 3°38.5′W Lt. Fl.(3) 10 sec. 25M. vis. from 184° to 068°. Not vis. to the westward N of a bearing of 067°. W. circular Tr. 62m. Horn 60 sec. Window in same Tr. F.R. 12M. showing over Skerries Bank from 210° to 255°. 55m. R.C. SKERRIES BANK By. Can.R. NE of Skerries Bank. Bell w.a.

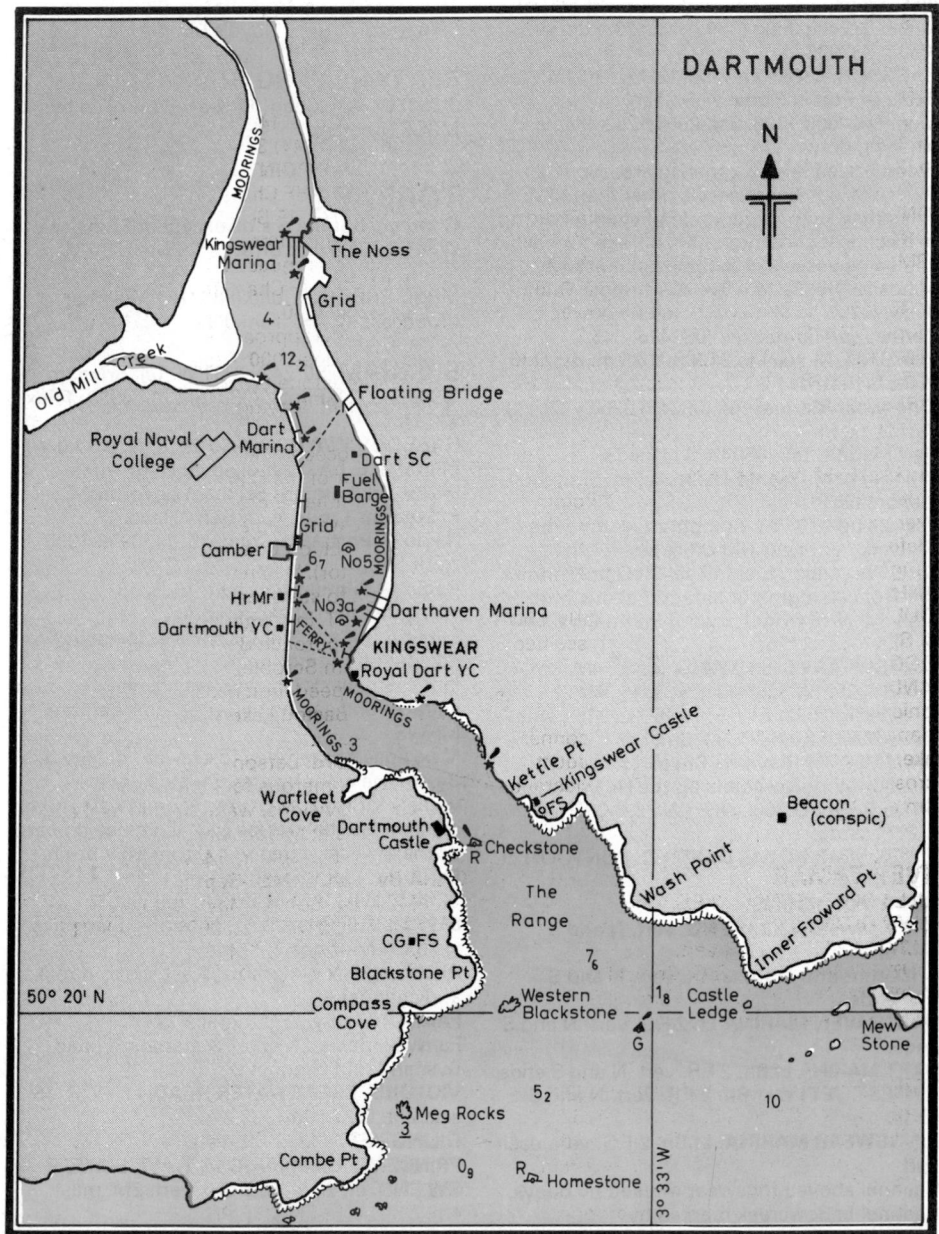

RIVER DART

HOMESTONE By. Can.R.
CASTLE LEDGE Lt.By. Fl.G. 5 sec. Conical G. Topmark Cone.
CHECKSTONE Lt.By. Fl. (2) R. 5 sec. Can.R.

DARTMOUTH 50°21′N 3°34′W. Tel:

Dartmouth (0803) 832337 & 833767;
(Emergency only — outside working hours):
(0803) 832408. Fax: (0803) 835430. Pilots:
(0803) 832908.
HARBOUR WAYPOINT. 50°19.0′N, 3°31.5′W.
Radio — Port & Pilots: VHF Chan. 11. Hrs:
Mon.-Fri. 0900-1700. Sat. 0900-1200. (Pilots
when on duty).
Entry: Speed limit 6 knots. In area No: 1-2
Bys. off Kingswear vessels other than H.M.
ships may keep to port side of channel owing
to local tidal conditions. Anchorage for yachts
and small vessels is to the east of fairway
opposite. No: 3a to 5 Bys. Dartmouth Quay
depth 6.3m.
Darthaven Marina. Tel: (080425) 545.
VHF Chan. M. Yachts 21.3m. × 3.7m. draught.
Visitors berths.
Kingswear Marina. Tel: (08043) 3351 × 39.
Yachts 12.1m.
Dart Marina. Tel: (08043) 3351 × 58.
VHF Chan. M. Yachts 18.2m. × 2m. draught.
Visitors berths.
Vessels up to 3.7m. draught may go to the
Embankment near HM office.
Facilities: Water, fuel (diesel) at Dart Marina.
Bn. Truncated granite pyramid about 24m.
high ½M. NNE from Forward Point. On E side
of Hr. entce., 177m.
KINGSWEAR Lt. Iso. W.R.G. 3 sec. 8M. 9m.
G.318°-325°; W.325°-331°; R.331°-340°.
KINGSWEAR. Lt. F.W. 9M. 107° to 116°. One
cable NW of Kettle Point. 6m.
DARTMOUTH (Bayards Cove). Lt. Fl. W.R.G. 2
sec. 6M. W. sector leads up the Hr. W. stripe
on Rock. 5m. G.280°-289°; W.289°-297°;
R.297°-shore.
KINGSWEAR ROYAL DART Y.C. PONTOON Lt.
F.G. vert.
FERRY PONTOONS.
  (Kingswear) Lt.Bn. 2 F.G. vert. N and S
  ends.
  (Dartmouth) Lt.Bn. 2 F.R. vert. N and S
  ends.
DARTHAVEN MARINA Lt. 2 F.G. vert. N and S
ends.
DART MARINA Lt.Bn. 2 F.R. vert. N and S ends.
R.N. EST. JETTY. Lt.Bn. 2 F.R. vert. N and S
ends.
KINGSWEAR MARINA. Lt.Bn. 2 F.G. vert. each
end.
Channel above Kingswear marked by buoys.
Channel in Bowcreek marked by
1 × starboard. Bn. & 5 × port Bns.

RACING BUOYS APPROACHES
DARTMOUTH. April-Oct. (1) 50°18.80′N,
3°35.25′W. (2) 50°18.68′N, 3°33.29′W. (3)
50°20.07′N, 3°31.42′W.

**INSHORE WAYPOINT OFF BERRY HD.
50°24.0′N, 3°27.5′W.**

BERRY HEAD 50°24′N, 3°28.9′W. Lt. Fl.(2)
15 sec. 18M. vis. from 100° to 023°. W. Tr.
58m. (Storm Sig.) Lloyd's Sig. Stn.

BERRY HEAD RG STN. 50°23.9′N,
3°29.0′W. VHF Chan. 16 & 67. Controlled by
MRSC Brixham.

TORBAY

Good anchorage S side except in SE gales.
WRECK. By. Pillar BRB. 50°25′N, 3°28.7′W.

MRSC BRIXHAM (0803) 882704. Weather
broadcast ev. 4h. from 0050.

BRIXHAM 50°24′N 3°31′W. Tel: Brixham
(08045) 3321. Pilots: (08045) 2214/4939. Telex:
42737.
HARBOUR WAYPOINT. 50°24.75′N, 3°31.0′W.
Pilotage: E.T.A. 12 h in advance to Trinity
Pilots, Brixham, for Brixham or Torquay.
P/Station: 1 mile N. of Berry Head.
Radio — Port: VHF Chan. 16, 14, 0930-1930
April-Sept.
Radio — Pilots: VHF Chan. 16, 9, 13,
10—when vessel expected.
Entry: 3 R. Balls/3 R. Lts. = Port closed due to
navigation hazard.
Inner harbour mostly dries with depth of 5.5m. in
entrance and depth of 4.3m. at some berths at
MHWS.
Max. speed 5 kts: keep to seaward of fairway
By. thence enter by appropriate fairway:
vessels for town dock area & breakwater hard
slipway use lifeboat fairway: illuminated board
warns of vessels departing from MFV basin.
Facilities: fuel (diesel), water.
PRINCE WILLIAM MARINA. Tel: (0803)
882711. VHF Chan. 37. 537 berths. Extensive
visitors moorings.
Anchorage: N of harbour. Keep clear of rocks
and channel.
FAIRWAY. Lt.By. Q.G. Conical G.
Fairway marked by port & starboard hand
Bys. and mid channel By.
VICTORIA BREAKWATER HEAD. Lt. Oc.R. 15
sec. 3M. W. Tr. 9m.
OILING JETTY Lt. 2 F.R. vert.
**PRINCE WILLIAM MARINA WAVE SCREEN
SW END.** Lt. 2x Fl. R. 5 sec. vert. 2M. mast
4m.
E. END Lt. 2x Fl. G. 5 sec. vert. 2M. mast 4m.

BRIXHAM NEW PIER HEAD. Q.G. 3M. G.
Metal structure. 6m.
EASTERN PIER HEAD. Lt. Q.
FISH BASIN E ARM. Lt. V.Q.
FISH MARKET JETTY. 2 F.G. vert. each end.

PAIGNTON 50°26'N 3°33'W. Tel: H.M.
(April-Sept) Paignton 557812. (Night Paignton
550405).
P/Station: Brixham.
Entry: Harbour dries. Depth of 3m. at MHWS.

PAIGNTON EAST QUAY Lt. Fl.R. 3M. Concrete
Col. 7m.
A By. Can.R. and flying 'N' Int. Code Flag is
periodically moored about 200m. N of the
Head of the E Jetty. When this By. is laid

Entry: 3 R. Balls or 3 R. Lts. = entrance closed.
No entry or departure, due to navigational
hazard.
BUNKERING FACILITY AT SOUTH QUAY.
QUEEN ANNE MARINE FUEL. VHF Chan. M.
Inner harbour dries. Depths of 3m. to 3.7m. at
MHWS.
Outer harbour. Haldon Pier. Depths 2.4m. to
3.9m. on N side.
Princess Pier. Depths 3.9m. on both sides.
Facilities: Fuel (diesel and petrol) at S Pier.
Water at Quays.
HALDON PIER HEAD Lt. Q.G. 6M. metal col.
9m.
PRINCESS PIER. Lt. Q.R. 6M. metal col. 9m.
MARINA E END. Lt. 2 F.R.Vert.
MARINA W END. Lt. 2 F.G.Vert.
SOUTH PIER. Lt. 2 F.G. vert. 5M. Iron structure
on Inner Hr. Pier. 6m.

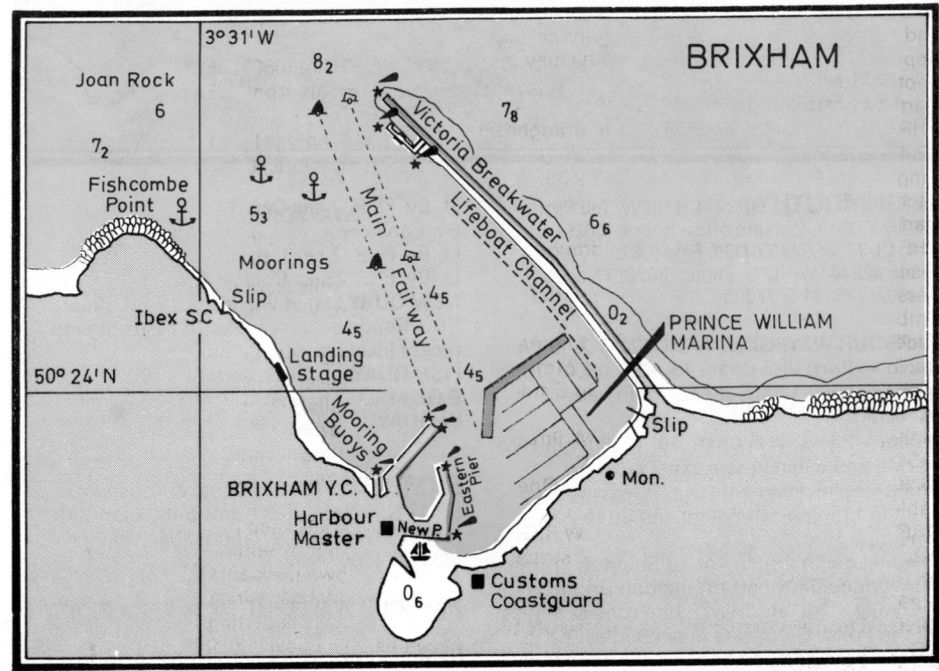

vessels entering or leaving Hr. should keep to
N of line joining the By. to the Head of the
Jetty. They should keep to the port side of the
Fairway from the 'N' flag By., entering and
leaving and proceed 'dead slow'. Bn. 6m.
square topmark R. 79m. E. of Hr. Entce.

TORQUAY 50°27'N, 3°32'W. Tel: Torquay
(0803) 22429.
HARBOUR WAYPOINT. 50°27.0'N, 3°31.0'W.
Radio — Port: VHF Chan. 14, 16, May-Sept.
0900-2200, March-April 0900-1700 Mon.-Fri.
Oct.-Feb. 0900-1700 Mon.-Fri.

ENTRANCE. Lt.By. Q.G. Conical G. Withdrawn
during winter, 1st October to 31st March.
MARINA Tel: (0803) 214624. 500 Berths.
Western side of outer harbour.

INSHORE WAYPOINT OFF ORESTONE.
50°27.0'N, 3°27.5'W.

BABBACOMBE 50°29'N, 3°31'W. Tel:
(0803) 22429.

HISTORIC WRECK. 50°32.92'N, 3°29.17'W.
200m. square.

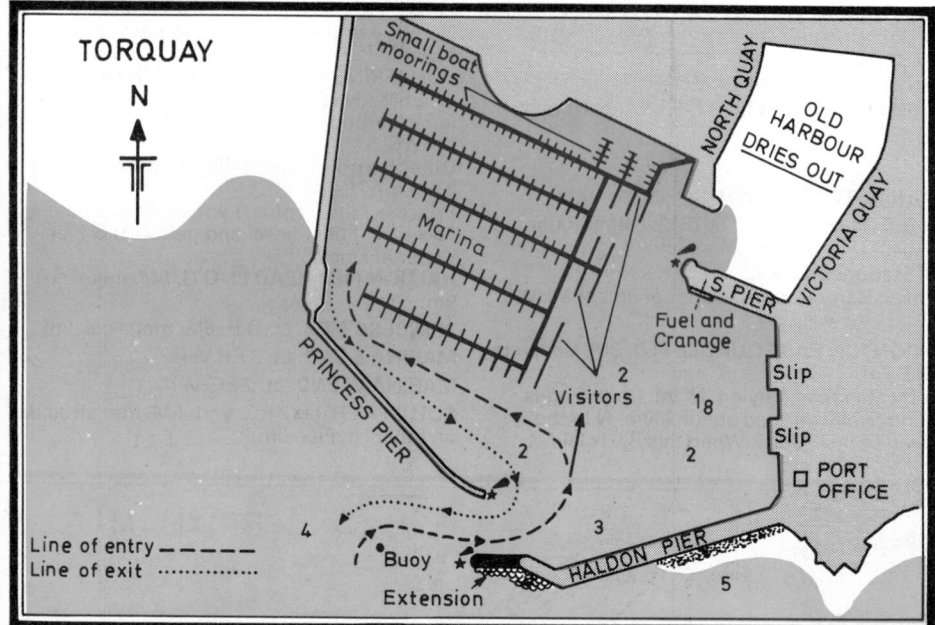

TEIGNMOUTH 50°32'N, 3°30'W. Tel: Port:
(0626) 772311. Outside office hours: (0626)
774348, 775858 & 779121. Fax: (0626) 770218.
Telex: 42840 WARD G. Pilots: (0626) 772256,
774902, 776134 & 772034.

HARBOUR WAYPOINT. 50°32.5'N, 3°27.5'W.
Radio — Port: VHF Chan. 16, 12— 0800-1700
Mon-Fri; 0900-1200 Sat and when vessel
expected.
Radio — Pilots: VHF Chan. 16, 12, 30 min-HW-
30 min and when vessel expected.
Entry: Vessel when entering or leaving
sounds 1 long blast. Patent slip up to 200
tons.
Channel depth 2m. to 4m. to Shaldon Bridge.
Drawbridge (in N part of Shaldon Bridge is
9m. wide × 2m. at MHWS. Tide runs at 4-5 kts
off the Point. Great care is needed as the
depths over, and positions of, the sandbanks
are constantly changing. Max. draught 5m.
MHWS.
Visitors mooring 1c. N of the Point.
THE DEN. Lts in Line. (Front) F.R. 6M. Stone
Tr. 10m. Vis. 225°-135°. **POWDERHAM**
TERRACE, (Rear) F.R. 3M. B. post 11m. In line
334° mark edge of Pole Sand.

GROYNE 14. Lt. Fl.G. 5 sec.

PIER HEAD. Lt. 2 F.G. Vert.

PHILLIP LUCETTE. Lt.Bn. Oc. R. 5.5 sec. 2M.
W.Bn.

DEN POINT. SW End Lt. Oc. G. 5 sec. F.G. vert.
△ on G. post.

Lt. By. Fl. R. 2 sec Can R.
By. Can R.
Lt. By. Fl. R. 2 sec Can R.
Lt. By. F. G. 2 sec. Conical G.
NEW QUAY Lts. in line (Front) F.Bu. (Rear)
F.Bu. Reported unreliable. To be used with
recent local knowledge only.
FISH QUAY. Lt. 2 F.G. vert.
E QUAY. Lt. 2 F.G. vert.
W QUAY. Lt. 2 F.G. vert.

EXMOUTH (Exeter Canal & Topsham).
50°37'N, 3°24'W. Tel: (Dock only) Exmouth
(0395) 272009. (River and Estuary Exeter
(0392) 74306.

HARBOUR WAYPOINT. 50°36.0'N, 3°22.0'W.

Radio — Port: VHF Chan. 16, 12, 6. Mon.-Fri.
0730-1630. and when vessels expected.
Radio — Pilots: VHF Chan. 16, 12, 9, 14, 6.
Entry: General speed limit of 10 kts through
the water except in areas and at times as
permitted by Bye-Laws to facilitate water
skiing, etc.
Exmouth Dock: Swing Bridge opened during
day-light hours. Draughts 4.6m. MHWS and
3.2m. at MHWN. Dock dries.
Exeter Canal: 37m. × 7.9m. × 3m. draught. M5
motorway bridge clearance 11m.

STRAIGHT POINT. 50°36.5'N, 3°21.7'W Lt. Fl.R.
10 sec. 7M. 246°-071°. Iron structure. 34m.

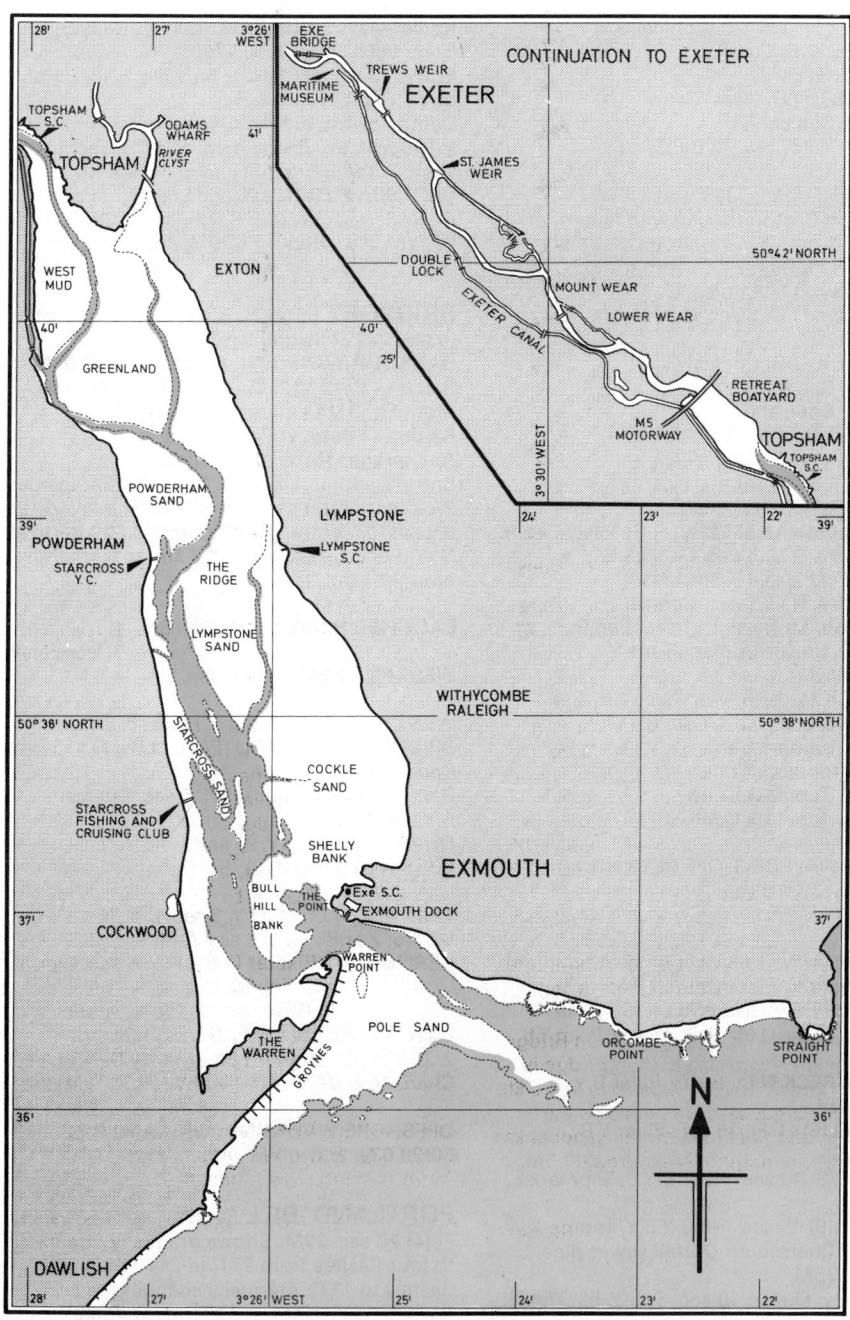

DNZ Lt.By. Fl.Y. 5 sec. Conical. Y. 50°36.10'N: 3°19.30'W.

DSZ Lt.By. Fl.Y. 5 sec. Conical Y. 50°36.80'N: 3°19.20'W.

EXE FAIRWAY. Lt.By. Fl. 10 sec. Spherical R.W. vert. stripes ᴍᴍ Bell.

No: 1 Lt.By. Q.G. Conical G.

No: 2 By. Can.R.

No: 3 Lt.By. Fl.G. 2 sec. Conical G.

No: 4 By. Can.R.

No: 5 By. Conical G.

No: 6 By. Can.R.

No: 7 Lt.By. Fl.G. 5 sec. Conical G.
No: 8 Lt.By. Q.R. Can.R.
No: 9 By. Conical G.
No: 10 Lt.By. Fl.R. 3 sec. Can.R.
No: 11 By. Conical G.
WARREN POINT No: 12 By. Can.R.

EXMOUTH. Ldg.Lts. 305° (rear). F.Y. 7M.
Flagstaff on Custom House with lantern on top, 10m. (front). F.Y. 7M. Iron Col. 2m.
EXMOUTH PIER Lt. 2 F.G. vert. grey col. 6m.
No: 13 Lt.By. Q.G. Conical G.
No: 15 Lt.By. Fl.G. 5 sec. Conical G.
Spit By. Can.R.
No: 17 Lt.By. Q.G. Conical G.
No: 14 By. Can.R.
No: 19 By. Conical G.
SHAGGLES By. Can.R.
No: 21 Lt.By. Q.G. Conical G.
P1. Lt. Fl.G. 5 sec Topmark △.
No: 25 Lt.By. Q.G. Conical G.
No: 16 (Powderham) Lt.By. Fl.R. 1 sec. Can.R.
No: 27 Lt.By. Fl.G. 5 sec. Conical G.
P3 Lt.By. Fl.G. 3 sec. Conical G.
No: 29 Lt.By. Fl.G. 1 sec. Conical G.
No: 16 (Nob) Lt. By. Fl.R. 1 sec. Can.R.
P5 Lt. Q.G. Bn.G. Topmark Cone.
By. Conical G.
TURF LOCK Lt. 2 F.R. vert. Grey Col. 6m.
TING TONG Lt.By. Q.R. Can. R.
P6 Bn. R. Topmark Can.
P9 Bn. G. Topmark Cone.
P11 Bn. G. Topmark Cone.
P13 Bn. G. Topmark Cone.

INSHORE WAYPOINT OFF BEER HD.
50°38.75´N, 3°06.0´W.

BEER. 50°42'N, 3°05'W Lt.Bn. F. Aluminium Col. with lantern near Church. 26m.
LYME BAY: BRETAGNE WRECK. 50°29.48´N 3°22.55´W. Lt.By. Q.(6)+ L.Fl. 15 sec. Pillar Y.B. Topmark S.
MUREE WRECK N Lt. By. Q. Pillar B.Y. Topmark N.
S Lt. By. Q.(6)+ L.Fl. 15 sec. Pillar Y.B. Topmark S.
E Lt. By. Q(3) 10 sec. Pillar B.Y.B. Topmark E. Racon.
W Lt.By. Q(9) 15 sec. Pillar Y.B.Y. Topmark W. Lyme Bay Charmouth Outfall sewer pipe extends 0.73M.
ODAS Lt.By. Fl.(5)Y. 10 sec. Sph.Y. 50°37.4´N; 2°43.6´W.
AXMOUTH PIER HEAD. Lt. Fl. 5 sec. 2M. △ on col. 7m.

LYME REGIS 50°43'N, 2°56'W. Tel: Lyme Regis (0297) 442137.
HARBOUR WAYPOINT. 50°42.75´N, 2°56.0´W.

Radio — Port: VHF Chan. 16, 14. 1 May-30 Sept. 0800-1100; 1500-1700.
Entry: 12 visitors berths on Victoria Pier. Hbr. dries. Enter 2½ h-HW-2½ h.
Depths of 4m. at MHWS in entrance and 2.7m. to 4.3m. inside Hr. at MHWS. Yachts 7.3m. × 1.9m. draught can go inside Hr.
VICTORIA PIER HEAD. Ldg.Lts. 296° (Front) Oc W.R. 8 sec. W.9M. R. 7M. 6m. R.296°-116° W.116°-296°. (Rear) F.G. 9M. 8m. on building.

BRIDPORT 50°42'N, 2°46'W. Tel: Bridport (0308) 23222 (Night: 24977).
HARBOUR WAYPOINT. 50°42.0´N, 2°47.0´W.
Radio — Port: VHF Chan. 16, 11. 0800-1700 Mon.-Fri. (H24 emergency only).
Radio — Pilots: VHF Chan. 09.
Anchorage: 1M. S of entrance.
Entry: Depth in entrance 1.5m. but Bar inside the outer entrance dries at MLWS. Basin dries except for centre. Max. draught 3.2m. Berth at N end of E Pier has depth 2.1m. to 3.5m. Max. draught 2.1m. to 3.5m.

EAST PIER HEAD. Lt. F.G. 2M. 3m. ⎫
                                           ⎬ Occasional.
WEST PIER HEAD. Lt. F.R. 2M. 3m. ⎭

WEST PIER ROOT. Lt. Iso. R. 2 sec. 5M. 9m.
BRIDPORT SEWER OUTFALL Lt.By. Fl.Y. 5 sec. Can.Y. ¾M. S of Entce.
Danger Zone Lt.Bys. (a) Fl. 5 sec. Conical R.Y.V.S. (b) Fl.Y. 3 sec. Can. Y.
ODAS Lt.By. Fl.(5)Y. 20 sec. Sph. Y.
BESSINGTON RANGE By. Barrel Y.

TRIPLANE A Lt.By. Fl.Y. 5 sec. Can. Y.
DZ No: 2 Lt.By. Fl.Y. 3 sec. Can. Y.
VERNON MINEFIELD Lt.By. Fl.Y. 5 sec. Can. Y.

GROVE POINT RG Stn. 50°32.9´N, 2°25.2´W. Coastguard Emergency DF Stn. VHF Chan. 16 & 67. Controlled by MRSC Portland.

OFFSHORE WAYPOINT PORTLAND BILL.
50°29.0´N, 2°27.0´W.

PORTLAND BILL 50°30.8'N, 2°27.3'W. Lt. Fl.(4) 20 sec. 29M. Shows gradually one flash to four flashes from 221° to 244°; then four flashes to 117°, gradually changing to one flash to 141°. Not vis. elsewhere. White circular Tr. with R. band near extremity of Bill. 43m. Dia. 30 sec. Window in same Lt.Ho. F.R. 13M. Vis. over Shambles Shoals from 271° to 291°. 19m. Conspicuous white beacon 18m. high at the point of the Bill.
Extreme caution necessary due to The Race (see Tidal notes).

W SHAMBLES. Lt.By. Q.(9) 15 sec. Pillar. Y.B.Y. Topmark W. Bell.
E SHAMBLES Lt.By. Q.(3) 10 sec. Pillar B.Y.B. Topmark E. w.a. Whis. 〰️.
TRIPLANE B. Lt.By. Fl. 10 sec. Sph.Y.

INSHORE WAYPOINT WEYMOUTH BAY. 50°35.0′N, 2°22.0′W.

MRSC PORTLAND (0305) 820441. Weather broadcast ev. 4h. from 0220.

PORTLAND 50°34′N 2°25′W. Tel: Naval

Base (0305) 820311 Ext. 2104. Pilots: (0305) 773118.
Radio — Port: C/s Portland Naval Base VHF Chan. 13. H24.
Pilots: Weymouth Hbr. Radio VHF Chan. 16, 12 0800-1700 Mon.-Fri. or as required.
Entry: Call QHM for permission to enter. Enter via North Ship Channel. Exit via East Ship Channel. Yachts to keep to N of line Fort Head/Chesil Beach to avoid HM ships. Keep clear of all v/s over 20m. LOA u/way in port limits.
Area prohibited to all merchant or private vessels except with specific permission. A line 325°T for 1050m. from E end of Inner Breakwater thence 251°T for 900m. thence 180°T to NE corner of Phoenix Pier thence from SE corner of Phoenix Pier 150°T for 280m. to W. Dolphin off Admiralty Slip at Castletown. Under no circumstances approach within 100m. of an H.M. ship. Permission to enter prohibited area call Q.H.M. on VHF Chan. 13.
Anchorage: Visiting yachts anchor in N part of Hbr. as allocated by QHM. Anchorage to the S of 50°34.5′N is prohibited.

OUTER BREAKWATER. Lt.Tr. 'D'. Oc. R. 30 sec. 5M. 12m. vis. over Hr. R. Iron Tr. on SW end. S Ship Chan. Entce. closed.
Lt.Bn. E. 2F. 2M. O on Bn. obsc. from sea.
Fort Lt.Bn. Q.R. 5M. vis. 013° to 268°. Iron Col. NW part of fort, 14m.

East ship Chan. lies between Fort Lt.Bn. and 'A' Head Lt.

NE BREAKWATER. Lt.Tr. 'A' Head. Fl.10 sec. 20M. on SE end of NE breakwater. 21m. White iron Tr. on N side of Gallery of 'A' Head Lt.Tr. Telephone for lifesaving only. Horn 10 sec.
'B' HEAD. Lt. Oc.R. 15 sec. 5M. Grey Col., 11m.
'C' HEAD. Lt. Oc.G. 10 sec. 5M. Grey Col., 11m.
North Ship Chan. is between 'B' and 'C' Head Lts.

TORPEDO PIER HEAD. Lt. Fl.G. 5 sec. 2M. Pedestal.
NAVAL AIR STATION. Lt. Oc. G. 15 sec. 10M. framework twr.

CAMBER PIER E ARM. Lt. 2 F.R. vert. 2M. Metal Col.
CAMBER PIER N ARM. Lt. 2 F.R. vert. 2M. Metal Col.
LOADING JETTY Lts. Q.

COALING PIER HEAD. Lt. V.Q.(3) 5 sec. 2M. on dolphin.
NE CORNER. Lt. F.R.
COALING PIER W END. Lt. Oc.G. 30 sec.
DEEP WATER BERTH Lts. 2F.R. Vert. each end.

Q. PIER. N CORNER. Lt. Fl.R. 5 sec. 5M. Metal frame Tr.
Q. PIER. S CORNER. Lt. Fl.G. 5 sec. 5M. Metal frame Tr.
Q. PIER. ELBOW. Lt. Fl. R. 2 sec. 2M. Metal frame Tr.

NAVAL AIR STATION Lt. Aero M(PO)R. 15m. Occas.

W. OF Q. PIER. Helicopter App. Control. Lt. Q.R. occas. 2M. Wooden pile 3m. not lit when Y. helicopter approach Lts. are on.

SMALL MOUTH Lt.Bn. L.Fl. 10 sec. 5M. W. □ on pile. 3m.
FERRYBRIDGE LDG. LTS. 288°02′ (Front) Q.G. 2M. Post 3m. (Rear) Iso.G. 4 sec. 2M. on bridge 5m.
WELWORTHY. Lt. Fl.(4) 10 sec. 5M. W. □ on pile. 3m.
NEWTONS COVE. D. G. Range Lt.By. Fl.Y. 2 sec. Can.Y. plus 4 Spar Bys. 120ft. square, 62m. to NW.
PORTLAND DEEP. D. G. Range Lt.By. Fl.Y. 10 sec. Can. & By. Can.Y. Topmark X.
STEMMING. Lt.By. Fl.Y. 5 sec. Can Y. 3.3M. S. of Durdle Door.
WEYMOUTH (SHALLOW). D.G. Range By. Can. Y. and Lt.By. Fl.Y. 5 sec. Can. Y.
PORTLAND NOISE RANGE. Lt.By. Fl.Y. 5 sec. Can. Y. & 3 Bys. Pillar Y.

WEYMOUTH 50°36′N, 2°27′W. Piermaster

Tel: (0305) 760276. HM Tel: (0305) 760620. Pilots: (0305) 773118. Customs: (0305) 774747.
HARBOUR WAYPOINT. 50°36.5′N, 2°26.0′W.
Radio — Port: VHF Chan. 16, 12. 0800-1700 (winter); 0700-2330 (summer) and as required.
Radio — Pilots: VHF Chan. 16, 9. P/V. VHF Chan. 16. When vessel expected. Send E.T.A 12 h. and 2 h. in advance.

Entry: Vessels up to 5.2m. draught enter/leave any time.
Visitors mooring (75) below Town Bridge.
Report to Piermaster on arrival.
Yacht Clubs: Royal Dorset (0305) 786258.
　　　　Weymouth S.C. (0305) 785481.
　　　　Weymouth Portland C.A. (0305) 833502.
Anchorages: Weymouth Roads between Nothe/Redcliffe Point 9-16m.
Signals: Shown from mast on S Pier and adjacent Weymouth Sailing Club.
2 F.R. over 1 G. Lt. = entrance foul, entry or departure forbidden.

Traffic Sigs 188m. SW Explos (3) 5 min. when V/l expected. Reed 15 sec. when British Rail vessel docking.
N PIER. Lt. 2 F.G. vert. 6M. 9m. Bell when vessels expected. Storm Sigs.
RO-RO FERRY TERMINAL Lt. 2 F.G. vert. each end. 2M. Dolphin.
BALLAST QUAY. Ldg. Lts. 237.5° (Front) F.R. 4M. W. △ on post. 5m. (Rear) F.R. 4M. W. △ on post. 7m.
ARISH MELL. Lt.By. Fl.Y. 5 sec. Can. Y.
WORBARROW BAY. Lt.By. Fl.Y. 5 sec. Can.Y. marks pipeline.
BINDON HILL Lt. Iso.R. 2 sec. Occasl.

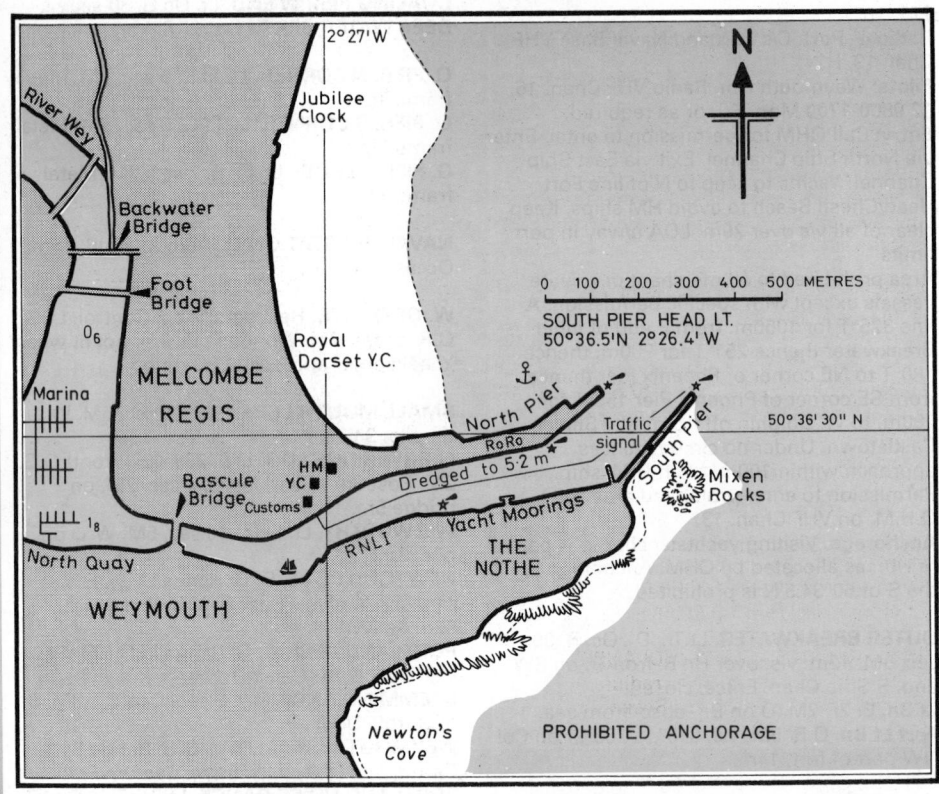

3 Fl.R. Lts. = Serious Emergency. Port Closed.
3 R. Lts. = vessel leaving; no app. vessel to obstruct ent.
3 G. Lts. = vessel app. from seaward, no vessel to leave harbour.
G/W/G Vert = Vessels to proceed with specific permission only.
Outer Harbour: 185 visitors berths.
No vessels, whether under oars, sails or power, to obstruct main channel.
Weymouth Bridge Signals: 3 R. Lts. Vert. = Bridge closed. 3 G. Lts. Vert. = Bridge open.
S PIER Lt. Q. 9M. White mast on platform.

Lulworth Cove Gunnery Range—Firing Danger Areas—Firing practice from sea and shore is carried out periodically between Lulworth Cove and Saint Alban's Head; the danger areas extend up to six miles offshore. When a danger area is in use, red flags are displayed and red lights exhibited, night and day, from Bindon Hill near Lulworth Cove, and Saint Alban's Head. Vessels may pass through the area but should endeavour to comply with advice from range safety vessels. The DZ buoys near Saint Alban's Ledge are targets for naval gunnery and, for

safety, vessels are advised to keep at least a mile clear of them. Keep watch on VHF Chan. 8 when firing in progress. For information of times, dates etc, ring Tel. No:
Naval Operations (H24) Portland 820311 Ext. 2358 or VHF Chan. 14.
Range Officer (During Firing) Bindon Abbey 462721 Ext. 819.
Guard Room (H24) Bindon Abbey 462721 Ext. 824.
Broadcast of Firing Times:
Radio Solent: 0745 hr.
2 Counties Radio: 0750, 0850 hr.
Portland Naval Base. VHF Chan. 13, 14. 0945, 1645 hr.

INSHORE WAYPOINT OFF ST. ALBANS HD. 50°30.5′N, 2°01.5′W.
ST. ALBANS HEAD Lt. Iso.R. 2 sec. Occas.
DZA Lt.By. Fl.Y. 2 sec. Can. Y.
DZB Lt.By. Fl.Y. 10 sec. Can. Y.
DZC Lt.By. Fl.Y. 5 sec. Can. Y.
Measured Distance: Anvil Point (near Durlston Head) 1M. 2 prs. W. iron masts. △ Topmark. 094°/274° Mag. 1 pr. E of Anvil Pt. Lt., other ¾M. West.

INSHORE WAYPOINT OFF ANVIL POINT. 50°35.0′N, 1°56.0′W.

ANVIL POINT 50°35.5′N, 1°57.5′W. Lt. Fl. 10 sec. 24M. vis. 237° to 076°. White Tr. 45m. shown H24.

PEVERIL LEDGE By. Can. R. Off Peveril Pt.

SWANAGE
Pier Lt. 2 F.R. vert. 3M. White mast with lantern, 6m. on N arm of Pier.

HISTORIC WRECK SITE STUDLAND BAY. 50°39.65′N, 1°54.80′W. 50m. radius.
ARTIFICIAL REEF (Fisheries Research) 50°39.69′N, 1°54.83′W.

POOLE 50°41′N 1°57′W. Tel: Poole (0202) 685261. Fax: (0202) 665703. Telex: 41134 PHC G. Pilots: (0202) 666401.
HARBOUR WAYPOINT. 50°39.0′N, 1°54.0′W.
Radio — Port: VHF Chan. 16, 14. H24.
Radio — Pilots: VHF Chan. 16, 14, 9, 6. H24.
Salterns Y.C. Marina (0202) 707321. Chan. M. Apr.-Oct. 0800-1600.
Cobbs Quay Marina Tel. No. (0202) 674299. 18.2m. × 1.8m. draught.
Sunseeker Marina Tel. No. (0202) 685335.
Fuel Barge Tel. No. (0202) 883152 VHF Channel 9,8,14,6,67,16. Also Chan. (M) 0830-1900 Summer. 0900-1700 Winter. Closed Jan-March. Other times by arrangement.

Harbour Entrance approach via the Swash Channel. Be aware of the Half Tide Training Bank on approach to the Harbour Entrance. Harbour Entrance very congested at peak entering and leaving times. The Middle Channel which is only 60m. wide is now used by the majority of Commercial Vessels, who must be given priority in use. Recreational craft advised to use the old Main Channel whenever possible.
Middle Ship Channel dredged to 5.2m.
Salterns Marina dredged to 1.5m. (Draught 1.8m.).
Swash Channel 5.2m. Buoyage extended.
Fuel barge at junction Brownsea Roads/Wych Channel near No. 50 By. Diesel, petrol, Calor, chandlery etc. Draught — generally 3.6m.-6.5m.
Lifting Bridge between Poole Town and Lower Hamworthy.
R.Lt.—do not approach bridge (vessels entitled to request bridge to be opened contact Poole Bridge on VHF Chan. 14.).
Bridge opening times: Mon.-Fri. 0930, 1130, 1430, 1630, 1830, 2130, 2330; Sat.-Sun. & Bank Hol. 0730, 0930, 1130, 1330, 1530, 1730, 1930, 2130, 2330/0630 opened on request.
Sandbanks Ferry when working displays 1 B. ball or W., G., R. Lts. vert. Ferry gives way to other vessels in Harbour. Sound 4 short blasts for ferry to keep clear. Allow enough time for ferry to manoeuvre.
Anchorage: South Deep. Visitors moorings at Town Quay.

SWASH CHANNEL

POOLE FAIRWAY Lt.By. L.Fl. 10 sec. Pillar R.W.V.S. Topmark Sph. Bell.
TRAINING BANK Lt.By. Fl.R. 4 sec. Can.R. marks seaward end of training wall on SW side of Swash Channel. 5 stakes with R. Can. Topmarks at intervals along Training Bank.

Bar No: 1 Lt.By. Q.G. Conical G. Bell.
No: 2 Lt.By. Fl.R. 2 sec. Can.R.
No: 3 By. Conical G.
No: 4 By. Can. R.
No: 5 By. Conical G.
No: 6 Punch & Judy By. Can. R.
No: 7 By. Conical G.
No: 8 By. Can. R.
No: 9 Lt.By. Fl.G. 5 sec. Conical G.
No: 10 Lt.By. Fl.R. 4 sec. Can. R.
No: 11 Lt.By. HOOK SANDS. Fl.G. 3 sec. Conical G.
No: 12 Channel Lt.By. Fl.R. 2 sec. Can. R. W of centre inner end Swash Channel.

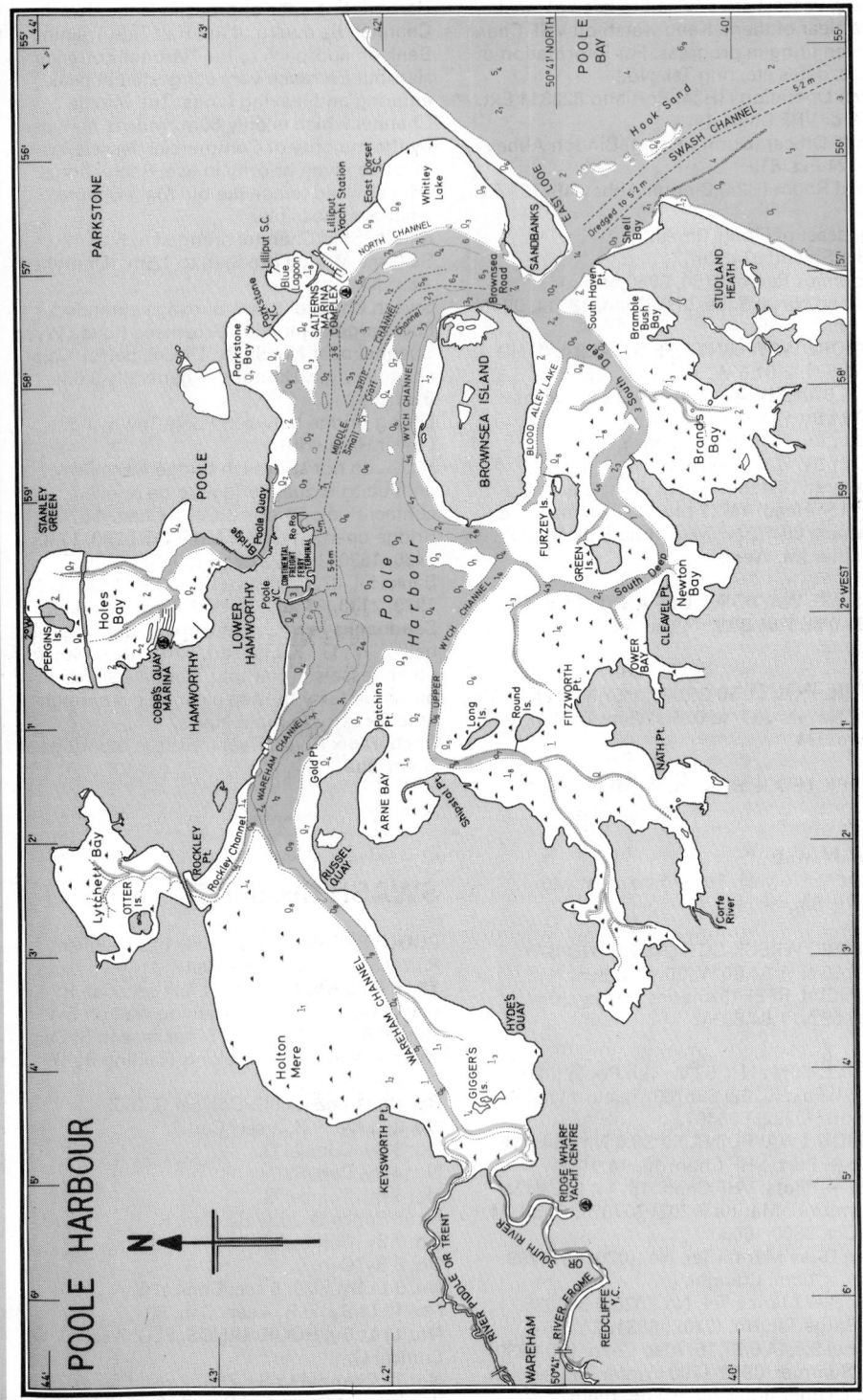

POOLE HARBOUR

N

No: 12A. By. Can.R.
No: 13 Lt.By. Fl.G. 5 sec. Conical G.
No: 14 Lt.By. Fl.R. 4 sec. Can. R.

SOUTH HAVEN POINT. Lt. Q.R. Ferry Landing.
Fl.R. on sides of ramp.
SAND BANKS. Lt.Bn. F.Or. 10M. vis. 315°-135°
4m. R.C.
FERRY LANDING. Lt. 2 F.G. vert. on W side of
Ramp. (When approaching signal 4 long
blasts.)

EAST LOOE CHANNEL

EAST LOOE Lt.By. Q.R. Can. R. marks E Looe
Chan.
EAST HOOK By. Can. R. marks E. side Hook
Sands.
HOOK SANDS Bn. B.Y. Topmark N.
EAST LOOE Lt.Bn. Oc.W.R.G. 6 sec. W.10M.,
R.6M., G.6M. Col. 9m. R.234°-294°; W.294°-
304°; G.304°-024°.
GROYNE S. End Lt. Fl.G. 3 sec. G △ on Bn.

N. HAVEN POINT. Lt.Bn. Q.(9) 15 sec.
Topmark W.
3 Cable Bns. Lt.F. between N Haven Pt. and
Brownsea Castle.
18a Lt.By. Fl. R. 4 sec. Can. R.
No. 18 Lt.By. Fl.R. 5 sec. Can. R.

SOUTH DEEP CHANNEL
No. 1 Pile Lt. Fl.G. 5 sec. Conical G.

No. 2 Pile. Can. R.
No. 3 Pile Lt. Fl.G. 5 sec. Conical G.
No. 4 Pile Lt. Fl.R. 5 sec. Can. R.
No. 5 Pile Lt. Fl.G. 5 sec. Conical G.
No. 6 Pile Lt. Fl.R. 5 sec. Can. R.
No. 7 Pile G. Conical G.
No. 8 Pile R. Can. R.
No. 9 Pile G. Conical G.
No. 10 Pile Lt. Fl.(2)R. 5 sec. Can. R.
No. 11 Pile Lt. Fl.(2)G. 5 sec. Conical G.
No. 12 Pile Lt. Fl.R. 5 sec. Can. R.
No. 13 Pile Lt. Fl.G. 5 sec. Conical G.
No. 14 Pile R. Can. R.
No. 15 Pile Lt. Fl.G. 5 sec. Conical G.
No. 16 Pile R. Can. R.
No. 18 Pile Lt. Fl.R. 5 sec. Can. R.
No. 19 Pile Lt. Fl.G. 5 sec. Conical G.
No. 20 Pile R. Can. R.

B.P. FURZEY ISLAND DEVELOPMENT
FURZEY ISLAND SLIPWAY Ldg.Lts. 305°
(Front) Fl.Y. 2 sec. 2M. 7m (Rear) Fl.Y. 2 sec.
2M. 9m.

BROWNSEA ROAD TO POOLE
TOWN (VIA NORTH CHANNEL)
No. 42 Lt.By. Q(3) 10 sec. Pillar B.Y.B.
Topmark E.
No: 19A Lt.By. Fl.G. 5 sec. Conical G.
SOUTH MIDDLE GROUND No: 20 Lt.By. Q.(6)
+L.Fl. 15 sec. Pillar Y.B. Topmark S.
No: 22 Lt.By. Fl.R. 4 sec. Can. R.

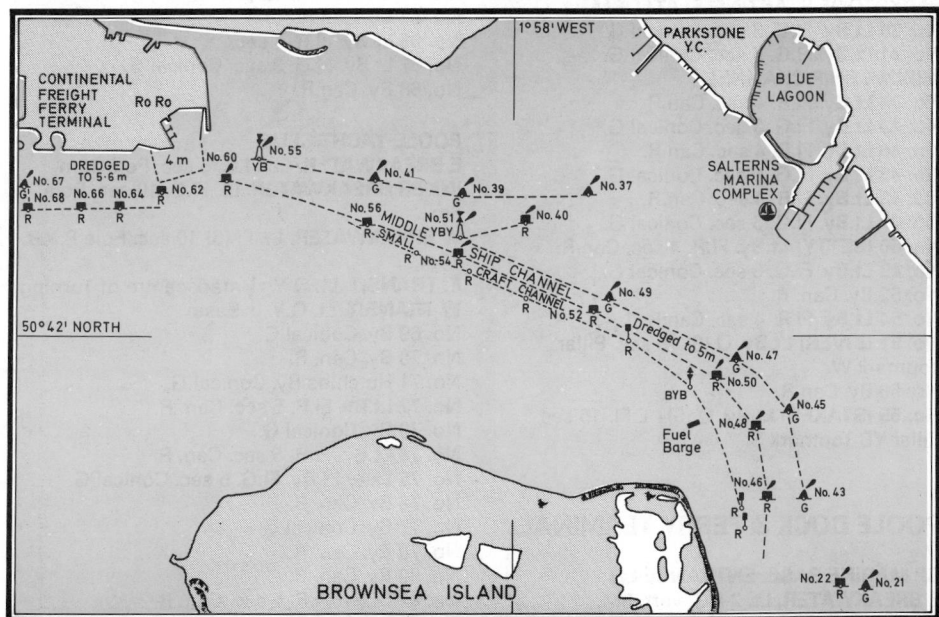

ROYAL MOTOR YACHT CLUB
E. BREAKWATER Lt. 2 F.G. vert. 2M.
W. BREAKWATER Lt. 2 F.G. vert.
No: 21 JACK JONES Lt.By. Fl.G. 5 sec. Conical
G.
No: 23 By. Conical G.
No: 26 By. Can. R.
BULLPIT Lt.Bn. Q.(9) 15 sec. Topmark W.
No: 28 By. Can. R.
No: 25 By. Conical G.
No: 30 BASKET BOOM Lt.By. Fl.R. 4 sec. Can.
R.
No: 27 By. Conical G.
No: 32 Lt.By. Fl.R. 4 sec. Can. R.
No: 29 Lt.By. Fl.G. 5 sec. Conical G.
No: 31 By. Conical G.

SALTERNS Lt.Bn. Q.(6) + L.Fl. 15 sec. Topmark
S.
POOLE HR. Y.C. & MARINA
INNER BREAKWATER. Lt. 2 F.G. vert. 3M.
OUTER BREAKWATER. Lt. 2 F.R. vert. 3M.
Channel By. Conical G.
Channel By. Can. R.
At the Marina, a "WAIT" sign lit orange
placed on S breakwater to warn small craft of
commercial vessels navigating in vicinity.
No: 33 By. Conical G.
No: 34 Lt.By. Fl.R. 4 sec. Can. R.
SALTERNS No: 36 Lt.By. Fl.R. 4 sec. Can. R.
No: 38 By. Barrel R.W. cheq.
No: 35 Lt.By. Fl.G. 5 sec. Conical G.
No: 38a Lt.By. Fl.R. 4 sec. Can. R.
No: 37 By. Conical G.
No: 40 Lt.By. Fl.R. 4 sec. Can. R.
PARKSTONE STARTING PLATFORM. Lt. Q.
No: 39 Lt.By. Fl.G. 3 sec. Conical G.
No: 41 Lt.By. Fl.G. 5 sec. Conical G.
MIDDLE SHIP CHANNEL
No: 44 Lt.By. Fl.R. 4 sec. Can.R.
No: 43 Lt.By. Fl.G. 3 sec. Conical G.
No: 46 Lt.By. Fl.R. 4 sec. Can.R.
No: 45 Lt.By. Fl.G. 5 sec. Conical G.
No: 48 Lt.By. Fl.R. 4 sec. Can.R.
No: 47 Lt.By. Fl.G. 3 sec. Conical G.
No: 50 (BETTY) Lt.By. Fl.R. 4 sec. Can.R.
No: 49 Lt.By. Fl.G. 5 sec. Conical G.
No: 52 By. Can. R.
No: 54 Lt.By. Fl.R. 4 sec. Can.R.
No: 51 (DIVER) Lt.By. Q.(9) 15 sec. Pillar
Topmark W.
No: 56 By. Can.R.
No: 55 (STAKES) Lt.By. Q.(6)+ L.Fl. 15 sec.
Pillar YB Topmark S.

POOLE DOCK & FERRY TERMINAL

BP MARINE BASE. ENTRANCE Lts.
E BREAKWATER. Lt. 2 F.G. vert. 6M.
W BREAKWATER. Lt. 2 F.G. vert. 6M.

HAMWORTHY, RO-RO FERRY TERMINAL. No.
1. W END. Lt. 2 F.G. vert. **E END** Lt. 2 F.G. vert.

TERMINAL No. 2 W END. Lt. 2 F.G. vert. **E**
END Lt. 2 F.G. vert.

TERMINAL No. 3 W END. Lt. 2 F.G. vert.

OYSTER BANK. Lt.Bn. Fl.(3)G. 5 sec. Pile E
side of Little Channel.

LITTLE CHANNEL (Speed limit 6 kts.) 3 x G.
Piles Topmark Conical G. mark E. side of
channel.

THE BRIDGE BETWEEN POOLE TOWN AND
HAMWORTHY has R. Or. and G. Traffic Lts.
Shown on NE and SW towers. A G. Lt. will be
exhibited when the bridge is completely lifted
and passage through the bridge is clear. A R.
Lt. will be exhibited to indicate that vessels
must not approach close to the bridge from the
direction in which the R. Lt. is visible. When a
Fl. Or. Lt. is exhibited it indicates that the bridge
is not completely lifted but vessels on the side
on which this Lt. is visible may pass through
the bridge with caution.

WAREHAM CHANNEL
No. 60 Lt.By. Fl.R. 4 sec. Can.R.
No. 62 Lt.By. Fl.R. 4 sec.
No. 64 By. Can.R.
No. 66 Lt.By. Fl.R. 4 sec.
No. 67 Lt.By. Fl.G. 3 sec. Conical G.
No. 68 By. Can.R.

POOLE YACHT CLUB
E BREAKWATER. Lt. Fl.G. 5 sec. Pole 10m.
INNER BREAKWATER. Lt. Fl.G. 10 sec. Pole
6m.
W BREAKWATER. Lt. Fl.(3) 10 sec. Pole B.Y.B.
10m.
E. TRANSIT. Lt. Q.Y. } mark centre of Turning
W TRANSIT. Lt. Q.Y. } Basin
No. 69 By. Conical G.
No. 70 By. Can. R.
No. 71 Hutchins By. Conical G.
No. 72 Lt.By. Fl.R. 5 sec. Can. R.
No. 73 By. Conical G.
No. 74 Lt.By. Fl.R. 5 sec. Can. R.
No. 75 Lake Lt.By. Fl.G. 5 sec. Conical G.
No. 76 By. Can. R.
No. 77 By. Conical G.
No. 78 By. Can. R.
No. 80 By. Can. R.
No. 82 Lt.By. Fl.R. 5 sec. Can. R.
No. 84 By. Can. R.

POOLE TO NEEDLES CHANNEL

POOLE HEAD By. Can. Y. marks sewer off Poole Head.
BRANKSOME CHINE By. Can. Y. marks sewer off Branksome.
ALUM CHINE By. Can. Y. marks pipes off Alum Chine.
WHITBREAD MARK YACHT RACING By. Can.Y.

BOURNEMOUTH 50°43′N, 1°52′W. Tel: Bournemouth 28282.
Entry Signals: R. flag at Bournemouth or Boscombe Pier at half mast—no entry on side indicated: R. Lt. (Night) — no entry.

HENGISTBURY HEAD. RG STN.
50°42.92′N, 1°45.56′W. Coastguard emergency DF Stn. VHF Chan. 16 & 67. Controlled by MRSC Portland.

INSHORE WAYPOINT OFF CHRISTCHURCH LEDGE. 50°41.0′N, 1°41.0′W.

CHRISTCHURCH 50°47′N, 1°50′W. Air Lt. Al.Fl.W.G. 10 sec. at Hurn Aerodrome.
Christchurch Harbour: Suitable for craft 25m. × 1.8m. draught. Harbour mostly dries. Reported that The Run (inner end entrance channel) dries at 0.6m. and ebb tide reaches 5 kts. Entry later than 30 mins. after 2nd HW inadvisable. Speed limit 4 kts.
Fuel, water available.

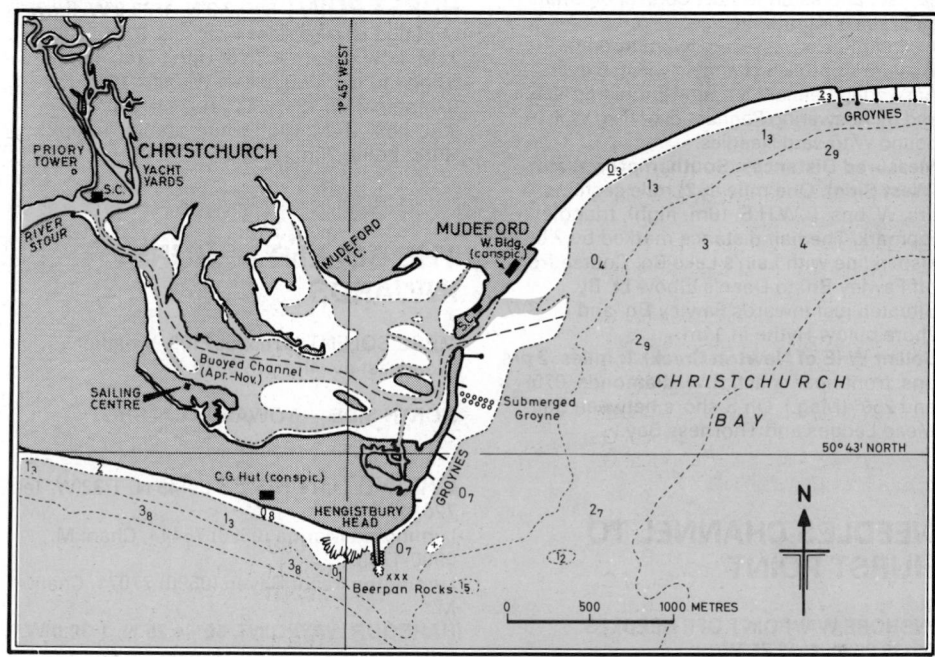

Bournemouth Pier: Depths 2.7m. to 3.4m. at outer end.

PIER HEAD. 2 F.R. vert. 2m. apart, white post, 8m. 1M. Horn(2) 120 sec. when ships expected.
BOURNEMOUTH PIER OUTFALL. By. Can. Y. marks drain pipes ¼M. E of Pier.

BOSCOMBE 50°43′N, 1°50′W
PIER HEAD. 2 F.R. vert. on R. Col. 7m. 1M. F.R. Lts. on hotel shown 289.5°, 0.51M. from Pier Lt.
BOSCOMBE PIER OUTFALL. By. Can. Y.

Lt.By. Fl.(2)R. 10 sec. Can.R. (May-Sept.).
LAMBETH By. Sph.Y. (April-October).
N HEAD. 50°42.6′N, 1°35.4′W Lt.By. Fl.(3)G. 10 sec. Conical G. marks W end N Chan. apprs. to the W Solent.

SOUTHAMPTON 50°54′N 1°24′W. HM. Tel: HM (0703) 330022. Ext. 2440 & 2478. VTS office. (0703) 339733. Pilots: (0703) 632345.
Telex: 477161 DHMSPR G.
Radio — Pilots: Office VHF Ch. 16, 9.
Vessels VHF Ch. 16, 6, 8, 9, 10, 12, 14, 18, 19, 24, 25, 26, 27.

VTS (for Southampton, Portsmouth and The Solent)
Port Radio: VHF Ch. 16, 12, 14, 18, 20, 22. H24.
Southampton Patrol: VHF Ch. 12, 16, 01-28, 60-88. H24. C/s SP.
Esso Fawley: VHF Ch. 16, 14, 19. H24.
All vessels to report to Southampton Radio before arrival/departure and at Reporting Points indicated on charts on VHF Chan. 12.
Radar Coverage: East Lepe to No Man's Land Fort.
Radar Assistance, Tidal Information, Wind and Weather information available on request.
Information Broadcasts VHF Chan 12 ev. even H+00 0600-2200 Fri.-Sun. plus B/Hol. Mon. Easter to 30 Sept. for small craft.
Southampton: All vessels over 20m length to contact and listen to Port Control on Chan 12 and report intentions.
All commercial vessels outward through Western Approach channel fly Flag E over Answering Pennant if bound E towards Nab. and fly Answering Pennant over Flag W if bound W toward Needles.
Measured Distances: Southampton Water (West Side). One mile in 2½ mile sections. 3 prs. W. bns. B.W.H.S. (6m. high), triangle topmark. The half distance marked by 2 bns. also in line with Lain's Lake Bn. Course from off Fawley Bn. to Dean's Elbow Lt. By. Situated just inwards Fawley Bn. and on SW shore below Hythe in 11m.
Solent W (E of Newton Creek) 1¼ miles. 2 prs bns. front near coast. R.W. diamonds. 070° and 250° (Mag.). On S shore between Salt Mead Ledges and Thorness Bay.

NEEDLES CHANNEL TO HURST POINT

INSHORE WAYPOINT OFF NEEDLES.
50°39.25′N, 1°37.75′W.

HISTORIC WRECK SITE NEEDLES. 50°39.7′N, 1°35.45′W, 75m. radius.

NEEDLES 50°39.7′N 1°35.4′W Lt.Ho. Oc.(2) 20 sec. W.R.G. W. 17M. R. 14M. G. 14M. R. 291°-300°. W. 300°-083°. R. 083°-212°. W. 212°-217°. G. 217°-224°. Circular granite Tr. R. band, gallery and R. lantern on extreme edge of Needles Rocks. 24m. Horn(2) 30 sec.

FAIRWAY. Lt.By. L.Fl. 10 sec. Pillar R.W.V.S. Topmark Sph. marks approach line for Hurst Point Lts. Whis. ᪐.

SW SHINGLES. Lt.By. Fl.R. 2½ sec. Pillar R. on S edge Shingles Bank. ᪐.
BRIDGE. Lt.By. V.Q(9) 10 sec. Pillar Y.B.Y. Topmark W. on extreme edge of reef. ᪐.
SHINGLES ELBOW. Lt.By. Fl.(2)R 5 sec. Can.R. marks Shingles Bank.
MIDDLE SHINGLES. Lt.By. Fl.(3)R. 10 sec. Can. R.
TOTLAND BAY PIER. Lt. 2 F.G. vert. 6m. end of Pier.
WARDEN LEDGE. Lt.By. Fl.G. 2½ sec. Conical G. marks bank off Warden Point. ᪐ Bell.
NE SHINGLES. Lt.By. Q.(3) 5 sec. Pillar B.Y.B. Topmark E.

INSHORE WAYPOINT OFF HURST POINT.
50°42.40′N, 1°32.50′W.

HURST POINT 50°42.3′N, 1°33.0′W. (Low Lt.) Ldg.Lts. 042°. Iso. 4 sec. vis. 029°-053°. 14M. Low square R.Tr. at Hurst Fort. 15m. (High Lt.) Iso. W.R. 6 sec. W. 080°-104° (Unintens) W. 234°-244°; R. 244°-250°; W. 250°-053°. 14M. High white circular Tr. on Hurst Point. 23m.

THE SOLENT — HURST INWARDS

MRSC SOLENT (0705) 552100. Weather broadcast ev. 4h from 0040.

NORTH SIDE — TOWARDS CALSHOT

LYMINGTON RIVER 50°45′N, 1°32′W. Tel: 72014.
Lymington Marina (0590) 75444. Chan. M. 0900-1700.
Lymington Yacht Haven (0590) 77071. Chan. M.
HARBOUR WAYPOINT. 50°44.25′N, 1°30.0′W.
Entry: Lymington Yacht Haven: 30.4m. × 2.4m. depth alongside.
Lymington Marina: 28.9m. × 3m. draught.
Town Quay: Depth alongside of 2m. Speed limit 6 knots.
Anchorage: Lymington Road in 7m.
LYMINGTON. Ldg.Lts. 318°30′ (Front) F.R. 8M. (Rear) F.R. 8M. vis. 308.5°-328.5°.
JACK IN THE BASKET. Lt.Bn. Fl.R. 2 sec. 9m. Topmark Can. ᪐.
CROSS BOOM No: 2 Lt.Bn. Fl.R. 2 sec. 3M. Topmark Can. 4m.
STAGE BOOM No: 1 Lt. Bn. Fl.G. 2 sec. 3M. Topmark Cone. 2m.
No: 3 Lt.Bn. Fl.G. 2 sec. 3M. Topmark Cone. 2m.

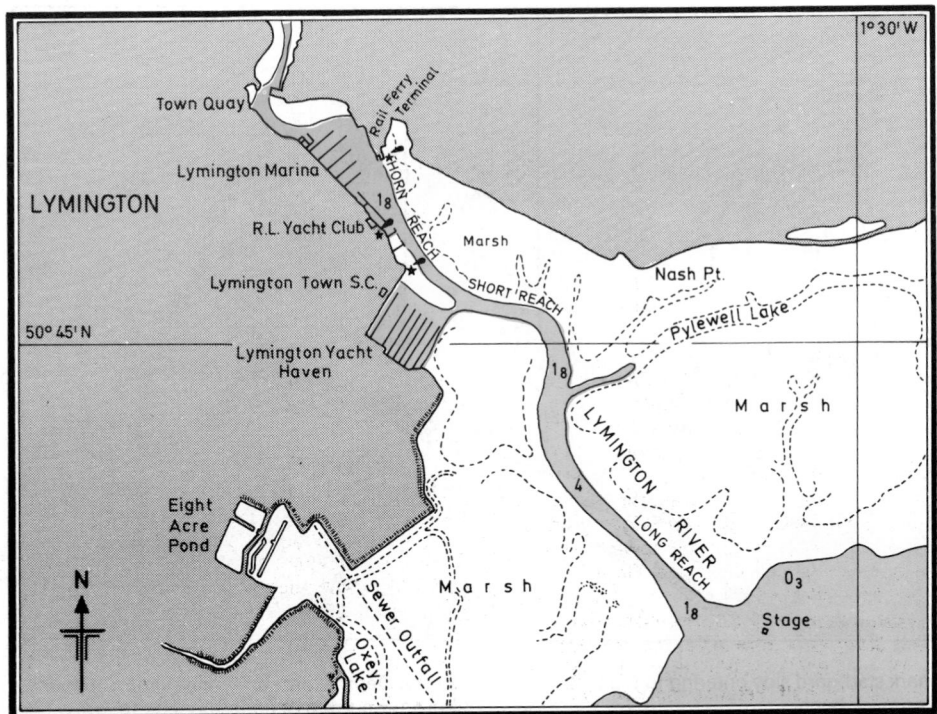

No: 7 Lt.Bn. Fl.G. 2 sec. 1M. Topmark Cone. 2m.
SEYMOURS POST. Lt.Bn. Fl.R. 2 sec. Topmark Can.
TAR BARREL. Lt.Bn. Fl.G. 2 sec.
ENTICOTT PILE. Lt.Bn. Fl.G. 2 sec. Topmark Cone.
COCKED HAT. Lt.Bn. Fl.R. 2 sec. 3M. Topmark Can. 3m.
CAGE BOOM No: 9 Lt.Bn. Fl.G. 2 sec. 3M. Topmark Cone. 4m.
No: 11 Lt.Bn. Fl.G. 2 sec.
HARPERS POST. Lt.Bn. Q.(3) 10 sec. 1M. B. □ and ○ on pile, 5m.
WAVESCREEN NE HEAD Lt. 2 F.R. vert.
BREAKWATER HEAD. Lt. 2 F.G. vert.

LYMINGTON YACHT HAVEN Ldg.Lts. 244° (Front) F.Y. R. ▽ on pile 4m. (Rear) F.Y. R. ▽ on pile 6m.
CAR FERRY PIER. Lt.Bn. 2 F.G. vert. Also V.Q.G.
INSHORE WAYPOINT OFF W LEPE. 50°45.0′N, 1°24.0′W.
WEST LEPE. Lt.By. Fl. R. 5 sec. Can. R. on edge of Lepe Middle Bank.
FRIGATE By. Sph.Y. (April-Oct.)
MUMM CHAMPAGNE By. Sph.Y. (April-Oct.)
PORSCHE By. Sph.Y. (April-Oct.)

INSHORE WAYPOINT OFF E LEPE. 50°45.8′N, 1°21.0′W.
EAST LEPE. Lt.By. Fl.(2)R. 5 sec. Can.R. Bell(2) 20 sec.
DURNS POINT. Obstr. Lt. Q. R. Dolphin.
MOTORTUNE. By. Sph. Y. (April-Oct.).

BEAULIEU RIVER Tel: (0590) 63200
HARBOUR WAYPOINT. 50°46.70′N, 1°21.60′W.
BEAULIEU SPIT. Lt.Bn. Fl.R. 5 sec. 3M. R. Dolphin, vis. 277°-037°. The Swatchway now closed to navigation. Use Main Channel.
Entry: V/ls with draught of 2m. or more should not cross the bar 1 h-LW-1 h (Springs) or in heavy weather.
Bar reported least depth 0.6m.
Bucklers Hard Marina 21.3m. × 2.1m. draught. Speed limit 5 kts. **Anchorage:** 1st Reach in lee of Gull Island.
Chan. marked by perches at intervals on either bank. Two leading marks in line bearing 337° lead in. Front seaward Transit Bn. R. with white triangular topmark close to the other R. port hand Bns. while Rear inland Transit Bn. is high up in trees W. of boat house.
Approach close to seaward Lt.Bn. leaving it and all 8 R. pile Bns. (with Can.R. topmarks) to port when entering.
7 G. pile Bns. (with Conical G. topmarks) also

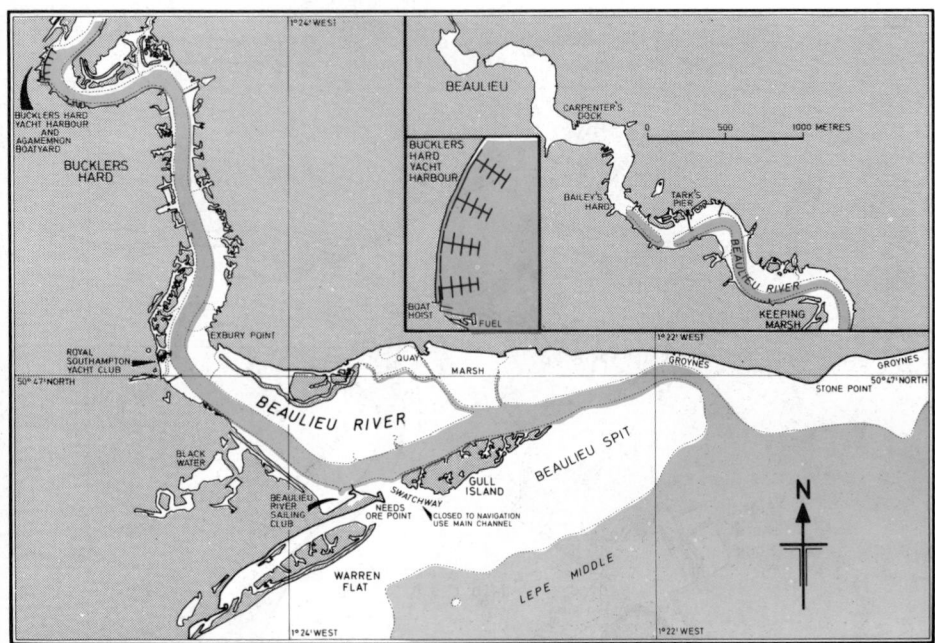

mark starboard side entering to the first approach bend.

All Chan. pile Bns. carry appropriate R.W. small reflectors as aid to navigation after dusk.

APPROACH CHANNEL No. 5, 9, 19 Lts. Fl.G. 4 sec.

APPROACH CHANNEL No. 12, 20 Lts. Fl.R. 4 sec.

BUCKLERS HARD MARINA Lt. 2 F.R. Vert. on pontoons A.C. and E.

No. 21 Lt. Fl.G. 4 sec.

SOUTH SIDE — TOWARDS CALSHOT

PORT VICTORIA PIER HEAD. Lt. 2 F.G. vert.
SCONCE. Lt.By. Q. Pillar B.Y. Topmark N Bell
NORTON SEWER By. Conical G., marks end of Norton sewer outfall.
BLACK ROCK. By. Conical G. marks Black Rock in Yarmouth Roads.

HISTORIC WRECK SITE. 50°42.52'N, 1°29.59'W, 50m. radius.

YARMOUTH HARBOUR (I.O.W.)

50°42'N, 1°30'W. Tel: 0983-760 321
Safety Signals: When harbour is full, signals shown from end ferry jetty. Illuminated notice 'Harbour Full' or R. flag by day, do not enter, anchor outside.

Entry: Depths: 2m. on leading line; 1.6m. in harbour entrance; generally 2m. to 4m. between bridges.
River Yar Bridge: clearance 2.2m. when closed. Opens 0830, 1015, 1215, 1415, 1715, 1815, 2015 1st April-30th September. Speed limit 4 knots.
Pier Lt. 2 F.R. vert. 2M. 5m. on G. Col. centre of Pier.
Lt. F. E and W ends. vis. 167.5°-192.5° occas.
HARBOUR. Ldg.Lts. 187°34'. (Front) 2 F.G. White ◊ B. Post. 5m. (Rear) F.G. 2M. W. ◊ B. Post 6m.
JETTY HEAD. Lt. 2 F.R. vert. 2M. W. Mast 4m. Second F.R. shown when Hbr. Full. 167.5°-192.5°.
Lt. Fl.G. 5 sec. 175°-060°.
FERRY TERMINAL. Lt. 2 F.R. vert. 2M. Dolphin 5m.
No: 1 MOORING Lt.By. Fl. 5 sec.
HAMSTEAD LEDGE. Lt.By. Fl.(2)G. 5 sec. Conical G.

INSHORE WAYPOINT OFF NEWTOWN. 50°44.0'N, 1°25.50'W.

NEWTOWN (I.O.W.)

NEWTOWN RIVER By. Can.R. at entce.
Newtown River: Depth of 0.9m. on the Bar with 1.2m. in River Entrance.
Anchorage: Clamerkin Lake and Clamerkin Lake/Newtown N Quay in 1.5m.
Facilities: Water, provisions available at N Quay and Lower Hampstead.

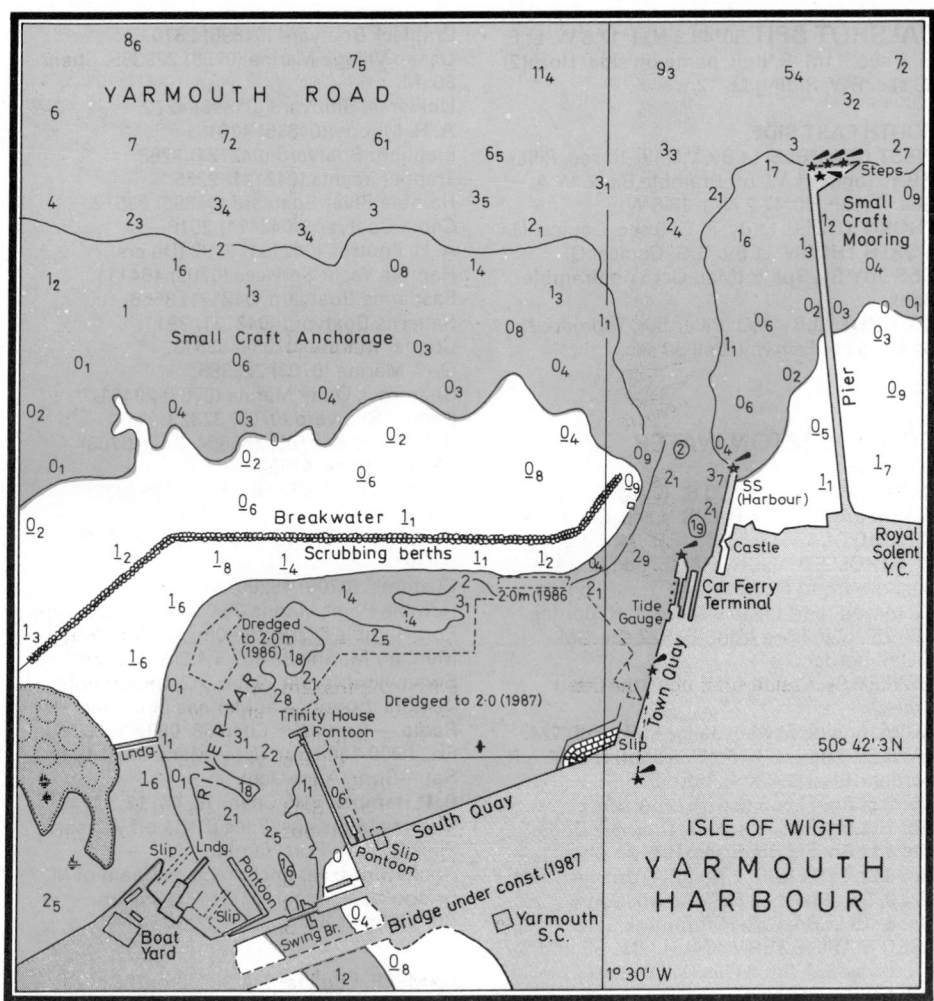

SALT MEAD. Lt.By. Fl.(3)G. 10 sec. Conical G. on N side of Salt Mead Ledges.
GURNARD LEDGE By. Conical. G. on N side.
GURNARD BAY. Keel By. Conical Y. (March-Oct.).
GURNARD. Lt.By. Q. Pillar B.Y. Topmark N.

DREDGED CHANNEL TO CALSHOT

ENTRY RESTRICTED Small craft under 20m. in length are not permitted to enter the area bounded by Bourne Gap By; Castle Point By; Reach By; Postn 50°47.89'N, 1°17.69'W; N Thorn By; Bourne Gap By., when vessels over 100m. in length are navigating the main channel between W Bramble By. (50°47.2'N, 1°18.6'W.) and Hook By. (50°49.5'N, 1°18.2'W.).

NORTHWEST SIDE
STANSORE POINT. 3 pile Bns. close S of Stansore Point, each with Qk.Fl.R.Lt. on R. Pile with W. band and R. ◇ marks cable. Keep clear, do not anchor. Gas mains dangerous.
NE GURNARD. Lt.By. Fl.(3)R. 10 sec. Can.R. 7 cables E of Stansore Point.
ROYAL THAMES By. Sph.Y. (Mar.-Oct.) Thorn Channel.
BOURNE GAP. Lt.By. Fl.R. 3 sec. Can.R. ⩙.
OUTFALL. Bn. Iso.R. 10 sec. 5M. Horn. 20 sec. ⩙. 4 F.R. one on each corner.
CALSHOT RADAR Bn. Close inshore E of Outfall Bn.
CALSHOT JETTY. Lt. 2 F.R. Vert.

CALSHOT SPIT 50°48.3′N, 1°17.5′W. Lt.F. Fl. 5 sec. 11M. R. hull, name on side. Horn(2) 60 sec. F.W. Riding Lt. 12m.

SOUTH EAST SIDE
WEST BRAMBLE. Lt.By. V.Q.(9) 10 sec. Pillar Y.B.Y. Topmark W. off Bramble Bank. W.A. Bell. Racon. 50°47.2′N, 1°18.6′W.
THORN KNOLL. Lt.By. Fl.G. 5 sec. Conical G.
NORTH THORN. Lt.By. Q.G. Conical G.
OSSORY By. Sph.Y (Mar.-Oct.) on Bramble Bank.
CALSHOT. Lt.By. V.Q. Pillar B.Y. Topmark N. on E side of Fairway. Bell 30 sec.

SOUTHAMPTON WATER
WEST SIDE
CASTLE POINT. Lt.By. I.Q.R. 10 sec. Can.R. ᰁ.
BLACK JACK. Lt.By. Fl.(2)R. 4 sec. Can.R. ᰁ.
CALSHOT CASTLE. Lt.Bn. F.R. 34m. Radar Tr.
CONTROLLED ANCHORAGE. Ldg.Lts. 326°07′. (Inshore front) Fl. 2 sec. 3M. Y. △ R. border. (Common rear) Fl.Or. 6 sec. Y. ◊ R. border. 327°25′. (Offshore front) Fl.R. 2 sec. 3M. Y O.R. border.
FAWLEY By. Can.R. off Entce. to Ashlett Creek.
AGWI. (inside Fawley Jetty) Lt.Bn. F.R. 2M.
FAWLEY. Ldg.Lts. 218°42′. (Front) Q.R. Y. △ R. border (Rear) Q.Y. ◊ R. border.
No: 2 Lt.Bn. Fl.R. 3 sec. R. □ on pile.
No: 1 Lt.Bn. Fl.G. 3 sec. G. Topmark Cone.
No: 4 Lt.Bn. Fl.(2)R. 5 sec. R. □ on pile.
No: 6 Lt.Bn. Fl.(3)R. 7 sec. R. □ on pile.
No: 3, 5 Lt.Bn. Q.G. G. Topmark Cone.
No: 8, 10 Lt.Bn. Q.R. R. Topmark Can.
ESSO MARINE TERMINAL. Lt.Bn. SE end. 2 F.R. vert. 10M. 9m. Whis.(2) 20 sec.
NW END. 2 F.G. vert.
FAWLEY Lt.By. Q.R. Can.R.
EAST SIDE
REACH. Lt.By. Fl.(3)G. 10 sec. Conical G. ᰁ.
HOOK. Lt.By. Q.G. Pillar G. Bell 15 sec. ᰁ. 50°49.5′N, 1°18.2′W.
BALD HEAD By. Conical G.
CHILLING By. Spherical B.
CORONATION. Lt.By. Fl.Y. 5 sec. Conical Y.
HAMBLE. Lt.By. Q.(6) + L.Fl. 15 sec. Pillar Y.B. Topmark S.

HISTORIC WRECK R. HAMBLE. 50°53.5′N, 1°17.22′W. Radius 75m.

RIVER HAMBLE (04895) 6387.
Hamble Point Marina (0703) 452464. Chan. M.
Stone Pier Yard. (04895) 4104.
Port Hamble (0703) 452741. Chan. M.
Mercury Yacht Hbr. (0703) 452741. Chan. M.

Crableck Boatyard (04895) 2570.
Ocean Village Marina (0703) 229385. Chan. 80. M.
Universal Shipyard (04895) 4272.
A. H. Moody (04895) 4261.
Elephant Boatyard (042121) 3268.
Trapper Yachts (042121) 2255.
Hamble River Boatyard (04895) 83572.
Cabin Boatyard (042121) 2516.
A. H. Foulkes (042121) 2182 (Divers).
Hamble Yacht Services (0703) 454111.
Eastlands Boatyard (042121) 3556.
Salterns Boatyard (042121) 3911.
Cougar Marine (0703) 453513.
O. V. Marina (0703) 229385.
Shamrock Quay Marina (0703) 29461.
Kemps Shipyard (0703) 32323.
B. P. Hamble (0703) 456654. Fax: (0703) 455578. Telex: 477504.
Warsash Divers Fareham 221125 (03295-4068).
Andark Ltd (Divers) (04895) 81755 (04892-6006).
Customs: (0703) 452007.
Hamble Point Marina 36.5m. × 3m. draught;
Port Hamble Marina 31.0m. × 3.6m. draught;
Mercury Marina 36.8m. × 4.5m. draught;
Swanwick Marina 19.8m. × 2.4m. draught.
Visitors moorings at Marinas or contact HM.
Radio — Port: VHF Chan 68. 0830-1700 Mon.-Fri.; 0900-1300 Sat. (Nov.-Mar.): 0900-1830 Sat.—Sun. (April-Oct.)
B. P. Hamble: VHF Chan. 16, 46, 12, 14, 19.
Visitors Moorings: Piles B1-B4 off Warsash; Piles 9-16 off Port Hamble.
Anchorages: No anchorage d/stream of M27.
Bridge clearances: M27: MHWS 4.3m. Bursledon: MHWS 4.0m. MLWS 8M.

HAMBLE. Ldg.Lts. 345°30′. (Front) Oc.(2)R. 12 sec. 2M. Pile 4m. (Rear) Q.R. 12M. White mast.
No. 1 Lt.Bn. Fl.G. 3 sec.
No. 2 Lt.Bn. Q.(3) 10 sec.
No. 3 Lt.Bn. Fl.(2)G. 5 sec.
No. 5 Lt.Bn. Fl.(3)G. 10 sec.
WARSASH. Ldg.Lts. 026°09′. (Front) Q.G.Pile B.W. cheq. 5m. 010°-040° (Rear) Iso. G. 6 sec. Bn. on Sailing Club. 12m. 022°-030°.
No: 6 Lt.Bn. Oc.(2)R. 12 sec. Dolphin R.
No. 7 Lt.Bn. Fl.G. 3 sec.
No. 8 Lt.Bn. Fl.R. 3 sec.
No. 9 Lt.Bn. Fl.(2)G. 5 sec.
No. 10 Lt.Bn. Fl.(2)R. 5 sec.
WARSASH JETTY Lt.Bn. 2 F.G. vert.
COUGAR MARINE PONTOON. Lt. 2 F.R. Vert.
Bl. Lt. Fl.R. 2 sec. Pile.
D9 Lt. Fl.G. 2 sec. Mooring Pile.
G20 Lt. Fl.R. 2 sec. Mooring Pile.
WARSASH SHORE Lt.Bn. Q.G. Pile G.
ROYAL THAMES Y.C. JETTY Lt.Bn. 2 F.G. vert.

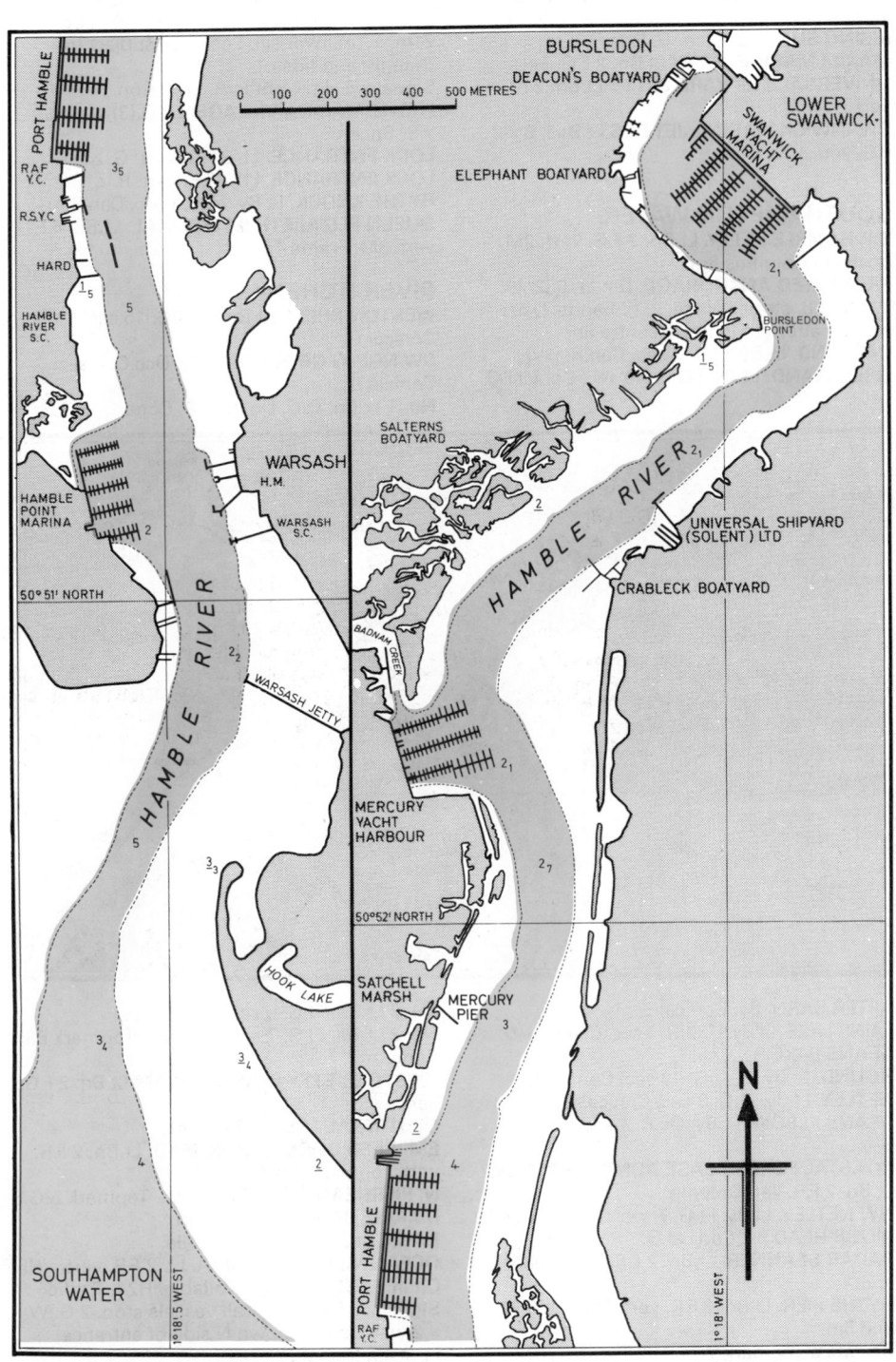

HARBOUR MASTER'S JETTY Lt.Bn. 2 F.G. vert.
RISING SUN Lt.Bn. Iso. G. 6 sec.
MAXIM MARINE JETTY Lt.Bn. 2 F.G. vert.
UNIVERSAL SHIPYARD JETTY Lt.Bn. 2 F.G. vert.
SWANWICK MARINA JETTIES Lt.Bns. 8 × 2 F.G. vert.

SOUTHAMPTON WATER

B.P. HAMBLE JETTY. Lt.Bn. 2 F.G. vert. 2M. posts on Dolphins 5m.
PROHIBITED ANCHORAGE. Dir. Lt. 032°49′. White △ B. stripe. White Tr. B. bands. Uses moiré pattern to indicate centre line.
CADLAND. Lt.By. Fl.R. 3 sec. Can.R. ∿.
GREENLAND. Lt.By. I.Q.G. 10 sec. Conical G. ∿.

HYTHE MARINA VILLAGE. (0703) 849263. VHF Ch. M. Approach channel 2.5m. Lock 21m. × 1m. over sill. Lock H24 subject to draught and tides.
Signals: G. Lt. = enter. R. Lt. = stop.
HYTHE MARINA VILLAGE. Lt. Q.(3) 10 sec. Y.B. Bn. ⊕
LOCK ENTRANCE. Lt. 2 F.G. vert. G. △
LOCK ENTRANCE. Lt. 2 F.R. vert. R. △
HYTHE KNOCK. Lt.By. Fl.R. 3 sec. Can.R. ∿.
QUEEN ELIZABETH II TERMINAL. Lt.Bn. 4 F.G. vert. 3M. Frame Tr.

RIVER ITCHEN

WESTON SHELF. Lt.By. Fl.(3)G. 15 sec. Conical G.
SWINGING GROUND. Lt.By. Occ.G. 4 sec. Conical G.
No: 1 Lt.Bn. Q.G. Dolphin B. Cone.

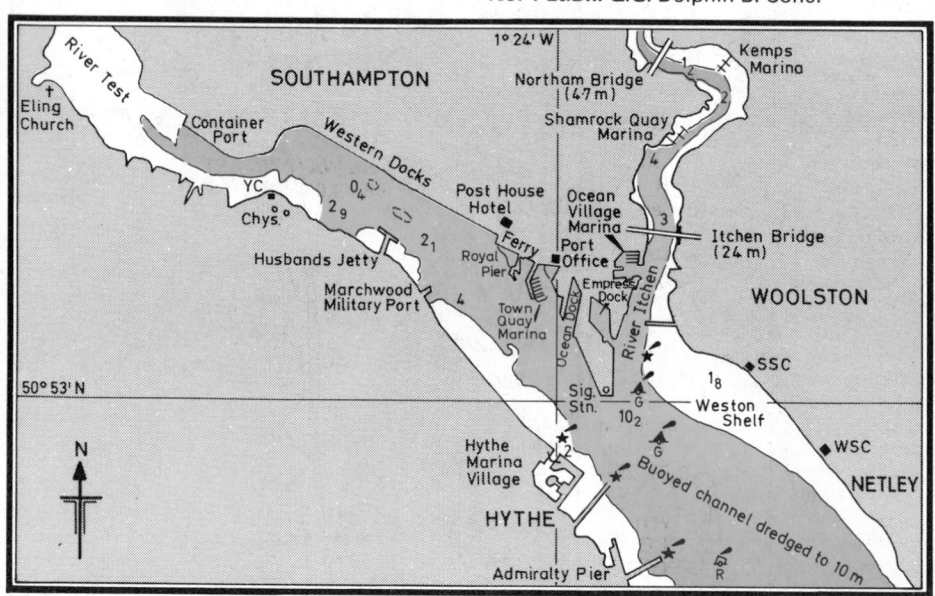

AFTER BARN. By. Conical G.
LAINS LAKE. Lt.By. Fl.(2)R. 4 sec. Can.R. ∿.
DEANS LAKE By. Can.R.
HOUND. Lt.By. Fl.(3)G. 10 sec. Conical G.
NETLEY. Lt.By. Fl.G. 3 sec. Conical G.
DEANS ELBOW. Lt.By. Oc.R. 4 sec. Can.R. ∿.
COASTAL FORCES BASE ADMIRALTY JETTY. Lt.Bn. 2 F.R. vert Dolphin.
NW NETLEY. Lt.By. Fl.G. 7 sec. Conical G. ∿.
MOOR HEAD By. Conical G.
RADAR SCANNER. Lt.Bn. 2 F.R. vert. each end.
HYTHE PIER. Lt.Bn. 2 F.R. vert. 5M. mast 12 and 5m.
Bn. Y.B.Y. Topmark W.
Bn. Y.B. Topmark S.

No: 2 Lt.Bn. Fl.G. 5 sec. 2M. E side.
No: 3 Lt.Bn. Fl.G. 7 sec. Dolphin. Topmark B. Cone.
WESTON JETTY DOWNSTREAM Lt.Bn. 2 F.G. vert.
UPSTREAM. Lt.Bn. 2 F.G. vert.
EMPRESS DOCK. S. PIERHEAD. Lt.Bn. 2 F.R. vert. Topmark ▽ R.
N. PIERHEAD Lt.Bn. 2 F.G. vert. Topmark △ G.
MARINE BASE. Lt. 2 F.R. vert.
BANK. Lt.Bn. Q.R. R. □ on pile.
OCEAN VILLAGE MARINA. Lt. 2 F.R. vert. VHF Chan. M. Other freq. available. H24. Traffic Signals: 3 F.R. vert. = all vessels stop. 2 G./W. = 2 way traffic (shown N side of entrance) First 4 h free of charge.
No: 4 Lt.Bn. Q.G. 2M. Pile G. Topmark Cone.

ITCHEN BRIDGE. Lt.Bn. 2 F.G. vert. E. Pier.
Ldg.Lts. 256°. (Front) F.R. Y. △ R. border. (Rear)
F.R. Y. ◇ R. border mark submarine pipeline.
CROSSHOUSE. Lt.Bn. Oc.R. 5 sec. 2M. R. □ on
R. Pile.
CHAPEL. Lt.Bn. Fl.G. 3 sec. 3M. Topmark Cone
also 2 F.R. vert. on Bns. A & C 80m. W.
Other Jetties have 2 F.R. or 2 F.G. vert. Lts.
No. 5 Lt.Bn. Fl.G. 3 sec. Topmark G. △
No. 6 Lt.Bn. Fl.R. 3 sec. Topmark R. □
No. 7 Lt.Bn. Fl.(2)G. 5 sec. Topmark G. △
No. 9 Lt.Bn. Fl.(4)G. 10 sec. Topmark G. △

RIVER TEST
LOWER FOUL GROUND. Lt.Bn. Fl.(2) R. 10
sec. R. Can.
UPPER FOUL GROUND. Lt.Bn. Fl.(2) R. 10 sec.
R. Can.
GYMP. Lt.By. Q.R. Can.R. 〰.
DIBDEN BAY. Lt.By. Q. Pillar B.Y. Topmark N.
GYMP ELBOW. Lt.By. Oc.R. 4 sec. Can.R.
SWINGING GROUND.
No: 2 Lt.By. Fl.(2) R. 10 sec. Can.R.
No: 4 Lt.By. Oc.R. 4 sec. Can.R.
No: 6 Lt.By. Fl.R. 3 sec. Can.R.
No: 8 Lt.By. Fl.(2)R. 10 sec. Can.R.
No: 10 Lt.By. Q.R. 〰.
No: 12 Lt.By. Fl.(2)R. 5 sec. 〰. Can. R.
No: 14 Lt.By. Oc.R. 4 sec. 〰.
No: 16 Lt.By. Fl.(3)R. 5 sec. Can.R.
ELING. Lt.By. Fl.R. 5 sec.
BURY. Lt.By. Fl.R. 5 sec. Can.R. 〰.
MARCHWOOD CHAN. Lt.By. Oc.(2) 10 sec.
Can.R.
CRACKNORE. Lt.By. Oc.R. 8 sec. Can.R.
TOWN QUAY. Ldg.Lts. 329°. (Front) 3 F.Y. 3M.
White △ G. border. (Rear) 3 F.Y. 2M. White ◇ R.
border on Royal Pier.
FERRY PONTOON Lt. 2 F.R. vert.
ROYAL PIER. SE HEAD Lt. 2 F.G. vert. 2M. 8m.
FERRY TERMINAL OUTER PONTOON HD. Lt.
2 F.G. vert.
MIDDLE SWINGING GROUND. Ldg.Lts. 336°.
(Front) Oc.G. 6 sec. B. △ White bands, R.
mast. B.Y. bands. (Rear) Oc.G. 6 sec. B. □ Y.
'X'.
Ldg.Lts. 069°30′ (Front) Fl.G. 1.3 sec. B. △
White bands, R. mast. B.Y. bands. (Rear) Fl.G.
1.3 sec. B. 'X' White bands, R. mast. Y.B.
bands.
MARCHWOOD MILITARY PORT JETTY. HEAD.
Lts.(×3) 2 F.R. vert.
HUSBANDS JETTY. Lt.Bn. 2 F.R. vert. 2M. off
jetty on dolphin.
FLOATING DOCK. Lt. 2 × 2 F.R. vert.
MARCHWOOD BASIN QUAY. Lt.Bn. 2 F.R.
vert.
UPPER SWINGING GROUND. Ldg.Lts. 011°
(Front) F.G. B. ▽ White bands, Y. mast, B.R.
bands. (Rear) F.G. B. 'X' White stripes, Y.

mast, B.R. bands.
RO/RO BERTH. Lt. 2 F.G. vert.
CONTAINER BERTH. Lt.Bn. 4 F.G. vert.
SLOWHILL COPSE APPROACH Lt. 2 F.R. vert.
N Dolphin.
Lt.Bn. F.W.G. G.208°-216°; W.216°-228°.
Ldg.Lts. 287°07′ (Front) A. Q. 17m. B. △ on Or.
Tr. Occl. 277°-297° (Rear) B. Q. 20m. B. ◇ on
Or. Tr.
BURY SWINGING GROUND Lts. F.R.G. 28m.
and Q. 25m. G.W.R. □ on Tr. Occl. R.147°-197°;
W.191°-203°; G. 197°-247°.
TRANSIT A Lt.Bn. F.R. R. △.
TRANSIT B. Lt.Bn. F.R. R. ◇ mark deep water
channel of swinging ground.

ISLE OF WIGHT — SOUTH & EAST COAST

NEEDLES TO ST. CATHERINE'S POINT

**OFFSHORE WAYPOINT ST. CATHERINE'S
POINT.** 50°33.0′N, 1°17.0′W.

ST. CATHERINE'S POINT 50°34.5′N,
1°17.8′W. Lt. Fl. 5 sec. 30M. White octagonal
Tr. and dwelling, 41m. Radio Bn. 257°-117°.
Window in same Tr. F.R. 17M. 099°-116°. 35m.
Experimental Lts. may be shown.

VENTNOR PIER. 50°35.4′N, 1°12.2′W Lt. 2 F.R.
vert. 3M. Mast on Pier Head, 10m.

STENBURY DOWN RG STN.
50°36.83′N, 1°14.53′W. Coastguard
Emergency DF Stn. VHF Chan. 16 & 67.
Controlled by MRSC Solent.

SANDOWN PIER. Lts. 2 F.R. vert. 2M. Pier
Head. 7 and 5m.

SHANKLIN PIER. Lts. 2 F.R. vert. 2M. Pier
Head, 7 and 5m. Bell (when vessels
expected). Pier destroyed.
W. PRINCESSA Lt.By. Q.(9) 15 sec. Pillar Y.B.Y.
Topmark W. marks Princessa Shoal, E of
Bembridge Down.
BEMBRIDGE LEDGE. Lt.By. Q.(3) 10 sec. Pillar
B.Y.B. Topmark E. off Bembridge Ledge.

ST. HELENS FORT 50°42.3′N, 1°05.0′W.
Lt. Fl.(3) 10 sec. 8M. Circular stone structure,
16m.
No: 4A By. Can.R. 232½°. 2.9 cables from Fort.

BEMBRIDGE (BRADING HAVEN)
Bembridge Marina (0983 87) 2973 & 2828.
Chan. M.
HARBOUR WAYPOINT. 50°42.0′N, 1°04.6′W.

New buoyed channel has been established
following dredging operations.
Marina 18.2m. × 1.8m. draught.
Facilities: Petrol and water at Red Wing Quay.
Anchoring not permitted in channel or
harbour.
Speed limit 6 kts. or less.
HARBOUR. Lt.Bn. Q. △ on pile NW of St.
Helens Fort. Tide Gauge

No. 2. By. Can. R.
No. 3. By. Conical G.
No. 4. By. Can. R.
No. 5. By. Conical G.
No. 6. By. Can. R.
No. 7. By. Conical G.
No. 8. By. Can. R.
No. 9. By. Conical G.
No. 9A By. Conical G
No. 10. By. Can. R.
No.10A. By. Can. R.
No. 11. By. Conical G.
No. 12. By. Can. R.
No. 13. By. Conical G.
No. 14. By. Can. R.
No. 15. By. Conical G.

NAB TOWER TO SPITHEAD

**INSHORE WAYPOINT OFF NAB TR. 50°40.0′N,
0°58.0′W.**

NAB TOWER 50°40.0′N, 0°57.1′W. Lt. Fl.(2)
10 sec. 19M. Tr. 27m. Horn(2) 30 sec. Fog Detr.
Lt. 6 Fl. ev. 4 mins. Vis. 300°-120°. RC. Racon.
Helopad.
SOLENT APPROACH CHANNEL. (N of Nab
Tr.).
Dredged to 14m. at L.W.O.S. for deep draught
tankers. W of Bullock Patch Lt.By.
OUTER NAB. Lt.By. Fl.Y. 2½ sec. Can. Y.
NAB No: 1 Lt.By. V.Q.(9) 10 sec. Pillar Y.B.Y.
Topmark W.
NAB No: 2 Lt.By. Fl.Y. 2½ sec. Conical Y.
NAB No: 3 Lt.By. Fl.Y. 2½ sec. Conical Y.

NEW GROUNDS. Lt.By. V.Q.(3) 5 sec. Pillar
B.Y.B. Topmark E.
NAB END WHISTLE. Lt.By. Fl.R. 5 sec. Pillar
R ﻌﻌ
DEAN TAIL. Lt.By. Fl.(3)G. 15 sec. Conical G.
NAB EAST. Lt.By. Fl.(2)R. 10 sec. Can.R.

DEAN ELBOW. Lt.By. Fl.G. 5 sec. Conical G.
WARNER. Lt.By. Q.R. Pillar R. ﻌﻌ
Whistle. Off E part of Warner Shoal.
HORSE ELBOW. Lt.By. Fl.(3)G. 10 sec.
Conical G. S of Horse Shoal.

HISTORIC WRECK SITE HORSE TAIL.
50°44.34′N, 1°02.23′W. 100m. radius.

NO MAN'S LAND FORT 50°44.4′N,
1°05.6′W Lt.Tr. Fl. 5 sec. 15M. Circular stone
structure N end No Man's Land Shoal, 21m.
HORSE SAND FORT 50°45.0′N,
1°04.3′W Lt.Tr. Fl. 10 sec. 15M. Circular
stone structure W end of Horse Sand, 21m.

**INSHORE WAYPOINT OFF HORSE SAND
FORT. 50°45.0′N, 1°05.0′W.**

SPITHEAD TO COWES

MINING GROUND NE. Lt.By. Fl.Y. 10 sec. Can.
Y. NW corner marked by By. G.W. Cheq.; SW
By. Can. Y. SE corner marked by By. Conical
G.W. Fishing and anchorage prohibited in
Mining Ground.
N STURBRIDGE. Lt.By. V.Q. Pillar B.Y.
Topmark N.
KEMPS By. Can. Y.

RYDE 50°44′N, 1°10′W
PIER Lts. 2 F.R. vert. on mast at Pier Head, 6m.
2 F.R. vert. on NW corner occas. 2 F.R. vert. on
N corner; F.Or. on N corner (in fog vis. 045°-
165° and 200°-320°). Siren(2) 60 sec. when
ferries expected.

WOOTTON CREEK. Tel. (0705) 812011.
Entry: Channel dredged to 3m. as far as Ferry
thence 2m. to Fishbourne, but reported as
drying at LWS. Speed limit 5 kts.
WOOTTON Bn.Lt. Q. 1M. B.Y. Beacon, N
topmark.
No. 1 Lt. Fl.(2)G. 5 sec.
No. 2 Lt. Fl.R. 5 sec.
No. 3 Lt. Fl.G. 3 sec.
No. 4 Lt. Fl.R. 2.5 sec.
No. 5 Lt. Fl.G. 2.5 sec.
No. 7 Lt. Bn. Q.G.
EAST SIDE JETTY HEAD Lt. 2 F.R. vert. 4m. In
fog F.Y. Vis. 195°-225°. Bell on request.
Lt. Oc.W.R.G. 10 sec. G. 220.8°-224.3°; W.
224.3°-225.8°; R. 225.8°-230.8°.
DOLPHIN B.Lt. Q ⚑ on Y. dolphin, B. top 3m.

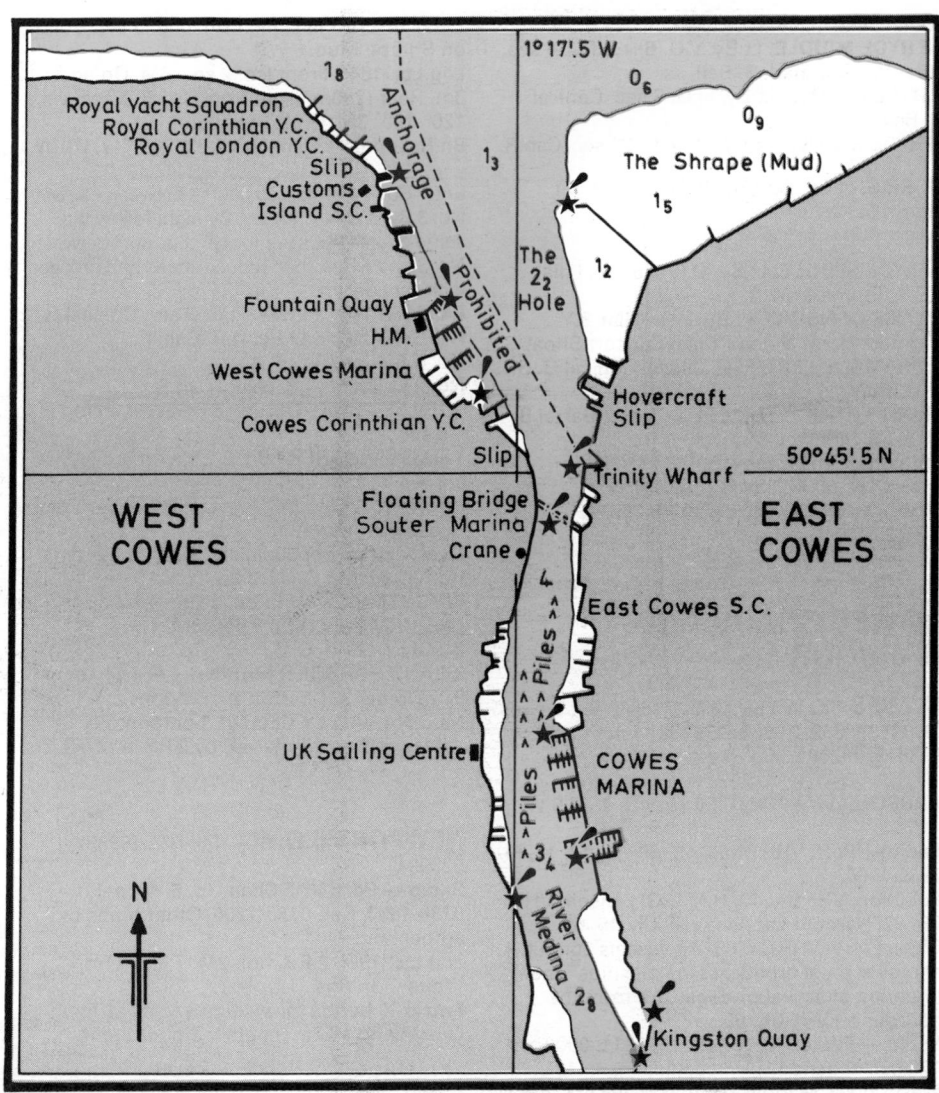

THE SOLENT — SPITHEAD TO COWES

NORTH SIDE
FORT GILKICKER. Oc.G. 10 sec. 3M. Storm
Sig. Lloyd's Sig. Stn.
LUCAS Lt.By. Fl.Y. 4 sec. Sph.Y. (May-Sept.).
STOKES BAY. By. Conical Y.
STOKES BAY OUTFALL. By. Conical G.
BROWNDOWN OUTFALL. Lt.By. Fl.G. 15 sec.
Conical G.
LEE OUTFALL Bn. G. marks outfall.
BOWRING ROSE By. Sph. Y. (March-Oct.).

E BRAMBLE. Lt.By. V.Q.(3) 5 sec. Pillar B.Y.B.
Topmark E. Bell.

INSHORE WAYPOINT OFF E BRAMBLE.
50°47.2′N, 1°13.2′W.

HILL HEAD. Lt.By. Fl.R. 2½ sec. Can.R.

SOUTH SIDE
MOTHER BANK. Lt.By. Fl.R. 3 sec. Can.R.
PEEL BANK. Lt.By. Fl.(2)R. 5 sec. Can.R. ⌁
DAKS-SIMPSON. By. Sph.Y. (Apr.-Oct.)
Racing mark.
NE RYDE MIDDLE. Lt.By. Fl.(2)R. 10 sec.
Can.R. ⌁ .

WOOTTON ROCKS. By. Can. R.
SE RYDE MIDDLE. Lt.By. V.Q.(6) + L.Fl. 10 sec. Pillar Y.B. Topmark S. Bell.
S RYDE MIDDLE. Lt.By. Fl.G. 5 sec. Conical G. Bell.
N RYDE MIDDLE. Lt.By. Fl.(4) R. 20 sec. Can.R.

NORRIS. Lt.By. Fl.(3)R. 10 sec. Can.R. off Norris Castle. 〰️

W RYDE MIDDLE. Lt.By. Q.(9) 15 sec. Pillar Y.B.Y. Topmark W.
PRINCE CONSORT. Lt.By. V.Q. Pillar B.Y. Topmark N. on N end Prince Consort Shoal.
S BRAMBLE. Lt.By. Fl.G. 2½ sec. Conical G. S. side Bramble Bank.
TRINITY HOUSE. Lt.By. Fl.Or. 2 sec. Barrel B. MDL By. Sph. Y. (Mar.-Oct.).
Prohibited Anchorage: 50°46.145′N 1°16.42′W; 50°46.234′N 1°16.834′W; 50°46.445′N 1°16.685′W; 50°46.355′N 1°16.285′W.

COWES ROADS AND HARBOUR

COWES (I.O.W.) 50°46′N 1°18′W. Tel: Cowes (0983) 293952. [(0983) 295733]: Pilot (0983) 293812; 292501.

HARBOUR WAYPOINT. 50°46.5′N, 1°17.5′W.

Radio — Port: VHF Chan. 16, 69, 11, 12, 14, M. 0830-1700.
Pollution: VHF Ch. 10; H.M.C.G. Liaison: VHF Ch. 67; Harbour Launch: VHF Ch. 16, 69; Chain Ferry: VHF Ch. 69. All vessels 30m LOA and over must broadcast to "all ships" their intention of arrival or departure from the harbour on VHF Ch. 69.
Radio — Pilots: VHF Chan. 16, 6, 11. 0900-1700, as required.
West Cowes Marina. Tel: (0983) 295724. (Chan. M) 0900-1700.
Entry: Vessels entering or leaving between May 1st and September 15th must keep on lanes of approach marked by pecked lines on charts.
Keep clear slipway close Kingston pontoon and Bys. R. Medina navigable to Newport by vessels 30.5m. × 2.1m. draught MHWS and 1.1m. MHWN.
Cowes max. size vessel 89m. × 5.3m. draught MHWS and 4.7m. MHWN.
Depth alongside U.K. Sailing Centre 2m.
Any vessel letting go an anchor in the Fairway or Roads must attach a watch buoy.
All vessels must contact the Chain Ferry on VHF Chan 69 to indicate their intentions.

EAST BREAKWATER. Lt.Bn. Fl.R. 3 sec. 3M. on Shrape Mud.
Ldg.Lts. 164°. Front Iso. 2 sec. 6M. On post 3m. Rear (290m. from front) Iso.R. 2 sec. vis. 120°-240° 3M. On Dolphin 5m.
Bn.R. Topmark Can. 50°45.635′N; 1°17.370′W.

Enter Cowes by day on course between Fairway No: 3 By. and No: 4 Lt.By. By night follow the same course but steer for Ldg.Lts. until between No: 3 and 4 Bys. then reduce speed and proceed with caution.
FAIRWAY NO: 3 Lt.By. Fl.G. 3 sec. Conical G.
FAIRWAY NO: 4 Lt.By. Q.R. Can. R.
No: 6 By Can. R.
No: 8 Lt.By. Fl.(2)R. 5 sec. Can R.
JUBILEE PONTOON Lts. 2 F.G. vert. In fog Fl. 1.5 sec.
TRINITY WHARF. Lt.Bn. 2 F.R. vert. on NW corner.
YACHT HAVEN MARINA. Lts. 2 F.G. vert. mark floating breakwaters.
Overhead power cable across River Medina from Kingston Quay, 35m.
KINGSTON QUAY. Lt.Bn. 2 F.R. vert.
MEDHAM Lt. V.Q.(3) 5 sec. 3M. 4m.
S FOLLY. Lt.Bn. Q.G.
ISLAND HARBOUR MARINA. Lock 24.4m. x 9.1m wide. 324 berths at pontoons.
MEDINA VALLEY CENTRE pontoon pier.
Jetties and berths marked by 2 F.R. or 2 F.G. Lts.

NEWPORT (I.O.W.). Tel: HM. (0983) 525994.
Radio — Port: VHF Chan. 16, 6. Mon.-Fri. 0730-1630, Sat. 0730-1200. Other times by agreement.
Ldg.Lts. 192°. 2 F.R. hor. 2M. 7 and 11m. White ◇ on Bns.
Entry: 30 berths for visiting yachts at Town Quay up to 48.7m length x 3m. draught.

APPROACHES TO PORTSMOUTH HARBOUR

PORTSMOUTH 50°48′N 1°06′W. Tel: Naval Base (0705) 822351 Ext. 22008. Commercial Port (0705) 297391 (Office Hours).
Pilots (0705) 297395. Telex 93121 10368 PM G. Fax: (0705) 861165.
Radio: (Q.H.M.) VHF Chan. 11 or Chan. 13 if so instructed by QHM.
(Harbour) VHF Chan. 11, 14.
Radio — Pilots: VHF Chan. 11, 14.
Camper & Nicholsons Marina (07017) 80221. (Chan. M).

Fareham Marina (0329) 234297. (Chan. M). 0900-1800.

Fareham Yacht Harbour (0329) 232854 (Chan. M) 0800-1800.

Entry: All vessels over 80grt maintain listening watch Ch. 11.

A yacht fitted with an engine must use it when entering/leaving harbour especially between S. Ballast Lt.By. and Southsea War Memorial.

All vessels over 20m. in length to listen on Chan. 11 or 13. Vessels under 20m in length ENTERING on the Portsmouth side should keep well to starboard, clear of the main approach channel. ALL vessels under 20m in length LEAVING harbour MUST use the boat channel.

All vessels under 20m in length should use the boat channel. It is 50m wide and extends from No. 4 By. to the N. End of H.M.S Dolphin, i.e. W of the W. limit of the dredged channel S of the entrance and W of a line from the NW corner of the dredged area to the Ballast By. At night keep in the RED sector of the harbour entrance Dir.Lt. Only enter or leave the boat channel at either end or to the W.

Tidal stream runs at approx. 5¼ kts max.

Speed limits: 10 kts in harbour. 12 kts within 900m. of any warship. 5kts in Wootton Creek.

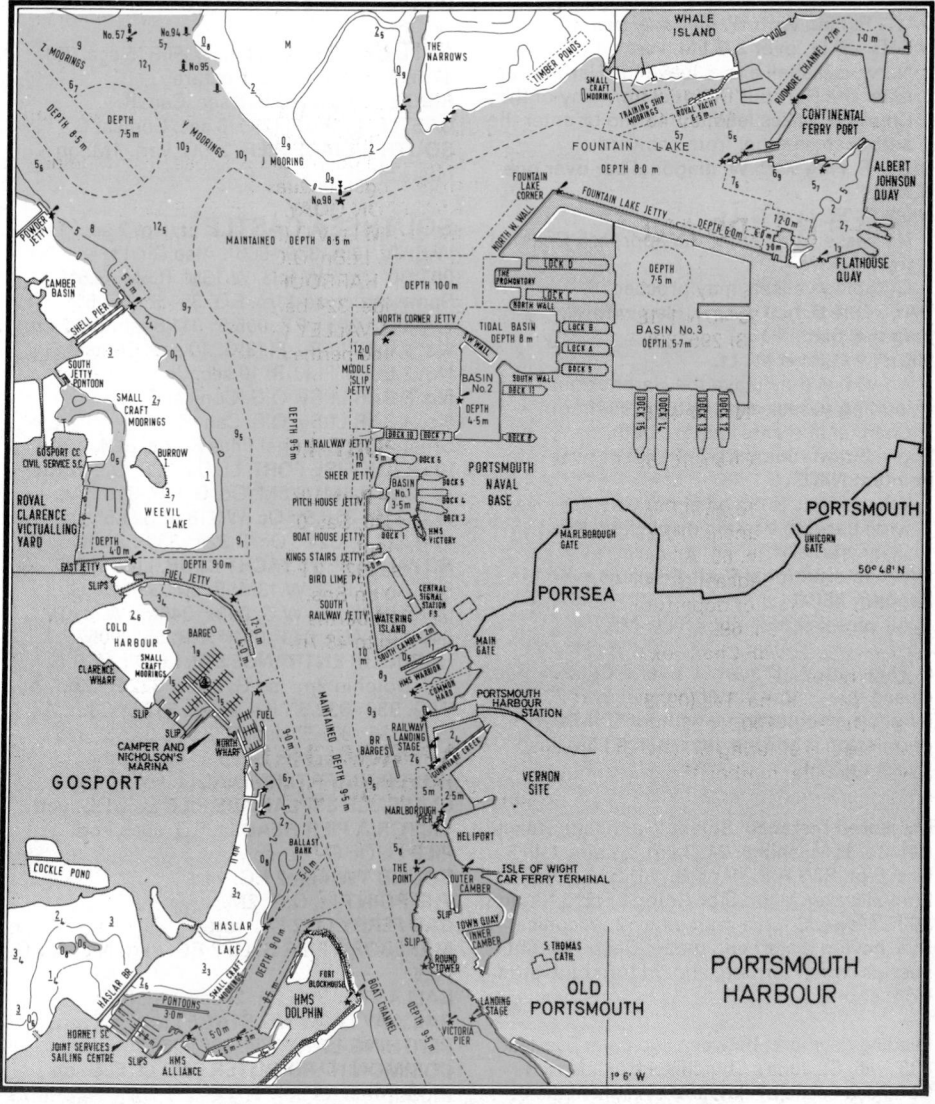

Water skiing: Prohibited except in designated areas at Lee on Solent & NW of Wootton Creek.
Board sailing: Prohibited South of 50°49'N in main channels.
Diving/Underwater swimming: Prohibited except under licence from QHM.

Signals: The following signals affecting traffic are hoisted by H.M. Ships or at Signal Stations at Portsmouth. All other signals are of purely Naval interest.

Signal and Meaning

DAY – R. Flag with W. diagonal bar.
NIGHT – R.Lt. over 2 G.Lts. vert.
   No vessel shall either leave the Harbour or enter the Harbour Channel from any of the Creeks or Lakes leading thereto or enter the approach channel from seaward.
DAY – R. Flag with W. diagonal bar over one R. ball
NIGHT – W. over G. Lt.
   No vessel shall enter the approach Channel from seaward.
   Outgoing vessels may proceed.
DAY – One B. ball over R. Flag with W. diagonal bar.
NIGHT – G. over W. Lt.
   No vessel may leave the Harbour but ingoing vessels may use the Harbour Channel and enter the Harbour.
DAY – International Code Pendant over Pendant NINE
   Vessels may proceed either way but give wide berth to vessels displaying 'Keep Clear' signal.
DAY – International Code Pendant over Pendant ZERO.
   All vessels KEEP CLEAR OF ME.

R. Flag with W. Diag/R.Lt. over 2 G. Lts. = Port closed due to low vis. No vessel over 20m in length may enter/leave without QHM's permission when vis. less than 0.25M. also B'cast on VHF.

Measured Distance: Solent (Spithead) Stokes Bay (for H.M. ships). 2437.6m. 2 pairs, tall bns. E pr. R.W.H.S. W pr. B.W.H.S. E pr. nr. Fort Gilkicker. W pr. S of Grange Fort 110° and 290° (Mag.). Course marked by 2 W. conical Bys. having a staff and globe. Deep draught vessels, when turning, should turn outwards from shore.

Leading daymarks between two outer Bys. lead 003° with St. Jude's Church spire in line with Southsea Castle by day, and by night in the white sector (between R. either side) of Southsea Castle Lt.

WEST SIDE
SADDLE. Lt.By. Q.G. Conical G.
MARY ROSE. By. Spherical Y. marking wreck.

HISTORIC WRECK SITE SPITHEAD.
50°45.8'N, 1°06.1'W. 300m. radius.
OUTER SPIT. Lt.By. Q.(6) + L.Fl. 15 sec. Pillar Y.B. Topmark S.
HORSE SAND. Lt.By. Fl.G. 2½ sec. Conical G.
〰〰.
SPIT REFUGE. Lt.By. Fl.R. 5 sec. Can. R. Bell 〰〰
BOYNE. Lt.By. Fl.G. 5 sec. Conical G.

SPIT SAND FORT Lt.Tr. Fl.R. 5 sec. 7M. 17m. Circular stone structure.
RIDGE. Lt.By. Fl.(2)R. 6 sec. Can. R.
CASTLE. Lt.By. Fl.(2)G. 6 sec. Conical G.
SOUTH PARADE PIER. 2 F.G. vert. 1M. on posts 5m.

SOUTHSEA CASTLE Lt. Iso. 2 sec. 11M. W.B. Tr. 16m. 339°-066°. Also Dir. Lt. 001°30' Dir. F.W.R.G. W.13M. R.5M. G.5M. Same structure 11m. F.G. 351.5°-357.5°. F.W. 000°-003°. F.R. 005.5°-011.5° shown 24 hr.
No: 1 (NB) Lt.By. Fl.(3)G. 10 sec. Conical G.
No: 2 Lt.By. Fl.(3)R. 10 sec. Can.R.
No: 3 BAR Lt.By. Q.G. Conical G.
No: 4 BAR Lt.By. Q.R. Can. R.
Small Boat Channel Piles BC2 & BC4.
BLOCKHOUSE FORT. Lt. Dir. 320° Dir. W.R.G. W.13M. R.5M. G.5M. Oc. G.310°-316°. Al. W.G.316°-318.5°; Oc. W.318.5°-321.5°. Al. W.R.321.5°-324°. Oc. R.324°-330°. Shown H24.
ROYAL ALBERT YACHT CLUB. Lt. Dir. 047°30'. F. & Al. W.R.G. W.13M; R.5M; G.5M. F.G. 037½°-043½°. Al. W.G. 043½°-046°; F.W. 046°-049°; Al. W.R. 049°-051½°; F.R. 051½°-057½°.
HARBOUR ENTRANCE DIR. Lt. Dir. W.R.G. 1M. Dolphin 2m. Iso.G. 2 sec. 322.5°-330°. Al. W.G. 330°-332.5°. Iso. 2 sec. 332.5°-335°. Al. W.R. 335°-337.5°. Iso. R. 2 sec. 337.5°-345°. Same structure as Gosport Fuel Jetty.
HOVERCRAFT TERMINAL Lt. F.Y.
CLARENCE ESPLANADE PIER Lt. 2 F.G. vert.
VICTORIA PIER HEAD Lt. F.G. each end.
PILE Lt. Oc.G. 15 sec.
ROUND TWR Lt. 2 F.G. vert.
THE POINT Lt. Q.G. 2M.
CAR FERRY Lt. 2 F.R. vert.
MARLBORO PIER S. Lt. 2 F.G. vert. **N** Lt. 2 F.G. vert.
BALLAST Lt.By. Fl.R. 2½ sec. Can.R.
RAILWAY LANDING STAGE Lt. 2 F.G. vert.
BERTHING Lt. F.Y. Vis. 308°-068°.
COMMON HARD OUTER END Lt. Fl.G. on tripod.

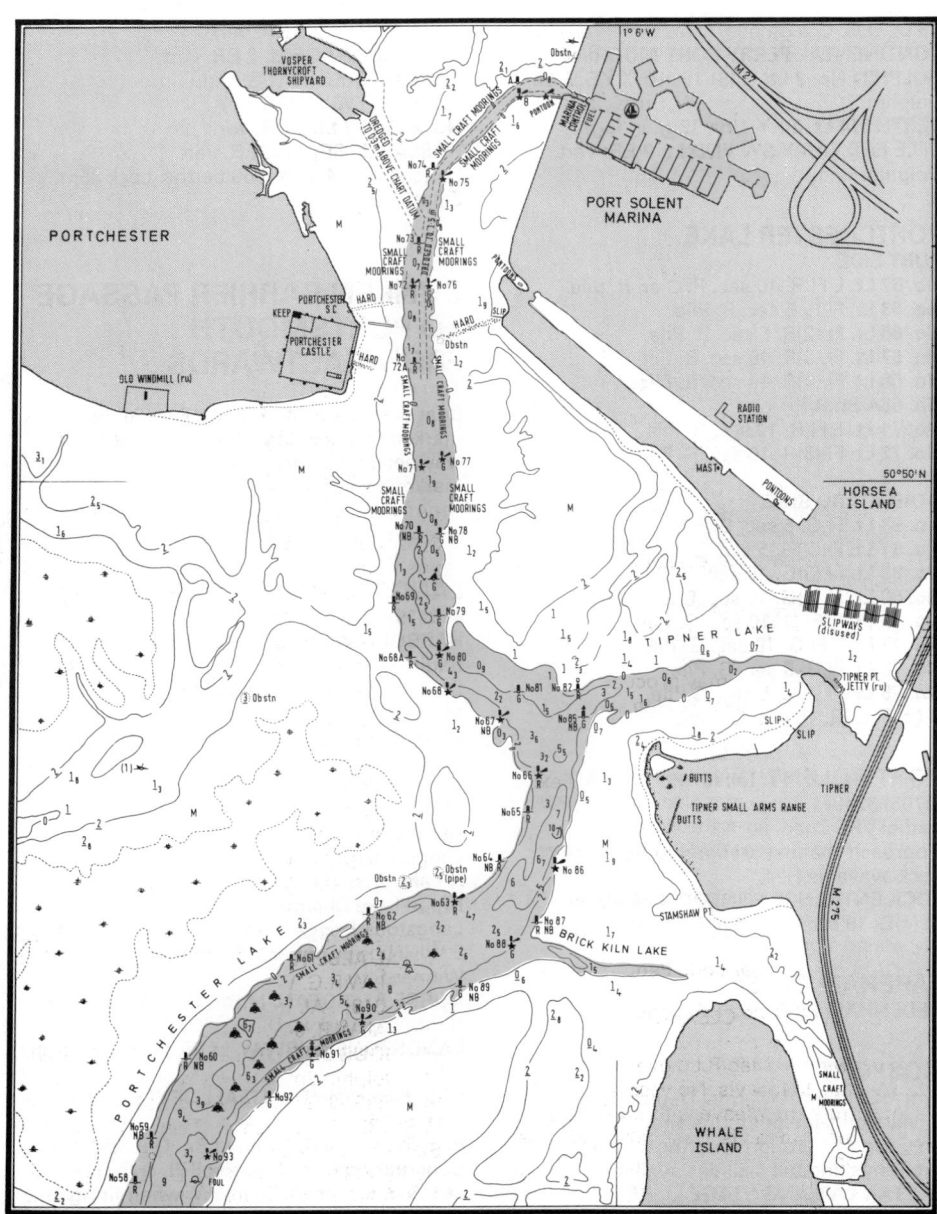

NORTH CORNER JETTY. Lt. Fl.G. 2 sec. 2M.
Roof of Bldg. 11m.
PILE 98 Lt. Q.(6) +L.Fl. 15 sec.
THE NARROWS. Lt. Q.R. Pile.
Lt. Fl.Y. 2 sec. Pile.
BASIN No. 2. DIR. Lt. Dir. uses Moire pattern
to indicate centre line.

FOUNTAIN LAKE.
FOUNTAIN LAKE CNR. Lt. 2 F.G. vert.

RUDMORE CHANNEL
C2 Lt. VQ(6) + L.Fl. 10 sec. ▽ on Y.B. pile.
C4 Lt. Q.R. R. ☐ on pile.
C1 Lt. Q.G. G. △ on pile 4m.
Wharf Lt. 2 F.G. vert.
C6 Bn. R. ☐ on pile.
C8 Lt. Fl.R. 5 sec. R. ☐ on pile.
C10 Lt. Q.(6) + L.Fl. 15 sec. ▽ on Y.B. pile 4m.
N. QUAY OIL BERTH Lt. 2 F.G. Vert. Dolphin.
C12 Lt. Q.R. R. ☐ on pile.

C5 Lt. Q.G. G △ on pile.
CONTINENTAL FERRY PORT MOORING
DOLPHIN No. 2 Lt. Q.(9) 15 sec. ⚑ Y.B.Y. on Dolphin.
BERTH 3/4 Lt. 2 F.Y. Hor. 13m. in fog.
MILE END QUAY SW END Lt. 2 F.R. vert. Dolphin.

PORTCHESTER LAKE
PORT SIDE
No. 57 Lt. L.Fl.R. 10 sec. R. □ on R. pile.
No. 63 Lt. Fl.R. 5 sec. R. Pile.
No. 66 Lt. Fl.(2)R. 5 sec. R. Pile.
No. 67 Lt. Fl.(3)R. 10 sec. R. Pile.
No. 68 Lt. Fl.(4)R. 10 sec, R. Pile.
No. 68A Bn.R.
No. 71 Lt. L.Fl.R. 10 sec. R. Pile.
No. 72 Lt. Fl.(3)R. 10 sec. R. Pile.

STARBOARD SIDE
No. 93 Lt. Fl.G. 5 sec. G. Pile.
No. 91 Lt. Fl.(2)G. 5 sec. G △ on G. Pile.
No. 86 Lt. Fl.(3)G. 10 sec. G. Pile.
No. 80 Lt. Fl.(4)G. 10 sec, G △ on G. Pile.
No. 79 Lt. F.(5)G. 10 sec. G. Pile.
No. 77 Lt. L.Fl.G. 10 sec. G. Pile
No. 76 Lt. Fl.G. 5 sec. G. Pile.
No. 75 Lt. Fl.(2)G. 5 sec. G Pile.
B Lt. Fl.(3)G. 10 sec. G. Pile.

PORT SOLENT Tel: (0705) 210765. Fax: (0705) 324241.
Radio: VHF Chan. 80, M.
Approach channel dredged to 1.5m at LW.
Lock available H24.
LOCK ENTRANCE PONTOON HEAD. Lt. Fl.(4)G. 10 sec.

FAREHAM CREEK
BEDENHAM PIER Lt. 2 F.R. vert.

GOSPORT
Entry: Cold Hr. Y. Marina. Depths 1.2m. to 2.5m. alongside pontoons and 1.2m. to 4.1m. on Gosport Borough moorings. Visitors moorings and full facilities available.
SULTAN LANDING STAGE Lt. F.R.
VOSPERS JETTY Lt. 2 F.R. vert. **ELBOW.** Lt. 2 F.R. vert.

PRIDDY'S HARD
POWDER JETTY Lt. 2 F.R. vert.
SHELL PIER Lt. 2 F.R. vert. on radar mast.

WEEVIL LAKE
ROLLING BRIDGE Lts. 4 F.R. Mark bridge opening.
ROYAL CLARENCE YARD Lt. 2 F.R. vert.

FUEL JETTY Lt. 2 F.R. vert.
LANDING STAGE Lt. 2 F.R. vert.
HASLAR LAKE Lt. Q.G. Dolphin.
No. 1 JETTY Lt. 2 F.R. vert.
No. 2 JETTY Lt. 2 F.R. vert.
HASLAR JETTY Lt. 2 F.R. vert.
Portchester Marina: 500 berths. Lock 35m. × 2-3m.

SUNKEN BARRIER PASSAGE TO PORTSMOUTH FROM EASTWARDS

Boat passage East of South Parade Pier marked by Piles. Main Passage about half way between shore and Horse Sand Fort marked by Lt.Bn. Qk.Fl.R. to seaward & Pile Topmark ◊ to Shoreward. Barrier marked elsewhere by Piles Y. Topmark X.

LANGSTONE HARBOUR Tel: (0705) 463419.
HARBOUR WAYPOINT. 50°46.0′N, 1°01.4′W.
Radio — Port: VHF 16. 12 Hours: 1 Apr.-30 Sept. 0830-1700; 1 Oct-31 Mar. 0830-1700 Mon-Fri; 0830-1300 Sat-Sun.
Entry: Bar reported least depth 1.7m.
Langstone (Glory Hole) Marina (Eastney): 336 berths, 2.3m. draught. Approach Channel 1m. MLWS. Automatic sill 1.6m. plus tide Holding Basin 2.5m. MLWS.
Langstone Channel depths 2m. to 4m.
N Lake dries but 3.7m. at MHWS.
Broad Lake Channel dredged to 1.8m.
Langstone Bridge: Vertical clearance 1.7m.
E WINNER By. Pillar Y.B. Topmark S. marks E Winner Shoal.
HORSE AND DEAN. Lt.Bn. Fl.(2) 5 sec. Pole B.R.B. Topmark Is. D.
LANGSTONE FAIRWAY. Lt.By. Fl. 10 sec. Sph. R.W.
EASTNEY POINT OUTFALL JETTY. Lt. 2 F.R. vert. 5M 5m.
EASTNEY POINT. Drain Lt.Bn. Q.R. 2M. Concrete Dolphin, 2m. also F.R. & Oc.(2)Y. 10 sec. & Y. Lts. on Tr. 500m. W. when firing in progress.
LANGSTONE MARINA situated N side of Eastney Point with 336 berths up to 2.3m draught. Entry/exit over sill 1.6m plus tide. Holding basin and jetty with depth 2.5m MLWS.
ROWAY WRECK PILE. Lt. Fl.(2) 5 sec. 1.2M. SSW of Eastney Point Drain Lt.
WATER INTAKE. Fl.R. 10 sec. Pile.
HAYLING ISLAND FERRY. Lt. 2 F.G. vert.
EASTNEY LANDING STAGE. Lts. Fl.R. 20 sec. each end. Dolphin.

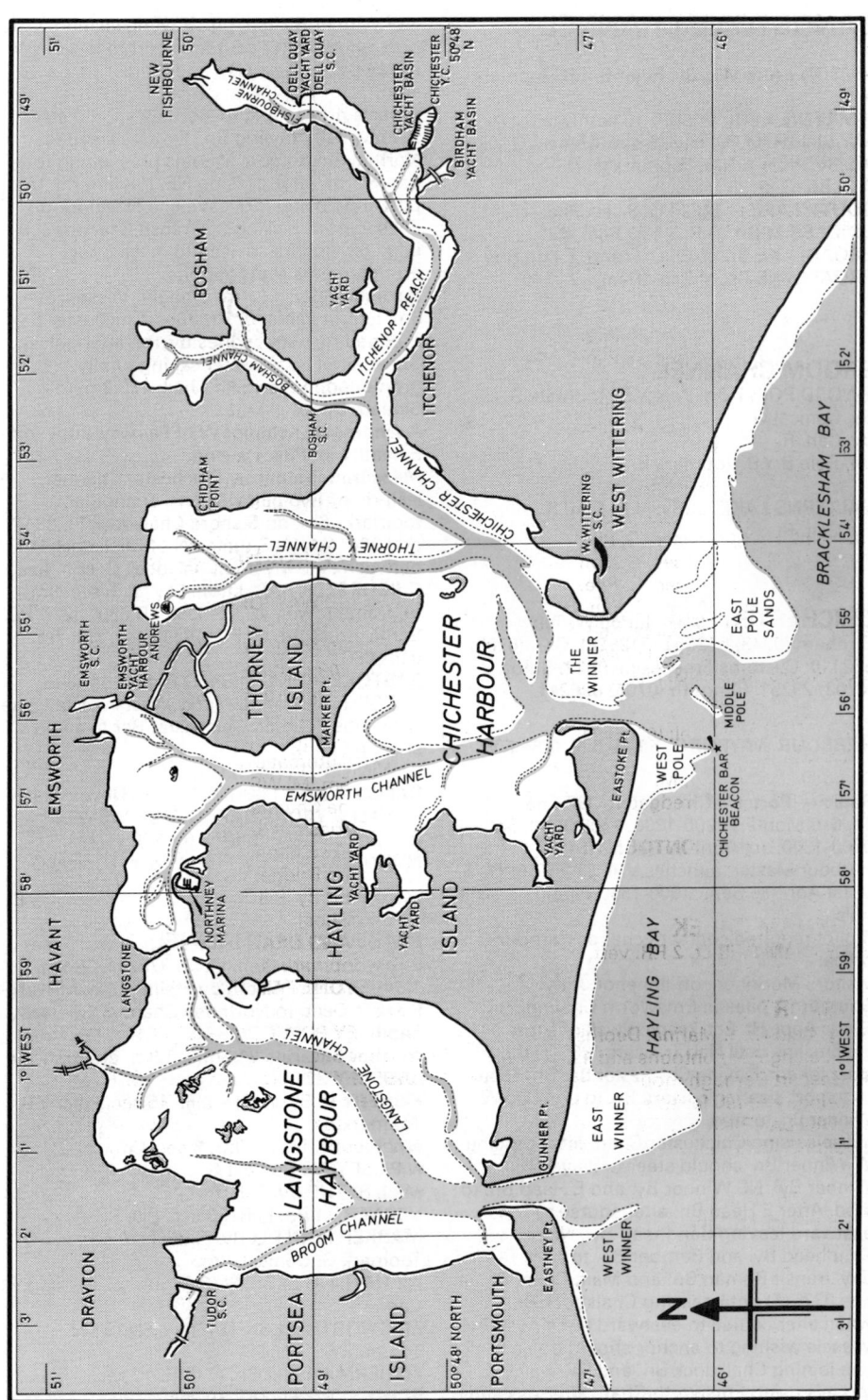

LANGSTONE CHANNEL

MILTON LAKE Wk. By. Pillar B.R.B. Topmark Is.D.
E MILTON. Lt.By. Fl.(4)R. 10 sec. Can.R.
NW SINAH. Lt.By. Fl.G. 5 sec. Conical G. Wk.By. Pillar B.R.B. Topmark Is. D.
A Lt.Bn. Q. R.
SOUTH LAKE Lt.Bn. Fl.G. 3 sec. Pile.
BINNESS Lt.Bn. Fl.R. 3 sec. Pile.
BROADLAKE Bn. Y. Pile. (Front). ⎱ Ldg.Bns.
BROADLAKE Bn. Y. Pile. (Rear). ⎰ 340°

BROOM CHANNEL

SWORD POINT Bn. Pole Y.B. Topmark S.
By. Conical G.
By. Can. R.
Bn. Pole B.Y.B. Topmark E.

SALTERNS LAKE. Lt.By. Fl.R. Can. R.
By. Can. R.

CHICHESTER 50°47′N 0°56′W. Tel:
Birdham (0243) 512301 (512524). C.G. (0705) 552110: Customs Freephone 9522: Soton (0703) 29251: P'mouth (0705) 826241.

HARBOUR WAYPOINT. 50°45.5′N, 0°56.5′W.

Radio — Port: c/s Chichester. VHF Chan. 16, 14, 6, 0 Mon-Fri 0900-1300, 1400-1730. Sat 0900-1300. 1st April-30 Sept.
Harbour Master launches VHF Chan. 16, 14, 6, 0. 1st April-30 Sept. 1000-1800 W/ends & Bank hols.
If pilot required contact Itchenor Harbour office.
Visitors Moorings: off Itchenor Jetty: Southern 5 piles in Emsworth Channel.
Entry: Appr. Hr. Ent. keeping well offshore on the 5m. line until Nab Tr. bears 186° (T) then steer for ent. leaving Chichester Bar Bn. about ½c. to port, passing E Stoke Bn. to port and W Winner Bn. to stbd.
Vessels using Chichester Chan. after passing W Winner Bn. should steer to leave NW Winner By., NE Winner By. and E Head Bn. to stbd. After E Head Bn. alter course to N eastward leaving Sandhead By., NE Sandhead By. and Camber Bn. to port. By day, transit Roman Bn. and Main Chan. Bn. in line 032° (T) until passing Chalkdock Bn. when alter course to eastward to Fairway By. Vessels wishing to anchor should do so S of line joining Chalkdock Bn. and Fairway By. Vessels using Emsworth Chan. after passing NW Winner By. to stbd., Hayling Island S.C. to port, should alter course to port to leave NW Pilsey By., N Pilsey By. and Marker Pt. Bn. to stbd.
Vessels proceeding to Northey should steer to leave NE. Hayling Bn., Sweare Deep Bn., Northey Bn. to port. Vessels proceeding to Emsworth, after passing NE. Hayling Bn. to port should steer to leave line of Mooring Piles to port, picking up Transit Beacons Ldg.Lts. Visitors advised to make prior arrangements for moorings.
Harbour: 30m. × 2.7m. draught. Vessels over 3m. length liable for Hr. dues. Chichester Bar dredged to 1.5m. (varies by 1m. after gales). Speed limit 8 kts (water ski-ing totally prohibited). Emsworth Channel 3.3m. to Sweare Deep.
Anchorages: Itchenor W of Fairway Buoy: off E head: E of Pilsey Island.
Measured Distances: Chichester Channel. Half-mile. Two pairs W. bns. Triangular topmarks 6m. on S shore Chalkdock Pt. 084° and 264° (Mag.) Situated N of Chalkdock Pt. between Fairway and Chalkdock G. con. bys.
CHICHESTER BAR. Lt.Bn. Fl.W.R. 5 sec. 8m. ☐ on frame tower. W.322°-080°; R.080°-322°. RC. Same structure. Lt. Fl.(2)R. 10 sec. 2M. 7m. 020°-080°.
EASTOKE POINT. Lt.Bn. Q.R. R. ☐ on R. Bn.
CHI-SPIT. By. Can.R. marks West Pole Tail, use with subsidiary Lt. Chichester Bar to avoid shoaling bank.
W WINNER. Lt.Bn. Q.G.
SANDY POINT. Lt.Bn. F. April to November.
SPARKES YACHT HARBOUR 2c WSW of Sandy Point with berths for 200 yachts.
NW WINNER. Lt.By. Fl.G. 10 sec. Conical G.

EMSWORTH CHANNEL

Emsworth Y. Hr. Tel: (0243) 375211. 18.2m. × 1.8m. draught. Depth over sills 1.5m. MHWN. Sweare Deep to Northney Channel 1m. least depth.
Northney Marina 21.3m. × 1.8m. draught. Tel: (0705) 466321.
FISHERY Lt.By. Q.(6) + L.Fl. 15 sec. Pillar Y.B. Topmark S.
NW PILSEY. Lt.By. Fl.G. 5 sec. Conical G.
N PILSEY By. Conical G.
MILL RYTHE By. Can. R.
VERNER. Lt.Bn. Fl.R. 10 sec. Pile R.
MARKER POINT Lt.By. Fl.(2)G. 10 sec. Topmark G. Conical, 8m.
NE HAYLING Lt.Bn. Fl.(2)R. 10 sec. Topmark R. Can.
EMSWORTH. Lt.Bn. Q.(6) + L.Fl. 15 sec. Topmark S.
FISHERMANS. Lt.Bn. Fl.(3)R. 10 sec.
ECHO. Lt.Bn. Fl.(3)G. 10 sec.

CHANNEL TO NORTHNEY MARINA
SWEARE DEEP Lt.Bn. Fl.(3)R. 10 sec. Topmark R. Can.
NORTHNEY Lt.Bn. Fl.(4)R. 10 sec. Topmark R. Can.
WEST CUT Bn. Y.B.Y. Topmark W.

CHICHESTER CHANNEL
N WINNER. Lt.By. Fl.(2)G. 10 sec. Conical G.
MID WINNER Lt.By. Fl.(3)G. 10 sec. Conical G.
STOCKER Lt.By. Fl.(3)R. 10 sec. Can.R.
NE WINNER. By. Conical G.
COPYHOLD By. Can.R. ⨺.
EAST HEAD. Lt.Bn. Fl.(4)G. 10 sec. G. Cone Topmark.
SANDHEAD. Lt.By. Fl.(4)R. 10 sec. Can.R.
NE SANDHEAD. Lt.By. Fl.R. 10 sec. Can.R.
PILSEY ISLAND. Lt.Bn. Fl.(2)R. 10 sec. For Thorney Channel.
THORNEY STARBOARD Lt.Bn. Fl.G. 5 sec. Pile Topmark Cone.
ROOKWOOD. By. Conical G.
CAMBER Lt.Bn. Q.(6) + L.Fl. 15 sec. Pole. Topmark S.
TRANSIT Bns. 032° (Front) Roman R. (Rear) Main W. Channel.
CHALKDOCK. Lt.Bn. Fl.(2)G. 10 sec.
FAIRWAY Lt.By. Fl.(3)G. 10 sec. Conical G.
DEEPEND Bn. Pole Y.B. Topmark S.

ITCHENOR
Birdham Pool Y. Basin. Tel: (0243) 512310. 16.7m. × 1.3m. draught.
Channel usable for craft up to 1.5m. draught 3 h.-HW-3 h.
Lock: 2/3 h.-HW-2/3 h. 0700-2200 but longer at W/ends.
ITCHENOR JTY. Lt.Bn. 2 F.G. vert.
BIRDHAM Lt.Bn. Fl.(4)G. 10 sec. Pile G.
Chichester Y. Basin Tel: (0243) 512731. 18.2m. × 1.8m. draught (maintained depth 2.1m.).
Channel: Depths 0.5m. to 1.5m.
Lock: Open 2 h.-HW-2 h. (Springs less at Neaps) 0700-2100 longer at W/ends and Hols.
Signals: — "Wait" on R. Board or "Enter" on G. Board both lit at night.
C.Y.B. Lt.Bn. Fl.G. 5 sec. Pile G.
CHICHESTER BASIN, Channel marked by Bns. Pole G.

CHANNEL TO DELL QUAY
COPPERAS By. Conical G.
D.Q.1. By. Can. R.
D.Q.2. By. Conical G.
D.Q.3. By. Conical G.
D.Q.4. By. Can. R.

HISTORIC WRECK SITE BRACKLESHAM BAY. 50°45.1'N, 0°51.47'W. 100m. radius.

SELSEY BILL. RG STN. 50°43'47"N, 0°48'08"W. Emergency D.F. Stn. VHF Chan. 16 & 67.
Controlled by MRSC Solent.

INSHORE WAYPOINT OFF PULLAR BY. 50°40.0'N, 0°50.0'W.

SELSEY BILL EASTWARDS
PULLAR By. Pillar Y.B.Y. Topmark W.
OUTER OWERS By. Pillar Y.B. Topmark S.

OFFSHORE WAYPOINT OFF OWERS. 50°35.5'N, 0°45.0'W.

OWERS 50°37.3'N, 0°40.6'W. Lt.Ho.By. Fl.(3) 20 sec. 22M. 12m. Horn (3) 60 sec.

THE LOOE CHANNEL

STREET By. Can. R.
BOULDER Lt.By. Fl.G. 2½ sec. Conical G.
MIXON Bn. B. with square cage, close S of Selsey Bill, marking Mixon Ridge.
SELSEY BILL. LB.Stn. F.R. occas.
EASTBOROUGH HEAD (East Bank) Lt.By.Q.(3) 10 sec. Pillar B.Y.B. Topmark E.

BOGNOR ROCKS Bys. Can. West one B. East one R. close together off Bognor Regis.

LITTLEHAMPTON OUTFALL. Lt.By. Fl.Y. 5 sec. Can. Y.

LITTLEHAMPTON 50°48'N, 00°32'W Tel: Littlehampton (0903) 721215/6. C.G. (0705) 552100. Customs: Brighton (0273) 592664.

HARBOUR WAYPOINT. 50°47.0'N, 0°32.5'W.

Radio — Pilots: VHF Chan. 16, 6 MF 2182, 2301, 2246, 2241. Hours: 3h. before H.W. to H.W. if in ballast. 2 h. before H.W. to H.W. if loaded. Only listens if ETA sent 12 h. in advance.
Littlehampton Marina (0903) 713553. Chan. M. 0800-1800.
Signals: Swing Bridge. Fl.G. Lt.—open. Fl.R. Lt.—closed.
Entry: Hbr. Speed limit 6½ kts. Water skiing/Board sailing prohibited. Flood tide rate 3 to 4 kts. Ebb Tide rate 2-5 kts. A training wall marked by poles runs to seaward off East Pier

submerged at half tide.
Max. vessel size 65m. × 3.8m. draught MHWN
and 5.0m. MHWS. Bar reported dries 0.4m.
with 1m. to 2m. in channel and off town.
Bridge: Clearance 9.4m. A.C.D. or 3.6m.
above MHWS. Tide boards either side of
bridge. Request to open by 1630 on day
BEFORE intended passage. No requests on
Sundays nor Bank holidays.
Facilities: water, provisions, diesel and petrol.
Fixed road bridge: clearance 3.6m. at MHWS.
Fixed rail bridge: clearance 3.0m. at MHWS.
Channel varies 1.2m. to 3.7m. as far as
Arundel.

WEST PIER Lt. 2 F.R. vert. 6M. R.Bn. 5m.
EAST PIER. Ldg.Lts. 346°. (Front) F.G. 7M. B.
metal Col. 6m. (Rear) Oc.W.Y. 7½ sec. 10M. W.
concrete Tr. 9m. W.287°-000°; Or.000°-042°.
NORFOLK WHF. Lt. Fl.G. 3 sec. 5M. B.Post 4m.
Vis. 335°-355°.
SWING BRIDGE. SW Fendering. 2 F.R. vert.
Fl.G. or Fl.R. Bridge Signals.
NE Fendering. 2 F.G. vert.

WORTHING PIER. 50°48.5′N, 0°22′W Lt. 2
F.R. vert. 1M. on post at Head. 6m. Bns. mark
sewer outfalls 2½M. W and 1½M. E of Pier.
E WORTHING OUTFALL. Lt.By. Fl.(2)R. 10 sec.
Can.R.

SHOREHAM 50°50′N 0°15′W Tel: (POIS)
Brighton (0273) 592366. Pilots (0273) 430921.
Fax: (0273) 592492. Telex: 878178.

HARBOUR WAYPOINT. 50°48.5′N, 0°15.0′W.

Radio — Port: VHF Chan. 16, 14, H24.
Radio — Pilots: VHF Chan. 16, 14. Tidal.
Signals: Tidal. By night: R. Lt.—tide level does
not exceed 2m. above chart datum.
G. Lt. when between 2-3m. water above chart
datum but not less than 2m.
W. Lt.—tide level more than 3m. above chart
datum.
International Port Traffic Signal shown by day
and night from Middle Pier Control, roof of
L/boat House and at locks. Signals on N Side
Control traffic using Prince George and
Signals on S Side, Prince Phillip Lock. Signals
are shown along E Arm for vessels entering
harbour and along Canal for vessels leaving.
Entry: Depths 1.7m. outside and 2m. inside
harbour, but unreliable due to silting. Above
Soldier's Point the flood and ebb streams set
along the axis of the channel. The ebb stream
combined with the river current can attain a
rate of 5 knots off Soldier's Point at Springs,
but owing to the increased depth and width
of the harbour entrance, the maximum rate
there is not more than 3 knots at Springs;
from 1½ hours after high water until one hour
before low water this ebb stream from the
harbour overcomes the last of the west-going

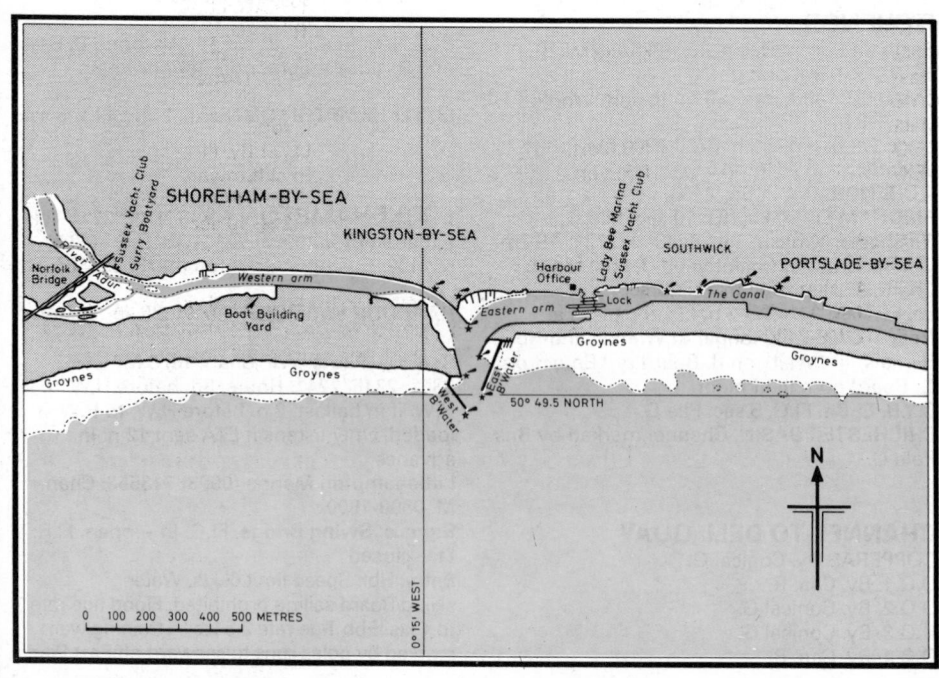

and the beginning of the east-going Channel streams which are therefore, not felt until well clear of the harbour.
IN EASTERN ARM OF HARBOUR there is practically no tidal stream at any time, even at the height of the flood.
Locks: Prince George: 73m. × 12.2m. × 6.9m. oversills at MHWS.
Prince Phillip: 73m. × 17.4m. × 8.9m. oversills at MHWS.
Both locks manned 4 h.-HW-4 h. but vessels can lock in/out thru Prince Phillip when tide serves.
Lock fee payable (valid one month) in addition to Marina charge. **Anchorage:** 1M. S of harbour with offshore winds.

W BREAKWATER HEAD. Lt. Fl.R. 5 sec. 7M. Concrete Col. 7m.
E BREAKWATER HEAD. Lt. Fl.G. 5 sec. 8M; Concrete Col. 7m. Siren 120 sec.
E SHOREHAM OUTFALL By. Pillar Y.B. Topmark S.
MIDDLE PIER. Ldg.Lts. 355° (Front) F.W.R.G. 10, 9, 9M; White Watch House, R. Base, 8m. Horn 20 sec. (Rear) Fl. 10 sec. 15M. Grey round stone Tr. 13m. Int. Port Traffic Signals. Tidal Signals.

WEST PIER HEAD. Lt. F.W.R. R. to seaward.
EAST PIER HEAD. Lt. F.W.G. G. to seaward.

EASTERN ARM
CANAL QUAY. W. End Lt. 2 F.R. vert. Wooden Mast.
CANAL QUAY. E. End Lt. 2 F.R. vert. Wooden Mast.
TEXACO WHARF. W End Lt. 2 F.R. vert.
TEXACO WHARF. Centre Lt. 2 F.R. vert.

WESTERN ARM
LIFEBOAT SLIP. Lt. 2 F.G. vert. Traffic Signals.
LIFEBOAT HOUSE. Lt. Oc.R. 3 sec.
KINGSTON WHARF. Lt. 2 F.G. vert.
RIVER ADUR BRIDGE. Lt. 2 F.R. vert. (S end) 2 F.G. vert. (N end).

SHOREHAM TO HASTINGS
Lt.By. Fl.Y. 5 sec. Pillar Y. 2½M. S of Shoreham.
Lt.By. Fl.Y. 10 sec. in position 50°47.8'N 0°11.20'W.

BRIGHTON
WEST PIER. Lt. Fl.R. 10 sec. 2M. Bell 13 sec. when vessels expected.

MARINE PALACE PIER. Lt. 2 F.R. vert. 2M. Mast on Hut.

HISTORIC WRECK SITE. 50°48.6'N, 0°6.5'W. 200m. × 150m. area.

BRIGHTON MARINA 50°49'N 00°06'W.
Tel: Brighton (0273) 693636. RC.

HARBOUR WAYPOINT. 50°48.0'N, 0°06.25'W.

Radio — Port: c/s Brighton Marina VHF. Ch. M for berthing, locking. c/s Brighton Control VHF. Ch. 16, 68, 11, for Traffic Control and Movements.
Entry: Traffic signals No. 1, 2, 2a of International Port Signals shown from end of entrance channel and control building.
Lock 100m. × 10m. × 1.8m. over sill. Manned 0800-2000, otherwise by arrangement.
Channel into Outer Harbour marked by Bys. Can.R. & Conical G. and Lt.Bys. Fl.R. 3 sec. Can.R. & Fl.G. 3 sec. Conical G. Channel dredged to 2.5m.
Lt.By. Fl.Y. 3 sec. Spar Y.
Lt.By. Fl.Y. 4 sec. Spar Y.
Lt.By. Fl.Y. 6 sec. Spar Y.
Lt.By. Fl.Y. 2 sec. Spar Y.
E. BREAKWATER Lt. Fl.(4)W.R. 20 sec. W.10M. R.8M. W. Pillar G. Stripes 16m. R.260°-295°; W.295°-100°. W. Lts. shown inside Breakwater walls.
E BREAKWATER HEAD. Lt. Q.G. 7M. 8m.
W BREAKWATER HEAD. Lt. Q.R. 7M. W. round. Twr. R. stripes 10m. Horn (2) 30 sec.
INNER HARBOUR ENTRANCE E SIDE. Lt. 2 F.G. vert.
N SIDE. Lt. 2 F.R. vert.
SEWER OUTFALL. Lt.By. Fl.Y. 5 sec. Can. Y. FRIARS 2 Bns. on cliff towards Newhaven.
LANGNEY POINT OUTFALL By. Can. R.
JEAN B Lt.By. Fl.(2)R. 10 sec.

NEWHAVEN RG STN. 50°46'54"N,
0°03'07"E. Emergency DF Stn. VHF Chan. 16 & 67. Controlled by MRSC Solent.

NEWHAVEN 50°46'N 0°04'E. Tel: Sig. Stn.
(0273) 513071. HM. (0273) 514131.
Newhaven Y.C. (0273) 513976. Yacht Harbour (0273) 513881.

HARBOUR WAYPOINT. 50°45.5'N, 0°01.0'E.

Radio — Port: VHF Chan. 16, 12—continuous.
Newhaven Marina (0273) 513881. Chan. M.
Signals: East Pier Inner.—G. Lt.

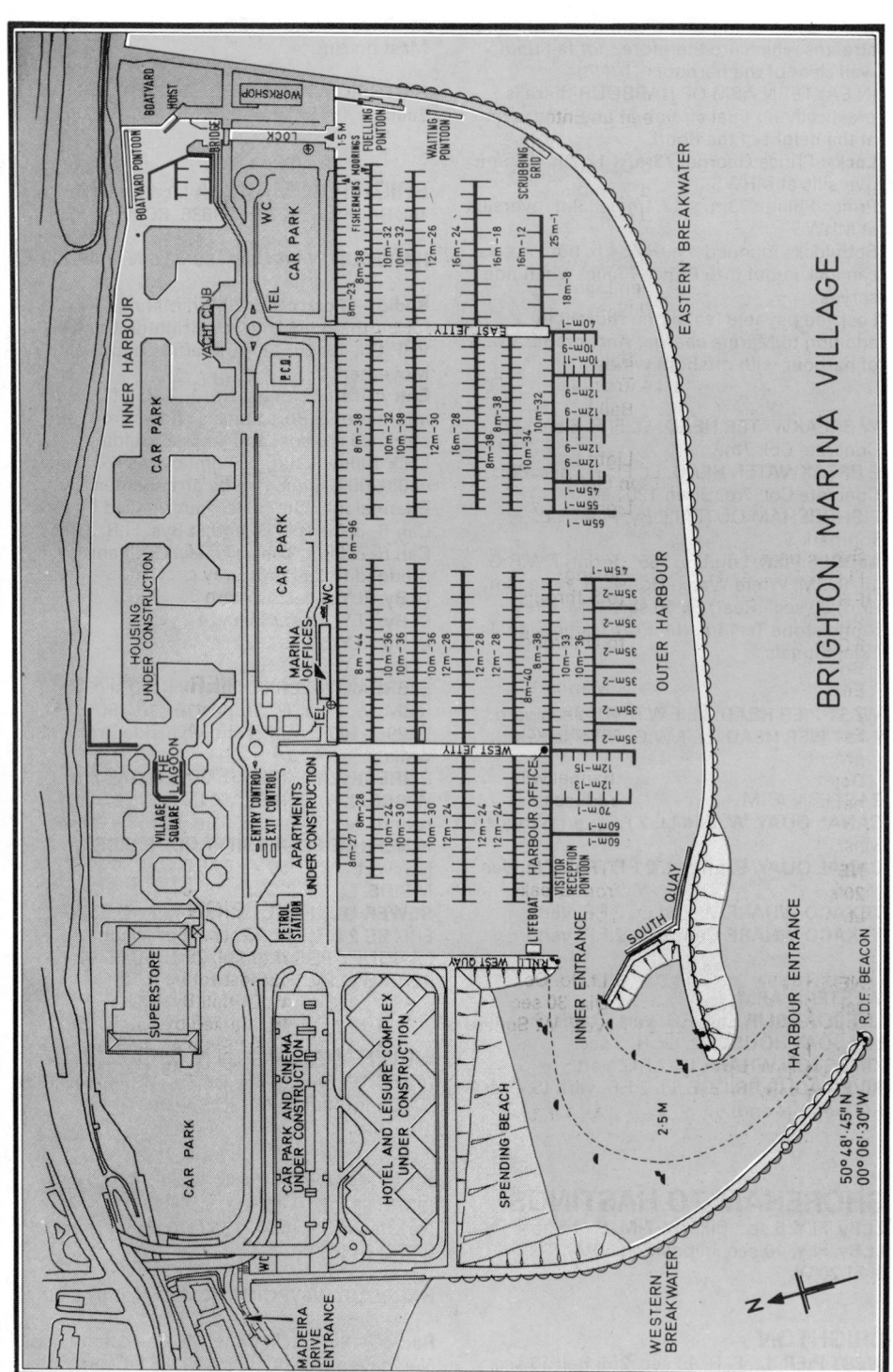

Newhaven. (Mast at base of Lt. Ho. West Pier).

Red Triangle
Red Ball } Entry only permitted DAY.
Green Lt. Entry only permitted NIGHT.

Red Ball
Red Triangle } Departure only permitted DAY.
Red Light. Departure only permitted NIGHT.

Red Ball. Entry and Departure permitted DAY.
Green Light }
Red Light. } Entry and Departure permitted NIGHT.

Red Ball
Red Triangle } Entry and Departure prohibited DAY.
Red Ball

Red Light
Green Light } Entry and Departure prohibited NIGHT.
Red Light

Swing Bridge

Fl.G. = Bridge opening or closing.
F.R. = Vessels may pass N to S through Bridge.
F.G. = Vessels may pass S to N through Bridge.
Entry: Newhaven Marine Y. Marina 15m. × 2.1m. draught. Visitors moorings.
Facilities: Fuel (diesel and petrol), water, provisions.
Depths: 5.5m. in entrance channel with 3m. between piers but siltation reduces depths.

NEWHAVEN LONG SEA OUTFALL. Lt. Fl.(5)Y. 20 sec. Spar Y. 190°×1.2M. from Breakwater Lt.

NEWHAVEN BREAKWATER Lt.Ho. Oc.(2) 10 sec. 12M. Concrete Tr. 17m. Dia. 30 sec.
WEST PIER S END. Lt. 2 F.R. vert. W. Square Bldg. RC.
N END. Lt. 2 F.R. vert.
INNER END. Lt. F.R.
EAST PIER. Lt. Iso.G. 5 sec. 6M. White structure on Head. 12m.
INNER END. Lt. 2 F.G. vert.
E QUAY S END. Lt. 2 F.G. vert.
NEWHAVEN MARINE YACHT MARINA. Lt. 2 F.R. vert. N & S in Sleepers Hole.
RAILWAY QUAY. Lt. 2 F.G. vert.
SWING BRIDGE. Lts. F.R.
RO-RO BERTH. Lt. 2 F.G. vert. Pontoon.
NORTH QUAY. Lt. 2 F.G. vert.
GREENWICH LANBY. 50°24.5'N 0°00'E/W. Fl. 5 sec. 21M. R. structure. 12m. diameter. Racon. Horn 30 sec.

BEACHY HEAD 50°44.0'N, 0°14.6'E. Lt. Fl.(2) 20 sec. 24M. Grey circular Tr. R.band and lantern. 32m. Horn 30 sec. Shown H24. Fog Detr. Lt. 4-7 Fl. ev. 4 mins. Vis. 085.5°-265.5°.

EASTBOURNE PIER. 50°46'N 0°18'E Lt. 2 F.R. vert. 2M. Metal post on Head, 8m.
EAST SOVEREIGN SHOALS By. Can.R. topmark. R.Can.
SOUTHERN HEAD SHOAL. Lt.By. Q. Spherical B. 9 cables NNW of Royal Sovereign Tr.

OFFSHORE WAYPOINT OFF ROYAL SOVEREIGN. 50°41.0'N, 0°26.0'E.

ROYAL SOVEREIGN 50°43.4'N, 00°26.1'E. Lt. Fl. 20 sec. 15M. W. Twr. on W. cabin on concrete Col. 28m. Dia.(2) 30 sec. Radio Bn. R. Fluorescent band 2m. wide.
PEVENSEY BAY. Outfall By. Can. R.
SHINGLE BANK. Marked by 4 x Bys. Sph. Y. (1) 49°45.7'N 0°35.1'E; (2) 49°44.5'N 0°37.2'E; (3) 49°42.7'N 0°31.1'E; (4) 49°44.7'N 0°31.1'E.

HASTINGS TO DUNGENESS

HISTORIC WRECK SITE BULVERHYTHE 50°50.7'N, 0°39.65'E. 100m. radius.

HASTINGS. 50°51'N, 0°35'E.
HASTINGS. Long Outfall Lt.By. Fl.Y 5 sec. Can. Y.
PIER. Lt. 2 F.R. vert. 5M. W. hut, 8m.
W BREAKWATER. Lt. Fl.R. 2½ sec. 4M. Mast, 5m.

Ldg.Lts. 356°18'. (Front) F.R. 4M. W. metal Col. 14m. (Rear) F.R. 4M. W. octagonal Tr. 55m.

FAIRLIGHT RG STN. 50°52.2'N, 0°38.8'E.
Coastguard Emergency DF Stn. VHF Chan. 16 & 67. Controlled by MRCC Dover.
HISTORIC WRECK SITE RYE 50°53.37'N, 0°41.77'E. 75m. radius.

RYE HARBOUR 50°56'N 0°47'E. Tel: Port:
(0797) 225225. Fax: (0797) 226711. Pilots: (0424) 812440. Rye S.C. (0424) 812446.
HARBOUR WAYPOINT. 50°54.0´N, 0°48.0´E.

Radio — Port: VHF Chan 16, 14. 0900-1700 also if commercial vessels moving.
Radio — Pilots: VHF Chan 16, 14 when vessel expected.
Entry: Speed limit 6 kts. Water skiing prohibited. Do not approach if wind force 6 or over from SE-S-SW. Depth over bar 4.8m. Springs 3.6m. Neaps. Access 3 h-HW-3 h. Tide runs 4-5 kts. at springs.
Tide Signal (Hbr. office):
  F.G. = 2-3m. on bar ⎫
  F. Purple = Over 3m. on a bar ⎭ night only
Traffic signals: By Day/Night Q.Y. = ship moving in/out; By day 1 B/Ball = vessel inwards; 2 B/Balls (Hor) = vessel outwards; 3 B/Balls (Triangle) = vessels in and out.
RYE FAIRWAY. Lt.By. L.Fl. 10 sec. Spherical R.W. vert. stripes. ⨎⨎. Appr. and Anche. By.
WEST GROYNE HEAD No. 2 Lt. Fl.R. 5 sec. 3M. Wooden Tripod 9m.
EAST ARM HEAD No. 1 Lt. Q.(9) 15 sec. 5M. G. Δ on post 9m.
WEST BANK No. 6 Lt. Q.R. 2M. R. Pile 3m. Further lights are shown upstream.
EAST BANK No. 3 Lt. Q.G. 2M. G. Δ on tripod 3m.
No. 10 Lt. Q.R.
No. 7 Lt. Q.G. 2M. G. Δ on pile 3m.
No. 18 Lt. Q.R. Pile.
No. 9 Lt. Q.G. 2M. G. Δ on piles 3m.
No. 11 Lt. Oc.W.G. 4 sec. W. 7M. G. 6M. G. Δ on dolphin 3m. W. 326°-331°, G. 331°-326°.
Tide and Traffic Signals.
No. 24 Lt. Q.R. Pile.
No. 26 Lt. Q.R. Pile.
No. 28 Lt. Q.R. Pile.
No. 30 Lt. Q.R. Pile.
No. 15 Lt. Q.G.
No. 36 Lt. Q.R. Pile.
No. 19 Lt. Q.G.
No. 25 Lt. Q.G.
No. 46 Lt. Q.R.
BULLOCK BANK. Lt.By. V.Q. Pillar B.Y. Topmark N. Whis.
OFFSHORE WAYPOINT OFF DUNGENESS. 50°53.0´N, 1°00.0´E.

DUNGENESS 50°54.8'N, 0°58.7'E. Lt. Fl. 10
sec. 27M. partially obsc. 078°-shore. B.Tr. W. bands. 40m. Horn(3) 60 sec. Shown H24.
Same structure F.R.G. 11M. R. 057°-073°; G. 073°-078°; R. 196°-216°. 37m. R.C.
Old Lt.Ho. can be seen about 2.5 cables W of above Lt.Ho. When in line 274°.
WATER INTAKE. Lt.By. Q. (6) + Lt. Fl. 15 sec. Pillar Y.B. Topmark S.
CS1. Lt.By. Fl.Y. 2½ sec. Pillar Y. Topmark X. Whis. 50°33.67'N 00°03.83'W.
CS2. Lt.By. Fl.Y. 5 sec. Pillar Y. Topmark X 50°39.10'N 00°32.70'E.
CS3. Lt.By. Fl.Y. 10 sec. Pillar Y. Topmark X. Bell. 50°52'N 01°02.30'E.
CS4. Lt.By. Fl.(4) Y. 15 sec. Pillar. Y. Topmark X. Whis. 51°08.58'N 01°34.03'E. Mark boundary between traffic lane for SW bound traffic and English Inshore Traffic Zone.

THE RIDGE (or Le Colbart)
COLBART N. Lt.By. V.Q. Pillar By. Topmark N.
LE COLBART SW. Lt.By. V.Q.(6) + L.Fl. 10 sec. Pillar Y.B. Topmark S. Whis.

FOLKESTONE 51°05'N, 1°12'E. Tel:
Folkestone (0303) 54947.

HARBOUR WAYPOINT. 51°04.25´N, 1°11.5´E.

Radio — Port: VHF Chan. 16, 22—as required. Operated by Sealink UK.
Radio — Pilots: VHF Chan. 9.
Entry: Extreme caution necessary when approaching or in Harbour or when crossing Entrances due to Cross Channel Ferries. Do not anchor within 1M. of Breakwater Head Lt. Outer Hr. — Berthing Signals: No. 1 Berth = 1 R./Y. ball or G. Lt.; No. 3 Berth = 3 R./Y. balls or 3 G. Lts. vert.; Traffic Signals: Blue flag/3 R. Lts. vert. = Ferry leaving. Port closed to other traffic.
Inner Hr. — Dries out with 4.5m. at MHWS over main part; 5/6m. at S Quay; 3m. at The Stade. Inner Hr. above the Railway Br. has 3.5m. at MHWS access restricted to craft with small air draught.

BREAKWATER HEAD. Lt. Fl.(2) 10 sec. 22M. Dia.(4) 60 sec. In fog Fl. 2 sec. 246°-306°. Intens 271.5°-280.5°.
No: 3 BERTH. Ldg.Lts. 295° (Front) F.R. (Rear) F.G. Occas.
INNER HARBOUR
EAST PIER HEAD. Lt. Q.G. on metal Col.
SOUTH QUAY. (Abnormal Load Berth) Lt. 2 F.R. vert. on aluminium Col.

FOLKESTONE & DOVER
Masters are warned of the high frequency of

the cross channel ferries entering and leaving these ports. Extreme caution is advised and a wide berth be given to the entrances.

DOVER STRAITS AND CHANNEL INFORMATION SERVICE.

Vessels in Dover Straits to listen on Chan. 16 and where possible Chan 11 for B'casts from Information Service.

Information on Large, Hampered or Rogue vessels, also information on safety generally in Straits. Chan 11 covers area.

Vessels either passing or entering Dover to call on VHF Chan 12 and give ETA at 3M. range then listen for Traffic Information.

(Dover English only otherwise English and French).

Information b'casts regarding safety of navigation. Bearing & Distance from St. Margarets Bay & Dungeness Radar Stns. via Dover C.G.

Sailing Vessels and Vessels under 20m long: allowed to use Inshore Traffic Zones and usually safer. If crossing Traffic Lanes must do so at right angles to general flow of Traffic. Keep Ships Head at right angles, regardless of tidal stream. Rule 10 applies. If you cannot comply with above easily and are fitted with engine — use it. Avoid Collision Risk but apply rules properly if Risk exists.

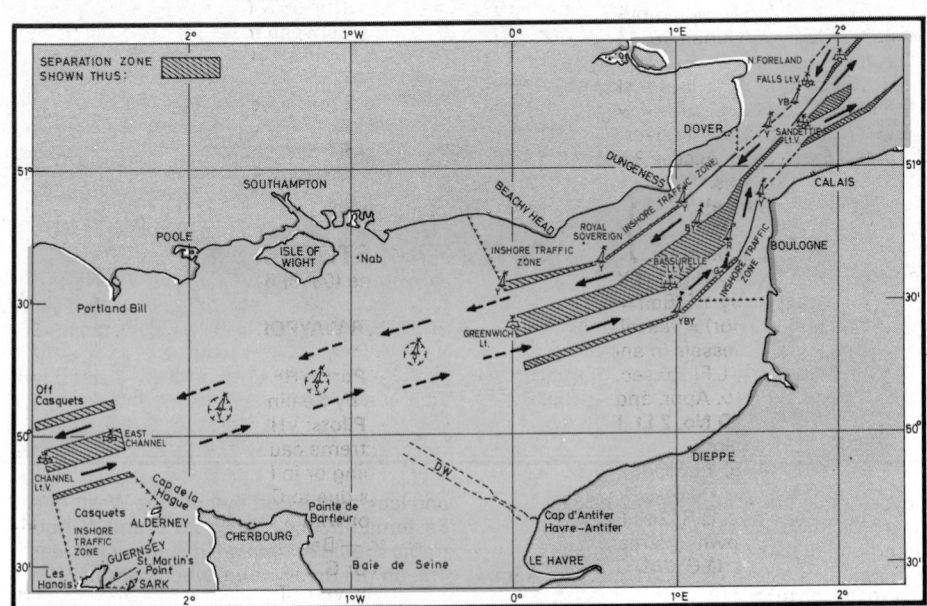

ENGLISH CHANNEL

Ushant Dover Strait Casquets. Ship Movement Report Scheme — Loaded oil gas and chemical carriers over 1600 GRT, vessels not under command or restricted by draught, or with defects to navigational aids, engines or steering to report position course speed destination draught and defects to:

Ouessant Traffic (Crossma), Chan. 11:16:79
Portland Coast Guard, Chan. 69:16.
Dover Coast Guard, Chan. 69:16:11:80.
Griz Nez Traffic (Crossma), Chan. 69:16:11:79.
Joburg Traffic (Crossma), Chan. 11:16:79.
B'cast: clear wx +(Restricted vis.)
Ushant H+10, H+40 (also H+25, H+55)
Joburg H+20, H+50 (also H+05, H+35)
Griz Nez H+10 (also H+25)
Dover H+40 (also H+55)

MRCC DOVER KENT (0304) 210008. Weather broadcast ev. 4h. from 0105.

DOVER RG STN. 51°07.94'N, 1°20.70'E.
Coastguard Emergency DF Stn. VHF Chan. 16 & 67. Controlled by MRCC Dover.

HISTORIC WRECK SITE DOVER. 51°07.6'N, 1°20.8'E. 150m. radius.

DOVER 51°07'N 1°20'E. Pilots & Port: Tel:
Dover (0304) 240400. Telex: 965619 (965620).
C.G. (0304) 852515.
Customs (0304) 240400 Ext. 312.
Wellington Docks (0304) 240400 Ext. 4531.

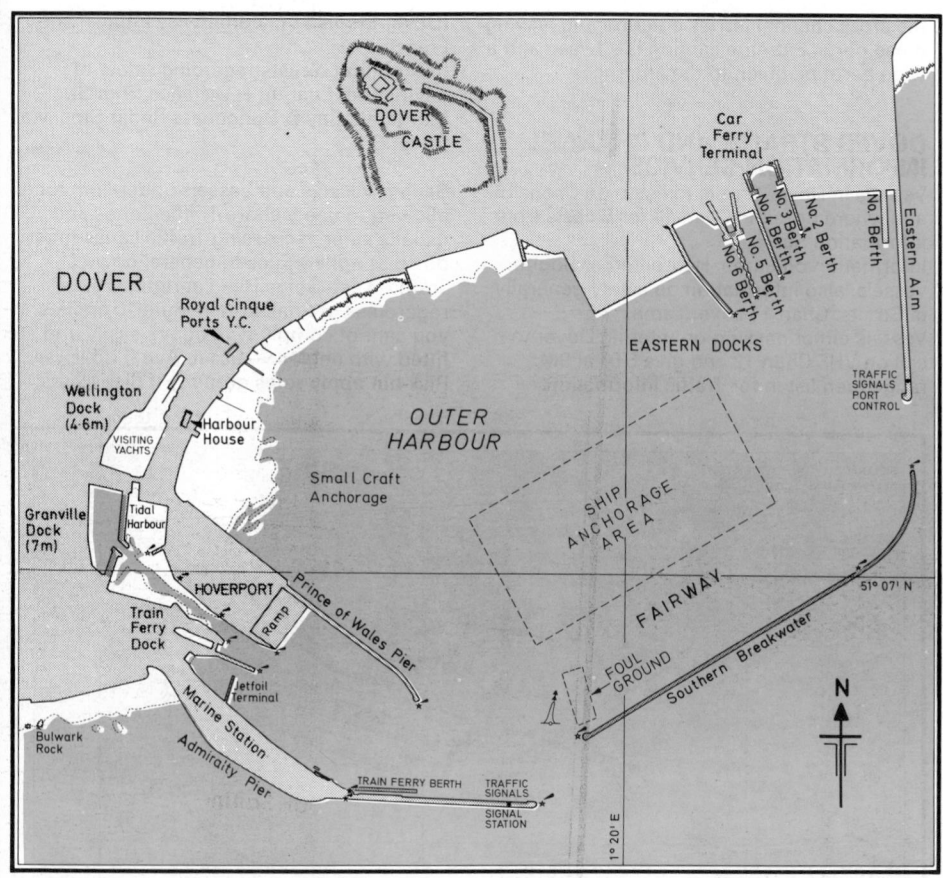

Royal Cinque Ports Y.C. (0304) 206262.
Dover Yacht Co. (0304) 201073. Geo.
Hammond (0304) 201201. Night: 203333.
Immigration Eastern Dk. (0304) 240123. Adm.
Pier (0304) 201913.

HARBOUR WAYPOINT. 51°06.5′N, 1°21.0′E.

Radio — Port: South end of Eastern Arm. VHF
Chan. 16, Cont. 74, 12.
Harbour Patrol, VHF Chan. 16,
12, 6.
Radio — Pilots: VHF Chan. 9.

**Entry Signals: DOVER HARBOUR TRAFFIC
CONTROL—**
Even though the Traffic Control Signal may
be exhibited for entry/departure, vessels
awaiting permission to proceed should keep
at a safe distance from the entrance until so
authorised.
Warning: Masters of vessels navigating in
the Dover Strait are warned of the high
frequency of cross-channel vessels entering

and leaving the Port by both the Western and
Eastern Entrances, and both E. and W. bound
traffic should maintain a distance of at least
1M. off the breakwaters when passing.

Communication with Port Control
Vessels fitted with VHF/RT—on Channel 74. If
not fitted Ch. 74, call on Ch. 16 and request to
use Ch. 12. ALL vessels must obtain permission
to enter or leave.

OUTER HARBOUR: Shown from Admiralty
Pier Extension for Western entrance and Port
Control for Eastern entrance.
Traffic Signals — apply to all vessels
including yachts — 3 F.R. Vert. Lts. = Vessels
shall not proceed. G./W./G. Vert. Lts. = Vessel
may proceed only when it has specific orders
to do so.
One way traffic only at both entrances.
Vessels without VHF make by Lamp SV = I
wish to enter: SW = I wish to leave: Port
Control replies 'OK' or 'Wait': Q. Fl = Keep
clear of entrance you are approaching.

ENTRY INTO OR EXIT FROM ENCLOSED DOCKS
Permission for entry into the enclosed docks must first be obtained from Port Control by ALL craft using VHF Ch. 74 or Ch. 12 or by contacting the Harbour Patrol Launch.
Berthing instructions for Wellington Dock will be given on arrival at the Dockmaster's Office, situated at the entrance to the Granville Dock on the Crosswall Quay. Dock gates approx. open 1½ h.-HW-1 h. approx. Yachtsmen intending to leave the Dock must report to the Dockmaster's office 2 hours before HW to pay their Harbour dues and receive sailing instructions.

NAVIGATIONAL WARNINGS Very frequent ferry, jetfoil and hovercraft movements through both entrances render small craft movements difficult. Strong tides across entrances and high walls will make entry under sail slow and hazardous — use of engine very strongly recommended. Observe traffic signals and follow instructions of Harbour Patrol Launch. Do not pass between buoy marking wreck inside Western Entrance and Southern Breakwater.

SHELTER The small craft anchorage is exposed to winds from NE through S to SW and in gales a heavy sea builds up. Visiting yachts should not be left unattended in the Outer Harbour. Craft are NOT permitted to berth or land personnel on the Prince of Wales Pier.
Speed limit 8 knots.
Entry: Depths: Channel to Granville Dock 5.8m. MHWS. Channel to Wellington Dock about 5.0m. MHWS. Wellington Dock 4.6m. MHWS and 3.4m. MHWN.

WELLINGTON DOCK Visiting yachts are normally berthed on the South and Western side of the Wellington Dock. On the Eastern side of the Wellington Dock, pontoon berths have been established and are for private use of Dover based yachts only.

DOCKING SIGNALS Docking signals for the Wellington Dock as for outer harbour. In addition, a small flashing amber lamp will be shown approximately 5 minutes before the bridge is swung.

ADMIRALTY PIER HEAD. Lt. Fl. 7.5 sec. 20M. W. Tr. Traffic Sig. Horn 10 sec.

INNER HARBOUR
PRINCE OF WALES PIER HEAD. Lt. V.Q.G. 4M. W. Tr. 14m. Docking Sig. Bell(2) 15 sec. & Fl.Y. 1.5 sec. Occas.
ADMIRALTY PIER No. 5 BERTH. Lt. 2 F.R. vert.

INNER. Lt. 2 F. Bu. vert.
TRAIN FERRY DOCK JETTY HEAD. Lt. Q.R. on post Bell(3) 10 sec.
JET FOIL TERMINAL BERTH. Dir Lt. Dir. Mo. (C) W.R.G. 8 sec. G.287°-291°; W.291°-293°; R.293°-297°.
JETTY HEAD. Lt. Iso. R. 2 sec.
TRAIN FERRY JETTY. Lt. Iso. G. 2 sec.
SOUTH PIER HEAD. Lt. 2 F.R. vert. Bn.
NORTH PIER EXTENSION. Lt. Q.G. & Fl. Y. 2.5 sec. Occas.
NORTH PIER HEAD. Lt. 3 F.G. vert. Bn.
NORTH PIER SPUR. Lt. Oc.G. on post.

TIDAL HARBOUR
DOLPHIN JETTY HEAD. Lt. Q.G.
CROSSWALL QUAY. Lt. F. 324°-333°. Marks channel to small craft emergency landing area.
SOUTHERN BREAKWATER
W HEAD. Lt. Oc.R. 30 sec. 18M. W. Tr.
KNUCKLE. Lt. Oc.W.R. 10 sec. W.15M. R.13M. W. Tr.
N HEAD. F.Y. 4M. on mast.
EASTERN ARM HEAD. Horn (2) 30 sec. Traffic and Port Control Signal Stn.

THE CAMBER
PIER A. WEST JETTY HEAD. Lt. Q.R. on mast.
PIER B. HEAD. Lt. Fl.(2)R. 5 sec. Siren 5 sec.
PIER C. Lt. Oc.R. 5 sec.
PIER D. Lt. Q.(6)+L.Fl. 15 sec. Siren (3) 20 sec. Occas.
DOLPHIN. Lt. Bn. Fl.R. 2 sec.

DOVER BLOCKSHIP. Lt.By. Q. Pillar B.Y. Topmark N.
DOVER WEST. Lt.By. Fl.Y. 4 sec. Sph. Y.
DOVER EAST. Lt.By. Fl.(4)Y. 6 sec. Sph. Y.
DOVER. Lt.By. Fl. Y. 4 sec. Sph. Y.

SOUTH FORELAND TO NORTH FORELAND

OFFSHORE WAYPOINT OFF S FORELAND. 51°08.0′N, 1°25.0′E.

SOUTH FORELAND 51°08.4′N, 1°22.4′E. Lt.Ho. W. sq. Tr.
DEAL PIER. Lt. 2 F.R.(Vert.) 5M. 7m.

Two Bys. Conical G. B1 and B2 mark Western side of Brake Sand and starboard side of Ramsgate Chan. from Southward, fitted ↯ and panels of fluorescent material.

SANDWICH HAVEN. (Richborough) 51°20′N 1°25′E
Entry: 2½ h. before to 2 h. after HW Dover on average according to draught.

Moorings 10m.×1.5m. draught at Sandwich Sailing and M.B. Club, also at Sandwich Marina 18m. × 2.1m. draught and at Sandwich Quay 18m. × 3m. draught. Vessels 55m. × 3m. draught can make Sandwich at MHWS. Reported all berths dry at LW.

RIVER STOUR channel marked by R. Can. & G. Conical bys. up to the Tripod marking entrance to R. Stour thence posts mark channel to Sandwich Haven.

PEGWELL BAY. Hoverport now maintenance area. Keep clear of ramps and flight path. Flights now infrequent.

SANDWICH APPROACH. Lt. Fl.(2)R. 10 sec. 4M. Tr. 3m. moved to meet changes in channel.

KIRSTEN SKOU WK. Lt.By. 51°03.8'N, 01°25.4'E. Q.(6) + L.Fl. 15 sec. Pillar Y.B. Topmark S.

Anchorage: Ramsgate Road ½M. S of Hbr. if winds WNW/NNE. Small craft anchor near Hbr. entrance S of line Quern By/S B'water in 2½m.—3½m. Approach channel 110m. wide.

Entry: Vessels should report to VTS office at Point Romeo 51°19.5'N 1°27.3'E i.e. 2½M from Channel Entrance Buoys. Report again at Point Romeo. ALL vessels including yachts much obtain permission (Ch.14) before entering main channel.

Inner Harbour: Traffic Signal (Int. Port Traffic Sigs.) No. 2 and 3. 500 berths 24m. × 2.4m. draught. Dock gates open 2 h.-HW-1 h. subject to weather conditions. ALL vesels must contact Port Control before entering and obey signals. Reception/waiting area on the pontoons at West Pier. Depths 6.5m. in entrance and 3m. at Royal Harbour (draught 6.5m. at HWS. Visitors berths available. Berths used for shelter or short stay in Outer

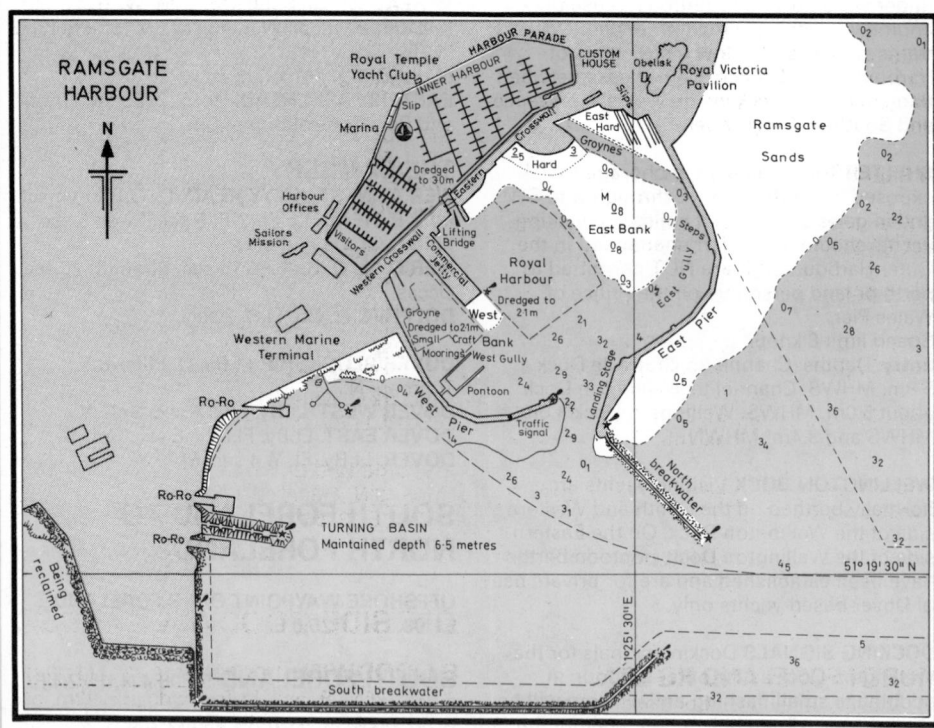

RAMSGATE HARBOUR

N

RAMSGATE 51°20'N 1°25'E. HM. (VTS) Tel: (0843) 592277. Telex: 965861 TDCHAR G. Fax: (0843) 590941.

OFFSHORE WAYPOINT RAMSGATE HARBOUR WAYPOINT. 51°19.5'N, 1°28.0'E.

Radio — Port: VHF Chan. 16, 14, H24.
Signals: West Pier: International Port Traffic Signals.

Harbour subject to rise and fall of tide and exposed in bad weather. Vessels must not be left unattended in Outer Harbour. Turning Basin dredged to 6.5m., may be less due to siltation.

E BRAKE. Lt.By. Q.(3) 10 sec. Pillar B.Y.B. Topmark E.
No. 1 Lt.By. Fl.G. 5 sec. Conical G.
No. 2 Lt.By. Fl.(4)R. 10 sec. Can.R.

No. 3 Lt.By. Fl.G. 2½ sec. Conical G.
No. 4 Lt.By. Q.R. Can.R.
QUERN. By. Pillar B.Y. Topmark N.
No. 5 Lt.By. Q.(6)+L.Fl. 15 sec. Pillar. Y.B.
Topmark S.
No. 6 Lt.By. Q. Pillar. B.Y. Topmark N.
Harbour Lt.By. Fl.G. Conical G.

OLD CUDD CHANNEL
Ldg.Lts. 291°34′ EAST PIER. Lt. (Front) Oc. 10
sec. 4M. vis. 250° to 195°. Metal Col. on Head.
8m. Port Sig. Bell 75m. NNE.

WEST PIER. Lt. (Rear) F.R. or G. 7M. Granite
circular Twr. on Head. 12m. also Tidal Lts.
256°-251°. G. when less than 3m. R. when
more than 3m. of water in entrance. Horn 600
sec. Traffic Signal sounded more frequently
when required.

SFB Lt.By. Fl. 10 sec. Pillar R.W.V.S.

WESTERN MARINE TERMINAL. Ldg.Lts. 270°
(Front) Dir. Oc.W.R.G. 10 sec. Bn. G.259°-269°;
W.269°-271°; R.271°-281° also Q.R. on Bn.
200m. SW (Rear) Oc. 5 sec. Bn.

N BREAKWATER HEAD. Lt. Q.G. G.W. Pillar.

S BREAKWATER HEAD. Lt. V.Q.R. R.W. Pillar.
RO-RO BERTH 2 & 3. Lt. 2 F.R. vert.

No. 1 BERTH. Lt. 2 F.R. vert. Dolphin.

COMMERCIAL JETTY. Lt. 2 F.R. vert.
RO-RO FERRY TERMINAL. Lt. 2 F.G. vert.

BROADSTAIRS PIER. 51°21′N, 1°27′E Lt. 2 F.R.
vert. 4M. SE end of Pier. 7m.

BROADSTAIRS KNOLL. Lt.By. Fl.R. 2.5 sec.
Can.R.

NORTH FORELAND OUTFALL (DIFFUSERS).
51°23′.57″N, 1°29′.88″E.

NORTH FORELAND RG STN.
51°22.57′N, 01°26.80′E. Controlled by MRCC
Dover.

OFFSHORE WAYPOINT OFF N FORELAND.
51°23.0′N, 1°29.0′E.

NORTH FORELAND 51°22.5′N, 1°26.8′E.
Lt. Fl.(5)W.R. 20 sec. W.21M. R.18M. W.
octagonal Twr. 57m. R.C. R.150°-200°. W.
Elsewhere.

VARNE 51°01.2′N, 1°24.0′E. Lanby. Fl.R. 20
sec. 19M. R. hull, 12m. Horn. 30 sec. Racon.
Situated 6M. SSE of Dover. Lit by day when
Fog Sig. operating.
S VARNE. Lt.By. Q.(6) + L.Fl. 15 sec. Pillar Y.B.
Topmark S. 〰. Whis.
E VARNE. Lt.By. Fl.R. 2½ sec. Can.R. 〰.

MID VARNE. Lt.By. Q.G. Conical G. 〰.

SOUTH FORELAND TO ELBOW — THROUGH THE DOWNS AND GULL STREAM

DEAL BANK. Lt.By. Q. R Can.R. off Deal
Castle.
GOODWIN FORK. Lt.By. Q.(6) + L.Fl. 15 sec.
Pillar Y.B. Topmark S. 〰. Bell.
DOWNS. Lt.By. Fl.(2)R. 5 sec. Can.R.
W GOODWIN. Lt.By. Fl.G. 5 sec. Conical G.
〰.
NW GOODWIN. Lt.By. Q.(9) 15 sec. Pillar
Y.B.Y. Topmark W. Bell w.a. 〰.
BRAKE. Lt.By. Fl.(4)R 15 sec. Can.R. Bell w.a.
N GOODWIN. Lt.By. Fl.G. 2½ sec. Conical G.
〰.
GULL STREAM. Lt.By. Q.R. Can.R.
GOODWIN KNOLL. Lt.By. Fl.(2)G. 5 sec.
Conical G. 〰.
GULL. Lt.By. V.Q.(3) 5 sec. Pillar B.Y.B.
Topmark E.
NE GOODWIN. Lt.By. Q.(3) 10 sec. Pillar B.Y.B.
Topmark E. Whis. Racon.
ELBOW. Lt.By. Q. Pillar B.Y. Topmark N. 〰.

HISTORIC WRECK SITE GOODWIN SANDS (1)
51°16.43′N, 1°30.52′E. (2) 51°15.76′N,
1°30.02′E. (3) 51°12.0′N, 1°30.56′E. 150m.
radius.

OUTSIDE GOODWIN SANDS

S GOODWIN 51°07.9′N, 1°28.6′E. Lt.F. Fl.(2)
30 sec. 25M. R. hull, Lt.Tr. amidships, 12m. off
SW end of Goodwin Sands. Nauto (2) 60 sec.
SW GOODWIN. Lt.By. Q.(6) + L.Fl. 15 sec.
Pillar Y.B. Topmark S.
S GOODWIN. Lt.By. Fl.(4)R. 15 sec. Can.R. 〰
SE GOODWIN Lt.By. Fl.(3)R. 10 sec. Can.R.
about 1M. W of E Goodwin Lt.V. 〰.

E GOODWIN 51°13.0′N, 1°36.3′E. Lt.F. Fl.
15 sec. 26M. R. hull, Lt.Tr. amidships, 12m.
about 1M. to Eastward of Goodwin Sands.
Horn 30 sec. Racon.

E GOODWIN Lt.By. Q.(3) 10 sec. Pillar B.Y.B. Topmark E.

SOUTH FALLS BANK
SOUTH FALLS Lt.By. Q(6)+L.Fl. 15 sec. Pillar Y.B. Topmark S.
FALLS Lt.F. 51°18.1'N, 1°48.5'E. Fl.(2) 10 sec. 24M. R. hull 12m. RC. Racon. Horn Mo.(N) 60 sec.
MID FALLS Lt.By. Fl.(3)R. 10 sec. Can. R.
DRILL STONE. 51°26'N, 1°43'E Lt.By. Q.(3) 10 sec. Pillar B.Y.B. Topmark E. ⌇⌇. Bell w.a. marks Drillstone Bank.
FALLS HEAD Lt.By. Q. Pillar B.Y. Topmark N.

LONDON Tel: (P.L.A.). Upper/Middle District 071-481 0720. Lower District (0474) 567684. Tilbury Dock Coordinator (0375) 859677. Thames Navigation Service (0474) 560311. Telex: 262880 PLATNS G. Fax: (0474) 352996. Contact T.N.S. for all pilotage orders. WOOLWICH RADIO (BARRIER) 081-855 0315. Telex: 896157 PLABAR G. Customs: 071-283 8633 Ext. 446. Customs: (0474) 563555.
Pilots: Gravesend. Tel: (0474) 567716. Telex: 96444 PILGRA G.
NE SPIT (RAMSGATE) (0843) 583786.
HARWICH (PLA) (0255) 241320.

Gravesend Radio. VHF Chan. 16, 12, 14, 18, 20, 9. Shore radar coverage—
Outer Estuary to Erith. For all Thames berthing information.
Radio Tide Gauges at: Walton, Margate, Shivering Sands, Southend and Tilbury. Contact Gravesend before entering/leaving and in Transit.
Woolwich Radio (Barrier Control). VHF Chan.14, 16, 22. Erith to London Bridge, and Barrier Shore radar.
Coverage: Erith-Greenwich.
Radio Tide Gauges: Woolwich.

TILBURY DOCK. VHF Chan. 4, 15, 17.

Thurrock Yacht Club. Tel: (0375) 373720. Chan. M.
Chelsea Boat Harbour. Tel: 071-351 4433. Chan. M.
St. Katherine Dock Marina. Tel: 071-488 2400. VHF Chan. 14, 6, 12, 80, 37. 2 h.-HW-1½ h. Winter 0800-1800. Summer 0600-2030. Lock 42m. × 7.9m. (Clear) × 5.4m. draught. (Sill dries 0.6m.).
Chiswick Quay Marina Tel: 081-994 8743.
Brentford Dock Marina. Tel: 081-568 0287. VHF Chan. 16, 14. (M) 1000-1800.
Swan Island Harbour Tel: 081-892 2861.
Greenwich Y.C. Tel: 081-858 7339.
Canal Basin Gravesend. (0474) 352392. Manned 0700-2100 ev. day. 2100-0700 at 24 h.

notice. Operates 1 h.-HW-1 h. July/Aug. Sat./Sun. every tide. Winter req. 2 h. notice.
South Dock Marina. Tel: 071-252 2244. VHF Chan. 80, 37(M). Lock available 2 h.—HW—2 h. 33m. × 6.6m. × sill 2.5m. ACD. 372 berths. H24.
Shellhaven. Tel: (0375) 653388. Fax: (0375) 653547. Telex: 897230 SHELL G.
Radio. VHF Chan. 19. H24.
King George Dock. Radio: VHF Chan. 68.
West India Dock. Radio VHF Chan. 68.
Vessels intending to overtake a Specified Vessel, between W. Blythe/SR No. 7, i.e. one carrying dangerous/low flash goods should inform Gravesend Radio and wait until all other vessels have been warned.

Vessels intending to Transit Southwark Br. should contact Woolwich radio at Tower or Waterloo Br. beforehand.

River Thames:
Speed limit 8 kts.
(a) Inshore off Southend from Shoeburyness to Canvey Point.
(b) In all creeks adjoining the Thames.
(c) Off Shellhaven and Coryton Oil jetties.
(d) Above Wandsworth.
Water ski areas: Off Shoeburyness Pier; S part of Hadleigh Ray to Tewkes/Benfleet Creek; Holehaven Creek (upper part).
Leigh Channel depth 1.8m.
Ray Gut depth 0.3m. to 4m.
S Benfleet: Road Bridge clearance 2.7m.
E Haven: Road Bridge clearance 3.6m.
Barking Creek dries 1.5m.
Richmond Lock 76m. × 8.1m. × 1.4m. Lower Sill (0.8m. upper sill).
Overhead cables. Safe clearance 15m.

BOW CREEK — TIDAL BARRIER
18m. × 9.1m. ht. at MHWS.

BARKING CREEK — TIDAL BARRIER —
    CLEAR Ht. 22m.
DARTFORD CREEK — BARRIER —
    CLEAR Ht. 120m.
EASTHAVEN CREEK — BARRIER —
    CLEAR Ht. 3.3m.
FOBBING CREEK — BARRIER —
    CLEAR Ht. 9.3m.
Creek Barriers show Fl.R. when closed.

River Thames — Thames Barrier Control.
Control Zone: Margaretness to Blackwall Point. Notice Boards with Lights at Thamesmead, Barking Power Stn., Brunswick Power Stn., Blackwall Point.

Amber Lt. = Proceed with extreme caution.
Red Lt. = Navigation within Zone prohibited.
Red St. Andrew's Crosses (Lit) from Piers =
    Barrier or Span Closed.
Green Arrows (Lit) from Piers = Span open.
Loud Hailers are fitted at certain points to
pass instructions. They may also transmit
Morse Signal "K". On hearing Morse Signal
(indicating Barrier Closure) Contact Woolwich
Radio if fitted VHF RT. If not fitted stop your
vessel, listen to voice instructions.
It is extremely dangerous to go through a
Span that is marked Closed (for navigation),
the gates may be in a semi-raised position.
Small Craft: Do not navigate above Thames
Refinery Jetty or below Gulf Oil Island unless
intending to pass through the Barrier.
ALL GATES CLOSED: No vessel to navigate
within 200m. of Barrier due to turbulence.

Depth over sills: Gate C, D, E, F = 5.8m. C.D.
B, G = 1.25m. C.D.

There is a large visitors centre on S Side
showing the working of the Thames Barrier.

Distances: The Lower River Thames.
There are 18 Reaches in the **Lower Thames**
between Sea Reach and the Upper Pool of
London — their names and Compass Courses
are shown below.
From Tower Bridge up river is 16½ miles, and
a vessel must pass under 28 bridges (or 29 if
not using Richmond half Tide Lock) to reach
Teddington Lock where the river ceases to
become Tidal.

The Upper River Thames. The total distance
from Teddington to Henley is 46 miles, to
Oxford is 93 miles, and to the source at
Lechlade a total of 124 miles.

T.W.A. (Thames Conservancy Division) Tel:
0734 593777.
Boat Licences. Tel: 081-940 8723.

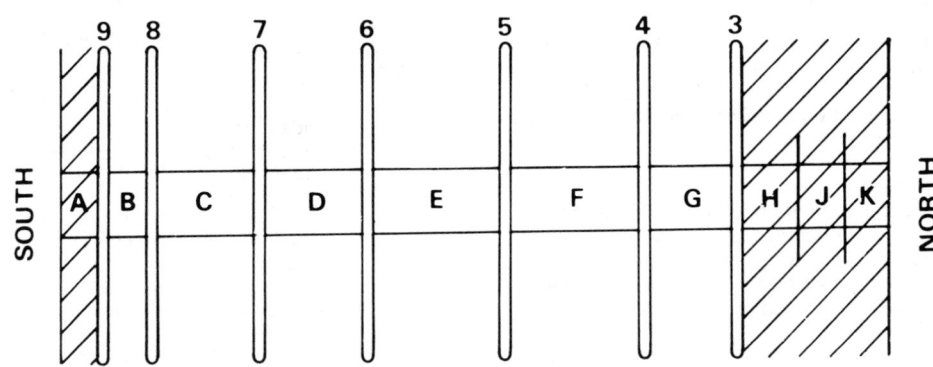

No.	Course Up	Name	From and To	Course Down
1	WNW	Sea Reach	No. 1 SR to No. 1 Mucking Buoy	ESE
2	SW	Lower Hope	No. 1 Mucking Buoy to Coalhouse Pt.	NE
3	WXN	Gravesend Reach	Coalhouse Point to Tilbury Ness	EXS
4	NXW	Northfleet Hope	Tilbury Ness to Broadness	SXE
5	WSW	St. Clements (or Fiddler) Reach	Broadness to Stone Ness	ENE
6	NWXN	Long Reach	Stone Ness to Crayfordness	SEXS
7	WXN½N	Erith Rands	Crayfordness to Coldharbour Point	EXS½S
8	NORTH	Erith Reach	Coldharbour Point to Jenningtree Pt.	SOUTH
9	NW½W	Half-way Reach	Jenningtree Point to Cross Ness	SE½E
10	W½N	Barking Reach	Cross Ness to Margaret Ness	E½S
11	SW½W	Gallions Reach	Margaret Ness to Gallions Point	NE½E
12	WXN½N	Woolwich Reach	Gallions Point to Hook Ness	EXS½S
13	NNW	Bugsby's Reach	Hook Ness to { Bow Creek (N) / Blackwall Pt. (S) }	SSE
14	SOUTH	Blackwall Reach	Bow Creek to Enderby's Wharf	NORTH
15	WXS to NW	Greenwich Reach	Enderby's Wharf to Deptford	EXN to SE
16	NW to NNE	Limehouse Reach	Deptford to Regents Canal Dock Entrance	SE to SSW
17	WSW	Lower Pool	Regents Canal Dock Entrance to Cherry Garden Pier	ENE
18	NW½W	Upper Pool	Cherry Garden Pier to London Bdge.	SE½E

Under the control of the Thames Water Authority no vessel is allowed in these waters without being registered and licensed by this body. There are about 90 bridges, and 52 locks to negotiate over its length.

From **Richmond** to **Staines** the Size of Locks is 53m. by 5.9m. width 1.8m. draught. Headway of Bridges 3.8m. From **Staines** to **Reading** app. 40m. by 5.3m. and draught 1.2m. and to Marlow 1.3m. thence to Reading. Headway of Bridges 3.7m. From **Reading** to **Oxford**, Locks 37m. by 5.3m. Draught 1.2m. by 3.2m. beam; **Oxford** up to **Lechlade** 33m. by 4.5m. Draught 1.1m. with 2.3m. Headway under bridges.

I. Figures on following page are generalisations: for detailed information consult PLA charts.

II. Take off about 1 metre from H.W. Springs to get H.W. Neaps. Add about 0.9 metre to L.W. Springs to get L.W. Neaps.

III. Two horizontal orange lights indicate the navigational arches.

IV. *Indicates distance below London Bridge to point starred.

Remarks

The depth of water given is the minimum in the centre half of the fairway in way of centre span within 50m. of the Bridge.
Trinity High Water is taken for these purposes as 3.5 metres above Ordnance Datum (Newlyn).
The depths and headways for Richmond Bridge, Richmond Railway Bridge and Twickenham Bridge are referred to the water level of 1.8 metres below T.H.W. maintained by the sluices at Richmond Footbridge, when they are closed during the low water period. The Richmond weir sluices are raised at about 2 hours before H.W. there and lowered at about 2 hours after. Passage through the navigation spans of Richmond Footbridge is available between these times.
Depths of water and headways are affected to a varying degree by the volume of upland water.
The above information has been supplied by the Port of London Authority and whilst every care is taken in the preparation of these tables, the Port Authority are not responsible for any inaccuracy.

Richmond Lock: available HW —2 h. to LW +4 h.

Richmond Footbridge—Low water details cover lock and approaches.

Kew Railway Bridge.—Depth shown is through span south of the centre arch.

Hammersmith Bridge.—Depths shown are in the maintained channel which is southward of the centre of the bridge where the headway is less than the maximum. Bridge sags slightly under heavy traffic. Gauge boards showing the headway at any moment are situated at the lower end of Chiswick Ait and at the lower end of Harrod's Quay.

Albert Bridge — Supporting Pier in centre of middle span reduces width to 55.5m. either side.

Tower Bridge. Signals: Bascules Closed 1 R. Lt. each side from piers.
Bascules open 1 G. Lt. each side from piers. Siren 20 sec. or Gong 30 sec.
To Open Bridge: Ring 071-407 0922 not less than 24 hr. in advance. All other signals discontinued.
Bridge Unable to Open: bridge closed signal plus 1.2m diam. B.W. diag. stripe disc each end of bascule. Disc lit at night.
In reduced vis: 'Bridge Open' sig. plus High Frequ. Sound for 10 sec. or in event of power failure a gong every 30 sec.
Except when "Bridge Unable to open" sig. displayed, the bridge will be opened in reduced vis. when the vessel is ready to pass through and on giving 1 Long 2 Short 1 Long Blast.
Craft drawing over 1.8m. should not attempt passage between Richmond and Putney at LW. Also note depth at LWS at London Bridge is only 1.8m.

Between Tower Bridge and Putney Bridge a High Intensity Isophase Lt will be shown on the up and down stream sides of certain arches of the bridges. This light when shown indicates that a vessel over 40m in length, or over 50 tons or a Tug and Tow is about to use the arch indicated. All other vessels or craft are to keep clear.

Sound Signals: River Thames

— · ·	Not under command or unable to manoeuvre*
· · · ·	(or more) I am doubtful if you are taking sufficient avoiding action.
· · · · ·	I am about to turn round, head to starboard.*
· · · · · ·	I am about to turn round, head to port.*

–	I am about to leave the dock, wharf or pier. Or enter Fairway.
– – .	I am overtaking to starboard.
– – . .	I am overtaking to port.
– . – .	I am in agreement with your intention to overtake.
	(*To be used also in fog).

GRAVESEND

. – – . –	I require a Pilot.
–	I wish to exchange Pilots.
– . . –	The River Pilot desires to land but I do **not** require a Channel Pilot.
– – . –	I require the attention of the Port Health Authority.

Vessels above Broadness Pt. of 8.5 metres draught and below Broadness Pt. of 9.2 metres draught and over should display a black cylinder or 3 R. Lts. (vert.).

Southend. Vessels about to enter or leave the designated anchorages or anchorage areas should indicate their intentions by sounding 5 or more short blasts on the whistle or siren. Small craft should then keep well clear.

RIVER THAMES BRIDGE HEIGHTS AND DEPTHS

Name of Bridge	TYPE	Headway of Centre Span above		Depth in Centre Span below Chart Datum	Tidal Levels above Chart Datum				Distance above London Bridge Sea Miles	Least Width Channel or Centre Span
					MEAN SPRINGS		MEAN NEAPS			
		Chart Datum	MHWS		HW	LW	HW	LW		
										m
Richmond	A	7.9	5.3	1.7	2.6	0	1.4	0	13.94	18
Richmond Rly.	A	7.9	5.3	2.5	2.6	0	1.4	0	13.64	30
Twickenham	A	8.5	5.9	2.3	2.6	0	1.4	0	13.61	31
Richmond Foot	A	9.7	4.9	0.8	4.8	0	3.6	0	13.45	20
Kew	A	10.6	5.3	1.3	5.3	0	4.1	0.1	11.31	41
Kew Railway	F	10.9	5.6	1.2	5.3	0	4.2	0.1	10.95	31
Chiswick	A	12.2	6.9	1.3	5.3	0	4.2	0.1	10.20	46
Barnes Rly.	A	10.9	5.4	1.1	5.5	0	4.3	0.2	9.53	37
Hammersmith	S	9.4	3.7	1.4	5.7	0	4.6	0.3	7.95	122
Putney	A	11.4	5.5	1.4	5.9	0.1	4.8	0.4	6.44	44
Fulham Rly.	F	12.8	6.9	1.6	5.9	0.1	4.8	0.4	6.30	43
Wandsworth	A	11.9	5.8	1.4	6.1	0.1	4.9	0.5	5.46	86
Battersea Rly.	A	12.2	6.1	2.0N 2.4S	6.1	0.1	4.9	0.5	4.85	42
Battersea	A	11.7	5.5	2.0	6.2	0.1	5.0	0.6	4.29	50
Albert	S	11.1	4.9	1.7S	6.2	0.1	5.1	0.6	4.06	117
Chelsea	S	12.9	6.6	2.2	6.3	0.2	5.2	0.7	3.41	101
Victoria Rly.	A	12.3	6.0	1.7N 2.1S	6.3	0.2	5.2	0.7	3.30	53
Vauxhall	A	12.1	5.6	1.3	6.5	0.2	5.3	0.8	2.52	46
Lambeth	A	13.1	6.5	1.6	6.6	0.3	5.5	0.9	2.11	50
Westminster	A	12.2	5.4	1.2N 1.4S	6.8	0.4	5.6	1.1	1.72	35
Charing X Rly.	F	13.8	7.0	2.2N 2.9S	6.8	0.4	5.6	1.1	1.38	47
Waterloo	A	15.3	8.5	1.8N 1.7S	6.8	0.4	5.6	1.1	1.13	73
Blackfriars	A	14.0	7.1	2.3N 1.5S	6.9	0.4	5.8	1.2	0.64	57
Blackfriars Rly.	A	13.9	7.0	2.3N 1.7S	6.9	0.4	5.8	1.2	0.60	57
Southwark	A	14.3	7.4	1.8N 3.6S	6.9	0.4	5.8	1.2	0.25	43
Cannon St. Rly.	F	14.0	7.1	2.4N 3.2S	6.9	0.4	5.8	1.2	0.16	41
London Bridge	A	16.0	8.9	1.8	7.1	0.5	5.9	1.3	0	100
Tower (down)	B	15.7	8.6	5.7	7.1	0.4	5.9	1.3	Below	61
Tower (up)		49.6	42.5						0.49	61

Chart Datum is the level of the Lowest Astronomical Tide (LAT).
A = Arched Bridge (Headway is measured exact centre of centre arch).
S = Suspension Bridge. B = Bascule Bridge. F = Flat Soffit Bridge.

22:72

Below London Bridge	Distance	Ruling Depth Below C/D	H.W. Springs Depth	L.W. Springs Depth	Least Width Channel or Centre Span
	miles	m	m	m	m
Tower Br./Thames Tunnel*	1.46*	4.0	11.0	4.3	116
Thames/Tunnel/Greenland Dk.*	2.96*	4.0	11.1	4.4	128
Greenland Dk./Charlton*	8.56*	4.6	11.6	5.0	137
Charlton/King George V. Dk.	9.26*	5.7	12.6	6.1	183
King George V. Dk./Dagenham*	12.26*	6.1	13.0	6.6	183
Dagenham/Coldharbour*	14.46*	6.7	13.2	7.3	183
Coldharbour/Gravesend*	22.76*	7.9	14.5	8.5	300
Gravesend/Thameshaven	31.16*	7.9	14.2	8.5	300
Thameshaven/No. 1 Sea Reach*	43.66*	9.6	15.7	10.2	300

* For Piers in the River Thames available to small craft see following pages.

British Waterways Board.
Licences required for all pleasure craft. Allow three weeks for issue. Apply to Craft Licencing Office, B.W.B, Willow Grange, Church Road, Watford WD1 3QA. Tel: (0923) 226422.
St. Pancras Y. Basin, B.W.B., 53 Clarendon Road, Watford, Herts. WD1 1LA. Tel: (0923) 31363.
Grand Union Canal (23.7m. × 4.3m. × 1.1m. draught × 2.3m. headroom).
Grand Union Canal, Brentford Locks. Tel: 081-560 1120.
Lee and Stort Navigations
Bow Locks Tel: 071-987 5661.
Lime House Basin Tel: 071-895 9930. 0800-1700.

Recommended max. craft size for canal 21.95m x 4.42m x 1.22m draught x 2.59m height. Best time to arrive is 3h.-HW. Lock not available 2h.-LW-2h. Larger craft should contact Dockmaster at least 24h. in advance for advice. Approx. lock size 7.6m x 27.5m x 6m at HW. Swing bridge can cause problems. Lock available 0800-1700 daily when tide serves.

HW at Lime House = HW London Bridge.

HW at Brentford = HW London Bridge + 1 h.

Thames Tidal Lock 101: 0600-2200 2 h.-HW-2 h.

Brentford Gauging Lock: 0700-1800 Mon.-Fri. 0600-2200 Sat./Sun./Bank Hol. 2 h.-HW-2 h.

Lime House Basin: 3 h.-HW.

Bow Locks: Mon.-Sat. 4 h.-HW-2 h. Sun/Bank Hol. 2 h.-HW-2 h.

Yacht Bunkers. There are very few places where petrol can be obtained. There are at present no fuelling places below Tower Bridge area. Always carry spare cans so that you can get fuel from riverside garages.

Bunkering facilities — normal hours but outside by prior arrangement.

Strand on the Green. Bassin & Arnolds 081-994 2431, only place supplying petrol.

Swan Island 081-892 2861.

Barge Freddy (Nr. Westminster Pier) Tel: 071-930 0068. VHF Chan. 14.

Barge Vogelzand (Nr. Lambeth Pier) Tel: 0836 501826. VHF Chan. 14.

Thames Refueller Bunker Barge 071-481 1774. Below Tower Bridge. VHF Chan. 14.

PIERS WHERE LANDING CAN BE MADE BY ARRANGEMENT

Richmond Landing Stage	South Side Above Bridge	081-940 2244	Summer only
St. Helena Pier	South Side Below Bridge		Private. Summer only
Kew Pier	South Side Below Bridge	081-940 3891 081-940 7632	
Hammersmith Pier	North Side Above Bridge	081-748 8607	Private
Putney Pier	South Side Above Bridge	081-788 5104	
Cadogan Pier	North Side Below Albert Bridge	071-352 4604	
Lambeth Pier	South Side	071-735 1680	*
Westminster Pier	North Side Below Bridge	071-930 8294	
Charing Cross Pier	North Side Below Bridge	071-839 5393	*
Festival Pier	South Side	071-261 0455	*
Tower Pier (Lower)	North Side Above Bridge	071-481 3800	
Tower Pier (Upper)		071-481 0720	

London Bridge City Pier	South Side Below Bridge	071-378 6770	Private
Cherry Garden Pier	South Side Below Tower Bridge	071-237 5134	Private*
Wapping (Tunnel) Pier	North Side	071-481 2711	Private
Greenland Pier	South Side Old Surrey Dock	071-515 1046	Private
West India Dock Pier	North Side Limehouse Reach	071-987 1185	Private
Greenwich Pier	South Side	081-858 0079	*
Barrier Gardens Pier	South Side Below Barrier	081-854 5555	Private*

*Locked out of hours.

All public Piers are fitted VHF Chan. 16, M and listen Chan. 14.

RIVER THAMES ESTUARY — INSHORE PASSAGES

Sand banks are continually changing in the Thames Estuary. It is inadvisable to use the short cuts across the swins unless you are very sure of the latest water available. South Channel/Horse and Gore Channel/Overland Passage/Four Fathoms Channel with generally min. depth 2m. Shoaling has occurred in Gore and South Chan. Keep to deepest charted water.
LONGNOSE. By. Can.R. topmark, Can. light reflective panels, marks Longnose Ledge.
FORENESS SEWER OUTFALL. By. Pillar B.Y. Topmark N.

INSHORE WAYPOINT FORENESS SEWER. 51°25.0′N, 1°26.2′E.

INSHORE WAYPOINT OFF E MARGATE. 51°27.5′N, 1°27.0′E.

MARGATE 51°23′N, 1°23′E
P/Station: NE Spit.
Radio — Pilots: VHF Chan. 16. 9—continuous.
Entry: Dries 2m. with approx. 4m. MHWS at head of Stone Pier.

PIER. Lt. Q.R. 18m.

PROMENADE PIER. Lt. 2 F.R. Vert. 4M. Flagstaff, 8m.

HORSE & GORE CHANNEL

INSHORE WAYPOINT E OF SE MARGATE. 51°24.0′N, 1°22.0′E.
SE MARGATE Lt.By. Q.(3) 10 sec. Pillar. B.Y.B. Topmark E. marks N Entce. to S Chan.
S MARGATE. Lt.By. Fl.G. 2½ sec. Conical G. ⩗.
INSHORE WAYPOINT S MARGATE. 51°23.8′N, 1°16.8′E.

MARGATE HOOK Bn. B. mast topmark S.
HOOK SPIT By. Conical G. Lt. reflective panels. ⩗

E LAST Lt.By. Q.R. Can.R. ⩗.
INSHORE WAYPOINT E LAST. 51°24.0′N, 1°12.6′E.
RECULVERS 2 square Trs. with wooden Bns. on cliffs.
BROOKSEND OUTFALL. By. Can.R.
SWALECLIFFE LONG OUTFALL By. Can.Y.

FOUR FATHOMS CHANNEL

MIDDLE SAND Bn. R.W. metal cylindrical mast. Topmark Sph. 10m.

INSHORE WAYPOINT SPANIARD. 51°26.0′N, 1°04.1′E.

SPANIARD Lt.By. Q(3) 10 sec. Pillar B.Y.B. Topmark E.
SPILE Lt.By. Fl.G. 2½ sec. Conical G.
INSHORE WAYPOINT SPILE. 51°26.1′N, 0°55.8′E.

HERNE BAY TO EAST SWALE RIVER

HERNE BAY PIER. 51°22.9′N, 1°07.0′E Lt. Q. 4M. on post at Head. 8m.

INSHORE WAYPOINT OFF WHITSTABLE/SWALE. 51°24.0′N, 1°02.0′E.

WHITSTABLE 51°22′N, 1°02′E. Tel: (0227) 274086.
Radio—Whitstable Harbour Radio. VHF Chan. 16, 12, 9—3 h.-HW-1 h., also 0800-1700.
Entry: F.R. below Entrance F. Lt. =entry prohibited.
Vessels should arrive at Whitstable Street By. 1½ h. before HW.
For Pilots contact Medway Navigation Service.
Anchorage: up to 3.5m. draught—½M. E of Street By.
Harbour dries with 92m. × 4.5m. draught MHWS and 3.6m. MHWN. Small craft are berthed at W end of S Quay and alongside the W wall.

WHITSTABLE OYSTER Lt.By. Fl.(2)R. 10 sec. Can. R.

NE ARM. Lt. F. 8M. on W. mast at Hr. Entce. On same structure, F.R. 5M. shown when entry or departure prohibited.

WEST QUAY. Lt. Fl.W.R.G. 5 sec. W.5M. R.3M. G.3M. Dolphin.

NE CORNER Lt. 2 F.G. vert. 2M. Pole 4m.

EAST QUAY. N End Lt. 2 F.R. 1M.
Ldg.Lts. 122.5° (Front) F.R. (Rear) F.R.

ENTRANCE TO EAST SWALE RIVER

WHITSTABLE STREET. 51°23.8′N, 1°01.7′E. Lt.By. V.Q. Pillar B.Y. Topmark N..
POLLARD SPIT. Lt.By. Q.R. Can.R.
COLUMBINE By. Conical G. 〰.
COLUMBINE SPIT By. Conical G.
HAM GAT By. Conical G.
SHELL NESS BEACON B. at Point.
SAND END. Lt.By. Fl.G. 5 sec. Conical G. 〰.
HORSE SAND. By. Conical G.

FAVERSHAM 51°19′N 0°54′E. Tel: Faversham (0795) 2916.
Pilotage: Pilots available via Medway Navigation Service.
Entry: Creek dries but Basin impounded by dock gates. Craft 43m. × 7m. × 3m. draught MHWS and 2m. draught MHWN.

FAVERSHAM SPIT ENTCE. By. Pillar By. Topmark N thence by.
No. 1, 3, 5, 7, 9, 11 Bys. Conical G.
No. 2, 4, 6, 8, 10, 12, 14, 16 Bys. Can.R.

QUEENS CHANNEL

MARGATE SAND Bn. B. Topmark. N. 11m (destroyed).
PAN SAND Bn. B. Topmark S. 15m. On Pan Sands.
S GIRDLER Bn. Triangle.

PRINCES CHANNEL

NE SPIT Lt.By V.Q.(3) 5 sec. 〰 Pillar B.Y.B. Topmark E.
E. MARGATE Lt.By. Fl.R. 2½ sec. Can.R.

INSHORE WAYPOINT OFF PRINCES CHAN. 51°29.0′N, 1°20.0′E.

TONGUE SAND TOWER. Lt.By. Fl.R. 1 sec. Spherical B.R.W.Hor. bands, marks Tongue Sand Tr.
NE TONGUE SAND TOWER Lt.By. Q. Pillar By.Topmark N
SW TONGUE SAND TOWER Lt.By. Q.(6) + L.Fl. 15 sec. Pillar Y.B. Topmark S. Bell 15 sec.
E TONGUE. Lt.By. Fl.(2)R. 5 sec. Can.R. 〰.
S SHINGLES. Lt.By. Q.(6) + L.Fl. 15 sec. Pillar Y.B. Topmark S. Bell. 〰.
N TONGUE. Lt.By. Fl.(3)R. 10 sec. Can.R. 〰.
SE GIRDLER. Lt.By. Fl.(3)G. 10 sec. Conical G. 〰.
W GIRDLER. Lt.By. Q.(9) 15 sec. Pillar Y.B.Y. Topmark W. Bell.
GIRDLER. Lt.By. Fl.(4)R. 15 sec. Can.R. 〰.

E. RED SANDS Lt.By. Fl.(2)R. 5 sec. Can. R. 〰.
SHIVERING SANDS Lt.By. Q(6)+ L.Fl. 15 sec. Pillar Y.B. Topmark S. Bell.

INSHORE WAYPOINT SOUTH OF SHIVERING SANDS TWRS. 51°29.5′N, 1°04.8′E.

HISTORIC WRECK SITE. SOUTH EDINBURGH. 51°31.73′N, 1°14.88′E. 100m. radius.

EDINBURGH CHANNELS

INSHORE WAYPOINT N OF OUTER TONGUE. 51°31.2′N, 1°26.4′E.

INSHORE WAYPOINT S OF OUTER TONGUE. 51°30.5′N, 1°26.4′E.

OUTER TONGUE. 51°30.78′N, 1°26.47′E. Lt.By. L. Fl. 10 sec. Pillar R.W.V.S. Topmark Sph. Whis. Racon.

INSHORE WAYPOINT OFF EDINBURGH CHAN. 51°31.0′N, 1°21.0′E.

NORTH EDINBURGH CHANNEL

EDINBURGH Lt.By. Q.R. Can.R. 〰.
N EDINBURGH No: 1 Lt.By. Q.(6) + L. Fl. 15 sec. Pillar Y.B. Topmark S. Bell.
PATCH Lt.By. Fl.(2)R. 5 sec. Can.R. 〰.
SE LONG SAND Lt.By. Q.G. Conical G.
N EDINBURGH No: 2 Lt.By. Fl.(3)R. 10 sec. Can.R. 〰.
N EDINBURGH No: 3 Lt.By. Q.(9) 15 sec. Pillar Y.B.Y. Topmark W.
N EDINBURGH No: 4 Lt.By. Fl.R.(4) 10 sec. Can.R. 〰. w.a. bell.
N EDINBURGH No: 5 Lt.By. Fl.G. 2½ sec. Conical G. 〰.

N EDINBURGH No: 6 Lt.By. Fl.(2)R. 5 sec. Can.R. ༺.
N EDINBURGH No: 7. Lt.By. Fl.(2)G. Conical G. ༺.
N EDINBURGH No: 8 Lt.By. Fl.(3)R. 10 sec. Can.R. ༺.
N EDINBURGH No: 9 Lt.By. Fl.(3)G. 10 sec. Conical G. ༺ w.a. bell.
SHINGLES PATCH. Lt.By. Q. Pillar B.Y. Topmark N.

INSHORE WAYPOINT SHINGLES PATCH. 51°33.4′N, 1°16.1′E.

KNOB CHANNEL

N SHINGLES. Lt.By. Fl.R. 2½ sec. Can.R.
TIZARD. Lt.By. Q.(6) + L.Fl. 15 sec. Pillar Y.B. Topmark S.
NW SHINGLES Bn. Topmark Can. on edge of Shingle Sands.
MID SHINGLES. Lt.By. Fl.(2)R. 5 sec. Can. R. ༺.
NE KNOB. Lt.By. Q.G. Conical G. ༺.
NW SHINGLES. Lt.By. V.Q. Pillar By. Topmark N.
SE KNOB. Lt.By. Fl.G. 5 sec. Conical G. ༺.
KNOB. Lt.By. Iso. 5 sec. H.F.P. Pillar. R.W.V.S. Topmark Sph.

INSHORE WAYPOINT N OF SHIVERING SANDS TWRS. 51°30.4′N, 1°04.9′E.
SHIVERING SANDS TOWERS N Lt.By. Q. Pillar B.Y. Topmark N.

OAZE DEEP TO THE GREAT NORE

Pilot boarding and landing area established N. of the Red Sand Towers. Extreme caution necessary in this area.

S OAZE. Lt.By. Fl.(2)G. 5 sec. Conical G. ༺.
INSHORE WAYPOINT S.W. OAZE. 51°28.8′N, 0°57.1′E.

INSHORE WAYPOINT N OF RED SAND TWRS. 51°29.3′N, 0°59.4′E.
N RED SAND TWRS. Lt.By. Fl.(3)R. 10 sec. Can.R. w.a. Bell.
S RED SAND TWRS. Lt.By. Q.G. Conical G.

SW OAZE. Lt.By. Q.(6) + L.Fl. 15 sec. Pillar Y.B. Topmark S. ༺.
INSHORE WAYPOINT W. OAZE. 51°28.8′N, 0°55.4′E.
W OAZE. Lt.By. V.Q.(9) 10 sec. Pillar Y.B.Y. Topmark W.

NORTH CHANNELS

SUNK 51°51′N, 1°35′E. Lt.F. Fl.(2) 20 sec. 24M. R.hull, Lt.Tr. amidships, 12m. Horn.(2) 60 sec. R.C. Racon.

BLACK DEEP TO KNOCK JOHN DEEP DRAUGHT CHANNEL

TRINITY. 51°49.0′N, 1°36.5′E Lt.By. Q.(6) + L.Fl. 15 sec. Pillar Y.B. Topmark S.

INSHORE WAYPOINT LONG SAND HEAD. 51°49.0′N, 1°40.0′E.

LONG SAND HEAD Lt.By. V.Qk.Fl. Pillar B.Y. Topmark N. Bell.
MI-AMIGO WK. By. 51°34.95′N, 1°17.35′E. Can.R.

INSHORE WAYPOINT BLACKDEEP CHANNEL. 51°46.0′N, 1°32.0′E.

B.D. No: 2 Lt.By. V.Q.(9) 10 sec. Pillar Y.B.Y. Topmark W.
B.D. No: 1 Lt.By. Fl.G. 5 sec. Conical G. ༺.
B.D. No: 4 Lt.By. Fl.(2)R. 5 sec. Can.R. ༺.
LONG SAND Bn. Topmark N.
B.D. No: 3 Lt.By. Fl.(3)G. 15 sec. Conical G. ༺.
INSHORE WAYPOINT B.D. No: 5. 51°39.2′N, 1°24.0′E.
B.D. No: 5 Lt.By. V.Q.(3) 5 sec. Pillar B.Y.B. Topmark E. Bell.
B.D. No: 6 Lt.By. Q.(9) 15 sec. Pillar Y.B.Y. Topmark W. ༺.
B.D. No: 7 Lt.By. Q.G. Conical G. ༺.
B.D. No: 8 Lt.By. Fl.R. 2½ sec. Can.R. ༺. NW LONG SAND Bn. Topmark N.
B.D. No: 9 Lt.By. Q.(6) + L.Fl. 15 sec. Pillar. Y.B. Topmark S. ༺.
B.D. No: 10 Lt.By. Q.R. Can.R. ༺.
INSHORE WAYPOINT B.D. No: 11. 51°34.1′N, 1°13.6′E.
B.D. No: 11 Lt.By. Fl.(3)G. 10 sec. Conical G. ༺.
B.D. No: 12 Lt.By. Fl.(4)R. 15 sec. Can.R. ༺.
INSHORE WAYPOINT K.J. No: 1. 51°33.6′N, 1°11.0′E.
KNOCK JOHN No: 1 Lt.By. Fl.G. 5 sec. Conical G. ༺.
KNOCK JOHN Lt.By. Fl.(2)R. 5 sec. Can.R. ༺.
KNOCK JOHN TOWERS. 51°34′N, 1°10′E. Twin concrete Trs. on Knock John Sands.
KNOCK JOHN No: 2 Lt.By. Fl.(3)R. 5 sec. Can.R. ༺.
KNOCK JOHN No: 3 Lt.By. Q.(6) + L.Fl. 15 sec. Pillar Y.B. Topmark S.

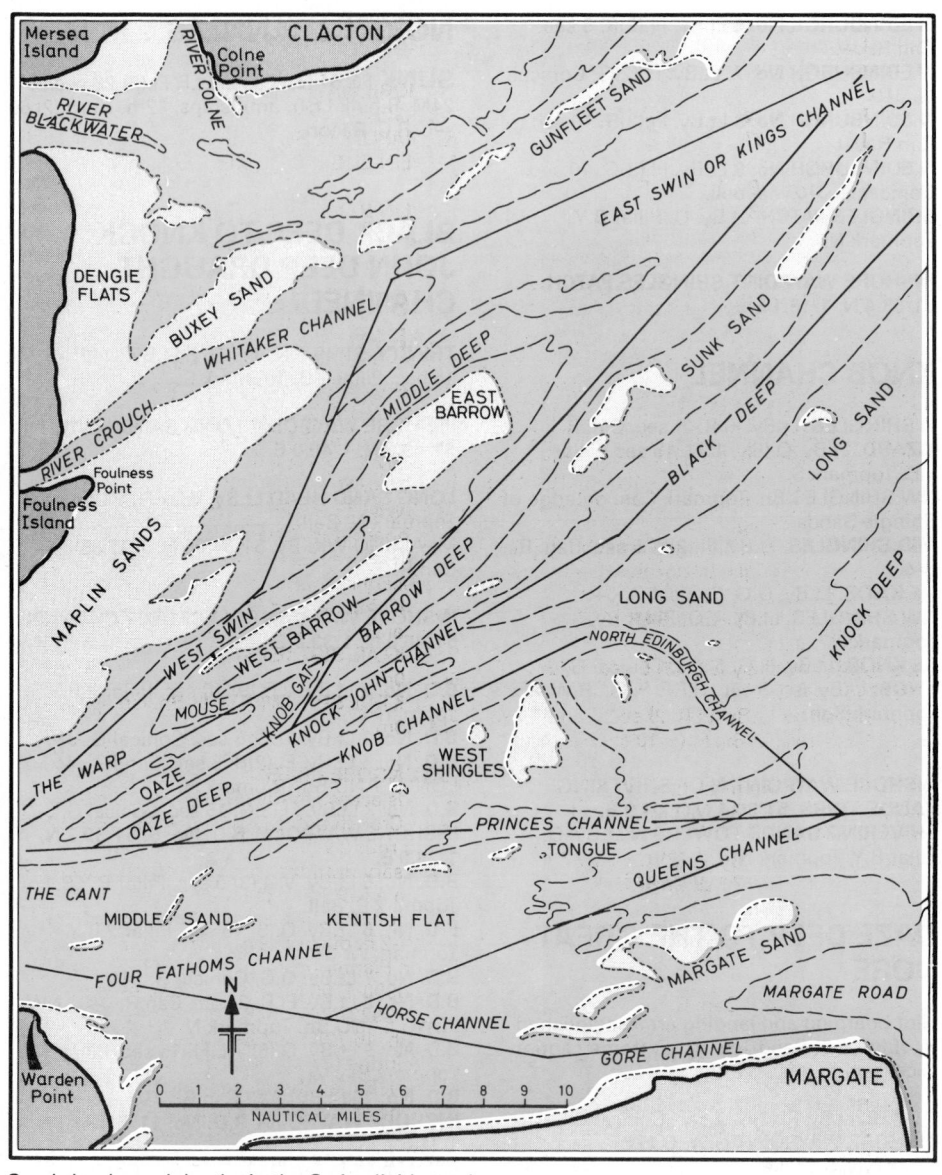

Sands banks and depths in the Swins liable to change.

KNOCK JOHN No: 4 Lt.By. L.Fl.R. 10 sec. Can.R. ⱴⱴ.
KNOCK JOHN No: 5 Lt.By. Fl.(3)G. 10 sec. Conical G. ⱴⱴ.
KNOCK JOHN No: 7 Lt.By. Fl.(4)G. 15 sec. Conical G. ⱴⱴ.

Special notice must be taken of new anchorages, especially those for deep draught vessels established off Harwich, near the Sunk and in Black Deep Channel.

BARROW DEEP

INSHORE WAYPOINT OFF SUNK HEAD.
51°46.0′N, 1°27.5′E.
SUNK HEAD TOWER. Lt.By. Q. Pillar B.Y. Topmark N. NE of Sunk Head T. ⱴⱴ. Not visible at LW.

W SUNK. Lt.By. Q.(9) 15 sec. Pillar Y.B.Y. Topmark W. ⱴⱴ.
LITTLE SUNK Bn. Triangle. ⱴⱴ.

Depths in the Chan. are constantly changing. Consult Thames Navigation Service, Gravesend for latest information.

INSHORE WAYPOINT BARROW DEEP CHANNEL. 51°42.0´N, 1°21.0´E.

No: 2 BARROW Lt.By. Fl.(2)R. 5 sec. Can.R.
No: 3 BARROW Lt.By. Q.(3) 10 sec. Pillar B.Y.B. Topmark E. Racon (B) Bell.
SUNK Bn. Triangle. 2M. S of Barrow Deep Lt.V.
No: 4 BARROW Lt.By. V.Q.(9) 10 sec. Pillar Y.B.Y. Topmark W.
No: 5 BARROW Lt.By. Fl.G. 10 sec. Conical G. ⏚.
No: 6 BARROW Lt.By. Fl.(4)R. 15 sec. Can.R. ⏚.
No: 7 BARROW Lt.By. Fl.G. 2½ sec. Conical G. ⏚.
E BARROW Bn. Topmark X.
SW SUNK Bn. Triangle.
No: 8 BARROW Lt.By. Fl.(2)R. 5 sec. Can.R. ⏚.
BARROW Bn. Triangle on Barrow Sands, 2M. NW of No: 9 Barrow Lt.By.
INSHORE WAYPOINT No: 9 BARROW. 51°34.4´N, 1°10.7´E.
No: 9 BARROW. Lt.By. V.Q.(3) 5 sec. Pillar B.Y.B. Topmark E.
No: 10 BARROW Lt.By. Fl.R. 2½ sec. Can.R. ⏚
No: 11 BARROW. Lt.By. Fl.G. 10 sec. Conical G. ⏚.
W BARROW Bn. Topmark E.
BARROW No: 12. Lt.By. V.Q.(3) 5 sec. Pillar B.Y.B. Topmark E.
BARROW No. 14. Lt.By. Fl.(2)R. 5 sec. Can. R.
INSHORE WAYPOINT SW BARROW. 51°31.7´N, 1°00.8´E.
SW BARROW. Lt.By. Q.(6)+L.Fl. 15 sec. Pillar B.Y. Topmark S.

N. OAZE Lt.By. Q./R. Can. R.

MOUSE CHANNEL & KNOB GAT

E MOUSE. Lt.By. Fl.G. 5 sec. Conical G.
KNOB GAT. Lt.By. V.Q.(9) 10 sec. Pillar Y.B.Y. Topmark W.
SE MOUSE. Lt.By. Q.G. Conical G.

KING'S CHANNEL OR EAST SWIN

GUNFLEET SPIT. Lt.By. Q.(6)+L.Fl. 15 sec. Pillar Y.B. Topmark S. ⏚ close S of old Gunfleet Lt.Ho. Bell w.a.
N MIDDLE By. Pillar Y.B. Topmark N.

S. WHITAKER Lt.By. Fl.(2)G. 10 sec. Conical G.
W HOOK MIDDLE By. Can.R. Topmark Can.

INSHORE WAYPOINT NE MAPLIN. 51°37´.4N, 1°05´.3E.
NE MAPLIN. Lt.By. Fl. G. 5 sec. Conical G. Bell.
MAPLIN EDGE. By. Conical G.

MAPLIN BANK. Lt.By. Fl.(3)R. 10 sec. Can.R. ⏚.

WEST SWIN CHANNEL TO WARPS

INSHORE WAYPOINT MAPLIN. 51°34.0´N,1°02.8´E.
MAPLIN. Lt.By. Q.(3) 10 sec. Pillar. B.Y.B. Topmark E.
WEST SWIN. By. Can.R.
SW SWIN. Lt.By. Fl.R. 5 sec. Can.R.
Pilot boarding and landing area established N. of N. Oaze Lt.By. Extreme caution necessary in this area.
BLACKTAIL SPIT. Lt.By. Fl.(3)G. 10 sec. Conical G.
BLACKTAIL SPIT (EAST). Lt.Bn. Iso. G. 5 sec. 5M. 10m.
BLACKTAIL SPIT (WEST). Lt.Bn. Iso. G. 10 sec. 5M. 10m.

HAVENGORE CREEK
Affords access to River Roach and thus the River Crouch and saves very small vessels going round Whitaker Bn. For vessels with necessary draught the Creek is approached at HW on a Northerly course between S and E Shoebury Bys. Havengore Bridge opened 2 h.-HW-2 h. during daylight hours. Phone Range Planning Officer (0702) 292271 Ext. 3211 0900-1700 Mon.-Fri. Bridge keeper (0702) 292271 Ext. 3436 at other times. Radio VHF Ch. 16.72 C/S Shoe Base (Range): Shoebridge (Bridge Keeper). Shoe Radar (Radar). Radar surveillance when range in use. The spans either side of the bascule are closed by a chain fence. A tide board gives headway under the bascule. Creek just above Bridge dries at 2.4m.

CAUTION—FIRING DANGER AREA
Experimental firing is frequently carried out off the Maplin and Foulness Sands. While this is in progress, no vessel may enter, or remain in the area.
Vessels wishing to navigate Havengore Creek may do so under the following conditions:
(1) When no R. flags are hoisted along the coast.
(2) When R. flags are hoisted — by special permission of Range Planning Office.

Obstructions to navigation, sometimes submerged, may be encountered within the area. Bns. of no navigational significance, with or without lights, may also be erected, River Thames inwards.
MAPLIN SANDS. SURVEY PLATFORM Lt.Bn. Gp.Fl.(2) 5 sec. metal frame Tr. 10m.

MEDWAY RIVER 51°27′N 0°45′E. Tel:
Sheerness (0795) 662211 — Medway Nav. Service. (0795) 663025, 662276. Telex: 96435 MEDOPS G. Fax: (0795) 666596.
Vessels to report to Medway radio on Chan. 74. Then listen on Chan. 12 to Gravesend radio, when inward and also when outward change to Chan. 12 on clearing the Medway By. Vessels report as follows: Medway By., No. 12 By., Upnor Jetty, Darnetness, Chatham Ness, when berthed or anchored and prior to leaving. Report at Queenboro' Spit if using Swale.

Radio — Port: Medway Radio. VHF Chan. 16, 74, 22, 73, 9—continuous. Pilots available via Medway Radio.

Tugs VHF Chan. 73.
B.P. Kent. Tel: (0634) 270710. Fax: (0634) 270509. Telex: 965584. VHF Chan. 16, 73.
Kings Ferry Bridge. VHF Chan. 10 cont.
Gillingham Marina. Tel: (0634) 280022. VHF Chan. M. 0830-1700 Summer only.
Medway Bridge Marina (0634) 43576. Chan. M. 0900-1800 Summer only.
Hoo Marina (0634) 250311.
Medway Pier Marina (0634) 51113. Chan. M.
Cuxton Marina (0634) 721941.
Elmhaven Marina (0634) 240489.
Allington Marina (0622) 52057.

Entry Signals: By day and night: Powerful light Fl. 7½ secs. Garrison Pt.—when V/Ls over 130m. in length underway in app. chan. or river.
Shown to seaward—vessel outward bound.
Shown to river—vessel inward bound.
Yachts should keep clear of Commercial Vessels.
R. Swale. Signal for Kings Ferry Bridge—sound 1 long and 4 short blasts or hoist flag or bucket.
Kings Ferry Bridge. Width 27.4 m. Clearance above Datum, bridge down 9m. Clearance above Datum, bridge up 34.4m. For actual clearance subtract height of tide. Depth of water below Datum 3.5m.
Rochester Bridge: Clearance H.W.S.T. 6m. Maximum rise and fall (Springs) 5.7m. Depth below Datum 1.5m.
Medway (M2 Motorway) Bridge clearance 16.7m MHWS.

Upnor Lock (No. 1 Basin Chatham) Chatham Maritime Marina Lock length 30m width 8.5 depth on sill MHWN 3.3m.
River Medway: Depths — Garrison Pt. to Pinup Rch. 6.2m. Gillingham Rch to Roch Br. 3.0m. Medway Lt. By. — Garrison Point 11m. Speed limits: 6 kts. W of Folly Pt. 8 kts. Queenborough Hr. and Swale.
Swale Depths — Queenborough — Kings Ferry Br. 3.5m. Kings Ferry Bridge Ht. 29m. (open) MHWS; 3.3m. (closed) MHWS. Tidal rate — Swale — 3-4 kts.
Stangate Creek Depths 3.6m. to 9m.
Halstow Creek dries 3m.
Colemouth Creek depth 0.3m.
East Hoo Creek depth 2.8m.
Half Acre Creek depth 4m.
Otterham, Bartlett, Rainham, S Yantlet Creeks — dry.
Rochester Bridge least depth 0.6m. Centre Span. Max. depth 2.1m. N Span. Clearance 5.9m. at MHWS.
Medway Bridge Marina 200+ Berths. 13.5m. × 1.7m. draught. Fuel, provisions, etc.
Cuxton Marina 20m. × 1.4m. draught. Fuel, etc.
Allington Marina 100 Berths. 18m. × 1.4m. Fuel, etc.
Measured Distance: Chatham Reach. ½M. 2 pairs W. bns. Triangular topmarks. 010° and 190° (Mag.). Small vessels not exceeding 8 knots. On marshes between Whitewall Creek and Chatham Ness on W. Bank Conspicuous.

INSHORE WAYPOINT MEDWAY. 51°28.8′N, 0°52.9′E.

OUTER BAR (MEDWAY). Lt.By. Mo (A) 6 sec. Pillar R.W.V.S. Topmark Sph. ⌣.
No: 1 Lt.By. Fl.G. 2½ sec. Conical G. ⌣.
No: 2 Lt.By. Q. Pillar B.Y. Topmark N.
No: 3 Lt.By. Fl.(3)G. 10 sec. Conical G. ⌣.
No: 4 Lt.By. Fl.R. 10 sec. Can.R. ⌣.
No: 5 Lt.By. Q.G. Conical G. ⌣.
No: 6 Lt.By. Q.R. Can.R. ⌣.
No: 7 Lt.By. Fl.G 10 sec. Conical G. ⌣.
No: 8 Lt.By. Fl.R. 5 sec. Can.R. ⌣.
RICHARD MONTGOMERY N. Lt.By. Fl. Y. 2½ sec. Can Y.
RICHARD MONTGOMERY E. Lt.By. Fl.(4)Y. 10 sec. Sph. Y.
RICHARD MONTGOMERY S. Lt.By. Fl. Y. 5. sec. Conical Y.
RICHARD MONTGOMERY W. Lt.By. Fl.(4)Y. 10 sec. Sph. Y. This wreck is dangerous.
Entry into area marked by buoys is totally prohibited.
No: 9 Lt.By. Fl.G. 5 sec. Conical G. ⌣.
No: 10 Lt.By. Q. Pillar B.Y. Topmark N. ⌣.
No: 11 Lt.By. Fl.(3)G. 10 sec. Conical G. ⌣.
GRAIN EDGE By. Conical G.

WEST CANT. Lt.By. Q.R. Can.R. ⌇⌇.
SEWER. Lt.By. Q. Pillar B.Y. Topmark N. marks end of pipeline.
GRAIN HARD. Lt.By. Fl.G. 5 sec. Conical G. ⌇⌇.

ISLE OF GRAIN. 51°26.6′N 0°43.5′E Lt.Bn.
Q.W.R.G. W.13M. R.7M. G.8M. R.220°-234°; G. to 241°; W. to 013°. R. metal framework Tr. R.W. diamond topmark. 20m.
G. sector enables vessels to anchor in Little Nore, clear of Fairway.

SHEERNESS (GARRISON POINT).
Traffic Sig. Fl. 7 sec. vis. 7M. (day), 10M. (night). Concrete building R.W.hor. bands. Also Storm Signals.

RO-RO BERTH NO: 10 Lt. 2 F.R. Vert. on dolphin. Horn (3) 30 sec.

NO: 1 BERTH (N End) 2 F.R. Vert.
RETRACTING PONTOON Lt. 2 F.R. Vert.
NO: 3 BERTH (S End) 2 F.R. Vert.
NO: 4 BERTH. Lt. 2 F.R. Vert. Dolphin.

RIVER SWALE
QUEENBOROUGH SPIT. Lt.By. Q.(3) 10 sec. Pillar B.Y.B. Topmark E.
OLD RAILWAY PIER. (QUEENBOROUGH POINT) DOLPHIN. Lt. Q.R.
DOLPHIN. Lt. Fl.R. 4 sec.
S No. 1 Lt.By. Fl.R. 3 sec. Can. R.
CONCRETE LIGHTER. Lt.Bn. Fl.G. 3 sec.
QUEENBOROUGH CREEK.
No: 1 By. Conical G. Topmark Cone G.
No: 2 By. Can R. Topmark Can R.
No: 3 By. Conical G. Topmark Cone G.
No: 4 By. Can R. Topmark Can R.
No: 5 By. Conical G. Topmark Cone G.
No: 6 By. Can R. Topmark Can R.
No. 5 Lt.By. Q. 5M. Lattice Tr. 16m. 163°-168°.
S No. 2 Lt.By. Fl.G. Conical G.
S No. 3 Lt.By. Fl.G. 2½ sec. Conical G.
RECLAMATION PIER (Lodon Hope). Lt. 2 F.R. vert. 2M. Dolphin 5m.
WASHER WHF. Lt. 2 F.R. vert. 2M. Col. 3m.
No. 1 Lt.Bn. Q.G.W. G.3M., W.5M., Lattice Tr. 10m. G.308°-320°; W.320°-350°; G.350°-015°.
LONG POINT No. 4 Lt.Bn. Iso.R. 3 sec. 3M. Lattice Tr. 10m.
No. 2 Lt.Bn. Q.G.W. G.3M., W.5M., Lattice Tr. 8m. G.253°-273°; W.273°-331°; G.331°-338°.
S No. 4 Lt.By. Fl.R. Can. R.
No. 3 Lt.Bn. Q.R.G.W. R.3M., G.3M., W.5M. Lattice Tr. 8m. R.183°-202°; G.202°-252°; W.252°-327°.
S No. 5 Lt.By. Fl.G. 5 sec. Conical G.
S No. 6 Lt.By. Fl.R. 5 sec. Can. R.
S No. 7 Lt.By. Fl.R. Can. R.

HORSE REACH OUTER. Ldg.Lts. 113° on W. Bank. (Front) Q.G. 5M. Topmark Cone on dolphin, 7m. (Rear) Fl.G. 3 sec. 6M. G. ▽ on dolphin, 10m.
HORSE REACH. Inner Ldg.Lts. 097°45′ on E Bank. (Front) Fl.(4)R. 5 sec. 5M. Topmark Can. on dolphin, 6m. (Rear) Fl.(2)R. 5 sec. 9M. Or. topmark upper half R. on metal Tr. 12m. vis. 094°-102°.
FERRY REACH NEATS COURT OUTFALL: Lt. Fl.(2)R. 10 sec. 3M. R. □ on.Bn.
KINGSFERRY BRIDGE. Ldg.Lts 147°33′ (Front) 2 F.G. vert. 7M. vis. 129°-160°. R.O., W. stripes on framework Tr. Traffic Sig. (Rear) 2 F. vert. 10M. vis. 129°-160°. B. ⅛ Y. stripes, on framework Tr. East Side 2 F.R. (vert.). West Side 2 F.G. (vert.).
S8 Lt.By. Q.R. Can R.
S9 Lt.By. Q.G. Conical G.
S10 Lt.By. Fl.R. 2 sec. Can R.
S11 Lt.By. Fl.G. 2 sec Conical G.
GROVEHURST DOCK. 2 F.G. vert. both ends of Coal Jetty.
KEMSLEY MILL INTAKE Lt.Bn. 2 F.G. vert. Topmark Cone. mark pipeline.
HARTY FERRY. Bn. R. Topmark Can. Scrubbing Dock.
Elmley By. Conical G. marks N. side of passage through causeway close W. of buoy.

MILTON CREEK ENTRANCE
N FERRY. By. Conical G.
S FERRY. By. Can.R.
No. 8, 6, 4, 2 Bys. Can.R.

CONYER CREEK
Entry: Dries 1m. but craft 15m. × 1.8m. draught (or 30m. × 3m. draught if with local pilot) accepted at Conyer Marine; Swale Marina 24m. × 2m. draught access 2 h.—HW—2 h.
SWALE MARINA. Tel: 0795 521562.
CONYER MARINE Tel: 0795 521276.
BY. Pillar B.Y.B. Topmark E. off Windmill Creek.
No. 1 By Conical G.

SHEERNESS TO ROCHESTER

ISLE OF GRAIN

POWER STN OUTFALL CHANNEL. Lt.Bn. Fl.(2) G. 10 sec. Topmark Cone.
POWER STATION. No: 1 Intake Lt. Bn. 2 F.G. vert. Topmark Cone. Horn 20 sec. No: 2 Intake Lt.Bn. 2 F.G. vert.
KENT REFINERY
JETTIES — Number 1-11 2 F.G. vert. Each End.

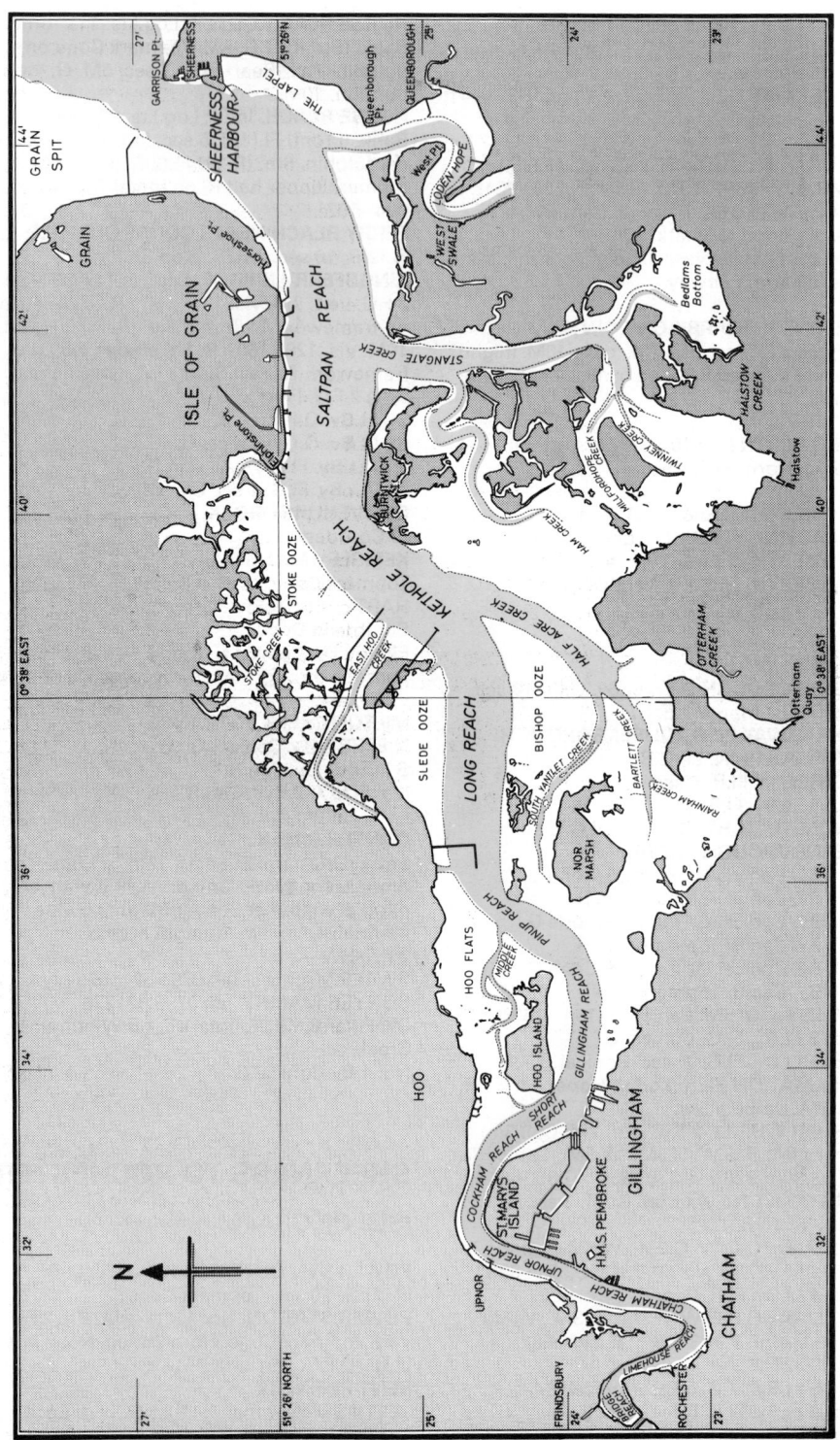

No: 1 COASTER JETTY. Lt. 2 F.G.vert. 3M. metal Col. each end.

N KENT. Lt.By. Q.G. Conical G. ⌇⌇ .
S KENT. Lt.By. Fl.R. 5 sec. Can.R. ⌇⌇ .
Z1 Lt.By. Fl.(2) Pillar B.R.B.
Z2 Lt.By. Q. Pillar B.Y.
VICTORIA. Lt.By. Fl.(3)G. 10 sec. Conical G. ⌇⌇ off Horseshoe Point.
No: 2 Lt. Mooring By. Q.R. Sph. Or.
No: 4 Lt. Mooring By. Q.R. Sph. Or.
Thames Estuary Lts. 2 F.G. vert. Caution necessary as very large vessels manoeuvring in this vicinity.
No: 12 Lt.By. Q.R. Can.R. ⌇⌇ On N. edge of Sharpness Shelf.
STANGATE SPIT Lt.By. V.Q.(3) 5 sec. Pillar. B.Y.B. Topmark E. Marks W side of Entce.
No: 14 Lt.By. Fl.R. 5 sec. Can.R. Off Sharpness Kethole Reach. ⌇⌇ .
No: 13 Lt.By. Fl.G. 5 sec. Conical G. ⌇⌇ marks Stoke Shoal.
STOKE By. Conical G.
BULWARK. Wreck Lt.By. Fl.(3)G. 15 sec. Conical G. ⌇⌇ W. Bulwark By. Can. R.
BEES NESS JETTY HEAD. Lt. 2 F.G.vert. 3M. Metal Col. on each of 2 dolphins.
HALF ACRE CREEK. (Enter E of No. 16 Lt.By.)
BARGE. Lt. Q.R. In Half Acre Creek.
OTTERHAM FAIRWAY. Lt.By. Mo(A) 3 sec. Pillar R.W.V.S.

OTTERHAM CREEK
No: 2 By. Can.R.
No: 4 By. Can.R.
No: 3 By. Conical G.
No: 6 By. Can.R.
No: 8 By. Can.R.
No: 10 By. Can.R.
MOTNEY HILL OUTFALL Lt.Bn. 2 F.R. vert. Topmark Can.
BARTLETT CREEK. Lt.By. Fl.(2)R. 5 sec. Can.R. R. Topmark.
RAINHAM CREEK (off BARTLETT CREEK).
RAINHAM CREEK. Lt.By. Fl.(2)R. 2 sec. Can.R.
By. Can.R.
By. Can.R.
Leads to Bloors Wharf.
SOUTH YANTLET CREEK (Leads from Half Acre Creek to Gillingham Reach.).
No: 1 By. Sph. R.W.
No: 2 By. Sph. R.W.
No: 3 By. Sph. R.W.
No: 4 By. Pillar. R.W.

LONG REACH
No: 8 Bn. (Rear) B.W. ◊ No: 7 Bn. (Front) B.W. △.
When in line form leading marks 088°-268°.

OAKHAM NESS JETTY. Lts. 2 F.G. vert. 3M. Metal Col. on dolphin.
No: 15 Lt.By. Fl.G. 10 sec. Conical G. ⌇⌇ off Oakham Ness.
No: 16 Lt.By. Fl.(2)R. 10 sec. Can.R. ⌇⌇ Off Bishop Spit.
No: 17 Lt.By. Fl.(3)G. 10 sec. Conical G. ⌇⌇ .
No: 18 Lt.By. Fl.R. 5 sec. Can.R. ⌇⌇ near Bishop Ness.
No: 19 Lt.By. Fl.G. 5 sec. Conical G. ⌇⌇ in Long Reach.
BISHOP NESS Bns. 2 B. near bank edge.
No: 20 Lt.By. Fl.(2)R. 10 sec. Can.R. ⌇⌇ Off Bishop Ness.
KINGSNORTH JETTY. Lt. 2 F.G. vert. 3M. Metal Col. each end.
No: 22 Lt.By. Fl.R. 5 sec. Can.R. ⌇⌇ near Darnett Ness.
No: 23 DARNETT NESS. Lt.By. I.Q.G. Conical G. ⌇⌇ off Hoo Flats.
DARNETT NESS. No: 6 Lt.Bn. 51°24'N, 0°36'E Q.R. 3M. R.W. cheq. metal. 12m. on edge of bank.
MIDDLE CREEK WEST HOO
No: 1 By. Conical G.
No: 2 By. Can.R.
No: 3 By. Conical G.
No: 4 By. Pillar Y.B. Topmark S.
No: 5 By. Can.R.
LONG REACH
No: 1 Bn. B.W. hor. bands and △ No: 2 Bn. B.W. vert. stripes and ◊ .
Form leading marks 088.5° or 268.5°.
No: 24 Lt.By. Fl.R. 5 sec. Can.R.
No: 25 Lt.By. Fl.(3). G. 10 sec. Conical G. ⌇⌇ off Folly Bank.
PINUP REACH
No: 5 Bn. (Rear) W. ◊ No: 3 Bn. (Front) B.W. hor. bands. surmounted by ▽. In line 096°30'
No: 5 Bn. (Rear) B.W. vert. stripes ◊.
Bns. No: 3 & 4 when in line form leading marks for Fairway. 207°.
Folly Point Bn. Topmark Cone.
GILLINGHAM REACH
Bns. No: 3 & 5 when in line form leading marks for fairway. 277°.
No: 26 Lt.By. Fl.(2)R. 10 sec. Can.R. ⌇⌇ .
No: 27 Lt.By. Fl.G. 10 sec. Conical G. ⌇⌇ off Middle Bank.
No: 28 Lt.By. Fl.R. 5 sec. Can.R.
No: 29 Lt.By. Fl.(3)G. 10 sec. Conical G.
No: 30 SHORT REACH. Lt.By. Fl.(2)R. 10 sec. Can.R.
No. 30A By. Can. R.
No: 31 Lt.By. I.Q.G. Conical G. ⌇⌇ .

Many unlighted mooring bys. in Reaches of River between Darnett Ness and Rochester.

CHATHAM DOCKYARD
BULLS NOSE
N SIDE of ENTCE. 2 F.R. vert. on post, 3m.
S SIDE of ENTCE. 2 F.G. vert. on post, 3m.
GILLINGHAM MARINA. Tel: (0634) 280024
VHF Chan. 37(M). Max. 20m. × 3m. draught.
Gillingham Marina Lock E Basin 4 h.-HW-4 h.
(0800-2100). W Basin Tidal 2 h. —HW—2 h.
approx. Deep water moorings if Basins not
accessible. Fuel (diesel), water, full facilities.
Visitors berths.
GILLINGHAM MARINA. Lt. 2 F.R. vert. Also
F.W. Lt. when depth exceeds 1m. at entrance
to creek.

SHORT REACH

Hoo Marina Tel: (0634) 250311. VHF Chan. M.
Chandlery, electricity, hoist, showers.
Basin dredged to 0.5m. Sill prevents it from
drying. 24m. × 2m. draught. 120 berths.
HOO MARINA W MOLE E HEAD Lt. 2 F.R. vert.
T MOLE W HEAD Lt. 2 F.G. vert.
E HEAD Lt. 2 F.R. vert.
JETTY HEAD Lt. 2 F.G. vert.
WAVE BAFFLE Lt. 2 F.G. vert.
UPNOR REACH
ARETHUSA VENTURE CENTRE. Lt. V.Q.(6) +
L.Fl. 10 sec. ⚓ on B.Y. Bn.
UPNOR JETTY. Lt.Bn. 2 F.G. vert.
No: 32. Lt.By. Q.R. Can R. 〰.
ST. MARY'S WHARF PONTOON Lt. 2 F.R. vert.
LANDING STAGE. Lt. 2 F.G. vert.

CHATHAM REACH
FOLLA WHARF. Lt. 2 F.G. vert.
THUNDERBOLT PIER. Lt. 2 F.R. vert.

SUN PIER. Lt. 2 F.R. vert. 8M. on metal cols.
CHATHAM NESS. Lt. Fl.G. 3 sec. G. Bn. 5m.
LIME HOUSE REACH. SHIP PIER HEAD Lt. 2
F.R. vert.
LASER QUAY. Lt. 2 F.G. vert S. and N. End.
BRIDGE REACH. STROOD PIER HEAD. Lt. 2
F.G. vert. Also F. 21m. from head.
ROCHESTER BRIDGE. Lts. Downstream SE
Side 2 F.G. vert. NW Side 2 F.R. vert.
Upstream Centre F.Y. Headroom under middle
arch 6m. above M.H.W.S.

WARPS TO SOUTHEND

NORE
S SHOEBURY. Lt.By. Fl.G. 5 sec. Conical G.
SHOEBURY. Bn. Fl.(3)G. 10 sec. Obstruction to
N of this Bn. Obstruction continues to shore.
GAP. Lt.Bn. Fl.Y. 2½ sec. marks gap in the
obstruction.
PHOENIX UNIT. Lt.Bn. Fl.(2) 10 sec.
WEST SHOEBURY. Lt.By. Fl.G. 2½ sec.
Conical G.
SOUTHEND SEWER OUTFALL. Lt.By. Fl.Y. 5
sec. Conical Y. & **Lt.By.** Fl.Y. 10 sec. Sph. Y.
Prohibited anchorage 100m. either side of
line joining the buoys.
LEES TR. On Isle of Grain close E of London
Stone at Entrance to Yantlet Creek.

SWATCHWAY
NORE SWATCH. Lt.By. Fl.(4)R. 15 sec. Can.R.
S side of Swatchway.
MID SWATCH. Lt.By. Fl.G. 5 sec. Conical G. N
side of Swatchway.
W NORE SAND. Lt.By. Fl.(3)R. 10 sec. Can.R.
E BLYTH. Lt.By. Fl.(2)R. 10 sec. Can.R.

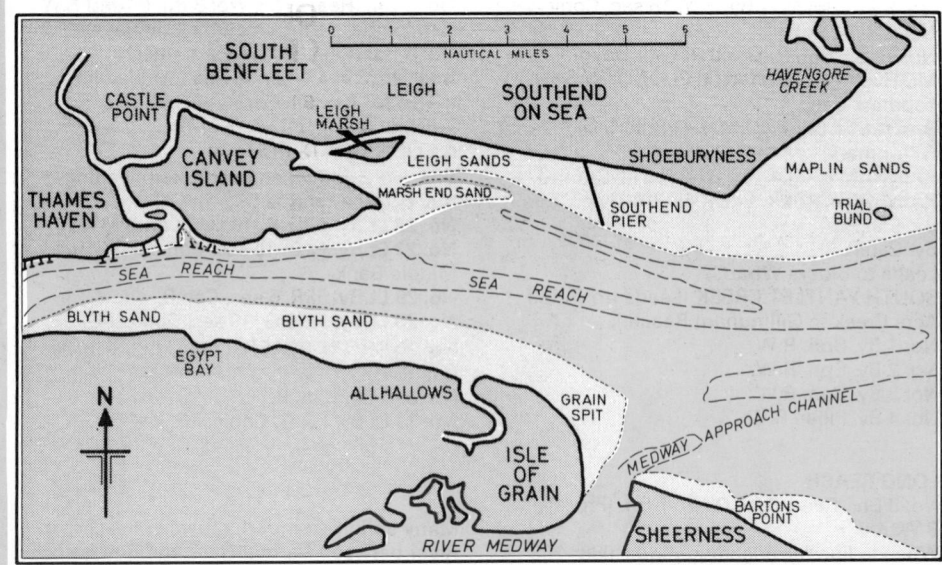

SEA REACH FROM GREAT NORE (YANTLET CHANNEL)

INSHORE WAYPOINT SEA REACH No. 1. 51°29.4′N, 0°52.9′E.

SEA REACH No: 1 Lt.By. Fl.Y. 2½ sec. Pillar Y. Topmark Sph. ⌇⌇ Marks E Entce. to Yantlet Dredged Chan. Racon.
SEA REACH No: 2. Lt.By. Iso. 5 sec. Pillar R.W.V.S. Topmark R. Sph.
SE LEIGH. Lt.By. Q.(6) + L.Fl. 15 sec. Pillar. Y.B. Topmark S.
SEA REACH No: 3. Lt.By. L.Fl. 10 sec. Sph. R.W.V.S.
SEA REACH No: 4. Lt.By. Fl.Y. 2½ sec. Pillar Y. Topmark X.
SEA REACH No: 5. Lt.By. Iso. 5 sec. Sph. R.W.V.S.
SEA REACH No: 6. Lt.By. Iso. 2 sec. Pillar. R.W.V.S. Topmark R. Sph.
SEA REACH No: 7. Lt.By. Fl.Y. 2½ sec. Pillar Y. Marks W end Yantlet Chan. Racon.

RIVER THAMES — SHOEBURYNESS

SHOEBURYNESS PIER. Lt. F.G. occas.
CORPORATION LOADING PIER. Lt. 2 F.G. vert. 2M. Mast 6 and 4m.

SOUTHEND PIER. Lt. 2 F.G. vert. 4M. E end, 7 and 5m.
W HEAD. Lt. 2 F.G. vert. 8M. B. mast, W. bands, 13m.
LEIGH DEPOSIT. Lt.By. Fl.Y. 15 sec. Conical Y. Topmark X.
LEIGH By. Conical G. fitted with Dayglo panels. Entce. to Chan. in 2m. M.L.W.S.

LEIGH. Ldg.Lts. 312°. (Front) F. 6M. G. metal Col. (Rear) F. 6M. G. metal Col.

W LEIGH MIDDLE. Lt.By. Q.G. Conical G.
CHAPMAN. Lt.By. Fl.(3)G. 10 sec. Conical G. marks explos anche. area. Bell(3).
MIDDLE BLYTH. Lt.By. Q. Pillar B.Y. Topmark N.
CANVEY ISLAND JETTY. Lt.Bn. 2 F.G. vert. Bell 10 sec.
HOLEHAVEN POINT Bn. B.
Powerful traffic Lts. Iso. 5 sec. shown up and down river at Holehaven and Scars Elbow when tankers berthing or unberthing. Occidental Jetty. Approach forms bridge over creek. Ht. 11.28m. above MHWS 17.35m. A.C.D.
HOLEHAVEN CORYTON No: 4 JETTY. 2 F.G. vert. on dolphin. Horn 20 sec.
Lts. 2 F.G. shown from each end of every jetty.
SHELLHAVEN 'A' JETTY. 2 F.G. Siren(3) 60 sec.

SHELLHAVEN DOLPHIN. 3 F.G. ▽.
On various piers and dolphins at Shellhaven, Thameshaven and Shelly Bay, 2 F.G. vert. are shown to mark ends.
WEST BLYTH. Lt.By. Fl.(4)R. 15 sec. Can.R. S of river.
MUCKING. No: 1 Lt.By. Q.G. Conical G. on N side. Bell.
LOWER HOPE. Lt.By. Fl.R. 5 sec. Can.R. N of Lower Hope Point.
MUCKING No: 3 Lt.By. Fl.G. 2½ sec. Conical G. NW of Lower Hope Point. Owing to shoaling on Mucking Flats, vessels are advised to keep to buoyed Fairway.
MUCKING JETTY. Lt. 2 F.G. vert.

LOWER HOPE POINT TO TRIPCOCK POINT

MUCKING No: 5 Lt.By. Fl.(3)G. 10 sec. Conical G.
SPOIL GROUND. Bys. Sph.Y.

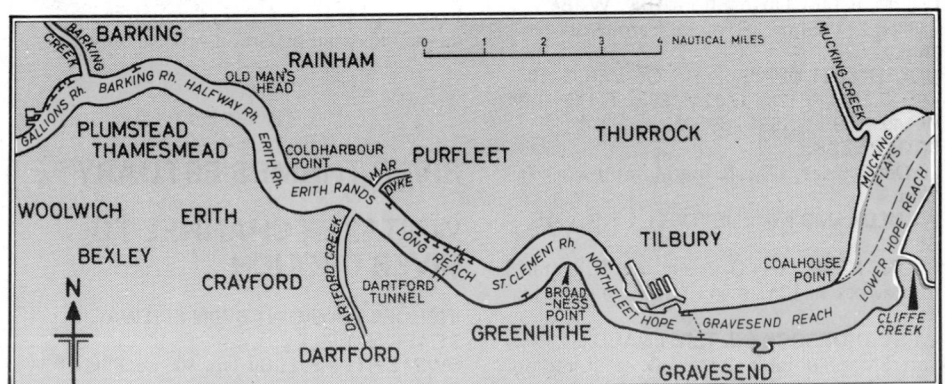

PUMP ASHORE UNIT. Lts. F.R.W.R. vert. also 2 F.G. vert. (offshore) and 2 F.R. vert. (on shore).

MUCKING No: 7 Lt.By. Fl.G. 5 sec. Conical G.

OVENS. Lt.By. Q.G. Conical G. ⌇⌇ On N side. w.a. Bell.

HIGHAM. Lt.By. Fl.(2)R. 5 sec. Can.R. ⌇⌇.

SHORNMEAD. Lt. Fl.(2)W.R.G. 10 sec. W.17M; R.13M; G.13M. G. Shore-080°; R.080°-085°; W.085°-088°; G.088°-141°; W.141°-205°; R.205°-213°. R. metal framework Tr.

TILBURY. Lt.By. Q.(6) + L.Fl. 15 sec. Pillar Y.B. Topmark S. Marks N bank of river.

JETTY. Lt. 2 F.G. vert. Jetty protrudes towards channel on North bank at Coalhouse Point.

SPOIL GROUND No: 1. Lt.By. Fl.Y. 5 sec. Conical Y.

SPOIL GROUND No: 2. Lt.By. Fl.Y. 10 sec. Conical Y.

TILBURY GENERATING STATION PIER. Lts. 2 F.G. vert. Siren (2) 60 sec.

GRAVESEND
TRINITY HOUSE PILOT STATION Lt. F.R.

TILBURY
LANDING STAGE. Lt. 2 F.G. vert. at E and W ends.
INNER SIDE. Lt. F.G. on dolphins, at rear of each end of stage. Bell(3) 30 sec.

TILBURY DOCKS. Lt.Bn. S side of Entce. 2 F.G. vert. 9m. N side of Entce. 2 F.G. vert. When in line with Tilbury Ness it marks N alignment of dredged Chan.

RIVER THAMES — ABOVE TILBURY

Main channel Lts. only shown. Wharves show 2 F.R. vert. or 2 F.G. vert.

NORTHFLEET LOWER Lt. Oc. W.R. 5 sec. W.17M; R.14M. Obsc. Shore-164°; W.164°-271°; R.271°-Shore. R. metal framework Tr. 16m.

NORTHFLEET UPPER. Lt.Ho. Oc. W.R.G. 10 sec. W.16M. R.12M. G.12M. 30m. R.126°-149°; W.149°-159°; G.159°-269°; W.269°-279°.

BROADNESS.
Lt. Oc. R. 5 sec. 12M. R. metal framework Tr. 12m.

WOULDHAMS No. 2 JETTY. Lt. 2 F.G. vert. Bell 55 sec.

STONE NESS. Lt. Fl.G. 2½ sec. 9M. R. metal framework Tr. 13m. also F.G. above main Lt. 3M.

WEST THURROCK OIL TERMINAL. Lt. 2 F.G. vert. 8m. on dolphin. 2 Lts. F.G. exhibited on extremities of jetty. Siren Mo(A) 30 sec.

LITTLEBROOK POWER STATION. Outfall Caisson Lt. Fl.(2) 10 sec. Horn 20 sec. Topmark Is. D.
Intake Caisson Lt. V.Qk.Fl. Topmark N.

CRAYFORD NESS. 51°29′N, 0°13′E. Lt.Ho. Fl. 5 sec. 14M. R. metal framework Tr. 16m. also F. 3M. 17m.

ERITH REACH
COLDHARBOUR POINT Fl.2½ sec. 7M. 11m. R.Tr.
DEEP WATER WHF. Lt. 2 F.R. vert. Siren (2) 30 sec.
COLDHARBOUR JTY. Lt. Q.G. 6M. 16m. 155°-354° Also 2 F.G. vert.
BELVEDERE POWER STATION. Lt. Fl.R. 2½ sec. on upstream end of jetty.

DAGENHAM

FORDS LANDING STAGE. Lt. 2 F.R. vert. Siren (2) 20 sec.
FORDS JETTY E END. Lt. 2 F.G. vert. 2M. Each end, 8 and 7m. Bell(3×3) 30 sec.
CROSS NESS. Lt.Bn. Fl. 5 sec. 2M. R. metal frame Tr. 6m.

MARGARET NESS or TRIPCOCK POINT. Lt. Fl.(2) 5 sec. R. metal framework Tr. on river bank, 11m.

WOOLWICH FERRY. Lts. 2 F.R. vert. (S Side) 2 F.G. vert. N Side of river.

LIME HOUSE REACH Lt. Q.R. R.□ on Bn.

TOWER BRIDGE Lts. F.R. when closed. F.G. when open. Fog signal. Horn 20 sec. Gong 30 sec. When bridge open.

THAMES TIDAL BARRIER. Lts. 3 F.R. △ shown from span A. H. J. K. Pass through those spans indicated by Green Arrows only.

RIVER THAMES ESTUARY

WHITAKER CHANNEL TO RIVER CROUCH

INSHORE WAYPOINT SWIN SPITWAY. 51°41.6′N, 1°08.4′E.
SWIN SPITWAY. Lt.By. Iso. 10 sec. Pillar. R.W. Bell.

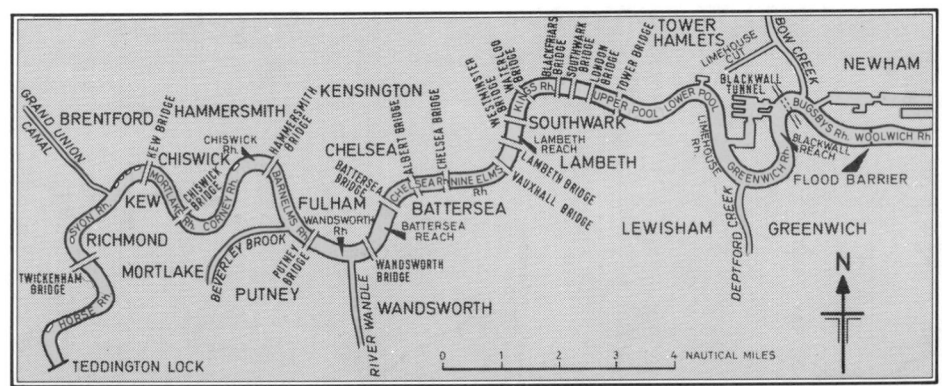

INSHORE WAYPOINT OFF WHITAKER.
51°41.6´N, 1°11.2´E.
WHITAKER. Lt.By. Q.(3) 10 sec. Pillar B.Y.B. Topmark E.
WHITAKER Bn. Topmark Is.D., tripod base, 12m. H.W.O.S.T.
Whitaker No. 1 Lt.By. Q(6) + L.Fl. 15 sec. Pillar. Y.B. Topmark S.
Whitaker No. 2 Lt.By. Fl.Y. 10 sec. Can Y.
Whitaker No. 3 Lt.By. Fl.Y. 5 sec. Conical Y.
Whitaker No. 4 Lt.By. Fl.Y. 10 sec. Conical Y.
Whitaker No. 5 Lt.By. Fl.Y. 5 sec. Conical Y.
Whitaker No. 6 Lt.By. Q. Pillar. B.Y. Topmark N.
Ridge Lt.By. Fl.R. 10 sec. Can R.
Swallow Tail By. Conical G.
Foulness Lt.By. Fl.(2)R. 10 sec. Can R.
South Buxey Lt.By. Fl.(3) G. 15 sec. Conical G.
Sunken Buxey Lt.By. Q. Pillar. By. Topmark N.
Buxey No. 1 Lt.By. V.Q.(6) + L.Fl. 10 sec. Pillar. Y.B. Topmark S.
Buxey No. 2 Lt.By. Fl.R. 10 sec. Can R.
Outer Crouch Lt.By. Fl.G. 5 sec. Conical G.
Crouch Lt.By. Fl.R. 10 sec. Can R.
Inner Crouch Lt.By. L.Fl. 10 sec. Sph. R.W. vert stripes.

RIVER CROUCH Tel: H.M. (0621) 783602.
Customs Ipswich (0473) 219481.
Burnham Yacht Harbour. Tel: (0621) 782150.
VHF Chan. 80M. 0900-1700.
Yacht Harbour available H24.
Essex Marina (0702) 258531. Chan. (M) — on Wallasea Island. Draught 9m. on outside arms with 1m. on inner arms.
N Fambridge Yacht Station Tel. (0621) 740370.
Westwick Marina Tel. (0621) 741268. Chan. (M) 1000-1700 18.3m. × 1.8m. draught.
Bridge Marsh Marine (0621) 740414.
Brandy Hole Yacht Station. (0702) 230248.
Anchorage: R. Crouch — Cliff Reach.
R. Roach — Between Branklet/Jubilee Bys.
Entry: Bar with 2-4m. across River S of Burnham. Craft drawing 5.2m. can reach

Baltic Wharf; drawing 3.5m. can reach Hullbridge; drawing 2.5m. can reach Battlebridge at MHWS.

HOLLIWELL. By. Sph. Y. (April-Oct).
REDWARD. By. Sph. Y. (April-Oct).
BRANKLET. By. Sph. Y. (April-Oct). Entrance R. Roach.

HORSE SHOAL Lt.By. Q. Pillar B.Y. Topmark N.

FAIRWAY NO. 1 Lt.By. Q.G. Conical G.
FAIRWAY NO. 3 Lt.By. Q.G. Conical G.
FAIRWAY NO. 5 Lt.By. Q.G. Conical G.

BURNHAM Y. Hr. Lt.By. L. Fl. 10 sec. Pillar R.W. vert. stripes.
BURNHAM Y. Hr. Lt.By. Fl. G. 10 sec. G. △ on spar.
BURNHAM Y. Hr. Lt.By. Fl. R. 10 sec. R. □ on spar.

FAIRWAY NO. 7 Lt.By. Q.G. Conical G.
FAIRWAY NO. 9 Lt.By. Q.G. Conical G.
FAIRWAY NO. 2 Lt.By. Q.R. Can R.
FAIRWAY NO. 11 Lt.By. Q.G. Conical G.
FAIRWAY NO. 13 Lt.By. Q.G. Conical G.
FAIRWAY NO. 15 Lt.By. Q.G. Conical G.

BURNHAM ON CROUCH.
ESSEX MARINA E. END Lt.Fl.R. 5 sec. **W. END** Lt. Fl.R 5 sec.
BALTIC WHF. Lt. 2 F.R. vert.
Bridge Marsh Marine (North Bank).
CANEWDON. By. Sph. Y. (April-Oct).
N Fambridge Yacht Station.
CLIFF REACH By. Sph. Y. (April-Oct).
Westwick Marina.
CLIFF BY. Sph. Y. (April-Oct).

RAY SAND CHANNEL
Dries at 1m. at S end.
BUXEY Bn. B.Y. Topmark N. 9m. on W side Buxey Sand.

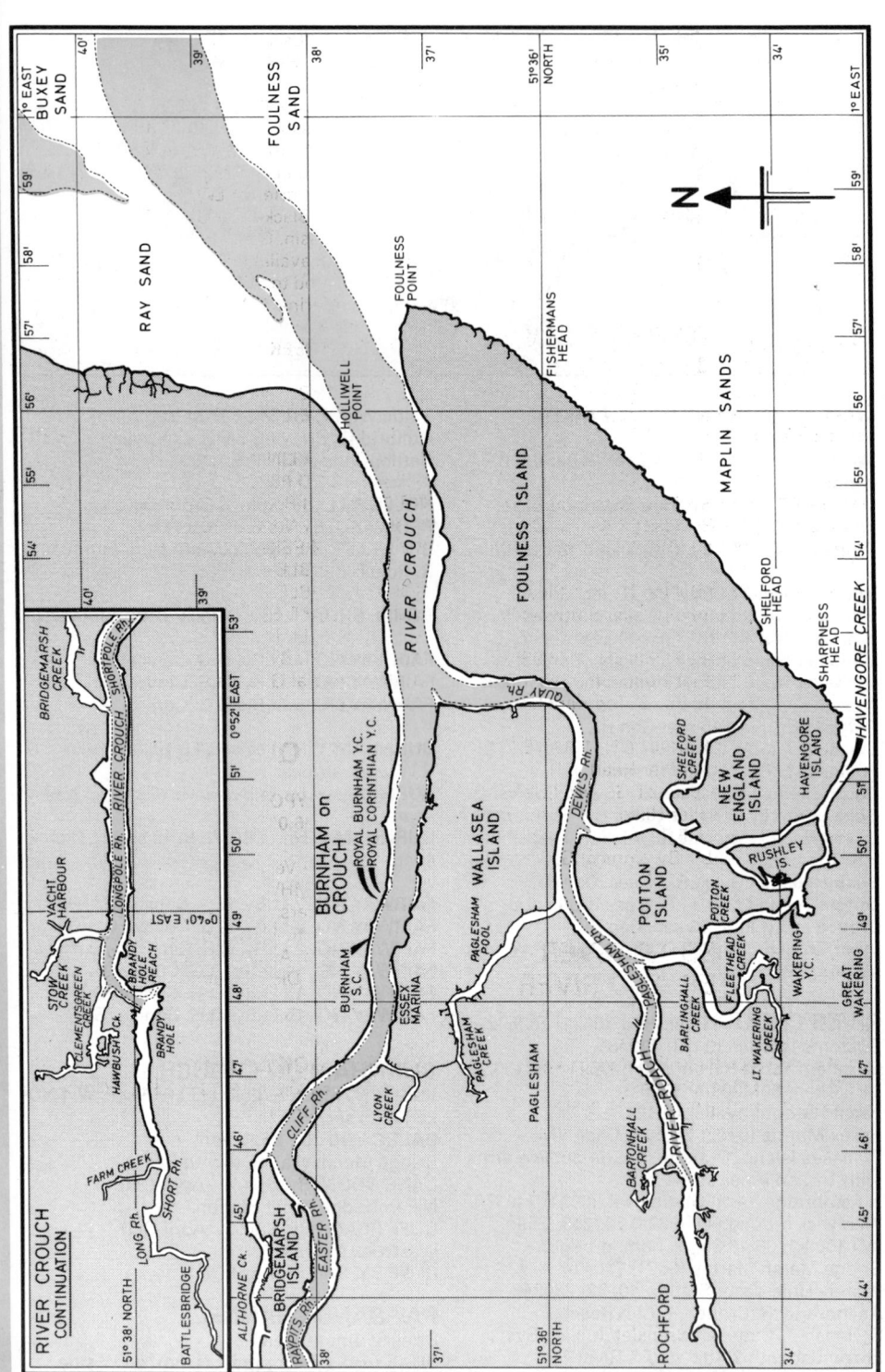

RIVER ROACH

JUBILEE. By. Sph. Y. (April-Oct).
ROACH. By. Sph. Y. (April-Oct).
WHITEHOUSE. By. Sph. Y. (April-Oct).
POTTON. By. Sph. Y. (April-Oct).
No. 1 By. Conical G.
No. 2 By. Can.R.
SHUTTLEWOODS BOATYARD. North Bank,
Paglesham.
No. 3 By. Conical G.

SUNK LT.F. TO RIVER COLNE & RIVER BLACKWATER

GOLDMER GAT AND WALLET

NE GUNFLEET. Lt.By. Q.(3) 10 sec. Pillar
B.Y.B. Topmark E.
WALLET No: 2 Lt.By. Fl.R. 5 sec. Can.R.
WALLET No: 4 Lt.By. Fl.(4)R. 10 sec. Can.R.
WALLET SPITWAY. Lt.By. L.Fl. 10 sec. Sph.
R.W.V.S. Bell.
SWIN SPITWAY. Lt.By. Iso. 10 sec. Pillar.
RWVS marks S. end of Wallet Spitway.

WALTON-ON-NAZE. 51°50.6′N, 1°16.9′E Lt.Bn.
2 F.G. vert. 3M. at Pier Head. 5m. Bell occas.
WALTON OUTFALL. Bn. G. Topmark Cone.

CLACTON-ON-SEA. 51°47.0′N, 1°09.6′E Lt.Bn.
2 F.G. vert. on post at Pier Head.
Reed(2) 120 sec. occas. 2 F.G. vert. Lt. also on
E and W corner of Pier Head.
BERTHING ARM. Lt. F.R.
CLACTON OUTFALL. By. Conical G.

APPROACHES TO RIVER BLACKWATER AND RIVER COLNE

KNOLL. Lt.By. Q. Pillar B.Y. Topmark N.
EAGLE. Lt.By. Q.G. Conical G.
N EAGLE By. Pillar B.Y. Topmark N.
NW KNOLL. Lt.By. Fl.(2)R. 5 sec. Can.R.
COLNE BAR Lt.By. Fl.(2)G. 5 sec. Conical G.
Topmark Cone. At entce. to River Colne.
BENCH HEAD. By. Conical G.
DENGIE MARSHES. Lt. Q.Y. 4M. Bn. 4m.
Occas.
ST. PETERS FLATS WAVEBREAK. Lt. 2 F.R.
vert. R. □ on Bn. mark wave break on Dengie
Flats (16 barges filled with gravel).
BRADWELL POWER STATION. 51°44′40″N,
0°53′40″E Lt. 2 F.R. at NE and SW ends.
BRADWELL CREEK Lt. Q.R.

MALDON (Essex) 51°43′N 0°46′E. H.M. Tel.
(0621) 53110. Heybridge Basin Lockkeeper
(0621) 53506.
Bradwell Marina (0621) 76235. Chan. (M). 280
Berths. Access 4 h.-HW-4 h. Springs.
Maylandsea Shipyard (0621) 740264.
River Blackwater — Channel to Maldon 3.4m.
at MHWS but dries at LW.
Chelmer and Blackwater Canal: Entered at
Heybridge Basin. Gates 7.9m. wide × 3.7m.
MHWS. Lock available for craft up to 1.8m.
draught ½ Flood to ½ Ebb and open 1½ h.-HW-1½ h.
Bradwell Marina 15m. × 1.8m. draught.

THIRSLET CREEK SPIT Lt.By. Fl.(3)G. 10 sec.
Spar. G.
MB By. Sph. B.
GOLD HANGER SPIT. No: 1 Lt.By. Fl.G. 5 sec.
Conical G.
MARCONI SAILING CLUB Lt. F. 7m. Post.
OSEA ISLAND PIER Lt. 2 F.G. vert.
No: 2 Lt.By. Fl.R. 3 sec. Can.R.
THE DOCTOR No: 3 By. Conical G.
SOUTHEY CREEK By. Can.R.
NORTH DOUBLE Lt.By. Fl.G. 3 sec. Conical G.
SOUTH DOUBLE By. Can.R.
HILLY POOL PT. By. Can.R.
HEYBRIDGE. Lt. Iso. G. 5 sec. 10m.
HERRINGS PT. By. Conical G.
Thence Conical G. & Can.R. Bys. to Maldon.

MERSEA QUARTERS

INSHORE WAYPOINT OFF R. BLACKWATER.
51°44.0′N, 1°06.0′E.

River Colne — Vessels up to 4.3m. can reach
Wivenhoe at MHWS.
Mersea Quarters: Depths 3.7m. to 6.1m.
Tollesbury Y. Hr. 15/16.5m. × 2.1m. draught.
Sill dries 2.3m. Available 2 h.-HWS-2 h. or
1 h.-HWN-1 h. Diesel, petrol, water, etc.
available.

RIVER BLACKWATER

Approach marked by NASS Lt.Bn. V.Q.(3) 5
sec. B.Y.B. Topmark E.

W. MERSEA

STONE HILL HARD, N. END. Lt. 2 F.G. vert.
Pontoon. S. END Lt. 2 F.G. vert Pontoon.
FAIRWAY. By. Sph. R.W.V.S.
No: 1 By. Conical G.
No: 2 Lt.By. Fl.R. 3 sec. Can.R.
No: 3 By. Conical G.
No: 4 By. Can.R.
No: 6 By. Can.R.
No: 5 By. Conical G.

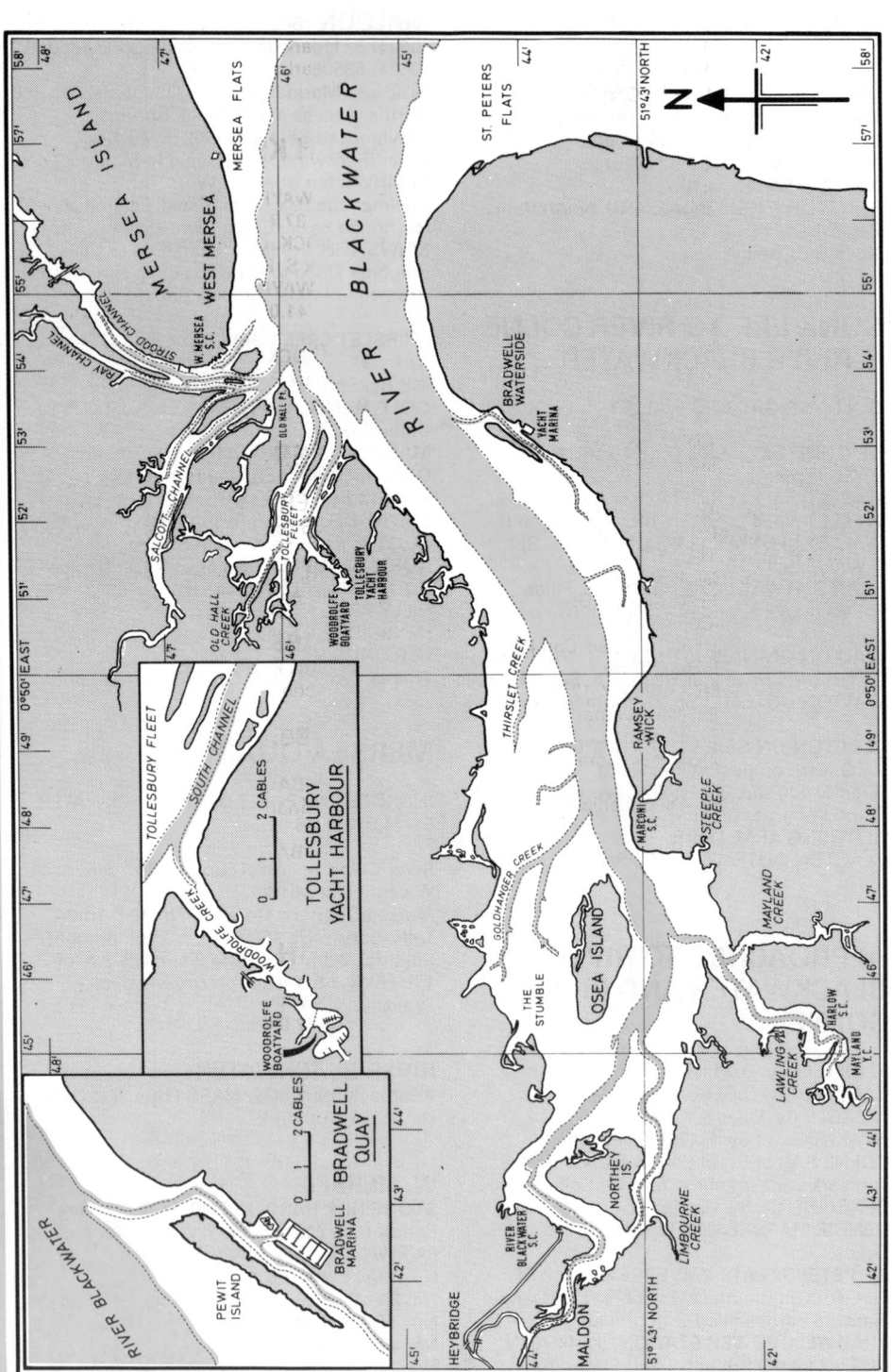

From No: 6 By.
THE NASS By. Can.R.
Thence seasonal Bys. Can.R. & Conical G.
mark S Channel to Tollesbury Yacht harbour.

COLNE RIVER 51°57'N 1°17'E
Measured Distance: River Colne. Outer ½M.
marks on E bank below Brightlingsea. Co.
351°(M) 171°(M).

COLCHESTER 51°53'N 0°53'E. Tel: (0206)
575858. Fax: (0206) 562410.
Radio — Port: VHF Chan. 16, 68, 11, 14—0900-
1700 LT. Mon.-Fri. otherwise 2 h.—HW—1 h.

COLNE POINT Bn. B. situated on Point.
INNER BENCH HEAD. Lt.By. Gp.Fl.(2)R. 5 sec.
Can.R. Topmark Can. on W entce. to Colne
River.
No: 1. By. Conical G.
No: 2 Lt.By. Fl.(2)R. 5 sec. Can.R.
No: 3. By. Conical G.
No: 8 Lt.By. Q.R. Can.R. ⌄⊥⌄ .
No: 9 Lt.By. Fl.G. 3 sec. Conical G.
No: 13 Lt.By. Q.G. Conical G.
LOWLANDS. Lt.By. Fl.(2)R. 5 sec. Can.R.
Marks wreck off Mersea Stone.
BATEMANS TOWER. Lt.Bn. F.Y. 12m.
COCUM HILLS. Bn. B.Y.B. Topmark E.
No: 12 Lt.By. Fl.R. 5 sec. Can.R.
No: 13A Lt.By. Fl.(2)G. 4 sec. Conical G.
No:14 By. Can.R.
No: 15 Lt.By. Fl.(2)G. 4 sec. Conical G.
No:16 By. Can.R.
No:18 Lt.By. Q.R. Can.R.
No: 17. By. Conical G.
No: 20 Lt.By. Q.R. Can.R.
No: 22 By. Can.R.
No: 19 Lt.By. Q.G. Conical G.
No: 24 Lt.By. Q.R. Can.R.
No: 21. By. Conical G.
BANK No: 23 Lt.Bn. Fl.G. 5 sec. 5m.

WIVENHOE YACHT CLUB. Lt.Bn. F.Y.
ROWHEDGE WHARF. Lt.Bn. F.Y.

BRIGHTLINGSEA CREEK ENTCE. Lt.By. Q.(6)
+ L.Fl. 15 sec. Pillar Y.B. Topmark S.
Lt.By. Fl.(2) 4 sec.
Lt.By. Fl.R. 2 sec.
Lt.By. Fl.(3)G. 5 sec. Conical G.

BRIGHTLINGSEA Tel: H.M. (0206 30)
2200. Port Office: (0206 30) 2370. Fax: (0206
30) 5243. Telex: 988795 HYTHE G.
Radio — Port: VHF Chan. 14. 0900-1700 or by
arrangement with (0836) 698927.

Ldg.Lts. 047°50'. (Front) F.R. post 5m. R.W.
stripe daymark. (Rear) F.R. on post 7m. R.W.
stripe daymark.

KENTISH KNOCK SANDS

OFFSHORE WAYPOINT SE OF S KNOCK.
51°34.0'N, 1°37.7'E.
SOUTH KNOCK. Lt.By. Q.(6) + Fl. 15 sec. Pillar.
Y.B. Topmark S. Bell.
OFFSHORE WAYPOINT KENTISH KNOCK.
51°38.0'N, 1°41.0'E.

KENTISH KNOCK Lt.By. Q.(3) 10 sec. Pillar
B.Y.B. Topmark E. Whis.

GALLOPER SANDS

S GALLOPER. Lt.By. 51°43.9'N, 1°56.5'E.
Q.(6) + L.Fl. 15 sec. Pillar Y.B. Topmark S. Whis.
Racon.
N GALLOPER. Lt.By. Q. Pillar B.Y. Topmark N.
⌄⊥⌄ marks N end of Shoal.

OUTER GABBARD 51°57.8'N, 2°04.3'E. Lt.
By. Q(3) 10 sec. Pillar B.Y.B. Topmark E.
w.a.whis. Racon.

INNER GABBARD

S INNER GABBARD. Lt.By. Q.(6) + L.Fl. 15 sec.
Pillar Y.B. Topmark S.

N INNER GABBARD. Lt.By. Q. Pillar B.Y.
Topmark N.

SHIPWASH SHOAL (Outside)

INSHORE WAYPOINT OFF S SHIPWASH.
51°53.0'N, 1°32.0'E.

S SHIPWASH. Lt.By. Q.(6) + L.Fl. 15 sec. Pillar
Y.B. Topmark S. ⌄⊥⌄ .
E SHIPWASH. Lt.By. V.Q.(3) 5 sec. Pillar B.Y.B.
Topmark E. on E side of Shoal.
N SHIPWASH. Lt.By. Q. Pillar B.Y. Topmark N.
⌄⊥⌄ on N side of Shoal. Bell w.a.

OFFSHORE WAYPOINT OFF SHIPWASH.
52°02.0'N, 1°43.0'E.

SHIPWASH 52°02.0'N, 1°42.1'E. Lt.F. Fl.(3) 20
sec. 24M. R. hull, Lt.Tr. amidships, 12m. Dia.(3)
60 sec.
WATCH By. Can.R. with reflective panels, 3.5
cables from Lt.F.

SHIPWAY

FORT MASSAC WRECK 51°53.4′N. 1°32.6′E.
E. Lt.By. V.Q.(3) 5 sec. Pillar B.Y.B. Topmark E.
W. Lt.By. V.Q.(9) 10 sec. Pillar Y.B.Y. Topmark
W.
SHIP HEAD. Lt.By. Fl.R. 2.5 sec. Can.R. — S
end of Shipwash Shoal.

SW SHIPWASH. Lt.By. L. Fl.R. 10 sec. H.F.P.
Pillar R.
NW SHIPWASH. Lt.By. Fl.R. 5 sec. Can.R.
Sunk Lt.F. marks S of Shipwash Shoal.
ROUGHS TOWER. SE Lt.By. Q.(3) 10 sec.
Pillar B.Y.B. Topmark E. Bell.
NW Lt.By. Q.(9) 15 sec. Pillar Y.B.Y.
Topmark W.
ROUGHS. Lt.By. V.Q. Pillar B.Y. Topmark N.
〰.
HA Lt.By. Iso 5 sec. Pillar. RWVS Whis.
S BAWDSEY. Lt.By. Q.(6)+L.Fl. 15 sec. Pillar
Y.B. Topmark S. Whis.
INSHORE WAYPOINT MID BAWDSEY.
51°59.0′N, 1°35.0′E.
MID BAWDSEY. Lt.By. Fl.(3)G. 10 sec.
Conical G.
INSHORE WAYPOINT NE BAWDSEY.
52°02.0′N, 1°37.5′E.
NE BAWDSEY. Lt.By. Fl.G. 10 sec. Conical G.
〰.

MEDUSA CHANNEL NORTHWARDS TO HARWICH

NAZE TOWER Bn. Castellated stone tower,
48m. on shore edge.
MEDUSA. Lt.By. Fl.G. 5 sec. Conical G.
STONE BANKS By. Can.R. Topmark Can.
SOUTH CORK. By. Pillar Y.B. Topmark S.

ENTRANCE TO HAMFORD WATERS

Hamford Waters: Keep to channel as banks
are steep-to. Whole area widely used by
yachts.
Tidemarsh Marina (Twizzle Creek) 16m. × 3m.
draught. Fuel, water, etc. available.
PYE END By. Pillar R.W. Topmark Sph.
Pye End and 7 other Bys. Can.R. mark Pye
Sands.
CRAB KNOLL By. Conical G.

MRSC THAMES (0255) 675518. Weather
broadcast ev. 4h. from 0010.

HARWICH 51°57′N 1°17′E. Tel: Harbour

Control (0255) 243000. H.M. (0255) 243030.
Fax: (0255) 241325. Telex: 98472 VTS. Fax:
(Enquiries) (0255) 240933. — Pilots: (0255)
243111. Fax: (0255) 241325. Telex: 98472
PILHAR G.
Radio — Port: Harwich Hbr. VHF Chan. 16, 71,
14, 11, 10, 9—continuous. Radar Chan. 14, 20
on request. All pilotage requests for Harwich,
Felixstowe and Cork, Ipswich, Colne,
Blackwater, Crouch and Roach also boarding
station for Thames & Medway. Vessels
damaged, listing more than 5° etc. get
permission to enter, leave, proceed. Vessels
over 50 GRT Listen Chan. 71.
Parkeston Quay. VHF Chan. 16,
18—continuous—for British Rail ferries only.
Pilots: (Shore Stn.) Chan. 16, 9—continuous.
P.V. VHF Chan. 16, 6, 71.
All vessels over 50 GRT should follow the
recommended routes, only deep draught
vessels using the Deep Water Route. Yachts
should follow the Yacht Track outside of Main
Channel, to the south and should, for their
own safety, avoid the Deep Water Channel W
of HA Lt.By. Inform Port Control of track to be
used. Water Ski area between Erwarton Ness
and Harkstead Point. Visitors moorings at
Harwich Quay at HW. Quay dries at LW.
Speed limit 8 kts. Harwich.

APPROACHES TO HARWICH HARBOUR

INSHORE WAYPOINT OFF WASHINGTON BY.
51°57.0′N, 1°27.0′E.
WASHINGTON. Lt.By. Q.G. Conical G. N of
Channel.
FELIXSTOWE LEDGE. Lt.By. Fl.(3) G. 10 sec.
Conical G.
WADGATE LEDGE. Lt.By. Fl.(4)G. 15 sec.
Conical G.
PLATTERS. Lt.By. Q.(6) + L.Fl. 15 sec. Pillar
Y.B. Topmark S.
ROLLING GROUND. Lt.By. Q.G. Conical G.

BEACH END. Lt.By. Fl.(2)G. 5 sec. Conical G.
〰 E side of river entce. Bell.
FORT Lt.By. Fl.(4)G. 15 sec. Conical G.
NW BEACH. Lt.By. Fl.(3) 10 sec. Conical G.
Bell.
LANDGUARD POINT Bn. G. on Point. Racon.

HARWICH DEEP WATER CHANNEL.
No: 1 Lt.By. Fl.Y. 2½ sec. Conical Y. Racon.
No: 2 Lt.By. Fl.(4)Y. 15 sec. Can.Y. Racon.
No: 3 Lt.By. Fl.Y. 2½ sec. Conical Y.

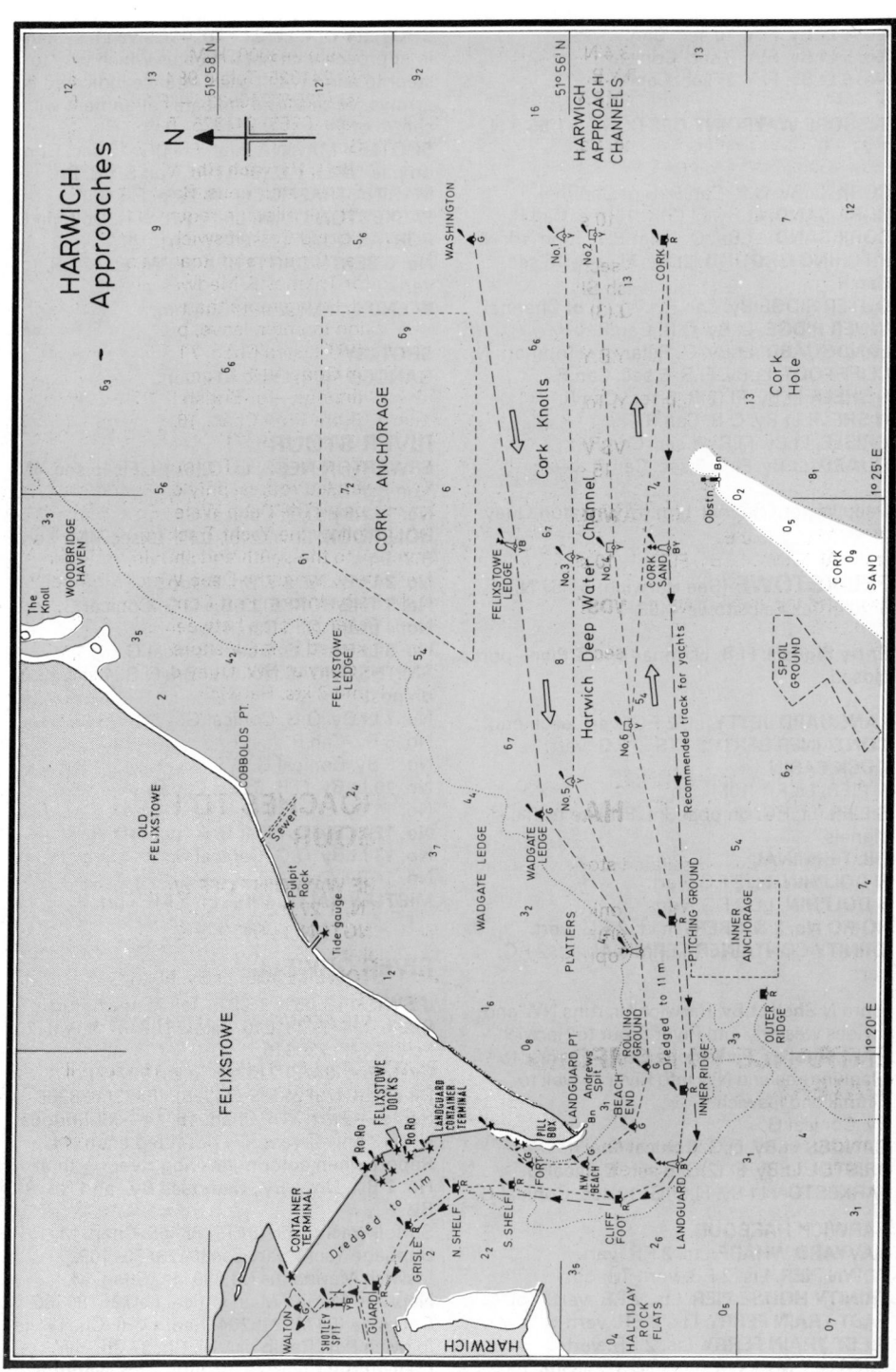

No: 4 Lt.By. Fl.Y. 10 sec. Can.Y.
No: 5 Lt.By. Fl.Y. 5 sec. Conical Y.
No: 6 Lt.By. Fl.Y. 2½ sec. Can.Y.

INSHORE WAYPOINT OFF CORK. 51°55.5′N,
1°27.7′E.

CORK. Lt.By. Q.R. Can.R. S of Channel.
CORK SAND. Lt.By. Fl.(3)R. 10 sec. Can R.
CORK SAND. Lt.Bn. Q. Pillar B.Y. Topmark N.
PITCHING GROUND. Lt.By. Fl.(4)R. 15 sec.
Can.R.
OUTER RIDGE By. Can.R. ⏦. S of Channel.
INNER RIDGE. Lt.By. Q.R. Can.R. ⏦.
LANDGUARD. Lt.By. Q. Pillar B.Y. Topmark N.
CLIFF FOOT. Lt.By. Fl.R. 5 sec. Can.R.
S SHELF. Lt.By. Fl.(2)R. 5 sec. Can.R.
N SHELF. Lt.By. Q.R. Can.R.
GRISLE. Lt.By. Fl.R. 2½ sec. Can.R.
GUARD. Lt.By. Fl.R. 5 sec. Can.R. ⏦.

Deep Water Channel 10m. to Parkston Quay.

FELIXSTOWE (See Harwich) 51°57′N,
1°20′E. Tel: Felixstowe 4433.

Entry Signals: Fl.R. Lt. inner end S Pier—port
closed.

LANGUARD JETTY. Lt. 2 F.G. vert. each end.
CONTAINER BERTHS LTS. 2 F.G. vert.
DOCK BASIN
N PIER. Lt. F.R. 10M. 3m.
S PIER. Lt. F.G. on post 3m. Private traffic
signals.
OIL TERMINAL
N DOLPHIN. Lt. 2 F.G. vert.
S DOLPHIN. Lt. 2 F.G. vert.
RO-RO No. 3 & 4 BERTH. Lt. 2 F.G. vert.
TRINITY CONTAINER TERMINAL. Lt. 2 F.G.
vert.

From N Shelf Lt.By. Harwich Hr. runs NW and
divides westerly into River Stour to Harwich
Town, Shotley, Parkestone Quay, up river to
Manningtree and NW into River Orwell to
Pinmill and Ipswich.
By. Conical G.
GANGES Lt.By. Q.G. Conical G.
BRISTOL Lt.By. Fl.(2)G. 5 sec. Conical G.
PARKESTON Lt.By. Fl.(3)G. 10 sec. Conical G.

HARWICH HARBOUR
NAVYARD WHARF. Lts. 2 F.R. vert.
TOWN PIER. Lts. 2 F.R. vert. Tripod.
TRINITY HOUSE PIER. Lts. 2 F.R. vert. Col.
EAST TRAIN FERRY. Lts. 2 F.R. vert.
WEST TRAIN FERRY. Lts. 2 F.R. vert.
SHOTLEY MARINA. Tel: (0473) 348908. Fax:
(0473) 348868.
Radio: VHF Chan. 80, 37(M).

SHOTLEY DIR. Lt. 339°30′. Passive Lt. system
in approach channel indicates which way to
steer to align with Lock Entrance indicated by
arrows, vertical line indicates alignment with
centre of Lock.
SHOTLEY MARINA E. Lt. Fl.(4)G. 15 sec. G. Δ
on pile. **W Lt.** V.Q.(3) 5 sec. ⴕ on B.Y.B. Bn.
MARINA TRAFFIC Lts. W Side. F.R.G.
PARKESTON QUAY. Lts. 2 F.R. vert. Dolphin B.
PORTAL QUAY. Lts. 2 F.R. vert.
No: 6 BERTH CAR FERRY TERM. Lts. 2 F.R.
vert.
W END Lt. Fl.R. 2 sec. Dolphin.

SHOTLEY
GANGES PIER. Lts. 2 F.G. vert.

RIVER STOUR
ERWARTON NESS. Lt. Q.(6) + L.Fl. 15 sec. 4M.
ⴕ on B.Y. Bn.
No: 1 Lt.By. Q.G. Conical G.
HOLBROOK. Lt. V.Q.(6)+L.Fl. 10 sec. 4M. ⴕ on
B.Y. Bn.
No: 2 Lt.Bn. Q. ⴕ Y. Bn. B. top.
No: 3 THE HORSE. Lt.By. Q.G. Conical G.
No: 4 Lt.By. Q.R. Can.R.
No: 5 Lt.By. Fl.G. 5 sec. Conical G.
SMITHS SHOAL No: 6. Lt.Bn. Fl.R. 4 sec. R. ☐
on post.
No: 7 Lt.By. Q.G. Conical G.
No: 8 By. Can.R.
No: 9 By. Conical G.
No. 10 Lt.By. Fl.R. 6 sec. Can.R.
No: 11 By. Conical G.
No. 12 Lt.By. Q. Pillar B.Y. Topmark N.
No: 13 Lt.By. Q.G. Conical G.
No. 14 By. Can.R.
MISTLEY BALTIC WHF. Lt. 2 F.R. vert.

RIVER ORWELL

IPSWICH 52°05′N 1°09′E. Tel: Ipswich Port
Radio. (0473) 231010. Telex: 988787 & 98642.
Fax: (0473) 230915.
Customs: (0473) 212388 Telex: 987172.
Divers: (0473) 59929 (70028); (0473) 688266.
Radio — Port: VHF Chan. 16, 14—continuous.
Use 12 only if vessel is not fitted chan. 14.
Report when entering/leaving river/berth at
No. 2 By., No. 4 By., Cathouse By., and No. 9
By.
Suffolk Yacht Hbr. (0473) 88465. Chan. M.
Debbage Yacht Services (0473) 601169.
Ipswich Marina (0473) 689111. Chan. M.
Neptune Marina Main Office. (0473) 780366.
Dockside (0473) 215204. Radio VHF Ch. 14 via
Ipswich Port Radio or VHF Ch. 37 2h.-HW
(daylight) for berth allocation (C/S. Neptune
Marina Berthing).
Peninsula B'yard (0473) 348812. Chan. M.

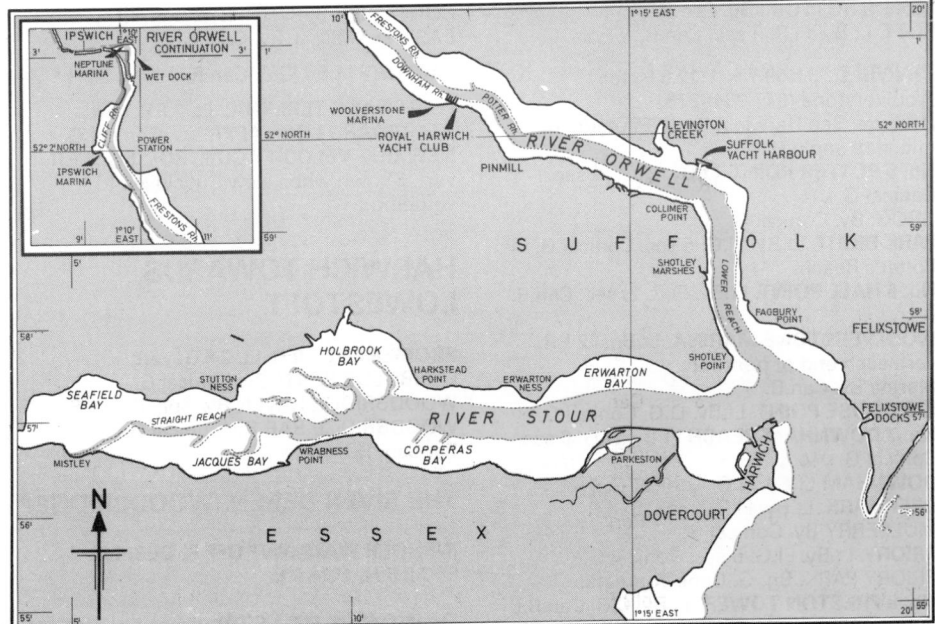

Wolverstone Marina (0473) 84206. Chan. M.
Shotley Point Marina. (0473) 348908. Chan.
M.

Entry: River Orwell Fairway clearance strictly
enforced owing to day and night shipping
movements. Visitors should contact Marina
for moorings due to congestion. All non-
commercial and leisure craft inward to
Ipswich Enclosed Dock must contact Neptune
Marina. Speed limit 6 kts.
Dredger shows B. ball on foul side by day. 3
Lts. in triangle apex up with R. Lt. on foul side
by night.
River Stour — craft with draughts up to 4m.
can reach Mistley and draughts up to 2m. can
reach Manningtree at MHWS but dry out at
LW.
Shotley Marina: Channel 2m. Lock.
River Orwell:
Collimer Point — Traffic Signal — Fl.Y. 2 sec.
shown when dangerous for vessels to
proceed beyond No. 5 Lt.By. River closed to
inward traffic for approx. 45 mins.
Suffolk Y. Hr. 15m. × 2m. draught. Diesel,
water, etc. available.
Woolverstone Marina 26m. × 2.4m. draught.
Diesel and petrol, water, etc. available.
Ipswich Marina 12m. × 1.8m. draught. Fuel,
etc. available.
Wet Dock — Lock 91m. × 15m. × 7.2m. on sill
at MHWS. Vessels 14.5m. beam × 5.5m.
draught. Lock available 2 h.-HW-1 h.; usually
open 1 h.-HW.
G. Lt. = Lock open. R. Lt. = Lock closed.

Neptune Marina 12m. × 3.3m. draught. Fuel,
etc. available.

BLOODY POINT TO IPSWICH

SHOTLEY SPIT. Lt.Bn. Q.(6) + L. Fl. 15 sec.
Pillar Y.B. Topmark S.
WALTON. Lt.By. Fl.(3) G. 10 sec. Conical G.
〰.
TELEGRAPH Bn. R.W. ◊ Topmark, opposite
Fagbury Pt.
TELEGRAPH N Bn. B.W. ◊ Topmark, Fagbury
Pt.
FAGBURY POINT. Lt.By. Fl.G. 2½ sec. Conical
G. 〰.
MARSH No. 1. Lt.By. Fl.G. 5 sec. Conical G.
TRIMLEY. Lt.By. Fl.G. 2½ sec. Conical G. 〰.
No: 2 Lt.By. Fl.R. 2½ sec. Can.R. 〰.
COLLIMER. Lt.By. Fl.R. 5 sec. Can.R. 〰.
Colimer Point. Water ski area eastwards
marked by Y.Bys.
ORWELL Lt.By. Fl.R. 2½ sec. Can.R. 51°58.14′N
1°16.65′E.
STRATTON. Lt.By. Fl.G. 5 sec. Conical G.
SUFFOLK YACHT HR. (LEVINGTON)
Ldg. Lts. (Front) Iso.Y. 1 sec. (Rear) Oc.Y. 3
sec.
No: 3 LEVINGTON CREEK. Lt.By. Fl.G. 2½ sec.
Conical G. 〰.
BAY. Lt.By. Fl.G. 5 sec. Conical G. 〰.
Broke Hall Hard Bn. Conical G.
BUTTERMAN'S BAY. No: 4 Lt.By. Q.R.

FOXE'S BOTTOM. By. Can.R.
BUTT. Lt.By. Fl.R. 5 sec. Can.R.

PINMILL. 51°59.7'N 1°12.8'E. Tel.
Woolverstone (047 384) 276.
Pilotage: See Harwich. Yacht Pilotage in Pin-
mill area apply H.M.
No: 5 POTTER POINT. Lt.By. Fl.G. 2½ sec.
Conical G. 〰.
GROG. By. Conical G.
PARK BIGHT. Lt.By. Fl.G. 5 sec. Conical G. in
Potter's Reach.
No: 6 HALL POINT. Lt.By. Fl.R. 2½ sec. Can.R.
〰.
WOOLVERSTONE MARINA. Lt.Bns. 2 F.R.
vert. each end of pontoon.
Marina By. Can.R.
CATHOUSE POINT. Lt.By. Q.G. Conical G.
No: 7 DOWNHAM REACH Lt.By. Fl.G. 5 sec.
Conical G. 〰.
DOWNHAM Lt.By. Q.G. Conical G. 〰.
DEER PARK. Lt.By. Fl.R. 5 sec. Can.R.
MULBERRY By. Conical G.
PRIORY. Lt.By. Fl.G. 5 sec. Conical G.
PRIORY PARK. Bn. G. Cone Topmark.
No: 8 FRESTON TOWER. Lt.By. Q.R. Can.R.
〰.
BRIDGEWOOD By. Conical G.
FRESTON REACH By. Can.R.,
HILL. Lt.By. Fl.R. 5 sec. Can.R.
No: 9 FRESTON REACH Lt.By. Fl.G. 2½ sec
Conical G. 〰.
REDGATE HARD By. Can.R.
POND OOZE By. Conical G.
Bridge Appr. East By. Conical G.
Bridge Appr. West By. Can.R.
HIGH MARSH. No: 10 By. Can.R. 〰.
No: 11 WHERSTEAD OOZE By. Conical G. 〰.
ORWELL BRIDGE CENTRE. Lt. F.Y. also 2 F.R.
vert. on Pier 9. 2 F.G. vert. on Pier 10. Lts.
shown on up and downstream sides.
By. Conical G. ⎫ mark approaches
By. Can.R.   ⎭ to Bridge.
RIVER ORWELL BRIDGE. Clearance above
MHWOST 38.8m.
Beware small pieces of debris falling. Sound
1 Long Blast when approaching.
SEWER JTY Lts. 2 F.G. vert.
SEWER By. Conical G.

WHERSTEAD OOZE By. Can.R.
EASTFEN Lt.By. Q.G. Conical G.
POWER STATION (W). Lt.By. Q.R. Can.R
POWER STATION. Lts. 2 F.G. vert. shown from
SE and NW corners.
In Long Reach there are mooring Bys. in Fair
way for large vessels.
FOXS MARINA (W Bank). Entrance Bns.
Can. R.
HEARTH By. Conical G.
No: 12 CLIFF REACH Lt.By. Fl.R. 5 sec.
Can.R. 〰.

CONTAINER BERTH. 2 Bys. Can.R.
EAST TERMINAL By. Can.R.

FACTORY Lt.By. Q.R. Can.R.

WEST BANK TERMINAL Lt. 2 F.R. vert.
STARBOARD LOCK APPR. By. Conical G.
NEW CUT VELOCITY CONTROL. Lts. 3 F.R.
vert. Shown when New Cut closed to
shipping.

HARWICH TOWARDS LOWESTOFT

PROMENADE PIER. Lt. 2 F.G. vert.
COBBOLDS POINT By. Conical G.
WOODBRIDGE HAVEN By. Sph. R.W.V.S.
WOODBRIDGE BAR By. Conical G.
By. Can. R.

THE RIVER DEBEN (WOODBRIDGE)

INSHORE WAYPOINT OFF R. DEBEN.
51°58.5'N, 1°24.5'E.

BAWDSEY RG. STN. 51°59.6'N 1°24.6'E.
Emergency DF Stn. VHF Chan. 16 & 67.
Controlled by MRSC Thames.

FELIXSTOWE FERRY. 51°59'N, 1°23'E. Tel:
(0394) 283469, 270853.
Radio: VHF Chan. 8.
Entry: Craft draught 3.5m. can reach
Woodbridge at MHWS (with 2.7m. draught at
MHWN) Bar constantly shifts and depths
vary. Reported depth 0.4m. H.M. will
lead/direct vessels over the bar on request.
Pilotage available for R. Deben.
Tide Mill Yacht Hr. (Woodbridge) 15m. × 2m.
draught. Tel: (0255) 62185.
Diesel, water etc. available.
Visitors moorings available in the River.
TIDE MILL. Y. Hr. Tel: (0394) 385745.
ROBERTSONS. Tel: (0394) 32305.

GROYNE Lt. Q.R.
ENTRANCE LDG.LTS. (Front) Fl. W. △ in R. ▯
(Rear) Fl.R. R. ▯ on post. Private, moved as
changes occur. May be replaced by Fl.Y.

FERRY LANDING
W SIDE. Lt. 2 F.R. vert.
E SIDE. Lt. (Bawdsey Jty). 2 F.G. vert.
Fairway By. has to be altered continually as
Chan. shifts.
HORSE SAND By. Can.R. marks NE end of
Horse Sand inside River Deben.
River Deben marked from Kirton Creek
inwards by No: 2 By. Can.R; No: 2A By.
Can.R.; No: 4 By. Can.R.; No: 6 By. Can.R; No:
1 By. Conical G; No: 3 By. Conical G; No: 8 By.

Can.R; No: 10 By. Can.R; No: 5 By. Conical G; No: 12 By. Sph. R; No: 7 By. Sph. G; No: 14 By. Sph. R; No: 9 By. Sph. G; No: 11 By. Sph. G; No: 13 By. Sph. G; No: 16 By. Sph. R.

CUTLER BANK
CUTLER By. Conical G. marks Cutler Bank.

WHITING BANK
SW WHITING By. Pillar Y.B. Topmark S. S End.
WHITING HOOK By. Can.R. W Side.
NE WHITING By. Pillar B.Y.B. Topmark E. N End.

ORFORDNESS TOWARDS LOWESTOFT

ORFORD HAVEN 52°05′N 1°32′E
Entry: Enter on flood. Do not enter in fog. Bar shifts. Entry dangerous without local knowledge.
Least depth over Bar reported as 2m. Keep towards mid channel to avoid mud flats.
From a position approx. 1c. S of Orford Haven By. steer 309°T (Hollesley Church). When Orford Bn. in line with large chimney to N steer 002°T until beam of ruined ramp, thence to close W of N Weir Point keeping to E side until abeam of Orford Bn.

ORFORD Bn. Topmark ◊ fluorescent Or. Ht. 4.5m.
ORFORD HAVEN. By. Sph. R.W.V.S. postn 52°01.78′N, 1°27.98′E.

INSHORE WAYPOINT OFF ALDEBURGH NAPES 52°10.0′N, 1°42.5′E.

ORFORDNESS 52°05.0′N 1°34.6′E. Lt.Ho. Fl. 5 sec. 30M. W. circular Tr., R. bands, 28m. Same structure F.R.G. R.14M. G.15M. 14m. R. shore-210°; R.038°-047°; G.047°-shore. Racon.
ALDEBURGH RIDGE By. Can.R.
SIZEWELL. Lt.By. Fl.R. 10 sec. Can.R.
SIZEWELL POWER STATION. Lt. 2 F.R. vert. shown from Head of both S and N pipelines.
COOLING WATER INTAKE Lt. Fl.R. 5 sec.
COOLING WATER OUTFALL. Lt. Fl. R. 5 sec.
Lt.By. Q.(3) 10 sec. Pillar. B.Y.B. Topmark E.
Lt.By. VQ(3) 5 sec. Pillar. B.Y.B. Topmark E.

SOUTHWOLD 52°20′N, 1°41′E. Tel: HM. (0502) 723502. Pilots: 723502 (Day), 722638 (Night).

HARBOUR WAYPOINT. 52°18.5′N, 1°41.5′E.

Radio — Port: VHF Chan. 16, 12. Hrs. 0800-1800.

Pilots: VHF Chan. 12. 16. 9. E.T.A. 12 h. and 2 h. in advance.
Signals: R. Flag or 3x Fl.R. Lts. Vert. = port closed.
Entry: Dangerous to enter with strong onshore wind and sea. Difficult entry at LW or with strong outgoing stream. Depths vary 1.3m-4.8m in channel and harbour. Bridge at Blythburgh clearance 2m at HW. Depths over Bar vary 0.7m-2.0m. Best time to enter between 2 and 3h. after LW.

Dir. Lt. 270° Dir.F.W.R.G.G. 267°-269°; W-271°; R-273°; shown when vessel berthing.
DOLPHIN. No. 2 Lt. 2 F.R. vert. 3M. Metal post on dolphin. 2m apart.

Lt.Ho. 52°19.6′N 1°41.0′E. Fl.(4) W.R. 20 sec. W.22M., R.22M., R.20M. W. circular Tr. 37m. R.204°-220°; W.220°-001°; R.001°-032.3°. Storm Sig.
N PIER. Lt. Fl.G. 1.5 sec. 4M. Metal Col. 4m. shows 3 Fl.R. 1.5 sec. vert. when Hr. inaccessible.
KNUCKLE Lt. 2 F.G. vert.
S PIER. Lt. Q.R. 2M.

INSHORE WAYPOINT OFF E. BARNARD Lt.By. 52°24.6′N, 01°46.4′E.
E BARNARD Lt.By. Q.(3) 20 sec. Pillar B.Y.B. Topmark E.
S NEWCOMBE. Lt.By. Fl.G. 2½ sec. Conical G.
PAKEFIELD. Lt.By. Fl.(2)G. 5 sec. Conical G.

INSHORE WAYPOINT OFF BENACRE NESS. 52°24.0′N, 1°50.0′E.

LOWESTOFT 52°29′N 1°45′E. Tel: HM. and Bridge Control (0502) 572286. Pilots (0502) 560277. Fax: Port Control (0502) 586375. HM. Oulton Broad (0502) 57496. C.G. (0502) 565356.

Radio — Port: VHF Chan. 16, 14,—continuous.
Radio — Pilots: VHF Chan. 16, 14 when vessel expected.
Entry: Sands are continually shifting. Beware shallows and drying areas, do not cross banks in bad weather or strong tidal conditions.
From the South: Waypoint off E. Barnard Lt.By. follow buoyed channel inshore of S. Newcombe and Pakefield buoys.
From the North and East: Waypoint E. of Corton Lt.By. then follow Holm Channel into Corton Road.
Vessels intending to pass close to entrance should always request details of traffic movements.

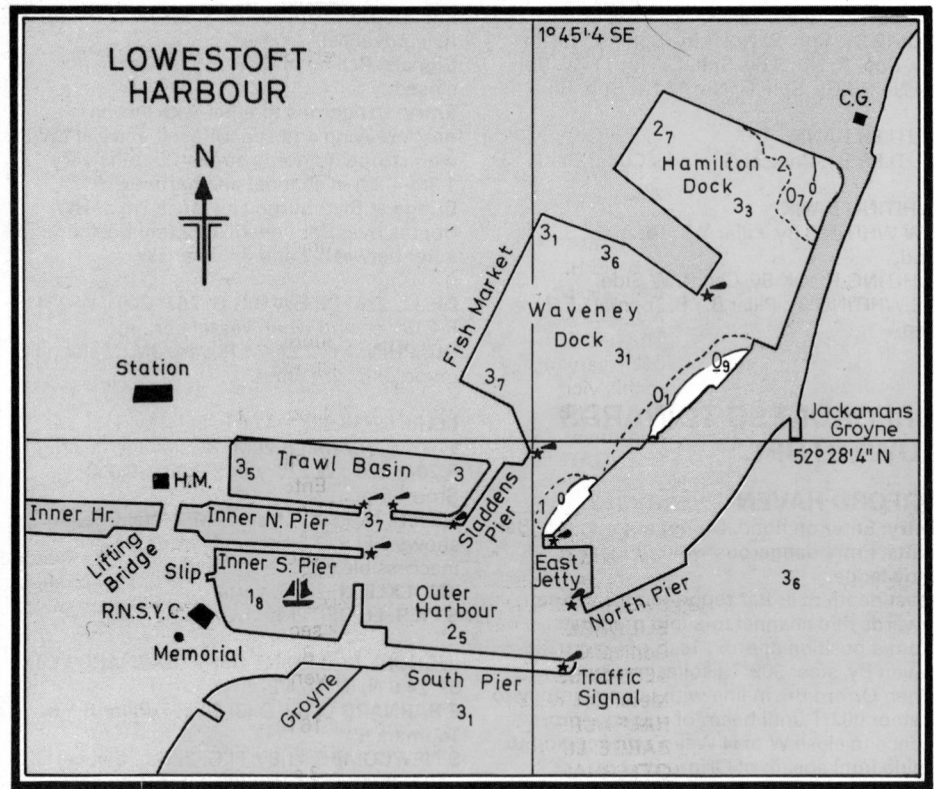

Inner Harbour Entry Signals: By day and night: no vessel to app. within 137m. of bridge until G. Lt. is shown on N Wall of ent. chan. When Lt. is exhibited vessels may enter or leave Inner Harbour through ent. chan.
Bridge to Inner Harbour opened:
May-Sept.—Mon.-Sat. 0700, 0930, 1900, 2100. Sun. 0730, 0930, 1400, 1900, 2100.
Oct.-April—Mon.-Sat. as above. Sun. and holidays: 0800 thence as above.
Harbour Entry Signals:
W. Fl. Lt. below fixed R. Lt. South Pier Lt. Ho.—vessels may proceed to sea but no vessel to enter Harbour. Otherwise vessels may enter but no vessel leave. Not visible between 232° to 286°T (from light). Maximum speed 4 knots. Recommended to arrive on Flood. Sail on the ebb.

Anchorage: N of line Lowestoft Lt. Ho. to W Holm By.
Measured Distance: Lowestoft (N of Town). 1M. 2 pairs bns. 2½ cables offshore. 171° and 351° (Mag.) N side Lowestoft Ness. S pair bns. just N of Lowestoft Lt. Ho.

LOWESTOFT Lt.Ho. Fl. 15 sec. 28M. W. Tr. on cliff, 37m. Partially obscured 347°-shore. Same structure. F.R. 18M. 30m. vis. 184°-217°.
W. HOLM. Lt.By. Fl.(3)G. 10 sec. Conical G.
LOWESTOFT SEWER INNER OUTFALL S. Lt.By. Q.(6) + L.Fl. 15 sec. Pillar Y.B. Topmark S. Bell.
LOWESTOFT SEWER INNER OUTFALL N. Lt.By. V.Q.(3) 5 sec. Pillar B.Y.B. Topmark E. Bell.
NESS Lt.By. Fl.R. 2½ sec. Can.R.

LOWESTOFT HARBOUR
LOWESTOFT ROADS, CLAREMONT PIER. Lt. 2 F.R. vert. 4M.
JACKAMANS GROYNE. Bn. Topmark R.

OUTER HARBOUR
S. PIER HEAD. Lt. Oc. R. 5 sec. 6M. W. Tr. on small pavilion, 12m. Pilot Stn. Traffic Sig. Reed(4) 60 sec.
N PIER HEAD. Lt. Oc. G. 5 sec. 8M. W. Tr. on small pavilion, 12m.

INNER HARBOUR
S PIER HEAD. Lt. 2 F.R. vert. 1M. metal Col.

N PIER HEAD. Lt. 2 F.Y. vert. 1M. metal Col. 6m.
LAKE LOTHING. Lt. 2 F.R. vert.
NEW JETTY HEAD, SLADDENS PIER. Lt. 2 F.G. vert.
ELBOW. Lt. F.Y.
E JETTY. Lt. 2 F.G. vert.
WAVENEY DOCK, SE CORNER. Lt. 2 F.R. vert.
N WALL, E END. Lt. 2 F.R. vert.

APPROACHES TO GREAT YARMOUTH

Great Yarmouth — Hewett and Corton Channels are closed and no longer marked. Approach via Holm Channel. Care should be taken to keep to the buoyed channel as depths are changing, generally for the worse. N Cross Sand and Middle Cross Sand — considerable changes are taking place to depths and shoal areas. Shoals are tending to extend N-NE.

OUTSIDE HOLM AND CORTON SAND

OFFSHORE WAYPOINT E. OF CORTON LT.BY. 52°31.0′N, 1°52.0′E.

CORTON. Lt.By. Q.(3) 10 sec. High focal plane B.Y.B. Topmark E. Whis. ᗑ . R/T. distress sig.

HOLM CHANNEL, YARMOUTH ROAD, CAISTER ROAD AND COCKLE GATWAY

SOUTH CORTON. Lt.By. Q.(6) + Lt.Fl. 15 sec. Pillar Y.B. Topmark S.
E HOLM. Lt.By. Fl.(3)R. 10 sec. Can.R.
HOLM. Lt.By. Fl.G. 2½ sec. Conical G.
HOLM SAND. Lt.By. Q. Pillar. B.Y. Topmark N.
NW HOLM. Lt.By. Fl.(4) G. 15 sec. Conical G.
W CORTON. Lt.By. Q.(9) 15 sec. Pillar Y.B.Y. Topmark W.
SW SCROBY. Lt.By. Fl.G. 2½ sec. Conical G.
SCROBY ELBOW. Lt.By. Fl.(2)G. 5 sec. Conical G. ᗑ . Bell.
OUTFALL (Obstn). Lt.By. Q.R. Can.R.
SOUTH CAISTER Lt.By. Fl.R. 2½ sec. Can.R.
MID CAISTER. Lt.By. Fl.(2)R. 5 sec. Can.R. ᗑ Bell w.a.
NW SCROBY. Lt.By. Fl.(3)G. 10 sec. Conical G. ᗑ .
N CAISTER. Lt.By. Fl.(3)R. 10 sec. Can.R. ᗑ . Whis.

N SCROBY. Lt.By. V.Q. Pillar. B.Y. Topmark N.
COCKLE. Lt.By. V.Q.(3) 5 sec. Pillar B.Y.B. Topmark E. ᗑ . Bell w.a.
AULD GARTH WRECK. By. Pillar B.Y.B.

MRCC YARMOUTH (0493) 851338. Weather broadcast ev. 4h. from 0040.

GREAT YARMOUTH 52°34′N 1°44′E. Tel: HM. (0493) 663476/661561/855151. Fax: (0493) 852480. Telex: 975102 GY PORT. Pilots: (0493) 855152. Telex: 975367 YHP LTS.

HARBOUR WAYPOINT. 52°34.0′N, 1°45.0′E.

Radio — Port: VHF Chan. 16, 12, 9, 11—continuous, also radar.
Radio: Havenbridge Ch. 12.
Radio — Pilots: VHF Chan. 16, 12, 9, 6. (Outside office hours contact Port Radio).
Signals: Owing to frequent movements of oil rig tenders, strict attention is necessary to Port Control Signals shown from Port Control Office and South Pier.
Control Tr. S. Pier.
3 F.R.Lts. vert. — do not enter. Tidal Lt. Q. Amber shown when tide flooding. Also shown by day.
Port Control Root of S Pier, showing up harbour. 3 R.Lts. vert. = no outward vessel to pass S of Lifeboat House.
Before leaving berth it is essential to check with harbour control as with full ebb tide under you, you may have difficulty in stopping. Do not come below passenger slip at N End Brush Quay. Best to enter on slack water or on young ebb. Exercise caution entering Gt. Yarmouth with onshore winds and ebb tide. In rough weather best to enter on flood tide but if you do make certain you turn to stem the tide well to seaward of your berth. **Keep well clear of Yarmouth Bridges.** Call **Gt. Yarmouth** Radio or contact H.M. before entering port or leaving berth to check it is safe to do so.

Reporting Points:
Ocean Term, E Quay.
Atlas Berth, Trinity Quay.
Turnaside Jetty, Bleydon Water.

Norfolk Broads:
Reached from Gt. Yarmouth or Lowestoft. Via Lowestoft to Oulton Broad, the S Rivers, the Waveney & Norwich. Via Gt. Yarmouth to River Yare, Breydon Water, River Bure and N Rivers and Broads.
Sea-going vessels proceed to Norwich via Gt. Yarmouth and Breydon Water. Distance 26M. in tidal waters. Depth 3.4m. at M.H.W.S. Max. length 46m.

Measured Distances: Breydon Water. ½M. Bns. for small craft.
River Waveney. 2 × ½M. with bns.

GORLESTON. 52°34′N, 1°44′E.
S PIER HEAD. Lt. Fl.R. 3 sec. 11M. C.G. Building. 11m. vis. 235°-340°. Horn(3) 60 sec.
HEAD. Lt. 2 F.R. vert. Coping of pier. 25m. NW. 2 F.R. vert.
Ldg.Lts. 264°. (Front) Oc. 3 sec. 10M. on Col. 6m. Tidal and Traffic Lts.

BRUSH. Lt.Ho. F.R. 6M. R. circular Tr. 20m. Pilots' lookout. Same structure (Rear) Oc. 6 sec. 10M. 7m.
N PIER. Lt. Q.G. 4M. R. metal Tr. 8m. vis. 176°-078°.
GROYNE HEAD. Lts. 3×2 F.G. vert.
HAVEN BRIDGE LTS. mark channel limit occas.
2 F.R. vert. and 2 F.G. vert. shown down stream. 1 F.R. marks centre of channel.
2 F.R. vert. and 2 F.G. vert. shown upstream. 1 F.R. marks centre of channel.
Haven Bridge opening section 26m, clearance 2.7m MHWS.
Signal: 3 R.Lts. vert. = traffic prohibited.

GREAT YARMOUTH
SOUTH DENES OUTFALL. Lt.Bn. Q.R. 2M. B.Y. △ 5m.
WELLINGTON PIER HEAD. Lt. 2 F.R. vert. 3M. post on shelter, 8m.
THE JETTY HEAD. Lt. 2 F.R. vert. 2M. on metal Col. 7m.
BRITANNIA PIER HEAD. Lt. F.R. vert. 4M. W. metal Col. 11m.

OUTSIDE CROSS SANDS

CROSS SAND
Lt.By. L.Fl. 10 sec. H.F.P. R.W.V.S. Racon.

OFFSHORE WAYPOINT OFF E CROSS SAND BY. 52°40.0′N, 1°55.0′E

E CROSS SAND Lt.By. Fl.(4)R. 15 sec. Can.R.
NE CROSS SAND. Lt.By. V.Q.(3) 5 sec. Pillar B.Y.B. Topmark E. ∿.
WINTERTON OLD. Lt.Ho. Racon.

OFFSHORE WAYPOINT OFF WINTERTON NESS. 52°45.0′N, 1°45.0′E

SMITH'S KNOLL 52°43.5′N, 2°18.0′E. Lt.F. Fl.(3) 20 sec. 23M. R. hull, Lt.Tr. amidships. 12m. Shown by day when fog sig. operating. Distress sig. R.C. Racon. Horn (3) 60 sec. WATCH By. Conical Y. ½M. W of Lt.V.

NEWARP 52°48.4′N, 01°55.8′E. Lt.F. Fl. 10 sec. 21M. R. hull, Lt.Tr. amidships, 12m. Shown H24. Horn 20 sec. H24. Racon.
WRECK BY. Pillar B.Y.B. Topmark E off Winterton Ness.
WINTERTON RIDGE
S WINTERTON RIDGE. Lt.By. Q.(6) + L.Fl. 15 sec. Pillar Y.B. Topmark S.
N WINTERTON RIDGE. Lt.By. Q. Pillar B.Y. Topmark N.
HAMMOND KNOLL
HAMMOND KNOLL. Lt.By. Q.(9) 15 sec. Pillar Y.B.Y. Topmark W.
HAISBOROUGH SAND
S HAISBRO' Lt.By. Q.(6) + L.Fl. 15 sec. Pillar Y.B. Topmark S. Bell.
MIDDLE HAISBRO' Lt.By. Fl.(2)G. 5 sec. Conical G.
N HAISBRO' Lt.By. Q. H.F.P. Pillar B.Y. Topmark N. Bell. Racon.

OWER BANK
DR1 Lt.By. L.Fl. 10 sec. H.F.P. R.W.V.S. Topmark Sph. Horn. 10 sec. ∿. This By. is in connection with the new deep draught route from N Hinder to Indefatigable Banks and German Bight. E of Well Bank.

TRIMINGHAM RG STN. 52°54.6′N, 1°20.7′E.
Emergency DF Stn. VHF Chan. 16 & 67. Controlled by MRCC Yarmouth.

CROMER TO HUNSTANTON POINT

HAPPISBURGH. 52°49.2′N, 1°32.3′E. Lt. Fl.(3) 30 sec. 14M. W. Tr. with R. bands. 41m.

OFFSHORE WAYPOINT OFF CROMER. 52°58.0′N, 1°22.0′E

CROMER 52°55.5′N, 1°19.1′E. Tel: Cromer (0263) 2507.
Lt.Ho. Fl. 5 sec. 23M. W. octagonal Tr. 84m. R.C. Racon.
LIFEBOAT HOUSE. Lt. 2 F.R. vert. 5M. Bl. and W. wooden building, 8m.
SHERINGHAM. Lt.Bn. F.R. 3M. R. post, 12m. shown till 2030.
SHERINGHAM SHOAL
E SHERINGHAM. Lt.By. Q.(3) 10 sec. Pillar B.Y.B. Topmark E. Horn. 10 sec.
W SHERINGHAM Lt.By. Q(9) 15 sec. Pillar Y.B.Y. Topmark W.
BLAKENEY OVERFALLS. Lt.By. Fl.(2)R. 5 sec. Can.R. Bell w.a.

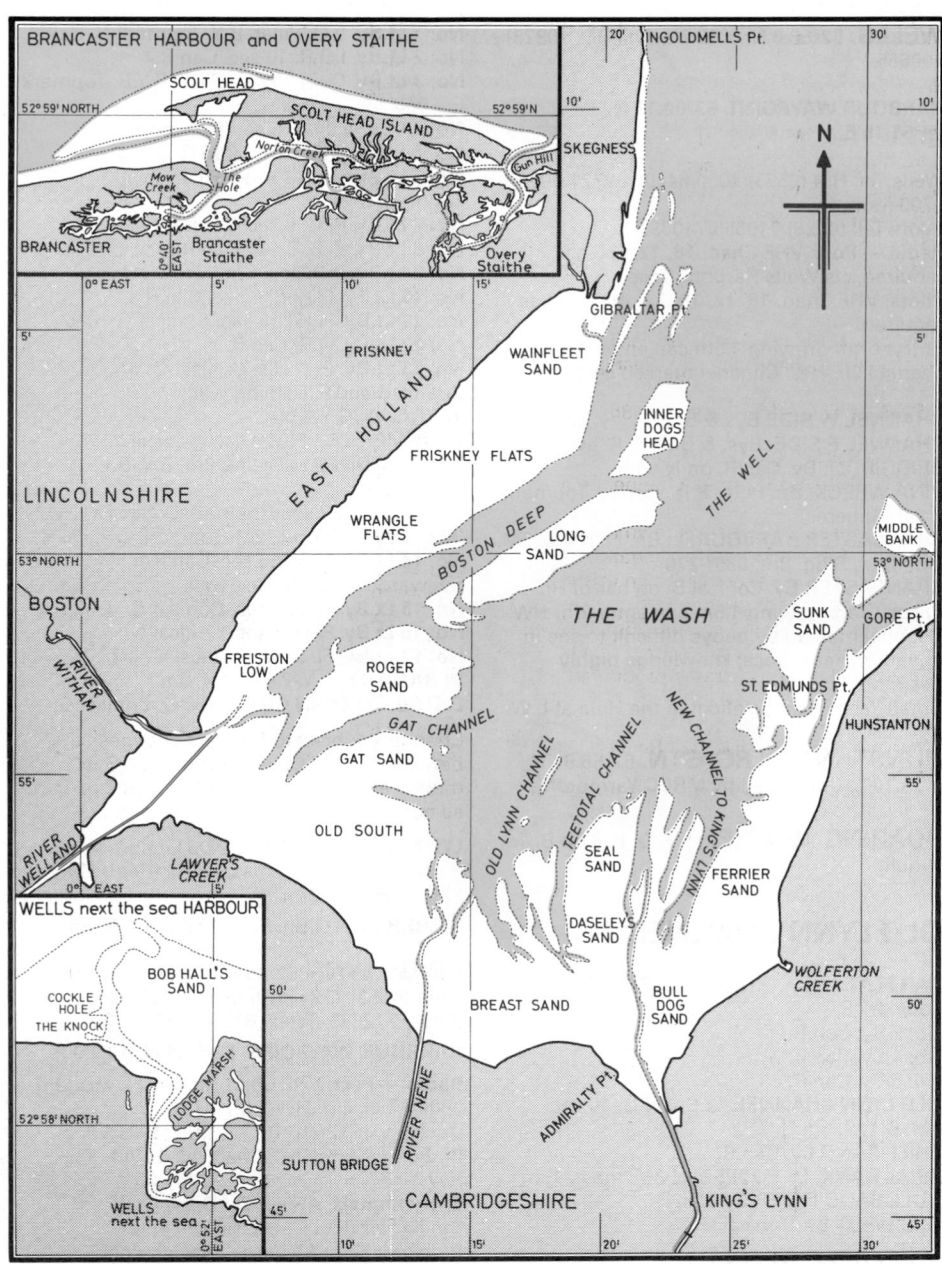

HJORDIS WRECK By. Conical G.
BLAKENEY No. 1 By. Conical G. Q. April-Oct.

BLAKENEY HARBOUR

HARBOUR WAYPOINT. 52°59.0´N, 0°59.0´E.
Blakeney Hbr. Pilot & Cruising Assoc.
Boatman. Tel. (0263) 740362.

Channel into Blakeney Hr. is buoyed.
Entry: Craft drawing 1.5m enter 2h.-HWS-2½h.
or 1½h.-HWN-1½h. Anchorage off Morston
Creek
Ldg. Bns. 170°. Or. moved as required by
changes in channel.

WELLS FAIRWAY Lt.By. Q. 53°00'.15N,
0°51'.12E.

WELLS. 52°58.6'N, 0°50.7'E. Tel: HM. (0328) 710655.

HARBOUR WAYPOINT. 53°00.17'N, 00°51.15'E.

Wells Tel: HM (0553) 4090/64402/62721 0900-1700 Mon.-Fri.
Pilots Tel: (0328) 710655/71039.
Radio — Port: VHF Chan. 16, 12, 6, 8 as required, c/s Wells Harbour Base.
Pilots: VHF Chan. 16, 12, 13. 2 h.-HW and as required.
Entry: Craft drawing 1.5m can enter Wells channel 2h.-HW. Channel marked by buoys.

CHANNEL W SIDE Bys & Bns. Fl. ev. sec.
CHANNEL E SIDE. Bys. & Bns. Fl.R. ev. sec.
BRIDGIRDLE By. Can.R. on N edge.
VINA WRECK. Bn. Pillar B.R. stripes. Topmark 2 × B. Spheres.
BRANCASTER HARBOUR. Lt.Bn. Fl. 5 sec. 3M.
Golf Club Bldg. 8m. 080°-270°.
BRANCASTER By. Conical B. on bar of Hr.
Entry: Craft drawing 1.5m can enter 2½h.-HW. Channel marked by buoys difficult to see in onshore winds. Local knowledge highly desirable.
Small Yachts can lie afloat in the Hole at L.W.

HUNSTANTON RG. STN. 52°56.94'N, 0°29.70'E. Controlled by MRCC Yarmouth.

ROARING MIDDLE. Lt. F. Q. B. ♿ on B. Tr. Y. hull.

OLD LYNN CHANNEL

BAR FLAT. Lt.By. Q.(3) 10 sec. Pillar B.Y.B. Topmark E.
No: 2 By. Can.R.
No: 4 By. Can.R.
No: 6 By. Can.R.
OLD LYNN CHANNEL. Lt.Bn. Fl.G. 10 sec. 1M. B. Col. 6m.
THIEF SAND By. Can.R.
TRIAL BANK. Lt. Fl.(2) 5 sec. 3M. mast. 13m.
HULL SAND INNER By. Can.R
OLD WEST By. Conical G.

Old Lynn Chan. upper end navigable only by light draught vessels with local knowledge.

CORK HOLE CHANNEL TO KING'S LYNN

SUNK. Lt.By. Qk.Fl.(9) 15 sec. Pillar Y.B.Y Topmark W.

No: 1 Lt.By. V.Q. Pillar. B.Y. Topmark N. Bell.
No: 2 Lt.By. I.Q.R. 10 sec. Can.R.
No: 3 Lt.By. Q.(3) 10 sec. Pillar B.Y.B. Topmark E. 〰〰
No: 3A Lt.By. Fl.G. 5 sec. Conical G.
No: 4 Lt.By. Fl.R. 5 sec. Can.R.
No: 5 Lt.By. Q.(3) 10 sec. Pillar. B.Y.B. Topmark E.
No: 7 Lt.By. Fl.G. 5 sec. Conical G.
No: 8 Lt.By. Fl.R. 5 sec. Can.R.
No: 9 Lt.By. Fl. 5 sec. Conical G. 〰〰 .
No: 10 Lt.By. Fl.(2)R. 6 sec. Can.R.
No: 11 Lt.By. Fl.(3) 10 sec. Conical G. 〰〰 .
No: 12 Lt.By. Q.R. Can.R.
No: 13 Lt.By. Fl. 1 sec. Conical G. 〰〰 .
Seaward end E Training wall.
W TRAINING WALL
W DUMP. Lt.By. Fl.Y. 4 sec. Conical Y.
WEST STONES Lt.Q. 2M. 3m. B.Y. Bn. Topmark N.
'B'Lt.Bn. Fl.Y. 2 sec. Topmark Conical Y. 2M.
'E' Lt.Bn. Fl.Y. 6 sec. 2M. Topmark Conical Y.
No: 14 Lt.By. Fl.R. 2.5 sec. Can.R.
Seaward end E Training wall.
No: 15 Lt.By. Fl.G. 3 sec. Conical G. 〰〰 .
No: 16 Lt.By. Fl.G. 3 sec. Conical G.
No: 17 Lt.By. Fl. 3 sec. Conical G. 〰〰 .
W BANK. Lt. Fl.Y. 2 sec. 4M. 3m.
ENTCE. TO LYNN CUT. Lt.By. Q. Conical G.

Channels subject to frequent changes between No: 7 Lt.By. and Lynn Cut. Bys. moved accordingly, with additional Bys. laid as necessary.

LYNN CUT. 52°47.0'N, 0°22.6'E Ldg.Lts. 155°. (Front) Q.R. 3M. on mast, 11m. (Rear) Q.R. 3M. on mast, 16m.

MARSH CUT Lt.Bn. Fl.G. 3 sec. Col. B. 3m.

KINGS LYNN 52°45'N 0°24'E. Tel: Kings Lynn (0553) 773411. Telex: 817588. Docks: (0553) 772636. Telex: 81368 ABP KL G.
HARBOUR WAYPOINT. 52°56.5'N, 0°23.0'E.
Radio — Port: VHF Chan. 16, 11, 14. Mon-Fri. 0800-1730. 4 h.-HW-1 h.
Docks. VHF Chan. 16, 14, 11. 2½ h.-HW-1 h.
Radio — Pilots: VHF Chan. 16, 11, 14. 3 h.-HW-1 h.
Entry Signals: Alexander Dock.
Bu. flag or R. Lt. — vessel can enter.
R. flag or G. Lt. — vessel leaving dock.

ALEXANDER DOCK ENTRANCE

S SIDE Siren 30 sec. at HW.
FERRY JETTY HEAD. Lt. Fl.Y. 2 sec. shown on Tide recorder on Ebb Tide.

CARTWRIGHTS JETTY E END. Lt. Q.G. G. tr. 3m.

WISBECH CHANNEL (RIVER NENE TO WISBECH)

ROARING MIDDLE. Lt. F. Thence.
BAR FLAT. By. Wisbech Pilots. Thence.
No: 1 Lt.By. Fl.G. 5 sec. Conical G. on W. side of Chan.
WESTMARK KNOCK. Lt.By. Fl.(2)R. 6 sec. Can.R. E side.
RAF No: 1 By. Conical Y.
RAF No: 2 By. Conical Y.
RAF No: 3 By. Conical Y.
RAF No: 4 Lt.By. V.Q.(3) 5 sec. Pillar B.Y.B. Topmark E.
FENLAND. Lt.By. Fl.(3)G. 10 sec. Conical G. ⎷⎷⎷.
DALE. Lt.Bn. Fl.G. 2 sec. Mast.
DOUBLE BRUSH. Lt.Bn. Qk.Fl.G. X. on Bn.
BIG TOM. Lt.Bn. Fl.(2)R. 10 sec. Bn.R.
WALKER. Lt.Bn. Fl.G. 5 sec.

RIVER NENE

W END. Lt. Fl.G. 5 sec. 3M. on B. mast, seaward end of wall.
MARSH. Lt. Q.R.
W BANK SCOTTISH SLUICE. Lt. Fl.G. & Q.G. vert. on mast.
E BANK, E CUT. Lt.Bn. Q.R.
W BANK, HARRIS. Lt.Bn. F. & Q. vert.
CROSS KEYS BRIDGE. Lt. Fl.R. Tr. Bridge sig. F.Lt. shown from each of two dolphins on bridge.
FOUL ANCHOR CORNER W SIDE. Lt. Fl. 5 sec. vert. & F. on mast.
FERRY CORNER. Lt. Fl. 5 sec. vert & F. on mast.
DAGLESS YACHT JETTY. Lt. 2 F.R. vert.

WISBECH 52°51'N 0°13'E. Tel: (0945) 582125/61369 0900-1700: (Night). Port: 582701 Pilots: 582870.

HARBOUR WAYPOINT. 52°55.5'N, 0°17.0'E.

Radio — Port: VHF Chan. 16, 14, 9. 0900-1700 and tidal when v/l expected.
Radio — Pilots: VHF Chan. 16, 9, 14 — 3 h. before to H.W. when vessels expected.
Entry Signals: Sutton Bridge. When app. bridge from either direction, normal Lts. bridge closed against traffic are 1 fixed R. Lt. on bridge tr. Preparatory signal for passage of river traffic, R. Lt. changes to Amber. When passage clear amber changes to G. The E and

W Dolphins of bridge are marked by fixed W. Lts.
Anchorage: Bar Flat By. to No. 1 By.

WISBECH
BATH COTTAGES. Lt. F.R.
SWINGING BERTH, NW CORNER. Lt. F.R.
PORT SUTTON BRIDGE 52°46'N, 0°12'E.
Tel: (0406) 351133. Fax: (0406) 350503.
Telex: 329194 Bridge.
Radio-Port: VHF Ch. 16.9
Entry: For pilotage see Wisbech.
SAND FLEET RANGE. By. Can.Y.

SKEGNESS TO BOSTON

SKEGNESS. By. Conical G.
WAINFLEET ROADS/SWATCHWAY.
WAINFLEET RANGE. Lt. U.Q.R. Control Tr. F.R. 3M. also shown on Trs. 2.3M. SW to 2.2M. NE when range operational.
SKEGNESS SOUTH By. Conical G.
WAINFLEET ROADS. By. Can.R.
INNER KNOCK. By. Can.R.
POMPEY. By. Conical G.
SWATCHWAY. By. Conical G.
PARLOUR CHANNEL (betw. Inner Dogs Head & Long Sand).

FREEMAN CHANNEL, LYNN WELL TO BOSTON DEEP

BOSTON ROADS. Lt.By. L.Fl. 10 sec. Sph. R.W.V.S.

P.I. By. Conical G.
P.A. By. Can.R.
P.B. By. Can.R.
LONGSAND. By. Conical G.⎫ off NW Longsand
FRISKNEY. By. Conical G. ⎭ Bank
SCULLRIDGE. By. Conical G. off Scullridge Bank.

BOSTON No: 1. Lt.By. Fl.G. 3 sec. Conical G. ⎷⎷⎷ on N side of Entce. to Chan.
ALPHA. Lt.By. Fl.R. 3 sec. Can.R. on S side Chan. Entce.
BRAVO. Lt.By. Fl.R. 6 sec. Can.R.
BOSTON No: 3. Lt.By. Fl.G. 6 sec. Conical G. ⎷⎷⎷.
CHARLIE. Lt.By. Fl.R. 3 sec. Can.R.
BOSTON No: 5. Lt.By. Fl.G. 3 sec. Conical G.
FREEMAN INNER. Lt.By. Q.(9) 15 sec. Pillar Y.B.Y. Topmark W.
DELTA. Lt.By. Fl.R. 6 sec. Can.R.
THENCE TO ECHO Lt.By.

Thence to Boston or River Welland via Lower Road.

HOLBEACH RANGE (Old S Middle)
No: 4 Lt.Bn. Fl.Y. 10 sec.
No: 3 Lt.Bn. Fl.Y. 5 sec.
NW END. Lt.Bn. Fl.R. 5 sec. Flagstaff.
SE END. Lt.Bn. Fl.R. 5 sec. Flagstaff.

BOSTON 52°58'N 0°01'W. Tel: H.M. (0205) 362328. Dock Office (0205) 365571. Telex: 378114 BOSDOCK. Pilots (0205) 362114.

HARBOUR WAYPOINT. 52°57.5'N, 0°17.0'E.

Radio — Port: c/s Boston Dock. VHF Chan. 16, 12 — Mon.-Fri. 0700-1700, also 3 h. before to 2 h. after HW. Maintain listening watch on Ch. 12 if seaward of Grand Sluice (Boston) or Bridge (Fosdyke), outwards to Welland Bn. or inwards from Golf Lt.By. Traffic Broadcast 2h - HW and at HW.
BOSTON GRAND SLUICE. VHF Chan. 73.
Radio — Pilots: Freeman Channel cutter, VHF Chan. 16, 12, MF 2182, 2241, 2246, 2301 kHz — 2½ h. before to 2 h. after H.W.
Entry Signals: Boston Dock.
Inward by Day: Bl. flag at mast head Dock Entrance — vessels may approach jetty or lock. Flag half mast — jetty or lock foul. No flag — gates closed. 2 Bl. flags — Proceed to S Roundhead.
Inward by Night: R. Lt. jetty end — lock not ready; vessels may come alongside jetty. G. Lt. — lower gates open, lock ready for entering. G. and R. Lts. together — level through, both gates open. Additional R. Lt. — jetty and lock foul. G. over 2 R. Lts. — Proceed to Roundhead.
Outward bound by Night: R. Lt. E end of Dock — lock foul, remain in berth. G. Lt. — approach lock. R. and G. Lts. — both gates open. Proceed.
Vessels fitted VHF call Dock Control for movement information and directions.
Boston Marina Tel: (0502) 64420.

LOWER ROAD
ECHO. Lt.By. Fl.R. 3 sec. Can.R.
BOSTON No: 7 Lt.By. Fl.G. 3 sec. Conical G. Edge of W bank of Lower Road.
FOXTROT. Lt.By. Fl.(2)R. 6 sec. Can.R.
BOSTON No: 9 Lt.By. Fl.G. 3 sec. Conical G.
GOLF. Lt.By. Fl.R. 3 sec. Can.R.
BOSTON No: 11 Lt.By. Fl.G. 6 sec. Conical G.
HOTEL. Lt.By. Fl.R. 3 sec. Can.R.
BOSTON No: 13 Lt.By. Fl.G. 6 sec. Conical G.
INDIA. Lt.By. Fl.R. 6 sec. Can.R
JULIET. Lt.By. Fl.R. 3 sec. Can.R.

BOSTON No: 15 Lt.By. Fl.G. 3 sec. Conical G. River Witham to Boston above Tabs Head Lt. marked by Beacons. W. Ldg.Lts. and Or. Turning Lts.
ENTCE. N SIDE, DOLLYPEG. Lt.Bn. Q.G. 1M. B. ∆ on Bn. ⌇⌇.
TABS HEAD. Lt. Q. W.G. W. shore-251°; G. 251°-shore. 1M. ⌇⌇. Tide gauge.
NEW CUT. Lt.Bn. Fl.G. 3 sec. B. ∆ topmark. Tidegauge.
NEW CUT. Ldg.Lts. 240°. (Front) F. 4M. (Rear) F. 4M. on masts.

RIVER WELLAND
FOSDYKE BRIDGE. 52°52'N, 0°02'W. Tel: 0205 85240.
Radio — Port: Call Sign: Fosdyke Radio VHF Chan. 16, 14. During ship movements on River Welland.

Tidal Streams
Fosdyke Wash –0345 Immingham = Flood begins
+0100 Immingham = Ebb begins.
Vessels drawing 3.7m can reach Fosdyke Bridge at HW Springs.
Vessels drawing 1.8m can reach Fosdyke Bridge at HW Neaps.
Vessels drawing 2.1m can reach Spalding at HW Springs.

FOSSDYKE & WITHAM (Manually operated locks).
TORKSEY (Tidal Lock). Tel: (042-771) 202. VHF Chan. 16 & 74. Contact Lock Keeper direct.
STAMP END LOCK. Tel: (0522) 25749. Mon.: 0800-1730. Tues.-Fri.: 0700-1730; Sat.: 0700-1200. Contact Lock Keeper direct outside these hours.
BOSTON (Tidal Lock). Tel: (0205) 64864. VHF Chan. 16 & 74. Vessels requested to book passage through lock at least 24 h. in advance.

WELLAND Lt. Bn. Q.R.
L1 Lt. Iso. G. 2 sec.
L2 Lt. Iso. R. 2 sec.
L3 Lt. Q.G.
L4 Lt. Q.R.
L5 Lt. Iso. G. 2 sec.
L6 Lt. Fl.(2)R. 6 sec.
L7 Lt. Q.G.
L8 Lt. Iso. G. 2 sec.
L8A Lt. Iso. R. 2 sec.
L9 Lt. Q.G.
L10 Lt. Q.R.
L12 Lt. 2 F.R. vert.
STONE JTY. Lt. 2 F.G. vert.

W RIDGE. Lt.By. Q.(9) 15 sec. Pillar Y.B.Y. Topmark W.
RACE BANK
S RACE. Lt.By. Q.(6) + L.Fl. 15 sec. Pillar Y.B. Topmark S. Bell.
N RACE. Lt.By. Fl.G. 5 sec. Conical G. off N end of bank. Bell.

OFFSHORE WAYPOINT OFF DOCKING SHOAL (THE WASH). 53°10.0′N, 0°38.0′E.

DOCKING SHOAL
E DOCKING. Lt.By. Fl.R. 2½ sec. Can.R.
N DOCKING. Lt.By. Q. Pillar B.Y. Topmark N.

INNER DOWSING SHOAL

OFFSHORE WAYPOINT OFF S INNER DOWSING. 53°12.0′N, 0°30.0′E.

INNER DOWSING 53°19.7′N, 0°34.0′E. Lt. Fl. 10 sec. 21M. R. Tr. on W. house, 41m. Horn 60 sec. Racon (Lts. Fl.R. 2 sec. each corner shown when Main Lt. inoperative).
S INNER DOWSING. Lt.By. Q.(6) + L.Fl. 15 sec. Pillar Y.B. Topmark S. Bell.
SCOTT PATCH. Lt.By. V.Q.(3) 5 sec. Pillar B.Y.B. Topmark E.

THE WELL (ENTRANCE TO THE WASH)

BURNHAM FLAT. Lt.By. V.Q.(9) 10 sec. Pillar Y.B.Y. Topmark W. ⌇⌇. Bell w.a.
N LYNN WELL Lt.By. L.Fl. 10 sec. H.F.P. Pillar R.W.V.S. Topmark Sph. w.a. whis.
LYNN KNOCK. Lt.By. Q.G. Conical G.

INSHORE WAYPOINT OFF WOOLPACK. 53°03.25′N, 0°29.4′E.
WOOLPACK Lt.By. Fl.R. 10 sec. Can.R. ⌇⌇.

INSHORE WAYPOINT OFF S OF WOOLPACK. 53°01.0′N, 0°26.0′E.

OUTER DOWSING SHOAL

DUDGEON 53°16.6′N, 1°17.0′E. Lt.V. Fl.(3) 30 sec. 25M. R. hull, Lt.Tr. amidships, 12m. Shown by day when fog sig. operating. Distress sig. R.C. Horn(4) 60 sec. Racon.
WATCH. By. 330° x 2.5 cables Can.R. with W. reflecting panels.
MIDDLE OUTER DOWSING. Lt.By. Fl.(3) G. 10 sec. Conical G.
N OUTER DOWSING. Lt.By. Q. Pillar B.Y. Topmark N.

DOWSING 53°34.0′N, 0°50.2′E. Lt.V. Fl.(2) 10 sec. 23M. R. hull, Lt.Tr. amidships, 12m. Shown by day when fog sig. operating. Distress sig. Horn (2) 60 sec. Racon.
DUDGEON SHOAL
E DUDGEON. Lt.By. Q.(3) 10 sec. Pillar B.Y.B. Topmark E. Bell.

NORTHWARDS to HUMBER

PROTECTOR OVERFALLS. Lt.By. Fl.R. 2½ sec. Can.R.
DZ No: 7 Lt.By. Fl.Y. 15 sec. Can.Y.
DZ No: 6 Lt.By. Fl.Y. 10 sec. Can.Y.
DZ No: 5 Lt.By. Fl.(4)Y. 20 sec. Can.Y.
DZ No: 4 Lt.By. Fl.Y. 5 sec. Can.Y.
DZ No: 3 Lt.By. Fl.Y. 2.5 sec. Can.Y.
DONNA NOOK. Bombing target. △ lattice Y.
DZ No: 2 Lt.By. Fl.Y. 10 sec. Can.Y.
DZ No: 1 Lt.By. Fl.Y. 15 sec. Can.Y.
ROSSE SPIT. Lt.By. Fl.(2) 5 sec. Can.R.

INSHORE WAYPOINT OFF ROSSE SPIT. 53°30.75′N, 0°18.0′E.

OFFSHORE WAYPOINT HUMBER. 53°37.0′N, 0°24.0′E.

HUMBER 53°35′N 0°23′E. Tel: V.T.S. (0482) 701787. H.M. (Hull) (0482) 27235. Telex: 597656 VTS HUM G. Pilots: (0964) 650392. Pilot Manager: (0482) 224026. Immingham Dock (0469) 73441. Telex: 52250. King George Dock (0482) 783538. Drypool Radio (0482) 222287. Booth Ferry Br. (0430) 430256. Tetney Oil Terminal (0472) 814101. Fax: (0472) 210275. Telex: 527055 COTH G.
Radio — Port: VTS Humber. VHF Chan. 16, 12 — continuous. Initial contact should be made with this station for all general, pilotage, berthing, navigational and tidal inf. and dual watch kept i.e. Chan. 12 + area Chan. or Chan. 16 + area Chan. River Humber approaches Chan. 12. Lower, Middle, Upper Humber Chan. 12. River Ouse, Chan. 14. R. Trent, Apex to Keadby Bridge, Chan. 8. R. Trent, Keadby Br. to Gainsborough, Chan. 6.
Grimsby Docks. VHF Chan. 16, 14, 18, 9 — continuous. Call Royal Dock Island.
Immingham Docks. VHF Chan. 16, 19, 22, 9 — continuous.
Saltend. VHF Chan. 16, 19 — continuous.
Hull, King George Dock. VHF Chan. 16, 9, 10, 20 — continuous.
River Hull Port Operations Service (Drypool Radio): VHF Chan. 16, 10, 14. Mon.-Sat. 2 h. before- 1 h. after HW Hull.
Albert Dock. VHF Chan. 16, 9. 4 h. before to 4 h. after HW Hull.

Blacktoft Jetty. VHF Chan. 14 — 3½ h. before to ¾ h. after H.W. Goole.

Goole Docks. VHF Chan. 16, 14 — continuous.

Viking Comm. Services. VHF Chan. 16, 9 — continuous.

Booth Ferry Bridge. VHF Chan. 9.

Selby Rail Bridge. VHF Chan. 9.

Selby Toll Bridge. VHF Chan. 9.

Tetney Base. VHF Chan. 16, 19, 48 — continuous.

Oil Base. VHF Chan. 9 — continuous.

Radio — Pilots: Spurn Pilots. VHF Chan. 16, 14 (Spurn) 11 (Hull Roads) H24.

Entry: Tide Surge Barrier River Hull Lts. Q.Fl.Y. and foghorn. When exhibited river is closed.

Signals: Immingham — Main signals No. 2 and 5 of International Port Traffic Signals shown at Albert Dock, King George Dock. Upstream Lt. Tower E side of Lock North End: 44m. above M.H.W. Downstream Lt. Tower office block Immingham Oil Terminal: 15 m. above M.H.W.

Daylight Lt.: 2 secs. on/2 secs. off/2 secs. on/4 secs. off — vessel ent./leaving or manoeuvring off Dock.

Night Lt. (Lower intensity): 2 secs. on/9 secs. off — vessel berthing or sailing from I.O.T. Jetty.

HUMBER (Salt End)

Signals: Salt End. Semaphore Arm lowered/G.Lt. = vessel may approach.

Semaphore Arm hor./R.G. Lt. = no vessel to approach. Vessel berthing/unberthing.

Hull Roads — CAUTION

Vessels warned not to anchor, from time of H.W. throughout the ebb, between the meridian of 0°17'W and a line running N and S through Alexandra Dock Gates.

Measured Distance: 2M. 1M. between each pair bns. 3 pairs bns. B. poles (12m. high) with black circular disc topmark. Course 112°-292' (Mag.). Off Sunk Spit (in Sunk Roads), 7M. above Spurn Point. Depth on course 6-12m.

HUMBER 53°36.72'N, 0°21.60'E. Lt.By. L.Fl. 10 sec. Pillar. R.W.V.S. Bell. Racon.

NORTH BINKS. Lt.By. Fl.Y. 2.5 sec. Conical Y. ᗜᔑ.

OUTER HAILE. Lt.By. Fl.(4)Y. 15 sec. Can. Y. ᗜᔑ.

SOUTH BINKS. Lt.By. Fl.Y. 5 sec. Conical Y.

OUTER BINKS No: 1 By. Pillar B.Y.B. Topmark E.

River Humber main appr. chan. is S of Spurn Lt.V. and Chequer No: 3 Lt.By. N of Bull Lt.V. and then inwards on the Killingholme Ldg.Lts. 292°T.

SPURN 53°33.5'N, 00°14.3'E. Lt.F. Q.(3) 10 sec. 8M. ᛜ on B. Twin Hull. Y.B. Tr. 10m. F. Riding Lt. Racon. Horn 20 sec.

EAST CHEQUER Lt.F. V.Q.(6) + Lt.Fl. 10 sec. Y.B. Topmark S. Horn 30 sec. ᗜᔑ.

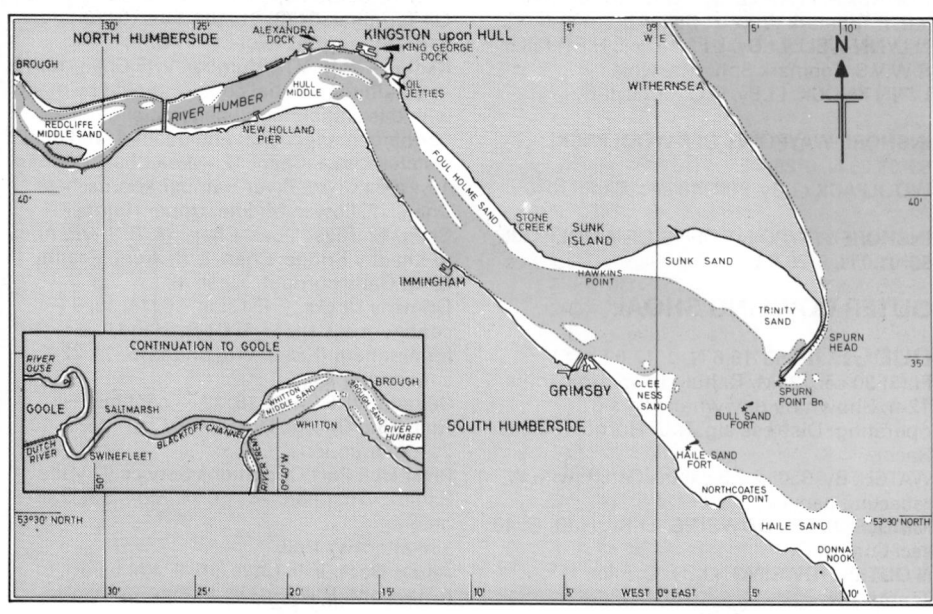

CHEQUER SHOAL. No: 3 Lt.By. Q.(6)+Lt.Fl. 15 sec. Pillar Y.B. Topmark S.
No: 3A BINKS. Lt.By. Fl.G. 4 sec. Conical G.
SPURN PT. Lt.Bn. Fl.G. 3 sec. 5M. 11m. Topmark Cone G.
MILITARY PIER HEAD. Lt. 2 F.G. vert. on mast.
PILOT JETTY Lt. 2 F.G. vert. each end.

HAILE SAND No: 2 Lt.By. Fl.(3)R. 10 sec. Can.R.
No: 2B Lt.By. Fl.R. 4 sec. Can.R.

TETNEY
MONO MOORING By. Lt.(2). V.Q.Y. vert. Can. Y. Horn Mo (A) 60 sec.

No: 2C Lt.By. Fl.R. 2 sec. Can.R.

BULL 53°33.8'N, 0°05.7'E. Lt. F. V.Q. 7M. Horn (2) 20 sec. B.Y. Topmark N.
BULL SAND FORT. Lt. Fl.(2) 5 sec. Topmark Is D. 4M. mast on fort. Horn 30 sec.
HAILE SAND FORT. Lt. Fl.R. 5 sec. 3M. mast on fort, 21 and 19m.
CLEETHORPES. 53°33'N, 0°00'E. Lt.Bn. 2 F.R. vert. 4M. 5 and 3m. on dolphin.
PIER HEAD. Lt. 2 F.R. vert.

No: 4 Lt.By. Fl.R. 4 sec. Can.R.
GATE No: 5 Lt.By. Fl.G. 4 sec. Conical G.
No: 5A Lt.By. Fl.G. 2 sec. Conical G.
CLEE NESS. No: 4A Lt.By. Fl.(2)R. 10 sec. Can.R. Bell w.a.
No: 4B Lt.By. Fl.R. 2 sec. Can.R.

NOTE: USE OF SUNK DREDGED CHANNEL BY PLEASURE CRAFT IS PROHIBITED

HAWKE CHANNEL AND SUNK ROAD

HAWKE Lt.F. V.Q.(3) 5 sec. B.Y.B. Topmark E.
Dolphin Lt.Bn. 2 F.G. vert. G. Cone Topmark.
No: 51 Lt.By. Q.G. Conical G.
No: 53 Lt.By. Fl.G. 4 sec. Conical G.
No: 54 Lt.By. Q.(3) 10 sec. Pillar B.Y.B. Topmark E.
No: 55 Lt.By. Q.(6) + L.Fl. 15 sec. Pillar Y.B. Topmark S.
No: 55A Lt.By. Fl.G. 4 sec. Conical G.
No: 56 Lt.By. Fl.(2)R. 6 sec. Can.R.
No: 56A Lt.By. Fl.R. 4 sec. Can.R.
No: 56B Lt.By. Fl.R. 4 sec. Can. R.
No: 57 Lt.By. Fl.G. 4 sec. Conical G.
No: 58 Lt.By. Fl.R. 4 sec. Can.R.
No: 59 Lt.By. Fl.G. 4 sec. Conical G.
No: 60 Lt.By. Fl.R. 4 sec. Can.R.

No: 61 Lt.By. Fl.G. 4 sec. Conical G.
No: 62 Lt.By. Fl.R. 4 sec. Can.R.
No: 63 Lt.By. Q.(9) 15 sec. Pillar Y.B.Y. Topmark W.

GRIMSBY 53°35'N, 0°04'W. Tel: Grimsby Port Manager (0472) 48111/59181. Dk.M. (0472) 42871. Telex: 52250 ABPGY G. Fax: (0472) 48275.
Entry Signals: Grimsby. Signals from mast on W side of 21 m. Lock (to seawards).
Dock Master requires 2 h. notice before moving.
Royal Dock. Incoming vessels.
International Port Traffic Signals shown 250m. SW.
G.W.G. = Vessel having D.M's permission by VHF may proceed.
R.R.R. = Vessels may not proceed.
Traffic is one way only.
GRIMSBY MARINA. Tel: (0472) 360404. VHF Chan. 18, 9. See Section 25.

Entered through Royal Dock, Union Dock and thence through Bridge with clear height 3.2m above dock H.W. Hours: 3½ h.-HW-2½ h. Craft up to 23.4m. × 4.5m. draught. Clearance under motorway bridge varies 3 m. to 6m.

Royal Dock Basin. Dredged Channel marked on Eastern edge by B. and W. Can. By. Western Limit marked by Leading Posts with Cross as Topmark, situated W side of 21 m. Lock.
Fish Docks. Incoming vessels.
Minimum depth water at which signals shown for vessels to enter Fish Docks is 5 m. on the 11 m. Lock Sill.
Signals made from mast on Fish Dock Is. W of 13m. Lock.
International Port Traffic Signals:
G.W.G. = V/l having D.M. permission by VHF may proceed.
R.R.R. = V/l may not proceed.
Above Lts. Oc. 10 sec. to distinguish from Royal Dock Lts.
RESTRICTED AREA OFF GRIMSBY 200m. RADIUS. 53°36.5'N, 0°05.48'W.
Lt.By. Fl.(3)Y. 9 sec. Can.Y.
If passage is made S of The Middle, course should be altered to pass S of No. 5 Gate Light-buoy (starboard hand) thence follow the marked channel S of Grimsby Middle. On approaching Middle No. 7 light-float (S cardinal) pass SW of it, then steer NW to the leading line alignment (292°) and adhere to it until abreast of Immingham Oil Terminal. When on passage in Grimsby Middle inward bound vessels must keep strictly to the N side of the channel and outward bound vessels strictly to the S side.

If using Hawke and Sunk channels, when approaching Spurn Head steer to pass E of Hawke light-float, thence being guided by the light-buoys. A depth of about 8.8m is usually maintained in the channel but consult chart regarding depths in Sunk Channel.

SEWER OUTFALL. Lt. 2 F.R. vert. 5M. on dolphin, 5 and 3m.
FISH DOCK.
E PIER. Lt. Iso.R. 4 sec. 8M. on brown metal Col. 10m. Horn 20 sec.
MIDDLE PIER HEAD. Lt. Fl.Y. 2½ sec. 8M. brown wooden mast, 10m.
W PIER Lt. Iso.G. 4 sec. 8M. brown wooden mast, 10m.
ROYAL DOCK
E PIER HEAD. Lt. Fl.(2)R. 6 sec. 8M. brown metal Col. 10m.
W PIER HEAD. Lt. Oc.G. 2 sec. 2M. brown metal Col. 7m. Bell. 10 sec.
NW ELBOW. Lt. Oc.G. 2 sec. 2M. brown metal Col. 12m.

S SHOAL Lt.By. Q.(6) + L.Fl. 15 sec. Pillar. Y.B. Topmark S.
LOWER BURCOM. No: 6 Lt.F. Fl.R. 4 sec. Bell. R. Hull.
MIDDLE No: 7 Lt.F. V.Q.(6) + L.Fl. 10 sec. Y.B. Topmark S. Horn. 20 sec.
No: 6A Lt.By. Fl.Y. 1.5 sec. Sph.Y.
No: 6B Lt.By. Fl.Y. 2 sec. Sph.Y
PYEWIPE OUTFALL. Lt.By. Fl.Y. 5 sec. Can Y.
MIDDLE BURCOM No: 8 Lt.By. Fl.(2)R. 6 sec. Can.R.
No: 7A Lt.F. Fl.G. 1.5 sec. Conical G. ⌄⌄⌄ .
UPPER BURCOM. No: 10 Lt.By. Fl.R. 4 sec. Can.R.
HOLME RIDGE. No: 9 Lt.By. Fl.G. 4 sec. Conical G. Bell w.a.
No: 10A Lt. F. Fl.(2)R. 6 sec. R. Hull. F. Riding Lt. Bell.
No: 9A Lt.By. Q.(6) + L.Fl. 15 sec. Pillar Y.B. Topmark S.
HOLME. No: 11 Lt.By. Fl.G. 4 sec. Conical G.
No: 11A Lt.By. Fl.(3)G. 9 sec. Conical G. ⌄⌄⌄ .

IMMINGHAM
IMMINGHAM OIL TERMINAL JETTY
SE END Lt. 2 Q.R. vert. on dolphin. Horn Mo.(N) 30 sec.
No: 2 BERTH, SE END. Lt. 2 F.R. vert.
No: 1 BERTH NW END. Lt. 2 F.R. vert. 2M. 5m.
NW END A1. Lt. 2 Q.R. vert. 5M. Dolphin.
FINGER PIER. Lt. F.R.
PASSAGE. Lt. F.R. each side of passage to shore side. F.G. each side of passage to N side.

IMMINGHAM DOCK.
E JETTY HEAD. Lt. 2 F.R. vert. 3M. R. metal framework Tr. 9 and 7m. Horn (2) 120 sec.
ELBOW. Lt. 2 F.R. vert. 5M. on Col. 8 and 6m. International Port Traffic Signals shown. Main Signals No. 2 and No. 5. Instructions for approaching Locks or berthing on E or W Jty given on Chan. 19 or 22 or by VTS Humber on Chan. 12.
W JETTY ELBOW. Lt. 2 F.R. vert. 3M. on Col. 8 and 6m.
W END. Lt. 2 F.R. vert. 5M.
No: 1 MOORING DOLPHIN. Lt. 2 F.R. vert 3M. Horn 25 sec.
FOUL HOLME CHANNEL
No: 71 HOLME DEPOSIT. Lt.By. Q.G. Conical G.
No: 71A Lt.By. Fl.G. 4 sec. Conical G.
No: 72 Lt.By. Fl.R. 4 sec. Can.R.
No: 73 Lt.By. Fl.G. 4 sec. Conical G.
CLAY HUTS No: 13 Lt.F. Iso. 2 sec. 9M. R.W.V.S. Topmark Sph. Bell w.a.
HOLME HOOK. No: 15 Lt.By. Fl.G. 4 sec. Conical G.
HALTON MIDDLE No: 15A. Lt.By. Q.G Conical G.

NORTH HOLME. No: 17 Lt.F. V.Q.(9) 10 sec. B. ⌶ on B.Y. hull.
PAULL SAND. No: 19 Lt.By. Fl.G. 4 sec. Conical G.
THORNGUMBALD CLOUGH. Ldg.Lts. 135°. (Front) Oc. 2 sec. 9M. W. Tr. 8m. vis. 130°-140°.
(Rear) Oc. 2 sec. 9M. R. Tr. on metal framework Tr. 13m. Synchronised with front, vis. 130°-140°.
No: 19A Lt.By. Fl.G. 2 sec. Conical G.

KILLINGHOLME 53°38.8'N, 0°12.9'W Ldg.Lts. 292°. (Front) Iso.R. 2 sec. 14M. W. Tr. 10m. vis. 287°-297°. (Rear) Oc.R. 4 sec. 14M. R. Tr. 21m. vis. 287°-297°.

S KILLINGHOLME
LPG JETTY. SE END. Lt. 2 Oc.R. 5 sec. vert.
NE END. Lt. 2 Oc.R. 5 sec. vert.
S DOLPHIN. Lt. 2 F.R. vert. Horn. Mo(G) 60 sec.
N DOLPHIN. Lt. 2 F.R. vert.
OIL JETTY HEAD SE END. Lt. 2 Q.R. vert, synchronized.
NW END. Lt. 2 Q.R. vert. synchro. Horn(3) 60 sec.
MOORING DOLPHINS. Lts. 2 F.R. vert.

SHOALING. Mariners are warned that changes are taking place in the area and they should navigate with caution.

N KILLINGHOLME

JETTY Lt. 2 F.G. vert. Mast 7m.
OIL JETTY, OFF S END. Lt. 2 F.R. vert. 2M. on dolphin, 15m. Horn(2) 30 sec. F.R. Lt. shown above each of two navigational spans for river craft..
OFF N END. Lt. 2 F.R. vert. 2M. on dolphin, 15m.

KILLINGHOLME No: 12. Lt.By. Q.R. Can.R.
SKITTER HAVEN. No: 14 Lt.By. Fl.R. 4 sec. Can.R.
SAND END. No: 16 Lt.F. Fl.R. 4 sec. 3M. R. hull. Bell w.a.
ELBOW. No: 18 Lt.By. Fl.R. 4 sec. Can.R.

SALT END

No: 3 BRANCH JETTY
SE END. Lt. 2 F.G. vert. on Bn., 7 and 5m.
DOLPHIN. Lt. 2 F.G. vert. 6m.
CENTRE. Lt. F.G. vis. 353°-127°. Traffic Sig. Horn Mo(U) 60 sec.
NW END. Lt. 2 F.G. vert. Horn Mo(U) 60 sec.
Lts in Line 000° (Front) Oc.Y. 4 sec. 9m. Y. 'X' on Bn. Downstream limit of dredged area (Rear) Oc.Y. 4 sec. 15m. Y. 'X' on Bn.

No: 1 JETTY
SE END. Lt. 2 F.G. vert.
CENTRE. Lt. F.G. on mast. vis. 333°-103°. Traffic Sig.
NW END. Lt. 2 F.G. vert. on Bn., 7 and 5m.
Lts in Line 104° (Front) Oc.Y. 6 sec, 9m. Y. 'X' on Bn. Upstream limit of dredged area (Rear) Oc.Y. 6 sec. 12m. Y. 'X' on Bn.

HALF TIDE WALL. Lt. 2 F.G. vert. 2M. 5 and 3m. G. Δ on structure.
No: 26A. Lt.By. Fl.R. 2 sec. Can.R.

ANSON. No: 20 Lt.By. Fl.R. 4 sec. Can.R.
HEBBLES. No: 21 Lt.By. Fl.G. 1½ sec. Conical G.
HOOK. No: 22 Lt.By. Fl.R. 4 sec. Can.R.
KING GEORGE DOCK. Entrance W Side. Fog Signal. Bell (3) 10 sec. Tr. Docking Signals.
E SIDE. Lt. V.Q.Y. Post Y. in line with Docking Sigs. mark E side of channel.
W SIDE. Lt. Q.Y. Post Y. in line with Docking Sigs. mark W side of channel.
W BULLNOSE. Lt. 2 F.G. vert.
KING GEORGE DOCK. Lt.Bn. F.R.G.Or. Sectors. on W side of Dock Entce. mark dredged area.
EAST MIDDLE. Lt.By. Q.R. Can.R.
HULL MIDDLE DEPOSIT. Lt.By. Fl.Y. 10 sec. Conical Y.
LOWER W MIDDLE. No: 24 Lt.By. Fl.R. 4 sec. Can.R.
UPPER W MIDDLE. No: 26 Lt.By. Fl.R. 4 sec 3M. Can.R.

HULL ROADS

Vessels are warned not to anchor from time of H.W. throughout the ebb, between the meridian of 0°17'W and a line running N and S through Alexandra Dock gates.

ALEXANDRA DOCK ENTRANCE Lts. in line 357° (Front) U.Q.Y. Y. Δ on post, 9m. Marks E. limit of dredged area. Shown when vessels berthing/unberthing. (Rear) U.Q.Y. Y. Δ on post 11m.

ALEXANDRA RIVER QUAY
SE CORNER. Lt. 2 F.G. vert. 2M. on mast, 5 and 4m.
W END. Lt. 2 F.G. vert. 2M. on mast, 5 and 4m.
VICTORIA PIER. E END. Lt. 2 F.G. vert. Q.Y. and Horn 2 sec. used for tidal surge barrier and swing bridge close by.
PUBLIC LANDING, SE CORNER. Lt. Oc.G. 3 sec. on dolphin.
W CORNER. Lt. 2 F.G. vert. on pile.
Hull Marina: Tel: (0482) 25048. Radio VHF Chan. M. Basin dries out. Lock gates open 3 h.-HW-3 h. Impounded water level 4.5m. Depth over sill at M.H.W.N. 3.9m.
MINERVA PIER. Lt. 2 F.G. vert.
RIVERSIDE QUAY. Lt. 2 F.G. vert. 5 and 3m.
No: 26A. Lt.By. Fl.R. 2½ sec. Can.R.
ST. ANDREW'S DOCK. (closed).
ENTRANCE, NE SIDE. Lt. 2 F.G. vert.
RIVER WALL, W END Lt. 2 F.G. vert. 2M. on mast 6 and 4m.
'T' JETTY Lt. 2 F.G. vert. each end.
Lts. and Lt.F. which mark chan. above Kingston upon Hull are moved as required by changes in the banks.
Vessels for New Holland follow buoyed channel N of Hull Middle, turn S after passing N Middle Lt.By.; W of New Holland Lt.F. (not charted).
NEW HOLLAND SHIPYARD JETTY. Lt. 2 F.R. vert.
NEW HOLLAND PIER
E HEAD. Lt. Fl.R. 3 sec. 7m.
MIDDLE. Horn 15 sec.
W HEAD. Lt. Fl.R. 3 sec. 7m.
DOCK ENTRANCE. Lts. 2 F.R. and 2 F.G. (Occas.).
No: 23 HESSLE SAND. Lt.F. Fl.G. 2 sec. G. hull. Bell w.a.
BARROW HAVEN. Lt.Bn. 2 F.R. vert.
No: 28. Lt.F. Fl.R. 4 sec. R. hull. Bell w.a.
No: 28A. Lt.F. Fl.R. 4 sec. R. hull. Bell w.a.
BARTON HAVEN
PIER EASTERN END. Lt. 2 F.R. vert.
WESTERN END. Lt. 2 F.R. vert.
HESSLE HAVEN
SHIPYARD. Lt. 2 F.G. vert.

HUMBER BRIDGE. Ht. 30m.
S TOWER PIER.
EASTERN END. Lt. 2 F.R. vert.
WESTERN END. Lt. 2 F.R. vert. Horn 20 sec.
BOAT JETTY. Lt. 2 F.R. vert.
N TOWER PIER.
BOAT JETTY. Lt. 2 F.G. vert. Horn (2) 20 sec.
Tide Gauge.

ANCHOLME CHANNEL.
CHALDERNESS. Lt.Bn. 2 F.R. vert. Tide gauge (illuminated).
No: 27 Lt.F. Fl.G. 2 sec. G. hull. Bell 20 sec.
No: 32 Lt.F. Fl.R. 2 sec. R. hull. Bell w.a.
No: 29 Lt.F. Fl.G. 4 sec. G. hull. Bell w.a.
No: 36 Lt.F. Fl.R. 4 sec. R. hull. Bell w.a.

JETTY. Lt.Bn. 2 F.G. vert. G. cone Topmark.
No: 31. Lt.F. Fl.G. 2 sec. G. Hull.
LOWER WHITTON Lt.F. Fl.(3)G. 10 sec. G. hull. Horn 15 sec.
JETTY Lt.Bn. 2 F.G. vert. G. cone Topmark.
No: 33 Lt.F. Fl.G. 2 sec. G. hull. Bell w.a.
No: 33A Lt.F. Fl.G. 4 sec. G. hull. Bell w.a.

BROUGH TIDE GAUGE DOLPHIN. Lt.Bn. 2 F.G. vert. Tide gauge (illuminated).
SLIPWAY. Lt.Bn. 2 F.G. vert.
MIDDLE WHITTON. Lt.F. Fl.(3)R. 10 sec. R. hull. Bell.
UPPER WHITTON. Lt.F. Fl.(2)R. 10 sec. R. hull. Horn(2) 40 sec.
No: 34 Lt.F. Fl.R. 4 sec. R. hull. Bell w.a.

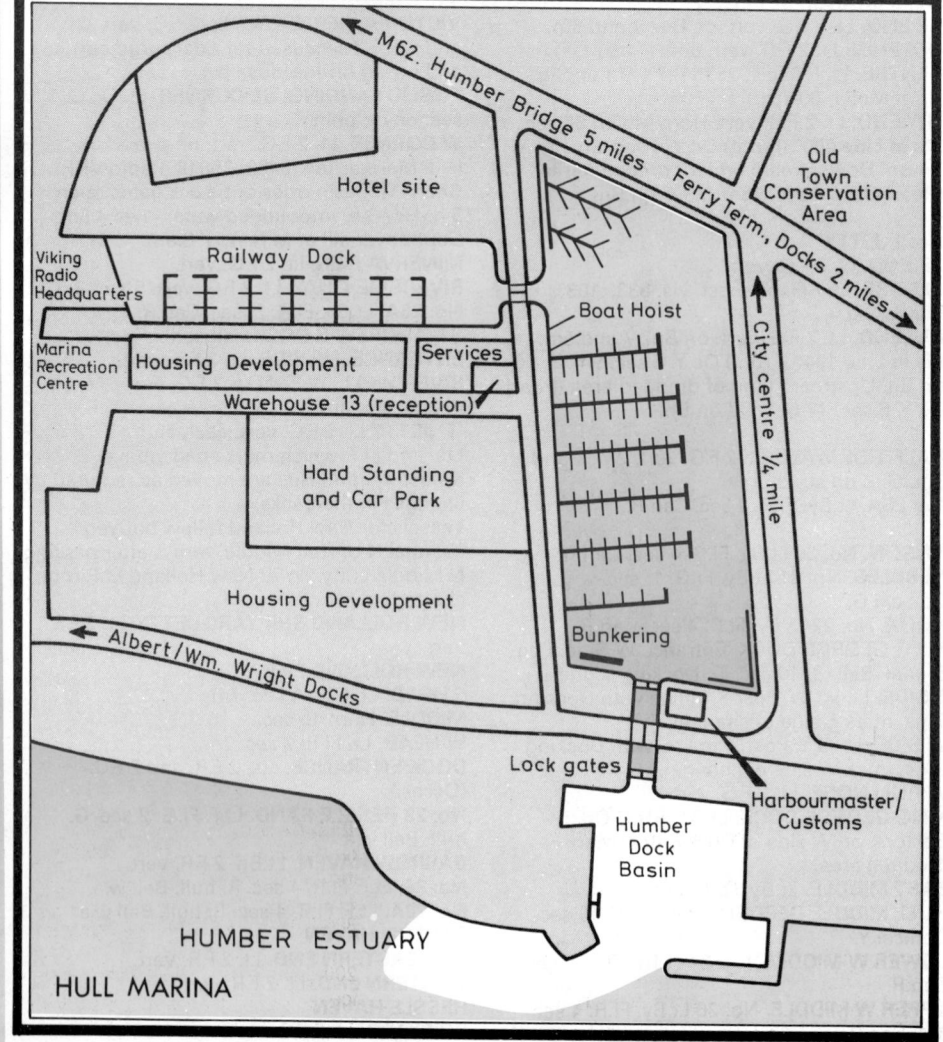

No: 40 E WALKER DYKE. Lt.Bn. Fl.R. 2 sec. on dolphin.
No: 42 W WALKER DYKE. Lt.Bn. Fl.R. 4 sec. on dolphin.

APEX. Lt.Ho. Fl.(3)W.R. 5 sec. R. steel Tr. on dolphin. Shows R. in direction of River Ouse and W. in direction of River Trent. Horn(2) 15 sec.

RIVER OUSE
FAXFLEET NESS. Lt.Bn. Fl.G. 6 sec. G. cone Topmark. Marks N side River Ouse Entce.
E OUSE. Lt.Bn. Q.R.
BISHOPSOIL. Lt.Bn. Q.G.
W OUSE. Lt.Bn. Fl.R. 4 sec.
BLACKTOFT JETTY. Lt.Bn. 2 F.G. vert. each end. Tide gauge.
BLACKTOFT. Ldg.Lts. 286° (Front) Fl.G. 2.5 sec. (Rear) Oc.G. 8 sec.
YOKEFLEET. No: 5 Lt. Q.G.
COMMONPIECE LANDING. No: 6 Lt. Fl.R. 2.5 sec.
YOKEFLEET CLOUGH. No: 7 Lt. Fl.G. 2.5 sec.
WHITGIFT MILL. No: 8 Lt. F.R.
WHITGIFT PIER No: 10 Lt. 2 F.R. vert.
WHITGIFT BIGHT No: 12 Lt. F.R.
COTNESS No: 9 Lt. Fl.G. 2.5 sec.
CRABLEY STAITH. No: 14 Lt. F.R.
COTNESS DRAIN. No: 11 Lt. Q.G.
REEDNESS. No: 17 Lt. Fl.R. 2.5 sec
No: 13 Lt. Fl.G. 4 sec.
GROVES STAITH No: 15 Lt. Fl.G. 2.5 sec.
LOWER SALTMARSHE. No: 17 Lt. Fl.G. 4 sec.
HALL STAITH. No: 19 Lt. Q.G.
UPPER SALTMARSH. No: 21 Lt. Fl.G. 4 sec. 2M. W. hut 5m.
BANK HOUSE STAITH. No: 23 Lt. Fl.G. 2.5 sec.
No: 25 Lt. Q.G.
SWINEFLEET ORCHARD. No: 18 Lt. F.R.
SWINEFLEET PIER. No: 20 Lt. 2 F.R. vert
SOUTH SWINEFLEET. No: 22 Lt. F.R.

GOOLE 53°42'N, 0°52'W. Tel: Goole (0405) 2691. Telex: 57626 ABPGO G.
Radio — Port: VHF Chan. 14. H24.
Entry Signals: Ocean Lock:
Ball/Diamond (R./G. Lt.) = Lock preparing for V/l to enter.
Diamond (G. Lt.) = Lock ready.
Diamond and Ball/Diamond (G./R./G. Lt.) = Vessel leaving and entering tideway.
Ocean Lock 2½ h.-HW-½ h. 7 days.
Victoria Lock 3¼ h.-HW Mon.-Fri.
Ouse Lock occasionally. Locks also available 0800-1615. Mon.-Fri.

Berthing facilities in Aire and Calder Canal entered through South Dock.
Waiting permitted at Blacktoft Jetty or Victoria Pier subject permission and payment.
GOOLE BIGHT. No: 24 Lt. F.R.
WEST GOOLE. No: 26 Lt. F.R.
ERNSHAW CLOUGH. No: 28 Lt. F.R.
LOWER EAST GOOLE. No: 27 Lt. Fl. G. 2.5 sec.
UPPER EAST GOOLE. No: 29 Lt. Q.G.
PORT OF GOOLE. No: 32 Lt. F.R.G. Siren 20 sec.
E. CHANNEL Ldg. Lts. 325° (Rear) F.R. 5M. W. mast. 7m. MIDDLE PIER (Common Front) F.R. 5M. W. mast 5m. W. CHANNEL Ldg. Lts. 334°30' (Rear) F.R. 5M. W. mast 7m.
SANDHALL REACH TRAINING WALL. No: 31 Lt. Fl. G. 2.5 sec.
UPPER SANDHALL. No: 33 Lt. Fl. G. 4 sec.
SANDHALL LODGE. No: 35 Lt. Q.G.

HOWENDYKE (2.5M upstream from Goole). Office hours Tel: (0430) 430646, Fax (0430) 431581. After hours Tel: (0405) 61873 or (0469) 60004. Telex: 57604 or 52156 HSLHOW G. Radio: VHF Ch. 09 (for mooring/unmooring only).

NOTTINGHAM
(British Waterways Board. Tel: 0602 862411)
Locks fitted VHF Chan. 16, 74 (working).

Lock	Tel. No
RIVER TRENT	
Gunthorpe	0602 663821
Newark Town	0636 702226
Newark Nether	0636 703830
Cromwell	0636 821213
Hours of opening: Mon. 0600-2100;	
Tues.-Sun. 0600-2200.	
Holme	0602 811197
Stoke	0602 878563
Hazleford	0636 830312
UPPER TRENT & RIVER SOAR	
Sawley	0602 735234
Cranfleet	0602 732490
Beeston	0602 254946
Meadow Lane	0602 862414
Redhill	05097 2359

CHESTERFIELD CANAL
West Stockwith (Tidal Lock)   0427 890204
Lock operational for periods for 7 h. per tide, 2½ h.-HW-4½ h.
Between 0800-2200 give as much notice as possible.
Between 2200-0800 lock must be booked 24 h. in advance.
Ansaphone when lock keeper absent.

CASTLEFORD

(British Waterways Board. Tel: 0977 554351. Associated British Ports.

Craft owners navigating in/out Goole Docks from lower Aire and Calder Navigation will not be charged by A.B.P. 3¼ h.-HW-½ h.

Locks fitted VHF Chan. 16 & 74:

Aldwarke, Barnby Dun, Birkwood, Bramwith, Bulkholme, Castleford, Doncaster, Ferrybridge, Fishpond, Frank Price, Keadby, Kilnhurst, Kings Road, Kippax, Kirk Lane Bridge, Knostrop, Leeds Section Office, Lemonroyd, Long Sandall, Mexborough Low & Top, Moors Bridge, Pollington, Rotherham Section, Selby, Skyehouse Road Bridge, Sprotbrough, Swinton Office, Sykehouse, Thorne, Tinsley Flight, Toplane Bridge, Vazon's Bridge, Waddington, Whitley, Woodlesford, Woodnock, Wykewell Bridge. Aire & Calder Navigation.

Goole to Leeds; Castleford to Wakefield (Broadreach Lock). All locks and bridges are manned.

Selby Lock. Tel: 0757 703182. Give ETA to lock keeper, preferably the day before arrival.

Keadby Lock. Tel: 0724 782205. Notify ETA to lock keeper giving 24 h. notice if possible.

RIVER TRENT

N TRENT. Lt.Bn. Fl.G. 8 sec.
S TRENT. Lt.Bn. V.Q.G. 2M. 4m. W. wooden pile on dolphin.
TRENT NESS. Lt. Fl.R. 2 sec.
FLATS. Lt.Bn. Q.R.
CLIFF END. Ldg.Lts. 152° (Front) No: 44 Q.R. (Rear) Q.
HILLSIDE. Lt. Fl.R. 2 sec.
GARTHORPE SHORE. Lt.Bn. Q.G.
DOLPHIN. Tide gauge.
JETTY. Lt. 2 F.G. vert.

BURTON STATHER JETTY. Lt. 2 F.R. vert.
SOLITARY HOUSE. Lt. Fl.R. 2 sec.
WATERTON. Lt.Bn. Q.G.
WADDINGTON. Lt.Bn. Q.G.
GRANGE. Lt. Q.R.
MERE DYKE. Lt. Q.G.
MAN REVAL. Lt. Q.G.

FLIXBOROUGH WHF. Lt. 2 F.R. vert.
PARKINGS. Lt. Q.R.
NEAP HOUSE NORTH. Lt. Fl.R. 2 sec. frame Tr. 4m.
NEAP HOUSE WHARVES. Lt. 2 F.R. vert.
GROVE WHARVES. Lt. 2 F.R. vert.
GROVE. Lt. Q.G.
AMCOTTS HOOK. Lt. Q.G.
BAR. Lt. Q.G.

KEADBY. Lt. Q.G. (Wharf Lt. 2 F.G. vert.).

GUNNESS WHARF. Lt. 2 F.R. vert.
KEADBY BRIDGE. Lt. 2 F.Y. vert. 2 F.G. vert. F.Y. 2 F.R. vert. Ht. 5.1m. Air draught boards illuminated.

COAST NORTHWARD FROM RIVER HUMBER

EASINGTON RG STN. 53°39'.09"N, 0°05'.54"E. Emergency DF Stn. VHF Chan. 16 & 67. Controlled by MRSC Humber.

NE OF SPURN HEAD
Lt.By. Q. Spherical R.W.B.hor. bands.
Lt.By. Q.R. Spherical R.W.B.hor. bands.
Lt.By. Q. Spherical R.W.B.hor. bands.
SOTA EDUARDO WK. N. Lt.By. Q. Pillar B.Y. Topmark N.
DUPLICATE N. Lt.By. Q. Pillar. B.Y. Topmark N.
S Lt.By. Q.(6) + L.Fl. 15 sec. Pillar Y.B. Topmark S.

CANADA/GEORGIOS Lt.By. V.Q.(3) 5 sec. Pillar B.Y.B. Topmark E.
DZ SOUTH Lt.By. Fl.Y. 2 sec. Can.Y.
DZ No: 5 Lt.By. Fl.Y. 5 sec. Can.Y.
DZ No: 4 Lt.By. Fl.Y. 10 sec. Can.Y.
DZ NORTH Lt.By. Fl.Y. 2 sec. Can.Y.
DZ No: 2 Lt.By. Fl.Y. 10 sec. Can.Y.
DZ No: 3 Lt.By. Fl.Y. 10 sec. Can.Y.

HORNSEA. Sewer Outfall Lt.By. Fl.Y. 20 sec. Can.Y.

BOMBING AREA. 53°56'N, 0°11'W Flagstaff. Lt. Fl.R. 5 sec. and 4 F.R. when air gunnery and bombing practice in progress.

INSHORE WAYPOINT BRIDLINGTON BAY. 54°02.5'N, 0°10.0'W.

MRSC HUMBER (0262) 672317. Weather broadcast ev. 4h. from 0340.

BRIDLINGTON 54°05'N, 0°11'W. Tel: Bridlington (0262) 670148.

HARBOUR WAYPOINT. 54°05.0'N, 0°10.0'W.

Radio Port: VHF Chan. 16, 12, 14.
Entry: Run in keeping N Pier Head Lt. 002°
Tidal signals shown from Sig.Stn. 50m. from S Pier Head: F.G. Lt. (No signal by Day) = Less than 2.7m. in harbour. F.R. Lt. (R. flag by Day) = More than 2.7m. in harbour. R. Flag over W. flag with Bl. circle = harbour not clear.

N PIER HEAD. Lt. Fl. 2 sec. 9M. Horn 60 sec.
S PIER HEAD. Lt. F.R. or G. 4M. Col. Tidal Lts.
Sig. Stn.
BRIDLINGTON OUTFALL. Lt.By. Fl.Y. 5 sec.
Can.Y.
SW SMITHIC. Lt.By. Q.(9) 15 sec. Pillar Y.B.Y.
Topmark W.
N SMITHIC. Lt.By. Q. Pillar B.Y. Topmark N.
Bell.
RANGE MARKER. By. 2 × DZ Lt.Bys. Q.Y. Sph.
Y.

**OFFSHORE WAYPOINT FLAMBOROUGH
HEAD. 54°07.0′N, 0°00.0′E/W.**

FLAMBOROUGH 54°07.0′N, 0°04.8′W.
Lt.Ho. Fl.(4) 15 sec. 29M. W. circular Tr. 65m.
Obscured within 8M. out to 1.5M. from coast
northward and in N part of Bridlington Bay.
R.C. Storm Sig. Horn.(2) 90 sec.

FLAMBOROUGH RG Stn. 54°07.1′N
0°05.0′W. Emergency DF Stn. VHF Chan. 16 &
67. Controlled by MRSC Humber.

PRODUCTION PLATFORMS — NORTH SEA

Main L. M(U) 15 sec. Secondary Lt. M(U)R. 15
sec. 1 each corner of platform synchronised.
Horn Mo(U) 30 sec.

The following are permanent oil and gas
installations in the North Sea. Safety zones of
radius 500m. have been established, centred
on each of them. Entry into these zones is
prohibited without authorisation except when
in distress. Closely integrated complexes
have only a single position listed. The
prudent yachtsman is advised to keep well
clear of these rigs in severe weather
conditions.

	°	′	°	′
Camelot Field	52	56.8N.,	02	09.3E.
Welland Gas Field				
53/4-A(B)	52	59.0N.,	02	44.2E.
Rijnfield				
P15-AC	52	17.5N.,	03	49.0E.
P15-B	52	18.5N.,	03	46.7E.
Mobil				
P12-SW	52	24.4N.,	03	45.6E.
P12-C	52	24.6N.,	03	51.7E.
P6B	52	44.3N.,	03	48.3E.
PC-A	52	45.3N.,	03	45.4E.

	°	′	°	′
Helmfield				
P6A	52	45.3N.,	03	45.4E.
Q1A	52	52.3N.,	04	08.5E.
Helder Field				
Q1	52	55.3N.,	04	05.9E.
Haven A	52	58.4N.,	04	06.4E.
Hoorn Field				
Q1	52	55.2N.,	04	09.0E.
BP Q8-A	52	35.7N.,	04	31.8E.
Amethyst Field				
A1D	53	36.6N.,	00	43.5E
A2D	53	37.3N.,	00	47.4E
Hewett Field				
48-29-A-FTP (B)	53	01.1N.,	01	47.8E.
48-29-B	53	03.3N.,	01	41.1E.
48-29-C	53	05.8N.,	01	45.9E.
52-5-A	53	00.0N.,	01	50.8E.
Clipper Field				
48-19-A	53	27.5N.,	01	43.9E
Vulcan Field				
48-25PUR	53	15.5N.,	01	58.3E
Barque Field				
48-13	53	36.7N.,	01	31.6E
Audrey Field				
48/15B-PXW	53	34.0N.,	01	58.3E
West Sole Field				
48-6-A PP	53	42.2N.,	01	09.0E.
48-6-B	53	43.1N.,	01	07.1E.
48-6-C	53	45.2N.,	01	04.9E.
Rough Field				
47-8-AD & AP	53	49.5N.,	00	28.3E.
47-3B	53	50.0N.,	00	26.5E.
Pickerill Field				
48/11-A	53	32.9N.,	01	04.7E.
Leman Field				
49-26-A (B)	53	05.4N.,	02	07.8E.
49-26-B	53	04.6N.,	02	11.1E.
49-26-BT	53	04.9N.,	02	10.9E.
49-26-C	53	05.8N.,	02	09.8E.
49-26-D	53	00.6N.,	02	11.2E.
49-26-E	53	03.1N.,	02	11.3E.
49-26-F	53	06.5N.,	02	04.0E.
49-26-G	53	07.1N.,	02	06.3E.
49-27-A	53	03.2N.,	02	14.0E.
49-27-B	53	03.1N.,	02	17.1E.
49-27-C	53	01.6N.,	02	15.4E.
49-27-D	53	01.0N.,	02	20.4E.
49-27-E	53	03.6N.,	02	12.7E.
49-27-F	53	02.5N.,	02	18.9E.
49-27-G	53	02.2N.,	02	22.9E.
49-27-H	53	00.2N.,	02	12.9E.
49-27-J	53	01.9N.,	02	13.2E.
Thames Gas Field				
49-28-4	53	05.5N.,	02	32.9E.
Sean Field				
49-25-A (PD)	53	11.3N.,	02	51.8E.
49-25-A (RD)	53	13.5N.,	02	49.7E.
Indefatigable Field				
49-18-A (B)	53	21.8N.,	02	34.1E.
49-18-B	53	23.5N.,	02	31.5E.

	°	′	°	′
49-19-M	53	21.2N.,	02	36.5E.
49-23-AT	53	19.3N.,	02	34.4E.
49-23-C	53	18.4N.,	02	34.0E.
49-23-D	53	18.1N.,	02	30.2E.
49-24-J	53	19.6N.,	02	37.9E.
49-24-K	53	16.8N.,	02	41.5E.
49-24-L	53	17.9N.,	02	37.2E.
49-24-N	53	17.3N.,	02	43.4E.
Viking Field				
49-12-A and				
F(B)	53	32.1N.,	02	15.5E.
49-17-B	53	26.9N.,	02	19.9E.
49-17-C	53	25.4N.,	02	22.6E.
49-17-D	53	26.5N.,	02	23.7E.
49-16-E	53	26.0N.,	02	09.3E.
49-17-G	53	26.9N.,	02	15.3E.
49-17-H	53	29.7N.,	02	19.5E.
Victor Field				
JD-49-22	53	19.6N.,	02	21.8E.
Vulcan Field				
49-21-PRD	53	14.8N.,	02	01.5E.
Valiant Field				
49-21-PTD	53	19.0N.,	02	05.8E.
49-16-PSB	53	21.4N.,	02	02.4E.
Vanguard Field				
49-16-PQD	53	22.6N.,	02	06.7E.
Loggs 49-16-CP				
49-16-PP	53	23.3N.,	02	00.4E.
Audrey Field				
Phillips 49-11A-				
PWD	53	32.4N.,	02	00.9E.
North Sea Range				
M1 Radio Tower	53	44.8N.,	02	33.5E
R1 Radio Tower	53	56.0N.,	02	24.0E
R2 Radio Tower	53	55.8N.,	02	51.0E
R3 Radio Tower	53	38.5N.,	02	56.8E
R4 Radio Tower	53	29.9N.,	02	30.8E
R5 Radio Tower	53	42.0N.,	02	08.5E
Nam Field				
K7FA1 (NETH)	53	34.3N.,	03	18.3E.
K8FA1 (NETH)	53	30.0N.,	03	22.2E.
K8FA2	53	30.9N.,	03	25.1E.
K8FA3	53	32.5N.,	03	25.4E.
K11FA1	53	27.0N.,	03	20.6E.
Noordwinning Field				
NW-K13-A	53	13.1N.,	03	13.2E.
NW-K13-B1	53	16.0N.,	03	07.0E.
NamField				
K14FA1	53	16.2N.,	03	37.8E.
K15FC-1	53	15.2N.,	03	45.8E.
Kotter	53	04.9N.,	03	57.9E.
K15FA1	53	14.9N.,	03	59.3E.
K14FB1	53	16.6N.,	03	52.4E.
K15-FG-1	53	18.4N.,	03	56.9E.
Placid Field				
K12A	53	28.6N.,	03	49.3E.
K9C-A	53	39.2N.,	03	52.4E.
K12C	53	27.6N.,	03	54.4E.
K-12D	53	25.3N.,	03	53.2E.
K-12BD	53	20.5N.,	03	53.8E.

	°	′	°	′
K-12E	53	28.5N.,	03	59.8E.
K-9AB-A	53	31.2N.,	03	59.6E.
L10A (NETH)	53	24.3N.,	04	12.2E.
L10-L	53	25.1N.,	04	11.1E.
L10B	53	27.5N.,	04	14.0E.
L10C	53	23.6N.,	04	12.1E.
L10D	53	24.6N.,	04	12.9E.
L10E	53	25.9N.,	04	14.2E.
L10F	53	23.2N.,	04	15.6E.
L10G	53	29.5N.,	04	11.8E.
L10K	53	29.6N.,	04	16.2E.
L11A	53	20.2N.,	04	22.7E.
Petroland Field				
L7-P (NETH)	53	32.3N.,	04	12.1E.
L7-CQ	53	32.3N.,	04	12.2E.
L7H	53	37.5N.,	04	08.7E.
L7-N	53	34.4N.,	04	10.6E.
L7-B	53	36.5N.,	04	12.4E.
L4-B	53	40.6N.,	04	00.1E.
L4-A	53	43.5N.,	04	06.0E.
L2-FA-1	53	57.7N.,	04	29.9E.
L7-A	53	36.0N.,	04	05.0E.
L8-A	53	35.1N.,	04	28.3E.
L8-H	53	33.8N.,	04	34.1E.
L8-G	53	34.9N.,	04	36.3E.
Namfield				
L13-FD-1	53	15.8N.,	04	14.9E.
Loggerfield	53	00.9N.,	04	13.0E.
UN-L/11B-PA	53	28.4N.,	04	29.5E.
Inschot. Platform	53	11.2N.,	05	10.0E.
Ameland Oost-2	53	59.0N.,	05	52.1E.
AWG1	53	29.6N.,	05	56.5E.
Cleeton Field				
42-29	54	02.0N.,	00	43.7E.
Raven Spurn Field				
South A 42/30-1	54	01.7N.,	00	58.1E.
South B	54	03.5N.,	00	54.0E.
ST2 43/26	54	03.3N.,	01	02.1E.
South C	54	04.9N.,	00	49.5E.
North CC 43/26	54	01.8N.,	01	06.2E.
Esmond Field				
Esmond 43-13				
CP CW	54	35.3N.,	01	25.0E.
Forbes Field				
43-8-AW	54	41.0N.,	01	29.8E.
Gordon Field				
43-15-BW 43-20	54	30.0N.,	01	56.5E.
GNSC-H7	54	30.6N.,	06	02.1E.
Ekofisk Booster				
36-22A-No.2	55	17.5N.,	00	12.3E.
(NOR)				
Dan Field A (D)	55	28.2N.,	05	08.0E.
B	55	28.2N.,	05	08.1E.
C	55	28.2N.,	05	08.2E.
E	55	28.9N.,	05	07.0E.
F	55	28.7N.,	05	06.4E.
Kraka Field	55	24.2N.,	05	04.8E.
Skojold Field (D)	55	32.0N.,	04	54.0E.
Tyra East Field	55	43.0N.,	04	48.0E.
Tyra West Field	55	43.0N.,	04	45.0E.

	°	′	°	′
Gorm Field A (D)	55	34.8N.,	04	45.5E.
B	55	34.7N.,	04	45.5E.
C	55	34.9N.,	04	45.6E.
D	55	34.8N.,	04	45.7E.
E	55	34.9N.,	04	45.7E.
F	55	34.8N.,	04	45.5E.
Dagmar Field	55	34.5N.,	04	37.2E.
Rolf Field	55	36.4N.,	04	45.5E.
GNSC-B11-(GF)	55	27.8N.,	04	33.0E.
Ekofisk Booster				
37-4A-No.1	55	54.0N.,	01	36.7E.
Auk Field				
30-16A-(B)	56	24.0N.,	02	03.8E.
Fulmar Field				
30-16-A (B)	56	29.5N.,	02	09.3E.
30-16-AQ	56	29.5N.,	02	09.2E.
30-16-SPM	56	28.6N.,	02	07.9E.
Clyde Field	56	27.2N.,	02	17.3E.
Argyll Field				
Deep Sea Pioneer	56	10.7N.,	02	46.9E.
30-24-SPM	56	10.5N.,	02	49.0E.
Eldfisk-2-7A	56	22.6N.,	03	16.0E.
(NOR)				
2-7-B	56	25.2N.,	03	13.1E.
2-7-FTP	56	22.5N.,	03	16.0E.
Edda Field				
2-7-C (NOR)	56	27.9N.,	03	06.3E.
Ekofisk Field				
2-4-A (NOR)	56	31.3N.,	03	13.4E.
2-4-B	56	33.9N.,	03	12.2E.
2-4-C	56	32.9N.,	03	12.9E.
2-4-D	56	33.8N.,	03	05.1E.
2-4-FTP	56	32.8N.,	03	13.0E.
2-4-H	56	32.8N.,	03	12.8E.
2-4-P	56	32.9N.,	03	12.8E.
2-4-Q	56	32.8N.,	03	12.9E.
2-4-R	56	33.0N.,	03	12.7E.
2-4-S	56	33.1N.,	03	12.8E.
2-4-T	56	32.9N.,	03	12.8E.
2-4-SPM1	56	32.1N.,	03	15.6E.
2-4-SPM2	56	33.6N.,	03	15.4E.
2-4-Flare 1	56	32.6N.,	03	13.1E.
2-4-Flare 2	56	33.1N.,	03	12.6E.
Albuskjell Field				
1-6-A (NOR)	56	38.5N.,	02	56.5E.
2.4.F	56	37.2N.,	03	03.2E.
Tor Field				
2-4-E (NOR)	56	38.5N.,	03	19.6E.
Gyda Field 2/1-D/P/Q	56	54.3N.,	03	05.2E.
Valhall Field				
2-8-QP (NOR)	56	16.7N.,	03	23.7E.
Hod Field	56	10.6N.,	03	27.6E.
Forties Field				
21-10-FA (B)	57	43.9N.,	00	58.4E.
21-10-FB	57	45.0N.,	00	54.9E.
21-10-FC	57	43.6N.,	00	50.8E.
21-10-FD	57	43.3N.,	00	54.2E.
21-10-FE	57	43.0N.,	01	01.9E.
Buchan Field				
21-1-A	57	54.2N.,	00	01.9E.
Kittiwake Field				
21/18	57	28.1N.,	00	30.7E.
Montrose Field				
22-17-A (B)	57	27.1N.,	01	23.1E.
Arbroath Field				
22-17-B	57	22.5N.,	00	23.0E.
Cod Field				
7-11-A (NOR)	57	04.2N.,	02	26.1E.
ULA Field				
7-12-D	57	06.7N.,	02	50.8E.
Beatrice Field				
11-30-A (B)	58	06.9N.,	03	05.2W.
11-30-B	58	08.9N.,	03	01.2W.
11-30-C	58	05.7N.,	03	09.1W.
Claymore Field				
14-19-A (B)	58	27.0N.,	00	15.2W.
Frigg Pipeline				
14-9-MCP-01	58	49.6N.,	00	17.2W.
Maureen Field				
16-29-A (B)	58	07.9N.,	01	42.1E.
16-29-SPM	58	07.0N.,	01	43.7E.
Balmoral Field				
Floating Prod. v/l	58	13.8N.,	01	06.5E.
Tartan Field				
15-16-A (B)	58	22.2N.,	00	04.4E.
Rob Roy and Ivanhoe Field				
15-21A	58	11.5N.,	00	06.8E.
Brae Field				
16-7-A	58	41.6N.,	01	16.9E.
16-7A Brae B	58	47.5N.,	01	20.8E.
Ekovisk Booster				
16-11-S	58	11.5N.,	02	28.4E.
Crawford Field				
North Sea Pioneer	59	07.6N.,	01	29.5E.
Beryl Field				
9-13-A (B)	59	32.8N.,	01	32.2E.
9-13-SPM3	59	32.1N.,	01	33.6E.
9-13-SPM2	59	33.2N.,	01	33.7E.
9-13-B	59	36.6N.,	01	30.7E.
Heimdal Field	59	34.4N.,	02	13.7E.
Frigg Field				
10-1-QP (B)	59	52.7N.,	02	03.9E.
10-1FP	59	52.9N.,	02	03.3E.
10-1-TP1	59	52.8N.,	02	03.9E.
10-1-CDP1	59	52.5N.,	02	03.6E.
25-1-DP2	59	53.2N.,	02	04.3E.
25-1-TCP2	59	52.8N.,	02	04.0E.
25-1-FCS	59	59.0N.,	02	15.0E.
Alwyn North Field				
3-9-A	60	48.6N.,	01	44.3E.
Heather Field				
2-5-A (B)	60	57.3N.,	00	56.3E.
Ninian Field				
3-8-Ninian South	60	48.3N.,	01	27.0E.
(B)				
3-3-Ninian				
Central	60	51.7N.,	01	28.2E.
3-3-Ninian North	60	54.7N.,	01	25.6E.

	° ′	° ′
Odin Field		
30-10 (NOR)	60 04.6N.,	02 09.9E.
Oseberg Field		
A+B	60 29.6N.,	02 49.7E.
C	60 36.5N.,	02 46.5E.
Veselfrikk		
Field A	60 47.0N.,	02 53.9E.
Troll Field 31/2-T1		
Petrojarl I.	60 46.0N.,	03 25.4E.
Thistle Field		
211-18-A (B)	61 21.9N.,	01 34.9E.
Dunlin Field		
211-23-A (B)	61 16.5N.,	01 35.9E.
Murchison Field		
211-19-A	61 23.6N.,	01 44.4E.
Magnus Field		
211-12-A (B)	61 37.2N.,	01 18.4E.
Eider Field		
211/16-A	61 21.4N.,	01 09.7E.
Tern Field		
210/25	61 16.6N.,	00 55.2E.
Cormorant Field		
211-26-A (B)	61 06.1N.,	01 04.4E.
North Cormorant		
211-21	61 14.4N.,	01 09.0E.
North West Hutton Field		
211-27-A	61 06.4N.,	01 18.6E.
211-28	61 04.1N.,	01 24.1E.
Brent Field		
211-29-B (B)	61 03.4N.,	01 42.8E.
211-29 Flare		
Stack 1	61 02.8N.,	01 45.4E.
211-29-A	61 02.1N.,	01 42.3E.
211-29C	61 05.8N.,	01 43.3E.
211-29D	61 07.9N.,	01 44.2E.
Spar	61 03.2N.,	01 40.1E.
Statfjord Field		
33-9-A (NOR)	61 15.3N.,	01 51.2E.
33-9-SPM	61 15.4N.,	01 52.4E.
33-12-SPM	61 13.5N.,	01 50.3E.
33-12-B	61 12.5N.,	01 49.8E.
33-9C	61 17.8N.,	01 54.2E.
Gullfaks Field		
34-10-A	61 10.6N.,	02 11.3E.
SPM-1	61 11.5N.,	02 09.4E.
34-10-B	61 12.2N.,	02 12.1E.
34-10-C	61 12.9N.,	02 16.4E.
34-10-SPM2	61 10.0N.,	02 13.8E.

WELLHEADS

Lt.Bys. Sph.Y. either Fl.Y. 5 sec. or Fl.Y. 2½ sec. or Fl.Y. 10 sec. or Fl.(4)Y. 15 sec. mark wellheads on Leman, Hewett, Indefatigable, Rough and Viking Gas Fields. All Wellheads are not marked.

FILEY 54°13′N, 0°17′W. Lt.Ho. F.R. 1M. G. iron Col. 31m. vis. 272°-308°. Storm sig. Fishing Lt.

FILEY BRIGG. Lt.By. Q.(3) 10 sec. Pillar B.Y.B. Topmark E. Bell.

SCARBOROUGH 54°17′N, 0°23′W. Tel: Lt. Ho. (0723) 360684. H.M. (0723) 373530.

HARBOUR WAYPOINT. 54°16.0′N, 0°21.0′W.

Radio — Port & Pilots: VHF Chan. 16, 12. H24. **Signals: Lt.Ho.Masthead.** B. ball — 4m. or more in Ent. R. flag — do not enter. Duty watch kept. **Vincent Pier Lt.** shown when more than 3.7m. on the Bar. Fixed Y. Lt. shown when less than 3.7m. on the Bar but more than 2m.
Berthing limited. Prior booking necessary.
OUTFALL Lt.By. Fl.R. 5 sec. Can R. Marks outfall and diffusers.
E PIER HEAD. Lt. Q.G. 3M. on mast, 8m.
W PIER HEAD. Lt. 2 F.R. vert. 4M. on watch hut, 5m. shown when 1.8m. water on bar.
LIGHTHOUSE PIER. Lt. Iso. 5 sec. 9M. W. round Tr. 17m. vis. 219°-039°. Shown when more than 3.7m. on the bar. Storm and tidal sig. Dia. 60 sec. Also F.Y. Vis. 233°-030° shown when more than 1.8m. and less than 3.7m. on bar.
SW CORNER. Lt. 2 F.G. vert. shown when more than 1.8m. on bar.
BRIDGE. Lt. 2 F.G. vert. shown when more than 1.8m. on bar.
E HARBOUR JETTY HD. Lt. 2 F.R. vert.

OFFSHORE WAYPOINT OFF WHITBY. 54°30.0′N, 0°30.0′W.

WHITBY RG STN. 54°29.35′N, 0°36.22′W. Coastguard Emergency DF Stn. VHF Chan. 16 & 67. Controlled by MRSC Humber.

WHITBY HIGH 54°28.6′N, 0°34.0′W. Lt.Ho. Iso. W.R. 10 sec. 23M. W. octagonal Tr. and dwellings, 73m. R.128°-143°; W.143°-319°.
WHITBY. Lt.By. Q. Pillar B.Y. Topmark N. Bell.

WHITBY 54°30′N, 0°37′W. Tel: (0947) 602354 & 603048. (Night 602147 & 603617).

HARBOUR WAYPOINT. 54°31.0′N, 0°37.0′W.

Radio — Port: VHF Chan. 16, 11, 12. Mon.-Fri. 0830-1730. Sat.-Sun. 1000-1230.
Radio — Pilots: VHF Chan. 16, 6, 11, 12. 2 h. HW-2 h.
Signals: All vessels over 30m. in length wishing to enter without pilot wait until
By day: B. ball } shown from top
By night: G.Lt. } W. Pier Lt.Ho.

Swing Bridge: Fixed G. Lts. — open. Fixed R. Lts. — closed.
If approaching from SE keep Whitby Rock By. to Port. Strong set across pierheads 2 h.-HW. Marina Max. LOA 18.2m, 2m. draught.

E PIER HEAD. Lt. F.R. 3M. on R. wooden house, 14m.
Ldg.Lts. 029°. (Front) F.Y. (Rear) F.Y.
W PIER HEAD. Lt. F.G. on G. wooden house, 14m. Traffic sig. 150m. S. Horn 30 sec.
NR CHURCH. Lt. F.R. 46m.
BOULBY. Lt.By. Fl.(4)Y. 10 sec. Can. Y.

SALTBURN PIER. By. Can.R. F.R.Lts. on radio mast 4.7M. ESE.
OUTFALL. Lt.By. Fl.Y. 10 sec. Pillar Y.

REDCAR (LUFFWAY) 54°37.1′N, 1°03.6′W. Ldg.Lts. 197°. (Front) F.R. 7M. on metal Col. 8m. (Rear) F.R. 7M. on metal Col. 12m. Vis. 182°-212°
OIL TERMINAL Lt.By. Q.R. indicates shoal line when in line with No: 14 Lt.By. Down river of berth.
HIGHSTONE LAID. Ldg.Lts. 247°. (Front) Oc.R. 2.5 sec. 7M. Col. 9m. Vis. 232°-262°. (Rear) Oc.R. 2.5 sec. 7M. Bldg. 11m. Vis. 232°-262°
SALT SCAR. Lt.By. Q. Pillar B.Y. Topmark N. Bell.

MIDDLESBROUGH

RIVER TEES 54°39′N, 1°08′W. Tel: Eston Grange (0642) 452541. Telex: 58145 HMTEES G.
Pilots: (0642) 242924 (590747).
Radio — Port: Tees Harbour Radio: VHF Chan. 16, 14, 22, 12, 11, 8 — continuous. Includes Port Information, operations, and harbour surveillance radar, covering River Tees, Tees Bay and approaches to Hartlepool and seawards for 24M.
Tees Pilots: VHF Chan. 16, 9 — continuous.
Entry Signals: South Gare Lt.Ho. *Traffic Signal* **Night:** 3 F.R. vert. Horn (2) 30 sec. — no vessel to enter app. chan. without H.M.'s permission. **Day:** (Shown from mast on H.M.C.G. Stn.) Fl. 1 sec. 345°-255°.
Best to enter ½ Flood — HW if weather bad. Caution necessary during NW, SE & E gales.
Tees Dock Radar Tower. Night: 3 Lts. vert. R./G./R. **Day:** Lt. Fl. ev. sec. — no vessel to enter Main Chan. to seaward without H.M.'s permission.
Deep draught signal for vessels over 9m. draught — B. cylinder 1.2m. long×0.6m. dia. or 3 R. Lts. vert. Small vessels must keep clear deep draught vessels.

Newport Bridge. (By night).
6 R. Lts. in pairs, vert. 2.4m. apart, on down and upstream face of bridge (2 R. Lts. Durham side; 2 R. Lts. Yorkshire side, 2 R. Lts. centre of main pier) — bridge closed. When all above Lts. show G. — bridge open.

TEES FAIRWAY.
Lt.By. Iso. 4 sec. Pillar R.W.V.S. Topmark Sph. Horn 5 sec.
Ldg.Lts. 210°04′ (Front) F.R. 13M. R.W. Tr. 18m. (Rear) F.R. 10M. Tr. 20m.

TEES NORTH. Lt.By. Fl.G. 5 sec. Conical G. ⌇⌇.
TEES SOUTH. Lt.By. Fl.R. 5 sec. Can.R. ⌇⌇.
No: 1 Lt.By. Q.G. Conical G. ⌇⌇.
No: 2 Lt.By. Q.R. Can.R. ⌇⌇.
No: 3 Lt.By. Fl.(3) G. 5 sec. Conical G. ⌇⌇.

S GARE 54°38.8′N, 1°08.1′W.
Lt.Ho. F.W.R. 12 sec. W.20M. R.17M. W. round Tr. 16m. W.020°-274°; R.274°-357°; Sig. Stn. Storm sig. Horn 30 sec.
No: 4 Lt.By. Fl.(3)R. 5 sec. Can.R. ⌇⌇.
No: 5 Lt.By. Iso.G. 2 sec. Conical G. ⌇⌇.
No: 6 By. Can.R. ⌇⌇.
No: 7 Lt.By. Fl.(3) G. 7½ sec. Conical G. ⌇⌇.
No: 8 By. Can.R. ⌇⌇.
No: 10 Lt.By. Iso.R. 1 sec. Can.R.

Ldg.Lts. 210° (Front) F.R. 13M. R. metal framework Tr. W. bands 18m. (Rear) F.R. 16M. R.W. Hor. bands framework Tr. 20m.

SEATON CHANNEL
DAYMARK BEACONS: On port hand the ½ tide training wall is marked by Bns. Can.R. On starboard hand Bns. surmounted by G. cones point upwards.

PHILLIPS APPROACH. Lt.By. Fl.Y. 2 sec. Conical Y.

No: 9 Lt.By. Q.G. Conical G. ⌇⌇.
Lt.By. Q.G. Conical G.
No: 11 Lt.By. Fl.Y. 5 sec. Conical G. ⌇⌇ marks N side Seaton Chan. Entce.
No: 12 Lt.By. Q.R. Can.R. ⌇⌇.
No: 13 Lt.Bn. I.Q.G. Col. G. Bell 15 sec.
No: 14 Lt.By. I.Q.R. 10 sec. Can.R. ⌇⌇.
No: 15 Lt.By. Fl.(2)G. 5 sec. Conical G. ⌇⌇.
No: 17 Lt.By. Fl.G. 5 sec. Conical G. ⌇⌇.
No: 19 Lt.By. Fl.(4)Y. 5 sec. Conical Y. ⌇⌇ marks downriver limit of turning circle.
No: 20 Lt.By. Oc.R. 10 sec. Can.R. ⌇⌇.
No: 21 Lt.By. Fl.Y. 2 sec. Conical Y. ⌇⌇ marks upriver limit of turning circle.
Lt.By. Fl. 1 sec. Conical G. marks top centre of turning circle.

No: 22 Lt.By. Fl.R. 2 sec. R. 2 Lt. Dolphins 2 F.R. vert. each — one each side of Chan. 6 cables W.
No: 23 Lt.By. Fl.(3)G. 5 sec. Conical G.
No: 25 Lt.Bn. Iso.G. 2 sec. 3M. 4m. B.W. vert. stripes.
No: 27 Lt.By. Q.G. Conical G.

MIDDLESBROUGH DOCK. Lt. 2 F.R. vert.
No: 25 Lt. Fl.(2) G. 5 sec. 3M. Pedestal W.B. vert. stripes 4m.

CLEVELAND TRANSPORTER BRIDGE
From landing stages at Middlesbrough and Port Clarence each side of river, Lts. 2 F.G. vert. are shown. Lts. 2 F. vert. shown from passenger car. CLEAR HEIGHT 49m.
No: 31 Lt. Iso. G. 2 sec. Bn. 4m.
TEES (NEWPORT) BRIDGE. Lts. F.G. (open) F.R. (closed) CLEAR HEIGHT (closed) 6.4m. (open) 36m.
VICTORIA BRIDGE. CLEAR HEIGHT 5.4m.

RIVER TEES — NORTHWARDS
LONG SCAR. Lt.By. Q.(3) 10 sec. Pillar B.Y.B. Topmark E. Bell w.a.
No: 1 Lt.By. Fl.G. 6 sec. Conical G.
No: 2 By. Can.R.
No: 3. Lt.By. Fl.(4)G. 5 sec. Conical G.
No: 4 Lt.By. Fl.(4)R. 5 sec. Can.R.
No: 5 By. Conical G.
No: 6 By. Can.R.

HARTLEPOOL 54°42'N, 1°11'W. Dock Tel: (0429) 266127

HARBOUR WAYPOINT. 54°41.5'N, 1°06.0'W.

Radio — Port: Hartlepool Radio. VHF Chan. 16, 12, 11 — continuous.
Hartlepool Pilots. VHF Chan. 16, 12, 6 — continuous.
Signals: Lt. F. Amber (day and night) — vessels may enter.
No light shown = vessels may leave.
Exhibited from mast close to front Ldg. lt.
Entry: E Arm of Victoria Dock dredged to 5m has pontoon for small craft.

THE HEUGH 54°41.8'N, 1°10.5'W Lt.
Fl.(2)W 10 sec. 19M. W. Tr. 19m.
OLD PIER HEAD. Lt. Q.G. 7M. B. framework Tr. 13m.
MIDDLETON BEACON. Lt. Q.R. R. □5m.
TOWN WALL Lt. 2 F.G. vert.
DIR. Lt. 324°53'. Dir. Iso. W.R.G. 3 sec. Tr. 42m G.323.2°-324.4°; W. 324.4°-325.4°; R. 325.4°-326.6°. 2 F.G. vert. mark pontoon 520m. SE.
PIPE JETTY HEAD. Lt. 2 F.R. vert. 1M. Bell 15 sec.

SEAHAM 54°50'N, 1°19'W. Tel: (091) 581 3246. Operations Office: (091) 581 3877. Telex: 537368 SEADOC G. Pilots: (091-581) 3246 (during tidal period). Customs: (091) 565 7113.

Radio — Port: VHF Chan. 16, 12 — H.M. 2½ h.-HW-1½ h. Ops Office Mon.-Fri. 0900-1700.
Radio — Pilot/Vessel: Chan. 16, 6, 12, when v/l expected.
Entry Signals: Harbour Off. S Dock.
R. square flag at half mast — half tide, vessels prepare to enter.
R. flag raised to masthead — vessels to enter.
R. Lt. shown at night.
Speed limit 5 kts. Small craft moor in N Dock (Dries). Larger craft moor in S Dock. Gates open 2½ h.-HW-½ h.

N PIER HEAD. Lt. Fl.G. 10 sec. 5M. W. metal Col. B. bands (frequently shows F. in bad weather). Dia. 30 sec., sounded from 2½ h.-HW-1½ h.
S PIER HEAD. Lt. 2 F.R. vert. 5M. on metal Col.
WAVE SCREEN HEAD. Lt. 3 F.R. 2M. △ on R. Col. 5m.
S DOCK ENTRANCE. Lts. N. Side. F.G. W. Col. S Side. F.R. W. Col.

SUNDERLAND 54°55'N, 1°21'W. Tel: (H.M.) Sunderland (091) 56 72626. Info Service (091) 51 42752. Pilots: (091) 56 72162.
Entry: Channel dredged to 7.8m. thence 7.6m. and 5.6m.

HARBOUR WAYPOINT. 54°55.0'N, 1°20.0'W.

Radio — Port: VHF Chan. 16, 14 — continuous. Radar advice on Chan. 14.
Pilots: VHF Chan. 16, 14 — H24.
Signals: Displayed at Old N Pier: 3 Fl.R. vert. = Danger. No vessel to enter or leave hr.
Displayed from Old N Pier and/or No. 3 Gate (for S Dock):
3 F.G. vert. = Vessels may pass inwards.
3 F.G. vert. (No. 3 Gate) = Vessels may pass outwards.
3 F.R. vert. (Old N Pier) = Vessels may pass outwards.
3 F.R. vert. (No. 3 Gate) = No vessels to pass in or out of S Dock.
No Signals = Dock Closed.
Anchorage: 1M. NE of Roker Lt.
HENDON ROCK. By. Can.R.

ROKER PIER HEAD 54°55.3'N, 1°21.0'W.
Lt. Fl. 5 sec. 23M. W. round Tr. R. bands and cupola. vis. 211°-357°. Horn 20 sec.
NEW S PIER. Lt. Fl. 10 sec. 9M. W. metal Tr. 14m.
S SIDE. OLD S PIER. HEAD. Lt. Fl.R. 5 sec. 2M. R. □ R. Tr. 20m.

OLD N PIER HEAD. Lt. Q.G. 8M. 12m. Horn 10 sec.
NORTH DOCK BASIN. Lt. Fl.G. 5 sec. G △ Bn.
TIDAL BASIN ENTCE. Lt. 2 F.R. vert. 2m. apart.
N DOCK, E PIER. HEAD. 2 F.G. vert. 2m. apart.

COAST LINE — NORTHWARDS FROM SUNDERLAND

OSLOFJORD/EUGENIA CHANDRIS. Lt.By. 55°00.26′N 1°23.58′W. Fl.(3)R. 10 sec. Can.R.

WHITBURN
Lt.By. Fl.Y. 2½ sec. Can.Y.
Lt.By. Fl.Y. 2½ sec. Can.Y.
FIRING RANGE
F.R. Lt. When firing taking place. (54°57.2′N, 01°21.3′W.)
F.R. Lt. When firing taking place. (54°57.7′N, 01°21.2′W.)

LIZARD POINT

INSHORE WAYPOINT OFF SOUTER POINT.
54°58.0′N, 1°20.0′W.

SOUTER 54°58.2′N, 1°21.7′W. Lt.Ho. F. W. Or. Tr. 43m. 230°-270°. Shown Sunrise + 1 h. — Sunset — 1 h. for calibrating D/F. RC.

MARCHELLER WRECK. Lt.By. V.Q. (3) 5 sec. Pillar Y.B. Topmark E. Wreck in position 54°59.8′N, 1°21.95′W.

TYNE RIVER 55°00′N, 1°27′W. Tel: (091) 257 2080 & 257 0407. Pilots: (091) 455 5656; Br. master: (091) 232 3830.

HARBOUR WAYPOINT. 55°01.0′N, 1°23.0′W.

Radio — Port: VHF Chan. 16, 12, 11, 14 — continuous.
This is the control station. Initial contact should be made and maintained with this station.
Harbour launch. VHF Chan. 16, 12, 6, 8, 11 — continuous.
Masters of vessels fitted with VHF R/T. and intending to enter, shift berth or leave port, to obtain permission from **Tyne Harbour Radio** before doing so. Vessel requiring H.M. sounds 3 short, 1 long blast.
Pilots: Launch VHF Chan. 16, 6, 8, 9, 12, 14 — continuous. Station VHF Chan. 16, 9. — continuous.
Entry: *Vessels entering warned to disregard line of leading Lts. as soon as they have*

passed between pierheads. Boat owners warned to keep at least 152m. from line of leading Lts. into port giving 305m. chan. for shipping for distance of at least 1M. out to sea.
Anchoring and fishing prohibited within the channel and within 6 cables radius of the Fairway By.
Signals: Tyne River/Dock signals — one way traffic system — shown from N. end Tyne Commissioners Quay, W end Engine House Quay, E end Riverside Quay, head of NW Quay:
3 R. Lts. vert = vessels may not proceed.
3 G. Lts. vert = vessels may proceed.
Newcastle Swing Bridge. Closed to river traffic from 0830-0900 and 1600-1800 local time Monday to Friday. Vessels may claim priority during these times if L.W. (for inward vessels) or H.W. (for outward vessels) coincides with the prohibited times.
Inward v/ls request priority from Tyne Hbr.
Radio: Outward v/ls request priority from Br. Master.
R. Lts. or Sound signal = Dangerous to approach.
G. Lts. = safe to approach.
Keep to centre of channel. Beware of Tidal set.

MRSC TYNE TEES (091) 257 2691. Weather broadcast ev. 4h. from 0150.

TYNEMOUTH RG STN. 55°01.06′N, 01°24.90′W. EMERGENCY C.G. D.F. VHF Chan 16 & 67. Controlled by MRSC Tyne/Tees.

ENTCE. N. PIER HEAD Lt.Ho. Fl.(3) 10 sec. 26M. Grey round masonry Tr. W. lantern, 26m. Horn 10 sec.
S PIER HEAD. Lt. Oc.W.R.G. 10 sec. W.13M. R.9M. G.8M. Grey round stone Tr. R.W. lantern, 15m. W.075°-161°; G.161°-179° over Bellhues Rk. W.179°-255°; R.255°-075°. Bell 10 sec.
BLACK MIDDENS No: 1 Lt.By. Q.G. Conical G. marks N side dredged Chan. ⌇⌇.
BLACK MIDDENS No: 2 Lt.By. Fl.(5)G. 15 sec. Conical G.
No: 1 GROYNE. Lt.Bn. Fl.G. 5 sec. 9M. on pole, 6m. ⌇⌇.
HERD SAND. Lt.By. Fl.(2)R. 10 sec. Can.R. ⌇⌇
HERD SAND GROYNE. Pile Structure. Oc.W.R. 10 sec. R. with W. lantern, 13m. Bell.

FISH QUAY. Ldg.Lts. 258°. (Front) F. 20M. W. square Tr. 25m. (Rear) 220m. from front. F. 20M. W. square Tr. 39m.
HOWDEN STAITH. Lt.Bn. 2 F.G. vert. 1M. at W. dolphin, 5 and 3m.

WILLINGTON QUAY. Lt. F. on Custom House Pontoon.
BILL POINT. NAVAL YARD. Lt. Fl.(2)G. 10 sec. 1M. Bn.
BILL QUAY POINT. Lt. Fl.(2)R. 10 sec. 3M. 6m. B.W. metal framework tower.
FRIARS GOOSE. S BANK. Lt. Fl.R. 5 sec. 3M. 6m. R. frame Tr. Traffic Signal 650m. NW.
VELVA LIQUIDS JETTY. Lt. 2 F.R. vert. each end.
ST. ANTHONY'S POINT. Lt.Bn. Fl.G. 5 sec. Also from extreme of Vickers Lt. 2 F.R.
HEWORTH SHORE. Lt. 2 F.R.
ST. PETER'S. N BANK. Lt.Bn. Fl.(3)G. 10 sec. G. pile structure with platform.

ST. PETER'S REACH

S BANK. Lt.Bn. 2 F.R. in pairs, to mark swinging area.
NEWCASTLE SWING BRIDGE. Lts. 2 F.G. vert. and 2 F.R. vert. N & S Channels marked by Lts.
METRO BRIDGE. N SIDE. Lt. F.G. on down and up stream sides.
METRO BRIDGE. S SIDE. Lt. F.R. on down and up stream sides.
KING EDWARD BRIDGE. Lt. 2 F.Y. vert. on centre Col.
NEW REDHEUGH BRIDGE Lt. F.G. 1M. marks N Pier.
Lt. F.R. 1M. marks S Pier.

COASTLINE & NORTHWARDS FROM RIVER TYNE

CULLERCOATS 55°02'N, 1°26'W. Ldg.Lts. (Front) F.R. 3M. on post, 27m. (Rear) F.R. 3M. on Col. 35m.
WHITLEY BAY. Lt.By. Fl.Y. 10 sec. Sph.Y.
DRURIDGE BAY. Lt. Fl.R. when air gunnery and bomb practice taking place.

BLYTH 55°07'N, 1°29'W. Tel: Blyth (0670) 352678. Fax: (0670) 368540. Telex: 537567.

OFFSHORE/HARBOUR WAYPOINT. 55°06.5'N, 1°28.0'W.

Radio — Port & Pilots: VHF Chan. 16, 12, 11. H24.
Harbour Patrol. VHF Chan. 16, 12, 10, 8, 6.
Radio — Pilots: VHF Chan. 16, 10, 8, 6. H24.
Measured Mile; Newbiggin, 11M. N of R. Tyne. 2 pairs lighted Marking Trs. 40m. and 46m. high. 177° and 357° (Mag). Depth 50m. between Blyth and Coquet Island Lt.Ho.

Measured Distance: St. Mary's Lt.Ho. to Coquet Island. Exact distance 16 nautical miles can be used to test vessel's speeds. Course 178° and 358° (Mag.). Depth 55m.
FAIRWAY. Lt.By. Fl.G. 3 sec. Conical G. SE of E Pier Head. Bell. Vessels entering or leaving pass to southward of this By.

E PIER HEAD 55°07.0'N, 1°29.1'W. Lt.Ho. Fl.(4) 10 sec. 21M. W. Tr. grey lantern, 19m. Lts. 2 F. occas. shown from each of measured mile Bns. 4M. N.
Same structure, Lt. F.R. 13M. 13m. vis. 152°-249°. Horn.(3) 30 sec.
Ldg.Lts. 324°. (Front) F.Bu. 10M. Or. ◇frame Tr. 11m. (Rear) F.Bu. 10M. Or. ◇frame Tr. 17m.
OUTER W PIER HEAD. Lt. 2 F.R. vert. 8M. W. metal framework Tr. 7m.
TRAINING WALL, S END. Lt. Fl.R. 6 sec. 1M. R. metal framework Tr. on dolphin, 6m.
W SIDE OF CHAN. Lt. 2 F.R. vert. on dolphin, 5 and 3m.
E SIDE OF CHAN. Lt. 2 F.G. vert. on dolphin, 5 and 3m.

S HARBOUR
INNER W PIER, N END. Lt. 2 Fl.(2)R. 6 sec. vert. 5M. W. metal structure, 5m.
WAVE TRAP. Lt. 2 F.G. vert.
PILOTS JETTY. Lt. 2 F.R. vert.

BLYTH SNOOK. Ldg.Lts. 338°. (Front) F.Bu. 5M. W. 6-sided Tr. 5m. (Rear) F.Bu. 5M. W. ∆ on mast, 11m.
E PIER N END. Lt. 2 Fl.(2)G. 6 sec. vert. 8M.
ALCAN TERMINAL. Lt. 2 F.G. vert.
WINTERBOURNE QUAY Ro-Ro- Pontoon. Lt. 2 F.R. vert.
WEST COALING STAITHS HEAD. Lt. 2 F.R. vert. 5M. 8m.
SOW AND PIGS ROCKS By. Can.R.
NEWBIGGIN BREAKWATER HEAD. Lt. Fl.G. 10 sec. 4M.

COQUET 55°20.0'N, 1°32.2'W. Lt.Ho. Fl.(3)W.R. 30 sec. W.23M. R.19M. W. square Tr. turreted parapet, lower half grey, 25m. R.330°-140°; W.140°-163°; R.163°-180°; W.180°-330°. Racon. Horn 30 sec.

OFFSHORE WAYPOINT. 55°21.5'N, 1°30.0'W.

COQUET CHANNEL — N CHANNEL

E SIDE
NE COQUET By. Can.R.
W SIDE
HAUXLEY By. Can.R. off Head.
PAN BUSH By. Can.R. off Warkworth.

AMBLE (WARKWORTH) 55°20'N, 1°34'W. Tel: Alnwick (0665) 710306.

HARBOUR WAYPOINT. 55°21.0'N, 1°34.0'W.

Radio — Port: VHF Chan. 16, 14. 0900-1700 Mon.-Fri.
Entry: Do not cross bar in bad weather. V/ls over 2m. draught cross bar 3 h.-HW-3 h.

WARKWORTH HARBOUR
AMBLE MARINA, Ch. M.
SEWER OUTFALL Lt.By. Fl.R. 10 sec. Can.R. Bell.
S BREAKWATER HEAD. Lt. Fl.R. 5 sec. 5M. W.R. Tr. 11m.
N BREAKWATER HEAD. Lt. Fl.G. 6 sec. 11M. W. metal framework Tr. R. bands. 10m.
BOULMER. Ldg.Lts. F. shown when lifeboat at sea.
BOULMER STILE By. Can.R. off Seaton Shad.
CRASTER. 55°28'N, 1°35'W Pier Bn. 'Little Car'.
NEWTON ROCKS By. Can.R. off Newton Pt. Rarnyard Shoal.
NORTH SUNDERLAND POINT By. Can.R.

NEWTON BY THE SEA R.G. STN.
55°31.03'N, 1°37.11'W. Emergency D.F. STN. VHF Chan. 16 & 67 controlled by MRSC Tyne/Tees.

N SUNDERLAND HARBOUR
Entry: Shown from NW Pier. R. Flag/Bl. Flag or shown from lighthouse R. Lt/G. Lt. = dangerous to enter.
BREAKWATER HEAD. Lt. Fl.R. 2.5 sec. metal tripod, 6m.
NW PIER HEAD. Lt. F.G. 3M. W. Tr. 11m. vis. 159°-294°. Traffic sig. Siren 90 sec. when vessels expected.
SHORESTON OUTCARS By. Can.R.

OFFSHORE WAYPOINT FARNE ISLANDS. 55°39.0'N, 1°32.0'W.

FARNE ISLANDS

LONGSTONE 55°38.6'N, 1°36.5'W. Lt. Fl. 20 sec. 24M. R.Tr. W. band, 23m. Distress sig. R.C. Horn(2) 60 sec.

FARNE ISLAND 55°36.9'N, 1°39.2'W. Lt. L.Fl.(2) W.R. 15 sec. W.13M. R.9M. W. round Tr. 27m. R.119°-277°; W.277°-119°

BLACK ROCK POINT, BAMBURGH
Lt.Ho. Oc.(2) W.R.G. 15 sec. W.17M. R.13M.

G.13M. W. Bldg. 12m. G.122°-165°; W.165°-175°; R.175°-191°; W.191°-238°; R.238°-275°; W.275°-289°; G.289°-300°.
SWEDMAN By. Conical G.
GOLDSTONE By. Conical G.
PLOUGH SEAT By. Can.R. on seaward side of Plough Rks.
Bn. marks inner side of Plough Rk.

HOLY ISLAND (Lindisfarne)

HOLY ISLAND HARBOUR Bns. 2 E and W on Old Law. 25 and 21m. Leading 260°.
RIDGE END By. Pillar. B.Y.B. Topmark E. close N of Holy I. bar.

When bar is passed Bn. on Heugh Hill brought in line with Church Belfry 310° leads up Holy Island Hr. 2.5m. H.W.O.S.T. on bar. When B.Bn. top is crossed over base, Hr. closed or dangerous to cross bar due to heavy sea.

EMANUEL Bn. white pointed top, 15m.

BERWICK 55°46'N, 1°59'W. Tel: Berwick (0289) 7404/6255.Telex: 53588 LINSAY.

HARBOUR WAYPOINT. 55°46.0'N, 1°57.0'W.

Radio — Port & Pilot: VHF Chan. 16, 12. Hrs. 0800-1700 Mon.-Fri. other times when v/s expected.
Entry: Vessels up to 4.5m draught can enter at HWS. Considered dangerous to enter or leave on ebb tide. Tweed Dock often congested, check berth available before entering.
Sandstell Point may shift during prolonged Easterly weather or River Spate water.
BREAKWATER HEAD. Lt. Fl. 5 sec. 10M. W. round stone Tr. R. cupola and base, 15m. vis. E of Seal Carr Ledges to shore.
Same structure Lt. F.G. vis. from inside Hr. Reed 60 sec. when fishing vessels at sea.
ROOT. Lt. F.R. 2m.
NR. ROOT. Lt. Q.R. 1M. on W. Col. 4m.
SPITTAL. Ldg.Lts. 207°. (Front) F.R. W. △ on W. mast, B. bands. 4m. (Rear) F.R. W. △ on W. mast, B. bands. 9m.
CARR ROCK JETTY. Lt. 2 F.R. vert. 2m.
TWEED DOCK, S PIER HEAD. Lt. 2 F.R. vert. 3m.

EAST COAST OF SCOTLAND

BURNMOUTH 55°50'N, 2°04'W. Ldg.Lts. (Front) F.R. 4M. W. post, 29m. (Rear) F.R. 4M. W. post, 35m.

INNER BASIN, W PIER ROOT. Lt. 2 F.G. vert. on wooden mast, 6m.

EYEMOUTH HARBOUR 55°52′N,
2°04′W. Tel: Eyemouth 223.
Radio — Port: VHF Chan. 16, 12.
Entry: Approach not advised if wind N-E. Port closed R. flag or R. Lt. Berthing limited for yachts. Tidal basin 0.9m LWS and 2.4m LWN. Max draught HWS 4.6m.
Ldg.Lts. 174°. (Front) F.G. 5M. Y. Col. 7m. (Rear) F.G. 4M. Y. Col. 10m.
E BREAKWATER HEAD. Lt. Iso. R. 2 sec. 8M. tripod, 8m.
LIFEBOAT HOUSE Siren 30 sec. when fishing vessels at sea.
ENTRANCE CHANNEL, E SIDE. Lt. 2 Q.R. 3M. R.W. cheq. posts, 3m.
W SIDE. Lt. Q.G. 1M. on B.W. cheq. post, 3m.

ST. ABBS. Ldg.Lts. (Front) 2 F.R. 1M. Tripod 4m. (Rear) 2 F.R. 1M. Tripod 8m.

ST. ABB'S RG STN. 55°54.49′N,
2°12.23′W. Controlled by MRSC Forth.

OFFSHORE WAYPOINT ST. ABBS HD. 55°55.0′N, 2°05.0′W.

ST. ABB'S HEAD 55°55.0′N, 2°08.3′W. Lt.
Fl. 10 sec. 29M. W. Tr. 68m. Racon. F. occas. on measured distance bns. 0.75M. WSW and 1.6M. W.
TORNESS POINT. Lt. Fl.R. 5 sec. 5M.

OFFSHORE WAYPOINT BARNES NESS. 56°00.0′N, 2°27.0′W.

BARNS NESS 55°59.2′N, 2°26.6′W. Lt. Iso.
4 sec. 10M. W. round Tr. 36m.

DUNBAR 56°00′N, 2°31′W. Tel: Dunbar
3206.

HARBOUR WAYPOINT. 56°00.75′N, 2°30.75′W.

BAYSWELL HILL. Ldg.Lts. 198° (Front) Oc.G. 6 sec. 3M. W. △ Or. Col. 15m. Intens. 188°-208° (Rear) Oc.G. 6 sec. 3M. W. ▽ Or. Col. 21m. Intens. 188°-208°.

VICTORIA HARBOUR. MIDDLE QUAY. Lt. Q.R. 3M. on Col. 6m. vis. over Hr. Entce.
S CARR Bn. B. Tr. with cross. 12m.

OFFSHORE WAYPOINT ISLE OF MAY. 56°10.0′N, 2°30.0′W.

MAY ISLAND (SUMMIT) 56°11.2′N,
2°33.3′W. Lt.Ho. Fl.(2) 15 sec. 22M. square Tr. on stone dwelling, 73m. Storm Sig. R.C.

TRIPLANE TARGET. Lt.By. Fl.Y. 3 sec. Sph. Y.
SPECIAL Lt.Bys. Fl.Y. 10 sec. Sph.Y. in positions — (1) 56°05.4′N, 2°40.5′W; (2) 56°04.8′N, 2°36.7′W.
Firth of Forth: Air Force Department Exercise Area joining positions:
(a) 56°35.00′N 1°30.00′W (b) 56°35.00′N 0°57.45′W (c) 56°26.13′N 0°36.00′W (d) 56°07.00′N 0°36.00′W (e) 56°02.00′N 1°30.00′W (f) 56°35.00′N 1°30.00′W

MRSC FORTH (0333) 50666. Weather broadcast ev. 4h. from 0205.

FIRTH OF FORTH S SIDE TO FORTH BRIDGE

INSHORE WAYPOINT SE OF BASS ROCK. 56°04.0′N, 2°37.0′W.

BASS ROCK 56°04.6′N, 2°38.3′W. Lt. Fl.(3)
20 sec. 10M. W. Tr. 46m. vis. 241°-107°.

N BERWICK

HARBOUR WAYPOINT. 56°04.0′N, 2°42.5′W.

OUTFALL SEWER Lt.By. Fl. Y. 5 sec. Sph. Y.

N PIER HEAD. Lt. F.W.R. 3M. on post, 7m. R. to seaward, W. over Hr. Extinguished when vessels cannot enter on account of bad weather. Storm sig.

FORTH (FIRTH OF) 56°04′N, 2°47′W. Tel:
Forth Navigation Service (031-553) 1151.
Pilots: (031 552) 1420. Fax: (031 553) 5428.
Telex: 727450 FORNAV G.
Radio — Port: Forth Navigation Service. VHF Chan. 16, 71, 12, 20 — continuous.
Radio — Pilots: VHF Chan. 16, 71, 12, 14.

INSHORE WAYPOINT N OF FIDRA. 56°06.0′N, 2°48.0′W.

FIDRA Lt.Ho. Fl.(4) 30 sec. 24M. W. Tr. 34m.
RC. Obscured by Bass Rk., Craig Leith and Lamb I.
WRECK. Lt.By. Fl.(2)R. 10 sec. Can.R.

PORT SETON 55°58′N, 2°57′W. Tel: Port
Seton 396.

HARBOUR WAYPOINT. 55°58.5′N, 2°58.0′W.

E PIER HEAD. Lt. Iso.W.R. 4 sec. W.10M, R.7M. R. shore-105°; W.105°-225°, R.225°-shore.
COCKENZIE JETTY HEAD. Lt. Q.R. 1M. Lantern, 6m.

FISHERROW E PIER HEAD. Lt. Oc. 6 sec. 6M. metal framework Tr. 5m.
Lt.By. Q. Pillar B.Y. Topmark N.
Lt.By. Fl.(3)G. 10 sec. Conical G. Bell.
KINGSTONE HUDDS. Lt.Bys. Fl.(5)Y. 20 sec. Sph. Y. postn. 56°06.20′N, 2°54.40′W. & 55°59.9′N, 3°09.2′W.
LEITH APPROACH. Lt.By. Fl.R. 5 sec. Can.R.

LEITH 55°59′N, 3°10′W. Tel: Leith (031-554) 3661. Telex: 72681 FORPOR G.

HARBOUR WAYPOINT. 56°00.0′N, 3°11.5′W.

Radio — Port: VHF Chan. 16, 12. H24.
Radio — Pilots: VHF Chan. 16, 14. H24.
Entry Signals: Ent. to Lock.
R. Lt. on both walls — Port closed.
G. Lt. on both walls — Lock opening.
2 G. Lts. on one wall — vessel to moor on that side.
Similar Lts. on Harbour side of Lock.
Refuge during E gales. Sheltered anchorage above Forth Bridge.
E BREAKWATER HEAD. Lt. Iso. R. 4 sec. 11M. R. lantern on concrete base, 7m. Horn 30 sec.
LEITH HBR. Lt.By. Fl.R. 4 sec. Pillar R.
W BREAKWATER HEAD. Lt. Fl.G. 6 sec.
LEAD-IN JETTY, OFF HEAD. Lt. Fl.R. 6 sec. on dolphin.
W PIER. Lt. Fl.R. 2 sec.

GRANTON 55°59′N, 3°13′W. Tel: Granton 3385.
Radio — Pilots: VHF Chan. 16, 14 — continuous.
Entry Signals: R. flag with W. cross shown from Middle Pier Head = do not enter.
OUTFALL By. Can W. Topmark X. 55°59.64′N 3°14.19′W marks outfall pipeline.

E BREAKWATER HEAD. Lt. Fl.R. 2 sec. 6M. on G. Tr. 5m.
W BREAKWATER HEAD. Lt. Fl.G. 2 sec. 7M. on W. Tr. 5m.
Crammond River: Bar 3m. A.C.D. open for keel boats against the wall or for shallow draught boats on drying berths.

FIRTH OF FORTH N SIDE TO FORTH BRIDGE

OFFSHORE WAYPOINT FIFENESS. 56°18.0′N, 2°30.0′W.

FIFENESS RG STN. 56°16.7′N, 2°35.2′W. Emergency DF Stn. VHF Chan. 16 & 67. Controlled by MRSC Forth.

FIFENESS. Lt.Ho. 56°16.7′N, 2°35.1′W. Iso. W.R. 10 sec. 21M. W. building. 12m. W.143°-147°; R.147°-217°; W.217°-023°. R.C.

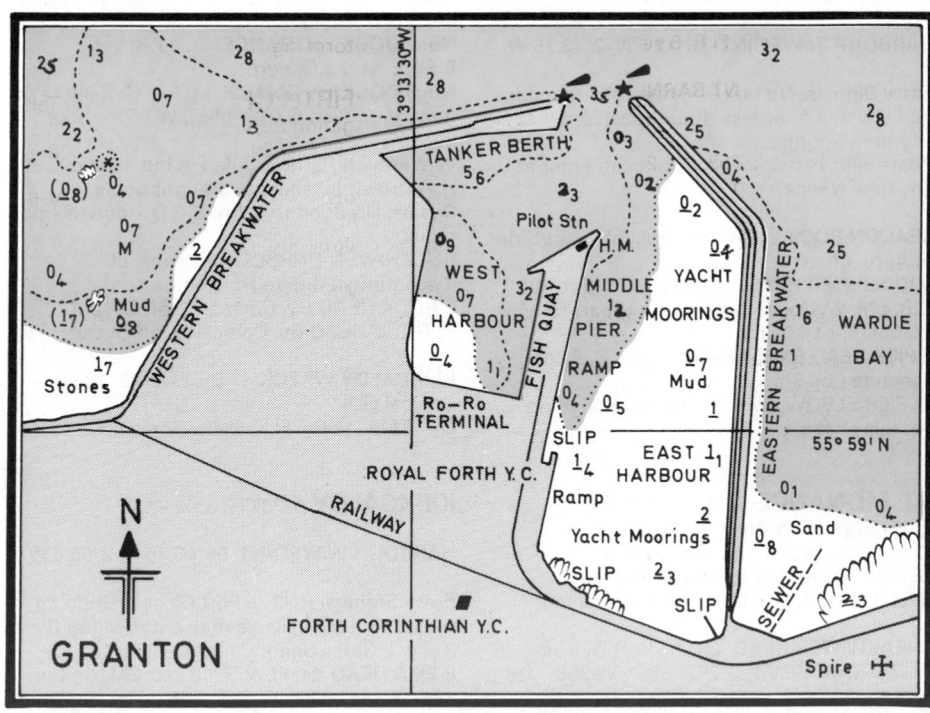

N CARR Lt.By. Q.(3) 10 sec. Pillar B.Y.B. Topmark E.
N CARR ROCK Bn. R. ball topmark. N of Fife Ness, 6m.

CRAIL HARBOUR Ldg.Lts. 295° (Front) F.R. 6M. stone Bn. 24m. Not shown when Hr. closed. (Rear) F.R. 6M. stone Bn. 30m.

ANSTRUTHER 56°13'N, 2°42'W.

HARBOUR WAYPOINT. 56°13.0'N, 2°41.5'W.

Leading lights shown 1st September to 1st May only, when fishing vessels are at sea and when inner harbour has 3m. of water.
Entry Signals: W. over G. Lts. shown W Pier when inner harbour has 3m. water and vessels expected. R. Lt. when entry prohibited.

W PIER HEAD. Lt. 2 F.R. vert. 6M. W. Tr. 11m. Traffic sig. Reed(3) 60 sec.
E PIER HEAD. Lt. Fl.G. 3 sec. 4M. on R. Col. 7m.
ROOT. Ldg.Lts. 019° (Front) F.G. 4M. on W. mast, 7m. (Rear) F.G. 4M. on W. mast, 11m.

PITTENWEEM 56°14'N, 2°43'W.

HARBOUR WAYPOINT. 56°12.5'N, 2°43.75'W.

Entry Signals: No Lts. — dangerous to enter. Boats with 3 ft. or less draught can enter at any time Springs. Boats with 7 ft. or less draught can enter at any time Neaps.

BEACON ROCK Lt.Bn. Q.R. 2M. 3m. Port Side of Appr. Chan.
MIDDLE PIER HEAD. Ldg.Lts. 037°. (Front) Q.R. 5M. W. Col. R. bands, 4m. (Rear) F.R. 5M. W. Col. R. bands, 8m.
E PIER HEAD EXTENSION. Lt. Oc.G. 6 sec. concrete Col. 5m.
W PIER ELBOW Horn 90 sec. when fishing vessels at sea.

ST. MONANCE 56°12'N, 2°36'W.
Entry Signals: W Pier.
G. Lt. = depth of 1.8m. in entrance.
G./R. Lt. = depth of 2.1m. in entrance.
R. Lt. below R. Ldg.Lt. = Entry prohibited.

BREAKWATER HEAD. Lt. Oc. W.R.G. 6 sec. W.7M. R.4M. G.4M. G.282°-355°; W.355°-026°; R.026°-038°

E PIER HEAD. Lt. 2 F.G. vert. 4M. W. tripod, 5m. Bell when fishing vessels expected.
W PIER, NR. HEAD. Lt. 2 F.R. vert. 4M. post on parapet, 5m.

INSHORE WAYPOINT SE OF ELIE NESS. 56°10.0'N, 2°47.0'W.

ELIE NESS 56°11'N, 2°49'W. Lt.Ho. Fl. 6 sec. 18M. W. Tr. 15m.
THILL ROCK By. Can.R.
EAST VOWS Bn. R. pyramid, open cage Topmark. 12m.

METHIL 56°11'N, 3°00'W. Tel: Leven 26725.

HARBOUR WAYPOINT. 56°10.5'N, 3°00.0'W.

Radio — Port: VHF Chan. 16, 14 — 3 h.-HW-1 h.
Entry Signals: R. Lt. over G. Lt. — dangerous to enter, bring up in Roads.
R. Lt. over W. Lt. — clear to come to No. 2 Dk.
R. Lt. = Remain in Roads until other signal.
Shown 3 h.-HW (until Dock gates closed)

SEWER OUTFALL. Lt. Fl. 3 sec. △ on B.Bn. Y. top.
WATER INTAKE TOWER. Lt. Q.G. 3M. 7m.
OUTER PIER HEAD. Lt. Oc.G. 6 sec. 5M. W. Tr. 8m. vis. 280°-100°.
No: 2 DOCK ENTRANCE. Lt. 2 F.R. vert.
E SIDE. Lt. 2 F.G. vert.
No: 3 DOCK ENTRANCE. Lt. F.W.G. Sectors on bollard on Pier. G.018°-065°; W.065°-about 208°.
W Wemyss: Partially filled in but available at H.W. for small shallow draught boats.
Dysart: Dredged to 0.7m. B.C.D. open to small boats.
BUCKHAVEN HARBOUR in ruins. Lt. discontinued due to Hr. silting.
E ROCK HEAD By. Conical G. off Dysart.
W ROCK HEAD By. Conical G. off Dysart.

KIRKCALDY WRECK. Lt.By. Fl.(3) G. 18 sec. Conical G.
OUTFALL. Lt.By. Fl.Y. 5 sec. Conical Y.

KIRKCALDY 56°07'N, 3°09'W.

HARBOUR WAYPOINT. 56°06.75'N, 3°08.0'W.

Entry Signals: R. Lt. = Port Closed. Bring up in Roads. G. Lt. = Vessels may enter. In fog Blast 3 sec. = Gates open. Channel clear.
E PIER HEAD. Lt. Fl.W.G. 10 sec. 8M. on Col. 10m. R.156°-336°; W.336°-156°.

SEWER OUTFALL. Bn. Y.
S PIER HEAD. Lt. 2 F.R. vert. 5M. on Col. 7m.
W PIER, INNER HEAD. Lt. F. on Col. 5m.
DOCK ENTCE. W SIDE. Lt. F.R. on Col. 6m.
Docking sig.
E SIDE. Lt. F.G. on Col. 6m. Tidal sig.

SANDEND. By. Conical G. near Burntisland.

BURNTISLAND 56°03′N, 3°14′W.
Radio — Pilots: VHF Chan. 16, 14, 9 —
continuous.
Entry Signals: R. Lt. = Port Closed. Bring up in
Roads until another
signal displayed.
G. Lt.   = Clear to enter E Dock.
A G. Lt over W. Lt. = A v/l proceeding to W
Dk. only may enter
outer hbr.
Shown 3 h.-HW until dock gates closed.
Measured Mile: S of Blae Rock — between
positions 56°02′N 3°11′W and 56°02′N 3°10′W.

W PIER, OUTER HEAD. Lt. Fl.(2)R. 6 sec. W.
Tr 7m.
E PIER, OUTER HEAD. Lt. Fl.(2)G. 6 sec. 5M.
W. Tr. 7m.
W PIER, INNER HEAD. Lt. 2 F.R. vert. 5M. R.
Tr. 4m.
E PIER, INNER HEAD. Lt. 2 F.G. vert. 5M. R.Tr.
6 and 5m.
W PIER, Lt.By. Fl.(2) 10 sec. Bu. W. Cheq.
D.G. RANGE. 2 x By. Sph. Or. 2 x Lt.By. Fl.
2 sec. Sph. Or.

INVERKEITHING HARBOUR
ST. DAVIDS. Lt.Bn. Dir. Lt. 098°; Dir. Fl.G. 5
sec. 7M. Or. Can. on pile 3m.
W NESS. Lt.By. Q.R. Spar R.

FIRTH OF FORTH — DEEP DRAUGHT CHANNELS

S CHANNEL
S CHANNEL APPROACH. Lt.By. L.Fl. 10 sec.
Sph. R.W.V.S.
NARROW DEEP. Lt.By. Fl.(2)R. 10 sec. Can.R.
NW side.
HERWIT ROCK. Lt.By. Fl.(3)G. 10 sec. Pillar. G.
Bell. Horn 45 sec.
N CRAIG By. Conical G. SE side.
CRAIG WAUGH By. Can.R.

INCHKEITH 56°02.0′N, 3°08.0′W. Lt.Ho. Fl.
15 sec. 22M. Grey stone Tr. 67m.
STELL POINT Horn 15 sec.
HAWKERAIG POINT. Ldg.Lts. 292° (Front) Q.
14M. W.Tr. 12m. Vis.282°-302° (Rear) Iso. 5
sec. 14M. W.Tr. 16m. Vis. 282°-302°.

Mortimers Deep — No vessel is allowed to
enter Mortimers Deep without approval from
Forth Navigation Service. Passage through
the area when tankers are berthed at Braefoot
Terminal or manoeuvring in area is
prohibited.

MORTIMERS DEEP CHANNEL
No: 1 Lt.By. Q.G. Conical G.
No: 2 Lt.By. Q.R. Can.R.
No: 3 Lt.By. Fl.(2)G. 5 sec. Conical G.
No: 4 Lt.By. Fl.(2) R. 5 sec. Can.R.
No: 5 Lt.By. Fl.G. 4 sec. Conical G.
No: 6 Lt.By. Fl.R. 4 sec. Can.R.
No: 7 Lt.By. Fl.(2)G. 5 sec. Conical G.
No: 8 Lt.By. Fl.R. 2 sec. Can.R.
No: 9 Lt.By. Q.G. Conical G.
No: 10 Lt.By. Fl.(2)R. 5 sec. Can.R.
No: 12 Lt.By. Q.R. Can.R.
No: 14 Lt.By. Q.(9) 15 sec. Pillar. Y.B.Y.
Topmark W.

BRAEFOOT TERMINAL: Radio: VHF Chan. 16,
15, 44, 48, 69, 73. Call 2 h. before ETA. ETA 72
h. in advance.
BRAEFOOT BAY TERMINAL. Ldg.Lts. 247°15′
(Front) Fl. 3 sec. 15M. △ post on dolphin
(Rear) Fl. 3 sec. 15M. ▽ post on gangway Vis.
237.2°-257.2°.
Ldg.Lts. 019°24′ Front F. 12 sec. Dolphin. & 2
F.G. vert. Rear Oc. 5 sec. Post.
MOORING AND BERTHING DOLPHIN. Lts. 2
F.G. vert.
PALLAS ROCK. Lt.By. V.Q.(9) 10 sec. Pillar.
Y.B.Y. Topmark W.
E GUNNET LEDGE. Lt.By. Q.(3) 10 sec. Pillar.
B.Y.B. Topmark E.
W GUNNET LEDGE. Lt.By. Q.(9) 15 sec. Pillar.
Y.B.Y. Topmark W.

INSHORE WAYPOINT S OF FAIRWAY BY.
56°03.0′N, 3°00.0′W.

N CHANNEL
FAIRWAY Lt.By. Iso. 2 sec. Sph. R.W.V.S.
Racon. Pilots may board here.
No: 1 Lt.By. Fl.G. 9 sec. Conical G.
No: 2 Lt.By. Fl.R. 9 sec. Can.R.
No: 3 Lt.By. Fl.G. 6 sec. Conical G.
No: 4 Lt.By. Fl.R. 6 sec. Can.R.
No: 5 Lt.By. Fl.G. 3 sec. Conical G.
No: 6 Lt.By. Fl.R. 3 sec. Can.R.
No: 7 Lt.By. Q.G. Conical G. Bell. Racon.
No: 8 Lt.By. Fl.R. 9 sec. Can.R.
No: 9 Lt.By. Fl.G. 6 sec. Conical G.
No: 10 Lt.By. Fl.R. 6 sec. Can.R.
No: 11 Lt.By. Fl.G. 3 sec. Conical G.
No: 12 Lt.By. Fl.R. 3 sec. Can.R.

OXCARS SPOIL GROUND Lt.By. Fl.Y. 5 sec.
Can. Y.

OXCARS 56°01.4′N, 3°16.7′W. Lt.Ho. Fl.(2)W.R. 7 sec. W.13M. R.12M. W. Tr. R. band. 16m. W.072°-087°; R.087°-196°; W.196°-313°; R.313°-072°. Bridge clearance gauge.

No: 13 Lt.By. Fl.G. 9 sec. Conical G.
No: 14 Lt.By. Fl.R. 9 sec. Can. R.

INCHCOLM E. Lt. Fl.(3) 15 sec. 10M. Grey Tr. 20m. partially obsc. 075°-145.5°. Horn (3) 45 sec.
S Ldg.Lts. 066° (Front) Q. 7M. W. Tr. 7m. (Common Rear) Iso 5 sec. 7M. W. Tr. 11m.
N Ldg.Lts. 076°45′ (Front) Q. 7M. 7m.

No: 15 Lt.By. Fl.G. 6 sec. Conical G.
No: 16 Lt.By. Fl.R. 3 sec. Can. R.
No: 17 Lt.By. Fl.G. 3 sec. Conical G.
No: 19 Lt.By. Fl.G. 9 sec. Conical G.

HOUND POINT TERMINAL Lts. F.R. 5M. 7m. Siren (3) 90 sec. on E Dolphin.

FORTH RAILWAY BRIDGE. Lt. 2 x 2 F.W. vert. 5M. 48m. Lt. 4 x 2 F.R. vert. 3M. 48m. on each side of bridge. Centres of spans marked by W. Lts. and ends of cantilevers by R. Lts. defining both N and S navigable Channels.

INCH GARVIE. 56°00′N, 3°23′W Lt.Bn. Fl. 5 sec. 11M. B. round Bn. W. lantern.

FORTH ROAD BRIDGE

N SUSPENSION TR. BASE. E SIDE. Lt. Iso.G. 4 sec. 7M. 7m. Same structure Aero Q.R. 11M. 155m. and 2 F.R. 7M. 109m.
W SIDE. Lt. Iso.G. 4 sec. 7M. Same structure 2 Aero F.R. 7M. 155m. and 2 F.R. 7M. 109m.
MAIN SPAN, N PART, E SIDE. Lt. Q.G. 6M. 50m. vis. downstream.

W SIDE. Lt. Q.G. 6M. 50m. vis. upstream.
CENTRE, E SIDE. Lt. Iso. 4 sec. 8M. 52m. vis. downstream.
W SIDE. Lt. Iso. 4 sec. 8M. 52m. vis. upstream.
S PART, E SIDE. Lt. Q.R. 6M. 50m. vis. downstream.
W SIDE. Lt. Q.R. 6M. 50m. vis. upstream.
S SUSPENSION TR. BASE, E SIDE. Lt. Iso. R. 4 sec. 7M. 7m. Same structure. Aero Q.R. and 2 F.R. Lts.
W SIDE. Lt. Iso. R. 4 sec. 7M. 7m.

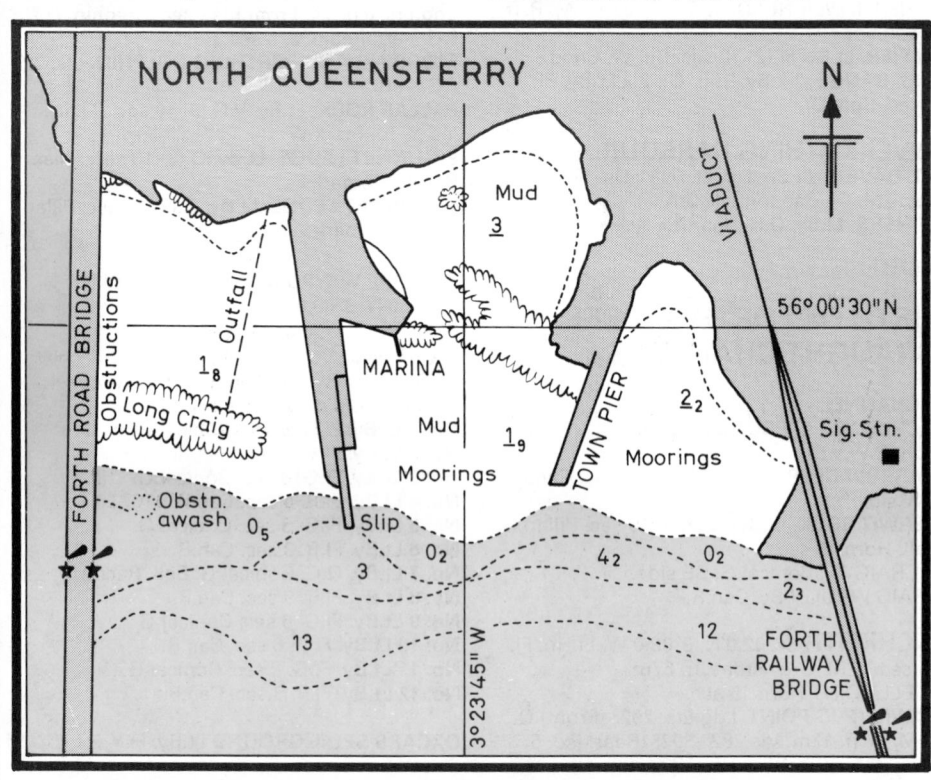

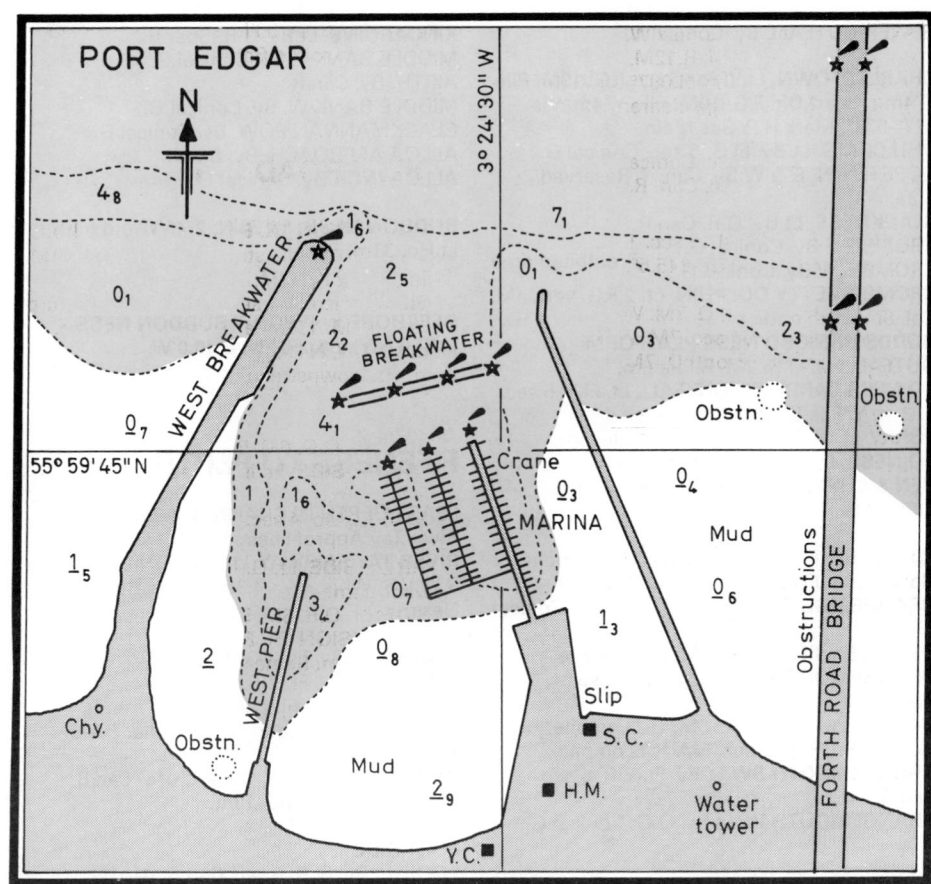

FORTH BRIDGE TO ALLOA

PORT EDGAR

Yacht Marina (031331)3330. VHF Chan. (M).
Apr.-Sept. 0900-1900. Oct.-Mar. 0900-1630.
Max. LOA 12m. 2.4m. draught.
W BREAKWATER. Lt. Dir. 244°. Dir.Fl.R. 4 sec.
11M. W. Tr. 4m. 4 × Q.Y. Lts. mark floating
breakwater. 2 × 2 F.R. vert. Lts. mark N end of
marina pontoons inside harbour.

BEAMER ROCK. Lt.Fl. 3 sec. 9M. W. Tr. R.
Band. 6m. Horn 20 sec.

ROSYTH 56°01'N, 3°27'W. Tel: (0383)
412121 Ext. 3187. Telex: 72157 ROSYTH G.
N Queensferry (Naval sig. stn. (0383) 412121
Ext. 3075).
Radio — Port: N Queensferry Naval sig. stn.
VHF Chan 16, 71, 74, H24. Rosyth Naval base
Q.H.M. VHF Chan. 73, 74 Mon.-Fri. 0730-1700.

ROSYTH DOCKYARD

MAIN CHANNEL Dir.Lt.Bn. "A" 323°30' Dir.
Oc.W.R.G. 9 sec. G.318°-322°; W.322°-325°;
R.325°-328°; shown H24. 4M. R. □ R.W. post.
B.W. diag. □ 7m.
Dir.Lt.Bn. "C" 115° Dir. Oc.W.R.G. 6 sec.
R.110°-114°; W.114°-116°; G.116°-120°, shown
H24. 4M. W. ▽ in R. Ⅱ on R.W. Bn. 7m.
Dir.Lt.Bn. "E" 295° Dir. Oc. 6 sec.
Floodlighting mast vis. 293.5°-296.5° 4M.
11m.
S ARM JETTY HEAD Lt. Fl.(2) W.R. 12 sec.
W.9M. R.6M. Brick Hut 5m. W.010°-280°;
R.280°-010°. Siren 20 sec. Occas.
MIDDLE JETTY HEAD Lt. F.G.R.G. vert.

No: 1 By. Conical G.
No: 2 Lt.By. Q.(3) 10 sec. Pillar B.Y.B.
Topmark E.
No. 3 Lt.By. Fl.G. 5 sec. Conical G.
No: 4 Lt.By. Fl.R. 3 sec. Can.R.
No. 5 Lt.By. Q.G. Conical G.
No: 6 Lt.By. Q.R. Can.R.

SEWER OUTFALL By. Conical Y.

CHARLESTOWN. Lt. (Front) Dir. F.G. 10M. Pile Y. 4m.; (Rear) Dir. F.G. 10M. Pile Y. 4m. Vis. 017°-037°. Mark H.P. Gas Main.
DHU CRAIG. Lt.By. Fl.G. 5 sec. Conical G.
HOPETOWN. E & W By. Can. Y. Reserved area.
BLACKNESS. Lt.By. Q.R. Can.R.
CROMBIE E By. Conical G. } Prohibited area
CROMBIE W By. Conical G.
CROMBIE JETTY DOLPHIN. Lt. 2 F.G. vert. 4M. Col. 8m. each end.
DODDS BANK BO'NESS PLATFORM OUTFALL. Lt. Q.R. 2M. R.Pile 3m.
BO'NESS CARRIDEN OUTFALL Lt. Fl.Y. 5 sec. Y. □ on Y. Pile Beacon.
TORRY. Lt. Fl.G. 10 sec. 7M. G. pile, 5m.
BO'NESS. Lt.By. Fl.R. 10 sec. Can.R.
HEN & CHICKENS. Lt.By. Fl.(3)G. 20 sec. Conical G.

No: 1 Lt.Bn. Fl.(3)R. 20 sec. 6M. R. □ on pile.
No: 2 Lt.Bn. Fl.G. 5 sec. 6M. G. □ on pile.
GRANGEMOUTH NE Lt.By. Fl.Y. 5 sec. Conical Y.
No: 3 Lt.Bn. Fl.R. 5 sec. 6M. R. □ on pile.
GRANGEMOUTH NW Lt.By. Fl.Y. 2 sec. Conical Y.
No: 4 Lt.Bn. Fl.G. 2 sec. 5M. G. □ on pile.
No: 5 Lt.Bn. Fl.R. 2 sec. 5M. R. □ on pile.
GRANGEMOUTH SW Lt.By. Fl.(2)R. 5 sec. Can.R.
GRANGEMOUTH W. Lt.By. Q.G. Conical G.

GRANGEMOUTH 56°02'N, 3°39'W. Tel: H.M. (0324) 486839. Port Office (0324) 482591. Telex: 777432 FOPALM G.
Radio — Port: VHF Chan. 16, 14 — H24.
Radio — Pilots: VHF Chan. 16, 14, 9 — H24.
Entry Signals: Traffic Signals shown from Outer Lock Entrance.
R. Lt.   = No vessel may approach.
G. Lt.   = Vessel may enter. Berth on side indicated by additional G. Lt.
Western Channel leads from Grange Docks through W Cut, spanned by a bridge, into Carron Dock depths of 7m.

EASTERN JETTY. Lt. Docking sig. Horn 30 sec.
LONGANNET POINT. Lt. Fl.G. 10 sec. 6M. 5m. Power Stn. Water Intake, E end Head.

INCH BRAKE. By. Conical G.

KINCARDINE
SWING BRIDGE. Lt. 2 F. one at centre of each span. F.R. Lts. mark each side of openings. 2 F.Or. vert. bridge open.

KINCARDINE. Lt.By. Q.R. Spar R.
MIDDLE BANK E. By. Conical G.
AIRTH. By. Can.R.
MIDDLE BANK W. By. Conical G.
CLACKMANNAN POW. By. Conical G.
ALLOA APPROACH. By. Can.R.
ALLOA INCH By. Conical G.

BUDDON NESS. 56°28'N, 2°45'W old high Lt.Ho. 31m. Racon.

OFFSHORE WAYPOINT BUDDON NESS (ABERTAY). 56°27.0'N, 2°40.0'W.

FIFENESS TO PERTH

LEAST DEPTH IN CHANNEL 4.8m.
River Tay Approaches
RIVER TAY FAIRWAY. Lt.By. L.Fl. 10 sec. Pillar R.W.V.S. Whis. ⌇ 4.35M. from Buddon Ness.

MIDDLE. Lt.By. Fl.(3)G. 18 sec. ⌇ Conical G.
MIDDLE. Lt.By. Fl.(2)R. 12 sec. ⌇ Can.R
ABERTAY. Lt.By. Fl.R. 6 sec. ⌇ Can.R.
ABERTAY. Lt.By. Q.(3) 10 sec. Pillar B.Y.B. Racon.
INNER. Lt.By. Fl.(2)R. 12 sec. ⌇ Can.R.
LUCKY Bn. B. stone, 13m.

PORT SIDE
POOL. Lt.By. Fl.R. 6 sec. Can.R. ⌇ .
SCALP. Lt.By. Fl.(2)R. 12 sec. Can.R. ⌇
CRAIG. Lt.By. Q.R. 1 sec. ⌇
NEWCOME. Lt.By. Fl.R. 6 sec. Can.R. ⌇
E DEEP. Lt.By. Q.R. Can.R. ⌇
W DEEP. Lt.By. Fl.R. 3 sec. Can.R. ⌇

STARBOARD SIDE
NORTH LADY. Lt.By. Fl.(3)G. 18 sec. ⌇ Conical G.
SOUTH LADY. Lt.By. Fl.(3)R. 18 sec. Can.R.
HORSE SHOE. Lt.By. V.Q.(6) + L.Fl. 10 sec. Pillar. Y.B. Topmark S.
HORSESHOE SEWER OUTFALL By. Conical Y.
TENTSMUIR PT. Lt. Fl.Y. 5 sec. Bn. Y. 198°-208°.
MONIFIETH. Lt. Fl.Y. 5 sec. Bn. Y. 018°-028° (mark gas pipeline).
BROUGHTY CASTLE. Lt. 2 F.G. vert. 9m. Lantern on G. post.
MIDDLE BANK. Lt.By. Q.(3) 10 sec. Pillar B.Y.B. Topmark E.
FOWLER ROCK By. Can.R. near Camperdown Dock Entce.
CALMAN ROCK Bn. Spar R. near Camperdown Dock Entce.

TAYPORT 56°27.2'N, 2°53.8'W. High Lt.Ho. Dir.Lt. 269°. Dir.Iso.W.R.G. 3 sec. W.22M. R.17M. G.16M. W. Tr. 24m. G.267°-268°; W.268°-270°; R.270°-271°.

DUNDEE 56°27'N, 2°58'W. Tel: Dundee (0382) 24121. Telex: 76644 DPA G.
Radio — Port: Dundee Harbour Radio. VHF. Chan. 16, 12, 14, 13, 11, 10 — continuous. All information relative to pilots and shipping movements are passed through this station.
Radio — Pilots: VHF Chan. 16, 6, 12.
Entry: Fl.R. Lt. shown from Port control near Camperdown Lock indicates no entry or exit from Camperdown Dock.

STANNERGATE SHELL OIL JETTY E. Lt. Fl.(4)G. 10 sec.
W Lt. Q.G. Siren 30 sec.

TIDAL BASIN
E BREAKWATER HEAD. Lt. 2 F.G. vert. 3M. metal Col. 5m.
W BREAKWATER HEAD. Lt. 2 F.R. vert. 4M. metal Col. 5m.

TAY ROAD BRIDGE
N NAVIGATION SPAN, NW SIDE. Lt. 2 F.G. vert. shown up and downstream. 4m.
CENTRE. Lt. V.Q. 27m. W. ▽, B. diagonal stripes.
CENTRE PIER. Lt. 2 F.Y. vert. 4m. Siren(2) 30 sec. shown up and downstream.
S NAVIGATION SPAN, CENTRE. Lt. V.Q. 28m. W. ▽, B. diagonal stripes.
SE SIDE. Lt. 2 F.R. vert. 4m. shown up and downstream.

TAY RAIL BRIDGE
Lts. 2 F.R. vert./2 F.G. vert./2 F. vert. shown up and downstream.
MY LORD BANK BYS. Nos: 1, 3, 5 Conical G. Nos: 2, 4, 6 Can.R.

PERTH HARBOUR Tel. Hr. Office (0738) 24056.
Radio — Port: VHF Chan. 9. If Pilot required contact Dundee.
FLISKE POINT. Bn. R. Col.
JOCKS HOLE. Lt.Bn. Q.R. 2M. 8m.
THE PEAT. Lt.Bn. Q.R. 2M. 8m.
CAIRNIE PIER. Lt. 2 F.G. vert. 2M. Col. 7m.
INCHYRA. Lt.Bn. Q.W.R. W.7M. R.5M. Post 3m. W.324.5°-022°; R.022°-087°; W.087°-144.5°.

PIPE LINE Lts. N Bank. Iso.G. 4 sec. 4M. Mast 4m.
S Bank. Iso.R. 4 sec. 4M. Mast 4m.
SLEEPLESS INCH OUT FALL. Lt.Bn. 2 F.R. vert. on Col. NE & NW side.
FRIARTON BRIDGE S PIER Lts. 2 F.R. vert.
NAVIGATION SPAN Lts. Q.
N PIER Lts. 2 F.G vert.

RIVER TAY NORTHWARD TO ABERDEEN

BELL ROCK 56°26.1'N, 2°23.1'W. Lt.Ho. Fl. 5 sec. 18M. W. round Tr. 28m. Racon.

OFFSHORE WAYPOINT W OF ARBROATH. 56°32.0'N, 2°33.0'W.

ARBROATH 56°33'N, 2°35'W. Tel: Arbroath 2166 (Night 3397).

HARBOUR WAYPOINT. 56°33.0'N, 2°34.0'W.

Entry Signals: All lights. G. — dangerous to enter.
Safety: L.B.S.

OUTFALL. Lt.By. Fl.Y. 3 sec. Can.Y.
Ldg.Lts. 299°15'. (Front) F.R. 5M. W. Col. 7m. (Rear) F.R. 5M. W. Col. 13m.
W BREAKWATER, E END. Lt. V.Q.(2) 6 sec. 4M. W. metal post, 6m.
E PIER, S ELBOW. Lt. Fl.G. 3 sec. Shows G. when unsafe to enter and F.R. Lt. when Hbr. closed. Siren(3) 60 sec.
ANNAT Lt.By. Fl.G. 3 sec. Conical G.

SCURDIE NESS 56°42.1'N, 2°26.1'W. Lt.Ho. Fl.(3) 20 sec. 23M. W. Tr. 38m. Racon.

OFFSHORE WAYPOINT W OF MONTROSE. 56°42.0'N, 2°21.0'W.

MONTROSE 56°42'N, 2°28'W. Tel: (0674) 72302 & 73153.

HARBOUR WAYPOINT. 56°42.0'N, 2°25.0'W.
Radio — Port & Pilots: VHF Chan. 16, 12 — H24.
Entry: Strong Tidal flow across entrance and in River. Channel protected by sandbanks to the N. Channel maintained to 5.5m. Dredged depth 6.5m. to 5.2m. but liable to silting.
Anchorage: 1-1½M. NE of Skurdie Ness Lt.

Lt.By. Q.R. Can.R.
Lt.By. Q.G. Conical G.
Ldg.Lts. 271°31'. (Front) F.R. 5M. W. & R. Tr.
11m. (Rear) F.R. 5M. W. Tr. 18m.
INNER Ldg.Lts. 264°58' (Front) F.G. 5M. Or. △
on Col. 21m. (Rear) F.G. 5M. Or. △ on Col.
33m.
Lt. Fl.G. 5 sec. G. Pole.
J. M. PIGGENS QUAY. Lt. 2 F.R. vert. 1M. Grey
Post 5m.

OFFSHORE WAYPOINT E OF JOHNSHAVEN.
56°48.0'N, 2°14.0'W.

JOHNSHAVEN 56°48'N, 2°20'W. Tel:
Benholm 207.
Ldg.Lts. 316°. (Front) F.R. R. structure, 5m.
(Rear) F.G. G. structure, 20m. shows R. when
unsafe to enter.

GOURDON HARBOUR 56°50'N, 2°17'W.
Ldg.Lts. 358° (Front) F.R. or G. 5M. W. Tr. 5m.
shows G. when unsafe to enter Hr. Storm sig.
Siren (2) 60 sec. when fishing vessels at sea.
(Rear) F.R. 5M. W. Tr. 30m.
W PIER, HEAD NO: 1. Lt. Fl.W.R.G. 3 sec.
W.9M. R.7M. G.7M. metal Col. 5m. G.shore-
344°; W.344°-354°; R.354°-shore.
E BREAKWATER, HEAD NO: 2. Lt. Q. 7M.
metal Col. 3m.

TOD HEAD 56°53.0'N, 2°12.8'W. Lt.Ho.
Fl.(4) 30 sec. 22M. W. Tr. 41m.

OFFSHORE WAYPOINT STONEHAVEN.
56°57.0'N, 2°07.0'W.

STONEHAVEN 56°58'N, 2°12'W. Tel:
Stonehaven 2963.
Signal: F.G. Lt. or B. Ball shown from S Pier
NE corner when S Harbour closed.

By. Can. R. in position 56°57.57'N, 2°11.95'W.

OUTER BREAKWATER HEAD. Lt. Iso. W.R.G. 4
sec. 9M. 7m. F.R. Lts. on radio mast 6.7m.
291°. G.214°-246°; W.246°-268°; R.268°-280°.
S PIER. NE CNR. Lt. F.G. Shown when unsafe
to enter harbour.
INNER HARBOUR, W SIDE. Ldg.Lts. 273°.
(Front) F. 5M. mast, 6m. for use only inside Hr.
(Rear) F.R. 5M. lantern on building, 8m.

GIRDLE NESS 57°08.3'N, 2°02.8'W. Lt.Ho.
Fl.(2) 20 sec. 22M. W. Tr. 56m. obscured by
Greg Ness when bearing more than 020°. R.C.
Racon. F.R. on radio mast 2.2M. SW.

INVERBERVIE RG STN. 56°51'.8N,
2°15'.66W. Emergency DF Stn. VHF Chan. 16
& 67. Controlled by MRCC Aberdeen.

OFFSHORE WAYPOINT ABERDEEN.
57°07.0'N, 2°00.0'W.

ABERDEEN FAIRWAY. Lt.By. L.Fl. 10 sec.
Sph.R.W.V.S. Racon.

MRCC ABERDEEN (0224) 592334. Weather
broadcast ev. 4h. from 0320.

ABERDEEN 57°08'N, 2°04'W. Tel: (0224)
592571 Pilots (0224) 593290. Telex: 73324.
Radio — Port: VHF Chan. 16, 12, 10, 11, 13 —
continuous.
Radio — Pilots: VHF Chan. 16, 12, 6 —
continuous.
Signals: *Port Control Tr.*
       G. Lt.   = no entry.
       R. Lt.   = no departure.
       R./G. Lt.   = port closed.
Entry: Depth 6m. but liable to silting.
Measured Mile: Aberdeen Bay N of Harbour.
2 Bns. each end of mile (brg. 274°). 184° Mag.
with bns. on Girdleness in line ahead. Depth
of over 9m.
In NNE & N gales there is less sea in harbour.
Avoid entering during NE gales.

DANGER ZONE. Marked by Lt.By. Fl.Y. 5 sec.
Can.Y. & Lt.By. Fl.Y. 10 sec. Can.Y. between
57°12.6'N 2°01.3'W and 57°13.4'N 2°00.7'W.

S BREAKWATER HEAD. Lt. Fl.(3)R. 8 sec. 7M.
W. Tr. 23m.
N PIER HEAD. Lt. Oc. W.R. 6 sec. 8M. W. Tr.
11m. W.145°-325°; R.325°-145°. Same
structure in fog Lt. F.Or. 10m. vis. 136°-336°;
Bell(3) 12 sec.

ABERCROMBY JETTY HEAD. Lt. Oc.G. 4 sec.
4M. △ G. Col. 5m.
S JETTY HEAD. Lt. Q.R. 4M. □ R. Col. 5m.
OLD S BREAKWATER. Lt. Q.R. 2M. □ on R.
Col.

TORRY. Ldg.Lts. 235°45' (Front) F.R. or G. 5M.
W. Tr. 14m. R. when entce. safe and G. when
dangerous to navigation. vis. 195°-279°.
(Rear) F.R. or G. 5M. W. Tr. 19m. vis. 195°-
279°.
LOWER JETTY. Lt. Q.G. △ G. Col.
NEW JETTY. Lt. Q.G. △ G. Col.
RIVER DON ENTRANCE Lt.Bn. Fl. 3 sec. 5M.
W.Tr. 16m.

ABERDEEN TO MORAY FIRTH

CRUDEN SKARES (SGEIR). Lt.By. Fl.R. 10 sec.
Can.R. ⌇⌇ Bell.

OFFSHORE WAYPOINT BUCHAN NESS.
57°28.0'N, 1°43.0'W.

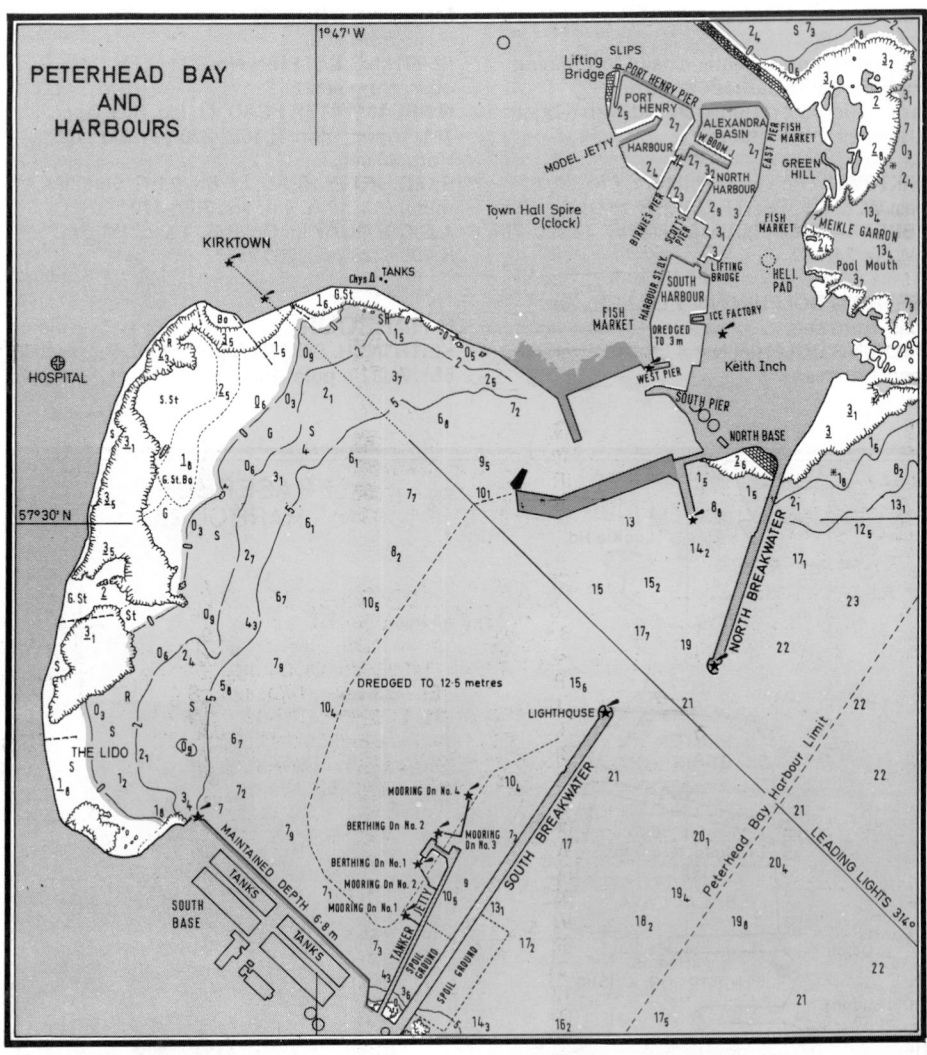

PETERHEAD BAY AND HARBOURS

BUCHAN NESS 57°28.2′N, 1°46.4′W.
Lt.Ho. Fl. 5 sec. 28M. W. Tr. R. bands, 40m.
Racon. Horn(3) 60 sec.
SANDFORD OUTFALL Lt.By. Fl.Y. 5 sec.
Can. Y.

PETERHEAD 57°30′N, 1°46′W. Peterhead
Bay. Tel: (0779) 74020. Mon-Fri 0900-1700.
(0779) 75281 outside office hours. Harbour.
Tel: (0779) 74281/3. H24. Fax: (0779) 75712.
Telex: 73749 PBMCG. Customs: (0779) 74867.

HARBOUR WAYPOINT. 57°29.0′N, 1°45.0′W.

Radio — Port: VHF Chan. 16, 14.
Radio — Pilots: VHF Chan. 14, 9.

Peterhead Asco N Base. Tel: (0779) 74161;
Fax: (0779) 77116.
Radio VHF Chan. 16, 11 as required.
Peterhead Asco S Base. Tel: (0779) 74712;
Fax: (0779) 70549; Telex: 73230 ASCO PE.
Radio VHF Chan. 16, 11. H24.
Entry: *Fishing Harbour signals* (on Control Tr.
over Hr. office on W Pier).

3 Fl.R. (hor)	Bay closed to inward traffic.
3 F.R. (hor)	Fishing Hr. closed to inward traffic.
2 Fl.R. (hor)	No exit from Bay to sea.
2 F.R. (hor)	No exit from Fishing Hr.
4 Fl.R. (hor)	Bay Hr. closed — No traffic movement permitted.
4 F.R. (hor)	Fishing Hr. closed.

When no signals showing, vessels may enter

or leave with permission from Control Tr, call on Chan. 16.
N Entrance permanently closed to shipping.
Outer part of N Harbour dries out.
Passage into Port Henry closed with a boom.
S Hr. caution necessary.

KIRKTOWN. Ldg.Lts. 314° (Front) F.R. 3M. R. mast W. △, 7m.(Rear) F.R. 3M. R. mast W. △, 9m.
S BREAKWATER HEAD. Lt. Fl.(2)R. 12 sec. 7M. B.W. Tr. 24m.

BERTHING DOLPHIN No: 1 Lt. 2 F.R. vert. obsc. from sea.
MOORING DOLPHIN No: 4 Lt. 2 F.R. vert. obsc. from sea.

MOORING DOLPHIN No: 1 Lt. 2 F.R. vert. obsc. from sea.
BERTHING DOLPHIN No: 2 Lt. 2 F.R. vert. obsc. from sea.
N BREAKWATER HEAD. Lt. Iso. R.G. 6 sec. 7M. Tripod, 19m. R.165°-230°; W.230°-165°. Horn 30 sec.
B.O.C. JETTY HEAD. Lt. Bn. 2 F.G. vert. 1M. W. metal Col. 11m. 9m. vis. 350°-170°
A.S.CO. QUAY Lt. Oc. R.G. 4 sec. 1M. 7m. R.195°-225°; G.225°-255°.

S HARBOUR
KEITH INCH. SOUTH QUAY. Lt. Fl. G. 2 sec. 5M. W.□ on pole 15m.

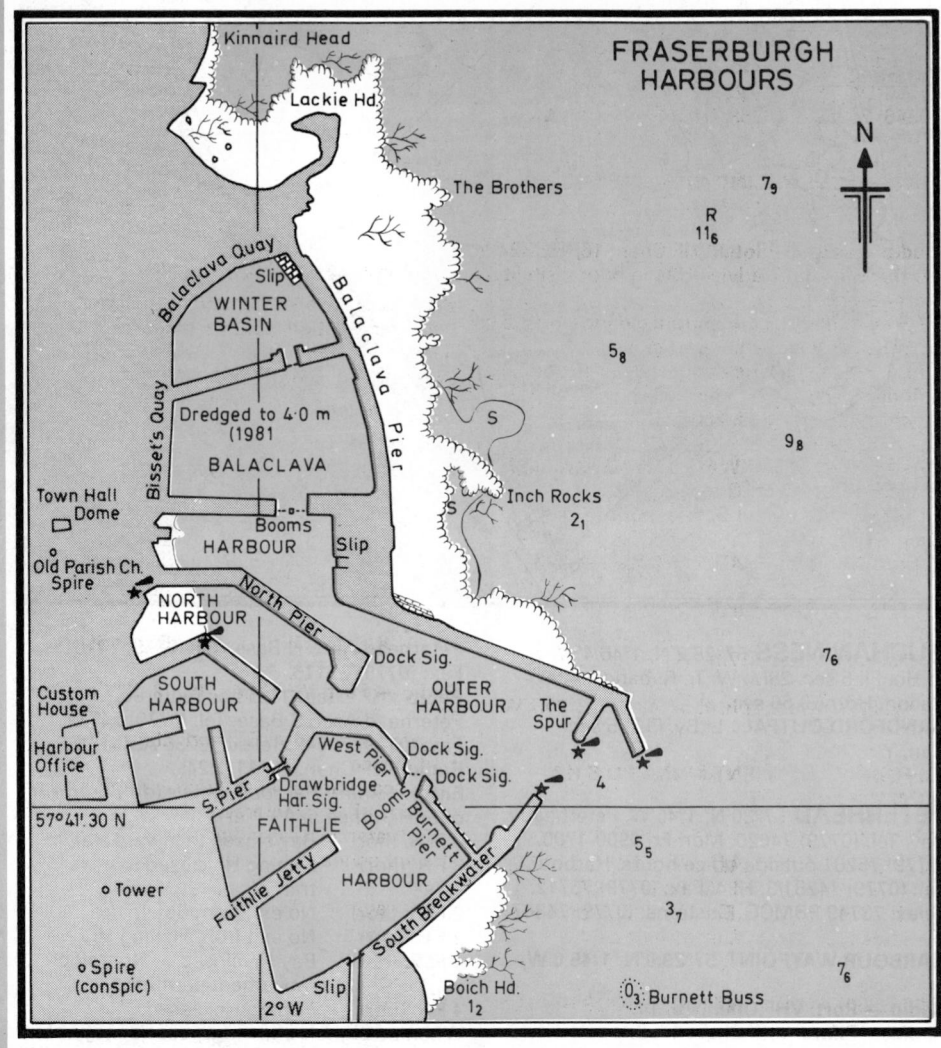

W PIER, ELBOW. Lt. Q.R. 2M. stone Tr. 7m.
vis. 000°-070°. Traffic sig. when fishing
vessels at sea.
KEITH INCH. Lt. 57°29.9'N, 1°46.2'W. Oc.
W.R.G. 6 sec. 12M. W. mast 16m. G.048.8°-
056.5°; W.056.5°-060.4°; R.060.4°-068.4°. H24.

OFFSHORE WAYPOINT RATTRAY HD.
57°37.0'N, 1°46.0'W.

RATTRAY HEAD 57°36.6'N, 1°48.9'W.
Lt.Ho. Fl.(3) 30 sec. 24M. white Tr. lower part
granite, upper brick, 28m. Horn(2) 45 sec. R.
Lts. on masts 2.5M. WNW & 2.2M. W. Racon.
MORMOND HILL. Lt. Aero Iso.R. 2 sec. radio
mast. Lt. Aero 2 F.R. vert.
CAIRNBULG BRIGGS. Lt.Bn. Fl. 3 sec. 5M. 9m.

FRASERBURGH 57°42'N, 2°00'W. Tel:
Fraserburgh (0346) 25858 & 25926. Pilots:
(0346) 26069 & 28868.

HARBOUR WAYPOINT. 57°47.0'N, 1°58.0'W.

Radio — Port & Pilots: VHF Chan. 16, 12. H24.
Radar will supply advice H24 in poor visibility.
Entry Signals:
W Pier. R. flag/R. Lt. = entrance dangerous. 2
B. Balls/2 R. Lts. vert. = Port closed.
Entry and anchorage dangerous in strong E'ly
Winds.
Anchorage: Pier Hds. 280°T. ½M.

BALACLAVA BREAKWATER HEAD. Lt. Fl.(2)G.
8 sec. 6M. Stone Tr. G.top. 26m.
SPUR HEAD. Lt. L. Fl.G. 6 sec. 5M. 'Slow'
board, 5m.
S BREAKWATER HEAD. Lt. Fl.R. 6 sec. 5M.
Col. 9m.
Ldg.Lts. 291°. Middle Jetty, Elbow (Front) Q.R.
5M. R.W. mast, 12m. N Pier, Root (Rear) Oc.
R. 6 sec. 5M. mast, 17m.

Lt.By. Fl. Y. 6 sec. Sph. Y. 57°43.8'N, 2°00.7'W.

OFFSHORE WAYPOINT KINNAIRD'S HD.
57°48.0'N, 2°00.0'W.

KINNAIRD'S HEAD 57°41.9'N, 2°00.1'W.
Lt.Ho. Fl. 15 sec. 25M. W. Tr. 37m. R.C.
GARDENSTOWN. Lt.Bn. F.W.R. 5M. on E Pier
Head. R.119°-214°; W. elsewhere.

OFFSHORE WAYPOINT N OF TROUP HEAD.
57°43.0'N, 2°18.0'W.

BANFF BAY

MACDUFF Tel: (0261) 32236 (Night (0261)
22014). Telex: 730148.

HARBOUR WAYPOINT. 57°41.0'N, 2°31.0'W.

Radio — Port & Pilots: VHF Chan. 16, 12. H24.
Anchorage: 1M. off on Ldg. Line.
LIGHTHOUSE PIER HEAD. Lt. Fl.(2) W.R.G. 6
sec. W.9M. R.7M. W. Tr. 12m. G. shore-115°;
W.115°-174°; R.174°-210°. Horn(2) 20 sec.
Ldg.Lts. 127° (Front) F.R. 3M. W. mast, B.
bands, 44m. shown 1 October to 1 March.
(Rear) F.R. 3M. W. mast, B. bands, 55m.
shown 1 October to 1 March.
W PIER HEAD. Lt. Q.G. 5M. 4m.
WHITEHILLS PIER HEAD. Lt. Fl.W. R. 3 sec.
W.9M. R.6M. W. Tr. 7m. R.132°-212°; W.212°-
245°.
PORTSOY PIER. Ldg.Lts. 160°. (Front) F. 5M.
Tr. 12m. (Rear) F.R. 5M. on mast, 17m.

WINDY HEAD RG STN. 57°38'55"0N
2°14'31"0W. Emergency DF Stn. VHF Chan. 16
& 67. Controlled by MRCC Aberdeen.

FINDOCHTY 57°42'N, 2°55'W.
Signals: Lts. on W Pier and Mast shown 1/8-
1/5 when enough water to enter. Day — R.
flag.
W PIER. Lt. F. 5M. W. Tr. Lt. F.R. 4M. on mast.
Shown 1 August to 1 May.

OFFSHORE WAYPOINT OFF PORTNOCKIE.
57°44.0'N, 2°51.0'W.

BUCKIE 57°41'N, 2°57'W. Tel: (0542) 31700.
Fax: (0542) 34742. Telex: 739148 SHARET G.

HARBOUR WAYPOINT. 57°41.5'N, 2°59.0'W.

Radio — Port: VHF Chan. 16, 12. H24 on Chan.
16.
Signals: 3 B. Balls/3 F.R. vert. Lts. at W Pier =
Port closed.
Entrance channel least depth 3.3m. Yachts
use No: 4 basin, entered by winding back the
breakwater access bridge, using a handle
stowed on jetty. Lifeboat is moored in No: 4
basin.
Anchorage: 1M. W of Mucks Lt.

W MUCK. Lt. Q.R. 7M. tripod, 5m. ⑂
unreliable in bad weather.
N BREAKWATER HEAD. Lt. 2 F.R. vert. 11M.
on Col. 7m.

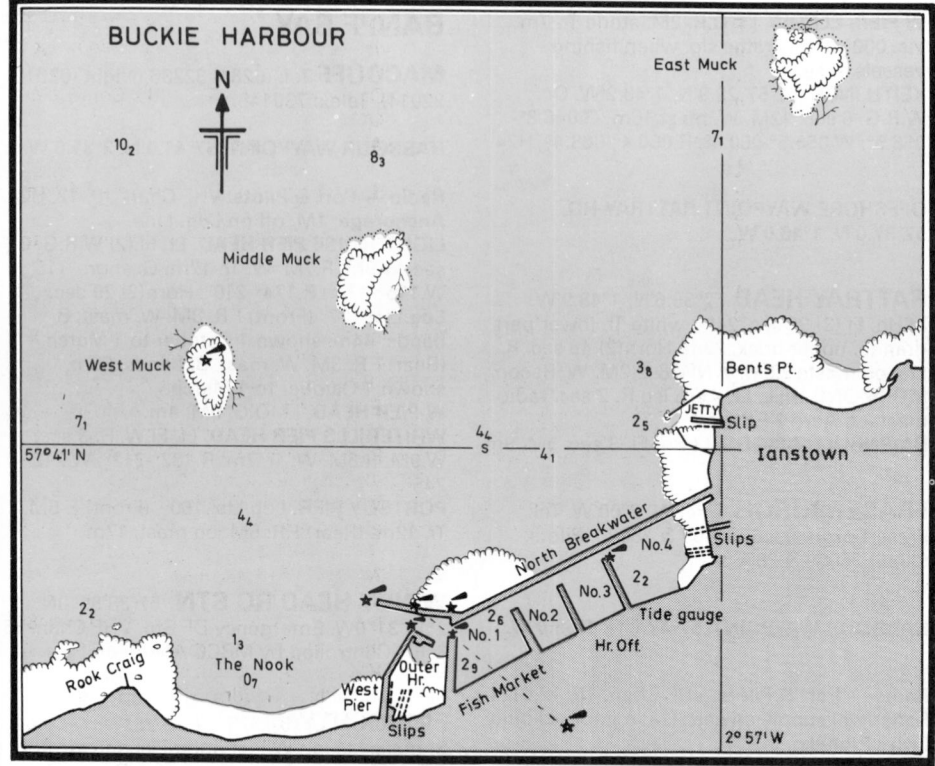

BUCKIE HARBOUR

N

East Muck

10₂

8₃

7₁

Middle Muck

West Muck

3₈   Bents Pt.

7₁

2₅   JETTY Slip

57°41' N

4₄ S   4₁   Ianstown

4₄

2₂

North Breakwater   No.4 Slips

No.3   2₂

2₆ No.2

Rook Craig   The Nook   1₃   No.1

0₇   Outer Hr.   2₉   Tide gauge

West Pier   Fish Market   Hr. Off.

Slips

2° 57' W

Ldg.Lts. 125°. (Front) Oc.R. 10 sec. 15M. W. Tr. 15m. Reserve Lt. F. Siren(2) 60 sec. (Rear) Iso.W.G. 2 sec. W.16M. G.12M. W. Col. 30m. G.090°-110°; W.110°-225°.
W PIER, NW CORNER. Lt. 2 F.G. vert. 9M. on Col. 4m. Tidal sig.

OFFSHORE WAYPOINT N OF LOSSIEMOUTH. 57°45.0'N, 3°17.0'W.

LOSSIEMOUTH 57°43'N, 3°17'W. Tel: (034-381) 3066.
Radio — Port & Pilots: VHF Chan. 16, 12. 0800-1700 and 1 h. before vessel expected.
Entry Signals: Dangerous to enter when winds ESE to N over force 5.
By day: B. Ball or shape at S Pier
By night: F.R. over Fl.R. Lt.
R. flag when cargo vessel leaving.
Strong cross tide at Hr. Entrance coming from River.
Anchorage: Lossiemouth Bay.

S PIER HEAD. Lt. Fl.R. 6 sec. 5M. mast, 11m. Entry and storm sig. 4 Lts. F.R. occas. shown about 5M. SE Siren 60 sec. when fishing vessels at sea.

MIDDLE JETTY. Ldg.Lts. 292°. (Front) F.R. mast, 5m. shown when safe to enter. (Rear) F.R. mast, 8m. (Fishing Lts).

COVESEA SKERRIES 57°43.5'N, 3°20.2'W. Lt.Ho. Fl. W.R. 20 sec. W.24M. R.20M. W. Tr. 49m. W.076°-267°; R.267°-282°.

HOPEMAN HARBOUR
Entry Signal: 2 R. Lts. vert. = vessel may enter.
S PIER HEAD. Lt. F.G. 4M. mast, 8m. F.R. Lts. on 4 radio masts 1.5M. E.
N QUAY, ELBOW. Ldg.Lts. 081°. (Front) F.R. 4m. (Rear) F.R. on post, 3m.

BURGHEAD 57°42'N, 3°30'W. Tel: Burghead (0343) 835337.
Radio — Port: VHF Chan. 16, 12, 9, 6 when vessels expected.
Radio — Pilots: VHF Chan. 16, 14. Working hours and when vessel expected.
Anchorage: In the Bay.

N BREAKWATER HEAD. Lt. Oc. 8 sec. 5M. concrete Tr. 7m. Storm sig. 5 F.R. Lts. on radio mast 1M. ESE.

SPUR HEAD. Lt. Q.R. 5M. wooden structure, 3m. vis. from SW only.
S PIER HEAD. Lt. Q.G. 5M. wooden structure, 3m. vis. from SW only.

NAIRN HARBOUR

Harbour Master Tel: (0667) 54704.
At present there are 40+ floating pontoons (6 for visitors) but a marina development is underway.
W PIER HEAD. Lt. Q.G. 1M. B. post, 5m.
E PIER HEAD. Lt. Oc. W.R.G. 4 sec. 5M. octagonal concrete Tr, 6m. G.shore-100°; W.100°-207°; R.207°-shore.

WHITENESS HEAD. McDERMOTT BASE. Dir. Lt. 142°30'. Dir. Iso. W.R.G. 4 sec. 6m. G.138°-141°; W.141°-144°; R.144°-147°.
CHANNEL ENTRANCE. Lt.By. Q.R. Pillar R.
CHANNEL ENTRANCE. Lt.By. Q.G. Pillar G.
Thence by Pillar Bys. R. & G.

APPROACHES TO INVERNESS FIRTH

SOUTH CHANNEL

RIFF BANK E. Lt.By. Fl.Y. 10 sec. Spherical Y. ⌇.
RIFF BANK S. Lt.By. Q.G. Conical G. marking S Middle edge.
RIFF BANK W Lt.By. Fl.Y. 5 sec. Sph.Y.
CRAIGMEE. Lt.By. Fl.R. 6 sec. Can.R. Fort George.

NORTH CHANNEL

NAVITY BANK. Lt.By. Fl.(3) G. 15 sec. Conical G. ⌇ on S edge.
RIFF BANK N. Lt.By. Fl.(2)R. 12 sec. Can.R. marking N edge of Riff Bank Middle.

INVERNESS FIRTH

INVERNESS 57°30'N, 4°14'W. Tel: (0463) 233291. Pilots: (0463) 235264. B.W. Canal: (0463) 233140.
Radio — Port: VHF Chan. 12, 16, 14. H24.
Radio — Pilots: VHF Chan. 12, 16, 6. 2 h.-HW-2 h. and when v/l expected.
Max. Air Draught Kessoch Road Br. — 27.4m.
Anchorage: Close NE of Munlochy By. & Kessoch Road W of Hbr. Entrance.
N & NE gales produce considerable sea.

CHANONRY POINT. Lt. Oc. 6 sec. 15M. W. Tr. 12m. vis. 148°-073°. F.R. Lts. on radio mast 6.1M. WNW.
CHANONRY NESS OUTFALL By. Conical Y.
NW SKATE BANK By. Can.R.
NE SKATE BANK By. Can.R.

AVOCH. Lt. 2 F.R. vert. 5M. concrete Col. 7m. when fishing vessels at sea.
Entry: Can be entered at HWS by craft up to 3m. draught.

MUNLOCHY SHOAL. Lt.By. L.Fl. 10 sec. Spherical R.W.V.S. ⌇ NE edge of Middle Bank.
PETTY BANK By. Can.R.
MEIKLE MEE. Lt.By. Fl.G. 6 sec. Conical G.
LONGMAN PT. Lt.Bn. Fl.W.R. 2 sec. W.5M. R.4M. R. conical metal Bn. 7m. W.078°-258°; R.258°-078°.
LONGMAN QUAY, 180m. × 4.5m. depth. Channel marked E side.
INNER Lt. Q.R. 4M. 3m.
TURNING Lt. Fl.R. 3 sec. 6M. 7m.
CRAIGTON POINT. Lt. Fl. W.R.G. 4 sec. W.11M. R.7M. G.7M. W.Bn. 6m. W.312°-048°; R.048°-064°; W.064°-085°; G.085°-shore.
KESSOCK ROAD BRIDGE. N Tr. Lts. Oc. G. 6 sec. 5M. NE/NW Tr. 28m. also Q.G. 3M. 3m. Aero Lts. F.R. on top of Tr. Y. Lts. mark bridge centre.
S Tr. Lts. Oc. R. 6 sec. 5M. SE/SW Tr. 28m. also Q.R. 3M. 3m. Aero Lt. F.R. on top of Tr.
OUTER BEACON Lt. Q.R.
INNER BEACON Lt. Q.R.
EMBANKMENT HEAD. Lt. Fl.G. 2 sec. 4M. G. Tr. 8m.
E SIDE. Lt.Bn. Fl.R. 3 sec. 6M. Y. △ Tr. 7m.
THORNBUSH WHARF, N END. Lt. Q.G. metal Col. 6m.
SLIPWAY HEAD. Lt. 2 F.G. vert. 4M. post, 4m.
NEW QUAY. N. End Lt. Q.R. 5M. Metal Col.
UPPER QUAY, N END. Lt. F. shed, 8m.
TRAINING WALL HEAD. Lt. Q.G. B. metal mast, W. bands, 5m.

CALEDONIAN CANAL

VHF Stations Chan. 16 & 74. Clachnaharry Sea Lock, Caledonian Canal, Dochgarroch Lock, Fort Augustus Lock, Laggan Lock, Corpach Lock.
Locks available 0800-1200, 1300-1700 (not Sunday). Unavailable 2h.-LW-2h. 45.72m x 10.67m x 4.1m.

CLACHNAHARRY

S TRAINING WALL HEAD. Lt. Iso. 4 sec. W. △ on W. mast, 5m. Traffic sig.

BONA FERRY, W SIDE. Lt. 2 F.R. vert. 5M. W. house, 6m. Not shown in summer.
FORT AUGUSTUS. Lt. 2 F.G. vert. 4M. W. Tr. 9m. vis. 202°-265°. Not shown in summer.
GAIRLOCHY. Lt. Fl. 3 sec. 4M. W. Tr. 7m. Not shown in summer.

OFFSHORE WAYPOINT CROMARTY FIRTH. 57°41.0′N, 3°53.0′W.

CROMARTY FIRTH Tel: Invergordon (0349) 852308.
Pilotage as for Invergordon.
FAIRWAY Lt.By. L.Fl. 10 sec. Sph. R.W.V.S. Racon.
CROMARTY BANK. Lt.By. Fl.(2)G. 10 sec. Conical G.
BUSS BANK. Fl.R. 3 sec. Can.R. off S Sutor Point.

CROMARTY Tel. No. Cromarty 502.

CROMARTY, THE NESS 57°41.0′N, 4°02.1′W. Lt. Oc. W.R. 10 sec. W.14M. R.11M. W. Tr. 18m. R.079°-088°; W.088°-275°. Obscured by N Sutor when bearing less than 253°. F.R. Lt. on mast 3.3M. SSW.
NIGG FERRY JETTY. Lt. 2 F.G. vert. 2M. 6m.
NIGG OIL TERM. JTY HD. Lt. Oc.G. 5 sec. 31m. 5M.
E & W DOLPHINS Lts. 2 F.G. vert.
BRITISH ALCAN JETTY
HEAD CENTRE. Lt. Q.G. 5M. mast on building, 17m.
E DOLPHIN. Lt. 2 F.G. vert. 2M. 5m.
W END. Lt. 2 F.G. vert. 2M. on dolphin, 5m.
NIGG SANDS E. Lt.By. Fl.(2)G. 10 sec. Conical G.
NATAL WK. Lt.By. Fl.(2) 12 sec. Pillar B.R.B. Topmark Is. D.
NIGG SANDS W. Lt.By. Fl.G. 3 sec. Conical G. ⌣
FAIRWAY, N BANK marked by No: 2, 3 and 4 Bns. without Topmark.
NEWHALL Lt.By. Fl.(2)R. 10 sec. Can.R. ⌣

INVERGORDON 57°41′N, 4°10′W. Tel: Port Mngr/Pilots: (0349) 852308. Telex: 75263.

HARBOUR WAYPOINT. 57°41.4′N, 4°09.0′W.

Radio — Port: Invergordon VHF Chan. 11, 16, 13. H24.
Radio — Pilots: c/s Invergordon Pilots. VHF Chan. 13, 16, 11. H24.
NE ADMIRALTY PIER. Lt.By. Fl.G. 2 sec. Conical G.

DOCKYARD PIER HEAD. Lt. Fl.(3)G. 10 sec. 4M. 15m.
OFF W END. Lt. 2 F.G. vert. on dolphin.
OFF E END. Lt. 2 F.G. vert. on dolphin.
INVERGORDON SUPPLY BASE. SE Lt. Iso.G. 4 sec. 6M. Grey mast 9m.
QUAY W END. Lt. Oc.G. 8 sec. 6M. Grey mast 9m.
QUEENS DOCK W ARM. Lt. Iso.G. 2 sec. 6M. Grey mast 9m.
DALMORE. EARTH EMBANKMENT. Lt. Fl.G. 4 sec. 4M. Tr. 8m.

ALNESS BAY
HIGHLAND DEEPHAVEN CAUSEWAY HEAD. Lt. Fl.G. 5 sec. 6M. Grey mast 9m.
ROSKEEN SEWER OUTFALL. Lt.By. Fl.Y. 5 sec. Conical Y.
THREE KINGS Lt.By. Q.(3) 10 sec. Pillar B.Y.B. Topmark E marks shoals 2M. S of Balintore.

OFFSHORE WAYPOINT TARBAT NESS. 57°53.0′N, 3°43.0′W.

TARBAT NESS 57°51.9′N, 3°46.5′W. Lt. Fl.(4) 30 sec. 24M. W. Tr. R. bands, 53m.
CADBOLL POINT. Lt.By. 'DZ' Fl.R. 5 sec.
TAIN FIRING RANGE. Lt. 2 F.R. vert. on mast occas.
Lt. 4 F. vert. Lt. 6 F.hor. Lt. F.R. on mast occas.
Lt.By. Fl.Y. 5 sec. Pillar Y.

DORNOCH FIRTH

OFFSHORE WAYPOINT DORNOCH FIRTH. 57°52.0′N, 3°53.0′W.

DORNOCH FIRTH BRIDGE
Lts. shown up/down stream.
SOUTH NAVIGATION SPAN
S.PIER. Lt. Iso R. 4 sec. 5M. R.□ 14m.
CENTRE. Lt. Iso R. 4 sec. 5M. W.O R. stripes 14m.
N. PIER. Lt. Q.Y. 5M. 14m.
CENTRE NAVIGATION SPAN
CENTRE. Lt. Iso 4 sec. 5M. W.O R. stripes 14m.
N. PIER. Lt. Q.Y. 5M. 14m.
NORTH NAVIGATION SPAN
CENTRE. Lt. Iso 4 sec. 5M. W.O R. stripes 14m.
N.PIER. Lt. Iso G. 4 sec. 5M. G.△ 14m.

CULLODEN ROCKS. By. Can.R. off Tarbat Ness.
TAIN BAR By. Sph.R.W.V.S. on bar at entce. to Dornoch Firth.
HELMSDALE. Ldg.Lts. 313°. (Front) F.R. or F.G. W. mast. Depth sig. (Rear) F.G. W. mast. (Front) R. = Hbr. Closed. G. = Hbr. open. NW PIER Horn 30 sec. when fishing vessels at sea.

BEN-A-CHIELT. Lt. Aero 5 F.R. vert. radio mast. Obstruction.
LYBSTER, S PIER HEAD. Lt. Oc.R. 6 sec. 3M. W. Tr. 10m. when fishing vessels at sea.
DORNOCH FIRTH BRIDGE 30m. navigational spans, clearance 11m.

HARBOUR WAYPOINT. 58°17.0′N, 3°17.0′W.

No: 3 Ra. Target. Lt.By. 57°58′N, 2°50′W. Fl.Y. 3 sec. Pillar Y.

CLYTHNESS 58°19.0′N, 3°13.0′W. Lt. Gp.Fl.(2) 30 sec. 16M. W. Tr. R. band, 45m.

OFFSHORE WAYPOINT CLYTHNESS. 58°18.0′N, 3°10.0′W.

OFFSHORE WAYPOINT ULBSTER HD. 58°22.0′N, 3°04.0′W.

WICK 58°26′N, 3°06′W. Tel: (0955) 2030.

HARBOUR WAYPOINT. 58°26.0′N, 3°03.0′W.

Radio — Port/Pilots: VHF Chan. 16, 14.

Entry Signals: Main harbour should never be app. for shelter in bad weather, as with winds from NE to S a heavy sea runs into harbour. Entry should not be attempted without pilot. **Lookout House, S Head.** (Flagstaff).

By day: B. ball
By night: 1 G. Lt. } harbour not accessible.

No vessel to enter or leave or attempt to do so until there is sufficient depth of water for vessel's draught. Signals indicating depth of water at ent. of harbour basins are hoisted on flagstaff at S Pier.
R. square flag: 2.4m. G. square flag: 2.7m. Y. square flag: 3m. R. Pennant: 3.3m. R. Pennant above square Y. flag: 3.6m.
When ent. obstructed, temporary B. ball or R. Lt. from S Pier Hd.
Dir.Lt. 290°30′ Dir. F. W.R.G. 4 sec. 10M. Col. N end of Bridge 9m. G.285°-289°; W.289°-291°; R.291°-295°

S PIER HEAD. Lt. Fl.W.R.G. 3 sec. 5M. W. octagonal Tr. 12m. Port sig. Bell(2) 10 sec. G.253°-269°; W.269°-286°; R.286°-329°.

Ldg.Lts. 234°. S Pier Root. (Front) F.R. on mast, 5m. (Rear) F.R. lantern on building, 8m. **HARBOUR QUAY.** Lt. F.Vi. marks end of Slipway. **N RIVER PIER.** Lt. 2 F.G. vert. 2M. Tripod. **S RIVER PIER.** Lt. 2 F.R. vert. 2M. Tripod.

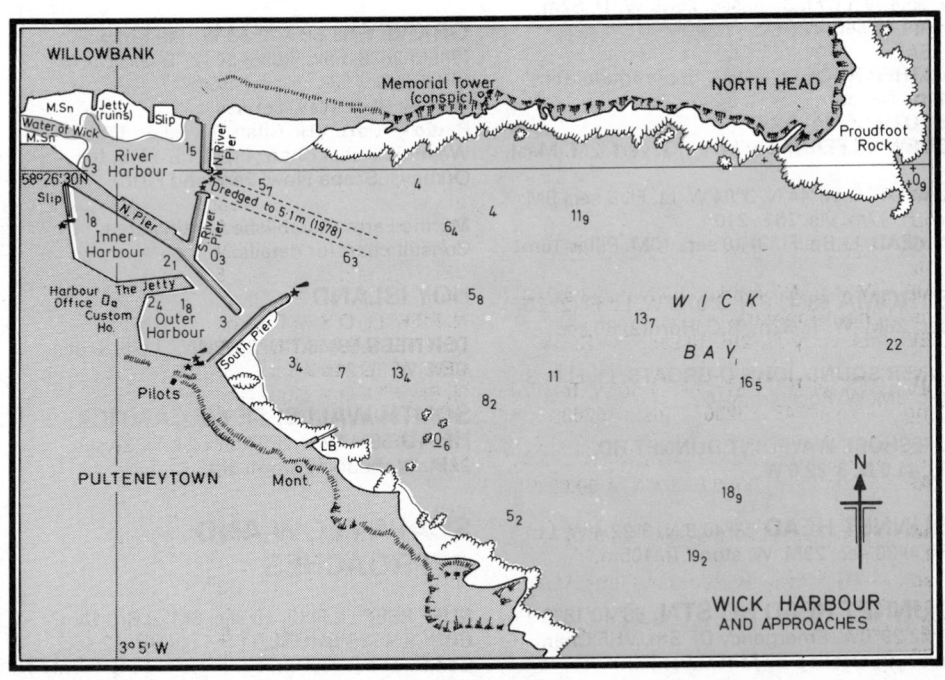

WICK HARBOUR
AND APPROACHES

OFFSHORE WAYPOINT NOSS HD. **58°28.0'N, 3°00.0'W.**

NOSS HEAD 58°28.8'N, 3°03.0'W. Lt. Fl.W.R. 20 sec. W.25M. R.21M. W. stone Tr, 53m. R.shore-191°; W.191°-shore.

THRUMSTER RG STN. 58°23.5'N, 3°07.25'W. Emergency DF Stn. VHF Chan. 16 & 67. Controlled by MRSC Pentland.

MRSC PENTLAND (0856) 3268. Weather broadcast ev. 4h. from 0135.

PENTLAND FIRTH

Note: Tidal streams with eddies and races run up to 16 knots with heavy turbulence and sudden changes between the main stream and the eddies. Headlands, islands, etc. should be given a wide berth.

OFFSHORE WAYPOINT DUNCANSBY HD. **58°39.0'N, 3°00.0'W.**

DUNCANSBY HEAD 58°38.6'N, 3°01.4'W. Lt. Fl. 12 sec. 17M. W. Tr. 67m. Racon.

PENTLAND SKERRIES 58°41.4'N, 2°55.4'W. Lt. Fl.(3) 30 sec. 25M. W. Tr. 52m. Horn 45 sec. W. Tr.

LOTHER ROCK Lt. Q. 6M. B. pyramidal Bn., 11m. Racon.
SOUTH RONALDSAY
BURWICK FERRY Jty Lt. 2 F.G. vert. 2M. Mast.

SWONA 58°44'N, 3°04'W. Lt. Fl. 8 sec. 9M. W. Tr. 17m. vis. 261°-210°.
N HEAD. Lt.Bn. Fl.(3) 10 sec. 10M. Pillar 16m.

STROMA 58°41.8'N, 3°07.0'W. Lt. Fl.(2) 20 sec. 26M. W. Tr. 32m. R.C. Horn(2) 60 sec.

INNER SOUND JOHN O-GROATS. Lt. Fl.R. 3 sec. 2M. W. Post. 4m. ᨦ.

OFFSHORE WAYPOINT DUNNET HD. **58°41.0'N, 3°22.0'W.**

DUNNET HEAD 58°40.3'N, 3°22.4'W. Lt. Fl.(4) 30 sec. 23M. W. stone Tr. 105m.

DUNNET HEAD RG STN. 58°40'18"0N, 3°22'29"0W. Emergency DF Stn. VHF Chan. 16 & 67. Controlled by MRSC Pentland.

THURSO BAY

SCRABSTER (Thurso) 58°37'N, 3°33'W. Tel: Thurso (0847) 62779/64618. Telex: 75449 THURSO G.
Radio — Port & Pilots: VHF Chan. 16, 12. 0800-2200.
Give 'Grounds' 58°37'35"0N, 3°30'00"W a wide berth.
Anchorage: ½M. NE-E of Thurso B'water.

HOLBORN HEAD 58°36.9'N, 3°32.4'W. Lt. Fl.W.R. 10 sec. W.15M. R.11M. W. Tr. 23m. W.198°-358°; R.358°-shore. F.R. Lts. on chy. 6.9M. 251°; F.R. Lts. on radio mast 4.7M. 262°.

THURSO BREAKWATER HEAD. Lt. Q.G. 6m. 4M. R. post shown 1 Sept.-30 Apr.

HARBOUR. Ldg.Lts. 195°. (Front) F.G. 4M. W. post, 5m. (Rear) F.G. 4M. W. mast, 6m.
SCRABSTER OUTER PIER HEAD. Lt. Q.G. 4M. Post 6m.
SCRABSTER PIER HEAD. Lt. 2 F.G. vert. 4M. W. post, 3m. shown 1 Aug.-31 May.
W PIER HEAD. Lt. 2 F.R. vert. 3M. concrete post, 3m. shown 1 Aug-31 May.

STRATHY POINT 58°36.0'N, 4°01.0'W. Lt. Fl. 20 sec. 27M. W. low Tr. on W. dwelling, 45m.

ORKNEY ISLANDS

ORKNEY 58°58'N, 2°58'W. Tel: Kirkwall (0856) 3636. Fax: (0856) 3012. Telex: 75475 SPLICE G.
Orkney Hbrs. Nav. Service
Radio — Port: VHF Chan. 16, 20, 9, 11. H24. Weather. F'cast Chan. 11, 0915, 1715, for Orkneys, Scapa Flow, Pentland Firth.

Marine Farms established in this area. Consult chart for details.

HOY ISLAND

TOR NESS 58°46.7'N, 3°17.6'W. Lt. Fl. 3 sec. 10M. W. Tr. 21m.

SOUTH WALLS, SE OF CANTICK HEAD 58°47.2'N, 3°07.8'W. Lt. Fl. 20 sec. 22M. W. Tr. 35m. Storm sig.

SCAPA FLOW AND APPROACHES

RUFF REEF Lt. Fl.(2) 10 sec. 6M. B.Bn. 10m.
CROCKNESS SHOAL. Lt.By. Fl.(2)R. 12 sec. Can.R. ᨦ.

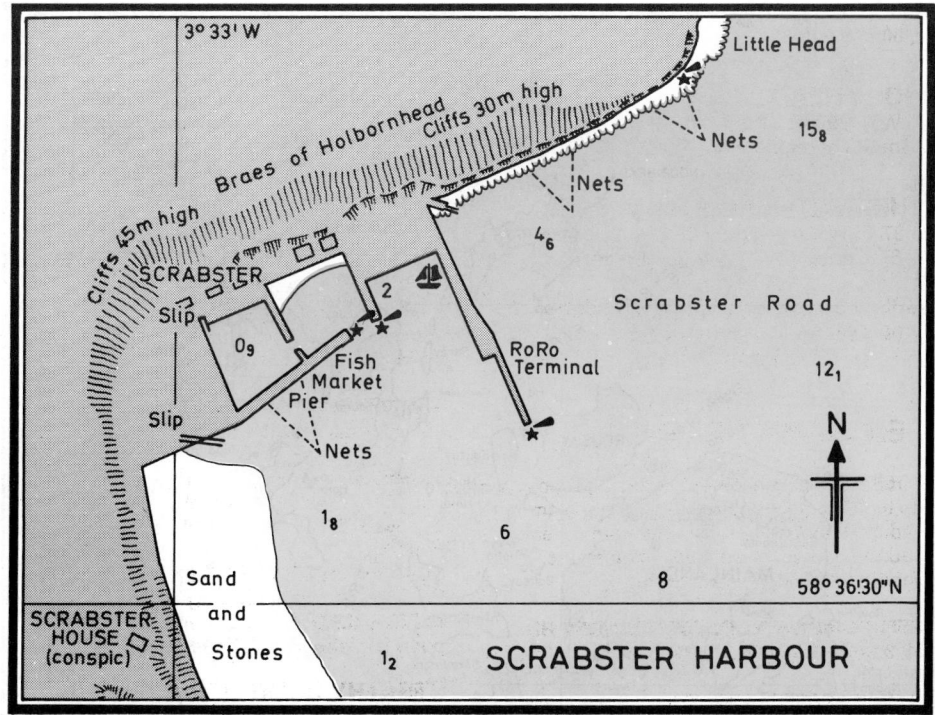

Map labels: 3°33'W · Little Head · Braes of Holbornhead · Cliffs 30m high · Nets · 15₈ · Cliffs 45m high · Nets · ⁴6 · SCRABSTER · Slip · 2 · Scrabster Road · 0₉ · Fish Market Pier · RoRo Terminal · 12₁ · Slip · Nets · N · 1₈ · 6 · 8 · 58°36'30"N · SCRABSTER HOUSE (conspic) · Sand and Stones · 1₂ · **SCRABSTER HARBOUR**

LYNESS HARBOUR
GUTTER SOUND WK. Lt.By. Fl.R. 6 sec. Can.R.
LONG HOPE, SOUTH NESS PIER HEAD. Lt. Fl.W.R.G. 3 sec. W.7M. R.5M. G.5M. W.Blg. 6m. G.082°-242°; W.242°-252°; R.252°-082°.

WIDEFORD HILL R.G. STN. 58°59.30'N, 3°01.4'W. Emergency D.F. STN. VHF Chan. 16 & 67 controlled by MRSC Pentland.

CAVA ISLAND 58°53.2'N, 3°10.6'W. Lt. Fl. 3 sec. 8M. W. Tr. 11m.
HOUTON BAY. Ldg.Lts. 316°02' (Front) Fl.G. 3 sec. R. △ on W. pole B. bands 8m. (Rear) F.G. R. △ on W. pole B. bands 16m. Vis. 312°-320°.
HOUTON BAY PIER HEAD. Lt. 2 F.R. vert. 4M.
RO-RO TERMINAL S END. Lt. Iso.R. 4 sec. 5M. Mast 7m.
RIDDOCK SHOAL. Lt.By. Fl.(2)R. 12 sec. Can.R. off Graemsay I.
PETER SKERRYS. Lt.By. Fl.G. 6 sec. Conical G. off Peterdown, in Bring Deeps.
HOXA HEAD Lt. Fl.W.R. 3 sec. W.9M. R.6M. W. Tr. 15m. W.026°-163°; R.163°-201°; W.201°-215°.
STANGER HEAD. Lt.Bn. Fl.R. 5 sec. 8M. Pillar 25m.

ROAN HEAD. Lt.Bn. Fl.(2)R. 6 sec. 7M. Pillar 12m.
NEVI SKERRY. Lt.Bn. Fl.(2) 6 sec. 6M. B.Bn. 7m.
THE GRINDS. Lt.By. Fl.(2)R. 10 sec. Can.R.
CALF OF FLOTTA. Lt.Bn. Q.R. 4M. Pillar 8m.

FLOTTA MARINE TERMINAL. Tel: Agent (0856) 2268/3462. Telex: 75212 OXYOPS G.
Radio — Port: VHF Chan. 16, 9, 11, 20. H24.
FLOTTA TERMINAL E END. Lt. 2 F.R. vert.
W END. Lt. 2 F.R. vert. Bell. 10 sec.
MOORING DOLPHIN E END. Lt. Q.R. 3M. 8m.
W END. Lt. Q.R. 3M. 8m.
4 MOORING. Lt.Bys. Fl. 5 sec.
SINGLE POINT MOORING TOWER No. 1 Lt.Bn. Fl.Y. 5 sec. 3M. 12m. Horn. Mo(A) 60 sec.
No. 2 Lt.Bn. Fl.(4)Y. 15 sec. 3M. 12m. Horn. Mo(N) 60 sec.
GIBRALTAR PIER. Lt. 2 F.G. vert. 3M. 3m.
GOLDEN WHF, N END. Lt. 2 F.R. vert. 3M. mast 7m.
LYNESS WHF, S END. Lt. 2 F.R. vert. 3M. mast 7m.
ST MARGARETS HOPE. (Needle Point Reef) Lt. Fl.G. 3 sec. on post, 2m. when vessels expected.
PIER HEAD. Lt. 2 F.G. vert. 4M. on Col. 6m. shown 15 July-15 April.

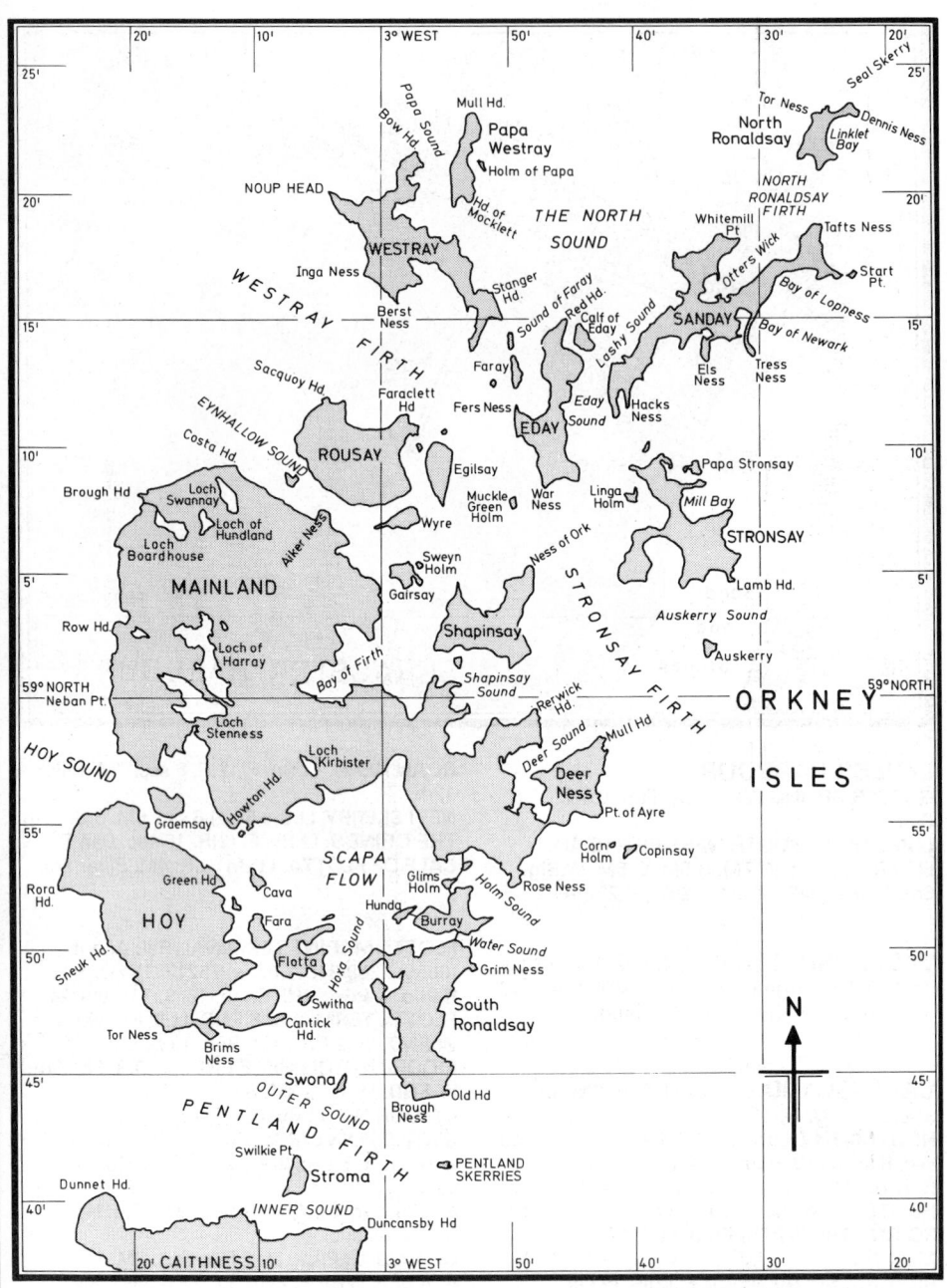

Ldg.Lts. 196° (Front) F.R. on post, 7m. when vessels expected. (Rear) F.R. on post, 11m. when vessels expected.

BARREL OF BUTTER Lt.Bn. Fl.(2) 10 sec. 7M. stone Twr 6m.

Lt.By. V.Q.(3) 5 sec. B.Y.B. Pillar Topmark E.

SCAPA PIER HEAD Tel: Kirkwall 634.
Lt. Fl.G. 3 sec. 8M. mast, 6m. F.R. Lts. mark radio masts 2.3M. SSE.
SCAPA SKERRY. Lt.By. Fl.(2)R. 12 sec. Can.R.

HOY SOUND

GRAEMSAY ISLAND. Ldg.Lts. 104°.
(Front) Iso. 3 sec. 15M. W. Tr. 17m. vis. 070°-255°. (Rear) Oc.W.R. 8 sec. W.20M. R.16M. W. Tr. 35m. R.097°-112°; W.112°-163°; R.163°-178°; W.178°-332°. Obscured on leading line with 0.5M.

SKERRY OF NESS Lt. Fl.W.G. 4 sec. W.7M. G. 4M. ▢ W. Tr. 6m. W.shore-090°; G.090°-shore.
BARR ROCK. Lt.By. Q. Pillar B.Y. Topmark N 1 cable N of Ebbing Eddy Rock.
STROMNESS APPROACH Lt.By. Qk.Fl.R. Fl.G. 3 sec. Conical G.
STROMNESS APPROACH. Lt.By. Q.R. Can.R.

STROMNESS (ORKNEYS) Tel: (0856) 850744.
Radio — Port: VHF Chan. 16, 12. 0900-1700. The Bush Overhead Power Line safe clearance 6.6m.

NL COMMISSIONERS PIER, SE CORNER. Lt. Iso. R. 6 sec. 5M. Tr. 15m.
Ldg.Lts. 317° (Front) F.R. 3M. W. Tr. 29m. 307°-327° shown H24. (Rear) F.R. 3M. W. Tr. 39m. 307°-327° shown H24.
N PIER HEAD. Lt. Fl.R. 3 sec. 3M. mast, 7m. shown 1 Aug-mid-May.

STRONSAY FIRTH

ROSE NESS. Lt. Fl. 6 sec. 8M. W. Bn. 24m.
ROSE NESS POINT. Bn. stone Tr. shaped with B. wooden cross.

COPINSAY 58°53.8'N, 2°40.2'W. Lt. Fl.(5) 30 sec. 21M. W. Tr. 79m. Horn(4) 60 sec.

AUSKERRY 59°01.6'N, 2°34.2'W. Lt. Fl. 20 sec. 18M. W. Tr. 34m.

HELLIAR HOLM, S END 59°01.2'N, 2°54.0'W. Lt. Fl.W.R.G. 10 sec. W.14M. R.10M. W. Tr. 18m. G.256°-276°; W.276°-292°; R.292°-098°; W.098°-116°; G.116°-154°.
BALFOUR PIER. Lt. Q.W.R.G. W.3M; R.2M; G.2M. 5m. G.shore-010°; W.010°-020°; R.020°-shore.
SCARGUN By. Conical G. ⌇⌇ in Kirkwall Bay.

MARINE FARMS are established in this area. Consult chart for details.

KIRKWALL (Orkneys) 58°59'N, 2°58'W. Tel: Kirkwall (0856) 2292.
Radio — Port: VHF Chan. 16, 12 — Hours: 0800-1700 and when vessel expected.

PIER N END. 58°59.2'N, 2°57.6'W. Lt. Iso. W.R.G. 4 sec. W.15M. R.13M. G.13M. G.153°-183°; W.183°-192°; R.192°-210°. metal Tr. 8m. shown 1 Aug.-30 April.
PIER E. END. Lt. 2 F.G. vert 3M. Mast 6m.
HARBOUR, N PIER. Lt. 2 F.R. vert.
W PIER HEAD. Lt. 2 F.G. vert.
Lt.By. Q. Pillar BY Topmark N.
VASA SKERRY Bn. B. iron frame, barrel shaped cage topmark, in Wide Firth.
Lt.By. Q.(6)+L.Fl. 15 sec. Pillar Y.B. Topmark S.
Lt.By. Q.(3) 10 sec. Pillar B.Y.B. Topmark E.
SEAL SKERRY Bn. R. iron frame, barrel shaped topmark, in Wide Firth, off Gairsa I.
GALT SKERRY. Lt.By. Q. Pillar B.Y. Topmark N off Galtness, Bell w.a.
THE GRAAND By. Pillar Y.B. Topmark S. off S end of Egilsay I.
EGILSAY PIER Lt. Fl.G. 3 sec. 4M. W. Col. 4m.

BROUGH OF BIRSAY 59°08.2'N, 3°20.3'W. Lt. Fl.(3) 25 sec. 18M. 52m. W. castellated Tr. and building.

STRONSAY
PAPA STRONSAY Lt. Iso. 4 sec. 9M. W. Tr. 8m.
No. 1 Lt.By. Fl.G. 5 sec. Conical G.
No. 2 Lt.By. Fl.R. 5 sec. Can.R.
No. 3 Lt.By. Fl.(2)G. 5 sec. Conical G.
No. 4 Lt.By. Fl.(2)R. 5 sec. Can.R.
NE CRAMPIE SHOAL By. Conical G. in Whitehall Hr.
WHITEHALL PIER, NR. HEAD. Lt. 2 F.G. vert. 4M. W. concrete Tr. 6m. shown 1st August to 30th April.

SANDAY
Overhead cable, safe clearance 5.4m. between Ouse Point and Elsness.
KETTLETOFT PIER HEAD. Lt. Fl.W.R.G. 3 sec. W.7M; R.5M; G.5M. W. Tr. 7m. W.351°-011°; R.011°-180°; G.180°-351°.
OTTERSWICK BAY By. Conical G. off Whitemill Pt.
'RIV' Bn. R. pyramid with cage, 12m.

START POINT 59°16.7'N, 2°22.5'W. Lt. Fl.(2) 20 sec. 19M. W. Tr. B. stripes, 24m.

EDAY ISLAND
CALF SOUND Lt. Iso W.R.G. 5 sec. W.8M. R.7M. G.6M. W. Tr. 8m. R.shore-216°; W.216°-223°; G.223°-302°; W.302°-307°.
BACKALAND PIER. Lt. Fl.R. 3 sec. 5M. 5m. vis. 192°-250°.

EDAY GRUNA. Lt.By. Q. Pillar B.Y. Topmark N in S Eday Sd.

WESTRAY

WESTRAY PIER (ORKNEYS)
Radio — Port: VHF Chan. 16, 14. As required.

NOUP HEAD 59°19.9'N, 3°04.0'W. Lt. Fl. 30 sec. 22M. W. Tr. 79m. vis. about 335°-242°; 248°-282°. Obscured by cliffs on easterly bearings within 0.8M. Partially obscured 240°-275°.
PAPA WESTRAY PIER HEAD. Lt. Fl.W.R.G. 5 sec. W.5M. R.3M. G.3M. White Building. 7m. G.306°-341°; W.341°-040°; R.040°-074°.
PIEROWALL E PIER. Lt. Fl.W.R.G. 3 sec. W.11M. R.7M. G.7M. mast, 7m. G.254°-276°; W.276°-291°; R.291°-308°; G.308°-215°.
WEST PIER Lt. 2 F.R. vert. 3M. mast.
EYNHALLOW SOUND. Lt.By. Q.(9) 15 sec. Pillar Y.B.Y. Topmark W.

NORTH RONALDSAY ISLAND

59°23.4'N, 2°22.8'W. Lt. Fl. 10 sec. 19M. R.brick Tr. 2 white bands, 43m RC. Racon.
NOUSTER PIER HEAD. Lt. Q.R. on post, 5m. shown 1st August to 30th April.
DENNIS HEAD Bn. old Lt.Ho.

FAIR ISLE, SHETLAND

SKADAN, S 59°30.9'N, 1°39.0'W. Lt. Fl.(4) 30 sec. 24M. W. Tr. 32m. vis. 260°-146°; but obscured close inshore from 260°-282°. Horn (2) 60 sec.

SKROO, N 59°32.3'N, 1°36.5'W. Lt. Fl.(2) 30 sec. 22M. W. Tr. 80m. Horn (3) 45 sec. Vis. 086.7°-358°.

MRSC SHETLAND (0595) 2976. Weather broadcast ev. 4h. from 0105.

SHETLAND ISLANDS E SIDE

COMPASS HEAD RG STN. 59°52.0'N, 1°16.3W. Emergency DF Stn. VHF Chan. 16 & 67. Controlled by MRSC Shetland.

SUMBURGH HEAD 59°51.3'N, 1°16.3'W. Lt. Fl.(3) 30 sec. 23M. W. Tr. 91m. R.C.

BROWNIES TAING (SHETLAND) Tel: (09505) 371.
Radio — Port: VHF Chan. 16, 12, 11 — 2 h. before vessel expected.

MOUSA, PERIE BARD 59°59.8'N, 1°09.4'W. Lt. Fl. 3 sec. 10M. W. Tr. 20m.

KIRKABISTER NESS, BRESSAY 60°07.2'N, 1°07.2'W. Lt. Fl.(2) 20 sec. 23M. W. Tr. 32m. RC.

LERWICK (Shetlands) 60°09¢N, 1°08¢W. Tel: HM. Lerwick (0595) 2828. Port Control/Pilots: (0595) 3462. Telex: 75496.
Radio — Port: VHF Chan. 16, 12 — H24.
Radio — Pilots: VHF Chan. 16, 6, 12 — 0800-1700 and when v/l expected.

TWAGEOS POINT. Lt. Fl. 6 sec. 6M. W. Bn. 8m.
MARYFIELD FERRY TERMINAL. Lt. Oc. W.R.G. 6 sec. 5M. W.008°-013°; R.013°-111°; G.111°-008°.
VICTORIA PIER HEAD. Lt. Fl.R. 3 sec. 1M. 5m.
N. JETTY. Lt. Q.R. 1M. 5m.
N HARBOUR. Lt.By. Q.R. Can. R.
OIL JETTY HEAD, SW CORNER. Lt. Fl. 3 sec. on post, 5m.

N NESS. Lt. Iso. W.G. 4 sec. 5M. on Col. 4m. G.158°-216°; W.216°-158°.
MIDDLE GROUND SW By. Can.R. at S end of shoal in Lerwick N Hr.
MIDDLE GROUND W. Lt.By. Fl.(2) 10 sec. Can.R. at NW end of shoal in Lerwick N Hr.
LOOFA BAA. Lt.Bn. Q.(6) + L.Fl. 15 sec. 5M. concrete Bn. 4m.
Channel dredged to 9m.
HOLMSGARTH QUAY HEAD. Lt. Q.G. 5M. W. Post. 4m.
HOLMSGARTH QUAY RO-RO Lt. Fl.R. 3 sec. 2M.
SHELL JETTY HEAD Lt. Q.(2)R. 8 sec. 2M. 5m.
GREMISTA MARINA S BREAKWATER. Lt. Iso.R. 4 sec. 2M. Post 4m.
N HARBOUR PIER Lt. F.R. & Fl.R. 3 sec. vert. 2M.
CRUESTER By. Conical G. on edge of shoals.
BAY OF HEOGAN PIER. 2 Ldg.Bns. in line 027° triangular mark deep water chan. into pier between Loofa Baa Bn. and Middle Ground SW By.
Lt.By. Q.G. Conical G.
Lt.By. Fl.G. Conical G.
Lt.By. Fl.R. Can.R.
Lt.By. Q.G. Conical G.

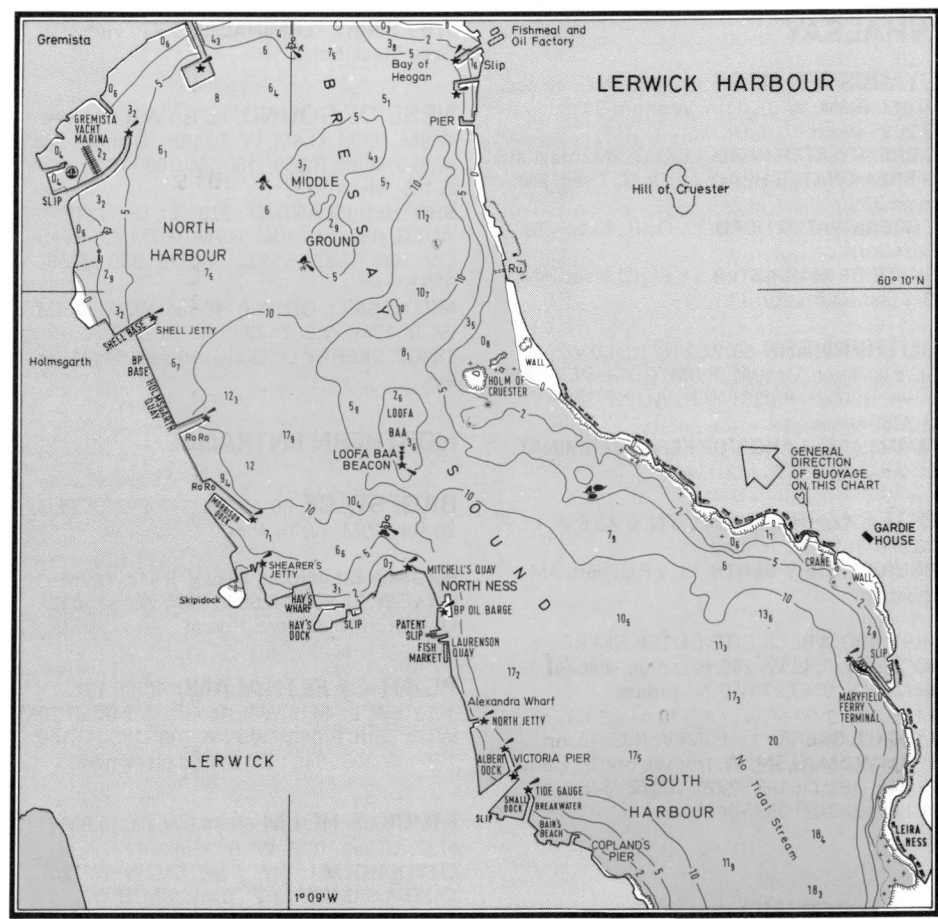

N APPR. TO LERWICK Lt.By. Q.(9) 15 sec.
Pillar Y.B.Y. Topmark W.
LERWICK S. Lt.By. L.Fl.G. Conical G.
LERWICK N. Lt.By. Fl.(2)G. 10 sec. Conical G.
Channel E. of Green Head and Point of
Scattland dredged to 6m.
POINT OF SCATTLAND B Lt.By. Q.R. Can.R.
N. ENTRANCE Dir.Lt. 215° Oc. W.R.G. 6 sec.
8M. △ Or. stripe. R.211°-214°; W.214°-216°;
G.216°-221°.
GREENHEAD Lt.Bn. Q.(4)R.10 sec. 3M. 4m.

MARINE FARMS are established in this area.
Consult chart for details.

BRESSAY SOUND PIER Lt. 2 F.G. vert.
HEOGAN NEW QUAY HEAD. Lt. Fl.G. 4 sec.
3M. W. Post 5m.

ROVA HEAD Lt. Fl.(3) W.R.G. 18 sec. W.8M.

R.7M. G.6M. W. Tr. 10m. R.shore-180°;
W.180°-194°; G.194°-213°; R.213°-241°;
W.241°-261.5°; G.261.5°-009°; W.009°-shore.
DALES VOE. Lt. Fl.(2)W.R.G. 8 sec. W.4M.
R.3M. G.3M. W. post, 5m. G.220°-227°;
W.227°-233°; R.233°-240°.
QUAY. Lt. 2 F.R. vert. Col. 9m.
LAXFIRTH PIER. Lt. 2 F.G. vert. 2M. Pole 4m.
WADBISTER VOE. Lt.By. Fl.(2). Spar R.B.
Topmark Is. D.
HOO STACK. Lt. Fl.(4)W.R.G. 12 sec. W.7M.
R.5M. G.5M. W. Tr. 40m. R.169°-180°; W.180°-
184°; G.184°-193°; W.193°-169°.
Dir. Lt. 182°. Dir. Fl.(4)W.R.G. 12 sec. W.9M.
R.6M. G.6M. Same structure. 33m. R.177°-
180°; W.180°-184°; G.184°-187°. Synchronised
with upper Lt.
MULL OF ESWICK Lt. Fl.W.R.G. 3 sec. W.9M.
R.6M. G.6M. W. Tr. 50m. R.shore-200°;
W.200°-207°; G.207°-227°; R.227°-241°;
W.241°-028°; R.028°-shore.
INNER VODER ROCK Bn. G. col. 5m.

WHALSAY

SYMBISTER NESS Lt. Fl.(2) W.G. 12 sec. W.8M. R.6M. W. Tr. 11m. W.shore-203°; G.203°-shore.
S BREAKWATER HEAD. Lt. Q.G. 2M. mast 4m.
N BREAKWATER HEAD. Lt. Oc.G. 7 sec. 3M. mast 3m.
E BREAKWATER HEAD. Lt. Oc.R. 7 sec. 3M. Post 3m.
SKATE OF MARRISTER. Lt. Fl.(G) 6 sec. 4M. G. mast on Platform.

SUTHERNESS 60°22.2'N, 1°00.0'W. Lt. Fl.W.G. 3 sec. W.10M. R.8M. G.7M. W. Tr. 8m. W.shore-038°; R.038°-173°; W.173°-206°; G.206°-shore.
MAIN LAND. LAXO VOE FERRY TERMINAL. Lt. 2 F.G. vert. 2M. mast. 4m.

OUT SKERRIES 60°25.5'N, 0°43.5'W. Lt. Fl. 20 sec. 20M. W. Tr. 44m.
BRURAY FERRY BERTH. Lt. 2 F.G. vert. 4M. mast 6m.

HISTORIC WRECK SITE OUTER SKERRIES. 60°25.2'N, 0°45'W. 250m. radius, also 60°25.5'N, 0°43.27'W 0.7c. radius.

MUCKLE SKERRY Lt. Fl.(2) W.R.G. 10 sec. W.7M. R.5M. G.5M. W. framework Tr. 13m. W.046°-192°; R.192°-272°; G.272°-348°; W.348°-353°; R.353°-046°.

YELL SOUND

MARINE FARMS are established in this area. Consult chart for details.

LUNNA HOLM 60°27.4'N, 1°02.4'W. Lt. Fl.(3)W.R.G. 15 sec. W.10M. R.7M. G.7M. W. Tr. 19m. R.shore-090°; W.090°-094°; G.094°-209°; W.209°-275°; R.275°-shore.

FIRTHS VOE. 60°27.2'N, 1°10.6'W. Lt. Oc.W.R.G. 8 sec. W.15M. R.10M. G.10M. W. Tr. 9m. W.189°-194°; G.194°-257°; W.257°-263°; R.263°-339°; W.339°-shore.
LINGA IS. Dir. Lt. Dir. Q(4)W.R.G. 8 sec. W.9M. R.9M. G.9M. Concrete col. 10m. R.145°-148°; W.148°-152°; G.152°-155°. Also Lt. Q(4)W.R.G. 8 sec. W.7M. R.4M. G.4M. 10m. R.052°-146°; G.154°-196°; W.196°-312°.
YELL ULSTA. Ferry Terminal Breakwater Head. Lt. Oc. R.G. 4 sec. R.5M. G.5M. Post 7m. G.shore-354°; R.004°-shore. Also Oc. W.R.G. 4 sec. W.8M. R.5M. G.5M. Same post G.shore-008°; W.008°-036°; R.036°-shore.

TOFT FERRY TERMINAL. Lt. 2 F.R. vert. 2M. Grey Mast. 5m.

NESS OF SOUND. Lt. Iso.W.R.G. 5 sec. W.9M. R.6M. G.6M. W. Tr. 18m. G.shore-345°; W.345°-350°; R.350°-160°; W.160°-165°; G.165°-shore.
BROTHER ISLAND. Dir.329°. Lt. Dir.Fl.(4) W.R.G. 8 sec. W.10M. R.7M. G.7M. Concrete Col. 16m. G.323.5°-328°; W.328°-330°; R.330°-333.5°.
MIO NESS Lt. Q(2)W.R. 10 sec. W.7M. R.4M. W. Tr. 12m. W.282°-238°; R.238°-282°.
TINGA SKERRY Lt. Q(2)G. 10 sec. 5M. W. Tr. 9m.

NORTHERN ENTRANCE

BAGI STACK 60°43.5'N, 1°7.4'W. Lt. Fl.(4) 20 sec. 10M. W. Tr. 45m.

GRUNEY ISLAND Lt. Fl.W.R. 5 sec. W.7M. R.4M. W. Tr. 53m. R.064°-180°; W.180°-012°. Obscured elsewhere. Racon.

POINT OF FETHALAND 60°38.1'N. 1°18'.6W. Lt. Fl.(3)W.R. 15 sec. W.24M. R.20M. W. Tr. 65m. R.080°-103°; W.103°-160°; R.160°-206°; W.206°-340°. Obscured elsewhere.

MUCKLE HOLM 60°34.9'N; 01°15.8'W. Lt. Fl.(2) 10 sec. 10M. W. Tr. 32m.
LITTLE HOLM Lt. Iso. 4 sec. 6M. W. Tr. 12m.
OUTER SKERRY Lt. Fl. 6 sec. 8M. B.W. Concrete Col. 12m.

QUEY FIRTH MINOR. Lt. 60°31.5'N, 1°19.5'W. Oc. W.R.G. 6 sec. W.12M. R.G.8M. W. Tr. 22m. W. from Land thru' S&W to 290°; G.290°-327°; W.327°-334°; R.334°-thru' N. to land.
COLLA FIRTH. PIER HEAD. Lt. 2 F.G. vert. 3M. Mast 6m.

LAMBA SOUTH Lt. Fl.W.R.G. 3 sec. W.8M. R.5M. G.5M. 30m. G.shore-288°; W.288°-293°; R.293°-327°; W.327°-044°; R.044°-140°; W.140°-shore.
Synchronised with above. Dir. 290°30'. Lt.Fl. W.R.G. 3 sec. W.10M. R.7M. G.7M. Col. 24m. G.285.5°-288°. W.288°-293°, R.293°-295.5°.
RUMBLE ROCKS Bn. Iso. B.R.B. Racon. at entce. to Yell Sound.

SULLOM VOE SHETLAND. Tel: H.M. (0806) 242551. Fax: (0806) 242237. Terminal Control (0806) 243000. Fax: (0806) 243200.

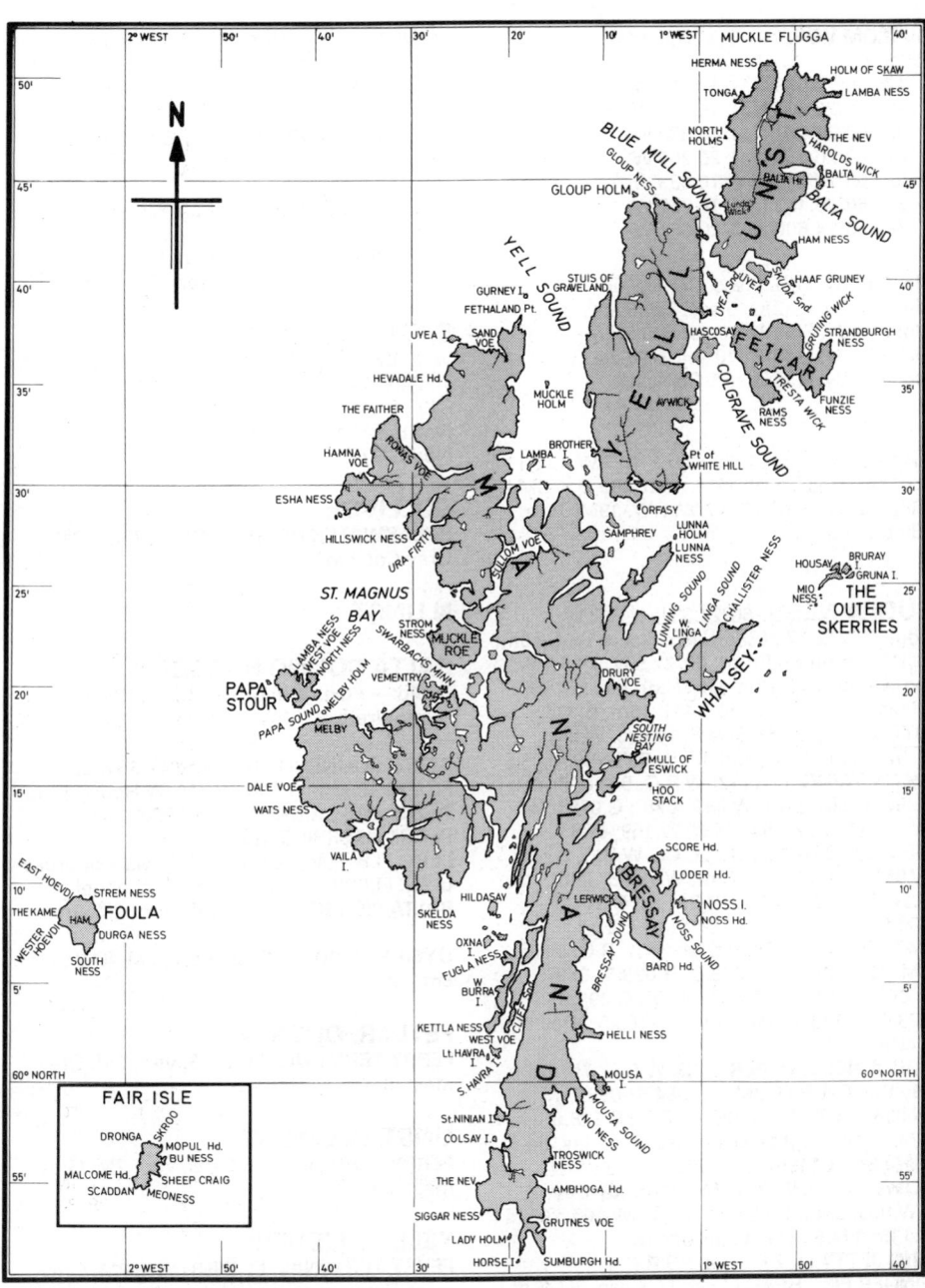

Telex: H.M. 75142 SULVOE G. Terminal: 75268.
Radio — Port: VHF Chan. 16, 12, 14, 20, 9, 10.
Radio — Pilots: VHF Chan. 14, 16.
Radio — Terminal: VHF Chan. 16, 19.
Radar: Surveillance maintained in Yell Sound and Sullom Voe.
Entry: Traffic movements, nav. info. Chan. 20

ev. 4h. from 0000h.
Reporting Points:
1½M. E of Point of Fethaland Lt. ½M. W of Muckle Holm Lt.
½M. E of Ness of Quey Firth Lt. ½M. W of Skaw Taing Lt.
1¼M. N of Mossbank Lt.
Local Wx. Msgs. on request.

SULLOM VOE. 7 Lt.Bys. Gp.Fl.(4)Y. 12 sec. Pillar Y.
1. 60°28.933'N, 1°17.317'W
2. 60°28.683'N, 1°18.617'W
3. 60°27.067'N, 1°18.833'W
4. 60°26.833'N, 1°20.200'W
5. 60°26.633'N, 1°16.833'W
6. 60°26.433'N, 1°19.350'W
7. 60°24.600'N, 1°20.667'W

No: 1 Lt.By. Fl.G. 2 sec. Conical G.
No: 2 Lt.By. Fl.(2)G. 5 sec. Conical G.
No: 3 Lt.By. Fl.(4)R. 10 sec. Can.R.
No: 4 Lt.By. Fl.(3)G. 10 sec. Conical G.
No: 5 Lt.By. Fl.G. 2 sec. Conical G.

GLUSS ISLE. 60°29.8'N, 1°19.3'W. Ldg.Lts. 194°44' (Front) F.W. 19M. 40m. (By Day 9M.). (Rear) 60°29.1'N, 1°19.7'W. F.W. 19M. 70m. (By Day 9M.).

FUGLA NESS. 60°27.3'N, 1°19.7'W. Ldg.Lts. 212°17'. (Rear). Iso. 4 sec. 14M. 46m. B. ▽ (Common Front) 60°27.5'N, 1°19.4'W. Iso. 4 sec. 14M. 28m. Or. □ Ldg.Lts. 202°55' (Rear) J2(E). Iso. 4 sec. 14M. 46m. B. ▽.
LITTLE ROE. Lt. Fl.(3)W.R. 10 sec. W.5M. R.4M. 17m. R.036°-095.5°; W.095.5°-036°.
SKAW TAING. Lt. Fl.(2) W.R.G. 5 sec. W.8M. R.5M. G.5M. 22m. W.049°-078°; G.078°-147°; W.147°-154°; R.154°-169°; W.169°-288°.
NESS OF BARDISTER. Lt. Oc. W.R.G. 8 sec. W.9M. R.7M. G.7M. 22m. W.180.5°-240°; R.240°-310.5°; W.310.5°-314.5°; G.314.5°-030.5°.
VATS HOULLANDS. Lt. Iso. W.Y. R.G. 3 sec. 6M. 75m. W.343.5°-029.5°; Y.029.5°-049°; G.049°-074.5°; R.074.5°-098.5°; G.098.5°-123.5°; Y.123.5°-148°; W.148°-163.5°. Day Light Occas.
SELLA NESS. UPPER Lt. Q. W.R.G. 7M. 15m. (By Day F.W.R.G. 2M.). G.084.5°-098.7°; W.098.7°-099.7°; W.126°-128.5°; R.128.5°-174.5°. Day Light Occas. also Obst. Lts. on Flare Stack 149m. 1M. NE.
LOWER Lt. Q. W.R.G. 7M. 11m. (By Day F.W.R.G. 2M.). G.084.5°-106.5°; W.106.5°-115°; R.115°-174.5°. Day Light Occas.
TUG JETTY Lt. 2 F.G. vert. 3M.
FINGER PIER HEAD Lt. Iso.G. 4 sec. 3M. Col. 4m.
GARTH PIER N ARM HEAD Lt. Fl.(2) G. 5 sec. 3M. Col. 4m.

SCATSTA NESS UPPER. Lt. Oc.W.R.G. 5 sec. 7M. 15m. (By day: F.W.R.G. 2M.) G.161.5°-187.2°; W.187.2°-188.2°; W.207.2°-208.2°; R.208.2°-251.5°.

LOWER. Lt. Oc.W.R.G. 5 sec. 7M. 10m. (By day: F.W.R.G. 2M.) G.161.5°-197.2°; W.197.2°-202.2°; R.202.2°-251.5°.

UNGAM ISLAND. Lt. V.Q.(2) 5 sec. 2M. W. Col. 2m.

COLBACK NESS JETTY. Lt. 2 F.R. vert. 3M. mast.
No: 1 JETTY E. Lt. 2 F.R. vert. Dolphin.
No: 4 JETTY N. Lt. 2 F.R. vert. Dolphin.

E YELL
WHITEHILL. Lt. Fl.W.R. 3 sec. W.9M. R.6M. W. Tr. 24m. W.shore-163°; R.163°-211°; W.211°-349°; R.349°-shore.
No: 1 JETTY Lt. 2 F.R. vert.
No: 4 JETTY Lt. 2 F.R. vert.

CULLIVOE
BREAKWATER HEAD. Lt. Oc. R. 7 sec. 2M. Grey Col. 5m.

N UNST

BALTA SOUND HARBOUR
Radio — Port: VHF Chan. 16, 20. Hrs. office or as required.

BALTA SOUND. 60°44.5'N, 0°47.6'W. Lt. Fl.W.R. 10 sec. W.10M. R.7M. W.House 17m. W.249°-010°; R.010°-060°; W.060°-154°.
BLACK SKERRIES. Bn. G.W.
Lt.By. Fl.R. 5 sec. Can.   } Mark approach
Lt.By. Fl.(3)R. 10 sec. Can.R. } channel
BALTA PIER HEAD. Lt. 2 F.G. vert. 2M. 7m.

UYEA SOUND. Lt. Fl.(2) 8 sec. 7M. R.W.Bn. 8m.

FETLAR. ODDSTA
FERRY TERMINAL. Lt. 2 F.G. vert. 2M. Grey mast. 6m.

UNST. BELMONT
FERRY TERMINAL. Lt. 2 F.G. vert. 2M. Grey mast. 6m.

YELL. GUTCHER
FERRY TERMINAL. Lt. 2 F.R. vert. 2M. Grey mast. 7m.

MUCKLE FLUGGA LT.
60°51.3'N 0°53.0'W. Fl.(2) 20 sec. 25M. W. Tr. 66m. R.C. Aux. Lt. F.R. 15M. Base of Tr. 52m. Vis. 276°-311°.

MARINE FARMS are established in this area. Consult chart for details.

SHETLAND ISLANDS w SIDE

ESHA NESS 60°29.3'N, 1°37.6'W Lt.Ho. Fl.
12 sec. 25M. W. square Tr. 61m.
HILLSWICK, S END OF NESS. Lt. Fl.(4) W.R.
15 sec. W.9M. R.6M. W. house, 34m. W.217°-
093°; R.093°-114°.
MUCKLE ROE, SWARBACKS MINN Lt. Fl.W.R.
3 sec. W.9M. R.6M. W. Tr. 30m. W.314°-041°;
R.041°-075°; W.075°-137°.
AITH BREAKWATER Lt. Q.G. 5M. G. Post 3m.
RNLI Berth.
SNARRA NESS. Lt. Oc. W.R.G. 8 sec. 2M.
Pedestal 30m. G. 149°-157°; W. 157°-165°; R.
165°-173°.
W. BURRA FIRTH TRANSPORT PIER HD. Lt.
Iso.G. 4 sec. 4M. Mast 4m.

VE SKERRIES 60°22.4'N, 1°48.7'W. Lt.
Fl.(2) 20 sec. 11M. W. Tr. 17m. Racon.

RAM'S HEAD Lt. Fl. W.R.G. 8 sec. W.6M.
R.9M. G.6M. W. house, 15m. G.265°-355°;
W.355°-020°; R.020°-090°; W.090°-136°.
VAILA PIER. Lt. 2 F.R. vert. building, 4m.

VAILA SOUND

MARINE FARMS established approaches to
Scalloway and Vaila Sound. Consult chart for
details.

SKELD VOE

SKELD PIER. Lt. 2 F.R. vert. 3M. W. Post. 4m.
SELI VOE. LEEANS PIER. Lt. 2 F.G. vert.
NORTH HAVRE. Lt. Fl.W.R.G. 12 sec. W.7M.
R.5M. G.5M. W. GRP Tr. 24m. G.001°-053.5°;
W.053.5°-060.5°; R.060.5°-182°; G.274°-334°;
W.334°-337.5°; R.337.5°-001°.
POINT OF THE PUND. Lt. Fl. W.R.G. 5 sec.
W.7M. R.5M. G5M. W. GRP. Tr. 20m. R.350°-
090°; G.090°-111°; R.111°-135°; W.135°-140°;
G.140°-177°; W.267°-350°.
Lt.By. Fl.(3)R. 8 sec. Can.R. 60°07.5'N,
1°18.63'W.
Lt.By. Fl.(3)G. 8 sec. Conical G. 60°07.45'N,
1°18.48'W.
Lt.By. Fl.(2)G. 6 sec. Conical G. 60°07.74'N,
1°17.69'W.

SCALLOWAY H.M. & Port Control. Tel:
(0806) 242551. Fax: (0806) 242237. Telex:
75142. Pier Master. Tel: (0595) 88574.
Radio — Port: VHF Chan. 16, 12, 9. Hours
0600-1800 Mon.-Fri., 0600-1230 Sat.
Radio — Pilots: VHF Chan. 16, 12, 9.

Entry: Up to date large scale charts advised.
Contact Port Control before arrival/departure.
Wind conditions at berth available on
request.
Anchorage: NE of Hildasay Island in N
Channel.
HARBOUR. 60°08.1'N, 1°16.4'W. Lt. Oc.
W.R.G. 10 sec. W.14M. R.11M. G.11M. B. Tr.
7m. G.045.7°-056.8°; W.056.8°-058.8°;
R.058.8°-069.9°. By day W.1M. R.1M. G.1M.
SCALLOWAY APPROACH. Lt.By. Fl.R. 2 sec.
Can.R.
Lt.By. Q. Pillar B.Y. Topmark N.
Lt.By. Fl.G. 2 sec. Conical G.
Lt.By. Fl.(2)G. 5 sec. Conical G.
Lt.By. Fl.(2)R. 5 sec. Can.R.   } off Blackness
Lt.By. Fl.(4)G. 10 sec. Conical G. } Pier.
**SCALLOWAY HBR. MOORES SLIPWAY JETTY
HEAD** Lt. 2 F.R. vert. 1M. Post. 4m.
BLACKNESS W PIER HEAD. Lt. 2 F.G. vert.
3M. Post. 6m.
E PIER HEAD. Lt. Oc.R. 7 sec. 3M. Post. 5m.
**CLIFT SOUND BRIDGE
CENTRE.** Lt. V.Q. 5M. 5m.
W PIER. Lt. 2 F.R. vert. 5M. 5m.
E PIER. Lt. 2 F.G. vert. 5M. 5m.
**LANG SOUND BRIDGE
CENTRE.** Lt. V.Q. 5M. 5m.
W PIER. Lt. 2 F.R. vert. 5M. 5m.
E PIER. Lt. 2 F.G. vert. 5M. 5m.
GALTA SKERRY Bn. W. concrete, with iron
cross.
FUGLA NESS. 60°06.4'N, 1°20.7'W. Lt.
Fl.(2)W.R.G. 10 sec. W.10M. R.7M. G.7M. W.
Tr. 20m. G.014°-032°; W.032°-082°; R.082°-
134°; W.134°-shore.
FOULA 60°06.8'N 2°03.7'W. Lt.Fl.(3) 15 sec.
18M. W. Tr. 36m.

NORTH COAST OF SCOTLAND

SULE SKERRY. 59°05.0'N, 4°24.3'W. Lt.Ho.
Fl.(2) 15 sec. 19M. W. Tr. 34m. RC. Racon.

SULA SGEIR. 59°05.6'N, 6°09.5'W. Lt. Fl.
15 sec. 11M. Sq.Tr. 74m.

RONA. (N Rona). Lt. Fl.(3) 20 sec. 24M. W.
Tr. 114m.

LOCH ERIBOLL WHITE HEAD
58°31.1'N, 4°38.8'W. Lt. Fl.W.R. 3 sec. W.13M.
R.12M. W. Tr. 18m. W.030°-172°; R.172°-191°;
W.191°-212°.

OFFSHORE WAYPOINT CAPE WRATH.
58°39.0'N, 5°00.0'W.

CAPE WRATH. 58°37.5'N, 5°00.0'W. Lt. Fl.(4) 30 sec. 24M. W. Tr. 122m. RC. Horn(3) 45 sec.

WEST COAST OF SCOTLAND

LOCH INCHARD

RUBHA NA LECAIG. Lt. Fl.(2) 10 sec. 8M. concrete pedestal, 30m.

KINLOCH BERVIE. 58°27.5'N, 5°03.0'W. Tel: 09 7182 235.
Radio — Port: VHF Chan. 6 as required.
LOCH BERVIE. Ldg.Lts. 327°. (Front) Oc.G. 8 sec. 9M. W. □, Or. △ inside, on framework Tr. 16m. (Rear) Oc. G. 8 sec. 9M. W. □, Or. ▽ inside, on framework Tr. 26m.
No: 1 Lt.Bn. Fl.R. 4 sec. 2M. R. Mast. 3m.
No: 2 Lt.Bn. Q.R. 2M. R. Mast. 3m.
No: 3 Lt.Bn. Fl.G. 4 sec. 2M. G. Mast. 3m.

OFFSHORE WAYPOINT SE OF RU STOER. 58°11.0'N, 5°30.0'W.

STOER HEAD 58°14.4'N, 5°24.0'W Lt. Fl. 15 sec. 24M. W. Tr. 59m.

LOCH A'CHAIRN BHAIN. KYLESKU BRIDGE. N SIDE
Lt. Q.R. 3M. Tr. 28m. each side.
S SIDE. Lt. Q.G. 3M. Tr. 28m. each side.
KYLESKU FISHING JTY Lt. 2 F.G. vert. 3M. Mast 6m.

LOCH INVER
GLAS LEAC. Lt. Fl.W.R.G. 3 sec. Grey concrete col. 7m. W.071°-080°; R.080°-090°; G.090°-103°; W.103°-111°; R.111°-243°; W.243°-251°; G.251°-071°.
AIRD GHLAS Lt.Bn. Q.G. 1M. B. Col. W. bands 3m.
CULAG HBR. BREAKWATER HEAD Lt.Bn. 2 F.G. vert. on pole.
SOYEA ISLAND Lt. Fl.(2) 10 sec. 6M. Grey Post 34m.

SUMMER ISLES
OLD DORNIE. NEW PIER HD. Lt. Fl.G. 3 sec. 5m.

INSHORE WAYPOINT OFF LOCH BROOM. 57°59.0'N, 5°29.0'W.

LOCH BROOM
RUBHA CADAIL Lt. Fl.W.R.G. 6 sec. W.9M. R.6M. G.6M. W. Tr. 11m. G. 311°-320°; W.320°-325°; R.325°-103°; W.103°-111°; G.111°-118°; W.118°-127°; R.127°-157°; W.157°-199°.

4 x Marine Farms established. Consult chart for details.

ULLAPOOL Tel: Ullapool (0854) 2091/2165.
Radio — Port: VHF Chan. 16, 12. 26 June-Nov/Dec. H24. Nov/Dec.-26 June 0900-1700.
ULLAPOOL POINT. Lt. Iso. R. 4 sec. 6M. Mast. 8m. Vis. 258°-110°.
PIER. Lt. 2 F.R. vert. metal col. 5m.
PIER EXTENSION SE CNR. Lt. Fl.R. 3 sec. 1M. Pole 6m.

CAILLEACH HEAD Lt. Fl.(2) 12 sec. 9M. W. Tr. 60m. vis. 015°-236°.

INSHORE WAYPOINT OFF LOCH EWE. 57°54.5'N, 5°43.5'W.

LOCH EWE
NATO POL PIER HEAD. Lt. Fl.G. 4 sec. & Dolphins Lts. Fl.G. 4 sec.

ISLE OF EWE SE

HARBOUR WAYPOINT. 57°52.0'N, 5°40.0'W.

FAIRWAY. Lt.By. L.Fl. 10 sec. Spherical R.W. vert. stripes ॴ.
No: 1 Lt.By. Fl.(3)G. 10 sec. Conical G.
'D' Lt.By. Fl.(2)R. 10 sec. Can.R.
'E' Lt.By. Fl.R. 2 sec. Can.R.
'F' Lt.By. Fl.(4)R. 10 sec. Can.R.

OFFSHORE WAYPOINT RUBH RE. 57°52.0'N, 5°51.0'W.

RUBHA REIDH 57°51.4'N, 5°48.6'W Lt. Fl.(4) 15 sec. 24M. W. Tr. 37m.

INSHORE WAYPOINT OFF LONGA ISLAND (LOCH GAIRLOCH). 57°43.0'N, 5°51.6'W.

LOCH GAIRLOCH
GLAS EILEAN. Lt. Fl.W.R.G. 6 sec. W.6M. R.4M. metal pedestal, concrete base, 9m. W.080°-102°; R.102°-296°; W.296°-333°; G.333°-080°.
GARELOCH PIER. Lt. Q.R. 9m.
HARBOUR WAYPOINT. 57°43.0'N, 5°43.0'W.
INSHORE WAYPOINT OFF RED POINT. 57°38.2'N, 5°52.0'W.
INSHORE WAYPOINT LOCH TORRIDON. 57°32.6'N, 5°40.0'W.
INSHORE WAYPOINT NW OF RONA. 57°36.0'N, 6°01.6'W.

RONA, NE POINT 57°34.7'N, 5°57.5'W Lt.
Fl. 12 sec. 19M. W. Tr. 69m. vis. 050°-358°.

LOCH A'BHRAIGE, SGEIR SHUAS. Lt. Fl.R. 2
sec. 3M. 6m. vis. 070°-199°.
JETTY SW. Lt. 2 F.R. vert.
Lt. Fl.R. 5 sec. 3M. R. Bn.
Ldg.Lts. 136°31' (Front) **No. 9 Lt.Bn.** Q.W.R.G.
W.4M. R.3M. W. and Or.Bn. W.135°-138°;
R.138°-318°; G.318°-135°. (Rear) **No: 10 Lt.Bn.**
Iso. 6 sec. 5M. W. Bn. 28m.
No: 1 Lt.Bn. Fl.G. 3 sec. 3M. Or.Bn. 91m.
RUBHA CHUILTAIRBH. Lt.Bn. Fl. 3 sec. 5M. W.
Bn. 6m.
No: 11 Lt.Bn. Q.Y. 4M. W. and Or.Bn. 6m.
No: 3 Lt.Bn. Fl.(2) 10 sec. 4M. W. and Or.Bn.
9m.
No: 12 Lt.Bn. Q.R. 3M. Or.Bn. 5m.
GARBH EILEAN, No: 8 SE POINT. Lt. Fl. 3 sec.
5M. W. Bn. 8m.

SOUND OF RAASAY

PORTREE. 57°25'N, 6°12'W. Tel: (0478) 2926.
Radio — Port: VHF Chan. 16, 8 as required.

HARBOUR WAYPOINT. 57°25.0'N, 6°08.5'W.

PIER HEAD. Lt.Bn. 2 F.R. vert. 4M. post 6m.
occas.
Mooring Lt.By. Fl. 2½ sec.

2 x Marine Farms established. Consult chart
for details.

RU NA LACHAN. 57°29.0'N, 5°52.0'W. Lt.
Oc. W.R. 8 sec. 21M. Metal Frame Tr. 17m.
W.337°-022°; R.022°-117°; W.117°-162°.
APPLECROSS. Lt.Bn. Fl.G. 3 sec. G. △ on post.

SKEIR TARRSUINN Bn. R. iron framework,
barrel shaped topmark, 9m. off NE end of
Scalpa I.
PABBA Bn. R. iron framework, barrel shaped
topmark, 9m. off SW end of Pabba I.
GULNARE ROCK By. Conical G. in Inner
Sound of Skye.

RAASAY SUISNISH Lt. 2 F.G. vert. 2M. Grey
mast. Raasay Pier.
Platform Const. ⎧ **Lt.By.** Fl.Y. 5 sec. Conical Y
Site ⎨ **Lt.By.** Fl.(4)Y. 10 sec. Conical Y.

SE POINT. EYRE POINT Lt. Fl.W.R. 3 sec.
W.9M. R.6M. W. Tr. 5m. W.215°-266°; R.266°-
288°; W.288°-063°.

ISLE OF SKYE

LOCH SLIGACHAN
SCONSER FERRY TERMINAL. Lt. Q.R. 3M.
Grey Post 8m.

INSHORE WAYPOINT SW OF CROWLIN.
57°19.2'N, 5°53.5'W.

CROWLIN, EILEAN BEG. Lt.Bn. Fl. 6 sec. 6M.
W. Bn. 32m.

PENFOLD ROCK By. Can.R. on E side.
JACKAL ROCK. By. Conical G.
MACMILLAN'S ROCK. Lt.By. Fl.(2)G. 12 sec.
Conical G. on NW end of Narrows.

INSHORE WAYPOINT LOCH CARRON.
57°21.4'N, 5°39.6'W.

LOCH CARRON
No. 1 Lt.By. Fl.G. 3 sec. Conical G.
No. 2 Lt.By. Fl.(2)R. 10 sec. Can.R.
No. 3 Lt.By. Fl.G. 5 sec. Conical G.
No. 4 Lt.By. Fl.R. 3 sec. Can.R.
No. 5 Lt.By. Q.R. Can.R.
No. 6 Lt.By. Fl.G. 3 sec. Conical G.
No. 7 Lt.By. Fl.(2)R. 10 sec. Can.R.

LOCH RERAIG. Dir. Lt. 065°. Dir. Fl.(3)W.R.G.
10 sec. W.6M. R.4M. G.4M. W. △ on concrete
base. G.060°-063°; W.063°-067°; R.067°-070°.
DUNCRAIG. Dir. Lt. 164°. Dir. Fl.(3)W.R.G. 10
sec. W.6M. R.4M. G.4M. W. △ on concrete
base. G.157°-162°; W.162°-166°; R.166°-171°.
LEACANASHIE. Dir. Lt. 042°30'. Dir.
Fl.(3)W.R.G. 10 sec. W.6M. R.4M. G.4M. W. △
on concrete base. G.318°-041°; W.041°-044°;
R.044°-050°.

FOUL GROUND. Lt.By. Fl.Y. 5 sec. Sph. Y.

INSHORE WAYPOINT KYLEAKIN. 57°17.2'N,
5°45.6'W.

KYLEAKIN
BOW ROCK By. Can.R. near W entce. to
Kyleakin.
CARRACH ROCK. Lt.By. Q.G. Conical G.

BLACK EYE. Lt.By. Fl.(2)R. 10 sec. Can.R.

EILEAN BAN Lt. Iso W.R.G. 4 sec. W.9M.
R.6M. G.6M. W. Tr. 16m. W.278°-282°; R282°-
096°; W.096°-132°; G.132°-182°. Racon.
ALLT-AN-AVAIG JTY. Lt. 2 F.R. vert. Vis. 075°-
270°.
S SHORE, FERRY SLIPWAY. Lt. Q.R. 2m. R.
and W. △. vis. in Kyle of Lochalsh.
MOORING DOLPHIN Lt. Q. 3M. Post 5m.

APPROACHES TO PLOCKTON

(a) By. Spar R.
(b) By. Spherical R.W.hor. bands.
(c) By. Spar B.
(d) By. Spar R.
(e) By. Spar B.
(f) By. Spherical R.W.hor. bands.
(g) By. Spar R.

STRING ROCK. Lt.By. Fl.R. 5 sec. Can.R. Lt.By. Fl.R. 4 sec. Can.R.

KYLE OF LOCHALSH

MARINE FARMS are established in this area. Consult chart for details.

FERRY TERMINUS PIER HEAD W SIDE. Lt. 2 F.G. vert. 5M. brown post, 6m.
E SIDE. Lt. 2 F.G. vert. 4M. brown post, 6m.
FISHERY PIER. Lt. Fl.G. 3 sec. 2M. Grey mast 6m.
BUTEC JETTY W. END. N. CORNER Lt. Oc.G. 6 sec. 3M. W. mast. 5m. Each End.
S. CORNER Lt. Oc.G. 6 sec. 3M. W.Post. 5m.
E. END. Lt. Oc.G. 6 sec. 3M. W. Post. 5m.
SGEIR-NA-CAILLICH. Lt.Bn. Fl.(2)R. 6 sec. 4M.
RACOON ROCK By. Conical G. In Loch Duich.

SOUND OF SLEAT

KYLE RHEA. 57°14.2'N, 5°39.9'W. Lt.Bn. Fl.W.R.G. 3 sec. W.11M. R.9M. G.8M. R.shore-219°; W.219°-228°; G.228°-338°; W.338°-346°; R.346°-shore.

SANDAIG ISLAND Lt. Fl. 6 sec. 8M. W. octagonal Tr. 12m.
ORNSAY, N END. Lt.Bn. Fl.R. 6 sec. 4M. W. tank on Grey stone Bn. 8m.

ORNSAY, SE END, ISLET 57°08.6'N, 5°46.4'W Lt. Oc. 8 sec. 15M. W. Tr. 18m. vis. 157°-030°. intens towards Sound of Sleat.
SGEIR UBLIHE. Bn. in Loch Hourn.
EILEAN IARMAIN. Lt. 2 F.R. vert. Post on Rock off pier.
ARMADALE BAY PIER CENTRE. Lt. Oc.R. 6 sec. 6M. building, 6m.

OFFSHORE WAYPOINT POINT OF SLEAT. 57°00.0'N, 6°01.0'W.

POINT OF SLEAT Lt. Fl. 3 sec. 9M. W. Tr. 20m.

OFFSHORE WAYPOINT SOUND OF SLEAT. 57°02.0'N, 5°56.0'W.

INSHORE WAYPOINT GLENELG BAY. 57°13.0'N, 5°38.8'W.

MALLAIG 57°00'N 5°49'W. Tel: (0687) 2154/2249.

HARBOUR WAYPOINT. 57°00.5'N, 5°50.5'W.

Radio — Port: VHF Chan. 16, 9. Mon.-Fri. 0900-1700.
NORTHERN PIER E END Lt. Iso. W.R.G. 4 sec. W.9M. R.6M. G.6M. Grey Tr. 6m. G.181°-185°; W.185°-197°; R.197°-201°. 3 F.R. vert. shown from same structure when vessels may not enter harbour.

SGEIR DHEARG. Lt. Fl. (2)W.G. 8 sec. 5M. Grey Bn. 6m. G.190°-055°; W.055°-190°.
ON REEF. Lt. 2 F.G. vert. 4M. B. Tr. 5m.

LOCH NEVIS

MARINE FARMS are established in this area. Consult chart for details.

OUTER HEBRIDES

OFFSHORE WAYPOINT BUTT OF LEWIS. 58°32.0'N, 6°11.0'W.

BUTT OF LEWIS 58°31.0'N, 6°15.7'W Lt. Fl. 5 sec. 25M. R.brick Tr. 52m. vis 056°-320°. RC. Horn(2) 30 sec. W. Tr.

TIUMPAN HEAD 58°15.6'N, 6°08.3'W Lt.Ho. Fl.(2) 15 sec. 25M. W. Tr. 55m.

BROAD BAY
TONG ANCHORAGE. Lts. in Line 320° (Front) Oc.R. 8 sec. 4M. 8m. (Rear) Oc.R. 8 sec. 4M. 9m.
EITSHAL RADIO MAST. Lts. 4 F.R. vert. 237m. to 357m.
HEN AND CHICKENS Bn. Pillar R. ball Topmark, off Chicken Head.
BIASTAN HOLM. Bn. Pillar R. 2m.

OFFSHORE WAYPOINT OFF STORNOWAY HR. 58°09.0'N, 6°17.0'W.

Emergency Coordination Centre (HMCG) Tel: (0851) 2013/2014.

MRSC STORNOWAY (0851) 2013. Weather broadcast ev. 4h. from 0110.

STORNOWAY 58°11'N, 6°22'W Tel:
Stornoway (0851) 2688

HARBOUR WAYPOINT. 58°11.0'N, 6°21.0'W.

Radio — Port: VHF Chan. 16, 12. H24.
CNOC NAN UAN. Lt. F.R. on Tr. conspicuous.

ARNISH POINT 58°11.5'N, 6°22.2'W.
Lt.Ho. Fl. W.R. 10 sec. 19M. W. round Tr. 17m.
vis. W.088°-198°; R.198°-302°; W.302°-013°.
ARNISH POINT REEF. Lt.By. Fl.(2) R. 6 sec.
Can.R. ʊⱴⱴ.
SANDWICK BAY. Lt.Bn. Oc. W.R.G. 6 sec. 9M.
Metal Pole 10m. G.334°-341°; W.341°-347°;
R.347°-354°.

SANDWICK RG STN. 58°12'39"0N
6°21'14"0W. Emergency DF Stn. VHF Chan. 16
& 67. Controlled by MRSC Stornoway.

STONY FIELD. 58°11.6'N, 6°21.3'W. Lt.Bn.
Fl.W.R.G. 3 sec. 11M. Metal Pole 8m. G.shore-
073°; R.073°-102°; W.102°-109°; G.109°-shore.
REEF ROCK. Lt.By. Q.R. Can.R.
EILEAN NA GOTHAIL. Lt. Fl.G. 6 sec. metal
col. 8m.
PATENT SLIP JETTY Lt.Bn. 2 F.G. vert.

No: 1 PIER 58°12.4'N, 6°23.3'W. Lt.Bn.
Q.W.R.G. 11M. Pole 8m. G.shore-335°;
W.335°-352°; R.352°-shore.
RO-RO JETTY Ldg.Lts. 325° (Front) F.G. Col.
3m. (Rear) F.G. Col. 3m.
SGEIRMORE Bn. G. cage Topmark, on N side
Stornoway Harbour.
SEID ROCKS Bn. R. iron framework, barrel
Topmark, off Seid Pt. S side of Loch.
SGEIR NA PACAID Bn. G. Entce. to Glumaig
Hr. W side.

LOCH ERISORT
TAVAG BEAG Lt. Fl. 3 sec. 3M. Col. 13m.
EILEAN CHALABRIGH Lt. Q.R. 3M. Col. 5m.

OFFSHORE WAYPOINT GOB NA MILAID.
58°01.0'N, 6°20.0'W.

MILAID POINT 58°01.0'N, 6°21.8'W Lt. Fl.
15 sec. 10M. W. Tr. 14M.
SKERGRAITCH Bn. R. pyramid, cage and
cross Topmark.

RUBH' UISENISH Lt. Fl. 5 sec. 11M. W. Tr.
24m.57°56.2'N, 6°28.2'W.
COMET ROCK. Lt.By. Fl.R. 6 sec. Can.R.
SHIANTS. Lt.By. Q.G. Conical G.

SKERINOE Lt.By. Fl.G. 6 sec. Conical G.

OFFSHORE WAYPOINT EILEAN GLAS.
57°51.0'N, 6°36.0'W.

EAST LOCH TARBERT

SCALPAY, EILEAN GLAS 57°51.4'N,
6°38.5'W Lt. Fl.(3) 20 sec. 23M. W. Tr. R.bands,
43m. R.C. Racon.
SGEIR GRIADACH. Lt.By. Q.(6) + L.Fl. 15 sec.
Pillar. Y.B. Topmark S.

INSHORE WAYPOINT EAST LOCH TARBERT.
57°50.1'N, 6°41.6'W.

N HARBOUR PIER. Lt.Bn. 2 F.G. vert. 6m. R. Δ
W. stripe on pole.
Lt.By. Fl.G. 2 sec. Conical G.
DUN COR MOR. Lt. Fl.R. 5 sec. W. Tr. 5M.
10m.

SGEIR GHLAS Lt. Iso.W.R.G. 4 sec. W.9M.
R.6M. G.6M. W. round concrete Tr. 12m.
G.282°-319°; W.319°-329°; R.329°-153°;
W.153°-164°; G.164°-171°.
PIER. Lt. Oc.W.R.G. 6 sec. 5M. 10m. G.090°-
298°; W.298°-306°; R.306°-090° when vessels
expected.
Lt. 2 F.G. vert. 5M. Col. 10m.
Lt. 2 F.G. vert. 5M. Col. 7m.

INSHORE WAYPOINT LOCH STOCKINISH.
57°47.4'N, 6°47.8'W.

INSHORE WAYPOINT LOCH FINSBAY.
57°45.5'N, 6°52.4'W.

INSHORE WAYPOINT BOISDALE/RODEL.
57°43.8'N, 6°56.0'W.

RODEL RG STN. 57°44.9'N, 6°57.4'W.
Controlled by MRSC Stornoway.

SOUND OF HARRIS

LEVERBURGH CHANNEL
PABBAY. Lt.By. Fl.R. 2 sec. Can.R.
RED ROCK Bn. B. pyramid shaped with cage,
on N side, 10m.
RUDH'AN LOSAID 2 W. Bns. 1½ cables NNE.
HEB. Bn. W. Stone. 16m.
DUBH SGEIR. Lt. Q.(2) 5 sec. 6M. R. W. Tr. 9m.
JANE TOWER. Lt. Q.(2)G. 5 sec. 4M. 6m.
Pedestal. Obsc. 273°-318°.
STUMBLES ROCK By. Can.R. on E side.

SGEIR MHIC COMA Lt.By. Fl.R. 2 sec. Can.R.
LEVERBURGH PIER Lt. Oc.W.R.G. 8 sec. 2M.
5m. G.305°-059°; W.059°-066°; R.066°-125°.
SGEIR VOLINISH Bn. R. iron framework, 9m.

STANTON CHANNEL
SAGHAY MOR. Bn. Cairn/Bn. W.R. stripe.
ENSAY. Bn. Cairn/Bn. W.R. stripe.
STROMSAY. Bn. Cairn/Bn. W.R. stripe.

COPE PASSAGE

COPE PASSAGE FAIRWAY. Lt.By. L.Fl. 10 sec.
Spherical R.W.V.S.
BAR Lt.By. Q.R. Can.R.
BAR Lt.By. Q.G. Conical G.
No: 12 Lt.By. Fl.R. 5 sec. Can.R
No: 10 Lt.By. Q.R. Can.R.
No: 9 Lt.By. Fl.G. 5 sec. Conical G.
No: 8 Lt.By. Fl.R. 5 sec. Can.R.
No: 7 Lt.By. Q.G. Conical G.
No: 6 Lt.By. Q.R. Can.R.
No: 5 Lt.By. Fl.G. 5 sec. Conical G.
No: 4 Lt.By. Fl.R. 5 sec. Can.R.
No: 3 Lt.By. Fl.G. 5 sec. Conical G.
No: 2 Lt.By. Q.R. Can.R.
No: 1 Lt.By. Q.G. Conical G.

BERNERAY BREAKWATER HEAD. Lt. Iso.R. 4
sec. 4M. Grey Col. 7m.
DROWNING ROCK Lt. Q.(2)G. 8 sec. 2M. G.
mast 2m.
REEF CHANNEL No: 1 Lt. Q.G. 4M. G. mast
2m.
REEF CHANNEL No: 2 Lt. Iso.G. 4 sec. 4M. G.
mast 2m.
EILEAN FUAM Lt.Bn. Q. 2M. 6m. W. Col.
BERNERAY. BORVE. FERRY TERMINAL. Lt. 2
F.G. vert. 3M. Slipway. 6m.
NORTH UIST. NEWTON JETTY. Lt.Bn. 2 F.R.
vert. 8M. 9m. Grey Col.
FERRY TERMINAL. Lt. 2 F.R. vert. 3M.
Slipway. 6m.

GRIMINISH HARBOUR
SGEIR DUBH MOR. Lt. Q.(2)G. 10 sec. 4M.
Pillar. Wind Generator 4m.
PIER HEAD. Lt. 2 F.G. vert. Grey Col. shown
Mar.-Oct.

OFFSHORE WAYPOINT OFF LOCH MADDY.
57°36.0'N, 7°04.0'W.

LOCH MADDY Tel: Port Manager (087)
63337/63282. Night: 63226. Telex: 777273.
Radio — Port: VHF Chan 16, 12.

WEAVER-S POINT. Lt. Fl. 3 sec. 7M. W. hut, 21m.
GLAS EILEAN MOR. Lt. Fl.(2) 6 sec.
aluminium col. 8m.
RUDNA NAM PLEAC Lt.Bn. Fl.R. 4 sec. 5M. W.
Post.
RUIGH LIATH. E ISLET. Lt. Q.G. wooden post,
6m.
By. Spar. R. Topmark Can.
VALLAQUIE ISLAND. Lt. Fl.(3)W.R.G. 8 sec.
W.7M. R.5M. G.5M. W. Pillar. 11m. G.shore-
205°; W.205°-210°; R.210°-240°; G.240°-254°;
W.254°-257°; R.257°-shore.
LOCHMADDY RO-RO PIER. Ldg.Lts. 298°
(Front) 2 F.G. vert. 4M. Col. 8m. (Rear) Oc. G.
8 sec. 4M. Col. on dolphin 10m. 284°-304°
KALLIN NO. 1. Lt.By. Fl.(2)R. 8 sec. Can.R.
KALLIN NO. 2. Lt.By. Fl.R. 5 sec. Can.R.
KALLIN NO. 3. Lt.By. Fl.G. 2 sec. Conical G.

GRIMSAY. KALLIN HARBOUR. BREAKWATER.
NE Cnr. Lt. 2 F.R. vert. 6m.

BENBECULA. SOUND OF FLODDAY.
Overhead cable, safe clearance 4.6m.

OFFSHORE WAYPOINT OFF LOCH CARNAN.
57°22.0'N, 7°11.0'W.

LOCH CARNAN
Ldg.Lts. 222°. (Front) Fl.R. 2 sec. 5M. W. ◊ on
post, 7m. (Rear) Iso. R. 10 sec. 5M. W. ◊ on
post, 11m.
LOCH CARNAN LANDFALL Lt.By. L.Fl. 10 sec.
Pillar R.W.V.S.
No: 1 Lt.By. Fl.G. 2½ sec. Conical G.
No: 2 Lt.By. Q.G. Conical G.
No: 3 Lt.By. Fl.R. 5 sec. Can.R.

INSHORE WAYPOINT OFF LOCH SKIPORT.
57°19.9'N, 7°12.6'W.

OFFSHORE WAYPOINT OFF USINISH LT.
57°18.0'N, 7°10.0'W.

SOUTH UIST

USINISH 57°17.9'N, 7°11.5'W Lt. Fl.W.R. 20
sec. W.19M. R.15M. W. Tr. 54m. W.193°-356°;
R.356°-013°.

OFFSHORE WAYPOINT OFF LOCH BOISDALE.
57°09.0'N, 7°14.0'W.

LOCH BOISDALE

MACKENZIE ROCK. Lt.By. Fl.(3)R. 15 sec.
Can.R. marks rock at entc. to Loch Boisdale.
CALVAY, E END. Lt. Fl.(2)W.R.G. 10 sec. W.7M.
R.4M. G.4M. W. Tr. W.111°-190°; G.190°-202°;
W.202°-286°; R.286°-111°.

GASAY ISLAND Lt. Fl.W.R. 5 sec. W.7M. R.4M. W. Tr. 10m. W.120°-284°; R.284°-120°.

N SIDE. Lt. Q.G. 3M. Post. 3m.
EILEAN DUBH Lt. Fl.(2)R. 5 sec. 3M. B. Col. 2m.
RO RO TERMINAL. HEAD. Lt. Iso. R.G. 4 sec. 2M. metal framework Tr. 12m. G.shore-283°; R.283°-shore and 2 F.G. vert.
SGOR ROCK. Lt.By. Fl.G. 3 sec. Conical G.

OFFSHORE WAYPOINT RUBHA NA-H ORDAIG. 57°06.4′N, 7°11.0′W.

SOUND OF ERISKAY
LUDAIG Dir.Lt. 297°02′. Dir Oc.W.R.G. 6 sec. W.7M. R.4M. G.4M. Col. 8m. G.287°-296°; W.296°-298°; R.298°-307°.
PIER Lt. 2 F.G. vert. 5M. Col.
STAG ROCK Lt. Fl.(2) 8 sec. 4M. Col. 7m.
BANK ROCK Lt. Q.(2) 4 sec. 4M. Col. 5m.
HAUN Dir.Lt. 235°59′. Dir.Oc.W.R.G. 3 sec. W.7M. R.4M. G.4M. Col. 9m. G.226°-234.5°; W.234.5°-237.5°; R.237.5°-246°.
PIER Lt. 2 F.R. vert. 5M. Col.
ERISKAY PIER. Lt. 2 F.G. vert. 5m.
ACAIRSEID MHOR. Ldg.Lts. 285° (Front) Oc. R. 6 sec. 4M. Grey Col. 9m. (Rear) Oc. R. 6 sec. 4M. Grey Col. 10m.

SOUTH UIST TO BENBECULA (WEST COAST)

SOUTH UIST. ROYAL ARTILLERY RANGE HEBRIDES. FALCONET TOWER Lt. F.R. 8M. Tr. 25m. (by day 3M.). Shown 1 hr. before firing starts. Changes to Iso.R. 2 sec. 15 min. before firing starts until completion. Seen by day. Similar Lts. shown 1.2M. NNW and 7.5M. SSW. Range extends 100M. NW of Uist. Most activity 30M. NW and SW of Ardivachar Point. Radar surveillance and patrols maintained.
C By. Conical G.
By. Conical G.
By. Can.R.
Lt.By. Fl.Y. 5 sec. Conical Y.
Lt.By. Fl.Y. 10 sec. Conical Y.
ARDIVACHAR POINT. Lt. F.R. 6M. 7m. shown as Falconet Tr. Lt.
RUBHA ARDVULE. Lt. F.R. 5M. 4m. shown as Falconet Tr. Lt.

SOUND OF BARRA
By. Conical G. 57°05.9′N, 7°19.5′W
Lt.By. Fl.R. 5 sec. Can.R. 57°05.75′N, 7°20.77′W.
Lt.By. Fl.(2) 10 sec. Pillar B.R. Topmark Is. D. 57°04.18′N, 7°23.58′W.

BINCH ROCK By. Pillar Y.B. Topmark S. 1½M. S of Eriskay I.
KATE BNS. FIARAY 1. W. Stone. 12m. ◊ topmark. 2. W. Stone. 6m. △ topmark.

OFFSHORE WAYPOINT HELLISAY ISLE. 57°00.0′N, 7°17.0′W.

CURACHAN. Lt.By. Q.(3) 10 sec. Pillar. B.Y.B. Topmark E.

ISLES OF BARRA. ARDVEENISH Lt. Oc. W.R.G. 6 sec. W. 9M. R. 6M. G. 6M. Grey col. 6m. G.300°-304°; W.304°-306°; R.306°-310°.

VATERSAY SOUND
BO-VIC-CHUAN. Lt.By. Q.(6) + L.Fl. 15 sec. Pillar Y.B. Topmark S off Barra I.

OFFSHORE WAYPOINT CASTLE BAY. 56°56.1′N, 7°22.6′W.

CASTLE BAY SOUTH. Lt.By. Fl.(2)R. 8 sec. Can.R. ⸰⸰ in Castle Bay. Racon.
SGEIR DUBH. Lt.Bn. Fl.(2)W.G. 6 sec. W.7M. G.5M. Col. on Tr. 6m. W.280°-180°; G.180°-280°.
SGEIR LIATH. Lt. Fl. 3 sec. 8M. W. building, 7m.
CASTLE HARBOUR 2 W. Ldg.Bns.

HARBOUR WAYPOINT. 56°56.1′N, 7°28.0′W.

SGEIR VICHALEN ROCK Bn. B. iron framework, barrel shape Topmark.
RUBHA GLAS. Ldg.Lts. 295°. (Front) F.G. 11M. Or. △ on W. Tr. 9m. (Rear) F.G. 11M Or. ▽ on W. Tr. 15m.
CASTLE BAY Lt. Fl.R. 5 sec. 3M. Col. 2m.
CASTLE BAY RO RO S. Lt. 2 F.G. vert. 3M. col. 7m.

BARRA RG STN. 57°00.80′N, 7°30.40′W. Controlled by MRSC Stornoway.

BARRA HEAD 56°47.1′N, 7°39.2′W Lt. Fl. 15 sec. 21M. W. stone Tr. 208m. vis. except where obscured by islands to NE. R.C.

FLANNAN ISLANDS
EILEAN MOR. 58°17.3′N, 7°35.4W. Fl.(2) 30 sec. 20M. W. Tr. 101m. obsc. in places by islands to W of Eilean Mor.

EAST LOCH ROAG
Overhead cable, clearance 5.7m.

AIRD LAIMISHADER. Lt. Fl. 12 sec. 8M. W. hut, 61m. obscured by land on certain bearings. F.R. Lts. on radio mast 7.5M. WSW. By. Conical G.
CARLOWAY PIER. Lt. 2 F.R. vert.
ARDVANICH POINT Lt. Fl.G. 3 sec. 2M. Pillar 2m.
TIDAL ROCK Lt. Fl.R. 3 sec. 2M. Col. 2m.
GREAT BERNERA KIRKIBOST JETTY Lt. 2 F.G. vert. 2M. Col. 6m.
GREINAM ISLAND. Lt.Bn. Fl.W.R. 6 sec. W.8M. R.7M. W. Bn. 8m. R.143°-169°; W.169°-143°.
RUBHA ARSPAIG JETTY Lt. 2 F.R. vert. 4M. mast.

WEST LOCH ROAG
LOCH MIAVAIG overhead cable safe clearance 8.3m.

ISLANDS WEST OF THE HEBRIDES

ST KILDA ISLAND. 57°48'N 08°33'W. Tel: (0870) 2384.
VILLAGE BAY. Lt.By. Q.G. Conical G.
Ldg.Lts. 270°(Front) Oc. 5 sec. 3M. Cairn; (Rear) Oc. 5 sec. 3M. Cairn.

ROCKALL ISLAND. Lt. 57°37.8'N, 13°41.3'W. Fl. 15 sec. 13M. R. Lantern. 19m. Unreliable due to weather damage.

MONACH ISLAND 57°32'N, 7°42'W. Disused Lt.Ho. R.brick. W side of Shillay Is. 47m. Racon.

ISLE OF SKYE (North & West)

OFFSHORE WAYPOINT EILEAN TRODDY. 57°44.6'N, 6°18.0'W.

EILEAN TRODDAY 57°43.6'N, 6°17.8'W. Lt.Ho. Fl.(2) W.R.G. 10 sec. W.12M. R.9M. G.9M. W. Bn. 49m. W.062°-088°; R.088°-130°; W.130°-322°; G.322°-062°.
SKEIR NA MULE Bn. B. pyramid shaped, cage and cross Topmark, 2.5M. N of Ru Hunish.

OFFSHORE WAYPOINT OFF LOCH SNIZORT. 57°40.0'N, 6°30.0'W.

INSHORE WAYPOINT UIG BAY. 57°34.4'N, 6°23.2'W.

UIG, KING EDWARD PIER HEAD. Lt. Iso.W.R.G. 4 sec. W.7M. R.4M. G.4M. Grey mast. 10m. W.180°-008°; G.008°-052°; W.052°-075°; R.075°-180°.
Lt. 2 F.R. vert. 4M. Grey mast 10m.
WATERNISH POINT. Lt.Bn. Fl. 20 sec. 8M. W. Tr. 21m.

OFFSHORE WAYPOINT WATERNISH POINT. 57°37.0'N, 6°39.0'W.
COMET ROCK. Lt.By. Fl.R. 6 sec. Can.R.

OFFSHORE WAYPOINT OFF LOCH DUNVEGAN. 57°32.8'N, 6°42.8'W.

LOCH DUNVEGAN

HARBOUR WAYPOINT. 57°27.5'N, 6°37.8'W.

UIGINISH POINT. Lt. Fl.W.G. 3 sec. W.7M. G.5M. W. hut, 14m. G.040°-128°; W.128°-306°. Obscured by Fiadhairt Point when bearing more than 148°.
PIER, N CORNER. Lt. 2 F.R. vert. 5M. on post, 4m. when vessel expected.
BO-NA-FAMACHD By. Conical G.

OFFSHORE WAYPOINT NEIST POINT. 57°24.5'N, 6°51.0'W.

NEIST POINT 57°25.4'N, 6°47.2'W Lt. Fl. 5 sec. 16M. W. Tr. 43m.

LOCH HARPORT
ARDTRECK POINT Lt. Iso 4 sec. 9M. small W. Tr. 17m.

THE SMALL ISLES

OFFSHORE WAYPOINT N OF CANNA. 57°06.0'N, 6°29.0'W.

SANDAY ISLAND
EAST END, CANNA. Lt.Bn. Fl. 6 sec. 8M. W. Bn. 32m. vis. 152°-061°.

HARBOUR WAYPOINT. 57°03.5'N, 6°28.5'W.

HUMLA ROCK. Lt.By. Fl.G. 6 sec. Conical G. 2½M. SW of Canna I.

INSHORE WAYPOINT NW OF POINT OF SLEAT. 57°04.0'N, 6°08.8'W.

INSHORE WAYPOINT LOCH EISHORT. 57°10.0'N, 5°56.4'W.

OIGH SGEIR, HYSKEIR 56°58.2′N,
6°40.9′W Lt.Ho. Fl.(3) 30 sec. 24M. W. Tr. 41m.
RC. Horn 30 sec.
EIGG ISLAND. Lt.Bn. Fl. 6 sec. 8M. W. Bn.
24m. vis. 181°-shore.
BO FASKADALE. Lt.By. Fl.(3)G. 18 sec. Conical
G. off rocks.

**OFFSHORE WAYPOINT N OF SOUND OF
ARISAIG. 56°53.0′N, 6°01.2′W.**

**INSHORE WAYPOINT SOUND OF ARISAIG.
56°50.6′N, 5°50.0′W.**

ARISAIG (LOCH NA CEALL)
Entry: Local knowledge is advisable.
Preferably use S. Channel ½-1 cable wide,
1.5m. depth. Very tortuous. Rocks marked by
perches. Large yacht centre with pier and
boatyard. N. Channel seldom used.

**OFFSHORE WAYPOINT S OF SOUND OF
ARISAIG. 56°48.0′N, 6°08.2′W.**

**OFFSHORE WAYPOINT ARDNAMURCHAN.
56°44.0′N, 6°14.0′W.**

ARDNAMURCHAN 56°43.6′N, 6°13.4′W.
Lt. Fl.(2) 20 sec. 24M. Grey granite Tr. 55m.
vis. 002°-217°. Horn (2) 20 sec.

**OFFSHORE WAYPOINT S OF
ARDNAMURCHAN. 56°42.0′N, 6°15.5′W.**

INNER HEBRIDES

CAIRNS OF COLL. SUIL GHORN. 56°42.2′N,
6°26.8′W. Lt. Fl.12 sec. 11M. Tr. 23m.
**OFFSHORE WAYPOINT ARINAGOUR.
56°36.0′N, 6°30.0′W.**

LOCH EATHARNA
ARINAGOUR PIER. Tel: (08793) 347. Out of
hours (08793) 359.
Radio — Port: VHF Chan. 31. Tx. 157.550. Rx.
162.150.
ARINAGOUR PIER HEAD. Lt. 2 F.R. vert. on
Col.
CHIEFTAIN ROCK. Lt.By. Fl.G. 6 sec. Conical
G.

**OFFSHORE WAYPOINT LOCH BREACHACHA.
56°33.8′N, 6°35.8′W.**

ROAN BOGHA. Lt.By. Q.(6) + L.Fl. 15 sec.
Pillar Y.B. Topmark S, in Gunna Sd.
PLACAID BO Lt.By. Fl.G. 4 sec. Conical G. in
Gunna Sd.

**OFFSHORE WAYPOINT GUNNA SOUND.
56°31.9′N, 6°40.2′W.**

TIREE ISLAND

GOTT BAY PIER. Tel: (08792) 337.
Radio — Port: VHF Chan. 31. Tx. 157.550. Rx.
162.150.

TIREE RG STN. 56°30.27′N, 6°57.80′W.
Emergency DF Stn. VHF Chan. 16 & 67.
Controlled by MRSC Oban.

**OFFSHORE WAYPOINT TIREE GOTT BAY.
56°30.0′N, 6°46.3′W.**

SCARINISH 56°30.0′N, 6°48.2′W. Lt. Fl. 3
sec. 16M. W. square Tr. 11m. vis. 210°-030°,
F.R. Lts. on radio Trs. 5.35M. 272° and 5.3M
276°.
Ldg.Lts. 286°30′. (Front) F.R. on Col. when
vessel expected. (Rear) F.R. on mast.

PASSAGE OF TIREE
Lt.By. Fl.(5)Y. 20 sec. Spar. Y.

SKERRYVORE 56°19.4′N, 7°06.9′W. Lt. Fl.
10 sec. 26M. Grey granite Tr. 46m. Racon.
Horn 60 sec.

DUBH ARTACH 56°08.0′N, 6°37.9′W. Lt.
Fl.(2) 30 sec. 20M. Grey granite Tr. R. band,
44m. Horn 45 sec.

**OFFSHORE WAYPOINT OFF CALIACH POINT.
56°37.0′N, 6°20.4′W.**

MARINE FARM established in this area.
Consult chart for details.

**OFFSHORE WAYPOINT SW OF STAFFA.
56°24.8′N, 6°22.3′W.**

**INSHORE WAYPOINT LOCH NA KEAL.
56°27.1′N, 6°10.1′W.**

LOCH LATHAICH (ROSS OF MULL)
EILEANAN NA LIATHANAICH. Lt. Fl.W.R. 6
sec. W.8M. R.6M. W. Bn. 12m. on SE extreme.
R.088°-108°; W. elsewhere.

**HARBOUR WAYPOINT BUNESSAN.
56°21.0′N, 6°16.0′W.**

LOCH SCRIDAIN
AIRD OF KINLOCH. Bn. W. mast △ topmark.

**OFFSHORE WAYPOINT NW OF IONA.
56°21.9′N, 6°25.1′W.**

SOUND OF IONA

Sound of Iona and Approaches have numerous shoal depths. Mariners are warned to exercise caution when navigating in this area.

IONA BANK By. Pillar Y.B. Topmark S on SW side of Sd.
BO-NA-SLIGINACH By. Conical G. marks rock on E side of Chan.
BOGHA CHOILTA By. Conical G.
RUADH SGEIR Bn. B. concrete Pillar with cross.
SGEIR-NA-BADH Stone Tr. nr. Earraid.

OFFSHORE WAYPOINT SW OF IONA. 56°17.0'N, 6°30.0'W.

OFFSHORE WAYPOINT S OF TORRAN ROCKS. 56°11.5'N, 6°27.0'W.

SOUND OF MULL

INSHORE WAYPOINT OFF ARDMORE POINT. 56°39.8'N, 6°07.4'W.

ARDMORE POINT. Lt.Bn. Fl.(2) 10 sec. 8M. 17m.
KILEHOAN. MINGARY PIER HEAD. Lt. Q.R. 3M. Grey post 8m.
NEW ROCKS. Lt.By. Fl.G. 6 sec. Conical G.

RUBHA NAN GALL 56°38.3'N, 6°03.9'W.
Lt. Fl.W. 3 sec. W.15M. R.13M. G.13M. W. Tr. 17m.

TOBERMORY
H.M. Tel: (0688) 2017.
Entry: Small craft anchorage S. end of bay in 7.3m. Several buoys for visiting yachts.

HARBOUR WAYPOINT TOBERMORY. 56°38.5'N, 6°03.0'W.

By. Can.Y. off Tobermory.
SKEIR-NA-FENNAG By. Conical G. off W end of Shoal, in Bunavulin Bay.
WRECK. Lt.By. Fl.(2)R. 10 sec. Can.R. 56°34.9'N, 5°59.1'W.
ANTELOPE ROCK By. Can.R. in Salen Bay.
BOGHA ROCK By. Conical G.
FIUNARY SPIT By. Conical G.
EILEANAN GLASA. Lt.Bn. Fl. 6 sec. 8M. W. Bn. 7m.

ARDTORNISH POINT Lt. Fl.(2) W.R.G. 10 sec. W.8M. R.5M. G.5M. W. Tr. 7m. G.shore-302°; W.302°-310°; R.310°-342°; W.342°-057°; R.057°-095°; W.095°-108°; G.108°-shore.

AVON ROCK By. Can.R.
YULE ROCKS By. Can.R.

LOCH ALINE
Ldg.Lts. 356° (Front) F. 2m. (Rear) F. 4m. H24.
SLIPWAY Lt. 2 F.R. vert.
Lt.By. Q.R. Can.R.
Lt.By. Fl.R. 2 sec. Can.R
Lt.By. Q.G. Conical G.

GLAS EILEANAN. GREY ROCKS Lt. Fl. 3 sec. 6M. W. round Tr. on W. masonry base, 10m.

CRAIGNURE PIER. Tel: (06802) 343. Out of hours (06802) 342. Telex: 77314.
Radio — Port: VHF Chan. 31. Tx. 157. 550. Rx. 162. 150. Hours as required.
CRAIGNURE. Ldg.Lts. 240°50'. (Front) F.R. concrete mast, 10m. (Rear) F.R. concrete mast, 12m. vis. 225.8°-255.8°, on request.

SANDA SHOAL By. Can.R. on N Bank of Loch Linnhe.
SGEIR-NAN-ROIN By. Conical G. off Lettermore Pt.
CULCHENNA. Lt.By. Fl.G. 6 sec. Conical G.

LOCH LEVEN
BALLACHULISH W HR. Lt. Fl.(2)G. 7 sec. 3M. G. Pole 3m.
KENTALLEN
SALACHAN POINT Bn. R. 9m. octagonal.

LOCH LINNHE
MARINE FARMS are established in this area. consult chart for details.
CHLOVOULIN. Lt.By. Fl.(2)R. 15 sec. Can.R. at head of Loch Linnhe.
CORRAN FLAT By. Can.R.

CORRAN POINT 56°43.3'N, 5°14.5'W. Lt.
Iso.W.R.G. 4 sec. W.10M. R.7M. W. Tr. 12m. R.shore-195°; W.195°-215°; G.215°-305°; W.305°-030°; R.030°-shore.
Lt. Fl.R. 5 sec. 3M. Grey mast. 7m.

CORRAN NARROWS, NE Lt. Fl. 5 sec. 4M. metal framework Tr. 4m. vis. S shore-214°.
CORRAN SHOAL. Lt.By. Q.R. Can.R.

FORT WILLIAM
LOCHABER POWER CO PIER. Lt. Fl.G. 2 sec. 4M.

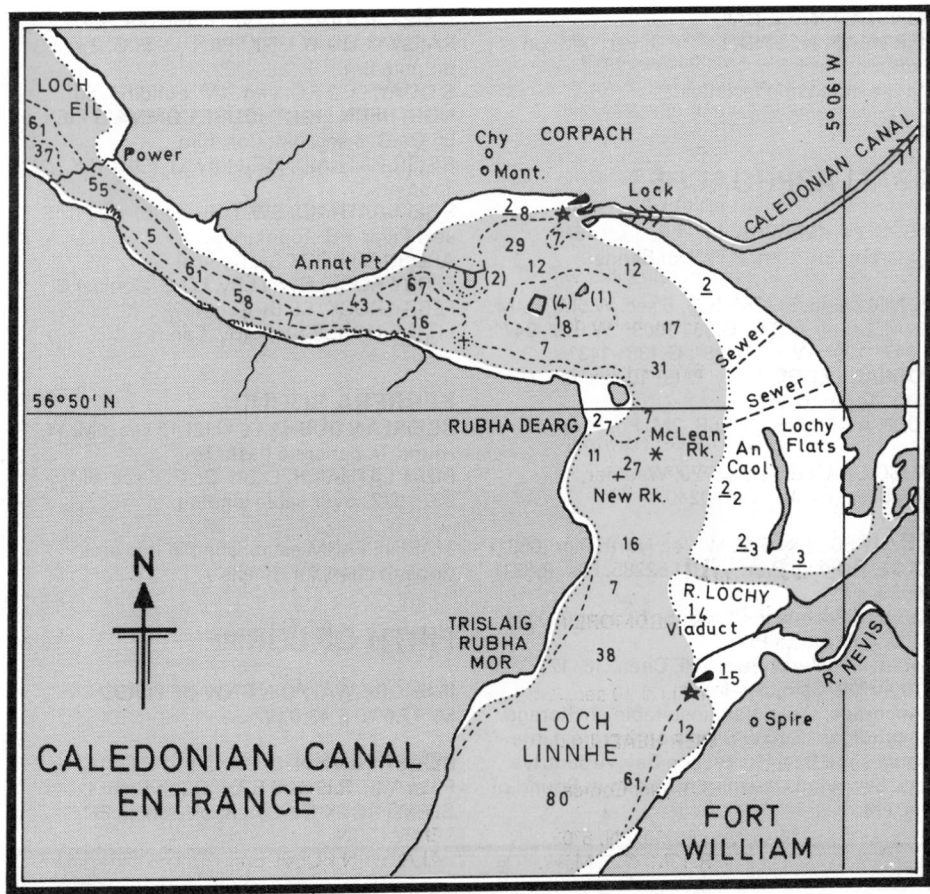

CALEDONIAN CANAL ENTRANCE

CORPACH (Caledonian Canal) 57°08′N 4°40′W. Tel: Lock Keeper (03977) 249. Pilot: (03977) 307.
Radio — Port & Pilots: VHF Chan. 16, 24. 0800-1700. Mon-Sat when lock manned.
Pilotage: Not Compulsory but available on request.
CORPACH. Lt. Iso.W.R.G. 4 sec. 5M. W. Tr. 6m. end of W sea lock entce. to Caledonian Canal. G.287°-310°; W.310°-335°; R.335°-030°.
GLENSANDA QUARRY BTH. SE. Lt. Fl.R. 3 sec. 4M. 4m.
NE Lt. Fl.R. 3 sec. 4M.
LOCHYFLAT S. Q.G. Conical G.
EILEAN-NA-CREICH. Lt.By. Fl.R. 3 sec. Can.R. ⌣⌣.
McLEAN ROCK. Lt.By. Fl.R. 12 sec. Can.R.

SGEIR BHUIDHE. Lt.Bn. Fl.(2) W.R. 7 sec. 9M. W. Bn. 7m. R.184°-220°; W.220°-184°.
APPIN POINT. Lt.By. Fl.G. 6 sec. Conical G.
BRANRA ROCK Bn. B.R.B. Topmark Is.D. 6m. nr. Port Appin.

LOCH CRERAN
Charted depths are based on old lead line surveys. Do not place undue reliance on these soundings and contours especially inshore.
AIRDS POINT. Lt.Bn. Fl.W.R.G. 2 sec. W.3M. R.1M. G.1M. R.Col. 2m. R.196°-246°; W.246°-258°; G.258°-041°; W.041°-058°; R.058°-093°.
ERISKA, NE POINT. Lt.Bn. Q.G. 2M. G.Col. 2m. vis. 128°-329°.
LOCH CRERAN Lt.By. Fl.G. 3 sec. Conical G.

LISMORE 56°27.4′N, 5°36.4′W. Lt. Fl. 10 sec. 19M. W. Tr. 31m. vis. 237°-208°.
LADY'S ROCK. Lt.Bn. Fl. 6 sec. 5M. R.round structure on W. Bn. 12m.

INSHORE WAYPOINT E OF LADY'S ROCK S END OF LISMORE. 56°27.0′N, 5°34.4′W.

DUART POINT. Lt. Fl.(3) W.R. 18 sec. W.5M. R.3M. Grey granite building, 14m. W.162°-261°; R.261°-275°; W.275°-353°; R.353°-shore.

DUNSTAFFNAGE BAY.
PIER HEAD, NE END. Lt. 2 F.G. vert. 2M. on pontoon, 4m.
Marina alongside facilities.

OBAN APPROACHES

N SPIT OF KERRERA. Lt. Fl.R. 3 sec. 5M.
Concrete Col. 10m. B.W. Hor.Bands.

DUNOLLIE Lt. Fl.(2)W.R.G. 6 sec. W.5M. R.4M.
G.4M. Stone Tr. 7m. G.351°-009°; W.009°-047°;
R.047°-120°; W.120°-138°; G.138°-143°.
CORRAN LEDGE. Lt.By. Q.(9) 10 sec. Pillar.
Y.B.Y. Topmark W.
RUBH A CRUIDH. Lt. Q.R. 2M. Post 3m.

MRSC OBAN (0631) 63720. Weather broadcast ev. 4h. from 0240.

OBAN 56°25'N 5°29'W. Tel: North Pier (0631)
62892. Railway Pier: (0631) 62285. Fax: (0631)
66588.
Radio — Port: VHF Chan. 16, 12. Hrs. 0900-
1700. Call: North Pier.
Radio — Railway Pier: VHF Chan. 16, 12.
0700-0100. Call: CAL-MAC.
Anchorage: Oban Bay unsuitable anchorage.
Anchorages — NW. Sound of Kerrera, Little
Horse-shoe Bay, Horseshoe Bay, Ardantrive
Bay. SW. winds frequently strong in Sound of
Kerrera.

N PIER, MIDDLE. Lt. 2 F.G. 5M. Col. 8m.
RAILWAY QUAY LINKSPAN. Lt. Fl.G. 2 sec.
dolphin 8m.
S QUAY. Lt. 2 F.G. vert. 4M. building, 5m.
NORTHERN LIGHTHOUSE COMMR'S PIER.
Lt. Oc.G. 6 sec. 3M. Col. 10m.
SGEIR-RATHAID, NE. Lt.By. Q. Pillar B.Y.
Topmark N.
SGEIR-RATHAID, SW. Lt.By. Q.(6) + L.Fl. 15
sec. Pillar Y.B. Topmark S.
ARDBHAN ROCK By. Conical G.
FERRY ROCK, NW. Lt.By. I.Q.G. Conical G.
FERRY ROCK, SE By Can.R.
LITTLE HORSE SHOE By. Can.R.

KERRERA SOUND
SGEIREAN DUBHA Lt. Fl.(2) 12 sec. 5M. W.
round Tr. concrete base, 7m.
PORT LATHAICH. Lt.Bn. Oc.G. 6 sec. 6M. vis.
037°-072° over cable landing.

MARINE FARM established in this area.
Consult chart for details.

FIRTH OF LORNE

INSHORE WAYPOINT NW OF FLADDA.
56°17.0'N, 5°43.0'W.

BOGHA NUADH. Lt.By. Q.(6) + L.Fl. 15 sec.
Pillar Y.B. Topmark S. off Dubh Sgair I.
BO NO ROCK By. Can.R. off Esdale Pt.

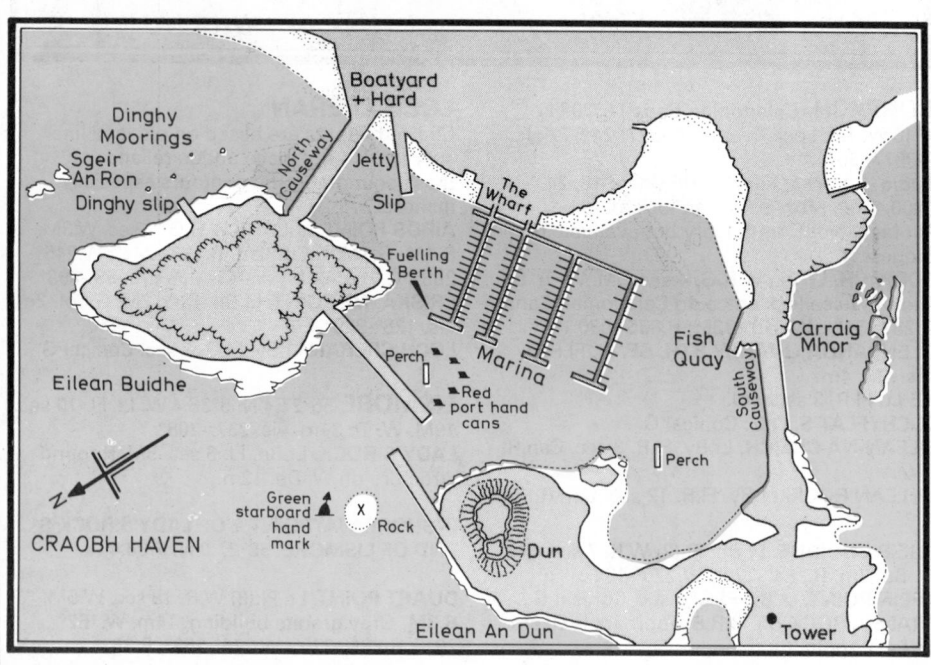

EASDALE HARBOUR

FLADDA 56°14.9'N, 5°40.8'W. Lt. Fl.(3) W.R.G. 18 sec. W.11M. R.9M. G.9M. W. Tr. 13m. R.169°-186°; W.186°-337°; G.337°-344°; W.334°-356°; R.356°-026°. Approaching from southward, faint Lt. varying with state of atmosphere will be seen when bearing more than 001°.

DUBH SGEIR. Lt. Fl. W.R.G. 6 sec. W.6M. R. 4M, G.4M.9m. W.000°-010°; R.010°-025°; W. 025°-215°; G.\215°-000°. RC. Racon. ARDLUING POINT By. Conical G. in Scarba Sd. S of Luing I.

Note: Off SW of Scarba and Camas nam Bairneach the eddy meets the main stream and can set up violent and dangerous turbulence and whirlpool known as The Hag several metres high and very noisy. The stream can reach 8½ knots.

CRAOBH HAVEN 56°12.7'N, 5°33.35'W

CRAOBH HAVEN MARINA. Tel: (08525) 222. Chan. (M).
Entry: Depths 5.5m. in entrance. Anchorage in harbour 9-14m.

COLONSAY

SCALASAIG Lt. Fl.(2) W.R.10 sec. W.8M. R.5M. G.5M. W. building, 8m. R.shore-230°; W.230°-337°; R.337°-354°.
PIER HEAD. Ldg.Lts. (Front) F.R. concrete Col. 8m. (Rear) F.R. concrete Col. 10m. on request.

LOCH MELFORT

FEARNACH BAY PIER LT. 2 F.R. vert. 3M. Mast 6m.
Kilmelford Yacht Haven. Tel: (08522) 248/279. Chan. (M) 1st May-30th Sept. 0830-1730. 1st Oct.-30th April (Tues.-Sat.) 0830-1730. Max. LOA 20m, draught 2.1m.

SOUND OF JURA

INSHORE WAYPOINT N OF REISA AN T-SRUITH. 56°09.0'N, 5°39.5'W.

REISA AN T-SRUITH. Lt.Bn. Fl.(2) 12 sec. 7M. W. Col. concrete base, 12m.

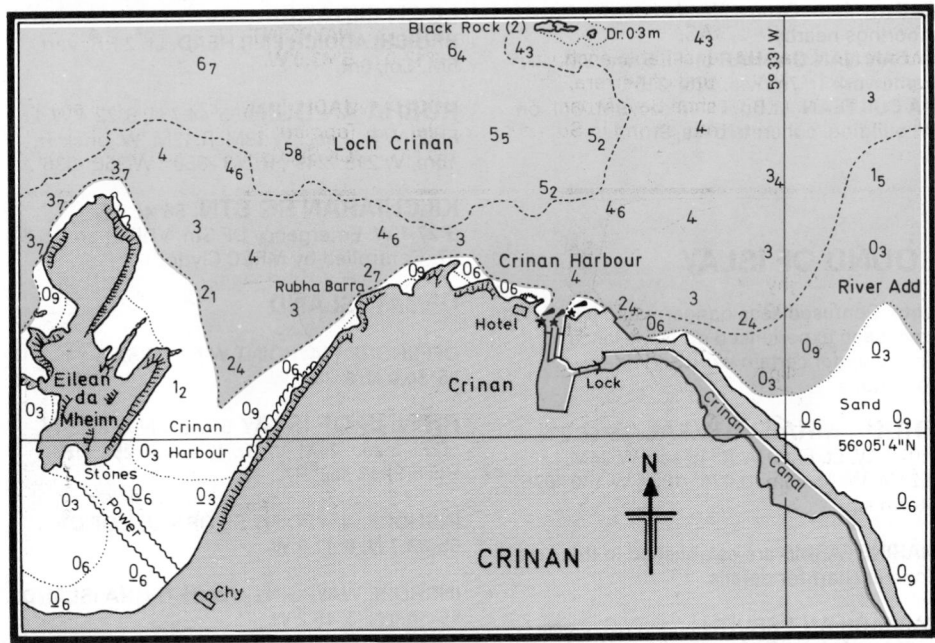

ENTRANCE By. Conical G.
CRAOBH HAVEN. Bn. G. marks submerged Rock.

THE GARVELLACHS. Lt.Bn. Fl. 6 sec. 9M. W. Bn. 21m. vis. 240°-215°.

CRINAN CANAL Tel: Ardrishaig 210.
VHF Stations Chan. 16 & 74. Sea Lock — Ardrishaig, Crinan Canal, Ardrishaig Lock, Oakfield Bridge, Cairbaan Lock, Dunardry Lock, Bellanoch Bridge, Crinan Bridge and Basin.

E OF LOCK ENTRANCE Lt. Fl.W.G. 3 sec. 4M. W. Tr. R. band, 8m. W.shore-146°; G.146°-shore.
SEA LOCK ENTCE. E WING. Lt. 2 F.R. vert. on post, 7m.
W WING. Lt. 2 F.G. vert. on post, 7m.

RUADH SGEIR. Lt.Bn. Fl. 6 sec. 8M. W. Tr. 13m.

INSHORE WAYPOINT W OF RUADH SGEIR. 56°04.5′N, 5°40.0′W.

LOCH CAOLISPORT

MARINE FARM established in this area. Consult chart for details.
POINT OF KNAPP. Bn. R.W.R. Topmark Cone.
SKERVUILE Lt. Fl. 15 sec. 9M. W. Tr. 22m

INSHORE WAYPOINT E OF SKERVUILLE. 55°52.0′N, 5°49.0′W.

NINE FEET ROCK. Lt.By. Q.(3) 10 sec. Pillar B.Y.B. Topmark E. in Lowlandman's Bay.
SMALL ISLES Bn. B. ball Topmark. S end of Sd.
LOCH CRAIGNISH.
Ardfern Yacht Centre Pier. Numerous moorings nearby.
EILEAN NAN GABHAR Lt. Fl. 5 sec. 8M. framework Tr. 7m. vis. 225°-010°.
NA CUILTEAN. Lt.Bn. Fl. 10 sec. 9M. Col. on W. building, concrete base, 9m.

SOUND OF ISLAY

Note: Confused seas dangerous to small craft have been experienced off N Entrance to Sound under certain wind and tide conditions.

RHUDA MHAIL RUVAAL. 55°56.2′N, 6°07.3′W. Lt. Fl.(3) W.R. 15 sec. W.24M. R.21M. W. Tr. 45m. R.075°-180°; W.180°-075°. Storm sig.

MARINE FARMS are established in this area. Consult chart for details.

CARRAGH AN T-SRUITH Lt. Fl.W.G. 3 sec. W.9M. G.6M. W. Tr. 8m. W.354°-078°; G.078°-170°; W.170°-185°.

CARRAIG MHOR Lt. Fl.(2) W.R. 6 sec. W.8M. R.6M. W. Tr. 7m. W.shore-175°; W.175°-347°; R.347°-shore.
BLACK ROCK. Lt.By. Fl.G. 6 sec. Conical G. ⨔ to S.

McARTHUR'S HEAD 55°45.9′N, 6°02.8′W, Lt. Fl.(2) W.R. 10 sec. W.14M. R.11M. W. Tr. 39m. W in Sd. of Islay from NE coast of Islay-159°; R.159°-244°; W.244°-E coast of Islay.
EILEAN A CHUIRN ISLAND. Lt.Bn. Fl.(3) 18 sec. 8M. W. Bn. 26m. Obscured when bearing more than 040°.

INSHORE WAYPOINT E OF PORT ELLEN. 55°36.0′N, 6°05.0′W.

OTTER ROCK. Lt.By. Q.(6) + L.Fl. 15 sec. Pillar Y.B. Topmark S.
PORT ELLEN. Lt.By. Fl.G. 6 sec. Conical G.

PORT ELLEN

HARBOUR WAYPOINT PORT ELLEN. 55°36.0′N, 6°11.0′W.

CARRAIG FHADA Lt. Fl.W.R.G. 3 sec. W.8M. R.6M. G.6M. W. square Tr. 19m. W.shore-248°; G.248°-311°; W.311°-340°; R.340°-shore.
RO-RO TERMINAL. Lt. 2 F.G. vert. on post on dolphin.

LOCH INDAAL

BRUICHLADDICH PIER HEAD. Lt. 2 F.R. vert. 5M. Col. 6m.

RUBHA AN DUIN 55°44.7′N, 6°22.4′W. Lt. Fl.(2) W.R. 7 sec. W.13M. R.12M. W. brick Tr. 15m. W.218°-249°; R.249°-350°; W.350°-036°.

KILCHIARAN RG STN. 55°46.0′N, 6°27.1′W. Emergency DF Stn. VHF Chan. 16 & 67. Controlled by MRCC Clyde.

ORSAY ISLAND

OFFSHORE WAYPOINT W OF ORSAY. 55°40.0′N, 6°34.0′W.

RHINNS OF ISLAY 55°40.4′N, 6°30.8′W. Lt. Fl. 5 sec. 24M. W. Tr. 46m. vis. 256°-184°. Horn(3) 45 sec. R.C.

INSHORE WAYPOINT SE OF MULL OF OA. 55°33.7′N, 6°17.9′W.

INSHORE WAYPOINT NW OF GIGHA ISLAND. 55°45.0′N, 5°49.2′W.

GIGHA SOUND

GIGULUM ROCK Lt.By. Q.(9) 15 sec. Pillar Y.B.Y. Topmark W. SE of Gigha I.
BADH ROCK By. Pillar Y.B.Y. Topmark W. ⨔ at N end of Sound.

CATH SGEIR. Lt.By. Q.(9) 15 sec. Pillar Y.B.Y. Topmark W. ∿ off SW coast of Gigha I. ARDMINISH BAY, Gigha, By. Can. R. marks rocks S end of bay.

INSHORE WAYPOINT W LOCH TARBERT. 55°45.0′N, 5°37.0′W.

WEST LOCH TARBERT
DUNSKEIG BAY Lt.Bn. Q.(2) 10 sec. 8M. metal mast. 11m.
EILEAN TRAIGHE. Lt.Bn. Q.R. ∿ 3M. R. Col. 3m.
CORRAN POINT. Lt.Q.G. 3M. G. Post. 3m.
SGEIR MHEIN. Lt. Q.R. 3M. R. Col. 3m.
BLACK ROCKS. Lt. Q.G. 3M. G. Post.
KENNACRAIG FERRY TERM. Lt. 2 F.G. vert.
KENNACOAY. Lt.By. Q.R. Can.R.
SGEIR LIATH. Lt. Fl.(2)R. 10 sec.

MACRIHANISH AIRFIELD. Lt. Aero Mo.(MH)R. occas.

OFFSHORE WAYPOINT MULL OF KINTYRE. 55°18.0′N, 5°50.0′W.

MULL OF KINTYRE 55°18.6′N, 5°48.1′W. Lt. Fl.(2) 20 sec. 29M. Y.Tr. on W. building, 91m. Vis. 347°-178°. Horn(N) 90 sec.
MACOSH ROCK. Lt.By. Fl.R. 6 sec. Can.R. ∿ N of Sanda Sound.

INSHORE WAYPOINT S OF SANDA ISLAND. 55°15.0′N, 5°37.0′W.

SANDA ISLAND 55°16.5′N, 5°34.9′W. Lt. Fl.W.R. 24 sec. W.19M. R.16M. W. Tr. 50m. R.245°-267°; W.267°-shore. Racon.
SANDA HARBOUR Bn. Pillar G. ball Topmark.
PATERSON'S ROCK. Lt.By. Fl.(3) R. 18 sec. Can R.

ARRANMAN BARRELS. Lt.By. Fl.(2)R. 12 sec. Can.R. ∿ N of Sanda Sound.

INSHORE WAYPOINT E OF SANDA ISLAND. 55°17.0′N, 5°30.0′W.

SEA TRAFFIC SEPARATION ROUTES
NORTH IRISH SEA — NORTH CHANNEL

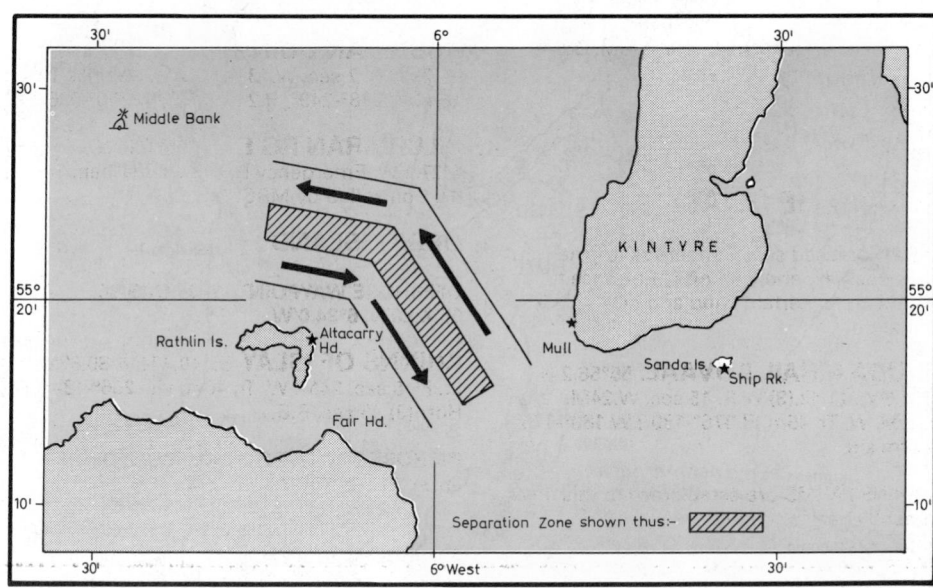

North and Westbound lane 2M. wide. Separation zone 2M. wide. East and Southbound lane 2M. wide. Inner limits: N and W lane Mull of Kintyre Lt.Ho. 057° — 2.5M. E and S lane Altacarry Lt.Ho. 214° — 2.5M.
Centre-line of separation zone joins following approx. positions: (a) 55°15.3′N., 5°55.4′W. (b) 55°22.8′N., 6°04.6′W. (c) 55°24.0′N., 6°15.0′W.
Note: Laden tankers of over 10,000 grt should avoid the areas between the traffic separation scheme and the Mull of Kintyre and between the traffic separation scheme and Rathlin Island.

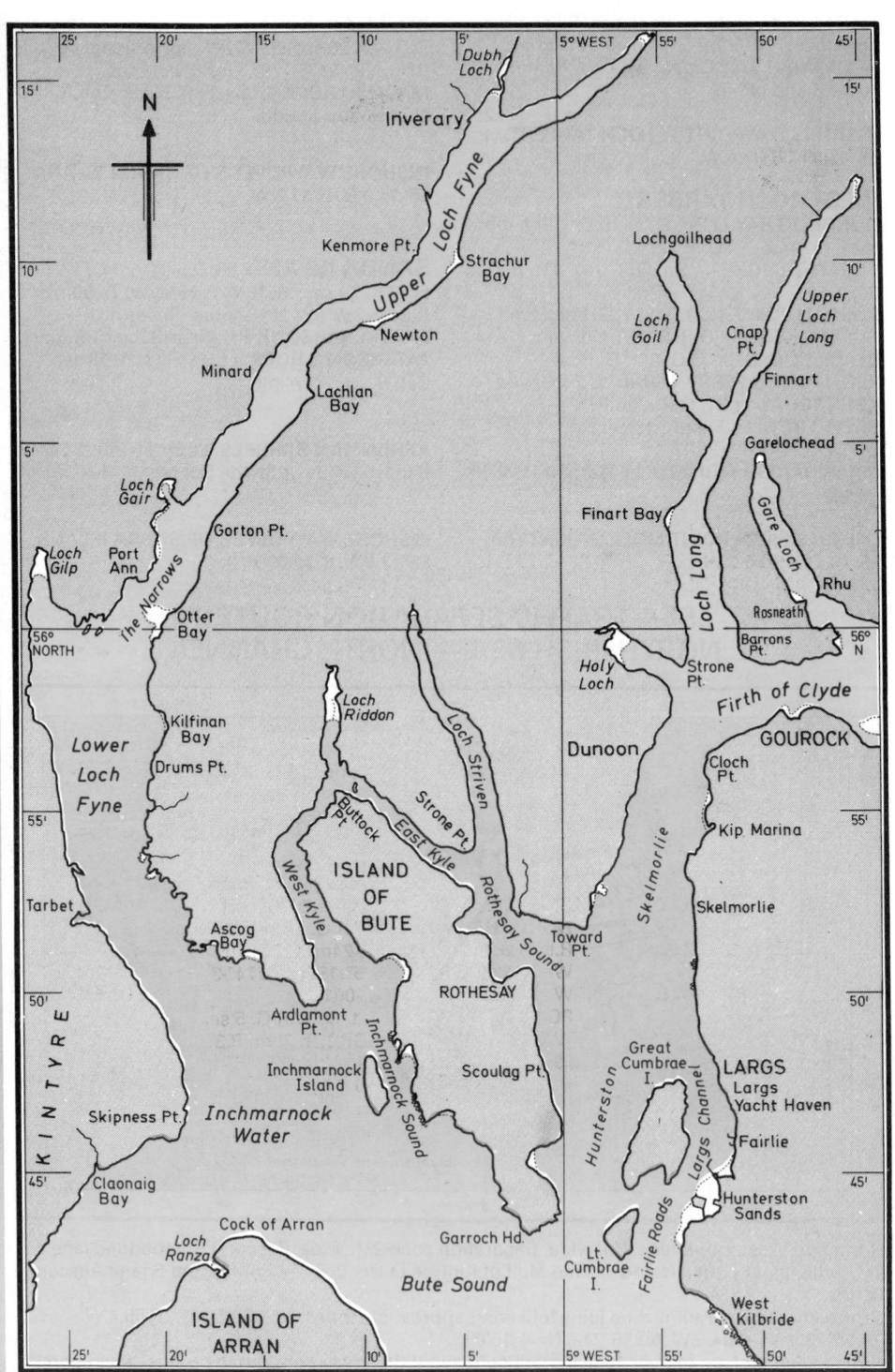

CAMPBELTOWN LOCH

INSHORE WAYPOINT CAMPBELTOWN LOCH.
55°26.0'N, 5°30.0'W.

DAVAAR 55°25.7'N, 5°32.4'W. Lt. Fl.(2) 10
sec. 23M. W. Tr. 37m. vis. 073°-330°. Siren (2)
20 sec.
MILLBEG BANK. Lt.By. Fl.G. 2 sec. Conical G.
opposite Millmore Bn.
MILLMORE Bn. W. concrete Bn. surmounted
by B. tank, 8m. on E end of Dorling.
'A' Lt.By. Fl.R. 10 sec. Can.R. S side chan. off
Millmore Bn.
'B' Lt.By. Fl.G. 6 sec. Conical G. off Trench Pt.
'C' Lt.By. Iso. 10 sec. Spherical R.W.V.S. on
Methe Bank.
TRENCH FLAT Bn. B. conical with ball.

KILKERRAN. Ldg.Lts. 240°30'. B(Front) F.Y.
6M. Y. △ on Bn. 7m. shown by day. A(Rear)
F.Y. 6M. Y. ▽ on Bn. 28m. shown by day.
KILKERRAN PIER. Lt. Q.R. 2M.

EMERGENCY COORDINATION CENTRE
(HMCG) Tel: (0586) 52770.

CAMPBELTOWN Tel: (0586) 52552.

HARBOUR WAYPOINT. 55°26.0'N, 5°33.0'W.

Radio — Port: VHF Chan. 16, 12, 14. 0845-
1645 Mon.-Thurs. 0845-1600 Fri.
P.O.L. DEPOT. VHF Chan. 16, 13.
Anchorages: Campbeltown Lock.
By. Conical G.
Yacht mooring pontoon dredged to 3m.

NEW QUAY HEAD. Lt. 2 F.R. vert. 4M. on
mast, 5m.
OLD QUAY HEAD. Lt. 2 F.G. vert. 4M. on Col.
7m. Storm sig.
2 Mooring Bys. 137m. apart. Submarine
telephone cable to shore.

SMERBY ROCKS By. Can.R.
Lt.By. Fl.(3) 15 sec. Spherical R.Y. hor. bands
〰 Bell.
OTTERARD ROCK. Lt.By. Q.(3) 10 sec. Pillar
B.Y.B. Topmark E.

INSHORE WAYPOINT CARRADALE BAY.
55°33.8'N, 5°27.2'W.

CARRADALE.
CRUBON ROCK. Lt.By. Fl.(2)R. 12 sec. Can.R.
〰 off Carradale Pt.

KILBRANNAN SOUND
PORT CRANNAICH PIER. Lt. Fl.R. 10 sec. 6M.
5m.

ARRAN ISLAND, W SIDE

LOCH RANZA
LAMONT SHELF. Lt.By. Fl.(2) 10 sec. Pillar
B.R.B. Topmark Is.D.

**INSHORE WAYPOINT NE OF SKIPNESS
POINT. 55°47.8'N, 5°17.5'W.**

SKIPNESS CALIBRATION RANGE Lt.
55°46.7'N, 5°19.0'W. Iso.R. 8 sec. 10M. Y.
◇Concrete building 7m. Vis. 292.2°-312.2°.
H24. Also Oc.(2)Y. 10 sec. 24M. shown when
range in use.
SKIPNESS POINT No: 51. Lt.By. Fl.R. 4 sec.
Can.R. off Skipness Pt.

MARINE FARM marked by 2 Lt.Bys. Fl.(4)Y. 12
sec. Can Y.

IRON ROCK LEDGES. Lt.By. Fl.G. 6 sec.
Conical G. 〰 off SW end of Arran I.

LOCH FYNE

SGAT MORE. 55°50.8'N, 5°18.4'W. Lt. Fl. 3
sec. 12M. W. round Tr. on concrete base, 9m.
PORTAVAIDIE BREAKWATER. Lt.Bn. 2 F.G.
vert. 4M. Pole.

EAST LOCH TARBERT
Entry: Tarbert or Fish Quay on SE side of
harbour has depths 1.8m. Yacht pontoon lies
SW of quay. SW part of quay has depths of
2.1m-2.5m. Area off quay is 3m.
MADADH MAOL. Lt. Fl.R. 2.5 sec. on Col. 4m.
EILEAN A CHOIC. Lt. Q.G. on Col. 3m.

ARDRISHAIG 56°01'N, 5°26'W.

INSHORE WAYPOINT ARDRISHAIG.
55°59.7'N, 5°26.1'W.

TIGN-N-COILLE No: 48. Lt.By. Fl.R. 4 sec.
Can.R.
SGEIR SCALOG No: 49 By. Conical G. on S
edge of shoal.
BREAKWATER HEAD. Lt. Fl.W.R.G. 6 sec. 4M.
W. Tr. 9m. G.287°-339°; W.339°-350°; R.350°-
035°. F.G. shown each side of entce. to Crinan
Canal lock. 2 F.G. vert. on pier 90m. NW F.R.
inner end of entce. lock on S side.

UPPER LOCH FYNE
THE NARROWS
'P'. Lt.By. Fl.R. 3 sec. Can.R.
OTTER SPIT. Lt. Fl.G. 3 sec. 8M. G. tank on
concrete pyramid, 7m.
GLAS EILEAN, S END. Lt.Bn. Fl.R. 5 sec. 7M.
Grey Col. on R. pedestal, 12m.
'Q' Lt.By. Fl.R. 3 sec. Can.R.

'X' Lt.By. Fl.R. 3 sec. Can.R.
SGEIR AN EIRIONNAICH. Lt.Bn. Fl.W.R. 3 sec.
8M. iron framework Tr. B.W. vert. stripes, 7m.
R.044°-087°; W.087°-192°; R.192°-210°;
W.210°-044°.

OTTER ROCK Bn. Spherical R. cage topmark.
FURNACE WHARF. Lt. 2 F.R. vert. 5M. Grey
Col. 9 and 7m.
TRANSIT. Ldg.Lts. 208°36' (Front) F. Bipod
(Rear) F. Bipod. Private. Occas.

MARINE FARMS are established in this area.
Consult chart for details.

ARRAN ISLAND, E SIDE

INSHORE WAYPOINT E OF PLADDA ISLAND.
55°26.0'N, 5°03.25'W.

PLADDA ISLAND 55°25.5'N, 5°07.3'W. Lt.
Fl.(3) 30 sec. 17M. W. Tr. 40m. R.C.

HOLY ISLAND

INSHORE WAYPOINT ENTRANCE LAMLASH.
55°32.4'N, 5°03.30'W.

PILLAR ROCK. 55°31.2'N, 5°03.8'W. Lt.
Fl.(2) 20 sec. 25M. 38m. R.G. VHF Radio Lt.Ho.

LAMLASH

HARBOUR WAYPOINT LAMLASH. 55°32.4'N,
5°05.75'W.

MARINE FARMS are established in this area.
Consult chart for details.

SW END 55°30.7'N, 5°04.1'W. Lt. Fl.G. 3 sec.
10M. W. Tr. 14m. vis. 282°-147°.
FULLARTON ROCK. Lt.By. Fl.(2)R. 12 sec.
Can.R. off Kingcross Pt.

HAMILTON ROCK SPIT. Lt.By. Fl.R. 6 sec.
Can.R. to be passed to Southward. At N
entce. to Lamlash Hr.

BRODICK
BRODICK BAY PIER Lt. 2 F.R. vert.
MOORING Lt.By. No: 1 Fl.Y. 4 sec.
MOORING Lt.By. No: 2 Fl.Y. 2 sec.

EMERGENCY COORDINATION CENTRE
(HMCG) Tel: (0475) 29014/29988. Telex:
777006.

MRCC CLYDE (0475) 29988. Weather
broadcast ev. 4h. from 0020.

FIRTH OF CLYDE

**INSHORE WAYPOINT R CLYDE. 55°41.0'N,
5°00.0'W.**

CLYDE RIVER 55°43'N 4°58'W. Tel: Estuary
Control (0475) 26221. Telex: 778976 CPALRS
G. Pilots Radio (0475) 34631. Finnart Oil
Terminal (0436) 810381. Fax: (0436) 810240.
Radio — Port: Clydeport Estuary Radio. VHF
Chan. 16, 14, 12 — continuous.
Radio — Pilots: VHF Chan. 16, 14. H24.
B.P. Finnart. VHF Chan. 16, 12, 19 —
continuous.
Signals (Day): Indicating Channel or
Destination of Large Vessels.
Pennant 1 = Firth of Clyde Channel.
Pennant 2 = Skelmorlie Channel
Pennant 3 = River Channel
Pennant 4 = Ardmore Channel (also Gareloch)
Pennant 5 = Loch Long Channel
Pennant 6 = Holy Loch
Pennant 7 = Kilcreggan Channel
1st Sub. = V/L. about to leave Channel to
anchor.
Port Closure Signals:
Rhu Narrows closed: R. Flag W. diag. bar —
R.G.G. Lts.
Faslane restricted area closed: Code Pennant
— No. 9 — G.G.G. Lts.
Submarines: Activity of submarines dived
and exercising below the surface east of line
joining Davaar Island Lt. and Killantringan Lt.
will be broadcast by Clyde Coastguard on
VHF Ch. 67 at 0220, 0620, 1020, 1420, 1820,
2220 (after the Weather Forecasts).
Measured Distances:
Firth of Clyde. 1M. 000°-180°T between and E
of Lt. Bys. 'I' and 'K' alongside Skelmorlie
Chan.
Loch Long and Loch Goil can be dangerous to
sailing craft because of sudden squalls, calms
and variable winds.
Arran NE 55°41½'N, 5°08½'W. 2M. 3 bns. upper
N end. 4 bns. in middle of 2M. 3 bns. S end
marking the limit of the second mile. 142°-
322°T. Lights occasionally shown from these
M.O.D. Bns. For large vessels 2M. QHM.,
telephone Helensburgh (0436) 4321, should
be contacted 10 days prior to using, who can
usually make arrangements for submarines
to keep clear of the measured distance.
Note. Owing to the Sannox Rock lying 3
cables offshore (1M. 3 cables S of the line of
the middle bns.) it is necessary to pass 7
cables (depth 128m.) off the land at the
Northern end and 1M. 3 cables (82m.) deep at
the Southern end, when on the correct
course. Bound N and coming on mile at S
end, in order to pass 7 cables off N end Bluff
of cliffs at N mile post must be kept 8° or 10°
on the port bow.

HUNTERSTON CHANNEL
HUN 14 Lt.By. Fl.R. 2 sec. Can.R.
HUN 13 Lt.By. Fl.G. 5 sec. Conical G.
HUN 12 Lt.By. Fl.R. 2 sec. Can.R.
HUN 11 Lt.By. Fl.G. 5 sec. Conical G.
BRIGURD OUTFALL Lt.By. Fl.Y. 5 sec.
Conical Y.
HUN 10 Lt.By. Fl.G. 3 sec. Conical G.
HUN 9 Lt.By. Fl.R. 4 sec. Can.R.
HUN 8 Lt.By. Fl.G. 3 sec. Conical G.
HUN 7 Lt.By. Fl.R. 2 sec. Can.R.
HUNTERSTON Lt.By. Q.G. Conical G.
FAIRLIE PATCH Lt.By. Fl.G. 1½ sec. Conical G.
HUN 5 Lt.By. Fl.G. 5 sec. Conical G.
HUN 4 Lt.By. Fl.R. 4 sec. Can.R.
HUN 3 Lt.By. Fl.R. 2 sec. Can.R.
HUN 2 Lt.By. Fl.G. 3 sec. Conical G.
HUN 1 Lt.By. Fl.(4)Y. 15 sec. Can.Y.

A1 MOORING Lt.By. Fl.Y. 2½ sec.

RUBHAN EUN 55°43.8'N, 5°00.2'W. Lt.
Fl.R. 6 sec. 8m 12M. on Isle of Bute.

LITTLE CUMBRAE
CUMBRAE ELBOW 55°43.3'N, 4°57.9'W. Lt. Fl.
3 sec. 23M. on tr. 31m. Horn(3) 40 sec. Vis
334°-210°.

GREAT CUMBRAE
PORTACHUR Lt.By. Fl.G. 3 sec. Conical G.
PORTACHUR POINT No. 38 By. Conical G.

MILLPORT EILEANS W END. Lt. Q.G. 2M. Post
5m. shown 1/9-30/4.
Ldg.Lts. 333° (Front) F.R. 5M. Col. 7m. (Rear)
F.R. 5M. Col. 9m.

FAIRLIE
HUNTERSTON ORE/COAL JETTY. Lts. 2 F.G.
vert. 5M. G. Col. 11m.
NATO PIER. Lts. 2 F.G. vert.

LARGS
LARGS YACHT HAVEN. Tel: (0475) 675333.
Fax: (0475) 672245. Telex: 777672 MCSTUG G.
Radio: VHF Chan. M. H24.
Berths for 550 yachts and 25 for visitors.
Repair facilities. Entrance and berthing area
dredged to 2m.

S BREAKWATER HEAD Lt. Oc.G. 10 sec.
Col.G.
Lt.By. Fl. 3 sec. Conical G.
Lt.By. Fl. 3 sec. Conical G.

ASCOG PATCHES. No. 13 Lt. Fl.(2) 10 sec. 5M.
8 on B.R. pile. 5m.
W BREAKWATER HEAD Lt. Oc.R. 10 sec. Col.
R.
MID CHANNEL Lt.By. L.Fl. 10 sec. Sph.
R.W.V.S.
PIER N END Lt. 2 F.G. vert. 5M.

TOWARD POINT 55°51.7'N, 4°58.7'W.
Lt.Fl. 10 sec. 21m. 22M. Horn 20 sec. W. Tr.
No: 34 By. Pillar B.Y.B. Topmark. E.

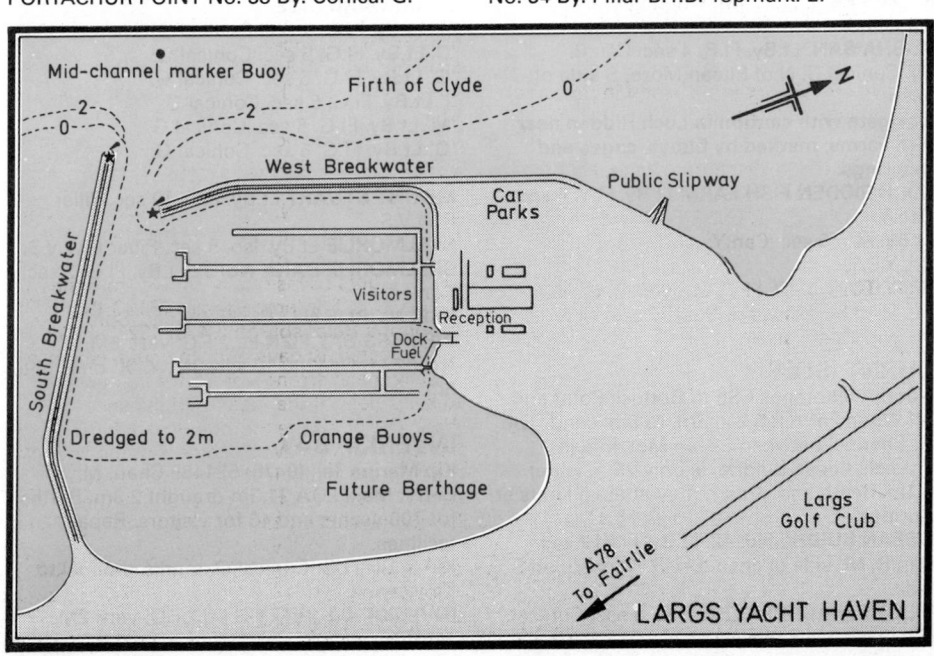

LARGS YACHT HAVEN

INSHORE WAYPOINT TOWARD POINT.
55°51.0'N, 4°58.0'W.

ROTHESAY 55°50'N 5°03'W. Tel: Rothesay
(0700) 3842.
Radio — Port: VHF Chan. 16, 12. Hours 0600-
2100 1 May-30 Sept.; 0600-1900 1 Oct.-30 Apr.
Entry: Rothesay Pier depths 2.2m. to 4.2m. on
N. side and 2m. to 2.8m. inside W. End. Inside
E. End are inner and outer harbours both
partly dry. Max. draught 2.5m.
Measured Distance: Firth of Clyde. (Kyles of
Bute, Rothesay Sound). ½M. 2 pairs bns.
Ardbeg Pt. ahead. 176° (Mag.). N pair bns on
Ardmeleish Pt.

N QUAY, E END. Lt. 2 F.G. vert. 5M. on Col.
7m.
W END. Lt. 2 F.R. vert. 5M. on Col. 7m.
CENTRE Bell when vessels expected.
ALBERT QUAY, NR. N END. Lt. 2 F.R. vert. 5M.
on Col. 8m.
BOGANY POINT No: 36 By. Can.R. off Bogany
Spit, in Rothesay Sd.
MOORING Lt.By. 'A' Fl.Y. 2 sec. Barrel B.

KYLES OF BUTE & ROTHESAY
ARDLAMONT POINT No: 47. Lt.By. Fl.R. 4 sec.
Can.R. off Ledge.
CARRY POINT No: 46. Lt.By. Fl.R. 4 sec.
Can.R.
KAMES PIER. Lt. F. 4M. when vessels
expected.
RUBHA BAN. Lt.By. Fl.R. 4 sec. Can.R.
By. Conical G. N of Eilean More, S side of
chan.
**Navigate with caution in Loch Ridden near
Fish Farms, marked by buoys, cages and
moorings.**
LOCH RIDDEN FISH FARM Lt.By. Fl.Y. 4 sec.
Can.Y.
Lt.By. Fl.Y. 6 sec. Can.Y.
Bn. Y.B.Y.
Bn. Y.B.Y.

BURNT ISLES
Note: Anchorages ESE of Buttock Point and
off Wood Farm Rock in 3m. to 5m. sand. The
N. Channel between Eilean Mor, Eilean
Fraoich, Eilean Buidhe, is only 25m. wide,
5.1m. depth and stream may attain 5 knots at
Springs.
EILEAN BUIDHE No: 42. Lt.By. Fl.R. 2 sec.
Can.R. NE side of chan. Bn. R.W. cheq. on S
side.
EILEAN FRAOICH. Lt.By. Fl.G. 3 sec. Conical
G.

CREYKE ROCK No: 45 By. Can.R. SW of rocks.
BEERE ROCK No: 44 By. Conical G. N edge.
WOOD FARM ROCK No: 43 By. Conical G. N
edge.
RUBHA BODACH. Lt.By. Fl.G. 3 sec. Conical
G.
ARDMALEISH POINT No: 41. Lt.By. Q. Pillar
B.Y. Topmark N.

LOCH STRIVEN
MARINE FARMS are established in this Area.
Consult chart for details.
Lt.Bys. (×2) Fl.(4)Y. 12 sec. Can.Y.
Lt.By. Fl.Y. 2½ sec. Conical Y.
Lt.By. Fl.Y. 2 sec. Conical Y. Near top of Loch.
LOCH STRIVEN JETTY Lts. 2 F.G. vert.
PL Lt.By. Fl.Y. 5 sec. Conical Y.
ARDYNE Lt.By. Fl.Y. 3 sec. Conical Y.
A.E. Lt.By. Fl.Y. 5 sec. Conical Y.
TOWARD BANK No: 35. Lt.By. Fl.G. 3 sec.
Conical G.

SKELMORLIE CHANNEL
(Deep draught vessels only)
PORT SIDE
'B' Lt.By. Fl.(4)Y. 10 sec. Sph. Y.
"D' Lt.By. Fl.R. 2 sec. Can.R.
'F' Lt.By. Fl.R. 4 sec. Can.R.
'H' Lt.By. Fl.R. 2 sec. Can.R.
'J' Lt.By. Fl.R. 2 sec. Can.R.
'L' Lt.By. Fl.R. 2 sec. Can.R.

STARBOARD SIDE
'A' Lt.By. Fl.G. 5 sec. Conical G.
'C' Lt.By. Fl.G. 5 sec. Conical G.
'G' Lt.By. Fl.G. 5 sec. Conical G.
'I' Lt.By. Fl.G. 5 sec. Conical G.
'M' Lt.By. Fl.G. 5 sec. Conical G.
'O' Lt.By. Fl.G. 5 sec. Conical G.

MOUNT STUART Lt.By. L.Fl. 10 sec. Pillar
R.W.V.S.
SKELMORLIE Lt.By. Iso. 5 sec. Pillar R.W.V.S.
SKELMORLIE BANK No: 32 Lt.By. Fl.G. 2 sec.
Conical G.
SKELMORLIE N Lt.By. Fl.Y. 3 sec. Sph. Y.
WEMYSS BAY PIER Lt. 2 F.G. vert. 5M.
No. 12 Lt. Oc.(2)Y. 10 sec. 3M. Y. 'X' on Y. pile.
5m.

INVERKIP BAY
Kip Marina Tel: (0475) 521485 Chan. M.
Entry: Max. LOA 21.3m draught 2.3m. Berths
for 700 yachts and 40 for visitors. Repair
facilities.
KIP Lt.By. Q.G. Conical G. marks channel to
Kip Marina.
INVERKIP OIL JETTY S Lt. 2 F.G. vert. 2M.
11m. Tr.

INVERKIP OIL JETTY N Lt. 2 F.G. vert. 2M. 11m. Tr.
LUNDERSTON BAY No. 8 Lt. Fl.(4)Y. 10 sec. 3M. Y 'O' on Y. Pile. 5m.

WARDEN BANK Lt.By. Fl.G. 2 sec. Conical G.
COWAL Lt.By. L.Fl. 10 sec. Pillar R.W.V.S.

THE GANTOCKS 55°56.5'N, 4°55.0'W. Lt. Fl.R. 2½ sec. 12m. 18M. W. Round Tr.
No: 31 By. Pillar B.Y. Topmark. N.
OUTFALL Bn.Y. Topmark Can.

DUNOON PIER. 55°57'N, 4°55'W.
Piermaster Tel: (0369) 2652.
Radio — Port: VHF Chan. 16, 31, 12. Mon.-Sat. 0700-2035, Sun. 0900-2015.
DUNOON BANK Lt.By. Q.(3) 10 sec. Pillar B.Y.B. Topmark. E.
DUNOON BANK By. Pillar Y.B.Y. Topmark. W.
DUNOON PIER S END Lt. 2 F.R. vert. 5m. 6M. Bell.
DUNOON PIER N END Lt. 2 F.R. vert. 5m. 6M.
CLOCH POINT Lt. Fl. 3 sec. 8M. B.W.Tr. 24m. Horn(2) 30 sec.
ASHTON Lt.By. Iso. 5 sec. Pillar R.W.V.S.
McINROYS POINT. Lt. 2 F.G. vert.
No: 5 Lt. Oc.(2)Y. 10 sec. 3M. Y. X on Y. pile 5m.

HOLY LOCH
HUNTERS QUAY. RO RO FERRY TERMINAL.
Lt. 2 F.R. vert.
HOLY LOCK PIER Lt. 2 F.R. vert 3M. Col. 6m.
No: 30 Lt.By. Q.(6) + L.Fl. 15 sec. Pillar Y.B. Topmark. S. off Strone Point.
WHITEFARLANE POINT Lt.By. Fl.R. 2 sec. Can.R.
GRAHAMS POINT Lt.By. Fl.G. 3 sec. Conical G. Keep out of Western Protected Area at all times and Eastern Protected Area when R./2 G. Lts. and R./W. flag shown from Floating Dock. Western Area is above Floating Dock.

LOCH LONG
LOCH LONG Lt.By. Oc. 6 sec. Pillar R.W.V.S.
BARONS POINT No. 3 Lt. Oc.(2)Y. 10 sec. 3M. Y. 'X' on Y. Pile.

RAVENROCK POINT 56°02.1'N, 4°54.3'W. Lt. Fl. 4 sec. 10M. W. Tr. on W. Col.
Dir.Lt. 204°. F.W.R.G. F.R.201½°-203°; Al.W.R.203°-205°.

COULPORT JETTY. Lt. 2 F.G. vert. Port Closure Signals.
COULPORT WORKS JETTY. Lts. 2 F.G. vert. 5M. W. Mast. 9m.

PORTDORNAIGE 56°03.7'N, 4°53.6'W. Lt. Fl. 6 sec. 11M. W. Col. Vis. 026°-206°.

CARRAIG NAN RON [Dog Rock]
56°06.0'N, 4°51.6'W. Lt. Fl. 2 sec. 11M. W. Col. 7m.

FINNART OCEAN OIL TERMINAL

CNAP POINT 56°07.4'N, 4°49.9'W. Ldg.Lts. 031°. (Front) Q. 10M. W. Col. (Rear) F. R. Ⅱ on W. Tr.
No: 2 JETTY N END Ldg.Lts. 066°. (Front) 2 F.G. vert. (Rear). Q.G. Vis. 051°-081°.
No: 2 JETTY S END Lt. 2 F.G. vert.
No: 3 JETTY NE END Ldg.Lts. 097°. (Front) 2 F.G. vert. (Rear) Q.G. Vis. 082°-112°.
No: 3 JETTY SW END Lt. 2 F.G. vert.
No: 4 Lt.By. Fl.R. 5 sec. Can.R.
No: 3 Lt.By. Fl.R. 3 sec. Can.R.
STRONE Lt. Fl.G. 3 sec. Tripod.

GLENMALLAN JETTY HEAD Lt. 2 F.G. vert. Port Closure Signals.
GLENMALLAN JETTY ELBOW Lt. 2 F.G. vert.

UPPER LOCH LONG
Lt.By. Fl.(4) Y. 10 sec. Conical Y.
Lt.By. Fl.(4) Y. 10 sec. Conical Y.
Lt.By. Fl.Y 5 sec. Conical Y.

GOUROCK
KEMPOCK POINT No. 4 Lt. Oc.(2)Y. 10 sec. 3M. Y. 'X' on Y. Pile. 5m
GOUROCK RAILWAY PIER Lt. 2 F.G. vert. 3M. Port closure signals on roof of Navy Bldgs 0.9M. E.

CARDWELL BAY
OUTFALL. Lt.By. Fl.(4)Y. 10 sec. Sph. Y.
No: 5 Lt.By. Fl.Y. 3 sec. Can. Y.
JETTY E. END Lt. Fl.R. 5 sec. 3M. Post 4m.
JETTY W. END. Lt. Fl.G. 5 sec. 3M. Post 4m.
RO-RO TERMINAL. Lt. 2 F.G. vert. 5M. Col.
WHITEFORELAND Lt.By. L.Fl. 10 sec. Pillar R.W.V.S.
No: 27 Lt.By. Fl.R. 2 sec. Can.R.
DIFFUSER Lt.By. Fl.Y. 3 sec. Sph. Y. marks diffuser and outfall postn. 55°58.37'N, 4°48.32'W off Ironotte Point.
ROSNEATH PATCH Lt. Fl.(2) 10 sec. 10M. Pile B.Y.B. Topmark Is.D.
GREENOCK ANCHORAGE Ldg. Lts. 196°. (Front) F.G. 12M. (Rear) F.G. 12M.

KILCREGGAN CHANNEL

KIL No: 1 Lt.By. Fl.G. 5 sec. Conical G.
KIL No: 2 Lt.By. Fl.R. 2 sec. Can. R.
KIL No: 3 Lt.By. Fl.G. 5 sec. Conical G.

ARDMORE CHANNEL To GARELOCH

ARD No: 4 Lt.By. Fl.R. 2 sec. Can.R.
ARD No: 5 Lt.By. Fl.G. 5 sec. Conical G.
ARD No: 8 Lt.By. Fl.R. 2 sec. Can.R.
ARD No: 10 Lt.By. Fl.R. 2 sec. Can.R.
No: 24 Lt.By. Fl.R. 5 sec. Can.R.
MOORING Lt.By. Fl. 2½ sec. Starb. side of channel.
ROW Lt.By. Fl.G. 5 sec. Conical G.

BEACON No. 7 N. 56°00.1'N, 4°45.3'W. Ldg. Lts. 356°18'. (Front) Oc. G. 6 sec. 3M. G. △ Pile 3m.
ARDENCAPLE CASTLE (centre) 2 F.G. vert. 12M. Stone Tr. NW Cnr. of Castle 26m. 335°-020° (Rear) F.G. 10M. Or. Daymark.
CAIRNDHU Lt.By. Fl.G. 2½ sec. Conical G.
Lt.By. Fl. 3 sec. Conical B.

GARELOCH

Overhead cable, safe clearance 4m.
BEACON No: 1 Lt. V.Q.(4)Y. 5 sec. 9m. X on Y. structure.
Dir. Lt. 080° Dir. Q. W.R.G. W.3M. R.2M. G.2M. G.077.5°-079.5°; W.079.5°-080.5°; R.080.5°-082.5°.
BEACON No. 8 N. Lt. Fl.Y. 3 sec. 3M. Y. 'X' on Y. Pile 3m.

RHU NARROWS

Note: Rhu Narrows and Faslane are restricted areas. Do not enter Faslane Protected Area. Clear areas when following signals shown:
Rhu Narrows: R. Flag with W. Bar or R. over 2 G. Lts. vert.
Faslane: Int. Code pendant over pendant 9 or 3 G. Lts. vert.
Shown at Faslane, Rhu, Rosneath Pt. Whiteforland Pt.

RHU POINT 56°00.9'N, 4°47.1'W. Lt. Q.(3) W.R.G. 6 sec. W.10M. R.7M. G.7M. Or. — on Tr. 9m. G.270°-000°; W.000°-114°; R.114°-188°. Shown H24.

RHU MARINA. Tel: (0436) 820238. Fax: (0436) 821039. Chan. M. Max. LOA 15.2m. draught 1.8m.

DIR. (Same Structure) Lt. 318° Dir. Oc.W.R.G. 6 sec. 14M. 5m. G.315.5°-317°; W.317°-319°; R.319°-323.5.°
RHU SOUTH. Lt.By. Fl.G. 3 sec. Conical G.
RHU NARROWS. Lt.By. Fl.G. Conical G.

'H' Lt.By. Q.R. Can. R.
Lt.By. Q.G. Conical G.
Floating Plant showing Sphere/Diamond/ Sphere (By Day); R./W./R. Lt. (By Night): Bell 5 sec. in 1 min. (In fog, etc.).

RHU MILITARY PORT. Ldg.Lts. 037°. (Front) F.G. (Rear) F.G. Port Closure signals shown from Root of jetty.

ROSNEATH. 56°00.6'N, 4°47.7'W. Dir. Lt. 290°42' Dir. Oc. W.R.G. 3 sec. 14M. G.288.2°-289.7°; W.289.7°-291.7°; R.291.7°-296.7°. Shown H24.
ROSNEATH Ldg. Lts. 290°42'. (Front) F.R. Or. ☐ on Tr. (Rear) F.R. Or. ☐ on Tr. Vis. 275.7°-305.7°.

CASTLE POINT. Lt. Fl.(2)R. 10 sec. 6M. R. mast 8m.
DG RANGE 56°00.4'N 4°47.33'W. Lt.By. Fl.Y. 3 sec. Barrel Y. and mooring bys.
ROSNEATH DG JETTY Lt. 2 F.R. vert.

ROSNEATH BAY 56°00.0'N, 4°47.1'W. Ldg. Lts. 163°24'. (Front) F.G. 12M. Vis. 149.4°-177.4°. (Rear) F.G. 12M. Vis. 149.4°-177.4°.
'S' Lt.By. Fl.Y. 3 sec. Barrel Y.

RHU SPIT Lt. Fl.2. 5 sec. 8M. W. Tr. G. bands 6m.

MAMBEG. 56°03.8'N, 4°50.4'W. Dir. Lt. 330°. Dir. Q.(4) W.R.G. 8 sec. 14M. W. Col. 6m. G.327.5°-329°; W.329°-331°; R.331°-332.5°. Shown H24.

FASLANE BASE

WHARF S ELBOW Lt. Fl.G. 5 sec.
FLOATING DOCK Lt. Fl.R. 5 sec.
MIDDLE Lt. 2 F.G. vert.
NORTH Lt. Q. W.R.G. W.9M. R.6M. G.6M. Grey Mast 14m. G.333°-084°; W.084°-161°; R.161-196°. Shown H24.
No. 7 BERTH. Lt. 2 F.G. vert. Grey mast 7m.
GARELOCHHEAD S FUEL JETTY. S Head Lt. 2 F.G. 10M. W. Tr. 10m.
N FUEL JETTY. Elbow Lt. 56°04.4'N 4°49.6'E. Iso.W.R.G. 4 sec. W.14M, W. Tr. 10m. G.351°-356°; W.356°-006°; R.006°-011°.
N HEAD. Lt. 2 F.G. 5M. W. Tr. 10m.

RIVER CLYDE

CLYDE PORT CONTAINER TERMINAL. Lt. Bn. Q.G. 8M. metal framework Tr. on Grey metal Col.
No: 1 Lt.By. Fl.G. 5 sec. Conical G.
No: 2 Lt.By. Fl.R. 2 sec. Can.R.
No: 3 Lt.By. Fl.G. 5 sec. Conical G.
No: 4 Lt.By. Fl.R. 2 sec. Can.R.
No: 5 Lt.By. Fl.G. 2 sec. Conical G.
No: 7 Lt.By. Fl.G. 2 sec. Conical G.
No: 8 Lt.By. Fl.R. 4 sec. Can.R.
No: 9 Lt.By. Fl.G. 2 sec. Conical G.
No: 12 Lt.By. Fl.R. 2 sec.
No: 14 By. Can.R.
No: 16 Lt.By. Fl.R. 4 sec. Can.R.
No: 20 Lt.By. Fl.R. 2 sec. Can.R.
GARVEL No: 24 Lt.By. Fl.R. 4 sec. Can.R.
No: 28 Lt.By. Fl.R. 2 sec. Can.R.
No: 30 Lt.By. Fl.R. 2 sec. Can.R.
No: 32 Lt.By. Fl.R. 2 sec. Can.R.
No: 34 Lt.By. Fl.R. 2 sec. Can.R.
No: 36 Lt.By. Fl.R. 4 sec. Can.R.
No: 40 Lt.By. Fl.R. 2 sec. Can.R.
No: 42 Lt.By. Fl.R. 4 sec. Can.R.

GREENOCK

A permit obtainable from Clyde Port Authority, 16 Robertson St., Glasgow. Tel: 041-221 8733 and 12 h. notice (contact Estuary Control Tel: (0475) 26221) is necessary to proceed up river from Greenock.

ANCHORAGE. 55°57.6'N, 4°46.5'W.
Ldg.Lts. 196°(Front) F.G. 12M. Y. Col. 7m. (Rear) F.G. 12M. Y. Col. 9m.
Ldg.Lts. 194°30' (Front) F.G. Bldg. 18m. (Rear) F.G. Pylon 33m.

VICTORIA HARBOUR ENTCE.
W SIDE. Lt. 2 F.G. vert. bracket on building, 5m.
GARVEL EMBANKMENT
W END. Lt. Oc.G. 10 sec. 4M. on mast.
E END MAURICE CLARKE POINT. Lt. Q.G. 2M. G. stone Tr. 7m. Traffic sig.

NEWARK CASTLE TO DUMBARTON

Note: Channel Newark Castle to Glasgow maintained 6.9m. to 8.2m.

PORT SIDE
PILLAR BANK No: 46 Lt.By. Fl.R. 2 sec. Can.R.
No: 48 Lt.By. Fl.R. 2 sec. Can.R.

CARDROSS Lt.By. Q.R. Pillar R
No: 52 Lt. Fl.R. 2 sec. Can.R.
HAVOCK No: 56 Lt.By. Fl.R. 2 sec. Can.R.
HELENSLEE No: 60 Lt.By. Fl.R. 4 sec. Can.R.
No: 64 Lt.By. Fl.R. 2 sec. Can.R.
No: 68 Lt.By. Fl.R. 4 sec. Can.R.
No: 70 By. Can.R.

STARBOARD SIDE
No: 13 Lt.By. Fl.G. 5 sec. Conical G.
No: 17 Lt.By. Fl.G. 5 sec. Conical G.
No: 21 Lt.By. Fl.G. 2 sec. Conical G.
No: 25 Lt.By. Fl.G. 5 sec. Conical G.
No: 29 Lt.By. Fl.G. 5 sec. Conical G.
GARMOYLE No: 33 Lt.By. Fl.G. 2 sec. Conical G.
No: 37 Lt.By. Fl.G. 5 sec. Conical G.
PUDDLE DEEP No: 39 Lt.By. Fl.G. 2 sec. Conical G.

LEVERN Bn. R. post. Entce. to Chan. to Dumbarton.

GLASGOW 55°56'N 4°41'W

Radio — Port: See Clyde River.
Radio — Pilots: See Clyde River.
Entry Signals: Customs Signal. Princes Pier. 1 long, 2 short and 2 short blasts.

DUMBARTON TO GLASGOW

PORT SIDE
ROCK No: 72 Lt.By. Fl.R. 2 sec. Can.R.
PETTY ROY PERCH R.
PETTY ROY No: 74 Lt.By. Fl.R. 4 sec. Can.R.

DUMBUCK Bn. R. Perch.
CRANNOG No: 76 Lt.By. Fl.R. 2 sec. Can.R.

MILTON No: 78 Lt.By. Fl.R. 2 sec. Can.R.
DUNGLASS. Lt.Bn. Fl.R. 2 sec. R. 10m.

BOWLING. Lt.Bn. Fl.R. 4 sec. R.W. cheq. 10m. on Pier Head, E side of Hr. Entce.
DONALD'S QUAY. Lt.Bn. Fl.R. 4 sec. R.W. cheq. R. base, 10m.
OLD KILPATRICK. Lt.Bn. Fl.R. 2 sec. R. 10m. Upstream of Bridge.
DUNTOCHER BURN. Lt.Bn. Fl.R. 2 sec. R. 10m.

DALMUIR (W). Lt. Fl.R. 2 sec. R. post, 10m.
DALMUIR (E). Lt.Bn. Fl.R. 4 sec. R. 10m
SLIPWAY N BANK Lt. Fl.R. 5 sec. 3M. R. Pole 5m.
CLYDEHOLME YARD. Lt. Fl.R. 4 sec. R. post.

STARBOARD SIDE
STEAMBOAT QUAY. 55°56.2′N, 4°41.4′W. Lt.
F.G. 12M. B.W. Cheq. Col. 12m. 210°-290°.
Traffic Sigs.
GARRISON. Lt.Bn. Fl.G. 5 sec. 8M. 10m.
Bn. G.
Bn. B.
Bn. B. (Mile Post 13).

DUMBUCK. Lt.Bn. Fl.G. 2 sec. G. Tr. 10m.
Bn. B.
Bn. B.
Bn. B. (Mile Post 13).

LONGHAUGH. Lt.Bn. Fl.G. 2 sec. G. with B.
base, 10m.
Bn. B.
No: 43 Lt.By. Fl.G. 5 sec. Conical G.
No: 45 Lt.By. Fl.G. 2 sec. Conical G.

No: 47 Lt.By. Fl.G. 2 sec. Conical G.

ST. PATRICK'S STONE. Lt.Bn. Fl.G. 5 sec.
Bn. G. 10m. Downstream of Bridge.
ERSKINE BRIDGE. E & W SIDES. Lts. 2 F.R.
vert. S Side. Lts. 2 F.G. vert.
ERSKINE. Fl.G. 5 sec. Bn. G. 10m.
RASHIELEE. Lt.Bn. Fl.G. 2 sec. G. 10m.

NEWSHOT. Lt.Bn. Fl.G. 5 sec. G. 10m.
ALGIES. Lt.Bn. Fl.G. 5 sec. G. 10m.
BLYTHSWOOD. Lt.Bn. Fl.G. 2 sec. G. 10m.
RENFREW (W). Lt. Fl.G. 5 sec. G. pole. 10m.
RENFREW (E). Lt. Fl.G. 5 sec. G. pole. 10m.
RENFREW FERRY. N SLIPWAY. Lt. 2 F.R.
vert. 2M. Dolphin.
S SLIPWAY. Lt. 2 F.G. vert. 2M. Dolphin.
BRAEHEAD. Lt.Bn. Fl.G. 2 sec. G. 10m.
SHIELDHALL. Lt. Fl.G. 2 sec. G. pole, 16m.
LINTHOUSE. Lt.Bn. Fl.G. 5 sec. G. 10m.
FAIRFIELD. Lt. Fl.G. 5 sec. G. pole, 10m.
WORKSHOPS. Lt. Fl.G. 5 sec. G. pole, 10m. 2
F.G. vert. & 2 F.R. vert. mark bridges
upstream.

GARDEN FESTIVAL SWING BRIDGE. Lt. Fl.R.
3 sec. 3M. R. □ on pile. 3m. marks N Channel
limit.
Lt. Fl.G. 3 sec. 3M. G. △ on pile. 3m. marks S
Channel limits.

CUSTOMS HOUSE QUAY. Lt. 2 F.R. vert. 1M.
post. 4m.
KINGSTON BRIDGE headroom 18/20m. at
H.W.O.S. tides between G. Lts. from bridge
24m. each side of centre line. Upstream 2 F.R.
vert. Downstream 2 F.G. vert.

INCHINNAN BRIDGE (PAISLEY). Lts. 2 F.
shown up and down river; R. bridge open; W.
bridge shut. On NW abutment Lt. F.R. bridge
shut; Lt. W., clear for navigation.

ARDROSSAN 55°39′N, 4°50′W. Tel: (0294)
63972. Telex: 777954 DOCARD G.

HARBOUR WAYPOINT. 55°37.5′N, 4°50.5′W.

Radio — Port: VHF Chan. 16, 12, 14.
Radio — Pilots: VHF Chan. 16, 6.
Signals: 3 R. Lts. (vert.) shown from Port
Control Tower on S side Montgomerie Pier
indicate Port Closed.
Entry: Least depth 5.2m. in entrance and 3-
5m. inside breakwater.
Anchorage: Fairlie Roads. Ardrossan Harbour
limited overnight or emergency anchorage
only. Cranes up to 32 tons available for lifting
yachts.
LIGHTHOUSE PIER HEAD. Lt. Iso.W.G. 4 sec.
9M. W. Tr. 11m. W.035°-317°; G.317°-035°.
DIR. Lt. 055° F.W.R.G. 9M. and F.R. 9M.
G.048½°-053½°; W.053½°-056½°; R.056½°-061°. F.R.
340°-130°.
N BREAKWATER HEAD. Lt. Fl.W.R. 2 sec. 5M.
R.gantry, 12m. R.041°-126°; W.126°-041°.
W CRINAN. Lt.By. Fl.R. 4 sec. Can.R. off W
Crinan Rk.
EAGLE ROCK. Lt.By. Fl.G. 5 sec. Conical G.
Ardrossan Approaches.

IRVINE 55°36′N 4°42′W. Tel: (0294) 78132
(Night: (0294) 87700).

HARBOUR WAYPOINT. 55°36.0′N, 4°42.5′W.

Radio — Port & Pilots: VHF Chan. 16, 12.
Mon.-Fri. 0800-1600.
Entry: Prior notice required for berthing.
Suitable for vessels up to 61m. 3.8m. draught.
Quays S. side depths 1-2m.

SPOIL GROUND. Lt.By. Fl.Y. 5 sec. Conical Y.
ENTRANCE, N SIDE. Lt.Bn. Fl.R. 3 sec. 5M.
wooden pile Bn. 9m.
S SIDE. Lt. Fl.G. 3 sec. 5M. G. Col. 6m.
Ldg.Lts. 051°. (Front) F.G. 5M. G. mast 10m.
vis. 019°-120°. (Rear) F.R. 5M. G. mast, 15m.
vis. 019°-120°.
IB-B Lt.By. Fl.Y. 3 sec. Conical Y. marks end of
pipeline.
OUTFALL IB-C Lt.By. Fl.Y. 5 sec. Conical Y.
GARNOCK VALLEY SEWER OUTFALL IB-D.
Lt.By. Fl.Y. 10 sec. Conical Y.

INSHORE WAYPOINT FIRTH OF CLYDE.
55°30.0′N, 4°51.0′W.

TROON 55°33′N 4°41′W. Tel: (0292) 313412.

HARBOUR WAYPOINT. 55°33.5′N, 4°42.5′W.

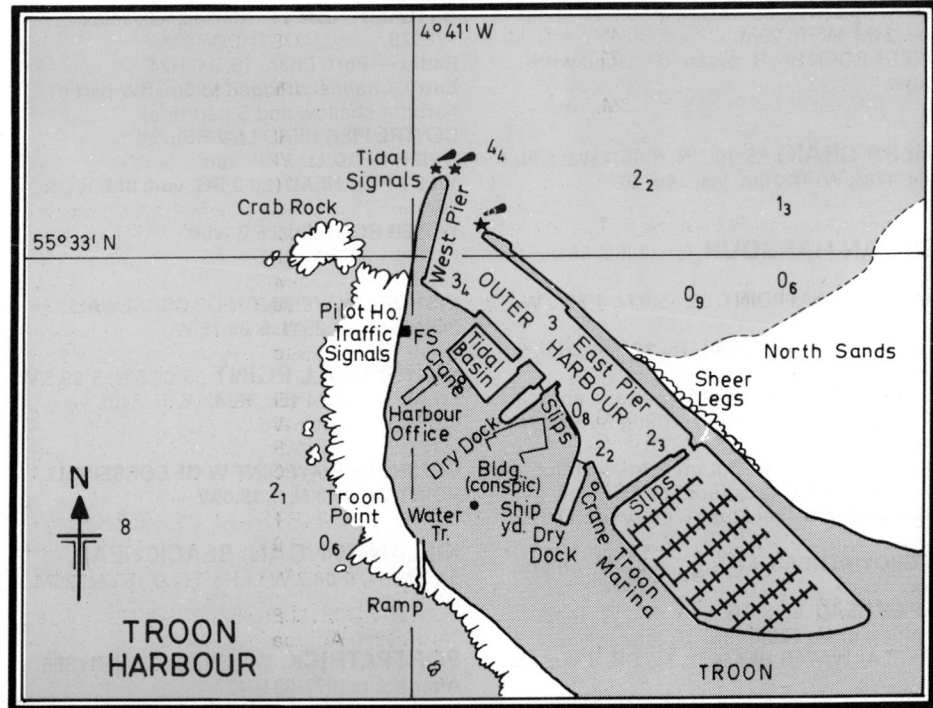

TROON HARBOUR

Radio — Port: VHF Chan. 16, 14. Mon-Thurs 0800-2400. Fri 0800-2300. Other times on request.
Troon Marina Tel: (0292) 315553 Chan. M.
Signals:
By day: 2 B. balls ⎫ Harbour blocked. Entry
By night: 2 R. Lts. vert. ⎰ and exit prohibited.
Berths available at Yacht Marina. Entrance 11m. wide, depth 2.6m. Max. LOA 37m. draught 3.7m.
W PIER HEAD. Lt. Oc.W.R. 6 sec. 5M. W. Tr. 11m. R.036°-090°; W.090°-036°. Siren 30 sec. 14m. SE Lt. Fl.W.G. 3 sec. 5M. post on dolphin, 7m. G.146°-318°; W.318°-146°.
E PIER HEAD. Lt. Fl. R. 10 sec. 3M. R.Col. 6m. obscured when bearing more than 199°.
LAPPOCK ROCK Bn. Tr. G.
LADY ISLE. Lt.Bn. Fl.(4) 30 sec. 8M. W. Bn. 19m.
MILL ROCK By. Can.R. off Troon.
TROON SPIT. Lt.By. Fl.G. 4 sec. Conical G. off Troon.

AYR 55°28′N 4°38′W. Tel: Ayr (0292) 281687 ext 34. Telex: 778853 KENNY G.

HARBOUR WAYPOINT. 55°28.25′N, 4°39.75′W.

Radio — Pilots: VHF Chan. 16, 14. 0800-2400.

Mon.-Thurs., 0800-2300 Fri. Sat./Sun. by arrangement.
Entry Signals: Day: 2 Black Balls — Port closed to inward vessels.
1 Black Ball — Shipping movements. Proceed with caution.
Night: 2 R. Lights — Port closed to inward vessels.
1 R. Light — Inward vessels to berth N side of River. Proceed with caution.
1 G. Light — prepare to berth in dock. Proceed with caution.
Entry: Least depth over bar 3.2m.
Anchorage: 2M. SW in E'ly winds or off Coast of Arran in SW/NW winds.

N BREAKWATER HEAD. Lt. Q.R. 5M. Tr. 7m.
S PIER HEAD. Lt. Q. 7M. R.Tr. W. lantern, vis. 012°-161°. Same structure Lt. F.G. vis. 012°-082° over St. Nicholas Rocks.
Ldg.Lts. 098°. (Front) F.R. 5M. R.Tr. W. lantern, 10m. Traffic sig. (Rear) Occ. R. 10 sec. 9M. R.Tr. W. lantern, 18m.
INNER ST. NICHOLAS ROCKS By. Conical G.
OUTER ST. NICHOLAS ROCKS. Lt.By. Fl.G. 2 sec. Conical G.

INSHORE WAYPOINT N OF TURNBERRY POINT. 55°21.8′N, 4°51.5′W.

TURNBERRY 55°19.0'N, 4°50.0'W. Lt. Fl. 15 sec. 24M. W. Tr. 29m.
BREST ROCK Bn. R. pyramid shaped with cage.

AILSA CRAIG 55°15.1'N, 5°06.4'W. Lt. Fl. 4 sec. 17M. W. Tr. 18m. vis. 145°-028°.

GIRVAN HARBOUR Tel: (0465) 3648.

HARBOUR WAYPOINT. 55°15.0'N, 4°52.0'W.

Radio — Port: VHF Chan. 16, 12. Mon.-Fri. 0900-1700.
Commercial fishing hbr. Access and approach hazardous in NW gales. Berthing for yachts limited.
Depths below Chart Datum 0.3m. to 1.5m.
Signals: 2 Black discs (hor.) or 2 F.R. Lts. (hor.) shown from S. Pier Quay = entry prohibited.

N GROYNE HEAD. Lt. Iso. 2 sec. 4M. on Col. 3m.
S PIER HEAD. Lt. 2 F.G. vert. 4M. W. Tr. 8m.
Traffic signals 220m. SE.
N BREAKWATER HEAD. Lt. Fl.(2)R. 6 sec. 4M. Pole. 7m.

LOCH RYAN

HARBOUR WAYPOINT LOCH RYAN. 55°02.0'N, 5°05.0'W.
MILLEUR POINT. Lt.By. Q. 10 sec. Pillar B.Y. Topmark N. 〰.
Lt.By. Fl.R. 5 sec. Can.R. 54°59'.48"0N, 05°02'.90"0W.
Lt.By. Fl.G. 5 sec. Conical G. 54°59'.23"0N, 05°03'.17"0W.

CAIRN RYAN

CAIRN POINT 54°58.5'N, 5°01.8'W. Lt. Fl.(2)R. 10 sec. 12M. W. Tr. 14m.
MOORING DOLPHIN. Lt. Fl.R. 5 sec. 5M. 5m.
BREAKWATER. Lt.Bn. 2 F.R. vert. 3M. 5m.
RAMP. TR. Lt. 2 F.G. vert. 2M. 5m.
SPIT OF SCAUR. Lt.By. Fl.G. 6 sec. Conical G. 〰.

STRANRAER APPROACH
No: 1 Lt.Bn. Oc.G. 6 sec. Pile G.
No: 3 Lt.Bn. Q.G. Pile G.
No: 5 Lt.Bn. Fl.G. 3 sec. Pile G.

STRANRAER Tel: (0776) 2460. Telex: 778125.
Radio — Port: Chan. 16, 14. H24.
Entry: Channel dredged to 5m. SW part of harbour shallow and S part dries.
CENTRE PIER HEAD Lt. 2 F.Bu. vert.
E PIER HEAD Lt. 2 F.R. vert.
WEST PIER HEAD. Lt. 2 F.G. vert. 4M. R.Col. 10m.
W PIER ROOT. Lt. 2 F.G. vert.

INSHORE WAYPOINT N OF CORSEWALL POINT. 55°01.25'N, 5°09.75'W.

CORSEWALL POINT 55°00.5'N, 5°09.5'W. Lt. Al.Fl.W.R. 74 sec. 18M. W. Tr. 34m. vis. 027°-257°. Storm sig.

OFFSHORE WAYPOINT W OF CORSEWALL POINT. 55°00.0'N, 5°19.0'W.

KILLANTRINGAN, BLACK HEAD 54°51.7'N, 5°08.7'W Lt.Ho. Fl.(2) 15 sec. 25M. W. Tr. 49m.

PORTPATRICK. Tel: Office (077-681) 355. After hours (077-681) 427.
Ldg.Lts. 050°30'(Front) F.G. 6m. Daymark R. ▯. Or. stripe. (Rear) F.G. on building, 8m. Daymark R. ▯. Or. stripe. Ldg. Lts. lead into outer harbour. Vessels must maintain the leading line to clear a rock shelf (Half Tide Rock) just inside entrance on port hand side when entering. The rock covers at half tide. Inner harbour lit by lights from M.O.D. berth. No vessel may lie even temporarily in or near berth reserved for M.O.D. Range Vessels or within swinging area of crane. Harbour used also by fishing vessels and users are recommended to contact H.M. on arrival. Depths. LW Springs 2m. over bar. HW Springs 5.5m. in harbour.
Portpatrick Harbour is difficult to enter or leave with wind from S thru' W to N.

CRAMMAG HEAD 54°39.9'N, 4°57.8'W. Lt. Fl. 10 sec. 18M. W. Tr. 35m.

OFFSHORE WAYPOINT MULL OF GALWAY. 54°36.0'N, 4°55.0'W.

MULL OF GALLOWAY 54°38.1'N, 4°51.4'W. Lt. Fl. 20 sec. 28M. W. Tr. 99m. vis. 182°-105°. Distress and storm sig.

PORT WILLIAM
Entry: Vessels up to 3m. draught can enter after half tide and moor at the quay. Harbour

dries. Soft mud. Do not enter from N or E as shoals extend from the pier.

PIER HEAD. Ldg.Lts. 105° (Front) Fl.G. 3 sec. 3M. Mast. 7m. (Rear) F.G. 2M. Bldg. 10m.
Lt. Q.R. 4M. on target ship 'F' 10.7M. N.
Lts. 3 F.R. on radio mast 16M. ENE.

LUCE BAY

DZ1 Lt.By. Fl.Y. 2 sec. Can. Y.
DZ2 Lt.By. Fl.Y. 6 sec. Can. Y.
DZ3 Lt.By. Fl.Y. 4 sec. Can. Y.
DZ4 Lt.By. Fl.Y. 2 sec. Can. Y.
DZ5 Lt.By. Fl.Y. 6 sec. Can. Y.
DZ6 Lt.By. Fl.Y. 4 sec. Can. Y.
DZ7 Lt.By. Fl.Y. 4 sec. Conical Y.
DZ8 Lt.By. Fl.Y. 2 sec. Conical Y.
DZ9 Lt.By. Fl.Y. 6 sec. Conical Y.
DZ10 Lt.By. Fl.Y. 4 sec. Conical Y.
DZ11 Lt.By. Fl.Y. 2 sec. Conical Y.

ISLE OF WHITHORN HARBOUR.
54°42'N 4°22'W.
Entry: Enter 2½ h. before to 2½ h. after H.W. Best refuge between Drummore and Kirkcudbright. Give Screen Rocks wide berth on ebb tide and keep at least 9m. off the Pier.
Lt. Q.G. 5M. Col. 8m.
Ldg.Lts. 335° (Front) Oc. R. 8 sec. 7M. Or. Mast. 7m. (Rear) Oc. R. 8 sec. 7M. Or. Mast. 9m.
Many facilities exist for yachts and fishing boats. The inner harbour can be entered + or — 2½ h. of H.W.

GARLIESTON 54°47'N 4°22'W.
PIER HEAD. Lt. 2 F.R. vert. 8M. on Col. 5m. Shown 1st Oct. to 3rd March, when vessels expected.

LITTLE ROSS 54°45.9'N, 4°05.0'W. Lt. Fl. 5
sec. 12M. W. Tr. 50m. Obscured in Wigtown Bay when bearing more than 103°.
LITTLE ROSS Bn. W.

KIRKCUDBRIGHT. 54°50'N, 4°03'W. Tel:
(0557) 31135.
Radio — Port: VHF Chan. 16, 12. 2 h.-HW-2 h.
Entry: Town Quay 5.2m. at HWS. Dries out to mud. Speed limit of 5 knots above No: 7 Lt.By.

KIRKCUDBRIGHT CHANNEL
No: 1 Lt.Bn. Fl.3 sec. 3M. 7m.
No: 2 Lt.By. Fl.(2)R. 6 sec. Can.R.
No: 3 Lt.By. Q.G. Conical G.

No: 4 Lt.By. Q.R. Can.R.
No: 7 Lt.By. Fl.(2)G. 6 sec. Conical G.
No: 10 Lt.By. Fl.(2)R. 6 sec. Can.R.
No: 11 Lt.By. Fl.G. 3 sec. Conical G.
No: 12 Lt.Bn. Fl.R. 3 sec. Perch 3m.
No: 13 Lt.By. Q.G. Conical G.
No: 14 Lt.Bn. Fl. 3 sec. Perch 5m.
No: 15 Lt.By. Fl.G. 3 sec. Conical G.
No: 17 Lt.By. Fl.(2) G. 6 sec.
No: 18 Lt.By. Fl.(2)R. 6 sec.
No: 19 Lt.By. Fl.G. 3 sec. Conical G.
No: 20 Lt.By. Q.R. Can.R.
No: 21 Lt.By. Q.G. Conical G.
No: 22 Lt.Bn. Fl.R. 3 sec. 2m.
No: 23 Lt.By. Fl.(2)G. 6 sec. Conical G.
No: 24 Lt.By. Q.R. Can R.
No: 26 Lt.By. Q.R. Can.R.

OUTFALL. Lt. Fl.Y. 5 sec. 2M. Y. Tr. 3m.
HESTAN ISLAND. Lt. Fl.(2) 10 sec. 7M. W. house, 38m.

PALNACKIE
Entry: Vessel must be at Bar, approx. 1M. NNE from Hestan Lt.Ho. about 2 h. before H.W. to berth Palnackie on same tide. If too late to make Palnackie but still enough water to enter river estuary, anchor inside where vessel will dry out at L.W. on soft bottom. Quay has depth of 4.6m. at HWS. Dries out.

ANNAN RIVER
Entry: Town Quay 3m. draught at HW. Dries out.
ANNAN, S END OF QUAY. Lt. 2 F.R. vert. 5M. on Col. 4m.
'A6' By. Can.B. is moved as required to mark Annan Chan.
Lt.Bn. Fl.R. 3 sec. 2M. 3m.
BARNKIRK POINT. Lt.Fl. 3 sec. 2M. 18m.

WEST COAST OF ENGLAND

SILLOTH 54°52'N 3°25'W. Tel: (06973) 31358. Fax: (06973) 32329. Pilots: (06973) 31215. Telex: 64327.
Radio — Port: VHF Chan. 16, 12, 2½ h.-HW-1½ h.
Radio — Pilots: VHF Chan. 16, 14, 2½ h.-HW-1½ h.
Entry Signals: Shown from Port Signal mast: Entry only when — By Day — Or. Signal Arm raised; By Night — Q. Blue Lt. Buoyed Channel 8M. in length. Because of tide range

navigable at HW only. Tidal Currents up to 5 kts.
Anchorage: In good weather — Workington. Best to arrive off Workington 2½-1½ h. before HW Silloth.

INSHORE WAYPOINT SOLWAY FIRTH. 54°42.5'N, 3°45.5'W.

SOLWAY FIRTH — SILLOTH CHANNEL
OUTER SOLWAY
SILLOTH (S.O.). Lt.By. Fl.(3)G. 10 sec. Conical G. Entce. to Silloth Chan. Bell.
MIDDLE. Lt.By. Fl.G. Conical G.
SOLWAY. Lt.By. Fl.G. 5 sec. Conical G. in Silloth Chan.
CORNER. Lt.By. Fl.G. 5 sec. Conical G.
S.3 By. Conical G.
S.5 By. Conical G.
BECKFOOT Lt.By. Fl.G. 10 sec. Conical G.

Note: Solway Firth. Banks and channels subject to frequent change. Buoyage is for use of pilots and does not necessarily mark the navigable channel. Use with extreme care and local knowledge.

SILLOTH
LEES SCAR. Lt. Q.G. 8M. W. Pile 11m. Vis. 005°-317°.
E COTE. Lt. F.G. 12M. W. Pile 15m.
GROYNE HEAD. Lt. 2 F.G. vert. 4M. Dolphin. 4m.
NEW DOCK CHANNEL Ldg. Lts. 115°15' (Front) F. W. mast. (Rear) F. W. mast. (Both vert. strip Lts).
OUTFALL Lt. 2 F.G. vert. G. Δ on Bn.
CARDURNOCK PERCH Mast with cage Topmark, marks W end of Brow Scar in Annan Channel.
'A2' By. Can.R. in Annan Channel.

MARYPORT 54°43'N 3°30'W. Tel: Maryport (0900) 2631.
Entry: Approach channel dries 2.8m. Bar dries 3.1m. Depth 5.3m. over bar MHWS.
S PIER HEAD. Lt. Fl. 1.5 sec. 4M. tripod, 10m.
TWO FEET BANK. By. Pillar Y.B.Y. Topmark W.
N WORKINGTON By. Pillar B.Y. Topmark N.
S WORKINGTON. Lt.By. Q.(6) + L.Fl. 15 sec. Pillar Y.B. Topmark S. Bell.

WORKINGTON 54°39'N 3°34'W. Tel: Dock Office: (0900) 602301. Fax: (0900) 604696. Telex: 64253 PTWKTN G. Pilots: (0900) 822631.

Entry: Best to arrive off Workington 2½-1½ h. before HW Silloth.
Radio — Port: VHF Chan. 16, 11, 14, 2½ h.-HW-2 h.
Radio — Pilots: VHF Chan. 16, 14, 2½ h.-HW-2 h.

Entry Signals:
By day: ball
By night: R. Lt. } from 2½ h.-HW-2 h.
By day: balls
By night: 2 R. Lts. } entry prohibited.

S PIER. Lt. Fl. 5 sec. 8M. R. brick building, 11m. C.G. Storm sig. Siren 20 sec.
HEAD. Lt. Q.G.
N JETTY HEAD. Lt. 2 F.R. vert. metal Col. 7m.
BUSH PERCH. Lt. Q.R. on metal mast.
Ldg.Lts. 131°49' (Front) F.R. 3M. W.Or. Tr. 10m. (Rear) F.R. 3M. W.Or. Tr. 12m.

HARRINGTON HARBOUR
Entry: 4M. N of Whitehaven. Used only by yachts and small craft. Dries at LW. Remains of N Breakwater marked by beacons.

WHITEHAVEN 54°33'N 3°36'W. Tel: Whitehaven (0946) 692435. Pilots: (0946) 827335.
Radio — Port: VHF Chan. 16, 12 — 2½ h.-HW-1½ h.
Radio — Pilots: VHF Chan. 16, 12.
Signals: At S side ent. to Queen's Dock — from 2½ h.-HW-1½ h.
By Day/Night = R. Ball/R. Lt. = Hbr. open: By Day/Night = 2 R. Balls/2 R. Lts = Hbr. closed. Dredger working in Hbr. or on Bar.
Entry: Harbour dries out. Reported depths: S Harbour 4.3m. Customs House and N Harbour 5.2m. at MHWS.
Anchorage: ½M. W-NW of Hbr. Best to arrive 2½ h.-HW-1½ h.

W PIER HEAD. Lt. Fl.G. 5 sec. 13M. W. round Tr. 16m
N PIER HEAD. Lt. 2 F.R. vert. 9M. W. round Tr. 8m.
N WALL QUAY HEAD. Lt. 2 F.R. vert. 2M. W. post, 8m.
OLD QUAY HEAD. Lt. 2 F.G. vert. 2M. W. post, 8m.

OFFSHORE WAYPOINT ST. BEE'S HEAD. 54°30.0'N, 3°42.0'W.

ST. BEES HEAD 54°30.8'N, 3°38.1'W. Lt. Fl.(2) 20 sec. 21M. W. round Tr. 102m. Obscured shore-340°. Shown H24.

Lts. F.R. on Tr. 14.6M. SSE.
CALDER HALL PWR. STN. OUTFALL. Bys. No.
1 and No. 2. Conical G.

RAVENGLASS
Harbour dries out 3 h.-HW-3 h. Craft up to
3.4m. draught can enter at H.W. and lie
aground.

ESKMEALS RANGE (MOD) 54°19.45′N,
03°24.7′W. Listens VHF Chan. 16 0800-1600
Mon.-Fri. Tx. All VHF Chan. Contact for any
'Range' information, programme etc. Also in
emergency.
Lt. F.G. on Blockhouse. Occas.

SELKER. Lt.By. Fl.(3)G. 15 sec. Conical G. off
Rocks. Bell.

Duddon Estuary should be approached with
care, especially on the ebb, as sandbanks not
constant. Do not attempt at neap tides, or
beyond 2 h.-HW-2 h. any time.

ISLE OF MAN — WEST SIDE

OFFSHORE WAYPOINT POINT OF AYRE.
54°27.0′N, 4°21.0′W.

POINT OF AYRE 54°24.9′N, 4°22.1′W. Lt.
Al.L.Fl.W.R. 60 sec. 19M. W. Tr. 2 R. bands,
32m. R.C. Racon.
54°25′N, 4°22′W. Lt.Ho. Fl. 3 sec. 8M. R. Tr.
lower part W., on B. base, 10m. Partially
obscured 335°-341°. Siren(3) 90 sec.

JURBY
CRONK Y CLIWE. Lt. 2 Fl.R. vert. 5 sec. on
mast, synchronised, 2m. apart, occas.

ORRISDALE. Lt. 2 Fl.R. vert. 5 sec. on mast,
synchronised, 2m. apart, occas.
NORTH DZ. Lt.By. Fl.Y. 10 sec. Conical Y.
Topmark X.
SOUTH DZ. Lt.By. Fl.Y. 10 sec. Conical Y.
Topmark X.
TARGET FLOATS Nos: 1, 2. Lts. Q.Y. Float Or.

PEEL (I.O.M.) 54°14′N, 4°42′W. Tel: Peel
(0624) 842338.

HARBOUR WAYPOINT. 54°14.0′N, 4°41.5′W.

Radio — Port: VHF Chan. 16, 12 when ship
expected.

Entry: Inner Harbour dries out approx. 2 h.-
LW-2 h. Any yachts proceeding to the
breakwater should contact H.M. as soon as
possible.
Craft 76.2m. × 4.3m. draught can lay
alongside Breakwater at MHWS. Craft 48m. ×
3m. draught MHWN (4m. MHWS) can enter
inner hr. and take the ground.
Anchorage: In Bay. NE of Groyne Lt.

PIER HEAD, E SIDE ENTCE. Lt. Oc.R. 7 sec.
5M. W. Tr. R. band, on office building, 8m. vis.
156°-249°.
GROYNE HEAD. Lt. Iso.R. 2 sec. 4m.
CASTLE JETTY HEAD. Lt. Oc.G. 7 sec. 4M. W.
Tr. G. band, 5m.
BREAKWATER HEAD. Lt. Oc. 7 sec. 6M. W. Tr.
11m. Bell(4) 12 sec. when vessels expected.
CORRIN Bn. Grey, near Peel.

PORT ERIN (I.O.M.)

HARBOUR WAYPOINT. 54°05.25′N, 4°47.0′W.

Anchorage: In Bay. W of ruined breakwater
(submerged at HW).

Ldg. Lts. 099°06′. (Front) F.R. 5M. W. Tr. R.
band, 10m. (Rear) F.R. 5M. W. Col. R. band, on
W. △, 19m.
RAGLAN PIER HEAD. Lt. Oc.G. 5 sec. 5M. W.
Tr. G. band, 8m.
PORT ERIN. By. Conical G. marks end of
demolished breakwater.

OFFSHORE WAYPOINT CALF OF MAN.
54°00.0′N, 4°51.0′W.

CALF OF MAN 54°03.2′N, 4°49.6′W. Lt. Fl.
15 sec. 28M. W. octagonal Tr. on granite
building, 93m. vis. 274°-190°. Horn 45 sec.

CHICKEN ROCK 54°02.3′N, 4°50.1′W. Lt.
Fl. 5 sec. 13M. granite Tr. 38m. Horn 60 sec.
THOUSLA ROCK Lt.Bn. Fl.R. 3 sec. 4M.
Octagonal Pillar 9m. on S side of Calf Sound.

EAST SIDE

PORT ST. MARY 54°04′N, 4°44′W. Tel: Port
St. Mary (0624) 833206.

HARBOUR WAYPOINT. 54°04.0′N, 4°43.0′W.

Entry: When app. from SW give Kallow Pt.
and Alfred Pier a berth of at least 2 cables
until head of Inner Pier is open N of the Head
of Alfred Pier. Round Inner Pier, keeping close
to it as possible.

Radio — Port: VHF Chan. 16, 12 — when vessels expected.
Port Information: Harbour dries out at 2m. Maximum draught 4m. at M.H.W.S.T. Yachts proceed to inner end of Breakwater and contact HM.
Anchorage: to seaward of Visitors moorings.

THE CARRICK. Lt. Q.(2) 5 sec. 7M. Pillar B.R.B. Topmark Is.D. 6m.
ALFRED PIER HEAD. Lt. Oc.R. 10 sec. 5M. W. Tr. R. band, 8m. Bell(3) 12 sec. when vessels expected.
INNER PIER HEAD. Lt. Oc.R. 3 sec. 5M. W. Tr. R. band, 8m.

CASTLETOWN (I.O.M.) 54°04'N 4°39'W.
Tel: (0624) 823549.
HISTORIC WRECK SITE CASTLETOWN 54°03.12'N, 4°37.72'W. 350m. radius.

HARBOUR WAYPOINT. 54°03.0'N, 4°39.0'W.

Radio — Port: VHF Chan. 16, 12 — when vessel expected.
Entry: Yachts berth 1½ h.-HW-1½ h. all berths dry out. Strong tide off Langness & Dreswich Points.
Anchorage: about 3c SE of Breakwater exposed to SW/SSE winds.

NEW PIER HEAD. Lt. Oc.R. 15 sec. 5M. W. Tr. R. band, 8m.
N SIDE ENTCE. Lt. Oc.G. 4 sec. W. metal post on concrete Col. G. band, 3m.
IRISH QUAY. Lt.Bn. Oc.R. 4 sec. 5M. W. Tr. R. band, 5m. vis. 142°-322°. 2 F.R. Lts. mark swing bridge 150m. NW.
LHEEAH-RIO ROCKS. Lt.By. Fl.R. 3 sec. Can.R. on SE edge. Bell.

INSHORE WAYPOINT LANGNESS POINT. 54°02.0'N, 4°37.0'W.

LANGNESS 54°03.5'N, 4°37.2'W. Lt. Fl.(2) 30 sec. 21M. W. Tr. 23m.
DERBY HAVEN. Lt. Iso.G. 2 sec. 5M. W. Tr. G. band, 5m.

INSHORE WAYPOINT DOUGLAS HEAD. 54°08.25'N, 4°26.25'W.

DOUGLAS HEAD 54°08.6'N, 4°27.9'W. Lt. Fl. 10 sec. 25M. W. Tr. 32m. Obscured when bearing more than 037°. F.R. Lts. on radio masts 1 and 3M. W.

DOUGLAS (I.O.M.) 54°09'N 4°29'W. Tel: (0624) 23813, 23817. Fax: (0624) 27238. Telex: 629335 IOMHAR G.

HARBOUR WAYPOINT. 54°09.0'N, 4°27.0'W.

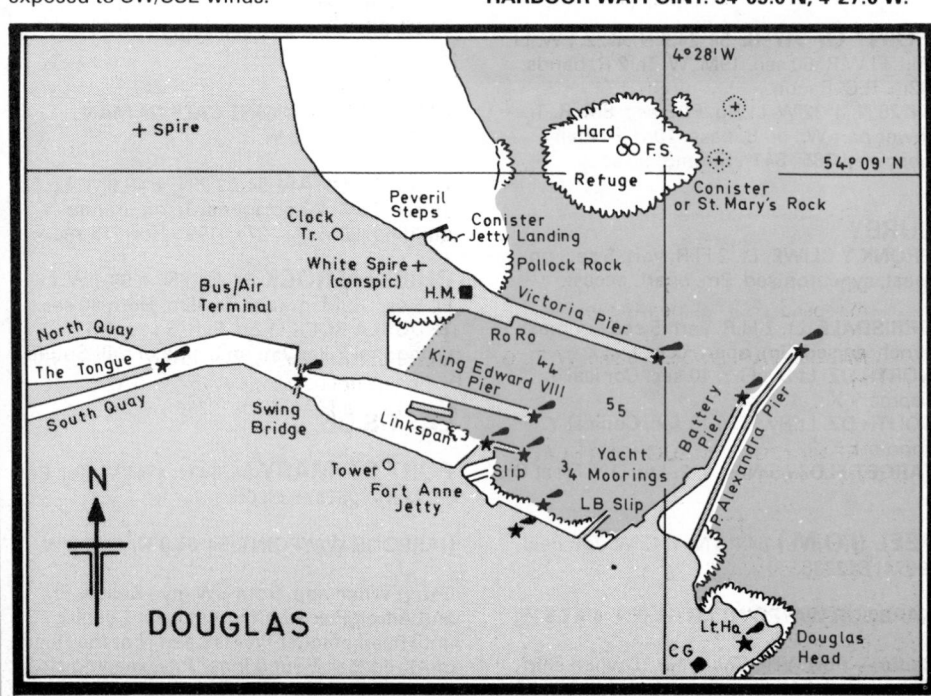

Mariners should have Chart No. 2696 (Fully Corrected).
Radio — Port: VHF Chan. 16, 12 — continuous.
Radar station at Douglas Head Lt.Ho. linked with Port radio station.
Information B'casts Chan. 12 at 0133, 0533, 0733, 0933, 1333, 1733, 2133.
Port Signals: Shown from mast at seaward end of Victoria Pier for vessels entering, leaving, manoeuvring in outer harbour.
   3 R. vert = Vessels not to proceed.
   G.W.R. vert. = Proceed only if specific
           permission given by VHF.
   3 G. vert. = All vessels may proceed.
   R. cross X = Vessels, unless specified, shall
           not proceed.
   W arrow → = Vessels may proceed in
           direction indicated.
Anchorages: as directed by Port Control.

PRINCESS ALEXANDRA PIER HEAD. Lt. Fl.R. 5 sec. 8M. R. mast 16m. Whis.(2) 40 sec.
BATTERY PIER. Lt. Q.R. 1M. W.R. Tr. 13m. 038°-218°. Ldg.Lts. 229° (Front) Oc. 10 sec. 5M. R.W. △ on mast for use W of 4°26'W only (Rear) Oc. 10 sec. 5M. W.R. ▽ on mast. 12m.
DOLPHIN. Lt. 2 F.R. vert. 038°-310°.
VICTORIA PIER HEAD. Lt. Oc.G. 8 sec. 3M. W. Col. 10m. 225°-327°. R.C. Int. Port Traffic Signals. Bell 2 sec.
FORT ANNE JETTY HEAD. Lt. Oc.R. 4 sec. W.R. Tr. 6m. 107°-297°.
ELBOW. Lt. Iso.R. 4 sec. W.R. Post. 5m. 095°-275°.
KING EDWARD VIII PIER. S SIDE HEAD. Lt. Oc.G. 4 sec. W. framework Tr. G. band, 6m. vis. 253°-005°.
INNER HARBOUR, TONGUE. Lt. Oc.R. 6 sec. W. post, R. band, 3m.
Lt.By. Q.(3)G. 5 sec. Conical G.
Lt.By. Fl.G. 3 sec. Conical G.
LAXEY
PIER HEAD. Lt. Oc.R. 3 sec. 5M. W. Tr. R. band, 7m. obscured when bearing less than 318°.
BREAKWATER HEAD. Lt. Oc.G. 3 sec. W. Tr. G. band, 7m.

OFFSHORE WAYPOINT MAUGHOLD HEAD. 54°17.25'N, 4°11.75'W.

MAUGHOLD HEAD 54°18.0'N, 4°19.0'W. Lt. Fl.(3) 30 sec. 22M. W. Tr. 65m.

SNAEFELL RG STN. 54°15.8'N, 4°27.6'W. Emergency DF Stn. VHF Chan. 16 & 67. Controlled by MRSC Liverpool.

RAMSEY (I.O.M.) 54°19'N 4°22'W. Tel: Ramsey (0624) 812245.

HARBOUR WAYPOINT. 54°19.25'N, 4°21.0'W.

Radio — Port: VHF Chan. 16, 12 — when vessels expected.
Entry: Hbr. dries out. Enter 2 h.-HW-2 h. Depth 6m. in channel MHWS and 5m. alongside the Piers and 4-5m. alongside the Quays MHWS. Max. size 61m. × 3m. draught MHWN (4m. draught MHWS).
Anchorage: 4 cables E of Pier Heads with Harbour Chan. open, outside N and S of extension of Iron Queens Pier. Harbour and Chan. dry out at L.W. Unfavourable weather conditions in winds SE to NE.
Queens Pier — landing prohibited.
Visitors Buoy — Sph. Y.

QUEENS PIER. Lt.By. Fl.R. 5 sec. Can.R.
S PIER HEAD. Lt. Oc.R. 5 sec. 4M. W. Tr. R. band, B. base, 8m. Bell(2) 10 sec. when vessels expected.
N PIER HEAD. Lt. Oc.G. 5 sec. 5M. W. Tr. B. base, 9m.
TOE OF MOORAGH BANK. Lt. Iso. G. 4 sec. W. post, Vi. band, on dolphin, 3m. For guidance of vessels inside Hr. Not vis. seaward.
SWING BRIDGE. Lts. 2 F.R. Hor.
WHITESTONE BANK Lt.By. Q.(9) 15 sec. Pillar Y.B.Y. Topmark W.
BAHAMA BANK. Lt.By. Q.(6) + L.Fl. 15 sec. Pillar Y.B. Topmark S. Bell.
KING WILLIAM BANK. Lt.By. Q.(3) 10 sec. Pillar B.Y.B. Topmark E.

APPROACHES TO BARROW

BARROW 54°06'N 3°14'W. Tel: Dock (0229) 22911 Hr.Mr. (0229) 20155.
Entry: Best to arrive 2 h.-HW.
Radio — Port: *Ramsden Radio.* VHF Chan. 16, 12 — continuous.
Ramsden Dock Radio. VHF Chan. 16 2 h.-HW.
Radio — Pilots: *Barrow Pilots.* VHF Chan. 16, 12, 9, 14. 6 and MF 2182, 2241 kHz — 3 h. before HW to HW.
Entry Signals: Ramsden Dock: R. flag or R. over W. Lts. — gates open and clear.
B. ball under R. flag or 2 R. Lts. — gates closed.
Walney Swing Bridge: G. Lt. — open R. Lt. — shut.

MORECAMBE BAY. Lt.By. Q.(9) 15 sec. Pillar Y.B.Y. Topmark W. w.a. whis.
LIGHTNING KNOLL Fairway Lt.By. L.Fl. 10 sec. Sph. R.W.V.S. Bell.

HALFWAY. Lt.By. Fl.R. 5 sec. Can.R. ᴠᴸᴸᴸ.
OUTER BAR. Lt.By. Fl.(4)R. 10 sec. Can.R. ᴠᴸᴸᴸ

BAR. Lt.By. Fl.(2)R. 5 sec. Can.R. cage
Topmark. on bar to Hr. Entce.

WALNEY RG STN. 54°06.58′N, 3°15.89′W.
emergency DF Stn. VHF Chan. 16 & 67.
Controlled by MRSC Liverpool.

WALNEY. 54°02.9′N, 3°10.6′W. Lt. Fl. 15 sec.
23M. stone Tr. 21m. obscured 122°-127° when
within 3M. of shore.
R.C. Storm sig.
HAWS POINT. Lt. Q.R. 6M. metal pile
structure, 8m. NE of point.
HAWS POINT EAST. Lt.By. Fl.G. 2.5 sec.
Conical G. ᴠᴸᴸᴸ.
SCAR. Lt.By. Fl.G. 5 sec. Conical G.
WALNEY CHANNEL. Ldg.Lts. 040°51′. No: 1
(Front) Q. 6M. B. pile structure, W. daymark,
6m. No: 2 (Rear) Iso. 2 sec. 6M. R. brick Col.
W. face, 12m.
No. 3A Lt. Q.G. 9M. 8m. Lt. in line with No. 4
Lt.Bn. marks E edge of approach channel.
RAMPSIDE SANDS. Ldg.Lts. 006°15′. No: 3
(Front) Q. 6M. B. pile structure, W. daymark,
6m. No: 4 (Rear) Iso. 2 sec. 6M. R. brick Col.
W. face, 14m.
BIGGAR SANDS. Ldg.Lts. 298°15′. No: 5
(Front) Q. 6M. B. pile structure, W. daymark,
6m. No: 6 (Rear) Iso. 2 sec. 6M. R. brick Col.
W. face, 19m.
No: A7 Lt. Q.G. 5M. Or. ◊.

DEEP WATER BERTH PLATFORM
Ldg.Lts. 153°45′. **No: A8** (Front) Q.R. 6M. 5m.
Or. ◊.
No: A9 (Rear) Iso. R. 2 sec. 8m. Or. ◊.
No: A10 Channel Lt. Q.R. 6M. 5m. marks
slipway.
Ldg.Lts. 143°22′. **No: A11** (Front) Q.R. 6M. 5m.
Or. ◊.
No: A12 (Rear) Iso. R. 2 sec. 6M. 8m. Or. ◊
Ldg.Lts. 118°15′.
No: A13 (Front) Q.R. 6M. 6m. Or.
No: A14. (Rear) Iso. R. 2 sec. 11m. Or.
PIKE STONES BED HOLLOW. Ldg.Lts. 043°30′
(Front) Fl.(4)Y. 5 sec. Pole Y. (Rear) Fl.(4)Y. 5
sec. Pole Y. mark gas pipe line.

RIDGE. Lt.By. Fl.R. 2½ sec. Can.R.
No: 1 Lt.By. Fl.G. 2.5 sec. Conical G.
No: 2 By. Can.R.
No: 3 By. Conical G.
No: 4 By. Can.R.
No: 5 By. Conical G.
No: 6 By. Can.R.
No: 7 By. Conical G.

No: 9 Lt.By. Fl.G. 5 sec. Conical G. ᴠᴸᴸᴸ.
No: 10 By. Can.R.
No: 11 By. Conical G.
No: 12 By. Can.R.
No: 13 Lt.By. Fl.G. 2½ sec. Conical G.
No: 14 By. Can.R.
No: 16 Lt.By. Fl.(2)R. 5 sec. Can.R.
No: 18 By. Can.R.
No: 20 Lt.By. Fl.(2)R. 5 sec. Can.R.
No: 22 By. Can.R.
No: 24 By. Can.R.

WEST PILE. Lt. Fl.R. 3 sec. 4M. W. daymark on
pile structure, 8m.
CONCRETE PIER HEAD. Lt.Bn. 2 F.G. vert.
No: 4 SLIPWAY. Lt. 2 F.R. vert. 4 and 2m.
Traffic sig. shown at Jubilee swing bridge
0.4M. NW. Outer extremity marked by Lt.By.
Q.G.
CARTMEL. Lt. F. 9M. 29m. Fishing Lt.

**INSHORE WAYPOINT R. LUNE. 53°55.5′N,
3°11.0′W.**

LUNE DEEPS

SHELL WHARF. Lt.By. Fl.G. 2½ sec. Conical G.
and Topmark. off W edge of Rossall Patches.
LUNE DEEP. Lt.By. Q.(6) + L.Fl. 15 sec. Pillar
Y.B. Topmark S. ᴠᴸᴸᴸ Whis. N side of Chan.
Racon.
DANGER PATCH. Lt.By. Fl.(3)R. 10 sec. Can.R.
ᴠᴸᴸᴸ off S edge. N side of Chan.
KING SCAR. Lt.By. Fl.(2)G. 5 sec. Conical G.
On N edge. S side of Chan.

RIVER WYRE CHANNEL

FLEETWOOD 53°55′N 3°00′W. Tel: HM.
(03917) 2323. Hbr. office: (03917) 70523. Telex:
677296 ABPFWD G. Fax: (03917) 77549.
Radio — Port: Fleetwood Docks. VHF Chan.
16, 12 — 2 h.-HW-1 h.
Fleetwood Hbr. Radio: VHF Chan. 16, 12, 11.
H24.
Radio — Pilots: VHF Chan. 16, 12.
Entry: Access to Harbour 4 h.-HW-4 h. No
moorings for visiting yachts in the docks.
Yachts use the river. Max. size at Wardleys
Y.C. 12.2m. × 2.4m. draught. Channel
maintained to dry 3m.
Signals: Storm cone shown from ent. to
Docks. Fl.Or. Lt. shown when large v/l in outer
channel or harbour.
Anchorage: SW of Fairway By.

No: 1 Lt.By. Q. ᴠᴸᴸᴸ Pillar B.Y. Topmark N.
Bell.
No: 3 Lt.By. Q.G. ᴠᴸᴸᴸ Conical G.

No: 4 Lt.By. Q.R. 〰 Can.R.
No: 5 Lt.By. Fl.G. 3 sec. Conical G.
No: 6 Lt.By. Fl.R. 3 sec. 〰 Can.R.
No: 7 Lt.By. Q.G. Conical G.
No: 8 Lt.By. Q.R. Can.R. 〰.
No: 9 By. Conical G.
No: 10 Lt.By. Fl.R. 3 sec.
No: 12 Lt.By. Q.R.
No: 13 By. Conical G.
No: 14 Lt.By. Fl.R. 3 sec.
No: 16 Lt.By. Q.R. 〰 Can.R.
No: 18 By. Can.R.

ESPLANADE. Ldg.Lts. (Front) Fl.Y. 2 sec. 8M.
buff coloured square Tr. R. lantern, B. base,
14m. (Rear) Fl.Y. 4 sec. 11M. buff coloured
square Tr. B. base, R. lantern, 28m. Vis. on
leading line only. Shown by day.
BLACK SCAR PERCH No: 11 Lt. Q.G. G. △ on
Bn. 4m. Horn 15 sec.
STEEP BREAST PERCH. Lt. Iso G. 2 sec. 2M.
platform on B. wooden post, B. base, 3m. in
line with Ldg.Lts.
VICTORIA PIER HEAD. Lt. 2 F.G. vert. 8 and
6m.
GROYNE. Lt. 2 F.G. vert. platform on post,
6m.
KNOTT END SAILING SCHOOL JETTY Lts. in
line 2 F. mark line of Jetty.

NEW HARBOUR BERTH
N DOLPHIN. Lt. 2 F.G. vert. 1M.
S DOLPHIN. Lt. 2 F.G. vert. 1M.
FERRY BERTH.
S SIDE. Lt. 2 F.G. vert. 1M. R. metal post, 6m.
R.N.L.I. BERTH. Lt. 2 F.G. vert. Also 2 F.G. vert.
on Survival Platform close N.
RO RO RAMP Lt.Bn. 2 F.G. (vert.) Horn (2) 30
sec. 3m.
BRIDGE SUPPORT Lt.Bn. 2 F.G. (vert.)

SLADE SLIP CORNER. Lt. 2 F.G. vert.

RIVER LUNE TO GLASSON DOCK & LANCASTER

GLASSON DOCK 53°59'N 2°53'W Tel:
(0524) 751724.
Radio — Ports & Pilots: VHF Chan. 16, 8, 2 h.-
HW.
Signals: B. Ball/R. Lt. = Gates not open.
R. flag/R. over W. Lt. = Gates open v/l may
enter.
R. Flag over B. Ball/2 F.R. vert. Lt. = Gates
open v/l leaving, others keep clear.
All yachts to keep clear of Commercial Traffic.
Glasson Dock. Dock entered through gate
15m. wide for vessels max. 85m x 14m x
4.57m draught at HWS. Enter ¾ h.-HW.

Glasson Basin Y. hr. — Max. 30.5m. × 3.7m.
draught.
River at Lancaster dries 4.3m.
Caution advised as training walls are
dangerous.
Inland Waterways. Glasson Dock, Lancaster
Canal. 24 hr. notice of arrival/departure
required. Ring Lock-keeper Galgate (0524)
751566. Also for use of Glasson Flight.
Anchorage: ¼M. SW of No. 1 By.

RIVER LUNE Lt.By. Q.(9) 15 sec. Pillar Y.B.Y.
Topmark W.
No: 2 Lt.By. Fl.(3)R. 10 sec. Can.R.
No: 4 Lt.By. Fl.(2)R. 5 sec. Can.R.
No: 3 Lt.By. Fl.(3)G. 10 sec. Conical G.
No: 6 Lt.By. Q.R. Can.R.
SOUTH BANK. Lt.By. Fl.(2)G. 4 sec. Conical G.
BAITHAVEN. Lt.By. Q. Can.R.
TOWN SCAR No: 8 By. Can.R.
No: 5 Lt.By. Q. Conical G.
No: 10 By. Can.R.
No: 7 By. Conical B.
CHADBURN SCAR. Lt.Q. Perch G.
No: 1 By. Can.R.
No: 2 By. Conical G. W Entce. to Dock.
No: 5 By. Conical G. E Entce. to Dock.
No: 14 Lt.By. Q. Can.R.
No: 3 By. Can.R.
No: 4 By. Can.R.
BASIL By. Can.R.
No: 20 Lt.By. Q. Can.R.
No: 22 By. Can.R.

RIVER LUNE. 53°58.9'N, 2°52.9'W. Ldg.Lts.
083°40'. Plover Scar (Front) Fl. 2 sec. 11M. W.
stone Tr. B. lantern, 6m. Cockersand Abbey
(Rear) F. 8M. R. framework Tr. 18m.
CROOK PERCH No: 7. Lt. Fl.G. 5 sec. 3M. G.
mast.
BRAZIL PERCH No: 16. Lt. Fl.(3)R. 10 sec. 3M.
R. mast.
GLASSON QUAY. Lt. F.G. 1M.
JTY. Lt. Fl.(2)R. 6 sec.
Starboard side of river marked by Bys. or
Perches G. and port side by Bys. or Perches
R.

APPROACHES TO HEYSHAM AND MORECAMBE

No: 1 Lt.By. Fl.G. 4 sec. Conical G.
No: 2 Lt.By. Fl.R. 4 sec. Can.R.
No: 3 Lt.By. Fl.(3)G. 8 sec. Conical G. Bell.
No: 5 Lt.By. Q.G. Conical G.
No: 6 Lt.By. Fl.R. 5 sec. Can.R.
No: 7 Lt.By. Fl.(3)G. 10 sec. Conical G.
No: 8 Lt.By. Fl.(2)R. 10 sec. Can.R.

HEYSHAM 54°01'N 2°55'W. Tel: (0524) 52373 & 52284. Fax: (0524) 53301. Telex: 65260 SELINK G.
Radio — Port: VHF Chan. 16, 14, 74 — continuous.
Radio — Pilots: VHF Chan. 16, 14, 9, 6; when vessel expected.
Entry: No berths or facilities for yachts. Port fully utilised by commercial craft.
Tides across Hbr. entrance can reach 3½-4 kts. spring tides.

S JETTY HEAD. Lt. 2 F.G. vert. 5M. W. frame. Tr. Siren. 30 sec.
SW QUAY. Ldg.Lts. 102°15'. (Front) F. Bu. 2M. Or.B. ◊post 11m. marks channel (Rear) F. Bu. 2M. Or.B. ◊post 14m.
S PIER HEAD. Lt. Oc.G. 7.5 sec. 6M. W. metal Tr. R. base, 9m.
S OUTFALL Lt. Fl.(2)G. 10 sec. 2M. Post 5m.
N OUTFALL. Lt.Bn. Fl.G. 5 sec. 2M. Post 5m.
N PIER HEAD. Lt. 2 F.R. vert. 2M. mast, 11m. obscured from seaward.
HEAVY LIFT RO-RO TERMINAL. Lts. F.G. on dolphins. 2 F.G. vert. on dolphins.
BRITISH GAS SUPPORT BASE. Lt. F.R. 6M. Radio mast 50m.
OCEAN OIL TERMINAL
Lt.By. Q.(9) 15 sec. Pillar Y.B.Y. Topmark W.
NW DOLPHIN. Lt.Bn. Fl.G. 4 sec. 2M.

GRANGE CHANNEL TO MORECAMBE

BAITING KNOT No. 2 By. Barrel R.

MORECAMBE

SEWER OUTFALL. Lt. Fl.G. 2 sec. 2M. metal framework Tr. 4m.
STONE PIER HEAD. Lt. F. stone Tr. 12m.
Ldg. Lts. 090°. (Front) F.R. 2M. G. mast, 10m. (Rear) F.R. 2M. G. mast, 14m.
CENTRAL PROMENADE PIER. Lt. 2 F.G. Vert. 4M. W. wooden Col. 9m.

MORECAMBE BAY (PRODUCTION PLATFORMS)
DP4. 53°52.6'N, 3°33.6'W.
DP8. 53°53.5'N, 3°37.3'W
DP8. Lt.By. Q.(9) 15 sec. Pillar Y.B.Y. Topmark W.
DP6. 53°51.9'N, 3°36.9'W.
DP6. Lt.By. V.Q.(9) 10 sec. Pillar Y.B.Y. Topmark W.

DP1. 280m. SSE of CPPI.
DP3. 3M. SSE of CPPI.
FLAME TRIPOD close W. of CPPI.
CPPI. 53°50.1'N, 3°34.9'W.
API. 53°50.7'N, 3°34.9'W.
MORECAMBE BAY GAS FIELD WELL HEAD.
Lt.Bys. V.Q.(9) 10 sec. Pillar. Y.B.Y. Topmark W. Q.(9) 15 sec. Pillar. Y.B.Y. Topmark W.
CLEVELEYS. Ldg.Lts. 091° (Front) F.Y. (Rear) F.Y.

BLACKPOOL

N PIER HEAD. Lt. 2 F.G. vert. 3M. 2m. apart.
CENTRAL PIER HEAD. Lt. 2 F.G. vert. 4M. metal triangular structure. 2m. apart.
Ldg.Lts. 089° (Front) 2 F.Y. (Rear) 2 F.Y.
S PIER HEAD. Lt. 2 F.G. vert. 4M. on building.
BELLA WK. Lt.By. V.Q.(9) 10 sec. Pillar Y.B.Y. Topmark W.

INSHORE WAYPOINT R. RIBBLE. 53°42.0'N, 3°09.0'W.

RIVER RIBBLE
Depths not maintained, S Training Wall broken, buoys and beacons unreliable.
GUT. Lt.By. L.Fl. 10 sec. Sph. R.W.V.S.

N TRAINING WALL
13M. Perch Lt. Fl.R. 5 sec. 3M. B.Tr. 6m.
11½M. Perch Lt. Fl.(2)R. 10 sec. R. □ on pile leads through gap in S Wall.
9⅞M. Perch Lt. Fl.R. 5 sec. 3M. Pile 6m.
8¾M. Perch Lt. Fl.R. 5 sec. 3M. Pile 6m.

S TRAINING WALL
14¼M. Perch Lt. Fl.G. 5 sec. 3M. B.Tr. 6m.
13¼M. Perch Lt. Fl.G. 5sec. 3M. B.Tr. 6m.
12½M. Perch Lt. Fl.G. 5 sec. 3M. B.Tr. 6m.
10M. Perch Lt. Fl.G. 5 sec. 3M. Pile 6m.
9¾M. Perch Lt. Fl.G. 5 sec. 3M. Pile 6m.
8¼M. Perch Lt. Fl.G. 5 sec. 3M. Pile 6m.
6M. Perch Lt. Fl.G. 5 sec. 3M. Pile 6m.
5M. Perch Lt. Fl.(2)G. 10 sec. 3M. Pile 6m.
3M. Perch Lt. Fl.G. 5 sec. 5M. Pile 6m.
2M. Perch Lt. Fl.G. 5 sec. 5M. Pile 6m.

PRESTON 53°41'N 3°12'W. Tel: Preston (0772) 726711.
Entry: Channel now runs through S Gut. Essential to ensure enough water before proceeding above Gut Lt.By. Access for yachts 2 h.-HW-2 h.

SOUTHPORT PIER HEAD Lt. 2 F.G. vert. 5M. W. post, 6m. vis. 033°-213°.
EL OSO. Lt.By. Q. Pillar. B.Y. Topmark N.

JORDAN'S SPIT. Lt.By. Q.(9) 15 sec. Pillar. Y.B.Y. Topmark W. ⌇⌇⌇ 10½M. from Southport Pier Lt.
Lt.By. Q. Pillar. B.Y. Topmark. N. marks obstruction.
SPOIL. Lt.By. Fl.Y. 3 sec. Pillar Y. N of Jordan's Spit.

INSHORE WAYPOINT ENE BAR LT. F
53°33.0'N 3°17.0'W.

MRSC LIVERPOOL (051) 931 3343. Weather broadcasts ev. 4h. from 0210.

LIVERPOOL 53°27'N 3°01'W. Tel: Mersey Radio (051) 200 2184. Telex: 626264 PTOPS G. Pilots (L'pool) (051) 200 2138, 2124, 2128 (Lynas) (0407) 830203.

Radio — Port: Mersey Radio. VHF Chan. 16, 12, 22, 19, 18, 9, 4. — continuous.
This is the control station for all radar, navigational, tidal and berthing information. Traffic Warning Lt. Q.Fl. Amber = large vessel entering approach channel inward.
Garston Dock. VHF Chan. 20. H24. Tel: (051) 427 5971. Telex: 628706 ABPGAR G.
Gladstone Dock. VHF Chan. 5 — continuous.
Alfred. VHF Chan. 5 — continuous.
Tranmere Stage. VHF Chan. 19 — continuous.
Langton. VHF Chan. 21 — continuous.
Manchester Ship Canal.
Eastham Lock. VHF Chan. 7, 14. Tel: (051) 327 1242.
AHM. (051) 327 1244. Pilots: (051) 327 1233.
Latchford Lock. VHF Chan. 20, 14. Tel: (0925) 35249.
Irlam, Barton, Mode Wheel Locks. VHF Chan. 18, 14. Tel: (061) 775 2014/789 1952/872 1368.
Hours continuous. Use Chan. 14 when underway.
Pilots: Seaforth VHF Chan. 12, 16, 11. P.V. Chan. 12, 11.
Pt. Lynas VHF Chan. 9, 16. P.V. Chan. 9, 16.

WEAVER NAVIGATION
Weston Point Dock. Tel: (09285) 72927. Telex: 43376.
Radio: VHF 14, 71, 73. H24 except 1800-1900.
Vessels intending to enter or leave should contact the Lock.
Port Information and **Entry Signals: River Mersey**
A general port sitrep on Chan. 9, 3 h. and 2 h. before H.W. also on request Chan. 4. All vessels over 50 GRT fitted VHF listen Chan. 12. All vessels report arrival at port limits and before departure. All vessels carrying dangerous goods or towing to report

intentions at Q2 Lt. F; Crosby Lt. F.; Brazil or C22 Lt. F.; Woodside Stage or Dukes By. Damaged vessels must report at time of incident and before entry. Vessels over 137m. report before swinging. No vessel to anchor inward of Ql.L.F. without permission. Owners of small craft are warned that exceptionally large oil tankers may be navigating in River Mersey, the sea channels or approaches and great care is necessary. Where such vessels exceed 198m. in length they will generally exhibit 4 R. Lts. spaced vert. 1m. apart, but this is not obligatory.
Gladstone Dock River Entrance. 3 F.G. vert. = Lock open. 3 F.R. vert. = lock closed.
Langton Dock River Entrance. W Bullnose: — Semi-Circle 10 F. Lts. G. when Lock open. R. when closed. 2 × 2 F.R. vert. Lts. 122m. S of Lock. 2 F.R. Lts. 213m. S of Lock. Dredging Limits 2 × ∆ 3 F.R. Lts.
Stallbridge Dock River Entrance. 6 F. Lts. Hor. W. when Lock open. R. when closed (Day: R./Bl. Hor. stripe flag).
Queen Elizabeth II Dock: — ∆ 3 F. Lts. G. when open R. when closed. Same ∆ 3 R. Fl. Lts.=Lock sluicing in progress.
Eastham Lock. Available 4 h. before and after H.W.: — Lt. Occ. 2 sec. W. when Lock open R. when closed. Also Lt. Occ.G. when water in Canal/River equal and gates open. Emergency Lt. Amber Fl. 6 sec. when 80 ft. Lock inoperative (Day 2 W. Hor. Discs.). Check on Chan. 14 before leaving berth.
Walton Lock for vessels up to 2.4m. draught.

LIVERPOOL (BRUNSWICK & COBURG DOCKS) MARINA ACCESS 2 h.-HW-2 h.
Canning Dock River Lock Signals (access to Albert Dock):
3 F.G. vert. Lts. = Entrance open.
3 F.R. vert. Lts. = Entrance closed.

NORTHWICH
(BRITISH WATERWAYS BOARD. Tel: (0606) 74321).

WEAVER NAVIGATION AND ANDERTON LIFT
Locks and bridges on the River Weaver are open from 0800-1630 Mon.-Thurs. (Fri. 0800-1530) except Bank Holidays. The Anderton Lift will be closed until further notice. Vessels wishing to enter the Manchester Ship Canal from Marsh Lock must obtain prior clearance from the Harbour Master (Tel: 061-872 2411 extn. 2188).
VHF Stations Chan. 16 & 74: Weston Point, Marsh Lock, Dutton Lock, Saltersford Lock, Anderton Depot.

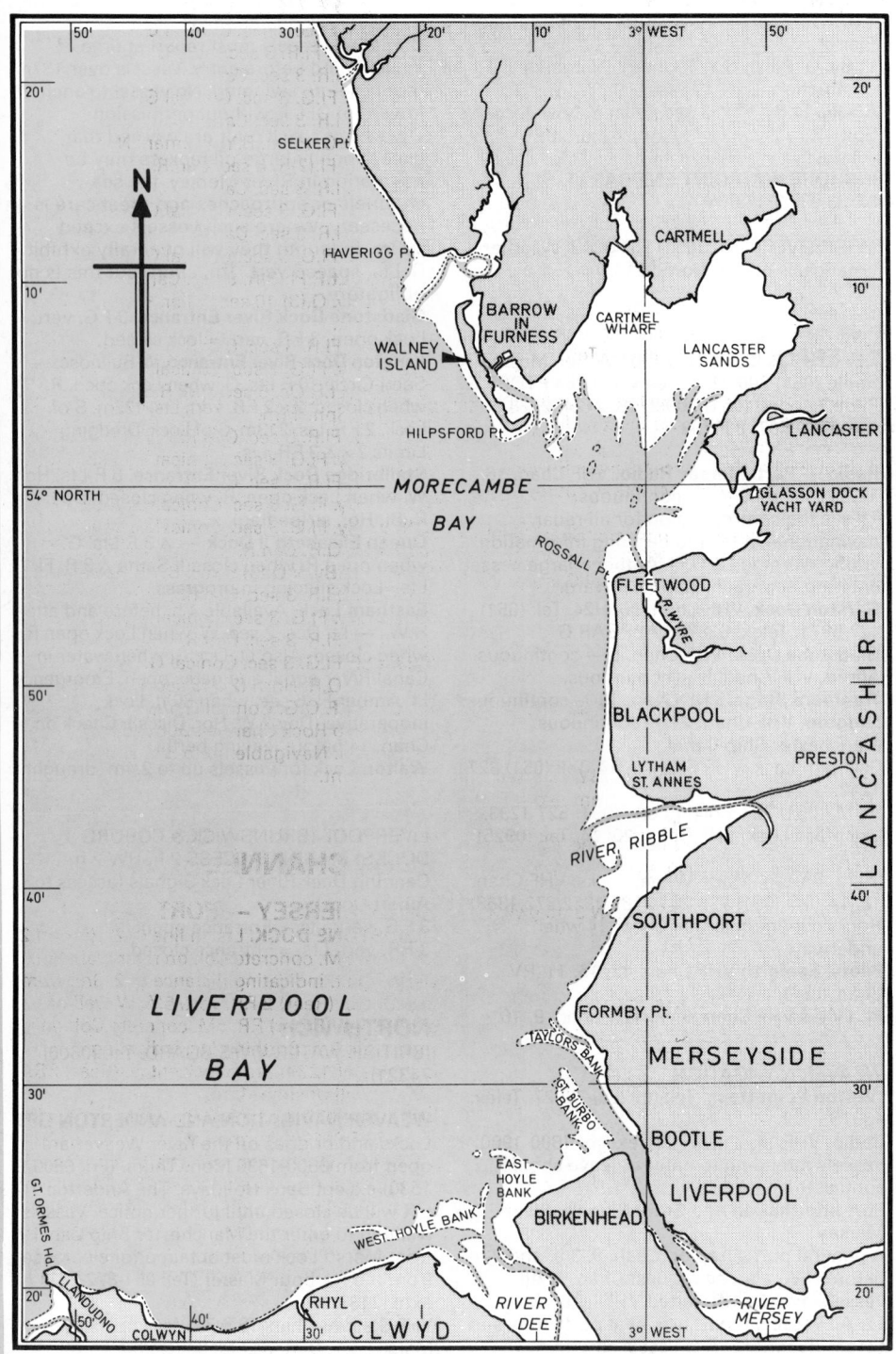

ELLESMERE PORT LOCKS
Key can be obtained from the entrance kiosk of the Ellesmere Port Boat Museum at the top of the lock flight.
Prior clearance must be obtained from the Harbour Master, Manchester Ship Canal at the Dock Office, Manchester for pleasure boats wishing to navigate the Ship Canal (Tel: 061-872 2411 extn. 2188).

WIGAN
(BRITISH WATERWAYS BOARD. Tel: (0942) 42239.)
LEEDS AND LIVERPOOL CANAL
Wigan Flight of Locks. Assistance up or down Wigan Flight may be available. Tel: (0942) 42239.
Stanley Dock Flight of Locks. 24 h. notice must be given. Tel: (0704) 893160 during normal working hours.
Tarleton Lock giving access to the Rufford Branch is tidal. Tel: (0704) 893160 or (077-473) 2250.
Bridgewater Canal. (Manchester Ship Canal Company). Tel: 061-872 2411, (extn. 2348).
Rochdale Canal. (Rochdale Canal Company). Tel: 061-236 2456.

RIVER MERSEY

OFFSHORE WAYPOINT BAR. 53°32.0′N, 3°24.0′W.

BAR. 53°32.0′N 03°20.9′W. LANBY. Fl. 5 sec. 21M. Lanby By. R. hull, metal framework Tr. 11m. Racon Horn 20 sec.
BURBO TWRS. Lt.By. Fl.(3)G. 9 sec. Conical G. marks remains of Burbo Twrs.

HARBOUR WAYPOINT 53°31.2′N 3°15.0′W.

QUEEN'S CHANNEL
'Q1' Lt.F. V.Q. Boat B.Y. Topmark N. ⌇.
'Q2' Lt.F. V.Q.R. Can.R.
'Q3' Lt.By. Fl.G. 3 sec. Conical G. ⌇.
'Q4' Lt.F. Q.R. Can.R.
'Q5' Lt.By. Q. Pillar B.Y. Topmark N.

FORMBY. Lt.F. Iso. 4 sec. 6M. R.W.V.S. Topmark Sph. 11m.
'Q6' Lt.F. Fl.R. 3 sec. Can.R. Bell.
'Q7' Lt.By. Fl.G. 3 sec. Conical G.
'Q8' Lt.F. Fl.R. 3 sec. Can.R.
'Q9' Lt.By. Fl.(3)G. 9 sec. Conical G. ⌇.
'Q10' Lt.F. Fl.R. 3 sec. Can.R.
'Q11' Lt.By. V.Q. Pillar. B.Y. Topmark N.
'Q12' Lt.F. Fl.R. 3 sec. Can.R.

CROSBY CHANNEL
'C1' Lt.By. Fl.G. 3 sec. Conical G. ⌇.
ALPHA Lt.F. Fl.R. 3 sec. Can.R.
'C2' Lt.F. Fl.R. 3 sec. Can.R.
'C3' Lt.By. Fl.G. 3 sec. Conical G. ⌇.
'C4' Lt.F. Fl.R. 3 sec. Can.R.
'C5' Lt.By. Q. Pillar. B.Y. Topmark N.
BETA Lt.F. Fl.(2)R. 6 sec. Can.R.
'C6' Lt.F. Fl.R. 3 sec. Can.R.
'C7' Lt.By. Fl.G. 3 sec. Conical G. ⌇.
'C8' Lt.F. Fl.R. 3 sec. Can.R.
'C9' Lt.By. Fl.G. 3 sec. Conical G. ⌇.
GAMMA Lt.F. Fl.(3)R. 9 sec. Can.R.
'C11' Lt.By. Q.(3) 10 sec. Pillar. B.Y.B. Topmark E.
'C10' Lt.F. Fl.R. 3 sec. Can.R.
'C13' Lt.By. Fl.G. 3 sec. Conical G. ⌇ Bell.
CROSBY. Lt.F. Oc. 5 sec. 8M. R.W.V.S. Topmark Sph. 11m.
'C12' Lt.F. Fl.R. 3 sec. Can.R.
'C15' Lt.By. Fl.G. 3 sec. Conical G. ⌇.
'C14' Lt.F. Fl.R. 3 sec. Can.R.
'C17' Lt.By. Fl.G. 3 sec. Conical G. ⌇.
'C19' Lt.By. Fl.G. 3 sec. Conical G. ⌇.
'C16' Lt.F. Q.R. Can.R.
BURBO Lt.By. V.Q.(3) 5 sec. B.Y.B. Topmark E.
'C18' Lt.F. Fl.R. 3 sec. Can.R.
'C21' Lt.By. Fl.G. 3 sec. Conical G. ⌇.
'C20' Lt.F. Fl.R. 3 sec. Can.R.
'C23' Lt.By. Fl.G. 3 sec. Conical G.
'C22' Lt.F. Q.R. Horn (2). 15 sec. Can.R.
BRAZIL Lt.F. Q.G. Conical G. indicates entrance to Rock Channel. Buoyed by Fishermen. Navigable up to 3 h. ebb. and 2m. draught.

ROCK CHANNEL

RIVER MERSEY — PORT SIDE
GLADSTONE DOCK. Lts. in line 072°. (Front) 2 F.R. vert. 5M. concrete Col. on river wall, 9m. Berthing Lt. indicating distance of 213m. from lock entce. (Rear) 2 F.R. vert. 5M. W wall of shed, 15m. (Front) F.R. 5M. concrete Col. on river wall, 9m. Berthing Lts. indicating distance of 122m. from lock entce. (Rear) F.R. 5M. W wall of shed, 15m.
Lts. in line 029°11′ (Front) 3 F.R. 8m. form of ▽ (Rear) 3 F.R. 12m. form of ▽.
LANGTON DOCK. Lts. in line 039°. (Front) 3 F.R. 3M. Col. 10m. (Rear) 3 F.R. 3M. Shed 15m.
Lts. in line 079°. (Front) F.R. 3M. (Rear) F.R. 3M. Berthing Lts. indicating distance of 213m. from lock entce.
Lts. in line 079°. (Front) 2 F.R. vert. 3M. (Rear) 2 F.R. vert. 3M. Berthing Lts. indicating distance of 122m. from lock entce.
Entry: 3 F.G. Lts. = Lock open.
          3 F.R. Lts. = Lock closed.

CANADA Lt.By. Fl.(2)R. 6 sec. Can.R.
SALISBURY DOCK Bell(4) 20 sec.
WATERLOO DOCK. Ldg.Lts. 151°. (Front) F.R.
Clear shoal water close W of dock wall.
Docking sig. (Rear) F.R.
Ldg.Lts. 174°. (Front) Q.R. Clear shoal water
in old entce. to Princes basin. (Rear) 2 F.R.
vert. 4M. metal Col. 8m.

**LIVERPOOL (PRINCES) LANDING STAGE, S
END.** Lt. 3 F.R. 4M. metal Col. in form of △. An
additional F.R. Lt. is shown when sluices are
open. Horn (3 × 3) 15 sec.
N END. Lt. 3 F.R. in form of △. Horn 20 sec.
DUKES. Lt.By. Fl.(2) R. Can.R. ⩔.
NORTH BRUNSWICK JETTY Bell(3) 20 sec.
from 2½h. before to 2h. after HW.
PLUCKINGTON BANK. Lt.By. V.Q.(9) 10 sec.
Pillar. Y.B.Y. Topmark W.
DINGLE OIL INSTALLATION. Lt. Fl.(4)Y. 12 sec.

GARSTON CHANNEL

'G1' Lt.By. Fl.G. 3 sec. Conical G. ⩔.
'G2' Lt.By. Fl.R. 3 sec. Can.R. ⩔.
'G3' Lt.By. Fl.G. 3 sec. Conical G. ⩔.
'G4' Lt.By. Fl.R. 3 sec. Can.R. ⩔ .
'G5' Lt.By. Fl.G. 3 sec. Conical G. ⩔.
'G6' By. Can.R.
'G7' Lt.By. Fl.G. 3 sec. Conical G. ⩔.
'G8' Lt.By. Fl.R. 3 sec. Can.R. ⩔ .
'G9' Lt.By. Fl.G. 3 sec. Conical G. ⩔.
'G11' Lt.By. Fl.G. 3 sec. Conical G. ⩔ .

GARSTON

E JETTY HEAD. Lt. 2 F.R. vert. 8M. ◊ on Grey
framework Tr. 11m. Bell 20 sec.
STALLBRIDGE DOCK. Ldg.Lts. 125°. (Front)
F.R. on Tr. 10m. By day F.R. Neon Ɩ. (Rear) F.R.
on Tr. 10m. By day Fr. Neon Ɩ.
When dock full or entce. obstructed 5 R. Lts.
hor. shown; when open to traffic 5 Lts. hor.
shown.
NW DOLPHIN. Lt. 2 F.G. vert. 9M. mast 12m.
Horn 11 sec. Entce. W Bullnose Lt. 2 F.G. vert.
3M. △ on Grey Tr. 10m.
W BULLNOSE DOCKING SIGNALS. F.W.R. 1M.
on mast. W. shown when dock open, R. when
closed.
GARSTON ROCKS By. Can.R.W. cheq.
Above Garston river almost dries.

RIVER MERSEY — STARBOARD SIDE

ROCK 53°27'N, 3°02'W. Lt.Ho. Unlit.

NEW BRIGHTON

TOWER. Lt.By. V.Q.(3) 5 sec. Pillar. B.Y.B.
Topmark E.
EGG. Lt.By. Fl.G. 3 sec. Conical G. ⩔.
BREAKWATER. Lt. 2 F.G. vert. 4M. mast △ G.
6m.
Lt. 2 F.G. vert. 6M. G. △ on mast 4m. ⎫ mark sea
Lt. 2 F.G. vert. 6M. G. △ on mast 4m. ⎭ defence
No: 5 Lt. Fl.G. G. △ 7m.
No: 2 Lt. Fl.G. 6m.
SEACOMBE FERRY. N CORNER. Lt. 3 F.G. 5M.
metal Col. 5m. in form of △.
30m. SSE Lt. F.Y. 6M. Tr. on roof, 8m.
S CORNER. Lt. 3 F.G. 5M. metal Col. 5m. in
form of △. Bell(3) 20 sec.

BIRKENHEAD

WOODSIDE LANDING STAGE, N END. Lt. 3
F.G. 4M. metal Col. 5m. in form of △.
S END. Lt. 2 F.G. vert. 7M. metal Col. 5m.
Bell(4) 15 sec.
CAMMELL LAIRD, SE CORNER. Lt. Fl.(2)G. 6
sec. 5M. W. structure, 5m.

TRANMERE TERMINAL
N DOLPHIN. Lt. Fl.G. 3 sec. 7M. 7m.
N STAGE, N END. Lt. 2 F.G. vert. 3M. Bell(2)
10 sec.
N STAGE, S END. Lt. 2 F.G. vert. 5M. 10m.
Bell.
S STAGE, N END. Lt. 3 F.G. △ 3M.
S STAGE, S END. Lt. 2 F.G. vert. 5M. 10m.

ROCK FERRY
JETTY HEAD, N END. Lt. Q.G. 6m.
S END. Lt. 2 F.G. vert. 6m.
S DOLPHIN. Lt. Fl.G. 3 sec. 5m.
DINGLE. Lt.By. Fl.(4)Or. 12 sec. Pillar Y.

BROMBOROUGH DOCK (closed)
RIVER WALL, N END. Lt. 3 F.G. △ 3M. metal
post and crossbar, 5m.
S END OF WALL. Lt. 3 F.G. metal post and
crossbar, in form of ▽.
BROMBOROUGH. Lt.By. Q.(3) 10 sec. Pillar
B.Y.B. Topmark E.

MANCHESTER 53°30'N 2°18'W.
Tel: 061-872 2411 Ext 2189.
Radio — Port and Canal: Eastham Locks: VHF
Chan. 7, 14. Stanlow Oil Dock: VHF Chan. 14,
20.
Latchford Locks: VHF Chan, 14, 20. Irlam
Locks: VHF Chan. 14, 18. Barton Locks: VHF
Chan. 14, 18. Modewheel Locks: VHF Chan.
14, 18. Call Chan. 14. H24.
Latchford, Irlam, Barton & Modewheel Locks:
either 45 ft Locks or 65 ft Lock available.

Modewheel Lock: Mon.-Thur. 0800-1200/1300-1700. Bank Hols: 0800-1200.
Fri. 0800-1200/1300-1500. Bank Hols: 0800-1200.
No. 6 Dock used for yachts.

EASTHAM CHANNEL
POWER STATION JETTY, NE CORNER. Lt. 2 F.G. vert.
SE CORNER. Lt. 2 F.G. vert. 5M. concrete post, 7m.
EASTHAM LOCKS
E DOLPHIN. Lt. Fl.(2)R. 6 sec. 8M. Perch, 5m.
CENTRE ISLAND Bell(4) when tide serves.
Traffic and water level sig.

APPROACHES TO MANCHESTER SHIP CANAL AND UPPER MERSEY

'E1' **Lt.By.** Fl.G. Conical G. ⌇.
'E2' **Lt.By.** Fl.R. Can.R. ⌇.
'E3' **Lt.By.** Fl.G. 3 sec. Conical G. ⌇.
'E4' **Lt.By.** Fl.R. Can.R. ⌇.
'E5' **Lt.By.** Fl.G. 3 sec. Conical G. ⌇.
'E6' **Lt.By.** Fl.R. Can.R. ⌇.
'E7' **Lt.By.** Fl.G. 3 sec. Conical G.

LIVERPOOL BAY
N WIRRAL. Lt.By. Fl.Y. 3 sec. Conical Y. ⌇ about 2¼M. seaward of old Leasowe Lt.Ho.
NEWCOMBE KNOLL WK. Lt.By. Q.(9) 15 sec. Pillar Y.B.Y. Topmark W.
HAMILTON Lt.By. Fl.(4)Y. 10 sec. Spar Y. Bell. 53°36.05'N, 3°27.23'W.
HAMILTON Lt.By. Fl.(4)Y. 10 sec. Spar Y. Bell. 53°31.68'N, 3°33.95'W.
Mark Wellheads in bay.

INSHORE WAYPOINT R. DEE. 53°26.5'N, 3°18.5'W.

N HOYLE Lt.By. V.Q. Pillar. B.Y. Topmark N.

HILBRE SWASH TO RIVER DEE
'HE2' **Lt.By.** Q.R. Can.R. ⌇.
'HE1' **Lt.By.** Q(3) 10 sec. Pillar B.Y.B. Topmark E. ⌇.
'HE4' By. Can.R.
'HE3' **Lt.By.** Fl.G. 2½ sec. Conical G.

SE HOYLE By. Can.R. in Welshman's Gut.
WELSHMAN. Lt.By. Q.(3) 10 sec. Pillar B.Y.B. Topmark E.
SELDOM SEEN By. Can.R.
Channels of River Dee change frequently, with consequent shifting of positions of Bys. marking Fairways. Pilots' services are advised.

APPROACHES TO RIVER DEE TO MOSTYN, CONNAH'S QUAY & CHESTER

INNER PASSAGE AND WELSH CHANNEL
W CONSTABLE Lt.By. V. Q.(9) 15 sec. Pillar Y.B.Y. Topmark W.

N RHYL. Lt.By. Q. Pillar. B.Y. Topmark N.
MIDDLE PATCH SPLIT. Lt.By. Fl.R. 5 sec. Can.R.
CHESTER FLAT Fl.(2)R. 5 sec. Can.R. BANK. By. Can.R.
S HOYLE Lt.By. Fl.(3)R. 10 sec. Can.R.
EARWIG. Lt.By. Fl.(2)G. 5 sec. Conical G. Bell. in Welsh Chan.
E HOYLE. Lt.By. Fl.(4)R. 15 sec. Can.R. in Welsh Chan.
TALACRE By. Conical G. ⌇.
AIR By. Conical G. ⌇.
DEE. Lt.By. Q.(6) + L.Fl. 15 sec. Pillar Y.B. Topmark S.

DEE RIVER 53°23'N 3°13'W

NE MOSTYN. Lt.By. Fl.(3)G. 10 sec. Conical G.
MOSTYN. Lt.By. Fl.(4)G. 15 sec. Conical G. ⌇.
Position may be changed without notice.
S SALISBURY By. Can.R.
BARRON HILL — mast on wreck.
HILBRE ISLAND, N END. Lt. Fl.R. 3 sec. 4M. W. frame Tr.

SHROPSHIRE UNION CANAL
RIVER DEE LOCKS — CHESTER
Passage is possible 1 h.-HW-1 h, at least 24 hours notice must be given to the Chester Section Inspector (Tel: Chester (0244) 372620). A charge is payable to cover the provision of staff to operate these locks. All boats entering the canal must be licensed in accordance with the Board's Bye-Laws.

MOSTYN DOCK & RIVER DEE.
53°19'N 3°16'W.
Tel: (0745) 560335. Fax: (0745) 560324. Telex: 61245 MOSDOC.

Entry: for River Dee, Shotton, Connahs Quay. Best arrive 2-2½ h. before H.W. Liverpool at Dee Buoy. Vessels up to 5.6m draught can reach Mostyn at HW Springs.
Radio — Ports & Pilots:.VHF Chan. 16, 14. 2 h.-HW or by arrangement.
Entry Signals:
By day: Large square R. flag ⎤ no vessel
By night: R. Lt. ⎦ to enter·
Anchorage: In 9m. LWST at Dee By: SE Air By. NE Mostyn By.

Gutway to Mostyn marked by 4×Lt. F.R. W. ◊ in inner Hr. form leading line.
MOSTYN TRAINING WALL HEAD. Lt. Fl.R. 1.3 sec. 4M. B. mast, 8m.
OUTER. Lt. F.W. W. Pile also 3×F.R. Lts. shown from piles in channel.
Ldg.Lts. 215°40′ (Front) F.R. W. ◊ B. mast. 12m. (Rear) F.R. W. ◊ B. mast. 22m.
N TRAINING WALL. Lt. Fl.R. 3 sec. 6M. on outer end E of Flint.
S TRAINING WALL. Lt. 2 F.G. vert. 6M. near outer end of wall.

SUMMERSBY WHARF. Lt. F.R.
CONNAHS QUAY. Lt. 2 F.R. vert.
DEE No: 1. By. Sph. R.W.V.S. thence Dee No. 2, 3, 4, 5, 6, 7, 8, 9, 10 By. Sph. R.W.V.S. marking the channel from Mostyn to Flint.

LLANDDULAS 53°18′N 3°39′W. Tel: (0492) 514577. H.M. (0492) 518202. Telex: 61553.
Radio — Port: VHF Chan. 16, 14. 4 h.-HW only when vessels expected.
Anchorage: 2M. N of Llysfaen Jetty.

RIVER CLWYD
RHYL. BREAKWATER HEAD. Lt. Q.R. 2M. on Bn. 7m.
LLANDDULAS LLYSFAEN JETTY Lt. Fl.G. 10 sec.
LLANDDULAS R.&G. Berthing Sig. shown when vessels expected.

RAYNES JETTY. 53°16′N, 3°40′W. Tel: Port Manager (0492) 517564 (518093).
Radio — Port: VHF Chan. 16, 14. 4 h.-HW only when vessel expected.
RAYNES QUARRY JTY. HEAD. Lt. 2 F.G. vert.

OFFSHORE WAYPOINT CONWY BAY (GT. ORMES HD.). 53°20.0′N, 3°58.0′W.

GREAT ORMES HEAD. RG STN.
53°19′59″N, 3°51′10″W. Emergency DF Stn. VHF Chan. 16 & 67. Controlled by MRSC Holyhead.

COLWYN BAY
LLANDUDNO PIER HEAD. Lt. 2 F.G. vert. 4M. mast, 8m.
A F.R. Lt. shown under the G. when vessels cannot go alongside pier.

OUTFALL By. Conical Y marks outfall pipe 53°19′.78N 3°53′82W.

CONWAY RIVER Tel: HM. (0492) 596253.
N Wales Cruising Club (0492) 593481.

HARBOUR WAYPOINT 53°18.1′N 3°55.75′W.

Radio — Port: VHF Chan. 16, 6, 8, 12, 14, 72. M. Hr. 1 April-30 Sept. 0900-1700, 1 Oct.-31 Mar. Mon.-Fri. 0900-1700.
N Wales Cruising Club Chan. M.
MAJOR CONSTRUCTION WORKS. Contact HM. for overnight berthing.
Quays dry at half tide. Depth 1.5m. at MHWS. Bridges have min. vert. clearance 5.5m.
FAIRWAY By. Sph.R.W.V.S.
No: 1 By. Conical G.
No: 2 By. Can.R.
No: 3 By. Conical G.
No: 4 By. Can.R.
No: 5 By. Conical G.
No: 6 By. Can.R.

RIVER ENTRANCE, S SIDE. Lt.Bn. Fl.W.R. 5 sec. 2M. B. metal Col. 5m. W.076°-088°; R.088°-171°; W.171°-319°; R.319°-076°.

BEAUMARIS 53°16′N 4°05′W
Pilotage: For Pilot for NE entrance Menai Strait give usual signals to Coast Guard at Pennon Pt. before entering Strait or inform Caernarvon 2902. E.T.A. 12 h. and 2 h. in advance. VHF Chan. 16 for expected ships.
P/Station: Beaumaris.
Measured Distance: Menai Strait NE Entrance, ½M. Square posts 15m. and 21m. apart on foreshore. 065° and 245° (Mag.) S of Beaumaris opposite Bangor. 4m. high.

APPROACHES TO MENAI STRAIT — NORTH END

TEN FEET BANK By. Can.R.
DINMOR BANK By. Conical G. off Dinmor Pt.
PERCH ROCK Bn. R. Can.R. Topmark, 8m. at entce. to Strait.

MENAI STRAIT

INSHORE WAYPOINT PUFFIN ISLAND 53°19.4′N 4°01.5′W.

SEA TRAFFIC SEPARATION ROUTES

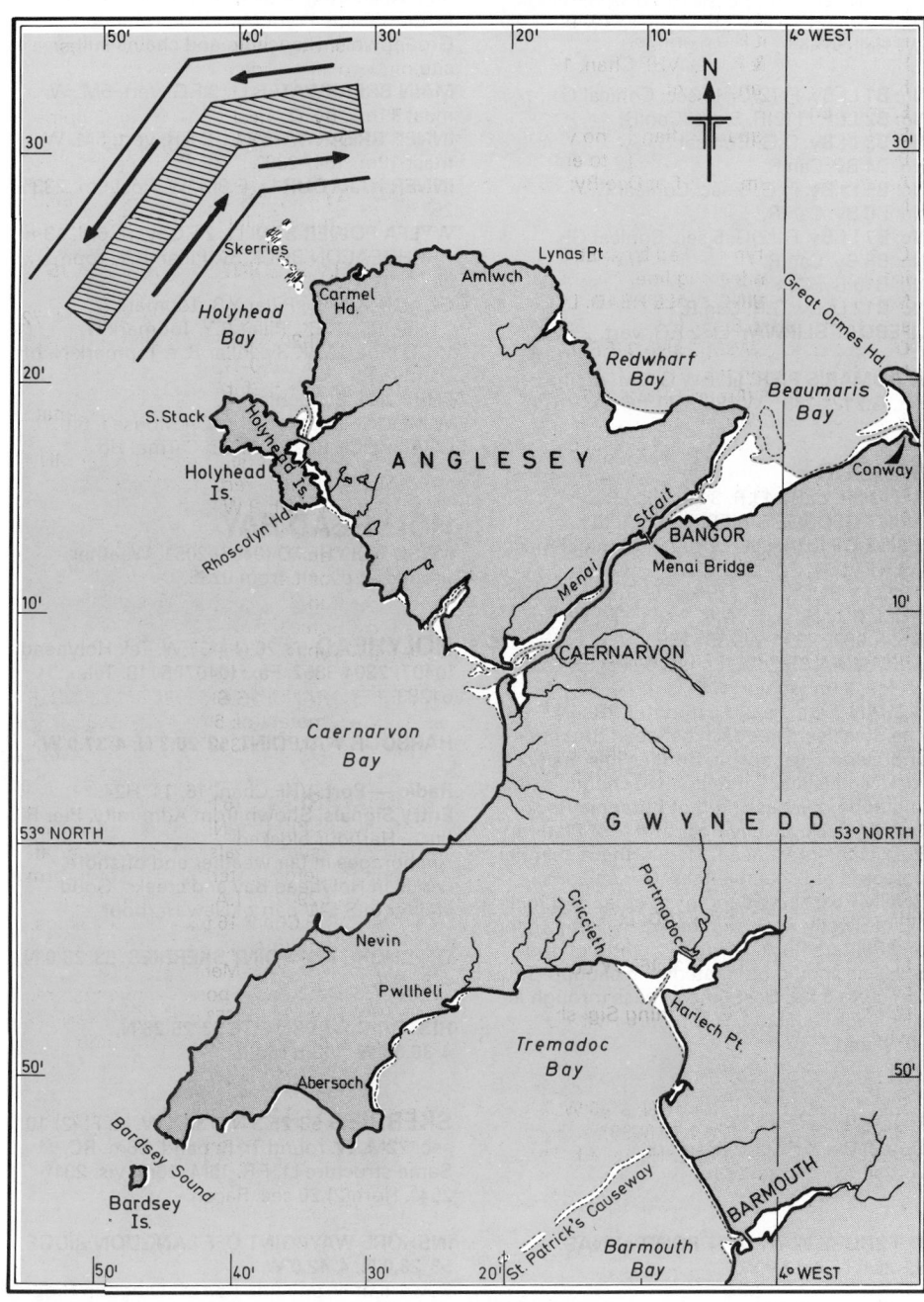

OFF SKERRIES, A SEPARATION ZONE 2M. WIDE IS CENTRED ON THE FOLLOWING POSITIONS:
(a) 53°22.8'N, 4°52.0'W; (b) 53°31.3'N, 4°41.7'W; (c) 53°32.1'N, 4°31.6'W.
A traffic lane 3M. wide on each side of separation zone.

TRWYN-DU 53°18.8'N, 4°02.4'W. Lt. Fl. 5.5 sec. 15M. W. round castellated Tr. B. bands, 19m. vis. 101°-023°. F.R. Lt. on radio mast 2M. SW Bell 30 sec.

No: B1 Lt.By. Fl.(2)G. 10 sec. Conical G.
No: B2 Lt.F. Fl.(2)R. 5 sec. Can.R.
No: B3 Lt.By. Q.G. Conical G.
No: B4 By. Can.R.
No: B5 Lt.By. Fl.G. 5 sec. Conical G.
No: B6 By. Can.R.
No: B7 Lt.By. Fl.(2)G. 5 sec. Conical G.
No: B8 By. Can R.
No: B10 By. Can.R.
No: B12 Lt.By. Q.R. Can.R.
LIFEBOAT SLIPWAY. Lt. 2 F.G. vert.

BEAUMARIS PIER. Lt. F.W.G. 6M. on mast, 5m. G.212°-286°; W.286°-041°; G.041°-071°.

BANGOR

BANGOR. Lt.By. Fl.R. 3 sec. Can.R.
SAINT GEORGE'S PIER. Lt. Fl.G. 10 sec.
E SIDE OF CHANNEL. Lt. Q.R. R. metal mast, 4m. vis. 064°-222°.
SWELLY ROCK. By. Conical G. Topmark 'SR'.
PRICE POINT. Lt. Fl.W.R. 2 sec. 3M. W. Bn. 5m. R.059°-239°; W.239°-259°.
BRITANNIA BRIDGE. Lt. Iso. 5 sec. SE span of bridge, 27m. above HW.
S CHAN. Ldg.Lts. 231°. (Front) F. (Rear) F.
The Swellies: The reach between Britannia and Menai Suspension Bridges has many rocks and islets. There are two channels, the southerly one passing S of Britannia Rock, Cribbin Rock, Swelly Rock and N of Platters Rock is the most used. The northern channel passes N of Britannia Rock, Gored Goch, Swelly Rock, between Ynys Beulas and rocks NE of Swelly Rock, and between Careg Halen and Platters Rock. Navigation through the Swellies should be treated with caution. Tides run up to 8 kts. Best time to pass through is HW Slack i.e. about 1½ h. before HW Holyhead.

REDWHARF BAY

Outfall Bn. Y. Pole ◊ Topmark.
Outfall By. Conical G.

OFFSHORE WAYPOINT POINT LYNAS.
53°28.0'N, 4°17.0'W.

POINT LYNAS 53°25.0'N, 4°17.3'W. Lt. Oc. 10 sec. 20M. W. castellated Tr. 39m. vis. 109°-315°. Horn 45 sec. Fog Detr. Lt.F. 213° 16M. R.C. Shown H24.
PILOT STN. JETTY Lt. 2 F.R. vert.

AMLWCH HARBOUR Available all states of tide. Anchoring and Fishing in vicinity of former Single Point Mooring prohibited. Groundwork of anchors and chains still in situ.
MAIN BREAKWATER Lt. 2 F.G. vert. 5M. W. mast 11m. 141°-271°.
INNER BREAKWATER Lt. 2 F.R. vert. 5M. W. mast 12m. 164°-239°.
INNER HARBOUR Lt. F. 8M. W. Post 9m. 233°-257°.
WYLFA POWER STN. Lt. 2 F.G. vert. 6M. 13m.
ARCHDEACON ROCK By. Pillar. B.Y. Topmark N.
COAL ROCK By. Pillar Y.B. Topmark S.
ETHEL ROCK By. Pillar B.Y. Topmark N.
VICTORIA BANK By. Pillar B.Y. Topmark N. off Camlyn Pt.
FURLONG By. Conical G.
W MOUSE Bn. W. globe. On Mouse I. 6m.
COAL ROCK Bns. 2 W., on Carmel Hd.

HOLYHEAD BAY

MRSC HOLYHEAD (0407) 2051. Weather broadcast ev. 4h. from 0235.

HOLYHEAD 53°20'N 4°37'W. Tel: Holyhead (0407) 2304/3852. Fax: (0407) 5118. Telex: 61283.

HARBOUR WAYPOINT. 53°20.3'N, 4°37.0'W.

Radio — Port: VHF Chan. 16, 14. H24.
Entry Signals: Shown from Admiralty. Pier R. Lts. = Harbour blocked.
Anchorages in fair weather and offshore winds in Holyhead Bay and creeks. Good shelter in S/SW part of New Harbour.

OFFSHORE WAYPOINT SKERRIES. 53°28.0'N, 4°37.0'W.

HISTORIC WRECK SITE 53°25.26'N, 4°36.66'W. 100m radius.

SKERRIES 53°25.3'N 4°36.4'W. Lt. Fl.(2) 10 sec. 22M. W. round Tr. R. band, 36m. RC. Same structure Lt. F.R. 16M. 26m. vis. 231°-254°. Horn(2) 20 sec. Racon.

INSHORE WAYPOINT OFF LANGDON RIDGE. 53°23.0'N, 4°42.0'W.
Beware of strong tide rips off Langdon Ridge.

LANGDON Lt.By. Q.(9) 15 sec. Pillar Y.B.Y. Topmark W.
BOLIVAR OR FENWICK ROCK By. Conical G. off S Porthwan Pt. in Church Bay.

WRECK. Lt.By. Fl.(2)R. 10 sec. Can.R.
CLIPERA ROCKS. Lt.By. Fl.(2)R. 15 sec. Can.R.
〰 Bell w.a.

HOLYHEAD NEW HARBOUR

BREAKWATER HEAD 53°19.8'N,
4°37.1'W. Lt.Ho. Fl.(3) 15 sec. 14M. W. square

stone Tr. B. band, 21m. F.R. Lt. on chimney
2M. SSE Siren 20 sec.
NE PLATTERS. Lt.By. Fl.(4)R. 15 sec. Can.R.
E PLATTERS. By. Conical G.
NW PLATTERS By. Can.R.
SKINNER. By. Conical G.

OLD HARBOUR APPROACH
YNYS HALEN (SALT ISLAND). Lt. Fl.Y. 3 sec.
PIEBIO ROCKS. By. Can.R.

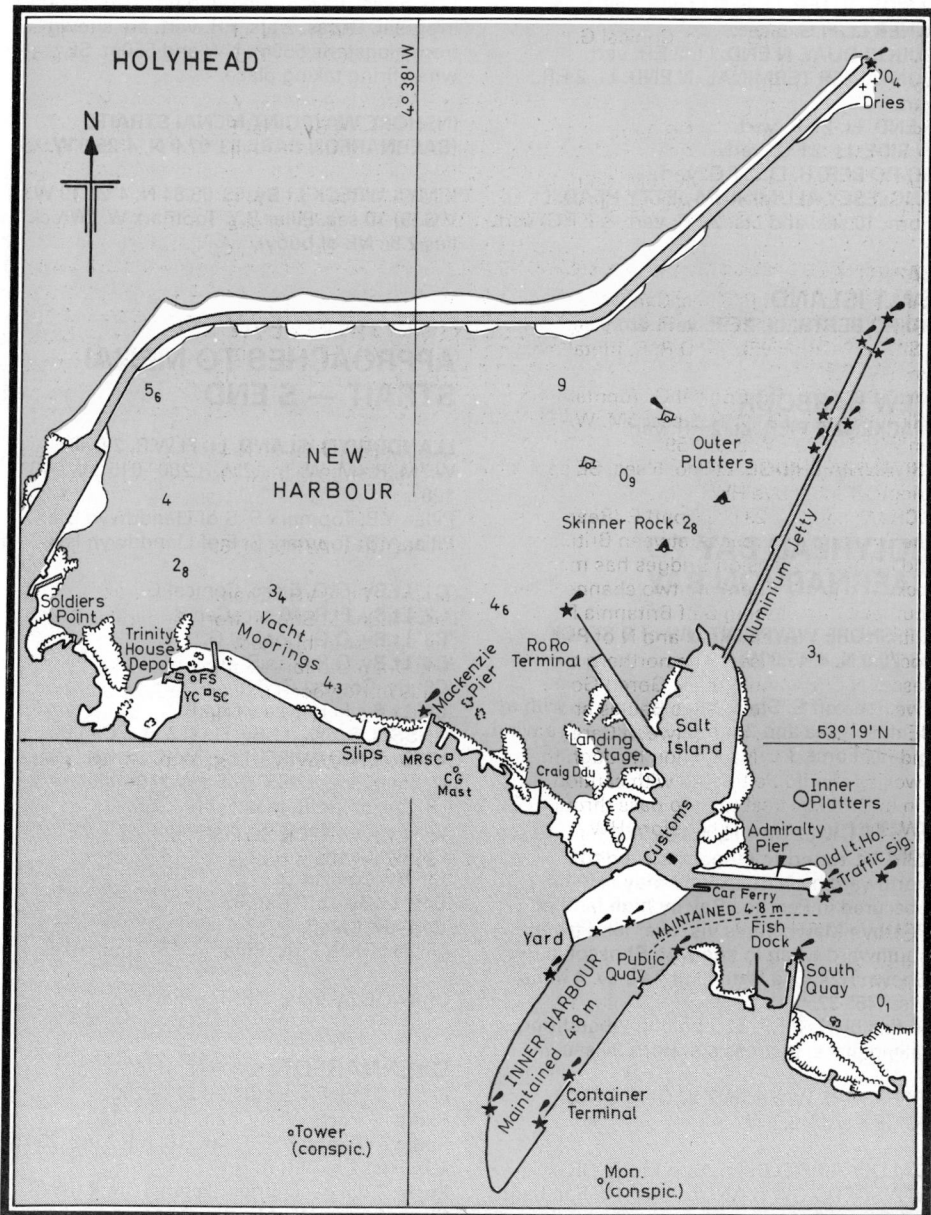

OLD HARBOUR
ADMIRALTY PIER DOLPHIN. Lt. 2 F.G. vert.
Bell. 1 sec.
ADMIRALTY PIER HEAD. Lt. F.R. 1M. W.Tr. 7m.
Vis. 184°-188° and Traffic Signal Lt. F.W.
shows R. when entrance impracticable.
S SPUR. Lt. 2 F.G. vert.
S QUAY. Lt. 2 F.R. vert.

INNER HARBOUR
N SIDE OUTER. Lt. Fl.G. 3 sec. Bell. 5 sec.
INNER Lt. Fl.G. 5 sec.
PUBLIC QUAY. N END. Lt. 2 F.R. vert.
CONTAINER TERMINAL. N END. Lt. 2 F.R.
vert.
S END. Lt. 2 F.R. vert.
W SIDE. Lt. 2 F.G. vert.
RO-RO BERTH. Lt. 2 F.G. vert.
ANGLESEY ALUMINIUM JETTY HEAD. Lt. Q.
Horn. 10 sec. and Lts. 2 F.R. vert. & 2 F.G. vert.

SALT ISLAND
RO-RO BERTH. Lt. 2 F.R. vert. 4m.

NEW HARBOUR
MACKENZIE PIER. Lt. 2 F.R. vert.

HOLYHEAD BAY TO CAERNARVON BAY

OFFSHORE WAYPOINT NW of S STACK.
53°20.0′N, 4°45.0′W.

The Race off S. Stack can reach 6 kts, with a
confused sea and 2m high breakers in a wind
of only Force 3.

S STACK 53°18.4′N, 4°41.9′W. Lt. Fl. 10 sec.
28M. W. round Tr. 60m. Obscured to
northward by N Stack, and may also be
obscured in Penrhos Bay by high land of
Penrhyn Mawr, but is vis. over land from
southward when in line with Rhoscolyn Bn.
Shown H24. Fog Detr. Lt. 4-7 Fl. ev. 4 mins.
Vis. 145°-325°.
R. flag by Day, F.R. Lt. at night, when firing
taking place. Distress sig. Horn 30 sec.

OFFSHORE WAYPOINT W OF S STACK
53°18.4′N 4°45.2′W.

VALLEY AIRFIELD. Lt. Aero Mo.(VY)R.
YNYSOEDD GWYLANOD Bn. R.W. hor. bands,
off Rhoscolyn.

OFFSHORE WAYPOINT WSW OF
RHOSCOLYN HEAD. 53°13.0′N, 4°46.0′W.

PORT TRECASTELL
An inlet 1½M. N of Ynys Meibion giving good
anchorage for small craft except with wind
SW-W.

YNYS MEIBION. 53°11.4′N, 4°30.2′W. Lt.
Fl.R. 5 sec. 10M. Tr. on building, 37m. Period
irregular. Occas. 2 Lts. F.R. vert. are shown
from Flagstaffs 550m. NW and 550m. SE
when firing taking place.

INSHORE WAYPOINT MENAI STRAITS
(CAERNARFON BAR). 53°07.0′N, 4°25.0′W.

KIMYA WRECK Lt.By. 53°08.84′N, 4°28.19′W.
V.Q.(9) 10 sec. Pillar B.Y. Topmark W. (Wreck
lies 2.5c NE of buoy).

APPROACHES TO MENAI STRAIT — S END

LLANDDWYN ISLAND. Lt. Fl.W.R. 2.5 sec.
W.7M. R.4M. W. Tr. 12M. R.280°-015°; W.015°-
120°.
Pillar. Y.B. Topmark S. S of Llanddwyn Isle.
Pillar. Y.B. Topmark S. E of Llanddwyn Isle.

'C1' Lt.By. Fl.G. 5 sec. Conical G.
'C2' Lt.By. Fl.R. 10 sec. Can.R.
'C3' Lt.By. Q.G. Conical G.
'C4' Lt.By. Q.R. Can.R.
'C5' By. Conical G.
'C6' Lt.By. Fl.R. 5 sec. Can.R.
MUSSEL BANK. Lt.By. Fl.(2) 5 sec. Can.R.
ABERMENAI POINT. Lt. Fl.W.R. 3.5 sec. 3M.
W. mast, 6m. R.065°-245°; W.245°-065°.
F.R. Lts. on radio mast 6.8M. SSE.
'C7' By. Conical G.
'C8' By. Can.R.
'C9' By. Conical G.
'C10' Lt.By. Q.R. Can.R.
'C12' By. Can.R.
AFON SEIONT. By. Pillar. B.Y.B. Topmark E.

CHANGE By Pillar Y.B. Topmark S.

CAERNARFON 53°09′N, 4°16′W. Tel:
(0286) 2118. Pilots: (0286) 2772/2902.
Radio — Ports: VHF Chan. 16, 12, 14.
Radio — Pilots: VHF Chan. 16. MF 2182, 2301
kHz. Hrs: 2 h. before H.W.,
Entry: Tidal basin dries. Depth 4.3m. MHWS.
Swing bridge W of Castle. 3 F.G. vert. = bridge

open. 3 F.R. vert. = bridge closed. Request for bridge to open = 1 long and 3 short blasts. Channel to Port Dinorwic generally depth 7m. but bar with least depth of 1.5m. (2.3m. within buoyed channel).
Measured Mile: Menai Strait (SW end) 2 pairs bns. No: C9 Con. B. buoy near centre of the run. 070°-250° (Mag.) 1M. below. Port Dinorwic. S Bn. is seaward of Llantair Ch. Belfry and the N end is in line with St. Mary's Church.

PILE PIER HEAD. Lt. 2 F.G. vert. 2M. W. Tr. B. stripes, 5m.
S PIER. Lt. 2 F.G. vert. 2M.

BUOYAGE DIRECTION REVERSED ABOVE CAERNARFON

'C13' By. Conical G.
'C11' By. Conical G.
'C14' By. Can.R.
'C9' By. Conical G.

HISTORIC WRECK SITE MENAI STRAIT 53°12.77'N, 4°11.72'W. 150m. radius.

PORT DINORWIC 53°11'N, 4°13'W.
Menai Marina Tel: (0248) 670441. VHF Chan. (M) 0800-1700.
Raybourne Marina. Tel: (0248) 670658.
Entry: Tidal basin dries, depth 4.3m. MHWS. Vaynol Dock (Marina) access 3 h.-HW-3 h. Max. 50m. × 4.6m. draught.

PIER HEAD. Lt. F.W.R. 2M. on post, 5m. R.225°-357°; W.357°-225°.
Lt.By. Fl.R. Can.R.
Lt.By. Fl.R. Can.R.

MENAI STRAIT TO BARDSEY ISLAND

Poole Lt. By. Fl.Y. 6 sec. Sph. Y. (April-Oct.).
CAREG-Y-CHWISLEN Bn.R. mast and globe.

PORTH DINLLEYN
Extensive yacht moorings including 6 for visitors. Max. draught 2.4m. Speed limit 8 kts in summer. Craft that can ground may find berth clear of private moorings.

HARBOUR WAYPOINT 52°57.3'N 4°34.2'W.

PORTH DINLLEYN Lt. F. R. on Point.

INSHORE WAYPOINT WNW OF THE TRIPODS
52°50.3'N 4°48.4'W.

CARDIGAN BAY
About 20 Target, mooring, marker buoys exist within 20M. of Peneribach. Some are lit.

OFFSHORE WAYPOINT W OF BARDSEY.
52°46.3'N, 4°51.5'W.

INSHORE WAYPOINT BARDSEY SOUND
52°46.8'N 4°48.7'W.
Note: Tide through Bardsey Sound runs at 5-6 knots.

OFFSHORE WAYPOINT S OF BARDSEY.
52°41.0'N, 4°52.5'W.

BARDSEY ISLAND; 52°45.0'N, 4°47.9'W.
Lt. Fl.(5) 15 sec. 26M. W. square Tr. R. bands, 39m. Horn Mo(N) 45 sec. Obscured by Bardsey I. 198°-250° and in Tremadoc Bay when bearing less than 260°. RC.

MYNYDD RHIW RG STN. 52°49'58"0N 4°37'45"0W. Emergency DF Stn. VHF Chan. 16 & 67. Controlled by MRSC Holyhead.

ST TUDWAL'S W ISLAND 52°47.9'N, 4°28.2'W. Lt. Fl.W.R. 20 sec. W.15M. R.13M. W. round Tr. 46m. W.349°-169°; R.169°-221°; W.221°-243°; R.243°-259°; W.259°-293°; R.293°-349°. Obscured by E Island 211°-231°. CARREG-Y-TRAI By. Can.R. Bell off SE part of S Tudwal's E Island.
TREMADOC BAY YACHT RACING By. Sph.Or. (May-Oct.).

INSHORE WAYPOINT SE OF ST. TUDWALS ISLAND 52°45.3'N 4°25.0'W.

ABERSOCH.
South Caernarfonshire Yacht Club. Tel: (075881) 2338. VHF Ch. M.
Visitors moorings 3c. SE of Y.C. Max. length 11m.

PWLLHELI. Tel: (0758) 3131.

HARBOUR WAYPOINT. 52°52.5'N, 4°22.5'W.

Entry: Bar and outer harbour dredged to 3m. Access 3 h.-HW-3 h. Max. 13.7m. × 1.8m. draught.
Visitors moorings available. Tidal stream Spring tides max. 3½ knots flood, 2 knots ebb.

OUTER No: 1 Lt.By. Q.G. Conical G.

APPROACH CHANNEL
No: 1 By. Conical G.
No: 2 By. Can.R.
No: 3 By. Conical G.
No: 4 By. Can.R.
No: 6 By. Can.R.
No: 8 By. Can.R.

GIMLET ROCK Bn. ball on S edge of shoal on N side of Pwllheli Hr.

CRIB GROYNE Lt. Q.R.
TRAINING ARM HEAD Lt. Q.G.
SEWER OUTFALL Lt. Fl. R. 2½ sec.
CHANNEL N. SIDE Lt. Fl.G. 2½ sec.
CHANNEL N. SIDE Lt. Fl.G. 5 sec.
CHANNEL N. SIDE Lt. Fl.G. 10 sec.
MARINA SE END Lt. 2 F.G. vert.
MARINA SW END Lt. 2 F.G. vert.

PORTHMADOG Tel: H.M. (0766) 512927.
Pilot: (0766) 75684.

HARBOUR WAYPOINT. 52°52.75′N, 4°11.0′W.

Radio — Port & Pilots: VHF Chan. 16, 12, 14. 0900-1715 when manned.
MADOC YACHT CLUB Chan. (M) and Chan. 16 when club open.
Entry: Yachts 12.2m. × 2.1m. draught at HWS. Craft able to take ground should berth alongside Madoc Y.C. If draught 1m. enter/leave 2½ h.-HW-2½ h. If draught nearly 3m. then enter/leave at HW. Contact H.M. in advance because of restricted and changeable approach conditions.
Anchorage: Porthmadog Fairway By. or St Tudwal's Roads.

FAIRWAY Lt.By. L.Fl. 10 sec. Pillar.

No: 1 By. Conical G.
No: 2 By. Can.R.
No: 3 By. Conical G.
No: 4 By. Can.R.
No: 5 By. Conical G.
No: 6 By. Cylindrical R.
No: 7 By. Conical G.

Chan. changes owing to shifting sands. Bys. at Porthmadog changed at short notice.

SHELL ISLAND. Lt. Fl.W.R.G. 4 sec. G.079°-124°; W.124°-134°; R.134°-179°. Shown 15.3-30/11.
MOCHRAS LAGOON. Sandy inlet, dries. Yachts can anchor in lagoon clear of

channels. Moorings available, Max. 12m. × 1m. draught, in the boat harbour.

INSHORE WAYPOINT SW OF CAUSEWAY.
52°40.0′N, 4°30.0′W.

CAUSEWAY Lt.By. Q.(9) 15 sec. Pillar. Y.B.Y. Topmark W. ᔓ Bell w.a. off W Prong of St Patrick's Causeway.

INSHORE WAYPOINT S OF SOUTH PRONG
52°40.5′N 4°20.0′W.

DIFFUSER SEWER. Lt.By. Fl.Y. 5 sec. Conical Y.
BARMOUTH OUTER Lt.By. L.Fl. 10 sec. Sph. R.W.V.S.
BAR By. Can.R.
No: 2 By. Can.R.
NORTH BANK Y PERCH Lt.Bn. Q.R. 5M. R. Tr. 4m.

HISTORIC WRECK SITE BARMOUTH 52°46.68′N, 4°07.4′W. 150m. radius.

BARMOUTH 52°43′N, 4°03′W. Tel: H.M.
(0341) 280671. Pilots: (0341) 250461.

HARBOUR WAYPOINT. 52°42.5′N, 4°05′W.

Radio — Port: VHF Chan. 16, 12. April-Sept. 0900-1700. Oct.-March 0900-1600.
Entry: Enter 3 h.-HW-2 h. but best time 1½ h.-HW. Visitors moorings available. Hr. Dries. Depth 3.8m. MHWS. Bar depth 0.3m. but changes considerably. Sea state and wind speeds for area 1M. off harbour available. Vessels over 14m LOA require special berthing arrangements.

YNYS Y BRAWD SE End Lt. Fl.R. 5 sec. 5M.
BREAKWATER SE W. post.
BREAKWATER, OFF SE END W. pole covered at certain times by tide.
BRIDGE. Lt. 2 F.R. Hor. NW End.
Additional Lts. shown by pilots at Barmouth when taking vessels into Hr.

INSHORE WAYPOINT W OF SARN-Y-BWCH.
52°35.0′N, 4°15.4′W.

SARN-Y-BWCH By. Pillar. Y.B.Y. Topmark W. PEN BWCH Bn. W. ◊, N of R. Dovey entce. By. Pillar. Y.B.Y. Topmark W.

ABERDOVEY 52°33′N, 4°02′W. Tel:
(065472) 626.

HARBOUR WAYPOINT. 52°31.75′N, 4°07.0′W.

Radio — Port: VHF Chan. 16, 12. 0900-1700 or as required by tide.
Safety: Inshore rescue boat.
Entry: Heavy silting reported E of Jetty. Aberdovey bar least depth 0.7m. Visiting yachts wait until half tide before entering. Max. 61m. × 4.6m. draught at HW.

OUTER FAIRWAY By. Sph. R.W.V.S.
BAR By. Conical G.
SOUTH PIT By. Conical G.
INNER By. Conical G.
The above Bys. at Aberdovey are shifted from time to time to meet changes in chan.
PATCHES By. Pillar Y.B.Y. Topmark W. off W edge of Cynfelin Patches.

INSHORE WAYPOINT E OF CYNFELIN PATCHES. 52°25.2′N, 4°18.5′W.

BORTH
Aber Leri Boatyard.

ABERYSTWYTH 52°24′N, 4°06′W. Tel: Hbr. Office: (0970) 611433. C.G.: (0970) 612220.

HARBOUR WAYPOINT. 52°24.5′N, 4°06.0′W.

Entry: Local knowledge essential. Tidal. Dries at L.W. suitable for craft able to take the ground. With up to 1m. draught can cross bar from 4 h.-HW-4 h. Flood tide flows 5 h. 30 min. and ebb tide 7 h. 00 min.
Anchorage: In fine weather about ½M. from S Pier in 9.5m. LW.

S BREAKWATER HEAD 52°24.4′N, 4°05.4′W. Lt. Fl.(2)W.G. 10 sec. 10M. B. metal col. 12m. G.030°-053°; W.053°-210°. 4 Lts. F.R. vert. on radio Tr. 2.8M. S.
Ldg.Lts. 138°. (Front) F.R. 5M. W. lantern, 4m. (Rear) F.R. 6M. W. post, 7m.
TIMBER JETTY HEAD Lt.Bn. Q.W.R. 4M. Metal Col. 9m. W.244°-141°; R.141°-175°.
Lt.By. Q.R. Y. Radar Target (P.A.)
Several lit and unlit Bys. and targets within 1M. radius.

ABERAERON 52°14′N, 4°16′W. Tel: Aberaeron 407.
Entry: Local knowledge necessary for entering.
S PIER. Lt. Fl.(3)G. 10 sec. 6M. 125°-200°.
N PIER. Lt. Fl.(4)R. 15 sec. 6M. 104°-178°.

NEW QUAY 52°13.0′N, 4°21.0′W.

HARBOUR WAYPOINT. 52°14.0′N, 4°21.0′W.
Entry: Hr. dries. Draught 2m. HWS. Visitors moorings in the bay.
NEW QUAY. By. Pillar B.Y. Topmark N.
PIER HEAD Lt. Fl.W.G. 3 sec. W.8M. R.5M. 12m. W.135°-252°; G.252°-295°.

CARDIGAN C.G. BUILDING Lt. 2 F.R. vert on wall. Lt. Fl.(2) 5 sec. 8 on B.R. Bn.

CARDIGAN

HARBOUR WAYPOINT. 52°07.75′N, 4°44.0′W.

Entry: Depths of 0.3m. over bar. Caution when crossing the bar, seas break especially on Spring ebb. Visitors moorings (mostly dry). Max. 12m. × 1.1m. draught.
AFON TYWI. Overhead cable safe clearance 7.4m.
CARDIGAN BRIDGE Lt. Iso.Y. 2 sec. Shown on up and downstream sides of bridge.
Aberporth Weather Forecast Stn. close N of Cardigan I.
CEMAES HEAD. Lt.By. Fl.(3) 20 sec. Sph. R.W.V.S.
PARROG HR. (for Newport). Mainly dries. Craft 9m. × 1.3m. draught at MHWS. Visitors moorings available.

CARDIGAN TO MILFORD HAVEN

WRECK. Lt.By. Q. Pillar. Topmark N.
WRECK. Lt.By. Q.(6)+L.Fl. 15 sec. Pillar. Topmark S.
Lt.By. Fl.(5)Y. 20 sec. Sph. Y. 52°10′N, 5°05′W.

FISHGUARD HARBOUR 52°01′N, 4°58′W. Tel: Fishguard (0348) 872881. Telex: 48167.

HARBOUR WAYPOINT. 52°02.0′N, 4°57.0′W.

Radio — Port & Pilots: VHF Chan. 16, 14 — continuous.
Fishguard Yacht Boat Co. (0348) 873377 Chan. M.
Fishguard Boat Yard (0348) 874590.
Anchorage: Fishguard Bay.

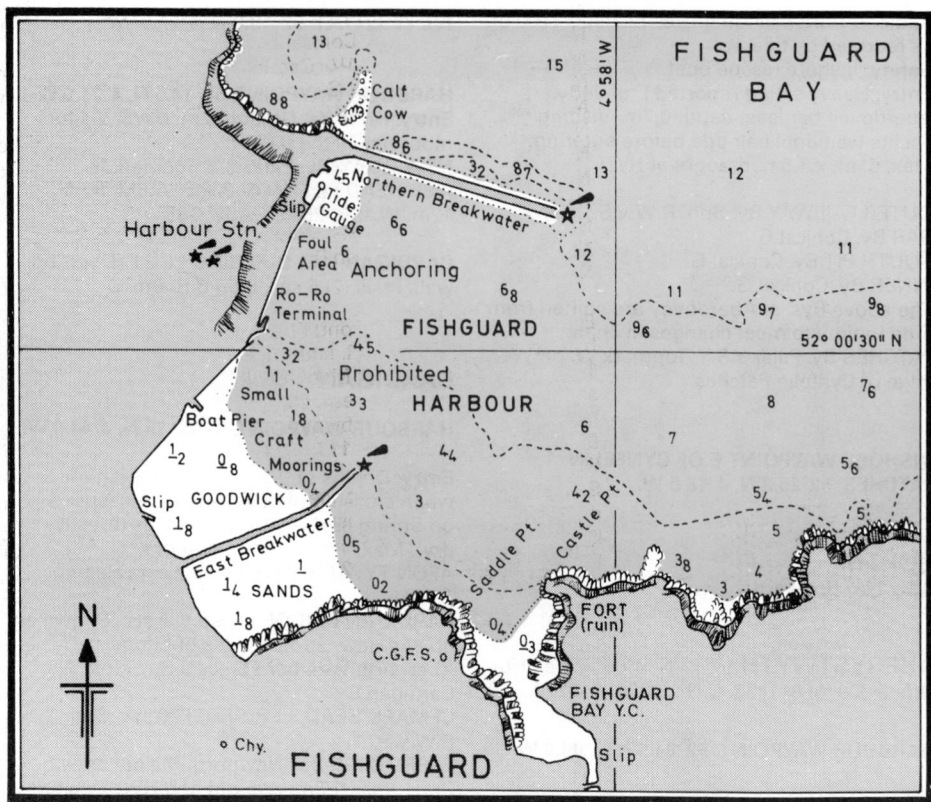

Entry: some visitors moorings at Aber Gwaun. Some yacht moorings in S part of Hr. Town — top of inlet dries. Depth 3m. at MHWS.

NORTHERN BREAKWATER HEAD.
52°00.7′N, 4°58.1′W. Lt. Fl.G. 5 sec. 13M. octagonal concrete Tr. 18m. Bell 10 sec.
E BREAKWATER HEAD Lt. Fl.R. 3 sec. 5M. metal framework Tr. 10m.
Ldg.Lts. 282°. (Front) F.G. 5M. W. ◊ on W. mast, 77m. (Rear) F.G. 5M. W. ◊ on W. mast, 89m.
PEN ANGLAS Bn. W., 4m. Dia. (2) 60 sec.

OFFSHORE WAYPOINT W OF STRUMBLE HEAD. 52°04.5′N, 5°17.5′W.

STRUMBLE HEAD 52°01.8′N, 5°04.3′W.
Lt. Fl.(4) 15 sec. 29M. W. round Tr. 45m. vis. 038°-257°. Shown H24.
Note: Tide reported at 6 kts. 1M. N of Strumble Head at Springs.

STRUMBLE HEAD TO MILFORD HAVEN

OFFSHORE WAYPOINT W OF S BISHOP.
51°51.0′N, 5°26.0′W.

S BISHOP 51°51.1′N, 5°24.6′W. Lt. Fl. 5 sec. 24M. W. round Tr. 44m. RC. Distress sig. Horn (3) 45 sec. H24.

OFFSHORE WAYPOINT S OF S BISHOP.
51°49.3′N, 5°24.5′W.

SOLVA.

HARBOUR WAYPOINT. 51°51.8′N, 5°11.5′W.

Only suitable for small craft. W. steel posts 2m. high have been erected. Post placed on each of islets at entce. N magnetic leads into Hr. keeping westernmost islet Black Rock a little to W which is the deeper water. Visitors moorings are available. Depths 5m. at MHWS. Hr. dries out.

ST. BRIDES BAY. Research area marked by Lt.Bys. (unreliable).
'B1' Lt.By. Fl.(4)Y. 10 sec. Can. Y.
'B2' Lt.By. Fl.Y. 20 sec. Conical Y.
'B3-B6' Lt.Bys. Fl.Y. 15 sec. Pillar Y.
'A1' Lt.By. Fl.(4)Y. 20 sec. Can. Y.
'A2' Lt.By. Fl.Y. 10 sec. Conical Y.
'A3-A6' Lt.Bys. Fl.Y. 15 sec. Pillar Y.
BRAWDY. Lt. Aero Mo.(BY)R. occas.

BROADHAVEN BAY

HARBOUR WAYPOINT. 51°47.2'N, 5°07.7'W.

APPROACHES TO BRISTOL CHANNEL

SMALLS 51°43.2'N, 5°40.1'W. Lt. Fl.(3) 15 sec. 25M. W. round Tr. R. bands. 38m. Racon. Same structure Lt. F.R. 13M. 33m. vis. 253°-285° over Hats and Barrels Rk. Horn(2) 60 sec.

OFFSHORE WAYPOINT NW OF SKOMER ISLAND. 51°45.3'N, 5°21.25'W.

SKOKHOLM ISLAND, SW END
51°41.6'N, 5°17.1'W. Lt. Fl.R. 10 sec. 17M. W. octagonal Tr. 54m. Partially obscured 226°-258°. Distress sig. Horn 15 sec. Shown H24.

OFFSHORE WAYPOINT SW OF SKOKHOLM ISLAND. 51°41.0'N, 5°18.0'W.

MILFORD HAVEN APPROACHES

MRSC MILFORD HAVEN. (06465) 218. Weather broadcast ev. 4h. from 0335.

MILFORD HAVEN 51°43'N, 5°03'W. Signal StationTel: (0646) 692342/3. Telex: 48575. H.M. Tel: (0646) 693091.

HARBOUR WAYPOINT. 51°40.5'N, 5°10.5'W.

Radio — Port: VHF Chan. 11, 12, 14, 16 — continuous. Radar surveillance.
B'casts: Local Weather Chan. 12, 14. 0300, 0900, 1500, 2100. Movement F'casts Chan 12. 0800-0830, 2000-2030.

ST GEORGE'S AND BRISTOL CHANNEL APPROACHES SEA TRAFFIC SEPARATION ROUTES

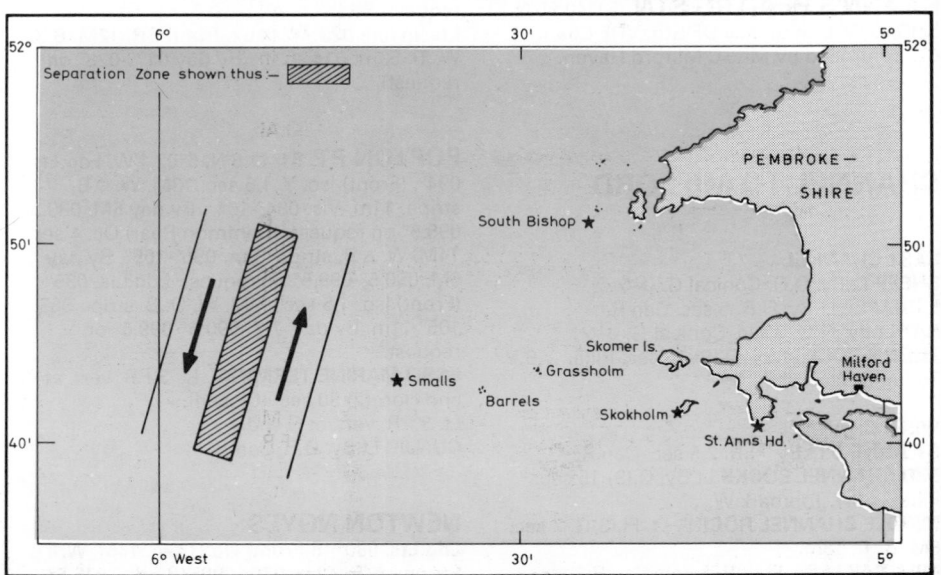

Northbound lane 3M. wide.   Separation zone 2M. wide.   Southbound lane 3M. wide.
Centre-line of separation zone centred on position 51°45'N., 5°53'W.
Tankers or any vessel over 500GRT must not use inshore traffic zone between The Smalls and Grassholm.

Harbour Patrol. VHF Chan. 12, 11 — continuous.
Call Milford Haven on app. and maintain listening watch for all navigational, shipping, tidal and weather information. Weather forecast Bristol Channel 0635, 1835.
Milford Docks. Tel. (0646) 692271. Telex: 48237. Chan. 9, 12, 14, 16. Hrs. 2 h.-HW.
Pembroke Dock. VHF Chan. 13. 0730-2300.
Radio — Pilots: VHF Chan. 16, 12 — also MF. 2182, 2241, 2246, 2301 kHz. H24.
Entry Signals: Milford Dock. 2 G. Lts. vert. or Bl. flag E side of lock — entry permitted. (In special cases when vessel allowed to pass out before entry signal shown, a second R. Lt. shown above R. Lt. on W Pier.)
Mariners are reminded that extremely large tankers manoeuvre in this port and must be given maximum sea room. Vessels restricted by their draught will sound 1 long, 2 short blasts in poor visibility and also show 3 R. Lts. (vert.) or a cylinder.
Anchorages: Dale Roads, Stack, Sandy Haven. Good shelter any time, any wind.

ST ANN'S HEAD 51°40.9′N, 5°10.4′W. Lt.
Fl.W.R. 5 sec. W.23M. R.22M. R.19M. W. octagonal Tr. 48m. W.230°-247°; R.247°-285°; R.(intens) 285°-314°; R.314°-332°; W.332°-124°; W.129°-131°. Ra. Horn(2) 60 sec.

ST ANN'S HEAD RG STN. 51°40.95′N,
5°10.55′W. Emergency DF Stn. VHF Chan. 16, 67. Controlled by MRSC Milford Haven.

CHANNEL TO MILFORD

EAST CHANNEL
SHEEP Lt.By. Q.G. Conical G. ᗡᗡ.
E CHAPEL Lt.By. Fl.R. 5 sec. Can.R.
RAT Lt.By. Fl.G. 5 sec. Conical G. ᗡᗡ.
THORN ROCK Lt.By. Q.(9) 15 sec. Pillar. Y.B.Y. Topmark W.

WEST CHANNEL
ST ANNE'S Lt.By. Fl.R. 2.5 sec. Can.R.
MID CHANNEL ROCKS Lt.By. Q.(9) 15 sec. Pillar. Y.B.Y. Topmark W.
MIDDLE CHANNEL ROCKS. Lt. Fl.(3)G. 7 sec. 8M. B. Tr. 18m.
MILL BAY Lt.By. Fl.(2)R. 5 sec. Can.R.
W CHAPEL Lt.By. Fl.G. 10 sec. Conical G.
W BLOCKHOUSE POINT. Lt. Q.W.R. W.9M. R.7M. R.W. Tr. 21m. W.220°-250°; R.250°-020°; W.020°-036°; R.036°-049°.

ANGLE Lt.By. V.Q. Pillar. B.Y. Topmark N.
W BLOCKHOUSE POINT. Ldg.Lts. 022°30′ (Front) F. 13M. B. ▯ W. Stripe. W. Tr. 004.5°-040.5° (By day on request).
WATWICK POINT. Lt. (Rear) F. 15M. B. ▯ W. stripe. 80m. 013.5°-031.5° (By day on request).
DALE FORT. Lt. Fl.(2) W.R. 5 sec. W.5M. R.3M. Col. 20m. R.222°-276°; W.276°-019°.
DALE ROADS. Lt.By. Fl.Y. 2.5 sec. mooring by. Y. marks 200m. prohibited area for anchoring or fishing.
DAKOTIAN. Lt.By. Q.(3) 10 sec. Pillar. B.Y.B Topmark E.
GREAT CASTLE HEAD. Lt. F. W.R.G. W.5M. R.3M. G.3M. W.B. Tr. 27m. R.243°-281°; G.281°-299°; W.299°-029°.
Ldg.Lts. 039°45′ (Front) Oc. 4 sec. 15M. Same structure 27m. 031.2°-048.2° (By day 032.2°-047.2° on request).
LITTLE CASTLE HEAD. Lt. (Rear) Oc. 8 sec. 15M. W. ▯ B. stripe. W. Tr. 53m. 031.2°-048.2° (By day 032.2°-047.2° on request).
BEHAR. By. Pillar. Y.B. Topmark S.
MONTREAL ROCK. By. Pillar. Y.B. Topmark S.
CHAPEL. Lt.By. Fl.G. 5 sec. Conical G.
STACK. Lt.By. Fl.R. 2.5 sec. Can.R.
S HOOK Lt.By. Q.(6)+L.Fl. 15 sec. Pillar. Y.B. Topmark S.
ESSO Lt.By. Q. Pillar. B.Y. Topmark N.
E ANGLE Lt.By. Fl.(3)G. 10 sec. Conical G.

Lts. in line 021°20′ (Aux. front) F.R. 12M. B◇ W. Tr. 53m. 014°-031° (By day 017°-028° on request).
Lts. in line 023°44′ (Aux. front) F.R. 12M. B. ◇ W. Tr. 53m. 014°-031° (By day 017°-028° on request).

POPTON PT. 51°41.6′N, 5°02.1′W. Ldg.Lts. 094°. (Front) Iso. Y. 1.5 sec. 13M. W. ◇ B. stripe. 11m. Vis. 084°-104°. By day 5M. 089.5°-098.5° on request. (Common Rear) Oc. 4 sec. 14M. W. △ B. stripe 19m. 085°-105°. By day 5M. 090.5°-099.5° on request. Ldg.Lts. 095° (Front) Iso. 1.5 sec. 14M. W. O. B. stripe 085°-105° 11m. By day. 7M. 090.5°-099.5° on request.
ESSO MARINE TERMINAL Lt. 3 F.R. vert. at W end Horn(2) 30 sec. (Closed).
Lt. 3 F.R. vert. at E end.
CUNJIC Lt.By. Q.R. Can.R.

NEWTON NOYES

Ldg.Lts. 080° (S Front) Oc. 3 sec. 14M. W. ▯ B. Stripe on Tr. 42m. 070°-090° (By day 075.5°-084.5° on request). (Common Rear) Oc. W.Y. 3 sec. W.14M. Y.13M. W. ▯ B. Stripe on Tr. 51m. W.070°-090°; Y.077°-097° (By day W.075.5°-084.5°; Y.082.5°-091.5° on request).

Ldg. Lts. 087° (N Front) Oc. Y. 3 sec. 13M. W. Tr. B. Stripe 41m. 077°-097°. (By day 082.5°-091.5° on request).

ELF MARINE TERMINAL
Tel: (0646) 690300. Fax: (0646) 697689.
Telex: 48468 ELF REF G.
Radio: VHF Chan. 14, 16, 18.
W END. Lt. 3 F.R. vert. Dolphin. 9m.
E END. Lt. 3 F.R. vert. Dolphin. 9m. Bell (2) 20 sec.
Ldg. Lts. 254° (Front) F.R. 2M. R. ▽W. Stripe. 4m. 234°-274°. (Rear) F.R. 2M. R. ▽W. Stripe. 5m. 234°-274°.

TEXACO TERMINAL
Tel: (0646) 641331.
Radio: VHF Chan. 14, 16, 21.
W END. Lt. 3 F.G. vert. 8m. Horn (3) 30 sec.
E END. Lt. 3 F.G. vert. 2M. Post on Dolphin. 8m. Bell 15 sec.
Ldg.Lts. 268° (Front) F.R. 1M. R. ▽ W. Stripe. 264°-272°. (Rear) F.R. 1M. R. ▽ W. Stripe. 8m. 264°-272°.

HUBBERSTON JTY HEAD. Lt. 2 F.R. vert. 10m.

MILFORD DOCK
HAKIN POINT OUTFALL. Lt.Bn. Fl.Y. 2½ sec. Topmark. Can.Y. 13m.
MILFORD DOCK ENTRANCE. By. Can.R.
MILFORD DOCK ENTRANCE. By. Conical G.
OUTFALL Lt.By. Q. Pillar. B.Y. Topmark N.
E PIER Ldg.Lts. 348°. (Front) F.G. on B. hut. 5m. (Rear) F.G. on B. Col. 20m. also 2 F.R. hor. Lts. shown from Chy. 0.61M. NE.
W PIER HEAD Lt. 2 F.R. vert. on W. mast. Docking sig.
Bl. Flag or 2 G. Lts. = Gates open, vessels may enter.
Signal arm lowered or 1 G. Lt. = vessels may leave.
WARDS PIER HEAD Lt. 2 F.R. vert.
MILFORD SHELF Lt.By. Fl.R. 2.5 sec. Can.R.
NEWTON NOYES PIER Lt. 2 F.R. vert. 1M. B. mast 8m.
GULF TERMINAL Lts. 3 F.R. vert.
Tel: (0646) 692461. Fax: (0646) 695837.
Telex: 48211 GORLMH G.
Radio: VHF Chan. 14, 16, 18.
GULF TERMINAL Ldg.Lts. 101°. Pennar (Front) Q. 6M. B. △. W. stripe. Llanreath (Rear) Iso. 4 sec. 10M. B. △ W. stripe. vis. 097°-105°.
Ldg.Lts. 102°. Wear Spit (Front) Q.R. 4M. R. ▯ W. stripe. SW Martello Tr. (Rear) Iso.R. 4 sec. 7M. W. stripe. vis. 098°-106°.
PENNAR OUTFALL CHANNEL. Lt. F. Y.
OUTFALL. Lt.By. Q. Pillar. B.Y. Topmark N.
PENNAR GUT By. Can.R.

PEMBROKE DOCK TO RIVER CLEDDAU

CARR SPIT No: 1 Lt.By. Fl.G. 2 sec. Conical G. and **CARR SPIT** No: 2 Lt.By. Q.G. Conical G. mark appr. to Pembroke Dock.
PEMBROKE DOCK Ldg.Lts. 153°. (Front) Q.G. W. ◊, B. stripe. (Rear) Q.G. W. ◊, B. stripe.
CARR JETTY. Lt. 2 F.G. vert.
FERRY TERMINAL Lts. 2 F.G. vert.
PORT OF PEMBROKE. (SW of RoRo Terminal in Pembroke Dock) 51°42'N, 4°57'W. Tel: Port Office (0646) 683981. Dock Master (Private) (0646) 690063; Mobile (0831) 482855. Fax: (0646) 687394. Telex: 48584 GOVAND G.
Radio: VHF Ch. 12, 68. Mon.-Fri. 0700-1900 or when vessel expected.
Ldg.Lts. 196° (Front) F.G. 4M. W. ▯ B. stripe. Occas. 192°-200°. (Rear) F.G. 10M. W. ▯ B. stripe. Occas. 192°-200°.
QUAY I. Lt. 2 F.G. vert.

NEYLAND POINT. Lt.By. Fl.(2)R. 10 sec. Can.R.
OUTFALL Bn. R. Bn. Can. Topmark.
DOCKYARD BANK No: 3 Lt.By. Fl.G. 10 sec. Conical G.
DOCKYARD BANK No: 4 Lt.By. Fl.(3)G. 15 sec. Conical G.
WESTFIELD PILL MARINA. APPROACH CHANNEL. Sill dries 2.2m, divides Marina into 2 areas.
    2 × By. Can.R.
    2 × By. Conical G.
CLEDDAU BRIDGE Lt. **N SIDE Lt.** 2 F.R. vert.
S SIDE Lt. 2 F.G. vert.
No: 8 Lt. F. Fl.(2)R. 10 sec.
Power cables, min. clearance 14m.

FISH FARM Lts. NW/SE End. 2 F.G. vert.

BRISTOL CHANNEL

TURBOT BANK. Lt.By. V.Q.(9) 10 sec. Pillar. Y.B.Y. Topmark W.

OFFSHORE WAYPOINT SW OF TURBOT BANK. 51°37.0'N, 5°10.0'W.

CROW ROCK Bn. Is.D. 9m. S of Linney Hd.

OFFSHORE WAYPOINT S OF LINNEY HD. 51°36.2'N, 5°04.0'W.

ST GOWAN 51°30.5'N, 4°59.8'W. Lt.V. Fl. 20 sec. 26M. R. hull, Lt.Tr. amidships, 12m. Shown by day when fog sig. operating. Distress sig. Horn(3) 60 sec. Racon(T).

OFFSHORE WAYPOINT S OF ST. GOWANS HD. 51°35.2'N, 4°55.75'W.

CALDY ISLAND 51°37.9'N, 4°41.0'W. Lt. Fl.(3) W.R. 20 sec. W.14M. R.12M. W. round Tr. 65m. R.173°-212°; W.212°-088°; R.088°-102°.

INSHORE WAYPOINT E OF CALDY ISLAND. 51°37.7'N, 4°39.0'W.

CALDY SOUND
SPANIEL By. Pillar. B.Y.B. Topmark E. off E End Caldy I.
N HIGH CLIFF By. Pillar B.Y. Topmark N. off N edge High Cliff Bk.
GILTAR PATCH By. Can.R. off Giltar Pt.
EEL SPIT POINT By. Conical G. off N End Caldy I.
WOOLHOUSE By. Pillar. Y.B. Topmark S. on S edge off Woolhouse Bk.

CARMARTHEN BAY

INSHORE WAYPOINT E OF TENBY. 51°39.3'N, 4°39.0'W.

WRECK By. Pillar Y.B. Topmark S. 51°40.7'N 4°34.36'W.

TENBY

HARBOUR WAYPOINT. 51°40.5'N, 4°41.4'W.

PIER HEAD Lt. F.R. 7M. metal mast, 7m.
NEAR HEAD. Lt. F. 1M. on metal post, 6m.
'DZ3' By. Sph. Y. ESE Caldy I.
'DZ1' By. Sph. Y. NE Caldy I.
'DZ2' Lt.By. Fl.Y. 2½ sec. Sph. Y.
'DZ4' Lt.By. Fl.Y. 5 sec. Sph. Y.
'DZ7' Lt.By. Fl.Y. 10 sec. Sph. Y.
'DZ5' Lt.By. Fl.Y. 2.5 sec. Sph. Y.
'DZ6' By. Sph. Y.
'DZ8' By. Conical Y.
'DZ9' By. Conical Y.
'DZ10' By. Conical Y.

SAUNDERSFOOT. Tel: (0834) 3313.
Entry: Hr. dries out. Draught up to 1m. at HW. For Marina see Section 25.
PIER HEAD. Lt. Fl.R. 5 sec. 7M. stone cupola, 6m.

A line 51°42.98'N, 4°41.33'W and 51°42.24'N, 4°41.47'W marked by Bys. Sph Y. from April to October. Speed limit 5 knots inshore of this line.

INSHORE WAYPOINT ENTRANCE TO R. TOWY (AFON TYWI). 51°41.75'N, 4°26.25'W.

RIVER TOWY TO CARMARTHEN

CARMARTHEN. 51°43'N, 4°42'W. Tel: (0267) 7472.
Entry: Max. draught 2m. from estuary to Carmarthen Quay.
River Towy Bys. shifted from time to time to mark Chan. as it frequently changes. Most Bys. have been withdrawn.
FERRYSIDE Bn. B. mast and ball, on E side of river.
Electric cables 24m. high, cross River Towy at Pibwr (4M. below Carmarthen).

INSHORE WAYPOINT ENTRANCE TO BURRY INLET. 51°37.0'N, 4°22.0'W.

BURRY INLET
BURRY PORT Lt.Bn. Q.R. Barrel Post.
W PIER Lt. F.R. Tr. 7m.
Burry Port dries out at LWST. Anchorage in 5m. LWST 1c. SW of Barrel Post running NE for 6c.
WHITEFORD Lt.Ho. Fl. 5 sec. 7M. Tr. 7m.

LLANELLI 51°40'N, 4°10'W. Tel: (0554) 741100.
Entry: N Dock capable of providing most facilities for yachts. Dries out at CD within 2M. of entrance. Best entry from 1½ h.-HW.

LLANELLI Chan. to dock through flats marked by Bns.

OFFSHORE WAYPOINT W OF W HELWICK. 51°31.25'N, 4°24.0'W.

W HELWICK Lt.By. Q.(9) 15 sec. Pillar. Y.B.Y. Topmark W. on W edge of shoal. Racon. Whis.

OFFSHORE WAYPOINT S OF WORMS HD. 51°30.6'N, 4°20.0'W.

E HELWICK PASS. Lt.By. V.Q.(3) 5 sec. Pillar B.Y.B. Topmark E. on E edge of shoals. Bell.

MIXON By. Can.R. on SW edge of Mixon Shoals. ∿ Bell.

PORT EYNON BAY
PRINCE IVANHOE WRECK. E By. Can.R.
S IVANHOE WRECK By. Can.R.

INSHORE WAYPOINT SE OF MUMBLES. 51°33.0'N, 3°56.5'W.

MUMBLES 51°34.0'N, 3°58.2'W. Lt. Fl.(4) 10 sec. 17M. W. octagonal Tr. 35m. Horn.(3) 60 sec. Fog Detr. Lt. Fl. 5 sec. duration ev. 5 mins. 334° arc 2½°.
RAILWAY PIER HEAD. Lt. 2 F.R. vert. 9M. W. framework Tr. 11m.
SW INNER GREEN GROUNDS. Lt.By. Q.(6)+L.Fl. 15 sec. Pillar. Y.B. Topmark S.
LEDGE. Lt.By. V.Q.(6)+L.Fl. 10 sec. Pillar. Y.B. Topmark S.
GROUNDS. Lt.By. V.Q.(3) 5 sec. Pillar. B.Y.B. Topmark E.
SPOIL GROUND Lt.By. Fl.Y. 2½ sec. Sph. Y.

APPROACHES TO SWANSEA

MRCC SWANSEA (0792) 366534. Weather broadcast ev. 4h. from 0005.

OUTER FAIRWAY. Lt.By. Q.G. Conical G. E side of Chan. ∿ Bell. Marks entce. to dredged Chan. to Swansea.
SWANSEA. Lt.By. Fl.G. 2.5 sec. Conical G. Bell. E side of Chan.

SWANSEA 51°37'N, 3°56'W. Tel: Swansea (0792) 650855 (Night 652601 Sat. & Sun.). Telex: 48150. Pilots: (0792) 654537.

HARBOUR WAYPOINT. 51°35.0'N, 3°56.5'W.

Radio — Port: VHF Chan. 14 — continuous.
Tugs: Ch. 69, 71 — continuous.
Radio.— Pilots: VHF Chan. 14, 16, 11, 12 — continuous but preferably 4 h. before to 4 h. after H.W.

SWANSEA MARITIME QUARTER
All pleasure craft must be under power in vicinity of harbour. Keep clear of commercial traffic. Max. speed 5 kts. Enter and leave keeping close to Western Breakwater.
Yacht Haven. Tel: (0792) 470310.
Radio: VHF Chan. 80. 0900-1700 Mon.-Fri. plus Lock Times. (plus 1 h. before evening lock at w/ends).
Lock: 3¾ h.-HW-3¼ h. 0800-2200 May-Sept. 0800-1700 Sept.-May. (0800-1900 Sept.-May at w/ends).
Lock operates on 30 min. cycle. Check on VHF Chan. 80.
Traffic Lts: 2 F.R. = Lock closed. Do not proceed.
R./G. Lt. = Free flow in operation proceed with caution.
R. Lt. = Normal Locking. Hold as required clear of Lock, proceed only if instructed.
G. Lt. = Proceed into lock as instructed.

TAWE RIVER BARRAGE
New barrage across River Tawe ½ mile upstream of ABP Docks.
Call Sign 'TAWE LOCK' VHF channel 18.
Lock operates 0700-2200 hrs. 4½ hrs. either side of high water.

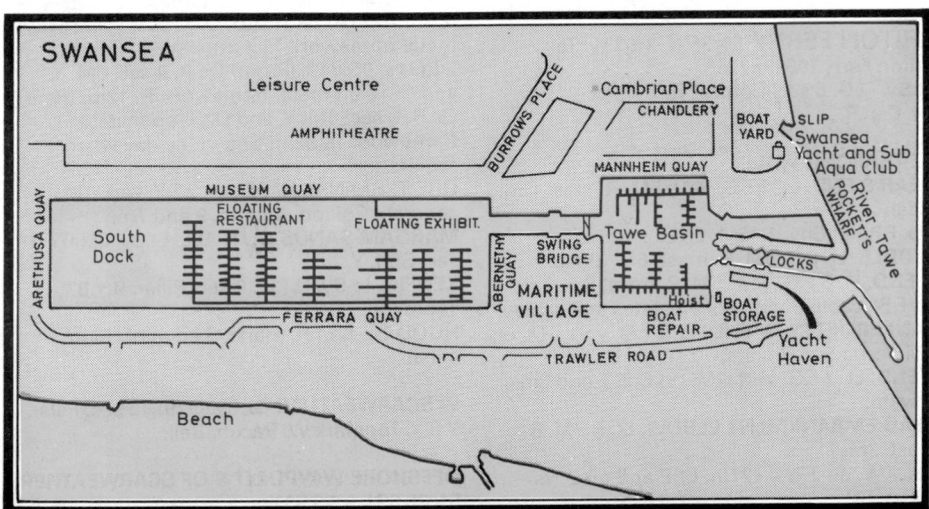

Max L.O.A. in lock 36.0m.
Max beam in lock 12.0m.

LOCK TRAFFIC SIGNALS.
2 F.R. — Lock closed.
R/G/ Lt. — Free flow in operation, proceed as instructed.
R. Lt. — Lock operating, standby.
G. Lt. — Proceed into the Lock.

Landing pontoon down stream. L.O.A. 32m
2 F.R.(vert) 2M. L.W.S.T.
No vessels must be left unattended at anytime.
Further information Tel: (0792) 470310.

W PIER HEAD. Lt. Fl.(2)R. 10 sec. 7M. metal Col. 11m. F.R. Lts. on radio mast 1.3M. NNE.
E BREAKWATER HEAD. Lt. 2 F.G. vert. 6M. W. framework Tr. 10m. Horn 30 sec. sounded at tide time.
Lts. in line 020°. Approach Jetty Head. (Front) 2 F.G. vert. 2M. 5m. mark E limit of dredged area. (Rear) F.G. 6M. Obscured when brg less than 020°.
CAR FERRY TERMINAL, S END. Lt. 2 F.G. vert. 4M. 9 and 6m.
SLIPWAYS. Lt. 2 F.G. vert. 4M. on B. mast.

RIVER NEATH
Approach buoys 3 × Can.R.

NEATH 51°36′N, 3°52′W. Tel: Port: (0639) 53486.
Radio — Pilots: VHF Chan. 16, 77. H24.
Depths to Briton Ferry. Dries 2.4m. with 6.1m. at MHWS and 4m. at MHWN.

BRITON FERRY 51°36′N, 3°52′W. Tel: Briton Ferry (0639) 2256.
Lt.By. Fl.G. 5 sec. Conical G.
By. Can.R.

SE TRAINING WALL
NEAR S END. Lt. 2 F.G. vert. 5M. R. mast, 6m. Tidal.
Lts. F.R. on Chy. 1.45M. ENE.
MIDDLE. Lt. F.G. 5M. R. mast, 6m. Tidal.
N END. Lt. 3 F.G. vert. 5M. R. mast, 6m. Tidal.
Lt. F.Bl. cable Bn. marks pipelines and cables.
TANKER JETTY, W END. Lt. 2 F.G. vert. 1M. on Col. 7 and 5m. Private.
E END. Lt. 2 F.G. vert. 1M. on Col. 7 and 5m. Private.
SLAG EMBANKMENT ELBOW. Lt. F. 7M. R. mast, 3m.
Lts. F.W. on 2 Trs. 427m. ESE and on 2 Trs. 305m. SE.

Bridges across River Neath marked by F.W., F.R. and F.G. Lts.
SPOIL GROUND. Lt.By. Fl.Y. 10 sec. Sph. Y.
Lt.By. Fl.G. 5 sec. Conical G.
OUTFALL. Lt.By. Fl.Y. 2.5 sec. Sph. Y.
OUTFALL. Lt.By. Fl.Y. 5 sec. Sph. Y.

PORT TALBOT CHANNEL TO NEW HARBOUR

PORT TALBOT 51°35′N, 3°49′W. Tel: Port Talbot (0639) 885171.
Radio — Port: VHF Chan. 16, 12 — H24. Call 'Port Talbot Harbour' for permission to enter Harbour.
Radio — Pilots: See Swansea.
Entry Signals: Dredgers will display R./W./f Lts. in vert. line and where necessary 2 B. balls by day or 2 R. Lts. by night to indicate foul side.
3 B. balls (3 G. Lts.) — vessels may enter.
3 R. Lts. — entry prohibited.
Anchorage: Off Mumbles. W. Oyster Ledge.

CABENDA. Lt.By. V.Qk.Fl.(6)+L.Fl. 10 sec. Pillar. Y.B. Topmark S.

No: 1 Lt.By. Fl.R. 5 sec. Can.R.
No: 2 Lt.By. Fl.G. 5 sec. Conical G. ᗡᖇ .
No: 3 Lt.By. Fl.R. 3 sec. Can.R. ᗡᖇ .
No: 4 Lt.By. Fl.G. 3 sec. Conical G. ᗡᖇ .

N BREAKWATER HEAD. Lt. Fl.(4)R. 10 sec. 3M. metal framework Tr. 11m.
S BREAKWATER HEAD. Lt. Fl.G. 3 sec. 3M. metal framework Tr. 11m.
Ldg.Lts. 059°49′ (Front) Oc.R. 4 sec. 6M. Y. and Or. ◊ on metal framework Tr. 12m. (Rear) Oc.R. 6 sec. 6M. Y. and Or. ◊ on metal framework Tr. 32m. Shown by day when required.
ORE TERMINAL HEAD. Lt. 2 F.Y. vert. 1M. concrete Col. on dolphin, 9 and 7m.
MARGAM SANDS OUTFALL. Lt.By. Fl.(4)Y. 15 sec. Sph. Y.
KENFIG. Lt.By. Q.(3) 10 sec. Pillar. B.Y.B. Topmark E.
HUGO By. Can.R. marks S edge of Hugo shoal.

W SCARWEATHER. Lt.By. Q.(9) 15 sec. Pillar. Y.B.Y. Topmark W. Racon. Bell.

OFFSHORE WAYPOINT S OF SCARWEATHER. 51°26.5′N, 3°55.5′W.

S SCARWEATHER. Lt.By. Q.(6) + L.Fl. 15 sec. Pillar Y.B. Topmark S.
E SCARWEATHER By. Pillar. B.Y.B. Topmark E.

PORTHCAWL 51°28'N, 3°42'W.

HARBOUR WAYPOINT. 51°27.5'N, 3°42.5'W.

Entry: Open drying out Harbour of refuge for any small boat up to 18m. long seeking shelter. Berth always available.
Coast Guard Station 1M. W of Porthcawl Lt.Ho.
Harbour ent. inside breakwater where tide gauge gives depth.
Anchorage: Unsafe during prevailing SW winds. Holding ground poor.

BREAKWATER HEAD. Lt. F.W.R.G. W.6M. R.4M. G.4M. W. 6-sided Tr. B. base, 10m. G.302°-036°; W.036°-082°; R.082°-122°. In line 094°15' with Saint Hilary Aero Lt. leads through Shord Chan.
FAIRY ROCK By. Pillar. Y.B.Y. Topmark W. on W end of shoal off Porthcawl.
TUSKER ROCK. Lt.By. Fl.(2)R. 5 sec. Can.R. ⩗⩗.

INSHORE WAYPOINT S. OF TUSKER ROCK 51°26.78'N 3°40.80'W.

W NASH. Lt.By. V.Q.(9) 10 sec. Pillar. Y.B.Y. Topmark W.
MIDDLE NASH By. Pillar Y.B. Topmark S. on S edge of shoal.

INSHORE WAYPOINT E OF NASH SAND. 51°24.45'N, 3°34.20'W.

E NASH. Lt.By. Q.(3) 10 sec. Pillar. B.Y.B. Topmark E.

OFFSHORE WAYPOINT S OF NASH POINT. 51°23.0'N, 3°33.0'W.

NASH 51°24.0'N, 3°33.1'W. Lt. Fl.(2) W.R. 10
sec. W.21M. R.20M. R.17M. W. round Tr. 56m. W.290°-097°; R.097°-100°; R. (intens) 100°-104°; R.104°-120°; W.120°-128°. Siren(2) 45 sec. RC.

SAINT HILARY 51°27.4'N, 3°24.1'W. Lt.Bn.
Aero. Q.R. 11M. Ro. mast. 346m. Also 4 F.R. vert.
BREAKSEA POINT. Lt.Bn. Fl.R. concrete Tr. **Lt.** F.R. on radio mast 2.7M. ENE.

OFFSHORE WAYPOINT S OF RHOOSE POINT. 51°22.0'N, 3°20.0'W.

BREAKSEA 51°19.9'N, 3°19.0'W. Lt.F. Fl. 15 sec. 15M. Horn (2) 30 sec. Racon.
MERKUR Lt.By. Fl.R. 2.5 sec. Can.R. ⩗⩗ Bell. S of Barry I.
W ONE FATHOM Lt.By. Q.(9) 15 sec. Pillar. Y.B.Y. Topmark W. W end One Fathom Bank.
N ONE FATHOM Lt.By. Q. pillar. B.Y. Topmark N.

WENVOE 51°27.5'N, 3°16.8'W. Lt. Aero Q. 12M. Radio mast 364m.

WELSH WATER. BARRY WEST Lt. By. Fl.R. 5 sec. Can R.

SOUTH EAST WALES PILOTS (Barry, Cardiff, Newport, River Usk). Tel: (0446) 732665, 735466. Telex 498180 SEWPIL G.
Radio: VHF Chan. 16, 6, 8, 9. Hours 4½-HW-3½h.

BARRY 51°23'N, 3°15'W. Tel: Barry (0446)
700311. Fax: (0446) 700100. Telex: 498421 ABPBY G.

HARBOUR WAYPOINT. 51°23.0'N, 3°15.5'W.

Radio — Port: *Barry Docks.* VHF Chan. 11, 16, 10 — 4 h.-HW-3 h.
Radio Pilots: See SE Wales Pilotage.
Signals:
W Jetty — 1 B. Ball or 1 R. Lt. = Passenger vessel may proceed from/to Passenger Pontoon.
W Jetty — 1 R. Flag or 1 G. Lt. = Vessel may enter Lady Windsor Lock from sea.
W & E Jetty — 1 R. Flag or R./G. Lt. = Vessel may enter No. 3 dock from sea.
Lady Windsor Lock/No. 3 Dock/Junction Cut (Within Docks):
1 R. Flag or 1 G. Lt. = Vessel may enter Lady Windsor or No. 3 Dock from No. 1 Dock or enter Junction Dock from No. 1 or No. 2 Dock.
1 Bu. Flag or 1 R. Lt. = Vessel may not enter from No. 1 Dock.
1 Bu. Flag or 1 R. Lt. (hand held) = Vessel to stop.
Entry: Lady Windsor Lock min. depth on sill 3.9m. Available approx. 3 h.-HW-3 h.
Yacht Club close to Lifeboat Slip. Obtain permission before approaching entrance, or entering Lady Windsor Lock, No. 3 Basin or junction cut.

(OLD HARBOUR) YORK ROCK. Lt. 2 F.G. vert. 5M. on Col. 5m. at head of breakwater.

BARRY DOCKS

W BREAKWATER HEAD. 51°23.4'N, 3°15.5'W. Lt. Fl. 2.5 sec. 10M. W. round Tr. 12m.
E BREAKWATER HEAD. Lt. Q.G. 8M. mast, 7m.
STEAMBOAT PIER HEAD. Lt. 2 F.R. vert. 6M. W. mast, 13m. Shown when vessels prohibited from entering or leaving Hr. Traffic sig.
LIFEBOAT SLIPWAY. Bn. Topmark R. Can.
LADY WINDSOR LOCK, ENTCE. Docking Signal — F.G. Lt. = v/l may enter.
MACKENZIE SHOAL. Lt.By. Q.R. Can.R. ᗢ SW of Flatholm I.
Lt.By. Fl.(5)Y. 20 sec. WNW of Steep Holm.

OFFSHORE WAYPOINT S OF FLATHOLM. 51°21.0'N, 3°07.0'W.

FLATHOLM 51°22.5'N, 3°07.0'W. Lt. Fl.(3) W.R. 10 sec. W.16M. R.13M. W. round Tr. 50m. H24. R.106°-140°; W.140°-151°; R.151°-203°; W.203°-106°. Distress sig. Horn. 30 sec.
WOLVES. Lt.By. V.Q. Pillar. B.Y. Topmark N.
RANIE. Lt.By. Fl.(2)R. 5 sec. Can.R. ᗢ off Lavernock Pt.
S CARDIFF. Lt.By. Q.(6)+L.Fl. 15 sec. Pillar Y.B. Topmark S. Bell.
MID CARDIFF. Lt.By. Fl.(3)G.15 sec. Conical G.
SEWER OUTFALL. Lt.By. Fl.(2)R. 10 sec. Can.R.
N CARDIFF. Lt.By. Q.G. Conical G.

EAST SIDE TO CARDIFF GROUNDS

MONKSTONE ROCK 51°24.8'N, 3°05.9'W. Lt. Fl.(2) 10 sec. 5M. R.Col. on round masonry Tr. 13m.
CARDIFF SPIT By. Can.R.
PENARTH HEAD. Lt.By. Fl.R. 1 sec. Can.R. ᗢ.

PENARTH 51°27'N, 3°10'W.

Portway Village Marina. Tel: (0222) 705021. Ch. M.

RIVER ELY. Ldg.Lts. 304° (Front) F. 2m. Or. ◊ (Rear) F. 6m. Or. ◊.
ELY TIDAL HBR. Ldg.Lts. 246°(Front) F. 5m. Or. ◊ (Rear) F. 8m. Or. ◊.
ELY. Lt.By. Fl.G. 5 sec. Conical G.
PROMENADE PIER, NR. HEAD. Lt. 2 F.R. vert. 3M. brown mast, 8 and 6m. Port sig. Reed Mo(BA) 60 sec.
BOAT CLUB PONTOON. Lt.Bn. Q.

APPROACHES TO AND CARDIFF DOCKS

OUTER WRACK. Lt.By. Q.(9) 15 sec. Pillar Y.B.Y. Topmark W. on E side of Chan. to Docks.
INNER WRACK. Lt.By. Fl.G. 2.5 sec. Conical G. on E side of Chan. to Docks.

CARDIFF 51°27.6'N, 3°09.9'W. Ldg.Lts. 349° (Front) F. 17M. 4m. (Rear) F. 17M. 24m.

RIVER TAFF CHANNEL

No. 1 By. Conical G.
No: 2 By. Conical G.
No: 3 By. Conical G.
No: 4 By. Can.R.

SE WALES PILOTAGE DISTRICT (For Barry, Cardiff, Newport, Gloucester, including Sharpness, Chepstow, Lydney). Tel: (04462) 732665 & 733730 & 735466. Telex: 498180 SEWPIL G. Telegraph: SEW PILOT.
Radio: VHF Chan. 16, 6, 8, 9, 11, 14.

CARDIFF 51°22'N, 3°07'W. Tel: Port (0222) 464544. Port Manager (0222) 461083. Fax: (0222) 471100. Telex: 498542 ABPCB G.

HARBOUR WAYPOINT OFF LAVERNOCK POINT. 51°23.75'N, 3°09.0'W.

Radio — Port: VHF Chan. 14, 16, 13. 4 h. before to 3 h. after HW.
Radio — Pilots: See SE Wales Pilotage.
Signals: Queen Alexandra Dock — Lock signals:
1 R. Fl.Lt. = Prepare to lock.
1 R. Lt. = Vessel may dock.
2 R. Lts. (vert.) = Outer half of lock only available.
3 R. Lts. △ = S Approach Jetty occupied.
Lock available 4 h.-HW-3 h. Depth over sill 12.8m. MHWS & 9.9m. at MHWN.

QUEEN ALEXANDRA DOCK ENTRANCE
S JETTY HEAD. Lt. 2 F.G. vert. Dia. 60 sec. occas. Traffic sig.
N JETTY, S END. Lt. 2 F.R. vert. Ely Hbr. Ldg.Lts. 304° (Front) F.W. Or. ◊ (Rear) F.W. Or. ◊. **Ldg.Lts.** 246° (Front) F.W. Or. ◊. (Rear) F.W. Or. ◊.
PETERSTONE FLATS 2 Bys. one conical, one can. shaped, B.Y. vert. stripes, mark sewer.
NEW PATCH By. Spherical R.W.Hor. bands.
WESTON. Lt.By. Fl.(2)R. 5 sec. Can.R. ᗢ E. of Flatholm.

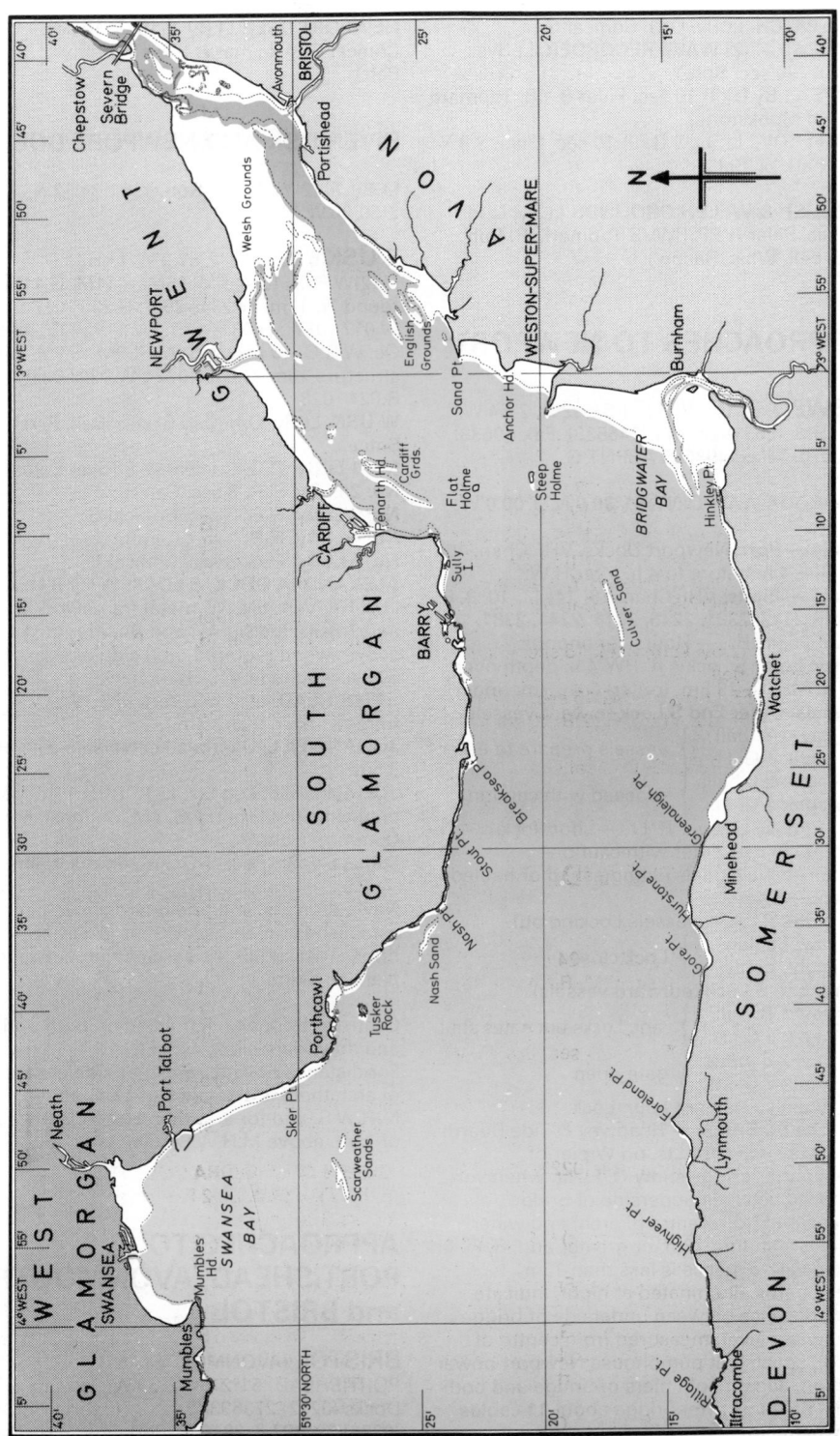

TAIL PATCH. Lt.By. Q.G. Conical G.
TAIL PATCH (2) WAVE RECORDER. Lt.Bys.
Fl.(5)Y. 20 sec. Sph.Y.
HOPE. Lt.By.Q.(3) 10 sec. Pillar B.Y.B. Topmark
E. E of Monkstone.
NW ELBOW. Lt.By. V.Q.(9) 10 sec. Pillar. Y.B.Y.
Topmark W. Bell.

ENGLISH & WELSH GROUNDS Lt.By. L. Fl.
10 sec. Pillar H.F.P. RWVS Topmark, R. Sph.
w.a. bell. Whis. Racon.

APPROACHES TO NEWPORT

NEWPORT (GWENT) 51°32'N, 2°54'W.
Tel: HM. (0633) 244411 (246538). Fax: (0633)
246070. Telex: 498585 ABPNT G.

HARBOUR WAYPOINT. 51°30.0'N, 3°00.0'W.

Radio — Port: Newport Docks. VHF Chan. 16,
11, 9 — 4 h. before to 4 h. after H.W.
Radio — Pilots: VHF Chan. 16, 14, 11, 10, 9, 8,
6. MF. 2182, 2301, 2246, 2016, 2241, 2381,
2527, 2534 kHz. — Hours continuous.
Entry: Enter S Lock 4 h.-HW-4 h. depth over
sill at MHWS 13.8m. (outer) & 10.7m. (inner).
Signals: Outer End S Lock (inward vessels).
By day: 1 B. ball ⎫
By night: 1 G. Lt. ⎬ vessels prepare to enter.
By night: 2 B balls ⎫
By night: 2 G. Lts. ⎬ proceed with caution.
By night: G. Lt. over R. Lt. — short lock
(122m.) in use, enter with caution.
When above signals extinguished or hauled
down — stop.
By night: R. Lt. — vessels Locking out.
By day: Bl. flag ⎫
By night: no lts. ⎬ Lock closed
Inner Ent. S Lock (outward vessels).
By day: 1 B. ball ⎫
By night: 1 G Lt. ⎬ apr. Locks but gates shut
By day: 2 B. balls ⎫
By night: 2 G. Lts. ⎬ gate open
No signals — do not appr. Lock.
George St. Bridge — Headway & Tide Boards.
Headway indicator Lts. on W pier of
Transporter bridge show G. Fl. Lt. when vert.
distance between underside of bridge
(measured from centre of arch) and water
level is statutory 13m. or greater and, R. Fl. Lt.
when vert. distance is less than 13m.
Tide boards, illuminated at night, indicate
vert. distance between underside of bridge
and water level (measured from centre of
arch); situated at pumphouse Newport power
station, and on both piers of bridge and both
piers of Transporter bridge about 11 cables
downstream.

NEWPORT DEEP. Lt.By. Fl.(3)G. 10 sec.
Conical G. ⌇⌇ marks SW extremity of Usk
Patch.

RIVER USK AND NEWPORT DOCKS

Lt.By. Fl.(2)Y. 15 sec. Sph. Y. 51°31.12'N,
2°59.30'W.

E USK 51°32.4'N, 2°57.9'W. Lt.Ho.
Fl.(2)W.R.G. 10 sec. W.15M. R.11M. G.11M. W.
round Tr. 11m. W.284°-290°; R.290°-017°;
W.017°-037°; G.037°-115°; W.115°-120° also Lt.
Oc. W.R.G. 10 sec. W.11M. R.9M. G.9M. same
structure 10m. G.018°-022°; W.022°-024°;
R.024°-028°.
W USK. Lt.By. Q.R. Can.R. ⌇⌇ Bell. River
Entce.
No: 1 Lt.By. Q.G. Conical G. E River Entce.
No: 2 Lt.By. Fl.R. 3 sec. Can.R.
No: 3 Lt.By. Fl.G. 3 sec. Conical G.
No: 4 Lt.By. Fl.R. 3 sec. Can.R.
No: 5 Lt.By. Fl.G. 3 sec. Conical G.
ALEXANDRA DOCK, S LOCK, W PIER HEAD.
Lt. 2 F.R. vert. 6M. W. metal framework Tr. 9
and 7m. Traffic sig. W. and Bu. dredging Lts.
shown when required on S side of river. Horn
60 sec. sounded 4 h.-HW-4 h.
E PIER HEAD. Lt. 2 F.G. vert. 6M. W.
framework Tr. 9 and 7m.
JULIANS PILL: Overhead cable safe clearance
3.8m.
JULIANS PILL. Ldg.Lts. 057°. (Rear) F.G. 4M.
on mast, 8m. (Front) F.G. 4M. on mast, 5m.
Common front.
Ldg.Lts. 149° (Rear) F.G. 4M. on mast, 9m.

Navigation Lts. and tide boards have been
established on and near George Street
bridge, which has a clear opening between
piers of 138m.

Centre of bridge arch marked on both upriver
and downriver sides with F.Y.
For distance of 45m. on either side of centre
of arch there is clearance of 13m. above
M.H.W.S. and for a further 22m. on either side
of 12m. above M.H.W.S.

APPROACHES TO PORTISHEAD, AVONMOUTH and BRISTOL

BRISTOL (AVONMOUTH AND
PORTISHEAD) 51°27'N, 2°35'W. Tel: City
Docks (0272) 273633. Bristol Floating Hbr.
(0272) 264797 & 297608. Port Operations

Service: (0272) 224494. Fax: (0272) 224762.
Pilots: (0272) 822257. (0272) 823884 for
yachts. <30m. L.O.A. if requiring a pilot.
Radio — Port: Avonmouth Radio. VHF Chan.
16, 12, 14, 9, 11 — continuous for vessels
Upper Bristol Channel, Severn Estuary, River
Avon to Black Rock.
Royal Edward Dock. VHF Chan. 16, 14, 12.
H24
Royal Portbury Dock. VHF Ch. 16, 14, 12. 4¼h.
HW-3½h.
City Docks Radio. VHF Chan. 16, 14, 11. From 3
h.-HW-1 h. for River Avon between Black Rock
and City Docks entrance. Call Dock Manager at
Black Rocks and Hotwells Pontoon for docking
instructions.
Portishead Dock Radio. VHF Chan. 16, 14, 12.
From 2½ h.-HW-1½ h. for vessels for Portishead
Docks.
Bristol Floating Harbour (Underfall Yard). VHF
Chan. 16, 73. 0800-1700 Mon.-Thurs. 0800-
1630 Fri. 0800-sunset weekends.
Radio — Pilots: Breaksea Stn.: VHF Chan. 16,
6, 8, 9, 12, 14.
Ilfracombe Stn.: VHF Chan. 16, 6, 8, 12, 14 by
arrangement.
Exempt vessels i.e. pleasure craft contact
Avonmouth Radio.
Entry: Signals for Princes Street and Redcliffe
Bridge = 1 short, 1 long blast. Manned 0600-
2300 summer, 0900-1645 winter.
Fog: The following fog warning signals for
the River Avon are exhibited from
Avonmouth Signal Station, when applicable,
during the period from 3 h.-HW-1 h.
Signal: A rectangle of W. fluorescent light =
Fog. The approximate range of visibility in
the River Avon is between ½ cable and 1 cable.
Two rectangles of W. fluorescent light
horizontally disposed 2-1m. apart = Dense
Fog. The approximate range of visibility in
the River Avon is less than ½ cable.
Limits on size: Max. 101.2m. × 14.9m. to City
Docks, but if over 99m. length, Mast Hd. 27m.
or draught over 2.7m. contact H.M.
Speed limits: Draught over 1.9m. 7 kts. over
ground. Draught up to 1.9m. 9kts. over
ground.

CITY DOCKS — STOP GATES. To prevent the
Floating Harbour becoming tidal on the top of
a Spring Tide, Stop Gates are placed across
the Junction Lock between Cumberland Basin
and the Floating Harbour, and across Netham
Lock whenever the tide reaches 9.1m. on the
outer sill at Cumberland Basin when the
predicted height of HW is 9.5m. or more.
Docking Signals: Docking signals are shown
from a mast on the Pier adjacent to the lower
pontoon, Hotwells, as follows:
A F.G. Lt. of high intensity directed down
stream. Ht. 2.7m. above Pier = Come ahead

with caution.
A F.R. Lt. of high intensity directed down
stream. Ht. 3.3m. above Pier = Bring up and
await orders.
These signals are repeated by all round lights
at the S end of the Pontoon.
RIVER AVON. Every vessel going down the
river against the Flood Tide is to stop above
the sharp bends when any vessels coming up
the river are rounding such bends, and so
avoid passing such vessels at these points in
the river.
No vessel, when being towed up the river, is
to cast off until within the Basin, or above the
Tongue Head, unless specifically ordered to
do so by the Dock Master.
**VESSELS ENTERING RIVER AVON BOUND
FOR BRISTOL CITY DOCKS.** Yachts and other
vessels bound for Bristol entering the River
Avon should make their destination known to
Avonmouth Signal Station in one of the
following ways:
By Day: By hoisting International Code
Alphabetical Flag 'R' prominently. (This signal
will not be acknowledged).
By Day or Night: By flashing morse Code
Letter R (· – ·) to the Signal Station repeatedly
until the Signal Station acknowledges either
by loud hailer or by repeating the signal by
light.
By Day or Night: By passing a message to the
effect by VHF Radio Telephone.
This is to ensure that the Dockmaster on duty
in the City Docks can be informed that the
vessel entering the river is definitely bound
for Bristol and not for Pill or Sea Mills. Unless
other special arrangements have been made
vessels should arrive off the Cumberland
Basin entrance not later than a quarter of an
hour after HW to allow time to proceed
through into the Floating Harbour.
VESSELS LEAVING THE CITY DOCKS. Vessels
leaving the City Docks should obtain details
of traffic in the river from the Dockmaster City
Docks, or by radio from the Avonmouth
Signal Station before proceeding from the
Cumberland Basin Locks. Thereafter they are
encouraged to report their positions from
time to time.
N. ELBOW Lt.By. Q.G. Conical G. Bell.
S MIDDLE Lt.By. Fl.(4)R. 15 sec. Can.R. on S
edge of W Middle Ground.
E MIDDLE Lt.By. Fl.R. 5 sec. Can.R.
CLEVEDON Lt.By. V.Q. Pillar. B.Y. Topmark N.
CLEVEDON PIER Lt. Fl.G. 10 sec. 3M. Post. 7m.
CLEVEDON PILL ENTRANCE Lt. Fl.G. 10 sec.
1M. G. Δ on post 2M. Shown 2 h.-H.W.-2 h.
WELSH HOOK Lt.By. Fl.(2)R. 5 sec. Can.R.
AVON Lt.By. Fl.G. 2½ sec. Conical G.
WALTON BAY. Old signal stn. Lt.Fl. 2½ sec.
2M. 35m.

NEWCOME Lt.By. Fl.(3)R. 10 sec. Can.R. 〰.
COCKBURN SHOAL Lt.By. Fl.R. 15 sec.
Can.R. 〰.

BLACK NORE POINT 51°29.1′N,
2°48.0′W. Lt. Fl.(2) 10 sec. 15M. W. round Tr.
11m. Vis. 044°-243°. Obscured by Sand Pt.
when bearing less than 049°.

PORTISHEAD POINT 51°29.6′N,
2°46.4′W. Lt. Q.(3) 10 sec. 16M. B. metal
framework Tr. W. concrete base. 9m. Vis.
060°-262°. Horn. 20 sec.
FIREFLY Lt.By. Fl.(2)G. 5 sec. Conical G. Off
Firefly Rocks.

PORTISHEAD 51°30′N, 2°46′W. Tel:
Portishead (0272) 842382.
Entry: R. Lts = Remain in Kings Road. G. Lts =
Entrance clear.
Port now closed to commercial traffic. Depths
no longer maintained.
PIER HEAD. Lt. Iso. G. 2 sec. 3M. W. Col. 5m.
Horn 15 sec. sounded when vessels expected.
LOCK, E SIDE. Lt. 2 F.R. vert. Col. Occas.
W SIDE. Lt. 2 F.G. vert. Col. Occas.
ROYAL PORTBURY OUTER. Lt.By. I.Q.G. 12
sec. Conical G.
MIDDLE. Lt.By. Fl.G. 5 sec. Conical G.
INNER. Lt.By. Fl.(3)G. 15 sec. Conical G.

PORTBURY WHARF 51°29.5′N, 2°44.1′W.
Ldg.Lts. 191°33′ (Front), Oc.G. 5 sec. 10M.
Grey mast 7m. Vis. 171½°-211½°. By day vis.
184½°-198½°. (Rear), Oc.G. 5 sec. 10M. Grey
mast. 12m. Vis. 171½°-211½°. By day vis. 184½°-
198½°.
SEABANK. Ldg.Lts. 102°59′ (Front) Oc.(2) 10
sec. 5M. Grey mast 13m. Vis. 086½°-119½°. By
day vis. 093°-113°. (Rear) Oc.(2) 10 sec. 5M.
Grey mast 16m. Vis. 086½°-119½°. By day vis.
093°-113°.

ROYAL PORTBURY DOCK. Tel: (0272) 823681
Ext. 4504, 4505.
Radio — Port: VHF Chan. 16, 14, 12. 2½ h.-HW-
1½ h.
Entry: R. Lts. = Wait in Kings Road. G. Lts. =
Enter.
PIER END. Lt. Fl.G. 15 sec. 6M. Grey Pillar 5m.
PIER CORNER. Lt. Fl.G. 3 sec. 7M. Grey Pillar
8m.
PIER KNUCKLE. Lt. Oc.G. 5 sec. 6M. Grey
Pillar 6m.

HARBOUR WAYPOINT KINGS RD. 51°29.5′N,
2°48.0′W.

AVONMOUTH. 51°30′N, 2°43′W. Tel:
(0272) 224494, 224761. Fax: (0272) 235320.
Telex: 44240 PBAAM G.

ROYAL EDWARD DOCK. Tel: (0272) 224433,
224434. Fax: (0272) 224435.
Radio — Port: VHF Chan. 16, 14, 12. H24.

N PIER HEAD. 51°30.5′N, 2°43.0′W. Lt. Fl.
10 sec. 10M. round stone Tr. 15m. Vis. 065°-
219°.
Ldg.Lts. 184°29′ (Front) Q.G. 6M. W. ▯ 5m. Vis.
129°-219°. (Rear) S Pier Lt. Oc. R.G. 30 sec.
10M. Round Stone Tr. 9m. R.294°-036°;
G.036°-194°. Bell. 10 sec.
KINGS ROAD. Ldg.Lts. 072°26′. (Front) Oc.R. 5
sec. 9M. vis. 062°-082°, W. obelisk, R. bands,
5m. (Rear) Q.R. 10M. 15m. vis. 066°-078°
B.W.Or. striped O.
ROYAL EDWARD LOCK. Lts. 2 F.R. vert. Col. N
side. 2 F.G. vert. Col. S side.
OIL JETTY HEAD. Lt. 2 F.G. vert.
GYPSUM EFFLUENT PIPE, INNER END. Lt.
Fl.Y. 3 sec. 2M. Y.Bn. 3M.
GYPSUM EFFLUENT PIPE. Lt.By. Fl.G. 5 sec.
Pillar G.

RIVER AVON

SWASH CHANNEL

AVONMOUTH DOCK ENTRANCE. Ldg.Lts.
127°10′ (Front) F.R. 3M. 7m. (Rear) F.R. 3M.
17m.

NELSON POINT CHANNEL

MONOLITHS Lt. Fl.R. 5 sec. 3M. W. ▯ B.W.
Col. 5m. 317°-137°.
SAINT GEORGE. Ldg.Lts. (Front) Oc.G. 5 sec.
1M. Or. Col. 6m. 158°-305°. (Rear) Oc.G. 5 sec.
1M. Or. Daymark W. Col. 9m. 158°-305°.
NELSON POINT. Lt. Fl.R. 3 sec. 3M. W. mast,
9m.
BROAD PILL. Lt. Q.Y. 1M. W. framework Tr.
11m.
AVONMOUTH BRIDGE NE. Lt. L.Fl.R. 10 sec.
3M.
SW. Lt. L.Fl.G. 10 sec. 3M.
SLUDGE LOADING QUAY. Lt. 2 F.R. vert. 2M.
Grey Col. 7m.
CUSTOM HOUSE. Lt. Fl. G. 2 sec. 1M. W.
Col. 5m.
ADAM AND EVE. Lt. Q(3)G. 6 sec. 1M. W. Col.
8m.
CHAPEL PILL. Lt. Q(2)G. 4 sec. 1M. W. Col. 7m.

HORSESHOE. Lt. (Upper) Q(3)R. 6 sec.. 1M. W. Col. 5m. (Lower) Fl. R. 2 sec. 1M. W. Col. 5m.
FIR TREE. Lt. Q(2)G. 4 sec. 1M. W. Col. 5m.
SEA MILLS Lt. Iso.R. 5 sec. 1M. W. Tr. 7m. Vis. 342°-148°.
MILES DOCK . (Lower) Lt. Q(3)G. 6 sec. 1M. W. Col. 5m. (Upper) Fl. G. 2 sec. 1M. W. Col. 7m.
LEIGH WOODS. (Lower) Lt. Q(2)G. 4 sec. 1M. W. Col. 5m. (Upper) Fl. G. 2 sec. 1M. W. Col. 5m.
BLACK ROCK. Lt. Fl. R. 2 sec.. 1M. W. Col. 5m.
ROUND POINT. Lt. Q(2)R. 4 sec. 1M. W. Col. 8m.
NIGHTINGALE VALLEY. Lt. Q(3)G. 6 sec. 1M. W. Col. 5m.

CUMBERLAND BASIN.
ENTRANCE, N SIDE. Lt. 2 F.R. vert.
ENTRANCE, S SIDE. Lt. 2 F.G. vert.
PLIMSOLL BRIDGE CENTRE. Lt.Bn. Iso. 5 sec.

AVON BRIDGE.
N SIDE. Lt. F.R. 1M.
CENTRE. Lt. Iso. 5 sec. 1M.
S SIDE. Lt. F.G. 1M.

RIVER SEVERN
BEDWIN SANDS. Lt.By. Fl.(3) 10 sec. Pillar B.Y.B. Topmark E.
No. 1 LOWER SHOOTS. Bn. △.
THE SHOOTS. Charston Rocks Lt. Fl. 5 sec. 9M. B.W. Tr. 5m. 203°-049°.
REDCLIFFE Ldg.Lts. 012°51' (Front) F. Bu. 8M. B. Tr. 16m. 358°-028° (Rear) F. Bu. 10M. mast 33m.
CHAPEL ROCK. Lt. Fl.W.R.G. 2.5 sec. W.8M. G.5M. B. Tr. W. lantern. W.213°-284°; R.284°-049°; W.049°-051.5°; G.051.5°-160°.

WYE BRIDGE. Lts. 2 Fl.Bu. hor. centre of span on up and downstream sides.

SEVERN BRIDGE. W.Tr. Lts. 3 Q. up and downstream. Horn(3) 45 sec.
CENTRE SPAN. Lt. Q.Bu. up and downstream.
E TR. Lts. 3 Q. up and downstream.

AUST. Lt. 2 Q.G. vert 6M. Power cable pylon 11.5m.
LYDE ROCK. Lt. Q.R. 2.6 sec. B.Tr. W. lantern, 5m.
SEDBURY. Lt. 2 F.R. vert. 3M. mast 10m.
SLIME ROAD. Ldg.Lts. 210°26'. (Front) F.Bu. 5M. W. hut, 9m. neon. (Rear) F.Bu. 5M. B. Tr. W. lantern 16m. neon.
INWARD ROCKS. Ldg.Lts. 252°28'. (Front) F. 6M. B. Tr. W. lantern, 6m. neon. (Rear) F. 2M. W. hut, mast, 13m. neon.
COUNTS. Lt.By. Q. Pillar. B. Topmark N.

SHEPERDINE. Ldg.Lts. 070°24'. (Front) F. 5M. B.Tr. W. lantern, 7m. neon. (Rear) F. 5M. B.Tr. W. lantern, 13m. neon. Bell(26) 60 sec.
NARLWOOD ROCKS. Ldg.Lts. 224°55'. (Front) Fl. 2 sec. 8M. Y.Bn. B.lantern, 5m. (Rear) Fl. 2 sec. 8M. Y.Bn. B.lantern, 9m.
LEDGES. Lt. F. Fl.(3)G. 10 sec. Boat G. Bell(2) 60 sec.
CONIGRE. Ldg.Lts. 077°30'. (Front) F.Vi. 8M. Tr. 21m. neon. (Rear) F.Vi. Tr. 29m. neon.
HILLS FLATS. Lt.By. Fl.G. 4 sec. Conical G.
HAYWARD ROCK. Lt. F. Q.G. Conical G.
FISHING HOUSE. Ldg.Lts. 217°41'. (Front) F. 2M. W. hut, 5m. neon. (Rear) F. 2M. W. hut, 11m. neon.
CONIGRE PILL POWER STATION, S END. Lt. 2 F.G. vert.
CENTRE. Lt. 2 F.G. vert. Siren(2) 30 sec.
N END. Lt. 2 F.G. vert.
BULL ROCK. Lt. Iso. 2 sec. 8M. G. mast 6m.

LYDNEY. 51°43'N, 2°31'W.
Tel: H.M: (0594) 516391. Dock Office: (0594) 842884. Yacht Club: (0594) 42573. Port Authority (N.R.A.) Severn/Trent Region: (0684) 850951.
Radio–Port: VHF Chan. 16: Working Channel.
Entry: 48h. notice required by telephone of entry/exit.
Traffic Signals: B. Ball = do not enter until outward vessel clear.
R. Lt. = Dock gates will not open on this tide.
Tidal Basin: Gates open 1 h.-HW. Entrance 10.1m. × depth over sill 7.3m. MHWS.
Dock: Lock 7.3m. × 4.1m. on sill. Thence via canal to upper dock.
Yacht Marina in docks.
PIER HEAD. Lt. F.W. or R. 6m tidal. Gong tidal.
BERKELEY PILL. Ldg.Lts. 187°46'. (Front) F.G. 2M. B.Tr. W. lantern, 5m. neon. (Rear) F.G. 2M. B.Tr. W. lantern, 11m. neon.
PANTHURST PILL. Lt. F.Bu. 1M. W. post, concrete hut, 6m. neon in form of X.

SHARPNESS 51°43'N, 2°29'W. Tel: Dursley
(0453) 811644. Telex: 43376 BWBSDS G.
Radio — Port: c/s Sharpness Control. VHF Chan. 16, 14. H24. Area covered: River Severn from seaward end Shoots Chan. to Sharpness, Gloucester and Sharpness Canal. Establish contact on app. to Shoots Chan.
Entry: B. Ball/R. Lts. = no entry. Port Closed. No Signal = entry for small vessels.
Yachts must not stay in Commercial Port.
S PIER HEAD. Lt. 2 F.G. vert. W. Post. 3M. 6m. Siren 20 sec.
N PIER HEAD. Lt. 2 F.R. vert. 3M. W. Pillar. 6m.
OLD ENTCE. S SIDE. Siren 5 sec. Tidal.

River Severn Locks (B.W.B.) Tel: (0452) 25524.
Operate 0800-1630 Winter. 0800-1915 Summer.
High/Low Level Bridges — Sharpness — advance booking through Lock-keeper Gloucester (0452) 25524 Ext. 249.
Sharpness Tidal Lock 24 h. notice as above. Open normally 2 h.-HW-1 h.
All Locks and Bridges fitted VHF Chan. 16, 74.

Sharpness: Docking Signals.
2 B. Balls or 2 R. Lts. (hor.) = Gates closed.
1 B. Ball or 1 R. Lt. = Entrance not clear.
1 G. Flag or 1 G. Lt. = Entrance clear for large vessels.
1 G. Flag/1 B. Ball or G. Lt./R. Lt. = Small vessels to dock BEFORE large ones.
2 G. Flags or 2 G. Lts. (hor.) = HW or tide ebbing.
Lock Gates open 2 h.-HW-½ h.
Sharpness/Gloucester Canal — Max. size vessel = 58m. × 8.8m. × 3.5m. draught.
Gloucester/Worcester — 41m. × 6.4m. × 2.4m. draught.
Worcester/Stourport — 27.4m. × 5.8m. × 1.8m. draught.

GLOUCESTER AREA
(British Waterways Board. Tel: (0452) 25524).
All the following operate on VHF Chan. 16 & 74.
Lincombe Lock (02993) 2887.
Holt Lock (0905) 620218.
Bever Lock (0905) 640275.
Diglis Lock (0905) 354280.
Upper Lode Lock (0684) 293138.

Gloucester Lock (0452) 25524, ext. 249.
Gloucester Lock (0452) 25525 (0.0.h.)
Hemstead Bridge (0452) 21880
Sellars Bridge (0452) 720251.
Junction Bridge (0452) 740444.

Cambridge Arm Bridge (045389) 272.
Patch Bridge (045389) 324.
Purton Bridge (0453) 811384.
Sharpness Marine (0453) 811476.
Splatt Bridge.

Sandfield Bridge.
Parkend Bridge.
Hardwicke Bridge.
Rea Bridge.
Sims Bridge.

BIRMINGHAM AREA
(British Waterways Board. Tel: (021-454) 7091).
Diglis Basin No. 1 & 2. VHF Chan. 16 & 74.
Stourport Basin No. 1 & 2. VHF Chan. 16 & 74.

Severn Bore: Starts about 2M above Sharpness reaching full undulation at about Longney. Front reaches 1-1.5m height. Strongest at about the 5th flood stream after the full or change of moon. Speed starts at about 5 kts. increasing to 14 kts. at Rosemary then decreasing. Boats can ride the wave if afloat and in mid-river but beware of violent breakers along the banks.

GLOUCESTER 51°52′N, 2°13′W.

Pilots Tel: Dursley (0453) 811323.
Telex: 498180 SEWPIL G.
Entry: Vessels for Chepstow check mast height, and whether masts can be lowered. BR. HT. Max. 52 ft, 15.8m. Above M.H.W.S. Vessels to be at Kings Road 2 h. before H.W. Sharpness to dock on that tide.
Radio — Pilots: VHF Chan. 16, 6, 8, 9, 11, 14. Hrs: Mon-Fri. 0900-1800.

WESTON-SUPER-MARE.

S PATCHES. Lt.By. Fl.(2) 5 sec. Pillar. B.R.B. Topmark 2 Sph. Bell.
PIER HEAD. Lt. 2 F.G. vert. W. post, 6 and 5m.
W CULVER. Lt.By. V.Q.(9) 10 sec. Pillar. Y.B.Y. Topmark W. on W end of Sands.
E CULVER. Lt.By. Q.(3) 10 sec. Pillar. B.Y.B. Topmark E. on E end of Sands.

INSHORE WAYPOINT BRIDGWATER BAY. 51°15.0′N, 3°08.5′W.

RIVER PARRETT TO BRIDGWATER

BRIDGWATER 51°21′N, 3°00′W. Pilots & Port: (0278) 782180.

Pilotage: 24 h. notice required at Gore By. or Barry Roads.
P/Station: Pilots board in vicinity of No: 7 By.
Radio — Port: VHF Chan. 16, 8. 3 h.-HW.
Entry: Bridgwater Bar dries 0.6m. Arrive at Gore By. between 2-3 h.-HW when enough water for draught up to 4.5m.

Gore Sand and Stert Flats – fishing stakes unmarked.

GORE. Lt.By. Iso. 5 sec. Sph. R.W.V.S. Bell. on N edge of Cobbler Patch. No: 1 Lt.By. Fl. 2.5 sec. Conical R.Y.
'DZ' No: 1 Lt.By. Fl.Y. 2½ sec. Conical Y.
'DZ' No: 2 Lt.By. Fl.Y. 10 sec. Conical Y.
HINKLEY POINT. Lt. 2 F.G. vert. 3M. on metal Col. 7 and 5m.

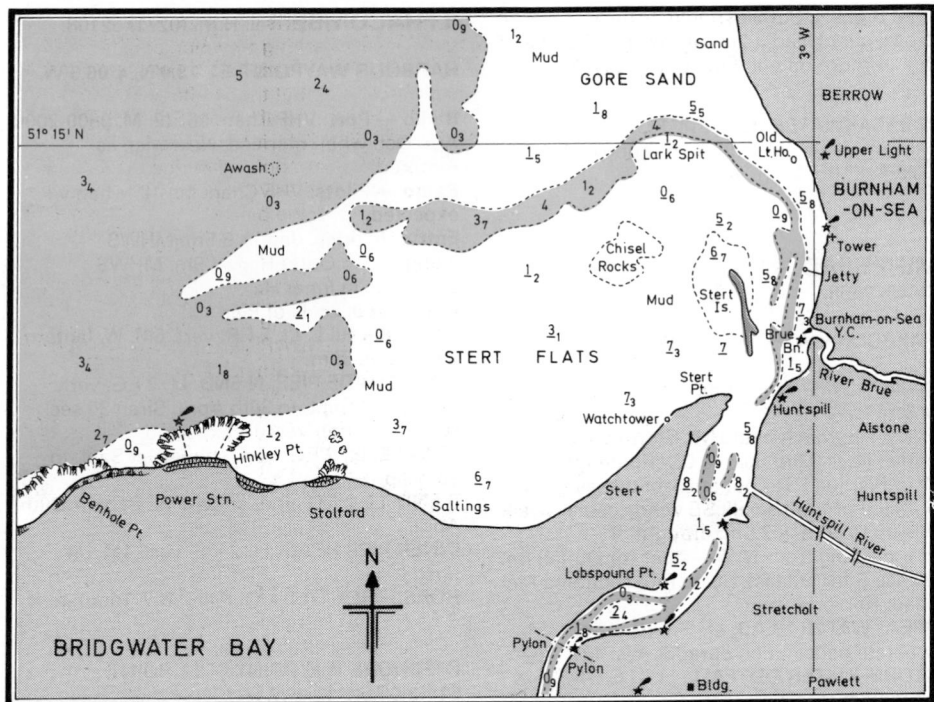

CHANNEL TO BURNHAM
No: 1 Lt.By. Q.R. Can.R.
No: 2 Lt.By. Fl.G. 5 sec. Conical G.
No: 4 Lt.By. Q.R. Can.R.
No: 7 Lt.By Fl.G. 5 sec. Conical G.
No: 9 By. Conical G.

BURNHAM ON SEA
ENTCE. 51°14.9′N, 2°59.9′W. Lt. Fl. 7.5 sec.
17M. W. square Tr. R. stripe, 28m. Vis. 074°-
164°. Dir.Lt. 078.5°. Dir. F.W.R.G. W.16M.
R.12M. G.12M. G.073°-077°; W.077°-080°;
R.080°-083°.
SEAFRONT. Ldg.Lts. (Front) F.R. 3M. concrete
Col. 6m. moved to meet changes in Chan.
(Rear) F.R. on Church Tr. 3M.
BRUE. Lt.Bn. Q.R. 3M. W. mast, R. bands, 4m.
STERT REACH. Lt. Fl. 3 sec. 7M. W.Col. 4m.
EAST DUNBALL POINT. Lt. Q.R. 2M. R.post,
W. bands, 5m.
COMBWICH REACH N. Lt. Q.R. 2M. R.post, W.
band, 5m.
COMBWICH WHARF. Lts. 2 F.G. vert. 3M.
dolphin.
COMBWICH REACH S. Lt. Q.R. 2M. R.Bn. W.
bands, 5m.
MARCHANTS REACH W SIDE. Lt. Fl.R. 2M.
R.Bn. W. bands, 5m.

WALPOLE SHELL MEX WHARF. Lt. 2 F.R. vert.
3M. Col. 5m.
NINE STREAMS POINT. Lt. Q.R. 2M. R.Bn. W.
stripes, 5m.
BIBBYS WHARF. Lt. 2 F.R. vert. 2M. wharf
face, 2m.
CUT POINT. Lt. Fl.G. 2M. B.post, W. bands,
5m.
'DZ' No: 2. Lt.By. Fl. 10 sec. Conical R.Y.
target.

LILSTOCK RANGE BYS.
Lt.By. Fl.(4)Y. 10 sec. Target Pillar Y.
Lt.By. Fl.Y. 2 sec. Conical Y.

WATCHET 51°11′N, 3°20′W. Tel: Watchet
(0984) 31264.

HARBOUR WAYPOINT. 51°11.5′N, 3°19.5′W.

Radio — Port: VHF Chan. 16, 9, 12, 14. 2 h.-
HW.
Entry: Hbr. dries 4m. Can take draught up to
5m. Depths cannot be relied on, allow 0.5m
underkeel clearance. Approach near HW.
Strong Tidal set across entrance. If bad
weather — Lt. & Signals not shown.

Tidal Signals: B. Ball shown from W Breakwater Head = 2m. or more on flood and 3m. or more on ebb tide. Entrance clear.

W BREAKWATER HEAD. Lt. F.G. 9M. R. 6-sided metal Tr. W. lantern, G. cupola, 9m.
E PIER. Lt.Bn. 2 F.R. vert. 3M.

MINEHEAD. 51°12.8′N, 3°28.3′W. Tel: (0643) 2566.

HARBOUR WAYPOINT. 51°13.75′N, 3°27.5′W.

Radio — Port: VHF Chan. 16, 12, 14 — 3 h. before HW.
Entry: Approach near HW. Storm water outfall rises 2.8m. above CD. Ruined Pier 1c. W of Pierhead. Do not attempt crossing outfall if ground swell. SE winds cause swell. V/ls up to 60m. × 2.5m. draught. If approaching from NW — steer for Outfall Bn. thence S for at least 1½c. before rounding Pier head. Hbr. dries out.
BREAKWATER HEAD. Lt. Fl.(2)G. 5 sec. 4M. concrete pedestal on parapet. Vis. 127°-262°.
STORM WATER OUTFALL. Lt. Q.G. 7M. G. Δ on Bn. 6m.

PORLOCK WEIR
Pool depth 1m at LW. Dock can take 3.7m draught at MHWS. Drying channel depth 5m at MHWS. Dock sill depth 4m at MHWS. About six small craft can lie afloat in the pool, others dry out on hard bottom in the dock.

OFFSHORE WAYPOINT FORELAND POINT. 51°16.0′N, 3°47.0′W.

LYNMOUTH FORELAND POINT
51°14.7′N, 3°47.1′W. Lt. Fl.(4) 15 sec. 26M. W. round Tr. 67m. Vis. 083°-275°. Storm sig. H24.
SAND RIDGE By. Conical G. on W edge.

LYNMOUTH.
Entry: Depth 4.6m. alongside MHWS.
RIVER TRAINING ARM. Lt. 2 F.R. vert. 5M. on Col. 6m.
HARBOUR ARM. Lt. 2 F.G. vert. 5M. on Col. 6m.
COPPERAS ROCKS By. Conical G. off Coombe Martin.

OFFSHORE WAYPOINT NE OF ILFRACOMBE. 51°13.75′N, 4°06.0′W.

ILFRACOMBE. Tel: H.M. (0271) 62108.

HARBOUR WAYPOINT. 51°13.0′N, 4°06.5′W.

Radio — Port: VHF Chan. 16, 12. M. 0800-2000 Apr.-Oct. when manned: Nov.-Mar. as required.
Radio — Pilots: VHF Chan. 16, 12, when v/l expected.
Entry: Hr. dries, depths 5.5m. MHWS alongside in Outer Hr. & 4.9m. MHWS alongside in Inner Hr.
Anchorage: 2c. N of Pier.
LANTERN HILL. Lt. 2 F.R. vert. 6M. W. lantern on chapel, 39m.
PROMENADE PIER, N END. Lt. 2 F.G. vert. shown 1st Sept. to 30th April. Siren 30 sec. sounded when vessels expected.
CENTRE. Lt. 2 F.G. vert. shown 1st Sept. to 30th April.
S END. Lt. 2 F.G. vert. shown 1st Sept. to 30th April.
INNER PIER HEAD. Lt. 2 F.G. vert. 1M. on post, 6m.
HORSESHOE. Lt.By. Q. Pillar. B.Y. Topmark N.

OFFSHORE WAYPOINT BULL POINT. 51°13.0′N, 4°13.0′W.

BULL POINT 51°12.0′N, 4°12.0′W. Lt. Fl.(3)
10 sec. 25M. W. round Tr. 47m. Storm sig. Obs. Shore-045°. Shown H24. Same structure Lt. F.R. 12M. 41m. Vis. 058°-096°.
MORTE STONE By. Conical G. ⫞ off Morte Pt.
BAGGY LEAP By. Conical G. off Baggy Pt.

OFFSHORE WAYPOINT BAGGY POINT. 51°10.0′N, 4°19.0′W.

BARNSTAPLE BAY

APPLEDORE & BIDEFORD Tel: H.M. (0237) 476711, ext. 317. Fax: (0234) 478849. Senior Pilot: (0237) 473806.
Radio — Pilots: VHF Chan. 16, 12. 2h.-HW Bideford.

BIDEFORD 51°03′N, 4°10′W. Tel: Bideford (02372) 73806.

HARBOUR WAYPOINT RIVER TAW. 51°05.0′N, 4°16.0′W.

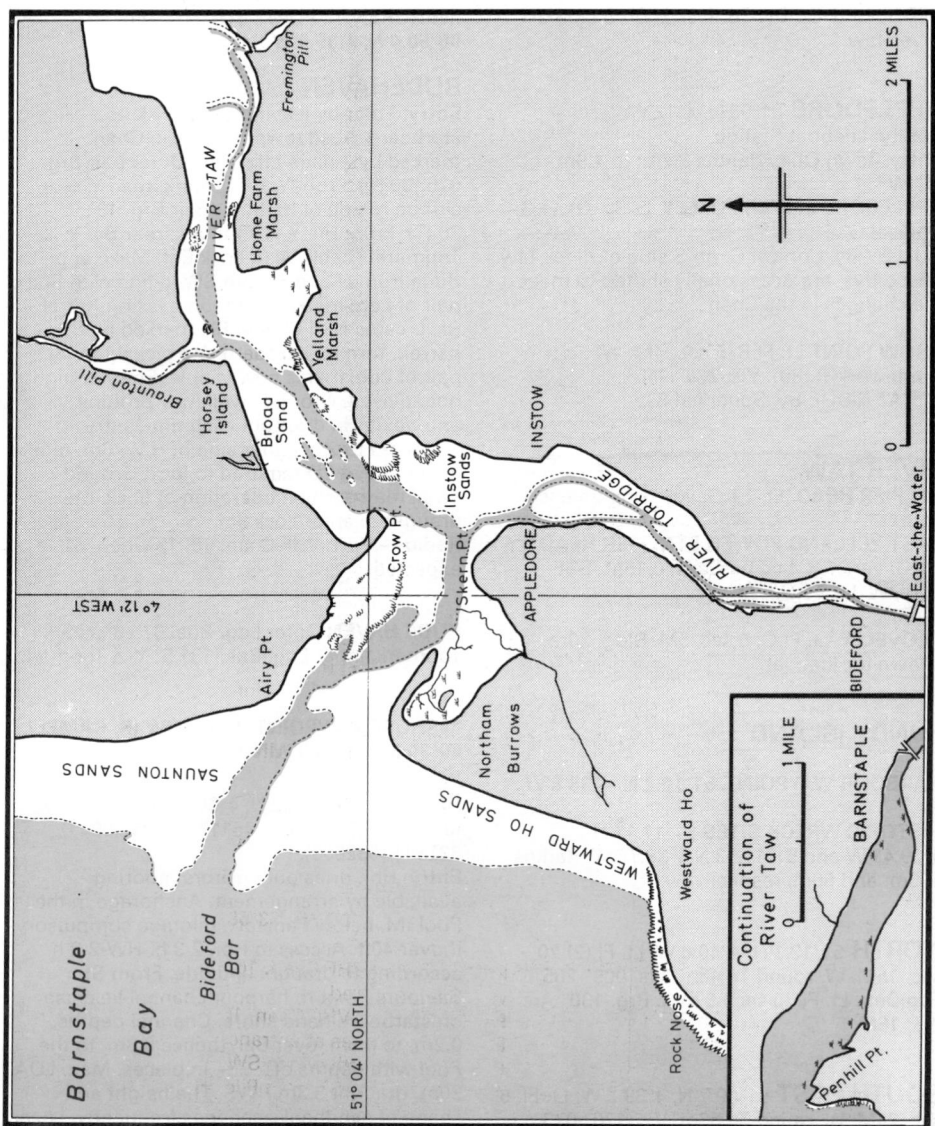

Radio — Pilots: VHF Chan. 16, 12. 2 h.-HW.
BRIDGE: Vert. Clearance 24m.
Anchorage: Good weather — Bideford
Fairway By. Bad weather — Clovelly Roads in
W/SW gales.
Entry: Bar dries. Ground swell causes steep
confused seas on the Bar, especially in NW
winds, making it impassable for yachts.
Tide can make 5 kts. off Skern Point at
Springs.

BIDEFORD FAIRWAY. Lt.By. L.Fl. 10 sec. Pillar.
R.W.V.S. Bell.

BIDEFORD — ENTRANCE TO RIVER TAW & TORRIDGE

INSTOW. 51°03.6′N, 4°10.6′W. Ldg.Lts.
118°. (Front) Oc. 6 sec. 15M. W. ◫ on W.
framework Tr. 22m. Vis. 103°-133°. Shown by
day. F.R. Lt. on radio masts 3M. NNW. F.R. Lt.
occas. on Heanton Punchardon Church
2.75M. NNE. (Rear) Oc. 10 sec. 15M. W. Tr.
38m. Vis. 103°-133°. Shown by day.
BAR. By. Conical G. Fluorescent panels.

MIDDLE RIDGE By. Conical G. on S side of River Taw.

APPLEDORE 51°03'N, 4°12'W.
Safety: Lifeboat Station.
Entry: Town Quay depths 3.7m. to 4.9m. MHWS.
APPLEDORE OUTER PULLEY. Lt.By. Qk.Fl.G. Conical G.
PULLEY By. Conical G. on S side of River Taw. These Bys. are occasionally shifted to meet the changes in the Chan.

CROW POINT Lt. Fl.R. 5 sec. 4M. W. framework Tr. 8m. Vis. 225°-045°.
SPRAT RIDGE By. Spherical R.

RIVER TAW
OIL PIER HEAD. Lt. 2 F.G. vert. one on each corner.
EAST YELLAND POWER STN. PIER HEAD. Lt. 2 F.G. vert. F.R. Lts. on Chys. 0.15M. SSE.
ELBOW. Lt. 2 F.G. vert.

CLOVELLY. Lt. Fl.G. 5 sec. 5M. Bldg. 30m. shown for lifeboat.

LUNDY ISLAND

HARBOUR WAYPOINT. 51°10.2'N, 4°38.8'W.

HISTORIC WRECK SITES 51°11.11'N 4°39.41'W and 51°11.03'N 4°38.78'W. Radius 100m. and 50m. respectively.

NORTH 51°12.1'N, 4°40.6'W. Lt. Fl.(2) 20 sec. 15M. W. round Tr. 48m. Vis. 009°-285°. Fog Detr. Lt. Fl. (5 sec.) 5 min. Brg. 130° Arc 2.5° 16M.

SOUTH EAST 51°09.7'N, 4°39.3'W. Lt. Fl. 5 sec. 24M. W. round Tr. 53m. Vis. 170°-073°. Distress sig. Horn 25 sec. RC.

HARTLAND POINT 51°01.3'N, 4°31.4'W. Lt. Fl.(6) 15 sec. 25M. W. round Tr. 37m. Horn 60 sec. Shown H24.

OFFSHORE WAYPOINT HARTLAND POINT. 51°02.0'N, 4°33.0'W.

HARTLAND RG STN. 51°01.2'N, 4°31.6'W. Emergency DF Stn. VHF Chan. 16 & 67. Controlled by MRSC Swansea.

INSHORE WAYPOINT BUDEHAVEN. 50°50.0'N, 4°35.5'W.

BUDEHAVEN Tel: (0288) 3111.
Entry: Enter by leaving Chapel Rk. to starboard, head towards Lock in Chan. marked by 2 pairs Ldg. Bns. Outer pair Brg. 075° 30'(T). Front Y. ◊ Topmark, rear, Y. ◊ on cliff on N side of Hr. Inner pair Brg. 131° 30'(T). Front Bn. Y. △ Topmark, rear Bn. Y. △ Topmark, ½ cable W of Lock Ent. Make appr. to Bude from N and S from SW in line with first pair of Ldg. marks . Imm. on passing Barrel Rk. (½ cable N of Chapel Rk. marked by Bn. barrel), turn to starboard and pick up inner pair of Ldg. marks now visible. Entry at night not advised. Ground swell may prohibit entry/exit. Hr. dries out each tide, entry restricted to 2 h. either side of H.W. 6m. min. water above CD required to lock. Ground swell may prohibit operation of Lock. Max. draught to enter Lock 3m.
Radio — Port: VHF Chan. 16, 12 when V/L expected.

BUDE HAVEN Outer Ldg. Bns. 075.5° Y. ◊ Topmark. Inner Ldg. Bns. 131.5° Y. △ Topmark.

INSHORE WAYPOINT PADSTOW (R. CAMEL). 50°35.5'N, 4°58.0'W.

PADSTOW 50°32'N, 4°56'W. Tel: Padstow (0841) 532239. Telex: 45117. Pilots: (0841) 532541 [532603].
Entry: Hbr. dries out. Visitors mooring available by arrangement. Anchorage in the Pool ¼M. below Padstow. Pilotage compulsory if over 40ft. Access to Hbr. 2-3 h.-HW-2-3 h. according to draught and tide. From St. Saviours Point to harbour channel lie close on starboard hand shore. Channel depths 0.2m. to 0.5m. over Bar, thence 0.8m. to the Pool with depths of 2.7m. in places. Max. LOA 30m, draught 3.3m HWS. The height and shape of sandbanks changes frequently. Local knowledge essential.
Radio — Pilots and Port: VHF Chan. 16, 14. 0830-1730 Mon.-Fri. also 2½ h.-HW-1½ h.

STEPPER POINT Lt. Fl. 10 sec. 4M. metal Col. 12m.
KETTLE ROCK. Lt. Q.G. 2m.
DOON BAR Lt.By. Fl.G. 5 sec. Conical G. W edge of Bk. in Chan.
GREENAWAY Lt.By. Fl.(2)R. 10 sec. Can.R.
ST SAVIOUR'S POINT. Lt. L.Fl.G. 10 sec. Topmark G. △.
N QUAY HEAD Lt. 2 F.G. vert. 2M. metal Col. 6m.

A F. Lt. is shown from heads of each of the inner quays.
S QUAY HEAD. Lt. 2 F.R. vert. 2M. metal Col. 7m.

TREVOSE HEAD RG STN 50°32′53″0N
5°01′55″0W. Emergency DF Stn. VHF Chan. 16 & 67. Controlled by MRCC Falmouth.
Lt.By. Fl.Y. 5 sec. pillar Y. ⩗. N of Trevose Hd.

OFFSHORE WAYPOINT TREVOSE HEAD.
50°33.0′N, 5°05.0′W.

TREVOSE HEAD 50°32.9′N, 5°02.1′W. Lt.
Fl. 5 sec. 25M. W. round Tr. 62m. Storm sig. Horn(2) 30 sec.

NEWQUAY (Cornwall) 50°25′N, 5°05′W. Tel:
H.M. (0637) 872809.

HARBOUR WAYPOINT. 50°26.0′N, 5°05.0′W.

Entry: Tidal and dries out at Springs. Access 4 h.-HW-4 h. Space is limited. Visitors moorings by arrangement. A ground swell causes heavy surf in Harbour at times. For Marina see Section 25.

N PIER HEAD Lt. 2 F.G. vert. 2M. bracket on wall 5m.
S PIER HEAD Lt. 2 F.R. vert. 2M. round stone Tr. 4m.

OFFSHORE WAYPOINT 6M. NW OF ST. AGNES HD. 50°22.5′N, 5°22.5′W.

TARGET Lt.Bys. 'A', 'C'. Fl. 1.5 sec. Spherical R.Y. vert. stripes approx. 6M. off St. Agnes Hd.
RADAR TRAINING No: 6. Lt.By. Fl.Y. 5 sec. Pillar. Y.
RADAR TRAINING No: 11. Lt.By. Fl.Y. 5 sec. Pillar. Y.
Lt.By. Fl.R. 2.5 sec. Pillar R.Y. NNW of Godrevy Lt.

GODREVY ISLAND 50°14.5′N, 5°23.9′W.
Lt. Fl.W.R. 10 sec. W.12M. R.9M. W. octagonal stone Tr. 37m. W.022°-101°; R.101°-145°; W.145°-272°.
Lts. 4 F.R. vert. shown on radio mast 6.5M. SE.
STONES Lt.By. Q. Pillar. B.Y. Topmark N. Bell. Whis.

5 perches mark W side of Chan. to Hayle Hr. Bar By. B. is at entce, also small By. Can.B. marking W Spit. 4 perches have F.Bu.Lts. not vis. from seawards.

HAYLE 51°11′N, 5°26′W.
Entry: Bar dries. Depth 5.5m. MHWS over Bar, harbour dries. Depth 4.6m. MHWS alongside. Hayle Hr. now closed to commercial traffic. Fishing vessels and other small craft may enter, crossing bar in favourable weather 1 h. — HW — 1 h. Position of bar frequently changes. Ldg.Lts. do not indicate deepest water.
HAYLE. Ldg.Lts. 180°. (Front) F. 4M. pile structure, R. and W. lantern, 17m. occas. (Rear) F. 4M. pile structure, R. and W. lantern, 23m. occas.
PERCH No: 4 Lt. F.G.
PERCH Lt. F.
PERCH Lt. F.
CHAPEL ANJOU POINT Lt. F. on Col.

OFFSHORE WAYPOINT NW OF ST. IVES.
50°15.75′N, 5°33.5′W.

ST. IVES 50°12′N, 5°20′W. Tel: H.M.
Penzance (0736) 795018.

HARBOUR WAYPOINT. 50°13.5′N, 5°28.0′W.

Radio — Port: VHF Chan. 16.
Entry: Drying Hbr. Remains of 'New Pier' SW of Smeatons Pier marked by buoy, submerged except at LW. Visitors moorings available contact H.M. Entrance depths 4.6m. MHWS and 2.7m. MHWN.

ST. IVES. By. Conical G. staff. SE end old breakwater.
SMEATONS E PIER HEAD Lt. 2 F.G. vert. W. round metal Tr. 8m.
W PIER HEAD Lt. 2 F.R. vert. 3M. Grey Col. 5m.

PORTREATH 50°12′N, 5°28′W.

HARBOUR WAYPOINT. 50°16.0′N, 5°18.0′W.

Entry: Entrance dangerous with heavy swell. Dries out. Access 2 h.-HW-2 h. Visitors moorings may be available.

PENDEEN RG STN. 50°08.6′N, 5°38.2′W.
Emergency DF Stn. VHF Chan. 16 & 67. Controlled by MRCC Falmouth.

OFFSHORE WAYPOINT N OF GURNARDS HD. **50°13.5'N, 5°37.5'W.**

OFFSHORE WAYPOINT W OF PENDEEN. **50°10.0'N, 5°43.0'W.**

PENDEEN 50°09.8'N, 5°40.2'W. Lt. Fl.(4) 15 sec. 27M. W. round Tr. 59m. Vis. 042°-240°; in bay between Gurnard Head and Pendeen, it shows to the coast. Siren 20 sec.
WELLHEAD Lt.By. 50°57.1'N, 6°46.9'W. Q.R. Spherical B.R.W. Hor. bands. Bell. ♪♪ .

OFFSHORE WAYPOINT W OF C. CORNWALL. **50°08.0'N, 5°45.0'W.**

OFFSHORE WAYPOINT OFF LANDS END. **50°03.0'N, 5°45.0'W.**

SOUTH COAST OF IRELAND

REPUBLIC OF IRELAND. DOCUMENTATION.
Fly Flag 'Q' and report to Customs or Civic Guard.
No passports necessary for U.K. citizens. Irish Tourist Board, 150 New Bond Street, London W1Y 0AQ. Tel: 01-493 3201.
Entry by Road: Ensure both craft and car are fully insured incl. craft when in the water! Temp. importation covered by Customs form 704A and 710 (up to six months).
Check Customs forms 142 & 142A for dutiable, prohibited or restricted goods.
Inland Waterways: Grand Canal/River Barrow. Speed limit 5 kmph, max. size 18.6m. × 3.9m. × 1.2m. draught × 2.74m. air draught. Lock permits required obtainable from Lock keepers.
River Shannon max. size 29m. × 5.8m. × 1m. draught × 2.1m. air draught. (least depth 1.3m.-1.5m.: lowest bridge 2.1m. MHWS — 3.65m. MHWN.)
Fuel: Petrol may be obtained from garages but diesel may be difficult. Water: Scarce in western regions. Fill up in Castletownbere, Kilronan, Killybegs.

FASTNET ROCK — EASTWARDS

OFFSHORE WAYPOINT S OF FASTNET. **51°22.0'N, 9°36.0'W.**

FASTNET 51°23.0'N, 9°36.0'W. Lt. Fl. 5 sec. 28M. Grey granite Tr. 49m. Horn (4) 60 sec., also shown in fog by day.
CLEAR ISLAND Wind motors established.

INSHORE WAYPOINT S OF C CLEAR. **51°24.4'N, 9°30.4'W.**

COPPER POINT LONG ISLAND E END. Lt. Q.(3) 10 sec. 8M. Pillar W. Topmark E. 16m.
AMELIA ROCK Lt.By. Fl.G. 3 sec. Conical G.
CUSH SPIT By. Conical G.

SCHULL HARBOUR. 51°31.6'N, 9°32.5'W. Ldg.Lts. 346°. (Front) Oc. 5 sec. 11M. W. mas* 5m. (Rear) Oc. 5 sec. 11M. W. mast 8m.
WRECK KOWLOON BRIDGE. 51°27.82'N, 9°13.77'W.
WRECK. Lt.By. Q.(6)+L.Fl. 15 sec. Pillar. Y.B. Topmark S.

BALTIMORE HARBOUR

HARBOUR WAYPOINT. **51°27.5'N, 9°23.0'W.**

BARRACK POINT Lt. Fl.(2)W.R. 6 sec. W.6M. R.3M. W. Tr. 40m. R.168°-294°; W.294°-038°. Occas.
LOT'S WIFE Tr. on Beacon Pt. E side of entce. to Hr.
LOO ROCK Lt.By. Fl.G. 3 sec. Conical G. on E side.
LOUSY ROCKS Perch Mast Y.B. Topmark S. 5m. on SE Rock.
WALLIS ROCK By. Can.R.

OFFSHORE WAYPOINT S OF TOE HEAD. **51°27.0'N, 9°11.0'W.**

CASTLE HAVEN, REEN POINT Lt. Fl.W.R.G. 10 sec. W.5M. R.3M. G.3M. W. Tr. 9m. G.shore-338°; W.338°-001°; R.001°-shore.

HARBOUR WAYPOINT. **51°30.0'N, 9°10.0'W.**

SKIDDY ISLAND Bn. Conical W. with R. band, on E side of entce. to Castle Haven.

INSHORE WAYPOINT E OF HIGH ISLAND. **51°30.6'N, 9°06.6'W.**

HARBOUR WAYPOINT GLANDORE. **51°32.0'N, 9°05.0'W.**

Glandore SW Perch. Mast G.
Glandore SE Perch. Mast R.
Glandore Mid. Perch. Mast G.
Glandore N Perch. Mast G.
Wind Rocks Perch. Mast G.

DANGER ROCK By. Pillar. B.Y. Topmark N. in Glandore Hr.

GALLEY HEAD 51°31.7′N, 8°57.1′W. Lt. Fl.(5) 20 sec. 28M. W. Tr. 53m. Vis. 256°-065°.

OFFSHORE WAYPOINT S OF GALLEY HEAD. 51°30.0′N, 8°57.0′W.

OFFSHORE WAYPOINT SE OF SEVEN HEADS. 51°33.5′N, 8°39.0′W.

CLONAKILTY HARBOUR Entce. marked by Perch.
FERRY POINT By. Conical B. in Courtmacsherry Bay.
BLACKTOM. By. Conical G.
COURTMACSHERRY Lt.By. Fl.G. 3 sec. Conical G. ᔐ at entce. to Courtmacsherry Hr.

COURTMACSHERRY HARBOUR

HARBOUR WAYPOINT. 51°37.0′N, 8°39.0′W.

LAND POINT Lt. Fl.(2) W.R. 5 sec. 5M. W. metal Col. 15m. W.315°-332°; R.332°-315°.

KINSALE HEAD GAS FIELD

MARATHON KINSALE B WEST. 51°21.6′N, 8°00.9′W. Lt. Mo.(U) 15 sec. 15M. & Mo(U)R. 15 sec. 3M. Horn. Mo.(U) 30 sec.
A EAST. 51°22.2′N, 7°56.7′W. Lt. as for B West.

OFFSHORE WAYPOINT S OF OLD HEAD OF KINSALE. 51°35.0′N, 8°31.0′W.

OLD HEAD OF KINSALE 51°36.3′N, 8°31.9′W. Lt. Fl.(2) 10 sec. 25M. B. Tr. 2 W. bands, 72m. on S Pt. Horn (3) 45 sec. R.C., also shown in fog by day.
BULMAN ROCK Lt.By. Q.(6)+L.Fl. 15 sec. Pillar. Y.B. Topmark S. off Entce. to Kinsale Hr.
CROHOGUE Lt.By. Fl.(3)R. 10 sec. Can.R.

KINSALE. 51°42′N, 8°31′W. Tel: H.M. (021) 772503. Night: 772256. Pilots: (021) 72300/72303. Telex: H.M. 28491.

HARBOUR WAYPOINT. 51°39.75′N, 8°30.25′W.

Radio — Port: VHF Chan. 16, 6, 14. H24.

CHARLESFORT Lt. Fl.W.R.G. 5 sec. W.9M. R.6M. G.6M. lantern on rampart of fort, 18m. G.348°-358°; W.358°-004°; R.004°-168°.
SPIT. Lt.By. Q.R. Can.R.
MARINA. Lt. 2 F.G. vert.
Above Charlesfort Chan. marked on W side by 3 Bys. Can.R.
SPUR Lt.By. Fl.(2)R. 6 sec. Can.R.

INSHORE WAYPOINT OFF ROBERTS HD. (CORK). 51°43.0′N, 8°16.5′W.

DAUNT ROCK Lt.By. Fl.(2)R. 6 sec. Can.R. ᔐ.
CORK. Lt.By. L.Fl. 10 sec. Pillar. R.W.V.S. Topmark Sph. Whis.

CORK 51°55′N, 8°30′W. Tel: Cork (021) 811380.

HARBOUR WAYPOINT. 51°47.5′N, 8°16.5′W.

Radio — Port: VHF Chan. 16, 14, 12 — continuous.
Radio — Pilots: VHF Chan. 16, 12, 6 — when on station.
Crosshaven Marina Tel. (021) 831161. Chan. (M) Mon.-Fri. 0900-1700.
Royal Cork Yacht Club Marina Tel. (021) 831440. Chan. (M) 0900-2300.

CAUTION — owing to their exposed positions, Bys. at entce. to Sound should not be relied upon. Vessels should navigate by Ldg.Lts.

THE SOUND TO DREDGED CHANNEL

ROCHE POINT 51°47.6′N, 8°15.3′W. Lt. Oc.W.R. 20 sec. W.20M. R.16M. W. Tr. 30m. R.shore-292°; W.292°-016°; R.016°-033°; W.(unintens) 033°-159°; R.159°-shore. Dia 30 sec. also shown by day in fog.
OUTER HARBOUR ROCK 'E2' Lt.By. Fl.R. 2.5 sec. Can.R.
CHICAGO KNOLL 'E1' Lt.By. Fl.G. 5 sec. Conical G.
'W2' Lt.By. Fl.R. 10 sec. Can.R.
W HARBOUR ROCK 'W1' Lt.By. Fl.G. 10 sec. Conical G. ᔐ.
'W4' Lt.By. Fl.R. 5 sec. Can.R.
'E4' Lt.By. Q. Pillar. B.Y. Topmark N.
No: 3 Lt.By. Fl.G. 2.5 sec. Conical G.
No: 6 Lt.By. Fl.R. 2.5 sec. Can.R. Turbot Bank.

WHITE BAY Ldg.Lts. 034°35'. (Front) Oc.R. 5 sec. 5M. W. hut, 11m. (Rear) Oc.R. 5 sec. 5M. W. hut, 21m. synchronized with front.

DREDGED CHANNEL TO COBH ROAD

FORT DAVIS 51°48.8'N, 8°15.8'W. Ldg.Lts. 354°05'. (Front) Oc. 5 sec. 10M. R. □ on metal framework Tr. 29m.
DOGNOSE LANDING QUAY (Rear) Oc. 5 sec. 10M. R. □ on Tr. 37m. Synchronized with front.
CURRAGHBINNEY Ldg.Lts. 252°. (Front). F. 3M. alum. Col. 10m. vis. 229.5°-274.5°. (Rear) F. 3M. alum. Col. 15m. vis. 229.5°-274.5°.
CROSSHAVEN MARINA. Lts. 2 F.R. vert. NE Corner. 2 F.R. vert. NW Corner.

RIVER OWENBOY
'C1' Lt.By. Fl.G. 10 sec. Conical G.
'C2' Bn. Pole B.
'C4' Lt.By. Fl.R. 10 sec. Can.R.
'C3' Lt.By. Fl.G. 10 sec. Conical G.

DOGNOSE No: 5 Lt.By. Fl.G. 5 sec. Conical G. on E side of Fairway.

No: 8 Lt.By. Fl.R. 5 sec. Can.R. on W. side of Chan. off Curlane Bk.
No: 10 Lt.By. Fl.R. 2.5 sec. Can.R.
No: 7 Lt.By. Fl.G. 2.5 sec. Conical G. off Black Rk. on E side of Chan.
No: 12 Lt.By. Fl.R. 5 sec. Can.R. on W side of Chan. off Spike I.
No: 14 Lt.By. Fl.R. 10 sec. Can.R. on W side of Chan. off Spike I.

COBH 51°50'N, 8°18'W.
Radio — Port: Whitegate Oil Wharf. VHF Chan. 16, 14.
Entry: N Side of Great Island (Cobh) isolated at HW. Passage between Daunt Rock & Roberts Head inadvisable in bad weather.

WHITEGATE MARINE TERMINAL JETTY. Lts. 2 F.G. vert.
No: 9 Lt.By. Fl.G. 5 sec. Conical G. off Entce. to E Chan.
No: 11 Lt.By. Fl.G. 10 sec. Conical G. on E side of Chan.
OUTER SPIT No: 16 Lt.By. Fl.R. 2 sec. Can.R.

SPIT BANK PILE 51°50.7'N, 8°16.4'W. Lt. Iso.W.R. 4 sec. W.10M. R.7M. W. house on R. piles, 10m. R.087°-196°; W.196°-221°; R.221°-358°.
No: 13 Lt.By. Fl.G. 2.5 sec. Conical G. on E side of Chan.

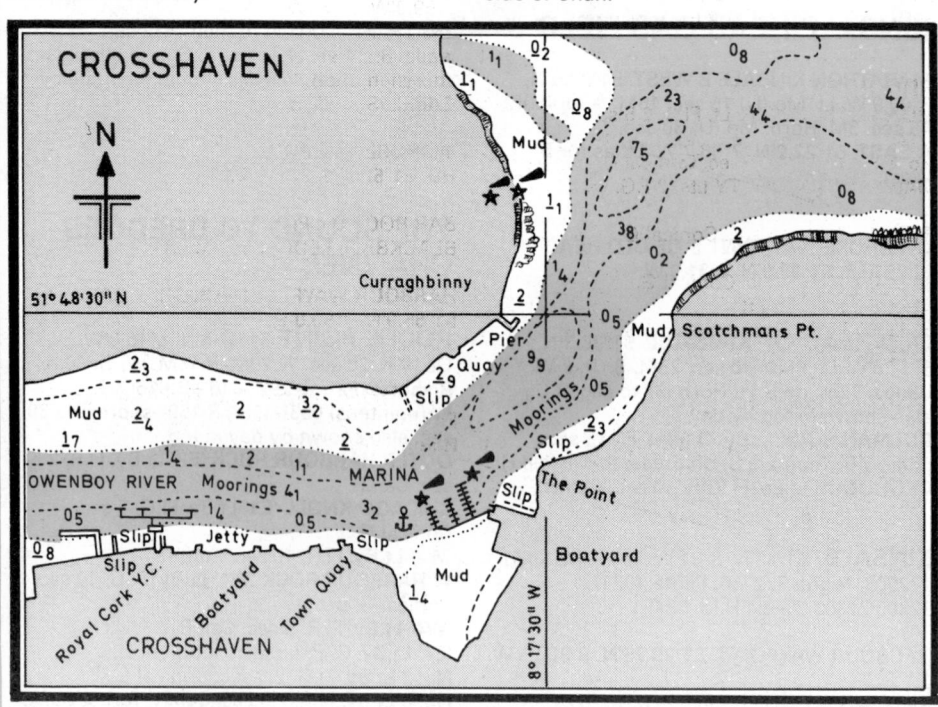

BAR ROCK No: 18 By. Pillar. Y.B. Topmark S. **No: 20 Lt.By.** Fl.R. 10 sec. Can.R. on N side of Spit Bk.
E PASSAGE E FERRY MARINA Lts. 2 F.R. vert. N & S ends.

SPIKE ISLAND
PIER HEAD Lt. 2 F.R. 2M. metal Col. 5m. 1 at either end.

HAULBOWLINE ISLAND
BASIN ENTCE. E SIDE Lt. 2 F.R. vert. on dolphin, 8m.
W SIDE Lt. 2 F.R. vert. on dolphin, 8m.
RINGASKIDDY BASIN ENTRANCE LTS. 2 F.R. vert. Pile.

WEST PASSAGE UP TO CORK

WHITE POINT No: 15 Lt.By. Fl.G. 5 sec. Conical G. on rocky shoals on N side of river.
BLACK POINT No: 17 Lt.By. Fl.G. 10 sec. Conical G. off Black Pt. on N side of river.
BALLYBRICKEN POINT JETTY. Lts. 3 F.R. vert.
MONKSTOWN PIER Lt. Fl.R. 2.5 sec. 4M. R. Tr. 4m. vis. 356°-209°.
VEROLME CORK DOCKYARD. Ldg.Lts. 029° (Front) 2 F.G. vert. (Rear) F.R.
FLOATING DOCK. Lts. 2 F.G. vert.

RIVER LEE
MONKSTOWN PIER. Lt. Fl.R. 2.5 sec. 4M. R. Tr. 4m. 356°-209°.
No: 21 Lt.By. Fl.G. 5 sec. Conical G.
MARINO POINT JETTY Lts. 2 F.G. vert.

R1 Lt.By. Fl.G. 2.5 sec. Conical G.
R2 Lt.By. Fl.R. Can.R.
R3 Lt.By. Fl.G. 5 sec. Conical G.
R4 Lt.By. Fl.R. Can.R.
R5 Lt.By. Fl.G. 2.5 sec. Conical G.
R6 Lt.By. Fl.R. Can.R.

R8 Lt.By. Fl.R. Can.R.

BARRY POINT OUTFALL. Bys. Conical G.
R10 Lt.By. Fl.R. Can.R.

R12 Lt.By. Fl.R. Can.R.
R7 Lt.By. Fl.G. 5 sec. Conical G.
R14 Lt.By. Fl.R. Can.R.
R16 Lt.By. Fl.R. Can.R.

R9 Lt.By. Fl.G. 5 sec. Conical G.
R11 Lt.By. Fl.G. 2.5 sec. Conical G.
R13 Lt.By. Fl.G. 5 sec. Conical G.

R18 Lt.By. Fl.R. Can.R.
CATTLE BERTH. Lt.Bn. Fl.G. 5 sec.
R20 Lt.By. Fl.R. Can.R.

R22 Lt.By. Fl.R. Can.R.
R24 Lt.By. Fl.R. Can.R.
R19 Lt.By. Fl.G. 5 sec. Conical G.
R21 Lt.By. Fl.G. 2.5 sec. Conical G.

TIVOLI 51°54.1'N, 8°26.0'W. Lt. Fl.G. 3 sec. 10M. Lantern on wall 3m. Vis. 275°-095°. on N side of Chan.
CORK, CUSTOM HOUSE Lt. 2 F.R. vert. 1M. bracket on corner of warehouse, 4m.

CORK HARBOUR TO DUNGARVAN HARBOUR

INSHORE WAYPOINT S OF POLLOCK ROCK. 51°46.0'N, 8°07.7'W.

POLLOCK ROCK. Lt.By. Fl.R. 6 sec. Can.R. Bell.
SMITHS. Lt.By. Fl.(3)R. 10 sec. Can.R. ⤳.

BALLYCOTTON ISLAND 51°49.0'N, 7°59.0'W. Lt. Fl.W.R. 10 sec. 22M. W.238°-063°; R.063°-238°. B. Tr. enclosed within W. walls, B.lantern. Horn (4) 90 sec. R.C., also shown in fog by day.
CAPEL ISLAND Bn. W. Tr. in Youghal Bay.

INSHORE WAYPOINT E OF KNOCKADOON HD. 51°52.5'N, 7°50.0'W.

BAR ROCK By. Pillar. Y.B. Topmark S.
BLACKBALL LEDGE. By. Can.R.

HARBOUR WAYPOINT YOUGHAL BAY. 51°55.0'N, 7°50.0'W.

YOUGHAL Tel: Pilots & Port (024) 92577. Fax: (024) 92747. Telex: 75888 YAWL.
Radio — Port: C/S. Greens Quay. VHF Chan. 16, 14. 3h-HW-3h.

YOUGHAL 51°56.5'N, 7°50.5'W. Lt. Fl.W.R. 2.5 sec. W.12M. R.9M. W. Tr. 24m. W.183°-273°; R.273°-295°; W.295°-307°; R.307°-351°; W.351°-003°.

INSHORE WAYPOINT E OF RAM HEAD. 51°56.0'N, 7°40.0'W.

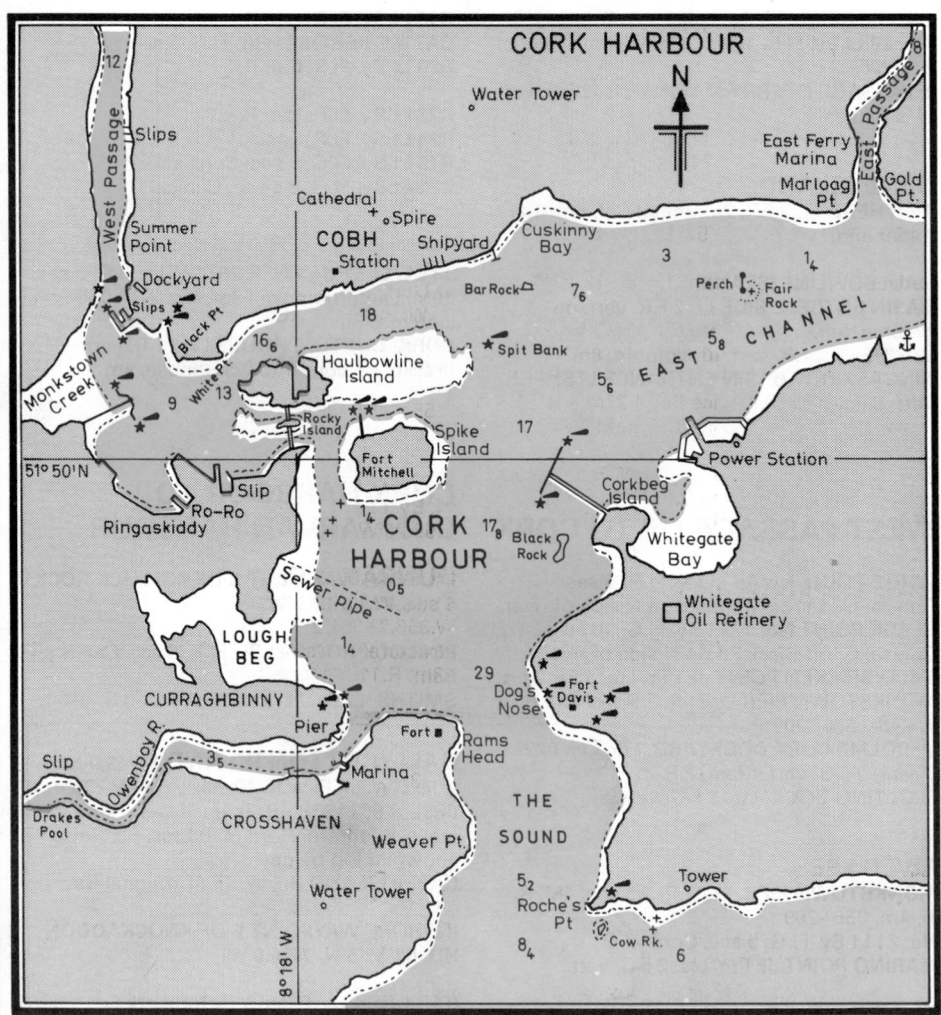

CORK HARBOUR

INSHORE WAYPOINT NE OF MINE HEAD.
52°00.0′N, 7°33.0′W.

MINE HEAD 51°59.6′N, 7°35.2′W. Lt. Fl.(4)
20 sec. 28M. W. Tr. B. band, 87m. vis. 228°-
shore.
HELVICK. Lt.By. Q.(3) 10 sec. Pillar. B.Y.B.
Topmark E.

BALLINACOURTY POINT 52°04.7′N,
7°33.1′W. Lt. Fl.(2) W.R.G. 10 sec. W.12M.
R.9M. G.9M. W. Tr. 16m. G.245°-274°; W.274°-
302°; R.302°-325°; W.325°-117°.
Port side of Chan. to Dungarvan marked by
Bys. Can.R. and starboard side marked by

Bys. Conical B. These Bys. are shifted from
time to time as Chan. changes.

INSHORE WAYPOINT OFF DUNGARVAN HR.
52°03.75′N, 7°31.5′W.

DUNGARVAN HARBOUR
BALLINACOURTY. Ldg.Lts. 083°. (Front) F. 2M.
W. Col. B. bands, 9m. (Rear) F. 2M. W. Col. B.
bands, 12m.
ESPLANADE. Ldg.Lts. (Front) F.R. 2M. on
post, 8m. (Rear) F.R. 2M. on mast, 9m.

INSHORE WAYPOINT OFF LOOKOUT POINT.
52°08.0′N, 6°58.0′W.

DUNGARVAN BAY TO WATERFORD

WATERFORD 52°09'N, 6°59'W. Tel: H.M. (051) 74907. Fax: (051) 74908. Pilots: (051) 74499.

HARBOUR WAYPOINT. 52°10.6'N, 6°56.2'W.

Radio — Ports: VHF Chan. 16, 14, 12. Mon.-Fri. 0900-1700.
Radio — Pilots: Dunmore E. VHF Chan. 16, 14. Mon.-Fri. 0900-1700 and when vessel expected.
Entry: Depth on Entrance Bar 4.27m. MLWST: Depth on Checkpoint Bar 3.35m. MLWST: Rise of Tide. 3.35m.-4.27m.
TRAMORE BAY Bns. W. end 3 W. Trs. one with man shaped topmark.
E END 2 Grey Trs. no Topmark.

WATERFORD HARBOUR

INSHORE WAYPOINT OFF HOOK HEAD.
52°07.2'N, 6°55.75'W.

HOOK HEAD 52°07.3'N, 6°55.7'W. Lt. Fl. 3 sec. 24M. W. Tr. 2 B. bands, 46m. Horn (2) 45 sec. Racon, also shown by day in fog.

DUNMORE EAST

E PIER HEAD. 52°08.9'N, 6°59.3'W. Lt. Fl.W.R. 8 sec. W.12M. R.9M. Grey granite Tr. W. lantern, 13m. W.225°-310°; R.310°-004°.
E BREAKWATER EXTENSION. Lt. Fl.R. 2 sec. 4M. 6m. vis. 000°-310°.
W WHARF. Lt. Fl.G. 2 sec. 4M. 6m. vis. 165°-246°.
DUNCANNON BAR
Lt. By. Fl.G. 2 sec. Conical G. 52°11.27'N 6°55.90'W.
Lt. By. Q.R. Can.R. 52°11.27'N 6°56.23'W.
Lt. By. Fl.G. 4 sec. Conical G. 52°12.00'N 6°56.00'W.
Lt. By. Fl.R. 3 sec. Can R. 52°12.00'N 6°56.20'W.

DUNCANNON. Dir. Lt. 357° Dir. Oc. W.R.G. 4 sec. W.11M. G.8M. R. 8M. G.353°-356.7°; W.356.7°-357.2°; R.357.2°-001°. Same structure Lt. Oc. W.R. 4 sec. W.9M. R.7M. 13m. R.119°-149°; W.149°-172.

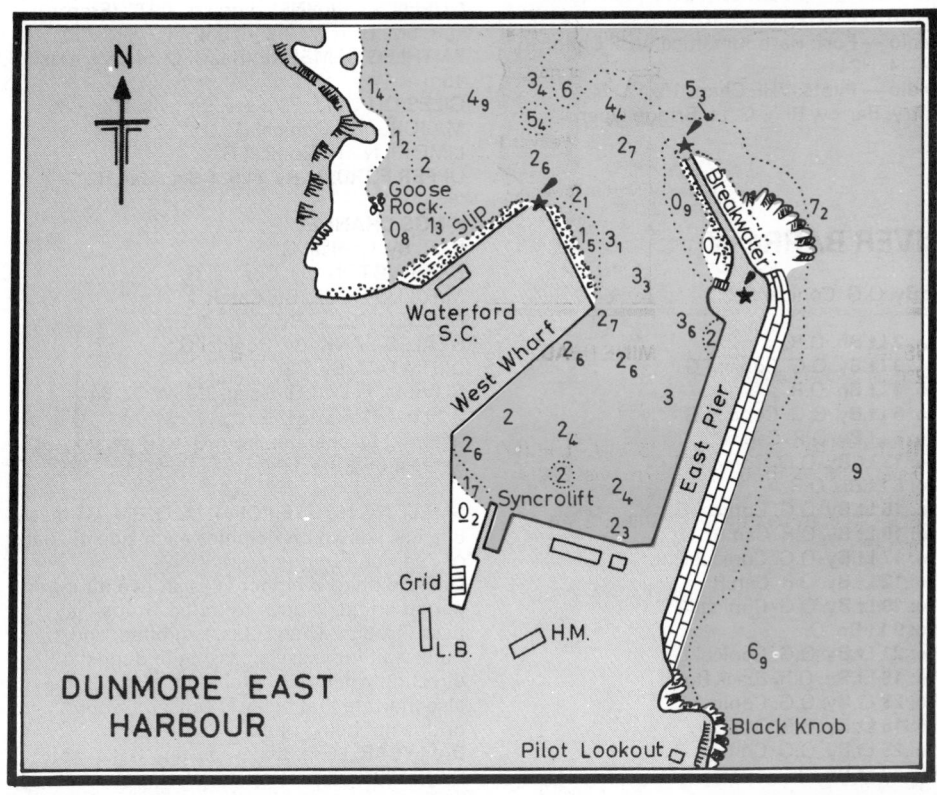

DUNMORE EAST HARBOUR

DUNCANNON SPIT Lt. By. Q.R. Can.R. W. of Spit.

DRUMROE BANK
LOWER. Lt.By. Fl.R. 3 sec. Can.R. off Duncannon Fort and E side of Drumroe Bk.
PASSAGE POINT, SPIT OF PASSAGE. Lt. Fl.W.R. 5 sec. W.6M. R.5M. R. pile structure, W. top, 7m. W.shore-127°; R.127°-302°.
SEEDES BANK. Lt.By. Fl.G. 3 sec. Conical G.
BARRON QUAY. Lt. Fl. 2 sec. W. Post. 3m.
CHEEK POINT. Lt. Q.W.R. 5M. W. mast, 6m. W.007°-289°; R.289°-007°.
SHEAGH. Lt. Fl.R. 3 sec. 3M. frame Tr. 29m. vis. 090°-325°.
KILMOKEA. Lt. Fl. 5 sec.
KILMOKEA POINT
GENERATING STATION JETTY. No: 4 Lt. 2 F.G. vert. on dolphin, 3M. 2m. apart.
E END. Lt. 2 F.G. vert. 3M.
W END. Lt. 2 F.G. vert. 3M.

No. 1 Lt.Bn. 2 F.G. vert. 3M. Dolphin. Railway Bridge Lts. 8 × F.R.

NEW ROSS 52°23'N, 6°56'W. Tel: H.M.
(051) 21841. Hbr. Office (051) 21303. Telex: 22626. (Pilots: 051-82206).
Radio — Port: Harbour Office. VHF Chan. 16, 12, 14. H24.
Radio — Pilots: VHF Chan. 16, 12, 14.
Entry: Barrow Br. = G. Lt. Bridge Open.

RIVER BARROW

Lt.By. Q.G. Conical G.

No: 2 Lt.Bn. Q.R.
No: 3 Lt.By. Q.G. Conical G.
No: 4 Lt.Bn. Q.R.
No: 5 Lt.By. Q.G. Conical G.
No: 6 Lt.By. Q.R. Can.R.
No: 13 Lt.By. Q.G. Conical G.
No: 8 Lt.Bn. Q.R.
No: 15 Lt.By. Q.G. Conical G.
No: 10 Lt.By. Q.R. Can.R.
No: 17 Lt.By. Q.G. Conical G.
No: 12 Lt.By. Q.R. Can.R.
No: 19 Lt.By. Q.G. Conical G.
No: 9 Lt.Bn. Q.
No: 21 Lt.By. Q.G. Conical G.
No: 16 Lt.Bn. Q.R. Black Rock.
No: 23 Lt.By. Q.G. Conical G.
No: 18 Lt.By. Q.R. Can.R.
No: 25 Lt.By. Q.G. Conical G.
No: 22 Lt.Bn. Q.R.

No: 29 Lt.By. Q.G. Pillar. G.
No: 25 Lt.Bn. Q.
No: 22 Lt.By. Q.R. Can.R

CAMLIN REACH Ldg.Lts. 095° (Front) F.R. (Rear) F.R.

RIVER SUIR TO WATERFORD

RAHEEN WHARF Lt. F.R.
NEW ROSS STAFFORDS WHARF Lt. F.
OIL JETTY S. Lt. F.G.
OIL JETTY N. Lt. F.G.
TOWN QUAY Lt. F.
SNOWHILL POINT. Ldg.Lts. 255°. (Front) Fl.W.R. 2.5 sec. 3M. W. mast, 5m. over The Bingledies, W. elsewhere.
GLASS HOUSE, FLOUR MILL (Rear). Q. 5M. W. framework Tr. 12m.
GURTEENS FLOATING JETTY. Lt. F.G.
BOLTON. Lt.By. Fl.R. 3 sec. Can.R.

QUEENS CHANNEL
LOWER BELLEVUE. Lt.By. Q.G. Conical G.
UPPER BELLEVUE. Lt.By. Fl.G. 4.5 sec. Conical G.
QUEEN'S CHANNEL. Ldg.Lts. 097°. (Front) Q.R. 5M. B. Tr. W. band, 8m. Vis. 030°-210°.
FAITHLEG DEMESNE (Rear). Q. 5M. W. mast, 15m.
GILES QUAY. Lt. Fl. 3 sec. 9m. vis. 255°-086°.
MAJORS. By. Conical G.
LIME KILN. By. Conical G.
UPPER FORD. Lt.By. Fl.R. 5 sec. Can.R.

KINGS CHANNEL
BAR. By. Conical G.
BARRINGTON. By. Conical G.
MAULUS ROCK. By. Can.R.
GOLDEN ROCK. By. Conical G.
NEALES BANK. By. Conical G.
DIRTY TAIL. By. Can.R.
COVE Lt. Fl.W.R.G. 6 sec. 2M. W. Tr. 6m. R.111°-161°; G.161°-234°; W.234°-111°. When entering Lt. changes from G. to R. when abreast of it.

SMELTING HOUSE POINT. Lt. Q. 3M. W. mast, 8m. Lts. shown on dolphins each side of span of Redmond bridge 1.3M. WNW.
On S dolphins a higher Lt. is shown during period bridge is open to traffic. Ships may pass through when G.Lts. exhibited, and must wait for vessels passing in opposite direction when R.Lt. exhibited; same Lt. may also indicate that delay is caused through bridge not being open.
BALLYCAR. Lt. Fl.R.G. 3 sec. 5m. G.127°-212°; R.212°-284°.

WATERFORD TO WEXFORD

**OFFSHORE WAYPOINT S OF CONINGBEG.
52°01.0'N, 6°40.0'W.**

CONINGBEG 52°02.4'N, 6°39.4'W. Lt.F.
Fl.(3) 30 sec. 24M. R.hull, lantern amidships,
12m. Shown by day when fog sig. operating.
Horn (3) 60 sec. Racon. Fog Detr. Lt. V.Q. on
Tr. 10m.

**OFFSHORE WAYPOINT E OF CONINGBEG.
52°02.7'N, 6°35.0'W.**

KILMORE, BREAKWATER HEAD. Lt. Q.R.G.
5M. pedestal, 6m. R.269°-354°; G.354°-003°;
R.003°-077°. Fishing.
BARRELS. Lt.By. Q.(3) 10 sec. Pillar. B.Y.B.
Topmark E. Horn (2) 10 sec.
FUNDALE ROCK By. Can.R.
S ROCK Lt.By. Q.(6)+L.Fl. 15 sec. Pillar. Y.B.
Topmark S.
CARNE PIER. Lt. Fl.R. 3 sec. Col. 6m.

EAST COAST OF IRELAND

**OFFSHORE WAYPOINT SSE OF TUSKAR
ROCK. 52°10.0'N, 6°10.0'W.**

TUSKAR ROCK 52°12.2'N, 6°12.4'W.
Lt.Ho. Q.(2) 7.5 sec. 28M. W. Tr. 33m. RC.
Racon. Horn (4) 45 sec. also shown by day in
fog.
LUCIFER. Lt.By. V.Q.(3) 5 sec. Pillar. B.Y.B.
Topmark E.
SPLAUGH ROCK Lt.By. Fl.R. 6 sec. Can.R. 〰
off S entce to S Shear Chan.
CARRIG ROCK Perch R. Topmark Can.R.
CALMINES Lt.By. Fl.R. 2 sec. Can.R. 〰 off
Calmines Bk.

ROSSLARE 52°15'N, 6°20'W. Tel: Rosslare
(053) 33114. Telex: 8730.
Radio — Port: VHF Chan. 16, 14, 6.

ROSSLARE PIER HEAD. 52°15.4'N,
6°20.2'W. Lt. Fl.W.R.G. 5 sec. W.13M. R.10M.
G.10M. R. metal Tr. 15M. G.098°-188°; W.188°-
208°; R.208°-246°; G.246°-283°; W.283°-286°;
R.286°-320°.
2 Bys. in Hr. used by B.R. steamers for
hauling off wires.
ROSSLARE Ldg.Lts. 124° (Front) F.R. 2M. 10m.
079°-169° (Rear) F.R. 2M. 12m. 079°-169°.
NEW FERRY PIER HEAD Lt. Q. 3M. 10m.
Ldg.Lts. 146° (Front) Oc. 3 sec. 3M. 11m.
(Rear) Oc. 3 sec. 3M. 13m.

HOLDENS BED AND LONG BANK

**INSHORE WAYPOINT APPROACH
ROSSLARE/WEXFORD. 52°15.0'N, 6°17.0'W.**

S LONG. Lt.By. V.Q.(6)+L.Fl. 10 sec. Pillar. Y.B.
Topmark S. Horn (2) 20 sec. on S extreme of
Holden's Bed Bk.
W HOLDENS Lt.By. Fl.(3)G. 10 sec. Conical G.
S HOLDENS Lt.By. Fl.(2)G. 6 sec. Conical G.
W LONG. Lt.By. Q.G. Conical G.
N LONG. Lt.By. Q. Pillar. B.Y. Topmark N. Horn
(3) 30 sec.
DOGGER BANK, E EDGE marked by 3 Bys.
Can.B. Southern-most By. marked by W.
band.
ROSSLARE POINT Marked by Perch, cage
topped.

WEXFORD Tel: Wexford 33205 (Pilot).
Entry: Chan. marked by large drums and
fishermans buffs. Enter to N of Bar By. and
Slaney Wreck. Depth 3.5m. at Bar and approx.
3m. in Chan. at H.W.O.S.T.
BLACK ROCK By. Conical B. above Wexford.
KILCOCK ROCK By. Can.B. above Wexford.

**OFFSHORE WAYPOINT E OF LUCIFER BANK.
52°21.0'N, 6°07.0'W.**

BLACKWATER BANK
S BLACKWATER. Lt.By. Q.(6)+L.Fl. 15 sec.
Pillar. Y.B. Topmark S. Horn (2) 30 sec.
SE BLACKWATER. Lt.By. Fl.R. 10 sec. Can.R.
E BLACKWATER. Lt.By. Q.(3) 10 sec. Pillar
B.Y.B. Topmark E. Horn (3) 20 sec.
N BLACKWATER. Lt.By. Q. Pillar. B.Y. Topmark
N.
W BLACKWATER. By. Conical G.

RUSK CHANNEL
No: 1 By. Conical G.
No: 2 By. Can.R.
No: 4 By. Can.R.
No: 6 By. Can.R.

GLASSGORMAN BANKS
E SIDE
No: 1 Lt.By. Fl.(2)R. 6 sec. Can.R.
No: 2 Lt.By. Fl.(4)R. 10 sec. Can.R.
ARKLOW HEAD, PIER HEAD. Lt. Oc.R. 10 sec.
9M. hut, 9m.
ROADSTONE BREAKWATER HEAD. Lt. Q.Y.

ARKLOW HARBOUR Tel: 0402-2466.

HARBOUR WAYPOINT. 52°47.5'N, 6°07.0'W.

Radio — Pilots: VHF Chan. 16. c/s Roadstone Jetty.

S PIER HEAD. 52°47.6'N, 6°08.4'W. Lt. Fl.W.R. 6 sec. 13M. metal framework Tr. 10m. R.shore-223°; W.223°-350°; R.350°-shore.
N PIER HEAD. Lt. L.Fl.G. 7 sec. 10M. 7m. vis. shore-287°.

OFFSHORE WAYPOINT S OF ARKLOW L.F. 52°38.0'N, 5°58.0'W.

ARKLOW 52°39.5'N, 5°58.1'W. Lanby By. Fl.(2) 12 sec. 16M. 12m. Horn Mo.(A) 30 sec. Racon.

INSHORE WAYPOINT NNW OF ARKLOW L.F. 52°41.8'N, 6°01.5'W.

ARKLOW BANK E SIDE
S ARKLOW Lt.By. V.Q.(6)+L.Fl. 10 sec. Pillar. Y.B. Topmark S.
ARKLOW No: 1 Lt.By. Fl.(3)R. 10 sec. Can.R.
ARKLOW No: 2 Lt.By. Fl.R. 6 sec. Can.R.
N ARKLOW Lt.By. Q. Pillar. B.Y. Topmark N. Horn. (2) 30 sec.

INSHORE WAYPOINT OFF THE CASTLE. 52°54.0'N, 5°58.0'W.

HORSE SHOE BANK. Lt.By. Fl.R. 3 sec. Can.R. ⨺ Bell. S of Wicklow Hd.

INSHORE WAYPOINT NE OF WICKLOW HD. 52°59.5'N, 5°58.0'W.

WICKLOW 52°58'N, 6°00'W. Tel: Hr. office (0404) 2455.

HARBOUR WAYPOINT. 52°59.5'N, 6°02.0'W.

Entry: H.W. difference minus 44 min. on Dublin. Spring Rise 2.5m. Neap Rise 2.0m. Harbour has 3.4m. L.W.O.S.T.
Radio — Port & Pilots: VHF Chan. 16, 2, 6, 7, 8, 26, 27, 28 when v/l expected.

WICKLOW HEAD 52°57.9'N, 5°59.8'W. Lt. Fl.(3) 15 sec. 26M. W. Tr. 37m. R.C.

WICKLOW Lt. By. Fl.(4) Y. 10 sec. Can. Y. marks sewer outfall.

WICKLOW HARBOUR
E PIER HEAD. Lt. Fl.W.R. 5 sec. 6M. W. Tr. R. base, gallery and cupola, 11m. R.136°-293°; W.293°-136°.
W PIER HEAD. Lt. Fl.G. 1.5 sec. 6M. metal Col. 5m.
W PACKET QUAY HEAD. Lt. Fl.W.G. 10 sec. 6M. metal Col. 5m. G.076°-256°; W.256°-076°.

INDIA BANK
S INDIA Lt.By. Q.(6)+L.Fl. 15 sec. Pillar Y.B. Topmark S.
N INDIA Lt.By. V.Q. Pillar. B.Y. Topmark N.

OFFSHORE WAYPOINT SE OF CODLING BANK. 53°04.0'N, 5°45.0'W.

CODLING 53°03.0'N, 5°40.7'W. Lanby By. Fl.4 sec. 15M. Lt. 12m. Horn 20 sec. Racon.
W CODLING. Lt.By. Fl.G. 10 sec. Conical G.
S CODLING. Lt.By. V.Q.(6)+L.Fl. 10 sec. Pillar Y.B. Topmark S.
E CODLING. Lt.By. Fl.(4)R. 10 sec. Can.R.
E KISH. Lt.By. Fl.(2)R. 10 sec. Can.R.
N KISH. Lt.By. V.Q. Pillar. B.Y. Topmark N.

OFFSHORE WAYPOINT NE OF KISH BANK LT. 53°20.0'N, 5°52.0'W.

KISH BANK 53°18.7'N, 5°55.3'W. Lt. Fl.(2) 30 sec. 28M. W. concrete Tr. R. band, 29m. Shown by day when fog sig. operating. Racon. R.C. Distress sig. Helicopter landing platform. Horn (2) 30 sec.

BENNET BANK. Lt.By. Q.(6)+L.Fl. 15 sec. Pillar. Y.B. Topmark S. Horn (3) 30 sec.

WICKLOW TO DUBLIN

BREACHES Lt.By. Fl.(2)R. 6 sec. Can.R. ⨺ off Breaches Shoal.

INSHORE WAYPOINT OFF MOULDITCH BANK. 53°08.3'N, 5°59.0'W.

MOULDITCH BANK Lt.By. Fl.R. 10 sec. Can.R.

BRAY HARBOUR. 53°13'N, 6°06'W.
BRAY OUTFALL. Lt.By. Fl.(4)Y. 10 sec. Can.Y. marks sewer outfall NE of N Pier.
MUGLINS. Lt. Fl. 5 sec. 8M. W. conical Tr. R. band. 14m.

DUN LAOGHAIRE 53°18'N, 6°07'W. Tel: Dublin (01) 801130.

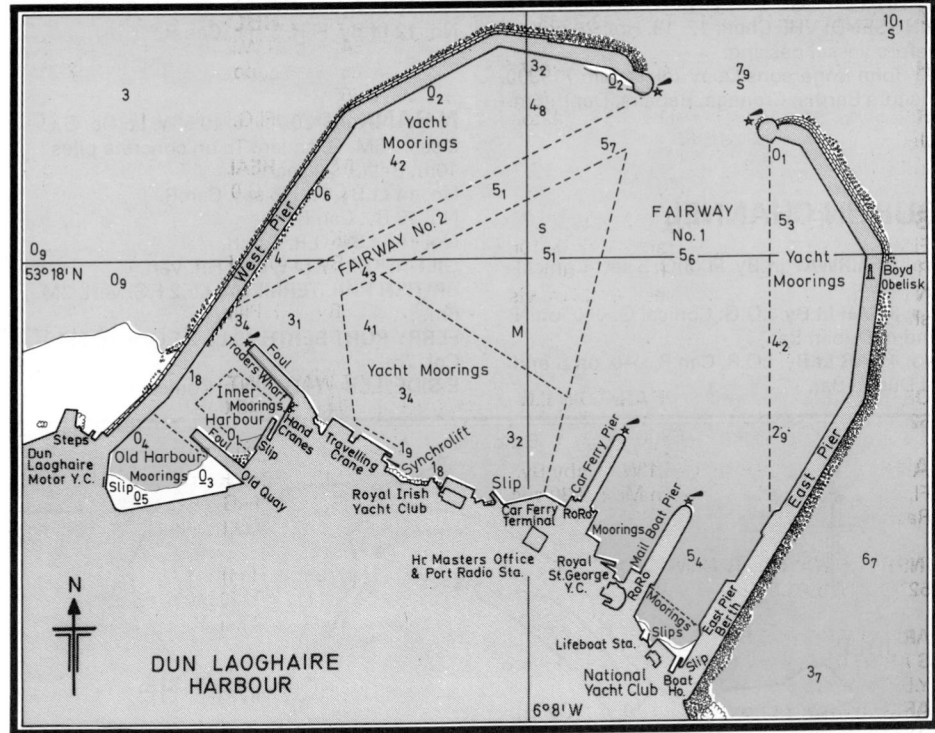

Radio — Port: VHF Chan. 16, 14. Mon.-Fri. 0900-1700.
Many unlit yacht racing marker buoys laid off harbour approaches April-Oct.
Entry: Fairway No: 1 dredged to 5.5m. but rock outcrops off Nos. 1&2 berths at 4.5m, in constant use by ferries. Flags MB3 flown from car ferry pier and high intensity Q.Y.Lt. also shown when ferry traffic imminent. Visiting yachts moor at shore end of Traders and Old Quay Wharves. Seaward ends of these wharves unsuitable or foul.

E BREAKWATER HEAD. 53°18.1′N,
6°07.6′W. Lt. Fl.(2) 15 sec. 22M. Granite Tr. W. lantern, 16m. Dia. 30 sec. Reserve Fog Sig. Bell 6 sec. from parapet of pier close to Lt.Ho. also shown by day in fog.
W BREAKWATER HEAD. Lt. Fl.(3)G. 7.5 sec. 7M. Granite Tr. W. lantern, 11m. vis. 188°-062°.
MAIL BOAT PIER HEAD. Lt. Fl.R. 3 sec. 1M. roof of pier, 9m.
CAR FERRY TERMINAL HEAD. Lt. Q.W.R. 3M. metal Col. 6m. R.030°-131°; W.131°-030°. Lt. Q.Y. Traffic signal 80m. SW.
TRADERS WHARF HEAD. Lt. 2 F.R. vert. 1M. on mast, 7m.

BURFORD BANK
S BURFORD. Lt.By. V.Q.(6)+L.Fl. 10 sec. Pillar. Y.B. Topmark S. Horn. 20 sec.
N BURFORD. Lt.By. Q. Pillar B.Y. Topmark N.

INSHORE WAYPOINT SE OF BAILY. 53°21.0′N, 6°01.0′W.

BAILY 53°21.7′N, 6°03.1′W. Lt. Fl. 20 sec. 27M. Granite Tr. Dia. 60 sec. SE point of Howth Peninsula, also shown by day in fog.

ROSBEG E. Lt.By. Q.(3) 10 sec. Pillar. B.Y.B. Topmark E.
KILLINEY BAY OUTFALL. Lt.By. Fl.Y. 3 sec. Can.Y.

DUBLIN 53°20′N, 6°09′W. Tel: Dublin (0001) 748771/722777. (Night 748779). Telex: 32508.

HARBOUR WAYPOINT. 53°20.6′N, 6°05.9′W.

Radio — Port: VHF Chan. 16, 12, 13, 14 — continuous. Weather forecasts available on request on Ch. 12.

LIFTING BRIDGE c/s E LINK (LOCATION RINGSEND) VHF Chan. 12, 13. Hrs: 20 mins before vessel passing.
Sir John Rogersons Quay Tel. Dublin 719300. Visitors Berths, Cranage, Repairs. Depth 6m.

DUBLIN CHANNEL

No: 1 FAIRWAY Lt.By. Fl.(3)G. 5 sec. Conical G.
No: 3 BAR Lt.By. I.Q.G. Conical G. ⩗ on N end of Dublin Bar.
No: 4 BAR Lt.By. I.Q.R. Can.R. ⩗ on S end of Dublin Bar.

No: 10 Lt.By. Fl.(2)R. 10 sec. ⩗ Can.R.
No: 12 Lt.By. Fl.R. 3 sec. Can.R.

N BANK. 53°20.7'N, 6°10.5'W. Lt. Oc. G. 8 sec. 16M. G. square Tr. on concrete piles, 10m. Bell(3) 20 sec.
No: 14 Lt.By. Fl.R. 5 sec. Can.R.
No: 16 By. Can.R.
No: 18 Lt.By. Q.R. Can.R.
OILTANKER JETTY. Lt. 2 F.R. vert.
BRITISH RAIL TERMINAL Lt. 2 F.G. vert. 2M. 6m.
FERRY PORT BERTH 49 Lt. 2 F.G. vert. 2M. Col. 7m.
E SIDE. Lt.By. Fl.G. 3 sec. Conical G.

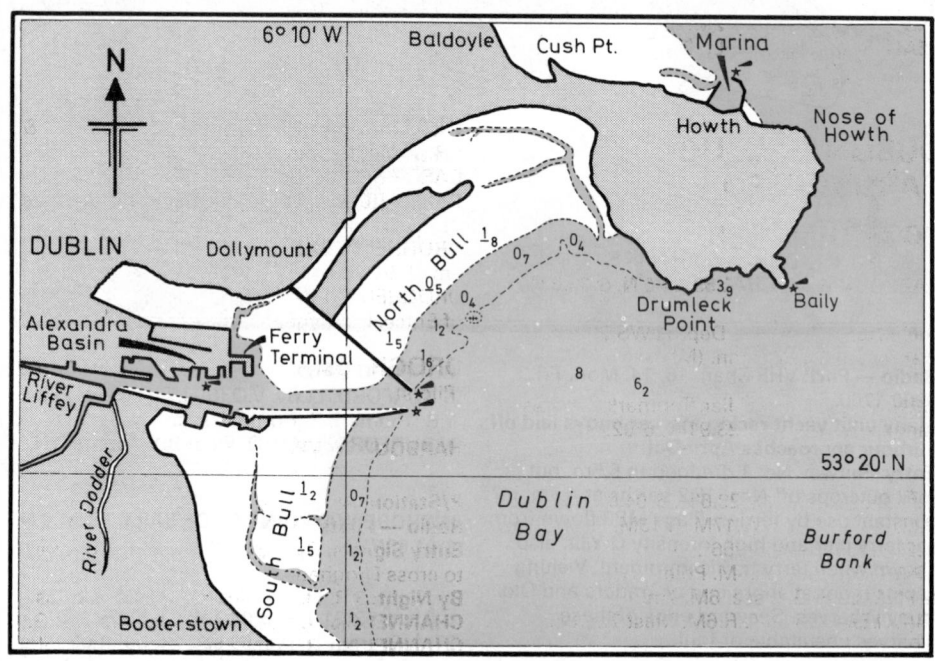

No: 5 BAR Lt.By. Fl.G. 2 sec. Conical G.
No: 6 BAR Lt.By. Fl.R. 2 sec. Can.R.
No: 5 Bn. B. stone.

POOLBEG. 53°20.5'N, 6°09.0'W. Lt. Oc.(2)R. 20 sec. 15M. R. round Tr. 20m. Horn(2) 60 sec.

N BULL WALL. 53°20.7'N, 6°08.9'W. Lt. Fl.(3) 10 sec. 15M. G. round Tr. 15m. Bell(4) 30 sec.
No: 7 Lt.By. Fl.G. 4 sec. Conical G.
No: 8 Lt.By. Fl.R. 5 sec. Can.R.
No: 9 Lt.By. Fl.G. 2 sec. Conical G.

W SIDE. Lt.By. V.Q.(6)+L.Fl. 10 sec. Spar. Y.B. Topmark S.
INNER W SIDE. Lt.By. Q.R. Spar R.
HEAD OF CULVERT. Lt. Iso.R. 4 sec. 4M. R. pedestal on dolphin 4m. vis. 098°-270°.
COAL QUAY. Lt. 2 F.R. vert. 2M. dolphin. 5m.
CAR FERRY TERMINAL JETTY HEAD Lt. 2 F.G. vert. 2M. 6m.
B. & I. FREIGHT TERMINAL HEAD Lt. 2 F.R. vert. 2M. 6m.
E SIDE. Lt.By. Fl.(3)G. 5 sec. Conical G.
W SIDE. Lt.By. Q.(6)+L.Fl. 15 sec. Spar Y.B. Topmark S.
INNER W SIDE. Lt.By. Q.R. Spar R.
S BANK QUAY. E End. Lt. Oc.R. 2 sec. 3M. R. square Tr. 7m. vis. 090°-290°.

ALEXANDRA BASIN

EASTERN BREAKWATER. 53°20.7'N, 6°12.1'W. Lt. Fl. 6 sec. 12M. B. square Tr. 15m. Bell(2) 15 sec. Hailing Station.
Lt.By. Fl.(2)G. 5 sec. Conical G.
EASTERN OIL JETTY. Lt. 2 F.G. vert. 2M. on Col. 6m.
WESTERN OIL JETTY. Lt. 2 F.G. vert. 2M. on Col. 7m.

N WALL QUAY. 53°20.7'N, 6°12.9'W. Lt. Fl. 2 sec. 10M. B. round Tr. W. bands, 12m. T.D. Bell 10 sec.
BULK JETTY OFF HEAD Lt. Fl.Y. 3 sec. 2M. Dolphin 6m.
ELBOW Lt. 2 F.G. vert. 2M. 6m.
LEAD IN JETTY HEAD Lt. 2 F.G. vert. 2M. 6m.

DUBLIN TO LOUGH CARLINGFORD

HOWTH HARBOUR

HARBOUR WAYPOINT. 53°24.0'N, 6°03.0'W.

Yacht Hbr. 200 berths, Depth LWS 2.4m. Marine Supt. VHF Chan. (M).

Lt.By. V.Q.(3) 5 sec. Pillar. Topmark E marks dangerous wreck 53°23.91'N, 6°02.07'W.

E PIER HEAD. 53°23.6'N, 6°04.0'W. Lt. Fl.(2) W.R. 7.5 sec. W.17M. R.13M. W. Tr. 13m. W.256°-295°; R.295°-256°.
E PIER EXT. Lt. Q.R. 4M. Pole.
W PIER. Lt. Fl.G. 3 sec. 6M. 7m.
TRAWLER PIER Lt. Q.R.6M. Mast 7m. 045°-270°.
MARINA PIER Lt. 2.F.R. vert.
HOWTH. Lt.By. Fl.G. 5 sec. Conical G.
S ROWAN Lt.By. Q.G. Conical G. off Howth Hr. 〰.
ROWAN ROCKS. Lt.By. Q.(3) 10 sec. Pillar B.Y.B. Topmark E.

DUBLIN AIRPORT Lt. Aero Al. Fl. W.G. 4 sec. 95m.

INSHORE WAYPOINT OFF MALAHIDE INLET. 53°27.9'N, 6°05.25'W.

BURRIN ROCK Perch B. off W end of Lambay I.
TAYLOR ROCK By. Conical G. off NW end of Lambay I.

INSHORE WAYPOINT E OF LAMBAY ISLAND. 53°29.5'N, 5°59.0'W.

ROCKABILL 53°35.8'N, 6°00.3'W. Lt. Fl.W.R. 12 sec. W.23M. R.19M. W. Tr. B. band, 45m. W.178°-329°; R.329°-178°. Horn.(4) 60 sec.

INSHORE WAYPOINT E OF ROCKABILL. 53°36.0'N, 5°58.0'W.

SKERRIES BAY PIER HEAD. Lt. Oc.R. 6 sec. 7M. W. Col. 7m. vis. 103°-154°.
GROSS ROCK. Lt.By. Fl.R. 10 sec. Can.R.

BALBRIGGAN 53°36.7'N, 6°10.7'W. Lt. Fl.(3) W.R.G. 20 sec. W.13M. R.10M. G.10M. W. Tr. 12m. G.159°-193°; W.193°-288°; R.288°-305°.

PLATIN 53°41.1'N, 6°23.4'W. Lt. Aero Q.R. & F.R. 11M. Chimney 81m.-149m.
CARDY ROCKS. Bn. R. Mast Topmark Can.
CARDY ROCKS. Lt.By. Q. Can.R. off Braymore Pt.
DROGHEDA. BAR. Lt. Q.R. 3M. R. metal Col. 6m. 〰.
DROGHEDA N BAR By. Conical B. on N side of Entce. to Boyne River.

DROGHEDA 53°43'N, 6°15'W. Tel: 041-8863 (Pilots)

HARBOUR WAYPOINT. 53°44.0'N, 6°12.0'W.

P/Station: At the Bar.
Radio — Pilots: VHF Chan. 16, 11.
Entry Signals: By Day: 3 R. shapes — unsafe to cross Drogheda Bar.
By Night: 3 R. Lts. vertical — unsafe to cross.
CHANNEL No. 1. Lt.By. Fl.G. 5 sec. Conical G.
CHANNEL No. 3. Lt.By. Fl.G. 2.5 sec. Conical G.
CHANNEL No. 2. Lt.By. Q.R. Can.R.
CHANNEL No. 4. Lt.By. Q.R. Can.R.

ENTRANCE 53°43.1'N, 6°14.9'W. Ldg.Lts. 248°. (Front) Oc. 12 sec. 15M. wooden framework Tr, W. lantern, 8m. vis. 203°-293°. (Rear) Oc. 12 sec. 17M. metal framework Tr. 12m. vis. 246°-252°.

N LIGHT 53°43.4'N, 6°15.2'W. Lt. Fl.R. 4 sec. 15M. Wood Tr. W. Lantern 7m. Vis. 282°-288°. Traffic Signals.
DROGHEDA BAR. Lt. Fl.(3)R. 5 sec. 3M. R. Col. 6m.

ALERIA Bn. Lt. Q.G. 3M. G. Bn. 11m.
LYONS. Lt. Fl.R. 2 sec. R. structure.
S BULL. Lt. Fl.R. 2 sec. R. structure. 2m.
N SIDE GREEN Bn. Lt. Q.(2)G. 3 sec. G. Bn. 2m.
MAIDEN Tr. Lt. Fl.R. 3 sec. R. structure. 2m.
BLUFF Bn. Lt. Fl.G. 2 sec. G. Post.
ROCK SHOT. Lt. Fl.G. 4 sec. G. structure. 2m.
GAUGE. Lt. Q.(2)G. 3 sec. 2m.
STAGE. Lt. Fl.G. 2 sec. G. structure.
LOWER CARRICK. Lt. Fl.R. 3 sec. R. structure. 2m.
CARRICK. Lt. Oc.R. 3 sec. R. Col. 2m.
QUAY NE CORNER. Lt. 2 F.R. vert. R. structure 3m.
NW CORNER. Lt. 2 F.R. vert. 3m.
CROOK PT. Lt. Q. 2m.
BARREL PERCH. Lt. Fl.R. 3 sec. 2m.
HOLE. Lt. Q.G. 2m.
S POINT. Lt. Q.R. 2m.
BIGHT. Lt. Fl.G. 3 sec. 2m.
SCARRA. Lt. Q.R. 2m.
BANKTOWN. Lt. Q.(2) 3 sec. 2m.
MORNINGTON PERCH. Lt. Q.(2) 3 sec. 2m.
QUEENSBORO. Lt. Fl.G. 2 sec. 2m.
STEWARTS BANK. Lt. Fl. 3 sec. 2m.
BRANIGANS POINT. Lt. Fl.G. 2 sec. 2m.
QUARRY. Lt. 2 F.R. vert. 3m.
MILESTONE. Lt. Q.R.
DONORS GREEN. Lt. F.G.
DUNANY Lt.By. Fl.R. 3 sec. Can.R. 〰 off E edge of Dunany Reefs in Dundalk Bay.

INSHORE WAYPOINT DUNDALK BAY. 53°56.0′N, 6°11.0′W.

DUNDALK 53°59′N, 6°18′W. Tel: H.M. (042) 34096.

HARBOUR WAYPOINT. 53°58.25′N, 6°17.0′W.

Radio — Port: VHF Chan. 16, 12. 3 h.-HW when v/l expected.
Radio — Pilots: VHF Chan. 16, 12, 6. 2 h.-HW.
Entry: Heavy seas at entrance in SE/E winds. Good shelter with winds SW/NW.
Anchorage: 2M. SE from Pile Lt.

N TRAINING WALL. HEAD. PILE.
53°58.5′N, 6°17.6′W. Lt. Fl.W.R. 15 sec. W.21M. R.18M. W. house on R. piles, 10m. W.124°-151°; R.151°-284°; W.284°-313°; R.313°-124°. Horn(3) 60 sec. also shown by day in fog.
Same structure Oc. G. 5 sec. vis. 331°-334°.
Same structure Fog Detr. Lt. V.Qk.Fl. 7m. 358°.

No: 1 Lt.Bn. Q.R. Y. ▯ on Bn.
No: 5 Lt.Bn. Q.G. concrete Col. G.
No: 7 Lt.Bn. Q.G. concrete Col. G.

No: 8 Lt.Bn. (Front) Fl.R. 3 sec. Can.R.
No: 9 Lt.Bn. Q.G. concrete Col. G.
No: 10 Lt.Bn. (Rear) Q.R. on pile.
No: 9A Lt. Bn. Q.G.
No: 6 Lt.Bn. Q.R. R. concrete Col.
No: 11 Lt.Bn. Q.G. concrete Col. G.
No: 4 Lt.Bn. Q.R. Bn.R.
No: 13 Lt.Bn. Q.G. concrete Col. G.
No: 12 Lt.Bn. Q.R. R. concrete Col.
No: 15 Lt. Bn. Q.G. concrete Col.
No: 14 Lt.Bn. Q.R. R. concrete Col.
Giles Quay Pier Lt.Bn. Fl.G. 3 sec.
No: 16 Lt.Bn. Q.R. concrete Col.
No: 18 Lt.Bn. Q.R. concrete Col.

IMOGENE ROCK Lt.By. Gp.Fl.(2)R. 10 sec. Can.R.

INSHORE WAYPOINT OFF CARLINGFORD LOUGH. 54°00.0′N, 6°00.0′W.

CARLINGFORD LOUGH 54°03′N, 6°11′W. Tel: Kilkeel 576.

HARBOUR WAYPOINT. 54°00.75′N, 6°04.2′W.

DUNDALK SAILING CLUB
Radio: VHF Chan. 16. M. 1300-1800 Sunday.
Entry: Hbr. dries at 1.5m. LAT. Hospital Bank dries at 1m. LAT.
Anchorage: 3c. S of Hbr. in 2m. LAT.
CARLINGFORD FAIRWAY. Lt.By. L.Fl. 10 sec. Sph..R.W.V.S. Whis.
HELLYHUNTER ROCK. Lt.By. Q.(6)+L.Fl. 15 sec. Pillar. Y.B. Topmark S. Horn (2) 20 sec. Entce. to Lough, N side.
No: 1 Lt.By. Fl.G. 5 sec. Pillar G. 〰.
No: 2 Lt. Fl.(2)R. 5 sec. 3M. '2' in R. ▯ pile. 4m.
No: 3 Lt.By. I.Q.G. 9 sec. Conical G. 〰.
No: 4 Lt.By. Fl.R. 3 sec. Can.R. 〰.

HAULBOWLINE ROCK 54°01.2′N, 6°04.7′W. Lt. Fl.(3) 10 sec. 20M. Grey granite Tr. 32m. also shown by day in fog. Reserve Lt. range 15M.
Same structure Fog Detr. Lt. Q. 26m. Vis. when bearing 330°.
TURNING LT. F.R. 9M. Same structure 21m. Vis. 196°-208°. Horn 30 sec.
No: 6 Lt.By. Fl.R. 5 sec. Can.R. 〰 marks Bk. off Block House I.
No: 5 Lt.By. Fl.G. 3 sec. Conical G. 〰 marks New England Rk. E side of Chan.
No: 7 Lt.By. Q.G. Conical G. 〰 on E side.

VIDAL BANK. 54°01.8′N, 6°05.4′W.
Ldg.Lts. 310°. (Front) Oc. 3 sec. 11M. G. house on piles, 7m. Vis. 295°-325°. H24.

GREEN ISLAND. (Rear) Oc. 3 sec. 11M. G. house on piles, 12m. Vis. 295°-325°. H24.
No: 9 Lt.By. I.Q.G. 9 sec. Conical G. ⌣⌣ marks Fraser Rk.
No: 8 HALPIN ROCK. Lt.By. Fl.R. 3 sec. Can.R. ⌣⌣.
EARL ROCK Bn. circular, staff and ball.

GREENORE Tel: Port (042) 73170. Fax: (042) 73567. Pilots (0806937) 725491. Telex: 43760.

GREENORE PIER. Lt. Fl.R. 7.5 sec. 5M. Concrete Col. 10m.
Radio — Port: VHF Chan. 16, 13. H24. c/s Ferry Greenore.
No: 11 Lt.By. Q.G. Conical G. ⌣⌣ E side of Fairway.
STALKA ROCK Perch, on Rk.
No: 10 WATSON ROCKS. Lt.By. Fl.R. 3 sec. Can.R. on E side of Chan.
No. 10A Lt.By. Fl.R. 3 sec. Can.R.
No: 11A Lt.By. Fl.G. 3 sec. Conical G.
CARLINGFORD QUAY. Lt. Fl. 3 sec. 2M. Col. 5m.
No: 12 Lt.By. Fl.R. Can.R. ⌣⌣ on W side of Chan.
No: 13 Lt.By. Q.G. Conical G. ⌣⌣ off Killowen Pt. on E side of Chan.

NEWRY RIVER

No: 15 Lt.By. I.Q.G. 11 sec. Conical G.
No: 14 Lt.By. I.Q.R. Can.R.
No: 17 Lt.By. Q.G. Conical G.
BLACK ROCK. Perch.
No: 16 Lt.By. Q. Can.R.

WARREN POINT. Tel: H.M. (069 372) 3381. Telex: 74660. Pilots: (06937) 62549.
Radio — Port: VHF Chan. 16, 12. H24.
Radio — Pilots: VHF Chan. 16, 12. H24.
Entry: Dredged depth approaches Warren Point 4.8m.
BREAKWATER HEAD. Lt. Fl.G. 3 sec. Col. 6m.
DEEP WATER QUAY Lt. Fl.G. 5 sec. 3M. R. post 5m.
NEWRY RIVER. Ldg.Lts. 310°25' (Front) Iso. 4 sec. 2M. Col. 5m. (Rear) Iso. 4 sec. 2M. Col. 15m.

LOUGH CARLINGFORD TO BELFAST LOUGH

KILKEEL HARBOUR
Radio — Port: VHF Chan. 16, 14, 12. 0900-2000 Mon.-Fri.

PIER HEAD. Lt. Fl.W.R. 2 sec. 8M. metal Col. 8m. R.296°-313°; W.313°-017°. Storm sig.
MEENEYS PIER HEAD. Lt. Fl.G. 3 sec. 2M. 6m.
ANNALONG, E BREAKWATER HEAD. Lt. Oc. W.R.G. 5 sec. 9M. metal framework Tr. 8m. G.204°-249°; W.249°-309°; R.309°-024°.

DUNDRUM 54°15'N, 5°51'W.
Entry Signals: Quay lights shown 2½ h. before to 2 h. after H.W. for local vesels. Channel Lts. only shown when vessels expected.
DUNDRUM BAR By. Conical G. on Bar to Hr. Entce.
DUNDRUM HARBOUR. F.R. Lt. shown on W side of appr. Chan. outside Hr. and 3 F.R. Lts. on W side of Chan. inside Hr. when local vessels expected. F.R. Lts. shown on flagstaffs on S and E sides of Entce. to Hr. when firing taking place.

ST. JOHN'S POINT 54°13.6'N, 5°39.5'W.
Lt. Fl.(2) 7.5 sec. 23M. B. round Tr. Y. bands, 37m. Same Tr. Auxiliary Lt. Fl.W.R. 3 sec. W.15M. R.11M. 14m. W.064°-078°; R.078°-shore. Shown by day when fog sig. operating. Horn(2) 60 sec. Fog.Detr. Lt. V.Q. 14m. 270°.
KILLOUGH WATER ROCK. Perch R. in Killough Hr.
KILLOUGH HARBOUR closed to navigation.

INSHORE WAYPOINT OFF ARDGLASS. 54°15.0'N, 5°34.75'W.

ARDGLASS 54°15'N, 5°37'W. Tel: Ardglass 291.
Radio Port & Pilots: VHF Chan. 16, 12, 14. 0900-1300. 1400-1700.
Entry: Fishing Hbr. Fleet arrives between 1730-2030. Berthing alongside not permitted between these hours. Vessels anchor off until 2100. Fuel, water, etc. available. In SE gales proceed to N Harbour and moor in Inner Dock (Gods Pocket).
Anchorages: Outside — S of fairway. Inside — between S and Inner Pier Lt.

INNER N PIER HEAD. Lt. Iso. W.R.G. 4 sec. W.8M. R.7M. G.5M. Tr. 10m. G.shore-310°; W.310°-318°; R.318°-shore.
OUTER PIER HEAD. Lt.Bn. Fl.R. 3 sec. 5M. 10m.
ARTOLE Bn. pyramid shaped, concrete B. globular Topmark, marks rocks. N side Ardglass Hr.
GUNS ISLAND Bn. W., obelisk shaped, Topmark Can.R. on S end.
ST. PATRICK'S ROCKS Mast R. Topmark Can. off Killard Pt.

STRANGFORD LOUGH (PORTAFERRY)
54°24'N, 5°21'W. Tel: Portaferry 297.

INSHORE WAYPOINT APPROACHES STRANGFORD LOUGH. 54°19.0'N, 5°28.0'W.

STRANGFORD HARBOUR 54°22'N
5°33'W. Tel: Port (039) 686637. Fax: (039) 686637. Pilots (0247) 728297.
Radio — Port: VHF Chan. 16, 12, 14, M. 0900-1700 Mon.-Fri.
Radio — Pilot: VHF Chan. 16.

STRANGFORD FAIRWAY. Lt.By. L.Fl. 10 sec. Sph. R.W.V.S. Topmark Sph. ⨇ Whis. off Entce. to Strangford Lough.
BAR PLADDY Lt.By. Q.(6)+L.Fl. 15 sec. Pillar. Y.B. Topmark S. off SE edge. In E Chan. to Strangford Lough.
PLADDY LUG Bn. Pillar W., in Strangford Lough.
DOGTAIL POINT. Ldg.Lts. 341° (Front) Oc.(4) 10 sec. 5M. 2m. (Rear) **GOWLANDS ROCK.** Oc.(2) 10 sec. 5M. 6m.
ANGUS ROCK Lt. Fl.R. 5 sec. 6M. Tr. 15m. H24.
SALT ROCK. Lt. Fl.R. 3 sec. 3M. 8m.
PORTAFERRY PIER HEAD. Lt. Oc. W.R. 10 sec. W.9M. R.6M. Or. mast, 9m. W.335°-005°; R.005°-017°; W.017°-128°.
STRANGFORD N. Ldg.Lts. 181°30'. (Rear) Oc. R. 10 sec. 6M. Or. mast, 12m. Vis. 178°-185°.

PIER HEAD, N. (Front) Oc. W.R.G. 10 sec. W.9M. R.6M. G.6M. Or. mast, 8m. G.173°-180°; W.180°-183°; R.183°-190°. Common front. Same structure E (Front) Oc.W.R.G. 5 sec. 6m. R.190°-244°; G.244°-252°; W.252°-260°; R.260°-294°. **E** Ldg.Lts. 256°. (Rear) Oc.R. 5 sec. 6M. Or. mast, 10m. Vis. 250°-264°. Bns. and Trs. mark various Rks. in Strangford Lough.
SWAN ISLAND. Lt.Bn. Fl.(2) W.R. 6 sec. W. masonry Col. 5m. W.115°-334°; R.334°-115°.
S PLADDY. Lt.Bn. Fl.(3) 10 sec.
N PLADDY. Lt.Bn. Q.
CHURCH POINT. Lt. Fl.(4)R. 10 sec. Beacon.
BALLYHENRY ISLAND. Lt. Q.G. 3M. 3m.

KILLYLEAGH
Radio — Port: VHF Chan. 16, 12 as required.
KILLYLEAGH TOWN ROCK. Lt.Bn. Qk. Fl.
LIMESTONE ROCK. Lt. Q.R. 3M. 3m.

OFFSHORE WAYPOINT NE OF S ROCK. 54°25.0'N, 5°20.0'W.

S ROCK 54°24.5'N, 5°21.9'W. Lt.F. Fl.(3)R. 30 sec. 20M. R.hull, 1 mast, lantern amidships,

12m. Shown by day when fog sig. operating. R.C. Racon. Horn(3) 45 sec. Fog. Detr. Lt. V.Qk.Fl. 10m.
BUTTER PLADDY By. Can.R. off E edge Butter Pladdy Shoal, SE of Kearney Pt.
S RIDGE By. Can. R. ⨇ off S Rk.
S ROCK Bn. W., old Lt.Ho.
N ROCK Bn. Pillar. R.
PLOUGH ROCK. Lt.By. Q.R. Can.R. ⨇ Bell.

PORTAVOGIE HARBOUR

HARBOUR WAYPOINT. 54°27.4'N, 5°24.5'W.

Radio — Port: VHF Chan. 16, 14. 0900-2000 Monday to Friday.

S PIER HEAD. Lt. Iso W.R.G. 5 sec. 9M. metal Tr. 9m. G.shore-258°; W.258°-275°; R.275°-348°.
W BREAKWATER HEAD. Lt. 2 F.G. vert. Post.
SKULMARTIN. Lt.By. L.Fl. 10 sec. Sph. R.W.V.S. Topmark Sph. Whis. 2.4M. from Ballywalter Pier Hd. Lt.
SKULMARTIN ROCK Mast R. Topmark Can. off Ballywalter.
BALLYWALTER BREAKWATER HEAD. Lt. Fl. W.R.G. 1.5 sec. 9M. metal Col. 5m. G.240°-267°; W.267°-277°; R.277°-314°.

DONAGHADEE 54°39'N, 5°32'W. Tel:
(0247) 882377 (Night: (0247) 771482).
Radio — Port: VHF Chan.16. Mon.-Fri. 0900-1700.
Entry: Harbour open to NE winds; strong swell if fresh. Vessels liable to drag. Harbour usually full, little room for visitors. Only power driven vessels capable of at least 10 knots should use passage through Donaghadee Sound as tidal stream makes 5 knots in places.

DONAGHADEE, S PIER HEAD.
54°38.7'N, 5°31.8'W. Lt. Iso. W.R. 4 sec. W.18M. R.14M. W. Tr. 17m. W.shore-326°; R.326°-shore. Siren 12 sec. when vessels expected.
GOVERNOR ROCKS. Lt.By. Fl.R. 3 sec. Can.R. ⨇ in Donaghadee Sd.
FORELAND ROCKS Mast R. Topmark Can. N of Foreland Pt.
DEPUTY REEF. Lt.By. Fl.G. 2 sec. Conical G. ⨇.
FORELAND SPIT. Lt.By. Fl.R. 6 sec. Can.R. ⨇ on N edge of Spit.
NINION BUSHES By. Can.R. at E end of Copeland Sd.

BELFAST LOUGH

OFFSHORE WAYPOINT NE OF MEW ISLAND.
54°42.0′N, 5°27.0′W.

MEW ISLAND, NE END 54°41.9′N,
5°30.7′W. Lt. Fl.(4) 30 sec. 30M. B. Tr. W. band,
37m. R.C.
S BRIGGS. Lt.By. Fl.(2)R. 10 sec. Can.R. 〰️.

ORLOCK POINT RG STN. 54°40.42′N
5°34.98′W. Emergency DF Stn. VHF Chan. 16
& 67. Controlled by MRSC Belfast.

BANGOR BAY. Lt.By. Q.R. Can.R.

BANGOR Tel: H.M. (0247) 472596. Marina
(0247) 453297. Fax: (0247) 453450.
Radio — Port: VHF Chan. 16, 11 when vessels
expected.
Radio — Marina: VHF Chan. 11, M. H24.
N PIER HEAD. Lt. Iso. R. 12 sec. 14M. Col. 9m.
Dir. Lt. 105° Dir. F.W.R.G. 12M. G. 093°-104.8°;
W. 104.8°-105.2°; R. 105.2°-117°.
PICKIE BREAKWATER HEAD Lt. 2 F.G. vert.
3M. 6m.
CENTRAL PIER HEAD Lt. Q. 2M. 4m.
CLOGHAN JETTY. Lt.By. Q.G. Conical G.
No: 1 Lt.By. I.Q.G. Conical G. Bell.
No: 5 Lt.By. Fl.(3)G. 7.5 sec. Conical G.
No: 6 Lt.By. Fl.(2)R. 5 sec. Can.R.
CLOGHAN JETTY. Lts. Fl.G. 3 sec. N & S ends.

KILROOT INTAKE & OUTFALL. Lt. Oc.G. 4 sec.
Post G.
UNLOADING JETTY. Lts. 2 F.G. vert. 2M. Mast
5m.
KILROOT POINT JETTY. Lts. Oc.G. 10 sec. Tr.
G.

MRSC BELFAST Tel: (0247) 88318. Weather
broadcast ev. 4h. from 0305.

INSHORE WAYPOINT BELFAST LOUGH.
54°43.2′N, 5°40.3′W.

BELFAST 54°46′N, 5°41′W. Tel: H.M. (0232)
234422/238506. Telex: 74204. (Pilots: (0232)
781143).
Radio — Port: Belfast Radio. VHF Chan. 16,
12, 8, 11, 14, 10. Continuous.
B.P. Belfast. VHF Chan. 16, 10, 9. Continuous.
Cloghan Point Term. VHF Chan. 16, 14, 10.
Kilroot Jetty, Co. Antrim. VHF Chan. 16, 14.
Royal N of Ireland Y.C. Tel: (02317) 2041. VHF
Chan. M.
Radio — Pilots: VHF Chan. 16, 12, 8, 10, 11,
14. Continuous.
Entry: Carrickfergus — when sufficient water
to enter square flag shown by day and
additional R. Lt. on W Pier Head by night.
E gales send in heavy seas, anchor further up
Lough in moderate depth with good holding.
Good shallow anchorage in Whitehouse and
Folly Roads.
Anchorage: E of No. 1 By.

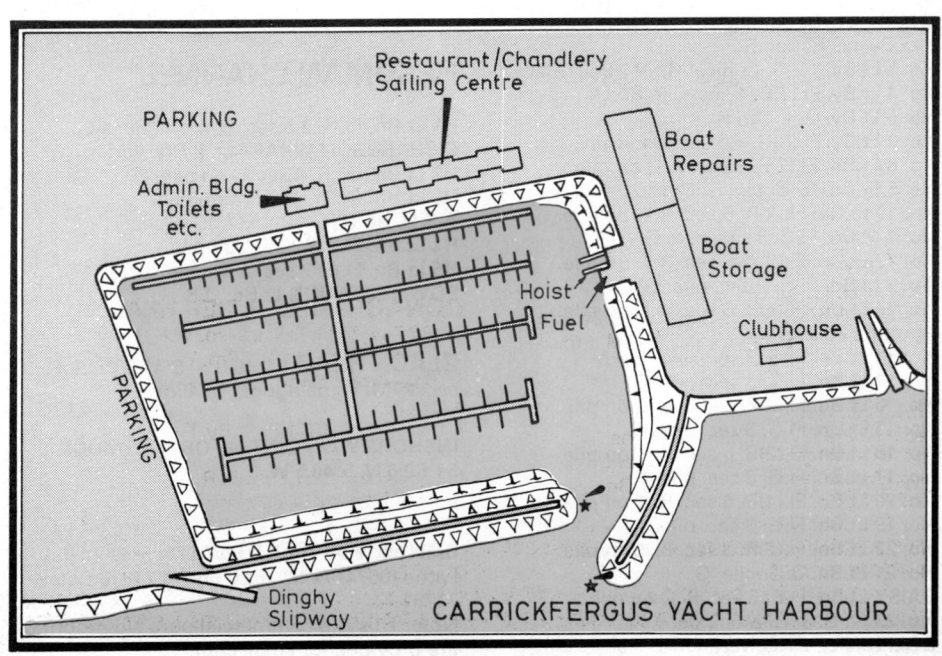

ROCKPORT SHOAL By. Can.R.
'X' By. Conical Y. off Ardnaloe House.
CARRICKFERGUS. Lt.By. Fl.R. 10 sec. Can.R.

CARRICKFERGUS HARBOUR Tel:
(09603) 62292
Radio — Port: VHF Chan. 16, 12, 14 — 2 h.
before to 1 h. after HW.
Radio — Pilots: VHF Chan. 16. H24.
Anchorage: 1M. E of No. 1 By.
E PIER HEAD. Lt. Fl.G. 7.5 sec. 2M. metal Col.
5m. 050°-255°.
W PIER HEAD. Lt. Fl.R. 7.5 sec. 2M. metal Col.
5m. 068°-256°.
MARINA E BREAKWATER HD. Lt. Q.G. 3M. G.
Pillar 8m.
W BREAKWATER HD. Lt. Q.R. 3M. R. Pillar
7m. 125°-065°.
CHIMNEY. Lt.Bn. Q.R.
Lt. F. marks sewage outfall E of Thompson's
Pt.
'102' By. Conical Y. lying W of Folly Roads.

SYDENHAM AERODROME 54°36.9'N,
5°52.5'W. Lt. Aero Mo(SD)G. 12M. 23m.

VICTORIA CHANNEL TO BELFAST

N Lt.By. I.Q.G. Conical G.
S Lt.By. I.Q.R. Can.R.
No: 1 Lt.By. I.Q.G. Conical G. 〰 Bell. (Pilots).
No: 4 Lt.By. Fl.(2)R. 4 sec. Can.R.
No: 6 Lt.By. Q.R. Can.R.
No: 3 Lt.By. Fl.(3)G. 7.5 sec. Conical G.
No: 8 Lt.Bn. Fl.(2)R. 6 sec. R. ☐ on pile.
No: 5 Lt.Bn. Q. G. pile G. Horn 20 sec.
No: 10 Lt.Bn. Fl.(2)R. 6 sec. R. ☐ on pile.
No: 7 Lt.Bn. Fl.G. 3 sec. pile. G.
No: 12 Lt.Bn. Fl.(2)R. 6 sec. R. ☐ on pile.
No: 9 Lt.Bn. Fl.G. 3 sec. pile. G.
No: 14 Lt.Bn. Fl.(4)R. 6 sec. R. ☐ on pile.
Nauto(2) 20 sec.
No: 11 Lt.Bn. Fl.G. 3 sec. pile. G.
No: 13 Lt.Bn. Fl.G. 3 sec. pile. G.
No: 16 Lt.Bn. Fl.(2)R. 6 sec. R. ☐ on pile.
No: 15 Lt.Bn. Fl.G. 3 sec. pile. G.
No: 18 Lt.Bn. Fl.(2)R. 6 sec. R. ☐ on pile.
No: 17 Lt.Bn. Fl.G. 3 sec. pile. G.
No: 20 Lt.Bn. Fl.(4)R. 6 sec. R. ☐ on pile.
No: 19 Lt.Bn. Fl.G. 3 sec. pile. G.
No: 22 Lt.Bn. Fl.(2)R. 3 sec. R. ☐ on pile.
No: 21 Lt.Bn. Q.G. pile G.
DAISY Lt.Bn. Fl.R. 5 sec. R. ☐ on pile.
No. 23 Lt. Q.G. G. ∆ on pile.
DOLPHIN Lt. 2 F.G. vert.

MUSGRAVE CHANNEL

M2 Lt.Bn. Fl.(4)R. 6 sec. R. ☐ on pile.
M1 Lt.Bn. Q.G. 2M. Pile G. 2m.
M3 Lt.Bn. Fl.G. 4 sec. 2M. Pile G. 2m.
E SIDE Lt.Bn. Fl.(2)R. 7.5 sec. 2M. pile, 2m.

E TWIN ISLAND Lt.Bn. Q.(6)R. 9 sec. R. ☐ on
pile.
DRYDOCK NW CORNER Horn(3) 15 sec.
Reserve fog sig. Bell.

W TWIN ISLAND
W TWIN Lt.Bn. Fl.G. 4 sec. 2M. G. ∆ Col. 10m.
SPENCER Lt.Bn. Fl.(2)G. 12 sec. 2M. Col. 10m.
THOMPSON DOCK Lt.Bn. Fl.R. 1.5 sec. 1M. Tr.
8m.
No: 10 SLIP 300m. of oil boom secured to 9
unlit buoys.
RIVER LAGAN BALLAST QUAY Lt. 2 F.R. vert.
1M. Tr. 6m.
ALBERT QUAY NE CORNER. Lt. Q.G.
S END BALLAST QUAY Lt. F.Bu. Col.
N QUEENS Lt. Fl.R. 5 sec. 2M. R. ☐ on pile,
7m.
S QUEENS Lt. Q.R. 2M. R. ☐ on pile, 7m.

DONEGAL QUAY
LIVERPOOL FERRY Lt. Fl.G. 2 sec.
ARDROSSAN FERRY Lt. Fl.(3)G. 6 sec.
LAGAN BRIDGE E SIDE Lt. F.G.
W SIDE Lt. F.G.

HERDMAN CHANNEL

H1 Lt.Bn. Fl.G. 2.5 sec. B. ∆ on Pile 〰.
RICHARDSON WHARF Lt. 2 F.G. vert.
H2 Lt.Bn. Oc.R. 4 sec. ☐ on pile.
H3 Lt.Bn. Oc.G. 4 sec. ∆ on pile.
A.S.N. BERTH Lt.Bn. Fl.(3)G. 6 sec.
H4 Lt.Bn. Fl.R. 4 sec. ☐ on pile.
H5 Lt.Bn. Fl.G. 2 sec. ∆ on pile.
POWER STATION Lt.Bn. Q.R.

BLACK HEAD 54°46.0'N, 5°41.3'W Lt. Fl. 3
sec. 27M. W. octagonal Tr. 45m.

INSHORE WAYPOINT NE OF PORTMUCK.
54°52.0'N, 5°40.5'W.

LARNE HARBOUR 54°51'N 5°47'W. Tel:
Larne (0574) 79221. Fax: (0574) 74610. Telex:
74781.
Note: This is a commercial port. No moorings
are provided for small craft.

HARBOUR WAYPOINT. 54°52.0′N, 5°47.5′W.

Radio — Port: VHF Chan. 16, 14 — Chan. 16 H24.

S HUNTER ROCK Lt.By. Q.(6) + L.Fl. 15 sec. Pillar. Y.B. Topmark S. Horn (3) 30 sec.
N HUNTER ROCK Lt.By. Q. Pillar. B.Y. Topmark N.
LARNE No: 1 Lt.By. Q.(3) 10 sec. Pillar. B.Y.B. Topmark E.
LARNE No: 3 Lt.By. Fl.(2)G. 6 sec. Conical G. ⌣⌣ off Sandy Pt.
BARR POINT Dia 30 sec. R. framework Tr. Reserve fog sig. horn.

CHAINE TOWER 54°51.3′N, 5°47.8′W. Lt. Iso.W.R. 5 sec. 11M. Grey Tr. 23m. W.230°-240°; R.240°-shore.

FERRIS POINT 54°51.1′N, 5°47.3′W. Lt.Ho. Iso.W.R.G. 10 sec. W.17M. R.13M. G.13M. Lantern above watch room on square W. Tr. 18m. W.345°-119°; G.119°-154°; W.154°-201°; R.201°-223° also shown by day in fog.

ENTRANCE 54°49.6′N, 5°47.7′W. Ldg.Lts 184°. (Front) No: 11. Oc. 4 sec. 12M. W. ◇, R. stripe, on R. pile structure. Vis. 179°-189°. (Rear) No: 12. Oc. 4 sec. 12M. W. ◇, R. stripe, on aluminium round Tr. 14m. Synchronised with front. Vis. 179°-189°.

No: 2 Lt.Bn. Fl.R. 3 sec. 4M. R. pile structure, 4m.
CONTINENTAL QUAY. Lt. 2 F.G. vert. 1M. on dolphin, 7 and 5m. Vis. 167°-240° occas. off NE corner of Hd.
No: 4 Lt.Bn. Fl.(2)R. 6 sec. 4M. R. pile structure, 4m.
LARNE No: 5 Lt.By. Q.G. Conical G. ⌣⌣.
LARNE No: 7 Lt.By. Q.G. Conical G. ⌣⌣.
S PIER HEAD. Lt. 2 F.R. vert. 5M. 4m.

BALLYLUMFORD
POWER STATION, JETTY, NW END Lt. 2 F.R. vert. 5M. on dolphin, 7m.
BERTH, NW END Lt. 2 F.R. vert. 5M. 7m.
SE END Lt. 2 F.R. vert. 5M. 7m. Dolphin R.
BALLYLUMFORD JETTY, NW END Lt. 2 F.R. vert. 2M. post on dolphin, 8m.
SE END. Lt. 2 F.R. vert. Dolphin R.
Ldg.Lts. 264° (Front) Oc. 6 sec. W. Pole.
(Rear) Oc. 6 sec. W. Pole.
Ldg.Lts. 310° (Front) Oc. 8 sec. W. Pole. ◇.
(Rear) Oc. 8 sec. W. Pole. ◇.

MAGHERAMORNE. Ldg.Lts. 177° (Front) Oc.R. 7 sec. Vis. 173°-181° (Rear) Oc. R. 12 sec. Vis. 162°-192°.
Lt. Fl.Y. 2 sec. Bn.

LOUGH LARNE TO RATHLIN ISLAND

MAIDENS 54°55.7′N, 5°43.6′W Lt. Fl.(3) 20 sec. 15M. W. Tr. B. band, 29m. Same structure, auxiliary Lt. Fl.R. 5 sec. 8M. 15m. Vis. 142°-182° over Russel and Highland Rks.

OFFSHORE WAYPOINT N OF MAIDENS. 54°58.0′N, 5°43.0′W.

MARINE FARMS are established in this area. Consult chart for details.

CARNLOUGH HARBOUR

N PIER. Lt. Fl.G. 3 sec. 5M. W.B. Col.
S PIER. Lt. Fl.R. 3 sec. 5M. W.B. Col.

RED BAY
PIER Lt. Fl. 3 sec. 5M. Pole 10m.

Marine Farm established in Red Bay. consult Chart for details.

HIGHLAND ROCK Mast R. Topmark Can.

NORTH COAST OF IRELAND

OFFSHORE WAYPOINT N OF TORR HD. 55°14.0′N, 6°03.0′W.

W TORR RG STN. 55°11.9′N, 6°05.6′W. Emergency DF Stn. VHF Chan. 16 & 67. Controlled by MRSC Belfast.

RATHLIN ISLAND

RUE POINT 55°15.5′N, 6°11.3′W. Lt. Fl.(2) 5 sec. 14M. W. octagonal concrete Tr. B. bands, 16m.

CHURCH BAY HMS DRAKE. By. Pillar. Y.B.
Topmark S.

OFFSHORE WAYPOINT NE OF ALTACARRY
HEAD. 55°19.0'N, 6°14.0'W.

RATHLIN E, ALTACARRY HEAD
55°18.1'N, 6°10.2'W. Lt. Fl.(4) 20 sec. 22M. W.
Tr. B. band, 74m. Vis. 110°-006° and 036°-058°.
RC.

RATHLIN W 55°18.1'N, 6°16.7'W Lt. Fl.R. 5
sec. 22M. W. Tr. lantern at base, 62m. Vis.
015°-225°. Shown by day when fog sig.
operating. Horn(4) 60 sec. Fog Detr. Lt. V.Q.
69m. 119°.
MANOR HOUSE PIER. Lt. Fl.(2)R. 6 sec. 4M.
Col. 5m.

RATHLIN ISLAND TO LOUGH FOYLE

BALLYCASTLE. Tel: Ballycastle 386.
PIER HEAD. Lt. L.Fl.W.R. 9 sec. 5M. Col. 6m.
R.110°-212°; W.212°-000°.

OFFSHORE WAYPOINT NNW OF BENBANE
HD. 55°16.0'N, 6°30.0'W.

INSHORE WAYPOINT N OF PORTRUSH.
55°13.5'N, 6°40.5'W.

PORTRUSH 55°13'N 6°39'W. Tel: H.M.
(0265) 822307.

HARBOUR WAYPOINT. 55°12.3'N, 6°40.5'W.

Radio — Port: VHF Chan. 16, 14. Mon.-Fri.
0900-1700 (extended June-Sept.). Sat.-Sun.
0900-1700 (June-Sept. only).
Entry: Water and Diesel available.
Anchorage: Sherry Roads.

Ldg.Lts. 028° (Front) F.R. 1M. 6m. (Rear) F.R.
1M. 8m.

THE STORKES Bn. R. Topmark Can.

N PIER HEAD. Lt. Fl.R. 3 sec. 3M. concrete
structure 6m. Vis. 220°-160°.
S PIER HEAD. Lt. Fl.G. 3 sec. 3M. concrete
structure. 6m. Vis. 220°-100°.
PORTSTEWART POINT. Lt. Oc.R. 10 sec. 5M. R.
square concrete hut, 21m. Vis. 040°-220°. Pilots'
sig.stn.

RIVER BANN

COLERAINE 55°10'N 6°46'W. Tel: Coleraine
(0265) 2012 (Night: Port Stewart (026-583)
2055) (or 3731).

HARBOUR WAYPOINT. 55°10.6'N, 6°46.6'W.

Radio — Port: VHF Chan. 16, 12. Mon.-Fri.
0900-1700 and when v/l expected.
Channel to Coleraine is maintained at 3.2m.
below C.D. River Entrance at 3.8m below C.D.

Ldg.Lts. 165°. (Front) Oc. 2M. W. metal Tr. 6m.
(Rear) Oc. 2M. W. metal Tr. 14m.
River marked by Lt.Bn. Fl.G. 5 sec. & Lt.Bn.
Fl.R. 5 sec.
W PIER, NR HEAD. Lt. Fl.G. 3 sec. G. metal
mast, 5m. occas.
E PIER HEAD. Lt. Fl.R. 5 sec. 2M. W. concrete
Tr. 6m.
BALLYAGHRAN. Lt. Fl.(2) R. 5 sec. □ on R. Bn.
TRIPOD. Lt. Fl.R. 3 sec. □ on R. Bn.
WEE BURN. Lt. Fl.G. 5 sec. △ on G. Bn.
OUTER COASTGUARD PORT. Lt. Fl.R. 5 sec. □
on R. Bn.
STARBOARD. Lt. Fl.(2) G 5 sec. △ on G. Bn.
INNER COASTGUARD PORT. Lt. Fl.R. 5 sec. □
on R. Bn.
STARBOARD. Lt. Fl.G. 5 sec. △ on G. Bn.
KENNEDYS STUMP. Lt. Fl.R. 5 sec. □ on R.
Bn.
OLD NOB. Lt. Fl.G. 5 sec. △ on G. Bn.
SANDHILLS. Lt. Fl.R. 5 sec. □ on R. Bn.
LT. Fl.G. 5 sec. △ on G. Bn.
POTTAGH PORT. Lt. Fl.R. 5 sec. R □ on Bn.
POTTAGH. Lt. Fl.G. 5 sec. △ on G. Bn.
GOLF LINKS. Lt. Fl.R. 5 sec. □ on R. Bn.
BANNBROOK. Lt. Fl.R. 5 sec. □ on R. Bn.
LT. Fl.G. 5 sec. △ on G. Bn.
QUARRY. Lt. Fl.G. 5 sec. △ on G. Bn.
LINTONS. Lt. Fl.R. 5 sec. □ on R. Bn.
SEATONS. Lt. Fl.G. 5 sec. △ on G. Bn.
LT. Fl.R. 5 sec. □ on R. Bn.
LT. Fl.G. 5 sec. △ on G. Bn.
CLARKES. Lt. Fl.R. 5 sec. □ on R. Bn. F.R. Lts.
mark outer pontoons at Coleraine Marina.
KENVARRA. Lt. Fl.R. 5 sec. □ on R. Bn.
F.G. on each side of Bascule Bridge. R. Lt. on
Trs.
OIL JETTY. S. END. Lt. Fl.G. 5 sec.
LOUGH NEAGH. OFF DUNMORE POINT. Lt. 2
F.R. (Hor.) Water Twr.

KINNEGO MARINA. Tel: (0762) 327573. VHF
Chan. 10.

LONDONDERRY (Lough Foyle) 55°00'N
7°19'W. Tel: H.M. (0504) 264884/263680. Hbr.
Radio: (0504) 363218. Pilots: (0003) 82402.

Radio — Port: VHF Chan. 16, 12, 14. H24.
Radio — Pilots: Lough Foyle. VHF Chan. 16, 12, 14. Mon.-Fri. 0800-1700.
Moville. VHF Chan. 16, 11, 12.
Entry: Anchorage Moville Bay in up to 18m. Entrance to R. Foyle approx. 1½c. wide. Call and maintain listening watch on VHF Chan. 14 which broadcasts information on shipping movements etc.

RIVER FOYLE. Foyle Bridge clearance 32m.

LOUGH FOYLE

OFFSHORE WAYPOINT OFF LOUGH FOYLE. 55°16.0'N, 6°52.5'W.

LOUGH FOYLE. Lt.By. L.Fl. 10 sec. Pillar. R.W.V.S. ʊʊ Whis. off Entce. to Lough.

INSHORE WAYPOINT ENTRANCE TO LOUGH FOYLE. 55°14.0'N, 6°53.0'W.

TUNS BANK. Lt.By. Fl.R. 3 sec. Can.R. ʊʊ On E side of Entce.

DUNAGREE POINT

INISHOWEN, W TOWER 55°13.6'N,
6°55.7'W. Lt.Ho. Fl.(2) W.R.G. 10 sec. W.18M. R.14M. G.14M. W. Tr. 2 B. bands, 28m. G.197°-211°; W.211°-249°; R. 249°-000°. Horn. (2) 30 sec. also shown by day in fog. Fog Detr. Lt. V.Q. 16m. 120°.
Note. Unlit Lt.Ho. exists close to NE of above Lt.Ho. on Dunagree Pt.

BLUICK ROCK Bn. G. △ Topmark Conical. N side of Chan.

WARREN POINT 55°13'N, 6°57'W. Tel:
Warren Point (069 372) 3381.
Radio — Port: VHF Chan. 16, 12 — continuous.
Radio — Pilots: VHF Chan. 16, 12 — continuous.
WARREN POINT 55°12.6'N, 6°57.1'W. Lt. Fl. 1.7 sec. 232°-061°. 10M. W.G. Tr. 9m.
MAGILLIGAN POINT. Lt.Bn. Q.R. 5M. on R. piles, 7m.
No: 1 Lt.By. Fl.R. 6 sec. Can.R. 4 cables from Magilligan Pt. Lt
McKINNEY'S BANK. Lt.Bn. Fl.R. 5 sec. 5M. on R. piles, 6m.
MOVILLE. Lt.Bn. Fl. W.R. 2.5 sec. 4M. Pile 11m. W. 240°-064°; R. 064°-240°.
GLENBURNIE. Lt. Fl.R. 2.5 sec. pile structure.
ST. BEDAN WK. Lt.By. Q. Pillar B.Y. Topmark N. off Carrickarory Pier.

SALTPANS. Lt.Bn. Fl.R. 2.5 sec. 3M. W. Lt.Ho. on Dunagree Pt. structure on R. piles, 5m. Nr. NE end of N Middle Bk.
GREAT MIDDLE BANK Perch B. ball Topmark, on edge.
CLARE. Lt.Bn. Q.R. 3M. W. structure on R. piles, 5m.

GREENORE POINT (FERRY)
Radio: VHF Chan. 16, 13. H24.

NE REDCASTLE. Lt.By. Fl. G. Conical. G.
REDCASTLE. Lt.Bn. Oc. G. 5 sec. 5M. G. hut. 5m.
VANCE. Lt.Bn. Fl.R. 5 sec. 3M. W. structure on R. piles. 5m.
DRUNG. Lt.By. Fl.R. 2 sec. Can.R.
ARGUS. Lt.By. Fl.(3)G. 10 sec. Conical G.
WHITECASTLE. Lt.Bn. Q.R. 9M. W. house on R. piles, 7m.
CABRY. Lt.Bn. Fl.G. 2.5 sec. 6M. G. structure on B. piles, 5m.

Port hand marks are R. and starboard hand are G.

QUIGLEYS POINT. Lt.Bn. Fl.R. 2 sec. 5M. W. structure on B. piles, 5m.
GREENBANK Lt.Bn. Q.G. 5M. G. structure on B. piles, 6m.
LEPERS POINT. Lt.Bn. Q.R. 3M. W. structure on R. piles, 5m.

TURE. Lt.Bn. Fl.R. 4 sec. 9M. W. house on R. piles, 7m.
AUGHT. Lt.Bn. Fl.G. 5 sec. 5M. G. structure on B. piles, 6m.
DRUMSKELLAN. Lt.Bn. Fl.G. 2.5 sec. 6M. G. structure on B. piles, 5m
LONGFIELD. Lt.Bn. Fl.R. 5 sec. 3M. W. structure on R. piles, 6m.
CRUMMIN POINT. Lt.Bn. Q.G. 5M. G. structure on B. piles, 6m.
WILLSBORO'. Lt.Bn. Fl.(2)R. 5 sec. 3M. R. piles, 5m.
BLACK BRAE. Lt.By. Q.R. Can.R.
KILDERRY. Lt.Bn. Fl.G. 2 sec. 5M. G. structure on B. piles, 6m.

MUFF. Lt. Fl.G. 2 sec. 3M. Pile G.
CONEYBURROW Lt. Fl.G. 2.5 sec. 3M. Pile G. 8m.

FAUGHAN Lt. Fl.R. 4 sec. 3M. W. structure on R. piles, 8m.
COOLKEERAGH WHARF.
NE END. Lt. Q.(2)R. 2 sec. **SW END.** Lt. Fl.R. 5 sec.
NE END. Lt. 2 F.R. vert. **SW END.** Lt. Fl.R. 2 sec.
JETTY. Lt. Fl.R. 2 sec.

RIVER FOYLE

CULMORE POINT Lt. Q. 5M. G. round Tr. on B. base, 6m.
CULMORE OUTFALL. By. Conical Y.
CULMORE BAY. Lt. Fl.G. 5 sec. 2M. W. Lantern G. Pile. 4m.
LISA HALLY Lt. Q.R.

BALLYNAGARD Lt. Fl. 3 sec. 3M. G. round house, W. lantern, 4m.
OTTER BANK Lt. Fl.R. 4 sec. 3M. W. structure on R. round Tr. 4m.
BROOK HALL. Lt.Bn. Q.G. 3M. G. structure on B. base, 4m.

MOUNTJOY. Lt.Bn. Q.R. 3M. W. structure on R. piles, 5m.
BOOM HALL. Bn. W.G.
Lt.By. Fl.R. 2 sec. Can.R.
FOYLE BRIDGE. Lts. F. each side mark centre.
W JETTY. Lt. V.Q.G. 3M. 8m.
E JETTY. Lt. V.Q.R. 3M. 8m.
CROOK. Lt.By. Q.G. Conical G.
ROSSES BAY CHANNEL. Ldg.Lts. 085°.
(Front) Oc.R. 5 sec. 3M. W. house on R. piles, 6m. **GRANSHA** (Rear) Fl.R. 5 sec. R.W. cheq. house, 16m.
Lt.By. Fl.G. 2 sec. Conical G.
CLOONEY POINT BANK. Lt.Bn. Fl.R. 4 sec. 3M. R. piles, 3m.
TALBOT. Bn. G.
PENNYBURN. Bn. Perch.

17S BERTH Lt. 2 F.G. vert.

ST. COLUMBS. Lt.Bn. Fl.R. 5 sec. 3M. W.R. piles, 3m.

ABERFOYLE Lt. Fl.R. 2 sec. 3M. W. structure on R. piles, 5m.
MIDDLE BANK No: 10. Lt.By. Fl. 1.5 sec. Conical R.Y. ⎈.
GLENGAD HEAD. Lt.By. Fl.R. 1.5 sec. Pillar R.Y. vert. stripes.

OFFSHORE WAYPOINT SW OF INISHTRAHULL. 55°24.5′N, 7°20.4′W.

INISHTRAHULL 55°25.8′N, 7°14.6′W. Lt.Fl.(3)15 sec. 25M. W. Tr. 59m. Racon.
Lt.By. Fl.R. 1.5 sec. Pillar R.Y. vert. stripes, SE of Inishtrahull.

OFFSHORE WAYPOINT TRAWBREAGA BAY. 55°20.75′N, 7°30.0′W.

LOUGH SWILLY TO BLOODY FORELAND (MULROY BAY)

INSHORE WAYPOINT LOUGH SWILLY. 55°14.5′N, 7°33.25′W.

LOUGH SWILLY
SWILLYMORE ROCKS Fl.G. 3 sec. Conical G. on W side ⎈

OFFSHORE WAYPOINT N OF FANAD HD. 55°17.5′N, 7°38.25′W.

FANAD HEAD 55°16.6′N, 7°37.9′W. Lt. Fl.(5) W.R. 20 sec. W.18M. R.14M. W. Tr. 39m. R.100°-110°; W.110°-313°; R.313°-345°; W.345°-100°.
Also F.R. on radio mast 3.08M. 200°.

DUNREE 55°11.9′N, 7°33.2′W. Lt. Fl.(2) W.R. 5 sec. W.12M. R.9M. house, 46m. R.320°-328°; W.328°-183°; R.183°-196°.
N COLPAGH ROCK. Lt.By. Fl.R. 6 sec. Can.R. on E side of Lough.
WHITE STRAND ROCKS. Lt.By. Fl.R. 10 sec. Can.R. on E side of Lough.

BUNCRANA PIER. 55°07.6′N, 7°27.8′W. Lt. Iso.W.R. 4 sec. W.14M. R.11M. on Col. 8m. R.shore-052° over Inch Spit; W.052°-139°; R.139°-shore over W. Strand Rk.
SALTPANS BANK. Lt.By. Q.(3) 10 sec. Pillar. B.Y.B. Topmark E on W side of Lough.
INCH SPIT. Lt.By. Fl.R. 3 sec. Can.R.
KINNEGAR SPIT. Lt.By. Fl.G. 10 sec. Conical G. on W side of Lough.
INCH FLATS. Lt.By. Fl.(2)R. 6 sec. Can.R. on E side of Lough.

RATHMULLEN PIER HEAD. Lt. Fl.G. 3 sec. 5M. G. Post vis. 206°-345°.
LIMEBURNER ROCK Lt. By. Q. Pillar B.Y. Topmark N. Whis.
RAVEDY ISLAND. Lt. Fl. 3 sec. 3M. concrete Tr. 9m. vis. 177°-357°.
DUNDOOAN ROCKS. Lt. Q.G. 1M. G. concrete Tr. 4m.
CRANNOGE POINT. Lt. Fl.G. 5 sec. 2M. G. concrete Tr. 5m.
LENAN ROCKS By. Conical R.

WEST COAST OF IRELAND
SHEEPHAVEN BAY

BAR ROCK Bn. Pillar. G.
DOWNINGS BAY PIER HEAD. Lt. Fl.R. 3 sec.
2M. on R. post, 5m. vis. 283°, through N till
obscured by Downies Point.
PORTNABLAGHY. Ldg.Lts. 125°15′ (Front) Oc.
6 sec. 2M. 7m. B.W. Col. (Rear) Oc. 6 sec. 2M.
12m. B.W. Col.

TORY ISLAND, NW POINT. 55°16.4′N,
8°14.9′W. Lt. Fl.(4) 30 sec. 30M. B. Tr. W. band,
40m. Vis. 302°-277°. R.C. Horn. 60 sec. also
shown by day in fog. Distress answering.
INISHBOFIN PIER. Lt. Fl. 8 sec. 3M. 3m.

INISHBOFIN BAY

BALLYNESS HARBOUR
Ldg.Lts. 119°29′ (Front) Iso. 4 sec. 1M. W.B.
Mast. 25m. (Rear) Iso. 4 sec. 1M. B.W. Mast.
26m.
**OFFSHORE WAYPOINT N OF BLOODY
FORELAND. 55°11.9′N, 8°16.0′W.**
BLOODY FORELAND. Lt. Fl.W.G. 7.5 sec.
W.6M. G.4M. W. concrete hut, 14m. W.062°-
232°; G.232°-062°.
GLASSAGH. Ldg.Lts. 137°25′ (Front) Oc. 8 sec.
3M. W.B. Col. 12m. (Rear) Oc. 8 sec. 3M. B.W.
Col. 17m.
INISHSIRRER, NW END. Lt. Fl. 3.7 sec. 4M. W.
Tr. 20m. vis. 083°-263°.
GOLA SPIT By. Can.R. in Gola Roads.
MIDDLE ROCK By. Can.R. in Gola Roads.
NICHOLAS ROCK. By. Pillar.

BUNBEG APPROACHES.
GOLA ISLAND. Ldg.Lts. 171°14′ (Front) Oc. 3
sec. 2M. W.B. Bn. 9m. (Rear) Oc. 3 sec. 2M.
B.W. Bn. 13m.
BO ISLAND E POINT. Lt. Fl.G. 3 sec. Bn. 3m.

GWEEDORE HARBOUR, BUNBEG
GUBNADOUGH Bys. 2 Conical B. off SW side
of Gola I.
INISHINNY. No: 1 Lt.Bn. Q.G. 1M. square G.
Col. with steps, 3m.
CARRICKBULLOG No: 2 Lt. Q.R. R. Tr.
No: 3 Bn. R. square Col. with steps, 3m.
INISHCOOLE. No: 4 Lt.Bn. Q.R. 1M. R. square
concrete Col. on base, with steps, 12m. neon.

YELLOW ROCKS. No: 6 Lt.Bn. Q.R. 1M.
square R. Col. with steps, 3m. neon.
MAGHERALOSK. No: 5 Lt.Bn. Q.G. 1M.
square G. Col. with steps, 4m. S.V.
CRUIT ISLAND OWEY SOUND Ldg.Lts.
068°20′ (Front) Oc. 10 sec. (Rear) Oc. 10 sec.
RINNALEA POINT. Lt.Fl. 7.5 sec. 9M. square
Tr. 19m. vis. 132°-167°.
Lt. F. shown at Hd. of Gortnasate Pier during
fishing season.
MULLAGHDOO Ldg.Lts. 184°20′ (Front) Iso 8
sec. W.Pole (Rear) Iso. 8 sec. W.Pole.

**OFFSHORE WAYPOINT NW OF ARAN I.
55°01.0′N, 8°35.0′W.**

ARANMORE, RINRAWROS POINT
55°00.9′N, 8°33.6′W. Lt. Fl.(2) 20 sec. 29M. W.
Tr. 71m. Obscured by land about 234°-007°
and when bearing about 013°.
Same structure, auxiliary Lt. Fl.R. 3 sec. 13M.
61m. vis. 203°-234°.
ARAN ROAD Perch, W. obelisk.
CARRICKBEALATROHA LOWER. Bn. Mast.
Y.B.Y. Topmark W.
LACKMORRIS. Bn. Mast. B.R.B. Topmark Is. D.
S CHANNEL. Bn. Mast R.

**OFFSHORE WAYPOINT W OF ARAN I.
54°58.8′N, 8°36.6′W.**

NORTH SOUND OF ARAN

BALLAGH ROCKS. Lt. Fl. 2.5 sec. 5M. W.B.
structure 13m.
FALLAGOWAN. Ldg.Lts. 186°. (Front) Oc. 8
sec. 3M. B. concrete Bn. W. band, 8m. (Rear)
Oc. 8 sec. 3M. B. concrete Bn. 17m.
BLACK ROCKS Lt. Fl.R. 3 sec. 1M. R. Col. 3m.
Base submerged at H.W.

RUTLAND NORTH CHANNEL

INISHCOO. Ldg.Lts. 119°18′. (Front) Iso. 6 sec.
1M. W. concrete Bn. B. band, 6m. (Rear) Iso. 6
sec. 1M. B. concrete Bn. Y. band, 11m.
CARRICKATINE. No: 2 Lt.Bn. Q.R. 1M. R.
concrete Bn. with steps, 4m. neon.
RUTLAND ISLAND. Ldg.Lts. 137°38′. (Front)
Oc. 6 sec. 1M. W. Bn. B. band, 8m. (Rear) Oc.
6 sec. 1M. B. Bn. Y. band, 14m.
INISHCOO. No: 4 Lt.Bn. Q.R. 1M. R. Bn.
NANCY'S ROCK. No: 1 Lt.Bn. Q.G. 1M. G. Bn.
No: 6 Lt.Bn. Q.R. 1M. R. Bn.

BURTON PORT. Ldg.Lts. 068°05'. (Front) F.G. 1M. Grey Bn. Y. band. (Rear) F.G. 1M. Grey Bn. Y. band.

BURTON PORT APPROACH
Lt.Bn. Fl. 5 sec.
Lt.Bn. Fl. 5 sec.
Lt.Bn. Fl.
Lt.Bn. Fl.R 5 sec.
Lt.Bn. Fl.R.

SOUTH SOUND OF ARAN

ILLANCRONE ISLAND. Lt. Fl. 5 sec. 6M. W. square Tr. 7m.
WYON POINT. Lt. Fl.(2) W.R.G. 10 sec. W.6M. R.3M. W. Tr. 8m. G.shore-021°; W.021°-042°; R.042°-121°; W.121°-150°; R.150°-shore.
TURK ROCK. Lt. Fl.G. 5 sec. 2M. square G.Tr. 3m.
AILEEN REEF. Lt. Q.R. 1M. R. square Bn. 4m.
CARRICKBEALATROHA UPPER. Lt. Fl. 5 sec. 2M. W. square brick Tr. 3m.

INSHORE WAYPOINT BOYLAGH BAY. 54°53.2'N, 8°27.0'W.

RUTLAND SOUTH CHANNEL

CORRENS ROCK. Lt. Fl.R. 3 sec. 2M. square R.Tr. 4m.
TEIGES ROCK. Lt. Fl. 3 sec. 2M. W. round Tr. 4m.
DAWROS HEAD. Lt. L.Fl. 10 sec. 4M. W.Col. 39m.

OFFSHORE WAYPOINT N OF MALIN MORE HD. 54°44.3'N, 8°47.9'W.

RATHLIN O'BIRNE, W SIDE 54°40.0'N, 8°50.0'W. Lt. Fl.W.R. 20 sec. W.22M. R.18M. W. Tr. 35m. R. 195°-307°; W.307°-195°.

OFFSHORE WAYPOINT SW OF RATHLIN O'BIRNE. 54°39.3'N, 8°51.6'W.

TEELIN HARBOUR Lt. Fl.R. 10 sec. R. post.

DONEGAL BAY

ST. JOHN'S POINT 54°34.2'N, 8°27.6'W. Lt. Fl. 6 sec. 14M. W. Tr. 30m.
BULLOCKMORE Lt.By. Q.(9) 15 sec. Pillar. Y.B.Y. Topmark W.

MARINE FARMS are established in this area. Consult chart for details.

INSHORE WAYPOINT SW OF ST. JOHN'S POINT. 54°33.4'N, 8°29.5'W.

KILLYBEGS HARBOUR 54°38'N, 8°26'W.
Tel: H.M. (073) 31032.
Radio — Port: VHF Chan. 16.

ROTTEN ISLAND 54°36.9'N, 8°26.3'W. Lt. Fl.W.R. 4 sec. W.15M. R.11M. W. Tr. 20m. W.255°-008°; R.008°-039°; W.039°-208°.
KILLYBEGS OUTER. Lt.By. V.Q.(6) + L.Fl. 10 sec. Pillar. Y.B. Topmark S.
KILLYBEGS INNER. Lt.By. Q. Pillar. B.Y. Topmark N.
By. Can.R.
Ldg.Lts. 338°. Pier Root. (Front) Oc.W. 8 sec. 2M. Y. ◊ on Bldg., 5m.
(Rear) Oc.R. 8 sec. 2M. Y. ◊ on Bldg., 7m.
W PIER HEAD. Lt. 2 F.R. vert.
BLACK ROCK JETTY. Lt.Bn. Fl.R.G. 5 sec. R.254°-204°; G.204°-254°.
Lt.By. Fl.R. Sph.

INSHORE WAYPOINT SW OF BALLYCONNELL POINT. 54°20.7'N, 8°42.8'W.
INSHORE WAYPOINT SLIGO BAY. 54°17.5'N, 8°38.75'W.

SLIGO 54°19'N 8°36'W. Tel: (071) 73157 (Pilots).
Radio — Pilots: VHF Chan. 16, 12, as required.

SLIGO BAY
WHEAT ROCK. Lt.By. Q.(6) + L.Fl. 15 sec. Pillar. Y.B. Topmark S. on N side of Sligo Bay.
RAGHLY LEDGE By. Can.R. N side of Sligo Bay. Temporarily discontinued.

BLACK ROCK 54°18.4'N, 8°37.0'W. Lt. Fl. 5 sec. 13M. W. Tr. B. band, 24m.
Same structure, auxiliary Lt. Fl.R. 3 sec. 5M. 12m. vis. 107°-130° over Wheat and Seal Rks.

LOWER ROSSES N OF POINT.
54°19.7'N, 8°34.4'W. Lt. Fl.(2) W.R.G. 10 sec. W.10M. R.8M. G.8M. G. Bungar Bank-066°; W.066°-070°; R.070°-Drumcliffe Bar. H24.
BUNGAR BANK. Lt.By. Fl.R. 7 sec. Can.R.
Mariners are cautioned against entering or leaving port without a pilot.

METAL MAN. Ldg.Lts. 125°. (Front) Fl. 4 sec. 7M. structure, 3m. H24.

OYSTER ISLAND. (Rear) Oc. 4 sec. 10M. Tr. 13m. NW Pt. H24.
OYSTER ISLAND, off NE POINT. Lt. Fl. 1.5 sec. 3M. △ on post, 4m.
BLENNICK ROCKS, W. Lt.Bn. Fl.R. 1.5 sec. 3M. on post, 4m.
E Lt.Bn. Fl.R. 3 sec. 3M. △ on post, 4m.
SEAL BANK, S SIDE. Lt.Bn. Fl. 3 sec. 3M. on post, 4m.
W TRAINING WALL. Lt.Bn. Fl. 1.5 sec. 3M. on post, 4m.
Also 3 Lts. 2 Fl. 3 sec. 3M. on posts, 4m. and 1 Fl. 1.5 sec. 3M. on post, 4m.
E TRAINING WALL. Lt.Bn. Fl.R. 1.5 sec. 3M. on post, 4m.
Also Lt. Fl.R. 1.5 sec. 3M. on post, 4m.
DEEP WATER QUAY, N END. Lt. F. 2M. on mast, 7m. when vessel expected.
UPPER QUAY, N END. Lt. F. 2M. on mast, 7m. when vessel expected.
S. Lt.Bn. F.R. 2M. on dolphin, 4m. when vessel expected.

INSHORE WAYPOINT N OF LENADOON POINT. 54°19.25′N, 9°02.25′W.

KILLALA BAY
CARRICKPATRICK. Lt.By. Q.(3) 10 sec. Pillar. B.Y.B. Topmark E.
KILLALA Lt.By. Fl.G. 6 sec. Conical G. 3M. from Inishcrone Lt.
INISHCRONE PIER ROOT. Lt. Fl. W.R.G. 1.5 sec. 2M. concrete Col. 8m. W.098°-116°; G.116°-136°; R.136°-187°.

INSHORE WAYPOINT KILLALA BAY. 54°13.8′N, 9°08.5′W.

KILLALA
RINNAUN POINT. Ldg.Lts. 230°. (Front) Oc. 10 sec. 5M. 7m. □ Concrete Tr. (Rear) Oc. 10 sec. 5M. 12m. □ Concrete Tr.

INCH ISLAND. Dir.Lt. 215°. Fl.W.R.G. 2 sec. 3M. 6m. □ Concrete Tr. G.205°-213°; W.213°-217°; R.217°-225°.

KILROE. Ldg.Lts. 196°. (Front) Oc. 4 sec. 2M. 5m. □ Concrete Tr. (Rear) Oc. 4 sec. 2M. 10m. □ Concrete Tr.

PIER Ldg.Lts. 236°. (Front) Iso. 2 sec. 2M. 5m. Or. □ on Concrete Tr. (Rear) Iso. 2 sec. 2M. 7m. Or. ◊ on pole.
KILLALA BAY BONE ROCK NE END Lt. Q. ⌁ on B.Y. Pillar. 7m.

INSHORE WAYPOINT N OF KILCUMMIN HD. 54°20.2′N, 9°13.5′W.

OFFSHORE WAYPOINT N OF THE STAGS. 54°22.9′N, 9°49.4′W.

BROADHAVEN
GUBACASHEL POINT 54°16.0′N, 9°53.3′W. Lt. Iso. W.R. 4 sec. W.12M. R.9M. W. Tr. 27m. W. shore (on the S side of Bay)-355°; R.355°-shore.
BALLYGLASS. Lt. Fl.G. 3 sec.

OFFSHORE WAYPOINT SW OF EAGLE I. 54°16.1′N, 10°10.0′W.

EAGLE ISLAND 54°17.0′N, 10°05.5′W. Lt. Fl.(3) 10 sec. 26M. W. Tr. 67m. R.C. Distress answering. H24.

BLACKROCK 54°04.0′N, 10°19.2′W. Lt. Fl.W.R. 12 sec. W.22M. R.16M. W. Tr. 86m. W.276°-212°; R.212°-276°.
BLACKSOD By. Can.R.

BLACKSOD PIER 54°05.9′N, 10°03.6′W. Lt. Fl.(2) W.R. 7.5 sec. W.12M. R.9M. W. Tr. on dwelling, 13m. R.189°-210°; W.210°-018°.
HEAD Lt. 2 F.R. vert. 3M. mast 6m.
CARRIGEENMORE Bn. Mast R.
ACHILL ISLAND RIDGE POINT. Lt. Fl. 5 sec. 5M. mast 21m.

OFFSHORE WAYPOINT W OF ACHILL HD. 53°58.2′N, 10°18.7′W.

ACHILL SOUND
INNISH BIGGLE Lt. Q.R.
SAULIA PIER. Lt. Fl.G. 3 sec. Col. 12m.
CARRIGEENFUSHTA Lt. Fl.G. 3 sec.
ACHILL SOUND Lt. Q.G.
WHITE STONE. Ldg.Lts. 330°. (Front) Oc. 4 sec. W. ◊ B. stripe on Pole. (Rear) Oc. 4 sec. W. ◊ B. stripe on pole.
Lt. Fl.R. 2 sec. Tr. R. 5m.
CARRIGIN-A-TSHRUTHA. Lt. Q.(2)R. 5 sec. on rock.

INSHORE WAYPOINT CLEW BAY. 53°48.5′N, 9°49.0′W.

CLEW BAY

WESTPORT (CO. MAYO) 53°48′N 9°31′W.

ACHILLBEG ISLAND, S POINT
53°51.5′N, 9°56.8′W. Lt. Fl.W.R. 5 sec. W.18M. R.18M. R.15M. W. round Tr. on square

building, 56m. R.262°-281°; W.281°-342°; R.342°-060°; W.060°-092°; R. (intens) 092°-099°; W.099°-118°. Obscured by Clare I. and The Bills.
PURTEEN PIER HEAD. Lt. Q.R.
CLARE ISLAND E PIER. Lt. Fl.R. 3 sec. 3M. 5m.
CLOUGHCORMAC By. Pillar. Y.B.Y. Topmark W. in Clew Bay.
DORINISH BAR. Lt.By. Fl.G. 3 sec. Conical G. S of Inishgort Lt.Ho.
DILLISH ROCKS Bn. Mast. Y.B. Topmark S. S of Inishgort Lt.Ho.

WESTPORT BAY

INISHGORT 53°49.6′N, 9°40.2′W. Lt. L.Fl. 10 sec. 10M. W. Tr. 11m. H24.
W PORT APPROACH Lt. Fl. 3 sec. G. Bn.
ROONAGH QUAY Ldg.Lts. 144°. (Front) Iso. 10 sec. 9m. (Rear) Iso 10 sec. 15m.
Also 2 F.R. Lts. on N side, when vessels entering or leaving.
Also 1 I.Q. 3 sec. 1M. conical stone Bn. 3m. and 1 F.Lt. on S side, when vessels entering or leaving.

OFFSHORE WAYPOINT W OF INISHTURK.
53°42.4′N, 10°19.6′W.

DONEE ISLAND Bn. on top of I. at Entce. to Killary Bay.
INISHBARNA Bn. in Killary Bay.

MARINE FARMS are established in this area. Consult chart for details.

INISHBOFIN
INISHLYON, LYON HEAD. Lt. Fl. W.R. 7.5 sec. W.7M. R.4M. W. post on concrete structure, 13m. W.036°-058°; R.058°-184°; W.184°-325°; R.325°-036°.
GUN ROCK. Lt. Fl.(2) 6 sec. 4M. W. Col. on W. hut, 8m. vis. 296°-253°, except where obscured by islands.

OFFSHORE WAYPOINT W OF INISHBOFIN.
53°35.9′N, 10°20.0′W.

CLEGGAN POINT. Lt. Fl.(3) W.R.G. 15 sec. W.6M. R.3M. G.3M. W. Col. on W. hut, 20m. W. shore-091°; R.091°-124°; G.124°-221°.
SEAL ROCK Bn. W., on the Carrickarone Rks. in Clifden Bay.
FISHING POINT. Bn. W., in Clifden Bay.

OFFSHORE WAYPOINT SLYNE HEAD.
53°24.0′N, 10°15.2′W.

SLYNE HEAD 53°24.0′N, 10°14.0′W. Lt. Fl.(2) 15 sec. 24M. B. Tr. 35m. R.C.

INISHNEE. Lt. Fl.(2) W.R.G. 10 sec. W.5M. R.3M. W. Col. on W. square concrete base, 9m. G.314°-017°; W.017°-030°; R.030°-080°; W.080°-194°.
CROAGHNAKEELA ISLAND. Lt. Fl. 3.7 sec. 5M. W. concrete Col. 7m. vis. 034°-045°; 218°-286°; 311°-325°.

OFFSHORE WAYPOINT W OF SKERD RKS.
53°14.8′N, 10°12.0′W.

GALWAY BAY
GENERAL — Cashla Bay — good small craft anch. Greatmans Bay — dries. Golam Hr. — sheltered. N Sound is main ent. — deep. Stormy weather — enter N and S Sound. Good small craft anch. — New Hr. — SE of N Bay — soft bottom. Gales W and SW — disturbed seas. Galway Bay — good shelter in prevailing SW and W'ly winds near Black Head. Anchor close to N coast when wind veers to NW.

Bn. 53°16.03′N 9°02.6′W. Topmark Conical G.
Bn. 53°15.23′N 9°01.11′W.
Bn. 53°14.28′N 9°01.78′W. Topmark N.
Bn. 53°15.10′N 9°04.94′W. Topmark S.

ROCK ISLAND, EERAGH, E SIDE
53°08.9′N, 9°51.4′W. Lt. Fl. 15 sec. 23M. W. Tr. 2 B. bands, 35m. vis. 297°-262°; distress sig.
Lt.By. Fl.(2) 7.5 sec. Can.R.
KIGGAUL BAY. Lt. Fl.W.R. 3 sec. W.5M. R.3M. metal Col. on stone Bn. 5m. W.329°-359°; R.359°-059° except where obscured by the W shore of the Bay.
CASHLA BAY. Lt. Fl.(3) W.R. 10 sec. W.6M. R.3M. W. metal Col. on concrete structure, 8m. W.216°-000°; R.000°-069°.
LION POINT. Dir. W.R.G. 4 sec. W.8½M. G.6M. R.6M. W. Col. 6.4m. G.357.5°-008.5°; W.008.5°-011.5°; R.011.5°-017.5°.
CANNON ROCK. Lt.By. Fl.G. 5 sec. Conical G.

INISHMORE, STRAW ISLAND
53°07.0′N, 9°37.9′W. Lt. Fl.(2) 5 sec. 17M. W. Tr. 9m. vis. except where obscured by land.
KILLEANEY BAR Lt.By. Fl.G. 3 sec. Conical G.
KILRONAN PIER HEAD. Lt. Fl.W.G. 1.5 sec. 3M. W. Col. 5m. G.240°-326°; W.326°-000°.
Ldg.Lts. 192°. Killeany Bay (Front) Oc. 5 sec. 3M. W. Col. on W. square base, 6m. vis. 142°-197°. (Rear) Oc. 5 sec. 2M. W. Col. on W. square base, 8m. vis. 142°-197°.

MARINE FARMS are established in this area. Consult chart for details.

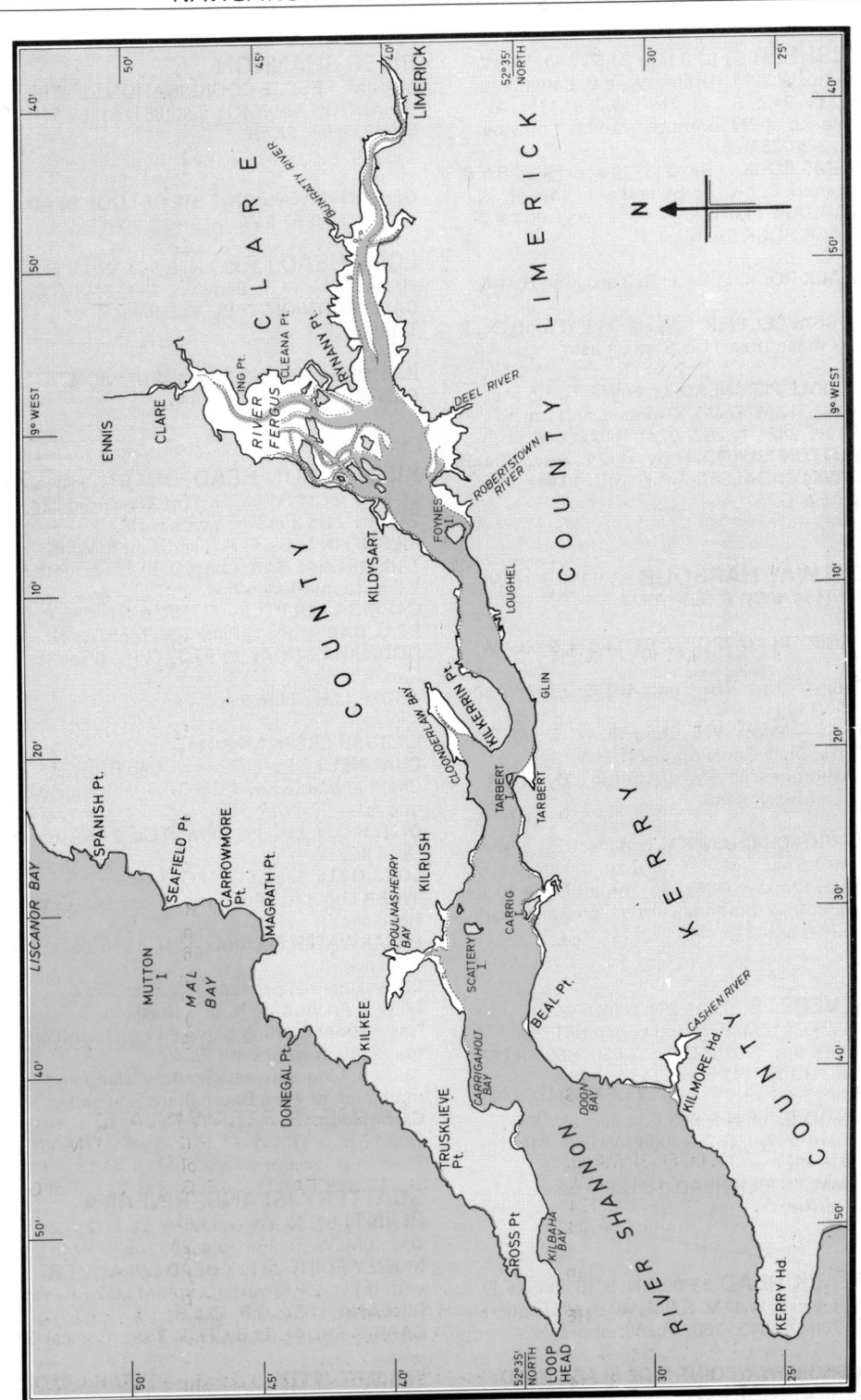

INISHEER 53°02.8'N, 9°31.5'W. Lt. Iso.W.R. 20 sec. W.20M. R.16M. W. Tr. B. band, 34m. W.231°-245°; R.245°-269°; W.269°-115°. At a distance of 7M. or more from Lt. it may be vis. 225°-231°.
FINNIS ROCK Lt.By. Q.(3) 10 sec. Pillar. B.Y.B. Topmark E. ᨪᨪ on SE end of Inisheer I.
MARGARETTA. Lt.By. Fl.G. 3 sec. Conical G.
BLACK ROCK Bn. Mast. R.

BLACK ROCK. Lt.By. Fl.R. 3 sec. Can.R. ᨪᨪ .

ROSSAVEEL PIER. Ldg.Lts. 116° (Front) Oc. 3 sec. mast. (Rear) Oc. 3 sec. mast.

SPIDDLE PIER HEAD. Lt. Fl.W.R.G. 7.5 sec. W.6M. R.4M. G.4M. Y. metal Col. 11m. G.102°-282°; W.282°-024°; R.024°-066°.
MUTTON ISLAND. Lt.By. Fl.(2)R. 6 sec. Can.R.
TAWIN SHOALS. Lt.By. Fl.(3)G. 10 sec. Conical G.

GALWAY HARBOUR 53°09'N, 9°16'W.
Tel: H.M. (091) 62329/61874.

HARBOUR WAYPOINT. 53°14.8'N, 9°03.4'W.

Radio — Port: VHF Chan. 16, 12. 2 h.-HW and 0900-1700.
Radio — Pilots: VHF Chan 16, 14, 11. 2 h.-HW.
Entry: Dock Gates open 2 h.-HW.
Anchorages: 5c. SW of Mutton I. By. & 2M. ESE of Black Head.

APPROACH CHANNEL. Ldg.Lts. 325°. (Front) Fl.R. 1.5 sec. 7M. R. ◊, Y. diagonal stripes, on mast, 12m. vis. 315°-345°. (Rear) Oc.R. 10 sec. 7M. R. ◊ , Y. diagonal stripes, on framework Tr. 20m. vis. 315°-345°.

LEVERETS. 53°15.2'N, 9°02.0'W. Lt.
Q.W.R.G. 10M. B. round concrete Tr. W. bands, 9m. G.015°-058°; W.058°-065°; R.065°-103°; G.103°-143.5°; W.143.5°-146.5°; R.146.5°-015°.
RINMORE. Lt. Iso. W.R.G. 4 sec. 5M. W. square Tr. 7m. G.359°-008°; W.008°-018°; R.018°-027°.
NIMMO'S PIER HEAD. Lt. Iso. Y. 6 sec. 6M. mast, 7m.

BLACK HEAD 53°09.2'N, 9°16.0'W. Lt. Fl.
W.R. 5 sec. W.11M. R.8M. W. square concrete Tr. 20m. W.045°-268°; R.268°-shore. H24.

INSHORE WAYPOINT N OF BLACK HEAD. 53°10.4'N, 9°16.0'W.

RIVER SHANNON
MARINE RESCUE COORDINATION CENTRE (SHANNON AIRPORT). Tel: (061) 61969 & 61219. Telex: 26262.

OFFSHORE WAYPOINT SW OF LOOP HEAD. 53°33.0'N, 9°57.6'W.

LOOP HEAD 52°33.7'N, 9°55.9'W. Lt. Fl.(4)
20 sec. 28M. W. Tr. 84m. vis. 280°-218°. R.C.
BALLYBUNNION. Lt.By. V.Q. Pillar B.Y. Topmark N.

INSHORE WAYPOINT BALLYBUNNION BANKS. 53°32.5'N, 9°47.0'W.

KILCREDAUN HEAD 53°34.8'N, 9°42.5'W.
Lt. Fl. 6 sec. 13M. W. Tr. 41m. Obscured 224°-247° by 24m. hill when within 1M.
KILSTIFFIN Lt.By. Fl.R. 3 sec. Can.R. Whis.
TAIL OF BEAL BAR. Lt.By. Q.(9) 15 sec. Pillar. Y.B.Y. Topmark N. Whis.
CARRIGA HOLT Lt.By. Fl.(2)R. 6 sec. Can.R.
BEAL BAR. Lt.By. Q.Pillar B.Y. Topmark N.
DOONAHA SHOAL. Lt.By. Fl.(3)R. 10 sec. Can.R.
ASDEE Lt.By. Fl.R. 3 sec. Can.R.

KILRUSH CREEK MARINA
CHANNEL Lt. By. Fl.R. 6 sec. Can.R. Channel marked by 4 Can R. and 4 Conical G. buoys.
OUTER Ldg. Lts. 355° (Front) Oc. 3 sec. (Rear) Oc. 3 sec.
LOCK GATE Sector Lt. Fl.G. 3 sec.
INNER Ldg. Lts. 070° (Front) Oc. 6 sec. (Rear) Oc. 6 sec.
BREAKWATER Sector Lt. Fl.G. 6 sec. covering entrance.
Entry: Channel dredged to 2.5m. below MLWS. Anchorage N. of Hog Island.
Navigation: Coming between Hog Island and mainland beware Wolf Rock. Approaching between Scattery Island and mainland, beware Baurnahard Spit and Carrigillaun.

SCATTERY ISLAND (RINEANA POINT) 52°36.3'N, 9°31.0'W. Lt. Fl.(2) 7.5
sec. 10M. W. Tr. 15m. vis. 208°-092°. H24.
MONEY POINT JETTY HEAD (W). Lt. 2 F.R. vert. (E) Lt. 2 F.R. vert. (Dolphin) Lt. 2 F.R. Vert.
RINEANA. Lt.By. Q.R. Can.R.
CARRIG SHOAL Lt.By. Fl.G. 3 sec. Conical G. ᨪᨪ .
TARBERT JETTY. Lt. 2 F.G. vert. 'T.' Hd. of Oil Jetty.

TARBERT ISLAND 52°35.5'N, 9°21.8'W.
Lt. Iso. W.R. 4 sec. W.14M. R.10M. W. round
Tr. 18m. W.069°-277°; R.277°-287°; W.287°-339°.
TARBERT. Ldg. Lts. 128°15' (Front) Iso. 2 sec.
3M. △ on W. metal frame Tr.
Vis. 123.2°-133.2°. (Rear) Iso. 5 sec. 3M.
G.W.V.S. Bn.
KILKERIN Lt.By. Fl.(2)R. 6 sec. Can.R.
GOREAN Lt.By. Fl.(2)G. 6 sec. Conical G.
BOLANDS ROCK Perch R.
BOLANDS Lt.By. Fl.R. 3 sec. Can.R.
CARRAIG FADA Lt.By. Fl.G. 5 sec. Conical G.

GARRAUNBAUN POINT Lt. Fl.(3) W.R. 10 sec.
W.8M. R.5M. W. square Col. 16m. R.shore-072°; W.072°-242°; R.242°-shore.
LOGHILL Lt.By. Fl.G. 3 sec. Conical G.
RINEALON POINT, RINALAN. Lt. Fl. 2.5 sec.
7M. B.W. metal Col. 7m. vis. 234°-088°.
BATTERY POINT. Lt.By. Q.(9) 15 sec. Pillar.
Y.B.Y. Topmark W. Foynes W Entce.
CARIGEEN ROCK By. Can.R. Foynes W Entce.
POULTALLIN. Lt.By. Fl.(3)G. 6 sec. Conical G.
Foynes E Entce.
ELBOW ROCK By. Can.R. Foynes E Entce.
LONG ROCK Lt.By. Fl.G. 5 sec. Conical G.

FOYNES OIL JTY MOORING. Lt.Bys. Q. Can.
B.

FOYNES HARBOUR

Radio — Port: VHF Chan. 16, 12, 13, as
required.
W CHANNEL. Ldg.Lts. 107°38'. Barneen Point
No: 1. (Front) Iso. W.R.G. 4 sec. B. △, W. Col.
3m. W.273.2°-038.2°; R.038.2°-094.2°;
G.094.2°-104.2°; W.104.2°-108.2°; R.108.2°-114.2°. E Jetty No: 2. (Rear) Oc. 4 sec. 10M. B.
△, W. Col. 16m.
COLLEEN POINT. No: 3 Lt. Q.G. 2M. G. Col.
2m.
WEIR POINT. No: 4 Lt. V.Q.(4)R. 10 sec. 2M. R.
Col. 2m.
TEN METRE By. Conical G.
STURAMUS Lt.By. Fl.(2)G. 6 sec. Conical G.
COHIRCON Lt.By. Fl.R. 3 sec. Can.R.
INISHMURRY. Lt.By. Q.R. Can.R.
AUGHINISH Lt.By. Q. Pillar B.Y. Topmark N.
EIGHT METRE Lt.By. Fl.G. 5 sec. Conical G.
CANON Lt.By. Fl.(2)R. 6 sec. Can.R.
CORK Lt.By. Fl.R. 5 sec. Can.R.
HERRING Lt.By. Fl.G. 3 sec. Conical G.

BEEVES ROCK 52°39.0'N, 9°01.3'W. Lt.
Fl.W.R. 5 sec. W.12M. R.9M. dark stone-coloured Tr. 12m. W.068°-091°; R.091°-238°;
W.238°-262°; W. (unintens) 262°-068°.

AUGHINISH MARINE TERM JTY. Lt. 2 F.G.
vert. (Each end).
SHANNON AIRPORT. Lt. Aero. Al. Fl.W.G. 7.5
sec. 40m.
FLATS Lt.By. Fl.G. 5 sec. Conical G.
CARRIGKEAL. Lt.By. Fl.G. 3 sec. Conical G.
DERNISH ISLAND PIER, W END. LT. 2 F.R.
vert. 2M. Col. 4m. **E END LT.** 2 F.R. vert. 2M.
Col. 5m.
E BREAKWATER HEAD Lt. Q.R. 1M. Col. 3m.
CARRIG BANK. Lt.By. Fl.(2)G. 6 sec. Conical·
G.
CONOR ROCK. Lt. Fl.R. 4 sec. 6M. W. metal
framework Tr. 6m. vis. 228°-093°.
BRIDGE Lt.By. Fl.G. 5 sec. Conical G.
FERGUS ROCK. Lt.By. Fl.R. 3 sec. Can.R.

N CHANNEL. Ldg.Lts. 093°. Tradree Rock
(Front) Fl.R. 2 sec. 5M. W. metal framework
Trs. 6m. vis. 246°-110°.
CAINS (QUAY) ISLAND (Rear) Iso. 6 sec. 5M.
W. concrete Tr. R. bands, 14m. vis. 327°-190°.
BIRD ROCK. Lt. Q.G. 5M. W. metal framework
Tr. 6m.
BUNRATTY Lt.By. Fl.G. 3 sec. Conical G.
GRASS ISLAND. Lt. Fl.G. 2 sec. 4M. W. metal
Col. B. bands, 6m.
LAHEENS ROCK. Lt. Q.R. 5M. W. metal pile
structure, 4m.
BATTLE. Lt.By. Fl.R. 4 sec. Can.R.
SLATE. Lt.By. Fl.(2)R. 6 sec. Can.R.
SPILLING ROCK. Lt. Fl.G. 5 sec. 5M. W. Pole.
5m.
GRAIG. Lt.By. Fl.R. 2 sec. Can.R.

N SIDE. Ldg.Lts. 061°. **CRAWFORD ROCK**
(Front) Fl.R. 3 sec. 5M. W. metal pile structure,
6m. **CRAWFORD NO: 2** (Rear) Iso. 6 sec. 5M.
W. wooden pile structure, 10m. Common
rear.
Ldg.Lts. 302°07'. Flagstaff Rock (Front) Fl.R. 2
sec. 5M. wooden pile structure, 7m.
SCARLETS. Lt.By. Fl.(2)G. 6 sec. Conical G.
THE WHELPS. Lt. Fl.G. 3 sec. 5M. W. metal
pile structure, 5m.
NEWTOWN. Lt.By. Fl.G. 5 sec. Conical G.
ARBANE. Lt.By. Fl.(2) R. 6 sec. Can.R.

Ldg.Lts. 106°28'. **MEELICK ROCK** (Front) Iso. 4
sec. 3M. W. metal pile structure, 6m.
MEELICK NO: 2 (Rear) Iso. 6 sec. 5M. W.
wooden pile structure, 9m.
HORRILS. Lt.By. Fl.R. 4 sec. Can.R.
MUCKINISH. Lt.By. Fl.(2)G. 6 sec. Conical G.
COOPER. Lt.By. Fl.G. 5 sec. Conical G.
COONAGH. Lt.By. Fl.R. 2 sec. Can.R.

Ldg.Lts. 146°. **BRAEMAR POINT** (Front) Iso. 4
sec. 5M. W. wooden pile structure, 5m.
BRAEMAR NO: 2 (Rear) Iso. 6 sec. 4M. W.
wooden pile structure, 6m.

TERVOE. Lt.By. Fl.R. 4 sec. Can.R.
COURTBRACK. Lt.By. Fl.(2) 6 sec. Can.R.
CLONMACKEN POINT. Lt. Fl.R. 3 sec. 4M. W.
wooden pile structure, 7m.
BALLINACURRA. Lt.By. Fl.G. 3 sec. Conical G.
SPILLANE'S TOWER. Lt. Fl. 3 sec. 6M. turret
on Tr. 11m.
BARRINGTONS. Lt.By. Fl.R. 4 sec. Can.R.

LIMERICK 52°35'N 9°43'W. Tel: H.M. (061)
315109. Telex: 70248. Pilots: (065) 51027.
Radio — Port: Limerick Harbour Radio. VHF
Chan. 16, 12, 13 — 0900-1700, also when vessels
expected.
Tarbet Oil Jetty. VHF Chan. 16, 12 — for
vessels berthing.
Radio — Pilots: Scattery Roads. VHF Chan.
16, 12, 6 — when vessels expected.
Anchorages: Limerick. Scattery Roads inside
Scattery Is. where pilot boards. Large ships
take pilot off Kilcredane and should discuss
anchorage if nec. by VHF with P.S.
Other safe anchorages on Shannon Estuary:
Tarbet. S of Stone Pier.
Red Gap. Labasheeda Bay.
Mount Trenchard. W of Foynes.
Beagh Castle. Off Fergus River Ent.
Glencloosagh Bay. W of Ardamore Pt.
Clondolaw. 1 M. N of Tarbet Is.

LIMERICK DOCK. Ldg.Lts. 098°30'. (Front) F. R.
◊ on Col. 8m. occas. (Rear) F. R. ◊ on Col. 7m.
occas.
N WHARF HEAD. Lt. 2. F.R. vert. on Col. 10m.
occas.
BRIDGE: Vertical clearance 3.3m.

INSHORE WAYPOINT OFF KERRY HD.
53°25.2'N, 9°57.4'W.

TRALEE BAY

FENIT 52°16'N 9°51'W. Tel: Tralee 36103.
Radio — Port & Pilots: VHF Chan. 16, 14 as
required.
Anchorage: 1M. W of Lt.Ho.

LITTLE SAMPHIRE ISLAND 52°16.2'N,
9°52.9'W. Lt. Fl.W.R.G. 5 sec. W.16M. R.13M.
G.13M. Bl. round stone Tr. 17m. R.262°-275°;
R.280°-090°; G.090°-140°; W.140°-152°; R.152°-
172°. Obscured elsewhere.

GREAT SAMPHIRE ISLAND 52°16.1'N
9°52.2'W Lt. Q.R. 3M. 15m Vis. 242°-097°.
FENIT PIER HEAD. Lt. 2 F.R. vert. 4M. on mast,
12m. Obscured 058°-148°.

BRANDON PIER HEAD. Lt. 2 F.G. vert. 4M. on
Col. 5m.

**OFFSHORE WAYPOINT W OF
INISHTEARAGHT.** 52°05.0'N, 10°44.0'W.

INISHTEARAGHT 52°04.5'N, 10°39.7'W.
Lt. Fl.(2) 20 sec. 27M. W. Tr. 84m. vis. 318°-
221°. Also shown by day in fog.

BLASKET SOUND Lt.By. Fl.(5)Y. 20 sec. Sph.Y.

INSHORE WAYPOINT SE OF GT. FROZE RK.
52°01.0'N, 10°38.4'W.

INSHORE WAYPOINT HEAD OF DINGLE BAY.
52°06.1'N, 10°02.0'W.

MARINE FARMS are established in this area.
Consult chart for details.

DINGLE HARBOUR
NE SIDE OF ENTRANCE. Lt. F.R. 6M. metal Tr.
20m.
PIER HEAD. Lt. 2 F.R. vert. 2M. on post, 4m.
Ldg.Lts. 182° (Front) Oc. 3 sec. (Rear) Oc. 3
sec.

INSHORE WAYPOINT NW OF BRAY HD.
51°54.4'N, 10°28.6'W.

VALENTIA 51°56'N 10°19'W. Tel: Valentia
24.

INSHORE WAYPOINT W OF BRAY HD.
51°53.0'N, 10°27.0'W.

FORT (CROMWELL) POINT 51°56.0'N,
10°19.3'W. Lt. Fl.W.R. 2 sec. W.17M. R.15M. W.
Tr. 16m. R.102°-304°; W.304°-351°. Obscured
from seaward by Doulus head when bearing
more than 180°.

Dir.Ldg.Lts. 141° (Front) Oc. W.R.G. 4 sec.
W.11M. R.8M. G.8M. W. Conical Tr. G.134°-
140°; W.140°-142°; R.142°-148°. (Rear) Oc. 4
sec. 5M. 43m. 133°-233°.
BEGINISH BAR CHANNEL Ldg.Lts. 019°
(Front). F.G. (Rear) F.G.
Ldg.Lts. 199° (Front) F.G. (Rear) F.G.

VALENTIA RIVER
Ldg.Lts. 101° (Rear) F.G. 430m. from front.
(Common Front) F.G.
Ldg.Lts. 233° (Rear) F.G. 300m. from front.
Ldg.Lts. 076° (Front) F.G. (Rear) F.G.

BALLYCARBERY SPIT Lt. Fl.R. 3 sec.
Ldg.Lts. 053° (Front) F.G. (Rear) F.G.
DANIELS ROCK Ldg. Lts. 034° (Front) F.R.
(Rear) F.R.
Ldg.Lts. 214° (Front) F.G. (Rear) F.G.
THE FOOT. Lt.By. Q.(3) 10 sec. Pillar. B.Y.B.
Topmark E.
HARBOUR ROCK Bn. Mast B.Y.B. Topmark E.
PORT MAGEE, W Bn. Mast. R.
PORT MAGEE, E Bn. Mast. R.

OFFSHORE WAYPOINT SW OF GT. SKELLIG.
51°45.0′N, 10°35.0′W.

SKELLIGS ROCK 51°46.2′N, 10°32.5′W. Lt.
Fl.(3) 10 sec. 27M. W. Tr. 53m. vis. 262°-115°.
Partially obscured by land within 6M. 110°-
115°.
DARRYNANE HARBOUR. Ldg.Lts. 034° (Front)
Oc. 3 sec. 4M. Bn. 10m. (Rear) Oc. 3 sec. 4M.
Bn. 16m.

KENMARE RIVER

INSHORE WAYPOINT ENTRANCE KENMARE
RIVER. 51°42.4′N, 10°04.8′W.

BUNAW. Ldg.Lts. 041°. (Front) Iso. Y. 8 sec.
9m. B. pole, Y. bands. (Rear) Iso. Y. 8 sec.
11m. B. pole Y. bands.
MAIDEN'S ROCK By. Conical G. off Rossmore
I.
BALLYCROVANE HBR. Lt. Fl.R. 3 sec.

OFFSHORE WAYPOINT W OF THE BULL.
51°35.0′N, 10°20.0′W.

BULL ROCK 51°35.5′N, 10°18.1′W. Lt. Fl. 15
sec. 23M. W. Tr. 83m. vis. 220°-186°. Shown
by day in fog.

BANTRY BAY

OFFSHORE WAYPOINT SSE OF DURSEY HD.
51°33.0′N, 10°13.0′W.

SHEEP'S HEAD. 51°32.5′N, 9°50.8′W. Lt.
Fl.(3) W.R. 15 sec. W.18M. R.15M. W. building,
83m. R.007°-017°; W.017°-212°.

BEARHAVEN W ENTRANCE

ARDNAKINNA POINT 51°37.1′N,
9°55.0′W. Lt. Fl.(2)W.R. 10 sec. W.17M, R.15M.

W. round Tr. 62m. R.319°-348°; W.348°-066°;
R.066°-shore.
F.R. Lt. on radio mast 3.45M. 295°.

COLT ROCK. Bn. Mast. R.

INSHORE WAYPOINT APPROACH TO
CASTLETOWN. 51°36.0′N, 9°56.0′W.

CASTLETOWN. 51°38.8′N, 9°54.3′W.
Dir.Lt. 024° Dir.Oc.W.R.G. 5 sec. W.14M.
R.11M. G.11M. W. concrete hut, R. stripe, 4m.
G.020.5°-024°; W.024°-024.5°; R.024.5°-027.5°.
PERCH ROCK. Lt.Bn. Q.G. 1M. W. concrete
col. B. bands, 4m.
CAMETRINGANE SPIT Lt. Q.R. Mast. R.
Ldg.Lts. 010°. (Front) Oc. 3 sec. 1M. W. ⌷, R.
stripe, R.W. cheq. sides, 4m. vis. 005°-015°.
(Rear) Oc. 3 sec. 1M. W. ⌷ R. stripe, 7m. vis.
005°-015°.
WALTER SCOTT. Lt.By. Q.(6)+L.Fl. 15 sec.
Pillar. Y.B. Topmark S.
HORNET ROCK. Lt.By. V.Q.(6)+L.Fl. 10 sec.
Pillar. YB. Topmark S.
GEORGE ROCK. Lt.By. Fl.(2) 10 sec. Pillar.
B.R.B. Topmark Is. D.
CARRICKAVADRA Bn. Mast. Y.B. Topmark S.
off E Pt.
BARDINI REEFER WK. Lt.By. Q. Pillar B.Y.
Topmark N.

MARINE FARMS are established in this area.
Consult chart for details.

ROANCARRIGMORE 51°39.1′N,
9°44.8′W. Lt. Fl.W.R. 3 sec. W.17M. R.14M. W.
round Tr. B. band, 17m. W.312°-050°; R.050°-
312°. Reserve Lt. Range 11M. and obscured
140°-220° in R. sector.

WHIDDY ISLAND CHANNEL

WHIDDY ISLAND
W. Clearing Lt. Oc. 2 sec. 3M. 3 ⌷ on W. mast,
22m. vis. 073°-106°.
SW DOLPHIN. Lt. Q.Y. 2M. metal mast on
dolphin, 10m. Horn 20 sec.
NE DOLPHIN. Lt. Q.Y. 2M. metal mast on
dolphin, 10m.

N BANTRY HARBOUR APPROACHES

BANTRY HARBOUR 51°40.8′N, 9°27.4′W. Tel:
H.M. Bantry 591.

HORSE. Lt.By. Fl.G. 6 sec. Conical G.
GURTEENROE. Lt.By. Fl.R. 3 sec. Can.R.
CHAPEL. Lt.By. Fl.G. 2 sec. Conical G.

OFFSHORE WAYPOINT S OF MIZEN HEAD.
51°26.0′N, 9°50.0′W.

MIZEN HEAD 51°26.9′N, 9°49.2′W. Lt. Iso.
4 sec. 16M. concrete platform and lantern,
52m. vis. 313°-133°. Racon.

CROOKHAVEN
BLACK HORSE Bn. Mast. B.Y. Topmark N.

INSHORE WAYPOINT CROOKHAVEN.
51°28.0′N, 9°40.0′W.

ROCK ISLAND POINT 51°28.6′N,
9°42.2′W. Lt. Fl.W.R. 8 sec. W.13M. R.11M. W.
Tr. 20m. Outside Hr. W. over Long I. Bay-281°;
R.281°-340°. Inside Hr. R.281°-348°; W.348°
towards N shore.

Visual Navigational Aids and Port Information

23

For France to Gibraltar and the Azores

NOTE: IN THIS SECTION WE DO NOT GIVE BUOYAGE EXCEPT FOR LARGE LANBY TYPE BUOYS.

Many continental ports have special entry and exit control signals which it is very necessary to observe, more particularly at ports like Boulogne, Calais and Oostende, where fast passenger carrying cross channel vessels enter at all times.

Storm signals Belgium and Netherlands as for France.

In most cases yachts are exempt from pilotage.

Sailing vessels must give way (also rowing boats) to other traffic and not tack across the fairway when other traffic is entering or leaving — applies especially in Calais, Oostende, Zeebrugge and Nieuwpoort. While in some ports it may not be compulsory for yachts to obey the entry and traffic signals shown, it is generally advisable to do so for your own safety unless directed by the Harbour Authority to ignore them.

Notes on passage planning and key documents required are kept at the Cruising Assoc (London) and are available for consultation.

FRENCH PORTS

Rules governing the passage of all vessels in French waters are now in force, especially in the following areas; Ushant, Cherbourg, St. Malo; Baie de Saint Brieuc, Dunkerque. Pleasure craft are generally exempt from the regulations which apply particularly to tankers. Pilotage and use of approach channels compulsory. Contact with Control Stations and listening on Chan. 16 compulsory.

GENERAL TRAFFIC, TIDAL AND DISTRESS PORT SIGNALS

Casualty: A Black Flag denotes a shipping casualty in the vicinity.

Storm Signals: Signals displayed for 24 hours.

Day/Night and Meaning

Cone point up } NW gale.
2 R.Lts. (vert.)

2 Cones point up (vert.) } NE gale.
R. over W.Lt.

Cone point down } SW gale.
2.W.Lts (vert.)

2 Cones point down (vert.) } SE gale.
W. over R.Lt.

Ball } Bad weather.
Red Lt.

2 Balls (vert.) } Storm or Strong gale.
2 R. Lts. (horiz.)

Black flag or cylinder   Wind veering.

2 Black flags or cylinders   Wind backing.

Black Cross } Force 12 probable.
R/G/R Lts. (vert)

Traffic Signals
Full Code

Shape	Light	
○ Ball	○ Red	} Entrance prohibited (emergency)
○ Ball	○ Red	
○ Ball	○ Red	
○ Ball	○ Red	} Entrance prohibited (normal)
△ Cone	○ White	
○ Ball	○ Red	
▽ Cone	○ Green	} Entrance and departure prohibited
△ Cone	○ White	
○ Ball	○ Red	
▽ Cone	○ Green	} Departure prohibited
△ Cone	○ White	
▽ Cone	○ Green	
Flag P		Lock Gates open.

Simplified Code in French Ports

Red flag or Red Lt.	Entrance prohibited.
Green flag or Green Lt.	Departure prohibited.
Red over Green Flag or Red over Green Lt.	Entrance and departure prohibited.

Tidal Signals: Depth above chart datum is indicated by units of 0.2m or 8in. The shapes or lights should be totalled up to give the depth.

Cone point down	Green Lt.	One unit (0.2m or 8in.).
Cylinder	Red Lt.	5 units (1m. or 3½ft.).
Ball	White Lt.	25 units (5m. or 16½ft.).

Shapes are displayed Cone — Cylinder — Ball from seaward and vertically if more than one shape:

Cone } Cylinder } Ball = 3 units 10 units 25 units
Cone } Cylinder }
Cone } = 38 units = 7.6m. or 25ft.

Blue pendant
    2 G.Lts. (horiz.)   Low water.
Elongated Cone (point up)
    G. over W.Lt.   Tide rising.
White flag Black St. Andrew's cross
    2 W. Lts. (horiz.)   High water.
Elongated Cone (point down)
    W. over G.Lt.   Tide falling.

Distress and Danger Signals from Lighthouses:

Ball over Cone (point down)
Ball over pendant =
Wreck drifting or aground in channel near lighthouse.

Cone (point down) over 2 balls
Pendant over 2 balls =
Drifting mine near lighthouse.

Cone (point up) over ball
Flag above ball =
Require immediate assistance, Personnel or Staff.

Ball over cone (point up)
Ball over flag =
Require immediate assistance, Material

Cone (point down) over Ball
Pendant over ball =
Require re-victualling.

Black flag =
Shipwreck in vicinity.

COAST GUARDS FRANCE: Authority: French Navy.
SAR CROSSMA (CAP GRIS NEZ & JOBURG) covers English Channel and Southern Nth Sea. VHF Chan. 11, 13, 16, also MF 2182 kHz.
SAR CROSSMA (d'ETEL & SOULAC) covers Atlantic Coast of France. VHF Chan. 13, 16, also MF 2182 kHz.
SAR CROSSO (CORSEN) covers NW Coast of France from Mont St Michel to Ile de Sein. VHF Chan. 11, 13, 16, also MF 2182, 2677 kHz. The above stations not only deal with search and rescue but also give information on weather and other matters affecting safety of navigation.

Life boats are maintained at all the major ports.

Call on 2182 kHz, or VHF Chan. 16 for assistance.

All foreign vessels 25m or over to listen VHF Chan. 16 when in French waters.

Unnecessary to fly Flag 'Q' unless you have goods to declare.

Passports for all.
Insurance Certificate.
Registration Certificate.

Certificate of Competence.

VISAS. No longer required for most foreigners, Yachtsmen who think they might still be affected, e.g. South Africans, should consult a French Consulate.

WARNING. It is reported that holidaymakers on French Coasts will be charged £60 if rescued and £600 if a helicopter is used.

French Tourist Office, 178 Piccadilly, London W1V 0AL. Tel: 071-491 7622.

ENTRY:

Provided no goods are carried which should be declared for customs purposes, yachts arriving on their own bottoms may enter the country without reporting to the authorities on arrival or departure.
If duty free supplies are required then the ships papers and Master's passport will be needed. Also it is advisable that all the crew should carry passports.
Yachts carrying fare paying passengers (possibly crew who are paying towards expenses) will be treated as commercial craft. Then five lists and two copies of the following will be required:
A complete crew list. A general declaration. A cargo manifest. Ships stores list (triplicate). A list of small parcels on board. These forms are available from H.M. Customs.
The yacht should enter France at a commercial port and will have to pay harbour dues on the commercial tariff.

Entry by Road:

Ensure craft and car fully insured — incl craft when in the water! Register on Small Ships Register. Carnet for any outboard engine (especially if craft not present) also for any boat over 12m. either with accommodation or requiring a 4 wheel trailer.
Max. dimensions: Width 2.5m., length (trailer) 11m., length (car) 11m. overall.
Temporary import licence from Customs (up to 6 months).
Inland Waterways — in busy commercial ports unless special small locks available for yachts, may be best to arrive/depart, to lock into system at weekend. Size is restricted particularly air draught.

Inland Waterways:

Main rivers and Canals — L38.5m × D1.8m. × B5m. × H3.5m.
Canal du Midi — L30m. × D1.6m. × B5.5m. × H3m.
Brittany Route — L25.8m × D1.2m. × B4.5m. × H2.5m. Summer depths may be 0.9m. or less! Seine (to Paris) — D3m. × H6m.

Canal du Nivernais — D1m. × H2.7m.
Canal de Bourgogne (Tunnel Pouilly en
Auxois) H3.1m.

Note: Times shown for lock available/lock
operating indicate when the lock will be
manned. Most ports lock individual or groups
of craft through, thus maintaining the water

level in the dock or basin at near constant
height. Some ports, however, lower the level
to an appropriate height, then leave the lock
gates open for vessels to pass through.
Traffic signals indicate whether the gates are
open. It will be obvious on approach whether
you have to wait in the lock to be locked
IN/OUT, or whether you can pass straight
through.

FRANCE — NORTH COAST

SANDETTIE. 51°09.4'N 1°47.2'E. Lt.F. Fl. 5
sec. 24M. R.hull, 12m. Horn 30 sec. Racon.
MPC Lt.By. Fl.Y. 2½ sec. 7M. Y 'X' on Y. HFPB
10m.
F3 Lanby 51°23.8'N, 2°00.6'E. Fl. 10 sec. 22M.
12m. Racon. Horn 10 sec.

OFFSHORE WAYPOINT DUNKERQUE LANBY.
51°03.0'N, 1°51.0'E.

DUNKERQUE Lanby. 51°03.1'N 1°51.8'E.
Fl. 3 sec. 20M. 10m. Racon. Fl. 2 sec. Riding
Lt. Q. in emergency.

INSHORE WAYPOINT OFF DUNKERQUE.
51°04.0'N, 2°21.0'E.

DUNKERQUE 51°02'N, 2°22'E.
Tel: (28) 65 99 22. Port Control (28) 29 70 70.
Fax: (28) 29 71 06. Central Hr. Office
(Dunkerque E) Tel: (28) 29 72 62.
Fax: (28) 29 72 75 Hr. Office (Dunkerque W)
Tel: (28) 29 72 79. Fax: (28) 29 72 76. Control
Tower (E) Tel: (28) 29 72 67. Fax: (28) 29 72 68.
Customs: (28) 66 87 14. Y.C. de la Mer du
Nord (28) 66 79 90. Y.C. de Dunkerque
(28) 66 11 06. Telex: Port Management 820055
PADDK F. Harbour Office: 130 972 F CAP DK.
Pilots: (28) 66 74 14. Fax: (28) 59 01 88. Telex:
820 902 F PILODUK DUNKQ. Deep Sea Pilots:
(28) 66 63 80. Telex: 130566 PILHAUT. Pilots
by helicopter. Tel: (21) 35 69 93.
A new buoyed channel has been laid for
vessels over 9m. draught. Recommended for
vessels with pilot only.
Radio — Port: VHF Chan. 16, 73, 12 —
continuous.
Radio — Pilots: VHF Chan. 16, 72. **Deep Sea**

Pilots: VHF Chan. 16, 72. H24.
Helicopter: VHF Chan. 16, 72. H24.
Signals: Full code shown from main Lt.Ho.
Additional signals:
3 F.R. vert. Lts. = Entry prohibited shown E
Harbour.
R./W./R. vert. Lts. = Entry prohibited shown E
Harbour.
G./W./G. vert. Lts. Exit prohibited shown E
Harbour.
R./W./R.+R. Lt. = Entry prohibited (except
Tankers) shown E Harbour.
R. Lt. = Entry prohibited shown W Harbour.
G. Lt. = Exit prohibited shown W Harbour.
R./G. Lt. = Entry/Exit prohibited.
Lock signals shown at Ecluse Watier, Trystram
and Charles de Gaulle Lock. Upper pair
indicate Charles de Gaulle. Middle pair
indicate Ecluse Watier. Lower pair indicates
Trystam.
F.G. and Fl.G.Lt. hor. = enter lock, moor near
Fl.Lt.
2 R. Lt. hor. = no entry.
3 Lt. △ W. 2 G.Lt. = enter, all gates open.
R./Fl.R. = Lock preparing for ship.
3 blasts = request Ecluse Watier gates open.
2 blasts = request Ecluse Trystam gates open.
5 blasts = request Bridge Mole No: 4 open.
4 blasts = request Bridge Mole No: 2 open.
2 long, 1 short blast = request Bridge Darse
No: 1 Bassin de la Marine open.
Yacht Club de Dunkerque has 120 visitors
pontoon berths in Bassin du Commerce.
Trystam lock opens daily 0800-1930. Sound
signal to Control Tower or VHF-radio call to
Capitainerie.
Entry: Port d'Echouage dredged 4.2m.; Bassin
de la Marine depth 3.5m.; Bassin de l'Arriere-
port depth 3m.; Bassin du Commerce
passage 13m. wide, depth 3m. to 3.6m.
Trystram Lock. 168m. × 25m. × 5m.
Good shelter in Roads. NE/NW winds cause
heavy seas at entrance. Best to enter 2 h.-HW-
1 h.

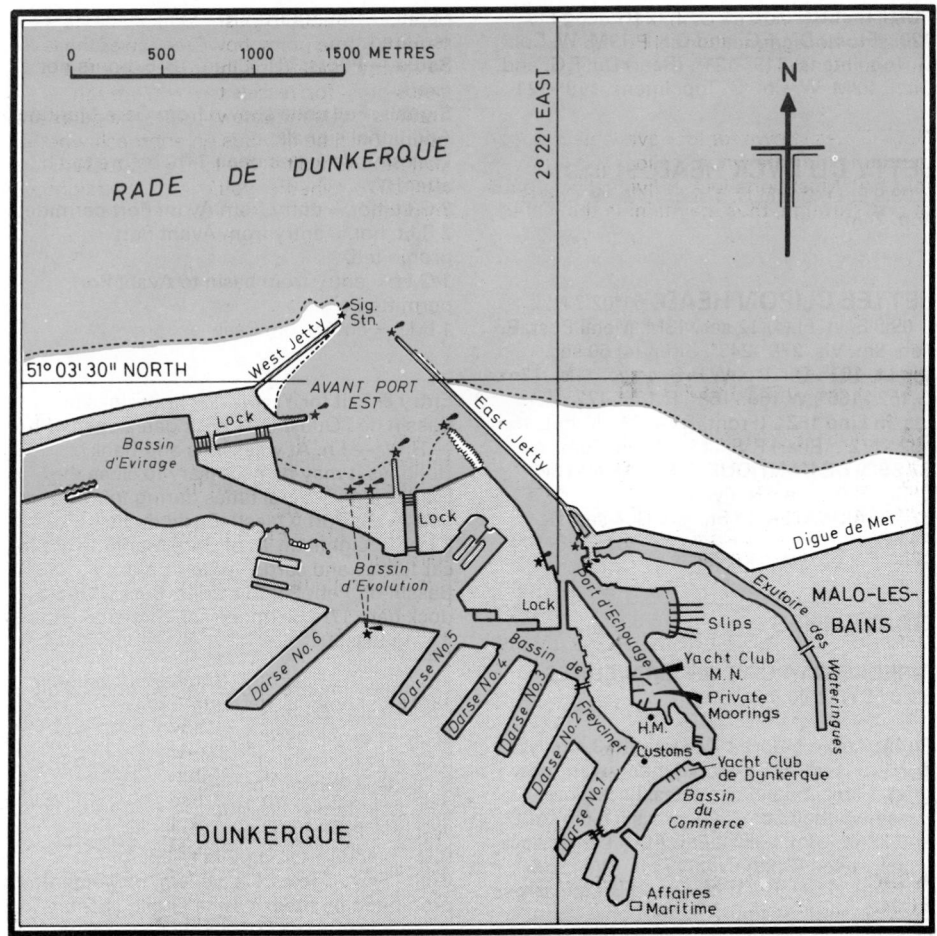

DUNKERQUE 51°03′N, 2°21.9′E. Lt.Ho.
Fl.(2) 10 sec. 29M. white Tr. B. top, 59m.
Obscured 094°-095.5°.

Ldg.Lts. 185° (Front) F.Vi. 6M. W. Metal Col. R.
Top. 5m Intens. 182.5°-187.5°.
(Common Rear) F.Vi. 8M. Metal Frame Tr.
22m. Intens. 183.5°-186.5°; 177.5°-180.5°.
Ldg.Lts. 179° (Front) F.Vi. 6M. W. Metal Col. G.
Top 5m. Intens 176.5°-181.5°.
JETEE E HEAD. Lt. Oc.(3)R. 12 sec. 9M. white
metal framework Tr. R. top, 11m. Horn(3) 30
sec.

JETEE, W HEAD. 51°03.7′N, 2°21.2′E. Lt. Oc.(1
+ 2) W.G. 12 sec. W.13M. G.9M. white Tr. R.
top, 35m. G.252°-310°; W.310°-252°. Sig.Stn.
Dia.(1 + 2) 60 sec.
Ldg.Lts. 137°. (Front) Oc.(2) 6 sec. 12M. W.
Col. R. Top 7m. (Rear) Oc.(2) 6 sec. 12M. W.
Col. R. Top 10m.

ANCIENNE JETTY WEST, Lt. Q. 13M. G. Tr.
10m. Horn 15 sec.

JETEE ECLUSE WATIER, HEAD. Lt. Fl.(3)G. 12
sec. 7M. G. Tr. 18m. (Aux. Lt. Fl.(3) 15 sec.)
Horn 10 sec.

ECLUSE CHAS. DE GAULLE. Lead-in-Jetty Lt.
Fl.G.4 sec. 7M. W.G. Tr. 10m. (Aux. Lt. Fl. 5
sec. 22M. 9m. 200°-080°.

BASSIN MARITIME. Ldg.Lts. 291°. (Front) Iso.
4 sec. B.W.Bn. (Rear) Iso. 4 sec. B.W.Bn.

BASSIN DE MARDYCK. Ldg.Lts. (Front) F.G.
(Rear) F.G.

PORT OUEST 51°02′N, 2°12′E.
Port Ouest is a Tanker Terminal and entry for
yachts is prohibited. Entrance near D.W. 13.
Lt.By.

PORT OUEST. 51°01.7'N, 2°12.0'E. Ldg.Lts. 120° (Front) Dir. F.G. and Dir. F. 19M. W. Col. G. Top. Intens. 119°-121°. (Rear) Dir. F.G. and Dir. F. 22M. W. Col. G. Top. Intens. 119°-121°.

JETTY DU DYCK HEAD. 51°02.3'N, 2°09.9'E. Lt. Bn. Fl.G. 4 sec. 10M. W. Col. G. Top. 24m.

JETTEE CLIPON HEAD. 51°02.7'N, 2°09.8'E. Lt. Fl.(4) 12 sec. 13M. Metal Post. R. Top. 8m. Vis. 278°-243°. Siren (4) 60 sec.
Dir. Lt. 167°. Dir. Iso. W.R.G. 4 sec. 11M. 12m. G.162°-166°; W.166°-168°; R.168°-172°.
Lts. in Line 162°. (Front) F.Vi. 3M. W. hut. 15m. 152°-172°. (Rear) F.Vi. 3M. W. hut. 20m.
BASSIN DE L'ANTIQUE. E BREAKWATER. Lt.Bn. Fl.R. 4 sec. R. Pylon.
W BREAKWATER. Lt.Bn. Iso. G. 4 sec. G. Pylon.

GRAVELINES

INSHORE WAYPOINT OFF GRAVELINES. 51°01.5'N, 2°05.0'E.

Entry: Arrive before HW; Draught 3.4m. HWS & 2.1m. HWN in Bassin Vauban; Avant-port dries 1.5m.; Tidal Basin dries; Locks into Bassin Vauban 28m. × 10m. × sill 0.6m. ACD and 28m. × 8m. × sill 0.6m. ACD. Larger Lock usually used; Open (Neaps) ¾ h.-HW-¾ h. & (Springs) 1½ h.-HW-1½ h.; Swing Bridge across Lock opened manually, cannot operate in strong NE or SW winds. Tide gauges indicate depths on sill. Entry to River Aa by gates 6m. × sill 1.2m. ACD.

JETEE, W. Lt. Fl.(2)W.G. 6 sec. W.9M. G.6M. W. Tr. G.Top. 14m. W.317°-327°; G.078°-085°; W.085°-244°.
JETTEE EST. Lt. Fl.(3)R. 12 sec. 4M. Tr. 8m.

WALDE. Lt. Fl.(3) 12 sec. 5M. W. hut on piles. 13m.

INSHORE WAYPOINT OFF CALAIS. 50°59.0'N, 1°45.0'E.

CALAIS 50°58'N 1°50'E. Tel: (21) 96 31 20/96 69 59. Telex: 160758 SERMAR. Pilots: (21) 96 40 18.
Radio — Port: VHF Chan. 16, 12 — continuous.
Carnot Lock: VHF Chan. 12, 16 as required.

Radio — Hoverport: VHF Chan. 20 as required.
Radio — Pilots: VHF Chan. 16, 6, hours not fixed.
Signals: Full code shown from Gare Maritime. Additional signals:
Lock signals, gates open 1½ h. before to ⅓ h. after HW.
2 G.Lt. hor. = entry from Avant Port permitted.
2 R.Lt. hor. = entry from Avant Port prohibited.
1 G.Lt. = entry from basin to Avant Port permitted.
1 R.Lt. = entry from Base

Entry & Exit for Yachts: Yacht basin is in Bassin de l'Ouest (The dock gates open 1½ h — H.W. — ½ h. At weekends and Bank Holidays it may be necessary to close the road bridge several times during this period) and Avant Port (Ouest), Basin du Petit Paradis. Lights on Tr. of Gare Maritime are for car ferries and cargo vessels only.
Bassin du Petit Paradis dries; Bassin Ouest dock gate 17m. × 2m. on sill. Signal to enter = 4 long blasts.

The following are shown *in addition* to Full Code Traffic Signals:
G.Lt. = Ferry entering.
R.Lt. = Ferry leaving.
R/G. Lts. = Tanker entering.
2 R.Lts. = Tanker leaving.
W. Lts. 3 Priority for small V/ls.
R.Lt. (below) = Dredger in Chan.
When Ferry/Tanker Lts. shown, movement prohibited by other V/ls including yachts.

CALAIS, N SIDE 50°57.7'N, 1°51.1'E. Lt. Fl.(4) 15 sec. 23M. white octagonal Tr. B. top, 59m. RC.
Obscured by cliffs of Cap Blanc-Nez when bearing less than 073°.
JETÉE, EST HEAD Lt. 50°58.4'N, 1°50.5'E. Fl.(2)R. 6 sec. 17M. Grey Tr. R. Top 12m. Reed (2) 40 sec. In fog Fl. (2) 6 sec. vert. on request.
JETÉE, W HEAD. Lt. Iso.G. 3 sec. 9M. white Tr G. top, 12m. Bell 5 sec. In fog Iso 3 sec. on request.
E SIDE. Lt. 2 F.Y. vert. 6m. Horn(4) 30 sec. within entce.
W SIDE. Dir. Lt. 294°30' Dir F.G. 14M. Grey Col. G. top. 5m. 291°-297° for use in berthing in Bassin Carnot. Occas.
GARE MARITIME. 50°58.0'N, 1°51.5'E. Lt. F.R. 14M. on Bn. 14m. Intens 115.5°-121.5°.
SANGATTE. Lt.Bn. Oc.W.G. 4 sec. W.9M. G.5M. W. Col. B. Top 13m. G.065°-089°; W. 089°-152°; G.152°-245°. Racon.

**OFFSHORE WAYPOINT CAP GRIS NEZ.
50°52.0′N, 1°32.0′E.**

CAP GRIS-NEZ 50°52.2′N, 1°35′E. Lt. Fl. 5 sec. 29M. white Tr. 72m. Obscured at cliffs of Cap Blanc-Nez and Cap d'Alprech 232°-005°. Siren 60 sec.

CAP GRIS NEZ RG STN. 50°52.12′N, 1°35.02′E. Emergency DF Stn. VHF Chan. 16, 11.

CAP GRIS NEZ SAR STN. Tel: Administration: (21) 874040. Operations: (21) 87 21 87. Fax: (21) 87 32 32. Telex: 130680 F CROSS GN & 130761 F CROSS GNI. Radio-VHF Chan. 16. H24. VHF Chan. 11. Info. bulletins ev. H + 10 for weather, traffic, obstructions etc. Forecasts on request. VHF

Chan. 13 & 121.5MHz. SAR Coordination. VHF Chan. 69, 79. CROSS Griz Nez. H 24. MF 2182kHz. Distress watch. H24.

CALAIS TO BOULOGNE

**INSHORE WAYPOINT APPROACHES
BOULOGNE. 50°45.0′N, 1°31.0′E.**

BOULOGNE 50°43′N 1°34′E. Tel: H.M. (21) 30 10 00. Control Tr. (21) 80 72 00. Telex: 110968. Pilots: (21) 31 36 08.
Radio — Port: VHF Chan. 16, 12 — continuous.
Radio — Pilots: VHF Chan. 12, 16 — continuous when on station.
Signals: Full code shown from W entrance to Darse Sarreg-Bournet for outer Hr. and from SW Jetty, Quai Gambetta, for inner Hr. Special signals alongside full code signals.

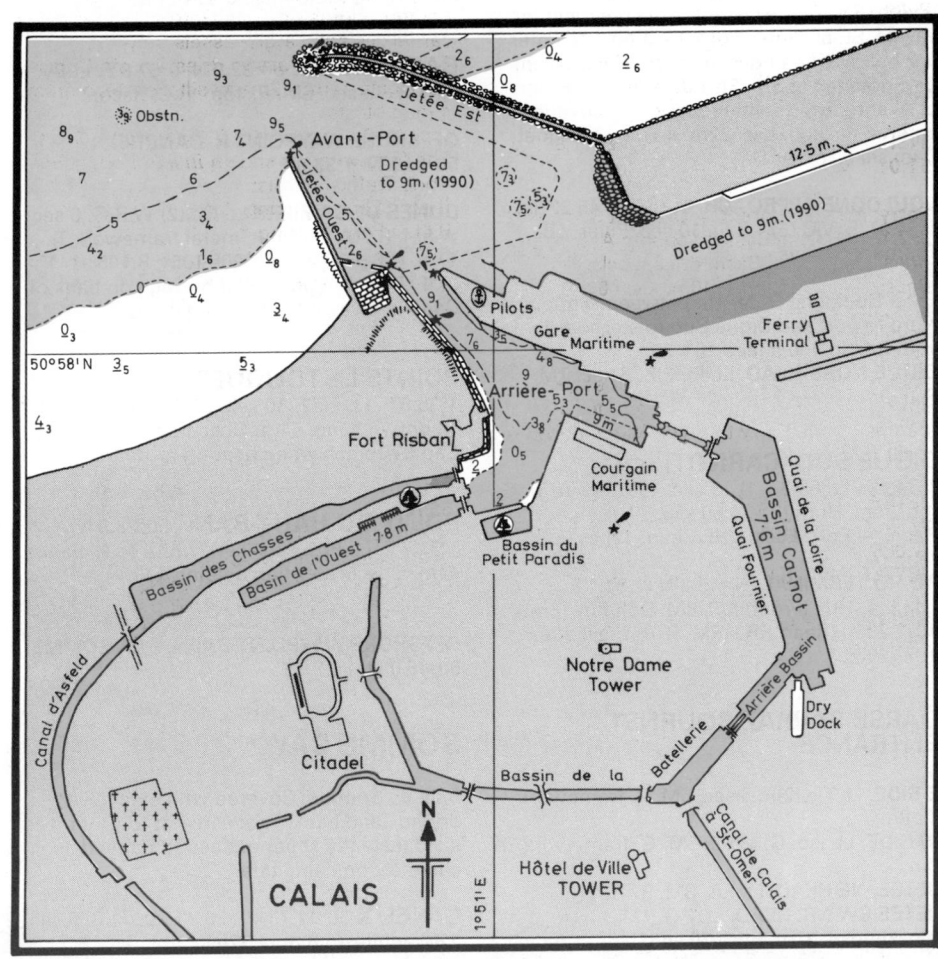

Additional G. Lt. indicates all vessels stop except one given permission to enter.
Additional R. Lt. indicates all vessels stop except one given permission to leave from outer Hr. Bassin Loubet and Port de Maree.
Additional 2 R. Lt. vert. indicates all vessels stop except one given permission to leave from Gare Maritime.
1 long, 2 short, 1 long blast = permission to enter or leave outer Hr. 2 long blasts = permission to enter or leave inner Hr.
Additional 2 R. Lt. indicates dredger working in channel. Vessels may proceed at own risk.
Bassin Loubet Lock   G. Lt. = enter.
                     R. Lt. = DO NOT enter.
Yacht Moorings: Port Marée (Quai Chauzy) Bassin Frederic-Sauvage.
Due to congestion yachts over 10m. in length must get permission to enter port.
Marguet Dam: 2 Blue Lts. = sluices open. V/ls. in Port Marée to double moorings.
Entry: Inner anchorage for vessels <60m. length. E of Digue Carnot. Area reserved for yachts. SE of Digue Nord. Best time to enter is 2 h.-HW when tides in hr. are slack. Avant-port dredged to 5m. Port de Marée in E Cnr. of Avant-port, Bassin Frederic — Sauvage entered through lock 22m. x 6m. × Marguet Dam sill 3.4m. ACD.

BOULOGNE APPROACH. Lt.By. 50°45′22″N, 1°31′07″E. V.Q.(6) + L.Fl. 10 sec. Pillar Y.B. Topmark S. whis.

Enter Boulogne Outer Hr. between Digue Nord to port and Digue Sud to starboard, with R.C. in line ahead 101°30′.
DIGUE NORD HEAD. Lt. Fl.(2)R. 6 sec. 7M. R.Tr. 9m.

DIGUE SUD (CARNOT) 50°44.5′N,
1°34.1′E. Lt. Fl.(2 + 1) 15 sec. 19M. white Tr. G. top, 26m. Horn (2 + 1) 60 sec.
Radio — Port: Lock: VHF Chan. 12, as required.
RO-RO TERMINAL. 50°43.7′N, 1°34.1′E. Ldg.Lts. 197° (Front) F.G. 8M. Dolphin 16m. 107°-287°. (Rear) F.R. 13M. R.W. mast 23m. 187°-207°.

DARSE SARRAZ-BOURNET, ENTRANCE

E SIDE. Lt. Oc.(2)R. 6 sec. 5M. R. framework Tr. 8m.
W SIDE. Lt. Iso. G. 4 sec. 5M. G. framework Tr. 8m.
JETEE, NE HEAD. Lt. F.R. 8M. R. Tr. 11m.
JETEE SW NR. HEAD. Lt. F.G. 4M. blockhouse, 17m. Horn 30 sec.

Ldg.Lts. 123°. **GARE MARITIME** (Front) F.G. 5M. white Col. R. bands, 4m.

QUAI GAMBETTA (Rear) F.R. 9M. grey metal framework Tr. R. top, on building, 44m. Intens 113°-133°.
F.R.W. vert. Lt. on each of 2 Trs. 1.2M. SE.
PETROLEUM WHARF. Lt. F.G.
PORT MAREE WHARF N. Lt. F.Vi.
S.Lt. F.Vi.

HOVERPORT N RAMP. Ldg.Lts. 119°30′. (Front) Dir. F.R. occas. ⌁⌁⌁ (Rear) Dir. F.R. occas. ⌁⌁⌁.

OFFSHORE WAYPOINT CAP D'ALPRECH.
50°43.0′N, 1°29.0′E.

CAP D'ALPRECH 50°42′N, 1°33.8′E. Lt.
Fl.(3) 15 sec. 23M. white Tr. B. top, 62m. R.C.
Lts. F.R. on radio mast 0.33M. ENE.

BASSURELLE 50°32.8′N, 0°57.8′E. Lt.By.
Fl.(4)R. 15 sec. 6M. R. 15m. R.C. Racon.

OFFSHORE WAYPOINT R. CANCHE.
50°34.5′N, 1°33.0′E.

DUNES DE CAMIERS Lt. Oc.(2) W.R.G. 6 sec. W.9M. R.7M. G.6M. R. metal framework Tr. 17m. G.015°-090°; W.090°-105°; R.105°-141°.
Lt. F.G. shown on wall of barrage on bank of Canche River, R.W. staff and cross.

POINTE LE TOUQUET 50°31.4′N,
1°35.6′E. Lt. Fl.(2) 10 sec. 25M. R. octagonal Tr. brown band, 54m. Obscured by cliffs of Cap d'Alprech when bearing more than 173°.

POINT DU HAUT-BANC 50°23.9′N,
1°33.7′E. Lt. Fl. 5 sec. 23M. white Tr. R. bands, 44m. Obscured when bearing 140°.

OFFSHORE WAYPOINT BAIE DE LA SOMME.
50°15.0′N, 1°27.0′E.

SOMME BAY

Baie de Somme: Covered with extensive drying sand bank. Take care not to ground as sand instantly shifting. Keep to buoyed channels on rising tide.

CAYEUX 50°11.7′N, 1°30.7′E. Lt. Fl.R. 5 sec. 22M. white Tr. R. top, 32m.

LE HOURDEL. Lt. Oc.(3) W.G. 12 sec. W.11M. G.9M. white Tr. G. top, 19m. W.053°-248°; G.248°-323°. Tidal Sig. Reed(3) 30 sec. **Entry:** Accessible draught 3m. HWS & 2.4m. HWN; Hr. dries. 5m.

PORT DU CROTOY
Entry: Accessible draught about 3m. HWS & 2m. HWN. Large marina close E of hr.
LE CROTOY. Lt. Oc.(2)R. 6 sec. 11M. white metal framework Tr. 19m. vis. 285°-135°.
YACHT HBR. W side JTY HD. Lt. Fl.R. 2 sec. 2M. R. Post 4m.
E SIDE. Lt. Fl.G. 2 sec. 2M. G. Post 4m.

INSHORE WAYPOINT APPROACHES ST. VALERY SUR SOMME. 50°13.0'N, 1°30.0'E.

ST. VALERY-SUR-SOMME
Entry: Accessible 50m. × 3.6m. draught at HW. Approach channel dries 5.8m.; Water starts to rise from 2 h.-HW; Marina on E side of hr. depths 2m. on pontoons. For Marina see Section 25.
Lt. Fl.R. 4 sec. 7M. white hut, G. top, on piles, 12m.
EMBANKMENT HEAD Lt.Bn. Fl.(3)G. 6 sec. 3M. B.W. Cheq. Bn. ᗺᖡ.
MOLE HEAD. Lt. Fl.R. 4 sec. 8M. white Tr. R. top, 9m.

AULT 50°06.3'N, 1°27.2'E. Lt. Oc.(3) W.R. 12 sec. W.18M. R.14M. white Tr. R. top, 95m. W.040°-175°; R.175°-220°.·

DIEPPE TO RIVER SOMME

OFFSHORE WAYPOINT NW OF LE TREPORT. 50°04.5'N, 1°21.0'E.

LE TREPORT Tel: Port & Pilots (35) 86 18 43.
HARBOUR WAYPOINT. 50°04.0'N, 1°22.0'E.
Radio — Port/Pilots: VHF Chan. 16, 12. 2 h.-HW.
Entry: Entrance channel dries 1.5m.; Avant-port dries; berths for yachts on Quai Bellot dry 3.5m.; Arriere-port entered through passage 16m. × sill 1.5m. ACD.: Swing Bridge (3 blasts to open): Bassin a Flot dock gate 14m. × sill 1.5m. ACD, depths 5m. in basin. Best time to enter port 2 h.-HW.
Anchorage: ½M-1M. from breakwater.

JETEE OUEST. 50°03.9'N, 1°22.2'E. Lt. Fl.(2)G. 10 sec. 24M. Tr. G. 15m. Reed Mo.(N) 30 sec. Sounded 2 h. before to 1 h. 45min. after H.W.
JETEE EST. Lt. Oc.R. 4 sec. 7M. Col. R. W. 8m. Port sig.
PENLY JETEE OUEST HEAD. Lt. Fl.(4)Y. 15 sec. 2M. Horn (2) 60 sec.

OFFSHORE WAYPOINT NNW OF DIEPPE. 49°57.0'N, 1°04.0'E.

DIEPPE 49°56'N 1°05'E. Tel: H.M. (35) 84 10 55. Telex: 180990 Cap Dieppe. Pilots: (35) 84 24 01.
Radio — Port: VHF Chan. 12, 16. H24.

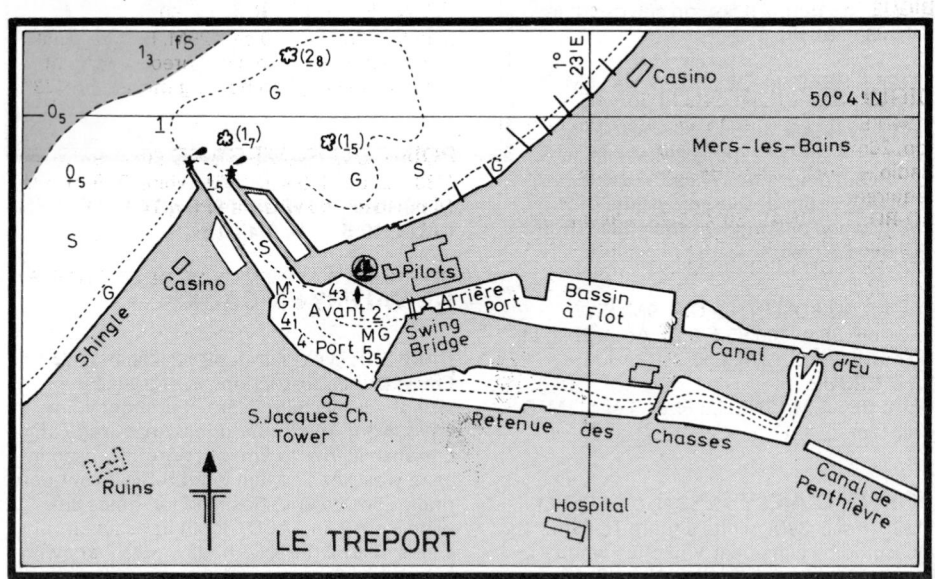

LE TREPORT

Radio — Pilot: VHF Chan. 16, 12, 2½ h. before to 1 h. after H.W. Also M.F. 2182 kHz.
Vessels less than 65m. in length and equipped with VHF do not need a pilot but they must inform the Port Captain of their E.T.A. at D1 By. at least 24 h. in advance of their arrival.
Following arrival in the roadstead ships which are exempt from pilotage must contact the Port Captain on Chan. 12 and listen out to receive instructions until arrival on the berth.
Signals: Request permission by VHF Chan. 12.
Simplified code shown from Bassin Duquesne, Arriere Port and Bassin du Canada. Full code shown from Jetee Ouest; W Side of Hbr.
R. Lt. = cross channel ferry leaving. G. Lt = cross channel ferry arriving (shown above normal signals).
W. Lt. = dock gates open. Shown above normal traffic signals.
2 R. Lt. = obstruction or dredger in channel. Shown above normal traffic signals.
Entry: Best to enter 2 h.-HW-1 h. due to strength of tidal stream across entrance. If necessary to enter outside this period keep close to jetty heads to allow for tidal set. If weather too bad for pilot to come out do not attempt to enter Hr.
Entrance channel dredged to 3.5m. to 4m.; Avant-port depths 3m. to 5m.; Y. berths in SW part near Jehan Ango Lock; Bassin Duquesne entered through Jehan Ango Lock 15m. × 3.5m. on sill, depth in basin 3m. to 5m.

JETEE E HEAD. Lt. Oc.(4)R. 12 sec. 8M. R. Tr. 19m.
JETEE W HEAD. 49°56.2′N, 1°05.0′E. Lt. Iso.W.G. 4 sec. W.12M. G.8M. white Tr. G. top on building, 11m. W.095°-164°; G.164°-095° but obscured by cliffs of P. d'Ailly when bearing less than 080°. Traffic sig. Reed 30 sec.

FALAIS DU POLLET. Lt. Q.R. 9M. R.W. structure 35m. 105.5°-170.5°. Aero Obst. Lt. on mast 199m. 5.7M. ESE.
LA MORGUE.
QUAI DE LA MARNE. Lt. Fl.Vi. 4 sec. 1M. R. Col. 12m.

POINTE D'AILLY 49°55′N, 0°57.6′E. Lt. Fl.(3) 20 sec. 30M. white square Tr. 95m. Obscured by cliffs near Veulettes when bearing less than 075°. R.C. Horn(3) 60 sec.

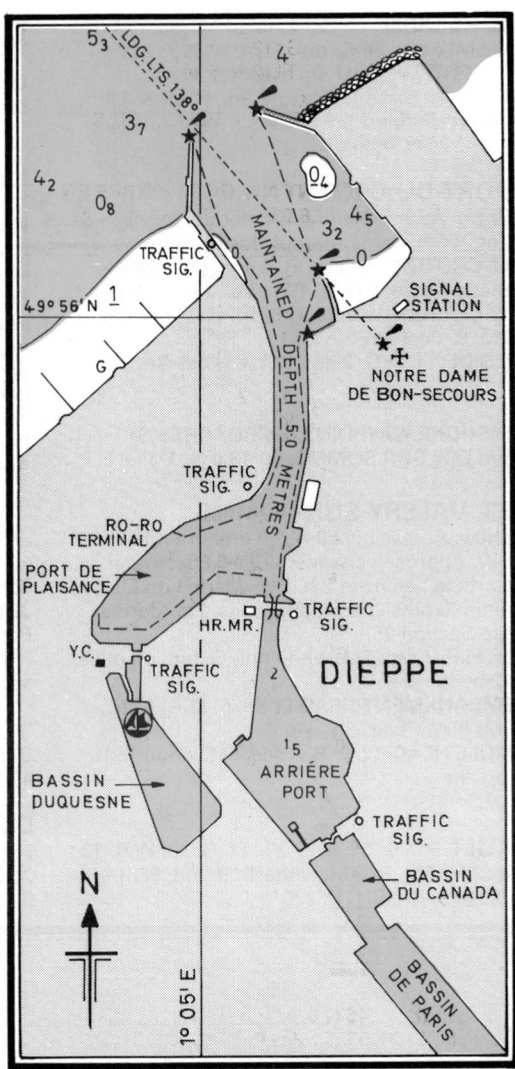

OFFSHORE WAYPOINT N OF ST. VALERY EN CAUX. 49°54.0′N, 0°43.0′E.

ST. VALERY-EN-CAUX

HARBOUR WAYPOINT. 49°52.5′N, 0°42.75′E.
Entry: Due to restrictions in entrance max. size of vessels 50m. × 8m. × draught 4.5m. HWS & 3m. HWN: Bar dries; Anchorage off entrance in 7m. to 9m. but normally used in calm weather or when wind S-SE: Avant-port dries 2.5m. to 3m.; Basin a Flot, gates 9m. wide × sill 3.3m. ACD, depth in basin 5m. Gates open 2 h.-HW-2 h. day tides. Vary with season at night.

JETEE OUEST. 49°52.5'N, 0°42.5'E. Lt. Oc.(1 + 2) G. 12 sec. 14M. Tr. G. 13m.
JETEE EST. HEAD. Lt. Fl.(2)R. 6 sec. Tr. R.

OFFSHORE WAYPOINT N OF VEULLETTES. 49°52.25'N, 0°36.6'E.

OFFSHORE WAYPOINT NW OF ST. PIERRE EN PORT. 49°50.0'N, 0°28.0'E.

during SW-N-NE winds. Dock gates open 1½ h.-HW. Best time to enter port is ½ h.-HW.

JETEE NORD 49°46'N, 0°21.8'E. Lt. Fl.(2) 10 sec. 16M. Grey Tr. R. Top. 15m. Obscured 234°-064° by cliffs of Pointe Fagnet and d'Etretat. Reed (2) 30 sec. sounded from 3h. before to 3h. after H.W.

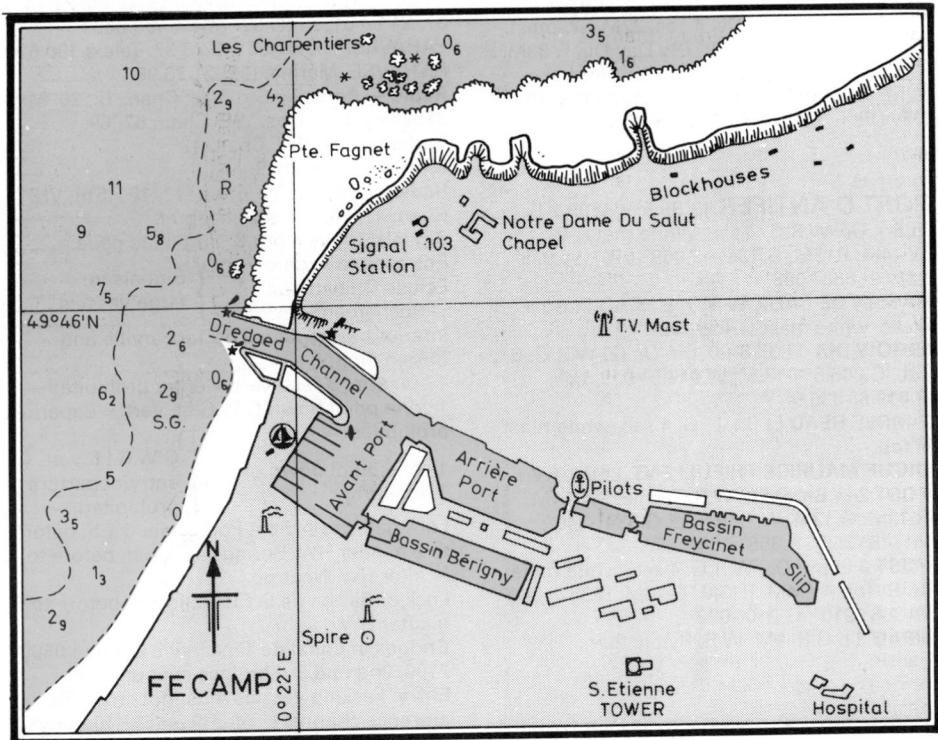

FECAMP 49°46'N 0°22'E. Tel: Pilots: 42 28 32. H.M. 28 25 53. Yacht Hbr. (35) 28 13 58.

HARBOUR WAYPOINT. 49°46.0'N, 0°21.0'E.

Radio-Port: VHF Chan. 16, 12, 3 h-HW also 0800, 1200, 1400, 1800.
Radio — Pilots: VHF Chan. 16, 12. 6 h-HW.
YACHT HARBOUR. VHF Chan. 9. 0800-2000 (local time).
Signals: Simplified code, also Flag P indicates dock gates of Bassin Berigny and Bassin Freycinet are open.
Entry: Enter on flood just before H.W. Approach made at angle 35°. Pass head of S Jetty 12m. off. When bows in slack water stern will be swung into line by E going stream. Pilots available 2½ h. before to 30 min. after HW. Entrance channel dredged to 1.1m. to 1.5m. but liable to siltation. Entry difficult

ROOT. Lt. Q.R. R. ○ on mast. 10m. In line 085° with Jetee Sud. Lt.
JETEE SUD HEAD. Lt. Q.G. 9M. Grey Tr. G. Top. 14m. vis. 072°-217°.
Dir. Lt. 085°. Dir. Oc. 4 sec. 16M. Same structure 7m. 083.5°-086.5°.

YPORT. Ldg.Lts. 165°. (Front) Oc. 4 sec. (Rear) Oc. 4 sec. Synchronised with front.

RIVER SOMME TO CAPE DE LA HEVE

HAVRE-ANTIFER Tel: (35) 22 81 40
Radio — Port: VHF Chan. 14, 67, 22.

OFFSHORE WAYPOINT N OF CAP D'ANTIFER. 49°45.0'N, 0°10.0'E.

CAP D'ANTIFER 49°41.1'N, 0°09.9'E. Lt. Fl. 20 sec. 29M. grey octagonal Tr. 128m. Obscured by cliffs of d'Etretat when bearing more than 222°, and by Cap de la Heve when bearing less than 021°. R.C.

PORT D'ANTIFER
APPROACH 49°38.3'N, 0°09.2'E. Ldg.Lts. 127°30' (Front) Dir. Oc. 4 sec. 22M. W. mast. G. Top. 105m. 127°-128° (By Day Dir. F. 33M. 126.5°-128.5° Occas.) (Rear) Dir. Oc. 4 sec. 22M. W. mast. G. Top. 124m. 127°-128° (By Day Dir. F. 33M. 126.5°-128.5° Occas.).

PORT D'ANTIFER 49°39.5'N, 0°09.2'E. Lt.Bn. Oc. W.R.G. 4 sec. White metal Tr. W.14M. R13M. G.13M. G.068°-078°; W.078°-088°; R.088°-098°.
BASSIN DE CAUX W MOLE HEAD Lt.Bn. Fl.R. 4 sec. white mast G.Top 12m.
ELBOW DIR. Lt. 018°30' Dir. Oc.(2) W.R.G. 6 sec. G.006.5°-017.5°; W.017.5°-019.5°; R.019.5°-036.5°.
E MOLE HEAD Lt.Bn. Fl.G. 4 sec. white mast R.top.
DIGUE MAURICE THIEULLENT. Lt.Bn. F.Vi.
POST 2 Lt.Bn. Oc.(2)W.R.G. 6 sec. W.14M. R.13M. G.13M. W.Tr. R.Top. G.334°-346°; W.346°-358°; R.358°-004°.
POST 3 Lt.Bn. Oc. W.R.G. 4 sec. white metal Tr. R. Top. W14M. R13M. G.13M. R.352°-358°; W.358°-010°; G.010°-022°.
HEAD. Lt. Q.R. 9M. W.R. Pylon. 20m.

OFFSHORE WAYPOINT NW OF CAP DE LA HEVE. 49°33.7'N, 0°00.0'E/W.

CAP DE LA HEVE TO LE HAVRE

L.H.A. LANBY. (LE HAVRE). 49°31'N 0°09.9'W. Fl.(2)R. 10 sec. 20M. W.R. By. 10m. R.C. Racon. Reserve Lt. 6M. Riding Lt. Q. Approach to main Chan. into Le Havre is from L.H. 2 By. thence on Ldg. Line of 107° through Entce. Chan. dredged to 15m.

OFFSHORE WAYPOINT OFF LE HAVRE. 49°29.0'N, 0°04.0'W.

CAP DE LA HEVE 49°30.8'N, 0°04.1'E. Lt. Fl. 5 sec. 26M. white octagonal Tr. R.Top. 123m. 225°-196°.

APPROACHES TO LE HAVRE AND HARBOUR

INSHORE WAYPOINT RIVER SEINE. 49°27.1'N, 0°01.2'E.

LE HAVRE 49°29'N 0°06'E. Tel: H.M. (35) 21 74 00. Port & Control Tr. (35) 21 74 00, 21 74 37, 21 80 01, 21 80 02. Telex: 190 663 F PAHAVRE. Pilots: (35) 42 28 32. Telex: 190 626 PILHAVRE. Marina: (35) 21 23 95.
Radio — Port: Sig.Stn. VHF Chan. 12, 20. MF 2182 kHz. Port Ops. VHF Chan. 67, 69. Radar advice: VHF Chan. 12. Marina VHF Chan. 9.
Radio — Pilots: VHF Chan. 12, 16 P.Stn. VHF Chan. 12, 20. P.V. & Helicopter.
Signals: Digue Nord & simplified code.
Entrance to Arriere Port ⎫
Ecluse Quinette de ⎬ Signals for
  Rochement ⎭ large vessels
Interior basins, Canal de Tancarville and Bassin du Roi:
1 hor. arm. 3 R.Lt. vert. = entry prohibited.
1 cone point down G.W.G.Lt. vert. = departure prohibited.

1 cone point down over ⎫ G.W.R.Lt. vert. =
1 hor. arm. ⎬ entry/departure
   ⎭ prohibited.
Lock gates to Arriere Port opened 1 h. before to 2 h. after HW. Springs and 1½ h. before to 1¼ h. after HW. Neaps.
Lock of Bassin de la Citadelle 3 h. before to 5 h. after HW.
Bridges in Canal de Tancarville opened 0500-2100, 2nd and 3rd bridges shut at 1930.
Entry: Passing vessels must not cross the entrance channel E. of LH9 and LH10 Lt.Bys. when other vessels are entering or leaving. Such vessels are not obliged to give way to the crossing vessel. Before attempting to cross the deep water channel, small craft **must** obtain permission and direction from port control on VHF Ch. 12.
Channel to Port du Plaisance (Anse de Joinville) Y. Hr. least depth 3m. Speed limit 3 kts. Easy access inside and N of Avant Port. Bassin de la Manche gives access to Bassin du Roi entered through Lock gate 8m. wide × Sill depth 1.1m. ACD. open 2½ h.-HW-½ h. thence to Bassin du Commerce through passage 11.7m. wide and depth 3.5m. ACD. Reserved for yachts.

ROUEN.
Staying in Rouen. There is nothing for the pleasure boat in the Maritime Port. The H.M. Office generally allows a stay of 48 hours in the St. Gervais basin which is enough time to

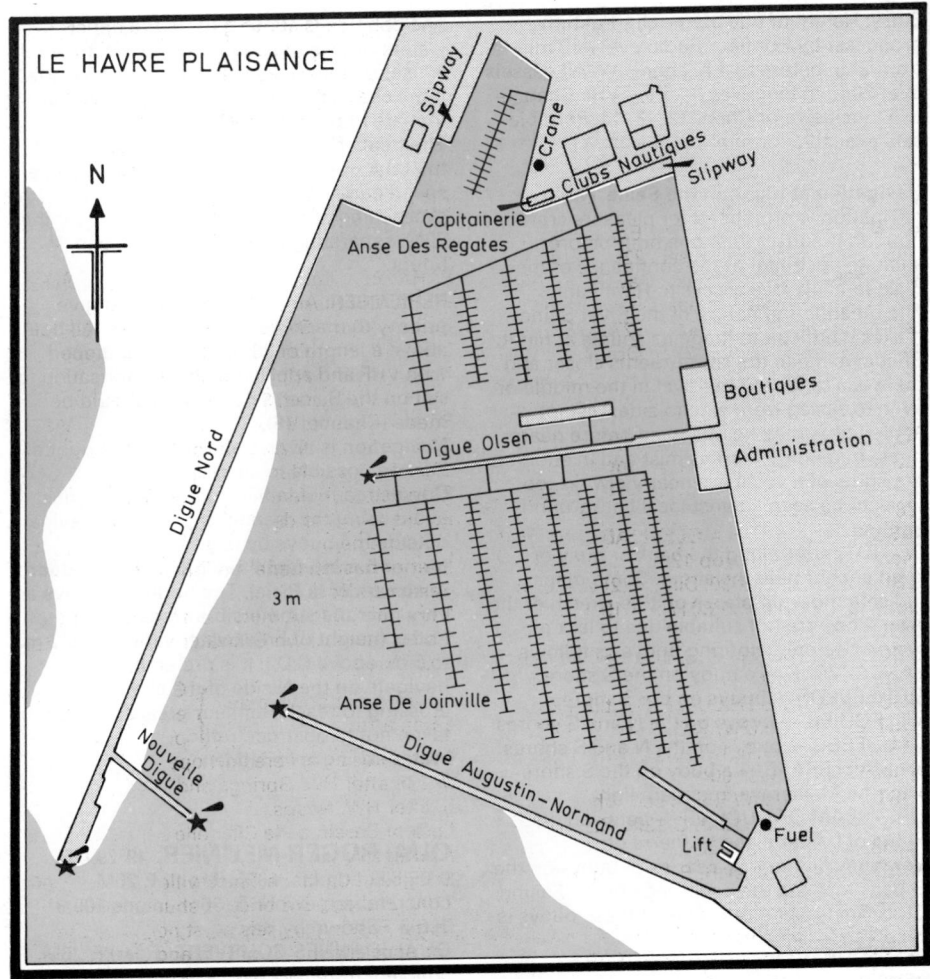

LE HAVRE PLAISANCE

N

Slipway
Crane
Clubs Nautiques
Slipway
Capitainerie
Anse Des Regates
Boutiques
Digue Nord
Digue Olsen
Administration
3 m
Anse De Joinville
Nouvelle Digue
Digue Augustin-Normand
Lift
Fuel

dismast or remast. Mooring is on a pontoon and the surface water is calm. One should beware of the problems inherent in large commercial ports.

Port offices open 24 hours throughout the year:

LE HAVRE   9 Boulevard Kennedy (opp. the Semaphore) Tel: (35) 21 33 30
VILLEQUIER Tel: (35) 96 20 77
ROUEN   21 Avenue du Mont Riboudet
            Tel: (35) 52 54 00
            Telex: 770865 CAPIPOR

From Rouen to Paris is 133M. There are 9 locks between Poses and Paris, depth 4m. speed limit 5½ kts. Inland waterways from Paris to River Schelde, Meuse, Rhine and Rhone. Max. length 37.5m. beam 5m. draught 1.7m. Check also that your 'Air Draught' is suitable for the bridges. Speed limit in canals is 3¼ kts.

Radio — Port: VHF Chan. 16, 73, 68 — continuous. B'cast Chan. 11 ev. H+00 in bad vis. Radar assistance VHF Chan. 15, 73.
Radio — Pilots: VHF Chan. 16, 73. MF 2182. WT. 500 kHz. H24.

SEINE RADAR
HONFLEUR RADAR. VHF Chan. 16, 11, 13, 71, 74. H.24. Rade de la Carosse to Courval Lt. Radicatel Radar Station.
VHF Chan. 11, 13, 73, 74 2 h. before to 2 h. after H.W. Le Havre, Risle River entrance to Courval Lt.

RIVER SEINE, ROUEN AND PARIS
Rouen Tel: Port Captain: (35) 88 81 55. Telex: Buropor Rouen 770865. Pilots: Rouen (35) 71 68 50. Telex: Rouen PILSEINE 770575. Caudebec 96 18 78. Le Havre: 21 33 30.

Entry: Height of tide above chart datum broadcast by Honfleur Radio every 10 min. from 2½ h. before to 4 h. after H.W. All vessels over 20m. in length to be fitted VHF Chan. 6 to 11 inclusive or Chan. 12, 13, 16. Portable sets available for hire.

Navigation at night on the Seine. Night navigation is prohibited for pleasure craft one hour after sunset until one hour before sunrise, upstream of the confluence of the Risle to allow free access to Honfleur. The meandering nature of the River Seine makes it difficult to judge its course at night. Shadows mean the shore seems closer and there is a tendency to travel in the middle or even to zigzag from side to side. Distant shore lights may be observed before nearer ones, frequently there is mist and in addition the lights of a yacht are nearly always too weak to be seen against local background lighting.
DO NOT moor along the bank or quay or even anchor near the shore. Some maps indicate mooring places on this stretch of the river. They are not suitable due to lack of water. Use only mooring buoys as follows:
TANCARVILLE — a buoy on the S shore.
QUILLEBEUF — buoys on the S shore.
VILLEQUIER — buoys on the N and S shores.
CAUDEBEC — buoys on the N and S shores.
LA MAILLERAYE — a buoy on the S shore near the Mailleraye upstream light.
UPSTREAM OF DUCLAIR — between the lights of L'Anerie and St Pierre de Varengeville there is a series of buoys on the S bank forming the anchorage of the Sailing Club 'Seine Maritime'. One of these buoys is reserved for visitors.
HENOUVILLE — a buoy on the N bank.
At St Georges Yacht Club.
Elsewhere there are often buoys near the ferryboat docks. Check with ferry crews first and vacate if necessary.
YOU MUST HOIST A POWERFUL MOORING LIGHT.

Special information. At Springs, the turn of tide between ebb and flood is instantaneous, and the flood tide is immediately very powerful. It is important to know this to avoid heart failure when you are at anchor at night.

Daytime Navigation. You will wish to cover the 70M. separating the roadstead and the port of Rouen in a single stretch by day. This is feasible at a speed of 5 kts. Going upstream pass the first channel buoys at LW Le Havre. It is still ebb tide but this will soon change to flood. The tide runs at approx. 2 kts. therefore time for the passage is about 10 hours.

The ebb tide is about 2 kts. in the upper waters of Villequier and 4 kts. downstream. It is useless to sail against it if the boat is slow. If the channel is reached after HW it will be too late to proceed upstream.
The tidal effect more or less balances out if the boat goes down river at a basic average speed equal to the surface speed. A yacht proceeding at a speed of 5 kts. will cover the 70M. separating Rouen from the sea in 14 hours.

REMEMBER: All pleasure craft must give priority to maritime and river traffic. All boats above a length of 20m. must be equipped with VHF and application for authorisation to sail on the Seine to Rouen Port should be made (Channel 16).
Navigation is always effected on the right as near as possible to shore.
Downstream of la Risle pleasure craft must avoid using the marked channel and navigate outside the buoys by day and night **(remembering night navigation is forbidden upstream of la Risle).** The Southern buoys are very near the submersible breakwater of Ratier (height of breakwater varies from 2 m. to 5 m. above C.D.). It is preferable to navigate on the N side of the channel. If crossing to reach Honfleur great care must be taken not to obstruct traffic.
Water ski-ing is forbidden.

QUAI ROGER MEUNIER. 49°29.0′N, 0°06.5′E. Ldg.Lts. 107°. (Front) F. 26M. concrete framework Tr. 36m. Intens 105.3°-103.3°. Shown by day.
QUAI JOANNES COURVERT. (Rear) F. 26M. concrete framework Tr. 78m. Intens 105.3°-108.3°. Shown by day.

Ldg.Lts. 090°. (Front) F.R. 18M. Tr. 21m. Intens 088.5°-091.5° occas. (Rear) F.R. 18M. Tr. on house, 43m. Intens 088.5°-091.5° occas.

DIGUE NORD HEAD. 49°29.2′N, 0°05.4′E. Lt. Fl.R. 5 sec. 21M. white Tr. R. top, 15m. Sig.Stn. Reed 15 sec.
DIGUE SUD HEAD. Lt. V.Q.(3) G. 2 sec. 13M. white Tr. G. top. 15m.
DIGUE SUD ELBOW. Dir.Lt. 270° Lt.Dir. Q.G. G.W. Structure.
YACHT HARBOUR DIQUE AUGUSTIN NORMAND. Lt. Q.(2)G. 5 sec.
BREAKWATER HEAD. Lt. Fl.(2)R. 6 sec. 3M. W. mast R. Top.
YACHT HARBOUR JETTY. Lt. Oc.G. 4 sec. G. Structure.

JETEE DU SEMAPHORE HEAD. Lt. Q.R. 7M.
W.R. mast. 9m. Bell 2½ sec.
QUAI ROGER MEUNIER. 49°29.0'N, 0°06.4'E.
Lt. Fl.(3) 15 sec. 24M. G. Tr. 4m. Fog only.

ARRIERE PORT
BASIN DE LA MANCHE JETTY HEAD. Lt.
Iso.R. 4 sec.
QUAI DE LA MARINE. Lt. V.Q.(9) 10 sec. 7M. ⌇
on Y.B.Y. Pylon. 7m.
2 Lt.Bns. F.Vi.

ECLUSE QUINETTE DE ROCHEMONT
N SIDE. Lt. F.R. or Fl.(2) 10 sec. in fog.
S SIDE. Lt.F.G. or Fl. 5 sec. in fog.

BASSIN THEOPHILE DUCROCQ
MCN Lt.By. Q.G. Pillar. G. NW of Mole
Central.
MCO Lt.By. Fl.R. 4 sec. Pillar. R. SW of Mole
Central.
MCS Lt.By. Oc.R. 4 sec. Pillar. R. S of Mole
Central.
MOLE NORD. Lt. Oc.(2)R. 6 sec. 5M. white Tr.
R. top, 7m. ⌇⌇. Horn(2) 20 sec.
MOLE SUD. Lt. Oc.(2)G. 6 sec. 5M. white Tr.
G. top, 7m. ⌇⌇.
DIR. Lt. 192°. Oc. W.R.G. Shown by day.
G.183°-190°; W.190°-194°; R.194°-201°.

Ldg. Lts. 106°. (Front) F.Vi. (Rear) F.Vi. vis. on
Ldg. Line.

BASSIN AUX PETROLES
BASSIN No: 1 Ldg.Lts. 154°. (Front) F.G.
(Rear) F.G.
BASSIN No: 2. Ldg.Lts. 154°. (Front) F.G.
(Rear) F.G.
Ldg.Lts. 171°. (Front) F.R. (Rear) F.R.
BASSIN No: 3. Ldg.Lts. 142°. (Front) F.G.
(Rear) F.G.
W SIDE. Lt. F.Vi.
E SIDE. Lt. F.Vi. W. Structure.
E SIDE. Lt. Q. on dolphin.
E SIDE. Lt. Fl.G. 4 sec. G. Pile.

DIGUE CHARLES LAROCHE. Dir.Lt. 119°30'.
Oc. W.R.G. 4 sec. 10M. 8m. G.118°-119°;
W.119°-120°; R.120°-121°.

NOUVEAU BASSIN RENE COTY
Ldg.Lts. 058°. (Front) F.Vi. (Rear) F.Vi.
Ldg.Lts. 147°. (Front) F.Vi. (Rear) F.Vi.
DARSE D'EL OCEAN Ldg.Lts. 159° (Front) Dir.
F.G. (Rear) Dir. F.G.

OFFSHORE WAYPOINT NW OF TROUVILLE.
49°23.2'N, 0°01.6'E.

TROUVILLE-DEAUVILLE 49°22'N
0°04'E. Tel: H.M. (31) 88 28 71 & 88 56 16.
Deauville Y.C. (31) 88 38 19. Customs: (31) 88
63 49.

HARBOUR WAYPOINT. 49°22.5'N, 0°04.0'E.

Radio — Yacht Hbr: VHF Chan. 9.
Signals: Simplified code shown from Pointe
de la Cahotte.
Letter P shown when gates opening later etc.
Entry: Basin de Yacht has 2m. above chart
datum.
Enter at slack H.W. Access to yacht harbour
difficult 1 h. before H.W.
Deauville lock gates open 4 h. before H.W.
Dover to H.W. but during very high tides
gates may open 15 min. later and close 15
min. earlier or 2 h-HW-2½ h (HW Trouville).
Max. length 65m. Max. draught 4.1m.
M.H.W.S. 2.8m. M.H.W.N.

E BREAKWATER HEAD. Lt. Fl.(4) W.R. 12 sec.
W.10M. R.7M. white metal framework Tr. R.
top, 14m. R. Shore-131°. W.131°-175°; R.175°-
131°.

Ldg.Lts. 148°. Jetee E Head (Front) Oc.R. 4
sec. 11M. white Tr. R. top, 11m. Unintens
330°-060°; intens 060°-150°. Reed(2) 30 sec.
Root. (Rear) Oc.R. 4 sec. 10M. white metal
framework Tr. R. top, 17m. Synchronised with
front. Vis. 120°-170°.

JETEE W. Lt.Bn. Fl. W.G. 4 sec. W.12M. G.9M.
W.005°-176°; G.176°-005°.
JETEE W NR. HEAD. Lt. Q.G. 7M. white Tr. G.
top, 11m.
BREAKWATER. Lt.Bn. Iso. G. 4 sec. 5M. Mast.
Seine Channel.

HONFLEUR 49°25'N 0°14'E. Tel: (31) 89 20
02. Telex: BURO PORT HONFL 170196.
Radio — Port: VHF Chan. 16, 12 2 hr. before to
4 hr. after HW Le Havre.
Radio — Pilots: VHF Chan. 16, 6 —
continuous.
Radar: VHF 16, 11, 71, 74. H24. Tide readings
Chan. 11 ev. 10 mins. 2 h. before to 3 h. after
HW.
Signals: Depth signals shown as per
standard, also at night a tidal light from Epi
de la Risberme showing F.W. every 48 secs.
with a R. Fl. = 1m. and G. Fl. = 0.2m.
Flag P or 3 F.W. Lt. vert. = gates to basins
open. Gates open at HW–1, HW, HW+1 (and
HW+2 daytime high season/weekends).
3 blasts = wish to enter Bassin de l'Est.
4 blasts = wish to enter Basin Carnot.
Enter basins if dock gates open, otherwise
wait in Avant Port.

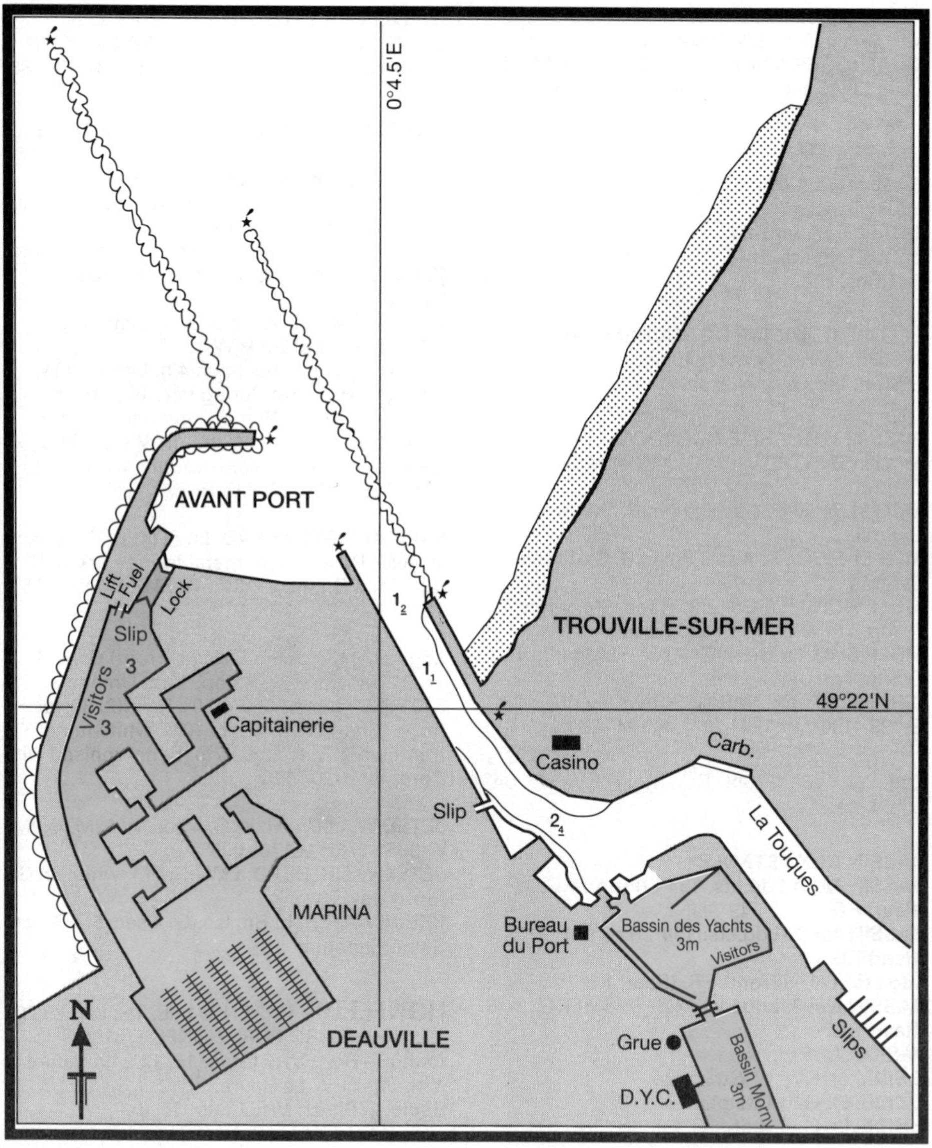

Entry: Approach channel dries at C.D.; Avant Port dries 1m. to 3m.; W. Lock 10.5m. × Sill dry 2.8m., thence into Bassin de l'Ouest (Vieux Bassin) depth 2.8m. for yachts; E Lock 16.3m. × Sill dry 1.3m. for other basins for commercial vessels.
Max. draught 6.4m. M.H.W.S. 3.9m. M.H.W.N.

DIGUE DU RATIER HD. PLATFORM A. Lt. V.Q. 8M. B. △ on Y. Platform 8m.

SPILLWAY. Lt. V.Q.(9) 10 sec. 6M. ⧗ Y.B., Bn. 15m.

FALAISE DES FONDS 49°25.5′N 0°12.9′E. Lt. Fl.(3)W.R.G. 12 sec. W.17M. R.13M. G.13M. W. Tr. 15m. G.040°-080°; R.080°-084°; G.084°-100°; W.100°-109°; R.109°-162°; G.162°-260°.

DIQUE EST. HEAD Lt. Q. 8M. B.W. Tr. 10m. Reed(5) 40 sec.

MOLE HEAD Lt. Oc.(2)R. 6 sec. W. Tr. 12m.

DIQUE OEST HEAD Lt. Q.G. 5M. G. Tr. 10m.

JETTY TRANSIT Lt. F.Vi. 1M. B.W. Tr. 10m.

QUAY Lts. 2 F.G. vert. Grey mast.

PONT DE NORMANDIE. Pillar N Lt. Fl.Y. 2.5 sec. 4M. Y. "X" on pile.

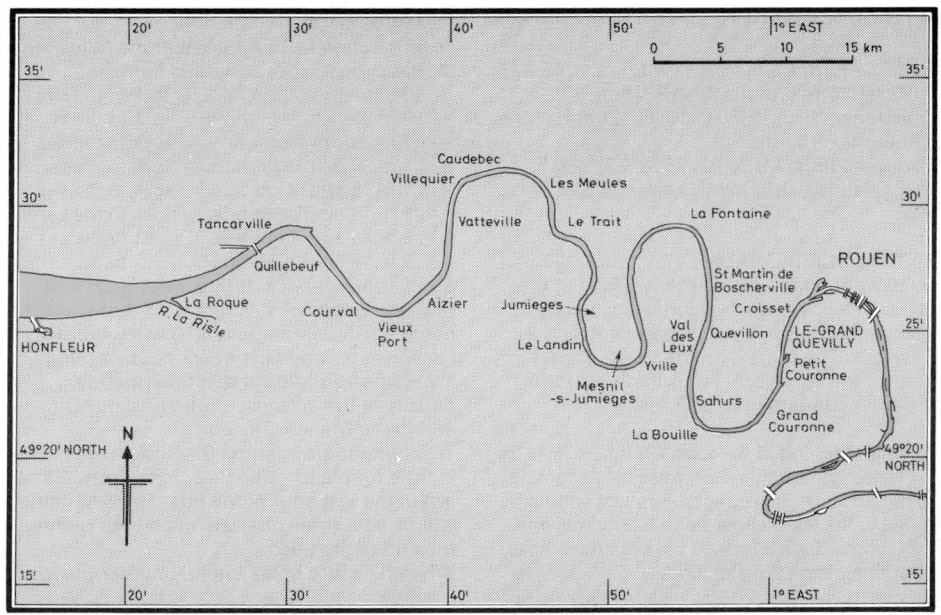

LA SEINE MARITIME
LA RISLE. Lt. Iso.G. 4 sec. 7M. white metal framework Tr. and hut, G. top. 11m. ⌇⌇.
TOURELLE YGOU. Lt. V.Q.R. 5M. R. pedestal on Tr. 7m. ⌇⌇.
LA ROQUE POINT. Lt. Q.G. 6M. white Col. G. top, 8m.
MARAIS-VERNIER. Lt. Fl.G. 4 sec. 5M. white Col. G. top, 8m.

TANCARVILLE 49°28'N 0°28'E
Radio — Port: VHF Chan. 16, 11 — continuous.
TANCARVILLE LOCK VHF Chan. 18.
Entry Signal: For vessels entering canal visible only from seaward.
2 R. flags/2 R. Lt. hor. = entrance prohibited
G. burgee/2 G. Lt. hor. = entrance permitted.
G. burgee over R. flag/G. over R.Lt. = entry and departure prohibited.
For vessels leaving canal visible only from Westward:
2 R. Lt. hor. = entry to lock prohibited. 2 G. Lt. hor. = entry to lock permitted.
3 blasts = request to open bridge. Maximum speed 5 kts. in the canal.

TANCARVILLE DIGUE NORD. Lt. Q.R. 6M. white Col. R. top. 9m. Aero Fl.R. 3 sec. on each of 2 bridge pillars.
BANC DE RADICATEL. Lt. Q.R. 6M. R.W. pylon.
SAINT JEAN DE FOLLEVILLE. Lt. Oc.R. 4 sec. 6M. W. pylon, R. top.

LILLEBONNE. Lt. Q.R. 6M. R.W. col.
QUILLEBOEUF. Lt. Q.G. 7M. W. Tower, G. top. Lts. shown upstream.

PORT JEROME 49°28'N, 0°33'E.
Radio: VHF Chan. 16, 73. H24.

OFFSHORE WAYPOINT N OF DIVES SUR MER. 49°19.5'N, 0°05.5'W.

DIVES-SUR-MER. 49°17.8'N, 0°05.2'W.

HARBOUR WAYPOINT DIVES SUR MER. 49°18.5'N, 0°05.5'W.

Entry: Access 2½ h.-HW-2½ h. Best time to enter at HW slack.
Lt. Oc.(2+1) W.R.G. 12 sec. W.12M. R.9M. G.9M. white hut, 6m. G.124°-154°; W.154°-157°;
R.157°-193°.

OFFSHORE WAYPOINT N OF OUISTREHAM. 49°20.0'N, 0°14.5'W.

CAEN-OUISTREHAM 49°17'N 0°15'W.
Tel: H.M. (31) 82 36 36. Telex: 772071. Pilots: (31) 97 16 81. Customs: (31) 97 18 62. SRCO Y.C. (31) 97 13 05.

HARBOUR WAYPOINT. 49°18.0′N, 0°14.75′W.

Radio — Port: Caen Port VHF Chan. 8, 68. MF 2182 kHz. Canal de Caen VHF Chan. 12; Ouistreham Port VHF 12, 16, 68. 2½ h.-HW-3 h. SRCO Y.C. VHF Chan. 9.
Radio — Pilots: MF 2182, 2506, 2321, 2157. VHF Chan. 16, 6, 12, 2½ h. before to 3 h. after HW.

ENTRY LOCK SIGNALS: Light panels, lighted by day and night during the working of the locks are shown on the control lock house. The panels on the Eastern part control the East lock. The panels on the Western part control the West lock. For meanings of the different combinations see below:

Normal Opening of the lock: About 2 h.-HW-3 h. **Entrance** prior to this is permissible according to dimensions and draught. Request should be made to the lock keeper on the previous tide, i.e. if you require a lock on the p.m. tide, make your request on the a.m. tide.

Pleasure-boats:
From 15 June to 15 September the following pleasure-boats lock service is enforced:
— , 3 h. before high-tide   lock to the sea
— , 2 h. 30 before high-tide   lock to the canal
— , 2 h. before high-tide   lock to the sea
— , 1 h. 30 before high-tide   lock to the canal
— , 1 h. 45 after high-tide   lock to the sea
— , 2 h. 15 after high-tide   lock to the canal
— , 2 h. 45 after high-tide   lock to the sea
— , 3 h. 15 after high-tide   lock to the canal
Similar lock-service during week-ends and holidays between 1 April and 15 June and between 15 September and 31 October. This is subject to modification without warning. Yachtsmen should consult the monthly notices in the entrance to the Harbour Office and in the Marina Office.
Throughout the year the free lock is opened, in time for pleasure boats coming from the sea in the last hour of the tide. The Sea-gate will be shut three quarters of an hour before the end of the tide.
When pleasure boats intend to enter the lock

No. 1	● Red ○ White ● Red		Entering the lock forbidden for all ships in the channel and outer port. Entering the lock permitted for all ships in the canal.
No. 2	● Green ○ White ● Green		Entering the lock forbidden for all ships in the canal. Entering the lock permitted for all ships in the channel and outer port.
No. 3	● Green ○ White ● Red		Entering the lock forbidden for all ships.
No. 4	● Green ○ White ● Red	○ White	Entering the lock forbidden. Derogation for ships less than 25m. length which see the signal.
No. 5	● Green ○ White ● Red	● Green	Entering the lock forbidden to permit the entry of a vessel specially authorised by the port officer.
No. 6	● Green ○ White ● Red	● Red	Entering the lock forbidden to permit the exit of a vessel specially authorised by the port officer.

The general rule is: Presence of a W. Lt. on the left or right of the number three signal: movement authorised for pleasure and fishing craft.
Absence of a W. Lt. on the left or right of the number three signal: movement forbidden for pleasure and fishing craft.
N.B. — A white light alone between two tides means: The lock will be opened 1 h. before usual time.

at the above mentioned hours and are still sailing in the neighbourhood of Orne mouth at the lock gates closing-time, they have to show the flag Q (Québec); They also must make arrangements for reaching the lock without loss of time.

Pleasure boats locking with merchant vessels must always enter the lock after these ships. The pleasure-boat harbour holds 650 mooring-berths. Slipway, force: 8 tons; draught: 1.8m. (6 feet).

Pleasure boats wharf:

A floating pontoon, 40m. long to the E of the entrance channel, is reserved for pleasure boats entering or leaving the port between two tides. Boats cannot occupy this pontoon more than 7 h. without special authorisation from the Port Office and must not be more than six abreast.

The outer channel, the swinging area and the car-ferry dock are dredged at 5.5m. under the chart datum level. The access to the W lock is dredged at 3m. under the chart datum level and the access to the E lock to chart datum level. Maximum draught authorised: 8.95m.

Canal: Maximum authorised draught (fresh water: 8.9m. from Ouistreham to Hérouville, 8.5m. from Hérouville to Calix. Depth of the canal: 9.9m. from Ouistreham to Calix. Width of bridges: Bénouville: 30m. Colombelles: 30m. Calix: 21, 76m.

Bassin St-Pierre: Accessible to ships with the following maximum dimensions: Length: 90m. Breadth; 12m. Draught; 4.2m. (fresh water).

The swing-bridge giving access to the Bassin St-Pierre is 12m. wide. The bassin measures 500m. × 50m. The western part of this basin is reserved for pleasure boats.

When loading at Berths A3/A6, it must be borne in mind that there is a stone ledge 2.7m. under the water, projecting 1m. from the quay.

Entry: Anchorage in Rade de Caen 7m. to 12m. W. Lock 225m. × 28.8m. × 3.25m. on sill. E. Lock 181m. × 18m. × 0.20m. on sill.

OUISTREHAM Tel: H.M. (31) 97 14 43.

MAIN. 49°16.8'N, 0°14.9'W. Lt. Oc.W.R. 4 sec. W.16M. R. 12M. white Tr. R. top. 37m. W.090°-115°; R.115°-151°; W.151°-090°.

OC. Lt.By. 49°19.9'N, 0°14.3'W. Iso. 4 sec. 4M. Pillar. R.W. Stripes. 8m. Topmark O. Whis.

ENROCHEMENTS EST. HEAD. Lt. Oc.(2)R. 6 sec. 8M. W. pylon R. Top 7m.

BANC DE L'ILE. Lt. Iso.G. 4 sec. 7M. W. Pylon G. Top.

Lt. VQ (3) R. 5 sec. 5M. R. Pylon.

Lt. VQ (3) G. 5 sec.

No: 4 By. Conical R.

JETEE W HEAD. Lt. !so.G. 4 sec. 6M. B. metal framework Tr. G. top, 12m. ᕙᕙ Horn 10 sec. sounded from 2½h. before to 3h. after H.W. also Lt. Iso. R. 4 sec. 100m. E.

JETEE E. 49°17.1'N, 0°14.8'W. Ldg.Lts. 185°. (Front) Dir. Oc.(3+1)R. 12 sec. 13M. white metal framework Tr. R. top. 10m. ᕙᕙ. Lt. V.Q.(3)Y. on dolphin 30m. W. (Rear) Dir.Oc.(3+1)R. 12 sec. 22M. Tripod. R. top. 30m. Synchronised with front. Intens 183°-187°.

RO-RO TERMINAL. Lt. Q.G. Dolphin.

TURNING AREA.

CENTRE LDG.LTS. 189°30' (Front) Dir. Q.Vi. (Rear) Dir. Q.Vi.

EAST LDG.LTS. 186°30' (Front) Q. (Rear) Q.

NORTH LDG.LTS. 278°30' (Front) Oc.G. 4 sec. (Rear) Oc.G. 4 sec.

CANAL DE CAEN Lt. Qk.Fl.R.

Lt. Oc.R. 4 sec.

Lt. Q.G.

Lt. Iso.G. 4 sec.

VIADUC DE CALIX Lt. Iso. 4 sec.

Lt. F.G. N Side.

Lt. F.R. S Side.

Lts. 2 F.R. mark locks to entce. to Caen Canal when gates open.

Lts. 2 F. when gates are closed.

PLATFORM. Lt. 2 Mo.(U) 15 sec. 13M. Y. hut on B. tripod. Horn. Mo.(U) 30 sec. 10M. Nth of Ouistreham.

COURSEULLES

Entry: Best time for entry is HW which stands for 1½ h.; Draught 3.5m. HWS; River Basin dries 3m.-3.5m.; Bridge opened 2/3 h.-HW-2/3 h; Y. Hr. above Bridge, depth maintained by sill 1.2m.-1.5m.; Dock gate 9.6m. wide × sill dry 2.3m.

JETEE E Lt. Fl.(2)R. 6 sec. 8M. Tr. R. 9m.

JETEE W Lt. Iso.W.G. 4 sec. W.9M. G.6M. G. Tr. 9m. W.135°-235°; G.235°-135°; Horn 30 sec. from 2 h. before to 2 h. after H.W.

OFFSHORE WAYPOINT N OF VER SUR MER. 49°23.5'N, 0°28.0'W.

POINTE DE VER 49°20.5'N, 0°31.1'W. Lt. Fl.(3) 15 sec. 26M. white square Tr. and dwelling, 42m. Obscured by cliffs of St. Aubin when bearing more than 275°. R.C.

PORT-EN-BESSIN. Tel: (31) 21 71 77.

Radio — Lock: VHF Chan. 18. 2 h-HW-2 h.

Entry: Anchorage off entrance in 3m. Entrance channel dries 2m. Access to Dock through passage 10m. wide. Max. draught 4.2m. M.H.W.S.

Ldg.Lts. 204°. (Front) Oc.(3) 12 sec. 9M. white metal framework Tr. 25m.
Siren 20 sec. from white hut, sounded over sector of 90° on each side of Ldg. line, continuous in W sector, interrupted in E. (Rear) Oc.(3) 12 sec. 10M. white house, 42m. Synchronised with front. R.C.
JETEE E HEAD. Lt. Oc.R. 4 sec. 6M. R. metal framework Tr. 14m.
JETTEE W HEAD. Lt. Fl.W.G. 4 sec. W.10M. G.7M. G. Tr. 14m. G.065°-114.5°; W.114.5:°-065°; Oc.(2)R. 6 sec. and Fl.(2)G. 6 sec. mark the heads of the piers.

OMAHA BEACH. Extensive wreck area off Arromanches.

GRANDCAMP — LES-BAINS

Entry: Entrance channel least width 18m. Lock gate (for Marina) 15m. wide × sill dry 2m. Open 2½ h.-HW-2½ h. Depth 2.5m. ACD. Visitors berths on N Pontoon.
PERRE. 49°23.4′N, 1°02.3′W. Lt. Oc. 4 sec. 13M. B. metal framework Tr. on white hut, 8m. Obscured when bearing more than 252°.

JETEE E HEAD. Lt. Oc.(2) R. 6 sec. R.8M. white Col. R. top, 10m. Siren Mo.(N) 30 sec.
JETEE W HEAD. Lt. Fl.G. 4 sec. 5M. Col. G.W. 8m.

MARESQUERIE. 49°23.2′N, 1°02.7′W. Lt. Oc. 4 sec. 12M. Grey Post. 28m. Vis. 090°-270°.
Ldg.Lts. 146° (Front) Q. 7M. Post 4m. (Rear) Q. 7M. Post. 4m.

INSHORE WAYPOINT OFF ISIGNY SUR MER. 49°25.0′N, 1°06.5′W.

ISIGNY-SUR-MER. 49°19.6′N, 1°06.8′W.
Entry: Dries, draught 4.2m. HWS and 2.2m. HWN. Neuf Quay dries 3m. Upper part dries 3.5m. Accessible for yachts 3 h.-HW-3 h. Petrol, diesel, water, etc. available.
Ldg.Lts. 172°30′. (Front) Dir.Oc.(2 + 1) 12 sec. 18M. white post on white hut, 7m. Intens 170.5°-174.5°. (Rear) Dir. Oc.(2 + 1) 12 sec. 18M. white metal framework Tr. on white hut, 19m. Synchronised with front. Intens 170.5°-174.5°.

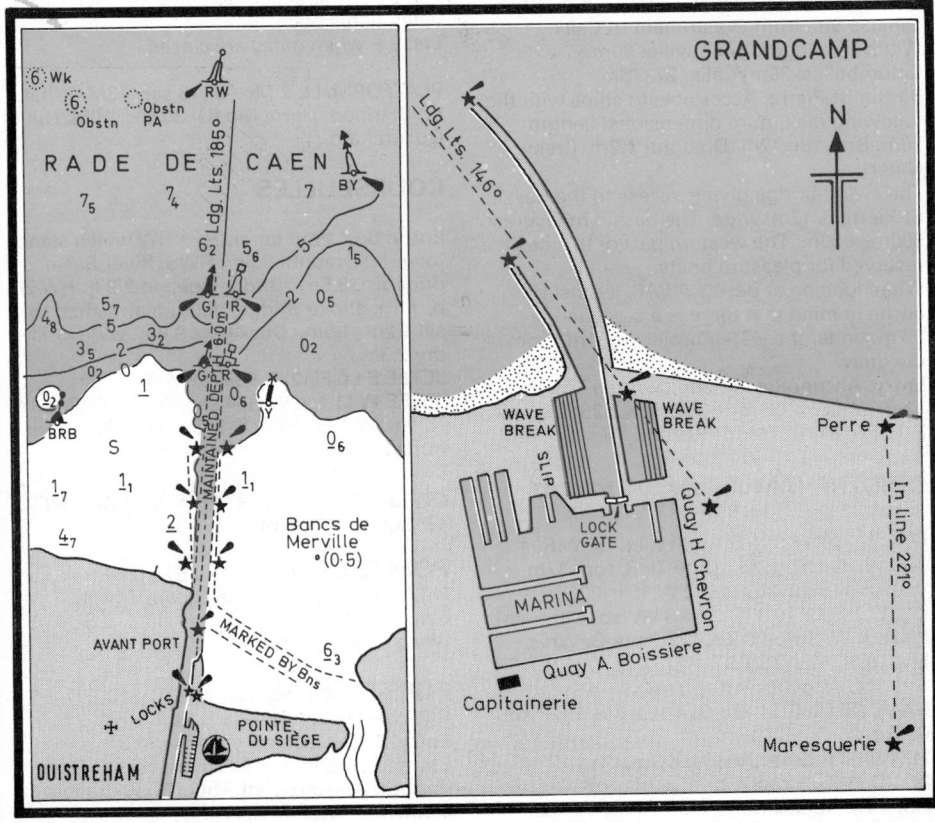

CARENTAN. 49°20.5′N, 1°11.2′W. Tel: (33) 42 24 44.
Radio — Port: VHF Chan. 9.
Entry: Chenal de Carentan dries 3.2m. Marina with 500 berths (55 for visitors).

Ldg.Lts. 209°30′. (Front) Dir.Oc.(3)R. 12 sec. 17M. white Col. R. top. 6m. Intens 208.7°-211.2°. (Rear) Oc.(3) 12 sec. 11M. white Col. G. top, 14m. Synchronised with front.

W.12M. R.9M. G.8M. white octagonal Tr. 90m. W.shore-316°; G.316°-321°; R.321°-342°; W.342°-shore.

INSHORE WAYPOINT OFF ST. VAAST DE LA HOGUE. 49°34.0′N, 1°14.5′W.

ST. VAAST 49°35.2′N, 1°15.4′W. Marina Tel: (33) 54 48 81.
Radio: Marina VHF Chan. 9 when lock open.

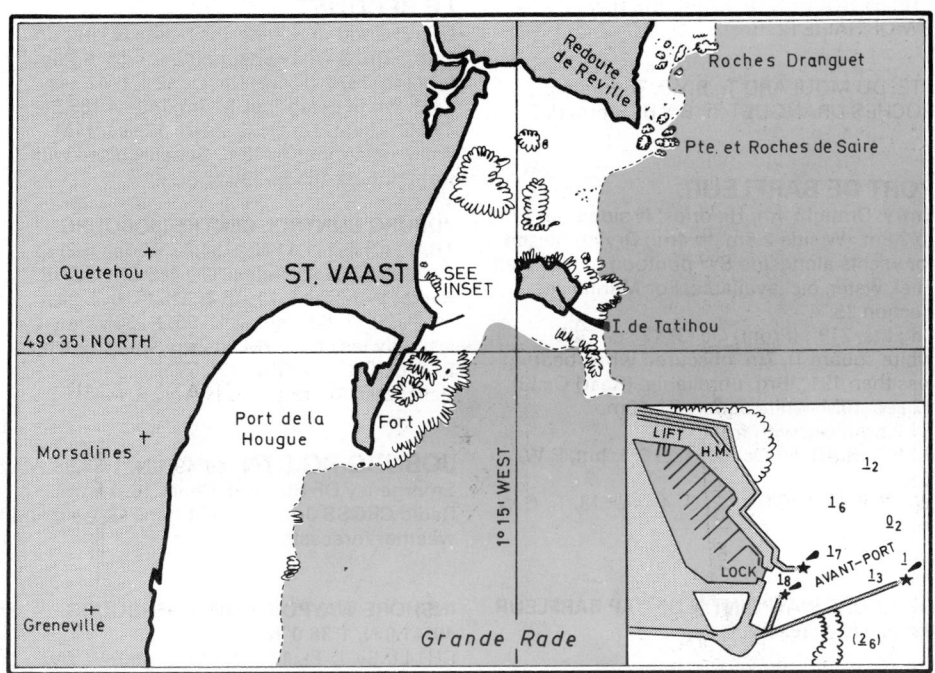

CHANNEL ENTRANCE W. Lt. Bn. Fl (3) G. 12 sec. G. △ on Bn.
E. Lt. Bn. Fl (3) R. 12 sec. R. □ on Bn.

ILES ST MARCOUF 49°29.9′N, 1°08.8′W Lt.Ho. V.Q.(3) 5 sec. 9M. Tr. B.Y.B. on fort, 18m.
Bn. Y.B. Topmark S. Cable W of Lt.Ho.

INSHORE WAYPOINT SE OF MORSALINES LT. 49°32.0′N, 1°15.5′W.

MORSALINES. Ldg.Lts. 267°47′. **LA HOUGUE** (Front) Oc. 4 sec. Brg. unreliable. 11M. white metal tripod, G. top, on hut, 9m. Obscured by Ile de Tatihou when bearing less than 228°. (Rear) Oc.(3 + 1) W.R.G. 12 sec.

Entry: Anchorages, Grande Rade in 14m. & Petite Rade in 2m. to 6m. Avant Port up to 4.6m. draught HWS & 3m. HWN. Inner Basin dries 2-3m. Drying berths on W and S sides. Y. hr. min depth 2.3m. Lock open 2h.15min–HW–3h. Signals: G.Lt. = gates open. R.Lt. = gates closed.

JETTY HEAD Lt. Oc.(2) W.R.G. 6 sec. W.11M. R.8M. G.8M. R.219°-237°; G.237°-310°; W.310°-350°; R.350°-040°.

NE SIDE, BREAKWATER HEAD. Lt. Iso.G. 4 sec. 5M. white pedestal, G. top, 6m.

SW SIDE, GROYNE HEAD. Lt. Oc.(4)R. 12 sec. 5M. white hut, R. top, 6m.

REVILLE

OFFSHORE WAYPOINT SE OF POINTE DE SAIRE. 49°34.5′N, 1°10.0′W.

POINTE DE SAIRE. 49°36.4′N, 1°13.8′W. Lt. Oc.(1 + 2) 12 sec. 13M. G. lantern on white roof, 11 m.
Obscured by Ile de Tatihou 017°-023° and 028°-036°.
PTE. ET ROCHES DE SAIRE Bn. R.W.
SW OF SAIRE Pt. Bn.

PTE. DU MOULARD Tr. B.Y.B. Topmark E.
ROCHES DRANGUET Tr. B.Y.B. Topmark E.

PORT DE BARFLEUR.

Entry: Draught 4m; Hr. dries; N side dries 2m. to 2.8m.; W side 2.8m. to 4m.; Drying berths for yachts alongside SW pontoon of NW Wall. Fuel, water, etc. available. For Marina see Section 25.
Ldg.Lts. 219°. (Front) Oc.(3) 12 sec. 10M. white square Tr. 7m. obscured when bearing less than 191°. Brg. unreliable. (Rear) Oc.(3) 12 sec. 10M. white square Tr. 13m. Synchronised with front.
E PIER HEAD. Lt. Oc.R. 4 sec. 6M. hut, R.W. 5m.
WEST PIER ROOT. Lt. Fl.G. 4 sec. 5M. Tr. G.W. 7m.

OFFSHORE WAYPOINT N OF CAP BARFLEUR. 49°45.0′N, 1°16.0′W.

CAP BARFLEUR 49°41.8′N, 1°15.9′W. Lt. Fl.(2) 10 sec. 27M. grey Tr. B. top. 72m. Obscured when bearing less than 088°. R.C. Sig.Stn. Reed(2) 60 sec.
RAZ DE BARFLEUR Bn. B.Y.B. Topmark E.
LES EQUETS. Lt.By. 49°43.7′N, 1°18.4′W. Q. 4M. Pillar. BY. 8m. Topmark ⯸.
BASSE DU RENIER. Lt.By. 49°44.9′N, 1°22.1′W. V.Q. 8M. Pillar. BY. 8m. Topmark ⯸ Whis.

ANSE DE VICQ. Ldg.Lts. 158°. (Front) F.R. 5M. white △, R. border, on metal framework Tr. 8m. (Rear) F.R. 5M. white ▽, R. border, on metal framework Tr. 14m.
NEVILLE POINT (BATTERY) Bn. B.Y. Topmark N.
ANSE DE ROUBARIL Bn. B.R.B.

OFFSHORE WAYPOINT N OF CAP LEVI. 49°45.0′N, 1°28.5′W.

CAP LEVI 49°41.8′N, 1°28.4′W. Lt. Fl.R. 5 sec. 20M. grey square Tr. 36m.
PORT DE LEVI.
Entry: Entrance 76m. wide. Quay on E side good drying out berths on sandy bottom.
Lt. F.W.R.G. W.11M. R.7M. G.6M. white wall, 7m. G.050°-109°; R.109°-140°; W.140°-shore.

LE BECQUET.

Entry: Good drying berths inside N jetty dry 1.4m.-3m. S Quay unsuitable for drying out.
Ldg.Lts. 187°. (Front) Dir. Oc.(2 + 1) 12 sec. 14M. white octagonal Tr. 7m. Intens 183.5°-190.5°. (Rear) Dir.Oc.(2 + 1)R. 12 sec. 11M. white octagonal Tr. 13m. Synchronised with front. Intens 183.5°-190.5°.

JOBURG CONTROL CENTRE (JOBOURG TRAFFIC) 49°41.11′N, 1°54.63′W. Tel: (33) 52 72 13 & 52 61 45. Telex: 170 465 CROSS JB.
Radio: VHF Chan. 11, 16 & 2182 kHz. B'cast ev. H+20, H+50 also ev. H+05, H+35 when visibility less than 2M. in English & French.
SAR COORDINATION 121.5 MHz.
Helicopter/Aircraft.

JOBURG RG STN. 49°49.1′N, 1°54.58′W. Emergency DF Stn. VHF Chan. 16, 11.
Radio CROSS Joburg VHF Chan. 13. Gale and weather forecasts.

INSHORE WAYPOINT OFF CHERBOURG. 49°41.0′N, 1°38.0′W.
CH1 Lt. By. L. Fl. 10 sec. 8M. O on R.W. By. 8m. Whis. 49°43.3′N 01°42.0′W.

CHERBOURG 49°39′N 1°34′W
Tel: (33) 53 75 16. VHF Chan. 9. Pilots: (33) 20 51 23. Telex: 170 952 PILCHER. Deep Sea Pilots: (33) 20 51 23. Telex: 171467 PILHAUT F.
Naval Port Radio: VHF Chan. 11.
Central Marine Operations. VHF Chan. 16.
Radio — Pilots: VHF Chan. 16, 12. H24. Deep Sea Pilots: VHF Chan. 16, 68. H24.
Signals: Wet dock — gate open 1 h. before to 1 h. after HW.
1 long blast = request swing bridge open. Orders given by loudspeaker. Also signals.
W./G.Lt. hor. = dock open, vessel can enter. No departure.
W/R.Lt. hor. = dock open, vessel can leave. No entry.
W.Lt.-G./R. Lt. hor. = dock closed, no entry or departure.

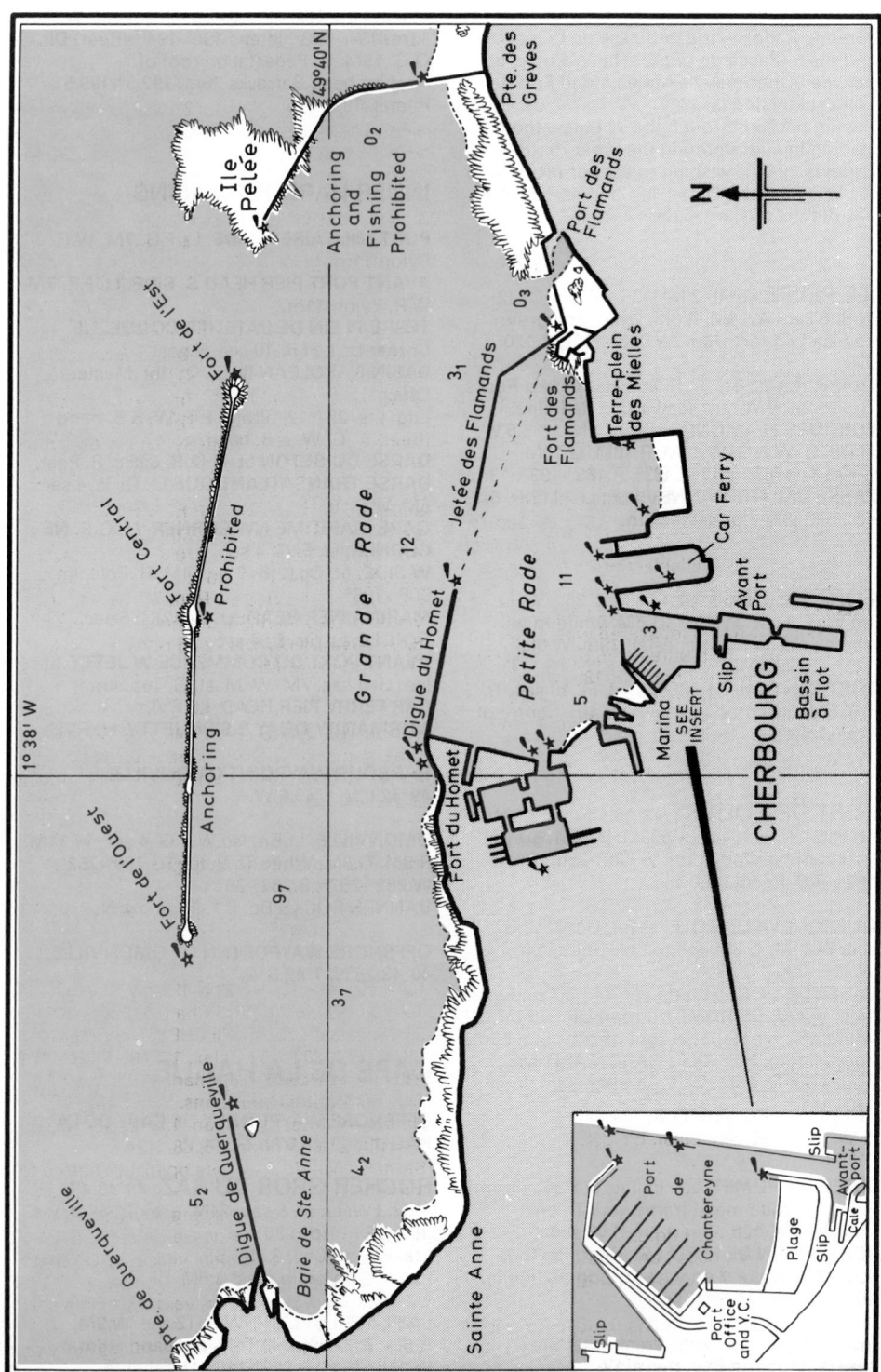

There are two entces. in the Outer Hr. (Grande Rade) — the W (Passe de L'Ouest) and the E (Passe de L'Est.). The W Entce. is between Querqueville Mole Lt. and Fort de L'Ouest Lt. Ldg.Lts. 141°.
Having passed through the W Entce. the leading line for entering the Inner Hr. (Petite Rade) is 124°. If wishing to anchor proceed to the W end of the Outer Hr. Chantereyne Y. Hr. has depths of 1.9m.-3.6m.

ILE PELEE 49°40.2'N, 1°35.1'W. Lt. Oc.(2) W.R. 6 sec. W.11M. R.8M. white and grey pedestal on fort, 18m. W.058°-120°; R.120°-058°.
Tromet Rocks, Bn. Tr. R. and Happetout Rocks, Tripod Bn. R.W. are seaward of Ile Pelee.
FORT DES FLAMONDS. 49°39.1'N, 1°35.6'W. Lt.Dir. Q. W.R.G. W.13M. R.10M. G.10M. G.173.5°-176°; W.176°-183°; R.183°-193°. 13m.
PASSE CABART-DANNEVILLE. Lt. Fl.(2)R. 6 sec. 5M. white pedestal, 5m.

FORT DE L'EST 49°40.3'N, 1°35.9'W. Lt. Iso.W.G. 4 sec. W.10M. G.6M. white metal framework Tr. and pedestal, 19m. W.008°-229°; G.229°-008°.
FORT CENTRAL. Lt. V.Q.(6) + L.Fl. 10 sec. Tr. Y.B. 8M. obscured to seaward, 4m. Centre of breakwater.

FORT DE L'OUEST 49°40.5'N, 1°38.9'W. Lt. Fl.(3) W.R. 15 sec. W.23M. R.19M. grey Tr. R. lantern, on fort, 19m. W.122°-355°; R.355°-122°. R.C. Reed(3) 60 sec.

QUERQUEVILLE MOLE. Lt.Bn. Oc.(3) W.G. 12 sec. W.11M. G.8M. white Col. G. top. 8m. W.120°-290°; G.290°-120°.
PASSE DE L'OUEST. Ldg.Lts. 140°30' and 142°. JETEE DE HOMET (Front) Dir.Q. 14M. white △S on parapet at roof of jetty, 5m. 63m. apart. Intens 138°-144°. **GARE MARITIME** (Rear) Dir. Q. 21M. W. ▽ on Bldg. 23m. Intens. 140°-142.5°.

JETEE DU HOMET. Lts. in line 124°30'. (Front) F.G. 9M. white metal framework Tr. on blockhouse, 10m. Reed(2 + 1) 60 sec.
TERRE-PLEIN DE MIELLES. (Rear) Iso.G. 4 sec. 12M. white ▽ on white tripod, B. bands, 16m. Intens 114.5°-134.5°.

Inside Digue de Homet Breakwater are several Mooring Bys. Barrel W.

Lts. in Line 192° (Front) Dir. Q.G. 14M. W. Col. 11m. 194°-198°. Intens 190°-194°. (Rear) Dir. Q.G. 15M. G. Pedestal on roof of Rochambeau Barracks 26m. 192.5°-199.5°. Intens. 189°-195°.

INNER HARBOUR BASINS

PORT MILITAIRE N SIDE. Lt. F.G. 7M. W.G. Pylon 11m.
AVANT PORT PIER HEAD S. SIDE. Lt. F.R. 7M. W.R. Pylon 11m.
TERRE-PLEIN DE L'ATELIER COQUE. NE **Corner** Lt. L.Fl.R. 10 sec. R post.
BASIN NAPOLEAN III. Lt. Q. Hbr. Masters Office.
Ldg. Lts. 257°12' (Front) F.G. W. △ B. band (Rear) F. G. W. △ B. band.
DARSE DU BETON Lt. Fl.(2)R. 6 sec. R. Post.
DARSE TRANSATLANTIQUE Lt. Oc.R. 4 sec. 5M. W.R. Tr.
GARE MARITIME NW CORNER. Lt. Q.R. **NE CORNER.** Lt. Fl.G. 4 sec.
W SIDE. Lt. Oc.(2)R. 6 sec. 4M. R. Pole 3m. 006°-186°.
MARINA PIER HEAD. Lt. Oc.(2)G. 6 sec.
E MOLE. Lt. Oc. R. 4 sec.
AVANT PORT DU COMMERCE W JETTY. Lt. Iso. G. 4 sec. 7M. W. Mast. G. Top. 4m.
CAR FERRY PIER HEAD. Lt. F.Vi.
NORMANDY QUAY E SIDE JETTY. Lt. F.Vi.

HARBOUR WAYPOINT OMONVILLE. 49°42.0'N, 1°49.6'W.

OMONVILLE. Lt.Bn. Iso.W.R.G. 4 sec. W.11M. R.8M. G.8M. White Tr. R. top. G.180°-252°; W.252°-262°; R.262°-287°.
BANNES ROCKS Bn. B.Y. Topmark N.

OFFSHORE WAYPOINT N OF OMONVILLE. 49°43.25'N, 1°49.5'W.

CAPE DE LA HAGUE

OFFSHORE WAYPOINT N OF CAPE DE LA HAGUE. 49°45.0'N, 1°57.0'W.

ROCHER GROS DU RAZ. 49°43.4'N, 1°57.3'W. Lt. Fl. 5 sec. 24M. grey Tr. 48m. vis. 354°-274°. Horn 30 sec.
Lts. F.R. on Chy. 3.8M. SE.
Lts. F.R. on radio mast 4.5M. SE.

LA PLATE Lt. Fl.(2+1)W.R. 12 sec. W.9M. R.6M. B. octagonal Tr. white band, 18m. W.115°-272°; R.272°-115°. Unreliable.

GOURY Ldg. Lts. 065°12' (Front) Q.R. 7M.R.☐ in W.☐ on pier 4m. (Rear) Q. 12M. W. Pylon 10m. Intens 057°-075°.

ENGLISH CHANNEL

SW CHANNEL LANBY 48°31.7'N, 5°49.1'W. Fl. 4 sec. 20M. R.W. By. 12m. RC Racon.
NE CHANNEL. Lt.By, 48°45.9'N, 5°11.6'W. L.Fl. 10 sec. 8M. RW. By. 9m. Racon. Whis.
CHANNEL. Lt.V. 49°54.4'N, 2°53.7'W. Fl. 15 sec. 25M. R. Hull 12m. RC. Racon. Horn. 20 sec.
E CHANNEL. Lt. By. 49°58.7'N, 2°29.9'W. Fl.Y. 5 sec. Pillar Y. w.a. whis. Racon.
EC1 Lt.By. 50°05.9'N, 1°48.3'W. Fl.Y. 2.5 sec. X on Y. HFP By. Racon. Whis.
EC2 Lt.By. 50°12.1'N, 1°12.4'W. Fl.(4)Y. 15 sec. X on Y. HFP By. Racon. Whis.
EC3 Lt.By. 50°18.3'N, 0°36.1'W. Fl.Y. 5 sec. X on Y. HFP By. Racon. Whis.

CHANNEL ISLANDS

REFER TO 22:63 FOR CHANNEL SEPARATION ROUTE

Situated between the Cherbourg Peninsula on the East, and the Casquets on the West, and extending Southwards into the Gulf of St. Malo, they cover the main islands of Alderney, Guernsey and Jersey, with other islands such as Sark and Herm, which may all be seen in detail on a large scale chart.

Safe berths can be found in St. Peter Port, Guernsey, Alderney and St. Helier, Jersey, with Cherbourg to the NE and St. Malo to the South.

The islands are fascinating but great care is necessary because of the very large rise and fall of tide (6-12m. approx.) and hence a very strong tidal stream at all times, especially in the Race of Alderney (11-12 knots) and, Swinge (8-9 knots).

Large scale charts and navigational knowledge of how to use them are essential. Tidal stream charts of the Channel Islands and Sailing Directions are most necessary. Excellent local sailing directions are available from the yacht clubs.

The relative lessening of Neap Tides should be chosen to visit the Islands if possible and,

clear weather is very necessary for safe navigation. On signs of fog ascertain your position most carefully and if practicable have a good anchorage thought out in advance and anchor in safety while the opportunity occurs. Have ample power available for safety too.

It is frequently advantageous to approach the islands by the Casquets and not the Race of Alderney, though on occasions Cherbourg makes a safe landfall from British waters before entering the islands. Watch the Tidal Stream Charts.

CHANNEL ISLANDS. DOCUMENTATION.

Customs clearance not needed if entering from U.K., but if from France then clear at Alderney, St. Peter Port, St. Helier or Gorey.

Fly Flag 'Q' and await clearance. At St. Peter Port, Customs will come to you by launch.

Passports for all desirable.

Registration for the vessel.

Jersey Tourist & Information Office, 35 Albemarle Street, London W1X 3FB. Tel: 071-493 5278.

Entry by road: Treat as if you are going to or coming from France. Ensure you are properly insured.

Jersey Tourist Information: 0534 78000.

Guernsey Tourist Information: 0481 23552.

Alderney Tourist Information: 0481-82 2994.

CASQUETS

NW TOWER 49°43.4'N, 2°22.7'W. Lt. Fl.(5) 30 sec. 25M. white Tr. 37m. the highest and NW of three Trs. Shown H24. R.C. Racon.
E TOWER Horn.(2) 60 sec.

ALDERNEY C.I.

OFFSHORE WAYPOINT OFF BRAYE HR. 49°44.5'N, 2°12.0'W.

BRAYE HR. 49°44'N, 2°12'W. Tel: (0481) 822620.
Mainbrayce Tel. (0481) 822772. Chan. (M) April-Sept. 0800-2000.

Radio — Port: VHF Chan. 16, 74, 12 0800-2200 daily (summer), 0800-1700 Mon.-Fri. (winter).
Entry: German Jetty demolished, cleared to depth of 4.5m. below datum. Due to tidal streams do not enter Alderney at night without local knowledge. Best to approach from NE. Care taken regarding set and drift due to strong tides. Little Crabby Harbour and Old Harbour dry. Depths 7-2m. on Admiralty Pier. Entry may only be registered at Braye with the Harbour Master (within 2 hours of arrival). Pick up yellow visitors buoys, 4 craft to a buoy. A charge is made. **Do not:** berth at quay, beach in Braye or Saye Bay, land at Longy Bay, land any animal, or moor to breakwater without permission. Keep to speed limit of 4 knots. Yachts late on tide unable to overcome the Race may anchor in Longy Bay and leave LW+2½h for Braye. Anchorages at: Braye, Saye Bay, Corblets Bay, Longy Bay, Telegraph Bay, Hannaine Bay, Platte Saline Bay.

QUENARD POINT 49°43.8'N, 2°09.8'W. Lt. Fl.(4) 15 sec. 18M. white round Tr. B. band,

37m. vis. 085°-027°. Siren(4) 60 sec. In line 111°4' with Chateau a l'Etoc Lt.

CHATEAU A L'ETOC. 49°44.0'N, 2°10.6'W. Lt. Iso. W.R. W.10M. R.7M. W. Col. 20m. R.071.1°-111.1°; W.111.1°-151.1°.

No. 1 Lt.By. Q.G. Conical G.
No. 2 Lt.By. Q.R. Can R.

BRAYE OLD PIER. 49°43.4'N, 2°11.8'W. Ldg.Lts. 215°. (Front) Q. 17M. W. Col. 8m. Intens. 210°-220°. (Rear) Iso. 10 sec. 18M. W. Col. 17m. Intens. 210°-220°.
QUAY HD. Lt. F.Y.

SARK

OFFSHORE WAYPOINT OFF SARK. 49°26.0'N, 2°19.0'W.

Anchorages: About 1½c. N of La Chapelle in 12m.; N of jetty in La Maseline in offshore winds and good weather; off Creux Hr.; 2c.

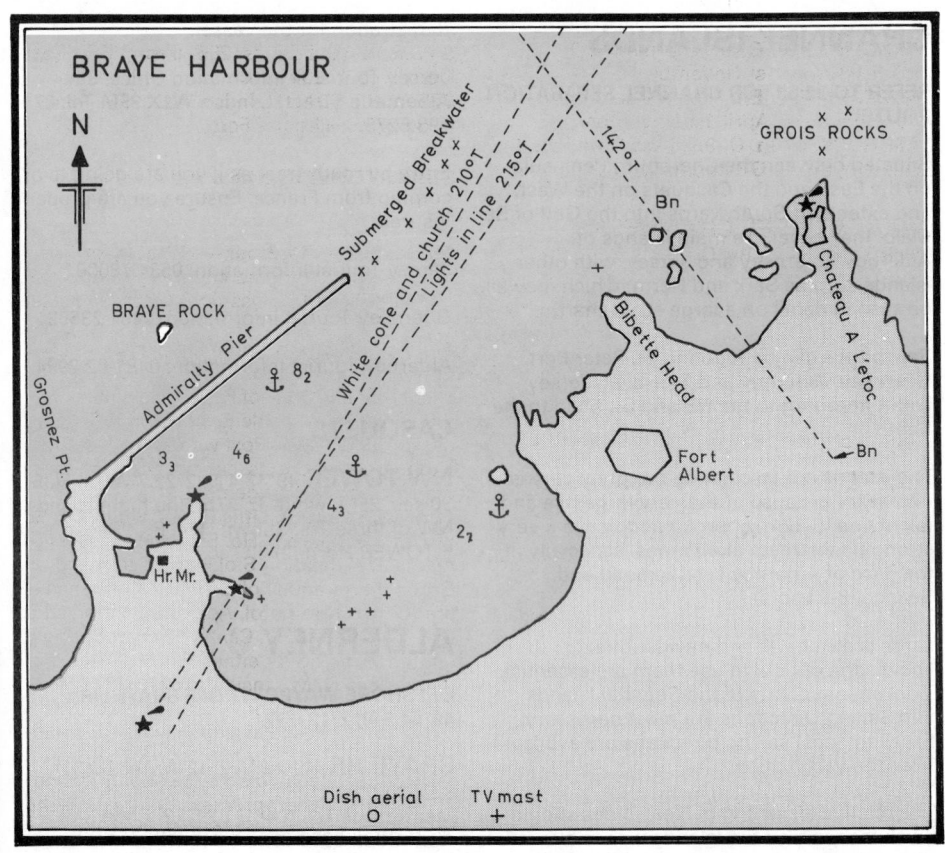

SSE of Point Chateau in 6-10m.; 1½c. N of Moie de Mouton; 2c. NNW & 1c. N of La Pointe de la Joue. Creux Hr. dries at MLWS.

POINT ROBERT 49°26.2'N, 2°20.7'W. Lt. Fl.(2) 5 sec. 18M. white octagonal Tr. 65m. vis. 138°-353°.
Distress sig. Horn(2) 60 sec.
FOUNIAIS. Bn. B.W. Topmark Can. W. "F".
CORBET DUNEZ. Lt. Fl.(4) W.R. 15 sec. 8M. W. Bn. 14m. W.057°-230°; R.230°-057°. Wind Generator nearby.
BIG RUSSEL NOIRE PUTE. Lt. Fl.(2)W. R. 15 sec. 6M. on rock. 8m. W.220°-040°; R.040°-220°.
BLANCHARD. Lt.By. Q.(3) 10 sec. Pillar. B.Y.B. Topmark E. Whis.

HERM
Entry: Speed limit 6 kts. in approaches to Herm. Hr. dries. Anchorage; Belvoir Bay at Neaps. S of Putrainez in NW winds; Rosiere in SW-N-ESE winds.

ALLIGANDE. Lt.Bn. Fl.(3)G. 5 sec. Topmark G. 'A'. Shown 1st April-1st November.
EPEC. Lt.Bn. Fl.G. 3 sec. Topmark G. 'E.' shown 1st April-1st November.
VERMERETTE. Lt.Bn. Fl.(2)Y. 5 sec. Topmark Y. 'V.' Shown 1st April-1st November.
GATE ROCK. Lt.Bn. Q.(9) 15 sec. ⅄ on Y.B. Bn.
GODFREY Bn. G 'GB' topmark.

GREAT RUSSEL CHANNEL
FOURQUIERES. Lt.By. Q. Pillar. BY. Topmark N.

GUERNSEY (C.I.)
RADIO MAST. 49°27.5'N, 2°34.8'W. Lt. F.R. 120m. Obstruction.

PLATTE FOUGERE, N END 49°30.9'N, 2°29.0'W. Lt. Fl.W.R. 10 sec. 16M. B.W. Tr. 15m. R.085°-155°. W.155°-085°. Racon. Nauto one blast ev. 45 sec. Also sounded if Lt. should fail.

OFFSHORE WAYPOINT LITTLE RUSSEL CHAN. 49°30.0'N, 2°29.0'W.

GRANDE ANFROQUE Bn. B.W. Hor. bands. Conspic. also Bn. W. Conspic.
TAUTENAY Lt.Bn. Q.(3)W.R. 6 sec. 7M. B.W. Vert stripes. 7m. W.050°-215°. R.215°-050°.
PETITE CANUPE Lt. Q.(6)+LFl. 15 sec. ⅄ on B. Bn. Y. top.

BEAUCETTE
Beaucette Yacht Marina. (0481) 45000 Chan. M.
Entry: Entrance 18m. wide. Sill dries 2.4m. Entry on Springs approx. 3½ h.-HW-3½ h. Normally depth inside of 1.2m. MLWN. Berths for yachts up to 13.7m. length. For Marina see Section 25.
Ldg.Lts. 276° (Front) F.R. W. Ů R. stripe. (Rear) F.R. R. Ů W. stripe.
PLATTE. Lt. Fl.W.R. 3 sec. W.7M. R.5M. G. conical stone Tr. 6m. R.024°-219°; W.219°-024°.
PETIT CANUPE. Bn. Y.B. Topmark S.
ROUSTEL, S END. Lt. Q. 7M. B.W.cheq. stone Tr. G. lantern, 8m.

ST. SAMPSON HARBOUR
Radio: VHF Chan. 12.
Entry: Hr. and approaches dry to 1c. outside. Entrance 36m. wide, depth 7.3m. at MHWS. 4.9m. to 5.2m. at MHWN.
CROCQ PIER HEAD. Lt. F.R. 5M. R.Col. 11m. 250°-340°. Traffic sig.
N PIER HEAD. Lt. F.G. 5M. on post, 3m. vis. 230°-340°.
S PIER HEAD. Ldg.Lts. 286° (Front) F.R. (Rear) F.G. Clock Tr. 230°-340°.
BREHON SHOAL Lt.Tr. Iso. 4 sec. 9M. 19m. large brown circular Fort.

CURRENT METER. Lt.By. Fl.(5)Y. 20 sec. Sph. Y.

St. Sampson's Harbour — Suitable for vessels up to 76m and 4m draught. Approach difficult owing to cross-tides. Passage ½ cable wide.
Entry signals from South Pier Head, R.Lt. = Entry/Exit prohibited.
Yacht Marina 2 c. S. of Fort Doyle. Entce. marked: (Front) N side R. stripe on W. background. (Rear) Post with W. vert. stripe and R. hor. bands. Lts. can be placed on these marks by prior arrangement.
Approach through Little Russel when 1M. SE of Platte Fougere Lt.Ho. Bring on to leading marks 277°, leading S of Petite Camp and Grune Pierre and N of Grune La Fosse and the rocks off Hometol. Appr. Chan. marked by Bys. Con. B. and By. Can.R. Entry at Springs limited to 3/4 hours either side HW. Tide gauges are placed inside and outside entce. Tide sets across Appr. Chan. but no set within 1 c. of entce. Vessel waiting can anchor NE of entce.
Services available: Inshore Lifeboat, Marine Ambulance, Recompression Centre, Breeches Buoy, Radar Rescue Co-ordination Unit.

GUERNSEY RG STN. 49°26.3'N,
2°35.8'W. Emergency DF Stn. VHF Chan. 16 &
67. Controlled by Guernsey.

ST. PETER PORT 49°27'N, 2°32'W. Tel:
Harbour Office: (0481) 20672. Telex: 4191488.
Marina Office: (0481) 25987.

HARBOUR WAYPOINT. 49°27.25'N, 2°31.25'W.

Radio — Port: VHF Chan. 12. Link call facility
Ch. 62

Signals: R. Lt. shown from Head of White
Rock Pier = Entry/Exit prohibited.
R.Lt. shown from New Jetty = Exit prohibited.
H.M. may permit movement 'against' these
signals at his discretion. All vessels over 13m.

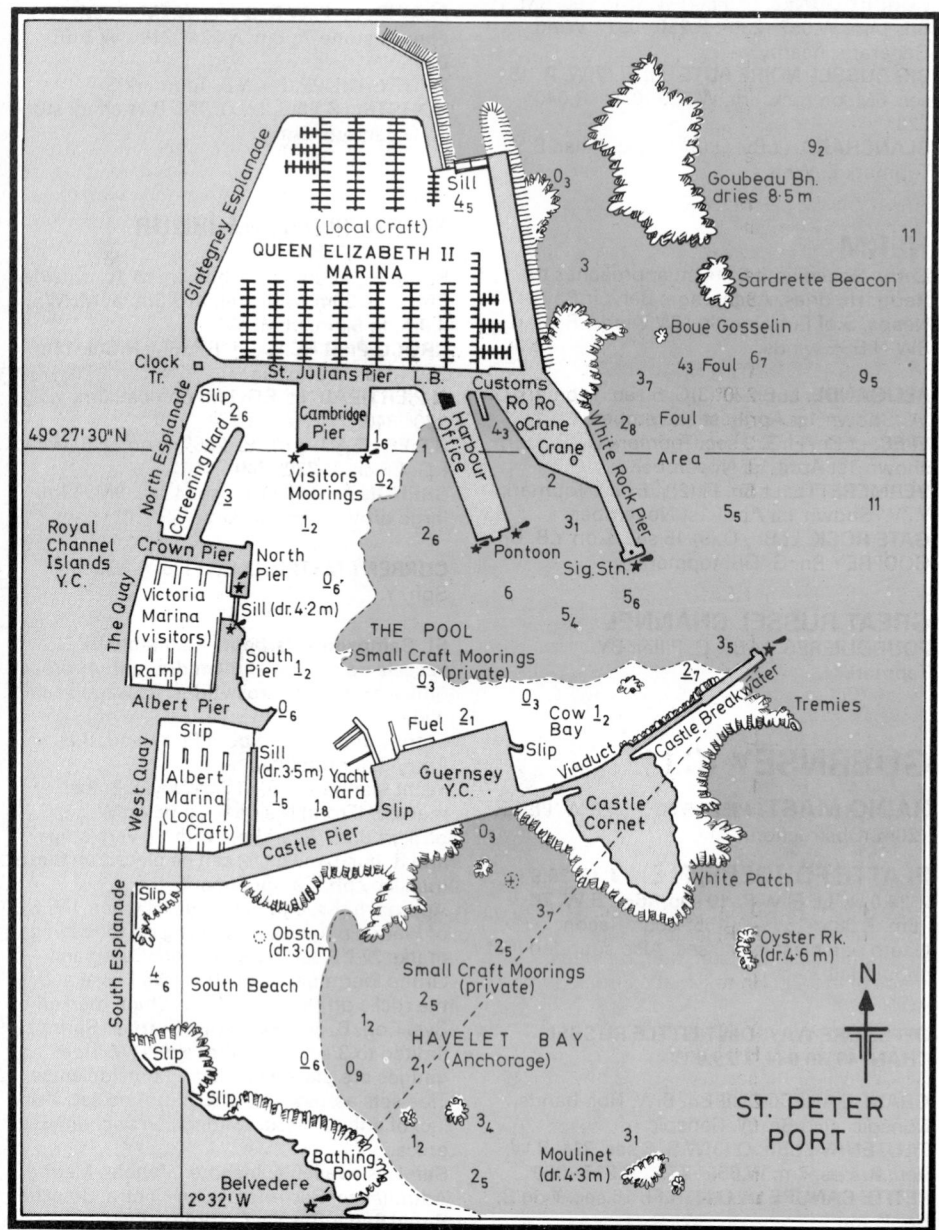

to obtain permission to move via St. Peter Port Radio. Vessels under 13m. in length, except those under sail, are exempt.
Entry: Depths 4.6m. in fairways, 5.4m. to 7.6m. in The Pool. Speed limit 6 kts. in entrance, 4 kts. elsewhere. Visitors moorings on Y, Bys. near Cambridge Pier. Max. draught 8.7m. M.H.W.S.

VICTORIA MARINA (Within St. Peter Port Harbour)
Entry: 2½ h. before — 2 h. after HW. All visitors met by Port Control Dory and advised entry and mooring availability. Contact Port Control (Ch. 12) ½ h. before arrival. Visitors only. 260 berths 13.5m LOA, 1.8m draught. Sill dries 4.1m. Pool: 120 fore and aft moorings, 18m LOA, 2m draught.
Queen Elizabeth II Marina. Used for permanently allocated local berths. No visitors. Local craft 20m LOA, 2.6m draught
Albert Marina. Local craft, 12m LOA, 2m draught. Sill dries 3.8m.

CASTLE BREAKWATER HEAD. 49°27.4′N, 2°31.4′W. Ldg.Lts. 220°. (Front) Al.W.R. 10 sec. 16M. dark round granite Tr. white on NE side, 14m. vis. 187°-007°. Unintens landward. Horn 15 sec. RC. Racon. Belvedere (Rear) Oc. 10 sec. 14M. white □, Or. stripe, on white Tr. 61m. vis. 179°-269°.

WHITE ROCK PIER HEAD. 49°27.4′N, 2°31.6′W. Lt. Oc.G. 5 sec. 14M. round stone Tr. 11m. Intens 174°-354°. Traffic sig.
NEW PIER HEAD. Lt. 2 F.G. 5M. 1m. one at each corner.
Lt. 2 F.G. vert. 7m.
ST. JULIANS EMPLACEMENT, NO: 7 BERTH, E END. Lt. F.G. 1M. on Col. 5m.
W END. Lt. F.G. 1M. on Col. 5m.
OLD HARBOUR, N PIER HEAD. Lt. F.G. 5M. on post, 3m.

SOUTH PIER HEAD. Lt. Oc.R. 5 sec. 14M. white framework Tr. R. lantern, 10m.
A retaining wall has been built between Pier Heads of the Old Hr. to Ht. of 4.2m. above C.D.
GOUBEAU Bn. Tr. Y. (G).
QUEEN ELIZABETH II MARINA. Dir. Lt. 270°. Dir. Oc. W.R.G. 10 sec. 6M. 5m. G.258°-268°; W.268°-272°; R.272°-282°.
RAFFEE. Lt.By. Q.(6) + L.Fl. 15 sec. Pillar Y.B. Topmark S.
Lt. Q.R. Pile R. marks N end of E mole.
Lt. Q.G. Pile G. marks S limit of rocks on N of Fairway.

Entry: Sill gates. Entry and exit via Starboard gate only. Port side gates always show F.R. Starboard gate: F.R. = no entry or exit. F.G. = tide 4.8m ACD gate open. Entry/Exit permitted. F.R./Fl. Amber = gate failed to open, no entry/exit. F.G./Fl. Amber = gates closing.

OFFSHORE WAYPOINT SE OF ST. MARTINS PT. 49°25.0′N, 2°31.0′W.

ST MARTIN'S POINT. 49°25.3′N, 2°31.7′W. Lt. Fl.(3) W.R. 10 sec. 14M. flat-roofed, white concrete building, 15m. R.185°-191°; W.191°-011°; R.011°-081°. Horn(3) 30 sec.
LONGUE PIERRE. Bn. Y. Topmark 'LP'.
LOWER HEADS. Lt.By. Q.(6)+L.Fl. 15 sec. Pillar. Y.B. Topmark S. Bell. E side of S Appr. to Little Russell Chan.

LES HANOIS 49°26.2′N, 2°42.1′W. Lt. Q.(2) 5 sec. 23M. grey round granite Tr. B. lantern, 30m. vis. 294°-237°. Distress sig. Horn(2) 60 sec. 4 F.R.Lts. on masts 1.27M. ESE.

JERSEY (C.I.)

SOREL POINT 49°15.7′N, 2°09.4′W. Lt. Fl.W.R. 7.5 sec. 15M. B.W.cheq. round concrete Tr. 50m. W.095°-112°; R.112°-173°; W.173°-230°; R.230°-269°; W.269°-273°.
Lts. F.R. on radio Tr. 1.25M. ESE.
DEMIE DE FREMONT By. Conical G. ⸎ close N of Rk.
BONNE NUIT BAY. Ldg.Lts. 223°. Pier Head (Front) F.G. 6M. 7m. (Rear) F.G. 6M. 34m.
ROZEL BAY. Dir. Lt. Dir. 245° F.W.R.G. 5M. 11m. G.240°-244°; W.244°-246°; R.246°-250°.
ECREVIERE. Lt.By. Q.(6)+L.Fl. 15 sec. Pillar. Y.B. Topmark S. ⸎ Bell. marks Chan. E of Ecreviere.

ST CATHERINES BREAKWATER HEAD. 49°13.4′N, 2°00.5′W. Lt. Fl. 1.5 sec. 13M. metal frame. Tr. 18m.
Good anchorage inside breakwater head.

GOREY 49°12′N, 2°01′W. Tel: Gorey (0534) 53616.
Radio-Port: VHF Chan. 74. 3 h. before to 3 h. after H.W. Summer only.
Entry: Dries 3m. to 5m. in harbour and at berths. Visitors moorings (dry).

PIER HEAD. Ldg.Lts. 298°. 49°11.9′N, 2°01.3′W. (Front) Oc.R.G. 5 sec. 12M. white metal framework Tr. 8m. R.304°-352°; G.352°-304°. (Rear) Oc.R. 5 sec. 8M. stone wall, 24m.
GOREY ROADS. Lt.By. Q.G. Conical G. ¾M. Pier Head.
GIFFARD By. Can.R. ⌇ close NE of Le Giffard Rk.
COCHON By. Can.R. ⌇ close NE of Cochon Rk.

INSHORE WAYPOINT VIOLET CHANNEL. 49°08.0′N, 1°56.5′W.

VIOLET CHANNEL. Lt.By. L.Fl. 10 sec. Pillar. R.W.V.S. Bell.
CANGER ROCK Lt.By. Q.(9) 15 sec. Pillar. Y.B.Y. Topmark W.

INSHORE WAYPOINT S OF CANGOR RK. 49°07.3′N, 2°00.3′W.

FROUQUIER AUBERT. Lt.By. Q.(6) + L.Fl. 15 sec. Pillar. Y.B. Topmark S.

LA GRÉVE D-AZETTE. 49°10.2′N, 2°05.0′W. Ldg.Lts. 082° (Front) Oc. 5 sec. 14M. R. 〇 W. Tr. 23m. Vis. 034°-129°. **MONTE UBÉ** (Rear) Oc.R. 5 sec. 12M. W. Tr. 46m. Vis. 250°-095°. Racon. Reserve Lt.

OFFSHORE WAYPOINT S OF ST. HELIER. 49°07.25′N, 2°07.0′W.

DEMIE DE PAS 49°09.1′N, 2°06.0′W. Lt. Mo.(D.) W.R. 12 sec. W.14M. R.10M. Y.B. Tr. name on side, 11m. R.130°-303°; W.303°-130°. ⌇ Horn(3) 60 sec. Racon.
HINGUETTE. Lt.By. Fl.(4)R. 15 sec. Can.R. close NE of Hinguette.
EAST ROCK By. Conical G. Q.G.
PLATTE. Lt.Bn. Fl.R. 1.5 sec. 5M. R. metal framework Tr. 6m.

SMALL ROADS
No: 2 Lt.By. Q.R. Can. R.

Ldg.Lts. 023°. 49°10.8′N, 2°06.8′W. **ALBERT PIER ELBOW** (Front) Oc.G. 5 sec. 11M. white bracket and lantern on sea wall, 8m.
ESPLANADE (Rear) Oc.R. 5 sec. 12M. R. 〇 on white framework Tr. 20m. Synchronised with front.

ST. HELIER 49°10′N, 2°07′W. Tel: St. Helier (0534) 34451. Telex: 4192028 PORJER G. Marina Office: (0534) 79549.

HARBOUR WAYPOINT. 49°09.2′N, 2°07.0′W.

Radio — Port/Marina Control: VHF Chan. 14. H24. NOTE: Chan. (80,37) M. NOT used in St. Helier.
Radio — Pilots: VHF Chan. 16, 14.
Entry: Victoria Pier Head.
F.G./Fl.G. Lt. — vessels may enter but no vessel to leave harbour.
F.R./Fl.R. Lt. — vessels may leave but no vessel to enter harbour.
R. and G. Lts. — no vessel to enter or leave unless instructed by radio to do so.
In addition to above an amber Lt. Q. indicates that power driven craft of 25m. in length or under may enter or leave contrary to the other signals displayed at the time. Such craft will keep to starboard side wherever practicable when passing between the Pier Heads. Speed limit 5 knots.
Before entering, leaving or shifting berth, all vessels must contact St. Helier Port Control when other shipping movements will be notified.
Seas break heavily when wind over tide. Heavy overfalls over submerged rocks and banks.
VICTORIA PIER HEAD Bell sounded in answer to vessels' fog sig. Traffic sig.

Ldg.Lts. 078° (Front) F.G. white Col. (Rear) F.G. white col.
YACHT HBR ENTRANCE. Lt.By. Q.R. Can. R. Lt.By. Q.G. Conical G.
BALEINE By. Conical G.
RUAUDIERE ROCK. Lt.By. Fl.G. 3 sec. Conical G. Bell. S of St. Aubin Bay, close NW of Ruaudiere Rk.
DIAMOND ROCK. Lt.By. Fl.(2)R. 6 sec. Can.R. close S of Diamond Rk.

ST AUBIN
Entry: Harbour dries. Visitors berths alongside N Pier. Anchorage E of Platte Rock Bn.

N PIER. 49°11.3′N, 2°09.9′W. Lt. Iso. R. 4 sec. 10M. on Col. 12m.
ST. AUBIN. Dir.Lt. 252°. Dir.F.W.R.G. Sectors, on same structure, 5m. G.246°-251°; W.251°-253°; R.253°-258°.
FORT PIER HEAD. Lt. Fl.(2) Y. 5 sec. 1M. 8m.
LES GRUNES DU PORT By. Can.R. E of Noirmont Pt.
LES FOURS. Lt.By. Q. Pillar. B.Y. Topmark N. 3 cables S of Noirmont Pt.Lt.

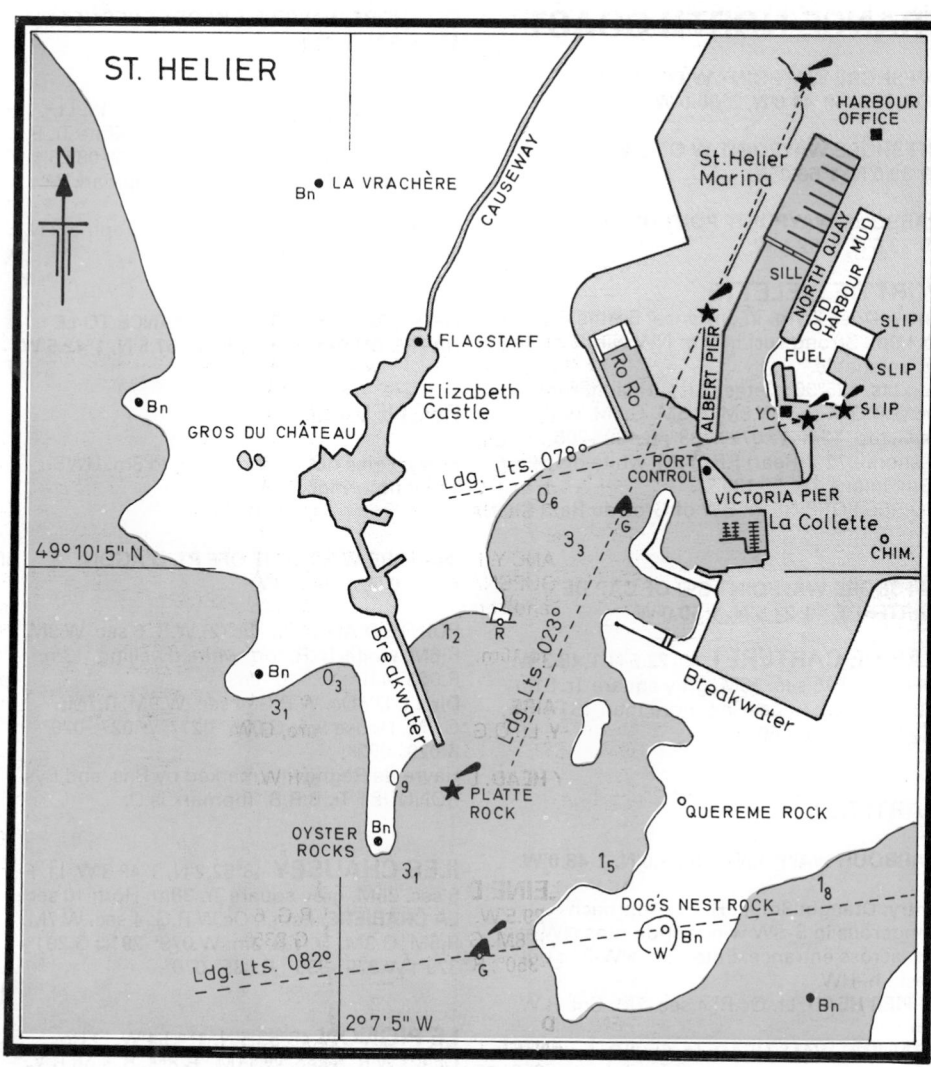

NOIRMONT POINT 49°10.0′N, 2°10.0′W.
Lt. Fl.(4) 12 sec. 13M. B.Tr. white band, 18m.
〰️.
PASSAGE ROCK. Lt.By. V.Q. Pillar. B.Y.
Topmark N. 〰️ Bell. Close NW of Passage Rk.

JERSEY RG STATION. 49°10.9′N
2°14.3′W. Emergency DF Stn. VHF Chan. 16,
82 & 67. Controlled by Jersey Radio.

OFFSHORE WAYPOINT SW OF CORBIERE PT.
49°10.0′N, 2°16.75′W.

LA CORBIERE 49°10.8′N, 2°14.9′W. Lt.
Iso.W.R. 10 sec. W.17M. R.16M. round stone

Tr. 36m. W shore-294°; R.294°-328°; W.328°-
148°; R.148°-shore. Horn Mo.(c) 60 sec. R.C.
Lt.Bn. F.R. vis. 331°-151° except where
obscured by 2 buildings.

OFFSHORE WAYPOINT W OF GROSNEZ PT.
49°15.5′N, 2°17.5′W.

GROSNEZ POINT. 49°15.5′N, 2°14.7′W.
Lt.Ho. Fl.(2) W.R. 15 sec. W.19M. R.17M. white
concrete hut, 50m. W.081°-188°; R.188°-241°.
Obs. elsewhere.
BANC DESORMES. Lt.By. Q.(9) 15 sec. Pillar.
Y.B.Y. Topmark W.

FRANCE NORTH COAST

OFFSHORE WAYPOINT W OF NEZ DE JOBURG. 49°41.0′N, 2°00.0′W.

OFFSHORE WAYPOINT W OF DIELETTE. 49°33.0′N, 1°56.0′W.

HARBOUR WAYPOINT PORT DE DIELETTE. 49°33.5′N, 1°52.5′W.

PORT DE DIELETTE.

Entry: Dries 2.1m. in entrance. Berths dry 4m. to 4.9m. Strong surf in S to NW winds make hr. untenable.
Ldg.Lts. 125°30′. Jetee Ouest Head (Front) Oc.W.R.G. 4 sec. W.8M. R.5M. G.5M. white Tr. G. top, 12m. W.072°-138°; R.138°-206°; G.shore-072°. (Rear) F.R. 11M. white dwelling, 23m. Intens 114.5°-136.5°.
NOIRES FORPINE Tr. SW of Gros du Raz.

OFFSHORE WAYPOINT SW OF CAP DE CARTERET. 49°21.5′N, 1°50.0′W.

CAP DE CARTERET 49°22.5′N 1°48.3′W. Lt. Fl.(2+1) 15 sec. 26M. grey square Tr. 81m. Obscured when bearing more than 161°. Sig.Stn. Horn(3) 60 sec.

CARTERET

HARBOUR WAYPOINT. 49°22.0′N, 1°48.0′W.

Entry: Draught 3m. at HWS. Approach dangerous in S-SW winds. Tide runs NW at 4 kts. across entrance. Enter 2 h.-HW-2 h. but best ½ h.-HW.
W PIER HEAD. Lt. Oc.R. 4 sec. 7M. Col. R.W. 6m.
TRAINING WALL HEAD. Lt. Fl.(2)G. 5 sec. W. mast. G. Top.

OFFSHORE WAYPOINT SW OF PORTBAIL. 49°18.5′N, 1°45.0′W.

PORT DE PORTBAIL

HARBOUR WAYPOINT. 49°18.8′N, 1°43.75′W.

Entry: Entrance dries 6m. Berths on SE side of quay dry ½ tide. Draught 3m. HWS.
Ldg.Lts. 042°. LA CAILLOURIE (Front) Q. 11M. W. Col. R. Top. 14m. (Rear) Q. 9M. white belfry, 20m.
TRAINING WALL HD Lt. Q.(2)R. 5 sec. R.W. mast 5M. 3m.

OFFSHORE WAYPOINT W OF SENEQUET. 49°06.0′N, 1°43.0′W.

LE SENEQUET 49°05.5′N, 1°39.7′W. Lt. Fl.(3) W.R. 12 sec. W.13M. R.10M. white Tr. B. base, 18m. R.083.5°-116.5°; W.116.5°-083.5°.
LE SENEQUET. By. Spar. Y.B.Y. Topmark W.

CHAUSSEE DES BOEUFS Tr. B.Y. Topmark N. Le Boeuf I.

OFFSHORE WAYPOINT ENTRANCE TO LE HAVRE DU REGNEVILLE. 48°57.5′N, 1°42.5′W.

REGNEVILLE

Entry: Dries out. Draught 2m. to 3m. HWS. Yacht moorings.

INSHORE WAYPOINT OFF PT. D'AGON. 49°00.0′N, 1°34.25′W.

POINTE D'AGON Lt. Oc.(2) W.R. 6 sec. W.9M. R.6M. white Tr. R. top, white dwelling, 13m. R.063°-110°; W.110°-063°.
Dir. Lt. Dir.Oc. W.R.G. 4 sec. W.9M; R.7M; G.7M. House 9m. G.025°-027°; W.027°-029°; R.029°-033°.
Havre de Regneville marked by Bns. and Bys.
RONQUET Tr. B.R.B. Topmark Is.D.

ILES CHAUSEY 48°52.2′N, 1°49.3′W. Lt. Fl. 5 sec. 25M. grey square Tr. 38m. Horn 10 sec.
LA CRABIERE. Est.Lt. Oc.W.R.G. 4 sec. W.7M. R.5M. G.3M. Tr. Y.B. 3m. W.079°-291°; G.291°-329°; W.329°-335°; R.335°-079°.

LE PIGNON 48°53.5′N, 1°43.4′W. Lt.Ho. Oc.(2) W.R. 6 sec. W.11M.; R.8M. B. ɵ on B.Y. Tr. R.005°-150°; W.150°-005°.

GRANVILLE 48°50′N 1°36′W. Tel: (33) 50 12 45 & (33) 50 17 75. Telex: Agent 170002. SCAC Granville.

HARBOUR WAYPOINT. 48°49.75′N, 1°36.5′W.

Radio — Port & Pilots: VHF Chan. 12, 16. 1½ h. before to 1 h. after HW.
Marina. VHF Chan. 9.
Herel Yacht Marina. Tel: (33) 50 20 06. Draught MHWN. 4.5m.
Access 3h-HW-3h. Yachts must ensure adequate depth of water over sill. Entry prohibited when Tide Gauge shows zero (0).

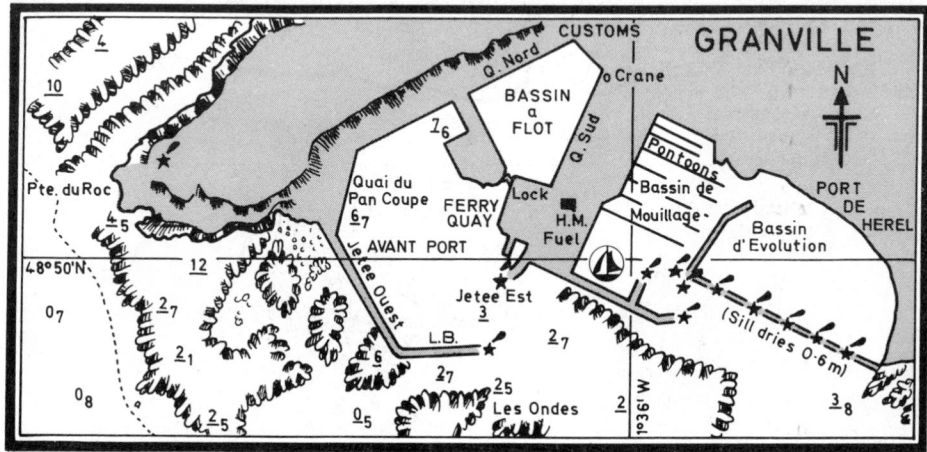

DIGUE PRINCIPALE. HEAD. Lt.Bn. Fl.R. 4 sec. 7M. W.Tr. R. Top. Horn. (2) 40 sec.
SECONDARY MOLE. Lt.Bn. Fl.G. 4 sec.
BASIN ENTRANCE W SIDE. Lt.Bn. Oc.R. 4 sec.
E SIDE. Lt.Bn. Oc.G. 4 sec.

OFFSHORE WAYPOINT W OF PTE DU ROC. 48°50.0′N, 1°38.0′W.

POINTE DU ROC 48°50.1′N, 1°36.8′W. Lt. Fl.(4) 15 sec. 23M. grey Tr. R. top, 49m. Sig.Stn.
TOURELLE FOURCHIE Horn(4) 60 sec.

E JETTY HEAD. Lt. Iso.G. 4 sec. Tr. G.W. 6M. 11m.
W JETTY HEAD. Lt. Iso.R. 4 sec. 6M. R. Tr. 12m.
LE LOUP. Lt. Fl.(2) 6 sec. Tr. B.R.B. Topmark Is.D. 11M.

PIERRE DE HERPIN 48°43.8′N, 1°48.9′W. Lt. Oc.(2) 6 sec. 15M. white Tr. B. top and base, 20m. Siren Mo(N) 60 sec.

CANCALE Lt. Oc.(3)G. 12 sec. 7M. white metal framework Tr. G. top, 12m. Obscured when bearing less than 223°.

OFFSHORE WAYPOINT ST. MALO. 48°41.5′N, 2°08.0′W.

ST. MALO APPROACHES

ST. MALO 48°39′N 2°01′W. Port Captain (99) 81 62 86. Pilots: (99) 81 61 66. Customs: (99) 81 74 56.

HARBOUR WAYPOINT. 48°39.4′N, 2°03.7′W.

Radio — Port: VHF Chan. 12, H24.
Les Sablons Yacht Hbr. VHF Chan. 9 0800-1200, 1400-1700.
Radio — Pilots: MF 2182, 2506, 2321 kHz. VHF Chan. 12, 3½ h.-HW-1½ h.
Signals: Simplified code shown from Ecluse du Naye. Also:
1 long blast = request bridge into Bassin Bouvet to open.
2 long blasts = request bridge into Bassin Duguay-Trouin to open.
Entry: Chenal de la Grande-Porte least depth 5.8m. Chenal de la Petite-Porte least depth 7.2m. Avant port dries in N part. Max. draught 9m.
Large Y. hr. in Anse des Bas-Sablons see section 25. Sill 2m. ACD. Tide Gauge on N side shows depth over sill.
Lock 160m. × 25m. × 1.7m. on sill. Available 2h.-HW-2h.
Arrive not later than HW-1 h.
Traffic Signals (shown N side of lock).

W. Lt-R. Lt.	= Gates open. Do not enter.
W. Lt.-G. Lt.	= Gates open. Do not leave.
W. Lt.-R./G. Lt.	= Gates open. Do not enter or leave.
R./G. Lt-G. Lt.	= No movements. Allow large vessel to enter.
R.-R./G. Lt.	= No movements. Allow large vessel to leave.

Many Bns. mark isolated Rks. at Apprs. to St. Malo. Largest scale charts essential.

LES COURTIS Lt. Fl.(3)G. 12 sec. 8M. Tr. 13m.
LA PLATE. Lt.Bn. V.Q. W.R.G. W.9M. R.6M. G.6M. ⌁ on B.Y. Tr. 11m. W.140°-203; R.203°-210°; W.210°-225°; G.225°-140°.

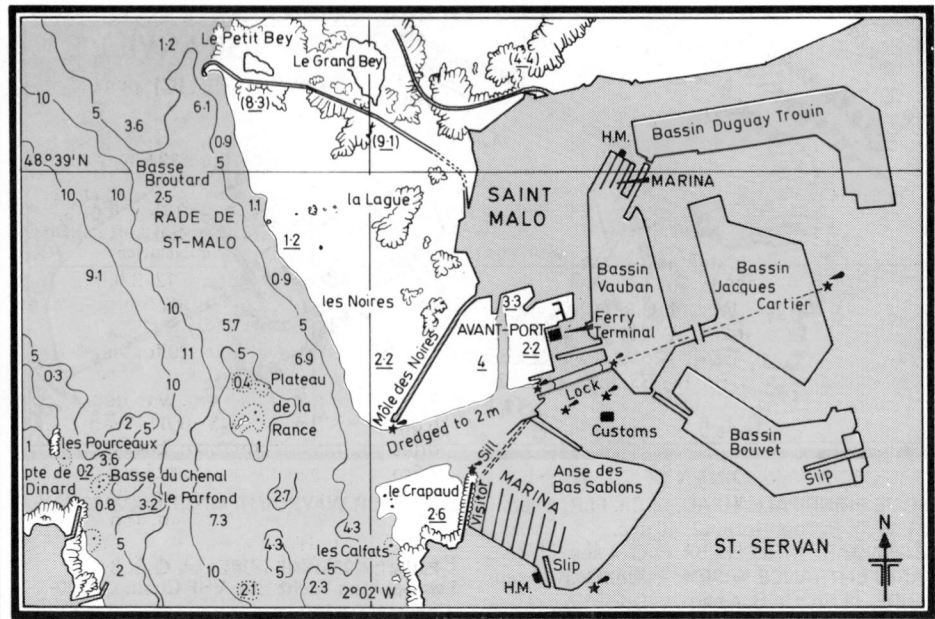

GRAND JARDIN Lt.Ho.
Radio: VHF Chan. 12, 16. 0800-1100, 1300-1700 (Except Sun.) & 1½ h.-HW-1½ h.

LE GRAND JARDIN. 48°40.2'N, 2°05.0'W.
Ldg.Lts. 089°. (Front) Fl.(2)R. 10 sec. 15M. grey Tr. 24m.
In line 130° with La Ballue leads through the Chan. of Petite Port. Obscured by Cap Frehel when bearing less than 097°, by lle de Cezembre 220°-233°, by Grande Conchee 241°-243°, by Grande Chevreun and Pointe du Meinga when bearing more than 251°. R.C.

ROCHEBONNE (Rear) Dir. F.R. 24M. white
square Tr. R. top, 40m. Intens 088.2°-089.7°.
LE BURON. Lt.Bn. Fl.(2)G. 6 sec. 8M. G. Tr. 14m.

MOLE DES NOIRES 48°38.6'N, 2°01.9'W.
Lt.Ho. Fl.R. 5 sec. 13M. Tr. R. 11m. Obscured 155°-159°; 171°-178° and when bearing more than 192°. Horn(2) 20 sec.

Ldg.Lts. 2 F.R. 071° mark axis of lock at Naye, 0.5M. ENE.

LES BAS-SABLONS. 48°38.2'N, 2°01.2'W.
Ldg.Lts. 129°. (Front) Dir. F.G. 16M. white square Tr. B. top, 20m. Intens 127.5°-130.5°.
LA BALLUE. (Rear) Dir. F.G. 25M. grey square Tr. 69m. Intens 127.5°-130.5°.

ECLUSE DU NAYE. Ldg.Lts. 071° (Front) F.R.
6M. Tr. 6m. (Rear) F.R. 8M. W. ○ R. Border on W. Col. 030°-120°.

Ldg.Lts. 071° (Front) F.Vi. W. □ R. stripe (Rear) F.Vi. W. □R. stripe mark S edge of dredged channel.

BAS SABLONS MARINA MOLE. Head. Lt.
Fl.G. 4 sec. 4M. Grey mast 7m.

LA RANCE RIVER
Estuary crossed by barrage. Lock at W end 65m. × 13m. × 2m. on sill. Operates 0430-2030 when tide >4m. Opened on the hour for 15 mins. Arrive 20 min. before the hour. Inform lockkeeper of draught and mast height. Night signal to open lock operates from dolphin nearest lock.
Traffic Signals: Ball/R. Lt. = No entry from N.
Cone ▽ /G. Lt. = no entry from S.
Canal to Rennes 25.8m. × 4.5m. × 1.3m. draught × 2.5m. height.
Entce. marked by Bns. Bn. Trs. and Bys. and Shoals and Rks. in river marked by Bns. and Bys.
Barrel in Fairway.
LA JUMENT. Lt. Fl.(5)G. 20 sec. 4M. G.Tr. 6m.
TIDAL BARRAGE NW WALL. Lt. Fl. G. 4 sec.
NE DOLPHIN. Lt. Fl.(2)R. 6 sec.

SAINT BRIAC
EMBOUCHURE DU FREMUR. 48°37.1'N, 2°08.2'W. Lt.Bn. Dir. 125°. Dir. Iso. W.R.G. 4 sec. W.14M. R.11M. G.11M. Col. 10m. G.121.5°-124.5°; W.124.5°-125.5°; R.125.5°-129.5°.

ST. CAST
Entry: Bay dries. Hr. depths 1m. to dry 2.5m. Y. Club and over 135 berths for yachts.
Lt. Iso. W.G. 4 sec. W.11M. G.8M. G.W. Structure. G. Coast-204°, W.204°-217°, G.217°-233°, W.233°-245°, G.245°-Coast.
LES BOURDINOTS. Bn. B.Y.B. Topmark E.

OFFSHORE WAYPOINT N OF CAP FREHEL. 48°42.0'N, 2°19.0'W.

CAP FREHEL 48°41'N, 2°19.2'W. Lt. Fl.(2) 10 sec. 29M. grey square Tr. 85m. Obscured by Pointe d'Erquy when bearing less than 071°. Siren(2) 60 sec. RC.

HARBOUR WAYPOINT ERQUY. 48°38.0'N, 2°29.5'W.

ERQUY
Entry: Good drying berths on Jetty dry 4m. to 5m. and on Quay dry 6.7m. Part of Hr. reserved for yachts.
MOLE S END Lt. 48°38.1'N, 2°28.8'W. Lt. Oc.(2 + 1) W.R.G. 12 Sec. W.11M. R.9M. G.9M. White Tr. R. top, 10m. R.055°-081°; W.081°-094°; G.094°-111°; W.111°-120°; R.120°-134°.
INNER JETTY HEAD Lt. Fl.R. 2.5 sec. 2M. W. Tr. R. Top. 10m.

OFFSHORE WAYPOINT N OF LA ROHEIN. 48°42.75'N, 2°35.0'W.

ROHEIN Lt. V.Q.(9) 10 sec. 9M. 13m. Tr. Y.B.Y.

INSHORE WAYPOINT NW OF PLATEAU DES JAUNES. 48°37.25'N, 2°35.5'W.

DAHOUET 48°34.9'N, 2°34.3'W.
Entry: Accessible for draughts 4.5m. HWS 2.5m. HWN. New (Outer) Quay dries 5.5m. Old (Inner) Quay dries 7m.
LA PETITE MUETTE Lt. Fl.W.R.G. 4 sec. W.9M. R.6M. G.6M. G. △ W. Tr. 10m. G.055°-114°; W.114°-146°; R.146°-196°. Lt. Fl.(2)G. 6 sec. 156°-286° 240m. SE.

INSHORE WAYPOINT N OF LE LEGUE. 48°34.5'N, 2°41.0'W.

LE LEGUE (ST. BRIEUC) 48°34'N 2°44'W. Tel: (96) 33 35 41.

HARBOUR WAYPOINT. 48°32.5'N, 2°42.5'W.

Radio — Port: C/S Legue Port. VHF Chan. 12, 16. 2 h.-HW-1½ h. Commercial port for St. Brieuc. Depth 4.8m.
Radio — Pilots: VHF Chan. 12. 2 h.-HW-1½ h. Channel is marked by Port & Starboard hand Bys. and Lt.Bys.
100-120 berths available (20 for visitors). 30 ton crane.
Entry: Channel dries 5.6m. with depths of 5.8m. MHWS and 3m. MHWN. Avant port dries 6m. Max. length 80m. Lock 85m. × 14m. × 5m. sill above chart datum. Lock opens — Ht. of tide St. Malo 9-10m. 1 h.-HW-1 h. 10-11m. 1¼ h.-HW-1½ h. 11-11.5m. 1½ h.-HW-1½ h. >11.5m. 2 h.-HW-2 h.
POINT À L'AIGLE JETTY Lt. Q.G. 8M. Tr. G.W. 13m.
CUSTOM HSE JTY. Lt. Iso. G. 4 sec. 7M. G.W. Col. 6m.
TRAHILLIONS Tr. B.Y. Topmark N.

INSHORE WAYPOINT BAIE DE ST. BRIEUC. 48°35.25'N, 2°42.75'W.

HARBOUR WAYPOINT BINIC. 48°36.0'N, 2°48.5'W.

BINIC 48°36.1'N, 2°49'W.
Entry: Avant-port dries 4m. at entrance and 6m. within. Good drying out berths. Best to enter either ½ tide or HW. Dock gate 10.5m. wide × 5.5m. on sill. Gate opened during working hours when tide >9.5m. Depth in dock 5.5m. to 7.5m. Alongside and mooring berths.
Lt. Oc.(3) 12 sec. 11M. white Tr. G. gallery 12m. Unintens. 020°-110°.

HARBOUR WAYPOINT PORTRIEUX. 48°38.75'N, 2°49.0'W.

PORTRIEUX 48°38.8'N, 2°49.4'W.
Entry: Berths dry 3m. to 5m. Max. draught 3.5m. M.H.W.S. to 2.5m. M.H.W.N. Length 47m.

PORT D'ECHOUAGE. MOLE N. HEAD Lt. Fl.G. 2.5 sec. 2M. W.G. Oct. Tr. 11m. Vis. 265°-155°.
MOLE S. HEAD Lt. Fl.R. 2.5 sec. 2M. R.W. Mast 9m.

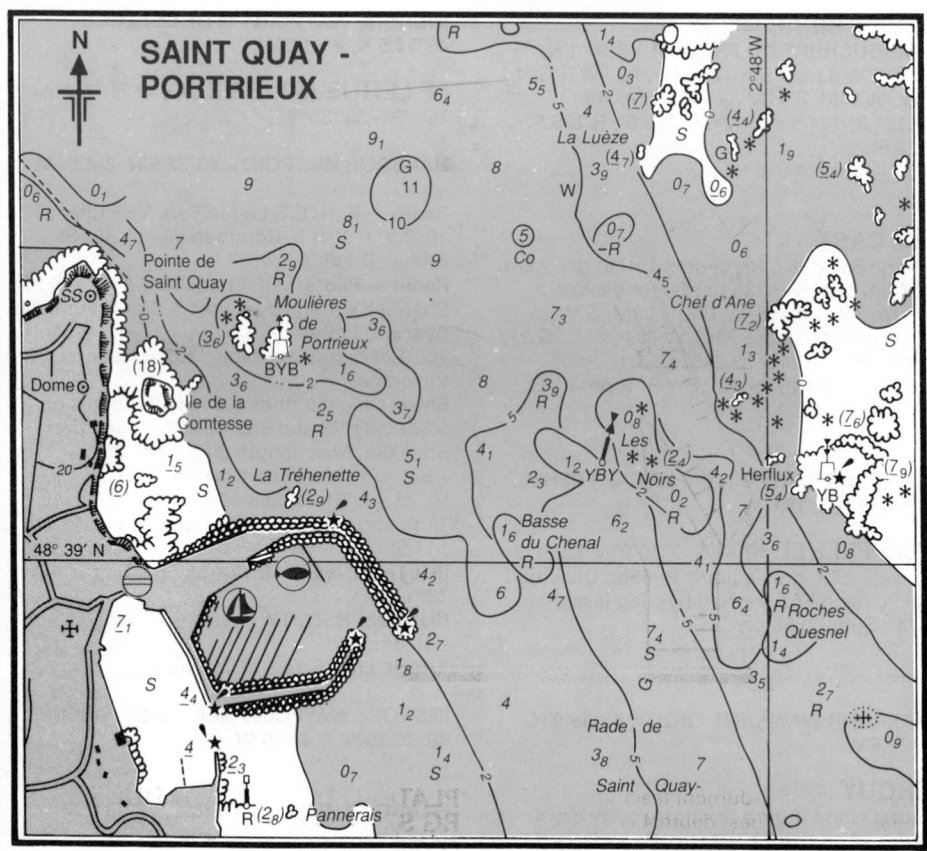

PORT EN EAU PROFONDE. MOLE HEAD Lt.
Fl.(3)G. 12 sec. G. Tr.
ELBOW Lt. 43°39.0′N, 2°49.1′W. Dir Iso.
W.R.G. 4 sec. W.15M. R.11M. G.11M. Concrete
Tr. W.159°-179°; G.179°-316°; W.316°-320.5°;
R.320.5°-159°. Reserve Lt. ranges 12-9M.
MOLE SE HEAD Lt. Ft.(3)R. 12 sec. 2M. R. Tr.

N and S passages through St. Quay Rocks to
Portrieux marked by Bys. Bns. and Trs.

ROCHES DE SAINT QUAY

ILE HARBOUR 48°40′N, 2°48.5′W. Lt.
Oc.(2) W.R.G. 6 sec. W.11M. R.8M. G.8M.
white square Tr. and dwelling, 16m. R.011°-
133°; R.–306°; G.–358°; W.–011°.

HERFLUX Dir. Lt. 130°. Dir. Fl.(2)W.R.G. 6 sec.
W.8M. R.6M. G.6M. ⚑ on B. Y. Tr. G.115°-125°;
W.125°-135°; R.135°-145°.

GRAND LEJON 48°45′N, 2°39.9′W. Lt.
Fl.(5) W.R. 20 sec. W.18M. R.14M. R.Tr. white
bands, 17m. R.015°-058°; W.058°-283°; R.283°-
350°; W.350°-015°. Helicopter landing
platform.
TOUR DE L'EAU Tr. B.W.

OFFSHORE WAYPOINT NE OF PAIMPOL.
48°51.0′N, 2°47.5′W.

ROCHE L'OST-PIC 48°46.8′N, 2°56.5′W. Lt.
Oc. W.R. 4 sec. W.11M. R.8M. white square Tr.
R. top, 20m. W.105°-116°; R.116°-221°;
W.221°-253°; R.253°-291°; W.291°-329°.
Obscured by islets near Brehat when bearing
less than 162°.
LE TAUREAU ROCK Tr. Bn. B.R.B. Topmark
Is.D.

PAIMPOL

INSHORE WAYPOINT OFF PAIMPOL.
48°47.4′N, 2°55.0′W.

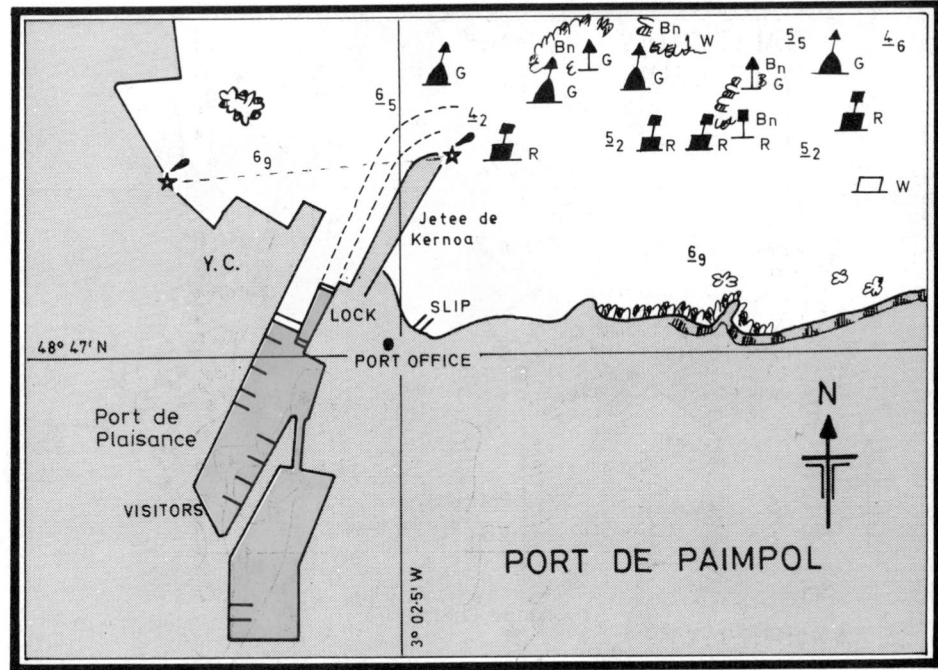

Entry: Chenal de la Jument least depth 1.2m.
Chenal de Brehat least depth 4.5m. Chenal du
Denou least depth 2.8m.
Channel from Rade de Paimpol to hr. dries
4.9m. Avant Port dries 5m. Dock Lock 60m. ×
11m. × 3.5m. outer sill (5m. Inner Sill). Yachts
usually lock in/out 1½ h.-HW-1½ h. Depth in
dock 3m. to 4.6m. Diesel , petrol, water, etc.
available.

POINTE DE PORZ-DON 48°47.5′N,
3°01.6′W. Lt. Oc.(2) W.R. 6 sec. W.15M. R.11M.
white house, 13m. W.269°-272°; R.272°-279°.

JETEE DE KERNOA. Ldg.Lts. 264°. (Front) F.R.
7M. white hut, R. top, 5m. vis. on leading line.
(Rear) F.R. vis. on leading line.

OFFSHORE WAYPOINT N OF LA HORAINE.
48°55.5′N, 2°55.0′W.

LA HORAINE 48°53.5′N, 2°55.3′W. Lt. Fl.(3)
12 sec. 10M. white octagonal Tr. B. diagonal
stripes, 11m.
ROCHE BARNOUIC Lt. V.Q.(3) 5 sec. 9M.
octagonal Tr. B.Y.B. 15m. Topmark E.
Apprs. to Anse de Paimpol marked by Bn. Trs.
and Bys.

PLATEAU DES ROCHES DOUVRES
RG STN. 49°06.5′N, 2°48.8′W. Emergency
DF Stn. VHF Chan. 16, 11.

OFFSHORE WAYPOINT N OF ROCHES
DOUVRES. 49°08.0′N, 2°53.0′W.

ROCHES DOUVRES 49°06.5′N, 2°48.8′W.
Lt. Fl. 5 sec. 29M. pink Tr. on dwelling with G.
roof, 60m. R.C. Siren 60 sec.

LES HEAUX DE BREHAT 48°54.5′N,
3°05.2′W. Lt. Oc.(3) W.R.G. 12 sec. W.15M.
R.12M. G.10M. grey Tr. 48m. R.227°-247°;
W.247°-270°; G.270°-302°; W.302°-227°.
Partially obscured by Ile de Brehat when
bearing more than 302°.

INSHORE WAYPOINT APPROACHES TO
LEZARDRIEUX. 48°51.5′N, 3°01.5′W.

ILE BREHAT

PAON ROCK 48°52′N, 2°59.2′W. Lt.
F.W.R.G. W.11M. R.8M. G.7M. Y. square
concrete framework Tr. on masonry base,
22m. W.033°-078°; G.078°-181°; W.181°-196°;
R.196°-307°; W.307°-316°; R.316°-348°.

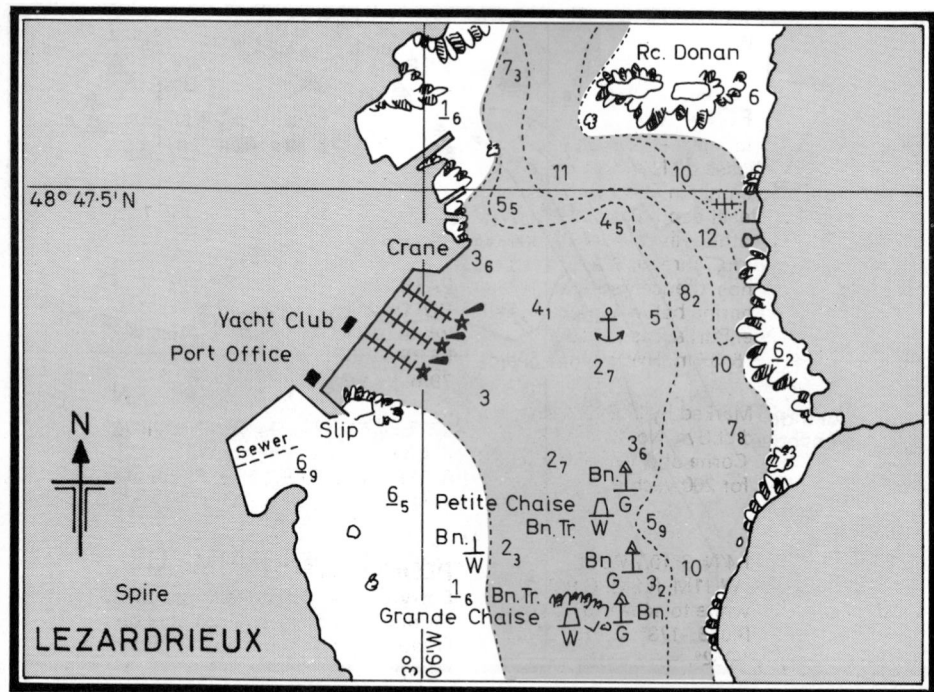

ROSEDO 48°51.5'N, 3°00.3'W. Lt. Fl. 5 sec. 23M. white Tr. 29m.

MEN-JOLIGUET 48°50.2'N, 3°00.2'W. Lt. Iso. W.R.G. 4 sec. W.13M. R.10M. G.8M. Tr. Y.B.Y. 6m. R.255°-279°; W.279°-283°; G.283°-175°.
CHENAL DU FERLAS ROCHE QUINONEC. Lt.Dir. Q.W.R.G. W.11M. R.9M. G.9M. 12m. Grey Col. G.254°-257°; W.257°-257.7°; R.257.7°-260.7°.
EMBOUCHURE DU TRIEUX. Lt. Dir. 271°. Fl.W.R.G. 2 sec. W.11M. R.9M. G.9M. G.267°-270°; W.270°-272°; R.272°-274°.

LE TRIEUX
(Riviere de Portrieux)

Entry: Grand Chenal least depth 6m. to Pointe Coatmer thence 3.2m. to Lezardrieux. Chenal de la Moisie depths <2m. Chenal du Ferlas depths about 2.4m. Lezardrieux draughts 8m. HWS. 6m. HWN. Y. Hr. berths on pontoons depths 1.8m. to 2.5m. also moorings in channel.

Portrieux 6M. above Lezardrieux draughts 4.5m. HWS and 3.2m. HWN. Lock 65m × 12m. x 3.5m. on sill. Lock used when tide <8.8m. otherwise entrance made direct. Gates open (day) 1 h.-HW-1 h. (night) when tide >8.8m. Depth in dock 3.9m.

ROCHER MEN-GRENN Lt. Q.(9) 15 sec. 8M. Tr. Y.B.Y. Topmark ⊠ 7m.

LA CROIX. Ldg.Lts. 225°. (Front) Oc. 4 sec, 19M. 2 Trs. joined 15m. Intens 215°-235°.

BODIC (Rear) Dir. Q. 22M, white house with G. gable, 55m. Intens 221°-229°.

COATMER. Ldg.Lts. 219°, (Front) F.R.G. R.9M. G.8M. white gable, 16m. R.200°-250°; G.250°-053°. (Rear) F.R. 9M. white gable, 50m. Vis. 197°-242°.

LES PERDRIX Lt. Fl.(2)W.G. 6 sec. W.9M. G.6M. G. Tr. 5m. G.165°-197°; W.197°-202.5°; G.202.5°-040°, also 3 × F.Bu. Lts. mark Marina pontoons 0.4M. SSW.

OFFSHORE WAYPOINT LA JUMENT. 48°55.5'N, 3°08.0'W.

OFFSHORE WAYPOINT R. DE TREGUIER.
48°54.75'N, 3°12.5'W.

RIVIERE DE TREGUIER

Entry: Approach channels — Grande Passe least depth 4.4m. Passe du Nord Est least depth 1.4m. but use only in good weather. Passe de la Gaine least depth 0.3m. use only by day, in good weather. River — least depth 3.2m. to Mouillage du Taureau, 2.6m. to Mouillage de Palamos, thence datum to Treguier. Large Y. marina below bridge. Fuel, water, etc. available. Port accessible for draughts 6m. HWS & 3.7m. HWN.

RIVER TREGUIER. Marked by Lt.Bys. No. 1-11, Fl.G. Conical G. and Lt.Bys. No. 2-12. Fl.R. Can.R. between La Corne and Treguier. Yacht Marina at Treguier for 200 yachts.

LA CORNE 48°51.4'N, 3°10.7'W. Lt. Fl.(3)W.R.G. 12 sec. W.11M. R.9M. G.9M. round masonry Tr. white to seaward, R. base, 15m. W.052°-059°; R.059°-173°; G.173°-213°; W.213°-220°; R.220°-052°.

GRANDE-PASSE. Ldg.Lts. 137°. **PORT DE LA CHAINE** (Front) Oc. 4 sec. 12M. white house, 12m. **SAINTE-ANTOINE** (Rear) Dir. Oc.R. 4 sec. 15M. white house, R. roof, 34m. Synchronised with front. Intens 134°-140°.

OFFSHORE WAYPOINT NW OF PORT BLANC.
48°53.25'N, 3°21.0'W.

HARBOUR WAYPOINT PORT BLANC.
48°51.25'N, 3°19.25'W.

PORT BLANC

LE VOLEUR. 48°50.2'N, 3°18.5'W. Lt. Fl. W.R.G. 4 sec. W.11M. R.10M. G.10M. W. Tr. 17m. G.140°-148°; W.148°-152°; R.152°-160°. Entce. to Port Blanc marked by white Tr. in Fairway, 150°, with Moulin de la Comtess (obsc. by trees) in line with white Tr. of Roche de Voleur.

OFFSHORE WAYPOINT NE OF ANSE DE PERROS. 48°52.0'N, 3°28.0'W.

HARBOUR WAYPOINT ANSE DE PERROS.
48°49.5'N, 3°25.25'W.

ANSE DE PERROS

PERROS-GUIREC

Entry: Y. Hr. dock gate 6m. width. Operates 2 h.-HWS-1 h. and 1 h.-HWN. A tide gauge indicates depth over sill.
PASSE DE L'OUEST. (KERJEAN). Lt.Bn. Dir. 143°30'. Dir. Oc.(2 + 1) W.R.G. 12 Sec. W.15M. R.13M. G.13M. W.Tr. Grey Top 78m. G.133.7°-143.2°; W.143.2°-144°; R.144°-154.3°.

PASSE DE L'EST. Ldg.Lts. 224°30'. **LE COLOMBIER** (Front) Dir.Oc.(4) 12 sec. 18M. white house, 28m. Intens 216.5°-232.6°.
KERPRIGENT. (Rear) Dir. Q. 22M. white Tr. 79m. Intens 221°-228°.

JETEE EST (LINKIN) HEAD. Lt. Fl.(2)G. 6 sec. 6M. white Tr. G. top, 4m.
MOLE OUEST HEAD. Lt. Fl.(2)R. 6 sec. 6M. white Tr. R. top, 4m.

PLOUMANACH

Entry: Entrance channel dries. Sill to Pool. Moorings in deep water in pool on trots. Good restaurants but no fuel or facilities except water.
PLOUMANACH 48°50.3'N, 3°29.0'W. Lt. Oc.W.R. 4 sec. W.14M. R.11M. pink square Tr. 26m. W.226°-242°; R.242°-226°. Obscured by Pointe de Tregastel when bearing less than 080°, partially obscured by Sept.-Iles 156°-207°, and by Ile Tome 264°-278°.
OFF PTE. MEAN RUZ Tr.R.
S OF ILE TOME Bn. B. W stripes.

TREGASTEL

Entry: Approx. 1M. W. of Ploumanach. 120 moorings (some visitors), mostly in deep water. 2 slipways available, or land on beach. Shops etc. available in nearby Staunes.

LES SEPT-ILES 48°52.8'N, 3°29.5'W. Lt. Fl.(3) 15 sec. 24M. grey Tr. and dwelling, 59m. Obscured by Ilot Rouzic and E end of Ile Bono 237°-241°, and in Baie de Lannion when bearing less than 039°.

OFFSHORE WAYPOINT CANAL DES SEPT ILES. 48°50.5'N, 3°36.0'W.

LES TRIAGOZ 48°52.3'N, 3°38.8'W. Lt. Oc.(2) W.R. 6 sec. W.15M. R.11M. grey Tr. R. Lantern. 31m. W.010°-339°; R.339°-010°. Obscured in places 258°-268° by Les Sept-Iles.

OFFSHORE WAYPOINT N OF PLATEAU DE LA MELOINE. 48°49.25'N, 3°45.0'W.

INSHORE WAYPOINT BAIE DE LANNION.
48°45.0'N, 3°43.0'W.

**Port de Locquirec and Port de Trebeurden.
See Section 25.**

BEC LEGUER 48°44.4'N, 3°32.9'W. Lt.
Oc.(4) W.R.G. 12 sec. W.12M. R.9M. G.8M. W
face of white house, R. lantern, 60m. G.007°-
084°; W.084°-098°; R.098°-129°.
Mouth of River to Lannion marked by R.Trs.
and R.Bns.
KINIERBEL Bn. B.W.
PTE. DE BIHIT Bn. B.

HARBOUR WAYPOINT RIVIERE DE LANNION.
48°44.5'N, 3°35.0'W.

LE YANDET
Entry: At entrance to Lannion River. Ample
water. Slipway. Steep climb to village. Good
restaurants. No facilities

LOCQUEMEAU
Entry: Only suitable for craft able to take
ground. Dries at LW. Poor holding ground.
Quay reserved for fishing boats.
LOCQUEMEAU. Ldg.Lts. 121° (Front) F.R. 6M.
white metal framework Tr. R. top, 21m. vis.
068°-228°. (Rear) Oc.(2 + 1)R. 12 sec. 7M.
white gabled house, 7m. Vis. 016°-232°.

INSHORE WAYPOINT BAIE DE MORLAIX.
48°44.0'N, 3°51.5'W.

ANSE DE PRIMEL. Ldg.Lts. 152° (Front) F.R.
5M. white □, R. stripe, on framework Tr. 35m.
vis. 134°-168°. (Rear) F.R. 5M. white □,
R. stripe, 56m.

PRIMEL
Entry: Busy fishing harbour. Use visitor's
moorings marked "Passager". Sufficient
water at Neaps. Some shops and
restaurants/bars.

HARBOUR WAYPOINT. 48°43.0'N, 3°49.9'W.

JETTY HEAD. Lt.Bn. Fl.G. 4 sec. W. Col. G.
top.

HARBOUR WAYPOINT RIVIERE MORLAIX.
48°41.6'N, 3°53.8'W.

MORLAIX
Entry: Baie de Morlaix. Grand Chenal least
depth 2m. Chenal Ouest de Richard least depth
5.8m. but due to tides do not use at night.

La Penze Riviere channel 1.5m. but dangerous.
Penpoul — Y. Hr. dries. Anchorage W of end
of slipway.
Morlaix — River dries 3.6m. (draughts 3m.
Neaps 5m. Springs) Avant Port dries
generally 3m.
Lock normally operates 1h.30min.-HW-1h but
exceptionally outside these times if more
than 2.5m over the sill.
Y. Berths at S end of dock. Tel: (98) 88-01-01.
Riviere de St. Pol marked by Bns. and Bn.Trs.
in Fairway.

ILE NOIRE. Ldg.Lts. 190°30' (Front) Oc.(2)
W.R.G. 6 sec. W.11M. R.8M. G.8M. white
square Tr. R. top, 15m. G.051°-135°; R.135°-
211°; W.211°-051°.

ILE LOUET. Ldg.Lts. 176° (Front) Oc.(3) W.G.
12 sec. W.13M. G.9M. white square Tr. 17m.
W.305°-244°; G.244°-305°; Vis. 139°-223° from
off shore, except where obscured by islands.
LA LANDE. 48°38.2'N, 3°53.1'W. (Rear) Fl. 5
sec. 23M. white square Tr. B. top, 85m.
Obscured by Pointe Annelouesten when
bearing more than 204°. Common rear.

LA MENK Lt. Q(9) W.R. 15 sec. W5M. R3M. ⅄
on Y.B. Tr. 6m.

INSHORE WAYPOINT GRAND CHENAL.
48°45.0'N, 3°55.0'W.

PORT DE ROSCOFF BLOSCON
JETTY. Lt. Fl.W.G. 4 sec. W.11M. G.8M. White
Col. G. top. W.210°-220°; G.220°-210°. R.C.

AR-CHADEN 48°44'N, 3°58.3'W. Lt. Q.(6) +
L.Fl.W.R. 15 sec. W.8M. R.5M. Tr. Y.B.
Topmark S. 12m. R.262°-288°; W.288°-294°;
R.294°-326°; W.326°-110°.

MEN-GUEN BRAS 48°43.8'N, 3°58.1'W.
Lt. Q.W.R.G. W.9M. R.6M. G.6M. Tr. B.Y.
Topmark N. 14m. W.068°-073°; R.073°-197°;
W.197°-257°; G257°-068°.

ROSCOFF. 48°43'N 3°58'W. Tel: 69 19 59.
Pilots: (98) 69 73 07. (Home). H.M. Bloscon
(98) 61 27 84. Vieux Port: (98) 69 76 37.
Customs: 61 27 86. Yacht Club 69 72 79.

HARBOUR WAYPOINT. 48°44.0'N, 3°58.0'W.

Radio — Ports and Pilots: VHF Chan. 12, 16. Hrs. May-Aug. 0700-1200; 1300-2200. Sept.-April 0800-1200, 1400-1800.
Entry: Old Harbour dries. Port de Bloscon depth 8m. RoRo Port.

ASTAN SHOAL Lt.By. V.Q.(3) 5 sec. Pillar. B.Y.B. Topmark E. Whis. E. of Ile de Batz.

Channel between Ile de Batz and mainland has B.Bns. on S side and R. OZBns. or Trs. on N side. Some have stripes and topmarks.

NW MOLE 48°43.6′N, 3°58.6′W. Ldg.Lts. 209°. (Front) Oc.(2 + 1) G.12 sec. 6M. white □, B. stripe, on white Col. G. top, 7m. vis. 078°-318°. (Rear) Oc.(2 + 1) 12 sec. 15M. grey square Tr. white on NE side, 24m. Synchronised with front. Vis. 062°-242°.
JETTY HD. Lt. F.Vi. 1M. W Purple Col. 5m.

OFFSHORE WAYPOINT N OF ILE DE BATZ. 48°47.0′N, 4°02.0′W.

PORTZ KERNOCH
Entry: Large harbour. Dries completely. Suitable only for craft able to take ground. Firm sand. Good shops.

ILE DE BATZ 48°44.8′N, 4°01.6′W. Lt. Fl.(4) 25 sec. 23M. grey Tr. 69m.
Auxiliary Lt. same structure, F.R. 7M. 66m. vis. 024°-059°.
SLIP Lt. V.Q.(6) + L.Fl. 10 sec. 6M. B.Y. Bn. 12m. Head of E Breakwater.

HARBOUR WAYPOINT MOGUERIEC. 48°43.0′N, 4°05.25′W.

PORT DE MOGUÉRIEC. Ldg.Lts. 162° (Front) Iso.W.G. 4 sec. W.11M. G.6M. White Tr. G. top W.158°-166°; G.166°-158°. (Rear) F.G. 7M. 22m. W. Col. G. top. Vis. 142°-182°.

OFFSHORE WAYPOINT N OF PONTUSVAL. 48°43.5′N, 4°19.25′W.

HARBOUR WAYPOINT PONTUSVAL. 48°41.0′N, 4°19.25′W.

PONTUSVAL 48°40.7′N, 4°20.8′W. Lt. Oc.(3) W.R. 12 sec. W.10M. R.7M. white square Tr. B. top, white dwelling, 16m. W. shore-056°; R.056°-096°. W.096°-shore. Q.Y & F.R.Lts. on Trs. 2.4M. S.
OFF PTE. DU PONTUSVAL Bn. B. in line with steeple of Plouneour Church 177°.

OFFSHORE WAYPOINT N OF ILE VIERGE. 48°40.75′N, 4°33.75′W.

ILE-VIERGE 48°38.4′N, 4°34.1′W. Lt. Fl. 5 sec. 29M. grey Tr. 77m. Siren 60 sec. R.C.

OFFSHORE WAYPOINT W OF LIBENTER SHOAL. 48°37.5′N, 4°39.0′W.

RIVIERE L' ABERVRACH. Tel: H.M. 04 91 62. Customs: 04 90 27. Y.C. 04 92 60.

HARBOUR WAYPOINT ENTRANCE TO L'ABERVRACH. 48°37.0′N, 4°35.7′W.

LE LIBENTER. 48°37.5′N, 4°38.4′W. Lt.By. Q.(9) 15 sec. 8M. Pillar. Y.B.Y. Topmark W. 8m. Whis. Marks Libenter Shoal.
Advisable to positively identify this buoy as Ldg.Lts. for Grand Chenal lie to the southward.
Grand Chenal de L'Abervrach marked by Bns. Port de L'Abervrach. Grand Chenal least depth 4.7m. decreasing to 3m. Chenal de la Pendante least depth 0.3m. Chenal de la Malouine least depth 3m. Good drying berths on E side of Mole dries 4.5m. Y. Hr. — pontoons and moorings least depth 2m. also anchorage. Fuel, water, provisions available.

1st Ldg.Lts. 100°. **ILE VRACH** (Front) Q. R. 7M. white square Tr. R.top white dwelling, 20m.
LANVAON (Rear) Dir. Q. 10M. grey square Tr. white on W side, 55m. Intens 090.5°-110.5°.

N BREAKWATER. N SIDE. 48°35.9′N, 4°33.9′W. Dir.Lts. 128°. Dir. Oc.(2) W.R.G. 6 sec. W.13M. R.11M. G.11M. W. structure. 9m. G.125.7°-127.2°; W.127.2°-128.7°; R.128.7°-130.2° and Bns. R.W.
BREAC'H VER. Lt. Fl.G. 2.5 sec. 4M. G. △ on Bn. 6m.

OFFSHORE WAYPOINT WNW OF CORN CARHAI. 48°35.5′N, 4°46.5′W.

CORN-CARHAI Lt. Fl.(3) 12 sec. 9M. white octagonal Tr. B. top, 17m.

HARBOUR WAYPOINT PORTSALL. 48°33.75′N, 4°45.75′W.

PORTSALL. 48°33.9′N, 4°42.3′W. Lt.Bn. Oc.(3+1) W.R.G. 12 sec. W.16M. R.13M. G.13M. white Col. R. top. 9m. G.058°-084°; W.084°-088°; R.088°-058°.

FRANCE WEST COAST

STIFF POINT 48°28.5'N, 5°03.4'W. Lt.
Fl.(2)R. 20 sec. 25M. two adjoining white Trs.
85m. Traffic Control Stn. Ldg.Lts. 293°30' with
Trezien Lt.

PORT DU STIFF. 48°28.2'N, 5°03.2'W.
MOLE ESTE. Lt. Q. W.R.G. W.10M. R.7M.
G.7M. W. Tr. G. Top 11m. G.251°-254°; W.254°-
264°; R.264°-267°.

CREACH 48°27.6'N, 5°07.8'W. Lt. Fl.(2) 10
sec. 33M. white Tr. B. bands, 70m. Obscured
247°-255°. R.C. Horn(2) 120 sec. Racon.

OFFSHORE WAYPOINT OFF USHANT.
48°36.0'N, 5°00.0'W.

CREACH POINT RG STN. 48°27.6'N,
5°07.8'W. Emergency DF Stn. VHF Chan. 16, 11.

NIVIDIC ROCK. Lt. V.Q.(9) 10 sec. 9M. W. Tr.
R bands. 28m. Obscured by Ouessant 225°-
290°. Unreliable. Helicopter landing platform.

OUESSANT (USHANT) Tel: (98) 89 31
31. Telex: 940086 CROCO A.
Vessel Traffic Management System.
Mandatory system including Yachts covering
Ushant separation scheme and Inshore Zone,
Chenal du Four, Chenal de la Helle, Passage
du Fromveur, Raz de Sein. Maintain listening
watch VHF Chan. 16.
Vessels permitted to use Inshore Zone
channels i.e. pleasure craft, report identity on
Chan. 16.
Ushant Control Centre. VHF Chan. 16, 13, 11.
MF 2182, 2677 kHz. H24. Also Chan. 68, 69,
79, 80. When 11 and 13 busy. SAR
Coordination 122.025 MHz. Infor. broadcasts
in English H+20, H+50 on Chan. 11. Shipping
and Safety Msgs. Inshore Zone and Passage
du Fromveur. Weather Msgs at 0150, 0450,
0750, 1050, 1350, 1650, 1950, 2250. Manche
Ouest, Ouest Bretagne, Nord Gascogne. Fog
Warnings ev. H+10 & H+40 when vis. <2M.
Saint Mathieu. VHF Chan. 16. Chenal de la
Helle or Chenal du Four. In emergency or
poor visibility radar assistance for small craft
in the Chenal du Four on Chan. 16. Working
Chan. 12.
Pointe du Raz. VHF Chan. 16 Raz de Sein.

LE STIFF SIGNAL & RADAR STN. c/s LE STIFF
VHF Chan. 16.

CROSSCO SAR STN. 48°25'N, 4°48'W.
Weather Msgs. Chan. 13 at 0900, 1600, 1900.
For Manche Ouest, Ouest Bretagne & Nord
Gascogne and at 0800, 1515, 1630, 1915, 1930
for Ile de Batz and Mont St. Michel.

LA JUMENT 48°25.4'N, 5°08.1'W. Lt.
Fl.(3)R. 15 sec. 22M. grey octagonal Tr. R. top,
36m. Obscured by Ouessant 199°-241°.
Danger sig. Horn (3) 60 sec.

PIERRE-VERTES LANBY. V.Q.(9) 10 sec. 8M.
9m. X on B.Y. By. Whis. ⌇⌇.

KEREON (MEN-TENSEL) 48°26.3'N,
5°01.6'W. Lt. Oc. (2 + 1)W.R. 24 sec. W.17M.
R.13M. grey Tr. 38m. W.019°-248°; R.248°-
019°. Danger sig. Siren (2 + 1) 120 sec.
MEN-KORN. Lt. V.Q.(3)W.R. 5 sec. 8M. B.Y.B.
Tr. Topmark E. 21m. W.145°-040°; R.040°-145°.

CHENAL DU FOUR (NORTH PART)

MARINE FARMS are established in this area.
Consult chart for details.

OFFSHORE WAYPOINT LE FOUR. 48°31.5'N,
4°49.25'W.

LE FOUR 48°31.4'N, 4°48.3'W. Lt. Fl.(5) 15
sec. 18M. grey Tr. 28m. Danger sig. Siren (3+2)
75 sec.

**OFFSHORE WAYPOINT CHENAL DE
L'ABERILDUT.** 48°28.0'N, 4°49.25'W.

HARBOUR WAYPOINT L'ANILDUT.
48°28.25'N, 4°47.0'W.

Entry: L'Aberildut. Bar depth 2m. Narrow
channel in middle has depths of 4.5m.

L'ABERILDUT 48°28.3'N, 4°45.6'W. Lt. Dir.
Oc.(2) W.R. 6 sec. W.25M. R.20M. white
buildings, 12m. W.081°-085°; R.085°-087°.
VALBELLE LANBY. FL.(2)R. 6 sec. 5M. 8m. R. ▯
on R. By. Whis.
LES PLATRESSES Lt. Fl.R.G. 4 sec. 5M. Tr. W.
17m. R.343°-153°; G.153°-333°.

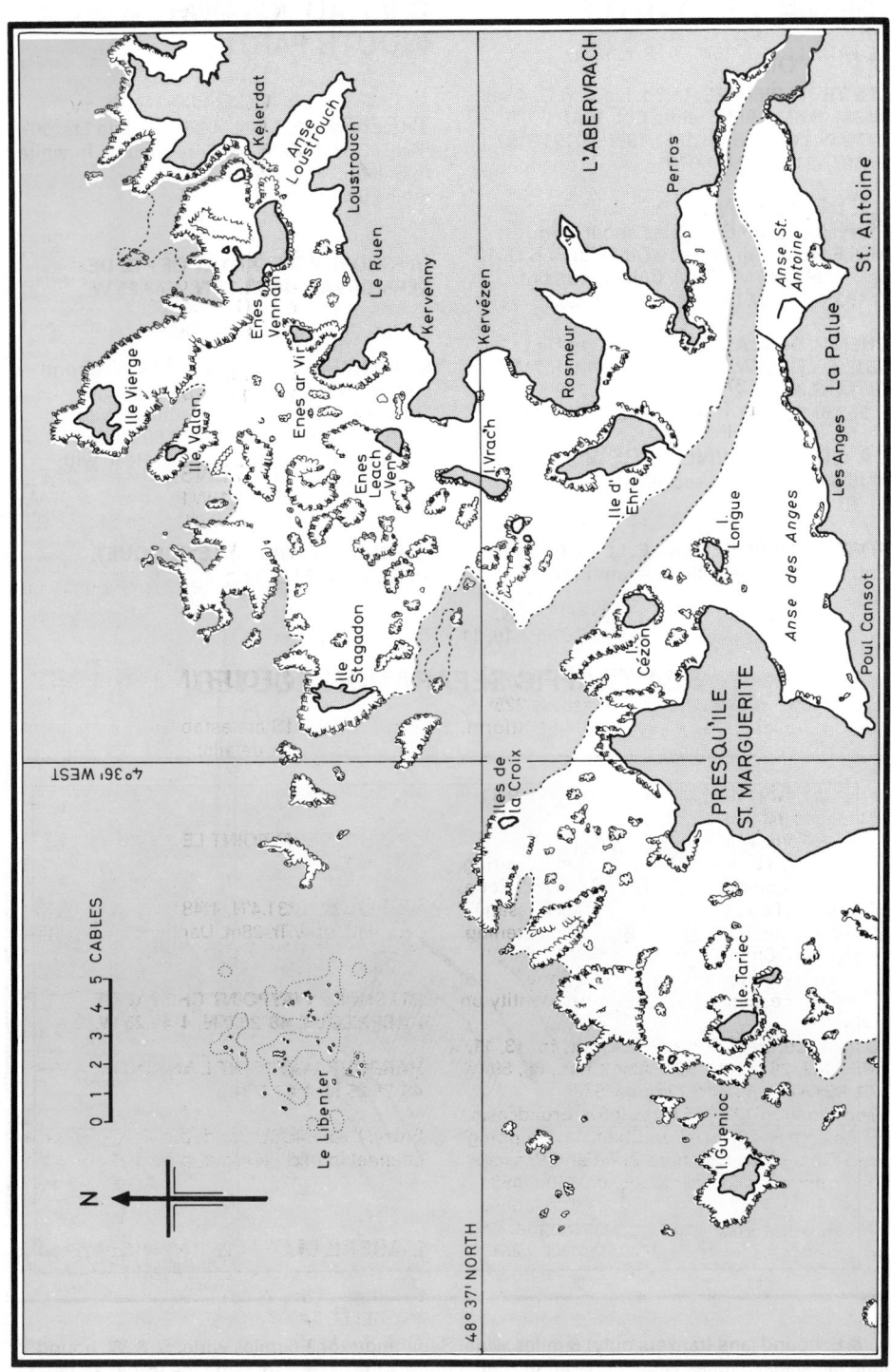

CHENAL DE LA HELLE

LE FAIX. Lt. V.Q. 10M. Tr. B.Y. 18m.

LES TROIS-PIERRES. Lt.Bn. Iso.W.R.G. 4 sec. W.9M. R.6M. G.6M. white Col. 15m. G.070°-147°; W.147°-185°; R.185°-191°; G.191°-197°; W.197°-213°; R.213°-070°.

ILE DE MOLENE

Entry: Ile de Molene. Dries about 1.5m.
MOLE HEAD. Dir.Lt. 191°. Dir.Fl.(3) W.R.G. 12 sec. W.9M. R.7M. G.7M. Col. on hut, 6m. G.183°-190°; W.190°-192°; R.192°-203°.

CHENAL DES LAS. Same structure Dir.Lt. 261°. Dir.Fl.(2) W.R.G. 6 sec. W.9M. R.7M. G.7M. G.252.5°-259.5°; W.259.5°-262.5°; R.262.5°-269.5°.

LA GRANDE VINOTIERE 48°22.0′N, 4°48.5′W.Lt. Oc.R. 6 sec. 8M. R. octagonal Tr. 15m.

PORT DU CONQUET MOLE. Lt. Oc.G. 4 sec.
Entry: Berths available in Avant Port.

CHENAL DU FOUR (SOUTH PART)

TREZIEN 48°25.4′N, 4°46.8′W. Ldg.Lts. 007° (Rear) Dir.Oc.(2) 6 sec. Grey circular Tr. white to S. 84m.
Intens 003°-011°.

OFFSHORE WAYPOINT W OF PTE DE KERMORVAN. 48°21.75′N, 4°49.25′W.

KERMORVAN. 48°21.7′N, 4°47.4′W. (Front) Fl. 5 sec. 22M. white square Tr. 20m. Obscured by Pte. de St. Mathieu when bearing less than 341°. Reed 60 sec. Front Ldg.Lt. 137.5° for Chenal de la Helle with Lochrist Lt.

HARBOUR WAYPOINT LE CONQUET. 48°21.5′N, 4°47.25′W.

SEA TRAFFIC SEPARATION ROUTES

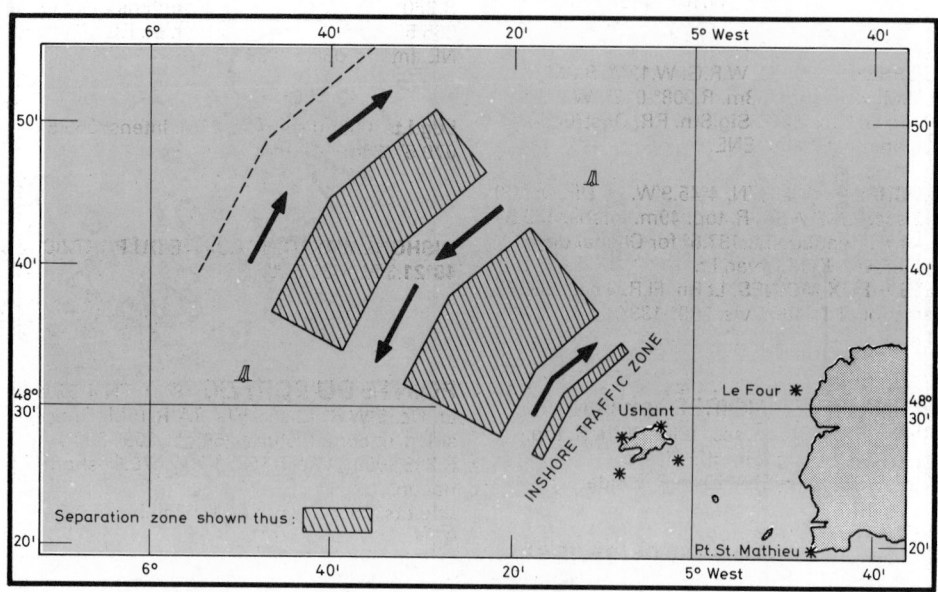

N. & E. bound lane (tankers only) 6 miles wide. Separation zone 6 miles wide. S. & W. bound lane (all ships) 5 miles wide. Separation zone 8 miles wide. N. & E. bound lane (other ships) 3 miles wide. Separation zone 1 mile wide borders Inshore Traffic Zone.

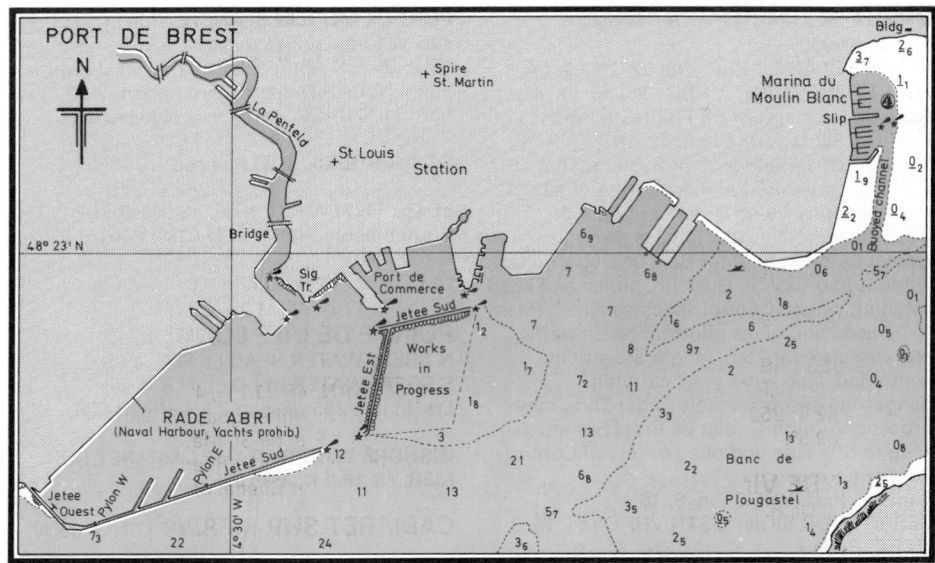

POINTE DE ST MATHIEU. 48°19.8′N, 4°46.3′W.
Ldg.Lts. 158°30′. With Kermorvan. (Rear) Fl.
15 sec. 29M. white Tr. R. top. 56m. Dir. F. 28M.
54m. Intens 157.5°-159.5°. R.C.
Lts. F.R. on radio mast 1.65M. ENE.

Lt.Bn. Q. W.R.G. W.14M. R.11M. G.11M. white
Tr. 26m. G.085°-107°; W.107°-116°; R.116°-
134°.

CORSEN. Lt. Dir.Q. W.R.G. W.12M. R.8M.
G.8M. white hut, 33m. R.008°-012°; W.012°-
015°; G. 015°-021°. Sig.Stn. F.R., Obstruction
Lt. on mast 400m. ENE.

LOCHRIST. 48°20.6′N, 4°45.9′W. Lt. Dir. Oc. (3)
12 sec. 22M. W. Tr. R. top, 49m. Intens. 135.5°-
140.5°. Rear Ldg.Lt. 137.5° for Chenal de la
Helle with Kermorvan Lt.
LES VIEUX-MOINES. Lt.Bn. Fl.R. 4 sec. 5M. R.
octagonal Tr. 16m. vis. 280°-133°.

LES PIERRES NOIRES 48°18.7′N,
4°54.9′W. Lt. Fl.R. 5 sec. 18M. W. Tr. R. top,
27m. Danger sig. Siren(2) 60 sec.
OFF BENIGUET ISLAND Tr. R. E side.

**OFFSHORE WAYPOINT SSE OF PTE DE ST.
MATHIEU.** 48°18.0′N, 4°45.5′W.

INSHORE WAYPOINT GOULET DE BREST.
48°18.0′N, 4°40.0′W.

GOULET DE BREST

POINTE DU PETIT MINOU 48°20.2′N
4°36.9′W. Lt. Fl.(2)W.R. 6 sec. W.19M. R.15M.
Grey round Tr. W. on SW side. R. Top. 32m.
W.070.5°-Shore; R.Shore-252°; W.252°-260°;
R.260°-307°; W.307°-015° (Unintens). W.015°-
065.5°. Siren 60 sec. Fog Detr. Lt. F.G. 420m.
NE. Intens. 036.5°-039.5°.

Ldg.Lts. 068° (Front). Q. 23M. Intens. 065.5°-
070.5°. 30m.

INSHORE WAYPOINT POINTE DU PORTZIC.
48°21.3′N, 4°32.5′W.

POINTE DU PORTZIC 48°21.6′N 4°32′W.
Lt. Oc.(2)W.R. 12 sec. W.19M. R.15M. Grey 8
sided Tr. 56m. R.shore-259°; W.259°-338°;
R.338°-000°; W.000°-065.5°; W.070.5°-shore.
Racon.
Ldg.Lts. 068° (Rear) Q. 23M. Intens. 065.5°-
071°.
Lt. Dir. Q.(6)+L.Fl. 6 sec. 24M. Same structure
54m. Intens. 045°-050°.
ROCHE MENGAM. Lt. Fl.(3)W.R. 12 sec.
W.8M. R.5M. R. Tr. B.Bands. R.034°-054°;
W.054°-034°. 11m.
CNEXO. Lt.Bn. Fl.R. 2 sec. 2M. Dolphin.

BREST 48°21'N 4°32'W. Tel. Pilots:
(98) 44 34 95.
MOULIN BLANC Y.HBR. (98) 02 20 02. LA
FORET-FOUESNANT Y.HBR. (98) 56 98 45.
Anse de Carmeret or off Pointe du Portzic Lt.
Radio — Pilots: VHF Chan. 12, 16.
Vessel Traffic Management System. This
controls movement and anchoring of all
vessels approaching Brest or in Baie de
Douarnenez. No vessel to pass through
Goulet de Brest or enter Baie de Douarnenez.
without permission. Give 1 h. notice and keep
listening watch. Control specifies which Pass
to be used and gives information on traffic,
etc. Vessels over 25m. length are strictly
controlled, also any vessel carrying
dangerous goods. Vessels under 25m. may
proceed through Goulet de Brest but must
keep to Stb. side and obey orders of Control
Post or patrol craft.
Radio — Port: VHF Chan. 8, 16.
CESAR TOUR SIGNAL STN VHF Chan. 16, 8.
c/s P.C. Rade.
MOULIN BLANC Y. HBR. VHF Chan. 9.
LA FORET-FOUESNANT VHF Chan. 9.
Major naval and commercial, and yachting
centre.
Depth 9.1m. to 10m.

PORT MILITAIRE
EAST JETTY. Lt. Q.G. 7M. Iron structure, G.W.
10m.
SOUTH JTY HEAD. Lt. Q.R. 7M. Mast, R.W.
10m. E end.

TERRE-PLEINE DU CHATEAU
48°22.9'N, 4°29.5'W. Lt. Dir. Oc.(2) W.R.G. 6
sec. W.11M. R.8M. G.8M. Roof. 19m. G.335°-
344°; W.344°-350°; R.350°-014°.

LA PENFOLD
E SIDE OF ENTCE. Lt. Iso.G. 3 sec. 7M. W. Tr.
G. Top 11m. 316°-180°.
W SIDE OF ENTCE. Lt. Iso.R. 3 sec. 7M. W. Tr.
R. Top 8m. 144°-350°.

Ldg.Lts. 314° (Front) Dir. Iso.R. 5 sec. (Rear)
Iso.R. 5 sec. Dir. 309°-319°.

COMMERCIAL PORT
E ENTRANCE S SIDE. Lt. Oc.(2)R. 6 sec. 5M.
Col. W. Tr. R.top 10m.
WEST JETTY HEAD. Lt. Iso.R. 4 sec. 7M. Col.
R.W. 10m.
EAST PIER. Lt. Oc.(2)G. 6 sec. G.W. Tr.
SOUTH JETTY Lt. Fl.G. 4 sec. 9M. W. Col. B.
Band. Vis. 022°-257°.

Lt. Oc.(3) R. 12 sec. R. □ on pile.

PORT DE MOULIN BLANC. E Side Lt. Fl.G. 2
sec. W Side Lt. Fl.R. 2 sec.
Y. Hr. (Brest) Approach Channel least depth
1.5m. N. BASIN depth 1.5m. to 2m. (450
berths). S BASIN depth 5m. (400 berths).

ST. NICHOLAS. Lt. Fl.R. 4 sec.

Lt. Dir. Fl.(2) W.R.G. 6 sec. W.9M. R.7M. G.7M.
Stonemasons Hut. R.014°-018°; W.018°-022°;
G.022°-026°.

POINTE DE L'ILE LONGUE
N BREAKWATER HEAD Lt. Fl.G. 4 sec.
S BREAKWATER HEAD Lt. Fl.R. 4 sec.
Lts. in line 265° (Front) 2 F.R. (Rear) Q.R.

**INSHORE WAYPOINT OFF CAMARET SUR
MER.** 48°18.0'N, 4°36.0'W.

CAMARET-SUR-MER. 48°17'N, 4°35'W

HARBOUR WAYPOINT. 48°17.0'N, 4°35.0'W.

Entry: Y. berths on pontoons on S side of N
Mole. Tel: (98) 27-95-99. Visitors berths
restricted. Fuel and water on end of quay S
side. Hr. dries except for area inside entrance
with access to berths with depth 1.5m.

SOUTH MOLE HEAD. Lt.Bn. Fl.(2)R. 6 sec. 8M.
R.Bn. 7m.

NORTH MOLE 48°16.9'N, 4°35.3'W. Lt.
Iso.W.G. 4 sec. W12M. G.9M. white Tr.
W.135°-182°; G.182°-027°. Head of Mole
marks anch.

POINTE DU TOULINGUET 48°16.8'N,
4°37.8'W. Lt. Oc.(3) W.R. 12 sec. W.15M.
R.12M. white square Tr. 49m. W.Shore-028°;
R.028°-090°; W.090°-Shore.

**OFFSHORE WAYPOINT BASSE DE LA
PARQUETTE.** 48°16.0'N, 4°45.25'W.

LA PARQUETTE. Lt. Fl.R.G. 4 sec. R.6M. G.5M.
Octagonal Tr. B.W. stripes, 18m. R.244°-285°;
G.285°-244°.

LE CHEVREAU Bn. 3m.
BASSE DU LIS LANBY. Lt.By. V.Q.(6) + L.Fl. 15
sec. 8M. Pillar. Y.B. 9m. Topmark S. Whis.

OFFSHORE WAYPOINT BASSE DU LIS.
48°13.0'N, 4°45.75'W.

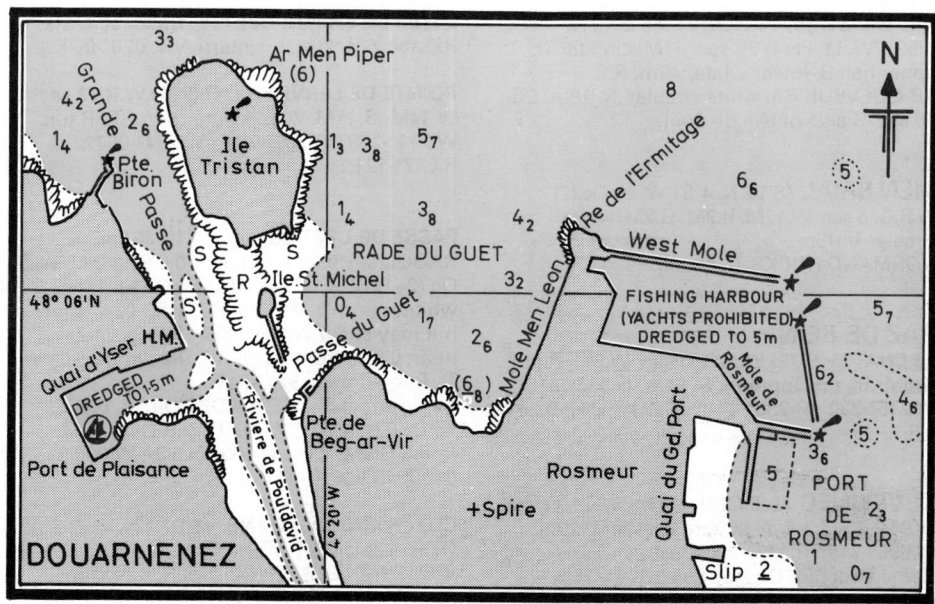

BAIE DE DOUARNENEZ

BASSE VIELLE LANBY. 48°08.3′N, 4°35.7′W
Fl.(2) 6 sec. 8M. 8 on B.R. By. 8m. Whis.

INSHORE WAYPOINT SE OF BASSE VIELLE.
48°07.5′N, 4°34.5′W.

**HARBOUR WAYPOINT MORGAT. 48°13.5′N,
4°28.75′W.**

POINTE DE MORGAT 48°13.2′N,
4°29.9′W. Lt. Oc.(4) W.R.G. 12 sec. W.15M.
R.11M. G.10M. R.W. Tr. 77m. W. Shore-281°;
G.281°-301°; W.301°021°; R.021°-043°.

MORGAT MOLE HEAD. Lt. Oc.(2) W.R. 6 sec.
W.9M. R.6M. W.R. Tr. 8m. W.007°-257°;
R.257°-007°.
Marina Lts. Fl.G. 4 sec. and Fl. R. 4 sec. on
pontoons 3.20m E.

INSHORE WAYPOINT NW OF DOUARNENEZ.
48°07.2′N, 4°21.25′W.

DOUARNENEZ. 48°06′N, 4°19′W

HARBOUR WAYPOINT. 48°06.2′N, 4°20.4′W.

Yachts should moor in Port de Rosmeur. The
fishing basin is reserved exclusively for
fishing boats.

ILE TRISTAN 48°06.2′N, 4°20.3′W. Lt.
Oc.(3) W.R. 12 sec. W.14M. R.11M. grey
circular Tr. white band, B. top, 36m.
BREAKWATER HEAD. Lt. Iso.G. 4 sec. 6M.
white pylon with G. top, 8m. N Hd.
SOUTH SIDE OF ENTRANCE. Lt. Oc.(2)R. 6
sec. 8M. white pylon with R. top, 6m. S. Hd.
ELBOW MOLE DE ROSMEUR HD. Lt. Oc.G. 4
sec. 6M. W. Tr. G. Top 6m. 170°-097°.
TREBOUL. Tel: Capt. du Port (98) 92-09-99. Y.
moorings 150 berths depth 1.5m. Visitors
moorings restricted. Diesel, fresh water,
provisions available.
TREBOUL Lt.Bn. Q.G. 6M. Col. G.W. 6m. P.
Biron Mole Head.

POINT DU MILLIER 48°05.9′N, 4°27.9′W.
Lt. Oc.(2) W.R.G. 6 sec. W.15M. G.11M.
R.12M. white Tr. 34m. G.080°-087°; W.087°-
113°; R.113°-120°; W.120°-129°; G.129°-148°;
W.148°-251°; R.251°-258°; Obsc. 255.5°-081.5°.

CHAUSSEE SEIN (THE SAINTS)

CHAUSSEE DE SEIN. LANBY. V.Q.(9) 10 sec.
Pillar. Y.B.Y. Topmark W.

AR-MEN ROCK 48°03.0′N, 4°59.9′W. Lt.
Fl.(3) 20 sec. 24M. circular Tr. upper half
white, 28m. Siren(3) 60 sec.

ILE DE SEIN, N POINT 48°02.6'N,
4°52.1'W. Lt. Fl.(4) 25 sec. 31M. circular Tr.
upper half B. lower white, 49m. R.C.
AR GUEVEUR Bn. white circular Tr. 18m. Dia.
60 sec. S side of Isle de Sein.

MEN BRIAL 48°02'N, 4°51'W. Lt. Oc.(2)
W.R.G. 6 sec. W.12M. R.9M. G.7M. white
circular Tr. 15m.
NORMAND ROCKS Tr. small.

RAZ DE SEIN
LE CHAT Lt. Fl.(2) W.R.G. 6 sec. W.9M. R.6M.
G.6M. Tr. Y.B. Topmark S. 24m. G.096°-215°;
W.215°-230°; R.230°-271°; G.271°-286°; R.286°-
096°.

TEVENNEC 48°04.3'N, 4°47.8'W. Lt. Q.W.R.
W.9M. R.6M. white square dwelling, 29m.
W.090°-345°; R.345°-090°.
Same structure Dir.Iso. 4 sec. 12M. 24m. vis.
325.5°-330.5°.

OFFSHORE WAYPOINT SE OF TEVENNEC.
48°04.0'N, 4°46.0'W.

LA VIEILLE 48°02.5'N, 4°45.4'W. Lt.
Oc.(2+1) W.R.G. 12 sec. W.15M. R.12M.
G.11M. grey square Tr. 33m. Siren(2+1) 60
sec. W.290°-298°; R.298°-325°; W.325°-355°;
G.355°-017°; W.017°-035°; G.035°-105°;
W.105°-123°; R.123°-158°; W.158°-205°.

LA PLATE Lt. V.Q.(9) 10 sec. 8M. ⊠ on Tr. Y.B.Y.
19m. Day.

OFFSHORE WAYPOINT W OF LA PLATE.
48°02.5'N, 4°46.0'W.

SOUTH TO ST. JEAN DE LUZ.

INSHORE WAYPOINT S OF AUDIERNE.
47°59.0'N, 4°33.2'W.

AUDIERNE

HARBOUR WAYPOINT. 48°00.0'N, 4°32.8'W.

Entry: Channel depth 0.5m. Max. draught
3.4m. Tide 5 kts. in river. Many yacht
moorings in outer harbour. Marina lies N. of
N. end of Ferry Quay with 120 berths.

JETÉE DE SAINTE-EVETTE. Head. Lt. Oc.(2)
R.6 sec. 6M. 2m. R. lantern. Vis. 090°-000°.

POINTE DE LERVILY. Lt. Fl.(2+1) W.R.12 sec.
W.14M. R.11M. 20m. White round Tr. R.top.
W.211°-269°; R.269°-294°; W.294°-087°;
R.087°-121°.

PASSE DE L'EST Ldg.Lts. 331°. **JETEE DE
RAOULIC.** Head. Front: 48°00.6'N, 4°32.5'W.
Oc.(2+1) W.G.12 sec. W.14M. G.9M. 11m.
white round Tr. W. shore-034°; G.034°-shore,
but may show W.037°-055°. Pilot signals.
Rear: 0.5M. from front. F.R. 9M. white 8-sided
Tr. R.top. Intens 321°-341°.
Same structure: **KERGADEC.** Dir. Lt. 006°.
48°01.0'N, 4°32.7'W. Dir.Q.W.R.G. W.12M.
R.9M. G.9M. 43m. G.000°-005.3°; W.005.3°-
006.7°; R.006.7°-017°.

COZ. FORNIC. GROYNE. 48°01.1'N, 4°32.3'W.
Oc.R. 4 sec. Grey mast.
VIEUX MOLE. GROYNE. Iso. R. 4 sec. on
mast.

PORS POULHAN
WEST SIDE OF ENT. Lt. Q.R. 7M. 14m. white
square Tr. R.lantern.

SAINT GUÉNOLÉ. 47°49'N, 4°22'W.
Radio — Port: VHF Chan. 12. 0900-1700.
Entry: Least depth 1.7m. Deepest Berth 3m.
Access difficult in winds SW/NW. Very
difficult in rough weather. Anchorage within
harbour NE of breakwater head in 2.5m. LW.

INSHORE WAYPOINT W OF ST. GUENOLE.
47°49.0'N, 4°24.25'W.

Ldg.Lts. 026°30'. Front: Q.R. 4M. 10m. mast.
Rear: 101m. from front. Q.R. 4M. 12m. mast.
Synchronised with front.

ROCHES DE GROUNILLI Ldg.Lts. 123°30'.
Front: 47°48.1'N, 4°22.5'W. F.G. 5M. 9m. white
Tr. B.bands. (Rear) 300m. from front. F.G. 5M.
13m. white Tr. B.bands.

Ldg.Lts. 055°24' (Front) Q. 2M. G.W. mast.
5m. (Rear) F.Vi. 1M. G.W. mast. 12m. Vis.
040°-070°.

POINT DE PENMARCH

**OFFSHORE WAYPOINT SSW OF PTE DE
PENMARCH. 47°45.0'N, 4°24.5'W.**

ECKMUHL 47°47.9'N, 4°22.4'W. Fl. 5 sec. 26M. 60m. grey 8-sided Tr. Siren 60 sec. RC.
LE MENHIR. Oc.(2) W.G. 6 sec. W.8M. G.4M. 19m. B. Tr. white base. G.135°-315°; W.315°-135°.
SCOEDEC. Lt. Fl.G. 2.5 sec. 5M. G.Tr. 6m.
LOCAREC. Lt. Iso.W.R.G. 4 sec. W.8M. R.5M. G.4M. 11m. white pedestal on rock. G.063°-068°; R.068°-274.5°; W.274.5°-281.5°; R.281.5°-298°; G.298°-337°; R.337°-063°.

KERITY
MENHIR. Lt. Fl(2) W.G. 6 sec. 2M. R. □ on Bn. 6m.
DETACHED BREAKWATER HEAD. Lt. Fl(2) G. 6 sec. 1M. G. mast. 5m.

OFFSHORE WAYPOINT SW OF GUILVINEC. 47°45.0'N, 4°22.0'W.

PORT DE GUILVINEC Tel: (98) 58 05 67 & 58 11 40.

HARBOUR WAYPOINT. 47°47.25'N, 4°17.5'W.

Radio: Port: VHF Chan 12.
Ldg.Lts. 053°. MOLE DE LECHIAGAT SPUR. (Front) 47°47.5'N, 4°17.0'W. Q. 10M. W. Pylon. 13m. 233°-066°. ROCHER LE FAOUTES (Middle) Q.W.G. W.14M. G.11M. R. O on W. Pylon. 17m. W.006°-293°; G.293°-006°. (Rear) Dir. Q. 8M. R. O on W. Pylon 26m. 051.5°-054.5°.
LOST MOAN. Lt. Fl.(3)W.R.G. 12 sec. W.8M. R.5M. G.4M. 7m. white Tr. R.top. G.014°-065°; R.065°-140°; W.140°-160°; R.160°-268°; W.268°-273°; G.273°-317°; W.317°-327°; R.327°-014°.
MÔLE DE LECHIAGAT. Head. Fl.G. 4 sec. 6M. 5m. white hut, G.top.
SPUR Lt. Fl.(2)G. 6 sec. 5M. G. struct. 4m. 078°-258°.
MOLE OUEST. Head. Lt. Fl.(2)R. 6 sec. 5M. 4m. White Tr. R.top.
PIER HEAD. Lt. Fl.R. 4 sec. 9M. R.mast 11m.
REISSANT ROCK Bn. Y.B.Tr. Topmark S.

OFFSHORE WAYPOINT SE OF LESCONIL. 47°45.0'N, 4°10.0'W.

LESCONIL

HARBOUR WAYPOINT. 47°47.5'N, 4°12.25'W.

MEN-AR-GROAS. 47°47.8'N, 4°12.7'W. Lt. Fl.(3)W.R.G. 12 sec. W.12M. R.9M. G.9M. 14m. white Tr. G. top. G.268°-313°; W.313°-333°; R.333°-050°.
E. BREAKWATER. Head. Lt. Q.G. 6M. 5m. G. structure.

W BREAKWATER. Head. Lt. Oc.R. 4 sec. 8M. R. Tripod 5m.

INSHORE WAYPOINT SE OF LOCTUDY. 47°49.25'N, 4°07.75'W.

HARBOUR WAYPOINT LOCTUDY. 47°50.0'N, 4°09.25'W.

LOCTUDY-LANGOZ. 47°50'N, 4°10'W.
Entry: Outer bar 0.7m. Deepest Berth 5m. Max. draught 5m. Springs 3.8m. Neaps. Dangerous seas break across bar in E winds. Tide 3kts. in entrance channel. Moorings for yachts W of Ile Trudy.
S.SIDE. Lt. 47°49.9'N, 4°09.6'W. Fl.(4) W.R.G. 12 sec. W.15M. R.11M. G.10M. 12m. white Tr. R.top. W.115°-257°; G.257°-284°; W.284°-295°; R.295°-318°; W.318°-328°; R.328°-025°.

LES PERDRIX. 47°50.3'N, 4°10.0'W. Lt. Fl. W.R.G. 4 sec. W.12M. R.9M. G.9M. B.W. cheq. Tr. 15m. G.090°-285°; W.285°-295°; R.295°-090°.
KAREK SAOZ. Lt. Q.R. 2M. R. Tr. 3m.
LE BLAS. Lt. Fl(3) G. 12 sec. 2M. G. △ on G. col. 7m.

BENODET, RIVIÈRE ODET

HARBOUR WAYPOINT BENODET. 47°51.5'N, 4°06.75'W.
Entry: Numerous yacht moorings Pointe du Coq to Anse de Penfoul. Marina at Penfoul 500 yachts. Also Sainte Marine marina on W. bank.

POINTE DU COQ. Ldg.Lts. 346°. Front: Oc.(2+1) G.12 sec. 13M. 11m. white round Tr. G. stripe. Intens 343°-349°.

PYRAMIDE. 47°52.5'N, 4°06.8'W. Common rear: Oc.(2+1) 12 sec. 15M. 48m. white Tr. G. top. Synchronised with front. Vis. 338°-016°.

POINTE DE COMBRIT. Ldg.Lts. 000°30'. Front: Oc.(3+1) W.R. 12 sec. W.12M. R.9M. 19m. white square Tr. and dwelling, grey corners. W.325°-017°; R.017°-325°. RC.
POINTE DU TOULGOET. Fl.R.2 sec.
PONT DE CORNOUAILLE. East: F.G. 2M. Green △ in white □. West: F.R. 3M. R. □ white border.

OFFSHORE WAYPOINT S OF PTE. DE MOUSTERLIN. 47°48.5'N, 4°02.25'W.

ÍLES DE GLÉNAN

ÍLE-AUX-MOUTONS 47°46.5'N, 4°01.7'W. Lt. Oc.(2) W.R.G.6 sec. W.15M. R.12M. G.10M. 18m White square Tr. and dwelling. W.035°-050°; G.050°-063°; W.063°-081°; R.081°-141°; W.141°-292°; R.292°-035°. Same structure: Dir.Oc.(2) 6 sec. 24M. 17m Synchronised with main light. Intens 278.5°-283.5°.
PENFRET 47°43.3'N, 3°57.2'W. Lt. Fl.R.5 sec. 21M. White square Tr. R. top. Same structure: Q. 12M. 34m. Vis. 295°-315°.
FORT CIGOGNE. Q.(2) R.G.5 sec. 2M. G.106°-108°; R.108°-262°; G.262°-268°; obscured 268°-106°. Shown in summer.
BEG MEIL QUAY HEAD. Lt. Fl.R. 2 sec. 2M. R.W. Col. 6m.

Generally channel 3m. 260 berths, some visitors moorings.

CONCARNEAU 47°52'N, 3°55'W. Tel: H.M. (98) 97 33 80. Pilots: (98) 58 85 05. Customs: (98) 97 01 73.

HARBOUR WAYPOINT. 47°51.25'N, 3°55.75'W.

Radio — Ports: VHF Chan. 16, 12. H24.
Radio — Pilots: VHF Chan. 16, 12 as required.
Entry: A yachting and fishing port. Outer Harbour used only by yachts. Yacht Hr. La Ronet-en-Fouesnant. Channel 1-2 marked by buoys and beacons, at mouth of Riviere de la Foret.

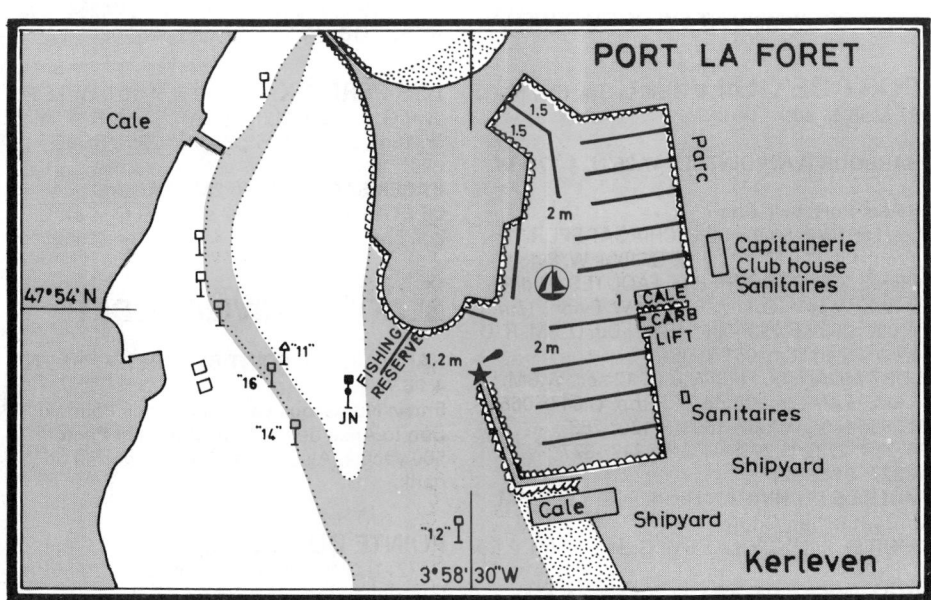

INSHORE WAYPOINT BAIE DE LA FORET. 47°50.0'N, 3°56.75'W.

PORT DE LA FORÊT — FOUESNANT

HARBOUR WAYPOINT. 47°53.25'N, 3°58.0'W.

CAP COZ. SHELTER MOLE. Fl.(2) R. 6 sec. 6M. 5m.
KERLEVEN. SHELTER MOLE. Head. Fl.G.4 sec. 5M. 5m.
INNER SHELTER MOLE. Head. Iso G. 4 sec. 4M. 5m.
Yacht Hbr. Tel: (98) 56 98 45. VHF Chan. 9.
Entry: Depth in Passage de Lanriec 2m.

LA CROIX. 47°52.2'N, 3°55.1'W. Ldg.Lts. 028°30'. Front: Oc.(3) 12 sec. 12M. 14m. white Tr. R. top. Vis. 006.5°-093°. **BEUZEC.** Rear: 1.34M from front. Q. 21M. 87m. Belfry. Intens 026.5°-030.5°.
LANRIEC. Lt. Q.G. 7M. 13m. White gable. Vis. 063°-078°.
LA MEDÉE. Fl.R.2½ sec. 4M. 6m. R.Tr.
PASSAGE DE LANRIEC. Oc.(2) W.R.6 sec. W.8M. R.6M. 4m. R.Tr. R.209°-354°; W.354°-007°; R.007°-018°. Also Lts. Fl.R. 4 sec and Q(6)+L. Fl.R. 10 sec. on W. side, Lts. Fl.G. 4 sec. and Fl.(2)G. 6 sec. on E. side of passage.
LE COCHON. Lt. Fl.(3)W.R.G. 12 sec. W.9M. R.6M. G.6M. 9m. G.Tr. G.048°-205°; R.205°-352°; W.352°-048°.
BASSE DU CHENAL. Lt. Q.R. 5M. R. Tr. 3m. 180°-163°.

BAIE DE POULDOHAN. Lt. Fl.G. 4 sec. 5M 6m. White square Tr. G. top. Vis. 053°-065°.

OFFSHORE WAYPOINT S OF PTE. DE TREVIGNON. 47°45.0′N, 3°50.0′W.

TRÉVIGNON

BREAKWATER. 47°47.6′N, 3°51.3′W. Lt. Oc.(3+1) W.R.G.12 sec. W.14M. R.11M. G.11M. 11m. White square Tr. G. top. W.004°-051°; G.051°-085°; W.085°-092°; R.092°-127°; R.322°-351°.
MOLE HEAD. Fl.G.4 sec. 7M.

W.10M. R.7M. G.6M. 38m. White round Tr. R. top. W. (unintens) 050°-140°; W.140°-296°; G.296°-303°; W.303°-311°; R.311°-328° over Les Verres; W.328°-050°. Obscured by Pointe de Beg-Morg when bearing less than 299°.

INSHORE WAYPOINT S OF PORT DE BRIGNEAU. 47°46.0′N, 3°39.5′W.

HARBOUR WAYPOINT BRIGNEAU. 47°46.6′N, 3°39.8′W.

Entry: Shelter for yachts in summer. Recommended shallow draught only.

BRIGNEAU. MOLE. Head. Lt. Oc.(2) W.R.G.6 sec. W.9M. R.6M. G.5M. 7m. White col. R. top.

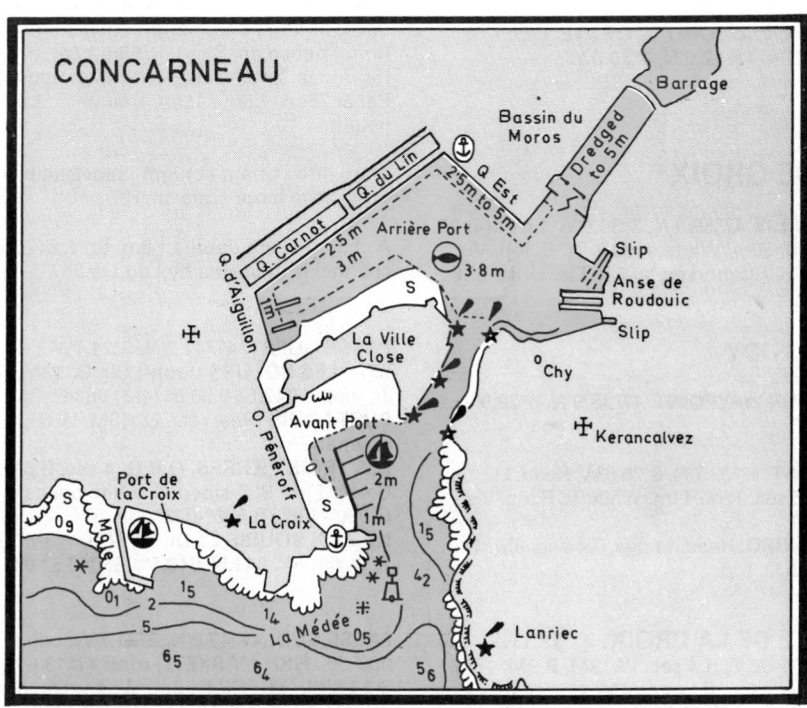

INSHORE WAYPOINT S OF PORT MANECH. 47°46.9′N, 3°44.0′W.

PORT MANECH

HARBOUR WAYPOINT. 47°47.9′N, 3°44.0′W.

Entry: Moorings for yachts in Pool between harbour and bar at entrance to L'Aven River. Good moorings beyond the bar and up the twin river at Belon.

POINTE DE \BEG-AR-VECHEN.
47°48.0′N, 3°44.4′W. Lt. Oc.(4) W.R.G.12 sec.

G.280°-329°; W.329°-339°; R.339°-034°.
MERRIEN. Lt. Q.R. 11M. 26m. White square Tr. R. top. Vis. 004°-009°.

DOËLAN

INSHORE WAYPOINT OFF DOËLAN. 47°45.75′N, 3°36.5′W.

Ldg.Lts. 47°46.3′N, 3°36.5′W. 014°. (Front) Oc.(3) W.G.12 sec. W.12M. G.8M. 20m. White Tr. G. band and lantern. W.shore-305°; G.305°-314°; W.314°-shore. (Rear) Q.R. 8M. 27m. White Tr. R. band and lantern.

INSHORE WAYPOINT OFF LE POLDU.
47°45.5'N, 3°32.75'W.

KERROC'H. 47°42.0'N, 3°27.7'W. Lt. Oc.(2)
W.R.G.6 sec. W.11M. R.9M. G.8M. 22m. Col.
R. Shore-302°; W.302°-096½°; R.096½°-112½°;
G.112½°-132°; R.132°-Shore.

LOMENER, ANSE DE STOLE
47°42.4'N, 3°25.5'W. Dir. Lt. 357°12', Dir.
Q.W.R.G. W.10M. R.8M. G.8M. W. Tr. R. top
18m. G.349.2°-355.2°; W.355.2°-359.2°;
R.359.2°-005.2°.

INSHORE WAYPOINT W OF PTE. DE
KERROC'H. 47°42.0'N, 3°30.0'W.

ÎLE DE GROIX

PEN MEN 47°38.9'N, 3°30.6'W. Lt. Fl.(4) 25
sec. 30M. 60m. White square Tr. B. top. Vis.
309°-275°. RC marked by F.R. Lts. close ESE.

PORT TUDY

HARBOUR WAYPOINT. 47°38.9'N, 3°26.5'W.

MÔLE EST. 47°38.7'N, 3°26.8'W. Head. Lt.
Fl.(2)R. 6 sec. 12M. 11m. White Tr. R.top. Vis.
112°-230°.
MÔLE NORD. Head. Lt. Iso.G.4 sec. 8M. 12m.
White Tr. G. top.

POINTE DE LA CROIX. 47°38.1'N,
3°25.0'W. Oc.W.R.4 sec. W.13M. R.9M. 16m.
White pedestal, R.lantern. W.169°-336°;
R.336°-345°; W.345°-353°.

POINTE DES CHATS 47°37.3'N, 3°25.3'W.
Lt. Fl.R.5 sec. 20M. 16m. White square Tr. and
dwelling. Vis. 199°-091°.

INSHORE WAYPOINT OFF LOMENER.
47°41.5'N, 3°25.5'W.

INSHORE WAYPOINT APPROACHES
LORIENT. 47°40.75'N, 3°25.0'W.

LORIENT 47°44'N, 3°21'W. H.M. Tel: (97) 37
11 86. Pilots: 37 14 80.

HARBOUR WAYPOINT. 47°41.9'N, 3°22.1'W.

Radio — Port: VHF Chan. 16, 11. Distress &
Rescue Chan. 12.
Radio — Pilots: VHF Chan. 16, 10, 8, 6. Hrs.
0600-1900 and 1 h. before E.T.A.
Entry: Simplified code applies. Yacht Hr. 2½c.
WNW of Pointe de l'Esperance. Outer part
depth 1.8m. Wet dock 4m. Large marina at
Kernevel.
Best time for entry/departure depends on
tidal stream at Passage de la Citadelle. i.e. 20
min.-HW Port Louis (normal) 30/45 min.-HW
when rivers flooding. For small vessels 1½ h.-
HW-1½ h. or LW when range above normal
otherwise any time.
Riviere and Canal du Blavet: enter NE of Rade
de Pen Marie. Channel dredged 3.5m. to
Rohu thence dry. Vessels 60m.×4m. draught
(Springs), 3m. (Neaps) can reach Hennebont.
Canal 25m.×4.5m.×1.3m. draught × 2.4m.
height.

Entry into Lorient at night inadvisable without
up-to-date large scale charts.

A channel with depth of 8m. to N. of existing
channel is indicated by Ldg.Lts 057°.

PASSE OUEST. 47°42.2'N, 3°21.7'W. Ldg.Lts.
057°. **LES SOEURS** (Front) Dir. Q. 13M. R.W.
Tr. Intens 042.5°-0.58.5° (4M) 058.5°-042.5°.
PORT LOUIS (Rear) Dir. Q. 18M. W.R.
daymark.
LES TROIS PIERRES. Q.R.G. 4 sec. R.6M.
G.6M. 11m. B. 8-sided Tr. white bands.
G.060°-196°; R.196°-002°.
ILE AUX SOURIS Lt. Dir. Q.W.G. W3M. G2M.
G.Tr. 6m. W. 041.5°-043.5°; G. 043.5°-041.5°.

PASSE SUD. 47°43.8'N, 3°21.7'W. Ldg.Lts.
008°30'. **FISH MARKET.** Front: 47°43.8'N,
3°21.8'W. Q.R. 15M. 16m. White □ on grey
metal framework Tr. Intens 006°-011°.
KERGROISE- LA PERRIÈRE. Rear: 515m. from
front. Q.R. 13M. 28m. R. □, white stripe, on
grey metal framework Tr. Synchronised with
front. Intens 005.5°-011.5°.

ÎLE SAINT-MICHEL. 47°43.5'N, 3°21.6'W.
Ldg.Lts. 016°. (Front): Dir. Oc.(3)G. 12 sec.
16M. 8m. White Tr. G.top. Intens. (Rear): Dir.
Oc.(3) G.015°-018° 12 sec. 16M. W.G. Tr. 12m.
Synchronised with front. Intens 014.5°-017.5°.
W. SIDE. LA PETITE JUMENT. Oc.R.4 sec. 6M.
5m. R. concrete Tr. Vis. 182°-024°.
TOURELLE DE LA CITADELLE. Oc.G.4 sec.
5M. 6m. B.W.cheq. concrete Tr. Vis. 009°-193°.

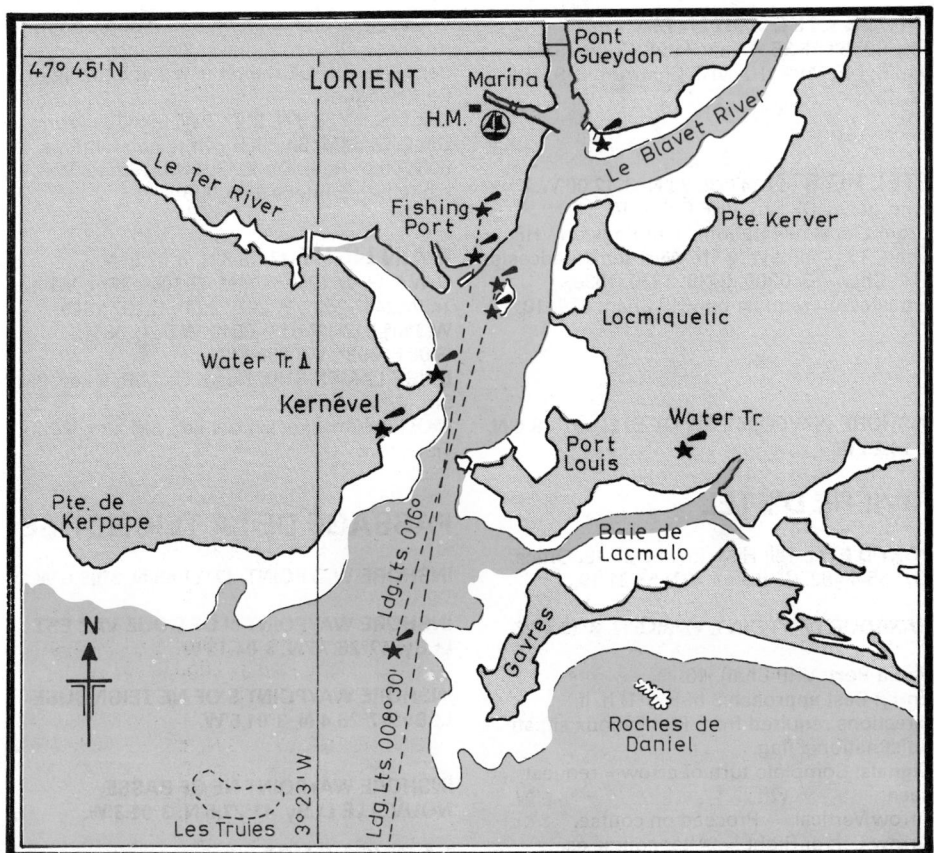

PORT-LOUIS. JETTY. Iso. G. 4 sec. 6M. 5m. W.
Tr. G. Top. Vis. 043°-301°
LE COCHON. Fl.R.4 sec. 6M. 5m. R.Tr.

KÉROMAN. SUBMARINE BASE. 47°43.6′N,
3°22.0′W. Ldg.Lts. 350°. Front: Oc.(2) R. 6 sec.
12M. 25m. R.W. hut. Intens 347.5°-352.5°.
Rear: Oc.(2) R.6 sec. 12M. 31m. R.metal
framework Tr. white bands. Synchronised
with front. Intens 347.5°-352.5°.
Ldg.Lts. 350° Occas. (Front) Dir. Q.G. 13M.
W.G. daymark. (Rear) Dir. Q.G. 13M. W.G.
daymark.
CITADELLE DE PORT LOUIS. Lt. Dir. Q.W.R.G.
W.7M. R. 5M. G. 5M. G. 168°-169.5°; W.169.5°-
170.5°; R.170.5°-173.5°. Occas.
The above Lts. for use of and at request of the
pilots.

FISHING HARBOUR. SE side of Entrance.
Fl.R.G. 4 sec. 6M. 6m. White Tr.G.top. G.000°-
235°; R.235°-360°.
Anchorage in 3m. NE of Citadel but
inadvisable overnight.

KERNEVEL. 47°43.0′N, 3°22.4′W. Ldg.Lts.
217°. Front: Dir. Q.R. 14M. 10m. R. □ on R.W.
metal framework Tr. Intens 215°-219°. F.R. on
each of 2 radio Trs. 0.16M. E. Rear: Dir. Q.R.
14M. 15m. White square Tr. R.top
Synchronised with front. Intens 215°-219°.
MARINA
E BREAKWATER HEAD. Lt. Fl.Y. 2.5 sec. 1M.
Mast Y. Top 3m.
S BREAKWATER HEAD. Lt. Q.R. 1M. Mast R.
Top 3m.
PENGARNE. Lt. Fl.G. 2.5 sec. 4M. G. Tr. 8m.
POINTE DE L'ESPÉRANCE. Dir.Lt. 037°15′.
Dir.Q.W.R.G. W.9M. R.7M. G.7M. W.col.
G.034.2°-036.7°; W.036.7°-037.2°; R.037.2°-
047.2°.
LANDING STAGE. Lt. Fl.(4) W.R. 15 sec. 6M.
7m. W. dolphin. R. Top. W.110°-347°; R.347°-
355°; W.355°-035°.
GUEYDON BRIDGE. Dir.Lt. 352°. Dir.Iso.
W.R.G.4 sec. W.9M. R.7M. G.7M. 6m. W.
masonry support. G.350°-351.5°; W.351.5°-
352.5°; R.352.5°-355.5°.

CROSS ÉTEL SAR STN.
Tel: (97) 52 35 35. Telex: 74 08 43 CROSS A.
Radio: MF 2182 kHz. VHF Chan. 16. 6, 9, 10, 12, 13.

ÉTEL RG STN. 47°39.80'N, 3°12.00'W.
Emergency DF Stn. VHF Chan. 16, 11.
Urgent local navigational warnings on VHF Chan. 13. Then every 2h. Weather Broadcasts VHF Chan. 13. 0300, 0730, 1330, 1830, repeated on request on VHF Chan. 6, 9, 10, 12.

INSHORE WAYPOINT SW OF ÉTEL. 47°38.0'N, 3°14.25'W.

RIVIÈRE D'ÉTEL

PORT D'ÉTEL Tel: H.M. (97) 55 35 19. Office: (97) 55 46 62. Customs: (97) 55 31 19.

HARBOUR WAYPOINT. 47°38.5'N, 3°13.0'W.

Radio-Port: VHF Chan. 16.
Entry: Best approach 3 h.-HW-1½ h. If directions required from Mat Fenoux sig.stn. hoist national flag.
Signals: Complete turn of arrow = request seen.
Arrow Vertical = Proceed on course.
Arrow Left or Right = Alter course as indicated.
Arrow Horizontal + ball = Bar not practicable.
R. Flag = Not enough water on the bar.
Operates 2 h.-HW-1½ h. Port Louis.

W. SIDE Ent. Oc.(2) W.R.G.6 sec. W.10M. R.7M. G.6M. 13m. R. metal framework Tr. W.022°-064°; R.064°-123°; W.123°-330°; G.330°-022°. 2 F.R. on radio mast 2.3M. NW. F.R. & F.W. on radio mast 2.4M. NW.
EPIC DE PLOUHINEC HEAD. Lt. Fl.R. 2.5 sec. 1M. Col. R.
PLATEAU DES BIRVIDEAUX. Lt. Fl.(2) 6 sec. 9M. 24m. B.8-sided masonry Tr. R.band, masonry base. Name on side.

OFFSHORE WAYPOINT SW OF QUIBERON. 47°27.5'N, 3°08.0'W.

PORT-MARIA

HARBOUR WAYPOINT. 47°28.25'N, 3°07.25'W.

Entry: Depths of 2/3m. in S part of harbour. Heavy swell from S makes entrance dangerous. Seek shelter in lee of Belle Ile or Port Haliguen.
Ldg.Lts. 47°28.6'N, 3°07.2'W. 006°30'. Front: Dir. Q.G. 14M. 5m. B.Tr. white band. Intens 005°-008°. Rear: Dir. Q.G. 14M. 13m. B.Tr. white band. Intens 005°-008°.

MAIN LIGHT 47°28.8'N, 3°07.5'W.
Q.W.R.G. W.15M. R.11M. G.10M. 28m. White Tr. W.246°-252°; W.291°-297°; G.297°-340°; W.340°-017°; R.017°-051°; W.051°-081°; G.081°-098°; W.098°-143°.
BRISE-LAMES SUD. Head. Oc.(2)R. 6 sec. 8M. 9m. White Tr. R. top.
MÔLE EST. Head. Iso.G.4 sec. 6M. 9m. White Tr. G. top.

PASSAGE DE LA TEIGNOUSE

INSHORE WAYPOINT. 47°27.65'N, 3°05.0'W.

INSHORE WAYPOINT N OF GOUE VAZ EST Lt.By. 47°26.75'N, 3°04.15'W.

INSHORE WAYPOINT S OF NE TEIGNOUSE Lt.By. 47°26.4'N, 3°01.5'W.

INSHORE WAYPOINT NE OF BASSE NOUVELLE Lt.By. 47°27.5'N, 3°01.3'W.

LA TEIGNOUSE. 47°27.5'N, 3°02.8'W.
Fl.W.R. 4 sec. W.15M. R.11M. W. Tr. R. Top. 19m. W033°-039°: R.039°-033°.
BASSE DU MILEU Lt.By. Fl.(2)G. 6 sec. 8M. 9m. Conical G.

PORT HALIGUEN 47°29'N, 3°06'W. Tel: (97) 50 20 56.

HARBOUR WAYPOINT. 47°29.4'N, 3°05.75'W.
Radio: VHF Chan. 9.
Entry: A yacht harbour, excellent for small craft. Old harbour dries. Yacht harbour depths 1.8m. to 3.4m. Moor stern on to pontoons.

MARINA OLD. BREAKWATER. Head. Lt. Fl.R. 2 sec. 5M. 10m. W. Tr. R.Top.

NEW BREAKWATER. 47°29.4'N, 3°06.0'W. Head. Lt. Oc.(2)W.R. 6 sec. W.12M. R.9M. W. Tr. R. Top. 10m. W.233°-240.5°; R.240.5°-299°; W.299°-306°; R.306°-233°.
NW MOLE. Head. Fl.G.2.5 sec. 1M. 6m. White col. B. top.
PIER HEAD. Fl. Vi. 2 sec. Purple Col. 5m.

BELLE ÎLE

POINTE DES POULAINS 47°23.3'N, 3°15.1'W. Lt. Fl. 5 sec. 23M. 34m. White square Tr. and dwelling. Vis. 023°-291°.

GOULPHAR 47°18.7'N, 3°13.7'W. Lt. Fl.(2) 10 sec. 24M. 87m. Grey Tr.

POINTE DE KERDONIS. 47°18.6'N, 3°03.6'W. Fl.(3) R.15 sec. 15M. 35m. White square Tr. and dwelling. Obscured by Pointes d'Arzic and de Taillefer 025°-129°.

LE PALAIS 47°21'N 3°09'W. Tel: H.M. (97) 31 42 90. Marina: (97) 52 83 17. YC (97) 31 85 16.

HARBOUR WAYPOINT. 47°20.9'N, 3°08.8'W.

Entry: Lock gates open 1 h.-HW-1 h.
Marina in Inner Basin 200 berths also visitors moorings.
JETÉE SUD. Oc.(2) R.6 sec. 8M. 11m. White round Tr. Obscured by Pointes de Kerdonis and de Taillefer 298°-170°.
JETÉE NORD. Fl.(2+1)G. 12 sec. 9M. 11m. White Tr. Obscured by Pointes de Kerdonis and de Taillefer 298°-168°.
SAUZON. Lt. Q.G. 10M. 9m. White Tr. G.top. 194°-045°.
JETTY NW. Head. Lt. Fl.G. 4 sec. 190°-078°.
JETTY SE. Head. Lt. Fl.R. 4 sec. 315°-272°.

RIVIÈRE DE CRAC'H

Ldg.Lts. 47°34.1'N, 3°00.4'W. 347°. Front: Q. W.R.G. W.10M. R.7M. G.7M. 10m. White truncated conical Tr. G.321°-345°; W.345°-013.5°; R.013.5°-080°. Rear: Q. 14M. 20m. White round Tr. G.top. Synchronised with front. Intens 337°-357°.

LA TRINITE-SUR-MER 47°35'N,
3°02'W. Tel: Marina (97) 55 71 49. YC (97) 55 73 48.

HARBOUR WAYPOINT. 47°33.7'N, 3°00.5'W.
Radio — Port: Yacht harbour VHF Chan. 9. Tel: 52 71 49.
900 berths (100 visitors) in Darse Nord, Centrale, Sud. Least depth entrance channel 3m. Deepest berth (Y.Hr.) 5m. Tide M.H.W.S. 5.4m. M.L.W.S. 0.7m.

Dir.Lt. 47°35.0'N, 3°01.0'W. 347°. Dir. Oc.W.R.G. 4 sec. W.14M. R.11M. G.11M. 9m. White Tr. G.345°-346°; W.346°-348°; R.348°-349°.
S. PIER. Head. Oc.(2) W.R.6 sec. W.10M. R.7M. W. Tr. R.top. R.090°-293.5°; W.293.5°-300.5°; R.300.5°-329°.
JETTY HEAD. Iso. 4 sec. 5M. W. Tr. R. Top 8m.

PORT-NAVALO 47°32.9'N, 2°55.1'W. Lt. Oc.(3) W.R.G.12 sec. W.15M. R.12M. G.11M. 32m. White Tr. and dwelling. W.155°-220°; G.317°-359°; W.359°-015°; R.015°-105°. Storm signals.

LE GRAND MOUTON. Lt. Q.G. 3M. G. Tripod 4m.

RIVIERE D'AURAY
LE GREGAN. Lt. Q.(6) + L.Fl. 15 sec. ⚑ on B.Y. Bn.
ROGUEDAS. Lt. Fl.G. 2.5 sec. 4M. 4m. Tr. G.

INSHORE WAYPOINT. 47°30.75'N, 2°58.0'W.

INSHORE WAYPOINT SE OF MEABAN Bn. 47°30.75'N, 2°55.3'W.

MORBIHAN
Tidal streams can attain 8 kts. at Springs inside the entrance and off Port Blanc, less in the upper reaches.
Caution: Fire fighting aircraft scoop water from corridors between Ile Aux Moines, Ile D'Arz, Ile Ilur, Ile Stiibiden, Ile Godec. Anchoring totally prohibited. Navigating prohibited as required without prior warning.

VANNES 47°39'N, 2°45'W.
Yacht Harbour. Tel: 97 54 16 08 or 97 54 00 47.
Radio: VHF Ch. 9.
Entry: Timetable for wet basin gate operation is available from Port Captain.
Tide levels MHWS/N 4.7-4.0m. MLWS/N 1.3-2.1m. Avant Port draught 4m. at mean tides. Lock sill 1m. A.C.D. width 10m.
Open by day 2h-HW-2h: Wet Dock depth 2m. Berths for 200 yachts at N. End.

CROUESTY EN ARZON 47°33'N, 2°54'W. Tel: Marina (97) 41 23 23.

HARBOUR WAYPOINT. 47°32.2'N, 2°54.8'W.

Entry: Yacht harbour N side of Petit Mont. Berths for 1000 yachts (approx. 100 visitors). Entrance channel dredged 1.7m. Basins 2m. M.H.W.S. 5.0m. M.L.W.S. 0.7m.

Ldg.Lts. 47°32.6'N, 2°53.9'W. 058°. (Front): Dir.
Q. 19M. R. Ⅱ W. stripe. W. Tr. 10m. Intens
056.5°-059.5°. (Rear): Dir. Q. 19M. W. Tr. 27m.
Intens. 056.5°-059.5°.
N. JETTY. Head. Oc.(2)R. 6 sec. 7M. 9m.
R.W.Tr.
S. JETTY. Head. Fl.G.4 sec. 7M. 9m. G.W.Tr.

**INSHORE WAYPOINT S OF ROC DE L'EPIEU
Bn.** 47°29.3'N, 2°52.85'W.

SAINT-JACQUES-EN-SARZEAU.
47°29.2'N, 2°47.5'W. Oc.(2) R. 6 sec. 6M. 5m.
White 8-sided Tr. R.top.

**INSHORE WAYPOINT S OF POINTE DE S.
JACQUES.** 47°28.0'N, 2°47.5'W.

ÎLE DUMET. Fl. (2+1) W.R.G. 15 sec. W.8M.
R.6M. G.6M. 14m. White col. G.top, on front.
G.090°-272°; W.272°-285°; R.285°-325°;
W.325°-090°.

INSHORE WAYPOINT S OF ILE DUMET.
47°24.2'N, 2°37.1'W.

RIVIÈRE DE PÉNERF

ENTRANCE. LE PIGNON. Fl.(3) W.R. 12 sec.
W.9M. R.6M. 6m. R.W.Tr. R.028°-167°; W.167°-
175°; R.175°-349°; W.349°-028°.

BASSE DE KERVOYAL Lt. Dir. Q.W.R. W8M.
R6M. ⚑ on Y.B. Tr. W.269°-271°; R.271°-269°.

**INSHORE WAYPOINT OFF ABBEY (LA
VILAINE).** 47°29.1'N, 2°33.8'W.

LA VILAINE ENTRANCE
Entry: Channel well marked. Barrage at Arzal.
Lock opens ev. h. 0700-2100. Marinas (above
Lock) at Port d'Arzal Camoel and La Roche
Bernard.

BASSE BERTRAND. Iso W.G.4 sec. W.8M.
G.4M. 7m. B.W.cheq. Tr. W.040°-054°; G.054°-
227°; W.227°-234°; G.234°-040°.

PENLAN. 47°31.0'N, 2°30.2'W. Oc.(2) W.R.G.
6 sec. W.13M. R.10M. G.8M. 21m. White Tr. R.
band and top, white dwelling. R.292.5°-025°;
G.025°-052°; W.052°-060°; R.060°-138°; G.138°-
218°.

POINTE DU SCAL. Oc.(3)G. 12 sec. 6M. 8m.
W. Tr. G. Top. Unintens when bearing more
than 207°.

INSHORE WAYPOINT OFF MESQUER.
47°29.95'N, 2°30.7'W.

MESQUER. JETTY. 47°25.3'N, 2°28.1'W.
Nr. Head. Oc.(3+1) W.R.G.12 sec. W.12M.
R.8M. G.7M. 7m. white col. and building.
W.067°-072°; R.072°-102°; W.102°-118°;
R.118°-293°; W.293°-325°; G.325°-067°.

INSHORE WAYPOINT OFF PIRIAC-SUR-MER.
47°23.4'N, 2°34.8'W.

PIRIAC-SUR MER. 47°23.0'N, 2°32.7'W.
INNER MOLE HD. Lt. Oc.(2) W.R.G.6 sec.
W.10M. R.7M. G.6M. 8m. White col. R.066°-
148°; G.148°-194°; W.194°-201°; G.201°-066°.
Siren 120 sec. Occas. 350m. SW.
PIPELINE. 47°22.2'N, 2°32.8'W. Oc.(2+1)
W.R.G.12 sec. W.12M. R.8M. G.8M. 14m.
White □, R. stripe. on R. metal framework Tr.
G.300°-036°; W.036°-068°; R.068°-120°.
BREAKWATER HEAD. Lt. Fl.G. 4 sec. 5M. W.
Tr. G. Top. 5m.
E BREAKWATER HEAD W. Lt. Fl.R. 4 sec. 5M.
W. Tr. R. Top. 4m.

**INSHORE WAYPOINT W OF POINTE DU
CASTELLI.** 47°22.5'N, 2°36.4'W.

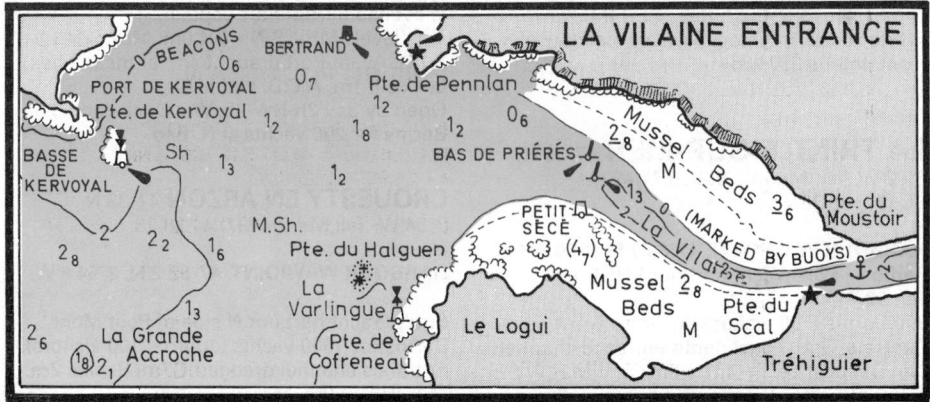

LA TURBALLE

Ldg.Lts. 006°30′. Front: Dir.F.Vi. 3M. 11m.
Metal mast. Intens 359°-004°. Rear: Dir.F.Vi.
3M. 19m. Metal framework. Intens 359°-004°.

JETÉE GARLAHY. 47°20.7′N, 2°31.0′W.
Fl.(4) W.R.12 sec. W.11M. R.8M. 13m. White
metal framework Tr. R.top. R.060°-315°;
W.315°-060°. Vis. 020°-134° from offshore.
DIGUE TOURLANDROUX. Fl.G. 4 sec. 4M.
8m. white pedestal. Siren 10 min.

LE FOUR 47°17.9′N, 2°33.0′W. Lt. Fl. 5 sec.
19M. 23m. B.W. Tr. G. Top. Iso W.4 sec. marks
swell gauge 2.6M. NNE.

**OFFSHORE WAYPOINT SW OF LE FOUR
(BASSE CAPELLA Lt.By.). 47°15.6′N, 2°44.8′W.**

**OFFSHORE WAYPOINT S OF LE FOUR (GOUE
VAS OU FOUR Lt.By.). 47°14.8′N, 2°38.2′W.**

ÎLE DE HOUAT

**OFFSHORE WAYPOINT S OF ILE DE HOUAT
(PT. DEFER Bn.). 47°21.4′N, 3°00.3′W.**

PORT DE SAINT-GILDAS. MÔLE NORD.
Oc.(2)W.G. 6 sec. W.8M. G.5M. 8m. White Tr.
G.top. W.168°-198°; G.198°-210°; W.210°-240°;
G.240°-168°.

ÎLE DE HÖEDIC

PORT DE L'ARGOL. 47°20.7′N, 2°52.5′W.
Lt. Fl.W.G.4 sec. W.11M. G.8M. white
pedestal. W.143°-163°; G.163°-183°; W.183°-
203°; G.203°-232°; W.102°-143°.

LES GRANDS CARDINAUX 47°19.3′N,
2°50.1′W. Fl(4) 15 sec. 15M. 28m. R. round
masonry Tr. White band. Obscured by Iles
d'Hoedic and de Houat 120°-143°. Danger
signals.

**INSHORE WAYPOINT W OF POINTE DU
CROISIC. 47°18.18′N, 2°34.8′W.**

LE CROISIC. 47°18′N, 2°31′W. Tel: H.M.
(40) 23 05 38. Marina (40) 23 10 95. YC (40) 23
04 76.
Entry: Inner harbours dry out.

HARBOUR WAYPOINT. 47°18.75′N, 2°31.45′W.

JETÉE DE TRÈHIC. HEAD. 47°18.5′N,
2°31.4′W. Iso W.G. 4 sec. W. 13M. G.8M. 12m.
Grey Tr. G. top. G.042°-093°; W.093°-137°;
G.137°-345°; Vis. 055°-160° from offshore.

Ldg.Lts. 47°18.0′N, 2°31.0′W. 156° Front:
Oc.(2+1) 12 sec. 18M. 10m. G.W.cheq.
topmark on white metal framework Tr. Intens
154°-158°. Rear: Oc.(2+1) 12 sec. 18M. 14m. G.
topmark, yellow diagonal stripes, on metal
framework Tr. Synchronised with front. Intens
154°-158°.

BASSE HERGO. Lt. Fl.G. 2.5 sec. 3M. G. △ on
G. Tr. 5m.

Ldg.Lts. 47°18.0′N, 2°31.2′W. 174°. Front: Q.G.
12M. W. □ G. stripe on G.W. structure 5m. Vis.
on leading line. G.W. Structure. Rear: Q.G.
12M. W. □ stripe on G.W. structure 8m. Vis.
on leading line. G.W. Structure.

Ldg.Lts. 47°17.9′N, 2°30.8′W. 134°30′, Front:
Dir. Q.R. 15M. R.W. □ on W. Pylon 6m. Intens.
132.5°-136.5°. Rear: Dir. Q.R. 15M. R.W. □ on
W. Pylon. 10m. Intens. 132.5°-136.5°.

LE GRAND MAHON. Fl.R. 2½ sec. 4M. 6m. R.
pedestal and base.

ESTUAIRE DE LA LOIRE

APPROACH SN 1. Lt.By. 47°00′N, 2°40′W. Lt.
Fl.10 sec. 8M. Pillar. R.W. 8m. Whis. Racon.
SN 2. Lt.By. 47°02.15′N, 2°33.45′W. Iso. 4 sec.
5M. Pillar. R.W. 8m. ⌇⌇

LA BANCHE 47°10.7′N, 2°28.0′W. Lt.
Fl.(2+1) W.R.15 sec. W.17M. R.12M. 22m. B.Tr.
white bands. R.266°-280°; W.280°-266°.

BAIE DU POULIGUEN

**INSHORE WAYPOINT APPROACHES
POULIGUEN. (S OF PTE VICHERIE).
47°14.95′N, 2°28.0′W.**

LE POULIGUEN. 47°16′N, 2°25′W. Tel: H.M.
(40) 42 33 74.
JETEE SUD. Lt. Q.R. 9M. 13m. White col. Vis.
outside bay 295°-339°.
Good facilities for yachts at La Baule YC 1½c
inside entrance on E Bank.
LES PETITS IMPAIRS. Fl.(2)G. 6 sec. 4M. 6m.
B.Tr. Vis. outside bay 293°-034°.

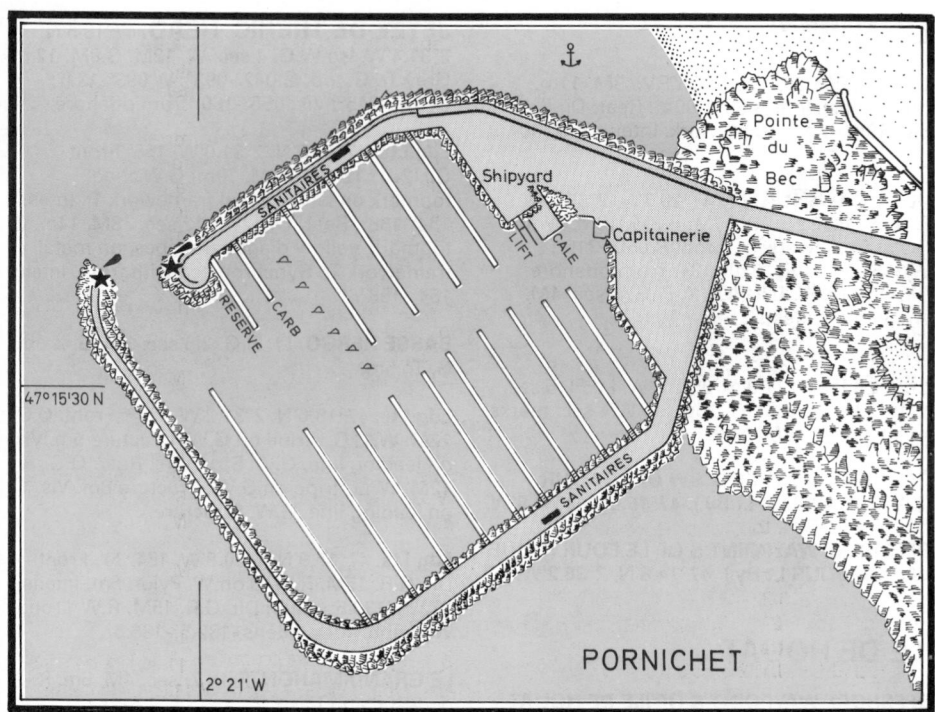

PORNICHET. 47°15.5'N, 2°21'W. Tel: H.M.
(40) 61 03 20. La Baule YC (40) 60 20 90. Yacht
Hr. (40) 61 03 20.

Radio: VHF Chan. 9.

HARBOUR WAYPOINT. 47°15.4'N, 2°22.85'W.

LA BAULE.
S BREAKWATER HEAD. 47°15.5'N, 2°21.1'W.
Lt. Iso.W.G. 4 sec. W.12M. G.9M. W.Tr.G.Top.
G.084°-081°; W.081°-084°.
Lt. Fl.G. 2 sec. 3M. B.G. Post 2m.

N BREAKWATER. Lt. Fl.R. 2 sec. 3M. B.R. Post
2m.
Yacht Hbr. Tel: (40) 61 03 20. VHF Chan. 9.
Up to 1100 berths for yachts up to 30.4m in
length. 150 berths for visitors. Keep to N of
buoy 1¾M. W of entrance or in W. sector of
Main Lt. Depths 3-3½m.

LE GRAND CHARPENTIER 47°12.8'N,
2°19.1'W. Lt. Q.W.R.G. W.15M. R.12M. G.10M.
22m. Grey Tr. G.020°-049°; W.049°-111°;
R.111°-310°; W.310°-020°. Helicopter landing
platform.

HARBOUR WAYPOINT LA LOIRE. 47°11.9'N,
2°17.4'W.

POINTE DE MINDEN MOLE WEST Lt. Fl. G.
2.5 sec. 2M. W. structure.

LE POINTEAU DIQUE SUD. 47°14.0'N,
2°11.0'W. Head. Fl.W.G. 4 sec. W.10M. G.6M.
4m. G. 054°-074°; W.074°-149°; G.149°-345°;
W.345°-054°.

SAINT MICHEL-CHEF-CHEF
PORT DE COMBERGE. JETEE SUD. Oc.W.G. 4
sec. W.9M. G.5M. 7m. White Tr. G.top. G.
Shore-123°; W.123°-140°; G.140°-shore.

PORT DE LA GRAVETTE DIQUE HEAD. Lt.
Fl.(3)W.G. 12 sec. W.8M. G.5M. W.Tr. G.Top.
W.124°-224°; G.224°-124°.

PORTCE 47°14.6'N, 2°15.4'W. Ldg.Lts.
025°30'. (Front) Dir. Q. 22M. W. Col. on
dolphin. 6m. Intens 024.7°-026.2°. (Rear)
Dir. Q. 27M. B. □ W. stripe on Tr. 36m. Intens
024°-027°.

POINT D'AIGUILLON 47°14.5'N, 2°15.8'W.
Lt. Oc.(4) W.R. 12 sec. W.15M. R.11M 27m. on
white Tr. W. (unintens) 207°-233° W.233°-293°;
W.297°-300°; R.300°-318°; W.318°-023°; W.023°-
089°.
LA COURONNEE. Lt.By. 47°07.6'N, 2°20.1'W.
Q.G. 6M. G. △ on G. HFPB 8m.

VILLÈZ-MARTIN. JETTY. 47°15.3'N,
2°13.7'W. Head. Fl.(2) 6 sec. 11M. 10m. Grey
round granite Tr. R. top.
LES MORÉES. Oc.(2) W.R. 6 sec. W.9M. R.6M.
G.5M. 12m. G. Tr. W.058°-224°; R.300°-058°.

SAINT NAZAIRE 47°16'N 2°13'W. Tel:
(40) 22 08 46.

JETÉE OUEST. Lt. Oc.(4)R. 12 sec. 8M. 11m.
White round Tr. R. top.
JETÉE EST. Lt. Oc.(4)G. 12 sec. 8M. 11m.
White round Tr. G. top.
OLD MOLE. 47°16.3'N, 2°11.8'W. Head.
Oc.(2+1) 12 sec. 12M. 18m. White round Tr. R.
top Weather and traffic signals.
MOLE HEAD Lt. Fl.Y. 2 sec. Y.mast.

OLD DOCK ENTRANCE, S. SIDE. 47°16.5'N,
2°11.9'W. Lt. Fl.(2)R. 6 sec. 10M. R. Tr. 9m.
CHANTIERS DE L'ATLANTIQUE. Lt.Bn. Fl.Bu.
2 sec. 1M. W. metal pylon on dolphin.
BRIDGE. Lt. Iso. 4 sec. Racon. 55m. Horn (2)
20 sec. Clearance 55m.
GRON Lt. Iso.R. 4 sec. 7M. post 6m.

LA LOIRE MARITIME

LOIRE 47°14'N, 2°18'W. Tel: Nantes (40) 89
47 46. Port de Trentemoult (Nantes) (40) 84
09 14.
St. Nazaire (40) 22 53 04. **Pilots:** Nantes (40)
69 29 00.
Radio — Ports: St. Nazaire VHF Chan. 16, 12.
H24.
Pointe de Chemoulin Signal Stn. VHF Chan. 16.
Nantes VHF Chan. 16, 12, 73. Hrs. 0700-1100;
1300-1700 (except Sundays). Tidal Info.
Chan. 73.
Radio — Pilots: VHF Chan. 16, 9, 6. H24. PV
2182 kHz.
Entry: Lock Signals. Vessels fly appropriate
Int. Code of Signal or 2 F.W. Lts. vert. Entry
prohibited = ball ½ mast. Entry & Dep.
prohibited = ball close up. Entry &
Dep. prohibited = ball over cone.
Tidal Info. ev. H+00, H+15, H+30, etc. VHF
Chan. 74. St. Nazaire to Nantes.

Least depth 5m. St. Nazaire to Nantes.
Channel well marked. Enter Canal Saint-Felix
through Malakoff Lock. Yachts enter St.
Nazaire through E Lock and berth at S end of
Bassin de Penhoet.
Navigation in La Loire Maritime is governed
by the height of tide needed for transit of
shallowest section. Tidal wave moves up river
at about 11kts. Ascend with flood as soon as
tide permits. Sailing from Nantes at 1 h.-HW,
vessels pass shallowest part at HW.

LE VILLAGE. No. 1 Lt. Q.R. 8M. White col. R.
top. 7m.

OILING JETTY. Oc. R. 4 sec. 9M. W.R. Tr. 10m.

DONGES. 47°18'N, 2°04'W. Tel: (40) 88 65 13.
Radio — Port: VHF Chan. 12, 16 as required.
SW. DOLPHIN Lt. Fl.G. 4 sec. 5M. 12m. G. Col.
NE. DOLPHIN. Iso. G. 4 sec. 5M. 12m. G.
Struc.
JETTY. Head. Fl.(2)R. 6 sec. 9M. 9m. R. Tr. Vis.
225°-135°.

PAIMBOEUF. MOLE. 47°17.4'N, 2°02.0'W.
Head. Oc.(3) W.G. 12 sec. W.11M. G.7M. 9m.
White round Tr. G. top. G.shore-123°; W.123°-
shore.
ÎLE DU PETIT CARNET. Fl.G. 2.5 sec. G.6M.
9m. White metal framework Tr. G. top.
Between Paimboeuf and Nantes, La Loire is
marked by Ldg.Lts. and by Occ.R. 4 sec. on N.
side and Occ.G. 4 sec. on S. side. These lights
are moved to meet changes in the channel.
Lts. Fl.(3)Y. 12 sec. on beacons mark outfall
200m. W. Q.(3)G. 5 sec. on T. Jetty 400m. E.

BAI DE BOURGNEUF

**INSHORE WAYPOINT SW OF PTE DE ST.
GILDAS. 47°07.7'N, 2°15.4'W.**

POINTE DE SAINT-GILDAS 47°08.0'N,
2°14.8'W. Lt. Q.W.R.G. W.11M. R.6M. G.6M.
23m. Metal framework Tr. on white house.
R.shore-308°; G.308°-078°; W.078°-088°;
R.088°-174°; W.174°-180°; G.180°-264°. RC.
Slip and moorings for yachts sheltered by a
jetty extending 3c. N from Pointe de Saint
Gildas.
La Gravette Hr. (2M. NE of Pointe de Saint
Gildas) 160 berths for yachts.

**OFFSHORE WAYPOINT 3.6M. N. OF ÎLE DU
PILIER Lt. 47°06.2'N, 2°21.3'W.**

ÎLE DU PILIER 47°02.6'N, 2°21.6'W. Fl.(3)
20 sec. 29M. 33m. Grey square Tr. RC. Same
structure: Q.R. 12M. 10m. Vis. 321°-034°.
Reed(3) 60 sec. RC.
BASSE DU MARTROGER. Q. W.R.G. W.8M.
R.5M. G.4M. 10m. B.Y. masonry Tr. G.033°-
055°; W.055°-060°; R.060°-095°; G.095°-124°;
W.124°-153°; R.153°-201°; W.201°-240°; R.240°-
033°. Topmark N.
LE PIERRE MOINE. Fl.(2) 6 sec. 5M. 14m.
B.Tr. R. bands.

PORNIC. 47°07'N, 2°07'W.

HARBOUR WAYPOINT. 47°06.4'N, 2°08.2'W.

YACHT HARBOUR. Tel: (40) 82 05 40.
Radio: VHF Chan. 9.
Entry: Entrance channel dries 1.3m. Berths for
900 yachts. Eastern pontoon for visitors.
Anchorage off Pornic in 3-5m. in sand and
mud.
Radio — Port: VHF Chan. 9. 0900-1200, 1400-
1800.
Radio — Pilots: VHF Chan. 12. H24.

JETÉE SW. Elbow. Fl.(2+1) 7 sec. 3M. 4m.
HEAD. Fl.(2)R. 6 sec. 2M. 4m.
JETÉE EST. Head. Fl.G. 2.5 sec. 2M. 4m.

POINTE DE NOVEILLARD. 47°06.6'N,
2°06.9'W. Oc.(3+1) W.R.G. 12 sec. W.14M.
R.10M. G.10M. 22m. White square Tr. G. top,
white dwelling. G. shore -051°; W.051°-079°;
R.079° -shore. Tidal signals.

POINTE DE GOURMALON. Lt. Fl.(2)G. 6 sec.
8M. W. mast. G. Top. 4m.
PORT DE PECHE N. Lt. Q.R. W. Post. 2m.;
S. Lt. Q.G. W. Post. 2m.
LA BERNERIE-EN-RETZ. Fl.R. 2 sec. 2M. 3m.
White support, R. top.
LE COLLET. Oc.(2) W.R. 6 sec. W.9M. R.6M.
7m. White hut, R. top. W.shore-093°; R.093°-
shore.

Ldg.Lts. 118°. (Front) Q.G. 6M. G.W. Tr. 4m.
(Rear) Q.G. 6M. G.W. Tr. 12m.

**INSHORE WAYPOINT BAIE DE BOURGNEUF.
47°03.4'N, 2°10.0'W.**

**INSHORE WAYPOINT N OF BC DE LA
BLANCHE BY. 47°04.9'N, 2°15.8'W.**

ÉTIER DES BROCHETS. 46°59.9'N,
2°01.9'W. Oc.(2+1) W.R.G. 12 sec. W.10M.
R.7M. G.6M. 8m. White col. G. top. G.071°-
091°; W.091°-102.5°; R.102.5°-116.5°; W.116.5°-
119.5°; R.119.5°-164.5°.

BEC DE L'EPOIDS. 46°56.4'N, 2°04.5'W.
Iso W.R.G. 4 sec. W.11M. R.8M. G.7M. 6m.
White square Tr. with gable. G.106°-113.5°;
R.113.5°-122°; G.122°-157.5°; W.157.5°-158.5°;
R.158.5°-171.5°; W.171.5°-176°.

PASSAGE DU GOIS

E SHORE. Lt. Fl.R. 4 sec. 6M. R. hut 6m.
Vis. 038°-218°.
E TURNING PT. Lt. Fl.2 sec. 6M. Grey
Pyramid 5m.
W TURNING PT. Lt. Fl. 2 sec. 3M. Grey
Pyramid 5m.
BASSOTIERE. Lt. Fl.G. 2 sec. 2M. W. Tripod.
G. Lantern. 7m. Vis. 180°-000°.

ÎLE DE NOIRMOUTIER

**OFFSHORE WAYPOINT W OF NOIRMOUTIER.
47°00.0'N, 2°24.9'W.**

POINTE DES DAMES 47°00.7'N 2°13.3'W.
Lt. Oc.(3) W.R.G. 12 sec. W.19M. R.15M. G.15M.
34m. White square Tr. and dwelling. G.016.5°-
057°; R.057°-124°; G.124°-165°; W.165°-191°;
R.191°-267°; W.267°-357°; R.357°-016.5°.
Obscured by the island 026°-036°.

PORT DE NOIRMOUTIER JETTY. Oc(2)R. 6
sec. 6M. 6m. White col. R. top.

PORT DE L'HERBAUDIERE. 47°01.7'N,
2°18.0'W. Tel: Port de Plaisance (51) 39 05 05.
Customs: (51) 39 06 80. YC (51) 39 30 46.
Radio: VHF Chan. 9.
Entry: Channel dredged to 1.3m. Deepest berths
3m. M.H.W.S. 5.4m. M.H.W.N. 4.0m. Marina in
SE part of harbour depths 2-3m. 500 berths, 100
for visitors. Initial call at pontoon at head of
central mole.

HARBOUR WAYPOINT. 47°02.1'N, 2°17.7'W.

JETÉE OUEST. 47°01.6'N, 2°17.9'W. Head.
Oc.(2+1) W.G.12 sec. W.10M. G.6M. 9m.
White metal col. and hut, G.top. W.187.5°-
190°; G.190°-187.5°. Reed 30 sec.
JETÉE EST. Head. Fl.(2)R. 6 sec. 5M. 8m. R.
mast.
EPIRON INTERIEUR HEAD Lt. Fl.R. 2 sec. 1M.
R. Box. 3m.

POINTE DE DEVIN. 46°59.1'N, 2°17.6'W.
Oc.(4) W.R.G.12 sec. W.11M. R.8M. G.8M.
10m. White col. and hut, G.top. G.314°-028°;
W.028°-035°; R.035°-134°
TOURELLE MILIEU. Lt. Fl.(4)R. 12 sec. 5M.
R.Tr. 6m.

OFFSHORE WAYPOINT CHAUSSEE DE
BOEUFS. 46°57.4′N, 2°26.3′W.

FROMENTINE

**HARBOUR WAYPOINT GOULET DE
FROMENTINE. 46°53.1′N, 2°11.6′W.**

POINTE NOTRE DAME-DE-MONTS.
46°53.3′N 2°08.6′W. Oc.(2) W.R.G. 6 sec.
W.13M. R.10M. G.10M. 21m. White Tr. G.000°-
043°; W.043°-063°; R.063°-073°; W.073°-094°;
G.094°-113°; W.113°-116°; R.116°-175°;
G.175°-196°; R.196°-230°.
Fl.W. Fl.R. and Fl.G. Lts. mark chan. between
Ile de Noirmoutier and mainland. Fl.R.2 sec.
marks N. side and Fl.G.2 sec. the S. side of
passage through bridge.

BRIDGE W END. 46°53.5′N, 2°09.0′W. Lt. 2 ×
Iso. 4 sec. 18M. Centre of bridge. 32m.
Lt. Iso. 4 sec. 18M. **E END.** 32m.

**INSHORE WAYPOINT PONT D'YEU.
46°45.5′N, 2°14.2′W.**

ILE D'YEU

MAIN LIGHT 46°43.1′N 2°22.9′W. Fl. 5 sec.
24M. 56m. White square Tr. Obsc. 257.5°-258°.
RC.
POINTE DU BUTTE. 0.8M. NW. Horn 60 sec.
LES CHIENS PERRINS. Lt. Q.(9) W.G. 15 sec.
W.8M. G.4M. 16m. Y.B.Y. Tr. Topmark W.
G.330°-350°; W.350°-200°.

PORT-JOINVILLE. 46°44′N, 2°21′W. Tel:
(51) 58 38 11. Customs (51) 58 37 28. Yacht
Harbour: 51 58 38 11.
Radio — Port: VHF Chan. 9.
Radio-Yacht Harbour: VHF Chan. 9.
Entry: Channel dredged to 1.5m. Channel to
Y. Hr. 2.5m. Max. draught 6.5m. H.W.S. 4.5m.
H.W.N. with winds NW/NE swell enters Hr.
Yacht Hr. is sheltered. Contact H.M. to arrange
berth. Enter wet basin 2h-HW-2h.

HARBOUR WAYPOINT. 46°44.2′N, 2°20.8′W.

JETÉE NW. 46°43.8′N, 2°20.7′W. Head.
Oc.(3) W.G.12 sec. W.11M. G.9M. 6m. White
8-sided Tr. G.top. G.shore-150°; W.150°-232°;
G.232°-279°; W.279°-285°; G.285°-shore. Tidal
signals. Horn (3) 30 sec.
QUAI DE CANADA. Ldg.Lts. 219° (Front) Q.R.
6M. Pylon 11m. 169°-269°. (Rear) Q.R. 6M.
mast 16m. 169°-269°.

HEAD. Lt. Iso.G. 4 sec. 7M. W.G. Tr. 20m.
GALIOTE JETTY ROOT. Lt. Fl.(2)R. 5 sec. 1M.

**OFFSHORE WAYPOINT N OF PT DES
CORBEAUX. 46°43.1′N, 2°15.0′W.**

INSHORE WAYPOINT. 46°42.4′N, 2°10.0′W.

POINTE DES CORBEAUX 46°41.4′N
2°17.1′W. Lt.Fl.(2+1) R.15 sec. 18M. 25m.
White square Tr. Obscured by high land of Ile
d'Yeu 083°-143°.
LA MEULE. Oc.W.R.G.4 sec. W.9M. R.6M.
G.6M. 9m. Grey Col. R.Top. G.007.5°-018°;
W.018°-027.5°; R.027.5°-041.5°.

SAINT JEAN DE MONTS. JETTY. Head. Lt.
Q.(2)R. 5 sec. 3M. 10m.

SAINT GILLES-SUR-VIE

HARBOUR WAYPOINT. 46°41.1′N, 1°58.1′W.
Entry: Sand Bar 0.5m. Channel 1.5m. H.W.S.
5.3m. H.W.N. 4.2m. L.W.S. 0.9m. L.W.N. 2.1m.
Max. 60m.×5.5m. Springs, 3.5m. Neaps.
Breakers form off entrance in onshore winds
and outgoing tide. Anchorage in fair weather SE
of Ldg.Lts. in 3-4m. Small yacht basin E of
Grande Mole depth 1m. Yacht Hr. with pontoons
600 yachts 5-25m. length 1.5m. depth.

POINTE DE GROSSE TERRE 46°41.6′N
1°58.0′W. Lt. Fl.(4) W.R
.12 sec. W.17M. R.13M. 25m. white truncated
conical Tr. W.290°-125°; R.125°-145°.
Ldg.Lts. 46°41.9′N, 1°56.8′W. 043°30′. Front:
Oc.(3+1) R.12 sec. 12M. 7m. White square Tr.
R.corners. Rear: Oc.(3+1) R.12 sec. 15M. 28m.
White square Tr. R.top. Synchronised with
front. Intens 033.5°-053.5°.
JETÉE DE BOISVINET. Fl.(2) W.R.6 sec. W.9M.
R.6M. 8m. R.col. R.045°-225°; W.225°-045°.
JETÉE DE LA GARENNE. Head. Q.W.G. W.9M.
G.6M. W.G.Tr. 8m. G.045°-335°; W.335°-045°.
Reed 20 sec.

L'ARMANDÈCHE 46°29.4′N 1°48.3′W. Lt.
Fl.(2+1) 15 sec. 23M. 42m. White 6-sided Tr.
R.top. Vis. 295°-130°.

LES BARGES 46°29.7′N 1°50.5′W. Lt. Fl.(2)
R.10 sec. 17M. 25m. Grey Tr. Helicopter landing
platform.

LA PETITE BARGE 46°28.9'N, 1°50.6W. Lanby. Q.(6) + L.Fl. 15 sec. 8M. 8m. Pillar Y.B.Y. 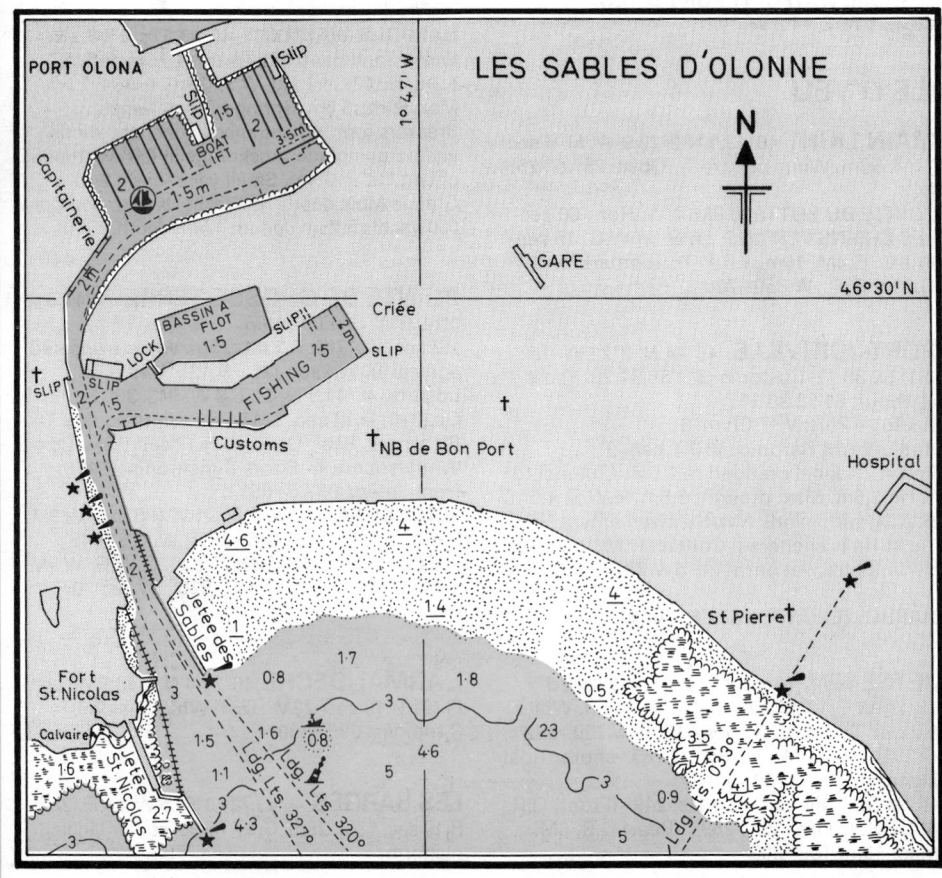. Whis.

INSHORE WAYPOINT S OF PETITE BARGE. 46°28.7'N, 1°50.9'W.

LES SABLES D'OLONNE Tel: Port: (51) 95 11 79. Pilots: (51) 32 60 97.

HARBOUR WAYPOINT. 46°28.1'N, 1°46.6'W.

Radio — Pilots: VHF Chan. 16 12. 0800-1800. Yacht Hbr. Tel: (51) 32 51 16. VHF Chan. 9. **Entry:** Entrance channel 0.5-1.5m. Y. Hr. 600 berths, 60 for visitors.

JETÉE SAINT NICOLAS. 46°29.2'N, 1°47.5'W. Head. U.Q.(2)R. 1 sec. 10M. 16m. White Tr. R.top Vis. 094°-043°. Horn(2) 30 sec.

Ldg.Lts. 320°. **JETÉE DES SABLES.** Head. Front: Q.G. 8M. 11m. white Tr. G.top. Partially or completely obscured when bearing more than 062°. Tidal signals.

TOUR DE LA CHAUME. 46°29.6'N, 1°47.8'W. Rear: Oc.(2+1) 12 sec. 13M. 33m. large grey square Tr. surmounted by white turret. R.C.

PASSE DU SW.

Ldg.Lts. 46°29.5'N, 1°46.3'W. 033°. Front: Iso.R. 4 sec. 16M. mast 14m. Rear: Iso.R. 4 sec. 16M. 33m. white square masonry Tr. Shown throughout 24 h.

Ldg.Lts. 327°. Front: F.R. 5M. 6m. R. Ⅱ. Rear: F.R. 11M. 9m. R. Ⅱ. Intens 323.5°-330.5°.

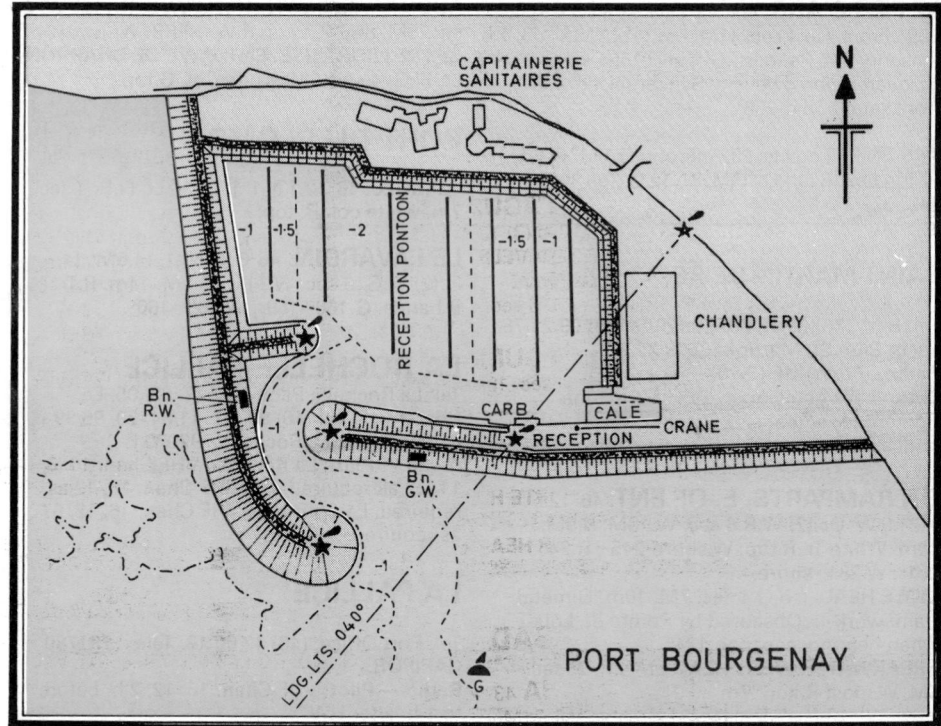

BOURGENAY. 46°26.5'N 01°40.8'W.
Tel: H.M. (51) 22 20 36.
Radio—Port: VHF Ch. 16, 9.
Entry: 510 pontoon berths with full facilities.

Ldg.Lts. 040° (Front) Q.G. 9M. G. Panel. (Rear)
Q.G. 9M. G. Panel.
DIQUE W HEAD Lt. Fl.R. 4 sec. 9M. R. Tr.
MOLE E HEAD Lt. Iso.G. 4 sec. 5M. Not vis. to
seaward.
BREAKWATER ELBOW Lt. Fl.(2)R. 6 sec. 5M.
Not vis. to seaward.

JARD-SU-MER. 46°24'N 01°36'W.
Tel: H.M. (51) 33 40 17.
Entry: Sandy bottom dries MLWS. 2 slips and
space for 200 yachts.

Ldg.Bns. 038° (Front) R.W. Pole (Rear). R.W.
Pole.
Entrance on Ldg. line marked by By. Conical
G. and By. Can.R.

PLATEAU DE ROCHEBONNE

ROCHEBONNE NW 46°12.9'N, 2°31.9'W. Lt.By.
Q.(9) 15 sec. 8M. ⵝ on B.Y. By. 8m. Whis. ⌇⌇⌇

ROCHEBONNE SW 46°10.1'N, 2°27.0'W. Lt.By.
Fl.(2)R. 6 sec. 5M. □ on R. By. 9m. ⌇⌇⌇
ROCHEBONNE SE 46°09.2'N, 2°21.2'W. Lt.By.
Q.(3) 10 sec. 8M. ⵟ on B.Y. By. 8m. Bell. ⌇⌇⌇
ROCHEBONNE NE 46°12.7'N, 2°25.0'W. Lt.By.
Iso.G. 4 sec. 5M. △ on G. By. 8m. ⌇⌇⌇

POINTE DU GROUIN-DU-COU

46°20.7'N, 1° 27.8'W. Lt. Fl.W.R.G. 5 sec.
W.22M., R.18M., G.16M. 29m. White square
Tr. R.034°-061°; W.061°-117°; G.117°-138°;
W.138°-034°. Sectors indeterminate.
Obscured by Ile de Re when bearing less than
034°.

LA TRANCHE-SUR-MER. PIER. Head. Fl.(2)R.
6 sec. 7M. 6m. R. Col.

ÎLE DE RÉ

**LES BALEINEAUX OR HAUT-BANC-
DU-NORD.** 46°15.8'N 1°35.2'W. Oc.(2)
6 sec. 13M. 23m. Pink Tr. R.Top.

LES BALEINES 46°14.7'N 1°33.7'W. Lt.
Fl.(4) 15 sec. 27M. 57m. Grey 8-sided Tr. and
dwelling. RC. Sig. Stn.

LE FIER D'ARS. 46°14.0'N, 1°28.8'W. Ldg.Lts. 265°. Front: Iso 4 sec. 11M. 5m. ☐ on W. masonry hut. Rear: Iso.G. 4 sec. 15M. 13m. G.square Tr. on dwelling. Synchronised with front. Intens 264°-266°.

ARS-EN-RÉ Ldg.Lts. 232°. (Front) Q. 9M. W.Col. R. Top 5m. (Rear) Q. 11M. W. Tr. G. Top 13m. 142°-322°.

SAINT-MARTIN DE RÉ

Tel: H.M. (46) 09 26 69. Customs (46) 09 21 78. Yacht Club St. Martin (46) 09 22 07.
Radio—Port: VHF Ch. 9.
Entry: Lock gates open 1h-HW-1h June-September and at HW October-May if 24h notice given.

ON RAMPARTS. E. OF ENT. 46°12.5'N, 1°21.9'W. Oc.(2) W.R.6 sec. W.13M. R.9M. 18m. White Tr. R.top. W.shore-245°; R.245°-281°; W.281°-shore.
MOLE HEAD. Iso.G.4 sec. 7M. 10m. G.metal framework Tr. Obscured by Pointe de Loix when bearing less than 124°.
BREAKWATER WEST HEAD Lt. Fl.R. 2½ sec. 4M. W. post R. top. 7m.

LA FLOTTE. Tel: (46) 09 67 66.

LA FLOTTE. 46°11.3'N, 1°19.3'W. Fl.W.G.4 sec. W.12M. G.7M. 10m. White round Tr. G.top. G.130°-205°; W.205°-220°; G.220°-257° also Moiré effect Dir. Lt. 212.5°. Horn(3) 30 sec. sounded by day for 2 h. before to 2 h. after HW.

RIVEDOUX-PLAGE Ldg.Lts. 200°. Front: Q.G. 5M. 6m. White Tr. G.top. Rear: Q.G. 5M. 9m. White and G.cheq. ☐
BRIDGE N SIDE. Lt. Iso. 4 sec. 8M. 34m. 061°-236° marks N-S passage.
BRIDGE S SIDE. Lt. Iso. 4 sec. 8M. 34m. 245°-059° marks S-N passage.
POINTE DE SABLANCEAUX. PIER. Q.Vi. 10m. white mast and hut, G.top.

CHAUVEAU 46°08.0'N 1°16.4'W. Lt. Oc.(2+1) W.R.12 sec. W.17M. R.13M. 23m. white round Tr. R.top. W.057°-094°; R.094°-104°; W.104°-342°; R.342°-057°. Partially obscured when bearing less than 202°.
CHANCHARDON. Fl.(2) W.R.4 sec. W.9M. R.6M. 15m. R.W. 8-sided Tr. R.118°-290°; W.290°-118°.

BUOY PA. 46°05.6'N, 1°42.4'W. Lt.By. Iso.W. 4 sec. 8M. 8m. R. ○ on R.W. HFPB. Whis. ⠿
SÈVRE NIORTAISE. ENT. PAVÉ DE CHARRON. Lt. Fl.G. 4 sec. 7M. white Col. G.top.

PORT DU PLOMB

W. MOLE. 46°12.1'N 1°12.2'W. Lt. Fl.R. 4 sec. 7m. white col. R. top.

LE LAVARDIN. 46°08.1'N, 1°14.5'W. Lt. Fl.(2) W.G. 6 sec. W.11M. G.8M. 14m. R.Tr. B.bands. G.160°-169°; W.169°-160°.

LA ROCHELLE-PALLICE

Tel: La Rochelle Pilot: (46) 42 63 05. La Charente Pilot: (46) 99 91 11/84 20 96/99 82 46. Telex: La Rochelle 792079 F.
Radio — Pilot: La Rochelle VHF Chan. 16, 6, 11, 12 as required. P.V. VHF Chan. 16, 12 as required. La Charente. VHF Chan. 16, 12, 67 as required.

LA PALLICE

Tel: Port Office: (46) 42 60 12. Telex: 791780 CAPIPOR.
Radio — Pilot: VHF Chan. 16, 12. 2 h. before to 1 h. after HW.
Lock gates open 2 h. before to 1 h. after HW. Signals as per Int. Code. Request made in advance to use lock.

MOLE D'ESCALE. 46°09.8'N 1°14.3'W. Head. Dir.Lt. 016°. Dir.Q.W.R.G. W.14M. R.13M. G.13M. 33m. Tr. on building. G.009°-014.7°; W.014.7°-017.3°; R.017.3°-031°. Sig.Stn.
SE CORNER. Oc.(2) R. 6sec. 6M. 7m. Caisson.
NW CORNER. Lt. Fl.G. 4 sec.

OIL JETTY. HEAD. Lt. Q.(6) + L.Fl. 15 sec. Y.B. Tr. also Fl.(5)Y. 20 sec. ½M. SE.

BASSIN CHEF-DE-BAIE JETÉE SUD HEAD Lt. Fl.(3)G. 12 sec. 9M. W. Tr. G. Top. 13m. Reed(3) 30 sec.

Ldg.Lts. 126° (Front) Q.G. 5M. G. ☐ W. stripe G.W. mast 10m. 110°-142°. (Rear) Q.G. 5M. G. ☐
G.W. mast. 29m. 116°-136°.

AVANT PORT
JETÉE NORD. HEAD. Oc.(2) R. 6 sec. 7M. Grey Tr. 10m. Intens 234°-144°. Unintens 144°-184°.
JETEE SUD. Lt. Iso.G. 4 sec. 7M. G. ▵ W. Bn. 6m.

BASIN Ldg.Lts. 085°. (Front) Q.R. 7M. R. Mast 21m. (Rear) Q.R. 7M; R.W. ☐ on W. Mast. R. Top.

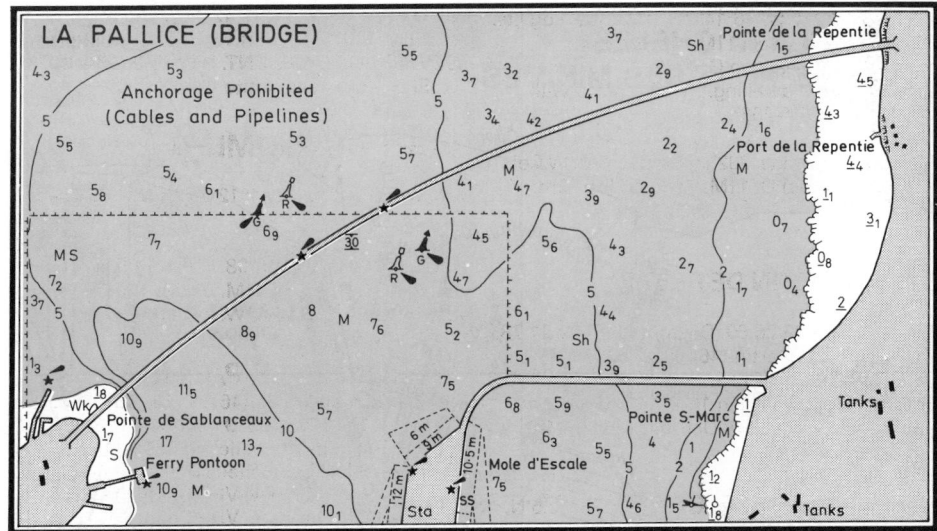

LA ROCHELLE

Large yacht harbour at Port des Minimes and moorings in tidal harbour. Port open 2h. before to 1h. after HW. Signals as per Int. Code must be obeyed. Red and blue lights control traffic through gates of Basins.

TOURELLE RICHELIEU Fl.(4) R. 12 sec. 9M. 10m. R.Tr. RC. F.R. Lts. on Tr. 1.2M WNW. Siren (4) 60 sec. sounded from 1 h. before to 1 h. after HW.

Ldg.Lts. 46°09.4'N, 1°09.1'W. 059°. Front: Q. (By Day Fl. 4 sec.) 14M. 15m. R.round Tr. white bands. Intens 056°-062°. Rear: Q. (By Day Fl. 4 sec.) 12M. 25m. White 8-sided Tr. G.top. Synchronised with front. Obscured 061°-065°.

LOCK. Ldg.Lts. 087°. Front: F.Vi. Intens. 084°-090°. Rear: F.Vi. Intens. 084°-090°.

PORT DE MINIMES (Yacht Harbour).

Tel: (46) 44 41 20. Customs: (46) 41 11 73. Doctor: (46) 44 08 20. Bassin Àflot (46) 41 32 05.
Radio: VHF Chan. 9. H24.
Entry: Bassin à Flot open 2 h.-HW-1 h.
W. MOLE. HEAD. Lt. Fl.G. 4 sec. Lt.Q. on prominent building.
E. MOLE. HEAD. Lt. Fl.(2) R. 6 sec.

LA CHARENTE

Pilotage compulsory in La Charente and all ports on the river. Speed limit 12 kts. No passing or overtaking on the bends. No navigation in fog when banks cannot be seen clearly.

ROCHEFORT. 45°56'N, 0°57'W. H.M. Tel: (46) 99 44 93. Y. Hr. Tel: (46) 84 30 30.
Port — Radio: VHF Chan. 16, 12.
Pilots — Radio: VHF Chan. 16, 67.
Y. Hr. — Radio: VHF Chan. 9. 1 h.-HW-1 h.
Martrou Bridge. VHF Chan. 16. 0500-2100 LT.
Entry: No. 1 Basin is yacht hr. 210 berths including visitors. Lock gates open 1½ h.-HW-1½ h. Lock 65m. × 8m. × sill depth 1.5m. A.C.D. Fuel available from pontoon on N side of entrance.

ÎLE D'AIX 46°00.6'N 1°10.7'W. Lt. Fl.W.R.5 sec. W. 23M. R.19M. 24m. Two white round Trs. R.top, one for light, the other to screen R. sector. R.103°-118°; W.118°-103°.

FORT DE LA POINTE. 45°58.0'N,

1°04.3'W. Ldg.Lts. 115°. Front: Q.R. 19M. 8m. White square Tr. R.top. Intens 113°-117°. Rear: Q.R. 20M. 21m. White square Tr. R.top. Intens 113°-117°.
AUX. Lt. Q.R. 8M. same structure 21m. 322°-067° over Port-des-Barques anchorage.

PORT NORD DE FOURAS

PIER. 45°59.8'N, 1°05.9'W. Head. Oc.(3+1) W.G.12 sec. W.11M. G.8M. 9m. White metal framework Tr. G.top. G.084°-127°; W.127°-084°.

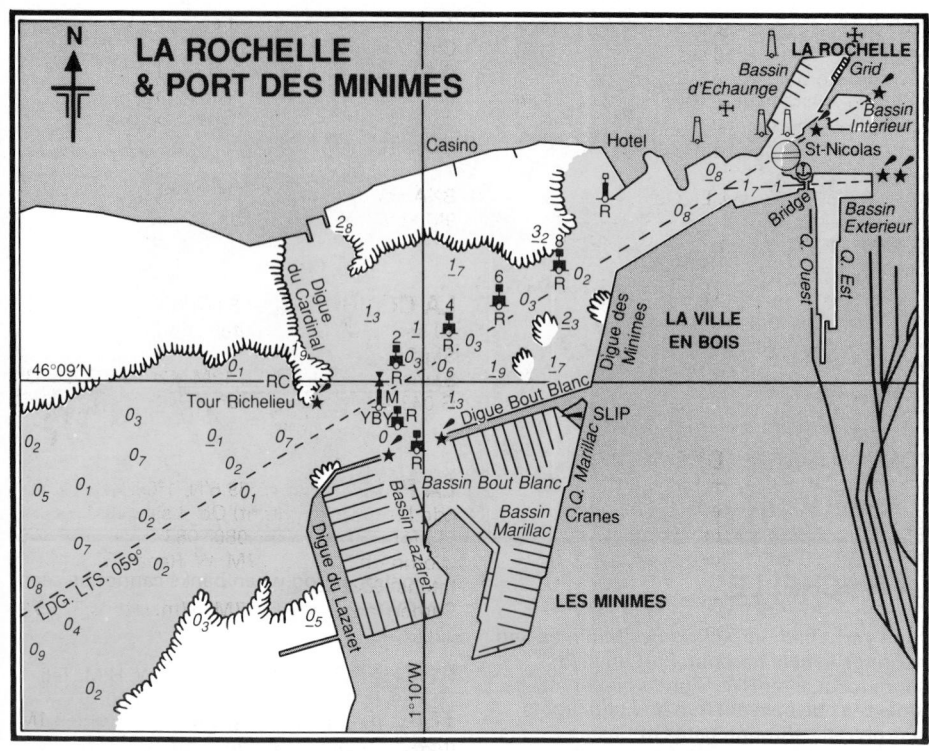

PORT SUD DE FOURAS

PASSE AUX FILLES Ldg.Lts. 042°30'.
Front: Oc.(2)R. 6 sec. Rear: Gp.Oc.(2)R. 6 sec.
Synchronised with front.
JETTY. Head. Fl. W.R. 4 sec. W.10M. R.7M.
R.117°-177°; W.177°-117°.

PORT-DES-BARQUES Ldg.Lts. 134°30'.
Front: Dir. Iso.G.4 sec. 7M. 5m. White square
Tr. Intens 125°-145°. Rear: Dir. Iso.G.4 sec. 8M.
13m. White square Tr. with B. gable, B.band
on W. side. Synchronised with front. Intens
125°-145°.
JETEE DE LA FUMEE HEAD. Lt. Q.G. 5M. G.
mast.

ÎLE D'OLERON

CHASSIRON 46°02.8'N 1°24.6'W. Lt. Fl. 10
sec. 28M. 50m. White round Tr. B.bands.
Partially obscured 297°-351°. Sig.Stn.
ROCHER D'ANTIOCHE. 46°04.0'N, 1°23.6'W.
Q. 11M. 21m. ☖ On B.Tr. Yellow band. ⌇.

ST. DENIS D'OLERON. 46°02.2'N 01°22'W.
Tel: H.M. (46) 47 97 97. Yacht Club de L'Ocean
(46) 47 93 64.
JETEE HEAD Lt. Fl.(2)W.G. 6 sec. W. 8M.
G. 5M. G. pole. W.277°-292°; G.-165°; Obsc
-205°; G.-277°.
Marina Port du Douhet. Tel: 46 76 71 13. 100
berths (10 visitors).
LA PÉRROTINE. Oc.(2)R. 6 sec. 6M. 8m. White
metal framework Tr. R.top. Obsc. by Pointe
des Saumonards when bearing less than
150°.
TOURELLE JULIAR. Q.(3) W.G. 10 sec.
W.11M. G.8M. ⊕ B.Y. Tr. 12m. W.147°-336°;
G.336°-147°.

LE CHATEAU Ldg.Lts. 319°. Front: Q.R.
7M. 11m. R. 0 on white Tr. Rear: Q.R. 7M. 24m.
White Tr. R.top.

PORT DE LA COTINIÈRE

APPROACH Dir.Lt. 048°. Dir.Oc.W.R.G.4 sec.
6M. 13m. White col. B. bands. G.033°-046°;
W.046°-050°; R.050°-063°.

ENTRANCE 45°54.8′N, 1°19.6′W. Ldg.Lts. 339°. Front: Dir.Oc.(2) 6 sec. 14M. 6m. White Tr. R.top. Horn (2) 20 sec. Sounded for 3 h. before to 3 h. after HW. Rear: Dir.Oc.(2) 6 sec. 12M. 14m. White metal framework Tr. R.bands. Synchronised with front. Intens 329°-349°.
GRAND JETÉE. Elbow. Lt. Oc.R. 4 sec. 8M. 11m. White Tr. R.top.
GRANDE JETÉE HEAD. Lt. Fl.R. 4 sec. 5M. W.R. Tr. 10m.
S JETTY. Head Lt. Iso. G. 4 sec. 6M. W.G. Tr. 9m.
ÉPI DU COLOMBIER. F.Bu. 6M. 6m. White Tr. Vi.top.
ST TROJAN Lt. Fl.G. 4 sec. 8m.

PONT DE LA SEUDRE. 45°47.9′N, 1°08.4′W. Down Stream Side: Q. 10M. 20m. Bridge structure, between piles 6 and 7. Vis. 054°-234°. Upstream side: Q. 10M. 20m. Bridge structure, between piles 6 and 7. Vis. 234°-054°.
POINTE DE MUS DE LOUP. Oc.G. 4 sec. 6M. 8m. House, white to seaward. Vis. 118°-147°.

LA GIRONDE 45°33′N 1°03′W Tel:
Le Verdon (56) 59 63 91/59 62 11, Ext. 235.
Pauillac (56) 09 01 60, Yacht Hbr.
(56) 54 12 16, Blaye (57) 42 13 63, Ambès
(56) 77 12 52, Bordeaux (56) 90 58 00 &
(56) 52 51 04. Telex: 570617 PABLV &
570428 CAPIPOR.
PILOTS BORDEAUX (56) 50 47 07.
Telex: 570505 PILOT BX F.
PILOTS VERDON (56) 09 63 85/09 63 87.
Telex: 550167 PILVDON F.

Radio — Port: Le Verdon. VHF Chan. 16, 12, 11, 14. H24.
Radar. VHF Chan. 16, 11, 12, 14. Advice etc in French.
Pauillac. VHF Chan. 16, 12. H24.
Pauillic Yacht Hbr. VHF Chan. 9.
Blaye. VHF Chan. 12. H24.
Ambès. VHF Chan. 12. H24.
Bordeaux. VHF Chan. 16, 12. H24.

Radio — Pilots: MF 2182 kHz. H24. VHF Chan. 16, 12, 6. H24.
Entry: Yacht moorings in Bonne Anse. Port de Royan — yacht moorings in northern part of harbour. Depths 0.6 m. to 2.4 m. Pauillac — yacht marina also at Goulée, St. Estephe, St. Georges de Didonne, Meschers sur Gironde, Talmont sur Gironde, Callonges, Les Portes Neuves, Freneau, Plassac.
Special attention to be paid to mooring lines at Bordeaux especially at LW.

Tidal Heights broadcast ev. 5 min. VHF Chan. 17.
Give La Mauvaise Bank N of Gironde entrance a wide berth. Advisable to enter by Grande Passe de L'Ouest except in NW gales.

BXA. 45°37.6′N, 1°28.6′W. Lt.By. Iso. 4 sec. 9M. R.W. V.S. 8m. Racon. Whis.

LA COUBRE 45°41.8′N 1°14.0′W. Lt. Fl.(2) 10 sec. 31M. 64m. white round Tr. R.top. RC. Sig.Stn.
Same structure: F.R.G. 12M. 42m. R.030°-043°; G.043°-060°; R.060°-110°.

LA PALMYRE. 45°39.6′N, 1°08.7′W. Ldg.Lts. 081°30′ (Front) Oc. 4 sec. 22M. Platform 21m. Intens 080°-083°. (Common Rear) Q. 27M. W. Radar Tr. 57m. Intens. 080°-083°.
Same structure: F.R. 17M. 57m. Intens 325.5°-328.5°.

TERRE-NÉGRE. Ldg.Lts. 327°. Front: 1.1M. from rear. Oc.(3) W.R.G.12 sec. W.17M. R.13M. G.12M. 39m. White Tr. R.top. on W. side. R.304°-319°; W.319°-327°; G.327°-000°; W.000°-004°; G.004°-097°; W.097°-104°; R.104°-116°.

CORDOUAN 45°35.2′N 1°10.4′W. Lt. Oc.(2+1) W.R.G.12 sec. W.21M. R.17M. G.17M. 60m. White conical Tr. dark grey band and top. W.014°-126°; G.126°-178.5°; W.178.5°-250°; W(unintens) 250°-267°; R(unintens) 267°-294.5°; R.294.5°-014°. Obscured in estuary when bearing more than 285°. Danger signals.

ROYAN 45°37.2′N 01°01.6′W.
Tel: H.M. (46) 38 72 72. Customs (46) 38 51 27.

JETÉE SUD Head. Lt. 45°37.1′N, 1°01.7′W. U.Q.(2)R. 1 sec. 12M. W.Tr. R. base. 11m. 199°-116°. Horn(2) 20 sec. sounded by day 2½ h.-HW-2 h.
MOLE NORD SPUR. Lt. Iso. 4 sec. Strip Lt.
JETÉE EST HEAD. Lt. Fl.G. 4 sec. 7M. W. Post. G. Top 2m. 311°-151°. F. strip Lt. on NW end of jetty.
NOUVELLE JETÉE. Lt. Oc.(2)R. 6 sec. 6M. W. Mast. R. Top. 8m.

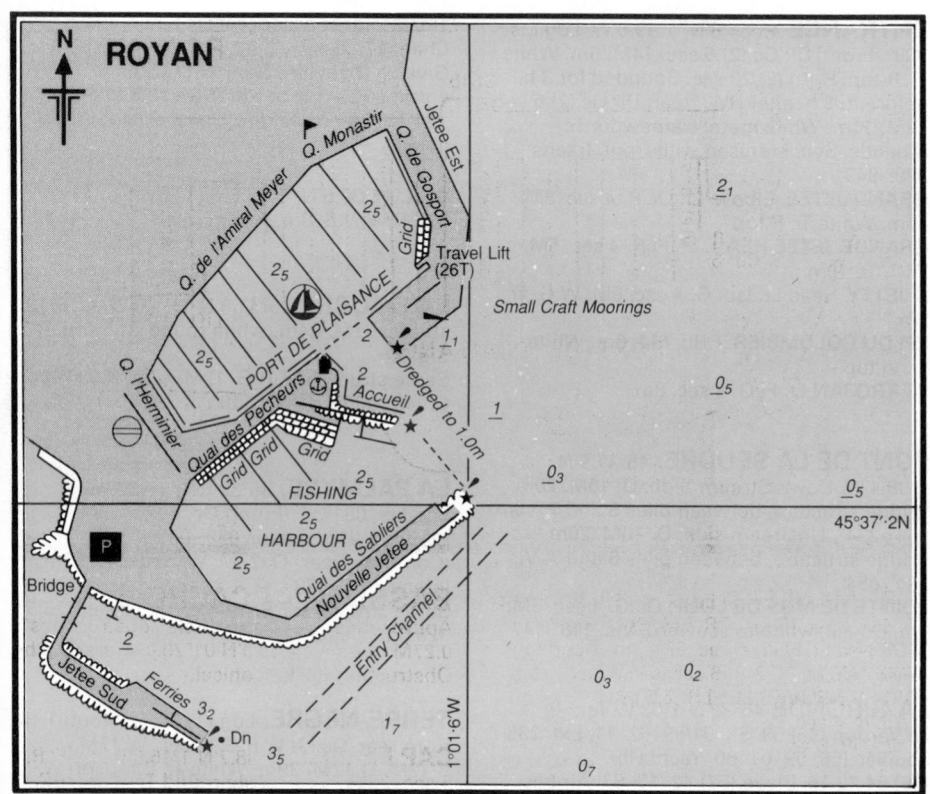

SAINT NICOLAS. 45°33.8'N, 1°04.9'W.
063°. 1st Ldg.Lts. Front: Q.G. 18M. 22m. White
square Tr. Intens 060°-066°.

POINTE DE GRAVE. Rear: Oc.W.R.G.4
sec. W.18M. R.12M. G.11M. 26m. White
square Tr. B.corners and top. W.033°-054°
Unintens; W.054°-233.5°; R.233.5°-303°;
W.303°-312°; G.312°-330°; W.330°-341°;
W.341°-025° Unintens.

LE CHAY. 45°37.4'N, 1°02.4'W. 041°. Ldg.Lts.
Front: Q.R. 16M. 33m. White Tr. R.top. Intens
039.5°-042.5°. Obscured 325°-335°. **SAINT-
PIERRE.** Rear: Q.R. 18M. 61m. Light-grey
water Tr. R.support. Intens 039°-043°.
POINTE DE GRAVE JETEE NORD HEAD.
Lt. Q. 2M. ᚼ B.Y. Bn. 6m.
SPUR Lt. Iso G. 4 sec. 2M. G. △ on G. mast
5m. Vis.173°-020°.

PORT-BLOC
ESTACADE NORD. Lt. Fl.G.4 sec. 6M. 8m.
White metal framework Tr. G.top. Lit by day in
fog.
ESTACADE SUD. Lt. Iso.R. 4 sec. 6M. 8m.
White Tr. R.top. Lit by day in fog

LE VERDON-SUR-MER

OIL PIER. 45°31.9'N, 1°02.1'W. Approach
Ldg.Lts. 171°30'. (Front) Dir. Q. 18M. 4m.
Also Fl.G. 2 sec. White △ B stripe on dolphin.
(Rear) Dir. Q. 20M. 16m. Also Fl.G. 2 sec. B.
support on platform.
POINTE DE LA CHAMBRETTE PIER. Lt. Fl.(3)
W.G.12 sec. W.8M. G.4M. 18m. White metal
framework Tr. G.top. W.172°-215°; G.215°-
172°.
MORTAGNE-LA-RIVE. Lt. Oc.R. 4 sec. 8M. 8m.
B. metal framework Tr. and pedestal.

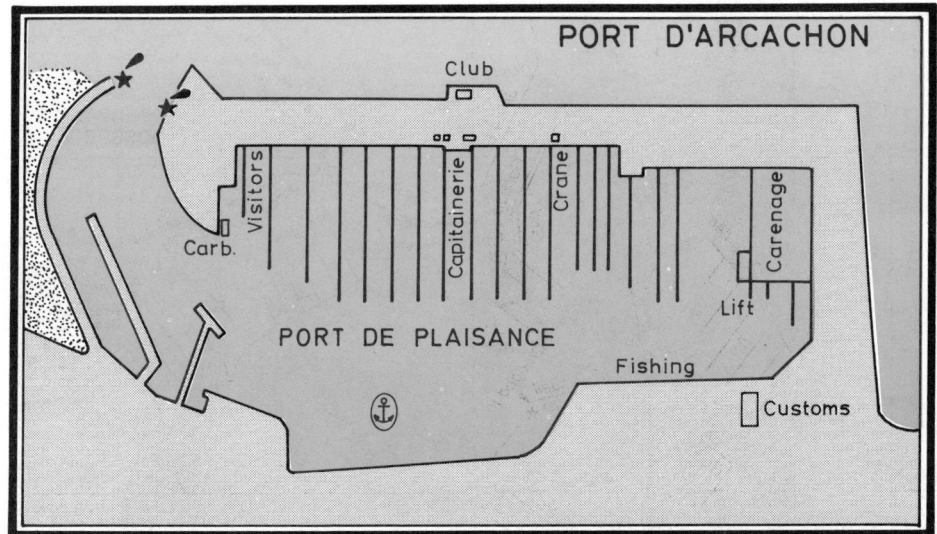

PORT MAUBERT. Ldg.Lts. 024°30′ (Front)
F.R. 5M. Post. (Rear) F.R. 5M. Post. 9m.
LAMENA. Lt. Fl.(2) 6 sec. 5M. 3m. Tidegauge.
VITREZAY. Lt. Fl.(2)R. 6 sec. 6M. 6m.
PORTES NEUVES Lt. Fl.R. 2.5 sec.
Lt. Oc.R. 4 sec.
Lt. Fl.(2)R. 6 sec.

TROMPELOUP. 45°13.7′N, 0°43.6′W.
Ldg.Lts. 159°30′. Front: Q. 19M. W. Tr. R.Top.
10m. Intens 157.5°-160.5°.
PATIRAS. N Point. Rear. Dir. Oc. 4 sec. 20M.
W. Tr. R. Top. 31m. Intens. 158.5°-160.5°.

PAUILLAC-TROMPELOUP
Yacht Hbr. Tel: (56) 59 12 16. VHF Chan.9.
PETROLEUM PIER. Lt. Fl.G. 4 sec. 5M. W. Tr.
G. top 17m. Reed 10 sec.
PUBLIC WHARF. Lt. **N END.** Fl.(2)G. 6 sec. 5M.
W. Tr. G. top.
Ldg.Lts. 45°11.9′N, 0°44.4′W. 180°.
PAUILLAC. Front: Iso R.4 sec. 17M. 3m. White
col. Intens 179°-181°. **ST. LAMBERT.** Rear: F.R.
17M. White and B.col. Intens 179°-181°.
PAUILLAC BREAKWATER ELBOW Lt. Fl.G. 4
sec. 5M. G. mast 7m. Lt. Q.G. marks end of
Breakwater.
ST. ANDRONY JETTY HEAD Lt. Oc.(2)R. 6 sec.
R. □ on Bn.
BLAYE. QUAY HEAD. Lt. Q.G. 7M. 7m. W. Col.
G. top. Above Blaye the chan. is marked by
G.Lts. on W. side and R.Lts. on E. side.

HOURTIN 45°08.8′N 1°09.7′W. Lt. Fl. 5 sec.
23M. 55m. R. square brick Tr.

BASSIN D'ARCACHON
Approaches — Danger. Circle "obstructions"
0.27M. radius 44°23.0′N 01°26.0′W marked by
Obstruction By. W. conical.

CAP FERRET 44°38.7′N 1°15.0′W. Lt. Fl.R.
5 sec. 26M. 53m. White round Tr. R.top. RC.
Same structure: Oc.(3) 12 sec. 14M. 46m. Vis.
045°-135°.
PORT DE LA VIGNE. Lt. Iso.R. 4 sec. 4M. W.
Post R. Top. 7m.

ARCACHON
W BREAKWATER. Lt. Q.G. 6M. G. mast.
E BREAKWATER. Lt. Q.R. 6M. R. mast.
LA SALIE. WHARF. 44°30.9′N, 1°15.6′W. Head.
Lt. Q.(9) 15 sec. 10M. 19m. Y.B.Y.
ATT-ARC. 44°34.7′N, 1°18.0′W. Lt.By. L. Fl.
10 sec. 5M. ○ on R.W. Pillar 8m.
EMISSAIRE 44°30.5′N, 1°17.6′W. Lt.By. Fl.(2) 6
sec. 5M. 8 on B.R. By. 8m.
ZDS 44°28.0′N, 1°19.3′W. Lt.By. Fl.(3)Y. 12 sec.
7M. X on Y. By. 8m.

SOULAC SAR STN. Tel: (56) 59 82 00.
Telex: 570512 CROSC C. Radio 2182 kHz. VHF
Chan. 16, 6, 9, 10, 12, 13. Weather B'casts.
VHF Chan. 13 at 0800, 1200, 1500, 2000 LT.
Nav. Warnings VHF Chan. 13. 0803, 1430, 1800
LT. Hours Mid June-Mid Sept. H24. Mid Sept.-
Mid June 0700-2200. Urgent navigational
warnings are broadcast on Chan. 13 ev. 2h.
while in force.

23:70   REED'S NAUTICAL ALMANAC

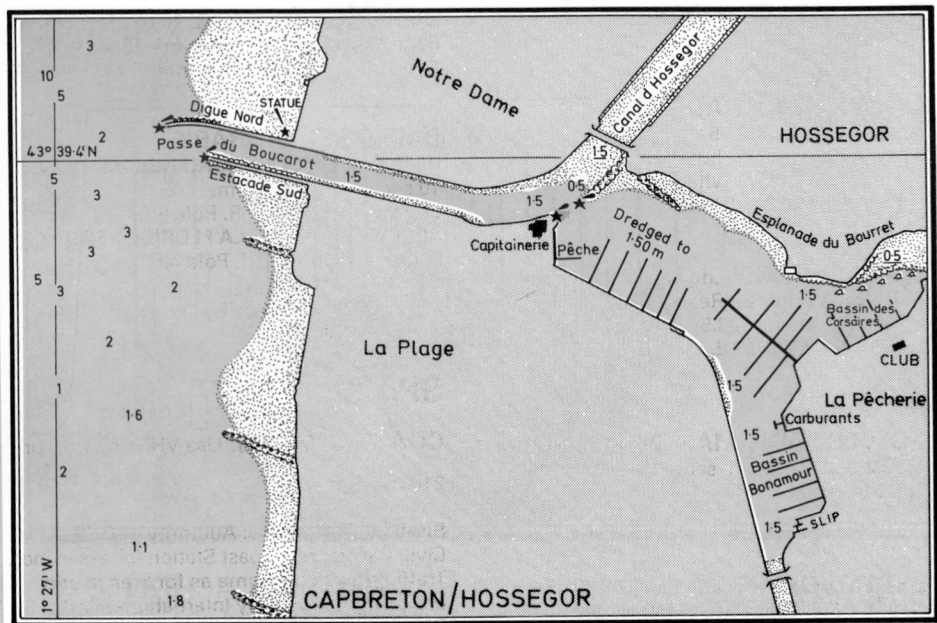

CONTIS 44°05.7′N 1°19.2′W. Lt. Fl.(4)25 sec. 23M. 50m. White round Tr. B.diagonal stripes. F.R. on radio mast 16.5M. NNE.

CAPBRETON Tel: (58) 72 25 26.
Radio — Port: VHF Chan. 9.
DIQUE NORD HEAD. 43°39.4′N, 1°26.8′W. Lt. Fl.(2)R. 6 sec. 10M. R.W. Tr. 13m. Horn 30 sec.
ESTACADE SUD. Lt. Iso. G.4 sec. 9M. 7m. Grey Tr.
BA 43°32.6′N, 1°32.8′W. Lt.By. L.Fl. 10 sec. 8M. ○ on R.W. By. 8m. Anchoring and fishing prohibited within 0.9M. of BA Lt.By.

L'ADOUR 43°31′N 1°30′W. Tel: H.M. Bayonne (59) 63 11 57. Telex: 550457. Pilots: (59) 63 16 18.
Radio — Port: Tour des Signaux. VHF Chan. 16, 12.
Bayonne Port. VHF Chan. 16, 12. H24. also provides Navigation Information for l'Adour.
Radio — Pilots: VHF Chan. 16, 12, 9. 0800-1200, 1400-1800 and when movement expected.
Vessel to keep listening watch within compulsory pilotage area.
Entry: Tidal streams set 2-5 kts. and during floods the ebb sets 6-7 kts. at Springs. Entry signals as per Int. Code. An additional White light at level of lowest Lt. indicates yachts may use entrance. Port d'Anglet yacht marina, Lt. at entrance and approach marked by beacons.

DIGUE DU LARGE. Head. Lt. Q.R. 7M. 11m. White square Tr. R.top.

BOUCAU. 43°31.9′N, 1°31.2′W. Ldg.Lts. 090°. Front: Q. 14M. 9m. White metal framework Tr. R.top. Intens 086.5°-093.5°. Rear: Q. 14M. 15m. White metal framework Tr. R.top. Intens 086.5°-093.5°.
JETÉE NORD. Head. Lt. Oc.(2)R. 6 sec. 5M. 12m. Mast.
JETÉE SUD. Head. Lt. Iso. G.4 sec. 7M. 9m. White Square Tr. G.top.
DIQUE EXTERIORE SUD. Lt. Q.(9) 15 sec. ⅄ on Y.B.Y. Tr.

ENTRANCE 43°31.7′N, 1°30.9′W. Ldg.Lts. 111°30′. Front: Dir. F.G. 14M. 6m. on hut. 109°-114°. Moved to meet changes in chan. Lit when chan. is practicable. Rear: Dir. F.G. 14M. 16m. white Tr. B.bands. 109°-114°.
TRAINING WALL NORD. Head. Lt. Fl.(2)R. 6 sec. 6M. W. Tr. R.top. 9m. Vis. 296°-091°.
TRAINING WALL. SOUTH. Lt. Fl.(2)G. 6 sec. 5M. W. col. G. Top. 7m. 205°-295°.
MARINA ENTRANCE. W SIDE. Lt. Fl.G. 2 sec. 3M. W Tr. G. Top. 5m.
E SIDE. Lt. F.R. Board. Strip light. 2m.
DIQUE BASSE E. SIDE. Lt. Fl.G. 4 sec. 4M. W. mast 3m.
DES FORGES QUAY Ldg.Lts. 322°30′. Front: Q.R. 6M. W. Tr. R. top. 15m. Vis. 188°-098°. Rear: Iso. R. 4 sec. 12M. Pylon 23m. Intens. 311°-331°.

POINTE DE BLANCPIGNON. Lt. F.G. 5M. 7m. White col.

LA FORME DE RADOUB 43°30.6'N, 1°29.7'W. Ldg.Lts. 205°. Front: Dir. F.G. 16M. 17m. White col. and hut. Intens. 203.5°-206.5°. Rear: Dir. F.G. 16M. White metal framework Tr. 24m. Intens 203.5°-206.5°.

BLANCPIGNON Ldg.Lts. 345°. Front: Q.G. 5M. 17m. White col. Rear: F.G. 10M. 16m. White hut. Intens 338.5°-352.2°.
PONT DE L'AVEUGLE. Lt. Q.G. 5M. 8m. White col.

POINTE SAINT-MARTIN 43°29.7'N, 1°33.2'W. Lt. Fl.(2) 10 sec. 31M. 73m. White Tr.B.top.

BIARRITZ.

BIARRITZ. 43°28.4'N, 1°31.2'W. Aero Mo(L) 7.5 sec. 80m. Partially obscured.
Ldg.Lts. 174°. Front: 43°29.1'N 1°33.9'W. Fl.R. 2 sec. Rear: 93m. from front. Fl.R. 2 sec.

GUETHARY Ldg.Lts. 133°. Front: Q.R. 11m. Rear: Q.R. 33m.

BAIE DE SAINT-JEAN-DE-LUZ

SAINTE-BARBE Ldg.Lts. 101°. Front: Dir. Oc.(3+1) R.12 sec. 18M. 30m. White △ on pole. Intens 095°-107°. Rear: Dir. Oc.(3+1) R.12 sec. 18M. 47m. B. ▽ W □ on Twr. Synchronised with front. Intens 095°-107°.
FINGER MOLE HEAD. Lt. Fl.Bu. 4 sec. 5M. W. Pedestal 3m.

ENTRANCE 43°23.3'N, 1°40.2'W. Ldg.Lts. 151°42'. Front: Dir. Q.G. 16M. 18m. White square Tr. R. stripe. Intens 149.5°-152° Rear: Dir. Q.G. 16M. 27m. White square Tr. G. stripe. Intens 149.7°-152.2°.
DIGUE DES CRIQUAS. Head. Lt. Iso.G. 4 sec. 9M. 11m. Grey square Tr. Horn 15 sec.

LE SOCOA. 43°23.8'N, 1°41.1'W. 138°. Ldg.Lts. Front: Q.W.R. W.12M. R.8M. 36m. White square Tr. B. stripe. R.264°-282°; W.282°-264°. Sig.Stn.

BORDAGAIN. Rear: Q. 20M. 67m. White 🏳, B. stripe, on metal framework Tr. Synchronised with front. Intens 135.5°-140.5°.

BAIE DE FONTARABIE
HENDAYE EPI SOCOBURU HEAD. Lt. L.Fl.R. 10 sec. 9M. R. Pole. 7m.
Lt. Fl.R. 2.5 sec. 2M. R. Pole 6m.
APPONTEMENT DE LA FLORIDE HEAD Lt. Fl.(3)R. 12 sec. 2M. R. Pole 4m.

SPAIN

COAST GUARDS. Use VHF Chan. 16 or 2182 KHz.

SPAIN, AZORES, etc: Authority — Guardia Civil, Call nearest Coast Station for assistance. Traffic signals are same as for France and are being replaced by International Port Signals.
There are numerous other stations.
Fly Flag 'Q' and report to Customs.
Passports for all.
Insurance Certificate.
Registration Certificate.

Spanish National Tourist Office, 57/58 St. James's Street, London SW1. Tel: 071-499 0901.

NORTH COAST

CABO HIGUER 43°23.6'N 1°47.4'W. Lt. Fl.(2) 10 sec. 23M. Stone Tr. W. Lantern. 63m. Vis. 072°-340°.

PUERTO DE FUENTERRABIA

TRAINING WALL. Lt. F.G. 3M. Masonry Col. 9m.
DIQUE NORTE ELBOW. Lt. F.G. 3M. Masonry Col. 7m.
CORNER. Lt. Fl.G. 3 sec. 3M. Masonry Col. 12m.
HEAD Lt. F.G. Metal post.
DIQUE SUR HEAD. Lt. F.R. 3M. Masonry Col. 7m.

PASAJES 43°20'N 1°56'W
Radio — Pilots: VHF Chan. 16, 14, 13, 12, 11. H24.

CABO LA PLATA 43°20.1'N 1°56.0'W Lt.
Oc. 4 sec. 13M. W. Castellated Bldg. 151m.
Vis. 285°-250°.
ARANDO GRANDE Lt. Fl.(2)R. 6 sec. 11M.
Masonry Tr. 10m.
SENOCOZULUA. W. SLOPE OF PUNTA DE
CRUCES Dir.Lt. 155.7°. Dir.Oc.(2) W.R.G. 12
sec. W.8M. R.4M. G.3M. W. Tr. 50m. G.129.5°-
154.5°; W.154.5°-157°; R.157°-190°.
Ldg.Lts. 43°20.0'N, 1°55.5'W. 154°49' (Front)
Q. 18M. Masonry Tr. 67m. (Rear) Oc.3 sec.
18M. Masonry Tr. 87m.
DIQUE DE SENOCOZULUA HEAD Lt. Fl.G. 3
sec. 9M. W. Col. 12m.
PUNTA DE LAS CRUCES 43°20.0'N, 1°55.4'W.
Lt. F.G. 11M. W. Col. 10m.
CASTILLO DE SANTA ISABEL. Lt. F.R. 8M.
Masonry Tr.
PUNTA DEL MIRADOR Q.R. 9M. Tr. 11m.
ERMITA DE SANTA ANA Iso.R. 4 sec. 9M. Hut
33m.
PUNTA TEODORO 43°19.9'N, 1°55.3'W. Lt.
Q.(4) 6 sec. 10M. Col. 20m.
PUNTA CALPARRA Lt. Fl.(3)G. 10 sec. 6M.
Col. 9m.

SAN SEBASTIAN

MONTE URGULL Fog Sig. Siren Mo(U) 60
sec.
ISLA DE SANTA CLARA SUMMIT Lt. Fl. 4 sec.
12M. Round Tr. 51m.

IGUELDO (SAN SEBASTIAN)
43°19.3'N 2°00.7'W.
Lt.Ho. Fl.(2 + 1) 15 sec. 36M. Round Tr. 131m.

LA CONCHA Ldg. Lts. 158° (Front) Fl.R. 1.5
sec. 10M. W.Or. Post 10m. Vis. 143°-173°
(Rear) Iso.R. 6 sec. 10M. W.Or. Post 17m. Vis.
154°-162°.
DARSENA DE LA CONCHA E. MOLE HEAD
Lt.F.G. Col.
DARSENA DE LA CONCHA W. MOLE HEAD
Lt. F.R. Col.
PUERTO DE ORIO W. side Lt. 5 F.
DIQUE DE ABRIGO HEAD Lt. Fl.R. 3 sec. 3M.
R. Col.
Lt. Fl(2)R. 6 sec. 3M. R. Col.
LEFT BANK Lt. Fl.G. 3 sec. 3M. G.W. Col.
Lt. Fl.(2)G. 6 sec. 3M. G.W. Col.
Lt. Fl.(3)G. 12 sec. 3M. G.W. Col.
Lt. Fl.G. 5 sec. 3M. G.W. Col.
MUELLE DE AZPURUA HEAD Lt. Q.G. W.G.
Col. 3m.

PUERTO DE GUETARIA

Radio Marina. MF 2182, 2700 kHz.

ISLA DE SAN ANTON N. END
(GUETARIA) 43°18.6'N 2°12.1'W Lt. Fl.(4)
15 sec. 29M. Oct.Tr. 91m.
SHELTER MOLE Lt. Iso.G. 3 sec. 5M. Tr. 8m.
ELBOW. Lt. Fl.G. 3 sec. 2M.
DIQUE NORTE HEAD. Lt. F.G. 2M. mast. 10m.
DIQUE DE ABRIGO S HEAD. Lt. F.R. Grey Tr.
11m.
ESPIGÓN SUR HEAD. Lt. F.R. 2M. mast 8m.

PUERTO DE ZUMAYA

ZUMAYA 43°18.1'N 2°15.1'W Lt. Oc.(1 + 3)
12 sec. 12M. Grey Octagonal Tr. 39m.
BREAKWATER HEAD Lt. Fl.G. 5 sec. 4M. Tr.
11m.
TRAINING WALL HEAD Lt. Fl.(2)R. 10 sec. 4M.
Tr. 6m.

PUERTO DE MOTRICO

MALECON DE PONIENTE HEAD Lt. F.G. 2M.
Mast 10m.
Ldg.Lts. 236°30'. **DIQUE DEL SUR HEAD**
(Front) F.R. 2M. Mast 10m. **ERMITA DE SAN**
MIGUEL (Rear) F.R. 2M. Tr. 63m.

PUERTO DE ONDARROA

NE BREAKWATER HEAD 43°19.5'N, 2°24.9'W.
Lt. Fl.(3)G. 8 sec. 12M. Grey Tr. 10m. Siren (3)
20 sec.
MOLE HEAD Lt. Fl.(2)R. 6 sec. 8M. Grey Tr.
7m.

INNER HARBOUR

N MOLE HEAD Lt. F.G. 5M. W. Mast 7m.
S MOLE HEAD Lt. F.R. 5M. W. Mast 7m.

PUNTA DE SANTA CATALINA
43°22.6'N 2°30.6'W Lt. Fl.(1 + 3) 20 sec. 24M.
Grey Octagonal Tr. 44m. Horn Mo (L) 20 sec.

PUERTO DE LEQUEITIO

ROMPEOLAS DE AMANDARRI HEAD Lt. Fl.G.
4 sec. 6M. Grey Tr. 10m.

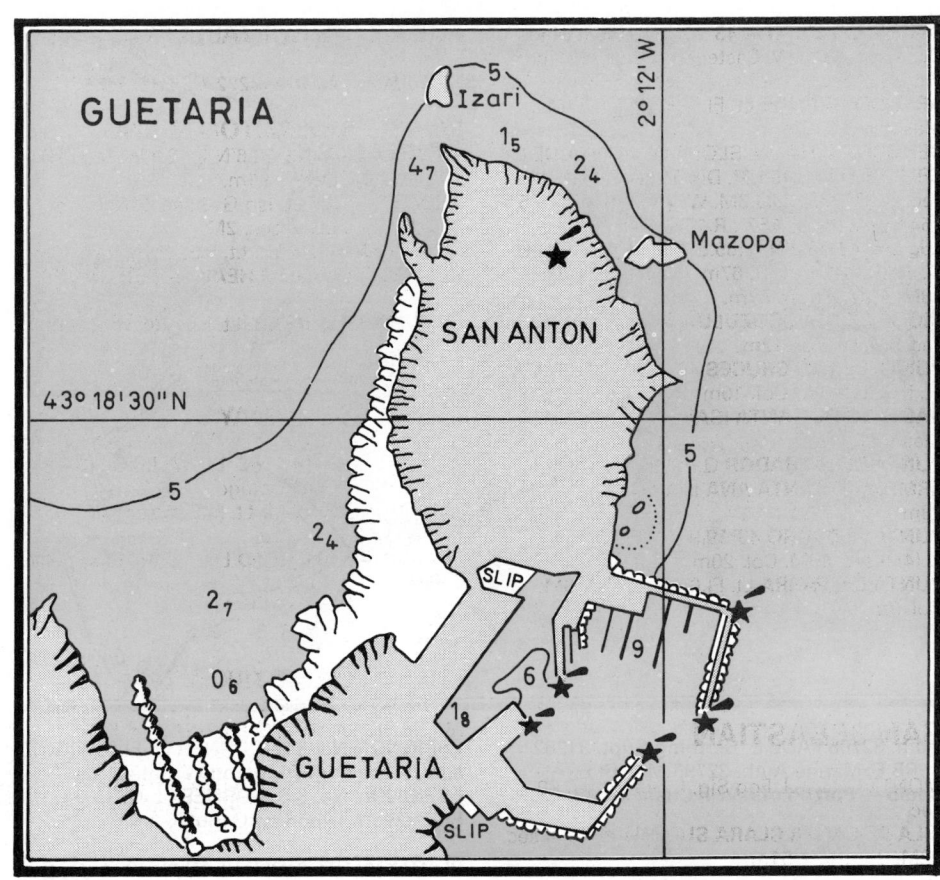

DIQUE AISLADO HEAD Lt. Fl.(2)R. 8 sec. 4M. Grey Tr. 5m.
MUELLE DEL TINGLADO HEAD Lt. F.G. 2M. Grey Col. 5m.
MUELLE SUR HEAD Lt. F.R. 2M. Green Col. 4m.

PUERTO DE ELANCHOVE

DIQUE SUR HEAD Lt. F.W.R. W.8M. R.5M. Green Col. 7m. W.000°-315°; R.315°-000°.
DIQUE NORTE HEAD Lt. Fl.G. 3 sec. 4M. Aluminium Tr. 8m.

PUERTO DE BERMEO

ROSAPE PUNTA LAMIAREN ENTRANCE S SIDE Lt. Oc.(2)W.R. 6 sec. W.9M. R.8M. W. Bldg. 36m. R. Coast-198.4°, W.198.4°-232°.
DIQUE ROMPEOLAS HEAD Lt. Fl.G. 4.5 sec. 5M. Tripod 9m.

SPUR HEAD Lt. F.G. 2M. Tr. 5m.
CONTRADIQUE HEAD. Lt. Fl.R. 3 sec. 3M. R. Post. 8m.
ESPIGON NORTE HEAD Lt. F.G. 3M. Tr. 5m.
ESPIGON SUR HEAD Lt. F.R. 5M. Tr. 5m.

OIL PRODUCTION INSTALLATIONS
PLATFORM GAVIOTA. 43°30.15′N, 41°42′W. Lt. Mo(U) 10 sec. 5M. Each Cnr. 25m. Horn.

CABO MACHICHACO 43°27.2′N 2°45.2′W Lt. Fl. 7 sec. 35M. Stone Tr. 120m. RC Siren (2) 60 sec.

PUERTO DE ARMINZA

TRAINING WALL N END Lt. Fl.(2)R. 8 sec. 5M. Tr. 7m.

BILBAO 43°21′N 3°02′W. Tel: Port Auth. 445 2000; Berthing Supt. 461 2626 & 461 3626; Marine Auth. 421 1132. Fax: Port Auth. 446 5409; Berthing Supt. 94-461 0672. Telex: Port

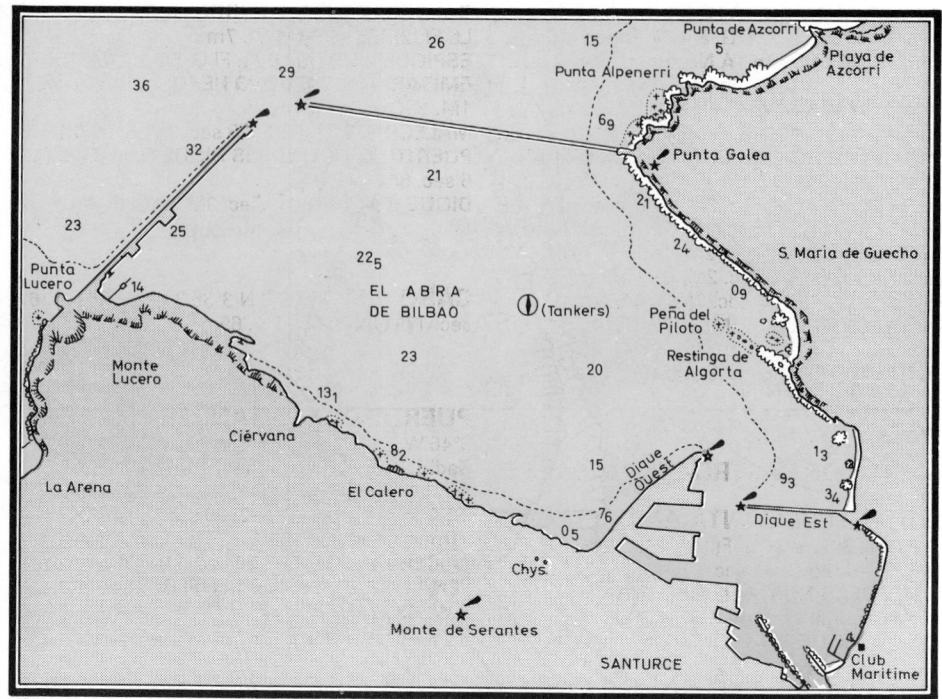

Auth. 32708 PADB E: Berthing Supt. 31282
JPRB E; Marine Auth. 32795 MARBI E.
Radio — Port/Pilots: VHF Chan. 16, 13, 12.
H24.

PUNTA GALEA 43°22.4′N 3°02.1′W Lt.
Fl.(3) 8 sec. 27M. Stone Tr. R.W. Top 82m. Vis.
011°-227°. Siren Mo(G) 30 sec.

DIQUE DE PUNTA GALEA Lt. Fl. R. 6 sec. 6M.
R. col. 19m.
CONTRAMUELLE DE ALGORTA HEAD Lt.
Fl.(4)R. 14 sec. 6M. R. Tr.
CONTRAMUELLE DE ALGORTA NEAR ROOT
Lt. 43°20.4′N 3°00.8′W. Q.W.R. 11M. W.R. Tr.
22m. W.119°-135°; R.135°-150°.

DIQUE DE PUNTA LUCERO HEAD 43°22.7′N,
3°04.9′W. Lt. Fl.G. 4 sec. 14M. 23m. Racon.

DIQUE DE SANTURCE W. HEAD Lt. Fl.(2)G. 12
sec. 6M. G. Tr. 26m.

ESPIGON No. 1 HEAD N CORNER Lt. Fl.(3) G.
10 sec. G. Tripod.
ESPIGON No. 1 S CORNER Lt. Fl.(4)G. 12 sec.
ESPIGON No. 2 HEAD N CORNER Lt.
Fl.(2+1)G. 15 sec. G.R. Col.
ESPIGON No. 2 S CORNER Lt. Fl. G. 4 sec. G.
Tripod.

ESPIGNON No. 3 N. CORNER Lt. Fl.(2+1)G. 15
sec. Framework Tripod on W. hut.
ESPIGNON No. 3 S. CORNER Lt. Q.G.
Framework Tripod on G. hut.

PORTUGALETE MOLE HEAD No. 3 Lt.
Fl.(2+1)G. 15 sec. G.R.Tr.

SANTURCE BOAT HARBOUR Lt. Oc. G. 4 sec.
G. col.
LA MOJIJONERA HEAD No. 4 Lt. Fl.(2) R. 6
sec. R. Tripod.

RIA DE NERVION

MUELLE DE LA BENEDICTA HEAD No. 5 Lt.
Fl.(2+1)G. 15 sec. G. R. Tripod.
DARSENA DE AXPE MORRO DEL FRAILE Lt.
Fl.(3)R. 8 sec. R. Tripod.
SUBMERGED MOLE HEAD Lt. Fl.(2+1)R. 15
sec. R. G. Tripod.

2nd Ldg.Lts. 115°. **MUELLE DE AXPE** EA
(Front) Iso. 2 sec. 5M. Grey ◇ Tripod 16m. EP
(Rear) Oc. 4 sec. 5M. Grey ◇ Tripod.

DARSENA DE PORTU BREAKWATER HEAD
No. 7 Lt. Fl.(2+1)G. 15 sec. 2M. G. and R.
Tripod. 10m.
No. 8 Lt. Fl.(4)R. 12 sec. 2M. Tripod 10m.

MUELLE DE ZORROZA HEAD No. 9 Lt. Fl.(2+1)G. 15 sec. 2M. G. and R. Tripod. 10m.
VUELTA DE ELORRIETA No. 10 Lt. Fl. R. 4 sec. 2M. R. Tripod. 10m.
CANAL DE DEUSTO Lt. Fl.(2+1) R. 15 sec. 2M. R. and G. Tripod. 10m.
EMBARCADERO Lt. Fl.G. 4 sec. Framework Tripod on G. hut.
No. 12 Lt. Fl.(2)R. 6 sec. 2M. R. Tripod 10m.
No. 13 Lt. Fl.(2)G. 6 sec. 1M. G. Tripod. 10m.
No. 15 Lt. Fl.(3)G. 8 sec. 2M. Tripod 11m.
No. 14 Lt. Fl.(3)R. 8 sec. 2M. R. Tripod. 10m.
No. 16 Lt. Fl.(4)R. 12 sec. 2M. Tripod 10m.
No. 18 Lt. Fl.R. 4 sec. 2M. R. Tripod. 10m.

MONTE SERANTES Lt. Aero Oc.R. 3 sec. 448m.

PUERTO DE CASTRO-URDIALES

CASTILLO DE SANTA ANA SE TWR.
43°23.1′N 3°12.9′W Lt. Fl.(4) 24sec. 20M. W. Tr. 46m. Siren Mo(C) 60 sec.
ROMPEOLAS NORTE HEAD Lt. Fl.G. 3 sec. 7M. Octagonal Tr. 12m.
CONTRADIQUE HEAD Lt. Q.(2)R. 6 sec. 5M. R. Tr. 8m.
FISHING BASIN. MUELLE NORTE. S END. Lt. F.G. 3M. Concrete Col. 6m.
MUELLE SW. N END. Lt. F.R. 2M. Concrete Col. 6m.

PUERTO DE LAREDO

ESPIGON NORTE HEAD Lt. F.R. 2M. Col. 9m.
ESPIGON SUR HEAD Lt. F.G. 2M. Col. 9m.

RIA DE SANTONA

PUNTA PESCADOR 43°27.9′N 3°26.1′W Lt. Fl.(3 + 1) 15 sec. 24M. Stone Tr. 37m.

PUNTA DEL CABALLO 43°27.1′N 3°25.5′W Lt. Oc.(4) 14 sec. 12M. Bl. Stone Tr. 24m. Vis. 169.5°-359°.

Ldg. Lts. 283°30′ **MUELLE DEL PASAJE** (Front) Fl. 2 sec. 9M. ▽ on Tr. 5m. **ON BRIDGE.** (Rear) Oc.(2) 5 sec. 14M. O on Tr. 12m. Vis. 279.5°-287.5°.

PUERTA DE SANTONA

BASIN W Side. Lt. F.R. 4M. Col. 6m.
BASIN E Side. Lt. F.G. 4M. Col. 6m.

DARSENA NUEVA ESPIGON NORTE HEAD. Lt. Fl.(2)R. 6 sec. 4M. Tr. 7m.
ESPIGON SUR HEAD Lt. Fl.G. 5 sec. 3M. 7m.
EMISARIO SUBMARINO HEAD. Lt. Fl.Y. 5 sec. 1M. Y.X. on Y. Tr. 4m.
MALECON N. Lt. Fl.R. 2.5 sec. 3M. R.Tr. 7m.
PUERTO DE COLINDRES DIQUE N. Lt. Fl.(2)R. 6 sec. 3M. W.R.Tr. 7m.
DIQUE S. Lt. Fl.G. 2.5 sec. 3M. W.G.Tr. 7m.

CABO AJO 43°30.8′N 3°35.3′W Lt. Oc.(3) 16 sec. 17M. R.W. Grey Tr. 69m.

PUERTO DE SANTANDER 43°28′N 3°46′W
Radio — Pilots: VHF Chan. 16, 14, 12, 9. H24.

ISLA MOURO Lt. Fl.(1+2) 20 sec. 11M. W.Tr. 37m.
LA CERDA Lt. Fl.(1+4) 20 sec. 11M. W.Tr. 22m.
PENA HORADADA No. 1 Lt. Fl.G. 6 sec. 9M. B.W. Cheq.Tr. 5m.

DARSENA DE MOLNEDO
W. MOLE HEAD Lt. F.R.
E MOLE HEAD Lt. F.G.
Ldg.Lts. 259°30′ (Front) Iso. 3 sec. 7M. Y.B.W. Tr. 22m. Vis. 183°-336°. (Rear) Oc. R. 4 sec. 7M. R.W. Grey Bldg. 33M. Vis. 256.5°-262.5°. To be used only W of Fondeadero Osa.

DARSENA DE MALIANO.
MUELLE DE MALIANO SE CORNER Lt. F.G.
W CORNER Lt. F.G.
S SPUR MOLE HEAD Lt. F.R.

Ldg.Lts. 274°30′(Front) F.R. Vis. 267°-282°. (Rear) F.R. Vis. 267°-282°.
LA COMBA Lt. Fl.(2) R. 12 sec. 5M. ∆ on R. 6-sided Tr. 12m.
No.3 MOLE. SE HEAD Lt. Fl.(2) G. 7 sec. 2M. G. post.
RIA DE ASTILLERO
ATRACADERO DE CALATRAVA NW HEAD. Lt. F.R. 3M. 7m. 135°-000°.
S HEAD. Lt. F.R. 3M. 7m. 135°-000°.
Lts. are shown upstream of this point.

CABO MAYOR 43°29.4′N 3°47.5′W Lt. Fl.(2) 10 sec. 21M. W.Octagonal Tr. 89m. RC. Horn (2) 40 sec.

RIA DE SUANCES

SUANCES PUNTA TORCO DE AFUERA 43°26.5'N 4°02.6'W Lt. Fl.(2+1) 24 sec. 22M. W.Tr. 33m. obs. close inshore by higher land 091°-113°.
Ldg.Lts. 146° **E MOLE** (Front) Q. 5M. W.Tr. 8m. **PUNTA MARZAN** (Rear) Iso. 4 sec. 5M. W.Tr. 12m.

PUERTO DE COMILLAS

Outer Ldg.Lts. 194° (Front) Iso. 2 sec. 4M. W.Col. 34m. (Rear) Oc. 4 sec. 4M. W.Col. 38m.

Inner Ldg.Lts. 245° (Front) Iso. 2 sec. 3M. Tr. 14m. (Rear) F.R. 5M. Tr. 18m.
BREAKWATER OUTER END Lt. F.G. 6M. Col. 5m.
CONTRADIQUE HEAD Lt. F.R. 11M. Col.

SAN VINCENTE DE LA BARQUERA

PUNTA SILLA 43°23.6'N 4°23.5'W Lt. Oc. 3.5 sec. 13M. W.Tr. 42m. Vis. 115°-250°. Horn Mo(V) 30 sec.
MALECON DEL OESTE HEAD Lt. Fl.W.G. 2 sec. W.7M. G.6M. G. Conical Tr. 7m. G.175°-235°; W.235°-045°.
ESCOLLERA DEL ESTE HEAD Lt. Fl.(2) R. 8 sec. 6M.
PUNTA DE LA ESPINA Lt. F.G. G. truncated masonry Tr.

PUNTA SAN EMETERIO TINA MAJOR 43°24.0'N 4°32.1'W. Lt. Fl. 5 sec. 20M. Bl.W.Tr. 66m.

LLANES PUNTA DE SAN ANTON
43°25.2'N 4°44.9'W Lt. Oc.(4) 15 sec. 15M. W.Octagonal Tr. 16m. RC.

PUERTO DE RIBADESELLA

SOMOS 43°28.4'N 5°5.0'W Lt. Fl.(1+2) 12 sec. 21M. Tr. 113m.
BREAKWATER HEAD Lt. Fl.(2) R. 6 sec. 5M. Tr. 10m. Vis. 117.3°-212.9° & 278.4°-212.9°.

PUERTO DE LASTRES

BREAKWATER HEAD Lt. Fl. G. 2.5 sec. 4M. Tr. 13m.

RIA DE VILLAVICIOSA

PUNTA ARICERAS TAZONES
43°32.9'N 5°24.0'W Lt. Oc.(3) 15 sec. 15M. Grey Y.Tr. 125m. Horn Mo(V) 30 sec.
DIQUE HEAD. Lt. Fl.G. 3 sec. 4M. Masonry Tr. 10m.

GIJON 43°33'N 5°40'W
Radio — Port: VHF Chan. 16, 14, 12, 11.
Radio — Pilots: VHF Chan. 16, 12.
Entry: Harbour signals as per Int. Code.

CABO DE TORRES 43°34.4'N 5°41.9'W Lt. Fl.(2) 10 sec. 18M. W.Octagonal Tr. 80m.
ZONA DE EL MUSEL. DIQUE EXTERIOR HEAD Lt. Fl.G. 3 sec. 6M. B.W.Col. 22m.
CONTRADIQUE DEL OESTE HEAD Lt. Fl.(3)G. 8 sec. 4M. Tr. 14m.
CONTRADIQUE DE LA OSA HEAD Lt. Fl.(4)R. 8 sec. 4M. Tr. 12m.
NUEVOS MUELLES DE LA OSA. Lt. F.R. 2M. W. Mast. 8m.
NTH CORNER. Lt. Fl.(2)R. 10 sec.
FINGER MOLE. Lt. Q.
WHARF ELBOW. Lt. F.R.
MUELLE DE RENDIELLO. Lt. F.R.
STH. HEAD. Lt. Fl.G. 4.5 sec.
DIQUE NORTE MUELLE DE LOS PORTICOS. HEAD. Lt. Oc.G. 2.5 sec. 5M. B.W.Tr. 8m.
DARSENAS DEL MUSEL ESPIGON 2 HEAD Lt. F.R. 2M. W.Tr. 4m.
ESPIGON 1 NW CORNER. Lt. F.R. 2M. R.Tr. 6m. **SE CORNER.** Lt. F.R. 2M. R. Col. 6m.
PANTALAN HEAD. Lt. F.R. 2M. W.Tr.
MUELLES LOCALES PIEDRA DEL SACRAMENTO Lt. Q.G. 4M. Octagonal Tr. 6m.

DIQUE DE LIQUERICA HEAD. Lt. Q.(2)R. 6 sec. 6M. W. Col. 7m.
MALECON DE FOMENTO HEAD Lt. Fl.G. 3 sec. 3M. Grey Col. 6m.

PUERTO DE CANDAS

PUNTA DEL CUERNO CANDAS
43°35.7'N 5°45.7'W Lt. Oc.(2) 10 sec 13M. R.W. Tr. 38m. Horn Mo(C) 60 sec.

CANAL DE EL CARRERO Ldg.Lts. 291°
PUNTA DEL CUERNO (Front) F.R. 3M. W.Col.
23m. (Rear) F.R. 3M. 62m.
MOLE HEAD Lt. F.G. 4M. Grey Tr. 9m.

PUERTO DE LUANCO.
Ldg.Lts. 255°. **MOLE HEAD** (Front) Fl.R. 3 sec.
4M. □ on wall 4m. (Rear) Occ.R. 8 sec. 4M. B.
mast. 8m.
MUELLE DEL GALLO HEAD Lt. Fl.G. 3 sec.
4M. Round Tr. 10m.

CABO PENAS 43°39.3′N 5°50.9′W Lt. Fl.(3)
15 sec. 21M. Grey Octagonal Tr. 116m. Siren
Mo(P) 60 sec.

RIA DE AVILES

AVILES 43°35′N 5°56′W. Tel: Pilots: 563013.
Radio — Pilots: VHF Chan. 16, 14, 12, 11. H24.
Entry: Flag S shown from pilot office Sarsena
de San Juan de Nieva = Vessel leaving, do
not enter. By night: 1 R. Lt. has same
meaning.
G. Lt = Vessel may enter Curva de Pachico
from W.
R. Lt. = Vessel may not enter Curva de
Pachico from W.
The above applies to all vessels.

PUNTA DEL CASTILLO. AVILES
43°35.7′N 5°56.7′W Lt. Oc.W.R. 4 sec. W.15M.
R.13M. W.Tr. 38m. R.091.5°-113°; W.113°-
091.5°. Siren Mo(A) 30 sec.
PUNTA DE LA FORCADA. Lt. Fl.R. 3 sec. 5M.
R. Tr. 23m.
ENTRANCE N. SIDE Lt. Fl.(2)R. 10 sec. 3M.
Tr. 9m.

ENTRANCE CHANNEL
ESCOLLERA NORTE Lt. 6 F.R. 4M. Concrete
Tr 11m.
ESCOLLERA SUR W. Lt. Fl.(2)G. 7 sec. 5M. G.
Tr. 10m. 100°-280°.
ESCOLLERA SUR E. Lt. 7 F.G. 3M. Col.
HEAD Lt. Fl.(3)G. 9 sec. 3M. G. Tr. 8m.
Lt.Bn. Fl.(2+1)G. 12 sec. 3M. Tr. 8m.
MUELLE DE RAICES Lt. N & S F.G. 3M. Tr.
10m.
MUELLE DE RAICES SPUR Lt. Fl.(4)G. 12 sec.
3M. G. △ W. Tr.
MUELLE DE ENDASA. Lt. N & S F.R. 3M.
Tr. 10m.
CANAL DE PEDRO MENENDEZ. N Lt. Fl.G. 2
sec. 3M. G. Tr. 6m.

Lt.Bn. Fl.R. 2 sec. 5M. R. Tr. 4m.
Lt.Bn. Fl.(2) R. 10 sec. 5M. R. Tr. 4m.
Lt.Bn. Fl.(2)G. 10 sec. 3M. G. Tr. 1m.
PUERTO PESQUERO Lt. 2×F.G.
MUELLES DE ENSIDESA. N Lt. F.R. 3M.
Tr. 10m.
WEST. Lt. Fl.(4)R. 11 sec. 3M. R. Tr. 8m.

PUERTO DE SAN ESTEBAN DE PRAVIA

W. BREAKWATER ELBOW 43°34.0′N 6°4.7′W
Lt. Fl.(2) 12 sec. 14M. B.W.Col. 13m. Horn
Mo(N) 30 sec.
HEAD Lt. Fl.G. 1.5 sec. 3M. B.Tr. 4m.
Ldg.Lts. 182° (Front) F.R. 3M. Col. 7m. (Rear)
F.R. 3M. W. □ R. bands. Col. 11m.
LEFT BANK TRAINING WALL SPUR Lt. Fl.G.
3 sec. 3M. Grey Tr. 2m.
TRAINING WALL Lt. 6 F.G.
Lts. in line. 202°30′ **PUERTO CHICO N SIDE**
(Front) F.Y. (Rear) F.Y.
SW CORNER Lt. F.Y.
BASIN ENTRANCE. ORE LOADING PIER Lt.
F.G.
MOLE HEAD Lt. Fl.R. 3 sec.

PUERTO DE CUDILLERO

PUNTA REBOLLERA 43°33.9′N 6°8.7′W
Lt. Oc.(4) 15 sec. 16M. W.Octagonal Tr. 31m.
Siren Mo(D) 30 sec.
DIQUE DEL ESTE HEAD Lt. F.R.
OLD DIQUE DEL OESTE Lt. F.G.

CABO VIDIO 43°35.6′N 6°14.7′W Lt. Fl. 5
sec. 18M. Tr. 98m. Siren Mo(V) 60 sec.

CABO BUSTO 43°34.1′N 6°28.2′W Lt. Fl.(4)
20 sec. 21M. W.Tr. 74m.

PUERTO DE LUARCA

PUNTA BLANCA 43°33.0′N 6°31.9′W Lt.
Oc.(3) 8 sec. 14M. W.Tr. 52m. Siren Mo(L) 30
sec.
DIQUE DEL CANOUCO HEAD Lt. V.Q.(2)R.
6 sec. 4M. W.R.Tr. 13m.
RIO NEGRO ENTRANCE Ldg.Lts. 170°(Front)
F.G. 2M. R.W.Col. 13m. (Rear) F.G. 2M.
R.W.Col. 21m.
DIQUE DEL OESTE HEAD Lt. Fl.G. 3 sec. 4M.
Tr. 8m.
MUELLE DEL PASO HEAD Lt. Fl(2)G. 7 sec.
1M. G. mast 7m.

PUERTO DE VEGA

PUNTA LAMA Lt. F.R. 6M. Grey Col. 12m.
NEW W MOLE HEAD Lt. F.G. 6M. Grey Col.
12m.

RIA DE NAVIA

CABO SAN AGUSTIN 43°33.8'N
6°44.1'W Lt. Oc.(2) 12 sec. 18M. B.W.Col. 82m.
PUERTO DE VIAVELEZ N JTY. Lt. Fl.(2)R. 5
sec. 4M. Tr. 10m.
S JTY. Lt. Fl.G. 3 sec. 4M. Tr. 10m.

ISLA TAPIA SUMMIT 43°34.4'N 6°56.8'W
Lt. Fl.(1+2) 19 sec. 18M. W.Tr. 22m.

PUERTO DE TAPIA

MALECON NORTE HEAD Lt. Fl.(2)R. 6 sec.
5M. Tr. 8m.
MALECON SUR HEAD Lt. Fl.G. 3 sec. 4M. Tr.
9m.

RIA DE RIBADEO

ISLA PANCHA 43°33.4'N 7°2.4'W Lt.
Fl.(3+1) 20 sec. 21M. W. Tr. 26m. Siren Mo.(R)
30 sec.
PUNTA DE LA CRUZ. Lt. Fl.(2) 7 sec. 5M. W.
Col. on Tr. 16m.

1st Ldg. Lts. 140° **PUNTA AEROJO** (Front)
Q.R. 6M. R. ◊ W. Tr. 18m. (Rear) Oc.R. 4 sec.
6M. R. ◊ W. Tr. 24m.

2nd Ldg. Lts. 205° **MUELLE DE GARCIA**
(Front) V.Q.R. 3M. R. ◊ W. Tr. 8m. (Rear) Oc.R.
2 sec. 3M. W. ▯ on structure. 18m.
PUNTA DE LAS CUEVAS Lt. Fl.(3)G. 9 sec.
5M. W. Col. 11m.
**MUELLE DE MIRASOL ESPIGON DE ABRIGO
HEAD** Lt. F.G.

RIA DE FOZ
BAJO LA RAPADOIRA Lt. Fl.G. 3 sec. 6M. W.
Tr. 10m.
TRAINING WALL HEAD. Lt. Q.G. 9M. Post 3m.
PIEDRA BURELA Lt. Q(3) 10 sec. 8M. Tr. 12m.
R. shore of Bajo Laxela, to Cabo Burela, W.
elsewhere.
PUERTO DE BURELA BREAKWATER HEAD Lt.
Fl.(4)G. 17 sec. 4M. Col. 16m.

SAN CIPRIAN
Radio — Port: VHF 16, 12.

PUNTA ATALAYA Lt. Fl.(4) 10 sec. 15M. W.Tr.
B.Stripes 39m.
ANXUELA JETTY HEAD Lt. Fl.G. 3 sec. 3M. W.
Col. 11m.
MOLE Lt. F.R. 3M. W. Col. 10m.
Dir. Lt. Dir. Q.W.R. 5M. 9m. R. ◊ on W. Tr.
R.178°-194° over Los Farallones. W. 194°
about 198°.

NEW PORT. Ldg.Lts. 203°55'(Front) Fl.(2)
6 sec. 4M. 25m. (Rear) Oc. 6 sec. 4M. 35m.
Ldg.Lts. 273°14' (Front) Fl.(2) 6 sec. 4M. 40m.
(Rear) Oc. 6 sec. 4M. 44m.
SOUTH BREAKWATER HEAD. Lt. Fl.(3)R.
8 sec. 5M.
NORTH BREAKWATER HEAD. Lt. Fl.(2)W.G.
8 sec. 5M. W.110°-180°; G.180°-110°.

PUNTA RONCADOIRA Lt. 43°44.1'N,
7°31.5'W. Fl. 7.5 sec. 21M. W.Tr. 92m.

RIA DE VIVERO

PUNTA FARO Lt. Fl.(2)R. 14 sec. 6M. W. Tr.
18m.
PUNTA SOCASTRO Lt. Fl.G. 7 sec. 6M. W.
Tr. 18m.

RIO LANDROVE

CILLERO PUNTA DEL PUNTAL MOLE HEAD
Lt. F.R.

RIA DEL BARQUERO

ISLA COELLEIRA OR CONEJERA Lt. Fl.(4) 24
sec. 10M. Grey Tr. 87m.
PUNTA DEL CASTRO Lt. Q.(2)R. 6 sec. 6M. W.
Tr. 14m.
PUNTA DE BARRA Lt. Fl.G. 3 sec. 6M. W.
Tr. 15m.

PUNTA ESTACA DE BARRES
43°47.2'N 7°41.1'W Lt. Fl.(2) 7.5 sec. 25M.
Octagonal Tr. 99m. RC obscured bearing
more than 291°. Siren Mo(B) 60 sec.
CABO ORTEGAL. Lt. Oc. 8 sec. 9M. 122m.

PUERTO DE CARINO

BREAKWATER HEAD Lt. Fl.G. 2 sec. 3M. W.
Tr. 12m.

PUNTA CANDELARIA 43°42.7'N 8°2.8'W
Lt. Fl.(3+1) 24 sec. 21M. Octagonal Tr. 88m.

RIA DE CEDEIRA

PUNTA PROMONTOIRO 43°39.1'N, 8°04.2'W.
Lt. Oc.(1 + 3) 16 sec. 11M. W. Tr. 24m.
DIQUE DE ABRIGO HEAD Lt. Fl.(2)R. 8 sec.
3M. W. Col. 10m.

CABO PRIOR 43°34.1'N 8°18.9'W Lt. Fl.(1
+ 2) 15 sec. 24M. Dark Tr. 107m. Siren Mo(P)
25 sec.

RIA DE EL FERROL DEL CAUDILLO

Radio: VHF Chan. 14, 16, 10, 11, 12, 13. H24.
Entry: Basin suitable for yachts and small
craft, Darsena de Curuxeiras, lies behind
Muelle de Concepcion Arenal.

CABO PRIORINA CHICO 43°27.5'N, 8°20.4'W.
Lt. Fl. 5 sec. 11M. W. Octagonal Tr. 34m. RC.
BATERIA DE SAN CRISTOBAL Lt. Oc.(2)W.R.
10 sec. 4M. W. Tr. 19m. W.048°-068°; R.068°-
048°.
Ldg.Lts. 085°25' **PUNTA DE SAN MARTIN** (Front)
Fl. 1.5 sec. 4M. W. Tr. 10m. (Rear) Oc. 4 sec. 4M.
W. Tr.
CASTILLO DE LA PALMA Lt. Oc.(1 + 2) 7 sec.
9M. Tr. 9m.
LA GRANA Oil Pier SW Head Lt. Q.R. 2M.
Mast 11m. NE Head Lt. IsoR. 2 sec. 2M. Mast
11m.
ESPIGON SUR. SE Corner Lt. Fl.(2)R. 7 sec.
3M. R.Col. 7m.
NUEVO MUELLE. SW CORNER Lt. Fl.(3)R.
9 sec. 3M. Col. 7m.
NW CORNER Lt. Fl.(3)R. 9 sec. 3M. R. Col. 7m.
MUELLE FERNANDEZ LADREDA CORNER
Lt. Fl.(4)G. 11 sec. 3M. G. Col. 7m.

DARSENA DE CURUXEIRAS

MUELLE DE CONCEPCION ARENAL HEAD W
Corner Lt. Fl.(4)R. 8 sec. 4M. W. Col. 6m.
ARSENAL ASTA DEL PARQUE Lt. Fl.(2+1)R.
12 sec. W. mast.
PIER HEAD Lt. Fl.R. 5 sec. 3M. Col. 8m.
DARSENA No. 1 WHARF HEAD Lt. F.G. 3M.
Col. 8m.
DARSENA No. 2 W MOLE HEAD Lt. Fl.(2+1)G.
12sec. 5M. Col. 7m..
MUELLE COMERCIAL HEAD Lt. Fl.G. 4 sec.
4M. W. Tr. 7m.
DOLPHIN Lt. Fl. 2 sec.
PIER E. Head Lt. F.W.G. vert. Centre Lt. F.R. W.
Head Lt. F.W.G. vert.
ASTILLEROS ASTANO MUELLE NOLL Lt.
Fl.(4)G. 11 sec. 3M. Grey Tr. 8m.
MUELLE No: 10 Lt. Fl.(2+1)G. 12 sec. 3M.
Grey Tr. 8m.
MUELLE No: 7 Lt. Fl(2).G. 7 sec. 3M. Grey
Tr. 8m.

RIA DE BETANZOS PUERTO DE SADA

Entry: Small marina in inner harbour at
Carcabeira.
MALECON NORTE HEAD Lt. Fl.(3)G. 9 sec.
4M. Tr. 6m.
ESCOLLO PULGUEIRA Lt. Fl.R. 3 sec. 4M. W.
Tr. 5m.
MALECON SUR Lt. F.R. 2M. Col. 6m. Vis. 156°-
268.5°.

PUERTO DE LA CORUNA

Tel: (981) 227402. Telex: 82364 JPCO E.
Radio — Port: VHF Chan. 16, 12.
Radio — Pilots: VHF Chan. 12.

TORRE DE HERCULES 43°23.2'N
8°24.3'W Lt. Fl.(4) 20 sec. 23M. Stone Tr.
104m. Siren Mo(L) 30 sec.RC.

PUNTA MERA Ldg. Lts., 108°30' (Front) F.R.
8M. W. Octagonal Tr. 55m. Vis. 026.8°-146.8°
(Rear) Oc.(2) 10 sec. 8M. W. Octagonal Tr.
79m. Vis. 357.5°-177.5°. Racon.

PUNTA FIAITEIRA Ldg. Lts., 182° (Front)
Iso.W.R.G. 2 sec. W.5M. R.4M. G.3M. R.W.
cheq. Sq. Tr. 28m. G.146.4°-180°; W.180°-184°;
R.184°-217.6°. (Rear) Oc.R. 4 sec. 4M. W. Tr.
53m.
DIQUE DE ABRIGO HEAD Lt. Fl.G. 3 sec. 4M.
Tr. 16m.
CASTILLO DE SAN ANTON Lt. Fl.(2)G. 6 sec.
8M. W. Tr. 15m.
Real Club Nautico de la Coruna situated close
N of marina.

MUELLE DE CENTENARIO

NW CNR. Lt. Q.R. 4M. R. Tr. 9m.
NE CNR. Lt. Fl.(3)R. 10 sec. 4M. R. Tr. 9m.
SE CNR. Lt. Fl.(3)G. 10 sec. 4M. G. Tr. 9m.
MUELLE DEL ESTE HEAD Lt. Fl.(2)R. 5 sec.
4M. Mast 11m.
DARSENA DE LA MARINA E Side Lt. F.G. 2M.
Mast 8m. W side Lt. F.R. 2M. Mast 8m.
Basin dredged to 2m.
MUELLE DE TRASATLANTICO HEAD N
CORNER Lt. Fl.(4)R. 8 sec. 4M. W. Tr. 8m.
S CORNER Lt. Fl.G. 3 sec. 4M. W. Tr. 8m.
OIL PIER HEAD Lt. Oc.(2)R. 4 sec. 4M. W. Twr.

PUERTO DE CAYON

ENTRANCE. Ldg. Lts. 147°10' (Front) Fl. 2 sec.
4M. W. Tr. 28m. (Rear) Oc. 4 sec. 4M. W. Tr.
54m.

PUERTO DE MALPICA Shelter Mole Lt. Fl.G.
3 sec. 4M. W. Col. 16m.

ISLAS SISARGAS 43°21.6'N 8°50.7'W Lt.
Fl.(3) 15 sec. 23M. W. Octagonal Tr. 108m.
Siren (3) 30 sec.

RIA DE CORME Y LAGE

PUNTA DEL RONCUDO 43°16.5'N, 8°59.5'W.
Lt. Fl. 6 sec. 10M. W. Tr. 36m.
PUNTA LAGE 43°13.9'N, 9°00.7'W. Lt. Fl.
(1 + 4) 14 sec. 11M. W. Tr. 64m.
PUERTO DE CORME MOLE HEAD Lt. Fl.(2)R.
5 sec. 4M. W. Tr. 13m.
PUERTO DE LAGE MOLE HEAD Lt. Fl.G. 3 sec.
4M. W. Tr. 16m.
MUELLE S HEAD. Lt. F.R.

CABO VILLANO 43°9.6'N 9°12.7'W Lt.
Fl.(2) 15 sec. 28M. Y./Grey Octagonal Tr.
102m. RC. Siren Mo (V) 60 sec. Racon.

WEST COAST

RIA DE CAMARINAS

S ENTRANCE. Ldg.Lts. 079°40'. **PUNTA
VILLUEIRA** (Front) Fl. 2 sec. 9M. Tr. 14m.
PUNTA DEL CASTILLO (Rear) Iso. 4 sec. 11M.
Tr. 25m. Vis. 078.2°-081.2°.

PUNTA DE LA BARCA Lt. Fl.(3 + 1) 10 sec. 7M.
Grey Tr. 11m.

PUNTA DE LAGO Lt. Oc.(2)W.R.G. 3.5 sec.
W.7M. R.5M. G.4M. Tr. 14m. W.029.5°-093°;
G.093°-107.8°; W.107.8°-109.1°; R.109.1°-
139.3°; W.139.3°-213.5°.

PUERTO DE CAMARINAS PIER HEAD Lt.
Fl.(3)R. 8 sec. 5M. Round Tr. 9m.
DIQUE DE ABRIGO HEAD Lt. Fl.(2)G. 10 sec.
3M.

SEA TRAFFIC SEPARATION ROUTES

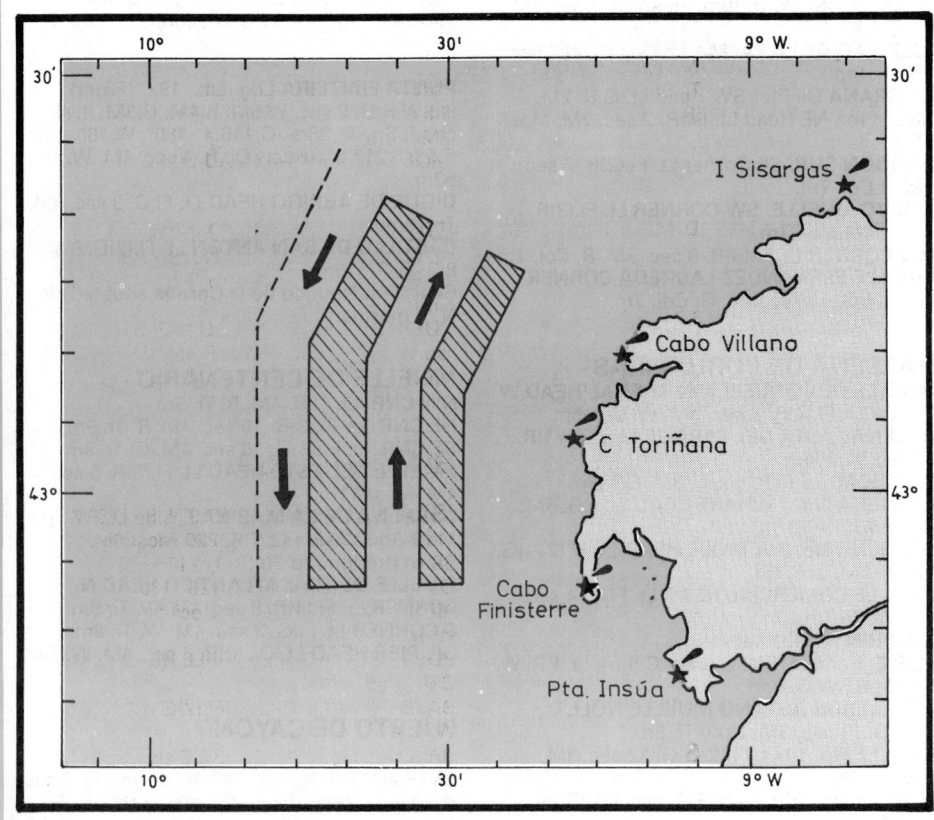

CABO TORINANA 43°3.2′N 9°17.9′W Lt. Fl. (2 + 1) 15 sec. 24M. W. Octagonal Tr. 63m. Vis. 340.5°-235.5°. Racon.

CABO FINISTERRE 42°52.9′N 9°16.3′W Lt. Fl. 5 sec. 23M. W. Octagonal Tr. 141m. RC obscured bearing more than 149°. Siren(2) 60 sec. Racon.

PUERTO DE FINISTERRE

MOLE HEAD Lt. Fl.R. 2 sec. 4M. R. Tr. 13m.
INNER ELBOW. Lt. Q.R. 1M. Tr. 8m.

RIA DE CORCUBION

CORCUBION. 42°57′N, 9°11′W. Tel: Pilots: (81) 745200/745419/745902.
Radio — Pilots: VHF Chan. 16, 14.
ISLOTE LOBEIRA GRANDE Lt. Fl.(3) 15 sec. 11M. R./Grey Octagonal Tr. 16m.
CARRUMEIRO CHICO Lt. Q.(2) 6 sec. 8 on B.R. Tr.
CABO CEE Lt. Fl.(4) 8 sec. 9M. Grey Octagonal Tr. 25m.
PUERTO DE CORCUBION MOLE HEAD Lt. Fl.(2)R. 8 sec. 5M. Grey Tr. 9m.
PUERTO DEL PINDO PIER Lt. F.G. 1M. Col. 8m.

PORTOCUBELO
DIQUE DE ABRIGO HEAD. Lt. Fl.G. 2 sec. 4M. Tr. 9m. 174°-067°.

PUNTA INSUA 42°46.3′N 9°7.6′W Lt. F.W.R. and Oc.(1+ 2) W.R. 20 sec. W.15M. R.14M. Tr. 26m. F.R.308°-012.5°. Oc.R.012.5°-044.5° over Bajos Mean Xinielana and Los Bruyos. Oc.044.5°-093° over Bayos de los Meixidos. F.W.093°-172.5° but obscured by high land 145°-172.5°.

RIA DE MUROS

MONTE LOURO PUNTA QUEIXAL Lt. Fl.(2+1) 12 sec. 12M. Tr. 25m. obscured by Monte Louro 081°-180°.
CABO REBURDINO Lt. Fl.(2)R. 6 sec. 9M. W.Tr. 16m. Vis. 168°-019°.

PUERTO DE MUROS

DIQUE EXTERIOR HEAD Lt. Fl.(4)R. 13 sec. 4M. W.Col. 8m.

MUELLE DEL NORTE HEAD Lt. F.G. 4M. Col. 6m.
MUELLE DEL ESTE HEAD Lt. F.R. 4M. Col. 6m.
PUERTO DE EL FREIJO MUELLE HEAD Lt. Fl.(2)R. 5 sec. 4M.

PUERTO DE NOYA

ESCOLLERA NORTE HEAD Lt. Fl.R. 5 sec. 4M. Tr. 7m.
SUD HEAD Lt. Fl.(2)G. 9 sec. 4M. Tr. 7m.
MUELLE DEL TESTAL HEAD Lt. Fl. 2 sec. 3M. W. Tr. 8m.
Ldg.Lts. 127° Mole (Front) F.R. 3M. Mast 9m. (Rear) F.R. 3M. Mast 12m.

PUERTO DE PORTOSIN
DIQUE DE ABRIGO HEAD. Lt. Fl.(2)G. 5 sec. 3M. Round Tr. 7m.
DIQUE MUELLE NE HEAD. Lt. Q.G. 1M. Round Tr. 6m.
CONTRADIQUE HEAD Lt. F.R. 3M. Tr. 8m.
PUNTA CABEIRO Lt. Fl.W.R.G. 4 sec. W.12M. R.7M. G.7M. W.Tr. 35m. R.054.5°-058.5°; G.058.5°-099.5°; W.099.5°-189.5°.

PUERTO DEL SON Ldg.Lts. 193.5° (Front) Fl.R. 2.5 sec. 7M. Grey Tr. 7m. (Rear) Oc.R. 5 sec. 7M. Grey Tr. 12m.
DIQUE DE ABRIGO HEAD Lt. F.G. on mast.

CABO CORRUBEDO 42°34.6′N 9°5.4′W Lt. Fl.(3+2)R. 20 sec. and Fl.(3)R. 20 sec. 15M. Grey Tr. 30m. Clear sector Fl.(3+2) 089.4°. Siren (3) 60 sec.
PUERTO DE CORRUBEDO MOLE HEAD Lt. Iso.W.R.G. 3 sec. W.7M. R.4M. G.4M. Tr. R.000°-016°; G.016°-352°; W.352°-000°.

RIA DE AROSA

ISLA SALVORA 42°27.9′N. 9°00.8′W Lt. Fl.(3+1) 20 sec. and Fl.(3) 20 sec. 21M. W.Tr. 38m. Clear sector Fl.(3+1) 217°-126°. Dangerous sector Fl.(3) 126°-160°.
PIEDRAS DEL SARGO E.Rock Lt. Q.G. 8M. W.Tr. 12m.
PUERTO DE AGUINO MOLE HEAD Lt. F.R. 4M. Col. 11m.
BAJO POMBEIRINO Lt. Fl.(2)G. 12 sec. 10M. W.Tr. 13m.
BAJO PRAGUERO Lt. Fl.G. 3 sec. 5M. W.Tr. 8m.
BAJO LOBEIRA DE CAMBADOS S.End Lt. Fl.(4)R. 12 sec. 6M. W.Tr. 9m.

BAJO GOLFEIRA Lt. Fl.(3)G. 12 sec. 5M. W.Tr. 9m.
BAJO CON DE ESTRO (PIEDRAS SALVORES) Lt. Fl.(3)G. 12 sec. 10M. Bn.
PUERTO EL GROVE N MOLE HEAD Lt. Oc.G. 2.5 sec. 3M. B.W.Cheq.Tr. 9m.
SANTO TOME WHARF Lt. F.G. 1M. Col. 5m.
PUERTO DE CAMBADOS SW BREAKWATER S HEAD Lt. Fl. 4.5 sec. 10M. W.Tr. 7m.
TRAGROVE BREAKWATER HEAD. Lt. Fl.(2)R. 7 sec. 3M. R.W. Cheq. Tr. 9m.
BAJO LA LOBA Lt. Q.G. 4M. W.Tr. 8m.
CONTRADIQUE Lt. Q.G.

ISLA RUA 43°32.9'N 8°56.4'W Lt. Fl.(2+1)W.R. 10 sec. 17M. Grey Tr. 24m. R.121.5°-211.5°; W.211.5°-121.5°.

PUERTO DE CASTINEIRAS
DIQUE DE ABRIGO HEAD. Lt. Oc. W.R.2sec. 3M. Round TR. 9M. W.263°-270°; R.270°-263°.

SANTA EUGENIA DE RIVIERA MOLE HEAD Lt. Fl.(2)R. 8 sec. 5M. Col. 10m.
BAJO LLAGAREOS DE TIERRA Lt. Q.R. 5M. W.Tr. 7m.
BAJO PIEDRA SECA Lt. Fl.(3)G 15 sec. 7M. W.Tr. 10m.

ISLA DE AROSA PUNTA DEL CABALLO 42°34.3'N 8°53.1'W Lt. Fl.(4) 8
sec. 10M. W.Octagonal Tr. 11m.
DIQUE MUELLE XUFRE HEAD. Lt. F.R. 4M. R. col. 9m.
BAJO SINAL DE OSTREIRA Lt. Fl.(3)R. 15 sec. 4M. R.Tr. 8m.
PUERTO DE PUEBLA DE CARAMINAL MOLE HEAD Lt. Fl.(2)R. 6 sec. 6M. Grey Tr. 7m.
DIQUE MUELLE HEAD. Lt. Oc.G. 2 sec. 4M. Round Tr. 8m.
PUERTO DE ESCARBOTE DIQUE HD. Lt. Fl.(3)W.R. 7 sec. 3M. Col. 7m. W.340°-010°; R.010°-340°.
PUERTO CABO CRUZ BREAKWATER HEAD Lt. F.G. Tripod 2m.
BAJO EL SEIJO Lt. Fl.(3)G. 10 sec. 7M. W.Tr.
PUERTO DE VILLANUEVA DE AROSA MOLE AT ENTRANCE Lt. Fl.(3+1)W.G. 10 sec. W.10M. G.7M. Tr. 7m. W.062.2°-104.1°; G.104.1°-062.2°.
PUERTO DE VILLAJUAN MOLE HEAD Lt. F.G. 3M. Col. 4m.

VILLAGARCIA
JETTY SW CNR. Lt. Fl.G. 1.5 sec. G.Bn.
NE CNR. Lt. Fl.R. 1.5 R.Bn.
Entry: Entrance channel 7m. with same depths alongside. Ample space for yachts to moor/anchor at or near Muelle de Ramel.
PUERTO DE CARRIL MOLE HEAD Lt. Q.G. 7M. Square Tr. 8m.

PUERTO DE RIANJO JTY. HD. Lt. Fl.G. 3 sec. 5M. Tr. 9m.
MUELLE DE SETEFOJAS HD. Lt. F.G. 2m. col. 4m.

RIA DE MARIN

ISLA ONS 42°22.9'N 8°56.2'W Lt. Fl.(4) 24 sec. 25M. Octagonal Tr. 126m.
PLAYA DEL CURRO Pier Lt. Q.R.2M. Grey Tr. 11m.
BAJO CAMOUCO Lt. Fl.(3)R. 18.4 sec. Tr. R. Top. 10m.
BAJO PICAMILLO Lt. Oc.(2)G. 6 sec. 10M. G.Col. 10m.
PORTONOVO MOLE HEAD Lt. Fl.(3)R. 6 sec. 4M. Col. 8m.
PUERTO DE SANQUENJO MOLE HEAD Lt. Fl.(4)R. 12 sec. 4M. Tr. 8m.

PUERTO DE RAJO
DIQUE MUELLE HEAD. Lt. Fl.(2)R. 8 sec. 3M. 9m.

PUNTA TENLO CHICO 42°24.5'N
8°42.5'W Lt. Oc.(3) 16 sec. 11M. Tr. 33m.

PONTEVEDRA

N MOLE HEAD Lt. Fl.(4)R. 15 sec. 4M. W.Tr. 5m.
S MOLE HEAD Lt. Fl.G. 3 sec. 6M. W.Tr. 5m.
N MOLE Lt. Fl.(2)R. 8 sec. 4M. W.Tr. 5m.
Lt. Fl.(4)R. 12 sec. 4M. W.Tr. 5m.

PUERTO DE COMBARRO
DIQUE MUELLE HEAD. Lt. Fl.(2)R. 8 sec. 7M. 3m.

PUERTO DE MARIN.
Tel: 986-882 140.
Radio: VHF Chan. 16, 6.

DIQUE OESTE HEAD Lt. Fl.(3)G. 7 sec. 7M. Tr. 7m.
MUELLE COMERCIAL NW Elbow Lt. Fl. 1.5 sec. 2M. Tr. 5m.
PUERTO PESQUERO N MOLE HEAD Lt. Fl.(2)R. 6 sec. 2M. Square Tr. 6m.

PUERTO DE BUEU

DIQUE MUELLE ESTE HEAD Lt. Fl.(2)R. 6 sec. 4M. Tr. 7m.
DIQUE NORTE HEAD Lt. Fl.G. 3 sec. 4M. Tr. 9m.
BAJO MOURISCA Lt. Fl.(2)G. 7 sec. Twr.
PUNTA COUSO 42°18.6'N, 8°51.3'W. Lt. Fl.(3)W.G. 9 sec. W.10M. G.8M. Tr. 18m. G.060°-096°; W.096°-190°; G.190°-000°.

DIQUE MUELLE DE ALDAN HEAD Lt. Fl.(2)R.
10 sec. 6M. R.W.cheq. Tr. 7m.
PUNTA ROBALEIRA 42°15.0'N, 8°52.4'W.
Lt. Fl.(2)W.R. 7.5 sec. W.11M. R.9M. R.Tr. 25m.
W.300.5°-321.5°; R. 321.5°-090°; R.115.5°-
170.5°. ᨑᨑ

CABO HOME Ldg.Lts. 129° (Front) Fl. 3 sec.
9M. R.W. Tr. 37m. Vis. 090°-180° **PUNTA
SUBRIDO** (Rear) Oc. 6 sec. 11M. R.W.Tr. 52m.
Vis. 090°-180°.

ISLAS CIES

MONTE AGUDO Lt. Fl.G. 5 sec. 9M. W.Tr.
24m. Vis. 146.5°-334°.
MONTE FARO 42°12.8'N, 8°54.9'W. Lt. Fl.(2)
8 sec. 22M. Tr. 185m. Obsc. 315°-016.5°.
PUNTA CANABAL Lt. Fl.(3+1) 22 sec. 11M.
W.Tr. 63m.
CABO VICOS Lt. Fl.(4)R. 14 sec. 9M. W.Tr.
92m. Vis. 210.5°-108°.
ISLOTE BOEIRA or AGOEIRA Lt. Fl.(2)R. 8 sec.
7M. W.Tr. 22m.

CABO ESTAY 42°11.1'N, 8°48.9'W. Ldg.Lts.
069°20' (Front) Iso. 2 sec. 18M. R.W.Tr. 16m. Vis.
066.3°-072.3°. Horn Mo(V) 60 sec. R.D., Racon.
(Rear) Oc. 4 sec. 18M. R.W.Tr. 49m. Vis. 066.3°-
072.3°.
PUNTA LAMEDA Lt. Fl.(2)G. 8 sec. 10M. W.Tr.
27m.
PUNTA BORNEIRA No: 6. Lt. Oc.(4)R. 10 sec.
8M. W.Tr. 11m.
DIQUE MUELLE DE CANIDO HEAD Lt. F.G.
3M. W.Tr. 10m.
ISLA TORALLA BRIDGE Lt. F. 2M. Lt. F.R. &
F.G. mark passage.
BAJO TOFINO No: 3. Lt. Fl.(4)G. 14 sec. 5M.
B.W.Tr. 9m.

PUERTO DE CANGAS

DIQUE EXTERIOR HEAD Lt. Fl.(1+2)R. 12 sec.
4M. R. Tr. 8m.
DIQUE MUELLE INTERIOR HEAD Lt. Q.G.R.
3M. W.Tr. 8m.
EL PEGO. Lt. Q.R. 3M. R.Tr. 7m.

PUERTO DE BOUZAS

FERRY NE CNR. Lt. Oc.(2)G. 10 sec. 4M.
G.W.Twr. 8m. 113°-336.5°.
E. CNR. Lt. F.G. 4M. G.W.Twr. 8m. 156.5°-
066.5°.
DIQUE MUELLE HEAD Lt. Fl.(3)G. 7.5 sec. 4M.
Tr. 8m. Vis. 101°-061°.
WATER TOWER OUTLET. Lt. F.G.

RIA DE VIGO

PUERTO DE VIGO 42°14'N 8°40'W
Radio — Pilots: VHF Chan. 16, 14.
Entry: Yacht moorings near passenger
terminal in centre of city.
DARSENA No: 4 MOLE HEAD Lt. Fl.(2)R. 5
sec. 4M. Tr. 8m. Vis. 094°-075°.
MUELLE DEL BERBES NE END Lt. Oc.(3)G. 12
sec. 5M. Tr. 8m.
MUELLE DE TRANSATLANTICOS W END Lt.
F.G. **E END** Lt. F.R.
MUELLE DE GUIXAR. Lt. Q.G. G. Post. 6m.

ENSENADA DE MOANA

EL CON PIER HEAD Lt. F.R. 4M. R.W. Col. 7m.
PUERTO DE MOANA BREAKWATER HEAD Lt.
F.R. 5M. R.W.Col. 8m.

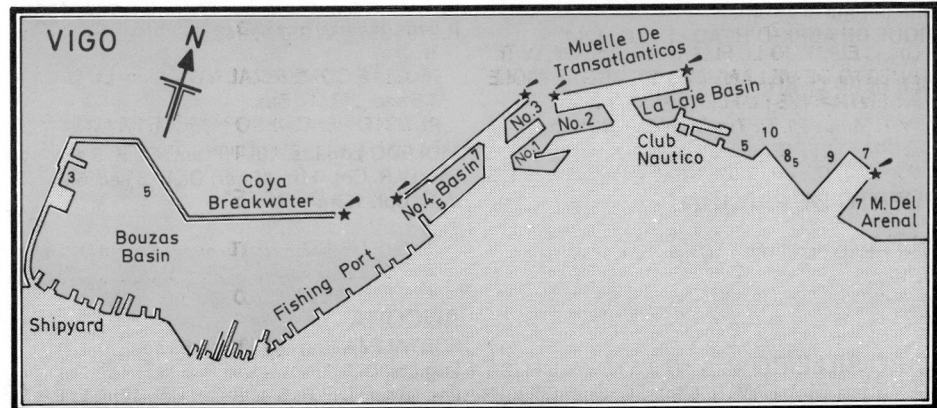

PUERTO DE MEIRA BREAKWATER HEAD Lt. Fl.R. 3 sec. 3M. Tr. 5m.
PUERTO DE MEIRA MOLE HEAD Lt. Fl. 3 sec. 4M. Col. 8m.

PUNTA AREINO LA GUIA 42°15.6'N 8°42.1'W Lt. Oc.(2+1) 20 sec. 15M. W.Tr. 35m.
DARSENA ETEA NW MOLE HEAD Lt. F.G. 2M. Post 4m.
E. MOLE Lt. F.R. 2M. Post 6m.
PUERTO DE DOMAYO MOLE HEAD Lt. Oc.R. 2.5 sec. 5M. W.Tr. R.Bands 3m. Vis. 074°-341°.
RANDE ORE BERTH Lt. 2 × F.G.
BRIDGE N PILLAR. W DOLPHIN. Lt. Fl.(4)R. 10 sec. 7M. Dolphin. 7m.
E DOLPHIN. Lt. Oc.(2)R. 8 sec. 7M. Dolphin. 7m.
S PILLAR. W DOLPHIN. Lt. Fl.(3)G. 7.5 sec. 7M. Dolphin. 7m.
E DOLPHIN. Lt. Oc.G. 5 sec. 7M. Dolphin. 7m.
ENSENADA DE SAN SIMON. MUELLE DE CRESANTES HEAD Lt. F.G.
LAS SERRALLEIROS. PEDRA QUE VOLE Lt. Fl.G. 4 sec. 7M. W.Tr. 10m.

ENSENADA DE BAYONA

CABEZO DE SAN JUAN Ldg.Lts. 083° (Front) Q.(2) 4 sec. 6M. 7m. Vis. 9M. 081.5°-084.5°. **PANJON** (Rear) Oc.R. 4 sec. 12M. W.Tr. 17m.

PUERTO DE BAYONA

Entry: Yacht Club and Marina SE of castle with depths of 2½-3m.
DIQUE DE ABRIGO HEAD Lt. Q.G. 12M. B.W.Cheq.Tr.
PIER HEAD Lt. F.R.

PUERTO DE PANJON

PIER HEAD Lt. Fl.(2)R. 10 sec. 5M. R.W. Cheq. Tr. 10m.

CABO SILLEIRO 42°6.2'N 8°53.8'W Lt. Fl.(2 + 1) 15 sec. 24M. R.W. Tr. 83m. RC. Siren(3) 30 sec.

PUERTO DE LA GUARDIA

PUNTA DEL JINETE Fog Sig. Siren Mo(L) 30 sec.
Ldg.Lts. 109° (Front) Fl.W.R.G. 2 sec. W.9M. R.8M. G.7M. Tr. 12m. G.000°-106°; W.106°-112°; R. 112°-180°. (Rear) Oc. 4 sec. 6M. Tr. 38m. Vis. 106°-112°.
MOLE HEAD Lt. Fl.G. 3 sec. 4M. W. Tr. 12m.
RIO MINHO. CAMPOSANCOS. MOLE HEAD Lt. Fl.R. 4 sec. 5M. Tr. 7m.

PORTUGAL

PORTUGAL. DOCUMENTATION.
Entry: Present ship's papers and passports to Maritime Police at first port of call. Pay fee. Receive Ship's Transit permit. Present these to Guarda Fiscal. Inform them if anything requires repair or of any crew changes. For parts a "Papel Selado" is purchased, for small parts okay to DIY, otherwise agent necessary. Papers must all be in Portuguese. For major repairs all these papers must be presented to the Alfandega (Customs) and to Junta Autonoma do Porto for berth space, estimates, etc. Passports for all.
Registration Certificate or International Certificate for Pleasure Navigation.
The Portuguese National Tourist Office, 1 New Bond Street, London W1. Tel: 071-493 3873.

COAST GUARDS: There is no C.G. Service in Portugal. Call nearest Coast Station for assistance.

RIO MINHO ENTRANCE. FORTE INSUA.
41°51.4'N, 8°52.5'W. Lt. Fl.W.R.G. 4 sec. W.12M. R.8M. G.8M. W. Tr. 16m. G.204°-270°; R.270°-357°; W.357°-204°.

MOLEDO Ldg.Lts. 100° (Front) Oc.R. 5 sec. 6M. W.R. Col. 11m. (Rear) Oc.R. 5 sec. 6M. W.R. Col. 15m.

ANCORA

FORTALEZA Fog Sig. Siren 60 sec.
Ldg.Lts. 071° (Front) L.Fl.R. 6 sec. 7M. Col. 6m. (Rear) L.Fl.R. 6 sec. 7M. Col. 10m. Lt F.R. shown from fortress when port closed.

PROMONTORIO DE MONTEDOR
41°44.9'N 8°52.5'W Lt. Fl.(2) 7.5 sec. 25M.
Sq. Tr. 101m. RC. Siren (3) 25 sec.

VIANA DO CASTELO Tel. No: 22.168
(Port) 22.697 (Pilots).
Radio Port: VHF Chan. 16, 11. MF 2182, 2484, 2657 kHz.
Pilots: VHF Chan. 16, 14. MF 2182, 2037, 2132, 2484 kHz.
Hrs: 2182 kHz on request. Chan. 16. Mon.-Fri. 0900-1200; 1400-1700.

RIO LIMA. BARRA SUL. 41°41.2'N, 8°50.3'W. Ldg. Lts. 012°30'
CASTELO DE SANTIAGO SW BATTERY (Front) Iso.R. 4 sec. 23M. R.W. Tr. 13m. Vis. 241°-151°.
SENHORA DA AGONIA (Rear) Oc.R. 6 sec. 21M. R.W. Tr. 31m. Vis. 005°-020°.
MOLHE DO BUGIO HEAD Lt. Fl.R. 5 sec. 6M. R.W. Tr. 9m. Siren 30 sec.
MOLHE EXTERIOR Lt. Fl. 3 sec. 5M. W.R. Tr. Siren(2) 60 sec.

NEIVA Ldg.Lts. (Front) Iso.G. 1.5 sec. 6M. Col. 13m. (Rear) Oc.G. 6 sec. 6M. Col. 19m.

ESPOSENDE

FORTE DE BARRA DO RIO CAVADO
41°32.5'N, 8°47.4'W. Lt. Fl. 5 sec. 21M. R. Tr. 20m. Siren 30 sec.

APULIA Ldg.Lts. 070° (Front) Fl. 3 sec. 8M. Col. 10m. Siren 75 sec. (Rear) Fl. 3 sec. 8M. Mast 12m.

A-VER-O-MAR Ldg.Lts. (Front) Fl.R. 5 sec. 3M. W. Tr. 13m. (Rear) Fl.R. 5 sec. 3M. W. Tr. 16m.

POVOA DE VARZIM

REGUFE 41°22.4'N, 8°45.2'W. Lt. Iso. 6 sec. 15M. R. Tr. 28m.
MOLHE NORTE HEAD 41°22.2'N, 8°46.2'W. Lt. Fl.R. 3 sec. 12M. Tr. 15m. Siren 30 sec.
MOLHE SUL HEAD Lt. L.Fl.G. 6 sec. Siren 40 sec.

CAXINAS Ldg.Lts. (Front) Oc.R. 5 sec. 6M. Col. 5m. (Rear) Oc.R. 5 sec. 8M. mast. 14m.

VILA DO CONDE

AZURARA 1st Ldg. Lts. 079° (Front) Iso.G. 4 sec. 5M. W.R. Tr. 9m. (Rear) Iso.G. 4 sec. 5M. W. Δ on bldg. 26m.
MOHLE NORTE HEAD Lt. Fl.R. 4 sec. 9M. Col. 8m. Siren 20 sec.
BARRA. RIO AVE ENTRANCE N SIDE. 2nd Ldg. Lts. 000° (Front) Oc.R. 3 sec. 6M. R. Col. 6m. (Rear) Oc.R. 3 sec. 6M. R. Col. 11m.

VILA CHA Ldg.Lts. (Front) Fl.R. 3 sec. 6M. W. Tr. 5m. (Rear) Fl.R. 3 sec. 6M. W. Tr. 11m.

ANGEIRAS

GUARITA Fog Sig. Siren 60 sec.

SHELTER ACCESS Ldg. Lts. 042°30' (Front) Oc.R. 6 sec. 5M. Post 4m. (Rear) Oc.R. 6 sec. 5M. Post 10m.
Ldg.Lts. 062°30'(Front) Oc.G. 5 sec. 6M. Col. 7m. (Rear) Oc.G. 5 sec. 6M. Col. 11m.
PEDRAS RUBRAS. AIRFIELD Lt. Aero Al.Fl.W.G. 10 sec. Tr. 90m.

LECA 41°12'N 8°42.6'W Lt. Fl. (3) 15 sec. 28M. B.W. Tr. 56m.
Pedra da Orca shoal 13¾c. S. of Light with less than 1.8m. Dangerous to small craft.

LEIXOES 41°11'N 8°43'W. Tel: Port: 995 30 00. Fax: 995 50 62. Telex: 22 674. Pilots: 995 26 09.
Radio — Port: VHF Chan. 16, 12, 1, 4, 9, 10, 11, 14, 18, 20, 61, 63, 67, 68, 69, 71, 79, 80, 84. H24.
Tugs. Chan. 9.
Radio — Pilots: VHF Chan. 16, 14. H24.
Entry: Porto de Servico in N corner of Hr. used by yachts.
R. Flag shown from H.M. Office = Vessel may enter.
B. Cyl. or G./R./G./ Lts. = Port closed.

OIL TERMINAL. QUEBRAMAR 41°10.3'N, 8°42.4'W. Lt. Fl.W.R. 5 sec. W.13M. R11M. Col. 23m. R.001°-180°; W.180°-001°. Siren 38 sec.

MOLHE SUL HEAD Lt. Fl.G. 4 sec. 5M. Tr. 16m. Siren 30 sec.
MOLHE NORTE INNER HEAD Lt. Fl.R. 4 sec. 3M. R. Hut 7m. Vis. 173°-353°.

High seas when wind E-SE and when SW-NW. Do not approach port.
Tidal streams about 8 kts. at Springs and ebb tide during floods about 15 knots.

RIO DOURO

Entry: Navigable by craft as far as Barca d'Alva 74M. from entrance. Channel narrow with rocky bottom. Entrance obstructed by sand banks and shoals. Depths on bar 4.9m HWN to 5.2m HWS. Freshets caused by rain or melting snow make currents of about 7 knots (but can reach 16 knots) between November and May, and depths may be 3½-4½m. above normal HW.
R.Flag shown from P/Station at Castelo de Foz = bar may be crossed.
Flag B hoisted half mast from Port Captain's office = river rising, current increasing.

ENTRANCE N SIDE MOLE HEAD
FELGUIERAS 41°08.7N, 8°40.6'W. Lt. Fl.R. 5 sec. 11M. Tr. 12m. Vis. 265°-134°. Siren (2) 30 sec. Reserve Lt. 7M.
BAR. Ldg. Lts. 078°30' **CAIS DA CANTEREIRA** (Front) Oc.R. 6 sec. 8M. W. Col. 10m. Reserve Lt. 4M.
SOBREIRAS (Rear) Oc.R. 6 sec. 8M. W. Col. 31m.

PRAIA DA AGUDA

Ldg. Lts. 068° (Front) Iso.G. 4 sec. 8M. W.G. Col. 15m. (Rear) Iso.G. 4 sec. 8M. W.G. Col. 19m.
FURADOURA. Lt. Fl. 4 sec. 8M. Col. 11m.

AVEIRO 40°39'N 8°45'W. Tel: H.M. 23657. Authority 24091/2. Telex: 37379 JAPA P. Pilots: 39429. Telex: 37338 INPPDA.
Radio — Port: MF 2182, 2484, 2657 on request through LEIXOES. Mon.-Fri. VHF Chan. 16, 11. Mon.-Fri. 0900-1200; 1400-1700.
Radio: Pilots: VHF Chan. 16, 14. 0800-1200, 1400-1800.
Entry: Bar with depth 5.8m but subject to great changes. Entrance ½c. wide at LW. Craft up to 2.4m draught can cross bar at ¾ flood.
Signals (from P/Station): Black Cyl. at masthead = Bar Closed.
Black Cyl. at ½ mast = Bar open with caution.
G/R/G Lts. = Bar closed.
Sailing vessels are towed across bar. Wait for tug. Motor vessels and small sailing craft not taking a tug remain outside until pilot boards from small boat.

AVEIRO 40°38.5'N, 8°44.8'W. Lt.Ho. Fl.(4) 15 sec. 25M. R.W. Tr. 65m. Rc.
Ldg. Lts. 065° (front) Oc.R.3 sec. 8M. mast 11m. (Rear) Oc.R. 6 sec. 8M. mast.
MOLHE NORTE HEAD Lt. Fl.R. 3 sec. 8M. R.W. Tr. 11m. Siren 15 sec..
MOLHE SUL HEAD Lt. Fl.G. 3 sec. 3M. Tr. 10m.
MOLHE CENTRAL Lt. L.Fl. G. 5 sec. 3M. W.G. Tr. 8m.
S. JACINTO TOPO N Lt. F.G. 3M. W.G. Tr. 6m.
TOPO S Lt. F.R. 4M. W.R. Tr. 6m.
TRIANGULO W Lt. Q. (2+1) G. 6 sec. 7M. G.R. Tr. 5m.
TRIANGULO N Lt. Fl. G. 3 sec. 7M. W.G. Tr. 4m.
TRIANGULO S Lt. Fl. R. 4 sec. 8M. W.R. Tr. 4m.
MONTE FARINHA Lt. Q.(2+1) R. 6 sec. 4M. R.G. Tr. 6m.
N COMMERCIAL WHARF. N END Lt. F.R. 4M. W.R. Tr. 7m.
S END Lt. F.G. 3M. W.G. Tr. 7m.
PRAIA DO PORTO. Lt. Q. (2+1) G. 6 sec. 3M. G.R. Tr. 7m.
TERMINAL SUL Lt. Q. (2+1) G. 6 sec. 3M. G.R. Tr. 6m.

CABO MONDEGO 40°11.4'N 8°54.2'W Lt. Fl. 5 sec. 28M. W Tr. 95m. RC. Siren 30 sec.

BUARCOS Lt. Iso. W.R.G. 6 sec. 11M. R.W. Tr. W.9M. R.6M. G.6M. G.004°-028°; W.028°-048°; R.048°-086°.

FIGUEIRA DA FOZ
Tel. No: Port: 22.356/22.366. Telex: 52339 PORFIG P. Pilots: 23.587.
Radio — Port: VHF Chan. 16, 11. Mon.-Fri. 0900-1200; 1400-1700. MF 2182, 2484, 2657 kHz on request.
Pilots: VHF Chan. 16, 14. Mon.-Fri. 0900-1200; 1400-1700.
Entry: Signals shown from Forte de Santa Catarina.
B. Ball/ G./R./G. Lts. = Entrance/Port Closed.
B. Ball (½ mast) = Entrance dangerous.
G./R.Fl./G. Lt. = Special care needed.

Doca Figueira used by yachts. Depths between Mole heads 5m reducing to 3.5m off Forte de Santa Catarina.

RIO MONDEGO MOLHE NORTE HEAD Lt. Fl.R. 6 sec. 6M. Tr. 12m. Siren 35 sec.

MOLHE SUL NEAR HEAD Lt. Fl.G. 6 sec. 7M. Tr. 12m.

ENTRANCE. Ldg. Lts. 073°36'. (Front) F.R. 6M. Col. 6m. (Rear) F.R. 6M. Col. 12m.

RETANCAO MARGINAL. N.Lt. Fl.R. 3 sec. 4M. W.R. Tr. 9m.
S.Lt. Fl.G. 3 sec. 4M. W.G. Tr. 8m.
DOCA DE RECREIO. W. MOLE HEAD Lt. F.R. 2M. R. Tr. 6m.
E. MOLE HEAD Lt. F.G. G. Tr. 6m.
CONFLUENCIA Lt. Fl.(3)G. 8 sec. 4M. G.R. Tr. 7m.
PORTO DE PESCA. N. MOLE HEAD Lt. F.G. 2M. G. Tr. 6m.
S. MOLE HEAD Lt. F.R. 2M. R. Tr. 6m.

PENEDO DA SAUDADE 39°45.8'N 9°1.8'W Lt. Fl. (2) 15 sec. 30M. Square Tr. 54m.

NAZARE SW CORNER OF MORRO DA NAZARE 39°36.2'N, 9°05.0'W. Lt. Oc. 3 sec. 14M. R. Lantern 36m. Vis. 282°-192°. Siren. 35 sec. Emergency Lt.F. 6M.
MOHLE NORTE. Lt. L.Fl.R. 5 sec. 9M. Round Tr. 14m.
MOHLE SUL. Lt. L.Fl.G. 5 sec. 8m. Round Tr. 14m.

SAO MARTINHO DO PORTO

PONTA DE SANTO ANTONIO Lt. Iso.R. 6 sec. 9M. R.W. Tr. 32m. Siren 30 sec.
CARREIRA DO SUL Ldg. Lts. 145° (Front) Iso.R. 1.5 sec. 6M. R.W. Tr. 9m. (Rear). Oc.R. 6 sec. 8M. R.W. Hut 16m.

FARILHAO ILHEU FARILHAO GRANDE.
39°28.6'N 9°32.6'W Lt. Fl. 15 sec. 13M. R. Tr. 99m.

ILHA BERLENGA 39°24.8'N 9°30.5'W Lt. Fl.(3) 20 sec. 27M. W. Tr. 112m. RC. Siren 28 sec. at N End.

CABO CARVOEIRO 39°21.5'N 9°24.4'W Lt. Fl.(3)R. 15 sec. 15M. W. Tr. 55m. RC. Siren 34 sec.

PENICHE

PENICHE DE CIMA Ldg. Lts. 215° (Front) L. Fl.R. 7 sec. 8M. R. Col. 9m. (Rear) L. Fl.R. 7 sec. 6M. Bldg. 13m.
MOLHE OESTE HEAD Lt. Fl.R. 3 sec. 9M. W.R. Tr. 12m. Siren 120 sec.
MOLHE LESTE HEAD Lt. 30°20.9'N, 9°22.4'W. Fl.G. 3 sec. 12M. W.G. Tr.
PORTO DAS BARCAS Lt. Fl.R. 6 sec. 6M. Bldg. 28m. Shown 15/3-15/10.
PORTO DINHEIRO Lt. Oc. 3 sec. 8M. Col. 18m. Shown 15/3-15/10.

ASSENTA.
39°03.4'N 9°24.8'W. Lt. L.Fl. 5 sec. 13M. W. Hut 74m. W. 15° over Landing place, R. elsewhere.

ERICEIRA
Lt. F.R. 6M. B. □ W. Turret 36m. Siren 70 sec.

CABO DA ROCA 38°46.8'N 9°29.8'W Lt. Fl.(4) 20 sec. 26M. W.Tr. 164m. RC Siren. 20 sec. Reserve Lt. range 22M. Fog Sig. Siren 20 sec.

CABO RASO FORTE DE SAO BRAS
38°42.5'N 9°29.1'W Lt. Fl.(3) 15 sec. 20M. R.Tr. 22m. Vis. 324°-189°. Horn (2) 60 sec.

LISBON 38°44'N 9°07'W. Tel: Port 362321/360727. Telex: 18529 P PORLI/S PORLI. Pilots: 613-311. Telex: 12771 PILOTS P.
Radio — Port: Port VHF Chan. 16, 11, 63. Intership Chan. 13.
OEIRAS SIG.STN. VHF Chan. 16, 11. H24. Portuguese only.
DOCA DE PESCA PEDROUCOS. VHF Chan. 3, 12. MF. 2037, 1863 kHz. H24 on 2037 kHz.
DOCA DE ALCANTARA LOCK. VHF Chan. 12, 5. Hrs. 0700, 0815, 0915, 1015, 1115, 1315, 1500, 1630, 1800.
ROCHA DRYDOCKS. VHF Chan. 14, 74.
ALFEITE SIG. STN. VHF Chan. 16, 11. H24 Info. weather Chan. 16. H+30 in Portuguese.
Radio — Pilots: Baia de Caiscas P/V.
West Mole Doca do Bom Successo VHF.
PILOT VESSEL VHF Chan. 16, 14.
PILOT OFFICE: VHF Chan. 16, 14. H24.
Entry: Vessel without a pilot speed limit 5 kts. Yacht harbours at Doca do Bom Successo, Doca de Belem and Doca Terreiro do Trigo.

SEA TRAFFIC SEPARATION ROUTES

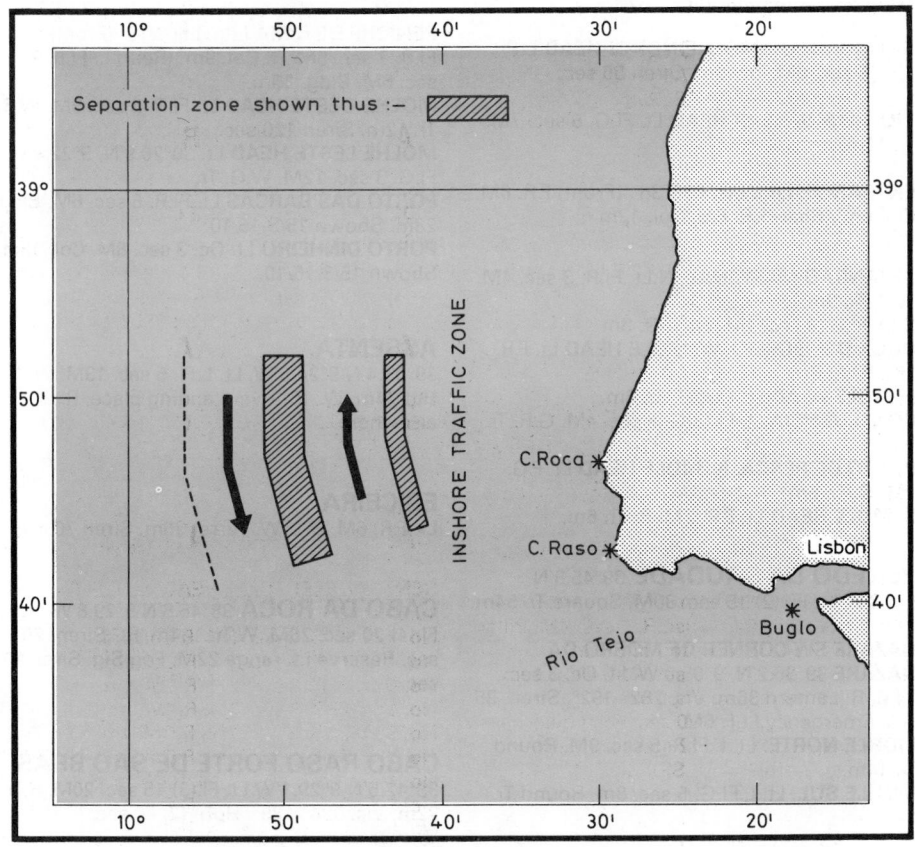

A separation zone 2 miles wide is centred on the following positions (a) 38°42.0′N 9°48.3′W (b) 38°47.0′N 9°50.0′W (c) 38°52.0′N 9°50.0′W with traffic lane, 4 miles wide, on each side. Separation zone, on eastern boundary of northbound traffic lane is 1 mile wide.

LISBON RIO TEJO

BARRA DO NORTE 38°41.3′N, 9°25.2′W. Ldg.Lts. 285°
FORTE DE SANTA MARTA (Front) Oc.W.R. 6 sec. W.18M. R.14M. W.Bl.Tr. 24m. R.233°-334°; W.334°-098°. Horn 10 sec.
NOSSA SENHORA DA GUIA (Rear) Iso.W.R. 2 sec. W.19M. R.16M. W. Octagonal Tr. 52m. W.326°-092°; R.278°-292°.

CASCAIS

Radio — Port: VHF Chan. 16, 11 & MF 2182, 2484, 2657 kHz. H24.
Entry: Excellent facilities for yachts. Special anchorage SE of Casa Seixas (1½c. SSW of Front Ldg. Lt.) 15th May-15th Oct. Approach by lighted channel.
PRAIA DA RIBEIRA Lt. Oc.R. 4 sec. 6M. Col. 6m. Vis. 251°-309°.
ALBATROZ Lt. Oc.R. 6 sec. 5M. Col. 12m.

FORTE DE SAO JULIAO 38°40.4′N, 9°19.4′W.
Lt. Oc.R. 5 sec. 14M. W.Tr. 38m.

**FORTE BUGIO SAO LOURENCO DA
BARRA** 38°39.5′N 9°17.9′W. Lt. Fl.G. 5 sec.
21M. Tr. 27m. Horn Mo(B) 30 sec.

BARRA DO SUL 38°41.8′N, 9°15.9′W Ldg.Lts.
047°
GIBRALTA (Front) Oc.R. 3 sec. 21M. W.Tr.
Floodlit 30m. Vis. 039.5°-054.5° shown H24
1/10-15/3 otherwise to 1 h. after sunrise.
ESTEIRO (Rear) Oc.R. 6 sec. 21M. R.W.Tr.
Floodlit 79m. Vis. 039.5°-054.5°.
EPAC PIER. Lt. Q. 4M. Col. 7m.
DOCA DE PEDROUCOS MOLHE OESTE HEAD
Lt. Fl.R. 6 sec. 2M. Tr. 12m.
MOLHE LESTE HEAD Lt. F.G. 4M. Tr. 12m.
PORTINHO DA COSTA NATO FUEL PIER W Lt.
F.G. 2M. Post 3m.; **E Lt.** F.G. 2M. Post 3m.
**DOCA DO BOM SUCESSO ENTRANCE W
SIDE** Lt. F.R. 6M. Tr. 9m.
E SIDE Lt. F.G. 6M. Tr. 9m.
DOCA DE BELEM ENTRANCE W SIDE Lt. F.R.
6M. Tr. 9m.
E SIDE Lt. F.G. 6M. Tr. 9m.
BRIDGE N PILLAR Lt. 2 Iso.R. 2 sec. 4M. Pillar
10m. Lt. Qk.Fl.R. marks top of pillar.
S PILLAR Lt. 2 Fl.(3)R. 9 sec. 4M. Pillar 10m.
Lt. Qk.Fl.R. marks top of pillar.
W SIDE Fog Sig. Horn 30 sec. each pillar.
E SIDE Fog Sig. Horn. 12 sec. each pillar.
DOCA DA MARINHA W SIDE Lt. F.R. 2M. Tr.
9m.
E SIDE Lt. F.G. 2M. Tr. 9m.
**DOCA DO TERREIRO DO TRIGO ENTRANCE
SW SIDE** Lt. F.R. 2M. Tr. 9m.
NE SIDE Lt. F.G⁻. 2M. Tr. 9m.

CANAL DO ALFEITE

Ldg.Lts. 223°30′ (Front) Oc.R. 3 sec. 7M. W.R.
Tr. 25m. (Rear) Oc.R. 6 sec. 7M. W.R. Tr. 35m.
E MOLE HEAD Lt. L.Fl.R. 5 sec. 8M. R.W. Col.
6m.
W MOLE HEAD Lt. L.Fl.G. 5 sec. 7M. W.G. Tr.
PONTE SPT Fog Sig. Siren 20 sec.

CALA DAS BARCAS

No. 2 Lt. Fl.R. 4 sec. 2M. Col. 5m.
No. 4 Lt. Fl.R. 6 sec. 2M. Col. 5m.
No. 6 Lt. Fl.(2)R. 12 sec. 2M. Col. 5m.
No. 8 Lt. Fl.R. 4 sec. 2M. Col. 5m.
No. 10 Lt. Fl.R. 6 sec. 2M. Col. 5m.

No. 1 Lt. Q.(3) 10 sec. 3M. Col. 5m.
No. 3 Lt. Fl.G. 6 sec. 2M. Col. 6m.
No. 5 Lt. Fl.(2)G. 12 sec. 2M. Col. 5m.
No. 12 Lt. Fl.(2)R. 12 sec. 2M. Col. 5m.

CANAL DO BARRIERO

No. 15 Lt. Fl.G. 4 sec. 2M. B.Col. 3m.
SIDERURGIA ENTRANCE CHANNEL Lt. Fl.G. 5
sec. 3M. B.Col. 5m.

CANAL DO SEIXAL

PILAR Lt. Fl.R. 3 sec. 6M. Col. 4m.
SECA Lt. Fl.G. 3 sec. 5M. Col. 6m.

CANAL DO MONTIJO

CENTRAL ELECTRICA HEAD. Lt. L.Fl.G.
10.5 sec. 3M.
No. 3 Lt. Fl.G. 3 sec. 2M. B.Col. 4m.
No. 4 Lt. Fl.R. 3 sec. 2M. R.Col. 4m.
No. 6 Lt. Fl.R. 3 sec. 2M. R.Col. 4m.
No. 8 Lt. Fl.R. 3 sec. 2M. R. Col. 4m.
No. 5 Lt. Fl.G. 3 sec. 2M. B.Col. 4m.
No. 7 Lt. Fl.G. 3 sec. 2M. B.Col. 4m.
No. 10 Lt. Fl.R. 3 sec. 2M. R.Col. 4m.
No. 9 Lt. Fl.G. 3 sec. 3M. B.Col. 4m.
No. 8A PIER HEAD. Lt. Fl.R. 6 sec. 3M. R. Col.
No. 11 Lt. Fl.G. 5 sec. 2M.
ALCOCHETE PONTE-CAIS Lt. F.R.G. 1M.
R.W.Col. 12m.

CHIBATA 38°38.5′N 9°13′W Lt. F.R. 15M.
Water Tr.

CABO ESPICHEL 38°24.8′N 9°19.9′W Lt.
Fl. 4 sec. 26M. W.Tr. 163m. Siren 31 sec.

ENSEADA DE SESIMBRA

FORTE DO CAVALO 38°26.0′N, 9°06.9′W.
Lt. Oc. 5 sec. 14M. R.Tr. 34m.

SESIMBRA Ldg.Lts. 004°(Front) L.Fl.R. 5
sec. 6M. W. Turret 8m. (Rear) F.R. 6M. NW
Corner of Fort 21m.

PORTO DE ABRIGO
BREAKWATER HEAD. Lt. Q.G. 2M.
PIER HEAD Lt. Fl.R. 3 sec. 3M. Tr. 12m.

MARCONI W Ldg.Lts. 030° (Front) Fl.R. 2.5 sec. 2M. W. △ 7m. (Centre) Fl.R. 3 sec. 2M. W. △ 148m. (Rear) Fl.R. 3.5 sec. 2M. W. △ 194m.

SERRA DE ACHADA MARCONI E Ldg.Lts. 360° (Front) Fl. 2.5 sec. 2M. W. △ 146m. (Centre) Fl. 3 sec. 2M. W. △ 259m. (Rear) Fl. 3.5 sec. 2M. W. △ 312m.

SETUBAL 38°30'N 8°55'W. Tel: Port Office 200 95/8. Port Captain 200 84, 324 43. Fax: 30992. Telex: 43 200 JAPS P. Pilots: 22914. Telex: 43271 INPP DS.
Radio — Port: VHF Chan. 16, 11. Mon.-Fri. 0900-1200, 1400-1700. MF 2182 kHz on request to Caiscais.

Radio — Pilots: VHF Chan. 16, 14.
Entry: Yachts moor at Doca de Recreo. Depth over bar +8m. Enter on flood tide only. Ebb tide attains 4 knots. Speed limit 10 knots.

FORTE DE OUTAO 38°29.2'N, 8°56.0'W.
Lt. Oc.R. 6 sec. 11M. W.Tr. 33m.
No. 2 Lt. Fl.(2)R. 10 sec. 9M. R.Bn. 14m. Racon.
No. 4 Lt. Fl.R. 4 sec. 4M. R.W. Cheq. Col. 14m.
No. 5 Lt. Fl.G. 4 sec. 4M. B.Bn. 14m.
ALBARQUEL Lt. Iso.R. 2 sec. 8M. R. Lantern.

FISHING BASIN E JETTY 38°31.1'N, 8°53.8'W. Ldg.Lts. 040° (Front) Oc.R. 3 sec. 14M. Grey Tr. 12m. **AZEDA** (Rear) Iso.R. 6 sec. 17M. R. Lantern 71m.

SEA TRAFFIC SEPARATION ROUTES

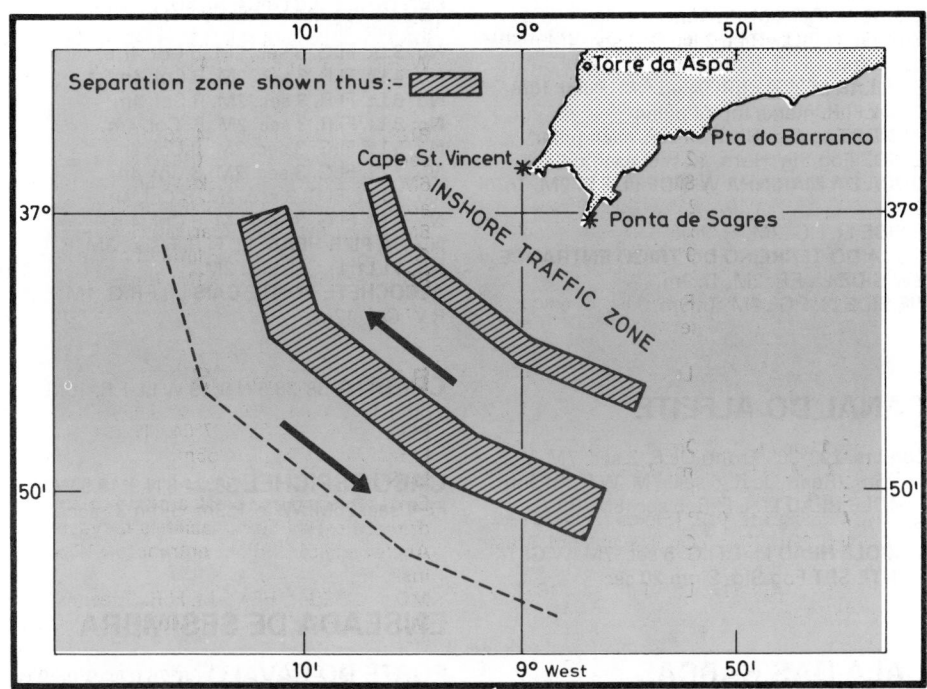

Separation zone 2 miles wide is centred on the following positions (a) 36°49.0'N, 8°56.5'W; (b) 36°51.0'N. 9°02.7'W; (c) 36°55.9'N, 9°10.5'W; (d) 37°00.0'N, 9°12.0'W; with traffic lane 3 miles wide, on each side. Separation zone on north-eastern boundary of north-westbound traffic lane is 1 mile wide.

ALGARVE EXPORTADOR Ldg.Lts. 295°06'.
(Front) Oc.R. 4 sec. 5M. Wall 14m.
ANUNCIADA (Rear) Iso.R. 4 sec. 5M. Church
Tr. 22m.

BALEIA PIER HEAD Lt. F.R. 3M.
CAIS DA SOCEL HEAD Lt. F.R. 5M.
SAPEC Lt. Fl.R. 3 sec. 3M. Col. on Sph. Tank
24m.
TROIA WHARF. N DOLPHIN. Lt. Fl.G. 5 sec.
5M. Mast 7m.
S DOLPHIN. Lt. Fl.(2)G. 10 sec. 5M. Mast. 7m.
TROIA Lt. Fl.Y. 3 sec. 6M. Col. Tidegauge.
PINHEIRO DA CRUZ. Lt. Fl. 3 sec. W.R. Col.
11m.

CABO DE SINES 37°57.5'N 8°52.7'W Lt.
Fl.(2) 15 sec. 24M. W.Tr. 40m.

PORTO DE SINES 37°57'N 8°52'W. Tel:
625001. Telex: 12027 SINMAR P.
Radio — Port: VHF Chan. 12, 68 0900-1200;
1400-1700. MF 2182, 2484, 2657 on request to
Caiscais.
Radio — Pilots: VHF Chan. 12, 14 on request.
Entry: Yacht harbour lies 1¼M. SE of Cabo de
Sines Lt.
MOLHE LESTE HEAD Lt. L.Fl.G. 8 sec. 6M.
G.W. Col. 16m.
ELBOW Lt. L.Fl.Y. 8 sec. 9M. Y. Col. 16m.
NE DIR. 37°56.9'N, 8°52.9'W. Lt. 021° Dir.
Oc.(2)W.R.G. 6 sec. W.8M. R.6M. G.6M. 16m.
G.003°-019°, W.019°-021°, R.021°-030°.
NW DIR. Lt. 348° Dir. Oc.W.R.G. 3 sec. W.8M.
R.6M. G.6M. 10m. G.340°-347°, W.347°-349°,
R.349°-356°.
PIER Ldg.Lts. 357°18' (Front) Iso.R. 6 sec. 5M.
17m. (Rear) Oc.R. 5.6 sec. 28m.

PORTO PESCA SINES Lt. Fl.R. 6 sec. 6M.
W.R. Tr.

POSTO 1 Dir. Lt. 268° Dir. Iso.W.R.G. 2 sec.
W.8M. R.6M. G.6M. 15m. R.257°-266°, W.266°-
270°, G.270°-286°.
CARVAO Ldg. Lts. 032° (Front) L.Fl.R. 5 sec.
5M. Mast 28m. (Rear) Oc.R. 6 sec. 5M. Mast
49m.
PONTA DE GAIVOTA. Lt. L.Fl. 7 sec. 13M.
R.W. Col. 19m.

PORTO COVO Lt. Fl.R. 4 sec. 5M. R.W. R.W.
Pyramid. 31m.

PORTINHO DO CANAL Ldg.Lts. 075° (Front)
Fl.R. 3 sec. 7M. Col. 4m. (Rear) Fl.R. 3 sec. 7M.
Col. 5m.

RIO MIRA ENTRANCE MILFONTES
37°43.1'N, 8°47.3'W. Lt. Fl. 3 sec. 10M. Turret
22m.

CABO SARDAO PONTA DO
CAVALEIRO 37°35.8'N 8°48.9'W Lt. Fl.(3) 15
sec. 23M. W.Tr. 69m.

PORTO DAS BARCAS

SADAO Ldg.Lts. (Front) Fl.G. 3 sec. 7M. R.W.
Col. shown 15/3-15/10. 38m. (Rear) Oc.G. 3
sec. 7M. R.W. Col. shown 15/3-15/10. 51m.

CABO SAO VICENTE 37°01.3'N 8°59.7'W
Lt. Fl. 5 sec. 32M. W.Tr. 84m. Siren 30 sec. RC.
SAGRES. Tel: H.M. 64210.
Radio — Port: VHF Chan. 16, 11. MF 2182,
2484, 2657. H24.

PONTA DE SAGRES 36°59.6'N 8°56.9'W.
Lt. Iso.R. 2 sec. 12M. W.Tr. 52m.
BALEEIRA MOLE. 37°00.6'N 8°58.4'W. Lt.
Fl.W.R. 4 sec. W.14M. R.11M. W. Tr. 12m.
W.254°-355°; R.355°-254°.

BURGAU Lts. in line 034°36'. (Front) Fl.R. 3
sec. 6M. R.W.Col. 64m. (Rear) Iso.R. 6 sec.
6M. R.W.Col. 76m. marks W limit of cable
area. Lts. in line 350°36' (Front) Fl.G. 3 sec.
5M. G.W.Col. 47m. (Rear) Iso.G. 6 sec. 5M.
G.W.Col. 71m. marks E limit of cable area.
POSTO Lt. L.Fl. 5 sec. 11M. 16m.

BAIA DE LAGOS

PONTA DA PIEDADE 37°04.8'N, 8°40.1'W.
Lt.Fl. 7 sec. 17M. Y.Tr. 55m.
LAGOS
Entry: Available to small craft up to 2m.
draught at HW. Good facilities for yachts.
Anchorage 5¾c. ESE of entrance in 16m (8m
inshore).
MOLHE OESTE HEAD Lt. Fl.R. 6 sec. 4M. W.Tr.
MOLHE LESTE HEAD Lt. Mo.(A)G. 10 sec. 3M.
W.G.Tr. 9m.

ALVOR Lt. F.R. 2M. R.Col. 31m.

River used as port of refuge by small craft up
to 3m. draught if unable to stay in Baia de
Lagos.

PORTO DE PORTIMAO. Tel: Port
Captain 23 111. Pilot 23 087. Telex: 589 03
BARLA P.
Radio — Port: VHF Chan. 16, 11. Mon.-Fri.
0900-1200, 1400-1700. MF 2182, 2484, 2657
kHz on request to Sagres.
Radio — Pilots: VHF Chan. 16, 14. H24.
Entry: Anchorage for yachts N of E
Breakwater. Good facilities.

PONTA DO ALTAR 37°06.4'N, 8°31.1'W. Lt.
L.Fl.R. 5 sec. 14M. W.Tr. 29m.
MOLHE OESTE HEAD Lt. Fl.R. 5 sec. 3M.
R.W.Tr. 9m.

MOLHE LESTE HEAD Lt. Fl.G. 5 sec. 2M. R.
Mast. 7m.
FERRAGUDO Ldg. Lts. 119°36' (Front) Oc.R. 5
sec. 8M. R.W. Col. 17m. (Rear) Oc.R. 7 sec.
8M. R.W. Col. 31m.

PORTIMAO Ldg. Lts. 319° (Front) F.R. 3M.
W.O. Tr. 10m. (Rear) F.R. 3M. B.W. △ Tr. 14m.
PRAIA DO CARVOEIRA Lt. L.Fl.R. 7 sec. 6M.
Col. 6m.

ALFANZINA 37°05'N 8°26'W Lt. Fl.(2) 15
sec. 29M. W. Tr. 56m.

ARMACAO DE PERA. Lt. Oc.R. 5 sec. 6M.
Bldg. 24m.
ALBUFEIRA PONTA DA BALEEIRA Lt. Oc. 6
sec. 4M. W.Tr. R. Bands. 30m.
PRAIA DA ALBUFEIRA E POINT OF BAY Lt.
Iso.R. 3 sec. 8M. R.W. Tr. 21m.

OLHOS DE AGUA Lt. L.Fl. 5 sec. 7M. R.W.
Col. 28m.

VILAMOURA. 37°04.4'N, 8°07.3'W. Lt. Fl.
10 sec. 19M. Naval Control Tr. 16m.
MARINA DE VILA MOURA W MOLE HEAD Lt.
Fl.R. 4 sec. 5M. Tr. 13m.
E MOLE HEAD Lt. Fl.G. 8 sec. 6M. Tr. 12m.
VILAMOURA MARINA. Tel: 32023. 35247.
Radio: MF 2182 kHz. VHF Chan. 16, 11, 12, 14,
30, 62, also CB Chan. 1. Hours: Mon.-Sat.
0800-1130. 1300-1700.
Berths: 1000 on catwalks or end on to jetty.
Depths: Outer Hbr. 4m. Inner Hbr. 2-3.3m.
Provisions: All grades fuel, food, water.
Repairs: Slipway, yard. 30T gantry crane.
Facilities: Showers, toilets, Doctor, chemist,
bank, etc.
Wx.F'cast: Area 50M. at 1000 hrs. daily

FARO Lt. Aero Al.Fl.W.G. 10 sec. W.11M.
G.8M. Octagonal Tr. 31m.
ANCAO ILHOTA DA COBRA Lt. F.G. 3M. Col.
5m.

BARRA DE FARO — OLHAO

FARO. Tel: 22.001. 22.034.
Radio — Port: VHF Chan. 16, 11. H24. MF
2182, 2484, 2657 kHz on request to Sagres.
Entry: Anchorage for yachts in 3.6m W of No:
15 By. Good facilities.
Tidal streams 6 knots at Springs.
Tidal Signals:
1 Ball = 3m.
2 Balls = 4m. etc.
Blue flag/R. pendant = tide falling.
R. pendant/Blue flag = tide rising.
R. pendant = channel closed.

BARRA NOVA Ldg. Lts. 021° (Front) Oc. 4 sec.
6M. R.W. Col. 8m. using Cabo de Santa Maria
as Rear Lt.

CABO DE SANTA MARIA 36°58.4'N,
7°51.8'W. Lt.Ho. Fl.(4) 17 sec. 25M. W. Tr.
49m. RC.
MOLHE OESTE HEAD Lt. Fl.R. 4 sec. 6M. W.
Tr. 8m.
MOLHE LESTE HEAD Lt. Fl.G. 4 sec. 6M. Col.
10m.
**ILHA DA CULATRA TRAINING WALL INNER
END** Lt. Oc.G. 5 sec. 3M. Col. 6m.

CANAL DE FARO

Ldg.Lts. 098° **MAR SANTO** (Front) Oc.R. 5 sec.
5M. Col. R.W.V.S. 8m. using Cabo de Santo
Maria as Rear Lt.
Ldg.Lts. 328° **CASA CUBICA** (Front) Iso.R. 6
sec. 6M. House 20m. **SANTA ANTONIO DO
ALTO** (Rear) Oc.R. 6 sec. 6M. Church 52m.

ILHA DA CULATRA

PONTE DO CARVO HEAD Lt. Fl. 6 sec. 6M. G.
Col. 6m.
PONTE CAIS PIER HEAD Lt. Oc.G. 4 sec. 5M.
G.Col. 5m.

CANAL DE OLHAO

GOLADA Ldg. Lts. 219°30'. (Front) L.Fl.R. 5
sec. 3M. R. Col. 5m. (Rear) Oc.R. 5 sec. 3M.
Col. 8m.

CAIS FAROL Lt. Fl.G. 3 sec. 7M. G. Col. 5m.
Ldg. Lts. 124°12' **ARRAIAIS** (Front) Iso.G. 1.5
sec. 5M. W. △ B. stripe. 7m. **OLD LIFEBOAT
HOUSE** (Rear) Oc.G. 3 sec. 2M. W. ▽ B. stripe.
8m.

MURTINAS Ldg. Lts. 352°30' (Front) L.Fl.R. 5
sec. 7M. Col. R.W.V.S. 6m. (Rear) L.Fl.R. 5 sec.
7M. Col. R.W.V.S. 12m.
MOLHE OESTE. Lt. Fl.R. 6 sec. 6M. octagonal
W.R. Tr.

CAIS PIER Ldg. Lts. 043°48' (Front) Iso.R. 6
sec. 7M. Bldg. 6m. **IGREJA** (Rear) Oc.R. 4 sec.
6M. Belfry 20m.

CANAL DA ASSETIA

MOINHO Ldg. Lts. (Front) L.Fl.R. 6 sec. 5M.
R.W. Col. 4m. Vis.100°-190°. Difficult to see.
Moved to meet changes in channel. (Rear)
300m. from front. L.Fl.R. 6 sec. 5M. R.W. Col.
11m.

Channels leading to Fuzeta and Tavira
available to small craft at HW only.

FUZETA

INEGRA. Lt. Oc.R. 3 sec. 5M. Belfry 31m.
LIVRAMENTO Ldg. Lts. **SAPAL** (Front) Oc.R. 5
sec. 7M. Col. R.W.V.S. 7m. **ARROTEIRA DE
BAIXO** (Rear) Oc. 5 sec. 9M. Col. R.W.V.S.
18m. Not used as Ldg.Lts. without local
knowledge.
W MOLE HEAD. Lt. Fl.R. 4 sec. 7M. Col.
R.W.V.S. 5m.
E MOLE HEAD. Lt. Fl.G. 4 sec. 5M. W.G. Tr.
7m.
BARRA. Lt. Fl.R. 4 sec. 4M. Col. 6m.

TAVIRA

BAR Ldg. Lts. **ARMACAO** (Front) Fl.R. 3 sec.
4M. R. Col. 3m. **FORTE** (Rear) Iso.R. 6 sec. 5M.
9m. 4M. R. Col. 3m.
W MOLE HEAD. Lt. Fl.R. 2.5 sec. 7M. Tr.
MOLHE LESTE. HEAD. Lt. Fl.G. 2½ sec. 6M. Tr.

BARRA NOVA DO COHICO Ldg. Lts.
PRAIA (Front) F. 4M. Col. 5m. **ALMARGEM**
(Rear) F. 4M. Col. 6m.

RIO GUADIANA

VILA REAL DE SANTO ANTONIO. Tel: 43035.
Radio — Port: VHF Chan. 16. Mon.-Fri. 0900-
1200, 1400-1700. MF 2182, 2484, 2657 kHz on
request to Sagres Mon.-Fri.
Entry: Navigable for over 25M with draught
of 5m. up to Pomarao and flat bottomed craft
to Mertola. Depth on the bar 4m. Tidal current
normally 1½ knots but increases considerably
in winter during floods. Yacht anchorage at
Odeleita 8M. above Ayamonte.
Anchorage: ½M. N of Ayamonte, Cannot land
at LW. Current 3 kts. May also anchor in
middle of Fishing Boat Basin.

VILA REAL DE SANTO ANTONIO
37°11.1'N 7°24.9'W. Lt. Fl.6.5 sec. 30M. B.W. Tr.
47m. RC.
W TRAINING WALL. Lt. Fl.R. 5 sec. 4M. R. Tr.

SPAIN

SOUTH COAST

DIQUE DE LEVANTE S END. Lt. Fl.G. 3 sec.
4M. Tr.
BALUARTE. Lt. Fl.G. 3 sec. 4M. B. Tr. 3m.

BARRA DE LA HIGUERITA
DIQUE DE PONIENTE HEAD Lt. Q.(2)R. 5 sec.
7M.
ISLA CHRISTINA Ldg. Lts. (Front) Q. (Rear) Fl.
4 sec. Tr.
DIQUE DE LEVANTE HEAD Lt. Fl.G. 3 sec. 6M.
Post 7m.
PANTALAN DEL MORAL. HEAD. Lt. F.

RIO PIEDRAS

ROMPIDO DE CARTAYA N BANK
37°12.9'N 7°7.6'W Lt. Fl.(2) 10 sec. 24M. B.W.
Col. 43m.

PUNTA UMBRIA. Tel: Y.C. 955 311966.
Radio — Port: VHF Chan. 9 as required.
BREAKWATER HEAD. Lt. V.Q.(6)+L.Fl. 10 sec.
3M. ⚓ on Y.B. Tr. 8m.
YACHT CLUB PIER Lt. F.W.R. Vert. 3M. Mast.
HARBOUR WORKS PIER Lt. F.W.R.Vert. 3M.
Mast.

**MUELLE DE LA CONTRADIA DE
PESCADORES** Lt. F.W.R. vert. 3M. Post.
BRIDGE 37°13.04'N, 6°57.81'W.
Drawbridge across Estero de Burro can be
opened by calling Huelva Pilots or Port.

PUERTO HUELVA 37°16'N 6°55'W
Radio — Pilots: VHF Chan. 16, 14, 12, 11. H24.
C/S. Huelva Barra Practicos or Huelva Puerto
Practicos.
Entry: Depths of 9m. at LW.
Anchorage: 3c. from root of Training Wall in
6m.

S.B.M. Lt.By. Fl.(3)Y. 12 sec. 5M. R.W. Siren 30
sec.

RIO ODIEL

PICACHO 37°08.2'N 6°49.5'W Lt. Fl.(2 + 4)
30 sec. 29M. R.W. Octagonal Tr. 49m.
DIQUE HEAD 37°06.5'N, 6°49.9'W. Lt.
Fl.(3+1)W.R. 20 sec. W.12M. R.9M. W.Twr.
R.band. 30m. W165°-100° R.100°-125°. Racon
(K).
CANAL DEL PADRE SANTO Ldg. Lts. 339°11'
(Front) Q. 5M. Tr. 46m. (Rear) Fl.R. 2 sec. 5M.
Tr. 52m.
MUELLE DE LA BARRA Lt. F.G.W.Vert. 1M.
Col. 5m.
MUELLE DE REINA SOFIA SE END Lt. F.W.G.
Vert. 3M. Col. on Dolphin 10m.
NW END Lt. F.W.G. Vert. 3M. Col. on Dolphin
10m.
**MUELLE DE ENERGIAS E INDUSTRIAS
ARAGONESAS SE END** Lt. F.W.G.Vert. 3M.
Col. 10m.
NW END Lt. F.W.G. Vert. 3M. Col. 10m.
MUELLE DE SALTES S END Lt. F.W.R. Vert.
N END Lt. F.W.R. Vert.
MUELLE DE MINERALES S END Lt. F.W.G.
Vert. 3M. Col. 7m.
N END Lt. F.W.G. Vert. 3M. Col. 7m.
PUENTE DEL TINTO S PASSAGE S SIDE Lt.
F.G. 3M. B.R. Pile vis. downstream. 2F. mark
centre of passage.
N SIDE Lt. F.R. 3M. R. Pile.
N PASSAGE S SIDE Lt. F.G. 3M. R. Pile vis.
upstream. 2F. Lts. mark centre of passage.
N SIDE Lt. F.R. 3M. B. Pile.

LA RABIDA
Radio — Port: VHF Chan. 16, 9.

MUELLE DE LA RABIDA HEAD Lt. F.W.G.Vert.
1M. B.W. Post 6m.

SMALL CRAFT QUAY. Lt. F.W.G. vert. 3M.
10m. each end.
**MUELLE DE FOSFORICO ESPANOL SA N
HEAD** Lt. 2 F. Vert. Col. also on S End.
MUELLE DE LA CAMPSA Lt. F.W.G.Vert. Col.
Bell.
PANTALAN FORET SA. Lt. 2 F.G. Vert. 3M. Col.
8m.
FACTORY PIER Lt. F.W.G.Vert.
MUELLE DE THARSIS Lt. 2F.R.

RIO GUADALQUIVIR

Entry: Proceeding up to Seville, arrive off
entrance before 1½h-HW to reach Locks on
flood tide. Craft of <2.5m draught and <7
knots should pass Bonanza ½h-LW. At 12
knots, passage to the Locks takes 4 hrs plus 1
hr to the city. Small craft can proceed above
the bridges at Seville.
When departing with draught <4.5m, leave
Seville 6 hr before HW Bonanza to make the
sea in about 6½ hr. Yachts may proceed
without a pilot. Tidal streams at the entrance
run at 3½ knots (Springs) and 1 knot (Neaps).
When in flood ebb tide reaches 6 knots. At
Bonanza the stream attains 1½-3 knots flood
and 2-3 knots ebb. During floods the rate in
the river can attain 8-10 knots.
P/Station: 2 M. N of Punta del Perro Lt. Ho.
Radio — Port: VHF Chan. 12.
Radio — Pilots: Chipiona. VHF Chan. 16, 9, 10,
12, 13, 14.
Bonanza. VHF Chan. 16, 9, 12, 14.
Seville. VHF Chan. 16, 9, 12, 14.

SANLUCAR DE BARRAMEDA

TORRE DE LA HIGUERA 37°00.6'N, 6°34.1'W.
Lt. Fl.(3) 20 sec. 20M. Tr. 46m.
BONANZA Lt. Fl. 5 sec. 7M. R. Tr. 22m.

NEW CANAL 36°47.9'N, 6°20.2'W. Ldg.Lts.
068°56' (Front) Q.G. 10M. R.W. struct. (Rear)
Oc.G. 4 sec. 10M. R.W. struct.
MUELLE DE BONANZA SHELTER MOLE S END
Lt. Q.R.G. 2M. B.W Col. 6m. G.023°-180°; R.
180°-023°.
N END Lt. Q.G. 7M. B.W. Col. 6m.
No. 2 (FAGINADO). Lt. Fl.(4)R. 8 sec. 3M. R.
Mast. 10m.
No. 5 (SAN CARLOS). Lt. Fl.(3)G. 7 sec. 4M.
Silver Mast. 10m.
No. 4 (MUELLE DE LA PLANCHA). Lt. Fl.(2)R.
6 sec. 3M. R.W. Mast. 10m.
No. 6 (MILLA MEDIDA) Lt. Fl.(4)R. 8 sec. 3M.
R. mast 10m.

No. 10 (CANO DE LA FIGUEROLA). Lt. Fl.(4)R. 8 sec. 3M. R. mast 10m.
No. 12 (CANO DE BRENES). Lt. Fl.(2)R. 6 sec. 3M. R. mast 10m.
No. 14 (PUNTAL). Lt. Fl.(4)R. 8 sec. 3M. R. mast 10m.
No. 13 (ESPARRAGUERA). Lt. Fl.(3)G. 7 sec. 4M. B. mast 10m.
No. 15 (SENO DE LA ESPARRAGUERA). Lt. Fl.G. 3 sec. 4M. B. mast 10m.
No. 17 (CANO QUERA). Lt. Fl.(3)G. 7 sec. 4M. B. mast 10m.
No. 19 (EL YESO). Lt. Fl.G. 3 sec. 4M. B. mast 10m.
No. 21 (TARFIA BAJA). Lt. Fl.(3)G. 7 sec. 4M. B. mast.
No. 23 (TORRE DE TARFIA). Lt. Fl.G. 3 sec. 4M. B. mast.
Ldg.Lts. 181°30′ (Front) Q.G. 6M. △ R.S. mast 10m. (Rear) Iso.G. 4 sec. 6M. ▽ R.S. mast 14m. vis. 166°-197°.
No. 24 (MATA ROJA). Lt. Fl.(2)R. 6 sec. 3M. S. mast 10m.
Ldg.Lts. 263° (Front) Q.R. 5M. S. mast 8m. (Rear) Iso.R. 4 sec. 5M. S. mast 12m. vis. 247°-278°.
No. 27 (VILLALON). Lt. Fl.G. 3 sec. 4M. B. mast.
No. 29 (EMBARCADERO CALLEJON DE LA MATA). Lt. Fl.(3)G. 7 sec. 4M. B. mast 10m.
No. 31 (PUNTA DEL CABALLO). Lt. Fl.G. 3 sec. 4M. B. mast 10m.
No. 33 (NUEVO BRAZO DEL ESTE). Lt. Fl.(3)G. 7 sec. 4M. B. mast 10m.
Ldg.Lts. 174°30′ (Front) Q.G. 4M. S. mast 8m. (Rear) Iso.G. 4 sec. 4M. Mast 12m. vis. 159°-190°.
No. 32 (LA LISA). Lt. Fl.(2)R. 6 sec. 3M. R. mast.
No. 39 (SUR CORTA DE LOS JERONIMOS). Lt. Fl.G. 3 sec. 4M. B. mast 10m.
No. 36 (PUNTA DEL MELONAR). Lt. Fl.(2)R. 6 sec. 3M. R. mast 10m.
No. 38 (OLIVILLOS SUR). Lt. Fl.(4)R. 8 sec. 3M. S. mast 10m.
No. 43 (OLIVILLOS SUR). Lt. Fl.G. 3 sec. 4M. S. mast 10m.
No. 40 (OLIVILLOS CENTRO-SUR). Lt. Fl.(2)R. 6 sec. 3M. R. mast 10m.
No. 45 (OLIVILLOS CENTRO). Lt. Fl.(3)G. 7 sec. 4M. S. mast 10m.
No. 42 (OLIVILLOS CENTRO). Lt. Fl.(4)R. 8 sec. 3M. S. mast 10m.
No. 47 (OLIVILLOS NORTE VERDE). Lt. Fl.G. 3 sec. 4M. S. mast 10m.
No. 44 (OLIVILLOS NORTE ROJA). Lt. Fl.(2)R. 6 sec. 3M. S. mast 10m.
No. 49 (LA COMPANIA). Lt. Fl.(3)G. 7 sec. 4M. B. mast 10m.
No. 46 (ISLETA SUR ROJA). Lt. Fl.(4)R. 8 sec. 3M. S. mast 10m.

No. 51 (ISLETA SUR VERDE). Lt. Fl.G. 3 sec. 4M. S. mast 10m.
No. 53 (ISLETA CENTRO VERDE). Lt. Fl.(3)G. 7 sec. 4M. B. mast 10m.
No. 55 (ISLETA NORTE VERDE). Lt. Fl.G. 3 sec. 4M. S. mast 10m.
No. 48 (ISLETA NORTE ROJA). Lt. Fl.(2)R. 6 sec. 3M. S. mast 10m.
Ldg.Lts. 210° (Front) F.R. 6M. △ on S. mast 10m. (Rear) F.R. 6M. ▽ on S. mast 14m. vis. 194.5°-225.5°.
No. 57 (GUINIGUADA). Lt. Fl.(3)G. 7 sec. 4M. B. mast 10m.
Ldg.Lts. 248° (Front) F.R. 6M. △ on S. mast 9m. (Rear) F.R. 6M. ▽ on S. mast 13m. vis. 232.5°-263.5°.
No. 59 (SAN CRISTOBAL). Lt. Fl.G. 3 sec. 4M. B. mast 9m.
No. 50 (HUERTA DE D. ISAIAS). Lt. Q.R. 3M. S. mast 9m.
MUELLE DE BUTANO W. Lt. Fl.G. 4 sec. R.W. Dolphin 9m.
E Lt. Fl.G. 4 sec. R.W. Dolphin 9m.
No. 61 (DESAGUE DEL COPERO). Lt. Fl.(3)G. 7 sec. 4M. B. mast 9m.
Ldg.Lts. 083° (Front) F.G. 6M. △ on S. mast 9m. (Rear) F.G. 6M. ▽ on S. mast 13m.
No. 63 (EJE SALIDA ESCLUSA). Lt. Fl.G. 3 sec. 4M. B. mast 13m.
SEVILLA No. 52 (DARSENA DEL BATAN). Lt. Fl.(4)R. 8 sec. 3M. R. mast 13m.
C.A.M.P.S.A. Lts. F.R. Dolphins.
BAJO SALMEDINA Lt. V.Q.(9) 10 sec. 5M. ⌇ on Y. Tr. B. Band 9m. ⌇

CHIPIONA PUNTA DEL PERRO
36°44.3′N 6°26.4′W Lt. Fl. 10 sec. 25M. Y. Tr. 67m.

BREAKWATER HEAD Lt. Q.G. 2M. B.W. Col. 6m.

ENTRANCE. LDG.LTS. 218°.
SPUR MOLE (Front) Q.R. 4M. △ R.W. Tr. 9m. (Rear) Iso.R. 4 sec. 4M. △ R.W. Tr. 11m.

PUERTO DE ROTA

Naval Base Radio: MF 2836, 2716 kHz. H24.

ROTA 36° 38.2′N 6°20.8′W Lt. Aero Al. Fl.W.G. 9 sec. 17M. R.W. Cheq. Water Tank 79m. Lt.Bn. Occ. 4 sec. 13M. R.W. Tr. 34m.
MOLE HEAD Lt. Fl.(3)R. 10 sec. 9M. R.W. Tr. 9m.

NAVAL AIR BASE SW BREAKWATER HEAD
Lt. Oc.(2)R. 6 sec. 4M. Col. 15m.
SE BREAKWATER HEAD Lt. Fl.(3)G. 7 sec. 8M.
Col. 13m.

Ldg. Lts. 345°30′ (Front) Q. 9M. B.W. ◊. Or. Tr.
13m. Vis. 335.5°-355.5°. (Rear) Oc. 3 sec. 11M.
B.W.O. Or. Tr. 26m. Vis. 335.5°-355.5°.

CADIZ 36°30′N 6°20′W
Radio — Pilots: VHF Chan. 16, 11, 12, 14. H24.
Entry: Yacht Harbour near Dique de San
Felippe. Outer harbour very shallow, liberally
covered with rocks, wrecks and shoal areas.
Canal Principal, least depth 10m. Canal Norte
least depth 8m. Canal Sur narrow and
dangerous, for vessels <2.5m draught
Anchorage: In Fishing Hbr. Also berthing. No
charge.

CASTILLO DE SAN SEBASTIAN
36°31.8′N 6°18.9′W. Lt. Fl.(2) 10 sec. 25M. Tr.
38m.

LAS PUERCAS No. 3 Lt. Q.(3)W.G. 9 sec.
W.8M. G.6M. B. Bn. 12m. W.107°-260.5°;
G.260.5°-107°.
BASIN MALECON DE SAN FELIPE HEAD Lt.
Fl.G. 3 sec. 4M. Tr. 10m.
MALECON DE LEVANTE HEAD Lt. Fl.R. 2 sec.
3M. Bn.
WARSHIP BERTH Lt. Q. 1M. R. ▯ Dolphin 3m.
MUELLE No. 3 N END Lt. F.G.
REAL NAUTICO SHELTER PIER. Lt. F.G.
MUELLE REINA SOFIA ELBOW. Lt. F.
MUELLE No. 2 N CORNER Lt. F.R. R. Col.
MUELLE CIUDAD Lt. Oc. 5 sec. 3M. R. △ Col.
27m.
MUELLE No. 5. Lt. F.G.
**PUERTO PESQUERO DIQUE DE PONIENTE
HEAD** Lt. Q.G. 3M. W. Tr. 5m.
DIQUE DE LEVANTE HEAD Lt. Q.R. 3M. W. Tr.
5m.
LA CABEZUELA MOLE Lt. Q.(3)R. 10 sec. 1M
W.R. Tr. 8m.
TANKER CLEANSING BERTH No. 1 DOLPHIN
Lt. Fl.(3)G. 10 sec. 3M. Grey Col.
W DOLPHIN Lt. Fl.(3)G. 8 sec.

INTERNATIONAL FREE ZONE.
Entrance Ldg. Lts. 210°30′. (Front) Iso. 2 sec.
3M. B. ◊. Mast 11m. Vis. 180.5°-240.5°. (Rear)
Iso. 6 sec. 3M. B. ◊. Mast 14m. Vis. 180.5°-
240.5°.
MUELLE DE PONIENTE NE CORNER Lt. F.G.
4M. B.W. Post 4m.
MUELLE DE RIBERA Lt. F.R. 3M. B. Post 4m.

**PUENTE JOSE LEON DE CARRANZA W SIDE
OF PASSAGE** Lt. 2F.G. 3M. Col.
E SIDE OF PASSAGE Lt. 2F.R. 3M. Col.
PUNTALES OUTER BREAKWATER HEAD Lt.
F.G. 6m. B. Post.
LA CLICA OUTER BERTH Lt. Q.G. 3M. W.G.
Bn.
INNER BERTH Lt. Fl.G. 3 sec. W.G. Bn.

PUERTO DEPORTIVO SHERRY.
36°34.75′N, 6°15.15′W. Tel: H.M. (956) 87 03
03. Fax: (956) 85 33 00. Telex: 76254 MPSM E.
Radio — Port: VHF Chan. 16, 9.
Depth in entrance 4.5m. (min.) and Inner
Harbour 3.4m. to 4.5m. Speed limit 2 kts.
Entrance difficult for low powered craft in SW
gales. Anchorage 200m. off E Head of Dique
de Levante in 4m.
DIQUE PONIENTE HEAD. Lt. Oc.R. 4 sec. 4M.
ANTEDARSENA ENTRANCE. Lt. Oc.G. 5 sec.
3M.
DARSENA INTERIOR ENTRANCE. Lt. Q.G. 1M.
ENTRANCE. Lt. Q.R. 1M.

PUERTO DE SANTA MARIA

Entry: Mainly commercial port. Channel
depth 4.5m. Quays on NW side have depths
of 1½-3m, those of SE side 3m.
ESCOLLERA DE LEVANTE HEAD Lt. Fl.(3)G.
11 sec. 4M. Tr. 9m.
NUEVO ESCOLLERO. Lt. Fl.(2) 8 sec. 3M. B.
Tr.
Ldg. Lts. 039°42′ **MUELLE COMERCIAL**
(Front) Q. 4M. Tr. 16m. (Rear) Iso. 4 sec. 4M.
Tr. 20m.
ESCOLLERA DE PONIENTE ROOT Lt. Q.R. 2M.
Tr.
ESCOLLERA DE PONIENTE HEAD. Lt. Fl.(2)R.
9 sec. 3M. R. Tr. 12m.
MUELLE PESQUERO SW END Lt. F.R.

CANAL DE SANCTI PETRI

Entry: A narrow winding channel. Bar depths
1.0-3.8m. Craft with 3m draught can cross bar
at HWS in calm weather. Channel least depth
0.3m. Zuazo Bridge vertical clearance 4m.

CASTILLO DE SANCTI PETRI Lt. Fl. 3 sec. 9M.
Tr. 18m.

COTO SAN JOSE 1st Ldg. Lts. 050°.
(Front) Q. 7M. (Rear) Iso. 4 sec. 7M.

BATERIA DE URRUTIA 2nd Ldg. Lts. 346°30'.
PUNTA DEL BOQUERON (Front) Q. (Rear) Iso.
4 sec.
CABO ROCHE. 36°17.8'N 6°08.3'W. Lt. Fl.(4) 24
sec. 20M. Brown. Tr. 44m.
PUERTO DE CONIL JETTY HEAD. Lt. Iso.R. 10
sec. 5M. R. Tr. 8m.

PUNTA PALOMA 36°03.9'N 5°43.1'W. Lt.
Fl.(2) 5 sec. 12M. Bldg. 44m. Vis. 323°-025°.

TARIFA 36°00.1'N 5°36.5'W. Lt. Fl.(3) 10 sec.
25M. W. Tr. 40m. RC Racon. Lt. (same
structure) F.R. 10M. 30m. Vis. 089°-113°.
Siren(3) 60 sec.

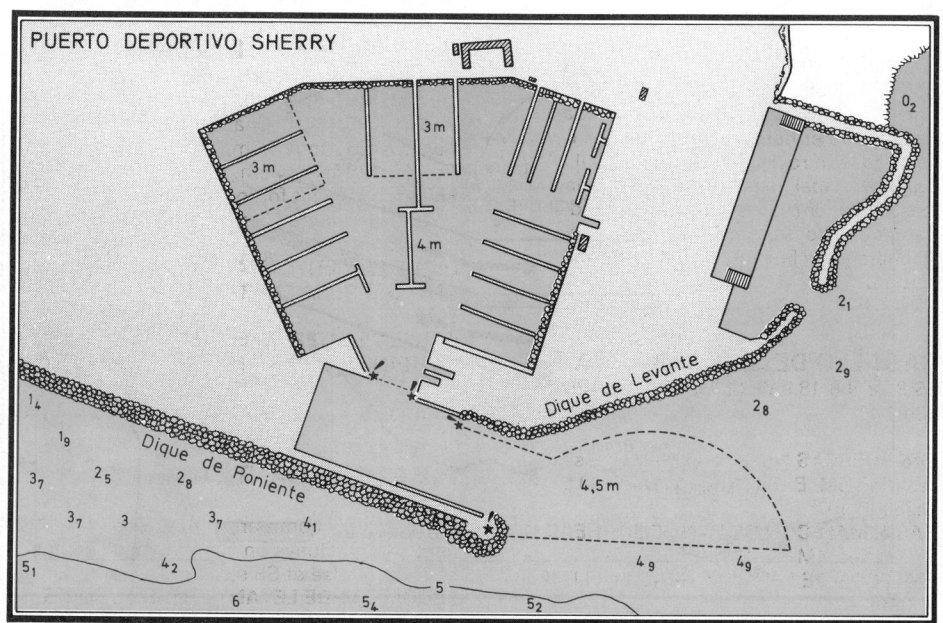

PUERTO DEPORTIVO SHERRY

CABO TRAFALGAR 36°10.7'N 6°02.1'W.
Lt. Fl.(2 + 1) 15 sec. 22M. W. Tr. 49m.

PUERTO DE BARBATE

BARBATE 36°11.3'N, 5°55.3'W. Lt. Fl.(2)W.R. 2
sec. W.10M. R.7M. R.W. Tr. 15m. W.281°-006°;
R. 006°-095°.
DIQUE DE PONIENTE HEAD Lt. Fl.(2)R. 6 sec.
6M. W.R. Tr. 12m.
Ldg. Lts. 297°30'. (Front) Q. 1M. W. Col. 2m.
(Rear) Q. R.W. Col. 7m.
CONTRA DIQUE HEAD Lt. Fl.G. 3 sec. 2M. Tr.
8m.

RIO DE BARBATE

E SIDE ENTRANCE Ldg. Lts. 058°30'.
(Front) Fl. 3 sec. 3M. Post 3m. (Rear) Fl. 3 sec.
3M. Post 6m.

PUNTA DE GRACIA CARAMINAL Lt. Oc.(2) 5
sec. 13M. Tr. 74m.

**STRAIT OF GIBRALTAR. TARIFA VESSEL
TRAFFIC SERVICE** 36°01'N, 5°35'W. Tel: (956)
684757, 684740. Fax: (956) 643606. Telex:
78262 CCTGE.
Radio: VHF Chan. 10, 16. H24.
Area: Strait of Gibraltar, Cape Espartel to
Punta Almina except area N of line 085° Punta
Carnero to Punta Almina.
Information VHF Chan 16, 10 anytime.
Vessel's initial report on Chan. 10. Navigation
information at H+15 on Chan 10 after
announcement on Chan. 16. Additional
broadcast when visibility less than 2M. Radar
surveillance 19M. radius. Assistance on
request.

PUERTO DE TARIFA

Entry: Inadvisable to attempt entry in heavy
E'ly or SW'ly winds due to narrow entrance
and eddies/breakers.
DIQUE DEL SAGRADO CORAZON HEAD Lt.
Fl.G. 3 sec. 4M. W. Tr. 10m. Vis. 249°-045°.

SEA TRAFFIC SEPARATION ROUTES
STRAIT OF GIBRALTAR

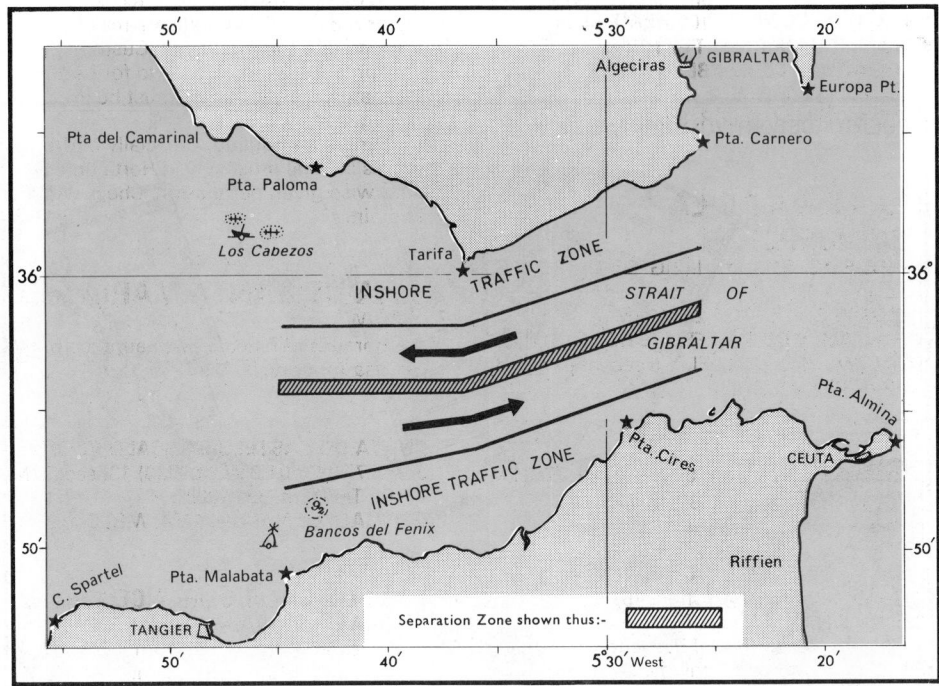

A Separation zone half a mile wide is centred on the following positions. (a) 35°59.09'N, 5°25.60'W; (b) 35°56.29'N, 5°36.40'W; (c) 35°56.29'N, 5°40.90'W. Eastbound lane is approx. 3¼ miles wide at its western extremity and approx. 1¾ miles wide at its eastern extremity.

MOLE No:1 CORNER Lt. Fl.R. 3M. Hut 6m
INNER SPUR HEAD Lt. Fl(2)G. 5 sec. 2M. G. Col. 5m.

PUNTA CARNERO 36°04.7'N 5°25.5'W. Lt. Oc.(1+3) W.R. 20 sec. W.16M. R.13M. Y. Tr. 42m. W.018°-325°; R.325°-018°. Siren Mo(K) 30 sec.

PUERTO DE ALGECIRAS —

LA LINEA. Tel: 652056.
Radio: VHF Chan. 16, 9, 12, 13 as required.

NORTH JETTY HEAD Lt. Fl.(2)R. 6 sec. 13M. W.R. Tr. 13m.
S JETTY Lt. F.G. 4M. B.W. Col. 9m.
N SIDE. Lt. Q.R. 2M. R. Tr.
NW CORNER. Lt. Q.R. 2M. R. Tr.

MUELLE DE NAVIO NORTH HEAD. Lt. Fl.(2+1)G. 8 sec. 4M. G.R. Pole 7m.
SOUTH. Lt. Fl.(2) G. 7 sec. 4M. G.W. Col.
MUELLE DE LA GALERA HEAD NW CORNER Lt. F.R. 1M. Col. 6m.
SE CORNER Lt. Fl.(3)G. 8 sec. 2M. Col. 6m.
MUELLE DE ISLA VERDE Lt. Fl.(3)R. 7 sec. 2M. mast 6m.
SMALL CRAFT BASIN PIER HEAD Lt. F.G. 1M. W. Col. 5m.
YACHT CLUB Lt. F.R.
MUELLE PESQUERO E CNR Lt. Fl.R. 3 sec. 4M. R.W. Post 4m.
W CNR. Lt. Fl.(2) R. 6 sec. 4M. W.R. Post 4m.
OIL PIPELINE Lt. 2 Fl.Y. Vert. B.Y. ◊
OIL TERMINAL JETTY CENTRE 36°10.7'N, 5°23.8'W. Lt. Q.(4) 14 sec. 10M. W. Col. 14m. Vis. 305°-105°.
E ARM HEAD Lt. Fl.(4)R. 8 sec. 4M. R.W. Col. 11m.

W ARM HEAD Lt. Fl.G. 3 sec. 4M. R.W. Col. 11m.
Ldg.Lts. 083°30′. (Front) Iso.G. 2 sec. Col. (Rear) Oc.G. 4 sec. Lead in 400m. off Jetty.
Ldg.Lts. 083°30′. (Front) Iso.R. 2 sec. (Rear) Oc.R. 4 sec. Lead in 100m off Jetty.
POWER STATION JETTY HEAD Lt. F.G.
ATRAQUES DE ALJIBES W DOLPHIN Lt. Fl.G. 5 sec. 2M. post 6m.
E DOLPHIN Lt. Q.(2)R. 8 sec. 2M. Post 6m.

LA LINEA DE LA CONCEPCION

DIQUE ABRIGO. Lt. Fl.(2)G. 6 sec. 4M. W.G. Tr. 4m.
ELBOW SW. Lt. Fl.Y. 2 sec. 4M. Y. Tr. 5m.
PANTALAN DE SAN FELIPE HEAD Lt. Fl.R. 3 sec. 2M. R. Col. 5m. Fl.R. 5 sec. marks Fish Farm 336° × 525m.

GIBRALTAR 36°08′N 5°22′W. Tel: H.M.

78134. Telex: 2130 GIBPOR GK.
Radio — Port: VHF Chan. 16, 6, 12, 13, 14. H24.
Lloyds Sign.Stn. VHF Chan. 16, 8, 14. H24.
Radio — Pilots: VHF Chan. 16, 12, 14.
Entry: Yacht berths at N Mole and yacht harbour NE of Root of Passenger Wharf and Marina near Main Runway.

EUROPA POINT. VICTORIA TR.

36°6.7′N 5°20.6′W. Lt. Iso. 10 sec. 21M. R.W. Tr. Vis. 197°-042°. 49m. Also Oc.R. 10 sec. 17M. 49m. Vis. 042°-067°. (Same structure) F.R.Lt. 17M. 44m. Vis. 042°-067°. Horn 20 sec.

SOUTH MOLE A HEAD 36°08.1N, 5°21.8′W. Lt. Fl. 2 sec. 15M. W. Tr. 18m. Horn 10 sec.
DETACHED MOLE B HEAD Lt. Q.R. 5M. Sq. Tr. 15m.
C HEAD Lt. Q.G. 5M. Sq. Tr. 15m.
NORTH MOLE WEST ARM D HEAD Lt. Q.R. 5M. Round Tr. 18m.
NORTH JETTY E HEAD Lt. F.R. 5M. Tr. 28m.
PASSENGER WHARF. Lt. F.G. on building.
CORMORANT CAMBER. Lt. 2 F.R. vert. 5m.
AUX. CAMBER W. ARM HEAD. Lt. 2 F.R.
COALING ISLAND NEW MOLE Lt.2 F.G. vert.
Lt. F. Aero 2 Q.Hor. Y. Hull.
AERO 36°08.7′N, 5°20.5′W. Lt. Aero Mo(GB)R. 10 sec. 30M. 405m.

AZORES

Entry: Present ship's papers and passports to Maritime Police. Pay fee. Receive Ship's

Transit permit. Then present these to Guarda-Fiscal. Inform them if anything requires repair or of any crew changes. For parts a "Papel Selado" is purchased, for small parts okay to D.I.Y., otherwise an agent is necessary. For major repairs all these papers must be presented to the Alfândega (Customs) and to the Junta Autónoma do Porto for berth space, estimates, etc. All papers must be in Portuguese.
To combat smuggling, especially of drugs, all yachts in Faial must stay in Horta unless otherwise given permission. Check with Port Captain.

ILHA DE SANTA MARIA 36°56′N, 25°01′W

Anchorages at Baie de Sao Laurenco or 5½c. E of Casa Andrade in 22m.

PONTA DO CASTELO GONCALO VELHO 36°55.7′N, 25°01.0′W. Lt. Fl.(3) 13½ sec. 27M. White Tr. 113m. 181°-089°.
ESPIGAO. Lt. Fl. 7 sec. 12M. W.R. Col. 206m.

BAIA DE SAO LOURENCO Ldg.Lts.

268° **CASA ANDRADE** (Front) L.Fl.R. 5 sec. 4M. Grey and blue house 23m. (Rear) Oc.R. 7.5 sec. 3M. White house 36m.
PONTA DO NORTE 37°00.7′N, 25°03.6′W. Lt. Fl.(4) 15 sec. 10M. White Tr.138m.

BAIA DOS ANJOS. FABRICA DOS ANJOS Lt. Fl. 4 sec. 4M. W.R. Col. 12m.
Ldg.Lts. 175° 37°00.2′N, 25°09.5′W. (Front) Fl. 3 sec. 10M. W.R. col. 12m. (Rear) L.Fl.6 sec. 10M. W.R. col. 20m.
CONTROL TOWER. 1M. NE OF PONTA CAGARRA 36°58.5′N, 25°09.7′W. Lt. Aero Al.Fl.W.G. 10 sec. 26M. 117m. 021°-121°.

VILA DO PORTO. Tel: 82.157.

Radio — Port: MF. 2182, 2484, 2657 kHz. Hours: 2182 kHz. 30 mins. at 1000 1300 1600 1900. Chan. 16; Mon.-Fri: 0900-1200, 1400-1700; (Sat. 0900-1200).
Port Captain's office is in fort overlooking the harbour.
Ldg.Lts. 017°45′ (Front) F.R. 6M. W.R. col. (Rear) F.R. 6M. W.R. col. 57m.
MOLE HEAD. Lt. L.Fl. 5 sec. 5M. R.W. Tr. 14m.
PONTA DE MALMERENDO 36°56.4′N, 25°09.4′W. Lt. Fl.(2) 10 sec. 10M. W. Bldg. R. Top. 49m. 282°-091°
ILHEUS DA FORMIGAS Lt. Fl.(2) 12 sec. 9M. Tr.22m.

ILHA DE SAO MIGUEL 37°49'N, 25°08'W
Anchorage for small vessels on the bank between Ilheu da Vila and main island.

PONTA DO ARNEL 37°49.3'N, 25°08.2'W. Lt. Fl. 5 sec. 25M. W.Oc.Tr. 66m 157°-355°.
POVOACAO, VARADOURO MOLE HEAD. Lt. Oc.R. 4 sec. 6M. W. Col. 8m.
RIBEIRA QUENTE Lt. Iso.R. 6sec. 7M. Mast 9m.
PONTA GARCA 37°42.8'N, 25°22.2'W. Lt. L.Fl.W.R. 5 sec. W.16M. R.13M. Grey Tr.100m. W.240°-080°; R.080°-100°. Red Sector covers Ilheu da Vila and Baixa da Lobeira.

VILLA FRANCA DO CAMPO 37°43'N, 25°26'W
Ldg.Lts. 316°30' (Front) Oc.G. 5 sec. 2M. Col. 7m. (Rear) Oc.G. 5 sec. 5M. White house 11m.
SLIPWAY Lt. L.Fl.R. 5 sec. 7M. Sq. Tr. 11m.

PORTO DA CALOURA 37°43'N, 25°30'W
MOLE S END Lt. Fl. 4 sec. 9M. White Col. 6m.
Ldg.Lts. 332°24' (Front) Oc.G. 3 sec. 5M. Post on rock 10m. (Rear) Oc.G. 3 sec. 5M. Post on rock 14m.
LAGOA. Lt. F.R. 3M. R. Post 8m.

PONTA DELGADA Tel: Port: 25.268, 23550. Telex: 8247 MRCC PD. Pilots: 23.550.
Radio — Port & Pilots: VHF Chan. 16, 11, 10, 12, 14. H24.
Anchorage for small vessels S of Molhe Salazar.
Entry Signals: Flag X/2 Gt.Lts. = movement or entry prohibited.
Small craft moor at quays near root of Molhe Salazar. Fresh water (to be chlorinated). Cranes up to 10 tons. Slip for small craft. Diesel fuel. Consul — consult Canadian Vice Consul.
BREAKWATER HEAD Lt. Oc.R. 3 sec. 9M. R.Tr. 14m.
1st. Ldg.Lts. 321° (Front) Iso.G. 5 sec. 8M. Col. on Y. house 14m. (Rear) Oc.G. 5 sec. 8M. Church 47m.
2nd. Ldg.Lts. 266° (Front) Oc.R. 6 sec. 9M. Fort Sao Bras 13m. (Rear) Oc.R. 6 sec. 9M. Fort 19m.
SANTA CLARA 37°43.9'N, 25°41.2'W. Lt. L.Fl. 5 sec. 15M. R.Tr. 26m. 282°-102°.
AIRPORT 37°44.6'N, 25°42.5'W. Lt. Aero Al.Fl.W.G. 10 sec. W.28M. G.23M. 83m. 282°-124°.

PONTA DA FERRARIA 37°51.2'N, 25°51.1'W. Lt. Fl.(3) 20 sec. 27M. White Tr. 106m. 339°-174°.

MOSTEIROS Lt. Oc.R. 3 sec. 6M. W. Col. R. Top. Post 270°-355°.
BRETANHA Lt. L.Fl. 6 sec. 10M. W. Post.
MORRO DAS CAPELAS Lt. Iso. R. 4 sec. 8M. R.Hut 114m. 153°-281°.

RABO DE PEIXE 37°49'N, 25°35'W
IGREJA DO BON JESUS Lt. Oc.G. 4 sec. 5M. Church Tr. 59m. 185°-220°.
HARBOUR SLIPWAY Lt. Oc.R. 3 sec. 6M. Post 8m. 059°-159°.
PONTO DO CINTRAO 37°50.7'N, 25°29.4'W. 4Lt. Fl.(2) 10 sec. 16M. Grey Tr. 117m.
PORT FORMOSO Lt. Fl.R. 4 sec. 3M. W. Hut.

ILHA TERCEIRA 38°47'N, 27°09'W

VILLA NOVA SLIPWAY Lt. Iso. 6 sec. 9M. Pyramid 10m.
LAGES 38°45.6'N, 27°04.8'W. Lt. Aero Al.Fl.W.G. 10 sec. W.28M. G.23M. Tr. 132m.

PRAIA DA VITÓRIA 38°44'N, 27°04'W
Anchorage for small vessels 2½c. NW of breakwater in 10m. Petroleum port. Supply base for airbase. Visiting yachtsmen are allowed to use Yacht Club facilities.
PONTA DO ESPIRITO SANTO MOLE HEAD Lt. Q.G. 4 sec. 5M. B.Col.11m.
MOLHE SUHL HEAD. Lt. Fl.R. 3 sec. 8M. on Tr.
SAO FERNANDO Lt. Oc.R. 3 sec. 6M. B.Pyramid 6m.

PONTA DAS CONTENDAS 38°38.6'N, 27°05.1'W. Lt.Fl.(4) W.R. 15 sec. 26M. W. Tr. 53m. W.220°-020°; R.020°-044°; W.044°-072°; R.072°-093°.
PORTO JUDEU Lt. Fl. 3 sec. 7M. Pyramid 27m.
MONTE BRASIL PONTA DO FAROL Lt. Oc.W.R. 10 sec. 8M. W.R. Col. 21m. W.295°-057°; R.191°-295°.

ANGRA DO HEROISMO 38°39'N, 27°13'W Tel: 22.051.
Radio — Port & Pilots: MF. 2182, 2484, 2657 kHz. Hours: 2182 kHz. 30 mins. at 1000 1300 1630. VHF Chan. 16, 11. Hours: Chan. 16 0800-2000.
Small Commercial Port. Lifeboat available. Small vessels may anchor 3¾c. SSE of Misericordia Church in 22m. Affected by heavy swells. Unprotected anchorage. Visiting yachtsmen are allowed to use Yacht Club facilities.
Ldg.Lts. 342° (Front) Fl.R. 4 sec. 5M. Church 29m. (Rear) Oc.R. 6 sec. 5M. Church 45m.

PORTO PIPAS MOLE HEAD Lt. Fl.G. 3 sec. 6M. B.Y.Cheq. Col. 14m. Also F.R. on factory roof.

SAO MATEUS — Lifeboat Station.
SAO MATEUS Lt. Iso.W.R.6 sec. W.10M. R.7M. W.Tr. 11m. W.296°-067°; R.270°-296°.
CINCO RIBEIRAS 38°40.6'N, 27°19.8'W. Lt. L.Fl. 6 sec. 12M. White pyramid 22m. Reserve Lt. 4M.

PONTA DA SERRETA 38°46.0'N, 27°22.5'W. Lt. Fl.(3) 15 sec. 21M. Col. 95m. 044°-203°.
BISCOITOS 38°48.1'N, 27°15.5'W. Lt. Oc. 6 sec. 12M. 13m.

ILHA GRACIOSA 39°01'N, 27°57'W
Radio — Port: MF. 2182, 2484, 2657 kHz. on request to Horta Radio. VHF Chan. 16, 11. Mon.-Fri. 0900-1200, 1400-1700.
Anchorages; SW of Ponta do Tufo in 24m; off Carpacho in 29m; 2½c NE of Fortun do Corpo Santo Lt. in 27m; 3¼c. SE of Vila de Praia Lt. in 13m.
Landings may be made at Porto de Calheta alongside quays with 3-4m. Ponta do Cais de Joao da Cruz; Cais de Negra; Cais de Praia. Lifeboat Station.
PONTA DO CARAPACHO. 39°00.8'N 27°57.4'W. Lt. Fl.(2) 10 sec. 15M. White Tr.190m. 165°-098°.
MOLE. Lt. Fl.G. 3 sec. 9M. W.G. Tr. 15m.
FORTIM DO CORPO SANTO Lt. L.Fl.R. 5 sec. 5M. R.Hut 13m.
PONTA DA BARCA 39°05.6'N, 28°03.0'W. Lt. Fl. 5 sec. 28M W.Tr.70m. 029°-031°; 035°-251°; 267°-287°.
FOLGA PIER Lt. L.Fl. 5 sec. 4M. Col. 30m.

ILHA DE SAO JORGE 38°33'N, 27°46'W
Anchorage: 3½c. S of Calheta Lt. or under Ilha do Pico.

BAIA DE VELAS
Anchorage: 2c. SSE of Baia de Velas Lt. in 24m.

PONTA DO TOPO 38°33.0'N, 27°45.9'W. Lt. Fl.(3) 17 sec. 20M. White Tr. 57m. 133°-033°.
PONTA DO JUNCA L Lt. Fl. 3 sec. 6M. R.W.Col. 71m.
CALHETA WHARF Lt. Oc.R. 3 sec. 6M. White Pedestal 17m.
URZELINA Lt. Fl. 6 sec. 4M. Post 9m.
QUEIMADA Lt. Fl. 5 sec. 10M. W.R. Col. 49m.

PORTA DAS VELAS 38°41'N, 28°12'W
Radio — Port: MF 2182, 2484, 2657 kHz. on

request to Horta Radio. VHF Chan. 16, 11. Mon.-Fri. 0900-1200, 1400-1700.
IN HARBOUR Lt. Oc.G. 3 sec. 5M. R.Hut 25m. Anchorage bearing 348°.
PIER HEAD Lt. Fl.R. 5 sec. 3M. R.Col. 6m.

ANCHORAGE. Lts. in line. 300° (Front) Iso.R. 5 sec. 6M. 2 R.Cols. 13m. **ERMIDA DO LIVRAMENTO** (Rear) Oc.R. 6 sec. 7M. Chapel 49m.

PONTA ROSAIS Lt. Fl.(2) 10 sec. 8M. Lookout Post 258m.

NORTE GRANDE Lt. Fl.6 sec. 12M. W.R. Tr.

ILHA DO PICO 38°32'N, 28°32'W

MADALENA. Tel: 62.203
Radio — Port: MF 2182, 2484, 2657 kHz. on request to Horta Radio. VHF Chan. 16, 11. Mon.-Fri. 0900-1200, 1400-1700.
Anchorage in Baia de Canas 2c. offshore in 40m. Landing close W of Ponta de San Antonio.

AREIA LARGA Ldg.Lts. 082°30' (Front) Oc.R. 3 sec. 7M. W.Col. 10m. (Rear) Oc.R. 3 sec. 6M. R. lantern on house 12m. Shown when suitable to enter.

MADALENA MOLE. 38°32.2'N, 28°32.0'W. Lt. Oc.R. 3 sec. 10M. R.W. Col. 11m. Vis. 010°-190°.

Ldg.Lts. 139°. (Front) Fl.G. 6 sec. 5M. Post 15m. (Rear) Fl.G. 6 sec. 5M. Post 20m.

CAIS DO PICO 38°32'N, 28°19'W. Lt. Oc.R.
6 sec. 6M. Hut 4m. Anchorage bearing 222°.
MOLE HEAD Lt. Fl.G. 3 sec. 2M. Col. Vis. 120°-130°.
PRAINHA Lt. Fl.R. 4 sec. 5M. B.W.Col. 14m. vis. 287°-128°.
SANTO AMARO Ldg.Lts. (Front) Oc.R. 6 sec. 7M. Col. 6m. (Rear) Oc.R. 6 sec. 3M. Col. 8m.

PONTA DA ILHA 38°24.8'N, 28°01.9'W. Lt. Fl.(3) 15 sec. 25M. White Tr. 28m. 166°-070°.

MANHENHA Ldg.Lts. (Front) Fl.R. 5 sec. 6M. Mast 13m. (Rear) Fl.R. 5 sec. 8M. House 20m.

CALHETA DE NESQUIM Ldg.Lts. (Front) Fl.R. 5 sec. 7M. Pedestal on rock 13m. (Rear) Fl.R. 5 sec. 7M. Col. 17m.

SANTA CRUZ DAS RIBEIRAS
Can accommodate small craft.
MOLE HEAD. 38°24.4'N, 28°11.2'W. Lt. Fl.R. 3 sec. 14M. W.R. Tr. 13m.

LAJES. Tel: 67.389.
Radio — Port: MF 2182, 2484, 2657 kHz. on request to Horta Radio. VHF Chan. 16, 11. Mon.-Fri. 0900-1200, 1400-1700. Lifeboat station.

SAN ROQUE DO PICO
Radio — Port: MF 2182, 2484, 2657 kHz. on request to Horta Radio. VHF Chan. 16, 11. Mon.-Fri. 0900-1200, 1400-1700.
CAIS PIER HEAD Lt. Fl.G. 5 sec. 2M. R.Col. 2m.
Ldg.Lts. 085° (Front) Oc. R. 6 sec. 3M. White Wall 16m. (Rear) Oc. R. 6 sec. 3M. Col. 21m.
PONTA SAO MATEUS 38°25.4'N, 28°27.0'W. Lt. Fl. 5 sec. 13M. White Tr. 33m. 284°-118°.

PORTO DO CALHAU. Ldg.Lts. 122° (Front) Oc.R. 3 sec. 3M. Post 10m. (Rear) Oc.R. 3 sec. 3M. Col. on house 12m.

ILHA DO FAIAL 38°36'N, 28°36'W

HORTA Tel: 22.813 (22.611 Pilots)
Radio — Port: MF. 2182, 2484, 2657 kHz. VHF Chan. 16, 11. H24.
Radio — Pilots: MF. 2182, 2484, 2657 on request. VHF Chan. 16, 11, 13. H24.
Commercial Port. Anchorage Baia da Horta or Leeward of Island in SW gales. Lifeboat station. Fresh water. Small repairs. Extensive marina development in progress.
PONTA DA RIBEIRINHA. 38°35.8'N, 28°36.2'W. Lt. Fl.(3) 20 sec. 29M. White Tr. 146m. 133°-001°.
HORTA BREAKWATER HEAD Lt. Fl.R. 3 sec. 9M. White Tr. 19m. 048°-017°.
BOA VIAGEM Lt. Iso.G. 1.5 sec. 5M. W.Y. Col. 12m.

Ldg.Lts. 196° (Front) Iso.G. 2 sec. 2M. Col. 6m. (Rear) Iso.G. 2 sec. 2M. Col. 9m.

FETEIRA Ldg.Lts. (Front) Oc.G. 6 sec. 5M. Col. 8m. (Rear) Oc.G. 6 sec. 5M. Col. 9m.

VALE FORMOSO 38°34.9'N, 28°48.7'W. Lt. L.Fl.(2) 10 sec. 11M. Tr. 113m.

ILHA DAS FLORES 39°27'N, 31°07'W

SANTA CRUZ. Tel: 22.224.
Radio — Port: MF. 2182, 2484, 2657 kHz. on request to. Horta Radio. VHF Chan. 16, 11. Anchorages in bay between Ponta Delgada and Ponta Ruiva in 35-40m. SE of Ilheu de Alvaro Rodrigues in 66m. Anchorage also in bay between Santa Cruz and Ponta da Caviera. Small craft 1¾c. off shore 5c. N of Pointa da Caveira in 27m. Landing place: Santa Cruz and Porta das Pocas.
SANTAS CRUZ PEDRA ACUCAREIRO. Lt. Fl.R. 5 sec. 4M. Tr. 12m. 156°-308°.

PORTO VELHO Ldg.Lts. 261°36' (Front) L.Fl.G. 5 sec. 6M. 13m. (Rear) L.Fl.G. 5 sec. 6M. 15m.

PORTO DAS POCAS 39°27'N, 31°07'W
Ldg.Lts. 284°36' (Front) Fl.R. 3 sec. 2M. Mast 7m. (Rear) Fl.R. 3 sec. 2M. Mast 16m. Lt. F.R. 2M. W. Tr. 17m.
SE POINT LAJES 39°22.5'N, 31°10.4'W. Lt. Fl.(3) 28 sec. 26M. Tr. 89m. 263°-054°.
W SIDE FAJA GRANDE Lt. Fl. 3 sec. 5M. R. Hut. 13m.
N SIDE PONTA DO ALBARNAZ 39°31.1'N, 31°13.9'W. Lt. Fl. 5 sec. 28M. White Tr. 87m. 035°-258°. Obsc. 204°-214°.

ILHA DO CORVO 39°30'N, 31°06'W

VILA NOVA
Radio — Port: MF. 2182, 2484, 2657 kHz. on request to Horta Radio. VHF Chan. 16, 11. Mon.-Fri. 0900-1200, 1400-1700.
Landing at Portinho da Casa. Temporary anchorage E of Ponta Negra Lt. 4c. off in 18m.
PONTA NEGRA Lt. Fl. 5 sec. 5M. White Tr. 22m.
CANTO DE CARNEIRA 39°43.0'N, 31°05.1'W. Lt. Oc. 5 sec. 10M. Grey Tr. 237m.

Visual Navigational Aids and Port Information

24

For Belgium thence North to Denmark

COAST OF BELGIUM NORTHWARDS

NOTE: WE DO NOT GIVE THE BUOYAGE FOR CONTINENTAL WATERS.

Coastguards:
Belgium: Constant Watch and Lifeboat stations at Nieuwpoort; Ostend; Zeebrugge.
Call nearest Coast Station VHF Chan. 16 or 2182 kHz for assistance.
Buoyage system continually altered and amended. Largest scale charts should be used.
Fly Flag 'Q' until cleared by Customs/Immigration.

Documentation:
Entry Form Benelux I, or Customs form C.1328.
Yacht registration certificate. Certificate of competence VHF R/T.
Tide Tables.
Int. Regs. for Preventing Collisions at Sea.
Registration Plate necessary if staying over two months.
Insurance (3rd Party and Rescue) taken out in UK.
Properly equipped including Lifesaving Appliances.
Passports.
Belgian National Tourist Office, 2 Gayton Road, Harrow, Middx. HA1 2XU. Tel: 081-861 3300.

Entry by Road:
Ensure craft and car fully insured.
No carnet necessary if proof of registration abroad carried, unless craft over 5.5m. in length.
Certificate for small craft engine can be got from Customs on arrival (deposit — refundable — may be required)

Inland Waterways:
Speed: The Meuse 15 km/h. Brussels/Charleroi canal 8 km/h. Nimy/Blaton/Peronnes canal 6km/h. River Lys 12 km/h. Ghent/Terneuzen 18 km/h.
Copies of regulations from Locks.
On the Meuse fly R. with W. □ centre to indicate yacht underway to Lock Keeper.

INSHORE WAYPOINT OFF NIEUWPOORT.
51°10.0'N, 2°42.5'E.

NIEUWPOORT 51°10'N 2°43'E. Tel: H.M. (058) 233045.
Radio—Port: VHF Chan. 16, 9, 19—continuous.
Radio—Pilots: VHF Chan. 9 H24.
Signals: Int. Port Traffic Sigs. Nos. 1, 2, 3 shown from Pilot Station W Pier.
Small craft: craft of 6m. or less overall or under oars, not to leave harbour if on shore wind force 3 or over or off shore wind of force 4 or over. Signal = 2 cones points together/Blue Fl. Lt.
Depth in channel 3m. LWS. Tide range 4m.-5m. Large yacht harbour.

NIEUWPOORT 51°09.3'N, 2°43.8'E Lt.Ho.
Fl.(2)R. 14 sec. 21M. R. circular Tr. white bands, 26m. Storm and tidal sig.
E PIER. Lt. F.R. 6M. white framework Tr. 12m. Horn Mo. (K) 30 sec.
W PIER HEAD. Lt. F.G. 6M. white iron Tr. 12m. Bell(2) 10 sec. R.C.
SALVAGE JETTY Lt. F.G. 4M. Post 3m.

NIEUWPOORT EILANDJE. Lt. Fl.G. 1.5 sec. 4M. Dolphin.
KROMME HOEK. Lt. F.R. 5M. Dolphin 5m. **Lt.** F.G. 4M. Dolphin 5m.

KATTESAS. Ldg.Lts. 175° (Front) F.R. 3m. Post 6m. (Rear) F.R. 3M. Post 9m.
QUAY N END. Lt. F.R. Dolphin.

INSHORE WAYPOINT OFF OSTEND.
51°15.0'N, 2°54.0'E.

OSTEND 51°14'N 2°55'E. Tel: (059) 701100. Telex: 82.125 LOODSW. B.
Radio—Port: VHF Chan. 9, 16 continuous.
Radio—Pilots: VHF Chan. 6, 16 continuous.
MERCATOR MARINA LOCK. Tel: (059) 705762.
Mercator Marina Lock. VHF Chan. 14. H24.
Signals: (Day and Night) Shown from East Pier. 51°14'30N, 02°55'30E.
Int. Port Traffic Sigs. No. 1, 2, 4, 5.
Fl.Y. Lt. and a R. Stoplight at the entrance Montgomerydok, vessels leaving the Montgomerydok, Fisherydok or Tidal dok have to stop and wait until both lights are extinguished.

2°45'E
51° 09'N
Water Tr.
Lt. Ho.
Sig. Stn.
ENTRANCE CHANNEL
Naval Basin
LB Slip
Mud
Slip
Yacht Harbour
Y.C.
South Basin
R. YZER
Fishing Harbour
N
NIEUWPOORT

0 500 1000 METRES
N
PASSE DIRECTE
2°55' EAST
Bredene Bad
51° 14' NORTH
Lt Ho.
N. Sea Y.C.
Montgomerydok
Lock
Mercator Yacht Harb.
Lifting Bridge
Lock
Vissershaven
Zeewezendok
Voorhaven
R. Ostend Y.C.
Spuikom
Vlotkom
Hourdok
Lock
Ostend-Bruges Canal
Doksluis
Zwaaidok Shipyards
OSTEND

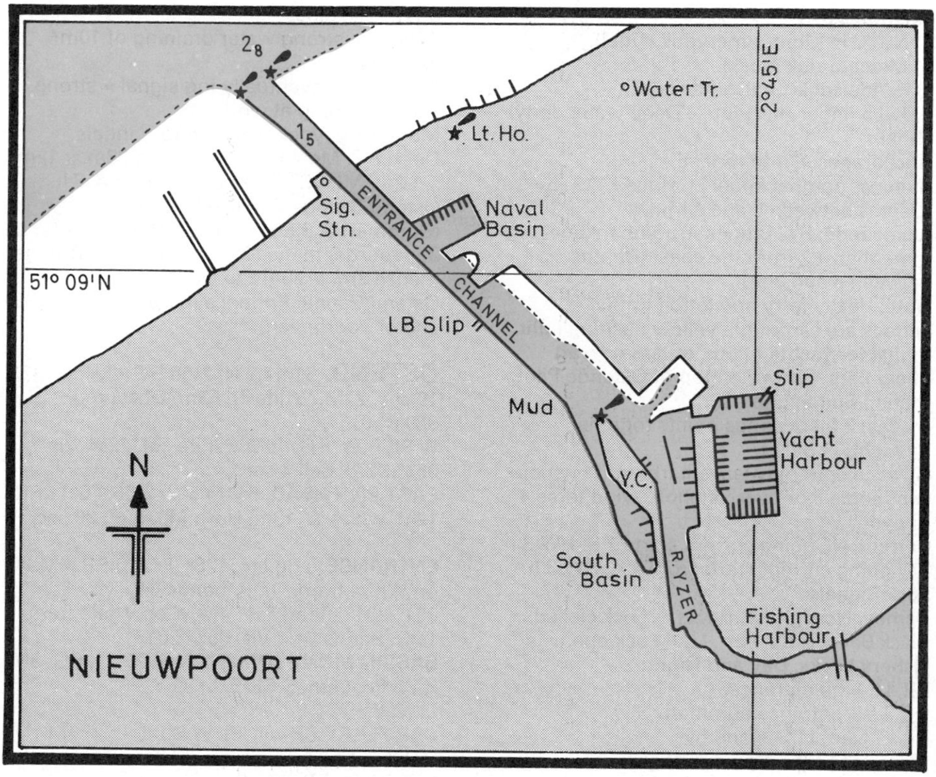

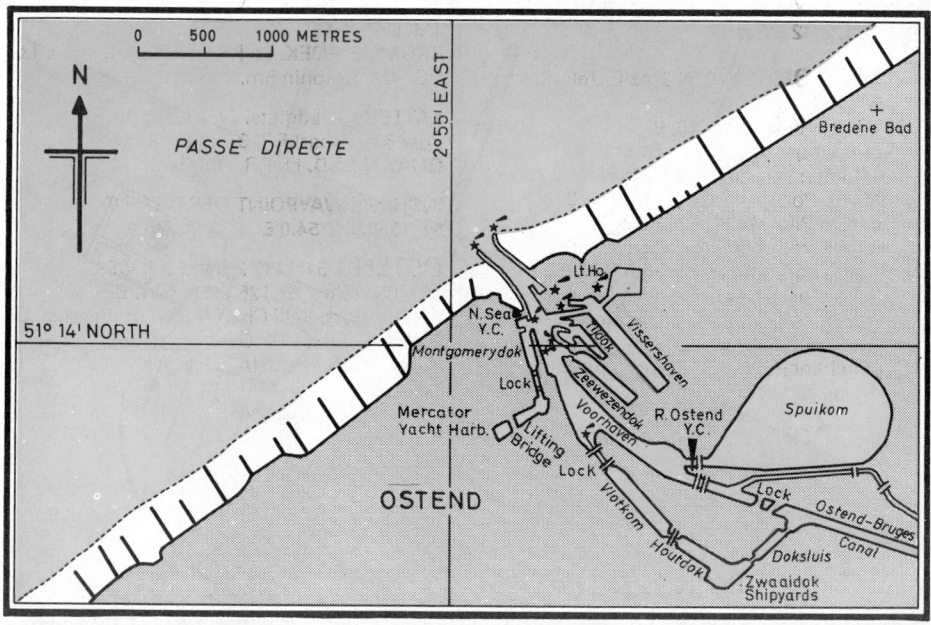

Yacht Basins:
a) NSYC in Montgomerydok (Tidal).
b) Mercatordok (Lock).
c) Handelsdokken (Demey Lock).
d) Ryco (Inner Harbour — Deep water Jetty) (Tidal).
Anchorages: Grote rede: E
Buitenstroombankboei Lt. House 129° Δ= 3'1
(Depths between 8 and 11m.).
Kleine rede: SW Binnenstroombankboei not more than 1'2 from the coast (Depths between 6 and 8m.).
Note: Heavy ferry and jetfoil traffic Jetfoils are carrying a yellow flashing light.
Signal for yachts of 6m. or less or craft under oars: Shown on top of Ostende Pilot Station Building (mast).
By day: 2 black cones points together.
By night: Fl.Bu. Lt.
No such craft may leave harbour if onshore wind force 3 or over, offshore wind force 4 or over.
Current: NE going current starts 2 h.-HW-3 h. SW going current starts from 4 h.-HW-3 h.
Lock Signals:
Demey: No signal/F. Bu. Lt. = Lock closed.
Black Ball/2 F. Bu. vert. Lt. = Lock open.
Fishery Locks. Day and Night:
F.R. Lt. = no entrance.
F.G. Lt. = entrance admitted.
F.R./G. vert. Lt. = stand by.
Mercator Locks. Day and Night:
F.R. Lt. = no entrance.
F.G. Lt. = entrance admitted.

Sas — Slijkens:
F.Or. Lt. = strong water draining of $10m^2$ expected.
F.R. Lt. plus eventually fog signal = strong water draining at work.
Montgomerydok (Leading to Handels Dokken & Mercator Y. hr.) Lock. 38m. × 12m. × 1.2m. MLWS. Gates open 3 h.-HW-3 h. Ostend-Brugge Canal: 6m. draught (Summer) & 5.5m. draught (Winter) as far as Zanvoorde; thence 3.8m. draught to Brugge; thence 2m. draught to Ghent (via Ghent-Ostend Canal). Entrance in Achterhaven (SE end of Voorhaven).

OSTEND. 51°14.2'N, 2°55.9'E. Lt.Ho. Fl.(3) 10 sec. 27M. White Tr. 63m. Obscured 069.5°-071°.
W PIER Lt. F.G. 10M. White col. 12m. Vis. 057°-327°. Bell 4 sec.
EAST PIER HEAD. 51°14.5'N, 2°55.1'E. Lt.F.R. 12M. white Tr. 13m. Horn Mo. (OE) 30 sec.

ENTRANCE. Ldg.Lts. 128° (Front) F.R. 4M. X on White frame Tr. R. bands $\nu\nu\nu$ vis. 051°-201° (Rear) F.R. 4M. X on White frame Tr. R. Bands $\nu\nu\nu$ Vis. 051°-201°.
BASSIN MONTGOMERY N SIDE. Lt. F.G. 3M. R.W. Post 5m. **S SIDE.** Lt. Q.Y.
Lt. Q.Y.
CAR FERRY CHANNEL W SIDE. Lt. F. 4M. Dolphin 5m.
E SIDE. Lt. F.R. 3M. Dolphin 5m.
DE MEY LOCK Lt. F.Bu.

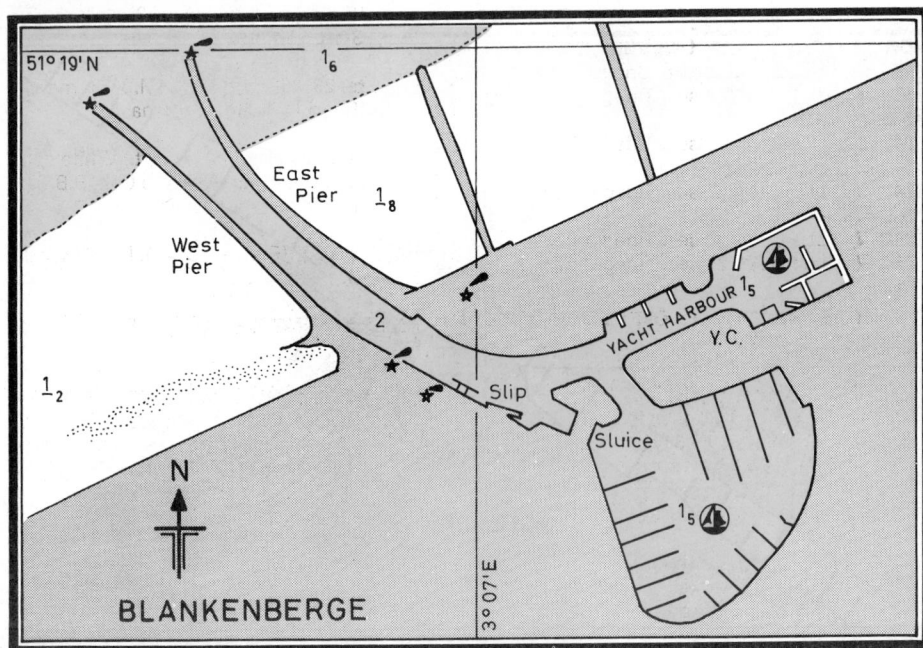

INSHORE WAYPOINT OFF BLANKENBERGE.
51°19.5′N, 3°06.0′E.

BLANKENBERGE.
Signals: Storm and Traffic Signals shown from Semaphore Mast near Lt.Ho.
2 B. Cones points together or Cont. Fl.Vi. Lt. = no boat under 5m. in length may leave Hbr.
Average Depth in entrance 1m. MLWS but Bar can be reduced to 0m. after SW gales but depths of 2m. have been reported in entrance.
Old and New Harbour have min. depth 2.2m.
Full provisions, water, fuel etc available.
Over 800 berths. Report to HM on arrival.
Cranes and repair facilities available.

COMTE JEAN JETTY 51°18.8′N,
3°06.9′E. Lt. Oc.(2) 8 sec. 20M. white stone Tr. B. top, 31m. Storm sig.
Ldg.Lts. 134° (Front) F.R. 3M. R. X on column (Rear) F.R. 3M. R. X on concrete mast.
W MOLE HEAD. Lt. F.G. 11M. 14m.
E PIER HEAD. Lt. F.R. 11M. white Tr. Bell(2) 15 sec. 290°-245°.
PROMENADE PIER HEAD. Lt. Fl.(3)Y. 20 sec.

OFFSHORE WAYPOINT
ZEEBRUGGE/SCHEUR CHANNEL.
51°24.5′N, 3°08.0′E.

SCHEUR CHANNEL
DROOGTE VAN SCHOONEVELD. Lt.Fl.(5)Y. 20 sec. 2M. Measuring Bn. on platform 12m.
MOW 0. Lt. Fl.(5)Y. 20 sec. Tidegauge Whis. 5 sec. Racon.
MOW 1. Lt. Fl.(5)Y. 20 sec. Tidegauge Whis. 5 sec.
MOW 3. Lt. Fl.(5)Y. 20 sec. Tidegauge Whis. 5 sec. Racon.
MOW 4. Lt. Fl.(5)Y. 20 sec. Tidegauge.
MOW 2. Lt. Fl.(5)Y. 20 sec. Tidegauge.

INSHORE WAYPOINT OFF ZEEBRUGGE.
51°22.0′N, 3°10.0′E.

ZEEBRUGGE 51°20′N, 3°12′E. Tel: H.M.
(050) 54 32 41. Port Control (050) 54 68 67.
Lockmaster (050) 54 32 31.
Fax: (050) 444224.H24.
Telex: 81201 PORZRG B. Pilots (050) 54 50 72.
Radio—Port: VHF Chan. 71 and 67 (for emergencies).
Radio—Pilots: VHF Chan. 9.
Signals: Signals for small craft shown from mast at Pilot Station prohibiting leaving if

wind force 3 or more if yacht 6m. in length or less. Int. Port Traffic Sigs. No. 2, 4, 5 shown from NE end of Leopold II Dam. Lt. Q.Fl.Y. (occas.) shown S side entrance to Visserhaven. Traffic prohibited from entering or leaving Visserhaven when light shown. Safeguard for traffic for W Sea Lock. W Sea Lock. 210m. × 19.7m. × 5.5m. on sill. Lock signals: B. Ball/G. over R.Lt. = lock being prepared. 2 B. balls/G.R.G.Lt. = lock ready.
Boudewijnkanaal (Baudouin Canal) from Inner Lt. to Brugge, depth 6-8m.
Brugge: Lock 115m. × 12m. × 4m. on sill connects to Ghent-Ostend Canal.

HEIST MOLE HEAD. 51°20.9′N,
3°12.3′E. Lt.Ho. Oc.W.R. 15 sec. W.20M. R.18M. 23m. Horn (3 + 1) 90 sec. W.068°-145°; R.145°-212°; W.212°-296°; R.C. Traffic Signals.
E OUTER BREAKWATER HEAD. Lt. Oc.R. 7 sec. 7M. 33m. 087°-281°. R. strip Lts to seaward.
W OUTER BREAKWATER HEAD. Lt. Oc. G. 7 sec. 7M. 33m. 057°-267° G. strip Lts to seaward. Horn (1+3) 90 sec.

Ldg.Lts. 136° (Front) Oc. 5 sec. 8M. R.W. Mast 22m. 131°-141°. H24 (Rear) Oc. 5 sec. 8M. R.W. Mast 45m. 131°-141°. H24.

Ldg.Lts. 154° (Front) Oc.W.R. 6 sec. 3M. Pylon. 20m. W.135°-160°; R.160°-169° (Day 150°-169°). (Rear) Oc. 6 sec. 3M. N.E. Cnr. of Bldg. 34m. 150°-162°.

Ldg.Lts. 235° (Front) Q.R. 5M. X on metal mast (Rear) Q.R. 5M. X on mast.

Ldg.Lts. 220° (Front) 2 F. (Vert.) White col. B. bands 2 neon (Rear) F. White Col. B.Bands. 1 neon.

Ldg.Lts. 032° (Front) F.G. 4M. Mast (Rear) F.G. 4M. mast.

MOLE KONINGSTRAAP. Lt. F.R.W. vert. 5M. mast 4m.

WESTHOOFD QUAY WALL NE Lt. F.G.
WESTHOOFD QUAY WALL NW Lt. F.R.

WESTHOOFD Ldg.Lts. 193° (Front) 2 F.R. (Vert.) W.col. R. bands (Rear) F.R. W.col. R.Bands.

WESTHOOFD Lt.Bn. Oc. 10 sec. 9M. Grey Tr. 7m.
E. TRAINING WALL Lt. F.R. 7M. Col. 6m.

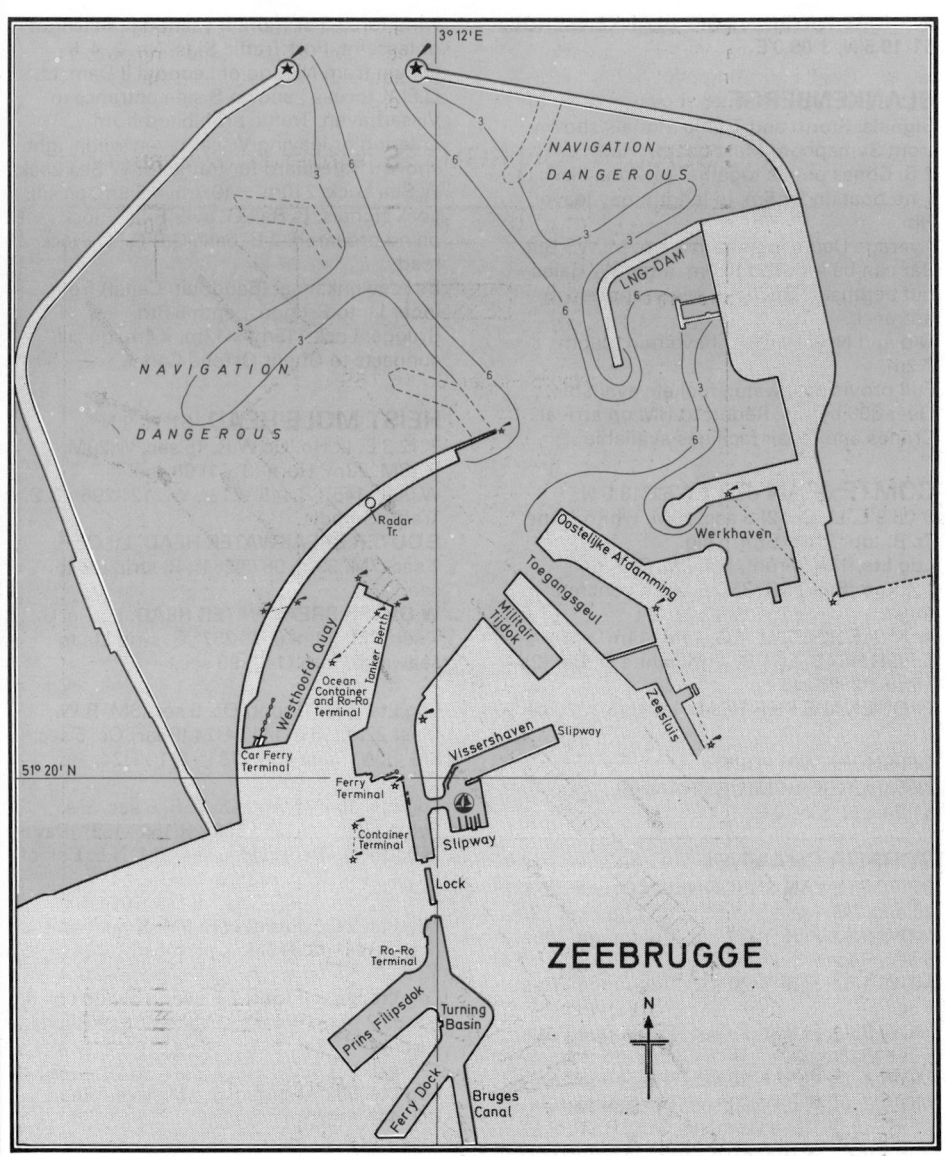

OFFSHORE WAYPOINT N OF WEST HINDER.
51°24.0'N, 2°26.0'E.

WEST HINDER 51°23'N, 2°26.3'E. Lt.V.
Fl.(4) 30 sec. 24M. R. hull, 14m. R.C. Siren(3)
30 sec. or Bell(3). S end of W Hinder Bk.

SCHELDE PILOT VESSEL
Station: Belgian P/Stn. "Wandelaar" 1½M. SE
of Akkaert Bank between SW Akkaert Lt. By.
and A1 Lt. By. Tel: (059) 701100. Telex: 82125

LOODSW B.
Radio: VHF Chan. 16, 65, 69—continuous.
Station: Netherlands P/Stn. "Steenbank" W
of Schouwen Bank Lt.By. Tel: 01 184 89601.
Telex: 37811 LWVL NL.
Radio: VHF Chan. 16, 14, 64—continuous.
Entry Signals: On approaching Pilot Vessel
show flag N or B for Dutch or Belgian pilot.
Pennant 1-6 indicating class of vessel; Flag
A — Antwerp, B — Breskins, G — Ghent,
H — Hansweerd, O — to sea thru' Oostgat,

S — Sloehaven, T — Terneuzen, V — Vlissingen, W — to sea via Wielingen, or show Pennant 7 or 8 indicating pilot not required for destination shown, or show Pennant 7 indicating pilot not required or is to be landed or show flag P indicating portable R/T required for passage Flushing to Antwerp.

SEA TRAFFIC SEPARATION ROUTES (SANDETTIE TO NOORD HINDER)

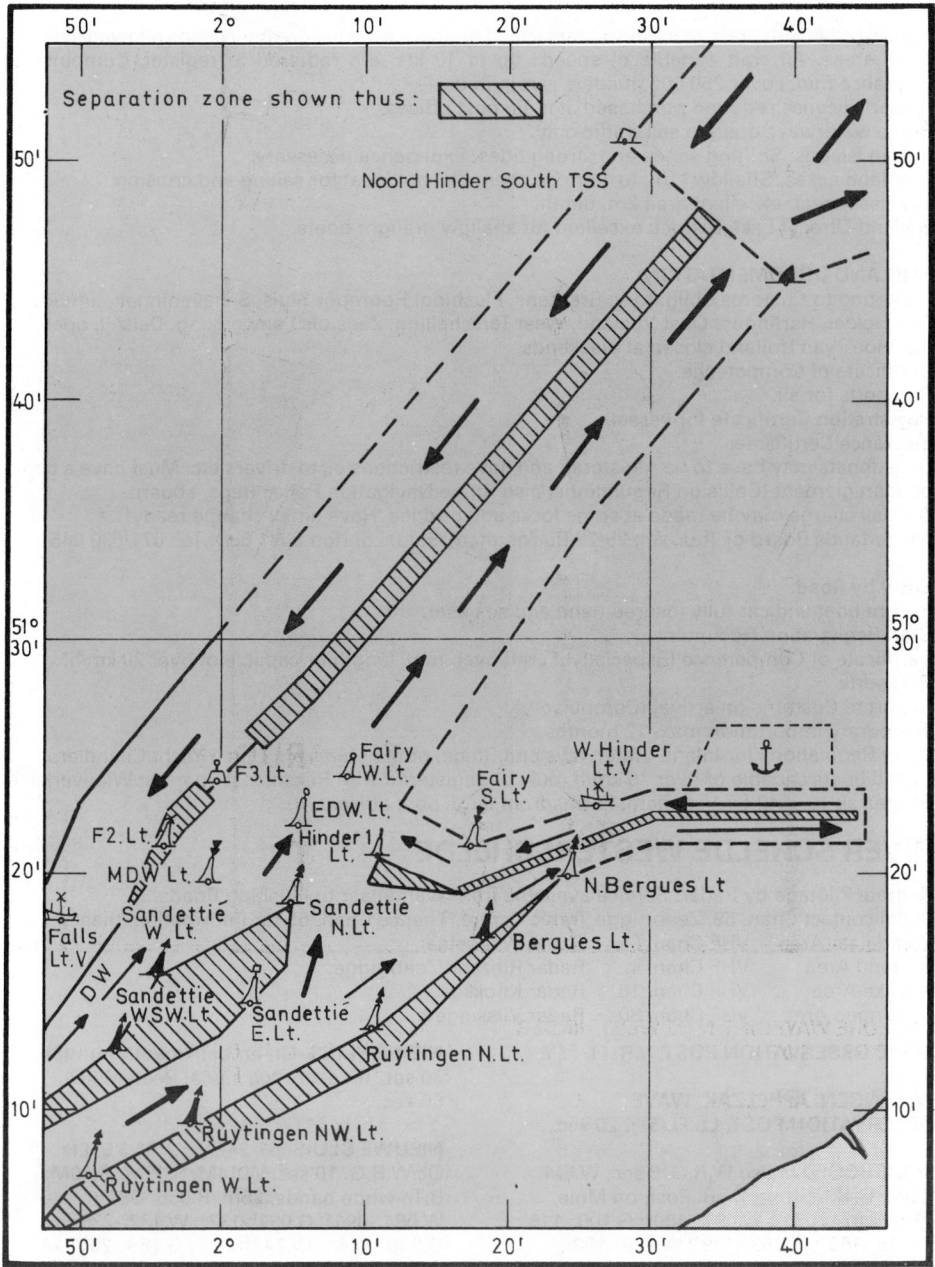

Routes indicated by broad arrows. Deep draught Tanker Route by thin arrows. Some buoys omitted.

COAST OF HOLLAND

Coastguards: Netherlands Coast Guard. H24 watch on 500 kHz. 2182 kHz, VHF Chan. 16.

Holland: Authority: Royal South Holland Society for Saving Shipwrecked Persons & Royal Nth & Sth Holland Life Saving Society. Motor lifeboats at Breskins; Burgsluis; Stellendam. Hook of Holland; Scheveningen. Inshore boats at Cadzand; Ouddorp; Terheiden; Katwijk aanZee.

Holland: Pleasure Craft: In inland waters speed limit is 6 to 9 kts., greater speeds allowed in large open areas. All craft capable of speeds up to 10 kts. are required to register. Compulsory insurance min. cover 250,000 guilders is required.
A yearly licence required purchased at main post offices.
Some waterways open to sail traffic only.
Frisian Islands: Shifting sands and strong tides. Experience necessary.
Friesland Lakes: Shallow (1m. to 1.6m. in channels) but ideal for sailing and cruising.
The Ijsselmeer: excellent area 2m. depth.
Holland-Utrecht Lake District: excellent for shallow draught boats.

HOLLAND DOCUMENTATION
Reporting to Customs obligatory: Breskens, Flushing, Roompot Sluis, Scheveningen, Ijmuiden, Den Helder, Harlingen, Oost Vlieland, West Terschelling, Zeesluis Lanwersoog, Delfzijl, open 24 hrs. Hoek Van Holland closed at weekends.
Certificate of Competence.
Passports for all.
Registration Certificate for vessel.
Insurance Certificate.
Speedboats may have to be registered and have restrictions as to drivers etc. Must have a copy of Vaareglement (Collision Regulations) also Rhine Navigation Police Regs. aboard.
A small charge may be made at some locks and bridges. Have small change ready!
Netherlands Board of Tourism, 25-28 Buckingham Gate, London SW1 6LD. Tel: 071-630 0451.

Entry by Road:
Ensure boat and car fully insured (land and sea use).
Craft Registration Document.
Certificate of Competence (Especially if craft over 15m. length or capable of over 20 km/h.
Passports.
Report to Customs on arrival (Compulsory).
Temporary importation max. 12 months.
Carry Regulations for Inland Waterways and Rhine, obtainable from Dutch Yacht Chandlers.
Speed boats capable of over 16 km/h must be registered with Rijksdienst voor het Wiegverkeer Skagerrak 10.9642 CZ Veendam. Forms from large post offices.

RIVER SCHELDE WESTERSCHELDE

Remote Pilotage by Radar: Service available from Wandelaar to Flushing Roads.
Initial contact Chan. 69. Zeebrugge Traffic Centre. Thence Chan. 65 for information, thence:

Wandelaar Area	VHF Chan. 65.	Radar Wandelaar.
Ribzand Area	VHF Chan. 4.	Radar Ribzand/Zeebrugge.
Knokke Area	VHF Chan. 16.	Radar Knokke.
Vlissingen Area	VHF Chan. 80.	Radar Vlissingen.

WAVE OBSERVATION POST. V.R. Lt. Fl.Y. 5 sec.
WIELINGEN. APPELZAK. WAVE OBSERVATION POST. Lt. Fl.(5)Y. 20 sec.

KRUISHOOFD Lt. Iso.W.R.G. 8 sec. W.8M. R.5M. G.4M. Stone Tr. B. Post, on Mole, 11m. R.074°-091°; W.091°-100°; G.100°-118°; W.118°-153°; R.153°-179°; W.179°-198°; G.198°-205°; W.205°-074°.

NIEWE SLUIS. On embankment. Horn (3) 30 sec. (Reserve fog signal Reed Mo(D) 60 sec.

NIEUWE SLUIS. 51°24.5'N, 3°31.3'E. Lts. Oc.W.R.G. 10 sec. W.14M. R.11M. G.10M. B.Tr. white bands, 26m. R.055°-084°; W.084°-091°; G.091°-132°; W.132°-238°; G.238°-244°; W.244°-258°; G.258°-264°; R.264°-292°; W.292°-055°.

OFFSHORE WAYPOINT DEURLOO CHANNEL. 51°31.0'N, 3°13.0'E.

WALCHEREN ISLAND

NOORDERHOOFD. Ldg.Lts. 149.5°. (Front) Oc.W.R.G. 10 sec. 13M. R. circular Tr. 18m. Telegraph Stn. R.353°-008°; G.008°-029°; W.029°-169°.

OFFSHORE WAYPOINT OOSTGAT CHANNEL. 51°35.5'N, 3°24.0'E.

WESTKAPELLE. (Rear) Fl. 3 sec. 28M. R. square superstructure, 50m. Obscured in parts by land. Common Rear.

ZOUTELANDE. Ldg.Lts. 326°. F.R. 13M. R.Bn. 20m. vis. 321°-352° in line with W Kapelle Lt.

MOLENHOOFD. Lt.Bn. Oc.W.R.G. 6 sec. R. 306°-328°; W.328°-347°; R.347°-008°; G.008°-031°; W.031°-035°; G.035°-140°; W.140°-169°. R.169°-198°.

KAAPDUINEN. 51°28.5'N, 3°31.0'E. Ldg.Lts. 130°. (Front) Oc. 5 sec. 13M. R.Y. square Tr. 26m. 115°-145°. (Rear) Oc. 5 sec. 13M. R.Y. square Tr. 35m.

FORT DE NOLLE. Lt.Bn. Fl.W.R.G. 2.5 sec. W.6M. R.4M. G.4M. R. column, 10m. R.293°-308°; W.308°-315.5°; G.315°-351°; R.351°-013°; G.013°-062°; R.062°-086°; W.086°-093°; G.093°-110°; W.110°-130°.

SCHELDE VESSEL TRAFFIC SERVICE

VHF sectors and areas are indicated on the charts. Communications in Dutch/English. With visibility more than 2000m all vessels fitted VHF should report as indicated. When visibility is less than 2000m, this will be broadcast and all vessels are to report and monitor frequencies as indicated.

ZEEBRUGGE TRAFFIC CENTRE. 51°20'N, 3°12'E. Tel: (050) 548200. Fax: (050) 547400. Telex: 81417. VHF Chan. 67(Emergency), 69, 65, 04(Radar). 19(Knokke Radar).

VLISSINGEN TRAFFIC CENTRE. 51°26'N, 3°35'E. Tel: (01184) 24790. Fax: (01184) 72503. Telex: 37874. VHF Chan. 14, 67(Emergency) 64, 21(Radar), 79(Oostgat Radar).

TERNEUZEN TRAFFIC CENTRE. 51°21'N 3°47'E. Tel: (01150) 82401. Fax: (01150)

30699. Telex: 55104. VHF Chan. 11, 14, 67(Emergency), 03(Radar).

HANSWEERT TRAFFIC CENTRE. 51°27'N 3°59'E. Tel (01130) 2751. Fax: (01130) 3311. Telex: 55109. VHF Chan 12, 67(Emengency), 65(Radar).

ZANDVLIET TRAFFIC CENTRE. 51°21'N 4°16'E. Tel: (03) 5686788. Fax: (03) 5680899. Telex: 33724. VHF Chan 12, 67(Emengency),

Vlissingen Radar	VHF Chan 21
Borssele Radar	VHF Chan 66
Terneuzen Radar	VHF Chan 3
Hansweert Radar	VHF Chan 65
Waarde Radar	VHF Chan 19
Saeftinge Radar	VHF Chan 21
Zandvliet Radar	VHF Chan 4
Kruisschans Radar	VHF Chan 3

FLUSHING 51°27'N 3°35'E. Tel: Port Authority: Flushing East (01184) 78741. Fax: (01184) 67020. Telex: 37865 HAVEN NL. Flushing (01184) 26000. Locks (01184) 12372.
Radio—Port: Flushing Locks. VHF Chan. 22. Port Information. VHF Chan. 9. Vlissingen Radio. VHF Chan. 14 B'cast H+50. Information: B'casts on movements, tides, visibility, weather, anchorages in Dutch and English:— ev. H + 5 and H + 55 on Chan. 3, 11 by Terneuzen.
Ev. H + 50 on Chan 14 by Vlissingen. Ev. H + 35 on Chan. 12 by Zandvliet.
Signals: R. Flag/R.Lt. near R.Hr.Lt.= port closed.
R. and G.Flag/R.G.Lt. near R.Hr.Lt. = port closed to vessels over 6m. draught.
Entry: Large Lock 138m. × 22.5m. × 5.4m. on sill. Small Lock 65m. × 8m. × 3m. on sill. Kanaal door Walcheren Lock (Flushing) — 35m. wide × 4.8m. on sill. Veere Locks 135m. × 19.3m. × 7.2m. on sill. 59m. × 7.4m. × 4.7m. on sill. Large and Small Lock at Flushing opened H24 provided Dock/River difference is less than 3m. (Flood) and 3.5m. (Ebb). Kanaal door Walcheren lock opened on request only. Sluicing signals: Blue Flag/ 3 F.R. △. Bridges — Flushing/Middelburg opened 0600-2000 Mon.-Fri. 0700-1000; 1700-2100 Sun. & Hols. Y. Hr. alongside entrance Kanaal door Walcheren Lock. Y. Hr. at Middelburge. Veerse Meer draught 3m. (Winter) 3.7m. (Summer) has extensive facilities for pleasure craft. Anchorage for small craft, Rammekens Road.

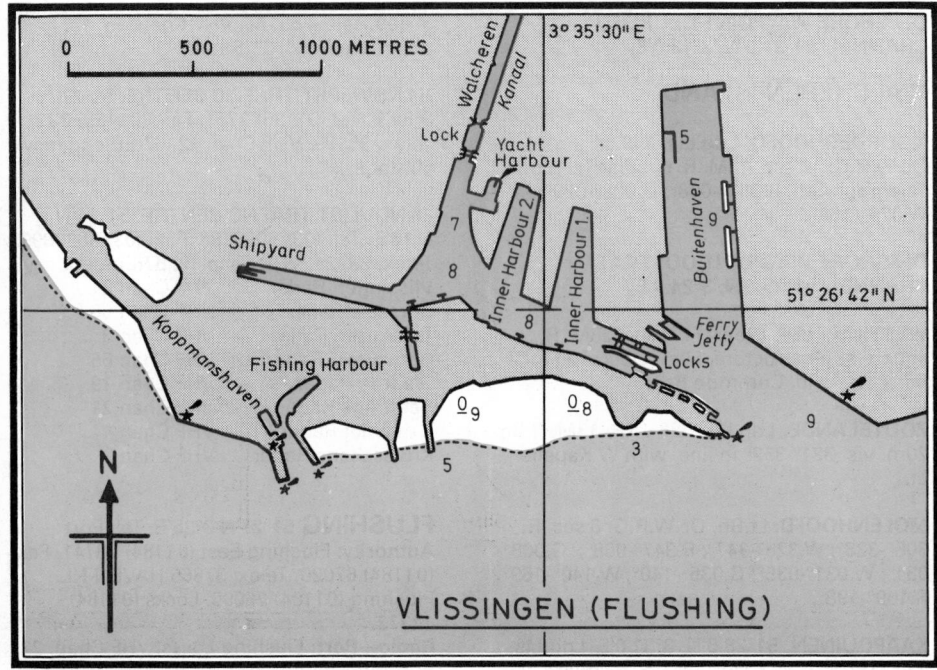

VLISSINGEN (FLUSHING)

FLUSHING

LEUGENAAR Ldg.Lts. 117° (Front) Oc.R. 5 sec. 7M. W.R. Pile 5m. Causeway submerged at H.W. **SARDIJNGEUL.** (Rear) Oc.W.R.G. 5 sec. W.12M. R.9M. G.9M. R. △ W. stripes on R.W. mast. post, 7m. R.245°-271°; G.271°-285°; W.285°-123°; R.123°-147°.

KOOPMANSHAVEN
W MOLE ROOT BOULEVARD DE RUYTER. 57°26.5'N, 3°34.5'E. Lt. Iso. W.R.G. 3 sec. W.12M. R.9M. G.8M. brown post, R. lantern, 14m. R.253°-270°; W.270°-059°; G.059°-071°; W.071°-077°; R.077°-101°; G.101°-110°; W.110°-114°.
PILOT SERVICE JETTY. Lt. F.R. 6M. on post. Tide Gauge. F.Y. shown in fog for incoming vessels.

EAST MOLE. Lt. F.G. 4M. on white mast.
BUITENHAVEN W MOLE HEAD. Lt. F.R. & Iso.W.R.G. 4 sec. 5M. Col. 10m. W.072°-021°; G.021°-042°; W.042°-056°; R.056°-072°. Traffic signals. Horn 15 sec.
E MOLE HEAD. Lt. F.G. 4m. Grey mast on Dolphin (in fog 2 F.Y.).

SCHONE WAARDIN. 51°26.6'N, 3°38.0'E. Lt. Oc.W.R.G. 9 sec. W.13M. R.10M. G.9M. R. metal mast R.248°-260°; G.260°-270°; W.270°-282.5°; G.282.5°-325°; W.325°-341°; G.341°-023°; W.023°-024°; G.024°-054°; R.054°-066°; W.066°-076.5°; G.076.5°-094°; W.094°-248°.

FLUSHING EAST (SLOEHAVEN) W MOLE HEAD. Lt. F.R. 5M. W. Col. 8m. (in fog F.Y.) Horn (2) 20 sec.
E MOLE HEAD. Lt. F.G. 4M. W. Col. 8m. (in fog 2 F.Y.).
Ldg.Lts. 023° (Front) Oc.R. 8 sec. 8M. G. Post 7m. By day 6M. vis. 015°-031°. (Rear) Oc.R. 8 sec. 8M. G. Post 12m. By day 6M. vis. 015°-031°.
QUARLESHAVEN. Ldg.Lts. 059° (Front) Oc.G. 5 sec. 12M. B. mast 8m. (Rear) Oc.G. 5 sec. 12M. B. mast 11m.
VAN CITTERSHAVEN DIR. LT. 125°. Dir. F.W.R.G. G.123.5°-124.4°; W.124.4°-124.6°; R.124.6°-125.4°.
Dir. Lt. 305° Dir. F.W.R.G.R. 303.5°-304.9°; W. 304.9°-305.1°; G. 305.1°-306.5°.

BRESKENS FERRY HARBOUR
W MOLE HEAD. Lt. F.G. 4M. B.W. mast 10m. ⌣⌣ (in fog F.Y.).
E MOLE HEAD. Lt. F.R. 5M. B.W. mast 10m. ⌣⌣ (in fog 2 F.Y.).

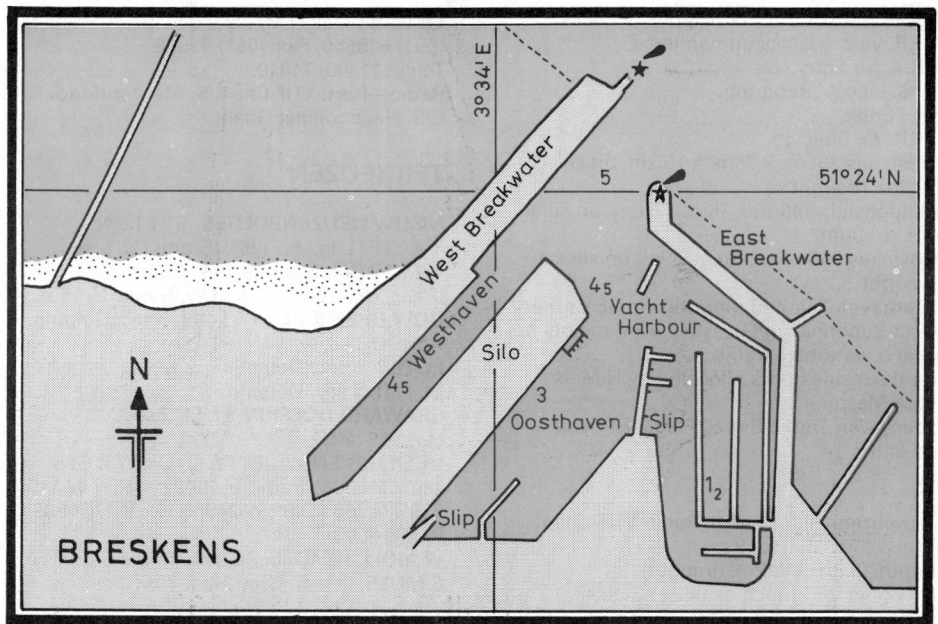

BRESKENS

BRESKENS

Yachts not allowed in Westhaven (Ferry Hr.).
Y. Hr. Berths 250 on pontoons. Depths 2.5m.
in Oosthaven.
W.MOLE. Lt. F.W.R.G. Grey mast. R.090°-
128°; W.128°-157°; R.157°-172°; W.172°-175°;
G.175°-296°; W.296°-300°; R.300°-008°;
G.008°-090°. Horn Mo(U) 30 sec.
E. MOLE. Lt. F.R. Grey mast, 5m. ⊔⊔⊔.

BORSSELE NOORDNOL PIER HEAD Lt.
Oc.W.R.G. 5 sec. 8m. R. mast W. bands.
R.305°-331°; W.331°-341°; G.341°-000°;
W.000°-007°; R.007°-023°; G.023°-054°;
W.054°-057°; G.057°-113°; W.113°-128°;
R.128°-155°; W.155°-305°.
BORSSELE. TOTAL JTY. NW END. Lt.
Oc.W.R 10 sec. mast R.135°-160°; W.160°-
135°.
BORSSELE EVERINGEN Lt. Iso.W.R.G. 4 sec.
W.R. structure. 9m. R.021°-026°; G.026°-080°;
W.080°-100°; R.100°-137°; W.137°-293°;
R.293°-308°; W.308°-344°; G.344°-357°;
W.357°-021°.
EVERINGEN. Lt. Fl.Y. 5 sec. Y. Pole.
BRAAKMAN Lt. Oc.W.R.G. 8 sec. W.7M.
R.5M. G.4M. 8m. B. Pedestal W. band.
R.116°-132°; W.132°-140°; G.140°-202°;
W.202°-116°.

BRAAKMANHAVEN

Radio—Port: VHF Chan. 6, 8, 11, 13, 34. c/o
DOW Chemical Terneuzen. Report as
follows: Approaching from W — At Flushing
to Vlissingen Radio on Chan 21. —
At Lt.By. 8 to Radar Terneuzen on Chan 3.
Approaching from E — At Hansweert to
Hansweert Radio on Chan. 65. — At
Terneuzen to Radar Terneuzen on Chan. 3.

Ldg.Lts. 191°. (Front) Iso. 4 sec. R. △ B.W.
Pile 7m. (Rear) Iso. 4 sec. R. ▽ B.W. Pile 9m.
Ldg. Lts. 211°30′. (Front) Oc.G. 4 sec. (Rear)
Oc.G. 4 sec.
W SIDE Lt. F.G. B.W. Pile. G. Top.
E SIDE Lt. F.R. R.W. mast. Traffic Signals.

TERNEUZEN 51°20′N 3°49′E. Tel: (01150)
95651. Fax: (01150) 20527. Telex: 55482.
Radio: VHF Chan.11—continuous. C/S
Havendienst Terneuzen. Vessel cannot enter
Ghent canal unless fitted with VHF Chan. 11.
Hoist letter P. Information B'cast ev. H+00.
Chan. 11 ev. H+05. Chan. 3.
Entry: 2 F.R. Lts at entrance West
Buitenhaven and Oost Buitenhaven = Basin
closed.

Locks: shown from both sides of Locks.
2 F.R. vert. = Locks unmanned.
F.R. = No Entry.
R./G. = Lock preparing.
G. = Enter.
3 F.R. Δ= Sluicing.
Westsluis 335m. × 38m. × 10.2m. on sill ×
12.2m. draught.
Middensluis 140m. × 18m. × 5.0m. on sill ×
6m. draught.
Oostsluis 258m. × 24m. × 3.9m. on sill × 4m.
draught.
Veerhaven: Limited moorings in SE Corner.
Oost Buitenhaven/Oostsluis used mainly for
inland waterway traffic.
Berths inside Locks allocated by H.M. or
Lock Master.
Veerhaven Traffic Sig: R. Flag/2 F.R. vert. =
no entry.

Terneuzen-Ghent Canal: Radio VHF Chan.
11.
Depth 13.5m. (12.2m. draught).
Draughts for branch canals at Sluiskil,
Driekwart, Sas Van Ghent limited 3.5m. to
5m.
Vessels must be fitted VHF Chan. 11.
Bridges: Least clearance 6.75m. Only
opened for vessels unable to proceed under
with gear lowered. Contact by VHF (Zelzate
— direct) via H.M.

Signals: As seen by approaching vessel.

Port: 2 F.R. vert. **Stb:** 2 F.R. vert. (no
passage, bridge unmanned.)
Port: 2 F.R. vert. **Centre:** F.Y. **Stb:** 2 F.R. vert.
(passage under br. only. — both ways.)
Port: F.R. **Stb:** F.R. (no passage.
Port: 2 F.R. vert. **Centre:** 2 F.Y. **Stb:**2 F.R. vert.
(passage under br. only.— one way.
br. unmanned.)
Port: F.R. **Centre:** 2 F.Y **Stb:** F.R. (passage
under br. only.— one way.)
Port: F.R. **Centre:** F.Y **Stb:** F.R. (passage
under br. only.— both ways.)
Port: F.R./F.G. **Stb:** F.R./F.G. (preparing br.—
no passage under.)
Port: F.G. **Stb:** F.G. (through passage.)

Zelzate Br. (additional sigs).
2 F.G. vert. = Passage to Br. permitted.
F.R./F.G. = Passage to Br. permitted if <16m.
beam.
2. F.R. vert. = Passage to Br. prohibited.
Bridges not opened until vessel within
500m.

GHENT. Tel: H.M. (091) 510457. Admin:
(091) 510550. Fax: (091) 51662.
Telex: 11460. 11019.
Radio—Port: VHF Chan. 5, 11—continuous.
C/S. Havendienst Ghent.

TERNEUZEN

NIEUW NEUZENPOLDER. 51°21.0'N,
3°47.3'E. Ldg.Lts. 125°. (Front) Oc. 5 sec.
13M. W.Col. B.bands. 5m.
(Rear) Oc. 5 Sec. 13M. B.W. frame Tr. 16m.
DOW CHEMICAL JTY. Lt. Fl. 3 sec. Dolphin.
Horn 15 sec.
Lt. Fl.R. 3 sec. Dolphin.
Lt. Fl.R. 3 sec. Dolphin.
SEAWARD DOLPHIN. Lt. Fl. 3 sec
Horn 15 sec.
VEER HAVEN W. JETTY. Lt. Oc. W.R.G. 5
sec. 9M. B.W. frame Tr. R.092°-115°; W.115°-
238°; G.238°-249°; W.249°-275°; R.275°-309°;
W.309°-003°.
W MOLE HEAD. Lt.Bn. F.G. Traffic Signals.
E MOLE. Lt. F.R. Grey Mast 7m.

WEST BUITENHAVEN

W MOLE HEAD. Lt. F.G. 4M. Mast 9m.
E MOLE HEAD. Lt. F.R. 5M. Mast 9m. Traffic
Signals.
Ldg.Lts. 192°30' (Front) Iso. 4 sec. 8M. Mast
10m. By day 6M. vis. 184.5°-200.5°. (Rear)
Iso. 4 sec. 8M. Mast 13m. By day 6M.

OOST BUITENHAVEN

W MOLE HEAD. Lt. F.G. 4M. Mast 9m. (In fog
F.Y.).
E MOLE HEAD. Lt. F.R. 5M. Mast 9m. Traffic
Signals. Channel to Ghent marked by Lts.

OTHENEPOLDER 51°20.2'N, 3°51.6'E. Lt.
Iso.W.R.G. 8 sec. W.12M. R.9M. G.9M. B.Tr.
11m. R.094°-113°; G.113°-124°; W.124°-127°;
R.127°-140°; G.140°-162°; W.162°-164°;
R.164°-184°; G.184°-201°; W.201°-204°;
R.204°-234°; W.234°-094°.

MARGARETHEPOLDER Lt. Oc.W.R.G. 9 sec.
W.6M. R.4M. G.4M. B.W.Tr. 8m.
R.059°-075.5°; W.075.5°-079°; G.079°-114°;
W.114°-169°; R.169°-210°; W.210°-Shore.

EENDRACHTPOLDER Ldg.Lts. 074°30'
(Front) Oc.W.R.G. 5 sec. W.8M. R.6M. G.5M.
B.W. mast, 8m. R.045°-064°; W.064°-107°;
G.107°-221°; W.221°-228°; R.228°-250°;
W.250°-045°. (Rear) Oc.5 sec. 6M. B.W. mast,
18m.

NORTH SHORE

ZUID BEVELAND

MIDDEL GAT CHANNEL (BAARLAND—HANSWEERT)
TIDE GAUGE. Lt. Fl.(5)Y. 20 sec. Y. Post.

HOEDEKENSKERKE DE VAL Lt. Iso. W.R.G.
2 sec. W.8M. R.5M. G.4M. R.W.Tr. 6m.
R.008°-034°; W.034°-201°; R.201°-206°;
W.206°-209°; G.209°-328°; W.328°-008°.

BIEZELINGSCHE HAM Lt. Oc.W.R. 7.5 sec.
W.9M. R.7M. R.W.Tr. 5m. W.176°-193°;
R.193°-221°; W.221°-045°.

JETTY HEAD Lt. F.R. 5M. R.W.Bn. 5m.

MIDDELGAT SCHORE Ldg.Lts. 021°30'
(Front) Oc.W.R.G. 4 sec. W.7M. R.5M. G.4M.
W.R.Tr. 9m. W.020°-027°; R.027°-048°;
W.048°-071°; G.071°-084°; W.084°-093°;
R.093°-105°; W.105°-124°; W.300°-316°;
R.316°-328°; W.328°-357°; G.357°-020°.
(Rear) Oc. 4 sec. W.R.mast, 18m.

TIDE GAUGE Lt. Fl.(5) Y. 20 sec. Y. post.

HANSWEERT
Entry: Y. Hr. in Zighaven (E side of entrance)
Fuel and water available either at berth or
from barges.
CANAL ENTRANCE W. SIDE Lt. Oc.W.R.G.
10 sec. W.9M. R.7M. G.6M. R.W.Tr. 9m.
R.288°-310°; W.310°-334°; G.334°-356.5°;
W.356.5°-044°; R.044°-061.5°; W.061.5°-073°;
G.073°-089°; R.089°-101.5°; G.101.5°-109°;
W.109°-114.5°; R.114.5°-127.5°,
W.127.5°-288°. Traffic Signals.
Lt. Iso. R. 4 sec.

E SIDE Lt. F.G. Grey Col, 6m. Horn (4) 30 sec.

HANSWEERT—ANTWERP

KRUININGEN FERRY HARBOUR W MOLE
HEAD Lt. F.R. Col. 7m. In fog F.Y. Horn
10 sec. ᾱ
E MOLE HEAD Lt. F.G. Col. 8m. In fog 2 F.G.

PERKPOLDER
W PIER HEAD Lt. F.G. B.W.Col. 8m. In fog
F.Y. Horn(2) 20 sec. ᾱ
E PIER HEAD Lt. F.R. B.W.Col. 8m. In fog F.Y.
ᾱ Fog Detr. Lt.

ZUIDERGAT
WALSOORDEN Lt. Iso.W.R.G. 4 sec. W.8M.
R.6M. G.5M. B.W.Dolphin, 9m. R.132°-172°;

W.-268°; G.-325°; W.-341°; R.-012°; W.-132°.

N MOLE HEAD Lt. F.G. Col. 5m. in fog F.Y.
S MOLE HEAD Lt. F.R. Col. 5m.

Ldg.Lts. 220° (Front) Oc. 3 sec. W. ᴫ col. 9m.
vis. 200°-240°. (Rear) Oc. 3 sec. R. ∇ on col.
vis. 200°-240°.

GROENENDIJK 51°22.3'N, 4°02.7'E.
Ldg.Lts. 167°30' (Front) Oc. W.R.G. 7 sec.
W.11M. R.8M. G.7M. W.B.Tr. 7m.
R.147°-162°; W.162°-190°; G.190°-239°;
W.239°-273°; R.273°-287°; W.287°-147°. By
day Oc. 7 sec. vis. 159.5°-175.5°; Obscured
over Schor van Baalhoek. (Rear) Oc. 7 sec.
14M. B.W. Mast 17m. By day 6M.
vis. 159.5°-175.5°.

BAALHOEK Lt. Iso.W.R.G. 4 sec. W.6M.
R.4M. G.4M. Col. 8m. R.107°-113°;
W.113°-123°; G.123°-147°; W.147°-231°;
G.231°-263°; W.263°-277°; R.277°-283°;
W.283°-107°.

SPEELMANSGAT Lt. Fl.(5) Y. 20 sec. ᾱ .

MARLEMONSCHE PLAAT Lt. Iso.W.R.G.
10 sec. W.6M. R.4M. G.4M. B.W.Col. 8m.
R.070°-082°; W.082°-088.5°; G.088.5°-151°;
W.151°-224°; R.224°-236°; W.236°-070°. ᾱ
Tide Gauge.
WESTKETEL Lt. Oc.W.R.G. 10 sec. W.8M.
R.5M. G.5M. R.Pedestal, 7m. R.231.5°-244°;
W.244°-253°; G.253°-301°; W.301°-039°;
R.039°-056°; W.056°-231.5°.

Ldg.Lts. 044° **MIDDENKETEL** (Front)
Iso.W.R. 3 sec. 6M. R.W.Pedestal, 7m.
R.248°-275°; W.275°-248°. **NOORDKETEL**
(Common Rear) Oc. 3 sec. 6M. R.Pedestal,
12m. **OOSTKETEL** Ldg.Lts. 317° (Front)
Q.W.R.G. W.6M. R.4M. G.4M. R.W.Pedestal,
6m. R.272°-301°; W.301°-322°; G.322°-053°;
W.053°-063°; R.063°-089°; W.089°-272°.

REIGERSBERGSCHE (BATH) Lt. Oc.W.R.G.
5 sec. W.7M. R.5M. G.4M. R.Pedestal, 5m.
W.075°-087°; R.087°-112°; W.112°-280°;
R.280°-342°; W.342°-349°; G.349°-075°.

ZUID SAAFTINGE Lt. Iso.W.R.G. 10 sec.
W.6M. R.4M. G.4M. B.W.Bn. R.157.5°-166°;
W.166°-246°; G.246°-293°; W.293°-325°;
R.325°-345.5°; W.345.5°-157.5°. Tide Gauge.

BELGIUM-SCHELDE

NOORD BALLASTPLAAT Lt. Fl.W.R.G. 4 sec.
W.9M. R.7M. G.6M. B.R.Bn. 6m. R.shore-
309°; W.309°-320°; G.320°-327°; W.327°-010°;
G.010°-045°; W.045°-101°; R.101°-shore.

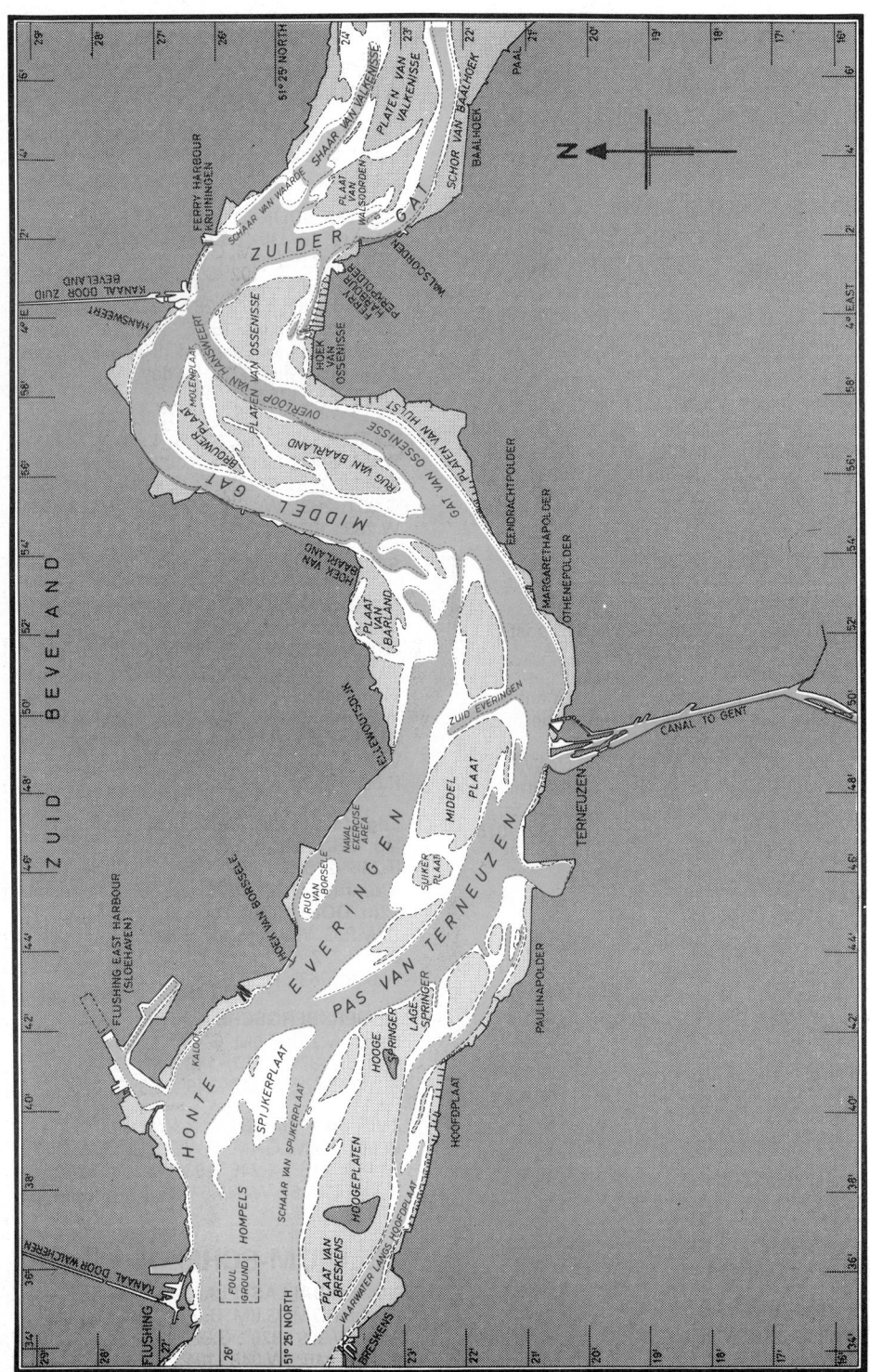

ZANDVLIET

ZANDVLIET Ldg.Lts. 118° (Front) Oc.W.R.G.
5 sec. W.9M. R.7M. G.6M. R.Tr. 12m.
R.shore-350°; W.350°-017°; G.017°-021°;
W.019°-088°; G.088°-109°; W.109°-125°;
R.125°-shore. (Rear) Oc. 5 sec. 9M.
R.W.mast, 19m.
BERENDRECHSLUIS Dir. Lt. 100°30′ 4m.
Uses moiré pattern to indicate centre line.
TOEGANGSAEUL ZEESLUIS Lt. F.G. 8M.
post.
ENTRANCE. N SIDE. Lt. F.R.

BALLASTPLAAT Ldg.Lts. 333°30′ (Front)
Iso.W.R.G. 4 sec. W.9M. R.7M. G.6M.
R.W.cheq. Ⅱ and G. ▽ Bn. 6m. R.shore-325°.
W.325°-353°; G.353°-092°; W.092°-116°;
R.116°-shore. By day 331°-336°;
(Rear) Iso.4 sec. R.mast. by day 331°-336°

PLAAT VAN DOEL
PROSPERPOLDER Lt. F.G. 4M. B.Tide Gauge
8m. and 2 F.R. vert.
OUDEN DOEL TRAINING WALL. Lt. Iso.
W.R.G. 4 sec. 9M. B.W. ☐ on B.Bn.
R.shore-201°; W.201°-266°; G.266°-315°;
W.315°-001°; R.001°-shore. R. Lts. on Power
Stn. 900m. SW.

DOEL Ldg.Lts. 185°30′ (Front) Fl.W.R.G.
3 sec. W.9M. R.7M. G.6M. 6m. R.shore-175°;
W.175°-202°; G.202°-304°; W.304°-330°;
R.330°-shore. By day 183°-188°. (Rear) Fl.
3 sec. 9M. 15m. By day 183°-185°.

JETTY HEAD Lt. Oc.W.R. 5 sec. W.9M. R.7M.
Y.B. ☐ on B.Tr. 10m. R.downstream-185°;
W.185°-334°; R.334°-upstream shore.
PLAAT VAN LILLO. Lts. 2 × 2 F.R.G.
LILLO LANDING STAGE Lt. Oc.W.R.G.
10 sec. W.9M. R.7M. G.6M. R ☐ on B.Bn. 6m.
R.shore-304°; W.304°-322°; G.322°-099°;
W.099°-148°; R.148°-shore.

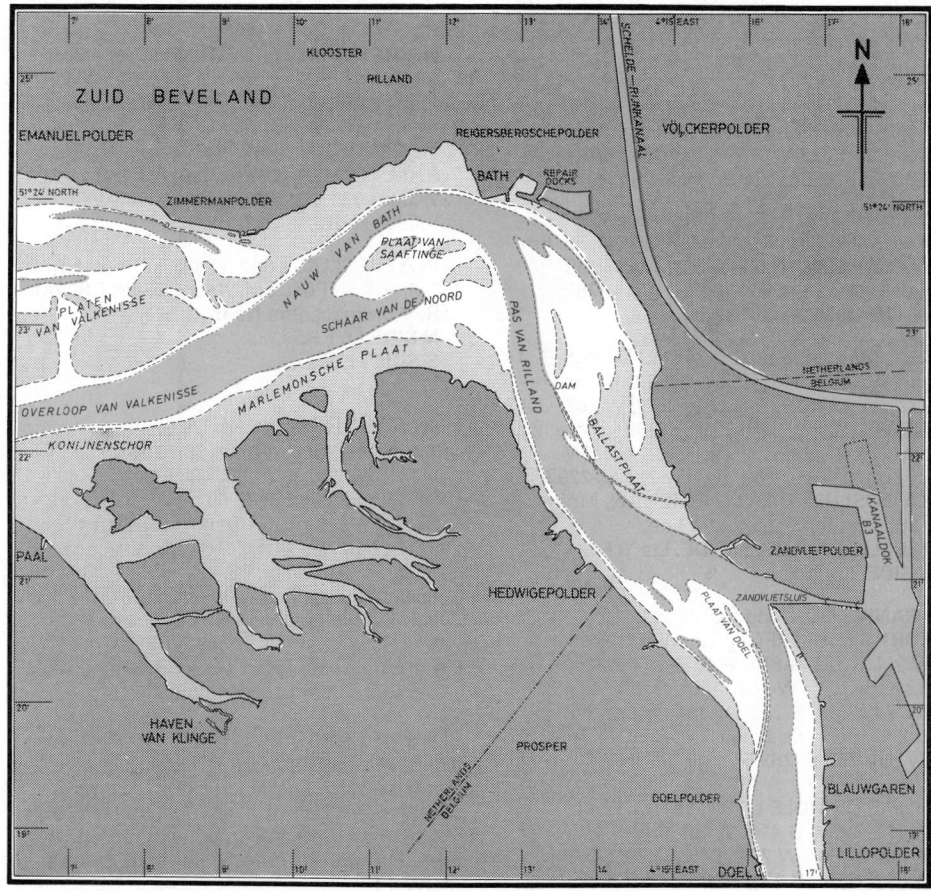

LIEFKENSHOEK Ldg.Lts. 283° (Front)
Oc.W.R.G. 3 sec. W.8M. R.6M. G.5M. B.W.Tr.
5m. R.shore-127°; W.127°-154°; G.154°-254°;
W.254°-289°; R.289°-shore. By day Oc. 3 sec.
280.5°-285.5°. (Rear) Oc. 3 sec. 9M. B.W.Mast,
11m. By day Oc. 3 sec. 280.5°-285.5°. Tide
gauge. Traffic Signals.

BELGISCHE SLUIS Lt. Fl.W.R.G. 3 sec.
W.9M. R.7M. G.6M. R.W. □ on B.Bn. 6m.
R.shore-317°; W.317°-338°; G.338°-345°;
W.345°-097°; R.097°-shore.

KRUISSCHANS Ldg.Lts. 112° (Front)
Oc.W.R.G. 5 sec. 9M. R. □ on B.Tr. 6m.
R.shore-001°; W.001°-015°; G.015°-108°;
W.108°-125°; R.125°-shore.
By Day F. 109.5°-114.5°. (Rear) Oc. 5 sec. 9M.
R.Y. □ on R.Post, 13m. By day F. 109.5°-
114.5°. Tide gauge.

BOUDEWIJNSLUIS N SIDE Lt. F.R. 7M.
Dolphin. 4m.

VAN CAUWELAERTSLUIS S SIDE Lt. F.G.
6M. Dolphin, 2m.

MEESTOOF

ANCHORAGE Ldg.Lts. 039° (Front)
F.G.R.vert. G.6M. R.7M. Dolphin, 5m. (Rear)
F.R.7M. R. □ on R.Col. 7m. Neon.

MEESTOOF Lt. F.R. Neon∇also Fl.W.R.G.
4 sec. W.9M. R.7M. G.6M. R.W. □ B.Bn. 6m.
W.shore-039°; R.039°-053°; W.053°-081°;
R.081°-095°; W.095°-151°; G.151°-175°;
W.175°-195°; R.195°-shore.

DE PAREL Ldg.Lts.227° (Front) Oc.W.R.G. 4
sec. W.9M. R.7M. G.6M. Y. □B.Bn. R.shore-
222°; W.222°-232°; G.232°-252°; W.252°-308°;
G.308°-320°; W.320°-339°; R.339°-shore. By
day 224.5°-229.5°. (Rear) Oc. 4 sec. 9M.
B. × on Y. post. 15m. By day 224.5°-229.5°.
KALLOSLUIS. Dir. Lt. 243°42' uses Moire
pattern to indicate centre line.
ZEESLUIS KALLO. N SIDE. Lts. 3 F.G.
S SIDE. Lts. 2 F.R.

KRANKELOON Ldg.Lts. 280°.
FORT S.MARIE (Front) Oc.W.R.G. 5 sec.
W.9M. R.7M. G.6M. W.B. □ on post, 6m.
R.shore-164°; W.164°-185°; G.185°-274°;
W.274°-285°; R.285°-shore. By day 277.5°-
282.5°.(Rear) Oc.5 sec. 7M. B.W. ▯ Y.Tr. 13m.
By day 277.5°-282.5°.

FILIP E OF MOLE Lt. L.Fl.W.R.G. 6 sec.
W.7M. R.5M. G.4M. □B.Bn. 6m.
R.shore-294°; W.294°-306°; G.306°-017°;
W.017°-125°; R.125°-153°.

BASIN ENTRANCE
SE SIDE Lt. F.R.   **NW SIDE** Lt. F.G.
E SIDE Lt. F.R.   **W SIDE** Lt. F.G.

BOERENSCHANS Ldg.Lts. 095° (Front) F.R.
8m. Neon△and Fl.W.R.G. 4 sec. W.9M. R.7M.
G.6M. R. □B.Bn. 6m. R.shore-321°; W.321°-
068°; G.068°-075°; W.075°-102°; R.102°-115°.
(Rear) F.R. Neon∇and Q. 5M. R.W. × R.Post,
12m.

PIJP TABAK Lt. F.Y. Neon∇and Oc.W.R.G.
5 sec. W.6M. R.4M. G.3M. Y. ∇B.W.Tr. 5m.
R.shore-142°; W.142°-260°; G.260°-288°;
W.288°-297°; R.297°-shore.

DRAAIENDE SLUIS Ldg.Lts. 141° (Rear) Q.
6M. B. × Y.mast, 12m. 113°-194°. (Common
Front) Oc.W.R.G. 5 sec. W. 7M. R.5M. G.4M.
W.B.Y. □ B.W. Post, 5m. R.shore-135°;
W.135°-228°; G.228°-263°; W.263°-274°;
R.274°-shore.

PIJP TABAK Ldg.Lts. 269°. (Rear) Q. 6M.
Y. × on B.Col. 12m.

OOSTERWEEL Lt. Q.W.R. W.5M. R.4M. R. □
on B.Bn. 6m. R.shore-281°; W.281°-084°;
R.084°-shore.

TIDE GAUGE Lt. Fl.W.R.G. 4 sec. W.5M.
R.4M. G.3M. R. □ on Tr. 7m. R.shore-308°;
W.308°-334°; G.334°-040°; W.040°-096°;
R.096°-shore.

ROYERSSLUIS Ldg.Lts. 091°. (Front) F.R.
2M. R. ▯ on Post, 5m. Neon. (Rear) F.R. 2M.
R. ∇ on mast, 9m. Neon.
N SIDE Lt. F.R.
S SIDE Lt. F.G.

ANTWERP 51°14'N 4°25'E.
Tel: Co-ordination (03) 568 70 65.
H.M. (03) 231 06 80 (541 08 50).
DK Pilots: (03) 568 68 09.
Radio—Port: Antwerpen Havendienst
VFH Chan. 18, 74. H24. Hr. Mr. VHF Chan. 63.
Bridges VHF Chan. 13.
Locks: Boudwijnsluis VHF Chan. 11.
Van Cauwelaersluis VHF Chan. 11.
Royersluis/Kattendijksluis VHF Chan. 22.
Kallosluis VHF Chan. 06/Zandvleitsluis/
Berendrechtsluis VHF Chan. 79.

YACHT HARBOUR Lt. F.W.R. 3M. B. ○ on
pile, 10m, W.shore-283°; R.283°-shore.
Imalso Y. Hr. Entered through lock gates.
Both gates open 1 h.-HW-1 h. (at HWS outer
gate may be closed to prevent too much
water entering). Inner gates shut HW+1 h. to
HW-1 h.

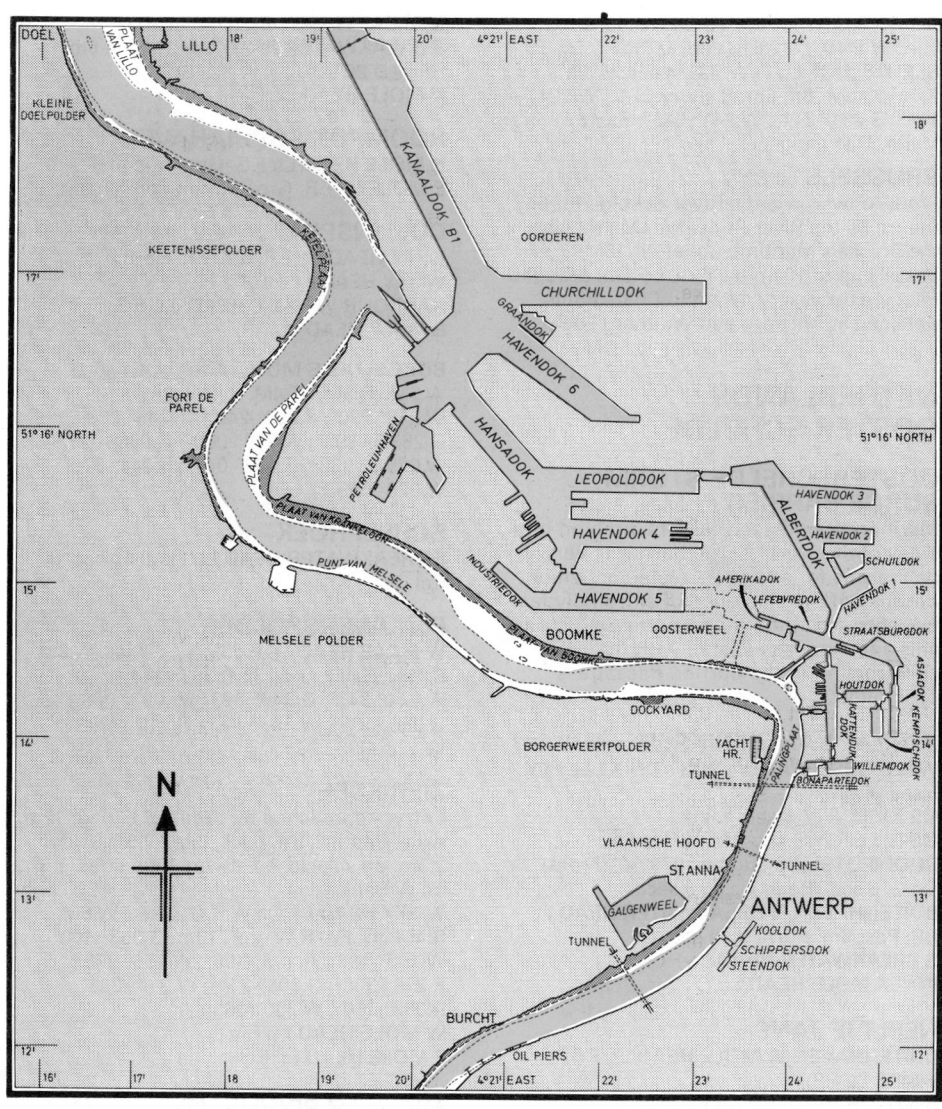

Depth on sill:
B. Ball or F. Lt. = 2.5m. to 3m.
2 B. Balls or 2 F. Lts. = 3m. to 3.5m.
3 B. Balls or 3 F. Lts. = 3.5m. to 3.8m.
Traffic signals:
R. Flag or R. Lt. = No entry.
G. Flag or G. Lt. = No exit.
Bu. Cone/Flag or Bu. Lt. = Approach channel closed.
Yacht Signals:
UH = Wish to enter under own power.
UP = Wish to enter immediately under own power as have emergency.

P = Wish to leave.
Z = Require tug assistance for entry.
Y. Hr. closed in winter except by arrangement.
All facilities available, fuels, water, etc.
Anchorage: 6½c. above/below St. Anna Pier. Three sections. Centre section for Govt. vessels only.

VLAAMSCHE HOOFD Lt. Oc.W.R. 5 sec. 3M. Dolphin. 4m. R.shore-202°; W.202°-022°; R.022°-shore.

RO-RO FERRY LANDING E END. Lt. 2 F.G. vert. **W END.** Lt. 2 F.R. vert.
SLEUTELHOF Lt. Fl.W.R.G. 4 sec. W.9M. R.7M. G.6M. Bn. 6m. R.shore-224°; W.224°-231°; G.231°-241°; W.241°-016°; R.016°-shore. Tide gauge.

BRUSSELS 50°52′N, 4°21′E.
From Antwerp via the River Schelde for 6M., thence by the River Rupel for 4M., then by the Brussels Maritime Canal for 18M. Vessels up to 104m by 15m. by 6m. draught. Pilotage necessary owing to Chan. Pilots obtained at Antwerp and Wintham Lock.

NETHERLANDS
OOSTER SCHELDE

OOSTERSCHELDE STORM
SURGE BARRIER 51°38′N, 3°42′E.
Mariners are advised that the area on both sides of the storm-surge barrier is very dangerous for all water-related activities because of the existence of extremely fast currents, mooring lines, submerged stone sills and work associated with the construction of the barrier. Passage is prohibited.

ZEEGAT VAN ZIERIKSEE
WAVE OBSERVATION POST OS X1 Lt. Fl.Y. 5 sec. Y. pile.
OS XV Lt. Fl.Y. 5 sec. Y. pile.
OS IV Lt. Fl.Y. 5 sec. 4M. Y. Pile 5m.
ROOMPOTSLUIS Ldg.Lts. 073°30′ (Front) Oc.G. 5 sec. (Rear) Oc.G. 5 sec.
BUITENHAVEN N BREAKWATER HEAD Lt. F.R. Post 6m. Horn(2) 30 sec.
S BREAKWATER HEAD Lt. F.G.
INNER MOLE HEAD Lt. Q.R.

NEELTJE JANS
BUITENHAVEN W MOLE HEAD Lt. F.G.
E SIDE Lt. F.R.
BINNENHAVEN W MOLE HEAD Lt. F.G.
E MOLE Lt. F.R.
BOUWPUT SCHAAR W SIDE Lt. F.G.
E SIDE Lt. F.R.

ROOMPOTSLUIS LOCK
VHF Chan. 18. All vessels except yachts less than 20m. in length to call Lock with details of ETA, etc.

HAVEN ROOMPOT
N BREAKWATER. HEAD. Lt. F.G.

ROOMPOTSLUIS
ROOMPOTSLUIS LOCK: 95m. × 14.5m. × 0.5m. draught at Datum Tide.

N BREAKWATER. ELBOW. Lt. F.G.
S BREAKWATER HEAD Lt. F.R. Post 5m. Horn(2) 30 sec.
N MOLE HEAD Lt. Q.G.

ROOMPOT SOPHIAHAVEN
N MOLE HEAD Lt. F.G. Grey hut 4m.
E MOLE Lt. F.R. Grey hut on dolphin 9m.

COLIJNSPLAT
E JTY HEAD Lt. F.R. 3M. Bn. Horn
W JTY HEAD Lt. F.G.
HARBOUR W MOLE HEAD Lt. F.G.
E MOLE HEAD Lt. F.R.

BURGSLUIS S MOLE HEAD Lt. F.W.R.G. W.8M., R.5M., G.4M. R. Col. 9m. W.218°-230°; R.230°-245°; W.245°-253.5°; G.253.5°-293°; W.293°-000°; G.000°-025.5°; W.025.5°-032°; G.032°-041°; R.041°-070°; W.070°-095°.

SCHELPHOEK
E BREAKWATER HEAD Lt. Fl.(2) 10 sec. B. Col. 7m.

FLAUWERSPOLDER
W MOLE HEAD Lt. Iso.W.R.G. 4 sec. W.6M., R.4M., G.4M. B.W. Tr. R.303°-344°; W.344°-347°; G.347°-083°; W.083°-086°; G.086°-103°; W.103°-110°; R.110°-128°; W.128°-303°.

ZIERIKSEE
Entry: Approached by canal 1½M. long, 12m. wide, depth 2.1m. Lock gate 12.5m. wide, 2.3m. on sill, closed at very high tides. Y. Hr. on W Bank.
W JTY HEAD Lt. Oc.W.R.G. 6 sec. W.6M., R.4M., G.4M. R.W. Col. 10m. G.063°-100°; W.100°-133°; R.133°-156°; W.156°-278°; R.278°-306°; G.306°-314°; W.314°-333°; R.333°-350°; W.350°-063°.
W MOLE HEAD Lt. F.G.
E MOLE HEAD Lt. F.G.

ZEELAND BRIDGE. Tel: 01110-3237.
Radio: VHF Chan. 18.
Zeeland Bridge: Opened, Mon.-Fri. only, for 30 minutes ev. odd H. 0700-2100.
Zeelandbrug Fixed Spans: clearance 15m. at Datum. centre arch (11m. close to pillars).
East Bound: pass between pillars 14-15 (from Roompot) and 40-41 (from Colijnsplaat)
West Bound: between 12-13 (from Roompot) and 38-39 (from Colijnsplatt).
F. Or. Lt. marks these spans. Tide gauge indicates clearance by each of these spans.

N PASSAGE N SIDE Lt. F.Y. **S SIDE** Lt. F.Y.
S PASSAGE N SIDE Lt. F.Y. **S SIDE** Lt. F.Y.

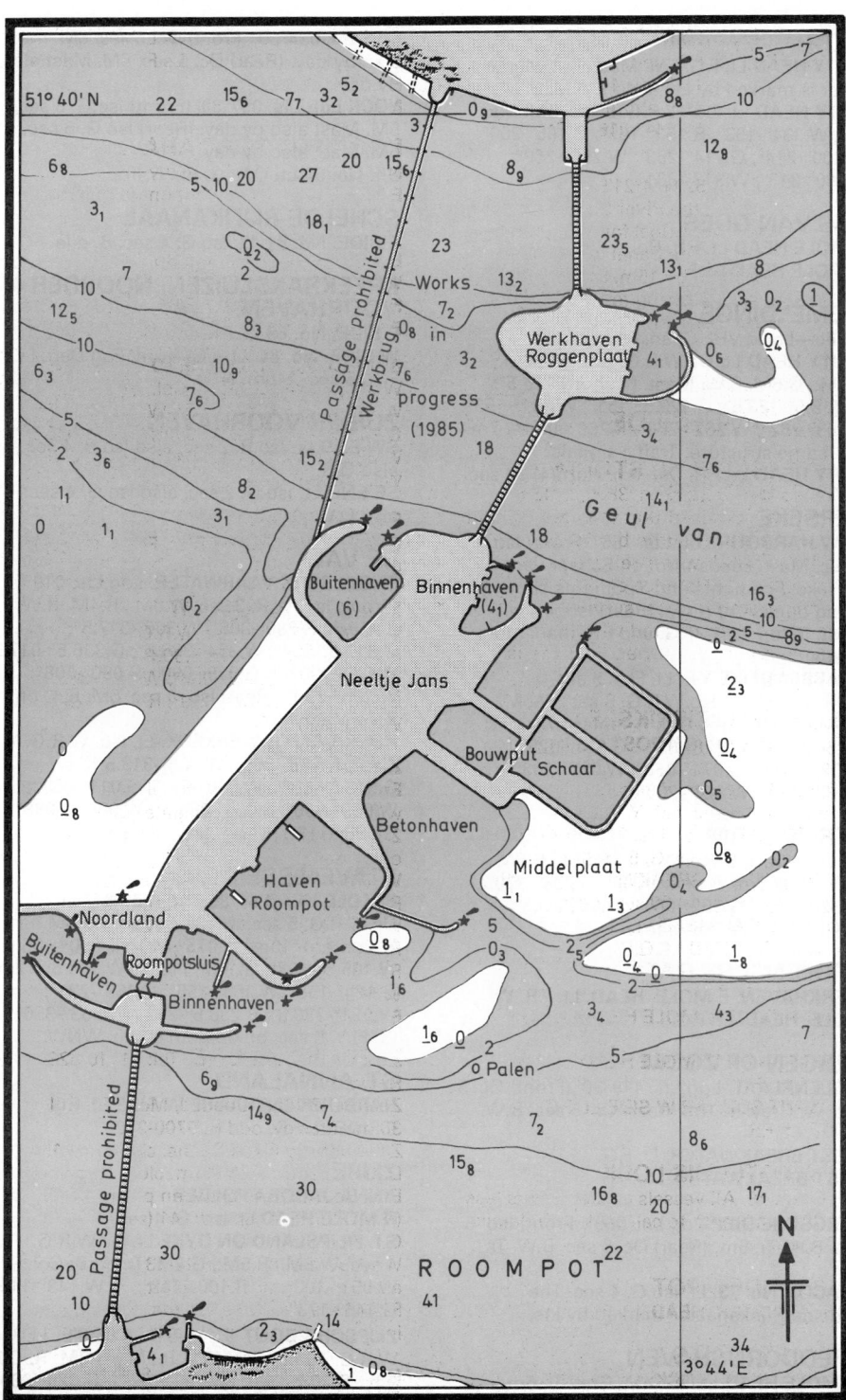

KATS
N JTY HEAD Lt. F.G. 5M. Mast 5m. Veerse Meer is marked by Lts. F.W. 1.15M. E.
S JTY HEAD Lt. Oc. W.R.G. 8 sec. 5M. Mast 5m. W.334°-153°; R.153°-165°; G.165°-200°; W.200°-214°; G.214°-258°; W.258°-260°; G.260°-313°; W.313°-331°.

SAS VAN GOES
S MOLE HEAD Lt. F.R. Col.
N MOLE HEAD Lt. F.G. Col.

WEMELDINGE
Radio—Lock: VHF Chan. 68.
W JTY HEAD Lt. Oc.W.R.G. 5 sec. W.9M., R.7M., G.6M. B.W. Mast. R. shore-116.5°; W.116.5°-123.5°; G.123.5°-151°; W.151°-153°; R.153°-262°; W.262°-266°; R.266°-shore. 7m. F.G. same structure. Traffic signals.
E JTY HEAD Lt. F.R. Col. 5m. Horn(4) 30 sec.

YERSEKE
NEW HARBOUR Ldg.Lts. 155° (Front) Iso. 4 sec. Mast. Leads through Schaar van Yerseke. Fog lights and Spotlights shown along outside of mole. (Rear) Iso. 4 sec. Mast. In fog 2 F.Y. (F.G. and F.R. mark mole heads).
KRABBENDIJKE Y.E. Lt. Fl.Y. 5 sec.
GORISHOEK Lt. Iso.W.R.G. 8 sec. W.6M., R.4M., G.4M. Grey Col. R. lantern 7m. R.260°-278°; W.278°-021°; G.021°-025°; W.025°-071°; G.071°-085°; W.085°-103°; R.103°-120°; W.120°-260°.

STRIJENHAM
Lt. Oc.W.R.G. 5 sec, W.8M., R.5M., G.5M. R.W. Mast 9m. W.shore-298°; R.298°-320°; W.320°-052°; G.052°-069°; W.069°-085°; R.085°-095°; W.095°-shore.

THOLENSCHE GAT
WERKHAVEN. E MOLE. HEAD. Lt. F.R. **W MOLE. HEAD.** Lt. F.G.

BERGEN OP ZOOM
MOLENPLAAT. Ldg.Lts. 119°30' (Front) Oc. 5 sec. W. Grey Tr. 7m. (Rear) Oc. 5 sec. B.W. Tr.
WEST BREAKWATER. Lt. F.G.
EAST BREAKWATER. Lt. F.R.

BERGSCHE DIEP Ldg.Lts. 065° (Front) Iso. 6 sec. B.W. Tr. 6m. (Rear) Oc. 5 sec. B.W. Tr. 9m.
BEACON No. 73. Lt. Iso.G. 4 sec. The Schelde-Rijnkanaal is marked by Lts.

THEODORUSHAVEN
W MOLE HEAD Lt. F.R. 4M. Grey Tr. 6m.
E MOLE HEAD Lt. F.G. 4M. Grey Tr. 6m.

Ldg.Lts. 034°30' (Front) Oc. 5 sec. 8M. mast also by day. (Rear) Oc. 5 sec. 8M. Mast also by day.
LOCK Ldg.Lts. 057°30' (Front) Iso.G. 6 sec. 5M. Mast also by day. (Rear) Iso.G. 6 sec. 5M. Mast also by day.
Bn. No. 54 Lt. Q.R. G. Bn. R. Top.

SCHELDE-RIJNKANAAL
E SIDE. No. 81. Lt. Iso.G. 4 sec. B. pile.

KREEKRAKSLUIZEN. NOORDER VOORHAVEN.
E SIDE. No. 69 Lt. F.R.
W SIDE. No. 64. Lt. F.G. Horn. Fog Detr. Lt. Fl.Y. 5 sec. 140m. N.

ZUIDER VOORHAVEN
SW END Lt. Iso.R. 2 sec, also Iso.R. 4 sec., also Q.R.
SE END Lt. Iso.G. 2 sec, also Iso.G. 4 sec., also Q.G.

DE VAL
ENGELSCHE VAARWATER. Ldg.Lts. 019° (Front) Iso. W.R. 3 sec. W.6M., R.4M. R.W. Col. 7m. R.290°-306°; W.306°-317.5°; G.317.5°-334°; W.334°-336.5°; G.336.5°-017.5; W.017.5°-026°; G.026°-090°; R.090°-108°; W.108°-290°. (Rear) Iso. 3 sec. 6M. B. □ on R.W. Mast 15m.
HOEK VAN OUWERKERK. Lt. Iso. W.R.G. 6 sec. R.268°-305°; W.305°-313.5°; G.313.5°-008°; W.008°-011°; G.011°-059°; W.059°-065°; R.065°-088.5°; W.088.5°-098°; G.098°-112°; R.112°-125°; W.125°-268°.

STAVENISSE
E MOLE HEAD 51°35.7'N, 4°00.3'E. Lt. Oc.W.R.G. 5 sec. W.12M., R.9M., G.8M. B. Tr. R. Lantern. 10m. W.075°-090°; R.090°-105.5°; W.105.5°-108°; G.108°-118.5°; W.118.5°-124°; G.124°-155°; W.155°-158°; G.158°-231°; W.231°-238.5°; R.238.5°-253°; W.253°-350°.
Lt. Fl.Y. 5 sec. on dolphin 800m. WNW.

ST. ANNALAND
HARBOUR ENTRANCE W SIDE Lt. F.G.
E SIDE Lt. F.R.

ZIJPE
ANNA JACOBA POLDER
N MOLE HEAD Lt. Iso. G. 4 sec.
ST. FILIPSLAND ON DYKE Lt. Oc.W.R.G. 4 sec. W.8M., R.5M., G.4M. Tr. on B. Col. 9m. W.051°-100°; R.100°-143°; W.143°-146°; G.146°-173°.
ZIJPSCHE BOUT 51°38.8'N, 4°05.8'E. Lt. Oc. W.R.G. 10 sec. W.12M., R.9M., G.8M. R. Col. 9m. R.208°-211°; W.211°-025°; G.025°-030°; W.030°-040°; R.040°-066°.

TRAMWEGHAVEN
S MOLE Lt. Iso.R. 4 sec. Bn. 7m. Siren 2 sec. In fog F.Y.

REFUGE HARBOUR
S MOLE Lt. F.R. Col. 7m. (in fog F.Y.).
N MOLE Lt. F.G. Col. 7m.
STOOFPOLDER 51°39.5′N, 4°06.4′E. Lt. Iso.W.R.G. 4 sec. W.12M., R.9M., G.8M. B. W. Tr. 10m. W.147°-154°; R.154°-226.5°; G.226.5°-243°; W.243°-253°; G.253°-259°; W.259°-263°; G.263°-270°; R.270°-283°; W.283°-008°.

KRAMMER
KRAMMER LOCKS. VHF Chan. 22. H24.

BRUNINISSE
GREVELINGENSLUIS S MOLE HEAD Lt. F.R. 4M. R. Bn.
N MOLE HEAD Lt. F.G. 3M. R. Bn.
Ldg.Lts. 281°. (Front) Oc. (Rear) F.
GREVELINGENDAM W BREAKWATER HEAD Lt. F.R.
E BREAKWATER HEAD Lt. F.G.
P.W. Lt. Fl.Y. 5 sec.
KRAMMERSLUIZEN S BREAKWATER HEAD Lt. F.G. on W side.
N BREAKWATER HEAD. Lt. F.R. Horn 20 sec.
JACHTENSLUIS
W SIDE. Lt. F.G.
E SIDE. Lt. F.R.
E SIDE. S BREAKWATER HEAD. Lt. F.R.
N BREAKWATER HEAD. Lt. F.G.
Horn (2) 24 sec.
S SIDE. Lt. F.R.
N SIDE. Lt. F.G.
Lights are shown upstream to Willemstad.

THE MAAS

ZEEGAT VAN BROUWERSHAVEN
WEST SCHOUWEN 51°42.6′N, 3°41.6′E. Lt.Fl.(2+1) 15 sec. 30M. Grey Tr. R. Stripes. 57m. Storm signals.
VERKLIKKER Lt.F.W.R. W.9M., R.7M. Tr. 13m. R.115°-127°; W.127°-169°; R.169°-175°; W.175°-115°.
WAVE OBSERVATION POST OS XIII Lt. Fl.Y. 5 sec.
OS XIV Lt. Fl.Y. 5 sec.
BG II Lt. Fl.Y. 5 sec.
BG V Lt. Fl.Y. 5 sec.
SPRINGER WORK HARBOUR E MOLE HEAD Lt. F.G.
W MOLE HEAD Lt. F.R.

KABBELAARSBANK NOORD HARBOUR
W MOLE HEAD Lt. F.G.
E MOLE HEAD Lt. F.R.

SCHARENDIJKE
W MOLE HEAD Lt. F.G. In fog F.Y.
E MOLE HEAD Lt. F.R.

MIDDEL PLAAT
WORK HARBOUR W MOLE HEAD Lt. F.R.
E MOLE HEAD Lt. F.G.

OSSEHOEK
HARBOUR W PIER HEAD Lt. F.G. 3M. W. ◻ on Tr. 6m.
E PIER HEAD. Lt. F.R. 4m. W. ◻ on Tr. 6m.

BROUWERSHAVEN
Ldg.Lts. 142° (Front) F. B.W. post. 5m. (Rear) F. B.W. mast 8m.

GEUL VAN BOMMENEDE
Ldg.Lts. 262° (Front) F. B.W. mast 5m. (Rear) F. B.W. mast 9m.
Lt. F.W.R.G. G.131°-142°; W.142°-163°; R.163°-264°; W.264°-131°.
GB11-RB2 Lt. Q.G. Bn.
G22-GB1 Lt. Q.R. Bn.

BOMMENEDE
WERKHAVEN E SIDE Lt. F.R.
W SIDE Lt. F.G.
G-14 Lt. Iso.R. 8 sec. Bn.
G6 Lt. Iso.R. 4 sec. Bn.

BRUINISSE
AQUA DELTA MARINA E BREAKWATER HEAD Lt. F.R.
W BREAKWATER Lt. F.G.
WERKHAVEN W MOLE HEAD Lt. F.G. 3M. Bn.
E MOLE HEAD Lt. Iso.R. 4 sec. 6M. Bn.
ELBOW Lt. F.R. 4M. Bn.

ZEEGAT VAN GOEREE

OUDDORP
W MOLE HEAD Lt. F.R. Post. 3m.
E MOLE HEAD Lt. F.G. Post. 3m.
WAVE OBSERVATION POST BG VIII Lt. Fl.Y. 5 sec.

GOEREE ISLAND, WESTHOOFD
51°48.8′N, 3°51.9′E. Lt. Fl.(3) 15 sec. 30M. R. square Tr. 54m. Storm Sig.

HINDER BANK

KWADE HOEK 51°50.3'N, 3°59.1'E. Lt. Iso. W.R.G. 4 sec. W.12M. R.9M. G.8M. 9m. Grey building. R.Top. W.235°-068°; R.068°-088°; G.088°-108°; W.108°-111°; R.111°-142°; W.142°-228°; R.228°-235°. F.R. on radio mast 4.2M. NE.

WAVE OBSERVATION POST HaX Lt. Fl.Y. 5 sec.
Ha 1 Lt. Fl.Y. 5 sec. 4M. Y. pile.

RAK VAN SCHEELHOEK

STELLENDAM

Stellendam. Lock 144m. × 16m. × 3.9m. on sill. Bridge clearance (Outer) 13m. (Inner) 6.5m. Inner Hr. depth 3.8m.
OUTER HARBOUR S MOLE HEAD Lt. F.R.
N MOLE Lt. F.G. Horn(2) 15 sec.
INNER HARBOUR E MOLE HEAD Lt. F.R.
W MOLE HEAD Lt. F.G.
COMPASS POLE Lt. F.
WAVE OBSERVATION POST E Lt. Fl.Y. 5 sec.

HARINGVLIET

HELIUSHAVEN

W JTY HEAD Lt. F.R. 4M. Col. 7m.
E JTY HEAD Lt. F.G. 3M. Col. 7m. Horn(3) 20 sec.

HELLEVOETSLUIS

COMMERCIAL HARBOUR

W SIDE Lt. Iso.W.R.G. 10 sec. W.11M., R.8M., G.7M. Y. Tr. R. Top. 16m. G.shore-275°; W.275°-295°; R.294°-316°; W.316°-036°; G.036°-058°; W.058°-095°; R.096°-shore.
W MOLE HEAD Lt. F.R. Col. 6m.
E MOLE HEAD Lt. F.G. Col. 6m. (in fog F.Y.).
HOORNSCHE HOOFDEN. WATCHHOUSE ON DYKE Lt. Oc.W.R.G. 5 sec. W.7M., R.5M., G.4M. Col. 7m. W.288°-297°; G.297°-313°; W.313°-325°; R.325°-335°; G.335°-344.5°; W.344.5°-045°; G.045°-055°; W.055°-131°; R.131°-N shore.

MIDDELHARNIS

W PIER HEAD Lt. F.W.R.G. W.8M., R.5M., G.4M. Col. 5m. W.144°-164.5°; R.164.5°-176.5°; G.176.5°-144°.
E PIER HEAD Lt. F.R. 5M. Col. 5m. (in fog F.Y.).
STAD AAN'T HARINGVLIET W JTY Lt. F.G. Post 6m.
DEN BOMMEL W MOLE HEAD Lt. F.G. Post. 5m.

NIEUWENDIJK

Ldg.Lts. 303°30' (Front) Iso.W.R.G. 6 sec. W.9M., R.7M., G.6M. B. Tr. Y. top. 8m. G.093°-100°; W.100°-103.5°; R.103.5°-113°; W.113°-093°. (Rear) F. 9M. B. Tr. Y. top. 11m.
GALATHEESE HAVEN. BREAKWATER. Lt. F.R. on post Fl.Y. 5 sec. mark Tidegauge 130m. SW.

DINTELSAS

E MOLE HEAD Lt. F.R. 7m. (in fog F.Y.), **W MOLE HEAD** Lt. F.G. 7m.

VOLKERAKSLUIZEN

Volkeraksluizen: 3 Locks; Jachtensluis 130m. × 16m. wide is NW of Sluice Lock. Bridge clearance 19m. VHF Chan. 22.
Signals: Fl. Lt. and F. Lt. indicate Lock to be used also illuminated boards showing Arrows and 'Sport' direct yachts to appropriate lock. Yacht lock closed 1st Nov.-1st March. Use main locks.

NOORDER-VOORHAVEN

W MOLE HEAD Lt. F.G. 4M. Col. 6m. (in fog F.Y.). ⅃⅃ Lts. F.R. and F.G. mark E Entrance to Yacht Lock 0.9M. **S SIDE** Lt. F.R. Pile 5m. (in fog F.Y.). ⅃⅃.
ZUIDER VOORHAVEN. W MOLE HEAD Lt. F.R. 5m. (in fog F.Y.). Horn 20 sec.
E MOLE HEAD Lt. F.G. 4m. (in fog F.Y.). Lts. F.R. and F.G. mark W Entrance to Yacht Lock 0.6M. N.
HELLEGAT YACHT LOCK Lt. Iso. 2 sec.

HOLLANDSCH DIEP

NUMANSDORP TRAMWEGHAVEN

W SIDE Lt. F.R. Tr. 9m. F.R. and F.Y. Lt. marks Bridge 0.5M. W.
E SIDE Lt. F.G. Mast 7m.

WILLEMSTAD
WERKHAVEN W MOLE HEAD Lt. F.G. 3M.
Col. 5m.
E MOLE HEAD Lt. F.R. 4M. Col. 5m.
W MOLE HEAD Lt. F.G. Post. 〰

NOORDSCHANS
W MOLE Lt. Iso.W.R.G. 4 sec. W.6M., R.4M.,
G.4M. Post 8m. W.shore-093°; R.093°-099°;
W.099°-164°; G.164°-171°; W.171°-175°;
R.175°-182°; W.182°-240°; R.240°-247°;
W.247°-shore.

STRIJENSAS
W DAM Lt. Oc.W.R. 5 sec. W.11M., R.9M., B.
Tr. Y. Top. 10m. W.196°-239°; R.239°-250°;
W.250°-065°;R.065°-069°.
W MOLE Lt. F.G.
S. BANK W SIDE Lt. F.G.
E SIDE Lt. F.R. and Lt. F.R.
ROODE VAART W SIDE Lt. F.G. 6M. Col.
E SIDE Lt. F.R.

MOERDIJK
W MOLE HEAD Lt. F.G. 1M. Col. 5m. (in fog
F.Y.)
E MOLE HEAD Lt. F.R. 1M. Col. 5m.
Navigation Spans in the Bridge 1M. NE
marked by F.Y. and F.R. Lts.

DORDSCHE KIL
S ENTRANCE E SIDE Lt. Iso.W.R.G. 6 sec.
R.238°-029°; W.029°-035°; G.035°-059°;
W.059°-065°; R.065°-170°. Wind generator
70m. ENE.
Channel banks marked by Lts. W side Iso.
G.; E side Iso.R.
YACHT HARBOUR E SIDE. Lt. F.G.
W SIDE Lt. F.R.
Ldg.Lts. 181° (Front) Iso. 8 sec. (Rear) Iso.
8 sec.
Ldg.Lts. 164° (Rear) Iso. 2 sec. (Common
Front) Iso. 2 sec. and Iso. 4 sec.
Ldg.Lts. 015° (Rear) Iso. 4 sec.
Ldg.Lts. 344° (Front) Iso. 2 sec. (Rear) Iso.
2 sec.
Ldg.Lts. 003°(Front) Iso. 8 sec. (Rear) Iso.
8 sec.
Ldg.Lts. 183° (Front) Iso. 8 sec. (Rear) Iso.
8 sec.
S GRAVENDEEL. S SIDE. Lt. F.R.
N SIDE Lt. F.G.

N ENTRANCE Ldg.Lts. 346°30′ (Front) Iso. 4
sec. Col. 14m. (Rear) Iso. 4 sec. Col. 16m.
Ldg.Lts. 166°30′ (Front) Iso. 4 sec. (Rear) Iso.
4 sec.

SCHROOTHAVEN
ENTRANCE S SIDE Lt. F.R.
N SIDE Lt. F.G.

HOOK OF HOLLAND AND EUROPOORT

HOOK OF HOLLAND ROADSTEAD (Traffic Control)
Coastal/Recreation Traffic crossing
roadstead. Call Maasmond Radar VHF Chan.
2. Follow track close W of line joining buoys
MV/MVN and Indusbank N. Before crossing
report name, position, course, maintain
listening watch. Cross under power and in
company when possible.

NOORD HINDER Lt V.52°00.1′N 2°51.2′E.
Fl.(2) 10 sec. 27M. R. Hull. 16m. Racon. Horn
(2) 30 sec. (Reserve Whis(2) 30 sec.)
PLATFORM EURO Lt. Mo(U) 15 sec. RW deck
House. Helopad. Horn Mo.(U) 30 sec.

**OFFSHORE WAYPOINT GOEREE, 51°55.0′N,
3°40.0′E.**

GOEREE 51°55.5′N, 3°40.2′E. Lt. Fl.(4)
20 sec. 28M. 32m. Storm sig. R.C. Racon.
Horn(4) 30 sec. Helopad.

MAASVLAKTE 51°58.2′N, 4°00.9′E. Lt.
Fl.(5) 20 sec. 28M. 66m. B. Octagonal
Concrete Tr. Or. bands. Vis. 340°-267°.

Vessels should not anchor in Chan. for deep
draught ships WSW and ESE of Maas Lt. By.
as this impeded their safe navigation. Use
anch. about 3M. SSE of Lt. By.

ZEELAND BRUG, OOSTERSCHELDE. Tel: 011 103237.
Radio—Port: VHF Chan. 18.

KREEKRAKSLUIZEN, SCHELDE, RIJNKANAAL. Tel: 011 35555.
Radio—Port: VHF Chan. 20.

SEA TRAFFIC SEPARATION ROUTES
NOORD HINDER TO EUROPOORT

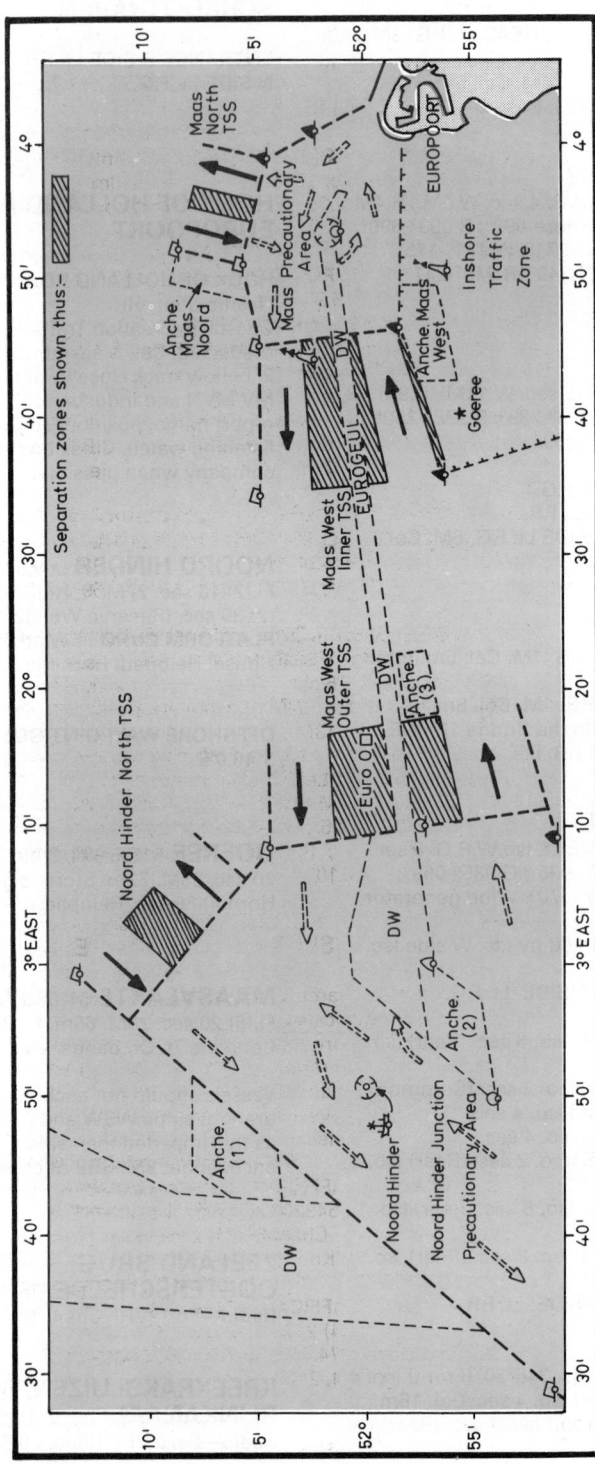

Separation zones shown thus:-

Anche. (1) For deep draught-vessels. Anche. (2) For deep-draught vessels which have to wait for a short period before entering DW-route. Anche. (3) For ships which on account of their draught cannot normally anchor in Maas West or Maas Noord anchorages.

INSHORE WAYPOINT EUROPOORT.
51°57.0′N, 3°58.0′E.

ROTTERDAM WATERWAY AND EUROPOORT

MAASMOND (ROTTERDAMSE WATERWEG)
51°59′N 4°07′E
Haven Coordinate Centrum.
Tel: (010) 4251400/4251410.
Emergencies (010) 4766766.
Fax: (010) 4771800, 4773489.
Telex: 24045, 27370. DRHCC NL:
Pilots HCC (010) 4251530, 4251538
(Rotterdam) H24: TCH (01740) 38309, 38820
(Hook of Holland) H24.
Fax: HCC (010) 4251557: TCH (01740) 38857.
Telex: 27482. VHF Chan. 11, 14. H24 [HCC].
Traffic Centre Oude Mass. Tel: (078) 132421
VHF Chan. 13, 19.
Traffic Centre Hoek Van Holland.
Tel: (01740) 38801, 38811.
Fax: (01740) 38864. VHF Chan. 13, 1, 2, 3,
65, 66. H24. [TCH].
Traffic Centre Botlek.
Tel: (010) 4724600, 4724610.
Fax: (010) 4724672. VHF Chan. 13, 61
80. H24. [VCB].
Traffic Centre Hartel. Tel: (010) 4383898.
VHF Chan. 5, 62. H24. [VPH].
Traffic Centre Stad.
Tel: (010) 4251700, 4251710.
Fax: (010) 4251722. VHF. Chan. 13, 60,
63. H24. [VCS].
Traffic Centre Maasboulevard.
Tel: (010) 4139575. VHF Chan. 21, 81 as
required. [VPM].
Each area divided into sectors:

Maasaanloop/		
Maas Approach	Chan. 01.	
Pilot Maas	Chan. 02.	
Maasmond/		TCH
Maas Entrance	Chan. 03.	
Waterweg	Chan. 65.	
Europoort	Chan. 66.	
Maasluis	Chan. 80.	VCB
Botlek	Chan. 61.	
Oude Maas	Chan. 62.	VPH
Hartel	Chan. 05.	
Eemshaven	Chan. 63.	
Waalhaven	Chan. 60.	VCS
Maasbruggen	Chan. 81.	
Brienenoord	Chan. 21.	VPM

Keep watch on Sector frequency: report
when changing sectors: Call Bridges on VHF
as you approach. Keep listening until past.
Botlekbrug Chan. 18. Spijkenisserbrug Chan.
18. Van Breinenoordbrug Chan. 20.
Alblasserdam Chan 22. Dordrecht Chan. 19.

Radio—Pilots: Maas Approach Chan. 1: Pilot
Maas Chan. 2. Maas Entrance Chan. 3. H24.
TRAFFIC SIGNALS — see Europoort.
Day and Night Signal at Arrival: Ocean
going ships bound for Europoort:
Day time — flag 5 over pennant 1;
Night time — G Lt, visible all around.
Tidal Signals: G. over W. Lt. = rising tide;
W. over G. Lt. = falling tide. Harbour
launches carry a Bu. Fl.Lt. and show a R. Lt.
or flag R.W.Bu. triangles. Vessels are to slow
down on observing such signals and stop if
the flag is raised and lowered or the R.Lt.
waved from side to side.

MAASLUIS (RADIO DIRKZWAGER) DEEP SEA PILOTS.
Tel: 010 4138178, 414422, 4135322.
Telex: 21058 DIRK NL.
Telegraph Stn. Rotterdam Dirkzwager.
Tel: 01899-19200. VHF Stn. Maasluis Radio
Dirkzwager. Tel: 010-144222.
Ship Reporting Stn. Tel: (010) 414 222.
Telex: SHIP/SHORE 26751 DIRK NL. Shore:
21058 DIRK NL.
Pilotage: Vessels bound for Europoort and
Botlek via Rotterdamsche Waterweg give
E.T.A. 6h. in advance to Maassluis or
Scheveningen. Vessels bound to Dordrecht
state destination.
Suitably equipped vessels can by prior
arrangement have the pilots brought off by
helicopter.
Radio: VHF Chan. 16, 14, 12—continuous.
Maasluis Radio Dirkzwager. Chan. 12.
Port information service for Rotterdamsche
Waterweg.

ROTTERDAM 51°55′N 4°30′E. See also
Maasmond
Entry: 16M. from the sea along the
Waterweg, access to Rhine, Ruhr, France,
Switzerland. Jachthaven is the yachting
basin at NE end of Westerkade.

DORDRECHT. Tel: (078) 142 372, 132421.
Telex: 27009 HAVEN NL.
Radio—Port: VHF Chan. 10, 13, 19. H24.
Radar Asst. Chan. 19.
Entry Signals: On the Rhine Flag H is shown
for other vessels to slow down.
Overtaking and overtaken vessels each
display a light blue flag until clear of each
other. One flag at jackstaff to indicate that
the vessel is overtaking, the other 2m. clear
of the starboard side to indicate to
oncoming traffic that it should pass on the
starboard side.
Volkeraksluizen. Telex: 54430.
Radio: VHF Chan. 18, 69. VHF not for use by
yachts.

NIEUWE NOORDERDAM HEAD. Lt.Bn.
F.R. 10M. Or.Tr. B.bands & in fog Alt. Fl.W.R.
8 sec. 278°-255°. 24m.
NIEUWE ZUIDERDAM HEAD. Lt.Bn. F.G.
10M. Or.Tr. B.bands & in fog. Alt. Fl.W.R.
8 sec.
330°-307°. 24m. Horn 10 sec.
WAVE RECORDING POST DK1. Lt. Fl.Y.
5 sec.
INNER PORT ENTRY NTH. Lt.Bn. Oc.R.
10 sec. Pole.
INNER PORT ENTRY STH. Lt.Bn. Oc.G.
10 sec. Pole.

MAASMOND 51°58.9′N, 4°04.9′E.
Ldg.Lts. 112° (Front) Iso. 4 sec. 21M.
W.Tr.B.bands 28m. 101°-123° (Rear) Iso.
4 sec. 21M. W.Tr. B.bands. 101°-123°. Shown
by day. For use of very deep draught
vessels.
Ldg.Lts. 107° (Front) Iso. R. 6 sec. 17M. R.Tr.
099.5°-114.5°. 29m (Rear) Iso. R. 6 sec. 17M.
R.Tr. 099.5°-114.5°. 43m Shown by day.
Ordinary draught vessels.

BERGHAVEN W. JETTY. Lt.Bn. F.R. Col. mast
above lantern.
E JETTY. Lt.Bn. F.G. Storm signals.

CALANDKANAAL. 51°57.6′N, 4°08.8′E.
Ldg.Lts. 116°. (Front) Oc. G. 6 sec. 17M.
W.Tr.R.bands. 108.5°-123.5°. (Rear) Oc. G. 6
sec. 17M. W.Tr.R.bands. 108.5°-123.5°.
B2-CA1 Lt. Iso. 2 sec. R.G. Post.

BEERKANAAL. Ldg.Lts. 192°30′ (Front) Iso.
G. 3 sec. (Rear) Iso. G. 3 sec. (By day Iso. 3
sec.).
Lt. Iso.G. 3 sec. Pedestal.

MISSISSIPPI HAVEN
E SIDE. Lt. Iso. W.R.G. 3 sec. R.W. Cheq. Col.
19m. G. 066.5°-068°; W.068°-071°; R.071°-
072.5°.
Ldg.Lts. 249°30′ (Front) Iso. W.R.G. 3 sec.
R.W. Cheq. Col. 19m. G. 247°-248°; W.248°-
251°; R.251°-252°. (Rear) Iso. 3 sec. R.W.
Cheq. Col. 23m. 242°-257°.

TRAFFIC SIGNALS AT HOOK OF HOLLAND
Traffic signals are shown from semaphores in the following positions:
North Bank: 51-58-54 N   04-06-50 E.
South Bank: 51-58-17 N   04-07-31 E.

Configuration may be shown as below:

NORTH BANK

Facing Seawards		Facing New Waterway and Europoort	
O	Marking position of signalstation Station in operation	O	Marking position of signalstation Station in operation
●●● O ●●●	Entrance into Maas Estuary prohibited	●●● O ●●●	Outgoing traffic from Maas Estuary prohibited
●● O ●●	Entrance into Europoort prohibited	●● O ●●	Outgoing traffic from Europoort prohibited
●● O ●●	Entrance into Rotterdam Waterway prohibited	●● O ●●	Outgoing traffic from N.W. prohibited
●● O ●●	Entrance into Oude Maas prohibited		

Facing Beerkanaal

O	Marking position of singalstation Station in operation
● O ●	Outgoing traffic from the Beerkanaal prohibited

O White Light   ● Red Light

CALANDKANAAL
ELBEHAVEN Lt. Fl. G. 5 sec.
BENELUXHAVEN. Lt. F.W.R.G. G.188.6°-190.6°; W.190.6°-192.3°; R.192.3°-194.9°.
Lt. Iso. W.R.G. 2 sec. G.178°-179.3°; W.179.3°-180.6°; R.180.6°-182.3°.
SCHEURHAVEN ENTRANCE W SIDE. Lt. F.R. Col. 7m.
PETROLEUM HAVEN No. 7. Lt. Iso. R. 4 sec. Col.

HOOK OF HOLLAND

ROTTERDAMSCHE WATERWEG
S SIDE. Lts. 20. G. Lts. B.O. on groynes and dolphins.
N SIDE. Lts. 20. R. Lts. 5M. R.O. on groynes and dolphins.
Lts. Fl.Y.

MAASSLUISSCHE SCHEUR
Ldg.Lts. 325°30′ (Front) L.Fl.R. 8 sec. 8M. R.O. on dolphin. (Rear) F.R. 10M. mast 9m. 322°-329°.
MAASLUIS W MOLE HEAD. Lt. F.R. Col. 6m.
E MOLE HEAD. Lt. F.G. Col. 6m.
BLANKENBURG. S SIDE OF DYKE HEAD.
Ldg.Lts. 282° (Front) Iso 4 sec. 13M. B.W. Tr. 9m. also by day. (Rear) Iso. 4 sec. 13M. B.W. Tr. 17m. 274.5°-289.5°.

BOTLEK HAVEN
W SIDE. Lt. F.G. Post 5m.
GEULHAVEN. N SIDE. Lt. F.R.
S SIDE. Lt. F.G.
WINDMILLHAVEN. DOCK ENTRANCE W SIDE. Lt. F.R.
E SIDE. Lt. F.G.

NIEUWE MAAS
1ST PETROLEUM HAVEN ENTRANCE. W SIDE. Lt. F.G.
E SIDE. Lt. F.R.

VLAARDINGEN
W MOLE HEAD. Lt. 2 F.R. vert mast 7m. Traffic Signals.
E MOLE HEAD. Lt. F.G. Col. 5m.
KONINGIN WILHELMINA HAVEN. W SIDE.
Lt. F.R. Mast 4m.
VULKAANHAVEN. Lt. F.R. Mast 6m. and F.G. on mast 6m.
2ND PETROLEUM HAVEN Lt. F.R. and F.G. Mast.
WILTONHAVEN. Lt. F.R. and F.G. Post.

HAVEN VAN MADROEL. Lts. F.R. & F.G.
EEMHAVEN. Lt. F.R. R.W. Mast.
PRINS JOHAN FRISOHAVEN. N SIDE. Lt. Q. Mast.
WILHELMINA HAVEN. W. Side Lt. F.R. **E. Side** Lt. F.G.
SPUIHAVEN. W SIDE. Lt. F.R.
VOORHAVEN. W SIDE. Lt. 2 F.R. vert.
E. SIDE. Lt. F.G.
MERWEHAVEN. E SIDE. Lt. F.G. Mast 6m.
LEKHAVEN. Lt. F.R. and F.G.
IJSELHAVEN. Lt. F.R. and F.G.
COMPASS DOLPHIN. Lt. F.l.R. dolphin.
Willemsbrug Bridge Centre Span clearance 10m.
Willemsbrug Railway Br. Span clearance 8m.

Koningshaven Depth 6m.
Railway Bridge clearance 45.4m. (raised) 7.9m. (lowered)
Road (Bascule) Bridge clearance 2.7m. (lowered)
Bridges opened for 20 mins on request — Signal – – – (3 long blasts) or by VHF or hailing.
Rail Traffic has priority.

Yacht harbours in Spuihaven and Veerhaven.

DELFSHAVEN
SCHIEMOND. E SIDE. Lt. F.G. Mast 6m.
SCHIEHAVEN. E SIDE. Lt. F.G. Col. 15m.
MAASHAVEN. W SIDE CHARLOIS. Lt. F.G.
LEUVEHAVEN. W SIDE. Lt. F.R. and F.G.
KONINGSHAVEN. ANTWERPSE HOOFD.
Lt. F.G. on mast.
NASSAUKADE. Lt. F.R.
MAASBRUGGEN. PIER. Lt. Iso.R. 4 sec.
VAN BRIENENOORD. N SIDE. Lt. Iso. 2 sec. R. ▽ above G. △ on R.G. Bn.
HOLLANDSCHE IJSEL. W END No. 4. Lt. Iso. 2 sec. R. ▽above G. △ on R.G. Bn.
Lt. L.Fl.G. 10 sec. G. △ on G. Bn.
No. 5 Lt. Iso.R. 4 sec.
No. 6 Lt. Iso.R. 4 sec.

OUDE MAAS
ENTRANCE END SIDE No. 1. Lt. Iso. 2 sec. R. ▽ above G. △ on R.G. Bn.

HUIS TE ENGELAND
Ldg.Lts. 51°52.9′N, 4°19.8′E. 157°30′ No. 2. (Front) Iso. 8 sec. 15M. Mast 13m. 150°-165°. (Rear) Iso. 8 sec. 15M. Bldg. 15m. 150°-165° (also shown by day).
HUIS TE ENGELAND. Lt. Iso.R. 4 sec. 4m. mast.

Bridges and Locks:
Botlekbrug clearance 44m. (open) 7m. (closed).
Spijkenisserbrug clearance 44m. (open) 11.2m. (closed).
Brielsebrug clearance 10m.
Calandbrug clearance 48m. (open).
Rozenburgsluis Br. (Bascule) clearance 3.5m. (lowered).
Voornsesluis Br. (Bascule) clearance 3.6m. (lowered).
Bridge Signals:
F.R. = No passage.
F.R./F.G. vert. = No passage. Permission given shortly.
F.G. = Through passage.

2 F.R. vert. = No passage. Br. non operational.
F.G.+ F.Y. = Passage under Br. both ways.
F.G.+2 F.Y. = Passage under Br. one way only.
Locks:
Rozenburgsluis 329m. × 24m. × 6.5m. on sill.
Voornesesluis 68m. × 7.5m. × 3.7m. on sill.
Voornesesluis gives access to Voedingkanaal and Brielse Meer. Depths 3.4m. to 4.8m. in canal.
Y. Hrs. at Rhoonsehaven; Heerjansdam, Puttershoek.

BOTLEKBRUG
Ldg.Lts. 51°51.6′N, 4°20.3′E. 161°30′. **No. 3** (Front) Iso. 2 sec. 13M. 14m. 154°-169°. **No. 4** (Rear) Iso. 2 sec. 16M. 17m. (also shown by day).
BRIDGE. 5 F. Lts. mark passage through lifting bridge.

HARTELKANAAL
S ENTRANCE. N SIDE. Lt. F.G.
S SIDE. Lt. F.R.G. R.shore-270°; G.270°-shore.
R. Lts. shown to Port & G. Lts. shown to Starboard.
S SIDE. Lt. F.R.

BRIELSE MEER

BRIELLE. BUITENHAVEN.
N HEAD. Lt. F.G.
S HEAD. Lt. F.R.
BRIDGE. 6 F. Lts. mark passage through lifting bridge.

ALLEMANSHAVEN
Ldg.Lts. 143° No. 6 (Front) Iso. 4 sec. 15M. 3m. 135.5°-150.5°. (Rear) Iso. 4 sec. 15M. 6m. 135.5°-150.5°.

SPIJKENISSE
N PIER HEAD. Lt. F.G.
S PIER HEAD. Lt. F.R.
No. 3 Lt. Iso.G. 4 sec. G. Δ on G. Bn.
No. 4 Lt. Iso.G. 4 sec. G. Δ on G. Bn.
No. 5 Lt. Iso.G. 4 sec. G. Δ on G. Bn.
BERENGAT. Lt. Iso.W.R.G. 6 sec. G.shore-114°; W.114°-119°; R.119°-158°; G.158°-shore.

JOHANNAPOLDER
OOST. Ldg.Lts. 51°50.7′N, 4°24.9′E. 082°30′ (Front) Iso. 2 sec. 15M. 13m. 075°-090°. (Rear) Iso. 2 sec. 17M. 16m. 075°-090°. (also shown by day).
No. 6 Lt. Iso.R. 4 sec. R. ▽ on R. Bn.
No. 8 Lt. Iso.R. 4 sec.
No. 9 S SIDE. Lt. Iso. 2 sec. R. ▽above G. Δ on R. W. Bn. Vis. 125°-345°.

JOHANNAPOLDER
WEST. Ldg.Lts. 51°50.7′N, 4°24.8′E. 300°30′ (Front) Iso. 8 sec. 15M. 13m. 293°-308°. (Rear) Iso. 8 sec. 15M. 18m. 293°-308°. (also shown by day).

GOIDSCHALXPOLDER
OOST. Ldg.Lts. 51°49.8′N, 4°27.1′E. 120°30′ (Front) Iso. 4 sec. 15M. 17m. 113°-128°. (Rear) Iso. 4 sec. 15M. 17m. 113°-128°. (also shown by day).
S SIDE No. 10. Lt. Iso.G. 4 sec. G. Δ on G. Bn.
TIDEGAUGE. Lt. Fl.Y. 5 sec.
WEST. Ldg.Lts. 51°49.9′N, 4°26.9′E. 257° (Front) Iso. 4 sec. 15M. 13m. 249.5°-264.5°. (Rear) Iso. 4 sec. 15M. 18m. 249.5°-264.5°. (also shown by day).
No. 11 Lt. Iso.R. 4 sec.

KOEDOOD
OOST. Ldg.Lts. 51°50.4′N, 4°30.5′E. 077°. (Front) Iso. 4 sec. 15M. 13m. 069.5°-084.5°. (Rear) Iso. 4 sec. 15M. 18m. 069.5°-084.5°. (also shown by day).
Ldg.Lts. 51°50.3′N, 4°29.8′E. 291°. No. 12 (Front) Iso. 6 sec. 15M. R. ▽ on R. Bn. 283.5°-298.5° also Iso.R. 6 sec. (Rear) Iso. 6 sec. 15M. 283.5°-298.5° (also shown by day).
No. 12A Lt. Iso.R. 4 sec.
No. 13 Lt. Iso.R. 4 sec. R. ▽ on R. Bn.
No. 14 Lt. Iso.R. 4 sec.

HEERJANSDAM
Ldg. Lts. 51°50.0′N, 4°33.1′E. 079°30′. (Front) Iso.W.R.G. 6 sec. 15M. R.296°-317°; W.317°-328°; G.328°-338°; R.338°-064°; W.064°-117°. (Rear) F. 15M. 072°-087° (also shown by day).

UILENVLIETSE HAVEN. Lt. Iso.W.R.G. 4 sec.
G.090°-109°; W.109°-117°; R.117°-139°.
Ldg.Lts. 347°. (Front) Iso. 6 sec. (Rear) F. Vis.
339.5°-354.5°.

PUTTERSHOEK
Lt. Iso.W.R.G. 6 sec. Post. G.157°-162°;
W.162°-166°; R.166°-213°; G.213°-284°;
R.284°-296°; W.296°-300°; G.300°-312°.
Lt. Iso.G. 4 sec. Post.
WEST. Ldg.Lts. 51°48.5'N, 4°34.5'E. 275°30'.
(Front) Iso. 4 sec. 15M. 12m. 267.5°-282.5°.
(Rear) Iso. 4 sec. 15M. 15m. 267.5°-282.5°.
(also shown by day).
Ldg.Lts. 292° (Front) Iso. 6 sec. (Rear) F. Vis.
284.5°-299.5°.
Ldg.Lts. 112°. (Front) Iso. 6 sec. (Rear) Iso.
6 sec.
SWINHAVEN. W SIDE. Lt. F.R.
E SIDE. Lt. F.G.
DRECHTHAVEN. W SIDE. Lt. F.R.
E SIDE. Lt. F.G.
DEVELHAVEN. W SIDE. Lt. F.R.
E SIDE. Lt. F.G.
No. 15 Lt. Iso.R. 4 sec. R. ▽ on R. Bn.
No. 15A Lt. Iso.G. 4 sec. 160m. SSW.
No. 16 Lt. Iso.G. 4 sec. G. △ on G. Bn.
No. 17 Lt. Iso.R. 4 sec. R. ▽ on R. Bn.
No. 18 Lt. Iso.G. 4 sec. G. △ on G. Bn.
No. 19 Lt. Iso.R. 4 sec. R. ▽ on R. Bn.
No. 20 Lt. Iso.G. 4 sec. G. △ on G. Bn.
No. 21 Lt. Iso.R. 4 sec. R. ▽ on R. Bn.
No. 22 Lt. Iso.R. 4 sec. R. ▽ on R. Bn.
DORDTSCHE KIL No. 1 Lt. Iso. 2 sec. R.
▽above G. △ on R.G. Bn.

KRABBEGEUL
KRABBEGORS. W SIDE. Lt. Iso.W.R.G. 6 sec.
R.336°-061°; G.061°-096°; W.096°-100°;
R.100°-126°; G.126°-242°.
S END. Lt. Iso.R. 4 sec. Post.

DORDRECHT
WILHELMINAHAVEN. N SIDE. Lt. F.R.G.
Post. G.295°-025°; R.025°-205°.
S SIDE. Lt. F.R.G. Post. R.340°-115°;
G.115°-290°.
JULIANAHAVEN. W SIDE. Lt. F.R.G. Post.
G.070°-205°; R.205°-340°.
No. II BASIN. Lt. F.G. Post.
No. II/III BASIN. Lt. F.R. Post.
No. I/II BASIN. Lt. F.R. Post.
UILENHAVEN. W SIDE. Lt. F.R.
E SIDE. Lt. F.G.

SCHEVENINGEN Tel: 070-514031.
Radio—Port: VHF Chan. 14—continuous.
Signals: Q.R.Lt. shown from fish market
indicates one or more vessels inward bound
in outer harbour.
R. over W. Lt. = entry prohibited.
W. over R. Lt. = departure prohibited.
Y.Fl.Lt. = large vessel entering or leaving.
Shown seaward for vessel leaving.
Landward for vessel entering.
Depth signals:
F.R. = Tide 5m. or more.
F.G./F.W. vert. = Rising tide.
F.W./F.G. vert. = Falling Tide.
Yacht facilities in 2nd Binnerhaven depth
2.9m.
Depth in Voorhaven 4.9m.

RADAR SCHEVENINGEN Tel: 070-
543525.
Radio—VHF Chan. 21, Range 9.5M. Advice
also obtainable through Scheveningen
Radio.

SCHEVENINGEN 52°06.3'N, 4°16.2'E.
Lt.Ho. Fl.(2) 10 sec. 29M. dark brown Tr.
48m. Storm Sig.Stn. 014°-244°.
Ldg.Lts. 156°. (Front) Iso. 4 sec. 13M. on
grey post, vis. day and night. (Rear) Iso.
4 sec. 13M. on grey post, vis. day and night.
FISHING HARBOUR
S PIER. Lt. F.G. 9M. B.Tr. Y bands R lantern
11m. Horn (3) 30 sec.
N PIER. Lt. F.R. B.Tr. Y bands R lantern 11m.
BUITENHAVEN S MOLE HEAD. Lt.Bn. Oc. G.
7.5 sec. 5M. 9m.
N MOLE HEAD. Lt.Bn. Oc. R. 7.5 sec. 5M.
9m.
Ldg.Lts. 131° (Front) Oc. G. 5 sec. 11M.
(Rear) Oc. G. 5 sec. 11M.
VOORHAVEN S SIDE. Lt.Bn. Oc. G. 7.5 sec.
4M.
N SIDE. Lt.Bn. Oc. R. 7.5 sec. 4M.
1ST VISSERHAVEN Lt. Q.Y. Shown when
vessels entering and leaving port.
3RD VISSERHAVEN JTY HEAD. Lt. Iso.R.
4 sec.
PROMENADE PIER. Lt.Bn. Iso. 5 sec. 5M.
Concrete Tr. 013°-253°.

NOORDWIJK AAN ZEE 52°14.9'N,
4°26.1'E. Lt. Oc.(3) 20 sec. 18M. white square
Tr. 32m.
SURVEY PLATFORM (NOORDWIJK) Lt.Bn.
Mo(U) 15 sec. Horn(U) 20 sec. Also F.R.

OFFSHORE WAYPOINT APPROACHES
IJMUIDEN. 52°30.0'N, 4°05.0'E.

INSHORE WAYPOINT OFF IJMUIDEN.
52°28.0'N, 4°31.0'E.

IJMUIDEN Tel: 02550-15703. Pilots Telex: 71169 PIVTS NL.
Radio—Port: VHF Chan. 9 from Lt. By. to Locks except when vis. <2000m then Chan. 19 from PV to Piers. H24.
North Sea Canal: VHF Chan. 11 from N Sea Lock to Km. 11.2. H24.
Radio—Pilots: VHF Chan. 12.
Harbour Radar: VHF Chan. 12 W of IJ muiden Lt. By. Chan. 19 Lt. By to Locks.
Signals: Frame positions as seen by incoming vessels:

1. Noordersluis.	2. Middensluis.	3. Zuidersluis.
4. Noorder Buitenkanaal.	9. Pilotage.	5. Zuider Buitenkanaal.
6. Seagoing vessels	7. Buitenhaven Hoogovens.	8. Fishing and coastal craft.

Frame No: 1: Fl.G.   = bound for Noordersluis. Lock preparing.
            F.G.   = Noordersluis ready.
            Fl.R.   = ships leaving Noordersluis.
            F.R.   = Noordersluis out of use.
Frame No: 2 & 3. as for Noordersluis but apply as indicated.
Frame No: 4: Fl.R.   = ships leaving Noorder Buitenkanaal.
            F.R.   = traffic prohibited.
Frame No: 5: as for No: 4, apply as indicated.
Frame No: 6: F.R.   = entry prohibited except with permission.
Frame No: 7: Fl.R.   = ship leaving Hoogovens Steel works.
            F.R.   = entry prohibited to Hoogovens Steel Works.
Frame No: 8: F.R.   = entry prohibited as indicated.
Frame No: 9: F.W.   = pilotage service normal.
            Fl.W.   = pilotage service suspended.
Frame positions as seen by outgoing vessels:

1. Zuider Buitenkanaal.	4. Pilotage.	2. Noorder Buitenkanaal.
	3. Buitenhaven Hoogovens.	

Frame No: 1: Fl.R.   = Inward vesel through Southern (Zuider) Outer Fairway.
            F.R.   = Zuider Buitenkanaal closed.
Frame No: 2: same meaning as No: 1, apply as indicated.
Frame No: 3: Fl.R.   = ship leaving Hoogovens Steelworks.
            F.R.   = entrance closed.
Frame No: 4: F.W.   = Pilotage service normal.
            Fl.W.   = Pilotage service suspended.

Iso.R. 3 sec. shown from entrance to Visserhaven and Haringhaven, also horn sounded when vessels cannot leave these basins.
Inward Vessels: 2 Oc. Hor. Lts. use N Lock.
Outward Vessels: 2 F.G./R. Lts. G./G. (Hor.) = normal.
R./G. Hor. = use N Lock: G./R. (Hor.) = use Middle Lock.
R./R. Hor. = entrance prohibited.
Also use loudspeakers to pass information.
3 F.R. Lts. = sluicing.
Small vessels use Zuidersluis or Kleenesluis.
Keep clear of pier heads, blocks of concrete up to 40m. off.
Minimum speed 6 kts or wait for LW.
Flood tide stronger than ebb. Flood flows until 2-3 h. after HW. Ebb strongest 2 h. after LW.
Best to enter IJmuiden 2-3 h. before HW and 2-3 h. after HW.
All yachts approach locks via Zuider Buitenkanal and report for clearance at

Customs Pier (port hand) 100m W of Zuidersluis. Kleinesluis used for yachts.
Vis. reports by C.G. IJmuiden Chan. 12 ev. H+00. Ch. 5 and 11 ev. H+30.
BEVERWIJK Radio-Port: VHF Chan. 71.

AMSTERDAM Tel: 020 221515.
Telex: 15480 HAVEN NL.
Radio—Port: VHF Chan. 16, 14. B'casts ev. H+00 when vis. less than 1000m.
It is prohibited to use Chan. M. in the Amsterdam area.

IJMUIDEN. 52°27.8'N, 4°34.5'E. Ldg.Lts. 100°30'. (Front) F.W.R. W.16M. R.13M. brown circular Tr. 32m. Storm and Sig.Stn. R.C. S side of Chan. W.050°-122°; R.122°-145°; W.145°-160°; by day F.W. 090.5°-110.5°. (Rear) Fl. 5 sec. 29M. R. circular Tr. 52m. 019°-199°. By day F.W. 090.5°-110.5°. Anchorage is prohibited on either side of dredged approach chan. for approx. ½M. N and S of Leading Line of entry 100°30'.

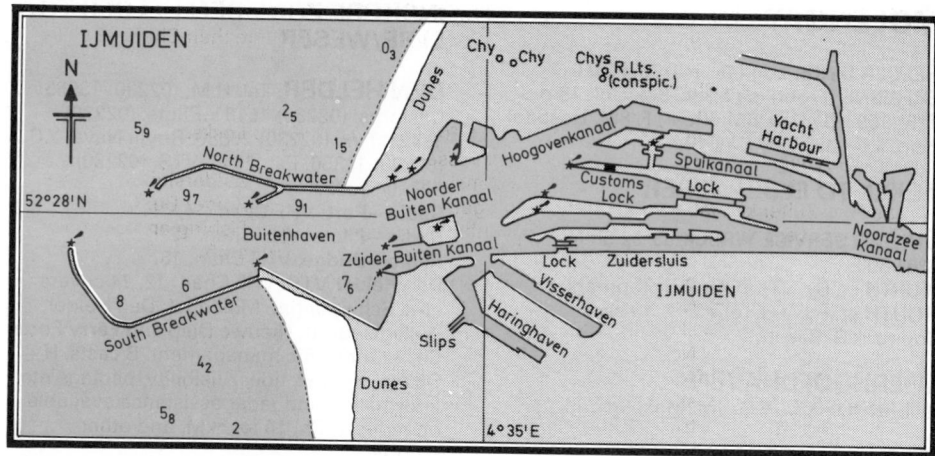

OUTER BREAKWATERS
SOUTH BREAKWATER HEAD. Lt. F.G. 10M. B.W. Tr. 14m. Horn(2) 30 sec. In fog Fl. 3 sec.
NORTH BREAKWATER HEAD. Lt. F.R. 10M. 14m.
SOUTH PIER. Lt. Q.G. 9M. B.W. Tr. 11m. In fog F.W. Vis. 263°-096°.
NORTH PIER. Lt. Q.R. 9M. Y. Tr. 11m. In fog F.W. Vis. 096°-295°.

ZUIDER BUITENKANAAL S SIDE. Lt.Bn. Iso. G. 3 sec. 4M. Bell 5 sec.
N SIDE. Lt.Bn. Iso. R. 3 sec. 5M.
Ldg.Lts. 069° (Front) Q. 354°-144° (Rear) Q. 024°-114°.
DOLPHIN. Lt. Oc. 4.5 sec.
N SIDE. Lt. Q. Dolphin. S.V. F.(Occas.) Lts. shown either side of lock entrances.

VISSERSHAVEN W SIDE. Lt.Bn. F.G. 085°-308°. Traffic Signals. In fog F.Y.
E SIDE. Lt.Bn. F.R. 284°-181°. In fog 2 F.Y.
NOORDER BUITENKANAAL S SIDE. Fort Eiland Lt.Bn. Iso G. 3 sec. Horn 15 sec.
Ldg.Lts. 077° (Front) Iso 3 sec. 031°-121°. G. Post (Rear) Iso. 3 sec. 031°-121° W.O. on G. column.

AVERIJHAVEN W MOLE. Lt.Bn. Iso. R. 3 sec. Harbour closed.
W SIDE. Lt.Bn. F.R.
E SIDE. Lt.Bn. F.G.
Ldg.Lts. 020° (Front) Q. (Rear) Q.

HOOGOVENHAVEN. Ldg.Lts. 065° (Front) Iso.G. 2 sec. Mast 11m. (Rear) Iso.G. 2 sec. Mast 16m.

AMSTERDAM ENTRANCE TO R. ELBE AND WESER

EGMOND AAN-ZEE 52°37.3'N, 4°37.6'E. Lt. Iso. W.R. 10 sec. W.18M. R.14M. Circular W.Tr. 36m. W.010°-175°; R.175°-188°.
TIDEGAUGE. Lt. Fl.(5)Y. 20 sec. Y. pile.

TEXEL 52°47.2'N, 4°06.5'E. Lt.V. Fl.(3 + 1) 20 sec. 26M. R. hull. W. band. R.C. 16m. Racon. Horn (3) 30 sec. or Whis.

ZEEGAT VAN TEXEL.
GROTE KAAP. Lt. Oc.W.R.G. 10 sec. W.11M. R.8M. G.8M. Brown Tr. 31m. G.041°-088°; W.088°-094°; R.094°-131°.

OFFSHORE WAYPOINT W OF SCHULPENGAT. 52°52.0'N, 4°32.0'E.

INSHORE WAYPOINT ENTRANCE TO SCHULPENGAT. 52°52.0'N, 4°37.0'E.

SCHULPENGAT. 53°00.9'N, 4°44.5'E. Ldg.Lts. 026°30' (Front) Iso 4 sec. 18M. Tr. Vis. 024.5°-028.5°. By Day 10M. 025°-028°.
DEN HOORN (Rear) Oc. 8 sec. 18M. Church Spire 024.5°-028.5°. By Day 10M. 025°-028°.
HUIS DUINEN. 52°57.2'N, 4°43.3'E. Lt. F.W.R. W.14M, R.11M. R. Tr. 27m. W.070°-113°; R.113°-158°; R.158°-208°.
TIDEGAUGE. Lt. Fl.(5)Y. 20 sec. Or. R. Tr.
KIJKDUIN. 52°57.4'N, 4°43.6'E. Lt. Fl.(4) 20 sec. 30M. Brown Tr. 56m.
SCHIBOLSNOL. 53°00.6'N, 4°45.8'E. Lt. F.W.R.G. W.15M. R.12M. G.11M. B. Tr. R. Top. 27m. W.338°-002°; G.002°-035°; W.035°-038°; R.038°-051°; W.051°-068.5°.

MOLENGAT

HELDER DYKE. Ldg.Lts. 141°30' **FORT ERFPRINS** (Front) Iso 5 sec. 8M. Col. 13m. 125°-159°. By Day. 6M. (Rear) F. 8M. Hospital 22m. 134°-150°. By Day. 6M.

TEXEL TO ELBE/WESER

VULEAN SERVICE WRECK 53°02.58'N 3°01.50'E.
NORTH Lt. By. V.Q. Pillar B.Y. Topmark.
SOUTH Lt. By. V.Q. (6) + L.Fl. 10 sec. Topmark S. Racon.

WIERHOOFDHAVEN
WIERHOOFD. Lt. F.G. 4M. Mast 9m.

FERRY. Ldg.Lts. 52°57.8'N, 4°46.8'E. 207° (Front) Iso. 2 sec. 14M. Mast 10m. 199°-215° (Rear) Iso. 2 sec. 14M. Mast 14m. 199°-215° (Shown also by day).
E SIDE. Lt. F.R. 5M. Grey Bn. R. Top 8m. 032°-233°.

BORKUMRIFF 53°47.5'N 6°22.1'E. Lt.V. Oc.(3) 15 sec. 21M. 20m. R. hull. W. Tr. R.C. Racon.

INSHORE ZONE DEN HELDER TO ELBE/WESER

DEN HELDER. Tel: H.M. (02230) 13955. Customs: (02230) 15181. Pilots: (02230) 17424, Fax: (02230) 25880. Royal Naval Y.C. (02230) 11366. Ext. 2645. VTS. (02230) 52770/52822.
Radio—Port: VHF Chan. 14, 16.
Radio—Pilots: VHF Chan. 12.
Radio—Bridge: VHF Chan. 18.
Den Helder VTS: VHF Chan. 12, 14 covers area Schulpengat, Molengat, Den Helder, Willemsnoord, Nieuwe Diep and Ferry Ports. Ch. 12 for traffic management. B'casts. H + 05 for weather, tides, visibility, pilotage etc. Information and radar assistance available on request. Ch. 14 for H.M. and other reports.
Traffic Lts. R/W/R vert. when shown from Port Coordination Centre indicate all vessels, unless with permission, are forbidden to enter or leave Willemsnoord Naval Port. Vessels must not stop in area 200m. either side of or within 1M. of line of lights
Entry: Den Helder is a Naval Port only. Merchant vessels may call only for shelter,

SEA TRAFFIC SEPARATION ROUTES
TEXEL TO HELGOLAND

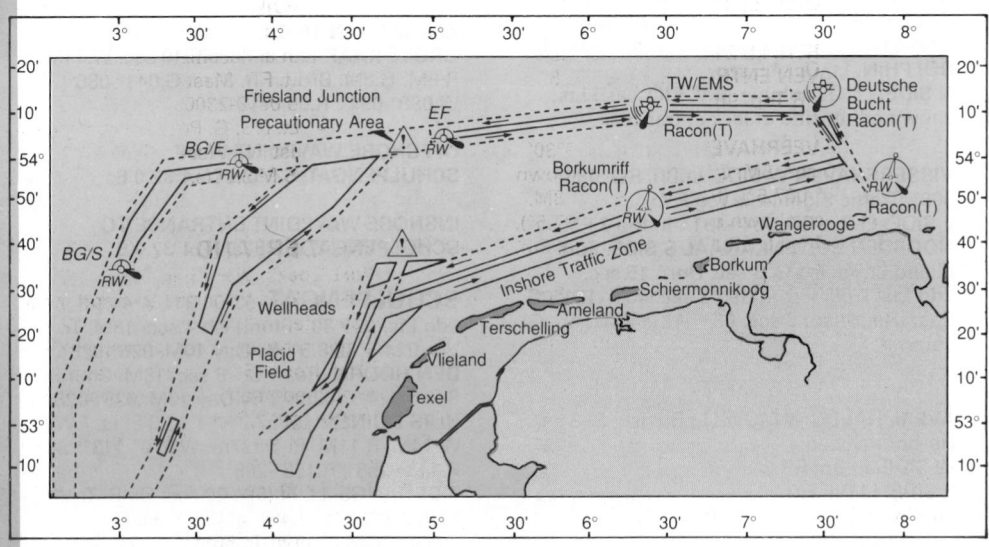

Important separation routes for vessels bound to rivers Weser and Jade and the Ports of Bremen, Bremerhaven and Wilhelmshaven. River Elbe not only has considerable traffic to Hamburg but gives access to Kiel Canal by which all traffic not using the Skagerrak gain access to the Baltic Sea.

repairs, provisions, Customs, water, changing crews, or for canal access to Alkmaar or Amsterdam. Harbour radar controls movement in poor visibility. Permission to enter should be obtained on VHF Chan. 14.

Yacht Hbr. situated in a basin close inside entrance to Bergehaven on W Side. All facilities available.

Outer Harbour: Visitors berths at R.N.Y.C. check with Club. (Daylight hours only).

Inner Harbour: Visitors berths available behind locks and at Y.C., check with Civil H.M. H24.

DEN HELDER. 52°57.4'N, 4°47.2'E.
Ldg.Lts. 191° (Front) Oc.G. 5 sec. 14M. Y △ R. Lantern. 16m. 161°-221°. (Rear) Oc.G. 5 sec. 14M. B △ R Tr. 161°-247°.

MALZWIN. Lt. Q.W.R. W.7M. R.5M. Mast 8m. R.165°-195°; W.195°-020°. (also shown by day 183°-199°).

MARINEHAVEN WILLEMSOORD. HARSSENS ISLAND. W BREAKWATER. HEAD. Lt. Q.G. Mast R. Top 12m. Horn 20 sec. (Ldg.Lts. 253°30' with Kijkduin Lt.).

W SIDE OF ENTRANCE. Lt. Fl.G. 5 sec. 4m. Col. R.Top 9m. 180°-067°.

MH4. Lt. Iso.R. 4 sec.

E SIDE OF ENTRANCE. Lt.Q.R. 4M. Col. R.Top. 9m.**SW POINT.** Lt. Oc.W.G. 5 sec. W.8M. G.4M. Col. R.Top 9m. W.259°-281°; G.281°-122°; W.190°-216°.

LOCK ENTRANCE. Lt. Oc.G. 13 sec. and Oc.R. 13 sec.

NR. No. 5 BERTH. Lt. 2 Fl.Y. Mooring Post.

RIJKSZEEHAVEN ENTRANCE. Lt. Oc.R. 5 sec. 4M. Mast R.Top. 9m.

T. HORNTJE VEERHAVEN. Ldg.Lts. 359°30' (Front) Iso. 5 sec. 8M. Col. 11m. (also shown by day 351.5°-007.5°). (Rear) Iso. 5 sec. 8M. Col. 18m. (also shown by day 351.5°-007.5°).

W MOLE HEAD. Lt. F.R. 5M. Mast. R.top. 8m. Horn (3) 20 sec.

E MOLE HEAD. Lt. F.G. 4M. Mast R.Top 8m. (in fog F.Y.).

MOK. 53°00.2'N, 4°46.9'E. Lt. Oc.W.R.G. 10 sec. W.10M. R.7M. G.6M. Col. 10m. R.229°-317°; W.317°-337°; G.337°-112°.

KOLK KM/RA2. Lt. Fl.(5)Y. 20 sec.
Ldg.Lts. 284°30'. (Front) Iso. 2 sec. 6M. Post R.Top 7m. (Rear) Iso. 8 sec. 6M. Post R.Top 10m. 224.5°-344.5°.

NIOZ BASIN. Ldg.Lts. 261°30'. (Front) F. 6M. 4m. 231.5°-291.5°. (Rear) F. 6M. Col. 6m. 231.5°-291.5°.

S MOLE HEAD. Lt. F.R. 4M. Col. 5m.
N MOLE HEAD. Lt. F.G. 3M. Col. 5m.

WADDENZEE
Waddenzee Vessel Traffic Information Service 53°21.69'N, 5°12.95'E. (Brandaris Lt.) Tel: (05620) 3100.

Radio: VHF Chan. 16, 4. H24.

Responsible for all navigational information and maritime coordination in the Waddenzee area.

MALZWIN KM/RA1. Lt. Fl.(5)Y. 20 sec. Post.

DEN OEVER
Radio—Port: Lock: VHF Chan. 20.

Entrance to outer harbour least depth 2.1 m. Lock entrance in Noorderhaven depth 3 m. open 0500-2100. Closed Sundays and Bank Holidays.

Ldg.Lts. 132° (Front) Oc. 10 sec. 7m. 127°-137°. (Rear) Oc. 10 sec. 127°-137°.

DETACHED BREAKWATER N HEAD Lt. L.Fl.R. 10 sec.

E HEAD. Lt. Q.R.

STEVINSLUIZEN E WALL Lt. Iso.W.R.G. 5 sec. W.10M., R.7M., G.7M. R. Tr. 15m. G.226°-231°; W.231°-235°; R.235°-290°; G.290°-327°; W.327°-335°; R.335°-345°. Horn(2) 30 sec.

W WALL Lt. Iso.W.R.G. 2 sec. G.195°-213°; W.213°-227°; R.227°-245°.

PIER HEAD Lt. F.G.

E WALL HEAD Lt. F.R.

NOORDEHAVEN N ENTRANCE Lt. F.G.

S ENTRANCE Lt. F.R.

TEXEL STROOM
OUDE SCHILDE: Large Yacht Harbour in Werkehaven with all facilities. Depth 3.8 m.

S MOLE HEAD Lt. F.R. Mast 7m. Horn(2) 30 sec. (sounded 0600-2300).

N MOLE HEAD Lt. F.G. G. Post 7m.

Lt. Oc. 6 sec. Mast 14m. (seen midway between N and S Mole Lts. leads into harbour).

KORNWERDERZAND
Radio—Port: Locks: VHF Chan. 18.

Entrance to Locks is through outer and inner harbour least depth 2.1m.

Swing bridge between outer and inner harbour. Headroom 5.8 m. when closed. Locks are opened at any time day or night. Maximum draught 2.8 m.

WEST Lt. Iso.R. 4 sec. 4M. Col. R. Top. 9m. 049°-229°.

ZUIDOOSTRAK ZR14. Lt. L.Fl.R. 8 sec. Pile R.

OUTER HARBOUR W MOLE HEAD Lt. F.G. Horn Mo(N) 30 sec.

E MOLE HEAD Lt. F.R.

W MOLE Lt. Iso.G. 6 sec.

SPUIHAVEN NOORD W MOLE HEAD. Lt. L.Fl.G. 10 sec.

BOONTJES BO 11-K2-2 Lt. Q. ≹ on Y. Bn. B. top.
BO28 Lt. Iso.R. 8 sec. R. Pile
BO39 Lt. Iso.G. 4 sec. G. Pile
BO40 Lt. Iso.R. 4 sec. G. Pile

TEXEL N POINT, EIERLAND
53°11.0'N, 4°51.4'E. Lt. Fl.(2) 10 sec. 29M. R. Tr. 52m. RC. Firing Area Danger Signals.
EIERLANDSCHE GRANDEN TIDEGAUGE Lt. Fl.(5)Y. 20 sec. 5M. Y. pile.
OFF W SIDE. Lt. Fl.(5)Y. 20 sec. Y. pile.
OFF VLIELAND TSS
VL CENTER. LANBY. Fl. 5 sec. Horn (2) 30 sec. Racon.

ZEEGAT VAN TERSCHELLING

TERSCHELLING
Zeegat Van Terschelling is the entrance between Vlieland and Terschelling giving access to West Terschelling, Harlingen, Den Oever, Kornwerderzand and Oude Schild Harbour.
Owing to the frequent changes in the channel, the buoys, lights etc. have to be altered at short notice. The chart should be used with extreme caution.

VLIELAND HARBOUR
Berths available for yachts. Least depth 2.4 m. Tide gauges at NE Corner of Basin. Provisions from village. Most facilities available.

VLIELAND 53°17.8'N, 5°03.6'E. Lt. Iso.W. 4 sec. 20M., Brown Tr. 53m.
E MOLE HEAD Lt. F.G. Post 4 m.
W MOLE HEAD Lt. F.R. Post.
Ldg.Lts. 276°30' (Front) F. 8M. (Rear) Oc. 10 sec. 8M.
VS12 Lt. Iso. R. 4 sec. R. □ on pile.
TG. Lt. Fl (5) Y. 20 sec. 5.5M. SSE.

TERSCHELLING BANDARIS TOWER 53°21.7'N, 5°12.9'E. Lt. Fl. 5 sec. 29M. Y. Tr. 55m.

WEST TERSCHELLINGHAVEN
3 small basins. Least depth 2.1 m. Secure on Western side of harbour.

W HARBOUR MOLE HEAD Ldg.Lts.
053° (Front) F.R. 5M. R.W. post. 5m. Horn 15 sec. On Dyke (Rear) Iso. 5 sec. 19M. Mast Y. Top. 14m. 045°-061° (intens 045°-052°).

SCHUITENGAT SG11 Lt. L.Fl.G. 5 sec. Pile G. ᘩᒲᒲ
E PIER HEAD Lt. F.G. 4M. G.W. Mast 5m. F. and L.Fl. 8 sec. and Q. Lts. mark pier Northwards.
Lt. Fl.(5)Y. 20 sec. Y. Pile. Tidegauge

HARLINGEN OUTER HARBOUR (VOORHAVEN) 53°10'N, 5°25'E.
Tel: (05178) 2512, Pilots (05178) 12993, Brandaris Tower (05620) 2341.
Radio—Port: VHF Chan. 11. Mon. 0001-Sat. 2200. Listen on Chan. 11.
Radio—Pilots: VHF Chan. 2. H24. MF 1657.5 kHz.
Entry: Vessels entering or leaving must report on Chan. 11. Entry/Departure prohibited when 2 F.R. Lts. shown from semaphore Tr.
Ldg.Lts. 112° (Front) Iso. 6 sec. 4M. B.W. Mast. 8m. 097°-127°. (Rear) Iso. 6 sec. 14M. B.W. Mast. 19m. 097°-127° (shown by day).
ZUIDHAVENDAM Lt. F.G. 7M. W.G. Col. 9m.
Lt. 53°10.5'N, 5°24.8'E. F.W.R. W.13M., R.10M., Tr. 20m. R.113°-116°; W.152°-068°.
P2 Lt. Fl.R. 2 sec.
P3 Lt. Iso.G. 4 sec. G. Post. ᘩᒲᒲ
P4 Lt. Iso.R. 4 sec.6M. Col. 6m.
P5 Lt. Fl.G. 2 sec. G. Post. ᘩᒲᒲ
P6 Lt. Fl.R. 2 sec. 6M. Col. 6m.
BS54 Lt. V.Q.R. R. Plle.
N MOLE HEAD Lt. Iso.R. 5 sec. 4M. Col. 8m.
PIER. Lt. F.R.
Ldg.Lt. (Rear) F.G. Tr. 5m. Seen midway between N and S Moles leads into harbour 170°.
OUDER ZUIDERHOOFD Lt. Iso.G. 6 sec. Dolphin 7m.

ZEEGAT VAN AMELAND
AMELAND. W END. 53°27.0'N, 5°37.6'E. Lt. Fl.(3) 15 sec. 30M. Brown W.Tr. 57m. Obsc. 070°-080°RC.
BORNDIEP. Lts. Fl.(5)Y. 20 sec. mark tide gauges 4.2M. NNW and 7.5M. SW.
BALLUMERBOCHT. Lt. Iso.R. 4 sec. 4M. Col. 5m.
MOLENGAT TIDEGAUGE. Lt. Fl.(5)Y. 20 sec. Y. Tr.
NES NIEUWE VEERDAM HEAD. Lt. Iso. 6 sec. 8M. Hut. 2m.
REEGEUL R3 Lt. Iso. G. 4 sec. G. port.
R5 Lt. Q.G. G. Post.
R7 Lt. L.Fl. G. 8 sec. G. Post.
MG28-R1 Lt. Q(6)+L.Fl. 15 sec.� on B.Bn.Y.top ᘩᒲᒲ
KG11 Lt. Fl.G. 2 sec. G. Post.
KG17 Lt. L.Fl.G. 8 sec. G. Post.
KG21 Lt. L.Fl.G. 5 sec. G. Post.

KG24 Lt. Iso R. 4 sec. R. Post.
KG30 Lt. Q.R. R. Pile.
KG32 Lt. Q.R. R. Post.
DG25 Lt. Q.G. G. Post.
KG37 Lt. L.Fl.G. 8 sec. G. Post.
DG29 Lt. L.Fl.G. 5 sec. G. Post.
DG33 Lt. Iso.G. 4 sec. G. Post.
DG38 Lt. Q.R. R. Post
HOLWERD. FERRY PIER HEAD. Lt. Oc. 6 sec. 6M. Col. R. Top 7m.

FREISCHE ZEEGAT
SCHIERMONNIKOOG. 53°29.2'N, 6°09.0'E. Lt. Fl.(4) 20 sec. 28M. Tr. (R. to seaward) 43m. also F.W.R. W.15M. R.12M. 28m. W.210°-221°; R.221°-230°. Lt. Fl.(5)Y. 20 sec. 7M. WNW.
ROODE HOOFD VS1. Lt. L.Fl.G. 7 sec. G. Pile.
VS3 Lt. Iso.G. 4 sec.
GROOTE SIEGE VS2. Lt. L.Fl.R. 7 sec. R. pile.
VS5 Lt. Fl.G. 4 sec. G. pile.
VS4 Lt. Fl.R. 4 sec. R. Pile.
VS7 Lt. L.Fl.G. 7 sec. G. pile.
FERRY PIER HEAD. Lt. F.
TIDEGAUGE. Lt. Fl.(5)Y. 20 sec. Pole.

LAUWERSOOG.
Tel: Port (05193) 9023. Locks: (05193) 9043.
Radio—Port: VHF Chan. 9. Mon. 0600-1700. Tues.-Wed. 0800-1700. Thurs-Sat. 0700-1500.
Radio—Locks: VHF Chan. 22. May-Sept: Mon.-Fri. 0700-2000. Sat. 0700-1900. Sun. 0900-1200, 1400-1830. Oct.-Apr. Mon.-Fri. 0700-1800. Sat. 0700-1700.
W MOLE HEAD. Lt. F.G. 3M. Col. (in fog F.Y.). Horn (2) 30 sec. Lts. Fl.Y. 10 sec. mark Firing Range limit 2M. ENE, Lts. Fl.R. when firing taking place.
E MOLE HEAD. Lt. F.R. 4M. Col.
MOLE HEAD. Lt. F.R.
LOCKS LEAD-IN JETTY. Lt. Iso. 4 sec. Also F.W. Lt.
BRAKZAND CHANNEL. Marked by R. & G. Lts.

ZOUTKAMP
N TRAINING WALL. F. & F.R. Lts shown from Lock.

GERMANY

Fly Flag 'Q' only if coming from outside the EEC or Scandinavia.
Fly 3rd Sub. pennant if passing through Kiel Canal without visiting Germany.
Report to Customs on arrival at Borkum, Norderney, Norddeich, Wilhelmshaven, Bremerhaven or Cuxhaven.
Registration Document and Charter Document.
Certificate of Competence for VHF R/T.
Passports.
Yacht Dues; Payable at either end of Kiel Canal.
Insurance Certificate.
Carry Int. Regs. for Preventing Collisions at Sea, German Collision Regs. and Rules for Kiel Canal even if you do not read German.
Treat the Elbe with great respect at night and on Ebb in westerly winds.
If under power and sail — Cone **MUST** be displayed.
German Tourist Office, 65 Curzon Street, London W1Y 7PE. Tel: 071-495 3990.
Entry by Road. Car and craft must be fully insured. Max. length of tow 18m. Temporary importation 12 months.
The North and West Frisian Islands have been designated a National Park. All vessels should keep to the buoyed and marked channels and fairways at half tide or less. (The channel width may vary from 25m. to 2M. due to bottom conditions.) Anchor anywhere at the side of the fairway provided you remain afloat at LW. Landing limited to designated places.

DIE EMS.

Tel: Pilots (04921) 24000. Telex: 27882
LOTSEN D. Reporting System. Tel: (04921)
8021. Telex: 27939.
Radio: Die Ems Information Service. VHF
Chan. 15, 18, 20, 21. H24. Broadcasts ev.
H+50 in German.

Radio—Port:	Westerems/	
	Randzel Gat	Chan. 18.
	Hubertgat/	
	Alte Ems	Chan. 18.
	Lt.By. 35-57	Chan. 20.
	Lt.By. 57-Lt.By. 86	Chan. 21.
	Lt.By. 86 to Leer	
	or Papenburg	Chan. 15.
	Emden Lock	Chan. 13.
	Nesserland Lock	Chan. 13.
	Jann-Berghaus	
	(Leer) Br.	Chan. 15.
	Leer Lock	
	(0700-2300)	Chan. 13.
	Freisen (Weener) Br.	Chan. 15.
	Papenburg Lock	Chan. 13.

Radio—Pilots: Chan. 12 H24. **Pilot Vessel:**
2182 1665 kHz VHF Chan. 16, 9.

HUBERTGAT TIDE GAUGE Lt. Fl.(5)Y. 20 sec.
5M. Y. Tr

DEUTSCHE BUCHT, EMS, JADE, WESER AND ELBE APPROACHES.

Reporting system VHF Chan. 79, 80, also
situation reports on VHF Chan. 79, 80, ev
H+00 for shipping, obstructions, wind, tide
and weather. Deutsche Bucht Pilots
(54°10.7'N 7°26.0'E) Tel: (04421) 202 027.
Telex: 253357 WHSMS D. Radio—VHF Chan.
16, 13, 9, 72. (Helicopter Service). Die Weser

Deep Sea Pilots. Bremerhaven Tel:
(04744) 5649. Telex: 1631 BTX D (commence
msg. with BTX 047445649 0001+):
Brake Tel: (04401) 4475, 3702.
Die Elbe Deep Sea Pilots Tel: (04834) 1705
Telex: 1631 BTXD (commence msg. with
BTX 048341705 0001+).

BORKUM

BORKUM GROSSER 53°35.4'N, 6°39.8'E. Lt.
Fl.(2) 12 sec. 24M. Brown Tr. 63m. (Same
structure) F.W.R.G. W.19M. R.15M. G.15M.
46m. G.107.4°-109°; W.109°-111.2°; R.111.2°-
112.6°.
BORKUM KLEINER 53°34.8'N, 6°40.1'E. Lt. F.
30M. R.W. Tr. 32m., also Fl. 3 sec., also Q.(4)
10 sec. Fl. 088°-089.9°. F.089.9°-090.9°. Ldg.
sector for Hubergat Q.(4) 090.9°-093°. RC.
FISCHERBALJE 53°33.2'N, 6°43.0'E. Lt.
Oc.(2)W.R.G. 16 sec. W.16M., R.12M., G.11M.
W. Tr. R. Top on Piles. 15m. R.260°-313°;
G.313°-014°; W.014°-068°. Ldg. sector for
Fischerbalje R.068°-123°. Fog Detr. Lt.

SCHUTZHAFEN BORKUM

W MOLE INNNER HEAD Lt. F.R. 4M. R.W.
Mast. 8m. Storm signals.
E MOLE HEAD Lt. F.G. 4M. B.W. Mast. 10m.
HORSBORNGAT Lt. Fl.(5)Y. 20 sec. Post.
BINNEN-RANDZEL Lt. F.W.R.G. W.7M.,
R.5M., G.4M. B. Grey Tr. 14m. W.318°-345°;
R.345°-015.8°; W.015.8°-033.5°; R.033.5°-
077.3°; W.077.3°-098°; G. 098°-122°.
TIDEGAUGE Lt. Fl.Y. 4 sec.
CAMPEN 53°24.4'N, 7°01.0'E Lt. F. 30M.
R.W.G. Tr. 62m., also Fl. 5 sec., also Fl.(4) 15
sec. Fl. 126.5°-127°; F.127°-127.3°; Fl.(4)
127.3°-127.8°.

EEMS HAVEN Tel. No: 05961-6142. Telex: 53299 HSDDZ.
Radio—Port: VHF Chan. 14. H24.
Radar: Assistance on request to Verkeersdienst DGSM. Regio Noord. Tel: (05960) 11180. Fax: (05960) 10306. Telex: 53785. VHF Chan. 14 or DELFZIJL P.V. VHF Chan. 16, 6. also VHF Chan. 4. H24 on request of pilot.
Ldg.Lts. 175° (Front) Iso. 4 sec. 8m. (Rear) Iso. 4 sec. 14m.
W MOLE HEAD Lt. F.G. 3M. 8m. Horn(2) 20 sec.
E MOLE HEAD Lt. F.R. 3M. 8m.
Ldg.Lts. 195° (Front) Iso.R. 4 sec. 8m. (Rear) Iso.R. 4 sec. 11m.
DOEKEGAT KANAAL W SIDE Lt. Q. 6m.
JULIANAHAVEN S SIDE ENTRANCE Lt. F.R.
N SIDE ENTRANCE Lt. F.G.
EMMAHAVEN N SIDE ENTRANCE Lt. F.G.
S SIDE ENTRANCE Lt. F.R.
WILHELMINAHAVEN S SIDE ENTRANCE Lt. F.G. 6m.
N SIDE Lt. F.R.

DOEKEGAT
WERKHAVEN S MOLE HEAD Lt. F.R.
N MOLE HEAD Lt. F.R.
TIDE GAUGE Lt. Fl.Y. 4 sec. 7M. Y. Tr. Also Tide Gauge ×2 Fl.(5)Y. 20 sec.

DELFZIJL Tel. No: (05960) 14966.
Telex: 53299 HSDDZ. (Pilots: (05960) 14988. Fax: (05960) 30424. Telex: 53785 DLWNO.
Radio—Port: Call sign Havendienst Delfzijl. VHF Chan. 14. Eemskanal Lockmaster's Office. VHF Chan. 11. H24 Mon.-Sat. Tel: 05960-13293.
WEIWERDER BRIDGE. VHF Chan. 22. Mon.-Sat. 0600-1400 otherwise Delfzijl. Tel: 05960-14116.
Heemskes Bridge c/s Delfzijl. Tel: (05960) 18700, 14966. VHF Channel 22. Mon. 0600-Sat. 1400. Other times contact Port Office on Chan. 14.
Radio—Pilots: MF 2182, 2391 for Dutch vessels, 1657 kHz. VHF Chan. 6, 16. Pilot Office. VHF Chan. 14 Cont. outward Chan. 6 inward.
Entry Signals: R. flag/R.Lt. = Entry prohibited.
R. flag/3 R.Lt. in △ = Sluicing at Eemskanaal Lock through gates.
B. flag/3 R.Lt. in △ over G.Lt. = Sluicing at Lock through draining sluices.
TIDE GAUGE Lt. Fl.(5)Y. 20 sec. Y. Pile.

ZEEHAVEN KANAAL
JETTY Lt. Q.
E ENTRANCE W MOLE HEAD Lt. F.G.
E MOLE HEAD Lt. F.R. Horn 15 sec.In fog F.Y. 〜〜〜
Ldg.Lts. 203° (Rear) F.R. No. 2A (Common Front) Q.R.
Ldg.Lts. 202°(Rear) F.R. 6m. 087°-117°.
No. 1A Lt. Fl.G. 2 sec.
No. 1B Lt. Fl.G. 5 sec.
No. 2B Lt. Fl.R. 5 sec.
No. 3 Lt. Fl.G. 5 sec.
No. 4 Lt. Fl.R. 5 sec.
No. 5 Lt. Fl.G. 2 sec.
No. 6 Lt. Fl.R. 5 sec.
No. 7 Lt. Q.G.
No. 8 Lt. Fl.R.
No. 9 Lt. Fl.G. 5 sec.
No. 10 Lt. Fl.R. 5 sec.
No. 11 Lt. Fl.G. 2 sec.
No. 12 Lt. Fl.(2)R. 2 sec.
No. 13 Lt. Fl.G. 5 sec.
No. 14 Lt. Fl.R. 2 sec.
No. 15 Lt. Fl.G. 5 sec.
No. 16 Lt. Fl.R. 5 sec.
No. 17 Lt. Q.G.
No. 18 Lt. (Eemskanal Lock SE).
No. 19 Lt. Fl.G. 2 sec.
No. 20 Lt. (Eemskanal Lock NW). F.G.
No. 21 Lt. (Balkenhaven E). Fl.G. 5 sec. Marina Entrance.
No. 23 Lt. (Balkenhaven W). Q.G.

KNOCK 53°20.4'N, 7°01.5'E Lt.F.W.R.G. W.12M., R.9M.,G.8M. Tr. 28m. W.270°-299°;R.299°-008.3°; G.008.3°-023°; W.023°-026.8°; R.026.8°-039°; W.039°-073°; R.073°-119°; W.119°-154°.
WYBELSUM Lt. F.W.R. W.6M., R.4M., R.W. Tr. 16m. W.295°-320°; R.320°-024°; W.024°-049°.

LOGUM
Ldg.Lts. 53°20.2'N, 7°08.0'E; 075°12' (Front) Oc.(2) 12 sec. 12M. R.W. Mast. 16m. (Rear) Oc.(2) 12 sec. 12M. R.W. Mast. 28m.

EMDEN
Ldg.Lts. 53°20.1'N, 7°12.2'E; 087°36' (Front) Oc. 5 sec. 12M. Mast. 14m. (Rear) Oc.5 sec. 12M. Mast. 30m.

OUTER HARBOUR
E PIER HEAD Lt. F.G. 5M. R.B. Tr. 7m.
W PIER HEAD Lt. F.R. 4M. R. Tr. 10m. Horn Mo(ED) 30 sec.
LOCK ENTRANCE W END N SIDE Lt. F.R. 1M. Post. 7m. 335°-095°.

S SIDE Lt. F.G. 1M. Post. 7m. 035°-155°.
E END N SIDE Lt. F.G. 1M. Post. 7m.
215°-335°.
S SIDE Lt. F.R. 1M. Post. 7m. 155°-275°.
NEUER BINNENHAFEN RO-RO TERMINAL
Lt. Iso. 4 sec. Dolphin.
OLHAFEN Lt. F. Dolphin.
NEUER BINNENHAFEN OUTER DOLPHIN Lt.
V.Q.(9) 10 sec. X on Y.B. dolphin.
PETKUM Lt. F.G. 1M. Dolphin 5m.
DITZUM ENTRANCE W SIDE Lt. F.G. ∆ on
dolphin.
E SIDE. Lt. F.R.

OLDERSUM
W MOLE HEAD Lt. F.R. 5M. R.W. Mast 6m.
E MOLE HEAD Lt. F.G. 3M. G.W. Mast 6m.
TIDEGAUGE Lt. Fl.Y. 4 sec. 5M. 9m.
108 Lt. Fl.(2)R. 9 sec. 3M. R. Tripod 5m.

LEDA
Ldg.Lts. 116°24' (Front) Iso. 4 sec. I.M.R.W.
mast 5m. (Rear) Iso. 4 sec. 1M. R.W. mast
6m.
No. 1 Lt. Fl.(2)G. 9 sec.
No. 2 Lt. Fl.R. 4 sec. 2M. R. mast. 5m.
No. 5 Lt. Fl.G. 4 sec. 1M. G. mast. 5m. Lts
shown upstream.
KIRCHBORGUM No. 121. Lt. Fl.(2)G. 9 sec.
Lts. shown upstream to Papenburg.

OSTER EMS
PLATFORM Lt. Mo(U) 15 sec.
LIEY Lt.Fl.Y. 4 sec. 3M. Y. Pole. 15m. Tide
Gauge
RESEARCH PLATFORM Lt. Mo(U) 15 sec.
9M. Mast on R.Y. Platform. 24m. Horn Mo(U)
30 sec.
TW/EMS. Lt.F. 54°10.0'N, 6°20.8'E. Oc. 5 sec.
17M. 12m. Racon. Horn Mo.(EM) 30 sec.
H24.
DEUTSCHE BUCHT 54°10.7'N, 7°26.0'E Lt.V.
Oc.(3) 15 sec. 17M. R. Hull. 12m. RC Racon.
Horn Mo(DB) 30 sec.

NORDERNEY
NORDERNEY 53°42.6'N, 7°13.8'E Lt. Fl.(3) 12
sec. 23M. R. Tr. 59m. Fishing harbour.
Ldg.Lts. 274°30' **W MOLE HEAD** (Front) Oc.
W.R. 4 sec. W.7M., R.4M. R.W. Tr. 10m.
W.062°-093°; R.093°-259.5°; W.259.5°-289.5°;
R.289.5°-062°. (Rear) Oc. 4 sec. 7M. Mast.
18m.
BALTRUM GROYNE HEAD Lt. Oc. W.R.G.
6 sec. W.6M., R.4M., G.3M. Mast 7m.
G.082.5°-098°; W.098°-103°; R.103°-082.5°.

NORDDEICH
W TRAINING WALL HEAD. Lt. F.G. 4M. R.W.
∆Tr. 8m. 327°-237°.
E TRAINING WALL HEAD Lt. F.R. 4M. Tr. 8m.
021°-327°,
Ldg.Lts. 144° (Front) Iso.W.R. 6 sec. W.6M.,
R.4M. Mast 6m. R.078°-122°; W.122°-150°.
(Rear) Iso. 6 sec. 6M. Mast. 9m.
Ldg.Lts. 350° (Front) Iso.W.R. 3 sec. W.6M.,
R.4M. Mast 5m. W.340°-022.5°;
R.022.5°-098°. (Rear) Iso. 3 sec. 6M. Mast. 8m.
Ldg.Lts. 170° (Front) Iso. 3 sec. 10M. O on
Grey Mast 12m. (Rear) Iso. 3 sec. 10M. Mast.
23m.
AERO Lt. Fl. 1.5 sec.
JUIST AERO Lt. Fl. 5 sec.
NESSMERSIEL MOLE N HEAD Lt. Oc. 4 sec.
5M. Mast 6m.

LANGEOOG
W MOLE HEAD Lt. Oc.W.R.G. 6 sec. W.7M.,
R.4M., G.3M. R. Mast 8m. G.064°-070°;
W.070°-074°; R.074°-326°; W.326°-330°;
G.330°-335°; R.335°-064°. Horn Mo(L) 30 sec.
(sounded 0730-1800).

BENSERSIEL
E TRAINING WALL HEAD Lt. Oc. W.R.G.
6 sec. W.5M., R.3M., G.2M. R.W. Mast 6m.
G.110°-119°; W.119°-121°; R.121°-110°.
Ldg.Lts. 138° (Front) Iso. 6 sec. 9M. Mast
7m. (Rear) Iso. 6 sec. 9M. Mast. 11m.
W MOLE HEAD Lt. F.G. 3M. Mast 5m.
E MOLE HEAD Lt. F.R. 4M. Mast 5m.
SPIEKEROOG Lt. F.R. 4M. Tr. 6m. 197°-114°.
TIDEGAUGE Lt. Fl.Y. 4 sec. Y.B. Pile.

NEUHARLINGERSIEL
TRAINING WALL HEAD Lt. Oc. 6 sec. 5M.
Mast 6m.
CAROLINENSIELER BALJE LEITDAMM. Lt.
L. Fl. 8 sec. 6M. G. Post. 7m.
HARLESIEL N MOLE HEAD Lt. Iso. R. 4 sec.
7M. Mast 6m.

RIVER JADE
Jade/Weser Pilots: Tel: (04421) 41900..
Fax: (04421) 41223. Telex: 253467.
Jade Reporting System.
Tel: (04421) 26311/18. Fax: (04421) 24037.
Telex: 253407.
Radio: Die Jade:
Wilhelmshaven. VHF Chan. 16, 11.
Wilhelmshaven Lock. VHF Chan. 16, 13.
Mon-Fri. 0500-1730. Sat. 0530-1500.
Sun & Hols 0700-1500.
Jade Revier. VHF Chan. 20, 63.

Jade Radar I. VHF Chan. 16, 63.
Jade Radar II. VHF Chan. 16, 20.
BRIDGES. VHF Chan. 11.
Jade Information Broadcasts ev. H+10 in
German. VHF Chan. 20.

WANGEROOGE. W END. 53°47.4'N, 7°51.5'E.
Lt. Fl.R. 5 sec. 23M. R.W. Tr. 60m. Same
structure. F.W.R.G. W.15M. R.11M. G.10M.
24m. R.002°-011°; W.011°-023°; G.023°-055°;
W.055°-060.5°; R.060.5°-065.5°;
W.065.5°-071°; G. (18M) 137°-142.5°;
W.(22M) 142.5°-152°. Ldg. Sector R. (17M)
152°-157.5° RC.
W BREAKWATER HEAD. Lt. F.R. 4M. R. mast.
3m.
O-DAMN. Lt. F.G. 5M. G. mast and lantern
3m.
AERO. Lt. Fl. 3 sec. 16m. Occas.

WANGEROOGE FAHRWASSER

MELLUMPLATE. Lt. 53°46.3'N, 8°05.6'E. Lt. F.
24M. R.W. sq. Tr, round base, 27m. also Fl.
4 sec. Fl. (4) 15 sec. Oc. W.R.G. 6 sec., Mo(A)
7.5 sec., Mo(N) 7.5 sec., Oc.R. 000°-006°;
Oc. 006°-037.6°; Oc. G. 037.6°-113.7°;
Fl. 113.7°-114.9°; Mo(A) 114.9°-115.7° Ldg.
sector, F. 115.7°-116°; Ldg. sector for outer
part of Wangerooge Fahrwasser, Mo(N)
116°-116.9°; Ldg. sector, Fl.(4)
116.9°-118.1°; Oc. R. 118.1°-168°;
Oc. 168°-183.5°; Oc. R. 183.5°-212°;
Oc. 212°-266°; Oc. R. 266°-280°;
Oc. 280°-000°; Helicopter landing platform.
MINSENER OOG. BUHNE A. N END.
53°47.3'N, 8°00.4'E. Lt. F. W.R.G. W.13M.
R.10M. G.9M. Sq. masonry Tr. 16m.
R.050°-055°; W.055°-130°; G.130°-138°;
W.138°-158°; R.158°-176°; W.176°-268°;
G.268°-303°; W.303°-050°.
OLDOOG, BUHNE C. 53°45.4'N, 8°01.4'E. Lt.
Oc. W.R.G. 4 sec. W.13M. R.10M. G.9M. B.W.
col. with sq. platform. W.153°-180°;
G.180°-203°; W.203°-232.5°; R.232.5°-274°;
W.274°-033°. Fog Det. Lt.
SCHILLIG. 53°41.8'N, 8°01.7'E. Lt. Oc.W.R. 6
sec. W.15M. R.12M. B.W. Tr. 15m.
W.195.8°-221°; R.221°-254.5°;
W.254.5°-278.3°.
HOOKSIELPLATE CROSS. Lt. Oc. W.R.G.
3 sec. W.7M. R.5M. G.4M. W.R. Tr. 25m.
R.345°-358.8°; W.358.8°-001.8°;
G.001.8°-012.4°; W.012.4°-020.5°;
R.020.5°-047.3°; W.047.3°-061.9°;
G.061.9°-079.7°; W.079.7°-092.5°;
R.092.5°-110.5°. Fog Det. Lt.
TOSSENS. 53°34.5'N, 8°12.4'E. Ldg. Lts.
146°. (Front) Oc. 6 sec. 20M. B.W. Tr. R.
lantern 15m. (Rear) Oc. 6 sec. 20M. R. Tr.
with three galleries. 51m. Helicopter
platform above lantern.

VOSLAPP. 53°37.3'N, 8°06.8'E. Ldg. Lts.
164°30'. (Front) Iso. 6 sec. 24M. R.W. Tr.
15m. ⌇ (Rear) Iso. 6 sec. 27M. W.R. Tr.
60m. Cross light F. W.R.G. W.9M. R.6M.
G.5M. same structure. 20m. W.200°-228°;
G.228°-248°; W.248°-269°; R.269°-310°.
NIEDERSACHSENBRUCKE. Ldg. Lts. 298°
(Front) F. 4M. W.R. Δ on Tr. 10m. Occas.
(Rear) F. 4M. W.R. ▽ on Tr. 13m. Occas.
JETTY. OFF N END. Fog signal on Dolphin
Horn Mo(IG) 30 sec.
ECKWARDEN. 53°32.5'N, 8°13.1'E Ldg. Lts.
154°.
SOLTHORNER WATT. (Front) Iso. W.R.G.
3 sec. W.19M. W.12M. R.9M. G.8M. R.W. Tr.
15m. R.346°-348°; W.348°-028°; R.028-052°;
W.(intens)052°-054°; Ldg. sector,
G.054°-067.5°; W.067.5°-110°; G.110°-152.6°;
W.(intens)152.6° — across fairway, with
undefined limit on E side of Ldg. line (Rear)
Iso. 3 sec. 21M. R. pyramidal Tr. and lantern
41m.
TANKER DISCHARGE JETTY N END. Fog
signal. Horn Mo(ML) 40 sec.
S END. 53°37.3'N, 8°08.6'E. Horn Mo(ML)
40 sec.
NWO TANKER PIER. N END. Fog signal.
Horn Mo(L) 30 sec.
ARNGAST. 53°28.9'N, 8°11.0'E. Lt. F.W.R.G.
W.21M. W.10M. R.16M. G.17M. G.7M. R.W.
Tr. 2 galleries 30m. Also Fl.W.G. 3 sec. Fl.(2)
9 sec. Oc. 6 sec. F.135°-142°. F.G.142°-150°;
F.150°-152°. F.G.152°-160.3°;
F.G.161.8°-174.6°. Fl.G.174.6°-175.5°. Fl.
(20M.) 175.5°-176.4°.; Oc. 176.4°-177.4°. Ldg.
sector. Fl.(2) 177.4°-180.5°. F.R. 180.5°-191°.
F.191°-198.3°. F.199.8°-213°. F.R. 213°-225°.
F.(10M.) 286°-303°. F.G. (7M.) 303°-314°.

WILHELMSHAVEN

NEUER VORHAFEN. 53°31.9'N, 8°09.7'E.
Ldg.Lts. 207°48'. (Front) Iso. 4 sec. 11M. B.
mast R. Lantern 17m. Lock Signals (Rear)
Iso. 4 sec. 11M. Y. Bldg. 23m.
W MOLE. HEAD. Lt. Oc. G. 6 sec. 4M. G.
mast 15m.
E MOLE. HEAD. Lt. Oc. R. 6 sec. 5M. R. mast
15m.
CROSS LIGHT. Oc. W.G. 3 sec. W.8M. G.5M.
Tr.12m. W.180°-235°; G.235°-271.5°;
W.271.5°-036°; G.036°-050°. Sig. Stn.
FLUTHAFEN. N MOLE. HEAD. Lt. F.W.G.
W.6M. G.3M. G. Tr. 9m. W.216°-280°;
G.280°-010°; W.010°-020°; G.020°-130°.
FLUTMOLE HEAD. Lt. F.R. 5M. R. mast on
platform 6m.
ALTERVORHAVEN. N MOLE HEAD. Lt. F.G.
3M. B. mast 6m.
S MOLE HEAD. Lt. F.R. 4M. R. mast 5m. Sig
Stn. F.W.R. and G. Lts. are shown in the
docks. Fog Det. Lt. close by.

RIVER WESER

Pilots. Tel: (0471) 42220. Fax: (0471) 413813.
Telex: 238605 WELTS D.
Radio-Pilots: VHF Chan. 6. 16 MF1665
2182kHz.
Reporting System:
Wasser und Schiffahrtsamt. Bremerhaven.
Tel: (0471) 48350. Fax: (0471) 4835200.
Telex: 238598.
Wasser und Schiffahrtsamt Bremen. Tel:
(0471) 555061. Fax: (0421) 553836.
Telex: 244837.
Bremerhaven Weser Revier

Weser Lt. By./No: 19 Lt. By. (inward)	Ch. 22
No: 19 Lt. By./No: 1 Lt. By. (outward)	Ch. 22
Schlusseltonne/Nordergrunde/	
No: 16-16A Lt By. (inward)	Ch. 22
No: 16-16A Lt. By./	
No: AI Lt. By. (outward)	Ch. 22
No: 19 Lt. By./No: 37 Lt. By.	Ch. 2
No: 37 Lt. By./No: 53 Lt. By.	Ch. 4
No: 53 Lt. By./No: 63 Lt. By.	Ch. 7
No: 63 Lt. By./No: 58 Lt. By.	Ch. 5
No: 58 Lt. By./No: 79 Lt. By.	Ch. 82
No: 79 Lt. By./No: 93 Lt. By.	Ch. 21
Bremen Weser Revier	
No: 93 Lt. By./No: 113 Lt. By.	Ch. 19
Hunte/Elsfleth	Ch. 19
No: 113 Lt. By./Lemwerder	Ch. 78
Lemwerder/Bremen	Ch. 81
Bremen Hunte Revier	
No: 1 Lt. By./AI Lt. By. (inward)	Ch. 22
Bremerhaven Front Lt. (outward)	Ch. 7
No: 56 Lt. By./Blexen (inward)	Ch. 5
No: 93 Lt. By. (outward)	Ch. 21
No: 93 Lt. By. (inward)	Ch. 19
Elsfleth Nautical School (outward)	Ch. 19
No: 111 By.	Ch. 19
Moorlosen Church	Ch. 81
Elsfleth/Oldenburg	Ch. 17
No: 1/A1 Lt. By.	Ch. 80

DIE WESER & DIE HUNTE RADAR STATIONS

Aussenweser
Alte Weser Radar Ch. 22. Neue Weser Lt. F.
to By. 21.
Alte Weser: Schlusseltonne By. to By.
16a/A16.
Hohe Weg Radar 1 Ch. 02 By. 19H/Rede to
By. 27; 2 Ch. 02 By. 27 to By. 37.
Robbenplate Radar 1 Ch. 04 By. 37 to By. 47;
2 Ch. 04 By. 47 to By. 53.
Blexen Radar Ch. 07 By. 53 to By. 63.
Unterweser
Luneplate Radar 1 Ch. 05 By. 63 to By. 58; 2
Ch. 82 By. 58 to By. 69.
Dedesdorf Radar Ch. 82 By. 69 to By. 79.
Sandstedt Radar Ch. 21 By. 79 to By. 87.
Harriersand Radar 1 Ch. 21 By. 87 to By. 93.
Harriersand Radar 2 Ch. 19 By. 93 - Km. 32.
Elsflether Sand Radar Ch. 19 Km. 32 - By. 113.
Ronnebeck Radar Ch. 78. By 113 - By 119.

Ritzelbuttelar Sand Radar Ch. 78. By. 119 -
By. 125. Schonebecker Sand Radar Ch. 78.
By. 125 - Km. 15. Ochtumer Sand Radar
Ch. 81. Km. 15 - Km. 11. Seehausen Radar
Ch. 81. Km. 11 - Km. 8 Lankenau Radar
Ch. 81. Km. 8 - Km. 4.
Weser Information Broadcasts (in German)
for visibility, weather, tides, obstructions
and shipping ev. H + 20 on VHF Chan. 2, 4,
5, 7, 21, 22, 82 by Bremerhaven Weser
Rivier; ev. H + 30 on Chan. 19, 78, 81 by
Bremen Weser Rivier and Chan. 17 by
Bremen Hunte Rivier.
Vessels in Die Hunte and/or approaching
Hunte Barrage listen and report on VHF
Chan. 10.
Numerous Groynes extend 340m. into River
Weser marked by Spar Bys. Topmark E on W
bank and Spar Bys. Topmark W on E bank.
Die Hunte navigable up to Oldenburg 12M
above Elsfleth. Der Kustenkanal gives
access to Die Ems. Depths above Elsfleth
2.2m MLW. Add 3.5m at Elsfleth and 2.4m at
Oldenburg for MHW. Flood barrage
downstream of Elsfleth: navigable width
26m in central openings.

WESER. Lt.By. 53°54.2'N, 7°50.0'E. Lt. Iso.
5 sec. Pillar R.W.V.S. Racon.
ALTE WESER. 53°51.9'N, 8°07.6'E. Lt.
F.W.R.G. W.22M. R.19M. G.17M. R.W. Tr. G.
Lantern, B. base. 33m. W.288°-352°;
 R.352°-003°; W.003°-017°. Ldg. Sector for
Alte Weser, G.017°-045°; W.045°-074°;
G.074°-118°; W.118°-123°. Ldg. sector for
Alte Weser R.123°-140°; G.140°-175°;
W.175°-183°; R.183°-196°; W.196°-238°. Fog
Det. Lt. RC. Horn Mo(AL) 60 sec.
TEGELER PLATE. N END. 53°47.9'N,
8°11.5'E. Lt. F.W.R.G. W.27M. R.17M. G.16M.
R. Tr. projecting gallery and W. lantern R.
Roof. 21m. W.329°-340°; R.340°-014°;
W.014°-100°; G.100°-116°; R.119°-123°;
G.123°-144°; R.147°-264°. Also Oc. 6 sec.
21M. Vis.116°-119° Ldg. sector for Neue
Weser. 144°-147° Ldg. sector for Alte Weser.
HOHE WEG. NE PART. 53°42.9'N, 8°14.7'E.
Lt. F.W.R.G. W.19M. R.16M. G.15M.
R. 8-sided Tr. 2 galleries, G. lantern. 29m.
W.102°-138.5°; G.138.5°-142.5°;
W.142.5°-145.5°; R.145.5°-184°;
W.184°-278.5°. Fog Det. Lt.
ROBBENNORDSTEERT, W SIDE OF SAND.
53°42.2'N, 8°20.5'E. Lt. F.W.R. W.10M. R.7M.
R. ▯ on R. col. on tripod. 11m. W.324°-356°;
R.356°-089°; W.089°-121°.

ROBBENPLATE

53°40.9'N, 8°23.0'E. Ldg.Lts. 122°18' (Front)
Oc. 6 sec. 17M. R. tripod and gallery. 15m.
(Rear) Oc. 6 sec. 18M. R. sq. Tr. 3 galleries,
G. Lantern. 37m. Vis.116°-125.5°. Fog Det. Lt.

WREMER LOCH. 53.38.5′N, 8°25.1′E. Ldg. Lts. 140°48′ (Front) Iso. W.R.G. 6 sec. W.12M. R.9M. G.8M. B.W. col. G. lantern. G.131°-139°; W.139°-142.5°; R.142.5°-183°; W.183°-300°; G.300°-303°; ↯↯ (Rear) Iso. 6 sec. 14M. B.W. col. G. lantern 31m. ↯↯.

DWARSGAT. 53°43.2′N 8°18.5′E. Ldg.Lts. 320°48′. (Front) Iso. 6 sec. 15M. ⅃ on R.W. mast 16m. (Rear) Iso. 6 sec. 17M. ⅃ on R. W. mast 35m.

LANGLÜTJENNNORDSTEERT. Lt. Fl. Y. 4 sec. 6M. Y. Tr. on tripod 10m.

LANGLÜTJEN. 53°39.6′N, 8°23.1′E. Ldg. Lts. 304°36′. (Front) Oc. W.R.G. 6 sec. W.12M. R.9M. G.8M. B. mast, B.W. gallery 15m. G.141°-145°; W.145°-211°; R.299°-303°; W.303°-306°; G.306°-309°. ↯↯ (Rear) Oc. 6 sec. 15M. B. mast, W. gallery 31m.

IMSUM
53°36.4′N, 8°30.6′E. Ldg. Lts. 124°36′. (Front) Oc. 6 sec. 13M. R. tripod with gallery, W. top. 15m. (Rear) Oc. 6 sec. 16M. R. ▽ on W. Tr. 39m.
CROSS LIGHT. F.W.R. W.9M. R.6M. R.W. lantern on R. mast 15m. W.343°-001°; R.001°-091°; W.091°-111°. Fog Det. Lt.
SOLTHORN. 53.38.3′N, 8°27.4′E. Ldg. Lts. 320°36′. (Front) Iso. 4 sec. 13M. R.W. mast, 2 galleries 15m. (Rear) Iso. 4 sec. 17M. R.W. mast, 2 galleries. 31m.
HOFE. 53°37.1′N 8°29.8′E Ldg. Lts. 330°48′. (Front) Oc. 6 sec. 18M. R.O. on R.W. mast 15m. (Cross Lt.) F.W.R. W.6M. R.4M. on same structure. W.346°-006°; R.006-093°; W.093°-105°. (Rear) Oc. 6 sec. 18M. R.O. on R.W. mast 35m.
WEDDEWARDEN AIRPORT. 53°34.9′N, 8°33.78′E. Lt. Aero Oc. R. 7 sec. 10M. R.W. Tr. 77m.
WATTINSEL, BRINKAMAHOF. Lt. F.Y. 8M. R. col. and platform. Floodlit 13m. Vis. 332°-147°. Fog Lt.
FEDDERWARDERSIEL. Lt. F.W.R.G. W.6M. R.4M. G.3M. B. mast on pedestal 9m. G.144°-153.5°; W.153.5°-157°; Outer Ldg. sector, R.157°-171°; W.171°-308°; R.308°-320°; W.320°-323°. Inner Ldg. sector, G.323°-326.5°; W.326.5°-144°.

BREMERHAVEN
FISCHERIEHAFEN. Ldg.Lts. 150°48′. (Rear) Oc. 6 sec. 18M. 2 R. ▽ on R.W. Mast 45m. (Common Front) 53°31.9′N, 8°34.6′E. Oc. 6 sec. 18M. R. ▽ on W. Mast 17m. F.Y. on Y. pile 206°.535m.

GEESTEMUNDE Ldg.Lts. 053°54′. (Rear) Oc. 6 sec. 11M. R. ▽ o R.W. Mast 27m. Vis. on leading line only.
NORDSCHLEUSE. W SIDE. Lt. F.R. 5M. R. mast and yard 12m. Vis. 184°-150°. F.W. on dolphins in Osthafen 0.73M. NE. F.W. on dolphin in Kaiserhafen II 0.55M. ESE. Horn Mo(NN) 30 sec.
E SIDE. Lt. F.G. 4M. R.B. mast 15m. Vis. 330°-184°.
KAISERSCHLEUSE. W SIDE. Lt. F.R. 5M. R. mast 14m.
E SIDE. Lt. F.G. 4M. R. Tr. G. lantern 10m. Vis. 058°-141°. Bell (4) 10 sec.
NEUER HAFEN. S MOLE. Ldg.Lts. 006° (Front) Iso. 4 sec. 6M. R.W. conical Tr. 15m. Vis. 001°-033°. (Rear) Iso. 4 sec. 6M. Brown sq. Tr. G. lantern 34m. Vis. 331°-041°.
DIE GEESTE. VORHAFEN. N MOLE HEAD. Lt. F.R. 5M. R. Tr. gallery and lantern 15m. Vis. 245°-166°. Fog Det. Lt. Horn Mo(GG) 60 sec.
S MOLE. HEAD. Lt. F.G. 5M. R.B. Tr. G. lantern 15m. Vis. 355°-265°.
FISCHERIEHAFEN II. Ldg.Lts. 183°54′ (Front) F. 4M. △ on mast 8m. (Rear) F. 5M. ▢ on mast 11m.

FLAGBALGERSIEL
REITSAND. Ldg. Lts. 233°54′ (Front) Oc. 6 sec. 15M. R.W. Tr. 18m. (Common Rear) 53°29.9′N, 8°29.9′E. Oc. 6 sec. 17M. R.W. Tr. 2 R. galleries and spire. 36m. Ldg.Lt. 005°18′ (Front) Oc. 6 sec. 15M. R.W. Tr., 1 gallery and spire 18m. Fog Det. Lt. UQ Bu. points SE.
Lt. Fl.Y. 4 sec. 6M. on dolphin 5m.
MIDGARD. Ldg.Lts. 216°36′ (Front) F.Y. 7M. W. △ B. border on Grey beacon 12m. Vis. 206°-216.6°. Occas. (Rear) F.Y. 7M. W. ▽ B. border on Grey beacon 14m. Vis. 209°-218°. Occas.
There is a yacht harbour close S of Midgard Pier.

TURNING BASIN. Lts. in line 120° (Front) F.Y. 7M. W.R. mast 12m. Vis. 095°-150°. (Rear) F.Y. 7M. W.R. mast 14m. Vis. 098°-145°.
Lts. in line 120° (Front) F.Y. 7M. W.R. mast 12m. Vis. 078°-157°. (Rear) F.Y. 7M. W.R. mast 14m. Vis. 082°-152°.
NORDENHAM. TIDE GAUGE. Lt. Fl.Y. Y. Bn. Floodlit.
GROSSENSIEL. 53°28.2′N, 8°28.8′E Ldg. Lts. 209°42′ (Front) Iso. 4 sec. 10M. W. Tr. 16m. Vis. 096°-276°. (Rear) Iso. 4 sec. 10M. B. Tr. 25m.
NORDENHAM. 53°27.9′N, 8°29.4′E. Ldg. Lts. 355°54′. (Front) Iso. 4 sec. 16M. △ on R.W. mast 15m. (Rear) Iso. 4 sec. 19M. ▽ on R.W. mast 41m.

GROSSER PATER. 53°19.8'N, 8°30.4'E.
Ldg.Lts. 175°54' (Front) Iso. 4 sec. 19M. W.
Tr. 15m. Structure partially obscured by
house. (Rear) Iso. 4 sec. 22M. W.R. Tr. 34m.
GROSSENSIEL HAFEN. N MOLE. HEAD. Lt.
F.G. 1M. B. mast, G. lantern 11m.
ZIEGLERPLATE. TIDE GAUGE. Km. 56.0 Lt.
F.Y. 8M. R. mast on dolphin 8m. Floodlit. SV.
ᨆ.

REIHERPLATE. 53°25.6'N, 8°29.2'E. Ldg.Lts.
185°18' (Front) Oc. 6 sec. 15M. B.W. Tr. B.R.
Base 14m. ᨆ. R. Lt. on chimney 300m.
WNW Fog Det. Lt. 1M. NNE. (Rear) Oc.
6 sec. 16M. B. sq. Tr. 27m.
STROHAUSERPLATE. W. TIDE GAUGE. Km
50.5 Lt. F.Y. 8M. B. mast on dolphin. Floodlit
8m.
E. Km. 50.5 Lt. F.Y. 8M. R. mast on dolphin
8m.
RECHTENFLETHE. Lt. F.Y. 8M. Pile. Floodlit.
8m.
WILHELMSPLATE. TIDE GAUGE. Km. 42.9
Lt. F.Y. 8M. R. mast on dolphin. Floodlit. 8m.

SANDSTEDT. 53°21.7'N, 8°30.7'E Ldg.Lts
021° (Front) Oc. 6 sec. 15M. R. Δ on W. Tr.
15m. (Rear) Oc. 6 sec. 15M. R. ▽ on R.W. Tr.
23m. Fog Det. Lt. 380m. SSE. Fl.Y. on tide
gauge 0.6M. WNW. F.Y. 0.6M. WSW.
Lts. in line (Front) F.Y. 7M. R.W. Bn. 12m.
Mark turning area. Vis. 033.6°-128.6°. (Rear)
F.Y. 7M. R.W. Bn. 14m. Vis. 040.6°-125.6°.
Lts. in line (Front) F.Y. 7M. R.W. Bn. 12m.
Mark turning area (Rear) F.Y. 7M. R.W. Bn.
14m.

BRAKE
DIR. Lt. Dir Iso., W.R.G. 4 sec. W.9M. R.7M.
G.6M. W. tripod 15m. R.345°-352.5°;
W.(intens)352.5°-356°; G.356°-360° (4°). R.
light on chimney 0.65M. N.

OSTERPATER. 53°17.3'N, 8°29.8'E. Ldg Lts.
173°42' (Front). Iso. 4 sec. 12M. R. Tr. with
gallery 14m. Fog Det. Lt. near Radar Tr.
700m. N. (Rear) Iso. 4 sec. 15M. R. Tr. 21m.
HARRIERSAND. 53°19'N, 8°29.8'E Ldg. Lts.
007°36' (Front) Oc. 6 sec. 11M. W. Tr. 11m.
(Rear) Oc. 6 sec. 15M. R. Tr. 22m.
HARRIERPLATE. Lt. F.Y. 8M. R. mast on
dolphin. Floodlit. 8m.
Ldg. Lts. 187°36'. **WATERPLATE.** (Front) Oc.
6 sec. 9M. W. pyramidal Tr. 15m.
SOLTPLATE (Common Rear). Oc. 6 sec. 9M.
B. pyramidal Tr. 31m.
Ldg. Lts. 327°54' **HOHENZOLLERN** (Front)
Oc. 6 sec. 9M. W. Tr. 14m.
ELFSLETHER SAND. N END. Lt. F.Y. 8M. mast
5m. F.Y. Lts. mark the banks of Die Hunte.

FÄHRPLATE. TIDE GAUGE. Lt. F.Y. 8M. Y.
mast on dolphin. Floodlit. 8m.
Ldg. Lts. 178°42' **HOHENZOLLERN** (Front)
Iso. 4 sec. 9M. W. Tr. 14m. Fog Det. Lt.
STEMPELSAND (Rear) Iso. 4 sec. 9M. B.
pyramidal Tr. 22m.
FARGE. Km. 26.45. **E SIDE. TIDE GAUGE.** Lt.
F.Y. 7M. R. mast on dolphin. Floodlit 8m.

BERNE. Ldg. Lts. 147°54' (Rear) Oc. 6 sec.
15M. W.R. mast with gallery 22m. (Common
front) 53°11.8'N, 8°31.1'E. Oc. 6 sec. 15M.
W.R. mast 15m.

JULIUSPLATE. Ldg. Lts. 299°36' (Rear) Iso.
4 sec. 15M. W.R. mast 29m.

LEMWERDER. 53°10.3'N, 8°35.4'E. Ldg. Lts.
119°36'. (Front) Iso. 4 sec. 15M. W.R. mast
15m. (Rear) Iso. 4 sec. 15M. W.R. mast 26m.
Km. 21.4 **W SIDE. TIDE GAUGE** Lt. F.Y. 7M.
B. mast on dolphin. Floodlit 8m.
E AND W SIDES. Km. 21-17.5 Lt. 18 F.Y. 7M.
on masts 8m. The Lts. at Km. 20.8, 19.8 and
18.5 show 2 F.Y. (vert).

There is a yacht harbour at Lemwerder and
a yacht basin, depth 2.8m, at Lesum.

LESUM. MOLE. HEAD. Lt. Q(9)W. 15 sec.
6M. Y.B. Tr. 14m. Aero Al. Fl. W.G. 5 sec
(Occas.) 30m, 0.8M. S.
Km. 17.5-9.8 Lt. 62 F.Y. 7M. on masts 8m.
The Lts. at Km. 16.8, 14.5, 13 and 11.5 show
2 F.Y. (vert). Fog Det. Lt. close S. of Km. 17.
Obstruction Lt. close W. of Km. 13.

BREMEN
INDUSTRIESCHLEUSE. N MOLE HEAD. Lt.
F.R. 4M. R. Tr. 14m.
S MOLE HEAD. Lt. F.G. 4M. R.B. Tr. G.
Lantern 12m.
Km. 9.5-6.0 Lt. 21 F.Y. 7M. on masts 8m. The
light at Km. 8.5 shows 2 F.Y. (vert). Fog Det.
Lt. SE of Km. 9.
SEEHAUSEN OST. Km. 7.8. **NEUSTÄDTER
HAFEN. TRAINING WALL. W END.** Lt. Iso. R.
3 sec. 8M. R. Tr. 14m.
WEST. Km. 7.8 Lt. F.G. 7M. G. Tr. 14m. Vis.
103°-013°.
**NEUSTÄDTER HAFEN. APPROACH AND
TURNING BASINS.** Lts. 22 F.Y. 5M. on masts
8m. 125m. apart.
SCHLAGEN. Ldg. Lts. 304°42' (Front) F.Y. 8M.
mast 8m. Intens. 299.7°-309.7°. (Rear) F.Y. 8M.
B.W. mast 11m. Vis. 299.7°-309.7°.
LANKENAU. N. Km. 6.3 Lt. F.G. 3M. Δ on G.
mast 10m. S. Km. 6.1 Lt. F.R. 3M. R. mast 10m.

UBERSEEHAFEN. N. MOLE. HEAD. Lt. F.R. 5M. R. Tr. 15m.
S. MOLE HEAD. Lt. F.G. 9M. Grey Tr. G. roof 14m. Vis. 334°-304°. Horn (10) 60 sec. Reserve fog signal Bell (10) 60 sec.
Km. 5.8-Km. 2.25 E & W Sides. Lts. 25 F.Y. 7M. on W. masts 8m. The Lts. Km. 4.87 and 3.8 show 2 F.Y. (vert).

EUROPAHAFEN. TURNING BASIN. LTS IN LINE 224°. (Front) F.Y. 7M. W. mast 8m. (Rear) F.Y. 7M. B.W. mast 10m. SV Vis. 164°-284°.
N SIDE ENTRANCE. Km. 4.05 Lt. F.R. 3M. R. mast 13m.
S. MOLE. HEAD. Lt. F.G. 3M. G. mast 13m.
Lt. F.Y. 7M. W. mast. Floodlit 8m.

HELGOLAND. 54°11'N, 7°54'E.
Radio—Port: VHF Chan. 16, 67. Mon.-Sat. 0700-2100 on request.
Radio—Pilots: VHF Chan. 16, 13.
Inner Roads — Little shelter from strong W or E winds.

HELGOLAND. Lt. 54°11.0'N, 7°53.0'E. Fl. 5 sec. 28M. Brown Sq. brick Tr. B. lantern W. Balcony 82m.

CABLE AREA. Lt. Oc.(3) W.R.G. 8 sec. W.6M. R.4M. G.4M. W.R. mast 18m. W.179°-185°; R.185°-190°; W.190°-196°; W.239°-244°; G.244°-280°; W.280°-285°.

VORHAFEN. OSTMOLE. S ELBOW. Lt. Oc. W.G. 6 sec. W.7M. G.4M. G. post 5m. W.203°-250°; G.250°-109°. Fog Det. Lt.
HEAD. Lt. F.G. 4M. G. post 7m. Vis. 289°-180°. Horn (3) 30 sec. on R.W. Tr.
SUDMOLE. HEAD. Lt. Oc.(2)R. 12 sec. 4M. Grey post, R. lantern 7m. Vis. 101°-334°.

BINNENHAFEN. W. PIER. Ldg.Lts. 302°12' (Front) Oc. R. 6 sec. 7M. △ 8m. (Rear) Oc. R. 6 sec. 7M. ▽ on W.R. mast 10m.
S SIDE ENTRANCE. Lt. F.W.R. W.7M. R.5M. R. col. 5m. R.040°-238°; W.238°-270°. Fog Det. Lt. 500m SW.
N SIDE ENTRANCE. Lt. F.W.G. W.7M. G.4M. G. col. 5m. W.248°-254°; G.254°-102°.

DUNE. 54°10.9'N, 7°54.9'E. Ldg.Lts. 020° (Front) Iso. 4 sec. 11M. R. △ on framework structure 11m. (Rear) Iso. W.R.G. 4 sec. W.13M. R.11M. G.9M. R.W. Tr. 17m. Synchronized with front. G.010°-018.5°; W.018.5°-021°; R.021°-030°; G.106°-125°; W.125°-130°; R.130°-144°.
DUNENHAFEN. W MOLE. HEAD. Lt. F.R. 5M. R. col. 5m. Vis. 294°-172° (238°).

DIE ELBE
Pilots & Reporting System:
Tel: (04852) 87295/87132. Mon.-Fri. 0730-1530.
Tel: (04852) 87295. After hours.
Telex: 28343 ELLOTS D.
Radio: VHF Chan. 16, 9 (8 for Pilot Vessels). Vessels over 50m. wishing to navigate the Elbe inform WSA Cuxhaven, Diechstrasse 12, 2190. Telex: 232205 24 h. before ETA.
Radar & Information Service:
River Elbe Approach. VHF Chan. 19.
Neuwerk Radar I. VHF Chan. 18.
Neuwerk Radar II. VHF Chan. 05.
Cuxhaven Radar. VHF Chan. 21.
Belum Radar. VHF Chan. 03.
Brunsbuttel Radar I. VHF Chan. 04.
Brunsbuttel Radar II. VHF Chan. 67.
Freiburg Radar I. VHF Chan. 18.
Freiburg Radar II. VHF Chan. 22.
Steindeich Radar. VHF Chan. 05.
Hetlingen Radar. VHF Chan. 21.
Information in English and German on navigational matters, weather, tides, etc. at every H+55 by Rivierzentrale Cuxhaven on Chan. 19, 18, 5, 21, 3 for E part Deutsche Bucht (approach to Belum Radar Sectors). Every H + 05 by Rivierzentrale Brunsbuttel on Chan. 4, 67, 18, 22, 5, 21 for Brunsbuttel to Hetlingen Radar Sectors.

ELBE. Lt. F. 54°00.0'N, 8°06.6'E. Iso. 10 sec. 17M. R. Hull and Lt. Tr. 12m. RC. Racon. Horn Mo(EL) 31 sec.

GROSSER VOGELSAND. 53°59.8'N, 8°28.7'E. Lt. Fl(3) 12 sec. 25M. Helicopter platform on R.W. Tr. 39m. Vis. 085.1°-087.1°. Also Iso. 3 sec. 26M. Vis. 087.1°-091.1°. Oc. 6 sec. 26M. Vis. 091.1°-095.1°. Fl.(4) 15 sec. 19M. Vis. 095.1°-101.9°. Fl.(4)R. 15 sec. 12M. Vis. 101.9°-105.1°. Fl.R. 3 sec. 15M. Vis. 113°-270°. Oc.(4)R. 18 sec. 9M. Vis. 322.5°-012°. Fog Det. Lt. RC. Horn Mo(VS) 30 sec.

NEUWERK. S SIDE. 53°55.0'N, 8°29.8'E. Lt. L. Fl.(3) W.R.G. 20 sec. Sq. brick Tr. with cupola. 38m. G.11M. 165.3°-215.3°; W.16M. 215.3°-238.8°; R.12M. 238.8°-321°; R.12M. 343°-100°.
GELB SAND TIDE GAUGE Lt. Fl.(5) Y. 20 sec.
MITTELPLATE. A Lt. F.R. 9M. R. dolphin 5m. F.G. on dolphin close by.

FRIEDRICHSKOOG. 54°00'N, 8°53'E.
Radio—Port: VHF Chan. 10. 2 h.-H.W.-2 h.
HARBOUR. Lt. F.W. 6M. B. 3 pile structure 7m. Horn Mo(F) 30 sec.
KLOTZENLOCH Lt. Fl.(5) Y. 20 sec. Y. Pile. Floodlit Tidegauge.

CUXHAVEN. 53°52'N, 8°42'E.
Tel: (04721) 38011. Telex: 232108 SNWCU D.
Radio—Port: VHF Chan. 12, 14, 16. H24.
Lt. 53°52.4'N, 8°42.6'E. F.W.R. W.8M. R.6M.
Dark R. round stone Tr. copper cupola 24m.
W.199.5°-245°; R.245°-285°; W.285°-290.3°.
Also Fl.(4) 12 sec. 290.3°-301°. Oc. 6 sec.
301°-310°. Fl.(5) 12 sec. 310°-318°. Fog Det.
Lt. Oc.(3)Y. on tidegauge 4M. NNW and
5.8M. N.R. Lt. on radio mast 3.2M. SW.

BAUMRÖNNE. Ldg.Lts. 151°12'. (Front) Fl.
3 sec. Iso. 4 sec. Fl.(2) 9 sec. Fl. 17M. 143.8°-
149.2°; Iso. 17M. 149.2°-154.2°. Fl.(2) 17M.
154.2°-156.7°.

ALTENBRUCH. 53°49.9'N, 8°45.5'E.
(Common Rear). Iso. 4 sec. 21M. B.W. Tr.
58m. Also Iso. 8 sec. 22M. Same structure
51m. Cross Lt. Oc. W.R. 3 sec. W.7M. R.5M.
Same structure 44m. W.201.9°-232.8°;
R.232.8°-247.2°; W.247.2°-254.6°.
53°50.1'N, 8°47.8'E. Ldg.Lts. 261° (Front) Iso.
8 sec. 19M. W.B. Tr. 19m. Common Front.
Also Iso. W.R.G. 8 sec. W.8M. R.9M. G.8M.
G.117.5°-124°; W.124°-135°; R.135°-140°.
WEHLDORF. 53°49.8'N, 8°48.2'E. Ldg.Lts.
130°48'. (Rear) Iso. 8 sec. 11M. W.B. Tr. 31m.

FERRY HARBOUR. W BREAKWATER. HEAD.
Lt. F.W.G. W.6M. G.3M. Col. G. Lantern 7m.
G.125°-349°; W.349°-125°.
PIER. HEAD. Lt. F.W.R. W.6M. R.4M. Col. R.
lantern 7m. R. 117°-336°; W.336°-117°.
YACHT HARBOUR. ENTRANCE. S SIDE. Lt.
F.W.R. 3M. Pile with R. platform 7m. W.056°-
120°; R.120°-272°; W.272°-295°. Shown 1/4-
31/10.
N SIDE. Lt. F.W.G. 3M. Pile with G. platform
7m. G.108°-340°; W.340°-108°. Shown 1/4-
31/10.

FISCHEREIHAFEN. W MOLE. HEAD. Lt.
F.W.G. W.4M. G.2M. Y. tripod, G. lantern 6m.
G.125°-344°; W.344°-125°.
E MOLE. HEAD. Lt. F.W.R. W.6M. R.4M. Y. Tr.
R. lantern 7m. W.008°-124°; R.124°-008°.

STEUBENHOFT. SE END. Lt. Oc.W.G. 4 sec.
W.5M. G.3M. G. Tr. 12m. G.122°-338°;
W.338°-122°.
TIDE GAUGE Lt. Fl.(5) Y. 20 sec. 084M. East.
AMERIKAHAFEN. MOLE. HEAD. Lt. F.R. 1M.
Grey Tr. 6m.
PIER III. HEAD. Lt. F.G. 1M. Grey Tr. 6m.
MEDEM. HADELNER KANAL. ENTRANCE.
Lt. Fl.(3) 12 sec. 5M. B. △ o platform with B.
Col. 6m.

BELUM. 53°50.1'N, 8°57.4'E. Ldg.Lts.
092°48'. (Rear) Iso. 4 sec. 18M. W.R. Tr. 45m.
(Common Front) 53°50.2'N, 8°56.2'E. Iso.
W.G. 4 sec. W.18M. G.10M. W.R. Tr. 23m. G.
S of 091°; W N of 091°. Also Iso. 4 sec. 18M.
same structure 23m.
OTTERNDORF. 53°49.6'N, 8°54.1'E. Ldg.Lts.
245°30' (Rear). Iso. 4 sec. 21M. W.R. Tr. 52m.
NORTHWARDS. TIDE GAUGE. Lt. Oc.(3)Y. ×
on Y. pile.

OSTE

OSTE BRIDGE. (Flood Barrage). 53°49'N,
9°02'E.
Tel: (04753) 422; Bridge (04752) 7121.
Radio: VHF Chan. 16, 69.
Request bridge opening VHF Chan. 69. From
Apr.-Sept. 1930-0730 and Oct.-Mar. H24
bridge opened by phone request only 1 h. in
advance.
**JUNCTION OF TRAINING DAMS OF DIE
ELBE AND DIE OSTE.** Lt. L.Fl. W.R.G. 8 sec.
W.7M. R.5M. G.4M. B.R. Tr. 11m. W.003°-
071°; G.071°-088°; W.088°-251°; G.251°-291°;
R.291°-003°. R. Lts. on 2 masts carrying wind
generators 5M. NNW.
BELUM OUTER DYKE. ROOT. Ldg. Lts.
129°54'. (Front) Iso. W.R. 6 sec. W.5M. R.3M.
W. mast 6m. W.091.5°-131°; R.131°-181.5°;
R.133°-181.5°. (Rear) F. 5M. R. Tr. 14m. Vis.
090°-180°.
LOCK. N SIDE. Lt. 2 F. 2M. 2 dolphins 5m.
S SIDE. Lt. 2 F. 2M. 2 dolphins 5m.

BALJE. 53°51.4'N, 9°02.7'E. Ldg.Lts. 081°.
(Front) Iso. W.G. 8 sec. W.17M. G.15M. W.R.
Tr. 24m. G.shore-080.5°; W.080.5°-shore.
(Rear) Iso. 8 sec. 21M. W.R. Tr. 54m. Also Oc.
W.R. 3 sec. W.5M. R.3M. W.180°-195°;
R.195°-215°; W.215°-223°.

BRUNSBUTTEL ELBE. Tel: (04852)
87265/87153. Telex: 28319 SMDKG D.
Radio—Port: VHF Chan. 11, 14, 16. H24.

DER NOORD-OSTSEE KANAL (KIEL CANAL)

OSTERMOOR. Tel: (04852) 8066.
Telex: 28347 EPORT D.
Radio—Port: Ostermoor. VHF Chan. 73. H24.
Breiholz. VHF Chan. 73. H24.
Radio—Pilots: (Elbe) Ostermoor. VHF Chan.
6, 9, 16. Breiholz. VHF Chan. 73.

BRUNSBÜTTEL KANAL
Vessels of not more than 50m. by 9m. by 3.1m. are Traffic Group 1. Speed limit 8 knots. Vessels with Pilot fly Flag H. Coasters without Pilot fly Flag N. Yachts without Pilots use Canal during Daylight only. Fly Flag N. Wait behind commercial vessels at locks. Moor only at Brunsbuttel Y. Hbr; Bridge at Duckerswisch ; Gieselau Lock; Obereider See; Borgstadt; Holtenau Y. Hbr. Water skiing is prohibited.
Vessels less than 300 GRT do not need a pilot.
Canal dues now paid only at Kiel-Holtenau Lock Kiosk. Have all vessel's documents ready for presentation.
Fuel available from B.P. Tiessen at Holtenau & Rensburg. English guide to Kiel Canal available from United Baltic Corporation, 21 Bury Street, London EC3. Tel: 071-283 1266.
Entrance Area: Signals shown from Canal Pilot House.

R. Lt.	=	No entry
W./R. Lt.	=	Prepare to enter.
G. Lt.	=	Vessels with pilot enter.
W./G. Lt.	=	Vessels without pilot enter.

Locks Signals

R. Lt.	=	No Entry.
W./R. Lt.	=	Prepare to enter.
G. Lt.	=	Vessels with pilot enter.
W./G. Lt.	=	Large vessels. Without pilot enter.
W./G./W. Lt.	=	Large vessels. Without pilot enter make fast on side of Lower W. Lt.
W. Lt.	=	Yachts may enter. (Reported as Isophase.)

Signals at Kiel are the same for entrance area and locks.
Sound signal for Neue Schleusen (Kiel) are only for piloted vessels. 3 sec. ev. 7 sec. enter right hand lock 2 sec. ev. 5 sec. enter Left hand lock.
Passage Signals. In Canal: 3 F.R. vert. = ALL vessels stop including yachts. Yachts may disregard all other signals.
Radio: Kiel Kanal I Chan. 13. Kiel Kanal II Chan. 2. Kiel Kanal III Chan. 3. Kiel Kanal IV (Holtenau Entrance) Chan. 12.
Information B'casts by Kiel Kanal II on VHF Chan. 2 at H+15, H+45 and Kiel Kanal III on VHF Chan. 3 at H+20, H+50 giving traffic reports weather, visibility. etc.

SCHLEUSENINSEL. 53°53.4′N, 9°08.5′E.
Ldg.Lts. 065°30′ (Front) Iso. 3 sec. Fl. 3 sec. 16M. R.W. Tr. 24m. Iso. to N of 063.3°. Fl. to

S of 063.3°. Oc.(3)Y. 12 sec. on tide gauge 1.2M. SSW. Lights are shown in Nord Ostsee Kanal.

INDUSTRIEGEBIET. 53°53.7′N, 9°09.9′E. (Rear) Iso. 3 sec. 21M. R.W. Tr. 46m.
ALTER HAFEN Ldg Lts. 012° (Front) Oc. (3) R. 10 sec. 2M. △ on mast 5m. (Rear) Oc. (3) R. 10 sec. 2M. ▽ on mast 7m.
ZWEIDORF. Lt. Oc.R. 5 sec. 3M. R. □ on W. framework Tr. 9m. Vis. 287°-107°. Fl.Y. 4 sec. on pile 400m. ESE.

ELBEHAFEN. 53°53.5′N, 9°10.1′E. Lts in line 000° (Front) L.Fl. 8 sec. 10M. W. ◇R. border on Grey mast 10m. (Rear) L.Fl.8 sec. 10M. W. ◇R. border on Grey mast 13m.
Lts in line 53°53.5′N, 9°11.2′E. 000° (Front) L.Fl. 8 sec. 10M. W. ◇R. border on Grey mast 10m. (Rear) L.Fl. 8 sec. 10M. W. ◇R. border on Grey mast 13m.

NEUE MÜNDUNG. S MOLE (MOLE 3). HEAD. Lt. 2 F.G. (vert.) 7M. W.B. Tr. G. lantern 15m. Vis. 275.5°-088.5°. Horn 10 sec. for the use of pilots.
N MOLE (MOLE 4). HEAD. 53°53.3′N, 9°07.6′E. Lt. F.W.R. (vert.) W.10M. R.8M. W.R. tripod 15m. R.275.5°-079°; W.079°-084°. Sig. Stn. Storm, port and pilotage signals.

ALTE MÜNDUNG. N MOLE (MOLE 2). HEAD. Lt. F.R. 4M. R. □ on tripod 14m. Vis. 278.5°-084.5°.
S MOLE (MOLE 1). HEAD. 53°53.3′N, 9°08.6′E. Lt. F.W.G. W.10M. G.6M. W.B. Tr. grey base 14m. G.264°-270.5°; W.270.5°-273°; G.273°-088°.

ST MARGARETHEN. Ldg.Lts. 311°48′. (Rear) Iso. 8 sec. 19M. R.W. Tr. 36m.

SCHEELENKUHLEN. 53°52.9′N, 9°15.7′E. (Common front) Iso. 8 sec. 18M. R.W. Tr. 20m. Fl.Y. 4 sec. on pile 380m. SSW.
Ldg.Lts. 089°12′. (Rear) Iso. 8 sec. 22M. R.W. Tr. 44m.

GLUCKSTADT. 53°48.4′N, 9°24.3′E. Ldg.Lts. 131°48′ (Front) Iso. 8 sec. 19M. W.R. Tr. 15m. (Rear) Iso. 8 sec. 21M. W.R. Tr. 30m. (Cross Lt.) Oc. W.R.G. 6 sec. W.4M. R.3M. G.2M. Same structure 15m. G.066°-085°; W.085°-107°; R.107°-114.5°.
OSTERENDE. 53°51.0′N, 9°20.5′E. Ldg.Lts. 115°48′. (Front) Iso. 4 sec. 11M. W.B. Tr. 20m. (Rear) Iso. 4 sec. 15M. W.B. Tr. 36m. Also L.Fl.W.R. 12 sec. W.7M. R.5M. Same structure 35m. R.034°-047°; W.047°-091.3; R.091.3°-104°.

HOLLERWETTERN. 53°50.5'N, 9°21.2'E.
Ldg.Lts. 340°30'. (Front) Iso. 4 sec. 19M. W.
sq. Tr. and dwelling with R. roof 21m.
BROKDORF. (Rear) Iso. 4 sec. 22M. W.R. Tr.
with 11m. mast 44m.

DIE STOR
STOR BRIDGE. 53°50'N, 9°24'E.
Radio: VHF Chan. 9, 16.

ENTRANCE. Ldg.Lts. 095°24'. (Front) Fl. 3
sec. 6M. R. Tr. 7m. Vis. 023.2°-123.3°. (Rear)
Fl. 3 sec. 6M. W. mast 12m. Vis. 024°-122.5°.
RHINPLATTE NORD. Lt. Oc.W.R.G. 6 sec.
W.6M. R.4M. G.3M. R. pedestal on dolphin
11m. G.122°-144°; W.144°-150°; R.150°-177°;
W.177°-122°. ⌇⌇
SÜDERELBE. S SIDE. WISCHHAFENER. Lt.
Oc.W.R.G 3 sec. W.4M. R.2M. G.2M. R.
pedestal 7m. G .086°-232.5°; W.232.5°-
236.5°; R.236.5°-266°; W.266°-086°.

RUTHENSAND
53°43.3'N, 9°25.5'E. Ldg.Lts. 161°36' (Front)
Oc.W.R.G. 6 sec. W.15M. R.12M. G.11M.
W.R. Tr. 15m. G.170°-176.1°; W.176.1°-177.6°;
R.177.6°-182°. Also Iso. 4 sec. 9M. Same
structure 11m. (Rear) Iso. 4 sec. 11M. W.R.
Tr. 30m.
RUTHENSTROM. Ldg.Lts. 196°54'. (Front)
Oc.G. 3 sec. 1M. Beacon 8m. (Rear) Oc.G. 3
sec. 1M. Beacon 11m.

GLUCKSTADT
N MOLE. Lt. Oc. W.R.G. 6 sec. W.8M. R.5M.
G.5M. W. Tr. 9m. R.330°-343°; W.343°-346°;
G.346°-145°; W.145°-150°; R.150°-170°.
HEAD. Lt. F.R. 4M. B. col. 5m.
S MOLE HEAD Lt. F.G.

KRAUTSAND
53°45.3'N, 9°23.3'E. Ldg.Lts. 302°42'. (Front)
Iso. 8 sec. 13M. R.W. Tr. and dwelling, B.
roof 20m. (Rear) Iso. 8 sec. 13M. W.R. 6-
sided framework Tr. 36m. Vis. 280°-310°.
RHINPLATTE SUD. Lt. L.Fl.W.R. 6 sec. W.5M.
R.3M. R. pedestal on dolphin 11m. R.065.2°-
170.5°; W.170.5°-329°; R.329°-341.4°;
W.341.4°-065.2°.
STEINDEICH. Lt. Oc.(2)W.R.G. 9 sec. W.9M.
R.6M. G.5M. W.R. Tr. 31m. R.299°-302°;
W.302°-305.8°; G.305.8°-316.2°; R.316.2°-
322.2°; W.322.2°-328°; G.328°-334.8°. Fog
Det. Lt. on tidegauge 280m. SE.

PAGENSAND
53°42.2'N, 9°30.3'E. Ldg.Lts. 134°12'. (Front)
Oc.W.R.G. 4 sec. W.12M. W.9M. R.6M. G.5M.
W.R. 6-sided Tr. and gallery 18m. R.345°-
356.5°; W.356.5°-020°; G.020°-075°. (Rear)

Oc. 4 sec. 13M. W.R. 6-sided Tr. with two
galleries 35m.

PAGENSAND NORD. Lt. Oc.(4)W.R.G. 15 sec.
W.7M. R.5M. G.4M. R.B. col. G. roof, stone
base 11m. W.044.2°-130.5°; R.130.5°-191.7°;
W.191.7°-276.7°; R.276.7°-324.5°; W.324.5°-
336°; G.336°-044.2°.

53°43.0'N, 9°29.4'E. Ldg.Lts. 345°18'. (Front)
Iso. 4 sec. 15M. W.R. Tr. 20m.
KOLLMAR. (Rear) Iso. 4 sec. 16M. W.R. Tr.
40m.
PAGENSAND MITTE. Lt. L.Fl.(2)W.R.G. 15
sec. W.9M. R.7M. G.5M. R.W. col. G. roof
11m. R.338°-346.5°; W.346.5°-104°; G.104°-
130°; W.130°-140°; R.140°-150°.
PAGENSAND SÜD. Lt. L.Fl.(4)W.R. 25 sec.
W.7M. R.5M. R.B. col. G. roof, stone base
11m. W.193°-157.5°; R.157.5°-193°.

PAGENSANDER NEBENELBE
DIE KRÜCKAU. S MOLE. HEAD. Lt. F.W.R.G.
W.6M. R.4M. G.3M. B. dolphin 8m. W.116.3°-
120.7°. Ldg. sector R.120.7°-225°; G.225°-
315°; R.315°-331.9°; W.331.9°-335.4°. Ldg.
sector G.335.4°-116.3°.

DIE PINNAU
N TRAINING WALL. HEAD. Lt. Oc.(2)W.R.G.
12 sec. W.6M. R.4M. G.3M. R. dolphin 8m.
G.049°-082.5°; W.082.5°-092.5° Ldg. sector;
R.092.5°-130°; G.130°-156.9°; W.156.9°-
161.6° Ldg. sector, R.161.6°-049°.
Ldg.Lts. 122°42'. (Front) Iso. 4 sec. 6M. W. △
R. border on mast 8m. (Rear) Iso. 4 sec. 6M.
W. ▽ R. border on mast 13m.

BÜTZFLETH ELBEHAFEN
N ENTRANCE. W SIDE. Lt. F.W.G. W.4M.
G.2M. on dolphin 6m. G.075°-345°; W.345°-
075°.

Lts. in line 225°18'. (Front) L.Fl. 8 sec. 2M. W.
◇B. border on mast 10m. Mark N limit of
berthing area. (Rear) Fl. 8 sec. 2M. W. ◇B.
border on mast 13m.
S ENTRANCE. W SIDE. Lt. F.W.R. W.4M.
R.2M. Col. 6m. W.075°-165°; R.165°-075°.
Ldg.Lts. 315°. (Rear) Fl.R. 8 sec. 4M. R.
lantern on B. mast 15m. Occas. (Common
front) L.Fl. 8 sec. 2M. W. ◇B. border on mast
10m. Mark S limit of berthing area. Also
Fl.R. 8 sec. 4M. same structure 9m. Occas.
Lts. in line 255°18'. (Rear) L.Fl. 8 sec. 2M. W.
◇B. border on mast 13m.

STADERSAND. 53°37'N, 9°32'E.
Radio: VHF Chan. 11, 12, 16. H24.

53°37.7'N, 9°31.7'E. Ldg.Lts. 165°18'. (Front)
Iso. 8 sec. 14M. W.R. Tr. 20m. (Rear) Iso.
8 sec. 16M. W.R. Tr. 40m. Fog Det. Lt.
BÜTZFLETHERSAND. 53°37.9'N, 9°31.5'E.
Ldg.Lts. 307°48'. (Front) Iso. 4 sec. 13M.
W.R. Tr. 20m. (Rear) Oc.W.R.G. 6 sec. 13M.
W.R. Tr. 33m. Also Oc.W.R.G. 6 sec. W.11M.
R.8M. G.7M. Same structure. G.181.8°-
191.8°; W.191.8°-193.7°; R.193.7°-220°.
JUELSSAND. NW END. 53°37.3'N, 9°33.4'E.
Lt. Oc.W.R.G. 6 sec. W.8M. R.6M. G.5M. W.
Tr. and dwelling B. roof 14m. R.301°-312.5°;
W.312.5°-318°; G.318°-338.1°.
TWIELENFLETH. 53°36.4'N, 9°33.5'E. Lt.
Oc.W.R.G. 6 sec. W.9M. R.6M. G.5M. W.B. Tr.
20m. G.137.3°-147.5°; W.147.5°-152.1°;
R.152.1°-159°. F.R. lights on overhead cables
1.04M. E and 0.7M. ESE.
MIELSTACK. 53°34.2'N, 9°38.6'E. Ldg.Lts.
136°18'. (Front) Oc. 4 sec. 12M. W. sq. Tr. R.
roof 13m. Vis. 126.5°-144.1°.
SOMFLETHERWISCH. (Rear) Oc. 4 sec. 13M.
W.R. 6-sided Tr. 32m. Vis. 127.5°-145.1°.
LÜHE. 53°34.3'N, 9°38.0'E. Ldg.Lts. 278°18'.
(Front) Iso. 3 sec. 12M. W.R. Tr. 16m. Vis.
265°-291°. **GRÜNENDEICH.** (Rear) Iso. 3 sec.
13M. W.R. 6-sided Tr. 36m. Vis. 271.3°-289°.

WEDEL. YACHT HARBOUR. W ENTRANCE.
Lt. F.R. 2M. F.G. 3M. 5m. Shown May-
October.
E ENTRANCE. 53°34.3'N, 9°40.8'E. Lt. F.R.
3M. F.G. 3M. 5m. Shown May-October.

SCHULAU. W MOLE. HEAD. Lt. F.R. 4M. R.
mast. 5m.
E MOLE. HEAD. Lt. F.G. 3M. G. mast. 5m.

WITTENBERGEN. 53°33.9'N, 9°45.2'E.
Ldg.Lts. 286°42'. (Front) Iso. 8 sec. 14M.
R.W. 6-sided framework Tr. 30m. **TINSDAL.**
(Rear) Iso. 8 sec. 16M. R.W. 6-sided Tr. with
11m. mast 55m.
SCHWEINESAND. Lt. Q.W. ⚓ on B.Y. Dolphin
8m.
FALKENSTEINER. Lt. Oc.W.R. 3 sec. W.6M.
R.4M. B.R. pile 6m. W.306°-318°;
R.318°-058°; W.058°-074.5°.
Lt. Fl.(2+1)G. 15 sec. 3M. G. and R. structure
on Dolphin 7m.

BLANKENESE. 53°33.5'N, 9°47.8'E. Ldg.Lts.
098°18'. (Front) Iso. 4 sec. 16M. W.R. Tr.
41m. (Rear) Iso. 4 sec. 20M. W.R. Tr. 84m.

ESTE LOCK
Radio: VHF Chan. 10, 16.

ENTRANCE N SIDE. Lt. Oc.W.R.G. 6 sec.
W.9M. R.7M. G.6M. W.B. Tr. 10m. G.119°-
196.8°; W.196.8°-200.1°; R.200.1°-298°.

HAMBURG. 53°32'N, 9°56'E.
Tel: Pilots: (040) 740 1680 & 740 2610.
Port Office: (040) 740 3151. Telex: 2174 999.
Harbour Traffic Control Centre: (040) 349
12327 and (040) 740 3151. Fax: (040) 740
3179. Telex: 2174 999. OHHND.
Radio-Port: VHF Chan. 14, 13, 06, 73. H24.
Radio—Pilots: VHF Chan. 67, 16. H24.
HAMBURG RADAR. VHF Chan. 3, 5, 7, 16,
19, 63, 80.
Radar Service: Vessels exempt from
compulsory pilotage MUST use this service
when Vis. <2000m.
Wedel-Tinsdale VHF Chan. 19.
Tinsdale-Seemannshoft VHF Chan. 3.
Seemannshoft-Toller Ort VHF Chan. 63, 7.
Kohlfleet, Parkhaven, Waltershofer,
Griesenwerder VHF Chan. 7.
Kohlbrand, Suderelde, Rethe VHF Chan. 80.
Norderelbe, E of Lotsenhoft, VHF Chan. 5.

HAMBURG ELBE PORT
Tel: (040) 740 2458, Telex: 212569 SMDH D.
Radio: VHF Chan. 12, 14, 16. H24.
Rethe Revier
Radio: VHF Chan. 13, 16.
Mon.-Sat. 0600-2100. Sun. and Bank
Holidays on request.
Suderelbe Revier Kattwyk Bridge.
Radio: VHF Chan. 13, 16. H24.
Harburg Lock
Radio: VHF Chan. 13, 16. H24.
Tiefstack Lock. Tel: (040) 78 68 91
Radio: VHF Chan 11.
NESS. MOLE. HEAD. Lt. Fl. 4 sec. 5M. ⚓ on
B.W. mast 8m.
GROSSSCHIFFSWARTEPLATZ. W. Lt.
Oc.(3)Y. 12 sec. 5M. Dolphin 6m.
E Lt. Oc.(3)Y. 12 sec. 5M. Dolphin 6m.

RÜSCHKANAL
ENTRANCE. E SIDE. Lt. F.R. 5M. Tr. 8m.
W SIDE. Lt. F.G. 4M. Tr. 10m.
FINKENWERDER. 53°32.6'N, 9°51.2'E.
Ldg.Lts. 273°06'. (Front) Oc.R. 5 sec. 10M. B.
∆ on R. mast 10m. (Rear) Oc.R. 5 sec. 10M.
B. ▽ on R. mast 16m.
STEENDIEKKANAL. W SIDE Lt. F.G. 2M.
dolphin 7m. **E. SIDE** Lt. F.R. 3M. dolphin 8m.
SPUNDWAND NW END Lt. F.G. 3M. 6m.
Also F.Y. on Middle and SE End.
SEEMANNSHÖFT. KÖHLFLEET. E SIDE. Lt.
Fl.(2)R. 5.5 sec. 4M. Grey Tr. 9m. Bell (1)
9 sec.
KÖHLFLEET. Ldg.Lts. 134°12' (Front) Oc.G. 5
sec. 8M. B. ∆ on R. mast 13m. (Rear) Oc.G. 5
sec. 8M. B. ▽ on R. mast. 20m.
KÖHLFLEET HAFEN. Lt. F.Y. 6M. Dolphin 5m.
Lt. Fl. Y. 4 sec. 2M. Dolphin 5m.
RO-RO TERMINAL. Lt. Iso.R. 2 sec. 3M. 7m.

DRADENAU HAFEN. NW CORNER. Lt. F.R. 4M. Dolphin 5m.
SW CORNER. Lt. F.G. 3M. 5m.
BUBENDEY-UFER. 53°32.4'N, 9°53.2'E. Ldg.Lts. 106°42' (Front) Iso. 8 sec. 16M. W.R. Tr. 20m. (Rear) Iso. 8 sec. 18M. W.R. Tr. 38m.

PARKHAFEN. ENTRANCE. W SIDE.
BUBENDEY-KAI. Lt. F.G. 4M. Grey Tr. 14m. Horn Mo(P) 60 sec.
WALTERSHOFER HÖFT. Lt. Oc.Y. 4 sec. 5M. Mast 6m.
GRIESENWERDERHÖFT. Lt. Fl.(2)Y. 5 sec. 2M. Dolphin 7m.
TUG BOAT STATION. W END. Lt. Oc.(2)Y. 9 sec. 4M. Dolphin 7m.
E END. Lt. Iso.Y. 4 sec. 4M. Dolphin 7m.

KÖHLBRAND AND SÜDER ELBE
KÖHLBRANDHÖFT. N END OF DYKE. Lt. Fl.(4)R. 15 sec. 6M. R. sq. Tr. 10m.
N Ldg.Lts. 143°36'. (Front) Fl.(2)R. 5 sec. 9M. △ on R. mast 12m. (Rear) Fl.(2)R. 5 sec. 9M. ▽ on R. mast 18m.
S Ldg.Lts. 001°30'. (Front) Fl.(2)R. 5 sec. 9M. △ 20m. (Rear) Fl.(2)R. 5 sec. 9M. ▽ 38m.
ALTENWERDER. Lt. 53°30.5'N, 9°56.4'E. F.W.R.G. W.12M. R.5M. G.4M. R. Tr. 10m. R.277°-332.2°; W.332.2°-337.6°; G.337.6°-349°.
N Ldg.Lts. 182°24'. (Front) Oc.G. 5 sec. 8M. Same structure. 10m. (Common rear) 53°30.4'N, 9°56.3'E. Oc.G. 5 sec. 8M. R. Tr. 19m. Also Oc. 5 sec. 13M. 19m.
S Ldg.Lts. 319°. (Front) Oc. 5 sec. 13M. R. Tr. 12m.
RETHE. Lt. Fl.Y. 1.5 sec. 5M. Dolphin 5m.
W SIDE. Lt. Fl.R. 4 sec. 4M. Dolphin 8m.
ALTENWERDER-ELLERHOLZ. 53°30.2'N, 9°56.5'E. Ldg.Lts. 175°. (Front) Oc.R. 5 sec. 10M. R. Tr. 10m. (Rear) Oc.R. 5 sec. 10M. R. Tr. 16m.
MOORBURGER WEIDE. Ldg.Lts. 139°. (Front) Oc.G. 5 sec. 8M. Mast 12m. (Rear) Oc.G. 5 sec. 8M. Mast 18m.
GROSSER KATTWYK. 53°30'.2N, 9°56.8'E. Ldg.Lts. 335°. (Front) Oc.R. 5 sec. 10M. Mast 11m. (Rear) Oc.R. 5 sec. 10M. Mast 18m.
MOORBURGER WEIDE. S DOLPHIN. Lt. Fl.Y. 4 sec. 5M. Dolphin 5m.

SEEHAFEN 4. Ldg.Lts. 155°. (Front) Oc.R. 5 sec. 6M. R. mast 11m. (Rear) Oc.R. 5 sec. 6M. R. mast 19m.

E SIDE. Lt. Oc.(4)R. 12 sec. 4M. Dolphin 8m.
W SIDE. Lt. F.G. 4M. Dolphin 8m.

BRUCKE 6 N DOLPHIN. Lt. Iso.Y. 4 sec. 3M. 9m.

S DOLPHIN. Lt. Iso.Y. 4 sec. 3M. 9m.

SEEHAFEN 3 E SIDE. Lt. Oc.(3)R. 10 sec. 3M. Dolphin 8m. **W SIDE.** Lt. F.G. 3M. Dolphin 8m
.
SEEHAFEN 2 E SIDE. Lt. Oc.(2)R. 9 sec. 4M. Dolphin 8m. **W SIDE.** Lt. F.G. 4M. Dolphin 8m.

SEEHAFEN 1 E SIDE. Lt. Oc.R. 3 sec. 4M. Dolphin 8m. **W SIDE.** Lt. F.G. 3M. Dolphin 8m.

HARBURG. VORHAFEN ZUR SCHLEUSE. E SIDE. Lt. F.W.R. W.6M. R.4M. R. Tr. 10m. R.009°-189°; W.189°-270°.

RETHE
RUGENBURGEN. Ldg.Lts. 322°54'. (Front) Oc.G. 5 sec. 7M. Tr. 12m. (Rear) Oc.G. 5 sec. 7M. Tr. 18m.
ENTRANCE POINT. S SIDE. Lt. F.R.G. R.4M. G.3M. R. sq. Tr. on cairn 10m. R.077°-156°; G.156°-323°.
KATHWYK RO-RO. Lt. Iso.Y. 4 sec. 2M. 3m.
NEUHÖFER HAFEN. N SIDE. Lt. F.Y. 5M. Dolphin 5m.
S SIDE. Lt. F.Y. 5M. Dolphin 5m.
KATTWYKHAFEN. NE DOLPHIN. Lt. F.Y. 3M. Dolphin 5m.
RETHEHÖFT. Lt. F.R.G. R.4M. G.3M. Mast 11m. R.334°-154°; G.154°-287°.

REIHERSTIEG
GETREIDESILO. Lt. F. 4M. Dolphin 6m. F.Y. on dolphin 500m. NW. F. on dolphin 650m. SE.
Ldg.Lts. 098°30'. (Front) F.R. 8M. R. mast 12m. (Rear) F.R. 8M. R. mast 15m.
KATTWYK (SANDORT) SÜDSPITZE. Lt. Oc.(2)R.G. 12 sec. R.4M. G.3M. R. Tr. 10m. G.185°-330°; R.330°-112.5°.

BÜSUM. 54°07'N, 8°52'E.
Tel: (0 48 34) 21 83.
Radio: VHF Chan. 11, 16. H24.

W SIDE OF FISHING HARBOUR. 54°07.7'N, 8°51.6'E. Lt. Oc.(2)W.R.G. 16 sec. W.16M. R.13M. G.12M. R.W. Tr. 22m. W.248°-317°; R.317°-024°; W.024°-084°; G.084°-091.5°; W.091.5°-093.5°. Ldg. sector for Su[di]der Piep; R.093.5°-097°; W.097°-148°.
W MOLE HEAD. 54°07.2'N, 8°51.6'E. Lt. Oc.(3)R. 12 sec. R. Dolphin 11m. F. Fog Det. Lt.
E MOLE. HEAD. Lt. Oc.(3)G. 12 sec. 8m. 54°07.5'N, 8°51.6'E. Ldg.Lts. 355°06'. (Front) Iso. 4 sec. 13M. B.W. mast 9m. (Rear) Iso. 4 sec. 13M. B.W. mast 12m.

DIE EIDER

ST PETER. 54°17.3'N, 8°39.2'E. Lt.
L.Fl.(2)W.R.G. 15 sec. W.15M. R.13M. G.11M.
R. Tr. B. lantern 23m. R.271°-294°;
W.294°-325°; R.325°-344°; W.344°-035°;
G.035°-056.5°; W.056.5°-068°; R.068°-091°;
W.091°-120; R.120°-130°.

EIDERDAMM. 54°16'N 8°50.8'E.
Radio—Port: VHF Chan. 14, 16. H24.
EIDERDAMM LOCK. Traffic Signals. 2 Long
blasts = Request Lock to open.

LOCK N MOLE. W END. Lt. Oc.(2)R. 12 sec.
4M. Mast 8m. Traffic Signals.
S MOLE. W END. Lt. Oc.G. 6 sec. 4M. Grey
Tr. 8m.

TONNING. 54°19'N 8°57'E.
Harbour has depths of 3m. at HW.

W MOLE. HEAD. Lt. F.R. 2M. R. col. 5m. Not
shown when navigation is closed by ice.
QUAY. Lt. F.G. 2M. Y. col. 5m. Not shown
when navigation is closed by ice.

DIE HEVER

WESTERHEVERSAND. 54°22.5'N, 8°38.5'E.
Lt. Oc.(3)W.R.G. 15 sec. W.21M. R.17M. G.
16M. R.W. Tr. 41m. W.012.2°-069°;
G. 069°-079.5°; R.079.5°-107°; W.107°-157°;
R.157°-169°; W.169°-206.5°; R.206.5°-218.5°;
W.218.5°-233°; R.233°-248°.

SÜDEROOGSAND. CROSS. 54°25.5'N,
8°28.7'E. Lt. Iso.W.R.G. 6 sec. W.15M. R.12M.
G.11M. B. structure. 18m. R.240°-244°;
W.244°-246°; G.246°-263°; W.263°-320°;
R.320°-338°; W.338°-013°; R.013°-048°;
W.048°-082.5°; R.082.5°-122.5°;
W.122.5°-150°.

HAFEN VON PELLWORM 54°31.3'N
8°41.2'E.
Harbour dries at LW with 2.8m. at MHW.

PELLWORM. S SIDE. 54°29.3'N, 8°39.1'E.
Ldg.Lts. 041°. (Front) Oc.W.R. 5 sec. W.24M.
W.11M. R.8M. Grey framework Tr. W. lantern
14m. W. (intens) on leading line,
W.303.5°-313.5°; R.313.5°-316.5°. (Rear)
54°29.8'N, 8°40.0'E. Oc. 5 sec. 25M. R.W. Tr.
38m. (Cross Lt.) Oc.W.R. 5 sec. Same
structure. 38m. R.11M. 122.6°-140°; W.14M.
140°-161.5°; R.11M. 161.5°-179.5°; W.14M.
179.5°-210.2°; R.6M. 255°-265.5°; W.8M.
265.5°-276°; R.6M. 276°-297°;
W.8M. 297°-307°.

FUHLE SCHLOT. STRUCKLAHNUNGSHÖRN.
W MOLE. HEAD. Lt. Oc. G. 6 sec. 2M. G.
mast 5m.

HUSUM 54°29'N, 9°03'E. LEITSTAND
SPERRWERK HUSUM (04841) 667218. WSA
TONNING (04861) 742/44. Fax: (04861) 6379.
Telex: 28412 WSA.
Radio—Port: VHF Chan. 11, 16.
Entry: Info. B'casts H+00 Chan. 11. 4 h.
—H.W. —2 h. Vessels over 9m. length or
3.4m. beam must report to Leitstand by VHF
or Tel. before entering Husumer Au. May
enter only when vis. exceeds 1000m (unless
piloted). All vessels to obtain permission to
transit from Buoy 61 to Husum. Draught up
to 4m. at H.W.

HUSUMER AU OUTER Ldg.Lts. 106°30'
(Front) Iso.R. 8 sec. 8M. R.W. mast 8m.
(Rear) Iso.R. 8 sec. 9M. Y. mast 17m. Storm
signals.
INNER. Ldg.Lts. 090°. (Front) Iso.G. 8 sec.
6M. R.W. mast 7m. (Rear) Iso.G. 8 sec. 6M.
R.W. mast 9m.

AMRUM HAFEN. 54°37.9'N, 8°22.9'E.
Ldg.Lts. 272°54.0' (Front) Iso.R. 4 sec. 10M.
W.R. mast 11m. **AMRUM.** (Rear) Fl.(3) 30
sec. 23M. R.W. Tr. 63m. Storm signals. Also
Iso.R. 4 sec. 15M. Same structure 33m.
WRIAKHÖRN. CROSS. 54°37.6'N, 8°21.2'E.
Lt. L.Fl.(2)W.R. 15 sec. W.9M. R.7M. Tr. 26m.
W.297.5°-319°; R.319°-343°; W.343°-014°;
R.014°-034°.
NEBEL. 54°38.8'N, 8°21.7'E. Lt. Oc.W.R.G. 5
sec. W.20M. R.15M. G.15M. R.W. Tr. 16m.
R.255.5°-258.5°; W.258.5°-260.5°;
G.260.5°-263.5°.
LANGENESS. NORDMARSCH. 54°37.6'N,
8°31.8'E. Lt. F.W.R.G. W.14M. R.11M. G.10M.
Dark brown round Tr. 14m. W.268°-279°;
R.279°-311°; W.311°-350°; G.350°-033°;
W.033°-045°; R.045°-064°; W.064°-123°;
R.123°-127°; W.127°-218°.

NIEBLUM. 54°41.1'N, 8°29.2'E. Lt.
Oc.(2)W.R.G. 10 sec. W.19M. R.15M. G.15M.
R.W. Tr. 11m. G.028°-031°; W.031°-032.5°;
R.032.5°-035.5°.
INSEL FÖHR. S POINT. OLHÖRN. 54°40.9'N,
8°34.1E. Lt. Oc.(4)W.R.G. 15 sec. W.13M.
R.10M. G.9M. R. Tr. Grey lantern 10m.
W.208°-250°; R.250°-281°; W.281°-290°;
G.290°-333°; W.333°-058°; R.058°-080°.

WYK FÖHR. 54°42'N, 8°35'E.
Radio: VHF Chan. 11, 16.

S MOLE. HEAD. Lt. Oc.(2)W.R. 12 sec. W.7M.
R.4M. W.R. mast 12m. W.220°-322°;
R.322°-220°.
OLAND. 54°40.5'N, 8°41.3'E. Lt. F.W.R.G.
W.13M. R.10M. G.9M. R. Tr. 7m. G.086°-093°;
W.093°-160°; R.160°-172°.

DAGEBÜLL
Lt. 54°44'N 8°41'E. Iso. W.R.G 8 sec. W.18M.
R.15M. G.15M. G. mast 23m. G.042°-043°;
W.043°-044.5°; R.044.5°-047°.
Lt. Q. (3) 10 sec. 2M. ♦ B.Y. Pole 7m.

AMRUM. W SIDE NORDDORF. 54°40.3'N,
8°18.6'E. Lt. Oc.W.R.G. 6 sec. W.15M. R.12M.
G.11M. W. round structure. R. lantern 22m.
W.009°-035°; G.035°-037°; W.037°-038°. Ldg.
sector: R.038.5°-090°; W.090°-156°;
R.156°-176.5°; W.176.5°-178.5°;
G.178.5°-188°; G.(unintens)188°-202° ;
W.(partially obscured)202°-230°

SYLT

HAFEN VON HORNUM 54°45'N 8°18'E.
Depths in Hbr. of 3m. to 4.5m. Pontoon for
yachts at N end of harbour.
54°44.8'N, 8°17.4'E. Ldg.Lts. 012°30' (Front)
Iso. 8 sec. 14M. R.W. Tr. 20m. (Rear) Iso.
8 sec. 18M. R.W. Tr. 45m.
HÖRNUM. 54°45.3'N, 8°17.5'E. Lt. Fl.(2)
9 sec. 20M. Same structure 48m.
N PIER. HEAD. Lt. F.G. 3M. G. post 6m. Vis.
024°-260°.
SCHUTZMOLE. HEAD. Lt. F.R. 4M. dolphin
7m. Mole floodlit.
Lt. Fl.Y. 4 sec. Y. pile.

KAMPEN. ROTE KLIFF. 54°56.8'N, 8°20.5'E.
Lt. Oc.(4)W.R. 15 sec. W.20M. R. 16M. W.B.
Tr. 62m. W.193°-260°; W.(unintens)260°-339°;
W.339°-165°; R.165°-193°. RC.
ELLENBOGEN. N END. LIST W. 55°03.2'N,
8°24.2'E. Lt. Oc.W.R.G. 6 sec. W.14M. R.11M.
G.10M. W. Tr. R. lantern 19m. R.040°-133°;
W.133°-196°; R.196°-210°; W.210°-227°;
R.227°-266.4°; W.266.4°-268°; G.268°-285°;
W.285°-310°; W.(unintens)310°-040°.

N SIDE. LIST OST. 55°03.0'N, 8°26.7'E. Lt.
Iso.W.R.G. 6 sec. W.14M. R.11M. G.10M.
W.R. Tr. 22m. W.(unintens)010.5°-098°;
G.098°-112°; W.112°-114°; R.114°-122°;
W.122°-262°; R.262°-278°; W.278°-296°;
R.296°-323.3°; W.323.3°-324.5°;
G.324.5°-350°; W.350°-010.5°.

LIST LAND. 55°01.1'N, 8°26.5'E. Lt.
Oc.W.R.G. 3 sec. W.12M. R.9M. G.8M. W.R.
mast 13m. W.170°-203°; G.203°-212°;
W.212°-215.5°; R.215.5°-232.5°;
W.232.5°-234°; G.234°-243°; W.243°-050°.
F.R. on mast 1M. WSW.

LIST HAFEN 55°01'N, 8°26'E.
Least depth 4m. in entrance. Draught up to
3m. in harbour. At Munkmarsch there is a
private yacht harbour. NOTE: The Lister Tief
Entrance approx. 55°08'N, 8°10'E 1.5M.
wide. Well lit and buoyed provides safer
access to Sylt and Rom (Germany and
Denmark). Depth 5m. on bar at MLW. In gale
conditions sea breaks to the W on 15m. line.

N MOLE. HEAD. Lt. F.G. 3M. G. mast 5m.
Vis. 218°038°. Storm signals.
S MOLE. HEAD. Lt. F.R. 3M. R. mast 5m.
Vis. 218°-353°.
NSB II Lt. By. Fl.(5) Y. 20 sec.

DENMARK

For Kiel Canal vessel must be registered.
Charter Party Document if on charter.
Certificate of Competency if over 20 Tonnes.
Passport for all aboard.
Carry Proof of ownership.
Temporary importation licence 3 months in any 6 months. Apply for residential licence if EEC National for longer periods.
If carrying more than Duty Free allowance: ¼ litre spirits, or 3 litres fortified wine, 4 litres wine, 60 cigarettes, or 100 grms tobacco, you must report at Customs Posts at: Esbjerg, Frederikshaven, Frederica, Haderslav, Holstebro, Horsens, Kolding, Randers, Skive, Sønderborg, Thisted, Vejle, Aalborg, Arhus, Odense, Svenborg, Copenhagen, Elsinore, Kalundborg, Korsør, Køge, Jøgem, Naestved, Nykøbing, Røbyhavn or Rønne.
Calor gas cylinders cannot be bought or exchanged but may be refilled.
Danish Tourist Board, Sceptre House, 169/173 Regent Street, London W1. Tel: 01-734 2637.
Entry by Road. Car and craft must be fully insured, also the trailer.
Temporary importation 12 months.
Use Danish charts and Harbour Pilots for Inland Waters. The Baltic, whilst Tideless, is affected by wind which can give a stream of about 2 kts and affect sea levels. If you run aground and the wind changes you can be stuck for some time.
By law you are required to have fully updated charts and navigational publications and be fully informed of all regulations etc.
Danish Embassy, 55 Sloane Street, London SW1. Tel: 071-235 1255.

NORTH SEA COAST

RØMØ DYB
Lt. Fl.(2)R. 10 sec. 2M. R. dolphin 3m.
Lt. Fl.R. 3 sec. 2M. R. dolphin 3m.
Lt. Fl.R. 5 sec. 2M. R. dolphin 3m.

RØMØ HAVN. 55°05′N, 8°34′E.
Radio: VHF Chan. 16, 10, 12, 13 on request.
Entry: Depths from 3.2m. to 4.2m.

S MOLE. HEAD. Lt. Fl.R. 3 sec. 2M. Grey framework Tr. 6m.
N MOLE. HEAD. Lt. Fl.G. 3 sec. 2M. Grey framework Tr. 6m.
INNER S MOLE. Lt. Fl.R. 5 sec. 1M. Col. 3m.
INNER N MOLE. Lt. Fl.G. 5 sec. 1M. Col. 3m.

GRÅDYB
SAEDENSTRAND. 55°29.8′N, 8°24.0′E. Ldg.Lts. 053°48′. (Front) Iso. 2 sec. 21M. Wooden building, B.W. stripe on roof. 12m. Vis. 051.8°-055.8°. Shown by day in poor visibility during ice season. (Middle) Iso. 4 sec. 21M. R.W. Tr. 26m. Vis. 051°-057°. (Rear) F. 18M. R. ⫞ on R. framework Tr. 36m. Vis. 052°-056°.
TIDE GAUGE. Lt. Fl.(5)Y. 20 sec. 4M. Y. mast 8m.
SOUTH. 55°28.7′N, 8°24.7′E. Ldg.Lts. 067°. (Front) F.G. 16M. Grey sq. wooden Tr. 10m. Shown by day in poor visibility during ice season. (Rear) F.G. 16M. Grey Tr. 21m.

SAEDDENSTRAND. N. 55°29.9′N, 8°23.8′E. Ldg.Lts. 049° (Front) F.R. 16M. W. mast 16m. Shown by day in poor visibility during ice season. (Rear) F.R. 16M. Grey concrete Tr. 27m.
JERG. Lt. Q. 6M. B.Y. Tr. 7m.
FOVRFELT N. Lt. Oc.(2)W.R.G. 6 sec. 5M. Y. Tr. 6m. G.066.5°-073°; W.073°-077°; R.077°-085.5°; G.327°-331°; W.331°-333.5°; R.333.5°-342°.
FOVRFELT. Lt. Fl.(2)R. 10 sec. 3M. R. Tr. 9m.
MEJLSAND. Lt. Fl.G. 5 sec. 5M. G. Tr. 6m.

ESBJERG 55°28′N, 8°26′E.
Tel: (05) 129200 (HM) (05) 121065 (Pilots).
Radio—Port: VHF Chan. 16, 12, 13. H24.
Radio—Pilots: VHF Chan. 16, 13. H24.
Yacht berths are in W part of Trafikhavn.
STRANDBY. SHELTER MOLE. NW CORNER. 55°28.8′N, 8°24.7′E. Lt. Oc.W.R.G. 5 sec. W.13M. R.9M. G.9M. W.R. building. 5m. G.101.7°-105.5°; W.105.5°-109.5°; R.109.5°-111.7°.
INDUSTRIFISKERIHAVEN. W MOLE. HEAD. Lt. Fl.R. 5 sec. 2M. R. post 4m. 192°-104°.
E MOLE. HEAD. Lt. Fl.G. 5 sec. 2M. G. post 4m. Vis. 030°-279°.
KONSUMFISKERIHAVN. W MOLE. HEAD. Lt. Fl.R. 3 sec. R. Tr. 4m. Vis. 203°-119°.
E MOLE. HEAD. Lt. Fl.G. 3 sec. G. Tr. 4m. Vis. 023°-256°.

MAIN LT. TRAFIKHAVN. NW CORNER.
55°28.3′N, 8°25.5′E. Lt. Oc.(2)W.R.G. 12 sec.
W.13M. R.9M. G.9M. W.R. Bldg. 5m.
G.118°-124.5°; W.124.5°-129°; R.129°-131°.
N MOLE. HEAD. Lt. F.R. 5M. R. conical
building. 7m. Vis. 232°-135°. Also shown by
day in poor visibility.
S MOLE. HEAD. Lt. F.G. 4M. G. conical
building 7m. Vis. 045°-276°.

SØNDREHAVN. W MOLE. HEAD. Lt. F.R. 4M.
R. post 8m.
E MOLE. HEAD. Lt. F.G. 4M. G. post 8m.
FAERGEHAVN. Lt. on pile.
LANDING STAGE. Lt. Fl.R. 3 sec. 2M.
Dolphin 4m.
Lt. Fl.R. 5 sec. 2M. Wooden dolphin 5m. R.
Lts. on chimney 0.5M. NNW.

FANØ
FANØ LO. W SIDE OF CHANNEL. Lt. Iso.
W.R.G. 4 sec. W.6M. R.3M. G.3M. G. Tr. 7m.
G.274°-303°; W.303°-313°; R.313°-342°;
W.342°-274°.
NAES SJORD. N. Lt. Fl.(3)R. 10 sec. 2M. R.
dolphin 3m.
S Lt. Fl.(2)R. 10 sec. 2M. R. dolphin 3m.
KREMER SAND N. Lt. Fl.G. 3 sec. 2M. G.
dolphin 3m.
S. Lt. F.G. on G. dolphin 2m.
RINDBY. Ldg.Lts. 181°. (Front) F. 5M. Grey Tr.
5m. Vis. 173°-189°. (Rear) F. 5M. Grey Tr.
12m. Vis. 173°-189°.
PAKHUSBANKEN. Lt. F.R.G. on W. mast 4m.
G.180°-242°; R.242°-332°.

NORDBY. 55°26.9′N, 8°24.5′E.
Small harbour for vessels up to 30m. in
length and 3.6m. draught.

NORDBY. Ldg.Lts. 216°. (Front) F.R. 2M. W. △
on mast 5m. Vis.136°-296°. (Rear) F.R. 2M.
W. ▽ on mast 7m. Vis.136°-296°.
POWER CABLE MAST. Lt. Fl.G. 3 sec. 1M. G.
△ on W. mast 1m.
Lt. L.Fl. 10 sec. 1M. 1m.
Lt. Fl.R. 3 sec. 1M. R. ▯ on W. mast 1m.

BLÅVANDSHUK. 55°33.5′N, 8°05.1′E. Lt.
Fl.(3) 20 sec. 23M. W. sq. Tr. 55m. RC.

SONDRE HAVNEBRO. Quay for fishing
vessels and yachts. Depths 1.6m. or 2.9m. at
MHW.

OKSBØL FIRING RANGE EKR/D77.
55°33.6′N, 8°04.7′E. Lt. Al.Fl.W.R. 4 sec.
W.16M. R.13M. Tr. 33m. By day Q.10M.
Shown when firing is in progress.
Lt. 55°37.3′N, 8°07.1′E. Al.Fl.W.R. 4 sec.
W.16M. R.13M. Tr. 35m. By day Q. 10M.
Shown when firing is in progress.

HVIDE SANDE 56°00′N, 8°07′E.
Radio—Port: VHF Chan. 16, 12, 13. As
required.
Pilots: VHF Chan. 6. H24.

HVIDE SANDE KANAL
56°00.1′N, 8°07.3′E. Lt. F. 14M. Grey Tr. 27m.

LEE MOLE. HEAD. Lt. Fl.R. 3 sec. 8M. R. hut
7m.
N MOLE. HEAD. Lt. Fl.R. 5 sec. 6M. Grey col.
10m. Also shown by day in poor visibility.
Horn 15 sec. Reserve fog signal Reed.
S MOLE. HEAD. Lt. Fl.R. 5 sec. 6M. Grey col.
10m. Also shown by day in poor visibility.
NORDHAVN. PIER. HEAD. Lt. F.G. 2M.
Galvanised pipe 4m.
INDUSTRIHAVN. SHELTER MOLE. Lt. 2 F.R.
2M. W. posts 3m. Vis. 035°-060°.
N INNER MOLE. HEAD. Lt. F.R. 3M. Grey col.
5m.
S INNER MOLE. HEAD. Lt. F.G. 2M. Grey col.
5m.
W BASIN. SHELTER MOLE. Lt. F.G. 2M. Grey
post 4m.
NEW ENTRANCE. E SIDE. Lt. F.R. 2M.
Galvanised pipe 4m.
W SIDE. Lt. F.G. 2M. Galvanised pipe 4m.
E BASIN. E PIER. Lt. F.R. 2M. Grey post 4m.

KAMMERSLUSE (giving access to
Ringkøbing Fjord). Depth over sill 4m.

LOCK ENTRANCE. Ldg.Lts. 291°36′. (Front)
F.R. 2M. R. △ on Grey Tr. 11m. Vis.208°-028°.
(Rear) F.R. 2M. R. ▽ on Grey Tr. 13m.
Vis.208°-028°.

FJORDHAVN. Ldg.Lts. 247° (Front) F.G. 5M.
R. △ on Grey mast 7m. (Rear) F.G. 4M. R. ▽
on Grey mast 9m.

LYNGVIG. HOLMLANDS KLIT. Lt. 56°03.0′N,
8°06.3′E. Fl. 5 sec. 22M. W. Tr. 53m.

RINGKØBING HAVN. 56°5.4′N,
8°14.4′E.
Yachts berth in Gamle Havn. Depth 2m.
Stavning Lystbådehavn is a yacht harbour in
Rinkøbing Fjord E side. Depth 1m. Speed
limit 2kts. Bork Havn, a yacht harbour, can
be used by vessels up to 10m. length, 3.5m.
beam, 1.3m. draught.

RINKØBING FJORD
W PIER. HEAD. Lt. F.R. Grey col. 5m.
S PIER. HEAD. Ldg.Lts. 042°. (Front) F.G. W.
△ on post. (Rear) F.G. W. ▽ on mast.

STAVNING LYSTBÅDEHAVN. Ldg.Lts. 049°
(Front) F. 3M. W. △ R. stripe on Grey metal
mast 6m. (Rear) F. 3M. W. ▽ R. stripe on
Grey metal mast. 10m.

SKAVEN LYSTBÅDEHAVN. Ldg.Lts. 129°.
(Front) F. 8M. W. △ R. stripe on G. metal
mast 6m. (Rear) F. 8M. W. ▽ R. stripe on G.
metal mast 11m.

NØRRE BORK. 55°50.7′N, 8°17.0′E. Ldg.Lts.
124°. (Front) F. 13M. W. △ R. stripe on Grey
Tr. 7m. (Rear) F. 13M. W. ▽ R. stripe on Grey
Tr. 10m.

TORSMINDE HAVN. 56°22′N, 8°07′E.
Radio: VHF Chan. 16, 12, 13. 0300-1300,
1400-2359.
Entry: Vessels advised to check depths and
current before entering channel. Must
obtain permission before using lock.
Vesthavn has depths of 3m. below Mean
Springs.

TORSMINDE. 56°22.6′N, 8°07.1′E. Lt. F. 14M.
Grey Tr. 30m.
N MOLE. Lt. Iso.R. 2 sec. 4M. Grey col. 8m.
Shown H24.
S MOLE. HEAD. Lt. Iso.G. 2 sec. 3M. Grey
mast 8m. Shown H24.
INSIDE HEAD. Siren 30 sec. Fishing on
request.
GROYNE. N HEAD. Lt. Fl.R. 3 sec. 4M. Grey
post 5m. H24.

W HARBOUR. W MOLE. HEAD. Lt. F.G. 2M.
Grey post 5m.
E MOLE. HEAD. Lt. F.R. 2M. Grey post 5m.
NW DOLPHIN. Lt. F.G. 4M. Grey post on
dolphin 5m.
SE DOLPHIN. Lt. F.G. 4M. Grey post on
dolphin 5m.
E. Ldg.Lts. 285°. (Front) F. B. △ (Rear) F. B. ▽.
LOCK. E SIDE. Lt. Iso. 4 sec. 4M. Grey mast
12m. Vis.020°-160°.
ROAD BRIDGE. Lt. Iso. 4 sec. 4M. 5m.
Vis.200°-340°.

BOVBJERG. 56°30.8′N, 8°07.3′E. Lt. L.Fl.(2)
15 sec. 16M. R. Tr. 62m.

LIMFJORD

THYBORØN KANAL

APPROACH. 56°42.5′N, 8°13.0′E. Lt. Fl.(3)
10 sec. 16M. Tr. 24m. Intens.023.5°-203.5°.
Shown by day in poor visibility. RC. Horn
30 sec.

AGGER TANGE. 56°43.0′N, 8°14.2°E. Ldg.Lts.
082°. (Front) Oc.W.R.G. 5 sec. W.11M. R.8M.
G.8M. R. hut conical top 8m.
G.074.5°-079.5°; W.079.5°-084.5°; R.084.5°-
089.5°. (Rear) Iso. 2 sec. 12M. R. ▽ on Grey
Tr. 17m. Vis.080°-084°.
LANGHOLM. 56°42.5′N, 8°14.6′E. Ldg.Lts.
120°. (Front) Iso. 2 sec. 11M. R. △ on R. hut.
7m. Vis.115°-125°. (Rear) Iso. 4 sec. 11M. R.
▽ on Grey Tr. 13m. Vis.115°-125°.
Lt. 56°42.4′N, 8°13.5′E. Oc.(2)W.R.G. 12 sec.
W.12M. R.9M. G.9M. W.R. Tr. 6m.
G.122.5°-146.5°; W.146.5°-150°;
R.150°-211.3°; G.211.3°-338°;
W.338°—340.5°; R.340.5°-344°.

THYBORØN. 56°42′N, 8°13.6′E. **Pilots** Tel:
(07) 831012.
Radio—Port: VHF Chan. 16, 12, 13. As
required.
Radio—Pilots: VHF Chan. 16, 12, 13. H24.
Controlling depth in Limfjord is 4m. Tidal
range less than 1m.
Boatyard and slip in Beddingshavn
(Thyborøn).

YDERHAVN. N MOLE. HEAD. Lt. Fl.G. 3 sec.
4M. G. pedestal 6m. Siren 20 sec.
S MOLE. HEAD. Lt. Fl.R. 3 sec. 4M. R.
pedestal 6m.

AGGER HAVN 56°46.6′N, 8°14.9°E.

N Pier depth 3.1m. ⎱ up to 25m.x6.2m.
S Pier depth 3.1m. ⎰   x3m. depth

Ldg.Lts. 298°. (Front) F.R. 1M. Or. △ on post
1m. (Rear) F.R. 1M. Or. ▽ on post 3m.

LEMVIG HAVN. 56°33.1′N, 8°18.5′E.
Tel: (07) 820106.
Approach through Lemvig depths 4.5m. at
entrance to 2.8m. off Lemvighavn. Yacht
Marina at Vinkel Hage depth at 3m. at
entrance and 2-3m. alongside piers.

SØJÅRD MARK. Ldg.Lts. 243°30′ (Front) F.R.
R. △ on W. beacon 20m. Neon. Vis. on
leading line only. Not shown when harbour
is closed by ice. (Rear) F.R. R. ▽ on W. mast.
30m. Neon. Vis. on leading line only. Not
shown when harbour is closed by ice.
MARINA. S MOLE. HEAD. Lt. F.R. 4M. Post
3m.
N MOLE. HEAD. Lt. F.G. 4M. Post 3m.
WEST OF HARBOUR. Ldg.Lts. 177°42′.
(Front) F.R. R. △ on W. Tr. 8m. Vis.153°-203°.
Not shown when harbour is closed by ice.
(Rear) F.R. R. ▽ on W. mast 20m. Vis.153°-
203°. Not shown when harbour is closed by
ice.

W MOLE. HEAD. Lt. F.G. 5M. Tr. 3m. Not shown when harbour is closed by ice.
GAMMELHAVEN. N MOLE. W END. Lt. F.R. 5M. 4m. Frame Tr. floodlit. Not shown when harbour is closed by ice.
TOFTUM. 56°33.2'N, 8°32.9'E. Lt. Iso. W.R.G. 4 sec. W.12M. R.8M. G.8M. W.R. house 24m. G.110°-120°; W.120°-137°; R.137°-144°; W.(unintens)190°-210°.

ODDESUND. 56°35'N, 8°34'E.
Radio (Bridge). VHF Chan. 16, 12, 13. As required.
Request Bridge open = Flag N or/and long + short blast, or W.Lt. in bow & long + short blast.

ODDESUND N-LIGE HAVN. 56°35'N, 8°33'E. Small harbour in Odby Bugt for fishermen and yachts by day. Depth in harbour 3m. Up to 15m. length.

ODDESUND BRO
PIER OF LIFTING SPAN No. 7. 56°34.8'N, 8°33.5'E. Lt. Iso. W.R.G. 2 sec. 11M. Engine House 10m. G.015.5°-032°; W.032°-052°; R.052°-068.5°. Traffic Signals. The navigable opening is marked by W.R.G. lights. Fog lights are shown on both sides of pillars 6 and 7. Siren 20 sec.
NORTH. 56°34.7'N, 8°33.5'E. Ldg.Lts. 218°30' (Front) Iso.G. 2 sec. 12M. Mast 13m. (Rear) Iso.G. 2 sec. 13M. Mast 16m.
SW. Ldg.Lts. 026°30'. (Front) Iso.G. 2 sec. 11M. Pier No. 7. 10m. (Rear) Iso.G. 2 sec. 12M. Pier No. 7 13m.
GRISETAAODDE. 56°34.9'N, 8°34.1'E. Lt. Oc.W.R.G. 5 sec. W.10M. R.7M. G.7M. W.R. Tr. 8m. R.053°-150°; G.150°-238°; W.238°-258°; R.258°-270°.

VENØ FISKERIHAVN
56°33'N 8°37'E. Depth in channel 2.2m. in harbour 2m.
Ldg.Lts. 051° (Front) F.R. 2M. W. Δ on post. 3m. Vis. on leading line. Occas. (Rear) F.R. 2M. W. ▽ on mast 4m. Vis. on leading line. Occas.

ASKAER ODDE. FERRY BERTH. N MOLE. HEAD. Lt. F.G. 1M. Grey post 3m. For use of ferries.

HOLSTEBRO-STRUER HAVN.
56°29.8'N, 8°36'E.
Radio: VHF Chan. 16, 12, 13. As required.

LYSTBÅDEHAVN. (2.5m. in W part, 2.5m.-3.5m. alongside shipyard) — yacht harbour inside Vestre Mole.

W MOLE. HEAD. Lt. Fl.G. 3 sec. 3M. W.G. post 5m.
N MOLE. HEAD. Lt. Fl.R. 3 sec. 2M. R.W. post 5m.
Ldg. Lts. 179°42'. (Front) F.R. 8M. R. Δ on Tr. 7m. (Rear) F.R. 8M. R. ▽ on Tr. 8m.
MARINA. N SHELTER MOLE. HEAD. Lt. Fl.R. 5 sec. 2M. Post 2m. Shown 1/4-15/11.
Lt. F.R. 2M. Post 2m. Shown 1/4-15/11.

HVIDSTENS HAGE
GYLDENDAL MARINA. Ldg.Lts. 023°18'. (Front) F.G. 4M. W.R. Δ on Grey Tr. 8m. (Rear) F.G. 4M. W.R. ▽ on Grey Tr. 9m.
SW MOLE. HEAD. Lt. F.R. 3M. Grey Tr. 4m. Mole Head floodlit.

JEGINDO FISKERIHAVN 56°39.1'N, 8°38.3'E.
Small fishing harbour. Depths 2.5m.

N BASIN. N MOLE Lt. F.G. 4M. G. mast 4m.
S MOLE Lt. F.R. 4M. R. mast 4m

SILLERSLEV HAVN 56°40.8'N, 8°43.9'E.
Small fishing harbour.
56°41.0'N, 8°44.0'E. Ldg.Lts. 030°30' Iso. 2 sec. 14M. W. House, R. band 10m. Vis.027.5°-033.5° (Rear) Iso. 4 sec. 14M. W.R. Tr. 28m. Vis.027.5°-033.5°.
W MOLE. HEAD. Lt. F.R. 2M. Grey post 3m.

SALLING SUND
LANGERODDE. 56°42.8'N, 8°50.1'E. Lt. Iso.W.R.G. 2 sec. W.14M. R.10M. G.10M. W.R. House 9m. G.036°-048°; W.048°-053°; R.053°-060°.
BRIDGE. PILE 8. SW. Lt. F.G. 5M. 5m. Vis.311°-131°.
PILE 9. SW. Lt. F.R. 5M. 5m. Vis.311°-131°.
NE. Lt. F.G. 5M. 5m. Vis.131°-311°. Siren 30 sec. Occas.
PILE 10. NE. Lt. F.R. 5M. 5m. Vis.131°-311°.

GLYNGORE HAVN 56°45.9'N, 8°51.9'E.
Owned by State Railways. Yacht berths in W side of Faergehavn. Depths 3.7m.

ON POINT. 56°45.9'N, 8°51.8'E. Lt. Oc.W.R.G. 5 sec. W.12M. R.8M. G.8M. W.R. Tr. 8m. G.021°-027°; W.027°-032°; R.032°-117°; G.117°-206°; W.206°-210°; R.210°-222°.
W MOLE HEAD Lt. F.G. 4M. G. post 4m.

NYKØBING 56°47.7'N, 8°52.0'E.
A yacht marina in Faergehavn. Depths 3.5m. and berths for yachts in Fiskerhavn. Depths 4.5m.

E. Ldg.Lts. 345° (Front) F.R. Y. △ on mast 6m.
Vis. on leading line. (Rear) F.R. Y. ▽ on mast
9m. Vis. on leading line.
W. Ldg.Lts. 323°36'. (Front) F.G. 2M. Y. △ on
mast 6m. (Rear) F.G. Y. ▽ on mast 14m.

LIVØ BREDNING
VODSTRUP. 56°48.4'N, 8°52.4'E. Lt.
Iso.W.R.G. 2 sec. W.12M. R.8M. G.8M. W.R.
House 16m. G.207°-210.5°; R.210.5°-213°;
G.213°-224°; W.224°-225.5°; R.225.5°-231°.

FUR. 56°50.3'N, 8°58.5'E. Lt. Oc.W.R.G. 5
sec. W.12M. R.8M. G.8M. W.R. House 13m.
G.162°-164.5°; R.164.5°-167.5°; G.167.5°-
208°; W.208°-214°; R.214°-222°.
FUR HAVN. ENTRANCE. E SIDE. Lt. F.G. 2M.
Grey post 3m.
W SIDE. Lt. F.R. 2M. Grey post 3m.
WHARF. Lt. F. 2M. Grey post 3m.

FEGGESUND
HAN NAES. Lt. Iso.W.R.G. 2 sec. 4M. R. post
15m. G.247°-289°, W.289°-297.5°,
R.297.5°-007°.
SKARREHAGE E. Ldg.Lts. 216°48'. (Front)
F.G. 4M. R. Tr. 16m.(Rear) F.G. 4M. R. Tr.
32m.
SKARREHAGE W. Ldg.Lts. 233°12'. (Front)
F.R. 4M. Tr. 3m. (Rear) F.R. 4M. Tr. 9m.
MALLE HAGE. Ldg.Lts. 262°30'. (Front) Iso.
2 sec. 6M. R. post 4m. (Rear) Iso. 4 sec. 6M.
R. post 13m.

VILSUND. 56°53'N, 8°38'E.
Radio: Bridge. VHF Chan. 16, 9, 12, 13.
0900-1700.
Entry: to request bridge opening at night —
call bridge-keeper during day.
VILSUND BRIDGE. N END. Lt. 2 F.R. 2 F.G.
4M. 3m. Traffic signals (1-3 F.R. vert.)

THISTED HAVN 56°57'N, 8°42'E.
Tel: (07) 923116.
Radio: VHF Chan. 16, 12, 13. As required.
Fiskerhavn depth 1m. to 2.9m.
THISTED BREDNING Lt. Aero 3 Fl.R. 1.5 sec.
Vert. 10M TV mast 183m.
N QUAY. Lt. F.R. 2M. Mast 8m. Vis.210°-050°.
W SHELTER MOLE. HEAD. Lt. Fl.R. 3 sec.
2M. R. col. 4m.
OUTER E MOLE. HEAD. Lt. Fl.G. 3 sec. 2M.
G. col. 4m.

ANNEKSHAVN. E MOLE. HEAD. Lt. Fl.G.
3 sec. 4M. G. post 5m.
W MOLE. HEAD. Lt. Fl.R. 3 sec. 4M. R. post
5m.

FUR HAVN
Fur Havn to Branden Faergebro Ferry.
VHF Chan. 16, 77.

NESS SUND
FERRY BERTH. E SIDE. Ldg.Lts. 100°24'.
(Front) F.G. 3M. Above bridge bascule 8m.
Shown from sunset to 2400 and from 0600
to sunrise. Occas. (Rear) F.G. 3M. Mast 9m.
Ldg.Lts. 291°48'. F.R. 3M. Above bridge
bascule 8m. Shown from sunset to 2400 and
from 0600 to sunrise. Occas. (Rear) F.R. 3M.
Mast 9m.

LØGSTØR. 56°58.2'N, 9°15.2'E.
Radio-Pilots: VHF Chan. 16, 12, 13.
Tel: Pilots: (08) 671075.
Channel from Løgstør to Alborg is 24M.
long controlling depth 4m.

LØGSTØR BREDNING
RØNBJERG HAVN. S MOLE. HEAD. Lt. F.G.
5M. Brown post 4m.
N MOLE. HEAD. Lt. F.R. 5M. Brown post 4m.

LØGSTØR. GRUNDE. 56°58.2'N,
9°15.2'E. Ldg.Lts. 079°. (Front) Iso. R.G. 2
sec. 13M. W. house, R. roof 9m. 7m. apart.
Each Lt. Vis.075°-083°. Lights are shown on
bridge 1.5M. N. (Rear) 56°58'N, 9°17.4'E. Iso.
4 sec. 17M. R.W. house with W. cross on
beacon 38m. The rear Lt. midway between
the front Lts. The rear Lt. in line with the G.
front Lt. indicates the S side, and in line with
the R. front Lt. the N side of the channel.
Vis.076.5°-081.5°.

AGGERSUND BROEN ROAD BRIDGE
Radio: VHF Chan. 16, 12, 13. As required.
Clearance under the bascule is 5.4m.
(centre).

GJOL has a fishery and yacht harbour,
depth 1m.

ATTRUP is a yacht harbour. Depth 2m. in
entrance. 1.2m. to 3m. in W part and less
than 1m. in E part.

ALBORG.
Tel: Pilots: (08) 120944 or 120609. H.M. (08)
122777.
Radio—Port: VHF Chan. 16, 12, 13. H24.
Radio—Pilots: VHF Chan. 16, 12, 13. As
required.
BRIDGE (LIMFJORDSBRO). VHF Chan. 16,
12, 13. As required.

VIRKSUND. 56°36'N, 9°18'E.
There is a yacht harbour on W side of
Virksund. Depth 2m. Max. length 12m.
Beam 4m.

VIRKSUND HAVN. Lt. F.R. 2M. R. dolphin.
F.R. Lock signals 0.1M. S.
E MOLE. Lt. F.G. 2M. G. post.

AGGERSUND. Lts. in line 135° (Front) F.R.
2M. ○ on mast 7m. Vis. 070°-200°. Mark
cable. Lts. are shown from the bridge
100m. W. (Rear) F.R.W. (vert.) R.2M.
W.3M. 8 on Tr. 12m. Vis.070°-200°.

HVALPSUND. 56°42'N, 9°12.1'E.
Yacht harbour has 175 berths, depth 3m.
Max. size 20m. × 5m. × 2m. draught.

YACHT HARBOUR. N MOLE. HEAD. Lt. Fl.R.
3 sec. 6M. Brown post 4m.
SUNDSØRE FERRY HARBOUR. Ldg.Lts.
291°18'. (Front) F.R. 3M. 10m. For use of
ferries. Shown from sunset to 2400 and
from 0600 to sunrise. (Rear) F.R. 3M. Mast
25m. For use of ferries. Occas. Shown from
sunset to 2400 and from 0600 to sunrise.
Lt. F.G. 4M. Post 4m. Shown from sunset to
2400 and from 0600 to sunrise. Siren 50 sec.
FISKENHAVN. Ldg.Lts. 201°24'. (Front) F.
5M. Ferry berth 10m. For use of ferries.
Shown from sunset to 2400 and from 0600
to sunrise. (Rear) F. 5M. Wooden mast 15m.
Shown from sunset to 2400 and from 0600
to sunrise.

N MOLE. HEAD. Lt. F.R. 3M. R. mast 4m. in
line 136.6° with F.R. on W. Mole leads clear
of Sundsøre Odde.
W MOLE. HEAD. Lt. F.G. 4M. G. mast 4m.
Shown from sunset to 2400 and from 0600
to sunrise. Fog Det. Lt. Siren 50 sec.
sounded 0600-2400.
Lt. F.R. 5M. B. mast 6m. Vis.117.5°-155.5°.
Shown from sunset to 2400 and from 0600
to sunrise.

SKIVE

YDNE HAVN CHANNEL
Ldg.Lts. 188°48' (Front) Iso. 2 sec. 6M. Or.R.
△ on Grey Tr. 6m. 068.8°-308.8° (Rear) Iso. 4
sec. 17M. Or.R. ▽ on grey Tr. 12m. 068.8°-
308.8°.

INDRE HAVN CHANNEL
Ldg.Lts. 228°33' (Front) Iso. R. 2 sec. 4M.
Or.R. △ on post 5m. 108.5°-348.5° (Rear) Iso.
R. 4 sec. 4M. Or.R. ▽ on post 7m. 108.5°-
348.5°.

SKIVE HAVN. 56°34.2'N, 9°3.2'E.
Tel: (07) 520068.
Radio—Port: VHF Chan. 16, 9, 12. 0700-1200,
1300-1615.
Large basin for yachts 2c. N of main harbour
entrance. Depth 2.5m.

S MOLE. HEAD. Lt. F.R. 4M. Grey Tr. 6m.
N MOLE. HEAD. Lt. F.G. 4M. post 6m.

NORTH SEA COAST

LODBJERG. Lt. Fl.(2) 20 sec. 23M. Round
granite Tr. 48m.
STENBJERG. Siren (2) 30 sec. Fishing.

VORUPØR
Ldg.Lts. (Front) Iso.R. 4 sec. 9M. R.W. Tr.
20m. Vis.22.5° on each side of alignment.
Leading Lts. to safest landing place. Moved
as the channel alters. (Rear) Iso.R. 4 sec. 9M.
R.W. Tr. 30m. Vis.22.5° on each side of
alignment.

MOLE. HEAD. Lt. Fl.G. 5 sec. 4M. Grey Tr.
6m.
AMTOFT BRO. 57°0.3'N, 8°56.7'E. Fishing
and yacht harbour. 2.5m. in entrance. 1.7m.
in yacht harbour.

KLITMØLLER
Ldg.Lts. 146° (Front) F.R. 4M. Mast 8m.
Vis.097°-210° Moved as the channel
changes. Fishing. (Rear) F.R. 4M. Mast 13m.
Vis.090°-202°. Fishing.
LANDING PLACE. Siren (2) 60 sec. Fishing.

HANSTHOLM HAVEN. 57°7.5'N,
8°35.5'E.
Tel: (07) 961017/961157.
Radio—Port & Pilots: VHF Chan. 16, 12, 13.

57°06.8'N, 8°36.0'E. Lt. Fl.(3) 20 sec. 26M. W.
8-sided Tr. 65m. Shown by day in poor
visibility. RC.

VESTMOLE. HEAD. Lt. Fl.G. 3 sec. 9M. G.
pillar. Floodlit 11m.
ØSTMOLE. HEAD. 57°07.7'N, 8°35.7'E. Lt.
Fl.R. 3 sec. 9M. R. pillar. Floodlit 11m.
57°07.1'N, 8°36.2'E. Ldg.Lts. 142°36'. (Front)
Iso. 2 sec. 13M. R. △ on mast 37m.
Vis.127.6°-157.6°. (Rear) Iso. 2 sec. 13M. R. ▽
on mast 45m.
VESTRE TVAERMOLE. HEAD. Lt. F.G. 6M. G.
col. Floodlit 6m.
ROOT. Horn 15 sec.
ØSTRE TVAERMOLE. HEAD. 57°07.4'N,
8°35.7'E. Lt. F.R. 6M. R. col. Floodlit 6m.

ROSHAGE. Lt. Fl. 5 sec. 6M. Tr. 7m.
LILDSTRAND. Ldg.Lts. 3 F. 7M. 7M. 8M. Wooden masts 12m. 12m. 22m. Vis.127°-149°. Fishing.
LANDING PLACE. Siren 30 sec. Grey mast. Fishing.

TRANUM. SIGNAL MAST. No. 1. 57°10.8′N, 9°26.7′E. Lt. Al.W.R. 4 sec. W.16M. R.13M. Tr. 20m. When firing is taking place. F.R. obstruction Lts. on masts. By day Fl.
No. 2 Lt. Al.W.R. 4 sec. Mast. When firing is taking place. By day Fl.
LØKKEN. LEE BREAKWATER. HEAD. Lt. Fl. 5 sec. 5M. Mast 5m.

HIRTSHALS HAVN. 57°35.6′N, 9°57.9′E.
Tel: (08) 941422.
Radio—Port & Pilots: VHF Chan. 16, 14. As required. Vessels up to 5.4m draught.

HIRTSHALS. 57°35.1′N, 9°56.6′E. Lt. F. Fl. 30 sec. Fl. 25M. F.18M. W round Tr. 57m. RC. A short eclipse may be seen before and after the 0.3 sec. flash.**SW OF LIGHTHOUSE.** Horn(2) 60 sec.

57°35.7′N, 9°57.7′E. Ldg.Lts. 166° (Front) Iso.R. 2 sec. 11M. R. △ on W. Mast 10m. Vis.156°-176°. RC. (Rear) Iso.R. 4 sec. 11M. R. ▽ on W. mast 18m. Vis.156°-176°.

OUTER SHELTER MOLE. HEAD. Lt. Fl.G. 3 sec. 6M. G. mast 14m. Horn 20 sec.

W MOLE. HEAD. Lt. Fl.G. 5 sec. 4M. G. mast 9m.
E MOLE. HEAD. Lt. Fl.R. 5 sec. 6M. R. mast 9m.

INNER HARBOUR. Lts. F.G. F.R. 4M. G.R. masts 6m.

Visual Navigational Aids and Port Information

25

SE Norway to Southern Baltic

NORWAY

DOCUMENTATION

Yachts should be registered.
All crew members must have valid passports.
Entry: Yachts must enter Norway at one of the following ports and report immediately to
Customs: Bergen, Haugesund, Stavanger, Egersund, Mandal, Kristiansand, Lillesand,
Fredrikstad, Tonsberg, Moss.
Yachts may remain in Norway for up to 12 months.
Norwegian Tourist Board, Charles House, 5 Lower Regent Street, London, S.W.1.
Tel: 071-839 6255.
Royal Norwegian Embassy, 25 Belgrave Square, London, S.W.1. Tel: 071-235 7151.

Yachtsmen. The Norwegian authorities have issued guidance for non-commercial foreign
pleasure craft as follows:
    Crews exempt from obtaining a visa may navigate outside Restricted Sea Areas without
permission. In Restricted Sea Areas they may navigate in the prescribed channels as per the
chart (with a State Pilot if the vessel is of more than 50 GRT). They may stop at recognised
towns and calling places, but not elsewhere, and may take part in regattas.
    Crews obliged to obtain a visa must comply with: Directions for Yachting Tours in
Norwegian Territorial Waters by Foreigners subject to Norwegian Visa Regulations (Royal
Norwegian Ministry of Justice).

Restricted Areas in Norwegian Territorial Waters
Kristiansand – all waters N of a line through:

Arosveten	58°04.0'N 7°50.0'E	Meholmskjaer	58°05.6'N 8°11.9'E
Songvar Lighthouse	58°00.9'N 7°49.0'E	Langbaen (Langbaskjaer)	58°06.4'N 8°15.4'E
Lille Svarten	58°02.9'N 8°01.4'E	Krygholmen, E extremity	58°07.2'N 8°14.4'E

Outer Oslofjorden – Langesundsfjorden – all waters N of a line through:

Norwegian border in	58°58.6'N 11°04.3'E	Svenner Light Tr.	58°58.1'N 10°09.1'E
Torbjornskjaer		Tvistein Lighthouse	58°56.2'N 9°56.6'E
Lighthouse	58°59.7'N 10°47.2'E	Mejulen Lt. Structure	58°57.7'N 9°41.6'E
Faerder Light Tr.	59°01.6'N 10°31.7'E	Position on shore in	58°57.9'N 9°41.9'E

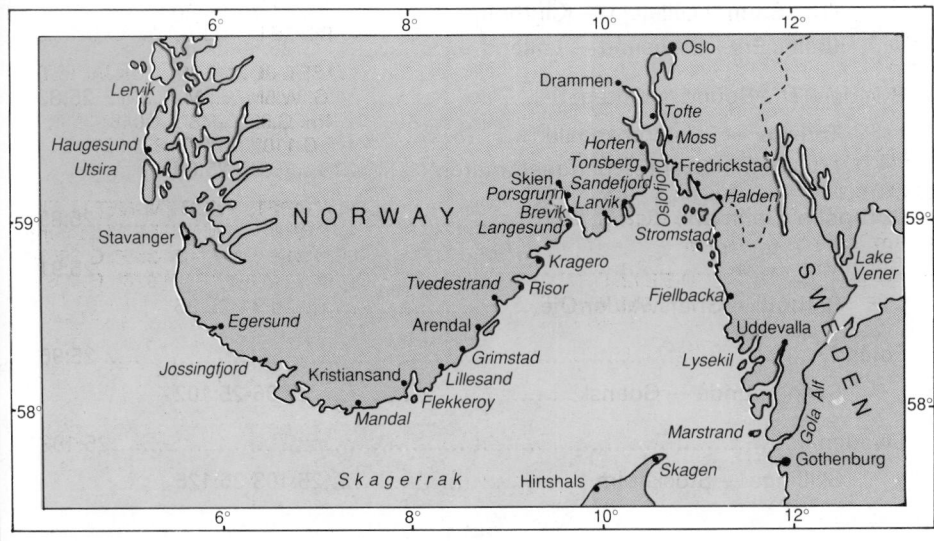

The main S.A.R. stations covered by this section are Kristiansand and Oslo. Local stations are at:

Brekkestø	58°12'N 8°21'E	Lyngør	58°38'N 9°08'E	Ule	59°01'N 10°11'E
Hesnesøy	58°20'N 8°39'E	Portør	58°48'N 9°26'E	Sandøysund	59°05'N 10°28'E
Merdø	58°25'N 8°48'E	Langesund	59°00'N 9°45'E	Herføl	59°00'N 11°03'E
Kilsund	58°33'N 8°59'E	Stavern	59°00'N 10°03'E		

Rescue services are organised by the Police through several agencies, i.e. Pilots, Customs, Navy, Rescue Associations etc.

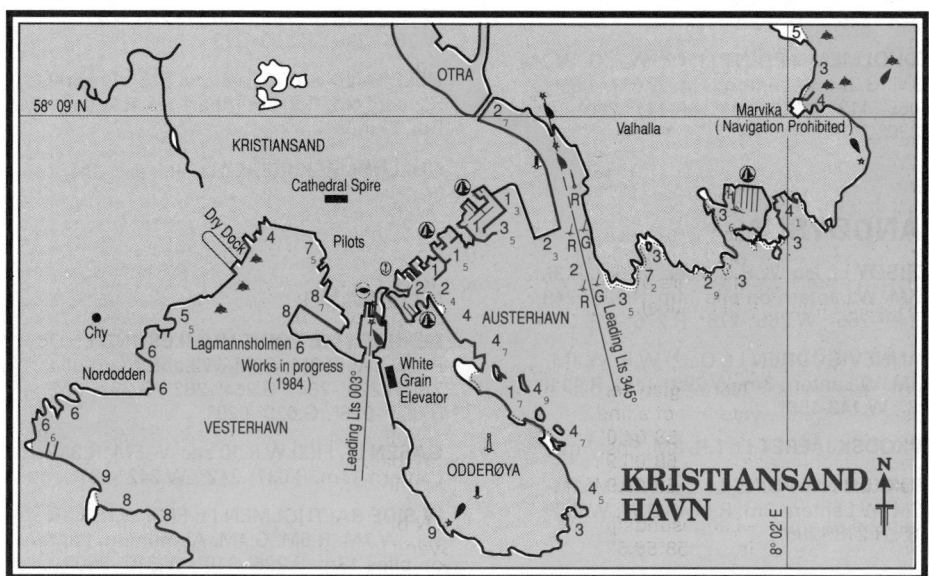

KRISTIANSAND 58°09'N 8°00'E
Tel: (042) 29552 (H.M.) (042) 24111 (Pilots)
Fax: (042) 22499. Telex: 21784 AGLOS N.
Radio-Port: VHF Chan. 12, 14, 16 H24.
Radio-Pilots: VHF Chan. 13, 12, 16 H24.
Entry: Large commercial port. Usually ice-free.

DYBINGEN Lt. Fl. R.3 sec. W.Lantern 6m.

FISKABUGTA ØGREY Ldg. Lts. 165° (Front) F.R. 4M. Post 5m. 075°-255°. (Rear) F.R.4M. Tr. 11m. 075°-255°. Private.

ODDERØYA 58°07.8'N 8°00.5'E Lt. Oc(2) W.R.G.8 sec. W.11M. R.9M. G.8M. W.R.Tr. Or.Lantern 12m. W.297°-299°; G.299°-320°; W.320°-330°; R.330°-000°; G.000°-078°; W.078°-134°; R.134°-143°.

FISHING HARBOUR Ldg. Lts. 003° (Front) F.R. 2M. Daymark on Fish Hall 8m. (Rear) F.R. 2M Daymark on Fish Hall 11m.

TOPDALSFJORDEN GLEODDEN Lt. Oc. W.R.G.6 sec. W.9M. R.6M. G.6M. W.Lantern 6m. G.181°-214°; W.214°-216°; R.216-010°; W.010°-020°; G.020°-040°.

OTRA (TORRIDALSELVA) Ldg. Lts. 345° (Front) F.R. (Rear) F.R.

VARODD BRIDGE Lts. 2 F.G. one either side.

VESTRE GABET. JØNGEHOLMSKJAERET Lt. Oc. W.R.G. W.5M. R.3M. G.3M. W.Lantern 4m. G.039°-048°; W.048°-053°; R.053°-110°; G.110°-125°; R.125°-201°; W.201°-209°.

FLEKKERØYGAPET. TORSTENSNET Lt. Fl. W.R.G.5 sec. W7M. R.5M. G.5M. W.Lantern 15M. R.266°-231.5°; W.231.5°-305°; G.305°-008.5°; W.008.5°-018°; R.018°-026°; G.026°-shore.

KRISTIANSANDSFJORDEN

GRONNINGEN 58°04.8'N 8°05.6'E Lt. Oc(3) W.R.G.12.5 sec. W.13M. R.12M. G.11M. W.Tr. W.House 19m. G.254°-274°; R.274°-310°; W.310°-030°; R.030°-122°; W.122°-140°; G.140°-165°. Horn 30 sec.

OKSØY 58°04.2'N 8°03.5'E Lt. Fl(2) 45 sec. 19M. W.R. Tr. 47m. RC. Racon AUX. Lt. F. 15M. Same structure 25m. 268°-273°.

KINN Lt. Oc(2) W.R.G.8 sec. W.7M. R.5M. G.5M. W.Lantern 8m. G.090°-094°; W.094°-112°; R.112°-152°; W.152°-184°; G.184°-200°; W.200°-205°; R.205°-220°; G.220°-245°; W.245°-256°; R.256°-307°; W.307°-321°; G.321°-325°.

LEDHOLMEN N POINT Lt. Oc. W.R.G. W.7M. R.3M. G.2M. W.Lantern 7m. W.037°-065°; G.065°-112°; W.112°-117°; R.117°-230°; G.230°-247°.

RANDØYSUN

TORSØY Lt. Iso. W.R.G.6 sec. W.6M. R.3M. G.3M. W.Lantern on pile 14m. R.135°-249°; G.249°-265°; W.265°-276°; R.276°-315°.

MANNEVIGODDEN Lt. Oc(2) W.R. W.4M. R.3M. W.Lantern 3m. W.290°-111°; R.111°-143°; W.143-156°.

KIRKODSKJAERET Lt. F.R. 3M. Post 5m.

STOKKEN NW POINT Lt. Oc. W.R. W.7M. R.2M. W.Lantern 3m. R.024°-207°; W.207°-218°; R.218°-285°.

RANSØYSUND

KVALSHOLMBAEN W OF KVALSHOLMEN Lt. Fl.3 sec. 2M. Lantern on piles 3m.

KVALSHOLMEN Ldg. Lts. 234° (Front) Oc. W.R.G.4 sec. W.6M. R.4M. G.4M. W.Lantern 8m. G.040°-046°; W.046°-051°; R.051°-227°; W.227°-239°; G.239°-245°.

NATVIGTANGEN (Common Rear) Oc(2) 8 sec. 7M. W.Lantern 22m. 230°-240°; 029°-035°. Intens on leading lines.

SVERVIKODDEN Ldg. Lts. 032° (Front) Oc. W.G.6 sec. W.7M. G.4M. W.Lantern 8m. W.029°-035°. Intens on leading line. G.220°-335°.

SPAGSNESSKJAER Lt. Oc(2) W.R.G.8 sec. W.7M. R.4M. G.4M. W.Lantern 5m. R.044°-098°; W.098°-108°; R. 108°-180°; G.180°-222°; R.222°-226°.

AGERØY. RABBODDEN Lt. Oc(2) W.R.G. W.4M. R.3M. G.2M. W.Lantern on piles 6m. G.238°-272°; W.272°-321°; R.321°-352°; G.352°-089°; R.089°-123°.

BREKKESTØ

REIERSKJAER Lt. F. W.R.G.5 sec. W.7M. R.4M. G.3M. W.Lantern on piles 9m. G.172°-201°; W.201°-228°; G.228°-248°; R.248°-293°; W.293°-333°; G.333°-045°; W.045°-052°; R.052°-060°.

VRAGHOLMSKJAERET Lt. Oc. W.R.G. W.7M. R.3M. G.2M. W.Lantern on piles 5m. W.086°-116°; R.256°-260°; G.260°-285°; W.285°-290°; R.290°-323°.

LILLESAND HAVN Ldg. Lts. 318° (Front) Iso. R.2 sec. 4M. Col. 7m (Rear) Iso. R.2. sec. 4M. Col. 27m.

GULLHOLMSKJAERET Lt. Fl.3 sec. 3M. Col. 5m.

LILLESAND

BERGSØY NE POINT HUMLESUND Lt. Oc. R.G.6 sec. R.3M. G2M. W.Lantern on piles 7m. R.220°-264°; G.264°-282°; R.282°-302°; R.007°-025°; G.025°-029°.

GASEN Lt. Fl(2) W.R.10 sec. W.5M. R.3M. Lantern 14m. R.037°-242°; W.242°-037°.

W SIDE SALTHOLMEN Lt. Fl(3) W.R.G.15 sec. W.7M. R.5M. G.4M. Aluminium Lantern on piles 13m. R.296°-310°; W.310°-330°; G.330°-359°; W.359°-003°; R.003°-011°; W.011°-045°.

HOMBORSUND

STORE GRONNINGEN S POINT 58°15.2'N 8°32.1'E. Lt. F. Fl(4) 60 sec. 14M. W. Tr. on house 22m.

HAVNESPYNTEN Lt. Oc. W.R.G. W.4M. R.3M. G.2M. W.Lantern 14m. W.222°-225°; R.225°-308°; W.308°-311°; G.311°-127°. G sector partly obscured by Homboroy and Sandholmen.

SUNDHOLMEN N POINT Lt. Oc(2) W.R.G. W.4M. R.3M. G2M. W.Lantern 9m. G.067°-077°; W.077°-080°; R.080°-204°; G.204°-308°.

HOMBORSUNDSLEIA Ldg. Lts. 042° **HESTRIGPYNTEN** (Front) Oc. W.R.G.6 sec. W.10M. R.9M. G.9M. W.Lantern 6M. G.325°-333°; W.333°-344°; R.344°-027°; W.027°-050°; G.050°-054°. **RAMSHANGEN** (Rear) Oc. 12M. W.Lantern 30m. 039°-045°. Intens on leading line.

GRIMSTAD

STANGHOLMEN Lt. Oc(2) W.R.G.9 sec.
W.6M. R.4M. G.3M. W.Lantern 11M. R.315°-327°; G.327°-334°; W.334°-346°; R.346°-002°;
G.002°-034°; R.034°-050°; W.050°-055°;
G.055°-091°; R.091°-149°; G.149°-171°.

RIVINGDYPET Lt. Fl. R.3 sec. 3M. Pile 7m.

RIVINGEN Lt. Oc(3) W.R.G. W.5M. R.3M.
G.3M. W.Lantern 12m. R.335°-347°; W.347°-351°; G.351°-162°; W.162°-177°; R.177°-189°.

RISHOLMEN NW POINT Lt. Fl.3 sec. 3M.
Lantern on Pedestal 7m.

ØSTRE TIVILLINGHOLMEN Ldg. Lts. 023°
(Front) Oc(2) W.R.G. W.5M. R.8M. G.2M.
W.Lantern 8m. R.020°-026°. Intens on
leading line. W.199°-208°; G.208°-282°;
G.340°-003°; **VESSØYHODET** (Rear) Oc. R.G.
W.13M. R.9M. G.8M. W.Lantern 21m.
R.108°-028° intens on leading line, G.289°-301°; R.301°-311°.

BJORØY NE POINT Lt. Iso. W.R.G.6 sec.
W.5M. R.3M. G3.M. W.Lantern 20M. R.198°-207°; W.207°-218°; G.218°-268°; W.268°-274°; R.274°-300°; W.300°-333°; G.333°-353°;
W.353°-013°; R.013°-025°.

SPAERHOLMEN Lt. Fl. W.R.G.5 sec. W.9M.
R.6M. G.6M. W.Lantern 9m. G.020°-022°;
W.022°-037°; R.037°-045°; W.045°-047°;
G.047°-051°; R.051°-211°; W.211°-222°;
G.222°-227°.

FEVIK Lt. Oc. R.G. R.3M. G.3M. W.Lantern
9m. G.223°-231°; R.231°-253°; G.253°-311;
R.311°-323°.

HESNES Ldg. Lts. 227° **HAHOLMEN** (Front)
Oc. W.R.G.6 sec. W.10M. R.7M. G.7M.
W.Lantern 5m. G.126°-218°; W.218°-230°;
R.230°-008°; W.008°-013°; G.013°-016°.
KVALØY (Rear) F. R.5M. W.Lantern 15m.
224°-230°. Intens on leading line.

KVALØY NW POINT. HESNESSUND ØSTRE
Lt. Oc. W.R.G. Sec. W.9M. R.7M. G6.M.
W.Lantern 4m. R.226°-235°; G.235°-241°;
W.241°-245°; R.245°-251°. G. from shore to
shore in **Hesnessund**.

HESNESØY W POINT HESNESSUND
VESTRE Lt. Oc. W.R.G.6 sec. W.9M. R.7M.
G.6m. W.Lantern 12m. R. from shore to
shore in **HESNESSUND** G.024°-035°;
W.035°-043°; R.043°-052°; W.150°-160°.

HESNESBREGEN Lt. Fl. W.R.15 sec. W.6M.
R.4M. Lantern on piles 13m. R.036°-232°;
W.232°-036°.

LEIHOLMSUND Ldg. Lts. 232° **LEIHOLMENS**
(Front) Oc. W.R.G. W.4M. R.3M. G.2M.
W.Lantern on piles 9m. R.220°-255.5°;
W.255.5°-259°; G.259°-269°; G.045.5°-049°;
R.049°-078°. **SALESKJAER** (Rear) Oc. R.G.
R.3M. G.2M. W.Lantern 3m. G. over
LEIHOLMSUND R.047°-112°.

GALTEN Lt. Fl. G.5 sec. 1M. W.Lantern on
bn. 5m.

ENTRANCE TO ARENDAL

ARENDAL 58°28'N 8°46'E
Tel: (041) 16154 (Port H.M.): (041) 23668
(Pilots).
Radio Port/Pilots VHF Chan. 12, 13, 16 H24.

TROMØYSUND BRONESET 58°28.1'N
8°49.9'E. Lt. Oc. W.R.G.6 sec. W.10M. R.7M.
G7M. W.Lantern 3m. R.064°-067°; W.067°-076°; G.076°-218°; W.218°-228°; R.228°-237°.

TROMØY BRIDGE Lt. 2 F. G. Vert. Centre
Span. SSE Lt. F. R.G. R. over shore (180°); G.
over Fairway (180°); NNW Lt. F. R.G. R. over
shore (180°). G. over fairway (180°).

TORUNGEN STORE TORUNGEN 58°23.8'N
8°47.9'E. Lt. Fl.20 sec. 18M W.R. Tr. 43M.
R.C. Racon.

LILLE TORUNGEN Lt. Oc(2) W.R.G.9 sec.
W.6M. R.4M. G.4M. W.Lantern on piles 9m.
R.154°-159°; W.159°-165°; W.165°-235°;
R.235°-252°; W.252°-261°; G.261°-296°;
W.296°-317°; R.317°-344°; W.344°-354°;
G.354°-047°; W.047°-049°; R.049°-115°.

MERDØY W POINT. Lt. Oc. W.R.G.6 sec.
W.9M. R.8MN. G.8M. W.Lantern 5m. R.317°-348°; G.348°-033°; W.033°-035°; R.035°-151°;
G.151°-180°.

SANDVIKODDEN 58°26.1'N 8°47.4'E. Lt.
Oc(3) W.R.G. W.12M. R.9M. G.8M.
W.Lantern 17m. R.170°-297°; G.297°-320°;
R.320°-344°; W.344°-001°; R.001°-005°.

HAHOLMBAEN Lt. Fl. G.3 sec. 1M. Lantern
7m.

LILLE SKOTHOLMEN Lt. Q. G.3M. Col. 7m.

GALTEN Lt. Fl. R.3 sec. 1M. Col. 3m.

TROMØYSUND

GITMERTANGEN Ldg. Lts. 222° **SOUTH** (Rear) Oc(2) 8 sec. 7M. Hut 26m 215°-230°. Intens on leading line. (Common Front) Oc.6 sec. 10M. W.Lantern on piles 9m. 136°-348°. Ldg. Lts 238° **NORTH** (Rear) Oc.6 sec. 10M. W. Lantern 21m. 233°-243°. Intens on leading line.

SKINDFELDTANGEN 58°31.0'N 8°57.2'E. Lt. Oc. W.R.G.6 sec. W.11M. R.8M. G.8M. W. Lantern 19m. R235°-263°; G.263°-300°; W.300°-307°; R307°-335°; W.335°-056°; G.056°-061°.

KJØRVIGPYNTEN Lt. Q. 3M. Lantern 5m.

FRISØY E POINT. Lt. Oc. W.R.G.6 sec. W10M. R.7M. G.7M. W.Lantern 5m. R.235°-239°; W.239°-243°; G.243°-049°; W.049°-053°; R.053°-063°;

BONDEN Lt. Fl. W.R.G.5 sec. W.7M. R.4M. G3M. W.Lantern on piles 14m. W.068°-075°; R.075°-229°; W.229°-238°; G.238°-068°.

TVEDSTRAND

KILSUND Ldg. Lts. 220° **FLOSTAØY NE POINT** (Rear) Oc(2) W.R.G.8 sec. W.10M. R.8M. G.8M. Lantern on store base 8m. W.shore-135°; R.135°-248°; G.248°-318°; W.318°-323°; R.323°-339°. **TVERDALSØY. HOLMESUNDSODDENN** (Common Front) Oc. W.R.G. W.4M. R.3M. G.3M. W.Lantern on piles 4m. W.013°-026°; R.026-051°; W.205°-226°; G.226°-013°. Ldg. Lts. 019° **OKSEFJORDEN** (Rear) Oc. W.R.G. W.4M. R.3M. G.2M. W.Lantern 9m. G.148°-156°; W.156°-157°; R.157°-226°; W.226°-046°.

RENDESKJAER Lt. Fl.3 sec. 3M. Lantern on piles 10m.

GRAVIKTANGEN Lt. Oc(3) W.R.G. W.7M. R.3M. G.2M. W.Lantern 7M. R.330°-344°; G.344°-110°; W.110°-127°; R.127°-151°.

SAGESUND Lt. Iso. W.R.G.4 sec. W.4M. R.3M. G.2M. W.Lantern 3m. R.346°-351°; W.351°-355°; G.355°-049°.

FURØYSUND Lt. Oc. W.R. W.4M. R.3M. W.Lantern 4m. W.158°-170°; R.170°-243°; W.243°-252°.

RAKENESTANGEN Lt. Iso. W.R.G.6 sec. W.4M. R.3M. G2M. W.Lantern 3m. R.310°-313°; W.313°-319°; G.319°-359°; R.359°-150°.

SANDØY W Point **HAVEFJORD** Lt. Oc(2) W.R.G. W.4M. R.3M. G.2M. W.Lantern 4m. G.352°-002°; W.002°-014°; R.014°-201°; G.201°-212°.

LYNGØRLEIA

LYNGOR KJEHOLMENS 58°38.1'N 9°09.4'E SW END Lt. F. Fl.60 sec. 14M. W.House. Tr. R. Band on S side. Dia(2) 90 sec.

TERNESKJAER Lt. Oc(2) R.G. R.3M. G.3M. W.Lantern on piles 6m. R.235°-246°; G.246°-045°; R.045°-053°; G.053°-065°.

BRENNINGSHOLMEN Ldg. Lts. 251° (Front) Oc. W.R.G.6 sec. W.10M. R.7M. G.7M. W.Lantern 11m. W.235°-339°; G.339°-045°; R.045°-058°. **TØKERSFJELL** (Rear) Oc(2) 8 sec. 7M. W.Lantern 21m. 246°-256°.

RUHOLMEN Lt. Oc(2) R.G. R.3M. G.2M. W.Lantern 3m. R.210°-235°; G.235°-258°; R.292°-043°; G.043°-066°.

JESØYSKJAER Lt. Oc. W.R.G. W.5M. R.3M. G.2M. W.Lantern 3m. G.195°-226°; R.226°-314°; W.314°-324°; R.324°-011°; G.011°-034°.

SONDELEDFJORDEN

HAVNES Lt. Fl. 4 sec. Pile 5m

RISØR

STANGHOLMEN 58°42.5'N 9°15.1'E. Lt. Oc. W.R.G.6 sec. W.10M. R.9M. G.8M. W.Lantern 9m. G.167°-184°; R.184°-253°; G.253°-322°; W.322°-349°; R.349°-011°.

SANDNESFJORDEN FURUØY 58°41.8'N 9°13.6'E. Lt. Oc(2) W.R.G.8 sec. W.10M. R.8M. G.8M. W.Lantern 13m. G.214-220°; W.220°-223°; R.223°-248°; W.248°-255°; G.255°-269°; W.269°-278°; R.278°-306°.

BJØRNSKJAER Lt. Oc(3) W.R.G.10 sec. W.9M. R.6M. G.6M. W.Lantern 8m. R.153°-207°; W.207°-215°; G.215°-008°; R.008°-024°; W.024°-040°; G.040-103°.

MIDTSKJAER Lt. Oc. R.G.6 sec. R.5M. G.5M. W.Lantern 4m. R.013°-025°; G.025°-050°; G.171°-194°; R.194°-212°.

SKOMAKERSKJAERET Lt. F.R. Cairn 5m.

RISØR Havn. Ldg. Lts. 351° (Front). F.R. 3M. Mast 12m (Rear) F.R. 3M Mast 21m.

BUVIKSUGGA Lt. Fl.3 sec. 3M. Cairn 7m.

GRØNHOLMGAPET

GRØNHOLMSKJAER Lt. Oc(2) W.R.G.9 sec. W.6M. R.4M. G.4M. W.Lantern on piles 7m. R.236°-253°; W.253°-263°; G.263°-073°; W.073°-078°; R.078°-093°.

KRAGERØFJORDEN

STRØMTANGEN 58°50.1'N 9°28.4'E. Ldg. Lts. 340° (Front) Oc. W.R.6 sec. W.10M. R.10M. W.Hut 8m. R.186°-322°; W.322°-346°. **STAVSENG** (Rear) Oc(2) W.R.G.8 sec. W.12M. R.9M. G.9M. W. Tr. on W.House 26m. W.335°-080°. Intens on leading line G.080°-094°; W.094°-105°; R.105°-108°; W.108°-119°.

BUTTEBAEN Lt. Oc. W.R.G.8 sec. W4M. R.3M. G.2M. W.Lantern on piles 4m. G.301°-311°; W.311°-318°; R.318°-071°; W.071°-075°; G.075°-151°; R.151°-172°; G.172°-183°.

TATOYKALVEN Lt. Fl.3 sec. Col.

KILSFJORDEN TATØY Lt. Fl. 5 sec. 3M. W.Lantern 9m.

ATANGEN Ldg. Lts. 329° (Front) F.R. (Rear) F.R.

KRAGERØ 58°52'N 9°25'E
Tel: (035) 81750
Radio Port: VHF Chan. 12, 13, 14, 16.

KRAGERØ 58°51.9'N 9°25.9'E Lt. Oc. W.R.G.6 sec. W.10M. R.7M. G.7M. W.Lantern 4m. G122°-146°; W.146°-171°; R.171°-189°; G.189°-193°; R.193°-206°; G.206°-353°; W.353°-029°.

SLEPA Lt. Fl. R.3 sec. 3M. Tripod 10m.

DJUPODDEN 58°51.5'N 9°35.4'E Ldg. Lts. 046° (Front) Oc. 10M. W.Lantern 14m. 042°-050°. Intens on leading line.
JOMFRUMLAND 58°51.8'N 9°36.3'E (Rear) F. Fl.15 sec 19M. W. Tr. 48m. Horn 30 sec.

LOVISENBERGSUNDET Ldg. Lts. 313° (Front) F.R. (Rear) F.R.

LANGARDSUND

KREPPA SW SIDE Lt. Fl. G.3 Sec. 1M. Pedestal 4m.

SUNDGARDSHOLMEN Lt. Oc. W.R.G.6 sec. W.4M. R.3M. G.2M. W.Lantern 4m. G.056°-064°; R.064°-248°; W.248°-251°; G.251°-261°.

SVANEFLEKKEN Lt. Fl. R.3 sec. 2M. Pedestal 4m.

SKJENSUND Lt. Oc. W.R.G.6 sec. W.4M. R.3M. G.2M. W.Lantern 5m. R.233°-251°; G.251°-280°; W.280°-306°; R.306°-070°; W.070°-072°; G.072°-082°.

TONERLEIA

SASTEINSUND KJELEN Lt. Fl.5 sec. 3M. Col. 6m.

MEJULEN NW SIDE Lt. Fl. W.R.G.5 sec. W.7M. R.5M. G.4M. W.Lantern on piles 6m. R.038°-049°; W.049°-058°; G.058°-224°; R.224°-230°.

DANHOLMEN Lt. Oc. W.R.G.6 sec. W.7M. R.5M. G.4M. W.Lantern 7m. G.220°-226°; W.226°-230°; R.230°-024°; W.024°-032°; G.032°-038°.

VITTENSKJUL Lt. Fl. W.R.G.5 sec. W.7M. R.4m. G.3M. W.Lantern 22m. G.221°-252°; W.252°-258.5°; R.258.5°-351.5°; G.351.5°-039°; W.039°-064°; R.064°-066°.

STORE FLUER Lt. Oc. W.R. W.4M. R.3M. W.Lantern 4m. W.071°-076°; R.076°-235°; W.235°-249°.

FOSSINGFJORD RISØY E POINT Lt. Oc(2) W.R.G. W.4M. R.3M. G.2M. W.Lantern 5M. G124°-134.5°; W.134.5°-148°; R.148°-271°; W.271°-279.5°; G.279.5°-287°.

FOSSINGFJORD Lt. Fl. W.R.5 sec. W.3M. R.2M. Pedestal 4m. W.123°-295°; R.295°-123°.

SKIENSELVA

KJØRBEKK Lt. Oc. R.6 sec. 7M. Hut on piles 5m. Vis. up and down river.

SVEA Lt. Oc. 6 sec. 8M. W.Hut 3m. Vis. up and down river.

SKIEN 59°13'N 9°37'E
Tel: (035) 95435
(Port): Telex 21160 STERM N
Radio Port: VHF Chan. 12, 14, 16, as required

SKIEN Ldg. Lts. 339° (Front) F.R. 3M. House 14m (Rear) F.R. 3M. Town Hall 24m.

Lt. Q.

PORSGRUND SELVA

TORSBERG 59°07.3'N 9°36.6'E Lt. Oc. W.R.G.6 sec. W.11M. R.9M. G9M. W.Lantern 9m. R.225°-226.5°; W.226.5°-310°; G.310°-335.5°; W.335.5°-341°; R.341°-011°; W.011°-053.5°; G.053.5°-066°.

PORSGRUNN 59°09'N 9°39'E
Tel: (035) 71233
Radio Port: VHF Chan. 12,14, 16 as required.
Bridge: VHF Chan. 12, 14 H24.

Porsgrunn Bridge –
Outward Bound vessel has priority.
In fog: Continuous sounding of fog horn =
Bridge cannot be opened.
Slow strokes of Bell = Inward vessels may
pass.
Continuous ringing of Bell= Outward
vessels may pass.
By Day and Night –
1 R.Lt. at N Bridge Head plus 2 Hor. R.Lts. in
middle of Bridge = Bridge cannot be
opened.
1 R.Lt. at N Bridge Head – Shown to Inward
Traffic = Do not pass.
1 G.Lt. at N Bridge Head – Shown to Inward
Traffic = May pass.
1 R.Lt. at N Bridge Head – Shown to
Outward Traffic = Do not pass.
1 G.Lt at N Bridge Head – Shown to
Outward Traffic = May pass.

VESTRE PORSGRUND 59°08.3'N 9°38.7'E.
Ldg. Lts. 045° (Front) F.R. 11M. W.Lantern
8m. Vis. only down river (Rear) F.R. 11M.
Hut 25m. Vis. only down river.

FRIERFJORDEN

FLAUØDDEN 59°03.3'N 9°40.2'E. Lt. Oc(2)
W.R.G. W.11M. R.8M. G.8M. W.Lantern 9m.
G.286°-295°; R.295°-028°; G.028°-086°;
W.086°-129°.

MIDTFJORDSKJER 59°03.3'N 9°39.4'E. Lt.
Oc(3) W.R.G.10 sec. W.11M. R.9M. G.9M. Tr.
10m. G.051.5°-138°; R.138°-159°; W.159°-
164.5°; G.164.5°-274°; W.274°-276.5°;
R.276.5°-018°; W.018°-051.5°.

SALTBUODDEN 59°04.9'N 9°38.9'E. Lt. Oc.
W.R.G.6 sec. W.11M. R.9M. G.9M.
W.Lantern 9m. G.333°-350°; W.350°-008°; R.
008°-132°; W.132°-156.5°; G.156.5°-180°.

ØVRE RINGSHOLMEN Lt. Fl.3 sec. 9M. Col.
10m.

FOLKVANG CANAL ENTRANCE.
E SIDE Lt. F.R.
W SIDE Lt. F.G.

KJEOYA Lt. Fl. G.3 sec.

LAUVOYANE Ldg. Lts. 309° (Front) F.R.
(Rear) F.R.

BREVIKFJORDEN

BREVIK 59°02'N 9°42'E
Tel: (03) 571519
(Port): (03) 571080 & 571088
(H.M.): (03) 571233
(Pilots): Fax (03) 571176. Telex 21783 TSENT
N.
Radio Port (Brevik Control) VHF Chan. 80,
12, 13, 14, 16 H24
Radio VTS (Sea Traffic Centre) VHF Chan.
80, 12, 13, 14, 16 H24
EMERGENCY COORDINATION CENTRE VHF
Chan. 80 (Brevik Control)

FIGGESKJER 59°00.8'N 9°45.2'E. Lt. Oc(2)
W.R.G.8 sec. W.11M. R.9M. G.9M.
W.Lantern on piles 9m. R.148°-152°; W.152°-
157°; G.157°-251°; R.251°-353°; G.353°-001°.

RAHOLMBAEN Lt. Fl(2) G.5 sec. 7M. Pillar
10m.

KUSKJERET Ldg.Lts. 194° (Front) F.R. 3M.
Post 4m. **HALDEN FISHING PIER** (Rear) F.R.
3M. Mast 7m.

BJORHØBAEN Lt. Iso. G.6 sec. Pillar
G.Band. Floodlit 10m.

SMAKKEBAEN Lt. Oc. G. 3M. Post 3m.

GJERMESHOLMEN Lt. Oc. R.G.6sec. R.9M.
G.9M. W.Lantern on piles 5m. G.111.5°-
121°; R.121°-202°; G.202°-281°; R.281°-
322.5°

STRØMTANGEN Lt. 2 F.G.Vert. 6M. Mast
9m.

KRABBERØDBOEN Lt. Fl. R.3 sec. 5M. Col.
8m.

LANGESUNDSBUKTA

FUGLØYSKJAER Lt. Fl. G.5 sec. 5M. Col.
11m.

LANGØYTANGEN 58°59.4'N 9°45.8'E. Lt.
Oc. W.R.G. W.13M. R.13M. G.13M. Tr. on
W.House 18m. G.216°-271°; W.271°-277°;
R.277°-315°; G.315°-340°; W.340°-010°;
R.010°-033°; W.033°-038°; G.038°-154°. R.C.
Horn(2) 60 sec.

MOLE HEAD Lt. Iso. G.4 sec. 2M. Col. 6m.

ARØY 58°59.9'N 9°47.9'E. Lt. Oc(3) W.R.G.10
sec.. W.11M. R.8M. G.8M. W.Lantern 22m.
G.343°-356°; W.356°-021°; R.021°-045°;
G.045°-137°; R.137°-149°.

KJORTINGEN 59°00.6'N 9°46.4'E. **NW** Lt.
Oc. W.R.G.6 sec. W.11M. R.8M. G.8M. Tr.
8m. W.135°-137°; G.137°-141°; R.141°-135°.

NE Lt. Iso. G.2 sec. 7M. Tr. 8m.
SE Lt. Oc(2) W.R.G.8 sec. W.10M. R.8M.
G.8M. Tr. 8m. W.337°-341°; R.341°-349°;
G.349°-140°; R.140°-203°; G.203°-337°.
SW Lt. Iso. R.2 sec. 7M. Tr. 8m.

KALVEN

AMLIROGNA 58°59.5'N 9°50.3'E. Lt. Oc(2)
W.R.G.8 sec. W.11M. R.9M. G.9M. Tr. 10m.
G.035°-078°; W.078°-088°; R.088°-149°;
W.149°-151.5°; G.151.5°-181.5°; R.181.5°-
250.5°; G.250.5°-279°.

LAMMØYBAEN Lt. Fl. R.5 sec. 7M. Pillar
10m.

SELSKJERBAEN Lt. Fl. R.3 sec. 7M. Pillar
10m.

HAØYTANGEN 58°00.5'N 9°49.5'E. Lt. Oc.
W.R.G.6 sec. W.11M. R.9M. G.9M. Tr. 11m.
R.304.5°-311°; R.311°-352°; G.352°-131°;
W.131°-133°; R.133°-144°.

VESTRE BRATTHOLMEN 59°02.0'N 9°46.6'E.
Lt. Oc(2) W.R.G.8 sec. W.11M. R.9M. G.9M.
Tr. 9m. R.282°-311.5°; W.311.5°-319.5°;
G.319.5°-121°; W.121°-132°; R.132°-143.5°.

KISTEHOLMEN Lt. Fl. G.3 sec. 7M. Pillar
11m.

BJØRKØYA Lt. Fl. R.3 sec. 7M. Pillar 10m.

RØODEN Lt. Oc. W.R.G.6 sec. W.11M. R.9M.
G.9M. Tr. 9m. R.264.5°-307.5°; W.307.5°-
311°; G.311°-065°; W.065°-070.5°; R.070.5°-
081.5°.

NEVLUNG HAVN

TVISTEIN 58°56.2'N 9°56.6'E. Lt. Fl. W.R.G.5
sec. W.13M. R.13M. G.12M. W.Building
17m. G.208°-249°; R.249°-265°; W.265°-095°;
R.095°-134°. Racon.

NEVLUNG HAVN 58°57.8'N 9°52.5'E. Lt.
Oc(2) W.R.G.8 sec. W.10M. R.7M. G.7M.
W.Lantern 9m. G.219.5°-229°; W.229°-263°;
R.263°-279°; W.279°-282°; G.282°-289°;
R.289°-295°; G.295°-333°; W.333°-338°;
R.338°-030°; W.030°-033°; G.033°-036.5°.

LARVIKSFJORDEN

SVENNOR KORPEKOLLEN 58°58.1'N
10°09.1'E. Lt. Oc(2) W.R.10 sec. W.18M.
R.17M. R.Tr. 40M. R.232°-261°; W.261°-059°;
R.059°-076°; W.076°-232°. Racon. Dia 60 sec.

STAVERNSODDEN S POINT OF ISLAND.
58°59.2'N 10°03.4'E. Lt. Oc(3) W.R.G.10 sec.
W.13M. R.10M. G.9M. W.house 44m. R.172°-
246°; G.246°-264°; W.264°-267°; R.267°-315°;
W.315°-346°; G.346°-043°.

VADHOLMEN 58°59.5'N 10°02.9'E. Lt. Oc.
W.R.G.6 sec. W.10M. R.8M. G.8M.
W.Lantern 7m. R.271°-189°; G.189°-202°;
W.202°-207°; R.207°-342°; W.342°-351.5°;
G.351.5°-359°.

OTERØY 59°01.7'N 10°04.4'E. Lt. Oc(2)
W.R.G.8 sec. W.10M. R.8M. G.8M.
W.Lantern 7m. G.220°-346°; W346°-356°;
R.356°-025°; G.025°-032°. Shown 1/7-10/6.

LARVIK 59°03'N 10°02'E

Tel: 034 86000
Radio Port: VHF Chan. 12, 14, 16 as
required.

LARVIK HAVN 59°02.9'N 10°01.7'E. Lt. Oc.
W.R.G.6 sec. W.10M. R.9M. G.9M.
Warehouse 8m. G.297°-316°; R.316°-332°;
W332°-337°; G.337°-352°; R.352°-012°.
Shown 1/7-10/6.

KENALKAIEN N. Lt. F.R. 048°-228°.

MOLE HEAD Lt. F.Y. 2M. Lantern. Shown
1/7-10/6.

TRANGSHOLMEN Lt. Fl.5 sec. 3M. Lantern
6m. Shown 1/7-10/6.

SANDEFJORDEN

HOLSKJAER 59°02.2'N 10°16.3'E. Lt. Oc.
W.R.G.6 sec. W.11M. R.8M. G.8M.
W.Lantern on Piles 11m. G.230°-267°;
R.267°-285°; G.285°-326°; R.326°-339°;
W.339°-344°; G.344°-002°; W.002°-004°;
R.004°-016°; W.016°-039°; G.039°-055°;
R.055°-160°; W.160°-164°; G.164°-180°.
Shown 1/7-10/6.

ASNESET ON POINT 59°05.7'N 10°14.6'E.
Lt. Oc. W.R.G.6 sec. W.10M. R.8M. G.8M.
W.Lantern 7m. R.335°-343°; G.343°-348°;
W.348°-353°; R.353°-006°; W.006°-161°;
R.161°-164°. Shown 1/7-10/6.

TRUBBERODDEN Lt. Oc(2) W.R.G.8 sec.
W.7M. R.5M. G.5M. W.Lantern 12M. G.175°-
190°; R.190°-252°; G.252°-264.5°; W.264.5°-
266°; R.266°-008°; G.008°-016°. Shown 1/7-
10/6.

TØNSBERG TØNNE Lt. F. R.3 sec. 3M.
Pedestal 22m. Shown 1/7-10/6.

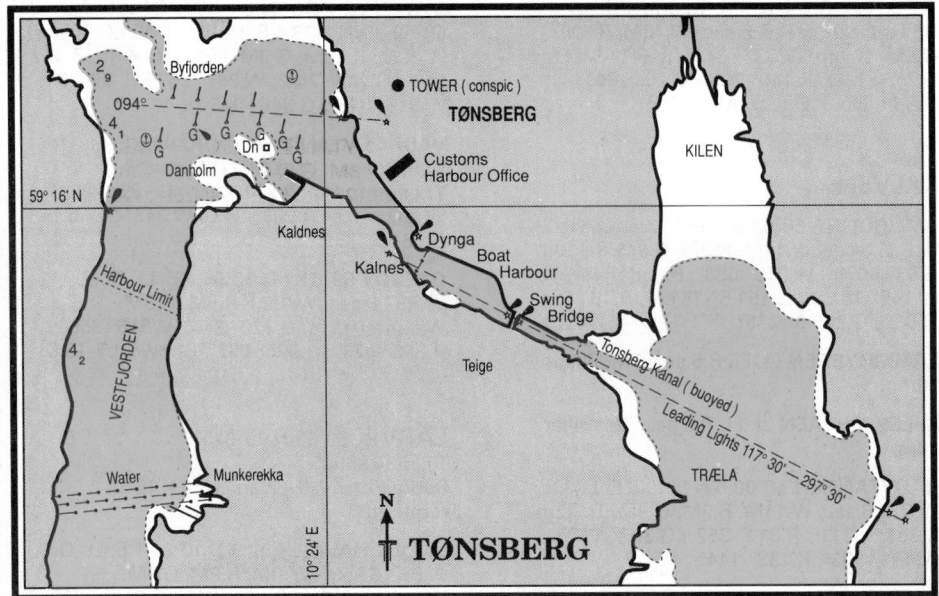

TØNSBERG HAVN

Swing Bridge across Kanal. Request opening by VHF or 1 long & 2 short blasts. G.Lt. (shown to Traffic) = Canal open. Bridge can be opened.
R.Lt. (Shown to Traffic) =Canal not clear. Bridge not open.
G.&R.l.t. = Canal open. Bridge closed. Gauges show clearance under closed bridge. Speed limit 3kts.

BRIDGE Ldg.Lts. 297°30' (Front) 2 F.R. 1 on each side of bridge.Shown when bridge closed. **KALNES** (Rear) Oc. R.G. Aluminium Lantern 8m. R. shore – 180°. G.180°-298°; R.298°-shore. Shown 1/7-10/6. Lights mark the channel.

DYNGA E SIDE OF CHANNEL. Lt. F .R.G. Col. G.329°-055°; R.055°-138°; G.138°-160°. Shown 1/7-10/6.

NORDBYEN Ldg. Lts. 094° (Front) Oc. W.R.G. W.9M. R.8M. G.8M. Aluminium Lantern 5m. G. Shore – 332°. W.332°-337°; R.337°-070°; G.070°-091.5°; W.091.5°-096.5°; R.096.5°-130°. Shown 1/7-10/6.
SLOTTSFJELLET (Rear) F.R. Post. Shown 1/7-10/6.

VESTFJORD

TINVIKSKJAER Lt. Iso. W.R.G.6 sec. W.6M. R.4M. G.4M. W.Lantern 4m. G.327°-332°; W.332°-354°; R.354°-102°; W.102°-107°;

G.107°-170°; W.170°-180°; R.180°-184°. In line 170° with Østre Vakerholmen Lt. leads through the middle of Haøysundet. Shown 1/7-10/6.

KAUSEN Lt. Iso. W.R.G.6 sec. W.6M. R.4M. G.4M. W.Lantern 4m. R.010°-023°; W.023°-210°; G.210°-216°. Shown 1/7-10/6.

FURUODDEN Lt. Oc. W.R.G.6 sec. W.6M. R.4M. G.4M. W.Lantern 3m. G.024°-030°; W.030°-032°; R.032°-063°; W.063°-068°; G.068°-179.5°; W.179.5°-186°; R.186°-193°. Shown 1/7-10/6.

MUNKERAEKKEN Lt. Oc. W.R.G.6 sec. W.7M. R.5M. G.5M. W.Lantern 2m. G.350°-358°; W.358°-005°; R.005°-178°; W.178°-185°; G.185°-201°. Shown 1/7-10/6.

SMØRBERG Lt. Oc. W.R.G.6 sec. W.9M. R.8M. G.8M. W.Lantern 7m. R.221°-294°; W.294°-359°; G.359°-003°. Shown 1/7-10/6.

TØNSBERGFJORD

BARKEVIK 59°06.1'N 10°23.0'E. Ldg. Lts. 018° (Front) Iso. 2 sec. 10M. W.Lantern 11m. 016°-023°. Intens on leading line (Rear) Oc. 6 sec. 17M. W.Lantern 42m. 016°-023°. Intens on leading line.

SVARTESKJAERSKATEN Lt. Fl.5 sec. 3M. Col. 4m. Shown 1/7-10/6.

ØSTRE VAKERHOLMEN Lt. Fl. W.R.G.3 sec. W6M. R.4M. G.3M. W.Lantern 6m. G.169°-172°; W.172°-002.5°; R.002.5°-006°. In line 170° with Tenvikskjaer Lt. leads through the middle of Haøysundet. Shown 1/7-10/6.

SALTBU 59°09.3'N 10°22.8'E. Lt. Oc. W.R.G.6 sec. W.11M. R.8M. G.8M. W.Lantern 9m. G.356°-358°; W.358°-171°' R.171°-180°.

SALTBUFLU Lt. Fl. G.5 sec. 1M. Col. 4m.

GRANABASUNDET Ldg. Lts. 210°30' (Front) Q. 7M. Pedestal 5m. (Rear) Iso. 4 sec. 7M. Pedestal 9m. 200°-220°. Intens on leading line.

LEIA

VASHOLMEN W SIDE. Lt. Fl. W.R.G.5 sec. W.7M. R.5M/ G.4M. W.Lantern 4m. R.009°-014°; W.014°-025°; G.025°-182.5°; W.182.5°-184°; R.184°-188°.

HVALØY N END. Lt. Fl. W.R.G.5 sec. W.6M. R.4M. G.3M. W.Lantern 5m. R.021°-024°; W.024°-029°; G.029°-144°; W.144°-156°; R.156°-183°; W.183°-187°; G.187°-273°; W.273°-275°; R.275°-277°; W.277°-281°; G.281°-293°.

SANDØYSUNDSLEIA

KRUKEPYNTEN Ldg. Lts. 345° (Front) Oc. W.R.G.6 sec. W.9M. R.8M. G.8M. W.Lantern 4m. G.170°-180°; W.180°-185.5°; R.185.5°-342°; W.342°-347°; G.347°-350°. Shown 1/7-10/6. **SANDVIKBERGET** 59°05.3'N 10°27.3'E (Rear) Oc. W.R.G.6 sec. W.10M. R.8M. G.8M. W.Lantern 10m. G.257°-267°; W.267°-274°; R.274°-308°; W.308°-347°. Shown 1/7-10/6.

KONGSHOLMEN E SIDE. Lt. Fl. W.R.G.5 sec. W.6M. R.4M. G.3M. W.Lantern 5M. G.184°-187°; W.187°-189°; R.189°-354°; W.354°-000°; G.000°-007°. Shown 1/7-10/6.

STORE FAERDER N POINT. Lt. Fl. W.R.G.5 sec. W7M. R.5M. G.4M. W.Lantern on wood structure 12m. G.039°-053°; W.053°-116°; R.116°-128°; W.128°-133°; G.133°-171°; R.171°-189°; W.189°-194°; G.194°-206°; W.206°-210°; R.210°-212°; W.212°-316°. Shown 1/7-10/6.

LAKSKJAER Lt. Fl(2) W.R.G.10 sec. W.7M. R.5M. G.4M. W.Lantern on piles 12m. R.169°-180°; G.180°-210°; W.210°-214°; R.214°-217°; W.217°-221°; G.221°-315°; R.315°-324°; W.324°-014°; G.014°-026°; R.026°-046°. Shown 1/7-10/6.

LILLE FAERDER 59°01.6'N 10°31.7'E. Lt. Fl(3) 30 sec. 19M. R.W. Tr. 47M.   R.C. Racon.

VRENGEN

MAKERØYTANGEN Lt. Oc. W.R.G.6 sec. W.8M. R.8M. G.8M. W.Lantern 4m. R.115°-123°; W.123°-253°; R.253°-268°; W.268°-308°; G.308°-319°.

BUERSTADBAEN Lt. Fl.5 sec. 3M. Col. 5m.

TUTEN 59°10.3'N 10°24.1'E. Lt. Oc. W.R.G.6 sec. W.11M. R.8M. G.8M. W.Lantern 14m. G.290°-302°; W.302°-060°; R.060°-067°. Lts. F.R. mark Vrengen Bridge 920m. 215°.

APPROACHES TO TØNSBERG

TØNSBERG 59°16'N 10°25'E
Tel: (033) 11278.
Radio-Port: VHF Chan. 12, 14, 16. Mon-Sat. 0600-2100. Sun. 0900-1700.

KALVETANGEN Lt. Oc. W.R.G.6 sec. W.8M. R.7M. G.7M. W.Lantern 3m. G.134°-156°; W.156°-169°; R.169°-282°; G.282°-307°. Shown 1/7-10/6.

ORSNES BREAKWATER HEAD Lt. F.

ØSTRE BUSTEIN Lt. Fl.5 sec. 3M. Pedestal 12m. Shown 1/7-10/6.

HOLLENDERBAEN 59°09.6'N 10°37.7'E. Lt. Oc(3) W.R.G.10 sec. W.14M. R.13M. G.12M. Structure 19m. W.316.5°-008°; R.008°-020°; G.020°-035°; W.035°-036.5°; R. 036.5°-105°; G.105°-156°; W.156°-170°; R.170°-200°; G.200°-230°; W.230°-240°; R.240°-274°; G.274°-279°; W.279°-285°; R.285°-291°; W.291°-301°; G.301°-316.5°. Racon.

FULEHUK Lt. Oc. R.6 sec. 7M. 10m.

HUIKJAELA Lt. Fl. W.R.G.5 sec. W.8M. R.5M. G.5M. W.Lantern on piles 9m. R.324°-339°; W.339°-358°; G.358°-133°; W.133°-136°; R.136°-142°.

LEISTEIN S POINT. Lt. Fl(2) W.R.G.10 sec. W.7M. R.5M. G.4M. W.Lantern on piles 8m. R.243°-255.5; W.255.5°-287°; G.287°-323°; W.323°-331°; R.331°-106°; W.106°-112°; G.112°-128°.

TØNSBERG EASTERN ENTRANCE

TØRGERSØY N POINT Lt. Fl. W.R.G.5 secs. W.7M. R.4M. G.3M. W.Lantern 5m. G.091°-098°; W.098°-143°; R.143°-243°; W.243°-282°; G.282°-288.5°.

NARVERØD 59°15.1'N 10°29.0'E Lt. Oc. W.R.G.6 sec. W.11M. R.8M .G.8M. W.Lantern 9m. G.218°-272°; W.272°-274°; R.274°-357°; W.357°-359°; G.359°-010°.

JERSØY Lt. Oc. W.R.G.6 sec. W.9M. R.8M. G.8M. W.Lantern 5m. R.266°-346°; W.346°-350°; G.350°-104°; R.104°-113°.

HUSOYSUND BREAKWATER HEAD Lt. F.

Ldg. Lts. 117°30' (Front) F.R. 4M. Post (Rear) F.R. 4M. Post.

OSLOFJORDEN

BASTØY NE POINT Lt. Oc(3) R.10 sec. 7M. 13m.

KJEMPA Lt. F.R.

S Point Lts F.R. mark W & NE limits of cable area between Bastøy and Asgardstrand

BASTØYBAEN Lt. Fl.3 sec. 3M. Post 4M. Shown 1/7-10/6.

ØSTENSKJAER 59°21.5'N 10°30.9'E Lt. Oc. W.R.G.6 sec. W.12M. R.9M. G.9M. Tr. W.Lantern 12m. G.242°-252°; W.252°-306°; R.306°-318°.5°; W.318.5°-341°; G.341°-031.5°; W.031.5°-168°; R.168°-194°. Shown 1/7-10/6.

MEFJORDBAEN 59°20.1'N 10°34.5'E Lt. Oc(2). W.R.G.8 sec. W.12M. R.12M. G.11M. Tr. 14m. W.165°-174.5°; R.174.5°-179°; G.179°-194°; W.194°-201.5°; R.201.5°-265°; G.265°-339°; W.339°-349°; R.349°-019°; G.019°-042°; R.042°-124°; G.124°-165°. Racon.

ASGARDSTRAND Lt. 2 F.R. Marks SW limit of cable area between Bastøy and Asgardstrand.

SLAGENSTANGEN 59°19'N 10°31'E
Radio-Port VHF Chan 11,12,13,14,16 as required.

SLAGENSTANGEN OIL PIER Ldg .Lts. 308° (Front) Q. (Rear) F.R. Shown 1/7-10/6.

HORTEN 59°25'N 10°30'E Tel. 41 421
Radio Pilots VHF chan 12.13.16 H24.

INNER HARBOUR Ldg. Lts. 187° (Front) Oc. W.R.6 sec. Tr. 6m. R.098°-278°; W.278°-098° (Rear) Oc R.6 sec. Tr. 16m.

DIRIKSBAEN Lt. Fl. G.3 sec. 3M. Col 6m.

CANAL MOLE ARM N END Lt. Oc.W.R.G.6 sec. W.9M. R.9M. G.9M. W Lantern 4m. G. Shore-187°; W.187°-217°; R.217°-258°; G.258°-273°; W.273°-322°; R.322°-357°; W.357°-010°; R.010°-038°. Shown 1/7-10/6. Horn 30 sec. Sounded by day in fog and by night when vessel expected.

RO RO JETTY S END Lt. Q.

HOLMESTRAND Ldg. Lts. 238° (Front) F.R.G. R.5M. G.4M. Post 10m. G.174°-256°; R.256°-343°. (Rear) F.R. Lantern 40m. 193°-283°.

MULODDEN Lt. Oc. W.R.G. W.9M. R.9M. G.9M. W.Lantern 5m. G.096°-148°; R.148°-151°; W.151°-156°; G.156°-186.5°; W.186.5°-192°; R.192°-276.5°; W.276.5°-291°; G.291°-313°.

DRAMSFJORDEN

STEINSBRATAN Lt. Oc. W.R.G.6 sec. W.9M. R.8M. G.8M. W.Lantern 4m. R.125°-136°; W.136°-280°; G.280°-289°; W.289°-311°; R.311°-317°.

FURUHOLMEN NE Lt. Fl.6 sec.

DRAMMEN 59°44'N 10°13'E. Tel. 81 88 90.
Radio Port VHF Chan 12,14,16. Mon-Fri 0630-2130; Sat 0630-1230.

HOLMEN Ldg. Lts. 268°30'. (Front) F.G. 3M. 7m. (Rear) F.G. 3M. 11m.

RISGARDEN MOLE HEAD Lt. Fl.2 sec. 6M. R.W. Lantern on Tr. 8m.

FLOATING DOCK E CORNER Lt. Q.R.

FLOATING DOCK W CORNER Lt. Fl. R.3 sec.

LIERSTRANDA SHELL OIL DEPOT Ldg. Lts. 335° (Front) F.R. 4M. Col. (Rear) F.R. 4 Col.

LINNESSTRANDA Ldg. Lts. 035° (Front) F.G. (Rear) F.G.

SANDEBUGTEN Ldg. Lts. 331°.
SELVIKBLINDA (Front) Fl. R.3 sec. Col. Shown when local vessels expected. F.R. Lts. in Line mark outlet 240m. NE. (Rear) F.R. Post.

SELVIKGRUNNEN Lt. Fl.2 sec. Col.

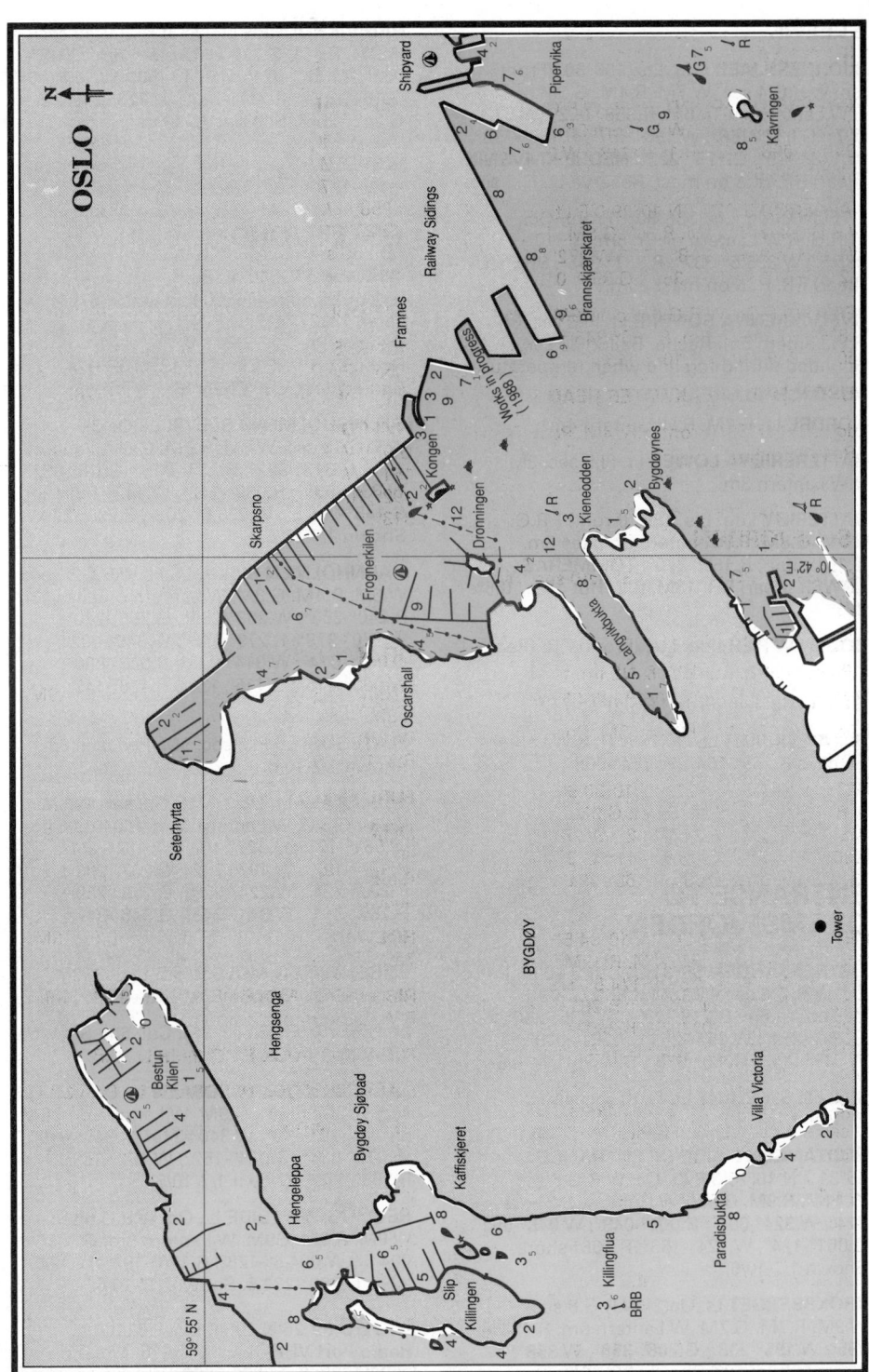

SVELVIK

BJORNESKJAER Ldg. Lts. 156°30' (Front) Iso. W.R.G.4 sec. W.7M. R.4M. G.3M. R.W.Lantern on Tr. 6m. R.358°-022°; W.022°-087°; G.087°-156°; W.156°-157°; R.157°-173°; W.173°-175°; G.175°-222°. **NEDRE KNIVSNIK** (Rear) F.R. R. Δ on mast. Reserve Lt. Fl.5 sec.

SVELNIK Ldg. Lts. 336°30'. (Front) Oc. W.R.G. R.W.Lantern on Tr. 8m. G.310°-335.5°; W.335.5°-337°; R.337°-345°. **BRENNA** (Rear) F.R. R. Δ on mast 26m.

SVELVIKRENNA SONDRE Lt. Fl.3 sec. 3M. R.W.Lantern 5m. Racon. Bell(2) 30 sec. Sounded during fog and when temperature below 0°C.

NORDRE Lt. F. 1M. R.W.Lantern 4m.

BATTERERIØYA LOWER Lt. Fl.5 sec. 3M. R.W.Lantern 3m.

BATTERIØY Ldg. Lts. 185° (Front) F.R.G. R.9M. G.8M. R.W.Lantern on piles 8m. G.151°-189°; R.189°-270°. **TØMMERAS LOWER** (Rear) F.R. 13M. R.W.Hut 15m. 165°-203°.

BOGEN W PIER Ldg. Lts. (Front) F.R. (Rear) F.R.

E PIER Ldg. Lts. (Front) F.R. (Rear) F.R.

BLINDESKJAER Lt. Oc(2) W.R. R.W.Lantern on piles R.159°-164°; W.164°-008°.

ENTRANCE TO DRAMSFJORDEN

ØSTNESTANGEN 59°31.2'N 10°31.0'E Lt. Oc. W.R.G.6 sec. W.10M R.8M. G.8M. W.Lantern 6m. R.219°-235°; W.235°-250°; G.250°-254°; W.254°-261°; R.261°-015°; W.015°-066°; G066°-078°. Shown 1/7-10/6.

MØLEN SW POINT Lt. Fl.10 sec. 4M. Pedestal 7m. Shown 1/7-10/6.

RØDTANGEN E SIDE OF ENTRANCE 55°31.7'N 10°25.3'E Lt. Oc. W.R.G.6 sec. W.11M. R.9M. G.9M. W.Hut 8m. G Shore-324°; W.324°-004°; R.004°-048°; W.048°-051°; G.051°-124°; W.124°-166°; R.166°-shore. Shown 1/7-10/6.

KROKSBERGET Lt. Oc(2) W.R.G.8 sec. W.9M. R.7M. G.7M. W.Lantern 6m. R.184°-195°; W.195°-208°; G.208°-358°; W.358°-008°; R.008°-018°. Shown 1/7-10/6.

RAMVIKHOLMEN Lt. Oc(3) W.R.G.10 sec. W.9M. R.7M. G.7M. W.Lantern 6m. G049°-052°; W.052°-074°; R.074°-150°; W.150°-164°; G.164°-217°; R.217°-223°; W.223°-242°; G.242°-255°. Shown 1/7-10/6.

OSLOFJORD

OSLO 59°57'N 10°40'E (Port): Tel. (02) 416860 Fax (02) 416751: Telex 121270 OSLO PORT (Pilots): Tel. 11 55 55 **Radio Port** VHF Chan 12,13,14,16 H24 **Radio Pilots** VHF Chan 16.

STEINSHOLMENS SLEVIK Lt. Oc(3) W.R.G.10 sec. W.8M. R.5M. G.5M. Lantern 12m. G.313°-322°; R.322°-015°; G015°-032°; W.032°-039°; R.039°-142°; W.142°-145°; G.145°-206.5°; W.206.5°-208°; R.208°-229°. Shown 1/7-10/6.

GARNHOLMEN S SIDE Lt. Fl. W.R.G.5 sec. W.6M. R.4M. G.3M. W.Lantern on piles 13m. R.240°-253°; W.253°-255°; G.255°-270°; W.270°-279°; R.279°-340°; W.340°-002°; G.002°-014°; W.014°-023°; R.023°-080°; W.080°-115°; G.115°-126°; R.126°-142°. Shown 1/7-10/6.

FLATEGURI Lt. Fl.3 sec. 5M. Pedestal 8m. Shown 1/7-10/6.

VESLEKALV Lt. Oc(2) W.R.G.8 sec. W.5M. R.3M. G.3M. W.Lantern 11m. R.040°-061°; W.061°-127°; G.127°-164°; W.164°-171°; R.171°-197°; W.197°-202°; G.202°-206°; R.206°-224°; W.224°-229°; G.229°-289°; R.289°-341°; W.341°-346°; G.346°-347°. Shown 1/7-10/6.

ENGELSVIKEN MOLE HEAD Lt. F.G. 3M. W.Lantern on tripod 8m. Shown 1/7-10/6.

Lt. Q(6) + L. Fl.15 sec. 3M. Col. 6m. Shown 1/7-10/6.

LARKOLLEN HUITNESBAEN Lt. Oc. W.R.G.6 sec. W.9M. R.9M. G.9M. W.Lantern on piles 5m. G.320°-340°; W.340°-344°; R.344°-019°; W.019°-034°; G.034°-152°; W.152°-159°; R.159°-176°. Shown 1/7-10/6.

REVLINGEN W SIDE Lt. Oc. W.R.G.6 sec. W.9M. R.9M. G9M. W.Lantern 5m. G.355°-004.5°; W.004.5°-128°; R.128°-194°; W.194°-229°; G.229°-231.5. Shown 1/7-10/6.

MOSS 59°26'N 10°40'E Tel. 51106 **Radio Port** VHF Chan 12,14,16. Mon-Fri 0800-1530; Sat 0800-1200.

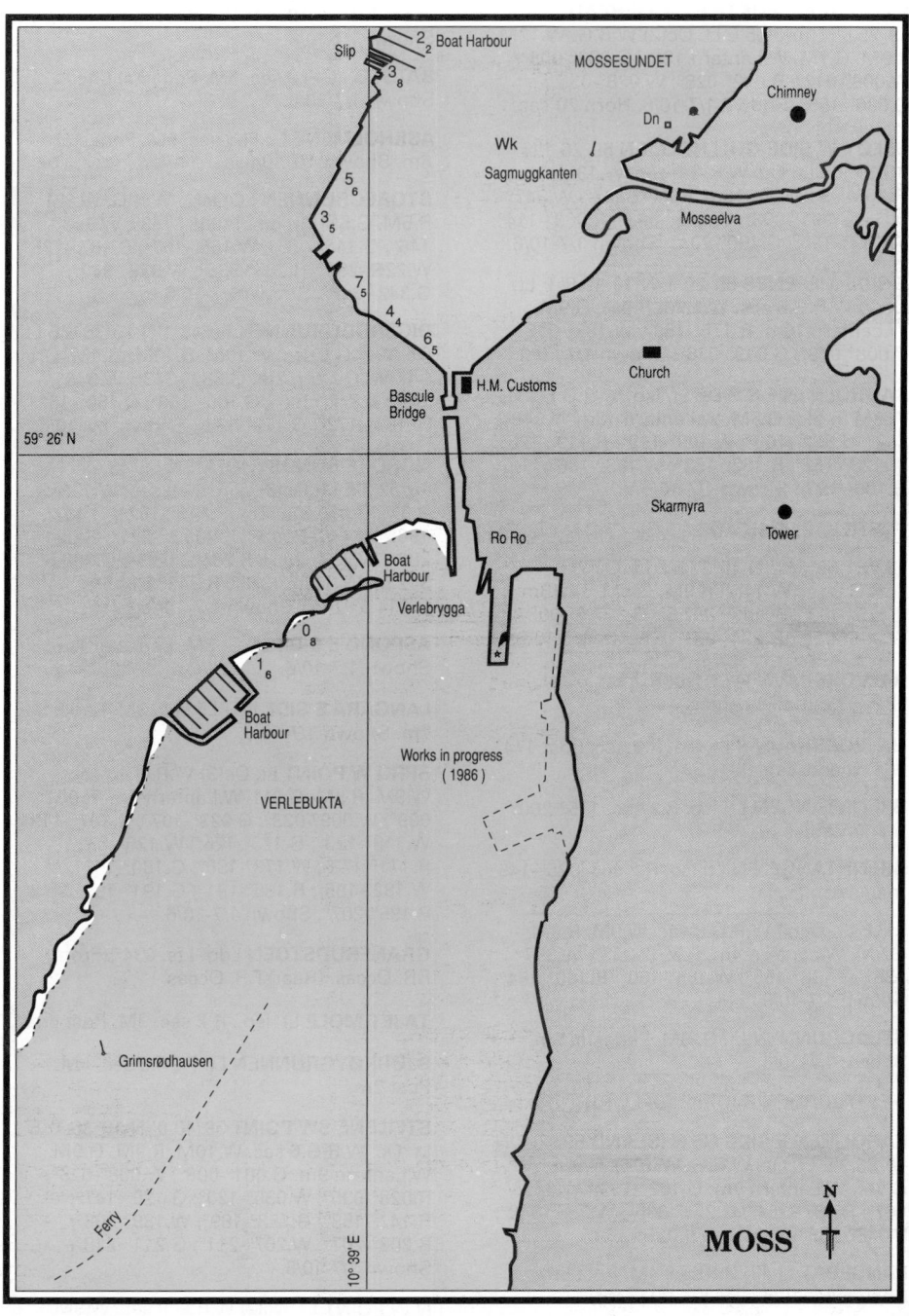

MOSS CANAL

MOSS VERLEBUKTA E MOLE HEAD
59°25.6'N 10°39.5'E Lt. Oc(2) W.R.G. W.12M.
R.9M. G.7M. W.Lantern 13m. G.202°-008°;
W.008°-012°; R.012°-028°; W.028°-036°;
G.036°-156°. Shown 1/7-10/6. Horn 20 sec.

JELØY W SIDE GULLHOLMEN 59°26.1'N
10°34.9'E Lt. Oc. W.R.G.6 sec. W.13M.
R.10M. G.9M. Tr. 16m. R.341°-347°; W.347°-
001°; G.001°-003°; W.003°-063°; R.063°-114°.
W.114°-190°; G.190°-204°. Shown 1/7-10/6.

E SIDE KIPPENES 59°29.2' N 10°40.8' E Lt.
Oc(2) W.R.G.8 sec. W.12M. R.9M. G.9M.
W.Lantern 10m. R.175°-183°; W.183°-008°;
R.008°-013°; G.013°-016°. Shown 1/7-10/6.

SAUHOLMENE S SIDE Lt. Iso. W.R.G.6 sec.
W.8M. R.5M. G.5M. W.Lantern 13m W.345°-
352°; G.352°-109°; W.109°-119°; R.119°-128°;
W.128°-162°; R.162°-183°; W.183°-186°;
G.186°-193°. Shown 1/7-10/6.

TOFTE W PIER HEAD Lt. F.G.

FILVET 59°34.2'N 10°37.5'E Lt. Oc(2)
W.R.G.8 sec W.11M. R.9M. G.8M. Tr. 13m
R.175°-183°; W.183°-337.5°; G.337.5°-008°;
W.008°-024°; R.024°-031°. Shown 1/7-10/6.

HALVORSHAVN N Lt. Iso. R.2 sec. Post
284°-033° marks cables.

HALVORSHAVN S Lt. Iso. R.2 sec. Post 174°-
284° marks cables.

BRENNTANGEN Lt. Iso. R.2 sec. 115°-200°
marks cables.

BRENNTANGEN N Lt. Iso. R.2 sec. 025°-145°
marks cables.

ELLE Lt. Oc(2) W.R.G.8 sec. W.9M. R.9M.
G.9M. W.Lantern 4m. R.351°-357°; W.357°-
138°; G.138°-155°; W.155°-160°; R.160°-164°.
Shown 1/7-10/6.

STEDGRUNNEN Lt. Q. 5M. Pedestal 5m.
Shown 1/7-10/6.

VESTFJORDEN BJORNNES Lt. F.R.

KAHOLMEN E SIDE OF N ISLAND 59°40.7'N
10°36.9'E Lt. Oc. W.R.G. W.10M. R.9M.
G.9M. W.Lantern 9m. G.162°-163°; W.163°-
167°; R.167°-264°; G.264°-336°; W.336°-348°;
R.348°-355°. Shown 1/7-10/6.

LANGEBAT Lt. Fl. G.3 sec. 4M. Post 5m.
Shown 1/7-10/6.

TRONSTADODDEN Ldg. Lts. 160° (Front)
Oc(2) W.R.G.8 sec. W.9M. R.7M. G.6M.
Lantern 12m. G.125°-159.5°; W.159.5°-161°;

R.161°-194.5°; G.194.5°-311°; W.311°-321°;
R.321°-325°. Shown 1/7-10/6. (Rear) Oc.
6sec. 12M. ▽ 18m 155°-165°. Intens 160°.
Shown 1/7-10/6.

BATSTØ Lt. Fl.3 sec. 6M. Pedestal 5m.
Shown 1/7-10/6.

ASKHOLMENE Lt. Fl.5 sec. 5M. Pedestal
8m. Shown 1/7-10/6.

STOREGRUNNEN Lt. Oc(2) W.R.G. W.8M.
R.5M. G.5M. Tr. 5m. R.068°-143°; W.143°-
146°; G.146°-165°; W.165°-167°; R.167°-225°;
W.225°-285°; R.285°-338°; W.338°-342°;
G.342°-348°. Shown 1/7-10/6.

DIGERUDGRUNNEN 59°43.1'N 10°35.6'E Lt.
Oc. W.R.G.6 sec. W.10M. R.10M. G.9M. Grey
Col. W. Ov. top 7m. G.332°-343°; W.343°-
347°; R.347°-106°; G.106°-160°; R.160°-168°;
W.168°-172°; G.172°-184°. Shown 1/7-10/6.

NORDRE SUNDBYHOLMEN 59°43.6'N
10°32.2'E Lt. Oc(3) W.R.G.10 sec. W.12M.
R.9M. G.9M. Tr. 11m. R.143°-182°; G.182°-
196°; W.196°-200.5°; R.200.5°-221°; G.221°-
283°; W.283°-285°; R.285°-308.5°; G.308.5°-
342.5°; W.342.5°-348°; R.348°-014.5°;
G.014.5°-143°. Shown 1/7-10/6.

ASPOND E SIDE Lt. Q. 3M. Pedestal 7m.
Shown 1/7-10/6.

LANGARA E SIDE Lt. Fl.5 sec. 3M. Pedestal
7m. Shown 1/7-10/6.

SPRO W POINT Lt. Oc(3) W.R.G.10 sec.
W.9M. R.9M. G.9M. W.Lantern 6m. R.001°-
009°; W.009°-023°; G.023°-107°; R.107°-119°;
W.119°-123°; G.123°-126°; W.126°-171°;
R.171°-173°; W.173°-180°; G.180°-182°;
W.182°-185°; R.185°-191°; G.191°-195°;
R.195°-207°. Shown 1/7-10/6.

GRANERUDSTOEN Ldg. Lts. 034° (Front)
F.R. Occas. (Rear) F.R. Occas.

TAJET MOLE Lt. Iso.. R.2 sec. 3M. Post 6m.

BJØRKØYGRUNNEN Lt. Fl. R.3 sec. 4M.
Post 2m.

STEILENE SW POINT 59°48.9' N 10°36.1° E
Lt. Oc. W.R.G.6 sec. W.10M. R.9M. G.9M.
W.Lantern 9m. G.001°-008°; W.008°-028°;
R.028°-035°; W.035°-120°; G.120°-147°;
R.147°-158°; G.158°-189°; W.189°-203°;
R.203°-207°; W.207°-211°; G.211°-218°.
Shown 1/7-10/6.

N W POINT Lt. Oc(2) W.R.G.8 sec. W.9M.
R.7M. G.7M. W.Lantern 5m. R.186°-206°;
W.206°-222°; G.222°-005°; W.005°-033°.
Shown 1/7-10/6.

GASUNGANE Lt. Fl. W.R.G.5 sec. W.7M. R.4M. G.3M. W.Lantern 5m. G.267°-355°; W.355°-001°; R.001°-011°; W.011°-059°; G.059°-146°; R.146°-215°; W.215°-224°; G.224°-236°. Shown 1/7-10/6.

HARAHOLMEN Ldg. Lts. 343°30' (Front) Q.R. 3M. Col. 3m. **BRØNNØYA NE POINT** (Rear) Fl. R.3 sec. 3M. Col. 8m.

KALVØYGRUNNEN Lt. Fl. G.3 sec. 3M. Col. 4m.

KALVØYA Ldg. Lts. 329° (Front) Q.R. 3M. Col. 5m. (Rear) Fl. R.3 sec. 4M. Col. 9m.

HØVIKODDEN Ldg. Lts. 011° (Front) Q. 5M. Col. 4m. (Rear) Fl.3 sec. 5M. Col. 11m.

ARNESFLUA GASØYA 59°51.0'N 10°35.7'E Lt. Iso. W.R.G.6 sec. W.10M. R.8M. G.8M. W.Lantern on piles. 7m. R.205°-226.5°; W.226.5°-254°; R.254°-261°; G.261°-320°; R.320°-011°; W.011°-020°; G.020°-044°; R.044°-052°. Shown 1/7-10/6.

ILDJERNSFLU 59°51.3'N 10°38.3'E Lt. Fl.5 sec. 10M. Tr. 9m. Shown 1/7-10/6.

NESODDEN Lt. Oc. W.R.G.6 sec. W.8M. R.8M. G.8M. W.Lantern on piles 3m. G.028°-032°; W.032°-037°; R.037°-042°; W.042°-045°; G.045°-050°; W.050°-056°; R.056°-171°; W.171°-216°; R.216°-228°; W.228°-244°; G.244°-259°; W.259°-261.5°; R.261.5°-271°. Shown 1/7-10/6.

SNARØYKILEN Lt. Fl. R.3 sec. 4M. Col. 5m.

LYSAKER MOLE HEAD Lt. F.R,. Shown 1/7-10/6. Ldg. Lts. 200m NE & 380m ENE mark anchoring and fishing prohibited area.

BYGDØY KILLINGEN BREAKWATER Lt. Iso. R.4 sec.

NORDRE LANGØYA Lt. Oc(2) W.R.G.9 sec. W.9M. W.Lantern 4m. R.060°-086.5°; W.086.5°-092°; G.092°-098°; W.098°-101°; R.101°-115°; W.115°-124°. G.124°-224°; R.224°-248.5°; Shown 1/7-10/6. Horn(3) 30 sec.

OSLO HAVN

RAUDEKKENE Lt. Oc. 5M. Col. 3m. Shown 1/7-10/6.

STANGSKJAERRABBEN Lt. O(3) W.R.G. W.9M. R.7M. G.6M. W.Lantern 4m. W.005°-066°; R.066°-072°; G.072°-077° W to east through Heggholmsundet. Shown 1/7-10/6. Horn(2) 30 sec.

HEGGHOLMEN Lt. Fl. G.2 sec. 9M. W.Hut 6m. 055°-246°. Shown 1/7-10/6. Horn 15 sec.

LINDØYA SE POINT Lt. Fl. R.3 sec. 6M. W.Lantern 3m. 242°-060°. Shown 1/7-10/6.

BLEIKØY NW POINT Lt. Oc. W.R. W.4M. R.3M. W.Lantern 3m. W.068°-085°; R.085°-183°; W.183°-239°. Shown 1/7-10/6.

KALVODDEN Lt. Iso. R.2 sec. 4M. Post 5m. Shown 1/7-10/6.

SJURSØYA BREAKWATER OFF NW HEAD Lt. Q.G. 3M. Col. 5m. Shown 1/7-10/6.

SANDTANGEN Lt. Fl.3 sec. 3M. Col. on piles 4m. Shown 1/7-10/6.

HOVEDØYA N SIDE Lts. in Line 216° (Front) F.R. (Rear) F.R. mark cables.

DYNA Lt. Oc(2) W.R.G. W.9M. R.9M. G.8M. W.House 6m. R. shore-241°; W.241°-261°; G.261°-040°; W.040°-051°; R.051°-062°. Shown 1/7-10/6. R.C. Horn 30 sec.

KOPPERNAGLEN Lt. Fl.3 sec. 3M. W.Lantern 3m. Shown 1/7-10/6. Horn 10 sec.

GALTEN Lt. Fl. G.3 sec. 1M. B.W. TR. 3M. Shown 1/7-10/6.

SORE KAVRINGDYNGA 59°53.9'N 10°43.6'E Lt. Oc(3) W.R.G. W.11M. R.8M. G.7M. W.R. Tr. 12m. G.044°-063°; W.063°-075°; R.075°-094°; W.094°-211°; G.211°-240°; W.240°-266°; R.266°-044°. Shown 1/7-10/6.

VIPPETANGEN JETTY II S HEAD Lt. F.G.

JETTY III S HEAD Lt. F.R.G. Vert.

KONGEN JETTY HEAD SE END Lt. F.

N.W. END Lt. F.

SARPSBORG

TORPEBERGET E SIDE Lt. Fl.5 sec. 3M. W. Col. 8m.

VISTERFLO W SIDE Lt. Fl. R.5 sec. 1M. W. Col. on Dolphin 4m.

RENUDTANGEN E SIDE Lt. Fl.3 sec. 3M. Post 4m. 035°-236°.

VESTENODDEN Lt. Fl. G.5 sec. Col.

GLOMMEN N SIDE HELLESKJAERET Lt. F.R.G. Col. R.000°-180°; G.180°-000°

KJELSEGRUNNEN S SIDE Lt. Fl.2 sec. 3M Col. 4m.

FREDERIKSTAD

GRESSVIKFLUA Ldg. Lts. 027°30' (Front) Oc. mast (Rear) Oc. mast

GRESSVIK Ldg Lts. 260° (Front) F.R. 1M. mast 8 m. (Rear) F.R. 1M. mast 12m.

KORSEPYNTEN Ldg . Lts. 076° (Front) F.G. 1M. mast 8m. (Rear) F.G. 1M. mast 15m.

FREDRIKSTAD W ENTRANCE

STRUTEN 59°07.0'N 10°44.7'E Lt. Oc. W.R.G.6 Sec. W.10M. R.7M. G.7M. Bn. 19m. G.319°-329°; W.329°-333°; R.333°-000.5°; W.000.5°-047°; G.047°-054°; W.054°-155°; R.155°-182°; G.182°-213°; W.213°-252°; R.252°-258.5°.

STRØMTANGEN 59°09.0'N 10°50.1'E Lt. Oc(2) W.R.G.8 sec. W.13M. R.13M. G.12M. W.House 15m. R.217.5-219°; W.219°-338°; R.338°-358°; G.358°-014°. R.014°-061°; W.061°-067°; G.067°-077°; W.077°-088°; R.088°-097°. Storm signals.

GASUNGANE Lt. Oc. W.R.G.6 sec. W.8M. R.5M. G.5M. W.Lantern on piles 6m. R.200°-217.5°; W.217.5°-219.5°; G.219.5°-000°; W.000°-020.5°; R.018°-032°.

KROSNESFJELLET Lt. Fl. R.5 sec. 2M. Post 3m.

HUTHOLMEN Lt. Q. 3M. Post.

KJØKØYSUND

ARISHOLMEN Lt. Iso. R.6 sec. 3M. Post 5m.

KALKGRUNNEN Lt. Iso. R.2 sec. 4M. Pedestal 8m.

HÅHOLMBÅEN Lt. Q. on Col.

KJØKØY 59°08.3'N 10°56.8'E Ldg. Lts. 061° (Front) F.R. 18M. Bn. 14m. (Rear) F.R. 18M. Bn. 28m. Vis on leading line.

RAKETANGEN Lt. F.R. 5M. Post 4m.

KJØKØYSKJAERET Lt. Iso. G.2 sec. 4M. Col. 5m.

TOMMERHELLA Lt. Fl. W.R.3 sec. W.3M. R.2M. Pedestal 12m. R.171°-205°; W.205°-171°.

LEIRA

STANGESKJAER Lt. Fl.5 sec. 3M. Pedestal 10m.

TENNESKJAER Lt. Oc. W.R.G.6 sec. W.9M. R.9M. G.9M. W.Lantern on piles 4m. R.083°-095°; W.095°-106°; G.106°-291°; W.291°-297°; R.297°-307°.

HVALER

ASMALSUND PIGSTENS 59°03.3'N 10°55.2'E Lt. Oc(3) W.R.G.10 sec. W.10M. R.8M. G.8M. W.Lantern 7m. R.338°-000°; W.000°-007°; G.007°-025°; W.025°-031°; R.031°-109°; G.148°-153°; W.153°-203°; R.203°-217°. Shown 1/7-10/6.

SKJELHOLM SKJELSBUSUND Lt. Oc(2) W.R.G.8 Sec. W.8M. R.5M. G.5M. W.Lantern 8m. W.110°-254°; R.319°-323°; W.323°-327°; G.327°-331°; W.331°-335°; R.335°-344°; G.344°-053°; W.053°-062; R.062°-087°. Shown 1/7-10/6.

UTGARDSKILEN Lt. Oc. W.R.G.6 sec. W.8M. R.5M. G.5M. W.Lantern on piles 6m. G.006°-028.5°; W.028.5°-038.5°; R.038.5°-184.5°; G.184.5°-195.5°. Shown 1/7-10/6.

W MOLE Lt. Iso. R.2 sec. 2M. Post 6m.

TORSKESKJAER Lt. Fl. G.3 sec. 3M. Col. 7m.

LYNGHOLM. PAPPERHAVN 59°06.5'N 10°50.2'E Lt. Oc(3) W.R.G.10 sec. W.12M. R.9M. G.9M. Hut 17m. G.011°-023°; W.023°-033°; R.033°-039°; W.039°-052°; G.052°-098°; R.098°-108°; W.108°-128°; G.128°-145°; W.145°-151°; R.151°-176°; W.176°-180°; G.180°-227°. Shown 1/7-10/6. Lt. F.R. shows towards Papperhavn.

FREDRIKSTAD 59°12'N 10°57'E
(Port): Tel. (032) 12319 & 16422
(Pilots): Tel. (032) 12416
Radio Port VHF Chan 12, 14, 16. 0600-1500.
Radio Pilots VHF Chan 13, 12, 16 as required.
Krakerøy Bridge VHF Chan 12, 14, 16 H24.

ALHUS Ldg. Lts. 356° (Front) Q. mast 6m. (Rear) Q. mast 12m. vis on leading line only.

Ldg Lts. 178° (Front) F.R. mast 17m (Rear) F.R. mast. vis on leading line only.

KALDERA 59°10.8'N 10°57.4'E Ldg. Lts. 352° (Front) Oc. W.R.G.6 sec. W.11M. R.9M. G.9M. W.Lantern 10m. G.158°-172°; W.172°-176°; R.176°-349°; W.349°-352°; G.352°-004°.
**WEST FREDRIKSTAD. KIRKETARNET.
VESTSIDENS CHURCH** (Rear) Oc. 12M. Tr. 40m.

VATERLAND Ldg. Lts. 355°30' (Front) F.R. mast 10m. vis. on leading line only. (Rear) F.R. mast 21m. Vis. on leading line only.

ISEGRAN Lt. Q.R. Col. Lts. F.G. mark bridge 6c. NE.

SMERTU Ldg. Lts. (Front) F.G. 1M. mast 7m. (Rear) F.G. 1M. mast 10m.

FREDRIKSTAD EASTERN ENTRANCE

BELGEN 59°8.1'N 10°58.2'E Lt. Oc(2) W.R.G.8 sec. W.10M. R.9M. G.9M. W.Lantern 7m. W.169°-182°; R.182°-298.5°; W.298.5°-316°; G.316°-326.5°; W.326.5°-347°; R.347°-019.5°; W.019.5°-150°; G.150°-169°.

KALKEGRUNNEN Lt. Fl. G.3 sec. 6M. Pedestal 5m.

FLYNDREGRUNNEN 59°09.3'N 10°57.7°E Lt. Oc(3) W.R.G.10 sec. W.10M. R.7M. G.7M. Floodlit Tr. 8m. G.044°-175°; R.175°-263°; G.263°-340°; W.340°-346°; R.346°-044°.

LØPEREN

HABUTANGEN Lt. Fl. R.3 sec. 5M. Col. 8m.

KVERNSKJAERGRUNNEN 59°02.2'N 10°58.6'E Lt. Oc. W.R.G.6 sec. W.10M. R.7M. G.7M. Floodlit Tr. 8m. R.016°-093°; G093°-171.5°; W.171.5°-174.5°; R.174.5°-210°; G.210°-359°; W.359°-016°.

DØDVIKPYNTEN Lt. Iso. R.G.2 sec. R.7M. G.7M. W.Lantern 4m. G.179°-212°; R.212°-006°.

LUBBEGRUNNEN 59°04.1'N 10°58.4'E Lt. Oc(3) W.R.G.10 sec. W.10M. 4.7M. G.7M. Floodlit Tr. 8m. G.026°-190°; W.190°-195.5°; R.195.5°-258°; G.258°-357°; W.357°-359°; R.359°-026°.

KUSKAER Lt. Fl. R.3 sec. 4M. Col. 5m.

E SIDE 59°04.9' N 10°58.5' E Lt. Oc. W.R.G.6 sec. W.10M. R.8M. G.8M. W.Lantern 8m. G.180°-183°; W.183°-187°; R.187°-000°; W.000°-006°; G.006°-007°.

LØPERUNGEN N END 59°05.2'N 10°58.8'E Ldg. Lts. 176° (Front) Oc(3) W.R.G.10 sec. W.12M. R.9M. G.9M. W.Lantern 14m. G.295°-332°; W332°-336°; R.336°-011°; W.011°-014°; G.014°-169°; W.169°-180°; R.180°-198°; W.198°-210°; G.210°-251°; **BRATHOLMEN W SIDE** (Rear) Oc(2) W.R.G.8 sec. W.12M. R.9M. G.9M. W.Lantern 27m. G.357°-058°; W.058°-076°; R.076°-170°; W.170°-187°; R.187°-198°; W.198°-202°; G.202°-221.5°.

TJELLHOLMGRUNNEN Lt. Fl. R.3 sec. 7M. Floodlit Tr. 8m.

LØPERUNGBOEN Lt. Fl. G.3 sec. 2M. Metal post, concrete base 6m.

VESTRE FUGLESKJAERGRUNNEN Lt. Fl. G.5 sec. 7M. Floodlit Tr. 8m.

FUGLETANGSKJAER Lt. Fl. R.5 sec. 5M. Pedestal 6m.

VIKER MOLE HEAD Lt. Iso. R.2 sec. 3M. Col. 4M. Shown 1/7-10/6.

GRAVNINGSUND KUSKJAER 59°01.5'N 11°06.2'E Lt. Oc. W.R.G.6 sec. W.10M. R.8M. G.8M. W.Lantern on piles 6 m. G. 062°-071.5°; W.071.5°-074.5°; R.074.5°-221°; W.221°-261°; G.261°-281°. Shown 1/7-10/6.

LAUERSVAELJEN

HOMLUNGEN 59°00.9'N 11°01.9' Lt. Oc. W.R.G.6 sec. W.12M. R10M. G.9M. Tr. Hut 13M. W.233°-083°; R.083°-094°; W.094°-096°; G.096°-117°.

BØRHOLMEN N POINT. Ldg. Lts. 096° (Front). Oc. W.R.G.6 sec. W.9M. R8M. G.8M. W.Lantern 4m. G.076°-084°; W.084°-215°; R.215°-236°; W.236°-245°; G.245°-252°. Shown 1/7-10/6. **SAUHOLMEN** (Rear) Oc(3) W.R.G. 10 sec. W.12M. R.9M. G.9M. W. Lantern 12m. G.075°-078°; W.078°-121°; R.121°-161°. Shown 1/7-10/6.

VIDGRUNNEN Lt. VQ(6) L. Fl.10 sec. Col. 10m.

TRESTEINENE Lt. Fl(2) W.R.G.10 sec. W.7M. R.7M. R.4M. G.4M. W.Lantern on piles 15m. W.032°-034°; G.034°-048°; R.048°-077°; G.077-091°; W.091°-118°; R.118°-273°; W.273°-280°; G. 280°-301°; W.301°-309°; R.309°-032°. Racon.

TORBJORNSKJAER 58°59.7'N 10°47.2'E Lt. Al. Oc. R.R.W.40 sec. W.15M. R15M. Tr. 26m.

RAMSØY W SIDE 59°07.0'N 11°01.0'E Lt. W.10M. R.8M. G.8M. Col. 7m. G.015°-021.5°; W.021.5°-025.5°; R.025.5°-110.5°; W.110.5°-132°; G.132°-152°.

RAMSØY N POINT Lt. Fl.3 sec. 3M. Pedestal 6m.

TERNESKJAERENE Lt. Oc(3) W.R.G.10 sec. W.9M. R.9M. G9M. W.Lantern on piles 5m. R.113°-125°; W.125°128°; G.128°-212°; R.212°-250°; W.250°-253°; G.253°-288°; W.288°-301°; R301°-345°; G.345°-056°; R.056°-059°. Shown 1/7-10/6.

IDEFJORDEN

FLOBERG 59°02.3'N 11°25.4'E Lt. Oc(2) W.R.G.8 sec. W.10M. R.8M. G.8M. W.Lantern 7 m. G.318.5°-334°; W.334°-157°; R.157°-163°. Shown 1/7-10/6.

HASLAUFLU 59°06.4'N 11°10.4'E Ldg. Lts. 016° (Front) Oc. W.R.G.6 sec. W.10M. R.9M. G.9M. W.Lantern on Bn. 7m. G.039°-334°; W.334°-007°; R.007°-015°; W.015°-039°; G.039°-140°; W.140°-213°; R.213°-218°. Shown 1/7-10/6. **HYKKELEN** (Rear) Oc. 6 sec. 14M. W.Lantern 18 m. 011°-021°. Intens on leading line. Shown 1/7-10/6.

KNUBBEN Lt. Fl.5 sec. 3M. W. Col.

STORTANGEN Lt. Fl. R.5 sec. 2M. W. Col.

LAUSKJAER W SIDE 59°06.5'N 11°06.7'E Ldg. Lts. 108° (Front) Oc. W.R.G.6 sec. W.10M. R.8M. G.8M. W.B.Lantern on pile 6 m. G.090°-098°; W.098°-114°; R.114°-176°; W.176°-317°; G.317°-325°; W.325°-336°; R.336°-350°; W.350°-353°; G.353°-005°. **SINGLØY** (Rear) Oc. 6 sec. 11M. W.B. lantern 17 m. 103°-113° Intens on leading line. Shown 1/7-10/6.

SVINESUND

SPONVIKSKANSEN N SIDE OF ENTRANCE 59°05.4'N 11°13.6'E Lt. Oc. W.R.G.6 sec. W.11M. R.8M. G.8M. W.Lantern 9m. G.239°-246.5°; R.246.5°-062.5°; W.062.5°-093°; R.093°-094.5°. Shown 1/7-10/6.

MOLODDEN Lt. Q.R. 2M. Tripod 5m. Shown 1/7-10/6.

BJALVARP Lt. Q.G. 2M. W.Lantern on Pedestal 6m.

RØRBEK Lt. Iso. R. 4 sec. 2M. Tripod 8m. 240°-000° approx. Shown 1/7-10/6.

SVINESUND Lt. Q.G. 2M. W.Lantern on Pedestal 5m.

BLASOPPYNTEN Lt. Fl. R. 3 sec. 2M. Tripod 8m. Shown 1/7-10/6.

KRAKENEBBET Lt. Q.R. 3M. Col 6m. Shown 1/7-10/6.

KNIVSØYHOLMEN S SIDE. Lt. Oc.(2) W.R.G 8 sec. W.8M. R.5M. G.5M. W.Lantern 9m. G. 222°-253°; W.253°-259.5°; R.259.5°-054.5°; W.054.5°-064°; G.064°-077°. Shown 1/7-10/6.

SVARTE JAN Lt. Q.G. 2M. W.Lantern on Pedestal 5m.

SKYSSKAFFEREN Lt. Oc. W.R.G.6 sec. W.9M. R.8M. G.8M. W.Lantern 4m. G.333°-338°; W.338°-341.5°; R.341.5°-127°; W.127°-133°; G.133°-166°; W.166°-172°; R.172°-181°. Shown 1/7-10/6.

HALDEN 59°07'N 11°23'E

Tel. (031) 83200.
Radio Port & Pilots. VHF Chan 12, 13, 14, 16 Mon.-Fri 0800-1530; Sat. 0800-1200.

HALDEN. HOLLENDEREN Lt. Fl. R.3 sec. Post shown 1/7-10/6.

Ldg Lts. 087° (Front) F.R. (Rear) F.R.

Ldg Lts. 024°22' (Front) F.R. (Rear) F.R.

SAEKKEN

SAEKKEFLUENE Lt. Fl.5 sec. 3M. Pedestal on Tripod 7m.

GLAN 58°59.6'N 11°04.4'E Lt. Oc. W.R.G.6 sec. W.10M. R.8M. G.8M. W.Lantern on piles 6m. R.259°-267°; W.267°-269°; G.269°-328°; W.328°-351°; R.351°-141°; G.141°-164°. Shown 1/7-10/6.

HERFOLRENNA Lt. Fl. G.3 sec. 3M. Col. 4m. Shown 1/7-10/6.

REIERTANGEN 59°01.0'N 11°06.9'E Lt. Oc. (2) W.R.G.8 sec. W.12M. R.9M. G.9M. W.Lantern 12m. G.200°-209°; W.209°-212°; R.212°-253°; W.253°-302°; R.302°-010°;' G.010°-018°; W.018°-029°; R.029°-034°.

KATTHOLMEN E SIDE. Lt. Fl. Lt. W.R.G.3 sec. W.6M. R.4M. G.3M. W. B.Lantern 8m. G.178°-205°; W.205°-225°; R.225°-297°; G.297°-023°; W.023°-026.5°; R.026.5°-055°; G.055°-083°.

SWEDEN

DOCUMENTATION

Yachts should be registered or carry International Certificate for Pleasure Navigation (available from Royal Yachting Association or Cruising Association) or a letter from the Secretary of a recognised yacht club, giving proof of ownership.

All crew members must have valid passport.

Yachts must report to Customs on arrival (hours Mon-Fri. 0800-1600) and enter/leave by certain ports. e.g:

W Coast: Halmstad, Gothenburg, Marstrand, Lysekil, Uddevalla, Stromstad.

S Coast: Karlskrona, Ronneby, Karlshamn, Simrishamn, Ystad, Malmo, Landskrona, Helsingborg.

E Coast: Kalmar, Norrkoping, Oxelosund, Nynashamn Sodertalje, Stockholm.

Gotland: Slite, Visby.

Swedish Tourist Board: 29/31 Oxford Street, London, W.1. Tel: 071-437 5816.

Swedish Embassy, 11 Montagu Place, London W1H 2AL. Tel: 071-724 2101.

Coastguard

C.G. Station: Stenungsund 58°05'N 11°45'E.

C.G. Station and craft: Stromstad 58°56'N 11°10'E; Grebbestad 58°41'N 11°15'E; Lysekil 58°16'N 11°26'E; Skarhamn 57°59'N 11°33'E; Marstrand 57°56'N 11°10'E.

Co-ordinating Centre and C.G. vessel: Gravarne 58°21'N 11°15'E

Yachts. The Swedish Touring Club (STF) has established a large number of Gasthamnar (guest harbours) along the coasts and in many inlets, lakes and canals. They are marked on Swedish charts with a red anchor and a similar sign is erected ashore to show the position of yacht berths. Fuel, water and provisions can usually be obtained either at the berths or close by. Toilet and refuse disposal arrangements are provided and at many harbours there are showers and coin-operated washing machines.

A booklet entitled "Gasthamnar", published (in Swedish) by STF, lists the yacht harbours by regions. It contains an English/Swedish glossary covering the more common terms in use, and includes useful chartlets showing the location of the harbours. Name and telephone number of the Harbour Warden are given for each Gasthamnar, as well as the relevant Swedish chart.

Regulations. Visiting yachts are expected to comply with normal seamanlike practice as regards mooring and fendering, to avoid discharging their toilets into harbour basins and to deposit refuse in places allocated ashore. Between 2200 and 0600 there is a 'silence' period.

Also listed and their locations shown on chartlets are the large numbers of huts, known as "Sopmajor" which have been erected on uninhabited islets off the coasts and in many inlets and lakes. They consist of a section for refuse disposal and another for (dry) toilets.

Radio. A number of base radio stations, operating on Channel 11A (27.095 MHz.) listen out for a period of 3 min. before each whole hour and half hour. Yachts in trouble can contact these stations before sending out an emergency call; those without radio equipment can call a base radio station through a number of auxiliary stations established in several harbours of refuge and other convenient places along the coast.

Emergency – Ambulances. The Swedish rescue organization can be alerted by telephoning 90 000 or through the base and auxiliary radio stations. Ambulance helicopters can land at a number of places and are located close to the auxiliary stations among the islands off the coast.

List of Gästhamnar

	Lat. N	Long. E
Nötholmen	58°52'.2	11°03'.5
Strömstad	58°56'	11°10'
Havstenssund	58°45'	11°11'
Resö	58°48'	11°10'
Sannäs	58°44'	11°15'
Kalvön	58°46'	11°09'
Grebbestad	58°41'	11°15'
Fjällbacka	58°36'	11°17'
Hamburgsund	58°33'	11°16'
Bovallstrand	58°29'	11°20'
Hunnesbostrand	58°26'	11°18'
Hasselösund	58°22'	11°14'
Smögen	58°21'	11°13'
Kungshamn	58°22'	11°15'
Malmön	58°21'	11°21'
Skalhamn	58°19'	11°24'
Valbodalen	58°17'	11°26'
Lysekil	58°16'	11°27'
Fiskebäckskil	58°15'	11°28'
Ellös	58°11'	11°28'
Gullholmen	58°11'	11°24'
Käringön	58°07'	11°22'
Stocken	58°09'	11°25'
Hälleviksstrand	58°07'	11°27'
Edshultshall	58°06'	11°28'
Mollösund	58°04'	11°28'
Björholmen	58°03'.1	11°31'.4
Kyrkesund N	58°02'	11°31'
Kyrkesund S	58°01'	11°31'
Skärhamn	57°59'	11°33'
Klädesholmen	57°57'	11°33'
Rönnäng	57°56'	11°35'
Mossholmen	57°57'.0	11°33'.6
Kongsviken	58°13'.5	11°35'.3
Nötesund	58°18'.1	11°42'.3
Henån	58°14'	11°41'
Marstrand	57°53'	11°36'
Nordön	57°53'.5	11°41'.3
Almön	58°03'.8	11°45'.5
Uddevalla	58°21'	11°55'
Åstol	57°55'	11°35'
Dyrön	57°56'	11°37'
Stenungsund	58°04'	11°49'
Ljungskile	58°13'	11°55'

SWEDEN – WEST COAST

TJURHOLMSKNAPPEN 58°58.5'N 11°05.9'E
Lt. Fl(2) W.R.G.6 sec. W.7M. R.5M. G.4M. W.
Tr. 14m. G.194°-236°; W.-323°; R.-356°; G.-
022.5°; W.-028°; R.-066°; G.-074°; W.-107°;
R.-117°.

APPROACHES TO STROMSTAD

LIKHOLMEN 58°55.5'N 11°06.8'E. Lt. Q.
W.R.G. W.6M. R.4M. G.3M. W.Lantern 8m.
G.197°-243°; W.-250°; R.-324°; G.-034°; W.-
036.5°; R.-058°; G.-069°; W.-075°; R.-092°.

HALSÖRHOLMEN 58°55.7'N 11°07.8'E. Fl.3
sec. 2M. W.Lantern on cairn 8m.

KRISTHÅLLAN 58°56.2'N 11°07.8'E. Lt. Fl(3)
W.R.G.9 sec. W.5M. R.3M. G.3M. W.Lantern
on pedestal 8m. G.285°-303°; W.-333°; R.-
033°; G.-096°; W.-100°; R.-107°.

STRÖMSTAD

Yacht harbour in Sodra Hamnen. 125/200
berths. Depths 2.5-8m.

58°56.2'N 11°09.4'E. Lt. Fl. W.R.G.3 sec.
W.6M. R.4M. G.3M. W.Lantern 7m.
G(unintens) 222°-233°; W(unintens) -242°;
R(unintens) -251°; G(unintens) -262°;
W(unintens) -272°; R(unintens) -353°;
W(unintens) -040.5°; G.-051°; W.-053°; R.-
078°.

SODRA LÅNGON 58°56.4'N 11°07.8'E. Ldg.
Lts. 161°30' (Front) Iso. W.R.G.4 sec. W.7M.
W.5M. R.3M. G.2M. W.Lantern on pedestal
5m. Intens on leading line, W.shore -220°;
G.220°-315°; W.-315°-321°; R.321°-340°.
58°56.1'N 11°08'. OE (Rear). Q.W.R. W.7M.
W.4M. R.4M. R.3M. W.Lantern on pedestal
15m. Intens on leading line, W.shore-180°;
R.180°-200°; W.200°-250°.

KLÖVNINGARNA 58°56.0'N 10°59.5'E. Ldg.
Lts. 053° (Front) Iso. W.R.G.4 sec. W.11M.
R.8M. G.7M. W.Tr. 12m. W.051°-059°; R.-
132°; G.-140.5°; W.-145°; R.-216°; G.-242°;
W.-225.5°; R.-327°; G.-051°. Racon. **NORD-
HÄLLSO** 58°58.1'N 11°04.8'E (Rear) 3.5M.
from front. Q.W.R.G. W.10M. W.9M. R.6M.
G.3M. W.Lantern 38m. W(intens) on leading
line, W.049°-057°; G.090°-115°; W.115°-122°;
R.122°-137.5°; W(unintens) 137.5°-203°.

KÅBBLINGARNA 58°54.9'N 11°05.6'E Lt. Fl.
W.R.G.3 sec. W.6M. R.4M. G.3M. R.Lantern
5m. R.187.5°-202°; G.-035°; W.-062°; R.-
075.5°

EKENAS HAMN

FISHING HARBOUR Ldg. Lts. 240° (Front)
F.G.6M.W. Δ on post 15m. Fishing. (Rear)
F.G.6M. W. ∇ on post 26m. Fishing.

W. BREAKWATER Ldg. Lts. 176° (Front)
F.R.3M. Col. 4m. Fishing. (Rear) F.R.3M. Col.
5m. Fishing.

SNEHOLM 58°53.6'N 11°04.0'E. Lt. Fl.
W.R.G.3 sec. W.8M. R.5M. G.4M. W. Tr.
B.Band 12m. G.123°-167°; W.-182°; R.-191°;
G.-248°; W.-250°; R.-292°; G.-335°; W.338°;
R.-347°; G.-033°.

VATTENHOLMEN 58°52.7'N 11°06.5'E. Lt.
Fl(2) W.R.G.6 sec. W.8M. R.6M. G.5M.
R.Lantern10m. G.337°-007°; W.-013°; R.-
017.3°; G.-103°; W.-115°; R.-150°.

APPROACHES TO KOSTERSUNDET

OTTERSTEN 58°51.5'N 11°00.0'E. Lt. Fl.
W.R.G.3 sec. W.6M. R.4M. G.3M. W.Lantern
9m. G.shore-095°; W.095°-103°; R.103°-119°.
Fishing.

STORA ÅRHOLMEN 58°52.2'N 10°59.9'E.
Lt. Fl(2) W.R.G. 6 sec. W.5M. R.3M. G.3M.
W.Lantern on pedestal 8m. G.shore-018°;
W.-021°; R.-107°; G.-201°; W.-205°; R. 205°-
shore. Fishing.

SIESÅDAN 58°52.6'N 11°00.5'E. Lt. Q.
W.R.G. W.3M. R.1M. G.1M. W.Lantern on
pedestal 5m. G.084°-129°; W.-136°; R.-166°;
W.-084°.

KOSTERSUNDET SÖDRA. Ldg. Lts. 015°
(Front) F.R.6M. W. ∆ , B.Border on post 12m.
Fishing. (Rear) F.R.6M. W. ▽ B.Border on
post 6m. Fishing.

SYDKOSTER GRÖNA Ldg. Lts. 223°30'
(Front) F.G.2M. Metal pillar 9m. (Rear)
F.G.2M. Metal pillar 9m.

NORDKOSTERS RÖDA Ldg. Lts. 251° (Front)
F.R.2M. Metal pillar 9m. (Rear) F.R.2M. Metal
pillar 14m.

KALVERÄNNAN

SKÅRESKÄR 58°50.5'N 11°02.7'E. Lt. Fl(4)
W.R.G. 12 sec. W.6M. R.4M. G.3M.
W.Lantern on pedestal 12m. W.042°-050°;
R.-106°; G.-188°; R.-264°; G.-042°. Fishing.

RUNDEGRÅ 58°51.2'N 11°02.8'E. Lt. Q.
W.R.G. W.5M. R.3M. G.3M. W.Lantern on
pedestal 8m. G.197°-225°; W.-240°; R.-288°;
G.-015°; W.-020°; R.-037°. Fishing.

VEDSKÄR 58°51.4'N 11°04.3'E. Lt. Fl.
W.R.G.6 sec. W.5M. R.3M. G.3M. W.Lantern
on pedestal 9m. G.003°-079°; W.-088°; R.-
186°; G.-257°; W.-312°; R.-003°. Fishing.

URSHOLMEN 58°50.2'N 10°59.5'E. Lt. L
Fl(2) W.R.G. 12 sec. W.17M. R.14M. G.13M.
W.Round Tr. B.Band 33m. W.036°-169°; R.-
174°; W.-337°; G.-341°; W.-349°; R.-036°.

SVANGEN 58°48.0'N 11°07.2'E. Lt. Fl.
W.R.G. 3 sec. W.16M. R.13M. G.12M.
W.Lantern 21m. R.302°-025°; G.-042°; W.-
047°; R.-076°; G.-107°; W.-108.5°; R.-136°; G.-
167.5°; W.-169.5°; R.-204°; W.-238°.

RAMSKÄR 58°45.6'N 10°59.7'E. Lt. Fl(3)
W.R.G. 9 sec. W.9M. R.6M. G.5M. W. Tr.
B.Band 19m. W.002°-046°; R.-078°; G.-108°;
W.-143°; R.-189°; G.-220°; W.-263°; G.-272°;
R.-279°; W.-338°; R.-346.5°; G.-002°. Racon.

BISSEN 58°48.2'N 11°09.6'E. Lt. Fl(2)
W.R.G. 6 sec. W.6M. R.4M. G.4M. R.Lantern
on Tr. 8m. G.shore-328°; W.-330°; R.-346°;
W(unintens)-125°; G.-140°; W.-143°; R.-156°.

HAVSTENSSUND Yacht harbour with 12
berths, depths 2-5m. also yacht harbour
with 25/30 berths. Depths 4-6m.

NW Approach to Havstenssund:

Reso (3c. ESE of Bissen Lt.)
Yacht harbour has 20 moorings in depths of
5m.

Sannas, entered through Sannasfjorden has
10 yacht moorings in depths of 3m.

SW Approach to Havstenssund:

Kalvon S side. Fishing harbour with 8/10
moorings for yachts. Buoyed channel with
depth of 3.6m.

58°45.2'N 11°10.8'E. Ldg. Lts. 013° (Front)
Iso. W.R.G. 4 sec. W.10M. R.7M. G.6M.
R.Lantern 11m. G. shore-012°; R.-040°; W.-
179°; G.-187°; W.-189°; R.-195°. 58°45.8'N
11°11.0'E. (Rear) Q.R.11M. R.Lantern 21m.
Vis. on leading line.

VÄCKER 58°42.9'N 11°09.8'E. Lt. Fl(4)
W.R.G. 12 sec. W.10M. R.7M. G.6M. W. Tr. R.
roof, B.Band, on grey conical base 15m.
Floodlit. W.016°-019°; R.-034°; G.-071°; W.-
085.5°; R.-099°; G.-285°; R.-344.5°; G.-016°.

APPROACHES TO GREBBESTAD

OTTERÖ 58°39.6'N 11°12.9'E. Lt. Fl(2)
W.R.G.6 sec. W.6M . R.4M. G.3M. W.Lantern
7m. G.055°-087°; W.-093°; R.-129°;
G(unintens)-221°.

SVINNÄS Ldg. Lts. 042° (Front) Q. W.R.G.
W.3M. R.6M. R.2M. G.2M. W. □ and lantern
on pedestal 5m. R(intens) on leading line.
G.235°-239°; W.-243°; R.-257°; R(unintens)-
040°. (Rear) Q.R.5M. W. □ and lantern on
pedestal 8m.

GREBBESTAD
60/80 yacht moorings in depths of 2-5m.

Ldg. Lts. 010°30' (Front) F.R.6M. W. ∆ and
lantern on pedestal 5m. F.R.Lt. on radio
mast 0.6M. W.N.W. (Rear) F.R.6M. ∇ and
lantern on pedestal 9m.

STANGESKÄR 58°39.7'N 11°11.7'E. Lt. Fl.
W.R.G.3 sec. W.9M. R.6M. G.5M. W.B. Tr.
8m. G.154.5°-159°; W.-161°; R.-243°; G.-
269.5°; W.-272°; R.-289°; G.-354°; W.-356°;
R.-065°.

DJUPSKÄR 58°38.3'N 11°11.8'E. Lt. Fl(3)
W.R.G.9 sec. W.8M. R.5M. G.4M. W.B.Tr.
9m. G.070°-123°; W.-126°; R.-145°; G.-178.5°;
W.-181°; R.-250°; G.-339°; W. -341.5°; R.-
070°.

BRÄMSKÄR 58°39.3'N 11°09.5'E. Lt. Fl.
W.R.G.6 sec. W.8M. R.6M. G.5M. W.Lantern
9m. G.002°-010°; W.-015°; R.-020°; G.-067.5°;
W.-097°; R.-118°; G.-255.5°; W.-258°; R.-272°;
G.-287.5°; W.-306°; R.-328°.

APPROACHES TO FJALLBACKA

SÖDRA SYSTER 58°35.6'N 11°09.4'E. Lt.
Fl(2) W.R.G.6 sec. W.6M. R.4M. G.3M. W.B.
Tr. 14m. W.004°-026°; R.-039°; G.-048°; W.-
072.5°; R.-085°; G.-117°; W.-162°; R.-219°; G.-
252.5°; W.-272°; R.-320°; G.-004°.

BRÄNDE HOLMEN 58°35.6'N 11°12.0'E. Lt.
Q. W.R.G. W.5M. R.3M. G.2M. W.Lantern
17m. G.251.5°-267.5°; W.-273°; R.-296°;
W(unintens)-050.5°; G.-093°; W.-097°; R.-
115°.

TRYBERGSHOLMEN 58°35.7'N 11°13.1'E. Lt.
Oc(2) W.R.G.9 sec. W.5M. R.3M. G.2M.
W.Lantern 6m. G.047.5°-063°; W.-072°; R.-
150°; G.-225°; W.-228°; R.-241°.

TESTHOLMEN 58°35.9'N 11°13.6'E. Lt.
Q.W.R.G. W.6M. R.4M. G.3M. W.Lantern 5m.
G.140°-155.5°; W.-157°; R.-213°; G.216.5°;
W.-319°; R.-327°.

LILLA KÖTTÖ 58°36.4'N 11°15.6'E. Lt. Fl.
W.R.G.3 sec. W.5M. R.3M. G.3M. W.Lantern
11m. G.302°-318.5°; W.-328°; R.-340°;
W(unintens)-071°; G.-086.5°; W.-092°; R.-
114°; W(unintens)-150°; G.-170°; W.-173°; R.-
178°.

VÄDERÖARNA

VÄDERÖBOD 58°32.6'N 11°02.0'E. Lt. L. Fl.
W.R.G.6 sec. W.16M. R.13M. G.12M. Or. Tr.
32m. Floodlit. R.145.5°-190°; R.(unintens)-
215°; R.-229°; G.-331°; W.-145.5°. Racon.

SKÄLHOLMEN 58°32.7'N 11°05.7'E. Lt. Fl.
W.R.G.6 sec. W.8M. R.6M. G.5M. W. Tr. 14m.
G.167°-184°; W.-187°; R.-208°; G.-218°; W.-
220°; R.-235°; G.-289°; W.-292°; R.-315°; G.-
324°; W.-328°; R.-353°; G.-002.5°; W.-008°;
R.-032°.

PLOGJÄRNET 58°34.4'N 11°04.2'E. Lt. Fl(3)
W.R.G.9 sec. W.6M. R.4M. G.4M. W.Lantern
9m. G.254°-271°; W.-280°; R.-357°; G.-072.5°;
W.-074.5°; R.-104°.

KALVÖSKÄR 58°35.1'N 11°15.2'E. Lt. Iso.
W.R.G.4 sec. W.6M. R.4M. G.3M. W.Lantern
4m. G.000°-016°; W.-019°; R.-068°; G.-133°;
W.-138°; R.-149°.

SANDVIKSHOLMEN 58°33.6'N 11°14.7'E. Lt.
Fl(2) W.R.G.6 sec. W.6M. R.4M. G.3M.
R.Lantern on Tr. 10m. G.014°-045.5°; W.-
048°; R.-122°; G.-190.5°; W.-193°; R.-242°.

SOTENS SVARTSKÄR 58°33.0'N 11°13.4'E.
Lt. Fl(3) W.R.G.9 sec. W.8M. R.6M. G.5M. W.
Tr. 7m. G.172.5°-210°; W.-217°; R.-302°; R.-
356°; G.-005°; W.-018.5°; R.-036.5°; G.-048°;
W.-051.5°; R.-063°.

LANGHOLMEN 58°31.9'N 11°13.6'NE. Ldg.
Lts. 006° (Front) Iso. W.R.G.4 sec. W.11M.
W.3M. R.2M. G.1M. W.Lantern 8m.
W.164.5°-087° (intens) on leading line,
G(unintens) 087°-130°; W(unintens) 130°-
150°; R(unintens) 150°-164.5°. 4 F.R. Lts. on
radio mast 2.23M ESE. **MÄKHOLMEN**
58°32.5'N 11°13.8'E (Rear) Q.10M.W. □ on
W.Pedestal 17m.

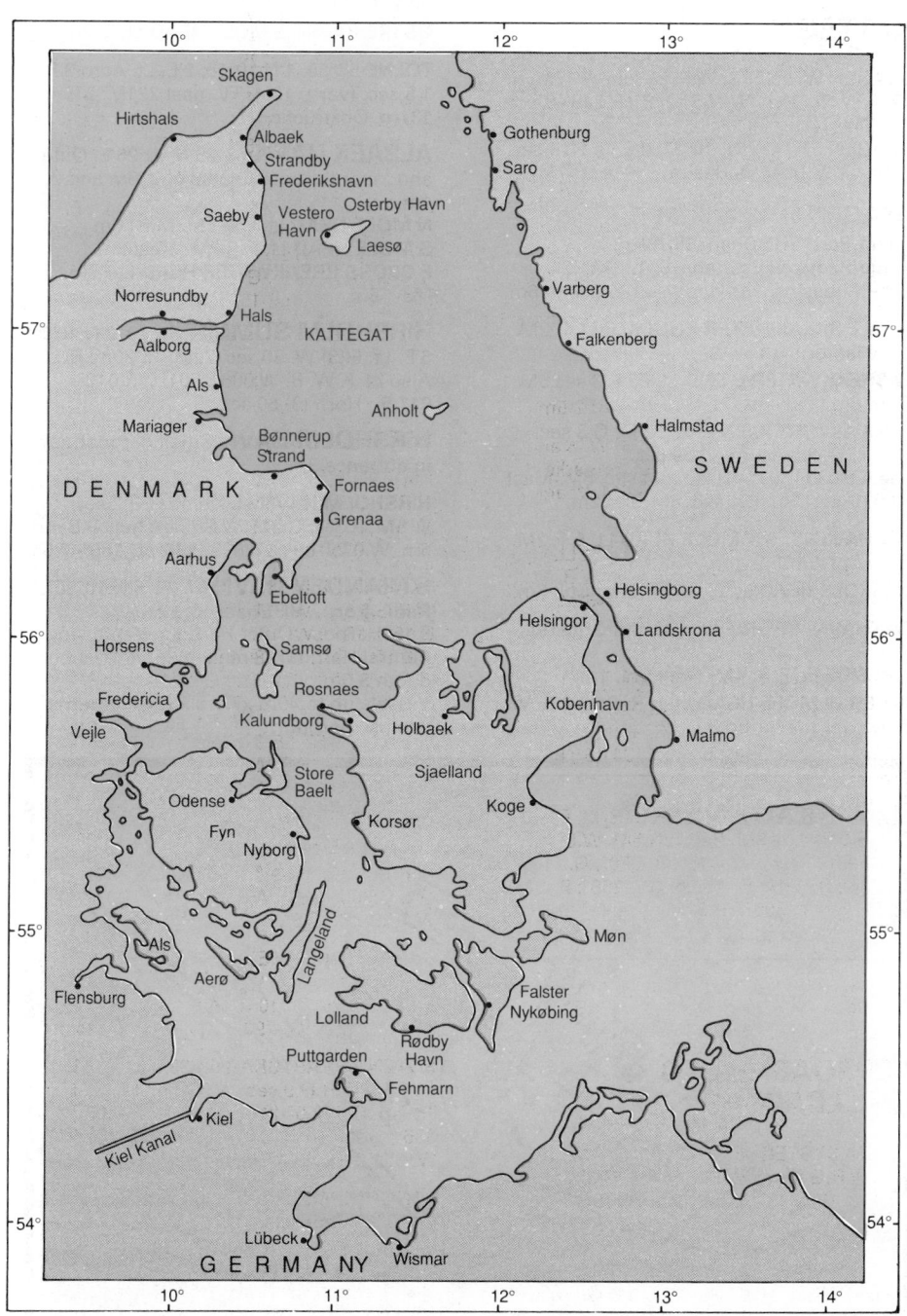

DENMARK

KATTEGAT

SKAGEN W. Lt. Fl(3) W.R.10 sec. W.17M. R. 12M. W. Tr. 31m. W.053°-248°; R.248°-323°. RC 50m. N.
SKAGEN 57°44. 2'N, 10°37. 9'E Lt. Fl. 4 sec. 23M. Grey Tr. 44m. Racon.

SKAGEN 57°43'N 10°36'E
Radio-Port: VHF Chan. 16, 12,13.
Radio-Pilots: VHF Chan. 16, 12, 13 H24.
Several basins with depths of 4. 5m. to 6m.

NEW E BREAKWATER KNUCKLE Lt. F. 2M. Grey lantern 4m.
W BREAKWATER E END Lt. Fl. R.3 sec.5M. R. Tr. 8m.
E BREAKWATER SW END Lt. Fl. G.3 sec. 5M. G. Tr. 8m. Horn (2) 30 sec. Ldg. Lts. 334° (Front) Iso. R.4 sec. 8M. Mast 13m. (Rear) Iso. R.4 sec. 8M. Tr. 22m.

FORHAVENS. SW MOLE HEAD Lt. F. R.2M. Grey Col. 5m.
NE MOLE HEAD Lt. F. G.2M. Grey Col. 5m.

OSTHAVN. SE SIDE Lt. F. G.4M. Grey Col. 4m.
NW SIDE Lt. F. R. 4M. Grey Col. 4m.
INNER W MOLE HEAD Lt. F. R. Post 6m. Vis. only over the harbour.

INNER E MOLE HEAD Lt. F. G. Post 6m. Vis only over the harbour.
ØSTRE BASIN. E MOLE HEAD Lt. F.

TOLNE 57°30. 1'N 10°18. 2'E. Lt. Aero 3 Fl. 1.5 sec. (vert). 12M. TV mast 221M. 215m. 137m. Obstruction.

ALBAEK HAVN 57°35'N 10°26'E. Outer and inner harbour depths of 2. 8m and 2. 4m.
N MOLE HEAD Lt. F. G.2M. Mast 6m.
S MOLE HEAD Lt. F. R.2M. Mast 6m.
E CROSS BREAKWATER HEAD Lt F.3M. Mast 5m.

HIRSHOLM SUMMIT 57°29. 2'N 10°37. 6'E. Lt. Fl(3) W. 30 sec. 22M. Tr. 30m. RC. Also Lt. F. W. R. W.006.5°-012°; R.012°-017.5°. Horn (3) 60 sec.

HIRSHOLM HAVN Small harbour depth in entrance 3m.

HIRSHOLM HAVN Lt. Iso. W.R.G.2 sec. W.5M. R.3M. G.3M. W.Square hut, G.Band 5m. W.075°-093°; R.093°-180°; G.180°-325°.

STRANDBY HAVN 57°29. 6'N 10°30.5'E
Radio-Port: VHF Chan. 16, 12.
Boat Harbour, Outer Harbour, depth 4m. Central Harbour depth 2m. Inner Harbour depth 3.5m.
Vessels up to 40m x7.5m.x3.5m. draught can use harbour.

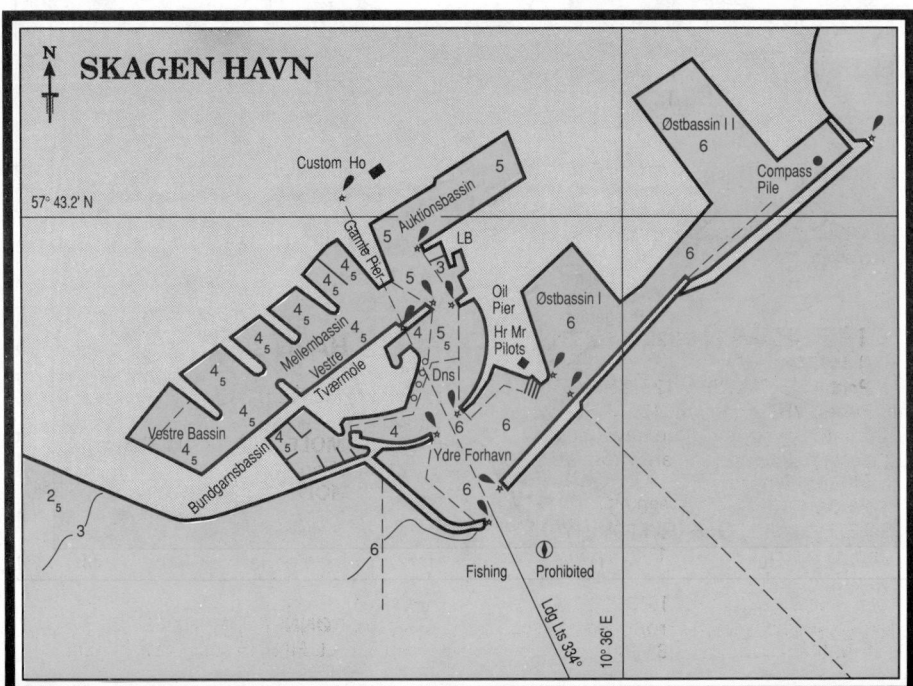

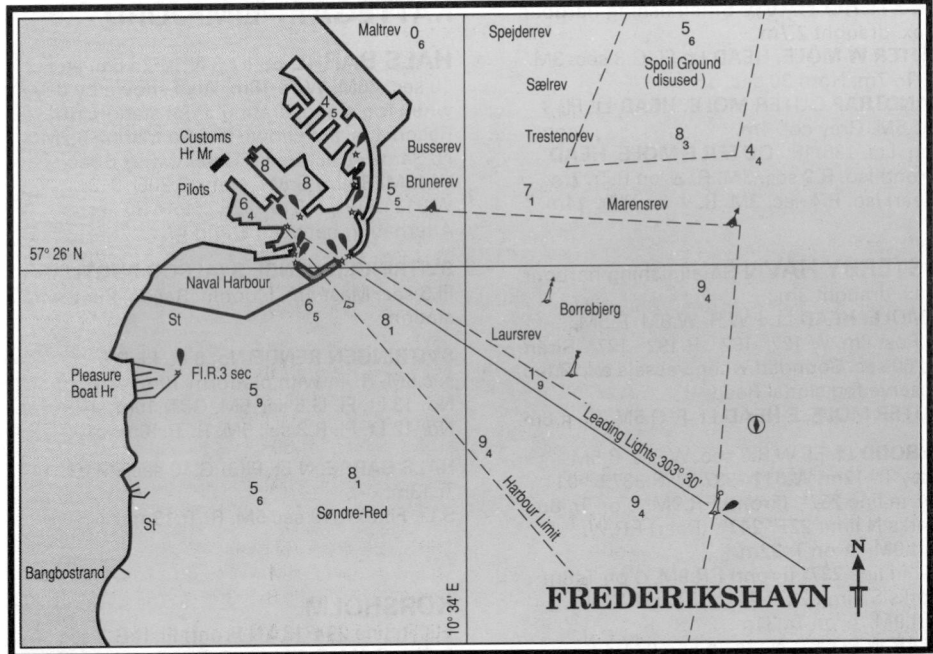

FREDERIKSHAVN

Ldg. Lts. 252° (Front) Iso. R.4 sec. 6M. R. Δ on Grey Tr. 8m. Vis. 184.5°-319.5°. (Rear) Iso. R.4 sec. 6M. R. ▽ on Grey Tr. 12m. Vis. 184.5°-319.5°.
N MOLE Lt. F. G.4M. G.Tr. 5m.
HEAD Lt. Fl. G.5 sec.5M. 10m. G. Tr. Siren 60 sec.
S MOLE Lt. F. R.4M. R.Tr.5m.
HEAD Lt. Fl. R.5 sec.5M. R.Tr. 10m.
BASIN ENTRANCE W Lt. F. G.4M.
G.structure 5m. Mole head illuminated. E Lt. F. R.4M. R. structure 5m.

RONNERNE. SOUTHWARDS MARINA MOLE HEAD Lt. Fl. G.3 sec. 4M. Grey mast. 4m. Mole head illuminated.

FREDERIKSHAVEN 57°26'N 10°33'E
Tel: (08) 441740
Radio-Port: VHF Chan. 16, 12 H24
Radio-Pilots: VHF Chan. 16, 12, 13 H24
A yacht harbour south of the naval base. Depths of 3m., in entrance and 1.5m. to 2.5m. within the harbour.
NE BREAKWATER HEAD 57°26.0'N 10°33.3'E. Lt. Iso W.G.2 sec. W.13M. G.9M. G.Tr. 8m. G.302°-271°; W.271°-278°. Siren (2) 30 sec. RC.
Ldg. Lts. 303°30' 57°26.0'N 10°33.2'E.
SW BREAKWATER HEAD (Front) Iso. R.2sec. 10M. R. Tr. 8m. Unintens 018°-108°.

S INNER MOLE (Rear) 57°26.1'N 10°32.8'E Iso. R.4 sec. 11M.Grey Tr. 30m. 297.5°-306.5°.
S INNER MOLE HEAD Lt. F. R.5M. R. Tr.5m.
N INNER MOLE HEAD Lt. F. G.5M. G. Tr.5m.
FLOATING DOCK No: 1. SE CORNER Lt. F. R.2M. 9m.
No: 2. NE CORNER Lt. F. R.2M. 10m.
NAVAL HARBOUR E CROSS MOLE Lt. Fl. R.5 sec. 4M.R. Tr. 4m. Vis. 006°-280°.
W CROSS MOLE Lt. Fl. G.5 sec. 4M.G. Tr. 4m. Vis. 129°-069°.
MARINA E MOLE Lt. Fl. R.3 sec. 3M. Mast 4m.
SOUTHWARD SBM Lt. Fl(2) 5 sec. 6M. Y. By. Racon.

SAEBY HAVN Small harbour. Depths 3.8m.
N OUTER MOLE. HEAD Lt. Fl. G.3 sec. Grey post 6m.
S OUTER MOLE. HEAD Lt. Fl. R.3 sec. Grey post 6m. Siren 60 sec.
INNER N MOLE. HEAD Lt. F.G. Grey post 7m.

LAESØ
NORDRE RØNNER. ON REEF 57°21.17'N 10°55.5'E. Lt. Fl(4) 15 sec. 14M. Tr. 16m.

VESTERO HAVN Small fishing harbour.
Max. draught 2.7m.
OUTER W MOLE. HEAD Lt. Fl. G.3 sec. 3M.
G. Tr. 7m. Horn 30 sec.
SANDTRAP OUTER MOLE. HEAD Lt. Fl. 3
sec.5M. Grey col. 4m.
Ldg. Lts. 136°18'. **OUTER E MOLE. HEAD**
(Front) Iso. R.2 sec. 3M. R. △ on R.Tr. 7m.
(Rear) Iso. R.4 sec. 3M. R. ▽ on R.Tr. 14m.

OSTERBY HAVN Small fishing harbour.
Max. draught 3m.
E MOLE. HEAD Lt. F.W.R. W.8M. R.5M.
W.Post 8m. W.127°-192°; R.192°-127°. Siren
(2) 60 sec. Sounded when vessels expected.
Reserve fog signal Reed.
OUTER MOLE. E HEAD Lt. F. G.5M. Post 6m.

SYRODD Lt. Fl. W.R.3 sec. W.8M. R.5M.
Grey Tr. 12m. W.011°-337.5°; R.337.5°-011°.
Lts. in line 237°. (Front) F.R.9M. O on Tr. 8m.
Marks N limit 227°-247°. (Rear) F.R.W.
vert.9M. ✤ on Tr.32m.
Lts. in line 237° (Front) F.R.9M. O on Tr.8m
Marks S. limit 227°-247°. (Rear) F.R.W.
vert.9M. ✤ on Tr. 31m.
NEAR W POINT. N Lts. in line 074°48'
(Front) F.R.9M. Tr. 8m. Mark cable extending
WSW. (Rear) 340m. from front. F.R.W.
vert.9M. Tr. 28m. S Lts. in line 071°24'
(Front) F.R.9M. Tr. 8m. Mark cable extending
WSW (Rear) 450m. from front. F.R.W.
vert.9M. Tr. 28m.

STENSNAES
N.Lts. in line 281°42' (Front) F.R.9M. Tr. 7m.
Mark cable extending ESE. (Rear) 240m.
from front. F.R.W. vert.9M. Tr.29m.
S.Lts. in line 286°42' (Front) F.R.9M. Tr. 8m.
Mark cable extending ESE. (Rear). 230m.
from front F.W.R. vert.9M ✤ on Tr. 30m.

LAESO RENDE 57°13.2'N 10°40.4'E Lt. L.
Fl(2) W.R.G.20 sec. W.18M. R.14M. G.14M.
B. Tr.25m. G.105.5°-179°; W.179°-203°;
R.203°-252°; G.252°-329.5°; W.329.5°-337°;
R.337°-105.5°. RC. Racon. Helicopter landing
platform. Horn (2) 20 sec.

ASAA HAVN 57°09'N 10°26'E
Small harbour. Depth in entrance and
harbour 2m.
W MOLE HEAD Lt. F.G.1M. Mast 4m. Shown
1/9-30/4. Siren 60 sec. when vessels
expected.
S MOLE HEAD Lt. F.R.1M. Mast 4m. Shown
1/9-30/4.
HOU. N MOLE Lt. Fl. G.3 sec. 4m. G. Pillar
3m.
INNER MOLE Lt. F.G.4M. G. Pillar 6m.

KATTEGAT – LIMFJORD

HALS BARRE 56°57.3'N 10°25.6'E. Lt. Fl.
10 sec. 26M. W.Tr. 18m. Also shown by day
when fog sig. operating. Pilot station. RC.
Racon. Lts. are shown from a Marina 6.2M
N. Same structure Lt. Oc(2) W.R.G.6 sec.
W.12M. R.8M. G.8M. 15m. G.305°-313°;
W.313°-319°; R.319°-325°. Horn 30 sec.
Alternating between E and W.

SVITRINGEN RENDE S (ALBOG BUGT) Lt.
Fl.3 sec. Mast 4m. Floodlit. Racon. Pilot
station

SVITRINGEN RENDE No: 8 Lt. Fl. R.3
sec.5M. R. Tr. with platform 10m. 〰
No: 13 Lt. Fl. G.5 sec.5M. G. Tr.10m. 〰
No: 12 Lt. Fl. R.3 sec.5M. R. Tr.10m. 〰

HALS BARRE. N Lt. Fl(3) G.10 sec.5M. G.
Tr.13m. 〰
S Lt. Fl (3) R.10 sec.5M. R. Tr.13m.〰

KORSHOLM
Lts. in line 294°18' (N Front) Fl. R.G.3 sec.
R.9M. G.4M. R.8-sided Tr.5m. R.139.5°-260°;
G.260°-298.5°. Intens 292.5°-296.5°. (S Front)
Fl. R.3 sec. R.8-sided Tr.5m. Vis.291.5°-
334.5°; Intens 292.5°-296.5°.

EGENSEKLOSTER PYNT. EGENSE (Rear)
56°58.9'N 10°18.2'E. Iso. 4 sec. 12M. R ▽ on
Tr. 20m. Midway between twin front lights.
Intens 291.5°-297.5°.

EGENSE FERRY BERTH. W MOLE HEAD
Horn (2) 20 sec.

HALS E 56°59.4'N 10°18.5'E. Ldg. Lts.
315°24'.

W MOLE HEAD (Front) Oc. W.R.G.5 sec.
W.14M. R.10M. G.10M. R.Hut 4m. G.311.5°-
315°; W.315°-316.5°; R.316.5°-321° H24.
(Rear) Iso. 4 sec. 13M. Grey mast 9m. H24.

HALS HAVN 56°59'N 10°19'E
Tel: Pilots (08) 251006, 251973.
Radio-Pilots: VHF Chan.16, 12, 13 as
required. Small harbour with depths of 3m
to 4m inside harbour.
W MOLE HEAD Lt. F.R. on post
E MOLE HEAD Lt. F.G. on post. Siren 30 sec.
FERRY BERTH. W MOLE HEAD Bell 15 sec.
on post.

Thence the Limfjord to Aalborg. A yacht
harbour is situated in the Badehavn and the
Marina Strandparken.

BLODEN

S Lts. in line 286° (Front) Iso. R.2 sec. 4M. R. △ W.Stripe on R. Tr. 13m. 275.5°-297.5° H24. (Common Rear) Iso. 4 sec. 6M. R. ▽ W. stripe on R. Tr.18m. 272°-294°. H24. N Lts. in line 279°30' (Front) Iso. G.2 sec. 3M. R. △ W.Stripe on R. Tr.13m. 268.5°-290.5°. H24.

HALS W 56°59.5'N 10°18.4'E. Ldg. Lts. 076°30' (Front) Iso. 2 sec. 14M. R. △ W.Stripe on R. Tr. 13m. 066.5°-086.5°. H24. (Rear) Iso. R.4 sec. 6M. R. ▽ W.Stripe on R. Tr. 19m. 066.5°-086.5°. H24.

EGENSEKLOSTER SKOV. Ldg. Lts. 116° (Front) Iso R.2 sec. 6M. R. △ W.Stripe on R. Tr. 13m. Vis 106°-126°. H24. (Rear) Iso. R.4 sec. 6M. R. ▽ W.Stripe on R. Tr. 19m. 106°-126°. H24.

SKELLET Ldg. Lts. 271° (Rear) Iso. G.4 sec. 3m. R. ▽ W.Stripe on R. Tr. 18m. 260°-282°. H24. (Common Front) Iso. G.2 sec. 3M. R. △ W. stripe on R. Tr. 13m. 260°-282°. H24. Same structure Iso. 2 sec. 8M. 13m. 131°-143°. H24.

FRYDENSTRAND Ldg. Lts. 137° (Rear). Iso. 4 sec. 8M. R. ▽ W. Stripe on R. Tr. 23m. 133°-141°. H24.

VESTERHASSING Lt. Iso. W.G.2 sec. 2M. R.W. ☐ on Tr. 13m. W.033°-048°; G.048°-033°. H24.

JETTY HEAD Lt. Fl.5 sec. 2M. B-pole 3m. H24.

CHRISTIANSHAB Lt. Iso. W.G.2 sec. 1M. R. ☐ W. stripe on Tr. 13m. W.037°-052°; G.052°-037°. H24.

GRØNLANDSHAVN Ldg. Lts. 240° (Front) F.R. 1M. R. △ W.Stripe on grey Tr. 28m. (Rear) F.R. 1M. R. ▽ W. stripe on grey Tr. 32m.

BREDHAGE. Ldg. Lts. 303°. (Front) Iso. 2 sec. 8M. R. △ W.Stripe on Tr. 13m. Vis. 299°-307°. H24. (Rear) Iso. 4 sec. 8M. R. ▽ W. stripe on R. Tr. 23m. 299°-307°. H24.

ENGHOLM. E 57°05.7'N 10°00.6'E. Ldg. Lts. 327°12' (Rear) Iso. 4 sec. 12M. R. ▽ W. stripe on R. Tr. 23m. Vis. 307°-347° H24.57°05.2'N 10°01.2'E. (Common Front) Iso. 2 sec. 12M. R. △ W.Stripe on R. Tr. 11m. 307°-347°. Same structure Iso. 2 sec. 8M. 10m. 044°-124°.

ESE Ldg. Lts. 083°36' (Rear) Iso. 4 sec. 8M. R. ▽ W.Stripe on R. Tr. 18m. 044°-124°. H24.

ENGHOLM. S Ldg. Lts. 301° (Front) Iso. R.2 sec. 4M. R. △ W. stripe on R. Tr. 13m. 290°-312°. H24. (Rear) Iso. R.4 sec. 4M. R. ▽ W.Stripe on R. Tr. 18m. 290°-312°. H24.

ENGHOLM SE 57°05.4'N 10°00.0'E. Ldg. Lts. 045°. Iso. R.2 sec. 11M. R. △ W.Stripe on R. Tr. 13m. 035°-055°. H24.57°05.5'N 10°00.3'E (Rear) Iso. R.4 sec. 11M. R. ▽ W.Stripe on R. Tr. 18m. 035°-055°.

ENGHOLM W Ldg. Lts. 024° (Front) Iso. 2 sec. 8M. R. △ W.Stripe on R. Tr. 13m. 018°-030°. H24. (Rear) Iso. 4 sec. 8M. R. ▽ W. stripe on R. Tr. 18m. 020°-028°. H24.

BOVET SE RØRLEDNING Lts. in line 322° (Front) F.Y. 1M. Y. ◊ on post 4m. 318°-326°. Mark pipeline crossing. (Rear) F.Y. 1M. Y. ◊ on mast 16m. 318°-326°.

ALBORG HAVN

SKUDEHAVN 57°03'.5N 9°53'.9E Ldg. Lts. 223° (Front) F.R. 12M. R. △ on warehouse 10m. Lts. are shown from Limfjord Bridge and the Railway Bridge. (Rear) F.R. 12M. R. ▽ on Tr. 12m.

AALBORG-EGHOLM FERRY Lt. F. on dolphin. Horn 12 sec. Also F. on dolphin. Bell 12 sec.

MARINA STRANDPARKEN W MOLE HEAD Lt. F.G. 4M. G.post 5m. Shown 1/4-15/11. E MOLE HEAD Lt. F.R. 4M. R.Post 5m. Shown 1/4-15/11.

NIBE. W SIDE Lt. Fl. (3) G.10 sec. 2M. G.post 2m. Shown 1/4-15/11. E SIDE Lt. Fl. (3) R.10 sec. 2M. R.Post 2m.

KATTEGAT

OSTER-HURUP

N MOLE HEAD Lt. F.G. 2M. W.Mast 5m. Shown 15/8-30/4. Siren 60 sec. when vessels expected. S MOLE HEAD Lt. F.R. 2M. W.Mast 5m. Shown 15/8-30/4.

MARIAGER FJORDE

Radio-Pilots: VHF Chan. 16, 12, 13. Vessels up to 5m. draught can reach Hobro Havn. Vessels wishing to have Hadsund Railway Bridge opened show Flag N. or W.Lt. and sound 1 long and 1 short blast. Yachts may have to wait if traffic is heavy. At Mariager Havn there is a yacht harbour with depths of 2m. to 2.3m.

ALS ODDE 56°42.7'N 10°20.9'E. (Front) Iso. G.2 sec. 10M. R. △ on Grey Tr. 7m. H24. (Rear) Iso. G.4 sec. 12M. R. ▽ on Grey Tr. 20m. H24.

MARIAGER FJORD ENTRANCE Ldg. Lts. 237° (Front) Iso. 2 sec. R. △ on Tr. 6m. Vis. on leading line (Rear) Iso. 4 sec. R. ▽ on Tr. 10m. Vis. on leading line. Ldg. Lts. 244° No: 2B (Front) Iso. R.2 sec. R. △ 6m. Further lights are shown in Mariager Fjord. No: 2A (Rear) Iso. R.4 sec. 3M. R. ▽ 10m.

ANHOLT
NEAR E END. ANHOLT 56°44.3'N 11°39.1'E. Fl.10 sec. 19M. R. Tr. 8m. Obsc. 053°-076° except when bearing 057° and 063°.

ANHOLT HAVN Small harbour max. draught 3m. 2 cones points together with B. ball or G.W.R. Lt. = no vessel to enter or leave.
OUTER N MOLE HEAD 56°42'.9N 11°30'.5E Lt. Iso. W.R.G.4 sec. W.14M. R.10M. G.10M. R. Tr. 8m. G.038°-112°; W.112°-130°; R.130°-135°; G.135°-160°; W.160°-164°; R.164°-038°. Fog Detector Lt. Horn (2) 30 sec. 0800-1600.
OUTER S MOLE HEAD Lt. F.G. 4M. G.Post 8m. Vis. 345°-260°. Two pontoon pierheads marked by F.W. Lts.
INNER N MOLE HEAD Lt. F.R.W.Post 6m. 254°-099°.
INNER S MOLE HEAD Lt. F.G.W.Post 6m. 354°-302°.

KATTEGAT – RANDERSFJORD

RANDERSFJORD Tel: (06) 485026.
Radio-Pilots: VHF Chan. 16, 6, 12.
Approach channel across Bar 5.8m depth.

UDBYHØJ. ELKER BAKKE 56°35.4'N 10°19.3'E Lt. Oc. W.R.G. 5 sec. W.15M. R.10M. G.10M. Gable of building 35m. G.194°-228°; W.228°°-232°; R.232°-254°; G.254°-276°; W.276°-279°; R.279°-289°.

OVER BARREN 56°36.1'N 10°20.5'E. Ldg. Lts. 253°06' (Front) Iso. 2 sec. 14M. R. △ on R.Mast 4m. 250.5°-255.5°. Intens on leading line. (Rear) Iso. 4 sec. 14M. R. ▽ on R.Mast 14m. 250.5°-255.5°. Intens on leading line.

OVER KIRKEGRUND W. Ldg. Lts. 281° (Front) Iso. R.2 sec.5M. R. △ on mast 4m. 269.5°-292.5°. Intens on leading line. (Rear) Iso. R.4 sec. 7M. R. ▽ on mast 9m. 278°-

284°.56°36.1'N 10°21.3'E. E Ldg. Lts. 101° (Front) Iso. R.2 sec. 11M. R. △ on mast 4m. 098.5°-103.5°. (Rear) Iso. R.4 sec. 11M. R. ▽ on mast 8m. 098°-103.5°.

ØEN MELBANK Lt. Fl(2) R.5 sec.5M. R.Col. 6m.

MELLEMPOLDE Lt. Fl(2) G.5 sec. 3M. G.Post on dolphin 4m.

UDBYHØJ
FISHING HARBOUR Lt. Oc(2) W.R.G.6 sec. 2M. G.Post on dolphin 4m. G.281°296°; W.296°-297°; R.297°-337°; G.337°-040°; W.040°-042°; R.042°-057°.
E MOLE HEAD Lt. F.G. 1M. Post 2m.
W MOLE HEAD Lt. F.R. 1M. Wpost 2m.
NORTH Ldg. Lts. 020° (Front) Iso. R.2 sec.5M. △ on W.Mast 5m. (Rear) Iso. R.4 sec.5M. ▽ on W.Mast 8m.
WEST Ldg. Lts. 052° (Front) Iso. W.R.G.2 sec. W.7M. R.5M. G.4M. R. △ on mast 9m. G.048°-056°; R. 056°-087°; W.087°-102°; R.102°-142°. (Rear) Iso. G.4 sec 5M. R. ▽ on mast 14m.

UDBY Ldg. Lts. 189°30' (Front) Iso. R.2 sec.5M. R. △ on W.Bn. 6m. (Rear) Iso. R.4 sec.5M. R. ▽ on W.Bn. 11m.

MØLLEGRUND Ldg. Lts. 232° (Front) Iso. G.2 sec.5M. R. △ on R.Bn. 6m. (Rear) Iso. G.4 sec.5M. R. ▽ on R.Bn. 10m.

SKALMSTRUP Ldg. Lts. 212° (Front) Iso. 2 sec. 7M. R. △ on Bn. 9m. 204.5°-219.5°. (Rear) Iso. 4 sec. 7M. R. ▽ on Bn. 20m. 204.5°-219.5°.

RAABY ODDE Ldg. Lts. 032° (Front) Iso. 2 sec. 7M. R. △ on Bn.5m. 024.4°-039.5°. (Rear) Iso. 4 sec. 7M. R. ▽ on Bn. 12m. 024.5°-039.5°.

KARE HOLM KANAL

N END E MOLE Lt. Fl. R.3 sec. 2M. R. ☐ on Bn.5m. Vis. 001°-081°.
W. MOLE Lt. Fl. G.3 sec. 2M. G. △ on Bn.5m. Vis. 181°-001°.

ØSTER-TØRSLEV Ldg. Lts. 001°24' (Front) Iso. 2 sec. 7M. R. △ on Bn.5m. 353.5°-008.5°. (Rear) Iso. 4 sec. 7M. R. ▽ on Bn. 12m. 353.5°-008.5°.

VEDERNE Ldg. Lts. 181°24' (Front) Iso. 2 sec. 8M. R. △ on R. Bn. 6m. (Rear) Iso. 4 sec. 8M. R. ▽ on R.Bn.12m.
Lt. Fl. G.3 sec. 2M. Post 2m.
Lt. Fl. R.3 sec. 2M. Post 2m.

VOER PIER HEAD Lt. F.R. 2M. Post 4m.

STØVRINGGAARD Lt. Iso. W.G.2 sec. W.5M. G.3M. Post 4m. G.190°-241°; W.241°-304°; G.304°-010°.

VOER Ldg. Lts. 017° (Front) Iso. R.2 sec. 8M. R. △ on R.Mast 6m. (Rear) 56°31'.2N 10°14'.3E. Iso. R.4 sec. 10M. R. ▽ on R.mast 12m.

UGGELHUSE Ldg. Lts. 197° (Front) Iso. R.2 sec. 9M. R. △ on R.Mast 12m. (Rear) Iso. R.4 sec. 9M. R. ▽ on R.Mast 32m.

VEDERNE Lt. Fl. R.3 sec. 2M. Dolphin 2m. Lt. Fl. R.3 sec. 2M. Dolphin 2m. No: 1 Lt. Fl. G.3 sec. 1M. Col. 2m. Fl. G.3 sec. Lts. mark channel to Randers Havn.

No: 2 Lt. Fl(2) R.5 sec. 1M. Col. 2m. Fl. R.3 sec. Lt. marks channel to Randers Havn.

HEVRING Mast 3 Lt. Al. W.R.4 sec. Mast (By day F.) When firing is taking place. F.R. obstruction lights on masts. R.Lt. on mast 1.3M NW. R.Lt. on Tr. 1.5M WSW.

E MOLE HEAD Lt.56°24.8'N 10°55.9'E. Lt. Iso. W.R.G.2 sec. W.10M. R.6M. G.4M. W.Tr. 8m. R.231°-245.5°; G.245.5°-270°; W.270°-305°; R.305°-331°; G.331°-351°; R.351°-003°.
N MOLE HEAD 56°24.7'N 10°55.7'E. Lt. Iso. W.R.G.4 sec. W.12M. R.8M. G.8M. R.Tr. 8m. R.187°205°; G.205°-219.5°; W.219.5°-226.5°; R.226.5°-235°.
SPUR MOLE HEAD Lt. Fl. G.5 sec. Tr.5m. 270°-180°.
MID MOLE HEAD Lt. F.G. Mast 5m. 129°-069°.

SYDHAVN. S QUAY. MOLE HEAD Lt. F.R.3M. Grey post 5m.

LYSTBADEHAVN. N BREAKWATER HEAD Lt. Fl. G.3 sec. 4M. W.Pyramid, G.Top 5m. Floodlit. Vis 028°-298°. H24.
S BREAKWATER HEAD Lt. Fl. R.3 sec. 4M. W.Pyramid, R.Top.5m. Floodlit. H24.

GLATVED LASTEANLAEG PIER HEAD Lt. Fl. G.3 sec. 4M. Post on dolphin 6m.

LYSEGRUND. SHOALEST PART Lt. Q (2) 5 sec.5M. B.R.Hut 10m.

HESSELØ 56°11.9'N 11°42.7'E. Lt. Fl(4) 20 sec. 18M. W.Tr. 40m.

KATTEGAT

BONNERUP
This is a fishing harbour. 5 small basins with depths of 3m. in entrance and 2m. to 2.8m. in four of the basins with 4m. in the largest.

E OUTER MOLE HEAD Lt. F.R.5M. Grey mast 6m. Siren 60 sec.
W OUTER MOLE HEAD Lt. F.G.5M. Grey mast 6m.

KNUDSHOVED. GERRILD. 56°31.7'N 10°49.9'E. Lt. Fl(4) W.G.20 sec. W.14M. G.11M. W.Tr. 27m. G.106.5°-128°; W.128°-295.5°.

FORNAES. ON POINT 56°26.6'N 10°57.5'E. Fl. 20 sec. 23M. Tr. 32m. Obscured to the Northward by Gjerrild klint and to the southward by Havknude.

GRENA HAVN 56°25'N 10°56'E
Tel: (06) 320550.
Radio-Port: VHF Chan. 16, 12, 13, 14.
Radio-Pilots: VHF Chan. 16, 12, 13 H24.
Small harbour N & S Basins. Depths of 4m. in N Basin where there is a jetty and slipway for small craft.

ISEFJORD

SPODSBJERG 55°58.6'N 11°51.4'E. Lt. Oc. W.R.G.5 sec. W.18M. R.11M. G.11M. W.Tr. 40m. G.shore-095°;W.095°-098°; R.098°-116°; G.116°-148°; W.148°-shore. Lt. on Tr. 5M ENE when firing taking place. Sig. Stn.

HUNDESTED HAVN
Radio-Port: VHF Chan. 16, 12, 13.
Radio-Pilots: VHF Chan. 16, 12.
Fishing and ferry harbour. Max. draught 5m.

OUTER HARBOUR. W MOLE HEAD Lt. F.R. Aluminium lantern. 6m. In fog F.Y.
E MOLE HEAD Lt. F.G. Grey pedestal 4m. Ldg. Lts. 017°18' (Front) Iso. R.2 sec. 4M. Mast 5m. Vis. 310°-084°. (Rear) Iso. R.4 sec. 4M. Tr. 6m. Vis. 310°-084°.

FERRY HARBOUR. N MOLE HEAD Lt. Fl. R.3 sec. 4M. Grey pedestal 5m. In fog F.Y. Fog Lt. F.Y. on Centre pier.
S MOLE 14m from Head Lt. Fl. G.3 sec. 4M. Grey lantern on pile 5m.

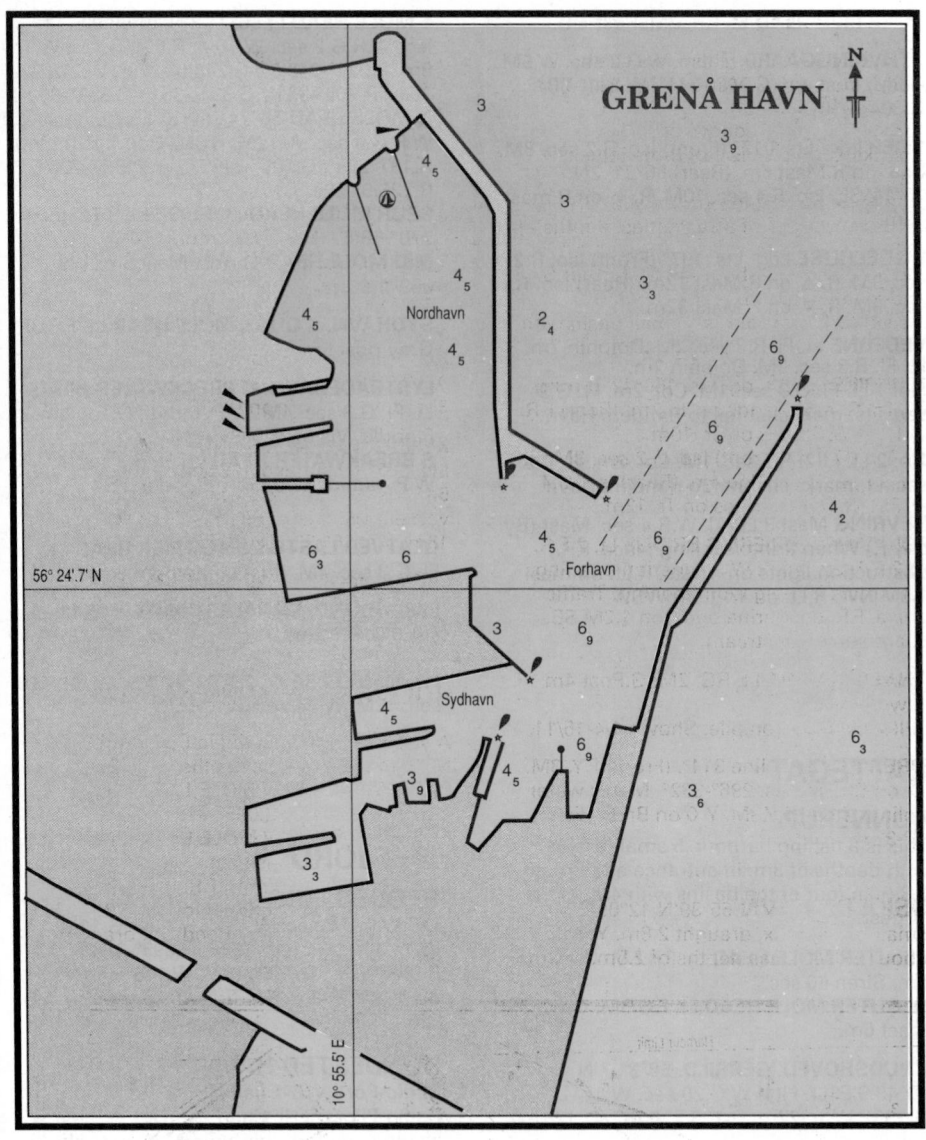

LYNAES HAVN 55°56'N 11°52'E.
Fishing and yacht harbour. Depths in yacht
harbour 2m. to 2.5m. Max. speed 3 kts.
GROYNE HEAD Lt. Oc(2) W.R.G.6 sec.
W.7M. R.5M. G.4M. R.8-sided wooden
structure 5m. W.000°-042°; R.042°-050°;
G.050°-146°; R.146°-340°; G.340°-000°.
Fl. R.3 sec. and Fl. G.3 sec. mark Marina
230m. NNE.
W MOLE HEAD Lt. F.R.2m. R.post 5m. Not
shown 0100-0500.

ROSKILDE FJORD

FREDERIKSWAERK HAVN 55°58'N
12°01'E
Old harbour has depths of 3.5m. Kronprins
Frederiks Bridge clearance 3.5m. at MWL.
For bridge to open show Flag N and sound
1 long, 1 short blast.
S MOLE HEAD Lt. Fl. G.5 sec. 3M. W.Tr. 4m.
N MOLE HEAD Lt. Fl. R.5 sec. 3M. W.Tr. 4m.

FREDERIKSSUND HAVN 55°50'N
12°03'E
Commercial harbour. There is a yacht
harbour close W. of Marbaek for craft 11m.
x 3.2m. x 2m. draught.
Marbaek Yacht Harbour (S of
Frederikssund) consists of three jetties,
depths up to 2.1m.
Danmarine Yacht Harbour (2¼ M.S. of
Marbaek) consists of three jetties, depths up
to 1.8m.
Yedderley Yacht Harbour (4½ M. further S.)
has depths up to 3m.
Herslev Yacht Harbour is a small basin with
depths of 2m.

FREDERIKSSUND Ldg. Lts. 160°42' (Front)
F.R. 3M. R. ∆ W.Bands on Tr. 7m. (Rear) F.R.
3M. R. ▽ W.Stripes on Tr. 10m.
Ldg. Lts. 172°30' (Front) Iso. G.2 sec. 3M. R.
∆ W.Stripes on bridge 4m. (Rear) Iso. G.4
sec. 3M. R. ▽ W. stripes on Tr. 12m.

KRONPRINS FREDERIKS BRIDGE Lt. 2 F.G.
and 2 F.R. Lts. mark W navigation opening.
R. Lts. mark E navigation opening. Traffic
signals. F.R. on Marina pontoon 1.2M SE.
Lts. are shown upstream.

KITNAES MARINA Lt. F.G. 2M. G.Post 4m.
Shown 1/4-15/11.
Lt. Fl(3) G.10 sec. on pile. Shown 1/4-15/11.

LEJRE VIG. Lts. in line 314°. (Front) F.Y. 3M.
Y. ◊ on Bn.3m. Vis. 296°-332°. Marks water
pipeline. (Rear) F.Y.3M. Y ◊ on Bn.5. Vis.
296°-332°.

ROSKILDE HAVN 55°39'N 12°05'E
A small basin, max. draught 2.8m. Yacht
harbour close W has depths of 2.5m. to 3m.

There is a boat pier close W of the yacht
harbour.
Ldg. Lts. 165° (Front) F.R. 4M. W. ∆ on Tr.
7m. (Rear) F.R. 4M. W. ▽ on Tr. 11m.
VEDDELED MARINA. N MOLE Lt. Fl. R.3 sec.
4M. R.post 2m.
S MOLE Lt. Fl. G.3 sec. 2M. G.Post 4m.
NØRREREV Lt. Fl. G.3 sec. Shown 1/5-15/10.

JAEGERSPRIS FIRING AREA. N LIMIT Lts. in
line 115°. **STOREHØJ** (Front) F.R. 3M. B. ∆
Y.Band on Bn.14m. Occas. Al.W.R.4 sec on
mast close by. (Rear) F.R. 3M. B. ▽ Y. band,
on Bn.25m. Occas. **S LIMIT.** Lts. in line
073°30'. **SØNDRE STRAUNDHUSE** (Front)
F.G. 3M. B. ∆ Y.Stripes on Bn.12m. Occas.
Al.W.R.4 sec on mast close by. (Rear) F.G.
3M. B. ▽ Y. band, on Bn.18m. Occas.

KYNDBYVAERKET. S END OF MOLE Ldg.
Lts. 165° (Front) Iso. R.2 sec. 7M. Grey post
5m. Vis. 161.5°-168.5°. Siren 30 sec. when
vessels expected. (Rear) Iso. R.4 sec. 7M. Tr.
18m. Vis. 161.5°-168.5°.

EJBY N. MOLE HEAD Lt. F.R. 3M. B.Post 6M.
Lt. Q. shown from mast 1.4M. W. when
firing taking place.

HOLBAEK HAVN 55°43'N 11°43'E

A yacht marina situated in Dragerup Vig 1½
M. E. of Holbaek has depths up to 2.8m.
BADEHAVNENS. W MOLE Lt. F.W.G.3M. Tr.
4m. W.315°-045°; G.045°-315°.
SKIBSHAVNENS W MOLE Lt. F.G.3M. G. Tr.
W.Band on grey base 5m.
Ldg. Lts. 241°30' (Front) F.R.4M. R. ∆ W.
bands on orange Tr. 9m. Floodlit. 230°-263°.
(Rear) F.R. 4M. R. ▽ W.Bands on orange Tr.
16m. 230°-263°.

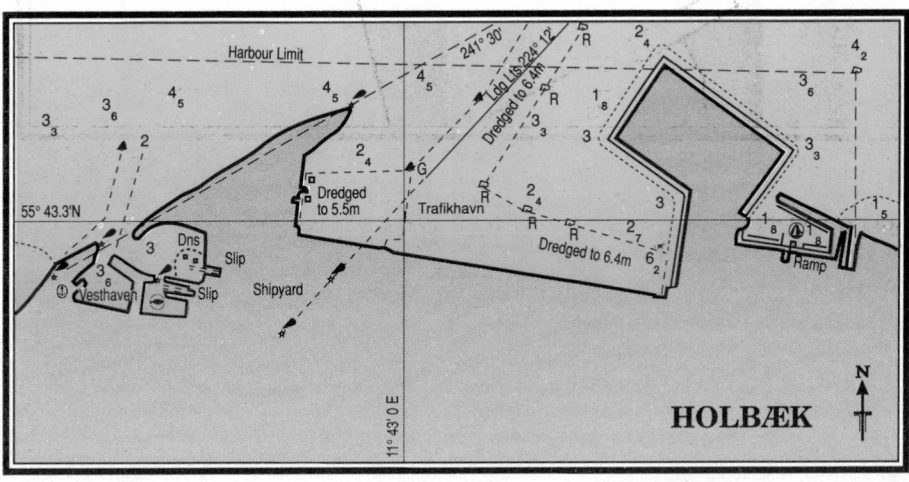

HOLBÆK

TRAFFIC HARBOUR Ldg. Lts. 224°12' (Front)
F.G.3M. W. △ R.Stripes on Tr. on
warehouse gable 14m. 214°-234°. (Rear)
F.G.3M. W. ▽ R.Stripes on Tr. 19m. 214°-
234°.
MARINA Lt. Iso. W.R.G.2 sec. W.4M. R.4M.
G.4M. G.Post 5m. W.105°-135°; R.135°-145°;
G.145°-105°.

HORBY. MARINA MOLE HEAD Lt. Oc.
W.R.G.10 sec. W.5M. R.4M. G.4M. R.W.Post
4m. G.309.5°-327°; W.327°-027.5°;R.027.5°-
309.5°.

ORØ Ldg. Lts. 061°30' (Front) F.R.4M. R. △
W. bands on Tr. 14m. (Rear) F.R.4M. R. ▽ W.
bands on Tr. 26m.
ORØ HAVN. PIER HEAD Lt. Oc. W.R.G.5 sec.
4M. R.post W. band 3m. W.150°-290°;
G.290°-065°; W.065°-092°; R.092°-150°.

ORØ VESTRE LØB

HØNSEHALSEN Lt Fl. W.R.G.3 sec. W.6M.
R.2M. G.2M. W.Tr. on 4 legs 5m. G.065°-
165°; W.165°-175°; R.175°-252°; G.252°-
338.5°; W.338.5°-343.5°; R.343.5°-065°.
Shown 1/8-15/5.

LØSERUP Lt. Oc W.R.G.5 sec. W.4M. R.Tr.
23m. G.180°-207°; W.207°-216°; R.216°-234°.
Shown 1/8-15/5.

KONGSØRE. NE MOLE HEAD Lt.
Al.Q.W.R.W. 3M. R.1M. Tr. 31m. Vis. 077°-
353°. Intens 170°-260°. Shown during
torpedo firing practice. Fl. W. Lts. are shown
on the target floats at other times.
MOLE Lt. F.G.4M. G.Tr. 4m.

NYKOBING HAVN 55°55'N 11°41'E
Small commercial harbour with yacht
harbour to SW.

MARINA. N SIDE Lt. F.G. 4M. Post 3m. Also
Lt. F.R.
S SIDE Lt. Fl. R.3 sec. 4M. Grey mast 4m.
Molehead floodlit.

RORVIG HAVN 55°57'N 11°46'E
Small fishing and yacht harbour. Depth in
channel 2.9m in yacht basin 1.4m.

SMALL CRAFT HARBOUR. N MOLE HEAD
Lt. F.G.

S MOLE HEAD Lt. F.R.

HJELM. SUMMIT 56°08.0'N 10°48.4'E.
Lt. Iso. W.R.G. 8 sec. W.18M. R.15M. G.15M.
W.Tr. 61m. G.016.5°-043°; W.043°-051°;
R.051°-068°; G.068°-088°; W.088°-091°;
R.091°-110°; W.110°-016.5°.

SWEDEN – WEST COAST

SOTEFJORDEN

On the E side of Hamburgsund near the ferry berth at Uddin there are 30/50 yacht moorings in depths of 4-5m. At Bovellstrand there are 30 yacht moorings in 4m. depth. At Hunnebostrand there are 125 yacht moorings in 3-4m. depth.

SÖÖ Ldg. Lts. 115°30' (Front) Q. 4M. Lantern on W.Pedestal 6m. Intens (7M) on leading line. **W SIDE** (Rear) Iso. W.R.G.4 sec. W.7M. R.5M. G.4M. R.Lantern on W. Tr. 14m. G.325°-356.5°; W.356.5°-000°; R.000°-036°; G.036°-098°; W.098°-118°; R.118°-122°; G.122°-184°. R. Lts. on radio mast 1.1M NE.

MJÖLSKAR Lt. Fl. W.R.G.3 sec. W.8M. R.5M. G.4M. W.B. Tr. grey conical base 14m. W.022°-025°; R.025°-169°; G.169°-194°; W.194°-196°; R.196°-355°; G.355°-022°.

SKARVASÄTT N END Lt. Fl(2) W.R.G.6 sec. W.8M. R.5M. G.4M. R.Lantern 14m. G(unintens) 011.5°-082.5°; R(unintens) 082.5°-148°; G.148°-162°; W.162°-167.5°; R.167.5°-176°; G.176°-183°.

TRYGGÖ Ldg. Lts. 016° (Front) Iso. R.4 sec. 8M Col. on W.Pedestal 7m. Vis. on leading line. (Rear) Q.R. 8M. Çol. on W.Pedestal 17m. Vis. on leading line.

BREVIKSUDDE 58°21.8'N 11°21.5'E Ldg. Lts. 074° (Front) Iso. W.R.G.3 sec. W.10M. R.7M. G.6M. W.Lantern 8m. G.336°-001°; W.001°-005°; R.005°-037°; G.037°-065.5°; W.065.5°-076.5°; R.076.5°-095.5°. (Rear) Q.8M. Lantern on W.Pedestal 25m. Vis. 028°-049.5°.

58°21.2'N 11°15.5'E Ldg. Lts. 279°. **KOLEBÄDAN.** (Front) Iso. W.R.G.3 sec. W.10M. R.7M. G.6M. W.Pedestal on B.W.base 6m. G.004.5°-084°; W.084°-087.5°; R.087.5°-179°; W.179°-004.5°. **SMÖGEN NÖRRA** (Rear) Oc.5 sec. 9M. Lantern on roof of pilot's look-out room 31m.

SMÖGEN

In the SW part of the harbour there are 300 yacht moorings in 2-4m. depth.

Ldg. Lts. 284° (Front) F.R. on post. Vis. on leading line only. (Rear) F.R. on post. Vis. on leading line only.

FISKETÄNGEN

There are 150 yacht moorings in 4-9m. depth. Ldg. Lts. 297°30' (Front) F.R.4M. W.Concrete Bn.13m. (Rear) F.R.4M. W.Concrete beacon 21m.

GRAVARNA

58°21.4'N 11°14.9'E. Ldg. Lts. 023°30' (Front) Iso. W.R.G.3 sec. W.14M. R.11M. G.10M. R.Lantern 15m. W(intens) on leading line, G.046°-055°; W.055°-058°; R.058°-069.5°. F.R. Lts. on radio masts 0.2M E. (Rear) Iso. 3 sec. 14M. R.Lantern 28m. Vis. on leading line.

BYTTERLOCKET Lt. Fl. R.3 sec. 1M. W.Structure on B.Cairn 4m.

FISHING HARBOUR Ldg. Lts. 349°30' (Front) F.G. 6M. W. △ on post 7m. Fishing. (Rear) F.G. 6M. W. ▽ on post 12m. Fishing.

FLÄTTARNA Lt. Fl(3) W.R.G.6 sec. W.6M. R.4M. G.3M. W.Lantern 8m. R.254°-258°; G.258°-262.5°; W.262.5°-281°; W(unintens) 281°-288°; R(unintens) 288°-335°; G.335°-343.5°; W.343.5°-345.5°; R.345.5°-358.5°; G.358.5°-046°; W.046°-060°; R.060°-066°; R(unintens) 066°-085°.

HATTEFLU Lt. Fl. W.R.G.3 sec. W.5M. R.4M. G.3M. W.Pedestal, B.Base 6m. G.038°-105.5°; W.105.5°-111.5°; R.111.5°-120°; W.120°-187.5°; W(unintens) 187.5°-252°.

PENGESKÄRSBADAN Lt. Q. W.R.G. W.5M. R.3M. G.2M. W.Pedestal, B.Base 7m. G.200°-234°; W.234°-238.5°; R.238.5°-200°.

ÄBYFJORD. ENTRANCE. HÄLLÖ

58°20.2'N 11°13.2'E. Lt. Fl.12 sec. 21M. W. Tr. Top 40m. Vis. about 183°-about 175°; Intens 345°-175°. Obscured 117°-119.5° within 2.5M. RC.

BROFJORDEN 58°21'N 11°26'E Tel: 0523 604 60. Telex: 42135. **Radio-Port:** VHF Chan. 16.1-28.60-88 H24. This is a large tanker port.

BRANDSKÄRSFLAK 58°17.6'N 11°18.8'E. Lt. Oc(2) W.R.G.8 sec. W.15M. R.14M. G.12M. W. Tr. G.Band, grey base 25m. Floodlit. R.227°-311°; G.311°-352°; R.352°-028°; G.028°-046°; W.046°-227°. Partly obscured 245°-256°. Racon. Helicopter landing platform.

DYNABROTT 58° 17.8'N 11°18.7'E. Lt. Oc. W.R.G.8 sec. W.15M. R.14M. G.12M. W. Tr. R.Band, grey base 25m. Floodlit. R.209°-216°; G.216°-225°; W.225°-052°; R.052°-078°; G.078°-209°. Helicopter landing platform. Partly obscured 060°-071°.

LINDHOLMEN MELLERSTA 58°19.5'N 11°22.8'E. Ldg. Lts. 050°30' (Front) Iso. 8 sec. 16M. R. Tr. 27m. Emergency Lt. Iso. R.8 sec. **FISKEBÄCKSVIK** 58°20.3'N 11°24.7'E (Rear) Iso. 8 sec. 17M. Orange pilot lookout Tr. 63m. Emergency Lt. Iso. R.8 sec.

LINDHOLMEN ÖSTRA 58°19.4'N 11°22.8'E. Lt. Iso. G.8 sec. 16M. R. Tr. 27m. In line 049°30' with Fiskebäcksvik, marks SE limit of channel as far as Stretudden Ldg. line.

VASTRA 58°19.5'N 11°22.7'E. Lt. Iso. R.8 sec. 16M. R. Tr. 27m. In line 051°30' with Fiskebäcksvik, marks NW limit of channel as far as Stretudden Ldg. line.

STRETUDDEN 58°20.6'N 11°24.5'E. Ldg. Lts. 046° (Front) Iso. 4 sec. 17M. W.Topmark on W.B. Tr. 35m. (Rear) 58°21.3'N 11°25.7'E. Iso. 4 sec. 18M. W.Topmark on W.B. Tr. 58m.

Lts. in line 150°. (Front) F.R. W. △ R.Border. Mark cable. (Rear) F.R. W. ▽ R.Border.

TÄN Lt. Q. W.R.G. W.8M. R.6M. G.5M. W. Tr. 12m. Floodlit. R.225°-259°, Obscured 259°-002°; G.002°-037.5°; W.037.5°-225°.

KÄVRA Lt. Fl. W.R.G.3 sec. W.9M. R.6M. G.5M. W. Tr. B.Base 10m. Floodlit. W.234°-046°; R.046°-096°; G.096°-149°; R.149°-170°, Obscured 170°-180°; G.180°-234°.

TINNHOLMEN Lt. Q. W.R.G. W.8M. R.5M. G.4M. W. Tr. 13m. R.009°-099°; G,099°-118.5°; W.118.5°-123°; R.123°-171°; G.171°-309°.

SVENSHOLMEN 58°18.7'N 11°22.0'E. Ldg. Lts. 087° (Front) Iso. W.R.G.3 sec. W.13M. R.10M. G.9M. 14m. G.047°-085.5°; W.085.5°-088.5°; R088.5°-098.5°; G.098.5°-154°; W.154°-168°; R.168°-243°; G.243°-313°. F.R. Lts. on chimney 2.7M NE. **RAMSVIK** 58°18.8'N 11°24.5'E (Rear) Oc.5 sec. 13M. Lantern on W ▯ 44m.

BLÄCKHALL 58°18.6'N 11°23.0'E. Lt. Fl(2) W.R.G.6 sec. W.10M. R.7M. G.6M. R.Lantern 9m. G.310°-322.5°; W.322.5°-327.5°; R.327.5°-020°; G.020°-113°; W.113°-121°; R.121°-150°.

HÄNGDYN Lt. Q. W.R.G. W.5M. R.3M. G.2M. R.Lantern on pedestal 5m. W.036°-039°; R.039°-264°; G.264°-036°.

GULSKAREN Lt. Fl(2) W.R.G.6 sec. W.8M. R.5M. G.4M. W. Tr. 9m. W.056.5°-059.5°; R.059.5°-132°; G.132°-141°; G(unintens) 141°-237°; W(unintens) 237°-258°; R(unintens) 258°-315°; R.315°-346.5°; G.346.5°-056.5°

VALBODALEN

Entered from N of Valbodalsholm the yacht harbour has 35 berths on a pontoon jetty in 4-5m depths.

GÄVEN Lt. Fl(3) W.R.G.9 sec. W.8M. R.6M. G.5M. R.Lantern on W. Tr. 27m. G(unintens) 234°-241°; W(unintens) 241°-261°; R(unintens) 261°-311°; G(unintens) 311°-002.5°; G.002.5°-024°; W.024°-030°; R.030°-041.5°; G.041.5°-053.5°; W.053.5°-061°; R.061°-110°; G.110°-122°.

STÄNGHOLMEN Lt. Iso. W.R.G.4 sec. W.6M. R.4M. G.3M. W.Lantern 6m. G.155°-163.5°; W.163.5°-165°; R.165°-245°; G.245°-293°; W.293°-328°; R.328°-011°.

FLATHOLMEN Lt. Fl. W.R.G.6 sec. W.9M. R.6M. G.5M. W.Lantern 10m. G.090.5°-094.5°; W.094.5°-096°; R.096°-112.5°; G.112.5°-129°; W.129°-138.5°; R.138.5°-200°; G.200°-257°; W.257°-265°; R.265°-304°; G.304°-335°.

FISKEBACKSIL

Close S of Fiskebacksil there are 30 yacht berths in depths of 3.5-4m.

Lts. in line 132° (Front) Iso. R.3 sec. 8M. Y. △ B.Border, on Y. Tr. 18m. Vis. on leading line. Mark water pipe. (Rear) Iso. R.3 sec. 8M. Y. ▽ B.Border, on Y. Tr. 40m. Vis. on leading line.

LYSEKIL Lts. in line 343° (Front) Iso. R.4 sec. 7M. Cable beacon 6m. Mark telephone cable. (Rear) Iso. R.4 sec. 7M. Cable beacon 31m.

SODRA HAMNEN

At the S end of Sodra Hamnen 2½ c N of Slaggabaden there are 60 yacht moorings in 1-10m. depth. In the Fishing Harbour 5½ c N of Slaggabaden there are 20 yacht moorings in 2-4m. depth. Yachts must not moor to fishing quay.

SLÄGGABÄDEN 58°16.0'N 11°26.4'E. Lt. L.
Fl. W.R.G.8 sec. W.10M. R.7M. G.6M. W. Tr.
grey base 7m. Floodlit. W.018°-020°; R.020°-
043°; G.043°-083°; W.083°-085°; R.085°-195°;
G.195°-226°; R.226°-248.5°; G.248.5°-261.5°;
W.261.5°-273°; R.273°-290.5°; G.290.5°-306°;
W.306°-316°; R.316°-352.5°; G.352.5°-018°.

LYSEKILS REDD Lt. Q. 4M. W.Pedestal 6m.

DEGAUSSING STATION. W DOLPHIN Lt. 2
F.R.vert. 2M. Post on dolphin.
E DOLPHIN Lt. 2 F.R. vert. 2M. Post on
dolphin.

GULLMAR FJORD

GULLMARSVIKEN Lt. Fl.3 sec. 3M. Lantern
on B.Perch 2m.

SKAFTO

GRÖTÖ SE POINT Lt. Fl. W.R.G.3 sec. W.6M.
R.4M. G.3M. W.Lantern 4m. G.173.5°-201°;
W.201°-205°; R.205°-236.5°; G.236.5°-295°;
W.295°-350.5°; R.350.5°-006°; G.006°-036°.

GRUNDSUND. PIER HEAD Lt. Oc(2) W.R.G.8
sec. W.6M. R.4M. G.3M. Grey Tr. 5m.
G.100°-132°; W.132°-160.5°; R.160.5°-171.5°.

ISLANDSBERG. SW PART Lt. Fl(4) W.R.G.12
sec. W.8M. R.5M. G.4M. R. Tr. 13m. G.shore-
031.5°; W.031.5°-034°; R.034°-038.5°;
R.044.5°-048°; G.048°-085.5°; R.085.5°-
125.5°; R.125.5°-181.5°; W.181.5°-185°;
R.185°-shore.

HÄTTAN 58°10.5'N 11°22.5'E. Lt. Fl(2)
W.R.G.6 sec. W.14M. R.11M. G.10M. B. Tr.
15m. G.020°-036°; W.036°-051.5°; R.051.5°-
077°; G.077°-116°; W.116°-124°; R.124°-
150.5°; G.150.5°-210°; W.210°-216°; R.216°-
226°.

FREDAGSHOLMEN. SW END Lt. Fl. W.R.G.3
sec. W.6M. R.4M. G.3M. R.Lantern 5m.
G.286.5°-294°; W.294°-300.5°; R.300.5°-
054.5°; G.054.5°-114.5°; W.114.5°-121.5°;
R.121.5°-136°.

ELLOS

Fishing village on E side of Ellosefjorden
with 15 yacht moorings in 2.5m depth.

GULLHOLMEN

Fishing harbour E side of N part of
Harmano. Speed limit 5 kts. Two basins.
Fixed bridge vertical clearance 1.7m, width
7.4m. There are 45 yacht moorings in 2m
depth.

ORNEKULLEN Ldg. Lts. 059° (Front) Iso. R.4
sec. W. ☐ on W.Mast 20m. Vis. on leading
line only. (Rear) Iso. R.4 sec. 9M. B.W. ☐ on
pedestal 32m. Vis. on leading line only.

HALLEN Ldg. Lts. 194° (Front) Iso. G.4 sec.
8M. W.Pedestal 5m. (Rear) Iso. G.4 sec. 8M.
W.Pedestal 9m. Vis. on leading line only.

TARNESKÄR Ldg. Lts. 239°30' (Front) Iso.
R.4 sec. 8M. W.Pedestal 5m. Vis. on leading
line only. (Rear) Iso. R.4 sec. 8M. White on
pedestal 7m. Vis. on leading line only.

FLATÖ Lt. Fl. W.R.G.3 sec. W.4M. R.2M.
G.2M. Lantern on W.Pedestal 10m. G.282°-
299.5°; W.299.5°-310°; R.310°-010°.

MORLANDA Lt. Fl(2) W.R.G.6 sec. W.6M.
R.4M. G.3M. W.Pedestal 6m. R.133°-142°;
G.142°-225°; W.225°-228°; R.228°-280°.

RÄVSNÄSUDDE 58°15.6'N 11°38.5'E. Ldg.
Lts. 047° (Front) Iso. 4 sec. 10M. W. ☐ on
W.Pedestal 14m. (Rear) Q. 10M. W. ☐ on
W.Pedestal 30m.

HJÄLTO Ldg. Lts. 261° (Front) Iso. 4 sec. 7M.
W.Pedestal 6m. (Rear) Q. 7M. W. ☐ on
W.Pedestal 10m.

SÄTEN Lt. Fl(2) W.R.G.6 sec. W.6M. R.4M.
G.3M. 7m. G.357°-039°; W.039°-048.5°;
R.048.5°-091°; G.091°-175.5°; W.175.5°-179°;
R.179°-190°.

HENAN

Lies at head of an inlet 1¼ M. S of Saten Lt.
Has 8 yacht moorings in 2.5m depth. Food,
fuel, fresh water available.

NOTESUND

5c E of Hogholmen Lt. Yacht harbour.

HOGHOLMEN Lt. Fl. W.R.G.3 sec. W.5M.
R.3M. G.3M. W. Tr. 6m. G.shore-230°;
W.230°-236°; R.236°-324°; G.324°-042°;
W.042°-056.5°; R,.056.5°-shore.

ÖSO Lt. Q. R.G. 2M. W.Pedestal 5M. G.107°-
280.5°; R.280.5°-349°.

MATTHOLME Lt. Fl. W.R.G.3 sec. W.4M.
R.2M. G.2M. W.Pedestal 5m. G.338°-089.5°;
W.089.5°-092.5°; R.092.5°-182.5°.

SANDVIKSKULLEN 58°18.1'N 11°44.0'E. Lt.
Fl(2) W.R.G.6 sec. W.10M. R.7M. G.6M.
W.Lantern 5m. G.shore-116°; W.116°-119°;
R.119°-205°; G.205°-246.5°; W.246.5°-249.5°;
R.249.5°-shore.

STANGEN Lt. Q. 4M. Lantern on W.GRP
structure 7m. Vis. 014°-257°.

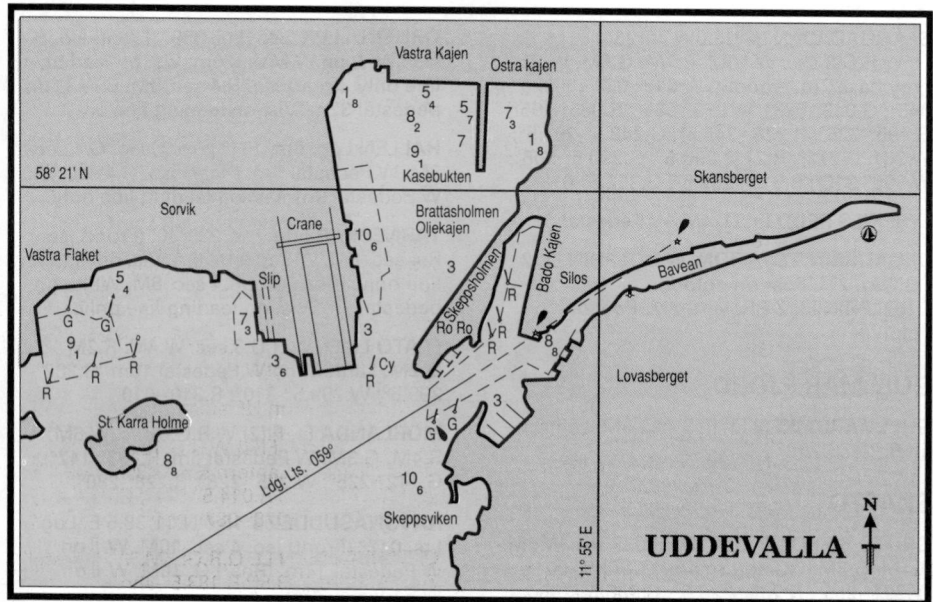

SUNNINGEN. N SIDE OF SOUND Lt. Fl.
W.R.G.3 sec. W.6M. R.4M. G.3M. Orange
structure 5m. G.233.5°-245.5°; W.245.5°-
071°; R.071°-083°. S SIDE OF SOUND Lt.
Fl(2) W.R.G.6 sec. W.6M. R.4M. G.3M.
Lantern on W.Pedestal 5m. G.052°-068°;
W.068°-242°; R.242°-247°; G.247°-253.5°.

UDDEVALLA 58°21'N 11°55'E
Tel: 0522 14770. Telex: 42269 UDDPORT S.
Radio-Port: VHF Chan. 16, 11, 14 as
required.

UDDEVALLA 58°22.4'N 11°49.4'E. Lt.
Aero Q. 21M. Mast 492m. Obstruction. Also
3 F.R. vert 6M.

58°20.7'N 11°54.8'E. Ldg. Lts. 059° (Front)
F.R. 10M. W. 18m. Vis. on leading line only.
(Rear) F.R. 9M. G.Lantern, W.Facing
alignment 35m. Vis. on leading line only.

STORE DEJE Lt. Q. 4M. Lantern on
W.Pedestal 6m.

SMÅHOLMARNA. SE POINT Lt. Fl. W.R.G.3
sec. W.6M. R.4M. G.3M. W.Lantern, R.Base
5m. R.160°-173.5°; G.173.5°-182.5°;
W.182.5°-218°; R.218°-292°; G.292°-333°;
W.333°-336°; R.336°-352°; G.352°-010°.

KOLLHOLM Lt. Iso. W.R.G.4 sec. W.6M.
R.4M. G.3M. W. Tr. 16m. G.152°-160°;
W.160°-165.5°; R.165.5°-169.5°; G.169.5°-
173.5°; W.173.5°-176°; R.176°-198°;
R(unintens) 198°-254°; G(unintens) 254°-
308.5°; G.308.5°-328°; W. 328°-332.5°;
R.332.5°-345°; G.345°-152°.

BJÖRNINGARNA Lt. Fl. W.R.G.3 sec. W.6M.
R.4M. G.3M. R.Lantern 4m. G.138.5°-157.5°;
W.157.5°-161°; R.161°-178°; W.178°-292°;
G.292°-331.5°; W.331.5°-336.5°; R.336.5°-
353°.

ASPHOLMEN. E POINT Lt. Fl(3) W.R.G.9 sec.
W.6M. R.4M. G.3M. W.Lantern, R.Base 5m.
G.124°-149°; W.149°-154°; R.154°-171°;
G.171°-186.5°; W.186.5°-316°; R.316°-331.5°;
G.331.5°-350°.

TVESTJÄRTEN Lt. Fl(2) W.R.6 sec. W.5M.
R.4M. W.Pedestal 5m. W.324.5°-196.5°;
R.196.5°-203.5°.

Ldg. Lts. 010°30' STRÖMHOLMEN (Rear) Fl.
W.R.G.3 sec. W.6M. R.4M. Lantern on
W.Pedestal 9m. G.163°-186.5°; W.186.5°-
014°; R.014°-029.5°. Kept open W of Rao.
Leads through channel W of Rao front light.

Ldg. Lts. 003°. STENSKÄRSRÄNNA (Front)
Q.R.G. R.3M. G.2M. Lantern on W.Pedestal
5m. R.354.5°-175°. Intens on leading line,
G.175°-189.5°. RAO (Common Rear) Iso.
W.G.5 sec. W.3M. G.8M. G.3M. R.Lantern
8m. G.345°-010°. Intens on leading line,
W.010°-198.5°. Ldg. Lts. 004°. RAO (Front)
Q.W. G.4M. W. △ on B.Pedestal 5m.
G.Northward, W.Southward.

JÄRNSKÄR Lt. Fl. W.R.G.3 sec. W.6M. R.4M.
G.3M. W.Lantern 5m. G.028°-050°; W.050°-
064°; R.064°-095°; G.095°-139.5°; W.139.5°-
148.5°; R.148.5°-226°; W.226°-277°.

KOLJEBERGSKIL Ldg. Lts. 093°30' (Front) Iso. R.3 sec. 6M. B.Hut, W.Gable, R.Band 11m. Vis. on leading line only. (Rear) Q.R.6M. B.Hut, W.Gable, R.Band 21m. Vis. on leading line only.

SÖRHALLSUDDE Ldg. Lts. 345° (Front) Iso. 4 sec. 9M. B.Hut, W.Gable, R.Band 7m. Vis. on leading line only. (Rear) Q.8M. B.Hut, W.Gable, R.Band 8m. Vis. on leading line only.

PORSNÄSUDDE Lt. Fl(2) W.R.G.6 sec. W.5M. R.5M. G.4M. R.Lantern 6m. G.315.5°-326.5°; W.326.5°-329°; R. 329°-139.5°; W.139.5°-165°. F.R. lights on radio mast 0.75M E.

KÄRINGÖ KUMMEL Lt. Iso. W.R.G.3 sec. W.7M. R.5M. G.4M. W.B. Tr. 9M. W.152°-173.5°; G.173.5°-209.5°;W.209.5°-212°; R.212°-237°; G.299°-310°; W.310°-316°; R.316°-322°.

KÄRINGÖ Lts. in line 193° (Front) F.R.7M. W. ◨R.Stripe 8m. Vis. on leading line only. Mark cable between Käringö and Oxskär. (Rear) F.R.7M. W. ◨R.Stripe 15m. Vis. on leading line only.

OXSKÄR Lt. Fl(3) W.R.G.9 sec. W.6M. R.4M. G.3M. W.Lantern 7m. G.326.5°-341°; W.341°-348°;R.348°-054.5°; W.054.5°-063°; G.240°-251°; R.251°-253°; G.253°-260°.

KRÄKSUNDSGAP. NORRA. SE POINT OF KRAKHOLM Lt. Q.4M. Lantern on W.Pedestal 4m.

SÖDRA. W POINT OF BRÅTÖ Lt. Fl(2) W.R.G.6 sec. W.8M. R.6M. G.5M. W. Tr. B.Conical base 13m. R.shore-358.5°; G.358.5°-045°; W.045°-050°; R.050°-078°; G.078°-093.5°; W.093.5°-118°; G.140°-195.5°; W.195.5°-220°; R.220°-243°; G.243°-253°.

KARINGON

There are 75 yacht moorings in 4m depth.

MASESKÄR 58°05.7'N 11°20.0'E. Lt. Fl(3) W.R.G. 30 sec. W.16M. R.13M. G.12M. R. ◨ on W.GRP Tr. 27m. W.012°-163°; R.163°-300°; G.300°-012°. Horn (2) 30 sec.

HALLEVIKSTRAND

There are 8 yacht moorings in 1.5m depth.

EDSHULTSHALL

75 yacht moorings in 4m depth. Fuel and fresh water available.

BRÅTÖ. SW POINT Lt. Fl(4) W.R.G.12 sec. W.6M. R.4M. G.3M. R.Lantern 7m. G.336.5°-350°; W.350°-355°; R.355°-090°; G.090°-132°; W.132°-137°; R.137°-shore.

MOLLOSUND

Moorings for 100 yachts in 4m depth. Fuel and fresh water available. Lt. Fl(2) W.R.G.6 sec. W.9M. R.6M. G.5M. R.Lantern 7m. G.shore-314°; W.314°-319.5°; R.319.5°-021°; G.021°-119.5°; W.119.5°-127.5°; R.127.5°-151.5°.

BJORHOLMEN

Yacht harbour on NE side of Bjorholmen.

LYR. W SIDE Lt. Fl(4) W.R.G.12 sec. W.5M. R.3M. G.3M. R.Lantern 5m. G.359°-009.5°; W.009.5°-014.5°; R.014.5°-021°; G.021°-072°; W.072°-078°; R.078°-087°.

OTTERHOLMEN Lt. Q.R.G. 2M. W.Pedestal 7m. G.shore-183.5°; R.183.5°-shore.

RÄBBEHUVUD. NW POINT Lt. Fl(2) W.R.G.6 sec. W.8M. R.5M. R.4M. G.4m. G.3M. W.B. Tr. 14m. G.009°-017.5°; W.017.5°-020°; R(unintens) 020°-105°; G(unintens) 105°-182.5°; W.182.5°-193.5°; R.193.5°-202°.

SÖDRA KYRKESUND 58°01.9'N 11°31.1'E. Ldg. Lts. 002°30' (Front) Iso. R.4 sec. 10M. W.Pedestal 21m. Vis. on leading line. 58°02.2'N 11°31.1'E (Rear) Q.R. 10M. W.Pedestal 30m. Vis. on leading line.

GÄSSKÄR. SW SIDE Lt. Fl(2) W.R.G.6 sec. W.6M. R.4M. G.3M. W.Lantern 4m. G.324.5°-334°; W.334°-340°; R.340°-070°; W.070°-132°; R.132°-148.5°.

Yacht harbours are established in the vicinity of Norra Kyrkesund Lt. and Södra Kyrkesund Lt. Also ¾ M. SSE of Svartskär.

NORRA KYRKESUND Ldg. Lts. 154°30' (Front) Iso. 4 sec. 6M. W.Pedestal, B.Base 5m. Vis. 135°-337°. (Rear) Q.W.R. W.8M. R.6M. Lantern on W.Pedestal 10m. W.147°-160°; R.160°-172°.

STAVSUNDSHÖLMEN Lt. Fl. R.G.3 sec. R.3M. G.2M. W.Pedestal 5m. G.Southward, R.Northward.

SANCT OLOVS. SVARTSKÄR Ldg. Lts. 006°30' (Front) Iso. W.R.G.4 sec. W.6M. R.4M. G.3M. R. Tr. 8m. W.342°-049°; W(unintens) 049°-119°; G.119°-155.5°; W.155.5°-169°; R.169°-178°; W(unintens) 178°-239°. F.R. Lts. on radio mast 1.05M N. (Rear) Q.13M. R.Lantern 25m. Vis. on leading line.

SKÄRHAMN

2 yacht harbours provide 40 moorings 3.5-4.4m. Boatyard and crane. Speed limit 3 kts. **SKÄR** Ldg. Lts. 050° (Front) Iso. W.R.G.3 sec. W.8M. W.5M. R.3M. G.3M. Lantern on W.Pedestal 7m. W.intens on leading line. G.170°-264°; W.264°-357°; R.357°-about 026°. **TJALLTANGEN HILL** (Rear) Oc.5 sec. 9M. W.Lantern 21m. Vis. 017°-099°.

EGGSKÄR Lt. Fl(2) W.R.G.6 sec. W.6M. R.4M. G.3M. W. Tr. 8m. R.017°-071.5°; G.071.5°-117°; W.117°-120°; R.120°-138.5°; G.138.5°-244°; R.244°-266.5°; G.266.5°-295°; W.295°-299°; R.299°-325°; G.325°-017°.

KLADESHOLMEN

Speed limit 5 kts. (3 kts. in harbour). W harbour has 25 yacht moorings in 3-4m depth. E harbour has 10 moorings. Bridge has vertical clearance of 1.4m.

KALVESUND (Ronnang old harbour)

20 yacht moorings with 2.7m draft.

MOSSHOLMEN

A yacht harbour lies close S of the oil jetty at Mossholmen.

TJÖRNEKALV Lts. in line 220°30' (Front) F.R. 8M. Lantern on W. △ B.Border 7m. Vis. on leading line. Mark cable between Tjörnekalv and Tjorn. (Rear) F.R. 8M. Lantern on W. ▽ B.Border 12m. Vis. on leading line.

ÄNGHOLMEN Ldg. Lts. 101°30' (Front) F.G. 2M. Post 4m. Fishing. (Rear) F.G. 2M. Post 13m. Fishing.

MARSTRANDSFJORD

HÄTTEBERGET 57°51.8'N 11°27.6'E. Lt. L. Fl(2) W.R.G.12 sec. W.21M. W.18M. R.18M. R.15M. G.18M. G.16M. B.R. Tr. 26m. W.(21M) 008°-110°; R.(18M) 110°-152°; G.(16M) 152°-225°; W.(18M) 225°-260°; R.(15M) 260°-346°; G.(18M) 346°-008°. Helicopter landing platform. Racon. RC. Horn 30 sec.

HAMNESKÄR Lt. F. 9M. Lattice mast 15m.

BERLIN. NW END Lt. Fl. W.R.G.3 sec. W.5M. R.3M. G.3M. R.Lantern 8m. G.330.5°-338.5°; W.338.5°-343°; R.343°-096.5°; G.096.5°-137°; W.137°-145°; R.145°-155°; G.155°-163°; W.163°-168.5°; R.168.5°-191°.

ÅSTOL 57°55.3'N 11°35.2'E. Lt. L. Fl. W.R.G.8 sec. W.12M. R.10M. G.8M. R.Lantern. Floodlit 7m. G.249°-262°; W.262°-264°; R.264°-271.5°; G.271.5°-281.5°; W.281.5°-294°; R.294°-029.5°; G.029.5°-040.5°; W.040.5°-062.5°; R.062.5°-083°; G.083°-090°.

Lts. in line 141° (Front) F.R. 8M. Lantern on W △, B. Border 7m. Mark cable between Åstol and Tjömekalv. (Rear) F.R. 8M. Lantern on W ▽, B.Border 12m.
FISHING HARBOUR Ldg. Lts. 257° (Front) F.G. 2M. W △ 5m. Fishing. (Rear) F.G. 2m W ▽ 7m. Fishing.

MARSTRANDSÖN

Entry: 150 yacht moorings in 2-4m depth. **NW END. SKALLEN** 57°53.5'N 11°33.7'E. Lt. Iso. W.R.G.4 sec. W.14M. R.11M. G.10M. W. Tr. 13m. G.034°-054°; W.054°-069°; R.069°-086°; G.086°-132°; W.132°-206.5°; R.206.5°-235°; G.235°-shore.

MARSTRAND 57°53.5'N 11°34.7'E. Lt. Fl(3) W.R.G.9 sec. W.10M. R.7M. G.6M. W.Lantern 7m. G.053°-091°, partially obscured 053°-083°; R.091°-148°; G.148°-160.5°; W.160.5°-163.5°; R.163.5°-171.5°.

MARSTRANDS HAMN. MALEPERTS. Lts. in line 345° (Front) F.R. 3M. Post 5m. Mark pipeline. (Rear) F.R. 3M. Post 7m.
ARVIDSVIK. Lts. in line 075° (Front) F.R. 3M. Post 5m. Mark pipeline. (Rear) F.R. 3M. Post 8m.

GRÅBERGET Lt. Fl(2) W.R.G.3 sec. W.6M. R.4M. G.3M. B. Tr. 8m. G.051°-052.5°; W.052.5°-054°; R.054°-067°; G.067°-099°; W.099°-103°; R.103°-147°; G.147°-209°; W.209°-223°; R.223°-234.5°.

MARSTRAND FISHING HARBOUR. E Ldg. Lts. 039° (Front) F.G. 2M. Post 5m. Vis. on leading line. Fishing. (Rear) F.G. 2M. Post 9m. Vis. on leading line. Fishing. W Ldg. Lts. 024° (Front) F.R. 2M. Post 7m. Vis. on leading line. Fishing. (Rear) F.R. 2M. Post on grey building 11m. Vis. on leading line. Fishing.

SÖDRA MEHOLM Lt. Fl(2) W.R.G.6 sec. W.5M. R.3M. G.3M. Lantern on W.Pedestal 8m. G.290.5°-073°; W.073°-256.5°; R.256.5°-290.5°.

NORRA MEHOLM Lt. Fl. W.R.G.3 sec. W.5M. R.3M. G.2M. Lantern on W.Pedestal 11m. W.266.5°-076°; R.076°-261.5°; G.261.5°-266.5°.

NORDHOLMARNA 57°54.6'N 11°38.0'E. Lt.
Oc(2) W.R.G.10 sec. W.10M. R.7M. G.6M.
W.Hut, G.Base. Floodlit 5m. R.055°-071°;
G.071°-111°; W.111°-227.5°; R.227.5°-242.5°;
G.242.5°-256.5°.

BACKEBÅDEN Lt. Fl. W.R.G.3 sec. W.9M.
R.7M. G.6M. R.Hut, W.Roof. Floodlit 7m.
R.110°-236.5°; G.236.5°-242.5°; W.242.5°-
110°.

HAKEFJORD

ÄLGØ Lt. Q. W.R.G. W.6M. R.4M. G.3M.
W.Lantern 7m. G.shore-081.5°; W.081.5°-
083.5°; R.083.5-200.5°; G.200.5°-212.5°;
W.212.5°-216°; R.216°-252.5°.

MITHOLMARNA Lt. Fl(4) W.R.G.12 sec.
W.6M. R.4M. G.3M. W.Lantern 7m. G.027°-
036.5°; W.036.5°-040.5°; R.040.5°-153.5°;
G.153.5°-205°; W.205°-207°; R.207°-219.5°.

WALLHAMN 58°01'N 11°42'E
Tel: 0304 60720.
Radio-Port: VHF Chan. 16, 6, 9.
58°00.7'N 11°42.2'E. Lts. in line 352°30'
(Front) F.R.10M. Tr. 27m. By day 3M.
(Rear)58°01'N 11°42.2'E. F.R. 10M. Tr.36m.
By day 3M. 58°00.7'N 11°42.3'E. Lts. in line
352°30' (Front) F.G. 10M. Tr. 27m. By day
3M. (Rear) 58°01.1'N 11°42.3'E. F.G. 10M. Tr.
36m. By day 3M.

VINTERHOLMEN Lt. Fl. W.R.G.3 sec. W.8M.
R.5M. G.4M. Tr. 11m. W.018°-021.5°;
R.021.5°-189°; G.189°-196°; W.196°-204.5°;
R.204.5°-335°; G.335°-018°.

BRATTOGRUNDET Lt. Fl. W.R.G.3 sec.
W.6M. R.4M. G.3M. Lantern on W.Pedestal,
grey base 5m. G.040°-194°; W.194°-199°;
R.199°-236°; G.236°-283°; W.283°-313°;
R.313°-040°. F.R. and F.G. on bridge 600m
NNE.

SNÖHOLMARNA Lt. Fl(2) W.R.G.6 sec.
W.6M. R.4M. G.3M. W.Lantern 4m. G.011.5°-
017.5°; W.017.5°-027.5°; R.027.5°-076.5°;
G.076.5°-137°; W.137°-143.5°; R.143.5°-
172.5°; G.172.5°-202°; R.202°-240.5°.

ALMON

Bridge between Kallon and Almon has
vertical clearance of 43m. Yacht harbour
situated at N End of Almon.

LERSKITEN Lt. Q. G.Pile 2m. R. Lts. on
chimney 420m. E and on mast 0.95M SE.

HAVDEN Ldg. Lts. 060° (Front) F.R. 7M. Y
△ B.Border 8m. On request. (Rear) F.R. 7M.
Y ▽ B.Border 13m. On request.
Ldg. Lts. 060° (Front) F.G. 6M. Y △ B.Border
6m. On request. (Rear) F.G. 6M. Y ▽
B.Border 9m. On request.

STENNUNGSUND 58°04'N 11°49'E
Radio-Port: VHF Chan. 16, 11 as required.
10/15 yacht moorings abreast the town in
3.1m. depth.
STENUNG Lts. in line 102°30' (Front) F.G.
6M. W △ B.Border on post 8m. On request.
(Rear) F.G. 6M. W ▽ B.Border on post 11m.
On request.

HOG. GREEN Ldg. Lts. 102° (Front) F.G.
7M. Y △ 16m. Vis. on leading line only. On
request. (Rear) F.G. 7M. Y ▽ on mast 23m.
Vis. on leading line only. On request.
RED Ldg. Lts. 102° (Front) F.R. 7M. Y △ on
mast 13m. Vis. on leading line only. On
request. (Rear)F.R. 7M Y ▽ on mast 18m.
Vis. on leading line only. On request.

GALTERÖN 58°06.3'N 11°48.4'E. Lt. Fl(2)
W.R.G.6 sec. W.10M. R.7M. G.6M.
W.Lantern 5m. G.009.5°-013.5°; W.013.5°-
115.5°; R.015.5°-028.5°; W(unintens) 028.5°-
178°; G.178°-217°; W.217°-223°; R.223°-234°.

HALSE NABB 58°07.4'N 11°49.8'E. Lt. Q.
W.R.G. W.10M. R.7M. G.6M. W.Hut, R.Roof
and base. Floodlit 5m. R.shore-040°;
W.040°-192°; G.192°-shore.

SUNDHOLMEN Lt. Fl(2) W.R.G.6 sec. W.5M.
R.3M. G.2M. Lantern on W.Pedestal 5m.
G.shore-000°; W.000°-188°; R.188°-270°.

SVANESUND

Entry: Yacht harbour situated 1c. SSW of
Svanesund light.

SVANESUND 58°08.4'N 11°50.2'E. Lt. Fl.
W.R.G.3 sec. W.10M. R.7M. G.6M. R. Tr. 5m.
G.191°-202°; W.202°-208°; R.208°-225.5°;
W(unintens) 225.5°-312°; G.312°-351°;
W.351°-008°; R.008°-shore.

DJURNÄSUDDE Lt. W. W.R.G. W.5M. R.3M.
G.2M. Lantern on W.Pedestal 5m. W.023°-
332°; R.332°-002°; G.002°-023°.

GRÖTA HOLME Lt. Fl(2) W.R.G.6 sec. W.7M.
R.5M. G.4M. Lantern on W.Pedestal 6m.
G.016°-034.5°; W.034.5-047.5°; R.047.5°-
090°; G.090°-170°; W.170°-174.5°; R.174.5°-
179°; G.179°-208°.

STRANDANAS Lt. Fl. W.R.G.3 sec. W.6M. W.2M. R.4M. G.3M. R.Lantern 4m. G.175°-178°; W.178°-185.5°; R.185.5°-242°; W(unintens) 242°-310°; G.310°-352°; W.352°-356°; R.356°-008°.

LJUNGSKILE

Entered 1M. ENE of Strandanas Lt. 9/25 yacht moorings in 2.5m. Boat crane (5 tons), ramp and boat yard, fuel, water etc.

RAMHOLMEN. SW SIDE Ldg. Lts. 312°30' (Front) Iso. 4 sec. 9M. W. □ on W.Pedestal 10m. Vis. on leading line only. (Rear) Q. 8M. B. □ on W.Pedestal 18m. Vis. on leading line only.

STORA SILLESUND Lt. Q. W.R.G. W.4M. R.2M. G.2M. B.W. Tr. 8m. G.shore-303.5°; W.303.5°-306°; R.306°-shore.

LEKSKÄR Lt. Fl(2) W.R.G. 6 sec. W.6M. R.4M. G.3M. W.Lantern 7m. G.312.5°-322°; W.322°-332.5°; R.332.5°-349°; W.009°-166°.

LÖNNBÄCKEN Lt. Fl. W.R.G.3 sec. W.8M. W.3M. R.5M. R.2M. G.4M. W.B. Tr. 12m. R.094°-119°; G.119°-147°; W.147°-150.5°; R.150.5°-213°; W(unintens) 213°-259°; R.(unintens) 259°-308.5°.

BJÖRLANDA. MARINA. Ldg. Lts. 099° (Front) F.R. 5M. R. Δ 8m. F.G. Ldg. Lts. 077° mark entrance channel. Shown 14/4-30/10. (Rear) F.R. 5M. R. ∇ 15m. Shown 14/4-30/10.

GÖTEBORG-TORSLANDA 57°43.6'N
11°48.7'E. Lt. Aero Fl. W.22 sec. 23M. Tr. 49m. Fl(6) 024°-048°; Fl(7) 048°-204°; Fl(6) 204°-228°; Fl(7) 228°-024°.

GÖTEBORG-SLÄTTADAMM Lt. 2 Aero F.R. 6M. Mast 139m. Obstruction.

GÖTEBORG-BISKOPSGÅRDEN
57°43.3'N 11°53.3'E. Lt. Aero Q.21M. Chimney 140m. Obstruction. F.R. Lts. on water tower 270m NE. Also 2 Aero F.R. 6M. and 4 Aero F.R. 7M. 110m.

STORA PÖLSAN Lt. L. Fl. W.R.G.8 sec. W.8M. W.7M. R.6M. R.5M. G.5M. G.4M. W.B. Tr. 18m. R.152.5°-208°; G.208°-275°; R.275°-278°; G.278°-304°; W.304°-308°; R.308°-344°; G.344°-350.5°; W.350.5°-152.5°.

SÄLÖKNAPP Lt. Fl(4) W.R.G.12 sec. W.6M. R.4M. G.3M. W.B. Tr. 7m. W.012°-019°; R.019°-085°; G.085°-188.5°; W.188.5°-191°; R.191°-265°; G.265°-012°.

SÄLO. SW SIDE Lt. Q. W.R.G. W.5M. R.3M. G.3M. W.Pedestal 8m. G.295°-333.5°; W.333.5°-339.5°; R.339.5°-025°; G.025°-150.5°; W.150.5°-153°; R.153°-163°. Lts. are shown in Norome Elfe.

NORDRE ÄLVS FJORD. STORA KALVEN Lt. Fl. W.R.G.3 sec. W.6M. R.4M. G.3M. W.Post 7ml. G.235-257°; W.257°-260°; R.260°-275°; G.275°-299.5°; W.299.5°-303°; R.303°-350°; G.350°-012°; W.012°-014.5°; R.014.5°-044°; G.044°-103°; W.103°-107°; R.107°-145°. Occas. Shown 15/4-30/10.

KÅKHOLMEN Ldg. Lts. 098° (Front) F.R. 6 M. W Δ on post 6m. Fishing. (Rear) F.R. 6M. W ∇ on post 11m. Fishing.

RÖRÖ

FISHING HARBOUR Ldg. Lts. 299° (Front) F.R. 3M. W Δ, B.Border 5m. Fishing. (Rear) F.R. 3M. W ∇, B.Border 15m. Fishing. Ldg. Lts. 329°30' (Front) F.G. 3M. W Δ 5m. Fishing. (Rear) F.G. 5M. W ∇ 15m. Fishing.

STORA OSET Lt. Fl(3) W.R.G.9 sec. W.8M. R.5M. G.4M. W.Lantern 12m. W.024°-048.5°; R.048.5°-062°; G.062°-089°; W.089°-120.5°; R.120.5°-163°; W(unintens) 163°-228°; G(unintens) 228°-254°; W(unintens) 254°-261°; R(unintens) 261°-280°; W(unintens) 280°-345°; G. 345°-024°.

HYPPELN Ldg. Lts. 305°30' (Front) F.G. 2M. R. Δ on col. 7m. Fishing. (Rear) F.G. 2M. R. ∇ on col. 11m. Fishing.

KÄLLÖ-KNIPPLAN. N BREAKWATER HEAD. Ldg. Lts. 334° (Front) F.G. W. Δ on col. 6m. Fishing. (Rear) F.G. W. ∇ on col. 12m. Fishing.

BJÖRKÖ. W SIDE 57°44.5'N 11°40.2'E. Ldg. Lts. 162°30' (Front) Iso. W.R.G.3 sec. W.11M. W.7M. R.5M. G.4M. R.Lantern 8m. G(unintens) 031°-100°; G.100°-112°; W.112°-119°; R.119°-128°; W(intens) on leading line. 57°44.2'N 11°40.4'E. (Rear) Iso. 3 sec. 11M. W.Lantern 32m. Vis. on leading line.

HÄLSÖ

E SIDE 57°44.0'N 11°39.8'E. Ldg. Lts 331°30' (Front) W.13M. W.10M. R.7M. G.6M. W. Tr. 7m. Intens W on leading line. G.168°-177°; W.177°-185°; R.185°-210°; G(unintens) 210°-239°; W(unintens)239°-257°; R(unintens) 257°-280°; W.280°-338°; G.338°-349°; W.349°-353°; R.353°-004°. 57°44.3'N 11°39.5'E. (Rear) Q.13M. W.Lantern 17m. Intens on leading line.

W Ldg. Lts. 298° (Front) F.R. 3M. Y. △ on mast 10m. Fishing. (Rear) F.R. 3M. Y. ▽ on mast 13m. Fishing.

LÅNGETÅNGE. Ldg. Lts. 050° (Front) F.R. 7M. W. △ on post 6m. (Rear) F.R. 7M. W. ▽ on post 11m.

HÖNÖ RÖD Ldg. Lts. 128° (Front) F.R. 7M. W. △ 6m. F.R. on radio mast O.3M SE. (Rear) F.R. 7M. W. ▽ 12m.

LILLA VARHOLMEN 57°42.2'N 11°42.5'E. Ldg. Lts. 314° (Front) Iso. 3 sec. 11M. W. ☐ on W. col. 20m. Vis. on leading line. 57°42.3'N 11°42.4'E. (Rear) Iso. W.R.G.3 sec. W.10M. R.5M. G.4M. W.Lantern 29m. W. on leading line; R.062°-079°; G.079°-106°; R.106°-116°. Lts. mark Bjorlanda Kile Marina 4.5M NE 14/4-30/10.

STORA VARHOLMEN 57°41.8'N 11°42.1'E. Lt. L. Fl(2) W.R.G.12 sec. W.13M. R.10M. G.9M. 15m. G.320.5°-326°; W.326°-340°; R.340°-352°; G.352°-005°; W.005°-007.5°; R.007.5°-036.5°; W(unintens) 036.5°-170°.

DANNEKROKEN Ldg. Lts. 172° (Front) Iso. R.3 sec. 8M. W. △ on mast 7m. (Rear) Iso. R.3 sec. 8M. W. ▽ on mast 11m.

TÅNGUDDEN. E SIDE OF HÖNÖ Lt. Iso. W.R.G.3 sec. W.7M. R.5M. G.4M. W.Lantern 5m. G.191°-306°; W.306°-309.5°; R.309.5°-326°.

ÖCKERÖ FISKEHAMN Ldg. Lts. 294° (Front) F.R. 2M. W. ▽ on post 6m. Fishing. (Rear) F.R. 2M. W. △ on post 11m. Fishing.

HÖNÖ HUVUD Lt. Fl(2) W.R.G.6 sec. W.8M. R.6M. G.5M. W.Lantern 19m. G.039°-062°; W.062°-148°; R.148°-206.5°; W.206.5°-277.5°; G.277.5°-312°; W.312°-318°; R.318°-333°.

ÄRTHOLMEN Lt. Q. W.R.G. W.6M. R.4M. G.3M. Lantern on pedestal 11m. G.315°-104.5°; W.104.5°-117.5°; R.117.5°-133°.

BENSKÄR Lt. Fl(3) W.R.G.9 sec. W.6M. R.4M. G.3M. Lantern on pedestal 10m. W.050°-094°; R.094°-179°; G.179°-050°.

KATTEGAT
HÖNÖLEDERNA

TYNNESKAR Lt. Fl. W.R.G.3 sec. W.6M. R.4M. G.3M. Lantern on W.Pedestal, B.Base 7m. G.036°-121.5°; W.121.5°-124°; R.124°-153°; G.153°-333°; R.333°-036°.

KLÅVA 57°40.8'N 11°38.7'E. Lt. Iso. W.R.G.4 sec. W.10M. R.8M. G.6M. W.Lantern 4m. G.277.5°-281.5°; W.218.5°-285°; R.285°-017°; G.017°-040°; W.040°-043.5°; R.043.5°-056.5°; G.056.5°-090°; R.090°-105°.

VINGA UNGAR Lt. Q. W.R.G. W.6M. R.4M. G.3M. Post 15m. G.000°-099°; R.099°-198.5°; G.198.5°-266.5°; W.266.5°-269°; R.269°-000° ﹏﹏

VINGA

VINGA 57°38.0'N 11°36.2'E. Lt. Fl(2) 30 sec. 25M. Grey stone Tr. 46m. Unintens on westerly bearings. Also shown by day 1/11-31/3. Sig. Stn. Traffic Signals.
E POINT 57°38.0'N 11°36.9'E. Ldg. Lts. 254° (Front) Oc. R.4 sec. 14M. 7M. W. Tr. 9m. Vis. 176°-276°; intens on leading line. Also shown by day 1/11-31/3. 57°38.0'N 11°36.5'E. (Rear) Oc. R.4 sec. 14M. 7M. R.House, B.Gable, W.Band on side facing alignment 19m. Synchronised with front. Vis. 186°-286°. Intens on leading line. Also shown by day 1/11-31/3.

VITEN 57°38.1'N 11°37.4'E. Lt. Iso. W.R.G.6 sec. W.11M. R.10M. R.8M. G.7M. G.6M. W.Lantern on W.Conical base. Floodlit. 11m. G.250°-292.5°; W.292.5°-296.5°; R.296.5°-307°; R(unintens) 307°-015°; G(unintens) 015°-094°; G.094°-103°; W.103°-117.5°; R.117.5°-126.5°; R(unintens) 126.5°-132°.

GÖTEBORG-BRUDAREMOSSEN
57°41.7'N 12°04.8'E. Lt. Aero Q. 21M. Mast on Tr. 440m. Also F.R. 6M.

TRUBADUREN 57°35.7'N 11°38.1'E. Lt. L. Fl(3) W.R.G.30 sec. W.20M. R.18M. R.17M. R.15M. G.17M. G.16M. G.14M. B. Tr. Or.Top on grey base. Floodlit. 24m. W(20M) 006°-130°; R(18M) 130°-140°; R(15M) 140°-160°; R(17M) 160°-163.5°; G(16M)163.5°-210°; G(14M) 210°-215°; W(20M) 215°-238°; G(17M) 238°-247.5°; G(16M) 247.5°-260°; G(14M) 260°-350°; G(17M) 350°-006°. RC. Racon. Helicopter landing platform. Same structure F.R. 13M. 18m. Vis. 064°-131°. Horn (4) 60 sec.

BUSKÄRS KNOTE Lt. Fl(3) W.R.G.9 sec. W.8M. R.5M. G.4M. Or. Tr. 12m. W.013°-029°; R.029°-088° (partially obscured 065°-080°; G.080°-181°); W.181°-191°; R.191°-212°; G.212°-235°; W.235°-239°; R.239°-270.5°; G.270.5°-013°. Racon.

GÖTEBORG APPROACHES

BÖTTÖ 57°38.9'N 11°43.2'E. Lt. Oc. W.R.5 sec. W.11M. R.8M. W. Tr. Floodlit. 12m. W.261°-247.5°; R.247.5°-261°. Horn (2) 30 sec.

VASSKÄREN 57°39.3'N 11°43.2'E. Lt. Iso. W.R.G.6 sec. W.15M. R.12M. G.10M. B. Tr. W.Top. Floodlit 15m. W.020°-040°; R.040°-065.5°; G.065.5°-268.5°; R.268.5°-276°; G.276°-020° ⨯/Also shown by day 1/11-31/3.

VASSKÄRSGRUND 57°39.2'N 11°43.4'E. Lt. I.V.Q. W.R.G.8 sec. W.13M. R.10M. G.9M. R. Tr. W.Top, R.Roof on grey plinth. Floodlit 11m. R.237°-239°; G.239°-254.5°; W.254.5°-260°; R.260°-277.5°; G.277.5°-316°; W.316°-090°; R.090°-097°. Racon.

BRANDNÄSBROTTEN Lt. Fl(2) W.R.G.6 sec. W.6M. R.4M. G.3M. W.GRP structure on G.Base 7m. G.047°-077°; W.077°-092.5°; R.092.5°-101°; W.101°-144°; W(unintens) 144°-236°; W.236°-249°; R.249°-325°.

GÄVESKÄR 57°39.7'N 11°46.3'E. Lt. Oc. W.R.G.10 sec. W.10M. R.8M. G.7M. W. Tr. Floodlit 10m. G.202°-224.5°; W.224.5°-235°; R.235°-243°; G.243°-267.5°; W.267.5°-068.5°; R.068.5°-077°. Also shown by day 1/11-31/3. Horn 30 sec.

FOTÖ Lts. in line 265° (Front) F.R.9M. Or.Structure 7m. Also shown by day 1/11-31/3. (Rear)F.R. 9M. 18m. Also shown by day 1/11-31/3.

Lts. in line 265° (Front) F.G. 9M. Or.Structure 7m. Also shown by day 1/11-31/3. (Rear) F.G. 9M. 18m. Also shown by day 1/11-31/3.

VALSKÄR Lt. Q. W.R. W.3M. R.1M. Lantern on W.Pedestal 4m. W.228°-064°; R.064°-101°.

SKÄDDAN Lt. Q.3M. Lantern on W.Pedestal 5m.

TANNESKÄR Lt. Iso. W.R.G.3 sec. W.7M. R.5M. G.4M. W.Lantern 9m. G.227°-233.5°; W.233.5°-238°; R.238°-249.5°; G.249.5°-256.5°; W.256.5°-259.5°; R.259.5°-285°; G.285°-359°.

MÅVHOLMSBÅDAN 57°40.4'N 11°42.6'E. Q.B. Tr. Or.Top. Floodlit 8M. Also shown by day 1/11-31/3. Racon ⨯/

DYNAN Lt. Q.5M. W. Tr. B.Band. Floodlit 7m.

HUNNEBÅDAN 57°40.8'N 11°49.6'E. Ldg. Lts. 083°30' (Front) Fl(2) W.R.G.6 sec.

W.10M. R.8M. G.6M. W. Tr. B.Conical base. Floodlit 6m. G.047.5°-058.5°; W.058.5°-071.5°; R.071.5°-074°; G.074°-083°; W.083°-289°; R.289°-047.5°. **STORA BILLINGEN** 57°41.1'N 11°53.0'E. (Rear) Iso. 4 sec. 14M. W.Lantern 24m. Also shown by day 1/11-31/3.

TORSVIKENS R. Lts. in line 356° 2 F.R. 2M. W. △ B.Border 9m. 11m. Marks W side of fairway.
G. Lts. in line 002° 2 F.G. 2M. W △ B.Border 9m. 11m. Marks E side of fairway.
Blue Lts. in line 100° 2 F. Bu. 1M. W △ B.Border 9m. 11m. Marks S side of harbour basin.

TORSHAMNEN R. Lts. in line 023° (Front) F.R. 7M. Or. △ B.Border, on post. F.Y. Lts. in line 356°. 160m. S. (Rear) F.R. 7M. Or. ▽ B.Border, on post.
G. Lts. in line 023°. (Front) F.G. 7M. Or. △ B.Border, on post. F.Y. Lts. in line 061.1° 130m. SSE. (Rear) F.G. 7M. Or. ▽ B.Border, on post.

HJÄRTHOLMEN Lts. in line 349° (Front) Q.R. 6M. W. △ on post 5m. Vis. on line. Mark W side of channel. Occas. F.R. on mast 260m. NW (Rear) Q.R 6M. W. ▽ on post 9m. Synchronised with front. Vis. on line. Occas.

RISHOLMEN Lts. in line 349° (Front) Q.G. 6M. Lantern on W. △ 7m. Vis. on line. Mark E side of channel. Occas. (Rear) Q.G. 6M. Lantern on W. ▽ 13m. Vis. on line. Occas.

KNIPPELHOLMEN 57°41.0'N 11°49.2'E. Lt. Iso. W.R.G.4 sec. 10M. W. Tr. B.Base 7m. G.249°-263°; W.263°-296.5°; R.296.5°-334°; G.334°-046.5°; W.046.5°-064°; R.064°-070°; G.070°-075°; W.075°-083°; R.083°-shore. Also shown by day 1/11-31/3.

VÄSTRA KNIPPELHOLMEN Horn (3) 30 sec. Or.Cairn. Floodlit.

ÄLVSBORGSHAMNEN Lts. in line 275° (Front) F.R. 2M. R. △ on mast 12m. Marks limit between 11m. and 9m. depths. (Rear) F.R. 2M. R. ▽ on mast 15m.

RO-RO Lts. in line 029° (Front) F.R. (Rear) F.R.

GÖTEBORS HAMN

SKANDIAHAMNEN R. Lts. in line 000°36' 2 F.R. 2M. Lantern on R. △ 20m. 23m. Marks approx. line between 11m. and 12m. depths off quay.

CARNEGIESKA BRUKET 57°41.4'N
11°54.3'E. Ldg. Lts. 080° (Front) Iso. R.3 sec.
11M. Tr. 48m. Vis. on leading line. Also
shown by day 1/11-31/3. 57°41.5'N
11°55.4'E (Rear) Iso. R.3 sec. 11M. Mast
77m. Vis. on leading line. Also shown by
day 1/11-31/3.

LILLA BILLINGEN. S SIDE OF CHANNEL Lt.
Fl(2) W.6 sec 7M. Dolphin 5m. Shown 6/7-
6/6.

SKEPPSBRON Lt. Fl(2) W.6 sec. 6M.
Dolphin 5m. Shown 6/7-6/6.

The opening of Hising swing bridge and
Götaälv lift bridge are marked by Lts. and
traffic signals are shown. The channel
upstream of Götaälv Bron is marked by Lts.
and floodlit dolphins.

FRIHAMNEN. BERTH 114 Lts. in line (Front)
F.R. Occas. (Rear) F.R.

GÖTEBORG. SW APPROACH

MORS MÖSSA Lt. Fl. W.R.G.3 sec. W.4M.
R.4M. G.2M. W.Pedestal, B.Base 7m.
G.286°-296°; W.296°-300.5°; R.300.5°-030°;
G.030°-098°; W.098°-116°; R.116°-129°.
Fishing.

STORA KANSÖ Lt. Iso. W.R.G.3 sec. W.5M.
R.4M. G.3M. W.Lantern on round hut,
R.Roof 11m. G.275°-281°; R.281°-295°;
W(unintens) 295°-024.5°; G(unintens)
024.5°-096°; G.096°-104°; W.104°-107°;
R.107°-115.5°; R(unintens) 115.5°-136.5°.
Fishing.

SVARTA BÅDEN Lt. Fl. W.R.G.6 sec. W.5M.
R.3M. G.3M. W.Pedestal 6m. G.shore-237°;
W.237°-243°; R.243°-315°; G.315°-046.5°;
W.046.5°-050.5°; R.050.5°-shore.

TÅNGEN Ldg. Lts. 203° (Front) F.R. 3M. Y. Δ
on post 11m. Fishing. (Rear) F.R. 3M. Y. ▽
on post 16m. Fishing.

KÅRHOLMESKÄR Lt. Fl. W.R.G.3 sec.
W.4M. R.3M. G.2M. W.Pedestal 8m. G.253°-
086°; W.086°-090°; R.090°-103°. Fishing.

DONSÖ SVARTSKÄR Lt. Fl(2) W.R.G.6 sec.
W.7M. R.5M. G.4M. W.Pedestal 11m.
W.043°-143.5°; R.143.5°-201.5°; G.201.5°-
261.5°; W.261.5°-266°; R.266°-345°; G.345°-
043°.

GÖTEBORG S APPROACH

TISLARNA 57°30.6'N 11°43.7'E. L. Fl(2)
W.R.15 sec. W.18M. R.15M. Y.Castellated
building 23m. R.100°-351°; W.351°-100°.

MATSKÄR Lt. Q. W.R.G. W.5M. R.3M.
G.3M. W.Pedestal 10m. G.214°-227°;
W.227°-237°; R.237°-302°; G.302°-003°;
W.003°-016°; R.016°-045°. Fishing.

VALÖ 57°33.1'N 11°48.3'E. Lt. Iso. W.R.G.4
sec. W.16M. R.13M. G.12M. W. Tr. G.Band
15m. R(unintens) 170°-174°; R.174°-178.5°;
G.178.5°-270°; W.270°-271.5°; R.271.5°-
291.5°; G.291.5°-344°; W.344°-345.5°;
R.345.5°-354.5°; G.354.5°-001.5°; W.001.5°-
066°; R.006°-033°; G.033°-039°.

RÄTTAREN Lt. Fl. W.R.G.3 sec. W.6M.
R.4M. G.3M. W.Structure on G.Base 5m.
G.205°-211.5°; W.211.5°-215.5°; R.215.5°-
327°; G.327°-350°; W.350°-357.5°; R.357.5°-
034°.

DONSÖHUVUD 57°35.7'N 11°49.1'E. Lt. Fl.
W.R.G.3 sec. W.10M. R.7M. G.6M.
W.Lantern 5m. G.185.5°-190°; W.190°-196°;
R.196°-315°; G.315°-023°; W.023°-025°;
R.025°-037.5°.

LILLA SJÖHOLMEN Lt. Fl. W.R.G.6 sec.
W.4M. R.2M. G.2M. W.Pedestal 6m. R.340°-
007°; G.007°-059°; W.059°-082°; R.082°-
165°. Fishing.

KNARRHOLMEN 57°37.2'N 11°49.5'E. Lt.
Fl(2) W.R.G.6 sec. W.10M. R.7M. G.6M.
R.Lantern 4m. G,000°-004.5°; W.004.5°-
005.5°; R.005.5°-032.5°; W(unintens) 032.5°-
142.5°; G.142.5°-164°; W.164°-166.5°;
R.166.5°-173°.

LILLA MOSSKULLEN Lt. Q. W.R.G. W.4M.
R.2M. G.2M. W.Pedestal 7m. G.277°-287°;
W.287°-296°; R.296°-020°; G.020°-103°;
W.103°-106°; R.106°-112°. Fishing.

SMÅSKÄREN Lt. Iso. W.R.G.3 sec. W.4M.
R.3M. G.2M. W.Pedestal. Floodlit 6m.
R.016°-090°; G.090°-171.5°; W.171.5°-188.5°;
R.188.5°-204°; G.204°-016°. Fishing.

RUMPEN Lt. Q.3M. W.Cairn, B.Band 3m.
Fishing.

GANLEBUKTEN. LÅNGHOLMEN Lt. Fl. R.3
sec. 1M. Dolphin 2m. Fishing. Shown 1/10-
31/3.

FISKEBÄCK. NORRA Ldg. Lts. 043°
(Front) F.G. 4M. Post 11m. (Rear) F.G. 4M.
Post 17m.

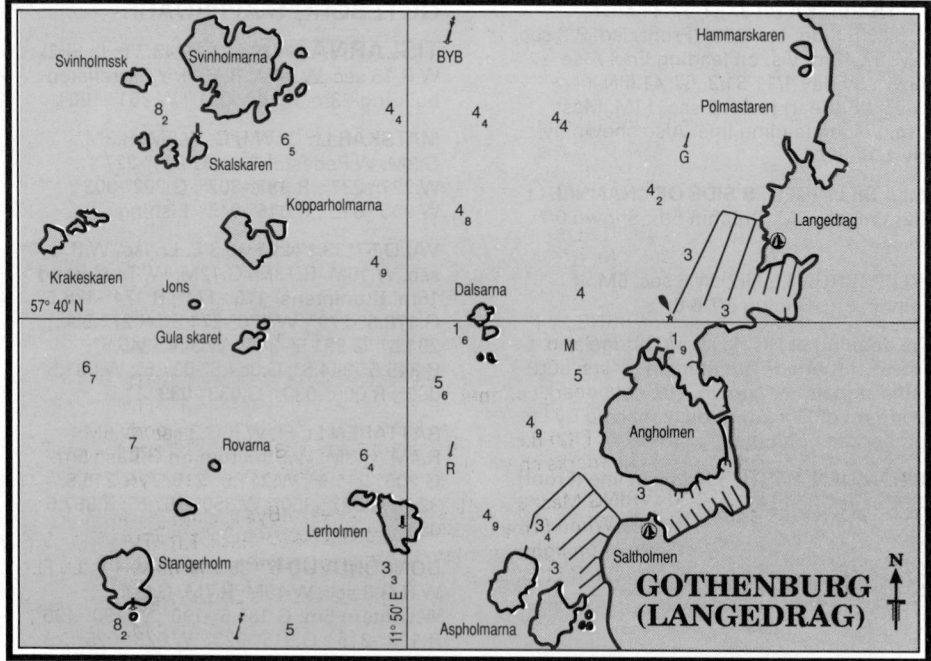

Svinholmssk Svinholmarna

8₂

6₅

Skalskaren

Kopparholmarna

Krakeskaren   Jons

57° 40' N

Gula skaret

6₇

7   Rovarna

6₄

Lerholmen

Stangerholm   3

8₂   5

BYB

4₄   4₄   4₄

Hammarskaren

Polmastaren

G

4₂

4₈

Langedrag

3

Dalsarna   4

1₆   1₉

M   5

5₆

4₉   Angholmen

R   3

4₉   3₄

3   Saltholmen

11° 50' E

Aspholmarna

GOTHENBURG
(LANGEDRAG)

N

LYGNSKÄR Lt. Fl. R.3 sec. 4M. R.Dolphin 5m. Fishing. F.R. Lts. on radio masts 4.4M ENE and 2.7M E.

Ldg. Lts. 098° (Front) F.R.6M. Y. ∆ on post on dolphin 4m. Fishing. (Rear) F.R.6M. Y. ▽ on mast 11m. Fishing.

SKIFTESKÄR Lt. Fl(3) W.R.G.9 sec. W.6M. R.4M. G.3M. Lantern on Or. Tr. 8m. R.097°-175°; G.175°-217°; W.217°-220.5°; R.220.5°-312.5°; G.312.5°-356.5°; W.356.5°-097°.

RIVÖ. E END Lt. Fl. W.R.G.3 sec. W.6M. R.4M. Q.3M. W.Wooden hut 2m. G.170°-174°; W.174°-183.5°; R.183.5°-199°; W(unintens) across the channel; G.326.5°-340°; W.340°-345.5°; R.345.5°-352°.

SMÖRBÅDEN Lt. Q. W.R.G. W.6M. R.4M. G.3M. Lantern on W.Pedestal 5m. G.001°-036°; W.036°-042.5°; R.042.5°-107.5°; G.107.5°-204°; W.204°-206°; R.206°-262°; G.262°-311.5°; W.311.5°-319°; R.319°-001°. Fishing.

LANGEDRAG. PIER HEAD Lt. Q. R.6M. Tr. 5m. Shown 1/5-31/10. Occas.

KUNGEN 57°27.0'N 11°50.1'E. Lt. Fl(3) W.R.G.9 sec. W.10M. R.8M. G.7M. W.B. Tr. 12m. G.008°-065°; W.065°-113.5°; R.113.5°-200°; G.200°-339°; W.339°-342°; R.342°-008°.

HALLANDS SVARTSKÄR 57°22.5'N 11°51.4'E. Lt. Fl. W.R.G.3 sec. W.10M. R.8M. G.7M. W.Tr. 10m. G.165°-174°; W.174°-179°; R.179°-197°; R(unintens) 197°-260°; G(unintens) 260°-264°; W(unintens) 264°-266°; R(unintens) 266°-287°; R.287°-295.5°; G.295.5°-324°; W.324°-328°; R.328°-340°; G.340°-353°; W.353°-000°; R.000°-017°.

MALÖ. S SIDE Lt. Fl(3) W.R.G.9 sec. W.8M. R.6M. G.5M. W.Tr. with grey base 10m. G316°-341°; W.341°-019°; R.019°-030°; G.030°-059.5°; W.059.5°-091°; R.091°-106°.

MALÖ HAMN. E SIDE OF SKALLANÄS ENTRANCE Lt. Fl(2) W.R.G.6 sec. W.7M. R.,5M. G.4M. W.Lantern 5m. G.342°-357°; W.357°-008.5°; R.008.5°-029°; G.029°-095°; W.095°-135°; R.135°-shore.

LILLELAND 57°18.4'N 11°55.6°E. Lt. Iso. W.R.G.3 sec. W.16M. R.13M. G.12M. B.W.Tr. and lantern, grey conical base. Floodlit 19m. G.235°-333°; W.333°-003°; R.003°-125°; G.125°-159.5°; W.159.5°-161°; R.161°-235°. Also shown by day 1/11-31/3.

NIDIGEN 57°18.2'N 11°54.2'E. Lt. Fl(2+1) W.R.27 sec. W.22M. R.18M. W.B.Tr. 25m. R. about 018°-about 039°; W. about 039°-about 018°. Also shown by day 1/11-31/3.

FLADEN 57°12.9'N 11°49.8'E. Lt. Iso. 8 sec. 20M. B.Tr. R.Top, grey base. Floodlit 24m. Racon. RC. Horn (3) 60 sec. Horns point N and E.

FJORDSKÄR Lt. Fl. W.R.G.3 sec. W.8M. W.6M. R.6M. R.4M. G.5M. G.3M. W.Lantern, grey stone base 10m. G.157°-194.5°; W.194.5°-201°; R.201°-318°; G.(intens) 318°-002.5°; W(intens) 002.5°-029°; R(intens) 029°-038.5°.

GOTTSKÄR Ldg. Lts. 313° (Front) F.R.3 M. W. Δ on post 8m. Fishing. (Rear) F.R. 3M. W. ▽ on mast 12m. Fishing.

KUNGSBACKA. W PIER Lt. Fl. W.R.G.3 sec. W.3M. R.1M. G.1M. Dolphin 6m. R.001°-090°; W.090°-270°; G.270°-357.5°; W.357.5°-001°. Shown 1/5-30/11.

BÅTFJORD

KROGSTADSUDDE Lt. Fl(4) W.R.G.12 sec. W.5M. R.3M. G.3M. W.Wooden Tr. 15m. G.039°-079°; W.079°-091.5°; R.091.5°-180°; W(unintens) 180°-shore. F.R. on chimney 1.2M. NNE Horn (2) 30 sec. Fishing.

RINGHALS RÖDA. KRAFTVERKSHAMN 57°15.2'N 12°07.7'E. Ldg. Lts. 056°24' (Front) Iso. 3 sec. 10M. R. ◊ W.Border, on post 5m. (Rear) Iso. 3 sec. 10M. R. ◊ W.Border, on post 8m.
Lts. in line 056°18' (Front) Iso. G.3 sec. 5M. R. Δ W.Border on pillar 3m. Marks S side of the channel. (Rear) Iso. G.3 sec. 5M. R. ▽ W.Border on pillar 6m.

Lts. in line 056°18' (Front) Iso. R.3 sec. 5M. R. Δ W.Border 3m. Marks N side of the channel. (Rear) Iso. R.3 sec. 5M. R. ▽ W.Border 6m.

BUAHAMN Ldg. Lts. 127° (Front) F.R.5M. W. Δ Or.Border, on mast 6m. Fishing. (Rear) F.R.5M. W. ▽ Or.Border, on mast 10m. Fishing.

OLAI RÖSE RÖDA Ldg. Lts. 307° (Front) F.G. 2M. W. Δ Or.Border, on mast 10m. (Rear) F.G. 2M. W. ▽ Or.Border, on mast 13m.

SALLEBACKA Ldg. Lts. 145° (Front) F.R. 3M. W. Δ on mast 6m. Fishing. (Rear) F.R. 3M. W. ▽ on mast 9m. Fishing.

KLÅBACK Lt. Fl(2) W.R.G.6 sec. W.7M. R.5M. G.4M. W.Lantern 14m. R.157°-314°; G.314°-333.5°; W.333.5°-157°.

GRIMETON 57°06.5'N 12°23.8'E. Lt. Aero Q.21M. Radio Tr. 290m. Obstruction. H24. Same structure 5 Aero F.R. vert. 6M.

Lt. 4 Aero F.R. 6M. SW and NE of six grey Trs. 158m. Obstruction.

VARBERG

VARBERG 57°07.1'N 12°14.5'E. Lts. in line 019°18' No. 1 (Front) Iso. 2 sec. 10M. W. Δ on post 10m. Marks E side of entrance channel. 57°07.6'N 12°14.7'E. No.3 (Rear) Iso. 2 sec. 10M. W. ▽ on post 14m.

VÄSTRA 57°07.1'N 12°14.4'E. Lts. in line 019°18' No.2 (Front) Iso. 2 sec. 10M. W. Δ on post 10m. Synchronised with Varberg No.1 Lt. Marks W side of entrance channel. 57°07.6'N 12°14.6'E. No.4 (Rear) Iso. 2 sec. 10M. W. ▽ on post 14m.

VARGBERGSRÄNNAN G. Lts. in line 064° (Front) Oc. G.4 sec. 6M. W. Δ on mast 15m. (Rear) Oc. G.4 sec. 6M. W. ▽ on mast 20m.
R. Lts. in line 069° (Front) Oc. R.4 sec. 6M. W. Δ on mast 15m. Synchronised with Vargbergsrännan Lt. (Rear) Oc. R.4 sec. 6M. W. ▽ on mast 20m.

SUBBEBERGET 57°05.3'N 12°14.4'E. Lt. L. Fl(2) W.R.G.30 sec. W.17M. R.14M. G.12M. W.Tr. 26m. G.342°-016.5; W.016.5°-113°; R.113°-157°; W.(unintens) 157°-shore.

TRÄSLÖV. S PIER HEAD Lt. Fl(3) W.R.G.9 sec. W.9M. R.7M. G.6M. Lantern on W.Pedestal. Floodlit. 9m. G.351°-058°; W.058°-091.5°; R.091.5°-119°.

GALTABÅCK

Ldg. Lts. 084°30' (Front) Iso. R.2 sec. 7M. Lantern on W.Pedestal 5m. Vis. on leading line, (unintens) 155°-172°. As required. (Rear) Iso. R.2 sec. 7M. W. ▽ on post 13m. Vis. on leading line. As required.

GLOMMEN. W BREAKWATER HEAD Lt. Fl. W.R.G.3 sec. W.6M. R.4M. G.3M. Lantern on W.Pedestal on base 9m. G.shore-021°; W.021°-028°; R.028°-036°; G.036°-056.5°; W.056.5°-075°; R.075°-shore. Horn Mo(N) 60 sec. Fishing.

MORUPS TÅNGE 56°55.5'N 12°21.8'E. Lt. Oc. W.R.G.8 sec. W.18M. R.15M. G.13M. B.Tr. 29m. G.shore-326°; W.326°-148.5°; R.148.5°-shore. Also shown by day 1/11-31/3. Racon.

FALKENBERGS HAMN

FALKENBERG 56°42.9'N 12°28.1'E. Lt. L. Fl. W.R.G.8 sec. W.11M. R.9M. G.8M. W.Tr. R.Bands. Floodlit. 11m. W(unintens) 200°-257°; R.257°-352°; G.352°-017°; W.017°-033°; R.033°-105°. Horn Mo(A) 30 sec.

OSTRA Lts. in line 032°30' (Front) Iso. 3 sec. 9M. W. △ R.Border on mast 12m. (Rear) Iso. 3 sec. 9M. W. ▽ R.Border on mast 18m.

VASTRA Lts. in line 032°30' (Front) Iso. 3 sec. 9M. W. △ R.Border on mast 12m. (Rear) Iso 3 sec. 9M. W. ▽ R.Border on mast 18m.

INNER G. Ldg. Lts. 061° (Front) Oc. G.4 sec. 8M. W. △ R.Border on mast 11m. (Rear) Oc. G.4 sec. 7M. W. ▽ R.Border on mast 15m.

INNER R. Ldg. Lts. 061° (Front) Oc. R.4 sec. 8M. W. △ R.Border on mast 11m. (Rear) Oc. R.4 sec. 7M. W. ▽ R.Border on mast 15m.

HALMSTAD 56°47.4'N 12°56.4'E. Lt. Aero V.Q. 21M. Radio mast 470m. Occas. Also 6 F.R. 6M.

KVIBILLE 56°45.0'N 12°48.8'E. Lt. Aero Q.21M. Tr. 184m. Occas. Also F.R. 6M.

SKALLKROKEN Ldg. Lts. 044° (Front) F.R. 4M. W. △ R.Border on post 4m. (Rear) F.R. 4M. W. ▽ R.Border on post 8m.

Ldg. Lts. 110° (Front) F.G. 2M. W. △ R.Border on post 3m. Pier head floodlit 300m W. (Rear) F.G. 2M. W. ▽ R. border on post 5m.

TYLÖGRUND 56°38.3'N 12°42.3'E. Lt. L. Fl(3) W.R.G. 30 sec. W.16M. R.13M. G.12M. R.Tr. W.Top 22m. R.141°-274°; G.274°-294°; W.294°-141°; R.141°-274°. Helicopter landing platform. V.Q. R.36m. 3M. Shown 3M NNW When firing taking place. Also shown by day 1/11-31/3.

GRÖTVIK. S. BREAKWATER HEAD Lt. Q. W.R.G. W.8M. R.6M. G.6M. Pedestal 6m. G.shore-312°; W.312°-019°; G.019°-043°; W.043°-077°; R.077°-shore.

HALMSTAD HAMN

BREAKWATER HEAD 56°38.9'N 12°50.3'E. Lt. Oc(2) W.R.G.12 sec. W.13M. R.10M. G.9M. R.Tr. 14m. W.018°-052°; R.052°-091°; W(unintens) 091°-270°; R.270°-312°; G.312°-018°. Breakwater Head 380m. SW floodlit. Lts. in line 037° 56°39.6'N 12°51.1'E (Front) Iso. 2 sec. 13M. W. △ on post 8m. Vis. in line only. Mark W side of channel. 56°39.7'N 12°51.1'E. (Rear) Iso. 2 sec. 13M. W. ▽ on post 13m. Vis in line only.

Lts. in line 037° 56°39.6'N 12°51.1'E. (Front) Iso. 2 sec. 13M. W. △ on post 2m. Synchronised with above 037° (Front) Lt. Vis. in line only. Mark E side of channel 56°39.6'N 12°51.1'E. (Rear) Iso. 2 sec. 13M. W. ▽ on post 8m. Vis. in line only.

OIL HARBOUR Ldg. Lts. 073° (Front) F.G. 6M. Or. △ on post 8m. (Rear) F.G. 6M. Or. ▽ on post 11m.

BÄSTAD Ldg. Lts. 219°. (Front) F.R. 9M. W. ◊ on post 8m. Vis. on leading line only. (Rear) F.R. 9M 12m. W. ◊ on post 12m. Vis. on leading line only.

DENMARK

LILLE BAELT

EBELTOFT VIG

EBELTOFT VIG HEAD 56°13.9'N 10°36.5'E Lt. Oc. W.R.G.5 sec. W.13M. R.10M. G.10M. W.Wood house, R.Band 13m. G.355°-357°; W.357°-358.5°; R.358.5°-005°; G.005°-008°; W.008°-008.5°; R.008.5°-010°.

Ldg. Lts. 026° (Front) F.R.4M. W. △ on framework Tr. 8m. (Rear) F.R.4M. W. ▽ on framework Tr. 9m.

PIER HEAD Lt. Fl.3 sec. 3M. Mast 9m.

EBELTOFT HAVN 56°12'N 10°40'E Yacht harbour in S Basin. Depth in entrance 3m. with 1.5-3m. inside. Ldg. Lts. 103°42' **W MOLE HEAD** (Front) F.R.5M. Col. 5m. (Rear) F.R.5M. Mast 18m. **NEAR ENTRANCE** Ldg. Lts. 143° (Front) F.G.2M. W, △ on B.Mast 5m. (Rear) F.G.2M. W.Mast 8m. **N MOLE HEAD** Lt. Fl.R.5 sec. 2M. W.Hut, R.Bands 6m. **W MOLE HEAD** Lt. Fl.G.5 sec. 2M. W.Hut, G.Bands 6m. **SKUDEHAVN** Lt. Fl.R.3 sec. 2M.W. Tr. R.Band 3m. Shown 1/4-15/11.

EBELTOFT FERRY HARBOUR

MOLE HEAD Lt. Fl.G.3 sec. 3M. Grey pedestal 4m. **BREAKWATER HEAD** Lt. Fl.R.3 sec. 3M. Grey pedestal 4m.

Ldg. Lts. 058°30' (Front) Iso. 2 sec.7M. Grey Tr. 10m 328.5°-148.5° (Rear) Iso. 4 sec. 7M. Grey Tr. 15m. 328.5°-148.5°.

HELGENAES. SLETTERHAGE sw

END 56°05.7'N 10°30.9'E Lt. Oc. W.R.G.10 sec. W.16M. R.12M. G.12M. W.Tr. 17m. R.251°-275°; G.275°-297°; W.297°-302°; R.302°-320.5°; G.320.5°-006°; R.006°-060°; G.060°-088°; W.088°-117°; R.117°-125°. RC. Horn Mo(A) 60 sec.

MARSELISBORG. LYSTBADHAVN

Lt. F.G.4M. G,mast 5m.

AARHUS 56°09'N 10°13'E Tel: (06) 133333. **Radio-Port:** VHF Chan. 16,12,13,H24. **Radio-Pilots:** VHF Chan. 16,6,12,13. Yachts lie in Lystbaade Fiskeri havn, bow on posts, stern to quay in depths of 2-3m.

OUTER HARBOUR 56°10.1'N 10°13.2'E Ldg. Lts. 295°06' (Front) Iso. 2 sec. 14M. Grey Tr. 28m. Intens 290°-300°. H24. **SE OF ST. JOHANNES CHURCH** 56°10.2'N 10°12.8'E (Rear) Iso. 4 sec. 14M. Grey Tr. 53m. Intens 290°-300°. H24.

ØSTRE MOLE ARM HEAD Lt. Fl.R.3 sec. 9M. Grey R,Tr. 16m. Fl.2 sec. 317m, 158m and R.Lts. on radio mast 3.8M. S. H24. Siren(2) 30 sec. Reserve fog signal Horn. SV shown when fog signal sounded.

VESTRE MOLE HEAD Lt. Fl.G.3 sec. 7M. Grey & G.Tr. 8m. H24.

ØSTRE MOLE HEAD Lt. F.R.7M. Grey & R.Tr. 6m. Vis. 026°-221°. H24. Bell. **SPUR HEAD** Lt Fl.G.5 sec. 6M. G.Tr. 6m. H24. Lts. in line 221°30' (Front) F. X on W. mast 5m. Marks NW side of channel to Basin 10, 2 F. Lts. in line mark SE side of channel. (Rear) F. X on W.Mast 21m. **E BREAKWATER N HEAD** Lt. Fl. R.5 sec 6M. R.Tr. Grey base 8m. Fog light. H24.

ØSTHAVN Ldg. Lts. 221°30'N (Front) Iso. G.2 sec. 6M. Tr. 18m. Vis. 210°-243°. H24. By day 2M. 217.5°-235.5°. (Rear) Iso. G.2 sec. 6M. Tr. 26m. 210°-243°. By day 2M. Vis. 217.5°-235.5°.

KALUNDBORG FERRY Ldg. Lts. 259° (Front) 2 F.G. hor. 5m. (Rear) F.G.House 15m.

BASIN 2. Bell 3 sec.

LYSTBAADE HAVN. E MOLE Lt. F.R. 6M. Grey Tr. R.band 6m. 000°-209.5°. H24.

SKØDSHOVED 56°11'N 10°23'E There is a small yacht harbour with depths to 1.5m. **BOAT HARBOUR. S MOLE HEAD** Lt. F.G. 4M. Grey post 5m. Shown 1/4-15/11.

KALVØ VIG

EGA MARINA

Depths 3.2m. in entrance and 2.2m-3.2m. alongside. Vessels up to 40m x 6m. x 3.1m. draught. **S MOLE HEAD** Lt. F.R. 4M. R.Post 4m. **N MOLE HEAD** Lt. F.G. 4M. G.Post 4m. **S MOLE HEAD** Lt. F.R. 4M. W.Cone shape, R.Top. Floodlit. Lt. F.G. 4M. W. ▯ G.Top. 5m. Floodlit.

STUDSTRUPVAERKETS HAVN

56°15'N 10°16'E A yacht harbour for vessels drawing up to 1.7m.

Ldg. Lts. 304° (Front) F.R. 5M. Or. △ on Tr. 42m. Vis 234°-014°. Aero Fl.2 sec. obstruction lights 192m 99m on chimney 300m SW. (Rear) F.R. 5M. Or. ▽ on house 49m.

NAPPENDAM

Yacht harbour on NE side of Egens Vig. Three basins, depths 3m in S Basin, 1.5-2.5m in Central Basin, 1-2.5m in N Basin.

S SHELTER MOLE HEAD Lt. F.R. 4M. W.Post 4 m. Shown 1/4-15/11.

RØNSTEN GRUND SE Lt. Fl(3) R.10 sec. 2M. Dolphin 2m. Shown 1/4-15/11.

NORSMINDE HAVN 56°01'N 10°16'E
Yacht harbour at entrance to Norminde Fjord. Several jetties with depths of 2.2m.

MARINA MOLE HEAD Lt. F.G. 4M. on post 3m.

TUNØ

TUNØ 55°57'N 10°26.7'E Lt. Oc. W.R.G.5 sec. W.12M. R.8M. G.8M. W. Church Tr. 31m. W (unintens) 072°-082°; G.095°-157°; W.157°-160°; R.160°-175°; G.175°-214°; W.214°-220°; R.220°-326°; G.326°-345°; W.345°-350°; R.350°-050°.

TUNO HAVN 55°57'N 10°27'E
Small harbour with depths of 3.2m.
S MOLE HEAD Lt. F.R. W.Post 3m. Shown 1/9-1/4 when vessels expected.

HOV HAVN 55°55'N 10°15'E
Small harbour, depths up to 3m. Ferry harbour to NE.
N MOLE ELBOW Lt. Oc. W.R.G.5 sec. W.8M. R.5M. G.5M. R.Tr. 5m. G.318°-328°; W.328°-335°; R.335°-345°.

FERRY HARBOUR. MOLE HEAD Lt. Oc(2) W.R.G.12 sec. W.7M. R.4M. G.4M. Mast 5m. W.199°-206°; R.206°-217°; G.217°-199°.

W MOLE HEAD Lt. F.R. W.Mast 8m. Shown 1/10-1/4.
Lt. Fl(3) G.10 sec. 2M. Dolphin 2m.
Lt. Fl. G.3 sec. 2M. Dolphin 2m.

SAMSØ

SAELVIG. PIER HEAD Lt. F.G. 4M. Mast 5m. F.R. obstruction lights on radio mast 0.5m SW.

LANGOR HAVN 55°55'N 10°38'E
Noted bird sanctuary. Quay with depths of 3m on S side and 2.4m on W side. Situated on E side of Samsø.

MARUP HAVN 55°56'N 10°33'E
Small harbour, max. draught 3m.

KOLBY KAAS HAVN.

N MOLE HEAD Lt. Fl. R.3 sec. 4M. Square Tr. 5m.
S MOLE HEAD Lt. Fl. G.3 sec. 3M. Square Tr. 5m. Siren(2) 28 sec. Sounded when mail steamer expected. Reserve fog signal Reed.

Ldg. Lts. 130° (Front) 2 F.G. hor. on ferry berth 5m. Shown when ferries expected. (Rear) F.G. Grey Tr. 12m. Seen midway between twin front Lts.

SAMSØ SW POINT. VESBORG 55°46.2'N 10°33'E Lt. Oc(2) 12 sec. 17M. W.Tr. 36m. 275°-149°. (in places 149°-169°).

LUSHAGE Lt. Fl.3 sec. 6M. Grey Tr. 5m. 204°-095°.

BALLEN HAVN 55°49'N 10°39'E
Yacht marina and commercial harbour. Depths 4m. in entrance, outer harbour 3m, inner harbour 2.6m.

S MOLE HEAD Lt. F.R. 4M. Grey mast 6m. 167°-289°.
N MOLE HEAD Lt. F.G. 2M. Grey mast 6m. 211°-336°.

ENDELAVE HAVN

E MOLE HEAD Lt. F.R. 5M. Mast 6m. 045°-270°.

Ldg. Lts. 165° (Front) F.7M. W.Mast 7m. 095°-235°. (Rear) F.7M. W.Mast 13m. 095°-235°.

HORSENS FJORD

HJARJNØ 55°49'N 10°03.9'E Ldg. Lts. 338°30' (Front) F.G. 10M. W.Wooden house 6m. 334.5°-342.5°. Fl(4) Y.10 sec. on E pile of Seafarm 1.2M. S. Fl. Y.3 sec. on outer piles of Seafarm 200m. NW. Shown 1/4-15/12. 55°49.8'N 10°03.7'E (Rear) F.G. 12M. Grey/Or.Tr. 18m. 334.5°-342.5°.

HALDRUP. Ldg. Lts. 320° NEAR VILLAGE (Front) F.R. 8M. W./Or.House 8m. 316°-324°; (Rear) F.R. 8M. W.R.House 18m. 316°-324°.

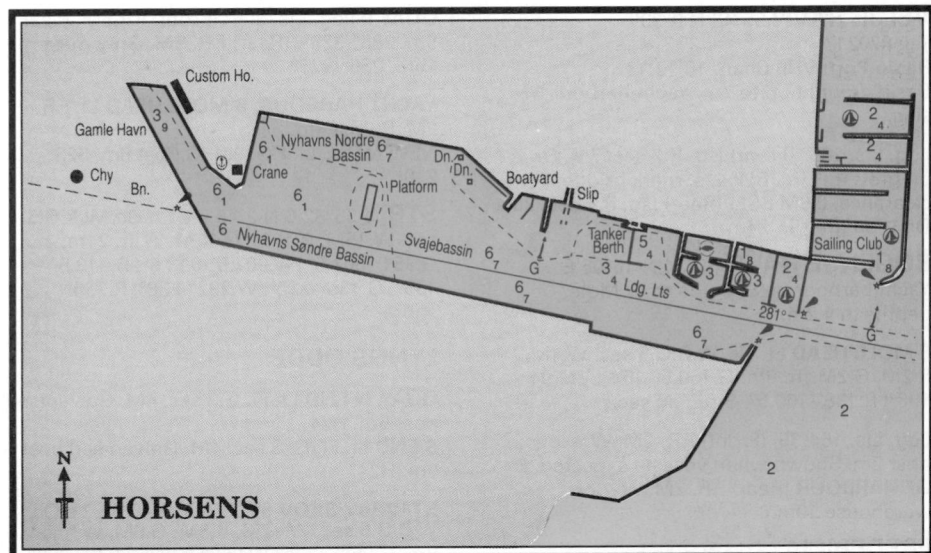

HORSENS

SEJET Ldg. Lts. 238°12'. **NEAR CHRISTIANSMINDE** (Front) F.G. 5M. W.House 3m. 228°-248°. (Rear) F.G. 5M. W.House 10m. 228°-248°.
HORSENS 55°51.5'N 9°51.6'E. Ldg. Lts. 281° **S SIDE OF HARBOUR** (Front) F.R. 10M. W.Building 12m. 191°-011°. 55°51.6'N 9°51.0'E (Rear) F.R. 10M. Or. ▽ on Tr. 22m. 191°-011°.

MARINA Lt. F.G. 2M. G.Post 3m. Shown 1/4-15/11.

HORSENS HAVN 55°51'N 9°52'E
Yacht Marina with four jetties N of root of N Harbour Mole. On N side of harbour inside entrance is a yacht harbour with depths of 1.8-3.1m.

N MOLE Lt. Fl. G.3 sec. 4M. G.Post on W.Hut 4m.
S MOLE Lt. Fl. R.3 sec. 4M. R.Post on W.Hut 4m.

JUELSMINDE HAVN 55°43'N 10°01'E
Radio-Pilots: VHF Chan. 16,12,13.
Small harbour with depths of 3.8m.

E MOLE HEAD Lt. Fl. R.5 sec. 4M. R.Pillar 5m.

FERRY HARBOUR Lt. Fl. R.3 sec. 2M. Tripod 4m.

Ldg. Lts. 179° (Front) F.G. 2M. △ on Tr. 10m. Vis. 169°-189° (Rear) F.G. 3M. ▽ on Tr. 14m. 169°-189°.

KORSHAVN Lt. Oc. W.R.G.5 sec. W.7M. R.3M. G.3M. R.Tr. 4 m. R.259°-292°; G.292°-

053°; W.053°-058°; R.058°-078°; W (unintens) 168°-213°.

ODENSE FJORD

ENEBAERODDE 55°31.0'N 10°33.7'E Lt. L. Fl. W.R.G.5 sec. W.11M. R.8M. G.8M. W.Tr. 13m. G.142°-164°; W.164°-180°; R.180°-028°; G.028°-082°.

GABET Ldg. Lts. 218° (Front) Iso. 2 sec. 5M. R △ on R.Mast 10m. 203°-233°. (Rear) Iso. 4 sec. 5M. R. ▽ on R.Mast 10m. 203°-233°. Odense Kanal is marked by lights.

SKOVEN Lt. Oc(2) W.R.G.6 sec. W.5M. R.3M. G.3M. Tr. 20m. G.134°-144°; W.144°-154°; R.154°-164°. H24.

BREGNØR. FISHING HARBOUR. N MOLE HEAD Lt. F.G. 3M. G.Pole 4m.

OTTERUP. YACHT HARBOUR. E MOLE HEAD Lt. F.W.R.G. 4M. Tr. 5m. G.023°-193.5°; W.193.5°-221.5°; R.221.5°-023°. Shown 1/4-15/11.

AEBELO. NW POINT 55°38.8'N 10°09.9'E Lt. Fl(2) 15 sec. 18M. Tr.20m. 016°-263°.

BREJNING

Yacht harbour 2M. WNW of Morkholts Hage. Basin depth 2m.

TRELDE NAES Lt. Iso. W.R.G.2 sec. W.8M. R.5M. G.5M. Tr. 26m. G.-shore-124°; W.124°-129°; R.129°-139°; W.139°-235°; R.235°-258°; G.258°-277°; W.277°-010°.

VELJE HAVN 55°43'N 9°33'E
Tel: 820217.
Radio-Port: VHF Chan. 16,12,13.
Basin draught up to 7m. Yacht harbour NE side.

Ldg. Lts. 288° (Front) Iso. R.2 sec. 7M. Or. △ on grey Tr. 17m. F.W. Lts. mark bridge, 40m clearance, 0.9M ESE. (Rear) Iso. R.4 sec. 8M. Or. ▽ on grey Tr. 24m.

BOGENSE HAVN 55°34'N 10°05'E
Yacht harbour on SW side of W Mole, depths to 4.2m.

E MOLE HEAD Lt. Oc. W.R.G.5 sec. W.4M. R.2M. G.2M. Tr. 6m. G.160.5°-194°; W.194°-198°; R.198°-160.5°. Siren 30 sec.

Ldg. Lts. 164°30' (Front) F.R. 2M. W △ on post 2m. Shown when vessels expected. **E OF HARBOUR** (Rear) F.R. 2M. W ▽ on warehouse 10m.

FREDERICIA 55°34'N 9°45'E
Tel: (05) 920168 (H.M.) 920959 (Pilots).
Radio-Port: VHF Chan. 16,12,13.
Radio-Pilots: VHF Chan. 16,12,13,H24.
Yacht harbour close SW of Mollebugthaven. Depth of 3m. in entrance and 1.5-3m. inside.

SHELL OIL PIER Lt. F.G. 4M. on dolphin 5m.
SKANSEODDE E Lt. Fl(2) R.G.5 sec. 5M. G.Mast. Floodlit 10m. R.073°-223°; G.223°-073°. Horn 30 sec. Racon.
QUAY Lt. F.G. 4M. G.Post 5m.
GAMLE HAVN. N MOLE KNUCKLE Lt. F.R. 2M. Post 5m.
FISKERIHAVN. E MOLE HEAD Lt. F.G. 2M. Grey mast 5m.
VESTHAVN. E MOLE HEAD Lt. Fl. G.3 sec. 2M. R.W.Tr. 4m.
W MOLE HEAD Lt. Fl. R.3 sec. R.Post 4m.

QUAY II Ldg. Lts. 305° (Front) F.R.5M. Pillar 5m. 285°-325°. (Rear) F.R. 5M. Grey mast 15m. 285°-325°.

YACHT HARBOUR. S MOLE HEAD Lt. F.R. 2M. R.Post 4m.
NEW MOLE Lt. F.G. 2M. G.Post 5m. 323°-210°.

STRIB 55°32.6'N 9°45.5'E Lt. Oc. W.R.G.5 sec. W.15M. R.12M. G.12M. W.Tr. 21m. G.351°-007.5°; W.007.5°-013.5°; R.013.5°-135°; G.135°-232°; W.232°-238°; R.238°-shore.

LYNGS ODDE

QUAY. N END Lt. Fl. G.3 sec. 4M. Galvanised post 5m. H24.
S END Lt. Fl. G.,3 sec. 4M. Galvanised post 5m. H24.

STAVRBY SKOV 55°31.0'N 9°45.6'E Lt. Oc. W.R.G.5 sec. W.12M. R.8M. G.8M. W.hut 9m. G.050°-068°; W.068°-079°; R.079°-090°. Fl. Y.3 sec. Lts. in line mark gas pipe line on N and S side of the bridge.

LILLE BAELT BRIDGE

W PILLAR. N SIDE Lt. F.G. 8M. 5m. 109°-019°. Horn(2) 40 sec. **S SIDE** Lt. F.G. 8M. 5m. 199°-109°.
CENTRE. N SIDE Lt. F. 12M. 50m. 109°-289°; **S SIDE** Lt. F. 12M. 50m. 289°-109°.
E PILLAR. N SIDE Lt. F.R. 8M. 5m. 019°-289°; **S SIDE** Lt. F.R. 8M. 5m. 289°-199°. Horn(2) 40 sec. sounded alternately with W.Pillar Horn.

MIDDELFART HAVN. W MOLE HEAD Lt. F.G. 3M. G.mast 5m. 120°-300°.

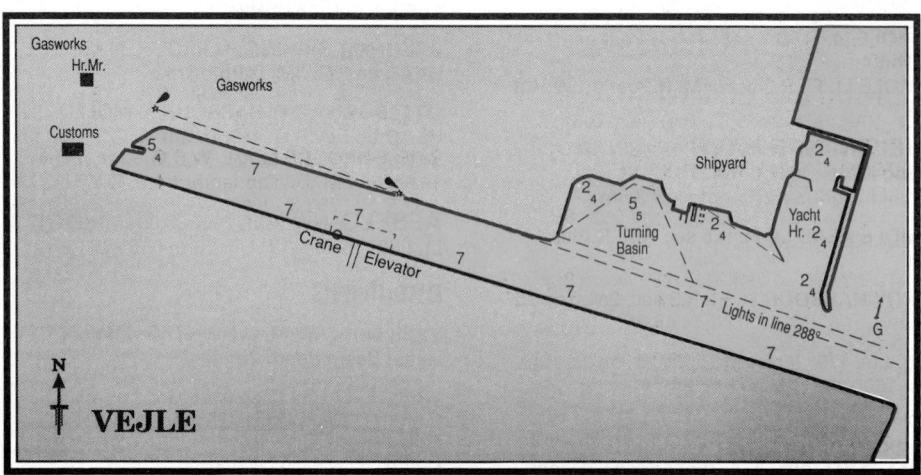

VEJLE

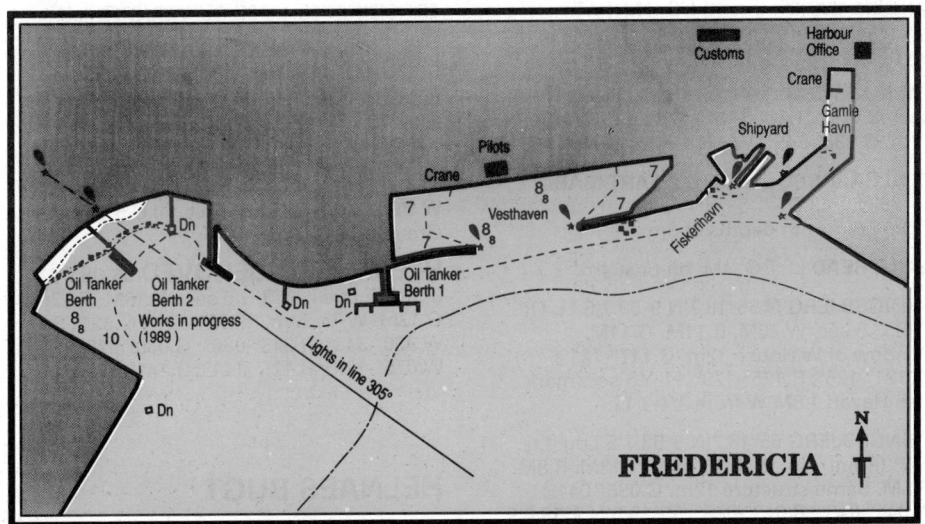

WEST LILLE BAELT BRIDGE

CENTRE. E SIDE Lt. Iso. 4 sec. 7M. 33m. 270°-335°.
W SIDE Lt. Iso. 4 sec. 7M. 33m. 097°-155°.
No: 1 PILLAR N SIDE Lt. 2 Fl. R.3 sec. 5M. 5m. 124°-213°.
No: 2 PILLAR S SIDE Lt. Fl. G.3 sec. 5M. 5m. 033°-124°. **N SIDE** Lt. 2 Fl. R.3 sec. 5M. 5m. 124°-304°.
No: 3 PILLAR S SIDE Lt. Fl. G.3 sec. 5M. 5m. 304°-124°. Siren 20 sec. Sounded alt E&W. **N SIDE** Lt. 2 Fl. R.3 sec. 5M. 5m. 213°-304°.
No: 4 PILLAR S SIDE Lt. 2 Fl. G.3 sec. 5M. 5m. 304°-033°.

BØRUP N 55°31.8'N 9°40.8'E Lt. Iso. W.R.G.4 sec. W.14M. R.9M. G.9M. W.Building, R.Band on W.Dwelling 9m. G.012°-027°; W.027°-036°; R.036°-042.5°.

GALSKLINT CABLE CROSSING N Lt. 3 Aero Q.R. 10M. mast 133m. 96m. 51m. **S.** Lt. 3 Aero Q.R. 10M. mast 131m. 93m. 49m.
SNOGHØJ 55°31.6'N 9°41.8'E Lt. Oc. W.R.G.5 sec. W.14M. R.9M. G.9M. W.R.House 6m. G.056°-063°; W.063°-067°; R.067°-074°.

BØRUP W 55°31.7'N 9°40.5'E Dir. Lt. 294.7° Dir. Iso. W.R.G.2 sec. W.14M. R.9M. G.9M. W.R.House 5m. G.290°-293.5°; W.293.5°-295°; R.295°-302°. Leads between Piers III and IV of Little Baelt Bridge.

DAMGAARD 55°31.7'N 9°40.3'E Dir. Lt. 294.2° Dir. Oc. W.R.G.5 sec. W.14M. R.9M. G.9M. W.R.House 7m. G.209-293.5°; 293.5°-

295°; R.295°-311°. Leads between Piers II and III of Little Baelt Bridge.

SKAEBAEK 55°30.7'N 9°37.1'E Lt. Oc(2) W.R.G.12 sec. W.14M. W.12M. R.10M. R.8M. G.10M. G.8M. Roof of factory 12m. G.035.5°-042.5°; W.042.5°-044°; R.044°-049°; G (intens) 309.5°-313°; W (intens) 313°-316°; R (intens) 316°-321°.

SKAERBAEKVAERKETS HAVN

Ldg. Lts. 330° (Front) F.R. 2M. W. ∆ on mast 7m. On request. (Rear) F.R. 2M. W. ∇ on mast 13m. On request.

SKAERBAEK HAVN

E MOLE HEAD Lt. F.G. Col. 4m.

Lts. in line 008° (Front) F.R. 4M. ○ on mast 10m. Mark cable. 55°30.9'N 9°36.6'E F.R.W. vert. R.14M. W.12KM. ⌘ on mast 4m.

DREJENSODDE Lt. Oc. W.R.G.5 sec. W.8M. R.4M. G.2M. G.Wooden hut 4m. G.243°-252.5°; W.252.5°-255°; R.255°-260.5°; G.260.5°-276°.

KOLDING HAVN

55°29.6'N 9°29.5'E Ldg. Lts. 267° (Front) F.R. 13M. Grey Tr. 10m. H24. (Rear) F.R.13M. Grey Tr. 17m. H24.

ENTRANCE. S SIDE Lt. Fl. R.3 sec. 2M. R.Pyramid 5m.
N SIDE Lt. Fl. G.3 sec. 2M. G.Pyramid 6m.

Ldg. Lts. 236°30' (Front) F.G. 2M. W.Tr. on pile 3m. 166.5°-306.5°. (Rear) F.G. 2M. W.Tr. on pile 6m 166.5°-306.5°.

FAENØ 55°28.5'N 9°42.2'E Lt. L. Fl. W.R.G.5 sec. W.11M. R.8M. G.8M. Gable of W.House 11m. G.338°-342°; W.342°-346°; R.346°-350°.

TEGLGARDSBUGT. MIDDLEFART MARINA 55°29'N 9°43'E
Eight piers with depths of 3m.

MOLE HEAD Lt. F.G. 4M. on post 4m.

TVINGSBJERG N 55°18.7'N 9°53.7'E Lt. Oc. W.R.G.5 sec. W.15M. R.11M. G.11M. Window of W.House 12m. G.117°-121°; W.121°-125°; R.125°-129°. Fl. Y.5 sec. mark Fish Haven 1.8M W from 1/4-1/12.

TVINGSBJERG 55°18.7'N 9°53.7'E Ldg. Lts. 042° (Front) Iso. W.R.G.2 sec. W.12M. R.8M. G.8M. Same structure 12m. G.036°-041°; W.041°-043°; R.043°-048°. 55°19.5'N 9°55.0'E (Rear) Iso. 4 sec 14M. W.R.Tr. 28m. 036°-048°.

ÅRØ. W SIDE Lt. Iso. W.R.G.2 sec. W.8M. R.5M. G.5M. W.R.Tr. 12m. R.306°-322°; G.322°-353°; W.353°-001°; R.001°-051°; G.151°-184°; W.184-187°; R.187°-193°. Obscured by buildings and trees 178°-180.5°.

ÅRØSUND HAVN

S MOLE HEAD 55°15.8'N 9°42.8'E Lt. Oc. W.R.G.5 sec. W.10M. R.8M. G.8M. W.Tr. 9m. G.126°-171°; R.171°-194°; G.194°-205°; W.205°-211°; R.211°-220°; G.220°-330°; W.330°-335°; R.335°-337°.
FERRY PIER HEAD Lt. F.R. 3M. Grey post 4m.
NEW S MOLE HEAD Lt. F.G. 2M. Post 4m.
PIER Lt. F.R. 2M. W.Post 4m.

BÅGØ 55°17.8'N 9°48.0'E Lt. Oc(2) W.R.G.6 sec. W.11M. R.7M. G.7M. W.Tr. 12m. W.081°-086.5°; R.086.5°-145°; G.145°-158°; W.158°-166°; R.166°-179°; G.179°-265°; R.265°-288°; G.288°-313.5°; W.313.5°-320.5°; R.320.5°-357.5°; G.357.5°-081°. Obscured by Bågø 195°-201°.

BÅGØ-ÅRO CABLE. Lts. in line 229° (Front) F.R. 4M. W ○ on mast 3m. Marks cable. (Rear) F.R.W. vert. 4M. W ⚲ on mast 10m.

ASSENS HAVN 55°16'N 9°53'E
Radio-Pilots: VHF Chan. 16,12,13.
Yacht harbour on W side of harbour, 9 piers, depths 2-3m.

55°16.2'N 9°53.1'E Lt. Oc. W.R.G.10 sec. W.14M. R.10M. G.10M. R.Structure 6m. G.155°-163°; W.163°-173°; R.173°-180°.

Ldg. Lts. 171°30' (Front) Iso. R.2 sec. 4M. R △ on Bn. 7m. Shown when vessels expected. (Rear) Iso. R.4 sec. 4M. R ▽ on Bn. 8m.

W BREAKWATER HEAD Lt. Fl. G.3 sec. 2M. Grey pedestal 5m.

HELNAES. LINDEHOVED 55°08.0'N
9°58.7'E Lt. Fl. W.R.G.5 sec. W.16M. R.12M. G.12M. W.Tr. 30m. R.302°-321°; G.321°-330°; W.330°-343°; R.343°-030°; G.030°-075°; W.075°-125°; R.125°-141°; G.141°-179°.

HELNAES BUGT

FALDSLED PIER. OFF HEAD Lt. F.G. 4M. G.pile 4m.

BØJDEN. FERRY HARBOUR Ldg. Lts. 138°42' (Front) F.R. 4M. Masts 6m. Shown when ferries are running. (Rear) F.R. 4M. Tr. 12m. Shown when ferries are running.

S MOLE HEAD Lt. Fl. G.3 sec. Grey Tr. 7 m. Siren 20 sec. Sounded when ferries are running.
N MOLE HEAD Lt. Fl. R.3 sec. Grey Tr. 7m.

HORNENAES Lts. in line 034° (Front) F.R. 5M. ○ on mast 15m. 334.6°-094.6°. Mark cable to Fynshav. (Rear) F.R.W. vert. 5M. ⚲ on mast 22m. 334.6°-094.6°.

LYØ REV Lt. Fl.5 sec. 2M. B.Mast 4m.

BJØRNØ 55°03.3'N 10°15.8'E Lt. Iso. W.R.G.4 sec. W.10M. R.7M. G.7M. W.R.Hut 6m. G.040°-052°; W.052°-060°; R.060°-071°.

FÅBORG FJORD

SISSERODDE. Ldg. Lts. 353° (Front) Iso. 2 sec. 9M. W.R.Hut 6m. 350°-356°. (Rear) Iso. 4 sec. 9M. W.R.Hut 10m. 350°-356°.

DYREBORG HAVN. E MOLE Lt. F.G. 2M. mast 6m.

ØSTERHEDE. Ldg. Lts. 046°36' (Front) F.G. 4M. R △ on W.R.Hut, 13m. 043.5°-049.5°. H24. (Rear) F.G. 4M. R. ▽ on brown mast 18m. 043.5°-049.5°. H24.

Lt. Fl.(2) 5 sec. on Tr. 4m. Shown 1/5-30/9.

FÅBORG HAVN. Ldg. Lts. 360°30'. **E**
MOLE HEAD (Front) F.R.G. 4M. R △ on grey
post 6m. G.002°-260°; R.260°-002°.
MUNKHOLM (Rear) F.R. 4M. R ▽ on
framework 11m. 224°-089°.

FERRY BERTH HEAD Lt. F.G. 2M. W. Col.
4m. 310°-110°.

MUNKE 55°01.4'N 10°16.4'E Lt. Iso. W.R.G.4
sec. W.14M. R.10M. G.10M. W.R.Hut 10m.
G.259°-264°; W.264°-268°; R.268°-273°.

NAKKEODDE 55°01.0'N 10°20.0'E Lt. Oc.
W.R.G.5 sec. W.11M. R.8M. G.8M. W.R.Hut
9m. G.116°-123°; W.123°-130°; R.130°-146°.

BALLEN. W MOLE HEAD Lt. F.R. 2M.
R.Mast, floodlit 5m. Floodlit mole head
close by.

Lts. in line 018° (Front) F.R. 2M. R ○, on
mast 8m. 003°-033°. Mark N end of power
cable. (Rear) F.R.W. vert. 2M. W ○, R.Border,
over W. ◊, R.Border, R.Stripe 12m. 10m.
003°-033°.

SKARØ HAVN. Lts. in line 214° (Front) F.R.
4M. 8M. 124°-304°. Mark S end of power
cable. H24. (Rear) F.R.W. vert. 4M. 12m.
124°-304°. H24.

FERRY PIER. NW CORNER Lt. Fl. R.3 sec.
4M. wooden mast 7m.

BAEKKEHAVE 55°01.1'N 10°32.7'E Lt. Oc.
W.R.G.5 sec. W.12M. R.8M. G.8M. W.R.hut
6m. G.095°-100°; W.100°-105°; R.105°-107°.

HØJESTENE LØB

VORNAES PYNT. Ldg. Lts. 040° (Front) F. R
△ on Tr. 7m 330°-110°. (Rear) F.R. ▽ on Tr.
18m. 330°-110°.

Lt. Fl(3) R.10 sec on R.Post.
Lt. Fl. G.3 sec. 2M. △ on G.Post 2m.
Lt. Fl(3) G.10 sec. 2M. △ on G.Post 2m.

DREJØ PIER Lt. F.B.Post. Shown from 1545-
0645, 1/9-31/3.

ÅLS

NORDBORG 55°04.7'N 9°42.7'E Lt. Oc.
W.R.G.5 sec. W.16M. R.11M. G.11M. Y.Tr.
27m G.065°-070°; W.070°-073°; R.073°-171°;
G.171°-184.5°; W.184.5°-236°; R.236°-259°.

TRANERODDE 55°02.8'N 9°51.2'E Lt. Iso.
W.R.G.2 sec. W.13M. R.10M. G.10M. W.R.Tr.
12m. R.131°-191°; G.191°-280°; W.280°-290°;
R.290°-301°.

TAKSENSAND 55°00.4'N 9°58.0'E Lt.
Oc(2) W.R.G.12 sec. W.15M. R.11M. G.11M.
W.Tr. 15m. G.127°-135°; W.135°-139°;
R.139°-174°; G.174°-186°; W.186°-323°.

FYNSHAV. FERRY HARBOUR 55°00'N
9°59'E
Yacht harbour is S of Ferry harbour
entrance. Depths of 2.4m. and 0.8-2.5m.
inside.

Ldg. Lts. 212°30' (Front) F.R. 6M. Mast 6m.
Shown when ferries running. (Rear) F.R. 6M.
Tr. 12m. Shown when ferries running.
S MOLE HEAD Lt. Fl. R.3 sec. Grey Tr. 7m.
Siren(2) 30 sec. Sounded when ferries
running.
N SIDE Lt. Fl. R.5 sec. 3M. Grey Tr. 7m.
N MOLE HEAD Lt. Fl. G.5 sec. 5M. Grey Tr.
7m.
Lts. in line 212°30' (Front) F.R. 5M.○ on
tripod 8 M 152.5°-272.5°. Mark cable to
Hornenaes. (Rear) F.R.W. vert. 5M. ℅ on
mast14m. 152.5°-272.5°.

MOMMARK HAVN 54°56'N 10°03'E
Ferry harbour used by fishing vessels and
yachts. Max. draught 3m.

E MOLE HEAD Lt. F.R. 2M. post 3m. Mole
heads floodlit.
SHELTER MOLE HEAD Lt. Fl. R.3 sec. 2M.
post 4m.

ABENRA HAVN 55°02'N 9°26'E
The yacht harbour is on W side of approach
to harbour. Depth 2.5m.
Radio-Pilots: VHF Chan. 16,12,13.

SØNDERSTRAND 55°01.8'N 9°25.4'E Lt.
Oc. W.R.G.5 Sec. W.15M. R.12M. G.12M.
Or.Wooden hut 4m. G.252°-255°; W.225°-
257°; R.257°-260°.

SONDERGYLLANDSKAJENS. SYDHAVN.
Ldg. Lts. 320°12' (Front) Iso. G.2 sec. 5M. R
△ on grey Tr. 10m. (Rear) Iso. G.4 sec. 5M. R.
▽ on grey Tr. 17m.

NYHAVN Ldg. Lts. 350°18' (Front) Iso. R.2
sec. 5M. Grey mast on Tr. 11m. (Rear) Iso.
R.4 sec. 5m. Grey mast on Tr. 19m.
Ldg. Lts. 027° (Front) F.6M. W. + on wooden
post 4m. (Rear) F.6M. W. + on wooden post
7m.
SMALL BOAT HARBOUR Lt. Fl. R.3 sec. 2M.
Board on pole 3m.

ENSTEDVAERKETS HAVN Lt. Fl. R.3
sec. 5M. Mast on mooring dolphin 6m.

Ldg. Lts. 55°01.4'N 9°25.8'E (Front) F.R. 10M.
R. ∆ on mast 10m. 239°-259°. H24. (Rear)
55°01.4'N 9°25.8'E F.R. 10M. R ▽ on mast
16m. 239°-259°.
Ldg. Lts. 154°18' (Front) F.G. 4M. R. ∆ on
mast 9m. 089.3°-219.3°. H24. (Rear) F.G. 4M.
R ▽ on building 10m. 089.3°-219.3°.
Lts. in line 242°30' (Front) F. 7M. W X on
mast 8m. Neon tubes in shape of X. Same
structure as Ldg. Lts. 249° (Front). 152.5°-
332.5°. H24. Marks dredged area limit.
(Rear) F.7M.W.X on mast 12m. Neon tubes
in shape of X. 152.5°-332.5°.
OIL PIER Lts. in line 260° (Front) F.7M.W.X
on mast 9m. Neon tubes in shape of X.
170°-350°. H24. Marks limit of dredged area.
(Rear) F.7M. W.X on mast 12m. Neon tubes
in shape of X. 170°-350°.

ALS FJORD

AUGUSTENBORG 54°57'N 9°52'E
On side of Fjord is a yacht harbour with four
piers with depths of 2.5m.

BALLEBRO 54°59.9'N 9°40.4'E. Lt. Iso.
W.R.G.2 sec. W.10M. R.7M. G.7M. W.R.Tr.
11m. G.128°-140°; W.140°-152°; R.152°-253°;
G.253°-262.5°; W.262.5°-274°; R.274°-283°.
Lts. in line 235° (Front) F.R.R. O, W.border
on W.Bn. Mark cable. (Rear) F.R.W. vert. R.
W. ℗ on W.Bn. 230°-240°.
Lts. in line 235° (Front) F.R. 2M. ○ on mast
6m. Mark cable. 230°-240°. (Rear) F.R.W.
vert. 2M. ℗ on mast 11m. 9m. 230°-240°.

AERØ

VITSO Lts. in line 077° (Front) F.R.R.O.
W.Border on mast 4m. Mark Cable. (Rear)
F.R.W. vert. R.W. ○ on mast 8m.

SKJOLDNAES 54°58.2'N 10°12.5'E Lt L.
Fl.30 sec. 20M Tr. 32m. Horn 60 sec. Signal
directed alternately N and S every other
minute.

SØBY HAVN. E MOLE HEAD Lt. Iso. W.R.2
sec. W.Tr. 6m. W.151°-255°; R.255°-151°;
Siren(2) 60 sec. Sounded for the use of
ferries.

AERØSKØBING HAVN Ldg. Lts. 196°18' W
MOLE HEAD (Front) F.G. 4M. R. ∆ on
G.Mast, W.Top 9m. Same structure FL. G.5
sec. 4M. 4m. (Rear) F.G. 4M. R. ▽ on W.Mast
14m.
DEJRØ Lt. Fl(2) R.5 sec. 2M. R.Dolphin 2m.
E MOLE HEAD Lt. Fl. R.5 sec. 4M. R.Post
4m.
MARINA MOLE HEAD Lt. Fl. R.3 sec. 2M.
R.Post 3m. Shown 1/4-15/11.
DETACHED SHELTER MOLE. S END Lt. Fl.
G.3 sec. 2M. G.Post. Floodlit. 3m. Shown
1/4-15/11.

VEJSNAES NAKKE Lt. Oc. W.R.G.5 sec.
W.7M. R.4M. G.4M. Grey Tr. 24m. W.007°-
210°; G.210°-252°; W.252°-337°; R.337°-352°;
G.352°-007°.

AERØ-LANGELAND. CABLE. Lts. in line
288°. (Front) F.R. 5M. R O, W.border, on
mast 5m. Marks cable. 219.8°-359.8° (Rear)
F.R.W. vert. W. 6M. R. 5M. R.W. ℗ on Tr.
13m. 219.8°-359.8°.

RISTINGE S. CABLE. Lts. in line 102°12'
(Front) F.R. 5M. R.O, W.Border on twin
masts 18m. 032.2°-172.2° (Rear) F.R.W. vert.
W. 6M. R. 5M. R.W. ℗ on twin masts 27m.
032.2°-172.2°.

MARSTAL HAVN. N Ldg. Lts. 254°
(Front) F.R. 5M. R ∆ on mast 5m. 184.8°-
324.8° (Rear) F.R. 5M. R ▽ on mast 11m.
184.8°-324.8°.

STEAMER PIER. S Ldg. Lts. 180° (Front) F.G.
2M. R ∆ on grey Tr. 8m. (Rear) F.G. 2M. R ▽
on grey Tr. 13m.

AERØ-HALMØ-BIRKHOLM CABLE.
BIRKHOLM Lts. in line (Front) F.R. 2M. R.O.
W.Border, on tripod 3m. Mark cable. (Rear)
F.R.W. vert. 2M. R.W. ℗ on Tr. 6m.

HUMMELVIG. Lts. in line 256° (Front) F.R.R.
O,W.Border on W.Bn. 5m. Mark cable.
(Rear) F.R.W. vert. R.W. ℗ on W.Bn. 9m.

GAMMEL-POL 54°52.9'N 10°04.2'E Lt. Oc(3)
W.R.G.15 sec. W.14M. R.10M. G.10M. W.R.
Col. 20m. W.166.5°-320°; R.320°-008°;
G.008°-036.5°; W.036.5°-049°; R.049°-166.5°.

GERMANY AND DENMARK

FLENSBURGER FJORD

Pilots: Tel. (0461) 25150.
Radio-Pilots: VHF Chan. 6,10,16.

ALS. S POINT. KEGNAES 54°51.2'N 9°59.3'E
Lt. Oc. W.R.G.5 sec. W.14M. R.10M. G.10M.
Y.Tr. 32m. R.217°-266.5°; G.266.5°-273°;
W.273°-289.5°; R.289.5°-337°; G.337°-026°;
W.026°-044°; R.044°-050.5°; G.050.5°-075°;
W.075°-080°; R.080°-102.5°.

FALSHOFT 54°46.2'N 9°58.0'E Lt. Oc(2)
W.R.G.16 sec. W.18M. R.14M. G.13M.
W.R.Tr. 25m. R.142°-154°; W.154°-159.5°;
G.159.5°-195°; R.195°-253°; W.253°-320.5°.
R.320.5°-347°.

KALKGRUND 54°49.6'N 9°53.4'E Lt.
F.W.R.G. W.19M. R.16M. G.15M. R.Tr. 2
W.Bands, 3 galleries. Floodlit 22m. W.022°-
070°; R.070°-083°; W.083°-132°; G.132°-158°;
W.158°-164°; R.164°-190°; W.190°-230°;
G.230°-258°; W.258°-265°; R.265°-287°;
W.295°-303°; R.314°-022°. Also Lt. Fl(2) 9
sec. 303°-314° and Fl(3) 12 sec. 287°-295°.
Racon. Fog. Det. Lt. Horn Mo(FS) 30 sec.

GELTING 54°45'N 9°53'E
Yacht harbour.
Ldg. Lts. 185° (Front) Oc. 6 sec. 8M. W. △,
R.Border on Tr. 13m. Occas. (Rear) Oc. 6
sec. 8M. W. ▽ R.Border on Tr. 18m. Occas.
MOLE Ldg. Lts. 208° (Front) Iso. 4 sec. 4M.
W △, R.Border on Tr. 13m. Occas. (Rear) Iso.
4 sec. 4M. W. ▽ R.Border on Tr. 16m. Occas.

JACHTHAFEN Ldg. Lts. 178°42' (Front) Iso.
G.4 sec. 6M. W. △ R.Border on post 4m.
Intens on leading line. (Rear) Iso. G.4 sec.
6M. W. ▽ R.Border on mast 6m. Intens on
leading line.

HØRUPHAVN. E SIDE Lt. Fl. G.3 sec. 4M.
W.Post 2m. **W SIDE** Lt. Fl. R.3 sec. 4M.
W.Post 2m.

ALS SUNDE

OSTERHAGE MARINA Lt. F.G. 4M. Pillar 4m.
E SIDE Lt. Fl. G.5 sec. 2M. G.Post 3m. 284°-
258°. ⌇⌇Bridge signals on Christian X
Bridge 400m. N.
W SIDE Lt. Fl. R.5 sec. 2M. R.Post 3m. 114°-
342°. ⌇⌇

Lts. in line 095° (Front) F.R. 2M. R
O,W.Border on Tr. 14m. Mark cable. (Rear)
F.R.W. vert. 2M. R.W. ⸰ on Tr. 24m. 19m.
Lts. in line 095° (Front) F.R. 2M. R
O,W.Border on Tr. 14m. Mark cable. (Rear)
F.R.W. vert. 2M. R.W. ⸰ on Tr. 24m.19m.

SOTTRUPSKOV Lt. Iso. W.R.G.4 sec. W.6M.
R.3M. G.3M. W.R.Pedestal 9m. G.151°-
192.5°; W.192.5°-201°; R.201°-238°. Fish
farms marked by Fl. Y.Lts. on piles 0.5M.E
and 0.75M SE during 1/3-1/12.

SONDERBORG HAVN 54°55'N 9°47'E
Te;l: (04) 422765.
Radio-Port & Pilots: VHF Chan. 16,12,13.
Quay on E side of harbour W of Customs
House reserved for passenger, fishing
vessels and yachts. Situated in Als Sunde,
through Als Fjord.

Christian X Bridge. Passage at W end 30m.
wide with mean vertical clearance of 5m.
Vessels needing bridge to open show - By
Day: Flag (or National Flag) at half mast and
sound 1 long, 1 short blast. At Night: show
W.Lt. at bow plus sound signal. Bridge
shows:
1 F.R. = passage prohibited.
2 Fl. R. = Vessel expected from N.
2 F.R. = Vessel from N. may pass through.
3 Fl. R. = Vessel expected from S.
3 F.R. = Vessel from S may pass through.
(One way traffic only).

LANGBALLIGAU Ldg. Lts. 177° (Front) Oc(2)
9 sec. 8M. Grey mast 6m. (Rear) Oc(2) 9 sec.
8M. Grey mast 10m.

NEUKIRCHEN 54°48.2'N 9°45.4'E Lt. Iso.
W.R.G.5 sec. W.14M. R.11M. R.5M. G.10M.
R.Building, W.Lantern 14m. W.125°-142°;
G.142°-193°; W.193°-197°; R.197°-210°;
W.210°-251°; R.251°-255°; R(unintens) 255°-
268°.

HOLNIS. SW OF POINT 53°51.7'N 9°34.5'E
Lt. F.W.R.G. W.13M. R.10M. G.9M. R.W.Tr.
and gallery 32m. R.053°-060°; W.060°-
066.5°; G.066.5°-091.5°; W.091.5°-189°;
R.189°-196°; W.196°-203°; R.203°-208°;
W(14M) 289.5°-297°; Also Lt. Fl.3 sec. 283°-
289.5° and Fl(4) 15 sec. 297°-302°.

SCHAUSENDE YACHT HARBOUR

¼M. SSW of Holnis Lt. Channel 2.3m. with
2.1-3m. at berths.

JACHTHAFEN Ldg. Lts. 121° (Front) F. 6M.
mast 4m. Intens on leading line (Rear) F.
6M. mast 6m. Intens on leading line.

SKODSBØL Ldg. Lts. 028° (Front) Iso. 2 sec. 7M. W.R.Tr. 11m. 008°-078° (Rear) 54°54.1'N 9°38.9'E Iso. 4 sec. 16M. R ◊ on W.Tr. 24m.

MARINA MINDE

NE side of Ruiknaes Bugt. Entrance depth 4m. with 3.5m. inside.

MOLE. OFF HEAD Lt. F.G. 4M. on floating breakwater 4m. Jetty head floodlit.

LÅGEMADE 54°54.1'N 9°36.9'E Ldg. Lts. 048° (Front) Iso. R.2 sec. 17M. 14M. W.R.Tr. 13m. 345°-052°. Intens 044°-052°. (Rear) Iso. R.4 sec. 17M. W.Tr. 26m. 041°-059°.

EGERNSUND. W SIDE OF ENTRANCE

Ldg. Lts. 335°30' (Front) F.R. W.Post 4m. (Rear) F.R. W.Post 6m.
BRIDGE. E SIDE. N SIDE OF CHANNEL Lt. F.G. 4M. 6m. 115°-295°.
S SIDE OF CHANNEL Lt. F.G. 4M. 6m. 295°-115°.
W SIDE. N SIDE OF CHANNEL Lt. F.R. 4M. 6m. 115°-295°.
S SIDE OF CHANNEL Lt. F.R. 4M. 6m. 295°-115°.
TOFT E Lt. Fl. R.3 sec. 2M. Dolphin 3m.

GRAASTEN. LANDING JETTY Ldg. Lts.

334° (Front) F.R. 3M. R ▵ on Tr. 5m. (Rear) F.R. 3M. R. ▽ on Tr. 8m. Ldg. Lts. 345°.

STEAMER PIER HEAD (Front) F.G. 3M G. ▵ on pile 5m. (Rear) F.G. 3M. G. ▽ on wooden pile 8m.

RINKENAES Ldg. Lts. 289°30' (Front) Iso. W.G.2 sec. W.7M. G.3M. W.R.Tr. 10 m. W.227°-312°; G.312°-004°. 54°53.6'N 9°33.8'E (Rear) Iso. 4 sec. 16M. R. ◊ on W.Tr. 30m. 281°-299°.

KOLLUND PIER 54°50'N 9°27'E

Owned by Customs Frontier Corps. Depth alongside 2.5m. Pile pier erected in summer for use of small craft on W side.

MURWIK N PIER. S END Lt. Oc. R.4 sec. 3M. W ◻ on grey mast 7m. Floodlit.
S PIER Lt. Oc. G.4 sec. 3M. W ▵ on grey mast on dolphin. 7m. Floodlit.

KIELSENG Ldg. Lts. 197° (Front) Oc. 4 sec. 7M. W.Mast 33m. Intens on leading line. (Rear) Oc. 4 sec. 7M. W.Mast 40m. Intens on leading line.

FLENSBURG HAFEN 54°48'N 9°26'E

The yacht harbour is inside Harniskai with depths of 6-8m.

54°48.3'N 9°26.1'E Ldg. Lts. 229° (Front) Iso. G.4 sec. 12M. W.Tr. 15m. H24. W.Lt. marks Jetty Head 560m. NNE. W.Lt. marks dolphin 350m. ENE. 54°48.3'N 9°26.1'E (Rear) Iso. G.4 sec. 13M. W.Tr. 19m. H24.

GERMANY

DIE SCHLEI

SCHLEIMÜNDE N MOLE HEAD 54°40.3'N
10°02.2'E
Lt. L. Fl(3) W.R.20 sec. W.14M. W.12M.
W.6M. R.10m. R.6M. W.B.Tr. 14m. Floodlit.
W(6M) 006°-100°; R(10M) 144.5°-201°;
W(14M) 201°-275°; W(12M) 275°-296°;
R(10M) 296°-006°. Storm signals. Fog Det.
Lt. 4 F. G. vert. Customs Lts. shown 1.7M
W.Horn Mo(SN) 30 sec.

Ldg. Lts. 107°30' (Front) Oc.4 sec. 9M.
W.Mast 6m. 040°-175°. (Rear) Oc.4 sec. 9M
W.Mast 8m. 040°-175°.

LOTSENINSEL 54°40.6'N 10°01.4'E Ldg. Lts.
093°42' (Front) Iso.4 sec. 11M. Δ on B.Mast
10m. Intens on leading line. 54°40.6'N
10°02.1'E (Rear) Iso.4 sec. 13M. ▽ on B.Mast
22m. Intens on leading line.

GRIMSNIS 54°40.6'N 9°56.6'E Ldg. Lts. 266°
(Front) Iso.4 sec. 11M. W.Mast 7m. Intens
on leading line. 54°40.6'N 9°56.1'E (Rear)
Iso.4 sec. 13M. W.Mast 16m. Intens on
leading line.

KAPPELN Ldg. Lts. 213° (Front) Oc.4 sec.
9M. W.Mast 8m. Intens on leading line.
(Rear) Oc.4 sec. 9M. W.Mast 11m. Intens on
leading line.

MAASHOLM W MOLE HEAD Lt. Q(2) R.5
sec. 3M. B. 4m.
E MOLE HEAD Lt. Fl. G.4sec. 3M. Bn. 4m.

OLPENITZ Ldg. Lts. 271°30' 54°39.3'N
10°01.9'E (Front) L. Fl. 8 sec. 13M W.Δ,
R.Border on grey mast 14m. Intens on
leading line. 54°39.4'N 10°01.8'E (Rear) L. Fl.
8 sec. 13M. W.▽, R.Border on grey mast
25m. Intens on leading line.
N MOLE HEAD Lt. F. G.3M. B.Mast 9m.
S MOLE HEAD Lt. F. R.3M. R.Mast 9m. Ldg.
Lts. 299°30' 54°39.8'N 10°01.9'E (Front) Iso.4
sec. 11M. W.Δ, R.Border, on grey mast 13m.
Intens on leading line. 54°39.8'N 10°01.9'E
(Rear) Iso.4 sec. 11M. W.▽, R.Border on grey
mast 20m. Intens on leading line.

DAMP YACHT HARBOUR

Numerous jetties for yachts. Depths 2.3-
3.7m.
N MOLE HEAD Lt. Fl. G.4 sec. 3M. W.
B.Mast on dolphin 8m. Platforms marked by
Mo(U) W.15 sec. and Fog sig. 2. 1M. ENE
and 1.9M. SE.

S MOLE HEAD Lt. Q(2) R.5 sec. 3M. W.
R.Mast on dolphin 8m.
Lt. Q. ⚓ on B. Y.Pile 6m.

ECKERNFÖRDE

54°27.6'N 9°50.6'E Dir. Lt. 242°15' Dir. Oc.
W.R.G.4 sec. W.12M. R.17M. G.17M. Grey
Tr. with two R.platforms 36m G.237°-242°;
W.242°-244.5°; R.244.5°-251°. Also Fl(2) 9
sec. 21M. 251°-268° and F.W.R. W.12M.
R.8M. W.180°-193°; R.193°-208°; W.208°-
237°.
HARBOUR ENTRANCE Lt. Oc. W.R.G.4 sec.
W.6M. R.4M. G.3M. R. W. Tr. 11m. W.195°-
251°; G.251°-293°; W.293°-315°; 315°-003°.
MOLE Lt. Fl. G.6 sec. 2M. Grey mast 8m.

KIELER FORDE

Tel: Pilots (0431) 30121. Deep Sea (0431)
362858. Telex: 299857 BWKI D.
Radio-Pilots: Kiel Lt. Tr. VHF Chan. 14, 16.
H24.
Radio-Pilots: Holtenau VHF Chan. 12, 16.
H24.
Olympia Hafen-Schilksee. Large yacht
harbour on W side with depths of 4m.
Wendtorf Marina near Stein. Channel has
depths of 2.8m.
Laboe Hafen. A yacht harbour close south
of town.

KIEL 54°20'N 10°10'E
Radio-Port: VHF Chan. 11, 16. H24.

KIEL REVIER
Radio-Port: VHF Chan. 22. H24.
Kiel with Holtenau is the port for Der Nord
Ostee Kanal.
Stickenhorn Mole 1¼M. WSW of
Frederichsort L. H. depths of 3-7m. H.Q. of
British Kiel Yacht Club which uses the 'T'
jetty. There is a yacht harbour 2c. ENE of
Atte Schleusen.
The Monkeberg Yacht Harbour is 1c. N of
Monkeberg jetty with depths of 5-8m. in the
entrance and 1-5m. within the harbour.
Wik Yacht Harbour is 1½c. S of Tirpitzmole
with depths of 3.3-4.5m.

KIEL 54°30.0'N 10°16.5'E Lt. Iso. W.R.G.6
sec. W.18M. R.15M. G.14M. W. round Tr. R.
gallery and base on caisson 29m. Floodlit.
R.071°-088°; W.088°-091.3°; G.091.3°-148.5°;
W.148.5°-220°; R.220°-246.5°; W.246.5°-295°;
R.295°-358°; W.358°-025.5°; G.025.5°-056°.
RC. Racon. Pilot Station. Fog. Det. Lt. Horn
Mo(KI) 30 sec.

BÜLK 54°27.3'N 10°12.0'E Lt. Fl. W.R.G.3 sec. W.14M. R.11M. G.10M. W. B. Tr. 2 galleries 29m. W.127°-146°; R146-213°; G.213°-228°; W.228°-235.5°; R.235.5°-238.5°; W.238.5°-262°; G.262°-043°.

STRANDER BUCHT. SCHILKSEE YACHT HARBOUR. MOLE ELBOW Lt. Oc. W.R.G.6 sec. W.8M. R.6M. G.5M. W. B.Mast 14m. G.170.5°-246°; W.246°-280.5°; R.280.5°-350.5°.

WENDTORF YACHT HARBOUR Ldg. Lts. 148° (Front) F. R.5M. Grey mast 8m. Fl. Y.5 sec. (occas) on tower 1.65M. NE. (Rear) F.R.5M. Grey mast 11m. No: 14 Lt. Fl. R4 sec. R.Pile with R.Ɖ

LABOE N MOLE HEAD Lt. Oc(4) W. R.15 sec. W.5M. R.6M. W. Tr. 7m. R.016°-070°; W.070°-162°; R.162°-200°.

JÄGERSBERG 54°23.6'N 10°12.5'E Ldg. Lt. 037° (Front) Oc.4 sec. 12M. W.Δ, R.Border on W.Mast, R.Lantern 15m. Intens on leading line **CROSS** Lt. Oc.W.R.4 sec.W.9M. R.7M. Same structure 14m. R.024°-032°; W.032-041°; W (unintens) 041°-134°; R.134°-149°; W.149°-179°. 54°23.8'N 10°12.7'E (Rear) Oc.4 sec. 12M. W. ▽ R.Border on W.Mast 25m. Intens on leading line.

FRIEDRICHSORT 54°23.5'N 10°11.7'E Lt. F.W.G. W.18M. W.9M. G.6M. G. Tr. on gallery and base 32m. Floodlit. W.(18M). 202°-209°; W.(9M). 224°-280°; G.280°-300°; W.(9M). 300°-032°; G.032°-090°. Also Fl(2) W.R.9 sec. W.17M. R.14M. W.209°-214°; R.214°-224°; Fl(3) W.G.12 sec. W.17M. G.13M. G.171.5°-188°; W.188°-195° and Oc.6 sec. 18M.195°-202°. Also shown by day when fog signal operating. Fog Det. Lt. Marina Breakwater, S. Head Lt. 1M. SW. F.R. on each of 3 radio masts 420m. 470m. and 530m. WNW. Horn Mo(F) 30 sec.

TIRPITZ HAFEN
Olympiahafen Dusternbrook is 1M.SSE of Tirpitz Hafen and consists of 3 basins for yachts. There are 2 yacht harbours between Bluchbrucke and Oslokai.

SCHEERMOLE HEAD Lt. Oc. G.4 sec. 3M. Mast 12m.

TIRPITZMOLE HEAD Lt. L. Fl(2) R.15 sec. 3M. R.Mast 11m. 144°-004°.

BLÜCHERBRÜCKE NE CORNER Lt. Oc(3) W.R.G.13 sec. W.5M. R.3M. G.3M. W.B. mast 15m. R.170°-200°; W.200°-259°; R.259°-303°; W.303°-308°; G.308°-001°; W.001°-027°; R.027°-049°. Storm signals.

HOLTENAU 54°22.6'N 10°08.7'E Lt. Aero Al. Fl. W.G.9 sec. W.12M. G.8M. Tr. 47m.

NORD-OSTSEE-KANAL

HOLTENAUER SCHLEUSEN N SIDE 54°22.2'N 10°09.4'E Lt. Oc(3) W.G.12 sec. W.11M. G.8M. R. Tr. 22m. G.217°-224°; W.224°-270°; G.270°-354°; G (unintens) 354°-012°; W (unintens) 012°-039°. 2 F.R. on chimneys 0.75M WSW. F. R. on church 340m. WNW. Lts. are shown in Nord-Ostsee Kanal.
S SIDE SCHEER HAFEN NORDMOLE Lt.Oc(2) W.R.9 sec. 9M.R W. Tr. grey lantern, masonry base 23m. R. (unintens 159°-192°; W.192°-214°; R.214°-288°; W.288°-302°; W. (unintens) 302°-003°.

HOLTENHAUER BRIDGE N SIDE Lt. 2 F. vert.
INNER SIDE Lt. 2 F. vert.

NEULAND 54°21.7'N 10°36.2'E Lt. Fl(4) W.R.30 sec. W.21M. R.18M. R. Tr. 40m. R.119°-128°; W.128°-229°; R.229°-255°; W.255°-299°; W (unintens) 299°-312°. RC.F.R. on chimney 1.5M. and on masts 0.6M. and 1.2M. WNW. Fl. Y. 5 sec. on Sig. Stn. 2. 3M. NW (occas).

FEHMARNBELT LANBY 54°35.9'N 11°09.0'E Oc.4 sec. 16M.R. conical structure on buoy 12m. Floodlit. RC. Racon. Emergency Lt. F.W.R.R. vert. 2 F.R. vert. shown if drifted off station. Horn Mo(FE) 30 sec. Horn Mo(D) 30 sec. sounded if drifted.

FEHMARN
54°31.7'N 11°03.5'E Lt. L. Fl. W.R.10 sec. W.18M. R.14M. Y. Tr. and dwelling, R.Lantern 16m. R.017°-054°; W.054°-200°; R.200°-231°; W.231°-254°; R.254°-260°.

PUTTGARDEN HAFEN 54°30'N 11°13'E
Radio-Port: VHF Chan.11, 16. H24.
Ldg. Lts. 205° (Front) Oc.W.R.G.4 sec. W.8M. R.6M. G.5M. W. R.Border on W. R.Mast 18m. G.146°-183°; W.183°-227°; R.227°-264°. (Rear) Oc.4 sec. 9M. W. ▽ R.Border, on W. R.Mast 29m.
W MOLE HEAD Lt. F. G.4M. B.Mast 7m.
E MOLE HEAD Lt. In fog F. R.4M. R.Mast 7m.

MARIENLEUCHTE 54°29.7'N 11°14.4'E
Lt. Fl(4) W. R.15 sec. W.22M. R.18M. R. W.
round Tr. with gallery 40m. R.118°-146°;
W.146°-173°; R.173°-223.3°; W.223.3°-333°.
R.C. Obstruction Lt. on mast 1.4M. W.

STABERHUK 54°24.4'N 11°18.8'E Lt. Oc(2)
W.G.16 sec. W.18M. G.14M. Y. Tr. R.Lantern
and dwellings 25m. W.175°-063.5°; G.063.5-
071.5°; W.071.5-090°.

Ldg. Lts. 305° **STRUKKAMPHUK** (Front)
Iso.W.R.3 sec. W.8M. W.3M. R.6M. W. round
Tr. 7m. W(8M) 292.5°-317.5°; W(3M) 317.5°-
037°; W(8M) 037°-157°; R(6M) 157°-177°.
54°26.6'N 11°01.1'E **FLÜGGE** (Rear) F.25M.
R.W. 8-sided Tr. R. Y. dwellings 37m. Intens
on leading line. Same structure Oc(4) 20
sec. 17M. 38m 245°-200°.

**FEHMARNSUND BRIDGE PIER VI N SIDE OF
PASSAGE** Lt. Oc. W.R.G.4 sec. W.8M. R.6M.
G.5M. Bridge pillar 23m. G.074.5°-086°;
W.086°-094°; R.094°-108°. Fog Det. Lt.
Racon. Horn Mo(F) 20 sec.

ORTH HAFEN
Small yacht harbour at Lemkenhafen in NE
corner of Orther Bucht through narrow
channel leading NE from Lemkenhafen Lt.
By.
Ldg. Lts. 348°30' (Front) F. R.6.M. B. Δ on
grey mast 6m. Intens on leading line. (Rear)
F.R.6M. B. ▽ on grey mast 11m. Intens on
leading line.

BURGSTAAKEN Ldg. Lts. 316° (Front) F.
R.7M. Grey Δ on grey mast 6m. Intens on
leading line. (Rear) F.R.7M. B. ▽ on B.Mast
13m. Intens on leading line.
PIER Ldg. Lts. 356°30' (Front) Iso. 8 sec. 9M.
R. Δ on mast 15m. (Rear) Iso.8 sec. 9M.. R. ▽
on mast 23m. Synchronised with front.
MOLE HEAD Lt. Oc(3) W.R.12 sec. W.8M.
R.5M. W.Mast, B.Platform 9m. R.252°-282°;
W. 282°-021°; R.021°-042°; W. 042°-186°.

HEILIGENHAFEN
Minor channel with depths of 3.3m. leading
W from No: 18 By. into yacht harbour
situated N of North Quay. Entrance floodlit.
Depths generally 2.3-4.3m.

S SIDE OF HEILI GREEDE 54°22.2'N
11°01.2'E Lt. Oc(2) W.R.G.9 sec. W.13M.
R.10M. G.9M. R. Tr. platform, W.Lantern,
R.W. dwelling 16m. G.100°-204°; W.204°-
212.2°; R.212.2°-250°. F.R. Lts. on Tr. 0.8M
SSW.

WARDER 54°22.6'N 10°59.1'E Ldg. Lts.
279°12' (Front) Iso. 3 sec. 17M. W Δ,
R.Border, on W.Mast 13m. 54°22'.6N
10°59.0'E. (Rear) Iso. 3 sec. 17M. W. ▽
R.Border, on W.Mast 18m. Schronised with
front.

DREDGED CHANNEL 54°22.4'N 10°59.6'E
Ldg. Lts. 268°30' (Front) Oc. 4 sec. 17M. W.
Δ, R.Border, on W.Mast 13m. 54°22.4'N-
10°59.5'E (Rear) Oc. 4 sec. 17M. W. ▽,
R.Border, on grey warehouse 19m.
Synchronised with front.

GROSSENBRODE
MOLE HEAD Lt. Oc. G.4 sec. 3M. B.Mast 9m.

DAHMESHÖVED 54°12.2'N 11°05.4'E Lt.
Fl(3) 12 sec. 23M. R.W.8-sided Tr. near Y.
building 33m. 176.3°-068-3°. Fog Det. Lt.

GRÖMITZ YACHT HARBOUR N MOLE HEAD
Lt. Oc. G.4 sec. 2NM. Post on dolphin 6m.

PELZERHAKEN 54°05.2'N 10°52.1'E Lt. Fl(2)
W.R.G.20 sec. W.14M. R.11M. G.9M. R. Tr.
W.Lantern and dwellings 21m. W.221°-
335°;R.335°-348°; W.348°-082°; G.082°-092°;
W.092°-101°. Obscured 242.5°-244° within
2M, partially obscured when bearing less
than 234°.

NEUSTADT 54°06'N 10°49'E
Tel: (0456) 16 12 36.
Radio-Port: VHF Chan. 11. Mon-Fri. 0900-
1200, 1300-1600.
A large yacht harbour situated 2c.S of
jetties in Neustadt Wiek. Buoyed channel
depth 2.7m. and 2.5m. alongside craft
jetties.

W SIDE OF HARBOUR 54°05.8'N 10°48.7'E
Ldg. Lts. 347°48' (Front) Oc.4 sec. 12M. W.
Δ, R.Border on mast 14m. Intens on leading
line. F. Y. Fog Det. Lt. on new mole head
190m. E. 54°05.8'N 10°48.7'E. (Rear) Oc. 4
sec. 12M. W. ▽, R.Border, on mast 19m.
Intens on leading line.

NEUSTADT-WIEK Ldg. Lts. 304° (Front)
Oc(3) 12 sec. 6M. W. Δ, R.Border on mast
11m. Intens on Ldg. line. Obstruction Lts. on
masts in this area. (Rear) Oc(3) 12 sec. 6M.
W. Δ, R.Border on mast 16m. Intens on Ldg.
line.

SEEBURG Ldg. Lts. 020°30' (Front) Iso.3 sec.
9M. W. Δ, R.Border on W.Mast on dolphin
13m. Intens on leading line. (Rear) Iso.3 sec.
9M. W. ▽, R.Border on W.Mast 16m. Intens
on leading line.

TRAVEMUNDE 53°57'N 10°51'E
Tel: Pilots (04502) 7117. Telex: 261419.
Radio-Port: VHF Chan. 16, 19. H24.
Radio-Pilots: VHF Chan. 16, 13. H24.

TRAVE REVIER: VHF Chan. 20. H24.

HERREN BRUCKE BRIDGE: VHF Chan. 13. H24.

LUBECK BRIDGE: VHF Chan. 18.

On N side of harbour between entrance and 3c. W are several jetties for yachts. Depths up to 10m.
Passethafen serves as a yacht harbour with depths of 4m.
There is a yacht harbour W of the Fishing Harbour at Siechenbucht.

TRAVEMÜNDE 53°57.8'N 10°53.0'E Lt. Fl. W.R.4 sec. W.19M. R.15M. Building 114m. R.165°-214°; W.214°-234°; R.234°-245°. RC.

N MOLE HEAD Lt. Oc.R.G.4 sec. R.6M. G.5M. W. B. Tr. 10m. Floodlit. R.123°-201°; G.201°-066°; Fog Det. Lt. Horn Mo(TD) 30 sec.

PRIWALL 53°57.5'N 10°53.2'E Ldg. Lts. 215°54' (Front) Oc(2) 9 sec. 17M. R. △ on W.R.Mast 14m. Intens on leading line. 53°57.3'N 10°53.0'E (Rear) Oc(2) 9 sec. 17M. R. ▽ on W. Tr. 24m. Intens on leading line.

DIE TRAVE
Bridge at Herrenbrucke clearance (closed) 22.75m. navigable width 56m.
Signals: 2 F.R.Hor. (and 2x3 long blasts in fog)=passage prohibited to ALL vessels.
Elbe-Lubeck Kanal connects Die Elbe/Die Trave. 7 locks (80mx12m). Depths 2.4m. to 3m. Bridges have clearance of 4.2m.

W SIDE Nos: 1-10 Lts. 10 F.Y.7M. W.Masts 12m.
E SIDE Nos: 1-17 Lts. 17 F.Y.7M. W. Trs. 12m.

The channel from Travemünde to Lübeck is marked by lights.

TARNEWITZ CENTRE MOLE ROOT Lt. Oc. W.R.3 sec. W.5M. R.3M. B.Mast with platform 7m.

HOHEN WIESCHENDORF 53°57.6'N 11°20.0'E Ldg. Lts. 180°18' (Front) Oc. 4 sec. 12M. B.W. Tr. W.Lantern 20m. 53°56.8'N 11°20.0'E (Rear) Oc. 4 sec. 13M. B. ▽ on B.W. Tr. 40m.

Ldg. Lts. 251°30' 53°56.9'N 11°20.9'E
JETTY (Front) Iso. 4 Sec. 12M. W. ▽ on B. Tr. 16m.
53°56.9'N 11°20.9'E (Rear) Iso. 4 sec. 12M. W. ▽ on B. Tr. 20m.

WOHLENBERG. PIER HEAD Lt. Oc. W.R.G.4 sec. W.6M. R.4M. G.3M. W.Mast 6m.

TIMMENDORF
There are 20 yacht moorings.

INSEL POEL. W POINT 53°59.6'N 11°22. 6'E Lt. F.W.R.G. W.16M. R.13M. G.11M. W.Round Tr. R.Top, W.Lantern, R.Cupola on grey dwelling 21m. R.049°-060° W.060°-069.5°; G.069.5-125.5°; W.125.5°-136.5°; R.136.5°-196°; G.196°-202.5°; W.202.5°-211.5°; R.211.5°-229°. Reserve Lt. range W14M. R.9M. G.9M. Pilots and warning signals. Horn 30 sec.

PILOT VESSEL HARBOUR Ldg. Lts. 055°24' (Front) Fl. 1.5 sec. when required by pilot vessel. (Rear) Fl. 1.5 sec. when required by pilot vessel.

WISMAR BUCHT

INSEL WALFISCH. Ldg. Lts. 123°54' (Rear) Oc(2). W.R.G.12 sec. W.9M. R.6M. G.5M. Grey Tr. with 2 galleries, W.Lantern, copper cupola 18m. G.056°-120°; W.120°-129°; R.129°-185°; W.185°-056°.

POEL (Common Front) F.6M. R.Pedestal on 8-sided concrete base, R.Lantern 6m. 53°57.9'N 11°24. 2'E Ldg. Lts. 339°30' (Rear) Q.13M. B. ○ on B. Tr. with 2 galleries 19m.

WENDORF Ldg. Lts. 159°30' (Front) Q. R.8M. B.Pedestal on 8-sided concrete base, B.Lantern 6m. (Rear) Q. R.8M. ◇ on B. Tr. 2 galleries 17m.

FLIEMSTORF Ldg. Lts. 330° (Front) Oc.3 sec. 10M. B.Pedestal on 8-sided concrete base, B.Lantern 6m. 53°56.3'N 11°24.8'E (Rear) Oc.3 sec. 13M. B. Tr. 2 galleries, 8-sided base 18m.

WISMAR 53°54'N 11°27'E
Tel: Port: 45300. Telex: 318882. H.M.: 45552. 2764. Telex: 318862. Pilots (Timmendorf): (00824) 95255.
Radio-Port: VHF Chan. 14, 12, 16. H24.
Radio-Pilots: VHF Chan. 12, 14, 16, H24.
Wismar-Wendorf yacht harbour with 20 visitors moorings is situated 1M.NNW.

Reporting System: Compulsory for all vessels over 17m. in length. Report to Traffic Control, VHF Chan. 14, 9, 12, 16 H24. on entering, leaving, manoeuvring. Information broadcasts Chan. 14 at 0630, 1930.
53°54. 0'N 11°27.1'E Ldg. Lts. 149°54' (Front) Oc. R.3 sec. 10M. B. △ on B. Tr. 2 galleries 27M. 53°53.7'N 11°27.4'E (Rear) Oc. R.3 sec. 10M. B. Tr. 46m.

W SIDE, DOLPHIN 63 Lt. L. Fl. G.8 sec. 5M. B.Pedestal on dolphin 5m.
W SIDE, DOLPHIN 65 Lt. L. Fl. G.4 sec. 6M. B.Pedestal on dolphin 5m.
E SIDE, DOLPHIN 56 Lt. Q. R.3M. R.Pedestal on dolphin 5m.

WERFT HAFEN. NE CORNER Lt. F. G.1M. B. Tr. 7m. F. R. on chimney 0.95M ESE. Lt. Oc. 2 sec. 2M. Dolphin.

KIRCHSEE FAHRWASSER
53°59.9'N 11°26.7'E No: 2 Ldg. Lts. 006°24' (Front) Oc(2) 10 sec. 10M. W. △ on R. Tr. 7m. 53°59.9'N 11°26.7'E (Rear) Oc(2) 10 sec. 10M. W. ▽ on R. Tr. 13m.

GOLWITZ
INSEL POEL. N SIDE 54°01.5'N 11°28.3'E Lt. Oc. W.R.G.5 sec. W.17M. R.13M. G.12M. R. Tr. on W.Building 13m. R.070°-084°; W.084°-087°; G.087°-097°; R.097°-126°.

GOLWITZ N Ldg. Lts. 165°06' (Front) Oc. 4 sec. 13M. W. △ on same structure 16m. 54°01'.0N 11°28'.5E Oc.4 sec. 13M. R. ▽ on R. Tr. 31m.

BUK 54°08.0'N 11°41.8'E Lt. L. Fl(4) W. R. 45 sec. W.24M. R.20M. R. W.Round Tr. brown cupola 95m. W.030°-040°; R.040°-073°; W.073°-265°. Shown 20/7-12/5.

MEASURED DISTANCE
MILE 3 54°08.5'N 11°43.3'E Lts. in line 180° (Front) Oc(3) 15 sec. 13M. R. △ on W. Tr. 54°07.8'N 11°43.3'E (Rear) Oc(3) 15 sec. 13M. R. ▽ on W. Tr.

MILE 2 54°08.0'N 11°45.0'E Lts. in line 180° (Front) Oc(2) 10 sec. 10M. R. △ on W. Tr. 54°07.6'N 11°45.0'E (Rear) Oc(2) 10 sec. 10M. R. ▽ on W. Tr.

MILE 1 54°08.4'N 11°46.7'E Lts. in line 180° (Front) Oc. 5 sec. 11M. R. △ on W. Tr. 54°08.0'N 11°46.7'E (Rear) Oc. 5 sec. 11M. R. ▽ on W. Tr.

STOLTERA 54°10.7'N 12°00.8'E Lt. F. 12M. R. ▽ on W. Tr. 30m. 108°-257°.

MARKGRAFENHEIDE Lt. Oc. 4 sec. 9M. W. Tr. 29m.

WARNEMUNDE HAFEN
Yacht moorings: 100.

W SIDE OF ENTRANCE 54°10.9'N 12°05.2'E Fl. (3+1) 24 sec. 20M. W. B.Round Tr. 2 galleries, copper cupola 34m. RC. F.R. on chimney 0.9M, 3.35M. and 4.55M. S. Upper gallery Lt. F. 120°-180°.

W MOLE HEAD Lt. F. G.5M. G. W.Conical Tr. and lantern, 2 galleries. Floodlit. 15m. W. reflector. Horn Mo (WN) 30 sec.

MIDDLE MOLE Lt. Iso. 4 sec. 8M. Y. 6-sided Tr. with platform. Floodlit. 15m.

MIDDLE MOLE HEAD 54°11.1'N 12°05.3'E Ldg. Lts. 175°48' (Front) Oc. 5 sec. 10M. Y. △ on R. W.Mast 10m.

ALTER STROM E SIDE 54°10.9'N 12°05.3'E (Rear) Oc. 5 sec. 13M. Y. ▽ on Y. Tr. 20m.

MIDDLE MOLE HEAD Lt. F. 4M. Dolphin 4m.

E FERRY BERTH. HEAD Lt. Oc. W. G.5 sec. W.5M. G.2M. B. Tr. 8m. Synchronised with Ldg. Lts. 175°48' (Front). G.071°-251°; W.251°-071°.

W FERRY BERTH Ldg. Lts. 168° (Front) Q.R. 6M. Grey mast 12m. For the use of ferries. (Rear) Q.R. 6M. Grey mast 14m.

E FERRY BERTH Ldg. Lts. 167°36' (Front). F.R. 3M. Centre of loading arch 14m. For the use of ferries (Rear) F. R.3M. R.Mast 19m.

OLD EAST MOLE. S END Lt. Fl(2+1) G.12 sec. 2M .G.R.Mast 7m. 340°-070°.

WARNEMUNDE SEEKANAL

WARNOW 54°10.5'N 12°06.0'E Ldg. Lts. 006°18' (Front) Oc(2) 9 sec. 10M. R. △ on R. Tr. 13m. 54°10'.6N 12°06'.0E (Rear) Oc(2) 9 sec. 10M. R. ▽ on R. Tr. 19m.

PETERSDORF 54°08.8'N 12°06.8'E Ldg. Lts. 161°30' (Front) Iso. R. 8 sec. 17M. W. △ B.Stripes, on B. Tr. 19m. 54°08'.2N 12°07.2'E (Rear) Iso. R.8 sec. 18M. B. Tr. 37m.

ENTRANCE E SIDE, NEW E MOLE HEAD Lt. F. R. 3M. R. W. Tr. 11m. 072°-252°. Q.(occas) on Pilot Station Building 550m SSE.

TOR 1. W SIDE Lt. Iso. 4 sec. 5M. G.Mast on dolphin.
TOR 2. E SIDE Lt. Iso. 4 sec. 5M. R.Mast on dolphin

TOR 3. **W SIDE** Lt. Iso. 4 sec. 5M. G.Mast on dolphin
TOR 4. **E SIDE** Lt. Iso. 4 sec. 5M. R.Mast on dolphin

NO: 5. **W SIDE** Lt. Oc. 4 sec. 5M. G.Mast on dolphin
NO: 6. **E SIDE** Lt. Oc. 4 sec. 5M. R.Mast on dolphin
NO: 7. **W SIDE** Lt. Oc. 4 sec. 5M. G.Mast on dolphin

ROSTOCK 54°09'N 12°08'E
Tel: H. M. 366 4255 (4256). Port Control 52446.
Agency 366 3950. Pilots (5001) 539/407.
Telex: H.M. Agency and Pilots: 31268 DD RCC ROS.
Radio-Port & Pilots: VHF Chan. 14, 12, 16. H24.
Reporting System: Compulsory all vessels over 30m. length. Report to Rostock Traffic Control Chan. 14, 9, 12, 22, 16. H24. on entering, leaving and manoeuvring.
Information B'casts. Chan. 14 at 0715, 1915.
Navigational advice Chan. 22.
Information for pleasure craft Chan. 14.
Yacht moorings: 20 at Rostock-Schmarl. 50 at Segelvereine in Rostock-Gehlsdorf.

UBERSEEHAFEN
PEEZ OIL HARBOUR 54°09.7'N 12°09.7'E
Ldg. Lts. 088°12' (Front) Iso. 4 sec. 10M. R. △ on Tr. 25m. 54°09.7'N 12°10.1'E. (Rear) Iso. 4 sec. 10M. R. ▽ on Tr. 35m.

W BASIN. NW CORNER Lt. F. G.2M. B.Mast 8m.
E MOLE HEAD Lt. F. R.3M. R.Mast 8m
PIER. N END Lt. F. R.9m. 105°-215° Occas.
S END Lt. F. R. 9m. 107°-217° Occas.

DIE-UNTER - WARNOW
W SIDE NO: 3 Lt. L. Fl. G.10 sec. 4M. G. platform on dolphin 6m.

E SIDE NO: 10 Lt. L. Fl(2) R.15 sec. 2M. R. platform on dolphin 7m. ⌇⌇

SCHMARL N. 54°08.4'N 12°05.2'E Ldg. Lts. 205°24' (Front) Oc. 3 sec. 10M. R. △ on B. W. Tr. 20m. 54°08.4'N 12°05.2'E. (Rear) Oc. 3 sec. 10M. R. ▽ on B. W. Tr. 16m.

W SIDE OF CHANNEL NO: 31 Lt. V. Q. (3) G.5 sec. 2M. G.Platform on dolphin 7m. ⌇⌇

E SIDE OF CHANNEL NO: 22 Lt. Q. R. 2M. R.Platform on dolphin 7m. F. R. on chimney 0.57M NW. ⌇⌇

MARIENEHE 54°06.6'N 12°05.3'E Ldg. Lts. 212°36' (Front) Q.10M. R. ◊ on W. Tr. on building 17m. 54°06.6'N 12°05.1E (Rear) Q.10M. R. ◊ on W. Tr. 26m.

OLDENDORF 54°07.5'N 12°06.2'E Ldg. Lts. 032°30' (Front) Fl. 4 sec. 10M. R. △ on R. Tr. 16m. 54°07.6'N 12°06.3'E (Rear) Fl. 4 sec. 10M. R. △ on R. Tr. 21m.

No: 28 Lt. L. Fl(2) R.15 sec. 2M. R.Platform on dolphin 7m.
No: 30 Lt. Q. R.8 M. R.Dolphin with platform 8m.

BRAMOW Dir. Lt. 216°30' Dir. Oc. W.R.G.2 sec. W.9M. R.5M. G.5M. W.Mast with platform. 12m. G.210.5°-214.5°; W.214.5°-218.5°; R.218.5°-222.5°.

No: 34 Lt. Fl. R.4 sec. 8M. R.Platform on dolphin 8m.
No: 43 Lt. L. Fl. G.10 sec. 4M. G.Dolphin 7m.
No: 49 Lt. L. Fl. G.10 sec. 4M. G.Dolphin 7m.

E SIDE OF CHANNEL No: 38 Lt. L. Fl(2) R.15 sec. 2M. R.Pedestal on dolphin 7m.
W SIDE OF CHANNEL No: 55 Lt. V. Q(9) G.10 sec. 2M. G.Dolphin 7m.
E SIDE OF CHANNEL No: 46 Lt. Fl(2) R.9 sec. 2M. R.Pedestal on dolphin 7m.

WUSTROW 54°20.2'N 12°22.6'E Lt. Oc(3) 12 sec. 16M. R.Square Tr. 2 W.Galleries and lantern, on NW corner of building 12m. F. R. on building 5.6M SSE. F. R. on radio mast 3.5M. NNE. Horn Mo(D)30 sec.

Yacht moorings: 25.

DARSSER ORT 54°28.4'N 12°30.2'E Lt. Fl(2+4) 22 sec. 20.M. R.Round Tr. brown cupola and dwelling 33m.

54°28.3'N 12°31.3'E Ldg. Lts. 256°12' (Front) Oc. 4 sec. 10M. R. △ on W. Tr. 9m. 54°28.2'N 12°31.1'E (Rear) Oc. 4 sec. 10M. R. ▽ on W. Tr. 13m.

Yacht moorings: 35.

S BREAKWATER HEAD Lt. F. R. 3M. R.W.Mast 5m.
Lt. F. G.Marks N Breakwater.
NE Lt. Fl. 4 sec. mast 8m. Tide gauge.

DENMARK

STORE-BAELT

ODDEN HAVN

Harbour can take vessels up to 30m x 3m.
draught. Small slip for craft up to 20 tons.
Yachts berth on S side of outer basin.

N MOLE HEAD Lt. Oc. W.R.G.5 sec. W.7M.
R.4M. G.4M. G.Tr. 10m. W.147°-270°; R.270°-
280°; G.280°-147°. Siren 30 sec. sounded
when vessels expected.

SJAELLANDS REV Lt. Fl.5 sec. 7M. R.Bn.
6m.

Refuge Tower on Yderrevet ½M. SSE of Lt.
with blankets, food and water. Flag for
distress signal.

SJAELLANDS REV N 56°06.1'N
11°12.2'E Lt. Iso. W.R.G.2 sec. W.22M.
R.17M. G.17M. W.R. Col. on round concrete
Tr. B.Base. Floodlit. 25m. G.025°-036°; W.-
039°; R.-062°; G.-074°; W.-077°; R.-105°; G.-
118°; R.-141°; G.-205°; W.-212°; R.-235°; G.-
256°; W.-283°; R.-317°; G.-350°; R.-025°. R.C.
Racon. Helicopter landing platform. Horn(2)
30 sec.

YDERFLAK Lt. Fl. W.R.G.3 sec. W.8M. R.5M.
G.5M. B.Tr. 10m. G.209°-231°; W.231°-259°;
R.259°-281.5°; W.281.5°-209°.

SJAELLANDS ODDE FERRY HARBOUR

Ldg. Lts. 007°48' (Front) Iso. 2 sec. 7M. Grey
Tr. 8m. 351.8°-023.8°. (Rear) Iso. 2 sec. 7M.
Grey Tr. 15m. 315.8°-023.8°.
W BREAKWATER HEAD Lt. Fl. R.3 sec. 3M.
Grey pedestal 4m.
E BREAKWATER HEAD Lt. Fl. G.3 sec. 3M.
Grey pedestal 4m.

SEJERØ

NW POINT 55°55.2'N 11°05.0'E Lt. Fl.(2) 15
sec. 17M. Y.Round Tr. 31m. Obsc. by land
when bearing 301°, 307°-311°, 316°-321°.

SEJERØ HAVN

W MOLE Lt. F.R. 4M. R.post 6m.
BREAKWATER HEAD Lt. F.G. 4M. G.Post 6m.
E HARBOUR. W MOLE HEAD Lt. F. Post 5m.

NEKSELØ Ldg. Lts. 175° (Front) Iso. 2 sec.
7M. W.R.Hut 18m. (Rear) Iso. 4 sec. 8M.
W.R.Hut 33m. 171°-179°.

HAVNSØ

There are 3 small craft jetties with depths of
2.2m. alongside.

N MOLE. E HEAD Lt. Oc. W.R.G.5 sec.
W.6M. R.4M. G.4M. G.Mast 6m. W.158°-
185°; R.185°-195°; G.195°-158°. Siren 30 sec.
sounded when vessels expected.

STARREKLINTE. MOLE HEAD Lt. Fl.3
sec. 2M. Post 4m.

JYDERUP 55°41.1'N 11°27.8'E Lt. Aero 4
Fl.1.5 sec. 12M. TV mast 331m. 301m. 204m.
136m.

RØSNAES

FISHING HARBOUR. N BREAKWATER HEAD
Lt. F.G. 2M. W.Post 5m. Siren 20 sec.

RØSNAES 55°44.6'N 10°52.2'E Lt. Fl.5
sec. 20M. W.Square Tr. 24m. Obsc. by land
from 260°-312° but may be seen between
hills when bearing 261° and from 308°-311°.
RC.

HATTERREV Lt. Fl. Y.3 sec. 5M. Y.Bn.
marked DW3 9m.

HATTER BARN Lt. Q.(4) Y.10 sec. 6M. Y.Bn.
marked DW6 9m.

RØSNAES PULLER Lt. Fl.(2) W.R.G.5 sec.
W.8M. R.5M. G.5M. R.Round Tr. on granite
base 13m. G.007°-019°; W.-030°; R.-054°; G.-
087°; W.-093°; R.-117°; G.-167°; W.-174°; R.-
286°; G.-352°; W.-358°; R.-007°.

ASNAES Lt. Fl.3 sec. 4M. W.R.pedestal 12m.

GISSELØRE. ON POINT Lt. Fl.3 sec. 7M.
W.Tr. 4m.

KALUNDBORG FJORD

55°39.9'N 11°04.8'E Lt. Oc. W.R.G.5 sec.
W.14M. R.10M. G.10M. Or.Tr. 13m. G.100°-
113.4°; W.113.4°-116.4°; R.116.4°-130°. H24.
Lt. Aero 3 Fl.2 sec. vert. chimney 224m.
55°39.7'N 11°05.0'E Lt. Fl.2 sec. 10M. grey
chimney 152m. Synchronised with Lt. Aero
3.

ASNAESVAERKET PIER. N Lt. Fl. G.3 sec.
2M. Bracket on pier 3m. H24. In fog 3 F. vert.
Siren 30 sec.

Ldg. Lts. 090°42' (Front) Iso. 2 sec. 3M. R. △
on W.Tr. 8m. Intens on leading line. H24.
(Rear) Iso. 4 sec. 3M. R. ▽ on W.Tr. 13m.
Intens on leading line. H24.

OIL PIER HEAD Lt. Fl. R.5 sec. 3M. Grey mast and platform 5m. H24.

KALUNDBORG 55°40'N 11°05'E
Tel: H.M. 53 51 01 88.
Pilots 53 51 02 00 & 53 51 05 97.
Radio-Port: VHF Chan. 16 0700-1600.
Radio-Pilots: VHF Chan. 16,6,12.
A channel close S of the W end of Vesthavn breakwater leads into a yacht harbour dredged to 2.5m.

N Ldg. Lts. 020°12' (Front) Iso. G.2 sec. 5M. R. Δ on Tr. 10m. H24. (Rear) Iso. G.4 sec. 5M. R. ▽ on Tr. 17m. H24.
S Ldg. Lts. 200°12' (Front) Iso. G.2 sec. 5M. R. Δ on mast on wall 15m. 130.2°-270.2°. H24. (Rear) Iso. G.4 sec. 5M. R. ▽ on oil tank 19m. 130.2°-270.2°. H24.
Dir. Lt. 200°12' Dir. Lt. Y. □ B.stripe. 198.2°-202.2°. Uses moiré pattern to indicate centre line.

VESTHAVN ENTRANCE. E SIDE Lt. F.G. 2M. mast 8m.
W MOLE HEAD Lt. F.R. 2M. pole 7m.

E HARBOUR. FERRY BERTH NW END Lt. Fl. G.3 sec. 3M. Hut on dolphin 6m.

ÅRHUS FERRY Ldg. Lts. 357° (Front) 2 F.R. hor. 1M. Ferry landing 8m. Occas. (Rear) F.R. 1M. Grey Tr. 12m. Occas.

W FERRY PIER Lt. F. Grey Tr.8m.
E PERRY PIER Lt. F. Grey Tr. 8m. In fog 3 F. Bell when ferries expected.

MULLERUP HAVN 55°30'N 11°11'E
Small harbour for vessels 38m. x 7m. x 3.4m. draught.

S MOLE HEAD Lt. Oc. W.R.G.5 sec. W.7M. R.4M. G.4M. W.mast 6m. G.025°-036.5°; W.-047.5°; R.-070.5°; G.-088.5°; W.-105°; R.104°-025°.
FISHING HARBOUR. S MOLE HEAD Lt. F.R.W. col. 4m. 202°-023°. Siren(2) 30 sec. when vessels expected.

ROMSØ TUE No: 24 Lt. Fl. W.R.G.3 sec. W.8M. R.6M. G.5M. G.Tr. 10m. G.051°-132°; W.-135°; R.-150°; G.-158°; W.169°; R.-300°; G.-325°; W.-332°; G.-051°. Racon.

KERTEMINDE HAVN 55°27'N 10°40'E
Yacht harbour has 7 piers with depths of 1.5-3m.

N MOLE HEAD Siren 20 sec. W.Square hut. Mole head floodlit.

MARINA BREAKWATER. OFF S END Lt. Fl. G.3 sec. 4M. dolphin 4m.
OFF N END Lt. Fl. R.3 sec. 4M. dolphin 4m.

Ldg. Lts. 253°24' (Front) Iso. R.2 sec. 4M. pillar 6m. 163.4°-343.4°. (Rear) Iso. R.4 sec. 4M. pillar 7m. 163.4°-343.4°.

MARINA Lt. F.G. 2M. Pole 3m.

SPROGØ HAVN. S MOLE HEAD Lt. Fl. R.3 sec. 4M. Grey mast 5m.

ØSTERRENDEN

SPROGØ NE W27 Lt. Fl.(2) R.G.10 sec. R.6M. G.5M. G.Tr. W.Lantern 10m. Floodlit. G.172°-001°; R.-009°; G.-090°; R.-172°.

HALSSKOV REV S S28 Lt. Fl. R.G.5 sec. R.6M. G.5M. Y.Tr. 10m. G.190°-313°; R.313°-190°. Racon.

ROUTE T

SPROGØ SE W29 Lt. Fl.(3) R.G.10 sec. R.6M. G.5M. G.Mast with platform 10m. G.195°-058°; R.058°-195°.

EGHOLM FLAK No: 30 Lt. Fl. R.G.3 sec. R.6M. G.5M. R.Mast with platform 10m. G.158°-345°; R.345°-158°.

VENGEANCEGRUND No: 31 Lt. Fl.(2) W.R.G.5 sec. W.8M. R.6M. G.5M. G.Mast with platform 10m. G.157°-305.5°; W.-309°; R.-314°; G.-355°; R.-157°.

AGERSO FLAK No: 34 Lt. Fl.(3) W.R.G.10 sec. W.8M. R.6M. G.5M. R.Mast with platform 10m. G.164°-050°; W.050°-060°; R.060°-164°. Racon.

HALSSKOV 55°20.3'N 11°06.0'E Lt. Oc. W.R.G.5 sec. W.14M. R.10M. G.10M. Tr. on W.Concrete base, B.Stripes 10m. W.037°-070°; R.-121°; G.-127°; W.-143°; R.-165°; W.-216.5°; G.-312°; R.-348°; G.-037°

HALSSKOV FERRY HARBOUR

Ldg. Lts. 043° (Front) F.G. 8M. Or. Δ on R.Tr. 8m. Shown by day in poor vis. 55°21.0'N 11°06.8'E (Rear) F.G. 10M. Or. ▽ on R.Tr. 25m. Shown by day in poor vis.

E MOLE HEAD Lt. Fl. G.3 sec. 5M. Grey Tr. 7m. Shown by day in poor vis.
W MOLE HEAD Lt. Fl. R.3 sec. 5M. Grey Tr. 7m.

FERRY BERTH MOLE HEAD Lt. Fl. G.5 sec. Grey post 6m.
FERRY HARBOUR E. Lt. F.R. 2M. Grey mast 6m. Shown by day in poor vis.
NW Lt. F.G. 2M. Grey mast 6m. Shown by day in poor vis.

KORSØR HAVN 55°20'N 11°08'E
Yacht harbour lies S of the Naval Base with depth of 2.9m. in entrance and 2.4-2.9m. alongside the piers.

NAVAL BASIN. MOLE HEAD Lt. Fl. G.5 sec. 3M. G.Mast

E FERRY BERTH. MOLE 55°20.2'N 11°08.2'E Ldg. Lts. 073°30' (Front) F.R. 11M. Or. ◬ on grey col. 8m. 068°-080°. Intens on leading line. H24. 55°20.2'N 11°08.4'E (Rear) F.R. 11M. Or. ▽ on grey col. 17m. 068°-080°. Intens on leading line. H24.

N MOLE HEAD Lt. Fl. R.3 sec. 4M. Tr. 5m. Fog. Lt. on mole.
DETACHED BREAKWATER N HEAD Lt. Fl. G.3 sec. 4M. Tr. 5m. Fog. Lt. on breakwater.
S HEAD Lt. F.R. 4M. Tr. on grey base 5m.
PLEASURE BOAT HARBOUR. N MOLE. S HEAD Lt. Oc. W.R.G.10 sec. W.4M. R.3M. G.2M. 5m. G.031.5°-061°; W.016°-110°; R.110°-031.5°. Shown 1/4-15/11.
S MOLE. N HEAD Lt. Fl. G.3 sec. 2M. G.mast 4m. Shown 1/4-15/11.

KNUDSHOVED 55°17.4'N 10°51.1'E Lt. Oc. W.R.G.10 sec. W.16M. R.11M. G.11M. W.Square Tr. 16m. W.155°-220°; G.-269°; W.-276°; R.-305.5°; G.-359°; W.-003.5°; R.-095°. Partly obsc. by houses from 072°-080°.

KNUDSHOVED FAERGEHAVN

55°17.8'N 10°50.8'E Ldg. Lts. 258° (Front) F.R. 10M. Or. ◬ on grey Tr. 8m. Shown by day in poor vis. A F.G. Lt. is shown close SSW and a F.R. Lt. close NW. 55°17.7'N 10°50.5'E (Rear) F.R. 10M. Or. ▽ on grey Tr. 25m. Shown by day in poor vis.

S MOLE HEAD Lt. Fl. R.3 sec. 5M. Grey Tr. on hut 7m. Shown by day in poor vis.
N MOLE HEAD Lt. Fl. G.3 sec. 5M. Grey Tr. 7m. Shown by day in poor vis.
FERRY PIER. NW Lt F.R. 2M. Grey mast 6m.
SSW Lt. F.G. 2M. Grey mast 6m.

NYBORG FJORD

Yachts must use special channel 3m. depth laid in summer leading W of Dynen and Avernakke Hage S Lts. into yacht harbour.

SLIPSHAVN Lt. Fl. G.3 sec. 7M. W.R. Tr. 10m. 259°-180°. Also in places 226°-251°.

LINDHOLM HAVN. Ldg. Lts. 059° (Front) Iso. R.2 sec. 4M. Or. ◬ on grey col. 8m. R. ◬ shown H24. (Rear) Iso. R.4 sec. 4M. Or. ▽ on grey Tr. 12m. R. ◬ shown H24.

NYBORG FJORD. Ldg. Lts. 310°30' (Front) Iso. 2 sec. 9M. W. ◯ on Bn. 4m. 216°-036° but obsc. in places. **JOMFRUHØJ** (Rear) Iso. 2 sec. 9M. W. ◯ on W.Bn. 13m. 216°-036° but obsc. in places.

HOLCKENHAVN. E. Lts. in line about 246° (Front) Iso. 2 sec. 6M. G.Pedestal on tripod 5m. 238.5°-253.5°. (Rear) Iso. 4 sec. 6M. G.Pedestal 6m. 238.5°-253.5°.

MARINA MOLE HEAD Ldg. Lts. 331°12' (Front) Oc. W.R.G.5 sec. W.9M. R.6M. G.6M. Or. ◬ on grey Tr. 6m. W.327.9°-334.7°; R.334.7°-338.2°; G.338.2°-327.9°. 55°18.4'N 10°47.4'E (Rear) Iso. 4 sec. 10M. Or. ▽ on grey mast 11m. 326.2°-336.2°.

S MOLE HEAD Lt. F.R. 4M. Grey post 5m.

DYNEN Lt. Fl. R.G.3 sec. R.6M. G.4M. dolphin 2m. For use of ferries. G.005.5°-152.5°; R.152.5°-005.5°.

AVERNAKKE HAGE S Lt. Fl. R.G.5 sec. 5M. dolphin 2m. For use of ferries. G.332.5°-152.5°; R.152.5°-332.5°.

VESTERHAVNS MOLE HEAD Lt. F.G. 1M. Grey mast 8m. Shows only to South.

NYBORG HAVN 55°18'N 10°47'E
Yacht harbour lies S of Fishing Harbour. Depth 3.5m. in entrance with 2.3-5m. alongside.

OUTER MOLE. E END Lt. F.R. 4M. Grey post 5m.

LUNDEBORG HAVN. MOLE HEAD Lt. F.G. W.Post 5m. Shown from sunset till midnight 1/8-31/3.

ELSEHOVED 55°06.1'N 10°46.6'E Lt. Oc. W.R.G.5 sec. W.12M. R.8M. G.8M. R.round Tr. 10m. G.188°-215°; W.215°-014°; R.014°-029°.

SVENDBORG SUND

Bratten. Yachts may berth on the W side of Nord Havn.
Svendborg. Yacht harbour lies ½M. NE Svendborg Sund Bridge consisting of yacht harbour and boat basin. Depths 3m.
Vindeby Marina. Depths of 2.5m. Current runs up to 4 kts. outside entrance.

ST. JORGENS. ON POINT 55°02.9'N 10°35.9'E Lt. Oc. W.R.G.5 sec. W.10M. R.7M. G.7M. W.R.Hut on wood piles 8m. G.053.5°-058.5°; W.058.5°-060.5°; R.060.5°-066°.

STRANDHUSE Lts. in line 322° (Front) F.R. 1M. ○ on W.Bn. 7m. Mark cable. (Rear) F.R.W. vert. 1M. ℅ on W.Bn. 10m.

KOGTVED. Lts. in line 328° (Front) F.R.W. ○ on Bn. Mark cable. (Rear) F.R.W. vert. W. ℅ on Bn.

TANKEFULD. Ldg. Lts. 269° (Front) F.R. 9M. W.R.Post 3m. (Rear) F.R. 9M. W.R.mast 5m.

VESTERRØN HAVN Lt. F.G. 3M. Grey mast 4m. Moleheads floodlit.

RANTZAUSMINDE. MARINA S MOLE HEAD Lt. F.R. 4M. post 5m.

BRATTEN W Ldg. Lts. 068°30' (Front) Iso. G.2 sec. 9M.W. △ on W.R.Mast 4m. (Rear) Iso. G.4 sec. 9M. W. ▽ on W.R.Mast 8m.

VINDEBYØRE 55°03.2'N 10°37.5'E Ldg. Lts. 061° (Front) Iso 2 sec. 13M. W.R.Post 4m. 55°03.3'N 10°37.6'E (Rear) Iso. 4 sec. 13M. W.R.Mast 10m.

BRIDGE PIER 11 Lt. 2 F.R. On NE and SE sides of bridge pier 3m.
PIER 12 Lt. 2 F.G. On NW and SW sides of bridge pier 3m.

BRATTEN E Ldg. Lts. 205° (Front) F.G. 9M. W. △ on W.R.Mast 9m. (Rear) F.G. 9M. W. ▽ on W.R.Mast 15m.

VINDEBY MARINA Lt. F.G. 4M. Grey Tr. 5M. Molehead floodlit.

SVENDBORG HAVN. GASVAERK Lt.
Oc. W.R.G.5 sec. W.6M. R.4M. G.4M. 8m. G.227°-232°; W.232°-237°; R.237°-252.5°; G.252.5°-289°.

FLOATING DOCK. S CORNER Lt. Q(6) + L. Fl.15 sec. 7M. 7m.
E POINT Lt. Fl. R.3 sec. 4M. post 6m.

KRISTIANSMINDE 55°03.6'N 10°38.2'E
½M. E of Svendborg Pier with depth 3m. for yachts.

55°03.6'N 10°38.5'E Ldg. Lts. 084° (Rear) F.13M R.W.Post 7m. 55°03.6'N 10°38.4'E (Common Front) F.W.R.G. W.12M. R.8M. G.8M. R.W.Post 4m. G.263°-082°; W.082°-090.5°; R.090.5°-175.5°. 55°03.6'N 10°38.3'E **N** Ldg. Lts. 346° (Rear) F.G. 10M. R.W.Post 7m.

SUDEMAE Ldg. Lts. 124°30' (Front) F.G. 8M. R.W.mast 5m. 121.5°-127.5°; (Rear) F.G. 8M. R.W.mast 8m. 121.5°-127.5°.

MÅRODDE 55°02.4'N 10°39.1'E Lt. F.W.R.G. 10M. W.R. col. 4m. G.000°-059°; R.059°-140°; G.140°-151°; W.151°-154°; R.154°-164°.

TROENSE 55°02.1'N 10°38.9'E Lt. F.W.R.G. W.10M. R8M. G.8M. W.R. col. 4m. G.118°-173°; W.173°-176°; R.176°-187°; G.187°-221°; R.221°-260°.

GRASTEN. W SIDE Ldg. Lts. 105° (Front) F.R.W.Mast 11m. (Rear) F.R.W.Mast 19m.

THURØ. W SIDE Ldg. Lts. 347° (Front) F.R.W. △ on W.Mast 4m. 335°-359°. (Rear) F.R.W. ▽ on W.Mast 7m. 335°-359°.

TAASINGE 55°01.7'N 10°39.5'E Ldg. Lts. 283°. (Front) Iso. R.2 sec. 11M. R. △ on R.W.Tr. 11m. 279°-287°. 55°01.7'N 10°39.3'E (Rear) Iso. R.4 sec. 11M. R. ▽ on R.W.Post 15m. 279°-287°.

OMØ

Yacht harbour lies on the E side of Omø Havn with depths of 2.5m.

N MOLE HEAD Lt. F.W.R.G. 4M. Grey col. 5m. W.146°-180°; R.180°-228°; G.228°-146°.

LANGELANDSØRE 55°09.6'N 11°08.1'E
Lt. Oc.(2) W.R.G.12 sec. W.18M. R.13M. G.13M. Y.Round Tr. 21m. G.266°-271°; W.-283°; R.-291°; G.-296°; W.-304.5°; R.-006°; G.-101°; W.-104°; R.-118°; G.-133°; W.-138.5°; R.-146°; G.-162°; W.-165.5°; R.-183°; G.-220°.

55°10.4'N 11°10.3'E Lts. in line 207°. F.R. 10M. W ○ on mast 5m. 177°-237°. Mark submarine cable to Agersø. (Rear) F.R.W. vert. 8M. W. ℅ on mast 14m. 177°-237°.

AGERSØ

Water level rises as much as 1.2m. in NE winds and lowers in SW winds.

N MOLE HEAD Lt. F.G. 2M. W. Col.
S MOLE HEAD Lt. Fl. R.3 sec. 3M. Metal mast 4m.
55°12.0'N 11°10.6'E Lt. Oc. W.R.G.5 sec. W.13M. R.9M. G.9M. W.Mast 11m. G.318°-328°; W.328°-332°; R.332°-032°; G.032°-060°.

AGERSØ SUND

SMÅLANDS FARVANDET. OIL TERMINAL
Lt. F.R. 4M. Mooring dolphin 5m.
Lt. F.R. 4M. Discharging platform 5m.
Lt. F.R. 4M. Mooring dolphin 5m.

LINDESKOV 55°16.2'N 11°14.6'E Ldg. Lts. 110° (Front) Iso. 2 sec. 20M. W.R.Tripod 7m. 107°-113°; H24. 55°16.1'N 11°15.0'E (Rear) Iso. 4 sec. 20M. W.R.Tr. 21m. 107°-113°.

GEDEHAVE W Ldg. Lts. 139°30' (Front) Iso. G.2 sec. 9M. W.R.Pedestal 6m. 136.5°-142.5°. H24. (Rear) Iso. G.4 sec. 9M. W.R.Tr. 16m. 136.5°-142.5°. H24.

HELLEHOLM 55°11.6'N 11°13.0'E Ldg. Lts. 173°30' (Front) Iso. 2 sec. 18M. W.R.Mast 7m. 170.5°-176.5°. H24. 55°11.2'N 11°13.0'E (Rear) Iso. 4 sec. 18M. W.R.Mast 17m. 170.5°-176.6° H24.

EGHOLM Ldg. Lts. 321° (Front) Iso. G.2 sec. 9M. W.R.Mast 5m. 318°-324°. H24. (Rear) Iso. G.4 sec. 9M. W.R.Tr. 17m. 318°-324°. H24.

AGERSO. **HELLEHOLM** 55°11.2'N 11°12.6'E Lt. Oc(3) W.R.G.15 sec. W.12M. R.8M. G.8M. W.Square Tr. 12m. R.170°-081°; G.-102°; W.-105°; R.-125°; Obsc. by Omø 036°-064°.

Lts. in line 260° (Front) F.R. 4M. ○ on mast 8m. Mark cable to Stignaes. (Rear) F.R.W. vert. 4M. ℅ on mast 14m.

STIGNAES

FERRY HARBOUR Ldg. Lts. 064° (Front) F.R. 5M. W.Post 4m. (Rear) F.R. 5M. W.Post 7m.

Lts. in line 080° (Front) F.R. 4M. ○ on mast 4m. Mark cable to Agersø. (Rear) F.R.W. vert. 4M. ℅ on mast 9m.

OIL PIER. S SIDE Lt. 2 F.R. hor. 1M. Grey masts 6m. N Lt. 335° -180°; S Lt. 270° -134° 20m. apart.
HEAD. CENTRE Lt. Oc. W.R.G.10 sec. W.4M. R.2M. G.2M. mast 12m. G.101.6° -108.3°; W.108.3° -115°; R.115° -121.6°. Occas.

SKAELSKØR FJORD

GEDEHAVE Ldg. Lts. 156° (Front) F.R. 4M. W. △ R.Stripes on mast 4m. (Rear) F.R. 4M. W. ▽ R.Stripes on mast 9m.

Lts. in line 033° (Front) F.R. 9M. W. ○ on mast 5m. 003° -063°. Mark cable to Stignaes. (Rear) F.R.W. vert. 10M. W. ℅ on mast 7m. 003° -063°.

LANGELAND

FRANKEKLINT Lt. Oc. R.G.5 sec. 7M. Gable of W.House 16m. G.039° -047°; R.047° -151°; G.151° -178°; R.178° -219°.

LOHALS HAVN 55° 08'N 10° 54'E Yacht harbour close S of ferry berth. Depth 2.5m.

S MOLE 55° 08.1'N 10° 54.2'E Lt. Iso. W.R.G.2 sec. W.12M. R.8M. G.8M. W.Square Tr. 8m. G.031° -095° ; W.095° -101°; R.101° -182°.
OUTER MOLE Lt. F.R. W.Post. Lt. F.G. 1M. B.Post 5m.

DAGELØKKE HAVN. S MOLE Ldg. Lts. 118° (Front) F.G. 4M. Grey mast 4m. Shown 15/8-14/4. (Rear) F.G. 4M. Gable of R.Warehouse 6m. Shown 15/8-14/4.

HOV 55° 08.8'N 10° 57.4'E Lt. Iso. W.R.G.4 sec. W.16M. R.12M. G.12M. R.W.Round Tr. 12m. R.210° -226.5°; G.-232.5°; W.-237°; R.-308.5°; G.-341°; W.-346°; R.010°.

SPODSBJAERG FERRY HARBOUR.
N MOLE HEAD Lt. Fl. G.3 sec. 2M. W.Tr. 5m.
S MOLE HEAD Siren 20 sec.
FISHING HARBOUR. S MOLE HEAD Lt. F.R. 4M. R.Post 5m. Shown when vessels expected.
LEE MOLE Lt. F.G. 4M. G.Post 5m.

Ldg. Lts. 286° 30' (Front) F.R. 4M. R. △ on grey Tr. 7m. Lead between mole heads. (Rear) F.R. 4M. R. ▽ on grey Tr. 9m.

ROUTE T

LANGELANDSBAELT. N DW40 Lt. Fl. R.G.3 sec. 5M. R.Mast, platform 10m. R.001.5°-180°; G.180° -001.5°.

BOSTRUP. E DW47 Lt. Fl. R.G.5 sec. 5M. G.Mast, platform 10m. R.009.5°-179°; G.179°-009.5°. Racon.

SPODSBJERG. SE Lt. Fl. W.R.G.3 sec. W.8M. R.5M. G.5M. Y.Mast with platform 10m. R.001.5°-217°; G.-231°; W.-235°; R.-240°; G.001.5°.

HØJBJERG. E DW55 Lt. Fl. R.G.5 sec. 5M. G.Mast, platform 10m. R. 002.5° -201°; G.201° -002.5°. Racon.

LANGELANDSBAELT. S DW54 Lt. Fl. R.G.3 sec. 5M. R.Mast, platform 10m. R.024.5°-181.5°; G.181.5°-024.5°. Racon.

RUDKØBING LØB

SIØ. **N** Ldg. Lts. 205° 24' (Front) Iso. 2 sec. 4M. R. △ W.Stripe on W.Mast 4m. (Rear) Iso. 4 sec. 4M. R. ▽ W.Stripe on grey Tr. 12m.
S Ldg. Lts. 032° 54' (Front) Iso. 2 sec. 6M. R. △ W.Stripe on grey mast 15m. (Rear) Iso. 4 sec. 6M. R. ▽ W.Stripe on grey Tr. 20m.

Lts. in line 119° (Front) F.R.W. ○ on post 8m. Mark cables. (Rear) F.R.W. vert. W ℅ on mast 10m.

Lts. in line 299° (Front) F.R. 1M. W ○ on mast 4m. (Rear) F.R.W. vert. 1M. W. ℅ on post 6m. 284° -314°.

NE. Ldg. Lts. 167° 36' (Front) Iso. G.2 sec. 4M. W. Δ Or.Border on mast 11m. (Rear) Iso. G.4 sec. 4M. W ▽ Or.Border on Tr. 17m.

N CHANNEL Lts. in line 139° (Front) F.R. W. ○ on Bn. Mark cable. (Rear) F.R.W. vert. W. ℅ on Bn.

RUDKOPING HAVN 54°56'N 10°43'E
Radio-Port & Pilots: VHF Chan. 16,9,12. Yacht harbour is close NE of fishing harbour. Depths 2.2m.

Ldg. Lts. 188°42' **N MOLE** (Front) F.R.R. Δ on grey mast 6m. **HARBOUR QUAY** (Rear) F.R. 4M. R. ▽ on Tr. 14m.

LANGELAND BRIDGE. PIER 11. N SIDE
Lt. Fl. G.3 sec. 4M. 3m. 123°-303°. Siren 30 sec.
S SIDE Lt. Fl. G.3 sec. 4M. 3m. 290°-110°. Synchronised with Pier 11. N Side.
PIER 12. N SIDE. Lt. Fl. R.3 sec. 4M. 3m. 110°-290° .
S SIDE Lt. Fl. R.3 sec. 4M. 3m. 303°-123°. Synchronised with Pier 12 N Side.
W. Ldg. Lts. 198° 12' S **MOLE HEAD** (Front) F.G. 4M. Grey Tr. 5m. (Rear) F.G. 4M. Roof of warehouse 6m.
N MOLE HEAD Lt. F.R. 4M. Grey Tr. 5m.
FISHING BASIN. W MOLE HEAD Lt. F.G. 4M. B.Post 4m.
MARINA. S MOLE HEAD Lt. Fl. G.3 sec. 2M. B.pile 3m. Shown 1/4-15/11.
OUTER MOLE. S END Lt. Fl. R.3 sec. 2M. W.Concrete pillar 1m. Shown 1/4-15/11.
S. Ldg. Lts. 053°42' (Front) F.R. 4M. R. Δ on grey mast 5m. (Rear) F.R. 4M. R. ▽ on Y.Silo 9m.

STRYNØ
PIER HEAD Lt. F.W.R.G. W.7M. R.4M. G.4M. Roof of R.Warehouse 5m. G.016°-246°; W.246°-355°; R.355°-016° H24.

Lts. in line 292° (Front) F.R. 8M. ○ on mast 6m. 274°-310° . Mark cable. (Rear) F.R.W. vert. 8M. ℅ on Tr. 10m. 274°-310°.

LANGELAND
KELDSNOR 54°43.9'N 10°43.4'E Lt. Fl(2) 20 sec. 25M. W.Square Tr. 39m. 200°-116° and in Marstal Bugt. Obsc. in places 098°-

135° when close to Langeland. F.R. on mast 1.2M. NNE shown during firing practice.
AUXILIARY Lt. Oc. W.R.G.5 sec. W.12M. R.9M. G.9M. Same structure 22m. G.218°-222°; W.222°-226°; R.226°-230°.

BAGENKOPHAVN. W SHELTER MOLE
HEAD Lt. Fl. G.3 sec. 4M. G.Tr. 6m. Siren 30 sec. Fishing.
INNER E MOLE Lt. Fl. R.3 sec. 4M. R.Tr. 6m.
INNER S MOLE HEAD Lt. Q. R. on pile.

Ldg. Lts. 102° 18' (Front) Iso. W.R.G.4 sec. W.8M. R.5M. G.5M. R. Δ on grey Tr. 10m. G.079°-099°; W.099°-106°; R.106°-126°. (Rear) Iso. 4 sec. 6M. R. ▽ on grey Tr. 13m. 077.3°-127.3°.

LOLLAND

TARS FERRY Ldg. Lts. 085° (Front) F.R. 8M. Or. Δ on grey mast 10m. (Rear) F.R. 8M. Or. ▽ on grey mast 14m.

PROTECTION MOLE Lt. Fl. R.3 sec. 3M. Grey pedestal.
S END Lt. Fl. G.3 sec. 3M. Grey pedestal 4m.

TÅRS FISH HARBOUR Ldg. Lts. 005° (Front) F.5M. R. Δ on post 4m. 275°-095°. (Rear) F. 5M. R ▽ on roof of building 5m. 275°-095°.

NAKSKOV FJORD

ALBUEN. NW PIER 54°50.2'N 10°57.8'E Lt. Iso. W.R.G.8 sec. W.11M. R.8M. G.8M. W.Round Tr. 11m. R.332.5°-053.5°; G.-108.5°; W.-163°; R.-283°.

ENCHØJE Ldg. Lts. 119°24' (Front) Iso. 2 sec. 8M. Or. Δ on Or.Tripod 16m. (Rear) Iso. 4 sec. 8M. Or. ▽ on Or.Tr. 22m.

S Ldg. Lts. 094°30' (Front) Iso. G.2 sec. 4M. R. Δ on pile 8m. (Rear) Iso. G.4 sec. 4M. R ▽ on Tr. 11m.
B. Lt. Fl.(2) R.5 sec. R.pile.

BOGO Ldg. Lts. 131°30' (Rear) F.G. 6M. Or. ▽ on Tr. 10m. Channel is marked by R.Lts. on the N side and G. Lts. on the S side. **RAMSØ** (Common Front) F.W.G. W.8M. G.6M. Or. Δ on concrete base 3m. W.259°-274°; G.274°-259°. **VESTEROODE** Ldg. Lts. 264° (Rear) F. 9M. Or. ▽ on Or.Tr. 10m.

ROSNAES Ldg Lts. 063°30' (Front) F.G. 5M. Or. Δ on grey mast 8m. 048.5°-078.5°. (Rear) F.G. 5M. Or. ▽ on Tr. 12m. 048.5°-078.5° .

NAKSKOV HAVN. FERRY BERTH Lt. Fl. R.3 sec. 1M. post 4m.

LANGØ Ldg. Lts. 176°30' (Front) F.R. 6M. Or. △ on R.Mast 8m. 161.5°-191.5°. (Rear) F.R. 6M Or. ▽ on Tr. 10m. 161.5°-191.5°.

LANGO HAVN Ldg. Lts. 169° (Front) F.G. Or. △ on post. 124° -214° . (Rear) F.G. Or. ▽ on post 124°-214°.

KARLY Lt. Fl. R.2 sec. 8M. Grey TV mast 174m. Obstruction. Same structure 3 F.R. vert. 2M. 155m. Obstruction.

KRANGENAES HAVN Ldg. Lts. 260° (Front) F.G. 5M. W. △ R.Bands on mast 4m. 150° - 340° . (Rear) F.G. 5M. W. ▽ R.Bands on grey Tr. 10m. 150° -340°.

Lts. in line 214° 30' (Front) F.R. 8M. ○ on mast 4m. 184.5°-244.5°. Mark cable to Fejo. (Rear) F.R.W. vert. 8M. ⸙ on mast 8m. 184.5°-244.5°.

ONSEVIG HAVN Ldg. Lts. 158° (Front) F.G. 4M. Wood mast 4m. **S MOLE** (Rear) F.G. 4M. Wooden mast 8m.

W MOLE HEAD Lt. F.R. 2M. mast 4m.

SMAALANDS FARVANDET

VEJRO NE POINT 55°02.4'N 11°22.2'E Lt. Oc. W.R.G.5 sec. W.16M. R.12M. G.12M. W.6-sided Tr. 19m. G.154°-194°; W.-215°; R.-240.5°; G.-270°; W.-278°; R.-287°; G.-304°; R.-320°; G.-079.5°; W.-089.5°; R.-106°; G.-143°; W.-146°; R.-154°; Obsc. by vegetation 330° - 063°.

SKALØ HAVN. W MOLE HEAD Lt. F. 2M. R.W.Tr. 3m.

VESTERBY HAVN Lt. F.R. 2M. Grey post 5m. 315°-135°.

FEJØ HAVN. W MOLE HEAD Ldg. Lts. 347° (Front) F.R. on warehouse. (Rear) F.R. on post.

DYBVIG HAVN E Lts. in line 227°30' (Front) F.R. 8M. ○ on mast 4m. 197.5° - 257.5°. Mark cable to Femø. (Rear) F.R.W. vert. 8M. ⸙ on mast 10m. 197.5° -257.5°.

FEMØ HAVEN. W MOLE Lt. F.R. Brown post 4m. 338°-146°.
ESE OF HARBOUR Ldg,. Lts. 098° (Front) F.Tripod 3m. (Rear) F.Tripod 6m.

ASKØ HAVN. E MOLE HEAD Lt. F.G. 4M. post 5m. Shown 1/8-1/5.
W MOLE HEAD Lt. F.R. 4M. post 5m. Shown 1/8-3/5.

BANDHOLM RENDE. Ldg. Lts. 313° (Front) Iso. 2 sec. 5M. W. △ on W.Mast 6m. 298°-328°. **LINDHOLM** (Rear) Iso. 4 sec. 5M. W. ▽ on W.Mast 15m. 298°-328°.

LOLLAND

BANDHOLM HAVN. N MOLE HEAD Lt. Fl. G.3 sec. 3M. B.Post 4m.
S MOLE HEAD Lt. Fl. R.3 sec. 3M. B.Post 4m.
E Ldg. Lts. 201° (Front) Iso. R.2 sec. 3M. △ on mast 8m. (Rear) Iso R.4 sec. 3M. Lantern on roof of castle 20m.

GULDBORG SUND

Lts. in line 245° (Front) F.R.W. ○ on Bn. Mark cable. (Rear) F.R.W. vert. W. ⸙ on Bn.

F.R. and F.G. mark E and W sides of Guldborg Bridge navigation channel. Traffic signals are shown.

LINDSTAAL Lts. in line 072°30' (Front) F.R. 8M. ○ on tripod 5m. 042.5°-102.5°. Mark cable. (Rear) F.R.W. vert. 8M. ⸙ on Tr. 10m. 042.5°-102.5°.

GRAENGE SKOVBY Lts. in line 219°30' (Front) F.R. 4M. Bn. 4m. Marks cable. (Rear) F.R.W. vert. 4M. Bn. 9m.

KING FREDERIK IX BRIDGE. E SIDE Lt. 2 F.R. 336°-156°. Traffic Signals.
W SIDE Lt. 2 F.G. 156°-336°. Siren 30 sec.

STORSTRØM

KARREBAESMINDE

NAESTVED (KARREBACK FJORD)
55°14'N 11°45'E
Tel: Port 53 72 00 56.
Pilots 53 72 73 66 & 53 74 23 97.
Radio-Port & Pilots: VHF Chan. 16,6,12.

Entrance to channel leading to Naestved on the River Susaa. Speed limit 6 kts. Yacht harbour lies SW of canal entrance with depths of 6m. Another yacht harbour lies ¼M. E of bridge with 3 jetties and depths of 2.5m.

Karresbaesminde Bridge: passage free ½h. before sunrise to ½h. after sunset (max. 0500-2100). A charge is made out of hours.

Width 23.3m. Clearance 2.5m. (bridge closed). Request for bridge opened = Flag N (½ mast) and 1 long 1 short blast or 1 W.Lt. at bow plus sound signal.

1 R.Lt. = passage prohibited.
2 R.Lt. = vessels from E passing.
3 R.Lt. = vessels from W passing.
Sound Signal = bridge cannot open.
Fl. Y.Lt. = yachts etc. to keep clear. Large vessel passing.

KARREBAESMINDE OUTER MOLE HEAD Lt. Oc. W.R.G.5 sec. W.6M. R4.M. G.4M. Grey Tr. 10m. G.326°-029°; W.029°-063°; R.063°-090°.
Lt. Fl. R.3 sec. 4M. Grey hut 4m.
S MOLE HEAD Lt. Fl. G.3 sec. 4M. Grey pedestal 4m.

F.R. and F.G. and Siren 30 sec. mark the navigational opening of Karrebaeksminde Bridge. Traffic signals.

MASNEDO W Ldg. Lts. 119° (Front) F.R. 8M. Grey mast 5m. (Rear) F.R. 8M. on building 16m.

MASNEDSUND Ldg. Lts. 113°30' (Front) F.G. 8M. On pier 3 of bridge 7m. (Rear) F.G.8M. Silo 22m.

Lights are shown from Masnedsund Bridge.

ORE. W OF VORDINBORG 55°00.4'N 11°52.3'E Lt. Iso W.R.G.4 sec. W.14M. R.10M. G.10M. W.R.Square Tr. 13m . G.050°-091°; W.091°-094°; R.094°-108°.

OREHOVED HAVN 54°57'N 11°51'E
Tel: H.M. 53 84 63 61. Port: 53 84 61 58 0900-1700 53 83 47 42 (O.O.H.) Fax: 53 84 64 47, Telex: 40104.
Radio-Port: VHF Chan. 16, 12, 13.
There are no facilities or berths for yachts.

Ldg. Lts. 272°30' (Front) Iso. R.2 sec. 2M. R. ∆ on post 7m. **PIER HEAD** 54°57.6'N 11°51.2'E (Rear) Iso W.R.G.4 sec. W.12M. R.8M. G.8M. W. Tr. 11m. G.110°-158°; W.158°-171°; R.171°-290°.

54°57'5N 11°50.9'E Lts. in line 211° (Front) F.R.10M. ○ on mast 10m. 161°-262°. Mark cable. 54°57.4'N 11°50.8'E (Rear) F.R.W.vert. 10M. ⅋ on mast 18m. 161°-261°.

MASNEDO 54° 59.3'N 11°52.9'E Lts. in line 031° (Front) F.R.10M. ○ on mast 11m. 341°-081°. Mark cable. 54°59.4'N 11°52.9'E (Rear) F.R.W. vert. 10M. ⅋ on mast 18m. 341°-081°.

STORSTRØM BRIDGE Lt. F.W.R.G.
Dolphin. The piers of the N and middle arch span are marked by F.R.G. Lts. 2 F.W. mark piers 900m. NE and SW.
PIER 22 Siren 30 sec.

MASNEDØ. E OF RAILWAY BRIDGE Ldg. Lts. 294°30' (Front) F.G. mast 2m. Not shown when channel blocked by ice. Traffic signals. Navigational opening of bridge is marked by Lts. (Rear) F.G. mast 8m.

ORINGE Ldg. Lts. 004° (Front) F.2M. mast 4m. 315°-045°. (Rear) F.2M. mast 9m. 315°-045°.

VORDINBORG ON QUAY Ldg. Lts.308° (Front) F.R.2M. Post 4m. 3 Fl.1.5 sec. on TV mast 3.7M NE. (Rear) F.R.2M. mast 8m.

VORDINGBORG TOWER Lt. F.R. 7M. Water Tr. 52m.

STEGE BUGT

STEGE HAVN N HARBOUR N MOLE HEAD Lt. F.R. W.Post 2m.
S MOLE HEAD Lt. F.G. W.Post 2m.

W SIDE OF HARBOUR Lt. Oc. W.R.G.5 sec. G.Square Tr. on warehouse 6m. G. 130°-138.5°; W.138.5°-145°; R. 145°-154°.

STOREBRO Lt. 2 F.R.2M. 1m. Marks E side of passage one each side. Iso. R.2 sec. indicates bridge open for passage. F.R. indicates passage may take place.
Lt. 2 F.G.2M. 1m. Marks W side of passage one each side.

NYORD HAVN. W MOLE Lt. F.R. 2M. B.Post 3m. Shown on dark nights when vessels expected.

LINDHOLM Lts. in line 281° (Front) F.R. 7M. W. ∆ on mast 3m. 251°-311°. Mark cable. F.R. and G. Lts. are shown for use of ferries (Rear) F.R.W. vert 10M. W. ⅋ on mast 11m. 251°-311°.

RØDSTENSNAKKE. Lts. in line 101° (Front) F.R. 9M. W. ○ on mast 4m. 071°-131°. Mark cable. (Rear) F.R.W. vert. 10M. W. ⅋ on mast 11m. 071°-131°.

KALEHAVE Lts. in line 331° (Front) F.R. ○ on mast. Mark cable to Koster. (Rear) F.R.W. vert. ⅋ on mast.
E MOLE HEAD Lt. F.G. 4M. mast 4m.
SW MOLE HEAD Lt. F.R. 4M. mast 4m.
W MOLE HEAD Lt. Fl. G.3 sec. 4M. mast 4m.

F.R. and F.G. Siren 30 sec on Ulvsund Bridge.

LYSTBÅDEHAVN MOLE HEAD Lt. Fl. G.5 sec. 3M. Galvanised steel pipe 3m. Lt. Fl. R.5 sec. 3M. Galavanised steel pipe 3m.
FERRY PIER Lt. 3.F.

SORTSØ GAB. FARO-FALSTER
BRIDGE. PILLAR 9 Lt. F.R.5M. R. □, W. border 4m. On upstream and down stream sides.
PILLAR 10 Lt. F.G.5M. G. △, in W. □ 4m. On upstream and downstream sides.
CENTRE SPAN Lt. F.7M. 30m. On upstream and down stream sides. Fog. Det. Lt. Horn (2) 30 sec. Sounded alternately.

FARO-SJAELLAND BRIDGE PILLAR
NO 5 SE SIDE Lt. F.R.4M. R. Ɖ, W.Border 4m.
N CHANNEL CENTRE SPAN Lt. F.6M. 24m.
PILLAR NO 6 NE SIDE Lt. F.G.4M. G. △, on W. Ɖ 4m.
SW SIDE Lt. F.R.4M. R. Ɖ, W.Border 4m.
S CHANNEL CENTRE SPAN Lt. F.6M. 24m.
PILLAR NO 7 NW SIDE Lt. F.G.4M. G. △, on W. Ɖ 4m.

GRONSUND

Lts. in line 086° (Front) F.R. 8M. R. ○, W.Border on mast 4m. 056°-116°. Mark cable to Falster. (Rear) F.R.W. vert 8M. R. ℅ on W.Border on mast 10m. 056°-116°.

BOGØ HAVN ENTRANCE CHANNEL W
SIDE Lt. Fl. R.3 sec. 2M. B.Post 2m. ⨱ Siren 30 sec.
E SIDE Lt. F.G.3M. B.Post. 2m. ⨱

Ldg. Lts. 353° (Front) F.G. Or. △ on mast 4m. (Rear) F.G.Or. ▽ on mast 7m.

STUBBEKØBING 54°53.5'N 12°01.6'E Lt. Iso. W.R.G.4 sec. W.14M. R.10M. G.10M. W. house, R. band 5m . G.147°-150°; W.150°-152°; R.152°-179°.

W MOLE HEAD Ldg. Lts. 176° (Front) F.G. post 3m. 086°-266°. Mark dredged channel. Shown when harbour is clear of ice. Siren 20 sec. Sounded 0700-2200 and when ships expected. (Rear) F.G. Grey Tr. 7m. 086°-266°.

THE SOUND
GILLELEJE HAVN
Yachts berth in the S basin situated in the NW corner of the inner harbour. Berths on the E side with depths generally of 2.5-3m.

W MOLE HEAD Lt. Fl. G.3 sec. Grey round Tr. 7m. Shown by day in poor vis. Siren 20 sec.
E MOLE HEAD Lt. Fl. R.3 sec. Grey square Tr. 7m. Shown by day in poor vis.
SPUR MOLE HEAD Lt. F.R.4M. post 4m.
N BASIN MOLE HEAD Lt. F.G.3M. Grey Tr. 7m. Shown by day in poor vis.
INNER N MOLE HEAD Lt. F.G. Grey tripod Tr. 8m. Shown by day in poor vis.

NAKKEHOVED 56°07.2'N 12°20.7'E Lt. Fl(3) 20 sec. 25M. W. square Tr. 54m. RC.

HORNBAEK HAVN

BREAKWATER HEAD Lt. F.l. G. 3 sec. 4M. G.Mast 7m.
E BREAKWATER HEAD Lt. F.l. R. 3 sec. 4M. R.Wooden mast 7m. Floodlit.
N MOLE HEAD Lt. F. G. 2M. G.Post 6m.

ELLEKILDE HAGE Lts. in line 231°18' (Front) F.R. 6M. R ○, W. border, on pylon 17m. 216.3°-246.3°. Marks cable area, S end. (Rear) F.R.W. vert. R.6M. W.7M.W.R. ℅ on pylon 30m. 216.3°-246.3°.

Lts. in line 231°18' (Front) F. R. 5M. R. ○, W. border, on pylon 14m. 216.3°-246.3°. Marks cable area. N end. (Rear) F.R.W. vert R.5M. W.6M. W.R. ℅ on pylon 29m. 216.3°-246.3°

JULEBAEK 56°03.7'N 12°34.4'E Lt. Oc. W.R.G.5 sec. W.15M. R.12M. G.12M. Or. lantern 8m. R.258°-278°; G.278°-288°; W.288°-290.5°; R.290.5°-303°.

HELSINGØR-MARIENLYST

Lts. in line 241°30' (Front) F.R.R. ○ on G. Tr. 24m. Mark N. cable. 186.5°-296-5°. (Rear) F.R.W. vert. W.7M. R.5M. R. ○ over W. ◊ on TV Tr. 38m.

Similar Bns. and Lts. mark end of N cable on Swedish shore.

Lts. in line 241°30' (Front) F.R.R. ○ on G. Tr. 23m. Mark cable. (Rear) F.R.W. vert. R. ○ over W. ◊ on G. Tr. 34m.

HELSINGOR 56°02'N 12°37'E
Tel: Port 49 21 05 15. Fax: 49 21 72 99. Pilots 31 38 67 00. Telex: 27515 SUNDET DK.
Radio-Port & Pilots: VHF Chan. 16, 12, 13. H24.
Yachts berth in the NW inner basin of the Nordhavn with depths of 3m. Yachts are prohibited in the Statshavn or commercial harbour.

GRØNNEHAVE Lts. in line 241° (Front) F.R.R. ○ on mast 10m. 186°-296°. Marks line of southern most cable. (Rear) F.R.W. vert. R. ○ over W. ◊ on mast 17m. 186°-296°.

LAPPESTENSBATTERI Lts. in line 229° (Front) F.R.R. ○ on grey Tr. 18m. Mark cable. (Rear) F.R.W. vert. R. ○ over W. ◊ on grey Tr. 34m .

Similar Bns. and Lts. mark the end of the cable on the Swedish shore.

Lts. in line 226°30' (Front) F.R.5M. R. ○ on grey Tr. 23m. Mark cable. (Rear) F.R. W. vert. 5M. R. ○ over W. ◊ on grey Tr. 32m.

NORDHAVN S MOLE HEAD Lt. Fl. R.3 sec. 3M. W. Tr. 4m.
N MOLE HEAD Lt. Fl. G.3 sec. 3M. W. Tr. 4m.
ELBOW Lt. Fl. 5 sec. 2M. Grey pillar 4m.
INNER Lt. Fl. R.5 sec. 3M. Grey pillar 3m.
BOAT PIER HEAD Lt. F.R. 3M. Galvanised pillar 2m.

INNER BOAT PIER HEAD Lt. F.G.3M. Galvanised pillar 2m.

KRONBORG 56°02.4'N 12°47.4'E Lt. Oc(2) W.R.G.6 sec. W.15M. R.12M. G.11M. NE Tr. of castle 34m. G.129°-137°; W.-145°; R.-161°; G.-214°; W.-311°; R.-349°; G.-352°; W.-356°; R.-017°; G.-027°. Obsc. by the SE Tr. of castle. Shows a faint W.Lt. between the R. and G. sectors. H24.

HELSINGØR HAVN
S PIER HEAD Lt. F.R.6M. R. round Tr. 7m. Obsc. when bearing less than 219°. Lt. F. marks end of pier. Horn 20 sec.
N MOLE HEAD Lt. F.G.6M. G. round Tr. 7m. Shown by day in poor vis. Lt. 2 F. mark end of pier.
FERRY BERTH Lt. F.R.3M. Mast 11m. For use of ferries. Lts. F.Y. F.R. or F.G. are shown at berth. Sodium fog Lts. shown from mole heads and DSB ferry berths.

Dir. Lt. 245° Dir. Lt. 1M. Uses moiré pattern to indicate centre line of berth. 243°-247°.

SNEKKERSTEN HAVN. S MOLE HEAD Lt. F.R.3M. post 4m.

ESPERGAERDE HAVN. S MOLE HEAD Lt. F.R.W.Lantern 3M. 172°-340°.

HUMIEBAEK HAVN. S MOLE HEAD Lt. F.R.2M. W. post 7m.

SLETTEN HAVN. S MOLE Lt. F.R.3M. Post 4m. 101°-349°.

NIVÅ HAVN. S MOLE Lt. F.R. R.Post 4m.

RUNSTED HAVN. S MOLE HEAD Lt. Oc. W.R.G.5 sec. W.8M. R.6M. G.6M. R.Mast 6m. R.050°-203°; G.203°-215°; W.215°-246°; R.246°-028°.

VEN

Swedish Island. Very popular resort and yachting centre.

Norreborgs Hamn on N side of island, depths of 2m.

Backviken on E side of Ven. Max draught 3m.

Kyrkbracken on W side of Ven. Largest of the 3 harbours. Entrance channel max. draught 2.3m. Depths inside generally 3m.

VEN 55°55.1'N 12°40.2'E Lt. L.Fl. W.R.G.10 sec. W.16M. R.13M. G.12M. W. R. Tr. 24m. G.000°-084°; W.-167°; R.-179°; G.-182°; W.-250°; R.-252°.

KYRKBACKEN MOLE HEAD 55°54.5'N 12°40'6E Lt. Iso W.R.G.4 sec. W.13M. R.10M. G.9M. W.Lantern on W. Base 7m. R.046°-075°; G.-093°; W.-103°; R.-132°; G.-157°; W.-323° but obscured by Ven about 158°- about 321°; G.-332°; W.-046°.

VENS SØDRA UDDE 55°53.5'N 12°42.8'E Lt. Oc(3) W.R.G.30 sec. W.16M. R.13M. G.12M. W. R. Tr. 35m. G. about 255°-266°; W.-287°; R.-332°; G.-347°; W.-003°; R.003°-about 065°.

BÄCKVIKEN. S BREAKWATER HEAD Lt. F.R.G.R.4M. G.3M. W. Tr. 3m. R.213°-356°; G.356°-213°.

HAKEN 55°54.6'N 12°43.7'E Lts. in line 245° (Front) Iso W.R.G.8 sec. W.16M. R.13M. R.17M. G.12M. W. Tr. R. dwellings 15m. R.136°-149°; G.-162°; W.-170.5°; R.-202°; R(unintens) -297°; R.-311°; G.-343°; W.-350.5°; R.-005°. Also shown by day 1/11-31/3. 55°54'6N 12°43'7E (Rear) F.R. 12M. Lantern on R. W. ◊, 22m. Vis. on leading line only. Mark power cable. The mainland end of cable is marked by Lts. at Rustningshamm.

VEDBAEK HAVN 55°51'N 12°34'E Depths 2.5m. A large basin accommodating 500 yachts. Entrance 20m. wide. Sea level lowered 0.6m. during SE and raised 0.9m. during NW gales.
N MOLE HEAD Lt. Fl. G.3 sec. 6M. G.Post 5m.
E MOLE HEAD Lt. Fl. R.3 sec. 6M. G.Post 5m.

There are numerous small harbous and marinas in this area:

SNEKKERSTEN HAVN 56°01'N 12°36'E
Depth 3m. Sea level drops 1m. during SE/S gales and rises 1m. Entrance 18m. wide, depth 2.8m.

ESPERGAEDE HAVN 56°00'N 12°34'E
Depth 2.4m. Entrance 15m. wide, depth 2.7m. marked by buoys.

HUMLEBAEK HAVN. 55°58'N 12°33'E
Depth 2.5m. Entrance 12m. wide, depth 2.5m. Sea level raised 1m. during S'ly gales, lowered 1m. during N'ly gales.

SLETTEN HAVN. 55°57'N 12°32'E
Depth 1.5m. Entrance 15m. wide. Sea level lowered 0.6m. during SE and raised during NW gales.

NIVÅ HAVN lies 7c SSW of Sletten Havn. Depth 2.5m. Harbour may only be used by day.

RUNGSTED HAVN 55°53'N 12°33'E
Yacht harbour with depths of 3m. in entrance, 2.5m. in N. basin and 2-2.5m. in S basin. Liable to silting. Anchoring prohibited throughout the harbour.

TARBAEK HAVN 55°47'N 12°36'E
Suitable for vessels up to 12m. x 3m. x 1.9m. draught. Entrance 15m. wide, 1.8m. depth. Sea level raises/lowers by 0.8m. during NW/SE winds.

S MOLE HEAD Lt. F.R. on mast 5m.

SKOVSHOVED HAVN
DETACHED BREAKWATER. N END Lt. Fl. R.3 sec. 2M. Grey post 5m.
S END Lt. Fl. G.3 sec. 2M. Grey post 5m.
N MOLE HEAD Lt. F.G.6M. Col. 6m.
S MOLE HEAD Lt. F.R.6M. Col. 6m.

HELLERUP YACHT HARBOUR 55°44'N 12°35'E
Only open 1st April-15th November. Depths 2.5m. Entrance channel marked by buoys. Entrance 15m. wide. Sea level lowered 1m. during S/SE and raised during N/NW gales.

E MOLE HEAD Lt. F.G. 4M. G. lantern 5m. 180°-090°. Shown 1/4-15/11.

GLADSAKSE 55°44.1'N 12°29.6'E Lt Aero 2 Fl. 2 sec. vert. 10M. TV mast 250m. 102m. apart.

TUBORG HAVN 55°44'N 12°35'E
Radio-Port: VHF. Chan. 16, 9, 12, 13. Commercial port owned by the Brewery.

55°43.6'N 12°35.1'E Ldg. Lts. 258° (Front) F.R. 10M. W. △ on Bn. 7m. 213°-303°. Extinguished when harbour cannot be entered.

55°43.6'N 12°34.9'E (Middle) F.R. 10M. W. ▽ on mast 13m. 213°-303°. Extinguished when harbour cannot be entered.

55°43.6'N 12°34.8'E (Rear) F.R. 10M. W. ◇ on gable of building 22m. 213°-303°. Extinguished when harbour cannot be entered. Fl.Lts. on mast 1.1M. WNW.

N MOLE HEAD Lt. Fl.3 sec. 4M. G. Tr. 5m. H24.
S MOLE HEAD Lt. Fl. R.3 sec. 4M. R. Tr. 5m. H24.

FLAKFORT
FORT. NW SIDE Lt. Fl(2) W.10 sec. 7M. Tripod 21m.

SALTHOLM BARAKKEBROEN Ldg. Lts. 116° (Front) Iso 2 sec. 4M. R. △ on mast 3m. Shown on arrival and departure of school boat. On request. (Rear) Iso 4 sec. 4M. R. ▽ on mast 5m.

MIDDLEGRUNDS FORT
WEST 55°43.3'N 12°39.9'E Lt. Oc. W.R.G.5 sec. W.15M. R.12M. G.12M. Or. block 11m. R.005°-069°; G.-128°; R.-173°; G.-184°; W.-193°; R.-225°. H24.

EAST 55°43.2'N 12°40'1E Lt. Oc(2) W.R.G.12 sec. W.15M. R.12M. G.12M. Or. block 11m. W.204.5°-245°; R.-290°; G.-334°; W.-350°; R.-056°. H24.

E MOLE HEAD Lt. F.G.2M. W.Mast 2m.
W MOLE HEAD Lt. F.R.2M. Post 2m.

Ldg. Lts. 000° (Front) F. 3M. W. △ 5m. When vessel expected. {(Rear) F. 3M. W. ▽ 6m.

KOBENHAVN 55°41'N 12°36'E
Tel: H.M. (Provestens Havn) 31 95 11 36.
Port: 33 14 43 40. Fax: 33 93 23 40. Telex: 15439 KHV DK. Pilots: 31 38 67 00. Telex: 27515 SUNDET DK.
Radio-Port: VHF Chan. 16, 9, 10, 12, 13, 14. H24.
Radio-Pilots: VHF Chan. 16, 8, 9, 10,12,13, 14. H24.
Knippelsbro Bridge Radio: VHF Chan. 16, 12, 13. H24.
Langebro Bridge Radio: VHF Chan. 16, 12, 13. H24.

A yacht marina is situated in the S. part of Kalkbraenderihavnen, depths of 4m. alongside the berths.

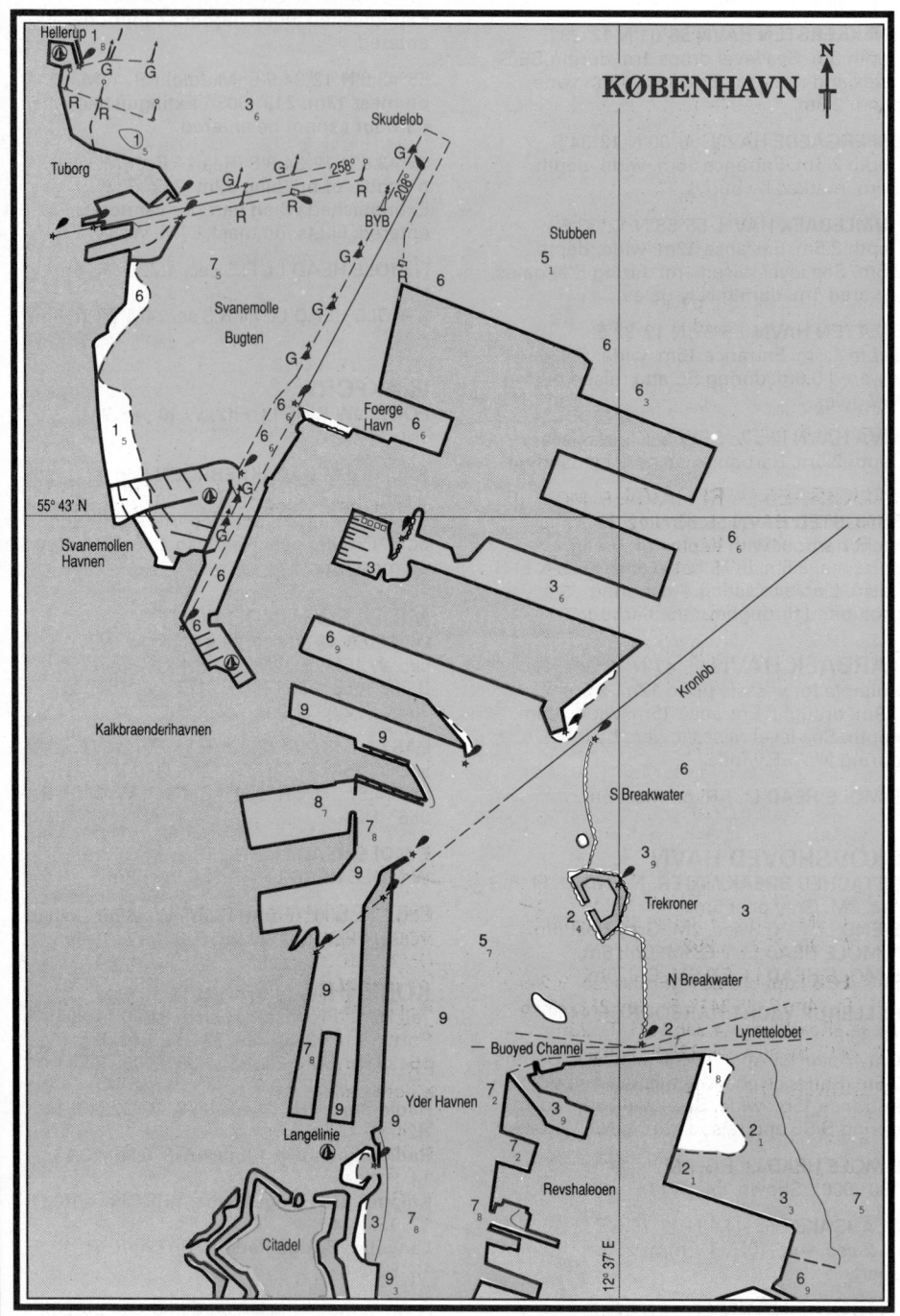

Knippelsbro and Langebro Bridges signals:
Flag N or 1 W. Lt. plus 1 long 1 short blast =
request to open.
1 R. Fl. Lt. = bridge closed.
2 R. Fl. Lt. = vessel from N expected.
2 R. F. Lt. = vessel from N may proceed.
3 R. Fl. Lt. = vessel from S expected.
3 R. F. Lt. = vessel from S may proceed.
2 R. F./3 R.F. Lt. = vessel from N and S
proceed
2 R. F./3 R. Fl. Lt. = vessel from N proceed.
Vessel from S. wait.
3 R. F./2 R.Fl. Lt. = vessel from S proceed.
Vessel from N. wait.

Clearance under Knippelsbro 5.4m.
Langebro 7m. Rail bridge (usually open)
1.5m.

Osthavenen (Amergervaeket)
Margaretheholmshavn. A large yacht
marina with marked channel and 8 piers.

KALKBRAENDERI HAVN. E. MOLE
55°43.2'N 12°35.8'E. Lts in line 208° (Front)
Iso. R.2 sec. 11M. R.W.Oval Tr. 5m. Intens
on leading line. 205.5°-210.5° .55°47.8'N
12°35.4'E. (Rear) Iso. R.4 sec. 11M. ▽ with
band on W.R. Tr. 12m. 205.5°-210.5°.

SVANEMOLLEHAVN. N MOLE HEAD Lt. Fl.
G.5 sec. 4 G. Tr. 5m.

TREKRONER. E SIDE OF BATTERY
55°42.2'N 12°37.0'E. Lt. Oc. W.RG.10 sec.
W.20M. R.16M. G.16M. W.Round Tr. 20m.
R.175°-195°; G.-207°; W.-210°; R.-214°; G.-
219.8°; W.-222.9°; R.-255°; G.-316.5°; W.-
320°; R.-336°.

SKUDELHAVN Lt. Iso. W.R.G.4 sec. W.7M.
R.5M. G.5M. Gable of house 6m. G.288.5°-
290°; W.290°-292°; R.292°-293.5°.

KRONLØB Ldg. Lts. 231° (Front) Iso. R.2 sec.
11M. Tr. 14m. 221°-241°. By day 2M. 226.5°-
235.5°. (Rear) Iso. R.4 sec.11M. Tr. 23m.
221°-241°. By day 2M. 226.5°-235.5°.

TREKRONER. BREAKWATER N END Lt. Fl.
R.3 sec. 7M. R.W.Round Tr. 7m. Shown by
day in poor vis. Racon. Horn 27 sec.

STUBBEN. BREAKWATER E END Lt. Fl. G.3
sec G.Round Tr. 7m. Shown by day in poor
vis.

LYNETTELBET. N BREAKWATER. S HEAD
Lt. Iso. W.R.G.4 sec. W.4M. R.2M. G.2M. G.
Tr. 6m. W.081°-089°; R.-094°; G.-263°; W.-
269.5°; R.-278°; G.-081°. Obsc. by buildings
287°-291°; 308°-318°.

KRONLØBSBASSIN. MOLE HEAD Lt. F.G.
6M. G.House 6m. The ferry berths 880m.
SW are marked by FR, FG and F.Lts. Bells
are sounded.

LYSTBÅDEHAVN Lt. F.G.G. pillar 3m. Shown
1/4-15/11.

BØMLØB. E SIDE. YDERHAVN. Lts. in line
194°48' (Front) Iso. R.2 sec. 2M. Pillar 6m.
178°-208°. (Rear) Iso. R.4 sec. 2M. Pillar 9m.
178°-208°.
R. and G. Lts. mark channel through
Knippelsbro and Langebro when bridges
are open.
E SIDE Lt. Fl. R.3 sec. Pillar 5m.Vis. over
harbour southward.

ENGHAVE BRYGGE Lt. Fl. G.3 sec. Mast on
dolphin 5m.

R. and G. Lts. mark channel when bridge is
open.

SLUSELØB Ldg. Lts. 203°30' (Front) Iso. R.2
sec. 4M. R. △, W.Stripes on mast 5m. (Rear)
Iso. R.4 sec. 4M. R. ▽, W.Bds on mast 11m.

FREDERIKSHOLMS LØB Ldg. Lts. 114°
(Front) Iso. 2 sec. 2M. R. △, W.Stripes 5m.
024°-204°. (Rear) Iso. 4 sec. 2M. R. ▽,
W.Stripes on mast 9m. 024°-204°.

TEGLVAERKSLOBETS Lt. F. W.R.G. W.7M.
R.5M. G.5M. on post 8m. G.034.3°-036.2°;
W.-036.2°-037.4°; R.037.4°-039.3°.
Ldg. Lts. 216°48' (Front) F.G.4M. warehouse
8m. 213.3°-220.3°. H.24. (Rear) F.G. 4M.
post on warehouse 11m. 213.3°-220.3°.

SYDHAVN. LOCK. N MOLE Lt. F.G. 2M. Post
3m. Occas.

PRØVESTENS HAVN. OIL JETTY.
ROOT. PRØVESTEN 55°41.0'N 12°38.3'E. Lt.
Oc(3) W.R.G.15 sec. W.13M. R.10M. G.10M.
W. Tr. R.W.Hut 10m. G.160°-168°; W.-171°;
R.-175°; G.-178.2°; W.-180.4°; R.-182.2°; G.-
203°.

F.R. and F.G. Lts. on posts in
Magretheholms Havn 0.6M. NW.

S HEAD Siren 45 sec.
N BREAKWATER. E HEAD Lt. Fl. G.3 sec.
5M. G. Tr. 6m.
S BREAKWATER. N HEAD Lt. Fl. R.3 sec.
5M. G. Tr. 6m.

OIL HARBOUR Ldg. Lts. 235° (Front) Iso.
R.2 sec. 2M. R. △ on R. Tr. 15m. 218°-258°.
(Rear) Iso. R.2 sec. 2M. R. ▽ on R. Tr. 20m.
218°-258°.

SUNDBY YACHT CLUB

Depths of 2m. Channel marked by buoys.

Ldg. Lts. 252° (Front) F.R.R. △ on W.Bn. 5m. (Rear) F.R.R. ▽ on W.Bn. 10m.

NORDRE RØSE. ON SHOAL 55°38.2'N
12°41.3'E. Lt. Oc(2) W.R.G.6 sec. W.18M. R.13M. G.13M. Round granite Tr. 14m. R.140°-157.5°; G.-176.5°; W.-181° over Hollaenderdybet, R.181°-339°; G.-351°; W.-352°; R.-358°; G.-030.5°. H.24. Horn Mo(A) 60 sec.

KASTRUP HAVN

Strand Park Marina situated 1/2 M. N of Kastrup. Channel marked by buoys. Depths 1.5m. to 3m. Vessels up to 15m. length.

STRAND PARK MARINA. S SHELTER MOLE HEAD Lt. Fl. R.3 sec. 4M. R.Pillar 4m. Floodlights show mole heads.
N SHELTER MOLE HEAD Lt. Fl. G.3 sec. 4M. G.Pillar 4m.
Ldg. Lts. 244°06' (Front) Iso. 2 sec. 5M. R. △ on Tr. 13m. 234.1°-254.1°. (Rear) Iso. 4 sec. 5M. R. ▽ on building 16m. 234.1°-254.1°.
N PIER HEAD Lt. F. G.2M. Grey post 3m.
S PIER HEAD Lt. F. R.2M. R.Post 3m.
YACHT HARBOUR. N PIER HEAD Lt. Fl. G.3 sec. 7M. Col. 3m.

AIRPORT. BÅDEHAVN. E MOLE HEAD Lt.
F.R. 2M. Grey post 3m.

REDNINGSHAVNEN Ldg. Lts. 220°38' (Front) Iso. G.2 sec. 7M. R. ▽, W. diagonal stripes, on mast 5m. 204.1°-237.1°. Shown when rescue vessels are at sea. (Rear) Iso. G.4 sec. 7M. R. ▽, W. diagonal stripes, on mast 7m. 204.1°-237.1°.
NE PIER HEAD Lt. Fl. G.3 sec. 2M. R.W.Pedestal 5m.

DRAGØR

Yacht harbour lies S of the Ferry Harbour. Enter between S end of long breakwater and a short breakwater extending NE from Dragor Fort. Sea level lowered 1m. in SE and raised 1.4m. in NE gales. Depths 4m. in outer harbour, 2.8m. in inner harbour.

FORT. SE CORNER 55°35.4'N 12°40.9'E Lt. Oc(2) W.R.G.12 sec. W.14M. R.10M. G.10M. Grey Bn. 6m. G.shore-194°; W.-199°; R.-201.5°; G.-280°; W.-309°; R.-336°; G.-shore. H.24.
S PIER HEAD Lt. F.R. 4M. Aluminium Tr. 7m. Also shown by day when fog signal operating. Horn 60 sec.
N PIER HEAD Lt. F.G 4M. Aluminium Tr. 6m.

Ldg. Lts. 253°30' (Front) Iso. R.2 sec. 3M. W. △ on post 4m. (Rear) Iso. R.2 sec. 3M. W. ▽ on mast 7m.

FERRY HARBOUR 55°35.6'N 12°40.9'E. Ldg. Lts. 228°30' (Front) Iso. 4 sec. 12M. Or. △ on aluminium Tr. 15m. 208.5°-248.5°. 55°35.6'N 12°40.8'E (Rear) Iso. 4 sec. 12M. Or. ▽ on aluminium Tr. 18m. Vis. 208.5°-248.5°.

N MOLE HEAD Lt. Fl. G.3 sec. 4M. Grey pedestal 4m.
E MOLE HEAD Lt. Fl. R.3 sec. 4M. Grey pedestal 4m.

YACHT HARBOUR. SHELTER MOLE HEAD Lt. F. R.3M. Grey col. concrete base 3m. Shown 1/4-15/11.

FERRY HARBOUR. E MOLE. S END Lt. F. G.3M. Grey col. concrete base 3m. Shown 1/4-15/11.

DROGDEN 55°32.2'N 12°42.8'E. Lt. Oc(3)
W.R.G.15 sec. W.18M. R.13M. G.13M. W.R.Square Tr. grey base 18m. R.009°-021°; G.-028.5°; W.-071°; R.-085°; G.-172°; W.-173°; R.-203°; G.-235.5°; R.-256.5°; G.-357.5°; W.-009°. H24. RC. Racon. Pilot station. Horn (3) 60 sec.

AVEDØREVAERKELS HAVN. W MOLE Lt. F. R.4M. Grey mast 9m.
E SECTOR Lt. Oc. W.R. G.10 sec. W.6M. R.5M. G.5M. Grey Tr. 37m. G.351.2°-355°; W.-357.5°; R.-001.2°. H24. By Day W.2M. R.1M. G.1M.
W SECTOR Lt. Oc. W.R.G.10 sec. W.6M. R.5M. G.5M. Grey Tr. 37m. G.348.7°-352.5°; W.-355°; R.-358.7°. H24. Synchronised with E Sector Lt. By Day: W.2M. R.1M. G.1M.

KALVEBOD

S Ldg. Lts. 012°24' (Front) Iso. 2 sec. 7M. R.W. △ on dolphin 4m. 282.4°-102.4°. (Rear) Iso. 4 sec. 7M. R.W. ▽ on W.Mast 8m. 282.4°-102.4°.

F.R. and F.G. Lts. on the bridge.

Lt. 2 Fl.2 sec. vert. 9M. Grey chimney 149m. H24.

BRØNDBYVESTER Lt. Q.G.

KØBENHAVN

FISKERHAVN Ldg. Lts. 316° (Front) F. R.1M. W. △ R. Bands on R.W.Pedestal 4m. 216°-056°. (Rear) F. R.1M. W. ▽ R.Bands on W.Mast 8m. 216°-056°.
N END Lt. F. W.R.G. 1M. post 3m. G.353°-006.5°; W.006.5°-009.5°; R.009.5°-023°. Shown 1/5-31/10 when vessels expected.

SLUSEHAVN. W MOLE HEAD Lt. F.G. G.Post 6m.
E MOLE HEAD Lt. F. R.4M. R.Mast 6m.
SJAELLANDSBRO. S MOLE Lt. Fl. R.3 sec. 2M. 3m.

F.R. and F.G. Lts. mark passage through bridge.

MOSEDE HAVN

Fishing and Yacht harbour off Mosede Klint. Channel marked by buoys. Entrance 20m. wide, depth 2.5m.
N MOLE HEAD Lt. Fl. G.3 sec. 1M. W.Pedestal 4m. Siren 30 sec. when vessels expected.
S MOLE HEAD Lt. Oc. W.R.G.10 sec. W.7M. R.4M. G.4M. W.Pedestal 4m. G.290°-306°; W.306°-316°; R.316°-290°.

KØGE HAVN

Køge Bugt Strandpark with marinas and recreational areas created between Hvidovre and position 2M. NW of Mosede Klint. About 1M. N of Køge there is a yacht harbour with depths of 3m
N PIER HEAD 55°27.3'N 12°11.9'E. Lt. Oc. W.R.G.10 sec. W.13M. R.9M. G.9M. G. Tr. 5m. Floodlit. G.234.5°-251.5°; W.251.5°-261.5; R.261.5°-270.3°.

Ldg. Lts. 248°42' (Front) F. G.5M. R. △ on pedestal 8m. (Rear) F. G.5M. R. △ on pedestal 11m.
S MOLE HEAD Lt. Fl. R.3 sec. 3M. R.Lantern 4m. H24. Siren (2) 30 sec.
TRANSVERSE MOLE HEAD Lt. Fl. R.5 sec. 2M. R.Hut 4M. H24.

NORDHAVN Ldg. Lts. 286°18' (Front) F. R.5M. R. △ on mast 10m. 276.3°-296.3°. (Rear) F. R.5M. R. ▽ on mast 15m. 276.3°-296.3°.
N MOLE HEAD Lt. Fl. G.5 sec. 3M. W.Lantern 4m. H24.
S MOLE HEAD Lt. Fl. R.5 sec. 3M. R.Lantern 4m. H24.

MARINA. S MOLE HEAD Lt. Fl. R.3 sec. 3M. R.Pedestal 5m. H24.
N MOLE HEAD Lt. Fl. G.3 sec. 2M. G.Pedestal 5m. H24.

BOGESKOV Ldg. Lts. 216° (Front) F. R.3M. R.W. △ 5m. (Rear) F.R.R.W. ▽ 2M.

STEVNS 55°17.5'N 12°27.5'E. Lt. . Fl. 25 sec. 26M. W.Round Tr. 64m. Obsc. by chimney when bearing 043°. RC.

STEVNS FIRING AREA 55°15.8'N 12°24.8'E. Lt. Al. Fl. W.R.4 sec. W.16M. R.13M. mast 31. When firing taking place. By day Q.10M.

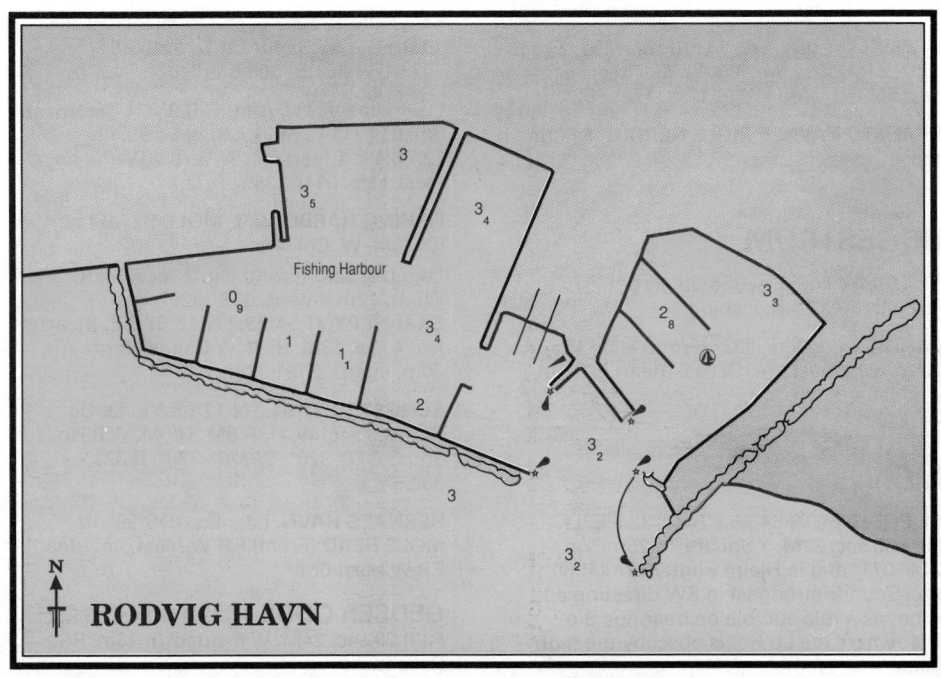

RODVIG HAVN

RØDVIG HAVN

Depth in entrance and S basin 1.7m. and 1.2-1.7m in N basin.
E MOLE HEAD Lt. Fl. G.3 sec. 3M. W.Pedestal 5m.
W MOLE HEAD Lt. Fl. R.3 sec. 3M. Grey conical concrete hut 5m. Siren 30 sec. Sounded as required.
CENTRE MOLE. SE END Lt. F. R.2M. Grey post 3m. Shown 15/8-15/5.
SW END Lt. F. G.2M. Grey post 3m. Shown 15/8-15/5.
SHELTER MOLE Lt. F. G.2 Grey post 3m.

FAKSE HAVN

Proceed through Industrihavn with depths of 4.2m. through narrow entrance into fish harbour 3m. and yacht harbour 2.5m. Sea level raised 1.5m in E'ly. and lowered in W'ly. gales. Speed limit 3 kts.
E PIER HEAD Lt. Fl. G.3 sec. 3M. G.Mast 8m. Siren (2) 60 sec. Sounded at night when vessels expected.

Ldg. Lts. 345°30' (Front) F. R.3M. R. △ on R.Bn. 10m. dg. Lts. obscured in Easterly sector by silos (Rear) F. R.3M. R. ▽ on R.Bn. 14m.

FEDDET 55°10.4'N 12°06.4'E. Ldg. ts. 251° (Front) Iso. 2 sec. 11M. W.Tr. 7m. Intens 246°-256°. (Rear) Iso. 4 sec. 11M. W. Tr. 13m. Intens 246°-256°.

RONEKLINT Ldg. Lts. 182° (Front) Iso. 2 sec. 7M. W.R.House 5m. 174°-190°. (Rear) Iso. 4 sec. 9M. Or. ◨ on W. Tr. 12m. 172°-192°.

PRAESTO HAVN. E MOLE HEAD Lt. F.R. on mast.

BØGESTRØM

STAVREBY Ldg. Lts. 356°30' (Front) F.R. Fishing. (Rear) F.R. Fishing.

SANDVIG Ldg. Lts. 233° (Front) F. R.1M. Grey △ on post 3m. Occas. (Rear) F. R.1M wooden hut 4m.

MØN

SE POINT. MON 54°56.8'N 12°32.5'E. Lt. Fl(4) 30 sec. 22M. Y.Square Tr. 25m. Vis. 214°-071° and in Hjelm Bugt. Horn (4) 60 sec. Sounds strongest in SW direction and is not as a rule audible on bearings S of 214° where the Lt. Ho. is obsc. by the high land.

NE POINT. HELLEHAVN NAKKE 55°00.5'N 12°31.4'E. Lt. Fl. W.R.G.5 sec. W.12M. R.8M. G.8M. R.W. Tr. 40m. G.140°-164°; W.164°-280°; R.280°-320°.

KLINTHOLM HAVN. N MOLE HEAD Lt. Fl. R.3 sec. 4M. on post 4m.
S MOLE HEAD Lt. Fl. G.3 sec. 4M. W.Pedestal 5m. Traffic signals 158m. 074°.
INNER MOLE HEAD Siren 30 sec. sounded when vessel expected.

BALTIC ENTRANCE

GRØNSUND

HESTEHOVED 54°50.1'N 12°10.0'E Lt. Oc(2) W.R.G.6 sec. W.13M. R.9M. G.9M. W.House 14m. R.216.5°-264°; G.-290°; W.-342°; R.-007°; G.-024°. RC.

HARBØLLE Ldg. Lts. 353°30' (Front). Iso. G.2 sec. 7M R. △, W.Bands, on grey Tr. 10m. Intens 347.5°-359.5°. (Rear) Iso. G.4 sec. 8M. R. ▽ W.Bands, on Tr. 21m. Intens 348.5°-358.5°.

54°53.4'N 12°08.2'E. Lt. Oc. W.R.G.10 sec. 10M. R. △ W.Bands on Tr. 6m. G.064°-101.5°; W.101.5°-106.5°; R.106.5°-117°.

Lts. in line 064° (Front) F. R.9M. ○ on mast 5m. 014°-114°. Mark cable. 54°53.4'N 12°08.4'E. (Rear) F.R. W.Vert. 10M. ⬡ on mast 11m. 014°-114°.

FISHING HARBOUR. E MOLE HEAD Lt. F. G.1M. W. Col. 4m.

Ldg. Lts. 324° (Front) Iso. 2 sec. 9M. R. △ on W. Tr. 12m. Intens. 319°-329°.
SKANSEPYNT 54°53.3'N 12°07.0'E. (Rear) Iso. 4 sec. 13M. R. ▽ W.Bands on grey Tr. 20m. Intens. 319°-329°.

BORGSTED 54°54.2'N 12°06.5'E. Lt. Oc. W.R.G.5 sec. W.11. R.8M. G.8M. W.R.House 3m. G.317°-320°; W.320°-323°; R.323°-332.5°.

HESNAES HAVN. Ldg. Lts. 018°30'. **W MOLE HEAD** (Front) F.R.W.Mast 5m. (Rear) F.R.W.Mast 6m.

GEDSER ODDE 54°33.9'N 11°57.9'E. Lt. Fl(3) 20 sec. 24M. W.6-sided Tr. 26m. RC. Racon.

RØDSAND RENDE

S END 54°32.8'N 11°56.2'E. Lt. Fl(3) R.10 sec. 10M. R.Pillar and lantern. 13m. Floodlit. Racon. Reserve light range 5M. Fog Det. Lt. Horn (3) 30 sec.
N END Lt. Fl. R.3sec. 8M. Grey post, round base 7m. ⌁

GEDSER HAVN

Ldg. Lts. 350°30' **E MOLE** (Front). Iso 2 sec. 7M. R. △ on W. Tr. 9m. Shows over Rødsand Rende. 344.5°-356.5°. (Rear) Iso. 4 sec. 7M. R. ▽ on Tr. 31m. 344.5°-356.5°. F.R. and F.G. (occas) Lts. are shown for use of ferries.
W MOLE HEAD Lt. F.R. Grey mast 7m. In fog F.Y.
E MOLE HEAD Lt. F.G. Hull 7m. In fog F.Y. Tidal stream signals. Bell. Sounded when ferries expected.

PLEASURE BOAT HARBOUR. N MOLE HEAD Lt. F. R.2M. Grey post 4m.
S MOLE HEAD Lt. F.G. 2M. Grey post 4m.

LOLLAND

NYSTED. SKANSEHAGE Lt. F.6M. Tripod 10m. Intens. 000°-005°.

RØDBY HAVN

Yachts berth on the N & E sides of Nordre Havn with depths of 5m. Ferries have priority over all vessels.

54°39.2'N 11°21.1'E. Ldg. Lts. 053°.
CENTRAL PIER HEAD (Front) Iso. R.2 sec. 10M. R. △ on R. Tr. 15m. Bell 1 sec. For use of ferries. 54°39.3'N 11°21.3'E (Rear) Iso. R.4 sec. 10M. W. ▽ on grey Tr. 25m.
W MOLE HEAD Lt. Fl. R.3 sec. 5M. R. Tr. 8m.
E MOLE HEAD Lt. Fl. G.3 sec. 5M. G. Tr. on hut 8m. Horn 20 sec.

SWEDEN

THE SOUND AND KATTEGAT

HALLANDS VÄDERÖ NW POINT
56°27.0'N 12°32.7'E Lt. Iso. 8 sec. 16M.
W.Round Tr.21m. Vis. about 335°-285°.

VINGASKÄR Lt. Fl(3) W.R.G.9 sec. W.6M.
R.4M. G.3M. W.Lantern 10m. G.164°-195°;
W.-218.5°; R.-286°; G.-348.5°; W.-046°; R.-
060.5°.

TOREKOV
The yacht harbour is NE of the pier with
depths of 1.5-3m. Entrance channel dredged
to 3m. and marked by buoys.

Ldg. Lts. 124°30' (Front) F.R.6M. W. Δ on
mast 8m. Vis. on leading line only. (Rear)
F.R.6M. W. ▽ on mast 10m. Vis. on leading
line only.

Lts. in line 088° (Front) F.G.4M. Cable Bn.
15m. Vis. on leading line only. Mark cable to
Vingaskär. (Rear) F.G.4M. Cable Bn. 25m.
Vis. on leading line only.

RAMSJÖ HAMN
RÖDA Ldg. Lts. 355° **ROMSIO** (Front)
F.R.2M. W. Δ on post 5m. Fishing. (Rear)
F.R.2M. W. ▽ on post 10m. Fishing.

GRÖNA Ldg. Lts. 326° (Front) F.G.2M. W. Δ
on post 5m. Fishing. (Rear) F.G.2M. W. ▽ on
post 11m. Fishing.

ÄNGELHOLM
BARKÅKRA 56°17.7'N 12°51.4'E Lt. Aero
Fl (7). 23M. on mast 56m.

SKÅLDERVIKEN Ldg. Lts. 099° (Front)
F.G.7M. on post 8m. Vis. on leading line
only. R. Lt. on mast 4M. S (Rear) F.G.7M. on
post 11m. Vis. on leading line only.

N PIER HEAD Lt. Fl. R.3 sec. 5M. on post
3m. Pierhead floodlit.
S PIER HEAD Lt. Fl(2) G.6 sec. 4M. on post
3m. Pierhead floodlit.

SVANSHALL Lt. F.W.R.G.W.7M. R.5M. G.4M.
W. Tr. 6m. R.129°-154°; G.154°-225°; W.225°-
270°; R.270°-300°. Fishing. Shown 15/7-15/5.

**ARILDSLÄGE. FISHING HARBOUR. OUTER
PIER HEAD** Lt. Iso. W.R.G.4 sec. W.9M.
R.6M. G.5M. W.Post 6m. G.shore –232°;
W.232°-250°; R.250°-shore. Fishing.

KULLEN. ON KULLABERG 56°18.1'N
12°27.4'E Lt. Fl. 5 sec. 27M. Grey Tr. and
Y.House 88m. Vis. about 332.5°-249.5°. Also
shown by day 1/11-31/3. RC. Horn (2) 60 sec.
200m. W.

VÄSTRA 56°18.2'N 12°27.4'E Lt. Oc(3)
W.G.20 sec. W.14M. G.10M. W.Lantern 12m.
G.335°-344°; W.344°-251.5°.

MÖLLE HAMN

OUTER MOLE HEAD 56°17.1'N 12°29.8'E Lt.
Fl. (2) W.R.G.6 sec. W.8M. R.5M. G.4M.
W.R.pedestal 6m. W.107°-116°; R.-180°; W.-
335°; R.-356°; G.-107°.

Ldg. Lts. 113° (Front) F.R.3M. Or. Δ on Col.
9m. (Rear) F.R.3M. Or. ▽ on Col. 10m.

NYHAMNSLÄGE Lt. Fl(3) W.R.G.9 sec.
W.8M. R.6M. G.5M. on post 6m. R.shore -
011°; G.-045.5°; W.-056°; R.-105°; G.-125°;
W.-137°; R.137°-shore.

HÖGANÄS
Facilities for yachts in the boat harbour E of
the loading pier in depths of 3m.

PIER HEAD Lt. Oc. W.R.G.6 sec. W.9M.
R.6M. G.5M. W.R. Tr. 12m. Floodlit. G.359°-
085.5°; W.085.5°-098°; R.098°-147.5°.

RÄNNA 56°11.8'N 12°33.5'E Ldg. Lts. 093°
(Front) Iso. 3 sec. 10M. R.W. Δ on pillar 16m.
56°11.8'N 12°33.6'E (Rear) Iso. 3 sec. 10M.
R.W. ▽ on pillar 21m.

LERBERGET. N PIER HEAD Lt. Fl. W.R.G.3
sec. W.6M R.4M. G.4M on post 3m.
G.shore-356°; R.-010°; G.-042°; W.-048°; R.-
065°; G.-108°; W.-113°; R.-143°; G.143°-
shore. Fishing. Shown 1/9-1/11 and at other
times when required. Traffic signals Horn
(4) 60 sec. Occas.

SVINBADAN 56°09.0'N 12°32.6'E Lt. Iso.
W.R.G.8 sec. W.17M. W.8M. R.17M. G.16M.
G.14M. B.Or. Tr. and lantern grey base. 24m.
Floodlit. G(14M)315°-329°; G(16M)-334°;
W(17M)-080°; R(17M)-095°; G(16M)-104°;
W(17M)-150°; R(17M)-157°; G(16M)-162°;
G(14M)-188°; W(8M)-315°. Helicopter
landing platform. Racon.

LJUNGBYHED 56°04'N 13°13'E Lt. Aero
Fl. 5 sec. 23M. on mast 80m.

VIKEN
3½ M.S of Hoganas, a yachting harbour and
resort. Depths 2m.

PIER HEAD 56°08.5'N 12°34.9'E Lt. Q.W.R.G.
W.10M. R.7M. G.6M. W.Lantern 8m.
G.shore-000°; W.000°-069°; R.069°-106°';
G.106°-121°.

KRISTINELUNDS Lts. in line 052° (Front) Iso.
R.6 sec. 7M. W. Δ, R.Border on pylon 19m.
Marks cable area N end. (Rear) Iso. R.6 sec.
7M. W. ▽ R.Border, on pylon 25m.

Lts, in line 052° (Front) Oc. R.5 sec. 7M. W.
Δ, R.Border on pylon 19m. Marks cable area
S end. (Rear) Oc. R.5 sec. 7M. W. ▽,
R.Border on pylon 29m. Lts. mark Danish
end.

DOMSTENS. OUTER BREAKWATER HEAD
Lt. F.R.4M. Lantern on wall 3m. Pier head
floodlit.

SOFIERO
N Lts. in line 046° (Front) Iso. R.4 sec. 7M.
W. ◊ on Bn. 22m. Vis. on leading line only.
Mark northern power cable. (Rear) Iso. R.4
sec. 7M. W. ◊ on Bn. 31m. Vis. on leading
line only.

S Lts. in line 050° (Front) Iso. G.4 sec. 6M.
W.Δ R.Border, on mast 15m. Vis. on leading
line only. Mark direction of southern power
cable. Similar Bns. and Lts. mark the end of
the cable on the Danish shore. (Rear) Iso.
G.4 sec. 6M. W. ▽, R.Border on mast 29m.
Vis. on leading line.

THE SOUND
PÅLSJÖ
N Lts. in line 061°30' (Front) Iso. G.4 sec.
6M. W. ◊ on mast 41m. Mark direction of
northern power cable. Vis. on leading line
only. (Rear) Iso. G.4 sec. 6M. W. ◊ on mast
49m. Vis. on leading line only.

S Lts. in line 061°30'. (Front) Iso. R.4 sec.
7M. W. Δ, R.Border on mast 26m. Mark
southern power cable. Vis. on leading line
only. (Rear) Iso. R.4 sec. 7M. W. ▽, R.Border
on mast 57m. Vis. on leading line only.

S Lts. in line 062° (Front) Iso. R.8 sec. 7M. ◊
on Bn. 8m. Vis. about 018°-about 108°. Mark
direction of southern telegraph cable. (Rear)
Iso. R.8 sec. 7M. ◊ Bn. 23m. Vis. about 018°-
about108°.

HELSINGBORG 56°03'N 12°41'E
Tel: Port (042) 10 63 22. Telex 722.15
HAMNEN S.
Pilots (042) 11 00 35.
Radio-Port: VHF Chan. 16, 11, 12.

Main yacht harbour is at Ra Hamn 3M. SSE
of the city centre.

Lts. in line 070° (Front) F.R. Marks outfall.
(Rear) F.R.

HELSINGBORG 56°02.6'N 12°41.4'E Lt.
Oc. W.R.G.15 sec. W.18M. R.15M. G.13M. Tr.
and R.House 17m. G.shore-000°; W.-011°;
R.-059°; G.-122°; W.-136.5°; R.-148.5°. Also
shown by day 1/11-31/3. Sig. Stn.

Lts. 3 F.R.vert. on radio mast 0.8M. NE.
V.Q. and F.R. on chimney 2.1M. SSE.

S ENTRANCE Ldg. Lts. 000°48' (Front) Q.
9M. R. Δ on post 11m. Vis. on leading line
only. Shown by day 1/11-31/3. (Rear) Q.9M.
R. ▽ on Tr. 16m. Vis. on leading line only.
Shown by day 1/11-31/3.

No: 5 Lt. F.R.3M. on post 6m. Horn Mo(K) 15
sec. 3 F.Y. hor. Lts. are shown for the use of
ferries close below the main Lt. Traffic Lts.
for the use of ferries. Also shown by day
1/11-31/3.
N ENTRANCE. N SIDE NO: 4 Lt. Q.R.8M.
W.Lantern 8m. In fog 3 F.vert. Horn (4) 60
sec.
S SIDE. DETACHED BREAKWATER. N END
No: 3 Lt. Q.G.7M. W.Lantern 8m.
S ENTRANCE. W SIDE. DETACHED
BREAKWATER S END No: 2 Lt. Iso. R.3 sec.
8M. W.Lantern 8m.
E SIDE No: 1 Lt. Iso. G.3 sec. 4M. W.Lantern
8m.

FERRY BERTHS. W BERTH Lt. 2 F.R.
Lt. F.R.
E BERTH Lt. 2 F.G.
Lt. F.G.

OUTFALLS Lts. in line 067° (Front) F.R.4M.
W. Δ, B.Bands, on lantern 9m. Mark the line
of the outfall pipe. R.Lts. on chimney 140m.
SW. (Rear) F.R.4M. W. ◊, B.Bands, on
lantern 13m.

VASTHAMNEN 56°-01.7'N 12°41.7'E
Ldg. Lts. about 003° (Front) Oc. R.4 sec.
12M. R. Δ, W.Stripe on Tr. 26m. 56°01.7'N
12°41.7'E (Rear) Oc. R.4 sec. 12M. R. Δ,
W.Stripe on Tr. 42m.

E BREAKWATER HEAD 56°01.6'N 12°14.8'E
Lt. Fl(3) G.10 sec. 10M. G.Tr. 15m.
Synchronised with W.Breakwater Lt.
W BREAKWATER HEAD 56°01.5'N 12°14.6'E
Lt. Fl(3) R.10 sec. 12M. R.Tr. 15m.
Synchronised with E Breakwater Lt.

SYDHAMN 56°01.6'N 12°42.1'E Ldg. Lts. 001°36' (Front) Iso. 3 sec. 12M. Or. Δ, R.Border on Tr. 22m. Vis. on leading line only. H24. F.R. on chimney 200m ENE. 56°01'.7N 12°42'.1E (Rear) Iso. 3 sec. 12M. Or. ▽, R.Border on Tr. 29m. Vis. on leading line only.

VÄSTRA. W BREAKWATER HEAD Lt. Q.R.8M. R.Tr. 12. ⌇⌇⌇ Also shown by day 1/11-31/3.
ÖSTRA. E BREAKWATER HEAD Lt. Q.G.6M. G.Tr. 12m. Also shown by day 1/11-31/3.

KOPPARVERKSHAMMEN. W ARM

HEAD Lt. Fl. R.3 sec. 6M. Metal Tr.W.Base. 5m. Floodlit. Also shown by day 1/11-31/3.
E ARM HEAD Lt. Fl. G.3 sec. 5M. G. □ on G.Tr.W.Base 7m. Floodlit. Also shown by day 1/11-31/3.

56°00.5'N 12°42.6'E Ldg. Lts. 349°30' (Front) Iso. 4 sec. 12M. Or. Δ, W.Border on W.B.Tr. 26m. Vis. on leading line only. Also shown by day 1/11-31/3. 56°00.6'N 12°42.6'E (Rear) Iso. 4 sec. 12M. Or. ▽, W.Border on warehouse 36m. Vis. on leading line only. Also shown by day 1/11-31/3.

Lts. in line 349°30' (Front) F.G.9M. G. Δ on building 23m. Mark E edge of channel. Also shown by day 1/11-31/3. (Rear) F.G.9M. G. ▽ on tank 28m. Also shown by day 1/11-31/3.

56°00.4'N 12°42.6'E Lts. in line 349°30' (Front) F.R.10M. R. Δ on Tr. 16m. Mark W edge of channel. Also shown by day 1/11-31/3. 56°00'.6N 12°42'.6E (Rear) F.R.10M. R. ▽ on warehouse 24m. Also shown by day 1/11-31/3.

Lts. in line 068° (Front) F.R.5M. W. Δ, R.Border 6m. Mark outfall pipe. (Rear) F.R.5M. W. ▽ R.Border 12m.

RÅÅ. PIER HEAD Lt. Q.W.R.G.W.9M. R.6M. G.5M. W.Lantern on Tr. 7m. G.shore-002°; W.002°-075°; R.075°-100°; G.100°-shore.
YACHT HARBOUR. BREAKWATER S HEAD Lt. F.R.6M. Post.4.
ÅLABODARNA. OUTER PIER HEAD Lt. Fl. W.R.G.1.5 sec. W.4M. R.2M. G.2M. W.Tr. 5m. R.129°-168°; W.168°-313°; G.313°-342°; W.342°-129°.

RUSTNINGSHAMN Lts. in line 065° (Front) F.R.8M. Lantern on R.W. ◊ 10 m. Vis. on leading line only. Mark power cable. (Rear) F.R.8M. Lantern on R.W. ◊ 25m. Vis. on leading line only.

BORSTAHUSEN. N PIER HEAD 55°53.7'N 12°48.2'E Lt. L. Fl. W.R.G.7.5 sec. W.10M. R.8M. G.6M. W.Pedestal 7m. R.356°-025.5°; G.-046°; W.-153°; R.-158°; R.-320°.

LANDSKRONA 55°52'N 12°50'E
Tel: Port (0418) 179 11.
Radio-Port: VHF Chan. 16, 12.

GRÄSRÄNNAN 55°51.7'N 12°48.0'E Lt. Oc. (2) W.R.G.7 sec. W.13M. R.10M. G.9M. W.Lantern, stone base 4m. G.105°-165°; W.-168°; R.-185°; G.-231°; G.shore-338°; W.-342°; R.-001.5°. Racon.

S Lts. in line 094° (Front) Oc. G.4 sec. 8M. W.Pedestal, G.Top, on dolphin 6m. Also shown by day 1/11-31/3. Mark S edge of channel. 55°52.0'N 12°49.6'E (Rear) Oc. G.4 sec. 10M. G. ◊ on mast 14m. 084°-104°. R.Lts. on radio mast 715m. SSE. Also shown by day 1/11-31/3.

55°51.9'N 12°49.4'E **GRÅEN** Ldg. Lts. 125° Oc. 4 sec. 13M. W. ▽, Or.Border on grey Col. 10m. 120°-130°. Also shown by day 1/11-31/3. 55°52.1'N 12°49.1'E (Common Front) Oc. W.R.G.4 sec. W.13M. R.10M. G.9m. W. Δ, Or.Border, on W. Hut, R.Top, on dolphin 6m. G.098°-120°; R.120°-130°; R.130°-098°. Also shown by day 1/11-31/3. 55°52.0'N 12°49.6'E N.Lts. in line 094° (Rear) Oc. R.4 sec. 10M. R. ◊ on building 14m. 084°-104°. Mark N edge of channel. Also shown by day 1/11-31/3.

LUNDÅKRAKAJEN Lts. in line 022° (Front) F.R. Occas. (Rear) F.R. Occas.

PINHATTAN 55°45.3'N 12°52.1'E Lt. L. Fl. W.R.G.8 sec. W.14M. R.11M. G.10M. Or. Tr. B.Top, W.Lantern 12m. Floodlit. G.000°-078°; W.-083°; R.-096.5°; G.-131°; W.-140.5°; R.-176°; G.-245°; R.-314°; G.-335.5°; W.-338°; R.-000°. Also shown by day 1/11-31/3. Racon.

BARSEBÄCKSHAMN 55°45'N 12°54'E
Entrance 40m. wide, depth 3.4m. Inner basin has yacht berths depth 2m. Outer basin has several pontoons for yachts, depths 2.7-3m.

Ldg. Lts. 088° **N MOLE HEAD** (Front) Iso. R.G.4 sec. R.6M. G.5M. W.B.Pedestal 5m. G.031.5°-070°; R.070°-031.5°. **ROOT** (Rear) F.R.4M. W. ▽ on Tr. 10m. Vis. on leading line only.

BARSEBÄCKSVERKET Ldg. Lts. 334° (Front) F.R.9M. Or. Δ on mast 6m. (Rear) F.R.9M. Or. ▽ on mast 12m.

VIKHÖGS Lt. F.W.R.G.W.7M. R.5M. G.4M. W.Lantern 4m. G.shore-002.5°; W.002.5°-060.5°; R.060.5°-shore. Fishing.

LOMMA. N PIER HEAD Lt. Fl. W.R.G.3 sec. W.6M. R.4M. G.3M. W.Lantern on R.Mast 8m. G.shore-050°; W.050°-095°; R.095°-119°; G.119°-shore.

OSKARSGRUNDET SYDVÄSTRE 55°34.6'N 12°49.0'E Lt. Oc. W.R.G.9 sec. W.16M. R.13M. G.12M. W.R.Tr. grey base. 11m. Floodlit. G.031°-049.5°; W.-054°; R.-066°; G.-088°; W.-094°; R.-144°; G.-192°; W.-235.5°; R.-237°; G.-251°; W.-256°; R.-280°; G.-346°; W.-349°; R.-031°. Also shown by day 1/11-31/3. Racon. In line 049°24' with Oskarsgrundet Nordöstra Lt. and Kalkgrundet Lt. Marks SE limit of Flintrannen. Horn 15 sec.

FLINTEN SYDVÄSTRE 55°35.2'N 12°50.0'E Lt. Iso. G.3 sec. 12M. W.G.Tr. on grey base 12m. Shown by day 1/11-31/3.

OSKARGRUNDET NORDÖSTRA

55°35.8'N 12°51.5'E Lt. Oc(2) W.R.G.9 sec. W.16M. R.13M. G.12M. W.Lantern and on R.Tr. grey base. 14m. Floodlit. W.049.5°-052.5°; R.-115°; W.-301°; R.-310°; G.-049.5°. Shown by day 1/11-31/3. Horn (2) 30 sec.

KALKGRUNDET 55°37.0'N 12°53.9'E Lt.

Oc. W.R.G.9 sec. W.16M. R.13M. G.12M. W.R.Tr. grey base 10m. Floodlit. W.049.5°-110°; R.-146°; G.-214.5°; W.-278.5°; R.-340°; G.-049.5°. Shown by day 1/11-31/3. Racon. Horn Mo(K) 60 sec.

MALMÖ 55°37'N 13°00'E

Tel: Port Authority (040) 34 44 00. Fax: (040) 11 11 74.
Port Control (040) 34 40 89 & 12 88 64.
Telex: 33275 MPORT S.
Pilots (040) 11 52 69 & 97 83 15. Fax: (040) 30 18 64. Telex: 32435 MLOTS S.
Radio-Port: VHF Chan. 14, 12, 16 H24.

VÅGBRYTARBANK 55°37.5'N 12°58.8'W Lt. Iso. W.R.G.10 sec. W.13M. R.10M. G.9M. W.Tr. 11m. G.041.5°-054.5°; W.-056.5°; R.-067°; G.-077.5°; W.-090°; R.-129°; G.-136.5°; W.-151°; R.-206°; G.-223°; G(unintens)-278°; W(unintens)-287°; R(unintens)-330°; G(unintens)-041.5°. Shown by day 1/11-31/3. Horn (2) 20 sec.

CENTRALHAMSRÄNNAN 55°37.0'N

12°59.8'E Ldg. Lts. 142°30' (Front) Oc. 5 sec. 18M. Or. △ on W.Tr. 13m. 55°36'.8N 13°00'.0E (Rear) Q.18M. Or. △ on W.Tr. 20m.

55°37.1'N 12°59.9'E Lts. in line 142°30' (Front) Oc. R.5 sec. 14M. W. ◇, Or.Border on W.Tr. 9m. Vis. on line only. Mark E edge of channel. 55°37.0'N 12°59.9'E (Rear) Q.R.14M. W. ◇, Or.Border on W.Tr. 12m. Vis. on line only.

No: 3 **BREAKWATER HEAD** Lt. Oc. W.R.G.3 sec. W.7M. R.5M. G.4M. W.Tr. 7m. G.147°-174°; W.-226.5°; R.-245°; G.-294°; W.-300°; R.-010°.

55°37.1'N 12°59.5'E No: 12 Lts. in line 143°30'. (Front) Oc. G.5 sec. 14M. G. △ on mast 8m. Mark W edge of channel. 55°37'.1N 12°59'.5E (Rear) Q.G. 14M. G. ▽ 16m.

E JETTY HEAD Lt. Q.Y. Occas.
W JETTY HEAD Lt. Q.Y. Occas.

FRIHAMNEN. DETACHED BREAKWATER

No: 5 **EAST HEAD** Lt. Q.G.4M. W.Pedestal 7m. 116°-300°.
N PIER HEAD No: 6 Lt. Q.R.5M. W.Pedestal 4m. 275.5°-115.5°.

55°36.9'N 13°00.5'E Ldg. Lts. 117° (Front) Iso. 4 sec. 15M. Or. △ on roof of house 24m. Vis. about 107°-about 123°. Intens on leading line. 55°36'.8N 13°00'.8E (Rear) Q.14M. Or ◇ on W.Tr. 32m. Vis. about 107°-about 123°. Intens on leading line.

INDUSTRIHAMNEN. DETACHED MOLE

55°37.5'N 13°01.3'E. Ldg. Lts. 082°30' (Front) Oc. 3 sec. 12M. Or. ◇ on W.Tr. 12m. 55°37.6'N 13°01.5'E (Rear) Oc. 3 sec. 12M. Or. ◇ on W.Tr. 20m.

N MOLE HEAD No: 11 Lt. Q.R.4M. Lantern on W.Pedestal.
S MOLE HEAD No: 10 Lt. Q.G.3M. Lantern on W.Pedestal 6m.
Lt. Oc. W.R.G.3 sec. W.9M. R.6M. G.5M. W.R.Tr. 24m. G.084°-103°; W.103°-108°; R.108°-about 140°.

NEW OIL HARBOUR 55°38.1'N 13°01.6'E Ldg. Lts. 132° (Front) Oc. 6 sec. 14M. Or. △ on Grey Tr. 22m. 55°37.9'N 13°02.0'E (Rear) Q.14M. Or. ▽ on Grey Tr. 35m.

Ldg. Lts. and Lts. in line also shown by day 1/11-31/3.

Lts. in line 132° (Front) Oc. G.6 sec. 6M. G. △ on Grey Tr. 22m. (Rear) Q.G.6M. G. ▽ on Grey Tr. 35m.

Lts. in line 132° (Front) Oc. R.6 sec. 6M. R. △ on Grey Tr. 22m. (Rear) Q.R.6M. R. ▽ on Grey Tr. 35m.

PILDAMMSSTADEN 55°34.8'N
12°59.4'E Lt. Aero V.Q.21M. On mast 103m.

LIMHAMN
LIMHAMN NORRA Lt. Oc. W.R.G.6 sec.
W.9M. R.7M. G.6M. W.R.Tr. 8m. R.142-175°;
G.-192°; W.-211.5°; R.-222°; G.-232°.
G(unintens)-013°. Shown by day 1/11-31/3.

OLJEHAMN Ldg. Lts. 205°30' (Front)
F.G.7M. Or. Δ on Grey Tr. 21m. Occas. (Rear)
F.G.7M. Or. ∇ on tank 26m. Occas.

CENTRALHAMN. VÄSTRA Lts. in line
201°30' (Front) Iso. G.3 sec. 8M. B.W. Δ on
grey Tr. 10m. Vis. on line only. Mark W edge
of channel. (Rear) Iso. G.3 sec. 8M. B.W. ∇
on Grey Tr. 20m. Vis. on line only.

ÖSTRA 55°35.7'N 12°56.0'E Lts. in line
200°30' (Front) Iso. R.3 sec. 10M. B.W. Δ on
Grey Tr. 10m. Synchronised with Vastra Lt.
Mark E edge of channel. 55°35.3'N 12°55.7'E
(Rear) Iso. R.3 sec. 10M. B.W. ∇ on Grey Tr.
on building 20m. F.R. obstruction Lts. 122m.
and 72m. on chimney 250m. NE.

SÖDRA 55°35.1'N 12°55.4'E Ldg. Lts. 097°
(Front) Q.R.10M. R. Δ B.Border on Tr. 8m.
Vis. on leading line only. V.Q.Y. ferry Lts.
100m. WNW and 370m. NE. Occas.
55°35'.1N 12°55'.5E (Rear) Iso. R.3 sec. 10M.
R. ∇, B.Border on Grey Tr. 11m. Vis. on
leading line only.

BÄTHAMN Ldg. Lts. 092° (Front) F.G.2M. R.
Δ on post 4m. (Rear) F.G.2M. R. ∇ on post
9m.

LERNACKEN 55°34.2'N 12°54.1'E Lt. Iso.
W.R.G.3 sec. W.16M. R.13M. G.12M.
W.Lantern, 24m. G. shore-009°; R.-022.5°;
G.-040°; W.-041.5°; R.-067°; G.-087°; W.-094°;
R.-125°; G.-154°; R.-167°; W.-194°; W.-203.5°;
R.-210°.

Ldg. Lts. about 149° (Front) Fl(2) R.6 sec.
7M. Or. Δ (Rear) Fl(2) R.6 sec. 7M. Or. ∇.

KLAGSHAMN
Ldg. Lts 076° (Front) Q. R. 2M. Or. Δ on Tr,
9m. (Rear) Oc. R.3 sec. 2M. Or. ∇ on Tr. 16m.

OUTER BREAKWATER INNER END Lt. Fl.(3)
R.G.9 sec. R.4M. G.3M. W. Tr. 11m. G.334°-
005°; R.-051°; G.-064°; R.-076°; G.-095°; R.-
141°; G.-155°; R.-167°.

Lts. in line 110° (Front) F.G.8M. W. Δ, R.
Border on Col. 8m. Mark pipeline. (Rear)
F.G.8M. W. ∇, R. border on building 14m.

SYDGAS 55°31'.2N 12°53'.7E Lts. in line
093° (Front) Iso. Y.4 sec. 10M. Y. ◊ on grey
mast 14m. Mark pipeline. 55°31.2'N

12°54.1'E (Rear) Q.Y.10M. Y. ◊ on grey mast
21m.

HOLLVIKEN CHANNEL
Yacht harbour lies near entrance to
Falsterbo Kanal, depths of 2.5m.

HOLLVIKEN 55°30.7'N 12°51.1'E Lt. Fl.(2)
W.R.G.6 sec. W.13M. R.19M. G.9M.
W.Lantern on G. Tr. W.Top. 9m Floodlit.
G.012.5°-117°; W.-019°; R.-057°; G.-064°; W.-
069°; R.-081°; G.-112.5°; R.-132°; G.-154°; W.-
157°; R.-163°; G.-172°; W.-180°; R.-193°; G.-
326°; W.334.5°; R.-012.5°. ⌁ Racon.
Reserve Lt.

HOLLREVET Lt. Q. 7M. G. Tr. 6m. In line
155° with Falsterbokanalen Lts. Nos. 4 and
6, indicates the W side of the dredged
channel.

FALSTERBOKANALEN
Tel: (040) 45 03 00
Radio-Port: VHF Chan. 16, 14, 13, 12.

N END E MOLE HEAD No 5: 55°24.9'N
12°56.1'E Lt.Oc.3 sec. 14M.B. ◊ on
W.Pedestal in front of Y. Ⅱ 6m. Floodlit. Vis.
when bearing 155°.
Nos. 3 and 5 and 4 and 6 are synchronised
and in line 155° mark the sides of the
dredged channel.

W MOLE HEAD No 6: 55°24.9'N 12°56.0'E
Lt.Oc.3 sec. 14M.B. ◊ on W.Pedestal in front
of Y. Ⅱ 6m. Floodlit. Vis. when bearing 155°

No: 3 55°24.1'N 12°56.8'E Lt.Oc.3 sec.
14M.B. Tr 24m. Vis. when bearing 155°.

No: 4 55°24.0'N 12°56.7'E Lt.Oc.3 sec.
13M.B. Tr 24m. Vis. when bearing 330°
(intens) and 155° (unintens).

S END E MOLE HEAD No 1: 55°23.6'N
12°57.2'E Lt.Oc.W.R.G.10 sec. 10 W.13M.
W.6M. R.10M. G.9M. W.Lantern 7m. R.
shore-303°; G.-328°; W.-333°; R.-007°; W.-
(unintens)-065°; R(unintens) 065°-canal. In
line 330° with No: 4 Lt. shown by day 1/11-
31/3.

W MOLE HEAD No 2: Lt. Fl. G.3.sec. 2M.
Lantern on W.Pedestal 6m.

SKANOR N MOLE HEAD 55°25.2'N
12°49.7'E Lt. L. Fl(2) R.G.10 sec. 10 R.10M.
G.9M. W.Tr. 7m. G.030°-063°; R.-130°; G.-
171°; R.171°-shore.

N BREAKWATER Ldg. Lts. 120° (Front) F.R.
R. Δ on post 5m. (Rear) F.R.R. ∇ on post 6m.

PIER HEAD Lt. F.G. Tr. 4m. White pier head
floodlit.

BALTIC SEA

POLLUTION

The Baltic is for all practical purposes virtually tideless. Differences in mean water levels are caused mainly by wind (gales) action. Therefore, the Authorities are vitally concerned about and intolerant of, any form of pollution. Do NOT allow oil, fuels, rubbish, plastics etc. etc. to go into the sea. Not only is it an offence under the MARPOL regulations, it is a filthy habit. Dispose of all rubbish ashore.

Gasthamners are located at:

South Coast	Gotland
Ystad	Burgsvik
Kåseberga	Klintrhamn
Skillinge	Visby
Simrishamn	Lickershamn
Kivik	Kappelshamn
Åhus	Ronehamn
Solvesborg	Ljugarn
Hållevik	Herrvik
Karlshamn	Katthammarsvik
Karön	Slite
Karlskrona	Valleviken
	Färösund
Karlmarsund & Öland	
Bergkvara	**Stockholm Skärgärd**
Kalmar	Nynäshamn
Mörbylanga	Dalarö
Färjestaden	Karlsund
Oskarshamn	Utö
Figeholm	Saltsjöbaden
Borgholm	Djurö
Sandvik	Geffoten
Byxelkrok	Vaxholm
Boda	Bosön
	Viggbyholm
East Coast	Islinge
Kråkelund to	Stockholm
Stockholm via	Furusund
Sodertalje	Nykvarn
Våstervik	Österskär
Gambleby	Gräddö
Loftahammar	Norrtälje
Valdemarsvik	Möja
Olsön	Ingmarsö
N. Finnö	
Söderköping	
Navekvarn	
Esteron	
Norrköping	
Oxelösund	
Nyköping	
Trosa	
Skansholmen	
Södertälje	

FALSTERBO UDDE 55°23.0'N 12°49.2'E Lt. Oc.5 sec. 10M. Yellowish grey round Tr. B.Band, on square base 24m. V. Q. R. on radar mast 1.6M. ENE shown during firing practice.

FALSTERBOREV 55°18'.5N 12°39'.5E Lt. Iso W.R.G. 8 sec. W.22M. R.19M. G. 18M. Or. B. Tr. grey base 29m. Floodlit. G. 220°-287°; W..-191°; R.-220°. RC. Racon. Horn (2) 30 sec.

SKÅRE

Yacht moorings available.

OUTER W PIER HEAD Lt. Q. W.R.G.6M. R.4M. G.4M. R. ☐ on W. Tr. 7m. G. shore-343°; W.343°-002°; R.002°-shore.

TRELLEBORGSRÄNNAN

TRELLEBORG 55°22'N 13°09'E
Tel: Port (041) 04 10 15.
Radio-Port: VHF Chan, 16, 9.

CHANNEL ENTRANCE 55°21.4'N 13°09.1'E Lt. Iso W.R.G.8 sec. W.16M. R.13M. G.12M. W.Lantern on B. W. Tr. on grey conical base. 12m. Floodlit. G.279°-311.5°; W.-060°; R.-082°; G.-099°; G(unintens)-110°; W(unintens)-279°. Also shown by day 1/11-31/3. Racon. ᴗᴥ F.G. and F. Y. Lts. are shown and fog signals sounded for the use of ferries.

W PIER HEAD W 55°22.0'N 13°09.2'E Lts. in line 014° (Front) Oc. Y. 4 sec. 15M. W. Δ on R. W. Tr. 12m. Vis. on line only. 55°22.3'N 13°09.4'E (Rear) Oc. Y. 4 sec. 15M. W. ▽ on R. W. Tr. 22m. Vis. on line only. R. Lt. on water tower 1.3M. NNE.

E. PIER HEAD E 55°22.0'N 13°09.3'E Lts. in line 014° (Front) Oc. Y. 4 sec. 15M. W. Δ on B. W. Tr. 12m. Floodlit. Vis. on line only. F.G. and F.Y. Lts. are shown and fog signals sounded for use of ferries. 3 F.R. vert on radio mast 1.8M NE. 55°22.3'N 13°09.5'E (Rear) Oc. Y. 4 sec. 15M. W. ▽ on R. W. Tr. 22m. Floodlit. Vis. on line only.

TRELLEBORG YTTRE ÖSTRA E PIER HEAD Lt. Fl(2) G.6 sec. 8M. Aluminium pedestal 8m. Horn(2) 30 sec.

TRELLEBORG YTTRE VÄSTRA W PIER HEAD Lt. Fl. R.3 sec. 9M. Aluminium pedestal 8m.

GISLÖV

INNER E PIER HEAD Ldg. Lts. 022°30' (Front) F. R. 7M. W. Δ, R.Border on Tr. 4m. Inner pierheads floodlit. (Rear) F.R. 7M. W. ▽, R. border on Tr. 11m.

W PIER HEAD Horn Mo (A) 60 sec. Fishing.

ÖSTRA TORP
Facilities for yachts available.

SMYGEHAMN Ldg. Lts. 003° (Front) F. R. 5M. R. Δ, on W. Structure 7m. Fishing. Shown 1/8-1/6, (Rear) F.R.5 M. R. ▽ on W. Structure. 10m. Fishing. Shown 1/8-1/6.

KULLAGRUND 55°17.9'N 13°19.5'E Lt. Iso W.R.G.4 sec. W.16M. R.13M. G.12M. W.Lantern on R. B. Tr. 18m. Floodlit. R.182°-244°; G.-270°; W.-105°; R.-119°; G.-182°. Racon. F. R. on water Tr. 5.5M N.

ABBEKÄS. N PIER Ldg. Lts. 297° (Front) F. R. 2M. R. Δ, on Pillar 8m. (Rear) F. R. 2M. R. ▽ W. on pillar 10m.

YSTAD 55°26'N 13°50'E
Tel: Port (041) 17 70 00 Ext. 260/263.
Radio-Port: VHF Chan. 16, 9.

Speed limit 5 kts. Depths 7.2m. in the entrance channel and main harbour. 50 yacht berths at W. Pier of small boat harbour in depths of 1.5-3m.

55°25.5'N 13°49.8'E. Ldg. Lts. 036° (Front) Iso. 4 sec. 15M. Or. Δ on Tr. 24m. 55°25.6'N 13°49.9'E. (Rear) Iso. 4 sec. 15M. Or. ▽ on Tr. 30m. Aero V.Q. 40m. 21M (occas.) on mast 4.7M. ENE

YTTRE VÄSTRA Lt. Fl. R.3 sec. 9M. W.Hut 8m. **YITTRE ÖSTRA** Lt. Fl(2) G.6 sec. 5M. W.Lantern 8m. Floodlighting at pier head.

YSTADS BÅTHAMN Ldg. Lts. 019° (Front) F.R. 2M. Or. Δ on mast 6m. (Rear) F.R. 2M. Or. ▽ on mast 11m.

KÅSEBERGA. N BREAKWATER PIER HEAD Lt. Q. W.R.G. W.5M. R.3M. G.2M. R. Tr. 8m. R.276°-288°; G.-302°; W.-035°; R.-065°. Horn Mo(R) 60 sec. Fishing.

SANDHAMMAREN 55°23.0'N 14°11.8'E. Lt. Fl. 5 sec. 22M. R. Tr. 31m. RC. F.R. on radio mast 0.8M. NNW.

DENMARK

BORNHOLM

RØNNE HAVN. 55°05.9'N 14°41.8'E Ldg. Lts. 064°30' (Front) Iso. 2 sec. 9M. Tr. 16m. 048°-081°. By day 2M. 062°-067°. 55°06.0'N 14°42.0'E (Rear) Iso. 4 sec. 9M. R.Mast 24m. 048°-081°. By day 2M. 062°-067°.

SHELTER MOLE HEAD Lt. Fl. G.3 sec. 8M. G. Tr. 11m. Floodlit. Horn 20 sec.
N SHELTER MOLE HEAD Lt. Fl. R.3 sec. 8M. R. Tr. 11m. Fog Det. Lt.

S BREAKWATER. W END Lt. F .G.6M. G.Square granite Tr. 9m. Floodlit. Fog. Det. Lt. F.R. Lts. on chimney 0.5M. ESE.

TRINDELEN BREAKWATER. S HEAD Lt. F. R.6M. R. Col. 8m. Floodlit. 185°-095°.
INNER MOLE HEAD Lt. F. R.5M. Grey round granite Tr. 11m.

NORREKAS
Situated N of Ronne Havn, yacht basin on E side of outer harbour for vessels of 15m. x 5m. x 2m. draught. Sea level lowered/raised 1m. by W/E and N gales respectively.

NORREKAS Lt. Oc. W.R.G.5 sec. W.6M. R.4M. G.4M. W.Hut, 2 R.Bands 5m. G.045°-090°; W.090°-105°; R.105°-180°.

HASLE HAVN 55°11'N 14°42'E
General depth 4m. Yacht moorings on E side of shelter mole in No: 5 basin. 100T. patent slip available.

Ldg. Lts. 097° (Front) Iso. W.R.G.4 sec. W.6M. R.4M. G.4M. R. △, W.Band, on Tr. 7m. G.085°-093°; W.093°-101°; R.101°-109°. (Rear) Iso. 4 sec. 7M. R. △ W.Band, on Tr. 11m. 007°-187°.

W MOLE HEAD Lt. Fl. G.3 sec. 3M. Tr. G.Base 6m. Mole head illuminated. Horn 15 sec.
N MOLE HEAD Lt. Fl. R.3 sec. 3M. Grey mast 6m.
INSIDE MOLE HEAD Lt. F. R.3M. Grey pedestal 3m.

TEGLKAAS BADEHAVN. E MOLE HEAD Lt. F. R.3M. Post 4m. Occas.

VANG. PIER HEAD Lt. Fl. G.5 sec. 4M. Tr. 5m.

VANG HAVN. N BREAKWATER HEAD
Ldg. Lts. 155° (Front) F. R.2M. W.Post 4m. 043°-267°. Shown when vessels expected. (Rear) F. R.2M. mast 8m. 043°-267°.

HAMMERHAVNEN. E OF HARBOUR Lt. Iso. W.R.G.2 sec. W.Wooden 12m. G.064°-073°; W.073°-077°; R.077°-086°.
N MOLE HEAD Lt. F. R. Tr. 7m.

HAMMERODDE 55°17.9'N 14°46.5'E Lt. Fl(2) 10 sec. 18M. W.Square Tr. 21m. 051°-300°, faintly visible elsewhere. Also shown by day when fog signal is operating. RC. East: Horn (3) 60 sec. West: Horn Mo(R) 60 sec. sounded alternately with E fog signal.

SANDVIG HAVN Ldg. Lts. 157°30' F. G.3M. post 3m. (Rear) F. G.3M. post 7m.

ALLINGE Ldg. Lts. 250° (Front) F. G.4M. post 5m. 174°-354°. 3 F.R. vert. 3m. 4M. indicates harbour closed. (Rear) F. G. Grey Tr. 174°-354°. Only shown when harbour accessible. Horn (2) 30 sec. sounded when vessel expected.

TEJN HAVN 55°14.9'N 14°50.4'E
The yacht harbour is in the northern most basin on the SE side of the harbour, with depths of 2.4-3.8m.

BREAKWATER HEAD Lt. Fl. R.3 sec. 3M. R. Tr. 8m.
SHELTER MOLE HEAD Lt. Oc. W.R.G.5 sec. W.7M. R.4M. G.4M. Tr. on building 9m. W.160°-204°; R.204°-238°; G.238°-160°.

Ldg. Lts. 144°24' (Front) Iso. G.2 sec. 2M. R. △ on Tr. 7m. 134.4°-154.4°. (Rear) Iso. G.4 sec. 2M. R. ▽ on Tr. 10m. 134.4°-154.4°.

GUDHJEM HAVN. N APPROACH Ldg. Lts. 120° (Front) F.R. on post 6m. Shown 1/8-1/4 when vessel expected and on dark nights in summer when local boats are at sea. (Rear) F. R. 2M.Or. ▽ on mast 8m.

S APPROACH Ldg. Lts. 202° (Front) F. R.2M. Or. △ on mast 12m. Shown when vessel expected and when local boats are at sea. Extinguished when harbour closed. (Rear) F. R.2M. Or. ▽ on mast 20m.

MELSTED HAVN Ldg. Lts. 208° (Front) F. on post 3m. 169°-315°. Shown when harbour is accessible and boats are at sea or vessels expected. (Rear) F. on post 5m. 169°-315°.

LISTED HAVN Ldg. Lts. 201°36' (Front) F. R.4M. R. △ W.Band on Tr. 9m. 131.6°-271.6°. (Rear) F. R.4M. R. ▽ W.Band on Tr. 11m. 131.6°-271.6°.

SVANEKE. SANDKAAS ODDE 55°07.9'N 15°09.2'E Lt. Fl(2) 20 sec. 21M. Grey square Tr. 20m. 135°-000°.
Lt. Iso. W.R.G.4 sec. 5M. W.Square wooden building, R.Band 6m. G.203.5-208.5°; W.208.5°-222°; R.222°-227°.

SVANEKE HAVN 55°08.2'N 15°08.9'E
Suitable for vessels 45m. x 8.5m. x 4m.
draught. 2 basins outer havn, depth 4.4m.
Inner havn depth 3.5m. reached through
lock gate.

Port closed signal = 1 B.Ball/3 F.R.vert Lts.
Lock closed signal = F. Lt. shown below
(Front) Ldg. Lt.

BREAKWATER OUTER END Lt. Fl. G.3 sec.
G. Col. 7m.

Ldg. Lts. 297° (Front) Iso. R.2 sec. Grey post
5m. Shown 15/8-1/5. (Rear) Iso. R.2 sec.
Grey post 6m. Shown 15/8-1/5.

ÅRSDALE HAVN Ldg. Lts. 248°30'
(Front) F.R. on mast, W. Δ 8m. Fishing.
(Rear) F.R. on mast, W. ∇ 16m. Fishing.

NEKSO HAVN 55°04'N 15°09'E
The smaller basin just S of Traffickhavn is
used by visiting yachts with depths of 3-
3.7m.

DETACHED BREAKWATER N END Lt. Fl. R.3
sec. R. Tr. 12m. Siren 30 sec. sounded when
vessels expected or boats at sea.
S MOLE NE HEAD Lt. F.R. R.Tripod 10m.
ENTRANCE W SIDE Lt. 3 F.R.vert. W.Silo
18m. Shown when lock gates closed.
**NEAR ENTRANCE TO SOUTHERN BOAT
HARBOUR** Ldg. Lts. 232° (Front) F.G.W. Tr.
9m. 130°-350°. (Rear) F.G. Gable of building
12m. 130°-350°.

SNOGEBAEK HAVN Ldg. Lts. 318°12'
(Front) F. R.2M. Grey mast 4m. 258.2°-
018.2° (Rear) F. R.2M. Grey mast 6m. 258.2°-
018.2°.

DUEODDE 54°59.5'N 15°04.6'E Lt. Fl(3) 10
sec. 20M. W.6-sided Tr. 48m. Horn (3) 120
sec. and 0.5M ENE Horn (3) 120 sec.
sounded alternately.

BAKKERNE Ldg. Lts. 011° (Front) F.
Shown when harbour accessible and boats
are at sea or vessels expected. (Rear) F.

ARNAGER HAVN. N MOLE HEAD Lt. F.
W.Post 5m. 276°-315°.

RONNE Lt. Aero Fl.3 sec. on Y.Airport
control Tr. 39m. Occas.

ÅRSBALLE 55°09.0'N 14°52.8'E Lt. Aero 2
Fl.2 sec. vert. 10M. TV mast 290m.
Obstruction.
4 Lts. Fl.1.5 sec. on TV Tr. 0.8M. NE.

CHRISTIANSO

The whole area within 1M. of the group is a
bird sanctuary. Speed limit 12 kts. and no
approach within 100m.of Graesholm and
Tat. Harbour between Christianso and
Frederikso is a good harbour of refuge
except in S'ly gales. Strong currents may be
encountered between the islets. Normally
the largest vessel to use Christianso
harbour is 20 tons. Harbour is divided by a
bridge, when open passage for vessels of
4m. draught. North harbour secure to ring
bolts in the rocks. South harbour,alongside
on E side in depths of 3m. Sea level can
lower by 0.4m. in SSW/W gales and raise by
0.6m. in N/E gales.

55°19.3'N 15°11.3'E Lt. Fl.5 sec. 19M. W.
on fort 29m. Obsc. when bearing 324°.
(NNE) Horn 60 sec. (SE) Horn 60 sec.
sounded alternately with NNE fog signal.

FREDERIKSØ Horn 60 sec. synchronised
with NNE fog signal.

CHRISTIANSØ HAVN. FREDERIKSHOLM Lt.
Iso. W.R.G.4 sec. W.7M. R.4M. G.4M.
W.R.House 7m. G.172°-186°; W.-194°; R.-
204°; G.-347°; W.-350°; R.-358°. Traffic
signals.

TAT Lt. Fl.3 sec. 7M. R.W.Tr. 7m.

GERMANY

BOCK 54°26.6'N13°02.0'E Ldg. Lts. 322°06' (Front) Oc. 6 sec. 13M. W.Tr. R.Lantern and gallery with W.Roof, grey stone base, W.Stripe 12m, 302°-342°. Synchronised with and on same leading line as Bessiner Haken Ldg. Lts.

54°26.9'N 13°01.6'E (Rear and Front) Oc. W.R.G.6 sec. W.13M. R.10M. G.9M. W.Tr. R.Lantern and gallery with W.Roof, grey stone base, W.Stripe 23m. W.089°-180°; R.-191°; W.-290°; G.-308°; W.-069°.

ZARRENZIN 54°25.6'N 13°01.0'E Ldg. Lts. 195°06' (Rear) Oc. 6 sec. 18M. W.R.Tr. R.Lantern and cupola 52m. Vis. on leading line only.

BARHÖFT

Boat harbour is used by Pilots/Customs/Yachts, depth about 2.1m. 25 moorings for yachts.

BOAT HARBOUR Ldg. Lts. 228°30' (Front) Oc. R.6 sec. 1M. W. △ on mast 9m. (Rear) Oc. R.6 sec. 1M. W. ▽ on mast 7m.

BESSINER HAKEN 54°22.1'N 13°07.9'E Oc. 6 sec. 12M. W △, R.Border, on W.R.Tr. 12m. 54°21.2'N 13°09.2'E (Rear) Oc. 6 sec. 14M. W. ◊ R.Border, on W.R.Tr. 30m. Vis. on leading line. Same leading line as Bock Ldg. Lts.

PAROW 54°21.7'N 13°05.2'E Ldg. Lts. 319° (Front) Oc(3) 15 sec. 10M. R.W. △ on grey Tr. 10m. F.R. Lt. on chimney 220m. N. 54°21.8'N 13°05.1'E (Rear) Oc(3) 15 sec. 10M. R.W. ▽ on grey Tr. 23m.

W MOLE Lt. F.R.

E MOLE Lt. F.G.

SCHWEDENSCHANZE 54°20.3'N 13°04.8'E Ldg. Lts. 271°06' (Front) Iso. 4 sec. 10M. △ on W.Tr. 5m. 54°20.3'N 13°04.8'E (Rear) Iso. 4 sec. 10M. ▽ on wall 9m.

STRALSUND

E MOLE Ldg. Lts. 181°06' (Front) Oc. G.5 sec. 5M. Grey Tr. 12m. 54°18.5'N 13°06.6'E (Rear) Oc. G.5 sec. 10M. Grey Tr. 23m.

For continuation South see Stralsund Lts.

HIDDENSEE

GELLEN 54°30.6'N 13°04.6'E Lt. Oc(2) W.R.G.10 sec. W.15M. R.11M. G.10M. W.Round Tr.R.Top, stone base 10m. R.013°-056°; W.-106°; R.-169°; W.-184°; R.-219°; G.-238°; W.013°.

NW SUMMIT DORNBUSCH 54°36.1'N 13°07.2'E Lt. L.Fl. W.R.10 sec. W.21M. R.15M. Grey Tr. 95m. R.023°-053°; W.053°-023°.

E END NEUENDORF Ldg. Lts. 286°36' (Front) F.R. 4M. W. △ on brown mast 6m. Occas. (Rear) F.R. 4M. W. ▽ on brown mast 12m. Occas.

LIBBEN FAHRWASSER

STOLPER HAKEN 54°32.9'N 13°08.8'E Ldg. Lts. 201°36' (Front) Oc. 6 sec. 10M. W. △ on W.Tr. 14m. 54°32.6'N 13°08.6'E (Rear) Oc 6 sec. 10M. W. ▽ on W.Tr. 27m.

POGENHOF 54°32.7'N 13°09.7'E Ldg. Lts. 178°30' (Front) Oc(2) 10 sec. 10M. W. △ on W.Tr. 12m. 54°32.5'N 13°09.6'E (Rear) Oc(2) 10 sec. 10M. W. ▽ on W.Tr. 20m.

HIDDENSEE 54°32.9'N 13°07.6'E Ldg. Lts. 260°42' (Front) Oc(3) 15 sec. 10M. W. △ on W.Tr. 14m. 54°32.9'N 13°06.9'E (Rear) Oc(3) 15 sec. 10M. W. ▽ on W.Tr. 27m.
Yacht moorings: 40.

VITTE Ldg. Lts. 289°30' (Front) F.R. 4M. mast 6m. (Rear) F.R. 4M. mast 12m.
Yacht moorings: 60.

RASSOWER STROM

RASSOW 54°32.9'N 13°11.5'E Ldg. Lts. 212°06' (Front) Oc(4) 15 sec. 10M. W. △ on W.Tr. 14m. 54°32.4'N 13°11.1'E (Rear) Oc(4) 15 sec. 10M. W. ▽ on W.Tr. 29m.

BUG. W MOLE HEAD Lt. F.R. 5M. R.Tr. 5m. **E MOLE HEAD** Lt. F.G. F.R. Lt. on chimney 0.5M. N.

VIEREGGE Ldg. Lts. 128°36' (Front) F.R. 8M. Grey mast 7m. (Rear) F.R. 8M. Grey mast 9m.

KAP ARKONA 54°40.9'N 13°26.1'E Lt. Fl(3) 17.1 sec. 22M. B.R. round Tr. with cupola. 75m.

RANZOW 54°35.2'N 13°38.2'E Lt. Fl.5 sec. 14M. W.Round Tr. 55m. 099°-297°. 2 F.R. Lts. on each of 3 radio masts 0.85M. WSW.

KOLLICKER ORT 54°33.8'N 13°40.8'E Lt. Fl. W.R.2 sec. W.10M. R.7M. W.Round Tr. 30m. W.166°-340°; R.340°-356°.

SASSNITZ 54°31'N 13°38'E
Tel: 2484.
Radio-Port: VHF Chan.14, 12, 16 H24.
Reporting System: Compulsory for all vessels over 17m. in length. VHF Chan. 14, 9, 12, 16 H24. Report on entering, leaving and manoeuvring.

Information Broadcasts: Chan. 14 at 0630 1830.
Yacht moorings: 40.

EAST PIER HEAD 54°30.4'N 13°38.4'E Lt. Oc. W.G.6 sec. W.10M. R.6M. W.8-sided Tr. R.Top 14m. G.200°-245°; W.245°-200°. 2 F.R. Lts. on the radio mast on Leuzberg 0.9M. NW.

FERRY BERTH No: 1 Ldg. Lts. 023°33' (Front) F.G. (Rear) F.G.

FERRY W BASIN 54°30.8'N 13°38.5'E Ldg. Lts. 018°42' (Front) Iso. 6 sec. 10M. W. △ R.Border on W.Tr. 20m. 54°30.9'N 13°38.5'E (Rear) Iso. 6 sec. 10M. W. ▽ R.Border on W.Tr. 24m.

Ldg. Lts. 007°30" (Front) Oc(2) 10 sec. 9M. R.Lantern on 4 legs 11m.
W MOLE Lt. F.R. 3M. Same structure 10m. (Rear) Oc(2) 10 sec. 9M. W. △ on grey Tr. 14m.

N LANDING PLACE Lt. F.R. 2M. on dolphin.
S LANDING PLACE Lt. F.R. on dolphin.
DEVIATION BEACON Lt. F.R. on dolphin.
FISHING PIER HEAD Lt. 2 F.G. vert. on dolphin.

PRORER WIEK

BINZ 54°24.5'N 13°35.7'E Lt. F.R. 10M. Chimney 56m. Obstruction.

PRORA 54°26.0'N 13°34.5'E Dir. Lt. 270°. Iso. W.R.G.8 sec. 23M. Grey 3-sided Tr. 2 galleries 35m. G.267°-268.5°; W.268.5°-271.5°; R.271.5°-273°. Racon. F.R. Lt. on chimneys 320m. NE and 0.75M. N. F.R. Lt. on mast 8.2M. SE.

MUKRAN 54°29.9'N 13°34.9'E Ldg. Lts. 337°24' (Front) Iso. G.8 sec. 16M. 12M. R. △ on grey 3-sided Tr. 2 galleries 49m. 54°30.2'N 13°34.7'E (Rear) Iso. G.8 sec. 17M. R. ▽ on grey 3-sided Tr. 2 galleries 68m. F.R. Lt. on radio mast 740m. NNW. F.R. Lt. on chimney 0.53M. SSW.

N MOLE Lt. Q.G. 6M. G.W.R.Tr. 17m. Lt. Iso. W.R.4 sec. W.6M. R.3M. W.Mast 12m. R.330°-008° W.008°-100°; R.100°-145°. White sector marks limits of turning basin. Lt. Iso W.R.4 sec. W.3M. R.2M. W.Mast 12m. W.045°-145°; R.145°-180°. White sector marks limit of turning basin.
BERTH 1 Lt. Iso. W.R.4 sec. W.6M. R.3M. R. △ on W.Mast 12m. W.225°-325°; R.325°-045°. White sector marks limit of turning basin.
BERTH 2 Lt. Iso. W.R.4 sec. W.6M. R.3M. R. △ on W.Mast 12m. R.225°-280°; W.280°-045°. White sector marks limit of turning basin.
PIER HEAD Lt. Iso. R.G.4 sec. R.6M. G.3M. 3-sided Tr. 25m. G.135°-315°; R.315°-135°. R.Sector marks Berth 1 area, G.Sector marks Berth 2 area.
Lt. Iso. W.R.4 sec. W.6M. R.3M. R. △ and lantern on W.Mast 12m. W.225°-325°; R.325°-045°.

GÖHREN 54°20.6'N 13°45.1'E Aero Lt. F.R. Obstruction.

STAHLBRODE

Ldt. Lts. 245°12' (Front) Oc. G.6 sec. 6M. R. △ on W.Tr. 18m. (Rear) Oc. G.6 sec. 6M. R. ▽ on W.Tr. 22m.

GLEWITZER FÄHRE Ldg. Lts. 065°12' (Front) Oc. G.6 sec. 6M. R. △ on W.Tr. 13m. (Rear) Oc. G.6 sec. 6M. R. ▽ on W.Tr. 16m.

MALTZIEN 54°14.2'N 13°21.4'E Ldg. Lts. 314°12' (Front) Oc. 6 sec. 11M. W.B. round Tr. 12m. (Rear) Oc. 6 sec. 7M. W. ◊, R.Border on W.Tr. 22m.

GRABOW Ldg. Lts. 099°12' (Front) Oc(2) R.10 sec. 7M. W. △, B.Border, on W.Tr. 12m.
PALMER ORT (Rear) Oc(2) R.10 sec. 7M. W. ⌐, B.Border, on W.Tr. 19m.

DEVIN Ldg. Lts. 293°12' (Front) Oc(2) 10 sec. 9M. W. ◊, R.Border, on W.Tr. 17m. H24. 54°16.6'N 13°09.7'E (Rear) Oc(2) 10 sec. 16M. W. ◊, R.Border, on W.R.Tr. 34m.

DRIGGE Ldg. Lts. 316°42' (Front) Oc(2) G.10 sec. 7M. W. ◊, R.Border on W.R.Tr. 15m. H24. (Rear) Oc(2) G.10 sec. 7M. W. △, R.Border, on W.R.Tr. 24m.

GUSTOW 54°17.9'N 13°11.7'E Ldg. Lts. 013°54' (Front) Oc. 6 sec. 10M. W. △, R.Border, on W. Tr. 10m. Occas. 54°18.0'N 13°11.8'E (Rear) Oc. 6 sec. 10M. W. ▽, R.Border, on W.Tr. 17m. Occas.

JETTY Dir. Lt. Dir. Oc. W.R.G.6 sec. W.3M. R.2M. G.1M. W.Mast 5m. G.342.6°-346.9°; W.346.9°-351.1°; R.351.1°-357°. Occas.

ANDERSHOF

Ldg. Lts. 195° (Front) Oc. G.6 sec. 5M. W. △, R.Border, on W.R.Tr. 22m. (Rear) Oc. G.6 sec. 7M. W. ▽, R.Border, on W.R.Tr. 39m.

54°16.4'N 13°07.5'E Ldg. Lts. 248°36' (Front) Oc. 6 sec. 10M. W. △, R.Border, on W.R.Tr. 22m. 54°16.3'N 13°07.2'E (Rear) Oc. 6 sec. 10M. W. over W. ⊐, R.Border, on W.R.Tr. 32m.

DÄNHOLM Ldg. Lts. 333°36' (Front) Oc. R.6 sec. 7M. Grey Tr. on B.Dolphin 12m. (Rear) Oc. R.6 sec. 7M. Grey Tr. 18M.

STRALSUND 54°18'N 13°06'E

Tel: Port 60 23 65. Pilots (0 08 21) 69 24 20. Telex: Port 318538. Pilots 317279.
Radio-Port: VHF Chan. 14, 12, 16 H24.
Radio-Pilots: VHF Chan. 12, 14, 16 H24.
Reporting System: Compulsory for all vessels over 20m. in length. VHF Chan. 14, 9, 12, 16 H24. Report on entering, leaving and manoeuvring.
Information Broadcast: Chan. 14 at 0635, 1835.
Yacht moorings: 100.

BRIDGE S SIDE Lt. Oc(2) W.R.G.10 sec. W.5M. R.4M. G.3M. Bridge span 12m. G.310°-322°; W.322°-339°; R.339°-351°.
N SIDE Lt. Oc(2) W.R.G.10 sec. W.5M. R.4M. G.3M. Bridge span 12m. G.114°-126°; W.126°-138°; R.138°-150°.

QUAY HEAD Ldg. Lts. 240°42' (Front) Oc(2) R.10 sec. 8M. Tr. 15m. (Rear) Oc(2) R.10sec. 8M. R.silo 23m.

Lts. mark the channel through the harbour.

N MOLE HEAD Lt. Q.G. 3M. Grey Bn. with platform on pivot 8m.
E MOLE HEAD Lt. Q.R. 3M. R.Tr. 5m.
N MOLE Lt. F.W.R.G. W.9M. R.5M. G.5M. B.W.Mast 14m. G.318.3°-322.3°; W.322.3°-326.3°; R.326.3°-330.3°.

ZIEGELGRABEN

BRIDGE Lt. F.R. 1M. Bridge structure 3m. Traffic signals. Also F.G. 1M. 3m.
E SIDE OF CHANNEL Lt. F.R. 4M. on dolphin.
W SIDE OF CHANNEL Lt. F.G. 4M. on dolphin.

GREIFSWALDER BODDEN

Yacht moorings: Griefswald-Ladebow 55, Griefswald-Stadt 50.

VILM Dir. Lt. 314°. Oc. W.R.G.4 sec. W.7M. R.4M. G.4M. W.Col. R.Lantern 23m. G.308°-312°; W.312°-316°; R.316°-320°.

LAUTERBACH S PIER HEAD Lt. Oc. W.R.G.6 sec. W.6M. R.4M. G.3M. W.Tr. 6m. R.276°-331°; G.-024°; W.-029°; R.-031.5°. F.R. Lt. on radio mast 1.9M. NW.
Yacht moorings: 80.

Ldg. Lts. 313°24' (Front) Oc(2) R.10 sec. W. △, R.Border, on W.Tr. 10m. (Rear) Oc(2) R.10 sec. W. ▽ , R.Border on W.Tr. 13m.

FALKENHAGEN Ldg. Lts. 269°48' (Front) Oc. 6 sec. 8M. W. ⫿, R.Border, on grey Tr. 14m. (Rear) Oc. 6 sec. 8M. W. ◊, R.Border, on grey Tr. 40m.

GAGER Ldg. Lts. 090°06' (Front) Oc. R.6 sec. 8M. R. △ on W.Tr. (Rear) Oc. R.6 sec. 8M. R. ▽ on W.Tr.
Yacht moorings: 35.

MOLE HEAD Lt. F.G. B.Col. on pedestal 8m.

BAABE Ldg. Lts. 047°36' (Front) F.R. 2M. W. △ on B.W.Mast 5m. (Rear) F.R. 2M. W. ▽ on B.W.Mast 7m.
Yacht moorings: 25.

GOBBIN 54°20.7'N 13°36.2'E Ldg. Lts. 076°06' (Front) Oc(3) 15 sec. 12M. W. ⫿, R.Border, on W.Tr. 14m. 54°20.9'N 13°37.3'E (Rear) Oc(3) 15 sec. 12M. R. ◊ on W.Tr. 32m.

LADEBOW 54°06.2'N 13°26.9'E Ldg. Lts. 208°24' (Front) Oc. R.6 sec. 10M. R. △ on W.Tr. 12m. 54°06.1'N 13°26.9'E (Rear) Oc. R.6 sec. 10M. R. ▽ on W.Tr. 17m.

HAFEN Fl. Lt. F.W.G. W.5M. G.2M. R.Lantern, B.Mast on pedestal 7m.

F2 Lt. F.W.G. W.5M. G.2M. R.Lantern, B.Mast on pedestal 7m.

F3 Lt. F. R.Lantern, B.Mast on pedestal 7m.

WIECK. N MOLE HEAD Lt. F. G.2M. G.Col. 4m.
Yacht moorings: 60.

ELDENA Ldg. Lts. 182°48' (Front) Oc(2) 10 sec. 5M. R.W. ⫿ on grey Tr. 13m. (Rear) Oc(2) 10 sec. 5M. W. ◊, R.Border, on grey Tr. 22m.

VIEROW Lt. Fl. W.R.G.4 sec. W.4M. R.2M. G.2M. mast 5m. On request. G.162.5°-172.5°; W.172.5°-176.5°; R.176.5°-186.5°.

RUDEN
Yacht moorings: 40.

N Dir. Lt. 090°. Dir. Oc. W.R.G.6 sec. W.7M. R.4M. G.4M. W.Tr. R.Lantern 25m. G.085°-089.5°; W.089.5°-090.5°; R.090.5°-095°.

E MOLE HEAD Lt. F.G. 2M. G.Tr. 6m. 260°-359°.

Ldg. Lts. 239°30' (Front) Oc. W.R.G.6 sec. W.9M. R.6M. G.5M. Grey round Tr. 8m. R.189°-207°; W.207°-250°; G.250°-349.3°; Lts. 2 Q.vert. on platforms 1.6M. SW, 2M W. (Rear) Oc. 6 sec. 11M. Grey Tr. 16m.

Dir. Lt. 320.5°. Oc. W.R.G.6 sec. W.5M. R.3M. G.2M. W.R.Mast 6m. G.313.8°-319°; W.319°-322°; R.322°-327.5°.

S POINT CROSS Lt. F.W.R. W.5M. R.3M. W.Tr. R.Lantern 5m. W.280°-290°; R.290°-005°; W.005°-015°.

PEENEMÜNDE Lt. Oc. W.R.G.6 sec. W.9M. R.6M. G.5M. W.R. round Tr. and Lantern 11m. G.190°-193°; W.-202°; R.-208°; G.094°-096°; W.-098°; R.-101°.

PEENESTROM

TONNENBANK 54°08.5'N 13°43.7'E Ldg. Lts. 206°36' (Front) Oc. 6 sec. 12M. W.Tr. R.Lantern 12m. F.R. Lt. on chimney 2M. W. 54°08.2'N 13°43.4'E (Rear) Oc. 6 sec. 12M. R. ◊ on W.Tr. 24m.

KNAAKRÜCKEN RINNE 54°08.9'N 13°45.8'E Ldg. Lts. 153°24' (Front) Oc. 6 sec. 13M. R. ∆ on W.Tr. 17m. F.R. Lt. on chimney 550m. SE. 54°08.5'N 13°46.2'E (Rear) Oc. 6 sec. 13M. R. ▽ on W.Tr. 33m.

PEENEMUNDE Ldg. Lts. 147°12' (Front) Oc(4) R.15 sec. 6M. W. ∆ R.Border, on W.Bn. 9m. (Rear) Oc(4) R.15 sec. 6M. W. ▽, R.Border, on W.Tr. 13m.

FREEST Ldg. Lts. 241°42' (Front) Oc.6 sec. 9M. R. ∆ on W.Tr. 15m. (Rear) Oc. 6 sec. 9M. R. ▽ on W.Tr. 19m.
Yacht moorings: 35.

54°08.3'N 13°43.7'E Lt. F.W.R.G. W.5M. R.3M. G.2M. W.Tr. R.Lantern 5m. G.255°-260.5°; W.260.5°-266°; R.266°-271.5°.

KRÖSLIN N Ldg. Lts. 169° (Front) Oc(3) 15 sec. 9M. R. ∆ on W.Tr. 10m. (Rear) Oc(3) 15 sec. 9M. R. ▽ on W.Tr. 18m.

KUHLER ORT Ldg. Lts. 129°30' (Front) Oc(3) 12 sec. 9M. W. ∆, B.Border on W.Bn. 8m. F.R. and F.G. on breakwaters 0.7M NNW. (Rear) Oc(3) 12 sec. 9M. W. ▽, B.Border on W.Bn. 12m.

KRÖSLIN 54°07.3'N 13°45.2'E Ldg. Lts. 225° (Front) Oc. 6 sec. 10M. W. ∆ R.Border, on W.Tr. 10m.54°07.3'. 3N 13°45.2'E (Rear) Oc. 6 sec. 10M. W. ▽, R.Border, on W.Tr. 12m.

WOTIG Ldg. Lts. 169° (Front) Oc. 6 sec. 9M. W. ∆, R.Border on W.Tr. 8m. (Rear) Oc. 6 sec. 9M. W. ▽, R.Border on W.Tr. 11m.

KRÖSLIN S Ldg. Lts. 315° (Front) Oc(2) 10 sec. 9M. W. ∆, R.Border on W.Tr. 8m. 54°07.8'N 13°45.6'E (Rear) Oc(2) 10 sec. 10M. W. ▽, B.Border on W.Tr. 13m.

New marina project at Kröslin.

HOLLENDORFER RACK Ldg. Lts. 117° (Front) Oc. 6 sec. 9M. W. ∆, B.Border on W.Tr. 8m. F.R. Lt. 550m. N. (Rear) Oc. 6 sec. 9M. W ▽, B.Border on W.Tr. 11m.

MÖLSCHOW Ldg. Lts. 160° (Front) Oc. 6 sec. 9M. W ∆, R.Border on W.Tr. 7M. (Rear) Oc. 6 sec. 9M. W. ▽, B.Border on W.Tr. 10m.

SANDHOF Ldg. Lts. 213° (Front) Oc. R.6 sec. 6M. W. ∆, R.Border on W.Tr. 11m. (Rear) Oc. R.6 sec. 6M. W. ▽, B.Border on W.Tr. 15m.

MAHLZOW Ldg. Lts. 030°18' (Front) Oc(3) 15 sec. 9M. W. ∆, R.Border on W.Tr. 15m. (Rear) Oc(3) 15 sec. 9M. W. ▽, R.Border on W.Tr. 20m.

54°03.5'N 13°47.8'E Ldg. Lts. 181° (Front) Oc(2) 10 sec. 10M. R. ∆ on W.Wood Bn. 11m. 54°03.5'N 13°47.8'E (Rear) Oc(2) 10 sec. 10M. R. ▽ on W.Tr. 19m.

F.R. and F.G. Lts. mark passage through Wolgast bridge.

WOLGAST 54°03'N 13°47'E
Tel: 26 90.
Radio-port: VHF Chan. 14, 12, 16. 0600-1800.
Reporting System: Compulsory for all vessels over 20m. in length. VHF Chan. 14, 9, 11, 16.H24. Report when entering, leaving and manoevring.
Information Broadcasts: Chan. 14 at 0715, 1715.
Navigational Advice: Chan. 22.
Yacht moorings: 50.

WOLGAST BRIDGE Lt. 2 F.G. 1M. and 2 F.R. 1M.

DOLPHIN No: 78. **E SIDE** Lt. Oc(4) R.9 sec. 2M. R.Dolphin 5m.
DOLPHIN No: 82 Lt. F.R. 2M. Dolphin 5m. 230° 115°.
DOLPHIN No: 84. **E SIDE** Lt. Fl. R.1.5 sec. 2M. R.Dolphin 5 m. 032°-253.5°.

HOHENDORF N Ldg. Lts. 206°30' (Front) Oc(4) 15 sec. 9M. W. △, R.Border on W.Tr. 10m. (Rear) Oc(4) 15 sec. 9M. W. ▽, B.Border on W.Tr. 15m.

Ldg. Lts. upstream are extinguished between 15/11-15/4 and shown only on request.

NEGENMARK Ldg. Lts. 160° (Front) Oc. 6 sec. 9M. W. △, R.Border, on W.Tr.10m. (Rear) Oc. 6 sec. 9M. W. ▽, B.Border on W.Tr. 15m.

HOHENDORF S Ldg. Lts. 286°30' (Front) Oc(2) R.10 sec. 7M. R. △, on W.Tr. 8m. (Rear) Oc(2) R.10 sec. 7M. R. ▽, on W.Tr. 21m.

SAUZIN 54°01.6'N 13°48.4'E Ldg. Lts. 321° (Front) Oc(3) 15 sec. 12M. R.W. ☐ on W.Tr. 9m. 54°02.3'N 13°47.5'E (Rear) Oc(3) 15 sec. 14M. R. ▽ on W.Tr. 28m.

GORMITZ Oc(2) W.R.G.7 sec. W.6M. R.4M. G.4M. G.026°-031°; W.031°-035°; R.035°-040°.

NETZELKOW 54°02.1'N 13°55.0'E Ldg. Lts. 016°30' (Front) Oc. 4 sec. 10M. W. △, R.Border on W.Tr. 7m. 54°02.3'N 13°55.3'E (Rear) Oc. 4 sec. 10M. W. ▽, R.Border on W.Tr. 14m.

RANKWITZ S 53°56.0'N 13°56.2'E Ldg. Lts. 141° (Front) Oc(4) 15 sec. 12M. W.Tr. 10m. 54°55.6'N 13°56.7'E Oc(4) 15 sec. 12M. R. ◇ on W.R.Tr. 25m.

N Ldg. Lts. 353°42' (Front) Oc. 6 sec. 9M. W. △, R.Border on W.Tr. 10m. (Rear) Oc. 6 sec. 9M. W. ▽, R.Border on W.Tr. 15m.

KRIENKE 53°55.3'N 13°56.1'E Ldg. Lts. 048°. (Front) Oc(2) 10 sec. 12M. W.Tr. 9m. 53°55.6'N 13°56.7'E (Rear) Oc(2) 10 sec. 15M. R. ◇ on W.R.Tr. 28m.

ZECHERIN 53°52.4'N 13°50.6'E Ldg. Lts. 228° (Front) Oc(3) 15 sec. 12M. R.W. ☐ on W.Tr. 10m. 53°52.0'N 13°50.0'E (Rear) Oc(3) 15 sec. 12M. R. ▽ on W.Tr. 22m.

PINNOW Ldg. Lts. 253°30' (Front) Oc(4) 15 sec. 9M. R. △, on W.Tr. 9m. (Rear) Oc(4) 15 sec. 9M. R. ▽ on W.Tr. 13m.

KLOTZOW Ldg. Lts. 015°30' (Front) Oc. 6 sec. 9M. W. △, R.Border on W.Tr. 9m. (Rear) Oc. 6 sec. 9M. W. ▽, R.Border on W.Tr. 14m.

JAHNKENORT Ldg. Lts. 213° (Front) Oc(2) 10 sec. 9M. W. △, R.Border on W.Tr. 10m. (Rear) Oc(2) 10 sec. 9M. W. ▽, B.Border on W.Tr. 16m

ANKLAMER E Ldg. Lts. 147°30' (Front) Oc(3) 15 sec. 9M. W. △, R.Border on W.Tr. 9m. (Rear) Oc(3) 15 sec. 9M. W. ▽, B.Border on W.Tr. 15m.

W. Ldg. Lts. 262°. (Front) Oc(4) 15 sec. 9M. W. △, B.Border on W.Tr. 10m. (Rear) Oc(4) 15 sec. 9M. W. ▽, B.Border on W.Tr. 14m.

KARNIN RAILWAY BRIDGE NW

APPROACH SW SIDE Lt. F.W.G. W.5M. G.3M. 5m. W.085°-113°; G.113°-220°.
NE SIDE Lt. F.R. 2M. 5m.
SE APPROACH SW SIDE Lt. F.R. 3M. 5m.
NE SIDE Lt. F.W.G. W.6M. G.3M. 5m. W.294°-308°; G.308°-025°.

ZECHERIN BRIDGE Lts. 2 F. R. and 2 F.G.

GREIFSWALDER OIE

Yacht moorings: 50.

54°15.0'N 13°55.5'E Lt. Fl. 3.8 sec. 26M. R.8-sided Tr. with 2 galleries, B.Lantern, brown cuppola 48m. Storm signals. F.R. Lt. on framework Tr. 12.4M. SSE and F.R. Lt. on chimney 10.3M. S.

OIE Lt. Oc. W.R.G.6 sec. W.5M. R.3M. G.2M. W.Hut 15m. G.102°-108°; W.-112°; R.-118°.

N MOLE HEAD Lt. F.R. R.Mast 6m. F.G. on Mole Head close S.

POLAND
SWINOUJSCIE (SWINEMUNDE)
53°55'N 14°17'E
Tel: Port 2001. Reporting/Information
Service 4903. Port Captain 3257.
Telex: Port 042 2316 ZPS PL. Port Captain
042 5476 KPSW PL.
Rescue Coordination Centre. Tel: 5924.
Telex 422632 PRO PL.
Radio-Port: VHF Chan. 12, 16.
Radio-Pilots: VHF Chan. 14, 12, 16 H24.
Information Broadcasts by Stettin on Chan.
8 at 0533 1133 1733 2333. By Police on
Chan. 12 ev. H+10. By Swinoujscie on Chan.
12 ev. H+20.

53°55.0'N 14°17.2'E **MAIN** Lt. Oc. W.R.5 sec.
W.25M. R.9M. Y.R.Round brick Tr. on square
building 68m. R.029°-057°; W.057°-280°. RC.

W MOLE HEAD MLYNY 53°55.7'N 14°16.8'E
Outer Ldg. Lts. 170°06' (Front) Oc.(3) 20 sec.
17M. W.Tr. 11m.
GALERIOWA 53°55'.4N 14°16.9'E. Oc(3) 20
sec. 17M. W. ∇ on W. round Tr. 3 galleries
23m.

E MOLE HEAD 53°56'.0N 14°16.8'E Lt. F.R.
11M. R. 8-sided.Tr. 13m. Reserve Lt. Fl. R. 3
sec. 6M. 6 F.Y. mark breakwater. Horn (3) 60
sec. Synchronised with Swinoujscie RC.

BASEN STOCZNIOWAY E. SIDE Lt. Oc(2)
G.10 sec. 2M. G. Col. on pyramidal base 4m.

N POINT Lt. F.G. 2M. W.Tr. with gallery 8m.
S POINT Lt. Oc. G.4 sec. 2M. G.Tr. with
gallery 7m. 3 F. R. vert. Lts. 300m. N, 450m.
NE mark overhead cable pylons.

ZATOKA POMORSKA Lt. F.W.R.G.W. 6M. R.
4M. G.4M. Building 9m. G.068.7°- 090.5°;
W.090.5°-103.7°; R.103.7°-125°.

NURT MIELINSKI
WYSPA MIELINO N END Lt. L. Fl.(2) R.G. 10
sec. R.3M. G.1M. + on R.Tr. with gallery
11m. R.267°-200°; G. 132°-300°.
RZEKA SWINA JETTY CPN-2 Lt. Oc. R.4 sec.
2M. post on dolphin 6m.
Lt. Oc. R. 4 sec. 2M. post on dolphin 6m.
Lt.Q. 5M. on dolphin 5m.
Lt.Q. (6) + L. Fl. 15 sec. 5M. �ⵊ on dolphin 5m.

SOUTH Ldg. Lts. 140° (Rear) F.6M. Or.Tr.
20m. 133°-147°. Emergency Lt.Oc. 6 sec.
5M. (Common front) Iso. 4 sec. 3M. W.Mast
15m. 133°-147°. Emergency Lt. Oc. 5 sec.
5M. Also Iso G. 4 sec. 5M. 15m. 341°-355°.
Emergency Lt.Oc. 5 sec. 5M.

NORTH Ldg. Lts. 348°20' (Rear) Oc.G. 4 sec.
5M. W. Or.Tr. 20m. 341°-355°. Emergency Lt.
Oc. 6 sec. 5M.

W SIDE Lt. 4 Oc.(2) R.15 sec. 3M. W.Tr. 9m.
4 Lts. mark W. side of Wyspa Miehn.

S END Lt. Oc. (2) R.15 sec. 3M. Double + on
R.Tr. 7m. 310°-240.5°.

PAPROTNO Ldg. Lts. 168°20' (Front) Oc. 5
sec. 5M. W.Tr. 15m. 161°-175°. Reserve
Lt.Oc.5 sec. (Rear) F. 5M. R.W. square Tr.
20m. 161°-175°. Reserve Lt. Oc. 6 sec.

WYSPA KARSIBOR N END Lt. L. Fl. (2)
W.R.G. 10 sec. 3M. + on cupola on R.Tr. 7m.
R.353°-169°; G.169°-283°; W.315°-330°.

BASIN ENTRANCE Lt. F.R. 3M. Col. 4m.
162°-196°.

W SIDE Lt. F.G. 3M. Col. 4m. 180°-214°.

KANAL PIASTOWSKI
KARSIBOR Ldg. Lts. 321°20' (Front) Oc. Y.5
sec. 5M. W.Round Tr. B.Top 15m. 320.2°-
323.2°. Reserve Lt. range 7M. (Rear) F.Y. 8M.
R. W.Tr. 39m. Reserve Lt. Oc.Y. 6 sec. range
8M.

W SIDE Lt. Oc.G. 5 sec. 3M. W.Tr. 9m.
3 Lts. mark W. side of channel between
Karsibor and Mielensky Paprotno Ldg. Lts.

PAPROTNO Lt. Oc.G. 5 sec. 3M. W.Tr. 10m.

BRAMA TOROWA No: 1E Lt. F. 7M. R.Round
Tr. 2 galleries 25m. 138.2°-145.2°; 318.2°-
325.2°.

W. Lt. F. 7M. G. round Tr. 2 galleries 25m.
138.2°-145.2°; 318.2°-325.2°. Also F. W. R.
3M. 23m. W.026.5°-036.5°; R. 036.5°-086°.
Horn Mo(K) 60 sec.

BRAMOWE **E MOLE HEAD** Lt. F. R. 4M.
Grey Tr. and gallery, granite base 14m.
Reserve Lt. Oc. R. 15 sec.

ZALEW WIELKI
BRAMA TOROWA No: 2 EAST 53°45.7'N
14°24.'4E Lt. L. Fl. 8 sec. 13M. R.Round Tr. 2
galleries on concrete base 25m. 136.5°-146°;
316.5-326°.
WEST 53°45.6'N 14°24.'2E Lt. L. Fl. 8 sec.
13M. G.Tr. with 2 galleries 25m. 136.5°-146°;
316.5°-326°. Same structure. Lt. Fl. W.R.G.4
sec. G. 104°-107°; W.107°-110°; R.110°-113°.

No: 3 EAST 53°42.9'N 14°28.3'E Lt. L. Fl. 5
sec. 13M. R.Round Tr. 2 galleries on
concrete base 25m. 136.5°-146°; 316.5-326°.
Also same structure Fl. W.R.G. 4 sec. W.6M.
R.4M. G.4M. 22m. G.179°-185°; W.185°-191°;
R.191°-197°; W.197°-223°.
WEST 53°42.8'N 14°28.'1E Lt. L. Fl. 5 sec.
13M. G.Round Bn., 2 galleries on concrete
base 25m. 136.5°-146°; 316.5°-326°.

SWINA
LUBIN Ldg. Lts. 300° (Front) Oc(2) 12 sec.
5M. W.Tr. 34m. (Rear) Oc(2) 12 sec. 5M. W.
▢, R.Border on W.Tr. 53m.

S MOLE Lt. F.G. 1M. Col. 7m.

WAPNICA N MOLE Lt. F.R. 1M. Col. 7m.

ZATOKA SKOSZEWSKA
Ldg. Lts. 081°20' (Front) Oc. 6 sec. 6M. R. ▢
on W.Tr. 21m. (Rear) Oc. 6 sec. 6M. R.Tr.
34m.

ZAGORZE Ldg. Lts.049° (Front) F.R. 5M. W.
▢ on W.Tr. 16m. (Rear) F.R. 5M. R.Tr. 25m.

PÓLWYSPU RÓW Lt. Fl. 5. sec. 6M. R. ○ on
R.Tr. 16m.

RZEKA DZIWNA GOLOGORA Ldg. Lts.001°
(Front) F. 5M. W.Tr. 15m. (Rear) F. 5M.
R.Building 18m.

ROZTOKA ODRZANSKA
WYSPA CHELMINEK N END Lt. F.R. 3M.
W.Tr.B.Top 13m.

S END Lt. F.R. 3M. R.Tr. 8m.

BRAMA TOROWA No: 4 KOPANICKA WEST
Lt. F. 7M. G.Round Tr. 25m. 138°-145.8°;
315.3°-322.8°. Reserve Lt. Oc. 5 sec.

EAST Lt. F. 7M. R.Tr. concrete base 25m.
137.3°-144.8°; 320.3°-327.8°. Horn Mo(N) 30
sec.

TRZEBIEZ Ldg. Lts. 150° (Front) Oc. Y. 8 sec.
7M. R. ▯ on W.Tr. 8m. (Rear) Oc. Y. 8 sec. 7M.
R. ▯ on Tr.

ENTRANCE N SIDE Lt. F.R. 2M. R.Tr. 6m.

BREAKWATER NW END Lt. F.G. 2M. Col.
7m.

SE END Lt. F.G. 2M. B.Tr. 6m.

S MOLE HEAD Lt. F.R. 2M. R.W.Tr. 6m.

Ldg. Lts. 301°12' (Front) Oc.5 sec. 4M. W. ▯
on B.Tr. 12m. (Rear) F.4M. W. ▽ on B.Tr.
16m.

STEPNICA, RAILWAY HARBOUR
Ldg. Lts. 066°36' (Front) Oc. R. 3 sec. 7M. W.
△ on Tr. 11m. (Rear) F.R. 7M. W.R. ▽, on grey
Tr. 15m.

N MOLE HEAD Lt. F.R. 2M. R.Mast 6m.
S MOLE HEAD Lt. F.G. 2M. G.Mast 6m.

BASEN RYBACKI BREAKWATER HEAD Lt.
F.R. 4M. Post 6m.

MANKOW Ldg. Lts. 141°20' (Front) Oc.5 sec.
7m. W.Round Tr. Or.Top 15m. 137.5°-146°.
ᗡᗞ Emergency Lt. Oc.15 sec. 2M. (Rear) F.
7M. W. triangular Tr. Or.Top 32m. 140°-143°.
Emergency Lt. Oc.15 sec. 3M.

STEPNICA Ldg. Lts. 348°06' (Front) Oc.(2)
15 sec. 5m. W.Round Tr.Or.Top 15m. 345.9°-
350.4°. (Rear) F.5M. W.round Tr.Or.Top 25m.
345.9°-350.4°.

ZULAWY Lt. F.W.R. W.2M. R.1M. W.Square
Tr. R.Top 12m. W.024.4°-046°; R.046°-098°
over Zakret Manków. W.098°-112.4°.
No: 26 Lt. Iso R.2 sec. 6M. Dolphin on R.
Round Tr. with gallery 8m. ᗡᗞ
Km. 44 Lt. Fl. G.4 sec. 5M. Dolphin 6m.
Marks gas pipeline.

RADUN Ldg. Lts. 168°06' (Front) Oc(2) 15
sec. 5NM W.Round Tr. with 2 galleries and
conical roof, Or.Top. 15m. 165.9°-170.4°.
Reserve Lt. Iso 4 sec. 6M. (Rear) F.5M. W.
square Tr. with 2 galleries and conical roof,
Or.Top 26m. 165.9°-170.4°. Reserve Lt. Iso. 8
sec. 6M.

WYSPA WIELKI KARW Lt. Q. Y. Bn. B.Top. 2
galleries.

KIELPINEK KREPA Ldg. Lts. 356°06' (Front)
Oc.5 sec. 5M. W.Round Tr. Or.Top 15m.
353.9°-358.4°. (Rear) F.5M. W.Square Tr.
Or.Top 26m. 353.9°-358.4°

DLUGI OSTROW S END Lt. Q. (6) + L. Fl. 15
sec. 6M. ⚡ on B.Round Tr. Y.Top with 2
galleries 8m.

RADUN ISLAND Lt. Fl. R.4 sec. 6M. W. R. Bn.
with 2 galleries.

E SIDE Lt. Fl. R.3 sec. 3M. R.W.Round
structure with gallery 8m.

DOMANCE CROSS Lt. F.W.R. W.2M. R.1M.
W. square Tr. and gallery, R.Top 12m.
W.191.8°-202.3°; R.202.3°-277.5° over bend
in channel; W.277.5°-292.5°. Emergency
Lt.Oc.4 sec. 2M.

Ldg. Lts. 176°06' (Front) Oc. Y. 5 sec. 5m. W. round Tr. with 2 galleries and conical roof, Or.Top 15m. F.G. on N. and S ends of tanker berths 200m. ENE. Emergency Lt. Oc. 15 sec. 4M. (Rear) Oc. Y. 5 sec. 5M. W.Tr. with 2 galleries and conical roof, Or.Top 26m. Emergency Lt. Oc. 15 sec. 4M.

INA N Ldg. Lts. 132°43' (Front) Oc.(2) 15 sec. 5m. W.Square Tr. B.Top 16m. Emergency Lt. Oc. 15 sec. 2M. (Common Rear) F.5M. W.Square Tr. B.Top 26m. Emergency Lt. Oc.15 sec. 2M.

S. Ldg. Lts. 018°12' (Front) Oc.(2) 15 sec. 5M. W.Square Tr. B.Top 15m. F. R. Lts. on power pylons 200m. W. 800m. WSW.

RYBI OSTROW Lt. V. Q. (6) + L. Fl. 10 sec. 4M. ⚓ on B.Dolphin, Y.Top 12m.

BABINA WYSPA MEWIEJ Lt. F.W.R. W.2M. R.1M. W.Square Tr. R.Top 12m. W.037.8°-058.4°; R.058.4°-133.7° over bend in channel; W.133.7°-154.2°.

RZEKA ODRA

OSTROW MNISI Lt. Q. ⚓ on Y.dolphin, B.Top.

WHYSPA KOPINA S POINT Lt. Iso R.4 sec. 2M. R.Tr. 7m.〰

W SIDE No: 45 Lt. Fl. G.4 sec. 3M. G. dolphin 8m.

E SIDE No: 46 Lt. Fl. R.4 sec. 3M. R.Dolphin 8m. 〰

INSKIE Lt. Oc.(3) W.R.13 sec. W.2M. R.1M. W.Square Tr. R.Top, conical roof 12m. W.011.3°-025.5°; R.025.5°-107° over bend in channel; W.107-118.1°.

W SIDE No: 47 Lt. Oc. G.4 sec. 3M. G. Dolphin 8m.

E SIDE No: 50 Lt. Fl.(2) R.6 sec. 3M. R. Dolphin 8m.

W SIDE No: 49 Lt. Fl.(2) G.6 sec. 3M. G. dolphin 8m. 〰

LAKI Ldg. Lts. 354° (Front) Oc. 5 sec. 5M. W. Round Tr. 2 galleries, Or.Top, conical roof 15m. (Rear) F.5M. W. square Tr. 2 galleries, Or.Top, conical roof 23m.

ZURAWI WYSPA N POINT Lt. Q. 2M. Y.Tr. B.Top, 2 galleries 12m.

BYKOWO Ldg. Lts. 174° (Front) Oc. 5 sec. 5M. W.Round Tr. Or.Top 15m. (Rear) F.5M. W.Square Tr. Or.Top 24m.

SWIETA Ldg. Lts. 198°12' (Front) Oc. 2 15 sec. 5M. W.Round Tr. B.Top 15m. Emergency Lt. Oc. 15 sec. 2M. (Rear) F.5M. W.Tr. B.Top 26m.

WYSPA ZURAWIA Lt. Q.(6) + L. Fl. 15 sec. B. Bn. Y.Top, 2 galleries.

No: 54 Lt. Fl. R. 2 sec. on dolphin.

No: 56 Lt. Fl.(2) R.6 sec.on dolphin.

No: 58 Lt. Fl.(3) R.8 sec.on dolphin.

No: 60 Lt. Q.R on dolphin.

No: 62 Lt. Fl. R.2 sec. on dolphin.

KRASNICA WHARF N END Lt. F.Bu. F.Bu. marks S end 400m/ SSW.

No: 64 Lt. Fl.(2) R.6 sec. on dolphin.

No: 66 Lt. Fl.(3) R.8 sec. on dolphin.

No: 68 Lt. Q. R. on dolphin.

No: 70 Lt. Iso R.2 sec. on dolphin.

NARBRZEZA GOCLAWSKIEGO N PART Lt. F.G.2M. Y. Post illuminated base. 4m.

WYSPA DEBINA Lt. Fl. R.4 sec. 5M. R.Tr. 6m.

SZCZECIN (STETTIN) 53°25'N 14°35'E
Tel: Port 430 31. H.M. 226 557. Ops. Dir. 47145. Deep Sea Pilots 44 745. Telex: Port 422108 ZP PL. Pilots 042 21 47. Emergency Coordination Centre Tel. 885 43.

BASEN SUM Lt. Fl. G.3 sec. 3M. B.Mast 9m.

LIGHTING AUTHORITIES BASIN ENTRANCE N SIDE Lt. Oc. G.4 sec. 2M. Col. 7m.
S SIDE Lt. F.G. 1M. Col. 7m.

JACHTOWE WHARF N END Lt. F.R. F.Bu. marks S end 250m. SSW.

PRZEKOP MIELENSKI E SIDE Lt. Fl. R.4.5 sec. 3M. Col. 6m.

For lights in Przekop Kielenski see below.

REKA ODRA BASEN OKO N SIDE Lt. F.G.
1M. Col. 7m.
S SIDE Lt. F.R. 1M. Col. 7m.
Lt. Fl. G.4 sec. 3m.
BASEN MLYNSKI Lt. F.Bu. 1M. Col. 7m.

WYSPA GRYFIA BASEN REMONTOWY
N SIDE Lt. F.R. 1M. Col. 7m.
S SIDE Lt. F.G. 1M. Col. 7m.
S END Lt. F.Bu. 1M. Col. 7m.

EWA NW END Lt. F.R. 1M. Col. 7m.
NE END Lt F.G. 1M. Col. 7m.

PORT CENTRALNY ENTRANCE W SIDE
FERRY LANDING Lt. F.G. 1M. Col. 9m.
BASEN WSCHODNI PIER E HEAD Lt. F.G.
1M. Col. 7m.
BASEN ZACHODNI PIER W HEAD Lt. F.R.
1M. Col. 7m.

KANAL PRZEMYSLOWY N END E SIDE Lt.
F.G. 1M. Col. 7m.

PRZEKOP MIELENSKI E SIDE Lt. F.R. 4M.
Post 8m.

Przekop Mielenski E side marked by 6 F.Y.
Lts. W side 8 F.Y. Lts.

**OSTROW GRABOWSKI. WYSPA WIDZKA
KEEPA N END** Lt. L.Fl(2) 14 sec. 1M. Col.
7m. F. Lt. 110m. SW and 80m. E.
Lt. Oc. 5 sec. 2M. Col. 8m.
W SIDE Lt. F.G. 1M. Col. 6m.
E SIDE S END Lt. F.R. 1M. Col. 6m.

ISLAND OF MIENIA Lt. Oc. R.4 sec. 4M. 5m.

RZEKA PARNICA Lt. F.G. 1M. woodpole 7m.

BASEN GORNICZY W SIDE CPN2 Lt. F.R.
1M. Col. 7m.
BASEN GORNOSLASKI PIER CPN1 Lt. F.G.
1M. Col. 7m.

BASEN NOTECKI W SIDE Lt. F.G. 1M. Col.
7m.
E SIDE Lt. F.R. 1M. Col. 7m.

BASEN WARTY ENTRANCE W SIDE Lt. F.G.
1M. Col. 7m.
E SIDE Lt. F.R. 1M. Col. 7m.

WALBRZYSKIM PIER Lt. F.R. 1M. Col. 7m.

BASEN GORNICZY TASMOWCA PIER
HEAD W SIDE Lt. F.R. 1M. Col. 7m.
E SIDE Lt. F.G. 1M. Col. 7m.
CHORZOWSKIEGO PIER HEAD Lt. F.R. 1M.
Col. 7m.
BYTOMSKIEGO PIER N CORNER Lt. F.G.
1M. Col. 7m.
F.R. Lts. 0.85M. W.
GLIWICKIEGO Lt. F.R. 1M. 7m.

KLEINES HAFF

ALTWARP No: 7 Lt. Fl. R.4 sec. 4M.
W.R.Lantern on B.Dolphin 5m. 153°-010°.
Indicates German-Polish border.

NOWE WARPNO MOLE HEAD Lt. F.W.R.G.
1M. W.Tr. 6m. G.152°-155°; W.155°-158°;
R.158°-161°; Whis 15 sec.
ELBOW Lt. F.G. 4M. Col. 7m.

UECKERMÜNDE W MOLE ROOT 53°45.2'N
14°04.3'E Lt. Oc. 6 sec. 13M. W.Square Tr.
11m. 113°-293°.

KAMP 53°50.4'N 13°50.6'E Ldg. Lts. 283°
(Front) Oc(3) 15 sec. 11M. R. ☐ on W.Tr. 9m.
F.R. Lts. mark overhead cables 650m. NNW.
53°50.5'N 13°50.5'E (Rear) Oc(3) 15 sec.
13M. Grey Tr. and gallery 25m.

KAMINKE Ldg. Lts. 017°36' (Front) Iso. 6
sec. 3M. Wooden Mast 8m. Occas. (Rear)
Iso. 6 sec. 3M. Wooden Mast 9m. Occas.

KIKUT 53°59.0'N 14°34.9'E Lt. Iso. 10 sec.
16M. Grey round stone Tr. W.Lantern 91m.
063°-241°. Reserve Lt. range 9M.

DZIWNOW

W MOLE NEAR ROOT Ldg. Lts. 142°30'
(Front) F. 3M. W. ◇, R.Border, on W.Tr. 8m.
(Rear) F. 3M. W. ☐ on W.R.Tr. 13m.

W MOLE HEAD Lt. F.G. 7M. Col. 10m.
Reserve Lt. F.11. G.5 sec. 4M.
E MOLE HEAD Lt. F.R. 7M. Col. 10m.
Reserve Lt. Fl. R.5 sec. 5M. Horn Mo(A) 60
sec.

BASEN ZIMOWY Lt. F.G. 1M. Col. 6m.
Lt. F.R. 1M. Col. 6m.

NIECHORZE 54°05.8'N 15°03.9'E Lt. Fl.10
sec. 20M. Grey 8-sided Tr. R.Stripes on
dwelling 63m.

MRZEZYNO Lt. Iso. R.G.6 sec. 5M.Tr. 7m.
G.106°-146°; R.146°-196°. Horn Mo(P) 60
sec.

W BREAKWATER ROOT Ldg. Lts. 180°48'
(Front) F. 4M. W. △, R.Border on W.Tr. 8m.
(Rear) F. 4M. W. ▽, R.Border on W.Tr. 10m.

E BREAKWATER HEAD Lt. F.R. 3M. W.R. Col.
with gallery 7m.
W BREAKWATER HEAD Lt. F.G. 3M. W.G.
Col. with gallery 7m.

DZWIRZYNO

KANAL RESKO W SIDE Lt. Oc. 8 sec. 6M.
Concrete Col. 13m. 152°-211°.
Dir. Lt. 180.2° Dir. F.W.R.G. W.5M. R.3M.
G.3M. Same structure 11M. G.152°-180°;
W.180°-180.5°; R.180.5°-211°.
E SIDE Horn(2) 60 sec.

KOLOBRZEG (KOLBERG) 54°11'N
15°34'E
Tel: 2703.
Radio-Port & Pilots: VHF Chan. 12, 14, 16
H24.

E MOLE NEAR ROOT 54°11.3'N 15°33.4'E Lt.
Fl.3 sec. 16M. R.Tr. B.Cupola 36m. RC.
Traffic Signals
HEAD Lt. Oc. R.4 sec. 7M. W. ○ on W.R. Col.
13m. Horn Mo(K) 30 sec.

W MOLE HEAD Lt. Oc. G.4 sec. 7M.
G.Round structure, 2 galleries 11m.
Emergency Lt. Oc. G.5 sec. 5M.

BASEN SPORTOWY N HEAD Lt. F.G.
S HEAD Lt. F.R.

BASEN RYBACKI N HEAD Lt. F.G.
S HEAD Lt. F.R.
Lt. F.G.

GASKI 54°14.7'N 15°52.5'E Lt. Oc(3) 15
sec. 23M. R.Round Tr.Brown dwelling 50m.

DARLOWO 54°26'N 16°23'E
Radio-Pilots: VHF Chan. 12, 14, 16.

E MOLE NEAR ROOT 54°26.5'N 16°22.9'E Lt.
L.Fl(2) 15 sec. 15M. R.Square Tr. W.Lantern
20m. 040°-220°.
HEAD Lt. F.R. 7M. Grey square Tr. 10m.

W MOLE HEAD Lt. F.G. 7M. Grey square Tr.
10m.

INNER W MOLE HEAD Lt. F.Bu. 3M. Col. 8m.
Horn Mo(R) 30 sec.

BASEN RYBACKI N MOLE HEAD Lt. F.R. 1M.
Col. 8m. Not visible from seaward.
S MOLE HEAD Lt. F.G. 1M. Col. 8m. Not
visible from seaward.

WITOWO 54°32'N 16°33'E.
Radio-Port: VHF Chan. 12, 16.

JAROSLAWIEC 54°32.5'N 16°32.7'E Lt.
Fl(2) 9 sec. 23M. B.Tr. near dwelling 50m.
Obsc. 065.5°-077.5° within 2.3M. RC.

USTKA 54°35'N 16°52'E
Radio-Port & Pilots: VHF Chan. 12, 14, 16.
0600-2200.
Station equipped with radar.

E SIDE OF RIVER 54°35.4'N 16°51.4'E Lt. Oc.
6 sec. 18M. Reddish-brown 8-sided stone Tr.
W.Cupola 22m. Storm signals.

E MOLE HEAD Lt. Iso. R.6 sec. 7M.
R.W.Mast 11m.
ROOT Lt. F.R. Col. 5m.

W MOLE HEAD Lt. Iso. G.6 sec. 7M. G.Mast,
W.Base 10m.

RIVER ENTRANCE W SIDE Lt. F.G. 1M. Col.
5m.

BASEN WEGLOWY N SIDE Lt. F.G. 1M. Col.
5m.
S SIDE Lt. F.R. 1M. Col. 5m.

BASEN REMONTOWY Lt. F.G. 1M. W.G. Col.
6m.

ROWY Ldg. Lts. 141° (Front) F.R. 2M. W. △
on concrete Col. 6m. (Rear) F.R. 2M. W. ▽
on concrete Col. 8m.

CZOLPINO 54°43.3'N 17°14.6'E Lt. Oc(2)
14 sec. 21M. Round brick Tr. B.Cupola 75m.

LEBA 54°46'N 17°33'E.
Radio-Port: VHF Chan. 12, 14, 16.
Navigational information available on
request.

E MOLE HEAD Lt. Fl. R.5 sec. 5M. W.R. Col.
and gallery 10m.
W MOLE HEAD Lt. F.G. 5M. W.G. Col. and
gallery 10m.

Ldg. Lts. 164°30' (Front) Oc. Y.10 sec. 6M. W.
△, R.Border on W.Tr. 7m. (Rear) Oc. Y.10 sec.
6M. W. △, R.Border on W.Tr. 11m. RC.

BASEN ZIMOWY N SIDE Lt. F.R. 1M. Grey
Col. 6m.
S SIDE Lt. F.G. 1M. Grey Col. 6m.

BASEN RYBACKI N SIDE Lt. F.R. 1M. W.G.
Col. 6m.
S SIDE Lt. F.G. 1M. Col. 5m.

STILO 54°47.3'N 17°44.2'E Lt. Fl(3) 12 sec.
23M. R.W.B. Col. 75m. 050.5°-290.5°.

ROZEWIE 54°49.8'N 18°20.4'E Lt. Fl.3 sec.
26M. R.Round Tr., 2 galleries. 83m. RC.

WLADYSLAWOWO 54°48'N 18°25'E
Radio-Port: VHF Chan. 10, 12, 71, 16.
MF. 2182 1634 kHz.
Information on latest depths to be obtained
from Harbour Master.

N MOLE HEAD 54°47.9'N 18°25.5'E Lt.
Al. W.G.W.G.W.G. W.16M. G.6M. Concrete
Tr. W.Lantern 13m. The White Lt. is obsc.
015.7°-109.1°. Reserve Lt. Mo(G) .25 sec.

E BREAKWATER Lt. F.W.R.G.W. 8M.Tr. 14m.
W.258.5°-261.5°.
E MOLE HEAD Lt. F.R. 3M. Mast 12m.

RIVER WHARF HEAD Lt. F.G. 2M. Col. 6m.

FISHERY BUILDING 54°47.8'N 18°24.8'E Lt.
F.R. 23M.Tr. 78m.

JASTARNIA 54°42.1'N 18°41.1'E Lt. Oc(2)
20 sec. 15M. W.R.Round Tr. and cupola
22m.

GORA SZWEDOW 54°37.7'N 18°49.3'E Lt.
Iso. 30 sec. 14M. Grey Tr. and gallery 34m.

HEL 54°36.1'N 18°48.9'E Lt. Iso. 10 sec.
17M. R.8-sided masonry Tr. 41m. 130°-080°.
RC. Storm signals.

HEL PORT

OUTER HARBOUR W MOLE HEAD Lt. Oc(2) R.12 sec. 6M. W.R.Tr. 9m.
S MOLE HEAD Lt. F.W.G. W.3M. Concrete Tr. on building 9m. W.280°-353°; G.353°-280°.

BASEN WEWNETRZNY W PIER HEAD Lt. F.R. 1M. W.R. Col. 6m.
E PIER HEAD Lt. F.G. 1M. Col. 6m.

JASTARNIA

Ldg. Lts. 000°24' (Front) Iso. Y.6 sec. 2M. Y. ◊, B.Border, on grey Tr. 10m. (Rear) F.Y. 2M. Y. ▽, B.Border, on grey Tr. 19m.

E BREAKWATER HEAD Lt. F.G. 2M.Tr. 9m.
W BREAKWATER HEAD Lt. F.R. 2M.Tr. 9m.
ENTRANCE W SIDE Lt. Fl(3) W.R.10 sec. W.8M. W.R. Col. concrete base 9m. R.083°-333°; W.333°-083°.

PUCK

Ldg. Lts. 238°18' (Front) F.R. 2M. R. ▢, W.Stripe on Tr. 13m. (Rear) F.R. 2M. R. ▢, W.Stripe on Tr. 24m.

No: 2 ENTRANCE Ldg. Lts. 186° (Front) Oc(2) 15 sec. 2M. ◊ on Col. 12m. (Rear) Oc(2) 15 sec. 2M. ◊ on Col. 18m.

ENTRANCE E SIDE Lt. F.R. 4M. Col. 6m.
W SIDE Lt. F.G. 4M. Col. 6m.

KUZNICA Ldg. Lts. 341° (Front) Oc. R.5 sec. 3M. W. ▯, R.Border on Tr. 14m. (Rear) F.R. 3M.Tr. 17m.

CYPEL RZUCEWSKI Lt. Fl(2) 6 sec. 6M. R.W.Tr. 9m.

REWA

Ldg. Lts. 172° (Front) Oc. 6 sec. 3M. ⚓ on Tr. 9m. (Rear) Oc. 6 sec. 3M. 6-sided topmark on Tr. 13m.

GDYNIA 54°32'N 18°33'E

Tel: Port 20 10 01. H.M. 20 28 53 & 21 66 36. Deep Sea Pilots 20 41 17, 20 37 04, 43 09 21. Telex: Port 054221 MPHG PL; Deep Sea Pilots 054301 MAG & 0512641.
Radio-Port & Pilots: VHF Chan. 12, 16 including Radar H24.
Harbour Master's Office: Chan. 12 H24.
Agency: Chan. 7.
Emergency Coordination Centre: GUM Radio Chan. 16. Tel: 21 61 62 H24. or Urzad Morski Gdynia. Tel: 20 69 11. Telex: 054285. Information broadcasts by GUM Radio Chan. 71 at 0005 0705 1305 1905. Station accepts Polish, German or English.

GDYNIA/GDANSK Reporting System Tel: Gdynia 21 07 05 & 21 54 28. Gdansk 43 73 71 & 43 07 10.
Gdynia VHF Chan. 12. Gdansk VHF Chan. 14 H24.

N BREAKWATER HEAD Lt. Fl. G.3 sec. 3M. B.Tr. 8m.

N DETACHED BREAKWATER N END Lt. Fl. R.3 sec. 3M. R.W.Tr. 10m.
S END Lt. Iso. G.4 sec. 8M. Concrete Tr. 15m. Reserve Lt. range 6M.

S DETACHED BREAKWATER N END 54°32.2'N 18°33.9'E Lt. Iso. R.4 sec. 10M. Round concrete Tr. 15m. Reserve Lt. range 6M.

S END Lt. Oc. G.10 sec. 9M. Concrete Tr. glass cupola 12m. Reserve Lt. range 5M. 2 F.R. Lts. on 2 radio masts 0.8M. NW.

54°32.3'N 18°33.1'E Ldg. Lts. 271°30' (Front) Iso. Y.4 sec. 17M. W.Tr. R.Stripe 15m. Shown by day. 54°32.3'N 18°32.1'E (Rear) Oc. Y.6 sec. 17M. W.Tr. R.Stripe 27m. Shown by day.

AWANPORT JETTY HEAD Lt. Iso. 2 sec. 2M.Tr. 6m.

BASEN XI E MOLE HEAD Lt. Oc. G.3 sec. B.Tr. 6m.
W MOLE HEAD Lt. Oc. R.3 sec. B.Tr. 6m.

BASEN 10 E MOLE HEAD Lt. Q.G. B.Tr. 6m.
W MOLE HEAD Lt. Q.R. B.Tr. 6m.

INNER MOLE HEAD Lt. Iso. 2 sec. 2M. Col. 4m.

AWANPORT FUEL BERTH Lt. F.R. 3M. Col. on dolphin 7m.
Lt. F.R. 3M. Col. on dolphin 7m.

NARBRZEZA FRANCUSKIE OFF HEAD Lt. F.R. 2M. W.Col. 6m.

BASEN III NARBRZEZA HOLENDERSKIEGO Lt. F.G. Grey Col. 7m.

NARBRZEZA SZWEDZKIEGO NE CORNER Lt. F.R. Col. 7m.

BASEN II NARBRZEZA SLASKIEGO Lt. F.G. Col. 7m.

NARBRZEZA ANGIELSKIEGO Lt. Q.R. 2M. R.Col. 4m.

BASEN I. ENTRANCE N SIDE PIER HEAD Lt. F.G. 2M. Post 6m.

NARBRZEZA POMORSKIE Lt. F.R. 2M. Col. 7m.

S ENTRANCE W SIDE NARBZEZA BENIOWSKIEGO Lt. F.R. 2M. Col. 7m.

INNER HARBOUR N SIDE Lt. Iso G.2 sec. 2M. Or. on Col. 6m.
S SIDE Lt. Oc. R.5 sec. 2M. Or. on Col. 7m.

BASEN 9 ENTRANCE W SIDE Lt. Q. 4M. dolphin 5m.

BASEN 10 E MOLE NARBRZEZA INDYJSKIEGO Lt. Oc. G.5 sec. 1M. Grey Col. 7m.

BASEN V ENTRANCE S SIDE Lt. Oc. R.5 sec. 1M. Grey Col. 7m.
N SIDE Lt. Oc. G.5 sec. 1M. Grey Col. 7m.

BASEN VI ENTRANCE S SIDE Lt. Q.R. 1M. R.Col. 6m.

BASEN VII DRY DOCK SE CORNER Lt. F.R. 1M. Col. 7m.
NW CORNER Lt. F.R. 1M. Col. 7m.

BASEN ZEGLARSKI E MOLE HEAD Lt. F.G. 2M. Concrete Col. 5m. Shown 15/4-15/11.

W MOLE HEAD Lt. F.R. 2M. Concrete Col. 5m. Shown 15/4-15/11.

SOPOT

MOLE ROOT 54°26.8'N 18°34.4'E Lt. Fl.4 sec. 17M. Bathing place turret 25m. 192.5°-307.5°.

PIER HEAD Lt. Fl. R.5 sec. 4M. Col. 6m. Shown 1/5-30/9.

GDANSK (DANZIG) 54°25'N 18°40'E
Nowy Port Tel. Port 43 92 00, 43 61 00.
H.M. 43 05 10, 43 07 10. Telex: 0512324.
Radio-Port: VHF Chan. 11, 14, 16.
Radio-H.M. Office: VHF Chan. 14.
Radio-Pilots: VHF Chan. 12, 14, 16 H24.
Port Polnocny
Radio-Pilots: VHF Chan. 14, 16.

NOWY PORT

BRZEZNO 54°24.6'N 18°38.6'E Ldg. Lts. 196 (Front) Iso. Y.4 sec. 13M. W. ∆, R.Border on W.Tr. 23m. 54°24.4'N 18°38.5'E (Rear) Iso. Y.4 sec. 13M. B. ▽ on Tr. 31m.

WESTERPLATTE 54°24.7'N 18°39.9'E Ldg. Lts. 147°42' (Front) Iso. G.4 sec. 12M. Two W.∆, upper with R.Border on W.Tr. 23m. 54°24.5'N 18°40.1'E (Rear) F.G. 12M. W. ▽ on grey Tr. B.Top. 35m.

W MOLE HEAD Lt. F.G. 7M. W.G.Tr. 11m. Floodlit.
E MOLE HEAD Lt. F.R. 7M. W.R.8-sided tower 13m.

KANAL PORTOWEGO Lt. F.Y. 1M. W.Col. 9m. 325°-135°.

Lt. Fl.1.5 sec. 8M. on dolphin 4m.

BASEN A. ZAWADZKIEGO ENTRANCE E SIDE Lt. F.R. 2M. Col. 8m.
W SIDE Lt. F.G. 2M. Col. 8m.

WYSPA OSTROW BASEN OSTROWICA I and II Lt. F.R. 2M. Col. 8m.

SIENNICKI BRIDGE NW SIDE N SIDE
Lt. Fl. R.3.5 sec. 1M. Dolphin 4m.
S SIDE Lt. Fl. G.3.5 sec. 1M. Dolphin 4m.

SE SIDE S SIDE Lt. Fl. R.3.5 sec. 1M. Dolphin 4m.
N SIDE Lt. Fl. G.3.5 sec. 1M. Dolphin 4m.

54°24.1'N 18°41.9'E Lt. Fl(3) 9 sec. 25M. Grey square Tr. with gallery on Port Captain's building 56m. Reserve Lt. range 16M.

PORT POLNOCNY

P1 Lt. Iso. G.6 sec. 5M. W.G.Dolphin 10 m.
P9 Lt. Mo(U) G.8 sec. 4M. W.G.Dolphin 10m.

LIQUID FUEL BASIN N BREAKWATER S ARM HEAD Lt. Oc. R.4 Sec. 4M. Mast 9M.
N ARM HEAD Lt. Iso. G.4 sec. 8M. Grey square concrete Tr. 12m.

SPUR HEAD Lt. Oc. G.4 sec. 4M. G.Col. 9m. 300°-120°.

Lt. Oc. 4 sec. 3M. Col. 7m.

N CORNER Lt. Oc. 4 sec. 3M. Col. 7m.

COAL PIER Lt. Oc. Y.3 sec. 4M. Dolphin 9m.

POMOST RUDOWY HEAD Lt. Fl.5 sec. 2M.

DETACHED BREAKWATER N HEAD Lt. Fl. R.4 sec. 6M. Grey concrete Tr. 12m.

SWEDEN

SKILLINGE

W BREAKWATER HEAD Ldg. Lts. 290°
(Front) Fl(2) W.R.G.6 sec. W.9M. R.6M.
G.5M. R. Δ on post 5m. G.247°-288°; W.288°-
293°. Horn Mo(N) 60 sec. (Rear) Fl(2) 6 sec.
9M. R. ∇ on mast 9m. Synchronised with
front. Vis. on leading line only.

BRANTEVIK Ldg. Lts. 253° (Front) F.R. on
post 7m. Fishing. Horn(4) 60 sec. (Rear) F.R.
on post 11m. Fishing.

SIMRISLUND Lts. in line 293° (Front) F.R. W.
Δ, R.Border 5m. Mark outfall pipe. (Rear)
F.R.W. ∇, R.Border 7m.

SIMRISHAMN

55°33.5'N 14°22.0'E Lt. Iso. W.R.G.6 sec.
W.13M. R.11M. G.9M. W.Tr. 16m. G.shore-
160°; W.-223°; G.-238°; W.-279°; R.-285°; W.-
355°; R.355°-shore. H24. 1/11-31/3. Horn 60
sec.

W PIER Ldg. Lts. 249°30' (Front) Q.R. 9M. R.
Δ on Tr. 10m. Vis. on leading line only.
(Rear) Q.R. 9M. R. ∇ on Tr. 12m.
Synchronised with front. Vis. on leading
line only.

BASKEMÖLLA Ldg. Lts. 195° (Front) F.R.
Wooden post 6m. Fishing. (Rear) F.R.
Wooden post 11m. Fishing.

STENSHUVUD 55°39.8'N 14°16.9'E Lt. Fl(2)
W.R.G.8 sec. W.11M. R.8M. G.7M. W.Tr.
13m. G.155°-180°; W.-311.5°; R.-322.5°; G.-
327.5°; W.332.5°; R.332.5°-shore. 2 F.R. Lts.
on radio mast 3.9M. WNW and F.R. on Tr.
6.5M. NNW.

KIVIK Ldg. Lts. 214° (Front) F.R.W. Δ on mast
6m. Fishing. (Rear) F.R.W. ∇ on mast 9m.
Fishing.

VITEMÖLLA Ldg. Lts. 210° (Front) F.G. Post
6m. Fishing. (Rear) F.G. Post 10m. Fishing.

HÖRBY Lt. Aero Q. 21M. Mast 480m.
Obstruction.

YNGSJÖ Ldg. Lts. 286° (Front) F.R. 5M. Mast
7m. (Rear) F.R. 5M. Mast 11m.

GROPAHÅLET N BREAKWATER Lt. Fl. G.3
sec. 2M. Post 3m.
S BREAKWATER Lt. Fl. R.3 sec. 2M. Post
3m.

ÅHUS

BÅKÖREN 55°56.6'N 14°20.5'E Ldg. Lts.
289°30' (Front) Q. 11M. R. Δ, on W.Tr. 6m.

Vis. on leading line only. 55°56.8'N 14°19.8E
(Rear) Oc. W.R.G.5 sec. W.14M. R.12M.
G.10M. R. ∇, on W.Tr. 15m. R.277°-280°; G.-
288.5°; W.-290.5°; R.-310°; G.-317°; R.-000°.

REVHAKEN Ldg. Lts. 246° (Front) Iso. 3 sec.
6M. R. Δ, on Tr. 7m. Vis. on leading line
only. (Rear) Q. 7M. R. ∇, on Tr. 14m. Vis. on
leading line only.

N Lts. in line 275° (Front) Iso. G.3 sec. 6M. R.
Δ, W.Base 7m. Floodlit. Marks N limit of
channel. **N MOLE HEAD** (Rear) Q.G. 6M. R.
∇, on Or.Tr. 12m. Floodlit.

S. Lts. in line 275° (Front) Iso. R.3 sec. 8M.
R. Δ, W.base 7m. Floodlit. Marks S limit of
channel. **S MOLE HEAD** (Rear) Q.R. 8M. R.
∇, on Or.Tr. 12m. Floodlit.

LÄGERHOLMEN 55°57.8'N 14°28.4'E Lt. Fl.
W.R.G.5 sec. W.13M. R.10M. G.9M. W.Tr.
17m. R.000°-035°; G.-056°; W.-085°;
R.(unintens)-114°; G.(unintens)-144°;
W.(unintens)-148°; R.(unintens)-192°;
G.(unintens)-196°; W.(unintens)-198°;
R.(unintens)-215°; R.-270°; G.-289°; W.-000°.

SÖLVESBORG

SILNÄSUDDE 55°59.8'N 14°36.9'E Lt. Fl(2)
W.R.G.6 sec. W.12M. R.9M. G.8M. R.W.Tr.
12m. R.shore-304°; G.-315°; W.-006°; R.-
017°; G.-056.5°; W.-079°; G.079°-shore. H24.
1/11-31/3.

TUNÖREN Lt. Iso. W.R.G.4 sec. W.7M. R.5M.
G.4M. W.Tr. 9m. G.202°-309°; W.-319°; R.-
359°; G.-120°; W.-132°; R.-202°.

SÖLVESBORG 56°02.0'N 14°35.4'E Ldg. Lts.
026° (Front) Oc. 6 sec. 10M. R. ◊ on W.Tr.
7m. Vis. on leading line only. 56°02.6'N
14°35.9'E (Rear) Q. 14M. R. ◊ on W.Tr. 17m.
Vis. on leading line only.

INRE REDDEN Ldg. Lts. 355°30' (Front) Q.R.
7M. R. Δ on mast 5m. Vis. on leading line
only. (Rear) Q.R. 7M. R. ∇ on mast 8m.
Synchronised with front. Vis. on leading
line only.

RÅDMANSHOLMEN Ldg. Lts. 019° (Front)
Iso. G.4 sec. 6M. R. Δ on W.Tr. 4m. Vis. on
leading line only. (Rear) Q.G. 5M. R. ∇ on
W.Tr. 7m. Vis. on leading line only.

VARSVRÄNNAN Ldg. Lts. 355°30' (Front)
F.R. 6M. R. Δ on mast 5m. Vis. on leading
line only. (Rear) F.R. 6M. R. ∇ on building
7m. Vis. on leading line only.

SÖLVESBORGRÄNNAN E SIDE No: 5 Lt.
Fl(2) G.6 sec. 1M. Dolphin 5m.
W SIDE No: 6 Lt. Fl. R.3 sec. 2M. Dolphin
5m.

INNERHAMNEN Ldg. Lts. 012° (Front) F.G. 5M. R. △ on mast 7m. Vis. on leading line only. (Rear) F.G. 5M. R. ▽ on mast 9m. Vis. on leading line only.

HERMANS HEJA Ldg. Lts. 108° (Front) F.G. 2M. Post, R. △ 5m. (Rear) F. G. 2M. Post, R. △ 8m.

SIGERSVIK Ldg. Lts. 053° (Front) F.R. 5M. Post, R. △ 5m. (Rear) F.R. 5M. Post, R. △ 8m.

EDENRYD Ldg. Lts. 330°30' (Front) F.G. 2M. R. △ on post 3m. (Rear) F.G. 2M. R. △ on post 8m.

TOSTEBERGA Ldg. Lts. 349° (Front) F.R. Post 4m. Fishing. (Rear) F.R. Post 7m. Fishing.

HÄLLEVIK

56°00.8'N 14°42.4'E Dir. Lt. 020°42' Dir. Iso. W.R.G.8 sec. W.13M. R.10M. G.9M. W.Tr. Copper Lantern 8m. G.338°-016.5°; W.016.5°-025°; R.025°-shore.

S BREAKWATER HEAD Lt. Fl(3) W.R.G.6 sec. W.9M. R.6M. G.5M. W.Tr. 9m. G.344°-013.5°; W.-024°; R.-043°; W.-223°. 2 F.R. Lts. 138m. 6M. on mast 1.6M. SSW.

TORSÖ Ldg. Lts. 346°30' (Front) F.R. 3M. Post 4m. Fishing. (Rear) F.R. 3M. Post 8m. Fishing.

NOGERSUND

E BREAKWATER HEAD Lt. F.G. 2M. W.Mast 5m.

W PIER HEAD Ldg. Lts. 008° (Front) F.R. 8M. R. △ on W.Tr. 7m. Vis. on leading line only. 56°00.2'N 14°44.3'E (Rear) F.R. 10M. R. ▽ on W.Tr. 12m. Vis. on leading line only.

HANÖ

BÖNSÄCKEN 56°01.1'N 14°50.3'E Lt. Fl(2) W.R.G.6 sec. W.10M. R.7M. G.6M. Grey Tr. 11m. G.000°-020°; W.-054°; R.-134°; G.-150°; W.-239°; R.-255°; G.-268°. H24. 1/1-31/3.

HANÖ SUMMIT 56°00.8'N 14°50.9'E Lt. Fl(3) 13.5 sec. 23M. W.Tr. 70m. R/T. for life-saving purposes.
N SIDE Horn(3) 60 sec.
S SIDE Horn Mo(K) 60 sec.

W SIDE Ldg. Lts. 124° **INNER PIER HEAD** (Front) F.R. 3M. R. △ on post 6m. Fishing. (Rear) F.R. 3M. R. ▽ on post 9m. Fishing.

S BREAKWATER HEAD Lt. F.G. 2M. Lantern 4m.

Lts. in line 122°30' (Front) F.G. 7M. R. ○, W.Border on post 11m. Vis. on bearing only. Mark power cable. (Rear) F.G. 7M. R. ⌀, W.Border, on post 26m. Vis. on bearing only.

Lts. in line 302°30' (Front) F.G. 7M. W. △, R.Border on mast 19m. Vis. on bearing only. Mark power cable. (Rear) F.G. 7M. W. ▽, R.Border, on mast 29m. Vis. on bearing only.

LISTERSHUVUD 56°02.2'N 14°47.1'E Lt. Iso. W.R.G.3 sec. W.10M. R.7M. G.6M. W.Lantern 12m. G.152°-191°; W.-206°; R.-229°; G.-244°; W.-274°; R.-286°; G.-319°; W.-348°; R.-004°; G.-017°.

HÖRVIK N PIER HEAD Lt. Fl. W.R.G.2 sec. W.5M. R.3M. G.2M. W.Tr. 6m. W.(unintens) 304°-101°; R.-167°; G.-194°; W.-203.5°; R.-281°. Fishing. Siren 60 sec. Fishing.

PUKAVIKSBUKTEN

BÅKNAHALL Lt. F.R. 3M. Or. □ on post 6m. Fishing. Shown 1/3-15/9.

SKÅPEHALE Lt. F.R. 3M. Or. □ on post 6m. Fishing. Shown 1/3-15/9.

NORJE Ldg. Lts. 272° (Front) F.R. 8M. W. △, B.Border on post 7m. (Rear) F.R. 8M. W. ▽, B.Border on post 14m.

LJUNGHOLMEN Ldg. Lts. 009° (Front) F.G. 6M. W. △, Or.Border on post 6m. (Rear) F.G. 6M. W. ▽, Or.Border on post 11m.

LÖRBY KLADD Lt. Fl. W.R.G.4 sec. W.6M. R.4M. G.3M. Lantern on grey base 6m. W.shore-243°; R.243°-249°; G.249°-287°. Fishing. Shown 1/4-30/9.

KROKÅS Ldg. Lts. 256° (Front) F.R. Post 9m. Fishing. (Rear) F.R. Post 14m. Fishing.

KARLSHAMN

VÄGGA SODRA. YTTRE ORTHOLMEN Lt. Fl(3) W.R.G.9 sec. W.6M. R.4M. G.3M. W.Mast 5m. R.009°-about 120°; W.about 120°-224°; R.224°-309°; G.309°-348°; W.348°-009°. Fishing.

VÄGGA FISHING HARBOUR Lt. Fl(2) W.R.G.8 sec. W.8M. R.6M. G.7M. W.Tr. 3m. G.338°-344°; W.-354°; R.-000°; W.(unintens) 000°-Fishing Harbour. Fishing. Shown 15/7-15/5.

ORTHOLMEN SW POINT 56°09.4'N 14°52.8'E Lt. Fl. W.R.G.3 sec. W.11M. R.8M. G.7M. W.Lantern 6m. G.323°-335.5°; W.-000°; R.-013°; G.(unintens)-143°; W.(unintens)-149°; R.(unintens)-163°.

56°09.8'N 14°52.2'E Ldg. Lts. 338° (Front)
Iso. R.2 sec. 10M. R. △, W.Border on
building 10m. Vis. on leading line only.
56°10.0'N 14°52.1'E (Rear) Iso. R.4 sec. 10M.
R. ▽, W.Border on Tr. 15m. Vis. on leading
line only.

SUTUDDEN Ldg. Lts. 318° (Front) Iso. G.3
sec. 8M. Or. △ on mast 18m. Vis. on leading
line only. (Rear) Q.G. 8M. Or. ▽ on mast
37m. Vis. on leading line only.

PIER HEAD Lt. F.R. 3M. Post 6m.

VINDHAMN Ldg. Lts. 206°30' (Front) F.R.
8M. Or. △ 14m. Vis. on leading line only.
(Rear) F.R. 8M. Or. ▽ 17m. Vis. on leading
line only.

KASTELLHOM PIER HEAD Lt. F.G. 3M. Post
6m.

NEW OIL HARBOUR GUNNÖN 56°09.0'N
14°46.7'E Lt. Iso. W.R.G.4 sec. W.14M.
R.11M. G.10M. △ on W.R. Col. 11m. G.274°-
294.5°; R.-306°; G.-322°; W.-327°; R.-340°; G.-
033°; R.-054°. H24. 1/11-31/3. R. Lt. on
chimney 0.8M. NNW.

KÖLÖ 56°09.3'N 14°49.6'E Ldg. Lts. 011°
(Front) Oc. W.R.G.6 sec. W.13M. R.10M.
G.9M. Or. △, R.Border on Col. 9m. R.353°-
003°; G.-010°; W.-014°; R.-016°; G.-052°; R.-
103°. F.R. Lts. on chimney 560m. E.
56°09.5'N 14°49.7'E (Rear) Q. 13M. Or. ▽,
R.Border on Col. 17m. H24. 1/11-31/3.

STILLERYD Ldg. Lts. 347° (Front) F.G. 7M.
Or. △, W.Border,. on pole 8m. (Rear) F.G.
7M. Or. ▽, W.Border, on pole 15m. R.Lt. on
chimney 550m. NE.

KARLSHAMN-GUNGVALLA
56°13.6'N 14°46.7'E Lt. Aero. Q. 21M. 405m.
Also 5 F.R. 6M. Obstruction.

BOKÖFJÄRDEN BAGGAHEGNA Lt. Fl. R.G.3
sec. R.3M. G.2M. Lantern on post. Or. ▯ 8m.
G.273°-297°; R.-331°; G.-343.5°; R.-351°; G.-
047°; R.-060°; R.-141°; R.-273°. Occas.

TÄRNÖ E POINT Lt. F.W.R.G. W.7M. R.5M.
G.4M. W.Lantern 5m. R.(unintens) 085°-
099°; G.(unintens) -129°; R.(unintens) -142°;
G.(unintens) -175°; R.(unintens) -179°;
G.(unintens) -262°; G.-291°; W.-333°; R.-352°.
Fishing.

TÄRNÖ S POINT 56°06.7'N 14°58.5'E Lt. Oc.
W.R.G.10 sec. W.13M. R.10M. G.9M.
W.Lantern 31m. G.240°-277°; W.-354°; R.-
026.5°; G.-041.5°; W.-044°; R.-098°; R.-135°.

VITÄSKAR Lt. Q.W.R.G. W6M. R.4M. G.3M.
W.Lantern 7m. G.122°-335°; W.-352°; R.-
122°. Fishing.

RONNEBY INLOPPET

GÅSFETEN 56°07.3'N 15°13.6'E Lt. L. Fl(2)
W.R.G.12 sec. W.11M. R.8M. G.7M. W.R.Tr.
12m. R.267°-297°; G.-001°; W.-048°; R.-198°.
〰Racon.

SAXEMARA W SIDE OF BUSSEKÄR
56°09.2'N 15°14.3'E Ldg. Lts. 018°30' (Front)
Iso. 4 sec. 15M. Brown Lantern, W. on side
facing alignment 4m. 56°09.8'N 15°14.7'E
(Rear) Q.11M. Brown Lantern, W.R.bands
on side facing alignment 10m.

SVANVIK SE SIDE OF FUNKO Ldg. Lts.
029°30' (Front) Iso. R.4 sec. 5M. W. △ on
Or.Pedestal 5m.
NW SIDE OF HARÖ (Rear) Q.R. 4M. W. ▽ on
Or.Pedestal 10m.

SVANVIKSUDDE Lt. Fl. W.R.G.3 sec. W.6M.
R.4M. G.4M. Grey Tr. 4m. G.260°-266°; W.-
269°; R.-275°.

STEKÖ S PART Lt. Fl. W.R.G.3 sec. W.7M.
R.4M. G.4M. W. ◇ on Or.Pedestal 4m.
G.051°-064.5°; W.-067°; R.-081°.

ASPAN 56°09.4'N 15°18.7'E Ldg. Lts. 087°
(Front) Iso. 4 sec. 15M. W.Lantern 3m. 071°-
173°. 56°09.4'N 15°19.2'E (Rear) Q. 11M.
W.Post 8m. 073°-101°.

SANDVIKEN Lt. Fl(4) W.R.G.12 sec. W.7M.
R.5M. G.5M. W. ◇ on Or.Pedestal 5m.
G.015°-030°; W.-033°; R.-037°.

RONNEBY Ldg. Lts. 358° (Front) F.R.W. △ on
post 14m (Rear) F.R. W. ▽ on post 18m.

RONNEBY KALLINGE 56°16'N 15°16'E Lt.
Aero Fl(7) 19 sec. 23M. W.Or.Tr. 98m.
Obstruction.

SALTÄRNA E POINT Lt. Fl(3) W.R.G.9 sec.
W.6M. R.4M. G.3M. W.Lantern 7m. G.348°-
002°; W.-017°; R.-029°.

MILLEGARNE SW POINT Lt. Fl. W.R.G.3 sec.
W.6M. R.4M. G.3M. W. ▯ on Tr. 8M. R.shore-
316°; G.-011°; W.-026°; R.-060°; R.(unintens)-
110°; W.(unintens)-shore. Fishing.

TVING 56°17.0'N 15°29.6'E Lt. Aero Q. 21M.
241m. Obstruction.

KARLSKRONA AND APPROACHES

VÄSTRA FÖRSÄNKNINGEN 56°06.5'N 15°34.8'E Lt. Q.W.R.G. W.12M. R.9M. G.8M. W.R.Dolphin 6m. Floodlit. W.003°-015.5°; R.-031°; G.-081°; R.-165.5°; G.-204°; W.-216.5°; R.-242°; G.-003°. Racon. H24. 1/11-31/3. V.Q.R. 0.5M ESE, shown when firing taking place.

KUNGSHOLMEN BREAKWATER HEAD Lt. Q.R.G. R.6M. G.5M. Tr. 5m. R.151.5°-204°; G.-151.5°.

ASPÖ DROTTNINGSKÄR Lt. F.G. 3M. W.Col. on W.Pedestal 3m. 233°-263°. Occas.

GODNATT 56°08.5'N 15°35.8'E Lt. Fl. W.R.G.3 sec. W.11M. R.8M. G.7M. Grey fort 20m. G.003°-013.5°; W.017.5°; R.-028.5°; G.-056°; R.-073.5°; G.079.5°; W.082.5°; R.-125.5°; G.-137°; W.139.5°; R.-144°; G.-189°; R.-197°; G.-234°; R.-242°; R.-302°; G.-330°; R.-003°.

BERGAHOLMEN Lt. Fl(3) W.R.G.9 sec. W.6M. R.4M. G.3M. Lantern on W.Pedestal 6m. G.006°-047°; W.-050°; R.-071°; G.-112°; R.-181°; G.-251°; R.-303°; G.-328°; W.-331°; R.-006°.

ÄSPESKÄR Lt. F.W.R.G. W.6M. R.4M. G.3M. Post 6m. G.304°-326°; W.-333°; R.-050.5°; G.-072°; W.-126°; R.-140°. Shown for local craft. 3 F.R. and 1 F.G.vert Lts. are shown close northward when firing taking place.

EKENNABBENS FISHING HARBOUR Ldg. Lts. 143° (Front) F.R. 2M. W. Δ on post 6m. Fishing. (Rear) F.R. 2M. W. ∇ on post 8m. Fishing.

TJURKÖ 56°06.3'N 15°38.0'E Ldg. Lts. 009° (Front) F.W.R.G. W.11M. R.8M. G.7M. W. Δ on post 7m. R.Shore-342°; G.-008°; W.-011°; R.-Shore. Fishing. 56°06.3'N 15°38.0'E (Rear) F.11M. W. ∇ on post 15m. Fishing.

DJUPASUND BRIDGE 56°06.4N 15°38.0'E Lt. Oc. W.R.G.4 sec. W.12M. R.9M. G.8M. Lantern on W.Pedestal 7m. G.shore-011.5°; W.-013.5°; R.-shore.

SALTÖHAMMAR OFF S POINT Lt. Q.W.R.G. W.5M. R.3M. G.3M. W.Lantern 3m. G.310°-320.5°; R.-329°; G.-012.5°; W.-015°; R.-029°; G.-053°; R.-141°; G.-221°.

BOLLÖARNO SW POINT BOLLÖ Lt. L. Fl. W.R.G.10 sec. W.7M. R.5M. G.4M. W. ▯ on Tr. 9m. R.009°-075°; G.-090°; G.(unintens)-155°; W.(unintens)-268°; R.(unintens)-313°; G.-349°; W.-009°. Fishing.

RÖNNESKÄR Lt. I.Q.W.R.G.6 sec. W.6M. R.4M. G.3M. W.Tr. 9m. R.(unintens) 197°-206°; G.(unintens)-212°; R.(unintens)-240°; G.(unintens)-252°; R.(unintens)-290°; R.-297°; G.-352°; W.014°; R.043°.

ASLA Lt. Fl(3) W.R.G.9 sec. W.6M. R.4M. G.3M. W.Lantern 6m. R.282°-299°; G.-328°; W.-025°; R.-097°; G.-116°; R.-197°. Fishing. Shown 15/7-15/5.

KÄSASKÄR Ldg. Lts. 355°30' (Front) Iso. 4 sec. 7M. Lantern on W.Pedestal 5m. Fishing. (Rear) Q. 6M. Mast 10m. Fishing.

RÖNNFJÄRDSLEDEN Ldg. Lts. 343° **HASSLÖ** (Front) Oc. R.3 sec. 6M. R. Δ on post 8m. (Rear) Oc. R.3 Sec. 6M. R. ∇ on post 12m.

GARPAVIKEN N BREAKWATER HEAD Lt. Q. 6M. Post 5m.

HASSLÖ JETTY E END Lt. F.

NW POINT Lt. F.W.R.G. W.5M. R.3M. G.3M. 3M. W.Lantern. G.000°-040°; W.-045°; R.-060°. Fishing.

W HÄSTHOLMEN Lt. F.R. building 4m. 216°-238°. Occas. Traffic signals shown and Lts. mark navigational openings of Hasslö swing bridge 370m. N.

KARLSKRONA Ldg. Lts. 012°30' **STUMHOLMEN** 56°09.5'N 15°36.0'E (Front) Iso. 8 sec. 15M. W.Round Tr. 22m. Vis. on leading line only. H24 1/11-31/3. 56°10.2'N 15°36.3'E (Rear) Iso. W.R.G.3 sec. W.15M. W.7M. R.5M. G.4M. W.Round Tr. 37m. W. intens on leading line. G.299°-311°; W.-316°; R.-322°; H24. 1/11-31/3.

LABORATORIEHOLMEN 56°09.7'N 15°36.3'E Lt. Iso. W.R.G.4 sec. W.10M. R.7M. G.6M. W.Tr. 11m. G.125°-147°; R.-160°; G.-240°; W.-247.5°; R.-260°; G.-281°; W.-283°; R.-313°; G.-326°; W.-338°; R.-350°.

KOFFERDIHAMNEN Ldg. Lts. 300° (Front) Q.R. 7M. Post 10m. Vis. on leading line only. (Rear) Q.R. 7M. Post 13m. Vis. on leading line only.

OIL HARBOUR CHANNEL VÄMÖVIKEN Ldg. Lts. 321° (Front) F.R. 7M. W. Δ, Or.Border on W.Dolphin 4m. (Rear) F.R. 7M. W. ∇, Or.Border on mast 7m.

KARLSKRONA OIL HARBOUR Ldg. Lts. 279°30' (Front) Iso. R.4 sec. 7M. W. Δ, Or.Border, on post 3m. (Rear) Iso. R.4 sec. 7M. W. ∇, Or.Border, on mast 6m.

VERKÖ 56°10.3'N 15°38.0'E Lt. Fl(2) W.R.G.6 sec. W.11M. R.8M. G.7M. W. ◐ on W.Tr. 8m. G.017°-023°; W.-029°; R.-035.5°.

NÄTTRABY Lt. Fl. R.3 sec. 8M. R.Tr. on dolphin 2m.

UTKLIPPANS HAMN

E ENTRANCE S PIER HEAD Lt. Fl. W.R.G.3 sec. W.4M. R.2M. G.2M. W.Col. on W.Pedestal 8m. G.239°-264°; W.-269°; R.-300°. Fishing.

W ENTRANCE N PIER HEAD Lt. Q.W.R.G. W.4M. R.2M. G.2M. W.Col. on W.Pedestal 8m. G.059°-089°; W.-134°; R.162°. Fishing.

UTKLIPPAN S ROCK 55°57.2'N 15°42.2'E Lt. Fl.15 sec. 23M. R.Tr. on old fort 31m. 1/11-31/3. RC. R/T. for life saving purposes. Same structure Iso. W.R.G.4 sec. W.16M. R.13M. R.12M. G.134°-140°; R.-189°; G.-233°; W.-240°; R.-299°; W.-134°. Horn(2) 30 sec.

UTLÄNGAN S POINT 56°00.8'N 15°47.4'E Lt. Oc(2) W.R.G.12 sec. W.15M. R.12M. G.10M. W.B.Tr. 13m. G.224.5°-232°; W.-011°; R.022.5°; G.-053°; W.-107.5°; R.-115°; G.-135°.

STENSHAMN

Ldg. Lts. 082° (Rear) F.G. 2M. Mast 9m. Fishing. (Common Front) F.G. 2M. Mast 7m. Fishing. Also F.R. 6M. 6m. Ldg. Lts. 178° (Rear) F.R. 6M. Mast 10m. Fishing.

FLÖTJEN Lt. Fl. W.R.G.3 sec. W.6M. R.4M. G.3M. W.Tr. 10m. R.337°-009.5°; G.-035°; W.052.5°; R.-111°; R.(unintens)-203°; G.(unintens)-273°; R.(unintens)-292°. Fishing.

FLUNDREBÅDAN Lt. Q.W.R.G. W.4M. R.3M. G.2M. Lantern on W.Pedestal 6m. R.334°-355°; G.-062°; W.-069°; R.-105°; G.-174°; W.-178°; R.-261°. Fishing.

UNGSKÄR S POINT Ldg. Lts. 300° (Front) F. Post 6m. Fishing. (Rear) F. Post 8m. Fishing.

LANGÖR

NW POINT LÅNGÖREN Ldg. Lts. 307° (Front) Iso. 4 sec. 7M. W. ◐ on Tr. 5m. Intens on leading line. (Rear) Q. 6M. W. ◐ on Tr. 8m.

Lt. V.Q.R. 1.4M. NNE shown when firing taking place.

NE POINT HOMMENABBEB Ldg. Lts. 160° (Front) Iso. R.4 sec. 5M. R. △, on Tr. 5m. Vis. on leading line only. (Rear) Fl(3) W.R.G.9 sec. W.6M. R.4M. G.3M. R. △ on Tr. 8m. R.intens on leading line, G.250°-286°; W.-320°; R.-002°.

TORHAMN E BREAKWATER HEAD Lt. Fl. W.R.G.3 sec. W.4M. R.3M. G.2M. W. ◐ on Tr. 6m. G.001°-009°; W.-016.5°; R.-044°.

The bridge between Möcklö and Senoren is marked by Q.R. and G.Lts. Traffic signals are shown.

KALMARSUND

SANDHAMNS Ldg. Lts. 342° **W PIER HEAD** (Front) F.R. 8M. W. △ on post 5m. Fishing. (Rear) F.R. 8M. W. ▽ on post 12m. Fishing. Horn 30 sec.

GRÖNHÖGEN Ldg. Lts. 056° (Front) Iso. R.3 sec. 9M. Y. △, R.Border, on post 8m. (Rear) Iso R.3 sec. 9M. Y. ▽, R.Border, on post 13m.

KRISTIANOPEL Ldg. Lts. 312° **WHARF ELBOW** (Front) F.R. 4M. W. △ on post 9m. Fishing. Shown 1/8-31/5. (Rear) F.R. 4M. W. ▽ on post 14m. Fishing. Shown 1/8-31/5.

UTGRUNDEN N END OF SHOAL 56°22.5'N 16°15.7'E Lt. L. Fl. W.R.G.8 sec. W.11M. R.8M. G.7M. B.W.Tr. and Lantern, grey conical base 26m. R,019°-096°; G.-153°; R.-166°; G.-185°; W.-192°; R.-265°; G.-292°; R.-316.5°; G.-349°; W.-019°. H24. 1/11-31/3. Racon. Horn 30 sec.

GARPEN 56°23.6'N 16°07.7'E Lt. Oc. W.R.G.8 sec. W.16M. R.13M. G.12M. Grey Tr. 27m. R.201°-210°; G.-253.5°; W.-270°; R.-307°; W.-004°; R.027°; W.(unintens) 088°-128.5°. H24. 1/11-31/3.

BERGKVARA DALSKÄR Ldg. Lts. 301° (Front) Iso. W.R.G.2 sec. W.8M. R.6M. G.4M. R. △ on grey Tr. 8m. G.294°-299°; W.-303°; R.-330°; G.-340°; W.-345°; R.-350°. (Rear) Iso. 2 sec. 9M. R. ▽ on grey Tr. 14m.

Ldg. Lts. 263°30' (Front) F.R. 4M. W. ☐ on cairn 9m. (Rear) F.R. 4M. B.W. ☐ over W △, on grey Tr. 15m.

Ldg. Lts. 331° (Front) F.G. 3M. Building 3m. (Rear) F.G. 3M. Building 5m.

DEGERHAMN Ldg. Lts. 018° (Front) Iso. 2 sec. 8M. Y. △, R.Border, on post 8m. (Rear) Iso. 2 sec. 8M. Y. ▽, R.Border, on post 16m.

Red Ldg. Lts. 018° (Front) F.R. 6M. W. Δ, B.Border 8m. (Rear) F.R. 6M. W. ∇, B.Border 12m.

Green Ldg. Lts. 018° (Front) F.G. 5M. W Δ, B.Border 8m. (Rear) F.G. 5M. W. ∇, B.Border 12m.

S Ldg. Lts. 052° (Front) Iso. 4 sec. 9M. W.Δ, B.Border, on mast 17m. Vis. on leading line only. (Rear) Q. 9M. W. ∇, B.Border, on mast 24m. Vis. on leading line only.

ÖLAND MÖRBYLÅNGA INLOPPET Ldg.
Lts. 127°30' (Front) F.R. 8M. Or. Δ, B.Border on roof of shed 9m. (Rear) F.R. 8M. Or. ∇, B.Border on Tr. 17m.

LÅNGVIKEN Ldg. Lts. 018° (Front) F.G. W. Δ, B.Border, on post 7m Fishing. (Rear) F.G. W. ∇, B.Border, on post 11m. Fishing.

ÄNGEN Ldg. Lts. 354° (Front) F.R.W. ○, B.Border on post 7m. Fishing. (Rear) F.G.W. ○, B.Border on post 9m. Fishing.

STENSÖ Ldg. Lts. 004° (Front) F.R. 2M. W. ◇, B.Border on post 7m. Fishing. (Rear) F.R. 2M. W. ◇, B.Border on post 10m. Fishing.

OUTER Ldg. Lts. 277° (Front) F.R. 5M. W. ◫, B.Border on post 6m. (Rear) F.R. W. ◫, B.Border on post 8m.

INNER Ldg. Lts. 292° (Front) F.G. 4M. W. Δ, B.Border on post 6m. (Rear) F.G. 4M. W. ∇, B.Border on post 8m.

KALMAR Lt. F.R. 7M. Cable beacon 13m. Vis. about 271°-about 284°.

SKANSGRUNDET 56°39.1'N 16°22.7'E
Lt. Oc(2) W.R.G.20 sec. W.15M. R.12M. G.11M. B.G.Tr. grey conical base, W.Lantern 18m. Floodlit. G.008°-019°; W.-024.5°; R.-032°; G.-058°; R.-150°; G.-197°; W.202.5°; R.-215°; G.-217°; R.-249°; G.-256°; R.-008°. H24. 1/11-31/3.

FÄRJESTADEN 56°39.0'N 16°28.1'E Ldg.
Lts. 103° (Front) Iso. 1.5 sec. 11M. W. Δ on post 4m. Vis. on leading line only. 56°39.0'N 16°28.2'E (Rear) Iso. 1.5 sec. 11M. W. ∇ on post 9m. Vis. on leading line only.

N BREAKWATER HEAD Lt. F.R. W.Post 4m.
S BREAKWATER HEAD Lt. F.G. W.Post 4m.

KALMAR HAMN ENTRANCE Ldg. Lts.
277° (Front) F.R. 8M. W. Δ, B.Border on post 8m. (Rear) F.R. 8M. W. ∇, B.Border on post 12m.

RO-RO BERTH Lt. F.

HUVUDET 56°40.1'N 16°23.3'E Lt. Q(3) W.R.G.4 sec. W.10M. R.7M. G.6M. R.Tr. 6m. Floodlit. W.007°-023°; R.-056°; G.-100°; R.-194°; G.-203°; W.-206°; R.-227°; W.(unintens)-317.5°; G.-007°.

W SIDE OF CHANNEL OSVALLSGRUNDET
56°40.3'N 16°23.6'E Lt. Fl. W.R.G.2 sec. W.10M. R.7M. G.6M. R.Tr. 6m. Floodlit. W.015.5°-022.5°; R.-127°; G.-203°; W.-209°; R.-215°; W.(unintens)-301.5°; R.-338°; G.-015.5°.

KULLÖ Ldg. Lts. 274°30' (Front) F.R. 6M. W. Δ on post 5m. (Rear) F.R. 6M. W. ∇ on post 6m.

ÄNGÖ BOAT HARBOUR Ldg. Lts. 248° (Front) F.G. 6M. W. Δ, B.Border on post 4m. (Rear) F.G. 6M. W. ∇, B.Border on post 6m.

SVENSKNABBEN Ldg. Lts. 251° (Front) F.R. 9M. W. Δ on post 5m. (Rear) F.R. 9M. W. ∇ on post 10m.

OLANDS BRIDGE CENTRE Lt. F. 3M.
39m. On N and S sides. Racon.
N SIDE W 56°40.7'N 16°23.9'E Lt. F.R. 13M. 36m.
E 56°40.7'N 16°23.9'E Lt. F.G. 12M. 36m.
S SIDE W 56°40.7'N 16°23.9'E Lt. F.R. 13M. 36m.
E 56°40.7'N 16°23.9'E Lt. F.G. 12M. 36m.

KRONGRUNDET 56°41.4'N 16°24.5'E Lt.
Oc(2) W.R.G.8 SEC. W.15M. W.10M. R.12M. G.10M. B.W.Tr. grey conical base, W.Lantern. 10m. Floodlit. W.023°-031°; R.-058°; G.-104°; W.-184°; R.-214°; G.-222.5°; W.(intens)-226.5°; R.-284°; G.-023°. H24. 1/11-31/3.

BERGA 56°41.7'N 16°20.5'E Lt. Aero V.Q.
22M. Water Tr. 71m. Obstruction.

MASKNAGGEN 56°43.8'N 16°29.0'E Lt. Q. W.R.G. W.14M. R.11M. G.10M. B.Tr. Or.Top, grey base. 10m. Floodlit. W.042°-047°; R.-072°; G.-124°; R.-190°; G.-224°; W.-231°; R.-238°; G.-042°. Whis.

ISPEUDDE 56°44.7'N 16°31.1'E Lt. L. Fl(2) W.R.G.12 sec. W.13M. R.10M. G.9M. W.Tr. 7m. G.044°-053°; W.-057°; R.070°; R.(unintens)-088°; G.(unintens)-150°; G.-166°; W.-191°; R.-198.5°.

STORA RÖR Ldg. Lts. 085° (Front) F.G. 7M. Or. Δ, R.Border on mast 7m. (Rear) F.G. 7M. Or. ∇, R.Border on mast 10m.

CABLE AREA Lts. in line 122° (Front) F.R. 9M. Y. ∆ on Y.Tr. 8m. Mark the SW limit of the cable area. Vis. on bearing only. (Rear) F.R. 9M. Y. ▽ on Y.Tr. 13m. Vis. on bearing only.

SKÄGGENÄS REVSUDDEN Ldg. Lts. 305° (Front) F.G. 7M. Or. ∆, R.Border on post 7m. (Rear) F.G. 7M. Or. ▽, R.Border on post 13m.

CABLE AREA Lts. in line 298° (Front) F.R. 9M. Y. ∆ on Y.Tr. 8m. Mark the NE limit of the cable area. Vis. on bearing only. (Rear) F.R. 9M. Y. ▽ on Y.Tr. 13m. Vis. on bearing only.

SILLÅSEN 56°45.8'N 16°29.9'E Lt. Iso. W.R.G.6 sec. W.16M. R.13M. G.12M. B.W.Tr. grey conical base 20m. Floodlit. R.008.5°-033°; G.-046°; R.-190.5°; G.-196.5°; W.-200°; R.-264.5°; G.-356°; W.-008.5°. H24. 1/11-31/3.

BORGHOLMS HAMN Ldg. Lts. 081° (Front) F.G. 2M. G.Tr. W.Top 7m. (Rear) F.G. 2M. G.Tr. W.Top 10m.

BORGHOLMS INLOPP Ldg. Lts. 111° (Front) F.R. 2M. W. ∆, R.Border on Tr. 7m. (Rear) F.R. 2M. W. ▽,R.Border on Tr. 13m.

BORGHOLM Lt. Oc. W.R.4 sec. W.9M. R.7M. W.Lantern 5m. W.shore-178°; R.178°-shore.

SLOTTSBREDAN 56°55.7'N 16°36.3'E Lt. Fl(2) W.R.G.6 sec. W.14M. R.11M. G.10M. B.G.Tr. and Lantern, grey conical base. 20m. Floodlit. W.018°-022°; R.-048°; G.-098°; R.-184°; G.-202°; W.-208°; R.-359°; G.-018°.

MÖNSTERÅSREDDEN Ldg. Lts. 309° (Front) Iso. W.R.G.4 sec. W.4M. R.2M. G.2M. Lantern on stone pedestal 3m. G.085°-100°; W.-114.5°; R.-132°; W.-085° (Rear) V.Q. 4M. Post 8m. Vis. 229°-317°.

MÖNSTERÅS INLOPP OKNÖ

57°00.2N 16°32.2'E Ldg. Lts. 270°30' (Front) Iso. 3 sec. 15M. Lantern on R.Pedestal 5m. Vis on leading line only. 57°00.2'N 16°31.9'E (Rear) Q. 15M. W. ⊓ on R.Pedestal 12m. Vis. on leading line only.

SANDVIK Ldg. Lts. 084° (Front) F.R. 7M. Y. ∆, R.Border on post 7m. (Rear) F.R. 7M. Y. ▽, R.Border on mast 11m.

DÄMMAN 57°03.4'N 16°41.7'E Lt. Iso. W.R.G.4 sec. W.16M. R.13M. G.12M. Or.B.Tr. grey base 20m. Floodlit G.010°-021°; W.-024.5°; R.-120°;G.-169°; W.-209°; R.-010°. H24. 1/11-31/3.

F.R. Fishing Ldg. Lts. 182° are shown at Svartö 4.2M. WNW and F.G. Fishing Ldg. Lts. 026° at Estenäs 3.2M. NW.

STORA JÄTTERSÖN Ldg. Lts. 189°30' (Front) Fl(2) W.R.G.3 sec. W.4M. R.3M. G.2M. Y. ∆, R.Border on post 8m. G.179.5°-187.5°; W.-192.5°; R.-208°; 57°05.8'N 16°33.4'E (Rear) Fl(2) 3 sec. 11M. Y. ▽, R.Border on mast 18m.

BOKÖSKÄR NORRA Lt. Fl. R.G.3 sec. R.4M. G.3M. Post 4m. G.358°-014°; R.-119°; G.-134.5°; R.-140.5°.

BOKÖSKÄR Ldg. Lts. 158° (Front) Iso. W.R.G.3 sec. W.7M. R.5M. G.4M. R. ∆ on post 4m. R.(unintens) 057°-135°; G.-155°; W.159.5°; R.-174°. **KUNGSHOLMEN** (Rear) Q. 7M. R. ▽ on R.W.Tr. 18m. Vis. on leading line only.

ÅSEHORN Ldg. Lts. 212° (Front) Oc. R.6 sec. 9M. R. ∆ on R.Tr. 23m. (Rear) Oc. R.6 sec. 9M. R. ▽ on R.Tr. 39m.

PÅSKALLAVIK Ldg. Lts. 269°30' (Front) F.R. 2M. ⊓ 6m. Fishing. (Rear) F.R. 2M. ⊓ 15m. Fishing.

RUNNÖ Ldg. Lts. 089° (Front) F.R. 2M. Post 6m. Fishing. (Rear) F.R. 2M. Post 11m. Fishing.

HORNSUDDE 57°11.8'N 16°54.6'E Lt. Mo(D) W.R.G.20 sec. W.12M. R.9M. G.8M. W.Lantern 10m. G.shore-022.5°; W.-194°; R.-shore.

BLÅ JUNGFRUN E SIDE Lt. L. Fl. W.R.8 sec. W.8M. R.6M. W.Tr. grey conical base 12m. W.169°-016.5°; R.016.5°-029.5°. **W SIDE** Lt. L. Fl(2) W.R.G.12 sec. W.8M. R.6M. G.5M. R.Tr. W.Top 11m. W.shore-012°; R.-050°; G.-099°; W.-102°; R.-135°; G.-182°; W.-211°; R.-shore.

BADHOLMEN SW POINT Dir. Lt. 284°12' Dir. Q.W.R.G. W.9M. R.6M. G.5M. W.Tr. 8m. G.245°-281°; W.-287°; R.-320°.

ARNEMAR 57°15.7'N 16°29.6'E Ldg. Lts. 245° (Front) Mo(N) W.R.G.10 sec. W.12M. R.9M. G.8M. R. ⊓ on pedestal 8m. R.211°-242°; G.-244°; W.-245.5°; R.-247°; G.-251.5°; R.-268.5°. H24. 1/11-31/3. 57°15.6'N 16°29.2'E (Rear) Mo(N) W.R.G.10 sec. W.12M. R.9M. G.8M. R. ⊓ on pedestal 15m. W. on leading line R.156°-171°; G.-191.5°; W.-195°; R.-215°. H24. 1/11-31/3.

OVÄDERSUDDEN 57°15.7'N 16°28.7'E Ldg. Lts. 234° (Front) Fl. W.R.G.3 sec. W.10M. R.7M. G.6M. Or. ∆ pole 6m. G.136°-232°; W.-236°; R.-244°; G.-251°. (Rear) F.G. 9M. Or. ▽ on post 12m.

GRIMSKALLEN 57°16.5'N 16°28.7'E N Ldg. Lts. 321°. (Rear) Q. 12M. R. ▽ on W.Tr. 24m. Vis. on leading line. H24. 1/11-31/3. 57°16.3'N 16°29.0'E (Common Front) Iso. W.R.G.4 sec. W.14M. W.12M. R.9M. G.8M. W.Lantern on R.Frame 11m. G.264.5°-270°; W.-272.5°; R.-293°; W.-326.5°; W.(intens) when bearing 321°. H24. 1/11-31/3. 57°16.3'N 16°28.4'E W Ldg. Lts. 271° (Rear) Q. 14M. R. ▽ on Tr. 30m. Vis. on leading line. H24. 1/11-31/3.

STÖTBOTTEN 57°16.5'N 16°33.4'E Lt. Iso. W.R.G.8 sec. W.13M. R.10M. G.9M. Tr. on grey base 12m. Floodlit. W.287°-289.5°; R.-313°; G.345.5°; R.-075.5°; G.-099°; R.-159°; G.-243°; R.-274.5°; G.-287°. Racon. F.W.Spotlight marks fairway limit. H24.

OSKARSHAMN TILLINGEO 57°17.0'N 16°31.1'E Ldg. Lts. 289°30' (Front) Oc. W.R.G.10 sec. W.14M. R.11M. R.10M. R. △ 7m. R.264°-282°; G.-288°; W.-290.5°; R.-318°; G.-339°; R.-020°. H24. 1/11-31/3. 57°17.1'N 16°30.4'E (Rear) Oc. 10 sec. 14M. R. ▽ 18m. H24. 1/11-31/3.

FINNREVET 57°16.7'N 16°38.5'E Lt. Fl(2) W.R.G.6 sec. W.16M. R.13M. G.12M. W.B.Tr. grey conical base. 14m. Floodlit. G.156°-215°; W.-228°; R.-239°; G.-253°; W.-264.5°; R.-290.5°; W.034.5°; R.-081.5°; G.-088°; W.-090°; R.-117°.

RÖDSKÄR Lt. Q.W.R.G. W.5M. R.3M. G.3M. W.Tr. 6m. G.235°-270°; W.-295°; R.-340°; G.-076.5°; W.-078°; R.-090°. Fishing.

TOKENÄSUDDE 57°19.4'N 17°00.0'E Lt. L. Fl. W.R.G.10 sec. W.12M. R.9M. G.8M. W.Lantern 7m. G.shore-042°; W.042°-190°; R.190°-shore.

BYXELKROK PIER HEAD Ldg. Lts. 125° (Front) F.G. 4M. R. △ on W.Post. 7m. Floodlit. (Rear) F.G. 4M. R. △ on hut 14m.

ÖLANDS SÖDRA GRUND 56°04.2'N 16°40.8'E Lt. Iso. 8 sec. 21M. B.R.Tr. grey base 33m. Floodlit. RC. Racon. Helicopter landing platform. A F. Lt. may be observed 090°-270°. Horn Mo(R) 30 sec.

EMMABODA 56°46'N 15°28'E Lt. Aero V. Q. 21M. Mast 530m. Obstruction.

ÖLAND

ÖLANDS SÖDRA UDEE 56°11.8'N
16°24.0'E Lt. Fl(2) 30 sec. 26M. W.B.Round stone Tr. 41m. Floodlit. H24. 1/11-31/3. RC. Same structure Lt. F.W.R.G. W.19M. R.15M. G.14M. 19m. G.153.5°-159°; W.159°-167.5°; R.167.5°-shore.

GRÄSGÅRD Ldg. Lts. 322°30' (Front) F.R.W. △ on W.Tr. 6m. Fishing. Horn 20 sec. (Rear) F.R.B. ▽ on B.Tr. 10m. Fishing.

SEGERSTAD 56°22.3'N 16°34.1'E Lt. L. Fl(3) W.R.G.20 sec. W.12M. R.10M. G.8M. W.Round stone Tr. 21m. G.shore-about 206°; W.206°-about 006°; R.006°-shore. H24. 1/11-31/3.

F.R. Fishing Ldg. Lts. 295° are shown at Skärlov.

BLÄSINGE FISKEHAMN Ldg. Lts. 310° (Front) F.R. 3M. W. △, B.Border on post 3m. (Rear) F.R. 3M. W. ▽, B.Border on post 6m.

KAPELLUDDEN 56°49.2'N 16°50.8'E Lt. L. Fl.10 sec. 12M. R.Tr. 30m. H24. 1/11-31/3. F.R. Lts. on radio mast 4M. WNW.

KÅREHAMN Ldg. Lts. 289° (Front) Iso. R.3 sec. 6M. W. △, R.Border on post 6m. Fishing. Shown 1/9-31/5. (Rear) Iso. R.3 sec. 6M. W. ▽, R.Border on mast 11m. Fishing. Shown 1/9-31/5.

HÖGBY 57°08.8'N 17°02.8'E Lt. L. Fl(2) 12 sec. 12M. W.Tr. 22m. H24. 1/11-31/3.

BÖDA S PIER HEAD 57°14.5'N 17°04.9'E Lt. F.W.R.G. W.6M. R.4M. G.3M. W. △, B.Border 4m. G.230°-312°; W.-319°; R.-340°. Fishing.

F.R. Fishing Ldg. Lts. 298° lead into harbour.

GRANKULLAVIKEN HAMN Ldg. Lts. 218° (Front) F.G. 9M. W. △, B.Border on mast 10m. Vis. on leading line only. (Rear) F.G. 9M. W. ▽, B.Border on mast 16m. Vis. on leading line only.

ÖLANDS NORRA UDDE 57°22.0'N
17°05.9'E Lt. Fl(4) 15 sec. 22M. W.Round stone Tr. 31m. Partially obscured 312°-054°. H24. 1/11-31/3. RC. 3 F.R. Lts. on radio mast 1.3M. SW. Same structure Lt. Iso. W.R.3 sec. W.13M. R.11M. 12m. W.182°-190°; R.190°-200°; W.200°-208.5°.

FÅRÖ

FÅRÖ NORSHOLM NE POINT Lt. Fl. W.R.G.3 sec. W.5M. R.3M. G.3M. W.Tr. 9m. G.000°-100°; W.-210°; R.-238°; G.-265.5°; W.-267°; R.-000°. Fishing.

FÅRÖ 57°57.7'N 19°21.1'E Lt. Iso. W.R.8 sec. W.16M. R.13M. W.Round stone Tr. 31m. R.008°-090°; W.-175°; R.-195°; W.-008°. Obscured by vegetation when bearing less than about 140°. H24. 1/11-31/ RC. Lts. Fl.1.5 sec. 10M. and 3 F.R. on mast close by.

BUNGEÖR 57°49.5'N 19°07.2'E Lt. L. Fl(2) W.R.G.15 sec. W.12M. R.10M. G.8M. W.B.Tr. 14m. G.201°-207°; R.-215°; G.-230°; W.-235.5°; R.-264°; G.-308°; W.-003°; R.-030°; G.-158.5°; R.-183°.

FÅRÖSUND

FÅRÖSUND SODRA Lt. Fl. W.R.G.3 sec. W.8M. R.5M. G.4M. R.Tr. 6m. W.(unintens) 227°-272°; R.(unintens)-290°; R.-303°; G.-344.5°; W.-350.5°; R.-002°; R.-133.5°; G.-142°; W.-147°; R.151.5°; G.-164°. 2 F.R. Lts. mark cable 1.3M NW.

FÅRÖSUND N 57°52.7'N 19°02.1'E Ldg. Lts. 179° (Front) Iso. 3 sec. 14M. W. △ on W.Pedestal 10m. Vis. on leading line only. 57°51.8'N 19°02.1'E (Rear) Iso. 3 sec. 14M. W. ▽ on W.Pedestal 25m. Vis. on leading line only.

HAUREVLAR Lt. Fl(4) W.R.G.5 sec. W.5M. R.3M. G.2M. Lantern on Or.Tr. on W.Pedestal 8m. R.250°-306°; G.-321°; W.-330°; R.-350°.

AURGRUND 57°55.6'N 19°02.6'E Lt. Oc. W.R.G.8 sec. W.14M. R.11M. G.10M. W.Tr. B.Top 12m. G.(unintens) 284.5°-012°; W.(unintens)-027°; R.(unintens)-076°; R.-104°; G.-141.5°; W.-199°; R.-218.5°; G.-226°. H24. 1/11-31/3.

SVINGRUND Lt. Fl(2) W.R.G.6 sec. W.7M. R.5M. G.4M. Or.B.Tr. 11m. G.000°-102°; W.-222°; R.-000°.

GRAUTEN E ROCK Lt. Fl(2) W.R.G.6 sec. W.8M. R.5M. G.4M. Or.Tr. 12m. R.051°-095°; G.-231°; W.-248°; R.-270°; W.-051°.

KYLLEJ Ldg. Lts. 331° (Front) F.R. 3M. W. △ on post 7m. Fishing. (Rear) F.R. 3M. W. ▽ on post 11m. Fishing.

SLITE HAMN

MAGÖ S END Lt. Fl(3) W.R.G.9 sec. W.8M. R.5M. G.4M. W.Tr. 13m. R.070°-107°; G.-112°; G.(unintens) 112°-242°; G.-263°; W.-070°.

GRUNDET SW END Lt. Fl(2) W.R.G.6 sec. W.6M. R.4M. G.3M. W.Lantern 4m. G.338.5°-001°; W.-012°; R.-032.5°; G.-137.5°; W.-139°; R.-149.5°; G.-160.5°; R.-167°.

Ldg. Lts. 320°30' (Front) Iso. R.4 sec. 8M. R. △ on Tr. 16m. (Rear) Iso. R.4 sec. 8M. R. ▽ on Tr. 20m.

LÄNNAHAMNEN Ldg. Lts. 331° (Front) F.G. 4M. Or. ◖ 5m. (Rear) F.G. 4M. Or. ◖ 7m.

BOTVALDEVIK Ldg. Lts. 255° (Front) F.R. 3M. W. △ on post 8m. Fishing. (Rear) F.R. 3M. W. ▽ on post 11m. Fishing.

ÖSTERGARN E END 57°26.6'N 18°59.4'E Lt. L. Fl(2) 15 sec. 16M. W.Round stone Tr. B.Band on upper part 36m. Vis. about 131°-about 081°. H24. 1/11-31/3. RC. Same structure F.R. 12M. 18m. Vis. 222°-272°.

W END Lt. Fl(2) W.R.G.6 sec. W.8M. R.5M. G.4M. W.Lantern 12m. G.332.5°-345°; W.-021°; R.-042.5°; W.(unintens)-087.5°; G.-111°; W.-113°; R.-139°; G.-156.5°; W.-190.5°; R.-205.5°.

KATTHAMMARSVIK Ldg. Lts. 188° (Front) F.R. 3M. W. △ on post 4m. Fishing. (Rear) F.R. 3M. W. ▽ on post 7m. Fishing.

HERRVIK W BREAKWATER HEAD Lt. Fl. W.R.G.2 sec. W.4M. R.2M. G.2M. Lantern on W.Pedestal 6m. G.124°-196°; W.-222°; R.-265°; W.-124°.

SYSNEUDD Ldg. Lts. 348° (Front) F.Post 18m. Fishing (Rear) F.Post 22m. Fishing.

LJUGARN NEAR MOLE Lt. Iso. W.R.G.4 sec. W.7M. R.5M. G.4M. W.Lantern 6m. W.251°-301°; R.-342°; G.-000°.

F.W. Ldg. Lts. 034° are shown when required for local fishing boats. F.W. Ldg. Lts. 358° are shown at Grynge, 5M. NE when fishing boats are at sea. F.W. Ldg. Lts. 342° are shown at Vitvär.

LAUS HOLMAR Lt. Fl. W.R.G.3 sec. W.6M. R.4M. G.3M. W.Tr. 8m. G.(unintens) 115°-119°; G.-211°; W.-021°; R.-030°; R.(unintens)-115°. Fishing.

F.W. Ldg. Lts. 271° are shown at Djaupdy 2M. SW.

NÄR 57°13.3'N 18°41.0'E Lt. Oc. W.R.8 sec. W.16M. R.13M. R.W.Round Tr. 21m. R.030°-058°; W.(unintens)-178°; W.-194°; R.-200°; W.-030°.

HÖRTE Ldg. Lts. 307° (Front) F.Mast 11m. Fishing. (Rear) F.Mast 15m. Fishing.

TOMTBOD Ldg. Lts. 346° (Front) F.Mast 10m. Fishing. (Rear) F.Mast 13m. Fishing.

NÄRSHAMN S PIER HEAD Lt. Q.W.R.G. W.8M. R.6M. G.5M. Tr. 6m. Floodlit. G.305°-344°; W.-358°; R.-038°. Fishing. Horn 30 sec. Fishing.

RONEHAMN

RONEHAMN Lt. Fl(3) W.R.G.9 sec. W.8M. R.5M. G.4M. B.W.Tr. grey base 10m. W.052°-057°; R.-076°; G.(unintens)-170°; R.(unintens)-224.5°; G.-243°; W.-266.5°; R.-350°; G.-052°.

Ldg. Lts. 325° (Front) F.R. 8M. W. Δ on post 8m. Vis. on leading line only. (Rear) F.R. 8M. W. ∇ on post 17m. Vis. on leading line only.

Ldg. Lts. 332°30' (Front) F.G. 7M. W. Δ on mast 11m. Vis. on leading line only. (Rear) F.G. 7M. W. ∇ on mast 18m. Vis. on leading line only.

FLUNTING Ldg. Lts. 345° (Front) F.Mast 8m. Fishing. (Rear) F.Mast 8m. Fishing.

FALUDDEN 56°59.8'N 18°23.7'E Lt. Oc(3) 15 sec. 17M. W.Tr. 10m. H24. 1/11-31/3. Lts. Fl.1.5 sec. 10M. and 3 F.R. on mast close by.

VÄNDBURG Ldg. Lts. 322° (Front) Q.R. 2M. W. Δ on mast 8m. Fishing. (Rear) Q.R. 2M. W. ∇ on mast 12m. Fishing.

FISHING HARBOUR Ldg. Lts. 222° (Front) F.G. 4M. W. Δ on mast 9m. (Rear) F.G. 4M. W. ∇ on mast 13m.

HELIGHOLMEN S END Lt. Fl(2) W.R.G.6 sec. W.8M. R.5M. G.4M. W.Tr. 13m. G.shore-255.5°; W.-041°; R.-shore.

HOBURG 56°55.3'N 18°09.3'E Lt. Fl.5 sec. 27M. W.Tr. B.Top 58m. Obsc. near coast by high cliffs at Hoburg. H24. 1/11-31/3. RC.

NÄSREVET Lt. Fl. W.R.G.3 sec. W.8M. R.5M. G.4M. R.Tr. W.Top, grey base 8m. R.299°-356°; G.-026°; W.-151°; R.-170°; G.-185°.

BURGSVIKEN

VALAR 57°01.9'N 18°13.0'E Lt. Oc(2) W.R.G.10 sec. W.13M. R.10M. G.9M. W.Tr. 7m. G.shore-065°; W.-091.5°; R.-185°; W.(unintens)-211°; R.(unintens)-230°. F.R. Lts. on radio masts 1.2M. ESE.

57°03.0'N 18°17.4'E Ldg. Lts. 073° (Front) Iso. 4 sec. 12M. Lantern on W.Pedestal, grey base 4m. Vis. on leading line only. 57°03.0'N 18°17.5'E (Rear) Iso. 4 sec. 12M. W. ▢ on mast 16m. Vis. on leading line only.

BURGSVIKS HAMN Ldg. Lts. 175° (Front) F.R. W. Δ on W.Mast 7m. (Rear) F.R. W. ∇ on W.Mast 10m.

STORA KARLSÖ W SIDE 57°17.5'N 17°57.8'E Lt. L. Fl(2) W.R. 12 sec. W.16M. R.13M. W.Tr. on dwelling 56m. W.340°-193°; R.-212°; W.-233°; R.-340°. RC.

F.W. Fishing Ldg. Lts. are shown at Djauvik, Valbyodar, Kovik and Vastegärn.

VARVSHOLMEN 57°24.0'N 18°11.6'E Ldg. Lts. 055° (Front) Iso. 4 sec. 11M. W.Col. 7m. Vis. on leading line only. 57°24.0'N 18°11.7'E (Rear) Iso. 4 sec. 11 M. W.Col. 12m. Vis. on leading line only.

VÄSTERGARN Ldg. Lts. 050° (Front) F.R. Post 3m. Fishing. (Rear) F.R. Post 7m. Fishing.

GNISVÄRD Ldg. Lts. 100° (Front) F.R. 4M. W. Δ on mast 4m. Fishing. Shown 1/7-30/4. (Rear) F.R. 4M. W. ∇ on mast 7m. Fishing. Shown 1/7-30/4.

FOLLINGBO 57°35.6'N 18°22.6'E Lt. Aero V.Q. 21M. Mast 243m. Obstruction.

VISBY

APPROACH 57°38.1'N 18°16.6'E Lt. Iso. W.R.G.4 sec. W.12M. R.9M. G.8M. W.Round structure 11m. Floodlit. R.077°-044°; G.-055°; W.-087°; R.-209°; G.-239°; W.-245°; R.-296°. RC. 2 F.R. Lts. on radio mast 2M. ENE.

N OUTER BREAKWATER HEAD Lt. Q.R. 9M. W.Tr. 9m. Floodlit.

OLD N BREAKWATER Ldg. Lts. 055° (Front) Oc. R.12 sec. Or. Δ, R.Band on pedestal. (Rear) Oc. R.12 sec. Or. ∇, R.Band on pedestal.

FLUNDREVIKEN Ldg. Lts. 096° (Front) F.R. 5M. R. Δ, W.Band on post 5m. Fishing. (Rear) F.R. 5M. R. ∇, W.Band on post 7m. Fishing.

SJÄLSÖ

Ldg. Lts. 099° (Front) F.R. W. Δ on mast 5m. Fishing. (Rear) F.R. W. ∇ on mast 10m. Fishing.

INNER Ldg. Lts. 038° (Front) F.G. W.Δ on mast 6m. Fishing. (Rear) F.G. W. ∇ on mast 10m. Fishing.

STENKYRKEHUK 57°49.2'N 18°27.8'E Lt. Oc(2) W.R.G.12 sec. W.10M. R.8M. G.7M. W.Round Tr. 42m. G.shore-037°; W.-220°; R.-shore. H24. 1/11-31/3.

IRE 57°49.0'N 18°37.0'E Lt. Aero 2 V.Q.vert. 22M. Radio Tr. 239m. Obstruction. Also 5 F.R. 6M.

LICKERSHAMN Ldg. Lts. 148° (Front) F.R. 2M. W. Δ on post 2m. Vis. on leading line only. Occas. (Rear) F.R. 2M. W. ∇ on mast 10m. Vis. on leading line only. Occas.

HALLSHUK 57°55.5'N 18°45.3'E Lt. L.
Fl(4) W.R.G.20 sec. W.15M. R.12M. G.10M.
W.Building 32m. G.110°-144°; W.-262°; R.-
291°. H24. 1/11-31/3.

KAPPELSHAMN 57°50.3'N 18°48.1'E Lt. Iso.
W.R.G.4 sec. W.12M. R.9M. G.8M. Tr. 11m.
W.(unintens) 109°-156.5°; G.-173°; W.-
180.5°; R.-196°.

STORUGNS INDUSTRIHAMN Ldg. Lts. 169°
(Front) F.R. 2M. 11m. (Rear) F.R. 2M. 16m.

GOTSKA SANDÖN

NW POINT 58°23.7'N 19°11.8'E Fl.5 sec.
24M. Brown wooden Tr. 42m. Partly obsc.
by vegetation about 280°-about 013°. H24.
1/11-31/3. RC. Also F.R. same structure 15M.
37m. 164°-186°.

HAMNUDDEN Lt. Fl(2) 6 sec. 8M. W.Round
Tr. 12m. 294°-161°.

KYRKUDDEN Lt. Fl(3) 9 sec. 8M. W.Round
Tr. 12m. 149°-037°.

SIMPEVARP 57°24.6'N 16°40.7'E Ldg. Lts.
267° (Front) Iso. R.4 sec. 12M. R. ☐, Y.Stripe,
on Tr. 11m. 57°24.6'N 16°40.4'E (Rear) Iso.
R.4 sec. 12M. R. ☐, Y.Stripe on Tr. 17m.

GRÖTTLAN 57°24.3'N 16°40.2'E Lt. Fl(2)
W.R.G.6 sec. W.10M. R.7M. G.6M. R.Lantern
on support 5m. Floodlit. G.182.5°-237°; W.-
245.5°; R.-252°; G.-264.5°; R.-351°. F.R. on
radio tower 0.6M. NNW.

SOEN Lt. Fl(3) W.R.G.9 sec. W.6M. R.4M.
G.3M. W.Lantern, R.Roof 5m. G.180°-199°;
W.-227°; R.-330°; G.-341°; W.-343°; R.-006°;
G.-029°.

GALTBÅDAN Lt. Q.W.R.G. W.4M. R.3M.
G.2M. Lantern on W.Pedestal 6m. G.003°-
008°; W.-011°; R.-073.5°; W.(unintens)-156°;
G.-169°; R.-177°.

EKÖ Lt. Iso. W.R.G.4 sec. W.6M. R.4M.
G.3M. W.Lantern 2m. G.170.5°-192°; W.-
205°; R.-226°; G.(unintens) 263.5°-298°;
G.348.5°-355.5°; W.-356.5°; R.-000°.

STRUPÖ LJUNGSKÅR 57°30.9'N 16°46.5'E
Lt. Fl(2) W.R.G.6 sec. W.11M. R.8M. G.7M.
W.Tr. B.Base. 13m. Floodlit. G.255°-271°; W.-
291°; R.-312°; G.-345°; R.-353°; G.-068°; R.-
099°.

VINÖKRÅKAN Lt. Fl. W.R.G.3 sec. W.7M.
R.5M. G.4M. W.R.Tr. B.Base 7m. Floodlit.
G.181°-273.5°; W.-276°; R.-305°; G.-349°.

MANNEN Lt. Iso. W.R.G.4 sec. W.7M. R.5M.
G.4M. W.Lantern, G.Top 5m. G.309°-322°;
W.-323°; R.-050°; G.-131°; W.-135°; R.-145°.

MELLANHÄLL Lt. Q.W.R.G. W.5M. R.3M.
G.3M. Lantern on W.Pedestal 5m. Floodlit.
R.237°-343°; G.-351°; W.-359°; R.-041°.

LILLA BERGÖ Lt. Fl. W.R.G.3 sec. W.6M.
R.4M. G.3M. W.Lantern 4m. Floodlit. G.084°-
218°; W.-228°; R.288.5°.

TUNNHOLMEN Lt. Fl(2) W.R.G.6 sec. W.6M.
R.4M. G.4M. W.Lantern 7m. Floodlit. G.354°-
080.5°; W.-083°; R.-173.5°; G.-206°; W.-
208.5°; R.-218°.

EKNÖ Ldg. Lts. 234° (Front) Iso. R.4 sec. 5M.
R. Δ on W.Pedestal 7m. Floodlit. (Rear) Iso.
R.4 sec. 7M. R. Δ on W.Pedestal 12m.
Floodlit.

ALHÄLLAN Lt. Fl(2) W.R.G.6 sec. W.7M.
R.5M. G.4M. W.Tr. B.Base 11m. G.053°-
066.5°; W.-068.5°; R.-089.5°; G.-125°;
W.(unintens)-163.5°; G.-190°; W.-192.5°; R.-
200°. A white beam is projected towards a
reflector on white concrete beacon on E
side of Förö.

BUSSGRUND Lt. Fl. W.R.G.3 sec. W.7M.
R.5M. G.4M. R.Tr. W.Top, grey base 9m.
G.170°-179°; W.-183°; R.-223°; G.-235°; R.-
254°; G.-357.5°; W.-359.5°; R.-007°.

BLOCKHOLMSUNDET

N SIDE No: 1 Lt. Iso. W.R.G.3 sec. W.6M.
R.4M. G.3M. G.Tr. grey base 5m. Floodlit.
G.280°-300°; W.-306°; R.-120°.
No: 2 Lt. Q.G. 3M. G.Pedestal, grey base
5m. Floodlit.

S SIDE No: 3 Lt. Q.R. 3M. R.Pedestal, grey
base 5m. Floodlit. Synchronised with No:2
Lt.
No: 4 Lt. Q.R. 3M. R.Pedestal, grey base 5m.
Floodlit. Synchronised with No: 2 Lt.

Q.G. and Q.R. Lts. mark fairway through
Stegenholms Channel. Bridge traffic signals
0.8M. WNW.

VÄSTERVIK

TREBRÖDERSSUND Lt. F.R. 4M. Pedestal
2m. /8-31/11.

VITUDDEN Lt. Oc. W.R.G.4 sec. W.9M.
R.6M. G.5M. W.Lantern 7m. R.324°-327°; G.-
330°; W.-333°; R.-344°; G.-347°; W.-350°; R.-
028°.

F.G. Lt. at each end of Gränsö Kanal 0.3M.
N.

BORGÖ Lt. Fl. W.R.G.4 sec. W.6M. R.4M.
G.3M. W.Lantern 5m. G.142°-154°; W.-158°;
R.-175°; G.-188°; R.-224°; G.-264°; R.-267°.
F.R. Lt. on radio mast 1.1M. WSW.

KORPHÄLLAN Ldg. Lts. 279° (Front)
Q.W.R.G. W.8M. R.6M. G.5M. W.Lantern 3m.
G.186°-190°; W.-236°; R.-254°; G.-268°;
G.(intens)-301°. (Rear) Iso. G.4 sec. 5M.
W.Lantern 7m. 260°-283°.

TALLSKARSHÅLET

GREEN Ldg. Lts. 205°06' **W SIDE OF
CHANNEL** (Front) Q. W.G. W.6M. G.3M.
R.W.Tr. 5m. G.138°-220°; W.320°-035°. (Rear)
Q.G. 3M. R.W.Tr. 16m. Vis. on leading line
only.

RED Ldg. Lts. 204°30' **E SIDE OF CHANNEL**
(Front) Q.R. 4M. Lantern on R.Pedestal 6m.
Vis. on leading line only. (Rear) Q.R. 5M.
Lantern on R.Pedestal 12m. Vis. on leading
line only.

HÄNDELÖPS Ldg. Lts. 320° (Front) F.R. 3M.
Post 7m. Fishing. (Rear) F.R. 3M. Post 13m.
Fishing.

IDÖ Lt. Fl(2) W.R.G.6 sec. W.9M. R.7M.
G.6M. G.Lantern, W.Top 4m. R.350°-359°;
G.-181.5°; W.-184°; R.-189°; G.-210°.

HAMNKLABBSHÄLLAN Lt. Fl(2) W.R.G.6
sec. W.7M. R.5M. G.4M. G.Tr. 8m. R.330.5°-
343.5°; G.-074°; W.-081.5°; R.-109°; G.-126°;
W.-134°; R.-139.5°.

Ldg. Lts. 236° **STICKSKÄR** (Front) Fl.
W.R.G.1.5 sec. W.7M. W.6M. R.4M. G.3M.
W.Tr. 10m. W.(intens) on leading line.
G.106°-108°; R.-122°; G.-189°; G.214°-229°;
W.-240°; R.-280°; G.-354°; W.-358°; R.-033°.
SPÄRÖ 57°42.8'N 16°43.9'E (Common Rear)
Iso. 6 sec. 14M. W.Tr. 36m. H24. 1/11-31/3. 2
F.R. Lts. on radio mast 2.3M. WNW. Ldg. Lts.
323° **IDÖ STÅNGSKÄR** (Front) Q.W.R.G.
W.8M. R.6M. G.5M. W.Lantern, R.Base 13m.
G.145°-150°; W.-152°; R.-158°; R.(unintens)-
302°; G.-321°; W.-324°; R.-338°.

KUNGSGRUNDET 57°41.2'N 16°54.5'E Lt. L.
Fl(2) W.R.G.15 sec. W.16M. R.13M. G.12M.
W.Lantern on B.R.Tr. 27m. R.005°-048°; G.-
088.5°; R.-122°; G.-193°; W.-005°; H24. 1/11-
31/3. RC. Racon. Helicopter landing platform
above lantern. Horn(2) 30 sec.

VÄSTERBÅDAN 57°44.8'N 16°44.6'E Lt. Oc.
W.R.G.10 sec. W.14M. R.11M. G.10M. R.Tr.
B.Base 14m. Floodlit. G.112°-133.5°; R.-157°;
R.(unintens)-220°; R.-258.5°; G.-268°; W.-
269.5°; R.-309°; G.-321°; R.-011°; G.-040°.
Racon.

SLADÖ ASK Lt. Q.W.R.G. W.7M. R.5M.
G.4M. W.Tr. R.Base 9m. R.180°-273°; G.-
012°; W.-017°; R.-042°.

FINNKARTEN Lt. Fl(4) W.R.G.10 sec. W.7M.
R.5M. G.4M. W.Tr. G.Base 10m. G.004°-020°;
W.-025°; R.-044°; G.-095°; R.-160°; G.-198°;
W.-201°; R.-220°.

ALESKÄR Lt. Fl. W.R.G.3 sec. W.8M. R.6M.
G.5M. W.Tr. B.Base 10m. R.170°-185°; G.-
278°; W.-297.5°; R.-311°; G.-322°; W.-328°;
R.-346°.

STORKLÄPPEN 57°50.6'N 16°51.0'E Lt. L. Fl.
W.R.G.10 sec. W.11M. R.8M. G.7M. Grey
and brown Tr. 20m. R.(unintens) 040°-063°;
G.(unintens)-130°; G.-199°; W.-344°; R.-040°.
H24. 1/11-31/3.

FINNHÄLLAN Lt. Fl. W.R.G.3 sec. W.8M.
R.6M. G.5M. R.Tr. W.Top, B.Base 9m.
G.173°-187°; W.-192°; R.-250°; G.-338°; W.-
342°; R.-356°.

HOMMELSKÄR Ldg. Lts. 353° (Front) Iso.
W.R.G.4 sec. W.6M. R.4M. G.3M. Lantern on
W.Hut, G.Band 5m. G.311°-332°; W.-343°; R.-
086°; G.-187°; W.-189°; R.-207°. **TORRÖUDD**
(Rear) Q.W.R.G. W.4M. R.2M. G.2M. Lantern
on W.Pedestal 7m. G.181°-194°; W.-207°; R.-
014°.

JÄRNKLINT Lt. Fl(2) W.R.G.6 sec. W.6M.
R.4M. G.3M. W.Lantern 6m. G.007°-020.5°;
W.-048°; R.090°; G.-142°; W.-145°; R.-180°.

GRINDÖ Lt. Q.W.R.G. W.5M. R.3M. G.3M.
W.Post on pedestal 9m. G.012°-030°; W.-
210°; R.-254°; G.-277°.

ALEN Ldg. Lts. 087° (Front) Q.W.R.G. W.4M.
R.3M. G.2M. W.Lantern on W.Pedestal 5m.
W.074°-087°; W.-091.5°; R.-224°; **TRÄDSKÄR**
(Rear) Iso. W.R.G.2 sec. W.6M. R.3M. G.3M.
Lantern on W.Pedestal 6m. W.069°-178.5°;
R.-268°; G.307°; W.-313°; R.-335°.

FÖREN Lt. Fl(2) W.R.G.6 sec. W.5M. R.3M.
G.3M. Lantern on W.Pedestal 6m. R.080°-
144°; G.-205°; W.-210°; R.-231°.

ERSKÄR Lt. Q.W.R.G. W.5M. R.4M. G.3M.
W.Lantern 9m. G.180°-210°; W.-214°; R.-
250°; G.-283°; W.-306°; R.106°; G.-113°; W.-
118°; R.-141°. Fishing.

PRICKHÄLLAN Lt. Fl(2) W.R.G.6 sec. W.6M. R.4M. G.3M. W.Tr. B.Base 6m. R.001.5°-045°; G.-140.5°; W.-155°; R.-255°; G.-359°; W.-001.5°.

TORSKKLABB Lt. Fl. W.R.G.3 sec. W.5M. R.3M. G.3M. W.Lantern 5m. G.186°-205°; W.-230°; R.-307°; G.-340°; W.-344.5°; R.005°.

ÅLGÅRDSUDDE Lt. L. Fl. W.R.G.8 sec. W.4M. R.3M. G.2M. Lantern on W.R.Pedestal 6m. G.shore-246°; R.-286°; G.-008°; W.-011°; R.-019.5°.

GRÅSKÄRSHÄLL Ldg. Lts. 178°30' (Front) Iso. W.R.G.4 sec. W.6M. R.4M. G.3M. W.Lantern 3m. G.315°-000°; W.-001°; R.-005°; G.-048°; R.-128°; G.-159°; W.-195°; **JUNGFRUSKÄR** (Rear) Q.W.R.G. W.7M. W.4M. R.3M. G.2M. W. □ on W.Pedestal 11m. G.345.5°-003°; W.-009°; R.-080°; W.-186.5°. Intens on leading line.

FLATVARP Ldg. Lts. 159° (Front) F.G. 4M. Y. △, R.Border on post 7m. Fishing. (Rear) F.G. 4M. Y. ▽, R.Border on post 11m. Fishing.

OLSKLABB Lt. Fl(2) W.R.G.6 sec. W.5M. R.3M. G.3M. Lantern on W.Pedestal 5m. R.273°-105°; G.-138°; W.-166°; R.-180.5°.

TORRÖ STICKSKÄR Lt. Fl(4) W.R.G.12 sec. W.6M. R.4M. G.4M. W.G.Tr. B.Base 7m. G.353°-017.5°; W.-026°; R.-120°; G.-174.5°; W.-195°; R.-223°.

TORRÖ Ldg. Lts. 222° (Front) Iso. 4 sec. 9M. W.R. daymark on W.Hut 6m. Vis. on leading line only. (Rear) Q. 9M. W.R. daymark on W.Hut 15m. Vis. on leading line only.

SVARTBÅDAN Lt. Fl(3) W.R.G.9 Sec. W.7M. R.5M. G.4M. W.R.Tr. B.Base 8M. G.150°-190°; R.-256°; G.-261°; W.-264°; R.-313°; G.-350°; W.-353°; R.-019°.

LJUSKLABB Lt. Q.W.R.G. W.5M. R.3M. G.3M. W.Lantern on W.Pedestal 9m. G.230°-246°; W.-249°; R.-272°; G.-300°; R.-004°. F.R. Lt. on radio mast 10.2M. NW.

HALSÖKLABB Lt. Fl. W.R.G.3 sec. W.6M. R.4M. G.3M. W.Lantern 12m. G.107°-240°; R.-305°; G.-347°; W.-354°; R.-107°.

HÄGERÖKARTEN Lt. Fl(4) W.R.G.12 sec. W.8M. R.5M. G.4M. W.Lantern on B.W.Tr. 10m. G.008°-038°; W.-043°; R.076°; G.-174.5°; W.-180.5°; R.-235°; G.-255°; W.-264°; R.-279°.

Ldg. Lts. 056° (Rear) F.R.House. For use of pilots. (Common Front) F.R.Post. Ldg. Lts. 086° (Rear) F.R.Post. For use of Pilots.

HÄRADSKÄR 58°09.0'N 16°59.5'E Lt. L. Fl(3) 20 sec. 18M. R.Tr. 36m. H24. 1/11-31/3.

SLATBAKEN

FÅRHOLMEN S POINT Lt. Fl(4) W.R.G.12 sec. W.5M. R.4M. G.3M. W.Lantern on W.G.Hut 6m. G.247°-254°; W.-256°; R.-010°; G.084°; W.-095°; R.-098°.

ETTERSUNDET ÖSTRA Lt. Fl. W.R.G.3 sec. W.4M. R.3M. G.2M. W.R.Lantern on dolphin 4m. R.089°-290°; G.-293°; W.-296°; R.-317°.

VÄSTRA Lt. Q.W.R.G. W.3M. R.2M. G.2M. W.G.Lantern on dolphin 4m. G.259°-108.5°; W.-115.5°; R.-133°.

HACKERSTAD Lt. Fl(2) W.R.G.6 sec. W.6M. R.4M. G.3M. W.Lantern 8m. G.shore-309°; W.-315°; R.-333°; W.(unintens)-077°; G.-098°; W.-102°; R.-120°.

LUNDBYNÄS Lt. Q.W.R.G. W.4M. R.2M. G.2M. Lantern on W.Pedestal 6m. G.281°-286.5°; W.-291°; R.-017°; G.-099°; W.-108°; R.-shore.

SÖDERKÖPING Lt. Fl. W.R.G.3 sec. W.6M. R.4M. G.3M. Tr. 7m. G.232°-252°; W.-254°; R.-255.5°. 1/8-31/10.

ÅDKOBB Lt. Fl(2) W.R.G.6 sec. W.5M. R.3M. G.3M. Lantern on W.Pedestal 5m. W.006°-009°; R.-130°; G.-171°; W.-173°; R.-268°; G.-006°.

LAMMSKÄR 58°24.0'N 16°57.2'E Ldg. Lts. 338°30' (Front) Iso. 4 sec. 12M R.W. □ on W.Structure 2m. 58°24.6'N 16°56.8'E (Rear) Q. 12M R.W. □ on W.Structure 9m. Intens on leading line.

HORVELSÖ Lt. Fl. W.R.G.3 sec. W.5M. R.4M. G.3M. W.Lantern 4m. G.155°-163°; W.-170°; R.-245°; G.-309°; W.-319°; R.-335°.

STORA HÖGHOLMEN Ldg. Lts. 006°30' (Front) Iso. 4 sec. 7M. W.R. daymark on W.Tr. 10m. 352°-115°. (Rear) Q. 6M. W.R. daymark on W.Hut 14m. 352°-178°.

SANDSÅNKAN 58°18.7'N 17°10.0'E Lt. L. Fl. W.R.G.10 sec. W.10M. R.7M. G.5M. B.Tr. with W.Lantern, grey conical base 15m. Wind generator. R.168.5°-183.5°; G.-211°; W.-330°; R.-357.5°; W.(unintens) 064°-110°.

ENSKÄR Lt. Fl. W.R.G.3 sec. W.6M. R.4M. G.3M. W.R.Hut 4m. G.167°-197°; W.-212°; R.-012°; G.-031°; W.-034°; R.-054°.

FÅGELÖN Lt. Q.W.R.G. W.3M. R.2M. G.2M. Lantern on W.Pedestal 6m. G.359°-015°; W.-018°; R.-099°; G.-187°; W.-192°; R.-199°.

BARÖSUND

SANDÖ 58°10.3'N 16°55.6'E Lt. L. Fl(2)
W.R.G.15 sec. W.11M. R.8M. G.7M. W.Tr.
B.Base 12m. G.319°-336.5°; W.-341°; R.-354°;
G.-015°; W.-018°; R.-039°; G.-127°; W.-144°;
R.-160°.

KVARNHOLMEN Lt. Fl(3) W.R.G.9 sec.
W.7M. R.5M. G.4M. W.R.Hut 5m. G.190°-
217°; R.-301°; G.-345.5°; W.-348.5°; R.-006°;
G.-049°; W.-051.5°; R.-081°.

KÄTTILÖ Lt. Fl. W.R.G.3 sec. W.6M. R.4M.
G.3M. W.Lantern 4m. G.161°-177.5°; W.-
181°; R.-330.5°; G.-335°; W.-337°; R.-345°.

ESPSKÄRSGRUND Lt. Fl(2) W.R.G.6 sec.
W.7M. R.5M. G.4M. W.G. Hut 4m. G.356.5°-
001°; W.-003.5°; R.-043°; G.-177°; R.-178°.

BERGHOLMEN Lt. Q.W.R.G. W.5M. R.3M.
G.3M. 3M. Lantern on W.Pedestal 11m.
R.255°-358°; G.-002°; W.-004°; R.-010°; G.-
013°.

STORA BOCKHOLM Ldg. Lts. 207° (Front)
Iso. 4 sec. 9M. W.R. daymark on W.Hut. 5m.
(Rear) Q. 9M. W.R. daymark on W.Hut 12m.
Vis. on leading line only.

SNUGGHOLMEN Lt. Fl(3) W.R.G.9 sec.
W.6M. R.5M. G.4M. W.R.Hut 7m. G.200°-
220°; W.-223°; R.-015°; G.-023°; W.-026°; R.-
shore.

NORRKÖPING

LINDÖKANALEN 58°37.0'N 16°14.7'E
N Ldg. Lts. 247° (Front) Iso. 3 sec. 14M. Or.
Δ, R.Border on W.Or.Tr. 8m. Vis. on leading
line only. R. Lts. on chimney 580m. NW.
58°36.9'N 16°14.3'E (Rear) Iso. 3 sec. 14M.
Or. ∇, R.Border on W.Or.Tr. 16m. Vis. on
leading line only.

58°37.0'N 16°14.6'E S Ldg. Lts. 247° (Front)
Iso. 3 sec. 14M. Or. Δ, R.Border on W.Or.Tr.
8m. Vis. on leading line only. 58°36.9'N
16°14.3'E (Rear) Iso. 3 sec. 14M. Or. ∇,
R.Border on W.Or.Tr. 16m. Vis. on leading
lines only.

N SIDE No: 2 Lt. Q.G. 3M. G.Dolphin 4m.

The channel is marked by lights.

MARIEBORG Ldg. Lts. 301°30' (Front) F.R.
7M. Δ on R.W.Tr. 21m. (Rear) F.R. 7M. ∇ on
R.W.Tr. 30m.

KARLSRO Lt. Q.G. 2M. on dolphin 3m.

ROSSVIKEN Ldg. Lts. 121°30' (Front) F.R.
4M. Or.Tr. 10m. (Rear) F.R. 4M. Or.Tr. 14m.

Q.R. and Q.G. Lts. and traffic signals on
Händelobrön 0.65M. NW. R. Lt. on
chimneys 0.95M. SW and 0.75M. SSW.

KUNGSÄNGEN 58°34.6'N 16°13.7'E Lt.
Aero Fl(3) 5 sec. 23M. Mast 59m.
Obstruction. 040°-055°; 241.5°-256.5°; Also
Aero Fl.5 sec. 055°-241.5°; 256.5°-040°.
F.R. Lt. on radio mast 1.3M. SSE.

BRÅVALLA 58°37'N 16°08'E Lt. Aero Fl(7)
19 sec. 23M. Mast 66m. Obstruction.

BRÅVIKEN

HARGÖKALV Lt. Fl(4) W.R.G.12 sec. W.9M.
R.7M. G.6M. W.Tr. R.Lantern 17m. Floodlit.
G.shore-270°; W.-276.5°; R.-286°; G.-299°; R.-
021°; G.-050°; W.-064°; R.-090°; G.-107°; W.-
111°; R.-122°.

LÖNÖ N SIDE 58°36.4'N 16°46.7'E Lt.
Fl. W.R.G.4 sec. W.10M. R.7M. G.6M.
W.Lantern, R.Roof 5m. Floodlit. G.shore-
106°; W.-109°; R.-126°; G.-139°; W.-195°; R.-
260°; G.-287°; W.-290.5°; R.-shore.

NÄVEKVARN 58°37.4'N 16°48.8'E Lt. Fl(2)
W.R.G.6 sec. W.10M. R.7M. G.6M. W.Hut,
G.Band 8m. Floodlit. G.shore-295°; W.-296°;
R.-315.5°; G.-336°; R.-000°; G.-069°; W.-
075.5°; R.-084°; G.-093°; W.-095°; R.-shore.

KARLSLUND Lt. Q.W.R.G. W.9M. R.7M.
G.6M. G.Hut, W.Roof and base 6m. Floodlit.
G.shore-280°; W.-282°; R.-330°; G.-022°; W.-
070°; R.-088°; G.-096.5°; W.-099°; R.-shore.

FÄRJESTADEN FERRY Ldg. Lts. 198° (Front)
F.G. 6M. Y. Δ, R.Border on building 7m.
Shown when required by ferries. (Rear) F.G.
6M. Y. ∇, R.Border on mast 10m.

SÄTERHOLMEN 58°38.4'N 16°35.6'E Lt. Fl(4)
W.R.G.12 sec. W.12M. R.9M. G.8M.
W.Lantern on pedestal 7m. Floodlit.
G.shore-280°; W.-281°; R.-284.5°; G.-288°;
W.-290°; R.-026°; G.-102.5°; W.-105°; R.-
shore.

KROKEK 58°40.4'N 16°28.2'E Lt. Aero V.Q.
21M. W.Or.Tr. 433m. Obstruction. Also 6
Aero F.R. 6m.

LÖVSGATA Lt. Fl(2) W.R.G.6 sec. W.9M.
R.7M. G.6M. W.Tr. G.Band 7m. Floodlit.
G.shore-286°; W.-288°; R.-302°; G.-069.5°;
W.-071.5°; R.-078°; G.-084°; W.-088°; R.-
shore.

ALGERSGRUND Lt. Q.W.R.G. W.9M. R.7M.
G.6M. Lantern on R.Pedestal 5m. Floodlit.
G.000°-083.5°; W.-272.5°; R.-000°.

STORA JUTEN 58°38.2'N 16°19.7'E Lt. Fl(3) W.R.G.9 sec. W.13M. R.10M. G.9M. R.Lantern on W.Tr. 6m. G.051°-065°; W.-070°; R.-138°; W.(unintens)-230.5°; R.(unintens)-243°; G.-251°; W.-254.5°; R.-282.5°.

BRAVIKEN NORTH Ldg. Lts. 275° (Front) F.R. 9M. Or. Δ, W.Bands on Or.W.Post 9m. V.Q. on chimney 500m WNW. (Rear) F.R. 9M. Or. ▽, W.Bands on Or.W.Post 15m.

SOUTH Ldg. Lts. 256° (Front) F.R. 3M. Or. Δ, W.Bands on Or.W.Post 14m. (Rear) F.R. 3M. Or. ▽, W.Bands on Or.W.Post 16m.

ESTERÖN Ldg. Lts. 076° (Front) F.R. 3M. Or. Δ, W.Bands on Or.W.Post. (Rear) F.R. 3M. Or. ▽, W.Bands on Or.W.Post 11m.

PAMPUSHAMNEN Ldg. Lts. 295° (Front) F.R. R. Δ on R.Post 15m. Marks centre of channel. (Rear) F.R. R. ▽ on R.Post 17m.

Lts. in line 295° (Front) F.G. G. Δ on G.Post 2m. Marks N side of channel. (Rear) F.G. G. ▽ on G.Post 3m.

FLÅSKÖSUND Lt. Fl. R.G.3 sec. R.4M. G.3M. W.G.Tr. 6m G.335°-060°; R.-155°; G.-170°.

FLÅSKÖGRUND Lt. Iso. W.R.G.4 sec. W.6M. R.4M. G.4M. W.R.Pillar 4m. G.130°-155°; W.-172°; R.-225°; W.-333°; R.-345°.

FLÄSKÖHALLAN Lt. Fl(3) W.R.G.9 sec. W.6M. R.4M. G.4M. W.G.Hut 4m. G.355°-002°; W.-013°; R.-155°.

BJÖRSKÄR Lt. Fl. W.R.G.3 sec. W.5M. R.3M. G.3M. W.Lantern 3m. G.058.5°-074.5°; W.-077°; R.-121°; G.-198°; W.-211°; R.-224°.

LÖNSHUVUD Lt. Fl(2) W.R.G.6 sec. W.7M. R.5M. G.4M. W.G.Hut 3m. G.shore-232°; W.-235.5°; R.-312°; G.-066.5°; W.068.5°; R.-072°.

JUNGFRUSALEN Lt. Q.W.R.G. 5.5M. R.3M. G.2M. Lantern on W.R.Hut 6m. W.014°-023°; R.-038°; G.-199°; W.-201°; R.-353°; G.-014°.

KOPPARHOLMEN W POINT Ldg. Lts. 016° Iso. W.R.G.4 sec. W.8M. R.6M. G.5M. Lantern on W.G.Hut 6m. G.000°-010°; W.-022°; R.-073°; G.-082°; W.087.5°; R.-122°; G.-172°; W.-177°; R.196°. **KUGGVIKSSKÄR** (Rear) Fl(4) W.R.G.6 sec. W.6M. R.4M. G.3M. W.Tr. 13m. R.307.5°-331°; G.-011°; W.-019°; R.-051°; G.-058.5°; R.-090°; R.-129°; W.-139°; R.253.5°.

SÖDRA LUNDA Lt. Fl. R.G.3 sec. R.4M. G.3M. On shed 5m. G.shore-349°; R.-090°; G.-173°; R.-shore.

ARKÖ ÖSTRA KOPPARHOLM 58°28.4'N 16°58.4'E Ldg. Lts. 292° (Front) W.R.G.2 sec. W.13M. W.7M. R.5M. G.4M W.Lantern, R. Ɖ, W.Stripe 8m. Floodlit. W.(intens) on leading line. G.119°-149°; W.-156.5°; R.-188°; R.(unintens)-230°. **KALEBO** 58°28.8'N 16°56.7'E (Rear) Oc. 6 sec. 16M. W.Lantern, R. Ɖ, W.Stripe 27m.

NORRA FÄLLBÄDAN 58°26.5'N 17°06.4'E Lt. Fl(3) W.R.G.9 sec. W.11M. R.8M. G.7M. B.Tr.W.Top, Y.Band, grey base. 16m. Wind generator. G.108.5°-114.5°; W.-116°; R.-122°; G.(unintens)-180°; R.(unintens)-240°; R.-245°; G.-253°; W.-315°; R.333.5°. ⨏

LISS LINDÖ Fl. W.R.G.3 sec. W.5M. R.3M. G.3M. W.Lantern 2m. G.120°-130.5°; W.-133.5°; R.-159°; W.(unintens)-289°; G.-308.5°; W.-322°; R.-shore.

ETTERGRUNDSHÄLLAN Lt. Oc. W.R.G.6 sec. W.8M. R.6M. G.5M. Lantern on W.R.Tr. 6m. G.132°-146°; W.-148°; R-315°.

GRÄNSÖSUND Ldg. Lts. 316° (Front) Iso. W.R.G.4 sec. W.6M. R.4M. G.3M. W.Lantern R&W Ɖ 4m. G.156°-169°; W.-171°; R.-245°; W.-335°. (Rear) Q. 7M. R.W. Ɖ on W.Hut 8m. Vis. on leading line only.

TROLLHOLMSHÄLLAN Lt. Fl(2) W.R.G.6 sec. W.5M. R.3M. G.3M. W.Lantern 3m. G.139°-155°; W.-157°; R.-209.5°; G.-330°; W.-333°; R.-139°.

NORRA GRÄNSÖ Lt. Fl. W.R.G.3 sec. W.5M. R.3M. G.3M. W.Pedestal 6m. R.355°-105°; G.-146°; W.-148.5°; R.-172°.

RAMSHOLMEN Ldg. Lts. 157° (Front) Q. 6M. W. Δ on mast 5m. (Rear) Oc. 3 sec. W. ▽ R.Border with R&W ☐ on W.Hut 9m. Vis. on leading line only.

FLÄSKÖ NE POINT Lt. Fl(2) R.G. 6sec. 2M. Lantern on W.R.Hut 6m. G.155°-240°; R.-335°; G.-350°.

BJÖRNÖ Ldg. Lts. 191° (Front) F.R. 4M. Or. Δ on mast 6m. (Rear) F.R. 4M. Or. ▽ on mast 11m.

BOSÖ STEN Lt. Fl(2) W.R.G.6 sec. W.6M. R.4M. G.3M. W.Lantern 4m. G.154°-170°; W.-172.5°; R.-238°; G.-288°; W.-295°; R.-341°. F.R. Lts. on chimneys and radio tower 0.7M. W.

MARÖ W POINT 58°33.6'N 16°54.9'E Ldg.
Lts. 203°30' (Front) Iso W.R.G.4 sec. W.11M.
W.6M. R.4M. G.3M. W.Lantern 5m. G.028°-
039.5°; W.-044°; R.-060.5°; G.(unintens)-118°;
W.(unintens)-203.5°; W.(intens) on leading
line. 58°33.0'N 16°54.4'E **EKÖ** (Rear)
Q.W.R.G. W.10M. W.5M. R.3M. G.3M. R. Ⅱ,
W.Stripe 14m. R.053°-063°; G.-083.5°; W.-
089°; R.-134°; G.(unintens)-144°; W.(intens)
on leading line.

LOGEGRUND Lt. Fl. G.3 sec. 2M.
W.G.Pedestal 3m.

KARTHÅLLAN Lt. Fl. W.R.G.3 sec. W.6M.
R.4M. G.3M. W.Tr. 10m. G.340°-345°; W.-
347°; R.-010°; G.-116°; R.-173°; G.-194°; W.-
197°; R.-203°; G.-281°. Fishing. 1/10-1/4.

MESEN 58°37.3'N 16°59.5'E Lt. Fl. W.R.G.3
sec. W.10M. R.7M. G.6M. W.Hut, R.Band
6m. R.062°-150°; G.-251°; W.-253°; R.-260°.

ÅLBÄCKSGRUND Lt. Fl(2) W.R.G.6 sec.
W.9M. R.7M. G.6M. W.G.Lantern 7m.
Floodlit. G.shore-267.5°; R.-000°; G.-062°;
W.-067.5°; R.-090°. R.Lt. on mast 2.45M. NW.

KUNGSHAMN 58°37.6'N 17°01.4'E Ldg. Lts.
069°30' (Front) Iso. W.R.G.4 sec. W.10M.
R.7M. G.6M. W.Lantern, R.Roof 11m.
Floodlit. G.255°-260°; W.-265°; R.-299°.
58°37.7'N 17°02.0'E (Rear) Q.W.R.G. W.10M.
R.7M. G.6M. W.Tr. R.Roof 19m. R.237°-247°;
G.-263°; W.-266.5°; R.-289°; G.-320°; W.-327°;
R.-001°; G.-027.5°; W.-shore.

FALKENS GRUND 58°37.9N 17°02.6'E Lt.
Fl(3) W.R.G.9 sec. W.10M. R.8M. G.6M. W.Tr.
R.Top on base. 11m. Floodlit. G.208°-255°;
W.-263°; R.-289°; G.-010°; R.-063°; G.-s077°;
W.-080.5°; R.-208°. ⌇

VINTERKLASEN Ldg. Lts. 213° (Front) F.R.
9M. 9m. 58°38.5'N 17°08.0'E (Rear) Mo(U)
W.R.G.10 sec. W.11M. R.8M. G.7M. W.Hut
R.Roof 17m. Floodlit. R.177°-248°; G.-301°;
W.-309°; R.-028°; G.-065°; W.-068°; R.-095°;
G.-141°.

GRÄSSKÄREN 58°37.1'N 17°14.4'E Lt.
L. Fl(2) W.R.G.15 sec. W.14M. R.11M.
G.10M. W.Tr. Or.Lantern 12m. Floodlit.
G.242.5°-263.5°; W.-267.5°; R.-284°; G.-301°;
W.-099°; R.-131°.

KOPPARNAGELN 58°36.8'N 17°17.5'E Lt.
Q.W.R.G. W.10M. R.7M. G.6M. B.W.Tr. 7m.
Floodlit. G.103°-250°; W.-258°; R.-103°. ⌇

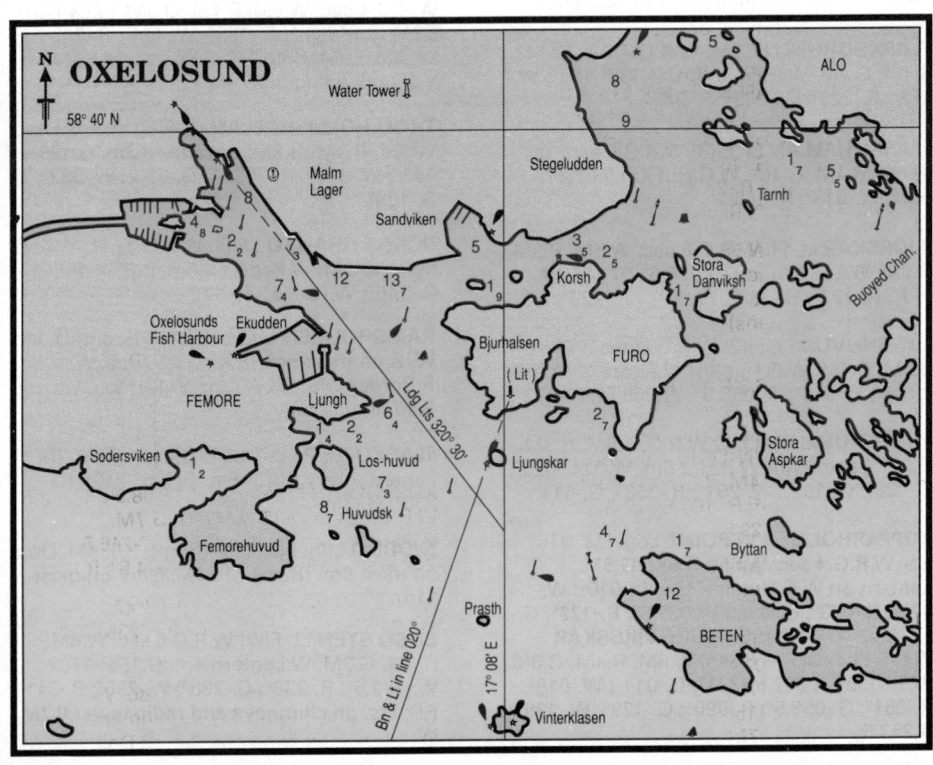

OXELÖSUND

OXELÖSUND 58°39.7'N 17°07.9'E Lt.
Q.W.R.G. W.10M. R.8M. G.7M. W.Lantern
4m. G.shore-282°; W.-308°; R.-348°; G.-
054.5°; W.-062°; R.-078°. 2 F.R. Lts. on
chimney 0.5M. N.

Ldg. Lts. 265° (Front) Q.G. 8M. Or. ∆ on post
7m. (Rear) Q.G. 8M. Or. ▽ on post 10m.

KORSHOLM 58°39.7'N 17°08.2'E Lt. Fl(2)
W.R.G.6 sec. W.10M. R.7M. G.6M.
W.Lantern 3m. Floodlit. G.075°-093°; W.-
099°; R.-170°; G.-238°; W.-244°; R.-259°; G.-
262°; W.-264°; R.-274°.

BETEN W SIDE 58°38.7'N 17°08.6'E Lt. Fl(2)
W.R.G.6 sec. W.13M. R.10M. G.8M.
W.Lantern 12m. Floodlit. G.shore-332.5°;
W.-343.5°; R.-028.5°; G.-063°; W.-066.5°; R.-
075°; G.086°-125°; W.-132°; R.-shore.

LJUNGSKÄR SW SIDE 58°39.2'N 17°07.9'E
Lt. Fl(4) W.R.G.12 sec. W.13M. R.10M. G.8M.
W.Tr. 7m. Floodlit. G.shore-323°; W.-327°;
R.-346°; G.-017.5°; W.-022.5°; R.-035°; G.-
050°; R.-071°; G.-134.5°; W.-142°; R.-shore.

OXELÖSUNDS HAMN Ldg. Lts.
320°30' (Front) Iso. R.4 sec. 9M. R. ∆, on
mast 6m. Vis. on leading line only. (Rear)
Iso. R.4 sec. 9M. R. ▽, on mast 10m. Vis. on
leading line only.

NORRA KRÄNKAN 58°37.0'N 17°23.4'E Lt.
Fl(3) W.R.G.9 sec. W.10M. R.8M. G.6M. W.Tr.
on grey conical base 12m. Floodlit. W.086°-
088.5°; R.-100°; G.-154.5°; W.-159°; R.-205°;
G.-207°; W.-210°; R.-242°; G.-261°; W.-288°;
R.-349°; G.-085.5°. Racon.

VÄSTRA KORPEN 58°36.3'N 17°19.6'E Lt.
Fl(4) W.R.G.12 sec. W.11M. R.8M. G.7M.
W.Tr. 8m. Floodlit. G.280°-312°; W.-321°; R.-
341.5°; W.(unintens)-074°; G.-105°; W.-111°;
R.-130°.

HÄVRINGE 58°36.3'N 17°19.3'E Ldg. Lts.
295°24' (Front) Iso. 3 sec. 14M. W. ☐ on
W.B.Pedestal 9m. Floodlit. Vis. on leading
line only. 58°36.3'N 17°19.1'E (Rear) Iso.
W.R.G.3 sec. W.14M. R.11M. G.10M. W.B.Tr.
23m. W.291°-314°; R.-109.5°; G.-138°; W.-
139°; R.-245°; G.-291°.

OSTÄKEN GUSTAF DALÉN 58°35.7'N
17°28.2'E Lt. Iso. W.R.G.8 sec. W.20M.
W.18M. R.18M. R.15M. G.17M. G.15M.
G.14M. B.Round Tr. R.Top, grey base 24m.
Floodlit. R(18M) 018°-045.5; G(17M)-050°;
G(14M)-131°; G(17M)-136°; W(18M)-176.5°;
R(18M)-181.5°; R(15M)-205°; G(15M)-210°;
G(14M)-232°; G(17M)-240°; R(18M)-249°;

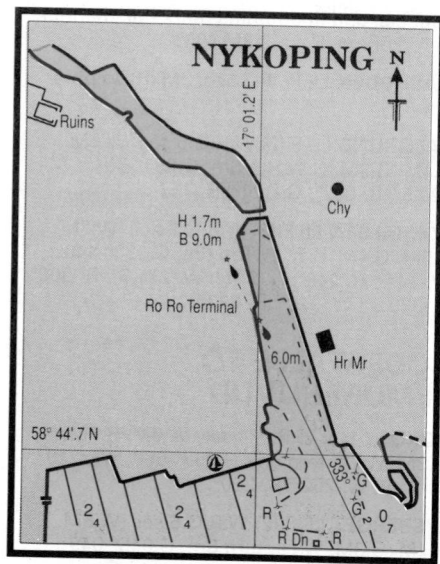

G(17M)-258°; W(20M)-017°. R.C. Racon.
H24.1/11-31/3. Horn(3) 30 sec. Horns point
NE and S.

HÄFRINGE-ÅLÖFJÄRD CHANNEL

LILLHAMMARSGRUND 58°39.8'N 17°20.3'E
Lt. Fl. W.R.G.3 sec. W.11M. R.9M. R.2M.
G.8M. W.Tr. R.Top, B.Base 11m. Floodlit.
G.101°-113.5°; W.-119.5°; R.-132°;
R.(unintens)-222°; G.-237°; W.-240°; R.-325°;
G.-345°. Racon.

NORRA MÅSKLUBBSHÅLLAN Lt. Q.W.R.G.
W.9M. R.6M. G.5M. G.1M. R.Structure 3m.
Floodlit. G.(unintens) 138°-266°; G.-275.5°;
W.-279°; R.-296°.

NORRA LILLHAMMARSGRUND 58°40.5'N
17°19.4'E Ldg. Lts. 301° (Front) Iso. 4 sec.
12M. R. Ⅱ, Y.Stripe on base 10m.
TRUTBÅDAN 58°41.4'N 17°16.2'E (Rear) Q.
12M. R. Ⅱ, Y.Stripe on Tr. 12m.

KORPHOLMEN 58°40.7'N 17°08.9'E Lt. Fl(2)
W.R.G.6 sec. W.10M. R.8M. G.7M.
W.Lantern 4m. Floodlit. G.231°-246.5°; W.-
249.5°; R.-258°; G.-002°; W.-004.5°; R.-059°.

NYKÖPING SKAVSTA 58°47.1'N
16°55.2'E Lt. Aero Fl(7) 19 sec. 23M. 2 masts
45m. Obstruction.

SJÖSA Ldg. Lts. 320° (Front) Iso. W.R.3 sec.
W.5M. R.4M. W. ∆ on G.Dolphin 4m. (Rear)
Q.W.R. W.5M. R.4M. W. ▽ on B.Dolphin 7m.

Ldg. Lts. and lit dolphins mark the channel to Nyköping. R. Lt. 2.3M NW.

NÄSUDDEN Lt. Fl. R.3 sec. 3M. R.Dolphin 4m.

SÄLGRUND Lt. Fl(2) W.R.G.6 sec. W.6M. R.4M. G.3M. G.W.Hut 6m. G.291°-301°; W.-320.5°; R.-052°; G.-121°; R.-157°.

KÖLHALSEN Lt. Fl(3) W.R.G.9 sec. W.7M. R.5M. G.4M. B.Tr. W.Top 6m. G.130°-140°; W.-144°; R.-248°; G.-277°; W.-281.5°; R.-300°; G.-320.5°; W.-322°; R.-337°.

SÖDERTÄLJE TO FEMÖREHUVUD

BOKÖ Lt. Iso. W.R.G.4 sec. W.6M. R.4M. G.3M. W.Lantern 5m. G.053°-060°; W.-229°; G.-249°; W.-252°; R.-260°.

LYSBERGET Lt. Fl(2) W.R.G.6 sec. W.6M. R.4M. G.3M. W.Lantern 8m. G.045°-049°; W.-051.5°; R.-063.5°.

BOCKHOLMEN Lt. Q.W.R.G. W.6M. R.4M. G.3M. W.G.Lantern on hut 4m. G.000°-006.5°; W.-001.5°; R.-051°; G.-179°; W.-182.5°; R.-200°.

TÖRNSKÄR Lt. Iso. W.R.G.4 sec. W.6M. R.4M. G.3M. W.G.Lantern on hut 5m. R.shore-150°; G.-171°; W.-173°; R.-188°; W.-226°; R.-shore.

SKVALLRAN Lt Fl(3) W.R.G.9 sec. W.7M. R.5M. G.4M. W.R.Tr. grey base 10m. G.189°-203°; W.-221°; R.-258°; G.-271°; W.-279.5°; R.-344°; G.-060°; W.-080°; R.-095°; R.(unintens)-116°.

ASKENSKALLEN Lt. Fl. W.R.G.3 sec. W.8M. R.6M. G.5M. W.G.Tr. 12m. G.091°-106°; W.-110°; R.-238°; G.-259°; W.-267°; R.-277°; G.-294°; R.-300°; G(unintens) 325°-335°; W(unintens)-000°; R(unintens)-010°.

GRÅSKÄR Lt. Q. 7M. Silver hut 10m. Shows in direction of Kockelskär Ldg. Lts.

YTTRE HALLOFJARDEN ASKÖN Ldg. Lts. 098° (Front) F.R. 4M. Or. △ on post 5m. (Rear) F.R. 4M. Or. ▽ on post 8m.

KOCKELSKÄR Ldg. Lts. 276° (Front) Iso. W.R.G.4 sec. W.7M. R.5M. G.4M. W.Tr. R.Base 7m. G.shore-275°; W.-277°; R.-308°; G.-359°; R.-018°. (Rear) Q. 10M R. □ on W.Tr. 20m. Vis. on leading line only.

KOCKELHÄLLAN Lt. Fl(3) W.R.G.9 sec. W.6M. R.4M. G.3M. W.G.Hut 5m. G.034°-054°; W.-077°; R.-133°; G.-170°; W.-174°; R.-194°; G.-265°; R.-276°.

HÖKÖ GUPA Lt. Fl. W.R.G.3 sec. W.6M. R.4M. G.3M. W.R.Lantern 5m. G.170°-177°; W.-180°; R.-210°; G.-228.5°; W.-236.5°; R.-265°; G.-318°; W.-327°; R.-shore.

TRÄTBÅDAN Lt. Fl(2) W.R.G.6 sec. W.7M. R.5M. G.4M. W.G.Tr. 7m. G.060.5°-G.068.5°; W.-071.5°; R.-088.5°; G.-157°; W.-160°; R.-167°; G.-267°.

HERRSÄTEN N SIDE OF STORA HERRSÄTEN Lt. Fl(4) W.R.G.12 sec. W.7M. R.5M. G.4M. W.G.Hut 5m. G.096.5°-100.5°; R.-112°; G.-129°; W.-139°; R.-222°;G.-238°; W.-242°; R.-267°.

SÄVÖSUND N SIDE OF LONGÖN 58°45.9'N 17°28.7'E Lt. Iso. W.R.G.3 sec. W.10M. R.7M. G.6M. W.G.Hut 3m. G.093°-102°; W.-109°; R.-147°; W.(unintens)-247°; R.-253°; G.-272°; W.-275°; R.-296°.

KÄLLVIK Lt. Fl. W.R.G.3 sec. W.9M. R.7M. G.6M. W.R.Hut 4m. Floodlit. G.315°-332.5°; W.-339.5°; R.-050°; G.-113.5°; W.125.5°; R.-134.5°.

Ldg. Lts. 042° **MÄRHOLMEN** (Front) Q.W.R. W.8M. R.6M. Lantern on W.R.Pedestal 6m. W.138°-270°; R.270°-leading line, R.(intens) on leading line.

BROMDAL (Rear) Iso. W.R.G.4 sec. W.9M. R.6M. G.5M. W. □ on W.R.Pedestal 13m. G.shore-323°; R.-000.5°; G.-026°; W.-032°; R.-086°.

STUDSVIK Lts. in line 249° (Front) F.R. 4M. W. △, B.Border 5m. Vis. on leading line only. Mark water intake. (Rear) F.R. 4M. W. ▽, B.Border 15m. Vis. on leading line only.

Lts. in line 328° (Front) F.R. 4M. W. △, B.Border 5m. Vis. on leading line only. Mark outfall pipe. R. Lt. on Tr. 400m. SW. (Rear) F.R. 4M. W. ▽, B.Border 7m. Vis. on leading line only.

BERGÖ SE POINT OF LILLA BERGÖ 58°45.1'N 17°24.7'E Lt. Fl. W.R.3 sec. W.10M. R.7M. W.Lantern 5m. Floodlit. W.194°-225°; R.225°-030° approx.

GRISKÄR Ldg. Lts. 314°36' (Front) Iso. W.R.G.4 sec. W.6M. R.4M. G.3M. W.Tr. R.Base 6m. G.153°-175°; W.-177.5°; R.-195°; G.-284°; W.-320°; 58°44.3'N 17°24.8'E (Rear) Q. 11M. R. Ⅱ, Y.Stripe on lantern on W.Pedestal 12m. Vis. on leading line only.

RINGSÖN Ldg. Lts. 338°30' (Front) Iso. W.R.G.4 sec. W.6M. R.4M. G.3M. R. Ⅱ, Y.Stripe on W.Tr. G.Base 9m. G.330°-332°; W.-342.5°; R.-046°; G.-117.5°; W.-125.5°; R.-140°. (Rear) Q. 10M. R. Ⅱ, Y.Stripe, Lantern on W.Pedestal 20m. Vis. on leading line only.

HARTSÖ STÅNGSKÄR Lt. Fl(4) W.R.G.12 sec. W.8M. R.6M. G.5M. W.Tr. B.Base 14m. G.003°-023°; W.-035°; R.-064.5°; G.-075°; W.-079°; R.-119°; G.-159°; W.-161.5°; R.-180°.

SKEPNA Lt. Fl. W.R.G.3 sec. W.6M. R.4M. G.3M. W.Hut 6m. G.270°-305°; W.-310°; R.-332°; G.-016°; W.-020°; R.090°.

LÅNGSKÄR Lt. Fl(2) W.R.G.6 sec. W.6M. R.4M. G.3M. W.Lantern 8m. G.096°-109.5°; W.-115°; R.-135°; W.(unintens)-215°; G.-230°; W.-234°; R.-245°.

LACKA TRUTBÅDE Lt. Fl. W.R.G.3 sec. W.6M. R.4M. G.3M. Lantern on brown pedestal 10m. G.080°-129.5°; W.-133.5°; R.-168°; G.-280°; W.-284°; R.-293°; G.-312°; W.-316°; R.-080°. Fishing. Shown 1/10-1/4.

ESPSKÄRSKLUBB Lt. Fl. R.G.3 sec. R.4M. G.3M. W.Hut 6m. G.215°-225°; R.-019°; G.-051°; R.-055°.

ÖRNSKLUBB Lt. Fl(2) R.G.6 sec. R.4M. G.3M. W.Hut 5m. G.122°-126°; R.-180°; G.-274°; R.-284°.

VÅLARÖ Lt. Q.R.G. R.4M. G.3M. W.Hut 5m. G.270°-305°; R.-000°; G.-055°; R.-064°.

STORA KAMPÅSEN Lt. Fl. W.R.G.3 sec. W.6M. R.4M. G.3M. Pylon with W.Hut 7m. G.shore-260°; W.-276°; R.-017°; G.-031°; R.-070°.

LEDSKÄR Lt. Iso. W.R.G.3 sec. W.7M. R.5M. G.4M. W.Lantern 7m. G.000°-033°; W.-052.5°; R.-088°; G.-112°; R.-178°; G.-197°; R.-230°; G.-309°; R.-000°.

Ldg. Lts. 246° **FLÄSKET** (Front) Q.9M. 4M. Lantern on W.G.Pedestal 5m. Intens on leading line. Traffic Lts. on bridge 1.6M NW. **KUNGSHATT** 59°17.9'N 17°54.5'E (Rear) Iso. 4 sec. 10M. W. ☐ on W.G.Pedestal 12m. Intens on leading line.

SÄTRA Lt. Fl. W.R.G.3 sec. W.4M. R.2M. G.2M. W.R.Pedestal 5m. G.shore-050°; W.-061°; R.-143°; G.-227°; W.-233°; R.-shore.

ESTBRÖTE Lt. Fl(2) W.R.G. 6 sec. W.5M. R.3M. G.3M. W.G.Pedestal 5m. G.181°-208°; W.-224°; R.-300°; G.-005°; W.-020°; R.-037°; G.-shore.

VÅRBY OIL HARBOUR Lts. in line about 200° (Front) F.R. 6M. Or. △. 6m. Mark E limit of dredged area. (Rear) F.R. 6M. Or. ▽. 9m.

Lts. in line about 170° (Front) F.G. 5M. Or. △ 6m. Mark W limit of dredged area. (Rear) F.G. 5M. Or. ▽. 9m.

SLAGSTA MARINA NORRA Lt. Q.G. 1M. G.Post 3m. Shown 1/4-30/11.

SODRA Lt. Q.R. 1M. R.Post 3m. Shown 1/4-30/11.

SLAGSTAHOLM Lt. Fl. W.R.G.3 sec. W.6M. R.4M. G.3M. W.R.Lantern 4m. G.070°-082°; W.-087°; R.-218.5°; G.-226°; W.-234.5°; R.-243.5°.

NORSBORG Lt. Fl(3) W.R.G.9 sec. W.6M. R.4M. G.3M. W.Lantern 4m. G.092°-105.5°; W.-110°; R.-180°; G.-253°; W.-255°; R.-shore.

VÅLLINGE Lt. Q.W.R.G. W.4m. R.2M. G.2M. W.Pedestal 5m. G.100°-118°; W.-125.5°; R.-187°; G.-260°; W.-267°; R.-285°.

BOCKHOLMSSUNDET

Ldg. Lts. 276°42' (Front) Iso. W.R.G.4 sec. W.6M. R.4M. G.3M. W.Lantern 4m. G.shore-124°; W.-127.5°; R.-196°; W.-shore. (Rear) V.Q. 7M. W. ☐ on pedestal 11m. Floodlit. Vis. on leading line only.

BOCKHOLMSSUND ÖSTRA Lt. Fl. W.R.G.3 sec. W.4M. R.3M. G.2M. Lantern on W.Pedestal 5m. Floodlit. G.shore-110°; W.-115.5°; R.-147°; W.-261°; R.-shore.

GÅSHOLM Lt. Fl(3) W.R.G.9 sec. W.5M. R.3M. G.3M. W. ☐ on W.Mast 8m. G.shore-126.5°; W.-136°; R.-199°; G.-307°; W.-320°; R.-shore.

Illuminated boards are shown on inland waters N and W.

BOCKHOLMSSÄTRA Lt. F.R.G. R. ☐ Y.Stripe on Tr. 8m. G.198°-245°; R.245°-shore.

LÅNGHÄLLSUDDE Lt. Fl. W.R.G.4 sec. W.6M. R.4M. G.3M. W.Lantern 4m. R.shore-055.5°; G.109.5°; W.-114°; R.-121.5°; G.-131.5°; W.-136°; R.-168°; G.-255°.

BORNHUVUD Lt. Iso. W.R.G.4 sec. W.7M. R.5M. G.4M. W.Hut, G.Daymark 7m. G.shore-345°; W.-348°; R.-130°; G.-160.5°; W.-173°; R.-shore.

VIKSBERG Lt. Fl(2) W.R.G.6 sec. W.6M. R.4M. G.3M. W.G.Lantern 3m. G.329°-336.5°; W.-339°; R.-006°; R.(unintens)-052°; W.(unintens)-097°; G.(unintens)-139°; G.-153°; W.-162.5°; R.-175°.

TEGELTORP Lt. Q.W.R.G. W.3M. R.2M.
G.2M. Lantern on W.Pedestal 5m. G.338°-
354.5°; W.-151°; R.-shore.

LANDSORT TO SÖDERTALJE

GRANKLUBBEN 58°47.9'N 17°45.2'E Lt. Iso.
W.R.G.3 sec. W.13M. R.10M. G.9M.
W.Lantern 13m. G.225°-298°; R.-312.5°; G.-
317.5°; W.-320°; R.-329.5°; G.-011°; W.-054°;
R.-075°.

RÖKOGRUNDET 58°47.2'N 17°46.8'E Lt.
Fl(4) W.R.G.12 sec. W.10M. R.7M. G.6M.
B.W.Tr. G.Lantern. 10m. Floodlit. G.024°-
088.5°; W.-090°; R.-107°; G.-164°; W.-169°;
R.-292°; G.-321°; W.-324.5°; R.-024°.

VÄSTRA RÖKO 58°47.4'N 17°47.0'E Lt.
Q.W.R.G. W.10M. R.7M. G.6M. W.Tr. 13m.
Floodlit. G.024°-084°; R.-114°; G.-151.5°; W.-
161.5°; R.-172°.

KOLGUSKÄR 58°48.2'N 17°46.7'E Lt. Fl(2)
W.R.G.6 sec. W.10M. R.7M. G.6M.
W.Lantern 10m. Floodlit. G.337°-001.5°; W.-
012°; R.-022°; G.-135°; W.-138°; R.-shore.

TORSKEN Lt. Q.W.R.G. W.9M. R.7M. G.6M.
Radar reflector on Or.Pedestal. 6m. Floodlit.
G.018.5°-155°; W.-169°; R.-248°; G.-307°; W.-
313°; R.-018.5°. ⚓

VATTKLUBBEN 58°49.4'N 17°44.5'E Lt. Iso.
W.R.G.6 sec. W.10M. R.8M. G.7M. W.Tr.
B.Diagonal stripes on lower part 10m.
Floodlit. G.305°-319.5°; W.-326°; R.-045°; G.-
125.5°; W.-135°; R.-163°; G.-219°; R.-240°.

SÖDRA BERGHOLMEN Lt. Fl. W.R.G.3 sec.
W.4M. R.3M. G.2M. Lantern on W.Pedestal
7m. G.206°-232°; W.-291°; R.-025°; G.-054°;
W.-060°; R.-078°; G.-148°. Occas.

KARINGHÄLLAN Lt. Fl(2) G.6 sec. 6M. G. □
on structure 7m. Floodlit. ⚓

FIFONG 58°50.6'N 17°43.5'E Lt. Fl(3)
W.R.G.9 sec. W.10M. R.7M. G.6M.
W.Lantern, Concrete base 7m. Floodlit.
G.164°-169.5°; W.-171.5°; R.-177°; G.-244.5°;
R.-312°; G.-350°; W.-359°; R.-004°; G.-016°.

FÅLLNÄSVIKEN SVARDSO Lt. Q.W.R.G.
W.4M. R.2M. G.2M. W.Lantern on pedestal
5m. G.shore-057°; W.-133°; R.-158°; G.-175°;
W.-186°; R.-shore. Shown 6/7-6/6.

Lts. in channel to Stora Vika are shown as
required.

STYRMANNEN Lt. Fl. W.R.G.3 sec. W.6M.
R.4M. G.3M. W.Lantern 5m. G.163°-191°;
W.-213.5°; R.-245°; R.-322°; G.-019.5°; W.-
022°; R.-042°. Shown 6/7-6/6. Occas.

STYVIKSUDD Lt. Fl(2) W.R.G.6 sec. W.5M.
R.3M. G.2M. Lantern on W.Pedestal 6m.
G.282°-009°; R.-016.5°; G.-143°; W.-148.5°;
R.-shore. Shown 6/7-6/6. Occas.

FRÖNÄS Lt. Fl. W.R.G.3 sec. W.4M. R.3M.
G.2M. Lantern on W.Pedestal 5m. G.shore-
154°; W.-190°; R.-270°; G.-325°; W.-335°; R.-
shore. Shown 6/7-6.6. Occas.

**W SIDE OF CHANNEL BREDSTÄKET No:
1(S)** Lt. F.R.G. R.5M. G.4M. R.Dolphin 4m.
Floodlit. G.090°-270°; R.270°-090°. Shown
6/7-6/6. Occas.

No: 2(N) Lt. F.R.G. R.5M. G.4M. R.Dolphin
6m. Floodlit. G.090°-270°; R.270°-090°.
Shown 6/7-6/6. Occas.

E SIDE OF CHANNEL No: 3(S) Lt. F.R.G.
R.5M. G.4M. W.Dolphin 4m. Floodlit. R.090°-
270°; G.270°-090°. Shown 6/7-6/6. Occas.

VIKA Lt. Iso. W.R.G.3 sec. W.8M. R.6M.
G.5M. W.Tr. 7m. G.shore-338°; W.-341°; R.-
000°; W.(unintens)-123°; R.-145°; G.-153°;
W.-158°; R.-shore. Shown 6/7-6/6. Occas.

GALKLUBB 58°52.8'N 17°43.1'E Lt. Iso.
W.R.G.8 sec. W.10M. R.7M. G.6M.
W.R.Lantern. 5m. Floodlit R.008°-081°; G.-
158°; W.-179.5°; R.-288°; G.-297°; W.-299°;
R.-347°; G.-357°; W.-008°.

SANKHÄLLAN 58°52.3'N 17°42.8'E Lt.
Q.W.R.G. W.10M. R.7M. G.6M. W.R.Lantern
6m. Floodlit. G.087°-181°; W.-184.5°; R.-193°;
G.-205.5°; W.-217°; R.-270°; G.-340°; W.-346°.
R.-087°.

SVARTHÄLL Lt. Fl(2) W.R.G.6 sec. W.8M.
R.5M. G.4M. Lantern on W.G.Hut 5m.
G.057°-069.5°; W.-071°; R.-159°; G.-217°; W.-
225°; R.-243°; G.-271°; R.-283°.

STENSKÄR 58°54.4'N 17°43.0'E Lt. Fl.
W.R.G.3 sec. W.10M. R.7M, G.6M.
W.R.Lantern 10m. Floodlit. G.153°-180°; W.-
184.5°; R.-284°; G.-347°; W.-354°; R.-002.5°;
G.-022°; W.-023.5°; R.-058°.

EGELSHOLM 59°00.5'N 17°42.9'E Lts. in line
172° (Front) Q.W.R.G. W.10M. R.7M. G.6M.
W.R.Lantern 3m. Floodlit. G.shore-170°; W.-
171.5°; R.-230°; G.-330.5°; W.-353.5°; R.-
shore.

REGARN N END (Rear) Iso. W.R.G.4 sec.
W.6M. R.4M. G.3M W.Lantern 6m. G.354°-
007°; W.-175°; R.-211°.

NÄSLANDET SEWAGE OUTFALL Lts. in line 008°. (Front) F.R. 7M. W. △, R.Border 7m. (Rear) F.R. 7M. W. ▽, R.Border 12m.

NOTHOLMEN 59°03.3'N 17°41.2'E Lt. Fl. W.R.G.3 sec. W.10M. R.7M. G.6M. W.Lantern on round hut, R.Roof 3m. Floodlit. G.119°-162°; W.-167°; R.-296.5°; G.-308°; W.-319°; R.-342°.

JARNAFJÄRDEN Lts. in line 100° (Front) F.R. 9M. △ 6m. Marks pipeline. (Rear) F.R. 9M. ▽ 9m.

SKJUTHOLMEN Lt. Q. 7M. Lantern on W.Pedestal 5m. Intens toward Brandalssund. Unintens 295°-350°.

BRANDALSSUND Lt. Fl. W.R.G.3 sec. W.5M. R.3M. G.3M. R.Dolphin 4m. G.shore-242°; W.-251.5°; R.-344°; G.-022°; W.-042°; R.-104°.

VIAD Ldg. Lts. 062° (Front) Iso. 4 sec. 7M. W.Tr. 7m. Vis. on leading line only. (Rear) Q. 6M. W.Tr. 18m. Vis. on leading line only.

HALLSFJÄRDEN Lt. Fl.3 sec. 8M. Lantern on W.Pedestal 4m.

FLÄSKLÖSA Lt. V.Q. 3M. W.Tr. 5m. Partially obscured by vegetation about 180°-about 335°.

Illuminated boards F.W. and F.Y. are shown marking the shore line.

HALLS HOLME 59°09.7'N 17°40.3'E Lt. Fl(2) W.R.G.6 sec. W.10M. R.7M. G.6M. W.Lantern on B.Pedestal 8m. G.shore-344°; W.-349.8°; R.-090°; G.-164.9°; W.-167.4°; R.-shore. R.Lt. on chimney 1M. NNW.

SÖDERTÄLJE SLUSS Ldg. Lts. (Front) F.R. on Tr. (Rear) F.R. on Tr.

No: 4 Lt. Oc(2) W.R.G.10 sec. W.6M. R.4M. G.3M. on Tr. 3m. G.001°-095°; R.-168.5°; G.-177.5°; W.-181°; R.-shore.

No: 5 Lt. F.R. 5M. on post 6m. Illuminated board 300m. W.

LANDSORT TO STOCKHOLM

ÖSTRA RÖKO Lt. Fl.(2) W.R.G.6 sec. W.6M. R.4M. G.3M. Lantern on W.G.Hut 8m. R.007.5°-026°; G.-036°; W.-043°; R.-059°; G.-076.5°; W.-084°; R.-129°; G.-143°; W.-148°; R.-211°; G.-219°; W.-222.5°; R.-246°; R.(unintens)-269°; G.(unintens)-354°; R.(unintens)-007.5° .

ÄLVSNABBEN KAPELLON Lt. Q.W.R.G. W.5M. R.5M. G.4M. R.W.Hut on W.Base 7m. R.shore-218°; G.-226°; W.-041°; R.-045°; G.-053°.

MYSINGEHOLM 59°00.2'N 18°15.7'E Lt. Iso. W.R.G.4 sec. W.13M. R.10M. G.9M. W.Tr. R.Roof 8m. Floodlit. G.005°-042°; W.-046°; R.-084°; G.-118°; R.-164°; G.-186°; W.-200°; R.-204.5°; G.-210°; W.-211.5°; R.-223°.

SÖDERHÄLL Lt. Fl(3) W.R.G.9 sec. W.9M. R.7M. G.6M. R.Hut 5m. Floodlit. G.153°-161°; W.-165°; R.-202.5°; G.-282.5°; W.-285°; R.-005°; G.-038.5°; R.-062°.

UTÖ FIRING RANGE 58°57.0'N 18°15.9'E Lt. V.Q.R. 12M. Lantern on building 69m. Vis. 278°-015°. Shown when firing taking place.

NÅSUDDEN Lt. Q. 3M. Tr. 2m. Vis. 155°-335°. On request.

Ldg. Lts. 158° (Front) F.R. 3M. W. △ on mast 6m. Vis. on leading line only. Occas. (Rear) F.R. 3M. W. ▽ on mast 11m. Vis. on leading line only. Occas.

LÅNGGARN Lt. I.Q. W.R.G.6 sec. W.9M. R.6M. G.5M. R.Tr. grey base 6m. Floodlit. G.206°-233°; W.-235.5°; R.-244°; G.-314.5°; R.-355°; G.-007°; W.-022°; R.-051°; G.-shore.

ORMSTA 59°07N 18°08'E Lt. Aero Q. 21M. Mast 89m. Obstruction. Also Lt. Aero F.R. 6M.

GÅLÖ Lt. Iso. W.R.G.8 sec. W.9M. R.7M. G.6M. R.Pedestal 4m. Floodlit. G.017°-042°; W.-050°; R.-140°; G.-282°; R.-017°.

KOÖN Lt. Q. 3M. Post 1m. Vis. 324°-144°. Occas.

TORRBÄNKEN E SIDE OF ISLAND Lt. Fl. W.R.G.3 sec. W.9M. R.7M. G.6M. R.Tr. 4m. Floodlit. G.(unintens) 213°-228°; G.-239°; W.-241.5°; R.-258°; R.(unintens)-273°; R.-285°; G.-326°; W.-342°; R.-000°.

KYCKLINGEN ON ROCK 59°06.4'N 18°22.6'E Lt. Iso. W.R.G.4 sec. W.10M. R.8M. G.7M. R.Tr. 10m. G.266°-245°; W.-248°; R.-266°.

ASPÖSKÄR 59°06.9'N 18°24.0'E Lt. Q.W.R.G. W.10M. R.7M. G.6M. Tr. on R.Hut 6m. G.329°-046°; W.-048°; R.-093°; G.-108°; W.-160°; R.-183°; G.-203°; W.-208°; R.-222°.

SEGELHOLM 59°06.8'N 18°24.7'E Lt. Fl(4) W.R.G.12 sec. W.10M. R.7M. G.6M. W.R.Hut 3m. Floodlit. G.058°-071°; W.-080°; R.-147°; G.-222°; W.-227.5°; R.-236.5°.

RIKSDALERSKÄRET 59°07.3'N 18°25.7'E Lt.
Fl(2) W.R.G.6 sec. W.10M. R.7M. G.6M.
W.R.Hut 4m. Floodlit. G.038°-053°; W.-
055.5°; R.-173°; G.-180°; W.-187.5°; R.-199°;
G.(unintens)-245°; W.(unintens)-250°;
R.(unintens)-254°.

TRATHOLMEN Ldg. Lts. 171° (Front) Q.Y.
1M. W. ∆ on floodlit support 3m. Shown
15/9-30/4. (Rear) Q.Y. 1M. W. ∇ on floodlit
support 6m. Shown 15/9-30/4.

JUTHOLMEN SW POINT 59°07.5'N
18°24.7'E Lt. Fl(2) W.R.G.6 sec. W.10M.
R.4M. G.6M. W.R.Hut 3m. Floodlit. G.349°-
030°; W.-038.5°; R.-044°; G.-095°; R.-110°;
W.-223.5°.

STENHOLMEN E SIDE OF KORSHOLM Lt.
Fl. W.R.G.3 sec. W.5M. R.3M. G.2M. Tr. on
R.Hut 5m. G.204°-214°; W.-222°; R.-282°.

GENBÖTE 59°07.9'N 18°26.0'E Lt. Iso.
W.R.G.3 sec. W.10M. R.7M. G.6M. W.R.Hut
24m. G.shore-006°; W.-015.5°; R.-038°; G.-
047.5°; W.-050.5°; R.-059°; W.(unintens)-
142°; G.(unintens)-185°; W.-212°; R.-234°; G.-
254°; W.-257.5°; R.-260°; G.-270°.

DALARÖ 59°08.1'N 18°25.4'E Lt. Fl(3)
W.R.G.9 sec. W.10M. R.7M. G.6M. R.Lantern
on grey stone base 4m. Floodlit. G.031°-
037°; W.-056°; G.-243.5°; W.-246°; R.-250°;
G.-263°; R.-031°.

V.Q.R. Lts. in line 331° mark telephone cable
between Dalarö and Aspö.

HUMMELKLÄPP 59°08.5'N 18°26.5'E Lt. Iso.
W.R.G.4 sec. W.11M. W.10M. R.8M. R.7M.
G.7M. G.6M. R.Tr. 6m. Floodlit. G.(intens)
247°-251°; W.(intens)-254.5°; R.(intens)-
282.5°; G.-302.5°; W.-310°; R.-343.5°; G.-
032°; W.-038°; R.-048.5°; G.-053.5°; W.-
055.5°; R.-066°. R.Lt. on mast 1M. N.

PILTHOLMSKNALL Lt. Fl(2) W.R.G.6 sec.
W.9M. R.6M. G.5M. G.W.Tr. 7m. R.030°-062°;
G.-067°; W.-071.5°; R.-213°; G.-249°; W.-253°;
R.-336°; G.-030°. ⌇⌇

ÖSTRA STENDÖRREN Lt. Fl(3) W.R.G.9 sec.
W.6M. R.4M. G.3M. R.Lantern 5m. G.208°-
224.5°; W.-229°; R.-238.5°; G.-355.5°; W.-
000°; R.-031° partially obscured 002°-007.5°.

BO Lt. Fl(2) 6 sec. 6M. W.G.Hut 2m.

BAGGEN OUTFALL Lts. in line 000° (Front)
F.R. 5M. W. ∆, R.Border on beacon 5m.
(Rear) F.R. 5M. W. ∇, R.Border on beacon
6m.

FJÄRDHÄLLAN ON E ROCK Lt. Fl. W.R.G.3
sec. W.8M. R.5M. G.4M. W.Round Tr. B.Base
8m. R.006°-031°; G.-063.5°; W.-069°; R.-109°;
G.-177°; R.-199°; G.-202°; W.-205°; R.-208°;
G.-245°; G.(unintens)-255°; W.(unintens)-
290°; W.-006°.

GRÖNÖ S ISLAND Lt. Iso W.R.G.4 sec.
W.6M. R.4M. G.3M. R.Tr. W.Top 7m.
G.shore-246°; W.-307.5°; R.-331°; G.-352°;
W.-358°; R.-015°; G.-053.5°; W.-079°; R.-092°.

KOFOTSGRUND Lt. I.Q. W.R.G.9 sec. W.6M.
R.4M. G.3M. G.Tr. W.Top, grey base 7m.
G.015°-035°; W.-038.5°; R.-049°; G.063.5°;
W.-066°; R.-075°; R.(unintens)-134°;
G.(unintens)-203°; G.-213°; W.-220°; R.-234°;
R.(unintens)-313°; G.(unintens)-015°.

KOFOTEN SE SIDE Lt. Fl. W.R.G.3 sec.
W.6M. R.4M. G.3M. Lantern on W.R.Hut 6m.
Floodlit. W.213°-000°; G.-030°; W.-044°; R.-
053°.

FRANSKA STENARNA Lt. Fl(2) W.R.G.6 sec.
W.7M. R.4M. G.4M. W.G.Lantern 5m.
G.035°-043.5°; W.-064°; W.(unintens)-210.5°;
W.-239.5°; W.(unintens)-305°; G.-313°; W.-
314.5°; R.-321°; W.(unintens)-035°.

TEGELHÄLLAN Lt. Fl(2) W.R.G.6 sec. W.7M.
R.5M. G.4M. Lantern on mast on W.R.Hut
7m. G.036°-111°; R.-169°; G.-202.5°; W.-209°;
R.-225°; G.-309°; W.-338.5°; R.-036°. F.R. Lts.
on radio mast 0.7M. W.

RUNÖ 59°17.8'N 18°43.1'E Lt. Fl. W.R.G.3
sec. W.10M. R.7M. G.6M. W.Lantern 6m.
Floodlit. G.201°-221°; W.-224°; G.-243.5°;
W.(unintens)-335°; G.-357.5°; W.-003°; R.-
019°.

LÅNGHOLMEN SW POINT Lt. Iso. W.R.G.4
sec. W.6M. R.4M. G.3M. Lantern on W.G.Hut
6m. G.031°-035°; W.-042°; R.-145°; G.-179.5°;
W.-194°; R.-204°; G.-212°; W.-214°; R.-222°;
G.-234°.

TROLLHARAN Lt. Q.W.R.G. W.5M. R.3M.
G.2M. W. on W.Tr. 12m. G.180°-202°; W.-
037.5°; R.-045°.

NYNAS CHANNELS

TREHÖRNINGEN 58°53.5'N 17°57.0'E Lt. I.Q.
W.R.G.6 sec. W.10M. R.8M. G.7M. W.Tr. 8m.
G.315°-358.5°; W.-359.5°; R.-025°.

BEDARÖ Ldg. Lts. 034°30' (Front) Oc.
W.R.G.4 sec. W.7M. R.5M. G.4M. W.Lantern
3m. G.020.5°-033.5°; W.-036°; R.-043°; G.-
163°; W.-177°; R.-195°; R.(unintens) 195°-
shore. (Rear) F.R. 6M. W. ∇ on post 7m. Vis.
on leading line only.

STATHMOS Lts. in line 315° (Front) F.R. 2M.
R. ∆ on pillar 8m. Mark outfall. (Rear) F.R.
2M. R. ∆ on pillar 11m.

BRUNSVIKSHOLMEN 58°55.1'N 17°58.8'E
Lt. Fl(2) W.R.G.6 sec. W.12M. R.9M. G.8M.
W.Tr. 8m. R.270°-279.5°; G.-296.5°; W.-
306.5°; R.-317°; G.-323°; W.-327°; R.-000°; G.-
039°; W.-043°; R.-047.5°. R.Lt. on chimneys
830m. and 0.52M. NW.

ÖRNGRUND 58°53.9'N 18°01.7'E Lt.
Q.W.R.G. W.10.M. R.8M. G.7M. B.R.GRP.Tr.
10m. W.010°-020.5°; R.-105°; G.-131.5°; W.-
147°; R.-195°; G.-232.5°; W.-246°; R.-290°; G.-
340°; W.-344.5°; R.-358°; G.-010°.

MÅSKNUV 58°51.4'N 18°01.1'E Lt. Mo(A)
W.R.G.8 sec. W.13M. R.10M. G.9M. W.Tr.
13m. G.008.5°-020°; W.-024°; R.-029°; W.-
156.5°; G.-171°; W.-182.5°; R.-188°; G.-
195.5°; W.-213°; R.-217.5°.

GUNNARSTENARNA Lt. L. Fl(2) W.R.G.15
sec. W.8M. R.6M. G.5M. W.Structure on
grey base 14m. R.000°-019°; G.-038°; R.-
102°; G.-142.5°; W.-152.5°; R.-180°; G.-235°;
W.-000°.

VIKSTEN SYDÖSTRA Lt. Q. 4M. W.Tr. 10m.
Vis. about 144°-about 188°.

VIKSTEN NORDVÄSTRA Lt. Fl(2) W.R.G.6
sec. W.8M. W.6M. R.5M. R.4M. G.4M. G.3M.
W.Lantern 17m. G.018°-025°; W.-029°; R.-
065°; G.-097°; W.-098°; R.-118°; G.-154°; R.-
187°; G.-201°; W.-208°; R.-216.5°.

SKRAPAN Lt. Fl(3) W.R.G.9 sec. W.8M.
R.5M. G.4M. B.W.Tr. W.Lantern 12m. G.001°-
037.5°; W.-051°; R.-060°; R.(unintens)-096°;
G.(unintens)-105°; G.-190.5°; W.-196°; R.-
228°; G.-246°; W.-274.5°; R.-291°; G.-310.5°;
W.-332°; R.-001°.

HERRHAMRALEDEN ÖLANDSSTEN Lt. I.Q.
W.R.G.6 sec. W.6M. R.4M. G.3M. Silver Hut
6m. G.220.5°-254°; W.254°-258.5°.

GRISBLÄNKAN Lt. Fl. W.R.G.3 sec. W.6M.
R.4M. G.3M. W.Pedestal, B.Base 10m..
G.057°-103°; R.-168°; G.-181°; R.-342°; G.-
347°; W.-357°; R.-057°.

F.R. Ldg. Lts. 500m. NE.

STORPELLES HOLME SW POINT Lt.
Q.W.R.G. W.5M. R.3M. G.3M. Col. 8m.
R.280°-303°; G.-354°; W.-359°; R.-080°; G.-
165°; W.-169°; R.-185°.

GRISSKÄR (SÖDRA KROKSKÄR) Lt.
Q.W.R.G. W.3M. R.2M. G.1M. Tr. 6m. G.335°-
355°; W.-359°; R.-011°; G.-138°; W.-139°; R.-
155°.

BOTTENHOLMEN S END Lt. Fl. W.R.G.4 sec.
W.3M. R.2M. G.1M. Tr. 5m. G.245°-264°; W.-
267°; R.-301°; G.-327°; W.-328.5°; R.-349.5°.

VÄSTRA KVARNHÄLLAN Lt. Q.W.R.G.
W.3M. R.2M. G.1M. Lantern on W.Pedestal
2m. G.143°-158°; W.-162°; R.-262°; G.-325°;
W.-333°; R.-349°; G.-004°; W.-007°; R.-025°.

TILLJANDERSKNALLT 58°45.5'N 17°49.7'E
Lt. L. Fl(2) W.R.G.12 sec. W.10M. R.8M.
G.7M. W.B.Tr. 14m. W.331°-338.5°; R.-029°;
G.-087°; R.-116.5°; G.-128.5°; W.-131°; R.-
153°; G.-190°; R.-218°; G.-250°; R.-313°; G.-
331°.

ÖJA

LANDSORT S POINT 58°44.4'N 17°52.1'E Lt.
Fl(1+4) 60 sec. 22M. W.Tr. R.Top 44m.
Unintens about 190°-about 197°. H24. 1/11-
31/3. RC. Same structure Lt. F. W.R.G.
W.14M. R.11M. G.10M. 27m. G.323.5°-351°;
W.-358°; R.-023°.

F.R. Ldg. Lts. 130° are shown for use of
pilots at entrance to West Pilot Harbour
540m. N.

F.R. Ldg. Lts. 288°30' are shown for use of
pilots 500m. N.

LANDSORTS BREDGRUND 58°43.9'N
17°52.7'E Lt. Iso. W.R.G.4 sec. W.16M.
R.13M. G.12M. Or.Tr. 19m. Floodlit. R.001°-
013°; G.-047.5°; W.-053°; R.-086°; G.-127°; R.-
159°; G.-177°; R.-210°; G.-217°; W.-219°; R.-
224°; G.-234°; R.-273°; G.-321.5°; R.-345°;
G.-356.5°;' W.-001°. Racon. H24. 1/11-31/3.
Horn(2) 60 sec on Tr.

SKEPPSKOBBEN Lt. F.Lantern on B.Base
4m. Fishing.

TORRMULEN Lt. Fl.5 sec. 3M. W.Lantern,
blue band on R.Base 6m. Fishing.

SKÖTRÖKAN SW POINT Lt. Fl. R.3 sec. 3M.
W.Pedestal, blue band 21m. Fishing.

VINDBÅDAN Lt. Fl. 3 sec. 3M. W.Tr. blue
band. Fishing.

HUVUDSKÄR 58°57.8'N 18°34.3'E Lt. Mo(N)
25 sec. 12M. W.B.Tr. 26m. Unintens 115°-
205°.

SÖDERNÄS Lt. Fl. W.R.G.3 sec. W.6M.
R.4M. G.3M. W.Lantern 6m. G.336°-055°;
W.-072°; R.-097°; G.-159°; W.-175°; R.-181°.

LAGNÖGRUNDET 59°21.5'N 18°25.1'E Lt.
Q(3) W.R.G.4 sec. W.10M. R.7M. G.6M.
W.Pedestal, B.Base 6m. Floodlit. G.105°-
135°; R.-187°; G.-269.5°; W.-300°; R.-105°. ﷽

TYNNINGÖ Lt. Fl(2) W.R.G.6 sec. W.6M. R.4M. G.3M. Grey Tr. W.Top. 5m. Floodlit. G.294°-306.5°; W.-312°; R.-343°; W.(unintens)-074°; G.-099°; W.-101°; R.-120°.

VÄRMDÖ-GARPEN Lt. Q.W.R.G. W.6M. R.4M. G.3M. W.Lantern 4m. Floodlit. R.102°-259°; G.-269°; W.-279.5°; R.-292°; G.-099°; W.-102°. F.W.Lt. 0.6M. ENE.

STOCKHOLM 59°20'N 18°05'E
Tel: Port 08 63 55 00 Pilots 08 666 66 22 Fax: 08 662 46 34.
Radio-Port: VHF Chan. 16, 12.
Radio-Pilots: VHF Chan. 16, 09.

KAKNÄS 59°20.1'N 18°07.8'E Lt. Aero VQ
and Q. 21M. Mast on Tr. 172m. Obstruction. Also 5 Aero F.R. Lts. 6M.

KUNGSHAMN Lt. Fl. W.R.G.3 sec. W.6M. R.4M. G.3M. W.Lantern 7m. W.shore-076.5°; G.-088.5°; W.-098°; R.-170°; W.-226°; R.-shore. Shown 6/7-6/6.

LIBERTUS Lt. Fl(3) W.R.G.9 sec. W.6M. R.4M. G.3M. W.Tr. 6m. G.102°-122°; W.-127°; R.-192°; W.-262°. Shown 6/7-6/6.

LILLA VÄRTAN No: 4 Lt. Q.R. 6M. Floodlit board on pole 6m. ᴠᴜᴠ

No: 5 Lt. Q.R. 6M. Flootlit board on pole 6m. ᴠᴜᴠ

No: 6 Lt. Q.R. 6M. Floodlit board on pole 6m. ᴠᴜᴠ

NYA LIDINGÖBRON Lt. Q.

BRUNNSVIKEN Lt. F.R. 3M.

TORSVIK Lt. Fl. W.R.G.3 sec. W.6M. R.4M. G.3M. W.Lantern 6m. G.010°-037°; W.-062°; R.-110°; G.-141°; W.-144.5°; R.-158°.

STORA FJÄDERHOLMEN Lt. 2 F.G. vert on post 8m. 2m apart. Shown 6/7-6/6.

BLOCKHUSUDDEN Lt. Fl(2) W.R.G.6 sec. W.6M. R.4M. G.3M. W.Tr. grey base 6m. W.shore-211°; R.-222°; G.-244°; W.-086.5°; R.-shore. Shown 6/7-6/6.

NACKA 59°17.9'N 18°10.6'E Aero V.Q.
21M. on mast 300m. Obstruction. Also 8 F.R. Lts. 6M. 250m. V.Q. Lts. on mast 250m. SE.

DANVIKS HEM. SEWAGE OUTFALL Lts. in line 178° (Front) F.R. 6M. W. △, R.Border 8m. (Rear) F.R. 6M. W. ▽, R.Border 12m.

DANVIKSKANALEN No: 1 W SIDE Lt.
Fl. G.2 sec. 8M. on post 10m. Vis. 150°-254°.

No: 2 E SIDE Lt. Fl. R.2 sec. 9M. on post 10m. Vis. 020°-043°.

HAMMARBYHAMNEN Lt. Fl. R.3 sec. 2M. W.Dolphin 4m. Shown 6/7-6/6.

ÅRSTAVIKEN No: 3 Lt. Fl(2) G.6 sec. 3M.
R.Dolphin 4m.

No: 8 S SIDE OF BRIDGE Lt. Fl. R.3 sec. 3M. W.Dolphin 4m.

No: 10 Lt. Fl(2) G.6 sec. 4M. B.R.Dolphin 4m.

Marinas and Yacht Harbours

26

VHF CHANNELS Marinas and Yacht Harbours use Ch. 80 (Tx 161.625 MHz. Rx 157.025 MHz) as a primary working channel with Ch. 37 (157.85 MHz) for use as an overload. Always call on Ch. 80 in the first instance, using Ch. 37 only if there is no reply.

South Coast

ST MARY'S, Isles of Scilly. H.M. Tel: (0720) 22768.
Berths: at quay only by order of H.M. St. Mary's Pool moors 180 yachts.
Facilities: Water 0830-1130, WCs, showers, garbage provisions, phone, fuel, chandlery, small slip, 6T crane, sailing club. Calor gas (Island Supply Stores).

NEWLYN HARBOUR, Penzance, Cornwall, TR18 5HW. Tel: (0736) 62523. Fax: (0736) 51614.
Call sign: Newlyn Harbour (Ch. 16, 12).
Berths: Overnight; alongside fishing vessels on W side Mary Williams Pier.
Facilities: electricity; water; refuse; diesel; petrol; Calor gas (Cosalt, Harbour Road); chandlery; charts; provisions; ice; phone; WCs; showers; launderette; restaurant; bar; mail. French & English spoken.

PENZANCE HARBOUR Wharf Road, Penzance, Cornwall, TR18 4AB. Tel: (0736) 66113.
Call sign: Penzance Harbour (Ch. 12, 16).
Open: Normal working hours. Wet Dock 2 hr.–HW–1 hr. 7 days a week under all conditions up to Force 10. Gates occasionally open longer for commercial craft so check on VHF.
Berths: 200 drying moorings plus up to 50 alongside berths in wet dock (available to visitors though numbers limited in drying moorings). Max. LOA 95m.
Facilities: fuel (diesel); chandlery; provisions; water; repairs; 10 ton mobile crane (plus 2 × 3 ton mobile in Penzance); storage (winter only); slipway; Calor gas (Bennetts, Market Jew Street); WC's, showers; hotels; restaurants; car hire.
Harbour Master: Capt. M. Tregoning.
Berthing Master: G. Gage.
Customs: Tel: R/T (0752) 220661.

HELFORD RIVER MOORINGS, Kernewas Farm, St Keverne, Helston, Cornwall, TR12 6RW. Tel: (0326) 280422. Office hours 1100-1200, 1500-1600.
Call sign: Mooring Officer Helford (Ch. M).
Berths: 370 moorings, 25 visitors on marked G. pick-up buoys.
Facilities: Helford River Sailing Club and Gweek Quay Boatyard nearby. Sea fishing.

FALMOUTH HARBOUR
VISITORS YACHT HAVEN, North Quay, Falmouth, TR11 5JT.
Tel: (0326) 312285/314379. Fax: 211352.
Call sign: Falmouth Harbour Radio (Ch. 16, 14, 13, 12.)
Open: Apr.-Oct. **Berths:** 40 alongside, swinging moorings also available. Max. draught 2m, LOA 12m.
Facilities: Fuel (diesel, petrol); water; washing and toilet facilities at near by Custom House Quay; chandlery; Calor gas (West Country Chandlers, 39 High Street); rigging; repairs; cranage; slipway.
Harbour Master: Capt. D. G. Banks.
Yacht Haven Supervisor: Vicki Ferguson.
Customs: Tel: R/T (0752) 220661.

GREENBANK HOTEL, Harbourside, Falmouth TR11 2SR. Tel: (0326) 312440. Telex: 45240.
Berths: 1 × visitors swinging mooring plus alongside mooring (limited).
Facilities: Water; showers and bathroom for visiting yachtsmen.
Proprietor: C. N. Gebhard.
Remarks: Approx. 6 ft of water 2 hr.–HW–2 hr.

ROYAL CORNWALL YACHT CLUB, Greenbank, Falmouth, Cornwall TR11 2SW.
Tel: (0326) 312126/311105. Fax: (0326) 211614.
Call sign: RCYC Ch. 80, 37 (M).
Open: Normal hours. **Berths:** 8 visitors swinging moorings (marked). Max. draught 1.75m, LOA 12m.
Facilities: Limited fuel; water alongside; boatman 1 May-30 Sept.; licensed bar/bar snacks; restaurant; showers.
Hon. Secretary: F. W. Jarrett.

PORT PENDENNIS MARINA 50°09'.0N 5°03'.6W. Tel: (0326) 211819 Fax: (0326) 212004.
Call Sign: Port Pendennis Ch.M.80.
Berths: No visitors moorings.
Remarks: Lock gate open 3h. - HW - 3h. Traffic lights.

Tidal Data — Section 21

FALMOUTH YACHT MARINA, North Parade, Falmouth, Cornwall TR11 2TD; located half a mile upstream from Greenbank Quay. Tel: (0326) 316620. Fax: (0326) 313939. **Call sign:** Falmouth Yacht Marina Ch. 80, 37 (M). **Open:** 24 hr. **Berths:** 335 pontoon (visitors approx. 100) to 65' LOA, depth 2m+. **Facilities:** fuel; electricity; chandlery; Calor gas: provisions; repair; storage; brokerage; Clubhouse; 30 tonne hoist; water; crane; parking; phone; launderette; security. **Managing Director:** Tim Grove (Quadrant Marine). **Remarks:** Dredged channel gives access up to 2m. draught at the lowest spring tides.

BOSUN'S LOCKER OF FALMOUTH, Upton Slip, Church St., Falmouth TR11 3DQ. Tel: (0326) 312414. (Night: 73652). Fax: (0326) 211414. **Open:** Normal hours. **Berths:** Max. draft 2m, LOA 11.5m. **Facilities:** Chandlery and foul weather clothing sales. Liferaft hire and servicing; Suzuki dealer and workshops; Calor/camping gas; brokerage and new boat sales; Admiralty charts; DTp Compass adjusters. **Managing Director:** Alan Hopton.

FALMOUTH BOAT CONSTRUCTION LTD, Little Falmouth Yacht Yard, Flushing, Falmouth, Cornwall TR11 5JT. Tel: (0326) 74309. **Open:** Mon.-Fri. 0730-1630. **Moorings:** 18 (Some visitors occasionally available). **Facilities:** 2 slipways undercover for craft to 75 feet LOA, 12T mobile hoist, repairs and total refits undercover. Storage; brokerage; cranage; resprays and osmosis treatments.

MYLOR YACHT HARBOUR LTD, Mylor, Falmouth, Cornwall, TR11 5UF. Tel: (0326) 72121. **Call sign:** Mylor Yacht Harbour Ch. 80, 37 (M). **Open:** Business hours. **Berths:** 215 moorings, 35 berths. **Facilities:** fuel (diesel, petrol, Calor gas); electricity; chandlery; provisions; showers; launderette; repairs; 25 ton boat hoist, 6 ton mobile crane; storage (for 300 boats on shore); brokerage; slipway. **Harbour Master:** Derek Rowe.

TRURO HARBOUR OFFICE, Town Quay, Truro, Cornwall TR1 2HJ. Tel: (0872) 72130. Administers moorings in the ports of Truro and Penryn. **Call sign:** Carrick One (Ch. 12, 16). **Open:** 0830-1730 Mon-Fri.

Berths: Town Quay, Truro (channel dries to mud). Max. draught 3.7m, LOA 50m. **Facilities:** water; refuse; petrol; Calor gas (Bennet, Newham); chandlery; charts; mail. Other facilities Truro Town. Yards at Penryn & Truro. **Harbour Master and Maritime Officer:** Capt. R. Bigwood.

PERCUIL BOATYARD, Percuil, Portscatho, Truro, Cornwall TR2 5ES. Tel: (087-258) 564. **Berths:** 80-90 moorings, 6' draught, 36' LOA. (some visitors).

MALPAS MARINE, Truro, Cornwall, TR1 1SQ. Tel: (0872) 71260. **Open:** 0900-1800. **Berths:** 30, 3 visitors, max. draught 2m, LOA 12m. **Facilities:** electricity; water; refuse; diesel; gas; chandlery; charts; WCs; showers; provisions; ice; phone; restaurant; café; bar; mail and phone nearby. Fibreglass repairs. 2T lift; slip; boat sales and hire. Spanish and English spoken.

CALSTOCK BOAT YARD, Lower Kelly, Calstock. Tel: (0822) 832502. **Berths:** 13 buoy & quayside drying. **Facilities:** fuel; boatyard; chandlery; slipway.

FOWEY HARBOUR, Albert Quay, Fowey, Cornwall PL23 1AJ. Tel: (0726) 832471/2. Fax: (0726) 833738. **Call sign:** Fowey Harbour Radio Ch. 12. (working). **Open:** 24 hr. Berths and visitors berths available. **Facilities:** fuel (diesel, petrol); chandlery; Calor gas (Troy Chandlery, Lostwithiel St.); provisions; repair; cranage. **Harbour Master:** Capt. M. J. Sutherland. **Customs:** Tel: R/T (0752) 220661.

LOOE, Harbour Office, The Quay, East Looe, Cornwall, PL13 1AQ. Tel: (05036) 2839... **Open:** Normal hours. **Berths:** 100 swinging and alongside (all drying). 2 visitors. **Facilities:** fuel (diesel, petrol); Calor gas (Harbour Chandlery); provisions (near by); repair; storage; slipway; cranage; water. **Harbour Master:** H. Butters. **Remarks:** Access 3 hr.–HW–3 hr.

LOOE, Norman Peam & Co. Ltd, Millpool Boatyard. Tel: (05036) 2244. **Open:** Normal hours. **Berths:** 250 buoy (drying). **Facilities:** fuel; chandler; boatyard; slipway.

SEAWARD MARINE ENTERPRISES,
Southdown Quay, Millbrook, Torpoint,
Cornwall PL10 1EZ. Tel: (0752) 823084.
Call sign: Ch. 16, 25.
Open: 24 hour.
Berths: 50 pontoon berths and 500 ft
quayside space.
Facilities: fuel; water; electricity; security
(boats and car-parking); clubhouse; showers.
Remarks: Easy access to River Tamar,
windsurfing and waterskiing.
Harbourmaster: Roger Seymour.

THE BALLAST POUND YACHT HARBOUR,
Torpoint, Cornwall. Tel: (0752) 813658.
Berths: 100 pontoon, 30 deep water, mud
berths. 10 visitors available.
Facilities: electricity; water; repair; storage (on
mud berths); brokerage; provisions; car hire
(nearby). Most requirements by arrangement.
Harbour Master: T. A. Mason.

TORPOINT YACHT HARBOUR, Torpoint.
Tel: (0752) 813658.
Berths: 20 quayside (drying), 16 buoy, 75
pontoon.
Facilities: fuel; yacht/boat club; slipway; Calor
gas (The Rural Calor Gas Centre, Gallows
Parks Works, Millbrook).

PLYMOUTH HARBOUR, Longroom, Plymouth,
Devon PL1 3RT. Tel: (0752) 663225.
Call sign: Longroom Port Control (Ch. 16, 14,
24 hr.)
Open: 24 hr. **Berths:** 1760 on buoys and
pontoons (over 20 visitors).
Facilities: fuel; Calor gas (Mashford, Cremyll
Ferry); chandlery; provisions (near by); repair;
slipping up to 100 ft × 150 tons; storage;
water.
Customs: Tel: R/T (0752) 220661

MAYFLOWER INTERNATIONAL MARINA,
Ocean Quay, Richmond Walk, Stonehouse,
Plymouth (E side of R. Tamar ent.), Devon PL1
4LS. Tel: (0752) 556633/567106. 24 hr.
personal service. Fax: (0752) 606896. Telex:
265451 MONREF G.
Call sign: Mayflower Marina. Ch. 80, 37 (M).
Open: 24 hr. **Berths:** 250 (visitors 30 for yachts
up to 100 ft.).
Facilities: fuel (petrol, diesel, calor
gas/camping gaz and paraffin); electricity;
chandlery; provisions (and off licence); crane
(2 ton); hoist (25 ton); bistro restaurant;

showers; laundrette; slipway; clubhouse and
bar; engineering; divers; electronics; rigging;
daily weather fax.
Harbour Master: Donald Bird.
Remarks: Yachtsmen qualify for discount on
visitors rates on production of a recent
berthing receipt from any of the following:
Brixham Yacht Marina, Darthaven Marina,
Falmouth Yacht Marina, Brest Marina,
Morgat, Cameret and La Forêt.

WEIR QUAY BOATYARD, Crab Pond, Bere
Alston, Yelverton. Tel: (0822) 840474.
Berths: 100
Facilities: water; boatyard; slipway.

QUEEN ANNE'S BATTERY MARINA,
Plymouth PL4 0LP. Tel: (0752) 671142.
Call sign: Q.A.B. Marina. Ch. M 80.
Open: 24 hr. – night and day staff.
Berths: 300 including 60 visitors' berths for
craft up to 100 ft. – draught to 15 ft. Access
directly onto Plymouth Sound.
Facilities: Fuel (petrol, diesel and gas): boat
hoist to 20 ton; slipway to 100 ft. craft; boat
repairs; electronic repairs; yacht charter;
sailing schools; brokerage; taxis; provisions;
laundry; telephones; water taxi to City Centre;
sail maker; rigger.
Royal Western Yacht Club welcomes visitors
by prior arrangement with the secretary on
(0752) 660077.

SKENTELBERY, K. R. & SONS, Laira Bridge
Boatyard, Plymouth, Devon. Tel: (0752)
402385.
Berths: 40.

R. BASTARD, Steer Point, Brixton, Nr.
Plymouth. Tel: (0752) 880104.
Berths: 70 buoy.
Facilities: slipway.

SUTTON HARBOUR CO, Harbour Office,
Sutton Harbour, Plymouth PL4 0ES.
Tel: (0752) 664186. Fax: (0752) 223521.
Call sign: Sutton Harbour. Ch. 16, 80, 37 (M).
Open: 24 hr. **Berths:** 350 (visitors available).
Facilities: fuel (diesel, petrol); chandlery;
provisions (near by); repair; cranage (limit 3
tons); slipway; water; electricity on pontoons;
brokerage; restaurants; laundrette; showers.
Berthing Masters: Victor Gray, Dennis Morris,
John Dare.

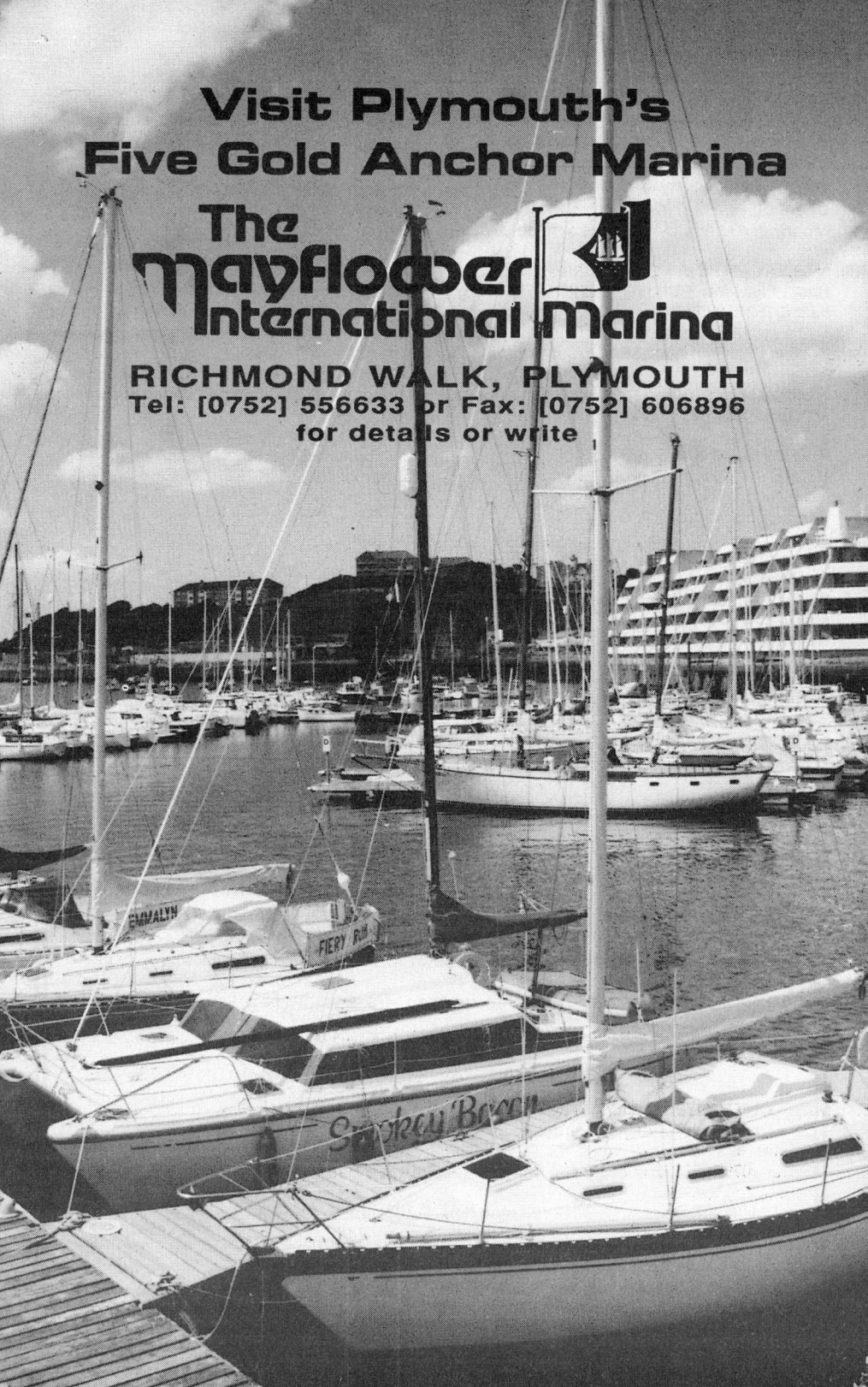

CLOVELLY BAY CO. LTD., Pier House, Turnchapel, Plymouth PL9 9TF.
Tel: (0752) 404231.
Call Sign: Clovelly Bay.
Open: All year, 24 hr.
Moorings: 30m+ LOA, visitors available.

MILLBAY MARINA VILLAGE, Great Western Road, Plymouth PL1 3EQ. Tel: (0752) 266785. Fax: (0752) 222513.
Call sign: Millbay Marina, Ch. 37.
Berths: 89, 25 visitors. Max. draught 6m, LOA 14m.
Facilities: electricity; water; TV aerial; phone; refuse; WCs; showers.

RIVER YEALM HARBOUR OFFICE, Yealm Hotel Drive, Newton Ferrers, Plymouth PL8 1BL, Devon. Tel: (0752) 872533.
Berths: 500 (approx.) 180 non-tidal (visitors 7 swinging, 5 anchored, 20 fore & af., 30 on pontoon). Max. draught 2.1m, LOA 12.8-21m.
Facilities: repairs; rigging service; scrubbing berths; chandlery; shops; restaurants; showers; yacht club.
Remarks: Access 6 hr.–HW–6 hr., but it is recommended that entry/departure is avoided 1 hr.-LWS-1 hr.
Harbour Master: M. J. Simpson.

SALCOMBE HARBOUR, Whitestrand, Salcombe, Devon TQ8 8BU. Tel: (054 884) 3791.
Call sign: Salcombe Harbour (Ch. 14).
Open: All the year round. Harbour launches on duty 0600-2100 (BST) in summer (VHF Ch. 14).
Berths: 300 (50 visitors), 2000 in Estuary.
Facilities: diesel, petrol, Calor gas (Salcombe House Boats); fresh water; chandlery; rigging; repairs; electronics; sails; engines; cranage; storage; brokerage; slipping; provisions; ice; shops; restaurants; hotels. Showers etc. at Salcombe Yacht Club and Island Cruising Club.
Harbour Master: Peter Hodges.
Assistant Harbour Master: Stan Turns.
Customs: Tel: R/T (0752) 220661
Remarks: Bar can be dangerous at Springs where there are strong onshore winds on the ebb tide.

WINTERS MARINE LTD, Lincombe, Salcombe. Tel: (054884) 3580.
Call sign: Ch. 16
Berths: 50 pontoon.
Facilities: boatyard, slipway; 20T hoist.

J. STONE & SON, Goodshelter, East Portlemouth, Salcombe. Tel: (054851) 242.
Berths: 90 buoy (some drying).
Facilities: boatyard; chandlery, yacht/boat club; slipway.

DART MARINA, Sand Quay, Dartmouth TQ6 0EA. Tel: (0803) 833351. Fax: (0803) 835150.
Call sign: Ch. 16, 37 (M). Dart Marina Control.
Open: 24 hr. **Berths:** 100 at staging (visitors available), plus 120 at Kingswear Marina.
Facilities: fuel (diesel, gas); electricity; chandlery; repair; cranage (limit 6 tons); slipways; provisions near by; winter/summer storage; brokerage; Dart Marina Hotel (3 star); restaurant; launderette. Showers; resident night security; slipway; plus at Kingswear Marina cranage (limit 1 × 60 tons, 2 × 5 tons, 1 × 15 tons travel hoist).
Director: Duncan Wills.

DARTMOUTH HARBOUR, The Old Post Office, South Embankment, Dartmouth, Devon. Tel: (0803) 832337.
Call sign: Dart Nav. (Ch. 11). **Open:** Mid May-end Sept., 7 days/week; Oct.-Mid May, normal working hours.
Berths: 550 (94 visitors).
Facilities: diesel available on barge in middle of harbour (Ch. 16). Chandlers and shops nearby; Calor gas (Battarbee, 2 Mansion House St.); repairs at local yards and specialists; cranage (2 ton mobile floating); slipway just below Higher Ferry. Fire boat.
Harbour Master: Capt. C. J. Moore.
Customs: Tel: R/T (0752) 220661.
Remarks: Outside normal hours use anchorage in emergency. Floating dry dock for yachts. Max. LOA 60 ft., Beam 15 ft 6 in. Tonnage 45t.

KINGSWEAR MARINA, Noss Works, Dartmouth. Tel: (0803) 833351.
Call Sign: Ch. 80 (M).
Berths: 140 pontoon & buoy.
Facilities: water; boatyard, chandlery; 60T crane.

DARTHAVEN MARINA, Kingswear, Devon TQ6 0BL. Tel: (080425) 545/brokerage by Ancasta Marine 498.
Call Sign: Darthaven Control Ch. 80, 37 (M).
Open: Winter: 0830-1800. June-Sept.: 0830-2130.
Berths: 235 (visitors available).
Facilities: electricity; chandlery services by J. W. & A. Upham Ltd., repair; storage; nearby restaurant and bars; brokerage; Calor gas;

camping gaz; travel hoist; laundrette; WC/showers.
Marina Managers: A. Henshaw & K. J. T. Holman.

DARTSIDE QUAY, Galmpton Creek, South Devon, TQ5 0EH. Tel: (0803) 845445. Fax: (0803) 843558.
Berths: 40. Visitors at quay and hardstanding. Max. draught 3m, LOA 20m.
Facilities: electricity; water; phone; refuse; chandlery/charts; WCs; repairs; 53T hoist; 6T crane; lift; slip; boat sales; lift-out & scrubbing grid; security.

DOLPHIN HAVEN, Torbay Boat Construction Co. Ltd, The Dolphin Shipyard, Galmpton, Brixham, Devon. Tel: (0803) 842424.
Berths: 100 (visitors 10).
Facilities: electricity; repairs; lift-out facilities; slipway; boat park; water.
Remarks: Access 3 hr.–HW–3 hr.

BRIXHAM HARBOUR, New Fish Quay, Brixham, Devon TQ5 8AJ. Tel: (08045) 3321.
Call Sign: Brixham Port. (Ch. 14, 16.) Pilots: Ch. 9.
Open: Winter 0900-1700 (weekdays); May-Sept. 0900-2000 (all week).
Berths: 400 moorings, different types permanently allocated, plus 600 in Outer Harbour SE Marina. Max. draught 7m, LOA 18m.
Facilities: Gas oil at E Quay Extension (long waits for visitors). Water; electricity; slip; provisions nearby; repairs; cranage (2 ton); winter boat storage; most services.
Harbour Master: Capt. R. Knowles.
Customs: Tel: R/T (0752) 220661.
Remarks: Outer harbour exposed to winds from NW & NE thru N above Force 5.

BRIXHAM MARINA, Brixham Yacht Harbour Ltd, Berry Head Road, Brixham. Tel: (0803) 882929.
Call sign: Brixham Marina, Ch. 37/80.
Berths: 539, 80 visitors, max. draught 4m, LOA 25m.
Facilities: electricity; water; telephone; refuse; Nearby — Diesel; gas; chandlery; charts; provisions; ice; WCs; showers; launderette; restaurant; café; bar; Yacht club; Sailing school; diving club; sea fishing; post; repairs; slip; boat sales; boat and car hire; careening; 24-hr security; storage.

TEIGNMOUTH, New Quay. Tel: (06267) 3165.
Berths: 110 buoy.
Facilities: boatyard; chandlery; yacht/boat club; slipway.

TORQUAY MARINA, Torquay, Devon TQ2 5EQ. Tel: (0803) 214624. Fax: 291634. **Berths:** 500 (visitors 60), max. draught 12m, LOA 22m. **Facilities:** chandlery; 24 h. security; restaurant; showers; WCs; launderette; slip; car park; brokerage. Access 24 hr. Fuel & cranage in harbour; Calor gas (The Boat Shop, Haldon Pier). **Customs:** Tel: (0752) 220661.

RIVER EXE.
Berths: 1000 buoy.
Facilities: various clubs; slipway.

RETREAT BOATYARD, Retreat Drive, Topsham, Exeter, Devon EX3 0LS. Tel: (0392) 874700/8745934. Fax: (0392) 876182.
Berths: 60 on moorings (some visitors). Calor gas available.

LYME REGIS HARBOUR, Lyme Regis, Dorset. Tel: (0297) 442137.
Call sign: Lyme Regis Harbour Radio. Ch. 16. **Open:** Normal working hr. **Berths:** 180 drying. 12 visitors alongside Victoria Pier.
Facilities: provisions near by; repairs; storage; slip; water; showers at LRSC, Chandler. **Harbour Master:** Lt.Cdr. J. R. Goslin, RN. **Remarks:** Drying harbour–entry 2½ hr.–HW–2½ hr. Use 5 red mooring buoys N of Harbour entrance marked W.D.D.C. to await tide.

WEYMOUTH HARBOUR. 20 Custom House Quay, DT4 8BQ. Tel: (0305) 206421. **Call sign:** Weymouth Harbour VHF Ch. 16, 12. **Open:** 24 hours.
Berths: Inner Harbour: 700 pontoons, chain and alongside. Outer Harbour: 185 Visitors in rafts on berths 4, 5, 6, 7, 8, and Cove Area pontoons. Draughts to 5.2m.
Facilities: Toilets and Ablutions for all visiting crews at No. 13 Custom House Quay (Pier Master). Fuel (Diesel supplies No. 5 Berth and Curtis Marine). Fresh water Pier Head No. 5 Berth and Wessex Water Authority. Repairs (GRP, wood, steel, marine engineers), crane hire, gas, diving equipment, public slipway (Inner Harbour).
Harbour Master: Capt. P. C. Tambling RD. **HM Customs:** Tel: R/T (03057) 74747. **Special Remarks:** Outer Harbour Entrance exposed to winds from NE to SE.

RIDGE WHARF YACHT CENTRE, Wareham, Dorset. (Poole Harbour, River Frome). Tel: (0929) 552650.
Open: Mon.-Fri. 0830-1730; W/E 1000-1300 and 1400-1600. **Berths:** 170.

Facilities: fuel; electricity; chandlery; Calor gas/Gaz; repair; cranage (travel hoist 20 tons); storage; brokerage; slipway. First Class winter lay up facilities.
Managing Director: Cmdr. R. T. Clarke.

POOLE HARBOUR, Harbour Commissioners, Harbour Office, Town Quay, Poole, Dorset BH15 1HG. Tel: (0202) 685261. Fax: (0202) 665703. Telex: 41134 PHC G.
Call sign: Poole Harbour Control, Ch. 14. **Open:** Harbour Office: Mon.-Fri. Winter 0900-1700. Town Quay: Summer daily 0800-2200. **Berths:** 100 quayside visitors only.
Facilities: boatyard, chandlery; yacht/boat club; slipway.

HARVEYS PLEASURE BOATS OF POOLE HARBOUR, Enefco House, Poole Quay, Poole, Dorset BH15 1HE.
Tel: (0202) 666226 and 700120.
Berths: 85 Swinging. Sheltered deepwater for craft 18-55 ft. (10 visitors).
Facilities: diesel; repairs; sail repairs; lift-out facilities; chandlery; boat park; water (within walking distance).

QUAY WEST MARINA, 23 West Quay Road, Poole BH15 1HX. Tel: (0202) 675071. **Open:** 0830-2030. **Berths:** 50.
Facilities: electricity; water; chandlery; provisions (shops near by); repairs; cranage; brokerage; laundrette, toilets/showers. **Harbour Master:** Jim Baker.
Customs: Tel: R/T (0703) 827350.

ARTHUR BRAY LTD, West Quay House, West Quay Road, Poole, Dorset BH15 1HT. Tel: (0202) 676469. Fax: (0202) 741656. **Berths:** Pontoon at Poole Quay; 110 Deepwater swinging moorings.
Facilities: International yacht brokerage; marine equipment to order. **Harbour Master:** Peter Burt.

COBBS QUAY MARINA, Hamworthy, Poole, Dorset BH15 4EL. Tel: (0202) 674299–Marina Office. 672588–Sales Office. 675469–Craning **Call sign:** C.Q. Base Ch. 80, 37 (M). **Open:** 24 hr. **Berths:** 600 marina berths, 100 quayside moorings (visitors available).
Facilities: diesel, petrol; electricity; chandlery; provisions (at club house); repair; cranage (limit 10 tons); slipping (limit 80 tons); storage (500 boats); brokerage, Sewerage disposal; Calor gas.

DAVIS'S BOATYARD, Cobbs Quay, Hamworthy, Poole. Tel: (0202) 674349. **Berths:** 82 pontoon + 16 alongside. **Facilities:** water; boatyard, slipway, 45T crane.

DORSET YACHT CO LTD, Lake Drive, Hamworthy, Poole BH15 4DT. Tel: (0202) 674531. Fax: 0202 677518.
Open: Mon.-Fri. 0900-1300 and 1400-1700. W/E 0900-1300.
Berths: 120 swinging moorings (visitors 6). Draught 2.4m. max. LOA 21m.
Facilities: fuel (petrol 4 star, diesel, oil); electricity; gas; provisions (shop near by); water; repair (all types); cranage by arrangement; storage up to 42 ft.; brokerage; slipway up to 85 ft. Hotels; restaurants; car hire–Poole town 1½ mile; on site club, licensed with food and visitor facilities.
Harbour Master: R. V. Culpan.

MITCHELL'S BOATYARD, Turks Lane, Parkstone, Poole, Dorset. Tel: (0202) 747857.
Berths: 36 pontoons, 148 swinging moorings (few visitors). Draught 1.2m. max. LOA 10m.
Facilities: launching and haul out service; slipway; repairs; pressure cleaning; undercover storage; showers; WCs.
Contact: Derek King.

LILLIPUT YACHT STATION, 324 Sandbanks Road, Lilliput, Poole, Dorset BH14 8HY. Tel: (0202) 707176.
Open: Mon.-Fri. 0900-1600. Other hr. by arrangement.
Moorings: swinging, deepwater and tidal. 600 ft. pier. Max. draught 1.8m, LOA 10m.
Facilities: water (Pier Head); slipway; outhauls up to 14 ft. craft; dinghy/outboard storage; lockers; some parking.
Manager: Miss M. F. Little.

SALTERNS MARINA, 40 Salterns Way, Lilliput, Poole, Dorset BH14 8JR.
Tel: (0202) 707321. Fax: (0202) 707488. Telex: 41259 SALTER G.
Call sign: Salterns Marina. Ch. 80, 37 (M).
Open: 24 hr. **Berths:** 220 (visitors available).
Facilities: fuel (diesel, petrol); electricity; chandlery; laundry; provisions (shops near by); new boat sales; repair; cranage; 40 tonne hoist; storage; brokerage; hotel; restaurant; yacht club.
Manageress: Miss B. H. James.

THE SANDBANKS YACHT CO LTD, 32 Panorama Road, Sandbanks, Poole, Dorset BH13 7RD. Tel: (0202) 707500.
Berths: 325 (chain swinging), 20 visitors. Max. draught 1.4m, LOA 9.75m.
Facilities: fuel (diesel, petrol); repairs; slipway; chandlery; boat park; water; toilets; boat hire; sales; storage; Calor gas.
Contact: G. N. & P. S. Seaton.
Remarks: Some berths dry out at low water.

CHRISTCHURCH MARINE LTD, River Avon, Christchurch, Dorset. Tel: (0202) 483250.
Open: Normal business hr. **Berths:** 90 (visitors by arrangement).
Facilities: fuel (diesel); electricity; chandlery; provisions (near by); water; repairs; slipping (limit 5 ft. draught); storage; brokerage; rigging service.
Harbour Master: H. T. Rossiter.
Customs: Tel: R/T (0703) 827350.

CHRISTCHURCH COUNCIL, Mudeford Quay, Christchurch. Tel: (0425) 274933.
Berths: 260 buoy (max. 30ft). No visitors.
Facilities: boatyard; water; chandlery, yacht/boat club, slipway.
Harbour Master: M. Hinton.

RIBS MARINE, Little Avon Marina, Christchurch. Tel: (0202) 477327.
Berths: 40 pontoon & quayside.
Facilities: boatyard, chandlery, water; slipway.

BOURNEMOUTH BOROUGH COUNCIL, Parks Dept. Town Hall, Bournemouth. Tel: (0202) 552066.
Berths: 136 quayside, buoy & pontoon (max. 30ft). No visitors.
Facilities: slipway.

LYMINGTON HARBOUR, Harbour Masters Office, Bath Road, Lymington, Hants. SO41 9SE.
Tel: (0590) 672014.
Open: Normal office hours plus week ends.
Berths: 700 permanent; 120 visitors available at Town Quay.
Facilities: All available ashore and at Marinas. Chandlery at Boat House, The Quay.
Harbour Master: F. V. Woodford.
Remarks: Lymington Harbour Commissioners River Authority–River limits include both marinas. Windsurfing and wet bikes forbidden.
Customs: Tel: R/T (0703) 827350.

ROYAL LYMINGTON YACHT CLUB, Lymington SO41 9SE.
Tel: (0590) 672677. Fax: (0590) 671642.
Berths: Available for members of reciprocating clubs, but very limited at summer weekends.
Facilities: All usual yacht club facilities.
Remarks: essential to telephone ahead. On arrival secure to 15-minute waiting berth. Contact boatman (steward after working hours) for berthing instructions.

LYMINGTON MARINA LTD, The Shipyard, Bath Road, Lymington, Hampshire. Tel: (0590) 673312-6.
Call sign: Lymington Marina, Ch. 80, 37 (M).
Open: 24 hr. **Berths:** 300 (visitors available). Yachts up to 110 ft. LOA.
Facilities: fuel (diesel, petrol); electricity; yacht/boat club; chandlery; repair; cranage (limit 40 tons travel lift, 15 ton Renner); storage; brokerage; Calor gas.
Head Dockmaster: Peter Crook.

LYMINGTON YACHT HAVEN, King's Saltern Road, Lymington, SO41 9QD. Tel: (0590) 677071. Fax: (0590) 678186. Telex: 477344.
Call sign: Lymington Yacht Haven Ch. 80, 37 (M).
Open: 24 hr. Office open every day 0800-2100 (Winter 0800-1800).
Berths: 575. Visitors berths available.
Facilities: diesel, petrol, water, electricity, Calor gas; chandlery, brokerage, 45 ton travel hoist; storage; repairs; gas; showers; laundrette. Engineer on stand-by at weekends.
Berthing Master: Jeremy Oakley.
Remarks: Transit daymarks (Red diamonds) and leading lights (Fixed amber) bearing 244° (T) at entrance to Haven.

KEYHAVEN, Lymington. Tel: (0590) 645695.
Berths: 400 buoy (most drying)
Facilities: boatyard; water; yacht/boat club; slipway; 10T crane.
River Warden: Tom Holt.

AQUABOATS LTD, Mill Lane, Lymington. Tel: (0590) 674266/7.
Open: Mon.-Fri. 0800-1630. **Berths:** 6 × ½ Tide pontoon.
Facilities: chandlery; provisions (nearby); repairs; cranage (1 × 12 ton mobile); storage.

BUCKLERS HARD, Harbourmaster's Office, Bucklers Hard, Beaulieu, Brockenhurst, Hampshire SO42 7XB. Tel: (0590) 616200, 616234.
Berths: 110 plus 30 pontoons and 100 pile moorings for visitors.
Facilities: fuel; boatyard; water; chandlery; yacht/boat club; slipway.
Access: governed by bar at entrance to Beaulieu River.
Harbour Master: W. H. J. Grindey.

HYTHE MARINA VILLAGE, Shamrock Way, Hythe, Southampton SO4 6AA. Tel: (0703) 207073. Fax: (0703) 842424. Telex: 47669 SHAMQY G.
Call sign: Hythe Marina Ch. 80, 37 (M).
Berths: 200 (25 visitors) on pontoons.
Max. draught LWS 1.2m, LOA 14.3m.
Facilities: Water, electricity, provisions, boatyard, fuel, chandlery, gas, security, repairs, rigging, telephone, lift, toilets, laundry, restaurant, wine bar.
Remarks: Lock operation may be subject to tidal conditions. Vessels restricted at low water can wait on waiting pontoon, with a depth alongside of 2m below chart datum.
Customs: Tel: (0703) 827350.

SHAMROCK QUAY, William Street, Northam, Southampton. Tel: (0703) 229461. Fax: (0703) 229461. Telex: 47669 SHAMQY G.
Call sign: VHF Ch. 80, 37 (M).
Berths: 300 (visitors welcome).
Facilities: water; electricity; provisions; boatyard; 50-ton hoist; chandlery; gas; security; repairs; rigging; telephone; toilets; showers; laundry; restaurant; wine bar.
Contact: J. Eads.

ITCHEN MARINE, America Wharf, Elm Street, Southampton. Tel: (0703) 631500.
Call Sign: Ch. 08.
Berths: 50 pontoon (drying).
Facilities: fuel; boatyard; 12T crane.

KEMPS SHIPYARD LTD, Kemps Quay, Quayside Road, Bitterne Manor, Southampton SO9 3FE. Tel: (0703) 632323. Fax: (0703) 226002. Tx: 477793 KEMPSA G.
Berths: 200 (visitors available). Draught 1.2-3.7m, max. LOA 30m.

TOWN QUAY MARINA, Harbour Board Office, Town Quay, Southampton. Tel: (0703) 23497.
Berths: many visitors berths.

OCEAN VILLAGE MARINA. MDL Estates Ltd, Marina Office, Channel Way, Canute Road, Southampton SO1 1JJ. Tel: (0703) 229385. Fax: (0703) 333384. Tx: 47669 SHAMQY G.
Call sign: Ocean Marina Ch. 80, 37 (M).
Open: 24 hr.
Berths: 400.
Facilities: toilets; showers; shops; restaurants; cinema; club.
Harbour Master: Adrian Smith. **Asst:** Patricia Matthews.

First Aid — Section 17

RIVER HAMBLE, Harbour Master's Office, Shore Road, Warsash, Hampshire SO3 6FR. Tel: (04895) 76387.
Call sign: Harbourmaster Ch. 16, 68. Marinas 80, 37 (M).
Moorings: Scrubbing piles, visitors moorings at Warsash (piles B1-B4) also 9-16 Port Hamble.
Facilities: mail; phone; water; fuel; bar; public hard; hards at Burlesdon, Swanwick, Hamble foreshore; piles at Salterns Boatyard Tel: (042121) 3911. Yard facilities at Hamble Yacht Services Tel: (0703) 45411. Fax: (0703) 455682. Also sailing clubs; sailmakers; divers; salvage; towing and maintenance.
Harbour Master: Capt. C. J. Nicholl, OBE. Tel: (04895) 82406. **Asst. Harbour Master:** Tel: Fareham (0329) 283944.
Customs: Tel: R/T (0703) 827350.

COUGAR QUAY, School Lane, Hamble, Hants. Tel: (0703) 453513.
Berths: 200 on dry land.
Facilities: Fuel, water, electricity, repairs, slipway, toilets, showers, telephone.

HAMBLE POINT MARINA, Hamble River, Southampton, Hampshire. Tel: (0703) 452464. Fax: (0703) 455206.
Call sign: Ch. 80, 37 (M).
Open: 24 hr. **Berths:** 220 (visitors available).
Facilities: fuel (diesel); electricity; chandlery; car park; club; extensive yard facilities; brokerage; water; continuous night security, wc/showers; Calor gas.
Supervisor: G. Whatley.
Dock Masters: D. Walters and A. Ramsey.

PORT HAMBLE. Tel: (0703) 452741
Call sign: Port Hamble Ch. 80, 37 (M).
Open: 24 hr. **Berths:** 340 (visitors available).
Facilities: fuel; electricity; chandlery; provisions; water; repairs; cranage (limit 40 tons); storage; brokerage; slipway; gas. Continuous night security, laying up facilities.
Contact: Dockmaster.

MERCURY YACHT HARBOUR, Satchell Lane, Southampton SO3 5NL. Tel: (0703) 452741. Fax: (0703) 455206. Telex: 47713.
Call Sign: Mercury Yacht Hr. Ch. 80 (M)
Berths: 340 pontoon.
Facilities: water; electricity; WCs; showers; security; club; chandlery; sales; yard.

FOULKES & SONS (RIVERSIDE BOATYARD), Blundell Lane, Bursledon, Southampton, Hants. Tel: 042-121 6349.
Berths: 25, 50 moorings midstream.
Facilities: pontoon; repairs; salvage; diving; towing; chandlery.

ELEPHANT BOATYARD. Tel: (042-121) 3268.
Facilities: pontoon; slip; repairs; bar nearby.

EASTLANDS. Tel: (042121) 3556.
Facilities; moorings; mud berths; haul out; repairs.

DEACONS BOATYARD LIMITED, Trapper Yachts, Bursledon Bridge, Southampton SO3 8AZ. Tel: (042-121) 2253. Fax: (042 121) 5665.
Berths: 150 (10 visitors).
Facilities: electricity; repairs; water; slipway; lift-out facilities; chandlery; boat park; toilets/showers.
Contact: Tim Ridgeway.

CABIN BOATYARD, Bridge Road, Bursledon, Hants. Tel: (042-121) 2516.
Berths: 126, 6 visitors.
Facilities: repairs (Electrical engineering and woodwork); slipway (up to 10 tons or 38ft); cranage(3 tons or 25ft); boat park; water; toilets; restaurant.

SWANWICK MARINA–A. H. MOODY & SON LTD, Swanwick, Southampton, Hants SO3 7ZL.
Tel: (0489) 885000 (after hours 85262)
Call sign: Swanwick Marina Ch. 80, 37 (M).
Open: 24 hr.
Berths: 375 (visitors berths usually available).
Max. draught 2.7m, LOA 21m.
Facilities: fuel; electricity; water; chandlery; hoists; storage; brokerage; repairs. Yard; Calor gas.
Open: Mon.-Fri 0730-1730. Sat. 0730-1200.
Dockmaster: P. Munnion.

R. K. MARINE, Hamble River Boatyard, Bridge Road, Swanwick, Southampton, Hants SO3 7EB. Tel: (04895) 83572/83585.
Berths: 35.
Facilities: yard; slip; engineers.
Contact: Mr. R. Kimish.

UNIVERSAL MARINA, Sarisbury Green, Southampton, Hants SO3 6ZN. Tel: (04895) 74272.
Berths: 400 pontoon
Facilities: repairs; 50T lift; storage; chandlery; slip; water; Calor gas.

STONE PIER YARD, Shore Road, Warsash, Hants SO3 9FR. Tel: (04898) 85400.
Facilities: pontoon; fuel; repairs; chandlery; refits.

Isle of Wight

BEMBRIDGE MARINA, Harbour Office, Bembridge, Isle of Wight.
Tel: (0983) 874436/872828.
Call sign: Bravo Hotel Lima Ch. M, 16.
Open: Normal working hours. **Berths:** 60 pontoon (visitors available).
Facilities: electricity; chandlery; water; provisions (near by); repair (local yards); storage. Fuel and chandlery available at local yards.
Berthing Master: Bob Green.

A.A. COOMBES, Embankment Road, Bembridge. Tel: (0983) 872296.
Berths: 72 buoy (drying, max. 30ft).
Facilities: boatyard, chandlery; yacht/boat club; slipway; 6T crane.

YARMOUTH HARBOUR, The Quay, Yarmouth, Isle of Wight PO41 0NT. Tel: (0983) 760321.
Open 24 hr. **Berths:** Fore and aft 250 available for visitors. Max. draught 2.1m, LOA 23m.
Facilities: fuel (diesel, petrol, calor gas); chandlery; provisions (near by); repair; storage; water. Yard facilities available near by, showers, WCs, barbecues.
Remarks: speed limit harbour approach – River Yar 4 knots.
Harbour Master: Captain N. W. Hunt.
Customs: Tel: R/T (0703) 827350.

HAROLD HAYLES LTD, The Quay, Yarmouth, Isle of Wight PO41 0RS. Tel: (0983) 760373. Fax: (0983) 760666.
Open: Weekdays: Sat. & Sun. a.m. Berths and visitors berths available.
Facilities: fuel (diesel, Calor gas); chandlery; repairs; slipways (limit 75 tons); storage; brokerage.
Managing Director: Colin Campbell.

COWES MARINA, Clarence Road, East Cowes, Isle of Wight PO31 7AS. Tel: (0983) 293983.
Call Sign: Ch. M
Open: Normal hours. **Berths:** 220 pontoon (visitors 80) max. draught 3m, LOA 30m.
Facilities: water; electricity; repairs; Calor gas.
Manager: D. H. Evans.

COWES HARBOUR, Harbour Office, Town Quay, Cowes, Isle of Wight.
Tel: (0983) 293952.
Call sign: Cowes Harbour Radio. VHF Ch. 16 (Working Ch. 69).
Open: Accessible to berths 24 hr. **Berths:** 1200 moorings. 800 visitors available (pontoon, swinging and pile) on application to Harbour Office.

Facilities: fuel (diesel, petrol); chandlery; water; electricity; repairs; cranage; slipway; provisions; showers; toilets; restaurant.
Harbour Master: Capt. H. N. J. Wrigley.
Customs: Tel: R/T (0703) 827350.

WEST COWES MARINA, High Street, Cowes, Isle of Wight PO31 7BD. Tel: (0983) 299975. Fax: (0983) 200332.
Call sign: Ch. 80.
Open: 24 hr. **Berths:** 220 visitors up to 27m.
Facilities: fuel (diesel); electricity; water; Calor gas; camping Gaz; ice; repair; cranage (limit 40 ton travel hoist; storage; brokerage; media centre.
Berthing Masters: Chris Brindle, Colin Peck.

CLUB U.K., Arctic Road, West Cowes, PO31 7PQ. Tel: (0983) 294941/290154.
Berths: up to 15.
Facilities: bar.
Remarks: Access S of floating bridge.
Manager: Brian Cole.

WOOTON CREEK FAIRWAYS ASSN., The Moorings, Wooton Bridge, Tel: (0983) 882763.
Berths: 200 buoy (drying, laid by owners).
Facilities: water; boatyard; chandlery; yacht/boat club & slipway.
Hon. Secretary: R. Perraton.

NEWPORT YACHT HARBOUR, Town Quay, Newport, Isle of Wight. Tel: (0983) 525994/520000 Ex. 2144.
Berths: 40 (40 visitors) up to 12m LOA, dries.
Facilities: water; provisions; boatyard; slipway; chandlery; electricity; gas; security; toilets; showers.
Harbour Master: W. G. Pritchett.

ISLAND HARBOUR, Mill Lane, Binfield, Newport, Isle of Wight PO30 2LA. Tel: (0983) 526020. Fax: (0983) 526001.
Call Sign: Island Harbour, Ch. 80, 37 (M).
Berths: 200 pontoons (visitors contact H.M.) Max draught 2m. L.O.A. 15m..
Facilities: fuel; water; power; showers; toilets; provisions; boatyard; slipway; gas; security; telephone; bar and restaurant; laundry.
Access: 3 hr.–HW–3 hr.

South Coast (continued)

CAMPER AND NICHOLSONS (MARINA) LTD, Mumby Road, Gosport, Hants PO12 1AH. Tel: (0705) 524811.
Call sign: Camper Base. VHF Ch. 80, 37 (M). If possible visitors should radio in advance.

Open: 24 hr. **Berths:** 350 (40 visitors available).
Facilities: fuel (petrol); electricity; chandlery; water; repairs; brokerage; launderette; yacht club; restaurant; toilets and showers.
Remarks: Access at all states of tide 2 metres.

HARDWAY MARINE, 95–99 Priory Road, Gosport, Hants PO12 4LF. Tel: (0705) 580420.
Berths: 100 (swinging mooring), 5 visitors.
Facilities: fuel (diesel); rigging service; sail repairs; scrubbing berths; chandlery; Calor gas.
Manager: S. Duncan-Brown.
Remarks: Access at all times

GOSPORT BOAT YARD, 5 Harbour Road, Gosport, Hants. Tel: (0705) 586216/526534.
Berths: 260 (20 mud berths).
Facilities: repairs; cranage; rigging service; slipway; boat park; water; showers/toilets.
Contact: Mrs. Smallwoods.
Remarks: Deep water access, jetty and free ferry service.

FAREHAM YACHT HARBOUR, Portsmouth Marine Engineering, Lower Quay, Fareham, Hants Tel: (0329) 232854/288221. Fax: (0329) 822140.
Call sign: Fareham Yacht Harbour Ch. 80, 37 (M).
Open: 0800-dusk, all week.
Berths: approx. 110 (some visitors). Max. LOA 10m.
Facilities: electricity; water; refuse; diesel; gas; WCs; showers; yacht club; 10T crane; boat sales; launching; dry berths; chandlery; repairs; brokerage. Some berths at Fareham Marine (0329 822445).
Manager; Dave Taylor.

FAREHAM MARINE, Lower Quay, Fareham. Tel: (0329) 822445.
Call Sign: Ch. 80.
Berths: 50 pontoon mostly drying.
Facilities: boatyard, slipway; chandlery.

WICORMARINE LTD, Portsmouth Harbour, Cranleigh Road, Portchester, Fareham PO16 9DR. Tel: (0329) 237112.
Call sign: Wicormarine Ch. 80, 37 (M).
Open: Normal hours. **Berths:** Various deepwater, tidal, jetty (visitors available).
Facilities: Fuel (diesel); water; gas; chandlery; limited provisions (shops 10 mins); repairs (all types); cranage; slipway; storage; Calor gas; brokerage.
Managing Director: C. M. Waddington.

PORTSMOUTH CAMBER, Port Managers Department, Harbour Office, George Byng Way, Continental Ferry Port, Portsmouth PO2 8SP. Tel: (0705) 297395.
Berths: Quayside. (Visitors as available.)
Customs: Tel: (0703) 827350.

PORT SOLENT, South Lockside, Portsmouth, Hants PO6 4TJ.
Tel: (0705) 210765. Fax: (0705) 324241.
Call Sign: Ch. 80, 37 (M).
Berths: 450 (50 visitors).
Facilities: electricity; water; phone; refuse; fuel; gas; chandlery; charts; provisions; ice; showers; WCs; launderette; 8 restaurants; 20 shops; bar; club & school; post; all repairs; 2T crane; 40T lift; slip; boat sales & hire; security; lift-out; storage; Calor gas.
Remarks: Access either side of HW. Full tidal access through locks. English, French spoken.

LANGSTONE MARINA, Fort Cumberland Road, Eastney, Portsmouth, Hants PO4 9RJ.
Tel: (0705) 822719.
Berths: 300, visitors, max. draught 1.5m all tides.
Facilities: showers; WCs; diesel; gas; 20T lift; security; storage; chandlery.
Remarks: sill gate in operation – therefore access only 3 hr.–HW–3 hr. Waiting pontoon.
Contact: Barry Moody.

LANGSTONE HARBOUR, Harbour Office, Ferry Road, Hayling Island, Hants PO11 0DG.
Tel: (0705) 463419.
Call sign: Ch. 16 Working Ch. 12 (office hours, essential traffic only).
Berths: 1500 buoy (some drying). By arrangement with harbour office, 6 visitors.
Facilities: fuel (diesel, petrol); slipway; boat park; water; toilets.
Remarks: Strong currents in and around entrance channel. Visitors are advised to contact the harbour office on, or prior to arrival.
Manager: Capt. P. Hausen.

HAYLING YACHT CO LTD, Mill Rythe Lane, Hayling Island, Hampshire. Tel: (0705) 463592.
Berths: 25 deep water/50 semi-deep water. Half tide (swinging moorings). 50 pontoon berths half-tide.
Facilities: diesel; repairs; slipway; lift-out facilities; water; boat park; chandlery; showers/toilets; Calor gas.
Contact: J. L. Blake.
Remarks: Dinghy access to yard 3 hr.–HW–3 hr.

SPARKES YACHT HARBOUR, 38 Wittering Road, Sandy Point, Hayling Island, Hants PO11 9SR. Tel: (0705) 463572/465741. Telex: 869488.
Call sign: Ch. 80, 37 (M).
Berths: 140 deep water max. draught 2.5m, LOA 18m, also 30 deep water and 75 dry berths at Sparkes Boatyard.
Facilities: chandlery; fuel (petrol & diesel); water; electricity; showers/toilets; car parking and restaurant.

NORTHNEY YACHT MARINA, Northney Road, Hayling Island, Hants PO11 0NH. Tel: (0705) 466321.
Call sign: Ch. 80, 37 (M) weekends.
Open: 24 hr. **Berths:** 228 (visitors available). Max. draught 1.8m, LOA 15m, all tides.
Facilities: fuel (diesel); electricity; chandlery; provisions (water & gas); repairs; cranage (limit 7 tons/40ft.); storage; showers; bar; brokerage.
General Manager: Dave Mitchell.

EMSWORTH YACHT HARBOUR, Thorney Road, Emsworth, Hampshire PO10 8PB. Tel: (0243) 375211.
Open: Mon.-Fri. 0800-1700. Sat. 0900-1600. Sun. 0900-1600.
Call sign: Ch. 80, 37 (M).
Berths: 200 (visitors available). Max. draught 1.6m, max. LOA 12m.
Facilities: fuel; electricity; repairs; cranage (limit 20 tons); storage; sail/rigging repairs; brokerage; Calor gas.
Harbour Master: Jenny Duxbury.
Remarks: Entrance to Marina over a sill, approx. 2 hr.–HW–2 hr.

THORNHAM MARINA, Thornham Lane, Prinsted, Emsworth, Hants PO10 8DD. Tel: (0243) 375335.
Berths: 33 swinging, 77 pontoon, 350 storage moorings.
Facilities: water; electricity; showers; toilets; engineering; club; restaurant; Calor gas.
Harbour Master: Mr. Titmarsh.

BURNES SHIPYARD, Old Bosham, Nr. Chichester, Sussex PO18 8LJ. Tel: (0243) 572239.
Berths: 100.
Facilities: repairs (both sail and engine); lift-out facilities; slipway; boat park; water (within walking distance); showers/toilets; shops; chandlery.
Contact: Mrs. D. Davies.
Remarks: Access 2-3-hr.–HW–2-3 hr.

ITCHENOR HARBOUR OFFICE, Chichester, W. Sussex. Tel: (0243) 512301.
Call Sign: Ch. 14
Berths: 530 buoy & pile (some drying).
Facilities: boatyard; chandlery; slipway.
Harbour Master: Capt. J. Whitney.

BIRDHAM SHIP YARD, Birdham Pool, Chichester, W Sussex PO20 7BG. Tel: (0243) 512310.
Open: Mon.-Fri. 0730-1700; Sat. 0900-2300.
Berths: 230.
Facilities: fuel (diesel, petrol); chandlery; repair; cranage (limit 3 tons); slipway (20 tons, up to 5 ft 6 in. draught); storage; brokerage.
Managing Director: M. R. Gardiner.
Remarks: Lock operates 3 hr.–HW–3 hr.

BOSHAM QUAY, Bosham. Tel: (0243) 573336.
Berths: 200 buoy, some drying
Facilities: boatyard, chandlery.

CHICHESTER YACHT BASIN, Birdham, Chichester Harbour, W Sussex PO20 7EJ. Tel: (0243) 512731
Call Sign: Chichester Yacht Basin, Ch. 80, 37(M).
Open: Apr.-Sept. Mon.-Fri. 0700-2100. W/E 0600-2200. Oct.-Mar. Mon.-Fri. 0800-1700. W/E 0800-1800.
Berths: 1129 (visitors 40).
Facilities: fuel (diesel, petrol); chandlery; showers; yacht club; provisions; repairs; travel hoist (limit 20 tons); electricity; sailing school; storage; brokerage.
Berthing Manager: John Haffenden.
General Manager: G. Martin.

BULLER A., Riverside Tea Gardens, Arundel, W. Sussex. Tel: 0903 882609.
Berths: 100 jetty (visitors available).

SHIP & ANCHOR MARINA, Ford, Nr. Arundel, Sussex BN18 0BJ. Tel: (0243) 551262.
Berths: 182 (32 pontoon, 150 boat park). Max. draught 1.2m. LOA 9.8m.
Facilities: repairs; lift-out facilities; slipway; water; chandlery; shop; restaurant; public house; showers/toilets.
Remarks: Access 4 hr.–HW–4 hr.

LITTLEHAMPTON SAILING & MOTOR CLUB LTD, 90/91 South Terrace, Littlehampton, W Sussex BN17 5LJ. Tel: (0903) 715859.
Berths: 70.
Secretary: A. T. Hawkes.

LITTLEHAMPTON MARINA, Ferry Road, River Arun, Littlehampton BN17 5DS. Tel: (0903) 713553.
Call sign: Littlehampton Marina Ch. 80, 37 (M).
Berths: 120 (visitors available). Draught 2.7m. max. LOA 18m.
Facilities: fuel; electricity; chandlery; repair; cranage/hoist (limit 16 tons); winch (limit 40 tons); storage; brokerage; slipway; compressed air for divers; caféteria; bar and restaurant afloat; toilets; showers; changing rooms.
Berthing Master: Chris Neale.
Customs: Tel: (0703) 827350.

ARUN YACHT CLUB LTD, Riverside West, Littlehampton BN17 5DL. Tel: (0903) 716016 – Office, 714533 – Members.
Berths: 115 (visitors 10). Dries out. Max. LOA 9m.
Facilities: water; electricity; slipway; bar; clubhouse; telephone; toilets; showers.

SURRY BOAT YARD LTD, Lower Brighton Road, Shoreham by Sea, Sussex BN43 6RN. Tel: (0273) 461491.
Open: 0800-1800.
Berths: 75 on pontoon and jetty (visitors if available).
Facilities: electricity; brokerage; slipway; pressure cleaning; water.
Berthing Master: A. R. Hornsby.
Remarks: Dries out at LW. All vessels take the ground.
Customs: Tel: (0703) 827350.

RIVERSIDE MARINE, The Boathouse, 41 Riverside Road, Shoreham Beach, West Sussex BN43 5RB. Tel: (0273) 453793.
Berths: mud, LOA over 30m.
Facilities: electricity; water; phone; refuse; multihull slip. Others locally.

LADY BEE MARINA. (The Canal, Shoreham Harbour), Albion Street, Southwick, Sussex. Tel: (0273) 591705.
Open: Mon.-Sat. 0830-1800. Sun. 0900-1300.
Call sign: Ch. 80, 37 (M).
Berths: 120 (visitors available).
Facilities: fuel (diesel); Calor, Gaz; electricity; chandlery; provisions near by; trailer slip; repairs; cranage (limit 40 ton mobile); storage; brokerage; restaurant, car park, showers, toilets, telephone. Sussex YC adjacent.
Remarks: Lockages for yachts. Lockages to be made available through the Prince George Lock as hereunder. The timings are approximate but will be adhered to as closely

as possible. Lock fee payable, valid for one month.
Outward: 3¾ h. and 1¾ h. before HW. ½ h. and 2¾ h. after HW.
Inward: 3¼ h. and 1¼ h. before HW. 1 h. and 3¼ h. after HW.
On tides where HW occurs on a **Saturday, Sunday** or **Bank Holiday** during the months of **April** to **October** inclusive, the schedule of lockages to be made available will be:
Outwards: 3¾ h., 2½ h. and 1 h. before HW. ¼ h., 1½ h. and 3 h. after HW.
Inward: 3¼ h., 2 h. and ½ h. before HW. ½ h., 1¾ h and 3¼ h. after HW.
Harbour Master: J. Robertson.

BRIGHTON MARINA VILLAGE, Brighton, E Sussex BN2 5UF.
Tel: (0273) 693636. Fax: (0273) 675082.
Call Sign: Brighton Control. VHF Listening watch. Ch. 16, 80, 37(M). Working Channels: Ch. 80, 37 (M), 11, 68.
Open: 24 hr. **Berths:** 1,800 Pontoon berths available all states of tide, visitors' berths. Max. draught 3m, LOA 30m.
Facilities: fuel (diesel, petrol); electricity; chandlery; provisions; repair; cranage (limit 60 tons); storage; brokerage; gas; water; phone; ice; WCs; showers; sailing school; sea fishing; mail; repairs; 15T hoist; 60T crane; car & boat hire; gardiennage; scrubbing grid. Yacht club and restaurant; launderette; security; Calor gas.
Harbour Manager: P. K. C. Simpson.
Deputy Harbour Manager: M. J. Shinn.
Customs: Tel: (0703) 229251.

NEWHAVEN MARINA, The Yacht Harbour, Newhaven, E. Sussex BN9 9BY.
Tel: (0273) 513881/2/3. Fax: (0273) 517990. (Emergency (0273) 516461).
Call Sign: Newhaven Marina Ch. 80, 37 (M).
Open: 24 hr. **Berths:** 550 (355 on pontoons) visitors available (max draught 2m, LOA 18m).
Facilities: fuel (diesel, petrol, gas); electricity; chandlery; provisions; repair; slipway 15T, 15m LOA: cranage (limit 12 tons); boat hoist 10T; storage; brokerage; launderette; yacht club; bar; restaurant.
Berthing Master: David Bourne.
Customs: Tel: (0273) 827350.

MEECHING BOATS, Denton Island, Newhaven, E Sussex BN9 9BA. Tel: (0273) 514907/514996.
Berths: 80. Pontoon moorings vessels up to draught 1.1m, LOA 11m.
Facilities: Small hard; water; electricity; repairs.

Open: Mon.-Fri. 0800-1200, 1300-1700. Sat. 1000-1200.
Remarks: Access to moorings 24 hr. Pontoons afloat 2 hr.–HW–2 hr.
Harbour Master: I. D. Johns.

CANTELL & SONS, Old Shipyard, Robinson Road, Newhaven, E Sussex BN9 9BL. Tel: (0273) 513375. Tx: 877838 CANTEL G.
Berths: 110 mud (some visitors).
Facilities: storage; chandlery.

NEW DEVELOPMENT (Opening 1993):
CRUMBLES HARBOUR VILLAGE, Pevensey Bay Rd, Eastbourne. Tel: (0323) 767066.
Berths: 600 pontoons.

RYE HARBOUR, Harbour Office, Camber, Rye, East Sussex. Tel: (0797) 225225.
Call sign: Ch. 14, Rye Harbour Radio 0900-1700 or when vessels expected.
Berths: 500 (mud berths).
Facilities: fuel (diesel, petrol); repairs; slipway; lift-out facilities; water; chandlery; boat park; showers/toilets; first aid.
Harbour Master: Capt. C. Bagwell.
Remarks: Access 2 hr.–HW–3 hr. Harbour runs dry.
Customs: Tel: (0304) 202441.

SANDROCK MARINE, Rock Channel, Rye, Sussex TN31 7HJ. Tel: (0797) 222679.
Berths: 9 mud, tidal.
Facilities: slip; water; electricity; diesel fuel; chandlery; engineering. Closed Thursday.
Harbour Master: Mr C. Bagwell.

H. J. PHILLIPS BOATBUILDERS, Rock Channel, Rye, Sussex TN31 7HJ. Tel: (0797) 223234/224479.
Open: 0800-1700.
Berths: 20 mud, access 2 hr.–HW–2 hr.
Facilities: slipway 20 tons; cranage 10 tons; water; electricity; repairs.
Harbour Master: D. J. Phillips.

FOLKESTONE HARBOUR, The Stade, Folkestone. Tel: (0303) 220801.
Call Sign: Ch. 22.
Berths: 70 buoy (drying).
Facilities: fuel; chandlery; Yacht/boat club; slipway.
Customs: Tel: R/T (0304) 202441.

**Radiobeacons — Section 19
Tidal Data — Section 21**

DOVER HARBOUR, Harbour House, Wellington Dock, Dover, Kent CT17 9BU. Tel: (0304) 240400. Fax: 240465.
Call sign: Dover Port Control (Ch. 16, 74, 12).
Open: Dock gates open 1 hr. either side HW. approx.
Berths: 150, some on pontoons. (Visitors available max. draught 5.3m, MHWN. LOA 90m.)
Facilities: fuel (diesel, petrol, gas); water; chandlery; repairs; slipway; hard; cranage at Dover Marine Supplies, 158/160 Snargate Street, Dover (Tel: (0304) 201677) and Dover Yacht Co in Wellington Dock. Tel: (0304) 201073; toilets/showers in Wellington Dock for visiting yachtsmen; Calor gas (Sharpe & Enright, Snargate Street).
Harbour Superintendent: Capt. Peter White.

SANDWICH MARINA, Sandwich, Kent. Tel: (0304) 613690.
Berths: 60 (pontoon berths). Max. draught 1.8m, LOA 18m.
Facilities: slipway; repairs; lift-out facilities; rigging service; water; boat park; toilets.

BOAT HOUSE MARINE SERVICES, Grove Ferry Road, Upstreet, Nr. Canterbury, Kent CT3 4BP. Tel: 0227 86345.
Berths: 50.
Facilities: slip.

HIGHWAY MARINA, Pillory Gate Wharf, Strand Street, Sandwich, Kent CT13 9EU. Tel: (0304) 613925. .
Berths: 40. (10 visitors at Town Quay). Max. draught 2m, LOA 10m.
Calor gas available.

RAMSGATE YACHT HARBOUR, Military Road, Ramsgate, Kent CT11 9LG. Tel: (0843) 592277/8/9.
Call sign: Ramsgate Harbour Radio. Ch. 16 & 14. Marina Ch. 14.

Open: 24 hr. **Berths:** 500 (300 visitors). LOA 110m, draught 4.8m (Harbour). LOA 30m, draught 3m (Marina). Access through lock 2h-HW-2h.
Facilities: fuel; electricity; chandlery; provisions; repair; slipway (limit 500 tons); cranage (limit 18 tons); storage; brokerage; first aid; showers/toilets.
Harbour Master: Capt. Jim Ewing.
General Manager: Commander C. H. Marsh.

WHITSTABLE YACHT CLUB, 3/4 Sea Wall, Whitstable, Kent CT5 1BX. Tel: (0227) 272942 (office), 272343 (members).
Call sign: Ch. 80, 37 (M).
Berths: 2 visitors moorings offshore.*
Facilities: bunk rooms; bar; clubhouse open 0900-2300. Refreshments (not Sun./Wed.).
Remarks: *Beware tide machine uncovers surrounded by 4 LWSG. marker buoys.
Customs: Tel: (0304) 202441.

HOLLOWSHORE SERVICES LTD., Hollowshore, Faversham. Tel: (0795) 532317.
Berths: 80 jetty (drying).
Facilities: fuel; boatyard; yacht/boat club; 5T crane.

YOUNGBOATS MARINE SERVICES, Oare Creek, Faversham, Kent ME13 7TX. Tel: (0795) 536176.
Berths: 120 (pontoon). Draught 1.2m, LOA 10m
Facilities: lift-out facilities; repairs; chandlery; Calor gas.
Harbour Master: T. J. Young.
Remarks: Access 1½ hr.–HW–1½ hr.

IRON WHARF BOATYARD, Faversham, Kent. Tel: (0795) 532020/537122.
Berths: 150. Max. draught 3m, LOA 27m.
Facilities: All facilities available.

BRENTS BOATYARD, The Old Shipyard, Upper Brents, Faversham, Kent ME13 7DR. Tel: (0795) 537809. Fax: (0795) 538656.
Berths: deep water, mud.
Facilities: water; electricity; toilets; crane; tug; storage; DIY.
Customs: Tel: (071) 865 5861.

SWALE MARINA, Conyer Wharf, Teynham, Sittingbourne, Kent ME9 9HP.
Tel: (0795) 521562.
Berths: 100 mud.
Open: Seven days a week. Calor gas.
Manager: R. Jarman.
Harbour Master: Butch Parry.
Remarks: Access 2 hr.–HW–2 hr.

CONYER MARINA, Conyer Quay, Teynham.
Tel: (0795) 521285.
Call Sign: Ch. 16, 80 (M).
Berths: 50 jetty (drying).
Facilities: fuel; boatyard; chandlery; yacht/boat club; slipway; 6T crane.

SWALE BOROUGH COUNCIL, Council Offices, Sheerness. Tel: (0795) 662051.
Berths: 138 buoy.
Facilities: boatyard; chandlery; yacht/boat club; slipway.
Contact: Peter Farbridge.

GILLINGHAM MARINA, River Medway, Kent ME7 1UB.
Tel: (0634) 280022. Fax: (0634) 280164.
Call sign: Gillingham Marina Lock. Ch. 80.
Berths: 500 (visitors berths usually available).
Facilities: pontoon berths, with electricity and water; chandlery; provisions; showers; toilets; repairs; boathoist; storage; brokerage; security; fuel; hoist; DIY; bar.
Access: E Basin Lock gates fully operational approx. 4 hr.–HW–4 hr. Between daylight hours 0800-2100 (max.). W Basin Tidal – access 2 hr.-HWS-2 hr.
Deep Water Moorings: For arrival and departure at other times.
Contact: Berthing Manager.

MEDWAY PIER MARINE LTD, Pier Head Building, Approach Rd, Gillingham, Kent.
Tel: (0634) 51113.
Berths: 45+ on pontoons.
Facilities: boatyard; chandlery; slipway 10T crane.

MEDWAY PORTS AUTHORITY, Sheerness Docks, Sheerness. Tel: (0795) 580003.
Call Sign: Ch. 74, 9
Berths: 100 buoy.

MACHIN KNIGHT & SONS LTD, Chatham Boatyard, No. 7 Covered Slip, Chatham Historic Dockyard, Kent ME4 4TE. Tel: (0634) 847103. Enquiries (081) 850 6300.
Open: 0730-1645 during summer.
Berths: 13 deepwater, 50 hard, 10 under cover. Moorings for all tides.
Facilities: storage; dry dock; draw dock; slipway.
Customs: Tel: (071) 865 5861.

MEDWAY BRIDGE MARINA, Manor Lane, Rochester, Kent ME1 3HS. Tel: (0634) 843576. Fax: (0634) 43820.
Open: 0900-1230 & 1330-1730.
Berths: 167 (20 visitors).
Facilities: bar and restaurant; (dry dock, slipways, transporter 16T); storage; boat sales; car park; chandlery; club; diy; food and wine; fuel (petrol and diesel), insurance; marine finance; repairs to engines, glassfibre; sails and covers and woodwork.
Remarks: Rochester Bridge: 22 ft. MHWS (air height).

CUXTON MARINA, Station Road, Cuxton, Rochester, Kent ME2 1AB. Tel: (0634) 721941.
Open: 24 hr. **Berths:** 150 (visitors accepted).
Facilities: fuel (diesel); electricity; repairs; cranage (limit 12 ton hoist); storage; brokerage; on site security; clubhouse facility.
Harbour Master: Mr Ian Pearson.
Remarks: Access deepwater moorings 5 hr.–HW–5 hr. Mud berths 3 hr.–HW–3 hr.

ELMHAVEN MARINA, Rochester Road, Halling, Rochester, Kent ME2 1AQ. Tel: (0634) 24089.
Berths: 30 + 6 walkway, 10 mud. 60 more at John Hawkins Marine. Tel: (0634) 242256.
Facilities: electricity; water; toilet; showers; crane; hard standing; phone.
Remarks: Restricted on LWS.
Contact: John Hawkins, Peter Braddon, Nigel Taylor.

ALLINGTON MARINA, Allington, Maidstone, Kent. Tel: (0622) 52057.
Berths: 100.
Facilities: fuel (petrol, diesel); electricity; repairs; slipway; cranage (10 ton); chandlery; toilets; water.
Contact: The Manager.
Remarks: Access through lock 3 hr.–HW–2 hr. Marina is non-tidal.

Tidal Data — Section 21

HOO MARINA, River Medway, Kent.
Tel: (0634) 250311.
Open: Mon.-Fri. 0900-1700. Sat. 0900-1700.
Berths: 100 floating berths, 125 mud berths.
Call sign: Ch. 80, 37 (M).
Facilities: electricity; repairs; service; cranage
(limit 20T); full security; storage; brokerage;
water; h.p. cleaning.
Harbour Master: S. R. Loosley.
Remarks: Access to floating berths up to
4hr.–HW–4 hr.

GRAVESHAM CANAL BASIN, Leisure
Services, Civic Centre, Gravesend, Kent, DA12
1AU. Tel: (0474) 337575. Lock office: (0474)
352392. Fax: (0474) 337453.
Berths: 100, 8 visitors, 1.2m draught, access 1
hr.–HW–1 hr.
Facilities: electricity; water; phone at office;
refuse; WCs; showers; yacht club; sailing
school; slip. Other facilities 10 min. walk.
Customs: Tel: (071) 865 5861.

London & Thames

GREENWICH YACHT CLUB, Riverway,
Greenwich, London, SE10 0BE.
Tel: Sec: 071-293 4316. Club: 071-858 7339.
Berths: 150, 8 visitors, max. draught 2m, LOA
12m.
Open: Tues., Thurs., Fri. 1930-2300. Sun.
1100-1500. Yard open most days.
Facilities: ice; phone; WCs; showers; bar;
clubhouse; 2T crane; slip; security; storage;
Calor gas (Benefactors, 275 Greenwich High
St.).
Secretary: Vic Webb.

TURNER MARINAS LTD, 57 Fitzroy Road,
London NW1 8TS. Tel: 071-722 9806.
Berths: 120. (visitors berths available by
appointment). On Regent's Canal.
Facilities: electricity; chandlery; toilets; water.
Managing Director: Mrs. M. F. Turner.
Remarks: Access from River Thames via
Limehouse or Brentford. Max. draught 1.4m,
LOA 23m.

THE MARINA AT SOUTH DOCK, South Lock
Office, Rope St. Plough Way, London SE16.
Tel: 071 252 2244.
Call Sign: Ch. 80 (M).
Berths: 300 pontoon.
Facilities: boatyard; yacht/boat club; slipway.

ST KATHARINE YACHT HAVEN, Ivory House,
St. Katharine-by-the-Tower, London E1 9AT.
Tel: 071-488 2400. Fax: 071-481 4515.
Call sign: St Katharine Ch. 80, 37 (M).
Open: 0600-2030 (Apr.-Aug.), 0800-1800
(Sept.-Mar.)
Berths: 150 pontoon (visitors available).
Facilities: electricity; water; showers; toilets;
laundrette; yacht club; restaurants; shops;
repairs; bar; chandlery; public transport.
Director: Miss C. Heptinstall.
Remarks: Entry 2 hr.–HW–1½ hr.
Customs: Tel: 071-865 5861.

CADOGAN PIER, Port of London Authority,
Piers & Moorings Section, Europe House,
World Trade Centre, London E1. Tel: 071 481
8484.
Berths: 40 pontoon.

CHELSEA HARBOUR MARINA, Lots Road,
London SW10 0XF. Tel: 071-351 4433. Fax:
071-352 1870.
Call sign: Chelsea Harbour Ch. 14, 80.
Open: 24 hr.
Berths: 63 pontoon(visitors available).
Facilities: 16/32 amp electricity; water;
provisions; chandlery; valeting; brokerage;
Yacht Club; showers; restaurants; car parking;
diesel and gas at Westminster; Calor gas
(Chelsea Boat Builders, Old Ferry Wharf, West
Brompton).
Harbour Master: Lt.Cdr. D. Pickett.
Remarks: Basin entry 2 hr.–HW–1½ hr.
(London Bridge + 20 mins.). Waiting pontoon
outside basin. Terminal for Riverbus.

CHISWICK QUAY MARINA, London W4 3UR.
Tel: 081-994 8743.
Berths: 56, 6-8 visitors, max. draught 1.5m,
LOA 15m, 2 hr.–HW–2 hr.
Facilities: electricity; water; refuse; phone;
WCs; mail; slip; security; dry berths. Others
available within ½ mile. Yard at Brentford (1
mile). French, Spanish, Italian spoken.

BRENTFORD DOCK MARINA, Justin Close,
Brentford, Middlesex TW8 8QA, at junction on
the Thames with Grand Union Canal.
Tel: 081-568 0287.
Call sign: Brentford Dock Marina Ch. 80, 37 (M).
Open: 1000-1800. **Berths:** 100 (15 visitors).
Facilities: electricity; chandlery; provisions;
repair; storage; brokerage; slipway nearby;
emergency fuel and gas; club restaurant;
brokerage. Visitor's berth with fuel and slip at
nearby Swan Island, Tel: 081-892 2861.

EEL PIE MARINE CENTRE, Eel Pie Island, Twickenham, Middx. Tel: 081 892 3626. **Facilities:** boatyard; chandlery; slipway.

TOUGH SHIPYARDS LTD., Teddington Wharf, Teddington, Middx. Tel: 081 977 4494. **Facilities:** boatyard; chandlery; YC.

THAMES (DITTON) MARINA LTD, Portsmouth Road, Thames Ditton, Surrey KT6 5QD. Tel: 081-398 6159/3900. Fax: 081-398 6438. **Open:** 7 days week. **Berths:** 156 (6 visitors). **Facilities:** petrol, diesel, Calor gas, water, electricity, repairs, 2 slipways, chandlery.

PORT HAMPTON, Lower Sunbury Road, Hampton, Middx. Tel: 081 979 8116. **Facilities:** fuel; boatyard; chandlery; yacht/boat club; slipway.

GEO WILSON & SONS, Ferry House, Thames St. Sunbury on Thames, Middx. Tel: 0932 782067 **Berths:** 100 mid-river.

WALTON MARINA, Walton Bridge, Walton on Thames, Surrey KT12 1QW. Tel: (0932) 226266. Fax: 240586. **Berths:** 180, 6 visitors. Max. draught 1m, LOA 9m. **Open:** Office 0900-1800. Access 24h. **Facilities:** electricity; water; refuse; gas; chandlery; phone; WCs; showers; café; repairs; 6T crane; slip; boat sales; gardiennage; lift-out. Others nearby. French and Spanish spoken.

SHEPPERTON MARINA, Felix Lane, Shepperton, Middlesex TW17 8NJ. Tel: (0932) 243722. **Open:** Summer 0900-1800. **Berths:** 280 (visitors limited). **Facilities:** provisions; water; gas; electricity. **Harbour Master:** Juliet Barber.

NAUTICALIA BOATYARD, Ferry Lane, Shepperton, Middx. Tel: 0932 254844. **Berths:** 40. **Facilities:** water; boatyard, chandlery.

EYOT HOWE LTD., D'Oyly Carte Island, Weybridge, Surrey. Tel: 0932 848586. **Berths:** 55 **Facilities:** water; boatyard; slipway.

PENTON HOOK MARINA, Staines Road, Chertsey, Surrey KT16 8PY. Tel: (0932) 568681. **Open:** 24 hr. **Berths:** 700 (visitors welcome). **Facilities:** fuel (petrol, diesel, gas); water; sewage and pump out points; electricity; chandlery; repair and maintenance; new boat sales; brokerage; trimmer; lift out and slipping; scrubbing; hard standing. Free colour brochure on request. **General Manager:** Richard Knights.

RACECOURSE YACHT BASIN (WINDSOR) LTD, Maidenhead Road, Windsor, Berks SL4 5HT. Tel: (0753) 851501. Fax: 898172. Tx: 849021 FRAN G. **Berths:** 170. **Facilities:** chandlery; repair; cranage (limit 15 tons); licensed club; boat sales; toilets and showers. **Harbour Master:** D. A. Beresford.

WINDSOR MARINA, Maidenhead Road, Oakley Green, Windsor, Berks. SL4 5TZ. Tel: (0753) 853911. Fax: (0753) 868195. **Berths:** 210 (visitors if available). **Facilities:** fuel; electricity; chandlery; provisions; boat repairs/engineering; cranage (limit 20 tons); storage; gas; fuel; slipway. **Harbour Master:** Roy Collins.

BRAY MARINA LTD, Monkey Island Lane, Bray, Berkshire, SL6 2EB. Tel: (0628) 23654. Fax: 773485.
Open: 0900-1730.
Berths: 375, some visitors. Max. draught 1.2m, LOA 13.6m.
Facilities: water, refuse; fuel; gas; chandlery; provisions; phone; WCs; showers; café; repairs; 10T crane; boat sales; security; lift-out; dry berths.

HARLEYFORD MARINA, Marlow, Buckinghamshire SL7 2DX. Tel: (06284) 71361 (24 hours). Tx: 847741.
Open: 0900-1730. **Berths:** 350 (visitors welcome).
Facilities: chandlery; electronics; provisions; licensed club; bottled gas; repair/servicing; cranage (limit 42 ft.); brokerage and new boat sales.

BOSSOM'S BOATYARD LTD, Medley, Oxford, OX2 0NL. Tel: (0865) 247780. Fax: 244163.
Berths: 55, 5 visitors, max. draught 2m, LOA 12m.
Facilities: phone; WCs; showers; repairs; hoist; slip; scrubbing grid; lift-out; dry berths.

East Coast

PORT OF LONDON AUTHORITY, Thames House, St. Andrews Rd, Tilbury.
Tel: (0375) 85200.
Berths: 80 buoy, privately laid. No visitors.
Facilities: yacht/boat club.

HALCON MARINE, The Point, Canvey Island, Essex. Tel: (0268) 511611.
Berths: 250 (jetty berths). 3 short-term deep water moorings by arrangement.
Facilities: diesel; water; repairs; rigging service; slipway; boat park; cranage; chandlery.
Remarks: Access approx. 2 hr.–HW–2 hr.

PITSEA MARINA, Wat Tyler Country Park, Watt Tyler Way, Pitsea, Basildon. Tel: (0268) 552044.
Berths: 100 jetty (drying).
Facilities: boatyard; chandlery; slipway.

DAUNTLESS COMPANY, Canvey Bridge, Canvey Island, Essex SS8 0QT. Tel: (0268) 793782.
Call sign: Ch. 80, 37 (M).
Berths: 350.
Open: 0800-1700.
Facilities: diesel; electricity; repairs; sail repairs; slipway; water; lift-out facilities; boat park; toilets.
Remarks: Access 2½ hr.–HW–2½ hr. Deep water berths max. draught 12 ft.
Contact: P. J. Lattimer.

SOUTHEND BOROUGH COUNCIL, Foreshore Office, Pier Hill, Southend. Tel: (0702) 611889.
Call Sign: Ch. 80 (M).
Berths: 3000 buoy (drying). No visitors berths.
Facilities: fuel, boatyard; chandlery; yacht/boat club; yard; slipway; 20T hoist.

SHUTTLEWOOD J. W. & SON LTD, Waterside, East End, Paglesham, Rochford, Essex. Tel: (0702) 258226.
Berths: 80 afloat, 30 tidal, all moorings.

SOUTH ESSEX SLIPWAYS LTD, Waterside Rd East End, Paglesham, Rochford, Southend. Tel: (0702) 258885.
Berths: 100 swinging moorings, some drying.
Facilities: water; boatyard; slipway; 10T crane.

ESSEX MARINA LTD, Wallasea Island, Nr. Rochford, Essex SS4 2HG.
Tel: (0702) 258531 (Marina Office). Fax: (0702) 258227. Tx: 995244 POLY G.
Call sign: Essex Marina, Ch. 80, 37 (M).
Open: Access at all times. **Berths:** 500 pontoon and swinging moorings (visitors welcome).
Facilities: fuel; repairs; travel hoist; electricity; engineering; toilet; showers; laundrette; security; brokerage; bars; restaurant.

BRANDY HOLE MARINE LTD, Pooles Lane, Hullbridge, Hockley, Essex SS5 6QB. Tel: (0702) 230248.
Berths: 120, 2 visitors. max. draught 1.5m, LOA 10m.
Open: 0800-2230.
Facilities: water; phone; refuse; diesel; WCs; showers; yacht club; all repairs; 5T lift; slip; scrubbing grid; dry berths; mud berths.

PETTICROW BOATYARD LTD, The Quay, Burnham-on-Crouch, Essex CM0 8AT. Tel: (0621) 782115.
Berths: 150 (swinging moorings).
Facilities: water; repairs; rigging service; brokerage; slipway; lift-out facilities; boat park; Interspray Centre.
Customs: (0473) 219481.

TUCKER BROWN & CO LTD, Burnham Yacht Harbour, Burnham-on-Crouch, Essex CM0 8BL. Tel: (0621) 782150.
Berths: 350 pontoon, 120 swinging, some visitors. Max. LOA 15m, draught 2.5m.
Facilities: repairs; sail repairs; rigging service; electricity; engineering; 30T hoist; slip; boat park; brokerage; chandlery; first aid; water.

BURNHAM YACHT HARBOUR MARINA LTD, Burnham on Couch. Tel: (0621) 782150.
Call Sign: Ch. 80 (M).
Berths: 120 buoy, 350 pontoon.
Facilites: water; fuel; boatyard; chandlery; slipway; 30T hoist.

R. J. PRIOR & SON (BURNHAM) LTD, Quayside, Burnham-on-Crouch, Essex. Tel: (0621) 782160.
Berths: 140 (15 visitors).Full tide moorings.
Facilities: diesel; repairs; rigging service; slipway; lift-out facilities; shop; restaurant; first aid; water and scrubbing posts.
Manager: Murray R. Prior.
Remarks: Access at all states of tide via floating Landing Jetty (pontoon) with power and water at head.

RICE & COLE LTD, Sea End Boathouse, Burnham-on-Crouch, Essex CM0 8AN. Tel: (0621) 782063.
Open: 0900-1730 daily. Calor gas.
Berths: 150.
Contact: W. Cole.

NORTH FAMBRIDGE YACHT STATION, North Fambridge, Essex CM3 6CR. Tel: (0621) 740370.
Berths: 150.
Facilities: diesel; water; repairs; slipway; crane; sailmakers; toilets/showers; provisions.

WEST WICK MOORINGS, Church Road, North Fambridge, Essex. Tel: (0621) 741268.
Call sign: Ch. 80, 37 (M).
Berths: 180 (4 visitors).
Facilities: diesel; water; electricity; repairs; slipway; crane; toilets/showers; provisions; telephone.

BRIDGEMARSH MARINE, Bridgemarsh Lane, Althorne. Tel: (0621) 740414.
Berths: 125 pontoon, 70 other.
Facilities: water; boatyard; yacht/boat club; slipway; 8 T crane.

BRADWELL MARINA, Bradwell-on-Sea, Nr. Southminster, Essex.
Tel: (0621) 76235/76391.
Call sign: Bradwell Marina Ch. 80, 37 (M).
Open: 0830-1700. **Berths:** 300 (visitors very welcome).
Facilities: fuel (diesel, petrol); water and electricity on all pontoons; chandlery; provisions (local shops); repairs; boat hoist (limit 16 tons displacement); shore storage; slipway and scrubbing posts; clubhouse, showers.
Dock Master: Roy Smith.
Remarks: Access unlimited but depth of water in Bradwell Creek at LW Springs is 2-3 feet.
Customs: Tel: (0473) 219481.

TOLLESBURY SALTINGS LTD, Sail Lofts, Woodrolfe Road, Tollesbury, Maldon. Tel: (0621) 868624.
Berths: 100 jetty (drying) & mud berths.
Facilities: water; yacht/boat club; slipway; 3T crane.

TOLLESBURY MARINA, The Yacht Harbour, Tollesbury. Tel: (0621) 869202.
Call Sign: Ch.80 (M).
Berths: 240 pontoon.
Facilities: water; fuel, boatyard; chandlery; yacht/boat club; slipway; 16T crane.

DAN WEBB & FEESEY, North Street, Maldon, Essex CM9 7AN, and The Shipyard, Marine Parade, Maylandsea, Essex CM3 6AN.
Tel: (0621) 740264.
Berths: 100 Maldon, 400 Mayland. Max. draught 2m, LOA 18m.
Facilities: fuel (diesel); electricity; water; repairs; rigging service; slipway; cranage; chandlery; boat park; toilets.

HEYBRIDGE, Lock House, Lock Hill, Heybridge Basin, Maldon. Tel: (0621) 853506.
Berths: 200 quayside.
Facilities: water; chandlery; yacht/boat club.
Harbour Master: Capt. C. Edmonds.

HOLT & JAMES WOODEN BOATS LTD, The Boatyard, Heybridge Basin, Maldon, Essex CM9 7RS. Tel: (0621) 854022.
Berths: 45 (2 visitors). Max. draught 2m, LOA 18m.

FAIRWAYS MARINE ENGINEERS LTD, Bath Place Wharf, Downs Road, Maldon, Essex CM9 7HU. Tel: (0621) 852866/859424. Fax: (0621) 850902.
Open: Mon.-Fri. 0900-1300, 1400-1730. Sat. 0900-1300.
Berths: 18 mudberths alongside jetties.
Facilities: chandlery; slip; engineering.
Directors: B. J. Walker, A. J. Tassier, T. H. Partington.

MALDON COUNCIL, Princes Road, Maldon.
Tel: (0621) 854477.
Call Sign: Ch. 16.
Berths: 500 buoy & jetty (drying).
Facilities: fuel; boatyard; chandlery; yacht/boat club.
River Bailiff: W. Johns.

THE YACHT HARBOUR, Woodrolfe Boatyard, Tollesbury, Maldon, Essex CM9 8SE.
Tel: (0621) 869202/868471.
Call sign: Tollesbury Marina Ch. 80, 37 (M) during working hours when tide serves.
Open: Normal working hours. **Berths:** 240 (visitors welcome). Draught 2m, Max. LOA 15m.
Facilities: fuel (diesel); chandlery; provisions (near by); repair; cranage; storage; water; yacht club with showers and restaurant; Calor gas (Tavern Garage, The Cause).
Remarks: Entry: 1-2 hr.–HW–1-2 hr. There are four moorings marked 'WB' on which yachts may wait for the tide, in the S Channel.

CLARK & CARTER LTD, 110 Coast Road, West Mersea, Essex CO5 8NB.
Tel: (0206) 382244. Fax: (0206) 384455.
Call Sign: Ch. 80 (M).
Berths: 250.
Facilities: boatyard; yacht club; slipway.
Customs: Tel: (0473) 219481.

L. H. MORGAN & SONS (MARINE) LTD, 32-42 Waterside, Brightlingsea, Essex CO7 0AX.
Tel: (020 630) 2003.
Open: Seven days.
Call sign: Ch. 8.
Berths: 28 Group A, 24 Group B.
Facilities: water; repairs; rigging service; chandlery; shop; boat park; Calor gas.
Manager: Steve Morgan.
Remarks: Group A access 6 hr.–HW–6 hr., Group B 4 hr.–HW–4 hr.

BRIGHTLINGSEA HARBOUR, Harbour Office, Waterside, Brightlingsea, Essex CO7 0AX.
Tel: (020 630) 2200.
Berths: 223 (25 pontoon, 78 swinging, 120 pile) (30 berths for visitors).
Facilities: fuel (petrol and diesel); repairs; slipway; cranage; water (walking distance); chandlery; boat park; shop; restaurant; showers/toilets.
Harbour Master: I. H. MacGregor.

ST OSYTH YACHT HARBOUR, St Osyth, Essex. Tel: (0255) 820005.
Open: 24 hr. **Berths:** Berthing and hard standing available (20 visitors approx).
Facilities: electricity; repair; cranage (by previous arrangement); storage; slipway 50 tons; showers/toilets; shop; restaurant.
Remarks: Creek well marked.

TITCHMARSH MARINA, Coles Lane, Walton-on-Naze, Essex CO14 8SL. Tel: (0255) 672185.
Open: Normal hours. **Berths:** 420 (visitors available).
Facilities: fuel (diesel); chandlery; 10 ton travel hoist also 35 ton travel lift; cranage; storage; repairs; winter berthing; engineering; Calor gas (French Marine).
Harbour Master/Manager: V. D. Titchmarsh.
Customs: Tel: (0473) 219481.

PIN MILL, Jack Ward & Son, Pin Mill, Ipswich, Suffolk IP9 1JN. Tel: (0473) 84276.
Berths: 100 (swinging). 6 visitors, and others as available.
Facilities: fuel (petrol and diesel); repairs; cranage; chandlery; water; first aid; shop; restaurant; showers/toilets.
Manager: A. Ward.

SHOTLEY POINT MARINA, Shotley Gate, Ipswich, Suffolk IP9 1QJ. Tel: (0473) 788982.
Call sign: VHF Ch. 80, 37 (M).
Open: 24 hr.
Berths: 350 pontoon. Visitors welcome.
Facilities: diesel; electricity; water; cranage; car parking; boat repairs; choice of restaurants and bars; luxury washrooms; provisions; chandlery; yacht sales and yacht brokerage.
Remarks: Access all states of the tide.

WOOLVERSTONE MARINA, M.D.L. (Marinas) Ltd, Woolverstone, Ipswich, Suffolk IP9 1AS. (River Orwell). Tel: (0473) 780206/354.
Call sign: Ch. 80, 37 (M).
Open: 24 hr. **Berths:** 200 (visitors available). 150 swinging moorings. Draught 2.4m, Max. LOA 27m.
Facilities: fuel (diesel, petrol); electricity; gas; chandlery; provisions; off licence; repairs; engineers; mobile crane; launderette; toilets; showers; storage; brokerage; club; restaurant.
Harbour Master/Manager: Miss J. Cracknell.

FOX'S MARINA IPSWICH LTD, The Strand, Wherstead, Ipswich, Suffolk. Tel: (0473) 689111.
Open: 24 hr. **Berths:** 100 pontoon, 12 half tide.
Facilities: fuel (diesel); electricity; chandlery; provisions; repair; cranage (limit 26 tons); storage; brokerage; 26-ton Renner boat hoist; workshops; restaurant; Calor gas.
Manager: M. K. Westmoreland.
Remarks: Marina access all states of the tide, up to 6 ft.

NEPTUNE MARINA, Neptune Quay, The Dock, Ipswich, Suffolk, IP4 1AX. Tel: Main Office: (0473) 780366, Dockside: (0473) 215204.
Call sign: VHF Chan. 14, 80.
Berths: Pontoon berths. Max. LOA 21m.
Facilities: electricity; water; telephone; cranage; repairs; rigging; sailmaking; storage; yacht delivery; shopping; restaurants; brokerage.
Remarks: Entry through lockgates 1 hr.-HW to HW Ipswich. Call Neptune Marina Berthing on Ch. M.

D. DEBBAGE YACHTING SERVICES, The Quay, New Cut West, Ipswich IP2 8HN. Tel: (0473) 601169.
Open: Mon.-Fri. 0800-1630.
Berths: 35.

Weather Services — Section 18

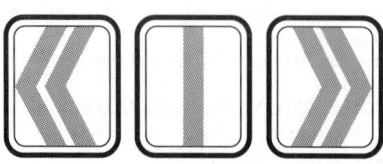

SHOTLEY POINT

Facilities

Harbour accessible at all times.
Channel dredged to 2m.
Locked entrance (30.30m X 9.09m)
available 24 hrs: 365 days.
Radar and VHF (Chs: 37;80) in
Control Tower; manned 24 hrs.
350 totally sheltered berths with
water and metered electricity;
30 ton travel lift; 10 ton crane; all
repairs; deisel.
Bar; restaurant; showers; shop;
chandlery; Yacht Club; car parks.
Transport to and from Continental
ferries at Harwich and Felixstowe.

THE FINEST WELCOME ON THE COAST

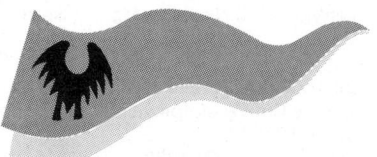

SHOTLEY POINT MARINA LIMITED

Shotley Gate, Ipswich, Suffolk IP9 1QJ
0473-788982

WHERRY QUAY, No. 1 Wherry Lane, Wherry Quay, Ipswich IP4 1LG. Tel: (0473) 230109. Fax: 232760.
Call sign: Ipswich Port Radio Ch. 14, 80, 37 (M).
Berths: visitors berths alongside quay in lock basin. Max. draught 6m, LOA 61m.
Facilities: water; electricity; all repairs; yacht club and bar; restaurant; laundry; showers/toilets; boat sales; tuition.
Remarks: Access 2 hr.-HW.

SUFFOLK YACHT HARBOUR, Stratton Hall, Levington, Ipswich (River Orwell) IP10 0LN. Tel: (0473) 659465.
Call sign: -SYH' – Ch. 80, 37 (M).
Open: 0800-1800.
Berths: 450 (visitors available).
Facilities: fuel (petrol, gas, oil); chandlery; provisions; repair; cranage; storage; brokerage; Calor gas.
Harbour Master: Jonathan J. Dyke.

FELIXSTOWE FERRY BOATYARD, Felixstowe, Suffolk. Tel: (0394) 282173.
Call sign: Deben Pilot. VHF listening on Ch. 8.
Open: 0800-1700. **Berths:** swinging moorings.
Facilities: fuel (diesel); electricity; chandlery; provisions; repairs (wood); cranage (limit 8 tons); storage 100 plus; Calor gas.
Harbour Master: C. Brinkley. Tel: 283469.
Customs: Tel: R/T (0473) 219481.

TIDE MILL YACHT HARBOUR, Woodbridge, Suffolk. Tel: (0394) 385745.
Open: 24 hr. **Berths:** 200 (30 visitors). Draught 2m, Max. LOA 16m.
Facilities: fuel (diesel); electricity; provisions; water; repair; cranage (15 ton); storage; brokerage; Slipway (20 ton); showers; barbecue.
Harbour Master: Richard Kember.
Remarks: Access over sill 3 hr.–HW–2 hr.
Customs: Tel: R/T (0473) 219481.

ROBERTSONS OF WOODBRIDGE (BOATBUILDERS) LTD, Lime Kiln Quay, Woodbridge, Suffolk IP12 1BD. Tel: (03943) 2305.
Berths: 100 (drying).
Facilities: gas; diesel; electricity; rigging service; slipway 70 tons; cranage; hoist 10 tons; chandlery; water; traditional boat building; repairs; swinging moorings; jetty berths; mud berths; showers/toilets.
Remarks: Access 3 hr.–HW–3 hr. depending on tide.

EVERSON AND SONS LTD, Phoenix Works, Riverside, Woodbridge, Suffolk IP12 1BD. Tel: (03943) 4358.
Open: 0830-1700.
Berths: 40. Dry at LW.
Facilities: boat builders; chandlers; engineers; Calor gas (Webb Bros. 30 Church Street).

WALDRINGFIELD BOATYARD LTD, The Quay, Waldringfield, Woodbridge, Suffolk IP12 4QZ. Tel: 047336 260.
Call sign: Ch. 80, 37 (M).
Open: 0800-2100 (summer).
Berths: 51 deepwater moorings, 25 half-tide.
Facilities: 40-ton crane; 60-ton slipway; Calor gas.
Harbour Master: R. B. Brown.

SLAUGHDEN QUAY, 32 Linden Road, Aldeburgh, Suffolk. Tel: (042885) 2896.
Berths: 100 swinging.
Facilities: petrol; diesel; repairs; rigging service; slipway; cranage; boat park; chandlery; first aid; shop; restaurant; water (within walking distance); showers/toilets; Calor gas (Aldenburgh Boatyard, Fort Green).
Contact: R. F. Upson.

SOUTHWOLD HARBOUR, Black Shore, Southwold, Suffolk. Tel: Office (0502) 724712.
Call sign: Southwold Port Radio (Ch. 16, 12).
Open: Harbour Office 0900-1730. **Berths:** 150 (20 visitors). Draught 2.2m+, LOA 15m.
Facilities: fuel; chandlery; provisions (nearby); repairs; cranage (10 tons); storage; Calor gas.
Pilot Service: (Ch. 12, 9).
Harbour Master: T. Chambers.

ROYAL NORFOLK AND SUFFOLK YACHT CLUB, Royal Plain, Lowestoft, Suffolk NR33 1AQ. Tel: (0502) 566726.
Open: Club 0730-2300. **Moorings:** 24 hr.
Berths: 80 (40 visitors).
Facilities: fuel; chandlery; repair; cranage (limit 2 tons). Clubhouse available to visiting yachts, showers, baths, meals, limited accommodation.
Secretary: Lt. Cdr. M. Dowsett.
Customs: Tel: R/T (0473) 219481.

LOWESTOFT CRUISING CLUB, 60 The Street, Lowestoft. Tel: (0502) 732348.
Berths: 60 pontoon.
Facilities: chandlery; yacht/boat club. Calor gas (Combined Gas Services, Norwich Road).

GREAT YARMOUTH HARBOUR, 20-21 South Quay, Great Yarmouth, Norfolk NR30 2RE. Tel: (0493) 855151. Fax: 852480. Telex: 975102 GYPORT G.
Open: 24 hr. **Berths:** 50 metres alongside at Town Hall Quay available for visitors.
Facilities: chandlery; provisions; repair; cranage (on request); fuel available on other quays; Calor gas.
Harbour Master: A. Goodlad.
Customs: Tel: R/T (0473) 219481.

BECCLES YACHT STATION, The Quay, Beccles, Suffolk NR34 9BH. Tel: (0502) 712225.
Berths: 109, 70 visitors. Max. draught 2m, LOA 16m.
Open: 1st April-31st Oct. 0900-1800.
Facilities: water; phone; refuse; provisions; WCs; launderette; crane; slip; others nearby; Calor gas (Hipperson, Gillingham Dam).

BURGH CASTLE MARINA, Nr. Great Yarmouth, Norfolk NR31 9PZ (River Waveney). Tel: (0493) 780331.
Open: 24 hr. **Berths:** 100 (10 visitors). Max. draught 1.5-2m, LOA 15-21m.
Facilities: fuel (diesel); electricity; chandlery; provisions; water; repair; cranage; storage; brokerage; slipway; hot showers; swimming pool; camping; pub; restaurant; D.I.Y. workshop for owners fittingout; Calor gas.
Harbour Master: Peter Oldman.
Remarks: Access to sea through Great Yarmouth Harbour (bridges will lift) at all states of tide.

BRUNDALL BAY MARINA, Riverside Estate, Brundall, Norwich. Tel: (0603) 716606. Fax: (0603) 716606.
Berths: 350, 25 visitors, max. draught 2m.
Open: 0800-1800.
Facilities: electricity; water; refuse; diesel; gas; chandlery; phone; launderette; restaurant; café; bar; sailing club & school; mail; all repairs; hoist; crane; lift; slip; sales & hire; scrubbing grid; gardiennage; security; lift-out; dry berths.

WELLS HARBOUR. Tel: (0328) 711744.
Call Sign: Ch. 16, 12.
Berths: 120 over 15ft, 70 under.
Facilities: fuel. boatyard; chandlery; yacht/boat club; slipway; 20T hoist.
Harbour Master: G. Walker.

STRATTON LONG MARINE, Westgate Street, Blakeney, Norfolk.
Tel: (0263) 740362 Blakeney Harbour Pilotage.
Open: 24 hr. **Berths:** usually available, some swinging.
Facilities: fuel; water; Calor gas and Gaz; chandlery; provisions; repairs (all types); cranage; storage; brokerage; slipway. Chandlery and marine facilities.
Contact: Stratton Long.
Remarks: Entry 3 hr.–HW–3 hr. Craft with draught up to 4 ft. can usually enter but more suitable if can take ground.

BRANCASTER HARBOUR, The Smithy, Brancaster Staithe, King's Lynn, PE31 8BJ. Tel: (0485) 210638.
Berths: 189 tidal moorings, 4 visitors, max. draught 1.2m, LOA 11m.
Facilities: electricity; water; phone; refuse; yacht club. Most others nearby; Calor gas (Links Garage).
Customs: Tel: (0473) 219481.

HARTFORD MARINA, Banks End, Wyton, Huntingdon. Tel: (0480) 454677/454678.
Berths: 200, for motor cruisers.
Facilities: water; electricity; gas; fuel; telephone; showers; toilets; slip; cranage; repairs; refuse disposal; yacht club; restaurant.
Remarks: The Marina is situated on the River Great Ouse.

BOSTON MARINA, 5 Witham Bank East, Boston. Tel: (0205) 64420.
Call Sign: Ch. 80 (M).
Berths: 50 jetty.
Facilities: fuel, chandlery; yacht/boat club.

ELY MARINA, (Loveys Marine), Waterside, Ely, Cambridgeshire CB7 4AU. Tel: (0353) 664622. On River Great Ouse–3 hrs. upstream Denver Lock.
Open: Normal hrs. **Berths:** visitors moorings available. Max. draught 1.4m, LOA 15m.
Facilities: fuel (petrol, diesel); gas; water; chandlery; provisions; repairs (all types); cranage (10 ton hoist); brokerage; slipway (day boats and small craft); antifouling; Interspray Centre; toilets & showers.

GRIMSBY MARINA LTD, Corporation Road, Grimsby, South Humberside.
Tel: (0472) 360404.
Call sign: Royal Dock (Ch. 18, 9.)
Open: 24 hr. **Berths:** 120 stern mooring to pontoon, 25 alongside. Max draught 3.7m, LOA 30.5m.
Entry is restricted to motor cruisers. Visiting yachts berth outside.

Facilities: fuel (diesel); electricity; chandlery; provisions (near by); repairs GRP/electronic/sails/engines/shafts/props. Shipwrights available; cranage (26.8 ton travel-lift/52 ft. LOA, 18 ft. beam); storage; brokerage; clubhouse; chandlers; Admiralty Charts; showers and phone.
Proprietor: G. D. Pinchbeck.
Remarks: Entrance 3½ hr.–HW–2½ hr.
Customs: Tel: (0472) 45441

HULL MARINA, Warehouse 13, Kingston Street, Hull HU1 2DQ. Tel: (0482) 25048.
Call sign: Hull Marina Ch. 80, 37 (M).
Open: 0800-2200 daily during B.S.T. 0800-1800 daily during G.M.T.
Berths: 290 (25 visitors on pontoons).
Facilities: water; electricity; fuel (gasoil and petrol); 50 ton hoist; pumpout facility; laundry services; customs clearance; bunkering facilities; WC's; showers. Hardstanding for 160 boats; repairs; chandlery; security; brokerage.
Marina Manager: Capt. R. B. Exley, RD, MNI.
Remarks: Access 3 hr.–HW–3 hr. (max. width 9m).
Customs: Tel: (0482) 796161.

SOUTH FERRIBY MARINA, Barton-on-Humber. Tel: (0652) 635620.
Call Sign: Ch. 80 (M).
Berths: 60 quayside.
Facilities: fuel; boatyard; chandlery; 10T crane.

NEWARK MARINA, 26 Farndon Road, Newark, Notts. Tel: (0636) 704022.
Open: 0900-1730 Tues. – Sat.1000-1700. Sun.
Berths: 75 (visitors generally available).
Facilities: chandlery; water; electricity; brokerage; repairs; gas.
Manager: Tom Mallett.

THE PARK YACHT CLUB, Park Marine Services, Trent Lane, Nottingham NG2 4DS. Tel: (0602) 506550. Fax: (0602) 506668.
Call Sign: Park Marine. Ch. 80, 37 (M).
Berths: 50 (some visitors). Max. draught 1.5m, LOA 16m.
Facilities: water; diesel; gas, chandlery; phone; restaurant; bar; mail; all repairs; slip; sales; security.

SAWLEY BRIDGE MARINA, Long Eaton, Nottingham NG10 3AE. Tel: (0602) 734278.
Call sign: High Water.
Open: 1000-1800 daily. **Berths:** 100 visitors
Facilities: fuel (petrol, gas, oil); electricity (on meter); chandlery; some provisions; water; repairs; cranage; storage; slipway; restaurant.
Harbour Master: Derrick Davison.

SHARDLOW MARINA, London Road, Shardlow, Derbyshire DE7 2HJ. Tel: (0332) 792832.
Berths: 350 (visitors 10). Max. draught 1.5m, LOA 18m.
Open: 0900-1700.
Facilities: electricity; water; phone; refuse; diesel; gas; chandlery; WCs; showers; mail; repairs; crane; slip; sales; car hire; scrubbing grid; security; lift-out; dry berths.

BRIDLINGTON HARBOUR, Harbour Office, North Pier, Bridlington YO16 4SJ.
Tel: (0262) 670148.
Call Sign: Ch. 16, 12.
Berths: 140.
Facilities: chandlery; water; yacht/boat club; slipway; 7T crane.
Harbour Master: P.H. Thornton.

SCARBOROUGH HARBOUR, 18 West Pier, Scarborough, North Yorkshire YO11 1PD.
Tel: (0723) 373530 (office hours); 360684 (other times).
Call sign: Ch. 16, 12.
Berths: 200 (10 visitors).
Facilities: fuel (petrol and diesel); repairs; slipway; cranage; restaurant; chandlery; shop; Calor gas (Appletons, 37 Columbus Ravine).
Customs: Tel: (0947) 602074.

WHITBY HARBOUR, Pier Road, Whitby.
Tel: (0947) 602354.
Call sign: Ch. 16, 11, 12.
Open: 0830-1700.
Berths: 260 pontoon, pile & buoy.
Facilities: fuel (diesel, petrol); water; gas; provisions (nearby); repair; cranage; storage; Calor gas (Collier & Son, New Quay Road).
Harbour Master: Capt. G. Cook. Tel: (0947) 602354.
Remarks: Access to upper harbour via swing bridge 2 hr.–HW–2 hr.
Customs: Tel: (0947) 602074

HARTLEPOOL YACHT HAVEN, Lock Office, Slake Terrace, Hartlepool, TS24 0RU.
Tel: (0429) 865744. Fax: (0429) 865947.
Call Sign: "Yacht Haven", Ch. 80 (M).
Remarks: Lock operates 4h-HW-4h. Channel dredged to –0.8 C.D. Lock signals: 2 R.Lts = closed. 1 R.Lt = in use, await instructions. 1 G.Lt = enter. 1 R./1 G.Lt. = free flow operating –proceed as directed.

HARTLEPOOL HARBOUR, Tees & Hartlepool Port Authority, Middleton Road, Hartlepool, Cleveland TS24 0SE. Tel: (0429) 266127. Fax: (0429) 222291. Tx: 58669 PORTHL G.
Call sign: Ch. 16, 12.

Open: 24 hr. **Berths:** limited in outer harbour, 400 available in Jackson and Coal Docks.
Facilities: fuel (diesel); gas; water; provisions (near by); repair; cranage; storage; Calor gas (Cairns, Andrew Street).
Harbour Master: Capt. A. Kirk.
Remarks: Inner Docks open 1 hr.–HW–1 hr., via N Basin and Central Dock.
Customs: Tel: (0429) 861390.

ST. PETERS MARINA, St. Peters Basin, Bottle House St., Newcastle upon Tyne. Tel: 091 265 4472.
Call Sign: Ch. 80 (M).
Berths: 140 pontoon.
Facilities: fuel; boatyard; chandlery; yacht/boat club.

FRIARS GOOSE WATER SPORTS CLUB, Green Lane, Riverside Park, Gateshead, Tyne & Wear NE10 0QH. Tel: (091) 4692545.
Berths: usually available.
Facilities: club house (except Sunday nights).
Contact: Steward during licensed hours.
Remarks: Accessible all times via pontoon. Eight miles upriver from harbour bar; Calor gas (Chambers, Hadrian Road.)
Customs: Tel: (091) 5657113.

HEBBURN MARINA, Prince Consort Rd, Hebburn. Tel: (091) 4835745.
Berths: 56 buoy.
Facilities: slipway; 8T crane.

ROYAL NORTHUMBERLAND YACHT CLUB (or BLYTH HARBOUR COMMISSION), South Harbour, Blyth, Northumberland.
Tel: (RNYC) 0670 353636,
(BHC) 0670 352678.
Call sign: Blyth Harbour Radio.
Open: Normal Hours. Closed Mon./Tues. Sep 30 to June 1.
Berths: 60 fore/aft moorings, 6 half tide cradles, jetty standings (limited visitors).
Facilities: fuel (diesel); chandlery; provisions (nearby); water; repairs; cranage; storage; bar; slipway and beaching; gas; toilets; showers; Calor gas (Davidson, 14 King Street).
Berthing Masters: (RNYC) D. T. Coussons.
Customs: Tel: Blyth (0670) 361521 Mon-Fri. N. Shields (091) 2579441.

BRAID MARINA – Camper & Nicholsons Marinas Ltd., The Braid, Amble, Morpeth, Northumberland NE65 0YP. Tel: (0665) 712168.
Call sign: Amble Marina Ch. 80, 37 (M).
Open: 24 hr. 365 days per year with security controlled access. **Berths:** 240, up to 80 ft. LOA: 8 ft 6 in. draught. Visitors berths available.
Facilities: showers/toilets; disabled toilets; launderette; telephone; fresh water and electricity on pontoons; fuel; chandlery; repairs; storage; Calor gas (Holborn, East Ord); lay up facilities; new yacht sales; brokerage; security controlled access.
Marina Manager: Simon Haigh.
Remarks: Access via sill 4 hr.–HW–4 hr.
Customs: Tel: (091) 5657113.

Scotland

COCKENZIE SLIP & BOATYARD, West Harbour, Cockenzie. Tel: (0875) 812150.
Berths: 6 moorings on chains, 4 alongside.

PORT EDGAR, South Queensferry, West Lothian, Scotland (Under Forth Road Bridge). Tel: (031) 331 3330.
Call sign: Port Edgar Ch. 80, 37 (M) – Apr.-Sept. 0900-1900. Oct.-Mar. 0900-1630).

Open: 0830-2200; Office: 0900-1215 & 1330-1930 Apr.-Aug.; 0900-1215 & 1330-1630 Sep.-Mar.; Sat. & Sun. 0900-1215 & 1330-1630 throughout the year.
Berths: 266 pontoon, 10 drying moorings, 24 all tides moorings (visitors available).
Facilities: fuel (diesel); electricity; chandlery; water; gas; repairs; cranage (limit 5 tons); storage; brokerage; boat hire; slip; caféteria; shops nearby; showers; Calor gas (Bosuns Locker, Port Edgar Marina).
Harbour Master: Garth Ridgers, MBE.
Customs: (0383) 4124475.

PORT O'LEITH MOTOR BOAT CLUB, 12 Pier Place, Newhaven, Edinburgh. Tel: 031 552 9577.
Berths: 25 quayside (drying).
Facilities: Yacht/boat yard; slipway.

FORTH YACHT MARINA, North Queensferry, Fife KY11 1HW. Tel: (0383) 416101/413700.
Open: Normal hours. **Berths:** 100 swinging moorings (visitors available).
Facilities: fuel (diesel); gas (near); water; provisions (nearby shops); repairs; cranage (15T); storage; slipway.
Remarks: Access 4 hr.–HW–4 hr.

ROYAL FORTH YACHT CLUB, Middle Pier, Granton, Edinburgh. Tel: 031 552 8560.
Berths: 120 buoy & pontoon for visitors.
Facilities: fuel; boatyard; chandlery; yacht/boat yard; slipway; 5T crane.

JOHNSHAVEN HARBOUR, Kincardineshire. Tel: (0224) 898287 (0800-1600).
Berths: On quays: 2 basins.
Facilities: fresh water; slipway; provisions in town.
Harbour Master: Richard McBay.
Remarks: Sheltered inner basin harbour dries out at LW, check with H.M. re: access. The very narrow entrance through a rocky foreshore can be difficult in winds from between NE and SE.

FORTH CORINTHIAN YACHT CLUB, 1, Granton Square, Granton, Edinburgh. Tel: 031 552 5939.
Berths: 45 buoy (drying).
Facilities: fuel; boatyard; chandlery, yacht/boat club; slipway.

GOURDON HARBOUR, by Montrose DD10 0LG. Tel: (0561) 61779 (Home).
Berths: Gutty Harbour (Main harbour is for fishing boats),.
Facilities: water, electricity, fuel, repairs and provisions (nearby).
Harbour Master: James Brown.

Remarks: There are protective storm gates. Both harbours dry out at low tide. Entrance to Gutty Harbour is rocky and can be difficult to navigate. Consult the H.M. re: arrival and access.
Customs: Tel: (0674) 74444.

ROYAL TAY YACHT CLUB, 34 Dundee Rd, Broughty Ferry, Dundee. Tel: (0382) 77516.
Call Sign: Ch. 80 (M).
Berths: 75 buoy.
Facilities: boatyard; yacht/boat club; slipway.

STONEHAVEN, Kincardineshire.
Tel: (0569) 62741.
Berths: On the quays. Also additional mooring chains in inner harbour.
Facilities: electricity, water, slipway, 1.5 ton crane for heavy weather booms only; sports and town nearby.
Harbour Master: Capt. John Lobban.
Remarks: In certain storm conditions only the inner basin is suitable for berthing and priority is given to local fishing boats. Both inner and outer basins dry out at LW but the cofferdam basin, an open area protected by the breakwater, has a depth of 1 m at MLWS.
Customs: Tel: (0224) 586258.

ROSEHEARTY, Aberdeenshire.
Tel: (03467) 292 (Home).
Berths: At quayside inside harbour. Also on outer breakwater in fairweather (short stay).
Harbour Master: Ian Downie.
Remarks: Harbour dries out at LW restricting access. The breakwater (though exposed to winds from between E and NE) can be used at all states of the tide. The harbour should not be approached in onshore winds. The adjacent port Rae should not be entered without local knowledge because of unmarked rocks.

PETERHEAD HARBOUR, West Pier, Peterhead, Aberdeenshire. Tel: (0779) 74281. Fax: 70741.
Telex: 73749 PBMCG.
Call sign: Ch. 16, 14.
Berths: Limited.
Facilities: water; fuel; chandlery; provisions; ice; sea fishing; repairs; 20T crane; car hire; Calor gas (Murisons, 28 Marischal Street).
Customs: Tel: (0779) 74867.

BANFF HARBOUR, 14 Scotstown, Banffshire, AB4 1LA.
Tel: (02612) 5093 (home).
Berths: 50. Alongside jetties. Max. draught 1.5m, LOA 11m.
Facilities: Fresh water at quays, fishing and sports complex; many facilities in town.
Harbour Master: Alasdair Galloway.

Remarks: The harbour is badly affected by sand. Channels have been dredged along some of the quays but even so passage by vessels is not possible at low tide. Visitors should check beforehand with H.M. as to accessibility. Dries at LWS.
Customs: Tel: (0346) 28033.

PORTSOY HARBOUR, Banffshire.
Tel: (02612) 5093 (Home).
Berths: 20. In the harbours. Max. draught 1.5m, LOA 8.5m.
Harbour Master: Alasdair Galloway.
Remarks: The new harbour is considerably larger but dries out. The old harbour is protected by a headland and the N Pier. No access to the sea at LW. Consult H.M.

CULLEN HARBOUR, Banffshire.
Tel: (0542) 41116 (Home).
Berths: On quays in inner basin.
Harbour Master: Henry Runcie.
Remarks: Harbour dries out at low tide. Accessible only about 4 hr.–HW–4 hr. for boats with draught of ¾ feet. Care needed in N to W winds.

PORTKNOCKIE, Banffshire, AB5 2LS.
Tel: (0542) 40705 (Home).
Berths: Two basins provide quayside mooring. Accessible all states of tide.
Facilities: Fresh water, electricity, slipway, provisions in town; toilets; children's pool.
Harbour Master: William Wilson.
Customs: Tel: (0261) 32217.

FINDOCHTY HARBOUR, Banffshire.
Tel: (0542) 40705 (Home).
Berths: 40 moorings on the quays in inner basin. There is a floating pontoon for deep-keel boats to 90 ft.
Facilities: water sports club; electricity; water; town nearby; camping.
Harbour Master: William Wilson.
Remarks: Dries out at low tide. Check with H.M. re: arrival times. Access 4 hr.–HW–4 hr.
Customs: Tel: (0542) 32254.

HOPEMAN HARBOUR, Morayshire.
Tel: (0343) 830650 (Home).
Berths: At quayside in Inner Basin only. Mooring chains are also fitted. Draught 1.5-2.7m.
Facilities: fresh water at quays; slipway; winch; provisions (nearby).
Harbour Master: Mrs Jean Amos.
Remarks: Entrance channel has 3.4m. water depth at HWS, but harbour dries out at LW. Check with H.M. re: arrival and access.
Customs: Tel: (0343) 7518.

FINDHORN, The Boatyard, Findhorn, Moray IV36 0YE. Tel: (0309) 30099.
Berths: visitors deep water moorings.
Facilities: fuel; repairs; chandlery; slipway; hoist (12T); yacht/boat club.
Access: 2 hr.–HW–2 hr.

NAIRN HARBOUR, Rhudal, Marine Road, IV12 4EA. Tel: (0667) 54704.
Berths: 80, 3 visitors, max. draught 2m, LOA 12m. Tidal 2 hr.–HW–2 hr.
Facilities: electricity; water; phone; refuse; fuel; gas; mail; provisions; WCs; showers; launderette; restaurant; bar; yacht club; sea fishing; minor repairs; slip; boat & car hire; scrubbing grid.

MUIRTOWN MARINA (INVERNESS) LTD, Muirtown Wharf, Caledonian Canal, Inverness IV3 5LS. Tel: (0463) 239745
Open: Normal hours. **Berths:** 25. Max. draught 4.6m.
Facilities: fuel (diesel); water; repair; cranage; storage; showers; toilets; electricity; Calor.
Remarks: At eastern end of Caledonian Canal. Entry via sea lock 4 hr.–HW–4 hr.
Berthing Master: R. J. Chisholm.

CALEY MARINA, Canal Road, Muirtown, Inverness IV3 6NF. Tel: (0463) 236539. Fax: (0463) 238323.
Open: 0830-1730 (Mon.-Sat.).
Berths: 50 pontoon (20 visitors available to order). Max. draught 3.7m.
Facilities: fuel (diesel); electricity; chandlery; provisions (nearby); water; repairs; cranage; storage; brokerage; slipway; gas nearby; showers; workshop; Calor gas (Black Park Filling Station, Clacknaharry).
Berthing Master: Tony Daly.
Remarks: At eastern end of Caledonian Canal. Max. draught 4m above Muirtown Locks. Access via sea lock 4 hr.–HW–4 hr.

LERWICK HARBOUR, Small Dock, Albert Buildings, Shetland Isles, ZE1 0LL. Tel: (0595) 3462. Fax: 5911. Telex: 75496.
Call sign: Lerwick Port Control, Ch. 16, 12.
Berths: 12 alongside quay, yachts tie up. Max. draught 6m.
Facilities: fuel; Calor gas (Rearo, Commercial Road); chandlery; provisions; ice; phone; WCs; showers; restaurant; café; bar; yacht club; sea fishing; mail; all repairs; 19T crane; slip; car hire.
Customs: Tel: (0595) 2835.

SLEAT MARINE SERVICES, Ardvasar, Isle of Skye IV45 8RU. Tel: 047 14 216.
Call sign: Sleat Marine Ch. 16.
Moorings: 8. Max. draught 3m, LOA 14m.
Facilities: diesel; water; some chandlery and repairs; slip for keel boats to 10 tons.
Remarks: Access by ferry pier Armadale Bay, by ferry from Mallaig, by road via Kyle of Lochalsh ferry.
Proprietor: John Mannall.

ARISAIG MARINE, Arisaig Harbour, Invernessshire PH39.
Tel: (068 75) 224 (day), 678 (night).
Call sign: Arisaig Harbour (Ch. 16).
Open: As required. **Berths:** 18 moorings (visitors 10).
Facilities: fuel (diesel, petrol); gas; water; electricity; chandlery; provisions; repair; cranage (limit 10 tons); winter storage; brokerage; slipway (to 25 m.); hotels; restaurants; shops; post office; railway station.
Harbour Master: Murdo M. Grant.
Remarks: Large sheltered anchorage with clearly marked entrance. Excellent base for Cruising Inner and Outer Hebrides.

BRITISH WATERWAYS BOARD, Corpach, Fort William. Tel: (03977) 249.
Call sign: Corpach Dock, Ch. 16, 74.
Open: 0800-1200; 1300-1630 Mon.-Sat.
Berths: Draft 4m (fresh water), LOA 62m.
Facilities: fuel (diesel, petrol, gas) by arrangement; provisions (near by) Calor gas (Macrae & Dick Ltd, Gordon Square).
Remarks: At western end of Caledonian Canal. Entry via sea lock 4 hr.-HWS-4 hr. Neaps: no tide restrictions.
Customs: Tel: (0397) 2948.

CRERAN MOORINGS, Barcaldine, Oban, Argyll PA37 1SG. Tel: (0631) 72265.
Open: April to end October.
Berths: Limited heavy swinging moorings. Max. LOA 12m.
Facilities: slipway; car/trailer park; camping; caravans; water; toilet; showers; snack bar.

AQUALINK, Gallanach Boatyard, Gallanach Rd, Gallanach, Oban. Tel: (0631) 66844.
Call Sign: Ch. 80 (M).
Berths: 18 buoy (max. 30ft).
Facilities: water; fuel; boatyard, chandlery, slipway; 10T crane.

DUNSTAFFNAGE YACHT HAVEN LTD, Oban, Argyll PA37 1PX. Tel: (0631) 66555, 65630.
Berths: 70.
Facilities: charter; school; workshop; stores; restaurant; pub; equipment hire; car park.
Harbour Master: Mr. T. I. McCall.
Calor gas (West Highland Gas Services, Soroba Road).

OBAN YACHT SERVICES LTD, Kerrera, Oban, Argyll PA34 4SX. Tel: (0631) 63666. Fax: (0631) 66593.
Call sign: Dirk (Ch. 16).
Berths: 10 visitors, swinging moorings, all draughts, all tides. Max. LOA 20m.
Facilities: fuel; gas; water; slipping; repairs; undercover storage.
Harbour Master: Douglas Craig.
Customs: Tel: (0631) 63079.

CLACHAN SEIL MARINE SERVICES, Strathnaver, Clachan Seil, Oban. Tel: 08523 444. **Berths:** 10 buoy.

ARDORAN MARINE, Lerags, Oban, Argyll PA34 4SE. Tel: (0631) 66123. Fax: (0631) 66611.
Call sign: Ch. 80, 37 (M).
Berths: 20 swinging moorings, pontoons for access to diesel and water.
Facilities: diesel; water; engine repairs; slip; crane; toilets; showers.
Remarks: Buoyed channel to Loch Feochan, access 2 hr.–HW–2 hr.
Harbour Master: Bill and Anne Robertson.

SCOTPORT (FAIRHURST & RAYMOND LTD) Balvicar, Seil, by Oban. Tel. (08523) 411/467.
Call sign: Ch. 80, 37 (M).
Berths: 30 (4 visitors).
Facilities: fuel; water; provisions; repairs; slipway; lift; chandlery; gas; security; toilets.

KILMELFORD YACHT HAVEN, Kilmelford by Oban, Argyll PA34 4XD. Tel: (08522) 248 and 279. Fax: (08522) 343.
Open: Mon.-Sat. 0830-1700. Sun. in season.
Berths: 50 swinging moorings to 50′ LOA– plus pier and pontoons and drying out grid.
Facilities: fuel (diesel); chandlery; provisions (nearby); water; cranage; storage up to 12′ beam, 12T; brokerage; slipway; gas; hotels and restaurants locally; workshop; all repairs.
Harbour Master: Nevin Blackwood.

MELFORT MARITIME, Fearnach Bay, Loch Melfort, Argyll.
Tel: (08522) 333. Fax: (08522) 329.
Berths: 35 moorings, 6 on pontoon (visitors available). Draught 3m, LOA 23m.
Facilities: Fuel; water, electricity, repairs, slipway, crane, WC, provisions; dry dock; showers; phone; storage; launderette.

CAMUS MARINE SERVICES AND CRAOBH HAVEN, Craignish, by Lochgilphead, Argyll PA31 8UD. Tel: (08525) 622/222. Telex: 799828 CAMUS G.
Call sign: Craobh Haven Marina, Ch. 16, 80, 37 (M).
Open: Mon.-Sat. 0830-1700, Sun. in season.
Berths: 200 serviced up to 24m LOA.
Facilities: fuel (diesel); water; electricity; WCs; showers; launderette; bar; boat sales; chandlery; provisions nearby; cranage; storage; slipway; hoist; Calor gas; hotels and restaurants nearby; brokerage; boatyard.
Manager: David Wilkinson.
Customs: (0631) 63079.

ARDFERN YACHT CENTRE, Loch Craignish,by Lochgilphead, Argyll PA31 8QN. Tel: (08525) 247/636. Fax: (08525) 624.
Berths: 70 moorings (visitors available). 400m of pontoons.
Facilities: fuel; water; electricity; provisions; repairs; slipway; lift; chandlery; gas; toilets; showers; brokerage; storage; engineering; hotel and launderette locally.
General Manager: D. M. Wilkie.

COLONSAY YACHT CLUB, The Hotel, Isle of Colonsay, Argyll PA61 7YP. Tel: (09512) 316. Fax: (09512) 353.
Berths: NW corner of pier (check for availability).
Facilities: All usual hotel services, battery charging, diesel, some gas, provisions nearby.
Remarks: S side pier kept clear for Ro-Ro. NW corner is drying harbour. No visitors at harbour wall.
Harbour Master: Finlay MacFadyen. Tel: (09512) 333.

CRINAN BOATS LTD, Crinan Harbour, Argyll, Scotland PA31 8SP. Tel: (0546 83) 232. Fax: (0546 83) 281.
Open: 0800-1800 in season.
Berths: 60 swinging moorings, replenishment pontoon at boatyard. Draught 2.4-3.7m, LOA 20m.
Facilities: fuel; chandlery; provisions; repair; water; engineering; showers; slipway (limit 20m, 60 tons); maintenance; laundry; chandlery; Calor gas.

TARBERT HARBOUR, Tarbert, Loch Fyne, Argyll PA29 6UQ. Tel: (0880) 820344.
Open: Normal working hours. **Berths:** 50 pontoon (visitors available). Max. draught 4.6m, LOA 14m.
Call sign: Ch. 16 (0900-1700).
Facilities: fuel (diesel, petrol, gas); repair; drying out berths; hotel; sailmaker; engineer; all town facilities nearby.
Customs: Tel: (0586) 52261.

MARA MARINE LTD, Tighnabruaich.
Tel: (0700) 811213.
Berths: 25 buoy.
Facilities: boatyard; slipway; 12T hoist.

LARGS YACHT HAVEN, Irvine Road, Largs, Ayrshire KA30 8EZ. Tel: (0475) 675333. Fax: (0475) 672245. Tx: 777672.
Call sign: Ch. 80, 37 (M).
Berths: 1550 (visitors available).
Facilities: fuel (diesel and petrol); water; electricity; repairs; 45-ton hoist; gas; brokerage; chandlery; toilets; showers. Sailing instruction; hard standing; yacht charterers; telephone; laundry; pub; shop; diving air compressor.
Contact: Carolyn Elder.

ROTHESAY HARBOUR, Rothesay, Bute PA20 9AQ.
Call sign: Ch. 16, 12.
Open: Normal working hours.
Berths: 50 alongside (visitors available). Some alongside berths dry out.
Facilities: fuel (diesel, petrol, gas); provisions (near by).
Harbour Master: Capt. A. Graham.

KIP MARINA HOLT LEISURE PARKS LTD, Inverkip, Renfrewshire, Scotland.
Tel: (0475) 521485. Fax: (0475) 521298.
Telex: 777582 Attn: KIP MARINA.
Call sign: Ch. 80, 37(M).
Open: 24 hr. **Berths:** 720 (visitors 40). All berths are walk on, sail at any state of the tide.
Facilities: fuel; electricity; water; chandlery; provisions; repairs; cranage 40 ton travel hoist; storage; brokerage; restaurant; bar; superloos and saunas; Calor gas.
Marina Master: Ian Smart.
Customs: Tel: Greenock (0475) 28311.

RHU MARINA, Rhu, Helensburgh, Dunbarton G84 8LH. Tel: (0436) 820238/820652.
Fax: (0436) 821 039.
Call sign: Ch. 80, 37 (M).
Open: Summer 0900-1800. Winter 1000-1700.
Berths: 120 pontoon, 50 swinging.
Facilities: fuel (diesel, gas); electricity by arrangement; water; chandlery; provisions (shops near by); repair; cranage; storage.

SILVERS MARINE, Silverhills, Rosneath, Helensburgh. Tel: (0436) 831222.
Call Sign: Ch. 80 (M).
Berths: 20 buoy.
Facilities: boatyard; chandlery; slipway; 18T hoist.

McGRUER & CO LTD, Rosneath, Helensburgh, Dunbartonshire, Scotland W84 0QL.
Tel: (0436) 831313.
Open: Normal working hours. **Berths:** 40 swinging. (Visitors available).
Facilities: provisions (near by); repair; cranage (25 ton hoist); 200 ft. slipway; Calor gas (United British Caravans).
Yacht Service Manager: S. Bates.

LOCH LOMOND MARINA, Balloch, Alexandria, Dunbartonshire. Tel: (0389) 52069.
Open: Summer 0930-2000. Winter 0930-1700.
Berths: 65. (visitors welcome).
Facilities: chandlery; repair; cranage; storage.
Harbour Master: Simon Kitchen.
Remarks: Max. draught in marina 1.2m due to channel in river.

DUNBARTON MARINA, Sandpoint, Woodyard Road, Dumbarton G82 4BG. Tel: (0389) 62396/31500. Fax: (0389) 32605.
Call sign: Ch. 80, 37 (M);
Berths: 200 winter storage.
Facilities: repairs; brokerage; crane 10 tons; chandlery; fuel (diesel); gas; engineering.
Harbour Master: George C. Hulley.

MODERN CHARTERS LTD, Victoria Place, Shore Road, Clynder, Dunbartonshire G84 0QD Tel: (0436) 831312.
Berths: 25 swinging moorings.
Facilities: fuel; water; gas; chandlery; fishing tackle; yacht charter/hire; public launching slip; post office and general store.
Harbour Master: Daniel Da Prato.

TROON MARINA, The Harbour, Troon, Strathclyde KA10 6DJ. Tel: (0292) 315553. Fax: (0292) 317294.
Call sign: Ch. 80, 37 (M).
Open: 24 hr. **Berths:** 340. All berths are walk on, sail at any state of the tide.
Facilities: fuel (diesel); electricity; water; chandlery; provisions; repairs; bar; restaurant, saunas, launderette; cranage (12 tons); storage; brokerage; slipway; boat park; first aid; toilets; showers.
Marina Manager: W. A. McCann.
Customs: Tel: (0292) 262088.

URR NAVIGATION TRUST, 52 High Street, Dalbeattie. Tel: (0556) 62249.
Berths: 150 buoy (drying).
Facilities: boatyard; chandlery, yacht/boat club; slipway.

ISLE OF WHITHORN HARBOUR, Dumfries DG1 2DD. Tel: (09885) 246.
Berths: 85 (20 visitors).
Facilities: fuel (petrol, diesel, oil); water; electricity; provisions; slipway; chandlery; gas; yacht club; telephone; toilets; showers; restaurant.
Remarks: Access 3 hr.–HW–3 hr.
Harbour Master: Mr. McWilliam.
Customs: Tel: (0671) 2718.

ROBERT HOUSTON, 13 North Crescent, Garlieston. Tel: (09886) 259.
Berths: 40 buoy (drying).

KIPPFORD, Kippford by Dalbeattie, Kirkcudbrightshire.
Open: Normal working hours. **Berths:** 300 drying moorings (some visitors available).
Facilities: fuel (diesel, petrol); chandlery; provisions (near by); repair; storage
Remarks: Access 2½ hr.–HW–2½ hr.

KIRKCUDBRIGHT, Harbour Office, Kirkcudbright. Tel: (0557) 31135.
Call Sign: Ch. 16, 12
Berths: 40 buoy (drying); 1 visitors buoy 2m LAT.
Facilities: boatyard, chandlery; yacht/boat yard; slipway
Harbour Master: Bill Morgan.

Isle of Man

PEEL HARBOUR, Harbour House, Crown Street, Peel. Tel: (0624) 842338.
Call sign: Peel Harbour, Ch. 16, 12.
Open: 0830-1630.
Berths: some 24 hr. at breakwater, inner harbour (2 visitors June-Sept.).
Facilities: fuel; stores; some repairs nearby; bar and showers at SC; Calor gas (Mill Road).
Remarks: Inner harbour dries out 3 hr.–LW–3 hr.
Harbour Master: Capt. C. A. Clague.

PORT ST MARY HARBOUR, Harbourmaster's House, Port St Mary. Tel: (0624) 833206.
Call sign: Port St Mary Harbour, Ch. 16, 12.
Berths: Inner Harbour (dries out), moorings, outer pier.
Facilities: diesel; water; slipways; cranes; engineer.
Remarks: Access to inner harbour 3 hr.–HW–3 hr. No mooring between piers.
Harbour Master: Capt. A. D. McKaig.

CASTLETOWN HARBOUR, Harbour Office, The Quay. Tel: (0624) 823549.
Call sign: Ch. 16, 12. **Open:** 3 hr.–HW–3 hr.
Berths: 20 (20 visitors), all drying. Max. draught 3m, LOA 15m.
Facilities: electricity; water; refuse; mail; sea fishing; 15T crane; 3 slips; car hire. Nearby–fuel; gas; provisions; phone; WCs; showers; launderette; restaurant.

DOUGLAS HARBOUR, Dept. Highways Ports & Properties, Harbours Division, Sea Terminal Building, Douglas. Tel: (0624) 23813. Fax: (0624) 27238. Tx: 629335 IOMHAR G.
Call sign: Douglas Harbour, Ch. 16, 12.
Berths: passenger/cargo/Ro-Ro, tankers, plus limited berthing for fishing vessels and pleasure craft in outer harbour.
Facilities: fuel (normal hours); water; chandlery; SC: showers available S Quay (Trafalgar House); Calor gas (J.R. Riley Ltd, 2 Quines Corner).
Remarks: inner harbour dries out. Bridge to it manned half flood to half ebb.
Harbour Master: Capt. D. M. Cowell.
Customs: Tel: (0624) 74321.

RAMSEY HARBOUR, Dept. Highways Ports & Properties, Harbour Office, East Quay, Ramsey. Tel: (0624) 812245.
Call sign: Ramsey Harbour, Ch. 16, 12.
Open: 0900-1600 and at tides when commercial vessels expected.
Berths: visitors at W Quay (immediately seaward of swing bridge).
Facilities: fuel; water; electricity; repairs; Calor gas (North Shore Road).
Remarks: Access 2 hr.–HW–2 hr.
Harbour Master: Capt. Michael Brew.

West Coast

NORSAIL LTD, Maryport Harbour, Maryport. Tel: (0900) 813331.
Call Sign: Ch. 80 (M).
Berths: 240 pontoon.
Facilities: fuel, boatyard, chandlery, yacht/boat club; slipway; 50T crane.

WHITEHAVEN HARBOUR, Whitehaven, Cumbria. Tel: (0946) 2435.
Open: Normal working hours. **Berths:** 70 fore and aft drying moorings (visitors available). Max. draught 1.5m, LOA 9m.
Facilities: fuel (diesel, petrol, gas); provisions (near by); storage.
Harbour Master: Capt. B. Ashbridge.
Remarks: Access 2½-3 hr.–HW–2½-3 hr.
Customs: Tel: (0900) 604611.

WALNEY CHANNEL. No Authority–all moorings laid by owners.
Berths: 300-400 buoy (most drying).
Facilities: boatyard; yacht/boat club; slipway; 13T crane.

GLASSON BASIN YACHT CO, Glasson Dock, Lancashire LA2 0AW. Tel: (0524) 751491.
Open: 7 days a week. Normal working hours.
Berths: 200 alongside and pontoon (visitors available).
Facilities: fuel (diesel); provisions; repair; chandlery; electricity; water; cranage; storage; boat park; slipway; brokerage; Calor gas.
Remarks: Access to locked basin –1 hr. to HW.
Customs: Tel: R/T (0524) 51013.

RIVER WYRE, Tel: (0253) 810797.
Berths: 85 buoy (some drying).
Facilities: yacht/boat club; slipway.
Harbour Master: Ted Boyd.

FLEETWOOD HARBOUR VILLAGE, Associated British Ports, Wyre Dock, Fleetwood, Lancashire FY7 6PP. Tel: (0253) 872323. Fax: (03917) 77549. Telex: 677296.
Call sign: Fleetwood Docks (Ch. 16, 12).
Open: 2 hr.–HW–2 hr. (winter), 3 hr.–HW–3 hr. (summer, weekends).
Berths: 74, 14 visitors. Max. draught 5m, LOA 12m.
Facilities: electricity; water; phone; refuse at berth; diesel; gas; chandlery; showers/WCs; launderette; most repairs; 10T crane; slip; security; lift-out; dry berths.
Contact: N. Pounder, Manager.

WARDLEYS MARINE, Wardleys Creek, Kiln Lane, Hambleton, Blackpool, Lancs. FY6 9DX. Tel: (0253) 700117.
Call sign: Ch. 16, 8.
Berths: 50 (some visitors). Dries out.
Facilities: water; electricity; slipway; chandlery; yacht club; toilets; car park; winter storage.
Access: Two miles S of Fleetwood on R. Wyre, access 2 hr.–HW–2 hr.
Harbour Masters: Mike and Anne Snowdon.

Telephone: 051-236 2776   Fax: 051-236 4577   Telex: 627424 DUBOIS G

DUBOIS PHILLIPS & McCALLUM LTD

ADMIRALTY CHART AGENTS

CHART CORRECTION SERVICE

NAUTICAL & TECHNICAL BOOKS & PUBLICATIONS

Oriel Chambers   Covent Garden   LIVERPOOL L2 8UD

SKIPPOOL, Wyre Borough Council, Civic Centre, Breck Road, Poulton-le-Fylde. Tel: (0253) 891000.
Berths: 114 pile (drying).
Facilities: boatyard; chandlery; slipway.

DOUGLAS BOATYARD, Becconsall Lane, Hesketh Bank, Preston, Lancs. (R. Douglas S side R. Ribble). Tel: (0772 81) 2462.
Open: Mon.-Fri. 1030-1230, 1330-1800, Sat.-Sun. 1400-1800. **Berths:** 80 (6 visitors).
Facilities: fuel (diesel, paraffin); water; gas; electricity; chandlery; charts; shops nearby; engineers; repairs; cranage 8T; storage (outside and under cover); slipway 30T.
Managing Director: D. M. Sheppard.
Remarks: Entry 2 hr.–HW–2 hr. Tidal berths.

PRESTON MARINA, Navigation Way, Ashton on Ribble, Preston. Tel: (0772) 733595.
Call Sign: Ch. 16, 14.
Berths: 100 pontoon, 18 buoy.
Facilities: fuel; boatyard; chandlery; yacht/boat club; 45T crane.

JAMES MAYOR & CO, Tarleton, Nr. Preston, Lancashire. Tel: (0772) 812250.
Open: Normal hours. **Berths:** 80 alongside in canal basin (visitors available). Max. draught 1.5m, LOA 21m.
Facilities: fuel (diesel); chandlery; provisions (near by); repair; cranage; storage.
Customs: Tel: (051) 933 7075.

ALBERT & CANNING DOCKS, Royal Liver Buildings, Pier Head, Liverpool L3 1JH. Tel: (051-236) 6090. Fax: (051-227) 3174.
Call sign: Canning River Ent., Ch. 80, 37 (M).
Berths: 12 pontoon, extensive quayside.
Facilities: some electricity; water; pump out; toilets; car park.
Remarks: Contact 24 hr. before entering, –2 hr. to HW. Max. draught 5m (tidal), LOA 55m.
Harbour Master: W. Broadbent.

BLUNDELLSANDS SAILING CLUB, Hightown, Liverpool. Tel: (051 929) 2101.
Berths: 50 buoy (drying, max. 30ft).
Facilities: yacht/boat club.

LIVERPOOL MARINA. Coburg Dock, Sefton Street, Liverpool. Tel: 051-709 0578.
Berths: 270+ (450 on completion).
Facilities: clubhouse, toilets/showers, water and electricity, security, slipway, repairs, chandlery.
Remarks: Access seawards via lock 2 hr.–HW–2 hr.

MANCHESTER YACHT HARBOUR, Trafford Road, Salford. Tel: 061-872 8041.
Berths: 80 (visitors 30). On Ship Canal.
Facilities: water; electricity; security; chandlery; toilets/showers.

FIDDLERS FERRY YACHT HAVEN, Penketh, Cheshire WA5 2UJ. Tel: (0925 72) 7519.
Call sign: 80, 37 (M).
Berths: 200. Max. draught 1.8m, LOA 18m.
Facilities: Boatyard; chandlery; 10 ton crane.
Remarks: Access 1½ hr.–HW–1½ hr.
Harbour Master: Mr E. Bergqvist.

Wales

DEGANWY YACHT SERVICES, The Quay, Deganwy, Gwynedd. Tel: (0492) 83869.
Open: Normal working hours. **Berths:** 400 (100 visitors).
Facilities: provisions (near by); cranage.
Remarks: Access 2 hr.–HW–2 hr.

CONWY HARBOUR, Aberconwy Council, The Quay, Conwy, Gwynedd. Tel: 0492-596253.
Call sign: Conwy Harbour (Ch. 16, 12, 14.) during working hours.
Open: Normal working hours. **Berths:** 408 swinging moorings drying (visitors available). Depths 1m (MLWS)-8m (MHWS) over bar. LOA at quay 40m and on moorings 15m.
Facilities: fuel (diesel, petrol, gas); chandlery; provisions (near by); repair; cranage; storage.
Harbour Master: Lt.Cdr. P. B. Halliday.
Remarks: Access to harbour 2-4 hr.–HW–2-4 hr. Major engineering work to build the Conwy tube tunnel is in progress. The clear channel through the harbour is marked by buoys.
KEEP TO NAVIGABLE CHANNEL.

BEAUMARIS AND MENAI BRIDGE HARBOUR, Council Offices, Llangefni, Anglesey LL77 7TW. Tel: (0248) 750057. Fax: (0248) 750032.
Call sign: Ch. 16 (intermittent daylight hours only).
Open: Normal working hours. **Berths:** 600 some drying (limited visitors available).
Facilities: fuel (diesel, petrol); chandlery; provisions (near by); repair.
Harbour Master: Capt. C. T. Hemingway.
Mooring Supervisor: M. Mothersole.

HOLYHEAD SAILING CLUB, Newry Beach, Holyhead, Anglesey, Gwynedd.
Tel: (0407) 762526.
Berths: 130 deep water moorings. LOA 17m.
Facilities: diesel; repairs; water; first aid; rigging service; cranage; slipway; boat park; chandlery; shop; showers/toilets; restaurants.
Remarks: access at all states of tide.

PORT DINORWIC YACHT HARBOUR LTD, Port Dinorwic, Gwynedd LL56 4JN.
Tel: (0248) 670559.
Harbour Office: (0248) 670010.
Call sign: Dinorwic Marine Ch. 80, 37 (M).
Open: 24 hr.
Berths: 100, (10 visitors).
Facilities: water; electricity; chandlery; repairs; crane; slipway; hardstanding; diesel; sail maker; provisions; yacht brokerage; telephone; car parking; clubhouse; toilets/showers; Calor gas (Menai Garage, Caernarfon Road).

ABERSOCH BOATYARD LTD, The Saltings, Abersoch, Pwllheli, Gwynedd LL53 7AR. Tel: (075881) 2213.
Open: Normal working hours. **Berths:** 200 deep water and swinging moorings (10 visitors).
Facilities: chandlery; repairs; storage.
Joint Harbour Masters: John Jones/Meirion Lloyd-James.

PWLLHELI HARBOUR, Pwllheli, Gwynedd.
Tel: (0758) 613131 Ext. 281.
Call sign: Ch. 16 (no watch kept).
Open: Normal working hours. **Berths:** 300 (visitors if available).
Facilities: fuel (diesel, petrol, gas); chandlery; provisions (near by); repair; cranage; storage; sailmaker; sailing clubs; engineering and electronic works; Calor gas (Caravan Park Shop).
Remarks: Access to harbour 3 hr.–HW–3 hr. Good shelter, but cuts up rough on bar if wind is SE (strong – gale force). Harbour speed limit 4 kts. Buoyed entrance and channel.

PWLLHELI MARINA, Glandon, Pwllheli, Gwynedd LL53 5YT. Tel: (0758) 701219.
Fax: (0758) 701443.
Call Sign: Hafan Pwllheli. Ch. 80 (M).
Open: 24h.
Berths: 265 (visitors available).
Facilities: water; electricity; slipway; toilets; showers; 24h. security. Nearby: diesel; petrol; chandlery; repairs; sailing clubs.
Remarks: Access to harbour 1m. at bar and channel at MLWS. Speed limit 6kn.
Manager: Will Williams.

PORTHMADOG HARBOUR, Porthmadog, Gwynedd LL49 9LU. Tel: (0766) 512927. Call HM on Ch. 16. Radio not permanently manned.
Open: Normal working hours. Pilotage compulsory for non-exempted vessels. **Berths:** 280 (visitors available). Max. draught 3.6m, LOA 60m.
Facilities: fuel (diesel, petrol); electricity on request; chandlery; provisions; water; cranage (3½ tons on quay); storage; brokerage; slipway; hotels; restaurants; Calor gas (Gwynedd Caravans, Snowdon St.).
Harbour Master: G. M. Bicks, Asst. H. M. D. Phillips, **Pilot:** R. A. Kyffin.
Remarks: Access: Vessels drawing 3'6" 2½ hr.–HW–2½ hr. Vessels drawing 5' 1½ hr.–HW–1½ hr. Vessels drawing over 5'–consult HM or Pilot (0766) 75684. Channel changes frequently. Sketch of Approaches Buoyage System available from H.M. 52p including postage. (For free amendment during season, call at Harbour Office).

BARMOUTH HARBOUR, The Quay, Barmouth, Gwynedd LL42 1HB. Tel: (0341) 280671.
Call sign: Barmouth Harbour, Ch. 16, 12.
Berths: 156, 6 visitors, max. draught 2m, LOA 12m.
Open: 2 hr.–HW–2 hr. over bar. Office: 0930-1630.
Facilities: electricity; water; phone; refuse; fuel; gas; chandlery; provisions; WCs; showers; launderette; restaurant; café; bar; yacht club; sea fishing; mail; minor repairs; slip; boat sales; car hire; lift-out; dry berths; Calor gas (LL Building Supplies, Church Street).

ABERDOVEY HARBOUR, Gwynedd. Tel: (0654) 767626.
Call sign: Aberdovey Harbour Ch. 16, 12.
Open: Daylight hours. **Berths:** 150 swinging moorings (visitors alongside wharf).
Facilities: fuel; chandlery; provisions (near by); repair; cranage; storage; Calor gas (Davey Marine, Penrhos Filling Station).
Harbour Master: J. A. Benbow.
Remarks: Entry to harbour restricted by bar–access 3 hr.–HW–3 hr. Heavy silting from Jetty eastwards.

ABERLERI BOATYARD, (F. L. Steelcraft), Pont Aberleri, Ynyslas, Borth, Dyfed. Tel: (0970) 871 713. Fax: (0970) 871 907. Telex: 35482.
Berths: 60 (visitors 5). Max. draught 3m, LOA 46m.
Facilities: water; electricity; boatyard; slipway; chandlery; security; toilets; steel and aluminium boat builders.

ABERYSTWYTH HARBOUR, Town Quay, Aberystwyth, Dyfed. Tel: (0970) 611433.
Call sign: Ch. 14 (within harbour).
Open: Normal working hours. **Berths:** 3 visitors at town quay.
Facilities: fuel (petrol), diesel at local garage; provisions (near by); Calor gas (Griffiths, Station Yard).
Harbour Master: Capt. W. J. Williams.
Remarks: Entry to harbour 3½ hr.–HW–3½ hr. in fair weather.
Customs: Tel: R/T (0222) 399123.

ABERAERON HARBOUR, Gwylan, Queen St., Aberaeron. Tel: (0545) 570407.
Berths: 80 Buoy (drying).
Facilities: crane; yacht/boat club; slipway.
Harbour Master: Vince Davies.

FISHGUARD HARBOUR, Dyfed SA64 0BU. Tel: (0348) 872881. Fax: 872699. Telex: 48167.
Call sign: Ch. 14.
Open: 24 hr. **Berths:** 170 deepwater moorings, 10 visitors. Max draught 6m..
Facilities: electricity; water; phone; refuse; WCs; showers; café; bar; mail; sea fishing; 25T crane; slip; security; lift-out; storage; repairs. Others nearby.
Harbour Master: S. Buhlman.
Remarks: Fishguard is a Sealink, British Ferries Terminal. Drying Harbour is in Lower Town which is suitable for bilge keel yachts. Goodwick Marine Services (Tel: 873479) can provide limited facilities.
Customs: Tel: R/T (0222) 399123.

DALE SAILING CO. LTD., Brunel Quay, Neyland, Milford Haven. Tel: (0646) 601636.
Berths: 100 buoy, 10 visitors.
Facilities: fuel; boatyard; chandlery; yacht/boat club; slipway; 30T hoist.

MILFORD HAVEN, Preseli District Council, Cumbria House, PO Box 14, Dyfed SA6 1TP. Port Operations Signal Station. Tel: (0646) 692342/3.
Call sign: Milford Haven Radio. Port Operations Ch. 12.
The Milford Haven Port Authority licenses a total of 1200 moorings. Visitors moorings are available at Dale; Gellyswick; Pennar Park Marina Company; and Lawrenny Yacht Station. Temporary moorings may also be available on application at other boat clubs.
Facilities: (available at most centres): moorings; fuel; water; repairs; haulage; gas; chandlery; provisions; Calor gas (54 Priory Road).
Harbour Master: Capt. J. E. Frost.
Tel: (0646) 693091.
Customs: Tel: R/T (0646) 681310.

NEW QUAY. Tel: (0545) 562047.
Berths: 250 buoy (drying).
Facilities: fuel; yacht/boat club; slipway.
Harbour Master: Dennis Leworthy.

**WESTFIELD PILL CAMPER & NICHOLSONS
(MARINAS) LTD,** Brunel Quay, Neyland,
Milford Haven SA73 1PY.
Tel: (0646) 601601.
Call Sign: Westfield Marina. Ch. 80, 37 (M).
Berths: 420 (30 visitors). Max. draught 2.1m,
LOA 18m.
Facilities: fuel; water, electricity, repairs,
slipway, chandlery; caféteria; laundrette;
toilets and showers; sailmakers; 24 hr.
security; Calor gas.
Remarks: Access all states of the tide. If
possible call in advance of arrival.
Manager: Govan Johns.

LAWRENNY YACHT STATION, Lawrenny
Quay, Kilgetty. Tel: (0646) 651212.
Call Sign: Ch. 80 (M).
Berths: 100 buoy.
Facilities: fuel. boatyard; chandlery;
yacht/boat club; slipway; 30T hoist.

RUDDERS BOATYARD, Badger Cottage, The
Hawn, Church Road, Burton, Dyfed SA73
1NU. Tel: (0646) 600288.
Berths: 36, 3 visitors. Max draught 3m, LOA
15m.
Facilities: electricity; water; refuse; phone;
WCs/showers; all repairs; slip; boat hire;
scrubbing grid; gardiennage; security; lift-out.
French spoken.

LLANELLI BOROUGH COUNCIL, Estates
Section, Ty Elwyn, Llanelli. Tel: (0554) 4315.
Berths: 265 buoy (drying).
Facilities: boatyard; chandlery; yacht/boat
club; slipway.

TENBY HARBOUR, Tenby, Dyfed.
Tel: (0834) 2717.
Open: Normal hours. **Berths:** 110 fore and aft
drying (visitors available).
Facilities: water; provisions (shops near by);
cranage; storage; Calor gas (Morris Bro. Bank
House, High Street).
Harbour Master: Alan Eagles.
Remarks: Access 2½ hr.–HW–2½ hr.

SAUNDERSFOOT HARBOUR, Saundersfoot,
Dyfed SA69 9HE. Tel: (0834) 812094. Marina
(0834) 812094.
Call sign: Ch. 16, 12. Marina Ch. 16, 11.
Open: Easter-Oct. till 2100. **Berths:** 200 (15
visitors) fore and aft and running moorings.
Facilities: water; chandlery; provisions (shops
near by); repair; cranage; slipway; (hotels,
restaurants, car hire near by). Arrangements
for fuel by request; car park; storage; 15 ton
haul-out; diesel; Calor gas (Frosts).
Harbour Master: C. G. Morgan.

BURRY PORT HARBOUR, Burry Port, Dyfed
SA16 0ER. Tel: (05546) 4315. Home: 5120.
Open: Normal hours. **Berths:** 260 moorings
drying out HW + 3 hr. 3 visitors moorings
available at Burry Port Yacht Services).
Facilities: fuel (diesel); water; chandlery;
provisions (shops near by); repair; storage;
Calor gas (Shoreline Caravan Park).
Harbour Superintendent: N. G. Hall.

SWANSEA YACHT HAVEN, Lockside,
Maritime Quarter, Swansea SA1 1WN.
Tel: (0792) 470310. Fax: 463948.
Call sign: Swansea Yacht Haven. Ch. 80. (M)
Open: 5 hr.–HW–5 hr. **Berths:** 365. Visitors
available, max. draught 3.7m, LOA 27m,
beam 8.5m in lock. Tawe Barrage construction
complete. See Section 22.
Facilities: fuel (diesel); water; electricity; gas;
chandlery; provisions (near by); ice; repairs
(near by); cranage (18T hoist); slipway (under

control Swansea Yacht and Sub Aqua Club
Tel: (0792) 654863; storage; brokerage;
showers; toilets; launderette; external waiting
area holding buoys; restaurants.
Customs: Tel: R/T (0222) 399123.
Manager: Mark Shenstone.

MONKSTONE CRUISING & SAILING CLUB,
Jersey Marine, Neath. Tel: (0792) 812229.
Berths: 60 poontoon.
Facilities: Yacht/boat club.

PORTHCAWL HARBOUR, Mid-Glamorgan.
Tel: (065671) 2756.
Berths: 33, 3 visitors, access 3 hr.–HW–3 hr.
Facilities: phone; WCs; showers; yacht club;
sea fishing; mail; slip; storage.

BARRY DOCK MARINE SERVICES LTD., The
Graving Dock, Barry. Tel: (0446) 746990.
Berths: 60 quayside.
Facilities: boatyard; 30T crane.

BARRY DOCK MARINE SERVICES LTD., The
Graving Dock, Barry. Tel: (0446) 746990.
Berths: 60 quayside.
Facilities: boatyard; 30T crane.

BARRY YACHT CLUB, Pier Head, Barry. Tel:
(0446) 73511.
Berths: 130 buoy (drying).
Facilities: fuel; boatyard; yacht/boat club;
slipway; 20T crane.

**RIVER ELY–PENARTH MOTOR BOAT &
SAILING CLUB,** Clubhouse, Ferry Road,
Grangetown, Cardiff, CF1 7JL. Tel: (0222)
226575.
Berths: 50, 16 visitors. Max draught 2m, LOA
12m. Access 2½ hr.–HW–2½ hr.
Facilities: electricity; water; refuse; phone;
chandlery; WCs/showers; restaurant;
clubhouse; sea fishing; slip; scrubbing grid;
lift-out; storage; provisions nearby; Calor gas
(S & M Boats).
Customs: Tel: (0222) 399123.

PORTWAY VILLAGE MARINA, Camper &
Nicholsons Ltd, Penarth, South Glamorgan.
Tel: (0222) 705021.
Call sign: Camper Base Ch. 80, 37 (M).
Berths: 400.
Facilities: Repairs; diesel; electricity; water;
chandlery; brokerage; laundrette; toilets and
showers; 24 hr. security and CCTV.
Remarks: Access by lock, approx. 8 hr. per
tide for 1.5 m. draught. If possible visitors
should call in advance of arrival.

SHARPNESS MARINE, The Old Dock,
Sharpness. Tel: (0453) 811476.
Berths: 80 jetty & quayside.
Facilities: water; fuel; boatyard; chandlery.

Severn & Avon

UPTON MARINA LTD, (Walton Marine Sales
Ltd), East Waterside, Upton-upon-Severn,
Worcs WR8 0PB.
Tel: (068 46) 4287/3111. Fax: (06846) 3325.
Call sign: Upton Marina Ch. 80, 37 (M).
Berths: 200. Draught 1.4m, air draught 4.9m,
LOA 15m.
Remarks: Access on R. Severn downstream
from Upton, NE bank.
Director/General Manager: M. J. Cook.

SANKEY MARINE, Worcester Road, Evesham,
Worcs WR11 4TA. Tel: (0386) 442338.
Berths: 55, 5 visitors.
Open: dawn to dusk.
Facilities: water; fuel; gas; chandlery; ice;
phone; WCs; showers; weekend
restaurant/bar; repairs; slip; boat sales; lift-
out; storage.

EVESHAM MARINA, Kings Road, Evesham.
Tel: (0386) 47813/48906. Fax: 44827
Open: 24 hr. **Berths:** 60 (10 visitors).
Facilities: fuel (diesel); electricity; chandlery;
provisions (shops near by); repair; cranage
(limit 20 tons); slip (70 ft. LOA); storage;
brokerage; charter.
Harbour Master: Bob Killick.

THE TEWKESBURY MARINA LTD, Bredon
Road, Tewkesbury, Glos GL20 5BY. Tel: (0684)
293737.
Open: 24 hr. **Berths:** 350–max. length 70 ft.,
draught 6 ft., air clearance 13 ft. (visitors 30).
Facilities: fuel (diesel, petrol); electricity;
chandlery; provisions (in town); repair;
cranage (limit 7 tons); slipways (limit 30 tons);
storage; brokerage; water.
Berthing Master: V. Clements.
Remarks: Entry for seagoing vessels subject
to headroom through Sharpness Docks on
River Severn.
Customs: Tel: (0453) 811302.

BRISTOL CITY DOCKS, Underfall Yard,
Cumberland Road, Bristol BS1 6XG.
Tel: (0272) 264797/264797.
Dockmaster: (0272) 273633 (Tidal).
Call sign: Ch. 73.
Open: Summer 0800-sunset. Winter -1700.
Berths: Some visitors. Max. draught 5.5m,
LOA 99m.
Harbour Master: Capt. R. M. Keyzor, MNI.
Remarks: Access via R. Avon. Pilot directions
essential. Contact HM on Ch. 14 before
approaching lock -3 hr. to HW.
Customs: Tel: R/T (0272) 235200.

BRISTOL MARINA LIMITED, Hanover Place,
Bristol. Tel: (0272) 25730.
Berths: 80 (pontoon), 100 (shore).
Facilities: fuel (diesel); water; electricity;
boatyard; slipway; lift; chandlery; gas;
security; repair; cranage (30 ton); storage;
brokerage; telephone; toilets; showers.

SALTFORD MARINA, The Shallows, Saltford,
Nr. Bristol BS18 3EZ. Tel: (0225) 872226.
Open: 0800-2000.
Berths: 100.
Facilities: electricity; chandlery; repair;
slipway (limit 25 ft.); storage; brokerage; 24
hr. security; pump out; bar and restaurant;
boat hire and sales; cranage; water; 50 dry
berths.

UPHILL BOAT SERVICES LTD, Uphill Wharf,
Weston-super-mare, Avon BS23 4XR. Tel:
(0934) 418617.
Berths: 70 plus pontoon moorings. Max.
draught 1.5m, LOA 12m.

Facilities: fuel; chandlery; slipways; storage;
engine servicing; sales.
Remarks: Access 2 hr.–HW–2 hr.
Harbour Master: R. M. Shardlow.
Customs: Tel: (0272) 23500.

Devon (North Coast)

WATERMOUTH HARBOUR, Watermouth
Cove, Ilfracombe. Tel: (0271) 865422.
Berths: 120 buoy (drying).
Facilities: Yacht/boat club, slipway; 11T crane.
Harbour Master: Michael Irwin.

ILFRACOMBE, Harbour Office, The Quay,
Ilfracombe. Tel: (0271) 863969.
Call Sign: Ch. 12, 80 (M).
Berths: 120 buoy (drying).
Facilities: boatyard; chandlery, yacht/boat
club; slipway; 3T crane.

INSTOW MARINE SERVICES, 12 Mollins
Garages, Quay Lane, Instow, Bideford. Tel:
(0271) 861081.
Berths: 100 buoy (drying).
Facilities: boatyard; chandlery; yacht/boat
club; slipway, 12T crane.

Cornwall (North Coast)

PADSTOW HARBOUR AND RIVER CAMEL,
Harbour Office, West Quay, Padstow, PL28
8AQ. Tel: (0841) 532239.
Call Sign: Padstow Harbour. Chan. 16, 14.
Harbour Office: Manned 0830-1730 weekdays
and 2½ hr.–HW–1½ hr.
Berths: Berths alongside in the Inner Harbour
for small craft. Access to harbour is 2-3
hr.–HW-2-3 hr. depending on draught via tidal
gate entrance. Vessels must not be left
unattended except in emergency. Vessels
may lay afloat (depending on draught) to
their own anchors in the channel below
moorings in the Pool, about a quarter of a
mile downstream.
Padstow Harbour: Limited afloat swinging
moorings for visiting craft up to
approximately 40 ft length, and drying
moorings for smaller craft are available on
the foreshore at Rock, across the estuary from
Padstow (daily ferry service).
Pilotage: Pilotage is compulsory for certain
vessels. Contact Harbour Office for details.
When approaching from seaward beware of

Newland Rock, Gulland Rock (unlit islands off the entrance), Gurley Rock, Chimney Rock, The Hen, Roscarrock and Villiers Rocks, also the wreck at about six cables west of Stepper Point, which do not dry but which can be dangerous near LW. Once inside the Headlands beware of heavy breaking seas on Doom Bar, especially during or after strong onshore winds. Channel over Doom Bar is marked by Greenaway (porthand) and Doom Bar (starboard hand) light buoys. From Ship-me-Pumps (St. Saviours Point) about a quarter of a mile downstream of Padstow Harbour, up to the harbour itself, the channel lies very close under western (starboard hand) shore. Lit by buoys/beacons. Channel dries at LW Springs. Onward passage is possible by small craft upstream to Wadebridge (about five miles) on Springs. Channel not marked. Local knowledge necessary.
Facilities: fuel (diesel); bulk ice; chandlery; general provisions and services; slipways for small craft up to about 30 ft LOA.
Harbour Master: J. Hinchliffe.
Customs: Tel: (0752) 220661.

NEWQUAY, Harbour Master:
Tel: (0637) 872809.
Call sign: Ch. 16, 14.
Open: 0800-1700.
Berths: Very limited, application to the H.M.
Facilities: fuel (diesel); gas; water; slipway; drying-out; marine services and chandlery.
Remarks: Care must be taken when approaching store-pot buoys in the bay. Draught 2m 2 hr.–HW–2 hr. Max. LOA 12m.

ST IVES HARBOUR, Smentons Pier, St Ives, Cornwall.
Tel: (0736) 795018.
Call sign: Ch. 16, 12.
Open: Normal hours.
Berths: 8.
Harbour Master: Eric Ward.
Remarks: Harbour dries. Access from half tide. Unsuitable in onshore winds or heavy swell.

PORTREATH HARBOUR ASSOCIATION.
Berths: Harbour basin – moor with warps to quay. Dries at LW. Harbour usable 2 hr.–HW–2 hr. plus 18 ft water at HW.
Facilities: fuel; water; toilets; slipway.

NEWQUAY HARBOUR. Tel: (0208) 872809.
Call Sign: Ch. 16, 12.
Berths: 75 buoy & quayside (drying).
Facilities: fuel; yacht/boat club; slipway.
Harbour Master: Capt. F. Sampson.

Ireland

ASTER BOATS LTD, Drinagh Harbour, South Shore, Clifden Bay, Clifden, Co. Galway, Ireland. Tel: (095) 21332.
Open: 0900-1800.
Berths: 14 visitors (swinging), 8 in Ardbear Bay.
Facilities: winter storage; fuel; water; electricity; repairs; slipway; pier; toilets; security; chandlery; transport; gas.

KILRUSH CREEK MARINA, Shannon Maritime Developments, Co. Clare, Ireland. Tel: (065) 52073. Fax: 061 361903. Telex: 72182.
Call Sign: Ch. 80.
Berths: 250 (40 visitors).
Facilities: Fuel; water; electricity; 30T hoist; slip; hard standing; repairs; WCs; showers; launderette; phone; bar; restaurant; workshop; provisions; security; chandlery; watersports.

KINSALE YACHT CLUB MARINA, Kinsale, Co. Cork, Ireland. Tel: (021) 772196.
Berths: 90 (30 visitors).
Facilities: fuel; gas; water; electricity; repairs; crane; slipway; chandlery; WC's; showers; phone; security; gourmet restaurants.

ROYAL CORK YACHT CLUB MARINA, Crosshaven, Co. Cork, Ireland.
Tel: (021) 831023.
Berths: 87 (visitors 10).
Facilities: fuel; water; electricity; telephone; toilets; showers; restaurant.

CROSSHAVEN BOATYARD, Crosshaven, Co. Cork, Ireland.
Tel: (021) 831161. Fax: 831603.
Berths: 100 (visitors 20).
Facilities: fuel; water; electricity; repairs; slipway; lift; chandlery; telephone; toilets.

EAST FERRY MARINA, Belgrove, Cobh, Co. Cork, Ireland. Tel: (021) 811342.
Call sign: Ch. 80, 37 (M).
Berths: 50 deep water. Draught 6m, LOA 24m.
Facilities: fuel; electricity; scrubbing pier; showers.
Harbour Master: Mr J. Butler.

Radiobeacons — Section 19

HOWTH YACHT CLUB MARINA, Howth, Dublin, Ireland. Tel: (01) 322141.
Call sign: Ch. 80, 37 (M).
Berths: 200 (at least 8 visitors available).
Facilities: water; slipway; chandlery; gas; petrol, diesel; electricity; first aid; cranage; toilets; showers.
Visitors may also tie up at Dun Laoghaire harbour nearby. (Tel: 801130). Max. draught 2.4m, facilities in town, 2.4T crane, slip 4T, car hire, security, lift-out, storage.
Customs: Tel: (0693) 772544.

Northern Ireland

COPELANDS MARINA, Donaghadee, Co. Down, N. Ireland. Tel: (0247) 882184.
Berths: 50 (visitors 3).
Facilities: fuel; water; electricity; lift; security; telephone; toilets.

BANGOR HARBOUR, North Down Borough Council, Town Hall, The Caastle, Bangor, Co. Down, N. Ireland BT20 4BT. Tel: (0247) 270371.
Berths: 125 (2 visitors). All tides. Max. draught 4m.
Harbour Master: Michael Fitzsimmons.

BANGOR MARINA, Co. Down, N. Ireland, BT20 5ED. Tel: (0247) 271529.
Berths: 300 pontoon, 24 hr. access, 300 sheltered moorings. Max. draught 2.9m, LOA 18m.
Facilities: water; electricity; diesel and petrol; WCs; showers; laundrette; provisions; chandlery; repairs; boat sales; parking; 45T hoist. Royal Ulster and Holyrood Y.C.s nearby.
Remarks: Lies at entrance to Belfast and Strangford Loughs.

CARRICKFERGUS MARINA, Rodgers Quay, Carrickfergus BT38 8BE, N. Ireland. Tel: 09603 66666.
Call sign: Carrickfergus Marina Ch. 80, 37 (M).
Berths: 300 (pontoons). Visitors available. Max. LOA 22m.
Open: 24 hours. Access at all states of the tide.
Facilities: fuel; water; electricity; slipway; repairs; boat storage; hoist; telephone; toilets; restaurant; snacks; electronics; brokerage; chandlery; upholstery; cruising school; sail repairs.
Marina Manager: John McCormick.

Volvo Penta service and parts centres around Britain

Volvo Penta service and parts centres offer you a wealth of practical help and experience.

New and reconditioned petrol and diesel engines, servicing and repairs, complete overhauls, installations, winterising, spring commissioning, exchange parts and propellers, engine and boat accessories, on board parts kits and a host of other marine equipment.

Volvo Penta. The greatest·name in marine power.

The South West

CHANNEL ISLANDS *Chicks Marine Ltd* Collings Road, St Peter Port, GUERNSEY Tel (0481) 723716/724536

CHANNEL ISLANDS *DK Collins* South Pier, St Helier, JERSEY Tel (0534) 32415

CORNWALL *Marine Engineering Co (Looe) Ltd* The Quay, EAST LOOE PL13 1AQ Tel (05036) 2887

CORNWALL *Penryn Marine* Mylor Yacht Harbour, NR FALMOUTH TR11 5UF Tel (0326) 76202

DEVON *Marine Engineering Co (Looe) Ltd* Seahorse Building, Queen Anne's Battery Marina, PLYMOUTH PL4 0LP Tel (0752) 226143

DEVON *Philip & Son Ltd* Noss Works, DARTMOUTH TQ6 0EA Tel (0803) 833351

DEVON *Pilkington Marine Engineering* 9 Pottery Units, Forde Road, Brunel Trading Estate, NEWTON ABBOT TQ12 4AD Tel (0626) 52663

DEVON *Retreat Boatyard (Topsham) Ltd* Retreat Boatyard, Topsham, EXETER EX3 0LS Tel (0392) 874720

DEVON *Starey Marine Services* Island Square, Island Street, SALCOMBE TQ8 8DP Tel (054884) 3655/2930

Wales

DYFED *Burry Port Yacht Services* The Harbour, BURRY PORT SA16 0ER Tel (05546) 2740

GLAMORGAN *Barry Marine (Swansea) Ltd* Unit 3 Fishmarket Quay, Swansea Marina, SWANSEA Tel (0792) 458057

GWYNEDD *Arfon Oceaneering* Victoria Dock Slipway, Balaclava Road, CAERNARFON LL55 1TG Tel (0286) 76055

GWYNEDD *Hookes Marine* Sarn Bach Road, ABERSOCH LL53 7ER Tel (075 881) 2458

PEMBROKESHIRE *Dale Sailing Co Ltd* Brunel Quay, Neyland, MILFORD HAVEN SA73 1PY Tel (0646) 601636

SOUTH GLAMORGAN *Cambrian and Westfleet* The Boatyard, Portway Village Marina, PENARTH CF6 1BW Tel (0222) 709983

Scotland

ARGYLL *Kilmelford Yacht Haven* Kilmelford, OBAN PA34 4XD Tel (085 22) 248

AYRSHIRE *Marine Sales (Engineering) Ltd* Largs Yacht Haven, Irvine Road, LARGS KA30 8EZ Tel (0475) 687139/687383

AYRSHIRE *Troon Marine Services Ltd* Harbour Road, TROON KA10 6DJ Tel (0292) 316180

GRAMPIAN *Henry Fleetwood & Sons Ltd* Baker Street, LOSSIEMOUTH IV31 6NZ Tel (034381) 3015

HIGHLANDS AND ISLANDS *Caley Marina* Canal Road, INVERNESS IV3 6NF Tel (0463) 236539

LOTHIAN *Port Edgar Marine Services Ltd* Port Edgar Marina, Shore Rd, South Queensferry, Nr EDINBURGH EH30 9SQ Tel (031-331) 1233

STRATHCLYDE *J N MacDonald & Co* 47-49 Byron Street, GLASGOW G11 6LP Tel (041 334) 6171

Northern Ireland

Robert Craig & Sons Ltd 15-21 Great Georges Street, BELFAST BT15 1BW Tel (0232) 232971

Republic of Ireland

Western Marine Ltd Bulloch Harbour, Dalkley, DUBLIN Tel 010 353 1 2800321 Fax (01) 2800327

The North

CUMBRIA *Waterhead Marine Ltd* AMBLESIDE LA22 0EX Tel (053 94) 32424

CUMBRIA *Windermere Aquatic Ltd* Glebe Road, BOWNESS-ON-WINDERMERE LA23 3HE Tel (09662) 2121

YORKSHIRE *Auto Unit Repairs (Leeds) Ltd* Henshaw Works, Yeadon, LEEDS LS19 7XY Tel (0532) 501222

Central

BERKSHIRE *D B Marine Engineering Ltd* Cookham Bridge, COOKHAM-ON-THAMES SL6 9SN Tel (06285) 26032

SURREY *Marlow Marine Services Ltd* Penton Hook Marina, Staines Road, CHERTSEY KT16 8PY Tel (0932) 568772

BUCKINGHAMSHIRE *Marlow Marine Services Ltd* Harleyford, MARLOW SL7 2DX Tel (06284) 71368

MIDDLESEX *Marlow Marine Services Ltd* Shepperton Marina, Felix Lane, SHEPPERTON TW17 8NJ Tel (0932) 247427

NORTHAMPTONSHIRE *C V S Pentapower* St. Andrews Road, NORTHAMPTON NN1 2LF Tel (0604) 38537/38409/36173

WORCESTERSHIRE *Upton Marina* Upton-on-Severn, WORCESTER WR8 0PB Tel (0684) 594540

The South East

LONDON *John A Sparks & Co Ltd* Ardwell Road, STREATHAM HILL SW2 4RT Tel 081-674 3434

KENT *John Hawkins Marine* Elmhaven Marina, Rochester Road (A228), Halling, ROCHESTER ME2 1AQ Tel (0634) 242256

SUSSEX *B A Peters plc* Birdham Pool, CHICHESTER PO20 7BG Tel (0243) 512831

SUSSEX *Felton Marine Engineering* Brighton Marina, BRIGHTON BN2 5UF Tel (0273) 601779

SUSSEX *Leonard Marine* The Old Shipyard, Robinson Road, NEWHAVEN BN9 9BL Tel (0273) 515987

The South

DORSET *Salterns Boatyard* 38 Salterns Way, Lilliput, POOLE BH14 8JR Tel (0202) 707321

DORSET *Poole Marine Services* Sunseeker International Marina, West Quay Road, POOLE BH15 1HX Tel (0202) 679577

HAMPSHIRE *Haven Boatyard Ltd* King's Saltern Road, LYMINGTON SO41 9QD Tel (0590) 677073/4/5

HAMPSHIRE *S.A.L. Marine* Mill Lane, LYMINGTON SO41 9AZ Tel (0590) 679588

HAMPSHIRE *R K Marine Ltd* Hamble River Boatyard, Bridge Road, Swanwick, SOUTHAMPTON SO3 7EB Tel (0489) 583572 or 583585

HAMPSHIRE *Motortech Marine Ltd* 5 The Slipway, Port Solent PORTSMOUTH PO6 4TR Tel (0705) 201171

ISLE OF WIGHT *Cowes Marine Services* White Gate Yard, Arctic Road WEST COWES PO31 7PG Tel (0983) 294861

ISLE OF WIGHT *Harold Hayles (Yarmouth IOW) Ltd* The Quay, YARMOUTH PO41 0RS Tel (0983) 760373

The East

BEDFORDSHIRE *Harry Kitchener Marine Ltd* Barkers Lane, BEDFORD MK41 9RL Tel (0234) 351931

ESSEX *Volspec Ltd* Woodrolfe Road, Tollesbury, MALDON CM9 8SE Tel (0621) 869756

ESSEX *French Marine Motors Ltd* 61/63 Waterside, BRIGHTLINGSEA CO7 0AX Tel (020630) 2133

HUMBERSIDE *SSS Marine* The Boatyard, Hull Marina, HULL HU1 2DQ Tel (0482) 227411 Tel (0482) 227464 spares

NORFOLK *Marinepower Engineering* Grange Walk, WROXHAM NR12 8RX Tel (0603) 782434

SUFFOLK *A D Truman Ltd* Old Maltings Boatyard, Oulton Broad, LOWESTOFT NR32 3PH Tel (0502) 565950

SUFFOLK *French Marine Motors Ltd* Suffolk Yacht Harbour, Levington, IPSWICH IP10 0LN Tel (0473) 659882

Commitment to care worldwide.

Volvo Penta centres for Commercial Operators around Britain

For operators of working craft including fishing boats, harbour launches, pilot and patrol craft, ferries and all general workboats, these are the specialist Volvo Penta Sales and Service Centres in Britain.

Owners of yachts and other leisure craft should refer to separate listing in this publication.

The South West

CHANNEL ISLANDS **Chicks Marine Ltd** Collings Road, St Peter Port, GUERNSEY Tel (0481) 723716/724536

CORNWALL **Marine Engineering Co (Looe) Ltd** The Quay, EAST LOOE PL13 1AQ Tel (05036) 2887

DEVON **E G Hubbard Marine Engineers** Furze Lane, BRIXHAM TQ5 8EE Tel (0803) 853327

DEVON **Marine Engineering Co (Looe) Ltd** Seahorse Building, Queen Anne's Battery Marina, PLYMOUTH PL4 0LP Tel (0752) 226143

DEVON **Philip & Son Ltd** Noss Works, DARTMOUTH TQ6 0EA Tel (0803) 833351

Wales

GLAMORGAN **John A Sparks & Co Ltd** Ipswich Road, CARDIFF CF3 7AQ Tel (0222) 492788

DYFED **Haven Maritime Ltd** 39/41 Front Street, PEMBROKE DOCK SA72 6JY Tel (0646) 686932

Scotland

BERWICKSHIRE **Coastal Marine Boatbuilders Ltd** Browns Bank, EYEMOUTH TD14 5DQ Tel (08907) 50328

GRAMPIAN **Henry Fleetwood & Sons Ltd** Baker Street, LOSSIEMOUTH IV31 6NZ Tel (034381) 3015

GRAMPIAN **Fettes & Rankine Engineering** 4 Albert Quay, ABERDEEN Tel (0224) 573343

GRAMPIAN **Northern Engineering Works** 22-30 Seagate, PETERHEAD AB4 6JP Tel (0779) 78691

GRAMPIAN **J S Pirie & Co** Harbour Road, FRASERBURGH Tel (03462) 3314

HEBRIDES **J Fleming Engineers Ltd** Goat Island, Stornoway, ISLE OF LEWIS PA87 2RS Tel (0851) 703488

SHETLAND **H N P Engineering Ltd** Commercial Road, LERWICK ZE1 0NJ Tel (0595) 2368

STRATHCLYDE **J N MacDonald & Co** 47-49 Byron Street, GLASGOW G11 6LP Tel (041 334) 6171

STRATHCLYDE **C McMillan** Kinloch Road, Campbeltown ARGYLL Tel (0586) 52832

Northern Ireland

Albert Annett & Sons The Harbour, KILKEEL Tel (06937) 62208

Robert Craig & Sons Ltd 15-21 Great Georges Street, BELFAST BT15 1BW Tel (0232) 232971

Republic of Ireland

Western Marine Ltd Bulloch Harbour, Dalkley, DUBLIN Tel 010 353 1 2800321

The North

MERSEYSIDE **James Troop & Co Ltd** Pleasant Hill Street, LIVERPOOL L8 5SZ Tel 051-709 0581

YORKSHIRE **Auto Unit Repairs (Leeds) Ltd** Henshaw Works, Yeadon, LEEDS LS19 7XY Tel (0532) 501222

Central

BERKSHIRE **D B Marine Engineering Ltd** Cookham Bridge, COOKHAM-ON-THAMES SL6 9SN Tel (06285) 26032

NORTHAMPTONSHIRE **C V S Pentapower** St Andrews Road, NORTHAMPTON NN1 2LF Tel (0604) 38537/38409/ 36173

The South East

LONDON **John A Sparks & Co Ltd** Ardwell Road, STREATHAM HILL SW2 4RT Tel 081-674 3434

SUSSEX **Felton Marine Engineering** Brighton Marina, BRIGHTON BN2 5UF Tel (0273) 601779

The South

HAMPSHIRE **R K Marine** Hamble River Boatyard, Bridge Road, Swanwick, SOUTHAMPTON SO3 7EB Tel (04895) 83572 or 83585

The East

ESSEX **Volspec Ltd** Woodrolfe Road, Tollesbury, MALDON CM9 8SE Tel (0621) 869756

ESSEX **French Marine Motors Ltd** 61/63 Waterside, BRIGHTLINGSEA CO7 0AX Tel (020630) 2133

NORFOLK **Prior Diesel Ltd** ABC Wharf, Southgates Road, GT YARMOUTH NR30 3LQ Tel (0493) 853241

HUMBERSIDE **Hall Brothers (Bridlington) Ltd** Bessingby Way, Bessingby Industrial Estate, BRIDLINGTON YO16 4SJ Tel (0262) 673346/676604

SOUTH HUMBERSIDE **Anglo Dansk Marine Eng Co Ltd** Robinson Lane, Fish Docks, GRIMSBY DN31 3SF Tel (0472) 351457/8/9

TYNE & WEAR **Royston Marine Eng Ltd** 40 Bell Street, Fish Quay, NORTH SHIELDS NE30 1HF Tel 091-259-5935 or 6797

Commitment to care worldwide.

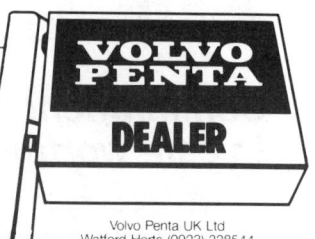

VOLVO PENTA

DEALER

Volvo Penta UK Ltd
Watford Herts (0923) 228544

KINNEGO MARINA, Oxford Island, Marina Office, Lurgan, Co Armagh, N. Ireland. Tel: (0762) 327573.
Call sign: Ch. 10, 16.
Open: April-Oct. 0900-2200; Nov.-Mar. 0900-1700.
Berths: 53, 20 moorings (5 visitors).
Remarks: Access via Coleraine Lower River Bawn to Lough Neagh system: masts stepped at Coleraine; draught 4 ft. 6 in.
Harbour Master: Mr Paddy Prunty.

COLERAINE MARINA, Coleraine, Co. Londonderry, N. Ireland. Tel: (0265) 44768.
Call sign: Ch. 37.
Berths: 59 (15 visitors). Max. draught 1.8m, LOA 12m.
Facilities: fuel; water; electricity; slipway; lift; chandlery; security; yacht club; telephone; toilets; showers.
Customs: Tel: (0265) 44803.

BALLYRONAN MARINA, Shore Road, Ballyronan, Magherafelt, N. Ireland. Tel: (06487) 63359/63441.
Open: Dawn to dusk all year.
Berths: 70.
Marina Manager: John Doyle.

BELGIUM

NIEUWPOORT HAVEN. Tel: (058) 233045.
Pilots: (058) 230000.
Call sign: Ch. 9.
Open: Normal hours. **Berths:** 2000 (including
visitors). Available at 1. Kon Yachtclub
Nieuwpoort. Tel: (058) 234413; 2. VVW Marina
(Novus Portus). Tel: (058) 235232. 3. W.S.K.
Lum. Tel: 23.36.41. Depths: Channel 2.5-3.5m.
Harbours: 2m, max. LOA 15m.
Facilities: clubs; shipyards; town nearby.
Customs: Tel: (058) 233451.

KONINKLIJKE YACHT CLUB NIEUWPOORT,
Krommehoek B 8450, Nieuwpoort.
Tel: 058/23.44.13.
Port: Vlotkom.
Berths: 485, max. LOA 17m.
Facilities: fuel; discount; shopping bikes;
water; gas; electricity; chandlery; repairs;
cranage 10T; slipway; duty-free; bar;
restaurant; weather forecast service;
children's playground; sanitary and showers.

OOSTENDE, Harbour Office B-8400.
Tel: (059) 32 16 69.
Call sign: Ch. 9, 16.
Customs: Wet dock, East Quay.
Tel: (059) 80 06 70.

MERCATOR MARINA, Slijkenseesteenweg 1,
B 8400 Oostende. Tel: (059) 705762 (Marina);
321665/321687 (Office).
Call sign: Mercator Yacht Harbour Ch. 14.
Open: 24 hours. **Berths:** 320 (visitors
available).
Facilities: fuel (diesel); electricity (220V
50kHz); chandlery; provisions; water; repairs;
storage; brokerage; slipway; showers; hotels;
restaurants; crane available in port.
Harbour Master/Director: R. Ghys.
Other Berthplaces: 1. North Sea Yacht Club
Ostend. Tel: (059) 702754. 30 visitors berths.
2. Royal Yacht Club Ostend. Tel: (059) 320307.
30 visitors berths.

NORTH SEA YACHT CLUB, Montgomerykaai
1, B 8400, Oostende, Belgium.
Tel: 059-702754.
Berths: 20 in summer (100 visitors). Max.
length 18m.

BLANKENBERGE, VVW Marina, Oude
Wenduinsesteenweg 4, B-8370 Blankenberge.
Tel: (050) 417536
Open: Normal hours. **Berths:** Visitors
available. Max. LOA 15m.
Facilities: fuel (diesel, petrol); water; gas;
electricity; chandlery; provisions (shops near
by); repairs (all types); cranage; (limit 10
tons); slipway; yacht club; bar; restaurant;
WCs; showers; phones; garbage;
gardiennage.

SCARPHOUT YACHT CLUB, Havenplein 1,
8370 Blankenberge, Belgium.
Tel: 050-411420.
Berths: 300, with 60 for visitors (max. length
13m.).

JACHTHAVEN HEERENLAAK, Heerenlaaweg
100, B 3680 Aldeneik-Maaseik, Belgium.
Tel: 011-566842.
Facilities: Campsite (354 places) next to
harbour.
Berths: 470 (max. length 15m). Draught 3.4m,
LOA 15m.

ROYAL BELGIAN SAILING CLUB, Rederskaai
1, B-8380-Zeebrugge, Belgium. Tel: Secretary
050-54.49.03. Clubhouse 050-54.41.97.
Berths: 100 (40 visitors). Max. length 16m.
Facilities: fuel (diesel, petrol); water; gas;
chandlery; provisions (shops near by); repairs
(all types); cranage (limit 5 tons mobile);
slipway. Yard facilities at Zeebrugge Harbour.
Tel: (050) 544903.
Harbour Master: T. Everaert.

JACHTHAVEN DE SPAANJERD, Maasdijk,
B3688 Ophoven-Kinrooi, Belgium.
Tel: 011-563125/567503.
Berths: 830, with 20 for visitors. Draught
3.4m, LOA 20m.

ANTWERP YACHT CLUB, Nieuw Lobroedok L
11, B 2008, Antwerp, Belgium.
Tel: 03-2350104.
Berths: 120 in summer, with 20 for visitors.

SCHMUGGELN SIE KEINE SÄUGETIERE

Durch das Einschmuggeln von Säugetieren auf die Britischen Inseln kann Tollwut eingeschleppt und damit das Leben von Menschen und Tieren gefährdet werden.

Nehmen Sie keine Haustiere mit, wenn Sie ins Ausland reisen.
Bringen Sie keine Säugetiere bei der Einreise mit.

Die Strafen sind hoch.

Wenn Sie ein Säugetier auf die Britischen Inseln einschmuggeln, können Sie zu einer Geldstrafe in unbegrenzter Höhe und zu einer Gefängnisstrafe von bis zu einem Jahr verurteilt werden.

Das Tier selbst muß möglicherweise getötet werden.

Dieses Gesetz gilt auch für gegen Tollwut geimpfte Säugetiere.

Jede Einfuhr eines Säugetieres muß zuvor genehmigt werden.

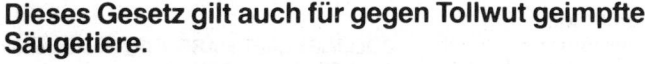

DIE 'REINZUBRINGEN IST WAHNSINN

Ministry of Agriculture, Fisheries and Food

HOLLAND

On arrival in Holland you are required to report to the nearest port with customs facilities, and to complete a declaration which will exempt you from import duties and taxes on the boat for a period of twelve months. This declaration is to be shown on all subsequent visits to Holland during that period. Once the twelve month period has elapsed, you are required to keep the boat out of Dutch waters for a further period of a day before a new declaration is granted. Navigation licence is compulsory for the Netherlands for ships longer than 15 metres and motorboats capable of a speed of more than 20 km per hour regardless of length.

Schelde Information Service:
Call sign: Ch. 12, 14.

BRESKENS, Westerschelde. Tel: Yachthaven (01172) 1902. **Customs:** Tel: (01172) 2610. **Open:** Normal hours. **Berths:** 500 (100 visitors).
Facilities: fuel (diesel, petrol); water; gas; electricity; chandlery; provisions (shops near by); repairs (all types); cranage (limit 25 tons); slipway.
Harbour Master: R. A. A. van Quekelberghe.

VLISSINGEN (Flushing), Yacht Harbour "De Schelde", S end of Walcheren Canal. Tel: Yachthaven (01184) 65912. **Customs:** Tel: (01184) 60.000
Call sign: (Locks) Ch. 22, Flushing-East Port Ch. 9, Post Vlissingen Ch. 21.
Open: Normal hours. **Berths:** Visitors available.
Facilities: fuel (diesel, petrol); water; gas; electricity; chandlery; provisions; repairs (all types); cranage/travel hoist; slipway (limit 15 tons).

MICHIEL DE RUYTER HAVEN, Ruyterplein 1, 4381 BZ. Tel: (01184) 14498. Fax: (01184) 14483. (Vlissingen Old Fishing Harbour).
Open: April-Sept., 0800-2200 (incoming), all day for departures.
Berths: 60 visitors. Max. draught 3m, LOA 16m. Sill-check tide gauge. Max. width at storm barrier 6m.
Facilities: diesel; petrol; water; gas; electricity; chandlery; provisions; all repairs; phone; WCs; showers; laundrette; restaurant; café; bar; yacht and diving clubs; mail.

W. V. ARNE YACHT HARBOUR, Oostwatering, Middelburg, Middle of Walcheren Canal. Tel: (01180) 27180 yacht harbour. Tel: (01180) 13852 yacht club.
Open: Normal hours.
Berths: Visitors available.
Facilities: Yacht club, toilets, showers, washing and drymachine, telefone, fuel (diesel, petrol), 2 × chandlery, provisions (shops near by in the centre) repairs (ask Harbourmaster).
Harbourmaster: H. Platteeuw.
Remarks: the bridge timings over Walcheren Canal are Monday till Saturday from 0600-2200. Sunday 0700-1100 and 1700-2100.

VEERE YACHT HARBOUR, Veerse Meer. N end of Walcheren Canal. Tel: (01181) 1484. **Open:** Normal hours. **Berths:** Visitors available.
Facilities: fuel (diesel, petrol); water; gas; electricity; chandlery; provisions (shops near by); repairs (all types); cranage (limit 12 ton travel hoist); slipways.
Harbour Master: G. v.d. Dussen. Tel: (01181) 1484.
Remarks: The Veerse Meer is 22 km long and 1.5 km wide at its broadest point. The draught depth is generally at least 3.50 m. but places where it is less than 1.50 m are clearly marked with stakes.

DELTA MARINA, Kortgene (Veerse Meer East) 4484 ZG. Tel: (01108) 1315. Fax: 01108-1477.
Open: 24 hours. **Berths:** 700 (visitors available).
Facilities: fuel (diesel, petrol); electricity; chandlery and supermarket; water; all repairs; 16 ton cranage; storage (on shore); brokerage; slipway; gas; restaurant.
Harbour Master: P. Kastelein.

COLIJNSPLAAT HARBOUR, Oosterschelde 4486 ZG. Tel: (01199) 762.
Open: 24 hr. **Berths:** Visitors available in yacht harbour.
Facilities: fuel (diesel, petrol); water; gas; electricity; provisions near by.
Harbour Master: D. Nonnekes.

Visual Navigational Aids for Holland — Section 24

BROUWERSHAVEN YACHT HARBOUR, Gravelingenmeer. Tel: (01119) 1330. **Open:** Normal hours. **Berths:** Visitors available.
Facilities: fuel (diesel, petrol); water; gas; electricity; chandlery; provisions (shops near by); repairs (all types); cranage (limit 9 tons); slipway; storage; brokerage.
Harbour Master: J. de Vos. Tel: (01119) 1330 (Home 1364).
Remarks: There is no direct access from the sea. The Gravelingenmeer, which is about 20 km long and 3-9 km wide can be reached via the lock at Bruinisse. Draught 2m, LOA 25m, width 7.5m.

AQUA-PESCH, MARINA STELLENDAM. Tel: 01879-2600. Stellendam outer harbour, seaside of lock, berth for visitors available. Yacht Harbour Office:
Open: 0930-1200, 1400-1730, 1830-2200.
Facilities: fuel on shore, water, camping gaz, electricity, repairs, hoist (limit 14m and 20 tons), slipway, storage, clubhouse with launderette and telephone; chandlery; charts.
Yacht Harbour Master: W. A. Pesch.
Customs: facilities are now available in Middelharnis through the Goereesesluis lock 10 miles up the Haringvliet. Staying overnight before clearance is permitted, providing clearance is obtained within 24 hours of arrival at Stellendam.

NOORDSCHANS YACHT HARBOUR. (Hollandsch Diep, 5 miles E of Willemstad). Tel: (01682) 3550.
Open: every day. **Berths:** 700 (visitors available).
Facilities: electricity; chandlery; water; all repairs; 30 ton mobile crane; restaurants.

SCHEVENINGEN MARINA, 2nd Harbour, Scheveningen. Tel: (Marina) (070) 3520017/275; (Harbour) (070) 3527721/722. Telex: 33378 GD HMW-NL. Fax: (070) 505764.
Open: all year round. **Berths:** 200 (visitors available).
Call sign: Ch. 14.
Facilities: fuel (diesel); electricity; chandlery; provisions; water; cranage; slipway; gas; WCs, showers, laundry; restaurants; hotels (near by); car hire. Repairs, cranage and Customs in harbour.
Berthing Master: R. Goudriaan.
Remarks: Scheveningen is a dangerous port of call when a strong wind is blowing from a NWly direction. There is no access to Dutch inland waters.

IJMUIDEN HARBOUR. Major fishing port. Entry to Noordzee Kanaal for Amsterdam. (18 miles). Tel: (02550) 19027.
Call sign: Seawards of fairway buoy, Ch. 12; fairway buoy-locks, Ch. 9; inside locks; Ch. 22 (IJmuiden Port). Locks – km pole 11.2, Ch. 11 (Nordzee Kanal). Km pole 13+, Ch. 14 (Amsterdam Port).
Open: 24 hr. **Berths:** Visitors short stay moorings available at Haringhaven and inside Zuidersluis (South Lock) Yacht harbour in 2nd side channel South from Noordzee Kanal, behind bridge.
Facilities: fuel; shops near by.
Remarks: IJmuiden is reasonably safe through the moles extending far out to sea. The IJmuiden locks give access to Dutch Inland waters.
Customs: Yachts must report to jetty 100m W of S Lock (N bank of Southern Outer Canal).

ROYAL NETHERLANDS YACHT CLUB (Koninklijke Nederlandsche Zeil – en Roeivereeniging). Tel: (02942) 1540. Muiden (entry to River Vecht/IJssellake).
Open: 24 hours. **Berths:** 140 (some visitors).
Facilities: fuel (diesel, gas); electricity (220V); chandlery and provisions near by; water; all repairs; cranage; brokerage (near by); slipway; clubhouse and restaurant – Tel: (02942) 1434 (manager).
Harbour Master: Th. A. Huisman, Chr. E. Eerden. Tel: (02942) 1450.

'TWELLEGEA JACHTHAVEN', Guiyet Amsterdam (North). Tel: (020) 320616.
Open: 24 hours. **Berths:** 80 (about 20 visitors), deep, open water.
Facilities: fuel (diesel); electricity; chandlery; water; engine and ship repairs; 30 ton crane plus mobile crane; storage; brokerage; gas; café/restaurant.
Harbour Master: J. Huisman.

PORT OF ZAANDAM, Port Control Authority, Municipality of Zaanstad, Westkade 2, 1506 BA Zaandam. Tel: (075) 512888/701701. Fax: 075 512311. Tx: 19110.
Open: 0600-2130 (week); 24 hr. (weekend).
Berths: Dirk Metselaarharbour, W. Thomassenharbour, draught 10m; Old Timber harbour (small slip), Isaac Bartharbour, draught 5-9m.
Facilities; water; provisions; repairs launch; towage; medical facilities; small slipway; dry dock; commercial shipping.
Remarks: All Zaandam harbours have a direct unrestricted connection with the North Sea Canal. Pilotage recommended.

ALKMAAR HARBOUR, Accijnstoren, Bierkade 26, 1811 NJ Alkmaar (on Great North Holland Canal, between Den Helder and Amsterdam). Tel: (072) 117135.
Berths: are available for visiting yachts.
Facilities: fuel, (diesel, petrol); water; chandlery; provisions; all repairs; cranage; storage; brokerage; gas.
Harbour Master: Th. Van der Meer.
Remarks: Locks and bridges in the Great North-Holland Canal are closed on: January 1st, Easter Sunday, and Christmas Day, on Sunday nights 2300-0500, Saturdays 1900-0700. On Sundays (June 1st to October 1st) only limited opening.

DEN HELDER. Het Nieuwe Diep 37A, 1781 AE Den Helder. Tel: 02230 13955. **Customs:** Tel: (02230) 15181. **Water Police:** (02230) 16767.
Emergency: 06-11 or 22222.
Immigration: Tel: 02230 57515.
Call sign: 'Den Helder Traffic Centre'. At all times permission to enter fairway and harbour should be obtained from Vessel Traffic Centre on Ch. 12.
Outer Harbour. A limited number of visitors berths are available at Royal Naval Yacht Club. Berths will be assigned by the yacht H.M. Tel: (02230) 52645. During daylight hours only.
Inner Harbours. (behind the locks.) Visitors berths available here and at **Yacht Clubs:** HWN. Tel: 24422; MWY. Tel: 17076/52173. Max. depth Westoever 4.6m, Oestoeverweg 3m, LOA 80m. If yachts cannot use Yacht Club berths due to length or draught, they should go to the civil port, jetty 32-39 (max. draught 6.8m, LOA 150m) or jetty 43-55 (Max. draught 5m, LOA 80m). Civil H.M.: Tel: (02230) 13955.
Open: 24 hours.
Facilities: All available.
Remarks: There are shipping links via the Noordhollands-Kanaal and the Zaan with Amsterdam, IJsselmeer and the Waddenzee.

JACHTHAVEN DEN HELDER, Watersport Village 1785 AZ. Tel: (02230) 37444.
Open: 0900-2400. **Berths:** 250 (visitors always available). Max. depth 2.4m (dredged).
Facilities: fuel (diesel); electricity; chandlery and shops; water; repairs; cranage; storage; several slipways; gas; pub-restaurant.

DEN OEVER – Western Sealock for entry to IJsselmeer. Tel: (02271) 1789 (Marina).
Call sign: Ch. 20.

Open: Lock – Mon.-Fri. and 2 hr. on Sat.
Marina: Normal hours. **Berths:** 210 (Summer) 230 (Winter), 60 visitors.
Facilities: fuel (diesel, petrol); water; electricity; chandlery; shops near by; repairs (all types); travel hoist; slipway.

OUDESCHILD, Nieuwe Jachthaven Texel. Tel: 02220 13608.
Berths: visiting yachts 230.
Remarks: Beware strong tidal current at harbour entrance. Draught up to 4.8m.

AANLOOPHAVEN, Vlieland. Tel: (05621) 1729.
Facilities: electricity; water; phone; fuel; gas; provisions; ice; WCs; showers; repairs; 10T crane; slip; launderette; restaurant; bar nearby. English, Dutch, German spoken. Max. draught 2.4m.

HARLINGEN, Waddenzee. Entry to the Van Harinxmakanaal on the west coast of Friesland.
Port Authority: Tel: (05178) 13041/92300.
Port Control: Tel: (05178) 12512.
Call Sign: Ch. 11.
Open: Mon.-Fri. 24 hr. Sat. 0000-2200. Sun. 0730-2200. 1 April-15 Oct.
Yacht Harbours: 1. Noorderhaven (in centre of town). Tel: (05178) 15666. **Berths:** 120 (visitors available); Inside the Tjerck Hiddeslocks: 2. HWSV. Tel: (05178) 16898. 100 visitors. 3. Jachtwerf Atlantic bv. Tel: (05178) 17658. 30 visitors.
Facilities: fuel (diesel, petrol); gas; water; provisions; repairs; dry-docking; cranage (40 tons); slipway; compass-adjuster; brokerage; customs; hotels, restaurants.
Remarks: Yachts can berth only in the Yacht harbours. When two red lights are showing from the semaphore, it is forbidden to enter or leave the port.

LAUWERSOOG, Jachthaven Noordergat. Tel: (05193) 9040.
Berths: 400, 60 visitors. Max. draught 3m, LOA 20m.
Facilities: All; 15T hoist; 1T crane; 15T lift. English, Dutch, German, Flemish spoken.

DELFZIJL, Z.V. Neptunus. Tel: (05960) 15004.
Berths: 100, up to 40 visitors. Max. draught 3m, LOA 16m.
Open: April-Sept. H.M. 0800-1100, 1700-2000.
Facilities: all nearby. English, French, Spanish, Dutch, German spoken.

The following harbours and marinas are situated within the **IJsselmeer** Sea. This is a freshwater inland sea. It is 31.25 miles long and 18 miles wide.

MEDEMBLIK.
Berths: Yachts proceed into the 2nd and 3rd harbours, via lifting road bridge. Opening times as follows: Mon.-Fri. 0800-2000; Sat.-Sun. 0730-2130.
Facilities: Fuel, water, repairs, WC/showers.
Remarks: You are not allowed to flush your toilets in the marina.

ENKHUISEN, Gemeentehaven Havenweg 3, 1601 GA, Enkhuizen.
Tel: 02280-12444.
Buyshaven: Tel: 02280-15660.
Compagnieshaven: Tel: 02280-13353.
Berths: In main harbour.
Facilities: Lift, chandler, WC/shower, washing machine, fuel, water, repairs.
Remarks: Approach to Enkhuisen is easy and well marked. In clear weather Zuidekerktoren is visible from quite a distance.

HOORN.
Berths: The Harbour Master will allocate berths in Gemeentehaven, Grashaven and Julianapark.
Facilities: Fuel, water, repairs, WC/shower, restaurant.
Remarks: It is possible to anchor on starboard hand, past the outer harbour entrance. Lock gates are always open. Depth reported as 2.6m.

MONNICKENDAM, (De Zeilhoek, Gouwzee, Van Goor), Hougedijk 6-7, 1145 PM, Katwoude. Tel: 02995 1463.
Berths: Berths in the three above marinas.
Facilities: Fuel, water, showers, toilets, washing machines, travel hoist (Van Goor), shops and restaurants, water sports centre, bar, security.

HEMMELAND, Monnickendam. Tel: (02995) 4677.
Open: 24 hours. **Berths:** 630 (20-200 visitors).
Facilities: electricity; water; 20 ton hoist; storage; slipway; further facilities in town.
Harbour Master: Jan Dykstra.

VOLENDAM.
Berths: Berthing is on the eastern end of outer wall.
Facilities: Harbour Master has key for water, showers & toilets.
Remarks: Dredged to 2.7m. and entrance is lit.

STICHTING YACHT HARBOUR, Andijk, Kerkbuurt. Tel: (02289) 3075.
Open: All year round. **Berths:** 650 (visitors available).
Facilities: fuel (diesel); electricity (220V); chandlery; provisions; water; 20 ton crane; storage; slipway; gas; laundry.
Harbour Master; H. Swagerman. Tel: (02289) 1481.

LEMMER, Vuurtorenweg 2, Lemmer (direct on IJsselmeer). Tel: (05146) 3000.
Open: every day.
Berths: 25 (visitors available).
Facilities: electricity; chandlery; provisions; water; all repairs; cranage; storage; slipway; gas.
Harbour Master: Karel Stillebroer.

STAVEREN: Jachthaven de Roggerbroek. Tel: 05194/1469.
Berths: There are plenty of berths available.
Facilities: Fuel, water, repairs and all the usual marina facilities.

HINDELOOPEN, Old Harbour, Jachthaven. Tel: 05142-2009.
Berths: In old inner harbour.
Facilities: Fuel; repairs; electricity.
Remarks: There is a marina on the port side of the entrance.

MAKKUM, Visserijhaven. Tel: 05158/1450.
Berths: 60 visitors berths available.
Facilities: Fuel, water, repairs, WC/showers.

KORNWERDERZAND – Eastern Sealock for entry to IJsselmeer. Tel: (05177) 441.
Call Sign: Ch. 18.
Open: 24 hr. **Berths:** Visitors available.
Facilities: water; provisions. Better facilities for yachts at Makkum Marina.

FRANCE

PORT AUTONOME DE DUNKERQUE.
Capitainerie, Terre-Plein Guillain, BP 6534,
59386 Dunkerque cedex 1. Tel: (28) 29 72 62.
Fax: (28) 29 72 75. Telex: 130972. Y.C.M.1. Tel:
(28) 66 79 90. Y.C.D. Tel: (28) 66 11 06.
Customs. Tel: (28) 66 87 14.
Call Sign: Dunkerque port, Ch. 73, 16.
Open: 24 hr. **Berths:** Visitors available in yacht
harbour on E side of Avant Port by Yacht Club
de la Mer du Nord. 120 visitors pontoons in
Bassin du Commerce from Yacht Club de
Dunkerque.
Facilities: fuel (diesel, petrol); water; gas;
electricity; chandlery; provisions (in town);
repairs; cranage.
Entry: Follow Eastern breakwater (Jetée Est)
to Avant Port. Sound signal to control tower
or VHF radio call to Dunkerque Port Ch. 73.

GRAVELINES. Capitainerie, 20 Bassin Vauban,
BP 235, 59820. Tel: (28) 23 13 42.
Call sign: Ch. 24, 61.
Berths: 450 (40 visitors) in Avant-Port. Await
HW to enter basin, pontoon berths available.
Facilities: water; electricity; toilets; cranage;
fuel.
Remarks: Entry difficult in fresh-strong winds.

CALAIS. Port de Plaisance, Bassin Ouest. Tel:
(21) 34 55 23.
Call Sign: Port Control Ch. 12.
Open: 24 hr. **Berths:** 350-400 (Visitors berths
available at yacht harbour in the Bassin de
l'Ouest open during normal hours). Lock 16m
wide; 8.4 deep.
Facilities: fuel (diesel); water; gas; chandlery;
provisions (shops near by); repairs; cranage;
slipway; electricity 220V 5A; oil dump.
Remarks: While waiting for lock to yacht
harbour to open craft can lie alongside the
quays at Eastern and southern sides of Avant
Port. Harbours dry out LW. Access to Canals,
Calais, Mediterranean.

BOULOGNE. Jetée Sud Ouest, BP 756, 62321
Boulogne. Port Captain. Tel: (21) 31 52 43
(24 hr.). Port de Plaisance. Tel: (21) 80 72 00.
Tx: 110 968 F.
Call Sign: Boulogne Port Ch. 12.
Open: 24 hr. **Berths:** Visitors' pontoons at
yacht harbour in inner harbour.
Facilities: Water; gas; electricity; provisions
(near by); showers; toilets.
Entry lights: Green over white over red
prohibits all movement in inner harbour.
Contact Port Control before sailing or entry.

PORT D'ETAPLES-SUR-MER. Tel: 21 94 74 26.
Berths: 116, 12 visitors, 1m draught.
Open: 2 hr–HW–2 hr.
Facilities: electricity; water; phone; gas;
chandlery; ice; WCs/showers; launderette;
restaurant; bar; yacht club; 3T crane; slip;
sailing school; 130T hoist; boat sales;
gardiennage; lift-out.
Remarks: follow buoyed channel, avoid SW
winds.

PORT DU TOUQUET, Baie de Canche.
Tel: (21) 051277.
Berths: 1m draught, all dry.
Facilities: water; club (Easter-Oct.); slip; 3T
crane; careening.

PORT DE PLAISANCE DU HOURDEL, 328 rue
Faidherbe, La Molliere, 80410 Cayeux sur
Mer. Tel: 22 26 61 78.
Berths: 70 moorings in Somme Bay.

CLUB NAUTIQUE DE LA BAIE DE SOMME,
Digue Mercier, 80550 Le Crotoy. Tel: 22 27 83
11/22 27 80 24 (Mairie).
Berths: 288.

ST VALERY-SUR-SOMME, Port de Plaisance
80230. Tel: 22 26 91 64.
Call sign: Ch. 9.
Open: Entrance to buoyed channel (5M long) -
3 hr.–HW. Max. draught 2m, LOA 15m.
Berths: 250 (30 visitors).
Facilities: fuel (petrol); water; chandlery;
provisions (shops near by); club; bar;
restaurant; showers; WCs; chandlery;
security.

LE TREPORT. Capitainerie, Quai Albert Couet.
Tel: (35) 86 17 91.
Call sign: Ch. 16, 12.
Berths: 5 (Before entering Bassin à Flot,
visitors to report to Capitainerie).
Facilities: water; ice; WCs; cranage; repairs;
mobile hoists; phone.
Customs: Tel: (35) 86 15 34.
Remarks: Enter Bassin à Flot 1½ hr.–HW–1½
hr. Lock shut at HW. Entry difficult in strong
winds.

DIEPPE, Capitainerie, Port de Commerce. Tel:
(35) 84 10 55. Yacht Harbour, Tel: (35) 84 32 99.
Call Sign: Port Control Ch. 12, 6, 16.
Open: 24 hr. **Berths:** 110 pontoon (visitors 20).
Facilities: fuel (diesel, petrol); water; gas;
electricity; chandlery; provisions (shops near
by); repairs; cranage; slipways; restaurants.
Remarks: Entry to yacht harbour at Bassin
Duquesne 2 hr.–HW–1 hr. Yachts must obey
traffic signals.

N'INTRODUISEZ PAS CLANDESTINEMENT DES ANIMAUX

L'entrée clandestine d'animaux dans les îles Britanniques pourrait introduire la rage et mettre ainsi en danger la vie de personnes et d'animaux.

Si vous allez à l'étranger, n'emmenez pas d'animaux familiers avec vous. Si vous arrivez dans les îles Britanniques, n'introduisez aucun animal.

Les sanctions sont sévères.

Si vous introduisez clandestinement un animal dans les îles Britanniques, vous pourriez être passible d'une amende d'un montant non limité et d'une peine atteignant jusqu'à un an de prison.

L'animal lui-même peut être détruit.

Cette loi s'applique même si l'animal est vacciné contre la rage.

Tout animal ne peut être importé que sous licence.

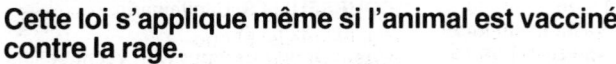

C'EST FOLIE DE L'INTRODUIRE

Ministry of Agriculture, Fisheries and Food

ST VALERY-EN-CAUX. Bureau du Port. Tel: (35) 97 01 30.
Open: 3 hr.–HW–3 hr.
Berths: 580 pontoon (50 visitors available).
Facilities: fuel (diesel, petrol); water; gas; electricity; chandlery; provisions; repairs; cranage; restaurants.

FECAMP. Yacht Harbour. Tel: (35) 28 13 58.
Call Sign: Port Control Ch. 12. Yacht Harbour Ch. 9.
Open: 24 hr. For craft with max. draught 2m, LOA 16m. Craft over this size consult H.M.
Berths: 530 pontoon berths (30 visitors) in Avant Port and Bassin Berigny. Outer half pontoon C in Avant Port is reserved for visitors.
Facilities: fuel (diesel); electricity; water; gas; chandlery; provisions; duty-free shop; repairs (GRP, wood); cranage (38 tons); storage; brokerage; slipway; hotels; restaurants.
Harbour Master: André Louis.

LE HAVRE, Port du Plaisance du Havre, Boulevard Clemenceau 76600. Tel:(35)212395. Port & Control Tower Tel:(35)217400.
Customs: Tel:(35)413351. Port Officer: Jean Ledantec Tel:(35)218041.
Call Sign: Port Control Ch. 12, Marina Ch. 9.
Open: 24 hr.
Berths: 960 (up to 100 visitors), 3m. depth, 5-18m. LOA.
Facilities: diesel; petrol (supply by credit card only); water; gas; electricity; chandlery; provisions; dry berths; WCs; showers; repairs (all types); cranage; slip; phone; fishing; clubs.
Remarks: construction of further 300 berths on Olsen quay.

HONFLEUR, Affaires Maritimes, place de L'ancien, Bassin du Centre. Tel: (31)892067. Capitainerie. Tel: (31)892002.
Call Sign: Port Control Ch. 11, 16.
Open: Drying harbour with yacht basin lock open at HW–1, HW, HW+1 (and HW+2 daytime high season/weekends).
Berths: 150 pontoon moorings (visitors 30).
Facilities: fuel (diesel, petrol); water; gas; provisions (shops nearby); repairs; cranage; storage; brokerage; slipway.

PORT DEAUVILLE MARINA, SER Port Deauville. Tel: (31) 98 30 01. 0900-1200, 1400-1800. (Closed Wednesday.)
Call Sign: Ch. 9.
Access: level 3-3$\frac{1}{2}$m.
Berths: 738 in marina (100 visitors available). (80 berths at Deauville-Trouville in summer.)
Customs: (31) 88 63 49.

Facilities: fuel (diesel); water; gas; electricity; chandlery; provisions (shops are nearer Trouville); repairs (all types). cranage (45 ton); slip; phone; ice; laundrette; showers; WCs.

DIVES-SUR-MER, Société Houlgataise des Regates de la Dives. Tel: (31) 91 47 10.
Berths: 150 moorings at Dives, 230 at Cabourg.
Facilities: water; showers; WCs; electricity; telephone; fuel; slipway.
Remarks: Passage hard on ebb tide when wind is NW-NE.

CAEN, Bassin St Pierre, 2 quai de la Londe, 14000 Caen, Calvados, Normandy. Tel: 31 93 74 47.
Call Sign: 12, 68.
Open: 0745-1230, 1400-1900.
Berths: 99 pontoons, 21 on quay (to 40m). LOA, 4m. draught). Some visitors.
Facilities: petrol; electricity; gas; ice; water; showers; WCs; diving air; slip; hoist; dry dock; rigging; repairs.
Contact: M. J. P. Allainguillaume.
Access: via Ouistreham canal (toll locks) 2 hr.–HW–3 hr. 14km. long, depth 5.5m. There is a speed limit of 7 knots.

OUISTREHAM RIVA BELLA, Capitainerie, BP 12, Port de Plaisance, 14650. Tel: (31) 97 14 43.
Call sign: Ch. 16, 12, 68. Ch. 9 0800-1200, 1430-1800.
Open: 24 hr. **Berths:** 650 pontoon moorings (visitors always available).
Facilities: fuel (diesel, petrol); water; gas; chandlery; provisions (shops near by); slipway; electricity; repairs.
Remarks: Dock gate opens – hr.–HW–3 hr. (Winter-3 hr. HW) weekends and 15 June-15 Sept. for pleasure craft. Yacht Club Tel: 31 97 13 05.

COURSEULLES. Capitainerie.
Tel: (31) 37 51 69.
Open: Drying harbour with yacht basins. Entry 2 hr.–HW–1 hr. Locks open 2 hr.–HW–2 hr.
Berths: 720 pontoon (visitors available).
Facilities: fuel (diesel, petrol); water; gas; electricity; chandlery; provisions (shops near by); WCs; showers; repairs (all types); slipway.

PORT EN BESSIN. Capitainerie.
Tel: (31) 21 70 49.
Open: Basin 2 hr.–HW–2 hr. Avant-Port 3 hr.–HW–3 hr.
Call sign: Ch. 18.
Berths: 36 (12 visitors) in Bassin a Flot.

Facilities: water; ice; electricity; WCs; showers; telephone; refuse; slipway; repairs; cranage (limit 6 tons); fuel.
Customs: Tel: (31) 21 71 09.
Remarks: Access very difficult in N-NE winds, dangerous in force 8-9.

GRANDCAMP-MAISY, Port Plaisance, Quai du Petit-Nice, 14450 Grandcamp-Maisy.
Tel: (31) 22 63 16.
Call sign: Ch. 9.
Open: Summer 0600-2200, Winter 0800-1700.
Berths: 292 pontoon berths in marina (25 visitors).
Facilities: fuel (diesel); water; gas; electricity; chandlery; provisions (shops near by); repair; cranage; storage; brokerage.
Harbour Master: M. R. Marion.
Remarks: Entry difficult in winds NW-NE 6-7.

ISIGNY SUR MER, Port de Plaisance, Mairie, rue Thiers, 14230 Isigny sur Mer. Tel: 31 22 00 40.
Berths: Pontoons to 150 metres. Moorings also at Grand Vey nearby.
Access: at rising tide.
Contact: M. Geiss.

PORT-CARENTAN, Port de Plaisance Cotentin, Capitainerie. Tel: (33) 42 24 44.
Customs: Tel: (33) 44 16 00.
Open: 2 hr.–HW–3 hr.
Call sign: Ch. 9.
Berths: 513 on pontoons (50 visitors). Max. draught 3m, LOA 35m, width 8m. Moorings also at Quinéville nearby.
Facilities: Water; electricity; WCs; showers; refuse; ice; cranage 50T; 16T lift; overwintering; slipway; fuel.

ST VAAST-LA-HOUGUE MARINA, Place Auguste-Contamine. Tel: (33) 54 48 81.
Call sign: Ch. 9.
Open: Entry 2¼ h.–HW–3 hr.
Berths: 665 (165 visitors).
Facilities: fuel (diesel, petrol); water; electricity; slipway; 15 ton crane; showers; toilets; Club Boutique.
Harbour Master: Jacques Simon.
Remarks: Warning, in certain conditions of neap tide and very high pressure, the closing time of the gate could be 1¼ hr earlier than the usual HW+3 hr.

BARFLEUR HARBOUR. Capitainerie.
Tel: (33) 54 08 29.
Open: 3 hr.–HW–3 hr.
Berths: 200 (visitors alongside always available).
Facilities: fuel (diesel, petrol); water; gas; electricity; chandlery; provisions (shops near by); repairs; cranage.
Remarks: Entry difficult in E and NE winds.

CHERBOURG. Capitainerie, Port Chantereyne.
Tel: (33) 53 75 16.
Call sign: Port Control Ch. 16. Chantereyne-Cherbourg Yacht Harbour Ch. 9.
Open: 24 hr. **Berths:** 613 in yacht harbour (70 visitors). Moorings also at Goury (Cap de la Hague).
Facilities: fuel (diesel, petrol); water; gas; electricity; chandlery; provisions; WCs; showers; repairs; cranage; slipway.

CHANNEL ISLANDS

BRAYE HARBOUR, Alderney, C.I.
Tel: (0481) 822620. Fax: (0481) 823699.
Call sign: Alderney Radio. Ch. 16, 74, 12. 0800-2200 (daily summer) 0800-1700 (Mon-Fri. winter).
Open: Harbour 24 hrs. **Berths:** 120. Visitors 80 (on yellow mooring buoys); pontoon.
Facilities: fuel (diesel, petrol); water; gas; provisions (3 min.); chandleries; repairs; refuse; launderette; cranage (12 ton limit); storage in winter; dinghy slipway; showers/toilets etc in Sailing Club, also showers and laundry facilities on main quay.
Remarks: Beaching and berthing on main quay is prohibited. Harbour taxi in operation. Do not exceed 4kts, in harbour.

MAINBRAYCE MARINE, Crabby Harbour, Braye, Alderney. Tel: (0481) 822772.
Call sign: Mainbrayce, Ch. 80, 37 (M).
Moorings: 100 swinging for visitors.
Facilities: water; gas; chandlery; repairs; 12T crane; water taxi to Braye 0800-2359.
Access: 2½ hr.–HW–2½ hr.

ST PETER PORT, Guernsey Harbour Office, White Rock. Tel: Harbour Office (0481) 20229. Fax: (0481) 714177. Telex: 4191488. Marinas. Tel: (0481) 25987.
Call sign: St Peter Port Radio (Ch. 78). Port control (Ch. 12). Link calls (Ch. 62). D.F. indicated bearings of vessels (Ch. 16, 67). Bearings are given from aerial position 49°26′27″N, 2°35′77″W.
Berths: 400 visitors in marinas or on waiting buoys. Max. draught 2.6m; LOA 20m.
Facilities: fuel (diesel, petrol, gas); water; electricity; chandlery; provisions; repair; slipways; cranage; careening; security; yacht club; telephone; toilets; showers; shop; laundry; restaurant; mail; refuse; bar; dining club; sailing school; boat sales; car hire; gardiennage; storage. French spoken.
Remarks: Entry to marinas 2½ hr.–HW–2½ hr. (use waiting pontoon). Advise Port Control ½ hr. before arrival. All visitors met by dory staff. Vessels of 3m+draught or 20m+LOA contact H.M. in advance.
Harbour Master: Captain T. A. Spencer.

BEAUCETTE YACHT MARINA, Beaucette Harbour, Vale, Guernsey, C.I.
Tel: (0481) 45000. Fax: (0481) 47071. Telex: 4191301.

Call sign: Beaucette Marina Ch. 80, 37 (M).
Open: 0800-2030 hrs. **Berths:** 150 including visitors. Max. LOA 18m.
Facilities: fuel; electricity; gas; water; bike hire; restaurant; car hire; showers; laundrette; repairs; slip; brokerage; bars; provisions.

GOREY HARBOUR, Gorey Pier, Gorey Harbour, Jersey, C.I. Tel: 0534 53616.
Berths: 220 (25 visitors).

ST HELIER HARBOUR AND MARINA, Upper Harbour Weighbridge, St Helier, Jersey, C.I. Tel: Harbour Office (0534) 34451. Fax: (0534) 69135. Telex: 4192028 PORJER G.
Tel: (0534) 79549 (Marina office).
Call sign: (Ch. 14) St Helier Port Control; (Ch. 16) Jersey Radio.
Open: 3 hr.–HW–3 hr. otherwise wait in holding area at entrance to La Collette basin. Harbour 24 hr. **Berths:** 400 (250 visitors).
Facilities: electricity; water; fuel; gas; chandlery; all repairs; 18T hoist; 30T crane; 18T lift; slip; boat sales and hire; car hire; scrubbing grid; lift-out; phone; refuse. In town: launderette; restaurant; bar; yacht club; mail; sea fishing. French spoken.

Remarks: Visitors are restricted to a duration of two weeks, which can be extended to three with the prior permission of the Harbour Master.
St Helier Marina lies within a busy commercial port. Care should therefore be exercised on arrival and departure by taking due note of signals from Port Control building (on stbd. hand when approaching).

LA COLLETTE YACHT BASIN, S Victoria Pier, St Helier, Jersey, C.I. Tel: (0534) 69147.
Open: 24 hr. **Berths:** 60, max. draught 1.8m, LOA 12m. Larger berths St Helier.
Facilities: gas; chandlery; provisions; ice; WCs; showers; phone; refuse; electricity; water. Others at St Helier Harbour.
Remarks: Basin close to St Helier approaches. Take due note of signals from Port Control building (stbd. hand when approaching). Holding area for St Helier Marina and Harbour is well marked.

FRANCE

PORT-BAIL. Bureau du Port. (33) 04 83 48.
Open: $2^1/_2$ hr.–HW–$2^1/_2$ hr. 15 June-31 Aug.
Call sign: Ch. 9.
Berths: 200 places (15 visitors). Moorings also at Pirou nearby.
Facilities: water; showers; slip; repairs; WCs; club.
Customs: Tel: (33) 54 90 08.

CLUB NAUTIQUE DE LA POINTE D'AGON, Mairie d'Agon-Coutainville, 50230 Agon-Coutainville. Tel: 33 47 21 14.
Berths: 150 (2 visitors). Moorings also at Regnéville nearby.
Facilities: Undergoing development; all facilities due in 1990.
Remarks: Access 5 hr. each tide.

GRANVILLE ST.-LÔ, BP 232, 50402 Granville. Tel: (33) 50 05 35. Port de commerce: 33 50 17 75.
Herel Yacht Harbour: Tel: (33) 50 20 06.
Call sign: Port Control Ch. 12, 16 ($1^1/_2$ hr.–HW–1 hr.) Yacht harbour Ch. 9.
Open: Access 3h-HW-3h. Yachts must ensure adequate depth of water over sill. Entry prohibited when tide gauge shows zero (O).
Berths: 1050 (150 visitors). Moorings also at Mont St-Michel nearby.
Facilities: fuel (diesel, petrol); water; gas; electricity; chandlery; provisions (shops near by); repairs; cranage; slipway.

PORT DE HEREL,
Capitainerie. Tel: 33 50 17 75 0800-1200 1400-2000 (out of season 1400-1800).
Port de Plaisance. Tel: 33 50 20 06.
Call Sign: Ch. 16, 12.
Berths: 1050 (max. LOA 15m.) 150 for visitors (on pontoons).
Facilities: water; electricity; WCs; showers: ice (at fishing port); 12T lift; 0.5 and 10T cranes; fuel (Port de Plaisance), gardiennage; Club Nautique.

PORT TREBEURDEN. Tel: (96) 23 64 00
Berths: 552. Open: 20 hours daily.
Facilities: water; electricity; telephone; crane; fuel; ice; parking; yacht and diving clubs; gardiennage; winter storage; security; chandlery; restaurants; WCs.
Note: the marina is due to open April 1992.

ST. MALO, Capitainerie du Port, Terre-plein des Ecluses, BP 121, 35402 St. Malo. Tel: 99 81 62 86. Fax: 99401170. Tx: 950197.
Call sign: VHF Chan. 12, 9 for Sablons Y. Hbr.
Yacht Club: Tel: 99 40 84 42.
Berths: 1216 berths available in Anse de Bas Sablons, St Servan, and 250 available in Bassin Vauban.
Facilities: fresh water; shower; telephone; electricity; ice; cranage; fuel; dry storage.
Access: $2^1/_2$ hr.–HW–$2^1/_2$ hr.
Remarks: Speed limited to 5 knots.

DAHOUET, Pleneuf Val-André 22370. Tel: 96 72 82 85.
Berths: 174, 313 pontoon, 15+ visitors. Max. draught 2.4m.
Open: $2^1/_2$ hr–HW–$2^1/_2$ hr.
Facilities: electricity; water; fuel; gas; chandlery; provisions; ice; phone; WCs; showers; restaurant; café; bar; yacht club; sailing school; sea fishing; repairs; 12T crane; boat sales; car hire; scrubbing grid; security; lift-out; storage. English spoken.

PORT-ST-BRIEUC-LE-LEGUÉ. Capitainerie. Tel: (96) 33 35 41.
Call sign: Ch. 12, 16.
Berths: 80-100 (15 visitors).
Facilities: fuel; ice; WCs; cranage (limit 6 tons).

PORT DE BINIC. Capitainerie. Tel: (96) 73 61 86.
Berths: 500.
Facilities: water; electricity; WC: shower; slipway; cranage (limit 12 tons).

PORT DE PONTRIEUX. Capitainerie, Kergoolat, 22260 Pontrieux.
Tel: (96) 95 60 72.
Call sign: Ch. 12, 16.
Berths: 100 (50 visitors).
Facilities: water; electricity; WCs; showers; telephone; refuse; crane; Club Nautique.

SAINT QUAY-PORTRIEUX.
Port d'Echouage Capitainerie. Tel: 96 70 95 31
Call Sign: Ch. 09
Berths: 500 (8 visitors - stay limited to 3 days July/Aug).
Facilities: water at quay; electricity; petrol; diesel; repairs; slip; crane; chandlery; WCs; showers.
Nouveau Port
Tel: 96 70 49 51. Fax: 96 70 42 96.
Call Sign: Ch.09.
Berths: 1000 (100 visitors). Moorings on floating pontoons.
Facilities: water; electricity; WCs; showers; mobile crane; fuel; chandlery; gardiennage; provisions (nearby).

PAIMPOL, Harbour Master. Tel: 96 20 47 65.
Berths: 270 (10 visitors on Pontoon A, plus others).
Facilities: Water. diesel, petrol, repairs, crane (6 tons), chandlery; ice.
Remarks: Good shelter from all winds, but Anse de Paimpol dries. Lock open 1½ hr.–HW to HW (Springs) 1 hr.–HW to HW (Neaps). Tel: 96 20 80 77.

PORT DE LEZARDRIEUX.
Tel: (96) 20 14 22/10 20.
Open: winter 0800-1200, 1330-1730. Summer: 0700-2200.
Call sign: Ch. 9.
Berths: On pontoons. Max. LOA 12m. Buoys for multihulls and large vessels.
Facilities: water; electricity; WCs; showers; (also for disabled); diesel 0830-1030, 1500-1630; telephone; crane; slipway.
Remarks: Port sheltered in all winds.

TREGUIER, Harbour Master. Tel: 96 92 42 37.
Berths: 200 (130 visitors in Marina).
Facilities: Water, electricity, repairs, crane, chandlery, petrol, food, post office.
Remarks: Shelter from most winds.

PORT BLANC. Capitainerie.
Tel: (96) 92 64 96.
Berths: Anchorage for 180 (30 visitors), most drying out.
Facilities: Water; electricity; refuse; WCs; cranage (limit 10 tons).

PORT DE PERROS-GUIREC. Capitainerie.
Tel: (96) 23 37 82.
Call sign: Ch. 9, 16.
Berths: 600 (50 visitors).
Facilities: water; electricity; fuel; WCs; showers. ice; cranage (limit 20 tons).
Remarks: Entrance dries.

PORT DE PLOUMANAC'H, Tel: (96) 91 44 31.
Call sign: Ch. 9, 16.
Berths: 150, 200 pontoons, 20 visitors.
Facilities: WCs; showers; other facilities at Perros-Guirec.
Remarks: Entry to moorings in pool, only when sufficient rise of tide above sill height allows. Entrance dries.

PORT DE LOCQUIREC. Bureau du Port, Mairie, 29241 Locquirec.
Tel: (98) 67 41 45.
Berths: 302 moorings.
Facilities: water; crane; repairs; shops; accommodation; telephone; electricity.

PORT DE PRIMEL-LE-DIBEN, Plougasnou. Bureau du Port. Tel: (98) 72 31 90.
Berths: Deep moorings available.
Facilities: water; telephone; crane; slipway; fuel.

MORLAIX. Tel: 98 88 54 92. Yacht Club: 98 62 13 14.
Call sign: Ch. 9, 16.
Berths: 130, 60 visitors.
Facilities: water; electricity; WCs; showers at Club house; Fuel 200m.
Access: Lock normally operates 1h. 30 min.– HW–1h. but exceptionally outside these times if more than 2.5m over the sill.

PORT DE ROSCOFF BLOSCON. Capitainerie.
Tel: 98 61 27 84. Fax: 98 61 11 81. Pilots: 98 69 73 07.
Call sign: Ch. 16, 12.
Berths: 100-150 (50 visitors).
Facilities: water; electricity; telephone; WCs; showers; fuel; crane.

RIVIERE L'ABERVRAC'H. Capitainerie.
Tel: 04 91 62.
Call sign: Ch. 9.
Berths: 80 (60 visitors).
Facilities: Water; electricity; WCs; showers; crane; fuel.

PORT DE PORTSALL. Affaires Maritimes, 29000. Tel: (98) 48 66 54.
Berths: Deep water moorings available.
Facilities: water; WCs; cranage (limit 1 ton); fuel.

PORT DU CONQUET. Affaires Maritimes, 12 rue Aristide Lucas, 29217 Le Conquet. Tel: (98) 89 00 05. Sauvetage: (98) 89 02 07 & (98) 89 31 31.
Berths: 200 in Avant-Port, max. draught 3m (E) to 4m (W).
Facilities: telephone; ice; slip; cranage (limit 15 tons); fuel; repairs.

BREST–Moulin-Blanc Marina. Port de Plaisance BP 411, 29275 Brest. Tel: (98) 02 20 02. Fax: 98 41 67 91.
Call Sign: Moulin Blanc Marina Ch. 16, 9.
Open: Winter 0830-1800. Summer 0800-2000.
Berths: 1200 (100 visitors) Access 24h.
Facilities: showers; WCs; bars; restaurant; duty-free; fuel (diesel, petrol); water; gas; electricity; chandler; provisions; repairs; cranage; dry dock (60m wide); storage; brokerage; slipway; restaurants; car hire; sailing school; launderette; ice; weather reports and forecasts; phone; change; English spoken.
Marina Director: H. Grall.

CAMARET MARINA (Styvel and La Pointe harbours). Tel: 98 27 95 99.
Berths: 365, 150 visitors.
Facilities: water; electricity; showers; WCs; slip; chandlers; ice; duty-free; restaurants in town.

MORGAT (CROZON) MARINA, Douarnenez Bay. Tel: 98 27 01 97.
Call sign: Ch. 9.
Berths: 525, 50 visitors.
Facilities: water; electricity; showers; crane; slip; launderette; 8T lift; phone; chandler; restaurants; fuel.

STE EWETT AUDIERNE, 29770 Esquibien. Tel: 98 70 00 28.
Berths: 152, 35 visitors. Max. draught 3m, LOA 12m.
Facilities: electricity; water; phone; TV aerial; fuel; gas; chandlery; provisions; WCs;

showers; launderette; restaurant; café; bar; sailing school and club; diving club; sea fishing; mail; repairs; slip; careening; security. English spoken.
Access: Outer harbour 24h. Marina (up river) 1h–HW–1h.

PORT DE SAINTE-MARINE, Combrit, 29120 Pont L'Abbé. Tel: (98) 56 38 72.
Call Sign: Ch. 9.
Berths: 720 (100 visitors). Max. draught 10m+, LOA 30m.
Facilities: water; electricity; WCs; showers; phone; slip; ice; 20 ton crane; refuse; provisions.
Remarks: Sainte Marine is on the opposite bank to and not far from Benodet.

BENODET – Port de Plaisance de Penfoul, 29118 Benodet. Tel: (98) 57 05 78.
Call Sign: Ch. 9.
Open: 0800-2000 (summer) 0800-1200, 1400-1800 (winter).
Berths: 402 (45 visitors) to 15m.
Facilities: Water; electricity; WCs; showers; fuel; slip; crane (10 tons); phone.
Customs: Tel: (98) 97 01 73.
Remarks: Access to the river is possible at all hours of the tide via canal. Speed limit 3 kts. Strong tidal currents.

PORT-LA-FORÊT, 29940 La Forêt-Fouesnant. Tel: 98 56 98 45. Fax: 98 56 81 31.
Call sign: Ch. 9.
Berths: 870, 100+ visitors. Max. LOA 30m.
Facilities: electricity; water; phone; fuel; gas; chandlery; provisions; ice; WCs; showers; launderette; restaurant; café; bar; sailing club and school; sea fishing; mail; repairs; 5T hoist; 2T crane; 30T travelift; slip; boat sales and hire; car hire; scrubbing grid; gardiennage; security; storage. English spoken.

PORT DE PLAISANCE DE CONCARNEAU,
Maison du Port, Mole Peneroff, 29110
Concarneau. Tel: 98 97 57 96.
Open: Summer 0730-1200, 1330-1930. Winter
0830-1200, 1330-1600.
Call sign: VHF Chan. 9.
Berths: 40 for visitors on pontoons.
Facilities: fuel; cranage; electricity; water;
showers; toilets; repairs.
Port Director: M. Didier Picard.
Remarks: Concarneau is an important fishing
port. Yachtsmen are reminded of rule 20 of
the 16th August 1965 decree, on going to sea,
which stipulates that priority given to sailing
yachts over motor vessels does not apply
when navigating the access channel.

LORIENT-KERNEVAL, Larmor Plage 56260.
Tel: 97 65 48 25. Fax: 97 33 63 56.
Call sign: Ch. 9.
Berths: 460, 60 visitors. Max. draught 4.5m,
LOA 25m.
Open: Office 0830-1230, 1400-1800 (winter);
0800-1230, 1330-2000 (July, August).
Facilities: electricity; water; repairs nearby;
crane 4T; travelift 25T; slip; scrubbing grid;
storage; gas; provisions; restaurant nearby.
Other facilities at Olarina. English spoken.

ETEL MARINA. Tel: 97 55 28 26 (summer)/97
55 28 26.
Call sign: Ch. 13.
Berths: 150, 15 visitors. Max draught LW
2.5m, LOA 18m.
Facilities: electricity; water; diesel and petrol;
phone; refuse; WCs; showers; sailing school
and diving club; minor repairs; 6T crane; 20T
hoist; sales; scrubbing grid; security; dry
berths. Nearby – chandler; ice; provisions;
restaurant; café; bar; slip.
Remarks: On River Etel 1M from sea, over
sand bank. Local knowledge needed for night
approaches. Access 2 hr–HW–1½ hr. Pilots 97
55 35 59.

LE PALAIS. Bureau de Port, 56360 Belle Ile,
Quai Bonnelle. Tel: (97) 31 42 90.
Call Sign: Ch. 16, 9.
Open: 24 hours. **Berths:** 100 in Avant Port. 100
in Bassin à Flot. Visitors stern to harbour wall
or on mooring buoys.
Facilities: Fuel; water; repairs; provisions;
WCs; showers; bank; refuse disposal; Post
Office; some restaurants.
Customs: Quai de l'Yser. Tel: (97) 31 85 95.
Remarks: Accessible in any conditions except
strong SE winds. Holding ground poor in
centre of harbour. Access to Bassin a Flot via
Lock 1h.30 min.–HW–1h. (0600-2200 LT) then
through lifting bridge.

LA TRINITÉ-SUR MER. Capitainerie, BP12,
56470 La Trinité. Tel: (97) 55 71 49.
Open: 24 hour. **Berths:** 930 on moorings and
pontoons.
Facilities: Chandlery; repairs; crane; 25T travel
hoist; sailmaker; provisions; Post Office; bank
(in town); launderette; restaurant.
Customs: La Trinite. Tel: (97) 55 73 46.
Remarks: Accessible in any conditions. Good
shelter except in strong SE to S winds when
La Vanererse sandbank covers.

VANNES, Port de Plaisance. Tel: 97 54 16 08.
Call sign: Ch. 9.
Berths: 250, 80 visitors. Max. draught 2.8m,
LOA 25m.
Open: Lock: between 0630 and 2200
according to tides. Office: 0900-1900
(summer); 0900-1200, 1330-1800 (winter).
Facilities: electricity; water; refuse; fuel; gas;
chandler; provisions; phone; WCs; showers;
launderette; restaurant; café; bar; sailing
school; diving club; mail; crane; slip; boat
sales and hire; car hire; scrubbing grid;
security; lift-out. English spoken. Customs.

ARZAL. Capitainerie, Le Vieux Chateau en
Camöel 56130, La Roche-Bernard.
Tel: (99) 90 05 86.
Berths: Available in the Marinas for visitors.
Facilities: Electricity; fuel; slip; crane; repairs;
provisions; WCs; showers.
Remarks: Accessible at all states of the tide.

LA ROCHE-BERNARD. Bureau du Port, 2 Quai
Saint-Antoine, Sagemor. Tel: (99) 90 62 17.
Berths: 250 – 200 on pontoons (20 visitors).
Facilities: electricity; fuel; water; slip; crane;
repairs; chandlery; bank; Post Office;
provisions; WCs; showers; restaurants (in
town).
Remarks: The attractive old port is to
starboard, and the new port is 180m further
upstream.

LA TURBALLE, Port de Plaisance. Tel: 40 62 80
40, summer: 40 23 41 65. Fax: 40 23 47 64.
Call sign: Ch. 9.
Berths: 260, 64 visitors. Max. draught 13m.
Facilities: electricity; water; gas; chandler;
provisions; ice; WCs; showers; phone;
restaurant; café; bar; club; sea fishing; mail;
140T lift; scrubbing grid; security (summer).

**For tidal coefficients based on
Brest see page 21:27**

PORNICHET-LA BAULE. Tel: 40 61 03 20.
Call sign: T.O.Z. 105.
Berths: 1150, 150 visitors. Max. draught 3.5m,
LOA 20m. Access to R. Pouliguen.
Facilities: electricity; water; phone; refuse;
fuel; gas; chandler; provisions; ice; phone;
WCs; showers, restaurant; café; bar; sea
fishing; repairs; hoist; lift; boat sales and hire;
car hire; scrubbing grid; security; lift-out;
storage. English, French and Spanish spoken.

PORNIC, BP22 La Noeveillard, 44210 Pornic.
Tel: (40) 82 05 40.
Call sign: VHF Ch. 9.
Berths: 754 (165 pontoon berths for visitors).
Facilities: Electricity; fuel; water; chandlery;
repairs; cranage; WCs; showers; Post Office;
provisions (in town); restaurants.
Harbour Master: Capt. Wiet.
Customs: Tel: (40) 82 03 17 (in town).
Remarks: Entry advisable 1 hr.–HW–1 hr.
Access hazardous in strong SW–E winds.

ILE D'YEU/PORT JOINVILLE, Capitainerie.
Tel: 51 58 38 11.
Call sign: VHF Ch. 9.
Berths: 140 (35 visitors).
Facilities: Water, electricity, WC/showers,
telephone, fuel, crane.
Remarks: Yachts may also use the wet basin.

PORT DE L'HERBAUDIERE, Port de Plaisance,
BP. 80, 85330, Noirmoutier en L'Ile. Tel: 51 39
05 05.
Call sign: VHF Ch. 9.
Berths: 490. Max. draught 3.5m, LOA 15m.
Facilities: Water, electricity, WC/showers,
crane, security, fuel, laundrette, chandler,
sailmaker, provisions.

PORT LA VIE, St-Gilles-Croix-de-Vie,
Captainerie Bd. de L'Egalite.
Tel: 51 55 30 83.
Call sign: VHF Ch. 9. (0600-2200 in season).
Berths: 700 (60 visitors).
Facilities: Water, electricity, WC/showers,
telephone, security, fuel.

PORT OLONA, LES SABLES-D'OLONNE, Quai
Alain Gerbaud, BP. 122, 85104. Tel: 51 32 51
16.
Call sign: VHF Ch. 9 & 16.
Berths: 1100 (110 visitors).
Facilities: Water, electricity, WC/showers,
telephone, fuel, security, travelift, laundrette,
plan to accommodate up to 20m. No entry
SE/SW force 8+.
Customs: Tel: 5132 0233.

PORT-BOURGENAY, Talmont-St-Hilaire 85440.
Tel: 51 22 20 36.
Call sign: Ch. 9, 16.
Berths: 510, 100 visitors. Max. draught 4.9m,
LOA 20m.
Facilities: electricity; water; TV aerial; phone;
fuel; gas; chandler; provisions; ice; WCs;
showers; launderette; restaurant; café; bar;
sea fishing; mail; repairs; 15T lift; slip; boat
sales and hire; car hire; scrubbing grid;
gardiennage; lift-out; storage. English, French
and Spanish spoken.

PORT DE JARD-SUR-MER, Capitainerie, Rue
du Cdt-Guilbaud. Tel: 51 33 40 17.
Open: 0830-1200, 1430-1800.
Berths: 375 (15 visitors).
Facilities: Water, WC, fuel, crane, phone, club,
electricity.
Access: 3 hr.–HW–3 hr.

L'AIGUILLON SUR MER, 85460 Vendée. Tel: 51
56 45 02.
Berths: 40 pontoon.
Facilities: Town nearby; restaurants;
campsites; sailing school; club.
Remarks: Access 2½ hr.–HW–2½ hr. Care
needed in any wind or bad weather. Avoid
oyster beds S of entrance in estuary.

PORT DE MARANS, 5 Rue de la Cloche, La
Rochelle. Tel: 46 41 92 33.
Berths: 50 (10 visitors).
Facilities: Water, electricity, WC/showers,
crane, fuel.

ARS-EN-RE, Bureau du Port, Sur Le Port
17590 Ars-en-Re. Tel: 46 29 25 10.
Call sign: VHF Ch. 9.
Open: 15 Jun-15 Sept. All day. Otherwise
weekdays: 0830-1230, 1400-1800.
Berths: 280. 3 hr–HW–3 hr. Max. draught
1.5m, LOA 15m. Visitors on Quai Nord
(marked).
Facilities: Water, electricity, crane, lift,
WC/showers.

SAINT-MARTIN-DE-RE, Ile de Ré 17590.
Tel: 46 09 26 69. Yacht Club: Tel: 46 09 22 07.
Berths: 250 (50 visitors).
Facilities: Water, electricity, WC/showers,
telephone, crane.

LA FLOTTE-EN-RE, Bureau du Port.
Tel: 46 09 67 66.
Berths: 100 (9 visitors).
Facilities: Water, electricity, WC/showers,
cranes, slip, fuel, security.
Remarks: Harbour dries out.

LA ROCHELLE-LES-MINIMES, Regie du Port de Plaisance at Capitainerie, Mole, Central B.P. 145 – 17005 La Rochelle. Tel: 46 44 41 20.
Call sign: VHF Ch. 9.
Berths: 3000 (300 visitors).
Facilities: Water, electricity, WC/shower, telephone, crane, fuel, travelift.

VIEUX-PORT DE LA ROCHELLE, Regie du Port de Plaisance. Tel: 46 41 68 73.
Berths: 200.
Facilities: Water, electricity.

PORT DE ROCHEFORT, Capitainerie.
Tel: 46 87 12 34.
Berths: 200 (20 visitors).
Facilities: Water, electricity, WC/shower, telephone, hoist, crane, fuel.

PORTS DE BOYARDVILLE ET DOUHET, Ile d'Oléron, apitainerie 17190 Boyardville.
Tel: 46 76 71 13. Yacht Club Tel: 59 63 16 22.
Berths: 100 (10 visitors).
Facilities: Water, electricity, slipway, security.

PORT DE MARENNES, Capitainerie, Av. des Martyrs-de-la-Resistance. Tel: 46 85 02 68.
Call sign: VHF Ch. 9.
Berths: 200 (10 visitors). Access via long canal.
Facilities: Water, electricity, crane, dry storage, security, fuel, telephone, WC/shower.

PORT DE ROYAN, Capitainerie, Quai de la Vieille Jetée, 17200 Royan.
Tel: 46 38 72 22.
Call sign: Ch. 9.
Berths: 620 (60 visitors). Max. draught 2.5m, LOA 23m.
Facilities: Water, electricity, WC/shower, telephone, crane, fuel, security.

MESCHERS-SUR-GIRONDE, Capitainerie, sur le Quai, Charente-Maritime 17132. Tel: 46 02 56 89.
Berths: 160 (max. length 8.45m.). 20 visitors on pontoons.
Facilities: Water; electricity; WC; telephone; security; customs; club.
Access: best from half tide to HW (possible to HW+4 hr.). No exit in SW blow.

MORTAGNE-SUR-GIRONDE, Capitainerie.
Tel: 46 90 63 15.
Berths: Berths available for visitors.
Facilities: Water, electricity, WC/shower, fuel, slipway, chandlery.

PORT DE BOURG-S/GIRONDE, Affaires Maritimes, Rue Franklin. Tel: 57 68 44 29.
Berths: 80 (6 visitors).
Facilities: Water, electricity, WC/shower, telephone, slipway, chandlery, fuel.

PORT-BLOC, Capitainerie, 33123 Le Verdon-S/Mer. Tel: 56 09 63 91.
Call sign: Ch. 12, 6, 16.
Berths: 150.
Facilities: Water, WC/shower, crane, fuel.

PORT LA VIGNE, Sté. Nautique de la Vigne, 33970, Cap Ferret. Tel: 56 60 54 36.
Berths: 260.
Facilities: Water, electricity, chandlery, WC/shower, crane, slip, fuel.

PORT D'ARCACHON, Capitainerie (Jetée du Port), Port de Plaisance, 33120 Arcachon.
Tel: 56 83 22 44.
Call Sign: VHF Ch. 9.
Berths: 1950 moorings, with 50 visitors.
Facilities: Water, electricity, fuel, telephone, crane, slipway, hoist, WC/shower, yacht club and school, boat hire, fishing, diving.

BÉTEY, Port de Plaisance, Andernos les Bains 33510.
Tel: 56 82 00 12.
Berths: 150 (some visitors available).
Facilities: Water, WC/shower, telephone, slipway, fuel (at Arcachon).

FONTAINE VIEILLE, Sté. Civile du Port Fontaine Vieille 33148, Lanton. Bureau de Port. Tel: 56 28 17 31.
Berths: 180 via canal.
Facilities: Water, fuel, security.

TAUSSAT-CASSY-LANTON, 33148 Lanton.
Tel: 56 82 93 09.
Berths: 200.
Facilities: Water, electricity, telephone, slipway, toilets, chandlery.

AUDENGE, Capitainerie. Tel: 56 26 82 47.
Berths: 84 (max. length 8m.).
Facilities: Water, electricity, WC/shower, slipway, fuel, telephone.

HOSSEGOR, Place de l'Hotel de Ville 40150.
Tel: 58 42 89 80.
Facilities: Waterskiing; windsurfing; sailing school; boat hire; fishing; surfing.

PORT DE PLAISANCE DE CAPBRETON, BP 49 40130. Tel: 58 72 21 23.
Call sign: Ch. 9.
Berths: 785 (max. length 18m, draught 2.5m), 75 visitors.
Open: 0700-2100. Out of season 0800-1800. Closed 1200-1400 daily.
Facilities: water; electricity; WC; shower; telephone; crane; security; hoist; fuel; ice; laundrette; restaurant; gas; repairs; sailing school; divers air.
Access: 3½ hr.HW-1 hr.

BAYONNE, Capitainerie, Allées Marines, 128 Av. de L'Adour. Tel: 59 63 11 57.
Berths: Visitors berths available.
Facilities: Water, electricity, fuel, crane.

PORT DU BRISE-LAMES/ANGLET, Bureau du Port (Plaisance), 118 Av. de L'Adour, 64600 Anglet. Tel: 59 63 05 45.
Berths: 385 on pontoons (58 visitors). Max. draught 2.5m, LOA 18m.
Facilities: Water, electricity, WC/shower, fuel, telephone, 13T. hoist, crane.

PORT DE ST-JEAN-DE-LUZ, Capitainerie de L'Arraldénia 64500. Tel: 59 47 26 81.
Berths: Visitors berths available.
Facilities: Water, electricity, WC/shower, fuel, crane, slipway, security.
Remarks: Navigating under sail is forbidden in the port.

PORT D'HENDAYE, Capitainerie, Port de la Floride, 12 rue des Aubépines, 64700. Tel: 59 20 16 97.
Berths: 250.
Facilities: water, WC/showers, telephone, slipway, cranage, security, fuel.

SPAIN

The Spanish N Coast is very rugged and exposed to wind and swell from N and W (SW and NW in summer) and, the shallow Continental Shelf can cause a choppy sea. There is little shelter in many ports along this coastline as they are open to N and E. The general direction of the current is westward, thence NW to the approaches to La Coruna. Spring tide ranges from 2.5m-4m.

FUENTERRABIA, Club Nautico.
Tel: 943 64 10 41.
Facilities: Water, electricity, crane, slipway.

PASAJES Port Office. Tel: 943 35 26 16.
Berths: Available in Darsena de Herrera.
Facilities: Water, electricity, cranes, radiotelephone, Yacht Club.

SAN SEBASTIAN, Club Nautico.
Tel: 943 42 35 74.
Berths: Anchorage in good weather.
Facilities: Water, electricity, showers, chandlery, slips, fuel, radiotelephone.
Remarks: Easy access and the bay is sheltered by the Isla Santa Clara.

GUETARIA, Club Nautico. Tel: 943 83 14 13.
Berths: 27. Anchorage at Motrico (10M).
Facilities: Water, diesel, slipway, repairs, chandlery.

LEKEITIO (Lequeitio), 48280 Vizcaya.
Tel: 684.05.00.
Berths: Mooring, next to S breakwater, or in the harbour on the quay.
Facilities: All usual facilities.
Remarks: Easy access, but with care in bad weather. The port is sometimes very crowded in summer.

BERMEO, Port Captain, Cofrida de Pescadores. Tel: 688 02 66.
Berths: Moor in ante puerto.
Facilities: Water, fuel, cranage, chandlery.
Remarks: Notable fishing port, provides good shelter.

PUERTO AUTONOMO DE BILBAO, Campo de Volantin 37, 48007 Bilbao.
Tel: 445 20.00/445 12.96. Club Maritimo.
Tel: 463 7600. Fax: 446 5409. Tx: 32708 PADB.
Berths: are available.
Facilities: Water, electricity, fuel.
Remarks: Port de Commerce offers all facilities, good port for winter laying up.

CASTRO URDIALES, Club Nautico.
Tel: 942 86 09 98.
Berths: On buoys near Yacht Club.
Facilities: Water, fuel, provisions, cranage, chandlery, small repairs.

LAREDO, Club Nautico. Tel: 942 60 58 12.
Berths: 300.
Facilities: Water, electricity, diesel, petrol, crane, slipway, repairs, chandlery.

SANTANDER (Ciudad), Pasea de Peveda 28.
Tel:. 21 20 58.
Call sign: VHF Ch. 16.
Berths: 250 (6-10 visitors).
Facilities: Water, electricity, showers, travelift, crane, security, fuel, chandlery.
Remarks: Shallows dangerous in bad weather.

SUANCES, Club Nautico. Tel: 942 81 09 33.
Berths: 80.
Facilities: Water, electricity, diesel, petrol, slipway, repairs, chandlery.

MARINA DEL CANTABRICO.
Berths: 450.
Facilities: Water, electricity, diesel, petrol, travelift, crane, repairs, chandlery.

VILLAVICIOSA, Club Nautico Albatros.
Tel: 985 89 17 02.
Berths: 20.
Facilities: Water, electricity, slipway, repairs.

GIJON, Real Club Astur de Regatas.
Tel: 985 32 42 02.
Facilities: Water, electricity, diesel, crane, slipway, repairs.

AVILES, Club Nautico Ensidesa.
Tel: 985 57 28 32.
Berths: 170.
Facilities: Water, travelift, crane 10T., repairs, chandler.

LUARCA, Club Nautico. Tel: 985 64 11 24.
Berths: 40.
Facilities: Water, electricity, diesel, crane, slipway, repairs.

NAVIA, Club Nautico. Tel: 985 63 00 94.
Facilities: Water, electricity, crane, slipway, repairs.

LA CORUNA, Port Captain. Tel: 22 60 01.
Call sign: VHF Ch. 16.
Berths: 50 berths for visitors.
Facilities: Water, electricity, fuel, WC/showers, chandlery, slipway, refuse disposal, telephone, crane.

VIGO, Port Captain, Tel: 21 13 26.
Call sign: VHF Ch. 16. 14.
Berths: In Darsena de Lage.
Facilities: Water, electricity, fuel, crane, provisions, chandlery.

PORTUGAL

LEIXOES, Port Captain. Tel: 995 17 06.
Call sign: VHF Ch. 16.
Berths: 60-70 (a few visitors berths are available).
Facilities: Water, showers, toilets, fuel, crane, chandlery.

CIUDADE DO PORTO, Port Captain. Tel: 282 66.
Call sign: VHF Ch. 12, 13, 16, 20, 67.
Berths: 9 visitors.
Facilities: Water, electricity, WC/showers, fuel, chandlery, crane.

FIGUEIRA DA FOZ, Doca de Recreio, 3080. Tel: (033) 22365/6. Fax: (033) 23945. Telex: 52339.
Max. draught 2.5m.
Facilities: fuel; gas; chandler; provisions; ice; phone; WCs; showers; launderette; restaurant; café; bar; mail; all repairs; slip; car hire; scrubbing grid.

PENICHE DE CIMA, Port Captain. Tel: 72 102.
Call sign: VHF Ch. 16, 11, 13.
Berths: Mooring along inside of breakwater.
Facilities: Water, fuel, slipway, security.
Remarks: Harbour liable to silting, anchorage difficult.

LISBON, Port Captain.
Tel: 60 81 01 and 60 81 04.
Call sign: VHF Ch. 16.
Berths: 270 (max. length 20m) at Doca do Bom Successo.
Facilities: Water, electricity, toilets, showers, telephone, diesel, crane, chandler, dry dock.
Remarks: Entering and leaving the harbour can be dangerous when a S-WNW gale is against the tide. This causes heavy seas.

PORTO DA BALEEIRA.
Fishing harbour, depth 6m, some construction under way.
Berths: Anchorage and berths at quay.
Facilities: water; fuel; provisions; repairs; dry dock; phone; showers; bars; restaurants; ice; fishing.

Anchorages also available on this coast at Belixe; Tonel (summer only: provisions, restaurants, bars, phones, ice); Zavial (restaurants); Salema (phones, showers, restaurants, bars. (Submerged rocks exist in depths less than 12m. Do not anchor close inshore). Burgau (restaurants, bars); Luz (showers, phone, restaurants, bars, Luz Bay Club: fishing).

PORTO DO LAGOS, (Tel: 62826).
Berths: berths and anchorage. Not sheltered
S/SE. Contact HM for entry.
Facilities: water; fuel at Solaria Quay; ice;
market; repairs; dry dock; phone; car rental;
fishing; club (Clube de Vela).

PORTIMÃO, Tel: 23111.
Call sign: Postradportimao. Ch. 16, 11.
Berths: Large sheltered anchorage in outer
basin (access all hours). Inner harbour for
supplies: contact HM. Speed limit 5 knots.
Marina and Ferry Terminal development
under way. Max. draught 7.6m, LOA 125m at
quay.
Facilities: fuel; water; ice; phone; car rental;
fishing; provisions; repairs; drydock; club
(Associação Naval Infante de Sagres).
Anchorage at Sagres (Tel: 64210).
Call sign: Radionavalsagres Ch. 16, 11.

Anchorages also available on this stretch of
coast at Praia da Rocha (not sheltered from
SW), restaurants, provisions, phones, car
rental, showers, bars, ice; Ponto do Altar (not
sheltered from S/SW; beware rocks); Alvor
(restaurants, bars, provisions, showers,
phones, car rental, ice). Entrance to Alvor
River over bar, marked only by changes in
water colour, and sandbanks; Carvoeiro (not
for bad weather), restaurants, bars,
provisions, showers, phone, car rental);
Armaçao de Pera (avoid rocks to W of line
taken S from fort); provisions, restaurants,
bars, phones, showers, ice, car rental;
Albufeira Bay (Tel: 54255) (sheltered from
WSW-ENE, best anchorage W of bay near
point); provisions, repairs, phones, ice,
showers, restaurants, bars, car rental; Olhos
de Agua (unsheltered); restaurant, provisions,
phones, showers, bar.

MARINA DE VILAMOURA, Vilamoura 8125.
Tel: (089) 32023/43/63. Fax: (089) 32033. Tx:
56843 MARINA P.
Call sign: Vilamoura Radio Ch. 16, 22.
Open: 15/6-14/9. offices: 0800-2000. Fuel:
0930-2000. 15/9-14/6 offices: 0900-1800 fuel:
0930-1900. Offices closed daily 1230-1400.
Berths: 1000. Max. draught 4m.
Facilities: water; electricity; fuel; phone; yacht
club; provisions; dry dock; shipyard; chandler;
showers; WCs; charter; car rental; ice; slip;
30T crane. Weather forecast 1000 LT on Ch.
20.

PORTO FARO/OLHAO, Faro: Tel: 803601/2/3.
Olhao: Tel: 713160.
Call sign: Postradfaro, Ch. 16, 11.
Faro is a commercial port, access to quays by
skiff only. Enter only on incoming tide.
Dangerous at night. Max. draught 6.1m, LOA
110m.
Olhao is a fishing port, being enlarged.
Facilities: provisions; phones; dry docks;
repairs; fuel; water; ice; car rental.
Anchorages on this stretch of coast at
Quarteira (not sheltered. Tel: 65214)
restaurants; provisions; phones; showers; ice;
bars; car rental. Praia de Faro (sheltered from
E). Rabo de Peixie on Ilha da Culatra
(sheltered from W and SW).

PORTO DE FUZETA, Tel: 93113.
Fishing port, constant change in depths
makes approach dangerous. Not
recommended for pleasure craft.
Facilities: fuel and water at inside wharf;
provisions; few repairs; phones; ice.

PORTO DE TAVIRA, Tel: 22438.
Berths: anchorage in Quatro Aguas
(sheltered).
Facilities: fuel and water at wharf. In town:
provisions; repairs; ice.

Anchorages are possible in front of almost all
the many beaches and towns on this part of
the coast. For shelter, Armona (summer
Facilities: restaurants; bars; showers) is
recommended.

VILA REAL DE SANTO ANTONIO, Ria
Guadiana, Tel: 43035.
Call sign: Postradvireal. Ch. 16, 11.
Facilities: fuel; water on dock; depth 2m.
Provisions; repairs; dry dock; showers;
phones; ice; car rental; club. Do not anchor
over ferry route. Contact HM for place at
dock. Navigation is not recommended
January-March (in swollen river) or at night.

SPAIN

COSTA DE LA LUZ

PUERTO DE AYAMONTE, Muelle de Portugal, Oficina del Puerto Ayamonte, Huelva. Tel: (955) 32 07 67.
Berths: 110, 100 visitors moorings, 2.5-5m depth in fishing harbour.
Facilities: petrol; diesel; water; dry berths; crane; slip; engine repairs; customs; parking. Chandler in town.

CLUB MARITIMO Y TENIS DE PUNTA UMBRIA, Almirante Pérez Guzmán, s/n, Punta Umbria, Huelva. Tel: (955) 31 18 99.
Berths: 175 moorings in harbour, depth 2m+ in Soya River.
Facilities: water; electricity; phone; petrol; diesel; dry berths; slip; restaurant; bar; customs; parking. Other facilities in town.

CLUB MARITIMO DE HUELVA, Avenida de Montenegro, s/n Huelva. Tel: (955) 24 76 27.
Berths: 250 moorings in harbour, 3m+ depth.
Facilities: water; electricity; diesel and petrol; phone in club; slip; engine repairs; dry berths; parking. Other services in town.

CLUB NAUTICO SEVILLA, Avenida Sanlúcar de Barrameda, Sevilla. Tel: (954) 45 47 77.
Berths: 90 (50 river up to 35m LOA, 40 smaller in dock). 90 visitors. 9 moorings.
Facilities: water; electricity; phone in club; petrol and diesel in port; restaurant and bar; ½T crane; slip; dry berths; engine repairs; customs; parking; chandler in town.

CLUB NAUTICO DE SANLUCAR DE BARRAMEDA, Bajo de Guía, s/n, San Lucar de Barrameda. Tel: (956) 36 19 93/36 01 44.
Call sign: Ch. 9.
Berths: 50 moorings up to 5m deep, 10-15m LOA. Not sheltered.
Access: 0900-2100, May-Sept.
Facilities: water; electricity; phone in club; parking; chandler in town; bar; café; restaurant.

REAL CLUB NAUTICO DE CADIZ, Playa de San Felipe s/n, Cádiz. Tel: (956) 21 32 62.
Berths: 175, 16m, LOA, depth 3.5-20m, 20 visitors.
Facilities: water; electricity; phone; petrol; diesel; 5T crane; slip; engine repairs; chandler; parking; fishing; restaurants; cafés; bar.

CLUB NAUTICO ALCAZAR, Plaza de San Lorenzo no. 2, Cádiz. Tel: (956) 23 69 14.
Berths: 256, 500 moorings, depth to 6m (dries out).
Facilities: water; electricity; phone in club; diesel; petrol; crane; slip; engine repairs; chandler in town; parking; restaurant; bar.

PUERTO SHERRY (REAL CLUB NAUTICO DEL PUERTO DE SANTA MARIA), Enrique Martinez no. 13, Puerto de Santa Maria, Cadiz. Tel: (956) 85 25 27.
Call sign: Ch. 9, 16.
Berths: 125, 20 visitors, 2-9m depth, to 50m LOA.
Facilities: water; phone in club; crane; slip; engine repairs; customs; chandler; parking; restaurant; café; bar; fishing; petrol and diesel in town.
Access: entrance to the totally sheltered port is on R. Guadalete and canal, two submerged breakwaters marked by buoys. Approach difficult in SW gale. Perceptible E and W going set along coast every 6 hr.

CLUB MARITIMO DEPORTIVO SANCTI-PETRI, C/Calleja, no. 1, Chiclana de la Frontera.
Berths: 90. 90 moorings, 10 visitors. Depth 3-15m.
Facilities: water; phone; dry berths; slip; engine repairs; customs; chandler; parking.

CLUB NAUTICO DEPORTIVO BARBATE, Puerto de la Albufera, Barbate. Tel: (956) 43 05 87.
Berths: 101, 10 visitors, 3-5m LOA, depth 4.5-9m.
Facilities: water; electricity; phone; diesel; petrol; customs; chandler. **In the port:** crane, slip, engine repairs, parking.

REAL CLUB NAUTICO DE ALGECIRAS, Paseo de la Conferencia, s/n, Algeciras. Tel: (956) 65 67 05/65 05 03.
Berths: 50 in port, 4m deep, 7-10m LOA.
Facilities: water; electricity; phone in club; slip; engine repairs; customs; parking. Petrol and diesel in port; chandler in town. Restaurant; café; bar.

GIBRALTAR

On arrival report to Yacht Reporting Station at Waterport, outside N end of main harbour, for customs, immigration, etc. Fly Flag 'Q'.

MARINA BAY, PO Box 373, Gibraltar. Tel: Gibraltar (350) 73300. Fax: (350) 74322. Telex: 2348 MBCL GK.
Call sign: Ch. 73.
Berths: 200. Max. draught 4m. Entrance safe in all winds.
Facilities: electricity, water, minor repairs, restaurants, bars nearby, gardiennage, 24 hour security, chandlery, WC's, showers.
All major repairs at Gun Wharf Yacht Centre (Tel: 72524): slip to 200T, duty free, provisions, charter, chart depot, chandlery, brokerage.

SHEPPARD'S MARINA & BOATYARD,
H. Sheppard & Co. Ltd., Waterport, Gibraltar. Tel: Gibraltar (350) 77183 or 75148. Telex: 2324 MARINA GK.
Open: Weekdays 0900-1300, 1430-1800; Saturdays 0900-1300. Piers open during all daylight hours.
Berths: 140. 24 visitors alongside pontoons. Max. draught 2.70m. Entrance safe in all winds.
Facilities: electricity, water, all repairs, 44 ton hoist, 5 ton crane, diesel, petrol, gardiennage, 24 hour security, chandlery, WC's, showers, brokerage, new boat sales, duty-free.

All major repairs at **Gun Wharf Yacht Centre** (Tel: 72524): 200T slip; duty-free; provisions; charter; chandlery; charts; brokerage; English and Spanish spoken.

AZORES
(Note: Anchorages not recommended in bad weather or without local knowledge or assistance.)

ILHA DE SANTA MARIA. Vila do Porto. Tel: 82 157.
Call sign: Port Captain, Ch. 16.
Tie up to pier with Captain's permission.
Facilities: water at ramp; provisions; gas; kerosene; ice; diesel in town (a climb away). Anchorage in Bay of São Lourenço.

ILHA DE SÃO MIGUEL. Ponta Delgada. Tel: Port: 25 268. Pilots: 23 550. Telex: 8247 MRCC PD.
Call sign: Ch. 16, 11. Pilots: Ch. 14.
Moor with permission of Port Captain at floating dock or at Guarda Fiscal fort, Molhe Salazar.
Facilities: provisions; gas; ice; kerosene; chandlery in town; 10T crane; slip. Yacht Club near fort has showers, mail service. Fuel and untreated water at sea wall.

ILHA TERCEIRA. Praia da Vitória, (38°44'N 27°04'W).
Call sign: Praia Port Control, Ch. 16.
Facilities: Yacht Club with showers; bar; restaurant; visiting yachtsmen may use the facilities.

ANGRA DO HEROISMO. (38°39'N 27°13'W). Tel: 22 051.
Call sign: Ch. 16, MF 2182 kHz.
Facilities: Fuel and water at dock. Yacht Club with showers, bar, restaurant. Visiting yachtsmen welcome. Ice, gas, provisions in town.

ILHA GRACIOSA. Santa Cruz. (39°01'N 27°57'W).
Call sign: Horta Radio, Ch. 16, 11. MF 2182.
Moor only with Port Captain's permission. Tie to dock.

ILHA DE SÃO JORGE. Velas. (38°41'N 28°12'W).
Call sign: Horta Radio. Ch. 16, 11.
Moorings sometimes available with Port Captain's permission. Fuel and water at quay. Water and provisions sparse in summer. Anchorage at Calheta.

ILHA DO FAIAL. Horta. (39° 27'N, 31°07'W). Tel: 22 813. Pilots: 22 611.
Call sign: Port Captain, Ch. 16, 2182 kHz. 24 hr. Pilots: Ch. 11, 13.
Facilities: Yacht Club; moorings and pier; 25T crane; repairs; water; launderette; restaurant and bar nearby. Anchor to leeward in SW gale or Baia do Horta. Extensive redevelopments reported. Commercial port. Lifeboat station.

Visual Navigational Aids for Azores — Section 23

Indices

27

	Page Number			Page Number	
	Tides	Lights and Port Information		Tides	Lights and Port Information
LONDON BRIDGE (S)	21:57	22:68	McARTHURS HEAD	—	22:158
	21:58-60		McDERMOTT BASE	21:104	22:133
LONDONDERRY (S)	21:247	22:230	MEDINA RIVER	21:209	22:49
	21:248-250		MEDWAY RIVER	21:44	22:78
LONG, LOCH	21:138	22:165	MEESTOOF	—	24:16
LONGSHIPS (LANDS END)	—	22:14	MEIKLE FERRY	21:104	—
LOOE	21:170	22:21	MELFORT, LOCH	21:133	22:157
LOOP HEAD	—	22:238	MELLON CHARLES	21:128	—
LOPEREN	—	25:19	MELLON, POINT	21:253	—
LORIENT	21:281	23:52	MEMMERT SAND	21:330	—
LOSSIEMOUTH	21:104	22:132	MENAI STRAIT	21:145	22:184
LOSTWITHIEL	21:170	—	MERSEY, RIVER	—	22:281
LOUGHROS MORE	21:257	—	MEW ISLAND	—	22:227
LOWER LARGO	21:95	—	METHIL	21:95	22:122
LOWESTOFT (S)	21:74	22:95	MEVAGISSEY	21:170	22:20
	21:71-73		MIDDLESBROUGH (S)	21:80	22:116
LUANCO	21:266	23:77		21:82-84	
LUARCA	21:266	23:77	MID YELL	21:105	—
LUCE BAY	—	22:171	MILAID POINT	—	22:149
LULWORTH COVE	21:186	22:34	MILFONTES	21:264	—
LUNDY ISLAND	21:157	22:210	MILFORD HAVEN (S)	21:157	22:193
LUNE RIVER	21:143	22:177		21:158-160	
LYBSTER	21:104	22:134	MILLPORT	21:138	—
LYDNEY	—	22:205	MINE HEAD	—	22:216
LYME REGIS	21:170	22:32	MINEHEAD	21:162	22:208
LYMINGTON	21:209	22:40	MINQUIERS, LES	21:218	—
LYNAES HAVN	—	25:32	MINSTERWORTH	21:162	—
LYNGORLEIA	—	25:6	MISTLEY	21:69	—
LYNGS ODDE	—	25:52	MIZEN HEAD	21:237	22:242
LYNHER RIVER	21:170	—	MOANA, ENSENADA DE	—	23:83
LYNMOUTH	21:162	22:208	MOELFRE	21:144	—
LYNESS	—	22:137			
LYSEBOTN	21:335	—	MOGUÉRIEC, PORT DE	—	23:41
LYSTBADEHAVN	—	24:54	MOIDART, LOCH	21:133	—
			MOLEDO	—	23:84
			MOLENE	21:281	23:44
			MOLENGAT	—	24:32
M			MÖLLE	—	25:82
			MOLLOSUND	—	25:39
			MØN	—	25:80
MAAS	21:311	24:21	MONSTERAS	—	25:109
MAASLUIS	21:311	24:25	MOMMARK HAVN	—	25:55
MAASMOND	—	24:25	MONACH ISLAND (Shillay)	—	22:152
MACDUFF	—	22:131	MONIFIETH	21:104	22:127
MACHRIHANISH	21:133	22:159	MONKSTONE ROCK	—	22:200
MADELENA	—	23:101	MONTIJO, CANAL DO	—	23:89
MAHNÖ	—	25:85	MONTROSE	21:104	22:127
MAIDEN ROCKS	—	22:229	MORBIHAN	21:281	23:55
MALAHIDE	21:237	22:223	MORECAMBE	21:143	22:178
MALDON	21:69	22:87	MORGAT	21:281	23:47
MALLAIG	21:133	22:148	MORLAIX	21:281	23:40
MAN, ISLE OF	21:144	22:173	MOSEDE	—	25:79
MANCHESTER	—	22:182	MOSS	—	25:14
MARGATE	21:44	22:73	MOSSHOLMEN	—	25:40
MARIAGER FJORDE	—	25:29	MOSTYN	21:144	22:183
MARIN, RIA DE	21:264	23:82	MOTRICO	—	23:72
MARINA MINDE	—	25:58	MOUNTS BAY	—	22:15
MARISTOW	21:170	—	MOUSA PERIE BARD LT.	—	22:140
MARQUIS, LE	21:266	—	MOUSEHOLE	21:170	22:15
MARSTAL	—	25:56	MOVILLE	21:247	22:230
MARSTRANDSON	—	25:40	MUCKLE FLUGGA	—	22:144
MARUP HAVEN	—	25:50	MUCKLE HOLM	—	22:142
MARYPORT	21:143	22:172	MUCKLE SKERRY	21:105	22:142
MAUGHHOLD HEAD	—	22:175	MUKRAN	—	25:92
MAY ISLAND	—	22:120	MULL SOUND	21:133	22:154

A

PERSONAL NOTES

PERSONAL NOTES

PLANNER

VIDEO SERIES

SOLENT TELE-PILOT

ISLE OF WIGHT (180 mins) All ports and rivers, plus a complete anti-clockwise passage from St.Catherine's Lt. House to the Needles and on back to St. Catherine's   **£39.50**

CHICHESTER HARBOUR - ENTRANCE (60 mins) Approach from Nab Tower via Ch.Bar Bn. and the Winner, including East Head, Sparkes Yacht Harbour and Mengham Rythe.   **£22.50**

CHICHESTER - INNER HARBOUR (180 mins) Total Inner Harbour, including all ports, passages and Marinas.   **£39.50**

LANGSTONE HARBOUR (60 mins) Approach from West via Fairway Buoy, including entrance, complete Inner Harbour and Marina.   **£22.50**

PORTSMOUTH HARBOUR (60 mins) Approach to busy entrance from South. Inner Harbour to Fareham and Portchester Lake, inc. Camper Nicholsons & Port Solent Marinas   **£22.50**

SOLENT PREVIEW (60 mins) Out-takes from the above five videos   **£16.50**

THAMES TELE-PILOT

THAMES ONE 'JOURNEY INTO THE TIDEWAY' (180 mins) River Wey/Shepperton to Tower Bridge, inc. Locks, Bridges, Marinas, Fog driftwood etc.   **£39.50**

THAMES TWO 'JOURNEY TO THE SEA' (180 mins) Tower Bridge to Medway, inc. Thames Barrier, Woolwich and Gravesend Radio.   **£39.50**

THAMES THREE 'JOURNEY OUT OF THE ESTUARY' (110 mins) River Medway to Ramsgate. A special Tele-Pilot exercise in NAVIGATION, CHARTWORK AND COASTAL PASSAGE PLANNING.   **£29.50**

RIVER MEDWAY (180 mins) A north east approach from the South Shoebury Buoy up to the M2 Motorway Bridge.   **£39.50**

HAVENGORE PASSAGE (120 mins) River Swale, River Crouch and River Roach   **£29.50**

CHANNEL TELE-PILOT

CHANNEL ONE 'THE SHORTER CROSSING' (120 mins) Ramsgate to Calais, a rough crossing   **£29.50**

CHANNEL THREE 'THE LONGER CROSSING' (180 mins) Poole to Alderney, Needles to Cherbourg to Alderney, inc. Alderney Race and Braye Harbour   **£39.50**

INDEX TO ADVERTISERS

INDEX TO ADVERTISERS

LEGAL NOTE

GENERAL ACKNOWLEDGEMENTS

Data and extracts from the Ephemeris of the Admiralty Nautical Almanac, Weather Forecast Area Charts and the plate of International Code Flags together with explanatory matter, are reproduced with the sanction of the Controller of H.M. Stationery Office. Phases of the Moon are reproduced with permission from data supplied by the Science and Engineering Research Council.

The Tidal Stream charts have all been based on Admiralty Tidal Stream Atlases, and acknowledgement is hereby given. Other information, such as Notices to Mariners, has also been used from Official sources.

Tidal Curve Diagrams are produced from portion(s) of BA Tide Tables, Vol.1 with the sanction of the Controller, H.M. Stationery office and of the Hydrographer of the Navy.

Cover. Britain and Europe image is reproduced with permission of National Remote Sensing Unit, Royal Aircraft Establishment, Farnborough.

The Publishers tender their grateful thanks, and would like to place on record their obligation to the Hydrographic Office, Ministry of Defence, the Controller of H.M. Stationery Office, the B.B.C., British Telecom, Meteorological Office, H.M. Coastguard, Trinity House, the Northern Lighthouse Board and Department of Transport, all of whom have given them every facility and who are ever ready to assist in the production of any work that will help seamen, also to Dr. R.C. Fisher who has contributed many valuable tables.

TIDAL PREDICTIONS — ACKNOWLEDGEMENTS

(a) Tidal predictions for River Tyne (N. Shields), Leith, Immingham, Holyhead, Avonmouth, Belfast, Aberdeen, Southampton, St. Helier, Milford Haven. Lowestoft, Walton-on-the-Naze, London Bridge, Shoreham, Galway, Reykjavik, Londonderry, Dover, Sheerness, Liverpool, Cobh, Antwerp (Prosperpolder), Inverness, Burnham-on-Crouch, Middlesbrough, Sunderland, are computed by the Proudman Oceanographic Laboratory, copyright reserved.

(b) Tidal predictions for Dublin are prepared by the Proudman Oceanographic Laboratory for the Dublin Port and Docks Board. Copyright reserved.

(c) Tidal predictions for Lerwick, Ullapool, Oban, Greenock, Falmouth, Plymouth, Dartmouth, Portland, Poole (Town Quay), Portsmouth and Gibraltar have been computed and supplied by the Hydrographer of the Navy and are Crown Copyright.

(d) Tidal predictions for Harlingen have been computed and supplied by Rijkswaterstaat, 's-Gravenhage.

(e) Tidal predictions for the following ports have been computed by the stated National Authority and supplied by The Hydrographer of the Navy.

Brest, St. Malo, Cherbourg, Dunkerque, Le Havre, Pointe de Grave (Service Hydrographique & Oceanographique de la Marine, Brest Cedex).
Flushing, Cuxhaven, Helgoland, Hook of Holland (Rijkswaterstaat, s'-Gravenhage).
Lisbon (Ministerio da Marinha, Lisbon).
Esbjerg (Meteorologisk Institut, Copenhagen),
Bergen (Norges Sjøkartverk, Stavanger).

Any infringement of these tables, either by appropriating or altering the Tide Tables, or otherwise, will be proceeded against under statute.

NEW FOR 1992

BEKEN OF COWES/REED'S NAUTICAL ALMANAC DESK DIARY
A5 week to view diary bound in blue leather. 184 pages including Keith Beken's personal selection from Beken's unique collection, weather forecast areas, coastal radio stations, Dover high water etc.

REED'S LOG BOOK FOR YACHTS
Suitable for power and sail. New layout - ideal for cruise planning.

REED'S MEDITERRANEAN NAVIGATOR
Published annually in November.
Companion volume to Reed's Almanac, covering the whole of the Mediterranean.

REED'S NAUTICAL ALMANAC AND COAST PILOT
The North American edition of Reed's, covering the Eastern Seaboard,
Gulf of Mexico and Caribbean.

*Available from all good nautical bookshops and chandlers,
or direct from the publishers.*

THOMAS REED
PUBLICATIONS LTD
Weir House, Hurst Road, East Molesey, Surrey KT8 9AQ U.K.
Tel: 081-941 8090 Fax: 081-941 8046 Telex: 883526 Reed G

ORDER FORM

REED'S Direct Mail Service

(Prices valid until September 30th 1992)

Please supply the items listed overleaf:

BLOCK CAPS PLEASE

Name ....

Address ....

....

.... Date ....

Signature ....

Please allow 28 days for delivery

Please charge my credit card

Card expiry date ....

Signed ....

Please find enclosed my cheque for £ ....
(Payable to Thomas Reed Publications Ltd)

Mail to:
REED'S DIRECT MAIL SERVICE,
THOMAS REED PUBLICATIONS LTD,
WEIR HOUSE,   **or telephone: 081-941-8090**
HURST ROAD, EAST MOLESEY,   **Fax: 081-941-8046**
SURREY KT8 9AQ.
UK.

Registered Office: 14 Hanover Square, London W1R 0BE. Reg. No. 2566249. England. VAT No. 577 0802 27

ORDER FORM

REED'S Direct Mail Service

(Prices valid until September 30th 1992)

QUANTITY	ITEM	UNIT PRICE	TOTAL inc. VAT & p&p.

Leather bound REED'S LOG BOOK and GUEST LOG IN SLIP CASE.
Gold block the following name(s) — max. 20 letters BLOCK CAPS.

QUANTITY	ITEM	UNIT PRICE	TOTAL inc. VAT & p&p.
....	☐☐☐☐☐☐☐☐☐☐☐☐☐☐☐☐☐☐☐☐	@ £45.00	£ ....
....	LEATHER SLEEVE FOR REED'S ALMANAC*	@ £17.50	£ ....
....	REED'S LEATHER BOUND LOG BOOK*	@ £22.50	£ ....
....	REED'S LEATHER BOUND GUEST LOG*	@ £22.50	£ ....
....	REED'S MARINE DISTANCE TABLES*	@ £19.50	£ ....
	(blocked as above)*		
....	REED'S MEDITERRANEAN NAVIGATOR 1992	@ £15.00	£ ....
....	REED'S N. AMERICAN EAST COAST ALMANAC 1992	@ £19.50	£ ....
....	ISLE OF WIGHT TELEPILOT VHS VIDEO	@ £39.50	£ ....
....	CHICHESTER HARBOUR (ENTRANCE) VHS VIDEO	@ £22.50	£ ....
....	CHICHESTER (INNER HARBOUR) VHS VIDEO	@ £39.50	£ ....
....	LANGSTONE HARBOUR VHS VIDEO	@ £22.50	£ ....
....	PORTSMOUTH HARBOUR VHS VIDEO	@ £22.50	£ ....
....	SOLENT PREVIEW	@ £16.50	£ ....
....	THAMES ONE VHS VIDEO	@ £39.50	£ ....
....	THAMES TWO VHS VIDEO	@ £39.50	£ ....
....	THAMES THREE VHS VIDEO	@ £29.50	£ ....
....	RIVER MEDWAY VHS VIDEO	@ £39.50	£ ....
....	HAVENGORE PASSAGE VHS VIDEO	@ £29.50	£ ....
....	CHANNEL ONE TELE-PILOT VHS VIDEO	@ £29.50	£ ....
....	CHANNEL THREE TELE-PILOT VHS VIDEO	@ £39.50	£ ....
....	BEKEN OF COWES 'BEAUTY OF SAIL' VHS VIDEO	@ £26.50	£ ....
....	KEYED-ALIKE LOCKS (Set of 5 – Standard)	@ £45.00	£ ....
....	KEYED-ALIKE LOCKS (Set of 4 – Medium)	@ £40.00	£ ....
....	KEYED-ALIKE LOCKS (Set of 4 – Small)	@ £35.00	£ ....
....	AFFIX	@ £17.50	£ ....
....	NAUTRACK WITH AFFIX	@ £35.00	£ ....
....	BEARING PLOTTER	@ £20.00	£ ....
....	BEARING PLOTTER WITH AFFIX	@ £32.00	£ ....
....	DME RANGE FINDER	@ £ 8.50	£ ....
....	COMPLEAT NAVIGATOR KIT	@ £57.50	£ ....
....	REED'S ALMANAC HOLDER (Teak)	@ £25.00	£ ....
....	REED'S ALMANAC HOLDER (Mahogany)	@ £22.50	£ ....

Prices quoted apply to UK and Eire only. Quotes for overseas orders by return post.

GRAND TOTAL £ ....